Whitaker's Almanack QUIZ

£2,000 worth of prizes to be won

QUIZ RULES

1 Employees of Whitaker or anyone else involved in the quiz and their families are excluded.

2 Entries are limited to one per person.

3 The closing date for entries is 31st January 1996 and all entries must be received by that date addressed to Whitaker's Almanack 1996 Quiz, 12 Dyott Street, London WC1A 1DF.

4 The first prize will be £1,000. There will be five prizes of £150 each and 10 runner-up prizes of a free copy of Whitaker's Almanack 1997 edition, on publication.

5 The prizes will be awarded to the first 16 correct entries that are drawn.

6 Prize winners will be notified by 1st March 1996. The names of winners may be published.

7 A list of prize winners and the correct answers to the questions will be available on request from Whitaker, 12 Dyott Street, London WC1A 1DF, after 1st March 1996. A stamped addressed envelope marked 'Prize Winners List' should accompany such requests.

8 In all matters concerning this quiz, the decision of the Editor will be final, and no correspondence will be entered into.

Name ....
(BLOCK LETTERS)

Address ....
(BLOCK LETTERS)

....

.... Postcode ....

Telephone No ....

Signed ....

QUIZ QUESTIONS

Give the answer and the number of the page in Whitaker's Almanack 1996 on which it appears

	Answer	Page No

1 Baroness Thatcher - Buckingham

   a) The Duchess of Kent - ? ....

   b) Betty Boothroyd - ? ....

   c) Rabbi J. Neuberger - ? ....

2 In which island group would you find

   a) Pukapuka? ....

   b) Banaba? ....

   c) Skara Brae? ....

3 What record is held by

   a) Dan O'Brien (USA)? ....

   b) Lord Egremont and the late Aga Khan? ....

   c) Cilaos, Isle de Réunion? ....

4 Who is

   a) Patriarch of Babilonia of the Chaldeans? ....

   b) the UK Territorial Commander? ....

   c) the Clerk of the Closet? ....

5 Fire £1,238m

   a) Education £m? ....

   b) Employment £m? ....

   c) Parish precepts £m? ....

6 What was first in 1801, missed in 1941 and last in 1991?

   ....

7 What have the following in common?

   a) Surrey Heath, Three Rivers, Vale Royal ....

   b) Stephen Joseph, Crucible, Nuffield ....

   c) The Second Mrs Kong and The Makropulos Case ....

	Answer	Page No

8 How many

a) sheriffdoms in Scotland ....

b) inches in an 'atlas' ....

c) elephants in Lane Xang ....

9 What should one 'Quit' at Victory House?

....

10 Which park

a) lies wholly in Dyfed? ....

b) includes the Cleveland Way? ....

c) is divided by The Broad Walk? ....

11 What is

a) the Dasht-e Lut? ....

b) the *Gorsedd*? ....

c) the Shinkansen? ....

12 In which city is

a) 'Eureka' in Discovery Road? ....

b) 'Zurich' in Stanhope Road? ....

c) 'Fish' in Cove Road? ....

13 Who is the father of

a) the Prince of the Asturias? ....

b) Columbus Taylor? ....

c) Birgitte van Deurs? ....

14 What first was achieved in 1995 by

a) Cpl Wayne Mills? ....

b) Pauline Clare? ....

c) Alison Hargreaves, alone and without oxygen? ....

QUIZ QUESTIONS

Give the answer and the number of the page in Whitaker's Almanack 1996
on which it appears

	Answer	Page No

15 What can be achieved by patrimony, by servitude or by redemption?

....

16 What links

    a) Kitty Godfree and Wallis Simpson? ....

    b) Elsie McKay and John Buchanan? ....

    c) Anita Gradin and Edith Cresson? ....

17 Which President's middle name is

    a) Gabriel? ....

    b) Rolihlahla? ....

    c) Saúl? ....

18 Which college is found at

    a) Stanford Hall, Loughborough? ....

    b) Mirfield, W. Yorks? ....

    c) Bramshill House, Basingstoke? ....

19 In which country is the national anthem

    a) La Concorde? ....

    b) The Hope? ....

    c) The Soldier's Song? ....

20 Ynys Môn = Anglesey

    a) Ceredigion = ? ....

    b) Cunninghame = ? ....

    c) Kyle and Carrick = ? ....

Whitaker, 12 Dyott Street, London WC1A 1DF

AN

Almanack

For the Year of Our Lord

1996

ESTABLISHED 1868

BY

JOSEPH WHITAKER, FSA

CONTAINING AN ACCOUNT OF THE

ASTRONOMICAL AND OTHER PHENOMENA

AND

A vast Amount of INFORMATION respecting the
GOVERNMENT, FINANCES, POPULATION,
COMMERCE, and GENERAL STATISTICS of
the various Nations of the WORLD
with an INDEX containing
nearly 10,000
References

LONDON

OFFICE: 12 DYOTT STREET
LONDON WC1A 1DF

The traditional design of the title page for Whitaker's Almanack which has appeared in each edition since 1868

Whitaker's Almanack

1996

J. WHITAKER & SONS LTD

12 DYOTT STREET · LONDON WCIA IDF

J. Whitaker and Sons Ltd
12 Dyott Street, London WC1A 1DF

Whitaker's Almanack published annually since 1868
© 128th edition J. Whitaker and Sons Ltd 1995

Standard edition (1280 pages)
Cloth covers
0 85021 254 5

Leather binding
0 85021 255 3

Designed by Douglas Martin
Jacket design by Carroll Associates
Typeset by Page Bros (Norwich) Ltd
Printed and bound in Great Britain by
Clays Ltd, part of St Ives PLC, Bungay, Suffolk

Contents

Preface	7
The Year 1996	9
Bank Holidays	10, 11
Astronomy	15
Data for 1996	16
Explanatory notes	71
Time Measurement and Calendars	81
Tidal Tables	96
Constants	96
Data for 1996	98
World Geographical Statistics	110
United Kingdom	118
Area and population	118
National flag	122
Royal Family	123
Households	125
Kings and Queens	134
Peerage	141
Orders of Chivalry	174
Baronetage and Knightage	177
Dames	209
Chiefs of Clans	212
Medals and Decorations	214
Forms of Address	217
Privy Council	218
Parliament	221
List of Members	231
By-elections	238
Constituencies	241
European Parliament	272
List of UK Members	272
UK constituencies	273
The Government	279
Government Departments and Public Offices	281
Law Courts and Offices	361
Tribunals	376
Police Service	380
Defence	384
Salaries and pensions	393
The Christian Churches	396
Other Faiths	430
Education	433
Directory of institutions	448
Independent schools	472
Social Welfare	483
National Health Service	483
National Insurance and benefits	486
War pensions	494
Water	496
Energy	498
Transport	501
Communications	510
Post	510
Telecommunications	512
Airmail and IDD codes	516
Weights and Measures	518
Development Corporations	524
Local Government	526
England	537
London	555
Wales	561
Scotland	565
Northern Ireland	571
Isle of Man	574
Channel Islands	575
Precedence	576
Conservation	578
Countryside conservation	578
Nature conservation	581
Wildlife conservation	583
Historic buildings	586
Museums and galleries	593
Sights of London	599
Hallmarks	604
Economic Statistics	606
Government finance	606
Trade	608
Cost of living	610
Finance	611
British currency	611
Investment business regulation	613
Banking	615
Mutual societies	621
National savings	626
Insurance	629
Stock Exchange	636
Stamp duties	637
Taxation	639
Legal Notes	653
Intellectual Property	677
Media	679
Broadcasting	679
The Press	685
Book Publishers	694
Annual reference books	697

CONTENTS CONTINUED

ORGANIZATIONS   700
Trade and employers' associations   700
Trade unions   702
National academies of scholarship   705
Research councils and associations   707
Sports bodies   713
Clubs   717
Societies and institutions   721

INTERNATIONAL ORGANIZATIONS   751

EUROPEAN UNION   774

COUNTRIES OF THE WORLD   783
Area and population   783
Antarctic   788
Currencies and exchange rates   790
Time zones   794
Countries A–Z   796

BRITISH DEPENDENT TERRITORIES   1071

THE YEAR 1994–5   1081
Events of the Year 1994–5   1081
   Illustrations
   Obituaries   1114
Archaeology   1118
Architecture   1123
Bequests to charity   1129
Broadcasting   1132
Conservation and heritage   1137
Dance   1143
Film   1148
Literature   1152
Nobel Prizes   1156
Opera   1157
Parliament   1162
   Public Acts of Parliament   1171
   White Papers, etc.   1174
The Queen's Awards   1178
Science and discovery   1181
Theatre   1192
Weather   1204
   Monthly data   1210
Sport   1216
   Sports records   1239

ABBREVIATIONS   1242

INDEX   1248
Stop-press   1278

Preface

TO THE 128TH ANNUAL VOLUME 1996

This 128th edition of Whitaker contains all the information on which its readers rely, as well as a number of new and revised items.

The structure of local government in Wales and Scotland changes radically in April 1996. Maps of the new local authority areas and lists of the new councils are included in the Local Government section. Changes affecting English councils in April 1995 and April 1996 are also summarized.

The legal requirement to use metric rather than imperial units of measurement for trading came into force just as this edition went to press. The new legal requirements, and the exceptions to them, are detailed in the Weights and Measures section.

Other new items include a new introduction to the Historic Buildings and Monuments section explaining how buildings are listed and monuments scheduled. In the Transport section the information pertaining to roads, vehicles and driving has been extensively revised and reorganized.

The information about the European Union and its main institutions now constitutes a separate section. The introduction has been revised, now including a summary table of statistics about member states and a chronology of the development of the Union.

As ever, we wish to thank the many organizations and individuals who have provided information for this edition; their assistance is invaluable and we are most grateful to them.

12 DYOTT STREET   HILARY MARSDEN
LONDON WCIA IDF   *Editor*
TEL 0171-836 8911

OCTOBER 1995

The Year 1996

CHRONOLOGICAL CYCLES AND ERAS

Dominical Letter	GF
Epact	10
Golden Number (Lunar Cycle)	II
Julian Period	6709
Roman Indiction	4
Solar Cycle	17

	Beginning
Japanese year Heisei 8	1 January
Regnal year 45	6 February
Chinese year of the Rat	19 February
Hindu new year	20 March
Indian (Saka) year 1918	22 March
Sikh new year	13 April
Muslim year AH 1417	19 May
Jewish year AM 5757	14 September
Roman year 2749 AUC	

RELIGIOUS CALENDARS

Epiphany	6 January
Makara Sankranti	15 January
Ramadan, first day	22 January
Vasant Panchami (Sarasvati-puja)	24 January
Mahashivaratri	17 February
Ash Wednesday	21 February
Holi	4 March
Ramanavami	28 March
Passover, first day	4 April
Good Friday	5 April
Easter Day (Western churches)	7 April
Baisakhi Mela (Sikh new year)	13 April
Easter Day (Greek Orthodox)	14 April
Idu-l-adha	c.30 April
Rogation Sunday	12 May
Ascension Day	16 May
Martyrdom of Guru Arjan Dev Ji	21 May
Feast of Weeks, first day	24 May
Pentecost (Whit Sunday)	26 May
Trinity Sunday	2 June
Corpus Christi	6 June
Raksha-bandhan	28 August
Janmashtami	4 September
Ganesh Chaturthi, first day	16 September
Yom Kippur (Day of Atonement)	23 September
Ganesh festival, last day	26 September
Feast of Tabernacles, first day	28 September
Navaratri festival, first day	13 October
Durga-puja	19 October
Sarasvati-puja	20 October
Dasara	21 October
Diwali (Hindu), first day	10 November
Diwali (Hindu), last day	12 November
Birthday of Guru Nanak Dev Ji	25 November
First Sunday in Advent	1 December
Chanucah, first day	6 December
Martyrdom of Guru Tegh Bahadur Ji	15 December
Christmas Day	25 December

CIVIL CALENDAR

Accession of Queen Elizabeth II	6 February
Duke of York's birthday	19 February
St David's Day	1 March
Prince Edward's birthday	10 March
Commonwealth Day	11 March
St Patrick's Day	17 March
Birthday of Queen Elizabeth II	21 April
St George's Day	23 April
Coronation of Queen Elizabeth II	2 June
Duke of Edinburgh's birthday	10 June
The Queen's Official Birthday	15 June
Princess of Wales' birthday	1 July
Queen Elizabeth the Queen Mother's birthday	4 August
Princess Royal's birthday	15 August
Princess Margaret's birthday	21 August
Lord Mayor's Day	9 November
Remembrance Sunday	10 November
Prince of Wales' birthday	14 November
Wedding Day of Queen Elizabeth II	20 November
St Andrew's Day	30 November

LEGAL CALENDAR

LAW TERMS

Hilary Term	11 January to 3 April
Easter Term	16 April to 24 May
Trinity Term	4 June to 31 July
Michaelmas Term	1 October to 21 December

QUARTER DAYS

England, Wales and Northern Ireland

Lady	25 March
Midsummer	24 June
Michaelmas	29 September
Christmas	25 December

TERM DAYS

Scotland

Candlemas	28 February
Whitsunday	28 May
Lammas	28 August
Martinmas	28 November
Removal Terms	28 May, 28 November

1996

JANUARY

Sunday		7	14	21	28
Monday	1	8	15	22	29
Tuesday	2	9	16	23	30
Wednesday	3	10	17	24	31
Thursday	4	11	18	25	
Friday	5	12	19	26	
Saturday	6	13	20	27	

FEBRUARY

Sunday		4	11	18	25
Monday		5	12	19	26
Tuesday		6	13	20	27
Wednesday		7	14	21	28
Thursday	1	8	15	22	29
Friday	2	9	16	23	
Saturday	3	10	17	24	

MARCH

Sunday		3	10	17	24	31
Monday		4	11	18	25	
Tuesday		5	12	19	26	
Wednesday		6	13	20	27	
Thursday		7	14	21	28	
Friday	1	8	15	22	29	
Saturday	2	9	16	23	30	

APRIL

Sunday		7	14	21	28
Monday	1	8	15	22	29
Tuesday	2	9	16	23	30
Wednesday	3	10	17	24	
Thursday	4	11	18	25	
Friday	5	12	19	26	
Saturday	6	13	20	27	

MAY

Sunday		5	12	19	26
Monday		6	13	20	27
Tuesday		7	14	21	28
Wednesday	1	8	15	22	29
Thursday	2	9	16	23	30
Friday	3	10	17	24	31
Saturday	4	11	18	25	

JUNE

Sunday		2	9	16	23	30
Monday		3	10	17	24	
Tuesday		4	11	18	25	
Wednesday		5	12	19	26	
Thursday		6	13	20	27	
Friday		7	14	21	28	
Saturday	1	8	15	22	29	

JULY

Sunday		7	14	21	28
Monday	1	8	15	22	29
Tuesday	2	9	16	23	30
Wednesday	3	10	17	24	31
Thursday	4	11	18	25	
Friday	5	12	19	26	
Saturday	6	13	20	27	

AUGUST

Sunday		4	11	18	25
Monday		5	12	19	26
Tuesday		6	13	20	27
Wednesday		7	14	21	28
Thursday	1	8	15	22	29
Friday	2	9	16	23	30
Saturday	3	10	17	24	31

SEPTEMBER

Sunday		1	8	15	22	29
Monday		2	9	16	23	30
Tuesday		3	10	17	24	
Wednesday		4	11	18	25	
Thursday		5	12	19	26	
Friday		6	13	20	27	
Saturday		7	14	21	28	

OCTOBER

Sunday		6	13	20	27
Monday		7	14	21	28
Tuesday	1	8	15	22	29
Wednesday	2	9	16	23	30
Thursday	3	10	17	24	31
Friday	4	11	18	25	
Saturday	5	12	19	26	

NOVEMBER

Sunday		3	10	17	24
Monday		4	11	18	25
Tuesday		5	12	19	26
Wednesday		6	13	20	27
Thursday		7	14	21	28
Friday	1	8	15	22	29
Saturday	2	9	16	23	30

DECEMBER

Sunday		1	8	15	22	29
Monday		2	9	16	23	30
Tuesday		3	10	17	24	31
Wednesday		4	11	18	25	
Thursday		5	12	19	26	
Friday		6	13	20	27	
Saturday		7	14	21	28	

PUBLIC HOLIDAYS

	England and Wales	Scotland	Northern Ireland
New Year	1 January	1, 2 January	1 January
St Patrick's Day	—	—	18 March
*Good Friday	5 April	5 April	5 April
Easter Monday	8 April	—	8 April
May Day	6 May	27 May	6 May
Spring	27 May	6 May	27 May
Battle of Boyne	—	—	12 July
Summer	26 August	5 August	26 August
*Christmas	25, 26 December	25, 26 December	25, 26 December

* In England, Wales, and Northern Ireland, Christmas Day and Good Friday are common law holidays
In the Channel Islands, Liberation Day (9 May) is a bank and public holiday

1997

JANUARY

Sunday	5	12	19	26
Monday	6	13	20	27
Tuesday	7	14	21	28
Wednesday	1	8	15	22	29
Thursday	2	9	16	23	30
Friday	3	10	17	24	31
Saturday	4	11	18	25

FEBRUARY

Sunday	2	9	16	23
Monday	3	10	17	24
Tuesday	4	11	18	25
Wednesday	5	12	19	26
Thursday	6	13	20	27
Friday	7	14	21	28
Saturday	1	8	15	22

MARCH

Sunday	2	9	16	23	30
Monday	3	10	17	24	31
Tuesday	4	11	18	25
Wednesday	5	12	19	26
Thursday	6	13	20	27
Friday	7	14	21	28
Saturday	1	8	15	22	29

APRIL

Sunday	6	13	20	27
Monday	7	14	21	28
Tuesday	1	8	15	22	29
Wednesday	2	9	16	23	30
Thursday	3	10	17	24
Friday	4	11	18	25
Saturday	5	12	19	26

MAY

Sunday	4	11	18	25
Monday	5	12	19	26
Tuesday	6	13	20	27
Wednesday	7	14	21	28
Thursday	1	8	15	22	29
Friday	2	9	16	23	30
Saturday	3	10	17	24	31

JUNE

Sunday	1	8	15	22	29
Monday	2	9	16	23	30
Tuesday	3	10	17	24
Wednesday	4	11	18	25
Thursday	5	12	19	26
Friday	6	13	20	27
Saturday	7	14	21	28

JULY

Sunday	6	13	20	27
Monday	7	14	21	28
Tuesday	1	8	15	22	29
Wednesday	2	9	16	23	30
Thursday	3	10	17	24	31
Friday	4	11	18	25
Saturday	5	12	19	26

AUGUST

Sunday	3	10	17	24	31
Monday	4	11	18	25
Tuesday	5	12	19	26
Wednesday	6	13	20	27
Thursday	7	14	21	28
Friday	1	8	15	22	29
Saturday	2	9	16	23	30

SEPTEMBER

Sunday	7	14	21	28
Monday	1	8	15	22	29
Tuesday	2	9	16	23	30
Wednesday	3	10	17	24
Thursday	4	11	18	25
Friday	5	12	19	26
Saturday	6	13	20	27

OCTOBER

Sunday	5	12	19	26
Monday	6	13	20	27
Tuesday	7	14	21	28
Wednesday	1	8	15	22	29
Thursday	2	9	16	23	30
Friday	3	10	17	24	31
Saturday	4	11	18	25

NOVEMBER

Sunday	2	9	16	23	30
Monday	3	10	17	24
Tuesday	4	11	18	25
Wednesday	5	12	19	26
Thursday	6	13	20	27
Friday	7	14	21	28
Saturday	1	8	15	22	29

DECEMBER

Sunday	7	14	21	28
Monday	1	8	15	22	29
Tuesday	2	9	16	23	30
Wednesday	3	10	17	24	31
Thursday	4	11	18	25
Friday	5	12	19	26
Saturday	6	13	20	27

PUBLIC HOLIDAYS

	England and Wales	Scotland	Northern Ireland
New Year	1 January	1, 2 January	1 January
St Patrick's Day	—	—	17 March
*Good Friday	28 March	28 March	28 March
Easter Monday	31 March	—	31 March
May Day	5 May	26 May	5 May
Spring	26 May	5 May	26 May
Battle of Boyne	—	—	14 July
Summer	25 August	4 August	25 August
*Christmas	25, 26 December	25, 26 December	25, 26 December

FORTHCOMING EVENTS 1996

This is the UN International Year for the Eradication of Poverty, the European Year of Lifelong Learning, and the Arts Council Year for Visual Arts, centred around the north of England
The European City of Culture is Copenhagen
* Provisional dates

5 – 14 January	London International Boat Show
	Earl's Court, London
14 – 17 March	Cruft's Dog Show
	National Exhibition Centre,
	Birmingham
14 March –	Ideal Home Exhibition
8 April	Earls Court, London
17 – 19 March	London International Book Fair
	Olympia, London
16 – 21 April	International Antiques Fair
	National Exhibition Centre,
	Birmingham
*24 April – 6	
October	Chichester Festival Theatre season
26 April – 5	
October	Pitlochry Festival Theatre season
*2 – 25 May	Mayfest 1996
	Glasgow
8 – 12 May	Royal Windsor Horse Show
	Home Park, Windsor
11 – 25 May	Sheffield Chamber Music Festival
17 May – 2 June	Bath International Festival
23 – 24 May	Chelsea Flower Show
	Royal Hospital, Chelsea
24 May – 2 June	Hay Festival of Literature
	Hay-on-Wye, Hereford
7 – 23 June	Aldeburgh Festival of Music
	and Arts, Suffolk
*9 June –	Royal Academy Summer Exhibition
18 August	Piccadilly, London
15 June	Trooping the Colour
	Horse Guards Parade, London
1 – 4 July	The Royal Show
	Stoneleigh Park, Kenilworth, Warks
5 – 14 July	York Early Music Festival
6 – 21 July	Cheltenham International Festival
	of Music
9 – 20 July	Royal Tournament
	Earls Court, London
10 – 14 July	Hampton Court Palace Flower Show
	East Molesey, Surrey
*11 – 20 July	Welsh Proms 1996
	St David's Hall, Cardiff
18 July –	Buxton Festival
4 August	Derbyshire
19 July –	Promenade Concerts season
14 September	Royal Albert Hall, London
2 – 24 August	Edinburgh Military Tattoo
	Edinburgh Castle
3 – 10 August	Royal National Eisteddfod of Wales
	Llandeilo
8 – 9 August	Battle of Flowers
	Jersey
11 – 31 August	Edinburgh International Festival
17 – 24 August	Three Choirs Festival
	Worcester
25 – 26 August	Notting Hill Carnival
	Notting Hill, London

30 August –	
3 November	Blackpool Illuminations
7 September	Braemar Royal Highland Gathering
	Aberdeenshire
9 – 13 September	TUC Annual Congress
	Blackpool
*14 – 22 September	Southampton International Boat Show
	Western Esplanade, Southampton
22 – 26 September	Liberal Democrat Conference
	Brighton
30 September –	Labour Party Conference
4 October	Blackpool
8 – 11 October	Conservative Party Conference
	Bournemouth
19 – 27 October	British International Motor Show
	National Exhibition Centre,
	Birmingham
3 November	London to Brighton Veteran Car
	Run
*7 – 24 November	London International Film Festival
9 November	Lord Mayor's Procession and Show
	City of London
10 – 12 November	CBI Annual Conference
	Harrogate
20 – 30 November	Huddersfield Contemporary Music
	Festival
24 – 27 November	Smithfield Show
	Earls Court, London

SPORTS EVENTS

20 January	Rugby Union: France v. England
	Parc des Princes, Paris
	Ireland v. Scotland
	Lansdowne Road, Dublin
3 February	Rugby Union: England v. Wales
	Twickenham, London
	Scotland v. France
	Murrayfield, Edinburgh
17 February	Rugby Union: Wales v. Scotland
	Cardiff Arms Park
	France v. Ireland
	Parc des Princes, Paris
2 March	Rugby Union: Ireland v. Wales
	Lansdowne Road, Dublin
	Scotland v. England
	Murrayfield, Edinburgh
16 March	Rugby Union: England v. Ireland
	Twickenham, London
	Wales v. France
	Cardiff Arms Park
6 April	Oxford and Cambridge Boat Race
	Putney to Mortlake, London
*20 April –	Snooker: World Professional
6 May	Championship
	Crucible Theatre, Sheffield
*21 April	Athletics: London Marathon
27 April	Rugby League: Challenge Cup
	Final
	Wembley Stadium, London
2 – 5 May	Badminton Horse Trials
	Badminton, Avon
4 May	Rugby Union: Pilkington Cup final
	Twickenham, London
11 May	Football: FA Cup final
	Wembley Stadium, London

18 May	Football: Scottish FA Cup final
	Hampden Park, Glasgow
19 May	Football: Welsh FA Cup final
	Cardiff Arms Park
23 May	Cricket: One-day International
	England v. India
	The Oval, London
25 May	Cricket: One-day International
	England v. India
	Headingley, Leeds
26 May	Cricket: One-day International
	England v. India
	Old Trafford, Manchester
3 – 8 June	Golf: British Amateur
	Championship
	Turnberry
6 – 10 June	Cricket: 1st Test Match
	England v. India
	Edgbaston, Birmingham
20 – 24 June	Cricket: 2nd Test Match
	England v. India
	Lord's, London
*24 June – 7 July	Lawn Tennis Championships
	Wimbledon, London
3 – 7 July	Henley Royal Regatta
	Henley-on-Thames
4 – 9 July	Cricket: 3rd Test Match
	England v. India
	Trent Bridge, Nottingham
13 July	Cricket: Benson & Hedges Cup
	final
	Lord's, London
*13 – 27 July	Shooting: NRA Imperial Meetings
	Bisley Camp, Woking, Surrey
*14 July	British Formula 1 Grand Prix
	Silverstone, Northants
18 – 21 July	Golf: Open Championship
	Royal Lytham and St Annes
19 July – 4 August	Olympic Games
	Atlanta, Georgia
25 – 29 July	Cricket: 1st Test Match
	England v. Pakistan
	Lord's, London
3 – 10 August	Yachting: Cowes Week
	Isle of Wight
8 – 12 August	Cricket: 2nd Test Match
	England v. Pakistan
	Headingley, Leeds
22 – 26 August	Cricket: 3rd Test Match
	England v. Pakistan
	The Oval, London
29 August	Cricket: One-day International
	England v. Pakistan
	Old Trafford, Manchester
31 August	Cricket: One-day International
	England v. Pakistan
	Edgbaston, Birmingham
1 September	Cricket: One-day International
	England v. Pakistan
	Trent Bridge, Nottingham
5 – 8 September	Eventing: Burghley Horse Trials
	Burghley, Lincs
7 September	Cricket: NatWest Trophy final
	Lord's, London
20 – 22 September	Golf: Solheim Cup
	St Pierre, Gwent
*24 – 29 October	Horse of the Year Show
	Wembley Arena, London

HORSERACING

14 March	Cheltenham Gold Cup
23 March	Lincoln Handicap
	Doncaster
30 March	Grand National
	Aintree
4 May	Two Thousand Guineas
	Newmarket
5 May	One Thousand Guineas
	Newmarket
7 June	The Oaks
	Epsom
8 June	The Derby
	Epsom
8 June	Coronation Cup
	Epsom
18 – 21 June	Royal Ascot
27 July	King George VI and Queen
	Elizabeth Diamond Stakes
	Ascot
14 September	St Leger
	Doncaster
5 October	Cambridgeshire Handicap
	Newmarket
19 October	Cesarewitch
	Newmarket

The horseracing fixtures are the copyright of the British Horse-racing Board

CENTENARIES OF 1996

1096	
*	First crusade to free the Holy Land begins
1496	
*	Santo Domingo (now capital of the Dominican Republic) founded, the first European town in the Americas
1596	
13 January	Jan van Goyen, Dutch artist, born
28 January	Sir Francis Drake, navigator, died
31 March	René Descartes, French philosopher, born
1796	
14 May	Edward Jenner carries out first vaccination against smallpox
25 June (os)/ 6 July (ns)	Nicholas I, Tsar of Russia 1825–55, born
21 July	Robert Burns, poet, died
10 November	Catherine II (the Great) of Russia died
1896	
1 January	Alfred Austin appointed Poet Laureate
5 January	Frederic, Lord Leighton, artist and President of the Royal Academy, died
20 February	Sir John Millais elected President of the Royal Academy
1 March	Battle of Adowa: Abyssinia defeated Italy
22 March	Thomas Hughes, novelist, died
4 April	National Portrait Gallery, London, opened
5 April	Modern Olympic Games revived at Athens
3 May	Dodie Smith, author, born
4 May	*Daily Mail* first published
7 May	Kitty Godfree, lawn tennis and badminton player, born
19 May	Clara Schumann, German musician, died
19 June	The Duchess of Windsor (Mrs Wallis Simpson) born
1 July	Harriet Beecher-Stowe, American anti-slavery novelist, died
19 July	A. J. Cronin, novelist, born
9 August	Jean Piaget, Swiss psychologist, born
24 September	F. Scott Fitzgerald, American novelist, born
3 October	William Morris, designer, poet and socialist, died
11 October	Dr E. W. Benson, Archbishop of Canterbury 1883–96, died
1 November	Edmund Blunden, poet and scholar, born
14 November	First London to Brighton 'Emancipation' car rally
16 November	Sir Oswald Mosley, politician and fascist, born
10 December	Alfred Nobel, Swedish chemist, died

CENTENARIES OF 1997

597	
*	St Augustine landed in England and converted the kingdom of Kent to Christianity
1497	
24 June	John Cabot, Italian explorer, discovered Newfoundland
1697	
18 October	Antonio Canaletto, Venetian artist, born
10 November	William Hogarth, painter and pictorial satirist, born
2 December	The rebuilt St Paul's Cathedral opened
1797	
31 January	Franz Schubert, Austrian composer, born
14 February	Battle of Cape St Vincent
2 March	Horace Walpole, politician and man of letters, died
27 March	Alfred, Comte de Vigny, French poet, born
8 July	Edmund Burke, statesman and political writer, died
30 August	Mary Wollstonecraft Shelley, novelist, born
10 September	Mary Wollstonecraft Godwin, writer, died
11 October	Battle of Camperdown
16 October	Earl of Cardigan, commander of the charge of the Light Brigade in the Crimean War, born
13 December	Heinrich Heine, German poet and journalist, born
1897	
8 January	Dennis Wheatley, novelist, born
12 January	Sir Isaac Pitman, inventor of phonetic shorthand system, died
19 February	Charles Blondin, tightrope walker famous for crossing Niagara Falls, died
3 April	Johannes Brahms, German composer, died
17 April	Thornton Wilder, American novelist and playwright, born
22 May	Blackwall Tunnel opened in London
27 May	Sir John Cockcroft, nuclear physicist and Nobel Prize winner, born
12 June	Leon Goossens, musician, born
12 June	Anthony Eden, Prime Minister 1955–7, born
21 July	Tate Gallery opened on Millbank
11 August	Enid Blyton, children's author and educationalist, born
3 September	Cecil Parker, film actor, born
25 September	William Faulkner, American novelist and Nobel Prize winner, born
29 October	Joseph Goebbels, Nazi leader, born
15 November	Aneurin Bevan, politician and Labour party leader, born
12 December	Royal Automobile Club founded under the name The Automobile Club of Great Britain

* exact date not known

Astronomy

The following pages give astronomical data for each month of the year 1996. There are four pages of data for each month. All data are given for 0h Greenwich Mean Time (GMT), i.e. at the midnight at the beginning of the day named. This applies also to data for the months when British Summer Time is in operation (for dates, *see* below).

The astronomical data are given in a form suitable for observation with the naked eye or with a small telescope. These data do not attempt to replace the *Astronomical Almanac* for professional astronomers.

A fuller explanation of how to use the astronomical data is given on pages 71–3.

CALENDAR FOR EACH MONTH

The calendar for each month shows dates of religious, civil and legal significance for the year 1996.

The days in bold type are the principal holy days and the festivals and greater holy days of the Church of England as set out in the calendar of the Alternative Service Book 1980, and the calendar of Sundays set out in the Book of Common Prayer. Observance of certain festivals and greater holy days is transferred if the day falls on a principal holy day. The calendar shows the date on which holy days and festivals are to be observed in 1996.

The days in small capitals are dates of significance in the calendars of non-Anglican denominations and non-Christian religions.

The days in italic type are dates of civil and legal significance. The royal anniversaries shown in italic type are the days on which the Union flag is to be flown.

The rest of the calendar comprises days of general interest and the dates of birth or death of well-known people.

Fuller explanations of the various calendars can be found under Time Measurement and Calendars (pages 81–9).

The zodiacal signs through which the Sun is passing during each month are illustrated. The date of transition from one sign to the next, to the nearest hour, is given under Astronomical Phenomena.

JULIAN DATE

The Julian date on 1996 January 0.0 is 2450082.5. To find the Julian date for any other date in 1996 (at 0h GMT), add the day-of-the-year number on the extreme right of the calendar for each month to the Julian date for January 0.0.

SEASONS

The seasons are defined astronomically as follows:

Spring from the vernal equinox to the summer solstice
Summer from the summer solstice to the autumnal equinox
Autumn from the autumnal equinox to the winter solstice
Winter from the winter solstice to the vernal equinox

The seasons in 1996 are:

Northern hemisphere

Vernal equinox	March 20d 08h GMT
Summer solstice	June 21d 02h GMT
Autumnal equinox	September 22d 18h GMT
Winter solstice	December 21d 14h GMT

Southern hemisphere

Autumnal equinox	March 20d 08h GMT
Winter solstice	June 21d 02h GMT
Vernal equinox	September 22d 18h GMT
Summer solstice	December 21d 14h GMT

The longest day of the year, measured from sunrise to sunset, is at the summer solstice. For the remainder of this century the longest day in the United Kingdom will fall each year on 21 June. *See also* page 81.

The shortest day of the year is at the winter solstice. For the remainder of this century the shortest day in the United Kingdom will fall on 21 December in 1996, 1997 and 2000, and on 22 December in 1998 and 1999. *See also* page 81.

The equinox is the point at which day and night are of equal length all over the world. *See also* page 81.

In popular parlance, the seasons in the northern hemisphere comprise the following months:

Spring	March April May
Summer	June July August
Autumn	September October November
Winter	December January February

BRITISH SUMMER TIME

British Summer Time is the legal time for general purposes during the period in which it is in operation (*see also* page 75). During this period, clocks are kept one hour ahead of Greenwich Mean Time. The hour of changeover is 01h Greenwich Mean Time. The duration of Summer Time in 1996 (subject to confirmation) is:

March 31 01h GMT to October 27 01h GMT

January 1996

FIRST MONTH, 31 DAYS. *Janus*, god of the portal, facing two ways, past and future

1	*Monday*	**The Naming of Jesus.** *Bank Holiday in the UK*	*week* 52 *day* 1
2	*Tuesday*	*Bank Holiday in Scotland.* Eleanor Rathbone d. 1946	2
3	*Wednesday*	William Joyce (Lord Haw Haw) exec. 1946	3
4	*Thursday*	Louis Braille b. 1809. T. S. Eliot d. 1965	4
5	*Friday*	Twelfth Night. Frederic, Lord Leighton d. 1896	5
6	*Saturday*	**The Epiphany.** Rudolf Nureyev d. 1993	6
7	*Sunday*	**1st S. after Epiphany.** Trevor Howard d. 1988	*week* 1 *day* 7
8	*Monday*	Robert Baden-Powell d. 1941. Chou En-lai d. 1976	8
9	*Tuesday*	Napoleon III d. 1873. Katherine Mansfield d. 1923	9
10	*Wednesday*	Dame Barbara Hepworth b. 1903. Frank Bridge d. 1941	10
11	*Thursday*	*Hilary Law Sittings begin.* Domenico Cimarosa d. 1801	11
12	*Friday*	Johann Pestalozzi b. 1746. Jack London b. 1876	12
13	*Saturday*	Jan van Goyen b. 1596. Stephen Foster d. 1864	13
14	*Sunday*	**2nd S. after Epiphany.** Edmund Halley d. 1742	*week* 2 *day* 14
15	*Monday*	Emma, Lady Hamilton d. 1815. Pres. Gamal Nasser b. 1918	15
16	*Tuesday*	Edward Gibbon d. 1794. Sir John Moore d. 1809	16
17	*Wednesday*	Leonhard Fuchs b. 1501. Adm. Lord Beatty b. 1871	17
18	*Thursday*	A. A. Milne b. 1882. Rudyard Kipling d. 1936	18
19	*Friday*	Gen. Robert E. Lee b. 1807. Sir Alfred Beit b. 1903	19
20	*Saturday*	George Burns b. 1896. George V d. 1936	20
21	*Sunday*	**3rd S. after Epiphany.** Benny Hill b. 1925	*week* 3 *day* 21
22	*Monday*	RAMADAN begins. ⚔ Rorke's Drift 1879	22
23	*Tuesday*	William Pitt (the Younger) d. 1806. Edvard Munch d. 1944	23
24	*Wednesday*	Pierre de Beaumarchais b. 1732. Sir Winston Churchill d. 1965	24
25	*Thursday*	**Conversion of St Paul.** Dorothy Wordsworth d. 1855	25
26	*Friday*	Australia Day. Edward G. Robinson d. 1973	26
27	*Saturday*	Lewis Carroll b. 1832. Kaiser Wilhelm II b. 1859	27
28	*Sunday*	**4th S. after Epiphany.** Sir Francis Drake d. 1596	*week* 4 *day* 28
29	*Monday*	Field Marshal Earl Haig d. 1928	29
30	*Tuesday*	Charles I exec. 1649. Francis Poulenc d. 1963	30
31	*Wednesday*	John Galsworthy d. 1933. Derek Jarman b. 1942	31

ASTRONOMICAL PHENOMENA

d	h	
2	16	Mercury at greatest elongation E.19°
4	07	Earth at perihelion (147 million km)
9	22	Mercury at stationary point
13	11	Mars in conjunction with Mercury. Mars 3° S.
16	03	Neptune in conjunction
18	20	Jupiter in conjunction with Moon. Jupiter 5° S.
18	22	Mercury in inferior conjunction
20	07	Mercury in conjunction with Moon. Mercury 2° S.
20	19	Sun's longitude 300° ≈
21	05	Mars in conjunction with Moon. Mars 6° S.
21	07	Uranus in conjunction
23	05	Venus in conjunction with Moon. Venus 4° S.
24	01	Saturn in conjunction with Moon. Saturn 4° S.
30	10	Mercury at stationary point

MINIMA OF ALGOL

d	h	d	h	d	h
3	08.6	14	19.8	26	07.1
6	05.4	17	16.7	29	04.0
9	02.2	20	13.5		
11	23.0	23	10.3		

CONSTELLATIONS

The following constellations are near the meridian at

	d	h		d	h
December	1	24	January	16	21
December	16	23	February	1	20
January	1	22	February	15	19

Draco (below the Pole), Ursa Minor (below the Pole), Camelopardus, Perseus, Auriga, Taurus, Orion, Eridanus and Lepus

THE MOON

Phases, Apsides and Node	d	h	m
○ Full Moon	5	20	51
☾ Last Quarter	13	20	45
● New Moon	20	12	50
☽ First Quarter	27	11	14
Apogee (406,528 km)	5	11	14
Perigee (357,246 km)	19	23	00

Mean longitude of ascending node on January 1, 202°

THE SUN

s.d. 16′.3

Day	Right Ascension	Dec. —	Equation of time	Rise 52°	Rise 56°	Transit	Set 52°	Set 56°	Sidereal time	Transit of First Point of Aries
	h m s	° ′	m s	h m	h m	h m	h m	h m	h m s	h m s
1	18 42 49	23 04	− 3 04	8 08	8 31	12 03	15 59	15 35	6 39 45	17 17 24
2	18 47 14	23 00	− 3 32	8 08	8 31	12 04	16 00	15 37	6 43 42	17 13 28
3	18 51 39	22 54	− 4 00	8 08	8 31	12 04	16 01	15 38	6 47 38	17 09 32
4	18 56 03	22 49	− 4 28	8 08	8 30	12 05	16 02	15 39	6 51 35	17 05 37
5	19 00 27	22 43	− 4 55	8 07	8 30	12 05	16 03	15 41	6 55 32	17 01 41
6	19 04 50	22 36	− 5 22	8 07	8 30	12 06	16 04	15 42	6 59 28	16 57 45
7	19 09 13	22 29	− 5 49	8 07	8 29	12 06	16 06	15 43	7 03 25	16 53 49
8	19 13 36	22 22	− 6 15	8 06	8 28	12 06	16 07	15 45	7 07 21	16 49 53
9	19 17 58	22 14	− 6 40	8 06	8 28	12 07	16 08	15 47	7 11 18	16 45 57
10	19 22 20	22 05	− 7 05	8 05	8 27	12 07	16 10	15 48	7 15 14	16 42 01
11	19 26 41	21 57	− 7 30	8 05	8 26	12 08	16 11	15 50	7 19 11	16 38 05
12	19 31 01	21 47	− 7 54	8 04	8 25	12 08	16 13	15 52	7 23 07	16 34 09
13	19 35 21	21 38	− 8 17	8 03	8 24	12 08	16 14	15 53	7 27 04	16 30 13
14	19 39 40	21 28	− 8 40	8 03	8 23	12 09	16 16	15 55	7 31 01	16 26 17
15	19 43 59	21 17	− 9 02	8 02	8 22	12 09	16 17	15 57	7 34 57	16 22 22
16	19 48 17	21 06	− 9 24	8 01	8 21	12 10	16 19	15 59	7 38 54	16 18 26
17	19 52 35	20 55	− 9 44	8 00	8 20	12 10	16 20	16 01	7 42 50	16 14 30
18	19 56 51	20 43	−10 05	7 59	8 19	12 10	16 22	16 02	7 46 47	16 10 34
19	20 01 08	20 31	−10 24	7 58	8 17	12 11	16 24	16 04	7 50 43	16 06 38
20	20 05 23	20 19	−10 43	7 57	8 16	12 11	16 25	16 06	7 54 40	16 02 42
21	20 09 38	20 06	−11 01	7 56	8 15	12 11	16 27	16 08	7 58 36	15 58 46
22	20 13 51	19 53	−11 18	7 51	8 13	12 11	16 29	16 10	8 02 33	15 54 50
23	20 18 05	19 39	−11 35	7 54	8 12	12 12	16 30	16 12	8 06 30	15 50 54
24	20 22 17	19 25	−11 51	7 52	8 10	12 12	16 32	16 15	8 10 26	15 46 58
25	20 26 28	19 11	−12 06	7 51	8 08	12 12	16 34	16 17	8 14 23	15 43 02
26	20 30 39	18 56	−12 20	7 50	8 07	12 12	16 36	16 19	8 18 19	15 39 07
27	20 34 49	18 41	−12 33	7 48	8 05	12 13	16 37	16 21	8 22 16	15 35 11
28	20 38 58	18 26	−12 46	7 47	8 03	12 13	16 39	16 23	8 26 12	15 31 15
29	20 43 06	18 10	−12 57	7 46	8 02	12 13	16 41	16 25	8 30 09	15 27 19
30	20 47 14	17 54	−13 08	7 44	8 00	12 13	16 43	16 27	8 34 05	15 23 23
31	20 51 20	17 38	−13 18	7 43	7 58	12 13	16 45	16 29	8 38 02	15 19 27

DURATION OF TWILIGHT (in minutes)

Latitude	52°	56°	52°	56°	52°	56°	52°	56°
	1 January		11 January		21 January		31 January	
Civil	41	47	40	45	38	43	37	41
Nautical	84	96	82	93	80	90	78	87
Astronomical	125	141	123	138	120	134	117	130

THE NIGHT SKY

Mercury reaches its greatest eastern elongation (19°) on the 2nd and is visible in the early evening for the first ten days of the month, low above the south-western horizon at the end of evening civil twilight. Mercury's magnitude fades from − 0.6 to +0.5 during this period.

Venus, magnitude − 4.0, is a brilliant evening object in the south-western sky and by the end of the month can still be seen for as long as three hours after sunset. The waxing crescent Moon will be seen near Venus on the evenings of the 22nd and 23rd.

Mars is too close to the Sun for observation.

Jupiter is not visible at first, but is emerging from the morning twilight and by the middle of the month it becomes visible for a short time above the south-eastern horizon before dawn. Its magnitude is − 1.8. Jupiter is in Sagittarius.

Saturn is visible as an evening object in the south-western sky, magnitude +1.2. The waxing crescent Moon passes 4° north of Saturn on the night of the 23rd to 24th.

THE MOON

Day	RA	Dec.	Hor. par.	Semi-diam.	Sun's co-long.	PA of Bright Limb	Phase	Age	Rise 52°	Rise 56°	Transit	Set 52°	Set 56°
	h m	°	'	'	°	°	%	d	h m	h m	h m	h m	h m
1	2 59	+14.9	54.9	15.0	31	252	80	9.9	13 18	13 03	20 59	3 48	4 02
2	3 49	+17.0	54.5	14.8	43	254	87	10.9	13 55	13 37	21 47	4 48	5 05
3	4 39	+18.4	54.2	14.8	56	256	93	11.9	14 36	14 18	22 35	5 43	6 02
4	5 29	+18.9	54.0	14.7	68	255	97	12.9	15 24	15 06	23 22	6 33	6 52
5	6 19	+18.6	53.9	14.7	80	245	99	13.9	16 17	16 00	—	7 17	7 35
6	7 08	+17.5	53.9	14.7	92	171	100	14.9	17 14	16 59	0 09	7 55	8 11
7	7 57	+15.6	54.0	14.7	104	123	99	15.9	18 15	18 02	0 56	8 28	8 41
8	8 45	+13.1	54.2	14.8	116	116	96	16.9	19 18	19 08	1 41	8 57	9 07
9	9 33	+10.0	54.5	14.8	128	115	91	17.9	20 22	20 16	2 26	9 22	9 30
10	10 19	+ 6.5	54.8	14.9	140	115	85	18.9	21 27	21 25	3 10	9 46	9 50
11	11 06	+ 2.6	55.3	15.1	153	115	78	19.9	22 34	22 35	3 54	10 09	10 10
12	11 53	- 1.4	55.9	15.2	165	114	69	20.9	23 42	23 47	4 39	10 32	10 30
13	12 42	- 5.4	56.6	15.4	177	113	59	21.9	—	—	5 25	10 57	10 51
14	13 32	- 9.3	57.4	15.7	189	111	49	22.9	0 53	1 01	6 14	11 25	11 15
15	14 25	-12.9	58.3	15.9	201	109	38	23.9	2 05	2 17	7 05	11 58	11 45
16	15 21	-15.8	59.2	16.1	213	106	27	24.9	3 18	3 34	8 01	12 38	12 21
17	16 21	-17.9	60.1	16.4	226	103	18	25.9	4 29	4 47	8 59	13 27	13 09
18	17 23	-18.8	60.8	16.6	238	100	10	26.9	5 35	5 54	10 01	14 27	14 09
19	18 26	-18.5	61.2	16.7	250	99	4	27.9	6 32	6 50	11 03	15 38	15 21
20	19 30	-16.8	61.4	16.7	262	114	1	28.9	7 21	7 36	12 05	16 56	16 42
21	20 32	-13.9	61.2	16.7	274	220	1	0.5	8 01	8 12	13 04	18 17	18 07
22	21 32	-10.1	60.7	16.5	287	240	3	1.5	8 34	8 42	14 00	19 37	19 31
23	22 29	- 5.8	59.9	16.3	299	243	9	2.5	9 04	9 07	14 54	20 56	20 54
24	23 23	- 1.3	59.0	16.1	311	245	16	3.5	9 30	9 30	15 44	22 11	22 13
25	0 15	+ 3.1	58.0	15.8	323	246	25	4.5	9 56	9 52	16 34	23 23	23 29
26	1 06	+ 7.3	57.1	15.6	335	248	35	5.5	10 23	10 15	17 21	—	—
27	1 56	+10.9	56.2	15.3	347	250	45	6.5	10 50	10 40	18 09	0 32	0 42
28	2 46	+14.0	55.5	15.1	360	252	55	7.5	11 21	11 07	18 56	1 38	1 51
29	3 36	+16.3	54.9	15.0	12	256	65	8.5	11 56	11 40	19 44	2 40	2 55
30	4 26	+17.9	54.4	14.8	24	259	74	9.5	12 36	12 18	20 31	3 37	3 54
31	5 16	+18.7	54.1	14.8	36	262	82	10.5	13 21	13 03	21 19	4 29	4 47

MERCURY

Day	RA	Dec.	Diam.	Phase	Transit	5° high 52°	5° high 56°
	h m	°	"	%	h m	h m	h m
1	20 06	-21.7	7	65	13 27	16 44	16 13
3	20 15	-20.9	7	58	13 28	16 50	16 22
5	20 22	-20.1	7	50	13 26	16 55	16 28
7	20 27	-19.3	8	41	13 22	16 57	16 32
9	20 29	-18.6	8	32	13 16	16 55	16 31
11	20 29	-18.0	9	22	13 07	16 49	16 26
13	20 25	-17.6	9	13	12 54	16 39	16 16
15	20 18	-17.4	10	6	12 38	16 24	16 02
17	20 08	-17.3	10	2	12 11	16 06	15 44
19	19 58	-17.5	10	1	12 02	15 46	15 24
21	19 47	-17.7	10	2	11 44	8 01	8 24
23	19 37	-18.0	10	7	11 27	7 46	8 09
25	19 29	-18.4	10	12	11 12	7 33	7 57
27	19 24	-18.7	9	19	10 59	7 23	7 48
29	19 22	-19.1	9	26	10 49	7 16	7 41
31	19 21	-19.4	9	32	10 42	7 11	7 37

VENUS

Day	RA	Dec.	Diam.	Phase	Transit	5° high 52°	5° high 56°
	h m	°	"	%	h m	h m	h m
1	21 03	-18.8	13	84	14 23	18 02	17 38
6	21 27	-16.9	13	83	14 28	18 21	18 00
11	21 51	-14.8	13	82	14 32	18 39	18 21
16	22 14	-12.6	14	80	14 36	18 56	18 41
21	22 37	-10.3	14	79	14 39	19 13	19 01
26	23 00	- 7.8	14	78	14 42	19 30	19 20
31	23 22	- 5.3	15	76	14 44	19 46	19 39

MARS

Day	RA	Dec.	Diam.	Phase	Transit	5° high 52°	5° high 56°
1	19 45	-22.3	4	99	13 05	16 15	15 42
6	20 02	-21.6	4	99	13 02	16 18	15 47
11	20 18	-20.8	4	100	12 58	16 21	15 52
16	20 34	-19.8	4	100	12 55	16 25	15 58
21	20 50	-18.8	4	100	12 51	16 29	16 04
26	21 06	-17.7	4	100	12 48	16 33	16 10
31	21 22	-16.5	4	100	12 44	16 37	16 17

SUNRISE AND SUNSET

	London		Bristol		Birmingham		Manchester		Newcastle		Glasgow		Belfast	
	0°05′	51°30′	2°35′	51°28′	1°55′	52°28′	2°15′	53°28′	1°37′	54°59′	4°14′	55°52′	5°56′	54°35′
	h m	h m	h m	h m	h m	h m	h m	h m	h m	h m	h m	h m	h m	h m
1	8 06	16 01	8 16	16 12	8 18	16 04	8 25	16 00	8 31	15 48	8 47	15 53	8 46	16 08
2	8 06	16 02	8 16	16 13	8 18	16 05	8 25	16 01	8 31	15 50	8 47	15 54	8 46	16 09
3	8 06	16 04	8 16	16 14	8 18	16 06	8 25	16 02	8 31	15 51	8 47	15 56	8 46	16 10
4	8 06	16 05	8 15	16 15	8 18	16 07	8 24	16 03	8 31	15 52	8 47	15 57	8 45	16 12
5	8 05	16 06	8 15	16 16	8 18	16 08	8 24	16 04	8 30	15 53	8 46	15 58	8 45	16 13
6	8 05	16 07	8 15	16 17	8 17	16 10	8 24	16 06	8 30	15 55	8 46	16 00	8 45	16 14
7	8 05	16 08	8 15	16 18	8 17	16 11	8 23	16 07	8 29	15 56	8 45	16 01	8 44	16 16
8	8 04	16 10	8 14	16 20	8 16	16 12	8 23	16 08	8 29	15 58	8 44	16 03	8 44	16 17
9	8 04	16 11	8 14	16 21	8 16	16 14	8 22	16 10	8 28	15 59	8 44	16 04	8 43	16 19
10	8 03	16 12	8 13	16 22	8 15	16 15	8 22	16 11	8 27	16 01	8 43	16 06	8 42	16 20
11	8 03	16 14	8 13	16 24	8 15	16 17	8 21	16 13	8 27	16 02	8 42	16 08	8 42	16 22
12	8 02	16 15	8 12	16 25	8 14	16 18	8 20	16 14	8 26	16 04	8 41	16 09	8 41	16 23
13	8 01	16 17	8 11	16 27	8 13	16 20	8 19	16 16	8 25	16 05	8 40	16 11	8 40	16 25
14	8 01	16 18	8 11	16 28	8 12	16 21	8 19	16 18	8 24	16 07	8 39	16 13	8 39	16 27
15	8 00	16 20	8 10	16 30	8 12	16 23	8 18	16 19	8 23	16 09	8 38	16 15	8 38	16 28
16	7 59	16 21	8 09	16 31	8 11	16 24	8 17	16 21	8 22	16 11	8 37	16 16	8 37	16 30
17	7 58	16 23	8 08	16 33	8 10	16 26	8 16	16 23	8 21	16 13	8 36	16 18	8 36	16 32
18	7 57	16 24	8 07	16 35	8 09	16 28	8 15	16 24	8 20	16 14	8 35	16 20	8 35	16 34
19	7 56	16 26	8 06	16 36	8 08	16 29	8 14	16 26	8 18	16 16	8 33	16 22	8 34	16 35
20	7 55	16 28	8 05	16 38	8 07	16 31	8 12	16 28	8 17	16 18	8 32	16 24	8 32	16 37
21	7 54	16 29	8 04	16 39	8 06	16 33	8 11	16 30	8 16	16 20	8 31	16 26	8 31	16 39
22	7 53	16 31	8 03	16 41	8 04	16 34	8 10	16 31	8 14	16 22	8 29	16 28	8 30	16 41
23	7 52	16 33	8 02	16 43	8 03	16 36	8 09	16 33	8 13	16 24	8 28	16 30	8 28	16 43
24	7 51	16 34	8 01	16 45	8 02	16 38	8 07	16 35	8 12	16 26	8 26	16 32	8 27	16 45
25	7 50	16 36	7 59	16 46	8 01	16 40	8 06	16 37	8 10	16 28	8 25	16 34	8 26	16 47
26	7 48	16 38	7 58	16 48	7 59	16 42	8 05	16 39	8 09	16 30	8 23	16 36	8 24	16 49
27	7 47	16 40	7 57	16 50	7 58	16 43	8 03	16 41	8 07	16 32	8 21	16 38	8 23	16 51
28	7 46	16 41	7 55	16 52	7 56	16 45	8 02	16 43	8 05	16 34	8 20	16 40	8 21	16 53
29	7 44	16 43	7 54	16 53	7 55	16 47	8 00	16 45	8 04	16 36	8 18	16 43	8 19	16 55
30	7 43	16 45	7 53	16 55	7 53	16 49	7 59	16 47	8 02	16 38	8 16	16 45	8 18	16 57
31	7 41	16 47	7 51	16 57	7 52	16 51	7 57	16 48	8 00	16 40	8 14	16 47	8 16	16 59

JUPITER

Day	RA	Dec.	Transit	5° high	
				52°	56°
	h m	° ′	h m	h m	h m
1	17 57.7	−23 11	11 17	8 15	8 51
11	18 07.5	−23 12	10 47	7 46	8 22
21	18 17.1	−23 10	10 17	7 16	7 51
31	18 26.3	−23 06	9 47	6 45	7 20

Diameters – equatorial 32″ polar 30″

SATURN

Day	RA	Dec.	Transit	5° high	
				52°	56°
	h m	° ′	h m	h m	h m
1	23 24.3	− 6 09	16 42	21 36	21 28
11	23 27.1	− 5 50	16 05	21 01	20 53
21	23 30.2	− 5 28	15 29	20 27	20 19
31	23 33.8	− 5 04	14 54	19 54	19 46

Diameters – equatorial 16″ polar 15″
Rings – major axis 37″ minor axis 1″

URANUS

Day	RA	Dec.	Transit	10° high	
				52°	56°
	h m	° ′	h m	h m	h m
1	20 06.5	−20 48	13 25	15 56	15 10
11	20 08.9	−20 41	12 48	15 21	14 35
21	20 11.3	−20 34	12 11	14 45	14 00
31	20 13.8	−20 26	11 34	14 09	13 25

Diameter 4″

NEPTUNE

Day	RA	Dec.	Transit	10° high	
				52°	56°
	h m	° ′	h m	h m	h m
1	19 46.0	−20 42	13 04	10 32	11 17
11	19 47.6	−20 38	12 26	9 53	10 38
21	19 49.2	−20 34	11 49	9 15	10 00
31	19 50.8	−20 30	11 11	8 36	9 21

Diameter 2″

February 1996

SECOND MONTH, 28 or 29 DAYS. *Februa*, Roman festival of Purification

1	*Thursday*	Dame Clara Butt b. 1873. Buster Keaton d. 1966	*week* 4 *day* 32
2	*Friday*	**Presentation of Christ.** James Joyce b. 1882	33
3	*Saturday*	Walter Bagehot b. 1826. Elizabeth Blackwell b. 1821	34
4	*Sunday*	**9th S. before Easter/Septuagesima**	*week* 5 *day* 35
5	*Monday*	Sir John Pritchard b. 1921	36
6	*Tuesday*	*Queen's Accession 1952.* Queen Anne I b. 1665	37
7	*Wednesday*	Daniel Malan d. 1959. Witold Lutoslawski d. 1994	38
8	*Thursday*	John Ruskin b. 1819. Sir Victor Gollancz d. 1967	39
9	*Friday*	Alban Berg b. 1885. Jim Laker b. 1922	40
10	*Saturday*	PAYE introduced 1944	41
11	*Sunday*	**8th S. before Easter/Sexagesima.**	*week* 6 *day* 42
12	*Monday*	Cotton Mather b. 1663. Lillie Langtry d. 1929	43
13	*Tuesday*	Eleanor Farjeon b. 1881. Richard Wagner d. 1883	44
14	*Wednesday*	St Valentine's Day. P.G. Wodehouse d. 1975	45
15	*Thursday*	Introduction of decimal currency in Britain 1971	46
16	*Friday*	Sir Geraint Evans b. 1922. John McEnroe b. 1959	47
17	*Saturday*	Ruth Rendell b. 1930. Graham Sutherland d. 1980	48
18	*Sunday*	**7th S. before Easter/Quinquagesima**	*week* 7 *day* 49
19	*Monday*	*Duke of York b. 1960. Chinese Year of the Rat*	50
20	*Tuesday*	Shrove Tuesday. Henry James Pye b. 1745	51
21	*Wednesday*	**Ash Wednesday.** Sir Frederick Banting b. 1941	52
22	*Thursday*	Amerigo Vespucci d. 1512. George Washington b. 1732	53
23	*Friday*	John Keats d. 1821. Dame Nellie Melba d. 1931	54
24	*Saturday*	Henry Cavendish d. 1810. Bobby Moore d. 1993	55
25	*Sunday*	**1st S. in Lent.** Sir John Tenniel d. 1914	*week* 8 *day* 56
26	*Monday*	Frank Bridge b. 1879. Everton Weekes b. 1925	57
27	*Tuesday*	German Reichstag burnt down 1933	58
28	*Wednesday*	Michel de Montaigne b. 1533. Linus Pauling b. 1901	59
29	*Tuesday*	Gioacchino Rossini b. 1792. E. F. Benson d. 1940	60

ASTRONOMICAL PHENOMENA

d   h
2   15   Saturn in conjunction with Venus. Saturn 1° S.
11 21   Mercury at greatest elongation W 26°.
15 14   Jupiter in conjunction with Moon. Jupiter 5° S.
17 04   Mercury in conjunction with Moon. Mercury 5° S.
19 05   Mars in conjunction with Moon. Mars 4° S.
19 09   Sun's longitude 330° ♓
20 16   Saturn in conjunction with Moon. Saturn 4° S.
22 05   Venus in conjunction with Moon. Venus 0°.04 N.

MINIMA OF ALGOL

d	h	d	h	d	h
1	00.8	12	12.1	23	23.3
3	21.6	15	08.9	26	20.2
6	18.4	18	05.7	29	17.0
9	15.2	21	02.5		

CONSTELLATIONS

The following constellations are near the meridian at

	d	h		d	h
January	1	24	February	15	21
January	16	23	March	1	20
February	1	22	March	16	19

Draco (below the Pole), Camelopardus, Auriga, Taurus, Gemini, Orion, Canis Minor, Monoceros, Lepus, Canis Major and Puppis

THE MOON

Phases, Apsides and Node	d	h	m
○ Full Moon	4	15	58
☾ Last Quarter	12	08	37
● New Moon	18	23	30
☽ First Quarter	26	05	52
Apogee (406,185 km)	1	15	32
Perigee (360,870 km)	17	08	34
Apogee (405,308 km)	29	07	01

Mean longitude of ascending node on February 1, 201°

THE SUN
s.d. 16'.2

Day	Right Ascension	Dec. —	Equation of time	Rise 52°	Rise 56°	Transit	Set 52°	Set 56°	Sidereal time	Transit of First Point of Aries
	h m s	° '	m s	h m	h m	h m	h m	h m	h m s	h m s
1	20 55 26	17 22	−13 28	7 41	7 56	12 14	16 47	16 32	8 41 59	15 15 31
2	20 59 31	17 05	−13 36	7 40	7 54	12 14	16 48	16 34	8 45 55	15 11 35
3	21 03 35	16 47	−13 43	7 38	7 52	12 14	16 50	16 36	8 49 52	15 07 39
4	21 07 38	16 30	−13 50	7 36	7 50	12 14	16 52	16 38	8 53 48	15 03 43
5	21 11 41	16 12	−13 56	7 35	7 49	12 14	16 54	16 40	8 57 45	14 59 47
6	21 15 42	15 54	−14 01	7 33	7 46	12 14	16 56	16 42	9 01 41	14 55 52
7	21 19 43	15 36	−14 05	7 31	7 44	12 14	16 58	16 45	9 05 38	14 51 56
8	21 23 43	15 17	−14 09	7 30	7 42	12 14	17 00	16 47	9 09 34	14 48 00
9	21 27 43	14 58	−14 12	7 28	7 40	12 14	17 01	16 49	9 13 31	14 44 04
10	21 31 41	14 39	−14 14	7 26	7 38	12 14	17 03	16 51	9 17 28	14 40 08
11	21 35 39	14 19	−14 15	7 24	7 36	12 14	17 05	16 53	9 21 24	14 36 12
12	21 39 36	14 00	−14 15	7 22	7 34	12 14	17 07	16 56	9 25 21	14 32 16
13	21 43 32	13 40	−14 15	7 20	7 32	12 14	17 09	16 58	9 29 17	14 28 20
14	21 47 28	13 20	−14 14	7 18	7 29	12 14	17 11	17 00	9 33 14	14 24 24
15	21 51 22	13 00	−14 12	7 17	7 27	12 14	17 13	17 02	9 37 10	14 20 28
16	21 55 16	12 39	−14 10	7 15	7 25	12 14	17 14	17 04	9 41 07	14 16 32
17	21 59 10	12 18	−14 06	7 13	7 22	12 14	17 16	17 07	9 45 03	14 12 37
18	22 03 02	11 57	−14 02	7 11	7 20	12 14	17 18	17 09	9 49 00	14 08 41
19	22 06 54	11 36	−13 58	7 09	7 18	12 14	17 20	17 11	9 52 56	14 04 45
20	22 10 46	11 15	−13 52	7 07	7 15	12 14	17 22	17 13	9 56 53	14 00 49
21	22 14 36	10 53	−13 47	7 05	7 13	12 14	17 24	17 15	10 00 50	13 56 53
22	22 18 26	10 32	−13 40	7 02	7 11	12 14	17 26	17 18	10 04 46	13 52 57
23	22 22 15	10 10	−13 33	7 00	7 08	12 13	17 27	17 20	10 08 43	13 49 01
24	22 26 04	9 48	−13 25	6 58	7 06	12 13	17 29	17 22	10 12 39	13 45 05
25	22 29 52	9 26	−13 16	6 56	7 03	12 13	17 31	17 24	10 16 36	13 41 09
26	22 33 39	9 04	−13 07	6 54	7 01	12 13	17 33	17 26	10 20 32	13 37 13
27	22 37 26	8 41	−12 57	6 52	6 58	12 13	17 35	17 28	10 24 29	13 33 17
28	22 41 12	8 19	−12 47	6 50	6 56	12 13	17 37	17 30	10 28 25	13 29 22
29	22 44 58	7 56	−12 36	6 48	6 53	12 13	17 38	17 33	10 32 22	13 25 26

DURATION OF TWILIGHT (in minutes)

Latitude	52°	56°	52°	56°	52°	56°	52°	56°
	1 February		11 February		21 February		28 February	
Civil	37	41	35	39	34	38	34	38
Nautical	77	86	75	83	74	81	73	81
Astronomical	117	130	114	126	113	125	112	124

THE NIGHT SKY

Mercury is unsuitably placed for observation throughout the month.

Venus, magnitude −4.1, continues to be visible as a brilliant evening object in the western sky for several hours after sunset. Venus and Saturn are near each other early in the month and Venus passes only 1°S. of Saturn on the 2nd. Venus is about 100 times brighter than Saturn. On the evenings of the 21st and 22nd the thin crescent Moon is near the planet.

Mars is unsuitably placed for observation.

Jupiter, magnitude −1.9, is visible as a morning object, low in the south-eastern sky before sunrise.

Saturn, magnitude +1.2, continues to be visible as an evening object in the south-western sky after sunset, though observers should not expect to see the rings as the Earth passes through the ring-plane on the 11th to 12th. By the end of the month Saturn will be lost to view in the gathering twilight.

Zodiacal Light. The evening cone may be observed in the western sky after the end of twilight from the 6th to the 20th. This faint phenomenon is only visible in good conditions, in the absence of both moonlight and artificial lighting.

THE MOON

Day	RA	Dec.	Hor. par.	Semi-diam.	Sun's co-long.	PA of Bright Limb	Phase	Age	Rise 52°	Rise 56°	Transit	Set 52°	Set 56°
	h m	°	′	′	°	°	%	d	h m	h m	h m	h m	h m
1	6 06	+18.7	54.0	14.7	48	265	88	11.5	14 12	13 54	22 06	5 15	5 33
2	6 55	+17.8	54.0	14.7	60	267	94	12.5	15 07	14 51	22 53	5 55	6 12
3	7 45	+16.2	54.1	14.7	72	265	97	13.5	16 07	15 53	23 39	6 30	6 44
4	8 33	+13.9	54.3	14.8	85	251	99	14.5	17 09	16 59	—	7 01	7 12
5	9 21	+10.9	54.5	14.9	97	157	100	15.5	18 13	18 06	0 24	7 28	7 36
6	10 08	+ 7.5	54.8	14.9	109	124	98	16.5	19 19	19 15	1 08	7 52	7 58
7	10 55	+ 3.7	55.2	15.0	121	118	95	17.5	20 25	20 25	1 53	8 16	8 18
8	11 42	− 0.2	55.7	15.2	133	116	90	18.5	21 33	21 36	2 38	8 39	8 38
9	12 31	− 4.3	56.2	15.3	145	114	83	19.5	22 42	22 49	3 23	9 04	8 59
10	13 20	− 8.2	56.8	15.5	157	112	74	20.5	23 52	—	4 11	9 30	9 22
11	14 11	−11.7	57.4	15.6	170	109	65	21.5	—	0 03	5 00	10 00	9 48
12	15 05	−14.8	58.1	15.8	182	106	54	22.5	1 03	1 17	5 52	10 36	10 21
13	16 02	−17.1	58.8	16.0	194	102	43	23.5	2 12	2 29	6 48	11 20	11 02
14	17 00	−18.4	59.5	16.2	206	98	32	24.5	3 18	3 36	7 45	12 12	11 54
15	18 01	−18.6	60.1	16.4	218	93	22	25.5	4 17	4 35	8 45	13 16	12 57
16	19 03	−17.5	60.5	16.5	230	90	13	26.5	5 08	5 25	9 45	14 28	14 12
17	20 04	−15.3	60.7	16.6	243	88	6	27.5	5 52	6 05	10 45	15 45	15 33
18	21 04	−12.0	60.7	16.5	255	91	2	28.5	6 29	6 38	11 42	17 06	16 57
19	22 03	− 7.9	60.4	16.5	267	164	0	0.0	7 00	7 06	12 37	18 26	18 22
20	22 59	− 3.5	59.8	16.3	279	236	2	1.0	7 29	7 31	13 30	19 44	19 44
21	23 53	+ 1.1	59.0	16.1	291	243	6	2.0	7 56	7 54	14 22	21 00	21 04
22	0 46	+ 5.4	58.2	15.8	304	246	12	3.0	8 23	8 18	15 12	22 12	22 20
23	1 38	+ 9.4	57.3	15.6	316	249	20	4.0	8 52	8 42	16 01	23 21	23 33
24	2 29	+12.7	56.4	15.4	328	252	29	5.0	9 22	9 10	16 49	—	—
25	3 20	+15.4	55.6	15.2	340	256	38	6.0	9 56	9 41	17 38	0 26	0 41
26	4 11	+17.3	55.0	15.0	352	260	48	7.0	10 34	10 17	18 26	1 27	1 43
27	5 01	+18.3	54.5	14.9	5	264	57	8.0	11 17	10 59	19 14	2 21	2 39
28	5 51	+18.6	54.2	14.8	17	267	67	9.0	12 06	11 48	20 01	3 10	3 28
29	6 41	+18.0	54.1	14.7	29	271	75	10.0	13 00	12 43	20 48	3 52	4 09

MERCURY

Day	RA	Dec.	Diam.	Phase	Transit	5° high 52°	5° high 56°
	h m	°	″	%	h m	h m	h m
1	19 22	−19.6	8	35	10 39	7 09	7 35
3	19 25	−19.9	8	41	10 34	7 06	7 33
5	19 29	−20.1	8	47	10 31	7 04	7 32
7	19 35	−20.3	7	51	10 29	7 04	7 31
9	19 42	−20.4	7	56	10 28	7 03	7 31
11	19 50	−20.4	7	59	10 29	7 04	7 32
13	19 59	−20.3	7	63	10 30	7 04	7 32
15	20 08	−20.2	7	66	10 31	7 05	7 32
17	20 18	−20.0	6	69	10 34	7 05	7 32
19	20 29	−19.7	6	71	10 36	7 05	7 32
21	20 39	−19.3	6	74	10 39	7 06	7 31
23	20 51	−18.8	6	76	10 43	7 05	7 30
25	21 02	−18.3	6	78	10 46	7 05	7 28
27	21 14	−17.6	6	80	10 50	7 04	7 27
29	21 26	−16.9	6	82	10 54	7 03	7 24
31	21 38	−16.1	5	83	10 58	7 02	7 22

VENUS

Day	RA	Dec.	Diam.	Phase	Transit	5° high 52°	5° high 56°
	h m	°	″	%	h m	h m	h m
1	23 26	− 4.7	15	76	14 44	19 49	19 42
6	23 48	− 2.1	15	74	14 46	20 05	20 00
11	0 09	+ 0.5	16	73	14 48	20 20	20 17
16	0 30	+ 3.1	16	71	14 49	20 35	20 34
21	0 51	+ 5.7	17	69	14 50	20 49	20 51
26	1 12	+ 8.2	17	67	14 52	21 04	21 07
31	1 33	+10.7	18	65	14 53	21 17	21 23

MARS

Day	RA	Dec.	Diam.	Phase	Transit	5° high 52°	5° high 56°
1	21 25	−16.3	4	100	12 43	16 38	16 18
6	21 41	−15.0	4	100	12 39	16 42	16 24
11	21 56	−13.7	4	100	12 34	16 46	16 30
16	22 11	−12.3	4	100	12 30	16 50	16 36
21	22 26	−10.9	4	100	12 25	16 54	16 41
26	22 41	− 9.4	4	100	12 20	16 58	16 46
31	22 56	− 7.9	4	100	12 15	17 02	16 51

SUNRISE AND SUNSET

	London		Bristol		Birmingham		Manchester		Newcastle		Glasgow		Belfast	
	0°05′	51°30′	2°35′	51°28′	1°55′	52°28′	2°15′	53°28′	1°37′	54°59′	4°14′	55°52′	5°56′	54°35′
	h m	h m	h m	h m	h m	h m	h m	h m	h m	h m	h m	h m	h m	h m
1	7 40	16 49	7 50	16 59	7 50	16 53	7 55	16 50	7 59	16 42	8 13	16 49	8 14	17 01
2	7 38	16 50	7 48	17 00	7 49	16 55	7 54	16 52	7 57	16 44	8 11	16 51	8 12	17 03
3	7 37	16 52	7 47	17 02	7 47	16 56	7 52	16 54	7 55	16 46	8 09	16 53	8 11	17 05
4	7 35	16 54	7 45	17 04	7 46	16 58	7 50	16 56	7 53	16 48	8 07	16 56	8 09	17 07
5	7 33	16 56	7 43	17 06	7 44	17 00	7 48	16 58	7 51	16 50	8 05	16 58	8 07	17 09
6	7 32	16 58	7 42	17 08	7 42	17 02	7 47	17 00	7 49	16 53	8 03	17 00	8 05	17 11
7	7 30	16 59	7 40	17 10	7 40	17 04	7 45	17 02	7 47	16 55	8 01	17 02	8 03	17 13
8	7 28	17 01	7 38	17 11	7 39	17 06	7 43	17 04	7 45	16 57	7 59	17 04	8 01	17 15
9	7 27	17 03	7 37	17 13	7 37	17 08	7 41	17 06	7 43	16 59	7 57	17 06	7 59	17 17
10	7 25	17 05	7 35	17 15	7 35	17 10	7 39	17 08	7 41	17 01	7 55	17 09	7 57	17 20
11	7 23	17 07	7 33	17 17	7 33	17 12	7 37	17 10	7 39	17 03	7 52	17 11	7 55	17 22
12	7 21	17 09	7 31	17 19	7 31	17 13	7 35	17 12	7 37	17 05	7 50	17 13	7 53	17 24
13	7 19	17 10	7 29	17 21	7 29	17 15	7 33	17 14	7 35	17 07	7 48	17 15	7 51	17 26
14	7 18	17 12	7 27	17 22	7 27	17 17	7 31	17 16	7 33	17 09	7 46	17 17	7 49	17 28
15	7 16	17 14	7 26	17 24	7 25	17 19	7 29	17 18	7 31	17 12	7 44	17 20	7 47	17 30
16	7 14	17 16	7 24	17 26	7 23	17 21	7 27	17 20	7 28	17 14	7 41	17 22	7 45	17 32
17	7 12	17 18	7 22	17 28	7 21	17 23	7 25	17 22	7 26	17 16	7 39	17 24	7 42	17 34
18	7 10	17 20	7 20	17 30	7 19	17 25	7 23	17 24	7 24	17 18	7 37	17 26	7 40	17 36
19	7 08	17 21	7 18	17 31	7 17	17 27	7 21	17 26	7 22	17 20	7 34	17 28	7 38	17 38
20	7 06	17 23	7 16	17 33	7 15	17 29	7 19	17 28	7 19	17 22	7 32	17 30	7 36	17 40
21	7 04	17 25	7 14	17 35	7 13	17 31	7 16	17 30	7 17	17 24	7 30	17 33	7 34	17 42
22	7 02	17 27	7 12	17 37	7 11	17 32	7 14	17 32	7 15	17 26	7 27	17 35	7 31	17 44
23	7 00	17 29	7 10	17 39	7 09	17 34	7 12	17 34	7 13	17 28	7 25	17 37	7 29	17 46
24	6 58	17 30	7 08	17 40	7 07	17 36	7 10	17 36	7 10	17 30	7 22	17 39	7 27	17 48
25	6 56	17 32	7 06	17 42	7 05	17 38	7 08	17 38	7 08	17 32	7 20	17 41	7 24	17 50
26	6 54	17 34	7 04	17 44	7 02	17 40	7 05	17 40	7 05	17 34	7 18	17 43	7 22	17 52
27	6 51	17 36	7 01	17 46	7 00	17 42	7 03	17 42	7 03	17 37	7 15	17 45	7 20	17 54
28	6 49	17 38	6 59	17 48	6 58	17 44	7 01	17 43	7 01	17 39	7 13	17 48	7 17	17 57
29	6 47	17 39	6 57	17 49	6 56	17 45	6 59	17 45	6 58	17 41	7 10	17 50	7 15	17 59

JUPITER

Day	RA	Dec.	Transit	5° high	
				52°	56°
	h m	° ′	h m	h m	h m
1	18 27.2	−23 05	9 44	6 42	7 17
11	18 36.0	−22 59	9 13	6 10	6 46
21	18 44.2	−22 52	8 42	5 38	6 13
31	18 51.7	−22 44	8 10	5 05	5 40

Diameters – equatorial 33″ polar 31″

SATURN

Day	RA	Dec.	Transit	5° high	
				52°	56°
	h m	° ′	h m	h m	h m
1	23 34.2	−5 01	14 50	19 51	19 43
11	23 38.2	−4 35	14 15	19 18	19 10
21	23 42.4	−4 07	13 40	18 45	18 38
31	23 46.8	−3 38	13 05	18 13	18 06

Diameters – equatorial 16″ polar 14″
Rings – major axis 36″ minor axis 0″

URANUS

Day	RA	Dec.	Transit	10° high	
				52°	56°
	h m	° ′	h m	h m	h m
1	20 14.0	−20 25	11 30	8 55	9 39
11	20 16.4	−20 18	10 53	8 17	9 00
21	20 18.7	−20 11	10 16	7 38	8 21
31	20 20.8	−20 04	9 39	7 00	7 42

Diameter 4″

NEPTUNE

Day	RA	Dec.	Transit	10° high	
				52°	56°
	h m	° ′	h m	h m	h m
1	19 50.9	−20 30	11 07	8 33	9 17
11	19 52.5	−20 26	10 29	7 54	8 38
21	19 53.9	−20 22	9 51	7 16	7 59
31	19 55.2	−20 19	9 13	6 37	7 20

Diameter 2″

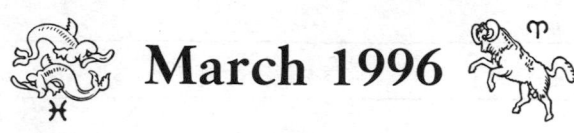

March 1996 ♈

THIRD MONTH, 31 DAYS. *Mars*, Roman god of battle

1	*Friday*	St David's Day. Lytton Strachey b. 1880	*week 8 day* 61
2	*Saturday*	Cardinal Archbishop Hume of Westminster b. 1923	62
3	*Sunday*	**2nd S. in Lent.** William Godwin b. 1756	*week 9 day* 63
4	*Monday*	Opening of the Forth Railway Bridge 1890	64
5	*Tuesday*	William Beveridge b. 1879. Sir Rex Harrison b. 1908	65
6	*Wednesday*	Elizabeth Barrett Browning b. 1806	66
7	*Thursday*	Sir Edwin Landseer b. 1802. Stevie Smith d. 1971	67
8	*Friday*	Ruggiero Leoncavallo b. 1858. Sir Thomas Beecham d. 1961	68
9	*Saturday*	Imogen Holst d. 1984. Prof C. Northcote Parkinson d. 1993	69
10	*Sunday*	**3rd S. in Lent.** *Prince Edward b. 1964*	*week 10 day* 70
11	*Monday*	Commonwealth Day. William Huskisson b. 1770	71
12	*Tuesday*	Cesare Borgia d. 1507. Gabriele d'Annunzio b. 1864	72
13	*Wednesday*	Joseph Priestley b. 1733. Earl Grey b. 1764	73
14	*Thursday*	Albert Einstein b. 1879. Karl Marx d. 1883	74
15	*Friday*	Lord Melbourne b. 1779. Sir Henry Bessemer d. 1898	75
16	*Saturday*	Georg Ohm b. 1787	76
17	*Sunday*	**4th S. in Lent.** St Patrick's Day. Mothering Sunday	*week 11 day* 77
18	*Monday*	*Bank Holiday in Northern Ireland*	78
19	*Tuesday*	**St Joseph of Nazareth.** Sir Richard Burton b. 1821	79
20	*Wednesday*	HINDU NEW YEAR. Henry IV d. 1413	80
21	*Thursday*	J. S. Bach b. 1685. Robert Southey d. 1843	81
22	*Friday*	Thomas Hughes d. 1896. Stephen Sondheim b. 1930	82
23	*Saturday*	Princess Eugenie of York b. 1990	83
24	*Sunday*	**5th S. in Lent.** Elizabeth I d. 1603	*week 12 day* 84
25	*Monday*	**The Annunciation.** Claude Debussy d. 1918	85
26	*Tuesday*	Robert Frost b. 1874. David Lloyd George d. 1945	86
27	*Wednesday*	James Callaghan b. 1912. Yuri Gagarin d. 1968	87
28	*Thursday*	Modest Mussorgsky d. 1881. Virginia Woolf d. 1941	88
29	*Friday*	⚔Towton Field 1461. John Major b. 1943	89
30	*Saturday*	Goya b. 1746. James Cagney d. 1986	90
31	*Sunday*	**Palm Sunday.** Andrew Marvell b. 1621	*week 13 day* 91

ASTRONOMICAL PHENOMENA

d h
- 4 14 Mars in conjunction
- 5 20 Pluto at stationary point
- 14 05 Jupiter in conjunction with Moon. Jupiter 5° S.
- 17 19 Saturn in conjunction
- 18 18 Mercury in conjunction with Moon. Mercury 4° S.
- 19 05 Mars in conjunction with Moon. Mars 3° S.
- 19 08 Saturn in conjunction with Moon. Saturn 3° S.
- 20 08 Sun's longitude 0°♈
- 22 02 Saturn in conjunction with Mars. Saturn 1° S.
- 23 03 Venus in conjunction with Moon. Venus 5° N.
- 23 09 Saturn in conjunction with Mercury. Saturn 0°.3 S.
- 24 03 Mars in conjunction with Mercury. Mars 0°.7 N.
- 28 08 Mercury in superior conjunction.

MINIMA OF ALGOL

d	h	d	h	d	h
3	13.8	15	01.1	23	15.6
6	10.6	17	21.9	26	12.4
9	07.5	20	18.7	29	09.2
12	04.3				

CONSTELLATIONS

The following constellations are near the meridian at

	d	h		d	h
February	1	24	March	16	21
February	15	23	April	1	20
March	1	22	April	15	19

Cepheus (below the Pole), Camelopardus, Lynx, Gemini, Cancer, Leo, Canis Minor, Hydra, Monoceros, Canis Major and Puppis

THE MOON

Phases, Apsides and Node	d	h	m
○ Full Moon	5	09	23
☾ Last Quarter	12	17	15
● New Moon	19	10	45
☽ First Quarter	27	01	31
Perigee (366,265 km)	16	05	38
Apogee (404,502 km)	28	02	38

Mean longitude of ascending node on March 1, 199°

THE SUN   s.d. 16'.1

Day	Right Ascension	Dec.	Equation of time	Rise 52°	Rise 56°	Transit	Set 52°	Set 56°	Sidereal time	Transit of First Point of Aries
	h m s	° '	m s	h m	h m	h m	h m	h m	h m s	h m s
1	22 48 43	−7 33	−12 24	6 45	6 51	12 12	17 40	17 35	10 36 19	13 21 30
2	22 52 28	−7 11	−12 13	6 43	6 48	12 12	17 42	17 37	10 40 15	13 17 34
3	22 56 12	−6 48	−12 00	6 41	6 46	12 12	17 44	17 39	10 44 12	13 13 38
4	22 59 55	−6 25	−11 47	6 39	6 43	12 12	17 46	17 41	10 48 08	13 09 42
5	23 03 39	−6 01	−11 34	6 37	6 41	12 11	17 47	17 43	10 52 05	13 05 46
6	23 07 21	−5 38	−11 20	6 34	6 38	12 11	17 49	17 45	10 56 01	13 01 50
7	23 11 04	5 15	11 06	6 32	6 36	12 11	17 51	17 47	10 59 58	12 57 54
8	23 14 45	−4 52	−10 51	6 30	6 33	12 11	17 53	17 49	11 03 54	12 53 58
9	23 18 27	−4 28	−10 36	6 28	6 30	12 10	17 54	17 52	11 07 51	12 50 03
10	23 22 08	−4 05	−10 21	6 25	6 28	12 10	17 56	17 54	11 11 48	12 46 07
11	23 25 49	−3 41	−10 05	6 23	6 25	12 10	17 58	17 56	11 15 44	12 42 11
12	23 29 30	−3 18	− 9 49	6 21	6 23	12 10	18 00	17 58	11 19 41	12 38 15
13	23 33 10	−2 54	− 9 33	6 18	6 20	12 09	18 01	18 00	11 23 37	12 34 19
14	23 36 50	−2 30	− 9 16	6 16	6 17	12 09	18 03	18 02	11 27 34	12 30 23
15	23 40 30	−2 07	− 9 00	6 14	6 15	12 09	18 05	18 04	11 31 30	12 26 27
16	23 44 10	−1 43	− 8 43	6 11	6 12	12 09	18 07	18 06	11 35 27	12 22 31
17	23 47 49	−1 19	− 8 26	6 09	6 10	12 08	18 08	18 08	11 39 23	12 18 35
18	23 51 28	−0 55	− 8 08	6 07	6 07	12 08	18 10	18 10	11 43 20	12 14 39
19	23 55 07	−0 32	− 7 51	6 05	6 04	12 08	18 12	18 12	11 47 17	12 10 43
20	23 58 46	−0 08	− 7 33	6 02	6 02	12 07	18 14	18 14	11 51 13	12 06 48
21	0 02 25	+0 16	− 7 16	6 00	5 59	12 07	18 15	18 16	11 55 10	12 02 52
22	0 06 04	+0 39	− 6 58	5 58	5 56	12 07	18 17	18 18	11 59 06	11 58 56
23	0 09 43	+1 03	− 6 40	5 55	5 54	12 07	18 19	18 20	12 03 03	11 55 00
24	0 13 21	+1 27	− 6 22	5 53	5 51	12 06	18 20	18 22	12 06 59	11 51 04
25	0 16 59	+1 50	− 6 04	5 51	5 49	12 06	18 22	18 25	12 10 56	11 47 08
26	0 20 38	+2 14	− 5 46	5 48	5 46	12 06	18 24	18 27	12 14 52	11 43 12
27	0 24 16	+2 37	− 5 27	5 46	5 43	12 05	18 26	18 29	12 18 49	11 39 16
28	0 27 55	+3 01	− 5 09	5 44	5 41	12 05	18 27	18 31	12 22 45	11 35 20
29	0 31 33	+3 24	− 4 51	5 41	5 38	12 05	18 29	18 33	12 26 42	11 31 24
30	0 35 11	+3 48	− 4 33	5 39	5 35	12 04	18 31	18 35	12 30 39	11 27 28
31	0 38 50	+4 11	− 4 15	5 37	5 33	12 04	18 32	18 37	12 34 35	11 23 33

DURATION OF TWILIGHT (in minutes)

Latitude	52°	56°	52°	56°	52°	56°	52°	56°
	1 March		11 March		21 March		31 March	
Civil	34	38	34	37	34	37	34	38
Nautical	73	81	73	80	74	82	76	84
Astronomical	112	124	113	125	116	129	120	136

THE NIGHT SKY

Mercury is too close to the Sun for observation.

Venus continues to be visible as a brilliant evening object in the western sky, magnitude −4.3. The thin crescent Moon will be seen near Venus on the evenings of the 22nd and 23rd.

Mars is in conjunction with the Sun on the 4th and therefore unsuitably placed for observation.

Jupiter continues to be visible as a conspicuous morning object, low in the south-eastern sky before sunrise, magnitude −2.1. Jupiter is in Sagittarius. On the morning of the 14th the Moon, just after Last Quarter, passes 5° north of the planet. The four Galilean satellites of Jupiter provide an interesting spectacle to the observer with a good pair of binoculars, providing that they are rigidly supported.

Saturn is in conjunction with the Sun on the 17th and is therefore too close to the Sun for observation.

Zodiacal Light. The evening cone may be observed stretching up from the western horizon, along the ecliptic, after the end of twilight, from the 7th to the 21st.

THE MOON

Day	RA	Dec.	Hor. par.	Semi- diam.	Sun's co- long.	PA of Bright Limb	Phase	Age	Rise 52°	Rise 56°	Transit	Set 52°	Set 56°
	h m	°	'	'	°	°	%	d	h m	h m	h m	h m	h m
1	7 30	+16.6	54.1	14.8	41	274	83	11.0	13 58	13 43	21 34	4 29	4 44
2	8 19	+14.5	54.3	14.8	53	277	89	12.0	14 59	14 47	22 20	5 02	5 14
3	9 07	+11.8	54.6	14.9	65	278	94	13.0	16 02	15 54	23 05	5 30	5 40
4	9 55	+ 8.5	55.0	15.0	77	276	98	14.0	17 08	17 03	23 50	5 56	6 02
5	10 42	+ 4.8	55.4	15.1	90	257	100	15.0	18 15	18 13	—	6 20	6 24
6	11 30	+ 0.9	55.9	15.2	102	130	100	16.0	19 23	19 25	0 35	6 44	6 44
7	12 19	− 3.2	56.3	15.4	114	116	97	17.0	20 32	20 38	1 21	7 09	7 05
8	13 08	− 7.1	56.8	15.5	126	112	93	18.0	21 43	21 52	2 09	7 35	7 28
9	14 00	−10.8	57.3	15.6	138	109	87	19.0	22 53	23 06	2 58	8 04	7 54
10	14 53	−14.0	57.8	15.8	150	105	79	20.0	—	—	3 49	8 38	8 25
11	15 48	−16.5	58.3	15.9	163	101	69	21.0	0 03	0 19	4 43	9 19	9 02
12	16 46	−18.0	58.7	16.0	175	97	58	22.0	1 09	1 26	5 39	10 08	9 50
13	17 45	−18.5	59.1	16.1	187	92	47	23.0	2 09	2 27	6 36	11 05	10 47
14	18 44	−17.8	59.5	16.2	199	87	36	24.0	3 01	3 18	7 34	12 12	11 55
15	19 44	−16.0	59.7	16.3	211	83	25	25.0	3 46	4 01	8 32	13 24	13 11
16	20 43	−13.2	59.9	16.3	223	80	16	26.0	4 24	4 36	9 28	14 41	14 31
17	21 40	− 9.5	59.8	16.3	236	77	8	27.0	4 58	5 05	10 23	15 59	15 53
18	22 36	− 5.3	59.6	16.2	248	78	3	28.0	5 27	5 31	11 16	17 17	17 15
19	23 30	− 0.9	59.1	16.1	260	87	0	29.0	5 55	5 55	12 08	18 33	18 36
20	0 24	+ 3.6	58.6	16.0	272	239	0	0.6	6 22	6 18	12 59	19 48	19 54
21	1 16	+ 7.7	57.9	15.8	285	249	3	1.6	6 50	6 43	13 49	21 00	21 10
22	2 09	+11.4	57.1	15.6	297	253	8	2.6	7 20	7 09	14 39	22 08	22 21
23	3 01	+14.4	56.3	15.3	309	256	14	3.6	7 53	7 39	15 28	23 12	23 28
24	3 52	+16.6	55.6	15.2	321	260	22	4.6	8 30	8 14	16 18	—	—
25	4 44	+17.9	55.0	15.0	333	264	31	5.6	9 12	8 54	17 06	0 10	0 28
26	5 35	+18.5	54.6	14.9	346	268	40	6.6	9 59	9 41	17 54	1 02	1 20
27	6 25	+18.1	54.3	14.8	358	273	50	7.6	10 51	10 34	18 42	1 48	2 05
28	7 14	+17.0	54.2	14.8	10	276	59	8.6	11 47	11 32	19 28	2 27	2 43
29	8 03	+15.2	54.3	14.8	22	280	68	9.6	12 46	12 34	20 13	3 01	3 14
30	8 51	+12.7	54.5	14.9	34	283	77	10.6	13 49	13 39	20 59	3 31	3 41
31	9 39	+ 9.6	54.9	15.0	46	285	84	11.6	14 53	14 47	21 43	3 58	4 05

MERCURY

Day	RA	Dec.	Diam.	Phase	Transit	5° high 52°	5° high 56°
	h m	°	"	%	h m	h m	h m
1	21 32	−16.5	5	82	10 56	7 02	7 23
3	21 44	−15.7	5	84	11 00	7 01	7 20
5	21 56	−14.8	5	86	11 05	6 59	7 17
7	22 08	−13.7	5	87	11 09	6 57	7 14
9	22 21	−12.6	5	89	11 14	6 55	7 10
11	22 34	−11.4	5	90	11 19	6 53	7 07
13	22 46	−10.2	5	92	11 24	6 50	7 03
15	22 59	− 8.8	5	93	11 29	6 48	6 59
17	23 13	− 7.4	5	95	11 35	6 45	6 54
19	23 26	− 5.9	5	96	11 40	6 42	6 50
21	23 40	− 4.3	5	97	11 46	6 39	6 46
23	23 53	− 2.6	5	98	11 52	6 36	6 42
25	0 07	− 0.9	5	99	11 58	6 33	6 37
27	0 21	+ 0.9	5	100	12 04	17 40	17 38
29	0 36	+ 2.7	5	100	12 11	17 56	17 56
31	0 50	+ 4.6	5	99	12 18	18 13	18 14

VENUS

Day	RA	Dec.	Diam.	Phase	Transit	5° high 52°	5° high 56°
	h m	°	"	%	h m	h m	h m
1	1 29	+10.2	18	66	14 52	21 15	21 20
6	1 49	+12.6	18	64	14 54	21 28	21 36
11	2 10	+14.9	19	61	14 55	21 42	21 51
16	2 31	+17.0	20	59	14 56	21 54	22 06
21	2 52	+19.0	21	57	14 57	22 07	22 20
26	3 13	+20.8	22	54	14 58	22 18	22 34
31	3 33	+22.4	23	52	14 59	22 29	22 46

MARS

Day	RA	Dec.	Diam.	Phase	Transit	5° high 52°	5° high 56°
1	22 53	− 8.2	4	100	12 16	17 01	16 50
6	23 08	− 6.6	4	100	12 11	17 04	16 55
11	23 22	− 5.1	4	100	12 06	17 08	17 00
16	23 37	− 3.5	4	100	12 01	17 11	17 05
21	23 51	− 1.9	4	100	11 55	17 14	17 09
26	0 05	− 0.4	4	100	11 50	17 16	17 13
31	0 19	+ 1.2	4	100	11 44	17 19	17 17

SUNRISE AND SUNSET

	London 0°05' 51°30'		Bristol 2°35' 51°28'		Birmingham 1°55' 52°28'		Manchester 2°15' 53°28'		Newcastle 1°37' 54°59'		Glasgow 4°14' 55°52'		Belfast 5°56' 54°35'	
	h m	h m	h m	h m	h m	h m	h m	h m	h m	h m	h m	h m	h m	h m
1	6 45	17 41	6 55	17 51	6 54	17 47	6 56	17 47	6 56	17 43	7 08	17 52	7 13	18 01
2	6 43	17 43	6 53	17 53	6 51	17 49	6 54	17 49	6 53	17 45	7 05	17 54	7 10	18 03
3	6 41	17 45	6 51	17 55	6 49	17 51	6 52	17 51	6 51	17 47	7 03	17 56	7 08	18 05
4	6 39	17 46	6 48	17 56	6 47	17 53	6 49	17 53	6 49	17 49	7 00	17 58	7 05	18 07
5	6 36	17 48	6 46	17 58	6 45	17 55	6 47	17 55	6 46	17 51	6 58	18 00	7 03	18 08
6	6 34	17 50	6 44	18 00	6 42	17 56	6 45	17 57	6 44	17 53	6 55	18 02	7 00	18 10
7	6 32	17 52	6 42	18 02	6 40	17 58	6 42	17 59	6 41	17 55	6 52	18 04	6 58	18 12
8	6 30	17 53	6 40	18 03	6 38	18 00	6 40	18 01	6 39	17 57	6 50	18 07	6 56	18 14
9	6 27	17 55	6 37	18 05	6 35	18 02	6 38	18 02	6 36	17 59	6 47	18 09	6 53	18 16
10	6 25	17 57	6 35	18 07	6 33	18 04	6 35	18 04	6 34	18 01	6 45	18 11	6 51	18 18
11	6 23	17 59	6 33	18 09	6 31	18 05	6 33	18 06	6 31	18 03	6 42	18 13	6 48	18 20
12	6 21	18 00	6 31	18 10	6 29	18 07	6 30	18 08	6 29	18 05	6 40	18 15	6 46	18 22
13	6 19	18 02	6 28	18 12	6 26	18 09	6 28	18 10	6 26	18 07	6 37	18 17	6 43	18 24
14	6 16	18 04	6 26	18 14	6 24	18 11	6 26	18 12	6 24	18 09	6 34	18 19	6 41	18 26
15	6 14	18 05	6 24	18 15	6 22	18 12	6 23	18 14	6 21	18 11	6 32	18 21	6 38	18 28
16	6 12	18 07	6 22	18 17	6 19	18 14	6 21	18 15	6 18	18 13	6 29	18 23	6 36	18 30
17	6 09	18 09	6 19	18 19	6 17	18 16	6 18	18 17	6 16	18 15	6 27	18 25	6 33	18 32
18	6 07	18 10	6 17	18 20	6 15	18 18	6 16	18 19	6 13	18 17	6 24	18 27	6 31	18 34
19	6 05	18 12	6 15	18 22	6 12	18 20	6 13	18 21	6 11	18 19	6 21	18 29	6 28	18 36
20	6 03	18 14	6 13	18 24	6 10	18 21	6 11	18 23	6 08	18 21	6 19	18 31	6 26	18 38
21	6 00	18 16	6 10	18 26	6 07	18 23	6 09	18 25	6 06	18 23	6 16	18 33	6 23	18 40
22	5 58	18 17	6 08	18 27	6 05	18 25	6 06	18 27	6 03	18 24	6 13	18 35	6 21	18 42
23	5 56	18 19	6 06	18 29	6 03	18 27	6 04	18 28	6 01	18 26	6 11	18 37	6 18	18 44
24	5 53	18 21	6 03	18 31	6 00	18 28	6 01	18 30	5 58	18 28	6 08	18 39	6 16	18 45
25	5 51	18 22	6 01	18 32	5 58	18 30	5 59	18 32	5 56	18 30	6 06	18 41	6 13	18 47
26	5 49	18 24	5 59	18 34	5 56	18 32	5 56	18 34	5 53	18 32	6 03	18 43	6 11	18 49
27	5 47	18 26	5 57	18 36	5 53	18 34	5 54	18 36	5 50	18 34	6 00	18 45	6 08	18 51
28	5 44	18 27	5 54	18 37	5 51	18 35	5 52	18 37	5 48	18 36	5 58	18 47	6 05	18 53
29	5 42	18 29	5 52	18 39	5 49	18 37	5 49	18 39	5 45	18 38	5 55	18 49	6 03	18 55
30	5 40	18 31	5 50	18 41	5 46	18 39	5 47	18 41	5 43	18 40	5 52	18 52	6 00	18 57
31	5 38	18 32	5 48	18 42	5 44	18 41	5 44	18 43	5 40	18 42	5 50	18 54	5 58	18 59

JUPITER

Day	RA	Dec.	Transit	5° high 52°	5° high 56°
	h m	° '	h m	h m	h m
1	18 51.0	−22 45	8 14	5 09	5 43
11	18 57.8	−22 37	7 41	4 35	5 09
21	19 03.7	−22 29	7 08	4 00	4 34
31	19 08.7	−22 22	6 33	3 25	3 58

Diameters – equatorial 36" polar 34"

SATURN

Day	RA	Dec.	Transit	5° high 52°	5° high 56°
	h m	° '	h m	h m	h m
1	23 46.3	− 3 41	13 08	8 01	8 07
11	23 50.8	− 3 12	12 33	7 23	7 29
21	23 55.4	− 2 42	11 59	6 46	6 51
31	0 00.0	− 2 13	11 24	6 09	6 14

Diameters – equatorial 16" polar 14"
Rings – major axis 36" minor axis 1"

URANUS

Day	RA	Dec.	Transit	10° high 52°	10° high 56°
	h m	° '	h m	h m	h m
1	20 20.6	−20 04	9 43	7 04	7 46
11	20 22.6	−19 58	9 05	6 26	7 07
21	20 24.3	−19 53	8 28	5 47	6 28
31	20 25.7	−19 48	7 50	5 08	5 49

Diameter 4"

NEPTUNE

Day	RA	Dec.	Transit	10° high 52°	10° high 56°
	h m	° '	h m	h m	h m
1	19 55.0	−20 19	9 17	6 41	7 24
11	19 56.2	−20 16	8 39	6 02	6 45
21	19 57.2	−20 13	8 01	5 23	6 06
31	19 57.9	−20 11	7 22	4 44	5 27

Diameter 2"

April 1996

FOURTH MONTH, 30 DAYS. *Asperire*, to open; Earth opens to receive seed

1	*Monday*	VAT introduced in the UK 1973	*week* 13 *day* 92
2	*Tuesday*	William Holman Hunt b. 1827	93
3	*Wednesday*	*Hilary Law Sittings end.* Leslie Howard b. 1893	94
4	*Thursday*	**Maundy Thursday.** PASSOVER begins	95
5	*Friday*	**Good Friday.** *Public Holiday in the UK*	96
6	*Saturday*	**Easter Eve.** Modern Olympic Games revived 1896	97
7	*Sunday*	**Easter Day** (Western churches)	*week* 14 *day* 98
8	*Monday*	*Bank Holiday in England, Wales and Northern Ireland*	99
9	*Tuesday*	Charles Baudelaire b. 1821. Lenin b. 1870	100
10	*Wednesday*	Gen. William Booth b. 1829. Antonia White d. 1980	101
11	*Thursday*	George Canning b. 1770. Sir Gerald du Maurier d. 1934	102
12	*Friday*	First manned space flight 1961	103
13	*Saturday*	Earl of Strafford b. 1593. Sir Arthur ('Bomber') Harris b. 1892	104
14	*Sunday*	**1st S. after Easter.** EASTER DAY (Greek Orthodox)	*week* 15 *day* 105
15	*Monday*	Matthew Arnold d. 1888. Kim Il Sung b. 1912	106
16	*Tuesday*	*Easter Law Sittings begin.* Ford Maddox Brown b. 1821	107
17	*Wednesday*	Diet of Worms 1521. Thornton Wilder b. 1897	108
18	*Thursday*	John Foxe d. 1587. Leopold Stokowski b. 1882	109
19	*Friday*	⚔Lexington 1775. Lord Berners d. 1950	110
20	*Saturday*	Canaletto d. 1768. Napoleon III b. 1808	111
21	*Sunday*	**2nd S. after Easter.** *Queen Elizabeth II b. 1926*	*week* 16 *day* 112
22	*Monday*	Sir Henry Campbell-Bannerman d. 1908	113
23	*Tuesday*	St George's Day. Cervantes d. 1616. Shakespeare d. 1616	114
24	*Wednesday*	Edmund Cartwright b. 1743. Bill Edrich d. 1986	115
25	*Thursday*	**St Mark.** Guglielmo Marconi b. 1874	116
26	*Friday*	Daniel Defoe d. 1731. Dame Cicely Courtneidge d. 1980	117
27	*Saturday*	Gen. Ulysses Grant b. 1822. Dashiel Hammett b. 1894	118
28	*Sunday*	**3rd S. after Easter.** League of Nations founded 1919	*week* 17 *day* 119
29	*Monday*	Jules Poincaré b. 1854. Sir Alfred Hitchcock d. 1980	120
30	*Tuesday*	Franz Lehár b. 1870. A. E. Housman d. 1936	121

ASTRONOMICAL PHENOMENA

d	h	
1	01	Venus at greatest elongation E. 46°
4	00	Total eclipse of Moon (*see* page 66)
10	16	Jupiter in conjunction with Moon. Jupiter 5° S.
15	22	Saturn in conjunction with Moon. Saturn 3° S.
17	05	Mars in conjunction with Moon. Mars 0°.5 S.
17	23	Partial eclipse of Sun (*see* page 66)
19	14	Mercury in conjunction with Moon. Mercury 5° N.
19	19	Sun's longitude 30° ♉
21	16	Venus in conjunction with Moon. Venus 9° N.
23	08	Mercury at greatest elongation E. 20°
29	10	Neptune at stationary point

MINIMA OF ALGOL

d	h	d	h	d	h
1	06.0	12	17.3	24	04.6
4	02.8	15	14.1	27	01.4
6	23.7	18	10.9	29	22.2
9	20.5	21	07.8		

CONSTELLATIONS

The following constellations are near the meridian at

	d	h		d	h
March	1	24	April	15	21
March	16	23	May	1	20
April	1	22	May	16	19

Cepheus (below the Pole), Cassiopeia (below the Pole), Ursa Major, Leo Minor, Leo, Sextans, Hydra and Crater

THE MOON

Phases, Apsides and Node	d	h	m
○ Full Moon	4	00	07
☾ Last Quarter	10	23	36
● New Moon	17	22	49
☽ First Quarter	25	20	40
Perigee (369,873 km)	11	02	47
Apogee (404,413 km)	24	22	26

Mean longitude of ascending node on April 1, 198°

THE SUN   s.d. 16′.0

Day	Right Ascension	Dec. +	Equation of time	Rise 52°	Rise 56°	Transit	Set 52°	Set 56°	Sidereal time	Transit of First Point of Aries
	h m s	° ′	m s	h m	h m	h m	h m	h m	h m s	h m s
1	0 42 29	4 34	−3 57	5 34	5 30	12 04	18 34	18 39	12 38 32	11 19 37
2	0 46 07	4 57	−3 39	5 32	5 27	12 04	18 36	18 41	12 42 28	11 15 41
3	0 49 46	5 20	−3 21	5 30	5 25	12 03	18 38	18 43	12 46 25	11 11 45
4	0 53 25	5 43	−3 04	5 28	5 22	12 03	18 39	18 45	12 50 21	11 07 49
5	0 57 04	6 06	−2 46	5 25	5 20	12 03	18 41	18 47	12 54 18	11 03 53
6	1 00 43	6 29	−2 29	5 23	5 17	12 02	18 43	18 49	12 58 14	10 59 57
7	1 04 23	6 51	−2 12	5 21	5 14	12 02	18 44	18 51	13 02 11	10 56 01
8	1 08 02	7 14	−1 55	5 19	5 12	12 02	18 46	18 53	13 06 08	10 52 05
9	1 11 42	7 36	−1 38	5 16	5 09	12 02	18 48	18 55	13 10 04	10 48 09
10	1 15 23	7 58	−1 22	5 14	5 07	12 01	18 50	18 57	13 14 01	10 44 14
11	1 19 03	8 20	−1 06	5 12	5 04	12 01	18 51	18 59	13 17 57	10 40 18
12	1 22 44	8 42	−0 50	5 10	5 02	12 01	18 53	19 01	13 21 54	10 36 22
13	1 26 25	9 04	−0 35	5 07	4 59	12 00	18 55	19 03	13 25 50	10 32 26
14	1 30 07	9 26	−0 20	5 05	4 57	12 00	18 56	19 05	13 29 47	10 28 30
15	1 33 49	9 47	−0 05	5 03	4 54	12 00	18 58	19 07	13 33 43	10 24 34
16	1 37 31	10 09	+0 09	5 01	4 51	12 00	19 00	19 09	13 37 40	10 20 38
17	1 41 13	10 30	+0 23	4 59	4 49	12 00	19 02	19 11	13 41 37	10 16 42
18	1 44 56	10 51	+0 37	4 56	4 47	11 59	19 03	19 13	13 45 33	10 12 46
19	1 48 40	11 12	+0 50	4 54	4 44	11 59	19 05	19 15	13 49 30	10 08 50
20	1 52 24	11 32	+1 03	4 52	4 42	11 59	19 07	19 17	13 53 26	10 04 54
21	1 56 08	11 53	+1 15	4 50	4 39	11 59	19 08	19 20	13 57 23	10 00 59
22	1 59 52	12 13	+1 27	4 48	4 37	11 58	19 10	19 22	14 01 19	9 57 03
23	2 03 38	12 33	+1 38	4 46	4 34	11 58	19 12	19 24	14 05 16	9 53 07
24	2 07 23	12 53	+1 49	4 44	4 32	11 58	19 13	19 26	14 09 12	9 49 11
25	2 11 09	13 13	+2 00	4 42	4 30	11 58	19 15	19 28	14 13 09	9 45 15
26	2 14 55	13 32	+2 10	4 40	4 27	11 58	19 17	19 30	14 17 06	9 41 19
27	2 18 42	13 51	+2 20	4 38	4 25	11 58	19 19	19 32	14 21 02	9 37 23
28	2 22 30	14 10	+2 29	4 36	4 22	11 57	19 20	19 34	14 24 59	9 33 27
29	2 26 18	14 29	+2 37	4 34	4 20	11 57	19 22	19 36	14 28 55	9 29 31
30	2 30 06	14 48	+2 46	4 32	4 18	11 57	19 24	19 38	14 32 52	9 25 35

DURATION OF TWILIGHT (in minutes)

Latitude	52°	56°	52°	56°	52°	56°	52°	56°
	1 April		11 April		21 April		30 April	
Civil	34	38	35	40	37	42	39	44
Nautical	76	85	79	90	84	96	89	105
Astronomical	121	137	128	148	138	167	152	200

THE NIGHT SKY

Mercury reaches greatest eastern elongation (20°) on the 23rd. It becomes visible in the western sky in the evenings after the first ten days of the month. This evening apparition is the most suitable one of the year for observers in the latitudes of the British Isles. Its magnitude ranges from −1.1 to +1.5. On the evening of the 19th the thin crescent of the Moon, barely two days old, will be seen to the left of Mercury.

Venus, magnitude −4.4, continues to be visible as a brilliant evening object. It completely dominates the western sky for several hours after sunset. Venus passes through its greatest eastern elongation (46°) on the 1st. Venus passes just south of the Pleiades during the first few days of April, being closest on the evenings of the 2nd and 3rd; on both occasions Venus is about 1° from Alcyone.

Towards the end of the month Scottish observers will have the unusual possibility of seeing Venus just above the north-western horizon *after* midnight.

Mars continues to be too close to the Sun for observation.

Jupiter, magnitude −2.3, is still a morning object, visible low in the south-eastern sky for several hours before sunrise.

Saturn remains unsuitably placed for observation.

THE MOON

Day	RA h m	Dec. °	Hor. par. ′	Semi-diam. ′	Sun's co-long. °	PA of Bright Limb °	Phase %	Age d	Rise 52° h m	Rise 56° h m	Transit h m	Set 52° h m	Set 56° h m
1	10 26	+ 6.1	55.4	15.1	59	287	91	12.6	16 00	15 57	22 29	4 23	4 27
2	11 14	+ 2.2	55.9	15.2	71	287	96	13.6	17 08	17 08	23 15	4 47	4 48
3	12 03	− 1.9	56.5	15.4	83	287	99	14.6	18 18	18 22	—	5 11	5 09
4	12 53	− 5.9	57.1	15.6	95	218	100	15.6	19 29	19 37	0 03	5 37	5 31
5	13 45	− 9.8	57.7	15.7	107	106	99	16.6	20 41	20 53	0 52	6 06	5 57
6	14 38	−13.2	58.2	15.8	119	103	95	17.6	21 53	22 08	1 44	6 39	6 26
7	15 34	−15.9	58.6	16.0	132	99	90	18.6	23 01	23 19	2 38	7 18	7 02
8	16 32	−17.7	58.9	16.0	144	95	82	19.6	—	—	3 34	8 05	7 47
9	17 31	−18.4	59.1	16.1	156	90	72	20.6	0 04	0 22	4 32	9 00	8 42
10	18 31	−18.0	59.2	16.1	168	86	61	21.6	0 59	1 16	5 30	10 04	9 46
11	19 30	−16.5	59.3	16.2	180	81	50	22.6	1 45	2 01	6 27	11 14	10 59
12	20 28	−14.0	59.3	16.1	192	77	39	23.6	2 25	2 37	7 22	12 27	12 16
13	21 24	−10.6	59.1	16.1	205	74	28	24.6	2 58	3 07	8 16	13 43	13 35
14	22 19	− 6.6	58.9	16.1	217	72	18	25.6	3 28	3 33	9 08	14 58	14 55
15	23 12	− 2.3	58.6	16.0	229	70	10	26.6	3 56	3 57	9 59	16 14	16 14
16	0 05	+ 2.0	58.2	15.9	241	70	5	27.6	4 22	4 20	10 49	17 28	17 32
17	0 57	+ 6.2	57.7	15.7	254	68	1	28.6	4 49	4 43	11 38	18 40	18 48
18	1 49	+10.1	57.2	15.6	266	310	0	0.0	5 18	5 09	12 28	19 50	20 01
19	2 41	+13.3	56.6	15.4	278	262	1	1.0	5 49	5 37	13 18	20 56	21 11
20	3 33	+15.8	56.0	15.2	290	263	5	2.0	6 25	6 10	14 08	21 58	22 14
21	4 25	+17.5	55.4	15.1	303	266	10	3.0	7 05	6 48	14 57	22 53	23 11
22	5 17	+18.4	54.9	15.0	315	270	16	4.0	7 50	7 32	15 46	23 42	23 59
23	6 08	+18.4	54.5	14.9	327	274	24	5.0	8 41	8 23	16 34	—	—
24	6 58	+17.5	54.3	14.8	339	278	33	6.0	9 35	9 19	17 21	0 24	0 40
25	7 47	+15.9	54.2	14.8	351	281	42	7.0	10 34	10 20	18 07	1 00	1 14
26	8 35	+13.6	54.3	14.8	4	284	51	8.0	11 34	11 23	18 52	1 31	1 43
27	9 22	+10.7	54.6	14.9	16	287	61	9.0	12 37	12 30	19 36	1 59	2 08
28	10 09	+ 7.4	55.0	15.0	28	289	70	10.0	13 42	13 38	20 21	2 24	2 30
29	10 56	+ 3.7	55.6	15.1	40	291	79	11.0	14 49	14 48	21 06	2 48	2 51
30	11 44	− 0.3	56.3	15.3	52	291	86	12.0	15 58	16 01	21 53	3 12	3 12

MERCURY

Day	RA h m	Dec. °	Diam. ″	Phase %	Transit h m	5° high 52° h m	5° high 56° h m
1	0 58	+ 5.5	5	99	12 21	18 21	18 23
3	1 13	+ 7.4	5	97	12 28	18 38	18 41
5	1 28	+ 9.3	5	95	12 35	18 55	19 00
7	1 42	+11.1	5	91	12 42	19 11	19 17
9	1 57	+12.8	6	86	12 49	19 27	19 35
11	2 11	+14.5	6	80	12 55	19 42	19 51
13	2 25	+16.0	6	74	13 01	19 55	20 06
15	2 38	+17.4	6	67	13 06	20 08	20 20
17	2 50	+18.6	7	60	13 10	20 18	20 31
19	3 01	+19.7	7	53	13 13	20 27	20 41
21	3 11	+20.5	7	46	13 14	20 33	20 48
23	3 20	+21.2	8	39	13 15	20 37	20 53
25	3 28	+21.7	8	33	13 14	20 39	20 55
27	3 34	+22.1	9	27	13 12	20 38	20 55
29	3 38	+22.2	9	22	13 08	20 35	20 52
31	3 42	+22.2	10	17	13 03	20 29	20 46

VENUS

Day	RA h m	Dec. °	Diam. ″	Phase %	Transit h m	5° high 52° h m	5° high 56° h m
1	3 37	+22.7	24	51	14 59	22 31	22 49
6	3 58	+24.1	25	48	14 59	22 40	22 59
11	4 17	+25.2	26	45	14 59	22 47	23 08
16	4 36	+26.2	28	42	14 58	22 52	23 14
21	4 54	+26.9	30	39	14 56	22 54	23 18
26	5 10	+27.4	32	35	14 52	22 53	23 18
31	5 24	+27.7	35	31	14 47	22 50	23 14

MARS

Day	RA h m	Dec. °	Diam. ″	Phase %	Transit h m	5° high 52° h m	5° high 56° h m
1	0 22	+ 1.5	4	100	11 43	6 08	6 10
6	0 36	+ 3.1	4	100	11 38	5 54	5 55
11	0 51	+ 4.6	4	100	11 32	5 41	5 40
16	1 05	+ 6.2	4	100	11 27	5 27	5 26
21	1 19	+ 7.6	4	100	11 21	5 14	5 11
26	1 33	+ 9.1	4	100	11 16	5 01	4 57
31	1 47	+10.5	4	99	11 10	4 49	4 43

SUNRISE AND SUNSET

	London		Bristol		Birmingham		Manchester		Newcastle		Glasgow		Belfast	
	0°05'	51°30'	2°35'	51°28'	1°55'	52°28'	2°15'	53°28'	1°37'	54°59'	4°14'	55°52'	5°56'	54°35'
	h m	h m	h m	h m	h m	h m	h m	h m	h m	h m	h m	h m	h m	h m
1	5 35	18 34	5 45	18 44	5 42	18 42	5 42	18 45	5 38	18 44	5 47	18 56	5 55	19 01
2	5 33	18 36	5 43	18 46	5 39	18 44	5 40	18 47	5 35	18 46	5 45	18 58	5 53	19 03
3	5 31	18 37	5 41	18 47	5 37	18 46	5 37	18 48	5 33	18 48	5 42	19 00	5 50	19 05
4	5 29	18 39	5 39	18 49	5 35	18 48	5 35	18 50	5 30	18 50	5 39	19 02	5 48	19 07
5	5 26	18 41	5 36	18 51	5 32	18 49	5 32	18 52	5 28	18 52	5 37	19 04	5 45	19 08
6	5 24	18 42	5 34	18 52	5 30	18 51	5 30	18 54	5 25	18 54	5 34	19 06	5 43	19 10
7	5 22	18 44	5 32	18 54	5 28	18 53	5 28	18 56	5 23	18 56	5 32	19 08	5 41	19 12
8	5 20	18 46	5 30	18 56	5 25	18 55	5 25	18 58	5 20	18 58	5 29	19 10	5 38	19 14
9	5 17	18 47	5 27	18 57	5 23	18 56	5 23	18 59	5 18	19 00	5 26	19 12	5 36	19 16
10	5 15	18 49	5 25	18 59	5 21	18 58	5 20	19 01	5 15	19 01	5 24	19 14	5 33	19 18
11	5 13	18 51	5 23	19 01	5 19	19 00	5 18	19 03	5 13	19 03	5 21	19 16	5 31	19 20
12	5 11	18 52	5 21	19 02	5 16	19 02	5 16	19 05	5 10	19 05	5 19	19 18	5 28	19 22
13	5 09	18 54	5 19	19 04	5 14	19 03	5 13	19 07	5 08	19 07	5 16	19 20	5 26	19 24
14	5 06	18 56	5 16	19 06	5 12	19 05	5 11	19 08	5 05	19 09	5 14	19 22	5 23	19 26
15	5 04	18 57	5 14	19 07	5 10	19 07	5 09	19 10	5 03	19 11	5 11	19 24	5 21	19 28
16	5 02	18 59	5 12	19 09	5 07	19 09	5 07	19 12	5 00	19 13	5 09	19 26	5 19	19 29
17	5 00	19 01	5 10	19 11	5 05	19 10	5 04	19 14	4 58	19 15	5 06	19 28	5 16	19 31
18	4 58	19 02	5 08	19 12	5 03	19 12	5 02	19 16	4 56	19 17	5 04	19 30	5 14	19 33
19	4 56	19 04	5 06	19 14	5 01	19 14	5 00	19 18	4 53	19 19	5 01	19 32	5 12	19 35
20	4 54	19 06	5 04	19 16	4 59	19 15	4 58	19 19	4 51	19 21	4 59	19 34	5 09	19 37
21	4 52	19 07	5 02	19 17	4 57	19 17	4 55	19 21	4 49	19 23	4 56	19 36	5 07	19 39
22	4 50	19 09	5 00	19 19	4 54	19 19	4 53	19 23	4 46	19 25	4 54	19 38	5 05	19 41
23	4 48	19 11	4 58	19 21	4 52	19 21	4 51	19 25	4 44	19 27	4 52	19 40	5 02	19 43
24	4 46	19 12	4 56	19 22	4 50	19 22	4 49	19 27	4 42	19 29	4 49	19 42	5 00	19 45
25	4 43	19 14	4 54	19 24	4 48	19 24	4 47	19 28	4 39	19 31	4 47	19 44	4 58	19 47
26	4 42	19 16	4 52	19 26	4 46	19 26	4 44	19 30	4 37	19 33	4 45	19 46	4 56	19 49
27	4 40	19 17	4 50	19 27	4 44	19 28	4 42	19 32	4 35	19 35	4 42	19 48	4 53	19 50
28	4 38	19 19	4 48	19 29	4 42	19 29	4 40	19 34	4 33	19 37	4 40	19 50	4 51	19 52
29	4 36	19 21	4 46	19 31	4 40	19 31	4 38	19 36	4 30	19 38	4 38	19 52	4 49	19 54
30	4 34	19 22	4 44	19 32	4 38	19 33	4 36	19 37	4 28	19 40	4 35	19 54	4 47	19 56

JUPITER

Day	RA	Dec.	Transit	5° high	
				52°	56°
	h m	° '	h m	h m	h m
1	19 09.1	−22 22	6 30	3 21	3 54
11	19 12.8	−22 16	5 54	2 45	3 18
21	19 15.2	−22 13	5 17	2 08	2 40
31	19 16.4	−22 12	4 39	1 29	2 02

Diameters – equatorial 40″ polar 37″

SATURN

Day	RA	Dec.	Transit	5° high	
				52°	56°
	h m	° '	h m	h m	h m
1	0 00.4	− 2 10	11 20	6 05	6 10
11	0 04.9	− 1 42	10 45	5 27	5 32
21	0 09.2	− 1 16	10 10	4 50	4 54
31	0 13.2	− 0 51	9 35	4 13	4 17

Diameters – equatorial 16″ polar 14″
Rings – major axis 36″ minor axis 2″

URANUS

Day	RA	Dec.	Transit	10° high	
				52°	56°
	h m	° '	h m	h m	h m
1	20 25.8	−19 48	7 46	5 05	5 45
11	20 26.9	−19 44	7 08	4 26	5 06
21	20 27.7	−19 42	6 29	3 47	4 27
31	20 28.2	−19 41	5 50	3 08	3 48

Diameter 4″

NEPTUNE

Day	RA	Dec.	Transit	10° high	
				52°	56°
	h m	° '	h m	h m	h m
1	19 58.0	−20 11	7 18	4 40	5 23
11	19 58.5	−20 09	6 40	4 01	4 44
21	19 58.8	−20 08	6 00	3 22	4 05
31	19 58.9	−20 08	5 21	2 43	3 25

Diameter 2″

May 1996

FIFTH MONTH, 31 DAYS. *Maia*, goddess of growth and increase

1	*Wednesday*	**SS Philip and James.** John Dryden d. 1700	*week* 17 *day* 122
2	*Thursday*	Jerome K. Jerome b. 1859. Bing Crosby b. 1904	123
3	*Friday*	Richard D'Oyly Carte b. 1844	124
4	*Saturday*	✗Tewkesbury 1471. E. Nesbit d. 1924	125
5	*Sunday*	**4th S. after Easter.** Napoleon Bonaparte d. 1821	*week* 18 *day* 126
6	*Monday*	*Bank Holiday in the UK.* Tony Blair b. 1953	127
7	*Tuesday*	Kitty Godfree b. 1896. Angela Carter b. 1940	128
8	*Wednesday*	Paul Gauguin d. 1903. Sir David Attenborough b. 1926	129
9	*Thursday*	Johann von Schiller d. 1805. Aldo Moro assass. 1978	130
10	*Friday*	Paul Revere d. 1818. Joan Crawford d. 1977	131
11	*Saturday*	Sir John Herschel d. 1871. Irving Berlin b. 1888	132
12	*Sunday*	**5th S. after Easter.** Florence Nightingale b. 1820	*week* 19 *day* 133
13	*Monday*	Dame Daphne du Maurier b. 1907	134
14	*Tuesday*	**St Matthias.** Robert Owen b. 1771	135
15	*Wednesday*	Edmund Kean d. 1833. Sir Tyrone Guthrie d. 1971	136
16	*Thursday*	**Ascension Day.** Henry Fonda b. 1905	137
17	*Friday*	Edward Jenner b. 1749. Dennis Potter b. 1935	138
18	*Saturday*	Pope John Paul II b. 1920. Fred Perry b. 1909	139
19	*Sunday*	**S. after Ascension Day.** Muslim New Year (1417)	*week* 20 *day* 140
20	*Monday*	Honore de Balzac b. 1799. John Clare d. 1864	141
21	*Tuesday*	Albrecht Dürer b. 1471. Andrei Sakharov b. 1921	142
22	*Wednesday*	Daniel Malan b. 1874. Max Wall d. 1990	143
23	*Thursday*	Thomas Hood b. 1799. Henrik Ibsen d. 1906	144
24	*Friday*	Feast of Weeks begins. *Easter Law Sittings end*	145
25	*Saturday*	Lord Lytton b. 1803. Igor Sikorsky b. 1889	146
26	*Sunday*	**Pentecost/Whit Sunday.** Queen Mary b. 1867	*week* 21 *day* 147
27	*Monday*	*Bank Holiday in the UK.* Amelia Bloomer b. 1818	148
28	*Tuesday*	Ian Fleming b. 1908. Patrick White b. 1912	149
29	*Wednesday*	T. H. White b. 1906. Sir William Gilbert d. 1911	150
30	*Thursday*	Christopher Marlowe d. 1593. Wilbur Wright d. 1912	151
31	*Friday*	Franz Joseph Haydn b. 1809. Prof. Rienhold Niebuhr d. 1971	152

ASTRONOMICAL PHENOMENA

d	h	
3	23	Mercury at stationary point
4	14	Venus at greatest brilliancy
4	16	Jupiter at stationary point
7	23	Jupiter in conjunction with Moon. Jupiter 5° S.
8	20	Uranus at stationary point
13	10	Saturn in conjunction with Moon. Saturn 3° S.
15	01	Mercury in inferior conjunction
16	04	Mars in conjunction with Moon. Mars 2° N.
17	05	Mercury in conjunction with Moon. Mercury 2° N.
20	01	Venus in conjunction with Moon. Venus 8° N.
20	06	Venus at stationary point
20	18	Sun's longitude 60° ♊
22	14	Pluto at opposition
27	19	Mercury at stationary point
29	10	Mars in conjunction with Mercury. Mars 3° N.

MINIMA OF ALGOL

Algol is inconveniently situated for observation during May.

CONSTELLATIONS

The following constellations are near the meridian at

	d	h		d	h
April	1	24	May	16	21
April	15	23	June	1	20
May	1	22	June	15	19

Cepheus (below the Pole), Cassiopeia (below the Pole), Ursa Minor, Ursa Major, Canes Venatici, Coma Berenices, Bootes, Leo, Virgo, Crater, Corvus and Hydra

THE MOON

Phases, Apsides and Node	d	h	m
○ Full Moon	3	11	48
☾ Last Quarter	10	05	04
● New Moon	17	11	46
☽ First Quarter	25	14	13
Perigee (366,505 km)	6	21	52
Apogee (405,106 km)	22	16	24

Mean longitude of ascending node on May 1, 196°

THE SUN
s.d. 15'.8

Day	Right Ascension	Dec. +	Equation of time	Rise 52°	Rise 56°	Transit	Set 52°	Set 56°	Sidereal time	Transit of First Point of Aries
	h m s	° '	m s	h m	h m	h m	h m	h m	h m s	h m s
1	2 33 55	15 06	+2 53	4 30	4 16	11 57	19 25	19 40	14 36 48	9 21 39
2	2 37 44	15 24	+3 00	4 28	4 13	11 57	19 27	19 42	14 40 45	9 17 44
3	2 41 34	15 42	+3 07	4 26	4 11	11 57	19 29	19 44	14 44 41	9 13 48
4	2 45 25	15 59	+3 13	4 24	4 09	11 57	19 30	19 46	14 48 38	9 09 52
5	2 49 16	16 16	+3 18	4 23	4 07	11 57	19 32	19 48	14 52 34	9 05 56
6	2 53 08	16 33	+3 23	4 21	4 05	11 57	19 34	19 50	14 56 31	9 02 00
7	2 57 00	16 50	+3 28	4 19	4 03	11 57	19 35	19 52	15 00 28	8 58 04
8	3 00 53	17 06	+3 31	4 17	4 00	11 56	19 37	19 54	15 04 24	8 54 08
9	3 04 46	17 22	+3 34	4 15	3 58	11 56	19 38	19 56	15 08 21	8 50 12
10	3 08 40	17 38	+3 37	4 14	3 56	11 56	19 40	19 58	15 12 17	8 46 16
11	3 12 35	17 54	+3 39	4 12	3 54	11 56	19 42	20 00	15 16 14	8 42 20
12	3 16 30	18 09	+3 40	4 11	3 52	11 56	19 43	20 01	15 20 10	8 38 24
13	3 20 26	18 24	+3 41	4 09	3 51	11 56	19 45	20 03	15 24 07	8 34 29
14	3 24 22	18 38	+3 41	4 07	3 49	11 56	19 46	20 05	15 28 03	8 30 33
15	3 28 19	18 53	+3 41	4 06	3 47	11 56	19 48	20 07	15 32 00	8 26 37
16	3 32 17	19 07	+3 40	4 04	3 45	11 56	19 49	20 09	15 35 57	8 22 41
17	3 36 15	19 20	+3 38	4 03	3 43	11 56	19 51	20 11	15 39 53	8 18 45
18	3 40 13	19 34	+3 36	4 01	3 41	11 56	19 52	20 13	15 43 50	8 14 49
19	3 44 13	19 47	+3 34	4 00	3 40	11 56	19 54	20 14	15 47 46	8 10 53
20	3 48 12	19 59	+3 30	3 59	3 38	11 57	19 55	20 16	15 51 43	8 06 57
21	3 52 13	20 12	+3 27	3 57	3 36	11 57	19 57	20 18	15 55 39	8 03 01
22	3 56 13	20 24	+3 22	3 56	3 35	11 57	19 58	20 20	15 59 36	7 59 05
23	4 00 15	20 35	+3 18	3 55	3 33	11 57	19 59	20 21	16 03 32	7 55 09
24	4 04 17	20 47	+3 12	3 54	3 32	11 57	20 01	20 23	16 07 29	7 51 14
25	4 08 19	20 58	+3 07	3 53	3 30	11 57	20 02	20 25	16 11 26	7 47 18
26	4 12 22	21 08	+3 00	3 51	3 29	11 57	20 03	20 26	16 15 22	7 43 22
27	4 16 25	21 18	+2 54	3 50	3 28	11 57	20 05	20 28	16 19 19	7 39 26
28	4 20 29	21 28	+2 47	3 49	3 26	11 57	20 06	20 29	16 23 15	7 35 30
29	4 24 33	21 38	+2 39	3 48	3 25	11 57	20 07	20 31	16 27 12	7 31 34
30	4 28 37	21 47	+2 31	3 47	3 24	11 58	20 08	20 32	16 31 08	7 27 38
31	4 32 42	21 55	+2 23	3 47	3 23	11 58	20 09	20 33	16 35 05	7 23 42

DURATION OF TWILIGHT (in minutes)

Latitude	52°	56°	52°	56°	52°	56°	52°	56°
	1 May		11 May		21 May		31 May	
Civil	39	45	41	49	44	53	46	57
Nautical	90	106	97	121	106	143	116	TAN
Astronomical	154	209	179	TAN	TAN	TAN	TAN	TAN

THE NIGHT SKY

Mercury is too close to the Sun for observation.

Venus, magnitude −4.5, continues to be visible as a brilliant evening object in the western sky. However, the time between sunset and Venus setting is decreasing quite markedly and by the end of the month Venus is unlikely to be seen for much more than a quarter of an hour after sunset. Observers with small telescopes will notice a significant change in the apparent shape and size of the planet during May. On the 1st it is one-third illuminated, with a diameter of 35 arcseconds; by the 31st it is an incredibly thin sliver, only 4 per cent illuminated but with a diameter of 55 arcseconds.

Mars remains too close to the Sun for observation.

Jupiter continues to be visible as a conspicuous object in the south-eastern sky, and by the end of the month is becoming visible low on the horizon by midnight. Jupiter's magnitude is −2.5.

Saturn, magnitude +1.0, very gradually becomes visible as a morning object during the month, when it may be seen low above the east-south-east horizon before the morning twilight renders observation impossible.

THE MOON

Day	RA	Dec.	Hor. par.	Semi- diam.	Sun's co- long.	PA of Bright Limb	Phase	Age	Rise 52°	Rise 56°	Transit	Set 52°	Set 56°
	h m	°	'	'	°	°	%	d	h m	h m	h m	h m	h m
1	12 34	− 4.4	57.0	15.5	65	292	93	13.0	17 09	17 16	22 42	3 37	3 33
2	13 25	− 8.4	57.8	15.7	77	293	97	14.0	18 22	18 32	23 33	4 05	3 57
3	14 19	−12.0	58.5	15.9	89	304	100	15.0	19 36	19 49	—	4 36	4 25
4	15 15	−15.1	59.1	16.1	101	82	100	16.0	20 48	21 04	0 28	5 13	4 59
5	16 14	−17.3	59.5	16.2	113	90	97	17.0	21 55	22 13	1 25	5 58	5 41
6	17 14	−18.4	59.8	16.3	125	88	92	18.0	22 54	23 12	2 24	6 52	6 33
7	18 15	−18.3	59.8	16.3	138	84	84	19.0	23 45	—	3 23	7 54	7 36
8	19 16	−17.0	59.7	16.3	150	80	75	20.0	—	0 01	4 22	9 04	8 48
9	20 15	−14.7	59.5	16.2	162	76	64	21.0	0 27	0 40	5 18	10 17	10 05
10	21 12	−11.5	59.2	16.1	174	73	53	22.0	1 02	1 12	6 13	11 32	11 24
11	22 06	− 7.7	58.8	16.0	186	70	41	23.0	1 33	1 39	7 05	12 47	12 43
12	22 59	− 3.5	58.4	15.9	199	69	30	24.0	2 00	2 03	7 55	14 01	14 01
13	23 51	+ 0.8	57.9	15.8	211	68	21	25.0	2 26	2 25	8 44	15 14	15 17
14	0 42	+ 5.0	57.4	15.6	223	67	13	26.0	2 52	2 48	9 33	16 26	16 33
15	1 33	+ 9.0	56.9	15.5	235	67	7	27.0	3 19	3 11	10 22	17 36	17 46
16	2 24	+12.4	56.4	15.4	248	65	2	28.0	3 49	3 38	11 11	18 43	18 56
17	3 16	+15.1	55.9	15.2	260	48	0	29.0	4 22	4 08	12 00	19 46	20 02
18	4 08	+17.1	55.4	15.1	272	292	0	0.5	5 00	4 43	12 50	20 44	21 02
19	5 00	+18.3	55.0	15.0	284	278	2	1.5	5 43	5 25	13 39	21 36	21 54
20	5 51	+18.5	54.6	14.9	297	278	6	2.5	6 31	6 13	14 27	22 21	22 38
21	6 41	+18.0	54.3	14.8	309	280	12	3.5	7 25	7 08	15 15	22 59	23 15
22	7 31	+16.6	54.2	14.8	321	283	19	4.5	8 22	8 07	16 01	23 32	23 45
23	8 19	+14.6	54.1	14.7	333	286	26	5.5	9 21	9 09	16 46	—	—
24	9 07	+11.9	54.3	14.8	345	288	35	6.5	10 23	10 14	17 31	0 01	0 11
25	9 53	+ 8.7	54.6	14.9	358	290	44	7.5	11 26	11 20	18 14	0 27	0 34
26	10 40	+ 5.2	55.0	15.0	10	292	54	8.5	12 31	12 29	18 58	0 51	0 55
27	11 27	+ 1.3	55.6	15.2	22	293	64	9.5	13 38	13 39	19 44	1 15	1 15
28	12 15	− 2.7	56.4	15.4	34	293	73	10.5	14 47	14 52	20 31	1 38	1 36
29	13 05	− 6.7	57.2	15.6	46	293	82	11.5	15 58	16 07	21 20	2 04	1 58
30	13 57	−10.5	58.1	15.8	59	292	89	12.5	17 12	17 24	22 13	2 33	2 23
31	14 52	−13.9	59.0	16.1	71	292	95	13.5	18 25	18 41	23 09	3 07	2 54

MERCURY

Day	RA	Dec.	Diam.	Phase	Transit	5° high 52°	5° high 56°
	h m	°	"	%	h m	h m	h m
1	3 42	+22.2	10	17	13 03	20 29	20 46
3	3 43	+22.1	10	13	12 57	20 21	20 37
5	3 44	+21.7	11	9	12 49	20 10	20 26
7	3 43	+21.3	11	6	12 40	19 58	20 13
9	3 40	+20.7	11	3	12 29	19 43	19 58
11	3 37	+19.9	12	2	12 18	19 28	19 41
13	3 33	+19.1	12	0	12 06	19 11	19 24
15	3 29	+18.3	12	0	11 54	4 53	4 40
17	3 25	+17.5	12	0	11 42	4 46	4 34
19	3 21	+16.6	12	2	11 31	4 38	4 28
21	3 18	+15.9	12	3	11 20	4 31	4 21
23	3 15	+15.3	12	5	11 09	4 24	4 15
25	3 13	+14.7	11	8	11 00	4 17	4 09
27	3 13	+14.4	11	11	10 52	4 11	4 02
29	3 13	+14.2	11	14	10 44	4 05	3 56
31	3 15	+14.1	10	18	10 38	3 59	3 50

VENUS

Day	RA	Dec.	Diam.	Phase	Transit	5° high 52°	5° high 56°
	h m	°	"	%	h m	h m	h m
1	5 24	+27.7	35	31	14 47	22 50	23 14
6	5 36	+27.8	38	26	14 39	22 42	23 07
11	5 45	+27.7	41	22	14 28	22 29	22 54
16	5 51	+27.4	44	17	14 13	22 12	22 36
21	5 52	+26.9	48	13	13 54	21 50	22 13
26	5 49	+26.2	51	8	13 31	21 21	21 43
31	5 42	+25.3	55	4	13 04	20 47	21 08

MARS

Day	RA	Dec.	Diam.	Phase	Transit	5° high 52°	5° high 56°
1	1 47	+10.5	4	99	11 10	4 49	4 43
6	2 02	+11.9	4	99	11 05	4 36	4 30
11	2 16	+13.2	4	99	10 59	4 24	4 16
16	2 30	+14.4	4	99	10 54	4 12	4 03
21	2 45	+15.6	4	99	10 49	4 00	3 51
26	2 59	+16.7	4	99	10 44	3 49	3 38
31	3 14	+17.8	4	99	10 39	3 38	3 26

SUNRISE AND SUNSET

	London		Bristol		Birmingham		Manchester		Newcastle		Glasgow		Belfast	
	0°05'	51°30'	2°35'	51°28'	1°55'	52°28'	2°15'	53°28'	1°37'	54°59'	4°14'	55°52'	5°56'	54°35'
	h m	h m	h m	h m	h m	h m	h m	h m	h m	h m	h m	h m	h m	h m
1	4 32	19 24	4 42	19 34	4 36	19 34	4 34	19 39	4 26	19 42	4 33	19 56	4 45	19 58
2	4 30	19 26	4 40	19 36	4 34	19 36	4 32	19 41	4 24	19 44	4 31	19 58	4 43	20 00
3	4 28	19 27	4 38	19 37	4 32	19 38	4 30	19 43	4 22	19 46	4 29	20 00	4 41	20 02
4	4 26	19 29	4 36	19 39	4 30	19 40	4 28	19 45	4 20	19 48	4 26	20 02	4 39	20 04
5	4 25	19 30	4 35	19 40	4 29	19 41	4 26	19 46	4 18	19 50	4 24	20 04	4 36	20 06
6	4 23	19 32	4 33	19 42	4 27	19 43	4 24	19 48	4 16	19 52	4 22	20 06	4 34	20 07
7	4 21	19 34	4 31	19 44	4 25	19 45	4 22	19 50	4 14	19 54	4 20	20 08	4 33	20 09
8	4 19	19 35	4 29	19 45	4 23	19 46	4 20	19 52	4 12	19 56	4 18	20 10	4 31	20 11
9	4 18	19 37	4 28	19 47	4 21	19 48	4 19	19 53	4 10	19 57	4 16	20 12	4 29	20 13
10	4 16	19 38	4 26	19 48	4 20	19 50	4 17	19 55	4 08	19 59	4 14	20 14	4 27	20 15
11	4 14	19 40	4 25	19 50	4 18	19 51	4 15	19 57	4 06	20 01	4 12	20 16	4 25	20 16
12	4 13	19 41	4 23	19 51	4 16	19 53	4 13	19 58	4 04	20 03	4 10	20 18	4 23	20 18
13	4 11	19 43	4 21	19 53	4 15	19 54	4 12	20 00	4 02	20 05	4 08	20 20	4 21	20 20
14	4 10	19 45	4 20	19 54	4 13	19 56	4 10	20 02	4 00	20 06	4 06	20 21	4 19	20 22
15	4 08	19 46	4 18	19 56	4 11	19 58	4 08	20 03	3 59	20 08	4 04	20 23	4 18	20 23
16	4 07	19 48	4 17	19 57	4 10	19 59	4 07	20 05	3 57	20 10	4 03	20 25	4 16	20 25
17	4 05	19 49	4 15	19 59	4 08	20 01	4 05	20 07	3 55	20 12	4 01	20 27	4 14	20 27
18	4 04	19 50	4 14	20 00	4 07	20 02	4 04	20 08	3 53	20 13	3 59	20 29	4 13	20 29
19	4 03	19 52	4 13	20 02	4 06	20 04	4 02	20 10	3 52	20 15	3 57	20 31	4 11	20 30
20	4 01	19 53	4 11	20 03	4 04	20 05	4 01	20 11	3 50	20 17	3 56	20 32	4 10	20 32
21	4 00	19 55	4 10	20 05	4 03	20 07	3 59	20 13	3 49	20 18	3 54	20 34	4 08	20 33
22	3 59	19 56	4 09	20 06	4 02	20 08	3 58	20 14	3 47	20 20	3 53	20 36	4 07	20 35
23	3 58	19 57	4 08	20 07	4 00	20 09	3 57	20 16	3 46	20 22	3 51	20 37	4 05	20 37
24	3 56	19 59	4 07	20 09	3 59	20 11	3 55	20 17	3 44	20 23	3 50	20 39	4 04	20 38
25	3 55	20 00	4 05	20 10	3 58	20 12	3 54	20 19	3 43	20 25	3 48	20 41	4 03	20 40
26	3 54	20 01	4 04	20 11	3 57	20 13	3 53	20 20	3 42	20 26	3 47	20 42	4 01	20 41
27	3 53	20 03	4 03	20 12	3 56	20 15	3 52	20 21	3 41	20 28	3 45	20 44	4 00	20 43
28	3 52	20 04	4 02	20 14	3 55	20 16	3 51	20 23	3 39	20 29	3 44	20 45	3 59	20 44
29	3 51	20 05	4 01	20 15	3 54	20 17	3 50	20 24	3 38	20 31	3 43	20 47	3 58	20 45
30	3 50	20 06	4 01	20 16	3 53	20 18	3 49	20 25	3 37	20 32	3 42	20 48	3 57	20 47
31	3 49	20 07	4 00	20 17	3 52	20 20	3 48	20 27	3 36	20 33	3 41	20 49	3 56	20 48

JUPITER

Day	RA	Dec.	Transit	5° high	
				52°	56°
	h m	° '	h m	h m	h m
1	19 16.4	− 22 12	4 39	1 29	2 02
11	19 16.2	− 22 13	3 59	0 50	1 23
21	19 14.7	− 22 17	3 19	0 10	0 43
31	19 11.9	− 22 24	2 36	23 24	0 02

Diameters – equatorial 43″ polar 41″

SATURN

Day	RA	Dec.	Transit	5° high	
				52°	56°
	h m	° '	h m	h m	h m
1	0 13.2	− 0 51	9 35	4 13	4 17
11	0 17.0	− 0 28	8 59	3 35	3 39
21	0 20.5	− 0 08	8 24	2 58	3 01
31	0 23.5	+ 0 10	7 47	2 20	2 23

Diameters – equatorial 16″ polar 15″
Rings – major axis 37″ minor axis 3″

URANUS

Day	RA	Dec.	Transit	10° high	
				52°	56°
	h m	° '	h m	h m	h m
1	20 28.2	− 19 41	5 50	3 08	3 48
11	20 28.3	− 19 41	5 11	2 29	3 09
21	20 28.0	− 19 42	4 32	1 49	2 30
31	20 27.5	− 19 44	3 52	1 10	1 50

Diameter 4″

NEPTUNE

Day	RA	Dec.	Transit	10° high	
				52°	56°
	h m	° '	h m	h m	h m
1	19 58.9	− 20 08	5 21	2 43	3 25
11	19 58.8	− 20 08	4 42	2 04	2 46
21	19 58.4	− 20 09	4 02	1 24	2 07
31	19 57.8	− 20 11	3 22	0 44	1 27

Diameter 2″

June 1996

SIXTH MONTH, 30 DAYS. *Junius*, Roman *gens* (family)

1	*Saturday*	Leslie Howard d. 1943. Helen Keller d. 1968	*week 21 day* 153
2	*Sunday*	**Trinity Sunday.** *Coronation Day 1953*	*week 22 day* 154
3	*Monday*	William Harvey d. 1657. Sydney Smith b. 1771	155
4	*Tuesday*	*Trinity Law Sittings begin.* Kaiser Wilhem II d. 1941	156
5	*Wednesday*	Orlando Gibbons d. 1625. Eleanor Farjeon d. 1965	157
6	*Thursday*	CORPUS CHRISTI. Count Camillo Cavour d. 1861	158
7	*Friday*	Robert the Bruce d. 1329. Dorothy Parker d. 1967	159
8	*Saturday*	Thomas Paine d. 1809. Sir John Millais b. 1829	160
9	*Sunday*	**2nd S. after Pentecost/1st S. after Trinity**	*week 23 day* 161
10	*Monday*	*Duke of Edinburgh b. 1921.* Judy Garland b. 1922	162
11	*Tuesday*	**St Barnabas.** Jacques Cousteau b. 1910	163
12	*Wednesday*	Harriet Martineau b. 1802. Charles Kingsley b. 1819	164
13	*Thursday*	Fanny Burney b. 1752. Thomas Arnold b. 1795	165
14	*Friday*	John McCormack b. 1884. Emmeline Pankhurst d. 1928	166
15	*Saturday*	*Queen's Official Birthday.* James Hunt d. 1993	167
16	*Sunday*	**3rd S. after Pentecost/2nd S. after Trinity**	*week 24 day* 168
17	*Monday*	John Wesley b. 1703. Charles Gounod b. 1818	169
18	*Tuesday*	Roald Amundsen d. 1928. Ethel Barrymore d. 1959	170
19	*Wednesday*	Mrs Wallis Simpson b. 1896. Sir James Barrie d. 1937	171
20	*Thursday*	Niccolò Machiavelli d. 1527. William IV d. 1837	172
21	*Friday*	Prince William of Wales b. 1982. Mary McCarthy b. 1912	173
22	*Saturday*	Giuseppe Mazzini b. 1805. Darius Milhaud d. 1974	174
23	*Sunday*	**4th S. after Pentecost/3rd S. after Trinity**	*week 25 day* 175
24	*Monday*	**St John the Baptist.** Juan Fangio b. 1911	176
25	*Tuesday*	George Orwell b. 1903. Alma-Tadema d. 1912	177
26	*Wednesday*	Pearl S. Buck b. 1892. Ford Madox Ford d. 1939	178
27	*Thursday*	⚔Dettingen 1743. Joseph Smith d. 1844	179
28	*Friday*	Archduke Ferdinand of Austria assass. 1914	180
29	*Saturday*	**St Peter.** Trades unions legalized 1871	181
30	*Sunday*	**5th S. after Pentecost/4th S. after Trinity**	*week 26 day* 182

ASTRONOMICAL PHENOMENA

d	h	
4	05	Jupiter in conjunction with Moon. Jupiter 5° S.
9	19	Saturn in conjunction with Moon. Saturn 3° S.
10	09	Mercury at greatest elongation W.24°
10	16	Venus in inferior conjunction
14	01	Mercury in conjunction with Moon. Mercury 0°.4 N.
14	02	Mars in conjunction with Moon. Mars 3° N.
15	10	Venus in conjunction with Moon. Venus 3° N.
15	19	Mars in conjunction with Mercury. Mars 3° N.
21	02	Sun's longitude 90° ♋.
23	09	Venus in conjunction with Mercury. Venus 2° S.
29	11	Mars in conjunction with Venus. Mars 4° N.

MINIMA OF ALGOL

Algol is inconveniently situated for observation during June.

CONSTELLATIONS

The following constellations are near the meridian at

	d	h		d	h
May	1	24	June	15	21
May	16	23	July	1	20
June	1	22	July	16	19

Cassiopeia (below the Pole), Ursa Minor, Draco, Ursa Major, Canes Venatici, Bootes, Corona, Serpens, Virgo and Libra

THE MOON

Phases, Apsides and Node	d	h	m
○ Full Moon	1	20	47
☾ Last Quarter	8	11	06
● New Moon	16	01	36
☽ First Quarter	24	05	23
Perigee (361,476 km)	3	16	23
Apogee (406,056 km)	19	06	33

Mean longitude of ascending node on June 1, 194°

THE SUN

s.d. 15′.8

Day	Right Ascension	Dec. +	Equation of time	Rise 52°	Rise 56°	Transit	Set 52°	Set 56°	Sidereal time	Transit of First Point of Aries
	h m s	° ′	m s	h m	h m	h m	h m	h m	h m s	h m s
1	4 36 48	22 04	+2 14	3 46	3 22	11 58	20 11	20 35	16 39 01	7 19 46
2	4 40 53	22 12	+2 05	3 45	3 21	11 58	20 12	20 36	16 42 58	7 15 50
3	4 45 00	22 19	+1 55	3 44	3 20	11 58	20 13	20 37	16 46 55	7 11 54
4	4 49 06	22 26	+1 45	3 44	3 19	11 58	20 14	20 39	16 50 51	7 07 59
5	4 53 13	22 33	+1 35	3 43	3 18	11 59	20 15	20 40	16 54 48	7 04 03
6	4 57 20	22 39	+1 24	3 42	3 17	11 59	20 16	20 41	16 58 44	7 00 07
7	5 01 28	22 45	+1 13	3 42	3 17	11 59	20 16	20 42	17 02 41	6 56 11
8	5 05 36	22 51	+1 02	3 41	3 16	11 59	20 17	20 43	17 06 37	6 52 15
9	5 09 44	22 56	+0 50	3 41	3 15	11 59	20 18	20 44	17 10 34	6 48 19
10	5 13 52	23 01	+0 38	3 40	3 15	11 59	20 19	20 45	17 14 30	6 44 23
11	5 18 01	23 05	+0 26	3 40	3 14	12 00	20 20	20 46	17 18 27	6 40 27
12	5 22 10	23 09	+0 14	3 40	3 14	12 00	20 20	20 46	17 22 24	6 36 31
13	5 26 19	23 13	+0 02	3 40	3 14	12 00	20 21	20 47	17 26 20	6 32 35
14	5 30 28	23 16	−0 11	3 39	3 13	12 00	20 21	20 48	17 30 17	6 28 39
15	5 34 37	23 19	−0 24	3 39	3 13	12 01	20 22	20 48	17 34 13	6 24 44
16	5 38 47	23 21	−0 37	3 39	3 13	12 01	20 22	20 49	17 38 10	6 20 48
17	5 42 56	23 23	−0 50	3 39	3 13	12 01	20 23	20 49	17 42 06	6 16 52
18	5 47 06	23 24	−1 03	3 39	3 13	12 01	20 23	20 50	17 46 03	6 12 56
19	5 51 16	23 25	−1 16	3 39	3 13	12 01	20 23	20 50	17 50 00	6 09 00
20	5 55 25	23 26	−1 29	3 40	3 13	12 02	20 24	20 50	17 53 56	6 05 04
21	5 59 35	23 26	−1 42	3 40	3 13	12 02	20 24	20 50	17 57 53	6 01 08
22	6 03 45	23 26	−1 55	3 40	3 13	12 02	20 24	20 51	18 01 49	5 57 12
23	6 07 54	23 25	−2 08	3 40	3 14	12 02	20 24	20 51	18 05 46	5 53 16
24	6 12 04	23 24	−2 21	3 41	3 14	12 02	20 24	20 51	18 09 42	5 49 20
25	6 16 13	23 23	−2 34	3 41	3 15	12 03	20 24	20 51	18 13 39	5 45 24
26	6 20 22	23 21	−2 47	3 41	3 15	12 03	20 24	20 50	18 17 35	5 41 29
27	6 24 31	23 19	−2 59	3 42	3 16	12 03	20 24	20 50	18 21 32	5 37 33
28	6 28 40	23 16	−3 11	3 43	3 16	12 03	20 24	20 50	18 25 29	5 33 37
29	6 32 49	23 13	−3 23	3 43	3 17	12 03	20 24	20 50	18 29 25	5 29 41
30	6 36 57	23 10	−3 35	3 44	3 18	12 04	20 23	20 49	18 33 22	5 25 45

DURATION OF TWILIGHT (in minutes)

Latitude	52°	56°	52°	56°	52°	56°	52°	56°
	1 June		11 June		21 June		30 June	
Civil	47	58	48	61	49	63	49	62
Nautical	117	TAN	125	TAN	128	TAN	125	TAN
Astronomical	TAN	TAN	TAN	TAN	TAN	TAN	TAN	TAN

THE NIGHT SKY

Mercury is unsuitably placed for observation throughout June.

Venus, magnitude −4.0, is moving rapidly towards the Sun, and is unlikely to be seen in the evening after the first four days of the month. During that time it will only be visible for a very short time, low above the western horizon after sunset. Venus moves quickly through inferior conjunction on the 10th and during the last ten days of the month it may be seen as a morning object, magnitude −4.2, low above the eastern horizon before dawn. It is interesting to note that at its next inferior conjunction in June (2004) Venus will transit the Sun's disk, and this will be visible from the British Isles!

Mars is still unsuitably placed for observation.

Jupiter, magnitude −2.7, is now visible for most of the night, as it approaches opposition in July. By the end of June it is visible low above the south-east horizon shortly after 21h. The gibbous Moon passes 5° north of Jupiter on the night of the 3rd to 4th.

Saturn is still visible in the south-eastern sky in the early mornings, magnitude +0.9. By the end of the month it is visible low above the eastern horizon shortly after midnight.

Twilight. Reference to the section above shows that astronomical twilight lasts all night for a period around the summer solstice (i.e. in June and July), even in southern England. Under these conditions the sky never gets completely dark as the Sun is always less than 18° below the horizon.

THE MOON

Day	RA		Dec.	Hor. par.	Semi- diam.	Sun's co- long.	PA of Bright Limb	Phase	Age	Rise		Transit		Set	
										52°	56°			52°	56°
	h	m	°	'	'	°	°	%	d	h m	h m	h m		h m	h m
1	15	50	−16.5	59.7	16.3	83	299	99	14.5	19 37	19 54	—		3 48	3 32
2	16	51	−18.1	60.3	16.4	95	30	100	15.5	20 42	21 00	0 08		4 38	4 20
3	17	53	−18.6	60.6	16.5	107	74	98	16.5	21 38	21 56	1 09		5 38	5 19
4	18	56	−17.7	60.6	16.5	120	76	93	17.5	22 25	22 40	2 11		6 47	6 30
5	19	57	−15.6	60.4	16.5	132	74	86	18.5	23 04	23 16	3 10		8 02	7 48
6	20	57	−12.6	60.0	16.4	144	71	77	19.5	23 37	23 45	4 07		9 19	9 09
7	21	53	− 8.8	59.5	16.2	156	69	66	20.5	—	—	5 01		10 36	10 30
8	22	48	− 4.6	58.8	16.0	168	67	55	21.5	0 06	0 10	5 53		11 51	11 49
9	23	40	− 0.3	58.1	15.8	181	67	44	22.5	0 32	0 32	6 43		13 05	13 06
10	0	31	+ 4.0	57.5	15.7	193	67	34	23.5	0 58	0 55	7 31		14 16	14 22
11	1	22	+ 7.9	56.9	15.5	205	68	24	24.5	1 24	1 17	8 19		15 26	15 35
12	2	12	+11.5	56.3	15.3	217	69	16	25.5	1 52	1 42	9 07		16 33	16 45
13	3	03	+14.4	55.7	15.2	230	70	9	26.5	2 24	2 10	9 56		17 37	17 52
14	3	54	+16.6	55.3	15.1	242	70	4	27.5	2 59	2 43	10 45		18 37	18 54
15	4	45	+18.0	54.9	15.0	254	63	1	28.5	3 39	3 22	11 34		19 31	19 49
16	5	36	+18.6	54.5	14.9	266	7	0	29.5	4 25	4 07	12 22		20 18	20 36
17	6	27	+18.3	54.3	14.8	279	298	1	0.9	5 17	4 59	13 10		20 59	21 16
18	7	17	+17.2	54.1	14.7	291	290	4	1.9	6 12	5 56	13 57		21 34	21 49
19	8	06	+15.4	54.0	14.7	303	290	8	2.9	7 11	6 58	14 43		22 05	22 16
20	8	53	+12.9	54.0	14.7	315	291	14	3.9	8 12	8 01	15 27		22 32	22 40
21	9	40	+ 9.9	54.2	14.8	328	292	21	4.9	9 14	9 07	16 11		22 56	23 02
22	10	26	+ 6.5	54.5	14.8	340	293	29	5.9	10 18	10 14	16 54		23 19	23 22
23	11	12	+ 2.8	55.0	15.0	352	293	38	6.9	11 22	11 22	17 38		23 42	23 41
24	11	59	− 1.1	55.6	15.1	4	293	48	7.9	12 29	12 32	18 23		—	—
25	12	47	− 5.1	56.3	15.3	16	293	58	8.9	13 37	13 44	19 10		0 06	0 02
26	13	37	− 8.9	57.2	15.6	29	292	68	9.9	14 48	14 58	19 59		0 32	0 25
27	14	29	−12.4	58.1	15.8	41	290	78	10.9	16 00	16 14	20 53		1 03	0 51
28	15	25	−15.4	59.1	16.1	53	288	86	11.9	17 12	17 29	21 50		1 39	1 24
29	16	24	−17.5	60.0	16.3	65	286	93	12.9	18 21	18 40	22 50		2 23	2 06
30	17	26	−18.5	60.7	16.5	77	289	98	13.9	19 23	19 42	23 52		3 18	2 59

MERCURY

Day	RA		Dec.	Diam.	Phase	Transit	5° high	
							52°	56°
	h	m	°	''	%	h m	h m	h m
1	3	16	+14.1	10	19	10 36	3 56	3 47
3	3	19	+14.3	10	23	10 31	3 50	3 42
5	3	23	+14.5	9	27	10 28	3 45	3 36
7	3	28	+14.9	9	31	10 25	3 40	3 31
9	3	35	+15.5	8	34	10 24	3 36	3 26
11	3	42	+16.0	8	38	10 23	3 32	3 22
13	3	50	+16.7	8	43	10 24	3 29	3 18
15	3	59	+17.5	7	47	10 25	3 26	3 14
17	4	09	+18.2	7	52	10 28	3 24	3 12
19	4	21	+19.0	7	56	10 31	3 23	3 09
21	4	33	+19.9	7	61	10 36	3 22	3 08
23	4	46	+20.7	6	66	10 41	3 23	3 08
25	5	00	+21.4	6	72	10 48	3 25	3 09
27	5	15	+22.1	6	77	10 56	3 28	3 11
29	5	31	+22.8	6	82	11 04	3 32	3 14
31	5	48	+23.3	5	87	11 13	3 38	3 20

VENUS

Day	RA		Dec.	Diam.	Phase	Transit	5° high	
							52°	56°
	h	m	°	''	%	h m	h m	h m
1	5	40	+25.0	55	3	12 58	5 15	4 55
6	5	29	+23.8	57	1	12 27	4 52	4 33
11	5	16	+22.5	58	0	11 54	4 28	4 11
16	5	03	+21.1	57	1	11 22	4 05	3 49
21	4	53	+19.8	55	4	10 53	3 42	3 28
26	4	46	+18.8	52	8	10 27	3 22	3 09
31	4	44	+18.1	48	12	10 05	3 03	2 51

MARS

Day	RA		Dec.	Diam.	Phase	Transit	5° high	
1	3	17	+18.0	4	99	10 38	3 36	3 24
6	3	32	+18.9	4	99	10 33	3 26	3 12
11	3	47	+19.8	4	98	10 28	3 16	3 02
16	4	01	+20.6	4	98	10 23	3 06	2 51
21	4	16	+21.3	4	98	10 18	2 57	2 41
26	4	31	+21.9	4	98	10 13	2 48	2 32
31	4	46	+22.5	4	98	10 09	2 40	2 23

SUNRISE AND SUNSET

	London		Bristol		Birmingham		Manchester		Newcastle		Glasgow		Belfast	
	0°05'	51°30'	2°35'	51°28'	1°55'	52°28'	2°15'	53°28'	1°37'	54°59'	4°14'	55°52'	5°56'	54°35'
	h m	h m	h m	h m	h m	h m	h m	h m	h m	h m	h m	h m	h m	h m
1	3 49	20 08	3 59	20 18	3 51	20 21	3 47	20 28	3 35	20 34	3 40	20 51	3 55	20 49
2	3 48	20 09	3 58	20 19	3 50	20 22	3 46	20 29	3 34	20 36	3 39	20 52	3 54	20 50
3	3 47	20 10	3 57	20 20	3 49	20 23	3 45	20 30	3 33	20 37	3 38	20 53	3 53	20 52
4	3 47	20 11	3 57	20 21	3 49	20 24	3 44	20 31	3 32	20 38	3 37	20 55	3 52	20 53
5	3 46	20 12	3 56	20 22	3 48	20 25	3 44	20 32	3 31	20 39	3 36	20 56	3 51	20 54
6	3 45	20 13	3 56	20 23	3 47	20 26	3 43	20 33	3 31	20 40	3 35	20 57	3 51	20 55
7	3 45	20 14	3 55	20 24	3 47	20 27	3 42	20 34	3 30	20 41	3 34	20 58	3 50	20 56
8	3 44	20 15	3 55	20 25	3 46	20 28	3 42	20 35	3 29	20 42	3 34	20 59	3 49	20 57
9	3 44	20 16	3 54	20 25	3 46	20 28	3 41	20 36	3 29	20 43	3 33	21 00	3 49	20 58
10	3 44	20 16	3 54	20 26	3 45	20 29	3 41	20 36	3 28	20 44	3 33	21 01	3 48	20 58
11	3 43	20 17	3 53	20 27	3 45	20 30	3 40	20 37	3 28	20 45	3 32	21 01	3 48	20 59
12	3 43	20 18	3 53	20 28	3 45	20 31	3 40	20 38	3 28	20 45	3 32	21 02	3 48	21 00
13	3 43	20 18	3 53	20 28	3 45	20 31	3 40	20 39	3 27	20 46	3 31	21 03	3 47	21 01
14	3 43	20 19	3 53	20 29	3 44	20 32	3 40	20 39	3 27	20 47	3 31	21 04	3 47	21 01
15	3 43	20 19	3 53	20 29	3 44	20 32	3 40	20 40	3 27	20 47	3 31	21 04	3 47	21 02
16	3 42	20 20	3 53	20 30	3 44	20 33	3 39	20 40	3 27	20 48	3 31	21 05	3 47	21 02
17	3 42	20 20	3 53	20 30	3 44	20 33	3 39	20 41	3 27	20 48	3 31	21 05	3 47	21 03
18	3 43	20 21	3 53	20 30	3 44	20 33	3 39	20 41	3 27	20 49	3 31	21 06	3 47	21 03
19	3 43	20 21	3 53	20 31	3 44	20 34	3 40	20 41	3 27	20 49	3 31	21 06	3 47	21 03
20	3 43	20 21	3 53	20 31	3 45	20 34	3 40	20 42	3 27	20 49	3 31	21 06	3 47	21 04
21	3 43	20 21	3 53	20 31	3 45	20 34	3 40	20 42	3 27	20 49	3 31	21 06	3 47	21 04
22	3 43	20 21	3 53	20 31	3 45	20 34	3 40	20 42	3 27	20 50	3 31	21 06	3 47	21 04
23	3 43	20 22	3 54	20 31	3 45	20 34	3 40	20 42	3 28	20 50	3 32	21 07	3 48	21 04
24	3 44	20 22	3 54	20 31	3 46	20 35	3 41	20 42	3 28	20 50	3 32	21 07	3 48	21 04
25	3 44	20 22	3 54	20 31	3 46	20 35	3 41	20 42	3 29	20 50	3 33	21 07	3 49	21 04
26	3 45	20 22	3 55	20 31	3 46	20 34	3 42	20 42	3 29	20 49	3 33	21 06	3 49	21 04
27	3 45	20 21	3 55	20 31	3 47	20 34	3 42	20 42	3 30	20 49	3 34	21 06	3 50	21 04
28	3 46	20 21	3 56	20 31	3 47	20 34	3 43	20 42	3 30	20 49	3 34	21 06	3 50	21 04
29	3 46	20 21	3 56	20 31	3 48	20 34	3 43	20 41	3 31	20 49	3 35	21 06	3 51	21 03
30	3 47	20 21	3 57	20 31	3 49	20 34	3 44	20 41	3 32	20 48	3 36	21 05	3 52	21 03

JUPITER

Day	RA	Dec.	Transit	5° high	
				52°	56°
	h m	° '	h m	h m	h m
1	19 11.6	−22 24	2 32	23 20	23 53
11	19 07.6	−22 32	1 49	22 38	23 12
21	19 02.8	−22 42	1 05	21 55	22 29
31	18 57.4	−22 50	0 20	21 12	21 46

Diameters – equatorial 46″ polar 44″

SATURN

Day	RA	Dec.	Transit	5° high	
				52°	56°
	h m	° '	h m	h m	h m
1	0 23.8	+ 0 11	7 44	2 16	2 19
11	0 26.4	+ 0 25	7 07	1 38	1 41
21	0 28.4	+ 0 36	6 30	1 00	1 03
31	0 29.9	+ 0 42	5 52	0 21	0 24

Diameters – equatorial 17″ polar 15″
Rings – major axis 39″ minor axis 4″

URANUS

Day	RA	Dec.	Transit	10° high	
				52°	56°
	h m	° '	h m	h m	h m
1	20 27.4	−19 45	3 48	1 06	1 46
11	20 26.5	−19 48	3 08	0 26	1 07
21	20 25.4	−19 52	2 27	23 42	0 27
31	20 24.0	−19 57	1 46	23 02	23 44

Diameter 4″

NEPTUNE

Day	RA	Dec.	Transit	10° high	
				52°	56°
	h m	° '	h m	h m	h m
1	19 57.8	−20 11	3 18	0 40	1 23
11	19 57.0	−20 13	2 38	0 01	0 44
21	19 56.1	−20 16	1 58	23 17	0 04
31	19 55.1	−20 18	1 18	22 37	23 20

Diameter 2″

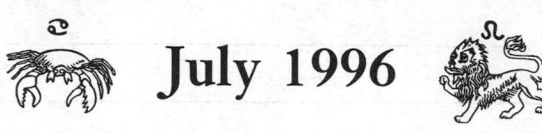

July 1996

SEVENTH MONTH, 31 DAYS. *Julius* Caesar, formerly *Quintilis*, fifth month of Roman pre-Julian calendar

1	*Monday*	*Princess of Wales b. 1961.* Juan Peron d. 1974	*week 26 day* 183
2	*Tuesday*	Sir Robert Peel d. 1850. Ernest Hemingway d. 1961	184
3	*Wednesday*	**St Thomas.** Tom Stoppard b. 1937	185
4	*Thursday*	William Byrd d. 1623. Marie Curie d. 1934	186
5	*Friday*	Phineas T. Barnum b. 1810. Cecil Rhodes b. 1853	187
6	*Saturday*	Tsar Nicholas I b. 1796. Beatrix Potter b. 1866	188
7	*Sunday*	**6th S. after Pentecost/5th S. after Trinity**	*week 27 day* 189
8	*Monday*	Count von Zeppelin b. 1838. Wilfred Rhodes d. 1973	190
9	*Tuesday*	Mrs Ann Radcliffe b. 1764. Ottorino Respighi b. 1879	191
10	*Wednesday*	Marcel Proust b. 1871. Joe Davis d. 1978	192
11	*Thursday*	⚔Courtrai 1302. Robert the Bruce b. 1274	193
12	*Friday*	*Bank Holiday in Northern Ireland*	194
13	*Saturday*	John Clare b. 1793. Lord Clark b. 1903	195
14	*Sunday*	**7th S. after Pentecost/6th S. after Trinity**	*week 28 day* 196
15	*Monday*	St Swithin's Day. Iris Murdoch b. 1919	197
16	*Tuesday*	Jean Corot b. 1796. Herbert von Karajan d. 1989	198
17	*Wednesday*	Charlotte Corday exec. 1793	199
18	*Thursday*	Jean Watteau d. 1721. W. M. Thackeray b. 1811	200
19	*Friday*	Edgar Degas b. 1834. A. J. Cronin b. 1896	201
20	*Saturday*	Francesco Petrarch b. 1304	202
21	*Sunday*	**8th S. after Pentecost/7th S. after Trinty**	*week 29 day* 203
22	*Monday*	**St Mary Magdalen.** ⚔Salamanca 1812	204
23	*Tuesday*	Marshal Philippe Pétain d. 1951	205
24	*Wednesday*	E. F. Benson b. 1867. Ernest Bloch b. 1880	206
25	*Thursday*	**St James.** Bill Bowes b. 1908	207
26	*Friday*	Carl Jung b. 1875. Lord Thorneycroft b. 1909	208
27	*Saturday*	Gertrude Stein d. 1946. James Mason d. 1984	209
28	*Sunday*	**9th S. after Pentecost/8th S. after Trinty**	*week 30 day* 210
29	*Monday*	William Wilberforce d. 1833. David Niven d. 1983	211
30	*Tuesday*	Thomas Gray d. 1771. Denis Diderot d. 1784	212
31	*Wednesday*	*Trinity Law Sittings end.* 'Gubby' Allen b. 1902	213

ASTRONOMICAL PHENOMENA

d	h	
1	10	Jupiter in conjunction with Moon. Jupiter 5° S.
2	07	Venus at stationary point
4	12	Jupiter at opposition
5	18	Earth at aphelion (152 million km)
7	03	Saturn in conjunction with Moon. Saturn 3° S.
11	09	Mercury in superior conjunction
12	09	Venus in conjunction with Moon. Venus 0°.4 S.
13	00	Mars in conjunction with Moon. Mars 5° N.
16	05	Mercury in conjunction with Moon. Mercury 6° N.
17	09	Venus at greatest brilliancy
18	18	Neptune at opposition
18	20	Saturn at stationary point
22	13	Sun's longitude 120° ♌
25	07	Uranus at opposition
28	15	Jupiter in conjunction with Moon. Jupiter 5° S.

MINIMA OF ALGOL

d	h	d	h	d	h
2	00.1	13	11.4	24	22.6
4	20.9	16	08.2	27	19.4
7	17.7	19	05.0	30	16.2
10	14.6	22	01.8		

CONSTELLATIONS

The following constellations are near the meridian at

	d	h		d	h
June	1	24	July	16	21
June	15	23	August	1	20
July	1	22	August	16	19

Ursa Minor, Draco, Corona, Hercules, Lyra, Serpens, Ophiuchus, Libra, Scorpius and Sagittarius

THE MOON

Phases, Apsides and Node	d	h	m
○ Full Moon	1	03	58
☾ Last Quarter	7	18	55
● New Moon	15	16	15
☽ First Quarter	23	17	49
○ Full Moon	30	10	35
Perigee (357,942 km)	1	22	17
Apogee (406,604 km)	16	13	48
Perigee (356,950 km)	30	07	41

Mean longitude of ascending node on July 1, 193°

THE SUN

s.d. 15′.8

Day	Right Ascension	Dec. +	Equation of time	Rise 52°	Rise 56°	Transit	Set 52°	Set 56°	Sidereal time	Transit of First Point of Aries
	h m s	° ′	m s	h m	h m	h m	h m	h m	h m s	h m s
1	6 41 05	23 06	−3 47	3 44	3 18	12 04	20 23	20 49	18 37 18	5 21 49
2	6 45 13	23 02	−3 58	3 45	3 19	12 04	20 23	20 48	18 41 15	5 17 53
3	6 49 21	22 57	−4 09	3 46	3 20	12 04	20 22	20 48	18 45 11	5 13 57
4	6 53 28	22 52	−4 20	3 47	3 21	12 04	20 22	20 47	18 49 08	5 10 01
5	6 57 35	22 47	−4 31	3 48	3 22	12 05	20 21	20 46	18 53 04	5 06 05
6	7 01 42	22 41	−4 41	3 48	3 23	12 05	20 21	20 45	18 57 01	5 02 09
7	7 05 48	22 35	−4 51	3 49	3 24	12 05	20 20	20 45	19 00 58	4 58 13
8	7 09 54	22 28	−5 00	3 50	3 26	12 05	20 19	20 44	19 04 54	4 54 18
9	7 14 00	22 21	−5 09	3 51	3 27	12 05	20 18	20 43	19 08 51	4 50 22
10	7 18 05	22 13	−5 18	3 52	3 28	12 05	20 18	20 42	19 12 47	4 46 26
11	7 22 10	22 06	−5 26	3 53	3 29	12 05	20 17	20 41	19 16 44	4 42 30
12	7 26 14	21 57	−5 34	3 55	3 31	12 06	20 16	20 40	19 20 40	4 38 34
13	7 30 18	21 49	−5 41	3 56	3 32	12 06	20 15	20 38	19 24 37	4 34 38
14	7 34 22	21 40	−5 48	3 57	3 34	12 06	20 14	20 37	19 28 33	4 30 42
15	7 38 25	21 31	−5 55	3 58	3 35	12 06	20 13	20 36	19 32 30	4 26 46
16	7 42 27	21 21	−6 01	3 59	3 37	12 06	20 12	20 34	19 36 27	4 22 50
17	7 46 29	21 11	−6 06	4 01	3 38	12 06	20 11	20 33	19 40 23	4 18 54
18	7 50 31	21 01	−6 11	4 02	3 40	12 06	20 10	20 32	19 44 20	4 14 58
19	7 54 32	20 50	−6 15	4 03	3 41	12 06	20 09	20 30	19 48 16	4 11 03
20	7 58 32	20 39	−6 19	4 05	3 43	12 06	20 07	20 29	19 52 13	4 07 07
21	8 02 32	20 27	−6 22	4 06	3 45	12 06	20 06	20 27	19 56 09	4 03 11
22	8 06 31	20 16	−6 25	4 07	3 46	12 06	20 05	20 25	20 00 06	3 59 15
23	8 10 29	20 03	−6 27	4 09	3 48	12 06	20 03	20 24	20 04 02	3 55 19
24	8 14 27	19 51	−6 28	4 10	3 50	12 06	20 02	20 22	20 07 59	3 51 23
25	8 18 25	19 38	−6 29	4 12	3 51	12 06	20 00	20 20	20 11 56	3 47 27
26	8 22 22	19 25	−6 29	4 13	3 53	12 06	19 59	20 18	20 15 52	3 43 31
27	8 26 18	19 12	−6 29	4 14	3 55	12 06	19 58	20 17	20 19 49	3 39 35
28	8 30 13	18 58	−6 28	4 16	3 57	12 06	19 56	20 15	20 23 45	3 35 39
29	8 34 08	18 44	−6 26	4 17	3 59	12 06	19 54	20 13	20 27 42	3 31 43
30	8 38 03	18 30	−6 24	4 19	4 00	12 06	19 53	20 11	20 31 38	3 27 48
31	8 41 56	18 15	−6 21	4 20	4 02	12 06	19 51	20 09	20 35 35	3 23 52

DURATION OF TWILIGHT (in minutes)

Latitude	52°	56°	52°	56°	52°	56°	52°	56°
	1 July		11 July		21 July		31 July	
Civil	48	61	46	58	44	53	41	49
Nautical	124	TAN	116	TAN	107	144	98	122
Astronomical	TAN	TAN	TAN	TAN	TAN	TAN	180	TAN

THE NIGHT SKY

Mercury passes through superior conjunction on the 11th and therefore remains too close to the Sun for observation.

Venus is rapidly moving away from the Sun and is visible as a brilliant morning object completely dominating the eastern sky for several hours before dawn, magnitude −4.5. Locating Venus in daylight is a challenge for keen-sighted naked-eye observers; it is even more interesting on the morning of the 12th when Venus rises shortly after the Moon, then a thin crescent only two days before New. Observers following it after sunrise will notice the gap between the two bodies steadily closing, an actual occultation occurring in daylight before 08h. (*See* page 66)

Mars, magnitude +1.5, very gradually emerges from the long morning twilight to be visible in the eastern sky for a short time before the sky gets too bright.

Jupiter reaches opposition on the 4th and is therefore visible in the southern skies throughout the hours of darkness. Its magnitude is −2.7. The Full Moon is near the planet on the 1st and again on the 28th.

Saturn, magnitude +0.8, is a morning object in the south-eastern sky in Cetus, though it is now rising in the east before midnight. On the morning of the 7th the Moon, at Last Quarter, passes 3° north of the planet.

Uranus is at opposition on the 25th, in Capricornus. Uranus is barely visible to the naked eye as its magnitude is +5.7, but it is readily located with only small optical aid.

Neptune is at opposition on the 18th, in Sagittarius. It is not visible to the naked eye as its magnitude is +7.9.

THE MOON

Day	RA	Dec.	Hor. par.	Semi-diam.	Sun's co-long.	PA of Bright Limb	Phase	Age	Rise 52°	Rise 56°	Transit	Set 52°	Set 56°
	h m	°	′	′	°	°	%	d	h m	h m	h m	h m	h m
1	18 30	−18.3	61.1	16.7	90	332	100	14.9	20 16	20 33	—	4 23	4 05
2	19 33	−16.7	61.3	16.7	102	59	99	15.9	21 01	21 14	0 54	5 37	5 22
3	20 35	−14.0	61.1	16.6	114	66	95	16.9	21 37	21 47	1 54	6 56	6 44
4	21 34	−10.4	60.6	16.5	126	67	88	17.9	22 09	22 14	2 52	8 16	8 08
5	22 31	− 6.2	59.9	16.3	138	66	79	18.9	22 37	22 39	3 46	9 35	9 31
6	23 26	− 1.7	59.1	16.1	151	66	69	19.9	23 04	23 02	4 38	10 52	10 52
7	0 18	+ 2.7	58.3	15.9	163	67	59	20.9	23 30	23 25	5 28	12 05	12 09
8	1 10	+ 6.8	57.4	15.6	175	68	48	21.9	23 58	23 49	6 17	13 17	13 24
9	2 01	+10.5	56.6	15.4	187	69	37	22.9	—	—	7 06	14 25	14 36
10	2 51	+13.6	55.9	15.2	200	72	28	23.9	0 28	0 16	7 54	15 30	15 44
11	3 42	+16.0	55.4	15.1	212	74	19	24.9	1 01	0 46	8 42	16 31	16 47
12	4 33	+17.7	54.9	15.0	224	77	12	25.9	1 40	1 23	9 31	17 26	17 44
13	5 24	+18.5	54.5	14.9	236	78	7	26.9	2 23	2 05	10 19	18 16	18 34
14	6 14	+18.4	54.2	14.8	249	77	3	27.9	3 12	2 54	11 07	18 59	19 16
15	7 04	+17.6	54.0	14.7	261	63	1	28.9	4 06	3 49	11 54	19 36	19 51
16	7 53	+16.0	53.9	14.7	273	335	0	0.3	5 03	4 49	12 40	20 08	20 21
17	8 41	+13.7	53.9	14.7	285	302	2	1.3	6 04	5 52	13 25	20 37	20 46
18	9 28	+10.9	54.0	14.7	298	296	5	2.3	7 05	6 57	14 09	21 02	21 09
19	10 15	+ 7.6	54.2	14.8	310	295	10	3.3	8 08	8 03	14 52	21 26	21 29
20	11 00	+ 4.0	54.5	14.9	322	295	16	4.3	9 12	9 10	15 36	21 48	21 49
21	11 46	+ 0.1	55.0	15.0	334	294	24	5.3	10 17	10 18	16 19	22 11	22 09
22	12 33	− 3.7	55.5	15.1	347	293	33	6.3	11 23	11 28	17 04	22 36	22 30
23	13 21	− 7.5	56.2	15.3	359	292	42	7.3	12 31	12 39	17 52	23 04	22 54
24	14 12	−11.1	57.0	15.5	11	290	53	8.3	13 40	13 52	18 42	23 36	23 23
25	15 05	−14.2	57.9	15.8	23	287	63	9.3	14 51	15 06	19 35	—	23 59
26	16 01	−16.6	58.9	16.0	35	284	74	10.3	15 59	16 17	20 32	0 15	—
27	17 00	−18.1	59.8	16.3	48	280	83	11.3	17 04	17 22	21 32	1 02	0 45
28	18 02	−18.5	60.6	16.5	60	277	91	12.3	18 01	18 19	22 34	2 01	1 42
29	19 05	−17.5	61.1	16.7	72	277	97	13.3	18 50	19 05	23 35	3 10	2 53
30	20 08	−15.4	61.4	16.7	84	294	100	14.3	19 32	19 43	—	4 26	4 12
31	21 09	−12.1	61.3	16.7	96	46	99	15.3	20 07	20 14	0 35	5 47	5 37

MERCURY

Day	RA	Dec.	Diam.	Phase	Transit	5° high 52°	5° high 56°
	h m	°	″	%	h m	h m	h m
1	5 48	+23.3	5	87	11 13	3 38	3 20
3	6 06	+23.7	5	91	11 23	3 46	3 27
5	6 25	+23.9	5	95	11 34	3 55	3 36
7	6 43	+24.0	5	98	11 45	4 05	3 46
9	7 02	+23.9	5	99	11 56	4 17	3 58
11	7 21	+23.6	5	100	12 07	19 43	20 01
13	7 40	+23.1	5	100	12 18	19 50	20 08
15	7 58	+22.4	5	99	12 28	19 56	20 12
17	8 15	+21.6	5	97	12 38	20 00	20 16
19	8 32	+20.7	5	95	12 46	20 03	20 17
21	8 49	+19.7	5	93	12 55	20 05	20 18
23	9 04	+18.6	5	90	13 02	20 05	20 18
25	9 19	+17.4	5	88	13 09	20 05	20 16
27	9 33	+16.1	5	85	13 15	20 04	20 14
29	9 47	+14.8	5	82	13 20	20 02	20 11
31	9 59	+13.5	6	80	13 25	20 00	20 07

VENUS

Day	RA	Dec.	Diam.	Phase	Transit	5° high 52°	5° high 56°
	h m	°	″	%	h m	h m	h m
1	4 44	+18.1	48	12	10 05	3 03	2 51
6	4 45	+17.7	44	17	9 46	2 47	2 35
11	4 49	+17.7	41	22	9 32	2 32	2 21
16	4 57	+17.8	38	26	9 20	2 20	2 08
21	5 08	+18.1	35	30	9 11	2 09	1 57
26	5 21	+18.5	32	34	9 05	2 00	1 48
31	5 36	+18.9	30	38	9 00	1 53	1 40

MARS

Day	RA	Dec.	Diam.	Phase	Transit	5° high 52°	5° high 56°
1	4 46	+22.5	4	98	10 09	2 40	2 23
6	5 01	+22.9	4	97	10 04	2 33	2 15
11	5 16	+23.3	4	97	9 59	2 26	2 08
16	5 31	+23.6	4	97	9 54	2 19	2 01
21	5 46	+23.7	4	97	9 49	2 13	1 54
26	6 01	+23.8	4	97	9 44	2 08	1 49
31	6 15	+23.9	4	96	9 39	2 03	1 44

SUNRISE AND SUNSET

	London		Bristol		Birmingham		Manchester		Newcastle		Glasgow		Belfast	
	0°05′	51°30′	2°35′	51°28′	1°55′	52°28′	2°15′	53°28′	1°37′	54°59′	4°14′	55°52′	5°56′	54°35′
	h m	h m	h m	h m	h m	h m	h m	h m	h m	h m	h m	h m	h m	h m
1	3 48	20 21	3 58	20 30	3 49	20 33	3 45	20 41	3 32	20 48	3 36	21 05	3 52	21 02
2	3 48	20 20	3 58	20 30	3 50	20 33	3 46	20 40	3 33	20 47	3 37	21 04	3 53	21 02
3	3 49	20 20	3 59	20 30	3 51	20 32	3 46	20 40	3 34	20 47	3 38	21 04	3 54	21 01
4	3 50	20 19	4 00	20 29	3 52	20 32	3 47	20 39	3 35	20 46	3 39	21 03	3 55	21 01
5	3 51	20 19	4 01	20 29	3 53	20 31	3 48	20 39	3 36	20 46	3 40	21 02	3 56	21 00
6	3 52	20 18	4 02	20 28	3 54	20 31	3 49	20 38	3 37	20 45	3 41	21 01	3 57	21 00
7	3 52	20 18	4 03	20 27	3 54	20 30	3 50	20 37	3 38	20 44	3 42	21 01	3 58	20 59
8	3 53	20 17	4 04	20 27	3 55	20 29	3 51	20 36	3 39	20 43	3 44	21 00	3 59	20 58
9	3 54	20 16	4 05	20 26	3 57	20 29	3 52	20 36	3 40	20 42	3 45	20 59	4 00	20 57
10	3 55	20 15	4 06	20 25	3 58	20 28	3 53	20 35	3 41	20 41	3 46	20 58	4 01	20 56
11	3 56	20 15	4 07	20 24	3 59	20 27	3 54	20 34	3 43	20 40	3 47	20 57	4 02	20 55
12	3 57	20 14	4 08	20 24	4 00	20 26	3 56	20 33	3 44	20 39	3 49	20 56	4 04	20 54
13	3 59	20 13	4 09	20 23	4 01	20 25	3 57	20 32	3 45	20 38	3 50	20 54	4 05	20 53
14	4 00	20 12	4 10	20 22	4 02	20 24	3 58	20 31	3 47	20 37	3 51	20 53	4 06	20 52
15	4 01	20 11	4 11	20 21	4 03	20 23	3 59	20 30	3 48	20 36	3 53	20 52	4 08	20 51
16	4 02	20 10	4 12	20 20	4 05	20 22	4 01	20 29	3 49	20 35	3 54	20 51	4 09	20 50
17	4 03	20 09	4 14	20 19	4 06	20 21	4 02	20 27	3 51	20 33	3 56	20 49	4 11	20 48
18	4 05	20 08	4 15	20 17	4 07	20 20	4 03	20 26	3 52	20 32	3 58	20 48	4 12	20 47
19	4 06	20 06	4 16	20 16	4 09	20 18	4 05	20 25	3 54	20 31	3 59	20 46	4 13	20 46
20	4 07	20 05	4 17	20 15	4 10	20 17	4 06	20 23	3 55	20 29	4 01	20 45	4 15	20 44
21	4 09	20 04	4 19	20 14	4 11	20 16	4 08	20 22	3 57	20 28	4 02	20 43	4 17	20 43
22	4 10	20 03	4 20	20 13	4 13	20 15	4 09	20 21	3 59	20 26	4 04	20 42	4 18	20 41
23	4 11	20 01	4 21	20 11	4 14	20 13	4 11	20 19	4 00	20 25	4 06	20 40	4 20	20 40
24	4 13	20 00	4 23	20 10	4 16	20 12	4 12	20 18	4 02	20 23	4 07	20 38	4 21	20 38
25	4 14	19 59	4 24	20 09	4 17	20 10	4 14	20 16	4 04	20 21	4 09	20 36	4 23	20 36
26	4 15	19 57	4 26	20 07	4 19	20 09	4 15	20 15	4 05	20 20	4 11	20 35	4 25	20 35
27	4 17	19 56	4 27	20 06	4 20	20 07	4 17	20 13	4 07	20 18	4 13	20 33	4 26	20 33
28	4 18	19 54	4 29	20 04	4 22	20 06	4 18	20 11	4 09	20 16	4 15	20 31	4 28	20 31
29	4 20	19 53	4 30	20 03	4 23	20 04	4 20	20 10	4 10	20 14	4 16	20 29	4 30	20 30
30	4 21	19 51	4 31	20 01	4 25	20 02	4 22	20 08	4 12	20 12	4 18	20 27	4 31	20 28
31	4 23	19 50	4 33	19 59	4 26	20 01	4 23	20 06	4 14	20 11	4 20	20 25	4 33	20 26

JUPITER

Day	RA	Dec.	Transit	5° high	
				52°	56°
	h m	° ′	h m	h m	h m
1	18 57.4	−22 50	0 20	3 24	2 50
11	18 51.9	−22 59	23 31	2 38	2 03
21	18 46.6	−23 07	22 46	1 52	1 17
31	18 41.9	−23 13	22 02	1 08	0 32

Diameters – equatorial 47″ polar 44″

SATURN

Day	RA	Dec.	Transit	5° high	
				52°	56°
	h m	° ′	h m	h m	h m
1	0 29.9	+ 0 42	5 52	0 21	0 24
11	0 30.7	+ 0 45	5 13	23 39	23 42
21	0 31.0	+ 0 43	4 34	23 00	23 03
31	0 30.6	+ 0 38	3 54	22 21	22 23

Diameters – equatorial 18″ polar 16″
Rings – major axis 41″ minor axis 4″

URANUS

Day	RA	Dec.	Transit	10° high	
				52°	56°
	h m	° ′	h m	h m	h m
1	20 24.0	−19 57	1 46	23 02	23 44
11	20 22.5	−20 02	1 06	22 22	23 04
21	20 20.8	−20 08	0 25	21 42	22 25
31	20 19.2	−20 13	23 40	21 02	21 45

Diameter 4″

NEPTUNE

Day	RA	Dec.	Transit	10° high	
				52°	56°
	h m	° ′	h m	h m	h m
1	19 55.1	−20 18	1 18	3 54	3 11
11	19 54.0	−20 22	0 37	3 13	2 30
21	19 52.9	−20 25	23 53	2 32	1 48
31	19 51.7	−20 28	23 12	1 51	1 07

Diameter 2″

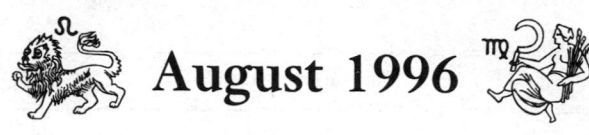

August 1996

EIGHTH MONTH, 31 DAYS. Julius, Caesar *Augustus*, formerly *Sextilis*, sixth month of Roman pre-Julian calendar

1	*Thursday*	⟋Minden 1759. Sir Frank Worrell b. 1924	*week* 30 *day* 214
2	*Friday*	Myrna Loy b. 1905. Enrico Caruso d. 1921	215
3	*Saturday*	Richard Arkwright d. 1792. Colette d. 1954	216
4	*Sunday*	**10th S. after Pentecost/9th S. after Trinity**	*week* 31 *day* 217
5	*Monday*	*Bank Holiday in Scotland.* Friedrich Engels d. 1895	218
6	*Tuesday*	**The Transfiguration.** Ben Jonson d. 1637	219
7	*Wednesday*	Sir Rabindranath Tagore d. 1941	220
8	*Thursday*	Princess Beatrice of York b. 1988	221
9	*Friday*	Izaak Walton b. 1593. Jean Piaget b. 1896	222
10	*Saturday*	Charles Keene b. 1823. James Whistler b. 1834	223
11	*Sunday*	**11th S. after Pentecost/10th S. after Trinity**	*week* 32 *day* 224
12	*Monday*	George Stephenson d. 1848. Thomas Mann d. 1955	225
13	*Tuesday*	John Ireland b. 1879. Florence Nightingale d. 1910	226
14	*Wednesday*	John Galsworthy b. 1867. Enzo Ferrari d. 1988	227
15	*Thursday*	*Princess Royal b. 1950.* T. E. Lawrence b. 1888	228
16	*Friday*	Peterloo Massacre 1819. Robert van Bunsen d. 1899	229
17	*Saturday*	Davy Crockett b. 1786. Rudolf Hess d. 1987	230
18	*Sunday*	**12th S. after Pentecost/11th S. after Trinity**	*week* 33 *day* 231
19	*Monday*	Orville Wright b. 1871. President Bill Clinton b. 1946	232
20	*Tuesday*	Duke of Buckingham b. 1592	233
21	*Wednesday*	*Princess Margaret b. 1930.* William IV b. 1765	234
22	*Thursday*	Jean-Honoré Fragonard d. 1806	235
23	*Friday*	Jo Richardson b. 1923. Oscar Hammerstein d. 1960	236
24	*Saturday*	**St Bartholomew.** Massacre of Huguenots, Paris 1572	237
25	*Sunday*	**13th S. after Pentecost/12th S. after Trinity**	*week* 34 *day* 238
26	*Monday*	*Bank Holiday in England, Wales and Northern Ireland*	239
27	*Tuesday*	Georg Hegel b. 1770. Theodore Dreiser b. 1871	240
28	*Wednesday*	Sir Edward Burne-Jones b. 1833	241
29	*Thursday*	John Locke b. 1632. Revd William Spooner d. 1930	242
30	*Friday*	Ernest Rutherford b. 1871	243
31	*Saturday*	Charles Baudelaire d. 1867. Henry Moore d. 1986	244

ASTRONOMICAL PHENOMENA

d	h	
3	11	Saturn in conjunction with Moon. Saturn 2° S.
10	04	Venus in conjunction with Moon. Venus 1° N.
10	12	Pluto at stationary point
10	20	Mars in conjunction with Moon. Mars 6° N.
16	18	Mercury in conjunction with Moon. Mercury 0°.3 N.
20	04	Venus at greatest elongation W. 46°
21	16	Mercury at greatest elongation E. 27°
22	20	Sun's longitude 150° ♍
24	22	Jupiter in conjunction with Moon. Jupiter 5° S.
30	19	Saturn in conjunction with Moon. Saturn 3° S.

MINIMA OF ALGOL

d	h	d	h	d	h
2	13.0	14	00.3	25	11.5
5	09.8	16	21.1	28	08.3
8	06.7	19	17.9	31	05.1
11	03.5	22	14.7		

CONSTELLATIONS

The following constellations are near the meridian at

	d	h		d	h
July	1	24	August	16	21
July	16	23	September	1	20
August	1	22	September	15	19

Draco, Hercules, Lyra, Cygnus, Sagitta, Ophiuchus, Serpens, Aquila and Sagittarius

THE MOON

Phases, Apsides and Node	d	h	m
☾ Last Quarter	6	05	25
● New Moon	14	07	34
☽ First Quarter	22	03	36
○ Full Moon	28	17	52
Apogee (406,465 km)	12	16	43
Perigee (358,786 km)	27	17	00

Mean longitude of ascending node on August 1, 191°

THE SUN

s.d. 15′.8

Day	Right Ascension	Dec. +	Equation of time	Rise 52°	Rise 56°	Transit	Set 52°	Set 56°	Sidereal time	Transit of First Point of Aries
	h m s	° ′	m s	h m	h m	h m	h m	h m	h m s	h m s
1	8 45 49	18 00	−6 18	4 22	4 04	12 06	19 50	20 07	20 39 31	3 19 56
2	8 49 42	17 45	−6 14	4 24	4 06	12 06	19 48	20 05	20 43 28	3 16 00
3	8 53 34	17 29	−6 09	4 25	4 08	12 06	19 46	20 03	20 47 25	3 12 04
4	8 57 25	17 13	−6 04	4 27	4 10	12 06	19 44	20 01	20 51 21	3 08 08
5	9 01 16	16 57	−5 58	4 28	4 12	12 06	19 43	19 59	20 55 18	3 04 12
6	9 05 06	16 41	−5 52	4 30	4 14	12 06	19 41	19 57	20 59 14	3 00 16
7	9 08 56	16 24	−5 45	4 31	4 16	12 06	19 39	19 54	21 03 11	2 56 20
8	9 12 45	16 07	−5 37	4 33	4 18	12 06	19 37	19 52	21 07 07	2 52 24
9	9 16 33	15 50	−5 29	4 35	4 19	12 05	19 35	19 50	21 11 04	2 48 28
10	9 20 21	15 33	−5 21	4 36	4 21	12 05	19 33	19 48	21 15 00	2 44 33
11	9 24 08	15 15	−5 11	4 38	4 23	12 05	19 31	19 45	21 18 57	2 40 37
12	9 27 55	14 57	−5 02	4 39	4 25	12 05	19 29	19 43	21 22 54	2 36 41
13	9 31 41	14 39	−4 51	4 41	4 27	12 05	19 27	19 41	21 26 50	2 32 45
14	9 35 27	14 20	−4 40	4 43	4 29	12 05	19 25	19 39	21 30 47	2 28 49
15	9 39 12	14 02	−4 29	4 44	4 31	12 04	19 23	19 36	21 34 43	2 24 53
16	9 42 57	13 43	−4 17	4 46	4 33	12 04	19 21	19 34	21 38 40	2 20 57
17	9 46 41	13 24	−4 04	4 48	4 35	12 04	19 19	19 31	21 42 36	2 17 01
18	9 50 24	13 05	−3 51	4 49	4 37	12 04	19 17	19 29	21 46 33	2 13 05
19	9 54 07	12 45	−3 38	4 51	4 39	12 04	19 15	19 27	21 50 29	2 09 09
20	9 57 50	12 25	−3 24	4 52	4 41	12 03	19 13	19 24	21 54 26	2 05 13
21	10 01 32	12 06	−3 09	4 54	4 43	12 03	19 11	19 22	21 58 23	2 01 18
22	10 05 13	11 45	−2 54	4 56	4 45	12 03	19 09	19 19	22 02 19	1 57 22
23	10 08 55	11 25	−2 39	4 57	4 47	12 03	19 07	19 17	22 06 16	1 53 26
24	10 12 35	11 05	−2 23	4 59	4 49	12 02	19 04	19 14	22 10 12	1 49 30
25	10 16 15	10 44	−2 07	5 01	4 51	12 02	19 02	19 12	22 14 09	1 45 34
26	10 19 55	10 23	−1 50	5 02	4 53	12 02	19 00	19 09	22 18 05	1 41 38
27	10 23 35	10 02	−1 33	5 04	4 55	12 01	18 58	19 07	22 22 02	1 37 42
28	10 27 14	9 41	−1 15	5 05	4 57	12 01	18 56	19 04	22 25 58	1 33 46
29	10 30 52	9 20	−0 57	5 07	4 59	12 01	18 53	19 02	22 29 55	1 29 50
30	10 34 30	8 59	−0 39	5 09	5 01	12 01	18 51	18 59	22 33 51	1 25 54
31	10 38 08	8 37	−0 20	5 10	5 03	12 00	18 49	18 56	22 37 48	1 21 59

DURATION OF TWILIGHT (in minutes)

Latitude	52°	56°	52°	56°	52°	56°	52°	56°
	1 August		11 August		21 August		31 August	
Civil	41	48	39	45	37	42	35	40
Nautical	97	120	89	106	83	96	79	89
Astronomical	177	TAN	153	205	138	166	127	147

THE NIGHT SKY

Mercury is too close to the Sun for observation.

Venus, magnitude −4.3, reaches its greatest western elongation (46°) on the 20th and continues to be visible as a magnificent object in the eastern sky in the mornings before sunrise. Venus is in the same area of the sky as Mars and by the end of the month the two planets are only a few degrees apart. On the morning of the 10th the old crescent Moon, four days before New, passes about 1° south of Venus.

Mars is visible as a difficult morning object in the eastern sky, magnitude +1.5. Mars is in Gemini, passing 6° south of Pollux at the end of the month.

Jupiter, magnitude −2.6, continues to be visible as a conspicuous object in the southern skies for most of the night. On the evening of the 24th the gibbous Moon passes 5° north of the planet.

Saturn is moving towards opposition next month so it is already visible in the southern skies for the greater part of the night. Its magnitude is +0.7.

Meteors. The maximum of the famous Perseid meteor shower occurs on the 12th. Conditions are very favourable because of the absence of moonlight.

THE MOON

Day	RA	Dec.	Hor. par.	Semi-diam.	Sun's co-long.	PA of Bright Limb	Phase	Age	Rise 52°	Rise 56°	Transit	Set 52°	Set 56°
	h m	°	'	'	°	°	%	d	h m	h m	h m	h m	h m
1	22 09	− 8.1	61.0	16.6	109	62	96	16.3	20 38	20 41	1 33	7 09	7 03
2	23 06	− 3.6	60.3	16.4	121	64	90	17.3	21 06	21 06	2 28	8 29	8 27
3	0 01	+ 1.0	59.5	16.2	133	66	82	18.3	21 34	21 30	3 20	9 47	9 49
4	0 54	+ 5.3	58.5	15.9	145	67	73	19.3	22 01	21 54	4 11	11 01	11 08
5	1 46	+ 9.3	57.6	15.7	157	70	63	20.3	22 31	22 20	5 01	12 13	12 22
6	2 38	+12.6	56.7	15.4	170	72	52	21.3	23 04	22 50	5 51	13 20	13 33
7	3 30	+15.3	55.9	15.2	182	75	42	22.3	23 41	23 25	6 39	14 23	14 39
8	4 21	+17.1	55.2	15.0	194	79	33	23.3	—	—	7 28	15 21	15 38
9	5 12	+18.2	54.7	14.9	206	82	24	24.3	0 22	0 05	8 17	16 12	16 30
10	6 02	+18.4	54.3	14.8	218	86	16	25.3	1 09	0 52	9 05	16 58	17 15
11	6 52	+17.8	54.1	14.7	231	88	10	26.3	2 01	1 44	9 52	17 37	17 53
12	7 41	+16.4	54.0	14.7	243	89	5	27.3	2 57	2 42	10 38	18 11	18 24
13	8 30	+14.3	53.9	14.7	255	87	2	28.3	3 57	3 44	11 23	18 41	18 51
14	9 17	+11.6	54.0	14.7	267	59	0	29.3	4 58	4 48	12 08	19 07	19 15
15	10 04	+ 8.5	54.2	14.8	280	314	1	0.7	6 01	5 54	12 51	19 31	19 36
16	10 50	+ 5.0	54.4	14.8	292	299	3	1.7	7 04	7 01	13 35	19 55	19 56
17	11 36	+ 1.2	54.8	14.9	304	296	7	2.7	8 09	8 09	14 18	20 18	20 16
18	12 22	− 2.6	55.2	15.0	316	294	12	3.7	9 14	9 18	15 03	20 42	20 37
19	13 10	− 6.4	55.7	15.2	329	292	19	4.7	10 21	10 28	15 49	21 08	21 00
20	13 59	−10.0	56.3	15.3	341	289	28	5.7	11 28	11 39	16 37	21 38	21 26
21	14 50	−13.2	57.0	15.5	353	286	38	6.7	12 36	12 50	17 28	22 13	21 58
22	15 44	−15.8	57.8	15.7	5	283	48	7.7	13 44	14 00	18 21	22 55	22 39
23	16 40	−17.5	58.6	16.0	17	279	59	8.7	14 48	15 06	19 18	23 47	23 29
24	17 39	−18.3	59.4	16.2	30	274	70	9.7	15 47	16 05	20 17	—	—
25	18 40	−17.9	60.1	16.4	42	270	80	10.7	16 38	16 55	21 16	0 49	0 31
26	19 41	−16.3	60.7	16.5	54	266	89	11.7	17 23	17 36	22 16	1 59	1 44
27	20 42	−13.6	61.0	16.6	66	265	95	12.7	18 01	18 11	23 14	3 17	3 05
28	21 42	−10.0	61.1	16.6	78	270	99	13.7	18 34	18 40	—	4 38	4 30
29	22 41	− 5.7	60.9	16.6	91	33	100	14.7	19 04	19 06	0 11	5 59	5 55
30	23 37	− 1.1	60.3	16.4	103	63	98	15.7	19 33	19 31	1 06	7 20	7 20
31	0 33	+ 3.5	59.6	16.2	115	67	93	16.7	20 02	19 56	1 59	8 38	8 42

MERCURY

Day	RA	Dec.	Diam.	Phase	Transit	5° high 52°	5° high 56°
	h m	°	"	%	h m	h m	h m
1	10 06	+12.8	6	79	13 27	19 58	20 05
3	10 18	+11.5	6	76	13 31	19 55	20 01
5	10 29	+10.1	6	74	13 35	19 51	19 56
7	10 40	+ 8.8	6	72	13 37	19 47	19 50
9	10 50	+ 7.4	6	69	13 40	19 42	19 45
11	11 00	+ 6.1	6	67	13 41	19 37	19 39
13	11 09	+ 4.8	6	64	13 43	19 32	19 32
15	11 18	+ 3.5	7	62	13 43	19 26	19 25
17	11 26	+ 2.3	7	59	13 43	19 20	19 18
19	11 34	+ 1.1	7	56	13 43	19 13	19 11
21	11 41	0.0	7	53	13 42	19 07	19 03
23	11 47	− 1.1	7	50	13 40	19 00	18 55
25	11 52	− 2.1	8	47	13 38	18 52	18 47
27	11 57	− 2.9	8	43	13 34	18 44	18 38
29	12 01	− 3.7	8	39	13 30	18 36	18 30
31	12 04	− 4.3	9	35	13 25	18 28	18 21

VENUS

Day	RA	Dec.	Diam.	Phase	Transit	5° high 52°	5° high 56°
	h m	°	"	%	h m	h m	h m
1	5 39	+18.9	30	38	8 59	1 52	1 39
6	5 56	+19.3	28	42	8 56	1 47	1 33
11	6 14	+19.6	26	45	8 55	1 44	1 30
16	6 33	+19.8	25	48	8 54	1 42	1 28
21	6 53	+19.8	23	51	8 55	1 42	1 28
26	7 14	+19.6	22	53	8 56	1 45	1 31
31	7 35	+19.3	21	56	8 58	1 48	1 35

MARS

Day	RA	Dec.	Diam.	Phase	Transit	5° high 52°	5° high 56°
1	6 18	+23.8	4	96	9 38	2 02	1 43
6	6 33	+23.8	4	96	9 33	1 57	1 38
11	6 47	+23.6	4	96	9 28	1 53	1 34
16	7 02	+23.3	4	96	9 22	1 49	1 31
21	7 16	+23.0	4	95	9 17	1 45	1 28
26	7 30	+22.6	4	95	9 11	1 42	1 25
31	7 43	+22.2	4	95	9 05	1 39	1 22

SUNRISE AND SUNSET

	London		Bristol		Birmingham		Manchester		Newcastle		Glasgow		Belfast	
	0°05′	51°30′	2°35′	51°28′	1°55′	52°28′	2°15′	53°28′	1°37′	54°59′	4°14′	55°52′	5°56′	54°35′
	h m	h m	h m	h m	h m	h m	h m	h m	h m	h m	h m	h m	h m	h m
1	4 24	19 48	4 34	19 58	4 28	19 59	4 25	20 04	4 16	20 09	4 22	20 23	4 35	20 24
2	4 26	19 46	4 36	19 56	4 29	19 57	4 27	20 03	4 17	20 07	4 24	20 21	4 37	20 22
3	4 27	19 45	4 37	19 54	4 31	19 56	4 28	20 01	4 19	20 05	4 26	20 19	4 38	20 20
4	4 29	19 43	4 39	19 53	4 33	19 54	4 30	19 59	4 21	20 03	4 27	20 17	4 40	20 18
5	4 30	19 41	4 40	19 51	4 34	19 52	4 32	19 57	4 23	20 01	4 29	20 15	4 42	20 16
6	4 32	19 39	4 42	19 49	4 36	19 50	4 33	19 55	4 25	19 59	4 31	20 13	4 44	20 14
7	4 33	19 38	4 44	19 47	4 37	19 48	4 35	19 53	4 26	19 57	4 33	20 11	4 45	20 12
8	4 35	19 36	4 45	19 46	4 39	19 46	4 37	19 51	4 28	19 54	4 35	20 09	4 47	20 10
9	4 37	19 34	4 47	19 44	4 41	19 44	4 38	19 49	4 30	19 52	4 37	20 06	4 49	20 08
10	4 38	19 32	4 48	19 42	4 42	19 42	4 40	19 47	4 32	19 50	4 39	20 04	4 51	20 06
11	4 40	19 30	4 50	19 40	4 44	19 40	4 42	19 45	4 34	19 48	4 41	20 02	4 53	20 04
12	4 41	19 28	4 51	19 38	4 46	19 38	4 44	19 43	4 36	19 46	4 43	20 00	4 54	20 02
13	4 43	19 26	4 53	19 36	4 47	19 36	4 45	19 41	4 38	19 44	4 45	19 57	4 56	19 59
14	4 44	19 24	4 55	19 34	4 49	19 34	4 47	19 39	4 39	19 41	4 47	19 55	4 58	19 57
15	4 46	19 22	4 56	19 32	4 51	19 32	4 49	19 37	4 41	19 39	4 49	19 53	5 00	19 55
16	4 48	19 20	4 58	19 30	4 52	19 30	4 51	19 35	4 43	19 37	4 51	19 50	5 02	19 53
17	4 49	19 18	4 59	19 28	4 54	19 28	4 52	19 32	4 45	19 35	4 53	19 48	5 04	19 51
18	4 51	19 16	5 01	19 26	4 56	19 26	4 54	19 30	4 47	19 32	4 55	19 45	5 05	19 48
19	4 52	19 14	5 03	19 24	4 57	19 24	4 56	19 28	4 49	19 30	4 56	19 43	5 07	19 46
20	4 54	19 12	5 04	19 22	4 59	19 22	4 58	19 26	4 51	19 28	4 58	19 41	5 09	19 44
21	4 56	19 10	5 06	19 20	5 01	19 20	4 59	19 24	4 53	19 25	5 00	19 38	5 11	19 41
22	4 57	19 08	5 07	19 18	5 02	19 18	5 01	19 21	4 54	19 23	5 02	19 36	5 13	19 39
23	4 59	19 06	5 09	19 16	5 04	19 15	5 03	19 19	4 56	19 20	5 04	19 33	5 15	19 37
24	5 00	19 04	5 10	19 14	5 06	19 13	5 04	19 17	4 58	19 18	5 06	19 31	5 16	19 34
25	5 02	19 02	5 12	19 11	5 07	19 11	5 06	19 14	5 00	19 16	5 08	19 28	5 18	19 32
26	5 04	18 59	5 14	19 09	5 09	19 09	5 08	19 12	5 02	19 13	5 10	19 26	5 20	19 29
27	5 05	18 57	5 15	19 07	5 11	19 06	5 10	19 10	5 04	19 11	5 12	19 23	5 22	19 27
28	5 07	18 55	5 17	19 05	5 12	19 04	5 11	19 08	5 06	19 08	5 14	19 21	5 24	19 25
29	5 08	18 53	5 18	19 03	5 14	19 02	5 13	19 05	5 07	19 06	5 16	19 18	5 26	19 22
30	5 10	18 51	5 20	19 01	5 16	19 00	5 15	19 03	5 09	19 03	5 18	19 16	5 27	19 20
31	5 12	18 48	5 22	18 58	5 17	18 57	5 17	19 00	5 11	19 01	5 20	19 13	5 29	19 17

JUPITER

Day	RA	Dec.	Transit	5° high	
				52°	56°
	h m	° ′	h m	h m	h m
1	18 41.5	−23 13	21 58	1 03	0 27
11	18 37.9	−23 18	21 15	0 19	23 39
21	18 35.4	−23 21	20 33	23 33	22 57
31	18 34.2	−23 23	19 53	22 52	22 16

Diameters – equatorial 45″ polar 42″

SATURN

Day	RA	Dec.	Transit	5° high	
				52°	56°
	h m	° ′	h m	h m	h m
1	0 30.5	+ 0 37	3 50	22 17	22 20
11	0 29.5	+ 0 28	3 10	21 37	21 40
21	0 27.9	+ 0 15	2 29	20 57	21 00
31	0 25.8	0 00	1 48	20 17	20 21

Diameters – equatorial 19″ polar 17″
Rings – major axis 43″ minor axis 4″

URANUS

Day	RA	Dec.	Transit	10° high	
				52°	56°
	h m	° ′	h m	h m	h m
1	20 19.0	−20 14	23 35	2 17	1 34
11	20 17.4	−20 19	22 55	1 35	0 52
21	20 15.9	−20 24	22 14	0 53	0 10
31	20 14.6	−20 28	21 33	0 12	23 24

Diameter 4″

NEPTUNE

Day	RA	Dec.	Transit	10° high	
				52°	56°
	h m	° ′	h m	h m	h m
1	19 51.6	−20 28	23 08	1 47	1 03
11	19 50.6	−20 31	22 28	1 06	0 22
21	19 49.6	−20 34	21 48	0 26	23 37
31	19 48.8	−20 36	21 07	23 41	22 56

Diameter 2″

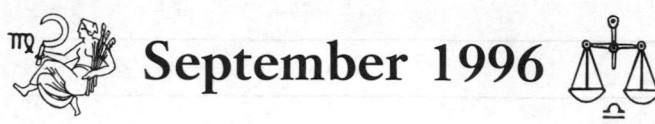

September 1996

NINTH MONTH, 30 DAYS. *Septem* (seven), seventh month of Roman pre-Julian calendar

1	Sunday	**14th S. after Pentecost/13th S. after Trinity**	*week 35 day 245*
2	Monday	Frederick Soddy b. 1877. J. R. R. Tolkien d. 1973	246
3	Tuesday	✗ Worcester 1651. Frank Capra d. 1991	247
4	Wednesday	Anton Bruckner b. 1824. Edvard Grieg d. 1907	248
5	Thursday	John Wisden b. 1826. Lord Delfont b. 1909	249
6	Friday	James II d. 1701. Henry Walford Davies b. 1869	250
7	Saturday	William Holman Hunt d. 1910	251
8	Sunday	**Blessed Virgin Mary. 15th S. after Pentecost/14th S. after Trinity**	*week 36 day 252*
9	Monday	William I d. 1087. John Curry b. 1949	253
10	Tuesday	Wilfred Scawen Blunt d. 1922	254
11	Wednesday	D. H. Lawrence b. 1885. Nikita Khrushchev d. 1971	255
12	Thursday	Maurice Chevalier b. 1888. Robert Lowell d. 1977	256
13	Friday	Arnold Schönberg b. 1874. William Heath Robinson d. 1944	257
14	Saturday	JEWISH NEW YEAR (5757). Dante Alighieri d. 1321	258
15	Sunday	**16th S. after Pentecost/15th S. after Trinity**	*week 37 day 259*
16	Monday	Bonar Law b. 1858. Peter Darrell b. 1929	260
17	Tuesday	Tobias Smollett d. 1771. Laura Ashley d. 1985	261
18	Wednesday	William Hazlitt d. 1830. Lord Berners b. 1883	262
19	Thursday	George Cadbury b. 1839. Dr Thomas Barnardo d. 1905	263
20	Friday	Mungo Park b. 1771. Stevie Smith b. 1902	264
21	Saturday	**St Matthew.** John McAdam b. 1756. H. G. Wells b. 1866	265
22	Sunday	**17th S. after Pentecost/16th S. after Trinity**	*week 38 day 266*
23	Monday	YOM KIPPUR. Wilkie Collins d. 1889	267
24	Tuesday	F. Scott Fitzgerald b. 1896. Dr Seuss d. 1991	268
25	Wednesday	Johann Strauss (the Elder) d. 1849	269
26	Thursday	T. S. Eliot b. 1888. George Gershwin b. 1898	270
27	Friday	Engelbert Humperdinck d. 1921	271
28	Saturday	FEAST OF TABERNACLES begins. Duke of Grafton b. 1735	272
29	Sunday	**St Michael and all Angels. 18th S. after Pentecost/17th S. after Trinity**	*week 39 day 273*
30	Monday	Deborah Kerr b. 1921. Donald Swann b. 1923	274

ASTRONOMICAL PHENOMENA

d	h	
3	08	Mars in conjunction with Venus. Mars 3° N.
3	15	Jupiter at stationary point
4	06	Mercury at stationary point
8	16	Mars in conjunction with Moon. Mars 6° N.
8	22	Venus in conjunction with Moon. Venus 3° N.
13	16	Mercury in conjunction with Moon. Mercury 3° S.
17	13	Mercury in inferior conjunction
21	05	Jupiter in conjunction with Moon. Jupiter 5° S.
22	18	Sun's longitude 180° ♎
26	17	Mercury at stationary point
26	19	Saturn at opposition
27	02	Saturn in conjunction with Moon. Saturn 3° S.
27	03	Total eclipse of Moon (*see* page 66)

MINIMA OF ALGOL

d	h	d	h	d	h
3	01.9	14	13.2	23	03.6
5	22.7	17	10.0	26	00.4
8	19.6	20	06.8	28	21.2
11	16.4				

CONSTELLATIONS

The following constellations are near the meridian at

	d	h		d	h
August	1	24	September	15	21
August	16	23	October	1	20
September	1	22	October	16	19

Draco, Cepheus, Lyra, Cygnus, Vulpecula, Sagitta, Delphinus, Equuleus, Aquila, Aquarius and Capricornus

THE MOON

Phases, Apsides and Node	d	h	m
☾ Last Quarter	4	19	06
● New Moon	12	23	07
☽ First Quarter	20	11	23
○ Full Moon	27	02	51
Apogee (405,707 km)	9	01	54
Perigee (363,072 km)	24	21	50

Mean longitude of ascending node on September 1, 190°

THE SUN

s.d. 15′.9

Day	Right Ascension	Dec.	Equation of time	Rise 52°	Rise 56°	Transit	Set 52°	Set 56°	Sidereal time	Transit of First Point of Aries
	h m s	° ′	m s	h m	h m	h m	h m	h m	h m s	h m s
1	10 41 46	+8 15	− 0 01	5 12	5 05	12 00	18 47	18 54	22 41 45	1 18 03
2	10 45 23	+7 54	+0 18	5 14	5 07	12 00	18 44	18 51	22 45 41	1 14 07
3	10 49 00	+7 32	+0 37	5 15	5 08	11 59	18 42	18 49	22 49 38	1 10 11
4	10 52 37	+7 10	+0 57	5 17	5 10	11 59	18 40	18 46	22 53 34	1 06 15
5	10 56 14	+6 47	+1 17	5 18	5 12	11 59	18 38	18 43	22 57 31	1 02 19
6	10 59 50	+6 25	+1 37	5 20	5 14	11 58	18 35	18 41	23 01 27	0 58 23
7	11 03 27	+6 03	+1 57	5 22	5 16	11 58	18 33	18 38	23 05 24	0 54 27
8	11 07 03	+5 40	+2 18	5 23	5 18	11 58	18 31	18 36	23 09 20	0 50 31
9	11 10 39	+5 18	+2 38	5 25	5 20	11 57	18 28	18 33	23 13 17	0 46 35
10	11 14 14	+4 55	+2 59	5 27	5 22	11 57	18 26	18 30	23 17 14	0 42 39
11	11 17 50	+4 32	+3 20	5 28	5 24	11 56	18 24	18 28	23 21 10	0 38 44
12	11 21 25	+4 09	+3 41	5 30	5 26	11 56	18 21	18 25	23 25 07	0 34 48
13	11 25 01	+3 46	+4 02	5 32	5 28	11 56	18 19	18 22	23 29 03	0 30 52
14	11 28 36	+3 23	+4 24	5 33	5 30	11 55	18 17	18 20	23 33 00	0 26 56
15	11 32 11	+3 00	+4 45	5 35	5 32	11 55	18 14	18 17	23 36 56	0 23 00
16	11 35 47	+2 37	+5 06	5 36	5 34	11 55	18 12	18 14	23 40 53	0 19 04
17	11 39 22	+2 14	+5 27	5 38	5 36	11 54	18 10	18 12	23 44 49	0 15 08
18	11 42 57	+1 51	+5 49	5 40	5 38	11 54	18 07	18 09	23 48 46	0 11 12
19	11 46 32	+1 27	+6 10	5 41	5 40	11 54	18 05	18 06	23 52 43	0 07 16
20	11 50 08	+1 04	+6 31	5 43	5 42	11 53	18 03	18 04	23 56 39	{ 0 03 20 / 23 59 24
21	11 53 43	+0 41	+6 53	5 45	5 44	11 53	18 00	18 01	0 00 36	23 55 29
22	11 57 18	+0 18	+7 14	5 46	5 46	11 53	17 58	17 58	0 04 32	23 51 33
23	12 00 54	− 0 06	+7 35	5 48	5 47	11 52	17 56	17 56	0 08 29	23 47 37
24	12 04 29	− 0 29	+7 56	5 50	5 49	11 52	17 53	17 53	0 12 25	23 43 41
25	12 08 05	− 0 53	+8 17	5 51	5 51	11 52	17 51	17 51	0 16 22	23 39 45
26	12 11 41	−1 16	+8 38	5 53	5 53	11 51	17 49	17 48	0 20 18	23 35 49
27	12 15 17	−1 39	+8 58	5 54	5 55	11 51	17 46	17 45	0 24 15	23 31 53
28	12 18 53	− 2 03	+9 18	5 56	5 57	11 51	17 44	17 43	0 28 11	23 27 57
29	12 22 29	− 2 26	+9 39	5 58	5 59	11 50	17 42	17 40	0 32 08	23 24 01
30	12 26 06	− 2 49	+9 58	5 59	6 01	11 50	17 39	17 37	0 36 05	23 20 05

DURATION OF TWILIGHT (in minutes)

Latitude	52°	56°	52°	56°	52°	56°	52°	56°
	1 September		11 September		21 September		30 September	
Civil	35	39	34	38	34	37	34	37
Nautical	79	89	76	84	74	82	73	80
Astronomical	127	146	120	135	115	129	113	126

THE NIGHT SKY

Mercury passes rapidly through inferior conjunction on the 17th and becomes visible in the mornings for the last few days of the month. It will be seen very low in the eastern sky around the time of beginning of morning civil twilight. Mercury's magnitude is around +0.5.

Venus is still visible as a brilliant object in the eastern sky before dawn, magnitude − 4.2. On the 3rd Venus is 3° south of Mars, but Mars continues to move away from the Sun and the separation of the two planets has increased to more than 10° by the end of September. At the very beginning of the month Venus is passing south of Castor and Pollux.

Mars, magnitude +1.5, continues to be visible as a morning object in the eastern sky for several hours before

sunrise. During the month Mars moves from Gemini into Cancer.

Jupiter continues to be visible as a conspicuous evening object in the south-western sky, magnitude − 2.4.

Saturn, magnitude +0.5, is at opposition on the 26th and is therefore visible in the southern skies throughout the hours of darkness. During the night of the 26th to 27th the Full Moon passes 3° north of Saturn.

Zodiacal Light. The morning cone may be seen stretching up from the eastern horizon along the ecliptic, before the beginning of morning twilight, from the 11th to the 25th.

THE MOON

Day	RA	Dec.	Hor. par.	Semi- diam.	Sun's co- long.	PA of Bright Limb	Phase	Age	Rise 52°	Rise 56°	Transit	Set 52°	Set 56°
	h m	°	′	′	°	°	%	d	h m	h m	h m	h m	h m
1	1 27	+ 7.7	58.7	16.0	127	70	86	17.7	20 32	20 22	2 51	9 53	10 01
2	2 20	+11.4	57.7	15.7	139	73	77	18.7	21 04	20 51	3 42	11 04	11 16
3	3 13	+14.3	56.8	15.5	152	76	68	19.7	21 40	21 25	4 33	12 11	12 25
4	4 05	+16.5	56.0	15.3	164	80	58	20.7	22 20	22 04	5 23	13 12	13 28
5	4 57	+17.8	55.3	15.1	176	84	48	21.7	23 06	22 48	6 12	14 06	14 24
6	5 48	+18.3	54.7	14.9	188	88	38	22.7	23 56	23 39	7 01	14 54	15 12
7	6 39	+17.9	54.4	14.8	200	91	29	23.7	—	—	7 48	15 36	15 52
8	7 28	+16.7	54.1	14.7	213	95	21	24.7	0 51	0 35	8 35	16 12	16 26
9	8 17	+14.9	54.0	14.7	225	98	14	25.7	1 49	1 35	9 20	16 43	16 55
10	9 04	+12.4	54.1	14.7	237	100	8	26.7	2 49	2 39	10 05	17 11	17 19
11	9 51	+ 9.3	54.3	14.8	249	101	4	27.7	3 52	3 44	10 49	17 36	17 42
12	10 38	+ 5.9	54.5	14.9	261	99	1	28.7	4 55	4 51	11 33	18 00	18 02
13	11 24	+ 2.2	54.8	14.9	274	9	0	0.0	6 00	5 59	12 17	18 23	18 23
14	12 11	− 1.7	55.2	15.0	286	296	1	1.0	7 06	7 08	13 01	18 47	18 43
15	12 59	− 5.5	55.7	15.2	298	291	4	2.0	8 12	8 18	13 47	19 13	19 06
16	13 48	− 9.1	56.1	15.3	310	288	9	3.0	9 20	9 29	14 35	19 42	19 31
17	14 38	−12.4	56.7	15.4	323	285	16	4.0	10 28	10 41	15 25	20 15	20 01
18	15 31	−15.1	57.2	15.6	335	282	24	5.0	11 35	11 50	16 17	20 54	20 38
19	16 26	−17.1	57.8	15.8	347	278	34	6.0	12 39	12 56	17 11	21 42	21 24
20	17 23	−18.1	58.4	15.9	359	273	45	7.0	13 38	13 56	18 07	22 38	22 20
21	18 22	−18.1	59.0	16.1	11	268	56	8.0	14 31	14 48	19 05	23 43	23 26
22	19 21	−16.9	59.6	16.2	24	264	67	9.0	15 16	15 31	20 02	—	—
23	20 20	−14.7	60.0	16.3	36	260	78	10.0	15 56	16 07	20 59	0 55	0 41
24	21 19	−11.5	60.3	16.4	48	257	87	11.0	16 30	16 38	21 55	2 12	2 02
25	22 16	− 7.5	60.4	16.5	60	254	94	12.0	17 01	17 05	22 50	3 31	3 25
26	23 13	− 3.1	60.2	16.4	72	254	98	13.0	17 30	17 30	23 44	4 51	4 49
27	0 09	+ 1.5	59.9	16.3	85	264	100	14.0	17 59	17 55	—	6 10	6 12
28	1 04	+ 5.9	59.3	16.1	97	71	99	15.0	18 29	18 21	0 37	7 27	7 33
29	1 58	+ 9.9	58.5	15.9	109	74	95	16.0	19 00	18 49	1 29	8 42	8 52
30	2 52	+13.2	57.7	15.7	121	77	90	17.0	19 36	19 22	2 21	9 52	10 05

MERCURY

Day	RA	Dec.	Diam.	Phase	Transit	5° high 52°	5° high 56°
	h m	°	″	%	h m	h m	h m
1	12 05	−4.6	9	33	13 22	18 23	18 16
3	12 06	−5.0	9	28	13 15	18 15	18 07
5	12 06	−5.1	9	24	13 06	18 06	17 58
7	12 05	−5.1	10	19	12 56	17 56	17 49
9	12 02	−4.8	10	14	12 45	17 47	17 40
11	11 57	−4.3	10	9	12 33	17 38	17 31
13	11 52	−3.5	10	5	12 19	17 29	17 23
15	11 45	−2.4	11	2	12 05	17 20	17 15
17	11 38	−1.2	10	1	11 50	6 29	6 34
19	11 32	+0.1	10	1	11 35	6 08	6 11
21	11 26	+1.4	10	3	11 22	5 48	5 50
23	11 21	+2.6	10	8	11 10	5 30	5 32
25	11 19	+3.5	9	14	11 01	5 16	5 16
27	11 19	+4.2	9	22	10 54	5 05	5 05
29	11 22	+4.6	8	31	10 49	4 58	4 58
31	11 27	+4.6	8	41	10 46	4 56	4 55

VENUS

Day	RA	Dec.	Diam.	Phase	Transit	5° high 52°	5° high 56°
	h m	°	″	%	h m	h m	h m
1	7 40	+19.2	21	56	8 58	1 49	1 36
6	8 02	+18.6	20	59	9 01	1 55	1 42
11	8 24	+17.9	19	61	9 03	2 02	1 50
16	8 47	+16.9	18	63	9 06	2 10	1 59
21	9 09	+15.7	18	65	9 09	2 20	2 10
26	9 32	+14.4	17	67	9 12	2 30	2 21
31	9 55	+12.8	16	69	9 15	2 41	2 34

MARS

Day	RA	Dec.	Diam.	Phase	Transit	5° high 52°	5° high 56°
1	7 46	+22.1	4	95	9 04	1 38	1 22
6	7 59	+21.5	4	94	8 57	1 35	1 19
11	8 13	+20.9	5	94	8 51	1 32	1 17
16	8 26	+20.3	5	94	8 44	1 30	1 15
21	8 38	+19.6	5	94	8 37	1 27	1 13
26	8 51	+18.8	5	93	8 30	1 24	1 11
31	9 03	+18.1	5	93	8 23	1 21	1 09

SUNRISE AND SUNSET

	London		Bristol		Birmingham		Manchester		Newcastle		Glasgow		Belfast	
	0°05′	51°30′	2°35′	51°28′	1°55′	52°28′	2°15′	53°28′	1°37′	54°59′	4°14′	55°52′	5°56′	54°35′
	h m	h m	h m	h m	h m	h m	h m	h m	h m	h m	h m	h m	h m	h m
1	5 13	18 46	5 23	18 56	5 19	18 55	5 18	18 58	5 13	18 58	5 22	19 11	5 31	19 15
2	5 15	18 44	5 25	18 54	5 21	18 53	5 20	18 56	5 15	18 56	5 24	19 08	5 33	19 12
3	5 16	18 42	5 26	18 52	5 22	18 50	5 22	18 53	5 17	18 53	5 26	19 05	5 35	19 10
4	5 18	18 39	5 28	18 49	5 24	18 48	5 24	18 51	5 19	18 51	5 28	19 03	5 37	19 07
5	5 20	18 37	5 30	18 47	5 26	18 46	5 25	18 49	5 21	18 48	5 30	19 00	5 38	19 05
6	5 21	18 35	5 31	18 45	5 27	18 43	5 27	18 46	5 22	18 46	5 31	18 58	5 40	19 02
7	5 23	18 33	5 33	18 43	5 29	18 41	5 29	18 44	5 24	18 43	5 33	18 55	5 42	19 00
8	5 24	18 30	5 34	18 40	5 31	18 39	5 31	18 41	5 26	18 41	5 35	18 52	5 44	18 57
9	5 26	18 28	5 36	18 38	5 32	18 36	5 32	18 39	5 28	18 38	5 37	18 50	5 46	18 55
10	5 27	18 26	5 38	18 36	5 34	18 34	5 34	18 36	5 30	18 36	5 39	18 47	5 48	18 52
11	5 29	18 24	5 39	18 33	5 35	18 32	5 36	18 34	5 32	18 33	5 41	18 44	5 49	18 50
12	5 31	18 21	5 41	18 31	5 37	18 29	5 38	18 32	5 34	18 30	5 43	18 42	5 51	18 47
13	5 32	18 19	5 42	18 29	5 39	18 27	5 39	18 29	5 35	18 28	5 45	18 39	5 53	18 45
14	5 34	18 17	5 44	18 27	5 40	18 25	5 41	18 27	5 37	18 25	5 47	18 37	5 55	18 42
15	5 35	18 14	5 45	18 24	5 42	18 22	5 43	18 24	5 39	18 23	5 49	18 34	5 57	18 40
16	5 37	18 12	5 47	18 22	5 44	18 20	5 45	18 22	5 41	18 20	5 51	18 31	5 59	18 37
17	5 39	18 10	5 49	18 20	5 45	18 18	5 46	18 19	5 43	18 18	5 53	18 29	6 00	18 35
18	5 40	18 07	5 50	18 17	5 47	18 15	5 48	18 17	5 45	18 15	5 55	18 26	6 02	18 32
19	5 42	18 05	5 52	18 15	5 49	18 13	5 50	18 14	5 47	18 13	5 57	18 23	6 04	18 30
20	5 43	18 03	5 54	18 13	5 51	18 10	5 52	18 12	5 49	18 10	5 59	18 21	6 06	18 27
21	5 45	18 00	5 55	18 10	5 52	18 08	5 53	18 10	5 50	18 07	6 01	18 18	6 08	18 24
22	5 47	17 58	5 57	18 08	5 54	18 06	5 55	18 07	5 52	18 05	6 03	18 15	6 10	18 22
23	5 48	17 56	5 58	18 06	5 55	18 03	5 57	18 05	5 54	18 02	6 04	18 13	6 11	18 19
24	5 50	17 54	6 00	18 04	5 57	18 01	5 59	18 02	5 56	18 00	6 06	18 10	6 13	18 17
25	5 52	17 51	6 02	18 01	5 59	17 59	6 00	18 00	5 58	17 57	6 08	18 07	6 15	18 14
26	5 53	17 49	6 03	17 59	6 01	17 56	6 02	17 57	6 00	17 55	6 10	18 05	6 17	18 12
27	5 55	17 47	6 05	17 57	6 02	17 54	6 04	17 55	6 02	17 52	6 12	18 02	6 19	18 09
28	5 56	17 44	6 06	17 54	6 04	17 51	6 06	17 52	6 03	17 49	6 14	18 00	6 21	18 07
29	5 58	17 42	6 08	17 52	6 06	17 49	6 07	17 50	6 05	17 47	6 16	17 57	6 23	18 04
30	6 00	17 40	6 10	17 50	6 07	17 47	6 09	17 48	6 07	17 44	6 18	17 54	6 24	18 02

JUPITER

Day	RA	Dec.	Transit	5° high	
				52°	56°
	h m	° ′	h m	h m	h m
1	18 34.1	− 23 23	19 49	22 48	22 12
11	18 34.5	− 23 24	19 10	22 09	21 33
21	18 36.2	− 23 23	18 33	21 32	20 56
31	18 39.2	− 23 21	17 57	20 56	20 20

Diameters – equatorial 41″ polar 38″

SATURN

Day	RA	Dec.	Transit	5° high	
				52°	56°
	h m	° ′	h m	h m	h m
1	0 25.6	− 0 02	1 44	20 13	20 17
11	0 23.1	− 0 20	1 02	19 33	19 37
21	0 20.4	− 0 39	0 20	18 52	18 56
31	0 17.5	− 0 57	23 33	18 12	18 16

Diameters – equatorial 19″ polar 17″
Rings – major axis 44″ minor axis 4″

URANUS

Day	RA	Dec.	Transit	10° high	
				52°	56°
	h m	° ′	h m	h m	h m
1	20 14.4	− 20 28	21 29	0 08	23 20
11	20 13.4	− 20 32	20 49	23 23	22 38
21	20 12.6	− 20 34	20 09	22 43	21 58
31	20 12.1	− 20 35	19 29	22 03	21 18

Diameter 4″

NEPTUNE

Day	RA	Dec.	Transit	10° high	
				52°	56°
	h m	° ′	h m	h m	h m
1	19 48.7	− 20 36	21 03	23 37	22 52
11	19 48.0	− 20 38	20 24	22 57	22 12
21	19 47.6	− 20 40	19 44	22 17	21 31
31	19 47.3	− 20 41	19 04	21 37	20 52

Diameter 2″

October 1996

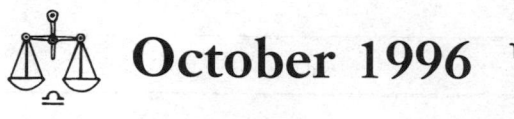

TENTH MONTH, 31 DAYS. *Octo* (eight), eighth month of Roman pre-Julian calendar

1	Tuesday	Michaelmas Law Sittings begin. Paul Dukas b. 1865	*week* 39 *day* 275
2	Wednesday	Graham Greene b. 1904. Sir Peter Medawar d. 1987	276
3	Thursday	William Morris d. 1896. James Herriot b. 1916	277
4	Friday	Sir Arthur Whitten Brown d. 1948	278
5	Saturday	Jacques Offenbach d. 1880	279
6	Sunday	**19th S. after Pentecost/18th S. after Trinity**	*week* 40 *day* 280
7	Monday	Edgar Allan Poe d. 1849. Marie Lloyd d. 1922	281
8	Tuesday	Great Fire of Chicago 1871. Willi Brandt d. 1992	282
9	Wednesday	Camille Saint-Saëns b. 1835. Alfred Dreyfus b. 1859	283
10	Thursday	Giuseppe Verdi b. 1813. Fridtjof Nansen b. 1861	284
11	Friday	James Joule d. 1889. Jean Cocteau d. 1963	285
12	Saturday	Gen. Robert E. Lee d. 1870	286
13	Sunday	**20th S. after Pentecost/19th S. after Trinty**	*week* 41 *day* 287
14	Monday	✗Hastings 1066. e.e.cummings b. 1894	288
15	Tuesday	Duchess of York b. 1959. Cole Porter d. 1964	289
16	Wednesday	Ridley and Latimer burned 1555	290
17	Thursday	Sir Philip Sidney d. 1586	291
18	Friday	**St Luke.** Charles Babbage d. 1871	292
19	Saturday	Leigh Hunt b. 1784. Jacqueline du Pré d. 1987	293
20	Sunday	**21st S. after Pentecost/20th S. after Trinity**	*week* 42 *day* 294
21	Monday	✗Trafalgar 1805. Dizzy Gillespie b. 1917	295
22	Tuesday	Franz Liszt b. 1811. Thomas Sheraton d. 1806	296
23	Wednesday	Douglas Jardine b. 1900. Dr W. G. Grace d. 1915	297
24	Thursday	Dame Sybil Thorndike b. 1882	298
25	Friday	Johann Strauss (the Younger) b. 1825	299
26	Saturday	William Temple d. 1944. Igor Sikorsky d. 1972	300
27	Sunday	**9th S. before Christmas/21st S. after Trinity**	*week* 43 *day* 301
28	Monday	**SS Simon and Jude.** John Smeaton d. 1792	302
29	Tuesday	Edmund Halley b. 1656. Wall Street crash 1929	303
30	Wednesday	Angelica Kauffmann b. 1741. Patrick Symons d. 1993	304
31	Thursday	Hallowmass Eve. John Evelyn b. 1620	305

ASTRONOMICAL PHENOMENA

d	h	
3	06	Mercury at greatest elongation W.18°
6	16	Neptune at stationary point
7	11	Mars in conjunction with Moon. Mars 5° N.
9	01	Venus in conjunction with Moon. Venus 3° N.
10	01	Uranus at stationary point
11	08	Mercury in conjunction with Moon. Mercury 2° N.
12	14	Partial eclipse of Sun (*see* page 66)
18	15	Jupiter in conjunction with Moon. Jupiter 5° S.
23	03	Sun's longitude 210 ♏
24	08	Saturn in conjunction with Moon. Saturn 3° S.

MINIMA OF ALGOL

d	h	d	h	d	h
1	18.0	13	05.3	24	16.5
4	14.9	16	02.1	27	13.3
7	11.7	18	22.9	30	10.2
10	08.5	21	19.7		

CONSTELLATIONS

The following constellations are near the meridian at

	d	h		d	h
September	1	24	October	16	21
September	15	23	November	1	20
October	1	22	November	15	19

Ursa Major (below the Pole), Cepheus, Cassiopeia, Cygnus, Lacerta, Andromeda, Pegasus, Capricornus, Aquarius and Piscis Austrinus

THE MOON

Phases, Apsides and Node	d	h	m
☾ Last Quarter	4	12	04
● New Moon	12	14	14
☽ First Quarter	19	18	09
○ Full Moon	26	14	11
Apogee (404,754 km)	6	17	56
Perigee (368,380 km)	22	08	53

Mean longitude of ascending node on October 1, 188°

THE SUN

s.d. 16'.1

Day	Right Ascension	Dec. −	Equation of time	Rise 52°	Rise 56°	Transit	Set 52°	Set 56°	Sidereal time	Transit of First Point of Aries
	h m s	° '	m s	h m	h m	h m	h m	h m	h m s	h m s
1	12 29 43	3 13	+10 18	6 01	6 03	11 50	17 37	17 35	0 40 01	23 16 10
2	12 33 20	3 36	+10 37	6 03	6 05	11 49	17 35	17 32	0 43 58	23 12 14
3	12 36 58	3 59	+10 56	6 05	6 07	11 49	17 32	17 29	0 47 54	23 08 18
4	12 40 36	4 22	+11 15	6 06	6 09	11 49	17 30	17 27	0 51 51	23 04 22
5	12 44 14	4 45	+11 33	6 08	6 11	11 48	17 28	17 24	0 55 47	23 00 26
6	12 47 53	5 08	+11 51	6 10	6 13	11 48	17 26	17 22	0 59 44	22 56 30
7	12 51 32	5 31	+12 08	6 11	6 15	11 48	17 23	17 19	1 03 40	22 52 34
8	12 55 12	5 54	+12 25	6 13	6 17	11 47	17 21	17 16	1 07 37	22 48 38
9	12 58 52	6 17	+12 42	6 15	6 19	11 47	17 19	17 14	1 11 34	22 44 42
10	13 02 32	6 40	+12 58	6 16	6 21	11 47	17 17	17 11	1 15 30	22 40 46
11	13 06 13	7 03	+13 13	6 18	6 23	11 47	17 14	17 09	1 19 27	22 36 50
12	13 09 55	7 25	+13 29	6 20	6 25	11 46	17 12	17 06	1 23 23	22 32 55
13	13 13 37	7 48	+13 43	6 22	6 28	11 46	17 10	17 04	1 27 20	22 28 59
14	13 17 19	8 10	+13 57	6 23	6 30	11 46	17 08	17 01	1 31 16	22 25 03
15	13 21 02	8 32	+14 11	6 25	6 32	11 46	17 06	16 59	1 35 13	22 21 07
16	13 24 46	8 54	+14 24	6 27	6 34	11 45	17 03	16 56	1 39 09	22 17 11
17	13 28 30	9 16	+14 36	6 28	6 36	11 45	17 01	16 54	1 43 06	22 13 15
18	13 32 14	9 38	+14 48	6 30	6 38	11 45	16 59	16 51	1 47 03	22 09 19
19	13 36 00	10 00	+14 59	6 32	6 40	11 45	16 57	16 49	1 50 59	22 05 23
20	13 39 45	10 22	+15 10	6 34	6 42	11 45	16 55	16 47	1 54 56	22 01 27
21	13 43 32	10 43	+15 20	6 36	6 44	11 45	16 53	16 44	1 58 52	21 57 31
22	13 47 19	11 04	+15 30	6 37	6 46	11 44	16 51	16 42	2 02 49	21 53 35
23	13 51 07	11 25	+15 38	6 39	6 48	11 44	16 49	16 39	2 06 45	21 49 40
24	13 54 55	11 46	+15 46	6 41	6 50	11 44	16 47	16 37	2 10 42	21 45 44
25	13 58 45	12 07	+15 54	6 43	6 53	11 44	16 45	16 35	2 14 38	21 41 48
26	14 02 34	12 28	+16 00	6 44	6 55	11 44	16 43	16 32	2 18 35	21 37 52
27	14 06 25	12 48	+16 06	6 46	6 57	11 44	16 41	16 30	2 22 32	21 33 56
28	14 10 16	13 08	+16 12	6 48	6 59	11 44	16 39	16 28	2 26 28	21 30 00
29	14 14 09	13 28	+16 16	6 50	7 01	11 44	16 37	16 26	2 30 25	21 26 04
30	14 18 02	13 48	+16 20	6 52	7 03	11 44	16 35	16 23	2 34 21	21 22 08
31	14 21 55	14 07	+16 23	6 53	7 05	11 44	16 33	16 21	2 38 18	21 18 12

DURATION OF TWILIGHT (in minutes)

Latitude	52°	56°	52°	56°	52°	56°	52°	56°
	1 October		11 October		21 October		31 October	
Civil	34	37	34	37	34	38	36	40
Nautical	73	80	73	80	74	81	75	83
Astronomical	113	125	112	124	113	124	114	126

THE NIGHT SKY

Mercury, magnitude −0.1 to −1.0, is visible in the eastern sky in the mornings low above the eastern horizon at the beginning of morning civil twilight. For observers in the British Isles this is the most suitable morning apparition of the year. However, Mercury passes through perihelion on the 2nd which is why its maximum elongation is only 18° and why the duration of visibility is relatively short. After the middle of the month Mercury is lost in the twilight as it moves back towards the Sun. On the morning of the 11th it may be possible to detect the thin sliver of the waning crescent Moon about 3° below the planet.

Venus, magnitude −4.1, continues to be visible as a brilliant object in the eastern sky in the early mornings before sunrise. On the mornings of the 3rd and 4th Venus is close to Regulus in Leo, passing only 0°.2 south of the star at 0h on the 4th (though it is then below the horizon). The old crescent Moon is near Venus on the morning of the 9th.

Mars continues to be visible as a morning object in the eastern sky, now visible shortly after 01h. Its magnitude is +1.4. Mars is moving steadily eastwards from Cancer into Leo, passing only 0°.2 south of Regulus on the 4th.

Jupiter, magnitude −2.2, continues to be visible in the south-western sky in the early part of the evening.

Saturn, being just past opposition, is still visible in the southern skies for most of the night. Its magnitude is +0.6.

THE MOON

Day	RA	Dec.	Hor. par.	Semi- diam.	Sun's co- long.	PA of Bright Limb	Phase	Age	Rise 52°	Rise 56°	Transit	Set 52°	Set 56°
	h m	°	'	'	°	°	%	d	h m	h m	h m	h m	h m
1	3 46	+15.7	56.8	15.5	133	81	82	18.0	20 15	19 59	3 13	10 57	11 13
2	4 39	+17.4	56.0	15.3	145	85	74	19.0	20 59	20 42	4 03	11 56	12 13
3	5 32	+18.2	55.4	15.1	158	89	65	20.0	21 49	21 31	4 53	12 48	13 05
4	6 23	+18.0	54.8	14.9	170	93	55	21.0	22 42	22 26	5 42	13 32	13 49
5	7 13	+17.1	54.4	14.8	182	97	45	22.0	23 39	23 25	6 30	14 11	14 26
6	8 02	+15.5	54.2	14.8	194	100	36	23.0	—	—	7 16	14 44	14 56
7	8 50	+13.1	54.2	14.8	206	103	27	24.0	0 39	0 27	8 01	15 13	15 22
8	9 37	+10.3	54.3	14.8	218	106	19	25.0	1 40	1 32	8 45	15 39	15 46
9	10 23	+ 7.0	54.5	14.9	231	108	12	26.0	2 43	2 38	9 29	16 03	16 07
10	11 10	+ 3.3	54.9	15.0	243	110	7	27.0	3 48	3 46	10 13	16 27	16 27
11	11 57	− 0.5	55.4	15.1	255	111	3	28.0	4 54	4 55	10 57	16 51	16 48
12	12 45	− 4.4	55.9	15.2	267	116	0	29.0	6 01	6 05	11 43	17 16	17 10
13	13 34	− 8.2	56.4	15.4	280	274	0	0.4	7 09	7 17	12 31	17 44	17 35
14	14 25	−11.6	56.9	15.5	292	280	2	1.4	8 18	8 30	13 21	18 16	18 04
15	15 18	−14.5	57.4	15.6	304	279	6	2.4	9 27	9 42	14 13	18 54	18 39
16	16 13	−16.7	57.8	15.8	316	275	13	3.4	10 33	10 50	15 07	19 39	19 22
17	17 10	−18.0	58.2	15.9	328	271	21	4.4	11 34	11 52	16 03	20 33	20 15
18	18 08	−18.2	58.6	16.0	341	267	31	5.4	12 28	12 46	17 00	21 34	21 17
19	19 07	−17.3	58.9	16.1	353	263	42	6.4	13 15	13 31	17 56	22 43	22 28
20	20 05	−15.4	59.2	16.1	5	258	53	7.4	13 55	14 08	18 52	23 56	23 45
21	21 02	−12.5	59.4	16.2	17	255	64	8.4	14 30	14 39	19 46	—	—
22	21 58	− 8.8	59.5	16.2	29	252	75	9.4	15 01	15 06	20 40	1 12	1 04
23	22 53	− 4.7	59.5	16.2	41	250	84	10.4	15 30	15 31	21 32	2 29	2 26
24	23 48	− 0.2	59.3	16.2	54	248	92	11.4	15 58	15 55	22 24	3 46	3 47
25	0 42	+ 4.2	59.0	16.1	66	246	97	12.4	16 26	16 20	23 16	5 03	5 07
26	1 36	+ 8.3	58.6	16.0	78	237	100	13.4	16 56	16 47	—	6 18	6 26
27	2 30	+11.9	58.0	15.8	90	99	100	14.4	17 30	17 17	0 08	7 31	7 42
28	3 24	+14.8	57.3	15.6	102	87	98	15.4	18 08	17 52	1 00	8 39	8 54
29	4 18	+16.9	56.6	15.4	114	88	93	16.4	18 50	18 33	1 52	9 42	9 59
30	5 12	+18.0	55.9	15.2	127	91	87	17.4	19 38	19 20	2 43	10 38	10 56
31	6 04	+18.3	55.3	15.1	139	94	80	18.4	20 31	20 14	3 33	11 27	11 44

MERCURY

Day	RA	Dec.	Diam.	Phase	Transit	5° high 52°	5° high 56°
	h m	°	"	%	h m	h m	h m
1	11 27	+ 4.6	8	41	10 46	4 56	4 55
3	11 33	+ 4.3	7	50	10 45	4 56	4 56
5	11 42	+ 3.7	7	59	10 46	5 00	5 01
7	11 52	+ 2.9	6	67	10 48	5 07	5 08
9	12 02	+ 1.8	6	75	10 51	5 15	5 17
11	12 14	+ 0.6	6	81	10 55	5 25	5 28
13	12 26	− 0.6	6	85	10 59	5 36	5 40
15	12 38	− 2.0	5	89	11 04	5 47	5 52
17	12 50	− 3.4	5	92	11 08	5 59	6 06
19	13 03	− 4.9	5	95	11 13	6 11	6 19
21	13 15	− 6.3	5	96	11 18	6 24	6 33
23	13 28	− 7.7	5	98	11 22	6 37	6 47
25	13 40	− 9.1	5	99	11 27	6 49	7 01
27	13 53	−10.5	5	99	11 31	7 02	7 15
29	14 05	−11.9	5	100	11 36	7 15	7 30
31	14 18	−13.2	5	100	11 41	7 27	7 44

VENUS

Day	RA	Dec.	Diam.	Phase	Transit	5° high 52°	5° high 56°
	h m	°	"	%	h m	h m	h m
1	9 55	+12.8	16	69	9 15	2 41	2 34
6	10 17	+11.1	16	71	9 18	2 53	2 47
11	10 40	+ 9.2	15	73	9 20	3 06	3 02
16	11 02	+ 7.2	15	74	9 23	3 19	3 16
21	11 24	+ 5.1	14	76	9 26	3 32	3 31
26	11 47	+ 2.9	14	78	9 28	3 46	3 47
31	12 09	+ 0.7	14	79	9 31	4 00	4 03

MARS

Day	RA	Dec.	Diam.	Phase	Transit	5° high 52°	5° high 56°
1	9 03	+18.1	5	93	8 23	1 21	1 09
6	9 15	+17.3	5	93	8 15	1 18	1 07
11	9 27	+16.4	5	92	8 07	1 15	1 04
16	9 39	+15.5	5	92	7 59	1 11	1 02
21	9 50	+14.6	5	92	7 51	1 08	0 59
26	10 01	+13.7	5	92	7 42	1 04	0 56
31	10 12	+12.8	5	91	7 33	1 00	0 53

SUNRISE AND SUNSET

	London		Bristol		Birmingham		Manchester		Newcastle		Glasgow		Belfast	
	0°05′	51°30′	2°35′	51°28′	1°55′	52°28′	2°15′	53°28′	1°37′	54°59′	4°14′	55°52′	5°56′	54°35′
	h m	h m	h m	h m	h m	h m	h m	h m	h m	h m	h m	h m	h m	h m
1	6 01	17 38	6 11	17 48	6 09	17 44	6 11	17 45	6 09	17 42	6 20	17 52	6 26	17 59
2	6 03	17 35	6 13	17 45	6 11	17 42	6 13	17 43	6 11	17 39	6 22	17 49	6 28	17 57
3	6 05	17 33	6 15	17 43	6 12	17 40	6 14	17 40	6 13	17 37	6 24	17 46	6 30	17 54
4	6 06	17 31	6 16	17 41	6 14	17 37	6 16	17 38	6 15	17 34	6 26	17 44	6 32	17 52
5	6 08	17 29	6 18	17 39	6 16	17 35	6 18	17 36	6 17	17 32	6 28	17 41	6 34	17 49
6	6 09	17 26	6 19	17 36	6 18	17 33	6 20	17 33	6 19	17 29	6 30	17 39	6 36	17 47
7	6 11	17 24	6 21	17 34	6 19	17 30	6 22	17 31	6 21	17 27	6 32	17 36	6 38	17 44
8	6 13	17 22	6 23	17 32	6 21	17 28	6 23	17 28	6 23	17 24	6 34	17 34	6 39	17 42
9	6 14	17 20	6 24	17 30	6 23	17 26	6 25	17 26	6 25	17 22	6 36	17 31	6 41	17 39
10	6 16	17 17	6 26	17 27	6 25	17 24	6 27	17 24	6 26	17 19	6 38	17 28	6 43	17 37
11	6 18	17 15	6 28	17 25	6 26	17 21	6 29	17 21	6 28	17 17	6 40	17 26	6 45	17 35
12	6 20	17 13	6 30	17 23	6 28	17 19	6 31	17 19	6 30	17 14	6 42	17 23	6 47	17 32
13	6 21	17 11	6 31	17 21	6 30	17 17	6 33	17 17	6 32	17 12	6 44	17 21	6 49	17 30
14	6 23	17 09	6 33	17 19	6 32	17 15	6 34	17 14	6 34	17 09	6 46	17 18	6 51	17 27
15	6 25	17 07	6 35	17 17	6 33	17 12	6 36	17 12	6 36	17 07	6 48	17 16	6 53	17 25
16	6 26	17 04	6 36	17 15	6 35	17 10	6 38	17 10	6 38	17 05	6 50	17 13	6 55	17 23
17	6 28	17 02	6 38	17 12	6 37	17 08	6 40	17 08	6 40	17 02	6 52	17 11	6 57	17 20
18	6 30	17 00	6 40	17 10	6 39	17 06	6 42	17 05	6 42	17 00	6 55	17 09	6 59	17 18
19	6 31	16 58	6 41	17 08	6 41	17 04	6 44	17 03	6 44	16 58	6 57	17 06	7 01	17 16
20	6 33	16 56	6 43	17 06	6 42	17 02	6 46	17 01	6 46	16 55	6 59	17 04	7 03	17 13
21	6 35	16 54	6 45	17 04	6 44	17 00	6 47	16 59	6 48	16 53	7 01	17 01	7 05	17 11
22	6 37	16 52	6 47	17 02	6 46	16 57	6 49	16 57	6 50	16 51	7 03	16 59	7 07	17 09
23	6 38	16 50	6 48	17 00	6 48	16 55	6 51	16 54	6 52	16 48	7 05	16 57	7 09	17 07
24	6 40	16 48	6 50	16 58	6 50	16 53	6 53	16 52	6 54	16 46	7 07	16 54	7 11	17 04
25	6 42	16 46	6 52	16 56	6 51	16 51	6 55	16 50	6 56	16 44	7 09	16 52	7 13	17 02
26	6 44	16 44	6 54	16 54	6 53	16 49	6 57	16 48	6 58	16 42	7 11	16 50	7 15	17 00
27	6 45	16 42	6 55	16 52	6 55	16 47	6 59	16 46	7 00	16 39	7 13	16 47	7 17	16 58
28	6 47	16 40	6 57	16 50	6 57	16 45	7 01	16 44	7 02	16 37	7 15	16 45	7 19	16 56
29	6 49	16 38	6 59	16 48	6 59	16 43	7 03	16 42	7 04	16 35	7 18	16 43	7 21	16 53
30	6 51	16 37	7 01	16 47	7 01	16 41	7 05	16 40	7 06	16 33	7 20	16 41	7 23	16 51
31	6 52	16 35	7 02	16 45	7 02	16 39	7 06	16 38	7 08	16 31	7 22	16 38	7 25	16 49

JUPITER

Day	RA	Dec.	Transit	5° high	
				52°	56°
	h m	° ′	h m	h m	h m
1	18 39.2	−23 21	17 57	20 56	20 20
11	18 43.4	−23 18	17 22	20 22	19 46
21	18 48.8	−23 13	16 48	19 49	19 13
31	18 55.1	−23 06	16 15	19 17	18 41

Diameters – equatorial 37″ polar 35″

SATURN

Day	RA	Dec.	Transit	5° high	
				52°	56°
	h m	° ′	h m	h m	h m
1	0 17.5	− 0 57	23 33	4 59	4 55
11	0 14.7	− 1 15	22 51	4 15	4 11
21	0 12.1	− 1 31	22 09	3 32	3 28
31	0 09.9	− 1 45	21 28	2 49	2 45

Diameters – equatorial 19″ polar 17″
Rings – major axis 44″ minor axis 3″

URANUS

Day	RA	Dec.	Transit	10° high	
				52°	56°
	h m	° ′	h m	h m	h m
1	20 12.1	−20 35	19 29	22 03	21 18
11	20 11.9	−20 36	18 49	21 23	20 38
21	20 12.2	−20 35	18 10	20 44	19 59
31	20 12.7	−20 33	17 32	20 06	19 21

Diameter 4″

NEPTUNE

Day	RA	Dec.	Transit	10° high	
				52°	56°
	h m	° ′	h m	h m	h m
1	19 47.3	−20 41	19 04	21 37	20 52
11	19 47.3	−20 41	18 25	20 58	20 12
21	19 47.6	−20 41	17 46	20 19	19 33
31	19 48.0	−20 40	17 07	19 40	18 55

Diameter 2″

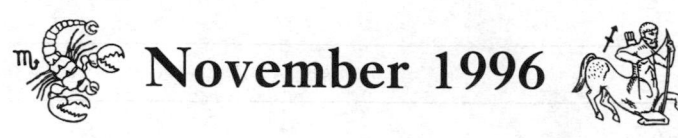

November 1996

ELEVENTH MONTH, 30 DAYS. *Novem* (nine), ninth month of Roman pre-Julian calendar

1	*Friday*	**All Saints.** Edmund Blunden b. 1896	*week* 43 *day* 306
2	*Saturday*	All Souls. Daniel Boone b. 1734	307
3	*Sunday*	**8th S. before Christmas/22nd S. after Trinity**	*week* 44 *day* 308
4	*Monday*	Felix Mendelssohn d. 1847	309
5	*Tuesday*	Vivien Leigh b. 1913. Lester Piggott b. 1935	310
6	*Wednesday*	Colley Cibber b. 1671. Adolphe Sax b. 1814	311
7	*Thursday*	Dame Joan Sutherland b. 1926	312
8	*Friday*	Prof. Christiaan Barnard b. 1922. Munich Putsch 1923	313
9	*Saturday*	Katharine Hepburn b. 1909. Dylan Thomas d. 1953	314
10	*Sunday*	**7th S. before Christmas/23rd S. after Trinity**	*week* 45 *day* 315
11	*Monday*	Armistice Day 1918. Denis Wheatley d. 1977	316
12	*Tuesday*	Gen. Thomas Fairfax d. 1671. Jill Tweedie d. 1993	317
13	*Wednesday*	Archbishop Carey b. 1935. George Grenville d. 1770	318
14	*Thursday*	*Prince of Wales b. 1948.* First London to Brighton car run 1896	319
15	*Friday*	William Pitt, Earl of Chatham b. 1708	320
16	*Saturday*	John Bright b. 1811. Sir Oswald Mosley b. 1896	321
17	*Sunday*	**6th S. before Christmas/24th S. after Trinity**	*week* 46 *day* 322
18	*Monday*	Sir William Gilbert b. 1836. Marcel Proust d. 1922	323
19	*Tuesday*	Thomas Shadwell d. 1692. Indira Gandhi b. 1917	324
20	*Wednesday*	*Queen's Wedding Day 1947.* Adm. Lord Jellicoe d. 1935	325
21	*Thursday*	François-Marie Voltaire b. 1694	326
22	*Friday*	Robert Clive d. 1774. Jack London d. 1916	327
23	*Saturday*	Boris Karloff b. 1887. Diana Quick b. 1946	328
24	*Sunday*	**5th S. before Christmas/25th S. after Trinity**	*week* 47 *day* 329
25	*Monday*	Isaac Watts d. 1748. Charles Kemble b. 1775	330
26	*Tuesday*	William Cowper b. 1731. Eugene Ionesco b. 1912	331
27	*Wednesday*	Fanny Kemble b. 1809. Alexander Dubcek b. 1921	332
28	*Thursday*	Jean-Baptiste Lully b. 1632. Alberto Moravia b. 1907	333
29	*Friday*	Louisa M. Alcott b. 1832. Graham Hill d. 1975	334
30	*Saturday*	**St Andrew.** Jonathan Swift b. 1667	335

ASTRONOMICAL PHENOMENA

d h
2 00 Mercury in superior conjunction
5 04 Mars in conjunction with Moon. Mars 4° N.
8 08 Venus in conjunction with Moon. Venus 1° N.
11 15 Mercury in conjunction with Moon. Mercury
4° S.
15 04 Jupiter in conjunction with Moon. Jupiter 5° S.
20 13 Saturn in conjunction with Moon. Saturn 3° S.
22 01 Sun's longitude 240°
25 00 Pluto in conjunction

MINIMA OF ALGOL

d	h	d	h	d	h
2	07.0	13	18.2	25	05.5
5	03.8	16	15.1	28	02.3
8	00.6	19	11.9	30	23.1
10	21.4	22	08.7		

CONSTELLATIONS

The following constellations are near the meridian at

	d	h		d	h
October	1	24	November	15	21
October	16	23	December	1	20
November	1	22	December	16	19

Ursa Major (below the Pole), Cepheus, Cassiopeia, Andromeda, Pegasus, Pisces, Aquarius and Cetus

THE MOON

Phases, Apsides and Node

	d	h	m
☾ Last Quarter	3	07	50
● New Moon	11	04	16
☽ First Quarter	18	01	09
○ Full Moon	25	04	10
Apogee (404,271 km)	3	13	38
Perigee (369,493 km)	16	04	34

Mean longitude of ascending node on November 1, 186°

THE SUN   s.d. 16'.2

Day	Right Ascension	Dec.	Equation of time	Rise 52°	Rise 56°	Transit	Set 52°	Set 56°	Sidereal time	Transit of First Point of Aries
	h m s	° '	m s	h m	h m	h m	h m	h m	h m s	h m s
1	14 25 50	14 27	+16 25	6 55	7 07	11 44	16 31	16 19	2 42 14	21 14 16
2	14 29 45	14 46	+16 26	6 57	7 10	11 44	16 29	16 17	2 46 11	21 10 20
3	14 33 41	15 05	+16 26	6 59	7 12	11 44	16 28	16 15	2 50 07	21 06 25
4	14 37 38	15 23	+16 26	7 01	7 14	11 44	16 26	16 13	2 54 04	21 02 29
5	14 41 36	15 42	+16 25	7 02	7 16	11 44	16 24	16 10	2 58 00	20 58 33
6	14 45 35	16 00	+16 22	7 04	7 18	11 44	16 22	16 08	3 01 57	20 54 37
7	14 49 34	16 18	+16 19	7 06	7 20	11 44	16 21	16 06	3 05 54	20 50 41
8	14 53 34	16 35	+16 16	7 08	7 22	11 44	16 19	16 05	3 09 50	20 46 45
9	14 57 36	16 52	+16 11	7 10	7 24	11 44	16 17	16 03	3 13 47	20 42 49
10	15 01 38	17 09	+16 06	7 11	7 27	11 44	16 16	16 01	3 17 43	20 38 53
11	15 05 41	17 26	+15 59	7 13	7 29	11 44	16 14	15 59	3 21 40	20 34 57
12	15 09 44	17 42	+15 52	7 15	7 31	11 44	16 13	15 57	3 25 36	20 31 01
13	15 13 49	17 59	+15 44	7 17	7 33	11 44	16 11	15 55	3 29 33	20 27 05
14	15 17 55	18 14	+15 35	7 18	7 35	11 44	16 10	15 53	3 33 29	20 23 10
15	15 22 01	18 30	+15 25	7 20	7 37	11 45	16 09	15 52	3 37 26	20 19 14
16	15 26 08	18 45	+15 15	7 22	7 39	11 45	16 07	15 50	3 41 23	20 15 18
17	15 30 16	19 00	+15 03	7 24	7 41	11 45	16 06	15 48	3 45 19	20 11 22
18	15 34 25	19 14	+14 51	7 25	7 43	11 45	16 05	15 47	3 49 16	20 07 26
19	15 38 34	19 28	+14 38	7 27	7 45	11 45	16 03	15 45	3 53 12	20 03 30
20	15 42 45	19 42	+14 24	7 29	7 47	11 46	16 02	15 44	3 57 09	19 59 34
21	15 46 56	19 55	+14 10	7 30	7 49	11 46	16 01	15 42	4 01 05	19 55 38
22	15 51 08	20 08	+13 54	7 32	7 51	11 46	16 00	15 41	4 05 02	19 51 42
23	15 55 20	20 21	+13 38	7 34	7 53	11 47	15 59	15 40	4 08 58	19 47 46
24	15 59 34	20 33	+13 21	7 35	7 55	11 47	15 58	15 38	4 12 55	19 43 50
25	16 03 48	20 45	+13 03	7 37	7 57	11 47	15 57	15 37	4 16 52	19 39 55
26	16 08 03	20 57	+12 45	7 38	7 58	11 47	15 56	15 36	4 20 48	19 35 59
27	16 12 19	21 08	+12 26	7 40	8 00	11 48	15 55	15 35	4 24 45	19 32 03
28	16 16 36	21 19	+12 06	7 42	8 02	11 48	15 54	15 34	4 28 41	19 28 07
29	16 20 53	21 29	+11 45	7 43	8 04	11 48	15 53	15 33	4 32 38	19 24 11
30	16 25 11	21 39	+11 24	7 45	8 06	11 49	15 53	15 32	4 36 34	19 20 15

DURATION OF TWILIGHT (in minutes)

Latitude	52°	56°	52°	56°	52°	56°	52°	56°
	1 November		11 November		21 November		30 November	
Civil	36	40	37	41	38	43	39	45
Nautical	75	84	78	87	80	90	82	93
Astronomical	115	127	117	130	120	134	123	137

THE NIGHT SKY

Mercury is unsuitably placed for observation.

Venus continues to be visible as a brilliant object in the eastern sky before dawn, magnitude −4.0. On the morning of the 8th the old crescent Moon, only three days before New, passes 1° south of the planet. Venus passes 4° north of Spica, in Virgo, on the 16th.

Mars, magnitude +1.1, continues to be visible as a morning object in Leo and crossing the meridian before dawn. The slight reddish tinge of the planet is a useful aid to its identification. The Moon, just after Last Quarter, passes 4° south of the planet on the morning of the 5th.

Jupiter is still visible low in the south-western sky in the early evening, though by the end of the month it is lost to view within an hour of sunset. Jupiter's magnitude is −2.0.

Saturn, magnitude +0.8, is an evening object in the south-western sky. Saturn is in Pisces. Last year the Earth passed through the plane of the rings, rendering them unobservable, but they are now gradually opening up, though the minor axis of the rings is only 2 arcseconds so observers with small telescopes will have some difficulty in detecting them.

THE MOON

Day	RA	Dec.	Hor. par.	Semi- diam.	Sun's co- long.	PA of Bright Limb	Phase	Age	Rise 52°	Rise 56°	Transit	Set 52°	Set 56°
	h m	°	′	′	°	°	%	d	h m	h m	h m	h m	h m
1	6 56	+17.6	54.8	14.9	151	98	72	19.4	21 27	21 12	4 22	12 08	12 24
2	7 46	+16.2	54.5	14.8	163	102	63	20.4	22 26	22 13	5 09	12 44	12 57
3	8 34	+14.1	54.3	14.8	175	105	53	21.4	23 27	23 17	5 55	13 14	13 25
4	9 21	+11.4	54.3	14.8	187	107	44	22.4	—	—	6 39	13 41	13 49
5	10 08	+ 8.2	54.4	14.8	200	110	35	23.4	0 29	0 22	7 23	14 06	14 11
6	10 54	+ 4.7	54.7	14.9	212	111	26	24.4	1 32	1 29	8 06	14 29	14 31
7	11 40	+ 0.9	55.2	15.0	224	112	18	25.4	2 37	2 37	8 50	14 53	14 51
8	12 28	− 3.0	55.8	15.2	236	113	11	26.4	3 44	3 47	9 36	15 17	15 13
9	13 16	− 6.9	56.4	15.4	248	114	5	27.4	4 52	4 59	10 23	15 44	15 36
10	14 07	−10.5	57.1	15.6	261	118	2	28.4	6 02	6 12	11 12	16 15	16 03
11	15 01	−13.7	57.7	15.7	273	162	0	29.4	7 13	7 26	12 05	16 51	16 36
12	15 56	−16.2	58.3	15.9	285	261	1	0.8	8 22	8 38	13 00	17 34	17 17
13	16 54	−17.8	58.7	16.0	297	266	4	1.8	9 26	9 44	13 56	18 25	18 07
14	17 53	−18.3	59.1	16.1	309	264	10	2.8	10 25	10 43	14 54	19 26	19 08
15	18 53	−17.7	59.3	16.1	322	260	18	3.8	11 15	11 31	15 52	20 33	20 18
16	19 52	−16.0	59.3	16.2	334	257	27	4.8	11 58	12 11	16 48	21 46	21 33
17	20 50	−13.3	59.3	16.2	346	253	38	5.8	12 34	12 44	17 43	23 01	22 52
18	21 46	− 9.9	59.2	16.1	358	251	50	6.8	13 05	13 12	18 36	—	—
19	22 40	− 5.9	59.0	16.1	10	249	61	7.8	13 34	13 37	19 27	0 17	0 11
20	23 34	− 1.5	58.8	16.0	22	247	72	8.8	14 01	14 00	20 18	1 32	1 31
21	0 26	+ 2.8	58.5	15.9	35	247	81	9.8	14 28	14 23	21 08	2 47	2 50
22	1 19	+ 7.0	58.1	15.8	47	246	89	10.8	14 56	14 48	21 59	4 01	4 07
23	2 12	+10.7	57.6	15.7	59	246	95	11.8	15 27	15 16	22 50	5 13	5 23
24	3 05	+13.9	57.2	15.6	71	241	98	12.8	16 02	15 48	23 41	6 22	6 36
25	3 59	+16.3	56.6	15.4	83	195	100	13.8	16 42	16 26	—	7 28	7 44
26	4 52	+17.8	56.1	15.3	95	109	99	14.8	17 28	17 10	0 33	8 27	8 45
27	5 45	+18.4	55.5	15.1	107	101	96	15.8	18 19	18 01	1 23	9 19	9 37
28	6 38	+18.1	55.1	15.0	119	101	92	16.8	19 14	18 57	2 13	10 05	10 21
29	7 29	+16.9	54.6	14.9	132	104	86	17.8	20 12	19 58	3 02	10 43	10 58
30	8 18	+15.0	54.4	14.8	144	106	79	18.8	21 13	21 01	3 48	11 15	11 28

MERCURY

Day	RA	Dec.	Diam.	Phase	Transit	5° high 52°	5° high 56°
	h m	°	″	%	h m	h m	h m
1	14 24	−13.8	5	100	11 43	7 33	7 51
3	14 36	−15.1	5	100	11 47	7 46	8 05
5	14 49	−16.3	5	100	11 52	7 59	8 19
7	15 01	−17.4	5	100	11 57	8 11	8 34
9	15 14	−18.5	5	99	12 02	15 39 15 14	
11	15 27	−19.5	5	99	12 06	15 36 15 09	
13	15 39	−20.4	5	99	12 11	15 34 15 05	
15	15 52	−21.3	5	98	12 16	15 32 15 01	
17	16 05	−22.1	5	97	12 21	15 30 14 57	
19	16 18	−22.9	5	97	12 26	15 29 14 54	
21	16 31	−23.5	5	96	12 31	15 28 14 51	
23	16 44	−24.1	5	95	12 37	15 29 14 48	
25	16 57	−24.6	5	94	12 42	15 29 14 47	
27	17 11	−25.0	5	92	12 47	15 31 14 47	
29	17 24	−25.4	5	91	12 53	15 33 14 47	
31	17 37	−25.6	5	89	12 58	15 36 14 49	

VENUS

Day	RA	Dec.	Diam.	Phase	Transit	5° high 52°	5° high 56°
	h m	° ′	″	%	h m	h m	h m
1	12 14	+ 0.2	14	79	9 32	4 03	4 06
6	12 36	− 2.0	13	81	9 34	4 18	4 23
11	12 59	− 4.3	13	82	9 37	4 33	4 40
16	13 21	− 6.6	13	84	9 40	4 49	4 58
21	13 45	− 8.9	12	85	9 44	5 04	5 16
26	14 08	−11.0	12	86	9 48	5 21	5 35
31	14 32	−13.1	12	87	9 52	5 38	5 54

MARS

Day	RA	Dec.	Diam.	Phase	Transit	5° high 52°	5° high 56°
1	10 14	+12.6	5	91	7 31	0 59	0 52
6	10 25	+11.7	6	91	7 22	0 55	0 49
11	10 35	+10.8	6	91	7 13	0 50	0 45
16	10 45	+ 9.9	6	91	7 03	0 45	0 41
21	10 55	+ 9.0	6	91	6 53	0 40	0 36
26	11 04	+ 8.1	6	90	6 43	0 34	0 31
31	11 13	+ 7.2	6	90	6 32	0 28	0 26

SUNRISE AND SUNSET

	London		Bristol		Birmingham		Manchester		Newcastle		Glasgow		Belfast	
	0°05′	51°30′	2°35′	51°28′	1°55′	52°28′	2°15′	53°28′	1°37′	54°59′	4°14′	55°52′	5°56′	54°35′
	h m	h m	h m	h m	h m	h m	h m	h m	h m	h m	h m	h m	h m	h m
1	6 54	16 33	7 04	16 43	7 04	16 38	7 08	16 36	7 11	16 29	7 24	16 36	7 27	16 47
2	6 56	16 31	7 06	16 41	7 06	16 36	7 10	16 34	7 13	16 27	7 26	16 34	7 29	16 45
3	6 58	16 29	7 08	16 39	7 08	16 34	7 12	16 32	7 15	16 25	7 28	16 32	7 31	16 43
4	6 59	16 28	7 09	16 38	7 10	16 32	7 14	16 30	7 17	16 23	7 30	16 30	7 33	16 41
5	7 01	16 26	7 11	16 36	7 12	16 30	7 16	16 28	7 19	16 21	7 32	16 28	7 35	16 39
6	7 03	16 24	7 13	16 34	7 13	16 29	7 18	16 27	7 21	16 19	7 35	16 26	7 37	16 37
7	7 05	16 23	7 15	16 33	7 15	16 27	7 20	16 25	7 23	16 17	7 37	16 24	7 39	16 36
8	7 07	16 21	7 16	16 31	7 17	16 25	7 22	16 23	7 25	16 15	7 39	16 22	7 41	16 34
9	7 08	16 19	7 18	16 30	7 19	16 24	7 24	16 21	7 27	16 13	7 41	16 20	7 43	16 32
10	7 10	16 18	7 20	16 28	7 21	16 22	7 26	16 20	7 29	16 11	7 43	16 18	7 45	16 30
11	7 12	16 16	7 22	16 27	7 23	16 20	7 28	16 18	7 31	16 10	7 45	16 16	7 47	16 28
12	7 14	16 15	7 23	16 25	7 24	16 19	7 29	16 16	7 33	16 08	7 47	16 14	7 48	16 27
13	7 15	16 13	7 25	16 24	7 26	16 17	7 31	16 15	7 35	16 06	7 49	16 13	7 50	16 25
14	7 17	16 12	7 27	16 22	7 28	16 16	7 33	16 13	7 37	16 04	7 51	16 11	7 52	16 23
15	7 19	16 11	7 29	16 21	7 30	16 14	7 35	16 12	7 39	16 03	7 53	16 09	7 54	16 22
16	7 20	16 09	7 30	16 19	7 31	16 13	7 37	16 10	7 41	16 01	7 55	16 08	7 56	16 20
17	7 22	16 08	7 32	16 18	7 33	16 12	7 39	16 09	7 43	16 00	7 57	16 06	7 58	16 19
18	7 24	16 07	7 34	16 17	7 35	16 10	7 40	16 07	7 45	15 58	7 59	16 04	8 00	16 17
19	7 25	16 06	7 35	16 16	7 37	16 09	7 42	16 06	7 47	15 57	8 01	16 03	8 02	16 16
20	7 27	16 04	7 37	16 15	7 38	16 08	7 44	16 05	7 48	15 55	8 03	16 01	8 04	16 14
21	7 29	16 03	7 39	16 13	7 40	16 07	7 46	16 04	7 50	15 54	8 05	16 00	8 06	16 13
22	7 30	16 02	7 40	16 12	7 42	16 06	7 48	16 02	7 52	15 53	8 07	15 59	8 08	16 12
23	7 32	16 01	7 42	16 11	7 43	16 04	7 49	16 01	7 54	15 51	8 09	15 57	8 09	16 11
24	7 34	16 00	7 43	16 10	7 45	16 03	7 51	16 00	7 56	15 50	8 11	15 56	8 11	16 09
25	7 35	15 59	7 45	16 09	7 47	16 02	7 53	15 59	7 58	15 49	8 13	15 55	8 13	16 08
26	7 37	15 58	7 46	16 09	7 48	16 01	7 54	15 58	7 59	15 48	8 15	15 53	8 15	16 07
27	7 38	15 58	7 48	16 08	7 50	16 01	7 56	15 57	8 01	15 47	8 17	15 52	8 16	16 06
28	7 40	15 57	7 50	16 07	7 51	16 00	7 58	15 56	8 03	15 46	8 18	15 51	8 18	16 05
29	7 41	15 56	7 51	16 06	7 53	15 59	7 59	15 55	8 05	15 45	8 20	15 50	8 20	16 04
30	7 43	15 55	7 52	16 05	7 54	15 58	8 01	15 55	8 06	15 44	8 22	15 49	8 21	16 03

JUPITER

Day	RA	Dec.	Transit	5° high	
				52°	56°
	h m	° ′	h m	h m	h m
1	18 55.8	−23 05	16 11	19 14	18 38
11	19 03.0	−22 55	15 39	18 43	18 08
21	19 11.0	−22 43	15 08	18 13	17 39
31	19 19.6	−22 28	14 37	17 45	17 11

Diameters – equatorial 34″ polar 32″

SATURN

Day	RA	Dec.	Transit	5° high	
				52°	56°
	h m	° ′	h m	h m	h m
1	0 09.7	− 1 46	21 24	2 45	2 40
11	0 07.9	− 1 55	20 43	2 03	1 59
21	0 06.8	− 2 01	20 02	1 22	1 17
31	0 06.2	− 2 02	19 23	0 43	0 37

Diameters – equatorial 19″ polar 17″
Rings – major axis 43″ minor axis 2″

URANUS

Day	RA	Dec.	Transit	10° high	
				52°	56°
	h m	° ′	h m	h m	h m
1	20 12.8	−20 32	17 28	20 02	19 18
11	20 13.7	−20 29	16 49	19 24	18 40
21	20 15.0	−20 25	16 11	18 47	18 03
31	20 16.6	−20 20	15 34	18 10	17 27

Diameter 4″

NEPTUNE

Day	RA	Dec.	Transit	10° high	
				52°	56°
	h m	° ′	h m	h m	h m
1	19 48.1	−20 40	17 03	19 36	18 51
11	19 48.8	−20 38	16 25	18 58	18 13
21	19 49.7	−20 36	15 46	18 20	17 35
31	19 50.8	−20 33	15 08	17 42	16 57

Diameter 2″

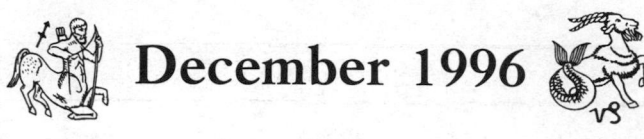

December 1996

TWELFTH MONTH, 31 DAYS. *Decem* (ten), tenth month of Roman pre-Julian calendar

1	Sunday	**Advent Sunday.** Queen Alexandra b. 1844	*week* 48 *day* 336
2	Monday	Edmond Rostand d. 1918. Stephen Potter d. 1969	337
3	Tuesday	Samuel Crompton b. 1753. John Flaxman d. 1826	338
4	Wednesday	John Gay d. 1732. Samuel Butler b. 1835	339
5	Thursday	Geraldus Mercator d. 1594. Claude Monet d. 1926	340
6	Friday	CHANUCAH begins. Henry VI b. 1421	341
7	Saturday	Lord Darnley b. 1545. Robert Graves d. 1985	342
8	Sunday	**2nd S. in Advent.** Mary, Queen of Scots b. 1542	*week* 49 *day* 343
9	Monday	Elisabeth Schwarzkopf b. 1915. Karl Barth d. 1968	344
10	Tuesday	Alfred Nobel d. 1896. Damon Runyon d. 1946	345
11	Wednesday	Sir Kenneth MacMillan b. 1929	346
12	Thursday	Gustave Flaubert b. 1821. Robert Browning d. 1889	347
13	Friday	Laurens van der Post b. 1906. L. P. Hartley d. 1972	348
14	Saturday	George Washington d. 1799. George VI b. 1895	349
15	Sunday	**3rd S. in Advent.** Izaak Walton d. 1683	*week* 50 *day* 350
16	Monday	Camille Saint-Saëns d. 1921. Glen Miller d. 1944	351
17	Tuesday	Sir Humphrey Davy b. 1778. Simón Bolivar d. 1830	352
18	Wednesday	Dorothy L. Sayers d. 1957. Bobby Jones d. 1971	353
19	Thursday	Emily Brontë d. 1848. Jean Genet b. 1910	354
20	Friday	Sir Robert Menzies b. 1894. Bill Brandt d. 1983	355
21	Saturday	*Michaelmas Law Sittings end.* Joseph Stalin b. 1879	356
22	Sunday	**4th S. in Advent.** Sir Henry Cotton d. 1987	*week* 51 *day* 357
23	Monday	Thomas Malthus d. 1834. Théophile Gautier d. 1872	358
24	Tuesday	Christmas Eve. King John b. 1167	359
25	Wednesday	**Christmas Day.** *Public Holiday in the UK*	360
26	Thursday	**St Stephen.** *Bank Holiday in the UK*	361
27	Friday	**St John the Evangelist.** Johann Kepler b. 1571	362
28	Saturday	**Holy Innocents.** Maurice Ravel d. 1937	363
29	Sunday	**1st S. after Christmas.** Christina Rossetti d. 1894	*week* 52 *day* 364
30	Monday	Sir Carol Reed b. 1906. Irving 'Swifty' Lazar d. 1993	365
31	Tuesday	John Wycliffe d. 1384. Henri Matisse b. 1869	366

ASTRONOMICAL PHENOMENA

d	h	
3	13	Saturn at stationary point
3	18	Mars in conjunction with Moon. Mars 3° N.
8	14	Venus in conjunction with Moon. Venus 2° S.
12	04	Mercury in conjunction with Moon. Mercury 7° S.
12	21	Jupiter in conjunction with Moon. Jupiter 5° S.
15	19	Mercury at greatest elongation E. 20°
17	18	Saturn in conjunction with Moon. Saturn 2° S.
21	14	Sun's longitude 270° ♑
23	20	Mercury at stationary point

MINIMA OF ALGOL

d	h	d	h	d	h
3	19.9	15	07.2	23	21.7
6	16.8	18	04.0	26	18.5
9	13.6	21	00.9	29	15.3
12	10.4				

CONSTELLATIONS

The following constellations are near the meridian at

	d	h		d	h
November	1	24	December	16	21
November	15	23	January	1	20
December	1	22	January	16	19

Ursa Major (below the Pole), Ursa Minor (below the Pole), Cassiopeia, Andromeda, Perseus, Triangulum, Aries, Taurus, Cetus and Eridanus

THE MOON

Phases, Apsides and Node	d	h	m
☾ Last Quarter	3	05	06
● New Moon	10	16	56
☽ First Quarter	17	09	31
○ Full Moon	24	20	41
Apogee (404,616 km)	1	10	28
Perigee (364,257 km)	13	04	08
Apogee (405,492 km)	29	05	18

Mean longitude of ascending node on December 1, 185°

THE SUN   s.d. 16′.3

Day	Right Ascension	Dec. −	Equation of time	Rise 52°	Rise 56°	Transit	Set 52°	Set 56°	Sidereal time	Transit of First Point of Aries
	h m s	° ′	m s	h m	h m	h m	h m	h m	h m s	h m s
1	16 29 29	21 48	+11 02	7 46	8 07	11 49	15 52	15 31	4 40 31	19 16 19
2	16 33 48	21 58	+10 39	7 47	8 09	11 50	15 51	15 30	4 44 27	19 12 23
3	16 38 08	22 06	+10 16	7 49	8 10	11 50	15 51	15 29	4 48 24	19 08 27
4	16 42 29	22 15	+ 9 52	7 50	8 12	11 50	15 50	15 28	4 52 21	19 04 31
5	16 46 50	22 22	+ 9 27	7 51	8 13	11 51	15 50	15 28	4 56 17	19 00 35
6	16 51 12	22 30	+ 9 02	7 53	8 15	11 51	15 50	15 27	5 00 14	18 56 40
7	16 55 34	22 37	+ 8 36	7 54	8 16	11 52	15 49	15 27	5 04 10	18 52 44
8	16 59 56	22 43	+ 8 10	7 55	8 18	11 52	15 49	15 26	5 08 07	18 48 48
9	17 04 20	22 49	+ 7 44	7 56	8 19	11 52	15 49	15 26	5 12 03	18 44 52
10	17 08 43	22 55	+ 7 17	7 57	8 20	11 53	15 49	15 26	5 16 00	18 40 56
11	17 13 07	23 00	+ 6 49	7 58	8 21	11 53	15 48	15 25	5 19 57	18 37 00
12	17 17 32	23 05	+ 6 21	7 59	8 23	11 54	15 48	15 25	5 23 53	18 33 04
13	17 21 57	23 09	+ 5 53	8 00	8 24	11 54	15 48	15 25	5 27 50	18 29 08
14	17 26 22	23 13	+ 5 24	8 01	8 25	11 55	15 48	15 25	5 31 46	18 25 12
15	17 30 47	23 16	+ 4 55	8 02	8 25	11 55	15 49	15 25	5 35 43	18 21 16
16	17 35 13	23 19	+ 4 26	8 03	8 26	11 56	15 49	15 25	5 39 39	18 17 20
17	17 39 39	23 21	+ 3 57	8 04	8 27	11 56	15 49	15 25	5 43 36	18 13 25
18	17 44 05	23 23	+ 3 28	8 04	8 28	11 57	15 49	15 26	5 47 32	18 09 29
19	17 48 31	23 25	+ 2 58	8 05	8 29	11 57	15 50	15 26	5 51 29	18 05 33
20	17 52 57	23 26	+ 2 28	8 05	8 29	11 58	15 50	15 26	5 55 26	18 01 37
21	17 57 23	23 26	+ 1 59	8 06	8 30	11 58	15 51	15 27	5 59 22	17 57 41
22	18 01 50	23 26	+ 1 29	8 06	8 30	11 59	15 51	15 27	6 03 19	17 53 45
23	18 06 16	23 26	+ 0 59	8 07	8 31	11 59	15 52	15 28	6 07 15	17 49 49
24	18 10 42	23 25	+ 0 29	8 07	8 31	12 00	15 52	15 29	6 11 12	17 45 53
25	18 15 09	23 23	0 00	8 08	8 31	12 00	15 53	15 29	6 15 08	17 41 57
26	18 19 35	23 22	− 0 30	8 08	8 32	12 01	15 54	15 30	6 19 05	17 38 01
27	18 24 01	23 19	− 1 00	8 08	8 32	12 01	15 55	15 31	6 23 01	17 34 05
28	18 28 27	23 17	− 1 29	8 08	8 32	12 02	15 55	15 32	6 26 58	17 30 10
29	18 32 53	23 13	− 1 58	8 08	8 32	12 02	15 56	15 33	6 30 55	17 26 14
30	18 37 18	23 10	− 2 27	8 08	8 32	12 03	15 57	15 34	6 34 51	17 22 18
31	18 41 44	23 05	− 2 56	8 08	8 31	12 03	15 58	15 35	6 38 48	17 18 22

DURATION OF TWILIGHT (in minutes)

Latitude	52°	56°	52°	56°	52°	56°	52°	56°
	1 December		11 December		21 December		31 December	
Civil	40	45	41	47	41	47	41	47
Nautical	82	93	84	96	85	97	84	96
Astronomical	123	138	125	141	126	142	125	141

THE NIGHT SKY

Mercury is unsuitably placed for observation.

Venus, magnitude −4.0, is still visible as a brilliant object in the south-eastern sky in the mornings before dawn. It is now moving more rapidly towards the Sun and consequently rising later and later until, by the end of December, observers in southern England will not be able to see it before 07h. Because of its southerly declination, those in Scotland will have to wait until nearly 08h. The old crescent Moon, only two days before New, passes 2° north of Venus on the 8th, while Venus itself passes 6° north of Antares on the morning of the 24th.

Mars continues to be visible as a morning object and by the end of the year is visible low above the eastern horizon shortly before midnight. When it rises on the last day of the month observers will notice the Moon, at Last Quarter, passing about 3°S. of the planet. During December Mars passes from Leo into Virgo.

Jupiter, magnitude −1.9, is only visible for a short time in the early evening, very low above the south-western horizon after sunset. By the middle of the month Jupiter is lost to view in the gathering dusk.

Saturn is still visible in the south-western sky in the evenings, but by the middle of the month it is too low in the western sky to be seen after midnight. Saturn's magnitude is +1.0. On the evening of the 17th the Moon, at First Quarter, passes 2° north of Saturn.

Meteors. The maximum of the well-known Geminid meteor showers occurs on the 13th. Conditions are favourable because of the absence of moonlight.

THE MOON

Day	RA	Dec.	Hor. par.	Semi- diam.	Sun's co- long.	PA of Bright Limb	Phase	Age	Rise 52°	Rise 56°	Transit	Set 52°	Set 56°
	h m	°	′	′	°	°	%	d	h m	h m	h m	h m	h m
1	9 06	+12.5	54.2	14.8	156	109	70	19.8	22 14	22 06	4 33	11 44	11 53
2	9 52	+ 9.5	54.2	14.8	168	111	61	20.8	23 17	23 11	5 17	12 09	12 16
3	10 38	+ 6.1	54.4	14.8	180	112	52	21.8	—	—	6 00	12 33	12 36
4	11 24	+ 2.5	54.8	14.9	192	113	43	22.8	0 20	0 18	6 43	12 56	12 56
5	12 10	− 1.4	55.3	15.1	205	113	33	23.8	1 25	1 26	7 27	13 19	13 16
6	12 58	− 5.2	55.9	15.2	217	113	24	24.8	2 32	2 37	8 13	13 44	13 38
7	13 47	− 9.0	56.7	15.5	229	113	16	25.8	3 40	3 49	9 00	14 12	14 02
8	14 39	−12.4	57.5	15.7	241	112	9	26.8	4 50	5 02	9 51	14 45	14 32
9	15 34	−15.2	58.4	15.9	253	113	4	27.8	6 01	6 16	10 45	15 25	15 09
10	16 31	−17.3	59.1	16.1	265	124	1	28.8	7 10	7 27	11 42	16 13	15 55
11	17 31	−18.4	59.7	16.3	278	222	0	0.3	8 13	8 32	12 42	17 11	16 52
12	18 33	−18.2	60.0	16.4	290	251	3	1.3	9 09	9 27	13 42	18 18	18 01
13	19 34	−16.8	60.2	16.4	302	253	7	2.3	9 57	10 11	14 41	19 31	19 17
14	20 34	−14.4	60.1	16.4	314	251	15	3.3	10 36	10 48	15 38	20 48	20 37
15	21 32	−11.0	59.9	16.3	326	249	24	4.3	11 10	11 18	16 32	22 05	21 58
16	22 28	− 7.1	59.5	16.2	339	248	35	5.3	11 39	11 44	17 25	23 21	23 19
17	23 22	− 2.7	59.0	16.1	351	247	46	6.3	12 07	12 07	18 16	—	—
18	0 15	+ 1.6	58.4	15.9	3	247	57	7.3	12 33	12 30	19 06	0 36	0 38
19	1 07	+ 5.8	57.9	15.8	15	247	67	8.3	13 01	12 54	19 55	1 50	1 55
20	1 59	+ 9.7	57.4	15.6	27	248	77	9.3	13 30	13 20	20 45	3 01	3 10
21	2 51	+13.0	56.8	15.5	39	250	85	10.3	14 03	13 49	21 35	4 11	4 23
22	3 43	+15.6	56.3	15.4	51	251	92	11.3	14 40	14 24	22 26	5 16	5 32
23	4 36	+17.4	55.9	15.2	64	250	96	12.3	15 22	15 05	23 16	6 18	6 35
24	5 29	+18.3	55.4	15.1	76	241	99	13.3	16 10	15 52	—	7 13	7 30
25	6 21	+18.4	55.0	15.0	88	165	100	14.3	17 03	16 46	0 06	8 01	8 18
26	7 12	+17.5	54.7	14.9	100	117	99	15.3	18 00	17 45	0 55	8 42	8 58
27	8 02	+15.9	54.4	14.8	112	112	96	16.3	19 00	18 47	1 43	9 17	9 30
28	8 51	+13.6	54.2	14.8	124	111	91	17.3	20 02	19 52	2 28	9 47	9 58
29	9 38	+10.8	54.1	14.7	136	112	85	18.3	21 04	20 57	3 13	10 13	10 21
30	10 24	+ 7.5	54.1	14.7	149	113	78	19.3	22 06	22 03	3 56	10 38	10 42
31	11 09	+ 3.9	54.3	14.8	161	113	69	20.3	23 09	23 09	4 39	11 00	11 02

MERCURY

Day	RA	Dec.	Diam.	Phase	Transit	5° high 52°	5° high 56°
	h m	°	″	%	h m	h m	h m
1	17 37	−25.6	5	89	12 58	15 36	14 49
3	17 50	−25.7	5	87	13 03	15 40	14 52
5	18 03	−25.8	5	85	13 08	15 45	14 57
7	18 15	−25.7	6	82	13 12	15 50	15 03
9	18 27	−25.6	6	79	13 17	15 56	15 10
11	18 39	−25.4	6	75	13 20	16 02	15 17
13	18 50	−25.0	6	70	13 23	16 09	15 26
15	19 00	−24.6	7	64	13 25	16 14	15 34
17	19 09	−24.2	7	58	13 25	16 20	15 41
19	19 16	−23.6	7	50	13 24	16 23	15 46
21	19 21	−23.1	8	42	13 20	16 24	15 50
23	19 23	−22.5	8	33	13 14	16 23	15 50
25	19 23	−21.9	9	23	13 05	16 18	15 46
27	19 19	−21.4	9	15	12 52	16 09	15 39
29	19 11	−21.0	10	7	12 36	15 56	15 27
31	19 02	−20.6	10	2	12 18	15 40	15 12

VENUS

Day	RA	Dec.	Diam.	Phase	Transit	5° high 52°	5° high 56°
	h m	°	″	%	h m	h m	h m
1	14 32	−13.1	12	87	9 52	5 38	5 54
6	14 56	−15.1	12	88	9 56	5 54	6 13
11	15 21	−16.9	12	89	10 01	6 12	6 33
16	15 46	−18.5	11	90	10 07	6 28	6 53
21	16 12	−19.9	11	91	10 13	6 45	7 12
26	16 38	−21.1	11	92	10 20	7 01	7 31
31	17 05	−22.0	11	93	10 27	7 15	7 47

MARS

Day	RA	Dec.	Diam.	Phase	Transit	5° high 52°	5° high 56°
1	11 13	+ 7.2	6	90	6 32	0 28	0 26
6	11 22	+ 6.4	7	90	6 21	0 22	0 20
11	11 31	+ 5.6	7	90	6 10	0 15	0 13
16	11 39	+ 4.8	7	90	5 58	0 07	0 06
21	11 46	+ 4.1	7	90	5 46	23 57	23 57
26	11 53	+ 3.5	8	91	5 34	23 47	23 48
31	12 00	+ 2.8	8	91	5 21	23 37	23 38

SUNRISE AND SUNSET

	London		Bristol		Birmingham		Manchester		Newcastle		Glasgow		Belfast	
	0°05'	51°30'	2°35'	51°28'	1°55'	52°28'	2°15'	53°28'	1°37'	54°59'	4°14'	55°52'	5°56'	54°35'
	h m	h m	h m	h m	h m	h m	h m	h m	h m	h m	h m	h m	h m	h m
1	7 44	15 55	7 54	16 05	7 56	15 57	8 02	15 54	8 08	15 43	8 23	15 48	8 23	16 03
2	7 45	15 54	7 55	16 04	7 57	15 57	8 04	15 53	8 09	15 42	8 25	15 48	8 24	16 02
3	7 47	15 54	7 56	16 04	7 59	15 56	8 05	15 53	8 11	15 42	8 27	15 47	8 26	16 01
4	7 48	15 53	7 58	16 03	8 00	15 56	8 06	15 52	8 12	15 41	8 28	15 46	8 27	16 01
5	7 49	15 53	7 59	16 03	8 01	15 55	8 08	15 51	8 14	15 40	8 30	15 46	8 29	16 00
6	7 50	15 52	8 00	16 02	8 03	15 55	8 09	15 51	8 15	15 40	8 31	15 45	8 30	15 59
7	7 52	15 52	8 01	16 02	8 04	15 55	8 10	15 51	8 16	15 39	8 32	15 44	8 31	15 59
8	7 53	15 52	8 03	16 02	8 05	15 54	8 12	15 50	8 18	15 39	8 34	15 44	8 33	15 59
9	7 54	15 52	8 04	16 02	8 06	15 54	8 13	15 50	8 19	15 39	8 35	15 44	8 34	15 58
10	7 55	15 51	8 05	16 02	8 07	15 54	8 14	15 50	8 20	15 38	8 36	15 43	8 35	15 58
11	7 56	15 51	8 06	16 01	8 08	15 54	8 15	15 50	8 21	15 38	8 37	15 43	8 36	15 58
12	7 57	15 51	8 07	16 01	8 09	15 54	8 16	15 50	8 22	15 38	8 39	15 43	8 37	15 58
13	7 58	15 51	8 08	16 01	8 10	15 54	8 17	15 50	8 24	15 38	8 40	15 43	8 38	15 58
14	7 59	15 51	8 09	16 01	8 11	15 54	8 18	15 50	8 24	15 38	8 41	15 43	8 39	15 58
15	8 00	15 51	8 10	16 02	8 12	15 54	8 19	15 50	8 25	15 38	8 42	15 43	8 40	15 58
16	8 00	15 52	8 10	16 02	8 13	15 54	8 20	15 50	8 26	15 38	8 42	15 43	8 41	15 58
17	8 01	15 52	8 11	16 02	8 14	15 54	8 20	15 50	8 27	15 38	8 43	15 43	8 42	15 58
18	8 02	15 52	8 12	16 02	8 14	15 55	8 21	15 50	8 28	15 39	8 44	15 43	8 43	15 58
19	8 03	15 53	8 12	16 03	8 15	15 55	8 22	15 51	8 28	15 39	8 45	15 44	8 43	15 59
20	8 03	15 53	8 13	16 03	8 16	15 55	8 22	15 51	8 29	15 39	8 45	15 44	8 44	15 59
21	8 04	15 54	8 14	16 04	8 16	15 56	8 23	15 52	8 30	15 40	8 46	15 45	8 44	16 00
22	8 04	15 54	8 14	16 04	8 17	15 56	8 23	15 52	8 30	15 40	8 46	15 45	8 45	16 00
23	8 05	15 55	8 14	16 05	8 17	15 57	8 24	15 53	8 30	15 41	8 47	15 46	8 45	16 01
24	8 05	15 55	8 15	16 05	8 17	15 58	8 24	15 53	8 31	15 42	8 47	15 46	8 46	16 01
25	8 05	15 56	8 15	16 06	8 18	15 58	8 25	15 54	8 31	15 42	8 47	15 47	8 46	16 02
26	8 06	15 57	8 15	16 07	8 18	15 59	8 25	15 55	8 31	15 43	8 48	15 48	8 46	16 03
27	8 06	15 57	8 16	16 08	8 18	16 00	8 25	15 56	8 31	15 44	8 48	15 49	8 46	16 04
28	8 06	15 58	8 16	16 08	8 18	16 01	8 25	15 56	8 32	15 45	8 48	15 50	8 46	16 05
29	8 06	15 59	8 16	16 09	8 18	16 02	8 25	15 57	8 32	15 46	8 48	15 51	8 46	16 06
30	8 06	16 00	8 16	16 10	8 18	16 03	8 25	15 58	8 32	15 47	8 48	15 52	8 46	16 07
31	8 06	16 01	8 16	16 11	8 18	16 04	8 25	15 59	8 31	15 48	8 47	15 53	8 46	16 08

JUPITER

Day	RA	Dec.	Transit	5° high	
				52°	56°
	h m	° '	h m	h m	h m
1	19 19.6	−22 28	14 37	17 45	17 11
11	19 28.7	−22 11	14 07	17 17	16 44
21	19 38.1	−21 51	13 37	16 50	16 18
31	19 47.8	−21 28	13 07	16 23	15 53

Diameters – equatorial 33" polar 31"

SATURN

Day	RA	Dec.	Transit	5° high	
				52°	56°
	h m	° '	h m	h m	h m
1	0 06.2	− 2 02	19 23	0 43	0 37
11	0 06.3	− 1 59	18 43	0 04	23 55
21	0 07.1	− 1 51	18 05	23 22	23 17
31	0 08.5	− 1 39	17 27	22 45	22 40

Diameters – equatorial 18" polar 16"
Rings – major axis 40" minor axis 2"

URANUS

Day	RA	Dec.	Transit	10° high	
				52°	56°
	h m	° '	h m	h m	h m
1	20 16.6	−20 20	15 34	18 10	17 27
11	20 18.4	−20 14	14 56	17 34	16 51
21	20 20.4	−20 07	14 19	16 57	16 15
31	20 22.6	−19 59	13 42	16 22	15 40

Diameter 4"

NEPTUNE

Day	RA	Dec.	Transit	10° high	
				52°	56°
	h m	° '	h m	h m	h m
1	19 50.8	−20 33	15 08	17 42	16 57
11	19 52.1	−20 30	14 30	17 05	16 20
21	19 53.5	−20 27	13 52	16 27	15 43
31	19 55.0	−20 23	13 14	15 50	15 06

Diameter 2"

RISING AND SETTING TIMES

TABLE 1. SEMI-DIURNAL ARCS (HOUR ANGLES AT RISING/SETTING)

Dec.	0° h m	10° h m	20° h m	30° h m	40° h m	45° h m	50° h m	52° h m	54° h m	56° h m	58° h m	60° h m	Dec.
0°	6 00	6 00	6 00	6 00	6 00	6 00	6 00	6 00	6 00	6 00	6 00	6 00	0°
1°	6 00	6 01	6 01	6 02	6 03	6 04	6 05	6 05	6 06	6 06	6 06	6 07	1°
2°	6 00	6 01	6 03	6 05	6 07	6 08	6 10	6 10	6 11	6 12	6 13	6 14	2°
3°	6 00	6 02	6 04	6 07	6 10	6 12	6 14	6 15	6 17	6 18	6 19	6 21	3°
4°	6 00	6 03	6 06	6 09	6 13	6 16	6 19	6 21	6 22	6 24	6 26	6 28	4°
5°	6 00	6 04	6 07	6 12	6 17	6 20	6 24	6 26	6 28	6 30	6 32	6 35	5°
6°	6 00	6 04	6 09	6 14	6 20	6 24	6 29	6 31	6 33	6 36	6 39	6 42	6°
7°	6 00	6 05	6 10	6 16	6 24	6 28	6 34	6 36	6 39	6 42	6 45	6 49	7°
8°	6 00	6 06	6 12	6 19	6 27	6 32	6 39	6 41	6 45	6 48	6 52	6 56	8°
9°	6 00	6 06	6 13	6 21	6 31	6 36	6 44	6 47	6 50	6 54	6 59	7 04	9°
10°	6 00	6 07	6 15	6 23	6 34	6 41	6 49	6 52	6 56	7 01	7 06	7 11	10°
11°	6 00	6 08	6 16	6 26	6 38	6 45	6 54	6 58	7 02	7 07	7 12	7 19	11°
12°	6 00	6 09	6 18	6 28	6 41	6 49	6 59	7 03	7 08	7 13	7 20	7 26	12°
13°	6 00	6 09	6 19	6 31	6 45	6 53	7 04	7 09	7 14	7 20	7 27	7 34	13°
14°	6 00	6 10	6 21	6 33	6 48	6 58	7 09	7 14	7 20	7 27	7 34	7 42	14°
15°	6 00	6 11	6 22	6 36	6 52	7 02	7 14	7 20	7 27	7 34	7 42	7 51	15°
16°	6 00	6 12	6 24	6 38	6 56	7 07	7 20	7 26	7 33	7 41	7 49	7 59	16°
17°	6 00	6 12	6 26	6 41	6 59	7 11	7 25	7 32	7 40	7 48	7 57	8 08	17°
18°	6 00	6 13	6 27	6 43	7 03	7 16	7 31	7 38	7 46	7 55	8 05	8 17	18°
19°	6 00	6 14	6 29	6 46	7 07	7 21	7 37	7 45	7 53	8 03	8 14	8 26	19°
20°	6 00	6 15	6 30	6 49	7 11	7 25	7 43	7 51	8 00	8 11	8 22	8 36	20°
21°	6 00	6 16	6 32	6 51	7 15	7 30	7 49	7 58	8 08	8 19	8 32	8 47	21°
22°	6 00	6 16	6 34	6 54	7 19	7 35	7 55	8 05	8 15	8 27	8 41	8 58	22°
23°	6 00	6 17	6 36	6 57	7 23	7 40	8 02	8 12	8 23	8 36	8 51	9 09	23°
24°	6 00	6 18	6 37	7 00	7 28	7 46	8 08	8 19	8 31	8 45	9 02	9 22	24°
25°	6 00	6 19	6 39	7 02	7 32	7 51	8 15	8 27	8 40	8 55	9 13	9 35	25°
26°	6 00	6 20	6 41	7 05	7 37	7 57	8 22	8 35	8 49	9 05	9 25	9 51	26°
27°	6 00	6 21	6 43	7 08	7 41	8 03	8 30	8 43	8 58	9 16	9 39	10 08	27°
28°	6 00	6 22	6 45	7 12	7 46	8 08	8 37	8 52	9 08	9 28	9 53	10 28	28°
29°	6 00	6 22	6 47	7 15	7 51	8 15	8 45	9 01	9 19	9 41	10 10	10 55	29°
30°	6 00	6 23	6 49	7 18	7 56	8 21	8 54	9 11	9 30	9 55	10 30	12 00	30°
35°	6 00	6 28	6 59	7 35	8 24	8 58	9 46	10 15	10 58	12 00	12 00	12 00	35°
40°	6 00	6 34	7 11	7 56	8 59	9 48	12 00	12 00	12 00	12 00	12 00	12 00	40°
45°	6 00	6 41	7 25	8 21	9 48	12 00	12 00	12 00	12 00	12 00	12 00	12 00	45°
50°	6 00	6 49	7 43	8 54	12 00	12 00	12 00	12 00	12 00	12 00	12 00	12 00	50°
55°	6 00	6 58	8 05	9 42	12 00	12 00	12 00	12 00	12 00	12 00	12 00	12 00	55°
60°	6 00	7 11	8 36	12 00	12 00	12 00	12 00	12 00	12 00	12 00	12 00	12 00	60°
65°	6 00	7 29	9 25	12 00	12 00	12 00	12 00	12 00	12 00	12 00	12 00	12 00	65°
70°	6 00	7 56	12 00	12 00	12 00	12 00	12 00	12 00	12 00	12 00	12 00	12 00	70°
75°	6 00	8 45	12 00	12 00	12 00	12 00	12 00	12 00	12 00	12 00	12 00	12 00	75°
80°	6 00	12 00	12 00	12 00	12 00	12 00	12 00	12 00	12 00	12 00	12 00	12 00	80°

TABLE 2. CORRECTION FOR REFRACTION AND SEMI-DIAMETER

	m	m	m	m	m	m	m	m	m	m	m	m	
0°	3	3	4	4	4	5	5	5	6	6	6	7	0°
10°	3	3	4	4	4	5	5	6	6	6	7	7	10°
20°	4	4	4	4	5	5	6	7	7	8	8	9	20°
25°	4	4	4	4	5	6	7	8	8	9	11	13	25°
30°	4	4	4	5	6	7	8	9	11	14	21	—	30°

NB: Regarding Table 1. If latitude and declination are of
the same sign, take out the respondent directly. If they are
of opposite signs, subtract the respondent from 12h.
Example:

Lat.	Dec.	Semi-diurnal arc
+52°	+20°	7h 51m
+52°	−20°	4h 09m

SUNRISE AND SUNSET

The local mean time of sunrise or sunset may be found by obtaining the hour angle from Table 1 and applying it to the time of transit. The hour angle is negative for sunrise and positive for sunset. A small correction to the hour angle, which always has the effect of increasing it numerically, is necessary to allow for the Sun's semi-diameter (16′) and for refraction (34′); it is obtained from Table 2. The resulting local mean time may be converted into the standard time of the country by taking the difference between the longitude of the standard meridian of the country and that of the place, adding it to the local mean time if the place is west of the standard meridian, and subtracting it if the place is east.

Example – Required the New Zealand Mean Time (12h fast on GMT) of sunset on May 23 at Auckland, latitude 36° 50′ S. (or minus), longitude 11h 39m E. Taking the declination as + 20°.6 (page 33), we find

	h	m
Tabular entry for 30° Lat. and Dec. 20°, opposite signs	+	5 11
Proportional part for 6° 50′ of Lat.	−	15
Proportional part for 0°.6 of Dec.	−	2
Correction (Table 2)	+	4
Hour angle	4	58
Sun transits (page 33)	11	57
Longitudinal correction	+	21
New Zealand Mean Time	17	16

MOONRISE AND MOONSET

It is possible to calculate the times of moonrise and moonset using Table 1, though the method is more complicated because the apparent motion of the Moon is much more rapid and also more variable than that of the Sun.

The parallax of the Moon, about 57′, is near to the sum of the semi-diameter and refraction but has the opposite effect on these times. It is thus convenient to neglect all three quantities in the method outlined below.

TABLE 3. LONGITUDE CORRECTION

X A h	40m m	45m m	50m m	55m m	60m m	65m m	70m m
1	2	2	2	2	3	3	3
2	3	4	4	5	5	5	6
3	5	6	6	7	8	8	9
4	7	8	8	9	10	11	12
5	8	9	10	11	13	14	15
6	10	11	13	14	15	16	18
7	12	13	15	16	18	19	20
8	13	15	17	18	20	22	23
9	15	17	19	21	23	24	26
10	17	19	21	23	25	27	29
11	18	21	23	25	28	30	32
12	20	23	25	28	30	33	35
13	22	24	27	30	33	35	38
14	23	26	29	32	35	38	41
15	25	28	31	34	38	41	44
16	27	30	33	37	40	43	47
17	28	32	35	39	43	46	50
18	30	34	38	41	45	49	53
19	32	36	40	44	48	51	55
20	33	38	42	46	50	54	58
21	35	39	44	48	53	57	61
22	37	41	46	50	55	60	64
23	38	43	48	53	58	62	67
24	40	45	50	55	60	65	70

Notation

φ	= latitude of observer
λ	= longitude of observer (measured positively towards the west)
T_{-1}	= time of transit of Moon on previous day
T_0	= time of transit of Moon on day in question
T_1	= time of transit of Moon on following day
δ_0	= approximate declination of Moon
δ_R	= declination of Moon at moonrise
δ_S	= declination of Moon at moonset
h_0	= approximate hour angle of Moon
h_R	= hour angle of Moon at moonrise
h_S	= hour angle of Moon at moonset
t_R	= time of moonrise
t_S	= time of moonset

Method

1. With arguments φ, δ_0 enter Table 1 on page 64 to determine h_0 where h_0 is negative for moonrise and positive for moonset.

2. Form approximate times from
$$t_R = T_0 + \lambda + h_0$$
$$t_S = T_0 + \lambda + h_0$$

3. Determine δ_R, δ_S for times t_R, t_S respectively.

4. Re-enter Table 1 on page 64 with
   (*a*) arguments φ, δ_R to determine h_R
   (*b*) arguments φ, δ_S to determine h_S

5. Form $t_R = T_0 + \lambda + h_R + AX$
   $$t_S = T_1 + \lambda + h_S + AX$$

   where $A = (\lambda + h)$

   and $X = (T_0 - T_{-1})$ if $(\lambda + h)$ is negative
   $X = (T_1 - T_0)$ if $(\lambda + h)$ is positive

   AX is the respondent in Table 3.

Example – To find the times of moonrise and moonset at Vancouver ($\varphi = +49°$, $\lambda = +8h\ 12m$) on 1996 January 19. The starting data (page 18) are

$$T_{-1} = 10h\ 01m$$
$$T_0 = 11h\ 03m$$
$$T_1 = 12h\ 05m$$
$$\delta_0 = -18°$$

1. $h_0 = 4h\ 32m$
2. Approximate values
   $t_R = 19d\ 11h\ 03m + 8h\ 12m + (-4h\ 32m)$
   $\quad = 19d\ 14h\ 43m$
   $t_S = 19d\ 11h\ 03m + 8h\ 12m + (+4h\ 32m)$
   $\quad = 19d\ 23h\ 47m$
3. $\delta_R = -17°.7$
   $\delta_S = -16°.8$
4. $h_R = -4h\ 34m$
   $h_S = +4h\ 39m$
5. $t_R = 19d\ 11h\ 03m + 8h\ 12m + (-4h\ 34m) + 9m$
   $\quad = 19d\ 14h\ 50m$
   $t_S = 19d\ 11h\ 03m + 8h\ 12m + (+4h\ 39m) + 33m$
   $\quad = 20d\ 00h\ 27m$

To get the LMT of the phenomenon the longitude is subtracted from the GMT thus:
Moonrise = 19d 14h 50m − 8h 12m = 19d 06h 38m
Moonset = 20d 00h 27m − 8h 12m = 19d 16h 15m

ECLIPSES AND OCCULTATIONS 1996

Eclipses

There will be four eclipses in 1996, two of the Sun and two of the Moon. (Penumbral eclipses are not mentioned in this section as they are too difficult to observe.)

1. A total eclipse of the Moon on April 3–4 is visible from the extreme western part of Australia, Indonesia, Asia, Indian Ocean, Africa, the Atlantic Ocean, Europe (including the British Isles), Iceland, Greenland, Antarctica, the Americas (except the western part of North America) and the eastern Pacific. The eclipse begins at 3d 22h 21m and ends at 4d 01h 59m. Totality lasts from 3d 23h 26m to 4d 00h 53m.

2. A partial eclipse of the Sun on April 17–18 is visible from New Zealand (except the extreme northern part), the southern Pacific Ocean and a small part of Antarctica. The eclipse begins at 17d 20h 31m and ends at 18d 00h 43m. At maximum eclipse 88 per cent of the Sun is obscured.

3. A total eclipse of the Moon on September 27 is visible from western Asia, the western Indian Ocean, Africa, Antarctica, Europe (including the British Isles), Iceland, Greenland, the Atlantic Ocean, the Americas and the Pacific Ocean (except the western part). The eclipse begins at 1h 12m and ends at 4h 36m. The total phase begins at 2h 19m and ends at 3h 29m.

4. A partial eclipse of the Sun on October 12 is visible from north-east Canada, Greenland, Iceland, Europe, extreme western Asia and North Africa. The eclipse begins at 11h 59m and ends at 16h 05m. From Greenwich the eclipse begins at 12h 59m and ends at 15h 31m, while from Edinburgh the eclipse begins at 12h 49m and ends at 15h 21m. As seen from the British Isles, about 60 per cent of the Sun is obscured at maximum.

Lunar Occultations

Observations of the times of occultations are made by both amateur and professional astronomers. Such observations are later analysed to yield accurate positions of the Moon; this is one method of determining the difference between ephemeris time and universal time.

Many of the observations made by amateurs are obtained with the use of a stop-watch which is compared with a time-signal immediately after the observation. Thus an accuracy of about one-fifth of a second is obtainable, though the observer's personal equation may amount to one-third or one-half of a second.

The list on page 67 includes most of the occultations visible under favourable conditions in the British Isles. No occultation is included unless the star is at least 10° above the horizon and the Sun sufficiently far below the horizon to permit the star to be seen with the naked eye or with a small telescope. The altitude limit is reduced from 10° to 2° for stars and planets brighter than magnitude 2.0 and such occultations are also predicted in daylight.

The column Phase shows (i) whether a disappearance (D) or reappearance (R) is to be observed; and (ii) whether it is at the dark limb (D) or bright limb (B). The column headed 'El. of Moon' gives the elongation of the Moon from the Sun, in degrees. The elongation increases from 0° at New Moon to 180° at Full Moon and on to 360° (or 0°) at New Moon again. Times and position angles (P), reckoned from the north point in the direction north, east, south, west, are given for Greenwich (lat. 51° 30', long. 0°) and Edinburgh (lat. 56° 00', long. 3° 12' west).

The coefficients a and b are the variations in the GMT for each degree of longitude (positive to the west) and latitude (positive to the north) respectively; they enable approximate times (to within about 1m generally) to be found for any point in the British Isles. If the point of observation is $\Delta\lambda$ degrees west and $\Delta\phi$ degrees north, the approximate time is found by adding $a.\Delta\lambda + b.\Delta\phi$ to the given GMT.

Example: the reappearance of ZC 50 on November 20 at Liverpool, found from both Greenwich and Edinburgh.

	Greenwich	Edinburgh
	°	°
Longitude	0.0	+ 3.2
Long. of Liverpool	+ 3.0	+ 3.0
$\Delta\lambda$	+ 3.0	− 0.2
Latitude	+ 51.5	+ 56.0
Lat. of Liverpool	+ 53.4	+ 53.4
$\Delta\phi$	+ 1.9	− 2.6
	h m	h m
GMT	24 01.3	23 47.1
$a.\Delta\lambda$	− 3.3	+ 0.2
$b.\Delta\phi$	− 6.1	+ 4.9
	23 51.9	23 52.2

If the occultation is given for one station but not the other, the reason for the suppression is given by the following code:

N = star not occulted

A = star's altitude less than 10° (2° for bright stars and planets)

S = Sun not sufficiently below the horizon

G = occultation is of very short duration

In some cases the coefficients a and b are not given; this is because the occultation is so short that prediction for other places by means of these coefficients would not be reliable.

Observers may like to note that ZC 692 = *Aldebaran* (occulted on October 1 and 29).

LUNAR OCCULTATIONS 1996

				El. of	GREENWICH				EDINBURGH			
Date	ZC No.	Mag.	Phase	Moon	UT	a	b	P	UT	a	b	P
				°	h m	m	m	°	h m	m	m	°
January	2	684	6.2	D.D.	147	21 5.9	G		15	N			
	25	136	6.3	D.D.	72	21 55.0	G		3	N			
	29	648	3.9	D.D.	118	23 7.8	G		23	N			
	29	653	4.8	D.D.	118	23 31.1	−1.0	−0.5	60	23 26.6	−1.0	0.0	47
February	1	944	5.7	D.D.	142	A				4 35.5	0.1	−1.2	69
	2	1073	6.0	D.D.	152	4 16.2	0.5	−2.7	155	4 5.6	0.3	−2.6	147
	2	1147	5.1	D.D.	158	17 10.4	G		158	17 7.9	−0.3	0.4	137
	22	214	6.4	D.D.	50	20 8.1	−0.4	−3.0	123	19 55.6	−0.5	−2.1	105
	25	609	7.5	D.D.	87	23 12.1	−0.1	−1.8	102	23 3.5	−0.3	−1.7	93
	27	878	5.5	D.D.	109	N				22 10.0	G		166
	28	1003	7.2	D.D.	118	18 54.6	−1.6	2.0	59	19 1.5	−1.3	3.3	40
	28	1011	7.4	D.D.	119	21 21.3	−1.9	0.7	59	21 20.9	−1.8	1.8	43
March	1	1147	5.1	D.D.	132	2 11.5	−0.3	−1.4	80	2 3.9	−0.4	−1.4	75
	1	1234	6.1	D.D.	139	19 3.0	G		30	N			
	1	1237	6.4	D.D.	140	N				20 20.4	G		183
	2	1341	4.3	D.D.	150	18 9.7	−0.7	1.7	87	18 16.6	−0.5	2.3	72
	25	814	5.3	D.D.	77	20 50.5	−1.0	−0.8	67	20 44.4	−1.1	−0.4	57
	26	944	5.7	D.D.	87	18 44.6	−1.8	1.0	58	S			
	26	961	6.2	D.D.	88	N				21 53.7	G		173
	26	975	6.8	D.D.	89	23 36.0	−0.3	−1.2	72	23 29.5	−0.4	−1.2	65
	28	1096	5.3	D.D.	100	0 16.2	0.2	−2.5	140	0 5.7	0.0	−2.4	134
	29	1309	5.7	D.D.	120	19 10.1	−1.7	1.0	80	19 11.0	−1.6	1.7	67
	29	1318	5.7	D.D.	121	22 2.8	−0.9	−2.3	139	21 50.3	−1.0	−1.8	131
	30	1332	5.7	D.D.	123	A				2 55.6	0.0	−1.4	76
	30	1410	5.3	D.D.	131	19 50.6	G		45	N			
	31	1519	6.5	D.D.	143	22 0.7	−1.8	−0.1	89	21 55.7	−1.6	0.3	81
April	1	1611	5.7	D.D.	154	19 29.0	−0.3	−2.6	173	19 20.7	−0.5	−0.8	154
	28	1577	7.1	D.D.	123	20 51.3	−2.4	1.0	61	20 50.4			49
	30	1787	6.0	D.D.	147	20 5.2	−1.2	0.4	108	S			
	30	1798	6.3	D.D.	148	22 36.9	−1.5	−0.8	108	22 29.8	−1.3	−0.5	104
May	1	1807	5.9	D.D.	150	2 18.8	G		174	2 4.7	−0.5	−2.5	166
	8	2826	4.0	R.D.	242	2 5.8	−1.2	1.2	253	2 7.5	−1.0	1.2	258
	22	1237	6.4	D.D.	60	21 7.8	0.0	−2.3	136	S			
	24	1440	6.7	D.D.	82	21 13.2	−1.3	−0.7	58	S			
June	26	2065	6.6	D.D.	123	22 36.9	−1.0	−2.3	159	22 24.6	−0.9	−1.8	152
	29	2361	4.9	D.D.	150	1 17.6	−0.8	−1.2	88	1 9.8	−0.8	−1.1	80
July	12	Venus	−4.5	D.B.	36	7 47.7	−1.1	+2.7	45	7 59.1	−0.7	+4.0	26
	12	Venus	−4.5	R.D.	36	8 55.5	−1.9	−1.0	299	8 43.0	−1.8	−2.3	320
August	24	2685	7.0	D.D.	125	20 12.9	−1.4	0.3	69	S			
	24	2687	6.5	D.D.	125	20 33.4	−1.6	−0.6	119	20 27.0	−1.3	−0.2	112
	26	3015	5.3	D.D.	154	22 39.7	G		148	22 25.9	−1.7	−0.8	129
September	25	3278	5.4	D.D.	152	2 3.9	−0.5	−0.7	65	1 59.8	−0.4	−0.4	51
October	1	692	1.1	R.D.	241	21 48.2	0.1	1.7	254	21 55.9	0.1	1.6	262
	5	1106	3.7	R.D.	276	1 40.9	−0.7	0.5	306	1 40.0	−0.7	0.0	323
	7	1341	4.3	R.D.	299	N				3 39.7	−0.3	3.8	225
	18	2745	6.9	D.D.	77	18 15.3	−1.6	−1.0	114	18 6.9	−1.4	−0.6	106
	23	3362	5.9	D.D.	134	1 22.5	−0.2	−0.1	43	1 22.4	−0.2	0.4	25
	29	650	5.7	D.D.	211	2 20.9	G		357	N			
	29	692	1.1	D.B.	214	8 31.5	0.5	−2.5	136	8 22.0	0.2	−2.3	126
	29	692	1.1	R.D.	215	A				9 6.4	0.0	−0.7	231
November	16	3015	5.3	D.D.	74	N				19 57.9	G		143
	20	50	6.0	D.D.	128	24 1.3	−1.1	−3.2	124	23 47.1	−0.9	−1.9	103
December	19	283	7.1	D.D.	122	21 58.8	−1.3	−0.7	83	21 52.9	−1.1	−0.2	68
	22	667	5.3	D.D.	156	19 22.9	G		144	19 17.0	−1.1	0.5	123
	26	1106	3.7	R.D.	195	R.B.				3 31.3	−1.7	0.8	225
	29	1428	3.8	R.D.	226	1 33.2	−1.7	1.4	259	1 33.6	−1.3	1.0	271

MEAN PLACES OF STARS 1996.5

Name	Mag.	RA h m	Dec. ° '	Spec. trum	Name	Mag.	RA h m	Dec. ° '	Spec. trum
α And *Alpheratz*	2.1	0 08.2	+29 04	A0p	γ Corvi	2.6	12 15.6	−17 31	B8
β Cassiopeiae *Caph*	2.3	0 09.0	+59 08	F5	α Crucis	1.0	12 26.4	−63 05	B1
γ Pegasi *Algenib*	2.8	0 13.1	+15 10	B2	γ Crucis	1.6	12 31.0	−57 06	M3
β Mensae	2.9	0 25.6	−77 16	G0	γ Centauri	2.2	12 41.3	−48 56	A0
α Phoenicis	2.4	0 26.1	−42 20	K0	γ Virginis	2.7	12 41.5	− 1 26	F0
α Cassiopeiae *Schedar*	2.2	0 40.3	+56 31	K0	β Crucis	1.3	12 47.5	−59 40	B1
β Ceti *Diphda*	2.0	0 43.4	−18 00	K0	ε Ursae Majoris *Alioth*	1.8	12 53.9	+55 59	A0p
γ Cassiopeiae*	Var.	0 56.5	+60 42	B0p	α Canum Venaticorum	2.9	12 55.9	+38 20	A0p
β Andromedae *Mirach*	2.1	1 09.5	+35 36	M0	ζ Ursae Majoris *Mizar*	2.1	13 23.8	+54 57	A2p
δ Cassiopeiae	2.7	1 25.6	+60 13	A5	α Virginis *Spica*	1.0	13 25.0	−11 09	B2
α Eridani *Achernar*	0.5	1 37.6	−57 15	B5	ε Centauri	2.6	13 39.7	−53 27	B1
β Arietis *Sheratan*	2.6	1 54.4	+20 47	A5	η Ursae Majoris *Alkaid*	1.9	13 47.4	+49 20	B3
γ Andromedae *Almak*	2.3	2 03.7	+42 19	K0	β Centauri *Hadar*	0.6	14 03.6	−60 21	B1
α Arietis *Hamal*	2.0	2 07.0	+23 27	K2	θ Centauri	2.1	14 06.5	−36 21	K0
α Ursae Minoris *Polaris*	2.0	2 28.0	+89 15	F8	α Bootis *Arcturus*	0.0	14 15.5	+19 12	K0
β Persei *Algol**	Var.	3 07.9	+40 57	B8	α Centauri *Rigil Kent*	0.1	14 39.3	−60 49	G0
α Persei *Mirfak*	1.8	3 24.1	+49 51	F5	ε Bootis	2.4	14 44.8	+27 05	K0
η Tauri *Alcyone*	2.9	3 47.3	+24 06	B5p	β UMi *Kochab*	2.1	14 50.7	+74 10	K5
α Tauri *Aldebaran*	0.9	4 35.7	+16 30	K5	γ Ursae Minoris	3.1	15 20.7	+71 51	A2
β Orionis *Rigel*	0.1	5 14.4	− 8 12	B8p	α CrB *Alphecca*	2.2	15 34.5	+26 44	A0
α Aurigae *Capella*	0.1	5 16.4	+46 00	G0	β Trianguli Australis	3.0	15 54.8	−63 25	F0
γ Orionis *Bellatrix*	1.6	5 24.9	+ 6 21	B2	δ Scorpii	2.3	16 00.1	−22 37	B0
β Tauri *Elnath*	1.7	5 26.1	+28 36	B8	β Scorpii	2.6	16 05.2	−19 48	B1
δ Orionis	2.2	5 31.8	− 0 18	B0	α Scorpii *Antares*	1.0	16 29.2	−26 25	M0
α Leporis	2.6	5 32.6	−17 49	F0	α Trianguli Australis	1.9	16 48.3	−69 01	K2
ε Orionis	1.7	5 36.0	− 1 12	B0	ε Scorpii	2.3	16 49.9	−34 17	K0
ζ Orionis	1.8	5 40.6	− 1 57	B0	α Herculis†	Var.	17 14.5	+14 24	M3
κ Orionis	2.1	5 47.6	− 9 40	B0	λ Scorpii	1.6	17 33.4	−37 06	B2
α Orionis *Betelgeuse**	Var.	5 55.0	+ 7 24	M0	α Ophiuchi *Rasalhague*	2.1	17 34.8	+12 34	A5
β Aurigae *Menkalinan*	1.9	5 59.3	+44 57	A0p	θ Scorpii	1.9	17 37.1	−43 00	F0
β CMa *Mirzam*	2.0	6 22.5	−17 57	B1	κ Scorpii	2.4	17 42.2	−39 02	B2
α Carinae *Canopus*	−0.7	6 23.9	−52 42	F0	γ Draconis	2.2	17 56.5	+51 29	K5
γ Geminorum *Alhena*	1.9	6 37.5	+16 24	A0	ε Sgr *Kaus Australis*	1.9	18 23.9	−34 23	A0
α Canis Majoris *Sirius*	−1.5	6 45.0	−16 43	A0	α Lyrae *Vega*	0.0	18 36.8	+38 47	A0
ε Canis Majoris	1.5	6 58.5	−28 58	B1	σ Sagittarii	2.0	18 55.0	−26 18	B3
δ Canis Majoris	1.9	7 08.2	−26 23	F8p	β Cygni *Albireo*	3.1	19 30.6	+27 57	K0
α Geminorum *Castor*	1.6	7 34.4	+31 54	A0	α Aquilae *Altair*	0.8	19 50.6	+ 8 52	A5
α CMi *Procyon*	0.4	7 39.1	+ 5 14	F5	α Capricorni	3.8	20 17.9	−12 33	G5
β Geminorum *Pollux*	1.1	7 45.1	+28 02	K0	γ Cygni	2.2	20 22.1	+40 15	F8p
ζ Puppis	2.3	8 03.5	−40 00	Od	α Pavonis	1.9	20 25.4	−56 45	B3
γ Velorum	1.8	8 09.4	−47 20	Oap	α Cygni *Deneb*	1.3	20 41.3	+45 16	A2p
ε Carinae	1.9	8 22.4	−59 30	K0	α Cephei *Alderamin*	2.4	21 18.5	+62 34	A5
δ Velorum	2.0	8 44.6	−54 42	A0	ε Pegasi	2.4	21 44.0	+ 9 52	K0
λ Velorum *Suhail*	2.2	9 07.9	−43 25	K5	δ Capricorni	2.9	21 46.8	−16 09	A5
β Carinae	1.7	9 13.2	−69 42	A0	δ Gruis	1.7	22 08.0	−46 59	B5
ι Carinae	2.2	9 17.0	−59 16	F0	δ Cephei†	3.7	22 29.0	+58 24	†
κ Velorum	2.6	9 22.0	−55 00	B3	β Gruis	2.1	22 42.5	−46 54	M3
α Hydrae *Alphard*	2.0	9 27.4	− 8 39	K2	α PsA *Fomalhaut*	1.2	22 57.5	−29 38	A3
α Leonis *Regulus*	1.3	10 08.2	+11 59	B8	β Pegasi *Scheat*	2.4	23 03.6	+28 04	M0
γ Leonis *Algeiba*	1.9	10 19.8	+19 52	K0	α Pegasi *Markab*	2.5	23 04.6	+15 11	A0
β Ursae Majoris *Merak*	2.4	11 01.6	+56 24	A0					
α Ursae Majoris *Dubhe*	1.8	11 03.5	+61 46	K0					
δ Leonis	2.6	11 13.9	+20 33	A3					
β Leonis *Denebola*	2.1	11 48.9	+14 35	A2					
γ Ursae Majoris *Phecda*	2.4	11 53.6	+53 43	A0					

*γ Cassiopeiae, 1995 mag. 2.5. β Persei, mag. 2.1 to 3.4.
α Orionis, mag. 0.1 to 1.2.
†α Herculis, mag. 3.1 to 3.9. δ Cephei, mag. 3.7 to 4.4,
Spectrum F5 to G0.

The positions of heavenly bodies on the celestial sphere are defined by two co-ordinates, right ascension and declination, which are analogous to longitude and latitude on the surface of the Earth. If we imagine the plane of the terrestrial equator extended indefinitely, it will cut the celestial sphere in a great circle known as the celestial equator. Similarly the plane of the Earth's orbit, when extended, cuts in the great circle called the ecliptic. The two intersections of these circles are known as the First Point of Aries and the First Point of Libra. If from any star a perpendicular be drawn to the celestial equator, the length of this perpendicular is the star's declination. The arc, measured eastwards along the equator from the First Point of Aries to the foot of this perpendicular, is the right ascension. An alternative definition of right ascension is that it is the angle at the celestial pole (where the Earth's axis, if prolonged, would meet the sphere) between the great circles to the First Point of Aries and to the star.

The plane of the Earth's equator has a slow movement, so that our reference system for right ascension and declination is not fixed. The consequent alteration in these quantities from year to year is called precession. In right ascension it is an increase of about 3 seconds a year for equatorial stars, and larger or smaller changes in either direction for stars near the poles, depending on the right ascension of the star. In declination it varies between $+20''$ and $-20''$ according to the right ascension of the star.

A star or other body crosses the meridian when the sidereal time is equal to its right ascension. The altitude is then a maximum, and may be deduced by remembering that the altitude of the elevated pole is numerically equal to the latitude, while that of the equator at its intersection with the meridian is equal to the co-latitude, or complement of the latitude.

Thus in London (lat. 51° 30′) the meridian altitude of Sirius is found as follows:

	°	′
Altitude of equator	38	30
Declination south	16	43
Difference	21	47

The altitude of Capella (Dec. $+46°\ 00'$) at lower transit is:

	°	′
Altitude of pole	51	30
Polar distance of star	44	00
Difference	7	30

The brightness of a heavenly body is denoted by its magnitude. Omitting the exceptionally bright stars Sirius and Canopus, the twenty brightest stars are of the first magnitude, while the faintest stars visible to the naked eye are of the sixth magnitude. The magnitude scale is a precise one, as a difference of five magnitudes represents a ratio of 100 to 1 in brightness. Typical second magnitude stars are Polaris and the stars in the belt of Orion. The scale is most easily fixed in memory by comparing the stars with Norton's *Star Atlas* (*see* page 71). The stars Sirius and Canopus and the planets Venus and Jupiter are so bright that their magnitudes are expressed by negative numbers. A small telescope will show stars down to the ninth or tenth magnitude, while stars fainter than the twentieth magnitude may be photographed by long exposures with the largest telescopes.

MEAN AND SIDEREAL TIME

Acceleration				Retardation			
h	m s	m s	s	h	m s	m s	s
1	0 10	0 00		1	0 10	0 00	
2	0 20	3 02	0	2	0 20	3 03	0
3	0 30	9 07	1	3	0 29	9 09	1
4	0 39	15 13	2	4	0 39	15 15	2
5	0 49	21 18	3	5	0 49	21 21	3
6	0 59	27 23	4	6	0 59	27 28	4
7	1 09	33 28	5	7	1 09	33 34	5
8	1 19	39 34	6	8	1 19	39 40	6
9	1 29	45 39	7	9	1 28	45 46	7
10	1 39	51 44	8	10	1 38	51 53	8
11	1 48	57 49	9	11	1 48	57 59	9
12	1 58	60 00	10	12	1 58	60 00	10
13	2 08			13	2 08		
14	2 18			14	2 18		
15	2 28			15	2 27		
16	2 38			16	2 37		
17	2 48			17	2 47		
18	2 57			18	2 57		
19	3 07			19	3 07		
20	3 17			20	3 17		
21	3 27			21	3 26		
22	3 37			22	3 36		
23	3 47			23	3 46		
24	3 57			24	3 56		

The length of a sidereal day in mean time is 23h 56m 04s.09. Hence 1h MT = 1h + 9s.86 ST and 1h ST = 1h − 9s.83 MT.

To convert an interval of mean time to the corresponding interval of sidereal time, enter the acceleration table with the given mean time (taking the hours and the minutes and seconds separately) and add the acceleration obtained to the given mean time. To convert an interval of sidereal time to the corresponding interval of mean time, take out the retardation for the given sidereal time and subtract.

The columns for the minutes and seconds of the argument are in the form known as critical tables. To use these tables, find in the appropriate left-hand column the two entries between which the given number of minutes and seconds lies; the quantity in the right-hand column between these two entries is the required acceleration or retardation. Thus the acceleration for 11m 26s (which lies between the entries 9m 07s and 15m 13s) is 2s. If the given number of minutes and seconds is a tabular entry, the required acceleration or retardation is the entry in the right-hand column above the given tabular entry, e.g. the retardation for 45m 46s is 7s.

Example – Convert 14h 27m 35s from ST to MT

	h	m	s
Given ST	14	27	35
Retardation for 14h		2	18
Retardation for 27m 35s			5
Corresponding MT	14	25	12

For further explanation, *see* pages 73–4.

ECLIPSES AND SHADOW TRANSITS OF JUPITER'S SATELLITES 1996

GMT	Sat.	Phen.
d h m		

FEBRUARY

26 06 32	I	Ec.D
27 05 53	I	Sh.E

MARCH

2 06 00	II	Sh.E
5 05 34	I	Sh.I
9 05 52	II	Sh.I
21 06 02	I	Sh.E
25 05 08	II	Ec.D
28 05 43	I	Sh.I

APRIL

5 04 55	I	Ec.D
6 04 09	III	Ec.R
6 04 18	I	Sh.E
12 03 34	IV	Ec.D
13 03 58	I	Sh.I
13 05 11	III	Ec.D
21 03 10	I	Ec.D
22 02 34	I	Sh.E
28 02 33	II	Sh.E
29 02 14	I	Sh.I
29 04 27	I	Sh.E

MAY

1 03 05	III	Sh.I
5 02 23	II	Sh.I
6 04 07	I	Sh.I
14 03 18	I	Ec.D
15 02 44	I	Sh.E
19 01 00	III	Ec.D
19 04 02	III	Ec.R
21 01 52	II	Ec.D
22 02 23	I	Sh.I
24 00 58	IV	Sh.E
30 01 33	I	Ec.D
30 02 05	II	Sh.E
31 01 00	I	Sh.E

JUNE

6 01 53	II	Sh.I
6 02 00	III	Sh.E
6 03 26	I	Ec.D
7 00 39	I	Sh.I
7 02 54	I	Sh.E
13 02 55	III	Sh.I
14 02 33	I	Sh.I
14 23 00	II	Ec.D
14 23 48	I	Ec.D
15 23 17	I	Sh.E
18 03 13	IV	Ec.D
22 01 37	II	Ec.D
22 01 42	I	Ec.D
22 22 56	I	Sh.I
23 01 12	I	Sh.E
23 23 03	II	Sh.I
30 00 51	I	Sh.I
30 03 07	I	Sh.E
30 22 04	I	Ec.D
30 22 50	II	Sh.I

JULY

1 00 50	III	Ec.D
1 01 37	II	Sh.E
5 00 10	IV	Ec.R
7 02 45	I	Sh.I
8 01 25	II	Sh.I
8 02 13	I	Ec.R
8 21 14	I	Sh.I
8 23 30	I	Sh.E
9 23 00	II	Ec.R
11 22 00	III	Sh.E
15 23 09	I	Sh.I
16 01 25	I	Sh.E
16 22 36	I	Ec.R
17 01 37	II	Ec.R
18 22 51	III	Sh.I
19 02 00	III	Sh.E
23 01 04	I	Sh.I
24 00 31	I	Ec.R
24 21 48	I	Sh.E
25 22 38	II	Sh.E
29 22 30	IV	Sh.I
31 21 28	I	Sh.I
31 23 43	I	Sh.E

AUGUST

1 20 54	I	Ec.R
1 22 25	II	Sh.I
5 23 58	III	Ec.R
7 23 23	I	Sh.I
8 22 48	I	Ec.R
9 20 07	I	Sh.E
10 22 49	II	Ec.R
15 19 53	IV	Sh.E
16 19 47	I	Sh.I
16 22 02	I	Sh.E
19 19 41	II	Sh.E
23 21 42	I	Sh.I
23 22 03	III	Sh.E
24 21 07	I	Ec.R
26 19 28	II	Sh.I
26 22 16	II	Sh.E
30 22 51	III	Sh.I

SEPTEMBER

1 20 21	I	Sh.E
2 22 04	II	Sh.I
4 19 59	II	Ec.R
8 20 02	I	Sh.I
8 22 17	I	Sh.E
9 19 26	I	Ec.R
9 21 16	IV	Ec.D
10 20 02	III	Ec.R
16 21 21	I	Ec.R
17 18 41	I	Sh.E
17 20 45	III	Ec.D
20 19 23	II	Sh.E
24 18 21	I	Sh.I
24 20 36	I	Sh.E
26 19 04	IV	Ec.R
27 19 10	II	Sh.I

GMT	Sat.	Phen.

OCTOBER

1 20 17	I	Sh.I
2 19 41	I	Ec.R
5 18 53	III	Sh.I
6 19 47	II	Ec.R
10 18 56	I	Sh.E
17 18 36	I	Sh.I
18 18 00	I	Ec.R
22 19 09	II	Sh.E
29 18 55	II	Sh.I

NOVEMBER

10 18 16	III	Sh.E
10 18 16	I	Ec.R
18 17 30	I	Sh.E
25 17 09	I	Sh.I

DECEMBER

2 16 36	II	Ec.R

Jupiter's satellites transit across the disk from east to west, and pass behind the disk from west to east. The shadows that they cast also transit across the disk. With the exception at times of Satellite IV, the satellites also pass through the shadow of the planet, i.e. they are eclipsed. Just before opposition the satellite disappears in the shadow to the west of the planet and reappears from occultation on the east limb. Immediately after opposition the satellite is occulted at the west limb and reappears from eclipse to the east of the planet. At times approximately two to four months before and after opposition, both phases of eclipses of Satellite III may be seen. When Satellite IV is eclipsed, both phases may be seen.

The times given refer to the centre of the satellite. As the satellite is of considerable size, the immersion and emersion phases are not instantaneous. Even when the satellite enters or leaves the shadow along a radius of the shadow, the phase can last for several minutes. With Satellite IV, grazing phenomena can occur so that the light from the satellite may fade and brighten again without a complete eclipse taking place.

The list of phenomena gives most of the eclipses and shadow transits visible in the British Isles under favourable conditions.

Ec. = Eclipse	R. = Reappearance
Sh. = Shadow transit	I. = Ingress
D. = Disappearance	E. = Egress

EXPLANATION OF ASTRONOMICAL DATA

Positions of the heavenly bodies are given only to the degree of accuracy required by amateur astronomers for setting telescopes, or for plotting on celestial globes or star atlases. Where intermediate positions are required, linear interpolation may be employed.

Definitions of the terms used cannot be given here. They must be sought in astronomical literature and textbooks. Probably the best source for the amateur is Norton's *Star Atlas and Reference Handbook* (Longman, 18th edition, 1989; £22.99), which contains an introduction to observational astronomy, and a series of star maps for showing stars visible to the naked eye. Certain more extended ephemerides are available in the British Astronomical Association Handbook, an annual popular among amateur astronomers (Secretary: Burlington House, Piccadilly, London WIV 9AG).

A special feature has been made of the times when the various heavenly bodies are visible in the British Isles. Since two columns, calculated for latitudes 52° and 56°, are devoted to risings and settings, the range 50° to 58° can be covered by interpolation and extrapolation. The times given in these columns are Greenwich Mean Times for the meridian of Greenwich. An observer west of this meridian must add his/her longitude (in time) and vice versa.

In accordance with the usual convention in astronomy, + and − indicate respectively north and south latitudes or declinations.

All data are, unless otherwise stated, for 0h Greenwich Mean Time (GMT), i.e. at the midnight at the beginning of the day named. Allowance must be made for British Summer Time during the period that this is in operation (*see* pages 15 and 75).

PAGE ONE OF EACH MONTH

The calendar for each month is explained on page 15.

Under the heading Astronomical Phenomena will be found particulars of the more important conjunctions of the Sun, Moon and planets with each other, and also the dates of other astronomical phenomena of special interest.

Times of Minima of Algol are approximate times of the middle of the period of diminished light.

The Constellations listed each month are those that are near the meridian at the beginning of the month at 22h local mean time. Allowance must be made for British Summer Time if necessary. The fact that any star crosses the meridian 4m earlier each night or 2h earlier each month may be used, in conjunction with the lists given each month, to find what constellations are favourably placed at any moment. The table preceding the list of constellations may be extended indefinitely at the rate just quoted.

The principal phases of the Moon are the GMTs when the difference between the longitude of the Moon and that of the Sun is 0°, 90°, 180° or 270°. The times of perigee and apogee are those when the Moon is nearest to, and farthest from, the Earth, respectively. The nodes or points of intersection of the Moon's orbit and the ecliptic make a complete retrograde circuit of the ecliptic in about 19 years. From a knowledge of the longitude of the ascending node and the inclination, whose value does not vary much from 5°, the path of the Moon among the stars may be plotted on a celestial globe or star atlas.

PAGE TWO OF EACH MONTH

The Sun's semi-diameter, in arc, is given once a month.

The right ascension and declination (Dec.) is that of the true Sun. The right ascension of the mean Sun is obtained by applying the equation of time, with the sign given, to the right ascension of the true Sun, or, more easily, by applying 12h to the column Sidereal Time. The direction in which the equation of time has to be applied in different problems is a frequent source of confusion and error. Apparent Solar Time is equal to the Mean Solar Time plus the Equation of Time. For example at noon on August 8 the Equation of Time is − 5m 33s and thus at 12h Mean Time on that day the Apparent Time is 12h − 5m 33s = 11h 54m 27s.

The Greenwich Sidereal Time at 0h and the Transit of the First Point of Aries (which is really the mean time when the sidereal time is 0h) are used for converting mean time to sidereal time and vice versa.

The GMT of transit of the Sun at Greenwich may also be taken as the local mean time (LMT) of transit in any longitude. It is independent of latitude. The GMT of transit in any longitude is obtained by adding the longitude to the time given if west, and vice versa.

LIGHTING-UP TIME

The legal importance of sunrise and sunset is that the Road Vehicles Lighting Regulations 1989 (SI 1989 No. 1796) make the use of front and rear position lamps on vehicles compulsory during the period between sunset and sunrise. Headlamps on vehicles are required to be used during the hours of darkness on unlit roads or whenever visibility is seriously reduced. The hours of darkness are defined in these regulations as the period between half an hour after sunset and half an hour before sunrise.

In all laws and regulations 'sunset' refers to the local sunset, i.e. the time at which the Sun sets at the place in question. This common-sense interpretation has been upheld by legal tribunals. Thus the necessity for providing for different latitudes and longitudes, as already described, is evident.

SUNRISE AND SUNSET

The times of sunrise and sunset are those when the Sun's upper limb, as affected by refraction, is on the true horizon of an observer at sea-level. Assuming the mean refraction to be 34′, and the Sun's semi-diameter to be 16′, the time given is that when the true zenith distance of the Sun's centre is 90° + 34′ + 16′ or 90° 50′, or, in other words, when the depression of the Sun's centre below the true horizon is 50′. The upper limb is then 34′ below the true horizon, but is brought there by refraction. It is true, of course, that an observer on a ship might see the Sun for a minute or so longer, because of the dip of the horizon, while another viewing the sunset over hills or mountains would record an earlier time. Nevertheless, the moment when the true zenith distance of the Sun's centre is 90° 50′ is a precise time dependent only on the latitude and longitude of the place, and independent of its altitude above sea-level, the contour of its horizon, the vagaries of refraction or the small seasonal change in the Sun's semi-diameter; this moment is suitable in every way as a definition of sunset (or sunrise) for all statutory purposes. (For further information, *see* footnote on page 72.)

TWILIGHT

Light reaches us before sunrise and continues to reach us for some time after sunset. The interval between darkness and sunrise or sunset and darkness is called twilight. Astronomically speaking, twilight is considered to begin or end when the Sun's centre is 18° below the horizon, as no light from the Sun can then reach the observer. As thus defined twilight may last several hours; in high latitudes at the summer solstice the depression of 18° is not reached, and twilight lasts from sunset to sunrise.

The need for some sub-division of twilight is met by dividing the gathering darkness into four stages.

(1) *Sunrise or Sunset*, defined as above
(2) *Civil twilight*, which begins or ends when the Sun's centre is 6° below the horizon. This marks the time when operations requiring daylight may commence or must cease. In England it varies from about 30 to 60 minutes after sunset and the same interval before sunrise
(3) *Nautical twilight*, which begins or ends when the Sun's centre is 12° below the horizon. This marks the time when it is, to all intents and purposes, completely dark
(4) *Astronomical twilight*, which begins or ends when the Sun's centre is 18° below the horizon. This marks theoretical perfect darkness. It is of little practical importance, especially if nautical twilight is tabulated

To assist observers the durations of civil, nautical and astronomical twilights are given at intervals of ten days. The beginning of a particular twilight is found by subtracting the duration from the time of sunrise, while the end is found by adding the duration to the time of sunset. Thus the beginning of astronomical twilight in latitude 52°, on the Greenwich meridian, on March 11 is found as 06h 23m − 113m = 04h 30m and similarly the end of civil twilight as 17h 58m + 34m = 18h 32m. The letters TAN (twilight all night) are printed when twilight lasts all night.

Under the heading The Night Sky will be found notes describing the position and visibility of the planets and other phenomena.

PAGE THREE OF EACH MONTH

The Moon moves so rapidly among the stars that its position is given only to the degree of accuracy that permits linear interpolation. The right ascension (RA) and declination (Dec.) are geocentric, i.e. for an imaginary observer at the centre of the Earth. To an observer on the surface of the Earth the position is always different, as the altitude is always less on account of parallax, which may reach 1°.

The lunar terminator is the line separating the bright from the dark part of the Moon's disk. Apart from irregularities of the lunar surface, the terminator is elliptical, because it is a circle seen in projection. It becomes the full circle forming the limb, or edge, of the Moon at New and Full Moon. The selenographic longitude of the terminator is measured from the mean centre of the visible disk, which may differ from the visible centre by as much as 8°, because of libration.

Instead of the longitude of the terminator the Sun's selenographic co-longitude (Sun's co-long.) is tabulated. It is numerically equal to the selenographic longitude of the morning terminator, measured eastwards from the mean centre of the disk. Thus its value is approximately 270° at New Moon, 360° at First Quarter, 90° at Full Moon and 180° at Last Quarter.

The Position Angle (PA) of the Bright Limb is the position angle of the midpoint of the illuminated limb, measured eastwards from the north point on the disk. The Phase column shows the percentage of the area of the Moon's disk illuminated; this is also the illuminated percentage of the diameter at right angles to the line of cusps. The terminator is a semi-ellipse whose major axis is the line of cusps, and whose semi-minor axis is determined by the tabulated percentage; from New Moon to Full Moon the east limb is dark, and vice versa.

The times given as moonrise and moonset are those when the upper limb of the Moon is on the horizon of an observer at sea-level. The Sun's horizontal parallax (Hor. par.) is about 9″, and is negligible when considering sunrise and sunset, but that of the Moon averages about 57′. Hence the computed time represents the moment when the true zenith distance of the Moon is 90° 50′ (as for the Sun) minus the horizontal parallax. The time required for the Sun or Moon to rise or set is about four minutes (except in high latitudes). *See also* page 65 and footnote below.

The GMT of transit of the Moon over the meridian of Greenwich is given; these times are independent of latitude but must be corrected for longitude. For places in the British Isles it suffices to add the longitude if west, and vice versa. For other places a further correction is necessary because of the rapid movement of the Moon relative to the stars. The entire correction is conveniently determined by first finding the west longitude λ of the place. If the place is in west longitude, λ is the ordinary west longitude; if the place is in east longitude λ is the complement to 24h (or 360°) of the longitude and will be greater than 12h (or 180°). The correction then consists of two positive portions, namely λ and the fraction λ/24 (or λ°/360) multiplied by the difference between consecutive transits. Thus for Sydney, New South Wales, the longitude is 10h 05m east, so λ=13h 55m and the fraction λ/24 is 0.58. The transit on the local date 1996 February 22 is found as follows:

		d	h	m
GMT of transit at Greenwich	Feb.	21	14	22
λ			13	55
0.58×(15h 12m−14h 22m)				29
GMT of transit at Sydney		22	04	46
Corr. to NSW Standard Time			10	00
Local standard time of transit		22	14	46

As is evident, for any given place the quantities λ and the correction to local standard time may be combined permanently, being here 23h 55m.

Positions of Mercury are given for every second day, and those of Venus and Mars for every fifth day; they may be interpolated linearly. The diameter (Diam.) is given in seconds of arc. The phase is the illuminated percentage of the disk. In the case of the inner planets this approaches 100 at superior conjunction and 0 at inferior conjunction. When the phase is less than 50 the planet is crescent-shaped or horned; for greater phases it is gibbous. In the case of the exterior planet Mars, the phase approaches 100 at conjunction and opposition, and is a minimum at the quadratures.

Since the planets cannot be seen when on the horizon, the actual times of rising and setting are not given; instead, the time when the planet has an apparent altitude of 5° has been tabulated. If the time of transit is between 00h and 12h

---

SUNRISE, SUNSET AND MOONRISE, MOONSET

The tables have been constructed for the meridian of Greenwich, and for latitudes 52° and 56°. They give Greenwich Mean Time (GMT) throughout the year. To obtain the GMT of the phenomenon as seen from any other latitude and longitude in the British Isles, first interpolate or extrapolate for latitude by the usual rules of proportion. To the time thus found, the longitude (expressed in time) is to be added if west (as it usually is in Great Britain) or subtracted if east. If the longitude is expressed in degrees and minutes of arc, it must be converted to time at the rate of 1° = 4m and 15′ = 1m.

A method of calculating rise and set times for other places in the world is given on pages 64 and 65 the time refers to an altitude of 5° above the eastern horizon; if between 12h and 24h, to the western horizon. The phenomenon tabulated is the one that occurs between sunset and sunrise. The times given may be interpolated for latitude and corrected for longitude as in the case of the Sun and Moon.

The GMT at which the planet transits the Greenwich meridian is also given. The times of transit are to be corrected to local meridians in the usual way, as already described.

PAGE FOUR OF EACH MONTH

The GMTs of sunrise and sunset for seven towns, whose adopted positions in longitude (W.) and latitude (N.) are given immediately below the name, may be used not only for these phenomena, but also for lighting-up times, which, under the Road Vehicles Lighting Regulations 1989, are from sunset to sunrise throughout the year. (*See* page 71 for a fuller explanation.)

The particulars for the four outer planets resemble those for the planets on Page Three of each month, except that, under Uranus and Neptune, times when the planet is 10° high instead of 5° high are given; this is because of the inferior brightness of these planets. The diameters given for the rings of Saturn are those of the major axis (in the plane of the planet's equator) and the minor axis respectively. The former has a small seasonal change due to the slightly varying distance of the Earth from Saturn, but the latter varies from zero when the Earth passes through the ring plane every 15 years to its maximum opening half-way between these periods. The rings were open at their widest extent in 1988.

TIME

From the earliest ages, the natural division of time into recurring periods of day and night has provided the practical time-scale for the everyday activities of the human race. Indeed, if any alternative means of time measurement is adopted, it must be capable of adjustment so as to remain in general agreement with the natural time-scale defined by the diurnal rotation of the Earth on its axis. Ideally the rotation should be measured against a fixed frame of reference; in practice it must be measured against the background provided by the celestial bodies. If the Sun is chosen as the reference point, we obtain Apparent Solar Time, which is the time indicated by a sundial. It is not a uniform time but is subject to variations which amount to as much as a quarter of an hour in each direction. Such wide variations cannot be tolerated in a practical time-scale, and this has led to the concept of Mean Solar Time in which all the days are exactly the same length and equal to the average length of the Apparent Solar Day.

The positions of the stars in the sky are specified in relation to a fictitious reference point in the sky known as the First Point of Aries (or the Vernal Equinox). It is therefore convenient to adopt this same reference point when considering the rotation of the Earth against the background of the stars. The time-scale so obtained is known as Apparent Sidereal Time.

Greenwich Mean Time

The daily rotation of the Earth on its axis causes the Sun and the other heavenly bodies to appear to cross the sky from east to west. It is convenient to represent this relative motion as if the Sun really performed a daily circuit around a fixed Earth. Noon in Apparent Solar Time may then be defined as the time at which the Sun transits across the observer's meridian. In Mean Solar Time, noon is similarly defined by the meridian transit of a fictitious Mean Sun moving uniformly in the sky with the same average speed as the true Sun. Mean Solar Time observed on the meridian of the transit circle telescope of the Old Royal Observatory at Greenwich is called Greenwich Mean Time (GMT). The mean solar day is divided into 24 hours and, for astronomical and other scientific purposes, these are numbered 0 to 23, commencing at midnight. Civil time is usually reckoned in two periods of 12 hours, designated a.m. (*ante meridiem*, i.e. before noon) and p.m. (*post meridiem*, i.e. after noon).

Universal Time

Before 1925 January 1, GMT was reckoned in 24 hours commencing at noon; since that date it has been reckoned from midnight. To avoid confusion in the use of the designation GMT before and after 1925, since 1928 astronomers have tended to use the term Universal Time (UT) or Weltzeit (WZ) to denote GMT measured from Greenwich Mean Midnight.

In precision work it is necessary to take account of small variations in Universal Time. These arise from small irregularities in the rotation of the Earth. Observed astronomical time is designated UT0. Observed time corrected for the effects of the motion of the poles (giving rise to a 'wandering' in longitude) is designated UT1. There is also a seasonal fluctuation in the rate of rotation of the Earth arising from meteorological causes, often called the annual fluctuation. UT1 corrected for this effect is designated UT2 and provides a time-scale free from short-period fluctuations. It is still subject to small secular and irregular changes.

Apparent Solar Time

As mentioned above, the time shown by a sundial is called Apparent Solar Time. It differs from Mean Solar Time by an amount known as the Equation of Time, which is the total effect of two causes which make the length of the apparent solar day non-uniform. One cause of variation is that the orbit of the Earth is not a circle but an ellipse, having the Sun at one focus. As a consequence, the angular speed of the Earth in its orbit is not constant; it is greatest at the beginning of January when the Earth is nearest the Sun.

The other cause is due to the obliquity of the ecliptic; the plane of the equator (which is at right angles to the axis of rotation of the Earth) does not coincide with the ecliptic (the plane defined by the apparent annual motion of the Sun around the celestial sphere) but is inclined to it at an angle of 23° 26′. As a result, the apparent solar day is shorter than average at the equinoxes and longer at the solstices. From the combined effects of the components due to obliquity and eccentricity, the equation of time reaches its maximum values in February (−14 minutes) and early November (+16 minutes). It has a zero value on four dates during the year, and it is only on these dates (approximately April 15, June 14, September 1, and December 25) that a sundial shows Mean Solar Time.

Sidereal Time

A sidereal day is the duration of a complete rotation of the Earth with reference to the First Point of Aries. The term sidereal (or 'star') time is a little misleading since the time-scale so defined is not exactly the same as that which would be defined by successive transits of a selected star, as there is a small progressive motion between the stars and the First Point of Aries due to the precession of the Earth's axis. This makes the length of the sidereal day shorter than the true period of rotation by 0.008 seconds. Superimposed on this steady precessional motion are small oscillations (nutation), giving rise to fluctuations in apparent sidereal time amounting to as much as 1.2 seconds. It is therefore customary to employ Mean Sidereal Time, from which these fluctuations have been removed. The conversion of GMT to Greenwich sidereal time (GST) may be performed by adding the value of the GST at 0h on the day in question (Page Two of each month) to the GMT converted to sidereal time using the table on page 69.

Example – To find the GST at August 8d 02h 41m 11s GMT

	h	m	s
GST at 0h	21	07	07
GMT	2	41	11
Acceleration for 2h			20
Acceleration for 41m 11s			7
Sum = GST =	23	48	45

If the observer is not on the Greenwich meridian then his/her longitude, measured positively westwards from Greenwich, must be subtracted from the GST to obtain Local Sidereal Time (LST). Thus, in the above example, an observer 5h east of Greenwich, or 19h west, would find the LST as 4h 48m 45s.

EPHEMERIS TIME

An analysis of observations of the positions of the Sun, Moon and planets taken over an extended period is used in preparing ephemerides. (An ephemeris is a table giving the apparent position of a heavenly body at regular intervals of time, e.g. one day or ten days, and may be used to compare current observations with tabulated positions.) Discrepancies between the positions of heavenly bodies observed over a 300-year period and their predicted positions arose because the time-scale to which the observations were related was based on the assumption that the rate of rotation of the Earth is uniform. It is now known that this rate of rotation is variable. A revised time-scale, Ephemeris Time (ET), was devised to bring the ephemerides into agreement with the observations.

The second of ET is defined in terms of the annual motion of the Earth in its orbit around the Sun (1/31556925.9747 of the tropical year for 1900 January 0d 12h ET). The precise determination of ET from astronomical observations is a lengthy process as the requisite standard of accuracy can only be achieved by averaging over a number of years.

In 1976 the International Astronomical Union adopted a new dynamical time-scale for general use whose scale unit is the SI second (*see* Atomic Time). ET is now of little more than historical interest.

TERRESTRIAL DYNAMICAL TIME

The uniform time system used in computing the ephemerides of the solar system is Terrestrial Dynamical Time (TDT), which has replaced ET for this purpose. Except for the most rigorous astronomical calculations, it may be assumed to be the same as ET. During 1996 the estimated difference TDT – UT is about 62 seconds.

ATOMIC TIME

The fundamental standards of time and frequency must be defined in terms of a periodic motion adequately uniform, enduring and measurable. Progress has made it possible to use natural standards, such as atomic or molecular oscillations. Continuous oscillations are generated in an electrical circuit, the frequency of which is then compared or brought into coincidence with the frequency characteristic of the absorption or emission by the atoms or molecules when they change between two selected energy levels. The National Physical Laboratory (NPL) routinely uses clocks of high stability produced by locking a quartz oscillator to the frequency defined by a caesium atomic beam.

International Atomic Time (TAI), established through international collaboration, is formed by combining the readings of many caesium clocks and was set close to the astronomically-based Universal Time (UT) near the beginning of 1958. It was formally recognized in 1971 and since 1988 January 1 has been maintained by the International Bureau of Weights and Measures (BIPM). The second markers are generated according to the International System (SI) definition adopted in 1967 at the 13th General Conference of Weights and Measures: 'The second is the duration of 9 192 631 770 periods of radiation corresponding to the transition between the two hyperfine levels of the ground state of the caesium-133 atom.'

Civil time in almost all countries is now based on Coordinated Universal Time (UTC), which was adopted for scientific purposes on 1972 January 1. UTC differs from TAI by an integer number of seconds (determined from studies of the rate of rotation of the Earth) and was designed to make both atomic time and UT accessible with accuracies appropriate for most users. The UTC timescale is adjusted by the insertion (or, in principle, omission) of leap seconds in order to keep it within ± 0.9 s of UT. These leap seconds are introduced, when necessary, at the same instant throughout the world, either at the end of December or at the end of June. So, for example, the 20th leap second occurs at 0h GMT on 1996 January 1. All leap seconds so far have been positive, with 61 seconds in the final minute of the UTC month. The time 23h 59m 60s UTC is followed one second later by 0h 0m 00s of the first day of the following month. Notices concerning the insertion of leap seconds are issued by the International Earth Rotation Service (IERS) at the Observatoire de Paris.

RADIO TIME-SIGNALS

UTC is made generally available through time-signals and standard frequency broadcasts such as MSF in the UK, CHU in Canada and WWV and WWVH in the USA. These are based on national time-scales that are maintained in close agreement with UTC and provide traceability to the national time-scale and to UTC. The markers of seconds in the UTC scale coincide with those of TAI.

To disseminate the national time-scale in the UK, special signals are broadcast on behalf of the National Physical Laboratory from the BT (British Telecom) radio station at Rugby. The signals are controlled from a caesium beam atomic frequency standard and consist of a standard frequency carrier of 60 kHz (MSF) which is switched off, after being on for at least half a second, to mark every second. In part of the first second of each minute the carrier is switched on and off at 100 bits/second to signal a binary coded decimal (BCD) message giving UTC time of day and calendar information. In the other seconds the carrier is always off for at least one tenth of a second at the start and then it carries an on-off code giving similar information for British clock time together with information identifying the start of the next minute. Changes to and from summer time are made following Government announcements. Leap seconds are inserted as announced by the IERS and information provided by them on the difference between UTC and UT is also signalled. Other broadcast signals in the UK include the BBC six pips signal, the BT Timeline ('speaking clock'), the NPL Truetime service for computers, and a coded time-signal on the BBC 198 kHz transmitters which is used for timing in the electricity supply industry. From 1972 January 1 the six pips on the

BBC have consisted of five short pips from second 55 to second 59 (six pips in the case of a leap second) followed by one lengthened pip, the start of which indicates the exact minute. From 1990 February 5 these signals have been controlled by the BBC with second markers referenced to the satellite-based US navigation system GPS (Global Positioning System) and time and day referenced to the MSF transmitter. Formerly they were generated by the Royal Greenwich Observatory. The BT Timeline is compared daily with the National Physical Laboratory caesium beam atomic frequency standard at the Rugby radio station. The NPL Truetime service is directly connected to the national time scale.

Accurate timing may also be obtained from the signals of international navigation systems such as the ground-based Loran-C or Omega, or the satellite-based American GPS or Russian GLONASS systems.

STANDARD TIME

Since 1880 the standard time in Britain has been Greenwich Mean Time (GMT); a statute that year enacted that the word 'time' when used in any legal document relating to Britain meant, unless otherwise specifically stated, the mean time of the Greenwich meridian. The system of standard time by zones based on Greenwich Mean Time has been gradually accepted since 1883. Now throughout the world a standard time which differs from that of Greenwich by an integral number of hours, either fast or slow, is used. The large territories of the United States and Canada are divided into zones approximately 7.5° on either side of central meridians. (For time zones of countries of the world, see Index.)

Variations from the standard time of some countries occur during part of the year; they are decided annually and are usually referred to as Summer Time or Daylight Saving Time.

At the 180th meridian the time can be either 12 hours fast on Greenwich Mean Time or 12 hours slow, and a change of date occurs. The internationally-recognized date or calendar line is a modification of the 180th meridian, drawn so as to include islands of any one group on the same side of the line, or for political reasons. The line is indicated by joining up the following co-ordinates:

Lat.	Long.	Lat.	Long.
60° S.	180°	48° N.	180°
51° S.	180°	53° N.	170° E.
45° S.	172.5° W.	65.5° N.	169° W.
15° S.	172.5° W.	75° N.	180°
5° S.	180°		

BRITISH SUMMER TIME

In 1916 an Act ordained that during a defined period of that year the legal time for general purposes in Great Britain should be one hour in advance of Greenwich Mean Time. The Summer Time Acts 1922 to 1925 defined the period during which Summer Time was to be in force, stabilizing practice until the Second World War.

During the war the duration of Summer Time was extended and in the years 1941 to 1945 and in 1947 Double Summer Time (two hours in advance of Greenwich Mean Time) was in force. After the war, Summer Time was extended each year in 1948–52 and 1961–4 by Order in Council.

Between 1968 October 27 and 1971 October 31 clocks were kept one hour ahead of Greenwich Mean Time throughout the year. This was known as British Standard Time.

The most recent legislation is the Summer Time Act 1972, which enacted that 'the period of summer time for the purposes of this Act is the period beginning at two o'clock,

Greenwich mean time, in the morning of the day after the third Saturday in March or, if that day is Easter Day, the day after the second Saturday in March, and ending at two o'clock, Greenwich mean time, in the morning of the day after the fourth Saturday in October.'

The duration of Summer Time can be varied by Order in Council and in recent years alterations have been made to bring the operation of Summer Time in Britain closer to similar provisions in other countries of the European Union; for instance, since 1981 the hour of changeover has been 01h Greenwich Mean Time.

The duration of Summer Time in 1996 and 1997 will be:

1996   31 March to 27 October
1997   30 March to 26 October

MEAN REFRACTION

Alt.	Ref.	Alt.	Ref.	Alt.	Ref.
° ′	′	° ′	′	° ′	′
1 20	21	3 12	13	7 54	6
1 30	20	3 34	12	9 27	5
1 41	19	4 00	11	11 39	4
1 52	18	4 30	10	15 00	3
2 05	17	5 06	9	20 42	2
2 19	16	5 50	8	32 20	1
2 35	15	6 44	7	62 17	0
2 52	14	7 54		90 00	
3 12					

The refraction table is in the form of a critical table (see page 69)

ASTRONOMICAL CONSTANTS

Solar parallax	8″.794
Astronomical unit	149597870 km
Precession for the year 1996	50″.291
Precession in right ascension	3s.075
Precession in declination	20″.043
Constant of nutation	9″.202
Constant of aberration	20″.496
Mean obliquity of ecliptic (1996)	23° 26′ 24″
Moon's equatorial hor. parallax	57′ 02″.70
Velocity of light in vacuo per second	299792.5 km
Solar motion per second	20.0 km
Equatorial radius of the Earth	6378.140 km
Polar radius of the Earth	6356.755 km
North galactic pole (IAU standard)	RA 12h 49m (1950.0). Dec. 27°.4 N.
Solar apex	RA 18h 06m Dec. +30°

Length of year (in mean solar days)

Tropical	365.24219
Sidereal	365.25636
Anomalistic (perihelion to perihelion)	365.25964
Eclipse	346.6200

Length of month (mean values)	d	h	m	s
New Moon to New	29	12	44	02.9
Sidereal	27	07	43	11.5
Anomalistic (perigee to perigee)	27	13	18	33.2

ELEMENTS OF THE SOLAR SYSTEM

Orb	Mean distance from Sun (Earth = 1)	km 10^6	Sidereal period days	Synodic period days	Incl. of orbit to ecliptic ° '	Diameter km	Mass (Earth = 1)	Period of rotation on axis days
Sun	—	—	—	—	—	1,392,530	332,946	25–35*
Mercury	0.39	58	88.0	116	7 00	4,879	0.0553	58.646
Venus	0.72	108	224.7	584	3 24	12,104	0.8150	243.017r
Earth	1.00	150	365.3	—	—	12,756e	1.0000	0.997
Mars	1.52	228	687.0	780	1 51	6,794e	0.1074	1.026
Jupiter	5.20	778	4,332.6	399	1 18	{142,984e / 133,708p	317.89	{0.410e
Saturn	9.54	1427	10,759.2	378	2 29	{120,536e / 108,728p	95.18	{0.426e
Uranus	19.18	2870	30,684.6	370	0 46	51,118e	14.54	0.718r
Neptune	30.06	4497	60,191.0	367	1 46	49,528e	17.15	0.671
Pluto	39.80	5954	91,708.2	367	17 09	2,302	0.002	6.387

e equatorial, *p* polar, *r* retrograde, * depending on latitude

THE SATELLITES

Name	Star mag.	Mean distance from primary	Sidereal period of revolution
EARTH		km	d
I Moon	—	384,400	27.322
MARS			
I Phobos	12	9,380	0.319
II Deimos	13	23,460	1.262
JUPITER			
XVI Metis	17	127,960	0.295
XV Adrastea	19	128,980	0.298
V Amalthea	14	181,300	0.498
XIV Thebe	16	221,900	0.675
I Io	5	421,600	1.769
II Europa	5	670,900	3.551
III Ganymede	5	1,070,000	7.155
IV Callisto	6	1,880,000	16.689
XIII Leda	20	11,094,000	239
VI Himalia	15	11,480,000	251
X Lysithea	18	11,720,000	259
VII Elara	17	11,737,000	260
XII Ananke	19	21,200,000	631r
XI Carme	18	22,600,000	692r
VIII Pasiphae	17	23,500,000	735r
IX Sinope	18	23,700,000	758r
SATURN			
XVIII Pan	—	133,600	0.575
XV Atlas	18	137,640	0.602
XVI Prometheus	16	139,350	0.613
XVII Pandora	16	141,700	0.629
XI Epimetheus	15	151,420	0.694
X Janus	14	151,470	0.695
I Mimas	13	185,520	0.942
II Enceladus	12	238,020	1.370
III Tethys	10	294,660	1.888
XIII Telesto	19	294,660	1.888
XIV Calypso	19	294,660	1.888
IV Dione	10	377,400	2.737
XII Helene	18	377,400	2.737
V Rhea	10	527,040	4.518
VI Titan	8	1,221,850	15.945

Name	Star mag.	Mean distance from primary	Sidereal period of revolution
SATURN		km	d
VII Hyperion	14	1,481,000	21.277
VIII Iapetus	11	3,561,300	79.330
IX Phoebe	16	12,952,000	550.5r
URANUS			
VI Cordelia	—	49,770	0.335
VII Ophelia	—	53,790	0.376
VIII Bianca	—	59,170	0.435
IX Cressida	—	61,780	0.464
X Desdemona	—	62,660	0.474
XI Juliet	—	64,350	0.493
XII Portia	—	66,090	0.513
XIII Rosalind	—	69,940	0.558
XIV Belinda	—	75,260	0.624
XV Puck	—	86,010	0.762
V Miranda	17	129,390	1.413
I Ariel	14	191,020	2.520
II Umbriel	15	266,300	4.144
III Titania	14	435,910	8.706
IV Oberon	14	583,520	13.463
NEPTUNE			
III Naiad	25	48,230	0.294
IV Thalassa	24	50,070	0.311
V Despina	23	52,530	0.335
VI Galatea	22	61,950	0.429
VII Larissa	22	73,550	0.555
VIII Proteus	20	117,650	1.122
I Triton	13	354,760	5.877
II Nereid	19	5,513,400	360.136
PLUTO			
I Charon	17	19,700	6.387

THE EARTH

The shape of the Earth is that of an oblate spheroid or solid of revolution whose meridian sections are ellipses not differing much from circles, whilst the sections at right angles are circles. The length of the equatorial axis is about 12,756 kilometres, and that of the polar axis is 12,714 kilometres. The mean density of the Earth is 5.5 times that of water, although that of the surface layer is less. The Earth and Moon revolve about their common centre of gravity in a lunar month; this centre in turn revolves round the Sun in a plane known as the ecliptic, that passes through the Sun's centre. The Earth's equator is inclined to this plane at an angle of 23.4°. This tilt is the cause of the seasons. In mid-latitudes, and when the Sun is high above the Equator, not only does the high noon altitude make the days longer, but the Sun's rays fall more directly on the Earth's surface; these effects combine to produce summer. In equatorial regions the noon altitude is large throughout the year, and there is little variation in the length of the day. In higher latitudes the noon altitude is lower, and the days in summer are appreciably longer than those in winter.

The average velocity of the Earth in its orbit is 30 kilometres a second. It makes a complete rotation on its axis in about 23h 56m of mean time, which is the sidereal day. Because of its annual revolution round the Sun, the rotation with respect to the Sun, or the solar day, is more than this by about four minutes (*see* page 73). The extremity of the axis of rotation, or the North Pole of the Earth, is not rigidly fixed, but wanders over an area roughly 20 metres in diameter.

TERRESTRIAL MAGNETISM

A magnetic compass points along the horizontal component of a magnetic line of force. These directions converge on the 'magnetic dip-poles', the places where a freely suspended magnetized needle would become vertical. Not only do these poles move with time, but their exact locations are ill-defined, particularly so in the case of the north dip-pole where the lines of force on the north side of it, instead of converging radially, tend to bunch into a channel. Although it is therefore unrealistic to attempt to specify the locations of the dip-poles exactly, the present approximate adopted positions are 79°.0 N., 105°.1 W. and 64°.7 S., 138°.6 E. The two magnetic dip-poles are thus not antipodal, the line joining them passing the centre of the Earth at a distance of about 1,250 km. The distances of the magnetic dip-poles from the north and south geographical poles are about 1,200 km and 2,800 km respectively.

There is also a 'magnetic equator', at all points of which the vertical component of the Earth's magnetic field is zero and a magnetized needle remains horizontal. This line runs between 2° and 10° north of the geographical equator in Asia and Africa, turns sharply south off the West African coast, and crosses South America through Brazil, Bolivia and Peru; it recrosses the geographical equator in mid-Pacific.

Reference has already been made to secular changes in the Earth's field. The following table indicates the changes in magnetic declination (or variation of the compass). Similar, though much smaller, changes have occurred in 'dip' or magnetic inclination. Secular changes differ throughout the world. Although the London observations

strongly suggest a cycle with a period of several hundred years, an exact repetition is unlikely.

London		Greenwich	
1580	11° 15' E.	1850	22° 24' W.
1622	5° 56' E.	1900	16° 29' W.
1665	1° 22' W.	1925	13° 10' W.
1730	13° 00' W.	1950	9° 07' W.
1773	21° 09' W.	1975	6° 39' W.

In order that up-to-date information on the variation of the compass may be available, many governments publish magnetic charts on which there are lines (isogonic lines) passing through all places at which specified values of declination will be found at the date of the chart.

In the British Isles, isogonic lines now run approximately north-east to south-west. Though there are considerable local deviations due to geological causes, a rough value of magnetic declination may be obtained by assuming that at 50° N. on the meridian of Greenwich, the value in 1996 is 3° 19' west and allowing an increase of 14' for each degree of latitude northwards and one of 28' for each degree of longitude westwards. For example, at 53° N., 5° W., declination will be about 3° 19' + 42' + 140', i.e. 6° 21' west. The average annual change at the present time is about 8' decrease.

The number of magnetic observatories is about 200, irregularly distributed over the globe. There are three in Great Britain, run by the British Geological Survey: at Hartland, north Devon; at Eskdalemuir, Dumfriesshire; and at Lerwick, Shetland Islands. The following are some recent annual mean values of the magnetic elements for Hartland.

Year	Declination West ° '	Dip or inclination ° '	Horizontal force gauss	Vertical force gauss
1955	10 30	66 49	0.1859	0.4340
1960	9 59	66 44	0.1871	0.4350
1965	9 30	66 34	0.1887	0.4354
1970	9 06	66 26	0.1903	0.4364
1975	8 32	66 17	0.1921	0.4373
1980	7 44	66 10	0.1933	0.4377
1985	6 56	66 08	0.1938	0.4380
1990	6 15	66 10	0.1939	0.4388
1994	5 42	66 08	0.1944	0.4394

The normal world-wide terrestrial magnetic field corresponds approximately to that of a very strong small bar magnet near the centre of the Earth, but with appreciable smooth spatial departures. The origin and the slow secular change of the normal field are not fully understood but are generally ascribed to electric currents associated with fluid motions in the Earth's core. Superimposed on the normal field are local and regional anomalies whose magnitudes may in places approach that of the normal field; these are due to the influence of mineral deposits in the Earth's crust. A small proportion of the field is of external origin, mostly associated with electric currents in the ionosphere. The configuration of the external field and the ionization of the atmosphere depend on the incident particle and radiation flux from the Sun. There are, therefore, short-term and non-periodic as well as diurnal, 27-day, seasonal and 11-year periodic changes in the magnetic field, dependent upon the position of the Sun and the degree of solar activity.

MAGNETIC STORMS

Occasionally, sometimes with great suddenness, the Earth's magnetic field is subject for several hours to marked disturbance. During a severe storm in 1989 the declination at Lerwick changed by almost 8° in less than an hour. In many instances such disturbances are accompanied by widespread displays of aurorae, marked changes in the incidence of cosmic rays, an increase in the reception of 'noise' from the Sun at radio frequencies, and rapid changes in the ionosphere and induced electric currents within the Earth which adversely affect radio and telegraphic communications. The disturbances are caused by changes in the stream of ionized particles which emanates from the Sun and through which the Earth is continuously passing. Some of these changes are associated with visible eruptions on the Sun, usually in the region of sun-spots. There is a marked tendency for disturbances to recur after intervals of about 27 days, the apparent period of rotation of the Sun on its axis, which is consistent with the sources being located on particular areas of the Sun.

ARTIFICIAL SATELLITES

To consider the orbit of an artificial satellite, it is best to imagine that one is looking at the Earth from a distant point in space. The Earth would then be seen to be rotating about its axis inside the orbit described by the rapidly revolving satellite. The inclination of a satellite orbit to the Earth's equator (which generally remains almost constant throughout the satellite's lifetime) gives at once the maximum range of latitudes over which the satellite passes. Thus a satellite whose orbit has an inclination of 53° will pass overhead all latitudes between 53° S. and 53° N., but would never be seen in the zenith of any place nearer the poles than these latitudes. If we consider a particular place on the earth, whose latitude is less than the inclination of the satellite's orbit, then the Earth's rotation carries this place first under the northbound part of the orbit and then under the southbound portion of the orbit, these two occurrences being always less than 12 hours apart for satellites moving in direct orbits (i.e. to the east). (For satellites in retrograde orbits, the words 'northbound' and 'southbound' should be interchanged in the preceding statement.) As the value of the latitude of the observer increases and approaches the value of the inclination of the orbit, so this interval gets shorter until (when the latitude is equal to the inclination) only one overhead passage occurs each day.

OBSERVATION OF SATELLITES
The regression of the orbit around the Earth causes alternate periods of visibility and invisibility, though this is of little concern to the radio or radar observer. To the visual observer the following cycle of events normally occurs (though the cycle may start in any position): invisibility, morning observations before dawn, invisibility, evening observations after dusk, invisibility, morning observations before dawn, and so on. With reasonably high satellites and for observers in high latitudes around the summer solstice, the evening observations follow the morning observations without interruption as sunlight passing over the polar regions can still illuminate satellites which are passing over temperate latitudes at local midnight. At the moment all satellites rely on sunlight to make them visible, though a satellite with a flashing light has been suggested for a future launching. The observer must be in darkness or twilight in order to make any useful observations and the durations of twilight and the sunrise, sunset times given on Page Two of each month will be a useful guide.

Some of the satellites are visible to the naked eye and much interest has been aroused by the spectacle of a bright satellite disappearing into the Earth's shadow. The event is even more interesting telescopically as the disappearance occurs gradually as the satellite traverses the Earth's penumbral shadow, and during the last few seconds before the eclipse is complete the satellite may change colour (in suitable atmospheric conditions) from yellow to red. This is because the last rays of sunlight are refracted through the denser layers of our atmosphere before striking the satellite.

Some satellites rotate about one or more axes so that a periodic variation in brightness is observed. This was particularly noticeable in several of the Soviet satellites.

Satellite research has provided some interesting results, including a revised value of the Earth's oblateness (1/298.2), and the discovery of the Van Allen radiation belts.

LAUNCHINGS
Apart from their names, e.g. Cosmos 6 Rocket, the satellites are also classified according to their date of launch. Thus 1961 α refers to the first satellite launching of 1961. A number following the Greek letter indicated the relative brightness of the satellites put in orbit. From the beginning of 1963 the Greek letters were replaced by numbers and the numbers by roman letters e.g. 1963–01A. For all satellites successfully injected into orbit the table gives the designation and names of the main objects (in the order A, B, C … etc.), the launch date and some initial orbital data. These are the inclination to the equator (i), the nodal period of revolution (P), the eccentricity (e), and the perigee height.

Although most of the satellites launched are injected into orbits less than 1,000 km high, there are an increasing number of satellites in geostationary orbits, i.e. where the orbital inclination is zero, the eccentricity close to zero, and the period of revolution is 1436.1 minutes. Thus the satellite is permanently situated over the equator at one selected longitude at a mean height of 35,786 km. This geostationary band is crowded. In one case there are four television satellites (Astra 1A, Astra 1B, Astra 1C and Astra 1D) orbiting within a few tens of kilometres of each other. In the sky they appear to be separated by only a few arc minutes.

ARTIFICIAL SATELLITE LAUNCHES 1994–5

Desig- nation	Satellite	Launch date	i	P	e	Perigee height
			°	m		km
1994–						
26	USA 103	May 3	64.4	717.9	0.710	1323
27	SROSS C2	May 4	46.0	95.1	0.014	430
28	MSTI 2	May 9	97.1	93.0	0.001	411
29	P91-A STEP-2	May 19	82.0	99.0	0.015	604
30	Gorizont 42	May 20	0.8	1436.0	0.000	35772
31	Progress M-23 rocket	May 22	51.6	88.6	0.003	185
32	Cosmos 2281 rocket	June 7	82.5	88.6	0.004	176
33	Foton 9 rocket	June 14	62.7	90.2	0.010	218
34	Intelsat 7-02 STRV-1A STRV-1B	June 17	0.0	1436.1	0.000	35776
35	UHF F/O F3	June 24	4.8	1436.1	0.000	35776
36	Soyuz TM-19 rocket	July 1	51.7	87.9	0.006	131
37	China FSW 2 rocket	July 3	62.8	89.5	0.011	176
38	Cosmos 2282	July 6	1.9	1436.1	0.001	35754
39	STS 65 Spacelab EDO	July 8	28.3	90.6	0.000	303
40	Panamsat 2 BS-3N	July 8	0.0	1436.1	0.000	35772
41	Nadezhda 4	July 14	82.9	104.7	0.004	951
42	Cosmos 2283 rocket	July 20	67.0	89.3	0.011	167
43	Apstar 1	July 21	0.0	1436.1	0.000	35785
44	Cosmos 2284 rocket	July 29	70.2	89.1	0.006	192
45	Cosmos 2285	August 2	74.0	105.0	0.003	974
46	P90-6 Apex	August 3	70.0	114.8	0.139	360
47	DBS 2	August 3	0.0	1436.1	0.000	35776
48	Cosmos 2286	August 5	63.4	717.8	0.732	747
49	Brasilsat B1 Turksat 1B	August 10	0.0	1436.1	0.000	35782
50	Cosmos 2287–9	August 11	64.8	675.7	0.001	19109
51	Molniya 3	August 23	63.0	717.7	0.736	622
52	Progress M-24 rocket	August 25	51.7	88.6	0.003	183
53	Cosmos 2290	August 26	64.8	90.3	0.016	181
54	USA 105	August 27	0.0	1436.1	0.000	35780
55	Optus B3	August 27	0.5	1436.2	0.003	35671
56	Kiku 6	August 28	13.2	861.8	0.502	8565
57	DMSP 23545	August 29	98.9	101.9	0.001	840
58	Telstar 402	September 9	6.6	621.6	0.727	201
59	STS-64 Spartan 201	September 9	57.0	89.7	0.001	252
60	Cosmos 2291	September 21	1.1	1436.2	0.001	35748
61	Cosmos 2292	September 27	83.0	108.9	0.103	400
62	STS-68 SRL-2 MAPS	September 30	57.0	88.9	0.001	213
63	Soyuz TM-20	October 3	51.6	92.4	0.000	390
64	Intelsat 703	October 6	0.0	1436.1	0.000	35779
65	Solidaridad 2 Thaicom 2	October 8	0.0	1436.1	0.000	35775
66	Okean-O1 No. 7	October 11	82.5	97.7	0.002	631
67	Ekspress	October 13	0.1	1436.0	0.000	35776
68	IRS-P2	October 15	98.7	101.3	0.000	818
69	Elektro	October 31	1.0	1436.1	0.000	35776
70	Astra 1D	November 1	0.0	1436.0	0.000	35773
71	Wind	November 1	19.6	221.0	0.828	48840
72	Cosmos 2293	November 2	65.0	92.8	0.001	402
73	STS-66 Cristas Spas	November 3	57.0	90.6	0.001	296
74	Resurs-O1 No. 3	November 4	98.0	98.0	0.000	660
75	Progress M-25	November 11	51.6	92.4	0.000	391
76	Cosmos 2294–6	November 20	64.9	675.7	0.003	19052
77	Cosmos 2297	November 24	71.0	102.0	0.001	845
78	Geo-IK	November 29	73.6	116.1	0.003	1480
79	Orion 1	November 29	0.0	1436.1	0.000	35775
80	DFH-3	November 29	0.2	1426.2	0.009	35225

Desig- nation	Satellite	Launch date	i	P	e	Perigee height
1994–			°	m		km
81	Molniya 1T	December 14	62.8	717.7	0.740	516
82	Luch	December 16	2.5	1436.1	0.001	35757
83	Cosmos 2298	December 20	74.0	100.8	0.002	785
84	DSP F17	December 22	0.0	1436.1	0.000	35780
85	Radio-Rosto RS-15	December 26	64.8	127.7	0.017	1881
86	Cosmos 2299-2304	December 26	82.6	114.0	0.001	1402
87	Raduga 32	December 28	1.4	1436.2	0.000	35784
88	Cosmos 2305	December 29	64.9	89.7	0.004	231
89	NOAA 14	December 30	98.9	102.0	0.001	847
1995–						
1	Intelsat 7F4, rocket	January 10	0.1	1436.4	0.002	35713
2	Tsikada, Faisat, Astrid, rocket	January 24	82.9	105.0	0.004	965
3	UHF Follow 4, rocket	January 26	5.0	1436.0	0.003	35647
4	Shuttle 63, Spartan 204, Oderacs 2a–f	February 3	51.6	92.3	0.000	386
5	Progress M26, rocket	February 15	51.6	92.4	0.000	391
6	Foton 10, rocket	February 16	62.7	90.3	0.011	218
7	Shuttle 67	March 2	28.5	90.6	0.000	280
8	Cosmos 2306, rocket	March 2	65.7	92.4	0.001	480
9	Cosmos 2307–2309, rocket	March 3	64.9	717.0	0.000	19100
10	Soyuz TM21, rocket	March 14	51.6	92.0	0.000	396

Astronomers Royal

Instituted in 1675, the title of Astronomer Royal was given to the director of the Greenwich Observatory until 1975. Currently it is an honorary title for an outstanding astronomer, who receives a stipend of approximately £100 a year.

John Flamsteed (1646–1719), appointed 1675
Edmund Halley (1656–1742), appointed 1720
James Bradley (1693–1762), appointed 1742
Nathaniel Bliss (1700–64), appointed 1762
Nevil Maskelyne (1732–1811), appointed 1765

John Pond (1767–1836), appointed 1811
Sir George Airy (1801–92), appointed 1835
Sir William Christie (1845–1922), appointed 1881
Sir Frank Dyson (1868–1939), appointed 1910
Sir Harold Jones (1890–1960), appointed 1933
Sir Richard Woolley (1906–86), appointed 1955
Sir Martin Ryle (1918–84), appointed 1972
Sir Francis Graham-Smith (1923–), appointed 1982
Sir Arnold Wolfendale (1927–), appointed 1991
Sir Martin Rees (1942–), appointed 1995

Time Measurement and Calendars

MEASUREMENTS OF TIME

Measurements of time are based on the time taken by the earth to rotate on its axis (day); by the moon to revolve round the earth (month); and by the earth to revolve round the sun (year). From these, which are not commensurable, certain average or mean intervals have been adopted for ordinary use.

THE DAY

The day begins at midnight and is divided into 24 hours of 60 minutes, each of 60 seconds. The hours are counted from midnight up to 12 noon (when the sun crosses the meridian), and these hours are designated a.m. (*ante meridiem*); and again from noon up to 12 midnight, which hours are designated p.m. (*post meridiem*), except when the 24-hour reckoning is employed. The 24-hour reckoning ignores a.m. and p.m., numbering the hours 0 to 23 from midnight.

Colloquially the 24 hours are divided into day and night, day being the time while the sun is above the horizon (including the four stages of twilight defined on page 72). Day is subdivided into morning, the early part of daytime, ending at noon; afternoon, from noon to about 6 p.m.; and evening, which may be said to extend from 6 p.m. until midnight. Night, the dark period between day and day, begins at the close of astronomical twilight (*see* page 72) and extends beyond midnight to sunrise the next day.

The names of the days are derived from Old English translations or adaptations of the Roman titles.

Sunday	Sun	Sol
Monday	Moon	Luna
Tuesday	Tiw/Tyr (god of war)	Mars
Wednesday	Woden/Odin	Mercury
Thursday	Thor	Jupiter
Friday	Frigga/Freyja (goddess of love)	Venus
Saturday	Saeternes	Saturn

THE MONTH

The month in the ordinary calendar is approximately the twelfth part of a year, but the lengths of the different months vary from 28 (or 29) days to 31.

THE YEAR

The equinoctial or tropical year is the time that the earth takes to revolve round the sun from equinox to equinox, i.e. 365.24219 mean solar days, or 365 days 5 hours 48 minutes and 45 seconds.

The calendar year usually consists of 365 days but a year containing 366 days is called bissextile (*see* Roman calendar, page 89) or leap year, one day being added to the month of February so that a date 'leaps over' a day of the week. In the Roman calendar the day that was repeated was the sixth day before the beginning of March, the equivalent of 24 February

A year is a leap year if the date of the year is divisible by four without remainder, unless it is the last year of the century. The last year of a century is a leap year only if its number is divisible by 400 without remainder, e.g. the years 1800 and 1900 had only 365 days but the year 2000 will have 366 days.

THE SOLSTICE

A solstice is the point in the tropical year at which the sun attains its greatest distance, north or south, from the Equator. In the northern hemisphere the furthest point north of the Equator marks the summer solstice and the furthest point south the winter solstice.

The date of the solstice varies according to locality. For example, if the summer solstice falls on 21 June late in the day by Greenwich time, that day will be the longest of the year at Greenwich though it may be by only a second, but it will fall on 22 June, local date, in Japan, and so 22 June will be the longest day there. The date of the solstice is also affected by the length of the tropical year, which is 365 days 6 hours less about 11 minutes 15 seconds. If a solstice happens late on 21 June in one year, it will be nearly six hours later in the next (unless the next year is a leap year), i.e. early on 22 June, and that will be the longest day.

This delay of the solstice does not continue because the extra day in leap year brings it back a day in the calendar. However, because of the 11 minutes 15 seconds mentioned above, the additional day in leap year brings the solstice back too far by 45 minutes, and the time of the solstice in the calendar is earlier, in a four-year pattern, as the century progresses. The last year of a century is in most cases not a leap year, and the omission of the extra day puts the date of the solstice later by about six hours too much. Compensation for this is made by the fourth centennial year being a leap year. The solstice has become earlier in date throughout this century and, because the year 2000 is a leap year, the solstice will get earlier still throughout the 21st century.

The date of the winter solstice, the shortest day of the year, is affected by the same factors as the longest day.

At Greenwich the sun sets at its earliest by the clock about ten days before the shortest day. The daily change in the time of sunset is due in the first place to the sun's movement southwards at this time of the year, which diminishes the interval between the sun's transit and its setting. However, the daily decrease of the Equation of Time causes the time of apparent noon to be continuously later day by day, which to some extent counteracts the first effect. The rates of the change of these two quantities are not equal or uniform; their combination causes the date of earliest sunset to be 12 or 13 December at Greenwich. In more southerly latitudes the effect of the movement of the sun is less, and the change in the time of sunset depends on that of the Equation of Time to a greater degree, and the date of earliest sunset is earlier than it is at Greenwich, e.g. on the Equator it is about 1 November.

THE EQUINOX

The equinox is the point at which the sun crosses the Equator and day and night are of equal length all over the world. This occurs in March and September.

DOG DAYS

The days about the heliacal rising of the Dog Star, noted from ancient times as the hottest period of the year in the northern hemisphere, are called the Dog Days. Their incidence has been variously calculated as depending on the Greater or Lesser Dog Star (Sirius or Procyon) and their duration has been reckoned as from 30 to 54 days. A generally accepted period is from 3 July to 15 August.

CHRISTIAN CALENDAR

In the Christian chronological system the years are distinguished by cardinal numbers before or after the birth of Christ, the period being denoted by the letters BC (Before Christ) or, more rarely, AC (*Ante Christum*), and AD (*Anno Domini* – In the Year of Our Lord). The correlative dates of the epoch are the fourth year of the 194th Olympiad, the 753rd year from the foundation of Rome, AM 3761 (Jewish chronology), and the 4714th year of the Julian period. The actual date of the birth of Christ is somewhat uncertain.

The system was introduced into Italy in the sixth century. Though first used in France in the seventh century, it was not universally established there until about the eighth century. It has been said that the system was introduced into England by St Augustine (AD 596), but it was probably not generally used until some centuries later. It was ordered to be used by the Bishops at the Council of Chelsea (AD 816).

THE JULIAN CALENDAR

In the Julian calendar (adopted by the Roman Empire in 45 BC, *see* page 89) all the centennial years were leap years, and for this reason towards the close of the 16th century there was a difference of ten days between the tropical and calendar years; the equinox fell on 11 March of the calendar, whereas at the time of the Council of Nicaea (AD 325), it had fallen on 21 March. In 1582 Pope Gregory ordained that 5 October should be called 15 October and that of the end-century years only the fourth should be a leap year (*see* page 81).

THE GREGORIAN CALENDAR

The Gregorian calendar was adopted by Italy, France, Spain and Portugal in 1582, by Prussia, the Roman Catholic German states, Switzerland, Holland and Flanders on 1 January 1583, by Poland in 1586, Hungary in 1587, the Protestant German and Netherland states and Denmark in 1700, and by Great Britain and Dominions (including the North American colonies) in 1752, by the omission of eleven days (3 September being reckoned as 14 September). Sweden omitted the leap day in 1700 but observed leap days in 1704 and 1708, and reverted to the Julian calendar by having two leap days in 1712; the Gregorian calendar was adopted in 1753 by the omission of eleven days (18 February being reckoned as 1 March). Japan adopted the calendar in 1872, China in 1912, Bulgaria in 1915, Turkey and Soviet Russia in 1918, Yugoslavia and Romania in 1919, and Greece in 1923.

In the same year that the change was made in England from the Julian to the Gregorian calendar, the beginning of the new year was also changed from 25 March to 1 January (*see* page 86).

THE ORTHODOX CHURCHES

Some Orthodox Churches still use the Julian reckoning but the majority of Greek Orthodox Churches and the Romanian Orthodox Church have adopted a modified 'New Calendar', observing the Gregorian calendar for fixed feasts and the Julian for movable feasts.

The Orthodox Church year begins on 1 September. There are four fast periods and, in addition to Pascha (Easter), twelve great feasts, as well as numerous commemorations of the saints of the Old and New Testaments throughout the year.

THE DOMINICAL LETTER

The dominical letter is one of the letters A–G which are used to denote the Sundays in successive years. If the first day of the year is a Sunday the letter is A; if the second, B; the third, C; and so on. A leap year requires two letters, the first for 1 January to 29 February, the second for 1 March to 31 December (*see* page 84).

EPIPHANY

The feast of the Epiphany, commemorating the manifestation of Christ, later became associated with the offering of gifts by the Magi. The day was of great importance from the time of the Council of Nicaea (AD 325), as the primate of Alexandria was charged at every Epiphany feast with the announcement in a letter to the churches of the date of the forthcoming Easter. The day was also of importance in Britain as it influenced dates, ecclesiastical and lay, e.g. Plough Monday, when work was resumed in the fields, fell on the Monday in the first full week after Epiphany.

LENT

The Teutonic word *Lent*, which denotes the fast preceding Easter, originally meant no more than the spring season; but from Anglo-Saxon times at least it has been used as the equivalent of the more significant Latin term Quadragesima, meaning the 'forty days' or, more literally, the fortieth day. Ash Wednesday is the first day of Lent, which ends at midnight before Easter Day.

PALM SUNDAY

Palm Sunday, the Sunday before Easter and the beginning of Holy Week, commemorates the triumphal entry of Christ into Jerusalem and is celebrated in Britain (when palm is not available) by branches of willow gathered for use in the decoration of churches on that day.

MAUNDY THURSDAY

Maundy Thursday is the day before Good Friday, the name itself being a corruption of *dies mandati* (day of the mandate) when Christ washed the feet of the disciples and gave them the mandate to love one another.

EASTER DAY

Easter Day is the first Sunday after the full moon which happens on, or next after, the 21st day of March; if the full moon happens on a Sunday, Easter Day is the Sunday after.

This definition is contained in an Act of Parliament (24 Geo. II c. 23) and explanation is given in the preamble to the Act that the day of full moon depends on certain tables that have been prepared. These tables are summarized in the early pages of the Book of Common Prayer. The moon referred to is not the real moon of the heavens, but a hypothetical moon on whose 'full' the date of Easter depends, and the lunations of this 'calendar' moon consist of twenty-nine and thirty days alternately, with certain necessary modifications to make the date of its full agree as nearly as possible with that of the real moon, which is known as the Paschal Full Moon. At present, Easter falls on one of 35 days (22 March to 25 April).

A FIXED EASTER

In 1928 the House of Commons agreed to a motion for the third reading of a bill proposing that Easter Day shall, in the calendar year next but one after the commencement of the Act and in all subsequent years, be the first Sunday after the second Saturday in April. Easter would thus fall on the second or third Sunday in April, i.e. between 9 and 15 April (inclusive). A clause in the Bill provided that before it shall come into operation, regard shall be had to any opinion expressed officially by the various Christian churches.

Efforts by the World Council of Churches to secure a unanimous choice of date for Easter by its member churches have so far been unsuccessful.

ROGATION DAYS

Rogation Days are the Monday, Tuesday and Wednesday preceding Ascension Day and from the fifth century were observed as public fasts with solemn processions and supplications. The processions were discontinued as religious observances at the Reformation, but survive in the ceremony known as 'beating the parish bounds'. Rogation Sunday is the Sunday before Ascension Day.

EMBER DAYS

The Ember Days at the four seasons are the Wednesday, Friday and Saturday (*a*) before the third Sunday in Advent, (*b*) before the second Sunday in Lent, and (*c*) before the Sundays nearest to the festivals of St Peter and of St Michael and All Angels.

TRINITY SUNDAY

Trinity Sunday is eight weeks after Easter Day, on the Sunday following Pentecost (Whit Sunday). Subsequent Sundays are reckoned in the Book of Common Prayer calendar of the Church of England as 'after Trinity'.

Thomas Becket (1118–70) was consecrated Archbishop of Canterbury on the Sunday after Whit Sunday and his first act was to ordain that the day of his consecration should be held as a new festival in honour of the Holy Trinity. This observance spread from Canterbury throughout the whole of Christendom.

MOVABLE FEASTS TO THE YEAR 2028

Year	Ash Wednesday	Easter	Ascension	Pentecost (Whit Sunday)	Sundays after Pentecost	Advent Sunday
1996	21 February	7 April	16 May	26 May	21	1 December
1997	12 February	30 March	8 May	18 May	22	30 November
1998	25 February	12 April	21 May	31 May	20	29 November
1999	17 February	4 April	13 May	23 May	21	28 November
2000	8 March	23 April	1 June	11 June	19	3 December
2001	28 February	15 April	24 May	3 June	20	2 December
2002	13 February	31 March	9 May	19 May	22	1 December
2003	5 March	20 April	29 May	8 June	19	30 November
2004	25 February	11 April	20 May	30 May	20	28 November
2005	9 February	27 March	5 May	15 May	22	27 November
2006	1 March	16 April	25 May	4 June	20	3 December
2007	21 February	8 April	17 May	27 May	21	2 December
2008	6 February	23 March	1 May	11 May	23	30 November
2009	25 February	12 April	21 May	31 May	20	29 November
2010	17 February	4 April	13 May	23 May	21	28 November
2011	9 March	24 April	2 June	12 June	18	27 November
2012	22 February	8 April	17 May	27 May	21	2 December
2013	13 February	31 March	9 May	19 May	22	1 December
2014	5 March	20 April	29 May	8 June	19	30 November
2015	18 February	5 April	14 May	24 May	21	29 November
2016	10 February	27 March	5 May	15 May	22	27 November
2017	1 March	16 April	25 May	4 June	20	3 December
2018	14 February	1 April	10 May	20 May	22	2 December
2019	6 March	21 April	30 May	9 June	19	1 December
2020	26 February	12 April	21 May	31 May	20	29 November
2021	17 February	4 April	13 May	23 May	21	28 November
2022	2 March	17 April	26 May	5 June	19	27 November
2023	22 February	9 April	18 May	28 May	21	3 December
2024	14 February	31 March	9 May	19 May	22	1 December
2025	5 March	20 April	29 May	8 June	19	30 November
2026	18 February	5 April	14 May	24 May	21	29 November
2027	10 February	28 March	6 May	16 May	22	28 November
2028	1 March	16 April	25 May	4 June	20	3 December

NOTES

Ash Wednesday (first day in Lent) can fall at earliest on 4 February and at latest on 10 March

Mothering Sunday (fourth Sunday in Lent) can fall at earliest on 1 March and at latest on 4 April

Easter Day can fall at earliest on 22 March and at latest on 25 April

Ascension Day is forty days after Easter Day and can fall at earliest on 30 April and at latest on 3 June

Pentecost (Whit Sunday) is seven weeks after Easter and can fall at earliest on 10 May and at latest on 13 June

Trinity Sunday is the Sunday after Whit Sunday

Corpus Christi falls on the Thursday after Trinity Sunday

Sundays after Pentecost – there are not less than 18 and not more than 23

Advent Sunday is the Sunday nearest to 30 November

EASTER DAYS AND DOMINICAL LETTERS 1500 TO 2033

Dates up to and including 1752 are according to the Julian calendar

		1500–1599	1600–1699	1700–1799	1800–1899	1900–1999	2000–2033
March							
d	22	1573	1668	1761	1818		
e	23	1505/16	1600	1788	1845/56	1913	2008
f	24		1611/95	1706/99		1940	
g	25	1543/54	1627/38/49	1722/33/44	1883/94	1951	
A	26	1559/70/81/92	1654/65/76	1749/58/69/80	1815/26/37	1967/78/89	
b	27	1502/13/24/97	1608/87/92	1785/96	1842/53/64	1910/21/32	2005/16
c	28	1529/35/40	1619/24/30	1703/14/25	1869/75/80	1937/48	2027/32
d	29	1551/62	1635/46/57	1719/30/41/52	1807/12/91	1959/64/70	
e	30	1567/78/89	1651/62/73/84	1746/55/66/77	1823/34	1902/75/86/97	
f	31	1510/21/32/83/94	1605/16/78/89	1700/71/82/93	1839/50/61/72	1907/18/29/91	2002/13/24
April							
g	1	1526/37/48	1621/32	1711/16	1804/66/77/88	1923/34/45/56	2018/29
A	2	1553/64	1643/48	1727/38	1809/20/93/99	1961/72	
b	3	1575/80/86	1659/70/81	1743/63/68/74	1825/31/36	1904/83/88/94	
c	4	1507/18/91	1602/13/75/86/97	1708/79/90	1847/58	1915/20/26/99	2010/21
d	5	1523/34/45/56	1607/18/29/40	1702/13/24/95	1801/63/74/85/96	1931/42/53	2015/26
e	6	1539/50/61/72	1634/45/56	1729/35/40/60	1806/17/28/90	1947/58/69/80	
f	7	1504/77/88	1667/72	1751/65/76	1822/33/44	1901/12/85/96	
g	8	1509/15/20/99	1604/10/83/94	1705/87/92/98	1849/55/60	1917/28	2007/12
A	9	1531/42	1615/26/37/99	1710/21/32	1871/82	1939/44/50	2023
b	10	1547/58/69	1631/42/53/64	1726/37/48/57	1803/14/87/98	1955/66/77	
c	11	1501/12/63/74/85/96	1658/69/80	1762/73/84	1819/30/41/52	1909/71/82/93	2004
d	12	1506/17/28	1601/12/91/96	1789	1846/57/68	1903/14/25/36/98	2009/20
e	13	1533/44	1623/28	1707/18	1800/73/79/84	1941/52	2031
f	14	1555/60/66	1639/50/61	1723/34/45/54	1805/11/16/95	1963/68/74	
g	15	1571/82/93	1655/66/77/88	1750/59/70/81	1827/38	1900/06/79/90	2001
A	16	1503/14/25/36/87/98	1609/20/82/93	1704/75/86/97	1843/54/65/76	1911/22/33/95	2006/17/28
b	17	1530/41/52	1625/36	1715/20	1808/70/81/92	1927/38/49/60	2022/33
c	18	1557/68	1647/52	1731/42/56	1802/13/24/97	1954/65/76	
d	19	1500/79/84/90	1663/74/85	1747/67/72/78	1829/35/40	1908/81/87/92	
e	20	1511/22/95	1606/17/79/90	1701/12/83/94	1851/62	1919/24/30	2003/14/25
f	21	1527/38/49	1622/33/44	1717/28	1867/78/89	1935/46/57	2019/30
g	22	1565/76	1660	1739/53/64	1810/21/32	1962/73/84	
A	23	1508	1671		1848	1905/16	2000
b	24	1519	1603/14/98	1709/91	1859		2011
c	25	1546	1641	1736	1886	1943	

HINDU CALENDAR

The Hindu calendar is a luni-solar calendar of twelve months, each containing 29 days, 12 hours. Each month is divided into a light fortnight (Shukla or Shuddha) and a dark fortnight (Krishna or Vadya) based on the waxing and waning of the moon. In most parts of India the month starts with the light fortnight, i.e. the day after the new moon, although in some regions it begins with the dark fortnight, i.e. the day after the full moon.

The new year begins in the month of Chaitra (March/April) and ends in the month of Phalgun (March). The twelve months, Chaitra, Vaishakh, Jyeshtha, Ashadh, Shravan, Bhadrapad, Ashvin, Kartik, Margashirsh, Paush, Magh and Phalgun, have Sanskrit names derived from twelve asterisms (constellations). There are regional variations to the names of the months but the Sanskrit names are understood throughout India.

Every lunar month must have a solar transit and is termed pure (shuddha). The lunar month without a solar transit is impure (mala) and called an intercalary month. An intercalary month occurs approximately every 32 lunar months, whenever the difference between the Hindu year of 360 lunar days (354 days 8 hours solar time) and the 365

days 6 hours of the solar year reaches the length of one Hindu lunar month (29 days 12 hours).

The leap month may be added at any point in the Hindu year. The name given to the month varies according to when it occurs but is taken from the month immediately following it. Leap months occur in 1996–7 (Ashadh) and 1999–2000 (Jyeshtha).

The days of the week are called Raviwar (Sunday), Somawar (Monday), Mangalwar (Tuesday), Budhawar (Wednesday), Guruwar (Thursday), Shukrawar (Friday) and Shaniwar (Saturday). The names are derived from the Sanskrit names of the Sun, the Moon and five planets, Mars, Mercury, Jupiter, Venus and Saturn.

Most fasts and festivals are based on the lunar calendar but a few are determined by the apparent movement of the Sun, e.g. Sankranti, which is celebrated on 14/15 January to mark the start of the Sun's apparent journey northwards and a change of season.

Festivals celebrated throughout India are Chaitra (the New Year), Raksha-bandhan (the renewal of the kinship bond between brothers and sisters), Navaratri (a nine-night festival dedicated to the goddess Parvati), Dasara (the victory of Rama over the demon army), Diwali (a festival of lights), Makara Sankranti, Shivaratri (dedicated to Shiva), and Holi (a spring festival).

Regional festivals are Durga-puja (dedicated to the goddess Durga (Parvati)), Sarasvati-puja (dedicated to the goddess Sarasvati), Ganesh Chaturthi (worship of Ganesh on the fourth day (Chaturthi) of the light half of Bhadrapad), Ramanavami (the birth festival of the god Rama) and Janmashtami (the birth festival of the god Krishna).

The main festivals celebrated in Britain are Navaratri, Dasara, Durga-puja, Diwali, Holi, Sarasvati-puja, Ganesh Chaturthi, Raksha-bandhan, Ramanavami and Janmashtami.

The dates of the main festivals in 1996 are given on page 9.

JEWISH CALENDAR

The story of the Flood in the Book of Genesis indicates the use of a calendar of some kind and that the writers recognized thirty days as the length of a lunation. However, after the diaspora, Jewish communities were left in considerable doubt as to the times of fasts and festivals. This led to the formation of the Jewish calendar as used today. It is said that this was done in AD 358 by Rabbi Hillel II, though some assert that it did not happen until much later.

The calendar is luni-solar, and is based on the lengths of the lunation and of the tropical year as found by Hipparchus (c.120 BC), which differ little from those adopted at the present day. The year AM 5756 (1995-6) is the 18th year of the 303rd Metonic (Minor or Lunar) cycle of 19 years and the 16th year of the 206th Solar (or Major) cycle of 28 years since the Era of the Creation. Jews hold that the Creation occurred at the time of the autumnal equinox in the year known in the Christian calendar as 3760 BC (954 of the Julian period). The epoch or starting point of Jewish chronology corresponds to 7 October 3761 BC. At the beginning of each solar cycle, the Tekufah of Nisan (the vernal equinox) returns to the same day and to the same hour.

The hour is divided into 1080 minims, and the month between one new moon and the next is reckoned as 29 days, 12 hours, 793 minims. The normal calendar year, called a Common Regular year, consists of 12 months of 30 days and 29 days alternately. Since twelve months such as these comprise only 354 days, in order that each of them shall not diverge greatly from an average place in the solar year, a thirteenth month is occasionally added after the fifth month of the civil year (which commences on the first day of the month Tishri), or as the penultimate month of the ecclesiastical year (which commences on the first day of the month Nisan). The years when this happens are called Embolismic or leap years.

Of the 19 years that form a Metonic cycle, seven are leap years; they occur at places in the cycle indicated by the numbers 3, 6, 8, 11, 14, 17 and 19, these places being chosen so that the accumulated excesses of the solar years should be as small as possible.

A Jewish year is of one of the following six types:

Minimal Common	353 days
Regular Common	354 days
Full Common	355 days
Minimal Leap	383 days
Regular Leap	384 days
Full Leap	385 days.

The Regular year has alternate months of 30 and 29 days. In a Full year, whether common or leap, Marcheshvan, the second month of the civil year, has 30 days instead of 29; in Minimal years Kislev, the third month, has 29 instead of 30. The additional month in leap years is called Adar I and precedes the month called Adar in Common years. Adar II is called Adar Sheni in leap years, and the usual Adar festivals are kept in Adar Sheni. Adar I and Adar II always have 30 days, but neither this, nor the other variations mentioned, is allowed to change the number of days in the other months, which still follow the alternation of the normal twelve.

These are the main features of the Jewish calendar, which must be considered permanent because as a Jewish law it cannot be altered except by a great Sanhedrin.

The Jewish day begins between sunset and nightfall. The time used is that of the meridian of Jerusalem, which is 2h 21m in advance of Greenwich Mean Time. Rules for the beginning of sabbaths and festivals were laid down for the latitude of London in the 18th century and hours for nightfall are now fixed annually by the Chief Rabbi.

JEWISH CALENDAR 5756-7

AM 5756 (756) is a Full Common year of 12 months, 51 sabbaths and 355 days. AM 5757 (757) is a Minimal Leap year of 13 months, 55 sabbaths and 383 days.

Jewish Month	AM 5756	AM 5757
Tishri 1	25 September 1995	14 September 1996
Marcheshvan 1	25 October	14 October
Kislev 1	24 November	12 November
Tebet 1	24 December	11 December
Shebat 1	22 January 1996	9 January 1997
Adar 1	21 February	8 February
†*Adar* II		10 March
Nisan 1	21 March	8 April
Iyar 1	20 April	8 May
Sivan 1	19 May	6 June
Tammuz 1	18 June	6 July
Ab 1	17 July	4 August
Elul 1	16 August	3 September

*Known as Adar Rishon in leap years
†Known as Adar Sheni in leap years

JEWISH FASTS AND FESTIVALS

For dates of principal festivals in 1996, *see* page 9

Tishri 1–2	Rosh Hashanah (New Year)
Tishri 3	*Fast of Gedaliah
Tishri 10	Yom Kippur (Day of Atonement)
Tishri 15–21	Succoth (Feast of Tabernacles)
Tishri 21	Hoshana Rabba
Tishri 22	Shemini Atseret (Solemn Assembly)
Tishri 23	Simchat Torah (Rejoicing of the Law)
Kislev 25	Chanucah (Dedication of the Temple) begins
Tebet 10	Fast of Tebet
†*Adar* 13	§Fast of Esther
†*Adar* 14	Purim
†*Adar* 15	Shushan Purim
Nisan 15–22	Pesach (Passover)
Sivan 6–7	Shavuot (Feast of Weeks)
Tammuz 17	*Fast of Tammuz
Ab 9	*Fast of Ab

*If these dates fall on the sabbath the fast is kept on the following day
†Adar Sheni in leap years
§This fast is observed on Adar 11 (or Adar Sheni 11 in leap years) if Adar 13 falls on a sabbath

THE MUSLIM CALENDAR

The Muslim era is dated from the *Hijrah*, or flight of the Prophet Muhammad from Mecca to Medina, the corresponding date of which in the Julian calendar is 16 July AD 622. Hijrah years (AH) are used principally in Iran, Turkey, Egypt, Malaysia, various Arab states and certain parts of India. The dating system was adopted about AD 639, commencing with the first day of the month Muharram. Muharram precedes the month in which the Hijrah took place and was recognized as the beginning of the year because it followed the month of pilgrimage.

The calendar is a lunar calendar and consists of twelve months containing an alternate sequence of 30 and 29 days, with the intercalation of one day at the end of the twelfth month at stated intervals in each cycle of 30 years. The object of the intercalation is to reconcile the date of the first day of the month with the date of the actual new moon.

Some adherents still take the date of the evening of the first physical sighting of the crescent of the new moon as that of the first of the month. For this reason, the beginning of a new month and the date of religious festivals can vary by a few days from the published calendars.

In each cycle of 30 years, 19 years are common and contain 354 days, and 11 years are intercalary (leap years) of 355 days, the latter being called *kabishah*. The mean length of the Hijrah years is 354 days 8 hours 48 minutes and the period of mean lunation is 29 days 12 hours 44 minutes.

To ascertain if a year is common or kabishah, divide it by 30: the quotient gives the number of completed cycles and the remainder shows the place of the year in the current cycle. If the remainder is 2, 5, 7, 10, 13, 16, 18, 21, 24, 26 or 29, the year is kabishah and consists of 355 days.

MUSLIM CALENDAR 1416–17

Hijrah year 1416 AH (remainder 6) is a common year; 1417 AH (remainder 7) is a kabishah year.

Month (length)	1416 AH	1417 AH
Muharram (30)	31 May 1995	19 May 1996
Safar (29)	30 June	18 June
Rabi' I (30)	29 July	17 July
Rabi' II (29)	28 August	16 August
Jumada I (30)	26 September	14 September
Jumada II (29)	26 October	14 October
Rajab (30)	24 November	12 November
Shaabân (29)	24 December	12 December
Ramadân (30)	22 January 1996	10 January 1997
Shawwâl (29)	21 February	9 February
Dhû'l-Qa'da (30)	21 March	10 March
Dhû'l-Hijjah (29 or 30)	20 April	9 April

MUSLIM FESTIVALS

Ramadan is a month of fasting for all Muslims because it is the month in which the revelation of the *Qur'an* (Koran) began. During Ramadan Muslims abstain from food, drink and sexual pleasure from dawn until after sunset throughout the month.

The two major festivals are *Idu-l-fitr* and *Idu-l-adha*. Idu-l-fitr marks the end of the Ramadan fast and is celebrated on the day after the sighting of the new moon of the following month. Idu-l-adha, the festival of sacrifice (also known as the great festival), celebrates the submission of the Prophet Ibrahim (Abraham) to Allah. Idu-l-adha falls on the tenth day of Dhul-Hijjah, coinciding with the day when those on *hajj* (pilgrimage to Mecca) sacrifice animals.

Other days accorded special recognition are:

Muharram 1	New Year's Day
Muharram 10	Ashura (the day Prophet Nuh left the Ark and Prophet Musa was saved from Pharaoh (Sunni), the death of the Prophet's grandson Husain (Shi'ite))
Rabi'u-l-Awwal (Rabi' I) 12	Mawlidu-n-Nabiyy (birthday of the Prophet Muhammad)
Rajab 27	Laylatu-l-Isra wa l-Miraj (Night of the Journey and Ascension)
Ramadân Odd-numbered nights in the last 10 of the month	Laylatu-l-Qadr (Night of Power)
Dhû'l-Hijjah 10	Idu-l-adha (Festival of Sacrifice)

THE SIKH CALENDAR

The Sikh calendar is a lunar calendar of 365 days divided into 12 months. The length of the months varies between 29 and 32 days.

There are no prescribed feast days and no fasting periods. The main celebrations are Baisakhi Mela (the new year and the anniversary of the founding of the Khalsa), Diwali Mela (festival of light), Hola Mohalla Mela (a spring festival held in the Punjab), and the Gurpurbs (anniversaries associated with the ten Gurus).

The dates of the major celebrations in 1996 are given on page 9.

CIVIL AND LEGAL CALENDAR

THE HISTORICAL YEAR

Before the year 1752, two calendar systems were in use in England. The civil or legal year began on 25 March and the historical year on 1 January. Thus the civil or legal date 24 March 1658 was the same day as the historical date 24 March 1659; and a date in that portion of the year is written as 24 March 165⅛ the lower figure showing the historical year.

THE NEW YEAR

In England in the seventh century, and as late as the 13th, the year was reckoned from Christmas Day, but in the 12th century the Church in England began the year with the feast of the Annunciation of the Blessed Virgin ('Lady Day') on 25 March and this practice was adopted generally in the 14th century. The civil or legal year in the British Dominions (exclusive of Scotland) began with Lady Day until 1751. But in and since 1752 the civil year has begun with 1 January. New Year's Day in Scotland was changed from 25 March to 1 January in 1600.

Elsewhere in Europe, 1 January was adopted as the first day of the year by Venice in 1522, German states in 1544, Spain, Portugal, and the Roman Catholic Netherlands in 1556, Prussia, Denmark and Sweden in 1559, France in 1564, Lorraine in 1579, the Protestant Netherlands in 1583, Russia in 1725, and Tuscany in 1751.

REGNAL YEARS

Regnal years are the years of a sovereign's reign and each begins on the anniversary of his or her accession, e.g. regnal year 45 of the present Queen begins on 6 February 1996.

The system was used for dating Acts of Parliament until 1962. The Summer Time Act 1925, for example, is quoted as 15 and 16 Geo. V c. 64, because it became law in the parliamentary session which extended over part of both of these regnal years. Acts of a parliamentary session during which a sovereign died were usually given two year numbers, the regnal year of the deceased sovereign and the regnal year of his or her successor, e.g. those passed in 1952 were dated 16 Geo. VI and 1 Elizabeth II. Since 1962 Acts of Parliament have been dated by the calendar year.

QUARTER AND TERM DAYS

Holy days and saints days were the usual means in early times for setting the dates of future and recurrent appointments. The quarter days in England and Wales are the feast of the Nativity (25 December), the feast of the Annunciation (25 March), the feast of St John the Baptist (24 June) and the feast of St Michael and All Angels (29 September).

The term days in Scotland are Candlemas (the feast of the Purification), Whitsunday, Lammas (Loaf Mass), and Martinmas (St Martin's Day). These fell on 2 February, 15 May, 1 August and 11 November respectively. However, by the Term and Quarter Days (Scotland) Act 1990, the dates of the term days were changed to 28 February (Candlemas), 28 May (Whitsunday), 28 August (Lammas) and 28 November (Martinmas).

RED-LETTER DAYS

Red-letter days were originally the holy days and saints days indicated in early ecclesiastical calendars by letters printed in red ink. The days to be distinguished in this way were approved at the Council of Nicaea in AD 325.

These days still have a legal significance, as judges of the Queen's Bench Division wear scarlet robes on red-letter days falling during the law sittings. The days designated as red-letter days for this purpose are:

Holy and saints days

The Conversion of St Paul, the Purification, Ash Wednesday, the Annunciation, the Ascension, the feasts of St Mark, SS Philip and James, St Matthias, St Barnabas, St John the Baptist, St Peter, St Thomas, St James, St Luke, SS Simon and Jude, All Saints, St Andrew

Civil calendar

The anniversaries of The Queen's accession, The Queen's birthday and The Queen's coronation, The Queen's official birthday, the birthday of the Duke of Edinburgh, the birthday of Queen Elizabeth the Queen Mother, the birthday of the Prince of Wales, St David's Day and Lord Mayor's Day

PUBLIC HOLIDAYS

Public holidays are divided into two categories, common law and statutory. Common law holidays are holidays 'by habit and custom'; in England, Wales and Northern Ireland these are Good Friday and Christmas Day.

Statutory public holidays, known as bank holidays, were first established by the Bank Holidays Act 1871. They were, literally, days on which the banks (and other public institutions) were closed and financial obligations due on that day were payable the following day. The legislation currently governing public holidays in the United Kingdom is the Banking and Financial Dealings Act 1971. It stipulates which days are to be public holidays in England, Wales, Scotland and Northern Ireland.

Certain holidays (indicated by * below) are granted annually by royal proclamation, either throughout the United Kingdom or in any place in the United Kingdom. The public holidays are:

England and Wales

*New Year's Day
Easter Monday
*The first Monday in May
The last Monday in May
The last Monday in August
26 December, if it is not a Sunday
27 December when 25 or 26 December is a Sunday

Scotland

New Year's Day, or if it is a Sunday, 2 January
2 January, or if it is a Sunday, 3 January
Good Friday
The first Monday in May
*The last Monday in May
The first Monday in August
Christmas Day, or if it is a Sunday, 26 December
*Boxing Day – if Christmas Day falls on a Sunday, 26 December is given in lieu and an alternative day is given for Boxing Day

Northern Ireland

*New Year's Day
17 March, or if it is a Sunday, 18 March
Easter Monday
*The first Monday in May
The last Monday in May
*12 July, or if it is a Sunday, 13 July
The last Monday in August
26 December, if it is not a Sunday
27 December if 25 or 26 December is a Sunday

For dates of public holidays in 1996 and 1997, see pages 10–11.

CHRONOLOGICAL CYCLES AND ERAS

SOLAR (OR MAJOR) CYCLE

The solar cycle is a period of twenty-eight years in any corresponding year of which the days of the week recur on the same day of the month.

METONIC (LUNAR, OR MINOR) CYCLE

In 432 BC, Meton, an Athenian astronomer, found that 235 lunations are very nearly, though not exactly, equal in duration to 19 solar years and so after 19 years the phases of the Moon recur on the same days of the month (nearly). The dates of full moon in a cycle of 19 years were inscribed in figures of gold on public monuments in Athens, and the number showing the position of a year in the cycle is called the golden number of that year.

JULIAN PERIOD

The Julian period was proposed by Joseph Scaliger in 1582. The period is 7980 Julian years, and its first year coincides with the year 4713 BC. The figure of 7980 is the product of the number of years in the solar cycle, the Metonic cycle and the cycle of the Roman indiction (28 × 19 × 15).

88   Time Measurement and Calendars

ROMAN INDICTION

The Roman indiction is a period of fifteen years, instituted for fiscal purposes about AD 300.

EPACT

The epact is the age of the calendar Moon, diminished by one day, on 1 January, in the ecclesiastical lunar calendar.

CHINESE CALENDAR

A lunar calendar was the sole calendar in use in China until 1911, when the government adopted the new (Gregorian) calendar for official and most business activities. The Chinese tend to follow both calendars, the lunar calendar playing an important part in personal life, e.g. birth celebrations, festivals, marriages; and in rural villages the lunar calendar dictates the cycle of activities, denoting the change of weather and farming activities.

The lunar calendar is used in Hong Kong, Singapore, Malaysia, Tibet and elsewhere in south-east Asia. The calendar has a cycle of 60 years. The new year begins at the first new moon after the sun enters the sign of Aquarius, i.e. the new year falls between 21 January and 19 February in the Gregorian calendar.

Each year in the Chinese calendar is associated with one of 12 animals: the rat, the ox, the tiger, the rabbit, the dragon, the snake, the horse, the goat or sheep, the monkey, the chicken or rooster, the dog, and the pig.

The date of the Chinese new year and the astrological sign for the years 1996–2000 are:

1996	19 February	Rat
1997	7 February	Ox
1998	28 January	Tiger
1999	16 February	Rabbit
2000	5 February	Dragon

COPTIC CALENDAR

In the Coptic calendar, which is used by part of the population of Egypt and Ethiopia, the year is made up of 12 months of 30 days each, followed, in general, by five complementary days. Every fourth year is an intercalary or leap year and in these years there are six complementary days. The intercalary year of the Coptic calendar immediately precedes the leap year of the Julian calendar. The era is that of Diocletian or the Martyrs, the origin of which is fixed at 29 August AD 284 (Julian date).

INDIAN ERAS

In addition to the Muslim reckoning there are six eras used in India. The principal astronomical system was the Kaliyuga era, which appears to have been adopted in the fourth century AD. It began on 18 February 3102 BC. The chronological system of northern India, known as the Vikrama Samvat era, prevalent in western India, began on 23 February 57 BC. The year AD 1996 is, therefore, the year 2053 of the Vikrama era.

The Saka era of southern India, dating from 3 March AD 78, was declared the national calendar of the Republic of India with effect from 22 March 1957, to be used concurrently with the Gregorian calendar. As revised, the year of the new Saka era begins at the spring equinox, with five successive months of 31 days and seven of 30 days in ordinary years, and six months of each length in leap years. The year AD 1996 is 1918 of the revised Saka era.

The Saptarshi era dates from the moment when the Saptarshi, or saints, were translated and became the stars of the Great Bear in 3076 BC.

The Buddhists reckoned from the death of the Buddha in 543 BC (the actual date being 487 BC); and the epoch of the Jains was the death of Vardhamana, the founder of their faith, in 527 BC.

JAPANESE CALENDAR

The Japanese calendar is essentially the same as the Gregorian calendar, the years, months and weeks being of the same length and beginning on the same days as those of the Gregorian calendar. The numeration of the years is different, for Japanese chronology is based on a system of epochs or periods, each of which begins at the accession of an Emperor or other important occurrence. The method is not unlike the former British system of regnal years, except that each year of a period closes on 31 December. The Japanese chronology begins about AD 650 and the three latest epochs are defined by the reigns of Emperors, whose actual names are not necessarily used:

Epoch

Taishō	1 August 1912 to 25 December 1926
Shōwa	26 December 1926 to 7 January 1989
Heisei	8 January 1989

The year Heisei 8 begins on 1 January 1996.

The months are not named. They are known as First Month, Second Month, etc., First Month being equivalent to January. The days of the week are Nichiyōbi (Sun-day), Getsuyōbi (Moon-day), Kayōbi (Fire-day), Suiyōbi (Water-day), Mokuyōbi (Wood-day), Kinyōbi (Metal-day), Doyōbi (Earth-day).

THE MASONIC YEAR

Two dates are quoted in warrants, dispensations, etc., issued by the United Grand Lodge of England, those for the current year being expressed as *Anno Domini* 1996 – *Anno Lucis* 5996. This *Anno Lucis* (year of light) is based on the Book of Genesis 1:3, the 4000 year difference being derived, in modified form, from *Ussher's Notation*, published in 1654, which places the Creation of the World in 4004 BC.

OLYMPIADS

Ancient Greek chronology was reckoned in Olympiads, cycles of four years corresponding with the periodic Olympic Games held on the plain of Olympia in Elis once every four years. The intervening years were the first, second, etc., of the Olympiad, which received the name of the victor at the Games. The first recorded Olympiad is that of Choroebus, 776 BC.

ZOROASTRIAN CALENDAR

Zoroastrians, followers of the Iranian prophet Zarathushtra (known to the Greeks as Zoroaster) are mostly to be found in Iran and in India, where they are known as Parsees.

The Zoroastrian era dates from the coronation of the last Zoroastrian Sasanian king in AD 631. The Zoroastrian calendar is divided into twelve months, each comprising 30 days, followed by five holy days of the Gathas at the end of each year to make the year consist of 365 days.

In order to synchronize the calendar with the solar year of 365 days, an extra month was intercalated once every 120 years. However, this intercalation ceased in the 12th century and the New Year, which had fallen in the spring, slipped back until it now falls in August. Because intercalation ceased at different times in Iran and India, there was one month's difference between the calendar followed in Iran (Kadmi calendar) and by the Parsees (Shenshai calendar).

In 1906 a group of Zoroastrians decided to bring the calendar back in line with the seasons again and restore the New Year to 21 March each year (Fasli calendar).

The Shenshai calendar (New Year in August) is mainly used by Parsees. The Fasli calendar (New Year, 21 March) is mainly used by Zoroastrians living in Iran, in the Indian subcontinent, or away from Iran.

THE ROMAN CALENDAR

Roman historians adopted as an epoch the foundation of Rome, which is believed to have happened in the year 753 BC. The ordinal number of the years in Roman reckoning is followed by the letters AUC (*ab urbe condita*), so that the year 1996 is 2749 AUC (MMDCCXLIX). The calendar that we know has developed from one said to have been established by Romulus using a year of 304 days divided into ten months, beginning with March. To this Numa added January and February, making the year consist of 12 months of 30 and 29 days alternately, with an additional day so that the total was 355. It is also said that Numa ordered an intercalary month of 22 or 23 days in alternate years, making 90 days in eight years, to be inserted after 23 February.

However, there is some doubt as to the origination and the details of the intercalation in the Roman calendar. It is certain that some scheme of this kind was inaugurated and not fully carried out, for in the year 46 BC Julius Caesar found that the calendar had been allowed to fall into some confusion. He sought the help of the Egyptian astronomer Sosigenes, which led to the construction and adoption (45 BC) of the Julian calendar, and, by a slight alteration, to the Gregorian calendar now in use. The year 46 BC was made to consist of 445 days and is called the Year of Confusion.

In the Roman (Julian) calendar the days of the month were counted backwards from three fixed points, or days, and an intervening day was said to be so many days before the next coming point, the first and last being counted. These three points were the Kalends, the Nones, and the Ides. Their positions in the months and the method of counting from them will be seen in the table below. The year containing 366 days was called *bissextillis annus*, as it had a doubled sixth day (*bissextus dies*) before the March Kalends on 24 February – *ante diem sextum Kalendas Martias*, or a.d. VI Kal. Mart.

Present days of the month	*March, May, July, October have thirty-one days*	*January, August, December have thirty-one days*	*April, June, September, November have thirty days*	*February has twenty-eight days, and in leap year twenty-nine*
1	Kalendis	Kalendis	Kalendis	Kalendis
2	VI	IV ⎤ ante	IV ⎤ ante	IV ⎤ ante
3	V ⎤ ante	III ⎦ Nonas	III ⎦ Nonas	III ⎦ Nonas
4	IV ⎱ Nonas	pridie Nonas	pridie Nonas	pridie Nonas
5	III ⎦	Nonis	Nonis	Nonis
6	pridie Nonas	VIII	VIII	VIII
7	Nonis	VII	VII	VII
8	VIII	VI ⎤ ante	VI ⎤ ante	VI ⎤ ante
9	VII	V ⎦ Idus	V ⎦ Idus	V ⎦ Idus
10	VI ⎤ ante	IV	IV	IV
11	V ⎦ Idus	III	III	III
12	IV	pridie Idus	pridie Idus	pridie Idus
13	III	Idibus	Idibus	Idibus
14	pridie Idus	XIX	XVIII	XVI
15	Idibus	XVIII	XVII	XV
16	XVII	XVII	XVI	XIV
17	XVI	XVI	XV	XIII
18	XV	XV	XIV	XII
19	XIV	XIV	XIII	XI
20	XIII	XIII	XII ⎤ ante Kalendas	X ⎤ ante Kalendas
21	XII	XII ⎤ ante Kalendas	XI ⎱ (of the month	IX ⎦ Martias
22	XI ⎤ ante Kalendas	XI ⎱ (of the month	X ⎦ following)	VIII
23	X ⎱ (of the month	X ⎦ following)	IX	VII
24	IX ⎦ following)	IX	VIII	*VI
25	VIII	VIII	VII	V
26	VII	VII	VI	IV
27	VI	VI	V	III
28	V	V	IV	pridie Kalendas
29	IV	IV	III	Martias
30	III	III	pridie Kalendas	
31	pridie Kalendas (Aprilis, Iunias, Sextilis, Novembris)	pridie Kalendas (Februarias, Septembris, Ianuarias)	(Maias, Quinctilis, Octobris, Decembris)	* (repeated in leap year)

Calendar for Any Year 1770–2033

To select the correct calendar for any year between 1770 and 2033,
consult the index below
* leap year

1770	C	1803	M	1836	L*	1869	K	1902	G	1935	E	1968	D*	2001	C
1771	E	1804	B*	1837	A	1870	M	1903	I	1936	H*	1969	G	2002	E
1772	H*	1805	E	1838	C	1871	A	1904	L*	1937	K	1970	I	2003	G
1773	K	1806	G	1839	E	1872	D*	1905	A	1938	M	1971	K	2004	J*
1774	M	1807	I	1840	H*	1873	G	1906	C	1939	A	1972	N*	2005	M
1775	A	1808	L*	1841	K	1874	I	1907	E	1940	D*	1973	C	2006	A
1776	D*	1809	A	1842	M	1875	K	1908	H*	1941	G	1974	E	2007	C
1777	G	1810	C	1843	A	1876	N*	1909	K	1942	I	1975	G	2008	F*
1778	I	1811	E	1844	D*	1877	C	1910	M	1943	K	1976	J*	2009	I
1779	K	1812	H*	1845	G	1878	E	1911	A	1944	N*	1977	M	2010	K
1780	N*	1813	K	1846	I	1879	G	1912	D*	1945	C	1978	A	2011	M
1781	C	1814	M	1847	K	1880	J*	1913	G	1946	E	1979	C	2012	B*
1782	E	1815	A	1848	N*	1881	M	1914	I	1947	G	1980	F*	2013	E
1783	G	1816	D*	1849	C	1882	A	1915	K	1948	J*	1981	I	2014	G
1784	J*	1817	G	1850	E	1883	C	1916	N*	1949	M	1982	K	2015	I
1785	M	1818	I	1851	G	1884	F*	1917	C	1950	A	1983	M	2016	L*
1786	A	1819	K	1852	J*	1885	I	1918	E	1951	C	1984	B*	2017	A
1787	C	1820	N*	1853	M	1886	K	1919	G	1952	F*	1985	E	2018	C
1788	F*	1821	C	1854	A	1887	M	1920	J*	1953	I	1986	G	2019	E
1789	I	1822	E	1855	C	1888	B*	1921	M	1954	K	1987	I	2020	H*
1790	K	1823	G	1856	F*	1889	E	1922	A	1955	M	1988	L*	2021	K
1791	M	1824	J*	1857	I	1890	G	1923	C	1956	B*	1989	A	2022	M
1792	B*	1825	M	1858	K	1891	I	1924	F*	1957	E	1990	C	2023	A
1793	E	1826	A	1859	M	1892	L*	1925	I	1958	G	1991	E	2024	D*
1794	G	1827	C	1860	B*	1893	A	1926	K	1959	I	1992	H*	2025	G
1795	I	1828	F*	1861	E	1894	C	1927	M	1960	L*	1993	K	2026	I
1796	L*	1829	I	1862	G	1895	E	1928	B*	1961	A	1994	M	2027	K
1797	A	1830	K	1863	I	1896	H*	1929	E	1962	C	1995	A	2028	N*
1798	C	1831	M	1864	L*	1897	K	1930	G	1963	E	1996	D*	2029	C
1799	E	1832	B*	1865	A	1898	M	1931	I	1964	H*	1997	G	2030	E
1800	G	1833	E	1866	C	1899	A	1932	L*	1965	K	1998	I	2031	G
1801	I	1834	G	1867	E	1900	C	1933	A	1966	M	1999	K	2032	J*
1802	K	1835	I	1868	H*	1901	E	1934	C	1967	A	2000	N*	2033	M

A

	January	February	March
Sun.	1 8 15 22 29	5 12 19 26	5 12 19 26
Mon.	2 9 16 23 30	6 13 20 27	6 13 20 27
Tue.	3 10 17 24 31	7 14 21 28	7 14 21 28
Wed.	4 11 18 25	1 8 15 22	1 8 15 22 29
Thur.	5 12 19 26	2 9 16 23	2 9 16 23 30
Fri.	6 13 20 27	3 10 17 24	3 10 17 24 31
Sat.	7 14 21 28	4 11 18 25	4 11 18 25

	April	May	June
Sun.	2 9 16 23 30	7 14 21 28	4 11 18 25
Mon.	3 10 17 24	1 8 15 22 29	5 12 19 26
Tue.	4 11 18 25	2 9 16 23 30	6 13 20 27
Wed.	5 12 19 26	3 10 17 24 31	7 14 21 28
Thur.	6 13 20 27	4 11 18 25	1 8 15 22 29
Fri.	7 14 21 28	5 12 19 26	2 9 16 23 30
Sat.	1 8 15 22 29	6 13 20 27	3 10 17 24

	July	August	September
Sun.	2 9 16 23 30	6 13 20 27	3 10 17 24
Mon.	3 10 17 24 31	7 14 21 28	4 11 18 25
Tue.	4 11 18 25	1 8 15 22 29	5 12 19 26
Wed.	5 12 19 26	2 9 16 23 30	6 13 20 27
Thur.	6 13 20 27	3 10 17 24 31	7 14 21 28
Fri.	7 14 21 28	4 11 18 25	1 8 15 22 29
Sat.	1 8 15 22 29	5 12 19 26	2 9 16 23 30

	October	November	December
Sun.	1 8 15 22 29	5 12 19 26	3 10 17 24 31
Mon.	2 9 16 23 30	6 13 20 27	4 11 18 25
Tue.	3 10 17 24 31	7 14 21 28	5 12 19 26
Wed.	4 11 18 25	1 8 15 22 29	6 13 20 27
Thur.	5 12 19 26	2 9 16 23 30	7 14 21 28
Fri.	6 13 20 27	3 10 17 24	1 8 15 22 29
Sat.	7 14 21 28	4 11 18 25	2 9 16 23 30

EASTER DAYS

March 26	1815, 1826, 1837, 1967, 1978, 1989
April 2	1809, 1893, 1899, 1961
April 9	1871, 1882, 1939, 1950, 2023
April 16	1775, 1786, 1797, 1843, 1854, 1865, 1911, 1922, 1933, 1995, 2006, 2017
April 23	1905

B (LEAP YEAR)

	January	February	March
Sun.	1 8 15 22 29	5 12 19 26	4 11 18 25
Mon.	2 9 16 23 30	6 13 20 27	5 12 19 26
Tue.	3 10 17 24 31	7 14 21 28	6 13 20 27
Wed.	4 11 18 25	1 8 15 22 29	7 14 21 28
Thur.	5 12 19 26	2 9 16 23	1 8 15 22 29
Fri.	6 13 20 27	3 10 17 24	2 9 16 23 30
Sat.	7 14 21 28	4 11 18 25	3 10 17 24 31

	April	May	June
Sun.	1 8 15 22 29	6 13 20 27	3 10 17 24
Mon.	2 9 16 23 30	7 14 21 28	4 11 18 25
Tue.	3 10 17 24	1 8 15 22 29	5 12 19 26
Wed.	4 11 18 25	2 9 16 23 30	6 13 20 27
Thur.	5 12 19 26	3 10 17 24 31	7 14 21 28
Fri.	6 13 20 27	4 11 18 25	1 8 15 22 29
Sat.	7 14 21 28	5 12 19 26	2 9 16 23 30

	July	August	September
Sun.	1 8 15 22 29	5 12 19 26	2 9 16 23 30
Mon.	2 9 16 23 30	6 13 20 27	3 10 17 24
Tue.	3 10 17 24 31	7 14 21 28	4 11 18 25
Wed.	4 11 18 25	1 8 15 22 29	5 12 19 26
Thur.	5 12 19 26	2 9 16 23 30	6 13 20 27
Fri.	6 13 20 27	3 10 17 24 31	7 14 21 28
Sat.	7 14 21 28	4 11 18 25	1 8 15 22 29

	October	November	December
Sun.	7 14 21 28	4 11 18 25	2 9 16 23 30
Mon.	1 8 15 22 29	5 12 19 26	3 10 17 24 31
Tue.	2 9 16 23 30	6 13 20 27	4 11 18 25
Wed.	3 10 17 24 31	7 14 21 28	5 12 19 26
Thur.	4 11 18 25	1 8 15 22 29	6 13 20 27
Fri.	5 12 19 26	2 9 16 23 30	7 14 21 28
Sat.	6 13 20 27	3 10 17 24	1 8 15 22 29

EASTER DAYS

April 1	1804, 1888, 1956
April 8	1792, 1860, 1928, 2012
April 22	1832, 1984

C

	January	February	March
Sun.	7 14 21 28	4 11 18 25	4 11 18 25
Mon.	1 8 15 22 29	5 12 19 26	5 12 19 26
Tue.	2 9 16 23 30	6 13 20 27	6 13 20 27
Wed.	3 10 17 24 31	7 14 21 28	7 14 21 28
Thur.	4 11 18 25	1 8 15 22	1 8 15 22 29
Fri.	5 12 19 26	2 9 16 23	2 9 16 23 30
Sat.	6 13 20 27	3 10 17 24	3 10 17 24 31

	April	May	June
Sun.	1 8 15 22 29	6 13 20 27	3 10 17 24
Mon.	2 9 16 23 30	7 14 21 28	4 11 18 25
Tue.	3 10 17 24	1 8 15 22 29	5 12 19 26
Wed.	4 11 18 25	2 9 16 23 30	6 13 20 27
Thur.	5 12 19 26	3 10 17 24 31	7 14 21 28
Fri.	6 13 20 27	4 11 18 25	1 8 15 22 29
Sat.	7 14 21 28	5 12 19 26	2 9 16 23 30

	July	August	September
Sun.	1 8 15 22 29	5 12 19 26	2 9 16 23 30
Mon.	2 9 16 23 30	6 13 20 27	3 10 17 24
Tue.	3 10 17 24 31	7 14 21 28	4 11 18 25
Wed.	4 11 18 25	1 8 15 22 29	5 12 19 26
Thur.	5 12 19 26	2 9 16 23 30	6 13 20 27
Fri.	6 13 20 27	3 10 17 24 31	7 14 21 28
Sat.	7 14 21 28	4 11 18 25	1 8 15 22 29

	October	November	December
Sun.	7 14 21 28	4 11 18 25	2 9 16 23 30
Mon.	1 8 15 22 29	5 12 19 26	3 10 17 24 31
Tue.	2 9 16 23 30	6 13 20 27	4 11 18 25
Wed.	3 10 17 24 31	7 14 21 28	5 12 19 26
Thur.	4 11 18 25	1 8 15 22 29	6 13 20 27
Fri.	5 12 19 26	2 9 16 23 30	7 14 21 28
Sat.	6 13 20 27	3 10 17 24	1 8 15 22 29

EASTER DAYS

March 25	1883, 1894, 1951
April 1	1866, 1877, 1923, 1934, 1945, 2018, 2029
April 8	1787, 1798, 1849, 1855, 1917, 2007
April 15	1770, 1781, 1827, 1838, 1900, 1906, 1979, 1990, 2001
April 22	1810, 1821, 1962, 1973

D (LEAP YEAR)

	January	February	March
Sun.	7 14 21 28	4 11 18 25	3 10 17 24 31
Mon.	1 8 15 22 29	5 12 19 26	4 11 18 25
Tue.	2 9 16 23 30	6 13 20 27	5 12 19 26
Wed.	3 10 17 24 31	7 14 21 28	6 13 20 27
Thur.	4 11 18 25	1 8 15 22 29	7 14 21 28
Fri.	5 12 19 26	2 9 16 23	1 8 15 22 29
Sat.	6 13 20 27	3 10 17 24	2 9 16 23 30

	April	May	June
Sun.	7 14 21 28	5 12 19 26	2 9 16 23 30
Mon.	1 8 15 22 29	6 13 20 27	3 10 17 24
Tue.	2 9 16 23 30	7 14 21 28	4 11 18 25
Wed.	3 10 17 24	1 8 15 22 29	5 12 19 26
Thur.	4 11 18 25	2 9 16 23 30	6 13 20 27
Fri.	5 12 19 26	3 10 17 24 31	7 14 21 28
Sat.	6 13 20 27	4 11 18 25	1 8 15 22 29

	July	August	September
Sun.	7 14 21 28	4 11 18 25	1 8 15 22 29
Mon.	1 8 15 22 29	5 12 19 26	2 9 16 23 30
Tue.	2 9 16 23 30	6 13 20 27	3 10 17 24
Wed.	3 10 17 24 31	7 14 21 28	4 11 18 25
Thur.	4 11 18 25	1 8 15 22 29	5 12 19 26
Fri.	5 12 19 26	2 9 16 23 30	6 13 20 27
Sat.	6 13 20 27	3 10 17 24 31	7 14 21 28

	October	November	December
Sun.	6 13 20 27	3 10 17 24	1 8 15 22 29
Mon.	7 14 21 28	4 11 18 25	2 9 16 23 30
Tue.	1 8 15 22 29	5 12 19 26	3 10 17 24 31
Wed.	2 9 16 23 30	6 13 20 27	4 11 18 25
Thur.	3 10 17 24 31	7 14 21 28	5 12 19 26
Fri.	4 11 18 25	1 8 15 22 29	6 13 20 27
Sat.	5 12 19 26	2 9 16 23 30	7 14 21 28

EASTER DAYS

March 24	1940
March 31	1872, 2024
April 7	1776, 1844, 1912, 1996
April 14	1816, 1968

E

	January	February	March
Sun.	6 13 20 27	3 10 17 24	3 10 17 24 31
Mon.	7 14 21 28	4 11 18 25	4 11 18 25
Tue.	1 8 15 22 29	5 12 19 26	5 12 19 26
Wed.	2 9 16 23 30	6 13 20 27	6 13 20 27
Thur.	3 10 17 24 31	7 14 21 28	7 14 21 28
Fri.	4 11 18 25	1 8 15 22	1 8 15 22 29
Sat.	5 12 19 26	2 9 16 23	2 9 16 23 30

	April	May	June
Sun.	7 14 21 28	5 12 19 26	2 9 16 23 30
Mon.	1 8 15 22 29	6 13 20 27	3 10 17 24
Tue.	2 9 16 23 30	7 14 21 28	4 11 18 25
Wed.	3 10 17 24	1 8 15 22 29	5 12 19 26
Thur.	4 11 18 25	2 9 16 23 30	6 13 20 27
Fri.	5 12 19 26	3 10 17 24 31	7 14 21 28
Sat.	6 13 20 27	4 11 18 25	1 8 15 22 29

	July	August	September
Sun.	7 14 21 28	4 11 18 25	1 8 15 22 29
Mon.	1 8 15 22 29	5 12 19 26	2 9 16 23 30
Tue.	2 9 16 23 30	6 13 20 27	3 10 17 24
Wed.	3 10 17 24 31	7 14 21 28	4 11 18 25
Thur.	4 11 18 25	1 8 15 22	5 12 19 26
Fri.	5 12 19 26	2 9 16 23 30	6 13 20 27
Sat.	6 13 20 27	3 10 17 24 31	7 14 21 28

	October	November	December
Sun.	6 13 20 27	3 10 17 24	1 8 15 22 29
Mon.	7 14 21 28	4 11 18 25	2 9 16 23 30
Tue.	1 8 15 22 29	5 12 19 26	3 10 17 24 31
Wed.	2 9 16 23 30	6 13 20 27	4 11 18 25
Thur.	3 10 17 24 31	7 14 21 28	5 12 19 26
Fri.	4 11 18 25	1 8 15 22 29	6 13 20 27
Sat.	5 12 19 26	2 9 16 23 30	7 14 21 28

EASTER DAYS

March 24	1799
March 31	1771, 1782, 1793, 1839, 1850, 1861, 1907
	1918, 1929, 1991, 2002, 2013
April 7	1822, 1833, 1901, 1985
April 14	1805, 1811, 1895, 1963, 1974
April 21	1867, 1878, 1889, 1935, 1946, 1957, 2019, 2030

F (LEAP YEAR)

	January	February	March
Sun.	6 13 20 27	3 10 17 24	2 9 16 23 30
Mon.	7 14 21 28	4 11 18 25	3 10 17 24 31
Tue.	1 8 15 22 29	5 12 19 26	4 11 18 25
Wed.	2 9 16 23 30	6 13 20 27	5 12 19 26
Thur.	3 10 17 24 31	7 14 21 28	6 13 20 27
Fri.	4 11 18 25	1 8 15 22 29	7 14 21 28
Sat.	5 12 19 26	2 9 16 23	1 8 15 22 29

	April	May	June
Sun.	6 13 20 27	4 11 18 25	1 8 15 22 29
Mon.	7 14 21 28	5 12 19 26	2 9 16 23 30
Tue.	1 8 15 22 29	6 13 20 27	3 10 17 24
Wed.	2 9 16 23 30	7 14 21 28	4 11 18 25
Thur.	3 10 17 24	1 8 15 22 29	5 12 19 26
Fri.	4 11 18 25	2 9 16 23 30	6 13 20 27
Sat.	5 12 19 26	3 10 17 24 31	7 14 21 28

	July	August	September
Sun.	6 13 20 27	3 10 17 24 31	7 14 21 28
Mon.	7 14 21 28	4 11 18 25	1 8 15 22 29
Tue.	1 8 15 22 29	5 12 19 26	2 9 16 23 30
Wed.	2 9 16 23 30	6 13 20 27	3 10 17 24
Thur.	3 10 17 24 31	7 14 21 28	4 11 18 25
Fri.	4 11 18 25	1 8 15 22 29	5 12 19 26
Sat.	5 12 19 26	2 9 16 23 30	6 13 20 27

	October	November	December
Sun.	5 12 19 26	2 9 16 23 30	7 14 21 28
Mon.	6 13 20 27	3 10 17 24	1 8 15 22 29
Tue.	7 14 21 28	4 11 18 25	2 9 16 23 30
Wed.	1 8 15 22 29	5 12 19 26	3 10 17 24 31
Thur.	2 9 16 23 30	6 13 20 27	4 11 18 25
Fri.	3 10 17 24 31	7 14 21 28	5 12 19 26
Sat.	4 11 18 25	1 8 15 22 29	6 13 20 27

EASTER DAYS

March 23	1788, 1856, 2008
April 6	1828, 1980
April 13	1884, 1952
April 20	1924

G

	January	February	March
Sun.	5 12 19 26	2 9 16 23	2 9 16 23 30
Mon.	6 13 20 27	3 10 17 24	3 10 17 24 31
Tue.	7 14 21 28	4 11 18 25	4 11 18 25
Wed.	1 8 15 22 29	5 12 19 26	5 12 19 26
Thur.	2 9 16 23 30	6 13 20 27	6 13 20 27
Fri.	3 10 17 24 31	7 14 21 28	7 14 21 28
Sat.	4 11 18 25	1 8 15 22	1 8 15 22 29

	April	May	June
Sun.	6 13 20 27	4 11 18 25	1 8 15 22 29
Mon.	7 14 21 28	5 12 19 26	2 9 16 23 30
Tue.	1 8 15 22 29	6 13 20 27	3 10 17 24
Wed.	2 9 16 23 30	7 14 21 28	4 11 18 25
Thur.	3 10 17 24	1 8 15 22 29	5 12 19 26
Fri.	4 11 18 25	2 9 16 23 30	6 13 20 27
Sat.	5 12 19 26	3 10 17 24 31	7 14 21 28

	July	August	September
Sun.	6 13 20 27	3 10 17 24 31	7 14 21 28
Mon.	7 14 21 28	4 11 18 25	1 8 15 22 29
Tue.	1 8 15 22 29	5 12 19 26	2 9 16 23 30
Wed.	2 9 16 23 30	6 13 20 27	3 10 17 24
Thur.	3 10 17 24 31	7 14 21 28	4 11 18 25
Fri.	4 11 18 25	1 8 15 22 29	5 12 19 26
Sat.	5 12 19 26	2 9 16 23 30	6 13 20 27

	October	November	December
Sun.	5 12 19 26	2 9 16 23 30	7 14 21 28
Mon.	6 13 20 27	3 10 17 24	1 8 15 22 29
Tue.	7 14 21 28	4 11 18 25	2 9 16 23 30
Wed.	1 8 15 22 29	5 12 19 26	3 10 17 24 31
Thur.	2 9 16 23 30	6 13 20 27	4 11 18 25
Fri.	3 10 17 24 31	7 14 21 28	5 12 19 26
Sat.	4 11 18 25	1 8 15 22 29	6 13 20 27

EASTER DAYS

March 23	1845, 1913
March 30	1777, 1823, 1834, 1902, 1975, 1986, 1997
April 6	1806, 1817, 1890, 1947, 1958, 1969
April 13	1800, 1873, 1879, 1941, 2031
April 20	1783, 1794, 1851, 1862, 1919, 1930, 2003, 2014, 2025

I

	January	February	March
Sun.	4 11 18 25	1 8 15 22	1 8 15 22 29
Mon.	5 12 19 26	2 9 16 23	2 9 16 23 30
Tue.	6 13 20 27	3 10 17 24	3 10 17 24 31
Wed.	7 14 21 28	4 11 18 25	4 11 18 25
Thur.	1 8 15 22 29	5 12 19 26	5 12 19 26
Fri.	2 9 16 23 30	6 13 20 27	6 13 20 27
Sat.	3 10 17 24 31	7 14 21 28	7 14 21 28

	April	May	June
Sun.	5 12 19 26	3 10 17 24 31	7 14 21 28
Mon.	6 13 20 27	4 11 18 25	1 8 15 22 29
Tue.	7 14 21 28	5 12 19 26	2 9 16 23 30
Wed.	1 8 15 22 29	6 13 20 27	3 10 17 24
Thur.	2 9 16 23 30	7 14 21 28	4 11 18 25
Fri.	3 10 17 24	1 8 15 22 29	5 12 19 26
Sat.	4 11 18 25	2 9 16 23 30	6 13 20 27

	July	August	September
Sun.	5 12 19 26	2 9 16 23 30	6 13 20 27
Mon.	6 13 20 27	3 10 17 24 31	7 14 21 28
Tue.	7 14 21 28	4 11 18 25	1 8 15 22 29
Wed.	1 8 15 22 29	5 12 19 26	2 9 16 23 30
Thur.	2 9 16 23 30	6 13 20 27	3 10 17 24
Fri.	3 10 17 24 31	7 14 21 28	4 11 18 25
Sat.	4 11 18 25	1 8 15 22 29	5 12 19 26

	October	November	December
Sun.	4 11 18 25	1 8 15 22 29	6 13 20 27
Mon.	5 12 19 26	2 9 16 23 30	7 14 21 28
Tue.	6 13 20 27	3 10 17 24	1 8 15 22 29
Wed.	7 14 21 28	4 11 18 25	2 9 16 23 30
Thur.	1 8 15 22 29	5 12 19 26	3 10 17 24 31
Fri.	2 9 16 23 30	6 13 20 27	4 11 18 25
Sat.	3 10 17 24 31	7 14 21 28	5 12 19 26

EASTER DAYS

March 22	1818
March 29	1807, 1891, 1959, 1970
April 5	1795, 1801, 1863, 1874, 1885, 1931, 1942, 1953, 2015, 2026
April 12	1789, 1846, 1857, 1903, 1914, 1925, 1998, 2009
April 19	1778, 1829, 1835, 1981, 1987

H (LEAP YEAR)

	January	February	March
Sun.	5 12 19 26	2 9 16 23	1 8 15 22 29
Mon.	6 13 20 27	3 10 17 24	2 9 16 23 30
Tue.	7 14 21 28	4 11 18 25	3 10 17 24 31
Wed.	1 8 15 22 29	5 12 19 26	4 11 18 25
Thur.	2 9 16 23 30	6 13 20 27	5 12 19 26
Fri.	3 10 17 24 31	7 14 21 28	6 13 20 27
Sat.	4 11 18 25	1 8 15 22 29	7 14 21 28

	April	May	June
Sun.	5 12 19 26	3 10 17 24 31	7 14 21 28
Mon.	6 13 20 27	4 11 18 25	1 8 15 22 29
Tue.	7 14 21 28	5 12 19 26	2 9 16 23 30
Wed.	1 8 15 22 29	6 13 20 27	3 10 17 24
Thur.	2 9 16 23 30	7 14 21 28	4 11 18 25
Fri.	3 10 17 24	1 8 15 22 29	5 12 19 26
Sat.	4 11 18 25	2 9 16 23 30	6 13 20 27

	July	August	September
Sun.	5 12 19 26	2 9 16 23 30	6 13 20 27
Mon.	6 13 20 27	3 10 17 24 31	7 14 21 28
Tue.	7 14 21 28	4 11 18 25	1 8 15 22 29
Wed.	1 8 15 22 29	5 12 19 26	2 9 16 23 30
Thur.	2 9 16 23 30	6 13 20 27	3 10 17 24
Fri.	3 10 17 24 31	7 14 21 28	4 11 18 25
Sat.	4 11 18 25	1 8 15 22 29	5 12 19 26

	October	November	December
Sun.	4 11 18 25	1 8 15 22 29	6 13 20 27
Mon.	5 12 19 26	2 9 16 23 30	7 14 21 28
Tue.	6 13 20 27	3 10 17 24	1 8 15 22 29
Wed.	7 14 21 28	4 11 18 25	2 9 16 23 30
Thur.	1 8 15 22 29	5 12 19 26	3 10 17 24 31
Fri.	2 9 16 23 30	6 13 20 27	4 11 18 25
Sat.	3 10 17 24 31	7 14 21 28	5 12 19 26

EASTER DAYS

March 29	1812, 1964
April 5	1896
April 12	1868, 1936, 2020
April 19	1772, 1840, 1908, 1992

J (LEAP YEAR)

	January	February	March
Sun.	4 11 18 25	1 8 15 22 29	7 14 21 28
Mon.	5 12 19 26	2 9 16 23	1 8 15 22 29
Tue.	6 13 20 27	3 10 17 24	2 9 16 23 30
Wed.	7 14 21 28	4 11 18 25	3 10 17 24 31
Thur.	1 8 15 22 29	5 12 19 26	4 11 18 25
Fri.	2 9 16 23 30	6 13 20 27	5 12 19 26
Sat.	3 10 17 24 31	7 14 21 28	6 13 20 27

	April	May	June
Sun.	4 11 18 25	2 9 16 23 30	6 13 20 27
Mon.	5 12 19 26	3 10 17 24 31	7 14 21 28
Tue.	6 13 20 27	4 11 18 25	1 8 15 22 29
Wed.	7 14 21 28	5 12 19 26	2 9 16 23 30
Thur.	1 8 15 22 29	6 13 20 27	3 10 17 24
Fri.	2 9 16 23 30	7 14 21 28	4 11 18 25
Sat.	3 10 17 24	1 8 15 22 29	5 12 19 26

	July	August	September
Sun.	4 11 18 25	1 8 15 22 29	5 12 19 26
Mon.	5 12 19 26	2 9 16 23 30	6 13 20 27
Tue.	6 13 20 27	3 10 17 24 31	7 14 21 28
Wed.	7 14 21 28	4 11 18 25	1 8 15 22 29
Thur.	1 8 15 22 29	5 12 19 26	2 9 16 23 30
Fri.	2 9 16 23 30	6 13 20 27	3 10 17 24
Sat.	3 10 17 24 31	7 14 21 28	4 11 18 25

	October	November	December
Sun.	3 10 17 24 31	7 14 21 28	5 12 19 26
Mon.	4 11 18 25	1 8 15 22 29	6 13 20 27
Tue.	5 12 19 26	2 9 16 23 30	7 14 21 28
Wed.	6 13 20 27	3 10 17 24	1 8 15 22 29
Thur.	7 14 21 28	4 11 18 25	2 9 16 23 30
Fri.	1 8 15 22 29	5 12 19 26	3 10 17 24 31
Sat.	2 9 16 23 30	6 13 20 27	4 11 18 25

EASTER DAYS

March 28	1880, 1948, 2032
April 4	1920
April 11	1784, 1852, 2004
April 18	1824, 1976

K

	January	February	March
Sun.	3 10 17 24 31	7 14 21 28	7 14 21 28
Mon.	4 11 18 25	1 8 15 22	1 8 15 22 29
Tue.	5 12 19 26	2 9 16 23	2 9 16 23 30
Wed.	6 13 20 27	3 10 17 24	3 10 17 24 31
Thur.	7 14 21 28	4 11 18 25	4 11 18 25
Fri.	1 8 15 22 29	5 12 19 26	5 12 19 26
Sat.	2 9 16 23 30	6 13 20 27	6 13 20 27

	April	May	June
Sun.	4 11 18 25	2 9 16 23 30	6 13 20 27
Mon.	5 12 19 26	3 10 17 24 31	7 14 21 28
Tue.	6 13 20 27	4 11 18 25	1 8 15 22 29
Wed.	7 14 21 28	5 12 19 26	2 9 16 23 30
Thur.	1 8 15 22 29	6 13 20 27	3 10 17 24
Fri.	2 9 16 23 30	7 14 21 28	4 11 18 25
Sat.	3 10 17 24	1 8 15 22 29	5 12 19 26

	July	August	September
Sun.	4 11 18 25	1 8 15 22 29	5 12 19 26
Mon.	5 12 19 26	2 9 16 23 30	6 13 20 27
Tue.	6 13 20 27	3 10 17 24 31	7 14 21 28
Wed.	7 14 21 28	4 11 18 25	1 8 15 22 29
Thur.	1 8 15 22 29	5 12 19 26	2 9 16 23 30
Fri.	2 9 16 23 30	6 13 20 27	3 10 17 24
Sat.	3 10 17 24 31	7 14 21 28	4 11 18 25

	October	November	December
Sun.	3 10 17 24 31	7 14 21 28	5 12 19 26
Mon.	4 11 18 25	1 8 15 22 29	6 13 20 27
Tue.	5 12 19 26	2 9 16 23 30	7 14 21 28
Wed.	6 13 20 27	3 10 17 24	1 8 15 22 29
Thur.	7 14 21 28	4 11 18 25	2 9 16 23 30
Fri.	1 8 15 22 29	5 12 19 26	3 10 17 24 31
Sat.	2 9 16 23 30	6 13 20 27	4 11 18 25

EASTER DAYS

March 28	1869, 1875, 1937, 2027
April 4	1779, 1790, 1847, 1858, 1915, 1926, 1999, 2010, 2021
April 11	1773, 1819, 1830, 1841, 1909, 1971, 1982, 1993
April 18	1802, 1813, 1897, 1954, 1965
April 25	1886, 1943

M

	January	February	March
Sun.	2 9 16 23 30	6 13 20 27	6 13 20 27
Mon.	3 10 17 24 31	7 14 21 28	7 14 21 28
Tue.	4 11 18 25	1 8 15 22	1 8 15 22 29
Wed.	5 12 19 26	2 9 16 23	2 9 16 23 30
Thur.	6 13 20 27	3 10 17 24	3 10 17 24 31
Fri.	7 14 21 28	4 11 18 25	4 11 18 25
Sat.	1 8 15 22 29	5 12 19 26	5 12 19 26

	April	May	June
Sun.	3 10 17 24	1 8 15 22 29	5 12 19 26
Mon.	4 11 18 25	2 9 16 23 30	6 13 20 27
Tue.	5 12 19 26	3 10 17 24 31	7 14 21 28
Wed.	6 13 20 27	4 11 18 25	1 8 15 22 29
Thur.	7 14 21 28	5 12 19 26	2 9 16 23 30
Fri.	1 8 15 22 29	6 13 20 27	3 10 17 24
Sat.	2 9 16 23 30	7 14 21 28	4 11 18 25

	July	August	September
Sun.	3 10 17 24 31	7 14 21 28	4 11 18 25
Mon.	4 11 18 25	1 8 15 22 29	5 12 19 26
Tue.	5 12 19 26	2 9 16 23 30	6 13 20 27
Wed.	6 13 20 27	3 10 17 24 31	7 14 21 28
Thur.	7 14 21 28	4 11 18 25	1 8 15 22 29
Fri.	1 8 15 22 29	5 12 19 26	2 9 16 23 30
Sat.	2 9 16 23 30	6 13 20 27	3 10 17 24

	October	November	December
Sun.	2 9 16 23 30	6 13 20 27	4 11 18 25
Mon.	3 10 17 24 31	7 14 21 28	5 12 19 26
Tue.	4 11 18 25	1 8 15 22 29	6 13 20 27
Wed.	5 12 19 26	2 9 16 23 30	7 14 21 28
Thur.	6 13 20 27	3 10 17 24	1 8 15 22 29
Fri.	7 14 21 28	4 11 18 25	2 9 16 23 30
Sat.	1 8 15 22 29	5 12 19 26	3 10 17 24 31

EASTER DAYS

March 27	1785, 1842, 1853, 1910, 1921, 2005
April 3	1774, 1825, 1831, 1983, 1994
April 10	1803, 1814, 1887, 1898, 1955, 1966, 1977
April 17	1870, 1881, 1927, 1938, 1949, 2022, 2033
April 24	1791, 1859, 2011

L (LEAP YEAR)

	January	February	March
Sun.	3 10 17 24 31	7 14 21 28	6 13 20 27
Mon.	4 11 18 25	1 8 15 22 29	7 14 21 28
Tue.	5 12 19 26	2 9 16 23	1 8 15 22 29
Wed.	6 13 20 27	3 10 17 24	2 9 16 23 30
Thur.	7 14 21 28	4 11 18 25	3 10 17 24 31
Fri.	1 8 15 22 29	5 12 19 26	4 11 18 25
Sat.	2 9 16 23 30	6 13 20 27	5 12 19 26

	April	May	June
Sun.	3 10 17 24	1 8 15 22 29	5 12 19 26
Mon.	4 11 18 25	2 9 16 23 30	6 13 20 27
Tue.	5 12 19 26	3 10 17 24 31	7 14 21 28
Wed.	6 13 20 27	4 11 18 25	1 8 15 22 29
Thur.	7 14 21 28	5 12 19 26	2 9 16 23 30
Fri.	1 8 15 22 29	6 13 20 27	3 10 17 24
Sat.	2 9 16 23 30	7 14 21 28	4 11 18 25

	July	August	September
Sun.	3 10 17 24 31	7 14 21 28	4 11 18 25
Mon.	4 11 18 25	1 8 15 22 29	5 12 19 26
Tue.	5 12 19 26	2 9 16 23 30	6 13 20 27
Wed.	6 13 20 27	3 10 17 24 31	7 14 21 28
Thur.	7 14 21 28	4 11 18 25	1 8 15 22 29
Fri.	1 8 15 22 29	5 12 19 26	2 9 16 23 30
Sat.	2 9 16 23 30	6 13 20 27	3 10 17 24

	October	November	December
Sun.	2 9 16 23 30	6 13 20 27	4 11 18 25
Mon.	3 10 17 24 31	7 14 21 28	5 12 19 26
Tue.	4 11 18 25	1 8 15 22 29	6 13 20 27
Wed.	5 12 19 26	2 9 16 23 30	7 14 21 28
Thur.	6 13 20 27	3 10 17 24	1 8 15 22 29
Fri.	7 14 21 28	4 11 18 25	2 9 16 23 30
Sat.	1 8 15 22 29	5 12 19 26	3 10 17 24 31

EASTER DAYS

March 27	1796, 1864, 1932, 2016
April 3	1836, 1904, 1988
April 17	1808, 1892, 1960

N (LEAP YEAR)

	January	February	March
Sun.	2 9 16 23 30	6 13 20 27	5 12 19 26
Mon.	3 10 17 24 31	7 14 21 28	6 13 20 27
Tue.	4 11 18 25	1 8 15 22 29	7 14 21 28
Wed.	5 12 19 26	2 9 16 23	1 8 15 22 29
Thur.	6 13 20 27	3 10 17 24	2 9 16 23 30
Fri.	7 14 21 28	4 11 18 25	3 10 17 24 31
Sat.	1 8 15 22 29	5 12 19 26	4 11 18 25

	April	May	June
Sun.	2 9 16 23 30	7 14 21 28	4 11 18 25
Mon.	3 10 17 24	1 8 15 22 29	5 12 19 26
Tue.	4 11 18 25	2 9 16 23 30	6 13 20 27
Wed.	5 12 19 26	3 10 17 24 31	7 14 21 28
Thur.	6 13 20 27	4 11 18 25	1 8 15 22 29
Fri.	7 14 21 28	5 12 19 26	2 9 16 23 30
Sat.	1 8 15 22 29	6 13 20 27	3 10 17 24

	July	August	September
Sun.	2 9 16 23 30	6 13 20 27	3 10 17 24
Mon.	3 10 17 24 31	7 14 21 28	4 11 18 25
Tue.	4 11 18 25	1 8 15 22 29	5 12 19 26
Wed.	5 12 19 26	2 9 16 23 30	6 13 20 27
Thur.	6 13 20 27	3 10 17 24 31	7 14 21 28
Fri.	7 14 21 28	4 11 18 25	1 8 15 22 29
Sat.	1 8 15 22 29	5 12 19 26	2 9 16 23 30

	October	November	December
Sun.	1 8 15 22 29	5 12 19 26	3 10 17 24 31
Mon.	2 9 16 23 30	6 13 20 27	4 11 18 25
Tue.	3 10 17 24 31	7 14 21 28	5 12 19 26
Wed.	4 11 18 25	1 8 15 22 29	6 13 20 27
Thur.	5 12 19 26	2 9 16 23 30	7 14 21 28
Fri.	6 13 20 27	3 10 17 24	1 8 15 22 29
Sat.	7 14 21 28	4 11 18 25	2 9 16 23 30

EASTER DAYS

March 26	1780
April 2	1820, 1972
April 9	1944
April 16	1876, 2028
April 23	1848, 1916, 2000

GEOLOGICAL TIME

The earth is thought to have come into existence approximately 4,600 million years ago, but for nearly half this time, the Archean era, it was uninhabited. Life is generally believed to have emerged in the succeeding Proterozoic era. The Archean and the Proterozoic eras are often together referred to as the Precambrian.

Although primitive forms of life, e.g. algae and bacteria, existed during the Proterozoic era, it is not until the strata of Palaeozoic rocks is reached that abundant fossilized remains appear, initially of small shellfish, followed by plants, primitive fishes and, in the Devonian period (c.400 million BC), land-living plants and amphibia.

Since the Precambrian, there have been three great geological eras:

PALAEOZOIC ('ancient life')
c.570–c.245 million BC

Cambrian – Mainly sandstones, slate and shales; limestones in Scotland. Shelled fossils and invertebrates, e.g. trilobites and brachiopods appear
Ordovician – Mainly shales and mudstones, e.g. in north Wales; limestones in Scotland
Silurian – Shales, mudstones and some limestones, found mostly in Wales and southern Scotland
Devonian – Old red sandstone, shale, limestone and slate, e.g. in south Wales and the West Country. 'The age of fishes' – proliferation of fish fossils. First traces of land-living life
Carboniferous – Coal-bearing rocks, millstone grit, limestone and shale
Permian – Marls, sandstones and clays. First large-scale appearance of reptile fossils

There were two great phases of mountain building in the Palaeozoic era: the Caledonian, characterized in Britain by NE–SW lines of hills and valleys; and the later Hercyian, widespread in west Germany and adjacent areas, and in Britain exemplified in E.–W. lines of hills and valleys.

The end of the Palaeozoic era was marked by the extensive glaciations of the Permian period in the southern continents and the decline of amphibians. It was succeeded by an era of warm conditions.

MESOZOIC ('middle forms of life')
c.245–c.65 million BC

Triassic – Mostly sandstone, e.g. in the West Midlands
Jurassic – Mainly limestones and clays, typically displayed in the Jura mountains, and in England in a NE–SW belt from Lincolnshire and the Wash to the Severn and the Dorset coast
Cretaceous – Mainly chalk, clay and sands, e.g. in Kent and Sussex

Giant reptiles were dominant during the Mesozoic era, but it was at this time that marsupial mammals first appeared, as well as *Archaeopteryx lithographica*, the earliest known species of bird. Coniferous trees and flowering plants also developed during the era and, with the birds and the mammals, were the main species to survive into the Cenozoic era. The giant reptiles became extinct.

CENOZOIC ('recent life')
from c.65 million BC

Palaeocene ⎫ The emergence of new forms of life, i.e.
Eocene   ⎭ existing species
Oligocene – Fossils of a few still existing species

Miocene – Fossil remains show a balance of existing and extinct species
Pliocene – Fossil remains show a majority of still existing species
Pleistocene – The majority of remains are those of still existing species
Holocene – The present, post-glacial period. Existing species only, except for a few exterminated by man

In the last 25 million years, from the Miocene through the Pliocene periods, the Alpine-Himalayan and the circum-Pacific phases of mountain building reached their climax. During the Pleistocene period ice-sheets repeatedly locked up masses of water as land ice; its weight depressed the land, and the locking-up of the water lowered the sea-level by 100–200 metres. The glaciations and interglacials of the Ice Age are difficult to date and classify, but recent scientific opinion considers the Pleistocene period to have begun approximately 1.64 million years ago. The last glacial retreat, merging into the Holocene period, was 10,000 years ago.

HUMAN DEVELOPMENT

Any consideration of the history of mankind must start with the fact that all members of the human race belong to one species of animal, i.e. *Homo sapiens*, the definition of a species being in biological terms that all its members can interbreed. As a species of mammal it is possible to group man with other similar types, known as the primates. Amongst these is found a sub-group, the apes, which includes, in addition to man, the chimpanzees, gorillas, orang-utans and gibbons. All lack a tail, have shoulder blades at the back, and a Y-shaped chewing pattern on the surface of their molars, as well as showing the more general primate characteristics of four incisors, a thumb which is able to touch the fingers of the same hand, and finger and toe nails instead of claws. The factors available to scientific study suggest that human beings have chimpanzees and gorillas as their nearest relatives in the animal world. However, there remains the possibility that there once lived creatures, now extinct, which were closer to modern man than the chimpanzees and gorillas, and which shared with modern man the characteristics of having flat faces (i.e. the absence of a pronounced muzzle), being bipedal, and possessing large brains.

There are two broad groups of extinct apes recognized by specialists. The ramapithecines, the remains of which, mainly jaw fragments, have been found in east Africa, Asia, and Turkey. They lived about 14 to 8 million years ago, and from the evidence of their teeth it seems they chewed more in the manner of modern man than the other presently living apes. The second group, the australo-pithecines, have left more numerous remains amongst which sub-groups may be detected, although the geographic spread is limited to south and east Africa. Living between 5 and 1.5 million years ago, they were closer relatives of modern man to the extent that they walked upright, did not have an extensive muzzle and had similar types of pre-molars. The first australopithecine remains were recognized at Taung in South Africa in 1924 and subsequent discoveries include those at the famous site of Olduvai Gorge in Tanzania. The most impressive discovery was made at Hadar in Ethiopia in 1974 when about half a skeleton, known as 'Lucy', was found.

Also in east Africa, between 2 million and 1.5 million years ago, lived a hominid group which not only walked upright, had a flat face, and a large brain case, but also made simple pebble and flake stone tools. On present evidence these habilines seem to have been the first people to make tools, however crude. This facility is related to the larger brain size and human beings are the only animals to make implements to be used in other processes. These early pebble tool users, because of their distinctive characteristics, have been grouped as a separate sub-species, now extinct, of the genus *Homo* and are known as *Homo habilis*.

The use of fire, again a human characteristic, is associated with another group of extinct hominids whose remains, about a million years old, are found in south and east Africa, China, Indonesia, north Africa and Europe. Mastery of the techniques of making fire probably helped the colonization of the colder northern areas and in this respect the site of Vertesszollos in Hungary is of particular importance. *Homo erectus* is the name given to this group of fossils and it includes a number of famous individual discoveries, e.g. Solo Man, Heidelberg Man, and especially Peking Man who lived at the cave site at Choukoutien which has yielded evidence of fire and burnt bone.

The well-known group Neanderthal Man, or *Homo sapiens neandertalensis*, is an extinct form of modern man who lived between about 100,000 and 40,000 years ago, thus spanning the last Ice Age. Indeed, its ability to adapt to the cold climate on the edge of the ice-sheets is one of its characteristic features, the remains being found only in Europe, Asia and the Middle East. Complete neanderthal skeletons were found during excavations at Tabun in Israel, together with evidence of tool-making and the use of fire. Distinguished by very large brains, it seems that neanderthal man was the first to develop recognizable social customs, especially deliberate burial rites. Why the neanderthalers became extinct is not clear but it may be connected with the climatic changes at the end of the Ice Ages, which would have seriously affected their food supplies; possibly they became too specialized for their own good.

The Swanscombe skull is the only known human fossil remains found in England. Some specialists see Swanscombe Man (or, more probably, woman) as a neanderthaler. Others group these remains together with the Steinheim skull from Germany, seeing both as a separate sub-species. There is too little evidence as yet on which to form a final judgement.

Modern Man, *Homo sapiens sapiens*, the surviving sub-species of *Homo sapiens*, had evolved to our present physical condition and had colonized much of the world by about 30,000 years ago. There are many previously distinguished individual specimens, e.g. Cromagnon Man, which may now be grouped together as *Homo sapiens sapiens*. It was modern man who spread to the American continent by crossing the landbridge between Siberia and Alaska and thence moved south through North America and into South America. Equally it is modern man who over the last 30,000 years has been responsible for the major developments in technology, art and civilization generally.

One of the problems for those studying fossil man is the lack in many cases of sufficient quantities of fossil bone for analysis. It is important that theories should be tested against evidence, rather than the evidence being made to fit the theory. The Piltdown hoax is a well-known example of 'fossils' being forged to fit what was seen in some quarters as the correct theory of man's evolution.

CULTURAL DEVELOPMENT

The Eurocentric bias of early archaeologists meant that the search for a starting point for the development and transmission of cultural ideas, especially by migration, trade and warfare, concentrated unduly on Europe and the Near East. The Three Age system, whereby pre-history was divided into a Stone Age, a Bronze Age and an Iron Age, was devised by Christian Thomsen, curator of the National Museum of Denmark in the early nineteenth century, to facilitate the classification of the museum's collections. The descriptive adjectives referred to the materials from which the implements and weapons were made and came to be regarded as the dominant features of the societies to which they related. The refinement of the Three Age system once dominated archaeological thought and remains a generally accepted concept in the popular mind. However, it is now seen by archaeologists as an inadequate model for human development.

Common sense suggests that there were no complete breaks between one so-called Age and another, any more than contemporaries would have regarded 1485 as a complete break between medieval and modern English history. Nor can the Three Age system be applied universally. In some areas it is necessary to insert a Copper Age, while in Africa south of the Sahara there would seem to be no Bronze Age at all; in Australia, Old Stone Age societies survived, while in South America, New Stone Age communities existed into modern times. The civilizations in other parts of the world clearly invalidate a Eurocentric theory of human development.

The concept of the 'Neolithic revolution', associated with the domestication of plants and animals, was a development of particular importance in the human cultural pattern. It reflected change from the primitive hunter/gatherer economies to a more settled agricultural way of life and therefore, so the argument goes, made possible the development of urban civilization. However, it can no longer be argued that this 'revolution' took place only in one area from which all development stemmed. Though it appears that the cultivation of wheat and barley was first undertaken, together with the domestication of cattle and goats/sheep in the Fertile Crescent, there is evidence that rice was first deliberately planted and pigs domesticated in south-east Asia, maize first cultivated in Central America and llamas first domesticated in South America. It has been recognized increasingly in recent years that cultural changes can take place independently of each other in different parts of the world at different rates and different times. There is no need for a general diffusionist theory.

Although scholars will continue to study the particular societies which interest them, it may be possible to obtain a reliable chronological framework, in absolute terms of years, against which the cultural development of any particular area may be set. The development and refinement of radio-carbon dating and other scientific methods of producing absolute chronologies is enabling the cross-referencing of societies to be undertaken. As the techniques of dating become more rigorous in application and the number of scientifically obtained dates increases, the attainment of an absolute chronology for prehistoric societies throughout the world comes closer to being achieved.

Tidal Tables

CONSTANTS

The constant tidal difference may be used in conjunction with the time of high water at a standard port shown in the predictions data (pages 98–109) to find the time of high water at any of the ports or places listed below.

EXAMPLE

Required time of high water at Stranraer at 2 January 1996
Appropriate time of high water at *Greenock*

Morning tide 2 January	0903 hrs
Tidal difference	−0020 hrs
High water at *Stranraer*	0843 hrs

The columns headed 'Springs' and 'Neaps' show the height, in metres, of the tide above datum for mean high water springs and mean high water neaps respectively.

* data very approximate
† data for first high water springs only
H. Harbour

Port	Diff.		Springs	Neaps
	h	m	m	m
Aberdeen	Leith	−1 19	4.3	3.4
Aberdovey	Liverpool	−3 01	5.0	3.5
Aberystwyth	Liverpool	−3 31	5.0	3.5
Aldeburgh	London	−3 05	2.8	2.7
Alloa	Leith	+0 49	5.6	4.2
Amlwch	Liverpool	−0 35	7.2	5.7
Anstruther Easter	Leith	−0 22	5.5	4.4
Antwerp (Prosperpolder)	London	+0 50	5.8	4.8
Appledore	Avonmouth	−1 16	7.5	5.2
Arbroath	Leith	−0 33	5.4	4.3
Ardrossan	Greenock	−0 15	3.2	2.6
*Arundel	London	−2 04	3.2	2.1
Avonmouth	Avonmouth	0 00	13.2	9.8
Ayr	Greenock	−0 25	3.0	2.5
Baie de Lampaul	London	+2 30	7.4	5.8
Ballycotton	Avonmouth	−1 47	4.2	3.2
Banff	Leith	−2 44	3.5	2.8
Bantry	Liverpool	+5 55	3.3	2.4
Bardsey Island	Liverpool	−3 20	4.4	3.2
Barmouth	Liverpool	−2 58	5.0	3.5
Barnstaple	Avonmouth	−1 01	4.1	1.4
Barrow (Docks)	Liverpool	0 00	9.3	7.1
Barry	Avonmouth	−0 22	11.4	8.5
Belfast	London	−2 47	3.5	3.0
Berwick	Leith	−0 03	4.7	3.8
Bideford	Avonmouth	−1 16	5.9	3.6
Blackpool	Liverpool	−0 10	8.9	7.0
Blacktoft	Hull	+0 31	5.7	4.0
Blakeney	Hull	+0 46	3.4	2.0
Blyth	Leith	+0 51	5.0	3.9
Boscastle	Avonmouth	−1 21	7.3	5.6
Boulogne	London	−2 44	8.9	7.2
Bovisand Pier	London	+3 55	5.3	4.3
Bowling	Greenock	+0 15	4.0	3.3
Braye (Alderney)	London	+5 33	6.2	4.7
Brest	London	+2 28	7.5	5.9
Bridgwater	Avonmouth	−0 22	4.6	1.7
Bridlington	Leith	+2 04	6.1	4.7
Bridport (W. Bay)	London	+4 37	4.1	3.0
Brighton	London	−2 51	6.6	5.0
Buckie	Leith	−2 56	4.1	3.2
Bude	Avonmouth	−1 34	7.7	5.8
Bull Sand Fort	Hull	−0 44	6.9	5.5
Burntisland	Leith	0 00	5.6	4.5
Calais	London	−2 04	7.2	5.9
Campbeltown	Greenock	+0 07	2.9	2.5
Cape Cornwall	Avonmouth	−2 31	6.0	4.3
Cardiff	Avonmouth	−0 15	12.2	9.2
Cardigan Port	Liverpool	−3 38	4.7	3.4
Carmarthen	Avonmouth	−0 49	2.6	0.4
Cayeux	London	−2 55	10.2	7.9
Chatham	London	−1 08	6.1	4.8
Chepstow	Avonmouth	+0 20	no data	
Cherbourg	London	−6 00	6.4	5.0
Chester	Liverpool	+1 05	4.0	1.7
Chichester H. (Entrance)	London	−2 40	4.9	4.0
†Christchurch H.	London	−5 08	1.8	1.4
Cobh	Liverpool	−5 55	4.2	3.2
Coulport	Greenock	−0 05	3.4	2.8
Coverack	Avonmouth	−2 02	5.3	4.2
Cowes	London	−2 38	4.2	3.5
Cromarty	Leith	−2 56	4.3	3.4
Cromer	Hull	+0 15	5.2	4.1
Dartmouth	London	+4 25	4.9	3.8
Deal	London	−2 37	6.1	5.0
Dieppe	London	−3 03	9.3	7.3
Dingle H.	Liverpool	+5 34	4.1	3.2
Donegal H.	Liverpool	−5 24	3.9	3.0
Douglas (IOM)	Liverpool	−0 04	6.9	5.4
Dover	London	−2 52	6.7	5.3
Duclair	London	−1 48	7.5	6.3
Duddon Bar	Liverpool	+0 03	8.5	6.6
Dunbar	Leith	−0 07	5.2	4.2
Dundalk (Sldr's Pt)	Liverpool	+0 21	5.1	4.2
Dundee	Leith	+0 11	5.4	4.3
Dungeness	London	−3 04	7.7	5.9
Dunkirk	London	−1 54	6.0	4.9
Eastbourne	London	−2 51	7.4	5.5
East Loch Tarbert	Greenock	+0 05	3.4	2.8
Exmouth Dock	London	+4 55	4.0	2.8
Eyemouth	Leith	−0 20	4.7	3.7
Falmouth	London	+3 35	5.3	4.2
Ferryside	Avonmouth	−0 59	6.7	4.5
Filey Bay	Leith	+1 51	5.8	4.9
Fishguard	Liverpool	−4 01	4.8	3.4
Folkestone	London	−3 04	7.1	5.7
Formby	Liverpool	−0 12	9.0	7.3
Fowey	London	+3 53	5.4	4.3
Fraserburgh	Leith	−2 29	3.7	2.9
†Freshwater	London	−4 48	2.6	2.3
Galway	Liverpool	−6 08	5.1	3.9
Glasgow	Greenock	+0 26	4.7	4.0
Goole	Hull	+1 00	5.7	3.7
Gorleston-on-Sea	London	−5 00	2.4	2.0
Granton	Leith	0 00	5.6	4.5
Granville	London	+4 32	13.0	9.8
Grimsby	Hull	−0 27	7.0	5.6
Hartlepool	Leith	+0 57	5.4	4.2
Harwich	London	−2 06	4.0	3.4
Hastings	London	−2 57	7.5	5.8
Haverfordwest	Liverpool	−4 51	2.2	0.3

Port	Diff. (h m)	Springs (m)	Neaps (m)
Hestan Islet	Liverpool +0 25	8.3	6.3
Holyhead	Liverpool −0 50	5.6	4.4
Hook of Holland	London −0 01	2.1	1.7
†Hurst Point	London −3 53	2.7	2.3
Ijmuiden	London +1 03	2.1	1.7
Ilfracombe	Avonmouth −1 12	9.2	6.9
Inveraray	Greenock +0 11	3.3	2.9
Invergordon	Leith −2 48	4.4	3.5
Ipswich	London −1 46	4.2	3.4
Itchenor	London −2 38	4.8	3.8
Kinsale	Liverpool −6 07	4.0	3.2
Kirkcudbright	Liverpool +0 15	7.5	5.9
Kirkwall	Leith −4 15	3.0	2.4
Knights Town	Liverpool +5 32	3.6	2.8
Lamlash	Greenock −0 26	3.2	2.6
Le Havre	London −3 55	7.9	6.6
Lerwick	Leith −3 48	2.2	1.6
Limerick Dock	Liverpool −4 27	6.1	4.6
Littlehampton (Entrance)	London −2 39	5.9	4.5
Lizard Point	Avonmouth −2 17	5.3	4.2
Llanddwyn Island	Liverpool −1 55	4.9	3.9
Llanelli	Avonmouth −0 57	7.8	5.8
Loch Moidart	Greenock +5 58	4.8	3.5
Londonderry	London −5 37	2.7	2.1
Looe	London +3 55	5.4	4.2
Lossiemouth	Leith −3 01	4.1	3.2
Lowestoft	London −4 25	2.4	2.1
Lulworth Cove	London +4 59	2.2	1.5
Lundy Island	Avonmouth −1 24	8.0	5.9
Lyme Regis	London +4 55	4.3	3.1
†Lymington	London −3 48	3.0	2.6
Margate	London −1 53	4.8	3.9
Maryport	Liverpool +0 24	8.6	6.6
Menai Bridge	Liverpool −0 30	7.3	5.8
Mevagissey	London +3 53	5.4	4.3
Middlesbrough	Leith +1 08	5.6	4.5
Milford Haven	Liverpool −5 08	7.0	5.2
Minehead	Avonmouth −0 40	10.6	7.9
Montrose	Leith −0 19	4.8	3.9
Morecambe	Liverpool +0 07	9.5	7.4
Mostyn Quay	Liverpool −0 17	8.5	6.4
Newburgh	Leith +0 48	4.1	3.0
Newcastle upon Tyne	Leith +0 53	5.3	4.1
Newhaven	London −2 46	6.7	5.1
Newlyn (Penzance)	Avonmouth −2 25	5.6	4.4
Newport (Gwent)	Avonmouth −0 15	12.1	8.8
Newquay	Avonmouth −1 59	7.0	5.3
New Quay, Cardigan Bay	Liverpool −3 31	4.9	3.4
North Shields	Leith +0 50	5.0	3.9
North Sunderland	Leith +0 04	4.8	3.7
Oban	Greenock +5 43	4.0	2.9
Old Lynn Road	Hull +0 07	7.3	5.8
Orford Ness	London −2 50	2.8	2.7
Ostend	London −1 32	5.1	4.2
Padstow	Avonmouth −1 46	7.3	5.6
Peel (IOM)	Liverpool −0 02	5.3	4.2
Peterhead	Leith −1 59	3.8	3.1
Plymouth	London +4 05	5.5	4.4
†Poole H. (Entrance)	London −5 18	2.0	1.6
Porlock Bay	Avonmouth −0 50	10.2	7.6
Porthcawl	Avonmouth −0 54	9.9	7.5
Portmadoc	Liverpool −2 46	5.1	3.4
Portland	London +5 09	2.1	1.4
Portpatrick	Liverpool +0 22	3.8	3.0
Portsmouth	London −2 38	4.7	3.8
Port Talbot	Avonmouth −0 54	9.6	7.3
Preston	Liverpool +0 10	5.3	3.3
Pwllheli	Liverpool −3 08	5.0	3.4
Ramsey (IOM)	Liverpool +0 10	7.6	5.9
Ramsgate	London −2 32	5.2	4.1
*Rosslare H.	Liverpool −5 24	1.9	1.4
Rosyth	Leith +0 09	5.8	4.7
Ryde	London −2 38	4.5	3.7
St Helier	London +4 48	11.0	8.1
St Ives	Avonmouth −1 56	6.6	4.9
St Malo	London +4 27	12.2	9.2
St Peter Port	London +4 54	9.3	7.0
Salcombe	London +4 10	5.3	4.1
Saltash	London +4 10	5.6	4.5
Scarborough	Leith +1 33	5.7	4.6
Scheveningen	London +1 02	2.2	1.8
Scrabster	Leith −6 06	5.0	4.0
Seaham	Leith +0 54	5.2	4.1
Selsey Bill	London −2 43	5.3	4.4
Sennen Cove	Avonmouth −2 31	6.1	4.8
Sharpness Dock	Avonmouth +0 42	9.3	5.6
Sheerness	London −1 19	5.8	4.7
Shoreham	London −2 44	6.3	4.9
Silloth	Liverpool +0 35	9.2	7.1
Southampton (1st high water)	London −2 54	4.5	3.7
Southend	London −1 23	5.8	4.7
Southwold	London −3 50	2.4	2.1
Stirling	Leith +1 15	2.9	1.6
Stonehaven	Leith −1 09	4.5	3.6
Stornoway	Liverpool −4 16	4.8	3.7
Stranraer	Greenock −0 20	3.0	2.4
Stromness	Leith −5 26	3.6	2.7
Sunderland	Leith +0 49	5.2	4.2
†Swanage	London −5 28	2.0	1.6
Swansea	Avonmouth −0 51	9.5	7.2
Tarn Point	Liverpool +0 05	8.3	6.4
Tay River (Bar)	Leith −0 19	5.2	4.2
Tees River (Entrance)	Leith +1 09	5.5	4.3
Teignmouth (Approaches)	London +4 37	4.8	3.6
Tenby	Avonmouth −1 06	8.4	6.3
Tilbury	London −0 49	6.4	5.4
Tobermory	Liverpool −5 11	4.4	3.3
Torquay	London +4 40	4.9	3.7
†Totland Bay	London −4 08	2.7	2.3
Troon	Greenock −0 25	3.2	2.6
Truro	London +3 43	3.5	2.4
Walton-on-Naze	London −2 10	4.2	3.4
Waterford	Liverpool −4 58	4.6	3.5
Weston-s.-Mare	Avonmouth −0 25	12.0	8.8
*Wexford H.	Liverpool −5 04	1.7	1.4
Whitby	Leith +1 23	5.6	4.3
Whitehaven	Liverpool +0 10	8.0	6.3
Wick	Leith −3 26	3.5	2.8
Wisbech Cut	Hull +0 03	7.0	5.1
Woolwich	London −0 20	7.0	5.9
Workington	Liverpool +0 21	8.1	6.3
Worthing	London −2 39	6.2	4.7
†Yarmouth (IOW)	London −3 43	3.1	2.5
Youghal	Liverpool −5 50	4.0	3.1

JANUARY 1996   *High water*   GMT

		LONDON BRIDGE *Datum of predictions 3.20 m below				AVONMOUTH *Datum of predictions 6.50 m below				LIVERPOOL *Datum of predictions 4.93 m below				HULL (*Albert Dock*) *Datum of predictions 3.90 m below			
		hr	m	hr	m	hr	m	hr	m	hr	m	hr	m	hr	m	hr	m
1	Monday	10 13	6.3	22 45	6.5	03 20	10.6	15 54	10.9	07 53	7.8	20 18	8.0	02 21	6.4	15 05	6.4
2	Tuesday	11 14	6.5	23 42	6.6	04 20	11.0	16 50	11.4	08 50	8.1	21 12	8.3	03 23	6.5	15 58	6.6
3	Wednesday	—	—	12 09	6.7	05 13	11.7	17 40	11.9	09 37	8.5	21 59	8.5	04 18	6.6	16 44	6.8
4	Thursday	00 33	6.7	12 57	6.7	06 00	12.2	18 25	12.3	10 19	8.8	22 39	8.7	05 07	6.7	17 26	7.0
5	Friday	01 17	6.6	13 39	6.6	06 42	12.6	19 06	12.5	10 56	9.0	23 16	8.9	05 50	6.8	18 03	7.1
6	Saturday	01 53	6.6	14 17	6.6	07 22	12.8	19 45	12.5	11 30	9.1	23 50	8.9	06 29	6.8	18 37	7.1
7	Sunday	02 26	6.6	14 52	6.6	07 59	12.7	20 21	12.4	—	—	12 04	9.1	07 05	6.9	19 10	7.2
8	Monday	02 57	6.6	15 26	6.7	08 34	12.5	20 55	12.2	00 23	8.9	12 39	9.1	07 39	6.9	19 42	7.2
9	Tuesday	03 31	6.7	16 01	6.7	09 06	12.3	21 25	12.0	00 58	8.8	13 13	9.0	08 13	6.9	20 14	7.2
10	Wednesday	04 06	6.6	16 37	6.7	09 35	12.1	21 54	11.9	01 32	8.8	13 48	8.9	08 47	6.9	20 48	7.1
11	Thursday	04 40	6.6	17 14	6.7	10 05	12.0	22 27	11.8	02 08	8.7	14 26	8.8	09 24	6.8	21 26	7.0
12	Friday	05 16	6.5	17 54	6.6	10 42	11.8	23 06	11.5	02 47	8.5	15 07	8.6	10 04	6.7	22 09	6.9
13	Saturday	05 56	6.4	18 39	6.5	11 26	11.5	23 53	11.1	03 31	8.2	15 55	8.3	10 50	6.5	22 58	6.6
14	Sunday	06 44	6.3	19 32	6.3	—	—	12 20	11.1	04 26	7.9	16 53	8.1	11 43	6.3	23 55	6.4
15	Monday	07 46	6.2	20 37	6.2	00 52	10.7	13 27	10.7	05 32	7.8	18 01	7.9	—	—	12 50	6.2
16	Tuesday	09 01	6.1	21 50	6.3	02 07	10.6	14 51	10.8	06 45	7.9	19 12	7.9	01 06	6.3	14 11	6.3
17	Wednesday	10 20	6.2	23 02	6.5	03 35	11.0	16 14	11.4	07 56	8.3	20 23	8.5	02 35	6.4	15 20	6.6
18	Thursday	11 32	6.5	—	—	04 50	11.9	17 21	12.3	09 00	8.9	21 27	9.0	03 51	6.7	16 18	7.1
19	Friday	00 05	6.8	12 34	6.9	05 50	12.9	18 18	13.2	09 55	9.5	22 22	9.5	04 52	7.1	17 10	7.5
20	Saturday	01 01	7.0	13 28	7.2	06 43	13.7	19 10	13.8	10 47	9.9	23 14	9.8	05 46	7.5	17 57	7.9
21	Sunday	01 51	7.2	14 20	7.4	07 33	14.3	20 00	14.2	11 36	10.2	—	—	06 36	7.7	18 43	8.1
22	Monday	02 40	7.3	15 09	7.5	08 21	14.6	20 47	14.3	00 02	10.0	12 24	10.3	07 23	7.9	19 28	8.2
23	Tuesday	03 26	7.4	15 57	7.6	09 07	14.5	21 30	14.1	00 50	9.9	13 11	10.3	08 08	7.8	20 13	8.2
24	Wednesday	04 10	7.3	16 41	7.5	09 50	14.2	22 10	13.6	01 36	9.8	13 56	10.0	08 52	7.6	20 57	8.0
25	Thursday	04 51	7.2	17 23	7.2	10 30	13.5	22 47	12.9	02 19	9.4	14 41	9.6	09 34	7.3	21 42	7.7
26	Friday	05 29	7.0	18 04	6.9	11 07	12.7	23 23	12.1	03 03	8.9	15 25	9.0	10 18	6.9	22 28	7.2
27	Saturday	06 07	6.8	18 46	6.6	11 46	11.7	—	—	03 48	8.4	16 13	8.4	11 06	6.5	23 20	6.7
28	Sunday	06 52	6.4	19 37	6.2	00 03	11.1	12 36	10.7	04 40	7.8	17 11	7.8	—	—	12 04	6.1
29	Monday	07 59	6.0	20 52	6.0	00 58	10.3	13 52	10.1	05 49	7.4	18 27	7.4	00 25	6.2	13 18	5.9
30	Tuesday	09 35	5.9	22 09	5.9	02 26	10.0	15 15	10.1	07 12	7.3	19 46	7.5	01 44	5.9	14 27	5.9
31	Wednesday	10 47	6.0	23 12	6.1	03 44	10.3	16 20	10.6	08 22	7.7	20 48	7.8	02 54	5.9	15 26	6.1

FEBRUARY 1996   *High water*   GMT

		LONDON BRIDGE				AVONMOUTH				LIVERPOOL				HULL (*Albert Dock*)			
		hr	m	hr	m	hr	m	hr	m	hr	m	hr	m	hr	m	hr	m
1	Thursday	11 46	6.2	—	—	04 44	11.0	17 15	11.2	09 15	8.1	21 38	8.2	03 54	6.0	16 17	6.4
2	Friday	00 07	6.3	12 36	6.4	05 36	11.7	18 02	11.9	09 59	8.6	22 21	8.6	04 45	6.2	17 01	6.6
3	Saturday	00 54	6.4	13 20	6.5	06 20	12.3	18 44	12.3	10 38	8.9	22 58	8.8	05 29	6.5	17 40	6.9
4	Sunday	01 33	6.5	13 57	6.5	07 01	12.7	19 24	12.5	11 14	9.1	23 33	8.9	06 07	6.7	18 15	7.0
5	Monday	02 07	6.5	14 32	6.6	07 39	12.8	20 01	12.6	11 47	9.2	—	—	06 43	6.8	18 48	7.2
6	Tuesday	02 41	6.7	15 06	6.8	08 15	12.7	20 36	12.5	00 06	9.0	12 20	9.2	07 17	7.0	19 21	7.2
7	Wednesday	03 15	6.7	15 42	8.9	08 48	12.7	21 07	12.5	00 39	9.0	12 53	9.2	07 51	7.1	19 54	7.3
8	Thursday	03 50	6.8	16 18	6.9	09 18	12.6	21 36	12.4	01 11	9.0	13 27	9.2	08 25	7.1	20 29	7.3
9	Friday	04 23	6.8	16 54	6.8	09 48	12.6	22 07	12.4	01 45	9.0	14 03	9.1	09 01	7.1	21 06	7.2
10	Saturday	04 57	6.7	17 31	6.7	10 23	12.4	22 44	12.1	02 21	8.8	14 41	8.9	09 39	6.9	21 48	7.1
11	Sunday	05 35	6.6	18 13	6.5	11 04	12.0	23 27	11.7	03 02	8.6	15 26	8.6	10 21	6.7	22 34	6.8
12	Monday	06 20	6.4	19 02	6.3	11 52	11.4	—	—	03 51	8.2	16 21	8.2	11 10	6.5	23 28	6.5
13	Tuesday	07 16	6.2	20 01	6.1	00 20	11.0	12 54	10.8	04 55	7.8	17 30	7.8	—	—	12 09	6.2
14	Wednesday	08 29	5.9	21 18	6.0	01 31	10.5	14 19	10.4	06 13	7.7	18 48	7.8	00 35	6.2	13 31	6.1
15	Thursday	09 57	6.0	22 40	6.2	03 08	10.5	15 55	10.9	07 34	8.0	20 09	8.1	02 13	6.2	14 53	6.4
16	Friday	11 18	6.3	23 48	6.5	04 33	11.4	17 09	11.9	08 45	8.6	21 17	8.8	03 38	6.5	15 57	6.8
17	Saturday	—	—	12 22	6.8	05 38	12.6	18 07	13.0	09 43	9.3	22 12	9.4	04 42	6.9	16 51	7.3
18	Sunday	00 45	6.8	13 16	7.1	06 31	13.6	18 57	13.8	10 34	9.9	23 01	9.8	05 37	7.3	17 41	7.7
19	Monday	01 36	7.1	14 05	7.3	07 19	14.3	19 44	14.3	11 21	10.2	23 47	10.0	06 25	7.6	18 26	8.1
20	Tuesday	02 22	7.3	14 52	7.5	08 05	14.7	20 28	14.4	—	—	12 06	10.4	07 08	7.8	19 11	8.2
21	Wednesday	03 06	7.4	15 36	7.6	08 48	14.6	21 09	14.3	00 30	10.0	12 50	10.3	07 49	7.8	19 53	8.2
22	Thursday	03 48	7.4	16 17	7.5	09 28	14.3	21 45	13.8	01 12	9.8	13 32	10.0	08 28	7.6	20 35	8.0
23	Friday	04 26	7.4	16 55	7.3	10 03	13.6	22 18	13.1	01 51	9.5	14 12	9.6	09 05	7.3	21 16	7.7
24	Saturday	05 03	7.2	17 30	7.0	10 35	12.8	22 47	12.3	02 30	9.0	14 52	9.0	09 41	6.9	21 57	7.1
25	Sunday	05 38	6.9	18 05	6.7	11 07	11.8	23 20	11.4	03 08	8.5	15 33	8.4	10 19	6.5	22 40	6.6
26	Monday	06 16	6.5	18 44	6.3	11 45	10.7	—	—	03 51	7.9	16 21	7.7	11 01	6.1	23 30	6.0
27	Tuesday	07 05	6.0	19 35	5.8	00 02	10.4	12 42	9.8	04 47	7.4	17 29	7.1	11 58	5.7	—	—
28	Wednesday	08 19	5.6	21 01	5.5	01 14	9.6	14 22	9.4	06 14	7.1	19 06	7.0	00 51	5.5	13 41	5.6
29	Thursday	10 14	5.6	22 35	5.6	03 00	9.7	15 47	9.9	07 46	7.3	20 20	7.4	02 21	5.4	14 51	5.7

JANUARY 1996   *continued*

		GREENOCK *Datum of predictions 1.62 m below			LEITH *Datum of predictions 2.90 m below			DUN LAOGHAIRE †Datum of predictions 0.20 m above		
			ht		ht		ht		ht		ht
		hr	m	hr	m	hr	m	hr	m	hr	m
1	Monday	09 03	3.1	21 48	3.1	11 19	4.7	23 43	4.8	08 30	3.7	20 47	3.6
2	Tuesday	10 09	3.2	22 46	3.2	—	—	12 15	4.9	09 25	3.8	21 41	3.7
3	Wednesday	10 59	3.3	23 34	3.2	00 36	4.8	13 05	5.0	10 10	3.9	22 26	3.7
4	Thursday	11 41	3.4	—	—	01 25	5.0	13 48	5.2	10 47	3.9	23 03	3.7
5	Friday	05 32	0.7	17 50	0.6	02 06	5.1	14 25	5.3	11 21	4.0	23 34	3.7
6	Saturday	06 07	0.6	18 22	0.6	02 43	5.1	14 58	5.4	11 51	4.0	—	—
7	Sunday	06 40	0.6	18 52	0.5	03 17	5.2	15 31	5.4	00 05	3.8	12 22	4.0
8	Monday	07 13	0.6	19 24	0.5	03 51	5.2	16 04	5.4	00 38	3.8	12 54	4.0
9	Tuesday	07 48	0.6	19 59	0.5	04 28	5.2	16 41	5.3	01 12	3.8	13 30	4.0
10	Wednesday	08 26	0.6	20 37	0.5	05 07	5.1	17 20	5.2	01 50	3.8	14 09	3.9
11	Thursday	09 06	0.7	21 19	0.5	05 48	5.1	18 02	5.1	02 33	3.7	14 53	3.9
12	Friday	09 51	0.7	22 07	0.5	06 32	5.0	18 46	4.9	03 18	3.7	15 39	3.8
13	Saturday	10 41	0.8	23 01	0.6	07 17	4.8	19 34	4.8	04 09	3.6	16 30	3.7
14	Sunday	11 39	0.9	—	—	08 07	4.7	20 28	4.7	05 06	3.5	17 27	3.6
15	Monday	00 01	0.7	12 44	1.0	09 04	4.7	21 32	4.7	06 10	3.5	18 34	3.6
16	Tuesday	08 05	2.9	20 16	3.0	10 12	4.7	22 45	4.8	07 19	3.6	19 46	3.6
17	Wednesday	09 31	3.0	21 41	3.1	11 22	4.9	23 55	5.0	08 23	3.7	20 52	3.8
18	Thursday	10 36	3.2	22 49	3.2	—	—	12 26	5.2	09 20	3.9	21 50	3.9
19	Friday	11 29	3.4	23 46	3.4	00 57	5.4	13 24	5.5	10 11	4.2	22 42	4.1
20	Saturday	—	—	12 17	3.6	01 53	5.6	14 15	5.8	10 58	4.3	23 29	4.2
21	Sunday	00 39	3.5	13 03	3.8	02 44	5.8	15 04	6.0	11 43	4.4	—	—
22	Monday	01 30	3.5	13 48	3.9	03 32	5.9	15 50	6.0	00 16	4.2	12 30	4.5
23	Tuesday	02 18	3.5	14 32	3.9	04 20	5.8	16 36	5.9	01 04	4.1	13 16	4.4
24	Wednesday	03 01	3.5	15 14	3.9	05 08	5.7	17 25	5.7	01 52	4.0	14 05	4.3
25	Thursday	03 42	3.5	15 55	3.8	05 58	5.4	18 15	5.5	02 43	3.9	14 57	4.1
26	Friday	04 23	3.4	16 38	3.7	06 48	5.1	19 07	5.2	03 37	3.7	15 52	3.9
27	Saturday	05 05	3.3	17 23	3.4	07 41	4.8	20 03	4.8	04 36	3.6	16 53	3.7
28	Sunday	05 50	3.2	18 12	3.2	08 37	4.6	21 04	4.6	05 39	3.5	18 00	3.5
29	Monday	06 40	3.0	19 12	2.9	09 37	4.4	22 09	4.4	06 46	3.4	19 09	3.4
30	Tuesday	07 43	2.9	21 12	2.8	10 41	4.4	23 13	4.4	07 49	3.5	20 14	3.4
31	Wednesday	09 27	3.0	22 28	2.9	11 42	4.6	—	—	08 49	3.6	21 15	3.5

NOTES:
*Difference of height in metres from Ordnance datum (Newlyn)
†Difference of height in metres from Ordnance datum (Dublin)
hr hour
m metres

FEBRUARY 1996   *continued*

		GREENOCK				LEITH				DUN LAOGHAIRE			
1	Thursday	10 34	3.1	23 18	3.0	00 11	4.6	12 37	4.8	09 41	3.7	22 04	3.5
2	Friday	11 21	3.3	—	—	01 02	4.7	13 24	5.0	10 23	3.8	22 42	3.6
3	Saturday	00 01	3.1	12 01	3.4	01 45	4.9	14 04	5.2	10 59	3.9	23 15	3.7
4	Sunday	00 41	3.1	12 36	3.4	02 22	5.1	14 39	5.3	11 30	4.0	23 44	3.7
5	Monday	01 16	3.1	13 05	3.4	02 56	5.2	15 13	5.4	11 59	4.0	—	—
6	Tuesday	01 46	3.1	13 35	3.5	03 30	5.2	15 46	5.4	00 12	3.8	12 29	4.0
7	Wednesday	02 13	3.1	14 08	3.5	04 06	5.3	16 21	5.4	00 44	3.8	13 03	4.0
8	Thursday	02 43	3.1	14 44	3.5	04 43	5.3	16 59	5.3	01 20	3.8	13 41	4.0
9	Friday	03 15	3.1	15 21	3.5	05 23	5.2	17 39	5.2	02 00	3.8	14 23	3.9
10	Saturday	03 50	3.1	15 59	3.5	06 05	5.1	18 21	5.1	02 45	3.8	15 08	3.9
11	Sunday	04 27	3.1	16 39	3.3	06 50	4.9	19 08	4.9	03 33	3.7	15 58	3.7
12	Monday	05 08	3.0	17 24	3.2	07 37	4.8	20 00	4.7	04 28	3.6	16 55	3.6
13	Tuesday	05 59	2.8	18 20	3.0	08 32	4.6	21 03	4.6	05 30	3.5	18 04	3.5
14	Wednesday	07 11	2.8	19 35	2.9	09 38	4.6	22 18	4.6	06 45	3.5	19 26	3.5
15	Thursday	09 02	2.8	21 24	2.9	10 54	4.7	23 36	4.8	08 00	3.6	20 38	3.6
16	Friday	10 19	3.1	22 40	3.1	—	—	12 05	5.0	09 03	3.8	21 40	3.8
17	Saturday	11 13	3.4	23 37	3.2	00 44	5.2	13 07	5.3	09 58	4.1	22 33	4.0
18	Sunday	—	—	12 02	3.6	01 41	5.5	14 01	5.7	10 46	4.2	23 20	4.1
19	Monday	00 29	3.3	12 49	3.7	02 31	5.7	14 49	5.9	11 30	4.3	—	—
20	Tuesday	01 16	3.4	13 33	3.8	03 17	5.8	15 34	6.0	00 01	4.1	12 13	4.4
21	Wednesday	01 59	3.5	14 15	3.9	04 00	5.8	16 17	5.9	00 44	4.1	12 56	4.3
22	Thursday	02 38	3.5	14 55	3.9	04 44	5.6	17 01	5.8	01 24	4.0	13 40	4.2
23	Friday	03 14	3.5	15 33	3.8	05 29	5.4	17 47	5.5	02 07	3.9	14 27	4.0
24	Saturday	03 51	3.5	16 11	3.6	06 14	5.1	18 34	5.1	02 53	3.7	15 15	3.8
25	Sunday	04 29	3.4	16 51	3.4	07 02	4.8	19 25	4.8	03 45	3.6	16 11	3.6
26	Monday	05 10	3.2	17 35	3.1	07 54	4.5	20 24	4.5	04 46	3.4	17 17	3.4
27	Tuesday	05 57	3.1	18 28	2.8	08 54	4.3	21 33	4.2	05 56	3.3	18 31	3.2
28	Wednesday	06 52	2.9	19 37	2.6	10 02	4.2	22 41	4.2	07 07	3.3	19 39	3.2
29	Thursday	08 06	2.8	22 04	2.7	11 08	4.4	23 43	4.4	08 12	3.4	20 43	3.3

MARCH 1996   *High water*   GMT

		LONDON BRIDGE *Datum of predictions 3.20 m below*				AVONMOUTH *Datum of predictions 6.50 m below*				LIVERPOOL *Datum of predictions 4.93 m below*				HULL (*Albert Dock*) *Datum of predictions 3.90 m below*			
		hr	ht m	hr	ht m	hr	ht m	hr	ht m	hr	ht m	hr	ht m	hr	ht m	hr	ht m
1	Friday	11 18	5.8	23 35	5.9	04 11	10.4	16 46	10.7	08 47	7.8	21 13	7.9	03 26	5.6	15 47	6.0
2	Saturday	—	—	12 09	6.1	05 06	11.2	17 35	11.6	09 34	8.3	21 56	8.4	04 19	6.0	16 33	6.4
3	Sunday	00 24	6.2	12 54	6.3	05 52	12.0	18 17	12.2	10 14	8.7	22 34	8.7	05 03	6.3	17 13	6.7
4	Monday	01 06	6.4	13 31	6.5	06 34	12.5	18 58	12.6	10 50	9.0	23 09	9.0	05 42	6.6	17 48	7.0
5	Tuesday	01 43	6.5	14 07	6.7	07 14	12.8	19 36	12.8	11 24	9.2	23 42	9.1	06 17	6.9	18 22	7.2
6	Wednesday	02 19	6.7	14 43	6.9	07 51	12.9	20 12	12.8	11 56	9.3	—	—	06 51	7.1	18 57	7.3
7	Thursday	02 55	6.9	15 19	7.0	08 26	12.9	20 44	12.8	00 14	9.2	12 30	9.3	07 26	7.2	19 32	7.4
8	Friday	03 31	7.0	15 57	7.0	08 57	13.0	21 15	12.9	00 48	9.2	13 04	9.3	08 01	7.3	20 09	7.4
9	Saturday	04 07	6.9	16 33	6.9	09 30	12.9	21 48	12.8	01 22	9.2	13 41	9.3	08 37	7.2	20 48	7.3
10	Sunday	04 42	6.9	17 10	6.8	10 06	12.8	22 25	12.5	01 59	9.1	14 21	9.0	09 15	7.0	21 31	7.1
11	Monday	05 20	6.7	17 50	6.5	10 46	12.3	23 07	11.9	02 39	8.8	15 05	8.7	09 57	6.8	22 18	6.8
12	Tuesday	06 03	6.4	18 35	6.2	11 32	11.5	23 58	11.1	03 28	8.4	16 00	8.1	10 44	6.5	23 12	6.4
13	Wednesday	06 56	6.1	19 31	5.9	—	—	12 32	10.7	04 31	7.9	17 11	7.7	11 43	6.2	—	—
14	Thursday	08 08	5.8	20 51	5.8	01 08	10.4	14 00	10.1	05 52	7.7	18 35	7.6	00 23	6.1	13 07	6.0
15	Friday	09 44	5.9	22 20	6.0	02 51	10.3	15 43	10.6	07 18	7.9	19 59	8.0	02 08	6.0	14 31	6.3
16	Saturday	11 06	6.3	23 30	6.4	04 19	11.2	16 55	11.7	08 31	8.5	21 05	8.6	03 28	6.4	15 37	6.7
17	Sunday	—	—	12 08	6.8	05 22	12.4	17 51	12.8	09 28	9.2	21 58	9.2	04 31	6.8	16 32	7.2
18	Monday	00 27	6.8	13 01	7.2	06 14	13.4	18 39	13.7	10 18	9.7	22 44	9.6	05 23	7.2	17 22	7.6
19	Tuesday	01 17	7.1	13 47	7.4	07 00	14.1	19 23	14.1	11 03	10.0	23 27	9.8	06 08	7.5	18 07	7.9
20	Wednesday	02 01	7.2	14 31	7.5	07 44	14.4	20 05	14.3	11 46	10.1	—	—	06 48	7.6	18 51	8.1
21	Thursday	02 44	7.3	15 12	7.5	08 25	14.4	20 43	14.1	00 07	9.8	12 27	10.0	07 26	7.6	19 33	8.0
22	Friday	03 24	7.4	15 51	7.4	09 03	14.0	21 18	13.6	00 46	9.6	13 06	9.7	08 01	7.5	20 13	7.8
23	Saturday	04 02	7.4	16 26	7.2	09 36	13.3	21 48	13.0	01 22	9.3	13 43	9.3	08 35	7.2	20 52	7.4
24	Sunday	04 38	7.2	16 58	7.0	10 05	12.6	22 15	12.2	01 58	9.0	14 20	8.8	09 08	6.9	21 30	6.9
25	Monday	05 13	6.9	17 31	6.7	10 34	11.7	22 44	11.4	02 34	8.5	14 59	8.3	09 42	6.5	22 08	6.4
26	Tuesday	05 50	6.5	18 08	6.3	11 07	10.8	23 20	10.5	03 14	8.0	15 43	7.7	10 18	6.1	22 50	5.9
27	Wednesday	06 33	6.1	18 53	5.9	11 52	9.8	—	—	04 03	7.5	16 40	7.1	11 02	5.8	23 47	5.4
28	Thursday	07 29	5.6	19 51	5.5	00 14	9.7	13 15	9.2	05 11	7.1	18 07	6.8	—	—	12 08	5.4
29	Friday	09 01	5.3	21 25	5.4	02 04	9.3	15 01	9.4	06 52	7.1	19 38	7.1	01 36	5.2	14 08	5.5
30	Saturday	10 37	5.6	22 50	5.6	03 30	9.9	16 08	10.3	08 07	7.5	20 37	7.6	02 50	5.4	15 11	5.8
31	Sunday	11 33	5.9	23 45	6.0	04 29	10.8	17 00	11.2	08 59	8.0	21 23	8.2	03 45	5.8	15 59	6.2

APRIL 1996   *High water*   GMT

		LONDON BRIDGE				AVONMOUTH				LIVERPOOL				HULL (*Albert Dock*)			
1	Monday	—	—	12 18	6.2	05 19	11.6	17 45	12.0	09 42	8.5	22 03	8.6	04 31	6.3	16 41	6.6
2	Tuesday	00 30	6.3	12 59	6.5	06 02	12.3	18 27	12.5	10 19	8.8	22 38	8.9	05 11	6.7	17 18	6.9
3	Wednesday	01 11	6.5	13 37	6.8	06 44	12.7	19 06	12.9	10 54	9.1	23 13	9.1	05 48	7.0	17 55	7.2
4	Thursday	01 50	6.8	14 15	7.0	07 23	13.0	19 44	13.1	11 28	9.3	23 47	9.3	06 24	7.3	18 32	7.4
5	Friday	02 29	7.0	14 55	7.1	08 00	13.1	20 19	13.2	—	—	12 04	9.4	07 00	7.4	19 11	7.5
6	Saturday	03 10	7.1	15 35	7.2	08 37	13.2	20 55	13.2	00 23	9.4	12 43	9.4	07 37	7.4	19 51	7.4
7	Sunday	03 50	7.1	16 14	7.0	09 14	13.2	21 32	13.1	01 01	9.3	13 23	9.3	08 15	7.3	20 33	7.3
8	Monday	04 30	7.0	16 53	6.8	09 52	13.0	22 11	12.7	01 41	9.2	14 06	9.0	08 55	7.1	21 18	7.1
9	Tuesday	05 11	6.8	17 33	6.5	10 34	12.4	22 54	12.1	02 25	8.9	14 54	8.6	09 38	6.9	22 08	6.7
10	Wednesday	05 55	6.5	18 16	6.2	11 22	11.6	23 46	11.2	03 16	8.5	15 50	8.1	10 28	6.5	23 06	6.3
11	Thursday	06 48	6.1	19 11	5.9	—	—	12 21	10.7	04 20	8.0	17 01	7.7	11 29	6.3	—	—
12	Friday	08 01	5.9	20 33	5.8	00 57	10.5	13 50	10.2	05 39	7.8	18 25	7.6	00 27	6.1	12 52	6.1
13	Saturday	09 32	6.0	21 59	6.0	02 39	10.4	15 24	10.6	07 01	8.0	19 43	8.0	02 00	6.1	14 10	6.3
14	Sunday	10 46	6.5	23 07	6.5	03 58	11.2	16 32	11.6	08 11	8.4	20 46	8.5	03 12	6.4	15 15	6.7
15	Monday	11 47	7.0	—	—	04 59	12.2	17 27	12.5	09 08	9.0	21 38	9.0	04 12	6.8	16 11	7.1
16	Tuesday	00 04	6.9	12 40	7.3	05 50	13.1	18 14	13.3	09 58	9.4	22 23	9.4	05 03	7.1	17 01	7.5
17	Wednesday	00 54	7.1	13 26	7.4	06 36	13.6	18 58	13.7	10 42	9.6	23 04	9.5	05 46	7.4	17 48	7.7
18	Thursday	01 39	7.2	14 08	7.4	07 19	13.9	19 39	13.8	11 24	9.7	23 42	9.5	06 24	7.5	18 31	7.8
19	Friday	02 21	7.2	14 48	7.3	08 00	13.8	20 16	13.6	—	—	12 03	9.6	07 01	7.4	19 13	7.7
20	Saturday	03 01	7.2	15 24	7.2	08 37	13.4	20 50	13.2	00 18	9.3	12 41	9.3	07 36	7.3	19 53	7.5
21	Sunday	03 40	7.2	15 58	7.1	09 10	12.9	21 21	12.7	00 54	9.1	13 17	9.0	08 09	7.1	20 31	7.1
22	Monday	04 16	7.1	16 30	6.9	09 40	12.3	21 49	12.1	01 29	8.9	13 53	8.7	08 41	6.9	21 07	6.7
23	Tuesday	04 52	6.8	17 03	6.7	10 09	11.6	22 17	11.4	02 05	8.6	14 31	8.3	09 13	6.6	21 43	6.3
24	Wednesday	05 29	6.5	17 40	6.4	10 40	10.9	22 49	10.7	02 45	8.2	15 13	7.8	09 47	6.3	22 22	5.9
25	Thursday	06 10	6.1	18 23	6.0	11 18	10.1	23 33	10.0	03 30	7.7	16 03	7.3	10 26	5.9	23 10	5.5
26	Friday	06 58	5.8	19 14	5.7	—	—	12 16	9.5	04 26	7.3	17 09	7.0	11 18	5.6	—	—
27	Saturday	07 59	5.6	20 20	5.6	00 47	9.5	13 52	9.5	05 42	7.1	18 36	7.0	00 25	5.3	12 42	5.5
28	Sunday	09 20	5.6	21 42	5.6	02 33	9.7	15 15	9.9	07 06	7.3	19 47	7.4	02 00	5.4	14 19	5.7
29	Monday	10 37	5.9	22 52	5.9	03 41	10.4	16 16	10.8	08 09	7.7	20 40	7.9	03 03	5.8	15 17	6.1
30	Tuesday	11 32	6.2	23 46	6.3	04 37	11.2	17 06	11.6	08 58	8.2	21 23	8.4	03 54	6.3	16 04	6.5

MARCH 1996   *continued*

		GREENOCK				LEITH				DUN LAOGHAIRE				NOTES:
		*Datum of predictions 1.62 m below				*Datum of predictions 2.90 m below				†Datum of predictions 0.20 m above				*Difference of height in metres from Ordnance datum (Newlyn)
		hr	ht m	hr	ht m	hr	ht m	hr	ht m	hr	ht m	hr	ht m	†Difference of height in metres from Ordnance datum (Dublin)
1	Friday	10 01	2.9	22 56	2.8	——	—	12 06	4.6	09 08	3.5	21 35	3.4	hr hour
2	Saturday	10 54	3.1	23 38	3.0	00 36	4.6	12 56	4.8	09 55	3.7	22 17	3.5	m metres
3	Sunday	11 35	3.2	——	—	01 20	4.8	13 38	5.0	10 32	3.8	22 50	3.6	
4	Monday	00 16	3.0	12 10	3.3	01 57	5.0	14 15	5.2	11 05	3.9	23 19	3.7	
5	Tuesday	00 51	3.0	12 39	3.3	02 31	5.2	14 49	5.3	11 33	3.9	23 44	3.8	
6	Wednesday	01 21	3.0	13 10	3.4	03 05	5.3	15 24	5.4	——	—	12 01	4.0	
7	Thursday	01 47	3.1	13 45	3.4	03 41	5.4	15 59	5.5	00 13	3.9	12 36	4.0	
8	Friday	02 15	3.1	14 21	3.5	04 18	5.4	16 37	5.4	00 50	3.9	13 15	4.0	
9	Saturday	02 47	3.2	14 59	3.5	04 57	5.3	17 17	5.3	01 31	3.9	13 57	4.0	
10	Sunday	03 21	3.2	15 37	3.4	05 39	5.2	18 00	5.2	02 15	3.9	14 44	3.9	
11	Monday	03 57	3.2	16 17	3.3	06 25	5.0	18 48	5.0	03 04	3.8	15 36	3.7	
12	Tuesday	04 37	3.0	17 02	3.1	07 14	4.8	19 42	4.8	03 58	3.6	16 36	3.6	
13	Wednesday	05 27	2.9	17 58	2.9	08 09	4.6	20 45	4.6	05 03	3.5	17 48	3.4	
14	Thursday	06 37	2.7	19 16	2.8	09 16	4.5	22 02	4.6	06 21	3.5	19 15	3.4	
15	Friday	08 40	2.8	21 17	2.8	10 33	4.6	23 25	4.8	07 41	3.6	20 29	3.6	
16	Saturday	10 01	3.0	22 31	3.0	11 48	4.9	——	—	08 49	3.7	21 32	3.7	
17	Sunday	10 56	3.3	23 25	3.2	00 33	5.1	12 51	5.2	09 46	4.0	22 25	3.9	
18	Monday	11 45	3.5	——	—	01 29	5.4	13 45	5.5	10 35	4.1	23 08	4.0	
19	Tuesday	00 13	3.3	12 31	3.6	02 16	5.6	14 32	5.7	11 18	4.2	23 46	4.0	
20	Wednesday	00 56	3.3	13 15	3.7	02 58	5.7	15 16	5.8	11 57	4.2	——	—	
21	Thursday	01 35	3.4	13 55	3.7	03 38	5.7	15 57	5.8	00 21	4.0	12 36	4.2	
22	Friday	02 11	3.5	14 33	3.7	04 18	5.6	16 38	5.6	00 57	3.9	13 16	4.1	
23	Saturday	02 45	3.5	15 10	3.6	04 57	5.4	17 19	5.4	01 35	3.8	13 59	3.9	
24	Sunday	03 20	3.5	15 46	3.5	05 38	5.1	18 01	5.1	02 16	3.7	14 45	3.7	
25	Monday	03 56	3.4	16 25	3.3	06 19	4.8	18 47	4.8	03 03	3.6	15 36	3.5	
26	Tuesday	04 36	3.3	17 08	3.0	07 05	4.6	19 40	4.4	03 56	3.4	16 37	3.3	
27	Wednesday	05 20	3.1	17 58	2.8	08 02	4.3	20 50	4.2	05 06	3.3	17 50	3.1	
28	Thursday	06 13	2.9	19 01	2.6	09 18	4.2	22 04	4.1	06 23	3.2	19 04	3.1	
29	Friday	07 18	2.8	21 02	2.6	10 29	4.2	23 09	4.3	07 32	3.3	20 08	3.2	
30	Saturday	08 48	2.8	22 21	2.7	11 29	4.4	——	—	08 31	3.4	21 02	3.3	
31	Sunday	10 11	2.9	23 05	2.9	00 02	4.5	12 21	4.7	09 21	3.5	21 45	3.5	

APRIL 1996   *continued*

		GREENOCK				LEITH				DUN LAOGHAIRE			
1	Monday	10 56	3.1	23 44	3.0	00 47	4.8	13 05	4.9	10 01	3.7	22 20	3.6
2	Tuesday	11 32	3.2	——	—	01 26	5.0	13 44	5.2	10 35	3.8	22 48	3.8
3	Wednesday	00 18	3.0	12 06	3.2	02 02	5.2	14 21	5.3	11 04	3.9	23 15	3.9
4	Thursday	00 49	3.1	12 42	3.3	02 38	5.4	14 59	5.5	11 34	4.0	23 45	4.0
5	Friday	01 18	3.1	13 20	3.4	03 15	5.5	15 37	5.6	——	—	12 10	4.0
6	Saturday	01 49	3.2	14 00	3.4	03 54	5.5	16 16	5.6	00 22	4.0	12 52	4.0
7	Sunday	02 22	3.3	14 40	3.4	04 34	5.4	16 59	5.5	01 05	4.0	13 37	4.0
8	Monday	02 58	3.3	15 20	3.4	05 17	5.3	17 44	5.3	01 52	4.0	14 27	3.9
9	Tuesday	03 35	3.3	16 03	3.3	06 04	5.1	18 34	5.1	02 43	3.9	15 22	3.8
10	Wednesday	04 17	3.1	16 51	3.1	06 56	4.9	19 30	4.8	03 40	3.7	16 26	3.6
11	Thursday	05 10	3.0	17 52	2.9	07 54	4.7	20 35	4.6	04 46	3.6	17 42	3.5
12	Friday	06 24	2.8	19 20	2.7	09 02	4.6	21 53	4.6	06 04	3.6	19 05	3.5
13	Saturday	08 19	2.8	21 06	2.8	10 19	4.7	23 13	4.8	07 24	3.6	20 17	3.6
14	Sunday	09 39	3.0	22 14	3.0	11 30	4.9	——	—	08 32	3.8	21 19	3.7
15	Monday	10 35	3.3	23 06	3.1	00 18	5.1	12 31	5.2	09 31	3.9	22 10	3.8
16	Tuesday	11 24	3.4	23 51	3.2	01 12	5.3	13 25	5.4	10 23	4.0	22 54	3.9
17	Wednesday	——	—	12 10	3.5	01 58	5.5	14 13	5.6	11 05	4.1	23 30	3.9
18	Thursday	00 32	3.3	12 53	3.5	02 39	5.5	14 56	5.6	11 42	4.1	——	—
19	Friday	01 09	3.4	13 34	3.5	03 16	5.5	15 36	5.6	00 01	3.9	12 18	4.0
20	Saturday	01 44	3.4	14 11	3.4	03 52	5.5	16 15	5.5	00 34	3.9	12 56	3.9
21	Sunday	02 18	3.5	14 48	3.4	04 28	5.3	16 53	5.3	01 09	3.8	13 36	3.8
22	Monday	02 53	3.5	15 24	3.3	05 04	5.1	17 32	5.1	01 48	3.8	14 19	3.7
23	Tuesday	03 28	3.4	16 03	3.1	05 41	4.9	18 13	4.8	02 32	3.7	15 07	3.5
24	Wednesday	04 06	3.3	16 46	3.0	06 23	4.7	18 59	4.5	03 19	3.5	16 01	3.3
25	Thursday	04 49	3.1	17 36	2.8	07 11	4.5	19 54	4.3	04 17	3.4	17 07	3.2
26	Friday	05 39	2.9	18 34	2.6	08 13	4.3	21 10	4.2	05 31	3.3	18 19	3.1
27	Saturday	06 39	2.8	19 42	2.6	09 36	4.2	22 21	4.3	06 47	3.2	19 26	3.2
28	Sunday	07 47	2.8	21 13	2.7	10 43	4.4	23 19	4.5	07 48	3.3	20 21	3.3
29	Monday	09 02	2.8	22 18	2.8	11 38	4.6	——	—	08 39	3.5	21 06	3.5
30	Tuesday	10 03	3.0	23 03	2.9	00 07	4.7	12 26	4.8	09 23	3.6	21 43	3.6

MAY 1996   *High water*   GMT

	LONDON BRIDGE *Datum of predictions 3.20 m below				AVONMOUTH *Datum of predictions 6.50 m below				LIVERPOOL *Datum of predictions 4.93 m below				HULL (*Albert Dock*) *Datum of predictions 3.90 m below			
	hr	ht m	hr	ht m	hr	ht m	hr	ht m	hr	ht m	hr	ht m	hr	ht m	hr	ht m
1 Wednesday	----	—	12 20	6.6	05 25	12.0	17 52	12.4	09 40	8.6	22 02	8.9	04 38	6.8	16 47	6.9
2 Thursday	00 33	6.6	13 04	6.9	06 10	12.6	18 34	12.9	10 20	9.0	22 41	9.2	05 19	7.1	17 29	7.2
3 Friday	01 18	6.9	13 47	7.1	06 53	13.0	19 15	13.3	10 59	9.2	23 19	9.4	05 57	7.4	18 10	7.4
4 Saturday	02 03	7.1	14 30	7.2	07 35	13.3	19 56	13.5	11 40	9.4	——	—	06 37	7.5	18 53	7.5
5 Sunday	02 48	7.3	15 14	7.2	08 17	13.4	20 37	13.5	00 00	9.5	12 24	9.4	07 16	7.5	19 37	7.5
6 Monday	03 34	7.3	15 58	7.1	09 00	13.4	21 19	13.4	00 43	9.5	13 09	9.3	07 57	7.4	20 22	7.3
7 Tuesday	04 20	7.2	16 40	6.9	09 43	13.1	22 02	13.0	01 28	9.4	13 56	9.1	08 40	7.3	21 11	7.1
8 Wednesday	05 05	6.9	17 22	6.5	10 28	12.6	22 48	12.3	02 16	9.1	14 47	8.8	09 26	7.0	22 04	6.8
9 Thursday	05 52	6.6	18 07	6.3	11 16	11.8	23 41	11.6	03 10	8.7	15 44	8.3	10 17	6.8	23 05	6.5
10 Friday	06 46	6.3	19 01	6.0			12 15	11.1	04 13	8.4	16 51	8.0	11 18	6.5	——	—
11 Saturday	07 55	6.2	20 18	6.0	00 50	10.9	13 34	10.6	05 24	8.1	18 06	7.8	00 21	6.3	12 33	6.4
12 Sunday	09 12	6.3	21 34	6.2	02 17	10.8	14 56	10.8	06 37	8.1	19 18	8.0	01 40	6.3	13 46	6.5
13 Monday	10 20	6.7	22 40	6.6	03 29	11.2	16 01	11.4	07 45	8.4	20 21	8.3	02 47	6.5	14 50	6.7
14 Tuesday	11 20	7.0	23 38	6.9	04 30	11.9	16 58	12.1	08 44	8.7	21 13	8.7	03 46	6.8	15 48	7.0
15 Wednesday	----	—	12 14	7.3	05 23	12.5	17 47	12.7	09 35	9.0	21 59	9.0	04 36	7.0	16 40	7.3
16 Thursday	00 30	7.1	13 03	7.3	06 10	12.9	18 31	13.1	10 21	9.2	22 41	9.1	05 20	7.2	17 28	7.4
17 Friday	01 18	7.1	13 46	7.2	06 54	13.1	19 12	13.2	11 03	9.2	23 18	9.1	06 00	7.3	18 13	7.4
18 Saturday	02 01	7.1	14 25	7.1	07 35	13.1	19 51	13.1	11 42	9.1	23 54	9.1	06 37	7.3	18 55	7.3
19 Sunday	02 42	7.0	15 01	7.0	08 13	12.8	20 26	12.8	——	—	12 18	9.0	07 13	7.2	19 34	7.1
20 Monday	03 20	7.0	15 33	6.9	08 48	12.5	20 59	12.5	00 29	9.0	12 54	8.8	07 47	7.1	20 12	6.9
21 Tuesday	03 57	6.9	16 05	6.8	09 20	12.0	21 29	12.0	01 05	8.8	13 30	8.6	08 19	6.9	20 47	6.6
22 Wednesday	04 33	6.7	16 39	6.6	09 50	11.6	21 59	11.5	01 42	8.6	14 07	8.4	08 50	6.7	21 22	6.3
23 Thursday	05 09	6.5	17 16	6.4	10 21	11.1	22 29	11.0	02 20	8.4	14 48	8.1	09 23	6.5	22 00	6.1
24 Friday	05 49	6.3	17 57	6.2	10 56	10.6	23 08	10.5	03 02	8.1	15 33	7.7	10 01	6.2	22 43	5.8
25 Saturday	06 32	6.1	18 43	6.0	11 41	10.1	——	—	03 51	7.7	16 26	7.4	10 46	6.0	23 38	5.7
26 Sunday	07 24	5.9	19 40	5.8	00 00	10.1	12 43	9.8	04 50	7.5	17 31	7.3	11 43	5.8	——	—
27 Monday	08 26	5.9	20 47	5.9	01 13	10.0	14 01	9.9	05 57	7.4	18 42	7.4	00 53	5.6	13 01	5.8
28 Tuesday	09 35	6.0	21 56	6.0	02 36	10.3	15 18	10.5	07 05	7.6	19 46	7.8	02 12	5.9	14 23	6.0
29 Wednesday	10 42	6.3	23 00	6.3	03 45	11.0	16 21	11.3	08 05	8.0	20 39	8.3	03 13	6.3	15 24	6.4
30 Thursday	11 40	6.6	23 56	6.6	04 44	11.7	17 15	12.1	08 58	8.5	21 26	8.8	04 04	6.7	16 17	6.8
31 Friday	----	—	12 31	6.9	05 36	12.5	18 04	12.8	09 46	8.9	22 10	9.2	04 50	7.1	17 05	7.1

JUNE 1996   *High water*   GMT

	LONDON BRIDGE				AVONMOUTH				LIVERPOOL				HULL (*Albert Dock*)			
	hr	ht m	hr	ht m	hr	ht m	hr	ht m	hr	ht m	hr	ht m	hr	ht m	hr	ht m
1 Saturday	00 48	6.9	13 20	7.2	06 25	13.0	18 50	13.4	10 33	9.2	22 55	9.5	05 33	7.4	17 52	7.4
2 Sunday	01 39	7.2	14 08	7.3	07 14	13.4	19 37	13.7	11 20	9.4	23 40	9.6	06 16	7.6	18 38	7.5
3 Monday	02 29	7.4	14 56	7.3	08 01	13.6	20 23	13.8	——	—	12 08	9.5	06 58	7.7	19 25	7.6
4 Tuesday	03 19	7.4	15 43	7.2	08 49	13.6	21 09	13.7	00 27	9.7	12 58	9.5	07 42	7.7	20 13	7.5
5 Wednesday	04 09	7.4	16 29	7.0	09 36	13.4	21 56	13.4	01 17	9.6	13 48	9.3	08 26	7.6	21 03	7.3
6 Thursday	04 57	7.2	17 13	6.8	10 22	13.0	22 43	12.9	02 08	9.4	14 39	9.1	09 14	7.4	21 56	7.0
7 Friday	05 46	6.9	17 58	6.6	11 09	12.4	23 33	12.2	03 02	9.1	15 33	8.7	10 05	7.2	22 53	6.8
8 Saturday	06 37	6.7	18 49	6.4	——	—	12 02	11.6	03 59	8.8	16 32	8.3	11 02	6.9	23 59	6.5
9 Sunday	07 37	6.5	19 54	6.3	00 33	11.5	13 07	11.1	05 01	8.5	17 38	8.0	——	—	12 07	6.7
10 Monday	08 44	6.5	21 05	6.4	01 46	11.1	14 20	10.8	06 08	8.2	18 46	7.9	01 09	6.4	13 17	6.6
11 Tuesday	09 50	6.6	22 11	6.6	02 56	11.1	15 26	11.0	07 15	8.2	19 51	8.1	02 15	6.4	14 23	6.7
12 Wednesday	10 52	6.9	23 12	6.8	03 57	11.4	16 25	11.4	08 17	8.3	20 48	8.3	03 15	6.6	15 24	6.8
13 Thursday	11 48	7.0	——		04 53	11.8	17 18	11.9	09 12	8.5	21 37	8.6	04 08	6.8	16 20	6.9
14 Friday	00 07	6.9	12 40	7.1	05 44	12.2	18 05	12.4	10 01	8.7	22 20	8.8	04 55	7.0	17 10	7.0
15 Saturday	00 58	6.9	13 25	7.0	06 29	12.4	18 48	12.7	10 44	8.8	22 58	8.9	05 37	7.1	17 56	7.0
16 Sunday	01 43	6.9	14 05	6.9	07 12	12.5	19 28	12.7	11 23	8.8	23 34	8.9	06 16	7.1	18 38	7.0
17 Monday	02 24	6.8	14 41	6.8	07 51	12.4	20 06	12.6	——	—	12 00	8.8	06 53	7.1	19 17	6.9
18 Tuesday	03 03	6.8	15 13	6.7	08 28	12.2	20 41	12.4	00 09	8.9	12 35	8.7	07 27	7.1	19 54	6.8
19 Wednesday	03 39	6.7	15 45	6.7	09 02	12.0	21 13	12.1	00 45	8.8	13 10	8.6	07 59	7.0	20 28	6.7
20 Thursday	04 14	6.7	16 19	6.6	09 34	11.7	21 44	11.8	01 21	8.7	13 46	8.5	08 31	6.9	21 02	6.5
21 Friday	04 50	6.6	16 56	6.5	10 05	11.4	22 13	11.5	01 58	8.6	14 24	8.3	09 03	6.8	21 37	6.4
22 Saturday	05 27	6.5	17 33	6.3	10 36	11.1	22 47	11.2	02 37	8.4	15 04	8.1	09 38	6.6	22 17	6.3
23 Sunday	06 08	6.3	18 15	6.2	11 14	10.8	23 30	10.9	03 19	8.2	15 49	7.9	10 19	6.4	23 03	6.1
24 Monday	06 53	6.2	19 04	6.1	——	—	12 02	10.5	04 09	7.9	16 43	7.6	11 08	6.2	——	—
25 Tuesday	07 48	6.2	20 05	6.1	00 26	10.6	13 03	10.4	05 07	7.8	17 46	7.6	00 00	6.0	12 07	6.1
26 Wednesday	08 51	6.2	21 12	6.2	01 34	10.5	14 16	10.5	06 10	7.7	18 52	7.8	01 13	6.0	13 21	6.1
27 Thursday	09 59	6.3	22 21	6.3	02 51	10.8	15 33	11.0	07 16	8.0	19 56	8.2	02 28	6.2	14 42	6.3
28 Friday	11 05	6.6	23 25	6.6	04 04	11.4	16 41	11.8	08 20	8.3	20 53	8.7	03 30	6.6	15 49	6.6
29 Saturday	——	—	12 04	6.9	05 08	12.2	17 39	12.6	09 18	8.8	21 45	9.2	04 23	7.0	16 45	7.0
30 Sunday	00 24	6.9	12 58	7.1	06 04	12.9	18 31	13.3	10 12	9.2	22 35	9.6	05 11	7.3	17 37	7.3

MAY 1996 *continued*

		GREENOCK				LEITH				DUN LAOGHAIRE				NOTES:
		*Datum of predictions 1.62 m below				*Datum of predictions 2.90 m below				†Datum of predictions 0.20 m above				*Difference of height in metres from Ordnance datum (Newlyn)
			ht		ht		ht		ht		ht		ht	
		hr	m	hr	m	hr	m	hr	m	hr	m	hr	m	†Difference of height in metres from Ordnance datum (Dublin)
1	Wednesday	10 49	3.1	23 40	3.0	00 50	5.0	13 09	5.1	10 00	3.8	22 15	3.8	hr hour
2	Thursday	11 31	3.2	———	—	01 31	5.2	13 52	5.4	10 34	3.9	22 46	3.9	m metres
3	Friday	00 15	3.1	12 14	3.3	02 11	5.5	14 33	5.5	11 10	4.0	23 21	4.1	
4	Saturday	00 51	3.2	12 57	3.3	02 51	5.6	15 15	5.7	11 49	4.1	———	—	
5	Sunday	01 27	3.3	13 41	3.4	03 32	5.6	15 58	5.7	00 00	4.1	12 35	4.1	
6	Monday	02 04	3.4	14 25	3.4	04 15	5.6	16 44	5.6	00 46	4.1	13 23	4.0	
7	Tuesday	02 42	3.4	15 10	3.3	05 00	5.5	17 32	5.4	01 34	4.1	14 16	3.9	
8	Wednesday	03 23	3.4	15 57	3.2	05 49	5.3	18 25	5.2	02 29	4.0	15 14	3.8	
9	Thursday	04 08	3.3	16 51	3.1	06 44	5.1	19 23	5.0	03 28	3.9	16 20	3.7	
10	Friday	05 03	3.1	17 56	2.9	07 44	4.9	20 27	4.8	04 35	3.8	17 33	3.6	
11	Saturday	06 17	3.0	19 15	2.8	08 51	4.8	21 40	4.7	05 50	3.7	18 48	3.6	
12	Sunday	07 53	2.9	20 40	2.8	10 02	4.8	22 51	4.8	07 05	3.7	19 56	3.6	
13	Monday	09 12	3.1	21 48	3.0	11 08	4.9	23 54	5.0	08 12	3.8	20 57	3.7	
14	Tuesday	10 11	3.2	22 41	3.1	———	—	12 08	5.1	09 12	3.9	21 50	3.8	
15	Wednesday	11 02	3.3	23 26	3.2	00 49	5.2	13 03	5.2	10 05	3.9	22 35	3.8	
16	Thursday	11 48	3.3	———	—	01 38	5.3	13 52	5.3	10 50	3.9	23 13	3.9	
17	Friday	00 07	3.2	12 33	3.3	02 20	5.4	14 37	5.4	11 28	3.9	23 43	3.9	
18	Saturday	00 45	3.3	13 14	3.3	02 57	5.4	15 17	5.4	———	—	12 01	3.9	
19	Sunday	01 20	3.4	13 52	3.2	03 31	5.4	15 55	5.3	00 12	3.9	12 37	3.8	
20	Monday	01 55	3.4	14 28	3.2	04 04	5.3	16 31	5.2	00 47	3.9	13 14	3.7	
21	Tuesday	02 29	3.5	15 05	3.1	04 38	5.2	17 08	5.0	01 25	3.8	13 55	3.7	
22	Wednesday	03 04	3.4	15 43	3.0	05 14	5.0	17 47	4.9	02 05	3.8	14 39	3.5	
23	Thursday	03 40	3.3	16 25	2.9	05 55	4.9	18 29	4.7	02 50	3.7	15 27	3.4	
24	Friday	04 20	3.2	17 13	2.8	06 41	4.7	19 16	4.6	03 39	3.5	16 20	3.3	
25	Saturday	05 07	3.0	18 05	2.7	07 31	4.5	20 09	4.4	04 36	3.4	17 22	3.2	
26	Sunday	06 01	2.9	19 02	2.7	08 30	4.4	21 13	4.4	05 41	3.3	18 29	3.2	
27	Monday	07 01	2.8	20 04	2.7	09 39	4.4	22 22	4.5	06 50	3.3	19 29	3.3	
28	Tuesday	08 07	2.8	21 13	2.7	10 45	4.6	23 20	4.7	07 48	3.4	20 19	3.5	
29	Wednesday	09 13	2.9	22 15	2.9	11 42	4.8	———	—	08 38	3.6	21 02	3.6	
30	Thursday	10 10	3.1	23 03	3.0	00 12	4.9	12 33	5.1	09 24	3.7	21 41	3.8	
31	Friday	11 01	3.2	23 46	3.1	01 00	5.2	13 22	5.3	10 06	3.9	22 21	4.0	

JUNE 1996 *continued*

		GREENOCK				LEITH				DUN LAOGHAIRE			
		hr	m	hr	m	hr	m	hr	m	hr	m	hr	m
1	Saturday	11 49	3.3	———	—	01 46	5.5	14 10	5.6	10 49	4.0	23 01	4.1
2	Sunday	00 28	3.3	12 37	3.3	02 30	5.6	14 57	5.7	11 33	4.1	23 43	4.2
3	Monday	01 09	3.4	13 26	3.3	03 15	5.7	15 43	5.8	———	—	12 20	4.1
4	Tuesday	01 51	3.5	14 15	3.4	03 59	5.8	16 31	5.8	00 30	4.3	13 11	4.1
5	Wednesday	02 33	3.6	15 05	3.3	04 47	5.7	17 21	5.6	01 21	4.2	14 05	4.0
6	Thursday	03 16	3.5	15 56	3.2	05 38	5.5	18 15	5.4	02 15	4.2	15 04	3.9
7	Friday	04 03	3.4	16 50	3.1	06 33	5.3	19 13	5.2	03 14	4.1	16 07	3.8
8	Saturday	04 57	3.3	17 48	3.0	07 33	5.1	20 13	5.0	04 19	4.0	17 14	3.7
9	Sunday	06 00	3.2	18 50	3.0	08 35	5.0	21 17	4.8	05 30	3.9	18 22	3.6
10	Monday	07 17	3.0	19 59	2.9	09 39	4.9	22 22	4.8	06 41	3.8	19 29	3.6
11	Tuesday	08 39	3.0	21 12	2.9	10 42	4.9	23 25	4.9	07 47	3.8	20 29	3.7
12	Wednesday	09 46	3.1	22 11	3.0	11 42	5.0	———	—	08 48	3.8	21 26	3.7
13	Thursday	10 41	3.1	23 01	3.1	00 22	5.0	12 39	5.0	09 44	3.8	22 13	3.8
14	Friday	11 30	3.1	23 45	3.2	01 15	5.1	13 32	5.1	10 31	3.8	22 53	3.8
15	Saturday	———	—	12 15	3.1	02 00	5.2	14 18	5.2	11 12	3.8	23 25	3.9
16	Sunday	00 24	3.3	12 58	3.1	02 39	5.3	14 59	5.2	11 44	3.8	23 54	3.9
17	Monday	01 01	3.3	13 36	3.0	03 13	5.3	15 35	5.2	———	—	12 17	3.7
18	Tuesday	01 35	3.4	14 12	3.0	03 45	5.3	16 10	5.1	00 27	3.9	12 52	3.7
19	Wednesday	02 08	3.4	14 47	3.0	04 18	5.2	16 45	5.1	01 02	3.9	13 29	3.7
20	Thursday	02 42	3.4	15 24	3.0	04 53	5.2	17 23	5.0	01 40	3.9	14 09	3.6
21	Friday	03 17	3.4	16 03	2.9	05 33	5.0	18 04	4.9	02 20	3.8	14 52	3.6
22	Saturday	03 55	3.3	16 45	2.9	06 16	4.9	18 47	4.8	03 05	3.7	15 38	3.5
23	Sunday	04 36	3.2	17 31	2.8	07 02	4.8	19 33	4.7	03 54	3.6	16 29	3.4
24	Monday	05 23	3.0	18 21	2.8	07 50	4.7	20 23	4.6	04 47	3.5	17 26	3.4
25	Tuesday	06 18	2.9	19 15	2.7	08 45	4.6	21 22	4.5	05 47	3.4	18 27	3.4
26	Wednesday	07 20	2.9	20 18	2.7	09 48	4.6	22 29	4.6	06 52	3.5	19 29	3.5
27	Thursday	08 29	2.9	21 29	2.8	10 56	4.7	23 32	4.8	07 55	3.6	20 24	3.6
28	Friday	09 37	3.0	22 31	3.0	11 59	5.0	———	—	08 52	3.7	21 14	3.8
29	Saturday	10 36	3.1	23 22	3.1	00 29	5.1	12 56	5.3	09 43	3.9	22 00	4.0
30	Sunday	11 30	3.2	———	—	01 22	5.4	13 50	5.6	10 32	4.0	22 45	4.2

JULY 1996　*High water*　GMT

		London Bridge				Avonmouth				Liverpool				Hull (*Albert Dock*)			
		*Datum of predictions 3.20 m below				*Datum of predictions 6.50 m below				*Datum of predictions 4.93 m below				*Datum of predictions 3.90 m below			
		hr	ht m	hr	ht m	hr	ht m	hr	ht m	hr	ht m	hr	ht m	hr	ht m	hr	ht m
1	Monday	01 19	7.2	13 48	7.3	06 57	13.4	19 21	13.8	11 04	9.5	23 24	9.8	05 56	7.6	18 26	7.6
2	Tuesday	02 12	7.4	14 38	7.3	07 48	13.7	20 11	14.1	11 54	9.6	—	—	06 41	7.9	19 14	7.7
3	Wednesday	03 04	7.5	15 27	7.4	08 38	13.9	20 59	14.1	00 14	9.9	12 45	9.7	07 26	8.0	20 02	7.7
4	Thursday	03 55	7.5	16 14	7.3	09 26	13.8	21 46	13.9	01 04	9.9	13 35	9.6	08 12	8.0	20 50	7.6
5	Friday	04 43	7.4	16 58	7.1	10 11	13.5	22 31	13.4	01 55	9.8	14 24	9.4	08 58	7.8	21 39	7.3
6	Saturday	05 30	7.2	17 41	6.9	10 55	12.9	23 16	12.7	02 45	9.5	15 13	9.0	09 46	7.6	22 30	7.0
7	Sunday	06 17	6.9	18 26	6.7	11 40	12.2	—	—	03 36	9.1	16 05	8.6	10 38	7.3	23 26	6.7
8	Monday	07 09	6.6	19 20	6.5	00 06	11.9	12 31	11.4	04 31	8.6	17 03	8.1	11 36	6.9	—	—
9	Tuesday	08 10	6.4	20 29	6.4	01 07	11.2	13 36	10.7	05 33	8.2	18 09	7.8	00 31	6.4	12 44	6.6
10	Wednesday	09 17	6.4	21 40	6.4	02 18	10.7	14 48	10.5	06 42	7.9	19 19	7.7	01 39	6.3	13 55	6.4
11	Thursday	10 21	6.5	22 46	6.5	03 25	10.7	15 52	10.8	07 50	7.9	20 22	8.0	02 42	6.3	15 01	6.4
12	Friday	11 21	6.7	23 45	6.7	04 25	11.0	16 50	11.3	08 50	8.1	21 16	8.3	03 39	6.5	16 00	6.5
13	Saturday	—	—	12 16	6.8	05 19	11.5	17 41	11.9	09 41	8.3	22 01	8.6	04 30	6.7	16 53	6.6
14	Sunday	00 38	6.7	13 04	6.8	06 07	11.9	18 26	12.3	10 26	8.6	22 41	8.8	05 15	6.9	17 40	6.7
15	Monday	01 25	6.7	13 46	6.7	06 50	12.2	19 07	12.6	11 06	8.7	23 18	8.9	05 55	7.0	18 21	6.8
16	Tuesday	02 07	6.7	14 22	6.7	07 31	12.3	19 46	12.6	11 42	8.7	23 52	9.0	06 32	7.1	18 58	6.8
17	Wednesday	02 44	6.7	14 54	6.7	08 09	12.3	20 23	12.5	—	—	12 17	8.7	07 06	7.1	19 32	6.8
18	Thursday	03 19	6.7	15 27	6.7	08 44	12.1	20 56	12.3	00 26	8.9	12 51	8.7	07 38	7.1	20 06	6.8
19	Friday	03 53	6.8	16 01	6.7	09 17	11.9	21 26	12.1	01 00	8.9	13 24	8.7	08 09	7.1	20 39	6.8
20	Saturday	04 28	6.7	16 35	6.6	09 46	11.8	21 54	11.9	01 34	8.8	13 59	8.6	08 41	7.0	21 13	6.8
21	Sunday	05 04	6.7	17 10	6.5	10 15	11.6	22 25	11.7	02 10	8.7	14 35	8.5	09 16	6.9	21 49	6.6
22	Monday	05 41	6.6	17 47	6.4	10 49	11.4	23 04	11.4	02 49	8.5	15 15	8.2	09 54	6.8	22 31	6.5
23	Tuesday	06 23	6.4	18 30	6.3	11 32	11.1	23 52	11.1	03 33	8.3	16 02	8.0	10 38	6.6	23 19	6.3
24	Wednesday	07 12	6.3	19 26	6.2	—	—	12 24	10.7	04 26	8.0	17 01	7.8	11 31	6.3	—	—
25	Thursday	08 12	6.2	20 33	6.1	00 53	10.7	13 31	10.5	05 29	7.8	18 10	7.8	00 20	6.1	12 36	6.1
26	Friday	09 22	6.2	21 47	6.2	02 09	10.6	14 55	10.7	06 39	7.8	19 21	8.0	01 42	6.1	14 04	6.1
27	Saturday	10 35	6.4	23 00	6.4	03 34	11.0	16 15	11.4	07 51	8.1	20 27	8.5	02 58	6.4	15 27	6.5
28	Sunday	11 41	6.7	—	—	04 48	11.8	17 20	12.4	08 58	8.6	21 26	9.1	03 58	6.8	16 30	6.9
29	Monday	00 05	6.8	12 39	7.0	05 49	12.7	18 16	13.3	09 57	9.1	22 19	9.7	04 50	7.3	17 24	7.3
30	Tuesday	01 03	7.1	13 31	7.2	06 44	13.4	19 08	14.0	10 50	9.5	23 09	10.0	05 38	7.7	18 14	7.6
31	Wednesday	01 57	7.4	14 20	7.3	07 35	13.9	19 58	14.4	11 40	9.8	23 58	10.2	06 24	8.0	19 02	7.8

AUGUST 1996　*High water*　GMT

		London Bridge				Avonmouth				Liverpool				Hull (*Albert Dock*)			
1	Thursday	02 48	7.5	15 08	7.4	08 24	14.1	20 45	14.5	—	—	12 29	9.9	07 09	8.2	19 47	7.9
2	Friday	03 37	7.6	15 53	7.4	09 10	14.1	21 30	14.3	00 46	10.2	13 16	9.8	07 54	8.3	20 31	7.8
3	Saturday	04 23	7.6	16 36	7.4	09 53	13.8	22 12	13.8	01 34	10.0	14 02	9.6	08 38	8.2	21 15	7.5
4	Sunday	05 07	7.4	17 16	7.2	10 33	13.2	22 52	13.0	02 21	9.7	14 46	9.2	09 24	7.9	21 59	7.2
5	Monday	05 49	7.1	17 56	6.9	11 11	12.4	23 32	12.0	03 07	9.2	15 32	8.7	10 11	7.5	22 47	6.8
6	Tuesday	06 32	6.7	18 40	6.6	11 51	11.4	—	—	03 56	8.6	16 22	8.1	11 03	6.9	23 45	6.3
7	Wednesday	07 23	6.3	19 40	6.2	00 18	11.0	12 43	10.6	04 52	8.0	17 24	7.6	—	—	12 07	6.4
8	Thursday	08 33	6.1	21 05	6.0	01 28	10.2	14 03	10.0	06 04	7.5	18 43	7.4	00 57	6.1	13 24	6.1
9	Friday	09 48	6.1	22 00	6.1	02 52	10.0	15 20	10.2	07 23	7.5	19 56	7.6	02 08	6.0	14 36	6.0
10	Saturday	10 53	6.2	23 22	6.3	03 58	10.3	16 23	10.7	08 28	7.7	20 54	8.0	03 10	6.2	15 39	6.1
11	Sunday	11 50	6.5	—	—	04 55	11.0	17 17	11.5	09 21	8.1	21 41	8.5	04 04	6.4	16 34	6.3
12	Monday	00 17	6.6	12 41	6.6	05 45	11.7	18 03	12.2	10 06	8.4	22 22	8.8	04 51	6.7	17 20	6.5
13	Tuesday	01 04	6.6	13 23	6.6	06 28	12.2	18 45	12.6	10 46	8.7	22 59	9.0	05 32	6.9	17 59	6.7
14	Wednesday	01 45	6.7	14 00	6.7	07 08	12.4	19 24	12.8	11 22	8.8	23 32	9.1	06 07	7.1	18 33	6.9
15	Thursday	02 21	6.7	14 33	6.7	07 46	12.5	20 01	12.7	11 55	8.8	—	—	06 41	7.2	19 07	7.0
16	Friday	02 55	6.8	15 06	6.8	08 22	12.4	20 35	12.5	00 04	9.1	12 28	8.8	07 13	7.3	19 39	7.1
17	Saturday	03 29	6.9	15 40	6.8	08 55	12.2	21 06	12.4	00 36	9.0	12 59	8.8	07 45	7.3	20 12	7.1
18	Sunday	04 04	6.9	16 13	6.7	09 24	12.1	21 33	12.2	01 09	9.0	13 32	8.8	08 18	7.2	20 46	7.0
19	Monday	04 39	6.8	16 46	6.6	09 52	12.0	22 04	12.1	01 43	8.9	14 06	8.7	08 52	7.2	21 21	6.9
20	Tuesday	05 14	6.7	17 21	6.5	10 25	11.8	22 41	11.8	02 19	8.7	14 43	8.5	09 30	7.0	22 00	6.7
21	Wednesday	05 53	6.5	18 02	6.4	11 05	11.5	23 25	11.3	03 01	8.5	15 28	8.2	10 13	6.8	22 45	6.5
22	Thursday	06 37	6.3	18 53	6.2	11 54	10.9	—	—	03 52	8.1	16 25	7.9	11 04	6.5	23 41	6.2
23	Friday	07 33	6.1	19 59	6.0	00 21	10.7	12 59	10.4	04 57	7.8	17 37	7.7	—	—	12 07	6.2
24	Saturday	08 45	5.9	21 18	6.0	01 39	10.3	14 27	10.3	06 12	7.6	18 55	7.9	01 00	6.0	13 42	6.1
25	Sunday	10 07	6.1	22 41	6.2	03 16	10.5	15 58	11.1	07 32	7.9	20 09	8.4	02 30	6.2	15 12	6.4
26	Monday	11 20	6.4	23 51	6.7	04 36	11.5	17 07	12.2	08 45	8.5	21 11	9.1	03 35	6.7	16 17	6.9
27	Tuesday	—	—	12 20	6.8	05 38	12.6	18 04	13.3	09 44	9.1	22 05	9.7	04 30	7.2	17 11	7.3
28	Wednesday	00 48	7.1	13 12	7.1	06 30	13.5	18 54	14.1	10 35	9.6	22 53	10.1	05 19	7.8	18 00	7.7
29	Thursday	01 40	7.4	13 59	7.3	07 19	14.0	19 41	14.6	11 23	9.9	23 40	10.3	06 05	8.2	18 44	7.9
30	Friday	02 28	7.6	14 45	7.5	08 05	14.3	20 26	14.7	—	—	12 08	9.9	06 49	8.4	19 26	8.0
31	Saturday	03 14	7.6	15 28	7.5	08 49	14.3	21 08	14.4	00 25	10.3	12 52	9.8	07 33	8.5	20 06	7.9

JULY 1996   *continued*

		GREENOCK *Datum of predictions 1.62 m below*				LEITH *Datum of predictions 2.90 m below*				DUN LAOGHAIRE †Datum of predictions 0.20 m above			
		hr	ht m	hr	ht m	hr	ht m	hr	ht m	hr	ht m	hr	ht m
1	Monday	00 09	3.3	12 23	3.3	02 12	5.7	14 40	5.8	11 20	4.1	23 29	4.3
2	Tuesday	00 55	3.5	13 16	3.3	02 59	5.8	15 29	5.9	—	—	12 07	4.2
3	Wednesday	01 40	3.6	14 08	3.3	03 45	5.9	16 18	5.9	00 15	4.4	12 58	4.1
4	Thursday	02 24	3.7	14 58	3.4	04 33	5.9	17 08	5.8	01 06	4.4	13 50	4.1
5	Friday	03 08	3.7	15 46	3.3	05 24	5.7	18 00	5.6	01 58	4.3	14 45	4.0
6	Saturday	03 53	3.6	16 34	3.3	06 18	5.6	18 54	5.3	02 55	4.2	15 43	3.8
7	Sunday	04 41	3.5	17 33	3.2	07 14	5.3	19 50	5.1	03 55	4.0	16 46	3.7
8	Monday	05 33	3.3	18 13	3.1	08 11	5.1	20 48	4.9	05 02	3.9	17 50	3.6
9	Tuesday	06 34	3.1	19 09	3.0	09 12	4.9	21 49	4.7	06 11	3.8	18 56	3.6
10	Wednesday	07 53	2.9	20 18	2.9	10 14	4.8	22 52	4.7	07 19	3.7	19 58	3.6
11	Thursday	09 21	2.9	21 38	2.9	11 17	4.8	23 53	4.8	08 23	3.6	20 57	3.7
12	Friday	10 25	3.0	22 37	3.0	—	—	12 16	4.8	09 22	3.6	21 48	3.8
13	Saturday	11 16	3.0	23 24	3.2	00 49	4.9	13 12	4.9	10 13	3.7	22 30	3.8
14	Sunday	—	—	12 02	3.0	01 39	5.1	13 59	5.0	10 53	3.7	23 05	3.9
15	Monday	00 06	3.2	12 44	3.0	02 19	5.2	14 39	5.1	11 25	3.7	23 34	3.9
16	Tuesday	00 44	3.3	13 22	3.0	02 54	5.3	15 14	5.2	11 56	3.7	—	—
17	Wednesday	01 17	3.3	13 57	3.0	03 26	5.3	15 47	5.2	00 05	3.9	12 29	3.7
18	Thursday	01 48	3.4	14 29	3.0	03 58	5.3	16 21	5.2	00 38	3.9	13 02	3.7
19	Friday	02 19	3.4	15 01	3.0	04 32	5.3	16 58	5.1	01 12	3.9	13 38	3.7
20	Saturday	02 53	3.4	15 35	3.0	05 09	5.2	17 37	5.1	01 50	3.9	14 17	3.7
21	Sunday	03 29	3.3	16 13	3.0	05 50	5.1	18 18	5.0	02 33	3.8	15 01	3.6
22	Monday	04 08	3.3	16 53	2.9	06 33	5.0	19 02	4.9	03 18	3.8	15 48	3.6
23	Tuesday	04 49	3.2	17 38	2.8	07 18	4.8	19 48	4.7	04 07	3.7	16 41	3.5
24	Wednesday	05 38	3.0	18 28	2.8	08 07	4.7	20 39	4.6	05 03	3.5	17 39	3.4
25	Thursday	06 36	2.9	19 30	2.7	09 06	4.6	21 42	4.6	06 08	3.5	18 47	3.5
26	Friday	07 48	2.8	20 49	2.8	10 16	4.7	22 54	4.7	07 22	3.5	19 52	3.6
27	Saturday	09 10	2.9	22 05	2.9	11 29	4.9	—	—	08 28	3.6	20 51	3.8
28	Sunday	10 20	3.1	23 03	3.2	00 01	5.0	12 35	5.2	09 27	3.8	21 43	4.0
29	Monday	11 19	3.2	23 53	3.4	01 01	5.3	13 32	5.5	10 19	4.0	22 30	4.2
30	Tuesday	—	—	12 13	3.3	01 54	5.7	14 25	5.8	11 07	4.1	23 16	4.4
31	Wednesday	00 41	3.5	13 05	3.4	02 43	5.9	15 14	6.0	11 53	4.2	23 59	4.5

NOTES:
*Difference of height in metres from Ordnance datum (Newlyn)
†Difference of height in metres from Ordnance datum (Dublin)
hr hour
m metres

AUGUST 1996   *continued*

		GREENOCK				LEITH				DUN LAOGHAIRE			
1	Thursday	01 27	3.7	13 56	3.4	03 30	6.0	16 01	6.0	—	—	12 40	4.2
2	Friday	02 11	3.8	14 42	3.4	04 16	6.0	16 49	5.9	00 47	4.4	13 28	4.1
3	Saturday	02 54	3.8	15 26	3.4	05 05	5.9	17 38	5.7	01 35	4.4	14 17	4.0
4	Sunday	03 36	3.7	16 07	3.4	05 55	5.7	18 29	5.4	02 27	4.2	15 10	3.8
5	Monday	04 18	3.6	16 49	3.3	06 47	5.4	19 20	5.1	03 23	4.0	16 07	3.7
6	Tuesday	05 03	3.4	17 33	3.2	07 42	5.1	20 15	4.8	04 25	3.8	17 10	3.6
7	Wednesday	05 53	3.1	18 21	3.1	08 41	4.8	21 15	4.6	05 36	3.6	18 17	3.5
8	Thursday	06 53	2.9	19 17	2.9	09 45	4.6	22 19	4.5	06 48	3.5	19 24	3.5
9	Friday	08 51	2.7	20 48	2.9	10 51	4.5	23 23	4.6	07 55	3.5	20 26	3.6
10	Saturday	10 11	2.8	22 12	3.0	11 54	4.6	—	—	08 59	3.5	21 21	3.7
11	Sunday	11 03	3.0	23 03	3.1	00 22	4.8	12 51	4.8	09 51	3.6	22 06	3.8
12	Monday	11 46	3.0	23 46	3.3	01 13	5.0	13 38	5.0	10 31	3.6	22 42	3.9
13	Tuesday	—	—	12 26	3.0	01 55	5.2	14 16	5.1	11 05	3.7	23 14	4.0
14	Wednesday	00 24	3.3	13 04	3.0	02 30	5.3	14 49	5.2	11 34	3.7	23 42	4.0
15	Thursday	00 57	3.3	13 37	3.0	03 02	5.4	15 21	5.3	—	—	12 02	3.8
16	Friday	01 25	3.3	14 05	3.0	03 34	5.4	15 54	5.3	00 10	4.0	12 33	3.8
17	Saturday	01 55	3.4	14 33	3.0	04 07	5.4	16 30	5.3	00 44	4.0	13 07	3.8
18	Sunday	02 28	3.4	15 04	3.1	04 44	5.3	17 08	5.3	01 20	4.0	13 45	3.8
19	Monday	03 04	3.4	15 38	3.1	05 23	5.2	17 49	5.2	02 01	3.9	14 28	3.8
20	Tuesday	03 41	3.4	16 15	3.1	06 04	5.1	18 31	5.0	02 46	3.8	15 14	3.7
21	Wednesday	04 20	3.2	16 55	3.0	06 49	5.0	19 16	4.9	03 35	3.7	16 04	3.6
22	Thursday	05 03	3.1	17 43	2.9	07 37	4.8	20 07	4.7	04 31	3.6	17 03	3.5
23	Friday	05 58	2.9	18 46	2.8	08 35	4.7	21 07	4.6	05 37	3.5	18 12	3.5
24	Saturday	07 12	2.8	20 16	2.8	09 46	4.6	22 22	4.7	06 58	3.5	19 28	3.6
25	Sunday	08 51	2.8	21 45	3.0	11 07	4.8	23 37	4.9	08 13	3.6	20 32	3.8
26	Monday	10 11	3.0	22 46	3.2	—	—	12 18	5.2	09 15	3.8	21 27	4.0
27	Tuesday	11 11	3.2	23 37	3.5	00 40	5.3	13 17	5.5	10 08	4.0	22 16	4.2
28	Wednesday	—	—	12 02	3.3	01 35	5.7	14 09	5.8	10 54	4.1	23 00	4.4
29	Thursday	00 24	3.6	12 51	3.4	02 24	5.9	14 56	6.0	11 37	4.2	23 42	4.5
30	Friday	01 10	3.8	13 37	3.5	03 10	6.1	15 41	6.0	—	—	12 19	4.2
31	Saturday	01 54	3.8	14 19	3.5	03 55	6.1	16 25	5.9	00 26	4.4	13 03	4.1

SEPTEMBER 1996 *High water* GMT

		LONDON BRIDGE *Datum of predictions 3.20 m below*				AVONMOUTH *Datum of predictions 6.50 m below*				LIVERPOOL *Datum of predictions 4.93 m below*				HULL (*Albert Dock*) *Datum of predictions 3.90 m below*			
		hr	ht m	hr	ht m	hr	ht m	hr	ht m	hr	ht m	hr	ht m	hr	ht m	hr	ht m
1	Sunday	03 58	7.6	16 10	7.5	09 29	13.9	21 48	13.8	01 10	10.0	13 34	9.5	08 16	8.3	20 46	7.6
2	Monday	04 39	7.4	16 49	7.3	10 05	13.2	22 23	12.9	01 52	9.6	14 15	9.1	08 59	8.0	21 25	7.3
3	Tuesday	05 17	7.1	17 26	7.0	10 38	12.4	22 56	11.9	02 34	9.1	14 55	8.6	09 43	7.5	22 06	6.8
4	Wednesday	05 52	6.7	18 04	6.6	11 11	11.4	23 32	10.8	03 18	8.4	15 39	8.1	10 30	6.8	22 52	6.3
5	Thursday	06 29	6.3	18 50	6.2	11 52	10.4	————		04 07	7.8	16 32	7.5	11 26	6.2	23 59	5.9
6	Friday	07 18	5.9	20 06	5.8	00 25	9.8	13 04	9.7	05 17	7.2	17 55	7.2	————		12 48	5.8
7	Saturday	09 01	5.7	21 49	5.7	02 14	9.4	14 48	9.7	06 50	7.1	19 24	7.3	01 30	5.7	14 08	5.7
8	Sunday	10 20	5.8	22 55	6.0	03 31	9.8	15 55	10.3	08 02	7.4	20 27	7.8	02 38	5.9	15 13	5.8
9	Monday	11 20	6.1	23 50	6.3	04 29	10.6	16 49	11.2	08 56	7.9	21 16	8.3	03 35	6.2	16 07	6.1
10	Tuesday	————		12 11	6.4	05 18	11.5	17 36	12.0	09 41	8.3	21 57	8.7	04 23	6.6	16 52	6.5
11	Wednesday	00 37	6.5	12 54	6.6	06 01	12.2	18 18	12.6	10 20	8.7	22 34	9.0	05 03	6.9	17 30	6.8
12	Thursday	01 18	6.7	13 32	6.7	06 41	12.6	18 58	12.9	10 56	8.9	23 07	9.1	05 39	7.1	18 05	7.0
13	Friday	01 53	6.8	14 06	6.8	07 19	12.7	19 35	12.9	11 28	9.0	23 38	9.1	06 12	7.3	18 37	7.2
14	Saturday	02 27	6.9	14 40	6.9	07 56	12.7	20 10	12.8	————		12 00	9.0	06 45	7.4	19 11	7.3
15	Sunday	03 02	7.0	15 15	6.9	08 29	12.5	20 42	12.6	00 09	9.1	12 31	9.0	07 19	7.4	19 44	7.3
16	Monday	03 37	7.0	15 50	6.9	08 59	12.4	21 11	12.5	00 42	9.1	13 04	9.0	07 53	7.4	20 18	7.3
17	Tuesday	04 13	7.0	16 24	6.8	09 29	12.3	21 44	12.4	01 17	9.0	13 39	8.9	08 30	7.3	20 54	7.1
18	Wednesday	04 48	6.8	17 00	6.6	10 04	12.1	22 22	12.1	01 55	8.9	14 17	8.7	09 09	7.1	21 33	6.9
19	Thursday	05 25	6.5	17 41	6.4	10 44	11.7	23 05	11.4	02 37	8.5	15 02	8.4	09 54	6.8	22 18	6.6
20	Friday	06 07	6.3	18 30	6.2	11 32	11.0	————		03 29	8.1	16 00	8.0	10 46	6.5	23 13	6.3
21	Saturday	06 58	6.0	19 33	5.9	00 00	10.6	12 36	10.3	04 36	7.7	17 13	7.7	11 53	6.1	————	
22	Sunday	08 10	5.8	20 57	5.9	01 18	10.0	14 11	10.1	05 56	7.5	18 37	7.8	00 31	6.1	13 36	6.1
23	Monday	09 43	5.9	22 25	6.2	03 06	10.3	15 46	10.9	07 22	7.8	19 54	8.3	02 05	6.2	14 58	6.4
24	Tuesday	10 59	6.3	23 35	6.7	04 24	11.3	16 53	12.1	08 33	8.4	20 56	9.0	03 12	6.7	16 01	6.9
25	Wednesday	11 59	6.8	————		05 23	12.5	17 47	13.3	09 29	9.1	21 48	9.6	04 08	7.3	16 54	7.4
26	Thursday	00 31	7.2	12 51	7.2	06 13	13.5	18 35	14.1	10 17	9.6	22 35	10.0	04 58	7.8	17 41	7.8
27	Friday	01 21	7.4	13 37	7.4	06 59	14.1	19 20	14.5	11 02	9.8	23 19	10.2	05 44	8.2	18 22	8.0
28	Saturday	02 06	7.6	14 20	7.5	07 42	14.3	20 03	14.5	11 45	9.8	————		06 28	8.4	19 02	8.0
29	Sunday	02 49	7.6	15 02	7.5	08 24	14.1	20 44	14.2	00 02	10.1	12 26	9.7	07 12	8.4	19 40	7.9
30	Monday	03 30	7.5	15 43	7.5	09 02	13.7	21 21	13.6	00 44	9.8	13 05	9.4	07 54	8.2	20 17	7.6

OCTOBER 1996 *High water* GMT

		LONDON BRIDGE				AVONMOUTH				LIVERPOOL				HULL (*Albert Dock*)			
1	Tuesday	04 09	7.4	16 22	7.3	09 36	13.1	21 54	12.7	01 23	9.4	13 43	9.1	08 35	7.8	20 53	7.3
2	Wednesday	04 43	7.1	16 59	7.0	10 07	12.3	22 24	11.8	02 02	8.9	14 20	8.6	09 17	7.3	21 29	6.8
3	Thursday	05 15	6.8	17 36	6.6	10 37	11.4	22 56	10.8	02 42	8.3	15 01	8.1	09 59	6.7	22 07	6.4
4	Friday	05 49	6.4	18 18	6.2	11 12	10.5	23 39	9.8	03 27	7.7	15 48	7.6	10 47	6.1	22 53	5.9
5	Saturday	06 30	6.0	19 11	5.7	————		12 09	9.6	04 25	7.2	16 54	7.2	11 57	5.6	————	
6	Sunday	07 27	5.6	20 54	5.5	01 04	9.1	14 06	9.4	05 58	6.9	18 35	7.1	00 28	5.6	13 31	5.5
7	Monday	09 30	5.5	22 17	5.7	02 54	9.4	15 20	10.0	07 25	7.1	19 50	7.5	01 59	5.7	14 38	5.7
8	Tuesday	10 40	5.8	23 14	6.1	03 55	10.2	16 16	10.9	08 23	7.6	20 43	8.0	02 59	6.0	15 32	6.0
9	Wednesday	11 34	6.2	————		04 45	11.2	17 04	11.7	09 09	8.2	21 25	8.5	03 48	6.4	16 17	6.5
10	Thursday	00 02	6.4	12 19	6.4	05 30	12.0	17 48	12.4	09 49	8.6	22 03	8.8	04 30	6.8	16 57	6.9
11	Friday	00 43	6.6	12 58	6.6	06 11	12.5	18 28	12.8	10 24	8.9	22 36	9.1	05 07	7.1	17 33	7.2
12	Saturday	01 20	6.8	13 35	6.8	06 50	12.8	19 07	12.9	10 57	9.1	23 09	9.2	05 42	7.4	18 08	7.4
13	Sunday	01 56	7.0	14 11	7.0	07 27	12.9	19 43	13.0	11 30	9.2	23 42	9.2	06 18	7.5	18 42	7.6
14	Monday	02 33	7.1	14 49	7.1	08 02	12.9	20 18	12.9	————		12 03	9.2	06 54	7.6	19 17	7.6
15	Tuesday	03 11	7.1	15 28	7.1	08 36	12.8	20 53	12.9	00 17	9.2	12 39	9.2	07 32	7.5	19 53	7.5
16	Wednesday	03 50	7.0	16 07	7.0	09 11	12.7	21 29	12.7	00 56	9.2	13 17	9.1	08 11	7.4	20 31	7.3
17	Thursday	04 27	6.8	16 47	6.8	09 48	12.5	22 09	12.3	01 37	8.9	13 59	8.9	08 54	7.2	21 11	7.0
18	Friday	05 05	6.5	17 29	6.5	10 30	11.9	22 54	11.6	02 23	8.6	14 47	8.6	09 41	6.9	21 58	6.7
19	Saturday	05 45	6.2	18 18	6.2	11 19	11.2	23 48	10.7	03 17	8.2	15 46	8.2	10 37	6.5	22 54	6.4
20	Sunday	06 33	6.0	19 19	6.0	————		12 23	10.5	04 23	7.7	16 58	7.9	11 49	6.2	————	
21	Monday	07 42	5.8	20 43	5.9	01 05	10.1	14 00	10.3	05 44	7.6	18 20	7.9	00 12	6.2	13 24	6.2
22	Tuesday	09 20	5.9	22 06	6.3	02 50	10.3	15 28	11.0	07 07	7.9	19 34	8.4	01 39	6.4	14 39	6.5
23	Wednesday	10 35	6.4	23 12	6.8	04 03	11.3	16 31	12.0	08 15	8.4	20 36	8.9	02 47	6.8	15 39	7.0
24	Thursday	11 35	6.8	————		05 01	12.3	17 25	13.0	09 10	9.0	21 29	9.4	03 44	7.3	16 32	7.4
25	Friday	00 09	7.2	12 28	7.2	05 50	13.2	18 13	13.7	09 57	9.4	22 15	9.8	04 36	7.7	17 17	7.7
26	Saturday	00 58	7.5	13 14	7.3	06 35	13.8	18 57	14.1	10 41	9.6	22 59	9.9	05 23	8.0	17 59	7.8
27	Sunday	01 43	7.5	13 58	7.4	07 18	14.0	19 40	14.1	11 21	9.6	23 40	9.8	06 08	8.2	18 37	7.9
28	Monday	02 25	7.4	14 40	7.4	07 58	13.8	20 20	13.8	————		12 00	9.5	06 52	8.1	19 15	7.8
29	Tuesday	03 04	7.3	15 20	7.3	08 36	13.5	20 57	13.2	00 19	9.5	12 37	9.3	07 34	7.9	19 51	7.6
30	Wednesday	03 40	7.2	15 59	7.2	09 10	12.9	21 29	12.5	00 57	9.2	13 14	9.0	08 14	7.6	20 26	7.3
31	Thursday	04 13	7.0	16 36	7.0	09 41	12.3	21 59	11.8	01 35	8.8	13 51	8.7	08 54	7.1	20 59	6.9

SEPTEMBER 1996 *continued*

	GREENOCK *Datum of predictions 1.62 m below*				LEITH *Datum of predictions 2.90 m below*				DUN LAOGHAIRE †Datum of predictions 0.20 m above			
	hr	m	hr	m	hr	m	hr	m	hr	m	hr	m
1 Sunday	02 35	3.8	14 58	3.5	04 40	6.0	17 10	5.7	01 10	4.3	13 47	4.0
2 Monday	03 14	3.8	15 35	3.5	05 27	5.7	17 57	5.4	01 57	4.2	14 35	3.9
3 Tuesday	03 53	3.6	16 13	3.5	06 17	5.4	18 46	5.1	02 49	4.0	15 27	3.7
4 Wednesday	04 33	3.4	16 55	3.3	07 09	5.0	19 39	4.8	03 48	3.7	16 25	3.6
5 Thursday	05 18	3.1	17 41	3.2	08 08	4.7	20 38	4.5	04 57	3.5	17 34	3.4
6 Friday	06 11	2.9	18 34	3.0	09 14	4.4	21 45	4.4	06 12	3.3	18 45	3.4
7 Saturday	07 28	2.7	19 42	2.9	10 23	4.4	22 52	4.5	07 25	3.3	19 50	3.5
8 Sunday	09 53	2.8	21 37	3.0	11 28	4.5	23 51	4.7	08 31	3.4	20 49	3.6
9 Monday	10 43	2.9	22 36	3.1	——	—	12 23	4.7	09 26	3.5	21 37	3.8
10 Tuesday	11 24	3.1	23 20	3.3	00 42	4.9	13 10	4.9	10 07	3.6	22 16	3.9
11 Wednesday	12 02	3.1	23 58	3.3	01 25	5.1	13 47	5.1	10 40	3.7	22 49	4.0
12 Thursday	——	—	12 37	3.2	02 01	5.3	14 20	5.3	11 10	3.8	23 18	4.0
13 Friday	00 29	3.3	13 10	3.2	02 34	5.4	14 52	5.4	11 36	3.8	23 44	4.0
14 Saturday	00 57	3.4	13 36	3.2	03 07	5.5	15 26	5.5	——	—	12 03	3.9
15 Sunday	01 29	3.4	14 03	3.2	03 41	5.5	16 02	5.5	00 14	4.0	12 37	3.9
16 Monday	02 03	3.5	14 33	3.3	04 18	5.5	16 40	5.4	00 52	4.0	13 16	3.9
17 Tuesday	02 40	3.5	15 07	3.3	04 57	5.4	17 20	5.3	01 33	4.0	13 58	3.9
18 Wednesday	03 17	3.4	15 42	3.2	05 39	5.3	18 03	5.2	02 18	3.9	14 45	3.8
19 Thursday	03 56	3.3	16 21	3.2	06 24	5.1	18 50	5.0	03 09	3.8	15 37	3.7
20 Friday	04 38	3.2	17 07	3.0	07 15	4.9	19 42	4.8	04 07	3.6	16 36	3.6
21 Saturday	05 32	3.0	18 11	2.9	08 14	4.7	20 43	4.6	05 18	3.5	17 46	3.5
22 Sunday	06 49	2.8	19 50	2.9	09 27	4.7	21 59	4.7	06 44	3.5	19 06	3.6
23 Monday	08 42	2.8	21 26	3.1	10 52	4.8	23 18	5.0	08 00	3.6	20 15	3.8
24 Tuesday	10 03	3.1	22 28	3.3	——	—	12 04	5.2	09 04	3.8	21 13	4.0
25 Wednesday	10 59	3.3	23 19	3.6	00 21	5.3	13 02	5.5	09 57	4.0	22 02	4.2
26 Thursday	11 47	3.4	——	—	01 16	5.7	13 51	5.8	10 42	4.1	22 46	4.3
27 Friday	00 06	3.7	12 32	3.5	02 04	5.9	14 36	5.9	11 23	4.2	23 26	4.4
28 Saturday	00 51	3.8	13 13	3.6	02 49	6.0	15 18	6.0	——	—	12 01	4.1
29 Sunday	01 33	3.8	13 52	3.6	03 32	6.0	15 59	5.9	00 06	4.4	12 40	4.1
30 Monday	02 13	3.8	14 28	3.7	04 15	5.9	16 41	5.7	00 48	4.2	13 19	4.0

NOTES:
*Difference of height in metres from Ordnance datum (Newlyn)
†Difference of height in metres from Ordnance datum (Dublin)
hr hour
m metres

OCTOBER 1996 *continued*

	GREENOCK				LEITH				DUN LAOGHAIRE			
1 Tuesday	02 51	3.7	15 04	3.7	04 59	5.6	17 23	5.4	01 32	4.1	14 02	3.9
2 Wednesday	03 28	3.6	15 41	3.6	05 44	5.3	18 08	5.1	02 20	3.9	14 50	3.8
3 Thursday	04 07	3.4	16 21	3.5	06 33	5.0	18 57	4.8	03 14	3.7	15 45	3.6
4 Friday	04 50	3.2	17 06	3.3	07 30	4.6	19 55	4.5	04 19	3.4	16 50	3.5
5 Saturday	05 42	2.9	17 58	3.2	08 37	4.4	21 06	4.4	05 34	3.3	18 03	3.4
6 Sunday	06 48	2.7	19 00	3.0	09 48	4.3	22 15	4.4	06 49	3.2	19 13	3.4
7 Monday	09 11	2.7	20 25	3.0	10 53	4.4	23 15	4.6	07 55	3.3	20 13	3.6
8 Tuesday	10 10	2.9	21 55	3.1	11 48	4.7	——	—	08 51	3.5	21 04	3.7
9 Wednesday	10 53	3.1	22 44	3.3	00 06	4.8	12 35	4.9	09 35	3.6	21 45	3.8
10 Thursday	11 31	3.2	23 22	3.3	00 50	5.1	13 13	5.1	10 12	3.8	22 21	3.9
11 Friday	12 06	3.3	23 55	3.4	01 28	5.3	13 48	5.3	10 42	3.9	22 51	4.0
12 Saturday	——	—	12 37	3.3	02 04	5.4	14 23	5.5	11 09	3.9	23 19	4.0
13 Sunday	00 27	3.4	13 06	3.3	02 39	5.6	14 58	5.6	11 36	4.0	23 49	4.1
14 Monday	01 02	3.5	13 34	3.4	03 16	5.6	15 35	5.6	——	—	12 09	4.1
15 Tuesday	01 40	3.5	14 06	3.4	03 54	5.6	16 14	5.6	00 28	4.1	12 49	4.1
16 Wednesday	02 19	3.5	14 41	3.5	04 35	5.6	16 55	5.5	00 11	4.0	13 33	4.0
17 Thursday	02 58	3.5	15 18	3.5	05 18	5.4	17 39	5.3	01 58	3.9	14 21	4.0
18 Friday	03 39	3.4	15 58	3.4	06 06	5.2	18 28	5.1	02 52	3.8	15 15	3.9
19 Saturday	04 24	3.2	16 46	3.2	07 00	5.0	19 23	4.9	03 54	3.7	16 16	3.8
20 Sunday	05 21	3.0	17 51	3.1	08 00	4.8	20 27	4.7	05 08	3.5	17 28	3.7
21 Monday	06 43	2.9	19 29	3.0	09 14	4.7	21 43	4.8	06 31	3.5	18 46	3.7
22 Tuesday	08 30	2.9	21 03	3.2	10 36	4.9	22 59	5.0	07 45	3.7	19 55	3.9
23 Wednesday	09 47	3.1	22 06	3.4	11 46	5.2	——	—	08 49	3.8	20 56	4.0
24 Thursday	10 41	3.3	22 58	3.6	00 01	5.3	12 43	5.5	09 42	4.0	21 48	4.2
25 Friday	11 27	3.5	23 45	3.7	00 55	5.6	13 31	5.7	10 28	4.1	22 33	4.2
26 Saturday	——	—	12 09	3.6	01 44	5.8	14 15	5.8	11 09	4.1	23 14	4.3
27 Sunday	00 30	3.7	12 49	3.6	02 28	5.9	14 56	5.8	11 45	4.1	23 51	4.2
28 Monday	01 13	3.7	13 25	3.7	03 11	5.8	15 34	5.7	——	—	12 19	4.1
29 Tuesday	01 52	3.7	14 01	3.7	03 51	5.7	16 12	5.6	00 31	4.1	12 57	4.1
30 Wednesday	02 30	3.6	14 37	3.8	04 32	5.5	16 50	5.4	01 13	4.0	13 37	4.0
31 Thursday	03 07	3.5	15 14	3.7	05 13	5.3	17 28	5.1	01 57	3.8	14 21	3.9

NOVEMBER 1996 *High water* GMT

		LONDON BRIDGE *Datum of predictions 3.20 m below				AVONMOUTH *Datum of predictions 6.50 m below				LIVERPOOL *Datum of predictions 4.93 m below				HULL (*Albert Dock*) *Datum of predictions 3.90 m below			
		hr	ht m	hr	ht m	hr	ht m	hr	ht m	hr	ht m	hr	ht m	hr	ht m	hr	ht m
1	Friday	04 45	6.8	17 13	6.6	10 11	11.5	22 30	11.0	02 13	8.3	14 30	8.3	09 33	6.6	21 33	6.6
2	Saturday	05 19	6.5	17 53	6.3	10 44	10.8	23 07	10.2	02 56	7.9	15 15	7.9	10 14	6.1	22 11	6.2
3	Sunday	05 59	6.1	18 40	5.9	11 27	10.0	—		03 45	7.4	16 08	7.5	11 04	5.7	23 01	5.8
4	Monday	06 47	5.8	19 38	5.6	00 03	9.5	12 48	9.4	04 51	7.0	17 20	7.2	—		12 24	5.5
5	Tuesday	07 54	5.5	21 01	5.6	01 45	9.2	14 29	9.6	06 22	7.0	18 48	7.3	00 38	5.6	13 48	5.6
6	Wednesday	09 32	5.6	22 18	5.8	03 07	9.8	15 33	10.4	07 35	7.4	19 54	7.7	02 09	5.8	14 48	5.9
7	Thursday	10 42	5.9	23 14	6.2	04 04	10.6	16 25	11.2	08 27	7.9	20 43	8.2	03 05	6.2	15 38	6.4
8	Friday	11 34	6.2	—		04 53	11.5	17 12	11.9	09 11	8.4	21 24	8.6	03 52	6.6	16 21	6.9
9	Saturday	00 01	6.5	12 19	6.5	05 37	12.2	17 56	12.5	09 49	8.8	22 02	9.0	04 33	7.0	17 01	7.3
10	Sunday	00 44	6.8	13 01	6.8	06 18	12.7	18 37	12.9	10 25	9.1	22 39	9.2	05 13	7.3	17 39	7.5
11	Monday	01 24	7.0	13 42	7.0	06 58	13.1	19 17	13.1	11 02	9.3	23 17	9.3	05 52	7.5	18 16	7.7
12	Tuesday	02 06	7.2	14 24	7.2	07 37	13.2	19 57	13.2	11 39	9.4	23 57	9.4	06 33	7.6	18 54	7.7
13	Wednesday	02 48	7.2	15 09	7.3	08 16	13.3	20 38	13.2	—		12 19	9.4	07 14	7.6	19 33	7.7
14	Thursday	03 30	7.1	15 54	7.2	08 57	13.2	21 19	13.0	00 40	9.3	13 03	9.4	07 58	7.5	20 13	7.5
15	Friday	04 12	6.9	16 38	7.0	09 39	12.9	22 03	12.6	01 26	9.1	13 49	9.2	08 44	7.3	20 57	7.3
16	Saturday	04 52	6.6	17 23	6.7	10 23	12.4	22 49	12.0	02 15	8.8	14 40	8.9	09 34	7.0	21 45	7.0
17	Sunday	05 33	6.3	18 12	6.4	11 13	11.7	23 41	11.3	03 09	8.4	15 37	8.6	10 31	6.7	22 41	6.8
18	Monday	06 19	6.1	19 11	6.2	—		12 14	11.1	04 12	8.0	16 43	8.3	11 41	6.5	23 51	6.6
19	Tuesday	07 25	6.0	20 26	6.2	00 50	10.6	13 39	10.8	05 26	7.8	17 57	8.2	—		12 59	6.4
20	Wednesday	08 55	6.1	21 41	6.4	02 21	10.6	15 00	11.1	06 42	7.9	19 09	8.3	01 09	6.6	14 10	6.6
21	Thursday	10 08	6.4	22 46	6.8	03 33	11.1	16 03	11.8	07 51	8.3	20 13	8.7	02 18	6.8	15 11	6.9
22	Friday	11 10	6.8	23 44	7.2	04 33	11.9	16 59	12.5	08 48	8.7	21 08	9.1	03 19	7.1	16 05	7.2
23	Saturday	—		12 04	7.1	05 25	12.6	17 49	13.1	09 37	9.1	21 56	9.3	04 13	7.5	16 52	7.4
24	Sunday	00 35	7.3	12 54	7.2	06 11	13.2	18 34	13.4	10 21	9.3	22 40	9.4	05 04	7.7	17 35	7.6
25	Monday	01 21	7.3	13 39	7.2	06 54	13.4	19 17	13.5	11 01	9.4	23 21	9.4	05 50	7.8	18 15	7.6
26	Tuesday	02 03	7.2	14 21	7.2	07 35	13.4	19 58	13.3	11 39	9.3	23 59	9.2	06 34	7.7	18 53	7.6
27	Wednesday	02 41	7.1	15 02	7.1	08 13	13.2	20 36	12.9	—		12 15	9.2	07 17	7.5	19 30	7.5
28	Thursday	03 16	7.0	15 40	7.0	08 49	12.8	21 10	12.4	00 36	9.0	12 51	9.1	07 56	7.3	20 04	7.3
29	Friday	03 48	6.9	16 17	6.9	09 21	12.3	21 41	11.9	01 12	8.8	13 28	8.9	08 34	7.0	20 35	7.1
30	Saturday	04 20	6.7	16 53	6.6	09 52	11.8	22 12	11.3	01 50	8.5	14 06	8.6	09 10	6.6	21 07	6.8

DECEMBER 1996 *High water* GMT

		LONDON BRIDGE				AVONMOUTH				LIVERPOOL				HULL (*Albert Dock*)			
		hr	ht m	hr	ht m	hr	ht m	hr	ht m	hr	ht m	hr	ht m	hr	ht m	hr	ht m
1	Sunday	04 55	6.5	17 31	6.4	10 24	11.2	22 45	10.8	02 29	8.2	14 47	8.3	09 46	6.3	21 42	6.5
2	Monday	05 34	6.3	18 13	6.2	10 59	10.6	23 25	10.2	03 13	7.8	15 33	7.9	10 26	6.0	22 24	6.2
3	Tuesday	06 17	6.0	19 01	6.0	11 46	10.1	—		04 05	7.5	16 27	7.6	11 17	5.8	23 17	6.0
4	Wednesday	07 10	5.8	19 58	5.9	00 21	9.8	12 59	9.8	05 08	7.2	17 32	7.5	—		12 27	5.7
5	Thursday	08 17	5.7	21 05	5.9	01 43	9.7	14 26	10.0	06 23	7.3	18 42	7.6	00 28	5.9	13 48	5.9
6	Friday	09 33	5.8	22 14	6.1	03 04	10.1	15 33	10.6	07 31	7.6	19 47	7.9	01 58	6.0	14 51	6.2
7	Saturday	10 40	6.1	23 15	6.4	04 06	10.9	16 30	11.4	08 26	8.1	20 40	8.3	03 04	6.3	15 43	6.7
8	Sunday	11 37	6.4	—		04 59	11.8	17 21	12.1	09 12	8.6	21 28	8.8	03 57	6.7	16 29	7.1
9	Monday	00 07	6.7	12 28	6.8	05 47	12.5	18 08	12.8	09 55	9.1	22 12	9.1	04 45	7.1	17 12	7.5
10	Tuesday	00 55	7.0	13 16	7.0	06 32	13.1	18 54	13.2	10 37	9.4	22 57	9.4	05 30	7.4	17 54	7.7
11	Wednesday	01 42	7.2	14 04	7.3	07 16	13.5	19 40	13.5	11 20	9.6	23 42	9.5	06 15	7.6	18 34	7.8
12	Thursday	02 28	7.3	14 53	7.4	08 01	13.7	20 26	13.6	—		12 05	9.7	07 01	7.7	19 16	7.8
13	Friday	03 14	7.2	15 42	7.4	08 46	13.7	21 12	13.5	00 29	9.5	12 52	9.7	07 47	7.7	19 59	7.8
14	Saturday	04 00	7.1	16 29	7.2	09 32	13.5	21 57	13.2	01 17	9.4	13 41	9.6	08 35	7.5	20 44	7.7
15	Sunday	04 43	6.9	17 16	7.0	10 17	13.2	22 42	12.7	02 07	9.2	14 31	9.4	09 25	7.3	21 32	7.5
16	Monday	05 26	6.6	18 04	6.7	11 05	12.6	23 30	12.0	02 59	8.9	15 24	9.1	10 19	7.0	22 25	7.2
17	Tuesday	06 10	6.4	18 57	6.5	11 59	11.9	—		03 55	8.5	16 23	8.7	11 19	6.8	23 26	6.9
18	Wednesday	07 05	6.3	20 01	6.4	00 27	11.3	13 07	11.3	04 59	8.1	17 28	8.4	—		12 26	6.6
19	Thursday	08 23	6.2	21 11	6.4	01 41	10.9	14 24	11.1	06 10	8.0	18 38	8.2	00 36	6.8	13 36	6.5
20	Friday	09 38	6.4	22 18	6.6	02 57	10.9	15 31	11.3	07 21	8.0	19 46	8.3	01 47	6.7	14 39	6.6
21	Saturday	10 44	6.6	23 18	6.9	04 01	11.3	16 31	11.7	08 24	8.3	20 47	8.6	02 52	6.8	15 36	6.8
22	Sunday	11 43	6.9	—		04 57	11.8	17 25	12.2	09 17	8.7	21 39	8.8	03 52	7.0	16 28	7.1
23	Monday	00 13	7.0	12 36	7.0	05 47	12.4	18 13	12.6	10 04	9.0	22 25	9.0	04 46	7.2	17 14	7.2
24	Tuesday	01 02	7.0	13 23	7.0	06 33	12.9	18 58	12.9	10 45	9.1	23 06	9.1	05 35	7.2	17 56	7.3
25	Wednesday	01 45	6.9	14 07	6.9	07 15	13.1	19 40	12.9	11 23	9.2	23 44	9.1	06 20	7.2	18 34	7.4
26	Thursday	02 24	6.8	14 47	6.9	07 55	13.1	20 18	12.8	11 59	9.2	—		07 01	7.2	19 11	7.3
27	Friday	02 58	6.8	15 24	6.8	08 31	12.9	20 53	12.5	00 19	9.0	12 34	9.1	07 39	7.0	19 44	7.3
28	Saturday	03 29	6.7	15 59	6.8	09 05	12.6	21 25	12.2	00 54	8.9	13 09	9.0	08 14	6.9	20 15	7.1
29	Sunday	04 01	6.7	16 34	6.7	09 36	12.2	21 55	11.8	01 29	8.7	13 45	8.9	08 47	6.7	20 46	7.0
30	Monday	04 35	6.6	17 09	6.6	10 06	11.8	22 24	11.4	02 06	8.5	14 23	8.7	09 20	6.6	21 19	6.9
31	Tuesday	05 12	6.4	17 47	6.4	10 35	11.3	22 57	11.0	02 45	8.3	15 02	8.4	09 56	6.4	21 57	6.6

NOVEMBER 1996 *continued*

		GREENOCK *Datum of predictions 1.62 m below				LEITH *Datum of predictions 2.90 m below				DUN LAOGHAIRE †Datum of predictions 0.20 m above				NOTES:
		hr	ht m	hr	ht m	hr	ht m	hr	ht m	hr	ht m	hr	ht m	
1	Friday	03 46	3.4	15 53	3.6	05 56	5.0	18 09	4.9	02 48	3.7	15 10	3.7	*Difference of height in metres from Ordnance datum (Newlyn)
2	Saturday	04 28	3.2	16 35	3.5	06 44	4.7	18 57	4.7	03 45	3.5	16 08	3.6	†Difference of height in metres from Ordnance datum (Dublin)
3	Sunday	05 18	3.0	17 24	3.3	07 42	4.5	20 03	4.5	04 53	3.3	17 16	3.5	hr hour
4	Monday	06 17	2.9	18 21	3.1	08 55	4.3	21 24	4.4	06 05	3.3	18 26	3.4	m metres
5	Tuesday	07 30	2.8	19 26	3.1	10 05	4.4	22 30	4.5	07 13	3.3	19 29	3.5	
6	Wednesday	09 10	2.9	20 42	3.1	11 03	4.6	23 24	4.7	08 10	3.5	20 24	3.6	
7	Thursday	10 10	3.1	21 50	3.2	11 53	4.8	—	—	08 57	3.6	21 10	3.7	
8	Friday	10 53	3.2	22 38	3.3	00 11	5.0	12 36	5.1	09 37	3.8	21 48	3.8	
9	Saturday	11 31	3.3	23 18	3.4	00 53	5.2	13 15	5.3	10 11	3.9	22 22	4.0	
10	Sunday	12 04	3.4	23 57	3.4	01 33	5.4	13 54	5.5	10 40	4.0	22 54	4.0	
11	Monday	—	—	12 36	3.5	02 13	5.6	14 33	5.7	11 11	4.1	23 28	4.1	
12	Tuesday	00 38	3.5	13 10	3.5	02 53	5.7	15 12	5.7	11 46	4.2	—	—	
13	Wednesday	01 20	3.5	13 46	3.6	03 34	5.8	15 53	5.7	00 09	4.1	12 28	4.2	
14	Thursday	02 02	3.5	14 23	3.7	04 17	5.7	16 35	5.6	00 55	4.1	13 14	4.2	
15	Friday	02 45	3.5	15 03	3.6	05 03	5.6	17 21	5.4	01 45	4.0	14 04	4.1	
16	Saturday	03 30	3.4	15 46	3.6	05 53	5.4	18 12	5.2	02 41	3.9	15 00	4.0	
17	Sunday	04 19	3.3	16 35	3.4	06 49	5.1	19 09	5.0	03 44	3.8	16 01	4.0	
18	Monday	05 18	3.1	17 38	3.3	07 50	4.9	20 13	4.9	04 56	3.7	17 10	3.9	
19	Tuesday	06 33	3.0	19 03	3.2	09 00	4.8	21 25	4.9	06 11	3.7	18 22	3.9	
20	Wednesday	08 02	3.0	20 33	3.3	10 14	4.9	22 36	5.0	07 24	3.7	19 32	3.9	
21	Thursday	09 19	3.2	21 41	3.4	11 21	5.1	23 38	5.2	08 28	3.8	20 36	4.0	
22	Friday	10 16	3.3	22 36	3.5	—	—	12 18	5.3	09 23	4.0	21 32	4.0	
23	Saturday	11 04	3.5	23 26	3.6	00 33	5.4	13 10	5.4	10 12	4.0	22 23	4.1	
24	Sunday	11 46	3.6	—	—	01 24	5.5	13 55	5.6	10 55	4.1	23 05	4.1	
25	Monday	00 11	3.6	12 26	3.6	02 10	5.6	14 36	5.6	11 31	4.1	23 41	4.0	
26	Tuesday	00 55	3.6	13 03	3.7	02 52	5.6	15 13	5.6	—	—	12 03	4.1	
27	Wednesday	01 35	3.5	13 39	3.8	03 31	5.5	15 48	5.5	00 16	4.0	12 38	4.1	
28	Thursday	02 12	3.5	14 15	3.8	04 09	5.4	16 22	5.4	00 55	3.9	13 15	4.0	
29	Friday	02 49	3.4	14 51	3.8	04 47	5.2	16 57	5.2	01 36	3.8	13 56	4.0	
30	Saturday	03 27	3.3	15 28	3.7	05 26	5.0	17 35	5.1	02 20	3.7	14 40	3.9	

DECEMBER 1996 *continued*

		GREENOCK				LEITH				DUN LAOGHAIRE			
1	Sunday	04 08	3.2	16 08	3.6	06 08	4.9	18 18	4.9	03 10	3.5	15 28	3.7
2	Monday	04 53	3.1	16 51	3.4	06 54	4.7	19 07	4.7	04 05	3.4	16 22	3.6
3	Tuesday	05 45	3.0	17 41	3.3	07 47	4.5	20 05	4.5	05 10	3.3	17 25	3.5
4	Wednesday	06 42	2.9	18 38	3.1	08 50	4.5	21 18	4.5	06 18	3.3	18 33	3.4
5	Thursday	07 46	2.9	19 40	3.1	10 01	4.5	22 29	4.6	07 20	3.4	19 33	3.5
6	Friday	09 00	3.0	20 48	3.1	11 02	4.7	23 26	4.8	08 13	3.5	20 26	3.6
7	Saturday	10 05	3.1	21 51	3.2	11 55	4.9	—	—	08 57	3.7	21 11	3.7
8	Sunday	10 52	3.3	22 44	3.3	00 16	5.0	12 42	5.2	09 36	3.9	21 52	3.9
9	Monday	11 33	3.4	23 31	3.4	01 04	5.3	13 27	5.4	10 13	4.0	22 31	4.0
10	Tuesday	—	—	12 12	3.5	01 49	5.5	14 11	5.7	10 49	4.2	23 13	4.1
11	Wednesday	00 17	3.5	12 51	3.6	02 33	5.7	14 53	5.8	11 28	4.3	23 55	4.2
12	Thursday	01 04	3.5	13 31	3.7	03 18	5.8	15 36	5.8	—	—	12 11	4.3
13	Friday	01 51	3.5	14 12	3.8	04 03	5.8	16 20	5.8	00 43	4.0	12 59	4.3
14	Saturday	02 37	3.5	14 54	3.8	04 50	5.7	17 07	5.6	01 33	4.1	13 49	4.3
15	Sunday	03 24	3.5	15 38	3.7	05 41	5.5	17 58	5.5	02 29	4.0	14 44	4.2
16	Monday	04 14	3.4	16 27	3.6	06 36	5.3	18 55	5.2	03 30	3.9	15 44	4.1
17	Tuesday	05 08	3.3	17 23	3.5	07 35	5.1	19 56	5.1	04 36	3.8	16 48	4.0
18	Wednesday	06 09	3.2	18 29	3.3	08 38	4.9	21 02	4.9	05 45	3.7	17 57	3.9
19	Thursday	07 17	3.1	19 52	3.2	09 44	4.8	22 09	4.9	06 56	3.7	19 08	3.8
20	Friday	08 38	3.1	21 13	3.2	10 50	4.9	23 12	5.0	08 00	3.8	20 14	3.8
21	Saturday	09 46	3.2	22 16	3.3	11 51	5.0	—	—	09 00	3.9	21 16	3.9
22	Sunday	10 40	3.3	23 10	3.4	00 11	5.1	12 47	5.2	09 53	3.9	22 10	3.9
23	Monday	11 26	3.5	23 58	3.4	01 06	5.2	13 36	5.3	10 39	4.0	22 55	3.9
24	Tuesday	—	—	12 07	3.6	01 54	5.2	14 19	5.4	11 18	4.1	23 31	3.9
25	Wednesday	00 42	3.4	12 46	3.6	02 36	5.3	14 56	5.4	11 50	4.1	—	—
26	Thursday	01 23	3.3	13 22	3.7	03 14	5.3	15 30	5.4	00 03	3.8	12 21	4.1
27	Friday	02 00	3.3	13 57	3.7	03 50	5.2	16 02	5.4	00 38	3.8	12 55	4.0
28	Saturday	02 34	3.3	14 31	3.7	04 24	5.2	16 34	5.3	01 14	3.8	13 31	4.0
29	Sunday	03 09	3.2	15 06	3.7	05 01	5.1	17 11	5.2	01 52	3.7	14 09	3.9
30	Monday	03 46	3.2	15 42	3.6	05 40	5.0	17 51	5.0	02 34	3.6	14 51	3.8
31	Tuesday	04 25	3.1	16 21	3.5	06 23	4.9	18 36	4.9	03 18	3.6	15 36	3.7

World Geographical Statistics

THE EARTH

The shape of the Earth is that of an oblate spheroid or solid of revolution whose meridian sections are ellipses, whilst the sections at right angles are circles.

DIMENSIONS

Equatorial diameter = 12,756.28 km (7,926.38 miles)
Polar diameter = 12,713.50 km (7,899.80 miles)
Equatorial circumference = 40,075.01 km (24,901.45 miles)
Polar circumference = 40,008.00 km (24,859.82 miles)

The equatorial circumference is divided into 360 degrees of longitude, which is measured in degrees, minutes and seconds east or west of the Greenwich meridian (0°) to 180° (the meridian 180° E. coinciding with 180° W.). This was internationally ratified in 1884.

Distance north and south of the Equator is measured in degrees, minutes and seconds of latitude. The Equator is 0°, the North Pole is 90° N. and the South Pole is 90° S. The Tropics lie at 23° 26′ N. (Tropic of Cancer) and 23° 26′ S. (Tropic of Capricorn). The Arctic Circle lies at 66° 34′ N. and the Antarctic Circle at 66° 34′ S. (NB The Tropics and the Arctic and Antarctic circles are of variable latitude due to the mean obliquity of the Ecliptic; the values given are for 1996.5.)

AREA, ETC.

The surface area of the Earth is 510,069,120 km^2 (196,938,800 miles^2), of which the water area is 70.92 per cent and the land area is 29.08 per cent.

The velocity of a given point of the Earth's surface at the Equator exceeds 1,000 miles an hour (24,901.45 miles in 24 hours, viz 1,037.56 mph); the Earth's velocity in its orbit round the Sun averages 66,629 mph (584,081.400 miles in 365.256363 days). The Earth is distant from the Sun 92,955,900 miles, on average.

Source: Royal Greenwich Observatory

OCEANS

AREA

	km^2	miles^2
Pacific	166,240,000	64,186,300
Atlantic	86,550,000	33,420,000
Indian	73,427,000	28,350,500
Arctic	13,223,700	5,105,700

GREATEST DEPTHS

Greatest depth location	metres	feet
Mariana Trench (Pacific)	10,924	35,840
Puerto Rico Trench (Atlantic)	8,605	28,232
Java Trench (Indian)	7,125	23,376
Eurasian Basin (Arctic)	5,450	17,880

SEAS

AREA

	km^2	miles^2
South China	2,974,600	1,148,500
Caribbean	2,515,900	971,400
Mediterranean	2,509,900	969,100
Bering	2,226,100	873,000
Gulf of Mexico	1,507,600	582,100
Okhotsk	1,392,000	537,500
Japan	1,015,000	391,100
Hudson Bay	730,100	281,900
East China	664,600	256,600
Andaman	564,880	218,100
Black Sea	507,900	196,100
Red Sea	453,000	174,900
North Sea	427,100	164,900
Baltic Sea	382,000	147,500
Yellow Sea	294,000	113,500
Persian Gulf	230,000	88,800

GREATEST DEPTHS

	Maximum depth	
	metres	feet
Caribbean	8,605	28,232
East China	7,507	24,629
South China	7,258	23,812
Mediterranean	5,150	16,896
Andaman	4,267	14,000
Bering	3,936	12,913
Gulf of Mexico	3,504	11,496
Okhotsk	3,365	11,040
Japan	3,053	10,016
Red Sea	2,266	7,434
Black Sea	2,212	7,257
North Sea	439	1,440
Hudson Bay	111	364
Baltic Sea	90	295
Yellow Sea	73	240
Persian Gulf	73	240

THE CONTINENTS

There are six geographic continents, though America is often divided politically into North and Central America, and South America.

AFRICA is surrounded by sea except for the narrow isthmus of Suez in the north-east, through which is cut the Suez Canal. Its extreme longitudes are 17° 20′ W. at Cape Verde, Senegal, and 51° 24′ E. at Ras Hafun, Somalia. The extreme latitudes are 37° 20′ N. at Cape Blanc, Tunisia, and 34° 50′ S. at Cape Agulhas, South Africa, about 4,400 miles apart. The Equator passes through the middle of the continent.

NORTH AMERICA, including Mexico, is surrounded by ocean except in the south, where the isthmian states of CENTRAL AMERICA link North America with South America. Its extreme longitudes are 168° 5′ W. at Cape Prince of Wales, Alaska, and 55° 40′ W. at Cape Charles,

Newfoundland. The extreme continental latitudes are Point Barrow, Alaska (71°22' N.) and 14°22' N. at Ocós in the south of Mexico. The West Indies, about 65,000 square miles in area, extend from about 27° N. to 10° N. latitude.

SOUTH AMERICA lies mostly in the southern hemisphere; the Equator passes through the north of the continent. It is surrounded by ocean except where it is joined to Central America in the north by the narrow isthmus through which is cut the Panama Canal. Its extreme longitudes are 34° 47' W. at Cape Branco in Brazil and 81° 20' W. at Punta Pariña, Peru. The extreme latitudes are 12° 25' N. at Punta Gallinas, Colombia, and 55° 59' S. at Cape Horn, Chile.

ANTARCTICA lies almost entirely within the Antarctic Circle (66° 34' S.) and is the largest of the world's glaciated areas. The continent has an area of about 5.5 million square miles, 99 per cent of which is permanently ice-covered. The ice amounts to some 7.2 million cubic miles and represents more than 90 per cent of the world's fresh water. The environment is too hostile for unsupported human habitation. *See also* pages 788–9.

ASIA is the largest continent and occupies almost a third of the world's land surface. The extreme longitudes are about 26° E. on the west coast of Asia Minor and 169° 40' W. at Mys Dežneva (East Cape), Russia, a distance of about 6,000 miles. Its extreme northern latitude is 77° 45' N. at Cape Čeljuskin, Russia, and it extends over 5,000 miles south to about 1° 15' N. of the Equator. The islands of Japan, the Philippines and Indonesia ring the continent to the east and south-east.

AUSTRALIA is the smallest of the continents and lies in the southern hemisphere. It is entirely surrounded by ocean. Its extreme longitudes are 113° 9' E. at Steep Point and 153° 38' E. at Cape Byron. The extreme latitudes are 10° 40' S. at Cape York and 39° S. at South East Point.

EUROPE, including European Russia, is the smallest continent in the northern hemisphere. Its extreme latitudes are 71° 11' N. at North Cape in Norway, and 36° 23' N. at Cape Matapan in southern Greece, a distance of about 2,400 miles. Its breadth from Cape da Roca in Portugal (9° 30' W.) in the west to the Urals in the east is about 3,300 miles. The division between Europe and Asia is generally regarded as the watershed of the Ural Mountains; down the Ural river to Gur'yev, Kazakhstan; across the Caspian Sea to Apsheronskiy Poluostrov, near Baku; along the watershed of the Caucasus Mountains to Anapa and thence across the Black Sea to the Bosporus in Turkey; across the Sea of Marmara to Çanakkale Boğazi (Dardanelles).

	Area km²	miles²
Asia	43,998,000	16,988,000
*America	41,918,000	16,185,000
Africa	29,800,000	11,506,000
Antarctica	c.13,600,000	c.5,500,000
†Europe	9,699,000	3,745,000
Australia	7,618,493	2,941,526

*North and Central America has an area of 24,255,000 km² (9,365,000 miles²)

†Includes 5,571,000 km² (2,151,000 miles²) of former USSR territory, including the Baltic states, Belarus, Moldova, the Ukraine, that part of Russia west of the Ural Mountains and Kazakhstan west of the Ural river. European Turkey (24,378 km²/9,412 miles²) comprises territory to the west and north of the Bosporus and the Dardanelles

GLACIATED AREAS

It is estimated that 15,600,000 km² (6,020,000 miles²) or 10.51 per cent of the world's land surface is permanently covered with ice.

	Area km²	miles²
South Polar regions	13,597,000	5,250,000
North Polar regions (incl. Greenland or Kalaallit Nunaat)	1,965,000	758,500
Alaska-Canada	58,800	22,700
Asia	37,800	14,600
South America	11,900	4,600
Europe	10,700	4,128
New Zealand	984	380
Africa	238	92

PENINSULAS

	Area km²	miles²
Arabian	3,250,000	1,250,000
Southern Indian	2,072,000	800,000
Alaskan	1,500,000	580,000
Labradorian	1,300,000	500,000
Scandinavian	800,300	309,000
Iberian	584,000	225,500

LARGEST ISLANDS

Island (and Ocean)	Area km²	miles²
Greenland (Kalaallit Nunaat) (Arctic)	2,175,500	840,000
New Guinea (Pacific)	792,500	306,000
Borneo (Pacific)	725,450	280,100
Madagascar (Indian)	587,040	226,658
Baffin Island (Arctic)	476,200	183,810
Sumatra (Indian)	427,350	165,000
Honshu (Pacific)	227,413	87,805
*Great Britain (Atlantic)	218,040	84,186
Ellesmere Island (Arctic)	212,745	82,119
Victoria Island (Arctic)	212,250	81,930
Sulawesi (Celebes) (Indian)	178,700	69,000
South Island, NZ (Pacific)	151,010	58,305
Java (Indian)	126,650	48,900
Cuba (Atlantic)	114,525	44,218
North Island, NZ (Pacific)	114,050	44,035
Newfoundland (Atlantic)	108,855	42,030
Luzon (Pacific)	105,880	40,880
Iceland (Atlantic)	103,000	39,770
Mindanao (Pacific)	95,247	36,775
Ireland (Atlantic)	82,462	31,839

*Mainland only

LARGEST DESERTS

	Area (approx.) km²	miles²
The Sahara (N. Africa)	9,000,000	3,500,000
Australian Desert	1,550,000	600,000
Arabian Desert	1,300,000	500,000
*The Gobi (Mongolia/China)	1,300,000	500,000
Kalahari Desert (Botswana/ Namibia/S. Africa)	583,000	225,000
Sonoran Desert (USA/ Mexico)	310,000	120,000
Namib Desert (Namibia)	310,000	120,000
†Kara Kum (Turkmenistan)	310,000	120,000
Thar Desert (India/ Pakistan)	260,000	100,000
Somali Desert (Somalia)	260,000	100,000
†Kyzyl Kum (Kazakhstan/ Uzbekistan)	260,000	100,000
Atacama Desert (Chile)	180,000	70,000
Dasht-e Lut (Iran)	52,000	20,000
Mojave Desert (USA)	35,000	13,500
Desierto de Sechura (Peru)	26,000	10,000

*Including the Takla Makan – 320,000 km² (125,000 miles²)
†Together known as the Turkestan Desert

DEEPEST DEPRESSIONS

	Maximum depth below sea level metres	feet
Dead Sea (Jordan/Israel)	395	1,296
Turfan Depression (Sinkiang, China)	153	505
Qattara Depression (Egypt)	132	436
Mangyshlak peninsula (Kazakhstan)	131	433
Danakil Depression (Ethiopia)	116	383
Death Valley (California, USA)	86	282
Salton Sink (California, USA)	71	235
W. of Ustyurt plateau (Kazakhstan)	70	230
Prikaspiyskaya Nizmennost' (Russia/Kazakhstan)	67	220
Lake Sarykamysh (Uzbekistan/ Turkmenistan)	45	148
El Faiyûm (Egypt)	44	147
Valdies peninsula, Lago Enriquillo (Dominican Republic)	40	131

The world's largest exposed depression is the Prikaspiyskaya Nizmennost' covering the hinterland of the northern third of the Caspian Sea, which is itself 28 m (92 ft) below sea level
Western Antarctica and Central Greenland largely comprise crypto-depressions under ice burdens. The Antarctic Wilkes subglacial basin has a bedrock 2,341 m (7,680 ft) below sea-level. In Greenland (lat. 73° N., long. 39° W.) the bedrock is 365 m (1,197 ft) below sea-level

LONGEST MOUNTAIN RANGES

Range (location)	Length km	miles
Cordillera de Los Andes (W. South America)	7,200	4,500
Rocky Mountains (W. North America)	4,800	3,000
Himalaya-Karakoram-Hindu Kush (S. Central Asia)	3,800	2,400
Great Dividing Range (E. Australia)	3,600	2,250
Trans-Antarctic Mts (Antarctica)	3,500	2,200
Atlantic Coast Range (E. Brazil)	3,000	1,900
West Sumatran-Javan Range (Indonesia)	2,900	1,800
Aleutian Range (Alaska and NW Pacific)	2,650	1,650
Tien Shan (S. Central Asia)	2,250	1,400
Central New Guinea Range (Irian Jaya/Papua New Guinea)	2,000	1,250

HIGHEST MOUNTAINS

The world's 8,000-metre mountains (with six subsidiary peaks) are all in the Himalaya-Karakoram-Hindu Kush range.

Mountain	Height metres	feet
Mt Everest*	8,848	29,028
K2 (Chogori)†	8,607	28,238
Kangchenjunga	8,597	28,208
Lhotse	8,511	27,923
Makalu I	8,481	27,824
Lhotse Shar	8,383	27,504
Dhaulagiri I	8,167	26,795
Manaslu I (Kutang I)	8,156	26,760
Cho Oyu	8,153	26,750
Nanga Parbat (Diamir)	8,125	26,660
Annapurna I	8,091	26,546
Gasherbrum I (Hidden Peak)	8,068	26,470
Broad Peak I	8,046	26,400
Shisha Pangma (Gosainthan)	8,046	26,398
Gasherbrum II	8,034	26,360
Annapurna East	8,010	26,280
Makalu South-East	8,010	26,280
Broad Peak Central	8,000	26,246

*Named after Sir George Everest (1790–1866), Surveyor-General of India 1830–43, in 1863. He pronounced his name Eve-rest
†Formerly Godwin-Austin

The culminating summits in the other major mountain ranges are:

Mountain (range or country)	Height metres	feet
Pik Pobeda (Tien Shan)	7,439	24,406
Cerro Aconcagua (Cordillera de Los Andes)	6,960	22,834
Mt McKinley, S. Peak (Alaska Range)	6,194	20,320
Kilimanjaro (Kibo) (Tanzania)	5,894	19,340
Hkakabo Razi (Myanmar)	5,881	19,296
Citlaltépetl (Orizaba) (Sierra Madre Oriental, Mexico)	5,699	18,700

Mountain (range or country)	Height	
	metres	feet
El'brus, *W. Peak* (Caucasus)	5,663	18,481
Vinson Massif (E. Antarctica)	4,897	16,067
Puncak Jaya (Central New Guinea Range)	4,884	16,023
Mt Blanc (Alps)	4,807	15,771
Klyuchevskaya Sopka (Kamchatka peninsula, Russia)	4,750	15,584
Ras Dashan (Ethiopian Highlands)	4,620	15,158
Zard Kūh (Zagros Mts, Iran)	4,547	14,921
Mt Kirkpatrick (Trans Antarctic)	4,529	14,860
Mt Belukha (Altai Mts, Russia/ Kazakhstan)	4,505	14,783
Mt Elbert (Rocky Mountains)	4,400	14,433
Mt Rainier (Cascade Range, N. America)	4,392	14,410
Nevado de Colima (Sierra Madre Occidental, Mexico)	4,268	14,003
Jebel Toubkal (Atlas Mts, N. Africa)	4,165	13,665
Kinabalu (Crocker Range, Borneo)	4,101	13,455
Kerinci (West Sumatran-Javan Range, Indonesia)	3,800	12,467
Jabal an Nabī Shu'ayb (N. Tihāmat, Yemen)	3,760	12,336
Teotepec (Sierra Madre del Sur, Mexico)	3,703	12,149
Thaban Ntlenyana (Drakensberg, South Africa)	3,482	11,425
Pico de Bandeira (Atlantic Coast Range)	2,890	9,482
Shishaldin (Aleutian Range)	2,861	9,387
Kosciusko (Great Dividing Range)	2,228	7,310

HIGHEST VOLCANOES

Volcano (last major eruption) and location	Height	
	metres	feet
Guallatiri (1993), Andes, Chile	6,060	19,882
Lascar (1991), Andes, Chile	5,990	19,652
Cotopaxi (1975), Andes, Ecuador	5,897	19,347
Tupungatito (1986), Andes, Chile	5,640	18,504
Nevado del Ruiz, Colombia (1985, 1992)	5,400	17,716
Sangay (1988), Andes, Ecuador	5,230	17,159
Guagua Pichincha (1988), Andes, Ecuador	4,784	15,696
Purace (1977), Colombia	4,756	15,601
Klyuchevskaya Sopka (1991), Kamchatka peninsula, Russia	4,750	15,584
Nevado de Colima (1991), Mexico	4,268	14,003
Galeras (1991), Colombia	4,266	13,996
Mauna Loa (1987), Hawaii Is.	4,170	13,680
Cameroon (1982), Cameroon	4,070	13,354
Acatenango (1972), Guatemala	3,960	12,992
Fuego (1991), Guatemala	3,835	12,582
Kerinci (1987), Sumatra, Indonesia	3,800	12,467
Erebus (1991), Ross Island, Antarctica	3,794	12,450
Tacana (1988), Guatemala	3,780	12,400
Santiaguito (1902, 1991), Guatemala	3,768	12,362
Rindjani (1966), Lombok, Indonesia	3,726	12,224
Semeru (1991), Java, Indonesia	3,675	12,060
Nyirgongo (1977), Zaïre	3,475	11,400

Volcano (last major eruption) and location	Height	
	metres	feet
Koryakskaya (1957), Kamchatka, Russia	3,456	11,339
Irazú (1992), Costa Rica	3,432	11,260
Slamet (1988), Java, Indonesia	3,428	11,247
Spurr (1953), Alaska, USA	3,374	11,069
Mt Etna (1169, 1669, 1993), Sicily, Italy	3,369	11,053
Raung, Java, Indonesia (1991)	3,322	10,932
Shiveluch (1964), Kamchatka, Russia	3,283	10,771
Turrialba (1992), Costa Rica	3,246	10,650
Agung (1964), Bali, Indonesia	3,142	10,308
Llaima (1990), Chile	3,128	10,239
Redoubt (1991), Alaska, USA	3,108	10,197
Tjareme (1938), Java, Indonesia	3,078	10,098
On-Taka (1991), Japan	3,063	10,049
Nyamuragira (1991), Zaïre	3,056	10,028
Iliamna (1978), Alaska, USA	3,052	10,016

OTHER NOTABLE VOLCANOES

	Height	
	metres	feet
Tambora (1815), Sumbawa, Indonesia	2,850	9,353
Mt St Helens (1980, 1986, 1991), Washington State, USA	2,530	8,300
Pinatubo (1991), Philippines	1,758	5,770
Hekla (1981, 1991), Iceland	1,491	4,892
Mt Pelée (1902), Martinique	1,397	4,583
Mt Unzen (1792, 1991), Kyushu, Japan	1,360	4,462
Vesuvius (AD 79, 1944), Italy	1,280	4,198
Kilauea (1993), Hawaii, USA	1,242	4,077
Stromboli (1993), Lipari Is., Italy	926	3,038
Krakatau (1883), Sunda Strait, Indonesia	804	2,640
Santorini (Thíra) (1628 BC), Aegean Sea, Greece	566	1,857
Vulcano (Monte Aria), Lipari Is., Italy	499	1,637
Tristan da Cunha (1961), South Atlantic	243	800
Surtsey (1963–7), off Iceland	173	568

LARGEST LAKES

The areas of some of these lakes are subject to seasonal variation.

	Area		Length	
	km^2	miles^2	km	miles
Caspian Sea, Iran/ Azerbaijan/Russia/ Turkmenistan/ Kazakhstan	371,000	143,000	1,171	728
*Michigan–Huron, USA/Canada	117,610	45,300	1,010	627
Superior, Canada/ USA	82,413	31,820	563	350

*Lakes Michigan and Huron are regarded as lobes of the same lake. The Michigan lobe has an area of 57,750 km^2 (22,300 miles^2) and the Huron lobe an area of 59,570 km^2 (23,000 miles^2)

	Area km²	miles²	Length km	miles
Victoria, Uganda/ Tanzania/Kenya	69,500	26,828	362	225
Aral Sea, Kazakhstan/ Uzbekistan	40,400	15,600	331	235
Tanganyika, Zaïre/ Tanzania/Zambia/ Burundi	32,900	12,700	675	420
†Baykal (*Baikal*), Russia	31,500	12,162	635	395
Great Bear, Canada	31,328	12,096	309	192
Malawi, Tanzania/ Malawi/ Mozambique	28,880	11,150	580	360
Great Slave, Canada	28,570	11,031	480	298
Erie, Canada/USA	25,670	9,910	388	241
Winnipeg, Canada	24,390	9,417	428	266
Ontario, Canada/USA	19,550	7,550	310	193
Balkhash, Kazakhstan	18,427	7,115	605	376
Ladozhskoye (*Ladoga*), Russia	17,700	6,835	200	124

UNITED KINGDOM (BY COUNTRY)

Lough Neagh, Northern Ireland	381.73	147.39	28.90	18.00
Loch Lomond, Scotland	71.12	27.46	36.44	22.64
Windermere, England	14.74	5.69	16.90	10.50
Lake Vyrnwy, Wales (artificial)	4.53	1.75	7.56	4.70
Llyn Tegid (*Bala*), Wales (natural)	4.38	1.69	5.80	3.65

†World's deepest lake (1,940 m/6,365 ft)

LONGEST RIVERS

River (source and outflow)	Length km	miles
Nile (*Bahr-el-Nil*) (R. Luvironza, Burundi – E. Mediterranean Sea)	6,670	4,145
Amazon (*Amazonas*) (Lago Villafro, Peru – S. Atlantic Ocean)	6,448	4,007
Mississippi-Missouri (R. Red Rock, Montana – Gulf of Mexico)	5,970	3,710
Yenisey-Angara (W. Mongolia – Kara Sea)	5,540	3,442
Yangtze-Kiang (*Chang Jiang*) (Kunlun Mts, W. China – Yellow Sea)	5,530	3,436
Ob'-Irtysh (W. Mongolia – Kara Sea)	5,410	3,362
Huang He (*Yellow River*) (Bayan Har Shan range, central China – Yellow Sea)	4,830	3,000
Zaïre (*Congo*) (R. Lualaba, Zaïre-Zambia – S. Atlantic Ocean)	4,700	2,920
Amur-Argun (R. Argun, Khingan Mts, N. China – Sea of Okhotsk)	4,670	2,903
Lena-Kirenga (R. Kirenga, W. of Lake Baykal – Arctic Ocean)	4,345	2,700
Mackenzie-Peace (Tatlatui Lake, British Columbia – Beaufort Sea)	4,240	2,635
Mekong (Lants'ang, Tibet – South China Sea)	4,184	2,600
Niger (Loma Mts, Guinea – Gulf of Guinea, E. Atlantic Ocean)	4,184	2,600

River (source and outflow)	Length km	miles
Rió de la Plata-Paraná (R. Paranáiba, central Brazil – S. Atlantic Ocean)	4,000	2,485
Murray-Darling (SE Queensland – Lake Alexandrina, S. Australia)	3,750	2,330
Volga (Valdai plateau – Caspian Sea)	3,690	2,293
Zambezi (NW Zambia – S. Indian Ocean)	3,540	2,200

OTHER NOTABLE RIVERS

St Lawrence (Minnesota, USA – Gulf of St Lawrence)	3,130	1,945
Ganges-Brahmaputra (R. Matsang, SW Tibet – Bay of Bengal)	2,900	1,800
Indus (R. Sengge, SW Tibet – N. Arabian Sea)	2,880	1,790
Danube (*Donau*) (Black Forest, SW Germany – Black Sea)	2,850	1,770
Tigris-Euphrates (R. Murat, E. Turkey – Persian Gulf)	2,740	1,700
Irrawaddy (R. Mali Hka, N. Burma – Andaman Sea)	2,090	1,300
Don (SE of Novomoskovsk – Sea of Azov)	1,969	1,224

BRITISH ISLES

Shannon (Co. Cavan, Rep. of Ireland – Atlantic Ocean)	386	240
Severn (Powys, Wales – Bristol Channel)	354	220
Thames (Gloucestershire, England – North Sea)	346	215
Tay (Perthshire, Scotland – North Sea)	188	117
Clyde (Lanarkshire, Scotland – Firth of Clyde)	158	98½
Tweed (Peeblesshire, Scotland – North Sea)	155	96½
Bann (Upper and Lower) (Co. Down, N. Ireland – Atlantic Ocean)	122	76

GREATEST WATERFALLS – BY HEIGHT

Waterfall (river and location)	Total drop metres	feet	Greatest single leap metres	feet
Angel (Carrao, Venezuela)	979	3,212	807	2,648
Tugela (Tugela, S. Africa)	947	3,110	410	1,350
Utigård (Jostedal Glacier, Norway)	800	2,625	600	1,970
Mongefossen (Monge, Norway)	774	2,540	—	—
Yosemite (Yosemite Creek, USA)	739	2,425	435	1,430
Østre Mardøla Foss (Mardals, Norway)	656	2,154	296	974
Tyssestrengane (Tysso, Norway)	646	2,120	289	948
Cuquenán (Arabopó, Venezuela)	610	2,000	—	—
Sutherland (Arthur, NZ)	580	1,904	248	815
*Kjellfossen (Naeröfjord, Norway)	561	1,841	149	490

*Volume often so low the fall atomizes into a 'bridal veil'

Waterfall (river and location)	Total drop		Greatest single leap	
	metres	feet	metres	feet

BRITISH ISLES (BY COUNTRY)

	metres	feet	
Eas a' Chuàl Aluinn (Glas Bheinn, Sutherland, Scotland)	200	658	
Powerscourt Falls (Dargle, Co. Wicklow, Rep. of Ireland)	106	350	
Pistyll-y-Llyn (Powys/ Dyfed border, Wales)	c.73	230–240	(cascades)
Pistyll Rhyadr (Clwyd/ Powys border, Wales)	71.5	235	(single leap)
Caldron Snout (R. Tees, Cumbria/Durham, England)	61	200	(cascades)

GREATEST WATERFALLS – BY VOLUME

Waterfall (river and location)	Mean annual flow	
	m³/sec	galls/sec
Boyoma (R. Lualaba, Zaïre)	c.17,000	c.3,750,000
Khône (Mekong, Laos)	11,500	2,530,000
Niagara (Horseshoe) (R. Niagara/Lake Erie–Lake Ontario)	3,000	670,000
Paulo Afonso (R. São Francisco, Brazil)	2,800	625,000
Urubupunga (Alto Paraná, Brazil)	2,800	625,000
Cataratas del Iguazú (R. Iguaçu, Brazil/Argentina)	1,725	380,000
Patos-Maribando (Rio Grande, Brazil)	1,500	330,000
Victoria (Mosi-oa-tunya) (R. Zambezi, Zambia/ Zimbabwe)	1,000	220,000
Churchill (R. Churchill, Canada)	975	215,000
Kaieteur (R. Potaro, Guyana)	660	145,000

TALLEST DAMS

	metres	feet
Rogun, Tajikistan	335	1,098
Nurek, Russia	300	984
Grand Dixance, Switzerland	285	935
*Longtan, China	285	935
Inguri, Russia	272	892
Chicoasén, Mexico	261	856
*Tehri, India	261	856

*Under construction

The world's most massive dam is the Syncrude Tailings dam in Alberta, Canada, which will have a volume of 540 million cubic metres/706 million cubic yards

TALLEST INHABITED BUILDINGS

Building and city	Height	
	metres	feet
Petronas Tower, Kuala Lumpur	450	1,476
Sears Tower, Chicago[1]	443	1,454
Tour Sans Fin, Paris	426	1,398
World Trade Center, New York[2]	417	1,368
Empire State Building, New York[3]	381	1,250
Amoco Building, Chicago	346	1,136
John Hancock Center, Chicago	343	1,127
Nation's Bank Tower, Atlanta	320	1,050
Chrysler Building, New York	319	1,046
Bank of China, Hong Kong[4]	315	1,033
First Interstate World Center, Los Angeles	310	1,017
Vegas World Tower	308	1,012
Central Plaza, Hong Kong[5]	306.5	1,005
Texas Commerce Tower, Houston	305	1,001

[1] With TV antennae 520 m/1,707 ft
[2] With TV antennae, 521.2 m/1,710 ft; second tower, 415 m/1,362 ft
[3] With TV tower (added 1950–1), 430.9 m/1,414 ft
[4] With steel mast, 367.4 m/1,205 ft
[5] With steel mast, 374 m/1,227 ft

TALLEST STRUCTURES

Structure and location	Height	
	metres	feet
*Warszawa Radio Mast, Konstantynow, Poland	646	2,120
KTHI-TV Mast, Fargo, North Dakota	629	2,063
CN Tower, Metro Centre, Toronto, Canada	555	1,822
Ostankino Tower, Moscow	537	1,762

*Collapsed during renovation, August 1991

LONGEST BRIDGES – BY SPAN

Bridge and location	Length	
	metres	feet

SUSPENSION SPANS

	metres	feet
Humber Estuary, Humberside, England	1,410	4,626
Verrazano Narrows, Brooklyn–Staten I, USA	1,298	4,260
Golden Gate, San Francisco Bay, USA	1,280	4,200
Mackinac Straits, Michigan, USA	1,158	3,800
Bosporus, Istanbul, Turkey	1,074	3,524
George Washington, Hudson River, New York City, USA	1,067	3,500
Ponte 25 Abril (Tagus), Lisbon, Portugal	1,013	3,323
Firth of Forth (road), nr Edinburgh, Scotland	1,006	3,300
Severn River, Severn Estuary, England	988	3,240

The Akashi-Kaikyo road bridge (1988–98) will have a main span of 1,990 m/6,528 ft and the Great Belt East Bridge, Denmark (due for completion 1997) will have a span of 1,624 m/5,328 ft

Bridge and location	Length	
	metres	feet

CANTILEVER SPANS

Pont de Québec (rail-road), St Lawrence, Canada	548.6	1,800
Ravenswood, W. Virginia, USA	525.1	1,723
Firth of Forth (rail), nr Edinburgh, Scotland	521.2	1,710
Minato, Osaka, Japan	510.0	1,673
Commodore Barry, Chester, Pennsylvania, USA	494.3	1,622
Greater New Orleans, Louisiana, USA	480.0	1,575
Howrah (rail-road), Calcutta, India	457.2	1,500

STEEL ARCH SPANS

New River Gorge, Fayetteville, W. Virginia, USA	518.2	1,700
Bayonne (Kill van Kull), Bayonne, NJ – Staten I, USA	503.5	1,652
Sydney Harbour, Sydney, Australia	502.9	1,650

The 'floating' bridging at Evergreen, Seattle, Washington State, USA, is 3,839 m/12,596 ft long
The longest stretch of bridgings of any kind are those between Mandeville and Jefferson, Louisiana, USA; the Lake Pontchartrain Causeway II 38.422 km/23.87 miles and Causeway I 38.352 km/23.83 miles

---

LONGEST VEHICULAR TUNNELS

Tunnel and location	Length	
	km	miles

*Seikan (rail), Tsugaru Channel, Japan	53.90	33.49
*Channel Tunnel, Cheriton, Kent – Sangatte, Calais	49.94	31.03
Moscow metro, Belyaevo – Bittsevsky, Moscow, Russia	37.90	23.50
Northern line tube, East Finchley – Morden, London	27.84	17.30
Oshimizu, Honshū, Japan	22.17	13.78
Simplon II (rail), Brigue, Switzerland – Iselle, Italy	19.82	12.31
Simplon I (rail), Brigue, Switzerland – Iselle, Italy	19.80	12.30
Shin-Kanmon (rail), Kanmon Strait, Japan	18.68	11.61
Great Appennine (rail), Vernio, Italy	18.49	11.49
St Gotthard (road), Göschenen – Airolo, Switzerland	16.32	10.14
Rokko (rail), Ōsaka – Kōbe, Japan	16.09	10.00

*Sub-aqueous

The longest non-vehicular tunnelling in the world is the Delaware Aqueduct in New York State, USA, constructed in 1937–44 to a length of 168.9 km/105 miles

BRITAIN – RAIL TUNNELS

	miles	yards
Severn, Bristol – Newport	4	484
Totley, Manchester – Sheffield	3	950
Standedge, Manchester – Huddersfield	3	66
Sodbury, Swindon – Bristol	2	924
Disley, Stockport – Sheffield	2	346
Ffestiniog, Llandudno – Blaenau Ffestiniog	2	338
Bramhope, Leeds – Harrogate	2	241
Cowburn, Manchester – Sheffield	2	182

The longest road tunnel in Britain is the Mersey Road Tunnel, 2 miles 228 yards long. The longest canal tunnel, at Standedge, W. Yorks, is 3 miles 330 yards long; it was closed in 1944 but is currently being restored

---

LONGEST SHIP CANALS

Canal (opening date)	Length		Min. depth	
	km	miles	metres	feet
White Sea-Baltic (formerly Stalin) (1933) Canalized river; canal	51.5 km/32 miles 227	141.00	5.0	16.5
*Suez (1869) Links Red and Mediterranean Seas	162	100.60	12.9	42.3
V. I. Lenin Volga-Don (1952) Links Black and Caspian Seas	100	62.20	n/a	n/a
Kiel (or North Sea) (1895) Links North and Baltic Seas	98	60.90	13.7	45.0
*Houston (1940) Links inland city with sea	91	56.70	10.4	34.0
Alphonse XIII (1926) Gives Seville access to sea	85	53.00	7.6	25.0
Panama (1914) Links Pacific Ocean and Caribbean Sea; lake chain, 78.9 km/49 miles dug	82	50.71	12.5	41.0
Manchester Ship (1894) Links city with Irish Channel	64	39.70	8.5	28.0
Welland (1931) Circumvents Niagara Falls and Rapids	45	28.00	8.8	29.0
Brussels (Rupel Sea) (1922) Renders Brussels an inland port	32	19.80	6.4	21.0

*Has no locks

The first section of China's Grand Canal, running 1,780 km/1,107 miles from Beijing to Hangchou, was opened AD 610
The longest boat canal in the world is the Volga-Baltic canal from Astrakhan to St Petersburg with 2,300 route km/1,850 miles

Distances from London by Air

The list of the distances in statute miles from London, Heathrow, to various cities (airport) abroad has been supplied by the publishers of *IATA/Serco-IAL Ltd Air Distances Manual*, Southall, Middx.

To	Miles
Abidjan	3,197
Abu Dhabi	3,425
Addis Ababa	3,675
Adelaide	10,111
Aden	3,670
Algiers	1,035
Amman (Queen Alia)	2,287
Amsterdam	230
Ankara (Esenboga)	1,770
Athens	1,500
Atlanta	4,198
Auckland	11,404
Baghdad (Saddam)	2,551
Bahrain	3,163
Baku	2,485
Bangkok	5,928
Barbados	4,193
Barcelona (Muntadas)	712
Basle	447
Beijing/Peking (Capital)	5,063
Beirut	2,161
Belfast (Aldergrove)	325
Belgrade	1,056
Berlin (Tegel)	588
Bermuda	3,428
Berne	476
Bogota	5,262
Bombay	4,478
Boston	3,255
Brasilia	5,452
Bratislava	817
Brisbane	10,273
Brussels	217
Bucharest (Otopeni)	1,307
Budapest	923
Buenos Aires	6,915
Cairo (International)	2,194
Calcutta	4,958
Calgary	4,357
Canberra	10,563
Cape Town	6,011
Caracas	4,639
Casablanca (Mohamed V)	1,300
Chicago (O'Hare)	3,941
Cologne	331
Colombo (Katunayake)	5,411
Copenhagen	608
Dakar	2,706
Dallas (Fort Worth)	4,736
Dallas (Lovefield)	4,732
Damascus (International)	2,223
Dar-es-Salaam	4,662
Darwin	8,613
Delhi	4,180
Denver	4,655

To	Miles
Detroit (Metropolitan)	3,754
Dhahran	3,143
Dhaka	4,976
Doha	3,253
Dubai	3,414
Dublin	279
Durban	5,937
Düsseldorf	310
Entebbe	4,033
Frankfurt (Main)	406
Freetown	3,046
Geneva	468
Gibraltar	1,084
Gothenburg (Landvetter)	664
Hamburg	463
Harare	5,156
Havana	4,647
Helsinki (Vantaa)	1,148
Hobart	10,826
Ho Chi Minh City	6,345
Hong Kong	5,990
Honolulu	7,220
Houston (Intercontinental)	4,821
Houston (William P. Hobby)	4,837
Islamabad	3,767
Istanbul	1,560
Jakarta (Halim Perdanakusuma)	7,295
Jeddah	2,947
Johannesburg	5,634
Kabul	3,558
Karachi	3,935
Kathmandu	4,570
Khartoum	3,071
Kiev (Borispol)	1,357
Kiev (Julyany)	1,337
Kingston, Jamaica	4,668
Kuala Lumpur (Subang)	6,557
Kuwait	2,903
Lagos	3,107
Larnaca	2,036
Lima	6,303
Lisbon	972
Lomé	3,129
Los Angeles (International)	5,439
Madras	5,113
Madrid	773
Malta	1,305
Manila	6,685
Marseille	614
Mauritius	6,075
Melbourne (Essendon)	10,504
Melbourne (Tullamarine)	10,499
Mexico City	5,529
Miami	4,414
Milan (Linate)	609
Minsk	1,176
Montego Bay	4,687
Montevideo	6,841
Montreal (Mirabel)	3,241
Moscow (Sheremetievo)	1,557
Munich (Franz Josef Strauss)	584

To	Miles
Muscat	3,621
Nairobi (Jomo Kenyatta)	4,248
Naples	1,011
Nassau	4,333
New York (J. F. Kennedy)	3,440
Nice	645
Oporto	806
Oslo (Fornebu)	722
Ottawa	3,321
Palma, Majorca (Son San Juan)	836
Paris (Charles de Gaulle)	215
Paris (Le Bourget)	215
Paris (Orly)	227
Perth, Australia	9,008
Port of Spain	4,404
Prague	649
Pretoria	5,602
Reykjavik	1,167
Rhodes	1,743
Rio de Janeiro	5,745
Riyadh	3,067
Rome (Fiumicino)	895
St John's, Newfoundland	2,308
St Petersburg	1,314
Salzburg	651
San Francisco	5,351
Sao Paulo	5,892
Sarajevo	1,017
Seoul (Kimpo)	5,507
Shanghai	5,725
Shannon	369
Singapore (Lunghua)	6,756
Sofia	1,266
Stockholm (Arlanda)	908
Suva	10,119
Sydney (Kingsford Smith)	10,568
Tangier	1,120
Tehran	2,741
Tel Aviv	2,227
Tokyo (Narita)	5,956
Toronto	3,544
Tripoli (International)	1,468
Tunis	1,137
Turin (Caselle)	570
Ulan Bator	4,340
Valencia	826
Vancouver	4,707
Venice (Tessera)	715
Vienna (Schwechat)	790
Vladivostok	5,298
Warsaw	912
Washington (Dulles)	3,665
Wellington	11,692
Yangon/Rangoon	5,582
Yokohama (Aomori)	5,647
Zagreb	848
Zürich	490

The United Kingdom

The United Kingdom comprises Great Britain (England, Wales and Scotland) and Northern Ireland. The Isle of Man and the Channel Islands are Crown dependencies with their own legislative systems, and not a part of the United Kingdom.

AREA AS AT 31 MARCH 1981

	Land miles^2	km^2	*Inland water miles^2	km^2	Total miles^2	km^2
United Kingdom	93,006	240,883	1,242	3,218	94,248	244,101
England	50,058	129,652	293	758	50,351	130,410
Wales	7,965	20,628	50	130	8,015	20,758
Scotland	29,767	77,097	653	1,692	30,420	78,789
†Northern Ireland	5,215	13,506	246	638	5,461	14,144
Isle of Man	221	572	—	—	221	572
Channel Islands	75	194	—	—	75	194

*Excluding tidal water
†Excluding certain tidal waters that are parts of statutory areas in Northern Ireland

POPULATION

The first official census of population in England, Wales and Scotland was taken in 1801 and a census has been taken every ten years since, except in 1941 when there was no census because of war. The last official census in the United Kingdom was taken on 21 April 1991 and the next is due in April 2001.

The first official census of population in Ireland was taken in 1841. However, all figures given below refer only to the area which is now Northern Ireland. Figures for Northern Ireland in 1921 and 1931 are estimates based on the censuses taken in 1926 and 1937 respectively.

Estimates of the population of England before 1801, calculated from the number of baptisms, burials and marriages, are:

1570	4,160,221	1670	5,773,646
1600	4,811,718	1700	6,045,008
1630	5,600,517	1750	6,517,035

Thousands	United Kingdom Total	Male	Female	England and Wales Total	Male	Female	Scotland Total	Male	Female	Northern Ireland Total	Male	Female
CENSUS RESULTS 1801–1991												
1801	—	—	—	8,893	4,255	4,638	1,608	739	869	—	—	—
1811	13,368	6,368	7,000	10,165	4,874	5,291	1,806	826	980	—	—	—
1821	15,472	7,498	7,974	12,000	5,850	6,150	2,092	983	1,109	—	—	—
1831	17,835	8,647	9,188	13,897	6,771	7,126	2,364	1,114	1,250	—	—	—
1841	20,183	9,819	10,364	15,914	7,778	8,137	2,620	1,242	1,378	1,649	800	849
1851	22,259	10,855	11,404	17,928	8,781	9,146	2,889	1,376	1,513	1,443	698	745
1861	24,525	11,894	12,631	20,066	9,776	10,290	3,062	1,450	1,612	1,396	668	728
1871	27,431	13,309	14,122	22,712	11,059	11,653	3,360	1,603	1,757	1,359	647	712
1881	31,015	15,060	15,955	25,974	12,640	13,335	3,736	1,799	1,936	1,305	621	684
1891	34,264	16,593	17,671	29,003	14,060	14,942	4,026	1,943	2,083	1,236	590	646
1901	38,237	18,492	19,745	32,528	15,729	16,799	4,472	2,174	2,298	1,237	590	647
1911	42,082	20,357	21,725	36,070	17,446	18,625	4,761	2,309	2,452	1,251	603	648
1921	44,027	21,033	22,994	37,887	18,075	19,811	4,882	2,348	2,535	1,258	610	648
1931	46,038	22,060	23,978	39,952	19,133	20,819	4,843	2,326	2,517	1,243	601	642
1951	50,225	24,118	26,107	43,758	21,016	22,742	5,096	2,434	2,662	1,371	668	703
1961	52,709	25,481	27,228	46,105	22,304	23,801	5,179	2,483	2,697	1,425	694	731
1971	55,515	26,952	28,562	48,750	23,683	25,067	5,229	2,515	2,714	1,536	755	781
1981	55,848	27,104	28,742	49,155	23,873	25,281	5,131	2,466	2,664	*1,533	750	783
1991	56,467	27,344	29,123	49,890	24,182	25,707	4,999	2,392	2,606	1,578	769	809
†RESIDENT POPULATION: PROJECTIONS (MID-YEAR)												
2001	59,800	29,475	30,325	52,989	26,148	26,841	5,143	2,508	2,636	1,667	819	848
2011	61,257	30,380	30,878	54,471	27,045	27,426	5,077	2,490	2,587	1,709	844	865
2021	62,146	30,883	31,263	55,320	27,518	27,802	5,051	2,486	2,565	1,775	879	896
2031	62,241	30,900	31,341	55,412	27,530	27,882	4,998	2,462	2,536	1,831	908	923

*Figures include 44,500 non-enumerated persons
† Projections are 1992 based

Source: HMSO – *Annual Abstract 1995*; OPCS – Census reports

ISLANDS: Census Results 1901-91

	Isle of Man Total	Male	Female	Jersey Total	Male	Female	*Guernsey Total	Male	Female
1901	54,752	25,496	29,256	52,576	23,940	28,636	40,446	19,652	20,794
1911	52,016	23,937	28,079	51,898	24,014	27,884	41,858	20,661	21,197
1921	60,284	27,329	32,955	49,701	22,438	27,263	38,315	18,246	20,069
1931	49,308	22,443	26,865	50,462	23,424	27,038	40,643	19,659	20,984
1951	55,123	25,749	29,464	57,296	27,282	30,014	43,652	21,221	22,431
1961	48,151	22,060	26,091	57,200	27,200	30,000	45,068	21,671	23,397
1971	56,289	26,461	29,828	72,532	35,423	37,109	51,458	24,792	26,666
1981	64,679	30,901	33,778	77,000	37,000	40,000	53,313	25,701	27,612
1991	69,788	33,693	36,095	84,082	40,862	43,220	58,867	28,297	30,570

* Population of Guernsey, Herm, Jethou and Lithou. Figures for 1901-71 record all persons present on census night; census figures for 1981 and 1991 record all persons resident in the islands on census night
Source: 1991 Census

RESIDENT POPULATION

MID-YEAR ESTIMATE

	1983	1993
United Kingdom	56,377,000	58,191,000
England	46,874,000	48,533,000
Wales	2,807,000	2,906,000
Scotland	5,153,000	5,120,000
Northern Ireland	1,543,000	1,632,000

Source: HMSO – *Annual Abstract of Statistics 1995*

BY AGE AND SEX 1993

Males	Under 16	65 and over
United Kingdom	6,140,000	3,692,000
England	5,089,000	3,103,000
Wales	309,000	203,000
Scotland	528,000	302,000
Northern Ireland	214,000	83,000

Females	Under 16	60 and over
United Kingdom	5,826,000	6,946,000
England	4,824,000	5,796,000
Wales	293,000	377,000
Scotland	504,000	609,000
Northern Ireland	204,000	163,000

Source: HMSO – *Population Trends 80*

BY ETHNIC GROUP (1991 CENSUS (GREAT BRITAIN))

Ethnic group	Estimated population	Percentage
Caribbean	500,000	16.6
African	212,000	7
Other black	178,000	5.9
Indian	840,000	27.9
Pakistani	477,000	15.8
Bangladeshi	163,000	5.4
Chinese	157,000	5.2
Other Asian	198,000	6.6
Other	290,000	9.6
Total ethnic minority groups	3,015,000	100
White	51,874,000	—
All ethnic groups	54,889,000	—

Source: HMSO – *Population Trends 72*

AVERAGE DENSITY *Persons per hectare*

	1981	1991
England	3.55	3.61
Wales	1.34	1.36
Scotland	0.66	0.65
Northern Ireland	1.12	1.11

Sources: OPCS – Census reports

IMMIGRATION 1993
Acceptances for settlement in the UK by nationality

Region	Number of persons
Europe: total	5,010
European Community	530
Other western Europe	3,230
Eastern Europe	1,250
Americas: total	7,660
USA	4,060
Canada	760
Africa: total	10,790
Asia: total	25,370
Indian sub-continent	14,090
Middle East	2,590
Australasia: total	2,650
Other	2,600
Stateless	1,570
Total	55,640
Foreign	24,580
Commonwealth	31,060
Old Commonwealth	3,420
New Commonwealth	27,650

Source: HMSO – *Annual Abstract of Statistics 1995*

LIVE BIRTHS AND BIRTH RATES 1993

	Live births	Birth rate*
United Kingdom	762,000	13.1
England and Wales	673,000	13.1
Scotland	63,000	12.4
Northern Ireland	25,000	15.3

*Live births per 1,000 population
Source: HMSO – *Annual Abstract of Statistics 1995*

LEGAL ABORTIONS 1993 (England and Wales)

Age group	Number
Under 16	3,080
16–19	25,800
20–34	109,700
35–44	18,800
45 and over	490
Age not stated	10
Total	157,800

Source: HMSO – Population Trends 80

BIRTHS OUTSIDE MARRIAGE (UK)

Age group	1981	1993
Under 20	30,000	44,000
20–24	33,000	84,000
25–29	16,000	64,000
Over 30	13,000	50,000
Total	91,000	242,000

Source: HMSO – Annual Abstract of Statistics 1995

MARRIAGE AND DIVORCE 1992

	Marriages	Divorces*
United Kingdom	356,013	—
England and Wales	311,564	160,385
Scotland	35,057	12,479
Northern Ireland	9,392	2,597

*Decrees absolute granted; in Northern Ireland, divorce petitions filed
Source: HMSO – Annual Abstract of Statistics 1995

DEATHS AND DEATH RATES 1993

Males	Deaths	Death rate*
United Kingdom	317,393	10.9†
England and Wales	279,158	—
Scotland	30,504	—
Northern Ireland	7,731	—
Females		
United Kingdom	340,459	11.0†
England and Wales	299,012	—
Scotland	33,545	—
Northern Ireland	7,902	—

* Deaths per 1,000 population
† 1992 figure
Sources: OPCS; Annual Report of the Registrar-General for Scotland 1993; Annual Report of the Registrar-General for Northern Ireland 1993; HMSO – Annual Abstract of Statistics 1995

INFANT MORTALITY 1993
Deaths of infants under 1 year of age per 1,000 live births

	Number
United Kingdom	6.3p
England and Wales	6.3
Scotland	6.5
Northern Ireland	6.0†

p provisional
† 1992 figure
Sources: HMSO – Population Trends 80; HMSO – Annual Abstract of Statistics 1995

EXPECTATION OF LIFE   LIFE TABLES 1990–92 (INTERIM FIGURES)

Age	England and Wales Male	Female	Scotland Male	Female	Northern Ireland Male	Female
0	73.4	79.0	71.4	77.1	72.3	77.6
5	69.1	74.6	67.1	72.6	68.0	73.3
10	64.2	69.6	62.2	67.7	63.0	68.4
15	59.3	64.7	57.3	62.7	58.1	63.4
20	54.5	59.8	52.5	57.8	53.3	58.5
25	49.7	54.8	47.7	52.9	48.6	53.6
30	44.9	49.9	43.0	48.0	43.8	48.7
35	40.1	45.1	38.3	43.2	39.1	43.8
40	35.4	40.2	33.5	38.4	34.4	39.0
45	30.7	35.5	29.0	33.7	29.7	34.3
50	26.2	30.9	24.6	29.1	25.2	29.7
55	21.9	26.4	20.4	24.7	21.0	25.3
60	17.9	22.1	16.6	20.6	17.0	21.0
65	14.3	18.1	13.2	16.8	13.6	17.2
70	11.2	14.5	10.4	13.4	10.6	13.6
75	8.6	11.2	8.0	10.4	8.2	10.4
80	6.4	8.4	6.0	7.8	6.1	7.8
85	4.8	6.1	4.5	5.6	4.5	5.7

Source: HMSO – Annual Abstract of Statistics 1995

DEATHS ANALYSED BY CAUSE 1993

	England & Wales*	Scotland	N. Ireland
TOTAL DEATHS	578,170	64,049	15,633
DEATHS FROM NATURAL CAUSES	562,442	61,560	14,994
Infections and parasitic diseases	3,406	340	55
Intestinal infectious diseases	198	19	—
Tuberculosis of respiratory system	315	45	9
Other tuberculosis, including late effects	169	42	6
Whooping cough	—	—	—
Meningococcal infection	173	13	4
Measles	4	—	—
Malaria	4	1	1
Syphilis	6	1	1
Neoplasms	142,446	15,619	3,655
Malignant neoplasm of stomach	7,347	766	194
Malignant neoplasm of trachea, bronchus and lung	32,603	4,299	812
Malignant neoplasm of breast	13,113	1,285	331
Malignant neoplasm of uterus	2,789	285	65
Leukaemia	3,555	288	84
Benign and unspecified neoplasms	1,892	121	81
Endocrine, nutritional and metabolic diseases and immunity disorders	7,918	775	75
Diabetes mellitus	6,266	513	44
Nutritional deficiencies	85	16	—
Other metabolic and immunity disorders	1,116	215	31
Diseases of blood and blood-forming organs	1,981	178	29
Anaemias	788	71	8
Mental disorders	7,719	1,322	56
Diseases of nervous system and sense organs	9,120	879	189
Meningitis	217	17	6
Diseases of the circulatory system	258,156	29,909	7,157
Rheumatic heart disease	1,833	201	47
Hypertensive disease	3,052	325	67
Ischaemic heart disease	146,432	16,925	4,245
Diseases of pulmonary circulation and other forms of heart disease	27,291	2,470	678
Cerebrovascular disease	61,173	8,392	1,722
Diseases of the respiratory system	90,870	8,409	2,756
Influenza	438	127	17
Pneumonia	54,597	4,495	1,814
Bronchitis, emphysema	6,183	424	151
Asthma	1,699	129	58
Diseases of the digestive system	18,422	2,162	445
Ulcer of stomach and duodenum	4,218	372	97
Appendicitis	124	8	1
Hernia of abdominal cavity and other intestinal obstruction	1,858	200	43
Chronic liver disease and cirrhosis	2,982	494	66
Diseases of the genito-urinary system	6,718	857	261
Nephritis, nephrotic syndrome and nephrosis	3,400	581	171
Hyperplasia of prostate	273	16	5
Complications of pregnancy, childbirth, etc.	27	7	—
Abortion	2	1	—
Diseases of the skin and subcutaneous tissue	1,017	100	33
Diseases of the musculo-skeletal system	3,424	269	35
Congenital anomalies	1,335	216	116
Certain conditions originating in the perinatal period	300	174	62
Birth trauma, hypoxia, birth asphyxia and other respiratory conditions	191	101	22
Signs, symptoms and ill-defined conditions	6,788	344	40
Sudden infant death syndrome	375	58	6
DEATHS FROM INJURY AND POISONING	15,728	2,489	639
All accidents	10,313	1,469	393
Motor vehicle accidents	2,969	407	147
Suicide and self-inflicted injury	3,540	615	129
All other external causes	1,875	405	117

*Some statistics for England and Wales have been recoded using a system last employed before 1983; the figures are therefore not directly comparable with 1983–1992 statistics

Sources: OPCS; General Register Office for Scotland; *Annual Report of the Registrar-General for Northern Ireland 1993*

The National Flag

The national flag of the United Kingdom is the Union Flag, generally known as the Union Jack. (The name 'Union Jack' derives from the use of the Union Flag on the jack-staff of naval vessels.)

The Union Flag is a combination of the cross of St George, patron saint of England, the cross of St Andrew, patron saint of Scotland, and a cross similar to that of St Patrick, patron saint of Ireland.

Cross of St George: cross Gules in a field Argent (red cross on a white ground).

Cross of St Andrew: saltire Argent in a field Azure (white diagonal cross on a blue ground).

Cross of St Patrick: saltire Gules in a field Argent (red diagonal cross on a white ground).

The Union Flag was first introduced in 1606 after the union of the kingdoms of England and Scotland under one sovereign. The cross of St Patrick was added in 1801 after the union of Great Britain and Ireland.

DAYS FOR FLYING FLAGS

The correct orientation of the Union Flag when flying is with the broader diagonal band of white uppermost in the hoist (i.e. near the pole) and the narrower diagonal band of white uppermost in the fly (i.e. furthest from the pole).

It is the practice to fly the Union Flag daily on some customs houses. In all other cases, flags are flown on government buildings by command of The Queen.

Days for hoisting the Union Flag are notified to the Department of National Heritage by The Queen's command and communicated by the department to the other government departments. On the days appointed, the Union Flag is flown on government buildings in the United Kingdom from 8 a.m. to sunset.

The Queen's Accession	6 February
Birthday of The Duke of York	19 February
*St David's Day (in Wales only)	1 March
Birthday of The Prince Edward	10 March
Commonwealth Day (1996)	11 March
Birthday of The Queen	21 April
*St George's Day (in England only)	23 April
Coronation Day	2 June
Birthday of The Duke of Edinburgh	10 June
The Queen's Official Birthday (1996)	15 June
Birthday of The Princess of Wales	1 July
Birthday of Queen Elizabeth the Queen Mother	4 August
Birthday of The Princess Royal	15 August
Birthday of The Princess Margaret	21 August
Remembrance Sunday (1996)	10 November
Birthday of The Prince of Wales	14 November
The Queen's Wedding Day	20 November
*St Andrew's Day (in Scotland only)	30 November
†The opening of Parliament by The Queen	
†The prorogation of Parliament by The Queen	

*Where a building has two or more flagstaffs, the appropriate national flag may be flown in addition to the Union Flag, but not in a superior position
†Flags are flown whether or not The Queen performs the ceremony in person. Flags are flown only in the Greater London area

FLAGS AT HALF-MAST

Flags are flown at half-mast on the following occasions:

(a) From the announcement of the death up to the funeral of the Sovereign, except on Proclamation Day, when flags are hoisted right up from 11 a.m. to sunset

(b) The funerals of members of the Royal Family, subject to special commands from The Queen in each case

(c) The funerals of foreign rulers, subject to special commands from The Queen in each case

(d) The funerals of Prime Ministers and ex-Prime Ministers of the United Kingdom, subject to special commands from The Queen in each case

(e) Other occasions by special command of The Queen

On occasions when days for flying flags coincide with days for flying flags at half-mast, the following rules are observed. Flags are flown:

(a) although a member of the Royal Family, or a near relative of the Royal Family, may be lying dead, unless special commands be received from The Queen to the contrary

(b) although it may be the day of the funeral of a foreign ruler

If the body of a very distinguished subject is lying at a government office, the flag may fly at half-mast on that office until the body has left (provided it is a day on which the flag would fly) and then the flag is to be hoisted right up. On all other government buildings the flag will fly as usual.

THE ROYAL STANDARD

The Royal Standard is hoisted only when The Queen is actually present in the building, and never when Her Majesty is passing in procession.

The Royal Family

ELIZABETH II, by the Grace of God, of the United Kingdom of Great Britain and Northern Ireland and of her other Realms and Territories Queen, Head of the Commonwealth, Defender of the Faith

Her Majesty Elizabeth Alexandra Mary of Windsor, elder daughter of King George VI and of HM Queen Elizabeth the Queen Mother
Born 21 April 1926, at 17 Bruton Street, London WI
Ascended the throne 6 February 1952
Crowned 2 June 1953, at Westminster Abbey
Married 20 November 1947, in Westminster Abbey, HRH The Duke of Edinburgh
Official residences: Buckingham Palace, London SW1; Windsor Castle, Berks; Palace of Holyroodhouse, Edinburgh
Private residences: Sandringham, Norfolk; Balmoral Castle, Aberdeenshire
Office: Buckingham Palace, London SW1A 1AA. Tel: 0171-930 4832

HUSBAND OF HM THE QUEEN

HRH THE PRINCE PHILIP, DUKE OF EDINBURGH, KG, KT, OM, GBE, AC, QSO, PC, Ranger of Windsor Park
Born 10 June 1921, son of Prince and Princess Andrew of Greece and Denmark (*see* page 135), naturalized a British subject 1947, created Duke of Edinburgh, Earl of Merioneth and Baron Greenwich 1947

CHILDREN OF HM THE QUEEN

HRH THE PRINCE OF WALES (Prince Charles Philip Arthur George), KG, KT, GCB and Great Master of the Order of the Bath, AK, QSO, PC, ADC(P)
Born 14 November 1948, created Prince of Wales and Earl of Chester 1958, succeeded as Duke of Cornwall, Duke of Rothesay, Earl of Carrick and Baron Renfrew, Lord of the Isles and Prince and Great Steward of Scotland 1952
Married 29 July 1981 Lady Diana Frances Spencer, now HRH The Princess of Wales (*born* 1 July 1961, youngest daughter of the 8th Earl Spencer and the Hon. Mrs Shand Kydd), *separated* 1992
Issue:
(1) HRH Prince William of Wales (Prince William Arthur Philip Louis), *born* 21 June 1982
(2) HRH Prince Henry of Wales (Prince Henry Charles Albert David), *born* 15 September 1984
Residences of the Prince of Wales: St James's Palace, London SW1; Highgrove, Doughton, Tetbury, Glos.
Residence of the Princess of Wales: Kensington Palace, London W8 4PU
Office: St James's Palace, London SW1A 1BS. Tel: 0171-930 4832

HRH THE PRINCESS ROYAL (Princess Anne Elizabeth Alice Louise), KG, GCVO

Born 15 August 1950, declared The Princess Royal 1987
Married (1) 14 November 1973 Captain Mark Anthony Peter Phillips, CVO (*born* 22 September 1948); marriage dissolved 1992; (2) 12 December 1992 Captain Timothy James Hamilton Laurence, MVO (*born* 1 March 1955)
Issue:
(1) Peter Mark Andrew Phillips, *born* 15 November 1977
(2) Zara Anne Elizabeth Phillips, *born* 15 May 1981
Residence: Gatcombe Park, Minchinhampton, Glos.
Office: Buckingham Palace, London SW1A 1AA. Tel: 0171-930 4832

HRH THE DUKE OF YORK (Prince Andrew Albert Christian Edward), CVO, ADC(P)
Born 19 February 1960, created Duke of York, Earl of Inverness and Baron Killyleagh 1986
Married 23 July 1986 Sarah Margaret Ferguson, now HRH The Duchess of York (*born* 15 October 1959, younger daughter of Major Ronald Ferguson and Mrs Hector Barrantes), *separated* 1992
Issue:
(1) HRH Princess Beatrice of York (Princess Beatrice Elizabeth Mary), *born* 8 August 1988
(2) HRH Princess Eugenie of York (Princess Eugenie Victoria Helena), *born* 23 March 1990
Residences: Buckingham Palace, London SW1; Sunninghill Park, Ascot, Berks.
Office: Buckingham Palace, London SW1 1AA. Tel: 0171-930 4832

HRH THE PRINCE EDWARD (Prince Edward Antony Richard Louis), CVO
Born 10 March 1964
Residence and Office: Buckingham Palace, London SW1A 1AA. Tel: 0171-930 4832

SISTER OF HM THE QUEEN

HRH THE PRINCESS MARGARET, COUNTESS OF SNOWDON, CI, GCVO, Royal Victorian Chain, Dame Grand Cross of the Order of St John of Jerusalem
Born 21 August 1930, younger daughter of King George VI and HM Queen Elizabeth the Queen Mother
Married 6 May 1960 Antony Charles Robert Armstrong-Jones, GCVO (*born* 7 March 1930, created Earl of Snowdon 1961, Constable of Caernarvon Castle); marriage dissolved 1978
Issue:
(1) David Albert Charles, Viscount Linley, *born* 3 November 1961, *married* 8 October 1993 the Hon. Serena Stanhope
(2) Lady Sarah Chatto (Sarah Frances Elizabeth), *born* 1 May 1964, *married* 14 July 1994 Daniel Chatto
Residence and Office: Kensington Palace, London W8 4PU. Tel: 0171-930 3141

MOTHER OF HM THE QUEEN

HM QUEEN ELIZABETH THE QUEEN MOTHER (Elizabeth Angela Marguerite), Lady of the Garter, Lady of the Thistle, CI, GMVO, GBE, Dame Grand Cross of the Order of

St John, Royal Victorian Chain, Lord Warden and Admiral of the Cinque Ports and Constable of Dover Castle
Born 4 August 1900, youngest daughter of the 14th Earl of Strathmore and Kinghorne
Married 26 April 1923 (as Lady Elizabeth Bowes-Lyon) Prince Albert, Duke of York, afterwards King George VI (*see* page 134)
Residences: Clarence House, St James's Palace, London SW1; Royal Lodge, Windsor Great Park, Berks; Castle of Mey, Caithness
Office: Clarence House, St James's Palace, London SW1A 1BA. Tel: 0171-930 3141

AUNT OF HM THE QUEEN

HRH PRINCESS ALICE, DUCHESS OF GLOUCESTER (Alice Christabel), GCB, CI, GCVO, GBE, Grand Cordon of Al Kamal
Born 25 December 1901, third daughter of the 7th Duke of Buccleuch and Queensberry
Married 6 November 1935 (as Lady Alice Montagu-Douglas-Scott) Prince Henry, Duke of Gloucester, third son of King George V (*see* page 134)
Residence and Office: Kensington Palace, London W8 4PU. Tel: 0171-937 6374

COUSINS OF HM THE QUEEN

HRH THE DUKE OF GLOUCESTER (Prince Richard Alexander Walter George), GCVO, Grand Prior of the Order of St John of Jerusalem
Born 26 August 1944
Married 8 July 1972 Birgitte Eva van Deurs, now HRH The Duchess of Gloucester, GCVO (*born* 20 June 1946, daughter of Asger Henriksen and Vivian van Deurs)
Issue:
(1)   Earl of Ulster (Alexander Patrick Gregers Richard), *born* 24 October 1974
(2)   Lady Davina Windsor (Davina Elizabeth Alice Benedikte), *born* 19 November 1977
(3)   Lady Rose Windsor (Rose Victoria Birgitte Louise), *born* 1 March 1980
Residence and Office: Kensington Palace, London W8 4PU. Tel: 0171-937 6374

HRH THE DUKE OF KENT (Prince Edward George Nicholas Paul Patrick), KG, GCMG, GCVO, ADC(P)
Born 9 October 1935
Married 8 June 1961 Katharine Lucy Mary Worsley, now HRH The Duchess of Kent, GCVO (*born* 22 February 1933, daughter of Sir William Worsley, Bt.)
Issue:
(1)   Earl of St Andrews (George Philip Nicholas), *born* 26 June 1962, *married* 9 January 1988 Sylvana Tomaselli, and has issue, Edward Edmund Maximilian George, Baron Downpatrick, *born* 2 December 1988; Lady Marina Charlotte Alexandra Katharine Windsor, *born* 30 September 1992; Lady Amelia Sophia Theodora Margaret Windsor, *born* 24 August 1995
(2)   Lady Helen Taylor (Helen Marina Lucy), *born* 28 April 1964, *married* 18 July 1992 Timothy Taylor, and has issue, Columbus George Donald Taylor, *born* 6 August 1994
(3)   Lord Nicholas Windsor (Nicholas Charles Edward Jonathan), *born* 25 July 1970
Residences: York House, St James's Palace, London SW1 1BQ; Crocker End House, Nettlebed, Oxon.

Office: York House, St James's Palace, London SW1A 1BQ. Tel: 0171-930 4872

HRH PRINCESS ALEXANDRA, THE HON. LADY OGILVY (Princess Alexandra Helen Elizabeth Olga Christabel), GCVO *Born* 25 December 1936
Married 24 April 1963 The Hon. Sir Angus Ogilvy, KCVO (*born* 14 September 1928, second son of 12th Earl of Airlie)
Issue:
(1)   James Robert Bruce Ogilvy, *born* 29 February 1964, *married* 30 July 1988 Julia Rawlinson, and has issue, Flora Alexandra Ogilvy, *born* 15 December 1994
(2)   Marina Victoria Alexandra, Mrs Mowatt, *born* 31 July 1966, *married* 2 February 1990 Paul Mowatt, and has issue, Zenouska May Mowatt, *born* 26 May 1990; Christian Alexander Mowatt, *born* 4 June 1993
Residence: Thatched House Lodge, Richmond Park, Surrey
Office: Buckingham Palace, London SW1A 1AA. Tel: 0171-930 1860

HRH PRINCE MICHAEL OF KENT (Prince Michael George Charles Franklin), KCVO
Born 4 July 1942
Married 30 June 1978 Baroness Marie-Christine Agnes Hedwig Ida von Reibnitz, now HRH Princess Michael of Kent (*born* 15 January 1945, daughter of Baron Gunther von Reibnitz)
Issue:
(1)   Lord Frederick Windsor (Frederick Michael George David Louis), *born* 6 April 1979
(2)   Lady Gabriella Windsor (Gabriella Marina Alexandra Ophelia), *born* 23 April 1981
Residences: Kensington Palace, London W8 4PU; Nether Lypiatt Manor, Stroud, Glos.
Office: Kensington Palace, London W8 4PU. Tel: 0171-938 3519

ORDER OF SUCCESSION

1   HRH The Prince of Wales
2   HRH Prince William of Wales
3   HRH Prince Henry of Wales
4   HRH The Duke of York
5   HRH Princess Beatrice of York
6   HRH Princess Eugenie of York
7   HRH The Prince Edward
8   HRH The Princess Royal
9   Peter Phillips
10   Zara Phillips
11   HRH The Princess Margaret, Countess of Snowdon
12   Viscount Linley
13   Lady Sarah Chatto
14   HRH The Duke of Gloucester
15   Earl of Ulster
16   Lady Davina Windsor
17   Lady Rose Windsor
18   HRH The Duke of Kent
19   Baron Downpatrick
20   Lady Marina Charlotte Windsor
21   Lady Amelia Windsor
22   Lord Nicholas Windsor
23   Lady Helen Taylor
24   Columbus Taylor
25   Lord Frederick Windsor
26   Lady Gabriella Windsor
27   HRH Princess Alexandra, the Hon. Lady Ogilvy
28   James Ogilvy
29   Flora Ogilvy
30   Marina, Mrs Paul Mowatt

Royal Households

THE QUEEN'S HOUSEHOLD

Lord Chamberlain, The Earl of Airlie, KT, GCVO, PC
Lord Steward, The Viscount Ridley, KG, GCVO, TD
Master of the Horse, The Lord Somerleyton, KCVO
Treasurer of the Household, The Rt. Hon. G. Knight, MP
Comptroller of the Household, T. Wood, MP
Vice-Chamberlain, T. Kirkhope, MP

Gold Sticks, Maj.-Gen. Lord Michael Fitzalan-Howard, GCVO, CB, CBE, MC; Gen. Sir Desmond Fitzpatrick, GCB, DSO, MBE, MC
Vice-Adm. of the United Kingdom, Adm. Sir James Eberle, GCB
Rear-Adm. of the United Kingdom, Adm. Sir Nicholas Hunt, GCB, LVO
First and Principal Naval Aide-de-Camp, Adm. Sir Jock Slater, GCB, LVO
Flag Aide-de-Camp, Adm. Sir Michael Boyce, KCB, OBE
Aides-de-Camp-General, Gen. Sir Charles Guthrie, GCB, LVO, OBE; Gen. Sir John Wilsey, KCB, CBE
Air Aides-de-Camp, Air Chief Marshal Sir Michael Graydon, GCB, CBE; Air Chief Marshal Sir William Wratten, KBE, CB

Mistress of the Robes, The Duchess of Grafton, GCVO
Ladies of the Bedchamber, The Countess of Airlie, DCVO; The Lady Farnham
Extra Lady of the Bedchamber, The Marchioness of Abergavenny, DCVO
Women of the Bedchamber, Hon. Mary Morrison, DCVO; Lady Susan Hussey, DCVO; Lady Dugdale, DCVO; The Lady Elton
Extra Women of the Bedchamber, The Hon. Mrs Van der Woude, CVO; Mrs John Woodroffe, CVO; Mrs Michael Wall, DCVO; Lady Abel Smith, DCVO; Mrs Robert de Pass
Equerries, Lt.-Col. Sir Guy Acland, Bt., MVO; Lt.-Cdr. T. Williamson; Capt. E. Macfarlane (temp.)
Extra Equerries, Vice-Adm. Sir Peter Ashmore, KCB, KCVO, DSC; Lt.-Col. The Lord Charteris of Amisfield, GCB, GCVO, QSO, OBE, PC; Maj.-Gen. Sir Simon Cooper, KCVO; Air Cdre the Hon. T. Elworthy, CVO, CBE; The Rt Hon. Sir Robert Fellowes, KCB, KCVO; Sir Edward Ford, KCB, KCVO, ERD; Rear-Adm. Sir John Garnier, KCVO, CBE; Rear-Adm. Sir Paul Greening, GCVO; Brig. Sir Geoffrey Hardy-Roberts, KCVO, CB, CBE; The Rt. Hon. Sir William Heseltine, GCB, GCVO, AC, CB; Lt.-Col. Sir John Johnston, GCVO, MC; Lt.-Col. A. Mather, OBE; Sir Peter Miles, KCVO; Lt.-Col. Sir John Miller, GCVO, DSO, MC; Air Cdre Sir Dennis Mitchell, KBE, CVO, DFC, AFC; The Lord Moore of Wolvercote, GCB, GCVO, CMG, QSO; Lt.-Gen. Sir John Richards, KCB, KCVO; Lt.-Col. W. H. M. Ross, CVO, OBE; Air Vice-Marshal Sir John Severne, KCVO, OBE, AFC; Lt.-Col. Sir Blair Stewart-Wilson, KCVO; Rear-Adm. Sir Richard Trowbridge, KCVO; Lt.-Col. G. West, CVO; Air Cdre Sir Archie Winskill, KCVO, CBE, DFC, AE; Rear-Adm. Sir Robert Woodard, KCVO

THE PRIVATE SECRETARY'S OFFICE

Buckingham Palace, London SWIA IAA
Private Secretary to The Queen, The Rt Hon. Sir Robert Fellowes, KCB, KCVO
Deputy Private Secretary, Sir Kenneth Scott, KCVO, CMG
Assistant Private Secretary, R. B. Janvrin, CVO

Special Assistant to the Private Secretary, S. Gimson
Press Secretary, C. V. Anson, LVO
Deputy Press Secretary, G. Crawford, LVO
Assistant Press Secretary, Miss P. Russell-Smith
Chief Clerk, Mrs G. S. Coulson, MVO
Secretary to the Private Secretary, Mrs J. Bean, LVO

THE QUEEN'S ARCHIVES

Round Tower, Windsor Castle, Berks
Keeper of The Queen's Archives, The Rt Hon. Sir Robert Fellowes, KCB, KCVO
Assistant Keeper, O. Everett, CVO
Registrar, Lady de Bellaigue, MVO

THE PRIVY PURSE AND TREASURER'S OFFICE

Buckingham Palace, London SWIA IAA
Keeper of the Privy Purse and Treasurer to The Queen, Maj. Sir Shane Blewitt, KCVO
Deputy Keeper of the Privy Purse and Deputy Treasurer, J. Parsons, LVO
Chief Accountant and Paymaster, D. Walker, LVO
Personnel Officer, Miss P. Lloyd
Land Agent, Sandringham, J. Major, FRICS
Resident Factor, Balmoral, P. Ord
Master of The Queen's Music, M. Williamson, CBE, AO
Poet Laureate, Ted Hughes, OBE
Keeper of the Royal Philatelic Collection, C. Goodwyn

FINANCE AND PROPERTY SERVICES

Director of Finance and Property Services, M. Peat, CVO
Deputy Director, Property Services, J. Tiltman
Superintending Architect, G. Sharpe

ROYAL ALMONRY

High Almoner, The Rt. Revd John Taylor
Hereditary Grand Almoner, The Marquess of Exeter
Sub-Almoner, Revd W. Booth
Secretary, C. Williams, RVM
Assistant Secretary, P. Hartley, LVO

THE LORD CHAMBERLAIN'S OFFICE

Buckingham Palace, London SWIA IAA
Comptroller, Lt.-Col. W. H. M. Ross, CVO, OBE
Assistant Comptroller, Lt.-Col. A. Mather, OBE
Secretary, P. D. Hartley, LVO
Assistant Secretary, J. Spencer, MVO
State Invitations Assistant, J. Hope
Permanent Lords-in-Waiting, Lt.-Col. The Lord Charteris of Amisfield, GCB, GCVO, OBE, QSO, PC; The Lord Moore of Wolvercote, GCB, GCVO, CMG, QSO
Lords-in-Waiting, The Viscount Boyne, KCVO; The Lord Camoys; The Viscount Long, CBE; The Lord Lucas of Crudwell; The Earl of Courtown
Baronesses-in-Waiting, The Baroness Trumpington; The Baroness Miller of Hendon, MBE
Gentlemen Ushers, Maj. N. Chamberlayne-Macdonald, LVO, OBE; Capt. M. Barrow, DSO, RN; Capt. M. Fulford-Dobson, RN; Lt.-Gen. Sir Richard Vickers, KCB, LVO, OBE; Air Vice-Marshal B. Newton, CB, OBE; Col. M. Havergal, OBE; Rear Adm. C. H. D. Cooke-Priest, CB; Air Vice-Marshal D. Hawkins, CB, MBE; Maj.-Gen. B. Pennicott, CVO

Extra Gentlemen Ushers, Maj. T. Harvey, CVO, DSO, ERD;
Maj.-Gen. Sir Cyril Colquhoun, KCVO, CB, OBE; Lt.-Col.
Sir John Hugo, KCVO, OBE; Vice-Adm. Sir Ronald
Brockman, KCB, CSI, CIE, CVO, CBE; Air Marshal Sir
Maurice Heath, KBE, CB, CVO; Sir James Scholtens,
KCVO; Sir Patrick O'Dea, KCVO; Adm. Sir David
Williams, GCB; H. Davis, CVO, CM; Maj.-Gen. R. Reid,
CVO, MC, CD; Lt.-Cdr. J. Holdsworth, CVO, OBE, RN; Col.
G. Leigh, CVO, CBE; Lt.-Cdr. Sir Russell Wood, KCVO,
VRD; Maj.-Gen. Sir Desmond Rice, KCVO, CBE; Lt.-Col.
Sir Julian Paget, Bt., CVO; S. W. F. Martin, CVO; J.
Haslam, CVO; Prof. Sir Norman Blacklock, KCVO, OBE,
FRCS; Air Marshal Sir Roy Austen-Smith, KBE, CB, CVO,
DFC; Vice-Adm. Sir David Loram, KCB, CVO; Sir Carron
Greig, KCVO, CBE; Gp Capt J. Slessor, CVO
Gentleman Usher to the Sword of State, Gen. Sir Edward
Burgess, KCB, OBE
Gentleman Usher of the Black Rod, Gen. Sir Edward Jones, KCB,
CBE
Serjeants-at-Arms, D. Walker, LVO; Maj. B. Eastwood, LVO,
MBE; P. Hartley, LVO
Marshal of the Diplomatic Corps, Vice-Adm. Sir James
Weatherall, KBE
Vice-Marshal, A. St J. H. Figgis, CMG
Constable and Governor of Windsor Castle, Gen. Sir Patrick
Palmer, KBE
Keeper of the Jewel House, Tower of London, Maj.-Gen. G. Field,
CB, OBE
Bargemaster, R. Crouch
Swan Warden, Prof. C. Perrins, LVO
Swan Marker, D. Barber
Superintendent of the State Apartments, St James's Palace, B.
Andrews, BEM

ECCLESIASTICAL HOUSEHOLD

THE COLLEGE OF CHAPLAINS

Clerk of the Closet, Rt. Revd Bishop of Chelmsford
Deputy Clerk of the Closet, Revd W. Booth
Chaplains to The Queen, Revd A. H. H. Harbottle, LVO; Ven.
D. N. Griffiths, RD; Revd Canon J. V. Bean; Revd K.
Huxley; Ven. P. Ashford; Revd Canon D. C. Gray, TD;
Revd Canon J. Hester; Revd S. Pedley; Revd Canon
M. A. Moxon; Revd Canon G. Murphy, LVO; Revd
D. J. Burgess; Revd E. R. Ayerst; Revd R. S. Clarke;
Revd Canon C. J. Hill; Revd Canon K. Pound; Revd
J. Haslam; Revd Canon G. Hall; Revd Canon A. C. Hill;
Revd J. C. Priestley; Revd Canon J. O. Colling; Revd
Canon G. Jones; Revd Canon D. G. Palmer; Revd
Canon D. H. Wheaton; Revd Canon P. Boulton; Revd
Canon R. A. Bowden; Revd Canon E. Buchanan; Revd J.
Robson; Revd Canon J. Stanley; Revd Canon
I. Hardaker; Revd Canon L. F. Webber; Ven. F. Bentley;
Revd D. Adams; Revd Canon J. Sykes; Revd Canon
I. Smith-Cameron
Extra Chaplains, Revd Canon J. S. D. Mansel, KCVO, FSA;
Preb. S. A. Williams, CVO; Ven. E. J. G. Ward, LVO; Revd
J. R W. Stott; Revd Canon A. D. Caesar, CVO; Revd
Canon E. James

CHAPELS ROYAL

Dean of the Chapels Royal, The Bishop of London
Sub-Dean of Chapels Royal, Revd W. Booth
Priests in Ordinary, Revd G. Watkins; Revd S. E. Young
Organist, Choirmaster and Composer, R. J. Popplewell, MVO,
FRCO, FRCM
Domestic Chaplain, Buckingham Palace, Revd W. Booth
Domestic Chaplain, Windsor Castle, The Dean of Windsor
Domestic Chaplain, Sandringham, Revd Canon G. R. Hall

Chaplain, Royal Chapel, Windsor Great Park, Revd Canon M.
Moxon
Chaplain, Hampton Court Palace, Revd Canon M. Moore
Chaplain, Tower of London, Revd Canon
J. G. M. W. Murphy, LVO
Organist and Choirmaster, Hampton Court Palace, R. Hill

MEDICAL HOUSEHOLD

Head of the Medical Household and Physician to The Queen,
R. Thompson, DM, FRCP
Physician, R. W. Davey, MB, BS
Serjeant Surgeon, B. T. Jackson, MS, FRCS
Surgeon Oculist, P. Holmes Sellors, LVO, BM, B.ch., FRCS
Surgeon Gynaecologist, M. E. Setchell, FRCS, FRCOG
Surgeon Dentist, N. A. Sturridge, CVO, LDS, BDS, DDS
Orthopaedic Surgeon, R. H. Vickers, MA, BM, B.ch., FRCS
Physician to the Household, J. Cunningham, DM, FRCP
Surgeon to the Household, A. A. M. Lewis, MB, FRCS
Surgeon Oculist to the Household, T. J. ffytche, MB, FRCS,
FRCophth.
Apothecary to The Queen and to the Household,
N. R. Southward, CVO, MB, B.chir.
Apothecary to the Household at Windsor, J. H. D. Briscoe, MB,
B.chir., D.obst.
Apothecary to the Household at Sandringham, I. K. Campbell,
MB, BS, FRCGP
Coroner of The Queen's Household, J. Burton, CBE, MB, BS

CENTRAL CHANCERY OF THE ORDERS OF KNIGHTHOOD
St James's Palace, London SW1A 1BS

Secretary, Lt.-Col. A. Mather, OBE
Assistant Secretary, Miss R. Wells, MVO

THE HONOURABLE CORPS OF GENTLEMEN-AT-ARMS
St James's Palace, London SW1A 1BS

Captain, The Lord Strathclyde, PC
Lieutenant, Col. T. A. Hall, OBE
Standard Bearer, Maj. Sir Fergus Matheson of Matheson, Bt.
Clerk of the Cheque and Adjutant, Lt.-Col. R. Mayfield, DSO
Harbinger, Maj. Sir Philip Duncombe, Bt.

Gentlemen of the Corps

Colonels, Sir Piers Bengough, KCVO, OBE; Hon. N. Crossley,
TD; T. Wilson; D. Fanshawe, OBE; J. Baker; R. ffrench
Blake; Sir William Mahon, Bt.; Sir Brian Barttelot, Bt.,
OBE; M. J. C. Robertson, MC
Lieutenant-Colonels, B. Lockhart; Hon. P. H. Lewis; R.
Macfarlane; Hon. G. B. Norrie; J. H. Fisher, OBE; R. Ker,
MC; P. Chamberlin
Majors, J. A. J. Nunn; I. B. Ramsden, MBE; M. J. Drummond-
Brady; A. Arkwright; G. M. B. Colenso-Jones; T. Gooch,
MBE; J. B. B. Cockcroft; C. J. H. Gurney; P. D. Johnson;
R. M. O. Webster
Captain, The Lord Monteagle of Brandon

THE QUEEN'S BODY GUARD OF THE YEOMEN OF THE GUARD
St James's Palace, London SW1A 1BS

Captain, The Lord Chesham
Lieutenant, Col. G. W. Tufnell
Clerk of the Cheque and Adjutant, Col. S. Longsdon
Ensign, Maj. C. Marriott
Exons, Maj. C. Enderby; Maj. M. T. N. H. Wills

MASTER OF THE HOUSEHOLD'S DEPARTMENT

BOARD OF GREEN CLOTH
Buckingham Palace, London SW1A 1AA
Master of the Household, Maj.-Gen. Sir Simon Cooper, KCVO
Deputy Master of the Household, Lt.-Col. Sir Guy Acland, Bt., MVO
Assistants to the Master of the Household, M. T. Parker, MVO; P. Jackson
Chief Clerk, M. C. W. N. Jephson, MVO
Chief Housekeeper, Miss H. Colebrook, MVO
Palace Steward, A. Jarred, MVO, RVM
Royal Chef, L. Mann, RVM
Superintendent, Windsor Castle, Maj. B. Eastwood, LVO, MBE
Superintendent, The Palace of Holyroodhouse, Lt.-Col. D. Anderson, OBE

ROYAL MEWS DEPARTMENT

Buckingham Palace, London SW1W 0QH
Crown Equerry, Lt.-Col. S. Gilbart-Denham, CVO
Veterinary Surgeon, P. Scott Dunn, LVO, MRCVS
Superintendent Royal Mews, Buckingham Palace, Maj. A. Smith, MBE
Comptroller of Stores, Maj. L. Marsham, MVO

THE ROYAL COLLECTION TRUST

St James's Palace, London SW1A 1BS
Director of Royal Collection and Surveyor of The Queen's Works of Art, Sir Geoffrey de Bellaigue, KCVO, FBA, FSA
Surveyor of The Queen's Pictures, C. Lloyd
Surveyor Emeritus of The Queen's Pictures, Sir Oliver Millar, GCVO, FBA, FSA
Librarian, The Royal Library, Windsor Castle, O. Everett, CVO
Deputy Surveyor of The Queen's Works of Art, H. Roberts, LVO, FSA
Librarian Emeritus, Sir Robin Mackworth-Young, GCVO, FSA
Director of Media Affairs, R. Arbiter
Curator of the Print Room, The Hon. Mrs Roberts, LVO
Administrator and Assistant to The Surveyors, D. Rankin-Hunt, MVO, TD
Assistant to The Surveyor of The Queen's Pictures, C. Noble, MVO
Senior Picture Restorer, Miss V. Pemberton-Pigott, MVO
Chief Restorer, Old Master Drawings, A. Donnithorne
Senior Furniture Restorer, E. Fancourt, MVO, RVM
Armourer, J. Jackson, RVM
Chief Binder, R. Day, MVO, RVM

ROYAL COLLECTION ENTERPRISES LTD

Managing Director, M. E. K. Hewlett
Financial Director, Mrs G. Johnson

ASCOT OFFICE

St James's Palace, London SW1A 1BS
Tel 0171-930 9882
Her Majesty's Representative at Ascot, Col. Sir Piers Bengough, KCVO, OBE
Secretary, Miss L. Thompson-Royds, MVO

THE QUEEN'S HOUSEHOLD IN SCOTLAND

Hereditary Lord High Constable, The Earl of Erroll
Hereditary Master of the Household, The Duke of Argyll

Lord Lyon King of Arms, Sir Malcolm Innes of Edingight, KCVO, WS
Hereditary Bearer of the Royal Banner of Scotland, The Earl of Dundee
Hereditary Bearer of the Scottish National Flag, The Earl of Lauderdale
Hereditary Keepers:
  Palace of Holyroodhouse, The Duke of Hamilton and Brandon
  Falkland Palace, N. Crichton-Stuart
  Stirling Castle, The Earl of Mar and Kellie
  Dunstaffnage Castle, The Duke of Argyll
  Dunconnel Castle, Sir Fitzroy Maclean, Bt., KT, CBE
Hereditary Carver, Maj. Sir Ralph Anstruther, Bt., GCVO, MC
Keeper of Dumbarton Castle, Brig. A. S. Pearson, CB, DSO, OBE, MC, TD
Governor of Edinburgh Castle, Maj.-Gen. J. Hall, OBE
Historiographer, Prof. T. C. Smout, FBA, FRSE, FSA SCOT.
Botanist, Prof. D. Henderson, CBE, FRSE
Painter and Limner, D. A. Donaldson, RSA, RP
Sculptor in Ordinary, Prof. Sir Eduardo Paolozzi, CBE, RA
Astronomer, Prof. J. Brown, PH.D., FRSE
Heralds and Pursuivants, see page 285

ECCLESIASTICAL HOUSEHOLD
Dean of the Chapel Royal, Very Revd W. J. Morris, KCVO, DD, LL.D
Dean of the Order of the Thistle, Very Revd G. I. Macmillan
Chaplains in Ordinary, Very Revd W. J. Morris, KCVO, DD, LL.D.; Revd J. McLeod; Very Revd G. I. Macmillan; Revd M. D. Craig; Very Revd W. B. R. Macmillan, LL.D, DD.; Very Revd J. L. Weatherhead, DD; Revd A. S. Todd, DD; Revd C. Robertson; Very Revd J. A. Simpson; Revd N. W. Drummond
Extra Chaplains, Very Revd R. W. V. Selby Wright, CVO, TD, DD, FRSE, FSA SCOT.; Very Revd W. R. Sanderson, DD; Revd T. J. T. Nicol, LVO, MBE, MC, TD; Very Revd Prof. J. McIntyre, CVO, DD, FRSE; Revd C. Forrester-Paton; Revd H. W. M. Cant; Very Revd R. A. S. Barbour, KCVO, MC, DD; Revd K. MacVicar, MBE, DFC, TD; Very Revd W. B. Johnston, DD; Revd A. J. C. Macfarlane; Revd M. I. Levison, DD; Rt. Revd J. Harkness, CB, OBE
Domestic Chaplain, Balmoral, Revd J. A. K. Angus, LVO, TD

MEDICAL HOUSEHOLD
Physicians in Scotland, P. Brunt, OBE, MD, FRCP; A. L. Muir, MD, FRCP
Surgeons in Scotland, J. Engeset, CH.M., FRCS; Prof. D. C. Carter MD, FRCS
Apothecary to the Household at Balmoral, D. J. A. Glass, MB, CH.B.
Apothecary to the Household at the Palace of Holyroodhouse, Dr J. Cormack, MD, FRCPE, FRCGP

THE QUEEN'S BODY GUARD FOR SCOTLAND

ROYAL COMPANY OF ARCHERS
Archers' Hall, Buccleuch Street, Edinburgh EH8 9LR
Captain-General and Gold Stick for Scotland, Col. the Lord Clydesmuir, KT, CB, MBE, TD
Captains, Maj. the Lord Home of the Hirsel, KT; The Duke of Buccleuch and Queensberry, KT, VRD; Maj. Sir Hew Hamilton-Dalrymple, Bt., KCVO; Maj. the Earl of Wemyss and March, KT
Lieutenants, The Earl of Airlie, KT, GCVO; Capt. Sir Iain Tennant, KT; Capt. N. E. F. Dalrymple-Hamilton, CVO, MBE, DSC, RN; The Marquess of Lothian, KCVO
Ensigns, Cdre Sir John Clerk of Penicuik, Bt., CBE, VRD; The Earl of Elgin and Kincardine, KT; Col. G. R. Simpson, DSO, LVO, TD; Maj. Sir David Butter, KCVO, MC

Brigadiers, The Earl of Minto, OBE; Maj.-Gen. Sir John Swinton, KCVO, OBE; Gen. Sir Michael Gow, GCB; The Hon. Lord Elliott, MC; Maj. the Hon. Sir Lachlan Maclean, Bt.; The Rt. Hon. Lord Younger of Prestwick, KCVO, TD; Capt. G. Burnet, LVO; The Duke of Montrose; Lt.-Gen. Sir Norman Arthur, KCB; The Hon. Sir William Macpherson of Cluny, TD; The Lord Nickson, KBE; Maj. the Lord Glenarthur; Earl of Dalkeith
Adjutant, Maj. the Hon. Sir Lachlan Maclean, Bt.
Surgeon, Dr P. A. P. Mackenzie, TD
Chaplain, Very Revd W. J. Morris, DD
President of the Council and Silver Stick for Scotland, Maj. Sir Hew Hamilton-Dalrymple, Bt., KCVO
Vice-President, Capt. Sir Iain Tennant, KT
Secretary, Capt. J. D. B. Younger
Treasurer, J. M. Haldane of Gleneagles

HOUSEHOLD OF THE PRINCE PHILIP, DUKE OF EDINBURGH

Treasurer, Sir Brian McGrath, KCVO
Private Secretary, Brig. M. G. Hunt-Davis, CBE
Equerry, Maj. A. C. Richards
Extra Equerries, J. B. V. Orr, CVO; The Lord Buxton of Alsa; Brig. C. Robertson, CVO
Temporary Equerries, Maj. J. Cosby; Capt. R. Goodfellow; Capt. the Hon. J. Geddes
Chief Clerk and Accountant, G. D. Partington

HOUSEHOLD OF QUEEN ELIZABETH THE QUEEN MOTHER

Lord Chamberlain, The Earl of Crawford and Balcarres, PC
Private Secretary, Comptroller and Equerry, Capt. Sir Alastair Aird, KCVO
Assistant Private Secretary and Equerry, Maj. R. Seymour, CVO
Treasurer and Equerry, Maj. Sir Ralph Anstruther, Bt., GCVO, MC
Equerry, Maj. C. Burgess (*temp.*)
Extra Equerries, Maj. Sir John Griffin, KCVO; The Lord Sinclair, CVO; Maj. W. Richardson, LVO; Maj. D. McMicking, LVO; Capt. A. Windham, LVO
Apothecary to the Household, Dr N. Southward, CVO, MB, B.chir.
Surgeon-Apothecary to the Household (*Royal Lodge, Windsor*), Dr J. Briscoe, D.obst.
Mistress of the Robes, vacant
Ladies of the Bedchamber, The Lady Grimthorpe, DCVO; The Countess of Scarbrough
Women of the Bedchamber, Dame Frances Campbell-Preston, DCVO; Lady Angela Oswald, LVO; The Hon. Mrs Rhodes; Mrs Michael Gordon-Lennox
Extra Women of the Bedchamber, Lady Jean Rankin, DCVO; Miss Jane Walker-Okeover; Lady Margaret Colville, CVO; Lady Elizabeth Basset, DCVO
Clerk Comptroller, M. Blanch, CVO
Clerk Accountant, J. P. Kyle, LVO
Information Officer, Mrs R. Murphy, LVO
Clerks, Miss F. Fletcher, LVO; Mrs W. Stevens

HOUSEHOLD OF THE PRINCE AND PRINCESS OF WALES

Private Secretary and Treasurer to the Prince of Wales, Cdr. R. J. Aylard, CVO, RN
Private Secretary to the Princess of Wales, P. Jephson, LVO
Deputy Private Secretary to The Prince of Wales, S. Lamport
Assistant Private Secretaries to The Prince of Wales, M. Butler; Dr M. Williams
Press Secretary to the Prince of Wales, A. Percival
Assistant Press Secretary to the Prince of Wales, Miss A. Henney
Press Secretary to the Princess of Wales, G. Crawford, LVO
Equerry to the Prince of Wales, Maj. P. J. Tabor
Extra Equerries to the Prince of Wales, The Hon. Edward Adeane, CVO; Maj.-Gen. Sir Christopher Airy, KCVO, CBE; Sqn. Ldr. Sir David Checketts, KCVO; Sir David Landale, KCVO; Sir John Riddle, Bt., CVO; G. J. Ward, CBE; Col. J. Q. Winter, LVO
Ladies-in-Waiting, Miss Anne Beckwith-Smith, LVO; Viscountess Campden; Mrs Max Pike; Mrs Duncan Byatt; Mrs James Lonsdale
Extra Lady-in-Waiting, Lady Sarah McCorquodale
Secretary to the Duchy of Cornwall and Keeper of the Records, J. N. C. James, CBE

HOUSEHOLD OF THE DUKE AND DUCHESS OF YORK

Private Secretary, Treasurer and Extra Equerry to the Duke and Duchess of York, Capt. R. N. Blair, RN
Comptroller and Assistant Private Secretary to the Duke and Duchess of York, Mrs Jonathan Mathias
Equerry to The Duke of York, Capt. D. H. Thompson

HOUSEHOLD OF THE PRINCE EDWARD

Private Secretary, Lt.-Col. S. G. O'Dwyer, LVO
Assistant Private Secretary, Mrs R. Warburton, MVO
Clerk, Miss L. Buggé

HOUSEHOLD OF THE PRINCESS ROYAL

Private Secretary, Lt.-Col. P. Gibbs, CVO
Assistant Private Secretary, The Hon. Mrs Louloudis
Ladies-in-Waiting, Lady Carew Pole, LVO; Mrs Andrew Feilden, LVO; The Hon. Mrs Legge-Bourke, LVO; Mrs William Nunneley; Mrs Timothy Holderness-Roddam; Mrs Charles Ritchie; Mrs David Bowes Lyon
Extra Ladies-in-Waiting, Miss Victoria Legge-Bourke, LVO; Mrs Malcolm Innes, LVO; The Countess of Lichfield

HOUSEHOLD OF THE PRINCESS MARGARET, COUNTESS OF SNOWDON

Private Secretary and Comptroller, The Lord Napier and Ettrick, KCVO
Lady-in-Waiting, The Hon. Mrs Whitehead, LVO
Extra Ladies-in-Waiting, Lady Elizabeth Cavendish, LVO; Lady Aird, LVO; Mrs Robin Benson, LVO, OBE; Lady

Juliet Townsend, LVO; Mrs Jane Stevens, LVO; The Hon.
Mrs Wills, LVO; The Lady Glenconner, LVO; The
Countess Alexander of Tunis, LVO; Mrs Charles
Vyvyan

HOUSEHOLD OF THE DUKE AND DUCHESS OF GLOUCESTER

Private Secretary, Comptroller and Equerry, Maj.
N. M. L. Barne
Assistant Private Secretary to the Duchess of Gloucester, Miss S.
Marland, LVO
Extra Equerry, Lt.-Col. Sir Simon Bland, KCVO
Ladies-in-Waiting, Mrs Michael Wigley, CVO; Mrs Euan
McCorquodale, LVO; Mrs Howard Page
Extra Ladies-in-Waiting, Miss Jennifer Thomson; The
Lady Camoys

HOUSEHOLD OF PRINCESS ALICE, DUCHESS OF GLOUCESTER

Private Secretary, Comptroller and Equerry, Maj.
N. M. L. Barne
Extra Equerry, Lt.-Col. Sir Simon Bland, KCVO
Ladies-in-Waiting, Dame Jean Maxwell-Scott, DCVO; Mrs
Michael Harvey
Extra Ladies-in-Waiting, Miss Diana Harrison; The Hon.
Jane Walsh, LVO; Miss Jane Egerton-Warburton, LVO

HOUSEHOLD OF THE DUKE AND DUCHESS OF KENT

Private Secretary, N. C. Adamson, OBE
Extra Equerries, Lt.-Cdr. Sir Richard Buckley, KCVO; Maj. J.
Stewart
Temporary Equerry, Capt. M. Barnett

Ladies-in-Waiting, Mrs Fiona Henderson, CVO; Mrs Colin
Marsh, LVO; Mrs Julian Tomkins; Mrs Peter Troughton;
Fiona, Lady Astor of Hever; Mrs Richard Beckett

HOUSEHOLD OF PRINCE AND PRINCESS MICHAEL OF KENT

Personal Secretary, Miss E. Moore-Searson
Equerry, J. Kennedy
Ladies-in-Waiting, The Hon. Mrs Sanders; Miss Anne
Frost; Mrs J. Fellowes

HOUSEHOLD OF PRINCESS ALEXANDRA, THE HON. LADY OGILVY

Comptroller and Private Secretary, Rear-Adm. Sir John
Garnier, KCVO, CBE
Extra Equerry, Maj. Sir Peter Clarke, KCVO
Lady-in-Waiting, Lady Mary Mumford, DCVO
Extra Ladies-in-Waiting, Mrs Peter Afia; Lady Mary
Colman; Lady Nicholas Gordon Lennox; The Hon.
Lady Rowley; Dame Mona Mitchell, DCVO

Royal Salutes

ENGLAND

A salute of 62 guns is fired on the wharf at the Tower of
London on the following occasions:
(a) the anniversaries of the birth, accession and
coronation of the Sovereign
(b) the anniversary of the birth of HM Queen Elizabeth
the Queen Mother
(c) the anniversary of the birth of HRH Prince Philip,
Duke of Edinburgh
A salute of 41 guns only is fired on extraordinary and
triumphal occasions, e.g. on the occasion of the Sovereign
opening, proroguing or dissolving Parliament in person, or
when passing through London in procession, except when
otherwise ordered.
A salute of 41 guns is fired from the two saluting stations
in London (the Tower of London and Hyde Park) on the
occasion of the birth of a Royal infant.
Constable of the Royal Palace and Fortress of London, Field
Marshal Sir John Stanier, GCB, MBE
Lieutenant of the Tower of London, Lt.-Gen. Sir Michael Gray,
KCB, OBE
Resident Governor and Keeper of the Jewel House, Maj.-Gen. G.
Field

Master Gunner of St James's Park, Gen. Sir Martin Farndale,
KCB
Master Gunner within the Tower, Col. O. Wingate

SCOTLAND

Royal salutes are authorized at Edinburgh Castle and
Stirling Castle, although in practice Edinburgh Castle is
the only operating saluting station in Scotland.
A salute of 21 guns is fired on the following occasions:
(a) the anniversaries of the birth, accession and coronation
of the Sovereign
(b) the anniversary of the birth of HM Queen Elizabeth
the Queen Mother
(c) the anniversary of the birth of HRH Prince Philip,
Duke of Edinburgh
A salute of 21 guns is fired in Edinburgh on the occasion
of the opening of the General Assembly of the Church of
Scotland.
A salute of 21 guns may also be fired in Edinburgh on the
arrival of HM The Queen, HM Queen Elizabeth the
Queen Mother, or a member of the Royal Family who is a
Royal Highness on an official visit.

Royal Finances

FUNDING

THE CIVIL LIST

The Civil List dates back to the late 17th century. It was originally used by the sovereign to pay the salaries of judges, ambassadors and other government offices as well as the expenses of the royal household. In 1760 on the accession of George III it was decided that the Civil List would be provided by Parliament in return for the King surrendering the hereditary revenues of the Crown. At that time Parliament undertook to pay the salaries of judges, ambassadors, etc. In 1831 Parliament agreed also to meet the costs of the royal palaces. Each sovereign has agreed to continue this arrangement.

The Civil List paid to The Queen is charged on the Consolidated Fund. Until 1972, the amount of money allocated annually under the Civil List was set for the duration of a reign. The system was then altered to a fixed annual payment for ten years but from 1975 high inflation made an annual review necessary. The system of payments reverted to the practice of a fixed annual payment for ten years from 1 January 1991.

The Civil List Acts provide for other members of the royal family to receive parliamentary annuities from government funds to meet the expenses of carrying out their official duties. Since 1975 The Queen has reimbursed the Treasury for the annuities paid to the Duke of Gloucester, the Duke of Kent and Princess Alexandra. Since April 1993 The Queen has reimbursed all the annuities except those paid to herself, Queen Elizabeth the Queen Mother and the Duke of Edinburgh.

The Prince of Wales does not receive a parliamentary annuity. He derives his income from the revenues of the Duchy of Cornwall and these monies meet the official and private expenses of the Prince of Wales and his family.

The annual payments for the years 1991–2000 are:

The Queen	£7,900,000
Queen Elizabeth the Queen Mother	643,000
The Duke of Edinburgh	359,000
*The Duke of York	249,000
*The Prince Edward	96,000
*The Princess Royal	228,000
*The Princess Margaret, Countess of Snowdon	219,000
*Princess Alice, Duchess of Gloucester	87,000
*The Duke of Gloucester	175,000
*The Duke of Kent	236,000
*Princess Alexandra	225,000
	10,237,000
*Refunded to the Treasury	1,515,000
Total	8,722,000

GRANT-IN-AID

Grant-in-aid from the Department of National Heritage is voted annually by Parliament to pay for the upkeep of the occupied royal palaces which are used as royal residences or for official or ceremonial purposes.

THE PRIVY PURSE

The funds received by the Privy Purse pay for official expenses incurred by The Queen as head of state and for some of The Queen's private expenditure. The revenues of the Duchy of Lancaster are the principal source of income for the Privy Purse. The revenues of the Duchy were retained by George III in 1760 when the hereditary revenues were surrendered in exchange for the Civil List.

PERSONAL INCOME

The Queen's personal income derives mostly from investments, and is used to meet private expenditure.

DEPARTMENTAL VOTES

Items of expenditure connected with the official duties of the royal family which fall on votes of government departments include:

Ministry of Defence – The Royal Yacht; The Queen's Flight
Foreign and Commonwealth Office – Marshal of the Diplomatic Corps; overseas visits at the request of government departments
Department of National Heritage – Royal palaces
Department of Transport – The Royal Train
HM Treasury – Central Chancery of the Orders of Knighthood

TAXATION

The sovereign is not legally liable to pay income tax, capital gains tax or inheritance tax. After income tax was reintroduced in 1842 some income tax was paid voluntarily by the sovereign but over a long period these payments were phased out. In November 1992 the Prime Minister announced that The Queen had offered to pay tax on a voluntary basis from 6 April 1993, and that the Prince of Wales also wished to pay tax on a voluntary basis on his income from the Duchy of Cornwall. (He was already taxed in all other respects.)

The provisions for The Queen and the Prince of Wales to pay tax were set out in a Memorandum of Understanding on Royal Taxation presented to Parliament on 11 February 1993. The main provisions are that The Queen will pay income tax and capital gains tax in respect of her private income and assets, and on the proportion of the income and capital gains of the Privy Purse used for private purposes. Inheritance tax will be paid on The Queen's assets, except for those which pass to the next sovereign, whether automatically or by gift or bequest. The Prince of Wales will pay income tax on income from the Duchy of Cornwall used for private purposes.

The Prince of Wales has confirmed that he intends to pay tax on the same basis following his accession to the throne.

Other members of the royal family are subject to tax as for any taxpayer.

Military Ranks and Titles

THE QUEEN

Lord High Admiral of the United Kingdom

Colonel-in-Chief
The Life Guards; The Blues and Royals (Royal Horse Guards and 1st Dragoons); The Royal Scots Dragoon Guards (Carabiniers and Greys); The Queen's Royal Lancers; Royal Tank Regiment; Corps of Royal Engineers; Grenadier Guards; Coldstream Guards; Scots Guards; Irish Guards; Welsh Guards; The Royal Welch Fusiliers; The Queen's Lancashire Regiment, The Argyll and Sutherland Highlanders (Princess Louise's); The Royal Green Jackets; Adjutant General's Corps; The Governor General's Horse Guards (of Canada); The King's Own Calgary Regiment; Canadian Forces Military Engineers Branch; Royal 22e Regiment (of Canada); Governor-General's Foot Guards (of Canada); The Canadian Grenadier Guards; Le Regiment de la Chaudiere (of Canada); 2nd Bn Royal New Brunswick Regiment (North Shore); The 48th Highlanders of Canada; The Argyll and Sutherland Highlanders of Canada (Princess Louise's); The Calgary Highlanders; Royal Australian Engineers; Royal Australian Infantry Corps; Royal Australian Army Ordnance Corps; Royal Australian Army Nursing Corps; The Corps of Royal New Zealand Engineers; Royal New Zealand Infantry Regiment; Royal New Zealand Army Ordnance Corps; Royal Malta Artillery; The Malawi Rifles

Affiliated Colonel-in-Chief
The Queen's Gurkha Engineers

Captain-General
Royal Regiment of Artillery; The Honourable Artillery Company; Combined Cadet Force; Royal Regiment of Canadian Artillery; Royal Regiment of Australian Artillery; Royal Regiment of New Zealand Artillery; Royal New Zealand Armoured Corps

Hon. Colonel
The Royal Mercian and Lancastrian Yeomanry

Patron
Royal Army Chaplains' Department

Air Commodore-in-Chief
Royal Auxiliary Air Force; Royal Air Force Regiment; Royal Observer Corps; Air Reserve (of Canada); Royal Australian Air Force Reserve

Commandant-in-Chief
Royal Air Force College, Cranwell

Hon. Air Commodore
RAF Marham

HM QUEEN ELIZABETH THE QUEEN MOTHER

Colonel-in-Chief
1st The Queen's Dragoon Guards; The Queen's Royal Hussars (Queen's Own and Royal Irish); 9th/12th Royal Lancers (Prince of Wales's); The King's Regiment; The Royal Anglian Regiment; The Light Infantry; The Black Watch (Royal Highland Regiment); Royal Army Medical Corps; The Black Watch (Royal Highland Regiment) of Canada; The Toronto Scottish Regiment; Canadian Forces Medical Services; Royal Australian Army Medical Corps; Royal New Zealand Army Medical Corps

Hon. Colonel
The Royal Yeomanry; A (London Scottish) Company, The London Regiment; Inns of Court and City Yeomanry

Commandant-in-Chief
Women in the Royal Navy; Women, Royal Air Force; Royal Air Force Central Flying School

HRH THE PRINCE PHILIP, DUKE OF EDINBURGH

Admiral of the Fleet
Field Marshal
Marshal of the Royal Air Force

Admiral of the Fleet, Royal Australian Navy
Field Marshal, Australian Military Forces
Marshal of the Royal Australian Air Force

Admiral of the Fleet, Royal New Zealand Navy
Field Marshal, New Zealand Army
Marshal of the Royal New Zealand Air Force

Captain-General, Royal Marines

Admiral
Royal Canadian Sea Cadets

Colonel-in-Chief
The Royal Gloucestershire, Berkshire and Wiltshire Regiment; The Highlanders (Seaforth, Gordons and Camerons); Corps of Royal Electrical and Mechanical Engineers; Intelligence Corps; Army Cadet Force; The Royal Canadian Regiment; The Royal Hamilton Light Infantry (Wentworth Regiment) (of Canada); The Cameron Highlanders of Ottawa; The Queen's Own Cameron Highlanders of Canada; The Seaforth Highlanders of Canada; The Royal Canadian Army Cadets; The Royal Australian Electrical and Mechanical Engineers; The Australian Cadet Corps; The Royal New Zealand Corps of Electrical and Mechanical Engineers

Deputy Colonel-in-Chief
The Queen's Royal Hussars (Queen's Own and Royal Irish)

Colonel
Grenadier Guards

Hon. Colonel
City of Edinburgh Universities Officers' Training Corps; The Trinidad and Tobago Regiment

Air Commodore-in-Chief
Air Training Corps; Royal Canadian Air Cadets

Hon. Air Commodore
RAF Kinloss

HRH THE PRINCE OF WALES

Captain, Royal Navy
Group Captain, Royal Air Force

Colonel-in-Chief
The Royal Dragoon Guards; The Cheshire Regiment;
The Royal Regiment of Wales (24th/41st Foot); The
Parachute Regiment; The Royal Gurkha Rifles; Army
Air Corps; The Royal Canadian Dragoons; Lord
Strathcona's Horse (Royal Canadians); Royal Regiment
of Canada; Royal Winnipeg Rifles; Air Reserve Group
of Air Command (of Canada); Royal Australian
Armoured Corps; The Royal Pacific Islands Regiment

Deputy Colonel-in-Chief
The Highlanders (Seaforth, Gordons and Camerons)

Colonel
Welsh Guards

Air Commodore-in-Chief
Royal New Zealand Air Force

Hon. Air Commodore
RAF Valley

HRH THE PRINCESS OF WALES

Colonel-in-Chief
The Light Dragoons; The Princess of Wales's Royal
Regiment (Queen's and Royal Hampshires); The
Princess of Wales's Own Regiment (of Canada); The
West Nova Scotia Regiment (of Canada); The Royal
Australian Survey Corps

Hon. Air Commodore
RAF Wittering

HRH THE DUKE OF YORK

Lieutenant-Commander, Royal Navy

Admiral
Sea Cadet Corps

Colonel-in-Chief
The Staffordshire Regiment (The Prince of Wales's);
The Royal Irish Regiment (27th (Inniskilling), 83rd,
87th and The Ulster Defence Regiment)

HRH THE PRINCESS ROYAL

Rear Admiral
Chief Commandant for Women in the Royal Navy

Colonel-in-Chief
The King's Royal Hussars; Royal Corps of Signals; The
Royal Scots (The Royal Regiment); The
Worcestershire and Sherwood Foresters Regiment
(29th/45th Foot); The Royal Logistic Corps; 8th
Canadian Hussars (Princess Louise's); Canadian Forces
Communications and Electronics Branch; The Grey
and Simcoe Foresters; The Royal Regina Rifle
Regiment; Royal Newfoundland Regiment; Royal
Australian Corps of Signals; Royal New Zealand Corps
of Signals; Royal New Zealand Nursing Corps

Affiliated Colonel-in-Chief
The Queen's Gurkha Signals; The Queen's Own
Gurkha Transport Regiment

Hon. Colonel
University of London Officers' Training Corps

Hon. Air Commodore
RAF Lyneham

Commandant-in-Chief
Women's Transport Service (FANY)

HRH THE PRINCESS MARGARET, COUNTESS OF SNOWDON

Colonel-in-Chief
The Royal Highland Fusiliers (Princess Margaret's
Own Glasgow and Ayrshire Regiment); Queen
Alexandra's Royal Army Nursing Corps; The Highland
Fusiliers of Canada; The Princess Louise Fusiliers (of
Canada); The Bermuda Regiment

Deputy Colonel-in-Chief
The Royal Anglian Regiment

Hon. Air Commodore
RAF Coningsby

HRH PRINCESS ALICE, DUCHESS OF GLOUCESTER

Air Chief Marshal

Colonel-in-Chief
The King's Own Scottish Borderers; Royal Australian
Corps of Transport; Royal New Zealand Corps of
Transport

Deputy Colonel-in-Chief
The King's Royal Hussars; The Royal Anglian
Regiment

Air Chief Commandant
Women, Royal Air Force

HRH THE DUKE OF GLOUCESTER

Deputy Colonel-in-Chief
The Royal Gloucestershire, Berkshire and Wiltshire
Regiment; The Royal Logistic Corps

Hon. Colonel
Royal Monmouthshire Royal Engineers (Militia)

Hon. Air Commodore
RAF Odiham

HRH THE DUCHESS OF GLOUCESTER

Colonel-in-Chief
Royal Australian Army Educational Corps; Royal New
Zealand Army Educational Corps

Deputy Colonel-in-Chief
Adjutant-General's Corps

HRH THE DUKE OF KENT

Field Marshal
Hon. Air Vice-Marshal

Colonel-in-Chief
The Royal Regiment of Fusiliers; The Devonshire and Dorset Regiment; The Lorne Scots (Peel, Dufferin and Hamilton Regiment)

Deputy Colonel-in-Chief
The Royal Scots Dragoon Guards (Carabiniers and Greys)

Colonel
Scots Guards

Hon. Air Commodore
RAF Leuchars

HRH THE DUCHESS OF KENT

Hon. Major-General

Colonel-in-Chief
The Prince of Wales's Own Regiment of Yorkshire

Deputy Colonel-in-Chief
The Royal Dragoon Guards; Adjutant-General's Corps; The Royal Logistic Corps

HRH PRINCE MICHAEL OF KENT

Major (retd), The Royal Hussars (Prince of Wales's Own)

Hon. Commodore
Royal Naval Reserve

HRH PRINCESS ALEXANDRA, THE HON. LADY OGILVY

Patron
Queen Alexandra's Royal Naval Nursing Service

Colonel-in-Chief
The King's Own Royal Border Regiment; The Queen's Own Rifles of Canada; The Canadian Scottish Regiment (Princess Mary's)

Deputy Colonel-in-Chief
The Queen's Royal Lancers; The Light Infantry

Deputy Hon. Colonel
The Royal Yeomanry

Patron and Air Chief Commandant
Princess Mary's Royal Air Force Nursing Service

The Royal Arms

ENGLAND

1st and 4th quarters (representing England) – Gules, three lions passant guardant in pale Or
2nd quarter (representing Scotland) – Or, a lion rampant within a double tressure flory counterflory Gules
3rd quarter (representing Ireland) – Azure, a harp Or, stringed Argent
The whole shield is encircled with the Garter

SCOTLAND

The Royal Arms shown with the Lion of Scotland in the 1st and 4th quarters, and the Lions of England in the 2nd quarter
The whole shield is encircled with the Thistle

SUPPORTERS (ENGLAND)

Dexter (right) – a lion rampant guardant Or, imperially crowned (shown in Scotland on the sinister)
Sinister (left) – a unicorn Argent, armed, crined, and unguled Or, gorged with a coronet composed of crosses patées and fleurs-de-lis, a chain affixed, passing between the forelegs, and reflexed over the back (shown in Scotland on the dexter and imperially crowned)

CRESTS

England – the Royal Crown Proper thereon a lion statant guardant Or imperially crowned also Proper
Scotland – upon an imperial crown Proper a lion sejant affrontée Gules imperially crowned Or, holding in the dexter paw a sword and in the sinister a sceptre erect, also Proper
Ireland – a tower triple-towered of the First, from the portal a hart springing Argent, attired and hooved Or

BADGES

England – the red and white rose united, slipped and leaved proper
Scotland – a thistle, slipped and leaved proper
Ireland – a shamrock leaf slipped Vert; also a harp Or, stringed Argent
United Kingdom – the rose of England, the thistle of Scotland, and the shamrock of Ireland engrafted on the same stem proper, and an escutcheon charged as the Union Flag (all ensigned with the Royal Crown)
Wales – upon a mount Vert a dragon passant, wings elevated Gules

The House of Windsor

King George V assumed by royal proclamation (17 June 1917) for his House and family, as well as for all descendants in the male line of Queen Victoria who are subjects of these realms, the name of Windsor.

KING GEORGE V (George Frederick Ernest Albert), second son of King Edward VII, *born* 3 June 1865; *married* 6 July 1893 HSH Princess Victoria Mary Augusta Louise Olga Pauline Claudine Agnes of Teck (Queen Mary, *born* 26 May 1867; *died* 24 March 1953); *succeeded* to the throne 6 May 1910; *died* 20 January 1936. *Issue:*

1. HRH PRINCE EDWARD Albert Christian George Andrew Patrick David, *born* 23 June 1894, *succeeded* to the throne as King Edward VIII, 20 January 1936; *abdicated* 11 December 1936; created *Duke of Windsor*, 1937; *married* 3 June 1937, Mrs Wallis Warfield (Her Grace The Duchess of Windsor, *born* 19 June 1896; *died* 24 April 1986), *died* 28 May 1972

2. HRH PRINCE ALBERT Frederick Arthur George, *born* 14 December 1895, *created* Duke of York 1920; *married* 26 April 1923, Lady Elizabeth Bowes-Lyon, youngest daughter of the 14th Earl of Strathmore and Kinghorne (HM Queen Elizabeth the Queen Mother, *see* page 123–4), *succeeded* to the throne as King George VI, 11 December 1936; *died* 6 February 1952, having had issue (*see* page 123)

3. HRH PRINCESS (Victoria Alexandra Alice) MARY (*Princess Royal*), *born* 25 April 1897, *married* 28 February 1922, Viscount Lascelles, later the 6th Earl of Harewood (1882–1947), *died* 28 March 1965. *Issue:*
  (1) George Henry Hubert Lascelles, 7th Earl of Harewood, KBE, *born* 7 February 1923; *married* (1) 1949, Maria (Marion) Stein (marriage dissolved 1967); *issue,* (*a*) David Henry George,

Viscount Lascelles, *born* 1950; (*b*) James Edward, *born* 1953; (*c*) (Robert) Jeremy Hugh, *born* 1955; (2) 1967, Mrs Patricia Tuckwell; *issue,* (*d*) Mark Hubert, *born* 1964
  (2) Gerald David Lascelles, *born* 21 August 1924, *married* (1) 1952, Miss Angela Dowding (marriage dissolved 1978); *issue,* (*a*) Henry Ulick, *born* 1953; (2) 1978, Mrs Elizabeth Colvin; *issue,* (*b*) Martin David, *born* 1962

4. HRH PRINCE HENRY William Frederick Albert, *born* 31 March 1900, *created* Duke of Gloucester, Earl of Ulster and Baron Culloden 1928, *married* 6 November 1935, Lady Alice Christabel Montagu-Douglas-Scott, daughter of the 7th Duke of Buccleuch (HRH Princess Alice, Duchess of Gloucester, *see* page 124); *died* 10 June 1974. *Issue:*
  (1) HRH Prince William Henry Andrew Frederick, *born* 18 December 1941; *accidentally killed* 28 August 1972
  (2) HRH Prince Richard Alexander Walter George (HRH The Duke of Gloucester), *see* page 124

5. HRH PRINCE GEORGE Edward Alexander Edmund, *born* 20 December 1902, *created* Duke of Kent, Earl of St Andrews and Baron Downpatrick 1934, *married* 29 November 1934, HRH Princess Marina of Greece and Denmark (*born* 30 November os, 1906; *died* 27 August 1968); *killed on active service,* 25 August 1942. *Issue:*
  (1) HRH Prince Edward George Nicholas Paul Patrick (HRH The Duke of Kent), *see* page 124
  (2) HRH Princess Alexandra Helen Elizabeth Olga Christabel (HRH Princess Alexandra, the Hon. Lady Ogilvy), *see* page 124
  (3) HRH Prince Michael George Charles Franklin (HRH Prince Michael of Kent), *see* page 124

6. HRH PRINCE JOHN Charles Francis, *born* 12 July 1905; *died*

Descendants of Queen Victoria

QUEEN VICTORIA (Alexandrina Victoria), *born* 24 May 1819; *succeeded* to the throne 20 June 1837; *married* 10 February 1840 (Francis) Albert Augustus Charles Emmanuel, Duke of Saxony, Prince of Saxe-Coburg and Gotha (HRH Albert, Prince Consort, *born* 26 August 1819, *died* 14 December 1861); *died* 22 January 1901. *Issue:*

1. HRH PRINCESS VICTORIA Adelaide Mary Louisa (Princess Royal) (1840–1901), *m.* 1858, Frederic (1831–88), Emperor of Germany March–June 1888. *Issue:*
  (1) HIM Wilhelm II (1859–1941), Emperor of Germany 1888–1918, *m.* (1) 1881 Princess Augusta Victoria of Schleswig-Holstein-Sonderburg-Augustenburg (1858–1921); (2) 1922 Princess Hermine of Reuss (1887–1947). *Issue:*
    (*a*) Prince Wilhelm (1882–1951), *Crown Prince* 1888–1918, *m.* 1905 Duchess Cecilie of Mecklenburg-Schwerin; *issue:* Prince Wilhelm (1906–40); Prince Louis Ferdinand (1907–94), *m.* 1938 Grand Duchess Kira (*see* page 135); Prince Hubertus (1909–50); Prince Friedrich Georg (1911–66); Princess Alexandrine Irene (1915–80); Princess Cecilie (1917–75)
    (*b*) Prince Eitel-Friedrich (1883–1942), *m.* 1906 Duchess Sophie of Oldenburg (marriage dissolved 1926)
    (*c*) Prince Adalbert (1884–1948), *m.* 1914 Duchess Adelheid of Saxe-Meiningen; *issue:* Princess Victoria Marina (1917–81); Prince Wilhelm Victor (1919–89)
    (*d*) Prince August Wilhelm (1887–1949), *m.* 1908 Princess Alexandra of Schleswig-Holstein-Sonderburg-Glücksburg (marriage dissolved 1920); *issue:* Prince Alexander (1912–85)
    (*e*) Prince Oskar (1888–1958), *m.* 1914 Countess von Ruppin; *issue:* Prince Oskar (1915–39); Prince Burchard (1917–88); Princess Herzeleide (1918–89); Prince Wilhelm (*b.* 1922)
    (*f*) Prince Joachim (1890–1920), *m.* 1916 Princess Marie of Anhalt; *issue:* Prince Karl Franz Joseph (1916–75)

  (*g*) Princess Viktoria Luise (1892–1980), *m.* 1913 Ernst, Duke of Brunswick 1913–18 (1887–1953); *issue:* Prince Ernst (1914–87); Prince Georg (*b.* 1915), *m.* 1946 Princess Sophie of Greece (*see* page 135) and has issue (two sons, one daughter); Princess Frederika (1917–81), *m.* 1938 Paul I, King of the Hellenes (*see* page 135); Prince Christian (1919–81); Prince Welf Heinrich (*b.* 1923)
  (2) Princess Charlotte (1860–1919), *m.* 1878 Bernhard, Duke of Saxe-Meiningen 1914 (1851–1914). *Issue:*
    Princess Feodora (1879–1945), *m.* 1898 Prince Heinrich XXX of Reuss
  (3) Prince Heinrich (1862–1929), *m.* 1888 Princess Irene of Hesse (*see* page 135). *Issue:*
    (*a*) Prince Waldemar (1889–1945), *m.* Princess Calixsta of Lippe
    (*b*) Prince Sigismund (1896–1978), *m.* 1919 Princess Charlotte of Saxe-Altenburg; *issue:* Princess Barbara (*b.* 1920); Prince Alfred (*b.* 1924)
    (*c*) Prince Heinrich (1900–4)
  (4) Prince Sigismund (1864–6)
  (5) Princess Victoria (1866–1929), *m.* (1) 1890, Prince Adolf of Schaumburg-Lippe (1859–1916); (2) 1927 Alexander Zubkov
  (6) Prince Joachim Waldemar (1868–79)
  (7) Princess Sophie (1870–1932), *m.* 1889 Constantine I (1868–1923), King of the Hellenes 1913–17, 1920–3. *Issue:*
    (*a*) George II (1890–1947), King of the Hellenes 1923–4 and 1935–47, *m.* 1921 Princess Elisabeth of Roumania (marriage dissolved 1935) (*see* page 135)
    (*b*) Alexander I (1893–1920), King of the Hellenes 1917–20, *m.* 1919 Aspasia Manos; *issue:* Princess Alexandra (1921–93), *m.* 1944 King Petar II of Yugoslavia (*see* page 135)
    (*c*) Princess Helena (1896–1982), *m.* 1921 King Carol of Roumania (*see* page 135), (marriage dissolved 1928)

(d) Paul I (1901–64), King of the Hellenes 1947–64, *m.* 1938 Princess Frederika of Brunswick (*see* page 134); *issue:* King Constantine II (*b.* 1940), *m.* 1964 Princess Anne-Marie of Denmark (*see* page 136), and has issue (three sons, two daughters); Princess Sophie (*b.* 1938), *m.* 1962 Juan Carlos I of Spain (*see* page 136); Princess Irene (*b.* 1942)
(e) Princess Irene (1904–74), *m.* 1939 4th Duke of Aosta; *issue:* Prince Amedeo (*b.* 1943)
(f) Princess Katherine (Lady Katherine Brandram) (*b.* 1913), *m.* 1947 Major R. C. A. Brandram, MC, TD; *issue:* R. Paul G. A. Brandram (*b.* 1948)
(8) Princess Margarethe (1872–1954), *m.* 1893 Prince Friedrich Karl of Hesse (1868–1940). *Issue:*
   (a) Prince Friedrich Wilhelm (1893–1916)
   (b) Prince Maximilian (1894–1914)
   (c) Prince Philipp (1896–1980), *m.* 1925 Princess Mafalda of Italy; *issue:* Prince Moritz (*b.* 1926); Prince Heinrich (*b.* 1927); Prince Otto (*b.* 1937); Princess Elisabeth (*b.* 1940)
   (d) Prince Wolfgang (*b.* 1896), *m.* (1) 1924 Princess Marie Alexandra of Baden; (2) 1948 Ottilie Möller
   (e) Prince Richard (1901–69)
   (f) Prince Christoph (1901–43), *m.* 1930 Princess Sophie of Greece (*see* below) and has issue (two sons, three daughters)

2. HRH PRINCE ALBERT EDWARD (HM KING EDWARD VII), *b.* 9 November 1841, *m.* 1863 HRH Princess Alexandra of Denmark (1844–1925), *succeeded* to the throne 22 January 1901, *d.* 6 May 1910. *Issue:*
   (1) Albert Victor, Duke of Clarence and Avondale (1864–92)
   (2) George (HM KING GEORGE V) (*see* page 134)
   (3) Louise (1867–1931) Princess Royal 1905–31, *m.* 1889 1st Duke of Fife (1849–1912). *Issue:*
      (a) Princess Alexandra, Duchess of Fife (1891–1959), *m.* 1913 Prince Arthur of Connaught (*see* page 136)
      (b) Princess Maud (1893–1945), *m.* 1923 11th Earl of Southesk (1893–1992); *issue:* The Duke of Fife (*b.* 1929)
   (4) Victoria (1868–1935)
   (5) Maud (1869–1938), *m.* 1896 Prince Carl of Denmark (1872–1957), later King Haakon VII of Norway 1905–57. *Issue:*
      (a) Olav V (1903–91), King of Norway 1957–91, *m.* 1929 Princess Märtha of Sweden (1901–54); *issue:* Princess Ragnhild (*b.* 1930); Princess Astrid (*b.* 1932); Harald V, King of Norway (*b.* 1937)
   (6) Alexander (6–7 April 1871)

3. HRH PRINCESS ALICE Maud Mary (1843–78), *m.* 1862 Prince Ludwig (1837–92), Grand Duke of Hesse 1877–92. *Issue:*
   (1) Victoria (1863–1950), *m.* 1884 *Admiral of the Fleet* Prince Louis of Battenberg (1854–1921), *cr.* 1st Marquess of Milford Haven 1917. *Issue:*
      (a) Alice (1885–1969), *m.* 1903 Prince Andrew of Greece (1882–1944); *issue:* Princess Margarita (1905–81) *m.* 1931 Prince Gottfried of Hohenlohe-Langenburg (*see* below); Princess Theodora (1906–69), *m.* Prince Berthold of Baden (1906–63) and has issue (2 sons, one daughter); Princess Cecilie (1911–37), *m.* George, Grand Duke of Hesse (*see* below); Princess Sophie (*b.* 1914), *m.* (1) 1930 Prince Christoph of Hesse (*see* above); (2) 1946 Prince George of Hanover (*see* page 134); Prince Philip, Duke of Edinburgh (*b.* 1921) (*see* page 123)
      (b) Louise (1889–1965), *m.* 1923 Gustaf VI Adolf (1882–1973), King of Sweden 1950–73
      (c) George, 2nd Marquess of Milford Haven (1892–1938), *m.* 1916 Countess Nadejda, daughter of Grand Duke Michael of Russia; *issue:* Lady Tatiana (1917–88); David Michael, 3rd Marquess (1919–70)
      (d) Louis, 1st Earl Mountbatten of Burma (1900–79), *m.* 1922 Edwina Ashley, daughter of Lord Mount Temple; *issue:* Patricia, Countess Mountbatten of Burma (*b.* 1924), Pamela (*b.* 1929)
   (2) Elizabeth (1864–1918), *m.* 1884 Grand Duke Sergius of Russia (1857–1905)
   (3) Irene (1866–1953), *m.* 1888 Prince Heinrich of Prussia (*see* page 134)
   (4) Ernst Ludwig (1868–1937), Grand Duke of Hesse 1892–1918, *m.* (1) 1894 Princess Victoria Melita of Saxe-Coburg (*see* below) (marriage dissolved 1901); (2) 1905 Princess Eleonore of Solms-Hohensolmslich. *Issue:*
      (a) Princess Elizabeth (1895–1903)

(b) George, Grand Duke of Hesse (1906–37), *m.* Princess Cecilie of Greece (*see* above), and had issue, 2 sons, accidentally killed with parents 1937
      (c) Ludwig, Grand Duke of Hesse (1908–68), *m.* 1937 Margaret, daughter of 1st Lord Geddes
   (5) Frederick William (1870–3)
   (6) Alix (Tsaritsa of Russia) (1872–1918), *m.* 1894 Nicholas II (1868–1918) Tsar of All the Russias 1894–1917, assassinated 16 July 1918. *Issue:*
      (a) Grand Duchess Olga (1895–1918)
      (b) Grand Duchess Tatiana (1897–1918)
      (c) Grand Duchess Marie (1899–1918)
      (d) Grand Duchess Anastasia (1901–18)
      (e) Alexis, Tsarevich of Russia (1904–18)
   (7) Marie (1874–8)

4. HRH PRINCE ALFRED Ernest Albert, Duke of Edinburgh, *Admiral of the Fleet* (1844–1900), *m.* 1874 Grand Duchess Marie Alexandrovna of Russia (1853–1920); succeeded as Duke of Saxe-Coburg and Gotha 22 August 1893. *Issue:*
   (1) Alfred (Prince of Saxe-Coburg) (1874–99)
   (2) Marie (1875–1938), *m.* 1893 Ferdinand (1865–1927), King of Roumania 1914–27. *Issue:*
      (a) Carol II (1893–1953), King of Roumania 1930–40, *m.* (2) 1921 Princess Helena of Greece (*see* page 134) (marriage dissolved 1928); *issue:* Michael (*b.* 1921), King of Roumania 1927–30, 1940–7, *m.* 1948 Princess Anne of Bourbon-Parma, and has issue (five daughters)
      (b) Elisabeth (1894–1956), *m.* 1921 George II, King of the Hellenes (*see* page 134)
      (c) Marie (1900–61), *m.* 1922 Alexander (1888–1934), King of Yugoslavia (*see* above); *issue:* Petar II (1923–70), King of Yugoslavia 1934–45, *m.* 1944 Princess Alexandra of Greece (*see* page 134) and has issue (Crown Prince Alexander, *b.* 1945); Prince Tomislav (*b.* 1928), *m.* (1) 1957 Princess Margarita of Baden (daughter of Princess Theodora of Greece and Prince Berthold of Baden, *see* above); (2) 1982 Linda Bonney; and has issue (three sons, one daughter); Prince Andrej (1929–90), *m.* (1) 1956 Princess Christina of Hesse (daughter of Prince Christoph of Hesse and Princess Sophie of Greece, *see* above); (2) 1963 Princess Kira-Melita of Leiningen (*see* below); and has issue (three sons, two daughters)
      (d) Prince Nicolas (1903–78)
      (e) Princess Ileana (1909–91), *m.* (1) 1931 Archduke Anton of Austria; (2) 1954 Dr Stefan Issarescu; *issue:* Archduke Stefan (*b.* 1932); Archduchess Maria Ileana (1933–59); Archduchess Alexandra (*b.* 1935); Archduke Dominic (*b.* 1937); Archduchess Maria Magdalena (*b.* 1939); Archduchess Elisabeth (*b.* 1942)
      (f) Prince Mircea (1913–16)
   (3) Victoria Melita (1876–1936), *m.* (1) 1894 Grand Duke Ernst Ludwig of Hesse (*see* above) (marriage dissolved 1901); (2) 1905 the Grand Duke Kirill of Russia (1876–1938). *Issue:*
      (a) Marie Kirillovna (1907–51), *m.* 1925 Prince Friedrich Karl of Leiningen; *issue:* Prince Emich (*b.* 1926); Prince Karl (*b.* 1928); Princess Kira-Melita (*b.* 1930), *m.* Prince Andrej of Yugoslavia (*see* above) (*b.* 1932); Princess Mechtilde (*b.* 1936); Prince Friedrich (*b.* 1938)
      (b) Kira Kirillovna (1909–67), *m.* 1938 Prince Louis Ferdinand of Prussia (*see* page 134); *issue:* Prince Friedrich Wilhelm (*b.* 1939); Prince Michael (*b.* 1940); Princess Marie (*b.* 1942); Princess Kira (*b.* 1943); Prince Louis Ferdinand (1944–77); Prince Christian (*b.* 1946); Princess Xenia (1949–92)
      (c) Vladimir Kirillovich (1917–92), *m.* 1948 Princess Leonida Bagration-Mukhransky; *issue:* Grand Duchess Maria (*b.* 1953), and has issue
   (4) Alexandra (1878–1942), *m.* 1896 Ernst, Prince of Hohenlohe Langenburg. *Issue:*
      (a) Gottfried (1897–1960), *m.* 1931 Princess Margarita of Greece (*see* above); *issue:* Prince Kraft (*b.* 1935), Princess Beatrix (*b.* 1936), Prince Georg Andreas (*b.* 1938), Prince Ruprecht (1944–); Prince Albrecht (1944–92)
      (b) Maria (1899–1967), *m.* 1916 Prince Friedrich of Schleswig-Holstein-Sonderburg-Glücksburg; *issue:* Prince Peter (1922–80); Princess Marie (*b.* 1924)
      (c) Princess Alexandra (1901–63)
      (d) Princess Irma (1902–86)
   (5) Princess Beatrice (1884–1966), *m.* 1909 Alfonso of Orleans, Infante of Spain. *Issue:*

(a) Prince Alvaro (b. 1910), m. 1937 Carla Parodi-Delfino; *issue:* Doña Gerarda (b. 1939); Don Alonso (1941–75); Doña Beatriz (b. 1943); Don Alvaro (b. 1947)
(b) Prince Alonso (1912–36)
(c) Prince Ataulfo (1913–74)

5. HRH Princess Helena Augusta Victoria (1846–1923), m. 1866 Prince Christian of Schleswig-Holstein-Sonderburg-Augustenburg (1831–1917). *Issue:*
(1) Prince Christian Victor (1867–1900)
(2) Prince Albert (1869–1931), Duke of Schleswig-Holstein 1921–31
(3) Princess Helena (1870–1948)
(4) Princess Marie Louise (1872–1956), m. 1891 Prince Aribert of Anhalt (marriage dissolved 1900)
(5) Prince Harold (12–20 May 1876)

6. HRH Princess Louise Caroline Alberta (1848–1939), m. 1871 the Marquess of Lorne, afterwards 9th Duke of Argyll (1845–1914); without issue

7. HRH Prince Arthur William Patrick Albert, Duke of Connaught, *Field Marshal* (1850–1942), m. 1879 Princess Louisa of Prussia (1860–1917). *Issue:*
(1) Margaret (1882–1920), m. 1905 Crown Prince Gustaf Adolf (1882–1973), afterwards King of Sweden 1950–73. *Issue:*
(a) Gustaf Adolf, Duke of Västerbotten (1906–47), m. 1932 Princess Sibylla of Saxe-Coburg-Gotha (*see* below); *issue:* Princess Margaretha (b. 1934); Princess Birgitta (b. 1937); Princess Désirée (b. 1938); Princess Christina (b. 1943); Carl XVI Gustaf, King of Sweden (b. 1946)
(b) Count Sigvard Bernadotte (b. 1907), m.; *issue:* Count Michael (b. 1944)
(c) Princess Ingrid (Queen Mother of Denmark) (b. 1910), m. 1935 Frederick IX (1899–72), King of Denmark 1947–72; *issue:* Margrethe II, Queen of Denmark (b. 1940); Princess Benedikte (b. 1944); Princess Anne-Marie (b. 1946), m. 1964 Constantine II of Greece (*see* page 135)
(d) Prince Bertil, Duke of Halland (b. 1912), m. 1976 Mrs Lilian Craig
(e) Count Carl Bernadotte (b. 1916), m. (1) 1946 Mrs Kerstin Johnson; (2) 1988 Countess Gunnila Bussler
(2) Arthur (1883–1938), m. 1913 HH the Duchess of Fife (*see* page 135). *Issue:*
Alastair Arthur, 2nd Duke of Connaught (1914–43)
(3) (Victoria) Patricia (1886–1974), m. 1919 Adm. Hon. Sir Alexander Ramsay. *Issue:*

Alexander Ramsay of Mar (b. 1919), m. 1956 Hon. Flora Fraser (Lady Saltoun)

8. HRH Prince Leopold George Duncan Albert, Duke of Albany (1853–84), m. 1882 Princess Helena of Waldeck (1861–1922). *Issue:*
(1) Alice (1883–1981), m. 1904 Prince Alexander of Teck (1874–1957), cr. 1st Earl of Athlone 1917. *Issue:*
(a) Lady May (1906–94), m. 1931 Sir Henry Abel-Smith, kcmg, kcvo, dso; *issue:* Anne (b. 1932); Richard (b. 1933); Elizabeth (b. 1936)
(b) Rupert, Viscount Trematon (1907–28)
(c) Prince Maurice (March–September 1910)
(2) Charles Edward (1884–1954), Duke of Albany (title suspended 1917, Duke of Saxe-Coburg-Gotha 1900–18, m. 1905 Princess Victoria Adelheid of Schleswig-Holstein-Sonderburg-Glücksburg. *Issue:*
(a) Prince Johann Leopold (1906–72), and has issue, including Ernst-Leopold (b. 1935) in whom is vested the right to petition for restoration of the Dukedom of Albany
(b) Princess Sibylla (1908–72) m. 1932 Prince Gustav Adolf of Sweden (*see* above)
(c) Prince Dietmar Hubertus (1909–43)
(d) Princess Caroline (1912–83), and has issue
(e) Prince Friedrich Josias (b. 1918), and has issue

9. HRH Princess Beatrice Mary Victoria Feodore (1857–1944), m. 1885 Prince Henry of Battenberg (1858–96). *Issue:*
(1) Alexander, 1st Marquess of Carisbrooke (1886–1960), m. 1917 Lady Irene Denison. *Issue:*
Lady Iris Mountbatten (1920–82), m.; *issue:* Robin A. Bryan (b. 1957)
(2) Victoria Eugénie (1887–1969), m. 1906 Alfonso XIII (1886–1941) King of Spain 1886–1931. *Issue:*
(a) Prince Alfonso (1907–38)
(b) Prince Jaime (1908–75), and has issue
(c) Princess Beatrice (b. 1909), and has issue
(d) Princess Maria (b. 1911), and has issue
(e) Prince Juan (1913–93) Count of Barcelona, and has issue: Princess Maria (b. 1936); Juan Carlos I, King of Spain (b. 1938), m. 1962 Princess Sophie of Greece (*see* page 135) and has issue (1 son, 2 daughters); Princess Margarita (b. 1939)
(f) Prince Gonzalo (1914–34)
(3) Major Lord Leopold Mountbatten (1889–1922)
(4) Maurice (1891–1914), died of wounds received in action

Kings and Queens

ENGLISH KINGS AND QUEENS 927 to 1603

HOUSES OF CERDIC AND DENMARK

Reign

927–939	Æthelstan Son of Edward the Elder, by Ecgwynn, and grandson of Alfred Acceded to Wessex and Mercia c.924, established direct rule over Northumbria 927, effectively creating the Kingdom of England *Reigned* 15 years
939–946	Edmund I *Born* 921, son of Edward the Elder, by Eadgifu *Married* (1) Ælfgifu (2) Æthelflæd *Killed* aged 25, *reigned* 6 years
946–955	Eadred Son of Edward the Elder, by Eadgifu *Reigned* 9 years
955–959	Eadwig *Born* before 943, son of Edmund and Ælfgifu *Married* Ælfgifu *Reigned* 3 years
959–975	Edgar I *Born* 943, son of Edmund and Ælfgifu *Married* (1) Æthelflæd (2) Wulfthryth (3) Ælfthryth *Died* aged 32, *reigned* 15 years
975–978	Edward I (the Martyr) *Born* c.962, son of Edgar and Æthelflæd *Assassinated* aged c.16, *reigned* 2 years
978–1016	Æthelred (the Unready) *Born* c.968/969, son of Edgar and Ælfthryth *Married* (1) Ælfgifu (2) Emma, daughter of Richard I, count of Normandy 1013–14 dispossessed of kingdom by Swegn Forkbeard (king of Denmark 987–1014) *Died* aged c.47, *reigned* 38 years
1016	Edmund II (Ironside) *Born* before 993, son of Æthelred and Ælfgifu *Married* Ealdgyth *Died* aged over 23, *reigned* 7 months (April–November)
1016–1035	Cnut (Canute) *Born* c.995, son of Swegn Forkbeard, king of Denmark, and Gunhild *Married* (1) Ælfgifu (2) Emma, widow of Æthelred the Unready Gained submission of West Saxons 1015, Northumbrians 1016, Mercia 1016, king of all

England after Edmund's death
King of Denmark 1019–35, king of Norway
1028–35
Died aged *c*.40, *reigned* 19 years

1035–1040   HAROLD I (Harefoot)
Born c.1016/17, son of Cnut and Ælfgifu
Married Ælfgifu
1035 recognized as regent for himself and his
brother Harthacnut; 1037 recognized as king
Died aged *c*.23, *reigned* 4 years

1040–1042   HARTHACNUT
Born c.1018, son of Cnut and Emma
Titular king of Denmark from 1028
Acknowledged king of England 1035–7 with
Harold I as regent; effective king after Harold's
death
Died aged *c*.24, *reigned* 2 years

1042–1066   EDWARD II (the Confessor)
Born between 1002 and 1005, son of Æthelred
the Unready and Emma
Married Eadgyth, daughter of Godwine, earl of
Wessex
Died aged over 60, *reigned* 23 years

1066   HAROLD II (Godwinesson)
Born c.1020, son of Godwine, earl of Wessex, and
Gytha
Married (1) Eadgyth (2) Ealdgyth
Killed in battle aged *c*.46, *reigned* 10 months
(January–October)

THE HOUSE OF NORMANDY

1066–1087   WILLIAM I (the Conqueror)
Born 1027/8, son of Robert I, duke of Normandy;
obtained the Crown by conquest
Married Matilda, daughter of Baldwin, count of
Flanders
Died aged *c*.60, *reigned* 20 years

1087–1100   WILLIAM II (Rufus)
Born between 1056 and 1060, third son of
William I; succeeded his father in England only
Killed aged *c*.40, *reigned* 12 years

1100–1135   HENRY I (Beauclerk)
Born 1068, fourth son of William I
Married (1) Edith or Matilda, daughter of
Malcolm III of Scotland (2) Adela, daughter of
Godfrey, count of Louvain
Died aged 67, *reigned* 35 years

1135–1154   STEPHEN
Born not later than 1100, third son of Adela,
daughter of William I, and Stephen, count of
Blois
Married Matilda, daughter of Eustace, count of
Boulogne
1141 (February–November) held captive by
adherents of Matilda, daughter of Henry I, who
contested the crown until 1153
Died aged over 53, *reigned* 18 years

THE HOUSE OF ANJOU (PLANTAGENETS)

1154–1189   HENRY II (Curtmantle)
Born 1133, son of Matilda, daughter of Henry I,
and Geoffrey, count of Anjou
Married Eleanor, daughter of William, duke of
Aquitaine, and divorced queen of Louis VII of
France
Died aged 56, *reigned* 34 years

1189–1199   RICHARD I (Coeur de Lion)
Born 1157, third son of Henry II
Married Berengaria, daughter of Sancho VI, king
of Navarre
Died aged 42, *reigned* 9 years

1199–1216   JOHN (Lackland)
Born 1167, fifth son of Henry II
Married (1) Isabella or Avisa, daughter of
William, earl of Gloucester (divorced)
(2) Isabella, daughter of Aymer, count of
Angoulême
Died aged 48, *reigned* 17 years

1216–1272   HENRY III
Born 1207, son of John and Isabella of
Angoulême
Married Eleanor, daughter of Raymond, count of
Provence
Died aged 65, *reigned* 56 years

1272–1307   EDWARD I (Longshanks)
Born 1239, eldest son of Henry III
Married (1) Eleanor, daughter of Ferdinand III,
king of Castile (2) Margaret, daughter of Philip
III of France
Died aged 68, *reigned* 34 years

1307–1327   EDWARD II
Born 1284, eldest surviving son of Edward I and
Eleanor
Married Isabella, daughter of Philip IV of France
Deposed January 1327, *killed* September 1327 aged
43, *reigned* 19 years

1327–1377   EDWARD III
Born 1312, eldest son of Edward II
Married Philippa, daughter of William, count of
Hainault
Died aged 64, *reigned* 50 years

1377–1399   RICHARD II
Born 1367, son of Edward (the Black Prince),
eldest son of Edward III
Married (1) Anne, daughter of Emperor Charles
IV (2) Isabelle, daughter of Charles VI of France
Deposed September 1399, *killed* February 1400
aged 33, *reigned* 22 years

THE HOUSE OF LANCASTER

1399–1413   HENRY IV
Born 1366, son of John of Gaunt, fourth son of
Edward III, and Blanche, daughter of Henry,
duke of Lancaster
Married (1) Mary, daughter of Humphrey, earl of
Hereford (2) Joan, daughter of Charles, king of
Navarre, and widow of John, duke of Brittany
Died aged *c*.47, *reigned* 13 years

1413–1422   HENRY V
Born 1387, eldest surviving son of Henry IV and
Mary
Married Catherine, daughter of Charles VI of
France
Died aged 34, *reigned* 9 years

1422–1471   HENRY VI
Born 1421, son of Henry V
Married Margaret, daughter of René, duke of
Anjou and count of Provence
Deposed March 1461, *restored* October 1470
Deposed April 1471, *killed* May 1471 aged 49,
reigned 39 years

THE HOUSE OF YORK

1461–1483   EDWARD IV
Born 1442, eldest son of Richard of York, who
was the grandson of Edmund, fifth son of Edward
III, and the son of Anne, great-granddaughter of
Lionel, third son of Edward III
Married Elizabeth Woodville, daughter of
Richard, Lord Rivers, and widow of Sir John
Grey
Acceded March 1461, *deposed* October 1470, *restored*
April 1471
Died aged 40, *reigned* 21 years

1483   EDWARD V
Born 1470, eldest son of Edward IV
Deposed June 1483, *died* probably July–September
1483, aged 12, *reigned* 2 months (April–June)

1483–1485   RICHARD III
Born 1452, fourth son of Richard of York and
brother of Edward IV
Married Anne Neville, daughter of Richard, earl
of Warwick, and widow of Edward, Prince of
Wales, son of Henry VI
Killed in battle aged 32, *reigned* 2 years

THE HOUSE OF TUDOR

1485–1509 HENRY VII
Born 1457, son of Margaret Beaufort, great-granddaughter of John of Gaunt, fourth son of Edward III, and Edmund Tudor, earl of Richmond
Married Elizabeth, daughter of Edward IV
Died aged 52, *reigned* 23 years

1509–1547 HENRY VIII
Born 1491, second son of Henry VII
Married (1) Catherine, daughter of Ferdinand II, king of Aragon, and widow of his elder brother Arthur (divorced) (2) Anne, daughter of Sir Thomas Boleyn (executed) (3) Jane, daughter of Sir John Seymour (died in childbirth) (4) Anne, daughter of John, duke of Cleves (divorced) (5) Catherine Howard, niece of the Duke of Norfolk (executed) (6) Catherine, daughter of Sir Thomas Parr and widow of Lord Latimer
Died aged 55, *reigned* 37 years

1547–1553 EDWARD VI
Born 1537, son of Henry VIII and Jane Seymour
Died aged 15, *reigned* 6 years

1553   JANE
Born 1537, daughter of Frances, daughter of Mary Tudor, the younger sister of Henry VIII, and Henry Grey, duke of Suffolk
Married Lord Guildford Dudley, son of the Duke of Northumberland
Deposed July 1553, *executed* February 1554 aged 16, *reigned* 14 days

1553–1558 MARY I
Born 1516, daughter of Henry VIII and Catherine of Aragon
Married Philip II of Spain
Died aged 42, *reigned* 5 years

1558–1603 ELIZABETH I
Born 1533, daughter of Henry VIII and Anne Boleyn
Died aged 69, *reigned* 44 years

BRITISH KINGS AND QUEENS SINCE 1603

THE HOUSE OF STUART

Reign
1603–1625 JAMES I (VI OF SCOTLAND)
Born 1566, son of Mary, queen of Scots and granddaughter of Margaret Tudor, elder daughter of Henry VII, and Henry Stewart, Lord Darnley
Married Anne, daughter of Frederick II of Denmark
Died aged 58, *reigned* 22 years
(*see also* page 140)

1625–1649 CHARLES I
Born 1600, second son of James I
Married Henrietta Maria, daughter of Henry IV of France
Executed 1649 aged 48, *reigned* 23 years

COMMONWEALTH DECLARED 19 May 1649
1649–53 Government by a council of state
1653–8 Oliver Cromwell, *Lord Protector*
1658–9 Richard Cromwell, *Lord Protector*

1660–1685 CHARLES II
Born 1630, eldest son of Charles I
Married Catherine, daughter of John IV of Portugal
Died aged 54, *reigned* 24 years

1685–1688 JAMES II (VII OF SCOTLAND)
Born 1633, second son of Charles I
Married (1) Lady Anne Hyde, daughter of Edward, earl of Clarendon (2) Mary, daughter of Alphonso, duke of Modena
Reign ended with flight from kingdom December 1688
Died 1701 aged 67, *reigned* 3 years

INTERREGNUM 11 December 1688 to 12 February 1689

1689–1702 WILLIAM III
Born 1650, son of William II, prince of Orange, and Mary Stuart, daughter of Charles I
Married Mary, elder daughter of James II
Died aged 51, *reigned* 13 years
and
1689–1694 MARY II
Born 1662, elder daughter of James II and Anne
Died aged 32, *reigned* 5 years

1702–1714 ANNE
Born 1665, younger daughter of James II and Anne
Married Prince George of Denmark, son of Frederick III of Denmark
Died aged 49, *reigned* 12 years

THE HOUSE OF HANOVER

1714–1727 GEORGE I (Elector of Hanover)
Born 1660, son of Sophia (daughter of Frederick, elector palatine, and Elizabeth Stuart, daughter of James I) and Ernest Augustus, elector of Hanover
Married Sophia Dorothea, daughter of George William, duke of Lüneburg-Celle
Died aged 67, *reigned* 12 years

1727–1760 GEORGE II
Born 1683, son of George I
Married Caroline, daughter of John Frederick, margrave of Brandenburg-Anspach
Died aged 76, *reigned* 33 years

1760–1820 GEORGE III
Born 1738, son of Frederick, eldest son of George II
Married Charlotte, daughter of Charles Louis, duke of Mecklenburg-Strelitz
Died aged 81, *reigned* 59 years

REGENCY 1811–20
Prince of Wales regent owing to the insanity of George III

1820–1830 GEORGE IV
Born 1762, eldest son of George III
Married Caroline, daughter of Charles, duke of Brunswick-Wolfenbüttel
Died aged 67, *reigned* 10 years

1830–1837 WILLIAM IV
Born 1765, third son of George III
Married Adelaide, daughter of George, duke of Saxe-Meiningen
Died aged 71, *reigned* 7 years

1837–1901 VICTORIA
Born 1819, daughter of Edward, fourth son of George III
Married Prince Albert of Saxe-Coburg and Gotha
Died aged 81, *reigned* 63 years

THE HOUSE OF SAXE-COBURG AND GOTHA

1901–1910 EDWARD VII
Born 1841, eldest son of Victoria and Albert
Married Alexandra, daughter of Christian IX of Denmark
Died aged 68, *reigned* 9 years

THE HOUSE OF WINDSOR

1910–1936 GEORGE V
Born 1865, second son of Edward VII
Married Victoria Mary, daughter of Francis, duke of Teck
Died aged 70, *reigned* 25 years

1936   EDWARD VIII
Born 1894, eldest son of George V
Married (1937) Mrs Wallis Warfield
Abdicated 1936, *died* 1972 aged 77, *reigned* 10 months (20 January to 11 December)

1936–1952 GEORGE VI
Born 1895, second son of George V
Married Lady Elizabeth Bowes-Lyon, daughter of 14th Earl of Strathmore and Kinghorne (*see also* pages 123–4)
Died aged 56, *reigned* 15 years

1952–   ELIZABETH II
Born 1926, elder daughter of George VI
Married Philip, son of Prince Andrew of Greece
(see also page 123)
WHOM GOD PRESERVE

KINGS AND QUEENS OF SCOTS 1016 TO 1603

Reign
1016–1034   MALCOLM II
Born c.954, son of Kenneth II
Acceded to Alba 1005, secured Lothian c.1016,
obtained Strathclyde for his grandson Duncan
c.1016, thus forming the Kingdom of Scotland
Died aged c.80, reigned 18 years
1034–1040   DUNCAN I
Son of Bethoc, daughter of Malcolm II, and
Crinan
Married a cousin of Siward, earl of Northumbria
Reigned 5 years
1040–1057   MACBETH
Born c.1005, son of a daughter of Malcolm II and
Finlaec, mormaer of Moray
Married Gruoch, granddaughter of Kenneth III
Killed aged c.52, reigned 17 years
1057–1058   LULACH
Born c. 1032, son of Gillacomgan, mormaer of
Moray, and Gruoch (and stepson of Macbeth)
Died aged c.26, reigned 7 months (August–March)
1058–1093   MALCOLM III (Canmore)
Born c.1031, elder son of Duncan I
Married (1) Ingiborg (2) Margaret (St Margaret),
granddaughter of Edmund II of England
Killed in battle aged c.62, reigned 35 years
1093–1097   DONALD III BÁN
Born c. 1033, second son of Duncan I
Deposed May 1094, restored November 1094,
deposed October 1097, reigned 3 years
1094   DUNCAN II
Born c.1060, elder son of Malcolm III and
Ingibiorg
Married Octreda of Dunbar
Killed aged c.34, reigned 6 months
(May–November)
1097–1107   EDGAR
Born c.1074, second son of Malcolm III and
Margaret
Died aged c.32, reigned 9 years
1107–1124   ALEXANDER I (The Fierce)
Born c.1077, fifth son of Malcolm III and
Margaret
Married Sybilla, illegitimate daughter of Henry I
of England
Died aged c.47, reigned 17 years
1124–1153   DAVID I (The Saint)
Born c.1085, sixth son of Malcolm III and
Margaret
Married Matilda, daughter of Waltheof, earl of
Huntingdon
Died aged c.68, reigned 29 years
1153–1165   MALCOLM IV (The Maiden)
Born c.1141, son of Henry, earl of Huntingdon,
second son of David I
Died aged c.24, reigned 12 years
1165–1214   WILLIAM I (The Lion)
Born c.1142, brother of Malcolm IV
Married Ermengarde, daughter of Richard,
viscount of Beaumont
Died aged c.72, reigned 49 years
1214–1249   ALEXANDER II
Born 1198, son of William I
Married (1) Joan, daughter of John, king of
England (2) Marie, daughter of Ingelram de Coucy
Died aged 50, reigned 34 years

1249–1286   ALEXANDER III
Born 1241, son of Alexander II and Marie
Married (1) Margaret, daughter of Henry III of
England (2) Yolande, daughter of the Count of
Dreux
Killed accidentally aged 44, reigned 36 years
1286–1290   MARGARET (The Maid of Norway)
Born 1283, daughter of Margaret (daughter of
Alexander III) and Eric II of Norway
Died aged 7, reigned 4 years
FIRST INTERREGNUM 1290–2
Throne disputed by 13 competitors. Crown
awarded to John Balliol by adjudication of
Edward I of England

THE HOUSE OF BALLIOL

1292–1296   JOHN (Balliol)
Born c.1250, son of Dervorguilla, great-great-
granddaughter of David I, and John de Balliol
Married Isabella, daughter of John, earl of Surrey
Abdicated 1296, died 1313 aged c.63, reigned 3 years
SECOND INTERREGNUM 1296–1306
Edward I of England declared John Balliol to
have forfeited the throne for contumacy in 1296
and took the government of Scotland into his
own hands

THE HOUSE OF BRUCE

1306–1329   ROBERT I (Bruce)
Born 1274, son of Robert Bruce and Marjorie,
countess of Carrick, and great-grandson of the
second daughter of David, earl of Huntingdon,
brother of William I
Married (1) Isabella, daughter of Donald, earl of
Mar (2) Elizabeth, daughter of Richard, earl of
Ulster
Died aged 54, reigned 23 years
1329–1371   DAVID II
Born 1324, son of Robert I and Elizabeth
Married (1) Joanna, daughter of Edward II of
England (2) Margaret Drummond, widow of Sir
John Logie (divorced)
Died aged 46, reigned 41 years
1332 Edward Balliol, son of John Balliol,
crowned King of Scots September, expelled
December
1333–6 Edward Balliol restored as King of Scots

THE HOUSE OF STEWART

1371–1390   ROBERT II (Stewart)
Born 1316, son of Marjorie, daughter of Robert I,
and Walter, High Steward of Scotland
Married (1) Elizabeth, daughter of Sir Robert
Mure of Rowallan (2) Euphemia, daughter of
Hugh, earl of Ross
Died aged 74, reigned 19 years
1390–1406   ROBERT III
Born c.1337, son of Robert II and Elizabeth
Married Annabella, daughter of Sir John
Drummond of Stobhall
Died aged c.69, reigned 16 years
1406–1437   JAMES I
Born 1394, son of Robert III
Married Joan Beaufort, daughter of John, earl of
Somerset
Assassinated aged 42, reigned 30 years
1437–1460   JAMES II
Born 1430, son of James I
Married Mary, daughter of Arnold, duke of
Gueldres
Killed accidentally aged 29, reigned 23 years
1460–1488   JAMES III
Born 1452, son of James II
Married Margaret, daughter of Christian I of
Denmark
Assassinated aged 36, reigned 27 years

1488–1513	JAMES IV
	Born 1473, son of James III
	Married Margaret Tudor, daughter of Henry VII of England
	Killed in battle aged 40, *reigned* 25 years
1513–1542	JAMES V
	Born 1512, son of James IV
	Married (1) Madeleine, daughter of Francis I of France (2) Mary of Lorraine, daughter of the Duc de Guise
	Died aged 30, *reigned* 29 years
1542–1567	MARY
	Born 1542, daughter of James V and Mary
	Married (1) the Dauphin, afterwards Francis II of France (2) Henry Stewart, Lord Darnley (3) James Hepburn, earl of Bothwell
	Abdicated 1567, prisoner in England from 1568, executed 1587, *reigned* 24 years
1567–1625	JAMES VI (and I of England)
	Born 1566, son of Mary, queen of Scots, and Henry, Lord Darnley
	Acceded 1567 to the Scottish throne, *reigned* 58 years
	Succeeded 1603 to the English throne, so joining the English and Scottish crowns in one person. The two kingdoms remained distinct until 1707 when the parliaments of the kingdoms became conjoined
	For British Kings and Queens since 1603, *see* pages 138–9

WELSH SOVEREIGNS AND PRINCES

Wales was ruled by sovereign princes from the earliest times until the death of Llywelyn in 1282. The first English Prince of Wales was the son of Edward I, who was born in Caernarvon town on 25 April 1284. According to a discredited legend, he was presented to the Welsh chieftains as their prince, in fulfilment of a promise that they should have a prince who 'could not speak a word of English' and should be native born. This son, who afterwards became Edward II, was created 'Prince of Wales and Earl of Chester' at the Lincoln Parliament on 7 February 1301.

The title Prince of Wales is borne after individual conferment and is not inherited at birth, though some Princes have been declared and styled Prince of Wales but never formally so created (*s.*). The title was conferred on Prince Charles by The Queen on 26 July 1958. He was invested at Caernarvon on 1 July 1969.

INDEPENDENT PRINCES AD 844 TO 1282

844–878	Rhodri the Great
878–916	Anarawd, son of Rhodri
916–950	Hywel Dda, the Good
950–979	Iago ab Idwal (or Ieuaf)
979–985	Hywel ab Ieuaf, the Bad
985–986	Cadwallon, his brother
986–999	Maredudd ab Owain ap Hywel Dda
999–1008	Cynan ap Hywel ab Ieuaf
1018–1023	Llywelyn ap Seisyll
1023–1039	Iago ab Idwal ap Meurig
1039–1063	Gruffydd ap Llywelyn ap Seisyll
1063–1075	Bleddyn ap Cynfyn
1075–1081	Trahaern ap Caradog
1081–1137	Gruffydd ap Cynan ab Iago
1137–1170	Owain Gwynedd
1170–1194	Dafydd ab Owain Gwynedd
1194–1240	Llywelyn Fawr, the Great
1240–1246	Dafydd ap Llywelyn
1246–1282	Llywelyn ap Gruffydd ap Llywelyn

ENGLISH PRINCES SINCE 1301

1301	Edward (Edward II)
1343	Edward the Black Prince, s. of Edward III
1376	Richard (Richard II), s. of the Black Prince
1399	Henry of Monmouth (Henry V)
1454	Edward of Westminster, son of Henry VI
1471	Edward of Westminster (Edward V)
1483	Edward, son of Richard III (d. 1484)
1489	Arthur Tudor, son of Henry VII
1504	Henry Tudor (Henry VIII)
1610	Henry Stuart, son of James I (d. 1612)
1616	Charles Stuart (Charles I)
*c.*1638 (*s.*)	Charles (Charles II)
1688 (*s.*)	James Francis Edward (The Old Pretender) (d.1766)
1714	George Augustus (George II)
1729	Frederick Lewis, s. of George II (d. 1751)
1751	George William Frederick (George III)
1762	George Augustus Frederick (George IV)
1841	Albert Edward (Edward VII)
1901	George (George V)
1910	Edward (Edward VIII)
1958	Charles Philip Arthur George

PRINCESSES ROYAL

The style Princess Royal is conferred at the Sovereign's discretion on his or her eldest daughter. It is an honorary title, held for life, and cannot be inherited or passed on. It was first conferred on Princess Mary, daughter of Charles I, in approximately 1642.

*c.*1642	Princess Mary (1631–60), daughter of Charles I
1727	Princess Anne (1709–59), daughter of George II
1766	Princess Charlotte (1766–1828), daughter of George III
1840	Princess Victoria (1840–1901), daughter of Victoria
1905	Princess Louise (1867–1931), daughter of Edward VII
1932	Princess Mary (1897–1965), daughter of George V
1987	Princess Anne (1950–), daughter of Elizabeth II

The Peerage
and Members of the House of Lords

The rules which govern the creation and succession of peerages are extremely complicated. There are, technically, five separate peerages, the Peerage of England, of Scotland, of Ireland, of Great Britain, and of the United Kingdom. The Peerage of Great Britain dates from 1707 when an Act of Union combined the two kingdoms of England and Scotland and separate peerages were discontinued. The Peerage of the United Kingdom dates from 1801 when Great Britain and Ireland were combined under an Act of Union. Some Scottish peers have received additional peerages of Great Britain or of the United Kingdom since 1707, and some Irish peers additional peerages of the United Kingdom since 1801.

The Peerage of Ireland was not entirely discontinued from 1801 but holders of Irish peerages, whether predating or created subsequent to the Union of 1801, are not entitled to sit in the House of Lords if they have no additional English, Scottish, Great Britain or United Kingdom peerage. However, they are eligible for election to the House of Commons and to vote in parliamentary elections, which other peers are not. An Irish peer holding a peerage of a lower grade which enables him to sit in the House of Lords is introduced there by the title which enables him to sit, though for all other purposes he is known by his higher title.

In the Peerage of Scotland there is no rank of Baron; the equivalent rank is Lord of Parliament, abbreviated to 'Lord' (the female equivalent is 'Lady'). All peers of England, Scotland, Great Britain or the United Kingdom who are 21 years or over, and of British, Irish or Commonwealth nationality are entitled to sit in the House of Lords.

No fees for dignities have been payable since 1937. The House of Lords surrendered the ancient right of peers to be tried for treason or felony by their peers in 1948.

HEREDITARY WOMEN PEERS

Most hereditary peerages pass on death to the nearest male heir, but there are exceptions, and several are held by women (*see* pages 149 and 161–2).

A woman peer in her own right retains her title after marriage, and if her husband's rank is the superior she is designated by the two titles jointly, the inferior one second. Her hereditary claim still holds good in spite of any marriage whether higher or lower. No rank held by a woman can confer any title or even precedence upon her husband but the rank of a hereditary woman peer in her own right is inherited by her eldest son (or in some cases daughter).

Since the Peerage Act 1963, hereditary women peers in their own right have been entitled to sit in the House of Lords, subject to the same qualifications as men.

LIFE PEERS

Since 1876 non-hereditary or life peerages have been conferred on certain eminent judges to enable the judicial functions of the House of Lords to be carried out. These Lords are known as Lords of Appeal or law lords and, to date, such appointments have all been male.

Since 1958 life peerages have been conferred upon distinguished men and women from all walks of life, giving them seats in the House of Lords in the degree of Baron or Baroness. They are addressed in the same way as heredi-

tary Lords and Barons, and their children have similar courtesy titles.

PEERAGES EXTINCT SINCE THE LAST EDITION

VISCOUNTCIES: Furness (*cr.* 1918)
BARONIES: Adrian (*cr.* 1955), Erskine of Rerrick (*cr.* 1964), Headley (*cr.* 1797 I.),
LIFE PEERAGES: Benson (*cr.* 1981), Bonham-Carter (*cr.* 1986), Brimelow (*cr.* 1976), Campbell of Eskan (*cr.* 1966); Ennals (*cr.* 1983); Goodman (*cr.* 1965), Joseph (*cr.* 1987), Kagan (*cr.* 1976), Lever of Manchester (*cr.* 1979), Morton of Shuna (*cr.* 1985), Mulley (*cr.* 1984), Pitt of Hampstead (*cr.* 1975), Reigate (*cr.* 1970), Schon (*cr.* 1976), Shackleton (*cr.* 1958), Taylor of Hadfield (*cr.* 1982), White of Hull (*cr.* 1991), Wilson of Rievaulx (*cr.* 1983)

DISCLAIMER OF PEERAGES

The Peerage Act 1963 enables peers to disclaim their peerages for life. Peers alive in 1963 could disclaim within twelve months after the passing of the Act (31 July 1963); a person subsequently succeeding to a peerage may disclaim within twelve months (one month if an MP) after the date of succession, or of reaching 21, if later. The disclaimer is irrevocable but does not affect the descent of the peerage after the disclaimant's death, and children of a disclaimed peer may, if they wish, retain their precedence and any courtesy titles and styles borne as children of a peer. The disclaimer permits the disclaimant to sit in the House of Commons if elected as an MP.

The following peerages are currently disclaimed:

EARLDOMS: Durham (1970); Home (1963); Selkirk (disclaimed by one claimant; *see* page 148)
VISCOUNTCIES: Camrose (1995); Hailsham (1963); Stansgate (1963)
BARONIES: Altrincham (1963); Archibald (1975); Merthyr (1977); Reith (1972); Sanderson of Ayot (1971); Silkin (1972)

PEERS WHO ARE MINORS (i.e. under 21 years of age)

EARLS: Craven (*b.* 1989)
BARONS: Elphinstone (*b.* 1980); Gretton (*b.* 1975); Lovat (*b.* 1977)

CONTRACTIONS AND SYMBOLS

S. Scottish title
I. Irish title
* The peer holds also an Imperial title, specified after the name by Engl., Brit. or UK
o there is no 'of' in the title
b. born
s. succeeded
m. married
w. widower or widow
M. minor
† heir not ascertained at time of going to press

Hereditary Peers

ROYAL DUKES

Style, His Royal Highness The Duke of ___
Style of address (formal) May it please your Royal Highness; *(informal)* Sir

Created	*Title, order of succession, name, etc.*	*Heir*
1947	*Edinburgh* (1st), The Prince Philip, Duke of Edinburgh, *(see* page 123)	The Prince of Wales
1337	*Cornwall,* Charles, Prince of Wales, *s.* 1952 *(see* page 123)	‡
1398	*Rothesay,* Charles, Prince of Wales, *s.* 1952 *(see* page 123)	‡
1986	*York* (1st), The Prince Andrew, Duke of York *(see* p. 123)	None
1928	*Gloucester* (2nd), Prince Richard, Duke of Gloucester, *s.* 1974 *(see* page 124)	Earl of Ulster *(see* page 124)
1934	*Kent* (2nd), Prince Edward, Duke of Kent, *s.* 1942 *(see* page 124)	Earl of St Andrews *(see* page 124)

‡ The title is not hereditary but is held by the Sovereign's eldest son from the moment of his birth or the Sovereign's accession

DUKES

Coronet, Eight strawberry leaves
Style, His Grace the Duke of ___
Wife's style, Her Grace the Duchess of ___
Eldest son's style, Takes his father's second title as a courtesy title
Younger sons' style, 'Lord' before forename and family name
Daughters' style, 'Lady' before forename and family name
For forms of address, *see* page 217

Created	*Title, order of succession, name, etc.*	*Heir*
1868 I.*	*Abercorn* (5th), James Hamilton (6th *Brit. Marq.,* 1790, and 14th *Scott. Earl,* 1606, both *Abercorn), b.* 1934, *s.* 1979, *m.*	Marquess of Hamilton, *b.* 1969.
1701 s.*	*Argyll* (12th), Ian Campbell (5th *UK Duke Argyll,* 1892), *b.* 1937, *s.* 1973, *m.*	Marquess of Lorne, *b.* 1968.
1703 s.	*Atholl* (10th), George Iain Murray, *b.* 1931, *s.* 1957	John *M., b.* 1929.
1682	*Beaufort* (11th), David Robert Somerset, *b.* 1928, *s.* 1984, *w.*	Marquess of Worcester, *b.* 1952.
1694	*Bedford* (13th), John Robert Russell, *b.* 1917, *s.* 1953, *m.*	Marquess of Tavistock, *b.* 1940.
1663 s.*	*Buccleuch* (9th) & *Queensberry* (11th) (1684), Walter Francis John Montagu Douglas Scott, KT, VRD (8th *Engl. Earl, Doncaster,* 1662), *b.*1923, *s.* 1973, *m.*	Earl of Dalkeith, *b.* 1954.
1694	*Devonshire* (11th), Andrew Robert Buxton Cavendish, MC, PC, *b.* 1920, *s.*1950, *m.*	Marquess of Hartington, *b.* 1944.
1900	*Fife* (3rd), James George Alexander Bannerman Carnegie (12th *Scott. Earl, Southesk,* 1633, *s.* 1992), *b.* 1929, *s.* 1959. *(see* page 135)	Earl of Southesk, *b.* 1961.
1675	*Grafton* (11th), Hugh Denis Charles FitzRoy, KG, *b.* 1919, *s.* 1970, *m.*	Earl of Euston, *b.* 1947.
1643 s.*	*Hamilton* (15th) & *Brandon* (12th) *(Brit.* 1711), Angus Alan Douglas Douglas-Hamilton *(Premier Peer of Scotland), b.* 1938, *s.* 1973	Marquess of Douglas and Clydesdale, *b.* 1978.
1766 I.*	*Leinster* (8th), Gerald FitzGerald *(Premier Duke and Marquess of Ireland;* 8th *Brit. Visct., Leinster,* 1747), *b.* 1914, *s.* 1976, *m.*	Marquess of Kildare, *b.* 1948.
1719	*Manchester* (12th), Angus Charles Drogo Montagu, *b.* 1938, *s.* 1985, *m.*	Viscount Mandeville, *b.* 1962.
1702	*Marlborough* (11th), John George Vanderbilt Henry Spencer-Churchill, *b.*1926, *s.* 1972, *m.*	Marquess of Blandford, *b.* 1955.
1707 s.*	*Montrose* (8th), James Graham (6th *Brit. Earl, Graham,* 1722), *b.* 1935, *s.*1992, *m.*	Marquess of Graham, *b.* 1973.
1483	*Norfolk* (17th), Miles Francis Stapleton Fitzalan-Howard, KG, GCVO, CB, CBE, MC *(Premier Duke;* 12th *Eng. Baron Beaumont,* 1309, *s.*1971; 4th *UK Baron Howard of Glossop,* 1869, *s.* 1972), *b.* 1915, *s.* 1975, *m.* Earl Marshal	Earl of Arundel and Surrey, *b.* 1956.
1766	*Northumberland* (11th), Henry Alan Walter Richard Percy, *b.* 1953, *s.*1988	Lord Ralph G. A. P., *b.* 1956.
1675	*Richmond* (10th) & *Gordon* (5th) *(UK* 1876), Charles Henry Gordon Lennox (10th *Scott. Duke, Lennox,* 1675), *b.* 1929, *s.* 1989, *m.*	Earl of March and Kinrara, *b.* 1955.
1707 s.*	*Roxburghe* (10th), Guy David Innes-Ker (5th *UK Earl, Innes,* 1837), *b.* 1954, *s.* 1974, *m. (Premier Baronet of Scotland)*	Marquess of Bowmont and Cessford, *b.* 1981.

Created	Title, order of succession, name, etc.	Heir
1703	*Rutland* (10th), Charles John Robert Manners, CBE, *b.* 1919, *s.* 1940, *m.*	Marquess of Granby, *b.* 1959.
1684	*St Albans* (14th), Murray de Vere Beauclerk, *b.* 1939, *s.* 1988, *m.*	Earl of Burford, *b.* 1965.
1547	*Somerset* (19th), John Michael Edward Seymour, *b.* 1952, *s.* 1984, *m.*	Lord Seymour, *b.* 1982.
1833	*Sutherland* (6th), John Sutherland Egerton, TD (5th *UK Earl, Ellesmere,* 1846, *s.* 1944), *b.* 1915, *s.* 1963, *m.*	Francis R. E., *b.* 1940.
1814	*Wellington* (8th), Arthur Valerian Wellesley, KG, LVO, OBE, MC (9th *Irish Earl, Mornington,* 1760), *b.* 1915, *s.* 1972, *m.*	Marquess of Douro, *b.* 1945.
1874	*Westminster* (6th), Gerald Cavendish Grosvenor, OBE, *b.* 1951, *s.* 1979, *m.*	Earl Grosvenor, *b.* 1991.

MARQUESSES

Coronet, Four strawberry leaves alternating with four silver balls
Style, The Most Hon. the Marquess (of) ___ . In Scotland the spelling 'Marquis' is preferred for pre-Union creations
Wife's style, The Most Hon. the Marchioness (of) ___
Eldest son's style, Takes his father's second title as a courtesy title
Younger sons' style, 'Lord' before forename and family name
Daughters' style, 'Lady' before forename and family name
For forms of address, *see* page 217

Created	Title, order of succession, name, etc.	Heir
1916	*Aberdeen and Temair* (6th), Alastair Ninian John Gordon (12th *Scott. Earl, Aberdeen,* 1682), *b.* 1920, *s.* 1984, *m.*	Earl of Haddo, *b.* 1955.
1876	*Abergavenny* (5th), John Henry Guy Nevill, KG, OBE, *b.* 1914, *s.* 1954, *m.*	Christopher G. C. N., *b.* 1955.
1821	*Ailesbury* (8th), Michael Sidney Cedric Brudenell-Bruce, *b.* 1926, *s.* 1974	Earl of Cardigan, *b.* 1952.
1831	*Ailsa* (8th), Archibald Angus Charles Kennedy (20th *Scott. Earl, Cassillis,* 1509), *b.* 1956, *s.* 1994	Lord David Kennedy, *b.* 1958.
1815	*Anglesey* (7th), George Charles Henry Victor Paget, *b.* 1922, *s.* 1947, *m.*	Earl of Uxbridge, *b.* 1950.
1789	*Bath* (7th), Alexander George Thynn, *b.* 1932, *s.* 1992, *m.*	Viscount Weymouth, *b.* 1974.
1826	*Bristol* (7th), (Frederick William) John Augustus Hervey, *b.* 1954, *s.* 1985	Lord F. W. C. Nicholas W. H., *b.* 1961.
1796	*Bute* (7th), John Colum Crichton-Stuart (12th *Scott. Earl, Dumfries,* 1633), *b.* 1958, *s.* 1993, *m.*	Earl of Dumfries, *b.* 1989.
1812	°*Camden* (6th), David George Edward Henry Pratt, *b.* 1930, *s.* 1983	Earl of Brecknock, *b.* 1965.
1815	*Cholmondeley* (7th), David George Philip Cholmondeley (11th *Irish Viscount, Cholmondeley,* 1661), *b.* 1960, *s.* 1990. *Lord Great Chamberlain*	Charles G. C., *b.* 1959.
1816 I.*	°*Conyngham* (7th), Frederick William Henry Francis Conyngham (7th *UK Baron, Minster,* 1821), *b.* 1924, *s.* 1974, *m.*	Earl of Mount Charles, *b.* 1951.
1791 I.*	*Donegall* (7th), Dermot Richard Claud Chichester, LVO (7th *Brit. Baron, Fisherwick,* 1790, 6th *Brit. Baron, Templemore,* 1831, *s.* 1953), *b.* 1916, *s.* 1975, *m.*	Earl of Belfast, *b.* 1952.
1789 I.*	*Downshire* (8th), (Arthur) Robin Ian Hill (8th *Brit. Earl, Hillsborough,* 1772), *b.* 1929, *s.* 1989, *m.*	Earl of Hillsborough, *b.* 1959.
1801 I.*	*Ely* (8th) Charles John Tottenham (8th *UK Baron, Loftus,* 1801), *b.* 1913, *s.* 1969, *m.*	Viscount Loftus, *b.* 1943.
1801	*Exeter* (8th), (William) Michael Anthony Cecil, *b.* 1935, *s.* 1988, *m.*	Lord Burghley, *b.* 1970.
1800 I.*	*Headfort* (6th), Thomas Geoffrey Charles Michael Taylour (4th *UK Baron, Kenlis,* 1831), *b.* 1932, *s.* 1960, *m.*	Earl of Bective, *b.* 1959.
1793	*Hertford* (8th), Hugh Edward Conway Seymour (9th *Irish Baron, Conway,* 1712), *b.* 1930, *s.* 1940, *m.*	Earl of Yarmouth, *b.* 1958.
1599 S.*	*Huntly* (13th), Granville Charles Gomer Gordon (*Premier Marquess of Scotland*) (5th *UK Baron, Meldrum,* 1815), *b.* 1944, *s.* 1987, *m.*	Earl of Aboyne, *b.* 1973.
1784	*Lansdowne* (8th), George John Charles Mercer Nairne Petty-Fitzmaurice, PC (8th *Irish Earl, Kerry,* 1723), *b.* 1912, *s.* 1944, *m.*	Earl of Shelburne, *b.* 1941.
1902	*Linlithgow* (4th), Adrian John Charles Hope (10th *Scott. Earl, Hopetoun* 1703), *b.* 1946, *s.* 1987, *m.*	Earl of Hopetoun, *b.* 1969.
1816 I.*	*Londonderry* (9th), Alexander Charles Robert Vane-Tempest-Stewart (6th *UK Earl, Vane,* 1823), *b.* 1937, *s.* 1955, *m.*	Viscount Castlereagh, *b.* 1972.
1701 S.*	*Lothian* (12th), Peter Francis Walter Kerr, KCVO (6th *UK Baron, Kerr,* 1821), *b.* 1922, *s.* 1940, *m.*	Earl of Ancram, MP, *b.* 1945.
1917	*Milford Haven* (4th), George Ivar Louis Mountbatten, *b.* 1961, *s.* 1970, *m.*	Earl of Medina, *b.* 1991.

Created	Title, order of succession, name, etc.	Heir
1838	*Normanby* (5th), Constantine Edmund Walter Phipps, (9th *Irish Baron, Mulgrave,* 1767), *b.* 1954, *s.* 1994, *m.*	Lord Justin, C.P., *b.* 1958.
1812	*Northampton* (7th), Spencer Douglas David Compton, *b.* 1946, *s.* 1978, *m.*	Earl Compton, *b.* 1973.
1825 I.*	*Ormonde* (7th), James Hubert Theobald Charles Butler, MBE (7th *UK Baron, Ormonde,* 1821), *b.* 1899, *s.* 1971, *w.*	None to Marquessate. To Earldoms of Ormonde and Ossory, Viscount Mountgarret, *b.* 1936 (*see* p. 151).
1682 S.	*Queensberry* (12th), David Harrington Angus Douglas, *b.* 1929, *s.* 1954	Viscount Drumlanrig, *b.* 1967.
1926	*Reading* (4th), Simon Charles Henry Rufus Isaacs, *b.* 1942, *s.* 1980, *m.*	Viscount Erleigh, *b.* 1986.
1789	*Salisbury* (6th), Robert Edward Peter Cecil, *b.* 1916, *s.* 1972, *m.*	Viscount Cranborne, PC, *b.* 1946 (*see also* Baron Cecil, page 154).
1800 I.*	*Sligo* (11th), Jeremy Ulick Browne (11th *UK Baron, Monteagle,* 1806), *b.* 1939, *s.* 1991, *m.*	Sebastian U. B., *b.* 1964.
1787	°*Townshend* (7th), George John Patrick Dominic Townshend, *b.* 1916, *s.* 1921, *w.*	Viscount Raynham, *b.* 1945.
1694 S.*	*Tweeddale* (13th), Edward Douglas John Hay (4th *UK Baron, Tweeddale,* 1881), *b.* 1947, *s.* 1979	Lord Charles D. M. H., *b.* 1947.
1789 I.*	*Waterford* (8th), John Hubert de la Poer Beresford (8th *Brit. Baron, Tyrone,* 1786), *b.* 1933, *s.* 1934, *m.*	Earl of Tyrone, *b.* 1958.
1551	*Winchester* (18th), Nigel George Paulet (*Premier Marquess of England*), *b.* 1941, *s.* 1968, *m.*	Earl of Wiltshire, *b.* 1969.
1892	*Zetland* (4th), Lawrence Mark Dundas (6th *UK Earl of Zetland,* 1838, 7th *Brit. Baron Dundas,* 1794), *b.* 1937, *s.* 1989, *m.*	Earl of Ronaldshay, *b.* 1965.

EARLS

Coronet, Eight silver balls on stalks alternating with eight gold strawberry leaves
Style, The Right Hon. the Earl (of) —
Wife's style, The Right Hon. the Countess (of) —
Eldest son's style, Takes his father's second title as a courtesy title
Younger sons' style, 'The Hon.' before forename and family name
Daughters' style, 'Lady' before forename and family name
For forms of address, *see* page 217

Created	Title, order of succession, name, etc.	Heir
1639 S.	*Airlie* (13th), David George Coke Patrick Ogilvy, KT, GCVO, PC, *b.* 1926, *s.* 1968, *m.* Lord Chamberlain	Lord Ogilvy, *b.* 1958.
1696	*Albemarle* (10th), Rufus Arnold Alexis Keppel, *b.* 1965, *s.* 1979	Crispian W. J. K., *b.* 1948.
1952	°*Alexander of Tunis* (2nd), Shane William Desmond Alexander, *b.* 1935, *s.* 1969, *m.*	Hon. Brian J. A., *b.* 1939.
1662 S.	*Annandale and Hartfell* (11th), Patrick Andrew Wentworth Hope Johnstone, *b.* 1941, *claim established* 1985, *m.*	Lord Johnstone, *b.* 1971.
1789 I.	°*Annesley* (10th), Patrick Annesley, *b.* 1924, *s.* 1979, *m.*	Hon. Philip H. A., *b.* 1927.
1785 I.	*Antrim* (9th), Alexander Randal Mark McDonnell, *b.* 1935, *s.* 1977, *m.* (*Viscount Dunluce*)	Hon. Randal A. St J. M., *b.* 1967.
1762 I.*	*Arran* (9th), Arthur Desmond Colquhoun Gore (5th *UK Baron Sudley,* 1884), *b.* 1938, *s.* 1983, *m.*	Paul A. G., CMG, CVO, *b.* 1921.
1955	°*Attlee* (3rd), John Richard Attlee, *b.* 1956, *s.* 1991, *m.*	None.
1714	*Aylesford* (11th), Charles Ian Finch-Knightley, *b.* 1918, *s.* 1958, *w.*	Lord Guernsey, *b.* 1947.
1937	°*Baldwin of Bewdley* (4th), Edward Alfred Alexander Baldwin, *b.* 1938, *s.* 1976, *m.*	Viscount Corvedale, *b.* 1973.
1922	*Balfour* (4th), Gerald Arthur James Balfour, *b.* 1925, *s.* 1968, *m.*	Eustace A. G. B., *b.* 1921.
1772	°*Bathurst* (8th), Henry Allen John Bathurst, *b.* 1927, *s.* 1943, *m.*	Lord Apsley, *b.* 1961.
1919	°*Beatty* (3rd), David Beatty, *b.* 1946, *s.* 1972, *m.*	Viscount Borodale, *b.* 1973.
1797 I.	*Belmore* (8th), John Armar Lowry-Corry, *b.* 1951, *s.* 1960, *m.*	Viscount Corry, *b.* 1985.
1739 I.*	*Bessborough* (11th), Arthur Mountifort Longfield Ponsonby (8th *UK Baron, Duncannon,* 1834), *b.* 1912, *s.* 1993, *m.*	Hon. Myles F. L. P., *b.* 1941.
1815	*Bradford* (7th), Richard Thomas Orlando Bridgeman, *b.* 1947, *s.* 1981, *m.*	Viscount Newport, *b.* 1980.
1677 S.	*Breadalbane and Holland* (10th), John Romer Boreland Campbell, *b.* 1919, *s.* 1959	None.
1469 S.*	*Buchan* (17th), Malcolm Harry Erskine, (8th *UK Baron Erskine* 1806), *b.* 1930, *s.* 1984, *m.*	Lord Cardross, *b.* 1960.

Created	Title, order of succession, name, etc.	Heir

1746   *Buckinghamshire* (10th), (George) Miles Hobart-Hampden, *b.* 1944, *s.*   Sir John Hobart, Bt., *b.* 1945.
1983, *m.*

1800   °*Cadogan* (7th), William Gerald Charles Cadogan, MC, *b.* 1914, *s.* 1933,   Viscount Chelsea, *b.* 1937.
m.

1878   °*Cairns* (6th), Simon Dallas Cairns, CBE, *b.* 1939, *s.* 1989, *m.*   Viscount Garmoyle, *b.* 1965.

1455 s. *Caithness* (20th), Malcolm Ian Sinclair, PC, *b.* 1948, *s.* 1965, *w.*   Lord Berriedale, *b.* 1981.

1800 I. *Caledon* (7th), Nicholas James Alexander, *b.* 1955, *s.* 1980, *m.*   Viscount Alexander, *b.* 1990.

1661   *Carlisle* (13th), George William Beaumont Howard (13th *Scott. Baron,* Hon. Philip C. W. *H., b.* 1963.
Ruthven of Freeland, 1651), *b.* 1949, *s.* 1994

1793   *Carnarvon* (7th), Henry George Reginald Molyneux Herbert, KCVO, Lord Porchester, *b.* 1956.
KBE, *b.* 1924, *s.* 1987, *m.*

1748 I.* *Carrick* (10th), David James Theobald Somerset Butler (4th *UK Baron,* Viscount Ikerrin, *b.* 1975.
Butler, 1912), *b.* 1953, *s.* 1992, *m.*

1800 I. °*Castle Stewart* (8th), Arthur Patrick Avondale Stuart, *b.* 1928, *s.* 1961, *m.* Viscount Stuart, *b.* 1953.

1814   °*Cathcart* (6th), Alan Cathcart, CB, DSO, MC (15th *Scott. Baron, Cathcart,* Lord Greenock, *b.* 1952.
1447), *b.* 1919, *s.* 1927, *m.*

1647 I. *Cavan.* The 12th Earl died in 1988. Heir had not established his claim Roger C. Lambart, *b.* 1944.
to the title at the time of going to press

1827   °*Cawdor* (7th), Colin Robert Vaughan Campbell, *b.* 1962, *s.* 1993, *m.* Hon. Frederick W. *C., b.* 1965.

1801   *Chichester* (9th), John Nicholas Pelham, *b.* 1944, *s.* 1944, *m.* Richard A. H. *P., b.* 1952.

1803 I.* *Clancarty* (9th), Nicholas Power Richard Le Poer Trench (8th *UK* None.
Visct. Clancarty, 1823), *b.* 1952, *s.* 1995

1776 I.* *Clanwilliam* (7th), John Herbert Meade (5th *UK Baron Clanwilliam,* Lord Gillford, *b.* 1960.
1828), *b.* 1919, *s.* 1989, *m.*

1776   *Clarendon* (7th), George Frederick Laurence Hyde Villiers, *b.* 1933, *s.* Lord Hyde, *b.* 1976.
1955, *m.*

1620 I.* *Cork* (14th) & *Orrery* (14th) (I. 1660), John William Boyle, DSC (10th Hon. John R. *B., b.* 1945.
Brit. Baron, Boyle of Marston, 1711), *b.* 1916, *s.* 1995, *m.*

1850   *Cottenham* (8th), Kenelm Charles Everard Digby Pepys, *b.* 1948, *s.* Viscount Crowhurst, *b.* 1983.
1968, *m.*

1762 I.* *Courtown* (9th), James Patrick Montagu Burgoyne Winthrop Stopford Viscount Stopford, *b.* 1988.
(8th *Brit. Baron, Saltersford,* 1796), *b.* 1954, *s.* 1975, *m.*

1697   *Coventry* (11th), George William Coventry, *b.* 1934, *s.* 1940, *m.* Viscount Deerhurst, *b.* 1957.

1857   °*Cowley* (7th), Garret Graham Wellesley, *b.* 1934, *s.* 1975, *m.* Viscount Dangan, *b.* 1965.

1892   *Cranbrook* (5th), Gathorne Gathorne-Hardy, *b.* 1933, *s.* 1978, *m.* Lord Medway, *b.* 1968.

1801   *Craven* (9th), Benjamin Robert Joseph Craven, *b.* 1989, *s.* 1990, *M.* Rupert J. E. *C., b.* 1926.

1398 s.* *Crawford* (29th) & *Balcarres* (12th) (s. 1651), Robert Alexander Lord Balniel, *b.* 1958.
Lindsay, PC (*Premier Earl on Union Roll,* 5th *UK Baron, Wigan,* 1826,
and *Baron Balniel* (life peerage), 1974, *b.* 1927, *s.* 1975, *m.*

1861   *Cromartie* (5th), John Ruaridh Blunt Grant Mackenzie, *b.* 1948, *s.* 1989, Viscount Tarbat, *b.* 1987.
m.

1901   *Cromer* (4th), Evelyn Rowland Esmond Baring, *b.* 1946, *s.* 1991, *m.* Viscount Errington, *b* 1994.

1633 s.* *Dalhousie* (16th), Simon Ramsay, KT, GCVO, GBE, MC (4th *UK Baron,* Lord Ramsay, *b.* 1948.
Ramsay, 1875), *b.* 1914, *s.* 1950, *m.*

1725 I.* *Darnley* (11th), Adam Ivo Stuart Bligh (20th *Engl. Baron, Clifton of* Lord Clifton, *b.* 1968.
Leighton Bromswold, 1608), *b.* 1941, *s.* 1980, *m.*

1711   *Dartmouth* (9th), Gerald Humphry Legge, *b.* 1924, *s.* 1962, *m.* Viscount Lewisham, *b.* 1949.

1761   °*De La Warr* (11th), William Herbrand Sackville, *b.* 1948, *s.* 1988, *m.* Lord Buckhurst, *b.* 1979.

1622   *Denbigh* (12th) & *Desmond* (11th) (I. 1622), Alexander Stephen William D. *F, b.* 1939.
Rudolph Feilding, *b.* 1970, *s.* 1995

1485   *Derby* (19th), Edward Richard William Stanley, *b.* 1962, *s.* 1994 Hon. Peter H. C. *S., b.* 1964.

1553   *Devon* (17th), Charles Christopher Courtenay, *b.* 1916, *s.* 1935, *m.* Lord Courtenay, *b.* 1942.

1800 I.* *Donoughmore* (8th), Richard Michael John Hely-Hutchinson (8th *UK* Viscount Suirdale, *b.* 1952.
Visct., Hutchinson, 1821), *b.* 1927, *s.* 1981, *m.*

1661 I.* *Drogheda* (12th), Henry Dermot Ponsonby Moore (3rd *UK Baron,* Viscount Moore, *b.* 1983.
Moore, 1954), *b.* 1937, *s.* 1989, *m.*

1837   *Ducie* (7th), David Leslie Moreton, *b.* 1951, *s.* 1991, *m.* Lord Moreton, *b.* 1981.

1860   *Dudley* (4th), William Humble David Ward, *b.* 1920, *s.* 1969, *m.* Viscount Ednam, *b.* 1947.

1660 s.* *Dundee* (12th), Alexander Henry Scrymgeour (2nd *UK Baron, Glassary,* Lord Scrymgeour, *b.* 1982.
1954), *b.* 1949, *s.* 1983, *m.*

1669 s. *Dundonald* (15th), Iain Alexander Douglas Blair Cochrane, *b.* 1961, *s.* Lord Cochrane, *b.* 1991.
1986, *m.*

1686 s. *Dunmore* (11th), Kenneth Randolph Murray, *b.* 1913, *s.* 1981, *w.* Viscount Fincastle, *b.* 1946.

1822 I. *Dunraven and Mount-Earl* (7th), Thady Windham Thomas None.
Wyndham-Quin, *b.* 1939, *s.* 1965, *m.*

1833   *Durham.* Disclaimed for life 1970 (*Antony Claud Frederick Lambton, b.* Hon. Edward R. *L.* (Baron Durham),
1922, *s.* 1970, *m.*) *b.* 1961.

Created	Title, order of succession, name, etc.	Heir
1837	*Effingham* (6th), Mowbray Henry Gordon Howard (16th *Engl. Baron, Howard of Effingham*, 1554), *b.* 1905, *s.* 1946, *m.*	Cdr. David P. M. A. *H., b.* 1939.
1507 s.*	*Eglinton* (18th) & *Winton* (9th) (1600), Archibald George Montgomerie (6th *UK Earl, Winton*, 1859), *b.* 1939, *s.* 1966, *m.*	Lord Montgomerie, *b.* 1966.
1733 i.*	*Egmont* (11th), Frederick George Moore Perceval (9th *Brit. Baron, Lovel* & *Holland*, 1762), *b.* 1914, *s.* 1932, *m.*	Viscount Perceval, *b.* 1934.
1821	*Eldon* (5th), John Joseph Nicholas Scott, *b.* 1937, *s.* 1976, *m.*	Viscount Encombe, *b.* 1962.
1633 s.*	*Elgin* (11th), & *Kincardine* (15th) (s. 1647), Andrew Douglas Alexander Thomas Bruce (4th *UK Baron, Elgin*, 1849), KT, *b.* 1924, *s.* 1968, *m.*	Lord Bruce, *b.* 1961.
1789 i.*	*Enniskillen* (7th), Andrew John Galbraith Cole (5th *UK Baron, Grinstead*, 1815) *b.* 1942, *s.* 1989, *m.*	Arthur G. *C., b.* 1920.
1789 i.*	*Erne* (6th), Henry George Victor John Crichton (3rd *UK Baron, Fermanagh*, 1876), *b.* 1937, *s.* 1940, *m.*	Viscount Crichton, *b.* 1971.
1452 s.	*Erroll* (24th), Merlin Sereld Victor Gilbert Hay, *b.* 1948, *s.* 1978, *m. Hereditary Lord High Constable and Knight Marischal of Scotland.*	Lord Hay, *b.* 1984.
1661	*Essex* (10th), Robert Edward de Vere Capell, *b.* 1920, *s.* 1981, *m.*	Viscount Malden, *b.* 1944.
1711	°*Ferrers* (13th), Robert Washington Shirley, PC, *b.* 1929, *s.* 1954, *m.*	Viscount Tamworth, *b.* 1952.
1789	°*Fortescue* (8th), Charles Hugh Richard Fortescue, *b.* 1951, *s.* 1993, *m.*	Hon. Martin D. *F., b.* 1924.
1841	*Gainsborough* (5th), Anthony Gerard Edward Noel, *b.* 1923, *s.* 1927, *m.*	Viscount Campden, *b.* 1950.
1623 s.*	*Galloway* (13th), Randolph Keith Reginald Stewart (6th *Brit. Baron, Stewart of Garlies*, 1796), *b.* 1928, *s.* 1978, *m.*	Andrew C. *S., b.* 1949.
1703 s.*	*Glasgow* (10th), Patrick Robin Archibald Boyle (4th *UK Baron, Fairlie*, 1897), *b.* 1939, *s.* 1984, *m.*	Viscount of Kelburn, *b.* 1978.
1806 i.*	*Gosford* (7th), Charles David Nicholas Alexander John Sparrow Acheson (5th *UK Baron, Worlingham*, 1835), *b.* 1942, *s.* 1966, *m.*	Hon. Patrick B. V. M. *A., b.* 1915.
1945	*Gowrie* (2nd), Alexander Patric Greysteil Hore-Ruthven, PC (3rd *UK Baron, Ruthven of Gowrie*, 1919), *b.* 1939, *s.* 1955, *m.*	Viscount Ruthven of Canberra, *b.* 1964.
1684 i.*	*Granard* (10th), Peter Arthur Edward Hastings Forbes, (5th *UK Baron, Granard*, 1806), *b.* 1957, *s.* 1992, *m.*	Viscount Forbes, *b.* 1981.
1833	°*Granville* (5th), Granville James Leveson-Gower, MC, *b.* 1918, *s.* 1953, *m.*	Lord Leveson, *b.* 1959.
1806	°*Grey* (6th), Richard Fleming George Charles Grey, *b.* 1939, *s.* 1963, *m.*	Philip K. *G., b.* 1940.
1752	*Guilford* (9th), Edward Francis North, *b.* 1933, *s.* 1949, *w.*	Lord North, *b.* 1971.
1619 s.	*Haddington* (13th), John George Baillie-Hamilton, *b.* 1941, *s.* 1986, *m.*	Lord Binning, *b.* 1985.
1919	°*Haig* (2nd), George Alexander Eugene Douglas Haig, OBE, *b.* 1918, *s.* 1928, *m.*	Viscount Dawick, *b.* 1961.
1944	*Halifax* (3rd), Charles Edward Peter Neil Wood (5th *UK Viscount, Halifax*, 1866), *b.* 1944, *s.* 1980, *m.*	Lord Irwin, *b.* 1977.
1898	*Halsbury* (3rd), John Anthony Hardinge Giffard, FRS, FEng., *b.* 1908, *s.* 1943, *w.*	Adam E. *G., b.* 1934.
1754	*Hardwicke* (10th), Joseph Philip Sebastian Yorke, *b.* 1971, *s.* 1974	Richard C. J. *Y., b.* 1916.
1812	*Harewood* (7th), George Henry Hubert Lascelles, KBE, *b.* 1923, *s.* 1947, *m.* (*see also* page 134)	Viscount Lascelles, *b.* 1950.
1742	*Harrington* (11th), William Henry Leicester Stanhope (8th *Brit. Viscount, Stanhope of Mahon*, 1717), *b.* 1922, *s.* 1929, *m.*	Viscount Petersham, *b.* 1945.
1809	*Harrowby* (7th), Dudley Danvers Granville Coutts Ryder, TD, *b.* 1922, *s.* 1987, *m.*	Viscount Sandon, *b.* 1951.
1605 s.	*Home*. Disclaimed for life 1963 (*see* Lord Home of the Hirsel, page 164)	Hon. David A. C. *D.-H.*, CBE, *b.* 1943.
1821	°*Howe* (7th), Frederick Richard Penn Curzon, *b.* 1951, *s.* 1984, *m.*	Charles M. P. *C., b.* 1967.
1529	*Huntingdon* (16th), William Edward Robin Hood Hastings Bass, *b.* 1948, *s.* 1990, *m.*	Hon. Simon A. R. H. *H. B., b.* 1950.
1885	*Iddesleigh* (4th), Stafford Henry Northcote, *b.* 1932, *s.* 1970, *m.*	Viscount St Cyres, *b.* 1957.
1756	*Ilchester* (9th), Maurice Vivian de Touffreville Fox-Strangways, *b.* 1920, *s.* 1970, *m.*	Hon. Raymond G. *F.-S., b.* 1921.
1929	*Inchcape* (4th), (Kenneth) Peter (Lyle) Mackay, *b.* 1943, *s.* 1994, *m.*	Viscount Glenapp, *b.* 1979.
1919	*Iveagh* (4th), Arthur Edward Rory Guinness, *b.* 1969, *s.* 1992	Hon. Rory M. B. *G., b.* 1974.
1925	°*Jellicoe* (2nd), George Patrick John Rushworth Jellicoe, KBE, DSO, MC, PC, FRS, *b.* 1918, *s.* 1935, *m.*	Viscount Brocas, *b.* 1950.
1697	*Jersey* (9th), George Francis Child Villiers (12th *Irish Visct., Grandison*, 1620), *b.* 1910, *s.* 1923, *m.*	Viscount Villiers, *b.* 1948.
1822 i.	*Kilmorey* (6th), Richard Francis Needham, PC, MP, *b.* 1942, *s.* 1977, *m.*	Viscount Newry and Morne, *b.* 1966.
1866	*Kimberley* (4th), John Wodehouse, *b.* 1924, *s.* 1941, *m.*	Lord Wodehouse, *b.* 1951.
1768 i.	*Kingston* (11th), Barclay Robert Edwin King-Tenison, *b.* 1943, *s.* 1948, *m.*	Viscount Kingsborough, *b.* 1969.
1633 s.*	*Kinnoull* (15th), Arthur William George Patrick Hay (9th *Brit. Baron, Hay of Pedwardine*, 1711), *b.* 1935, *s.* 1938, *m.*	Viscount Dupplin, *b.* 1962.

Created	Title, order of succession, name, etc.	Heir
1677 s.*	*Kintore* (13th), Michael Canning William John Keith (3rd *UK Viscount Stonehaven*, 1938), *b.* 1939, *s.* 1989, *m.*	Lord Inverurie, *b.* 1976.
1914	°*Kitchener of Khartoum* (3rd), Henry Herbert Kitchener, TD, *b.* 1919, *s.* 1937	None.
1756 I.	*Lanesborough* (9th), Denis Anthony Brian Butler, TD, *b.* 1918, *s.* 1950	None.
1624 s.	*Lauderdale* (17th), Patrick Francis Maitland, *b.* 1911, *s.* 1968, *m.*	Viscount Maitland, *b.* 1937.
1837	*Leicester* (7th), Edward Douglas Coke, *b.* 1936, *s.* 1994, *m.*	Viscount Coke, *b.* 1965.
1641 s.	*Leven* (14th) & *Melville* (13th) (s. 1690), Alexander Robert Leslie Melville, *b.* 1924, *s.* 1947, *m.*	Lord Balgonie, *b.* 1954.
1831	*Lichfield* (5th), Thomas Patrick John Anson, *b.* 1939, *s.* 1960	Viscount Anson, *b.* 1978.
1803 I.*	*Limerick* (6th), Patrick Edmund Pery, KBE (6th *UK Baron, Foxford*, 1815), *b.* 1930, *s.* 1967, *m.*	Viscount Glentworth, *b.* 1963.
1572	*Lincoln* (18th), Edward Horace Fiennes-Clinton, *b.* 1913, *s.* 1988, *m.*	Hon. Edward G. *F.-C.*, *b.* 1943.
1633 s.	*Lindsay* (16th), James Randolph Lindesay-Bethune, *b.* 1955, *s.* 1989, *m.*	Viscount Garnock, *b.* 1990.
1626	*Lindsey* (14th) *and Abingdon* (9th) (1682), Richard Henry Rupert Bertie, *b.* 1931, *s.* 1963, *m.*	Lord Norreys, *b.* 1958.
1776 I.	*Lisburne* (8th), John David Malet Vaughan, *b.* 1918, *s.* 1965, *m.*	Viscount Vaughan, *b.* 1945.
1822 I.*	*Listowel* (5th), William Francis Hare, GCMG, PC, (3rd *UK Baron, Hare*, 1869), *b.* 1906, *s.* 1931, *m.*	Viscount Ennismore, *b.* 1964.
1905	*Liverpool* (5th), Edward Peter Bertram Savile Foljambe, *b.* 1944, *s.* 1969	Viscount Hawkesbury, *b.* 1972.
1945	°*Lloyd George of Dwyfor* (3rd), Owen Lloyd George, *b.* 1924, *s.* 1968, *m.*	Viscount Gwynedd, *b.* 1951.
1785 I.*	*Longford* (7th), Francis Aungier Pakenham, KG, PC (6th *UK Baron, Silchester*, 1821; 1st *UK Baron, Pakenham*, 1945), *b.* 1905, *s.* 1961, *m.*	Thomas F. D. *P.*, *b.* 1933.
1807	*Lonsdale* (7th), James Hugh William Lowther, *b.* 1922, *s.* 1953, *m.*	Viscount Lowther, *b.* 1949.
1838	*Lovelace* (5th), Peter Axel William Locke King (12th *Brit. Baron, King*, 1725), *b.* 1951, *s.* 1964, *m.*	None.
1795 I.*	*Lucan* (7th), Richard John Bingham (3rd *UK Baron, Bingham*, 1934), *b.* 1934, *s.* 1964, *m.*	Lord Bingham, *b.* 1967.
1880	*Lytton* (5th), John Peter Michael Scawen Lytton (18th *Engl. Baron, Wentworth*, 1529), *b.* 1950, *s.* 1985, *m.*	Viscount Knebworth, *b.* 1989.
1721	*Macclesfield* (9th), Richard Timothy George Mansfield Parker, *b.* 1943, *s.* 1992, *m.*	Hon. J. David G. *P.*, *b.* 1945.
1800	*Malmesbury* (6th), William James Harris, TD, *b.* 1907, *s.* 1950, *w.*	Viscount FitzHarris, *b.* 1946.
1776 & 1792	*Mansfield and Mansfield* (8th), William David Mungo James Murray (14th *Scott. Visct., Stormont*, 1621), *b.* 1930, *s.* 1971, *m.*	Viscount Stormont, *b.* 1956.
1565 s.	*Mar* (14th) & *Kellie* (16th) (s. 1616), James Thorne Erskine, *b.* 1949, *s.* 1994, *m.*	Hon. Alexander D. *E.*, *b.* 1952.
1785 I.	*Mayo* (10th), Terence Patrick Bourke, *b.* 1929, *s.* 1962	Lord Naas, *b.* 1953.
1627 I.*	*Meath* (14th), Anthony Windham Normand Brabazon (5th *UK Baron, Chaworth*, 1831), *b.* 1910, *s.* 1949, *m.*	Lord Ardee, *b.* 1941.
1766 I.	*Mexborough* (8th), John Christopher George Savile, *b.* 1931, *s.* 1980, *m.*	Viscount Pollington, *b.* 1959.
1813	*Minto* (6th), Gilbert Edward George Lariston Elliot-Murray-Kynynmound, OBE, *b.* 1928, *s.* 1975, *m.*	Viscount Melgund, *b.* 1953.
1562 s.*	*Moray* (20th) Douglas John Moray Stuart (12th *Brit. Baron, Stuart of Castle Stuart*, 1796), *b.* 1928, *s.* 1974, *m.*	Lord Doune, *b.* 1966.
1815	*Morley* (6th), John St Aubyn Parker, *b.* 1923, *s.* 1962, *m.*	Viscount Boringdon, *b.* 1956.
1458 s.	*Morton* (22nd), John Charles Sholto Douglas, *b.* 1927, *s.* 1976, *m.*	Lord Aberdour, *b.* 1952.
1789	*Mount Edgcumbe* (8th), Robert Charles Edgcumbe, *b.* 1939, *s.* 1982	Piers V. *E.*, *b.* 1946.
1831	*Munster* (7th), Anthony Charles FitzClarence, *b.* 1926, *s.* 1983, *w.*	None.
1805	°*Nelson* (9th), Peter John Horatio Nelson, *b.* 1941, *s.* 1981, *m.*	Viscount Merton, *b.* 1971.
1660 s.	*Newburgh* (12th), Don Filippo Giambattista Camillo Francesco Aldo Maria Rospigliosi, *b.* 1942, *s.* 1986, *m.*	Princess Donna Benedetta F. M. *R.*, *b.* 1974.
1827 I.	*Norbury* (6th), Noel Terence Graham-Toler, *b.* 1939, *s.* 1955, *m.*	Viscount Glandine, *b.* 1967.
1806 I.*	*Normanton* (6th), Shaun James Christian Welbore Ellis Agar (9th *Brit. Baron, Mendip*, 1794, 4th *UK Baron, Somerton*, 1873), *b.* 1945, *s.* 1967, *m.*	Viscount Somerton, *b.* 1982.
1647 s.	*Northesk* (14th), David John MacRae Carnegie, *b.* 1954, *s.* 1994, *m.*	Lord Rosehill, *b.* 1980.
1801	*Onslow* (7th), Michael William Coplestone Dillon Onslow, *b.* 1938, *s.* 1971, *m.*	Viscount Cranley, *b.* 1967.
1696 s.	*Orkney* (8th), Cecil O'Bryen Fitz-Maurice, *b.* 1919, *s.* 1951, *w.*	O. Peter *St John*, *b.* 1938.
1925	*Oxford and Asquith* (2nd), Julian Edward George Asquith, KCMG, *b.* 1916, *s.* 1928, *m.*	Viscount Asquith, OBE, *b.* 1952.
1929	°*Peel* (3rd), William James Robert Peel (4th *UK Viscount Peel*, 1895), *b.* 1947, *s.* 1969, *m.*	Viscount Clanfield, *b.* 1976.
1551	*Pembroke* (17th) & *Montgomery* (14th) (1605), Henry George Charles Alexander Herbert, *b.* 1939, *s.* 1969	Lord Herbert, *b.* 1978.
1605 s.	*Perth* (17th), John David Drummond, PC, *b.* 1907, *s.* 1951, *m.*	Viscount Strathallan, *b.* 1935.

Created	Title, order of succession, name, etc.	Heir
1905	*Plymouth* (3rd), Other Robert Ivor Windsor-Clive (15th *Engl. Baron, Windsor*, 1529), *b.* 1923, *s.* 1943, *m.*	Viscount Windsor, *b.* 1951.
1785 I.	*Portarlington* (7th), George Lionel Yuill Seymour Dawson-Damer, *b.* 1938, *s.* 1959, *m.*	Viscount Carlow, *b.* 1965.
1689	*Portland* (11th), Count Henry Noel Bentinck, *b.* 1919, *s.* 1990, *m.*	Viscount Woodstock, *b.* 1953.
1743	*Portsmouth* (10th), Quentin Gerard Carew Wallop, *b.* 1954, *s.* 1984, *m.*	Viscount Lymington, *b.* 1981.
1804	*Powis* (8th), John George Herbert (9th *Irish Baron, Clive*, 1762), *b.* 1952, *s.* 1993, *m.*	Viscount Clive, *b.* 1979.
1765	*Radnor* (8th), Jacob Pleydell-Bouverie, *b.* 1927, *s.* 1968, *m.*	Viscount Folkestone, *b.* 1955.
1831 I.*	*Ranfurly* (7th), Gerald Françoys Needham Knox (8th *UK Baron, Ranfurly*, 1826), *b.* 1929, *s.* 1988, *m.*	Edward J. K., *b.* 1957.
1771 I.	*Roden* (10th), Robert John Jocelyn, *b.* 1938, *s.* 1993, *m.*	Viscount Jocelyn, *b.* 1989.
1801	*Romney* (7th), Michael Henry Marsham, *b.* 1910, *s.* 1975, *m.*	Julian C. M., *b.* 1948.
1703 s.*	*Rosebery* (7th), Neil Archibald Primrose (3rd *UK Earl, Midlothian*, 1911), *b.* 1929, *s.* 1974, *m.*	Lord Dalmeny, *b.* 1967.
1806 I.	*Rosse* (7th), William Brendan Parsons, *b.* 1936, *s.* 1979, *m.*	Lord Oxmantown, *b.* 1969.
1801	*Rosslyn* (7th), Peter St Clair-Erskine, *b.* 1958, *s.* 1977, *m.*	Lord Loughborough, *b.* 1986.
1457 s.	*Rothes* (21st), Ian Lionel Malcolm Leslie, *b.* 1932, *s.* 1975, *m.*	Lord Leslie, *b.* 1958.
1861	°*Russell* (5th), Conrad Sebastian Robert Russell, FBA, *b.* 1937, *s.* 1987, *m.*	Viscount Amberley, *b.* 1968.
1915	°*St Aldwyn* (3rd), Michael Henry Hicks Beach, *b.* 1950, *s.* 1992, *m.*	Hon. David S. *H. B.*, *b.* 1955.
1815	*St Germans* (10th), Peregrine Nicholas Eliot, *b.* 1941, *s.* 1988	Lord Eliot, *b.* 1966.
1660	*Sandwich* (11th), John Edward Hollister Montagu, *b.* 1943, *s.* 1995, *m.*	Viscount Hinchingbrooke, *b.* 1969.
1690	*Scarbrough* (12th), Richard Aldred Lumley (13th *Irish Visct., Lumley*, 1628), *b.* 1932, *s.* 1969, *m.*	Viscount Lumley, *b.* 1973.
1701 s.	*Seafield* (13th), Ian Derek Francis Ogilvie-Grant, *b.* 1939, s. 1969, *m.*	Viscount Reidhaven, *b.* 1963.
1882	*Selborne* (4th), John Roundell Palmer, KBE, FRS, *b.* 1940, *s.* 1971, *m.*	Viscount Wolmer, *b.* 1971.
1646 s.	*Selkirk*. The 10th Earl died November 1994. The succession lies between Alastair Douglas-Hamilton (Master of Selkirk) and Lord James Douglas-Hamilton, MP. A decision by the Lord Lyon King of Arms is expected in late 1995; Lord James Douglas-Hamilton disclaimed the earldom in November 1994	
1672	*Shaftesbury* (10th), Anthony Ashley-Cooper, *b.* 1938, *s.* 1961, *m.*	Lord Ashley, *b.* 1977.
1756 I.*	*Shannon* (9th), Richard Bentinck Boyle (8th *Brit. Baron Carleton*, 1786), *b.* 1924, *s.* 1963	Viscount Boyle, *b.* 1960.
1442	*Shrewsbury* & *Waterford* (22nd) (I. 1446), Charles Henry John Benedict Crofton Chetwynd Chetwynd-Talbot (*Premier Earl of England and Ireland*; 7th *Earl Talbot*, 1784), *b.* 1952, *s.* 1980, *m.*	Viscount Ingestre, *b.* 1978.
1961	*Snowdon* (1st), Antony Charles Robert Armstrong-Jones, GCVO, *b.* 1930, *m.* (*see also* page 123).	Viscount Linley, *b.* 1961 (*see also* page 123).
1880	°*Sondes* (5th), Henry George Herbert Milles-Lade, *b.* 1940, *s.* 1970, *m.*	None.
1765	°*Spencer* (9th), Charles Edward Maurice Spencer, b. 1964, *s.* 1992, *m.*	Viscount Althorp, *b.* 1994.
1703 s.*	*Stair* (13th), John Aymer Dalrymple, KCVO, MBE. (6th *UK Baron, Oxenfoord*, 1841), *b.* 1906, *s.* 1961, *m.*	Viscount Dalrymple, *b.* 1961.
1984	*Stockton* (2nd), Alexander Daniel Alan Macmillan, *b.* 1943, *s.* 1986	Viscount Macmillan of Ovenden, *b.* 1974.
1821	*Stradbroke* (6th), Robert Keith Rous, *b.* 1937, *s.* 1983, *m.*	Viscount Dunwich, *b.* 1961.
1847	*Strafford* (8th), Thomas Edmund Byng, *b.* 1936, *s.* 1984, *m.*	Viscount Enfield, *b.* 1964.
1606 s.*	*Strathmore* & *Kinghorne* (18th), Michael Fergus Bowes Lyon (16th *Scottish Earl, Strathmore*, 1677, & 18th *Kinghorne*, 1606; 5th *UK Earl, Strathmore & Kinghorne*, 1937), *b.* 1957, *s.* 1987, *m.*	Lord Glamis, *b.* 1986.
1603	*Suffolk* (21st) & *Berkshire* (14th) (1626), Michael John James George Robert Howard, *b.* 1935, *s.* 1941, *m.*	Viscount Andover, *b.* 1974.
1955	*Swinton* (2nd), David Yarburgh Cunliffe-Lister, *b.* 1937, *s.* 1972, *m.*	Hon. Nicholas J. *C.-L.*, *b.* 1939.
1714	*Tankerville* (10th), Peter Grey Bennet, *b.* 1956, *s.* 1980	Revd the Hon. George A. G. *B.*, *b.* 1925.
1822	°*Temple of Stowe* (8th), (Walter) Grenville Algernon Temple-Gore-Langton, *b.* 1924, *s.* 1988, *m.*	Lord Langton, *b.* 1955.
1815	*Verulam* (7th), John Duncan Grimston (11th *Irish Visct., Grimston*, 1719; 16th *Scott. Baron, Forrester of Corstorphine*, 1633), *b.* 1951, *s.* 1973, *m.*	Viscount Grimston, *b.* 1978.
1729	°*Waldegrave* (13th), James Sherbrooke Waldegrave, *b.* 1940, *s.* 1995, *m.*	Viscount Chewton, *b.* 1986.
1759	*Warwick* (8th) & °*Brooke* (8th) (*Brit.* 1746), David Robin Francis Guy Greville, *b.* 1934, *s.* 1984	Lord Brooke, *b.* 1957.
1633 s.*	*Wemyss* (12th) & *March* (8th) (s. 1697), Francis David Charteris, KT (5th *UK Baron, Wemyss*, 1821), *b.* 1912, *s.* 1937, *m.*	Lord Neidpath, *b.* 1948.
1621 I.	*Westmeath* (13th), William Anthony Nugent, *b.* 1928, *s.* 1971, *m.*	Hon. Sean C. W. *N.*, *b.* 1965.
1624	*Westmorland* (16th), Anthony David Francis Henry Fane, *b.* 1951, *s.* 1993, *m.*	Hon. Harry St C. *F.*, *b.* 1953.

Created	Title, order of succession, name, etc.	Heir
1876	*Wharncliffe* (5th), Richard Alan Montagu Stuart Wortley, *b*. 1953, *s*. 1987, *m*.	Viscount Carlton, *b*. 1980.
1801	*Wilton* (7th), Seymour William Arthur John Egerton, *b*. 1921, *s*. 1927, *m*.	Baron Ebury, *b*. 1934 (*see* page 155).
1628	*Winchilsea* (16th) & *Nottingham* (11th) (1681), Christopher Denys Stormont Finch Hatton, *b*. 1936, *s*. 1950, *m*.	Viscount Maidstone, *b*. 1967.
1766 I.	°*Winterton* (8th), (Donald) David Turnour, *b*. 1943, *s*. 1991, *m*.	Robert C. *T.*, *b*. 1950.
1956	*Woolton* (3rd), Simon Frederick Marquis, *b*. 1958, *s*. 1969, *m*.	None.
1837	*Yarborough* (8th), Charles John Pelham, *b*. 1963, *s*. 1991, *m*.	Lord Worsley, *b*. 1990.

COUNTESSES IN THEIR OWN RIGHT

Style, The Right Hon. the Countess (of) —
Husband, Untitled
Children's style, As for children of an Earl
For forms of address, *see* page 217

Created	Title, order of succession, name, etc.	Heir
1643 s.	*Dysart* (11th in line), Rosamund Agnes Greaves, *b*. 1914, *s*. 1975	Lady Katherine *Grant of Rothiemurchus*, *b*. 1918.
1633 s.	*Loudoun* (13th in line), Barbara Huddleston Abney-Hastings, *b*. 1919, *s*. 1960, *m*.	Lord Mauchline, *b*. 1942.
c.1115 s.	*Mar* (31st in line), Margaret of Mar (*Premier Earldom of Scotland*), *b*. 1940, *s*. 1975, *m*.	Mistress of Mar, *b*. 1963.
1947	°*Mountbatten of Burma* (2nd in line), Patricia Edwina Victoria Knatchbull, CBE, *b*. 1924, *s*. 1979, *m*.	Lord Romsey, *b*. 1947 (*see also* page 153).
c.1235 s.	*Sutherland* (24th in line), Elizabeth Millicent Sutherland, *b*. 1921, *s*. 1963, *m*.	Lord Strathnaver, *b*. 1947.

VISCOUNTS

Coronet, Sixteen silver balls
Style, The Right Hon. the Viscount —
Wife's style, The Right Hon. the Viscountess —
Children's style, 'The Hon.' before forename and family name
In Scotland, the heir apparent to a Viscount may be styled 'The Master of — (title of peer)'
For forms of address, *see* page 217

Created	Title, order of succession, name, etc.	Heir
1945	*Addison* (4th), William Matthew Wand Addison, *b*. 1945, *s*. 1992, *m*.	Hon. Paul W. *A.*, *b*. 1973.
1946	*Alanbrooke* (3rd), Alan Victor Harold Brooke, *b*. 1932, *s*. 1972	None.
1919	*Allenby* (3rd), Lt.-Col. Michael Jaffray Hynman Allenby, *b*. 1931, *s*. 1984, *m*.	Hon. Henry J. H. *A.*, *b*. 1968.
1911	*Allendale* (3rd), Wentworth Hubert Charles Beaumont, *b*. 1922, *s*. 1956	Hon. Wentworth P. I. *B.*, *b*. 1948.
1642 s.	of *Arbuthnott* (16th), John Campbell Arbuthnott, CBE, DSC, FRSE, *b*. 1924, *s*. 1966, *m*.	Master of Arbuthnott, *b*. 1950.
1751 I.	*Ashbrook* (10th), Desmond Llowarch Edward Flower, KCVO, MBE, *b*. 1905, *s*. 1936, *m*.	Hon. Michael L. W. *F.*, *b*. 1935.
1917	*Astor* (4th), William Waldorf Astor, *b*. 1951, *s*. 1966, *m*.	Hon. William W. *A.*, *b*. 1979.
1781 I.	*Bangor* (8th), William Maxwell David Ward, *b*. 1948, *s*. 1993, *m*.	Hon. E. Nicholas *W.*, *b*. 1953.
1925	*Bearsted* (4th), Peter Montefiore Samuel, MC, TD, *b*. 1911, *s*. 1986, *m*.	Hon. Nicholas A. *S.*, *b*. 1950.
1963	*Blakenham* (2nd), Michael John Hare, *b*. 1938, *s*. 1982, *m*.	Hon. Caspar J. *H.*, *b*. 1972.
1935	*Bledisloe* (3rd), Christopher Hiley Ludlow Bathurst, QC, *b*. 1934, *s*. 1979	Hon. Rupert E. L. *B.*, *b*. 1964.
1712	*Bolingbroke* (7th) & *St John* (8th) (1716), Kenneth Oliver Musgrave St John, *b*. 1927, *s*. 1974	Hon. Henry F. *St J.*, *b*. 1957.
1960	*Boyd of Merton* (2nd), Simon Donald Rupert Neville Lennox-Boyd, *b*. 1939, *s*. 1983, *m*.	Hon. Benjamin A. *L.-B.*, *b*. 1964.

Created	Title, order of succession, name, etc.	Heir
1717 I.*	*Boyne* (10th), Gustavus Michael George Hamilton-Russell, KCVO (4th UK Baron, Brancepeth, 1866), b. 1931, s. 1942, m.	Hon. Gustavus M. S. H.-R., b. 1965.
1929	*Brentford* (4th), Crispin William Joynson-Hicks, b. 1933, s. 1983, m.	Hon. Paul W. J.-H., b. 1971.
1929	*Bridgeman* (3rd), Robin John Orlando Bridgeman, b. 1930, s. 1982, m.	Hon. William O. C. B., b. 1968.
1868	*Bridport* (4th), Alexander Nelson Hood (7th Duke of Brontë in Sicily, 1799, and 6th Irish Baron Bridport, 1794), b. 1948, s. 1969, m.	Hon. Peregrine A. N. H., b. 1974
1952	*Brookeborough* (3rd), Alan Henry Brooke, b. 1952, s. 1987, m.	Hon. Christopher A. B., b. 1954.
1933	*Buckmaster* (3rd), Martin Stanley Buckmaster, OBE, b. 1921, s. 1974	Hon. Colin J. B., b. 1923.
1939	*Caldecote* (2nd), Robert Andrew Inskip, KBE, DSC, FEng., b. 1917, s. 1947, m.	Hon. Piers J. H. I., b. 1947.
1941	*Camrose*. Disclaimed for life 1995 (see Baron Hartwell, page 164)	Hon. Adrian M. Berry, b. 1937.
1954	*Chandos* (3rd), Thomas Orlando Lyttelton, b. 1953, s. 1980, m.	Hon. Oliver A. L., b. 1986.
1665 I.	*Charlemont* (14th), John Day Caulfeild (18th Irish Baron, Caulfeild of Charlemont, 1620), b.1934, s.1985, m.	Hon. John D. C., b. 1966.
1921	*Chelmsford* (3rd), Frederic Jan Thesiger, b. 1931, s.1970, m.	Hon. Frederic C. P. T., b. 1962.
1717 I.	*Chetwynd* (10th), Adam Richard John Casson Chetwynd, b. 1935, s. 1965, m.	Hon. Adam D. C., b. 1969.
1911	*Chilston* (4th), Alastair George Akers-Douglas, b. 1946, s. 1982, m.	Hon. Oliver I. A.-D., b. 1973.
1902	*Churchill* (3rd), Victor George Spencer (5th UK Baron Churchill, 1815), b. 1934, s. 1973	None to Viscountcy. To Barony, Richard H. R. S., b. 1926.
1718	*Cobham* (11th), John William Leonard Lyttelton (8th Irish Baron, Westcote, 1776), b. 1943, s. 1977	Hon. Christopher C. L., b. 1947.
1902	*Colville of Culross* (4th), John Mark Alexander Colville, QC (13th Scott. Baron, Colville of Culross, 1604), b. 1933, s. 1945, m.	Master of Colville, b. 1959.
1826	*Combermere* (5th), Michael Wellington Stapleton-Cotton, b. 1929, s. 1969, m.	Hon. Thomas R. W. S.-C., b. 1969.
1917	*Cowdray* (4th), Michael Orlando Weetman Pearson (4th UK Baron, Cowdray, 1910), b. 1944, s. 1995, m.	Hon. Charles A. P., b. 1956.
1927	*Craigavon* (3rd), Janric Fraser Craig, b. 1944, s. 1974	None.
1886	*Cross* (3rd), Assheton Henry Cross, b. 1920, s. 1932	None.
1943	*Daventry* (3rd), Francis Humphrey Maurice FitzRoy Newdegate, b. 1921, s. 1986, m.	Hon. James E. F. N., b. 1960.
1937	*Davidson* (2nd), John Andrew Davidson, b. 1928, s. 1970, m.	Hon. Malcolm W. M. D., b. 1934.
1956	*De L'Isle* (2nd), Philip John Algernon Sidney, MBE, (7th Baron De L'Isle and Dudley, 1835), b. 1945, s. 1991, m.	Hon. Philip W. E. S., b. 1985.
1776 I.	*De Vesci* (7th), Thomas Eustace Vesey (8th Irish Baron, Knapton, 1750), b. 1955, s. 1983, m.	Hon. Oliver I. V., b. 1991.
1917	*Devonport* (3rd), Terence Kearley, b. 1944, s. 1973	Chester D. H. K., b. 1932.
1964	*Dilhorne* (2nd), John Mervyn Manningham-Buller, b. 1932, s. 1980, m.	Hon. James E. M.-B., b. 1956.
1622 I.	*Dillon* (22nd), Henry Benedict Charles Dillon, b. 1973, s. 1982	Hon. Richard A. L. D., b. 1948.
1785 I.	*Doneraile* (10th), Richard Allen St Leger, b. 1946, s. 1983, m.	Hon. Nathaniel W. R. St J. St L., b. 1971.
1680 I.*	*Downe* (11th), John Christian George Dawnay (4th UK Baron, Dawnay, 1897), b. 1935, s. 1965, m.	Hon. Richard H. D., b. 1967.
1959	*Dunrossil* (2nd), John William Morrison, CMG, b. 1926, s. 1961, m.	Hon. Andrew W. R. M., b. 1953.
1964	*Eccles* (1st), David McAdam Eccles, CH, KCVO, PC, b. 1904, m.	Hon. John D. E., CBE, b. 1931.
1897	*Esher* (4th), Lionel Gordon Baliol Brett, CBE, b. 1913. s. 1963, m.	Hon. Christopher L. B. B., b. 1936.
1816	*Exmouth* (10th), Paul Edward Pellew, b. 1940, s. 1970, m.	Hon. Edward F. P., b. 1978.
1620 S.	*Falkland* (15th), Lucius Edward William Plantagenet Cary (Premier Scottish Viscount on the Roll), b. 1935, s. 1984, m.	Master of Falkland, b. 1963.
1720	*Falmouth* (9th), George Hugh Boscawen (26th Eng. Baron, Le Despencer, 1264), b. 1919, s. 1962, m.	Hon. Evelyn A. H. B., b. 1955.
1720 I.*	*Gage* (8th), (Henry) Nicolas Gage, (7th Brit. Baron, Gage, 1790), b. 1934, s. 1993, m.	Hon. Henry W. G., b. 1975.
1727 I.	*Galway* (12th), George Rupert Monckton-Arundell, b. 1922, s. 1980, m.	Hon. J. Philip M., b. 1952.
1478 I.*	*Gormanston* (17th), Jenico Nicholas Dudley Preston (Premier Viscount of Ireland; 5th UK Baron, Gormanston, 1868), b. 1939, s. 1940, w.	Hon. Jenico F. T. P., b. 1974.
1816 I.	*Gort* (9th), Foley Robert Standish Prendergast Vereker, b. 1951, s. 1995, m.	Hon. Nicholas L. P. V., b. 1954.
1900	*Goschen* (4th), Giles John Harry Goschen, b. 1965, s. 1977, m.	None.
1849	*Gough* (5th), Shane Hugh Maryon Gough, b. 1941, s. 1951	None.
1937	*Greenwood* (2nd), David Henry Hamar Greenwood, b. 1914, s. 1948	Hon. Michael G. H. G., b. 1923.
1929	*Hailsham*. Disclaimed for life 1963 (see Lord Hailsham of St Marylebone, page 164)	Rt. Hon. Douglas M. Hogg, QC, MP, b. 1945.
1891	*Hambleden* (4th), William Herbert Smith, b. 1930, s. 1948, m.	Hon. William H. B. S., b. 1955.
1884	*Hampden* (6th), Anthony David Brand, b. 1937, s. 1975, m.	Hon. Francis A. B., b. 1970.
1936	*Hanworth* (2nd), David Bertram Pollock, b. 1916, s. 1936, m.	Hon. David S. G. P., b. 1946.
1791 I.	*Harberton* (10th), Thomas de Vautort Pomeroy, b. 1910, s. 1980, m.	Hon. Robert W. P., b. 1916.

Created	Title, order of succession, name, etc.	Heir
1846	*Hardinge* (6th), Charles Henry Nicholas Hardinge, *b.* 1956, *s.* 1984, *m.*	Hon. Andrew H. *H., b.* 1960.
1791 I.	*Hawarden* (9th), (Robert) Connan Wyndham Leslie Maude, *b.* 1961, *s.* 1991, *m.*	Hon. Thomas P. C. *M., b.* 1964.
1960	*Head* (2nd), Richard Antony Head, *b.* 1937, *s.* 1983, *m.*	Hon. Henry J. *H., b.* 1980.
1550	*Hereford* (18th), Robert Milo Leicester Devereux (*Premier Viscount of England*), *b.* 1932, *s.* 1952	Hon. Charles R. de B. *D., b.* 1975.
1842	*Hill* (8th), Antony Rowland Clegg-Hill, *b.* 1931, *s.* 1974, *m.*	Peter D. R. C. *C.-H., b.* 1945.
1796	*Hood* (7th), Alexander Lambert Hood (7th *Irish Baron, Hood,* 1782), *b.* 1914, *s.* 1981, *m.*	Hon. Henry L. A. *H., b.* 1958.
1956	*Ingleby* (2nd), Martin Raymond Peake, *b.* 1926, *s.* 1966, *m.*	None.
1945	*Kemsley* (2nd), (Geoffrey) Lionel Berry, *b.* 1909, *s.* 1968, *m.*	Richard G. *B., b.* 1951.
1911	*Knollys* (3rd), David Francis Dudley Knollys, *b.* 1931, *s.* 1966, *m.*	Hon. Patrick N. M. *K., b.* 1962.
1895	*Knutsford* (6th), Michael Holland-Hibbert, *b.* 1926, *s.* 1986, *m.*	Hon. Henry T. *H.-H., b.* 1959.
1945	*Lambert* (3rd), Michael John Lambert, *b.* 1912, *s.* 1989, *m.*	None.
1954	*Leathers* (2nd), Frederick Alan Leathers, *b.* 1908, *s.* 1965, *m.*	Hon. Christopher G. *L., b.* 1941.
1922	*Leverhulme* (3rd), Philip William Bryce Lever, KG, TD, *b.* 1915, *s.* 1949, *w.*	None.
1781 I.	*Lifford* (9th), (Edward) James Wingfield Hewitt, *b.* 1949, *s.* 1987, *m.*	Hon. James T. W. *H., b.* 1979.
1921	*Long* (4th), Richard Gerard Long, CBE, *b.* 1929, *s.* 1967, *m.*	Hon. James R. *L., b.* 1960.
1957	*Mackintosh of Halifax* (3rd), (John) Clive Mackintosh, *b.* 1958, *s.* 1980, *m.*	Hon. Thomas H. G. *M., b.* 1985.
1955	*Malvern* (3rd), Ashley Kevin Godfrey Huggins, *b.* 1949, *s.* 1978	Hon. M. James *H., b.* 1928.
1945	*Marchwood* (3rd), David George Staveley Penny, *b.* 1936, *s.* 1979, *m.*	Hon. Peter G. W. *P., b.* 1965.
1942	*Margesson* (2nd), Francis Vere Hampden Margesson, *b.* 1922, *s.* 1965, *m.*	Capt. Hon. Richard F. D. *M., b.* 1960.
1660 I.*	*Massereene* (14th) & *Ferrard* (7th) (1797), John David Clotworthy Whyte-Melville Foster Skeffington (7th *UK Baron, Oriel,* 1821), *b.* 1940, *s.* 1992, *m.*	Hon. Charles J. C. W.-M. F. *S., b.* 1973.
1802	*Melville* (9th), Robert David Ross Dundas, *b.* 1937, *s.* 1971, *m.*	Hon. Robert H. K. *D., b.* 1984.
1916	*Mersey* (4th), Richard Maurice Clive Bigham, *b.* 1934, *s.* 1979, *m.*	Hon. Edward J. H. *B., b.* 1966.
1717 I.*	*Midleton* (12th), Alan Henry Brodrick (9th *Brit. Baron, Brodrick of Peper Harow,* 1796), *b.* 1949, *s.* 1988, *m.*	Hon. Ashley R. *B., b.* 1980.
1962	*Mills* (3rd), Christopher Philip Roger Mills, *b.* 1956, *s.* 1988, *m.*	None.
1716 I.	*Molesworth* (11th), Richard Gosset Molesworth, *b.* 1907, *s.* 1961, *w.*	Hon. Robert B. K. *M., b.* 1959.
1801 I.*	*Monck* (7th), Charles Stanley Monck (4th *UK Baron, Monck,* 1866), *b.* 1953, *s.* 1982 (does not use title)	Hon. George S. *M., b.* 1957.
1957	*Monckton of Brenchley* (2nd), Maj.-Gen. Gilbert Walter Riversdale Monckton, CB, OBE, MC, *b.* 1915, *s.* 1965, *m.*	Hon Christopher W. *M., b.* 1952.
1946	*Montgomery of Alamein* (2nd), David Bernard Montgomery, CBE, *b.* 1928, *s.* 1976, *m.*	Hon. Henry D. *M., b.* 1954.
1550 I.*	*Mountgarret* (17th), Richard Henry Piers Butler (4th *UK Baron, Mountgarret,* 1911), *b.* 1936, *s.* 1966, *m.*	Hon. Piers J. R. *B., b.* 1961.
1952	*Norwich* (2nd), John Julius Cooper, CVO, *b.* 1929, *s.* 1954, *m.*	Hon. Jason C. D. B. *C., b.* 1959.
1651 S.	*of Oxfuird* (13th), George Hubbard Makgill, *b.* 1934, *s.* 1986, *m.*	Master of Oxfuird, *b.* 1969.
1873	*Portman,* (9th), Edward Henry Berkeley Portman, *b.* 1934, *s.* 1967, *m.*	Hon. Christopher E. B. *P., b.* 1958.
1743 I.*	*Powerscourt* (10th), Mervyn Niall Wingfield (4th *UK Baron, Powerscourt,* 1885), *b.* 1935, *s.* 1973, *m.*	Hon. Mervyn A. *W., b.* 1963.
1900	*Ridley* (4th), Matthew White Ridley, KG, GCVO, TD, *b.* 1925, *s.* 1964, *m.* *Lord Steward*	Hon. Matthew W. *R., b.* 1958.
1960	*Rochdale* (2nd), St John Durival Kemp, *b.* 1938, *s.* 1993, *m.*	Hon. Jonathan H. D. *K., b.* 1961.
1919	*Rothermere* (3rd), Vere Harold Esmond Harmsworth, *b.* 1925, *s.* 1978, *m.*	Hon. H. Jonathan E. V. *H., b.* 1967.
1937	*Runciman of Doxford* (3rd), Walter Garrison Runciman (Garry), CBE, FBA (4th *UK Baron, Runciman,* 1933), *b.* 1934, *s.* 1989, *m.*	Hon. David W. *R., b.* 1967.
1918	*St Davids* (3rd), Colwyn Jestyn John Philipps (20th *Engl. Baron Strange of Knokin,* 1299, 8th *Engl. Baron Hungerford,* 1426, and *De Moleyns,* 1445), *b.* 1939, *s.* 1991, *m.*	Hon. Rhodri C. *P., b.* 1966.
1801	*St Vincent* (7th), Ronald George James Jervis, *b.* 1905, *s.* 1940, *m.*	Hon. Edward R. J. *J., b.* 1951.
1937	*Samuel* (3rd), David Herbert Samuel, PH.D., *b.* 1922, *s.* 1978, *m.*	Hon. Dan J. *S., b.* 1925.
1911	*Scarsdale* (3rd), Francis John Nathaniel Curzon (7th *Brit. Baron, Scarsdale,* 1761), *b.* 1924, *s.* 1977, *m.*	Hon. Peter G. N. *C., b.* 1949.
1905	*Selby* (4th), Michael Guy John Gully, *b.* 1942, *s.* 1959, *m.*	Hon. Edward T. W. *G., b.* 1967.
1805	*Sidmouth* (7th), John Tonge Anthony Pellew Addington, *b.* 1914, *s.* 1976, *m.*	Hon. Jeremy F. *A., b.* 1947.
1940	*Simon* (3rd), Jan David Simon, *b.* 1940, *s.* 1993, *m.*	None.
1960	*Slim* (2nd), John Douglas Slim, OBE, *b.* 1927, *s.* 1970, *m.*	Hon. Mark W. R. *S., b.* 1960.
1954	*Soulbury* (2nd), James Herwald Ramsbotham, *b.* 1915, *s.* 1971, *w.*	Hon. Sir Peter E. *R.,* GCMG, GCVO, *b.* 1919.

Created	Title, order of succession, name, etc.	Heir
1776 I.	*Southwell* (7th), Pyers Anthony Joseph Southwell, *b.* 1930, *s.* 1960, *m.*	Hon. Richard A. P. S., *b.* 1956.
1942	*Stansgate.* Disclaimed for life 1963 (*Rt. Hon. Anthony Neil Wedgwood Benn,* MP, *b.* 1925, *s.* 1960, *m.*)	Stephen M. W. B., *b.* 1951.
1959	*Stuart of Findhorn* (2nd), David Randolph Moray Stuart, *b.* 1924, *s.* 1971, *m.*	Hon. J. Dominic S., *b.* 1948.
1957	*Tenby* (3rd), William Lloyd George, *b.* 1927, *s.* 1983, *m.*	Hon. Timothy H. G. L. G., *b.* 1962.
1952	*Thurso* (3rd), John Archibald Sinclair, *b.* 1953, *s.* 1995, *m.*	Hon. James A. R. S., *b.* 1984.
1983	*Tonypandy* (1st), (Thomas) George Thomas, PC, *b.* 1909	None.
1721	*Torrington* (11th), Timothy Howard St George Byng, *b.* 1943, *s.* 1961, *m.*	John L. B., MC, *b.* 1919.
1936	*Trenchard* (3rd), Hugh Trenchard, *b.* 1951, *s.* 1987, *m.*	Hon. Alexander T. T., *b.* 1978.
1921	*Ullswater* (2nd), Nicholas James Christopher Lowther, PC, *b.* 1942, *s.* 1949, *m.*	Hon. Benjamin J. L., *b.* 1975.
1621 I.	*Valentia* (15th), Richard John Dighton Annesley, *b.* 1929, *s.* 1983, *m.*	Hon. Francis W. D. A., *b.* 1959.
1964	*Watkinson* (1st), Harold Arthur Watkinson, CH, PC, *b.* 1910, *m.*	None.
1952	*Waverley* (3rd), John Desmond Forbes Anderson, *b.* 1949, *s.* 1990	None.
1938	*Weir* (3rd), William Kenneth James Weir, *b.* 1933, *s.* 1975, *m.*	Hon. James W. H. W., *b.* 1965.
1983	*Whitelaw* (1st), William Stephen Ian Whitelaw, KT, CH, MC, PC, *b.* 1918, *m.*	None.
1918	*Wimborne* (4th), Ivor Mervyn Vigors Guest (5th *UK Baron, Wimborne,* 1880), *b.* 1968, *s.* 1993	Hon. Julian J. G., *b.* 1945.
1923	*Younger of Leckie* (3rd), Edward George Younger, OBE, TD, *b.* 1906, *s.* 1946, *w.*	Baron Younger of Prestwick, KCVO, TD, PC, *b.* 1931 (*see* page 166).

BARONS/LORDS

Coronet, Six silver balls
Style, The Right Hon. the Lord ___. In the Peerage of Scotland there is no rank of Baron; the equivalent rank is Lord of Parliament (*see* page 141) and Scottish peers should always be styled 'Lord', never 'Baron'
Wife's style, The Right Hon. the Lady ___
Children's style, 'The Hon.' before forename and family name
In Scotland, the heir apparent to a Lord may be styled 'The Master of ___ (title of peer)'
For forms of address, *see* page 217

Created	Title, order of succession, name, etc.	Heir
1911	*Aberconway* (3rd), Charles Melville McLaren, *b.* 1913, *s.* 1953, *m.*	Hon. H. Charles M., *b.* 1948.
1873	*Aberdare* (4th), Morys George Lyndhurst Bruce, KBE, PC, *b.* 1919, *s.* 1957, *m.*	Hon. Alastair J. L. B., *b.* 1947.
1835	*Abinger* (8th), James Richard Scarlett, *b.* 1914, *s.* 1943, *m.*	Hon. James H. S., *b.* 1959.
1869	*Acton* (4th), Richard Gerald Lyon-Dalberg-Acton, *b.* 1941, *s.* 1989, *m.*	Hon. John C. F. H. L.-D.-A., *b.* 1966.
1887	*Addington* (6th), Dominic Bryce Hubbard, *b.* 1963, *s.* 1982	Hon. Michael W. L. H., *b.* 1965.
1907	*Airedale* (4th), Oliver James Vandeleur Kitson, *b.* 1915, *s.* 1958	None.
1896	*Aldenham* (6th), and *Hunsdon of Hunsdon* (4th) (1923), Vicary Tyser Gibbs, *b.* 1948, *s.* 1986, *m.*	Hon. Humphrey W. F. G., *b.* 1989.
1962	*Aldington* (1st), Toby Austin Richard William Low, KCMG, CBE, DSO, TD, PC, *b.* 1914, *m.*	Hon Charles H. S. L., *b.* 1948.
1945	*Altrincham.* Disclaimed for life 1963 (*John Edward Poynder Grigg, b.* 1924, *s.* 1955, *m.*)	Hon. Anthony U. D. D. G., *b.* 1934.
1929	*Alvingham* (2nd), Maj.-Gen. Robert Guy Eardley Yerburgh, CBE, *b.* 1926, *s.* 1955, *m.*	Capt. Hon. Robert R. G. Y., *b.* 1956.
1892	*Amherst of Hackney* (4th), William Hugh Amherst Cecil, *b.* 1940, *s.* 1980, *m.*	Hon. H. William A. C., *b.* 1968.
1881	*Ampthill* (4th), Geoffrey Denis Erskine Russell, CBE, PC, *b.* 1921, *s.* 1973	Hon. David W. E. R., *b.* 1947.
1947	*Amwell* (3rd), Keith Norman Montague, *b.* 1943, *s.* 1990, *m.*	Hon. Ian K. M., *b.* 1973.
1863	*Annaly* (6th), Luke Richard White, *b.* 1954, *s.* 1990, *m.*	Hon. Luke H. W., *b.* 1990.
1949	*Archibald.* Disclaimed for life 1975 (*George Christopher Archibald, b.* 1926, *s.* 1975, *m.*)	None.
1885	*Ashbourne* (4th), Edward Barry Greynville Gibson, *b.* 1933, *s.* 1983, *m.*	Hon. Edward C. d'O. G., *b.* 1967.
1835	*Ashburton* (7th), John Francis Harcourt Baring, KG, KCVO, *b.* 1928, *s.* 1991, *m.*	Hon. Mark F. R. B., *b.* 1958.
1892	*Ashcombe* (4th), Henry Edward Cubitt, *b.* 1924, *s.* 1962, *m.*	Mark E. C., *b.* 1964.
1911	*Ashton of Hyde* (3rd), Thomas John Ashton, TD, *b.* 1926, *s.* 1983, *m.*	Hon. Thomas H. A., *b.* 1958.
1800 I.	*Ashtown* (7th), Nigel Clive Crosby Trench, KCMG, *b.* 1916, *s.* 1990, *w.*	Hon. Roderick N. G. T., *b.* 1944.

Created	Title, order of succession, name, etc.	Heir
1956	*Astor of Hever* (3rd), John Jacob Astor, *b.* 1946, *s.* 1984, *m.*	Hon. Charles G. J. A., *b.* 1990.
1789 I.*	*Auckland* (9th), Ian George Eden (9th *Brit. Baron, Auckland,* 1793), *b.* 1926, *s.* 1957, *m.*	Hon. Robert I. B. *E., b.* 1962.
1313	*Audley* (25th), Richard Michael Thomas Souter, *b.* 1914, *s.* 1973, *m.*	Three co-heiresses.
1900	*Avebury* (4th), Eric Reginald Lubbock, *b.* 1928, *s.* 1971, *m.*	Hon. Lyulph A. J. *L., b.* 1954.
1718 I.	*Aylmer* (13th), Michael Anthony Aylmer, *b.* 1923, *s.* 1982, *m.*	Hon. A. Julian *A., b.* 1951.
1929	*Baden-Powell* (3rd), Robert Crause Baden-Powell, *b.* 1936, *s.* 1962, *m.*	Hon. David M. *B.-P., b.* 1940.
1780	*Bagot* (9th), Heneage Charles Bagot, *b.* 1914, *s.* 1979, *m.*	Hon. C. H. Shaun *B., b.* 1944.
1953	*Baillieu* (3rd), James William Latham Baillieu, *b.* 1950, *s.* 1973, *m.*	Hon. Robert L. *B., b.* 1979.
1607 S.	*Balfour of Burleigh* (8th), Robert Bruce, FRSE, *b.* 1927, *s.* 1967, *m.*	Hon. Victoria B., *b.* 1973.
1945	*Balfour of Inchrye* (2nd), Ian Balfour, *b.* 1924, *s.* 1988, *m.*	None.
1924	*Banbury of Southam* (3rd), Charles William Banbury, *b.* 1953, *s.* 1981, *m.*	None.
1698	*Barnard* (11th), Harry John Neville Vane, TD, *b.* 1923, *s.* 1964	Hon. Henry F. C. *V., b.* 1959.
1887	*Basing* (5th), Neil Lutley Sclater-Booth, *b.* 1939, *s.* 1983, *m.*	Hon. Stuart W. *S.-B., b.* 1969.
1917	*Beaverbrook* (3rd), Maxwell William Humphrey Aitken, *b.* 1951, *s.* 1985, *m.*	Hon. Maxwell F. *A, b.* 1977.
1647 S.	*Belhaven and Stenton* (13th), Robert Anthony Carmichael Hamilton, *b.* 1927, *s.* 1961, *m.*	Master of Belhaven, *b.* 1953.
1848 I.	*Bellew* (7th), James Bryan Bellew, *b.* 1920, *s.* 1981, *m.*	Hon. Bryan E. *B., b.* 1943.
1856	*Belper* (4th), (Alexander) Ronald George Strutt, *b.* 1912, *s.* 1956	Hon. Richard H. *S., b.* 1941.
1938	*Belstead* (2nd), John Julian Ganzoni, PC, *b.* 1932, *s.* 1958	None.
1421	*Berkeley* (18th), Anthony Fitzhardinge Gueterbock, OBE, *b.* 1939, *s.* 1992, *m.*	Hon. Thomas F. *G., b.* 1969.
1922	*Bethell* (4th), Nicholas William Bethell, *b.* 1938, s. 1967, *m.*	Hon. James N. *B., b.* 1967.
1938	*Bicester* (3rd), Angus Edward Vivian Smith, *b.* 1932, *s.* 1968	Hugh C. V. *S., b.* 1934.
1903	*Biddulph* (5th), (Anthony) Nicholas Colin Maitland Biddulph, *b.* 1959, *s.* 1988, *m.*	Hon. William I. R. *M. B., b.* 1963.
1938	*Birdwood* (3rd), Mark William Ogilvie Birdwood, *b.* 1938, *s.* 1962, *m.*	None.
1958	*Birkett* (2nd), Michael Birkett, *b.* 1929, *s.* 1962, *m.*	Hon. Thomas *B., b.* 1982.
1907	*Blyth* (4th), Anthony Audley Rupert Blyth, *b.* 1931, *s.* 1977, *m.*	Hon. Riley A. J. *B., b.* 1955.
1797	*Bolton* (7th), Richard William Algar Orde-Powlett, *b.* 1929, *s.* 1963, *m.*	Hon. Harry A. N. *O.-P., b.* 1954.
1452 S.	*Borthwick* (23rd), John Henry Stuart Borthwick, TD, *b.* 1905, *claim succeeded* 1986, *w.*	Master of Borthwick, *b.* 1940.
1922	*Borwick* (4th), James Hugh Myles Borwick, MC, *b.* 1917, *s.* 1961, *m.*	Hon. George S. *B., b.* 1922.
1761	*Boston* (10th), Timothy George Frank Boteler Irby, *b.* 1939, *s.* 1978, *m.*	Hon. George W. E. B. *I., b.* 1971.
1942	*Brabazon of Tara* (3rd), Ivon Anthony Moore-Brabazon, *b.* 1946, *s.* 1974, *m.*	Hon. Benjamin R. *M.-B., b.* 1983.
1880	*Brabourne* (7th), John Ulick Knatchbull, CBE, *b.* 1924, *s.* 1943, *m.*	Lord Romsey, *b.* 1947 (*see* page 149).
1925	*Bradbury* (3rd), John Bradbury, *b.* 1940, *s.* 1994, *m.*	Hon. John *B., b.* 1973.
1962	*Brain* (2nd), Christopher Langdon Brain, *b.* 1926, *s.* 1966, *m.*	Hon. Michael C. *B.,* DM, FRCP, *b.* 1928.
1938	*Brassey of Apethorpe* (3rd), David Henry Brassey, OBE, *b.* 1932, *s.* 1967, *m.*	Hon. Edward *B., b.* 1964.
1788	*Braybrooke* (10th), Robin Henry Charles Neville, *b.* 1932, *s.* 1990, *m.*	George *N., b.* 1943.
1957	*Bridges* (2nd), Thomas Edward Bridges, GCMG, *b.* 1927, *s.* 1969, *m.*	Hon. Mark T. *B., b.* 1954.
1945	*Broadbridge* (3rd), Peter Hewett Broadbridge, *b.* 1938, *s.* 1972, *m.*	Martin H. *B., b.* 1929.
1933	*Brocket* (3rd), Charles Ronald George Nall-Cain, *b.* 1952, *s.* 1967, *m.*	Hon. Alexander C. C. *N.-C., b.* 1984.
1860	*Brougham and Vaux* (5th), Michael John Brougham, CBE, *b.* 1938, *s.* 1967	Hon. Charles W. *B., b.* 1971.
1945	*Broughshane* (2nd), Patrick Owen Alexander Davison, *b.* 1903, *s.* 1953, *w.*	Hon. W. Kensington *D.,* DSO, DFC, *b.* 1914.
1776	*Brownlow* (7th), Edward John Peregrine Cust, *b.* 1936, *s.* 1978, *m.*	Hon. Peregrine E. Q. *C., b.* 1974.
1942	*Bruntisfield* (2nd), John Robert Warrender, OBE, MC, TD, *b.* 1921, *s.* 1993, *m.*	Hon. Michael J. V. *W., b.* 1949.
1950	*Burden* (3rd), Andrew Philip Burden, *b.* 1959, *s.* 1995.	Hon. Fraser W. E. *B., b.* 1964.
1529	*Burgh* (7th), Alexander Peter Willoughby Leith, *b.* 1935, *s.* 1959, *m.*	Hon. A. Gregory D. *L., b.* 1958.
1903	*Burnham* (6th), Hugh John Frederick Lawson, *b.* 1931, *s.* 1993, *m.*	Hon. Harry F. A. *L., b.* 1968.
1897	*Burton* (3rd), Michael Evan Victor Baillie, *b.* 1924, *s.* 1962, *m.*	Hon. Evan M. R. *B., b.* 1949.
1643	*Byron* (13th), Robert James Byron, *b.* 1950, *s.* 1989, *m.*	Hon. Charles R. G. *B., b.* 1990.
1937	*Cadman* (3rd), John Anthony Cadman, *b.* 1938, *s.* 1966, *m.*	Hon. Nicholas A. J. *C., b.* 1977.
1796	*Calthorpe* (10th), Peter Waldo Somerset Gough-Calthorpe, *b.* 1927, *s.* 1945, *m.*	None.
1945	*Calverley* (3rd), Charles Rodney Muff, *b.* 1946, *s.* 1971, *m.*	Hon. Jonathan E. *M., b.* 1975.
1383	*Camoys* (7th), (Ralph) Thomas Campion George Sherman Stonor, *b.* 1940, *s.* 1976, *m.*	Hon. R. William R. T. *S., b.* 1974.
1715 I.	*Carbery* (11th), Peter Ralfe Harrington Evans-Freke, *b.* 1920, *s.* 1970, *m.*	Hon. Michael P. *E.-F., b.* 1942.
1834 I.*	*Carew* (7th), Patrick Thomas Conolly-Carew (7th *UK Baron, Carew,* 1838), *b.* 1938, *s.* 1994, *m.*	Hon. William P. *C.-C., b.* 1973.

Created	Title, order of succession, name, etc.	Heir
1916	Carnock (4th), David Henry Arthur Nicolson, *b.* 1920, *s.* 1982	Nigel *N.*, MBE, *b.* 1917.
1796 I.*	Carrington (6th), Peter Alexander Rupert Carington, KG, GCMG, CH, MC, PC (6th Brit. Baron, Carrington, 1797), *b.* 1919, *s.* 1938, *m.*	Hon. Rupert F. J. *C.*, *b.* 1948.
1812 I.	Castlemaine (8th), Roland Thomas John Handcock, MBE, *b.* 1943, *s.* 1973, *m.*	Hon. Ronan M. E. *H*., *b.* 1989.
1936	Catto (2nd), Stephen Gordon Catto, *b.* 1923, *s.* 1959, *m.*	Hon. Innes G. *C.*, *b.* 1950.
1918	Cawley (3rd), Frederick Lee Cawley, *b.* 1913, *s.* 1954, *m.*	Hon. John F. *C.*, *b.* 1946.
1603	Cecil, a subsidiary title of the Marquess of Salisbury. His heir Viscount Cranborne, PC, was given a Writ in Acceleration in this title to enable him to sit in the House of Lords whilst his father is still alive (*see also* page 144)	
1937	Chatfield (2nd), Ernle David Lewis Chatfield, *b.* 1917, *s.* 1967, *m.*	None.
1858	Chesham (6th), Nicholas Charles Cavendish, *b.* 1941, *s.* 1989, *m.*	Hon. Charles G. C. *C.*, *b.* 1974.
1945	Chetwode (2nd), Philip Chetwode, *b.* 1937, *s.* 1950, *m.*	Hon. Roger *C.*, *b.* 1968.
1945	Chorley (2nd), Roger Richard Edward Chorley, *b.* 1930, *s.* 1978, *m.*	Hon. Nicholas R. D. *C.*, *b.* 1966.
1858	Churston (5th), John Francis Yarde-Buller, *b.* 1934, *s.* 1991, *m.*	Hon. Benjamin F. A. *Y.-B.*, *b.* 1974.
1946	Citrine (2nd), Norman Arthur Citrine, *b.* 1914, *s.* 1983, *w.*	Hon. Ronald E. *C.*, *b.* 1919.
1800 I.	Clanmorris (8th), Simon John Ward Bingham, *b.* 1937, *s.* 1988, *m.*	Robert D. de B. *B.*, *b.* 1942.
1672	Clifford of Chudleigh (14th), Thomas Hugh Clifford, *b.* 1948, *s.* 1988, *m.*	Hon. Alexander T. H. *C.*, *b.* 1985.
1299	Clinton (22nd), Gerard Nevile Mark Fane Trefusis, *b.* 1934, *title called out of abeyance* 1965, *m.*	Hon. Charles P. R. F. *T.*, *b.* 1962.
1955	Clitheroe (2nd), Ralph John Assheton, *b.* 1929, *s.* 1984, *m.*	Hon. Ralph C. *A.*, *b.* 1962.
1919	Clwyd (3rd), (John) Anthony Roberts, *b.* 1935, *s.* 1987, *m.*	Hon. J. Murray *R.*, *b.* 1971.
1948	Clydesmuir (2nd), Ronald John Bilsland Colville, KT, CB, MBE, TD, *b.* 1917, *s.* 1954, *m.*	Hon. David R. *C.*, *b.* 1949.
1960	Cobbold (2nd), David Antony Fromanteel Lytton Cobbold, *b.* 1937, *s.* 1987, *m.*	Hon. Henry F. L. *C.*, *b.* 1962.
1919	Cochrane of Cults (4th), (Ralph Henry) Vere Cochrane, *b.* 1926, *s.* 1990, *m.*	Hon. Thomas H. V. *C.*, *b.* 1957.
1954	Coleraine (2nd), (James) Martin (Bonar) Law, *b.* 1931, *s.* 1980, *w.*	Hon. James P. B. *L.*, *b.* 1975.
1873	Coleridge (5th), William Duke Coleridge, *b.* 1937, *s.* 1984, *m.*	Hon. James D. *C.*, *b.* 1967.
1946	Colgrain (3rd), David Colin Campbell, *b.* 1920, *s.* 1973, *m.*	Hon. Alastair C. L. *C.*, *b.* 1951.
1917	Colwyn (3rd), (Ian) Anthony Hamilton-Smith, CBE, *b.* 1942, *s.* 1966, *m.*	Hon. Craig P. *H.-S.*, *b.* 1968.
1956	Colyton (1st), Henry Lennox d'Aubigné Hopkinson, CMG, PC, *b.* 1902, *m.*	Alisdair J. M. *H.*, *b.* 1958.
1841	Congleton (8th), Christopher Patrick Parnell, *b.* 1930, *s.* 1967, *m.*	Hon. John P. C. *P.*, *b.* 1959.
1927	Cornwallis (3rd), Fiennes Neil Wykeham Cornwallis, OBE, *b.* 1921, *s.* 1982, *m.*	Hon. F. W. Jeremy *C.*, *b.* 1946.
1874	Cottesloe (5th), Cdr. John Tapling Fremantle, *b.* 1927, *s.* 1994, *m.*	Hon. Thomas F. H. *F.*, *b.* 1966.
1929	Craigmyle (3rd), Thomas Donald Mackay Shaw, *b.* 1923, *s.* 1944, *m.*	Hon. Thomas C. *S.*, *b.* 1960.
1899	Cranworth (3rd), Philip Bertram Gurdon, *b.* 1940, *s.* 1964, *m.*	Hon. Sacha W. R. *G.*, *b.* 1970.
1959	Crathorne (2nd), Charles James Dugdale, *b.* 1939, *s.* 1977, *m.*	Hon. Thomas A. J. *D.*, *b.* 1977.
1892	Crawshaw (4th), William Michael Clifton Brooks, *b.* 1933, *s.* 1946	Hon. David G. *B.*, *b.* 1934.
1940	Croft (2nd), Michael Henry Glendower Page Croft, *b.* 1916, *s.* 1947, *w.*	Hon. Bernard W. H. P. C. *C.*, *b.* 1949.
1797 I.	Crofton (7th), Guy Patrick Gilbert Crofton, *b.* 1951, *s.* 1989, *m.*	Hon. E. Harry P. *C.*, *b.* 1988.
1375	Cromwell (7th), Godfrey John Bewicke-Copley, *b.* 1960, *s.* 1982, *m.*	Hon. Thomas D. *B.-C.*, *b.* 1964.
1947	Crook (2nd), Douglas Edwin Crook, *b.* 1926, *s* 1989, *m.*	Hon. Robert D. E. *C.*, *b.* 1955.
1920	Cullen of Ashbourne (2nd), Charles Borlase Marsham Cokayne, MBE, *b.* 1912, *s.* 1932, *m.*	Hon. Edmund W. M. *C.*, *b.* 1916.
1914	Cunliffe (3rd), Roger Cunliffe, *b.* 1932, *s.* 1963, *m.*	Hon. Henry *C.*, *b.* 1962.
1927	Daresbury (3rd), Edward Gilbert Greenall, *b.* 1928, *s.* 1990, *m.*	Hon. Peter G. *G.*, *b.* 1953.
1924	Darling (2nd), Robert Charles Henry Darling, *b.* 1919, *s.* 1936, *m.*	Hon. R. Julian H. *D.*, *b.* 1944.
1946	Darwen (3rd), Roger Michael Davies, *b.* 1938, *s.* 1988, *m.*	Hon. Paul *D.*, *b.* 1962.
1932	Davies (3rd), David Davies, *b.* 1940, *s.* 1944, *m.*	Hon. David D. *D.*, *b.* 1975.
1812 I.	Decies (7th), Marcus Hugh Tristram de la Poer Beresford, *b.* 1948, *s.* 1992, *m.*	Hon. Robert M. *D. de la P. B.*, *b.* 1988.
1299	de Clifford (27th), John Edward Southwell Russell, *b.* 1928, *s.* 1982, *m.*	Hon. William S. *R.*, *b.* 1930.
1851	De Freyne (7th), Francis Arthur John French, *b.* 1927, *s.* 1935, *m.*	Hon. Fulke C. A. J. *F.*, *b.* 1957.
1821	Delamere (5th), Hugh George Cholmondeley, *b.* 1934, *s.* 1979, *m.*	Hon. Thomas P. G. *C.*, *b.* 1968.
1838	de Mauley (6th), Gerald John Ponsonby, *b.* 1921, *s.* 1962, *m.*	Col. Hon. Thomas M. *P.*, TD, *b.* 1930.
1937	Denham (2nd), Bertram Stanley Mitford Bowyer, KBE, PC, *b.* 1927, *s.* 1948, *m.*	Hon. Richard G. G. *B.*, *b.* 1959.
1834	Denman (5th), Charles Spencer Denman, CBE, MC, TD, *b.* 1916, *s.* 1971, *w.*	Hon. Richard T. S. *D.*, *b.* 1946.
1885	Deramore (6th), Richard Arthur de Yarburgh-Bateson, *b.* 1911, *s.* 1964, *m.*	None.
1887	De Ramsey (4th), John Ailwyn Fellowes, *b.* 1942, *s.* 1993, *m.*	Hon. Freddie J. *F.*, *b.* 1978.

Created	Title, order of succession, name, etc.	Heir
1264	*de Ros* (28th), Peter Trevor Maxwell, *b.* 1958, *s.* 1983, *m.* (*Premier Baron of England*)	Hon. Finbar J. *M.*, *b.* 1988.
1881	*Derwent* (5th), Robin Evelyn Leo Vanden-Bempde-Johnstone, LVO, *b.* 1930, *s.* 1986, *m.*	Hon. Francis P. H. *V.-B.-J.*, *b.* 1965.
1831	*de Saumarez* (7th), Eric Douglas Saumarez, *b.* 1956, *s.* 1991, *m.*	Hon. Victor T. *S.*, *b.* 1956.
1910	*de Villiers* (3rd), Arthur Percy de Villiers, *b.* 1911, *s.* 1934	Hon. Alexander C. *de V.*, *b.* 1940.
1930	*Dickinson* (2nd), Richard Clavering Hyett Dickinson, *b.* 1926, *s.* 1943, *m.*	Hon. Martin H. *D.*, *b.* 1961.
1620 I.*	*Digby* (12th), Edward Henry Kenelm Digby (6th *Brit. Baron, Digby*, 1765), *b.* 1924, *s.* 1964, *m.*	Hon. Henry N. K. *D.*, *b.* 1954.
1615	*Dormer* (16th), Joseph Spencer Philip Dormer, *b.* 1914, *s.* 1975	Geoffrey H. *D.*, *b.* 1920.
1943	*Dowding* (3rd), Piers Hugh Tremenheere Dowding, *b.* 1948, *s.* 1992	Hon. Mark D. J. *D.*, *b.* 1949.
1800 I.	*Dufferin and Clandeboye.* The 10th Baron died in 1991. Heir had not established his claim to the title at the time of going to press	Sir John Blackwood, Bt., *b.* 1944.
1929	*Dulverton* (3rd), (Gilbert) Michael Hamilton Wills, *b.* 1944, *s.* 1992, *m.*	Hon. Robert A. H. *W.*, *b.* 1983.
1800 I.	*Dunalley* (7th), Henry Francis Cornelius Prittie, *b.* 1948, *s.* 1992, *m.*	Hon. Joel H. *P.*, *b.* 1981.
1324 I.	*Dunboyne* (28th), Patrick Theobald Tower Butler, VRD, *b.* 1917, *s.* 1945, *m.*	Hon. John F. *B.*, *b.* 1951.
1802	*Dunleath* (5th), Michael Henry Mulholland, *b.* 1915, *s.* 1993, *w.*	Hon. Brian H. *M.*, *b.* 1950.
1439 I.	*Dunsany* (19th), Randal Arthur Henry Plunkett, *b.* 1906, *s.* 1957, *m.*	Hon. Edward J. C. *P.*, *b.* 1939.
1780	*Dynevor* (9th), Richard Charles Uryan Rhys, *b.* 1935, *s.* 1962	Hon. Hugo G. U. *R.*, *b.* 1966.
1857	*Ebury* (6th), Francis Egerton Grosvenor, *b.* 1934, *s.* 1957, *m.*	Hon. Julian F. M. *G.*, *b.* 1959.
1963	*Egremont* (2nd), & *Leconfield* (7th) (1859), John Max Henry Scawen Wyndham, *b.* 1948, *s.* 1972, *m.*	Hon. George R. V. *W.*, *b.* 1983.
1643	*Elibank* (14th), Alan D'Ardis Erskine-Murray, *b.* 1923, *s.* 1973, *m.*	Master of Elibank, *b.* 1964.
1802	*Ellenborough* (8th), Richard Edward Cecil Law, *b.* 1926, *s.* 1945, *m.*	Maj. Hon. Rupert E. H. *L.*, *b.* 1955.
1509 S.*	*Elphinstone* (19th), Alexander Mountstuart Elphinstone (5th *UK Baron Elphinstone*, 1885), *b.* 1980, *s.* 1994, *M.*	Hon. Angus J. *E.*, *b.* 1982.
1934	*Elton* (2nd), Rodney Elton, TD, *b.* 1930, *s.* 1973, *m.*	Hon. Edward P. *E.*, *b.* 1966.
1964	*Erroll of Hale* (1st), Frederick James Erroll, TD, PC, *b.* 1914, *m.*	None.
1627 S.	*Fairfax of Cameron* (14th), Nicholas John Albert Fairfax, *b.* 1956, *s.* 1964, *m.*	Hon. Edward N. T. *F.*, *b.* 1984.
1961	*Fairhaven* (3rd), Ailwyn Henry George Broughton, *b.* 1936, *s.* 1973, *m.*	Capt. James H. A. *B.*, *b.* 1963.
1916	*Faringdon* (3rd), Charles Michael Henderson, *b.* 1937, *s.* 1977, *m.*	Hon. James H. *H.*, *b.* 1961.
1756 I.	*Farnham* (12th), Barry Owen Somerset Maxwell, *b.* 1931, *s.* 1957, *m.*	Hon. Simon K. *M.*, *b.* 1933.
1856 I.	*Fermoy* (6th), Patrick Maurice Burke Roche, *b.* 1967, *s.* 1984	Hon. E. Hugh B. *R.*, *b.* 1972.
1826	*Feversham* (6th), Charles Antony Peter Duncombe, *b.* 1945, *s.* 1963, *m.*	Hon. Jasper O. S. *D.*, *b.* 1968.
1798 I.	*ffrench* (8th), Robuck John Peter Charles Mario ffrench, *b.* 1956, *s.* 1986, *m.*	Hon. John C. M. J. F. *ff.*, *b.* 1928.
1909	*Fisher* (3rd), John Vavasseur Fisher, DSC, *b.* 1921, *s.* 1955, *m.*	Hon. Patrick V. *F.*, *b.* 1953.
1295	*Fitzwalter* (21st), (Fitzwalter) Brook Plumptre, *b.* 1914, *title called out of abeyance*, 1953, *m.*	Hon. Julian B. *P.*, *b.* 1952.
1776	*Foley* (8th), Adrian Gerald Foley, *b.* 1923, *s.* 1927, *m.*	Hon. Thomas H. *F.*, *b.* 1961.
1445 S.	*Forbes* (22nd), Nigel Ivan Forbes, KBE (*Premier Lord of Scotland*), *b.* 1918, *s.* 1953, *m.*	Master of Forbes, *b.* 1946.
1821	*Forester* (8th), (George Cecil) Brooke Weld-Forester, *b.* 1938, *s.* 1977, *m.*	Hon. C. R. George *W.-F.*, *b.* 1975.
1922	*Forres* (4th), Alastair Stephen Grant Williamson, *b.* 1946, *s.* 1978, *m.*	Hon. George A. M. *W.*, *b.* 1972.
1917	*Forteviot* (4th), John James Evelyn Dewar, *b.* 1938, *s.* 1993, *m.*	Hon. Alexander J. E. *D.*, *b.* 1971.
1951	*Freyberg* (3rd), Valerian Bernard Freyberg, *b.* 1970, *s.* 1993	None.
1917	*Gainford* (3rd), Joseph Edward Pease, *b.* 1921, *s.* 1971, *m.*	Hon. George *P.*, *b.* 1926.
1818 I.	*Garvagh* (5th), (Alexander Leopold Ivor) George Canning, *b.* 1920, *s.* 1956, *m.*	Hon. Spencer G. S. de R. *C.*, *b.* 1953.
1942	*Geddes* (3rd), Euan Michael Ross Geddes, *b.* 1937, *s.* 1975, *m.*	Hon. James G. N. *G.*, *b.* 1969.
1876	*Gerard* (5th), Anthony Robert Hugo Gerard, *b.* 1949, *s.* 1992, *m.*	Hon. Rupert B. C. *G.*, *b.* 1981.
1824	*Gifford* (6th), Anthony Maurice Gifford, QC, *b.* 1940, *s.* 1961, *m.*	Hon. Thomas A. *G.*, *b.* 1967.
1917	*Gisborough* (3rd), Thomas Richard John Long Chaloner, *b.* 1927, *s.* 1951, *m.*	Hon. T. Peregrine L. *C.*, *b.* 1961.
1960	*Gladwyn* (1st), (Hubert Miles) Gladwyn Jebb, GCMG, GCVO, CB, *b.* 1900, *w.*	Hon. Miles A. G. *J.*, *b.* 1930.
1899	*Glanusk* (4th), David Russell Bailey, *b.* 1917, *s.* 1948, *m.*	Hon. Christopher R. *B.*, *b.* 1942.
1918	*Glenarthur* (4th), Simon Mark Arthur, *b.* 1944, *s.* 1976, *m.*	Hon. Edward A. *A.*, *b.* 1973.
1911	*Glenconner* (3rd), Colin Christopher Paget Tennant, *b.* 1926, *s.* 1983, *m.*	Hon. Charles E. P. *T.*, *b.* 1957.
1964	*Glendevon* (1st), John Adrian Hope, ERD, PC, *b.* 1912, *m.*	Hon. Julian J. S. *H.*, *b.* 1950.
1922	*Glendyne* (3rd), Robert Nivison, *b.* 1926, *s.* 1967, *m.*	Hon. John *N.*, *b.* 1960.
1939	*Glentoran* (3rd), (Thomas) Robin (Valerian) Dixon, CBE, *b.* 1935, *s.* 1995, *m.*	Hon. Daniel G. *D.*, *b.* 1959.
1909	*Gorell* (4th), Timothy John Radcliffe Barnes, *b.* 1927, *s.* 1963, *m.*	Hon. Ronald A. H. *B.*, *b.* 1931.

Created	Title, order of succession, name, etc.	Heir
1953	*Grantchester* (3rd), Christopher John Suenson-Taylor, *b.* 1951, *s.* 1995, *m.*	Hon. Jesse D. *S.-T.*, *b.* 1977.
1782	*Grantley* (8th), Richard William Brinsley Norton, *b.* 1956, *s.* 1995	Hon. Francis J. H. *N.*, *b.* 1960.
1794 I.	*Graves* (9th), Evelyn Paget Graves, *b.* 1926, *s.* 1994, *m.*	Hon. Timothy E. *G.*, *b.* 1960.
1445 S.	*Gray* (22nd), Angus Diarmid Ian Campbell-Gray, *b.* 1931, *s.* 1946, *m.*	Master of Gray, *b.* 1964.
1950	*Greenhill* (3rd), Malcolm Greenhill, *b.* 1924, *s.* 1989	None.
1927	*Greenway* (4th), Ambrose Charles Drexel Greenway, *b.* 1941, *s.* 1975, *m.*	Hon. Mervyn S. K. *G.*, *b.* 1942.
1902	*Grenfell* (3rd), Julian Pascoe Francis St Leger Grenfell, *b.* 1935, *s.* 1976, *m.*	Francis P. J. *G.*, *b.* 1938.
1944	*Gretton* (4th), John Lysander Gretton, *b.* 1975, *s.* 1989, *M.*	None.
1397	*Grey of Codnor* (5th), Charles Legh Shuldham Cornwall-Legh, CBE, AE, *b.* 1903, *title called out of abeyance* 1989, *w.*	Hon. Richard H. *C.-L.*, *b.* 1936.
1955	*Gridley* (2nd), Arnold Hudson Gridley, *b.* 1906, *s.* 1965, *m.*	Hon. Richard D. A. *G.*, *b.* 1956.
1964	*Grimston of Westbury* (2nd), Robert Walter Sigismund Grimston, *b.* 1925, *s.* 1979, *m.*	Hon. Robert J. S. *G.*, *b.* 1951.
1886	*Grimthorpe* (4th), Christopher John Beckett, OBE, *b.* 1915, *s.* 1963, *m.*	Hon. Edward J. *B.*, *b.* 1954.
1945	*Hacking* (3rd), Douglas David Hacking, *b.* 1938, *s.* 1971, *m.*	Hon. Douglas F. *H.*, *b.* 1968.
1950	*Haden-Guest* (4th), Peter Haden Haden-Guest, *b.* 1913, *s.* 1987, *m.*	Hon. Christopher *H.-G.*, *b.* 1948.
1886	*Hamilton of Dalzell* (4th), James Leslie Hamilton, *b.* 1938, *s.* 1990, *m.*	Hon. Gavin G. *H.*, *b.* 1968.
1874	*Hampton* (6th), Richard Humphrey Russell Pakington, *b.* 1925, *s.* 1974, *m.*	Hon. John H. A. *P.*, *b.* 1964.
1939	*Hankey* (2nd), Robert Maurice Alers Hankey, KCMG, KCVO, *b.* 1905, *s.* 1963, *m.*	Hon. Donald R. A. *H.*, *b.* 1938.
1958	*Harding of Petherton* (2nd), John Charles Harding, *b.* 1928, *s.* 1989, *m.*	Hon. William A. J. *H.*, *b.* 1969.
1910	*Hardinge of Penshurst* (3rd), George Edward Charles Hardinge, *b.* 1921, *s.* 1960, *m.*	Hon. Julian A. *H.*, *b.* 1945.
1876	*Harlech* (6th), Francis David Ormsby-Gore, *b.* 1954, *s.* 1985, *m.*	Hon. Jasset D. C. *O.-G.*, *b.* 1986.
1939	*Harmsworth* (3rd), Thomas Harold Raymond Harmsworth, *b.* 1939, *s.* 1990, *m.*	Hon. Dominic M. E. *H.*, *b.* 1973.
1815	*Harris* (6th), George Robert John Harris, *b.* 1920, *s.* 1984	Derek M. *H.*, *b.* 1916.
1954	*Harvey of Tasburgh* (2nd), Peter Charles Oliver Harvey, *b.* 1921, *s.* 1968, *w.*	Charles J. G. *H.*, *b.* 1951.
1295	*Hastings* (22nd), Edward Delaval Henry Astley, *b.* 1912, *s.* 1956, *m.*	Hon. Delaval T. H. *A.*, *b.* 1960.
1835	*Hatherton* (8th), Edward Charles Littleton, *b.* 1950, *s.* 1985, *m.*	Hon. Thomas E. *L.*, *b.* 1977.
1776	*Hawke* (11th), Edward George Hawke, TD, *b.* 1950, *s.* 1992, *m.*	None.
1927	*Hayter* (3rd), George Charles Hayter Chubb, KCVO, CBE, *b.* 1911, *s.* 1967, *m.*	Hon. G. William M. *C.*, *b.* 1943.
1945	*Hazlerigg* (2nd), Arthur Grey Hazlerigg, MC, TD, *b.* 1910, *s.* 1949, *w.*	Hon. Arthur G. *H.*, *b.* 1951.
1943	*Hemingford* (3rd), (Dennis) Nicholas Herbert, *b.* 1934, *s.* 1982, *m.*	Hon. Christopher D. C. *H.*, *b.* 1973.
1906	*Hemphill* (5th), Peter Patrick Fitzroy Martyn Martyn-Hemphill, *b.* 1928, *s.* 1957, *m.*	Hon. Charles A. M. *M.-H.*, *b.* 1954.
1799 I.*	*Henley* (8th), Oliver Michael Robert Eden (6th *UK Baron, Northington,* 1885), *b.* 1953, *s.* 1977, *m.*	Hon. John W. O. *E.*, *b.* 1988.
1800 I.*	*Henniker* (8th), John Patrick Edward Chandos Henniker-Major, KCMG, CVO, MC (4th *UK Baron, Hartismere,* 1866), *b.* 1916, *s.* 1980, *m.*	Hon. Mark I. P. C. *H.-M.*, *b.* 1947.
1886	*Herschell* (3rd), Rognvald Richard Farrer Herschell, *b.* 1923, *s.* 1929, *m.*	None.
1935	*Hesketh* (3rd), Thomas Alexander Fermor-Hesketh, PC, *b.* 1950, *s.* 1955, *m.*	Hon. Frederick H. *F.-H.*, *b.* 1988.
1828	*Heytesbury* (6th), Francis William Holmes à Court, *b.* 1931, *s.* 1971, *m.*	Hon. James W. *à C.*, *b.* 1967.
1886	*Hindlip* (6th), Charles Henry Allsopp, *b.* 1940, *s.* 1993, *m.*	Hon. Henry W. *A.*, *b.* 1973.
1950	*Hives* (2nd), John Warwick Hives, CBE, *b.* 1913, *s.* 1965, *m.*	Matthew P. *H.*, *b.* 1971.
1912	*Hollenden* (3rd), Gordon Hope Hope-Morley, *b.* 1914, *s.* 1977, *m.*	Hon. Ian H. *H.-M.*, *b.* 1946.
1897	*HolmPatrick* (4th), Hans James David Hamilton, *b.* 1955, *s.* 1991, *m.*	Hon. Ion H. J. *H.*, *b.* 1956.
1933	*Horder* (2nd), Thomas Mervyn Horder, *b.* 1910, *s.* 1955	None.
1797 I.	*Hotham* (8th), Henry Durand Hotham, *b.* 1940, *s.* 1967, *m.*	Hon. William B. *H.*, *b.* 1972.
1881	*Hothfield* (6th), Anthony Charles Sackville Tufton, *b.* 1939, *s.* 1991, *m.*	Hon. William S. *T.*, *b.* 1977.
1597	*Howard de Walden* (9th), John Osmael Scott-Ellis, TD (5th *UK Baron, Seaford,* 1826), *b.* 1912, *s.* 1946, *m.*	To Barony of Howard de Walden, four co-heiresses. To Barony of Seaford, Colin H. F. *Ellis*, *b.* 1946.
1930	*Howard of Penrith* (2nd), Francis Philip Howard, *b.* 1905, *s.* 1939, *m.*	Hon. Philip E. *H.*, *b.* 1945.
1960	*Howick of Glendale* (2nd), Charles Evelyn Baring, *b.* 1937, *s.* 1973, *m.*	Hon. David E. C. *B.*, *b.* 1975.
1796 I.	*Huntingfield* (7th), Joshua Charles Vanneck, *b.* 1954, *s.* 1994, *m.*	Hon. Gerard C. A. *V.*, *b.* 1985.
1866	*Hylton* (5th), Raymond Hervey Jolliffe, *b.* 1932, *s.* 1967, *m.*	Hon. William H. M. *J.*, *b.* 1967.
1933	*Iliffe* (2nd), Edward Langton Iliffe, *b.* 1908, *s.* 1960, *m.*	Robert P. R. *I.*, *b.* 1944.
1543 I.	*Inchiquin* (18th), Conor Myles John O'Brien, *b.* 1943, *s.* 1982, *m.*	Murrough R. *O'B.*, *b.* 1910.
1962	*Inchyra* (2nd), Robert Charles Reneke Hoyer Millar, *b.* 1935, *s.* 1989, *m.*	Hon. C. James C. H. *M.*, *b.* 1962.

Created	Title, order of succession, name, etc.	Heir
1964	*Inglewood* (2nd), (William) Richard Fletcher-Vane, *b.* 1951, *s.* 1989, *m.*	Hon. Henry W. F. *F.-V.*, *b.* 1990.
1919	*Inverforth* (4th), Andrew Peter Weir, *b.* 1966, *s.* 1982	Hon. John V. *W.*, *b.* 1935.
1941	*Ironside* (2nd), Edmund Oslac Ironside, *b.* 1924, *s.* 1959, *m.*	Hon. Charles E. G. *I.*, *b.* 1956.
1952	*Jeffreys* (3rd), Christopher Henry Mark Jeffreys, *b.* 1957, *s.* 1986, *m.*	Hon. Arthur M. H. *J.*, *b.* 1989.
1906	*Joicey* (5th), James Michael Joicey, *b.* 1953, *s.* 1993, *m.*	Hon. William J. *J.*, *b.* 1990.
1937	*Kenilworth* (4th), (John) Randle Siddeley, *b.* 1954, *s.* 1981, *m.*	Hon. William R. J. *S.*, *b.* 1992.
1935	*Kennet* (2nd), Wayland Hilton Young, *b.* 1923, *s.* 1960, *m.*	Hon. W. A. Thoby *Y.*, *b.* 1957.
1776 I.*	*Kensington* (8th), Hugh Ivor Edwardes (5th *UK Baron, Kensington*, 1886), *b.* 1933, *s.* 1981, *m.*	Hon. W. Owen A. *E.*, *b.* 1964.
1951	*Kenswood* (2nd), John Michael Howard Whitfield, *b.* 1930, *s.* 1963, *m.*	Hon. Michael C. *W.*, *b.* 1955.
1788	*Kenyon* (6th), Lloyd Tyrell-Kenyon, *b.* 1947, *s.* 1993, *m.*	Hon. Lloyd N. *T.-K.*, *b.* 1972.
1947	*Kershaw* (4th), Edward John Kershaw, *b.* 1936, *s.* 1962, *m.*	Hon. John C. E. *K.*, *b.* 1971.
1943	*Keyes* (2nd), Roger George Bowlby Keyes, *b.* 1919, *s.* 1945, *m.*	Hon. Charles W. P. *K.*, *b.* 1951.
1909	*Kilbracken* (3rd), John Raymond Godley, DSC, *b.* 1920, *s.* 1950	Hon. Christopher J. *G.*, *b.* 1945.
1900	*Killanin* (3rd), Michael Morris, MBE, TD, *b.* 1914, *s.* 1927, *m.*	Hon. G. Redmond F. *M.*, *b.* 1947.
1943	*Killearn* (2nd), Graham Curtis Lampson, *b.* 1919, *s.* 1964, *m.*	Hon. Victor M. G. A. *L.*, *b.* 1941.
1789 I.	*Kilmaine* (7th), John David Henry Browne, *b.* 1948, *s.* 1978, *m.*	Hon. John F. S. *B.*, *b.* 1983.
1831	*Kilmarnock* (7th), Alastair Ivor Gilbert Boyd, *b.* 1927, *s.* 1975, *m.*	Hon. Robin J. *B.*, *b.* 1941.
1941	*Kindersley* (3rd), Robert Hugh Molesworth Kindersley, *b.* 1929, *s.* 1976, *m.*	Hon. Rupert J. M. *K.*, *b.* 1955.
1223 I.	*Kingsale* (35th), John de Courcy (*Premier Baron of Ireland*), *b.* 1941, *s.* 1969	Nevinson R. *de C.*, *b.* 1920.
1682 S.*	*Kinnaird* (13th), Graham Charles Kinnaird (5th *UK Baron, Kinnaird*, 1860), *b.* 1912, *s.* 1972, *m.*	None.
1902	*Kinross* (5th), Christopher Patrick Balfour, *b.* 1949, *s.* 1985, *m.*	Hon. Alan I. *B.*, *b.* 1978.
1951	*Kirkwood* (3rd), David Harvie Kirkwood, PH.D., *b.* 1931, *s.* 1970, *m.*	Hon. James S. *K.*, *b.* 1937.
1800 I.	*Langford* (9th), Col. Geoffrey Alexander Rowley-Conwy, OBE, *b.* 1912, *s.* 1953, *m.*	Hon. Owain G. *R.-C.*, *b.* 1958.
1942	*Latham* (2nd), Dominic Charles Latham, *b.* 1954, *s.* 1970	Anthony M. *L.*, *b.* 1954.
1431	*Latymer* (8th), Hugo Nevill Money-Coutts, *b.* 1926, *s.* 1987, *m.*	Hon. Crispin J. A. N. *M.-C.*, *b.* 1955.
1869	*Lawrence* (5th), David John Downer Lawrence, *b.* 1937, *s.* 1968	None.
1947	*Layton* (3rd), Geoffrey Michael Layton, *b.* 1947, *s.* 1989, *m.*	Hon. David *L.*, MBE, *b.* 1914.
1839	*Leigh* (5th), John Piers Leigh, *b.* 1935, *s.* 1979, *m.*	Hon. Christopher D. P. *L.*, *b.* 1960.
1962	*Leighton of St Mellons* (2nd), (John) Leighton Seager, *b.* 1922, *s.* 1963, *m.*	Hon. Robert W. H. L. *S.*, *b.* 1955.
1797	*Lilford* (7th), George Vernon Powys, *b.* 1931, *s.* 1949, *m.*	Hon. Mark V. *P.*, *b.* 1975.
1945	*Lindsay of Birker* (3rd), James Francis Lindsay, *b.* 1945, *s.* 1994, *m.*	Hon. Thomas M. *L.*, *b.* 1915.
1758 I.	*Lisle* (7th), John Nicholas Horace Lysaght, *b.* 1903, *s.* 1919, *m.*	Patrick J. *L.*, *b.* 1931.
1850	*Londesborough* (9th), Richard John Denison, *b.* 1959, *s.* 1968, *m.*	Hon. James F. *D.*, *b.* 1990.
1541 I.	*Louth* (16th), Otway Michael James Oliver Plunkett, *b.* 1929, *s.* 1950, *m.*	Hon. Jonathan O. *P.*, *b.* 1952.
1458 S.*	*Lovat* (16th), Simon Fraser, (5th *UK Baron, Lovat*, 1837), *b.* 1977, *s.* 1995, *M.*	Jack *F.*, *b.* 1984.
1946	*Lucas of Chilworth* (2nd), Michael William George Lucas, *b.* 1926, *s.* 1967, *m.*	Hon. Simon W. *L.*, *b.* 1957.
1663	*Lucas* (11th) & *Dingwall* (8th) (*Scottish Lordship* 1609), Ralph Matthew Palmer, *b.* 1951, *s.* 1991, *m.*	Hon. Lewis E. *P.*, *b.* 1987
1929	*Luke* (2nd), Ian St John Lawson-Johnston, KCVO, TD, *b.* 1905, *s.* 1943, *m.*	Hon. Arthur C. St J. *L.-J.*, *b.* 1933.
1914	*Lyell* (3rd), Charles Lyell, *b.* 1939, *s.* 1943	None.
1859	*Lyveden* (6th), Ronald Cecil Vernon, *b.* 1915, *s.* 1973, *m.*	Hon. Jack L. *V.*, *b.* 1938.
1959	*MacAndrew* (3rd), Christopher Anthony Colin MacAndrew, *b.* 1945, *s.* 1989, *m.*	Hon. Oliver C. J. *M.*, *b.* 1983.
1776 I.	*Macdonald* (8th), Godfrey James Macdonald of Macdonald, *b.* 1947, *s.* 1970, *m.*	Hon. Godfrey E. H. T. *M.*, *b.* 1982.
1949	*Macdonald of Gwaenysgor* (2nd), Gordon Ramsay Macdonald, *b.* 1915, *s.* 1966, *m.*	None.
1937	*McGowan* (3rd), Harry Duncan Cory McGowan, *b.* 1938, *s.* 1966, *m.*	Hon. Harry J. C. *M.*, *b.* 1971.
1922	*Maclay* (3rd), Joseph Paton Maclay, *b.* 1942, *s.* 1969, *m.*	Hon. Joseph P. *M.*, *b.* 1977.
1955	*McNair* (3rd), Duncan James McNair, *b.* 1947, *s.* 1989, *m.*	Hon. Thomas J. *M.*, *b.* 1990.
1951	*Macpherson of Drumochter* (2nd), (James) Gordon Macpherson, *b.* 1924, *s.* 1965, *m.*	Hon. James A. *M.*, *b.* 1979.
1937	*Mancroft* (3rd), Benjamin Lloyd Stormont Mancroft, *b.* 1957, *s.* 1987, *m.*	None.
1807	*Manners* (5th), John Robert Cecil Manners, *b.* 1923, *s.* 1972, *m.*	Hon. John H. R. *M.*, *b.* 1956.
1922	*Manton* (3rd), Joseph Rupert Eric Robert Watson, *b.* 1924, *s.* 1968, *m.*	Maj. Hon. Miles R. M. *W.*, *b.* 1958.
1908	*Marchamley* (4th), William Francis Whiteley, *b.* 1968, *s.* 1994	None.
1964	*Margadale* (1st), John Granville Morrison, TD, *b.* 1906, *w.*	Hon. James I. *M.*, TD, *b.* 1930.
1961	*Marks of Broughton* (2nd), Michael Marks, *b.* 1920, *s.* 1964	Hon. Simon R. *M.*, *b.* 1950.
1964	*Martonmere* (2nd), John Stephen Robinson, *b.* 1963, *s.* 1989	David A. *R.*, *b.* 1965.

Created	Title, order of succession, name, etc.	Heir
1776 I.	*Massy* (9th), Hugh Hamon John Somerset Massy, *b.* 1921, *s.* 1958, *m.*	Hon. David H. S. *M.*, *b.* 1947.
1935	*May* (3rd), Michael St John May, *b.* 1931, *s.* 1950, *m.*	Hon. Jasper B. St J. *M.*, *b.* 1965.
1928	*Melchett* (4th), Peter Robert Henry Mond, *b.* 1948, *s.* 1973	None.
1925	*Merrivale* (3rd), Jack Henry Edmond Duke, *b.* 1917, *s.* 1951, *m.*	Hon. Derek J. P. *D.*, *b.* 1948.
1911	*Merthyr.* Disclaimed for life 1977 (*Trevor Oswin Lewis, Bt.*, CBE, *b.* 1935, *s.* 1977, *m.*)	David T. *L.*, *b.* 1977.
1919	*Meston* (3rd), James Meston, *b.* 1950, *s.* 1984, *m.*	Hon. Thomas J. D. *M.*, *b.* 1977.
1838	*Methuen* (7th), Robert Alexander Holt Methuen, *b.* 1931, *s.* 1994, *m.*	Christopher P. M. C. *Methuen-Campbell*, *b.* 1928.
1711	*Middleton* (12th), (Digby) Michael Godfrey John Willoughby, MC, *b.* 1921, *s.* 1970, *m.*	Hon. Michael C. J. *W.*, *b.* 1948.
1939	*Milford* (3rd), Hugo John Laurence Philipps, *b.* 1929, *s.* 1993, *m.*	Hon. Guy W. *P.*, *b.* 1961.
1933	*Milne* (2nd), George Douglass Milne, TD, *b.* 1909, *s.* 1948, *m.*	Hon. George A. *M.*, *b.* 1941.
1951	*Milner of Leeds* (2nd), Arthur James Michael Milner, AE, *b.* 1923, *s.* 1967, *m.*	Hon. Richard J. *M.*, *b.* 1959.
1947	*Milverton* (2nd), Revd Fraser Arthur Richard Richards, *b.* 1930, *s.* 1978, *m.*	Hon. Michael H. *R.*, *b.* 1936.
1873	*Moncreiff* (5th), Harry Robert Wellwood Moncreiff, *b.* 1915, *s.* 1942, *w.*	Hon. Rhoderick H. W. *M.*, *b.* 1954.
1884	*Monk Bretton* (3rd), John Charles Dodson, *b.* 1924, *s.* 1933, *m.*	Hon. Christopher M. *D.*, *b.* 1958.
1885	*Monkswell* (5th), Gerard Collier, *b.* 1947, *s.* 1984, *m.*	Hon. James A. *C.*, *b.* 1977.
1728	*Monson* (11th), John Monson, *b.* 1932, *s.* 1958, *m.*	Hon. Nicholas J. *M.*, *b.* 1955.
1885	*Montagu of Beaulieu* (3rd), Edward John Barrington Douglas-Scott-Montagu, *b.* 1926, *s.* 1929, *m.*	Hon. Ralph *D.-S.-M.*, *b.* 1961.
1839	*Monteagle of Brandon* (6th), Gerald Spring Rice, *b.* 1926, *s.* 1946, *m.*	Hon. Charles J. S. *R.*, *b.* 1953.
1943	*Moran* (2nd), (Richard) John (McMoran) Wilson, KCMG, *b.* 1924, *s.* 1977, *m.*	Hon. James M. *W.*, *b.* 1952.
1918	*Morris* (3rd), Michael David Morris, *b.* 1937, *s.* 1975, *m.*	Hon. Thomas A. S. *M.*, *b.* 1982.
1950	*Morris of Kenwood* (2nd), Philip Geoffrey Morris, *b.* 1928, *s.* 1954, *m.*	Hon. Jonathan D. *M.*, *b.* 1968.
1945	*Morrison* (2nd), Dennis Morrison, *b.* 1914, *s.* 1953	None.
1831	*Mostyn* (5th), Roger Edward Lloyd Lloyd-Mostyn, MC, *b.* 1920, *s.* 1965, *m.*	Hon. Llewellyn R. L. *L.-M.*, *b.* 1948.
1933	*Mottistone* (4th), David Peter Seely, CBE, *b.* 1920, *s.* 1966, *m.*	Hon. Peter J. P. *S.*, *b.* 1949.
1945	*Mountevans* (3rd), Edward Patrick Broke Evans, *b.* 1943, *s.* 1974, *m.*	Hon. Jeffrey de C. R. *E.*, *b.* 1948.
1283	*Mowbray* (26th), *Segrave* (27th) (1283), & *Stourton* (23rd) (1448), Charles Edward Stourton, CBE, *b.* 1923, *s.* 1965, *m.*	Hon. Edward W. S. *S.*, *b.* 1953.
1932	*Moyne* (3rd), Jonathan Bryan Guinness, *b.* 1930, *s.* 1992, *m.*	Hon. Jasper J. R. *G.*, *b.* 1954.
1929	*Moynihan.* Barony dormant since the 3rd Baron died in November 1991. His trustees recognized Daniel Antony Patrick Berkeley Moynihan, (*b.* January 1991) as the financial heir of the 3rd Baron but the succession to the title is not settled	
1781 I.	*Muskerry* (9th), Robert Fitzmaurice Deane, *b.* 1948, *s.* 1988, *m.*	Hon. Jonathan F. *D.*, *b.* 1986.
1627 S.	*Napier* (14th) & *Ettrick* (5th) (*UK* 1872), Francis Nigel Napier, KCVO, *b.* 1930, *s.* 1954, *m.*	Master of Napier, *b.* 1962.
1868	*Napier of Magdala* (6th), Robert Alan Napier, *b.* 1940, *s.* 1987, *m.*	Hon. James R. *N.*, *b.* 1966.
1940	*Nathan* (2nd), Roger Carol Michael Nathan, *b.* 1922, *s.* 1963, *m.*	Hon. Rupert H. B. *N.*, *b.* 1957.
1960	*Nelson of Stafford* (3rd), Henry Roy George Nelson, *b.* 1943, *s.* 1995, *m.*	Hon. Alistair W. H. *N.*, *b.* 1973.
1959	*Netherthorpe* (3rd), James Frederick Turner, *b.* 1964, *s.* 1982, *m.*	Hon. Andrew J. E. *T.*, *b.* 1993.
1946	*Newall* (2nd), Francis Storer Eaton Newall, *b.* 1930, *s.* 1963, *m.*	Hon. Richard H. E. *N.*, *b.* 1961.
1776 I.	*Newborough* (7th), Robert Charles Michael Vaughan Wynn, DSC, *b.* 1917, *s.* 1965, *m.*	Hon. Robert V. *W.*, *b.* 1949.
1892	*Newton* (5th), Richard Thomas Legh, *b.* 1950, *s.* 1992, *m.*	Hon. Piers R. *L.*, *b.* 1979.
1930	*Noel-Buxton* (3rd), Martin Connal Noel-Buxton, *b.* 1940, *s.* 1980, *m.*	Hon. Charles C. *N.-B.*, *b.* 1975.
1957	*Norrie* (2nd), (George) Willoughby Moke Norrie, *b.* 1936, *s.* 1977, *m.*	Hon. Mark W. J. *N.*, *b.* 1972.
1884	*Northbourne* (5th), Christopher George Walter James, *b.* 1926, *s.* 1982, *m.*	Hon. Charles W. H. *J.*, *b.* 1960.
1866	*Northbrook* (6th), Francis Thomas Baring, *b.* 1954, *s.* 1990, *m.*	None.
1878	*Norton* (8th), James Nigel Arden Adderley, *b.* 1947, *s.* 1993, *m.*	Hon. Edward J. A. *A.*, *b.* 1982.
1906	*Nunburnholme* (4th), Ben Charles Wilson, *b.* 1928, *s.* 1974	Hon. Charles T. *W.*, *b.* 1935.
	Oaksey, see *Trevethin and Oaksey*	
1950	*Ogmore* (2nd), Gwilym Rees Rees-Williams, *b.* 1931, *s.* 1976, *m.*	Hon. Morgan *R.-W.*, *b.* 1937.
1870	*O'Hagan* (4th), Charles Towneley Strachey, *b.* 1945, *s.* 1961	Hon. Richard T. *S.*, *b.* 1950.
1868	*O'Neill* (4th), Raymond Arthur Clanaboy O'Neill, TD, *b.* 1933, *s.* 1944, *m.*	Hon. Shane S. C. *O'N.*, *b.* 1965.
1836 I.*	*Oranmore and Browne* (4th), Dominick Geoffrey Edward Browne (2nd *UK Baron Mereworth*, 1926), *b.* 1901, *s.* 1927, *m.*	Hon. Dominick G. T. *B.*, *b.* 1929.
1933	*Palmer* (4th), Adrian Bailie Nottage Palmer, *b.* 1951, *s.* 1990, *m.*	Hon. Hugo B. R. *P.*, *b.* 1980.
1914	*Parmoor* (4th), (Frederick Alfred) Milo Cripps, *b.* 1929, *s.* 1977	M. Anthony L. *C.*, CBE, DSO, TD, QC, *b.* 1913.

Created	Title, order of succession, name, etc.	Heir

1937 Pender (3rd), John Willoughby Denison-Pender, b. 1933, s. 1965, m. Hon. Henry J. R. D.-P., b. 1968.
1866 Penrhyn (6th), Malcolm Frank Douglas-Pennant, DSO, MBE, b. 1908, s. 1967, m. Hon. Nigel D.-P., b. 1909.
1603 Petre (18th), John Patrick Lionel Petre, b. 1942, s. 1989, m. Hon. Dominic W. P., b. 1966.
1918 Phillimore (5th), Francis Stephen Phillimore, b. 1944, s. 1994, m. Hon. Tristan A. S. P., b. 1977.
1945 Piercy (3rd), James William Piercy, b. 1946, s. 1981 Hon. Mark E. P. P., b. 1953.
1827 Plunket (8th), Robin Rathmore Plunket, b. 1925, s. 1975, m. Hon. Shaun A. F. S. P., b. 1931.
1831 Poltimore (7th), Mark Coplestone Bampfylde, b. 1957, s. 1978, m. Hon. Henry A. W. B., b. 1985.
1690 S. Polwarth (10th), Henry Alexander Hepburne-Scott, TD, b. 1916, s. 1944, m. Master of Polwarth, b. 1947.
1930 Ponsonby of Shulbrede (4th), Frederick Matthew Thomas Ponsonby, b. 1958, s. 1990 None.
1958 Poole (2nd), David Charles Poole, b. 1945, s. 1993, m. Hon. Oliver J. P., b. 1972.
1852 Raglan (5th), FitzRoy John Somerset, b. 1927, s. 1964 Hon. Geoffrey S., b. 1932.
1932 Rankeillour (4th), Peter St Thomas More Henry Hope, b. 1935, s. 1967 Michael R. H., b. 1940.
1953 Rathcavan (3rd), Hugh Detmar Torrens O'Neill, b. 1939, s. 1994, m. Hon. François H. N. O'N., b. 1984.
1916 Rathcreedan (3rd), Christopher John Norton, b. 1949, s. 1990, m. Hon. Adam G. N., b. 1952.
1868 I. Rathdonnell (5th), Thomas Benjamin McClintock–Bunbury, b. 1938, s. 1959, m. Hon. William L. M.-B., b. 1966.
1911 Ravensdale (3rd), Nicholas Mosley, MC, b. 1923, s. 1966, m. Hon. Shaun N. M., b. 1949.
1821 Ravensworth (8th), Arthur Waller Liddell, b. 1924, s. 1950, m. Hon. Thomas A. H. L., b. 1954.
1821 Rayleigh (6th), John Gerald Strutt, b. 1960, s. 1988, m. Hon. John F. S., b. 1993.
1937 Rea (3rd), John Nicolas Rea, MD, b. 1928, s. 1981, m. Hon. Matthew J. R., b. 1956.
1628 S. Reay (14th), Hugh William Mackay, b. 1937, s. 1963, m. Master of Reay, b. 1965.
1902 Redesdale (6th), Rupert Bertram Mitford, b. 1967, s. 1991 None.
1940 Reith. Disclaimed for life 1972 (Christopher John Reith, b. 1928, s. 1971, m.) Hon. James H. J. R., b. 1971.
1928 Remnant (3rd), James Wogan Remnant, CVO, b. 1930, s. 1967, m. Hon. Philip J. R., b. 1954.
1806 I. Rendlesham (8th), Charles Anthony Hugh Thellusson, b. 1915, s. 1943, w. Hon. Charles W. B. T., b. 1954.
1933 Rennell (3rd), (John Adrian) Tremayne Rodd, b. 1935, s. 1978, m. Hon. James R. D. T. R., b. 1978.
1964 Renwick (2nd), Harry Andrew Renwick, b. 1935, s. 1973, m. Hon. Robert J. R., b. 1966.
1885 Revelstoke (5th), John Baring, b. 1934, s. 1994 Hon. James C. B., b. 1938.
1905 Ritchie of Dundee (5th), (Harold) Malcolm Ritchie, b. 1919, s. 1978, m. Hon. C. Rupert R. R., b. 1958.
1935 Riverdale (2nd), Robert Arthur Balfour, b. 1901, s. 1957, w. Hon. Mark R. B., b. 1927.
1961 Robertson of Oakridge (2nd), William Ronald Robertson, b. 1930, s. 1974, m. Hon. William B. E. R., b. 1975.
1938 Roborough (3rd), Henry Massey Lopes, b. 1940, s. 1992, m. Hon. Massey J. H. L., b. 1969.
1931 Rochester (2nd), Foster Charles Lowry Lamb, b. 1916, s. 1955, m. Hon. David C. L., b. 1944.
1934 Rockley (3rd), James Hugh Cecil, b. 1934, s. 1976, m. Hon. Anthony R. C., b. 1961.
1782 Rodney (10th), George Brydges Rodney, b. 1953, s. 1992 Nicholas S. H. R., b. 1947.
1651 S.* Rollo (13th), Eric John Stapylton Rollo (4th UK Baron, Dunning, 1869), b. 1915, s. 1947, m. Master of Rollo, b. 1943.
1959 Rootes (3rd), Nicholas Geoffrey Rootes, b. 1951, s. 1992, m. William B. R., b. 1944.
1796 I.* Rossmore (7th), William Warner Westenra (6th UK Baron, Rossmore, 1838), b. 1931, s. 1958, m. Hon. Benedict W. W., b. 1983.
1939 Rotherwick (2nd), (Herbert) Robin Cayzer, b. 1912, s. 1958, w. Hon. H. Robin C., b. 1954.
1885 Rothschild (4th), (Nathaniel Charles) Jacob Rothschild, b. 1936, s. 1990, m. Hon. Nathaniel P. V. J. R., b. 1971.
1911 Rowallan (4th), John Polson Cameron Corbett, b. 1947, s. 1993, m. Hon. Jason W. P. C. C., b. 1972.
1947 Rugby (3rd), Robert Charles Maffey, b. 1951, s. 1990, m. Hon. Timothy J. H. M., b. 1975.
1919 Russell of Liverpool (3rd), Simon Gordon Jared Russell, b. 1952, s. 1981, m. Hon. Edward C. S. R., b. 1985.
1876 Sackville (6th), Lionel Bertrand Sackville-West, b. 1913, s. 1965, m. Hugh R. I. S.-W., MC, b. 1919.
1964 St Helens (2nd), Richard Francis Hughes-Young, b. 1945, s. 1980, m. Hon. Henry T. H.-Y., b. 1986.
1559 St John of Bletso (21st), Anthony Tudor St John, b. 1957, s. 1978 Edmund O. St J., WS, b. 1927.
1887 St Levan (4th), John Francis Arthur St Aubyn, DSC, b. 1919, s. 1978, m. Hon. O. Piers St A., MC, b. 1920.
1885 St Oswald (5th), Derek Edward Anthony Winn, b. 1919, s. 1984, m. Hon. Charles R. A. W., b. 1959.
1960 Sanderson of Ayot. Disclaimed for life 1971 (Alan Lindsay Sanderson, b. 1931, s. 1971, m.) Hon. Michael S., b. 1959.
1945 Sandford (2nd), Revd John Cyril Edmondson, DSC, b. 1920, s. 1959, m. Hon. James J. M. E., b. 1949.
1871 Sandhurst (5th), (John Edward) Terence Mansfield, DFC, b. 1920, s. 1964, m. Hon. Guy R. J. M., b. 1949.
1802 Sandys (7th), Richard Michael Oliver Hill, b. 1931, s. 1961, m. The Marquess of Downshire (see page 143).
1888 Savile (3rd), George Halifax Lumley-Savile, b. 1919, s. 1931 Hon. Henry L. T. L.-S., b. 1923.
1447 Saye and Sele (21st), Nathaniel Thomas Allen Fiennes, b. 1920, s. 1968, m. Hon. Richard I. F., b. 1959.

Created	Title, order of succession, name, etc.	Heir
1932	Selsdon (3rd), Malcolm McEacharn Mitchell-Thomson, b. 1937, s. 1963, m.	Hon. Callum M. M. M.-T., b. 1969.
1489 s.	Sempill (21st), James William Stuart Whitemore Sempill, b. 1949, s. 1995, m.	Master of Sempill, b. 1979.
1916	Shaughnessy (3rd), William Graham Shaughnessy, b. 1922, s. 1938, m.	Hon. Michael J. S., b. 1946.
1946	Shepherd (2nd), Malcolm Newton Shepherd, PC, b. 1918, s. 1954, m.	Hon. Graeme G. S., b. 1949.
1964	Sherfield (1st), Roger Mellor Makins, GCB, GCMG, FRS, b. 1904, w.	Hon. Christopher J. M., b. 1942.
1902	Shuttleworth (5th), Charles Geoffrey Nicholas Kay-Shuttleworth, b. 1948, s. 1975, m.	Hon. Thomas E. K.-S., b. 1976.
1950	Silkin. Disclaimed for life 1972 (Arthur Silkin, b. 1916, s. 1972, m.)	Hon. Christopher L. S., b. 1947.
1963	Silsoe (2nd), David Malcolm Trustram Eve, QC, b. 1930, s. 1976, m.	Hon. Simon R. T. E., b. 1966.
1947	Simon of Wythenshawe (2nd), Roger Simon, b. 1913, s. 1960, m.	Hon. Matthew S., b. 1955.
1449 s.	Sinclair (17th), Charles Murray Kennedy St Clair, CVO, b. 1914, s. 1957, m.	Master of Sinclair, b. 1968.
1957	Sinclair of Cleeve (3rd), John Lawrence Robert Sinclair, b. 1953, s. 1985	None.
1919	Sinha (4th), Susanta Prasanna Sinha, b. 1953, s. 1989, m.	Hon. A. K. S., b. 1930.
1828	Skelmersdale (7th), Roger Bootle-Wilbraham, b. 1945, s. 1973, m.	Hon. Andrew B.-W., b. 1977.
1916	Somerleyton (3rd), Savile William Francis Crossley, KCVO, b. 1928, s. 1959, m. Master of the Horse	Hon. Hugh F. S. C., b. 1971.
1784	Somers (9th), Philip Sebastian Somers Cocks, b. 1948, s. 1995	†
1780	Southampton (6th), Charles James FitzRoy, b. 1928, s. 1989, m.	Hon. Edward C. F., b. 1955.
1959	Spens (3rd), Patrick Michael Rex Spens, b. 1942, s. 1984, m.	Hon. Patrick N. G. S., b. 1968.
1640	Stafford (15th), Francis Melfort William Fitzherbert, b. 1954, s. 1986, m.	Hon. Benjamin J.B. F., b. 1983.
1938	Stamp (4th), Trevor Charles Bosworth Stamp, MD, FRCP, b. 1935, s. 1987, m.	Hon. Nicholas C. T. S., b. 1978.
1839	Stanley of Alderley (8th) & Sheffield (8th) (1738 I.), Thomas Henry Oliver Stanley (7th UK Baron Eddisbury, 1848), b. 1927, s. 1971, m.	Hon. Richard O. S., b. 1956.
1318	Strabolgi (11th), David Montague de Burgh Kenworthy, b. 1914, s. 1953, m.	Andrew D. W. K., b. 1967.
1954	Strang (2nd), Colin Strang, b. 1922, s. 1978, m.	None.
1955	Strathalmond (3rd), William Roberton Fraser, b. 1947, s. 1976, m.	Hon. William G. F., b. 1976.
1936	Strathcarron (2nd), David William Anthony Blyth Macpherson, b. 1924, s. 1937, m.	Hon. Ian D. P. M., b. 1949.
1955	Strathclyde (2nd), Thomas Galloway Dunlop du Roy de Blicquy Galbraith, PC, b. 1960, s. 1985, m.	Hon. Charles W. du R. de B. G., b. 1962.
1900	Strathcona and Mount Royal (4th), Donald Euan Palmer Howard, b. 1923, s. 1959, m.	Hon. D. Alexander S. H., b. 1961.
1836	Stratheden (6th) & Campbell (6th) (1841), Donald Campbell, b. 1934, s. 1987, m.	Hon. David A. C., b. 1963.
1884	Strathspey (6th), James Patrick Trevor Grant of Grant, b. 1943, s. 1992, m.	Hon. Michael P. F. G., b. 1953.
1838	Sudeley (7th), Merlin Charles Sainthill Hanbury-Tracy, b. 1939, s. 1941	D. Andrew J. H-T., b. 1928.
1786	Suffield (11th), Anthony Philip Harbord-Hamond, MC, b. 1922, s. 1951, m.	Hon. Charles A. A. H.-H., b. 1953.
1893	Swansea (4th), John Hussey Hamilton Vivian, b. 1925, s. 1934, m.	Hon. Richard A. H. V., b. 1957.
1907	Swaythling (4th), David Charles Samuel Montagu, b. 1928, s. 1990, m.	Hon. Charles E. S. M., b. 1954.
1919	Swinfen (3rd), Roger Mynors Swinfen Eady, b. 1938, s. 1977, m.	Hon. Charles R. P. S. E., b. 1971.
1935	Sysonby (3rd), John Frederick Ponsonby, b. 1945, s. 1956	None.
1831 I.	Talbot of Malahide (10th), Reginald John Richard Arundell, b. 1931, s. 1987, m.	Hon. Richard J. T. A., b. 1957.
1946	Tedder (3rd), Robin John Tedder, b. 1955, s. 1994, m.	Hon. Benjamin J. T., b. 1985.
1884	Tennyson (5th), Cdr. Mark Aubrey Tennyson, DSC, b. 1920, s. 1991, m.	Lt.-Cdr. James A. T., DSC, b. 1913.
1918	Terrington (4th), (James Allen) David Woodhouse, b. 1915, s. 1961, m.	Hon. C. Montague W., DSO, OBE, b. 1917.
1940	Teviot (2nd), Charles John Kerr, b. 1934, s. 1968, m.	Hon. Charles R. K., b. 1971.
1616	Teynham (20th), John Christopher Ingham Roper-Curzon, b. 1928, s. 1972, m.	Hon. David J. H. I. R.-C., b. 1965.
1964	Thomson of Fleet (2nd), Kenneth Roy Thomson, b. 1923, s. 1976, m.	Hon. David K. R. T., b. 1957.
1792	Thurlow (8th), Francis Edward Hovell-Thurlow-Cumming-Bruce, KCMG, b. 1912, s. 1971, w.	Hon. Roualeyn R. H.-T.-C.-B., b. 1952.
1876	Tollemache (5th), Timothy John Edward Tollemache, b. 1939, s. 1975, m.	Hon. Edward J. H. T., b. 1976.
1564 s.	Torphichen (15th), James Andrew Douglas Sandilands, b. 1946, s. 1975, m.	Douglas R. A. S., b. 1926.
1947	Trefgarne (2nd), David Garro Trefgarne, PC, b. 1941, s. 1960, m.	Hon. George G. T., b. 1970.

Created	Title, order of succession, name, etc.	Heir
1921	*Trevethin* (4th), *and Oaksey* (2nd) (1947), John Geoffrey Tristram Lawrence, OBE, *b.* 1929, *s.* 1971, *m.*	Hon. Patrick J. T. *L.*, *b.* 1960.
1880	*Trevor* (4th), Charles Edwin Hill-Trevor, *b.* 1928, *s.* 1950, *m.*	Hon. Marke C. *H.-T.*, *b.* 1970.
1461 I.	*Trimlestown* (20th), Anthony Edward Barnewall, *b.* 1928, *s.* 1990, *m.*	Hon. Raymond C. *B.*, *b.* 1930.
1940	*Tryon* (3rd), Anthony George Merrik Tryon, *b.* 1940, *s.* 1976, *m.*	Hon. Charles G. B. *T.*, *b.* 1976.
1935	*Tweedsmuir* (2nd), John Norman Stuart Buchan, CBE, FRSE, *b.* 1911, *s.* 1940, *m.*	Hon. William de l'A. *B.*, *b.* 1916.
1523	*Vaux of Harrowden* (10th), John Hugh Philip Gilbey, *b.* 1915, *s.* 1977, *m.*	Hon. Anthony W. *G.*, *b.* 1940.
1800 I.	*Ventry* (8th), Andrew Wesley Daubeny de Moleyns, *b.* 1943, *s.* 1987, *m.*	Hon. Francis W. *D. de M.*, *b.* 1965.
1762	*Vernon* (10th), John Lawrance Vernon, *b.* 1923, *s.* 1963, *m.*	Col. William R. D. *Vernon-Harcourt*, OBE, *b.* 1909.
1922	*Vestey* (3rd), Samuel George Armstrong Vestey, *b.* 1941, *s.* 1954, *m.*	Hon. William G. *V.*, *b.* 1983.
1841	*Vivian* (6th), Nicholas Crespigny Laurence Vivian, *b.* 1935, *s.* 1991, *m.*	Hon. Charles H. C. *V.*, *b.* 1966.
1934	*Wakehurst* (3rd), (John) Christopher Loder, *b.* 1925, *s.* 1970, *m.*	Hon. Timothy W. *L.*, *b.* 1958.
1723	*Walpole* (10th), Robert Horatio Walpole (*8th Brit. Baron Walpole of Wolterton*, 1756), *b.* 1938, *s.* 1989, *m.*	Hon. Jonathan R. H. *W.*, *b.* 1967.
1780	*Walsingham* (9th), John de Grey, MC, *b.* 1925, *s.* 1965, *m.*	Hon. Robert *de G.*, *b.* 1969.
1936	*Wardington* (2nd), Christopher Henry Beaumont Pease, *b.* 1924, *s.* 1950, *m.*	Hon. William S. *P.*, *b.* 1925.
1792 I.	*Waterpark* (7th), Frederick Caryll Philip Cavendish, *b.* 1926, *s.* 1948, *m.*	Hon. Roderick A. *C.*, *b.* 1959.
1942	*Wedgwood* (4th), Piers Anthony Weymouth Wedgwood, *b.* 1954, *s.* 1970, *m.*	John *W.*, CBE, MD, FRCP, *b.* 1919.
1861	*Westbury* (5th), David Alan Bethell, CBE, MC, *b.* 1922, *s.* 1961, *m.*	Hon. Richard N. *B.*, MBE, *b.* 1950.
1944	*Westwood* (3rd), (William) Gavin Westwood, *b.* 1944, *s.* 1991, *m.*	Hon. W. Fergus *W.*, *b.* 1972.
1935	*Wigram* (2nd), (George) Neville (Clive) Wigram, MC, *b.* 1915, *s.* 1960, *w.*	Maj. Hon. Andrew F. C. *W.*, MVO, *b.* 1949.
1491	*Willoughby de Broke* (21st), Leopold David Verney, *b.* 1938, *s.* 1986, *m.*	Hon. Rupert G. *V.*, *b.* 1966.
1946	*Wilson* (2nd), Patrick Maitland Wilson, *b.* 1915, *s.* 1964, *w.*	None.
1937	*Windlesham* (3rd), David James George Hennessy, CVO, PC, *b.* 1932, *s.* 1962, *w.*	Hon. James R. *H.*, *b.* 1968.
1951	*Wise* (2nd), John Clayton Wise, *b.* 1923, *s.* 1968, *m.*	Hon. Christopher J. C. *W.*, PH.D., *b.* 1949.
1869	*Wolverton* (7th), Christopher Richard Glyn, *b.* 1938, *s.* 1988	Hon. Andrew J. *G.*, *b.* 1943.
1928	*Wraxall* (2nd), George Richard Lawley Gibbs, *b.* 1928, *s.* 1931	Hon. Sir Eustace H. B. *G.*, KCVO, CMG, *b.* 1929.
1915	*Wrenbury* (3rd), Revd John Burton Buckley, *b.* 1927, *s.* 1940, *m.*	Hon. William E. *B.*, *b.* 1966.
1838	*Wrottesley* (6th), Clifton Hugh Lancelot de Verdon Wrottesley, *b.* 1968, *s.* 1977	Hon. Stephen J. *W.*, *b.* 1955.
1919	*Wyfold* (3rd), Hermon Robert Fleming Hermon-Hodge, ERD, *b.* 1915, *s.* 1942	None.
1829	*Wynford* (8th), Robert Samuel Best, MBE, *b.* 1917, *s.* 1943, *m.*	Hon. John P. R. *B.*, *b.* 1950.
1308	*Zouche* (18th), James Assheton Frankland, *b.* 1943, *s.* 1965, *m.*	Hon. William T. A. *F.*, *b.* 1984.

BARONESSES/LADIES IN THEIR OWN RIGHT

Style, The Right Hon. the Lady ___, *or* The Right Hon. the Baroness ___, according to her preference. Either style may be used, except in the case of Scottish titles (indicated by s.), which are not baronies (*see* page 141) and whose holders are always addressed as Lady
Husband, Untitled
Children's style, As for children of a Baron
For forms of address, *see* page 217

Created	Title, order of succession, name, etc.	Heir
1455	*Berners* (16th in line), Pamela Vivien Kirkham, *b.* 1929, *title called out of abeyance* 1995, *m.*	Hon. Rupert W. T. *K.*, *b.* 1953.
1529	*Braye* (8th in line), Mary Penelope Aubrey–Fletcher, *b.* 1941, *s.* 1985, *m.*	Two co-heiresses.
1321	*Dacre* (27th in line), Rachel Leila Douglas-Home, *b.* 1929, *title called out of abeyance*, 1970, *w.*	Hon. James T. A. *D.-H.*, *b.* 1952.
1332	*Darcy de Knayth* (18th in line), Davina Marcia Ingrams, *b.* 1938, *s.* 1943, *w.*	Hon. Caspar D. *I.*, *b.* 1962.
1439	*Dudley* (14th in line), Barbara Amy Felicity Hamilton, *b.* 1907, *s.* 1972, *m.*	Hon. Jim A. H. *Wallace*, *b.* 1930.

Created	Title, order of succession, name, etc.	Heir
1490 s.	*Herries of Terregles* (14th in line), Anne Elizabeth Fitzalan-Howard, *b.* 1938, *s.* 1975, *m.*	Lady Mary *Mumford*, cvo, *b.* 1940.
1602 s.	*Kinloss* (12th in line), Beatrice Mary Grenville Freeman-Grenville, *b.* 1922, *s.* 1944, *m.*	Master of Kinloss, *b.* 1953.
1681 s.	*Nairne* (12th in line), Katherine Evelyn Constance Bigham (*Katherine, Viscountess Mersey*), *b.* 1912, *s.* 1944, *w.*	The Viscount Mersey, *b.* 1934 (*see* page 151).
1445 s.	*Saltoun* (20th in line), Flora Marjory Fraser, *b.* 1930, *s.* 1979, *m.*	Hon. Katharine I. M. I. F., *b.* 1957.
1628	*Strange* (16th in line), (Jean) Cherry Drummond of Megginch, *b.* 1928, title called out of abeyance, 1986, *m.*	Hon. Adam H. D. of M., *b.* 1953.
1544/5	*Wharton* (11th in line), Myrtle Olive Felix Robertson, *b.* 1934, title called out of abeyance, 1990, *m.*	Hon. Myles C. D. R., *b.* 1964.
1313	*Willoughby de Eresby* (27th in line), (Nancy) Jane Marie Heathcote-Drummond-Willoughby, *b.* 1934, *s.* 1983	Two co-heiresses.

Life Peers

Between 1 September 1994 and 31 August 1995, the conferment of ten life peerages was announced, two under the Appellate Jurisdiction Act 1876 and eight under the Life Peerages Act 1958:

LAW LORDS: Rt. Hon. Sir Johann Steyn; Rt. Hon. Sir Leonard Hoffmann

NEW YEAR'S HONOURS (30 December 1994): The Hon. Mrs Sarah Hogg; Mrs Elizabeth Smith; The Rt. Hon. David Hope; The Rt. Hon. Robert McConnell

QUEEN'S BIRTHDAY HONOURS (17 June 1995): Sir James Blyth; Sir John Cuckney; The Most Revd Robert Eames; *The Most Revd and Rt. Hon. John Habgood

*No title gazetted at time of going to press

1994	*Nicholls of Birkenhead*, Donald James Nicholls, PC, *b.* 1933, *m.*
1994	*Nolan*, Michael Patrick Nolan, PC, *b.* 1928, *m.* Lord of Appeal in Ordinary
1986	*Oliver of Aylmerton*, Peter Raymond Oliver, PC, *b.* 1921, *m.*
1980	*Roskill*, Eustace Wentworth Roskill, PC, *b.* 1911, *m.*
1977	*Scarman*, Leslie George Scarman, OBE, PC, *b.* 1911, *m.*
1992	*Slynn of Hadley*, Gordon Slynn, PC, *b.* 1930, *m.* Lord of Appeal in Ordinary
1995	*Steyn*, Johan van Zyl Steyn, PC, *b.* 1932, *m.*
1982	*Templeman*, Sydney William Templeman, MBE, PC, *b.* 1920, *w.*
1964	*Wilberforce*, Richard Orme Wilberforce, CMG, OBE, PC, *b.* 1907, *m.*
1992	*Woolf*, Harry Kenneth Woolf, PC, *b.* 1933, *m.* Lord of Appeal in Ordinary

CREATED UNDER THE APPELLATE JURISDICTION ACT 1876 (AS AMENDED)

BARONS

Created

1986	*Ackner*, Desmond James Conrad Ackner, PC, *b.* 1920, *m.*
1981	*Brandon of Oakbrook*, Henry Vivian Brandon, MC, PC, *b.* 1920, *m.*
1980	*Bridge of Harwich*, Nigel Cyprian Bridge, PC, *b.* 1917, *m.*
1982	*Brightman*, John Anson Brightman, PC, *b.* 1911, *m.*
1991	*Browne-Wilkinson*, Nicolas Christopher Henry Browne-Wilkinson, PC, *b.* 1930, *m.* Lord of Appeal in Ordinary
1957	*Denning*, Alfred Thompson Denning, PC, *b.* 1899, *w.*
1986	*Goff of Chieveley*, Robert Lionel Archibald Goff, PC, *b.* 1926, *m.* Lord of Appeal in Ordinary
1985	*Griffiths*, (William) Hugh Griffiths, MC, PC, *b.* 1923, *m.*
1995	*Hoffmann*, Leonard Hubert Hoffmann, PC, *b.* 1934, *m.*
1988	*Jauncey of Tullichettle*, Charles Eliot Jauncey, PC, *b.* 1925, *m.* Lord of Appeal in Ordinary
1977	*Keith of Kinkel*, Henry Shanks Keith, PC, *b.* 1922, *m.* Lord of Appeal in Ordinary
1979	*Lane*, Geoffrey Dawson Lane, AFC, PC, *b.* 1918, *m.*
1993	*Lloyd of Berwick*, Anthony John Leslie Lloyd, PC, *b.* 1929, *m.* Lord of Appeal in Ordinary
1992	*Mustill*, Michael John Mustill, PC, *b.* 1931, *m.* Lord of Appeal in Ordinary

CREATED UNDER THE LIFE PEERAGES ACT 1958

BARONS

Created

1988	*Alexander of Weedon*, Robert Scott Alexander, QC, *b.* 1936, *m.*
1976	*Allen of Abbeydale*, Philip Allen, GCB, *b.* 1912, *m.*
1961	*Alport*, Cuthbert James McCall Alport, TD, PC, *b.* 1912, *w.*
1992	*Amery of Lustleigh*, Julian Amery, PC, *b.* 1919, *w.*
1965	*Annan*, Noël Gilroy Annan, OBE, *b.* 1916, *m.*
1992	*Archer of Sandwell*, Peter Kingsley Archer, PC, QC, *b.* 1926, *m.*
1992	*Archer of Weston-super-Mare*, Jeffrey Howard Archer, *b.* 1940, *m.*
1988	*Armstrong of Ilminster*, Robert Temple Armstrong, GCB, CVO, *b.* 1927, *m.*
1992	*Ashley of Stoke*, Jack Ashley, CH, PC, *b.* 1922, *m.*
1993	*Attenborough*, Richard Samuel Attenborough, CBE, *b.* 1923, *m.*
1974	*Balniel*, The Earl of Crawford and Balcarres, *see* page 145
1982	*Bancroft*, Ian Powell Bancroft, GCB, *b.* 1922, *m.*
1974	*Banks*, Desmond Anderson Harvie Banks, CBE, *b.* 1918, *m.*
1974	*Barber*, Anthony Perrinott Lysberg Barber, TD, PC, *b.* 1920, *m.*

1992   *Barber of Tewkesbury,* Derek Coates Barber, *b.* 1918, *m.*

1983   *Barnett,* Joel Barnett, PC, *b.* 1923, *m.*

1982   *Bauer,* Prof. Peter Thomas Bauer, D.SC., FBA, *b.* 1915

1967   *Beaumont of Whitley,* Revd Timothy Wentworth Beaumont, *b.* 1928, *m.*

1979   *Bellwin,* Irwin Norman Bellow, *b.* 1923, *m.*

1981   *Beloff,* Max Beloff, FBA, *b.* 1913, *m.*

1971   *Blake,* Robert Norman William Blake, FBA, *b.* 1916, *w.*

1994   *Blaker,* Peter Allan Renshaw Blaker, KCMG, PC, *b.* 1922, *m.*

1978   *Blease,* William John Blease, *b.* 1914, *m.*

1995   *Blyth of Rowington,* James Blyth, *b.* 1940, *m.*

1980   *Boardman,* Thomas Gray Boardman, MC, TD, *b.* 1919, *m.*

1976   *Boston of Faversham,* Terence George Boston, QC, *b.* 1930, *m.*

1984   *Bottomley,* Arthur George Bottomley, OBE, PC, *b.* 1907, *m.*

1972   *Boyd-Carpenter,* John Archibald Boyd-Carpenter, PC, *b.* 1908, *m.*

1992   *Braine of Wheatley,* Bernard Richard Braine, PC, *b.* 1914, *w.*

1987   *Bramall,* Edwin Noel Westby Bramall, KG, GCB, OBE, MC, *Field Marshal, b.* 1923, *m.*

1976   *Briggs,* Asa Briggs, FBA, *b.* 1921, *m.*

1975   *Brookes,* Raymond Percival Brookes, *b.* 1909, *m.*

1979   *Brooks of Tremorfa,* John Edward Brooks, *b.* 1927, *m.*

1974   *Bruce of Donington,* Donald William Trevor Bruce, *b.* 1912, *m.*

1976   *Bullock,* Alan Louis Charles Bullock, FBA, *b.* 1914, *m.*

1988   *Butterfield,* (William) John (Hughes) Butterfield, OBE, DM, FRCP, *b.* 1920, *m.*

1985   *Butterworth,* John Blackstock Butterworth, CBE, *b.* 1918, *m.*

1978   *Buxton of Alsa,* Aubrey Leland Oakes Buxton, MC, *b.* 1918, *m.*

1987   *Callaghan of Cardiff,* (Leonard) James Callaghan, KG, PC, *b.* 1912, *m.*

1984   *Cameron of Lochbroom,* Kenneth John Cameron, PC, *b.* 1931, *m.*

1981   *Campbell of Alloway,* Alan Robertson Campbell, QC, *b.* 1917, *m.*

1974   *Campbell of Croy,* Gordon Thomas Calthrop Campbell, MC, PC, *b.* 1921, *m.*

1987   *Carlisle of Bucklow,* Mark Carlisle, QC, PC, *b.* 1929, *m.*

1983   *Carmichael of Kelvingrove,* Neil George Carmichael, *b.* 1921

1975   *Carr of Hadley,* (Leonard) Robert Carr, PC, *b.* 1916, *m.*

1987   *Carter,* Denis Victor Carter, *b.* 1932, *m.*

1977   *Carver,* (Richard) Michael (Power) Carver, GCB, CBE, DSO, MC, *Field Marshal, b.* 1915, *m.*

1990   *Cavendish of Furness,* (Richard) Hugh Cavendish, *b.* 1941, *m.*

1982   *Cayzer,* (William) Nicholas Cayzer, *b.* 1910, *m.*

1964   *Chalfont,* (Alun) Arthur Gwynne Jones, OBE, MC, PC, *b.* 1919, *m.*

1985   *Chapple,* Francis (Frank) Joseph Chapple, *b.* 1921, *w.*

1978   *Charteris of Amisfield,* Martin Michael Charles Charteris, GCB, GCVO, OBE, PC, Royal Victorian Chain, *b.* 1913, *m.*

1963   *Chelmer,* Eric Cyril Boyd Edwards, MC, TD, *b.* 1914, *m.*

1987   *Chilver,* (Amos) Henry Chilver, FRS, FEng., *b.* 1926, *m.*

1977   *Chitnis,* Pratap Chidamber Chitnis, *b.* 1936, *m.*

1992   *Clark of Kempston,* William Gibson Haig Clark, PC, *b.* 1917, *m.*

1979   *Cledwyn of Penrhos,* Cledwyn Hughes, CH, PC, *b.* 1916, *m.*

1990   *Clinton-Davis,* Stanley Clinton Clinton-Davis, *b.* 1928, *m.*

1978   *Cockfield,* (Francis) Arthur Cockfield, PC, *b.* 1916, *w.*

1987   *Cocks of Hartcliffe,* Michael Francis Lovell Cocks, PC, *b.* 1929, *m.*

1980   *Coggan,* Rt. Revd (Frederick) Donald Coggan, PC, Royal Victorian Chain, *b.* 1909, *m.*

1964   *Collison,* Harold Francis Collison, CBE, *b.* 1909, *m.*

1987   *Colnbrook,* Humphrey Edward Gregory Atkins, KCMG, PC, *b.* 1922, *m.*

1981   *Constantine of Stanmore,* Theodore Constantine, CBE, AE, *b.* 1910, *w.*

1992   *Cooke of Islandreagh,* Victor Alexander Cooke, OBE, *b.* 1920, *m.*

1991   *Craig of Radley,* David Brownrigg Craig, GCB, OBE, *Marshal of the Royal Air Force, b.* 1929, *m.*

1987   *Crickhowell,* (Roger) Nicholas Edwards, PC, *b.* 1934, *m.*

1978   *Croham,* Douglas Albert Vivian Allen, GCB, *b.* 1917, *w.*

1995   *Cuckney,* John Graham Cuckney, *b.* 1925, *m.*

1974   *Cudlipp,* Hugh Cudlipp, OBE, *b.* 1913, *m.*

1979   *Dacre of Glanton,* Hugh Redwald Trevor-Roper, *b.* 1914, *m.*

1993   *Dahrendorf,* Ralf Dahrendorf, KBE, PH.D., D. phil., FBA, *b.* 1929, *m.*

1986   *Dainton,* Frederick Sydney Dainton, PH.D., SC.D., FRS, *b.* 1914, *m.*

1983   *Dean of Beswick,* Joseph Jabez Dean, *b.* 1922

1993   *Dean of Harptree,* (Arthur) Paul Dean, PC, *b.* 1924, *m.*

1986   *Deedes,* William Francis Deedes, MC, PC, *b.* 1913, *m.*

1991   *Desai,* Prof. Meghnad Jagdishchandra Desai, PH.D., *b.* 1940, *m.*

1970   *Diamond,* John Diamond, PC, *b.* 1907, *m.*

1993   *Dixon-Smith,* Robert William Dixon-Smith, *b.* 1934, *m.*

1967   *Donaldson of Kingsbridge,* John George Stuart Donaldson, OBE, *b.* 1907, *w.*

1988   *Donaldson of Lymington,* John Francis Donaldson, PC, *b.* 1920, *m.*

1985   *Donoughue,* Bernard Donoughue, D.phil., *b.* 1934.

1987   *Dormand of Easington,* John Donkin Dormand, *b.* 1919, *m.*

1994   *Dubs,* Alfred Dubs, *b.* 1932, *m.*

1995   *Eames,* Robert Henry Alexander Eames, PH.D., *b.* 1937, *m.*

1992   *Eatwell,* John Leonard Eatwell, *b.* 1945, *m.*

1983   *Eden of Winton,* John Benedict Eden, PC, *b.* 1925, *m.*

1992   *Elis-Thomas,* Dafydd Elis Elis-Thomas, *b.* 1946, *m.*

1985   *Elliott of Morpeth,* Robert William Elliott, *b.* 1920, *m.*

1981   *Elystan-Morgan,* Dafydd Elystan Elystan-Morgan, *b.* 1932, *m.*

1980   *Emslie,* George Carlyle Emslie, MBE, PC, FRSE, *b.* 1919, *m.*

1992   *Ewing of Kirkford,* Harry Ewing, *b.* 1931, *m.*

1983   *Ezra,* Derek Ezra, MBE, *b.* 1919, *m.*

1983 *Fanshawe of Richmond*, Anthony Henry Fanshawe Royle, KCMG, *b.* 1927, *m.*
1992 *Finsberg*, Geoffrey Finsberg, MBE, *b.* 1926, *m.*
1983 *Fitt*, Gerard Fitt, *b.* 1926, *m.*
1979 *Flowers*, Brian Hilton Flowers, FRS, *b.* 1924, *m.*
1967 *Foot*, John Mackintosh Foot, *b.* 1909, *m.*
1982 *Forte*, Charles Forte, *b.* 1908, *m.*
1989 *Fraser of Carmyllie*, Peter Lovat Fraser, PC, QC, *b.* 1945, *m.*
1974 *Fraser of Kilmorack*, (Richard) Michael Fraser, CBE, *b.* 1915, *m.*
1982 *Gallacher*, John Gallacher, *b.* 1920, *m.*
1992 *Geraint*, Geraint Wyn Howells, *b.* 1925, *m.*
1975 *Gibson*, (Richard) Patrick (Tallentyre) Gibson, *b.* 1916, *m.*
1979 *Gibson-Watt*, (James) David Gibson-Watt, MC, PC, *b.* 1918, *m.*
1992 *Gilmour of Craigmillar*, Ian Hedworth John Little Gilmour, PC, *b.* 1926, *m.*
1994 *Gladwin of Clee*, Derek Oliver Gladwin, CBE, *b.* 1930, *m.*
1977 *Glenamara*, Edward Watson Short, CH, PC, *b.* 1912, *m.*
1987 *Goold*, James Duncan Goold, *b.* 1934, *w.*
1976 *Grade*, Lew Grade, *b.* 1906, *m.*
1983 *Graham of Edmonton*, (Thomas) Edward Graham, *b.* 1925, *m.*
1967 *Granville of Eye*, Edgar Louis Granville, *b.* 1899, *m.*
       Gray of Contin, James (Hamish) Hector Northey
1983   Gray, PC, *b.* 1927, *m.*
1974 *Greene of Harrow Weald*, Sidney Francis Greene, CBE, *b.* 1910, *m.*
1974 *Greenhill of Harrow*, Denis Arthur Greenhill, GCMG, OBE, *b.* 1913, *m.*
1975 *Gregson*, John Gregson, *b.* 1924
1968 *Grey of Naunton*, Ralph Francis Alnwick Grey, GCMG, GCVO, OBE, *b.* 1910, *m.*
1991 *Griffiths of Fforestfach*, Brian Griffiths, *b.* 1941, *m.*
1970 *Hailsham of St Marylebone*, Quintin McGarel Hogg, KG, CH, PC, FRS, *b.* 1907, *m.*
1994 *Hambro*, Charles Eric Alexander Hambro, *b.* 1930, *m.*
1983 *Hanson*, James Edward Hanson, *b.* 1922, *m.*
1974 *Harmar-Nicholls*, Harmar Harmar-Nicholls, *b.* 1912, *m.*
1974 *Harris of Greenwich*, John Henry Harris, *b.* 1930, *m.*
1979 *Harris of High Cross*, Ralph Harris, *b.* 1924, *m.*
1968 *Hartwell*, (William) Michael Berry, MBE, TD, *b.* 1911, *w.*
1974 *Harvington*, Robert Grant Grant-Ferris, AE, PC, *b.* 1907, *m.*
1993 *Haskel*, Simon Haskel, *b.* 1934, *m.*
1990 *Haslam*, Robert Haslam, *b.* 1923, *w.*
1992 *Hayhoe*, Bernard John (Barney) Hayhoe, PC, *b.* 1925, *m.*
1992 *Healey*, Denis Winston Healey, CH, MBE, PC, *b.* 1917, *m.*
1984 *Henderson of Brompton*, Peter Gordon Henderson, KCB, *b.* 1922, *m.*
1979 *Hill-Norton*, Peter John Hill-Norton, GCB, *Admiral of the Fleet*, *b.* 1915, *m.*
1979 *Holderness*, Richard Frederick Wood, PC, *b.* 1920, *m.*
1991 *Hollick*, Clive Richard Hollick, *b.* 1945, *m.*
1990 *Holme of Cheltenham*, Richard Gordon Holme, CBE, *b.* 1936, *m.*
1974 *Home of the Hirsel*, Alexander Frederick Douglas-Home, KT, PC, *b.* 1903, *w.*

1979 *Hooson*, (Hugh) Emlyn Hooson, QC, *b.* 1925, *m.*
1995 *Hope of Craighead*, (James Arthur) David Hope, PC, *b.* 1938, *m.*
1974 *Houghton of Sowerby*, (Arthur Leslie Noel) Douglas Houghton, CH, PC, *b.* 1898, *m.*
1992 *Howe of Aberavon*, (Richard Edward) Geoffrey Howe, PC, QC, *b.* 1926, *m.*
1992 *Howell*, Denis Herbert Howell, PC, *b.* 1923, *m.*
1978 *Howie of Troon*, William Howie, *b.* 1924, *m.*
1961 *Hughes*, William Hughes, CBE, PC, *b.* 1911, *w.*
1966 *Hunt*, (Henry Cecil) John Hunt, KG, CBE, DSO, *b.* 1910, *m.*
1980 *Hunt of Tanworth*, John Joseph Benedict Hunt, GCB, *b.* 1919, *m.*
1978 *Hutchinson of Lullington*, Jeremy Nicolas Hutchinson, QC, *b.* 1915, *m.*
1982 *Ingrow*, John Aked Taylor, OBE, TD, *b.* 1917, *m.*
1987 *Irvine of Lairg*, Alexander Andrew Mackay Irvine, QC, *b.* 1940, *m.*
1968 *Jacques*, John Henry Jacques, *b.* 1905, *m.*
1988 *Jakobovits*, Immanuel Jakobovits, *b.* 1921, *m.*
1987 *Jay*, Douglas Patrick Thomas Jay, PC, *b.* 1907, *m.*
1987 *Jenkin of Roding*, (Charles) Patrick (Fleeming) Jenkin, PC, *b.* 1926, *m.*
1987 *Jenkins of Hillhead*, Roy Harris Jenkins, OM, PC, *b.* 1920, *m.*
1981 *Jenkins of Putney*, Hugh Gater Jenkins, *b.* 1908, *w.*
1987 *Johnston of Rockport*, Charles Collier Johnston, TD, *b.* 1915, *m.*
1991 *Judd*, Frank Ashcroft Judd, *b.* 1935, *m.*
1980 *Keith of Castleacre*, Kenneth Alexander Keith, *b.* 1916, *m.*
1985 *Kimball*, Marcus Richard Kimball, *b.* 1928, *m.*
1983 *King of Wartnaby*, John Leonard King, *b.* 1918, *m.*
1993 *Kingsdown*, Robert (Robin) Leigh-Pemberton, KG, PC, *b.* 1927, *m.*
1994 *Kingsland*, Christopher James Prout, TD, PC, QC, *b.* 1942
1965 *Kings Norton*, Harold Roxbee Cox, PH.D., FEng., *b.* 1902, *m.*
1975 *Kirkhill*, John Farquharson Smith, *b.* 1930, *m.*
1974 *Kissin*, Harry Kissin, *b.* 1912, *m.*
1987 *Knights*, Philip Douglas Knights, CBE, QPM, *b.* 1920, *m.*
1991 *Laing of Dunphail*, Hector Laing, *b.* 1923, *m.*
1990 *Lane of Horsell*, Peter Stewart Lane, *b.* 1925, *w.*
1992 *Lawson of Blaby*, Nigel Lawson, PC, *b.* 1932, *m.*
1993 *Lester of Herne Hill*, Anthony Paul Lester, QC, *b.* 1936, *m.*
1982 *Lewin*, Terence Thornton Lewin, KG, GCB, LVO, DSC, *Admiral of the Fleet*, *b.* 1920, *m.*
1989 *Lewis of Newnham*, Jack Lewis, FRS, *b.* 1928, *m.*
1974 *Lovell-Davis*, Peter Lovell Lovell-Davis, *b.* 1924, *m.*
1979 *Lowry*, Robert Lynd Erskine Lowry, PC, PC(NI), *b.* 1919, *m.*
1984 *McAlpine of West Green*, (Robert) Alistair McAlpine, *b.* 1942, *m.*
1988 *Macaulay of Bragar*, Donald Macaulay, QC, *b.* 1933, *m.*
1975 *McCarthy*, William Edward John McCarthy, D.Phil., *b.* 1925, *m.*
1976 *McCluskey*, John Herbert McCluskey, *b.* 1929, *m.*
1989 *McColl of Dulwich*, Ian McColl, FRCS, FRCSE, *b.* 1933, *m.*
1995 *McConnell*, Robert William Brian McConnell, PC (NI), *b.* 1922, *m.*
1966 *McFadzean*, William Hunter McFadzean, KT, *b.* 1903, *m.*

1991   *Macfarlane of Bearsden*, Norman Somerville Macfarlane, FRSE, *b*. 1926, *m*.
1978   *McGregor of Durris*, Oliver Ross McGregor, *b*. 1921, *m*.
1982   *McIntosh of Haringey*, Andrew Robert McIntosh, *b*. 1933, *m*.
1991   *Mackay of Ardbrecknish*, John Jackson Mackay, *b*. 1938, *m*.
1979   *Mackay of Clashfern*, James Peter Hymers Mackay, PC, FRSE, *b*. 1927, *m. Lord High Chancellor.*
1988   *Mackenzie-Stuart*, Alexander John Mackenzie Stuart, *b*. 1924, *m*.
1974   *Mackie of Benshie*, George Yull Mackie, CBE, DSO, DFC, *b*. 1919, *m*.
1982   *MacLehose of Beoch*, (Crawford) Murray MacLehose, KT, GBE, KCMG, KCVO, *b*. 1917, *m*.
1991   *Marlesford*, Mark Shuldham Schreiber, *b*. 1931, *m*.
1981   *Marsh*, Richard William Marsh, PC, *b*. 1928, *m*.
1985   *Marshall of Goring*, Walter Charles Marshall, CBE, FRS, *b*. 1932, *m*.
1987   *Mason of Barnsley*, Roy Mason, PC, *b*. 1924, *m*.
1980   *Matthews*, Victor Collin Matthews, *b*. 1919, *m*.
1981   *Mayhew*, Christopher Paget Mayhew, *b*. 1915, *m*.
1985   *Mellish*, Robert Joseph Mellish, PC, *b*. 1913, *m*.
1993   *Menuhin*, Yehudi Menuhin, OM, KBE, *b*. 1916, *m*.
1992   *Merlyn-Rees*, Merlyn Merlyn-Rees, PC, *b*. 1920, *m*.
1978   *Mishcon*, Victor Mishcon, *b*. 1915, *m*.
1981   *Molloy*, William John Molloy, *b*. 1918
1992   *Moore of Lower Marsh*, John Edward Michael Moore, PC, *b*. 1937, *m*.
1986   *Moore of Wolvercote*, Philip Brian Cecil Moore, GCB, GCVO, CMG, PC, *b*. 1921, *m*.
1990   *Morris of Castle Morris*, Brian Robert Morris, D.Phil., *b*. 1930, *m*.
1971   *Moyola*, James Dawson Chichester-Clark, PC (NI), *b*. 1923, *m*.
1985   *Murray of Epping Forest*, Lionel Murray, OBE, PC, *b*. 1922, *m*.
1979   *Murton of Lindisfarne*, (Henry) Oscar Murton, OBE, TD, PC, *b*. 1914, *m*.
1994   *Nickson*, David Wigley Nickson, KBE, FRSE, *b*. 1929, *m*.
1975   *Northfield*, (William) Donald Chapman, *b*. 1923
1973   *O'Brien of Lothbury*, Leslie Kenneth O'Brien, GBE, PC, *b*. 1908, *m*.
1976   *Oram*, Albert Edward Oram, *b*. 1913, *m*.
1971   *Orr-Ewing*, (Charles) Ian Orr-Ewing, OBE, *b*. 1912, *m*.
1992   *Owen*, David Anthony Llewellyn Owen, CH, PC, *b*. 1938, *m*.
1991   *Palumbo*, Peter Garth Palumbo, *b*. 1935, *m*.
1992   *Parkinson*, Cecil Edward Parkinson, PC, *b*. 1931, *m*.
1975   *Parry*, Gordon Samuel David Parry, *b*. 1925, *m*.
1990   *Pearson of Rannoch*, Malcolm Everard MacLaren Pearson, *b*. 1942, *m*.
1979   *Perry of Walton*, Walter Laing Macdonald Perry, OBE, FRS, FRSE, *b*. 1921, *m*.
1987   *Peston*, Maurice Harry Peston, *b*. 1931, *m*.
1983   *Peyton of Yeovil*, John Wynne William Peyton, PC, *b*. 1919, *m*.
1994   *Phillips of Ellesmere*, Prof. David Chilton Phillips, KBE, FRS, *b*. 1924, *m*.
1992   *Plant of Highfield*, Prof. Raymond Plant, PH.D., *b*. 1945, *m*.
1959   *Plowden*, Edwin Noel Plowden, GBE, KCB, *b*. 1907, *m*.
1987   *Plumb*, (Charles) Henry Plumb, MEP, *b*. 1925, *m*.
1981   *Plummer of St Marylebone*, (Arthur) Desmond (Herne) Plummer, TD, *b*. 1914, *m*.

1990   *Porter of Luddenham*, George Porter, OM, FRS, *b*. 1920, *m*.
1992   *Prentice*, Reginald Ernest Prentice, PC, *b*. 1923, *m*.
1987   *Prior*, James Michael Leathes Prior, PC, *b*. 1927, *m*.
1975   *Pritchard*, Derek Wilbraham Pritchard, *b*. 1910, *m*.
1982   *Prys-Davies*, Gwilym Prys Prys-Davies, *b*. 1923, *m*.
1987   *Pym*, Francis Leslie Pym, MC, PC, *b*. 1922, *m*.
1982   *Quinton*, Anthony Meredith Quinton, FBA, *b*. 1925, *m*.
1994   *Quirk*, Prof. (Charles) Randolph Quirk, CBE, FBA, *b*. 1920, *m*.
1978   *Rawlinson of Ewell*, Peter Anthony Grayson Rawlinson, PC, QC, *b*. 1919, *m*.
1976   *Rayne*, Max Rayne, *b*. 1918, *m*.
1983   *Rayner*, Derek George Rayner, *b*. 1926
1987   *Rees*, Peter Wynford Innes Rees, PC, QC, *b*. 1926, *m*.
1988   *Rees-Mogg*, William Rees-Mogg, *b*. 1928, *m*.
1991   *Renfrew of Kaimsthorn*, (Andrew) Colin Renfrew, FBA, *b*. 1937, *m*.
1979   *Renton*, David Lockhart-Mure Renton, KBE, TD, PC, QC, *b*. 1908, *w*.
1990   *Richard*, Ivor Seward Richard, PC, QC, *b*. 1932, *m*.
1979   *Richardson*, John Samuel Richardson, LVO, MD, FRCP, *b*. 1910, *w*.
1983   *Richardson of Duntisbourne*, Gordon William Humphreys Richardson, KG, MBE, TD, PC, *b*. 1915, *m*.
1987   *Rippon of Hexham*, (Aubrey) Geoffrey (Frederick) Rippon, PC, QC, *b*. 1924, *m*.
1992   *Rix*, Brian Norman Roger Rix, CBE, *b*. 1924, *m*.
1961   *Robens of Woldingham*, Alfred Robens, PC, *b*. 1910, *m*.
1992   *Rodger of Earlsferry*, Alan Ferguson Rodger, PC, QC, FBA, *b*. 1944, *Lord Advocate*
1992   *Rodgers of Quarry Bank*, William Thomas Rodgers, PC, *b*. 1928, *m*.
1977   *Roll of Ipsden*, Eric Roll, KCMG, CB, *b*. 1907, *m*.
1991   *Runcie*, Rt Revd Robert Alexander Kennedy Runcie, MC, PC, Royal Victoria Chain, *b*. 1921, *m*.
1975   *Ryder of Eaton Hastings*, Sydney Thomas Franklin (Don) Ryder, *b*. 1916, *m*.
1962   *Sainsbury*, Alan John Sainsbury, *b*. 1902, *w*.
1989   *Sainsbury of Preston Candover*, John Davan Sainsbury, KG, *b*. 1927, *m*.
1987   *St John of Fawsley*, Norman Antony Francis St John-Stevas, PC, *b*. 1929
1985   *Sanderson of Bowden*, Charles Russell Sanderson, *b*. 1933, *m*.
1979   *Scanlon*, Hugh Parr Scanlon, *b*. 1913, *m*.
1978   *Sefton of Garston*, William Henry Sefton, *b*. 1915, *m*.
1994   *Shaw of Northstead*, Michael Norman Shaw, *b*. 1920, *m*.
1959   *Shawcross*, Hartley William Shawcross, GBE, PC, QC, *b*. 1902, *w*.
1994   *Sheppard of Didgemere*, Allan John George Sheppard, *b*. 1932, *m*.
1980   *Sieff of Brimpton*, Marcus Joseph Sieff, OBE, *b*. 1913, *m*.
1971   *Simon of Glaisdale*, Jocelyn Edward Salis Simon, PC, *b*. 1911, *m*.
1991   *Skidelsky*, Robert Jacob Alexander Skidelsky, D.Phil., *b*. 1939, *m*.
1978   *Smith*, Rodney Smith, KBE, FRCS, *b*. 1914, *m*.
1965   *Soper*, Revd Donald Oliver Soper, PH.D., *b*. 1903, *m*.

1990   *Soulsby of Swaffham Prior*, Ernest Jackson Lawson Soulsby, PH.D., *b.* 1926, *m.*
1983   *Stallard*, Albert William Stallard, *b.* 1921, *m.*
1991   *Sterling of Plaistow*, Jeffrey Maurice Sterling, CBE, *b.* 1934, *m.*
1987   *Stevens of Ludgate*, David Robert Stevens, *b.* 1936, *m.*
1992   *Stewartby*, (Bernard Harold) Ian (Halley) Stewart, RD, PC, FBA, FRSE, *b.* 1935, *m.*
1981   *Stodart of Leaston*, James Anthony Stodart, PC, *b.* 1916, *w.*
1983   *Stoddart of Swindon*, David Leonard Stoddart, *b.* 1926, *m.*
1969   *Stokes*, Donald Gresham Stokes, TD, FEng., *b.* 1914, *w.*
1971   *Tanlaw*, Simon Brooke Mackay, *b.* 1934, *m.*
1978   *Taylor of Blackburn*, Thomas Taylor, CBE, *b.* 1929, *m.*
1992   *Taylor of Gosforth*, Peter Murray Taylor, PC, *b.* 1930, *w.*, *Lord Chief Justice of England*
1968   *Taylor of Gryfe*, Thomas Johnston Taylor, FRSE, *b.* 1912, *m.*
1992   *Tebbit*, Norman Beresford Tebbit, CH, PC, *b.* 1931, *m.*
1987   *Thomas of Gwydir*, Peter John Mitchell Thomas, PC, QC, *b.* 1920, *w.*
1981   *Thomas of Swynnerton*, Hugh Swynnerton Thomas, *b.* 1931, *m.*
1977   *Thomson of Monifieth*, George Morgan Thomson, KT, PC, *b.* 1921, *m.*
1962   *Todd*, Alexander Robertus Todd, OM, D.SC., D.Phil., FRS, *b.* 1907, *w.*
1990   *Tombs*, Francis Leonard Tombs, FEng., *b.* 1924, *m.*
1994   *Tope*, Graham Norman Tope, CBE, *b.* 1943, *m.*
1981   *Tordoff*, Geoffrey Johnson Tordoff, *b.* 1928, *m.*
1993   *Tugendhat*, Christopher Samuel Tugendhat, *b.* 1937, *m.*
1990   *Varley*, Eric Graham Varley, PC, *b.* 1932, *m.*
1985   *Vinson*, Nigel Vinson, LVO, *b.* 1931, *m.*
1990   *Waddington*, David Charles Waddington, GCVO, PC, QC, *b.* 1929, *m.*
1990   *Wade of Chorlton*, (William) Oulton Wade, *b.* 1932, *m.*
1992   *Wakeham*, John Wakeham, PC, *b.* 1932, *m.*
1992   *Walker of Worcester*, Peter Edward Walker, MBE, PC, *b.* 1932, *m.*
1974   *Wallace of Campsie*, George Wallace, *b.* 1915, *m.*
1974   *Wallace of Coslany*, George Douglas Wallace, *b.* 1906, *m.*
1989   *Walton of Detchant*, John Nicholas Walton, TD, FRCP, *b.* 1922, *m.*
1992   *Weatherill*, (Bruce) Bernard Weatherill, PC, *b.* 1920, *m.*
1977   *Wedderburn of Charlton*, (Kenneth) William Wedderburn, FBA, QC, *b.* 1927, *m.*
1976   *Weidenfeld*, (Arthur) George Weidenfeld, *b.* 1919, *m.*
1980   *Weinstock*, Arnold Weinstock, *b.* 1924, *m.*
1978   *Whaddon*, (John) Derek Page, *b.* 1927, *m.*
1974   *Wigoder*, Basil Thomas Wigoder, QC, *b.* 1921, *m.*
1985   *Williams of Elvel*, Charles Cuthbert Powell Williams, CBE, *b.* 1933, *m.*
1992   *Williams of Mostyn*, Gareth Wyn Williams, QC, *b.* 1941, *m.*
1969   *Wilson of Langside*, Henry Stephen Wilson, PC, QC, *b.* 1916, *m.*
1992   *Wilson of Tillyorn*, David Clive Wilson, GCMG, PH.D., *b.* 1935, *m.*
1985   *Wolfson*, Leonard Gordon Wolfson, *b.* 1927, *m.*

1991   *Wolfson of Sunningdale*, David Wolfson, *b.* 1935, *m.*
1994   *Wright of Richmond*, Patrick Richard Henry Wright, GCMG, *b.* 1931, *m.*
1987   *Wyatt of Weeford*, Woodrow Lyle Wyatt, *b.* 1918, *m.*
1978   *Young of Dartington*, Michael Young, PH.D., *b.* 1915, *w.*
1984   *Young of Graffham*, David Ivor Young, PC, *b.* 1932, *m.*
1992   *Younger of Prestwick*, George Kenneth Hotson Younger, KCVO, TD, PC, *b.* 1931, *m.*

BARONESSES

Created
1967   *Birk*, Alma Birk, *b.* 1921, *m.*
1987   *Blackstone*, Tessa Ann Vosper Blackstone, PH.D., *b.* 1942
1987   *Blatch*, Emily May Blatch, CBE, PC, *b.* 1937, *m.*
1990   *Brigstocke*, Heather Renwick Brigstocke, *b.* 1929, *w.*
1964   *Brooke of Ystradfellte*, Barbara Muriel Brooke, DBE, *b.* 1908, *w.*
1982   *Carnegy of Lour*, Elizabeth Patricia Carnegy of Lour, *b.* 1925
1990   *Castle of Blackburn*, Barbara Anne Castle, PC, *b.* 1910, *w.*
1992   *Chalker of Wallasey*, Lynda Chalker, PC, *b.* 1942, *m.*
1982   *Cox*, Caroline Anne Cox, *b.* 1937, *m.*
1990   *Cumberlege*, Julia Frances Cumberlege, CBE, *b*, 1943, *m.*
1978   *David*, Nora Ratcliff David, *b.* 1913, *w.*
1993   *Dean of Thornton-le-Fylde*, Brenda Dean, *b.* 1943, *m.*
1974   *Delacourt-Smith of Alteryn*, Margaret Rosalind Delacourt-Smith, *b.* 1916, *m.*
1978   *Denington*, Evelyn Joyce Denington, DBE, *b.* 1907, *m.*
1991   *Denton of Wakefield*, Jean Denton, CBE, *b.* 1935
1990   *Dunn*, Lydia Selina Dunn, DBE, *b.* 1940, *m.*
1990   *Eccles of Moulton*, Diana Catherine Eccles, *b.* 1933, *m.*
1972   *Elles*, Diana Louie Elles, *b.* 1921, *m.*
1975   *Faithfull*, Lucy Faithfull, OBE, *b.* 1910
1974   *Falkender*, Marcia Matilda Falkender, CBE, *b.* 1932
1994   *Farrington of Ribbleton*, Josephine Farrington, *b.* 19–, *m.*
1974   *Fisher of Rednal*, Doris Mary Gertrude Fisher, *b.* 1919, *w.*
1990   *Flather*, Shreela Flather, *b.* 19–, *m.*
1981   *Gardner of Parkes*, (Rachel) Trixie (Anne) Gardner, *b.* 1927, *m.*
1993   *Gould of Potternewton*, Joyce Brenda Gould, *b.* 1932, *m.*
1991   *Hamwee*, Sally Rachel Hamwee, *b.* 1947
1991   *Hilton of Eggardon*, Jennifer Hilton, QPM, *b.* 1936
1995   *Hogg*, Sarah Elizabeth Mary Hogg, *b.* 1946, *m.*
1990   *Hollis of Heigham*, Patricia Lesley Hollis, D.Phil., *b.* 1941, *m.*
1985   *Hooper*, Gloria Dorothy Hooper, *b.* 1939
1965   *Hylton-Foster*, Audrey Pellew Hylton-Foster, DBE, *b.* 1908, *w.*
1991   *James of Holland Park*, Phyllis Dorothy White (P. D. James), OBE, *b.* 1920, *w.*
1992   *Jay of Paddington*, Margaret Ann Jay, *b.* 1939
1979   *Jeger*, Lena May Jeger, *b.* 1915, *w.*
1967   *Llewelyn-Davies of Hastoe*, (Annie) Patricia Llewelyn-Davies, PC, *b.* 1915, *w.*
1978   *Lockwood*, Betty Lockwood, *b.* 1924, *w.*

1979 *McFarlane of Llandaff,* Jean Kennedy McFarlane, *b.* 1926
1971 *Macleod of Borve,* Evelyn Hester Macleod, *b.* 1915, *w.*
1991 *Mallalieu,* Ann Mallalieu, QC, *b.* 1945, *m.*
1970 *Masham of Ilton,* Susan Lilian Primrose Cunliffe-Lister, *b.* 1935, *m.* (*Countess of Swinton*)
1993 *Miller of Hendon,* Doreen Miller, MBE, *b.* 1933, *m.*
1982 *Nicol,* Olive Mary Wendy Nicol, *b.* 1923, *m.*
1991 *O'Cathain,* Detta O'Cathain, OBE, *b.* 1938, *m.*
1989 *Oppenheim-Barnes,* Sally Oppenheim-Barnes, PC, *b.* 1930, *m.*
1990 *Park of Monmouth,* Daphne Margaret Sybil Désirée Park, CMG, OBE, *b.* 1921
1991 *Perry of Southwark,* Pauline Perry, *b.* 1931, *m.*
1974 *Pike,* (Irene) Mervyn (Parnicott) Pike, DBE, *b.* 1918
1981 *Platt of Writtle,* Beryl Catherine Platt, CBE, FEng., *b.* 1923, *m.*
1994 *Rawlings,* Patricia Elizabeth Rawlings, *b.* 1939
1974 *Robson of Kiddington,* Inga-Stina Robson, *b.* 1919, *w.*

1979 *Ryder of Warsaw,* Margaret Susan Cheshire (Sue Ryder), CMG, OBE, *b.* 1923, *w.*
1991 *Seccombe,* Joan Anna Dalziel Seccombe, DBE, *b.* 1930, *m.*
1971 *Seear,* (Beatrice) Nancy Seear, PC, *b.* 1913
1967 *Serota,* Beatrice Serota, DBE, *b.* 1919, *m.*
1973 *Sharples,* Pamela Sharples, *b.* 1923, *m.*
1995 *Smith of Gilmorehill,* Elizabeth Margaret Smith, *b.* 19–, *w.*
1974 *Stedman,* Phyllis Stedman, OBE, *b.* 1916, *w*
1992 *Thatcher,* Margaret Hilda Thatcher, OM, PC, FRS, *b.* 1925, *m.*
1994 *Thomas of Walliswood,* Susan Petronella Thomas, OBE, *b.* 19–, *m.*
1980 *Trumpington,* Jean Alys Barker, PC, *b.* 1922, *w.*
1985 *Turner of Camden,* Muriel Winifred Turner, *b.* 1927, *m.*
1985 *Warnock,* Helen Mary Warnock, DBE, *b.* 1924, *m.*
1970 *White,* Eirene Lloyd White, *b.* 1909, *w.*
1993 *Williams of Crosby,* Shirley Vivien Teresa Brittain Williams, PC, *b.* 1930, *m.*
1971 *Young,* Janet Mary Young, PC, *b.* 1926, *m.*

Lords Spiritual

The Lords Spiritual are the Archbishops of Canterbury and York and 24 diocesan bishops of the Church of England. The Bishops of London, Durham and Winchester always have seats in the House of Lords; the other 21 seats are filled by the remaining diocesan bishops in order of seniority. The Bishop of Sodor and Man and the Bishop of Gibraltar are not eligible to sit in the House of Lords.

ARCHBISHOPS

Style, The Most Revd and Right Hon. the Lord Archbishop of __
Addressed as Archbishop, *or* Your Grace

Introduced to House of Lords
1991 *Canterbury* (103rd), George Leonard Carey, PC, PH.D., *b.* 1935, *m. Consecrated Bishop of Bath and Wells* 1987, *trans.* 1991
1973 *York* (96th)-*elect,* David Michael Hope, PC, D.Phil., *b.* 1940, *cons.* 1985, *elected* 1985, *trans.* 1991, 1995

BISHOPS

Style, The Right Revd the Lord Bishop of __
Addressed as My Lord
elected=date of election as diocesan bishop

Introduced to House of Lords
1990 *London* (132nd)-*elect,* Richard John Carew Chartres, *b.* 1947, *cons.* 1992, *m.*
1994 *Durham* (93rd), (Anthony) Michael (Arnold) Turnbull, *b.* 1935, *m., cons.* 1988, *elected* 1988, *trans.* 1994
1982 *Winchester* (96th)-*elect,* Michael Charles Scott-Joynt, *b.* 1943, *cons.* 1987, *m.*
1979 *Chichester* (102nd), Eric Waldram Kemp, DD, *b.* 1915, *m., cons.* 1974, *elected* 1974

1980 *Liverpool* (6th), David Stuart Sheppard, *b.* 1929, *m., cons.* 1969, *elected* 1975
1984 *Ripon* (11th), David Nigel de Lorentz Young, *b.* 1931, *m., cons.* 1977, *elected* 1977
1985 *Chelmsford* (7th), John Waine, *b.* 1930, *m., cons.* 1975, *elected* 1978, *trans.* 1986
1985 *Sheffield* (5th), David Ramsay Lunn, *b.* 1930, *cons.* 1980, *elected* 1980
1985 *Newcastle* (10th), Andrew Alexander Kenny Graham, *b.* 1929, *cons.* 1977, *elected* 1981
1987 *Worcester* (111th), Philip Harold Ernest Goodrich, *b.* 1929, *m., cons.* 1973, *elected* 1982
1987 *Chester* (39th), Michael Alfred Baughen, *b.* 1930, *m., cons.* 1982, *elected* 1982
1988 *Southwark* (7th), Robert Kerr Williamson, *b.* 1932, *m., cons.* 1984, *elected* 1984, *trans.* 1991
1989 *Lichfield* (97th), Keith Norman Sutton, *b.* 1934, *m., cons.* 1978, *elected* 1984
1989 *Peterborough* (36th), William John Westwood, *b.* 1925, *m., cons.* 1975, *elected* 1984
1989 *Portsmouth* (7th), Timothy John Bavin, *b.* 1935, *cons.* 1974, *elected* 1985 (retires Sept. 1995)
1989 *Exeter* (69th), (Geoffrey) Hewlett Thompson, *b.* 1929, *m., cons.* 1974, *elected* 1985
1990 *Bristol* (54th), Barry Rogerson, *b.* 1936, *m., cons.* 1979, *elected* 1985
1991 *Coventry* (7th), Simon Barrington-Ward, *b.* 1930, *m., cons.* 1985, *elected* 1985
1991 *Norwich* (70th), Peter John Nott, *b.* 1933, *m., cons.* 1977, *elected* 1985
1992 *St Edmundsbury and Ipswich* (8th), John Dennis, *b.* 1931, *m., cons.* 1979, *elected* 1986
1993 *Lincoln* (70th), Robert Maynard Hardy, *b.* 1936, *m., cons.* 1980, *elected* 1987
1993 *Oxford* (41st), Richard Douglas Harries, *b.* 1936, *m., cons.* 1987, *elected* 1987
1994 *Birmingham* (7th), Mark Santer, *b.* 1936, *w., cons.* 1981, *elected* 1987

Bishops awaiting seats, in order of seniority

Southwell (9th), Patrick Burnet Harris, *b.* 1934, *m., cons.* 1973, *elected* 1988

Blackburn (7th), Alan David Chesters, *b.* 1937, *m.*, *cons.* 1989, *elected* 1989

Carlisle (65th), Ian Harland, *b.* 1932, *m.*, *cons.* 1985, *elected* 1989

Truro (13th), Michael Thomas Ball, *b.* 1932, *cons.* 1980, *elected* 1990

Ely (67th), Stephen Whitefield Sykes, *b.* 1939, *m.*, *cons.* 1990, *elected* 1990

Hereford (103rd), John Keith Oliver, *b.* 1935, *m.*, *cons.* 1990, *elected* 1990

Leicester (5th), Thomas Frederick Butler, *b.* 1940, *m.*, *cons.* 1985, *elected* 1991

Bath and Wells (77th), James Lawton Thompson, *b.* 1936, *m.*, *cons.* 1978, *elected* 1991

Wakefield (11th), Nigel Simeon McCulloch, *b.* 1942, *m.*, *cons.* 1986, *elected* 1992

Bradford (8th), David James Smith, *b.* 1935, *m.*, *cons.* 1987, *elected* 1992

Manchester (10th), Christopher John Mayfield, *b.* 1935, *m.*, *cons.* 1985, *elected* 1993

Salisbury (77th), David Staffurth Stancliffe, *b.* 1942, *m.*, *cons.* 1993, *elected* 1993

Gloucester (39th), David Edward Bentley, *b.* 1935, *m.*, *cons.* 1986, *elected* 1993

Guildford (8th), John Warren Gladwin, *b.* 1942, *cons.* 1994, *elected* 1994, *m.*

Rochester (106th), Michael James Nazir-Ali, PH.D., *b.* 1949, *cons.* 1984, *elected* 1995, *m.*

Derby (6th), Jonathan Sansbury Bailey, *b.* 1940, *cons.* 1992, *m.*

St Albans (9th), Christopher William Herbert, *b.* 1944, *m.*

COURTESY TITLES

From this list it will be seen that, for example, the Marquess of Blandford is heir to the Dukedom of Marlborough, and Viscount Amberley to the Earldom of Russell. Titles of second heirs are also given, and the courtesy title of the father of a second heir is indicated by *; e.g. Earl of Burlington, eldest son of *Marquess of Hartington For forms of address, *see* page 217

MARQUESSES

*Blandford – *Marlborough, D.*
Bowmont and Cessford – *Roxburghe, D.*
Douglas and Clydesdale – *Hamilton, D.*
*Douro – *Wellington, D.*
Graham – *Montrose, D.*
Granby – *Rutland, D.*
Hamilton – *Abercorn, D.*
*Hartington – *Devonshire, D.*
*Kildare – *Leinster, D.*
Lorne – *Argyll, D.*
*Tavistock – *Bedford, D.*
*Worcester – *Beaufort, D.*

EARLS

Aboyne – *Huntly, M.*
Altamont – *Sligo, M.*
Ancram – *Lothian, M.*
Arundel and Surrey – *Norfolk, D.*
*Bective – *Headfort, M.*
*Belfast – *Donegall, M.*
Brecknock – *Camden, M.*
Burford – *St Albans, D.*
Burlington – *Hartington, M.*
*Cardigan – *Ailesbury, M.*
Compton – *Northampton, M.*
*Dalkeith – *Buccleuch, D.*
Dumfries – *Bute, M.*
*Euston – *Grafton, D.*
Glamorgan – * *Worcester, M.*
Grosvenor – *Westminster, D.*
*Haddo – *Aberdeen and Temair, M.*
Hillsborough – *Downshire, M.*
Hopetoun – *Linlithgow, M.*
March and Kinrara – *Richmond, D.*
*Mount Charles – *Conyngham, M.*
Mornington – *Douro, M.*
Offaly – * *Kildare, M.*
Ronaldshay – *Zetland, M.*
*St Andrews – *Kent, D.*
*Shelburne – *Lansdowne, M.*
*Southesk – *Fife, D.*
Sunderland – * *Blandford, M.*

*Tyrone – *Waterford, M.*
Ulster – *Gloucester, D.*
*Uxbridge – *Anglesey, M.*
Wiltshire – *Winchester, M.*
Yarmouth – *Hertford, M.*

VISCOUNTS

Althorp – *Spencer, E.*
Amberley – *Russell, E.*
Andover – *Suffolk and Berkshire, E.*
Anson – *Lichfield, E.*
Asquith – *Oxford & Asquith, E.*
Boringdon – *Morley, E.*
Borodale – *Beatty, E.*
Boyle – *Shannon, E.*
Brocas – *Jellicoe, E.*
Calne and Calstone – * *Shelburne, E.*
Campden – *Gainsborough, E.*
Carlow – *Portarlington, E.*
Carlton – *Wharncliffe, E.*
Castlereagh – *Londonderry, M.*
Chelsea – *Cadogan, E.*
Chewton – *Waldegrave, E.*
Chichester – * *Belfast, E.*
Clanfield – *Peel, E.*
Clive – *Powis, E.*
Coke – *Leicester, E.*
Corry – *Belmore, E.*
Corvedale – *Baldwin of Bewdley, E.*
Cranborne – *Salisbury, M.*
Cranley – *Onslow, E.*
Crichton – *Erne, E.*
Crowhurst – *Cottenham, E.*
Dalrymple – *Stair, E.*
Dangan – *Cowley, E.*
Dawick – *Haig, E.*
Deerhurst – *Coventry, E.*
Drumlanrig – *Queensberry, M.*
Dunwich – *Stradbroke, E.*
Dupplin – *Kinnoull, E.*
Ebrington – *Fortescue, E.*
Ednam – *Dudley, E.*
Emlyn – *Cawdor, E.*
Encombe – *Eldon, E.*
Ennismore – *Listowel, E.*
Enfield – *Strafford, E.*
Erleigh – *Reading, M.*
Errington – *Cromer, E.*
Fincastle – *Dunmore, E.*
FitzHarris – *Malmesbury, E.*

Folkestone – *Radnor, E.*
Forbes – *Granard, E.*
Garmoyle – *Cairns, E.*
Garnock – *Lindsay, E.*
Glandine – *Norbury, E.*
Glenapp – *Inchcape, E.*
Glentworth – *Limerick, E.*
Grimstone – *Verulam, E.*
Gwynedd – *Lloyd George of Dwyfor, E.*
Hawkesbury – *Liverpool, E.*
Hinchingbrooke – *Sandwich, E.*
Ikerrin – *Carrick, E.*
Ingestre – *Shrewsbury, E.*
Ipswich – *Euston, E.*
Jocelyn – *Roden, E.*
Kelburn – *Glasgow, E.*
Kingsborough – *Kingston, E.*
Knebworth – *Lytton, E.*
Lascelles – *Harewood, E.*
Lewisham – *Dartmouth, E.*
Linley – *Snowdon, E.*
Loftus – *Ely, M.*
Lowther – *Lonsdale, E.*
Lumley – *Scarbrough, E.*
Lymington – *Portsmouth, E.*
Macmillan of Ovenden – *Stockton, E.*
Maidstone – *Winchilsea and Nottingham, E.*
Maitland – *Lauderdale, E.*
Malden – *Essex, E.*
Mandeville – *Manchester, D.*
Medina – *Milford Haven, M.*
Melgund – *Minto, E.*
Merton – *Nelson, E.*
Moore – *Drogheda, E.*
Newport – *Bradford, E.*
Newry and Mourne – *Kilmorey, E.*
Parker – *Macclesfield, E.*
Perceval – *Egmont, E.*
Petersham – *Harrington, E.*
Pollington – *Mexborough, E.*
Raynham – *Townshend, M.*
Reidhaven – *Seafield, E.*
Ruthven of Canberra – *Gowrie, E.*
St Cyres – *Iddesleigh, E.*
Sandon – *Harrowby, E.*
Savernake – * *Cardigan, E.*
Slane – * *Mount Charles, E.*
Somerton – *Normanton, E.*
Stopford – *Courtown, E.*
Stormont – *Mansfield, E.*
Strathallan – *Perth, E.*

Stuart – *Castle Stewart, E.*
Suirdale – *Donoughmore, E.*
Tamworth – *Ferrers, E.*
Tarbat – *Cromartie, E.*
Vaughan – *Lisburne, E.*
Villiers – *Jersey, E.*
Weymouth – *Bath, M.*
Windsor – *Plymouth, E.*
Wolmer – *Selborne, E.*
Woodstock – *Portland, E.*

BARONS (LORD ___)

Aberdour – *Morton, E.*
Apsley – *Bathurst, E.*
Ardee – *Meath, E.*
Ashley – *Shaftesbury, E.*
Balgonie – *Leven & Melville, E.*
Balniel – *Crawford and Balcarres, E.*
Berriedale – *Caithness, E.*
Bingham – *Lucan, E.*
Binning – *Haddington, E.*
Brooke – *Warwick, E.*
Bruce – *Elgin, E.*
Buckhurst – *De La Warr, E.*
Burghley – *Exeter, M.*
Cardross – *Buchan, E.*
Carnegie – * *Southesk, E.*
Clifton – *Darnley, E.*
Cochrane – *Dundonald, E.*
Courtenay – *Devon, E.*
Dalmeny – *Rosebery, E.*
Doune – *Moray, E.*
Downpatrick – * *St Andrews, E.*
Eliot – *St Germans, E.*
Eskdail – * *Dalkeith, E.*
Formartine – * *Haddo, E.*
Gillford – *Clanwilliam, E.*
Glamis – *Strathmore, E.*
Greenock – *Cathcart, E.*
Guernsey – *Aylesford, E.*
Hay – *Erroll, E.*
Herbert – *Pembroke, E.*
Howland – *Tavistock, M.*
Hyde – *Clarendon, E.*
Inverurie – *Kintore, E.*
Irwin – *Halifax, E.*
Johnstone – *Annandale and Hartfell, E.*
Kenlis – * *Bective, E.*
Langton – *Temple of Stowe, E.*
La Poer – * *Tyrone, E.*
Leslie – *Rothes, E.*
Leveson – *Granville, E.*
Loughborough – *Rosslyn, E.*
Maltravers – * *Arundel and Surrey, E.*
Mauchline – *Loudoun, C.*

Medway – *Cranbrook, E.*
Montgomerie – *Eglinton and Winton, E.*
Moreton – *Ducie, E.*
Naas – *Mayo, E.*
Neidpath – *Wemyss & March, E.*

Norreys – *Lindsey & Abingdon, E.*
North – *Guilford, E.*
Ogilvy – *Airlie, E.*
Oxmantown – *Rosse, E.*
Paget de Beaudesert – *Uxbridge, E.*

Porchester – *Carnarvon, E.*
Ramsay – *Dalhousie, E.*
Romsey – *Mountbatten of Burma, C.*
Rosehill – *Northesk, E.*
Scrymgeour – *Dundee, E.*
Seymour – *Somerset, D.*

Strathnaver – *Sutherland, C.*
Wodehouse – *Kimberley, E.*
Worsley – *Yarborough, E.*

PEERS' SURNAMES WHICH DIFFER FROM THEIR TITLES

The following symbols indicate the rank of the peer holding each title:

C. Countess
D. Duke
E. Earl
M. Marquess
V. Viscount
* Life Peer
Where no designation is given, the title is that of an hereditary Baron or Baroness

Abney-Hastings – *Loudoun, C.*
Acheson – *Gosford, E.*
Adderley – *Norton*
Addington – *Sidmouth, V.*
Agar – *Normanton, E.*
Aitken – *Beaverbrook*
Akers-Douglas – *Chilston, V.*
Alexander – *A. of Tunis, E.*
Alexander – *A. of Weedon*
Alexander – *A. of Caledon, E.*
Allen – *A. of Abbeydale*
Allen – *Croham*
Allsopp – *Hindlip*
Amery – *A. of Lustleigh*
Anderson – *Waverley, V.*
Annesley – *Valentia, V.*
Anson – *Lichfield, E.*
Archer – *A. of Sandwell*
Archer – *A. of Weston-super-Mare*
Armstrong – *A. of Ilminster*
Armstrong-Jones – *Snowdon, E.*
Arthur – *Glenarthur*
Arundell – *Talbot of Malahide*
Ashley – *A. of Stoke*
Ashley-Cooper – *Shaftesbury, E.*
Ashton – *A. of Hyde*
Asquith – *Oxford & Asquith, E.*
Assheton – *Clitheroe*
Astley – *Hastings*
Astor – *A. of Hever*
Atkins – *Colnbrook*
Aubrey-Fletcher – *Braye*
Bailey – *Glanusk*
Baillie – *Burton*
Baillie Hamilton – *Haddington, E.*
Baldwin – *B. of Bewdley, E.*

Balfour – *B. of Inchrye*
Balfour – *Kinross*
Balfour – *Riverdale*
Bampfylde – *Poltimore*
Banbury – *B. of Southam*
Barber – *B. of Tewkesbury*
Baring – *Ashburton*
Baring – *Cromer, E.*
Baring – *Howick of Glendale*
Baring – *Northbrook*
Baring – *Revelstoke*
Barker – *Trumpington*
Barnes – *Gorell*
Barnewall – *Trimlestown*
Bathurst – *Bledisloe, V.*
Beauclerk – *St Albans, D.*
Beaumont – *Allendale, V.*
Beaumont – *B. of Whitley*
Beckett – *Grimthorpe*
Bellow – *Bellwin*
Benn – *Stansgate, V.*
Bennet – *Tankerville, E.*
Bentinck – *Portland, E.*
Beresford – *Decies*
Beresford – *Waterford, M.*
Berry – *Camrose, V.*
Berry – *Hartwell*
Berry – *Kemsley, V.*
Bertie – *Lindsey, E.*
Best – *Wynford*
Bethell – *Westbury*
Bewicke-Copley – *Cromwell*
Bigham – *Mersey, V.*
Bigham – *Nairne*
Bingham – *Clanmorris*
Bingham – *Lucan, E.*
Blackwood – *Dufferin & Clandeboye*
Bligh – *Darnley, E.*
Blyth – *B. of Rowington*
Bootle-Wilbraham – *Skelmersdale*
Boscawen – *Falmouth, V.*
Boston – *B. of Faversham*
Bourke – *Mayo, E.*
Bowes Lyon – *Strathmore, E.*
Bowyer – *Denham*
Boyd – *Kilmarnock*
Boyle – *Cork & Orrery, E.*
Boyle – *Glasgow, E.*
Boyle – *Shannon, E.*
Brabazon – *Meath, E.*
Braine – *B. of Wheatley*
Brand – *Hampden, V.*
Brandon – *B. of Oakbrook*
Brassey – *B. of Apethorpe*

Brett – *Esher, V.*
Bridge – *B. of Harwich*
Bridgeman – *Bradford, E.*
Brodrick – *Midleton, V.*
Brooke – *Alanbrooke, V.*
Brooke – *Brookeborough, V.*
Brooke – *B. of Ystradfellte*
Brooks – *B. of Tremorfa*
Brooks – *Crawshaw*
Brougham – *Brougham and Vaux*
Broughton – *Fairhaven*
Browne – *Kilmaine*
Browne – *Oranmore and Browne*
Browne – *Sligo, M.*
Bruce – *Aberdare*
Bruce – *Balfour of Burleigh*
Bruce – *B. of Donington*
Bruce – *Elgin and Kincardine, E.*
Brudenell-Bruce – *Ailesbury, M.*
Buchan – *Tweedsmuir*
Buckley – *Wrenbury*
Butler – *Carrick, E.*
Butler – *Dunboyne*
Butler – *Lanesborough, E.*
Butler – *Mountgarret, V.*
Butler – *Ormonde, M.*
Buxton – *B. of Alsa*
Byng – *Strafford, E.*
Byng – *Torrington, V.*
Callaghan – *C. of Cardiff*
Cameron – *C. of Lochbroom*
Campbell – *Argyll, D.*
Campbell – *Breadalbane and Holland, E.*
Campbell – *C. of Alloway*
Campbell – *C. of Croy*
Campbell – *Cawdor, E.*
Campbell – *Colgrain*
Campbell – *Stratheden and Campbell*
Campbell-Gray – *Gray*
Canning – *Garvagh*
Capell – *Essex, E.*
Carington – *Carrington*
Carlisle – *C. of Bucklow*
Carmichael – *C. of Kelvingrove*
Carnegie – *Fife, D.*
Carnegie – *Northesk, E.*
Carr – *C. of Hadley*
Cary – *Falkland, V.*
Castle – *C. of Blackburn*
Caulfeild – *Charlemont, V.*
Cavendish – *C. of Furness*

Cavendish – *Chesham*
Cavendish – *Devonshire, D.*
Cavendish – *Waterpark*
Cayzer – *Rotherwick*
Cecil – *Amherst of Hackney*
Cecil – *Exeter, M.*
Cecil – *Rockley*
Cecil – *Salisbury, M.*
Chalker – *C. of Wallasey*
Chaloner – *Gisborough*
Chapman – *Northfield*
Charteris – *C. of Amisfield*
Charteris – *Wemyss and March, E.*
Cheshire – *Ryder of Warsaw*
Chetwynd-Talbot – *Shrewsbury, E.*
Chichester – *Donegall, M.*
Chichester-Clark – *Moyola*
Child Villiers – *Jersey, E.*
Cholmondeley – *Delamere*
Chubb – *Hayter*
Clark – *C. of Kempston*
Clegg-Hill – *Hill, V.*
Clifford – *C. of Chudleigh*
Cochrane – *C. of Cults*
Cochrane – *Dundonald, E.*
Cocks – *C. of Hartcliffe*
Cocks – *Somers*
Cokayne – *Cullen of Ashbourne*
Coke – *Leicester, E.*
Cole – *Enniskillen, E.*
Collier – *Monkswell*
Colville – *Clydesmuir*
Colville – *C. of Culross, V.*
Compton – *Northampton, M.*
Conolly-Carew – *Carew*
Constantine – *C. of Stanmore*
Cooke – *C. of Islandreagh*
Cooper – *Norwich, V.*
Corbett – *Rowallan*
Courtenay – *Devon, E.*
Cox – *Kings Norton*
Craig – *C. of Radley*
Craig – *Craigavon, V.*
Crichton – *Erne, E.*
Crichton-Stuart – *Bute, M.*
Cripps – *Parmoor*
Crossley – *Somerleyton*
Cubitt – *Ashcombe*
Cunliffe-Lister – *Masham of Ilton*

Cunliffe-Lister – *Swinton, E.*
Curzon – *Howe, E.*
Curzon – *Scarsdale, V.*
Cust – *Brownlow*
Dalrymple – *Stair, E.*
Daubeny de Moleyns – *Ventry*
Davies – *Darwen*
Davison – *Broughshane*
Dawnay – *Downe, V.*
Dawson-Damer – *Portarlington, E.*
Dean – *D. of Beswick**
Dean – *D. of Harptree**
Dean – *D. of Thornton-le-Fylde**
Deane – *Muskerry*
de Courcy – *Kingsale*
de Grey – *Walsingham*
Delacourt-Smith – *Delacourt Smith of Alteryn**
Denison – *Londesborough*
Denison-Pender – *Pender*
Denton – *D. of Wakefield**
Devereux – *Hereford, V.*
Dewar – *Forteviot*
De Yarburgh-Bateson – *Deramore*
Dixon – *Glentoran*
Dodson – *Monk Bretton*
Donaldson – *D. of Kingsbridge**
Donaldson – *D. of Lymington**
Dormand – *D. of Easington**
Douglas – *Morton, E.*
Douglas – *Queensberry, M.*
Douglas-Hamilton – *Hamilton, D.*
Douglas-Hamilton – *Selkirk, E.*
Douglas-Home – *Dacre*
Douglas-Home – *Home of the Hirsel**
Douglas-Pennant – *Penrhyn*
Douglas-Scott-Montagu – *Montagu of Beaulieu*
Drummond – *Perth, E.*
Drummond of Megginch – *Strange*
Dugdale – *Crathorne*
Duke – *Merrivale*
Duncombe – *Feversham*
Dundas – *Melville, V.*
Dundas – *Zetland, M.*
Eady – *Swinfen*
Eccles – *E. of Moulton**
Eden – *Auckland*
Eden – *E. of Winton**
Eden – *Henley*
Edgcumbe – *Mount Edgcumbe, E.*
Edmondson – *Sandford*
Edwardes – *Kensington*
Edwards – *Chelmer**
Edwards – *Crickhowell**
Egerton – *Sutherland, D.*
Egerton – *Wilton, E.*

Eliot – *St Germans, E.*
Elliot-Murray-Kynynmound – *Minto, E.*
Elliott – *E. of Morpeth**
Erroll – *E. of Hale*
Erskine – *Buchan, E.*
Erskine – *Mar & Kellie, E.*
Erskine-Murray – *Elibank*
Evans – *Mountevans*
Evans-Freke – *Carbery*
Eve – *Silsoe*
Ewing – *E. of Kirkford**
Fairfax – *F. of Cameron*
Fane – *Westmorland, E.*
Farrington – *F. of Ribbleton**
Feilding – *Denbigh, E.*
Fellowes – *De Ramsey*
Fermor-Hesketh – *Hesketh*
Fiennes – *Saye & Sele*
Fiennes-Clinton – *Lincoln, E.*
Finch Hatton – *Winchilsea, E.*
Finch-Knightley – *Aylesford, E.*
Fisher – *F. of Rednal**
Fitzalan-Howard – *Herries of Terregles*
Fitzalan-Howard – *Norfolk, D.*
FitzClarence – *Munster, E.*
FitzGerald – *Leinster, D.*
Fitzherbert – *Stafford*
Fitz-Maurice – *Orkney, E.*
FitzRoy – *Grafton, D.*
FitzRoy – *Southampton*
FitzRoy Newdegate – *Daventry, V.*
Fletcher-Vane – *Inglewood*
Flower – *Ashbrook, V.*
Foljambe – *Liverpool, E.*
Forbes – *Granard, E.*
Fox-Strangways – *Ilchester, E.*
Frankland – *Zouche*
Fraser – *F. of Carmyllie**
Fraser – *F. of Kilmorack**
Fraser – *Lovat*
Fraser – *Saltoun*
Fraser – *Strathalmond*
Freeman-Grenville – *Kinloss*
Fremantle – *Cottesloe*
French – *De Freyne*
Galbraith – *Strathclyde*
Ganzoni – *Belstead*
Gardner – *G. of Parkes**
Gathorne-Hardy – *Cranbrook, E.*
Gibbs – *Aldenham*
Gibbs – *Wraxall*
Gibson – *Ashbourne*
Giffard – *Halsbury, E.*
Gilbey – *Vaux of Harrowden*
Gilmour – *G. of Craigmillar**
Gladwin – *G. of Clee**
Glyn – *Wolverton*
Godley – *Kilbracken*
Goff – *G. of Chieveley**
Gordon – *Aberdeen, M.*

Gordon – *Huntly, M.*
Gordon Lennox – *Richmond, D.*
Gore – *Arran, E.*
Gough-Calthorpe – *Calthorpe*
Gould – *G. of Potternewton**
Graham – *G. of Edmonton**
Graham – *Montrose, D.*
Graham-Toler – *Norbury, E.*
Grant of Grant – *Strathspey*
Grant-Ferris – *Harvington**
Granville – *G. of Eye**
Gray – *G. of Contin**
Greaves – *Dysart, C.*
Greenall – *Daresbury*
Greene – *G. of Harrow Weald**
Greenhill – *G. of Harrow**
Greville – *Warwick, E.*
Grey – *G. of Naunton**
Griffiths – *G. of Fforestfach**
Grigg – *Altrincham*
Grimston – *G. of Westbury*
Grimston – *Verulam, E.*
Grosvenor – *Ebury*
Grosvenor – *Westminster, D.*
Gueterbock – *Berkeley*
Guest – *Wimborne, V.*
Guinness – *Iveagh, E.*
Guinness – *Moyne*
Gully – *Selby, V.*
Gurdon – *Cranworth*
Gwynne Jones – *Chalfont**
Hamilton – *Abercorn, D.*
Hamilton – *Belhaven and Stenton*
Hamilton – *Dudley*
Hamilton – *H. of Dalzell*
Hamilton – *Holm Patrick*
Hamilton-Russell – *Boyne, V.*
Hamilton-Smith – *Colwyn*
Hanbury-Tracy – *Sudeley*
Handcock – *Castlemaine*
Harbord-Hamond – *Suffield*
Harding – *H. of Petherton*
Hardinge – *H. of Penshurst*
Hare – *Blakenham, V.*
Hare – *Listowel, E.*
Harmsworth – *Rothermere, V.*
Harris – *H. of Greenwich**
Harris – *H. of High Cross**
Harris – *Malmesbury, E.*
Harvey – *H. of Tasburgh*
Hastings Bass – *Huntingdon, E.*
Hay – *Erroll, E.*
Hay – *Kinnoull, E.*
Hay – *Tweeddale, M.*
Heathcote-Drummond-Willoughby – *Willoughby de Eresby*
Hely-Hutchinson – *Donoughmore, E.*
Henderson – *Faringdon*

Henderson – *H. of Brompton**
Hennessy – *Windlesham*
Henniker-Major – *Henniker*
Hepburne-Scott – *Polwarth*
Herbert – *Carnarvon, E.*
Herbert – *Hemingford*
Herbert – *Pembroke, E.*
Herbert – *Powis, E.*
Hermon-Hodge – *Wyfold*
Hervey – *Bristol, M.*
Hewitt – *Lifford, V.*
Hicks Beach – *St Aldwyn, E.*
Hill – *Downshire, M.*
Hill – *Sandys*
Hill-Trevor – *Trevor*
Hilton – *H. of Eggardon**
Hobart-Hampden – *Buckinghamshire, E.*
Hogg – *Hailsham of St Marylebone**
Holland-Hibbert – *Knutsford, V.*
Hollis – *H. of Heigham**
Holme – *H. of Cheltenham**
Holmes à Court – *Heytesbury*
Hood – *Bridport, V.*
Hope – *Glendevon*
Hope – *H. of Craighead**
Hope – *Linlithgow, M.*
Hope – *Rankeillour*
Hope Johnstone – *Annandale and Hartfell, E.*
Hope-Morley – *Hollenden*
Hopkinson – *Colyton*
Hore Ruthven – *Gowrie, E.*
Houghton – *H. of Sowerby**
Hovell-Thurlow-Cumming-Bruce – *Thurlow*
Howard – *Carlisle, E.*
Howard – *Effingham, E.*
Howard – *H. of Penrith*
Howard – *Strathcona*
Howard – *Suffolk and Berkshire, E.*
Howe – *H. of Aberavon**
Howells – *Geraint**
Howie – *H. of Troon**
Hubbard – *Addington*
Huggins – *Malvern, V.*
Hughes – *Cledwyn of Penrhos**
Hughes-Young – *St Helens*
Hunt – *H. of Tanworth**
Hutchinson – *H. of Lullington**
Ingrams – *Darcy de Knayth*
Innes-Ker – *Roxburghe, D.*
Inskip – *Caldecote, V.*
Irby – *Boston*
Irvine – *I. of Lairg**
Isaacs – *Reading, M.*
James – *J. of Holland Park**
James – *Northbourne*
Jauncey – *J. of Tullichettle**
Jay – *J. of Paddington**
Jebb – *Gladwyn*

Jenkin – *J. of Roding**
Jenkins – *J. of Hillhead**
Jenkins – *J. of Putney**
Jervis – *St Vincent, V.*
Jocelyn – *Roden, E.*
Johnston – *J. of Rockport**
Jolliffe – *Hylton*
Joynson-Hicks – *Brentford, V.*
Kay-Shuttleworth – *Shuttleworth*
Kearley – *Devonport, V.*
Keith – *K. of Castleacre**
Keith – *K. of Kinkel**
Keith – *Kintore, E.*
Kemp – *Rochdale, V.*
Kennedy – *Ailsa, M.*
Kenworthy – *Strabolgi*
Keppel – *Albemarle, E.*
Kerr – *Lothian, M.*
Kerr – *Teviot*
King – *Lovelace, E.*
King – *K. of Wartnaby**
King-Tenison – *Kingston, E.*
Kirkham – *Berners*
Kitchener – *K. of Khartoum, E.*
Kitson – *Airedale*
Knatchbull – *Brabourne*
Knatchbull – *Mountbatten of Burma, C.*
Knox – *Ranfurly, E.*
Laing – *L. of Dunphail**
Lamb – *Rochester*
Lambart – *Cavan, E.*
Lambton – *Durham, E.*
Lampson – *Killearn*
Lane – *L. of Horsell**
Lascelles – *Harewood, E.*
Law – *Coleraine*
Law – *Ellenborough*
Lawrence – *Trevethin and Oaksey*
Lawson – *Burnham*
Lawson – *L. of Blaby**
Lawson-Johnston – *Luke*
Legge – *Dartmouth, E.*
Legh – *Grey of Codnor*
Legh – *Newton*
Leigh-Pemberton – *Kingsdown**
Leith – *Burgh*
Lennox-Boyd – *Boyd of Merton, V.*
Le Poer Trench – *Clancarty, E.*
Leslie – *Rothes, E.*
Leslie Melville – *Leven and Melville, E.*
Lester – *L. of Herne Hill**
Lever – *Leverhulme, V.*
Leveson-Gower – *Granville, E.*
Lewis – *L. of Newnham**
Lewis – *Merthyr*
Liddell – *Ravensworth*
Lindesay-Bethune – *Lindsay, E.*
Lindsay – *Crawford, E.*
Lindsay – *L. of Birker*

Littleton – *Hatherton*
Llewelyn-Davies – *Hemphill*
Llewelyn-Davies of Hastoe*
Lloyd – *L. of Berwick**
Lloyd George – *Lloyd George of Dwyfor, E.*
Lloyd George – *Tenby, V.*
Lloyd-Mostyn – *Mostyn*
Loder – *Wakehurst*
Lopes – *Roborough*
Low – *Aldington*
Lowry-Corry – *Belmore, E.*
Lowther – *Lonsdale, E.*
Lowther – *Ullswater, V.*
Lubbock – *Avebury*
Lucas – *L. of Chilworth*
Lumley – *Scarbrough, E.*
Lumley-Savile – *Savile*
Lyon-Dalberg-Acton – *Acton*
Lysaght – *Lisle*
Lyttelton – *Chandos, V.*
Lyttelton – *Cobham, V.*
Lytton Cobbold – *Cobbold*
McAlpine – *M. of West Green**
Macaulay – *M. of Bragar**
McClintock-Bunbury – *Rathdonnell*
McColl – *M. of Dulwich**
Macdonald – *M. of Gwaenysgor*
Macdonald of Macdonald – *Macdonald*
McDonnell – *Antrim, E.*
Macfarlane – *M. of Bearsden**
McFarlane – *M. of Llandaff**
McGregor – *M. of Durris**
McIntosh – *M. of Haringey**
Mackay – *Inchcape, E.*
Mackay – *M. of Ardbrecknish**
Mackay – *M. of Clashfern**
Mackay – *Reay*
Mackay – *Tanlaw**
Mackenzie – *Cromartie, E.*
Mackie – *M. of Benshie**
Mackintosh – *M. of Halifax, V.*
McLaren – *Aberconway*
MacLehose – *M. of Beoch**
Macleod – *M. of Borve**
Macmillan – *Stockton, E.*
Macpherson – *M. of Drumochter*
Macpherson – *Strathcarron*
Maffey – *Rugby*
Maitland – *Lauderdale, E.*
Makgill – *Oxfuird, V.*
Makins – *Sherfield*
Manners – *Rutland, D.*
Manningham-Buller – *Dilhorne, V.*
Mansfield – *Sandhurst*
Marks – *M. of Broughton*
Marquis – *Woolton, E.*
Marshall – *M. of Goring**
Marsham – *Romney, E.*

Martyn-Hemphill – *Hemphill*
Mason – *M. of Barnsley**
Maude – *Hawarden, V.*
Maxwell – *de Ros*
Maxwell – *Farnham*
Meade – *Clanwilliam, E.*
Mercer Nairne Petty-Fitzmaurice – *Lansdowne, M.*
Millar – *Inchyra*
Miller – *M. of Hendon**
Milles-Lade – *Sondes, E.*
Milner – *M. of Leeds*
Mitchell-Thomson – *Selsdon*
Mitford – *Redesdale*
Monckton – *M. of Brenchley, V.*
Monckton-Arundell – *Galway, V.*
Mond – *Melchett*
Money-Coutts – *Latymer*
Montagu – *Manchester, D.*
Montagu – *Sandwich, E.*
Montagu – *Swaythling*
Montagu Douglas Scott – *Buccleuch, D.*
Montagu Stuart Wortley – *Wharncliffe, E.*
Montague – *Amwell*
Montgomerie – *Eglinton, E.*
Montgomery – *M. of Alamein, V.*
Moore – *Drogheda, E.*
Moore – *M. of Lower Marsh**
Moore – *M. of Wolvercote**
Moore-Brabazon – *Brabazon of Tara*
Moreton – *Ducie, E.*
Morris – *Killanin*
Morris – *M. of Castle Morris**
Morris – *M. of Kenwood*
Morrison – *Dunrossil, V.*
Morrison – *Margadale*
Mosley – *Ravensdale*
Mountbatten – *Milford Haven, M.*
Muff – *Calverley*
Mulholland – *Dunleath*
Murray – *Atholl, D.*
Murray – *Dunmore, E.*
Murray – *Mansfield and Mansfield, E.*
Murray – *M. of Epping Forest**
Murton – *M. of Lindisfarne**
Nall-Cain – *Brocket*
Napier – *Napier and Ettrick*
Napier – *N. of Magdala*
Needham – *Kilmorey, E.*
Nelson – *N. of Stafford*
Nevill – *Abergavenny, M.*
Neville – *Braybrooke*
Nicholls – *N. of Birkenhead**
Nicolson – *Carnock*
Nivison – *Glendyne*
Noel – *Gainsborough, E.*
North – *Guilford, E.*

Northcote – *Iddesleigh, E.*
Norton – *Grantley*
Norton – *Rathcreedan*
Nugent – *Westmeath, E.*
O'Brien – *Inchiquin*
O'Brien – *O'Brien of Lothbury**
Ogilvie-Grant – *Seafield, E.*
Ogilvy – *Airlie, E.*
Oliver – *O. of Aylmerton**
O'Neill – *Rathcavan*
Orde-Powlett – *Bolton*
Ormsby-Gore – *Harlech*
Page – *Whaddon**
Paget – *Anglesey, M.*
Pakenham – *Longford, E.*
Pakington – *Hampton*
Palmer – *Lucas & Dingwall*
Palmer – *Selborne, E.*
Park – *P. of Monmouth**
Parker – *Macclesfield, E.*
Parker – *Morley, E.*
Parnell – *Congleton*
Parsons – *Rosse, E.*
Paulet – *Winchester, M.*
Peake – *Ingleby, V.*
Pearson – *Cowdray, V.*
Pearson – *P. of Rannoch**
Pease – *Gainford*
Pease – *Wardington*
Pelham – *Chichester, E.*
Pelham – *Yarborough, E.*
Pellew – *Exmouth, V.*
Penny – *Marchwood, V.*
Pepys – *Cottenham, E.*
Perceval – *Egmont, E.*
Percy – *Northumberland, D.*
Perry – *P. of Southwark**
Perry – *P. of Walton**
Pery – *Limerick, E.*
Peyton – *P. of Yeovil**
Philipps – *Milford*
Philipps – *St Davids, V.*
Phillips – *P. of Ellesmere**
Phipps – *Normanby, M.*
Plant – *P. of Highfield**
Platt – *P. of Writtle**
Pleydell-Bouverie – *Radnor, E.*
Plummer – *P. of St Marylebone**
Plumptre – *Fitzwalter*
Plunkett – *Dunsany*
Plunkett – *Louth*
Pollock – *Hanworth, V.*
Pomeroy – *Harberton, V.*
Ponsonby – *Bessborough, E.*
Ponsonby – *de Mauley*
Ponsonby – *P. of Shulbrede*
Ponsonby – *Sysonby*
Porter – *P. of Luddenham**
Powys – *Lilford*
Pratt – *Camden, M.*
Preston – *Gormanston, V.*
Primrose – *Rosebery, E.*
Prittie – *Dunalley*
Prout – *Kingsland**
Ramsay – *Dalhousie, E.*
Ramsbotham – *Soulbury, V.*
Rawlinson – *R. of Ewell**

Rees-Williams – *Ogmore*
Renfrew – *R. of Kaimsthorn**
Rhys – *Dynevor*
Richards – *Milverton*
Richardson – *R. of Duntisbourne**
Rippon – *R. of Hexham**
Ritchie – *R. of Dundee*
Robens – *R. of Woldingham**
Roberts – *Clwyd*
Robertson – *R. of Oakridge*
Robertson – *Wharton*
Robinson – *Martonmere*
Robson – *R. of Kiddington**
Roche – *Fermoy*
Rodd – *Rennell*
Rodger – *R. of Earlsferry**
Rodgers – *R. of Quarry Bank**
Roll – *R. of Ipsden**
Roper-Curzon – *Teynham*
Rospigliosi – *Newburgh, E.*
Rous – *Stradbroke, E.*
Rowley-Conwy – *Langford*
Royle – *Fanshawe of Richmond**
Runciman – *R. of Doxford, V.*
Russell – *Ampthill*
Russell – *Bedford, D.*
Russell – *de Clifford*
Russell – *R. of Liverpool*
Ryder – *Harrowby, E.*
Ryder – *R. of Eaton Hastings**
Ryder – *R. of Warsaw**
Sackville – *De La Warr, E.*
Sackville-West – *Sackville*
Sainsbury – *S. of Preston Candover**
St Aubyn – *St Levan*
St Clair – *Sinclair*
St Clair-Erskine – *Rosslyn, E.*
St John – *Bolingbroke and St John, V.*
St John – *St John of Blesto*
St John-Stevas – *St John of Fawsley**
St Leger – *Doneraile, V.*
Samuel – *Bearsted, V.*
Sanderson – *S. of Ayot*
Sanderson – *S. of Bowden**
Sandilands – *Torphichen*
Saumarez – *De Saumarez*
Savile – *Mexborough, E.*
Scarlett – *Abinger*
Schreiber – *Marlesford**
Sclater-Booth – *Basing*
Scott – *Eldon, E.*
Scott-Ellis – *Howard de Walden*
Scrymgeour – *Dundee, E.*
Seager – *Leighton of St Mellons*
Seely – *Mottistone*
Sefton – *S. of Garston**
Seymour – *Hertford, M.*
Seymour – *Somerset, D.*
Shaw – *Craigmyle*
Shaw – *S. of Northstead**
Sheppard – *S. of Didgemere**

Shirley – *Ferrers, E.*
Short – *Glenamara**
Siddeley – *Kenilworth*
Sidney – *De L'Isle, V.*
Sieff – *S. of Brimpton**
Simon – *S. of Glaisdale**
Simon – *S. of Wythenshawe*
Sinclair – *Caithness, E.*
Sinclair – *S. of Cleeve*
Sinclair – *Thurso, V.*
Skeffington – *Massereene, V.*
Slynn – *S. of Hadley**
Smith – *Bicester*
Smith – *Hambleden, V.*
Smith – *Kirkhill**
Smith – *S. of Gilmorehill**
Somerset – *Beaufort, D.*
Somerset – *Raglan*
Souter – *Audley*
Spencer – *Churchill, V.*
Spencer-Churchill – *Marlborough, D.*
Spring Rice – *Monteagle of Brandon*
Stanhope – *Harrington, E.*
Stanley – *Derby, E.*
Stanley – *Stanley of Alderley & Sheffield*
Stapleton-Cotton – *Combermere, V.*
Sterling – *S. of Plaistow**
Stevens – *S. of Ludgate**
Stewart – *Galloway, E.*
Stewart – *Stewartby**
Stodart – *S. of Leaston**
Stoddart – *S. of Swindon**
Stonor – *Camoys*
Stopford – *Courtown, E.*
Stourton – *Mowbray*
Strachey – *O'Hagan*
Strutt – *Belper*
Strutt – *Rayleigh*
Stuart – *Castle Stewart, E.*
Stuart – *Moray, E.*
Stuart – *S. of Findhorn, V.*
Suenson-Taylor – *Grantchester*
Taylor – *Ingrow**
Taylor – *T. of Blackburn**
Taylor – *T. of Gosforth**
Taylor – *T. of Gryfe**
Taylour – *Headfort, M.*
Temple-Gore-Langton – *Temple of Stowe, E.*
Tennant – *Glenconner*
Thellusson – *Rendlesham*
Thesiger – *Chelmsford, V.*
Thomas – *T. of Gwydir**
Thomas – *T. of Swynnerton**
Thomas – *T. of Walliswood**
Thomas – *Tonypandy, V.*
Thomson – *T. of Fleet*
Thomson – *T. of Monifieth**
Thynn – *Bath, M.*
Thynne – *Bath, M.*
Tottenham – *Ely, M.*
Trefusis – *Clinton*
Trench – *Ashtown*

Trevor-Roper – *Dacre of Glanton**
Tufton – *Hothfield*
Turner – *Netherthorpe*
Turner – *T. of Camden**
Turnour – *Winterton, E.*
Tyrell-Kenyon – *Kenyon*
Vanden-Bempde-Johnstone – *Derwent*
Vane – *Barnard*
Vane – *Inglewood*
Vane-Tempest-Stewart – *Londonderry, M.*
Vanneck – *Huntingfield*
Vaughan – *Lisburne, E.*
Vereker – *Gort, V.*
Verney – *Willoughby de Broke*
Vernon – *Lyveden*
Vesey – *De Vesci, V.*
Villiers – *Clarendon, E.*
Vivian – *Swansea*
Wade – *W. of Chorlton**
Walker – *W. of Worcester**
Wallace – *W. of Campsie**
Wallace – *W. of Coslany**
Wallop – *Portsmouth, E.*
Walton – *W. of Detchant**
Ward – *Bangor, V.*
Ward – *Dudley, E.*
Warrender – *Bruntisfield*
Watson – *Manton*
Wedderburn – *W. of Charlton**
Weir – *Inverforth*
Weld-Forester – *Forester*
Wellesley – *Cowley, E.*
Wellesley – *Wellington, D.*
Westenra – *Rossmore*
White – *Annaly*
White – *James of Holland Park**
Whiteley – *Marchamley*
Whitfield – *Kenswood*
Williams – *W. of Crosby**
Williams – *W. of Elvel**
Williams – *W. of Mostyn**
Williamson – *Forres*
Willoughby – *Middleton*
Wills – *Dulverton*
Wilson – *Moran*
Wilson – *Nunburnholme*
Wilson – *W. of Langside**
Wilson – *W. of Tillyorn**
Windsor – *Gloucester, D.*
Windsor – *Kent, D.*
Windsor-Clive – *Plymouth, E.*
Wingfield – *Powerscourt, V.*
Winn – *St Oswald*
Wodehouse – *Kimberley, E.*
Wolfson – *W. of Sunningdale**
Wood – *Halifax, E.*
Wood – *Holderness**
Woodhouse – *Terrington*
Wright – *W. of Richmond**
Wyatt – *W. of Weeford**
Wyndham – *Egremont & Leconfield*

Wyndham-Quin – *Dunraven, E.*
Wynn – *Newborough*
Yarde-Buller – *Churston*
Yerburgh – *Alvingham*
Yorke – *Hardwicke, E.*
Young – *Kennet*
Young – *Y. of Dartington**
Young – *Y. of Graffham**
Younger – *Y. of Leckie, V.*
Younger – *Y. of Prestwick**

Orders of Chivalry

THE MOST NOBLE ORDER OF THE GARTER (1348)

KG

Ribbon, Blue

Motto, Honi soit qui mal y pense
(*Shame on him who thinks evil of it*)

The number of Knights Companions is limited to 24

SOVEREIGN OF THE ORDER
The Queen

LADIES OF THE ORDER
HM Queen Elizabeth the Queen
Mother, 1936
HRH The Princess Royal, 1994

ROYAL KNIGHTS
HRH The Prince Philip, Duke of
Edinburgh, 1947
HRH The Prince of Wales, 1958
HRH The Duke of Kent, 1985

EXTRA KNIGHTS COMPANIONS AND
LADIES
HRH Princess Juliana of the
Netherlands, 1958
HRH The Grand Duke of
Luxembourg, 1972
HM The Queen of Denmark, 1979
HM The King of Sweden, 1983
HM The King of Spain, 1988
HM The Queen of the Netherlands,
1989

KNIGHTS AND LADY COMPANIONS
The Earl of Longford, 1971
The Marquess of Abergavenny, 1974
The Duke of Grafton, 1976
The Lord Hunt, 1979
The Duke of Norfolk, 1983
The Lord Lewin, 1983
The Lord Richardson of
Duntisbourne, 1983
The Lord Carrington, 1985
The Lord Callaghan of Cardiff, 1987
The Viscount Leverhulme, 1988
The Lord Hailsham of St
Marylebone, 1988
Lavinia, Duchess of Norfolk, 1990
The Duke of Wellington, 1990
Field Marshal Lord Bramall, 1990
Sir Edward Heath, 1992
The Viscount Ridley, 1992
The Lord Sainsbury of Preston
Candover, 1992
The Lord Ashburton, 1994
The Lord Kingsdown, 1994

Sir Ninian Stephen, 1994
The Baroness Thatcher, 1995
Sir Edmund Hillary, 1995

Prelate, The Bishop of Winchester
Chancellor, The Lord Carrington, KG,
GCMG, CH, MC
Register, The Dean of Windsor
Garter King of Arms, P. Gwynn-Jones,
LVO
Gentleman Usher of the Black Rod, Gen.
Sir Edward Jones, KCB, CBE
Secretary, D. H. B. Chesshyre, LVO

THE MOST ANCIENT AND MOST NOBLE ORDER OF THE THISTLE (REVIVED 1687)

KT

Ribbon, Green

Motto, Nemo me impune lacessit (*No
one provokes me with impunity*)

The number of Knights is limited to 16

SOVEREIGN OF THE ORDER
The Queen

LADY OF THE THISTLE
HM Queen Elizabeth the Queen
Mother, 1937

ROYAL KNIGHTS
HRH The Prince Philip, Duke of
Edinburgh, 1952
HRH The Prince of Wales, Duke of
Rothesay, 1977

KNIGHTS
The Lord Home of the Hirsel, 1962
The Earl of Wemyss and March, 1966
The Earl of Dalhousie, 1971
The Lord Clydesmuir, 1972
Sir Donald Cameron of Lochiel, 1973
The Lord McFadzean, 1976
The Hon. Lord Cameron, 1978
The Duke of Buccleuch and
Queensberry, 1978
The Earl of Elgin and Kincardine,
1981
The Lord Thomson of Monifieth,
1981
The Lord MacLehose of Beoch, 1983
The Earl of Airlie, 1985
Capt. Sir Iain Tennant, 1986
The Viscount Whitelaw, 1990
Sir Fitzroy Maclean of Dunconnel,
1993

Chancellor, The Duke of Buccleuch
and Queensberry, KT, VRD

Dean, The Very Revd G. I. Macmillan
Secretary and Lord Lyon King of Arms, Sir
Malcolm Innes of Edingight, KCVO,
WS
Usher of the Green Rod, Rear-Adm. D.A.
Dunbar-Nasmith, CB, DSC

THE MOST HONOURABLE ORDER OF THE BATH (1725)

GCB *Military*   GCB *Civil*

GCB   Knight (or Dame) Grand
       Cross
KCB   Knight Commander
DCB   Dame Commander
CB   Companion

Ribbon, Crimson

Motto, Tria juncta in uno (*Three joined
in one*)

Remodelled 1815, and enlarged many
times since. The Order is divided into
civil and military divisions. Women
became eligible for the Order from 1
January 1971

THE SOVEREIGN

GREAT MASTER AND FIRST OR
PRINCIPAL KNIGHT GRAND
CROSS
HRH The Prince of Wales, KG, KT,
GCB

Dean of the Order, The Dean of
Westminster
Bath King of Arms, Air Chief Marshal
Sir David Evans, GCB, CBE
Registrar and Secretary, Rear-Adm.
D. E. Macey, CB
Genealogist, P. Gwynn-Jones, LVO
Gentleman Usher of the Scarlet Rod, Air
Vice-Marshal Sir Richard Peirse,
KCVO, CB
Deputy Secretary, The Secretary of the
Central Chancery of the Orders of
Knighthood
Chancery, Central Chancery of the
Orders of Knighthood, St James's
Palace, London SW1A 1BH

THE ORDER OF MERIT
(1902)

OM *Military*   OM *Civil*

OM

Ribbon, Blue and crimson

This Order is designed as a special distinction for eminent men and women without conferring a knighthood upon them. The Order is limited in numbers to 24, with the addition of foreign honorary members. Membership is of two kinds, military and civil, the badge of the former having crossed swords, and the latter oak leaves

THE SOVEREIGN

HRH The Prince Philip, Duke of
  Edinburgh, 1968
Dame Veronica Wedgwood, 1969
Sir Isaiah Berlin, 1971
Sir George Edwards, 1971
Sir Alan Hodgkin, 1973
The Lord Todd, 1977
Revd Prof. Owen Chadwick, KBE,
  1983
Sir Andrew Huxley, 1983
Sir Michael Tippett, 1983
Frederick Sanger, 1986
Air Cdre Sir Frank Whittle, 1986
The Lord Menuhin, 1987
Prof. Sir Ernst Gombrich, 1988
Dr Max Perutz, 1988
Dame Cicely Saunders, 1989
The Lord Porter of Luddenham, 1989
The Baroness Thatcher, 1990
Dame Joan Sutherland, 1991
Prof. Francis Crick, 1991
Dame Ninette de Valois, 1992
Sir Michael Atiyah, 1992
Lucien Freud, 1993
The Lord Jenkins of Hillhead, 1993
Honorary Members, Mother Teresa,
  1983; Nelson Mandela, 1995

Secretary and Registrar, Sir Edward
  Ford, KCB, KCVO, ERD
Chancery, Central Chancery of the
  Orders of Knighthood, St James's
  Palace, London SW1A 1BH

THE MOST EXALTED ORDER OF THE STAR OF INDIA (1861)

GCSI   Knight Grand Commander
KCSI   Knight Commander
CSI   Companion

Ribbon, Light blue, with white edges
Motto, Heaven's Light our Guide

THE SOVEREIGN
Registrar, The Secretary of the
  Central Chancery of the Orders of
  Knighthood
No conferments have been made
  since 1947

THE MOST DISTINGUISHED ORDER OF ST MICHAEL AND ST GEORGE (1818)

GCMG   KCMG

GCMG Knight (or Dame) Grand
        Cross
KCMG Knight Commander
DCMG Dame Commander
CMG   Companion

Ribbon, Saxon blue, with scarlet centre
Motto, Auspicium melioris aevi (*Token of a better age*)

THE SOVEREIGN

GRAND MASTER
HRH The Duke of Kent, KG, GCMG,
GCVO, ADC

Prelate, The Rt. Revd the Bishop of
  Coventry
Chancellor, Sir Anthony Acland, GCMG,
  GCVO
Secretary, Sir John Coles, KCMG
Registrar, Sir John Graham, Bt., GCMG
King of Arms, Sir Oliver Wright, GCMG,
  GCVO, DSC
Gentleman Usher of the Blue Rod, Sir John
  Margetson, KCMG
Dean, The Dean of St Paul's
Deputy Secretary, The Secretary of the
  Central Chancery of the Orders of
  Knighthood
Chancery, Central Chancery of the
  Orders of Knighthood, St James's
  Palace, London SW1A 1BH

THE MOST EMINENT ORDER OF THE INDIAN EMPIRE (1868)

GCIE Knight Grand Commander
KCIE Knight Commander
CIE   Companion

Ribbon, Imperial purple
Motto, Imperatricis auspiciis (*Under the auspices of the Empress*)

THE SOVEREIGN

Registrar, The Secretary of the
  Central Chancery of the Orders of
  Knighthood

No conferments have been made
  since 1947

THE IMPERIAL ORDER OF THE CROWN OF INDIA
(1877) FOR LADIES

CI

Badge, the royal cipher in jewels
  within an oval, surmounted by an
  heraldic crown and attached to a
  bow of light blue watered ribbon,
  edged white
The honour does not confer any rank
  or title upon the recipient
No conferments have been made
  since 1947

HM The Queen, 1947
HM Queen Elizabeth the Queen
  Mother, 1931
HRH The Princess Margaret,
  Countess of Snowdon, 1947
HRH Princess Alice, Duchess of
  Gloucester, 1937

THE ROYAL VICTORIAN ORDER (1896)

GCVO   KCVO

GCVO Knight or Dame Grand
        Cross
KCVO Knight Commander
DCVO Dame Commander
CVO   Commander
LVO   Lieutenant
MVO   Member

Ribbon, Blue, with red and white edges
Motto, Victoria

THE SOVEREIGN
GRAND MASTER
HM Queen Elizabeth the Queen
  Mother

Chancellor, The Lord Chamberlain
Secretary, The Keeper of the Privy
  Purse
Registrar, The Secretary of the
  Central Chancery of the Orders of
  Knighthood
Chaplain, The Revd J. Robson
Hon. Genealogist, D. H. B. Chesshyre,
  LVO

THE MOST EXCELLENT ORDER OF THE BRITISH EMPIRE (1917)

GBE   KBE

The Order was divided into military and civil divisions in December 1918

GBE   Knight or Dame Grand Cross
KBE   Knight Commander
DBE   Dame Commander
CBE   Commander
OBE   Officer
MBE   Member

Ribbon, Rose pink edged with pearl grey with vertical pearl stripe in centre (military division); without vertical pearl stripe (civil division)
Motto, For God and the Empire

THE SOVEREIGN

GRAND MASTER
HRH The Prince Philip, Duke of Edinburgh, KG, KT, OM, GBE, PC, FRS

Prelate, The Bishop of London
King of Arms, Adm. Sir Anthony Morton, GBE, KCB
Registrar, The Secretary of the Central Chancery of the Orders of Knighthood
Secretary, Sir Robin Butler, GCB, CVO
Dean, The Dean of St Paul's
Gentleman Usher of the Purple Rod, Sir Robin Gillett, Bt., GBE, RD
Chancery, Central Chancery of the Orders of Knighthood, St James's Palace, London SW1A 1BH

ORDER OF THE COMPANIONS OF HONOUR (1917)

CH

Ribbon, Carmine, with gold edges

This Order consists of one class only and carries with it no title. The number of awards is limited to 65 (excluding honorary members)

Anthony, Rt. Hon. John, 1981
Ashley of Stoke, The Lord, 1975
Astor, Hon. David, 1993
Baker, Dame Janet, 1993
Baker, Rt. Hon. Kenneth, 1992
Brenner, Sydney, 1986
Brooke, Rt. Hon. Peter, 1992

Carrington, The Lord, 1983
Casson, Sir Hugh, 1984
Cledwyn of Penrhos, The Lord, 1976
de Valois, Dame Ninette, 1981
Eccles, The Viscount, 1984
Fraser, Rt. Hon. Malcolm, 1977
Freud, Lucian, 1983
Gielgud, Sir John, 1977
Glenamara, The Lord, 1976
Gorton, Rt. Hon. Sir John, 1971
Guinness, Sir Alec, 1994
Hailsham of St Marylebone, The Lord, 1974
Hawking, Prof. Stephen, 1989
Healey, The Lord, 1979
Houghton of Sowerby, The Lord, 1967
Jones, James, 1977
Jones, Prof. Reginald, 1994
King, Rt. Hon. Tom, 1992
Lange, Rt. Hon. David, 1989
Lasdun, Sir Denys, 1995
Milstein, César, 1994
Mott, Sir Nevill, 1995
Owen, The Lord, 1994
Pasmore, Victor, 1980
Perutz, Prof. Max, 1975
Powell, Anthony, 1987
Powell, Sir Philip, 1984
Pritchett, Sir Victor, 1992
Runciman, Hon. Sir Steven, 1984
Rylands, George, 1987
Sanger, Frederick, 1981
Sisson, Charles, 1993
Smith, Sir John, 1993
Somare, Rt. Hon. Sir Michael, 1978
Talboys, Rt. Hon. Sir Brian, 1981
Tebbit, The Lord, 1987
Tippett, Sir Michael, 1979
Trudeau, Rt. Hon. Pierre, 1984
Watkinson, The Viscount, 1962
Weight, Prof. Carel, 1994
Whitelaw, The Viscount, 1974
Widdowson, Dr Elsie, 1993
Honorary Members, Lee Kuan Yew, 1970; Dr Joseph Luns, 1971

Secretary and Registrar, The Secretary of the Central Chancery of the Orders of Knighthood

THE DISTINGUISHED SERVICE ORDER (1886)

DSO

Ribbon, Red, with blue edges

Bestowed in recognition of especial services in action of commissioned officers in the Navy, Army and Royal Air Force and (since 1942) Mercantile Marine. The members are Companions only. A Bar may be awarded for any additional act of service

THE IMPERIAL SERVICE ORDER (1902)

ISO

Ribbon, Crimson, with blue centre

Appointment as Companion of this Order is open to members of the Civil Services whose eligibility is determined by the grade they hold. The Order consists of The Sovereign and Companions to a number not exceeding 1,900, of whom 1,300 may belong to the Home Civil Services and 600 to Overseas Civil Services. The Prime Minister announced in March 1993 that he would make no further recommendations for appointments to the Order.

Secretary, Sir Robin Butler, GCB, CVO
Registrar, The Secretary of the Central Chancery of the Orders of Knighthood, St James's Palace, London SW1A 1BH

THE ROYAL VICTORIAN CHAIN (1902)

It confers no precedence on its holders

HM THE QUEEN
HM Queen Elizabeth the Queen Mother, 1937
HRH Princess Juliana of the Netherlands, 1950
HM The King of Thailand, 1960
HIH The Crown Prince of Ethiopia, 1965
HM The King of Jordan, 1966
HM King Zahir Shah of Afghanistan, 1971
HM The Queen of Denmark, 1974
HM The King of Nepal, 1975
HM The King of Sweden, 1975
The Lord Coggan, 1980
HM The Queen of the Netherlands, 1982
Gen. Antonio Eanes, 1985
HM The King of Spain, 1986
HM The King of Saudi Arabia, 1987
HRH The Princess Margaret, Countess of Snowdon, 1990
The Lord Runcie, 1991
The Lord Charteris of Amisfield, 1992
HE François Mitterrand, 1992
HE Richard von Weizsäcker, 1992
HM The King of Norway, 1994

Baronetage and Knightage

BARONETS

Style, 'Sir' before forename and surname, followed by 'Bt.'
Wife's style, 'Lady' followed by surname
For forms of address, *see* page 217

There are five different creations of baronetcies: Baronets of England (creations dating from 1611); Baronets of Ireland (creations dating from 1619); Baronets of Scotland or Nova Scotia (creations dating from 1625); Baronets of Great Britain (creations after the Act of Union 1707 which combined the kingdoms of England and Scotland); and Baronets of the United Kingdom (creations after the union of Great Britain and Ireland in 1801).

Badge of Baronets of the United Kingdom   *Badge of Baronets of Nova Scotia*

Badge of Ulster

The patent of creation limits the destination of a baronetcy, usually to male descendants of the first baronet, although special remainders allow the baronetcy to pass, if the male issue of sons fail, to the male issue of daughters of the first baronet. In the case of baronetcies of Scotland or Nova Scotia, a special remainder of 'heirs male and of tailzie' allows the baronetcy to descend to heirs general, including women. There are four existing Scottish baronets with such a remainder, one of whom, the holder of the Dunbar of Hempriggs creation, is a Baronetess.

The Official Roll of Baronets is kept at the Home Office by the Registrar of the Baronetage. Anyone who considers that he is entitled to be entered on the Roll may petition the Crown through the Home Secretary. Every person succeeding to a baronetcy must exhibit proofs of succession to the Home Secretary. A person whose name is not entered on the Official Roll will not be addressed or mentioned by the title of baronet in any official document, nor will he be accorded precedence as a baronet.

BARONETCIES EXTINCT SINCE THE LAST EDITION
Erskine (*cr.* 1961) by the death of Lord Erskine of Rerrick; Flavelle (*cr.* 1917); Llewellyn (*cr.* 1959); Stapleton (*cr.* 1679); Throckmorton (*cr.* 1642); Waller (*cr.* 1815)

Registrar of the Baronetage, R. M. Morris
Assistant Registrar, Mrs F. G. Bright
Office, Home Office, 50 Queen Anne's Gate, London SWIH 9AT. Tel: 0171-273 3498

KNIGHTS

Style, 'Sir' before forename and surname, followed by appropriate post-nominal initials if a Knight Grand Cross, Knight Grand Commander or Knight Commander

Wife's style, 'Lady' followed by surname
For forms of address, *see* page 217
The prefix 'Sir' is not used by knights who are clerics of the Church of England, who do not receive the accolade. Their wives are entitled to precedence as the wife of a knight but not to the style of 'Lady'.

ORDERS OF KNIGHTHOOD
Knight Grand Cross, Knight Grand Commander, and Knight Commander are the higher classes of the Orders of Chivalry (*see* pages 174–6). Honorary knighthoods of these Orders may be conferred on men who are citizens of countries of which The Queen is not head of state. As a rule, the prefix 'Sir' is not used by honorary knights.

KNIGHTS BACHELOR

The Knights Bachelor do not constitute a Royal Order, but comprise the surviving representation of the ancient State Orders of Knighthood. The Register of Knights Bachelor, instituted by James I in the 17th century, lapsed, and in 1908 a voluntary association under the title of The Society of Knights (now The Imperial Society of Knights Bachelor by Royal Command) was formed with the primary objects of continuing the various registers dating from 1257 and obtaining the uniform registration of every created Knight Bachelor. In 1926 a design for a badge to be worn by Knights Bachelor was approved and adopted; in 1974 a neck badge and miniature were added.

Knight Principal, Sir Conrad Swan, KCVO
Chairman of Council, The Lord Lane of Horsell
Prelate, Rt. Revd and Rt. Hon. The Bishop of London
Hon. Registrar, Sir Kenneth Newman, GBE, QPM
Hon. Treasurer, Sir Douglas Morpeth, TD
Clerk to the Council, R. M. Esden
Office, 21 Old Buildings, Lincoln's Inn, London WC2A 3UJ

LIST OF BARONETS AND KNIGHTS
Revised to 31 August 1995

Peers are not included in this list

†	Not registered on the Official Roll of the Baronetage at the time of going to press
( )	The date of creation of the baronetcy is given in parenthesis
I	Baronet of Ireland
NS	Baronet of Nova Scotia
S	Baronet of Scotland

If a baronet or knight has a double barrelled or hyphenated surname, he is listed under the final element of the name
A full entry in italic type indicates that the recipient of a knighthood died during the year in which the honour was conferred. The name is included for purposes of record

Abal, Sir Tei, Kt., CBE
Abbott, Sir Albert Francis, Kt., CBE
Abbott, Vice-Adm. Sir Peter Charles, KCB
Abdy, Sir Valentine Robert Duff, Bt. (1850)
Abel, Sir Seselo (Cecil) Charles Geoffrey, Kt., OBE
Abeles, Sir (Emil Herbert) Peter, Kt.
Abercromby, Sir Ian George, Bt. (s. 1636)
Abraham, Sir Edward Penley, Kt., CBE, FRS
Acheson, Prof. Sir (Ernest) Donald, KBE
Ackers, Sir James George, Kt.
†Ackroyd, Sir Timothy Robert Whyte, Bt. (1956)
Acland, Sir Antony Arthur, GCMG, GCVO
Acland, Lt.-Col. Sir (Christopher) Guy (Dyke), Bt., MVO (1890)
Acland, Sir John Dyke, Bt. (1644)
Acland, Maj.-Gen. Sir John Hugh Bevil, KCB, CBE
Adam, Sir Christopher Eric Forbes, Bt. (1917)
Adams, Sir Philip George Doyne, KCMG
Adams, Sir William James, KCMG
Adamson, Sir (William Owen) Campbell, Kt.
Adrien, Hon. Sir Maurice Latour-, Kt.
Adye, Sir John Anthony, KCMG
Agnew, Sir Crispin Hamlyn, Bt. (s. 1629)
Agnew, Sir John Keith, Bt. (1895)
Agnew, Sir (William) Godfrey, KCVO, CB
Aiken, Air Chief Marshal Sir John Alexander Carlisle, KCB
Ainsworth, Sir (Thomas) David, Bt. (1916)
Aird, Capt. Sir Alastair Sturgis, KCVO
Aird, Sir (George) John, Bt. (1901)
Airey, Sir Lawrence, KCB
Airy, Maj.-Gen. Sir Christopher John, KCVO, CBE
Aitchison, Sir Charles Walter de Lancey, Bt. (1938)
Aitken, Sir Robert Stevenson, Kt., MD, D.phil.
Akehurst, Gen. Sir John Bryan, KCB, CBE
Albert, Sir Alexis François, Kt., CMG, VRD
Albu, Sir George, Bt. (1912)
Alcock, Air Chief Marshal Sir (Robert James) Michael, KBE, CB
Aldous, Rt. Hon. Sir William, Kt.
Alexander, Sir Charles Gundry, Bt. (1945)
Alexander, Sir Claud Hagart-, Bt. (1886)
Alexander, Sir Douglas, Bt. (1921)
Alexander, Sir (John) Lindsay, Kt.
Alexander, Prof. Sir Kenneth John Wilson, Kt.

Alexander, Sir Michael O'Donal Bjarne, GCMG
Alexander, Sir Norman Stanley, Kt., CBE
†Alexander, Sir Patrick Desmond William Cable-, Bt. (1809)
Allan, Sir Anthony James Allan Havelock-, Bt. (1858)
Allard, Sir Gordon Laidlaw, Kt.
Allen, Prof. Sir Geoffrey, Kt., ph.D., FRS
Allen, Sir John Derek, Kt., CBE
Allen, Hon. Sir Peter Austin Philip Jermyn, Kt.
Allen, Sir Richard Hugh Sedley, KCMG
Allen, Sir William Guilford, Kt.
Allen, Sir (William) Kenneth (Gwynne), Kt.
Alleyne, Sir George Allanmoore Ogarren, Kt.
Alleyne, Revd Sir John Olpherts Campbell, Bt. (1769)
Alliance, Sir David, Kt., CBE
Allinson, Sir (Walter) Leonard, KCVO, CMG
Alliott, Hon. Sir John Downes, Kt.
Allison, Air Marshal Sir John Shakespeare, KCB, CBE
Alment, Sir (Edward) Anthony John, Kt.
Althaus, Sir Nigel Frederick, Kt.
Ambo, Rt. Revd George, KBE
Amet, Hon. Sir Arnold Karibone, Kt.
Amies, Sir (Edwin) Hardy, KCVO
Amis, Sir Kingsley William, Kt., CBE
Amory, Sir Ian Heathcoat, Bt. (1874)
Anderson, Sir John Anthony, KBE
Anderson, Maj.-Gen. Sir John Evelyn, KBE
Anderson, Sir John Muir, Kt., CMG
Anderson, Hon. Sir Kevin Victor, Kt.
Anderson, Vice-Adm. Sir Neil Dudley, KBE, CB
Anderson, Prof. Sir (William) Ferguson, Kt., OBE
Anderton, Sir (Cyril) James, Kt., CBE, QPM
Andrew, Sir Robert John, KCB
Andrews, Sir Derek Henry, KCB, CBE
Andrews, Hon. Sir Dormer George, Kt.
Angus, Sir Michael Richardson, Kt.
Annesley, Sir Hugh Norman, Kt., QPM
Anson, Vice-Adm. Sir Edward Rosebery, KCB
Anson, Sir John, KCB
Anson, Rear-Adm. Sir Peter, Bt., CB (1831)
Anstey, Brig. Sir John, Kt., CBE, TD
Anstruther, Maj. Sir Ralph Hugo, Bt. GCVO, MC (s. 1694)
Antico, Sir Tristan Venus, Kt.
†Antrobus, Sir Edward Philip, Bt. (1815)
Appleyard, Sir Leonard Vincent, KCMG
Appleyard, Sir Raymond Kenelm, KBE
Arbuthnot, Sir Keith Robert Charles, Bt. (1823)

Arbuthnot, Sir William Reierson, Bt. (1964)
Archdale, Capt. Sir Edward Folmer, Bt., DSC, RN (1928)
Archer, Gen. Sir (Arthur) John, KCB, OBE
Arculus, Sir Ronald, KCMG, KCVO
Armitage, Air Chief Marshal Sir Michael John, KCB, CBE
Armour, Prof. Sir James, Kt., CBE
Armstrong, Sir Andrew Clarence Francis, Bt., CMG (1841)
Armytage, Sir John Martin, Bt. (1738)
Arnold, Rt. Hon. Sir John Lewis, Kt.
Arnold, Sir Malcolm Henry, Kt., CBE
Arnold, Sir Thomas Richard, Kt., MP
Arnott, Sir Alexander John Maxwell, Bt. (1896)
Arnott, Prof. Sir (William) Melville, Kt., TD, MD
Arrindell, Sir Clement Athelston, GCMG, GCVO, QC
Arthur, Lt.-Gen. Sir (John) Norman Stewart, KCB
Arthur, Sir Stephen John, Bt. (1841)
Ash, Prof. Sir Eric Albert, Kt., CBE, FRS, FEng.
Ashburnham, Sir Denny Reginald, Bt. (1661)
Ashe, Sir Derick Rosslyn, KCMG
Ashley, Sir Bernard Albert, Kt.
Ashmore, Admiral of the Fleet Sir Edward Beckwith, GCB, DSC
Ashmore, Vice-Adm. Sir Peter William Beckwith, KCB, KCVO, DSC
Ashworth, Sir Herbert, Kt.
Aske, Revd Sir Conan, Bt. (1922)
Askew, Sir Bryan, Kt.
Asscher, Prof. (Adolf) William, Kt., MD, FRCP
Aston, Sir Harold George, Kt., CBE
Aston, Hon. Sir William John, KCMG
Astor, Hon. Sir John Jacob, Kt., MBE
Astwood, Hon. Sir James Rufus, KBE
Astwood, Lt.-Col. Sir Jeffrey Carlton, Kt., CBE, ED
Atcherley, Sir Harold Winter, Kt.
Atiyah, Sir Michael Francis, Kt., OM, ph.D., FRS
Atkinson, Air Marshal Sir David William, KBE
Atkinson, Sir Frederick John, KCB
Atkinson, Sir John Alexander, KCB, DFC
Atkinson, Sir Robert, Kt., DSC, FEng.
Attenborough, Sir David Frederick, Kt., CVO, CBE, FRS
Atwell, Sir John William, Kt., CBE, FRSE, FEng.
Atwill, Sir (Milton) John (Napier), Kt.
Audland, Sir Christopher John, KCMG
Audley, Sir George Bernard, Kt.
Auld, Rt. Hon. Sir Robin Ernest, Kt.
†Austin, Sir Anthony Leonard, Bt. (1894)
Austin, Vice-Adm. Sir Peter Murray, KCB
Austin, Air Marshal Sir Roger Mark, KCB, AFC

Aykroyd, Sir James Alexander Frederic, Bt. (1929)
Aykroyd, Sir William Miles, Bt., MC (1920)
Aylmer, Sir Richard John, Bt. (I. 1622)
Bacha, Sir Bhinod, Kt., CMG
Backhouse, Sir Jonathan Roger, Bt. (1901)
Bacon, Sir Nicholas Hickman Ponsonby, Bt. *Premier Baronet of England* (1611 and 1627)
Bacon, Sir Sidney Charles, Kt., CB, FEng.
Baddeley, Sir John Wolsey Beresford, Bt. (1922)
Baddiley, *Prof.* Sir James, Kt., Ph.D., D.SC., FRS, FRSE
Badenoch, Sir John, Kt., DM, FRCP
Badger, Sir Geoffrey Malcolm, Kt.
Bagge, Sir (John) Jeremy Picton, Bt. (1867)
Bagnall, *Field Marshal* Sir Nigel Thomas, GCB, CVO, MC
Bailey, Sir Alan Marshall, KCB
Bailey, Sir Brian Harry, Kt., OBE
Bailey, Sir Derrick Thomas Louis, Bt., DFC (1919)
Bailey, *Prof.* Sir Harold Walter, Kt., D.Phil., FBA
Bailey, Sir John Bilsland, KCB
Bailey, Sir Richard John, Kt., CBE
Bailey, Sir Stanley Ernest, Kt., CBE, QPM
Baillie, Sir Gawaine George Hope, Bt. (1823)
Baines, *Prof.* Sir George Grenfell-, Kt., OBE
Baird, Sir David Charles, Bt. (1809)
Baird, *Lt.-Gen.* Sir James Parlane, KBE, MD
Baird, Sir James Richard Gardiner, Bt., MC (s. 1695)
Baird, *Vice-Adm.* Sir Thomas Henry Eustace, KCB
Bairsto, *Air Marshal* Sir Peter Edward, KBE, CB
Baker, Sir Robert George Humphrey Sherston-, Bt. (1796)
Baker, *Hon.* Sir (Thomas) Scott (Gillespie), Kt.
Balchin, Sir Robert George Alexander, Kt.
Balcombe, *Rt. Hon.* Sir (Alfred) John, Kt.
Balderstone, Sir James Schofield, Kt.
Baldwin, Sir Peter Robert, KCB
Ball, *Air Marshal* Sir Alfred Henry Wynne, KCB, DSO, DFC
Ball, Sir Charles Irwin, Bt. (1911)
Ball, Sir Christopher John Elinger, Kt.
Ball, *Prof.* Sir Robert James, Kt., Ph.D.
Bamford, Sir Anthony Paul, Kt.
Banham, Sir John Michael Middlecott, Kt.
Bannerman, Sir David Gordon, Bt., OBE. (s. 1682)
Bannister, Sir Roger Gilbert, Kt., CBE, DM, FRCP
†Barber, Sir (Thomas) David, Bt., (1960)

Barbour, *Very Revd* Sir Robert Alexander Stewart, KCVO, MC
Barclay, Sir Colville Herbert Sanford, Bt. (s. 1668)
Barclay, Sir Peter Maurice, Kt., CBE
Barclay, Sir Roderick Edward, GCVO, KCMG
Barder, Sir Brian Leon, KCMG
Barker, Sir Alwyn Bowman, Kt., CMG
Barker, Sir Colin, Kt.
Barker, Sir Harry Heaton, Kt., KBE
Barker, *Hon.* Sir (Richard) Ian, Kt.
Barlow, Sir Christopher Hilaro, Bt. (1803)
Barlow, Sir (George) William, Kt., FEng.
Barlow, Sir John Kemp, Bt. (1907)
Barlow, Sir Thomas Erasmus, Bt., DSC (1902)
Barnard, Sir Joseph Brian, Kt.
Barnes, Sir James George, Kt., MBE
Barnes, Sir Kenneth, KCB
Barnewall, Sir Reginald Robert, Bt. (I. 1623)
Baron, Sir Thomas, Kt., CBE
Barraclough, *Air Chief Marshal* Sir John, KCB, CBE, DFC, AFC
Barraclough, Sir Kenneth James Priestley, Kt., CBE, TD
Barran, Sir David Haven, Kt.
Barran, Sir John Napoleon Ruthven, Bt. (1895)
Barratt, Sir Lawrence Arthur, Kt.
Barratt, Sir Richard Stanley, Kt., CBE, QPM
Barrett, *Lt.-Gen.* Sir David William Scott-, KBE, MC
Barrett, *Lt.-Col.* Sir Dennis Charles Titchener, Kt., TD
Barrett, Sir Stephen Jeremy, KCMG
Barrington, Sir Alexander (Fitzwilliam Croker), Bt. (1831)
Barrington, Sir Nicholas John, KCMG, CVO
Barron, Sir Donald James, Kt.
Barrow, *Capt.* Sir Richard John Uniacke, Bt. (1835)
Barrowclough, Sir Anthony Richard, Kt., QC
Barry, Sir (Lawrence) Edward (Anthony Tress), Bt. (1899)
Bartlett, Sir John Hardington, Bt. (1913)
Barton, *Prof.* Sir Derek Harold Richard, Kt., FRS, FRSE
Barttelot, *Col.* Sir Brian Walter de Stopham, Bt., OBE (1875)
Barwick, *Rt. Hon.* Sir Garfield Edward John, GCMG
Batchelor, Sir Ivor Ralph Campbell, Kt., CBE
Bate, Sir David Lindsay, KBE
Bate, Sir (Walter) Edwin, Kt., OBE
Bateman, Sir Cecil Joseph, KBE
Bateman, Sir Geoffrey Hirst, Kt., FRCS
Bateman, Sir Ralph Melton, KBE
Bates, Sir Geoffrey Voltelin, Bt., MC (1880)
Bates, Sir (John) Dawson, Bt., MC (1937)

Batho, Sir Peter Ghislain, Bt. (1928)
Bathurst, *Admiral of the Fleet* Sir (David) Benjamin, GCB
Bathurst, Sir Frederick Peter Methuen Hervey-, Bt. (1818)
Bathurst, Sir Maurice Edward, Kt., CMG, CBE, QC
Batten, Sir John Charles, KCVO
Battersby, *Prof.* Sir Alan Rushton, Kt., FRS
Battishill, Sir Anthony Michael William, KCB
Batty, Sir William Bradshaw, Kt., TD
Baxendell, Sir Peter Brian, Kt., CBE, FEng.
Bayliss, *Prof.* Sir Noel Stanley, Kt., CBE
Bayliss, Sir Richard Ian Samuel, KCVO, MD, FRCP
Bayly, *Vice-Adm.* Sir Patrick Uniacke, KBE, CB, DSC
Bayne, Sir Nicholas Peter, KCMG
Baynes, Sir John Christopher Malcolm, Bt. (1801)
Bazley, Sir Thomas Stafford, Bt. (1869)
Beach, *Gen.* Sir (William Gerald) Hugh, GBE, KCB, MC
Beale, *Lt.-Gen.* Sir Peter John, KBE, FRCP
Beament, Sir James William Longman, Kt., SC.D., FRS
Beattie, *Hon.* Sir Alexander Craig, Kt.
Beattie, *Hon.* Sir David Stuart, GCMG, GCVO
Beauchamp, Sir Christopher Radstock Proctor-, Bt. (1745)
Beaumont, *Capt.* the Hon. Sir (Edward) Nicholas (Canning), KCVO
Beaumont, Sir George (Howland Francis), Bt. (1661)
Beaumont, Sir Richard Ashton, KCMG, OBE
Beavis, *Air Chief Marshal* Sir Michael Gordon, KCB, CBE, AFC
Becher, Sir William Fane Wrixon, Bt., MC (1831)
Beck, Sir Edgar Charles, Kt., CBE, FEng.
Beck, Sir Edgar Philip, Kt.
Beckett, *Capt.* Sir (Martyn) Gervase, Bt., MC (1921)
Beckett, Sir Terence Norman, KBE, FEng.
Bedingfeld, *Capt.* Sir Edmund George Felix Paston-, Bt. (1661)
Beecham, Sir Jeremy Hugh, Kt.
Beecham, Sir John Stratford Roland, Bt. (1914)
Beeley, Sir Harold, KCMG, CBE
Beetham, *Marshal of the Royal Air Force* Sir Michael James, GCB, CBE, DFC, AFC
Beevor, Sir Thomas Agnew, Bt. (1784)
Begg, Sir Neil Colquhoun, KBE
Beith, Sir John Greville Stanley, KCMG
Belch, Sir Alexander Ross, Kt., CBE, FRSE

Beldam, *Rt. Hon.* Sir (Alexander) Roy (Asplan), Kt.
Belich, Sir James, Kt.
Bell, Sir Brian Ernest, KBE
Bell, Sir (George) Raymond, KCMG, CB
Bell, Sir John Lowthian, Bt. (1885)
Bell, *Hon.* Sir Rodger, Kt.
Bell, Sir Timothy John Leigh, Kt.
Bell, Sir (William) Ewart, KCB
Bell, Sir William Hollin Dayrell Morrison-, Bt. (1905)
Bellew, Sir Henry Charles Grattan-, Bt. (1838)
Bellinger, Sir Robert Ian, GBE
Bellingham, Sir Noel Peter Roger, Bt. (1796)
Bengough, *Col.* Sir Piers, KCVO, OBE
Benn, Sir (James) Jonathan, Bt. (1914)
Bennett, Sir Charles Moihi Te Arawaka, Kt., DSO
Bennett, *Air Vice-Marshal* Sir Erik Peter, KBE, CB
Bennett, *Rt. Hon.* Sir Frederic Mackarness, Kt.
Bennett, Sir Hubert, Kt.
Bennett, *Hon.* Sir Hugh Peter Derwyn, Kt.
Bennett, Sir John Mokonuiarangi, Kt.
Bennett, *Gen.* Sir Phillip Harvey, KBE, DSO
Bennett, Sir Reginald Frederick Brittain, Kt., VRD
Bennett, Sir Ronald Wilfrid Murdoch, Bt. (1929)
Benson, Sir Christopher John, Kt.
Bentley, Sir William, KCMG
Benyon, Sir William Richard, Kt.
Beresford, Sir (Alexander) Paul, Kt., MP
Berger, *Vice-Adm.* Sir Peter Egerton Capel, KCB, MVO, DSC
Berghuser, *Hon.* Sir Eric, Kt., MBE
Berlin, Sir Isaiah, Kt., OM, CBE
Berman, Sir Franklin Delow, KCMG
Bernard, Sir Dallas Edmund, Bt. (1954)
Berney, Sir Julian Reedham Stuart, Bt. (1620)
Berrill, Sir Kenneth Ernest, GBE, KCB
Berriman, Sir David, Kt.
Berry, *Prof.* Sir Colin Leonard, Kt., FRCPath.
Berthon, *Vice-Adm.* Sir Stephen Ferrier, KCB
Berthoud, Sir Martin Seymour, KCVO, CMG
Best, Sir Richard Radford, KCVO, CBE
Bethune, Sir Alexander Maitland Sharp, Bt. (s. 1683)
Bethune, *Hon.* Sir (Walter) Angus, Kt.
Bett, Sir Michael, Kt., CBE
Bevan, Sir Martyn Evan Evans, Bt. (1958)
Bevan, Sir Timothy Hugh, Kt.
Beveridge, Sir Gordon Smith Grieve, Kt., FRSE, FEng., FRSA
Beverley, *Lt.-Gen.* Sir Henry York La Roche, KCB, OBE, RM

Beynon, *Prof.* Sir (William John) Granville, Kt., CBE, Ph.D., D.SC., FRS
Bibby, Sir Derek James, Bt., MC (1959)
Bickersteth, *Rt. Revd* John Monier, KCVO
Biddulph, Sir Ian D'Olier, Bt. (1664)
Bide, Sir Austin Ernest, Kt.
Bidwell, Sir Hugh Charles Philip, GBE
Biggam, Sir Robin Adair, Kt.
Biggs, *Vice-Adm.* Sir Geoffrey William Roger, KCB
Biggs, Sir Norman Paris, Kt.
Bilas, Sir Angmai Simon, Kt., OBE
Billière, *Gen.* Sir Peter Edgar de la Cour de la, KCB, KBE, DSO, MC
Bing, Sir Rudolf Franz Josef, KBE
Bingham, *Hon.* Sir Eardley Max, Kt., QC
Bingham, *Rt. Hon.* Sir Thomas Henry, Kt.
Birch, Sir John Allan, KCVO, CMG
Birch, Sir Roger, Kt., CBE, QPM
Bird, Sir Richard Geoffrey Chapman, Bt. (1922)
Birkin, Sir John Christian William, Bt. (1905)
Birkin, Sir (John) Derek, Kt., TD
Birkmyre, Sir Archibald, Bt. (1921)
Birley, Sir Derek Sydney, Kt.
Birrell, Sir James Drake, Kt.
Birtwistle, Sir Harrison, Kt.
Bishop, Sir Frederick Arthur, Kt., CB, CVO
Bishop, Sir George Sidney, Kt., CB, OBE
Bishop, Sir Michael David, Kt., CBE
Bisson, *Rt Hon.* Sir Gordon Ellis, Kt.
Black, *Prof.* Sir Douglas Andrew Kilgour, Kt., MD, FRCP
Black, Sir James Whyte, Kt., FRCP, FRS
Black, *Adm.* Sir (John) Jeremy, GBE, KCB, DSO
Black, Sir Robert Brown, GCMG, OBE
Black, Sir Robert David, Bt. (1922)
Blackburne, *Hon.* Sir William Anthony, Kt.
Blacker, *Gen.* Sir (Anthony Stephen) Jeremy, KCB, CBE
Blacker, *Gen.* Sir Cecil Hugh, GCB, OBE, MC
†Blackett, Sir Hugh Francis, Bt. (1673)
Blacklock, *Surgeon Capt. Prof.* Sir Norman James, KCVO, OBE
Blackman, Sir Frank Milton, KCVO, OBE
Blackwell, Sir Basil Davenport, Kt., FEng.
Blackwood, Sir John Francis, Bt. (1814)
Blair, Sir Alastair Campbell, KCVO, TD, WS
Blair, *Lt.-Gen.* Sir Chandos, KCVO, OBE, MC
Blair, Sir Edward Thomas Hunter, Bt. (1786)
Blake, Sir Alfred Lapthorn, KCVO, MC
Blake, Sir Francis Michael, Bt. (1907)
Blake, Sir Peter James, KBE

Blake, Sir (Thomas) Richard (Valentine), Bt. (i. 1622)
Blaker, Sir John, Bt. (1919)
Blakiston, Sir Ferguson Arthur James, Bt. (1763)
Bland, Sir (Francis) Christopher (Buchan), Kt.
Bland, Sir Henry Armand, Kt., CBE
Bland, *Lt.-Col.* Sir Simon Claud Michael, KCVO
Blelloch, Sir John Nial Henderson, KCB
Blennerhassett, Sir (Marmaduke) Adrian Francis William, Bt. (1809)
Blewitt, *Maj.* Sir Shane Gabriel Basil, KCVO
Blofeld, *Hon.* Sir John Christopher Calthorpe, Kt.
Blois, Sir Charles Nicholas Gervase, Bt. (1686)
Blomefield, Sir Thomas Charles Peregrine, Bt. (1807)
Bloomfield, Sir Kenneth Percy, KCB
Blosse, *Capt.* Sir Richard Hely Lynch-, Bt. (1622)
Blount, Sir Walter Edward Alpin, Bt., DSC (1642)
Blunden, Sir George, Kt.
†Blunden, Sir Philip Overington, Bt. (i. 1766)
Blunt, Sir David Richard Reginald Harvey, Bt. (1720)
Boardman, *Prof.* Sir John, Kt., FSA, FBA
Bodilly, *Hon.* Sir Jocelyn, Kt., VRD
Bodmer, Sir Walter Fred, Kt., Ph.D., FRS
Body, Sir Richard Bernard Frank Stewart, Kt., MP
Boevey, Sir Thomas Michael Blake Crawley-, Bt. (1784)
Bogarde, Sir Dirk (Derek Niven van den Bogaerde), Kt.
Boileau, Sir Guy (Francis), Bt. (1838)
Boles, Sir Jeremy John Fortescue, Bt. (1922)
Boles, Sir John Dennis, Kt., MBE
Bolland, Sir Edwin, KCMG
Bollers, *Hon.* Sir Harold Brodie Smith, Kt.
Bolton, Sir Frederic Bernard, Kt., MC
Bona, Sir Kina, KBE
Bonallack, Sir Richard Frank, Kt., CBE
Bond, Sir Kenneth Raymond Boyden, Kt.
Bond, *Prof.* Sir Michael Richard, Kt., FRCPsych., FRCPGlas., FRCSE
Bondi, *Prof.* Sir Hermann, KCB, FRS
Bonham, *Maj.* Sir Antony Lionel Thomas, Bt. (1852)
Bonsall, Sir Arthur Wilfred, KCMG, CBE
Bonsor, Sir Nicholas Cosmo, Bt., MP (1925)
Boolell, Sir Satcam, Kt.
Boon, Sir Peter Coleman, Kt.
Boord, Sir Nicolas John Charles, Bt. (1896)
Boorman, *Lt.-Gen.* Sir Derek, KCB
Booth, Sir Angus Josslyn Gore-, Bt. (i. 1760)

Booth, Sir Christopher Charles, Kt., MD, FRCP

Booth, Sir Douglas Allen, Bt. (1916)

Booth, Sir Gordon, KCMG, CVO

Booth, Sir Michael Addison John Wheeler-, KCB

Booth, Sir Robert Camm, Kt., CBE, TD

Boothby, Sir Brooke Charles, Bt. (1660)

Boreel, Sir Francis David, Bt. (1645)

Boreham, *Hon.* Sir Leslie Kenneth Edward, Kt.

Bornu, The Waziri of, KCMG, CBE

Borrie, Sir Gordon Johnson, Kt., QC

Borthwick, Sir John Thomas, Bt. MBE (1908)

Bossom, *Hon.* Sir Clive, Bt. (1953)

Boswall, Sir (Thomas) Alford Houstoun-, Bt. (1836)

Boswell, *Lt.-Gen.* Sir Alexander Crawford Simpson, KCB, CBE

Bosworth, Sir Neville Bruce Alfred, Kt., CBE

Bottomley, Sir James Reginald Alfred, KCMG

Boughey, Sir John George Fletcher, Bt. (1798)

Boulton, Sir Clifford John, GCB

Boulton, Sir (Harold Hugh) Christian, Bt. (1905)

Boulton, Sir William Whytehead, Bt., CBE, TD (1944)

Bourn, Sir John Bryant, KCB

Bourne, Sir (John) Wilfrid, KCB

Bovell, *Hon.* Sir (William) Stewart, Kt.

Bowater, Sir Euan David Vansittart, Bt. (1939)

Bowater, Sir (John) Vansittart, Bt. (1914)

Bowden, Sir Andrew, Kt., MBE, MP

Bowden, Sir Frank, Bt. (1915)

Bowen, Sir Geoffrey Fraser, Kt.

Bowen, Sir Mark Edward Mortimer, Bt. (1921)

Bowen, *Hon.* Sir Nigel Hubert, KBE

†Bowlby, Sir Richard Peregrine Longstaff, Bt. (1923)

Bowman, Sir Jeffery Haverstock, Kt.

†Bowman, Sir Paul Humphrey Armytage, Bt. (1884)

Bowmar, Sir Charles Erskine, Kt.

Bowness, Sir Alan, Kt., CBE

Bowness, Sir Peter Spencer, Kt., CBE

Boxer, *Air Vice-Marshal* Sir Alan Hunter Cachemaille, KCVO, CB, DSO, DFC

Boyce, *Vice-Adm.* Sir Michael Cecil, KCB, OBE

Boyce, Sir Robert Charles Leslie, Bt. (1952)

Boyd, Sir Alexander Walter, Bt. (1916)

Boyd, Sir John Dixon Iklé, KCMG

Boyd, Sir (John) Francis, Kt.

Boyd, The Hon. Sir Mark Alexander Lennox-, Kt., MP

Boyd, *Prof.* Sir Robert Lewis Fullarton, Kt., CBE, D.SC., FRS

Boyes, Sir Brian Gerald Barratt-, KBE

Boyle, Sir Stephen Gurney, Bt. (1904)

Boyne, Sir Henry Brian, Kt., CBE

Boynton, Sir John Keyworth, Kt., MC

Boyson, *Rt. Hon.* Sir Rhodes, Kt., MP

Brabham, Sir John Arthur, Kt., OBE

Bradbeer, Sir John Derek Richardson, Kt., OBE, TD

Bradbury, *Surgeon Vice-Adm.* Sir Eric Blackburn, KBE, CB

Bradford, Sir Edward Alexander Slade, Bt. (1902)

Bradley, Sir Burton Gyrth Burton-, Kt., OBE

Bradman, Sir Donald George, Kt.

Bradshaw, Sir Kenneth Anthony, KCB

Bradshaw, *Lt.-Gen.* Sir Richard Phillip, KBE

Brain, Sir (Henry) Norman, KBE, CMG

Braithwaite, Sir (Joseph) Franklin Madders, Kt.

Braithwaite, Sir Rodric Quentin, GCMG

Bramall, Sir (Ernest) Ashley, Kt.

Bramley, *Prof.* Sir Paul Anthony, Kt.

Brancker, Sir (John Eustace) Theodore, Kt., QC

Branigan, Sir Patrick Francis, Kt., QC

Braithwaite, *Rt. Hon.* Sir Nicholas Alexander, Kt., OBE

Bray, Sir Theodor Charles, Kt., CBE

Brennan, *Hon.* Sir (Francis) Gerard, KBE

Brett, Sir Charles Edward Bainbridge, Kt., CBE

Brickwood, Sir Basil Greame, Bt. (1927)

Bridges, *Hon.* Sir Phillip Rodney, Kt., CMG

Brierley, Sir Ronald Alfred, Kt.

Bright, Sir Graham Frank James, Kt., MP

Bright, Sir Keith, Kt.

Brinckman, Sir Theodore George Roderick, Bt. (1831)

Brisco, Sir Donald Gilfrid, Bt. (1782)

Briscoe, Sir John Geoffrey James, Bt. (1910)

Brise, Sir John Archibald Ruggles-, Bt., CB, OBE, TD (1935)

Bristow, *Hon.* Sir Peter Henry Rowley, Kt.

Brittan, *Rt. Hon.* Sir Leon, Kt., QC

Brittan, Sir Samuel, Kt.

Britton, Sir Edward Louis, Kt., CBE

Broackes, Sir Nigel, Kt.

†Broadbent, Sir Andrew George, Bt. (1893)

Brocklebank, Sir Aubrey Thomas, Bt. (1885)

Brockman, *Vice-Adm.* Sir Ronald Vernon, KCB, CSI, CIE, CVO, CBE

Brodie, Sir Benjamin David Ross, Bt. (1834)

Brogan, *Lt.-Gen.* Sir Mervyn Francis, KBE, CB

Bromhead, Sir John Desmond Gonville, Bt. (1806)

Bromley, Sir Rupert Charles, Bt. (1757)

Bromley, Sir Thomas Eardley, KCMG

Brook, Sir Robin, Kt., CMG, OBE

†Brooke, Sir Alistair Weston, Bt. (1919)

Brooke, Sir Francis George Windham, Bt. (1903)

Brooke, *Hon.* Sir Henry, Kt.

Brooke, Sir Richard Neville, Bt. (1662)

Brookes, Sir Wilfred Deakin, Kt., CBE, DSO

Brooksbank, Sir (Edward) Nicholas, Bt. (1919)

Broom, *Air Marshal* Sir Ivor Gordon, KCB, CBE, DSO, DFC, AFC

Broomfield, Sir Nigel Hugh Robert Allen, KCMG

Broughton, *Air Marshal* Sir Charles, KBE, CB

†Broughton, Sir David Delves, Bt. (1661)

Broun, Sir Lionel John Law, Bt. (s. 1686)

Brown, Sir Allen Stanley, Kt., CBE

Brown, Sir (Arthur James) Stephen, KBE

Brown, Sir (Austen) Patrick, KCB

Brown, *Adm.* Sir Brian Thomas, KCB, CBE

Brown, *Lt.-Col.* Sir Charles Frederick Richmond, Bt. (1863)

Brown, Sir (Cyril) Maxwell Palmer, KCB, CMG

Brown, *Vice-Adm.* Sir David Worthington, KCB

Brown, Sir Derrick Holden-, Kt.

Brown, Sir Douglas Denison, Kt.

Brown, *Hon.* Sir Douglas Dunlop, Kt.

Brown, Sir (Frederick Herbert) Stanley, Kt., CBE, FEng.

Brown, *Prof.* Sir (George) Malcolm, Kt., FRS

Brown, Sir George Noel, Kt.

Brown, Sir John Douglas Keith, Kt.

Brown, Sir John Gilbert Newton, Kt., CBE

Brown, Sir Mervyn, KCMG, OBE

Brown, *Hon.* Sir Ralph Kilner, Kt., OBE, TD

Brown, Sir Robert Crichton-, KCMG, CBE, TD

Brown, *Rt. Hon.* Sir Simon Denis, Kt.

Brown, *Rt. Hon.* Sir Stephen, Kt.

Brown, Sir Thomas, Kt.

Brown, Sir William Brian Piggott-, Bt. (1903)

Browne, *Rt. Hon.* Sir Patrick Reginald Evelyn, Kt., OBE, TD

Brownrigg, Sir Nicholas (Gawen), Bt. (1816)

Browse, *Prof.* Sir Norman Leslie, Kt., MD, FRCS

Bruce, Sir (Francis) Michael Ian, Bt. (s. 1628)

Bruce, Sir Hervey James Hugh, Bt. (1804)

Bruce, *Rt. Hon.* Sir (James) Roualeyn Hovell-Thurlow-Cumming-, Kt.

Brunner, Sir John Henry Kilian, Bt. (1895)

Brunton, Sir (Edward Francis) Lauder, Bt. (1908)

Brunton, Sir Gordon Charles, Kt.
Bryan, Sir Arthur, Kt.
Bryan, Sir Paul Elmore Oliver, Kt.,
  DSO, MC
Bryce, *Hon.* Sir (William) Gordon,
  Kt., CBE
Bryson, *Adm.* Sir Lindsay Sutherland,
  KCB, FEng.
Buchan, Sir John, Kt., CMG
Buchanan, Sir Andrew George, Bt.
  (1878)
Buchanan, Sir Charles Alexander
  James Leith-, Bt. (1775)
Buchanan, *Prof.* Sir Colin Douglas,
  Kt., CBE
Buchanan, *Vice-Adm.* Sir Peter
  William, KBE
Buchanan, Sir Robert Wilson
  (Robin), Kt.
Buchanan, Sir (Ranald) Dennis, Kt.,
  MBE
Buck, Sir (Philip) Antony (Fyson),
  Kt., QC
Buckley, *Rt. Hon.* Sir Denys Burton,
  Kt., MBE
Buckley, Sir John William, Kt.
Buckley, *Lt.-Cdr.* Sir (Peter) Richard,
  KCVO
Buckley, *Hon.* Sir Roger John, Kt.
Bulkeley, Sir Richard Thomas
  Williams-, Bt. (1661)
Bull, Sir Simeon George, Bt. (1922)
Bullard, Sir Julian Leonard, GCMG
Bullus, Sir Eric Edward, Kt.
Bulmer, Sir William Peter, Kt.
Bultin, Sir Bato, Kt., MBE
Bunbury, Sir Michael William, Bt.
  (1681)
Bunbury, Sir (Richard David)
  Michael Richardson-, Bt. (I. 1787)
Bunch, Sir Austin Wyeth, Kt., CBE
Bunyard, Sir Robert Sidney, Kt., CBE,
  QPM
Burbidge, Sir Herbert Dudley, Bt.
  (1916)
Burbury, *Hon.* Sir Stanley Charles,
  KCMG, KCVO, KBE
Burdett, Sir Savile Aylmer, Bt. (1665)
Burgen, Sir Arnold Stanley Vincent,
  Kt., FRS
Burgess, *Gen.* Sir Edward Arthur, KCB,
  OBE
Burgess, Sir (Joseph) Stuart, Kt., CBE,
  ph.D., FRSC
Burgh, Sir John Charles, KCMG, CB
Burke, Sir James Stanley Gilbert, Bt.
  (I. 1797)
Burke, Sir (Thomas) Kerry, Kt.
Burley, Sir Victor George, Kt., CBE
Burman, Sir (John) Charles, Kt.
Burnet, Sir James William Alexander
  (Sir Alastair Burnet), Kt.
Burnett, *Air Chief Marshal* Sir Brian
  Kenyon, GCB, DFC, AFC
Burnett, Sir David Humphery, Bt.,
  MBE, TD (1913)
Burnett, Sir John Harrison, Kt.
Burnett, Sir Walter John, Kt.
Burney, Sir Cecil Denniston, Bt.
  (1921)

Burns, Sir Terence, GCB
Burns, *Maj.-Gen.* Sir (Walter Arthur)
  George, GCVO, CB, DSO, OBE, MC
Burrell, Sir John Raymond, Bt. (1774)
Burrenchobay, Sir Dayendranath,
  KBE, CMG, CVO
Burrows, Sir Bernard Alexander
  Brocas, GCMG
Burston, Sir Samuel Gerald Wood,
  Kt., OBE
Burt, *Hon.* Sir Francis Theodore Page,
  KCMG
Burton, Sir Carlisle Archibald, Kt.,
  OBE
Burton, Sir George Vernon Kennedy,
  Kt., CBE
Burton, Sir Michael St Edmund,
  KCVO, CMG
Bush, *Adm.* Sir John Fitzroy Duyland,
  GCB, DSC
Butler, *Rt. Hon.* Sir Adam Courtauld,
  Kt.
Butler, Sir Clifford Charles, Kt., ph.D.,
  FRS
Butler, Sir (Frederick) (Edward)
  Robin, GCB, CVO
Butler, Sir Michael Dacres, GCMG
Butler, Sir (Reginald) Michael
  (Thomas), Bt. (1922)
Butler, *Hon.* Sir Richard Clive, Kt.
†Butler, Sir Richard Pierce, Bt. (1628)
Butt, Sir (Alfred) Kenneth Dudley, Bt.
  (1929)
Butter, *Maj.* Sir David Henry, KCVO,
  MC
Butterfield, *Hon.* Sir Alexander Neil
  Logie, Kt.
Buxton, *Hon.* Sir Richard Joseph, Kt.
Buxton, Sir Thomas Fowell Victor,
  Bt. (1840)
Buzzard, Sir Anthony Farquhar, Bt.
  (1929)
Byatt, Sir Hugh Campbell, KCVO, CMG
Byers, Sir Maurice Hearne, Kt., CBE,
  QC
Byford, Sir Lawrence, Kt., CBE, QPM
Cable, Sir James Eric, KCVO, CMG
Cadbury, Sir (George) Adrian
  (Hayhurst), Kt.
Cadell, *Vice-Adm.* Sir John Frederick,
  KBE
Cadogan, *Prof.* Sir John Ivan George,
  Kt., CBE, FRS, FRSE
Cahn, Sir Albert Jonas, Bt. (1934)
Cain, Sir Edward Thomas, Kt., CBE
Cain, Sir Henry Edney Conrad, Kt.
Caine, Sir Michael Harris, Kt.
Caines, Sir John, K B
Cairncross, Sir Alexander Kirkland,
  KCMG
Calcutt, Sir David Charles, Kt., QC
Calderwood, Sir Robert, Kt.
Caldwell, *Surgeon Vice-Adm.* Sir (Eric)
  Dick, KBE, CB
Callard, Sir Eric John, Kt., FEng.
Callaway, *Prof.* Sir Frank Adams, Kt.,
  CMG, OBE
Calley, Sir Henry Algernon, Kt., DSO,
  DFC
Calne, *Prof.* Sir Roy Yorke, Kt., FRS

Calthorpe, Sir Euan Hamilton
  Anstruther-Gough-, Bt. (1929)
Cameron of Lochiel, Sir Donald
  Hamish, KT, CVO, TD
Cameron, Sir (Eustace) John, Kt., CBE
Cameron, *Hon.* Sir John, KT, DSC, QC
  (Lord Cameron)
Cameron, Sir John Watson, Kt., OBE
Campbell, Sir Alan Hugh, GCMG
Campbell, Sir Colin Moffat, Bt., MC
  (s. 1668)
Campbell, *Prof.* Sir Colin Murray, Kt.
Campbell, *Prof.* Sir Donald, Kt., CBE,
  FRCS, FRCPGlas.
Campbell, Sir Ian Tofts, Kt., CBE, VRD
Campbell, Sir Ilay Mark, Bt. (1808)
Campbell, Sir Lachlan Philip
  Kemeys, Bt. (1815)
Campbell, Sir Matthew, KBE, CB, FRSE
Campbell, Sir Niall Alexander
  Hamilton, Bt. (1831)
Campbell, Sir Robin Auchinbreck, Bt.
  (s. 1628)
Campbell, Sir Thomas Cockburn-,
  Bt. (1821)
Campbell, *Hon.* Sir Walter Benjamin,
  Kt.
Campbell, *Hon.* Sir William Anthony,
  Kt.
Campion, Sir Harry, Kt., CB, CBE
†Carden, Sir Christopher Robert, Bt.
  (1887)
Carden, Sir John Craven, Bt. (I. 1787)
Carew, Sir Rivers Verain, Bt. (1661)
Carey, Sir Peter Willoughby, GCB
Carlill, *Vice-Adm.* Sir Stephen Hope,
  KBE, CB, DSO
Carlisle, Sir James Beethoven, GCMG
Carlisle, Sir John Michael, Kt.
Carlisle, Sir Kenneth Melville, Kt., MP
Carmichael, Sir David Peter William
  Gibson-Craig-, Bt. (s. 1702 and
  1831)
Carmichael, Sir John, KBE
Carnac, *Revd Canon* Sir (Thomas)
  Nicholas Rivett-, Bt. (1836)
Carnegie, *Lt.-Gen.* Sir Robin
  Macdonald, KCB, OBE
Carnegie, Sir Roderick Howard, Kt.
Carnwath, Sir Andrew Hunter, KCVO
Carnwath, Sir Robert John Anderson,
  Kt., CVO
Caro, Sir Anthony Alfred, Kt., CBE
Carpenter, *Very Revd* Edward
  Frederick, KCVO
Carpenter, *Lt.-Gen.* the Hon. Sir
  Thomas Patrick John Boyd-, KBE
Carr, Sir (Albert) Raymond
  (Maillard), Kt.
Carr, *Air Marshal* Sir John Darcy
  Baker-, KBE, CB, AFC
Carrick, *Hon.* Sir John Leslie, KCMG
Carrick, Sir Roger John, KCMG, LVO
Carsberg, *Prof.* Sir Bryan Victor, Kt.
Carswell, *Rt. Hon.* Sir Robert Douglas,
  Kt.
Carter, Sir Charles Frederick, Kt., FBA
Carter, Sir Derrick Hunton, Kt., TD
Carter, Sir John, Kt., QC
Carter, Sir John Alexander, Kt.

Carter, Sir Philip David, Kt., CBE
Carter, Sir Richard Henry Alwyn, Kt.
Carter, Sir William Oscar, Kt.
Cartland, Sir George Barrington, Kt., CMG
Cartledge, Sir Bryan George, KCMG
Cary, Sir Roger Hugh, Bt. (1955)
Casey, Rt. Hon. Sir Maurice Eugene, Kt.
Cash, Sir Gerald Christopher, GCMG, GCVO, OBE
Cass, Sir Geoffrey Arthur, Kt.
Cass, Sir John Patrick, Kt., OBE
Cassel, Sir Harold Felix, Bt., TD, QC (1920)
Cassels, Field Marshal Sir (Archibald) James Halkett, GCB, KBE, DSO
Cassels, Sir John Seton, Kt., CB
Cassels, Adm. Sir Simon Alastair Cassillis, KCB, CBE
Cassidi, Adm. Sir (Arthur) Desmond, GCB
Casson, Sir Hugh Maxwell, CH, KCVO, PPRA, FRIBA
Cater, Sir Jack, KBE
Cater, Sir John Robert, Kt.
Catford, Sir (John) Robin, KCVO, CBE
Catherwood, Sir (Henry) Frederick (Ross), Kt., MEP
Catling, Sir Richard Charles, Kt., CMG, OBE
Cato, Hon. Sir Arnott Samuel, KCMG
Cave, Sir Charles Edward Coleridge, Bt. (1896)
Cave, Sir (Charles) Philip Haddon-, KBE, CMG
Cave, Sir Robert Cave-Browne-, Bt. (1641)
Cawley, Sir Charles Mills, Kt., CBE, ph.D.
Cayley, Sir Digby William David, Bt. (1661)
Cayzer, Sir James Arthur, Bt. (1904)
Cazalet, Hon. Sir Edward Stephen, Kt.
Cazalet, Sir Peter Grenville, Kt.
Cecil, Rear-Adm. Sir (Oswald) Nigel Amherst, KBE, CB
Chacksfield, Air Vice-Marshal Sir Bernard Albert, KBE, CB
Chadwick, Revd Prof. Henry, KBE
Chadwick, Hon. Sir John Murray, Kt., ED
Chadwick, Sir Joshua Kenneth Burton, Bt. (1935)
Chadwick, Revd Prof. (William) Owen, OM, KBE, FBA
Chan, Rt. Hon. Sir Julius, GCMG, KBE
Chance, Sir (George) Jeremy ffolliott, Bt. (1900)
Chandler, Sir Colin Michael, Kt.
Chandler, Sir Geoffrey, Kt., CBE
Chaney, Hon. Sir Frederick Charles, KBE, AFC
Chaplin, Sir Malcolm Hilbery, Kt., CBE
Chapman, Sir David Robert Macgowan, Bt. (1958)
Chapman, Sir George Alan, Kt.
Chapman, Sir Sidney Brookes, Kt., MP

Chapple, Field Marshal Sir John Lyon, GCB, CBE
Charlton, Sir Robert (Bobby), Kt., CBE
Charnley, Sir (William) John, Kt., CB, FEng.
Chataway, Rt. Hon. Sir Christopher, Kt.
Chatfield, Sir John Freeman, Kt., CBE
Chaytor, Sir George Reginald, Bt. (1831)
Checketts, Sqn. Ldr. Sir David John, KCVO
Checkland, Sir Michael, Kt.
Cheetham, Sir Nicolas John Alexander, KCMG
Cheshire, Air Marshal Sir John Anthony, KBE, CB
Chessells, Sir Arthur David (Tim), Kt.
Chesterman, Sir (Dudley) Ross, Kt., ph.D.
Chesterton, Sir Oliver Sidney, Kt., MC
Chetwood, Sir Clifford Jack, Kt.
Chetwynd, Sir Arthur Ralph Talbot, Bt. (1795)
Cheung, Sir Oswald Victor, Kt., CBE
Cheyne, Sir Joseph Lister Watson, Bt., OBE (1908)
Chichester, Sir (Edward) John, Bt. (1641)
Chilcot, Sir John Anthony, KCB
Child, Sir (Coles John) Jeremy, Bt. (1919)
Chilton, Brig. Sir Frederick Oliver, Kt., CBE, DSO
Chilwell, Hon. Sir Muir Fitzherbert, Kt.
Chinn, Sir Trevor Edwin, Kt., CVO
Chipperfield, Sir Geoffrey Howes, KCB
Chitty, Sir Thomas Willes, Bt. (1924)
Cholmeley, Sir Montague John, Bt. (1806)
Christie, Sir George William Langham, Kt.
Christie, Hon. Sir Vernon Howard Colville, Kt.
Christie, Sir William, Kt., MBE
Christopherson, Sir Derman Guy, Kt., OBE, D.phil., FRS, FEng.
Chung, Sir Sze-yuen, GBE, FEng.
Clapham, Sir Michael John Sinclair, KBE
†Clark, Sir Jonathan George, Bt. (1917)
Clark, Sir Francis Drake, Bt. (1886)
Clark, Sir John Allen, Kt.
Clark, Prof. Sir John Grahame Douglas, Kt., CBE
Clark, Sir John Stewart-, Bt., MEP (1918)
Clark, Sir Robert Anthony, Kt., DSC
Clark, Sir Robin Chichester-, Kt.
Clark, Sir Terence Joseph, KBE, CMG, CVO
Clark, Sir Thomas Edwin, Kt.
Clarke, Hon. Sir Anthony Peter, Kt.
Clarke, Sir (Charles Mansfield) Tobias, Bt. (1831)

Clarke, Prof. Sir Cyril Astley, KBE, MD, SC.D., FRS, FRCP
Clarke, Sir Ellis Emmanuel Innocent, GCMG
Clarke, Sir Jonathan Dennis, Kt.
Clarke, Maj. Sir Peter Cecil, KCVO
Clarke, Sir Robert Cyril, Kt.
Clarke, Sir Rupert William John, Bt., MBE (1882)
Clay, Sir Richard Henry, Bt. (1841)
Clayton, Sir David Robert, Bt., (1732)
Clayton, Sir Robert James, Kt., CBE, FEng.
Cleaver, Sir Anthony Brian, Kt.
Cleminson, Sir James Arnold Stacey, KBE, MC
Clerk, Sir John Dutton, Bt., CBE, VRD (s. 1679)
Clerke, Sir John Edward Longueville, Bt. (1660)
Clifford, Sir Roger Joseph, Bt. (1887)
Clothier, Sir Cecil Montacute, KCB, QC
Clucas, Sir Kenneth Henry, KCB
Clutterbuck, Vice-Adm. Sir David Granville, KBE, CB
Coates, Sir David Frederick Charlton, Bt. (1921)
Coates, Sir Ernest William, Kt., CMG
Coats, Sir Alastair Francis Stuart, Bt. (1905)
Coats, Sir William David, Kt.
Cobban, Sir James Macdonald, Kt., CBE, TD
Cobham, Sir Michael John, Kt., CBE
Cochrane, Sir (Henry) Marc (Sursock), Bt. (1903)
Cockburn, Sir John Elliot, Bt. (s. 1671)
Cockcroft, Sir Wilfred Halliday, Kt., D.phil.
Cockerell, Sir Christopher Sydney, Kt., CBE, FRS
Cockram, Sir John, Kt.
Cockshaw, Sir Alan, Kt., FEng.
Codrington, Sir Simon Francis Bethell, Bt. (1876)
Codrington, Sir William Alexander, Bt. (1721)
Coghill, Sir Egerton James Nevill Tobias, Bt. (1778)
Cohen, Sir Edward, Kt.
Cohen, Sir Ivor Harold, Kt., CBE, TD
Cohen, Sir Stephen Harry Waley-, Bt. (1961)
Coldstream, Sir George Phillips, KCB, KCVO, QC
Cole, Sir (Alexander) Colin, KCB, KCVO, TD
Cole, Sir David Lee, KCMG, MC
Cole, Sir (Robert) William, Kt.
Coles, Sir (Arthur) John, KCMG
Colfox, Sir (William) John, Bt. (1939)
Collett, Sir Christopher, GBE
Collett, Sir Ian Seymour, Bt. (1934)
Collins, Hon. Sir Andrew David, Kt.
Collins, Sir Arthur James Robert, KCVO
Collins, Sir John Alexander, Kt.
Collyear, Sir John Gowen, Kt., FEng.

Colman, *Hon.* Sir Anthony David, Kt.
Colman, Sir Michael Jeremiah, Bt.
(1907)
Colquhoun, *Maj.-Gen.* Sir Cyril
Harry, KCVO, CB, OBE
Colquhoun of Luss, Sir Ivar Iain, Bt.
(1786)
Colt, Sir Edward William Dutton Bt.
(1694)
Colthurst, Sir Richard La Touche, Bt.
(1744)
Colvin, Sir Howard Montagu, Kt.,
CVO, CBE, FBA
Compston, *Vice-Adm.* Sir Peter
Maxwell, KCB
Comyn, *Hon.* Sir James, Kt.
Conant, Sir John Ernest Michael, Bt.
(1954)
Condon, Sir Paul Leslie, Kt., QPM
Connell, *Hon.* Sir Michael Bryan, Kt.
Conran, Sir Terence Orby, Kt.
Cons, *Hon.* Sir Derek, Kt.
†Constable, Sir Frederick
Strickland-, Bt. (1641)
Cook, *Prof.* Sir Alan Hugh, Kt.
Cook, Sir Christopher Wymondham
Rayner Herbert, Bt. (1886)
Cooke, Sir Charles Fletcher-, Kt., QC
Cooke, *Lt.-Col.* Sir David William
Perceval, Bt. (1661)
Cooke, Sir Howard Felix Hanlan, ON,
GCMG, GCVO, CD
Cooke, *Rt. Hon.* Sir Robin Brunskill,
KBE
Cooksey, Sir David James Scott, Kt.
Cooley, Sir Alan Sydenham, Kt., CBE
Coop, Sir Maurice Fletcher, Kt.
Cooper, *Rt. Hon.* Sir Frank, GCB, CMG
Cooper, Sir (Frederick Howard)
Michael Craig-, Kt., CBE, TD
Cooper, *Gen.* Sir George Leslie
Conroy, GCB, MC
Cooper, Sir Louis Jacques Blom-, Kt.,
QC
Cooper, Sir Patrick Graham Astley,
Bt. (1821)
Cooper, Sir Richard Powell, Bt.
(1905)
Cooper, *Maj.-Gen.* Sir Simon
Christie, KCVO
Cooper, Sir William Daniel Charles,
Bt. (1863)
Coote, Sir Christopher John, Bt.,
Premier Baronet of Ireland (I. 1621)
Copas, *Most Revd* Virgil, KBE, DD
Cope, *Rt. Hon.* Sir John Ambrose, Kt.,
MP
Copisarow, Sir Alcon Charles, Kt.
Corbet, Sir John Vincent, Bt., MBE
(1808)
Corbett, *Maj.-Gen.* Sir Robert John
Swan, KCVO, CB
Corby, Sir (Frederick) Brian, Kt.
Corfield, *Rt. Hon.* Sir Frederick
Vernon, Kt., QC
Corfield, Sir Kenneth George, Kt.,
FEng.
Corley, Sir Kenneth Sholl Ferrand,
Kt.

Cormack, Sir Magnus Cameron, KBE
Cormack, Sir Patrick Thomas, Kt., MP
Corness, Sir Colin Ross, Kt.
Cornford, Sir (Edward) Clifford, KCB,
FEng.
Cornforth, Sir John Warcup, Kt., CBE,
D.Phil., FRS
Corry, Sir William James, Bt. (1885)
Cortazzi, Sir (Henry Arthur) Hugh,
GCMG
Cory, Sir (Clinton Charles) Donald,
Bt. (1919)
Cossons, Sir Neil, Kt., OBE
Cotter, *Lt.-Col.* Sir Delaval James
Alfred, Bt., DSO (I. 1763)
Cotterell, Sir John Henry Geers, Bt.
(1805)
Cotton, Sir John Richard, KCMG, OBE
Cotton, *Hon.* Sir Robert Carrington,
KCMG
Cottrell, Sir Alan Howard, Kt., Ph.D.,
FRS, FEng.
†Cotts, Sir Richard Crichton
Mitchell, Bt. (1921)
Coulson, Sir John Eltringham, KCMG
Couper, Sir (Robert) Nicholas
(Oliver), Bt. (1841)
Court, *Hon.* Sir Charles Walter
Michael, KCMG, OBE
Coutts, Sir David Burdett Money-,
KCVO
Couzens, Sir Kenneth Edward, KCB
Covacevich, Sir (Anthony) Thomas,
Kt., DFC
Coward, *Vice-Adm.* Sir John Francis,
KCB, DSO
Cowdrey, Sir (Michael) Colin, Kt.,
CBE
Cowen, *Rt. Hon. Prof.* Sir Zelman,
GCMG, GCVO, QC
Cowie, Sir Thomas (Tom), Kt., OBE
Cowperthwaite, Sir John James, KBE,
CMG
Cox, Sir Alan George, Kt., CBE
Cox, *Prof.* Sir David Roxbee, Kt., FRS
Cox, Sir (Ernest) Gordon, KBE, TD,
D.Sc., FRS
Cox, Sir Geoffrey Sandford, Kt., CBE
Cox, Sir (George) Trenchard, Kt.,
CBE, FSA
Cox, *Vice-Adm.* Sir John Michael
Holland, KCB
Cradock, *Rt. Hon.* Sir Percy, GCMG
Craig, Sir (Albert) James (Macqueen),
GCMG
Craufurd, Sir Robert James, Bt. (1781)
Craven, *Air Marshal* Sir Robert
Edward, KBE, CB, DFC
Crawford, *Prof.* Sir Frederick
William, Kt., FEng.
Crawford, Sir (Robert) Stewart,
GCMG, CVO
Crawford, *Vice-Adm.* Sir William
Godfrey, KBE, CB, DSC
Crawshay, *Col.* Sir William Robert,
Kt., DSO, ERD, TD
Creagh, *Maj.-Gen.* Sir (Kilner) Rupert
Brazier-, KBE, CB, DSO
Cresswell, *Hon.* Sir Peter John, Kt.

Crichton, Sir Andrew James
Maitland-Makgill-, Kt.
Crill, Sir Peter Leslie, Kt., KBE
Cripps, Sir Cyril Humphrey, Kt.
Crisp, Sir (John) Peter, Bt. (1913)
Critchett, Sir Ian (George Lorraine),
Bt. (1908)
Critchley, Sir Julian Michael
Gordon, Kt., MP
Croft, Sir Owen Glendower, Bt.
(1671)
Croft, Sir Thomas Stephen Hutton,
Bt. (1818)
†Crofton, Sir Hugh Denis, Bt. (1801)
Crofton, *Prof.* Sir John Wenman, Kt.
Crofton, Sir Malby Sturges, Bt. (1838)
Croker, Sir Walter Russell, KBE
Crookenden, *Lt.-Gen.* Sir Napier, KCB,
DSO, OBE
Cross, *Air Chief Marshal* Sir Kenneth
Brian Boyd, KCB, CBE, DSO, DFC
Crossland, *Prof.* Sir Bernard, Kt., CBE,
FEng.
Crossland, Sir Leonard, Kt.
Crossley, Sir Nicholas John, Bt.
(1909)
Crouch, Sir David Lance, Kt.
Cruthers, Sir James Winter, Kt.
Cubbon, Sir Brian Crossland, GCB
Cubitt, Sir Hugh Guy, Kt., CBE
Cullen, Sir (Edward) John, Kt., F.Eng.
Cumming, Sir William Gordon
Gordon-, Bt. (1804)
Cuninghame, Sir John Christopher
Foggo Montgomery-, Bt. (NS 1672)
†Cuninghame, Sir William Henry
Fairlie-, Bt. (S. 1630)
Cunliffe, Sir David Ellis, Bt. (1759)
Cunningham, Sir Charles Craik, GCB,
KBE, CVO
Cunningham, *Lt.-Gen.* Sir Hugh
Patrick, KBE
Cunynghame, Sir Andrew David
Francis, Bt. (S. 1702)
Curle, Sir John Noel Ormiston, KCVO,
CMG
Curran, Sir Samuel Crowe, Kt., D.Sc.,
Ph.D., FRS, FRSE, FEng.
†Currie, Sir Donald Scott, Bt. (1847)
Currie, Sir Neil Smith, Kt., CBE
Curtis, Sir Barry John, Kt.
Curtis, Sir (Edward) Leo, Kt.
Curtis, *Hon.* Sir Richard Herbert, Kt.
Curtis, Sir William Peter, Bt. (1802)
Curtiss, *Air Marshal* Sir John Bagot,
KCB, KBE
Curwen, Sir Christopher Keith, KCMG
Cuthbertson, Sir Harold Alexander,
Kt.
Cutler, Sir (Arthur) Roden, VC, KCMG,
KCVO, CBE
Cutler, Sir Charles Benjamin, KBE, ED
Cutler, Sir Horace Walter, Kt., OBE
Dacie, *Prof.* Sir John Vivian, Kt., MD,
FRS
Dalais, Sir Adrien Pierre, Kt.
Dale, Sir William Leonard, KCMG
Dalrymple, *Maj.* Sir Hew Fleetwood
Hamilton-, Bt., KCVO (S. 1697)

Dalton, Sir Alan Nugent Goring, Kt., CBE
Dalton, *Vice-Adm.* Sir Geoffrey Thomas James Oliver, KCB
Daly, *Lt.-Gen.* Sir Thomas Joseph, KBE, CB, DSO
Dalyell, Sir Tam, Bt., MP (NS 1685)
Daniel, Sir Goronwy Hopkin, KCVO, CB, D.Phil.
Daniel, Sir John Sagar, Kt., D.SC.
Daniell, Sir Peter Averell, Kt., TD
Danks, Sir Alan John, KBE
Darby, Sir Peter Howard, Kt., CBE, QFSM
Darell, Sir Jeffrey Lionel, Bt., MC (1795)
Dargie, Sir William Alexander, Kt., CBE
Dark, Sir Anthony Michael Beaumont-, Kt.
Darling, Sir Clifford, GCVO
Darling, Sir James Ralph, Kt., CMG, OBE
Darling, *Gen.* Sir Kenneth Thomas, GBE, KCB, DSO
Darlington, *Rear-Adm.* Sir Charles Roy, KBE
Darvall, Sir (Charles) Roger, Kt., CBE
Dashwood, Sir Francis John Vernon Hereward, Bt., *Premier Baronet of Great Britain* (1707)
Dashwood, Sir Richard James, Bt. (1684)
Daunt, Sir Timothy Lewis Achilles, KCMG
David, Sir Jean Marc, Kt., CBE, QC
David, *His Hon.* Sir Robin (Robert) Daniel George, Kt., QC
Davidson, Sir Robert James, Kt., FEng.
Davie, Sir Antony Francis Ferguson-, Bt. (1847)
Davies, *Air Marshal* Sir Alan Cyril, KCB, CBE
Davies, *Hon.* Sir (Alfred William) Michael, Kt.
Davies, Sir Alun Talfan, Kt., QC
Davies, *Prof.* Sir David Evan Naughton, Kt., CBE, FRS, FEng.
Davies, Sir David Henry, Kt.
Davies, *Hon.* Sir (David Herbert) Mervyn, Kt., MC, TD
Davies, *Vice-Adm.* Sir Lancelot Richard Bell, KBE
Davies, Sir Oswald, Kt., CBE
Davies, Sir Peter Maxwell, Kt., CBE
Davies, Sir Victor Caddy, Kt., OBE
Davis, Sir Charles Sigmund, Kt., CB
Davis, Sir Colin Rex, Kt., CBE
Davis, *Hon.* Sir (Dermot) Renn, Kt., OBE
Davis, Sir (Ernest) Howard, Kt., CMG, OBE
Davis, Sir John Gilbert, Bt. (1946)
Davis, Sir Rupert Charles Hart-, Kt.
Davis, *Hon.* Sir Thomas Robert Alexander Harries, KBE
Davison, *Rt. Hon.* Sir Ronald Keith, GBE, CMG
Dawbarn, Sir Simon Yelverton, KCVO, CMG

Dawson, Sir Anthony Michael, KCVO, MD, FRCP
Dawson, *Hon.* Sir Daryl Michael, KBE, CB
Dawson, Sir Hugh Michael Trevor, Bt. (1920)
Dawtry, Sir Alan (Graham), Kt., CBE, TD
Day, Sir Derek Malcolm, KCMG
Day, Sir (Judson) Graham, Kt.
Day, Sir Michael John, Kt., OBE
Day, Sir Robin, Kt.
Deakin, Sir (Frederick) William (Dampier), Kt., DSO
Deane, *Hon.* Sir William Patrick, KBE
Dearing, Sir Ronald Ernest, Kt., CB
de Bellaigue, Sir Geoffrey, KCVO
Debenham, Sir Gilbert Ridley, Bt. (1931)
de Deney, Sir Geoffrey Ivor, KCVO
Deer, Sir (Arthur) Frederick, Kt., CMG
de Hoghton, Sir (Richard) Bernard (Cuthbert), Bt. (1611)
De la Bère, Sir Cameron, Bt. (1953)
de la Rue, Sir Andrew George Ilay, Bt. (1898)
Dellow, Sir John Albert, Kt., CBE
Delve, Sir Frederick William, Kt., CBE
de Montmorency, Sir Arnold Geoffroy, Bt. (I. 1631)
Denholm, Sir John Ferguson (Ian), Kt., CBE
Denman, Sir (George) Roy, KCB, CMG
Denny, Sir Anthony Coningham de Waltham, Bt. (I. 1782)
†Denny, Sir Charles Alistair Maurice, Bt. (1913)
Dent, Sir John, Kt., CBE, FEng.
Dent, Sir Robin John, KCVO
Denton, *Prof.* Sir Eric James, Kt., CBE, FRS
Derbyshire, Sir Andrew George, Kt.
Derham, Sir Peter John, Kt.
de Trafford, Sir Dermot Humphrey, Bt. (1841)
Deverell, Sir Colville Montgomery, GBE, KCMG, CVO
Devesi, Sir Baddeley, GCMG, GCVO
De Ville, Sir Harold Godfrey Oscar, Kt., CBE
Devitt, Sir Thomas Gordon, Bt. (1916)
de Waal, Sir (Constant Henrik) Henry, KCB, QC
Dewey, Sir Anthony Hugh, Bt. (1917)
Dewhurst, *Prof.* Sir (Christopher) John, Kt.
d'Eyncourt, Sir Mark Gervais Tennyson-, Bt. (1930)
Dhenin, *Air Marshal* Sir Geoffrey Howard, KBE, AFC, GM, MD
Dhrangadhra, HH the Maharaja Raj Saheb of, KCIE
Dibela, *Hon.* Sir Kingsford, GCMG
Dickenson, Sir Aubrey Fiennes Trotman-, Kt.
Dickinson, Sir Harold Herbert, Kt.
Dickinson, Sir Samuel Benson, Kt.
Dilbertson, Sir Geoffrey, Kt., CBE

Dilke, Sir John Fisher Wentworth, Bt. (1862)
Dillon, *Rt. Hon.* Sir (George) Brian (Hugh), Kt.
Dillon, Sir John Vincent, Kt., CMG
Dillon, Sir Max, Kt.
Diver, *Hon.* Sir Leslie Charles, Kt.
Dixon, Sir Jonathan Mark, Bt. (1919)
Djanogly, Sir Harry Ari Simon, Kt., CBE
Dobbs, *Capt.* Sir Richard Arthur Frederick, KCVO
Dobson, *Vice-Adm.* Sir David Stuart, KBE
Dobson, Sir Denis William, KCB, OBE, QC
Dobson, *Gen.* Sir Patrick John Howard-, GCB
Dodds, Sir Ralph Jordan, Bt. (1964)
Dodson, Sir Derek Sherborne Lindsell, KCMG, MC
Dodsworth, Sir John Christopher Smith-, Bt. (1784)
Doll, *Prof.* Sir (William) Richard (Shaboe), Kt., OBE, FRS, DM, MD, D.SC.
Dollery, Sir Colin Terence, Kt.
Donald, Sir Alan Ewen, KCMG
Donald, *Air Marshal* Sir John George, KBE
Donne, *Hon.* Sir Gaven John, KBE
Donne, Sir John Christopher, Kt.
Dookun, Sir Dewoonarain, Kt.
Dorey, Sir Graham Martyn, Kt.
Dorman, *Lt.-Col.* Sir Charles Geoffrey, Bt., MC (1923)
Dougherty, *Maj.-Gen.* Sir Ivan Noel, Kt., CBE, DSO, ED
Doughty, Sir William Roland, Kt.
Douglas, Sir (Edward) Sholto, Kt.
Douglas, Sir Robert McCallum, Kt., OBE
Douglas, *Hon.* Sir Roger Owen, Kt.
Douglas, *Rt. Hon.* Sir William Randolph, KCMG
Dover, *Prof.* Sir Kenneth James, Kt., D.Litt., FBA, FRSE
Dowell, Sir Anthony James, Kt., CBE
Down, Sir Alastair Frederick, Kt., OBE, MC, TD
Downes, Sir Edward Thomas, Kt., CBE
Downey, Sir Gordon Stanley, KCB
Downs, Sir Diarmuid, Kt., CBE, FEng.
Downward, Sir William Atkinson, Kt.
Dowson, Sir Philip Manning, Kt., CBE, ARA
Doyle, Sir Reginald Derek Henry, Kt., CBE
D'Oyly, Sir Nigel Hadley Miller, Bt. (1663)
Drake, Sir (Arthur) Eric (Courtney), Kt., CBE
Drake, *Hon.* Sir (Frederick) Maurice, Kt., DFC
Dreyer, *Adm.* Sir Desmond Parry, GCB, CBE, DSC
Drinkwater, Sir John Muir, Kt., QC
Driver, Sir Antony Victor, Kt.
Driver, Sir Eric William, Kt.
Drummond, Sir John Richard Gray, Kt., CBE

Drury, Sir (Victor William) Michael, Kt., OBE
Dryden, Sir John Stephen Gyles, Bt. (1733 and 1795)
du Cann, *Rt. Hon.* Sir Edward Dillon Lott, KBE
Duckworth, *Maj.* Sir Richard Dyce, Bt. (1909)
du Cros, Sir Claude Philip Arthur Mallet, Bt. (1916)
Duff, *Rt. Hon.* Sir (Arthur) Antony, GCMG, CVO, DSO, DSC
Duffell, *Lt.-Gen.* Sir Peter Royson, KCB, CBE, MC
Duffus, *Hon.* Sir William Algernon Holwell, Kt.
Duffy, Sir (Albert) (Edward) Patrick, Kt., PH.D.
Dugdale, Sir William Stratford, Bt., MC (1936)
Dunbar, Sir Archibald Ranulph, Bt. (s. 1700)
Dunbar, Sir David Hope-, Bt. (s. 1664)
Dunbar, Sir Drummond Cospatrick Ninian, Bt., MC (s. 1698)
Dunbar, Sir James Michael, Bt. (s. 1694)
Dunbar of Hempriggs, Dame Maureen Daisy Helen (Lady Dunbar of Hempriggs), Btss. (s. 1706)
Duncan, Sir James Blair, Kt.
Duncombe, Sir Philip Digby Pauncefort-, Bt. (1859)
Dunham, Sir Kingsley Charles, Kt., PH.D., FRS, FRSE, FEng.
Dunlop, Sir Thomas, Bt. (1916)
Dunlop, Sir William Norman Gough, Kt.
Dunn, *Air Marshal* Sir Eric Clive, KBE, CB, BEM
Dunn, *Air Marshal* Sir Patrick Hunter, KBE, CB, DFC
Dunn, *Rt. Hon.* Sir Robin Horace Walford, Kt., MC
Dunne, Sir Thomas Raymond, KCVO
Dunnett, Sir Alastair MacTavish, Kt.
Dunnett, Sir (Ludovic) James, GCB, CMG
Dunning, Sir Simon William Patrick, Bt. (1930)
Dunphie, *Maj.-Gen.* Sir Charles Anderson Lane, Kt., CB, CBE, DSO
Dunstan, *Lt.-Gen.* Sir Donald Beaumont, KBE, CB
†Duntze, Sir Daniel Evans, Bt. (1774)
Dupre, Sir Tumun, Kt., MBE
Dupree, Sir Peter, Bt. (1921)
Durand, Sir Edward Alan Christopher David Percy, Bt. (1892)
Durant, Sir (Robert) Anthony (Bevis), Kt., MP
Durham, Sir Kenneth, Kt.
Durie, Sir Alexander Charles, Kt., CBE
Durkin, *Air Marshal* Sir Herbert, KBE, CB
Durrant, Sir William Alexander Estridge, Bt. (1784)

Duthie, *Prof.* Sir Herbert Livingston, Kt.
Duthie, Sir Robert Grieve (Robin), Kt., CBE
Duval, Sir (Charles) Gaetan, Kt.
Duxbury, *Air Marshal* Sir (John) Barry, KCB, CBE
Dyer, *Prof.* Sir (Henry) Peter (Francis) Swinnerton-, Bt., KBE, FRS (1678)
Dyke, Sir David William Hart, Bt. (1677)
Dyson, *Hon.* Sir John Anthony, Kt.
Earle, Sir (Hardman) George (Algernon), Bt. (1869)
East, Sir (Lewis) Ronald, Kt., CBE
Easton, Sir Robert William Simpson, Kt., CBE
Eaton, *Adm.* Sir Kenneth John, GBE, KCB
Eberle, *Adm.* Sir James Henry Fuller, GCB
Ebrahim, Sir (Mahomed) Currimbhoy, Bt. (1910)
Eccles, Sir John Carew, Kt., D.phil., FRS
Echlin, Sir Norman David Fenton, Bt. (I. 1721)
Eckersley, Sir Donald Payze, Kt., OBE
Edge, *Capt.* Sir (Philip) Malcolm, KCVO
†Edge, Sir William, Bt. (1937)
Edmonstone, Sir Archibald Bruce Charles, Bt. (1774)
Edwardes, Sir Michael Owen, Kt.
Edwards, Sir Christopher John Churchill, Bt. (1866)
Edwards, Sir George Robert, Kt., OM, CBE, FRS, FEng.
Edwards, Sir (John) Clive (Leighton), Bt. (1921)
Edwards, Sir Llewellyn Roy, Kt.
Edwards, *Prof.* Sir Samuel Frederick, Kt., FRS
Egan, Sir John Leopold, Kt.
Egerton, Sir John Alfred Roy, Kt.
Egerton, Sir (Philip) John (Caledon) Grey-, Bt. (1617)
Egerton, Sir Seymour John Louis, GCVO
Egerton, Sir Stephen Loftus, KCMG
Eggleston, *Hon.* Sir Richard Moulton, Kt.
Eichelbaum, *Rt. Hon.* Sir Thomas, GBE
Eliott of Stobs, Sir Charles Joseph Alexander, Bt. (s. 1666)
Ellerton, Sir Geoffrey James, Kt., CMG, MBE
Elliot, Sir Gerald Henry, Kt.
Elliott, Sir Clive Christopher Hugh, Bt. (1917)
Elliott, Sir David Murray, KCMG, CB
Elliott, *Prof.* Sir John Huxtable, Kt., FBA
Elliott, Sir Randal Forbes, KBE
Elliott, *Prof.* Sir Roger James, Kt., FRS
Elliott, Sir Ronald Stuart, Kt.
Ellis, Sir John Rogers, Kt., MBE, MD, FRCP
Ellis, Sir Ronald, Kt., FEng.

Ellison, *Col.* Sir Ralph Harry Carr-, Kt., TD
Elphinstone, Sir John, Bt. (s. 1701)
Elphinstone, Sir (Maurice) Douglas (Warburton), Bt., TD (1816)
Elton, Sir Arnold, Kt., CBE
Elton, Sir Charles Abraham Grierson, Bt. (1717)
Elwes, Sir Jeremy Vernon, Kt., CBE
Elwood, Sir Brian George Conway, Kt., CBE
Elworthy, Sir Peter Herbert, Kt.
Elyan, Sir (Isadore) Victor, Kt.
Emery, *Rt. Hon.* Sir Peter Frank Hannibal, Kt., MP
Empson, *Adm.* Sir (Leslie) Derek, GBE, KCB
Engineer, Sir Noshirwan Phirozshah, Kt.
Engle, Sir George Lawrence Jose, KCB, QC
English, Sir Cyril Rupert, Kt.
English, Sir David, Kt.
English, Sir Terence Alexander Hawthorne, KBE, FRCS
Epstein, *Prof.* Sir (Michael) Anthony, Kt., CBE, FRS
Ereaut, Sir (Herbert) Frank Cobbold, Kt.
Errington, *Col.* Sir Geoffrey Frederick, Bt. (1963)
Errington, Sir Lancelot, KCB
Erskine, Sir (Thomas) David, Bt. (1821)
Esmonde, Sir Thomas Francis Grattan, Bt. (I. 1629)
Espie, Sir Frank Fletcher, Kt., OBE
Esplen, Sir John Graham, Bt. (1921)
Eustace, Sir Joseph Lambert, GCMG, GCVO
Evans, Sir Anthony Adney, Bt. (1920)
Evans, *Rt. Hon.* Sir Anthony Howell Meurig, Kt., RD
Evans, *Air Chief Marshal* Sir David George, GCB, CBE
Evans, *Air Chief Marshal* Sir David Parry-, GCB, CBE
Evans, *Hon.* Sir Haydn Tudor, Kt.
Evans, Sir Richard Mark, KCMG, KCVO
Evans, Sir Robert, Kt., CBE, FEng.
Evans, Sir (Robert) Charles, Kt.
Evans, Sir (William) Vincent (John), GCMG, MBE, QC
Eveleigh, *Rt. Hon.* Sir Edward Walter, Kt., ERD
Everard, *Maj.-Gen.* Sir Christopher Earle Welby-, KBE, CB
Everard, Sir Robin Charles, Bt. (1911)
Everson, Sir Frederick Charles, KCMG
Every, Sir Henry John Michael, Bt. (1641)
Ewans, Sir Martin Kenneth, KCMG
Ewart, Sir (William) Ivan (Cecil), Bt., DSC (1887)
Ewbank, *Hon.* Sir Anthony Bruce, Kt.
Ewin, Sir (David) Ernest Thomas Floyd, Kt., OBE, MVO
Ewing, *Vice-Adm.* Sir (Robert) Alastair, KBE, CB, DSC

Ewing, Sir Ronald Archibald Orr-, Bt.
(1886)
Eyre, Sir Graham Newman, Kt., QC
Eyre, *Maj.-Gen.* Sir James Ainsworth
Campden Gabriel, KCVO, CBE
Eyre, Sir Reginald Edwin, Kt.
Faber, Sir Richard Stanley, KCVO,
CMG
Fadahunsi, Sir Joseph Odeleye, KCMG
Fagge, Sir John William Frederick,
Bt. (1660)
Fairbairn, *Hon.* Sir David Eric, KBE,
DFC
Fairbairn, Sir (James) Brooke, Bt.
(1869)
Fairclough, Sir John Whitaker, Kt.,
FEng.
Fairgrieve, Sir (Thomas) Russell, Kt.,
CBE, TD
Fairhall, *Hon.* Sir Allen, KBE
Fairweather, Sir Patrick Stanislaus,
KCMG
Falconer, *Hon.* Sir Douglas William,
Kt., MBE
Falk, Sir Roger Salis, Kt., OBE
Falkiner, Sir Edmond Charles, Bt.
(I. 1778)
Fall, Sir Brian James Proetel, GCVO,
KCMG
Falle, Sir Samuel, KCMG, KCVO, DSC
Fareed, Sir Djamil Sheik, Kt.
Farmer, Sir (Lovedin) George
Thomas, Kt.
Farndale, *Gen.* Sir Martin Baker, KCB
Farquhar, Sir Michael Fitzroy Henry,
Bt. (1796)
Farquharson, *Rt. Hon.* Sir Donald
Henry, Kt.
Farquharson, Sir James Robbie, KBE
Farr, Sir John Arnold, Kt.
Farrer, Sir (Charles) Matthew, GCVO
Farrington, Sir Henry Francis
Colden, Bt. (1818)
Fat, Sir (Maxime) Edouard (Lim
Man) Lim, Kt.
Faulkner, Sir (James) Dennis
(Compton), Kt., CBE, VRD
Fawcus, Sir (Robert) Peter, KBE, CMG
Fawkes, Sir Randol Francis, Kt.
Fay, Sir (Humphrey) Michael
Gerard, Kt.
Fayrer, Sir John Lang Macpherson,
Bt. (1896)
Fearn, Sir (Patrick) Robin, KCMG
Feilden, Sir Bernard Melchior, Kt.,
CBE
Feilden, Sir Henry Wemyss, Bt.,
(1846)
Feldman, Sir Basil Samuel, Kt.
Fell, Sir Anthony, Kt.
Fell, Sir David, KCB
Fellowes, *Rt. Hon.* Sir Robert, KCB,
KCVO
Fenn, Sir Nicholas Maxted, GCMG
Fennell, *Hon.* Sir (John) Desmond
Augustine, Kt., OBE
Fennessy, Sir Edward, Kt., CBE
†Ferguson, Sir Ian Edward Johnson-,
Bt. (1906)

Fergusson of Kilkerran, Sir Charles,
Bt. (s. 1703)
Fergusson, Sir Ewan Alastair John,
GCMG, GCVO
Fergusson, Sir James Herbert
Hamilton Colyer-, Bt. (1866)
Feroze, Sir Rustam Moolan, Kt., FRCS
Ferris, *Hon.* Sir Francis Mursell, Kt.,
TD
ffolkes, Sir Robert Francis Alexander,
Bt, OBE (1774)
Field, Sir Malcolm David, Kt.
Fielding, Sir Colin Cunningham, Kt.,
CB
Fielding, Sir Leslie, KCMG
Fiennes, Sir John Saye Wingfield
Twisleton-Wykcham-, KCB, QC
Fiennes, Sir Ranulph Twisleton-
Wykeham-, Bt., OBE (1916)
Figg, Sir Leonard Clifford William,
KCMG
Figgess, Sir John George, KBE, CMG
Figures, Sir Colin Frederick, KCMG,
OBE
Fingland, Sir Stanley James Gunn,
KCMG
Finlay, Sir David Ronald James Bell,
Bt. (1964)
Finley, Sir Peter Hamilton, Kt., OBE,
DFC
Firth, *Prof.* Sir Raymond William, Kt.,
ph.D., FBA
Fish, Sir Hugh, Kt., CBE
Fisher, Sir George Read, Kt., CMG
Fisher, *Hon.* Sir Henry Arthur Pears,
Kt.
Fisher, Sir Nigel Thomas Loveridge,
Kt., MC
Fison, Sir (Richard) Guy, Bt., DSC
(1905)
†Fitzgerald, *Revd* (Sir) Daniel Patrick,
Bt. (1903)
FitzGerald, Sir George Peter
Maurice, Bt., MC (*The Knight of
Kerry*) (1880)
FitzHerbert, Sir Richard Ranulph, Bt.
(1784)
Fitzpatrick, *Gen.* Sir (Geoffrey
Richard) Desmond, GCB, DSO, MBE,
MC
Fitzpatrick, *Air Marshal* Sir John
Bernard, KBE, CB
Flanagan, Sir James Bernard, Kt., CBE
Fletcher, Sir Henry Egerton Aubrey-,
Bt. (1782)
Fletcher, Sir James Muir Cameron,
Kt.
Fletcher, Sir Leslie, Kt., DSC
Fletcher, *Air Chief Marshal* Sir Peter
Carteret, KCB, OBE, DFC, AFC
Floissac, *Hon.* Sir Vincent Frederick,
Kt., CMG, OBE, QC
Floyd, Sir Giles Henry Charles, Bt.
(1816)
Foley, *Lt.-Gen.* Sir John Paul, KCB, OBE,
MC
Foley, Sir (Thomas John) Noel, Kt.,
CBE
Follett, *Prof.* Sir Brian Keith, Kt., FRS
Foot, Sir Geoffrey James, Kt.

Foots, Sir James William, Kt.
Forbes, *Hon.* Sir Alastair Granville,
Kt.
Forbes, *Maj.* Sir Hamish Stewart, Bt.,
MBE, MC (1823)
Forbes of Craigievar, Sir John
Alexander Cumnock, Bt. (s. 1630)
Forbes, *Vice-Adm.* Sir John Morrison,
KCB
Forbes, *Hon.* Sir Thayne John, Kt.
†Forbes of Pitsligo, Sir William
Daniel Stuart-, Bt. (s. 1626)
Ford, Sir Andrew Russell, Bt. (1929)
Ford, Sir David Robert, KBE, LVO, OBE
Ford, *Maj.* Sir Edward William
Spencer, KCB, KCVO
Ford, *Air Marshal* Sir Geoffrey
Harold, KBE, CB, FEng.
Ford, *Prof.* Sir Hugh, Kt., FRS, FEng.
Ford, Sir James Anson St Clair-, Bt.
(1793)
Ford, Sir John Archibald, KCMG, MC
Ford, Sir Richard Brinsley, Kt., CBE
Ford, *Gen.* Sir Robert Cyril, GCB, CBE
Foreman, Sir Philip Frank, Kt., CBE,
FEng.
Forman, Sir John Denis, Kt., OBE
Forrest, *Prof.* Sir (Andrew) Patrick
(McEwen), Kt.
Forrest, *Rear-Adm.* Sir Ronald
Stephen, KCVO
Forster, Sir Archibald William, Kt.,
FEng.
Forster, Sir Oliver Grantham, KCMG,
MVO
Forte, Hon. Sir Rocco John Vincent,
Kt.
Forwood, Sir Dudley Richard, Bt.
(1895)
Foster, *Prof.* Sir Christopher David,
Kt.
Foster, Sir John Gregory, Bt. (1930)
Foster, Sir Norman Robert, Kt.
Foster, Sir Robert Sidney, GCMG,
KCVO
Foulis, Sir Ian Primrose Liston-, Bt.
(s. 1634)
Foulkes, Sir Nigel Gordon, Kt.
Fowden, Sir Leslie, Kt., FRS
Fowke, Sir David Frederick
Gustavus, Bt. (1814)
Fowler, Sir (Edward) Michael
Coulson, Kt.
Fowler, *Rt. Hon.* Sir (Peter) Norman,
Kt., MP
Fox, Sir (Henry) Murray, GBE
Fox, Sir (John) Marcus, Kt., MBE, MP
Fox, *Rt. Hon.* Sir Michael John, Kt.
Fox, Sir Paul Leonard, Kt., CBE
France, Sir Arnold William, GCB
France, Sir Christopher Walter, GCB
Francis, Sir Horace William
Alexander, Kt., CBE, FEng.
Frank, Sir Douglas George Horace,
Kt., QC
Frank, Sir (Frederick) Charles, Kt.,
OBE, FRS
Frank, Sir Robert Andrew, Bt. (1920)
Frankel, Sir Otto Herzberg, Kt., D.SC.,
FRS

Franklin, Sir Eric Alexander, Kt., CBE
Franklin, Sir Michael David Milroy, KCB, CMG
Franks, Sir Arthur Temple, KCMG
Fraser, Sir Angus McKay, KCB, TD
Fraser, Sir Charles Annand, KCVO
Fraser, *Gen.* Sir David William, GCB, OBE
Fraser, *Air Marshal Revd* Sir (Henry) Paterson, KBE, CB, AFC
Fraser, Sir Ian, Kt., DSO, OBE
Fraser, Sir Ian James, Kt., CBE, MC
Fraser, Sir (James) Campbell, Kt.
Fraser, *Prof.* Sir James David, Bt. (1943)
Fraser, Sir William Kerr, GCB
Frederick, Sir Charles Boscawen, Bt. (1723)
Freeland, Sir John Redvers, KCMG
Freeman, Sir James Robin, Bt. (1945)
Freeman, Sir Ralph, Kt., CVO, CBE, FEng.
Freer, *Air Chief Marshal* Sir Robert William George, GBE, KCB
Freeth, *Hon.* Sir Gordon, KBE
French, *Hon.* Sir Christopher James Saunders, Kt.
Frere, *Vice-Adm.* Sir Richard Tobias, KCB
Fretwell, Sir (Major) John (Emsley), GCMG
Freud, Sir Clement Raphael, Kt.
Froggatt, Sir Leslie Trevor, Kt.
Froggatt, Sir Peter, Kt.
Frossard, Sir Charles Keith, KBE
Frost, Sir David Paradine, Kt., OBE
Frost, *Hon.* Sir (Thomas) Sydney, Kt.
Fry, Sir Peter Derek, Kt., MP
Fry, *Hon.* Sir William Gordon, Kt.
Fryberg, Sir Abraham, Kt., MBE
Fuchs, Sir Vivian Ernest, Kt., Ph.D.
Fuller, *Hon.* Sir John Bryan Munro, Kt.
Fuller, Sir John William Fleetwood, Bt. (1910)
Fung, *Hon.* Sir Kenneth Ping-Fan, Kt., CBE
Furness, Sir Stephen Roberts, Bt. (1913)
Gadsden, Sir Peter Drury Haggerston, GBE, FEng.
Gage, *Hon.* Sir William Marcus, Kt.
Gainsford, *Prof.* Sir Ian Derek, Kt., DDS
Gairy, *Rt. Hon.* Sir Eric Matthew, Kt.
Gaius, *Rt. Revd* Saimon, KBE
Gallwey, Sir Philip Frankland Payne-, Bt. (1812)
Gam, *Rt. Revd* Sir Getake, KBE
Gamble, Sir David Hugh Norman, Bt. (1897)
Garden, *Air Marshal* Sir Timothy, KCB
Gardiner, Sir George Arthur, Kt., MP
Gardner, Sir Douglas Bruce Bruce-, Bt. (1945)
Gardner, Sir Edward Lucas, Kt., QC
Garland, *Hon.* Sir Patrick Neville, Kt.
Garland, *Hon.* Sir Ransley Victor, KBE
Garlick, Sir John, KCB
Garner, Sir Anthony Stuart, Kt.

Garnier, *Rear-Adm.* Sir John, KCVO, CBE, LVO
Garrett, *Hon.* Sir Raymond William, Kt., AFC
Garrick, Sir Ronald, Kt., CBE, FEng.
Garrioch, Sir (William) Henry, Kt.
Garrod, *Lt.-Gen.* Sir (John) Martin Carruthers, KCB, OBE
Garthwaite, Sir (William) Mark (Charles), Bt. (1919)
Gaskell, Sir Richard Kennedy Harvey, Kt.
Gatehouse, *Hon.* Sir Robert Alexander, Kt.
Geddes, Sir (Anthony) Reay (Mackay), Kt.
George, Sir Arthur Thomas, Kt.
George, Sir Richard William, Kt.
Gerken, *Vice-Adm.* Sir Robert William Frank, KCB, CBE
Gery, Sir Robert Lucian Wade-, KCMG, KCVO
Gethin, Sir Richard Joseph St Lawrence, Bt. (I. 1665)
Ghurburrun, Sir Rabindrah, Kt.
Gibb, Sir Francis Ross (Frank), Kt., CBE, FEng.
Gibbings, Sir Peter Walter, Kt.
Gibbon, *Gen.* Sir John Houghton, GCB, OBE
Gibbons, Sir (John) David, KBE
Gibbons, Sir William Edward Doran, Bt. (1752)
Gibbs, *Hon.* Sir Eustace Hubert Beilby, KCVO, CMG
Gibbs, *Rt. Hon.* Sir Harry Talbot, GCMG, KBE
Gibbs, Sir Roger Geoffrey, Kt.
Gibbs, *Field Marshal* Sir Roland Christopher, GCB, CBE, DSO, MC
†Gibson, Revd Sir Christopher Herbert, Bt. (1931)
Gibson, *Revd* Sir David, Bt. (1926)
Gibson, *Vice-Adm.* Sir Donald Cameron Ernest Forbes, KCB, DSC
Gibson, *Rt. Hon.* Sir Peter Leslie, Kt.
Gibson, *Rt. Hon.* Sir Ralph Brian, Kt.
Giddings, *Air Marshal* Sir (Kenneth Charles) Michael, KCB, OBE, DFC, AFC
Gielgud, Sir (Arthur) John, Kt., CH
Giffard, Sir (Charles) Sydney (Rycroft), KCMG
Gilbert, *Air Chief Marshal* Sir Joseph Alfred, KCB, CBE
Gilbert, Sir Martin John, Kt., CBE
†Gilbey, Sir Walter Gavin, Bt. (1893)
Giles, *Rear-Adm.* Sir Morgan Charles Morgan-, Kt., DSO, OBE, GM
Gill, Sir Anthony Keith, Kt., FEng.
Gillett, Sir Robin Danvers Penrose, Bt., GBE, RD (1959)
Gillmore, Sir David Howe, GCMG
Gilmour, *Col.* Sir Allan Macdonald, KCVO, OBE, MC
Gilmour, Sir John Edward, Bt., DSO, TD (1897)
Gina, Sir Lloyd Maepeza, KBE
Gingell, *Air Chief Marshal* Sir John, GBE, KCB, KCVO

Girolami, Sir Paul, Kt.
Girvan, *Hon.* Sir Frederick Paul, Kt.
Gladstone, Sir (Erskine) William, Bt. (1846)
Glasspole, Sir Florizel Augustus, GCMG, GCVO
Glen, Sir Alexander Richard, KBE, DSC
Glenn, Sir (Joseph Robert) Archibald, Kt., OBE
Glidewell, *Rt. Hon.* Sir Iain Derek Laing, Kt.
Glock, Sir William Frederick, Kt., CBE
Glover, *Gen.* Sir James Malcolm, KCB, MBE
Glover, Sir Victor Joseph Patrick, Kt.
Glyn, Sir Alan, Kt., ERD
Glyn, Sir Anthony Geoffrey Leo Simon, Bt. (1927)
Glyn, Sir Richard Lindsay, Bt. (1759 and 1800)
Goad, Sir (Edward) Colin (Viner), KCMG
Godber, Sir George Edward, GCB, DM
Goff, Sir Robert (William) Davis-, Bt. (1905)
Gold, Sir Arthur Abraham, Kt., CBE
Gold, Sir Joseph, Kt.
Goldberg, *Prof.* Sir Abraham, Kt., MD, DSC, FRCP
Golding, Sir John Simon Rawson, Kt., OBE
Goldman, Sir Samuel, KCB
Goldsmith, Sir James Michael, Kt.
Gombrich, *Prof.* Sir Ernst Hans Josef, Kt., OM, CBE, Ph.D., FBA, FSA
Gooch, Sir (Richard) John Sherlock, Bt. (1746)
Gooch, Sir Trevor Sherlock (Sir Peter), Bt. (1866)
Goodall, Sir (Arthur) David Saunders, GCMG
Goodenough, Sir Richard Edmund, Bt. (1943)
Goodhart, Sir Philip Carter, Kt.
Goodhart, Sir Robert Anthony Gordon, Bt. (1911)
Goodhart, Sir William Howard, Kt., QC
Goodhew, Sir Victor Henry, Kt.
Goodison, Sir Alan Clowes, KCMG
Goodison, Sir Nicholas Proctor, Kt.
Goodman, Sir Patrick Ledger, Kt., CBE
Goodson, Sir Mark Weston Lassam, Bt. (1922)
Goodwin, Sir Matthew Dean, Kt., CBE
Goold, Sir George Leonard, Bt. (1801)
Gordon, Sir Alexander John, Kt., CBE
Gordon, Sir Andrew Cosmo Lewis Duff-, Bt. (1813)
Gordon, Sir Charles Addison Somerville Snowden, KCB
Gordon, Sir Keith Lyndell, Kt., CMG
Gordon, Sir (Lionel) Eldred (Peter) Smith-, Bt. (1838)
Gordon, Sir Robert James, Bt. (s. 1706)
Gordon, Sir Sidney Samuel, Kt., CBE

Gordon Lennox, Lord Nicholas Charles, KCMG, KCVO

†Gore, Sir Nigel Hugh St George, Bt. (I. 1622)

Gorham, Sir Richard Masters, Kt., CBE, DFC

Goring, Sir William Burton Nigel, Bt. (1627)

Gorst, Sir John Michael, Kt., MP

Gorton, *Rt. Hon.* Sir John Grey, GCMG, CH

Goschen, Sir Edward Christian, Bt., DSO (1916)

Gosling, Sir (Frederick) Donald, Kt.

Goswell, Sir Brian Lawrence, Kt.

Goulding, Sir (Ernest) Irvine, Kt.

Goulding, Sir (William) Lingard Walter, Bt. (1904)

Gourlay, *Gen.* Sir (Basil) Ian (Spencer), KCB, OBE, MC, RM

Gourlay, Sir Simon Alexander, Kt.

Govan, Sir Lawrence Herbert, Kt.

Gow, *Gen.* Sir (James) Michael, GCB

Gow, Sir Leonard Maxwell Harper, Kt., MBE

Gowans, Sir James Learmonth, Kt., CBE, FRCP, FRS

Gowans, *Hon.* Sir (Urban) Gregory, Kt.

Graaff, Sir de Villiers, Bt., MBE (1911)

Grabham, Sir Anthony Henry, Kt.

Graham, Sir Alexander Michael, GBE

Graham, Sir Charles Spencer Richard, Bt. (1783)

Graham, Sir James Bellingham, Bt. (1662)

Graham, Sir James Thompson, Kt., CMG

Graham, Sir John Alexander Noble, Bt., GCMG (1906)

Graham, Sir John Moodie, Bt. (1964)

Graham, Sir Norman William, Kt., CB

Graham, Sir Peter, KCB, QC

Graham, Sir Peter Alfred, Kt., OBE

Graham, *Lt.-Gen.* Sir Peter Walter, KCB, CBE

†Graham, Sir Ralph Stuart, Bt. (1629)

Graham, *Hon.* Sir Samuel Horatio, Kt., CMG, OBE

Grandy, *Marshal of the Royal Air Force* Sir John, GCB, GCVO, KBE, DSO

Grant, Sir Archibald, Bt. (s. 1705)

Grant, Sir Clifford, Kt.

Grant, Sir (John) Anthony, Kt., MP

Grant, Sir (Matthew) Alistair, Kt.

Grant, Sir Patrick Alexander Benedict, Bt. (s. 1688)

Gray, Sir John Archibald Browne, Kt., SC.D., FRS

Gray, *Vice-Adm.* Sir John Michael Dudgeon, KBE, CB

Gray, Sir John Walton David, KBE, CMG

Gray, *Lt.-Gen.* Sir Michael Stuart, KCB, OBE

Gray, Sir Robert McDowall (Robin), Kt.

Gray, Sir William Hume, Bt. (1917)

Gray, Sir William Stevenson, Kt.

Graydon, *Air Chief Marshal* Sir Michael James, GCB, CBE

Grayson, Sir Jeremy Brian Vincent Harrington, Bt. (1922)

Green, Sir Allan David, KCB, QC

Green, Sir (Edward) Stephen (Lycett), Bt., CBE (1886)

Green, *Hon.* Sir Guy Stephen Montague, KBE

Green, Sir Kenneth, Kt.

Green, Sir Owen Whitley, Kt.

Green, Sir Peter James Frederick, Kt.

Greenaway, Sir John Michael Burdick, Bt. (1933)

Greenborough, Sir John, KBE

Greenbury, Sir Richard, Kt.

Greene, Sir (John) Brian Massy-, Kt.

Greengross, Sir Alan David, Kt.

Greening, *Rear-Adm.* Sir Paul Woollven, GCVO

Greenwell, Sir Edward Bernard, Bt. (1906)

Gregson, Sir Peter Lewis, KCB

Greig, Sir (Henry Louis) Carron, KCVO, CBE

Grenside, Sir John Peter, Kt., CBE

Grey, Sir Anthony Dysart, Bt. (1814)

Grierson, Sir Michael John Bewes, Bt. (s. 1685)

Grierson, Sir Ronald Hugh, Kt.

Grieve, *Prof.* Sir Robert, Kt.

Griffin, *Adm.* Sir Anthony Templer Frederick Griffith, GCB

Griffin, *Maj.* Sir (Arthur) John (Stewart), KCVO

Griffin, Sir (Charles) David, Kt., CBE

Griffiths, Sir Eldon Wylie, Kt.

Griffiths, Sir John Norton-, Bt. (1922)

Grimwade, Sir Andrew Sheppard, Kt., CBE

Grindrod, *Most Revd* John Basil Rowland, KBE

Grinstead, Sir Stanley Gordon, Kt.

Grose, *Vice-Adm.* Sir Alan, KBE

Grotrian, Sir Philip Christian Brent, Bt. (1934)

Grove, Sir Charles Gerald, Bt. (1874)

Grove, Sir Edmund Frank, KCVO

Grugeon, Sir John Drury, Kt.

Grylls, Sir (William) Michael (John), Kt., MP

Guinness, Sir Alec, Kt., CH, CBE

Guinness, Sir Howard Christian Sheldon, Kt., VRD

Guinness, Sir Kenelm Ernest Lee, Bt. (1867)

Guise, Sir John Grant, Bt. (1783)

Gujadhur, Sir Radhamohun, Kt., CMG

Gull, Sir Rupert William Cameron, Bt. (1872)

Gumbs, Sir Emile Rudolph, Kt.

Gunn, *Prof.* Sir John Currie, Kt., CBE

Gunn, Sir Robert Norman, Kt.

Gunn, Sir William Archer, KBE, CMG

†Gunning, Sir Charles Theodore, Bt. (1778)

Gunston, Sir John Wellesley, Bt. (1938)

Gurdon, *Prof.* Sir John Bertrand, Kt., D.Phil., FRS

Guthrie, *Gen.* Sir Charles Ronald Llewelyn, GCB, LVO, OBE

Guthrie, Sir Malcolm Connop, Bt., (1936)

Guy, *Gen.* Sir Roland Kelvin, GCB, CBE, DSO

Habakkuk, Sir John Hrothgar, Kt., FBA

Hackett, *Gen.* Sir John Winthrop, GCB, CBE, DSO, MC

Hadfield, Sir Ronald, Kt., QPM

Hadlee, Sir Richard John, Kt., MBE

Hadley, Sir Leonard Albert, Kt.

Hague, *Prof.* Sir Douglas Chalmers, Kt., CBE

Halberg, Sir Murray Gordon, Kt., MBE

Hale, *Prof.* Sir John Rigby, Kt.

Hall, Sir Arnold Alexander, Kt., FRS, FEng.

Hall, Sir Basil Brodribb, KCB, MC, TD

Hall, *Air Marshal* Sir Donald Percy, KCB, CBE, AFC

Hall, Sir Douglas Basil, Bt., KCMG (s. 1687)

Hall, Sir Ernest, Kt., OBE

Hall, Sir (Frederick) John (Frank), Bt. (1923)

Hall, Sir John, Kt.

Hall, Sir John Bernard, Bt. (1919)

Hall, Sir Peter Edward, KBE, CMG

Hall, Sir Peter Reginald Frederick, Kt., CBE

Hall, Sir Robert de Zouche, KCMG

Hall, *Brig.* Sir William Henry, KBE, DSO, ED

Halliday, *Vice-Adm.* Sir Roy William, KBE, DSC

Hallinan, Sir (Adrian) Lincoln, Kt.

Halpern, Sir Ralph Mark, Kt.

Halsey, *Revd* Sir John Walter Brooke, Bt. (1920)

Halstead, Sir Ronald, Kt., CBE

Ham, Sir David Kenneth Rowe-, GBE

Hambling, Sir (Herbert) Hugh, Bt. (1924)

Hamburger, Sir Sidney Cyril, Kt., CBE

Hamer, *Hon.* Sir Rupert James, KCMG, ED

Hamill, Sir Patrick, Kt., QPM

Hamilton, *Rt. Hon.* Sir Archibald Gavin, Kt.

Hamilton, Sir Edward Sydney, Bt. (1776 and 1819)

Hamilton, Sir James Arnot, KCB, MBE, FEng.

Hamilton, Sir Malcolm William Bruce Stirling-, Bt. (s. 1673)

Hamilton, Sir Michael Aubrey, Kt.

Hamilton, Sir (Robert Charles) Richard Caradoc, Bt. (s. 1646)

Hammett, *Hon.* Sir Clifford James, Kt.

Hammick, Sir Stephen George, Bt. (1834)

Hampel, Sir Ronald Claus, Kt.

Hampshire, Sir Stuart Newton, Kt., FBA

Hancock, Sir David John Stowell, KCB

Hancock, *Air Marshal* Sir Valston Eldridge, KBE, CB, DFC

Hand, *Most Revd* Geoffrey David, KBE

Handley, Sir David John Davenport-, Kt., OBE

Hanham, Sir Michael William, Bt., DFC (1667)

Hanley, Sir Michael Bowen, KCB

Hanmer, Sir John Wyndham Edward, Bt. (1774)

Hannam, Sir John Gordon, Kt., MP

Hannay, Sir David Hugh Alexander, GCMG

Hanson, Sir Anthony Leslie Oswald, Bt. (1887)

Hanson, Sir (Charles) John, Bt. (1918)

Hanson, Sir John Gilbert, KCMG, CBE

Happold, Prof. Sir Frank, Kt, FEng.

Hardcastle, Sir Alan John, Kt.

Harders, Sir Clarence Waldemar, Kt., OBE

Hardie, Sir Charles Edgar Mathewes, Kt., CBE

Hardie, Sir Douglas Fleming, Kt., CBE

Harding, Sir Christopher George Francis, Kt.

Harding, Sir George William, KCMG, CVO

Harding, Marshal of the Royal Air Force Sir Peter Robin, GCB

Harding, Sir Roy Pollard, Kt., CBE

Hardman, Sir Henry, KCB

Hardy, Sir David William, Kt.

Hardy, Sir James Gilbert, Kt., OBE

Hardy, Sir Rupert John, Bt. (1876)

Hare, Sir Philip Leigh, Bt. (1818)

Harford, Sir (John) Timothy, Bt. (1934)

Hargroves, Brig. Sir Robert Louis, Kt., CBE

Harington, Gen. Sir Charles Henry Pepys, GCB, CBE, DSO, MC

Harington, Sir Nicholas John, Bt. (1611)

Harland, Air Marshal Sir Reginald Edward Wynyard, KBE, CB

Harman, Gen. Sir Jack Wentworth, GCB, OBE, MC

Harman, Hon. Sir Jeremiah LeRoy, Kt.

Harmsworth, Sir Hildebrand Harold, Bt. (1922)

Harpham, Sir William, KBE, CMG

Harris, Prof. Sir Alan James, Kt., CBE, FEng.

Harris, Sir Anthony Kyrle Travers, Bt. (1953)

Harris, Prof. Sir Charles Herbert Stuart-, Kt., CBE, MD

Harris, Prof. Sir Henry, Kt., FRCP, FRCPath., FRS

Harris, Lt.-Gen. Sir Ian Cecil, KBE, CB, DSO

Harris, Sir Jack Wolfred Ashford, Bt. (1932)

Harris, Air Marshal Sir John Hulme, KCB, CBE

Harris, Sir Philip Charles, Kt.

Harris, Sir William Gordon, KBE, CB, FEng.

Harrison, Prof. Sir Donald Frederick Norris, Kt., FRCS

Harrison, Sir Ernest Thomas, Kt., OBE

Harrison, Sir Francis Alexander Lyle, Kt., MBE, QC

Harrison, Surgeon Vice-Adm. Sir John Albert Bews, KBE

Harrison, Hon. Sir (John) Richard, Kt., ED

Harrison, Hon. Sir Michael Guy Vicat, Kt.

Harrison, Sir Michael James Harwood, Bt. (1961)

Harrison, Prof. Sir Richard John, Kt., FRS

Harrison, Sir (Robert) Colin, Bt. (1922)

Harrison, Sir Terence, Kt., FEng

Harrop, Sir Peter John, KCB

Hartley, Air Marshal Sir Christopher Harold, KCB, CBE, DFC, AFC

Hartley, Sir Frank, Kt., CBE, Ph.D.

Hartopp, Sir John Edmund Cradock-, Bt. (1796)

Hartwell, Sir (Francis) Anthony Charles Peter, Bt. (1805)

Harvey, Sir Charles Richard Musgrave, Bt. (1933)

Haselhurst, Sir Alan Gordon Barraclough, Kt., MP

Haskard, Sir Cosmo Dugal Patrick Thomas, KCMG, MBE

Haslam, Hon. Sir Alec Leslie, Kt.

Haslam, Rear-Adm. Sir David William, KBE, CB

Hassan, Sir Joshua Abraham, GBE, KCMG, LVO, QC

Hassett, Gen. Sir Francis George, KBE, CB, DSO, MVO

Hastings, Sir Stephen Lewis Edmonstone, Kt., MC

Hatty, Hon. Sir Cyril James, Kt.

Haughton, Sir James, Kt., CBE, QPM

Havelock, Sir Wilfrid Bowen, Kt.

Hawkins, Sir Arthur Ernest, Kt.

†Hawkins, Sir Howard Caesar, Bt. (1778)

Hawkins, Sir Paul Lancelot, Kt., TD

Hawley, Sir Donald Frederick, KCMG, MBE

†Hawley, Sir Henry Nicholas, Bt. (1795)

Haworth, Sir Philip, Bt. (1911)

Hawthorne, Prof. Sir William Rede, Kt., CBE, SC.D., FRS, FEng.

Hay, Sir David Osborne, Kt., CBE, DSO

Hay, Sir David Russell, Kt., CBE, FRCP, MD

Hay, Sir Hamish Grenfell, Kt.

Hay, Sir James Brian Dalrymple-, Bt. (1798)

†Hay, Sir John Erroll Audley, Bt. (s. 1663)

†Hay, Sir Ronald Frederick Hamilton, Bt. (s. 1703)

Haydon, Sir Walter Robert, KCMG

Hayes, Sir Brian David, GCB

Hayes, Sir Claude James, KCMG

Hayes, Vice-Adm. Sir John Osier Chattock, KCB, OBE

Hayr, Air Marshal Sir Kenneth William, KCB, KBE, AFC

Hayward, Sir Anthony William Byrd, Kt.

Hayward, Sir Jack Arnold, Kt., OBE

Haywood, Sir Harold, KCVO, OBE

Hazell, Sir Quinton, Kt., CBE

Head, Sir Francis David Somerville, Bt. (1838)

Healey, Sir Charles Edward Chadwyck-, Bt. (1919)

Heap, Sir Desmond, Kt.

Heap, Sir Peter William, KCMG

Heath, Rt. Hon. Sir Edward Richard George, KG, MBE, MP

Heath, Sir Mark Evelyn, KCVO, CMG

Heath, Air Marshal Sir Maurice Lionel, KBE, CB, CVO

Heathcote, Brig. Sir Gilbert Simon, Bt., CBE (1733)

Heathcote, Sir Michael Perryman, Bt. (1733)

Heatley, Sir Peter, Kt., CBE

Heaton, Sir Yvo Robert Henniker-, Bt. (1912)

Heiser, Sir Terence Michael, GCB

Hellaby, Sir (Frederick Reed) Alan, Kt.

Henderson, Sir Denys Hartley, Kt.

Henderson, Sir (John) Nicholas, GCMG, KCVO

Henderson, Sir William MacGregor, Kt., D.SC., FRS

Henley, Sir Douglas Owen, KCB

Henley, Rear-Adm. Sir Joseph Charles Cameron, KCVO, CB

Hennessy, Sir James Patrick Ivan, KBE, CMG

†Henniker, Sir Adrian Chandos, Bt. (1813)

Henry, Sir Denis Aynsley, Kt., OBE, QC

Henry, Rt. Hon. Denis Robert Maurice, Kt.

Henry, Hon. Sir Geoffrey Arama, KBE

Henry, Sir James Holmes, Bt., CMG, MC, TD, QC (1923)

Henry, Hon. Sir Trevor Ernest, Kt.

Hepburn, Sir John Alastair Trant Kidd Buchan-, Bt. (1815)

Herbecq, Sir John Edward, KCB

Herbert, Adm. Sir Peter Geoffrey Marshall, KCB, OBE

Hermon, Sir John Charles, Kt., OBE, QPM

Heron, Sir Conrad Frederick, KCB, OBE

Hervey, Sir Roger Blaise Ramsay, KCVO, CMG

Heseltine, Rt. Hon. Sir William Frederick Payne, GCB, GCVO

Hetherington, Sir Arthur Ford, Kt., DSC, FEng.

Hetherington, Sir Thomas Chalmers, KCB, CBE, TD, QC

Heward, Air Chief Marshal Sir Anthony Wilkinson, KCB, OBE, DFC, AFC

Hewetson, Sir Christopher Raynor, Kt., TD

Hewett, Sir Peter John Smithson, Bt., MM (1813)

Hewitt, Sir (Cyrus) Lenox (Simson), Kt., OBE
Hewitt, Sir Nicholas Charles Joseph, Bt. (1921)
†Heygate, Sir Richard John Gage, Bt. (1831)
Heyman, Sir Horace William, Kt.
Heywood, Sir Peter, Bt. (1838)
Hezlet, *Vice-Adm.* Sir Arthur Richard, KBE, CB, DSO, DSC
Hibbert, Sir Jack, KCB
Hibbert, Sir Reginald Alfred, GCMG
Hickey, Sir Justin, Kt.
Hickman, Sir (Richard) Glenn, Bt. (1903)
Hidden, *Hon.* Sir Anthony Brian, Kt.
Hielscher, Sir Leo Arthur, Kt.
Higgins, Sir Christopher Thomas, Kt.
Higgins, *Hon.* Sir Malachy Joseph, Kt.
Higgins, *Rt. Hon.* Sir Terence Langley, KBE, MP
Higginson, Sir Gordon Robert, Kt., PH.D., FEng.
Higgs, Sir (John) Michael (Clifford), Kt.
Highgate, Sir James Brown, Kt., CBE
Hildyard, Sir David Henry Thoroton, KCMG, DFC
Hill, Sir Alexander Rodger Erskine-, Bt. (1945)
Hill, Sir Arthur Alfred, Kt., CBE
Hill, Sir Brian John, Kt.
Hill, Sir James Frederick, Bt. (1917)
Hill, Sir John McGregor, Kt., PH.D., FEng.
Hill, Sir John Maxwell, Kt., CBE, DFC
†Hill, Sir John Rowley, Bt. (I. 1779)
Hill, *Vice-Adm.* Sir Robert Charles Finch, KBE, FEng.
Hillary, Sir Edmund, KG, KBE
Hillhouse, Sir (Robert) Russell, KCB
Hills, Sir Graham John, Kt.
Hine, *Air Chief Marshal* Sir Patrick Bardon, GCB, GBE
Hines, Sir Colin Joseph, Kt., OBE
Hinsley, *Prof.* Sir Francis Harry, Kt., OBE, FBA
Hirsch, *Prof.* Sir Peter Bernhard, Kt., PH.D., FRS
Hirst, *Rt. Hon.* Sir David Cozens-Hardy, Kt.
Hirst, Sir Michael William, Kt.
Hoare, Sir Peter Richard David, Bt. (1786)
Hoare, Sir Timothy Edward Charles, Bt. (I. 1784)
Hobart, Sir John Vere, Bt. (1914)
Hobday, Sir Gordon Ivan, Kt.
Hobhouse, Sir Charles John Spinney, Bt. (1812)
Hobhouse, *Rt. Hon.* Sir John Stewart, Kt.
Hockaday, Sir Arthur Patrick, KCB, CMG
Hockley, *Gen.* Sir Anthony Heritage Farrar-, GBE, KCB, DSO, MC
Hodge, Sir John Rowland, Bt., MBE (1921)
Hodge, Sir Julian Stephen Alfred, Kt.

Hodges, *Air Chief Marshal* Sir Lewis MacDonald, KCB, CBE, DSO, DFC
Hodgkin, *Prof.* Sir Alan Lloyd, OM, KBE, FRS, SC.D.
Hodgkin, Sir Gordon Howard Eliot, Kt., CBE
Hodgkinson, *Air Chief Marshal* Sir (William) Derek, KCB, CBE, DFC, AFC
Hodgson, Sir Maurice Arthur Eric, Kt., FEng.
Hodgson, *Hon.* Sir (Walter) Derek (Thornley), Kt.
Hodson, Sir Michael Robin Adderley, Bt. (I. 1789)
Hoffenberg, *Prof.* Sir Raymond, KBE
Hogg, *Maj.* Sir Arthur Ramsay, Bt., MBE (1846)
Hogg, Sir Christopher Anthony, Kt.
Hogg, Sir Edward William Lindsay-, Bt. (1905)
Hogg, *Vice-Adm.* Sir Ian Leslie Trower, KCB, DSC
Hogg, Sir John Nicholson, Kt., TD
Holcroft, Sir Peter George Culcheth, Bt. (1921)
Holden, Sir David Charles Beresford, KBE, CB, ERD
Holden, Sir Edward, Bt. (1893)
Holden, Sir John David, Bt. (1919)
Holder, Sir John Henry, Bt. (1898)
Holder, *Air Marshal* Sir Paul Davie, KBE, CB, DSO, DFC, PH.D.
Holderness, Sir Richard William, Bt. (1920)
Holdgate, Sir Martin Wyatt, Kt., CB, PH.D.
Holdsworth, Sir (George) Trevor, Kt.
Holland, *Hon.* Sir Alan Douglas, Kt.
Holland, *Hon.* Sir Christopher John, Kt.
Holland, Sir Clifton Vaughan, Kt.
Holland, Sir Geoffrey, KCB
Holland, Sir Guy (Hope), Bt. (1917)
Holland, Sir Kenneth Lawrence, Kt., CBE, QFSM
Holland, Sir Philip Welsby, Kt.
Holliday, *Prof.* Sir Frederick George Thomas, Kt., CBE, FRSE
Hollings, *Hon.* Sir (Alfred) Kenneth, Kt., MC
Hollis, *Hon.* Sir Anthony Barnard, Kt.
Hollom, Sir Jasper Quintus, KBE
Holloway, *Hon.* Sir Barry Blyth, KBE
Holm, Sir Carl Henry, Kt., OBE
Holman, *Hon.* Sir (Edward) James, Kt.
Holmes, *Prof.* Sir Frank Wakefield, Kt.
Holmes, Sir Maurice Andrew, Kt.
Holmes, Sir Peter Fenwick, Kt., MC
Holroyd, *Air Marshal* Sir Frank Martyn, KBE, CB, FEng.
Holt, *Prof.* Sir James Clarke, Kt.
Holt, Sir Michael, Kt., CBE
Home, Sir William Dundas, Bt. (s. 1671)
Honeycombe, *Prof.* Sir Robert William Kerr, Kt., FRS, FEng.
Honywood, Sir Filmer Courtenay William, Bt. (1660)

Hood, Sir Harold Joseph, Bt., TD (1922)
Hookway, Sir Harry Thurston, Kt.
Hoole, Sir Arthur Hugh, Kt.
Hooper, *Hon.* Sir Anthony, Kt.
Hope, Sir (Charles) Peter, KCMG, TD
Hope, Sir John Carl Alexander, Bt. (s. 1628)
Hopkin, Sir David Armand, Kt.
Hopkin, Sir (William Aylsham) Bryan, Kt., CBE
Hopkins, Sir Anthony Philip, Kt., CBE
Hopkins, Sir Michael John, Kt., CBE, RA, RIBA
Hopwood, *Prof.* Sir David Alan, Kt., FRS
Hordern, *Rt. Hon.* Sir Peter Maudslay, Kt., MP
Horlick, *Vice-Adm.* Sir Edwin John, KBE, FEng.
†Horlick, Sir James Cunliffe William, Bt. (1914)
Hornby, Sir Derek Peter, Kt.
Hornby, Sir Simon Michael, Kt.
Horne, Sir Alan Gray Antony, Bt. (1929)
Horsfall, Sir John Musgrave, Bt., MC, TD (1909)
Horsley, *Air Marshal* Sir (Beresford) Peter (Torrington), KCB, CBE, MVO, AFC
†Hort, Sir Andrew Edwin Fenton, Bt. (1767)
Hosker, Sir Gerald Albery, KCB, QC
Hoskyns, Sir Benedict Leigh, Bt. (1676)
Hoskyns, Sir John Austin Hungerford Leigh, Kt.
Hotung, Sir Joseph Edward, Kt.
Houghton, Sir John Theodore, Kt., CBE, FRS
†Houldsworth, Sir Richard Thomas Reginald, Bt. (1887)
Hounsfield, Sir Godfrey Newbold, Kt., CBE
House, *Lt.-Gen.* Sir David George, GCB, KCVO, CBE, MC
Houssemayne du Boulay, Sir Roger William, KCVO, CMG
Howard, Sir (Hamilton) Edward de Coucey, Bt., GBE (1955)
Howard, *Prof.* Sir Michael Eliot, Kt., CBE, MC
Howard, *Maj.-Gen.* Lord Michael Fitzalan-, GCVO, CB, CBE, MC
Howard, Sir Walter Stewart, Kt., MBE
Howell, Sir Ralph Frederic, Kt., MP
Howells, Sir Eric Waldo Benjamin, Kt., CBE
Howlett, *Gen.* Sir Geoffrey Hugh Whitby, KBE, MC
Hoyle, *Prof.* Sir Fred, Kt., FRS
Hoyos, *Hon.* Sir Fabriciano Alexander, Kt.
Huddie, Sir David Patrick, Kt., FEng.
Hudson, Sir Havelock Henry Trevor, Kt.
Hudson, *Lt.-Gen.* Sir Peter, KCB, CBE
Huggins, *Hon.* Sir Alan Armstrong, Kt.

Hugh-Jones, Sir Wynn Normington, Kt., MVO
Hughes, Sir David Collingwood, Bt. (1773)
Hughes, *Prof.* Sir Edward Stuart Reginald, Kt., CBE
Hughes, Sir Jack William, Kt.
Hughes, *Air Marshal* Sir (Sidney Weetman) Rochford, KCB, CBE, AFC
Hughes, Sir Trevor Denby Lloyd-, Kt.
Hughes, Sir Trevor Poulton, KCB
Hugo, *Lt.-Col.* Sir John Mandeville, KCVO, OBE
Hull, *Prof.* Sir David, Kt.
Hulse, Sir (Hamilton) Westrow, Bt. (1739)
Hume, Sir Alan Blyth, Kt., CB
Humphreys, Sir Olliver William, Kt., CBE
Humphreys, Sir (Raymond Evelyn) Myles, Kt.
Hunn, Sir Jack Kent, Kt., CMG
Hunt, Sir David Wathen Stather, KCMG, OBE
Hunt, Sir John Leonard, Kt., MP
Hunt, *Adm.* Sir Nicholas John Streynsham, GCB, LVO
Hunt, Sir Peter John, Kt., FRICS
Hunt, Sir Rex Masterman, Kt., CMG
Hunt, Sir Robert Frederick, Kt., CBE, FEng.
Hunter, *Hon.* Sir Alexander Albert, KBE
Hunter, Sir Alistair John, KCMG
Hunter, Sir Ian Bruce Hope, Kt., MBE
Hunter, *Prof.* Sir Laurence Colvin, Kt., CBE, FRSE
Hurrell, Sir Anthony Gerald, KCVO, CMG
Hutchinson, *Hon.* Sir Ross, Kt., DFC
Hutchison, *Lt.-Cdr.* Sir (George) Ian Clark, Kt., RN
Hutchison, *Rt. Hon.* Sir Michael, Kt.
Hutchison, Sir Peter, Bt., CBE (1939)
Hutchison, Sir Peter Craft, Bt. (1956)
Hutton, *Rt. Hon.* Sir (James) Brian Edward, Kt.
Huxley, *Prof.* Sir Andrew Fielding, Kt., OM, FRS
Huxtable, *Gen.* Sir Charles Richard, KCB, CBE
Hyatali, *Hon.* Sir Isaac Emanuel, Kt.
Hyslop, Sir Robert John (Robin) Maxwell-, Kt.
Ibbs, Sir (John) Robin, KBE
Imbert, Sir Peter Michael, Kt., QPM
Imray, Sir Colin Henry, KBE, CMG
Inge, *Field Marshal* Sir Peter Anthony, GCB
Ingham, Sir Bernard, Kt.
Ingilby, Sir Thomas Colvin William, Bt. (1866)
Inglis, Sir Brian Scott, Kt.
Inglis of Glencorse, Sir Roderick John, Bt. (s. 1703)
Ingram, Sir James Herbert Charles, Bt. (1893)
Ingram, Sir John Henderson, Kt., CBE
Inkin, Sir Geoffrey David, Kt., OBE

†Innes, Sir David Charles Kenneth Gordon, Bt. (NS 1686)
Innes of Edingight, Sir Malcolm Rognvald, KCVO
Innes, Sir Peter Alexander Berowald, Bt. (s. 1628)
Inniss, *Hon.* Sir Clifford de Lisle, Kt.
Irvine, Sir Donald Hamilton, Kt., CBE, MD, FRCGP
Irvine, *Dr* Sir Robin Orlando Hamilton, Kt.
Irving, *Prof.* Sir Miles Horsfall, Kt., MD, FRCS, FRCSE
Isaacs, Sir Kendal George Lamon, KCMG, CBE, QC
Isham, Sir Ian Vere Gyles, Bt. (1627)
Jack, *Hon.* Sir Alieu Sulayman, Kt.
Jack, Sir David, Kt., CBE, FRS, FRSE
Jack, Sir David Emmanuel, GCMG, MBE
Jackson, *Air Chief Marshal* Sir Brendan James, GCB
Jackson, Sir (John) Edward, KCMG
Jackson, *Hon.* Sir Lawrence Walter, KCMG
Jackson, Sir Michael Roland, Bt. (1902)
Jackson, Sir Nicholas Fane St George, Bt. (1913)
Jackson, Sir Robert, Bt. (1815)
Jackson, *Gen.* Sir William Godfrey Fothergill, GBE, KCB, MC
Jackson, Sir William Thomas, Bt. (1869)
Jacob, Sir Isaac Hai, Kt., QC
Jacob, *Hon.* Sir Robert Raphael Hayim (Robin), Kt.
Jacobi, Sir Derek George, Kt., CBE
Jacobi, *Dr* Sir James Edward, Kt., OBE
Jacobs, Sir David Anthony, Kt.
Jacobs, *Hon.* Sir Kenneth Sydney, KBE
Jacobs, Sir Piers, KBE
Jacobs, Sir Wilfred Ebenezer, GCMG, GCVO, OBE, QC
Jacomb, Sir Martin Wakefield, Kt.
Jaffray, Sir William Otho, Bt. (1892)
James, Sir Cynlais Morgan, KCMG
James, Sir Gerard Bowes Kingston, Bt. (1823)
James, Sir Robert Vidal Rhodes, Kt.
James, Sir Stanislaus Anthony, GCMG, OBE
Jamieson, *Air Marshal* Sir David Ewan, KBE, CB
Jansen, Sir Ross Malcolm, KBE
Jardine, Sir Andrew Colin Douglas, Bt. (1916)
Jardine, *Maj.* Sir (Andrew) Rupert (John) Buchanan-, Bt., MC (1885)
Jardine of Applegirth, Sir Alexander Maule, Bt. (s. 1672)
Jarratt, Sir Alexander Anthony, Kt., CB
Jawara, *Hon.* Sir Dawda Kairaba, Kt.
Jay, Sir Antony Rupert, Kt., CVO
Jeewoolall, Sir Ramesh, Kt.
Jefferson, Sir George Rowland, Kt., CBE, FEng.
Jefferson, Sir Mervyn Stewart Dunnington-, Bt. (1958)
Jeffreys, *Prof.* Sir Alec John, Kt., FRS

Jeffries, *Hon.* Sir John Francis, Kt.
Jehangir, Sir Hirji, Bt. (1908)
Jejeebhoy, Sir Rustom, Bt. (1857)
Jellicoe, Sir Geoffrey Alan, Kt., CBE, FRIBA
Jenkins, Sir Brian Garton, GBE
Jenkins, Sir Michael Romilly Heald, KCMG
Jenkins, Sir Owain Trevor, Kt.
Jenkinson, Sir John Banks, Bt. (1661)
†Jenks, Sir Maurice Arthur Brian, Bt. (1932)
Jennings, *Prof.* Sir Robert Yewdall, Kt., QC
Jephcott, Sir (John) Anthony, Bt. (1962)
Jessel, Sir Charles John, Bt. (1883)
Jewkes, Sir Gordon Wesley, KCMG
Joel, *Hon.* Sir Asher Alexander, KBE
John, Sir Rupert Godfrey, Kt.
Johns, *Air Chief Marshal* Sir Richard Edward, KBE, CBE, LVO
Johnson, *Rt. Hon.* Sir David Powell Croom-, Kt., DSC, VRD
Johnson, *Gen.* Sir Garry Dene, KCB, OBE, MC
Johnson, Sir John Rodney, KCMG
†Johnson, Sir Patrick Eliot, Bt. (1818)
Johnson, Sir Peter Colpoys Paley, Bt. (1755)
Johnson, *Hon.* Sir Robert Lionel, Kt.
Johnson, Sir Ronald Ernest Charles, Kt., CB
Johnson, Sir Vassel Godfrey, Kt., CBE
Johnston, Sir (David) Russell, Kt., MP
Johnston, Sir John Baines, GCMG, KCVO
Johnston, *Lt.-Col.* Sir John Frederick Dame, GCVO, MC
Johnston, *Lt.-Gen.* Sir Maurice Robert, KCB, OBE
Johnston, Sir Thomas Alexander, Bt. (s. 1626)
Johnston, Sir William Robert Patrick Knox- (Sir Robin), Kt., CBE, RD
Johnstone, Sir (George) Richard Douglas, Bt. (s. 1700)
Johnstone, Sir (John) Raymond, Kt., CBE
Jolliffe, Sir Anthony Stuart, GBE
Jones, *Gen.* Sir (Charles) Edward Webb, KCB, CBE
Jones, Sir Christopher Lawrence-, Bt. (1831)
Jones, Sir David Akers-, KBE, CMG
Jones, *Air Marshal* Sir Edward Gordon, KCB, CBE, DSO, DFC
Jones, Sir (Edward) Martin Furnival, Kt., CBE
Jones, Sir Ewart Ray Herbert, Kt., D.SC., ph.D., FRS
Jones, Sir Francis Avery, Kt., CBE, FRCP
Jones, Sir Gordon Pearce, Kt.
Jones, Sir Harry Ernest, Kt., CBE
Jones, Sir James Duncan, KCB
Jones, Sir (John) Derek Alun-, Kt.
Jones, Sir John Henry Harvey-, Kt., MBE
Jones, Sir (John) Kenneth (Trevor), Kt., CBE, QC

Jones, Sir John Lewis, KCB, CMG
Jones, Sir John Prichard-, Bt. (1910)
Jones, Sir Keith Stephen, Kt.
Jones, *Hon.* Sir Kenneth George
  Illtyd, Kt.
Jones, *Air Marshal* Sir Laurence
  Alfred, KCB, CB, AFC
Jones, Sir (Owen) Trevor, Kt.
Jones, Sir (Peter) Hugh (Jefferd)
  Lloyd-, Kt.
Jones, Sir Richard Anthony Lloyd,
  KCB
Jones, Sir Robert Edward, Kt.
Jones, Sir Simon Warley Frederick
  Benton, Bt. (1919)
Jones, Sir (Thomas) Philip, Kt., CB
Jones, Sir (William) Emrys, Kt.
Jones, *Hon.* Sir William Lloyd Mars-,
  Kt., MBE
†Joseph, *Hon.* Sir James Samuel, Bt.
  (1943)
Joughin, Sir Michael, Kt., CBE
Jowitt, *Hon.* Sir Edwin Frank, Kt.
Judge, *Hon.* Sir Igor, Kt.
Jugnauth, *Rt. Hon.* Sir Anerood, KCMG,
  QC
Jungius, *Vice-Adm.* Sir James George,
  KBE
Junor, Sir John Donald Brown, Kt.
Jupp, *Hon.* Sir Kenneth Graham, Kt.,
  MC
Kaberry, *Hon.* Sir Christopher
  Donald, Bt. (1960)
Kalo, Sir Kwamala, Kt., MBE
Kan Yuet-Keung, Sir, GBE
Kapi, *Hon.* Sir Mari, Kt., CBE
Kaputin, Sir John Rumet, KBE, CMG
Katsina, The Emir of, KBE, CMG
Katz, Sir Bernard, Kt., FRS
Kausimae, Sir David Nanau, KBE
Kavali, Sir Thomas, Kt., OBE
Kawharu, *Prof.* Sir Ian Hugh, Kt.
Kay, *Prof.* Sir Andrew Watt, Kt.
Kay, *Hon.* Sir John William, Kt.
Kay, *Hon.* Sir Maurice Ralph, Kt.
Kaye, Sir David Alexander Gordon,
  Bt. (1923)
Kaye, Sir Emmanuel, Kt., CBE
Kaye, Sir John Phillip Lister Lister-,
  Bt. (1812)
Keane, Sir Richard Michael, Bt.
  (1801)
Keatinge, Sir Edgar Mayne, Kt., CBE
Keeble, Sir (Herbert Ben) Curtis,
  GCMG
Keene, *Hon.* Sir David Wolfe, Kt.
Keith, *Prof.* Sir James, Kt.
Kellett, Sir Stanley Charles, Bt. (1801)
Kelly, *Rt. Hon.* Sir (John William)
  Basil, Kt.
Kelly, Sir William Theodore, Kt., OBE
Kemball, *Air Marshal* Sir (Richard)
  John, KCB, CBE
Kemp, Sir (Edward) Peter, KCB
Kendrew, Sir John Cowdery, Kt., CBE,
  SC.D., FRS
Kenilorea, *Rt. Hon.* Sir Peter, KBE
Kennard, *Lt.-Col.* Sir George Arnold
  Ford, Bt. (1891)

Kennaway, Sir John Lawrence, Bt.
  (1791)
Kennedy, Sir Clyde David Allen, Kt.
Kennedy, Sir Francis, KCMG, CBE
Kennedy, *Hon.* Sir Ian Alexander, Kt.
Kennedy, Sir Ludovic Henry
  Coverley, Kt.
†Kennedy, Sir Michael Edward, Bt.,
  (1836)
Kennedy, *Rt. Hon.* Sir Paul Joseph
  Morrow, Kt.
Kennedy, *Air Chief Marshal* Sir
  Thomas Lawrie, GCB, AFC
Kennedy-Good, Sir John, KBE
Kenny, Sir Anthony John Patrick, Kt.,
  D.phil., D.Litt., FBA
Kenny, *Gen.* Sir Brian Leslie Graham,
  GCB, CBE
Kent, Sir Harold Simcox, GCB, QC
Kenyon, Sir George Henry, Kt.
Kermode, Sir (John) Frank, Kt., FBA
Kermode, Sir Ronald Graham Quale,
  KBE
Kerr, *Hon.* Sir Brian Francis, Kt.
Kerr, *Adm.* Sir John Beverley, GCB
Kerr, Sir John Olav, KCMG
Kerr, *Rt. Hon.* Sir Michael Robert
  Emanuel, Kt.
Kerruish, Sir (Henry) Charles, Kt.,
  OBE
Kerry, Sir Michael James, KCB, QC
Kershaw, Sir (John) Anthony, Kt., MC
Keswick, Sir John Chippendale
  Lindley, Kt.
Kidd, Sir Robert Hill, KBE, CB
Kikau, *Ratu* Sir Jone Latianara, KBE
Killen, *Hon.* Denis James, KCMG
Killick, Sir John Edward, GCMG
Kilpatrick, *Prof.* Sir Robert, Kt., CBE
Kimber, Sir Charles Dixon, Bt. (1904)
Kinahan, Sir Robert George
  Caldwell, Kt., ERD
King, Sir Albert, Kt., OBE
King, *Gen.* Sir Frank Douglas, GCB,
  MBE
King, Sir John Christopher, Bt. (1888)
King, *Vice-Adm.* Sir Norman Ross
  Dutton, KBE
King, Sir Richard Brian Meredith,
  KCB, MC
King, Sir Wayne Alexander, Bt.
  (1815)
Kingman, *Prof.* Sir John Frank
  Charles, Kt., FRS
Kingsland, Sir Richard, Kt., CBE, DFC
Kingsley, Sir Patrick Graham Toler,
  KCVO
Kinloch, Sir David, Bt. (s. 1686)
†Kinloch, Sir David Oliphant, Bt.
  (1873)
Kipalan, Sir Albert, Kt.
Kirby, *Hon.* Sir Richard Clarence, Kt.
Kirkpatrick, Sir Ivone Elliott, Bt.
  (s. 1685)
Kirkwood, *Hon.* Sir Andrew Tristram
  Hammett, Kt.
Kirwan, Sir (Archibald) Laurence
  Patrick, KCMG, TD
Kitcatt, Sir Peter Julian, Kt., CB

Kitson, *Gen.* Sir Frank Edward, GBE,
  KCB, MC
Kitson, Sir Timothy Peter Geoffrey,
  Kt.
†Kleinwort, Sir Richard Drake, Bt.
  (1909)
Klug, Sir Aaron, Kt.
Knight, Sir Allan Walton, Kt., CMG
Knight, Sir Arthur William, Kt.
Knight, Sir Harold Murray, KBE, DSC
Knight, *Air Chief Marshal* Sir Michael
  William Patrick, KCB, AFC
Knill, Sir John Kenelm Stuart, Bt.
  (1893)
Knill, *Prof.* Sir John Lawrence, Kt.,
  FEng.
Knott, Sir John Laurence, Kt., CBE
Knowles, Sir Charles Francis, Bt.
  (1765)
Knowles, Sir Leonard Joseph, Kt., CBE
Knowles, Sir Richard Marchant, Kt.
Knox, Sir Bryce Muir, KCVO, MC, TD
Knox, Sir David Laidlaw, Kt., MP
Knox, *Hon.* Sir John Leonard, Kt.
Knox, *Hon.* Sir William Edward, Kt.
Koraea, Sir Thomas, Kt.
Kornberg, *Prof.* Sir Hans Leo, Kt.,
  D.SC., SC.D., PH.D., FRS
Korowi, Sir Wiwa, GCMG
Krusin, Sir Stanley Marks, Kt., CB
Kulukundis, Sir Elias George
  (Eddie), Kt., OBE
Kurongku, *Most. Revd* Peter, KBE
Labouchere, Sir George Peter, GBE,
  KCMG
Lacon, Sir Edmund Vere, Bt. (1818)
Lacy, Sir Hugh Maurice Pierce, Bt.
  (1921)
Lacy, Sir John Trend, Kt., CBE
Laddie, *Hon.* Sir Hugh Ian Lang, Kt.
Laidlaw, Sir Christophor Charles
  Fraser, Kt.
Laing, Sir (John) Maurice, Kt.
Laing, Sir (William) Kirby, Kt., FEng.
Laird, Sir Gavin Harry, Kt., CBE
Lake, Sir (Atwell) Graham, Bt. (1711)
Laker, Sir Frederick Alfred, Kt.
Lakin, Sir Michael, Bt. (1909)
Laking, Sir George Robert, KCMG
Lamb, Sir Albert (Larry), Kt.
Lamb, Sir Albert Thomas, KBE, CMG,
  DFC
Lambert, Sir Anthony Edward, KCMG
Lambert, Sir John Henry, KCVO, CMG
†Lambert, Sir Peter John Biddulph,
  Bt. (1711)
Lampl, Sir Frank William, Kt.
Landale, Sir David William Neil,
  KCVO
Landau, Sir Dennis Marcus, Kt.
Lane, Sir David William Stennis
  Stuart, Kt.
Lang, *Lt.-Gen.* Sir Derek Boileau, KCB,
  DSO, MC
Langham, Sir James Michael, Bt.
  (1660)
Langley, *Maj.-Gen.* Sir Henry
  Desmond Allen, KCVO, MBE
Langrishe, Sir Hercules Ralph Hume,
  Bt. (I. 1777)

Lankester, Sir Timothy Patrick, KCB
Lapsley, *Air Marshal* Sir John Hugh, KBE, CB, DFC, AFC
Lapun, *Hon.* Sir Paul, Kt.
Larcom, Sir (Charles) Christopher Royde, Bt. (1868)
Large, Sir Peter, Kt., CBE
Larmour, Sir Edward Noel, KCMG
Lasdun, Sir Denys Louis, Kt., CH, CBE, FRIBA
Latey, *Rt. Hon.* Sir John Brinsmead, Kt., MBE
Latham, *Hon.* Sir David Nicholas Ramsey, Kt.
Latham, Sir Michael Anthony, Kt.
Latham, Sir Richard Thomas Paul, Bt. (1919)
Latimer, Sir (Courtenay) Robert, Kt., CBE
Latimer, Sir Graham Stanley, KBE
Laucke, *Hon.* Sir Condor Louis, KCMG
Lauder, Sir Piers Robert Dick-, Bt. (s. 1690)
Laughton, Sir Anthony Seymour, Kt.
Laurantus, Sir Nicholas, Kt., MBE
Laurence, Sir Peter Harold, KCMG, MC
Laurie, Sir Robert Bayley Emilius, Bt. (1834)
Lauti, *Rt. Hon.* Sir Toaripi, GCMG
Lavan, *Hon.* Sir John Martin, Kt.
Law, *Adm.* Sir Horace Rochfort, GCB, OBE, DSC
Lawes, Sir (John) Michael Bennet, Bt. (1882)
Lawler, Sir Peter James, Kt., OBE
Lawrence, Sir David Roland Walter, Bt. (1906)
Lawrence, Sir Guy Kempton, Kt., DSO, OBE, DFC
Lawrence, Sir Ivan John, Kt., QC, MP
Lawrence, Sir John Patrick Grosvenor, Kt., CBE
Lawrence, Sir John Waldemar, Bt., OBE (1858)
Lawrence, Sir William Fettiplace, Bt. (1867)
Laws, *Hon.* Sir John Grant McKenzie, Kt.
Lawson, Sir Christopher Donald, Kt.
Lawson, *Col.* Sir John Charles Arthur Digby, Bt., DSO, MC (1900)
Lawson, Sir John Philip Howard-, Bt. (1841)
Lawson, *Hon.* Sir Neil, Kt.
Lawson, *Gen.* Sir Richard George, KCB, DSO, OBE
Lawton, *Prof.* Sir Frank Ewart, Kt.
Lawton, *Rt. Hon.* Sir Frederick Horace, Kt.
Layard, *Adm.* Sir Michael Henry Gordon, KCB, CBE
Layden, Sir John (Jack), Kt.
Layfield, Sir Frank Henry Burland Willoughby, Kt., QC
Lazarus, Sir Peter Esmond, KCB
Lea, *Vice-Adm.* Sir John Stuart Crosbie, KBE
Lea, Sir Thomas William, Bt. (1892)
Leach, *Admiral of the Fleet* Sir Henry Conyers, GCB

Leach, Sir Ronald George, GBE
Leahy, Sir Daniel Joseph, Kt.
Leahy, Sir John Henry Gladstone, KCMG
Learmont, *Gen.* Sir John Hartley, KCB, CBE
Leask, *Lt.-Gen.* Sir Henry Lowther Ewart Clark, KCB, DSO, OBE
Leather, Sir Edwin Hartley Cameron, KCMG, KCVO
Leaver, Sir Christopher, GBE
Le Bailly, *Vice-Adm.* Sir Louis Edward Stewart Holland, KBE, CB
Le Cheminant, *Air Chief Marshal* Sir Peter de Lacey, GBE, KCB, DFC
Lechmere, Sir Berwick Hungerford, Bt. (1818)
Ledger, Sir Frank, (Joseph Francis), Kt.
Ledwidge, Sir (William) Bernard (John), KCMG
Lee, Sir Arthur James, KBE, MC
Lee, *Air Chief Marshal* Sir David John Pryer, GBE, CB
Lee, *Brig.* Sir Leonard Henry, Kt., CBE
Lee, Sir Quo-wei, Kt., CBE
Lee, *Col.* Sir William Allison, Kt., OBE, TD
Leeds, Sir Christopher Anthony, Bt. (1812)
Lees, Sir David Bryan, Kt.
Lees, Sir Thomas Edward, Bt. (1897)
Lees, Sir Thomas Harcourt Ivor, Bt. (1804)
Lees, Sir (William) Antony Clare, Bt. (1937)
Leese, Sir John Henry Vernon, Bt. (1908)
Le Fanu, *Maj.* Sir (George) Victor (Sheridan), KCVO
le Fleming, Sir Quintin John, Bt. (1705)
Legard, Sir Charles Thomas, Bt. (1660)
Legg, Sir Thomas Stuart, KCB, QC
Leggatt, *Rt. Hon.* Sir Andrew Peter, Kt.
Leggatt, Sir Hugh Frank John, Kt.
Leggett, Sir Clarence Arthur Campbell, Kt., MBE
Leigh, Sir Geoffrey Norman, Kt.
Leigh, Sir Richard Henry, Bt. (1918)
Leighton, Sir Michael John Bryan, Bt. (1693)
Leitch, Sir George, KCB, OBE
Leith, Sir Andrew George Forbes-, Bt. (1923)
Le Marchant, Sir Francis Arthur, Bt. (1841)
Le Masurier, Sir Robert Hugh, Kt., DSC
Lemon, Sir (Richard) Dawnay, Kt., CBE
Leng, *Gen.* Sir Peter John Hall, KCB, MBE, MC
Lennard, *Revd* Sir Hugh Dacre Barrett-, Bt. (1801)
Leon, Sir John Ronald, Bt. (1911)
Leonard, *Rt. Revd and Rt. Hon.* Graham Douglas, KCVO

Leonard, *Hon.* Sir (Hamilton) John, Kt.
Lepping, Sir George Geria Dennis, GCMG, MBE
Le Quesne, Sir (Charles) Martin, KCMG
Le Quesne, Sir (John) Godfray, Kt., QC
Leslie, Sir Colin Alan Bettridge, Kt.
Leslie, Sir John Norman Ide, Bt. (1876)
†Leslie, Sir (Percy) Theodore, Bt. (s. 1625)
Leslie, Sir Peter Evelyn, Kt.
Lethbridge, Sir Thomas Periam Hector Noel, Bt. (1804)
Leupena, Sir Tupua, GCMG, MBE
Levene, Sir Peter Keith, KBE
Lever, Sir (Tresham) Christopher Arthur Lindsay, Bt. (1911)
Levey, Sir Michael Vincent, Kt., MVO
Levine, Sir Montague Bernard, Kt.
Levinge, Sir Richard George Robin, Bt. (I. 1704)
Levy, Sir Ewart Maurice, Bt. (1913)
Lewando, Sir Jan Alfred, Kt., CBE
Lewinton, Sir Christopher, Kt.
Lewis, Sir David Courtenay Mansel, KCVO
Lewis, Sir Kenneth, Kt.
Lewthwaite, *Brig.* Sir Rainald Gilfrid, Bt., CVO, OBE, MC (1927)
†Ley, Sir Ian Francis, Bt. (1905)
Leyland, Sir Philip Vyvyan Naylor-, Bt. (1895)
Lickiss, Sir Michael Gillam, Kt.
Lickley, Sir Robert Lang, Kt., CBE, FEng.
Lidderdale, Sir David William Shuckburgh, KCB
Liggins, *Prof.* Sir Graham Collingwood, Kt., CBE, FRS
Lightbown, Sir David Lincoln, Kt., MP
Lighthill, Sir (Michael) James, Kt., FRS
Lightman, *Hon.* Sir Gavin Anthony, Kt.
Lighton, Sir Thomas Hamilton, Bt. (I. 1791)
Lim, Sir Han-Hoe, Kt., CBE
Linacre, Sir (John) Gordon (Seymour), Kt., CBE, AFC, DFM
Lindop, Sir Norman, Kt.
Lindsay, Sir James Harvey Kincaid Stewart, Kt.
Lindsay, *Hon.* Sir John Edmund Frederic, Kt.
Lindsay, Sir Ronald Alexander, Bt., (1962)
Lipworth, Sir (Maurice) Sydney, Kt.
Lithgow, Sir William James, Bt. (1925)
Little, *Most Revd* Thomas Francis, KBE
Littler, Sir (James) Geoffrey, KCB
Livesay, *Adm.* Sir Michael Howard, KCB
Llewellyn, Sir Henry Morton, Bt., CBE (1922)
Llewelyn, Sir John Michael Dillwyn-Venables-, Bt. (1890)
Lloyd, Sir Ian Stewart, Kt.

Lloyd, Sir (John) Peter (Daniel), Kt.
Lloyd, Sir Nicholas Markley, Kt.
Lloyd, *Rt. Hon.* Sir Peter Robert
    Cable, Kt., MP
Lloyd, Sir Richard Ernest Butler, Bt.
    (1960)
Loader, Sir Leslie Thomas, Kt., CBE
Loane, *Most Revd* Marcus Lawrence,
    KBE
Lobo, Sir Rogerio Hyndman, Kt., CBE
Lock, *Cdr.* Sir (John) Duncan, Kt.
Lockhart, Sir Simon John Edward
    Francis Sinclair-, Bt. (s. 1636)
Loder, Sir Giles Rolls, Bt. (1887)
Lodge, Sir Thomas, Kt.
Lofthouse, Sir Geoffrey, Kt., MP
Logan, Sir Donald Arthur, KCMG
Logan, Sir Raymond Douglas, Kt.
Lokoloko, Sir Tore, GCMG, GCVO, OBE
Lombe, *Hon.* Sir Edward Christopher
    Evans-, Kt.
Longden, Sir Gilbert James Morley,
    Kt., MBE
Longmore, *Hon.* Sir Andrew
    Centlivres, Kt.
Loram, *Vice-Adm.* Sir David Anning,
    KCB, MVO
Lorimer, Sir (Thomas) Desmond, Kt.
Lovell, Sir (Alfred Charles) Bernard,
    Kt., OBE, FRS
Lovelock, Sir Douglas Arthur, KCB
Loveridge, Sir John Warren, Kt.
Lovill, Sir John Roger, Kt., CBE
Low, Sir Alan Roberts, Kt.
Low, Sir James Richard Morrison-,
    Bt. (1908)
Lowe, *Air Chief Marshal* Sir Douglas
    Charles, GCB, DFC, AFC
Lowe, Sir Thomas William Gordon,
    Bt. (1918)
Lowry, Sir John Patrick, Kt., CBE
Lowson, Sir Ian Patrick, Bt. (1951)
Lowther, *Maj.* Sir Charles Douglas,
    Bt. (1824)
Loyd, Sir Francis Alfred, KCMG, OBE
Loyd, Sir Julian St John, KCVO
Lu, Sir Tseng Chi, Kt.
Lucas, Sir Cyril Edward, Kt., CMG, FRS
Lucas, Sir Thomas Edward, Bt. (1887)
Luce, *Rt Hon.* Sir Richard Napier, Kt.
Luckhoo, Sir Lionel Alfred, KCMG,
    CBE, QC
Lucy, Sir Edmund John William
    Hugh Cameron-Ramsay-Fairfax,
    Bt. (1836)
Luddington, Sir Donald Collin
    Cumyn, KBE, CMG, CVO
Lumsden, Sir David James, Kt.
Lus, *Hon.* Sir Pita, Kt., OBE
Lush, *Hon.* Sir George Hermann, Kt.
Lushington, Sir John Richard
    Castleman, Bt. (1791)
Luttrell, *Col.* Sir Geoffrey Walter
    Fownes, KCVO, MC
Lyell, *Rt. Hon.* Sir Nicholas Walter,
    Kt., QC, MP
Lygo, *Adm.* Sir Raymond Derek, KCB
Lyle, Sir Gavin Archibald, Bt. (1929)
Lyons, Sir Edward Houghton, Kt.
Lyons, Sir James Reginald, Kt.

Lyons, Sir John, Kt.
McAdam, Sir Ian William James, Kt.,
    OBE
Macadam, Sir Peter, Kt.
McAlpine, Sir William Hepburn, Bt.
    (1918)
†Macara, Sir Hugh Kenneth, Bt.
    (1911)
Macartney, Sir John Barrington, Bt.
    (i. 1799)
McAvoy, Sir (Francis) Joseph, Kt., CBE
McCaffrey, Sir Thomas Daniel, Kt.
McCall, Sir (Charles) Patrick Home,
    Kt., MBE, TD
McCallum, Sir Donald Murdo, Kt.,
    CBE, FEng.
McCamley, Sir Graham Edward, Kt.,
    MBE
McCarthy, *Rt. Hon.* Sir Thaddeus
    Pearcey, KBE
McClellan, *Col.* Sir Herbert Gerard
    Thomas, Kt., CBE, TD
McClintock, Sir Eric Paul, Kt.
McColl, Sir Colin Hugh Verel, KCMG
McCollum, *Hon.* Sir William, Kt.
McConnell, Sir Robert Shean, Bt.
    (1900)
McCorkell, *Col.* Sir Michael William,
    KCVO, OBE, TD
McCowan, *Rt. Hon.* Sir Anthony
    James Denys, Kt.
McCowan, Sir Hew Cargill, Bt.
    (1934)
McCrea, *Prof.* Sir William Hunter,
    Kt., FRS
McCrindle, Sir Robert Arthur, Kt.
McCullough, *Hon.* Sir (Iain) Charles
    (Robert), Kt.
McCusker, Sir James Alexander, Kt.
MacDermott, *Rt. Hon.* Sir John Clarke,
    Kt.
McDermott, Sir (Lawrence) Emmet,
    KBE
MacDonald, *Gen.* Sir Arthur Leslie,
    KBE, CB
McDonald, *Air Marshal* Sir Arthur
    William Baynes, KCB, AFC
McDonald, Sir Duncan, Kt., CBE, FEng.
Macdonald of Sleat, Sir Ian Godfrey
    Bosville, Bt. (s. 1625)
Macdonald, Sir Kenneth Carmichael,
    KCB
Macdonald, *Vice-Adm.* Sir Roderick
    Douglas, KBE
McDonald, Sir Tom, Kt., OBE
McDonald, *Hon.* Sir William John
    Farquhar, Kt.
MacDougall, Sir (George) Donald
    (Alastair), Kt., CBE, FBA
McDowell, Sir Eric Wallalce, Kt., CBE
McDowell, Sir Henry McLorinan,
    KBE
Mace, *Lt.-Gen.* Sir John Airth, KBE, CB
McEwen, Sir John Roderick Hugh,
    Bt. (1953)
McFarland, Sir John Talbot, Bt.
    (1914)
Macfarlane, Sir (David) Neil, Kt.
Macfarlane, Sir George Gray, Kt., CB,
    FEng.

McFarlane, Sir Ian, Kt.
McGeoch, *Vice-Adm.* Sir Ian Lachlan
    Mackay, KCB, DSO, DSC
McGrath, Sir Brian Henry, KCVO
Macgregor, Sir Edwin Robert, Bt.
    (1828)
MacGregor of MacGregor, Sir
    Gregor, Bt. (1795)
McGregor, Sir Ian Alexander, Kt.,
    CBE, FRS
MacGregor, Sir Ian Kinloch, Kt.
McGrigor, *Capt.* Sir Charles Edward,
    Bt. (1831)
McIntosh, *Vice-Adm.* Sir Ian Stewart,
    KBE, CB, DSO, DSC
McIntosh, Sir Ronald Robert
    Duncan, KCB
McIntyre, Sir Donald Conroy, Kt.,
    CBE
McIntyre, Sir Meredith Alister, Kt.
McKaig, *Adm.* Sir (John) Rae, KCB, CBE
Mackay, Sir (George Patrick)
    Gordon, Kt., CBE
McKay, Sir John Andrew, Kt., CBE
Mackechnie, Sir Alistair John, Kt.
McKee, *Maj.* Sir (William) Cecil, Kt.,
    ERD
McKellen, Sir Ian Murray, Kt., CBE
McKenzie, Sir Alexander, KBE
Mackenzie, Sir Alexander Alwyne
    Henry Charles Brinton Muir-, Bt.
    (1805)
Mackenzie, *Vice-Adm.* Sir Hugh
    Stirling, KCB, DSO, DSC
†Mackenzie, Sir (James William)
    Guy, Bt. (1890)
Mackenzie, *Gen.* Sir Jeremy John
    George, KCB, OBE
†Mackenzie, Sir Peter Douglas, Bt.
    (s. 1673)
†Mackenzie, Sir Roderick McQuhae,
    Bt. (s. 1703)
McKenzie, Sir Roy Allan, KBE
Mackeson, Sir Rupert Henry, Bt.
    (1954)
Mackie, Sir Maitland, Kt., CBE
MacKinlay, Sir Bruce, Kt., CBE
McKinnon, Sir James, Kt.
McKinnon, *Hon.* Sir Stuart Neil, Kt.
Macklin, Sir Bruce Roy, Kt., OBE
Mackworth, *Cdr.* Sir David Arthur
    Geoffrey, Bt. (1776)
McLaren, Sir Robin John Taylor,
    KCMG
MacLaurin, Sir Ian Charter, Kt.
Maclean, Sir Donald Og Grant, Kt.
Maclean of Dunconnell, Sir Fitzroy
    Hew, Bt., KT, CBE (1957)
McLean, Sir Francis Charles, Kt., CBE
MacLean, *Vice-Adm.* Sir Hector
    Charles Donald, KBE, CB, DSC
Maclean, Sir Lachlan Hector Charles,
    Bt. (NS 1631)
Maclean, Sir Robert Alexander, KBE
McLennan, Sir Ian Munro, KCMG, KBE
McLeod, Sir Charles Henry, Bt.
    (1925)
McLeod, Sir Ian George, Kt.
MacLeod, Sir (John) Maxwell
    Norman, Bt. (1924)

Macleod, Sir (Nathaniel William) Hamish, KBE

McLintock, Sir Michael William, Bt. (1934)

Maclure, Sir John Robert Spencer, Bt. (1898)

McMahon, Sir Brian Patrick, Bt. (1817)

McMahon, Sir Christopher William, Kt.

Macmillan, Sir (Alexander McGregor) Graham, Kt.

MacMillan, Lt.-Gen. Sir John Richard Alexander, KCB, CBE

McMullin, Rt. Hon. Sir Duncan Wallace, Kt.

Macnaghten, Sir Patrick Alexander, Bt. (1836)

McNamara, Air Chief Marshal Sir Neville Patrick, KBE

Macnaughton, Prof. Sir Malcolm Campbell, Kt.

McNee, Sir David Blackstock, Kt., QPM

McNeice, Sir (Thomas) Percy (Fergus), Kt., CMG, OBE

MacPhail, Sir Bruce Dugald, Kt.

Macpherson, Sir Ronald Thomas Steward (Tommy), CBE, MC, TD

Macpherson of Cluny, Hon. Sir William Alan, Kt., TD

McQuarrie, Sir Albert, Kt.

MacRae, Sir (Alastair) Christopher (Donald Summerhayes), KCMG

Macrae, Col. Sir Robert Andrew Scarth, KCVO, MBE

Macready, Sir Nevil John Wilfrid, Bt. (1923)

Mactaggart, Sir John Auld, Bt. (1938)

Macwhinnie, Sir Gordon Menzies, Kt., CBE

McWilliams, Sir Francis, GBE, FEng.

Madden, Adm. Sir Charles Edward, Bt., GCB (1919)

Maddocks, Sir Kenneth Phipson, KCMG, KCVO

Maddox, Sir John Royden, Kt.

Madel, Sir (William) David, Kt., MP

Madigan, Sir Russel Tullie, Kt., OBE

Magnus, Sir Laurence Henry Philip, Bt. (1917)

Maguire, Air Marshal Sir Harold John, KCB, DSO, OBE

Mahon, Sir (John) Denis, Kt., CBE

Mahon, Sir William Walter, Bt. (1819)

Maiden, Sir Colin James, Kt., D.phil.

Main, Sir Peter Tester, Kt., ERD

Maini, Sir Amar Nath, Kt., CBE

Maino, Sir Charles, KBE

Mais, Hon. Sir (Robert) Hugh, Kt.

†Maitland, Sir Charles Alexander, Bt. (1818)

Maitland, Sir Donald James Dundas, GCMG, OBE

Makins, Sir Paul Vivian, Bt. (1903)

Malcolm, Sir David Peter Michael, Bt. (s. 1665)

Malet, Sir Harry Douglas St Lo, Bt. (1791)

Mallaby, Sir Christopher Leslie George, GCVO, KCMG

Mallinson, Sir William John, Bt. (1935)

Malone, Hon. Sir Denis Eustace Gilbert, Kt.

Mamo, Sir Anthony Joseph, Kt., OBE

Mance, Hon. Sir Jonathan Hugh, Kt.

Manchester, Sir William Maxwell, KBE

Mander, Sir Charles Marcus, Bt. (1911)

Manduell, Sir John, Kt., CBE

Mann, Rt. Hon. Sir Michael, Kt.

Mann, Rt. Revd Michael Ashley, KCVO

Mann, Sir Rupert Edward, Bt. (1905)

Mansel, Revd Canon James Seymour Denis, KCVO

Mansel, Sir Philip, Bt. (1622)

Mansfield, Vice-Adm. Sir (Edward) Gerard (Napier), KBE, CVO

Mansfield, Prof. Sir Peter, Kt., FRS

Mansfield, Sir Philip (Robert Aked), KCMG

Mantell, Hon. Sir Charles Barrie Knight, Kt.

Manton, Sir Edwin Alfred Grenville, Kt.

Manzie, Sir (Andrew) Gordon, KCB

Mara, Rt. Hon. Ratu Sir Kamisese Kapaiwai Tuimacilai, GCMG, KBE

Margetson, Sir John William Denys, KCMG

Marjoribanks, Sir James Alexander Milne, KCMG

Mark, Sir Robert, GBE

Markham, Sir Charles John, Bt. (1911)

Marking, Sir Henry Ernest, KCVO, CBE, MC

Marling, Sir Charles William Somerset, Bt. (1882)

Marr, Sir Leslie Lynn, Bt. (1919)

Marriner, Sir Neville, Kt., CBE

Marriott, Sir Hugh Cavendish Smith-, Bt. (1774)

Marriott, Sir John Brook, KCVO

Marsden, Sir Nigel John Denton, Bt. (1924)

Marshall, Sir Arthur Gregory George, Kt., OBE

Marshall, Sir Colin Marsh, Kt.

Marshall, Sir Denis Alfred, Kt.

Marshall, Prof. Sir (Oshley) Roy, Kt., CBE

Marshall, Sir Peter Harold Reginald, KCMG

Marshall, Sir Robert Braithwaite, KCB, MBE

Marshall, Sir (Robert) Michael, Kt., MP

Martell, Vice-Adm. Sir Hugh Colenso, KBE, CB

Martin, Vice-Adm. Sir John Edward Ludgate, KCB, DSC

Martin, Prof. Sir (John) Leslie, Kt., ph.D.

Martin, Prof. Sir Laurence Woodward, Kt.

Martin, Sir (Robert) Bruce, Kt., QC

Marychurch, Sir Peter Harvey, KCMG

Masefield, Sir Peter Gordon, Kt.

Masire, Sir Ketumile, GCMG

Mason, Hon. Sir Anthony Frank, KBE

Mason, Sir (Basil) John, Kt., CB, D.SC., FRS

Mason, Prof. Sir David Kean, Kt., CBE

Mason, Sir Frederick Cecil, KCVO, CMG

Mason, Sir Gordon Charles, Kt., OBE

Mason, Sir John Charles Moir, KCMG

Mason, Sir John Peter, Kt., CBE

Mason, Prof. Sir Ronald, KCB, FRS

Matane, Sir Paulias Nguna, Kt., CMG, OBE

Mather, Sir (David) Carol (Macdonell), Kt., MC

Mather, Sir William Loris, Kt., CVO, OBE, MC, TD

Mathers, Sir Robert William, Kt.

Matheson, Sir (James Adam) Louis, KBE, CMG, FEng.

Matheson of Matheson, Sir Fergus John, Bt. (1882)

Matthews, Sir Peter Alec, Kt.

Matthews, Sir Peter Jack, Kt., CVO, OBE, QPM

Matthews, Sir Stanley, Kt., CBE

Maud, The Hon. Sir Humphrey John Hamilton, KCMG

†Maxwell, Sir Michael Eustace George, Bt. (s. 1681)

Maxwell, Sir Nigel Mellor Heron-, Bt. (s. 1683)

May, Hon. Sir Anthony Tristram Kenneth, Kt.

May, Rt. Hon. Sir John Douglas, Kt.

May, Sir Kenneth Spencer, Kt., CBE

Mayhew, Rt. Hon. Sir Patrick Barnabas Burke, Kt., QC, MP

Maynard, Hon. Sir Clement Travelyan, Kt.

Maynard, Air Chief Marshal Sir Nigel Martin, KCB, CBE, DFC, AFC

Medlycott, Sir Mervyn Tregonwell, Bt. (1808)

Megarry, Rt. Hon. Sir Robert Edgar, Kt., FBA

Megaw, Rt. Hon. Sir John, Kt., CBE, TD

Meinertzhagen, Sir Peter, Kt., CMG

Melhuish, Sir Michael Ramsay, KBE, CMG

Mellon, Sir James, KCMG

Melville, Sir Harry Work, KCB, ph.D., D.SC., FRS

Melville, Sir Leslie Galfreid, KBE

Melville, Sir Ronald Henry, KCB

Mensforth, Sir Eric, Kt., CBE, F.Eng.

Menter, Sir James Woodham, Kt., ph.D., SC.D., FRS

Menteth, Sir James Wallace Stuart-, Bt. (1838)

Menzies, Sir Peter Thomson, Kt.

Meyer, Sir Anthony John Charles, Bt. (1910)

Meyjes, Sir Richard Anthony, Kt.

Meyrick, Sir David John Charlton, Bt. (1880)

Meyrick, Sir George Christopher Cadafael Tapps-Gervis-, Bt. (1791)

Miakwe, Hon. Sir Akepa, KBE

Michael, Sir Peter Colin, Kt., CBE
Middleton, Sir George Humphrey, KCMG
Middleton, Sir Lawrence Monck, Bt. (1662)
Middleton, Sir Peter Edward, GCB
Miers, Sir (Henry) David Alastair Capel, KBE, CMG
Milbank, Sir Anthony Frederick, Bt. (1882)
Milburn, Sir Anthony Rupert, Bt. (1905)
Miles, Sir Peter Tremayne, KCVO
Miles, Sir William Napier Maurice, Bt. (1859)
Millais, Sir Geoffrey Richard Everett, Bt. (1885)
Millar, Sir Oliver Nicholas, GCVO, FBA
Millar, Sir Ronald Graeme, Kt.
Millard, Sir Guy Elwin, KCMG, CVO
Miller, Sir Donald John, Kt., FRSE, FEng.
Miller, Sir Douglas Sinclair, KCVO, CBE
Miller, Sir Hilary Duppa (Hal), Kt.
Miller, Sir (Ian) Douglas, Kt.
Miller, Sir John Holmes, Bt. (1705)
Miller, Lt.-Col. Sir John Mansel, GCVO, DSO, MC
Miller, Sir (Oswald) Bernard, Kt.
Miller, Sir Peter North, Kt.
Miller, Sir Ronald Andrew Baird, Kt., CBE
Miller, Sir Stephen James Hamilton, KCVO, MD, FRCS
Miller of Glenlee, Sir Stephen William Macdonald, Bt. (1788)
Millett, Rt. Hon. Sir Peter Julian, Kt.
Millichip, Sir Frederick Albert (Bert), Kt.
Milling, Air Marshal Sir Denis Crowley-, KCB, CBE, DSO, DFC
Mills, Vice-Adm. Sir Charles Piercy, KCB, CBE, DSC
Mills, Sir Frank, KCVO, CMG
Mills, Sir John Lewis Ernest Watts, Kt., CBE
Mills, Sir Peter Frederick Leighton, Bt. (1921)
Milman, Lt.-Col. Sir Derek, Bt. (1800)
Milne, Sir John Drummond, Kt.
Milner, Sir (George Edward) Mordaunt, Bt. (1717)
Milnes Coates, Sir Anthony Robert, Bt. (1911)
Mitchell, Air Cdre Sir (Arthur) Dennis, KBE, CVO, DFC, AFC
Mitchell, Sir David Bower, Kt., MP
Mitchell, Sir Derek Jack, KCB, CVO
Mitchell, Prof. Sir (Edgar) William John, Kt., CBE, FRS
Mitchell, Rt. Hon. Sir James FitzAllen, KCMG
Mitchell, Hon. Sir Stephen George, Kt.
Moate, Sir Roger Denis, Kt., MP
Mobbs, Sir (Gerald) Nigel, Kt.
Moberly, Sir John Campbell, KBE, CMG
Moberly, Sir Patrick Hamilton, KCMG

Moffat, Lt.-Gen. Sir (William) Cameron, KBE
Mogg, Gen. Sir (Herbert) John, GCB, CBE, DSO
Moir, Sir Ernest Ian Royds, Bt. (1916)
Moller, Hon. Sir Lester Francis, Kt.
†Molony, Sir Thomas Desmond, Bt. (1925)
Monck, Sir Nicholas Jeremy, KCB
Monro, Sir Hector Seymour Peter, Kt., MP
Montgomery, Sir (Basil Henry) David, Bt. (1801)
Montgomery, Sir (William) Fergus, Kt., MP
Mookerjee, Sir Birendra Nath, Kt.
Moollan, Sir Abdool Hamid Adam, Kt.
Moollan, Hon. Sir Cassam (Ismael), Kt.
Moon, Sir Peter Wilfred Giles Graham-, Bt. (1855)
†Moon, Sir Roger, Bt. (1887)
Moore, Sir Francis Thomas, Kt.
Moore, Sir Henry Roderick, Kt., CBE
Moore, Hon. Sir John Cochrane, Kt.
Moore, Maj.-Gen. Sir (John) Jeremy, KCB, OBE, MC
Moore, Sir John Michael, KCVO, CB, DSC
Moore, Prof. Sir Norman Winfrid, Bt. (1919)
Moore, Sir Patrick William Eisdell, Kt., OBE
Moore, Sir William Roger Clotworthy, Bt., TD (1932)
Morauta, Sir Mekere, Kt.
Mordaunt, Sir Richard Nigel Charles, Bt. (1611)
Moreton, Sir John Oscar, KCMG, KCVO, MC
Morgan, Maj.-Gen. Sir David John Hughes-, Bt., CB, CBE (1925)
Morgan, Sir John Albert Leigh, KCMG
Morison, Hon. Sir Thomas Richard Atkin, Kt.
Morland, Hon. Sir Michael, Kt.
Morland, Sir Robert Kenelm, Kt.
Morpeth, Sir Douglas Spottiswoode, Kt., TD
Morris, Air Marshal Sir Arnold Alec, KBE, CB, FEng.
Morris, Sir (James) Richard (Samuel), Kt., CBE, FEng.
Morris, Sir Keith Elliot Hedley, KBE, CMG
Morris, Sir Robert Byng, Bt. (1806)
Morris, Very Revd Sir William James, KCVO, Ph.D.
Morrison, Hon. Sir Charles Andrew, Kt.
Morrison, Sir Howard Leslie, Kt., OBE
Morritt, Hon. Sir (Robert) Andrew, Kt., CVO
Morrow, Sir Ian Thomas, Kt.
Morse, Sir Christopher Jeremy, KCMG
Morton, Adm. Sir Anthony Storrs, GBE, KCB
Morton, Sir (Robert) Alastair (Newton), Kt.

Moseley, Sir George Walker, KCB
Moser, Prof. Sir Claus Adolf, KCB, CBE, FBA
†Moss, Sir David John Edwards-, Bt. (1868)
Mostyn, Gen. Sir (Joseph) David Frederick, KCB, CBE
†Mostyn, Sir William Basil John, Bt. (1670)
Mott, Sir John Harmer, Bt. (1930)
Mott, Sir Nevill Francis, Kt., CH, FRS
†Mount, Sir (William Robert) Ferdinand, Bt. (1921)
Mountain, Sir Denis Mortimer, Bt. (1922)
Mowbray, Sir John, Kt.
Mowbray, Sir John Robert, Bt. (1880)
Muir, Sir Laurence Macdonald, Kt.
†Muir, Sir Richard James Kay, Bt. (1892)
Muirhead, Sir David Francis, KCMG, CVO
Mulcahy, Sir Geoffrey John, Kt.
Mullens, Lt.-Gen. Sir Anthony Richard Guy, KCB, OBE
Mummery, Hon. Sir John Frank, Kt.
Munn, Sir James, Kt., OBE
Munro, Sir Alan Gordon, KCMG
Munro, Sir Alasdair Thomas Ian, Bt. (1825)
Munro, Sir Ian Talbot, Bt. (s. 1634)
Munro, Sir Sydney Douglas Gun-, GCMG, MBE
Muria, Hon. Sir Gilbert John Baptist, Kt.
Murley, Sir Reginald Sydney, KBE, TD, FRCS
Murphy, Sir Leslie Frederick, Kt.
Murray, Rt. Hon. Sir Donald Bruce, Kt.
Murray, Sir Donald Frederick, KCVO, CMG
Murray, Sir James, KCMG
Murray, Sir John Antony Jerningham, Kt., CBE
Murray, Prof. Sir Kenneth, Kt., FRCPath., FRS, FRSE
Murray, Sir Nigel Andrew Digby, Bt. (s. 1628)
Murray, Sir Patrick Ian Keith, Bt. (s. 1673)
†Murray, Sir Rowland William Patrick, Bt. (s. 1630)
Mursell, Sir Peter, Kt., MBE
Musgrave, Sir Christopher Patrick Charles, Bt. (1611)
Musgrave, Sir Richard James, Bt. (i. 1782)
Musson, Gen. Sir Geoffrey Randolph Dixon, GCB, CBE, DSO
Myers, Sir Kenneth Ben, Kt., MBE
Myers, Sir Philip Alan, Kt., OBE, QPM
Myers, Prof. Sir Rupert Horace, KBE
Mynors, Sir Richard Baskerville, Bt. (1964)
Nabarro, Sir John David Nunes, Kt., MD, FRCP
Naipaul, Sir Vidiadhar Surajprasad, Kt.
Nairn, Sir Michael, Bt. (1904)

Nairn, Sir Robert Arnold Spencer-, Bt. (1933)

Nairne, *Rt. Hon.* Sir Patrick Dalmahoy, GCB, MC

Naish, Sir (Charles) David, Kt.

Nalder, *Hon.* Sir Crawford David, Kt.

Nall, Sir Michael Joseph, Bt., RN (1954)

†Napier, Sir Charles Joseph, Bt. (1867)

Napier, Sir John Archibald Lennox, Bt. (s. 1627)

Napier, Sir Oliver John, Kt.

Neal, Sir Eric James, Kt., CVO

Neal, Sir Leonard Francis, Kt., CBE

Neale, Sir Gerrard Anthony, Kt.

Neave, Sir Paul Arundell, Bt. (1795)

Nedd, *Hon.* Sir Robert Archibald, Kt.

Neill, *Rt. Hon.* Sir Brian Thomas, Kt.

Neill, Sir Francis Patrick, Kt., QC

Neill, *Rt. Hon.* Sir Ivan, Kt., PC(NI)

†Nelson, Sir Jamie Charles Vernon Hope, Bt. (1912)

Nelson, *Air Marshal* Sir (Sidney) Richard (Carlyle), KCB, OBE, MD

Nepean, *Lt.-Col.* Sir Evan Yorke, Bt. (1802)

Neubert, Sir Michael John, Kt., MP

Nevile, *Capt.* Sir Henry Nicholas, KCVO

Neville, Sir Roger Albert Gartside, Kt., VRD

New, *Maj.-Gen.* Sir Laurence Anthony Wallis, Kt., CB, CBE

Newall, Sir Paul Henry, Kt., TD

Newington, Sir Michael John, KCMG

Newman, Sir Francis Hugh Cecil, Bt. (1912)

Newman, Sir Geoffrey Robert, Bt. (1836)

Newman, *Hon.* Sir George Michael, Kt.

Newman, Sir Jack, Kt., CBE

Newman, Sir Kenneth Leslie, GBE, QPM

Newman, *Vice-Adm.* Sir Roy Thomas, KCB

Newman, *Col.* Sir Stuart Richard, Kt., CBE, TD

Newns, Sir (Alfred) Foley (Francis Polden), KCMG, CVO

Newsam, Sir Peter Anthony, Kt.

Newton, Sir (Charles) Wilfred, Kt., CBE

Newton, Sir (Harry) Michael (Rex), Bt. (1900)

Newton, Sir Kenneth Garnar, Bt., OBE, TD (1924)

Newton, Sir (Leslie) Gordon, Kt.

Ngata, Sir Henare Kohere, KBE

Niall, Sir Horace Lionel Richard, Kt., CBE

Nichol, Sir Duncan Kirkbride, Kt., CBE

Nicholas, Sir David, Kt., CBE

Nicholas, Sir Herbert Richard, Kt., OBE

Nicholas, Sir John William, KCVO, CMG

Nicholls, *Air Marshal* Sir John Moreton, KCB, CBE, DFC, AFC

Nicholson, Sir Bryan Hubert, Kt.

†Nicholson, Sir Charles Christian, Bt. (1912)

Nicholson, *Hon.* Sir David Eric, Kt.

Nicholson, *Rt. Hon.* Sir Michael, Kt.

Nicholson, Sir Paul Douglas, Kt.

Nicholson, Sir Robin Buchanan, Kt., Ph.D., FRS, FEng.

Nicoll, Sir William, KCMG

Nicolson, Sir David Lancaster, Kt, FEng.

Nield, Sir Basil Edward, Kt., CBE, QC

Nightingale, Sir Charles Manners Gamaliel, Bt. (1628)

Nightingale, Sir John Cyprian, Kt., CBE, BEM, QPM

Nimmo, *Hon.* Sir John Angus, Kt., CBE

Nixon, Sir Edwin Ronald, Kt., CBE

Nixon, *Revd* Sir Kenneth Michael John Basil, Bt. (1906)

Noble, Sir David Brunel, Bt. (1902)

Noble, Sir Iain Andrew, Bt., OBE (1923)

Noble, Sir (Thomas Alexander) Fraser, Kt., MBE

Nombri, Sir Joseph Karl, Kt., ISO, BEM

Norman, Sir Arthur Gordon, KBE, DFC

Norman, Sir Mark Annesley, Bt. (1915)

Norman, Sir Robert Henry, Kt., OBE

Norman, Sir Robert Wentworth, Kt.

Norman, Sir Ronald, Kt., OBE

Normanton, Sir Tom, Kt., TD

Norris, *Air Chief Marshal* Sir Christopher Neil Foxley-, GCB, DSO, OBE

Norris, Sir Eric George, KCMG

North, Sir Thomas Lindsay, Kt.

North, Sir (William) Jonathan (Frederick), Bt. (1920)

Norton, *Vice-Adm. Hon.* Sir Nicholas John Hill-, KCB

Norwood, Sir Walter Neville, Kt.

Nossal, Sir Gustav Joseph Victor, Kt., CBE

Nott, *Rt. Hon.* Sir John William Frederic, KCB

Nourse, *Rt. Hon.* Sir Martin Charles, Kt.

Nugent, Sir John Edwin Lavallin, Bt. (I. 1795)

Nugent, *Maj.* Sir Peter Walter James, Bt. (1831)

Nugent, Sir Robin George Colborne, Bt. (1806)

Nursaw, Sir James, KCB, QC

Nuttall, Sir Nicholas Keith Lillington, Bt. (1922)

Nutting, *Rt. Hon.* Sir (Harold) Anthony, Bt. (1903)

Oakeley, Sir John Digby Atholl, Bt. (1790)

Oakes, Sir Christopher, Bt. (1939)

Oakshott, *Hon.* Sir Anthony Hendrie, Bt. (1959)

Oates, Sir Thomas, Kt., CMG, OBE

Oatley, Sir Charles William, Kt., OBE, FRS, FEng.

Obolensky, *Prof.* Sir Dimitri, Kt.

O'Brien, Sir Frederick William Fitzgerald, Kt.

O'Brien, Sir Richard, Kt., DSO, MC

O'Brien, Sir Timothy John, Bt. (1849)

O'Brien, *Adm.* Sir William Donough, KCB, DSC

O'Connell, Sir Maurice James Donagh MacCarthy, Bt. (1869)

O'Connor, *Rt. Hon.* Sir Patrick McCarthy, Kt.

O'Dea, Sir Patrick Jerad, KCVO

Odell, Sir Stanley John, Kt.

Ogden, Sir (Edward) Michael, Kt., QC

Ogilvie, Sir Alec Drummond, Kt.

Ogilvy, *Hon.* Sir Angus James Bruce, KCVO

Ogilvy, Sir Francis Gilbert Arthur, Bt. (s. 1626)

Ognall, *Hon.* Sir Harry Henry, Kt.

Ohlson, Sir Brian Eric Christopher, Bt. (1920)

Okeover, *Capt.* Sir Peter Ralph Leopold Walker-, Bt. (1886)

Olewale, *Hon.* Sir Niwia Ebia, Kt.

Oliphant, Sir Mark (Marcus Laurence Elwin), KBE, FRS

O'Loghlen, Sir Colman Michael, Bt. (1838)

Olver, Sir Stephen John Linley, KBE, CMG

O'Neil, *Hon.* Sir Desmond Henry, Kt.

Ongley, *Hon.* Sir Joseph Augustine, Kt.

Onslow, *Rt. Hon.* Sir Cranley Gordon Douglas, KCMG, MP

Onslow, Sir John Roger Wilmot, Bt. (1797)

Oppenheim, Sir Alexander, Kt., OBE, D.SC., FRSE

Oppenheim, Sir Duncan Morris, Kt.

Oppenheimer, Sir Michael Bernard Grenville, Bt. (1921)

Oppenheimer, Sir Philip Jack, Kt.

Opperman, *Hon.* Sir Hubert Ferdinand, Kt., OBE

Orde, Sir John Alexander Campbell-, Bt. (1790)

O'Regan, *Hon.* Sir John Barry, Kt.

O'Regan, *Dr* Sir Stephen Gerard (Tipene), Kt.

Orlebar, Sir Michael Keith Orlebar Simpson-, KCMG

Ormond, Sir John Davies Wilder, Kt., BEM

Orr, Sir David Alexander, Kt., MC

Orr, Sir John Henry, Kt., OBE, QPM

Osborn, Sir John Holbrook, Kt.

Osborn, Sir Richard Henry Danvers, Bt. (1662)

Osborne, Sir Peter George, Bt. (I. 1629)

Osifelo, Sir Frederick Aubarua, Kt., MBE

Osman, Sir (Abdool) Raman Mahomed, GCMG, CBE

Osmond, Sir Douglas, Kt., CBE

Osmond, Sir (Stanley) Paul, Kt., CB

Oswald, *Admiral of the Fleet* Sir (John) Julian Robertson, GCB

Otton, Sir Geoffrey John, KCB
Otton, *Rt. Hon.* Sir Philip Howard, Kt.
Oulton, Sir Antony Derek Maxwell, GCB, QC
Outram, Sir Alan James, Bt. (1858)
Overall, Sir John Wallace, Kt., CBE, MC
Owen, Sir Geoffrey, Kt.
Owen, Sir Hugh Bernard Pilkington, Bt. (1813)
Owen, Sir Hugo Dudley Cunliffe-, Bt. (1920)
Owen, *Hon.* Sir John Arthur Dalziel, Kt.
Owo, The Olowo of, Kt.
Oxburgh, *Prof.* Sir Ernest Ronald, KBE, Ph.D., FRS
Oxford, Sir Kenneth Gordon, Kt., CBE, QPM
Packard, *Lt.-Gen.* Sir (Charles) Douglas, KBE, CB, DSO
Padmore, Sir Thomas, GCB
Page, Sir (Arthur) John, Kt.
Page, Sir Frederick William, Kt., CBE, FEng.
Page, Sir John Joseph Joffre, Kt., OBE
Paget, Sir Julian Tolver, Bt., CVO (1871)
Paget, Sir Richard Herbert, Bt. (1886)
Pain, *Lt.-Gen.* Sir (Horace) Rollo (Squarey), KCB, MC
Pain, *Hon.* Sir Peter Richard, Kt.
Paine, Sir Christopher Hammon, Kt., FRCP, FRCR
Palin, *Air Chief Marshal* Sir Roger Hewlett, KCB, OBE
Palliser, *Rt. Hon.* Sir (Arthur) Michael, GCMG
Palmar, Sir Derek James, Kt.
Palmer, Sir (Charles) Mark, Bt. (1886)
Palmer, *Gen.* Sir (Charles) Patrick (Ralph), KBE
Palmer, Sir Geoffrey Christopher John, Bt. (1660)
Palmer, *Rt. Hon.* Sir Geoffrey Winston Russell, KCMG
Palmer, Sir John Chance, Kt.
Palmer, Sir John Edward Somerset, Bt. (1791)
Palmer, *Maj.-Gen.* Sir (Joseph) Michael, KCVO
Palmer, Sir Reginald Oswald, GCMG, MBE
Pantlin, Sir Dick Hurst, Kt., CBE
Paolozzi, Sir Eduardo Luigi, Kt., CBE, RA
Parbo, Sir Arvi Hillar, Kt.
Parish, Sir David Elmer Woodbine, Kt., CBE
Park, *Hon.* Sir Hugh Eames, Kt.
Parker, Sir (Arthur) Douglas Dodds-, Kt.
Parker, Sir Eric Wilson, Kt.
Parker, *Hon.* Sir Jonathan Frederic, Kt.
Parker, Sir Peter, KBE, LVO
Parker, Sir Richard (William) Hyde, Bt. (1681)
Parker, *Rt. Hon.* Sir Roger Jocelyn, Kt.
Parker, *Vice-Adm.* Sir (Wilfred) John, KBE, CB, DSC

Parker, Sir William Peter Brian, Bt. (1844)
Parkes, Sir Edward Walter, Kt., FEng
Parkinson, Sir Nicholas Fancourt, Kt.
Parsons, Sir Anthony Derrick, GCMG, MVO, MC
Parsons, Sir (John) Michael, Kt.
Parsons, Sir Richard Edmund (Clement Fownes), KCMG
Partridge, Sir Michael John Anthony, KCB
Pascoe, *Gen.* Sir Robert Alan, KCB, MBE
Pasley, Sir John Malcolm Sabine; Bt. (1794)
Paterson, Sir Dennis Craig, Kt.
Paterson, Sir George Mutlow, Kt., OBE, QC
Paterson, Sir John Valentine Jardine, Kt.
Patnick, Sir (Cyril) Irvine, Kt., OBE, MP
Paton, Sir (Thomas) Angus (Lyall), Kt., CMG, FRS, FEng.
Pattie, *Rt. Hon.* Sir Geoffrey Edwin, Kt., MP
Pattinson, Sir (William) Derek, Kt.
Pattullo, Sir (David) Bruce, Kt., CBE
Paul, Sir John Warburton, GCMG, OBE, MC
Paul, *Air Marshal* Sir Ronald Ian Stuart-, KBE
Payne, Sir Norman John, Kt., CBE, FEng.
Peach, Sir Leonard Harry, Kt.
Peacock, *Prof.* Sir Alan Turner, Kt., DSC
Pearce, Sir Austin William, Kt., CBE, Ph.D., FEng.
Pearce, Sir (Daniel Norton) Idris, Kt., CBE, TD
Pearce, Sir Eric Herbert, Kt., OBE
Pearman, *Hon.* Sir James Eugene, Kt., CBE
Pearse, Sir Brian Gerald, Kt.
Pearson, Sir Francis Nicholas Fraser, Bt. (1964)
Pearson, *Gen.* Sir Thomas Cecil Hook, KCB, CBE, DSO
Peart, *Prof.* Sir William Stanley, Kt., MD, FRS
Pease, Sir (Alfred) Vincent, Bt. (1882)
Pease, Sir Richard Thorn, Bt. (1920)
Peat, Sir Gerrard Charles, KCVO
Peat, Sir Henry, KCVO, DFC
Peck, Sir Edward Heywood, GCMG
Peckham, *Prof.* Sir Michael John, Kt., FRCP, FRCPGlas., FRCR, FRCPath.
Pedder, *Air Marshal* Sir Ian Maurice, KCB, OBE, DFC
Peek, Sir Francis Henry Grenville, Bt. (1874)
Peek, *Vice-Adm.* Sir Richard Innes, KBE, CB, DSC
Peel, Sir John Harold, KCVO
Peel, Sir (William) John, Kt.
Peierls, Sir Rudolf Ernst, Kt., CBE, D.SC., D.Phil., FRS
Peirse, Sir Henry Grant de la Poer Beresford-, Bt. (1814)
Peirse, *Air Vice-Marshal* Sir Richard Charles Fairfax, KCVO, CB

Pelgen, Sir Harry Friedrich, Kt., MBE
†Pelly, Sir Richard John, Bt. (1840)
Pemberton, Sir Francis Wingate William, Kt., CBE
Penrose, *Prof.* Sir Roger, Kt., FRS
Percival, *Rt. Hon.* Sir (Walter) Ian, Kt., QC
Pereira, Sir (Herbert) Charles, Kt., D.SC., FRS
Perring, Sir Ralph Edgar, Bt. (1963)
Perris, Sir David (Arthur), Kt., MBE
Perry, Sir David Howard, KCB
Perry, Sir (David) Norman, Kt., MBE
Perry, Sir Michael Sydney, Kt., CBE
Pestell, Sir John Richard, KCVO
Peterkin, Sir Neville, Kt.
Peters, *Prof.* Sir David Keith, Kt., FRCP
Petersen, Sir Jeffrey Charles, KCMG
Petersen, Sir Johannes Bjelke-, KCMG
Peterson, Sir Christopher Matthew, Kt., CBE, TD
Petit, Sir Dinshaw Manockjee, Bt. (1890)
Peto, Sir Henry George Morton, Bt. (1855)
Peto, Sir Michael Henry Basil, Bt. (1927)
Petrie, Sir Peter Charles, Bt., CMG (1918)
Pettigrew, Sir Russell Hilton, Kt.
Pettit, Sir Daniel Eric Arthur, Kt.
Philips, *Prof.* Sir Cyril Henry, Kt.
Phillips, Sir Fred Albert, Kt., CVO
Phillips, Sir Henry Ellis Isidore, Kt., CMG, MBE
Phillips, Sir Horace, KCMG
Phillips, *Hon.* Sir Nicholas Addison, Kt.
Phillips, Sir Peter John, Kt., OBE
Phillips, Sir Robin Francis, Bt. (1912)
Pickering, Sir Edward Davies, Kt.
†Pickthorn, Sir James Francis Mann, Bt. (1959)
Pidgeon, Sir John Allan Stewart, Kt.
Piers, Sir Charles Robert Fitzmaurice, Bt. (I. 1661)
Pigot, Sir George Hugh, Bt. (1764)
Pigott, Sir Berkeley Henry Sebastian, Bt. (1808)
Pike, Sir Michael Edmund, KCVO, CMG
Pike, Sir Philip Ernest Housden, Kt., QC
Pilditch, Sir Richard Edward, Bt. (1929)
Pile, Sir Frederick Devereux, Bt., MC (1900)
Pile, Sir William Dennis, GCB, MBE
Pilkington, Sir Antony Richard, Kt.
Pilkington, Sir Thomas Henry Milborne-Swinnerton-, Bt. (s. 1635)
Pill, *Rt. Hon.* Sir Malcolm Thomas, Kt.
Pillar, *Adm.* Sir William Thomas, GBE, KCB
Pindling, *Rt. Hon.* Sir Lynden Oscar, KCMG
Pinker, Sir George Douglas, KCVO
Pinsent, Sir Christopher Roy, Bt. (1938)

Pippard, *Prof.* Sir (Alfred) Brian, Kt., FRS

Pirie, *Gp Capt* Sir Gordon Hamish, Kt., CVO, CBE

Pitakaka, Sir Moses Puibangara, GCMG

Pitblado, Sir David Bruce, KCB, CVO

Pitcher, Sir Desmond Henry, Kt.

Pitman, Sir Brian Ivor, Kt.

Pitoi, Sir Sere, Kt., CBE

Pitt, Sir Harry Raymond, Kt., PH.D., FRS

Pitts, Sir Cyril Alfred, Kt.

Plastow, Sir David Arnold Stuart, Kt.

†Platt, Sir (Frank) Lindsey, Bt. (1958)

Platt, Sir Harold Grant, Kt.

Platt, *Prof.* Hon. Sir Peter, Bt. (1959)

Playfair, Sir Edward Wilder, KCB

Pliatzky, Sir Leo, KCB

Plowman, *Hon.* Sir John Robin, Kt., CBE

Plumb, *Prof.* Sir John Harold, Kt.

Pohai, Sir Timothy, Kt., MBE

Pole, Sir (John) Richard (Walter Reginald) Carew, Bt. (1628)

Pole, Sir Peter Van Notten, Bt. (1791)

Pollen, Sir John Michael Hungerford, Bt. (1795)

Pollock, Sir George Frederick, Bt. (1866)

Pollock, Sir Giles Hampden Montagu-, Bt. (1872)

Pollock, *Admiral of the Fleet* Sir Michael Patrick, GCB, MVO, DSC

Ponsonby, Sir Ashley Charles Gibbs, Bt., KCVO, MC (1956)

Pontin, Sir Frederick William, Kt.

Poore, Sir Herbert Edward, Bt. (1795)

Pope, *Vice-Adm.* Sir (John) Ernle, KCB

Pope, Sir Joseph Albert, Kt., D.SC., PH.D.

Popplewell, *Hon.* Sir Oliver Bury, Kt.

†Porritt, Sir Jonathon Espie, Bt. (1963)

Portal, Sir Jonathan Francis, Bt. (1901)

Porter, Sir John Simon Horsbrugh-, Bt. (1902)

Porter, Sir Leslie, Kt.

Porter, *Air Marshal* Sir (Melvin) Kenneth (Drowley), KCB, CBE

Porter, *Rt. Hon.* Sir Robert Wilson, Kt., PC(NI), QC

Posnett, Sir Richard Neil, KBE, CMG

Potter, *Hon.* Sir Mark Howard, Kt.

Potter, *Maj.-Gen.* Sir (Wilfrid) John, KBE, CB

Potts, *Hon.* Sir Francis Humphrey, Kt.

Pound, Sir John David, Bt. (1905)

Pountain, Sir Eric John, Kt.

Powell, Sir (Arnold Joseph) Philip, Kt., CH, OBE, RA, FRIBA

Powell, Sir Charles David, KCMG

Powell, Sir Nicholas Folliott Douglas, Bt. (1897)

Powell, Sir Richard Royle, GCB, KBE, CMG

Power, Sir Alastair John Cecil, Bt. (1924)

Poynton, Sir (Arthur) Hilton, GCMG

Prance, *Prof.* Sir Ghillean Tolmie, Kt., FRS

Prendergast, Sir (Walter) Kieran, KCVO, CMG

Prentice, *Hon.* Sir William Thomas, Kt., MBE

Prescott, Sir Mark, Bt. (1938)

Preston, Sir Peter Sansome, KCB

Preston, Sir Ronald Douglas Hildebrand, Bt. (1815)

Prevost, Sir Christopher Gerald, Bt. (1805)

Price, Sir Charles Keith Napier Rugge-, Bt. (1804)

Price, Sir David Ernest Campbell, Kt.

Price, Sir Francis Caradoc Rose, Bt. (1815)

Price, Sir Frank Leslie, Kt.

Price, Sir (James) Robert, KBE

Price, Sir Leslie Victor, Kt., OBE

Price, Sir Norman Charles, KCB

Price, Sir Robert John Green-, Bt. (1874)

Prickett, *Air Chief Marshal* Sir Thomas Other, KCB, DSO, DFC

Prideaux, Sir Humphrey Povah Treverbian, Kt., OBE

†Primrose, Sir John Ure, Bt. (1903)

Pringle, *Air Marshal* Sir Charles Norman Seton, KBE, FEng.

Pringle, *Hon.* Sir John Kenneth, Kt.

Pringle, *Lt.-Gen.* Sir Steuart (Robert), Bt., KCB, RM (S. 1683)

Pritchard, Sir Neil, KCMG

Pritchett, Sir Victor Sawdon, Kt., CH, CBE

Proby, Sir Peter, Bt. (1952)

Prosser, Sir Ian Maurice Gray, Kt.

Proud, Sir John Seymour, Kt.

Pryke, Sir David Dudley, Bt. (1926)

Pugh, Sir Idwal Vaughan, KCB

Pugsley, *Prof.* Sir Alfred Grenvile, Kt., OBE, D.SC., FRS, FEng.

Pullen, Sir William Reginald James, KCVO

Pullinger, Sir (Francis) Alan, Kt., CBE

Pumphrey, Sir (John) Laurence, KCMG

Purchas, *Rt. Hon.* Sir Francis Brooks, Kt.

Purves, Sir William, Kt., CBE, DSO

Purvis, *Vice-Adm.* Sir Neville, KCB

Puttnam, Sir David Terrance, Kt., CBE

Quicke, Sir John Godolphin, Kt., CBE

Quigley, Sir (William) George (Henry), Kt., CB, PH.D.

Quilliam, *Hon.* Sir (James) Peter, Kt.

Quilter, Sir Anthony Raymond Leopold Cuthbert, Bt. (1897)

Quinlan, Sir Michael Edward, GCB

Quinton, Sir James Grand, Kt.

Radcliffe, Sir Sebastian Everard, Bt. (1813)

Radford, Sir Ronald Walter, KCB, MBE

Radzinowicz, *Prof.* Sir Leon, Kt., LL D

Rae, *Hon.* Sir Wallace Alexander Ramsay, Kt.

Raeburn, Sir Michael Edward Norman, Bt. (1923)

Raeburn, *Maj.-Gen.* Sir (William) Digby (Manifold), KCVO, CB, DSO, MBE

Raffray, Sir Piat Joseph Raymond Andre, Kt.

Raikes, *Vice-Adm.* Sir Iwan Geoffrey, KCB, CBE, DSC

Raison, *Rt. Hon.* Sir Timothy Hugh Francis, Kt.

Ralli, Sir Godfrey Victor, Bt., TD (1912)

Ramdanee, Sir Mookteswar Baboolall Kailash, Kt.

Ramphal, Sir Shridath Surendranath, GCMG

Ramphul, Sir Baalkhristna, Kt.

Ramphul, Sir Indurduth, Kt.

Ramsay, Sir Alexander William Burnett, Bt. (1806)

Ramsay, Sir Allan John (Hepple), KBE, CMG

Ramsay, Sir Thomas Meek, Kt., CMG

Ramsbotham, *Gen.* Sir David John, GCB, CBE

Ramsbotham, *Hon.* Sir Peter Edward, GCMG, GCVO

Ramsden, Sir John Charles Josslyn, Bt. (1689)

Ramsey, Sir Alfred Ernest, Kt.

Randle, *Prof.* Sir Philip John, Kt.

Ranger, Sir Douglas, Kt., FRCS

Rank, Sir Benjamin Keith, Kt., CMG

Rankin, Sir Alick Michael, Kt., CBE

Rankin, Sir Ian Niall, Bt. (1898)

Rasch, *Maj.* Sir Richard Guy Carne, Bt. (1903)

Rashleigh, Sir Richard Harry, Bt. (1831)

Ratford, Sir David John Edward, KCMG, CVO

Rattee, *Hon.* Sir Donald Keith, Kt.

Rattle, Sir Simon Dennis, Kt., CBE

Rault, Sir Louis Joseph Maurice, Kt.

Rawlins, *Surgeon Vice-Adm.* Sir John Stuart Pepys, KBE

Rawlinson, Sir Anthony Henry John, Bt. (1891)

Read, *Air Marshal* Sir Charles Frederick, KBE, CB, DFC, AFC

Read, *Gen.* Sir (John) Antony (Jervis), GCB, CBE, DSO, MC

Read, Sir John Emms, Kt.

†Reade, Sir Kenneth Ray, Bt. (1661)

Reay, *Lt.-Gen.* Sir (Hubert) Alan John, KBE

Redgrave, *Maj.-Gen.* Sir Roy Michael Frederick, KBE, MC

Redmayne, Sir Nicholas, Bt. (1964)

Redmond, Sir James, Kt., FEng.

Redwood, Sir Peter Boverton, Bt. (1911)

Reece, Sir Charles Hugh, Kt.

Reece, Sir James Gordon, Kt.

Reed, *Hon.* Sir Nigel Vernon, Kt., CBE

Rees, Sir (Charles William) Stanley, Kt., TD

Rees, Sir David Allan, Kt., PH.D., D.SC., FRS

Rees, *Prof.* Sir Martin John, Kt., FRS

Reeve, Sir Anthony, KCMG, KCVO

Reeves, *Most Revd* Paul Alfred, GCMG, GCVO
Reffell, *Adm.* Sir Derek Roy, KCB
Refshauge, *Maj-Gen.* Sir William Dudley, Kt., CBE
Reid, Sir Alexander James, Bt. (1897)
Reid, Sir (Harold) Martin (Smith), KBE, CMG
Reid, Sir Hugh, Bt. (1922)
Reid, Sir Norman Robert, Kt.
Reid, Sir Robert Paul, Kt.
Reiher, Sir Frederick Bernard Carl, KBE, CMG
Reilly, Sir (D'Arcy) Patrick, GCMG, OBE
Reilly, *Lt.-Gen.* Sir Jeremy Calcott, KCB, DSO
Renals, Sir Stanley, Bt. (1895)
Rennie, Sir John Shaw, GCMG, OBE
Renouf, Sir Clement William Bailey, Kt.
Renouf, Sir Francis Henry, Kt.
Renshaw, Sir (Charles) Maurice Bine, Bt. (1903)
Renwick, Sir Richard Eustace, Bt. (1921)
Renwick, Sir Robin William, KCMG
Reporter, Sir Shapoor Ardeshirji, KBE
Reynolds, Sir David James, Bt. (1923)
Reynolds, Sir Peter William John, Kt., CBE
Rhodes, Sir Basil Edward, Kt., CBE, TD
Rhodes, Sir John Christopher Douglas, Bt. (1919)
Rhodes, Sir Peregrine Alexander, KCMG
Rice, *Maj.-Gen.* Sir Desmond Hind Garrett, KCVO, CBE
Rice, Sir Timothy Miles Bindon, Kt.
Richard, Sir Cliff, Kt., OBE
Richards, Sir (Francis) Brooks, KCMG, DSC
Richards, *Lt.-Gen.* Sir John Charles Chisholm, KCB, KCVO, RM
Richards, Sir Rex Edward, Kt., D.SC., FRS
Richardson, Sir Anthony Lewis, Bt. (1924)
Richardson, *Rt. Hon.* Sir Ivor Lloyd Morgan, Kt.
Richardson, Sir (John) Eric, Kt., CBE
Richardson, Sir Michael John de Rougemont, Kt.
Richardson, *Lt.-Gen.* Sir Robert Francis, KCB, CVO, CBE
Richardson, Sir Simon Alaisdair Stewart-, Bt. (s. 1630)
Riches, Sir Derek Martin Hurry, KCMG
Riches, *Gen.* Sir Ian Hurry, KCB, DSO
Richmond, Sir Alan James, Kt.
Richmond, *Rt. Hon.* Sir Clifford Parris, KBE
Richmond, Sir John Frederick, Bt. (1929)
Richmond, *Prof.* Sir Mark Henry, Kt., FRS
Rickett, Sir Denis Hubert Fletcher, KCMG, CB

Rickett, Sir Raymond Mildmay Wilson, Kt., CBE, Ph.D.
Ricketts, Sir Robert Cornwallis Gerald St Leger, Bt. (1828)
Riddell, Sir John Charles Buchanan, Bt., CVO (s. 1628)
Ridley, Sir Adam (Nicholas), Kt.
Ridsdale, Sir Julian Errington, Kt., CBE
Rigby, *Lt.-Col.* Sir (Hugh) John (Macbeth), Bt. (1929)
Riley, Sir Ralph, Kt., FRS
Rimer, *Hon.* Sir Colin Percy Farquharson, Kt.
Ring, Sir Lindsay Roberts, GBE
Ringadoo, *Hon.* Sir Veerasamy, GCMG
Ripley, Sir Hugh, Bt. (1880)
Risk, Sir Thomas Neilson, Kt.
Rix, *Hon.* Sir Bernard Anthony, Kt.
Rix, Sir John, Kt., MBE, FEng.
Roberts, Sir Bryan Clieve, KCMG, QC
Roberts, *Hon.* Sir Denys Tudor Emil, KBE, QC
Roberts, Sir Derek Harry, Kt., CBE, FRS, FEng.
Roberts, Sir (Edward Fergus) Sidney, Kt., CBE
Roberts, Sir Frank Kenyon, GCMG, GCVO
Roberts, *Brig.* Sir Geoffrey Paul Hardy-, KCVO, CB, CBE
Roberts, Sir Gilbert Howland Rookehurst, Bt. (1809)
Roberts, Sir Gordon James, Kt., CBE
Roberts, *Rt. Hon.* Sir (Ieuan) Wyn Pritchard, Kt., MP
Roberts, Sir Samuel, Bt. (1919)
Roberts, Sir Stephen James Leake, Kt.
Roberts, Sir William James Denby, Bt. (1909)
Robertson, Sir John Fraser, KCMG, CBE
Robertson, Sir Lewis, Kt., CBE, FRSE
Robertson, *Prof.* Sir Rutherford Ness, Kt., CMG
Robins, Sir Ralph Harry, Kt., FEng.
Robinson, Sir Albert Edward Phineas, Kt.
†Robinson, Sir Christopher Philipse, Bt. (1854)
Robinson, Sir John James Michael Laud, Bt. (1660)
Robinson, *Rt. Hon.* Sir Kenneth, Kt.
Robinson, Sir Niall Bryan Lynch-, Bt., DSC (1920)
Robinson, Sir Wilfred Henry Frederick, Bt. (1908)
Robotham, *Hon.* Sir Lascelles Lister, Kt.
Robson, *Prof.* Sir James Gordon, Kt., CBE
Robson, Sir John Adam, KCMG
Roch, *Rt. Hon.* Sir John Ormond, Kt.
Roche, Sir David O'Grady, Bt. (1838)
Rodgers, Sir (John Fairlie) Tobias, Bt. (1964)
Rodrigues, Sir Alberto Maria, Kt., CBE, ED
Roe, *Air Chief Marshal* Sir Rex David, GCB, AFC
Rogers, Sir Frank Jarvis, Kt.

Rogers, *Air Chief Marshal* Sir John Robson, KCB, CBE
Rogers, Sir Richard George, Kt., RA
Roll, *Revd* Sir James William Cecil, Bt. (1921)
Rooke, Sir Denis Eric, Kt., CBE, FRS, FEng.
Ropner, Sir John Bruce Woollacott, Bt. (1952)
Ropner, Sir Robert Douglas, Bt. (1904)
Roscoe, Sir Robert Bell, KBE
Rose, *Rt. Hon.* Sir Christopher Dudley Roger, Kt.
Rose, Sir Clive Martin, GCMG
Rose, Sir David Lancaster, Bt. (1874)
Rose, *Gen.* Sir (Hugh) Michael, KCB, CBE, DSO, QGM
Rose, Sir Julian Day, Bt. (1872 and 1909)
Rosier, *Air Chief Marshal* Sir Frederick Ernest, GCB, CBE, DSO
Ross, Sir Archibald David Manisty, KCMG
Ross, Sir (James) Keith, Bt., RD, FRCS (1960)
Ross, *Lt.-Gen.* Sir Robert Jeremy, KCB, OBE
Rosser, Sir Melvyn Wynne, Kt.
Rossi, Sir Hugh Alexis Louis, Kt.
Roth, *Prof.* Sir Martin, Kt., MD, FRCP
Rothnie, Sir Alan Keir, KCVO, CMG
Rothschild, Sir Evelyn Robert Adrian de, Kt.
Rougier, *Hon.* Sir Richard George, Kt.
Rous, *Lt.-Gen.* the Hon. Sir William Edward, KCB, OBE
Rowe, Sir Jeremy, Kt., CBE
Rowell, Sir John Joseph, Kt., CBE
Rowland, *Air Marshal* Sir James Anthony, KBE, DFC, AFC
Rowlands, *Air Marshal* Sir John Samuel, GC, KBE
Rowley, Sir Charles Robert, Bt. (1836)
Rowley, Sir Joshua Francis, Bt. (1786)
Rowling, *Rt. Hon.* Sir Wallace Edward, KCMG
Roxburgh, *Vice-Adm.* Sir John Charles Young, KCB, CBE, DSO, DSC
Royden, Sir Christopher John, Bt. (1905)
Rumbold, Sir Henry John Sebastian, Bt. (1779)
Rumbold, Sir Jack Seddon, Kt.
Runchorelal, Sir (Udayan) Chinubhai Madhowlal, Bt. (1913)
Runciman, *Hon.* Sir James Cochran Stevenson (Sir Steven Runciman), Kt., CH
Rusby, *Vice-Adm.* Sir Cameron, KCB, MVO
Russell, Sir Charles Ian, Bt. (1916)
Russell, *Hon.* Sir David Sturrock West-, Kt.
Russell, Sir George, Kt., CBE
Russell, Sir George Michael, Bt. (1812)
Russell, *Prof.* Sir Peter Edward Lionel, Kt., D.Litt., FBA

Russell, Sir (Robert) Mark, KCMG
Russell, Sir Spencer Thomas, Kt.
Russell, Rt. Hon. Sir (Thomas) Patrick, Kt.
Rutter, Sir Frank William Eden, KBE
Rutter, Prof. Sir Michael Llewellyn, Kt., CBE, MD, FRS
Ryan, Sir Derek Gerald, Bt. (1919)
Rycroft, Sir Richard Newton, Bt. (1784)
Ryrie, Sir William Sinclair, KCB
Sabola, Hon. Sir Joaquim Claudino Gonsalves-, Kt.
Sachs, Hon. Sir Michael Alexander Geddes, Kt.
Sainsbury, Sir Robert James, Kt.
Sainsbury, Rt. Hon. Sir Timothy Alan Davan, Kt., MP
St Aubyn, Sir (John) Arscott Molesworth-, Bt. (1689)
St George, Sir George Bligh, Bt. (I. 1766)
St Johnston, Sir Kerry, Kt.
Sainty, Sir John Christopher, KCB
Sakzewski, Sir Albert, Kt.
Salt, Sir Patrick MacDonnell, Bt. (1869)
Salt, Sir (Thomas) Michael John, Bt. (1899)
Sampson, Sir Colin, Kt., CBE, QPM
Samuel, Sir Jon Michael Glen, Bt. (1898)
Samuelson, Sir (Bernard) Michael (Francis), Bt. (1884)
Samuelson, Sir Sydney Wylie, Kt., CBE
Sandberg, Sir Michael Graham Ruddock, Kt., CBE
Sanders, Sir John Reynolds Mayhew-, Kt.
Sanders, Sir Robert Tait, KBE, CMG
Sanderson, Sir Frank Linton, Bt. (1920)
Sarei, Sir Alexis Holyweek, Kt., CBE
Sarell, Sir Roderick Francis Gisbert, KCMG, KCVO
Sargant, Sir (Henry) Edmund, Kt.
Saunders, Hon. Sir John Anthony Holt, Kt., CBE, DSO, MC
Saunders, Sir Peter, Kt.
Sauzier, Sir (André) Guy, Kt., CBE, ED
Savage, Sir Ernest Walter, Kt.
Savile, Sir James Wilson Vincent, Kt., OBE
Saville, Rt. Hon. Sir Mark Oliver, Kt.
Say, Rt. Revd Richard David, KCVO
Schiemann, Rt. Hon. Sir Konrad Hermann Theodor, Kt.
Schneider, Rt. Hon. Sir Lancelot Raymond Adams-, KCMG
Scholey, Sir David Gerald, Kt., CBE
Scholey, Sir Robert, Kt., CBE, FEng.
Scholtens, Sir James Henry, KCVO
Schubert, Sir Sydney, Kt.
Schuster, Sir (Felix) James Moncrieff, Bt., OBE (1906)
Scipio, Sir Hudson Rupert, Kt.
Scoon, Sir Paul, GCMG, GCVO, OBE
Scopes, Sir Leonard Arthur, KCVO, CMG, OBE

Scott, Sir Anthony Percy, Bt. (1913)
Scott, Sir (Charles) Peter, KBE, CMG
Scott, Sir David Aubrey, GCMG
Scott, Sir Dominic James Maxwell-, Bt. (1642)
Scott, Sir Ian Dixon, KCMG, KCVO, CIE
Scott, Sir James Jervoise, Bt. (1962)
Scott, Sir Kenneth Bertram Adam, KCVO, CMG
Scott, Sir Michael, KCVO, CMG
Scott, Rt. Hon. Sir Nicholas Paul, KBE, MP
Scott, Sir Oliver Christopher Anderson, Bt. (1909)
Scott, Prof. Sir Philip John, KBE
Scott, Rt. Hon. Sir Richard Rashleigh Folliott, Kt.
Scott, Sir Robert David Hillyer, Kt.
Scott, Sir Walter John, Bt. (1907)
Scott, Rear-Adm. Sir (William) David (Stewart), KBE, CB
Scowen, Sir Eric Frank, Kt., MD, D.SC., LL D., FRCP, FRCS
Scrivenor, Sir Thomas Vaisey, Kt., CMG
Seale, Sir John Henry, Bt. (1838)
Seaman, Sir Keith Douglas, KCVO, OBE
†Sebright, Sir Peter Giles Vivian, Bt. (1626)
Seccombe, Sir (William) Vernon Stephen, Kt.
Secombe, Sir Harry Donald, Kt., CBE
Seconde, Sir Reginald Louis, KCMG, CVO
Sedley, Hon. Sir Stephen John, Kt.
Seely, Sir Nigel Edward, Bt. (1896)
Seeto, Sir Ling James, Kt., MBE
Seeyave, Sir Rene Sow Choung, Kt., CBE
Seligman, Sir Peter Wendel, Kt., CBE
Sergeant, Sir Patrick, Kt.
Series, Sir (Joseph Michel) Emile, Kt., CBE
Serpell, Sir David Radford, KCB, CMG, OBE
Seton, Sir Iain Bruce, Bt. (s. 1663)
†Seton, Sir James Christall, Bt. (s. 1683)
Severne, Air Vice-Marshal Sir John de Milt, KCVO, OBE, AFC
Seymour, Cdr. Sir Michael Culme-, Bt., RN (1809)
Shakerley, Sir Geoffrey Adam, Bt. (1838)
Shakespeare, Sir William Geoffrey, Bt. (1942)
Shapland, Sir William Arthur, Kt.
Sharp, Sir Adrian, Bt. (1922)
Sharp, Sir George, Kt., OBE
Sharp, Sir Kenneth Johnston, Kt., TD
Sharp, Sir Milton Reginald, Bt. (1920)
Sharp, Sir Richard Lyall, KCVO, CB
Sharpe, Hon. Sir John Henry, Kt., OBE
Shattock, Sir Gordon, Kt.
Shaw, Sir Brian Piers, Kt.
Shaw, Sir (Charles) Barry, Kt., CB, QC
Shaw, Sir (George) Neville Bowan-, Kt.
Shaw, Prof. Sir John Calman, Kt., CBE, FRSE

Shaw, Sir (John) Giles (Dunkerley), Kt., MP
Shaw, Sir John Michael Robert Best-, Bt. (1665)
Shaw, Sir Neil McGowan, Kt.
Shaw, Sir Robert, Bt. (1821)
Shaw, Sir Roy, Kt.
Shaw, Sir Run Run, Kt., CBE
Sheehy, Sir Patrick, Kt.
Sheen, Hon. Sir Barry Cross, Kt.
Sheffield, Sir Reginald Adrian Berkeley, Bt. (1755)
Shehadie, Sir Nicholas Michael, Kt., OBE
Sheil, Hon. Sir John, Kt.
Sheldon, Hon. Sir (John) Gervase (Kensington), Kt.
Shelley, Sir John Richard, Bt. (1611)
Shelton, Sir William Jeremy Masefield, Kt.
Shepheard, Sir Peter Faulkner, Kt., CBE
Shepherd, Sir Peter Malcolm, Kt., CBE
Shepperd, Sir Alfred Joseph, Kt.
Sherlock, Sir Philip Manderson, KBE
Sherman, Sir Alfred, Kt.
Sherman, Sir Louis, Kt., OBE
Shersby, Sir (Julian) Michael, Kt., MP
Shields, Sir Neil Stanley, Kt., MC
Shields, Prof. Sir Robert, Kt., MD
Shiffner, Sir Henry David, Bt. (1818)
Shillington, Sir (Robert Edward) Graham, Kt., CBE
Shock, Sir Maurice, Kt.
Short, Brig. Sir Noel Edward Vivian, Kt., MBE, MC
Shuckburgh, Sir Rupert Charles Gerald, Bt. (1660)
Siaguru, Sir Anthony Michael, KBE
Sich, Sir Rupert Leigh, Kt., CB
Siddall, Sir Norman, Kt., CBE, FEng.
Sidey, Air Marshal Sir Ernest Shaw, KBE, CB, MD
Sie, Sir Banja Tejan-, GCMG
Simeon, Sir John Edmund Barrington, Bt. (1815)
Simmons, Air Marshal Sir Michael George, KCB, AFC
Simmons, Sir Stanley Clifford, Kt., FRCS, FRCOG
Simon, Sir David Alec Gwyn, Kt., CBE
Simonet, Sir Louis Marcel Pierre, Kt., CBE
Simpson, Hon. Sir Alfred Henry, Kt.
Simpson, Sir William James, Kt.
Sinclair, Sir Clive Marles, Kt.
Sinclair, Sir George Evelyn, Kt., CMG, OBE
Sinclair, Sir Ian McTaggart, KCMG, QC
Sinclair, Air Vice-Marshal Sir Laurence Frank, GC, KCB, CBE, DSO
Sinclair, Sir Patrick Robert Richard, Bt. (s. 1704)
Sinclair, Sir Ronald Ormiston, KBE
Singer, Prof. Sir Hans Wolfgang, Kt.
Singer, Hon. Sir Jan Peter, Kt.
Singh, Hon. Sir Vijay Raghubir, Kt.
Singhania, Sir Padampat, Kt.
Sinnamon, Sir Hercules, Kt., OBE

Sitwell, Sir (Sacheverell) Reresby, Bt. (1808)

Skeet, Sir Trevor Herbert Harry, Kt., MP

Skeggs, Sir Clifford George, Kt.

Skingsley, *Air Chief Marshal* Sir Anthony Gerald, GBE, KCB

Skinner, Sir (Thomas) Keith (Hewitt), Bt. (1912)

Skipwith, Sir Patrick Alexander d'Estoteville, Bt. (1622)

Skyrme, Sir (William) Thomas (Charles), KCVO, CB, CBE, TD

Slack, Sir William Willatt, KCVO, FRCS

Slade, Sir Benjamin Julian Alfred, Bt. (1831)

Slade, *Rt. Hon.* Sir Christopher John, Kt.

Slaney, *Prof.* Sir Geoffrey, KBE

Slater, *Adm.* Sir John (Jock) Cunningham Kirkwood, GCB, LVO

Sleight, Sir Richard, Bt. (1920)

Sloan, Sir Andrew Kirkpatrick, Kt., QPM

Sloman, Sir Albert Edward, Kt., CBE

Smallwood, *Air Chief Marshal* Sir Denis Graham, GBE, KCB, DSO, DFC

Smart, *Prof.* Sir George Algernon, Kt., MD, FRCP

Smart, Sir Jack, Kt., CBE

Smedley, *Hon.* Sir (Frank) Brian, Kt.

Smedley, Sir Harold, KCMG, MBE

Smiley, *Lt.-Col.* Sir John Philip, Bt. (1903)

Smith, Sir Alan, Kt., CBE, DFC

Smith, Sir Alexander Mair, Kt., Ph.D.

Smith, Sir Andrew Colin Hugh-, Kt.

Smith, *Lt.-Gen.* Sir Anthony Arthur Denison-, KBE

Smith, Sir Charles Bracewell-, Bt. (1947)

Smith, Sir Christopher Sydney Winwood, Bt. (1809)

Smith, *Prof.* Sir Colin Stansfield, Kt., CBE

Smith, Sir Cyril, Kt., MBE

Smith, *Prof.* Sir David Cecil, Kt., FRS

Smith, *Air Chief Marshal* Sir David Harcourt-, GBE, KCB, DFC

Smith, Sir David Iser, KCVO

Smith, Sir Douglas Boucher, KCB

Smith, Sir Dudley (Gordon), Kt., MP

Smith, *Maj.-Gen.* Sir (Francis) Brian Wyldbore-, Kt., CB, DSO, OBE

Smith, *Prof.* Sir Francis Graham-, Kt., FRS

Smith, Sir Geoffrey Johnson, Kt., MP

Smith, Sir Howard Frank Trayton, GCMG

Smith, Sir John Alfred, Kt., QPM

Smith, *Prof.* Sir John Cyril, Kt., CBE, QC, FBA

Smith, Sir John Hamilton-Spencer-, Bt. (1804)

Smith, Sir John Jonah Walker-, Bt. (1960)

Smith, Sir John Kenneth Newson-, Bt. (1944)

Smith, Sir John Lindsay Eric., Kt., CH, CBE

†Smith, Sir John Rathbone Vassar-, Bt. (1917)

Smith, Sir Joseph William Grenville, Kt., MD, FRCP

Smith, Sir Leslie Edward George, Kt.

Smith, *Rt. Hon.* Sir Murray Stuart-, Kt.

Smith, Sir Raymond Horace, KBE

Smith, Sir Robert Courtney, Kt., CBE

Smith, Sir Robert Hill, Bt. (1945)

Smith, *Prof.* Sir Roland, Kt.

Smith, *Air Marshal* Sir Roy David Austen-, KBE, CB, CVO, DFC

Smith, Sir (Thomas) Gilbert, Bt. (1897)

Smith, *Adm.* Sir Victor Alfred Trumper, KBE, CB, DSC

†Smith, Sir (William) Antony (John) Reardon-, Bt. (1920)

Smith, Sir (William) Richard Prince-, Bt. (1911)

Smithers, Sir Peter Henry Berry Otway, Kt., VRD, D.Phil.

Smyth, Sir Thomas Weyland Bowyer-, Bt. (1661)

Smyth, Sir Timothy John, Bt. (1955)

Snelling, Sir Arthur Wendell, KCMG, KCVO

Soame, Sir Charles John Buckworth-Herne-, Bt. (1697)

Sobers, Sir Garfield St Auburn, Kt.

Solomon, Sir David Arnold, Kt., MBE

Solomon, Sir Harry, Kt.

Solti, Sir Georg, KBE

Somare, *Rt. Hon.* Sir Michael Thomas, GCMG, CH

Somers, *Rt. Hon.* Sir Edward Jonathan, Kt.

Somerset, Sir Henry Beaufort, Kt., CBE

Somerville, *Brig.* Sir John Nicholas, Kt., CBE

Somerville, Sir Quentin Charles Somerville Agnew-, Bt. (1957)

Sopwith, Sir Charles Ronald, Kt.

Soutar, *Air Marshal* Sir Charles John Williamson, KBE

South, Sir Arthur, Kt.

Southby, Sir John Richard Bilbe, Bt. (1937)

Southern, Sir Richard William, Kt., FBA

Southern, Sir Robert, Kt., CBE

Southey, Sir Robert John, Kt., CMG

Southgate, Sir Colin Grieve, Kt.

Southgate, Sir William David, Kt.

Southward, Sir Leonard Bingley, Kt., OBE

Southward, Sir Ralph, KCVO, FRCP

Southwood, *Prof.* Sir (Thomas) Richard (Edmund), Kt., FRS

Southworth, Sir Frederick, Kt., QC

Souyave, *Hon.* Sir (Louis) Georges, Kt.

Sowrey, *Air Marshal* Sir Frederick Beresford, KCB, CBE, AFC

Sparkes, Sir Robert Lyndley, Kt.

Sparrow, Sir John, Kt.

Spearman, Sir Alexander Young Richard Mainwaring, Bt. (1840)

Spedding, *Prof.* Sir Colin Raymond William, Kt., CBE

Speed, Sir (Herbert) Keith, Kt., RD, MP

Speed, Sir Robert William Arney, Kt., CB, QC

Speelman, Sir Cornelis Jacob, Bt. (1686)

Speight, *Hon.* Sir Graham Davies, Kt.

Speir, Sir Rupert Malise, Kt.

Spencer, Sir Derek Harold, Kt., QC, MP

Spicer, Sir James Wilton, Kt., MP

Spicer, Sir Nicholas Adrian Albert, Bt., MB (1906)

Spiers, Sir Donald Maurice, Kt., CB, TD

Spooner, Sir James Douglas, Kt.

Spotswood, *Marshal of the Royal Air Force* Sir Denis Frank, GCB, CBE, DSO, DFC

Spratt, *Col.* Sir Greville Douglas, GBE, TD

Spring, Sir Dryden Thomas, Kt.

Spry, *Hon.* Sir John Farley, Kt.

Stabb, *Hon.* Sir William Walter, Kt., QC

Stainton, Sir (John) Ross, Kt., CBE

Stakis, Sir Reo Argiros, Kt.

Stallard, Sir Peter Hyla Gawne, KCMG, CVO, MBE

Stamer, Sir (Lovelace) Anthony, Bt. (1809)

Stanbridge, *Air Vice-Marshal* Sir Brian Gerald Tivy, KCVO, CBE, AFC

Stanier, Sir Beville Douglas, Bt. (1917)

Stanier, *Field Marshal* Sir John Wilfred, GCB, MBE

Stanley, *Rt. Hon.* Sir John Paul, Kt., MP

†Staples, Sir Thomas, Bt. (I. 1628)

Stark, Sir Andrew Alexander Steel, KCMG, CVO

Starke, *Hon.* Sir John Erskine, Kt.

Starkey, Sir John Philip, Bt. (1935)

Starrit, Sir James, KCVO

Statham, Sir Norman, KCMG, CVO

Staughton, *Rt. Hon.* Sir Christopher Stephen Thomas Jonathan Thayer, Kt.

Staveley, Sir John Malfroy, KBE, MC

Staveley, *Admiral of the Fleet* Sir William Doveton Minet, GCB

Stear, *Air Chief Marshal* Sir Michael James Douglas, KCB, CBE

Steel, Sir David Edward Charles, Kt., DSO, MC, TD

Steel, *Rt. Hon.* Sir David Martin Scott, KBE, MP

Steel, *Maj.* Sir (Fiennes) Michael Strang, Bt. (1938)

Steele, Sir (Philip John) Rupert, Kt.

Steere, Sir Ernest Henry Lee-, KBE

Stenhouse, Sir Nicol, Kt.

Stening, *Col.* Sir George Grafton Lees, Kt., ED

Stephen, *Rt. Hon.* Sir Ninian Martin, KG, GCMG, GCVO, KBE

Stephens, Sir Robert Graham, Kt.

Stephenson, Sir Henry Upton, Bt. (1936)

Stephenson, *Rt. Hon.* Sir John
Frederick Eustace, Kt.
Sternberg, Sir Sigmund, Kt.
Stevens, Sir Laurence Houghton, Kt.,
CBE
Stevenson, *Vice-Adm.* Sir (Hugh)
David, KBE
Stevenson, Sir Simpson, Kt.
Stewart, Sir Alan, KBE
Stewart, Sir Alan d'Arcy, Bt. (I. 1623)
Stewart, Sir David James
Henderson-, Bt. (1957)
Stewart, Sir David John Christopher,
Bt. (1803)
Stewart, Sir Edward Jackson, Kt.
Stewart, *Prof.* Sir Frederick Henry,
Kt., Ph.D., FRS, FRSE
Stewart, Sir Houston Mark Shaw-,
Bt., MC, TD (s. 1667)
Stewart, Sir James Douglas, Kt.
Stewart, Sir James Moray, KCB
Stewart, Sir (John) Simon (Watson),
Bt. (1920)
Stewart, Sir Robertson Huntly, Kt.,
CBE
Stewart, Sir Robin Alastair, Bt. (1960)
Stewart, Sir Ronald Compton, Bt.
(1937)
Stewart, Prof. Sir William Duncan
Paterson, Kt., FRS, FRSE
Stibbon, *Gen.* Sir John James, KCB, OBE
Stirling, Sir Alexander John Dickson,
KBE, CMG
Stirling, Sir Angus Duncan Aeneas,
Kt.
Stockdale, Sir Arthur Noel, Kt.
Stockdale, Sir Thomas Minshull, Bt.
(1960)
Stocker, *Rt. Hon.* Sir John Dexter, Kt.,
MC, TD
Stoddart, *Wg Cdr.* Sir Kenneth
Maxwell, KCVO, AE
Stoker, *Prof.* Sir Michael George
Parke, Kt., CBE, FRCP, FRS, FRSE
Stokes, Sir John Heydon Romaine,
Kt.
Stone, Sir Alexander, Kt., OBE
Stones, Sir William Frederick, Kt.,
OBE
Stonhouse, Sir Philip Allan, Bt. (1628)
Stonor, *Air Marshal* Sir Thomas
Henry, KCB
Storey, *Hon.* Sir Richard, Bt. (1960)
Stormonth Darling, Sir James
Carlisle, Kt., CBE, MC, TD
Stott, Sir Adrian George Ellingham,
Bt. (1920)
Stow, Sir Christopher Philipson-, Bt.,
DFC (1907)
Stow, Sir John Montague, GCMG,
KCVO
Stowe, Sir Kenneth Ronald, GCB, CVO
Stracey, Sir John Simon, Bt. (1818)
Strachey, Sir Charles, Bt. (1801)
Straker, Sir Michael Ian Bowstead,
Kt., CBE
Strawson, *Prof.* Sir Peter Frederick,
Kt., FBA
Street, *Hon.* Sir Laurence Whistler,
KCMG

Streeton, Sir Terence George, KBE,
CMG
Stringer, Sir Donald Edgar, Kt., CBE
Strong, Sir Roy Colin, Kt., Ph.D., FSA
Stronge, Sir James Anselan Maxwell,
Bt. (1803)
Stroud, *Prof.* Sir (Charles) Eric, Kt.,
FRCP
Strutt, Sir Nigel Edward, Kt., TD
Stuart, Sir James Keith, Kt.
Stuart, Sir Kenneth Lamonte, Kt.
†Stuart, Sir Phillip Luttrell, Bt. (1660)
Stubblefield, Sir (Cyril) James, Kt.,
D.SC., FRS
Stubbs, Sir James Wilfrid, KCVO, TD
Stubbs, Sir William Hamilton, Kt.,
Ph.D.
Stucley, *Lt.* Sir Hugh George
Coplestone Bampfylde, Bt. (1859)
Studd, Sir Edward Fairfax, Bt. (1929)
Studd, Sir Peter Malden, GBE, KCVO
Studholme, Sir Henry William, Bt.
(1956)
Stuttaford, Sir William Royden, Kt.,
CBE
Style, *Lt.-Cdr.* Sir Godfrey William,
Kt., CBE, DSC, RN
†Style, Sir William Frederick, Bt.
(1627)
Suffield, Sir (Henry John) Lester, Kt.
Sugden, Sir Arthur, Kt.
Sullivan, Sir Desmond John, Kt.
Sullivan, Sir Richard Arthur, Bt.
(1804)
Summerfield, *Hon.* Sir John
Crampton, Kt., CBE
Sutherland, *Prof.* Sir James
Runcieman, Kt., FBA
Sutherland, Sir John Brewer, Bt.
(1921)
Sutherland, Sir Maurice, Kt.
Sutherland, *Prof.* Sir Stewart Ross, Kt.,
FBA
Sutherland, Sir William George
MacKenzie, Kt.
Suttie, Sir (George) Philip Grant-, Bt.
(s. 1702)
Sutton, Sir Frederick Walter, Kt., OBE
Sutton, *Air Marshal* Sir John Matthias
Dobson, KCB
Sutton, Sir Richard Lexington, Bt.
(1772)
Swaffield, Sir James Chesebrough,
Kt., CBE, RD
Swaine, Sir John Joseph, Kt., CBE
Swallow, Sir William, Kt.
Swan, Sir Conrad Marshall John
Fisher, KCVO, Ph.D.
Swan, Sir John William David, KBE
Swann, Sir Michael Christopher, Bt.,
TD (1906)
Swanwick, Sir Graham Russell, Kt.,
MBE
Swartz, *Hon.* Sir Reginald William
Colin, KBE, ED
Sweetnam, Sir (David) Rodney,
KCVO, CBE, FRCS
Swinburn, *Lt.-Gen.* Sir Richard Hull,
KCB

Swinson, Sir John Henry Alan, Kt.,
OBE
Swinton, *Maj.-Gen.* Sir John, KCVO,
OBE
Swire, Sir Adrian Christopher, Kt.
Swire, Sir John Anthony, Kt., CBE
Swiss, Sir Rodney Geoffrey, Kt., OBE
Swynnerton, Sir Roger John Massy,
Kt., CMG, OBE, MC
Sykes, Sir Francis John Badcock, Bt.
(1781)
Sykes, Sir John Charles Anthony le
Gallais, Bt. (1921)
Sykes, *Prof.* Sir (Malcolm) Keith, Kt.
Sykes, Sir Richard, Kt.
Sykes, Sir Tatton Christopher Mark,
Bt. (1783)
Symington, *Prof.* Sir Thomas, Kt., MD,
FRSE
Symons, *Vice-Adm.* Sir Patrick
Jeremy, KBE
Synge, Sir Robert Carson, Bt. (1801)
Tait, *Adm.* Sir (Allan) Gordon, KCB,
DSC
Tait, Sir James Sharp, Kt., D.SC., LL D.,
Ph.D.
Tait, Sir Peter, KBE
Talbot, *Vice-Adm.* Sir (Arthur Allison)
FitzRoy, KBE, CB, DSO
Talbot, *Hon.* Sir Hilary Gwynne, Kt.
Talboys, *Rt. Hon.* Sir Brian Edward,
CH, KCB
Tancred, Sir Henry Lawson-, Bt.
(1662)
Tangaroa, *Hon.* Sir Tangoroa, Kt., MBE
Tange, Sir Arthur Harold, Kt., CBE
Tapsell, Sir Peter Hannay Bailey, Kt.,
MP
†Tate, Sir (Henry) Saxon, Bt. (1898)
Taukala, Sir David Dawea, Kt., MBE
Tavaiqia, *Ratu* Sir Josaia, KBE
Tavare, Sir John, Kt., CBE
Taylor, *Lt.-Gen.* Sir Allan Macnab,
KBE, MC
Taylor, Sir (Arthur) Godfrey, Kt.
Taylor, Sir Cyril Julian Hebden, Kt.
Taylor, Sir Edward Macmillan
(Teddy), Kt., MP
Taylor, Sir John Lang, KCMG
Taylor, Sir Nicholas Richard Stuart,
Bt. (1917)
Taylor, *Prof.* Sir William, Kt., CBE
Teagle, *Vice-Adm.* Sir Somerford
Francis, KBE
Tebbit, Sir Donald Claude, GCMG
Te Heuheu, Sir Hepi Hoani, KBE
Telford, Sir Robert, Kt., CBE, FEng.
Temple, Sir Ernest Sanderson, Kt.,
MBE, QC
Temple, Sir Rawden John Afamado,
Kt., CBE, QC
Temple, *Maj.* Sir Richard Anthony
Purbeck, Bt., MC (1876)
Templeton, Sir John Marks, Kt.
Tenison, Sir Richard Hanbury-, KCVO
Tennant, *Capt.* Sir Iain Mark, KT
Tennant, Sir Anthony John, Kt.
Tennant, Sir Peter Frank Dalrymple,
Kt., CMG, OBE

Teo, Sir Fiatau Penitala, GCMG, GCVO, ISO, MBE

Terry, Sir Michael Edward Stanley Imbert-, Bt. (1917)

Terry, *Air Chief Marshal* Sir Peter David George, GCB, AFC

Tetley, Sir Herbert, KBE, CB

Tett, Sir Hugh Charles, Kt.

Thatcher, Sir Denis, Bt., MBE, TD (1990)

Thesiger, Sir Wilfred Patrick, KBE, DSO

Thomas, Sir Derek Morison David, KCMG

Thomas, Sir Frederick William, Kt.

Thomas, Sir (Godfrey) Michael (David), Bt. (1694)

Thomas, Sir Jeremy Cashel, KCMG

Thomas, Sir (John) Alan, Kt.

Thomas, Sir John Maldwyn, Kt.

Thomas, *Prof.* Sir John Meurig, Kt., FRS

Thomas, Sir Keith Vivian, Kt.

Thomas, Sir Robert Evan, Kt.

Thomas, *Hon.* Sir Swinton Barclay, Kt.

Thomas, Sir William James Cooper, Bt., TD (1919)

Thomas, Sir (William) Michael (Marsh), Bt. (1918)

Thomas, *Adm.* Sir (William) Richard Scott, KCB, KCVO, OBE

Thompson, Sir Christopher Peile, Bt. (1890)

Thompson, Sir Donald, Kt., MP

Thompson, Sir Gilbert Williamson, Kt., OBE

Thompson, *Surgeon Vice-Adm.* Sir Godfrey James Milton-, KBE

Thompson, *Vice-Adm.* Sir Hugh Leslie Owen, FEng.

Thompson, Sir (Humphrey) Simon Meysey-, Bt. (1874)

Thompson, *Prof.* Sir Michael Warwick, Kt., D.SC

Thompson, Sir Paul Anthony, Bt. (1963)

Thompson, Sir Peter Anthony, Kt.

Thompson, Sir Richard Hilton Marler, Bt. (1963)

Thompson, Sir (Thomas) Lionel Tennyson, Bt. (1806)

Thomson, Sir Adam, Kt., CBE

Thomson, Sir Evan Rees Whitaker, Kt.

Thomson, Sir (Frederick Douglas) David, Bt. (1929)

Thomson, Sir John, KBE, TD

Thomson, Sir John Adam, GCMG

Thomson, Sir John (Ian) Sutherland, KBE, CMG

Thomson, Sir Mark Wilfrid Home, Bt. (1925)

Thomson, Sir Thomas James, Kt., CBE, FRCP

Thorn, Sir John Samuel, Kt., OBE

Thorne, *Maj.-Gen.* Sir David Calthrop, KBE, CVO

Thorne, Sir Neil Gordon, Kt., OBE, TD

Thorne, Sir Peter Francis, KCVO, CBE

Thornton, Sir (George) Malcolm, Kt., MP

Thornton, *Lt.-Gen.* Sir Leonard Whitmore, KCB, CBE

Thornton, Sir Peter Eustace, KCB

Thorold, Sir Anthony Henry, Bt., OBE, DSC (1642)

Thorpe, *Hon.* Sir Mathew Alexander, Kt.

Thouron, Sir John Rupert Hunt, KBE

Thwaites, Sir Bryan, Kt., PH.D.

Thwin, Sir U, Kt.

Tibbits, *Capt.* Sir David Stanley, Kt., DSC

Tickell, Sir Crispin Charles Cervantes, GCMG, KCVO

Tidbury, Sir Charles Henderson, Kt.

Tikaram, Sir Moti, KBE

Tims, Sir Michael David, KCVO

Tindle, Sir Ray Stanley, Kt., CBE

Tippet, *Vice-Adm.* Sir Anthony Sanders, KCB

Tippett, Sir Michael Kemp, Kt., OM, CH, CBE

†Tipping, Sir David Gwynne Evans-, Bt. (1913)

Tirvengadum, Sir Harry Krishnan, Kt.

Titman, Sir John Edward Powis, KCVO

Tod, *Air Marshal* Sir John Hunter Hunter-, KBE, CB

Todd, *Prof.* Sir David, Kt., CBE

Todd, Sir Ian Pelham, KBE, FRCS

Todd, *Hon.* Sir (Reginald Stephen) Garfield, Kt.

Tollemache, Sir Lyonel Humphry John, Bt. (1793)

Tololo, Sir Alkan, KBE

Tomkins, Sir Alfred George, Kt., CBE

Tomkins, Sir Edward Emile, GCMG, CVO

Tomkys, Sir (William) Roger, KCMG

Tomlinson, *Prof.* Sir Bernard Evans, Kt., OBE

Tooley, Sir John, Kt.

Tooth, Sir (Hugh) John Lucas-, Bt. (1920)

ToRobert, Sir Henry Thomas, KBE

Tory, Sir Geofroy William, KCMG

Touche, Sir Anthony George, Bt. (1920)

Touche, Sir Rodney Gordon, Bt. (1962)

Tovey, Sir Brian John Maynard, KCMG

ToVue, Sir Ronald, Kt., OBE

Towneley, Sir Simon Peter Edmund Cosmo William, KCVO

Townsend, *Rear-Adm.* Sir Leslie William, KCVO, CBE

Townsing, Sir Kenneth Joseph, Kt., CMG

Traill, Sir Alan Towers, GBE

Trant, *Gen.* Sir Richard Brooking, KCB

Travers, Sir Thomas à'Beckett, Kt.

Treacher, *Adm.* Sir John Devereux, KCB

Trehane, Sir (Walter) Richard, Kt.

Trelawny, Sir John Barry Salusbury-, Bt. (1628)

Trench, Sir Peter Edward, Kt., CBE, TD

Trescowthick, Sir Donald Henry, KBE

Trethowan, *Prof.* Sir William Henry, Kt., CBE, FRCP

Trevelyan, Sir George Lowthian, Bt. (1874)

Trevelyan, Sir Norman Irving, Bt. (1662)

Trewby, *Vice-Adm.* Sir (George Francis) Allan, KCB, FEng.

Trezise, Sir Kenneth Bruce, Kt., OBE

Trippier, Sir David Austin, Kt., RD

Tritton, Sir Anthony John Ernest, Bt. (1905)

†Trollope, Sir Anthony Simon, Bt. (1642)

Trotter, Sir Ronald Ramsay, Kt.

Troubridge, Sir Thomas Richard, Bt. (1799)

Troup, *Vice-Adm.* Sir (John) Anthony (Rose), KCB, DSC

Trowbridge, *Rear-Adm.* Sir Richard John, KCVO

Truscott, Sir George James Irving, Bt. (1909)

Tuck, Sir Bruce Adolph Reginald, Bt. (1910)

Tucker, *Hon.* Sir Richard Howard, Kt.

Tuckey, *Hon.* Sir Simon Lane, Kt.

Tuita, Sir Mariano Kelesimalefo, Kt., OBE

Tuite, Sir Christopher Hugh, Bt., PH.D. (1622)

Tuivaga, Sir Timoci Uluiburotu, Kt.

Tuke, Sir Anthony Favill, Kt.

Tupper, Sir Charles Hibbert, Bt. (1888)

Turbott, Sir Ian Graham, Kt., CMG, CVO

Turing, Sir John Dermot, Bt. (s. 1638)

Turnberg, *Prof.* Sir Leslie Arnold, Kt., MD, FRCP

Turnbull, Sir Richard Gordon, GCMG

Turner, Sir Colin William Carstairs, Kt., CBE, DFC

Turner, *Hon.* Sir Michael John, Kt.

Turnquest, Sir Orville Alton, GCMG, QC

Tuti, *Revd* Dudley, KBE

Tuzo, *Gen.* Sir Harry Craufurd, GCB, OBE, MC

Tweedie, *Prof.* Sir David Philip, Kt.

Tyree, Sir (Alfred) William, Kt., OBE

Tyrwhitt, Sir Reginald Thomas Newman, Bt. (1919)

Udoma, *Hon.* Sir (Egbert) Udo, Kt.

Unsworth, *Hon.* Sir Edgar Ignatius Godfrey, Kt., CMG

Unwin, Sir (James) Brian, KCB

Ure, Sir John Burns, KCMG, LVO

Urquhart, Sir Brian Edward, KCMG, MBE

Urwick, Sir Alan Bedford, KCVO, CMG

Usher, Sir Leonard Gray, KBE

†Usher, Sir (William) John Tevenar, Bt. (1899)

Ustinov, Sir Peter Alexander, Kt., CBE

Utting, Sir William Benjamin, Kt., CB

Vallance, Sir Iain David Thomas, Kt.

Vallat, Sir Francis Aimé, GBE, KCMG, QC

Vallings, *Vice-Adm.* Sir George Montague Francis, KCB

Vanderfelt, Sir Robin Victor, KBE

van der Post, Sir Laurens Jan, Kt., CBE

Vane, Sir John Robert, Kt., D.phil., D.SC., FRS

Vanneck, *Air Cdre* Hon. Sir Peter Beckford Rutgers, GBE, CB, AFC

van Straubenzee, Sir William Radcliffe, Kt., MBE

Vasquez, Sir Alfred Joseph, Kt., CBE, QC

Vaughan, Sir Gerard Folliott, Kt., MP, FRCP

Vavasour, *Cdr.* Sir Geoffrey William, Bt., DSC, RN (1828)

Veale, Sir Alan John Ralph, Kt., FEng.

Verco, Sir Walter John George, KCVO

†Verney, Sir John Sebastian, Bt. (1946)

Verney, *Hon.* Sir Lawrence John, Kt., TD

Verney, Sir Ralph Bruce, Bt., KBE (1818)

Vernon, Sir James, Kt., CBE

Vernon, Sir Nigel John Douglas, Bt. (1914)

Vernon, Sir (William) Michael, Kt.

Vesey, Sir (Nathaniel) Henry (Peniston), Kt., CBE

Vestey, Sir (John) Derek, Bt. (1921)

Vial, Sir Kenneth Harold, Kt., CBE

Vick, Sir (Francis) Arthur, Kt., OBE, ph.D.

Vickers, *Lt.-Gen.* Sir Richard Maurice Hilton, KCB, MVO, OBE

Victoria, Sir (Joseph Aloysius) Donatus, Kt., CBE

Vincent, *Field Marshal* Sir Richard Frederick, GBE, KCB, DSO

Vincent, Sir William Percy Maxwell, Bt. (1936)

Vinelott, *Hon.* Sir John Evelyn, Kt.

Vines, Sir William Joshua, Kt., CMG

Vyvyan, Sir John Stanley, Bt. (1645)

Waddell, Sir Alexander Nicol Anton, KCMG, DSC

Waddell, Sir James Henderson, Kt., CB

Wade, *Prof.* Sir Henry William Rawson, Kt., QC, FBA

Wade, *Air Chief Marshal* Sir Ruthven Lowry, KCB, DFC

Waite, *Rt. Hon.* Sir John Douglas, Kt.

Wake, Sir Hereward, Bt., MC (1621)

Wakefield, Sir (Edward) Humphry (Tyrell), Bt. (1962)

Wakefield, Sir Norman Edward, Kt.

Wakefield, Sir Peter George Arthur, KBE, CMG

Wakeford, *Air Marshal* Sir Richard Gordon, KCB, OBE, MVO, AFC

Wakeley, Sir John Cecil Nicholson, Bt., FRCS (1952)

†Wakeman, Sir Edward Offley Bertram, Bt. (1828)

Walford, Sir Christopher Rupert, Kt.

Walker, *Revd* Alan Edgar, Kt., OBE

Walker, *Gen.* Sir Antony Kenneth Frederick, KCB

Walker, Sir Baldwin Patrick, Bt. (1856)

Walker, Sir (Charles) Michael, GCMG

Walker, Sir Colin John Shedlock, Kt., OBE

Walker, Sir David Alan, Kt.

Walker, Sir Gervas George, Kt.

Walker, *Rt. Hon.* Sir Harold, Kt., MP

Walker, Sir Harold Berners, KCMG

Walker, *Maj.* Sir Hugh Ronald, Bt. (1906)

Walker, Sir James Graham, Kt., MBE

Walker, Sir James Heron, Bt. (1868)

Walker, *Air Marshal* Sir John Robert, KCB, CBE, AFC

Walker, *Lt.-Gen.* Sir Michael John Dawson, KCB, CBE

Walker, Sir Michael Leolin Forestier-, Bt. (1835)

Walker, Sir Patrick Jeremy, KCB

Walker, *Hon.* Sir Robert, Kt.

Walker, *Gen.* Sir Walter Colyear, KCB, CBE, DSO

Wall, *Hon.* Sir Nicholas Peter Rathbone, Kt.

Wall, Sir Patrick Henry Bligh, Kt., MC, VRD

Wall, Sir Robert William, Kt., OBE

Wallace, Sir Ian James, Kt., CBE

Waller, *Hon.* Sir (George) Mark, Kt.

Waller, *Rt. Hon.* Sir George Stanley, Kt., OBE

Waller, Sir (John) Keith, Kt., CBE

Waller, Sir Robert William, Bt. (I. 1780)

Walley, Sir John, KBE, CB

Wallis, Sir Peter Gordon, KCVO

Wallis, Sir Timothy William, Kt.

Walmsley, *Vice-Adm.* Sir Robert, KCB

Walsh, Sir Alan, Kt., D.SC., FRS

Walsh, *Prof.* Sir John Patrick, KBE

†Walsham, Sir Timothy John, Bt. (1831)

Walter, Sir Harold Edward, Kt.

Walters, *Prof.* Sir Alan Arthur, Kt.

Walters, Sir Dennis Murray, Kt., MBE

Walters, Sir Frederick Donald, Kt.

Walters, Sir Peter Ingram, Kt.

Walters, Sir Roger Talbot, KBE, FRIBA

Walton, Sir John Robert, Kt.

Wan, Sir Wamp, Kt., MBE

Wanstall, *Hon.* Sir Charles Gray, Kt.

Ward, *Rt. Hon.* Sir Alan Hylton, Kt.

Ward, Sir Joseph James Laffey, Bt. (1911)

Ward, *Maj.-Gen.* Sir Philip John Newling, KCVO, CBE

Ward, Sir Timothy James, Kt.

Wardale, Sir Geoffrey Charles, KCB

Wardlaw, Sir Henry (John), Bt. (s. 1631)

Wardle, Sir Thomas Edward Jewell, Kt.

Waring, Sir (Alfred) Holburt, Bt. (1935)

†Warmington, Sir Marshall Denham Malcolm, Bt. (1908)

Warner, Sir (Edward Courtenay) Henry, Bt. (1910)

Warner, Sir Edward Redston, KCMG, OBE

Warner, Sir Frederick Archibald, GCVO, KCMG

Warner, *Prof.* Sir Frederick Edward, Kt., FRS, FEng.

Warner, Sir Gerald Chierici, KCMG

Warner, *Hon.* Sir Jean-Pierre Frank Eugene, Kt.

Warnock, Sir Geoffrey James, Kt.

Warren, Sir Brian Charles Pennefather, Bt. (1784)

Warren, Sir (Frederick) Miles, KBE

Warren, Sir (Harold) Brian (Seymour), Kt.

Warren, Sir Kenneth Robin, Kt.

Wass, Sir Douglas William Gretton, GCB

Waterhouse, *Hon.* Sir Ronald Gough, Kt.

Waterlow, Sir Christopher Rupert, Bt. (1873)

Waterlow, Sir (James) Gerard, Bt. (1930)

Waters, *Gen.* Sir (Charles) John, GCB, CBE

Waters, Sir Thomas Neil Morris, Kt.

Wates, Sir Christopher Stephen, Kt.

Watkins, *Rt. Hon.* Sir Tasker, VC, GBE

Watson, Sir Bruce Dunstan, Kt.

Watson, Sir Duncan Amos, Kt., CBE

Watson, Sir (James) Andrew, Bt. (1866)

Watson, Sir John Forbes Inglefield-, Bt. (1895)

Watson, Sir Michael Milne-, Bt., CBE (1937)

Watson, Sir (Noel) Duncan, KCMG

Watson, *Vice-Adm.* Sir Philip Alexander, KBE, MVO

Watt, *Surgeon Vice-Adm.* Sir James, KBE, FRCS

Watt, Sir James Harvie-, Bt. (1945)

Watts, Sir Arthur Desmond, KCMG

Watts, *Lt.-Gen.* Sir John Peter Barry Condliffe, KBE, CB, MC

Wauchope, Sir Roger (Hamilton) Don-, Bt. (s. 1667)

Way, Sir Richard George Kitchener, KCB, CBE

Weatherall, *Prof.* Sir David John, Kt., FRS

Weatherall, *Vice-Adm.* Sir James Lamb, KBE

Weatherstone, Sir Dennis, KBE

Weaver, Sir Tobias Rushton, Kt., CB

Webb, Sir Thomas Langley, Kt.

Webber, Sir Andrew Lloyd, Kt.

Webster, *Very Revd* Alan Brunskill, KCVO

Webster, *Vice-Adm.* Sir John Morrison, KCB

Webster, *Hon.* Sir Peter Edlin, Kt.

Wedderburn, Sir Andrew John Alexander Ogilvy-, Bt. (1803)

Wedgwood, Sir (Hugo) Martin, Bt. (1942)

Weekes, Sir Everton DeCourcey, KCMG, OBE

Weinberg, Sir Mark Aubrey, Kt.

Weir, Sir Michael Scott, KCMG

Weir, Sir Roderick Bignell, Kt.

Welby, Sir (Richard) Bruno Gregory, Bt. (1801)

Welch, Sir John Reader, Bt. (1957)

Weldon, Sir Anthony William, Bt. (I. 1723)

Wellings, Sir Jack Alfred, Kt., CBE

Wells, Sir Charles Maltby, Bt., TD (1944)

Wells, Sir John Julius, Kt.

Westbrook, Sir Neil Gowanloch, Kt., CBE

Westerman, Sir (Wilfred) Alan, Kt., CBE

Weston, Sir Michael Charles Swift, KCMG, CVO

Weston, Sir (Philip) John, KCMG

Whalen, Sir Geoffrey Henry, Kt., CBE

Wheeler, Sir Frederick Henry, Kt., CBE

Wheeler, Sir Harry Anthony, Kt., OBE

Wheeler, *Air Chief Marshal* Sir (Henry) Neil (George), GCB, CBE, DSO, DFC, AFC

Wheeler, *Rt. Hon.* Sir John Daniel, Kt., MP

Wheeler, Sir John Hieron, Bt. (1920)

Wheeler, *Hon.* Sir Kenneth Henry, Kt.

Wheeler, *Lt.-Gen.* Sir Roger Neil, KCB, CBE

Wheler, Sir Edward Woodford, Bt. (1660)

Whent, Sir Gerald Arthur, Kt., CBE

Whishaw, Sir Charles Percival Law, Kt.

Whitaker, *Maj.* Sir James Herbert Ingham, Bt. (1936)

White, Sir Christopher Robert Meadows, Bt. (1937)

White, *Hon.* Sir Christopher Stuart Stuart-, Kt.

White, Sir David Harry, Kt.

White, Sir George Stanley James, Bt. (1904)

White, *Wg Cdr.* Sir Henry Arthur Dalrymple-, Bt., DFC (1926)

White, *Adm.* Sir Hugo Moresby, GCB, CBE

White, *Hon.* Sir John Charles, Kt., MBE

White, Sir John Woolmer, Bt. (1922)

White, Sir Lynton Stuart, Kt., MBE, TD

White, *Adm.* Sir Peter, GBE

White, Sir Thomas Astley Woollaston, Bt. (1802)

Whitehead, Sir John Stainton, GCMG, CVO

Whitehead, Sir Rowland John Rathbone, Bt. (1889)

Whiteley, Sir Hugo Baldwin Huntington-, Bt. (1918)

Whiteley, *Gen.* Sir Peter John Frederick, GCB, OBE, RM

Whitfield, Sir William, Kt., CBE

Whitford, *Hon.* Sir John Norman Keates, Kt.

Whitley, *Air Marshal* Sir John René, KBE, CB, DSO, AFC

Whitmore, Sir Clive Anthony, GCB, CVO

Whitmore, Sir John Henry Douglas, Bt. (1954)

Whittle, *Air Cdre* Sir Frank, OM, KBE, CB, FRS, FEng.

Whittome, Sir (Leslie) Alan, Kt.

Wickerson, Sir John Michael, Kt.

Wicks, Sir James Albert, Kt.

Wicks, Sir Nigel Leonard, KCB, CVO, CBE

Wigan, Sir Alan Lewis, Bt. (1898)

Wiggin, Sir Alfred William (Jerry), Kt., TD, MP

†Wiggin, Sir Charles Rupert John, Bt. (1892)

Wigram, *Revd Canon* Sir Clifford Woolmore, Bt. (1805)

Wilbraham, Sir Richard Baker, Bt. (1776)

Wilford, Sir (Kenneth) Michael, GCMG

Wilkes, *Gen.* Sir Michael John, KCB, CBE

Wilkins, Sir Graham John, Kt.

Wilkinson, Sir (David) Graham (Brook) Bt. (1941)

Wilkinson, *Prof.* Sir Denys Haigh, Kt., FRS

Wilkinson, *Prof.* Sir Geoffrey, Kt., FRS

Wilkinson, Sir Peter Allix, KCMG, DSO, OBE

Wilkinson, Sir Philip William, Kt.

Wilkinson, Sir William Henry Nairn, Kt.

Willatt, Sir (Robert) Hugh, Kt.

Willcocks, Sir David Valentine, Kt., CBE, MC

Williams, Sir Alastair Edgcumbe James Dudley-, Bt. (1964)

Williams, Sir Alwyn, Kt., PH.D., FRS

Williams, Sir Arthur Dennis Pitt, Kt.

Williams, Sir (Arthur) Gareth Ludovic Emrys Rhys, Bt. (1918)

Williams, *Prof.* Sir Bruce Rodda, KBE

Williams, *Adm.* Sir David, GCB

Williams, *Prof.* Sir David Glyndwr Tudor, Kt.

Williams, Sir David Innes, Kt.

Williams, *Hon.* Sir Denys Ambrose, KCMG

Williams, Sir Donald Mark, Bt. (1866)

Williams, *Prof.* Sir (Edward) Dillwyn, Kt., FRCP

Williams, *Hon.* Sir Edward Stratten, KCMG, KBE

Williams, *Prof.* Sir Glanmor, Kt., CBE, FBA

Williams, Sir Henry Sydney, Kt., OBE

Williams, Sir John Robert, KCMG

Williams, Sir (Lawrence) Hugh, Bt. (1798)

Williams, Sir Leonard, KBE, CB

Williams, Sir Osmond, Bt., MC (1909)

Williams, Sir Peter Watkin, Kt.

Williams, *Prof.* Sir Robert Evan Owen, Kt., MD, FRCP

Williams, Sir (Robert) Philip Nathaniel, Bt. (1915)

Williams, Sir Robin Philip, Bt. (1953)

Williams, Sir (William) Maxwell (Harries), Kt.

Williamson, *Marshal of the Royal Air Force* Sir Keith Alec, GCB, AFC

Williamson, Sir (Nicholas Frederick) Hedworth, Bt. (1642)

Willink, Sir Charles William, Bt. (1957)

Willis, *Hon.* Sir Eric Archibald, KBE, CMG

Willis, *Vice-Adm.* Sir (Guido) James, KBE

Willis, *Air Chief Marshal* Sir John Frederick, KCB, CBE

Willison, *Lt.-Gen.* Sir David John, KCB, OBE, MC

Willison, Sir John Alexander, Kt., OBE

Wills, Sir David Seton, Bt. (1904)

Wills, Sir (Hugh) David Hamilton, Kt., CBE, TD

Wills, Sir John Vernon, Bt., TD (1923)

Wilmot, Sir Henry Robert, Bt. (1759)

Wilmot, *Cdr.* Sir John Assheton Eardley-, Bt., MVO, DSC, RN (1821)

Wilsey, *Gen.* Sir John Finlay Willasey, KCB, CBE

Wilson, Sir Alan Herries, Kt., FRS

Wilson, *Lt.-Gen.* Sir (Alexander) James, KBE, MC

Wilson, Sir Anthony, Kt.

Wilson, *Vice-Adm.* Sir Barry Nigel, KCB

Wilson, *Lt.-Col.* Sir Blair Aubyn Stewart-, KCVO

Wilson, Sir Charles Haynes, Kt.

Wilson, Sir David, Bt. (1920)

Wilson, Sir David Mackenzie, Kt.

Wilson, Sir Geoffrey Masterman, KCB, CMG

Wilson, Sir James William Douglas, Bt. (1906)

Wilson, Sir John Foster, Kt., CBE

Wilson, Sir John Gardiner, Kt., CBE

Wilson, *Brig.* Sir Mathew John Anthony, Bt., OBE, MC (1874)

Wilson, *Hon.* Sir Nicholas Allan Roy, Kt.

Wilson, Sir Patrick Michael Ernest David McNair-, Kt., MP

Wilson, Sir Reginald Holmes, Kt.

Wilson, Sir Robert, Kt., CBE

Wilson, Sir Robert Donald, KBE

Wilson, *Rt. Revd* Roger Plumpton, KCVO, DD

Wilson, Sir Roland, KBE

Wilson, *Air Chief Marshal* Sir (Ronald) Andrew (Fellowes), KCB, AFC

Wilson, *Hon.* Sir Ronald Darling, KBE, CMG

Wilton, Sir (Arthur) John, KCMG, KCVO, MC

Wiltshire, Sir Frederick Munro, Kt., CBE

Wingate, *Capt.* Sir Miles Buckley, KCVO

Winnington, Sir Francis Salwey William, Bt. (1755)

Winskill, *Air Cdre* Sir Archibald Little, KCVO, CBE, DFC

Winterbottom, Sir Walter, Kt., CBE

Wiseman, Sir John William, Bt. (1628)

Wolfendale, *Prof.* Sir Arnold Whittaker, Kt., FRS

Wolfson, Sir Brian Gordon, Kt.

Wolseley, Sir Charles Garnet Richard Mark, Bt. (1628)

†Wolseley, Sir James Douglas, Bt. (I. 1745)

Wolstenholme, Sir Gordon Ethelbert Ward, Kt., OBE

Wombwell, Sir George Philip Frederick, Bt. (1778)

Womersley, Sir Peter John Walter, Bt. (1945)

Woo, Sir Leo Joseph, Kt.

Wood, Sir Alan Marshall Muir, Kt., FRS, FEng.

Wood, Sir Andrew Marley, KCMG

Wood, Sir Anthony John Page, Bt. (1837)

Wood, Sir David Basil Hill-, Bt. (1921)

Wood, Sir Frederick Ambrose Stuart, Kt.

Wood, Sir Ian Clark, Kt., CBE

Wood, *Prof.* Sir John Crossley, Kt., CBE

Wood, *Hon.* Sir John Kember, Kt., MC

Wood, Sir Martin Francis, Kt., OBE

Wood, Sir Russell Dillon, KCVO, VRD

Wood, Sir William Alan, KCVO, CB

Woodard, *Rear Adm.* Sir Robert Nathaniel, KCVO

Woodcock, Sir John, Kt., CBE, QPM

Woodfield, Sir Philip John, KCB, CBE

Woodhead, *Vice-Adm.* Sir (Anthony) Peter, KCB

Woodhouse, *Rt. Hon.* Sir (Arthur) Owen, KBE, DSC

Wooding, Sir Norman Samuel, Kt., CBE

Woodroffe, *Most Revd* George Cuthbert Manning, KBE

Woodroofe, Sir Ernest George, Kt., PH.D.

Woodruff, *Prof.* Sir Michael Francis Addison, Kt., D.SC., FRS, FRCS

Woods, Sir Colin Philip Joseph, KCVO, CBE

Woods, *Rt. Revd* Robert Wilmer, KCMG, KCVO

Woodward, *Hon.* Sir (Albert) Edward, Kt., OBE

Woodward, *Adm.* Sir John Forster, GBE, KCB

Woolf, Sir John, Kt.

Woollaston, Sir (Mountford) Tosswill, Kt.

Wordie, Sir John Stewart, Kt., CBE, VRD

Worsley, *Gen.* Sir Richard Edward, GCB, OBE

Worsley, Sir (William) Marcus (John), Bt. (1838)

Worsthorne, Sir Peregrine Gerard, Kt.

Wraight, Sir John Richard, KBE, CMG

Wratten, *Air Chief Marshal* Sir William John, KBE, CB, AFC

Wraxall, Sir Charles Frederick Lascelles, Bt. (1813)

Wrey, Sir George Richard Bourchier, Bt. (1628)

Wrigglesworth, Sir Ian William, Kt.

Wright, Sir Allan Frederick, KBE

Wright, Sir Denis Arthur Hepworth, GCMG

Wright, Sir Edward Maitland, Kt., D.phil., LL D., D.SC., FRSE

Wright, *Hon.* Sir (John) Michael, Kt.

Wright, Sir (John) Oliver, GCMG, GCVO, DSC

Wright, Sir Paul Hervé Giraud, KCMG, OBE

Wright, Sir Peter Robert, Kt., CBE

Wright, Sir Richard Michael Cory-, Bt. (1903)

Wrightson, Sir Charles Mark Garmondsway, Bt. (1900)

Wynn, Sir David Watkin Williams-, Bt. (1688)

Yacoub, *Prof.* Sir Magdi Habib, Kt., FRCS

Yang, *Hon.* Sir Ti Liang, Kt.

Yapp, Sir Stanley Graham, Kt.

Yardley, Sir David Charles Miller, Kt., LL.D.

Yarranton, Sir Peter George, Kt.

Yarrow, Sir Eric Grant, Bt., MBE (1916)

Yellowlees, Sir Henry, KCB

Yocklunn, Sir John (Soong Chung), KCVO

Yoo Foo, Sir (François) Henri, Kt.

Youens, Sir Peter William, Kt., CMG, OBE

Young, Sir Brian Walter Mark, Kt.

Young, Sir Colville Norbert, GCMG, MBE

Young, *Lt.-Gen.* Sir David Tod, KBE, CB, DFC

Young, *Rt. Hon.* Sir George Samuel Knatchbull, Bt., MP (1813)

Young, *Hon.* Sir Harold William, KCMG

Young, Sir John Kenyon Roe, Bt. (1821)

Young, *Hon.* Sir John McIntosh, KCMG

Young, Sir Leslie Clarence, Kt., CBE

Young, Sir Norman Smith, Kt.

Young, Sir Richard Dilworth, Kt.

Young, Sir Robert Christopher Mackworth-, GCVO

Young, Sir Roger William, Kt.

Young, Sir Stephen Stewart Templeton, Bt. (1945)

Young, Sir William Neil, Bt. (1769)

Younger, *Maj.-Gen.* Sir John William, Bt., CBE (1911)

Zeeman, *Prof.* Sir (Erik) Christopher, Kt., FRS

Zeidler, Sir David Ronald, Kt., CBE

Zoleveke, Sir Gideon Pitabose, KBE

Zunz, Sir Gerhard Jacob (Jack), Kt., FEng.

Zurenuoc, Sir Zibang, KBE

Dames Grand Cross and Dames Commanders

Style, 'Dame' before forename and surname, followed by appropriate post-nominal initials. Where such an award is made to a lady already in enjoyment of a higher title, the appropriate initials follow her name
Husband, Untitled
For forms of address, *see* page 217

Dame Grand Cross and Dame Commander are the higher classes for women of the Order of the Bath, the Order of St Michael and St George, the Royal Victorian Order, and the Order of the British Empire. Dames Grand Cross rank after the wives of Baronets and before the wives of Knights Grand Cross. Dames Commanders rank after the wives of Knights Grand Cross and before the wives of Knights Commanders

Honorary Dame Commanders may be conferred on women who are citizens of countries of which The Queen is not head of state

---

LIST OF DAMES   *Revised to 31 August 1995*

Women peers in their own right and life peers are not included in this list
If a dame has a double barrelled or hyphenated surname, she is listed under the final element of the name

HM Queen Elizabeth the Queen Mother, KG, KT, CI, GMVO
HRH The Princess Royal, GCVO
HRH The Princess Margaret, Countess of Snowdon, CI, GCVO
HRH The Duchess of Gloucester, GCVO
HRH Princess Alice, Duchess of Gloucester, GCB, CI, GCVO, GBE
HRH The Duchess of Kent, GCVO
HRH Princess Alexandra of Kent, GCVO
Abaijah, Dame Josephine, DBE
Abel Smith, Lady, DCVO
Abergavenny, The Marchioness of, DCVO
Airlie, The Countess of, DCVO
Albemarle, The Countess of, DBE
Anderson, *Brig.* Hon. Dame Mary Mackenzie (Mrs Pihl), DBE
Anelay, Dame Joyce Anne, DBE
Anglesey, The Marchioness of, DBE
Anson, Lady (Elizabeth Audrey), DBE
Anstee, Dame Margaret Joan, DCMG
Arden, *Hon.* Dame Mary Howarth (Mrs Mance), DBE
Baker, Dame Janet Abbott (Mrs Shelley), CH, DBE
Ballin, Dame Reubina Ann, DBE
Barnes, Dame (Alice) Josephine (Mary Taylor), DBE, FRCP, FRCS
Barrow, Dame Jocelyn Anita (Mrs Downer), DBE
Barrow, Dame (Ruth) Nita, GCMG
Barstow, Dame Josephine Clare (Mrs Anderson), DBE
Basset, Lady Elizabeth, DCVO
Bean, Dame Majorie Louise, DBE
Beaurepaire, Dame Beryl Edith, DBE
Bergquist, *Prof.* Dame Patricia Rose, DBE
Berry, Dame Alice Miriam, DBE
Blaize, Dame Venetia Ursula, DBE
Blaxland, Dame Helen Frances, DBE

Booth, *Hon.* Dame Margaret Myfanwy Wood, DBE
Bottomley, Dame Bessie Ellen, DBE
Bowman, Dame (Mary) Elaine Kellett-, DBE, MP
Boyd, Dame Vivienne Myra, DBE
Bracewell, *Hon.* Dame Joyanne Winifred (Mrs Copeland), DBE
Brain, Dame Margaret Anne (Mrs Wheeler), DBE
Brazill, Dame Josephine (Sister Mary Philippa), DBE
Bridges, Dame Mary Patricia, DBE
Brown, Dame Beryl Paston, DBE
Brown, Dame Gillian Gerda, DCVO, CMG
Browne, Lady Moyra Blanche Madeleine, DBE
Bryans, Dame Anne Margaret, DBE
Bryce, Dame Isabel Graham, DBE
Buttfield, Dame Nancy Eileen, DBE
Byford, Dame Hazel, DBE
Bynoe, Dame Hilda Louisa, DBE
Cartland, Dame Barbara Hamilton, DBE
Cartwright, Dame Mary Lucy, DBE, SC.D., D.PHIL., FRS
Cartwright, Dame Silvia Rose, DBE
Casey, Dame Stella Katherine, DBE
Cayford, Dame Florence Evelyn, DBE
Charles, Dame (Mary) Eugenia, DBE
Chesterton, Dame Elizabeth Ursula, DBE
Clark, *Prof.* Dame (Margaret) June, DBE, ph.D.
Clay, Dame Marie Mildred, DBE
Clayton, Dame Barbara Evelyn (Mrs Klyne), DBE
Cleland, Dame Rachel, DBE
Coles, Dame Mabel Irene, DBE
Coll, Dame Elizabeth Anne Loosemore Esteve-, DBE
Cookson, Dame Catherine Ann, DBE
Corsar, The Hon. Dame Mary Drummond, DBE
Coulshed, Dame (Mary) Frances, DBE, TD
Crowe, Dame Sylvia, DBE
Daws, Dame Joyce Margaretta, DBE
Dell, Dame Miriam Patricia, DBE

Dench, Dame Judith Olivia (Mrs Williams), DBE
de Valois, Dame Ninette, OM, CH, DBE
Digby, Lady, DBE
Donaldson, Dame (Dorothy) Mary (Lady Donaldson of Lymington), GBE
Doyle, *Air Comdt.* Dame Jean Lena Annette Conan (Lady Bromet), DBE
Drake, *Brig.* Dame Jean Elizabeth Rivett-, DBE
Dugdale, Kathryn, Lady, DCVO
Dumont, Dame Ivy Leona, DCMG
Ebsworth, *Hon.* Dame Ann Marian, DBE
Emerton, Dame Audrey Caroline, DBE
Engel, Dame Pauline Frances (Sister Pauline Engel), DBE
Evison, Dame Helen June Patricia, DBE
Fenner, Dame Peggy Edith, DBE, MP
Fitton, Dame Doris Alice (Mrs Mason), DBE
Fookes, Dame Janet Evelyn, DBE, MP
Fraser, Dame Dorothy Rita, DBE
Friend, Dame Phyllis Muriel, DBE
Frost, Dame Phyllis Irene, DBE
Fry, Dame Margaret Louise, DBE
Gallagher, Dame Monica Josephine, DBE
Gardiner, Dame Helen Louisa, DBE, MVO
Gibbs, Dame Molly Peel, DBE
Giles, *Air Comdt.* Dame Pauline (Mrs Parsons), DBE, RRC
Golding, Dame (Cecilie) Monica, DBE
Goodman, Dame Barbara, DBE
Gordon, Dame Minita Elmira, GCMG, GCVO
Gow, Dame Jane Elizabeth (Mrs Whiteley), DBE
Grafton, The Duchess of, GCVO
Green, Dame Mary Georgina, DBE
Grey, Dame Beryl Elizabeth (Mrs Svenson), DBE
Grimthorpe, The Lady, DCVO
Guilfoyle, Dame Margaret Georgina Constance, DBE
Guthardt, *Revd Dr* Dame Phyllis Myra, DBE

Haig, Dame Mary Alison Glen-, DBE
Hale, *Hon.* Dame Brenda Marjorie (Mrs Farrand), DBE
Hall, Dame Catherine Mary, DBE
Hammond, Dame Joan Hood, DBE
Harper, Dame Elizabeth Margaret Way, DBE
Harris, Dame (Muriel) Diana Reader-, DBE
Heilbron, *Hon.* Dame Rose, DBE
Henderson, Dame Louise Etiennette Sidonie, DBE
Henrison, Dame Anne Elizabeth Rosina, DBE
Herbison, Dame Jean Marjory, DBE, CMG
Hercus, *Hon.* Dame (Margaret) Ann, DCMG
Hetet, Dame Rangimarie, DBE
Higgins, *Prof.* Dame Rosalyn, DBE, QC
Hill, Dame Elizabeth Mary, DBE
Hill, *Air Cdre* Dame Felicity Barbara, DBE
Hiller, Dame Wendy (Mrs Gow), DBE
Hird, Dame Thora (Mrs Scott), DBE
Howard, Dame (Rosemary) Christian, DBE
Hunter, Dame Pamela, DBE
Hurley, *Prof.* Dame Rosalinde (Mrs Gortvai), DBE
Hussey, Lady Susan Katharine, DCVO
Isaacs, Dame Albertha Madeline, DBE
James, Dame Naomi Christine (Mrs Haythorne), DBE
Jenkins, Dame (Mary) Jennifer (Lady Jenkins of Hillhead), DBE
Jessel, Dame Penelope, DBE
Jones, Dame Gwyneth (Mrs Haberfeld-Jones), DBE
Kekedo, Dame Mary, DBE, BEM
Kekedo, Dame Rosalina Violet, DBE
Kelleher, Dame Joan, DBE
Kettlewell, *Comdt.* Dame Marion Mildred, DBE
Kilroy, Dame Alix Hester Marie (Lady Meynell), DBE
Kirby, Dame Georgina Kamiria, DBE
Kirk, Dame (Lucy) Ruth, DBE
Knight, Dame (Joan Christabel) Jill, DBE, MP
Kramer, *Prof.* Dame Leonie Judith, DBE
Lamb, Dame Dawn Ruth, DBE
Lancaster, Dame Jean, DBE
Lewis, Dame Edna Leofrida (Lady Lewis), DBE
Lister, Dame Unity Viola, DBE
Litchfield, Dame Ruby Beatrice, DBE
Lloyd, *Prof.* Dame June Kathleen, DBE, FRCP
Lowrey, *Air Comdt.* Dame Alice, DBE, RRC
Lympany, Dame Moura, DBE
Lynn, Dame Vera (Mrs Lewis), DBE
Mackinnon, Dame (Una) Patricia, DBE
Macknight, Dame Ella Annie Noble, DBE, MD
McLaren, Dame Anne Laura, DBE, FRCOG, FRS
Macmillan of Ovenden, Katharine, Viscountess, DBE

Major, Dame Malvina Lorraine (Mrs Fleming), DBE
Mann, Dame Ida Caroline, DBE, D.SC., FRCS
Markova, Dame Alicia, DBE
Martin, Rosamund Mary Holland-, Lady, DBE
Metge, *Dr* Dame (Alice) Joan, DBE
Miller, Dame Mabel Flora Hobart, DBE
Miller, Dame Mary Elizabeth Hedley-, DCVO, CB
Mitchell, Dame Mona, DCVO
Mitchell, *Hon.* Dame Roma Flinders, DBE
Mitchell, Dame Wendy, DBE
Morrison, *Hon.* Dame Mary Anne, DCVO
Mueller, Dame Anne Elisabeth, DCB
Muldoon, Thea Dale, Lady, DBE, QSO
Mumford, Lady Mary Katharine, DCVO
Munro, Dame Alison, DBE
Murdoch, Dame Elisabeth Joy, DBE
Murdoch, Dame (Jean) Iris (Mrs Bayley), DBE
Murray, Dame (Alice) Rosemary, DBE, D.phil.
Ollerenshaw, Dame Kathleen Mary, DBE, D.phil.
Oxenbury, Dame Shirley Anne, DBE
Park, Dame Merle Florence (Mrs Bloch), DBE
Paterson, Dame Betty Fraser Ross, DBE
Peake, *Air Cdre* Dame Felicity Hyde, DBE, AE
Penhaligon, Dame Annette (Mrs Egerton), DBE
Plowden, The Lady, DBE
Poole, Dame Avril Anne Barker, DBE
Porter, Dame Shirley (Lady Porter), DBE
Prendergast, Dame Simone Ruth, DBE
Prentice, Dame Winifred Eva, DBE
Preston, Dame Frances Olivia Campbell-, DCVO
Price, Dame Margaret Berenice, DBE
Purves, Dame Daphne Helen, DBE
Pyke, Lady, DBE
Quinn, Dame Sheila Margaret Imelda, DBE
Railton, Dame Ruth (Mrs King), DBE
Rankin, Lady Jean Margaret Florence, DCVO
Raven, Dame Kathleen Annie (Mrs Ingram), DBE
Restieaux, *Dr* Dame Norma Jean, DBE
Riddelsdell, Dame Mildred, DCB, CBE
Ridley, Dame (Mildred) Betty, DBE
Ridsdale, Dame Victoire Evelyn Patricia (Lady Ridsdale), DBE
Rigg, Dame Diana, DBE
Robertson, *Comdt.* Dame Nancy Margaret, DBE
Roe, Dame Raigh Edith, DBE
Rue, Dame (Elsie) Rosemary, DBE
Rumbold, *Rt. Hon.* Dame Angela Claire Rosemary, DBE, MP
Salas, Dame Margaret Laurence, DBE

Salmond, *Prof.* Dame Mary Anne, DBE
Saunders, Dame Cicely Mary Strode, OM, DBE, FRCP
Schwarzkopf, Dame Elisabeth Friederike Marie Olga Legge-, DBE
Scott, Dame Catherine Campbell, DBE
Scott, Dame Jean Mary Monica Maxwell-, DCVO
Scott, Dame Margaret, (Dame Catherine Margaret Mary Denton), DBE
Shenfield, Dame Barbara Estelle, DBE
Sherlock, *Prof.* Dame Sheila Patricia Violet, DBE, MD, FRCP
Sloss, *Rt. Hon.* Dame (Ann) Elizabeth (Oldfield) Butler-, DBE
Smieton, Dame Mary Guillan, DBE
Smith, *Hon.* Dame Janet Hilary (Mrs Mathieson), DBE
Smith, Dame Margaret Natalie (Maggie) (Mrs Cross), DBE
Smith, Dame Margot, DBE
Snagge, Dame Nancy Marion, DBE
Soames, Mary, Lady, DBE
Spark, Dame Muriel Sarah, DBE
Steel, *Hon.* Dame (Anne) Heather (Mrs Beattie), DBE
Stephens, *Air Comdt.* Dame Anne, DBE
Stewart, Dame Muriel Acadia, DBE
Sutherland, Dame Joan (Mrs Bonynge), OM, DBE
Szaszy, Dame Miraka Petricevich, DBE
Taylor, Dame Jean Elizabeth, DCVO
Te Atairangikaahu, Te Arikinui, Dame, DBE
Te Kanawa, Dame Kiri Janette (Mrs Park), DBE
Thorneycroft, Carla, Lady, CBE
Tilney, Dame Guinevere (Lady Tilney), DBE
Tinson, Dame Sue, DBE
Tizard, Dame Catherine Anne, GCMG, DBE
Tokiel, Dame Rosa, DBE
Tyrwhitt, *Brig.* Dame Mary Joan Caroline, DBE, TD
Uatioa, Dame Mere, DBE
Uvarov, Dame Olga, DBE
Varley, Dame Joan Fleetwood, DBE
Wagner, Dame Gillian Mary Millicent (Lady Wagner), DBE
Wall, (Alice) Anne, (Mrs Michael Wall), DCVO
Wallace, Dame (Georgina Catriona Pamela) Augusta, DBE
Warburton, Dame Anne Marion, DCVO, CMG
Warwick, Dame Margaret Elizabeth Harvey Turner-, DBE, FRCP, FRCPEd.
Waterhouse, Dame Rachel Elizabeth, DBE, ph.D.
Wedgwood, Dame (Cicely) Veronica, OM, DBE
Weston, Dame Margaret Kate, DBE
Williamson, Dame (Elsie) Marjorie, DBE, ph.D.
Winstone, Dame Dorothy Gertrude, DBE, CMG

The Military Knights of Windsor

The Military Knights of Windsor take part in all ceremonies of the Noble Order of the Garter and attend Sunday morning service in St George's Chapel, Windsor Castle, as representatives of the Knights of the Garter. The Knights receive a small stipend in addition to their army pensions and quarters in Windsor Castle.

The Knights of Windsor were originally founded in 1348 after the wars in France to assist English knights, who, having been prisoners in the hands of the French, had become impoverished by the payments of heavy ransoms. When Edward III founded the Order of the Garter later the same year, he incorporated the Knights of Windsor and the College of St George into its foundation and raised the number of Knights to 26 to correspond with the number of the Knights of the Garter. Known later as the Alms Knights or Poor Knights of Windsor, their establishment was reduced under the will of King Henry VIII to 13 and Statutes were drawn up by Queen Elizabeth I.

In 1833 King William IV changed their designation to The Military Knights and granted them their present uniform which consists of a scarlet tail-coat with white cross sword-belt, crimson sash and cocked hat with plume. The badges are the Shield of St George and the Star of the Order of the Garter.

Governor, Maj.-Gen. Peter Downward, CB, DSO, DFC
Military Knights, Brig. A. L. Atkinson, OBE; Brig. J. F. Lindner, OBE, MC; Maj. W. L. Thompson, MVO, MBE, DCM; Maj. L. W. Dickerson; Maj. J. C. Cowley, DCM; Lt.-Col. N. L. West; Maj. G. R. Mitchell, MBE, BEM; Lt.-Col. R. L. C. Tamplin; Maj. P. H. Bolton, MBE; Lt.-Col. H. R. Rogers, MBE, Brig. T. W. Hackworth, OBE; Maj. R. J. Moore
Supernumerary, Brig. A. C. Tyler, CBE, MC

The Order of St John

THE MOST VENERABLE ORDER OF THE HOSPITAL OF ST JOHN OF JERUSALEM (1888)

GCStJ   Bailiff/Dame Grand Cross
KStJ   Knight of Justice/Grace
DStJ   Dame of Justice/Grace
ChStJ   Chaplain
CStJ   Commander
OStJ,   Officer
SBStJ   Serving Brother
SSStJ   Serving Sister
EsqStJ Esquire

Mottoes, Pro Fide *and* Pro Utilitate Hominum

The Order of St John, founded in the early 12th century in Jerusalem, was a religious order with a particular duty to care for the sick. In Britain the Order was dissolved by Henry VIII in 1540 but the British branch was revived in the early 19th century. The branch was not accepted by the Grand Magistracy of the Order in Rome but its search for a role in the tradition of the Hospitallers led to the founding of the St John Ambulance Association in 1877 and later the

St John Ambulance Brigade; in 1882 the St John Ophthalmic Hospital was founded in Jerusalem. A royal charter was granted in 1888 establishing the British Order of St John as a British Order of Chivalry with the Sovereign as its head.

Admission to the Order is conferred in recognition of service, usually in St John Ambulance. Membership does not confer any rank, style, title or precedence on a recipient.

SOVEREIGN HEAD OF THE ORDER
HM The Queen

GRAND PRIOR
HRH The Duke of Gloucester, GCVO

Lord Prior, The Lord Vestey
Prelate, The Rt. Revd M. A. Mann, KCVO
Chancellor, Prof. A. R. Mellows, TD
Bailiff of Egle, The Lord Remnant
Headquarters, St John's Gate, Clerkenwell, London ECIM 4DA

Chiefs of Clans and Names in Scotland

Only chiefs of whole Names or Clans are included, except certain special instances (marked *) who, though not chiefs of a whole name, were or are for some reason (e.g. the Macdonald forfeiture) independent. Under decision (*Campbell-Gray*, 1950) that a bearer of a 'double or triple-barrelled' surname cannot be held chief of a part of such, several others cannot be included in the list at present.

THE ROYAL HOUSE: HM The Queen

AGNEW: Sir Crispin Agnew of Lochnaw, Bt., 6 Palmerston Road, Edinburgh EH9 1TN

ANSTRUTHER: Sir Ralph Anstruther of that Ilk, Bt., KCVO, MC, Balcaskie, Pittenweem, Fife

ARBUTHNOTT: The Viscount of Arbuthnott, CBE, DSC, Arbuthnott House, Laurencekirk, Kincardineshire AB30 1PA

BARCLAY: Peter C. Barclay of that Ilk, 28A Gordon Place, London W8 4JF

BORTHWICK: The Lord Borthwick, TD, Crookston, Heriot, Midlothian EH38 5YS

BOYD: The Lord Kilmarnock, 194 Regent's Park Road, London NW1 8XP

BOYLE: The Earl of Glasgow, Kelburn, Fairlie, Ayrshire KA29 OBE

BRODIE: Ninian Brodie of Brodie, Brodie Castle, Forres, Morayshire IV36 0TE

BRUCE: The Earl of Elgin and Kincardine, KT, Broomhall, Dunfermline, Fife KY11 3DU

BUCHAN: David S. Buchan of Auchmacoy, Auchmacoy House, Ellon, Aberdeenshire

BURNETT: J. C. A. Burnett of Leys, Crathes Castle, Banchory, Kincardineshire

CAMERON: Sir Donald Cameron of Lochiel, KT, CVO, TD, Achnacarry, Spean Bridge, Inverness-shire

CAMPBELL: The Duke of Argyll, Inveraray, Argyll PA32 8XF

CARMICHAEL: Richard J. Carmichael of Carmichael, Carmichael, Thankerton, Biggar, Lanarkshire

CARNEGIE: The Duke of Fife, Elsick House, Stonehaven, Kincardineshire AB3 2NT

CATHCART: Maj.-Gen. The Earl Cathcart, CB, DSO, MC, Moor Hatches, West Amesbury, Salisbury SP4 7BH

CHARTERIS: The Earl of Wemyss and March, KT, Gosford House, Longniddry, East Lothian EH32 0PX

CLAN CHATTAN: M. K. Mackintosh of Clan Chattan, Maxwell Park, Gwelo, Zimbabwe

CHISHOLM: Alastair Chisholm of Chisholm (*The Chisholm*), Silver Willows, Beck Row, Bury St Edmunds

COCHRANE: The Earl of Dundonald, Lochnell Castle, Ledaig, Argyllshire

COLQUHOUN: Sir Ivar Colquhoun of Luss, Bt., Camstraddan, Luss, Dunbartonshire G83 8NX

CRANSTOUN: David A. S. Cranstoun of that Ilk, Corehouse, Lanark

CRICHTON: vacant

DARROCH: Capt. Duncan Darroch of Gourock, The Red House, Branksome Park Road, Camberley, Surrey

DEWAR: Kenneth Dewar of that Ilk and Vogrie, The Dower House, Grayshott, Nr. Hindhead, Surrey

DRUMMOND: The Earl of Perth, PC, Stobhall, Perth PH2 6DR

DUNBAR: Sir James Dunbar of Mochrum, Bt., Bld 848 C.2, 66877 Flugplatz, Ramstein, Germany

DUNDAS: David D. Dundas of Dundas, 8 Derna Road, Kenwyn 7700, South Africa

DURIE: Raymond V. D. Durie of Durie, Court House, Pewsey, Wilts

ELIOTT: Mrs Margaret Eliott of Redheugh, Redheugh, Newcastleton, Roxburghshire

ERSKINE: The Earl of Mar and Kellie, Erskine House, Kirk Wynd, Clackmannan FK10 4JF

FARQUHARSON: Capt. A. Farquharson of Invercauld, MC, Invercauld, Braemar, Aberdeenshire AB35 5TT

FERGUSSON: Sir Charles Fergusson of Kilkerran, Bt., Kilkerran, Maybole, Ayrshire

FORBES: The Lord Forbes, KBE, Balforbes, Alford, Aberdeenshire AB33 8DR

FORSYTH: Alistair Forsyth of that Ilk, Ethie Castle, by Arbroath, Angus DD11 5SP

FRASER: The Lady Saltoun, Cairnbulg Castle, Fraserburgh, Aberdeenshire AB43 5TN

*FRASER (OF LOVAT): The Lord Lovat, Balblair House, Beauly, Inverness-shire IV4 7AZ

GAYRE: Lt.-Col. Robert Gayre of Gayre and Nigg, Minard Castle, Minard, Inverary, Argyll PA32 8YB

GORDON: The Marquess of Huntly, Aboyne Castle, Aberdeenshire

GRAHAM: The Duke of Montrose, Buchanan Auld House, Drymen, Stirlingshire

GRANT: The Lord Strathspey, The House of Lords, London SW1A 0PW

GRIERSON: Sir Michael Grierson of Lag, Bt., 40C Palace Road, London SW2 3NJ

HAIG: The Earl Haig, OBE, Bemersyde, Melrose, Roxburghshire

HALDANE: Martin Haldane of Gleneagles, Gleneagles, Auchterarder, Perthshire

HANNAY: Ramsey Hannay of Kirkdale and of that Ilk, Cardoness House, Gatehouse-of-Fleet, Kirkcudbrightshire

HAY: The Earl of Erroll, Woodbury Hall, Sandy, Beds

HENDERSON: John Henderson of Fordell, 7 Owen Street, Toowoomba, Queensland, Australia

HUNTER: Pauline Hunter of Hunterston, Plovers Ridge, Lon Cecrist, Treaddur Bay, Holyhead, Gwynedd

IRVINE OF DRUM: David C. Irvine of Drum, 20 Enville Road, Bowden, Altrincham, Cheshire WA14 2PQ

JARDINE: Sir Alexander Jardine of Applegirth, Bt., Ash House, Thwaites, Millom, Cumbria LA18 5HY

JOHNSTONE: The Earl of Annandale and Hartfell, Raehills, Lockerbie, Dumfriesshire

KEITH: The Earl of Kintore, The Stables, Keith Hall, Inverurie, Aberdeenshire AB51 0LD

KENNEDY: The Marquess of Ailsa, Cassillis House, Maybole, Ayrshire

KERR: The Marquess of Lothian, KCVO, Ferniehurst Castle, Jedburgh, Roxburghshire TN8 6NX

KINCAID: Mrs Heather V. Kincaid of Kincaid, 4 Watling Street, Leintwardine, Craven Arms, Shropshire

LAMONT: Peter N. Lamont of that Ilk, St Patrick's College, Manly, NSW 2095, Australia

LEASK: Madam Leask of Leask, 1 Vincent Road, Sheringham, Norfolk

LENNOX: Edward J. H. Lennox of that Ilk, Pools Farm, Downton on the Rock, Ludlow, Shropshire

LESLIE: The Earl of Rothes, Tanglewood, West Tytherley, Salisbury, Wilts SP5 1LX

LINDSAY: The Earl of Crawford and Balcarres, PC, Balcarres, Colinsburgh, Fife

LOCKHART: Angus H. Lockhart of the Lee, Newholme, Dunsyre, Lanark

LUMSDEN: Gillem Lumsden of that Ilk and Blanerne, Kinderslegh, Bois Avenue, Chesham Bois, Amersham

MACALESTER: William St J. S. McAlester of Loup and Kennox, 2 Avon Road East, Christchurch, Dorset

McBAIN: J. H. McBain of McBain, 7025, North Finger Rock Place, Tucson, Arizona, USA

MALCOLM (MACCALLUM): Robin N. L. Malcolm of Poltalloch, Duntrune Castle, Lochgilphead, Argyll

MACDONALD: The Lord Macdonald (*The Macdonald of Macdonald*), Kinloch Lodge, Sleat, Isle of Skye

*MACDONALD OF CLANRANALD: Ranald A. Macdonald of Clanranald, Wester Lix Cottage, Killin, Perthshire

*MACDONALD OF SLEAT (CLAN HUSTEAIN): Sir Ian Bosville Macdonald of Sleat, Bt., Thorpe Hall, Rudston, Driffield, N. Humberside YO25 OJE

*MACDONELL OF GLENGARRY: Air Cdre Aeneas R. MacDonell of Glengarry, CB, DFC, Elonbank, Castle Street, Fortrose, Ross-shire IV10 8TH

MACDOUGALL: vacant

MACDOWALL: Fergus D. H. Macdowall of Garthland, 16 Tower Road, Nepean, Ontario, Canada

MACGREGOR: Sir Gregor MacGregor of MacGregor, Bt., Bannatyne, Newtyle, Blairgowrie, Perthshire PH12 8TR

MACINTYRE: James W. MacIntyre of Glenoe, 15301 Pine Orchard Drive, Apartment 3H, Silver Spring, Maryland, USA

MACKAY: The Lord Reay, House of Lords, London SW1

MACKENZIE: The Earl of Cromartie, Castle Leod, Strathpeffer, Ross-shire IV14 9AA

MACKINNON: Madam Anne Mackinnon of Mackinnon, 16 Purleigh Road, Bridgwater, Somerset

MACKINTOSH: Lt.-Cdr. L. R. D. Mackintosh of Mackintosh, OBE (*The Mackintosh of Mackintosh*), Moy Hall, Inverness IV13 7YQ

MACLACHLAN: Madam Marjorie MacLachlan of MacLachlan, Castle Lachlan, Argyll

MACLAREN: Donald MacLaren of MacLaren and Achleskine, Achleskine, Kirkton, Balquidder, Lochearnhead

MACLEAN: The Hon. Sir Lachlan Maclean of Duart, Bt., Arngask House, Glenfarg, Perthshire PH2 9QA

MACLENNAN: vacant

MACLEOD: John MacLeod of MacLeod, Dunvegan Castle, Isle of Skye

MACMILLAN: George MacMillan of MacMillan, Finlaystone, Langbank, Renfrewshire

MACNAB: J. C. Macnab of Macnab (*The Macnab*), Leuchars Castle Farmhouse, Leuchars, Fife KY16 OEY

MACNAGHTEN: Sir Patrick Macnaghten of Macnaghten and Dundarave, Bt., Dundarave, Bushmills, Co. Antrim

MACNEACAIL: Iain Macneacail of Macneacail and Scorrybreac, 12 Fox Street, Ballina, NSW, Australia

MACNEIL OF BARRA: Ian R. Macneil of Barra (*The Macneil of Barra*), Kisimul Castle, Barra

MACPHERSON: The Hon. Sir William Macpherson of Cluny, TD, Newtown Castle, Blairgowrie, Perthshire

MACTHOMAS: Andrew P. C. MacThomas of Finegand, c/o The Clan MacThomas Society, 19 Warriston Avenue, Edinburgh

MAITLAND: The Earl of Lauderdale, 12 St Vincent Street, Edinburgh

MAKGILL: The Viscount of Oxfuird, Hill House, St Mary Bourne, Andover, Hants SP11 6BG

MAR: The Countess of Mar, St Michael's Farm, Great Witley, Worcs WR6 6JB

MARJORIBANKS: Andrew Marjoribanks of that Ilk

MATHESON: Maj. Sir Fergus Matheson of Matheson, Bt., Old Rectory, Hedenham, Bungay, Suffolk NR35 2LD

MENZIES: David R. Menzies of Menzies, 20 Nardina Crescent, Dalkeith, Western Australia

MOFFAT: Madam Moffat of that Ilk, St Jasual, Bullocks Farm Lane, Wheeler End Common, High Wycombe

MONCREIFFE: vacant

MONTGOMERIE: The Earl of Eglinton and Winton, The Dutch House, West Green, Hartley Wintney, Hants

MORRISON: Dr Iain M. Morrison of Ruchdi, Magnolia Cottage, The Street, Walberton, Sussex

MUNRO: Hector W. Munro of Foulis, TD, Foulis Castle, Evanton, Ross-shire IV16 9UX

MURRAY: The Duke of Atholl, Blair Castle, Blair Atholl, Perthshire

NESBITT (OR NISBET): Robert Nesbitt of that Ilk, Upper Roundhurst Farm, Roundhurst, Haslemere, Surrey

NICOLSON: The Lord Carnock, 90 Whitehall Court, London SW1A 2EL

OGILVY: The Earl of Airlie, KT, GCVO, PC, Cortachy Castle, Kirriemuir, Angus

RAMSAY: The Earl of Dalhousie, KT, GCVO, GBE, MC, Brechin Castle, Brechin, Angus DD7 6SH

RATTRAY: James S. Rattray of Rattray, Craighall, Rattray, Perthshire

ROBERTSON: Alexander G. H. Robertson of Struan (*Struan-Robertson*), The Breach Farm, Goudhurst Road, Cranbrook, Kent

ROLLO: The Lord Rollo, Pitcairns, Dunning, Perthshire

ROSE: Miss Elizabeth Rose of Kilravock, Kilravock Castle, Croy, Inverness

ROSS: David C. Ross of that Ilk, The Old Schoolhouse, Fettercairn, Kincardineshire

RUTHVEN: The Earl of Gowrie, PC, Castlemartin, Kilcullen, Co. Kildare, Republic of Ireland

SCOTT: The Duke of Buccleuch and Queensberry, KT, VRD, Bowhill, Selkirk

SCRYMGEOUR: The Earl of Dundee, Birkhill, Cupar, Fife

SEMPILL: The Lord Sempill, East Lodge, Druminnor, Rhynie, Aberdeenshire AB5 4LT

SHAW: John Shaw of Tordarroch, Newhall, Balblair, By Conon Bridge, Ross-shire

SINCLAIR: The Earl of Caithness, Churchill, Chipping Norton, Oxford OX7 5UX

SKENE: Danus Skene of Skene, Nether Pitleur, Strathmiglo, Fife

STIRLING: Fraser J. Stirling of Cader, 17 Park Row, Farnham, Surrey

STRANGE: Maj. Timothy Strange of Balcaskie, Little Holme, Porton Road, Amesbury, Wilts

SUTHERLAND: The Countess of Sutherland, House of Tongue, Brora, Sutherland

SWINTON: John Swinton of that Ilk, 123 Superior Avenue SW, Calgary, Alberta, Canada

TROTTER: Alexander Trotter of Mortonhall, Charterhall, Duns, Berwickshire

URQUHART: Kenneth T. Urquhart of Urquhart, 507 Jefferson Park Avenue, Jefferson, New Orleans, Louisiana 70121, USA

WALLACE: Ian F. Wallace of that Ilk, 5 Lennox Street, Edinburgh EH4 1QB

WEDDERBURN OF THAT ILK: The Master of Dundee, Birkhill, Cupar, Fife

WEMYSS: David Wemyss of that Ilk, Invermay, Forteviot, Perthshire

Decorations and Medals

VICTORIA CROSS (VC), 1856
GEORGE CROSS (GC), 1940

British Orders of Knighthood, etc.
BARONET'S BADGE
KNIGHT BACHELOR'S BADGE

Decorations
CONSPICUOUS GALLANTRY CROSS (CGC), 1995
ROYAL RED CROSS Class I (RRC), 1883. For ladies
DISTINGUISHED SERVICE CROSS (DSC), 1914. For all
    ranks for actions at sea
MILITARY CROSS (MC), December 1914. For all ranks for
    actions on land
DISTINGUISHED FLYING CROSS (DFC), 1918. For all
    ranks for acts of gallantry when flying in active
    operations against the enemy
AIR FORCE CROSS (AFC), 1918. For all ranks for acts of
    courage when flying, although not in active operations
    against the enemy
ROYAL RED CROSS Class II (ARRC)
ORDER OF BRITISH INDIA
KAISAR-I-HIND MEDAL
ORDER OF ST JOHN

Medals for Gallantry and Distinguished Conduct
UNION OF SOUTH AFRICA QUEEN'S MEDAL FOR
    BRAVERY, in Gold
DISTINGUISHED CONDUCT MEDAL (DCM), 1854
CONSPICUOUS GALLANTRY MEDAL (CGM), 1874
CONSPICUOUS GALLANTRY MEDAL (FLYING)
GEORGE MEDAL (GM), 1940
QUEEN'S POLICE MEDAL FOR GALLANTRY
QUEEN'S FIRE SERVICE MEDAL FOR GALLANTRY
ROYAL WEST AFRICAN FRONTIER FORCE
    DISTINGUISHED CONDUCT MEDAL
KING'S AFRICAN RIFLES DISTINGUISHED CONDUCT
    MEDAL
INDIAN DISTINGUISHED SERVICE MEDAL
UNION OF SOUTH AFRICA QUEEN'S MEDAL FOR
    BRAVERY, in Silver
DISTINGUISHED SERVICE MEDAL (DSM), 1914
MILITARY MEDAL (MM), 1916
DISTINGUISHED FLYING MEDAL (DFM), 1918
AIR FORCE MEDAL (AFM)
CONSTABULARY MEDAL (IRELAND)
MEDAL FOR SAVING LIFE AT SEA
SEA GALLANTRY MEDAL
INDIAN ORDER OF MERIT (Civil)
INDIAN POLICE MEDAL FOR GALLANTRY
CEYLON POLICE MEDAL FOR GALLANTRY
SIERRA LEONE POLICE MEDAL FOR GALLANTRY
SIERRA LEONE FIRE BRIGADES MEDAL FOR GALLANTRY
COLONIAL POLICE MEDAL FOR GALLANTRY (CPM)
QUEEN'S GALLANTRY MEDAL, 1974
ROYAL VICTORIAN MEDAL (RVM), Gold, Silver and
    Bronze
BRITISH EMPIRE MEDAL (BEM), (formerly the Medal of
    the Order of the British Empire, for Meritorious Service;

also includes the Medal of the Order awarded before 29
    December 1922)
CANADA MEDAL
QUEEN'S POLICE (QPM) AND QUEEN'S FIRE SERVICE
    MEDALS (QFSM) FOR DISTINGUISHED SERVICE
QUEEN'S MEDAL FOR CHIEFS

War Medals and Stars (in order of date)

Polar Medals (in order of date)

IMPERIAL SERVICE MEDAL

Police Medals for Valuable Service
BADGE OF HONOUR

Jubilee, Coronation and Durbar Medals

KING GEORGE V, KING GEORGE VI AND QUEEN
    ELIZABETH II LONG AND FAITHFUL SERVICE MEDALS

Efficiency and Long Service Decorations and Medals
MEDAL FOR MERITORIOUS SERVICE
ACCUMULATED CAMPAIGN SERVICE MEDAL
THE MEDAL FOR LONG SERVICE AND GOOD CONDUCT
    (Military)
NAVAL LONG SERVICE AND GOOD CONDUCT MEDAL
ROYAL MARINES MERITORIOUS SERVICE MEDAL
ROYAL AIR FORCE MERITORIOUS SERVICE MEDAL
ROYAL AIR FORCE LONG SERVICE AND GOOD CONDUCT
    MEDAL
MEDAL FOR LONG SERVICE AND GOOD CONDUCT
    (ULSTER DEFENCE REGIMENT)
POLICE LONG SERVICE AND GOOD CONDUCT MEDAL
FIRE BRIGADE LONG SERVICE AND GOOD CONDUCT
    MEDAL
COLONIAL POLICE AND FIRE BRIGADES LONG SERVICE
    MEDALS
COLONIAL PRISON SERVICE MEDAL
HONG KONG DISCIPLINED SERVICES MEDAL
ARMY EMERGENCY RESERVE DECORATION (ERD), 1952
VOLUNTEER OFFICERS' DECORATION (VD)
VOLUNTEER LONG SERVICE MEDAL
VOLUNTEER OFFICERS' DECORATION for India and the
    Colonies
VOLUNTEER LONG SERVICE MEDAL for India and the
    Colonies
COLONIAL AUXILIARY FORCES OFFICERS' DECORATION
COLONIAL AUXILIARY FORCES LONG SERVICE MEDAL
MEDAL FOR GOOD SHOOTING (Naval)
MILITIA LONG SERVICE MEDAL
IMPERIAL YEOMANRY LONG SERVICE MEDAL
TERRITORIAL DECORATION (TD), 1908
EFFICIENCY DECORATION (ED)
TERRITORIAL EFFICIENCY MEDAL
EFFICIENCY MEDAL
SPECIAL RESERVE LONG SERVICE AND GOOD CONDUCT
    MEDAL
DECORATION FOR OFFICERS, ROYAL NAVY RESERVE
    (RD), 1910
DECORATION FOR OFFICERS, RNVR (VRD)
ROYAL NAVAL RESERVE LONG SERVICE AND GOOD
    CONDUCT MEDAL
RNVR LONG SERVICE AND GOOD CONDUCT MEDAL
ROYAL NAVAL AUXILIARY SICK BERTH RESERVE LONG
    SERVICE AND GOOD CONDUCT MEDAL

ROYAL FLEET RESERVE LONG SERVICE AND GOOD
  CONDUCT MEDAL
ROYAL NAVAL WIRELESS AUXILIARY RESERVE LONG
  SERVICE AND GOOD CONDUCT MEDAL
AIR EFFICIENCY AWARD (AE), 1942
ULSTER DEFENCE REGIMENT MEDAL
THE QUEEN'S MEDAL. For champion shots in the RN,
  RM, RNZN, Army, RAF
CADET FORCES MEDAL, 1950
COASTGUARD AUXILIARY SERVICE LONG SERVICE
  MEDAL (formerly Coast Life Saving Corps Long
  Service Medal)
SPECIAL CONSTABULARY LONG SERVICE MEDAL
ROYAL OBSERVER CORPS MEDAL
CIVIL DEFENCE LONG SERVICE MEDAL
AMBULANCE SERVICE (EMERGENCY DUTIES) LONG
  SERVICE AND GOOD CONDUCT MEDAL
RHODESIA MEDAL
ROYAL ULSTER CONSTABULARY SERVICE MEDAL
SERVICE MEDAL OF THE ORDER OF ST JOHN
BADGE OF THE ORDER OF THE LEAGUE OF MERCY
VOLUNTARY MEDICAL SERVICE MEDAL, 1932
WOMEN'S VOLUNTARY SERVICE MEDAL
COLONIAL SPECIAL CONSTABULARY MEDAL

Foreign Orders, Decorations and Medals (in order of date)

THE VICTORIA CROSS (1856)
FOR CONSPICUOUS BRAVERY

VC

Ribbon, Crimson, for all Services (until 1918 it was blue for
the Royal Navy)

Instituted on 29 January 1856, the Victoria Cross was
awarded retrospectively to 1854, the first being held by Lt.
C. D. Lucas, RN, for bravery in the Baltic Sea on 21 June
1854 (gazetted 24 February 1857). The first 62 Crosses
were presented by Queen Victoria in Hyde Park, London,
on 26 June 1857.
  The Victoria Cross is worn before all other decorations,
on the left breast, and consists of a cross-pattée of bronze,
one and a half inches in diameter, with the Royal Crown
surmounted by a lion in the centre, and beneath there is
the inscription *For Valour.* Holders of the VC receive a tax-
free annuity of £100 (under review), irrespective of need
or other conditions. In 1911, the right to receive the Cross
was extended to Indian soldiers, and in 1920 to Matrons,
Sisters and Nurses, and the staff of the Nursing Services
and other services pertaining to hospitals and nursing, and
to civilians of either sex regularly or temporarily under
the orders, direction or supervision of the Naval, Military,
or Air Forces of the Crown.

SURVIVING RECIPIENTS OF THE VICTORIA CROSS
as at 31 August 1995

Agansing Rai, *Havildar,* MM (Gurkha Rifles)
  1944 *World War*
Ali Haidar, *Jemadar* (Frontier Force Rifles)
  1945 *World War*
Annand, *Capt.* R. W. (Durham Light Infantry)
  1940 *World War*

Bhan Bhagta Gurung, *Capt.* (2nd Gurkha Rifles)
  1945 *World War*
Bhandari Ram, *Capt.* (Baluch R.)
  1944 *World War*
Chapman, *Sgt.* E. T., BEM (Monmouthshire R.)
  1945 *World War*
Cruickshank, *Flt. Lt.* J. A. (RAFVR)
  1944 *World War*
Cutler, Sir Roden, AK, KCMG, KCVO, CBE (Australia)
  1941 *World War*
Fraser, *Lt.-Cdr.* I. E., DSC (RNR)
  1945 *World War*
Gaje Ghale, *Subedar* (Gurkha Rifles)
  1943 *World War*
Ganju Lama, *Jemadar,* MM (Gurkha Rifles)
  1944 *World War*
Gardner, *Capt.* P. J., MC (RTR)
  1941 *World War*
Gian Singh, *Jemadar* (Punjab R.)
  1945 *World War*
Gould, *Lt.* T. W. (RN)
  1942 *World War*
Hinton, *Sgt.* J. D. (NZMF)
  1941 *World War*
Jamieson, *Maj.* D. A., CVO (R. Norfolk R.)
  1944 *World War*
Kenna, *Pte.* E. (Australian M. F.)
  1945 *World War*
Kenneally, *C-Q-M-S* J. P. (Irish Guards)
  1943 *World War*
Lachiman Gurung, *Rifleman* (Gurkha Rifles)
  1945 *World War*
Learoyd, *Wg Cdr.* R. A. B. (RAF)
  1940 *World War*
Merritt, *Lt.-Col.* C. C. I., CD (S. Saskatchewan R.)
  1942 *World War*
Norton, *Capt.* G. R., MM (SAMF)
  1944 *World War*
Payne, *WO* K. (Australian Army)
  1969 *Vietnam*
Porteous, *Col.* P. A. (RA)
  1942 *World War*
Rambahadur Limbu, *Lt.,* MVO (Gurkha Rifles)
  1965 *Sarawak*
Reid, *Flt. Lt.* W. (RAFVR)
  1943 *World War*
Smith, *Sgt.* E. A., CD (Seaforth Highlanders of Canada)
  1944 *World War*
Smythe, *Capt.* Q. G. M. (SAMF)
  1942 *World War*
Speakman-Pitt, *Sgt.* W. (Black Watch)
  1951 *Korea*
Tulbahadur Pun, *WOI* (Gurkha Rifles)
  1944 *World War*
Umrao Singh, *Sub-Major* (IA)
  1944 *World War*
Watkins, *Maj. Rt. Hon.* Sir Tasker, GBE (Welch R.)
  1944 *World War*
Wilson, *Lt.-Col.* E. C. T. (E. Surrey R.)
  1940 *World War*

THE GEORGE CROSS (1940)
FOR GALLANTRY

GC

Ribbon, Dark blue, threaded through a bar adorned with laurel leaves

Instituted 24 September 1940 (with amendments, 3 November 1942).

The George Cross is worn before all other decorations (except the VC) on the left breast (when worn by a woman it may be worn on the left shoulder from a ribbon of the same width and colour fashioned into a bow). It consists of a plain silver cross with four equal limbs, the cross having in the centre a circular medallion bearing a design showing St George and the Dragon. The inscription *For Gallantry* appears round the medallion and in the angle of each limb of the cross is the Royal cypher 'G VI' forming a circle concentric with the medallion. The reverse is plain and bears the name of the recipient and the date of the award. The cross is suspended by a ring from a bar adorned with laurel leaves on dark blue ribbon one and a half inches wide.

The cross is intended primarily for civilians; awards to the fighting services are confined to actions for which purely military honours are not normally granted. It is awarded only for acts of the greatest heroism or of the most conspicuous courage in circumstances of extreme danger. From 1 April 1965, holders of the Cross have received a tax-free annuity of £100 (under review).

The royal warrant which ordained that the grant of the Empire Gallantry Medal should cease authorized holders of that medal to return it to the Central Chancery of the Orders of Knighthood and to receive in exchange the George Cross. A similar provision applied to posthumous awards of the Empire Gallantry Medal made after the outbreak of war in 1939. In October 1971 all surviving holders of the Albert Medal and the Edward Medal exchanged those decorations for the George Cross.

SURVIVING RECIPIENTS OF THE GEORGE CROSS
as at 31 August 1995

If the recipient originally received the Empire Gallantry Medal (EGM), the Albert Medal (AM) or the Edward Medal (EM), this is indicated by the initials in parenthesis.

Archer, *Col.* B. S. T., GC, OBE, ERD, 1941
Atkinson, T., GC (EGM), 1939
Baker, J. T., GC (EM), 1929
Bamford, J., GC, 1952
Beaton, J., GC, CVO, 1974
Biggs, *Maj.* K. A., GC, 1946
Bridge, *Cdr.* J., GC, GM, 1944
Butson, *Col.* A. R. C., GC, CD, MD (AM), 1948
Bywater, R. A. S., GC, GM, 1944
Errington, H., GC, 1941
Fairfax, F. W., GC, 1953
Farrow, K., GC (AM), 1948
Flintoff, H. H., GC (EM), 1944
Gledhill, A. J., GC, 1967
Gregson, J. S., GC (AM), 1943
Hawkins, E., GC (AM), 1943
Hodge, *Capt.* A. M., GC, VRD (EGM), 1940
Johnson, *WO1* (*SSM*) B., GC, 1990

Kinne, D. G., GC, 1954
Lowe, A. R., GC (AM), 1949
Lynch, J., GC, BEM (AM), 1948
McClymont, J. M., GC (EGM), 1940
Malta, GC, 1942
Manwaring, T. G., GC (EM), 1949
Moore, R. V., GC, 1940
Moss, B., GC, 1940
Naughton, F., GC (EGM), 1937
Nix, F. E., GC (EM), 1944
Patton, The Hon. John, GC, CBE, 1940
Pearson, Miss J. D. M., GC (EGM), 1940
Pratt, M. K., GC, 1978
Purves, Mrs M., GC (AM), 1949
Raweng, Awang anak, GC, 1951
Riley, G., GC (AM), 1944
Rimmer, R., GC (EGM), 1931
Rowlands, *Air Marshal* Sir John, GC, KBE, 1943
Sinclair, *Air Vice-Marshal* Sir Laurence, GC, KCB, CBE, DSO, 1941
Stevens, H. W., GC, 1958
Stronach, *Capt.* G. P., GC, 1943
Styles, *Lt.-Col.* S. G., GC, 1972
Sylvester, W. G., GC (EGM), 1940
Taylor, *Lt.-Cdr.* W. H., GC, MBE, 1941
Walker, C., GC, 1972
Walker, C. H., GC (AM), 1942
Walton, E. W. K., GC (AM), 1948
Wilcox, C., GC (EM), 1949
Wiltshire, S. N., GC (EGM), 1930
Yates, P. W., GC (EM), 1932

Forms of address

It is only possible to cover here the forms of address for peers, baronets and knights, their wife and children, and Privy Counsellors. Greater detail should be sought in one of the publications devoted to the subject.

Both formal and social forms of address are given where usage differs; nowadays, the social form is generally preferred to the formal, which increasingly is used only for official documents and on very formal occasions.

F— represents forename
S— represents surname

BARON – *Envelope (formal)*, The Right Hon. Lord —; *(social)*, The Lord —. *Letter (formal)*, My Lord; *(social)*, Dear Lord —. *Spoken*, Lord —.

BARON'S WIFE – *Envelope (formal)*, The Right Hon. Lady —; *(social)*, The Lady —. *Letter (formal)*, My Lady; *(social)*, Dear Lady —. *Spoken*, Lady —.

BARON'S CHILDREN – *Envelope*, The Hon. F— S—. *Letter*, Dear Mr/Miss/Mrs S—. *Spoken*, Mr/Miss/Mrs S—.

BARONESS IN OWN RIGHT – *Envelope*, may be addressed in same way as a Baron's wife or, if she prefers *(formal)*, The Right Hon. the Baroness —; *(social)*, The Baroness —. Otherwise as for a Baron's wife.

BARONET – *Envelope*, Sir F—S—, Bt. *Letter (formal)*, Dear Sir; *(social)*, Dear Sir F—. *Spoken*, Sir F—.

BARONET'S WIFE – *Envelope*, Lady S—. *Letter (formal)*, Dear Madam; *(social)*, Dear Lady S—. *Spoken*, Lady S—.

COUNTESS IN OWN RIGHT – As for an Earl's wife.

COURTESY TITLES – The heir apparent to a Duke, Marquess or Earl uses the highest of his father's other titles as a courtesy title. (For list, *see* pages 169–70.) The holder of a courtesy title is not styled The Most Hon. or The Right Hon., and in correspondence 'The' is omitted before the title. The heir apparent to a Scottish title may use the title 'Master' (*see* below).

DAME – *Envelope*, Dame F—S—, followed by appropriate post-nominal letters. *Letter (formal)*, Dear Madam; *(social)*, Dear Dame F—. *Spoken*, Dame F—.

DUKE – *Envelope (formal)*, His Grace the Duke of —; *(social)*, The Duke of —. *Letter (formal)*, My Lord Duke; *(social)*, Dear Duke. *Spoken (formal)*, Your Grace; *(social)*, Duke.

DUKE'S WIFE – *Envelope (formal)*, Her Grace the Duchess of —; *(social)*, The Duchess of —. *Letter (formal)*, Dear Madam; *(social)*, Dear Duchess. *Spoken*, Duchess.

DUKE'S ELDEST SON – *see* Courtesy titles.

DUKE'S YOUNGER SONS – *Envelope*, Lord F—S—. *Letter (formal)*, My Lord; *(social)*, Dear Lord F—. *Spoken (formal)*, My Lord; *(social)*, Lord F—.

DUKE'S DAUGHTER – *Envelope*, Lady F—S—. *Letter (formal)*, Dear Madam; *(social)*, Dear Lady F—. *Spoken*, Lady F—.

EARL – *Envelope (formal)*, The Right Hon. the Earl (of) —; *(social)*, The Earl (of) —. *Letter (formal)*, My Lord; *(social)*, Dear Lord —. *Spoken (formal)*, My Lord; *(social)*, Lord —.

EARL'S WIFE – *Envelope (formal)*, The Right Hon. the Countess (of) —; *(social)*, The Countess (of) —. *Letter (formal)*, Madam; *(social)*, Lady —. *Spoken (formal)*, Madam; *(social)*, Lady —.

EARL'S CHILDREN – *Eldest son, see* Courtesy titles. *Younger sons*, The Hon. F—S— (for forms of address, *see* Baron's children). *Daughters*, Lady F—S— (for forms of address, *see* Duke's daughter).

KNIGHT (BACHELOR) – *Envelope*, Sir F—S—. *Letter (formal)*, Dear Sir; *(social)*, Dear Sir F—. *Spoken*, Sir F—.

KNIGHT (ORDERS OF CHIVALRY) – *Envelope*, Sir F—S—, followed by appropriate post-nominal letters. Otherwise as for Knight Bachelor.

KNIGHT'S WIFE – As for Baronet's wife.

LIFE PEER – As for Baron or for Baroness in own right.

LIFE PEER'S WIFE – As for Baron's wife.

LIFE PEER'S CHILDREN – As for Baron's children.

MARQUESS – *Envelope (formal)*, The Most Hon. the Marquess of —; *(social)*, The Marquess of —. *Letter (formal)*, My Lord; *(social)*, Dear Lord —. *Spoken (formal)*, My Lord; *(social)*, Lord —.

MARQUESS'S WIFE – *Envelope (formal)*, The Most Hon. the Marchioness of —; *(social)*, The Marchioness of —. *Letter (formal)*, Madam; *(social)*, Dear Lady —. *Spoken*, Lady —.

MARQUESS'S CHILDREN – *Eldest son, see* Courtesy titles. *Younger sons*, Lord F—S— (for forms of address, *see* Duke's younger sons). *Daughters*, Lady F—S— (for forms of address, *see* Duke's daughter).

MASTER – The title is used by the heir apparent to a Scottish peerage, though usually the heir apparent to a Duke, Marquess or Earl uses his courtesy title rather than 'Master'. *Envelope*, The Master of —. *Letter (formal)*, Dear Sir; *(social)*, Dear Master of —. *Spoken (formal)*, Master, or Sir; *(social)*, Master, or Mr S—.

MASTER'S WIFE – Addressed as for the wife of the appropriate peerage style, otherwise as Mrs S—.

PRIVY COUNSELLOR – *Envelope*, The Right (or Rt.) Hon. F—S—. *Letter*, Dear Mr/Miss/Mrs S—. *Spoken*, Mr/Miss/Mrs S—. It is incorrect to use the letters PC after the name in conjunction with the prefix The Right Hon., unless the Privy Counsellor is a peer below the rank of Marquess and so is styled The Right Hon. because of his rank. In this case the post-nominal letters may be used in conjunction with the prefix The Right Hon.

VISCOUNT – *Envelope (formal)*, The Right Hon. the Viscount —; *(social)*, The Viscount —. *Letter (formal)*, My Lord; *(social)*, Dear Lord —. *Spoken*, Lord —.

VISCOUNT'S WIFE – *Envelope (formal)*, The Right Hon. the Viscountess —; *(social)*, The Viscountess —. *Letter (formal)*, Madam; *(social)*, Dear Lady —. *Spoken*, Lady —.

VISCOUNT'S CHILDREN – As for Baron's children.

The Privy Council

The Sovereign in Council, or Privy Council, was the chief source of executive power until the system of Cabinet government developed in the 18th century. Now the Privy Council's main functions are to advise the Sovereign and to exercise its own statutory responsibilities independent of the Sovereign in Council (*see also* page 221).

Membership of the Privy Council is automatic upon appointment to certain government and judicial positions in the United Kingdom, e.g. Cabinet ministers must be Privy Counsellors and are sworn in on first assuming office. Membership is also accorded by The Queen to eminent people in the UK and independent countries of the Commonwealth of which Her Majesty is Queen, on the recommendation of the British Prime Minister. Membership of the Council is retained for life, except for very occasional removals.

The administrative functions of the Privy Council are carried out by the Privy Council Office (*see* pages 337–8) under the direction of the Lord President of the Council, who is always a member of the Cabinet.

Lord President of the Council, The Rt. Hon. Antony Newton, OBE, MP
Clerk of the Council, N. H. Nicholls, CBE

MEMBERS *as at 31 August 1995*

HRH The Duke of Edinburgh, 1951
HRH The Prince of Wales, 1977

Aberdare, Lord, 1974
Ackner, Lord, 1980
Adams-Schneider, Sir Lancelot, 1980
Airlie, Earl of, 1984
Aitken, Jonathan, 1994
Aldington, Lord, 1954
Aldous, Sir William, 1995
Alebua, Ezekiel, 1988
Alison, Michael, 1981
Alport, Lord, 1960
Amery of Lustleigh, Lord, 1960
Ampthill, Lord, 1995
Anthony, Douglas, 1971
Archer of Sandwell, Lord, 1977
Armstrong, Ernest, 1979
Arnold, Sir John, 1979
Ashdown, Paddy, 1989
Ashley of Stoke, Lord, 1979
Atkins, Robert, 1995
Auld, Sir Robin, 1995
Avonside, Lord, 1962

Azikiwe, Nnamdi, 1960
Baker, Kenneth, 1984
Balcombe, Sir John, 1985
Barber, Lord, 1963
Barnett, Lord, 1975
Barwick, Sir Garfield, 1964
Beckett, Margaret, 1993
Beith, Alan, 1992
Beldam, Sir Roy, 1989
Belstead, Lord, 1983
Benn, Anthony, 1964
Bennett, Sir Frederic, 1985
Bevins, John, 1959
Biffen, John, 1979
Bingham, Sir Thomas, 1986
Birch, William, 1992
Bird, Vere, 1982
Bisson, Sir Gordon, 1987
Blair, Anthony, 1994
Blaker, Lord, 1983
Blatch, Baroness, 1993
Bolger, James, 1991
Booth, Albert, 1976
Boothroyd, Betty, 1992
Boscawen, Hon. Robert, 1992
Bottomley, Lord, 1952
Bottomley, Virginia, 1992
Boyd-Carpenter, Lord, 1954
Boys, Michael, 1989
Boyson, Sir Rhodes, 1987
Braine, Lord, 1985
Brandon of Oakbrook, Lord, 1978
Brathwaite, Sir Nicholas, 1991
Bridge of Harwich, Lord, 1975
Brightman, Lord, 1979
Brittan, Sir Leon, 1981
Brooke, Peter, 1988
Brown, Sir Simon, 1992
Brown, Sir Stephen, 1983
Browne, Sir Patrick, 1974
Browne-Wilkinson, Lord, 1983
Buckley, Sir Denys, 1970
Butler, Sir Adam, 1984
Butler-Sloss, Dame Elizabeth, 1988
Caithness, Earl of, 1990
Callaghan of Cardiff, Lord, 1964
Cameron of Lochbroom, Lord, 1984
Campbell of Croy, Lord, 1970
Canterbury, The Archbishop of, 1991
Carlisle of Bucklow, Lord, 1979
Carr of Hadley, Lord, 1963
Carrington, Lord, 1959
Carswell, Sir Robert, 1993
Casey, Sir Maurice, 1986
Castle of Blackburn, Baroness, 1964
Cato, Robert, 1981
Chalfont, Lord, 1964
Chalker of Wallasey, Baroness, 1987
Chan, Sir Julius, 1981
Channon, Paul, 1980
Charteris of Amisfield, Lord, 1972
Chataway, Sir Christopher, 1970
Clark, Hon. Alan, 1991
Clark, Helen, 1990

Clark of Kempston, Lord, 1990
Clarke, Kenneth, 1984
Cledwyn of Penrhos, Lord, 1966
Cockfield, Lord, 1982
Cocks of Hartcliffe, Lord, 1976
Coggan, Lord, 1961
Colman, Fraser, 1986
Colnbrook, Lord, 1973
Colyton, Lord, 1952
Compton, John, 1983
Concannon, John, 1978
Cooke, Sir Robin, 1977
Cooper, Sir Frank, 1983
Cope, Sir John, 1988
Corfield, Sir Frederick, 1970
Cowen, Sir Zelman, 1981
Cradock, Sir Percy, 1993
Cranborne, Viscount, 1994
Crawford and Balcarres, Earl of, 1972
Crickhowell, Lord, 1979
Croom-Johnson, Sir David, 1984
Cumming-Bruce, Sir Roualeyn, 1977
Cunningham, Jack, 1993
Davies, Denzil, 1978
Davison, Sir Ronald, 1978
Dean of Harptree, Lord, 1991
Deedes, Lord, 1962
Dell, Edmund, 1970
Denham, Lord, 1981
Denning, Lord, 1948
Devonshire, Duke of, 1964
Diamond, Lord, 1965
Dillon, Sir Brian, 1982
Donaldson of Lymington, Lord, 1979
Dorrell, Stephen, 1994
Douglas, Sir William, 1977
du Cann, Sir Edward, 1964
Duff, Sir Antony, 1980
Dunn, Sir Robin, 1980
Eccles, Viscount, 1951
Eden of Winton, Lord, 1972
Eggar, Timothy, 1995
Eichelbaum, Sir Thomas, 1989
Emery, Sir Peter, 1993
Emslie, Lord, 1972
Erroll of Hale, Lord, 1960
Esquivel, Manuel, 1986
Evans, Sir Anthony, 1992
Eveleigh, Sir Edward, 1977
Farquharson, Sir Donald, 1989
Fellowes, Sir Robert, 1990
Ferrers, Earl, 1982
Floissac, Sir Vincent, 1992
Foot, Michael, 1974
Forsyth, Michael, 1995
Foster, Derek, 1993
Fowler, Sir Norman, 1979
Fox, Sir Michael, 1981
Fraser, Malcolm, 1976
Fraser of Carmyllie, Lord, 1989
Freeman, John, 1966
Freeman, Roger, 1993
Freeson, Reginald, 1976
Gairy, Sir Eric, 1977

Garel-Jones, Tristan, 1992
Gault, Thomas, 1992
Georges, Telford, 1986
Gibbs, Sir Harry, 1972
Gibson, Sir Peter, 1993
Gibson, Sir Ralph, 1985
Gibson-Watt, Lord, 1974
Gilbert, John, 1978
Gilmour of Craigmillar, Lord, 1973
Glenamara, Lord, 1964
Glendevon, Lord, 1959
Glidewell, Sir Iain, 1985
Goff of Chieveley, Lord, 1982
Goodlad, Alastair, 1992
Gorton, Sir John, 1968
Gowrie, Earl of, 1984
Gray of Contin, Lord, 1982
Griffiths, Lord, 1980
Gummer, John, 1985
Habgood, Rt Revd John, 1983
Hague, William, 1995
Hailsham of St Marylebone, Lord, 1956
Hamilton, Sir Archie, 1991
Hanley, Jeremy, 1994
Harrison, Walter, 1977
Harvington, Lord, 1971
Hattersley, Roy, 1975
Hayhoe, Lord, 1985
Healey, Lord, 1964
Heath, Sir Edward, 1955
Henry, Sir Denis, 1993
Herbison, Margaret, 1964
Heseltine, Michael, 1979
Heseltine, Sir William, 1986
Hesketh, Lord, 1991
Higgins, Sir Terence, 1979
Hirst, Sir David, 1992
Hobhouse, Sir John, 1993
Hoffmann, Lord, 1992
Hogg, Hon. Douglas, 1992
Holderness, Lord, 1959
Home of the Hirsel, Lord, 1951
Hope of Craighead, Lord, 1989
Hordern, Sir Peter, 1993
Houghton of Sowerby, Lord, 1964
Howard, Michael, 1990
Howe of Aberavon, Lord, 1972
Howell, David, 1979
Howell, Lord, 1976
Hughes, Lord, 1970
Hunt, David, 1990
Hunt, Jonathan, 1989
Hurd, Douglas, 1982
Hutchison, Sir Michael, 1995
Hutton, Sir Brian, 1988
Ingraham, Hubert, 1993
Jauncey of Tullichettle, Lord, 1988
Jay, Lord, 1952
Jellicoe, Earl, 1963
Jenkin of Roding, Lord, 1973
Jenkins of Hillhead, Lord, 1964
Jones, Aubrey, 1955
Jopling, Michael, 1979
Jugnauth, Sir Anerood, 1987
Kaufman, Gerald, 1978
Keith of Kinkel, Lord, 1976
Kelly, Sir Basil, 1984
Kenilorea, Sir Peter, 1979
Kennedy, Sir Paul, 1992

Kerr, Sir Michael, 1981
King, Thomas, 1979
Kingsdown, Lord, 1987
Kingsland, Lord, 1994
Kinnock, Neil, 1983
Knight, Gregory, 1995
Lamont, Norman, 1986
Lane, Lord, 1975
Lang, Ian, 1990
Lange, David, 1984
Lansdowne, Marquess of, 1964
Latey, Sir John, 1986
Lauti, Sir Toaripi, 1979
Lawson of Blaby, Lord, 1981
Lawton, Sir Frederick, 1972
Leggatt, Sir Andrew, 1990
Leonard, Rt. Revd Graham, 1981
Lilley, Peter, 1990
Listowel, Earl of, 1946
Llewelyn-Davies of Hastoe, Baroness, 1975
Lloyd of Berwick, Lord, 1984
Lloyd, Sir Peter, 1994
Longford, Earl of, 1948
Louisy, Allan, 1981
Lowry, Lord, 1974
Luce, Sir Richard, 1986
Lyell, Sir Nicholas, 1990
Mabon, Dickson, 1977
McCarthy, Sir Thaddeus, 1968
McCowan, Sir Anthony, 1989
MacDermott, Sir John, 1987
MacGregor, John, 1985
MacIntyre, Duncan, 1980
Mackay of Clashfern, Lord, 1979
McKay, Ian, 1992
McKinnon, Donald, 1992
Maclean, David, 1995
McMullin, Sir Duncan, 1980
Major, John, 1987
Manley, Michael, 1989
Mann, Sir Michael, 1988
Mara, Ratu Sir Kamisese, 1973
Marsh, Lord, 1966
Mason of Barnsley, Lord, 1968
Maude, Hon. Francis, 1992
Mawhinney, Brian, 1994
May, Sir John, 1982
Mayhew, Sir Patrick, 1986
Megarry, Sir Robert, 1978
Megaw, Sir John, 1969
Mellish, Lord, 1967
Mellor, David, 1990
Merlyn-Rees, Lord, 1974
Millan, Bruce, 1975
Millett, Sir Peter, 1994
Mitchell, Sir James, 1985
Molyneaux, James, 1983
Monro, Sir Hector, 1995
Moore of Lower Marsh, Lord, 1986
Moore, Michael, 1990
Moore of Wolvercote, Lord, 1977
Morris, Alfred, 1979
Morris, Charles, 1978
Morris, John, 1970
Morris, Michael, 1994
Morritt, Sir Robert, 1994
Moyle, Roland, 1978
Murray, Hon. Lord, 1974
Murray, Sir Donald, 1989

Murray of Epping Forest, Lord, 1976
Murton of Lindisfarne, Lord, 1976
Mustill, Lord, 1985
Nairne, Sir Patrick, 1982
Namaliu, Rabbie, 1989
Needham, Richard, 1994
Neill, Sir Brian, 1985
Newton, Antony, 1988
Nicholls of Birkenhead, Lord, 1995
Nicholson, Sir Michael, 1995
Nolan, Lord, 1991
Nott, Sir John, 1979
Nourse, Sir Martin, 1985
Nutting, Sir Anthony, 1954
Oakes, Gordon, 1979
O'Brien of Lothbury, Lord, 1970
O'Connor, Sir Patrick, 1980
O'Donnell, Turlough, 1979
O'Flynn, Francis, 1987
Oliver of Aylmerton, Lord, 1980
Onslow, Sir Cranley, 1988
Oppenheim-Barnes, Baroness, 1979
Orme, Stanley, 1974
Otton, Sir Philip, 1995
Owen, Lord, 1976
Paeniu, Bikenibeu, 1991
Palliser, Sir Michael, 1983
Palmer, Sir Geoffrey, 1986
Parker, Sir Roger, 1983
Parkinson, Lord, 1981
Patten, Christopher, 1989
Patten, John, 1990
Patterson, Percival, 1993
Pattie, Sir Geoffrey, 1987
Percival, Sir Ian, 1983
Perth, Earl of, 1957
Peyton of Yeovil, Lord, 1970
Pill, Sir Malcolm, 1995
Pindling, Sir Lynden, 1976
Portillo, Michael, 1992
Powell, Enoch, 1960
Prentice, Lord, 1966
Prescott, John, 1994
Price, George, 1982
Prior, Lord, 1970
Puapua, Tomasi, 1982
Purchas, Sir Francis, 1982
Pym, Lord, 1970
Raison, Sir Timothy, 1982
Ramsden, James, 1963
Rawlinson of Ewell, Lord, 1964
Redwood, John, 1993
Rees, Lord, 1983
Renton, Lord, 1962
Renton, Timothy, 1989
Richard, Lord, 1993
Richardson, Sir Ivor, 1978
Richardson of Duntisbourne, Lord, 1976
Richmond, Sir Clifford, 1973
Rifkind, Malcolm, 1986
Rippon of Hexham, Lord, 1962
Robens of Woldingham, Lord, 1951
Roberts, Sir Wyn, 1991
Robinson, Sir Kenneth, 1964
Roch, Sir John, 1993
Rodger of Earlsferry, Lord, 1992
Rodgers of Quarry Bank, Lord, 1975
Rose, Sir Christopher, 1992
Roskill, Lord, 1971

Ross, *Hon.* Lord, 1985
Rowling, Sir Wallace, 1974
Rumbold, Dame Angela, 1991
Runcie, Lord, 1980
Russell, Sir Patrick, 1987
Ryder, Richard, 1990
Sainsbury, Hon. Sir Timothy, 1992
St John of Fawsley, Lord, 1979
Sandiford, Erskine, 1989
Saville, Sir Mark, 1994
Scarman, Lord, 1973
Schiemann, Sir Konrad, 1995
Scott, Sir Nicholas, 1989
Scott, Sir Richard, 1991
Seaga, Edward, 1981
Seear, Baroness, 1985
Shawcross, Lord, 1946
Shearer, Hugh, 1969
Sheldon, Robert, 1977
Shephard, Gillian, 1992
Shepherd, Lord, 1965
Shore, Peter, 1967
Simmonds, Kennedy, 1984
Simon of Glaisdale, Lord, 1961
Sinclair, Ian, 1977
Slade, Sir Christopher, 1982
Slynn of Hadley, Lord, 1992
Somare, Sir Michael, 1977
Somers, Sir Edward, 1981

Stanley, Sir John, 1984
Staughton, Sir Christopher, 1988
Steel, Sir David, 1977
Stephen, Sir Ninian, 1979
Stephenson, Sir John, 1971
Stewartby, Lord, 1989
Steyn, Lord, 1992
Stocker, Sir John, 1986
Stodart of Leaston, Lord, 1974
Stott, Lord, 1964
Strathclyde, Lord, 1995
Stuart-Smith, Sir Murray, 1988
Talboys, Sir Brian, 1977
Taylor of Gosforth, Lord, 1988
Tebbit, Lord, 1981
Templeman, Lord, 1978
Thatcher, Baroness, 1970
Thomas of Gwydir, Lord, 1964
Thomas, Sir Swinton, 1994
Thomson, David, 1981
Thomson of Monifieth, Lord, 1966
Thorpe, Jeremy, 1967
Tizard, Robert, 1986
Tonypandy, Viscount, 1968
Trefgarne, Lord, 1989
Trumpington, Baroness, 1992
Ullswater, Viscount, 1994
Varley, Lord, 1974
Waddington, Lord, 1987

Waite, Sir John, 1993
Wakeham, Lord, 1983
Waldegrave, William, 1990
Walker, Sir Harold, 1979
Walker of Worcester, Lord, 1970
Waller, Sir George, 1976
Ward, Sir Alan, 1995
Watkins, Sir Tasker, 1980
Watkinson, Viscount, 1955
Weatherill, Lord, 1980
Wheeler, Sir John, 1993
Whitelaw, Viscount, 1967
Wilberforce, Lord, 1964
Williams, Alan, 1977
Williams of Crosby, Baroness, 1974
Wilson of Langside, Lord, 1967
Windlesham, Lord, 1973
Wingti, Paias, 1987
Withers, Reginald, 1977
Woodhouse, Sir Owen, 1974
Woolf, Lord, 1986
Wylie, *Hon.* Lord, 1970
York, The Archbishop of, 1991
Young, Baroness, 1981
Young, Sir George, 1993
Young of Graffham, Lord, 1984
Younger of Prestwick, Lord, 1979
Zacca, Edward, 1992

The Privy Council of Northern Ireland

The Privy Council of Northern Ireland had responsibilities in Northern Ireland similar to those of the Privy Council in Great Britain until the Northern Ireland Act 1974 instituted direct rule and a UK Cabinet minister became responsible for the functions previously exercised by the Northern Ireland government.

Membership of the Privy Council of Northern Ireland is retained for life. The postnominal initials PC(NI) are used to differentiate its members from those of the Privy Council.

MEMBERS *as at 31 August 1995*

Bailie, Robin, 1971
Bleakley, David, 1971
Bradford, Roy, 1969
Craig, William, 1963
Dobson, John, 1969
Kelly, Sir Basil, 1969
Kirk, Herbert, 1962
Long, William, 1966
Lowry, The Lord, 1971
McConnell, The Lord, 1964
McIvor, Basil, 1971

Morgan, William, 1961
Moyola, The Lord, 1966
Neill, Sir Ivan, 1950
Porter, Sir Robert, 1969
Simpson, Robert, 1969
Taylor, John, MP, 1970
West, Henry, 1960

Parliament

The United Kingdom constitution is not contained in any single document but has evolved in the course of time, formed partly by statute, partly by common law and partly by convention. A constitutional monarchy, the United Kingdom is governed by Ministers of the Crown in the name of the Sovereign, who is head both of the state and of the government.

The organs of government are the legislature (Parliament), the executive and the judiciary. The executive consists of HM Government (Cabinet and other Ministers) (*see* pages 279–80), government departments (*see* pages 281–360), local authorities (*see* Local Government), and public corporations operating nationalized industries or social or cultural services (*see* pages 281–360). The judiciary (*see* Law Courts and Offices) pronounces on the law, both written and unwritten, interprets statutes and is responsible for the enforcement of the law; the judiciary is independent of both the legislature and the executive.

THE MONARCHY

The Sovereign personifies the state and is, in law, an integral part of the legislature, head of the executive, head of the judiciary, the commander-in-chief of all armed forces of the Crown and the 'Supreme Governor' of the Church of England. The seat of the monarchy is in the United Kingdom. In the Channel Islands and the Isle of Man, which are Crown dependencies, the Sovereign is represented by a Lieutenant-Governor. In the member states of the Commonwealth of which the Sovereign is head of state, her representative is a Governor-General; in United Kingdom dependencies the Sovereign is usually represented by a Governor, who is responsible to the British Government.

Although the powers of the monarchy are now very limited, restricted mainly to the advisory and ceremonial, there are important acts of government which require the participation of the Sovereign. These include summoning, proroguing and dissolving Parliament, giving royal assent to bills passed by Parliament, appointing important office-holders, e.g. government ministers, judges, bishops and governors, conferring peerages, knighthoods and other honours, and granting pardon to a person wrongly convicted of a crime. An important function is appointing a Prime Minister, by convention the leader of the political party which enjoys, or can secure, a majority of votes in the House of Commons. In international affairs the Sovereign as head of state has the power to declare war and make peace, to recognize foreign states and governments, to conclude treaties and to annex or cede territory. However, as the Sovereign entrusts executive power to Ministers of the Crown and acts on the advice of her Ministers, which she cannot ignore, in practice royal prerogative powers are exercised by Ministers, who are responsible to Parliament.

Ministerial responsibility does not diminish the Sovereign's importance to the smooth working of government. She holds meetings of the Privy Council, gives audiences to her Ministers and other officials at home and overseas, receives accounts of Cabinet decisions, reads dispatches and signs state papers; she must be informed and consulted on every aspect of national life; and she must show complete impartiality.

COUNSELLORS OF STATE

In the event of the Sovereign's absence abroad, it is necessary to appoint Counsellors of State under letters patent to carry out the chief functions of the Monarch, including the holding of Privy Councils and giving royal assent to acts passed by Parliament. The normal procedure is to appoint as Counsellors three or four members of the royal family among those remaining in the United Kingdom.

In the event of the Sovereign on accession being under the age of eighteen years, or at any time unavailable or incapacitated by infirmity of mind or body for the performance of the royal functions, provision is made for a regency.

THE PRIVY COUNCIL

The Sovereign in Council, or Privy Council, was the chief source of executive power until the system of Cabinet government developed. Now its main function is to advise the Sovereign to approve Orders in Council and to advise on the issue of royal proclamations. The Council's own statutory responsibilities (independent of the powers of the Sovereign in Council) include powers of supervision over the registering bodies for the medical and allied professions. A full Council is summoned only on the death of the Sovereign or when the Sovereign announces his or her intention to marry. (For full list of Counsellors, *see* pages 218–20)

There are a number of advisory Privy Council committees, whose meetings the Sovereign does not attend. Some are prerogative committees, such as those dealing with legislative matters submitted by the legislatures of the Channel Islands and the Isle of Man or with applications for charters of incorporation; and some are provided for by statute, e.g. those for the universities of Oxford and Cambridge and the Scottish universities.

The Judicial Committee of the Privy Council is the final court of appeal from courts of the United Kingdom dependencies, courts of independent Commonwealth countries which have retained the right of appeal, courts of the Channel Islands and the Isle of Man, some professional and disciplinary committees, and church sources. The Committee is composed of Privy Counsellors who hold, or have held, high judicial office, although usually only three or five hear each case.

Administrative work is carried out by the Privy Council Office under the direction of the Lord President of the Council, a Cabinet Minister.

PARLIAMENT

Parliament is the supreme law-making authority and can legislate for the United Kingdom as a whole or for any parts of it separately (the Channel Islands and the Isle of Man are Crown dependencies and not part of the United Kingdom).

The main functions of Parliament are to pass laws, to provide (by voting taxation) the means of carrying on the work of government and to scrutinize government policy and administration, particularly proposals for expenditure. International treaties and agreements are by custom presented to Parliament before ratification.

Parliament emerged during the late 13th and early 14th centuries. The officers of the King's household and the King's judges were the nucleus of early Parliaments, joined by such ecclesiastical and lay magnates as the King might summon to form a prototype 'House of Lords', and occasionally by the knights of the shires, burgesses and proctors of the lower clergy. By the end of Edward III's reign a 'House of Commons' was beginning to appear; the first known Speaker was elected in 1377.

Parliamentary procedure is based on custom and precedent, partly formulated in the Standing Orders of both Houses (see Standing Orders, page 227), and each House has the right to control its own internal proceedings and to commit for contempt. The system of debate in the two Houses is similar; when a motion has been moved, the Speaker proposes the question as the subject of a debate. Members speak from wherever they have been sitting. Questions are decided by a vote on a simple majority. Draft legislation is introduced, in either House, as a bill. Bills can be introduced by a Government Minister or a private Member, but in practice the majority of bills which become law are introduced by the Government. To become law, a bill must be passed by each House (for parliamentary stages, see Bill, page 225) and then sent to the Sovereign for the royal assent, after which it becomes an Act of Parliament.

Proceedings of both Houses are public, except on extremely rare occasions. The minutes (called Votes and Proceedings in the Commons, and Minutes of Proceedings in the Lords) and the speeches (The Official Report of Parliamentary Debates, Hansard) are published daily. Proceedings are also recorded for transmission on radio and television and stored in the Parliamentary Recording Unit before transfer to the National Sound Archive. Television cameras have been allowed into the House of Lords since January 1985 and into the House of Commons since November 1989; committee meetings may also be televised.

By the Parliament Act of 1911, the maximum duration of a Parliament is five years (if not previously dissolved), the term being reckoned from the date given on the writs for the new Parliament. The maximum life has been prolonged by legislation in such rare circumstances as the two world wars (31 January 1911 to 25 November 1918; 26 November 1935 to 15 June 1945). Dissolution and writs for a general election are ordered by the Sovereign on the advice of the Prime Minister. The life of a Parliament is divided into sessions, usually of one year in length, beginning and ending most often in October or November.

THE HOUSE OF LORDS
London SW1A OPW
Tel 0171-219 3000

The House of Lords consists of the Lords Spiritual and Temporal. The Lords Spiritual are the Archbishops of Canterbury and York, the Bishops of London, Durham and Winchester, and the 21 senior diocesan bishops of the Church of England. The Lords Temporal consist of all hereditary peers of England, Scotland, Great Britain and the United Kingdom who have not disclaimed their peerages, life peers created under the Life Peerages Act 1958, and those Lords of Appeal in Ordinary created life peers under the Appellate Jurisdiction Act 1876, as amended (law lords). Disclaimants of a hereditary peerage lose their right to sit in the House of Lords but gain the right to vote at parliamentary elections and to offer themselves for election to the House of Commons (see also page 141). Those peers disqualified from sitting in the House include:

– aliens, i.e. any peer who is not a British citizen, a Commonwealth citizen (under the British Nationality Act 1981) or a citizen of the Republic of Ireland
– peers under the age of 21
– undischarged bankrupts or, in Scotland, those whose estate is sequestered
– peers convicted of treason

Peers who do not wish to attend sittings of the House of Lords may apply for leave of absence for the duration of a Parliament.

Until the beginning of this century the House of Lords had considerable power, being able to veto any bill submitted to it by the House of Commons, but those powers were greatly reduced by the Parliament Acts of 1911 and 1949 (see page 226).

Combined with its legislative role, the House of Lords has judicial powers as the ultimate Court of Appeal for courts in Great Britain and Northern Ireland, except for criminal cases in Scotland. These powers are exercised by the Lord Chancellor and the law lords.

Members of the House of Lords are unpaid. However, they are entitled to reimbursement of travelling expenses on parliamentary business within the UK and certain other expenses incurred for the purpose of attendance at sittings of the House, within a maximum for each day of £71.50 for overnight subsistence, £32.00 for day subsistence and incidental travel, and £31.00 for secretarial costs, postage and certain additional expenses.

COMPOSITION as at 11 July 1995

Archbishops and Bishops, 25
Peers by succession, 755 (17 women)
Hereditary Peers of first creation (including the Prince of Wales), 15
Life Peers under the Appellate Jurisdiction Act 1876, 24
Life Peers under the Life Peerages Act 1958, 374 (65 women)
Total 1,193
Of whom:
Peers without Writs of Summons, 82 (4 minors)
Peers on leave of absence from the House, 74

STATE OF PARTIES as at 11 July 1995

About half of the members of the House of Lords take the whip of one of the political parties. The other members sit on the cross-benches or as independents.

Conservative, 476
Labour, 112
Liberal Democrats, 52
Cross-bench, 288
Other (including Bishops), 265 (of whom 156 are ineligible to attend)

OFFICERS

The House is presided over by the Lord Chancellor, who is ex officio Speaker of the House. A panel of deputy Speakers is appointed by Royal Commission. The first deputy Speaker is the Chairman of Committees, appointed at the beginning of each session, a salaried officer of the House who takes the chair in committee of the whole House and in some select committees. He is assisted by a panel of deputy chairmen, headed by the salaried Principal Deputy Chairman of Committees, who is also chairman of the European Communities Committee of the House.

The permanent officers include the Clerk of the Parliaments, who is in charge of the administrative staff collectively known as the Parliament Office; the Gentleman Usher of the Black Rod, who is also Serjeant-at-Arms in attendance upon the Lord Chancellor and is responsible for security and for accommodation and services in the House of Lords; and the Yeoman Usher who is Deputy Serjeant-at-Arms and assists Black Rod in his duties.

Speaker (£17,659), The Lord Mackay of Clashfern, PC
    Private Secretary, M. E. Ormerod
Chairman of Committees (£50,080), The Lord Boston of Faversham, QC
Principal Deputy Chairman of Committees (£46,101), The Lord Tordoff
Clerk of the Parliaments (£98,957), Sir Michael Wheeler-Booth, KCB
Clerk Assistant and Principal Finance Officer (£67,500–£98,000), J. M. Davies
Reading Clerk and Clerk of Public Bills (£57,000–£84,500), P. D. G. Hayter, LVO
Counsel to Chairman of Committees (£57,000–£84,500), D. Rippengal, CB, QC; Sir James Nursaw, KCB, QC: Mrs E. Denza, CMG
Assistant Counsel (£40,117–£58,729), N. J. Adamson, CB, QC
Principal Clerks (£48,819–£84,500), J. A. Vallance White (*Judicial Office and Fourth Clerk at the Table*); M. G. Pownall (*Clerk of the Journals*); B. P. Keith (*Private Bills*); D. R. Beamish (*Committees*); R. H. Walters, D.phil.
Chief Clerks (£40,117–£58,729), Dr F. P. Tudor; T. V. Mohan; E. C. Ollard
Senior Clerks (£27,613–£41,788), Mrs M. E. Ollard (*seconded as Secretary to the Leader of the House and Chief Whip*); A. Makower; E. J. J. Wells; S. P. Burton; J. L. Goddard
Clerks (£15,172–£26,365), Mrs M. B. Bloor; D. J. Batt; Dr C. A. Mylne; Miss L. Mouland
Clerk of the Records (£40,117–£58,729), D. J. Johnson, FSA
Deputy Clerk of the Records (£31,258–£50,655), S. K. Ellison
Establishment Officer, R. H. Walters, D.phil.
Deputy Establishment Officer (£27,613–£41,788), G. Embleton
Accountant (£27,613–£50,655), C. Preece
Assistant Accountant (£21,789–£28,116), Miss J. M. Lansdown
Computer Executive (£27,613–£41,788), Ms S. C. White
Internal Auditor (£27,613–£41,788), C. H. Rogers
Staff Adviser (£27,613–£41,788), D. A. W. Dunn, ISO
Judicial Taxing Clerk (£21,789–£28,116), C. G. Osborne
Librarian (£40,177–£58,729), D. L. Jones
Deputy Librarian (£31,258–£50,655), P. G. Davis, ph.D.
Senior Library Clerk (£27,613–£41,788), Miss I. L. Victory, ph.D.
Examiners of Petitions for Private Bills, B. P. Keith; R. J. Willoughby
Gentleman Usher of the Black Rod and Serjeant-at-Arms (£57,000–£84,500), Gen. Sir Edward Jones, KCB, CBE
Yeoman Usher of the Black Rod and Deputy Serjeant-at-Arms (£27,613–£41,788), Air Vice-Marshal D. R. Hawkins, CB, MBE
Administration Officer (£27,613–£41,788), Brig. A. J. M. Clark
Staff Superintendent, Maj. A. M. Charlesworth
Shorthand Writer (fees), Mrs P. J. Woolger
Editor, Official Report (*Hansard*), (£37,817–£55,312), Mrs M. E. Villiers
Deputy Editor, Official Report (£28,310–£45,767), G. R. Goodbarne

THE HOUSE OF COMMONS
London SW1A 0AA
Tel 0171-219 3000

The members of the House of Commons are elected by universal adult suffrage. For electoral purposes, the United Kingdom is divided into constituencies, each of which returns one member to the House of Commons, the member being the candidate who obtains the largest number of votes cast in the constituency. To ensure equitable representation the four Boundary Commissions keep constituency boundaries under review and recommend any redistribution of seats which may seem necessary because of population movements, etc. The number of seats was raised to 640 in 1945, then reduced to 625 in 1948, and subsequently rose to 630 in 1955, 635 in 1970, 650 in 1983 and 651 in 1992. Of the present 651 seats, there are 524 for England, 38 for Wales, 72 for Scotland and 17 for Northern Ireland.

ELECTIONS

Elections are by secret ballot, each elector casting one vote; voting is not compulsory. When a seat becomes vacant between general elections, a by-election is held.

British subjects and citizens of the Irish Republic can stand for election as Members of Parliament (MPs) provided they are 21 or over and not subject to disqualification. Those disqualified from sitting in the House include:

– undischarged bankrupts
– people sentenced to more than one year's imprisonment
– clergy of the Church of England, Church of Scotland, Church of Ireland and Roman Catholic Church
– members of the House of Lords
– holders of certain offices listed in the House of Commons Disqualification Act 1975, e.g. members of the judiciary, Civil Service, regular armed forces, police forces, some local government officers and some members of public corporations and government commissions

For entitlement to vote in parliamentary elections, *see* Legal Notes section.

A candidate does not require any party backing but his or her nomination for election must be supported by the signatures of ten people registered in the constituency. A candidate must also deposit with the returning officer £500, which is forfeit if the candidate does not receive more than 5 per cent of the votes cast. All election expenses at a general election, except the candidate's personal expenses, are subject to a statutory limit of £4,330, plus 3.7 pence for each elector in a borough constituency or 4.9 pence for each elector in a county constituency.

See pages 231–7 for an alphabetical list of MPs, pages 241–71 for the results of the last General Election, and pages 238–9 for the results of recent by-elections.

STATE OF PARTIES *as at 28 July 1995*
Conservative, 327 (18 women)
Elected as Conservative but has resigned the whip, 1
Labour, 270 (38 women)
Liberal Democrats, 24 (3 women)
Plaid Cymru, 4
Scottish Nationalist, 4 (2 women)
Democratic Unionist, 3
Social Democratic and Labour, 4
Ulster Unionist, 9
United Kingdom Unionist, 1
The Speaker and three Deputy Speakers, 4 (2 women)
Total, 651 (63 women)

BUSINESS

The week's business of the House is outlined each Thursday by the Leader of the House, after consultation between the Chief Government Whip and the Chief Opposition Whip. A quarter to a third of the time will be taken up by the Government's legislative programme, and the rest by other business, e.g. question time. As a rule, bills likely to raise political controversy are introduced in the Commons before going on to the Lords, and the Commons claims exclusive control in respect of national taxation and expenditure. Bills such as the Finance Bill, which imposes taxation, and the Consolidated Fund Bills, which authorize expenditure, must begin in the Commons. A bill of which the financial provisions are subsidiary may begin in the Lords; and the Commons may waive its rights in regard to Lords' amendments affecting finance.

The Commons has a public register of MPs' financial and certain other interests; this is published annually as a House of Commons paper. Members must also disclose any relevant financial interest or benefit in a matter before the House when taking part in a debate, in certain other proceedings of the House, or in consultations with other MPs, with Ministers or civil servants.

MEMBERS' PAY AND ALLOWANCES

Since 1911 members of the House of Commons have received salary payments; facilities for free travel were introduced in 1924. Members are entitled to claim income tax relief on expenses incurred in the course of their parliamentary duties. Salary rates since 1911 are as follows:

1911	£400 p.a.	1980 June	£11,750 p.a.
1931	360	1981 June	13,950
1934	380	1982 June	14,510
1935	400	1983 June	15,308
1937	600	1984 June	16,106
1946	1,000	1985 Jan	16,904
1954	1,250	1986 Jan	17,702
1957	1,750	1987 Jan	18,500
1964	3,250	1988 Jan	22,548
1972 Jan	4,500	1989 Jan	24,107
1975 June	5,750	1990 Jan	26,701
1976 June	6,062	1991 Jan	28,970
1977 July	6,270	1992 Jan	30,854
1978 June	6,897	1994 Jan	31,687
1979 June	9,450	1995 Jan	33,189

In 1969 MPs were granted an allowance for secretarial and research expenses. In 1987 this became known as the Office Costs Allowance. From April 1995 the allowance is £42,754 a year.

Since 1972 MPs can claim reimbursement for the additional cost of staying overnight away from their main residence while on parliamentary business. This is currently £11,661 a year and since 1984 has been non-taxable.

From 1980 provision was made enabling each MP in receipt of Office Costs Allowance to contribute sums to an approved pension scheme for the provision of a pension, or other benefits, for or in respect of persons whose salary is met by him/her from the Office Costs Allowance.

The net cost of travel allowances for 1994–5 was stated in June 1995 to be £8,885,199.

MEMBERS' PENSIONS

Pension arrangements for MPs were first introduced in 1964. The arrangements currently provide a pension of one-fiftieth of salary for each year of pensionable service with a maximum of two-thirds of salary at age 65. Pension is payable normally at age 65, for men and women, or on later retirement. Pensions may be paid earlier, e.g. on ill-health

retirement. The widow/widower of a former MP receives a pension of five-eighths of the late MP's pension. Pensions are index-linked. Members currently contribute 6 per cent of salary to the pension fund; there is an Exchequer contribution, currently slightly more than the amount contributed by MPs.

The House of Commons Members' Fund provides for annual or lump sum grants to ex-MPs, their widows or widowers, and children whose incomes are below certain limits. Alternatively, payments of £2,070 a year to ex-MPs with at least ten years' service and who left the House of Commons before October 1964, and £1,294 a year to their widows or widowers are made as of right. Members contribute £24 a year and the Exchequer £215,000 a year to the fund. The net assets of the fund as at 30 September 1994 amounted to £2,551,631.

OFFICERS AND OFFICIALS

The House of Commons is presided over by the Speaker, who has considerable powers to maintain order in the House. A deputy, the Chairman of Ways and Means, and two Deputy Chairmen may preside over sittings of the House of Commons; they are elected by the House, and, like the Speaker, neither speak nor vote other than in their official capacity.

The staff of the House are employed by a Commission chaired by the Speaker. The heads of the six House of Commons departments are permanent officers of the House, not MPs. The Clerk of the House is the principal adviser to the Speaker on the privileges and procedures of the House, the conduct of the business of the House, and committees. The Serjeant-at-Arms is responsible for security, ceremonial, and for accommodation in the Commons part of the Palace of Westminster.

Speaker (£67,819), The Rt. Hon. Betty Boothroyd, MP for West Bromwich West
Chairman of Ways and Means (£55,292), The Rt. Hon. Michael Morris, MP for Northampton South
First Deputy Chairman of Ways and Means (£51,621), Sir Geoffrey Lofthouse, MP for Pontefract and Castleford
Second Deputy Chairman of Ways and Means (£51,621), Dame Janet Fookes, DBE, MP for Plymouth Drake

OFFICES OF THE SPEAKER AND CHAIRMAN OF WAYS AND MEANS

Speaker's Secretary (£40,185–£58,729), N. Bevan, CB
Chaplain to the Speaker, The Revd Canon D. Gray, TD
Secretary to the Chairman of Ways and Means, (£27,676–£41,860), Ms L. M. Gardner

DEPARTMENT OF THE CLERK OF THE HOUSE

Clerk of the House of Commons (£98,958), D. W. Limon, CB
Clerk Assistant (£67,500–£81,400), W. R. McKay
Clerk of Committees (£67,500–£81,400), C. B. Winnifrith
Principal Clerks (£48,797–£58,729)
  Public Bills, R. B. Sands
  Table Office, G. Cubie
  Journals, A. J. Hastings
  Private Bills, R. J. Willoughby
  Select Committees, D. G. Millar
  Domestic Committees, M. R. Jack, PH.D.
  Overseas Office, R. W. G. Wilson
  Standing Committees, W. A. Proctor
  Second Clerk of Select Committees, Ms H. E. Irwin
  Financial Committees, Mrs J. Sharpe
Deputy Principal Clerks (£44,500–£58,729), S. A. L. Panton; Ms A. Milner-Barry; F. A. Cranmer; R. J. Rogers; C. R. M. Ward, PH.D.; D. W. N. Doig; D. L. Natzler; E. P. Silk; A. R. Kennon; L. C. Laurence Smyth; S. J. Patrick;

D. J. Gerhold; C. J. Poyser; D. F. Harrison; S. J. Priestley;
A. H. Doherty; P. A. Evans; R. I. S. Phillips; R. G. James,
ph.d.; D. R. Lloyd; Ms P. A. Helme; B. M. Hutton
Senior Clerks (£27,676–£41,860), J. S. Benger, d.phil.;
Ms E. C. Samson; N. P. Walker; M. D. Hamlyn; Mrs E. J.
Flood; P. C. Seaward, d.phil.; C. G. Lee; C. D. Stanton;
A. Y. A. Azad; C. A. Shaw; Ms L. M. Gardner; K. J. Brown;
D. Steel (*acting*); P. Bolton (*acting*); Mrs E. A. J. Attridge
(*acting*); A. M. Kidner (*acting*)
Clerks of Domestic Committees (£27,676–£41,860), P. G.
Moon; M. Clark
Examiners of Petitions for Private Bills, R. J. Willoughby; B. P.
Keith
Registrar of Members' Interests, R. J. Willoughby
Taxing Officer, R. J. Willoughby

Vote Office
Deliverer of the Vote (£40,185–£58,729), H. C. Foster
Deputy Deliverers of the Vote (£27,676–£41,860), J. F. Collins
(*Distribution*); F. W. Hallett (*Production*)

Speaker's Counsel
Speaker's Counsel (£54,131–£64,283), J. S. Mason, cb
Speaker's Counsel (European legislation) (£54,131–£64,283),
T. J. G. Pratt, cb
Speaker's Assistant Counsel (£40,185–£58,729), A. Akbar

Department of the Serjeant-at-Arms
Serjeant-at-Arms (£55,000–£66,000), P. N. W. Jennings
Deputy Serjeant-at-Arms (£40,185–£58,729), M. J. A.
Cummings
Assistant Serjeant-at-Arms (£31,330–£50,632), P. A. J.
Wright
Deputy Assistant Serjeant-at-Arms (£27,676–£41,860), J. M.
Robertson

Parliamentary Works Directorate
Director of Works (£52,537–£58,729), H. P. Webber
Deputy Director of Works (£40,185–£58,729), B. C. Sewell

Information Systems Office
Information Systems Officer (£40,185–£58,729), R. S. Morgan

Department of the Library
Librarian (£55,000–£66,000), Miss J. B. Tanfield
Deputy Librarian (£48,797–£58,729), Miss P. J. Baines
Assistant Librarians (£40,185–£58,729), S. Z. Young; K. G.
Cuninghame
Deputy Assistant Librarians (£31,330–£50,632), Mrs J. M.
Wainwright; C. C. Pond, ph.d.; Mrs C. B. Andrews;
R. C. Clements; Mrs J. M. Lourie; R. J. Ware, d.phil.; C. R.
Barclay; Mrs J. M. Fiddick; Mrs C. M. Gillie; R. J.
Twigger; Mrs G. L. Allen
Senior Library Clerks (£27,676–£41,860), Ms F. Poole; T. N.
Edmonds; R. J. Cracknell; Miss O. M. Gay; Miss E. M.
McInnes; B. K. Winetrobe; Miss M. Baber; Ms A. Walker;
Mrs H. V. Holden; Miss J. Seaton; Mrs P. L. Carling;
A. J. L. Crompton; Miss P. J. Strickland; Miss V. A. Miller;
Ms H. M. Jeffs; M. P. Hillyard; S. A. Wise (*acting*); Ms J.
Roll

Department of Finance and Administration
Director of Finance and Administration (£55,000–£66,000),
J. Rodda
Accountant (£48,797–£51,333), A. R. Marskell
Deputy Accountant (£31,330–£50,632), M. Fletcher
Head of Establishments Office (£48,797–£58,729), B. A.
Wilson
Deputy Head of Establishments Office (£31,330–£50,632), J. A.
Robb

Head of Finance Office (£40,185–£58,729), M. J. Barram
Staff Inspector (£31,330–£50,632), R. C. Collins

Department of the Official Report
Editor (£48,797–£58,729), I. D. Church
Deputy Editor (£40,185–£58,729), P. Walker
Principal Assistant Editors (£31,330–£50,632), J. Gourley;
W. G. Garland; Miss H. Hales; Miss L. Sutherland
Assistant Editors (£31,330–£47,032), Miss V. Grainger; Miss
V. A. A. Clarke; S. Hutchinson; Miss C. Fogarty; Miss
V. A. Widgery; Ms K. Stewart; P. Hadlow

Refreshment Department
Director of Catering Services (£40,185–£58,729), Mrs S. J.
Harrison
Catering Accountant (£27,676–£41,860), D. R. W. Wood
Operations Manager (£27,676–£41,860), N. M. Hutson

PARLIAMENTARY INFORMATION

The following is a short glossary of aspects of the work of
Parliament. Unless otherwise stated, references are to
House of Commons procedures.

Adjournment Debate – Usually a half-hour debate
introduced by a back-bencher at the end of business for
the day. The subjects raised are often local or personal
issues.

Bill – Proposed legislation is termed a bill. The stages of
a public bill (for private bills, *see* page 226) in the House of
Commons are as follows:
First Reading: There is no debate at this stage, which
nowadays merely constitutes an order to have the bill
printed
Second Reading: The debate on the principles of the bill
Committee Stage: The detailed examination of a bill, clause
by clause. In most cases this takes place in a standing
committee, or the whole House may act as a committee. A
special standing committee may take evidence before
embarking on detailed scrutiny of the bill. Very rarely, a
bill may be examined by a select committee (*see* page 227)
Report Stage: Detailed review of a bill as amended in
committee
Third Reading: Final debate on a bill
Public bills go through the same stages in the House of
Lords, except that in almost all cases the committee stage is
taken in committee of the whole House.
A bill may start in either House, and has to pass through
both Houses to become law. Both Houses have to agree the
same text of a bill, so that the amendments made by the
second House are then considered in the originating
House, and if not agreed, sent back or themselves amended,
until agreement is reached.

Chiltern Hundreds – A legal fiction, a nominal office
of profit under the Crown, the acceptance of which requires
an MP to vacate his seat. The Manor of Northstead is
similar. These are the only means by which an MP may
resign.

Closure and Guillotine – To prevent deliberate
waste of time of either House, a motion may be made that
the question be now put. In the House of Commons, if the
Speaker decides that the rights of a minority are not being
prejudiced and 100 members support the closure motion in
a division, if carried, the original motion is put to the House
without further debate.

The guillotine represents a more rigorous and systematic application of the closure. Under this system, a bill proceeds in accordance with a rigid timetable and discussion is limited to the time allotted to each group of clauses. The closure is hardly ever used in the Lords, and there is no procedure for a guillotine. The completion of business in the Lords is ensured by agreement from all sides of the House.

CONSOLIDATED FUND BILL – A bill to authorize issue of money to maintain Government services. The bill is dealt with without debate.

DELEGATED LEGISLATION – Many statutes empower Ministers to make delegated legislation, with little or no reference back to Parliament, usually by means of Statutory Instruments. These fall into four broad categories:
Affirmative Instruments, which are subject to approval by resolutions of both Houses before they can come into or remain in force
Negative Instruments, which are subject to annulment by resolution of either House
General Instruments, which include those not required to be laid before Parliament and those which are required to be so laid but are not subject to approval or annulment
Special Procedure Orders, against which parties outside Parliament may lodge petitions

DISSOLUTION – Parliament comes to an end either by dissolution by the Sovereign, on the advice of the Prime Minister, or on the expiration of the term of five years for which the House of Commons was elected. Dissolution is normally effected by a royal proclamation.

EARLY DAY MOTION – A motion put on the notice paper by an MP without in general the real prospect of its being debated. Such motions are expressions of back-bench opinion.

EMERGENCY DEBATE – In the Commons a method of obtaining prompt discussion of a matter of urgency is by moving the adjournment under Standing Order No. 20 for the purpose of discussing a specific and important matter that should have urgent consideration. A member may ask leave to make this motion by giving written notice to the Speaker, usually before 12 noon, and if the Speaker considers the matter of sufficient importance and the House agrees, it is discussed usually at 7 p.m. on the following day.

FATHER OF THE HOUSE – The Member whose continuous service in the House of Commons is the longest. The present Father of the House is the Rt. Hon. Sir Edward Heath, KG, MBE, MP, elected first in 1950.

GENERAL SYNOD MEASURE – A measure passed by the national assembly of the Church of England under the Church of England Assembly (Powers) Act 1919. These measures are considered by the Joint Ecclesiastical Committee, who make a report. They are then considered by both Houses and, if approved, sent for the royal assent.

HANSARD – The official report of debates in both Houses (and in standing committees) published by HMSO, normally on the day after the sitting concerned.

HOURS OF MEETING – The House of Commons meets Monday to Thursday at 2.30 p.m., and on Friday at 9.30 a.m. Some changes – Wednesday sittings beginning at 10 a.m. and some Fridays without sittings – were introduced as an experiment during the 1994–5 session. The House of Lords normally meets at 2.30 p.m. Monday to Wednesday and at 3 p.m. on Thursday. In the latter part of the session, the House of Lords sometimes sits on Fridays at 11 a.m.

HYBRIDITY – A public bill which is considered to affect specific private or local interests, as distinct from all such interests of a single category, is called a hybrid bill and is subject to a special form of scrutiny to enable people affected to object. In the House of Lords, affirmative instruments (*see* Delegated Legislation above) may also be treated as hybrid.

LEADER OF THE OPPOSITION – In 1937 the office of Leader of the Opposition was recognized and a salary was assigned to the post. Since January 1995 the salary has been £64,257 (including parliamentary salary of £24,985). The present Leader of the Opposition is the Rt. Hon. Tony Blair, MP.

THE LORD CHANCELLOR – The Lord High Chancellor of Great Britain is (*ex officio*) the Speaker of the House of Lords. Unlike the Speaker of the House of Commons, he is a member of the Government, takes part in debates and votes in divisions. He has none of the powers to maintain order that the Speaker in the Commons has, these powers being exercised in the Lords by the House as a whole. The Lord Chancellor sits in the Lords on one of the Woolsacks, couches covered with red cloth and stuffed with wool. If he wishes to address the House in any way except formally as Speaker, he leaves the Woolsack.

NAMING – When a member has been named by the Speaker for a breach of order, i.e. contrary to the practice of the House, called by surname and not addressed as the 'Hon. Member for... (her/his constituency)', the Leader of the House moves that the offender 'be suspended from the service of the House' for (in the case of a first offence) a period of five sitting days. Should the member offend again, the period of suspension is increased.

OPPOSITION DAY – A day on which the topic for debate is chosen by the Opposition. There are twenty such days in a normal session. On seventeen days, subjects are chosen by the Leader of the Opposition; on the remaining three days by the leader of the next largest opposition party.

PARLIAMENT ACTS 1911 AND 1949 – Under these Acts, bills may become law without the consent of the Lords.
Since at least the 18th century the Commons has had the privilege of having bills concerned with supply (i.e. taxation and money matters) passed without amendment by the Lords, though until 1911 the Lords retained the right to reject such bills outright.
By the Parliament Act 1911, a bill which has been endorsed by the Speaker of the House of Commons as a money bill, and has been passed by the Commons and sent up to the Lords at least one month before the end of a session, can become law without the consent of the Lords if it is not passed by them without amendment within a month.
Under the Parliament Acts 1911 and 1949, if the Lords reject any other public bill (except one to prolong the life of a Parliament) which has been passed by the Commons in two successive sessions, then that bill shall (unless the Commons direct to the contrary) become law without the consent of the Lords. The Lords have power, therefore, to delay a public bill for thirteen months from its first second reading in the House of Commons.

PRIME MINISTER'S QUESTIONS – The Prime Minister answers questions from 3.15 to 3.30 p.m. on Tuesdays and Thursdays. Nowadays the 'open question' predominates. Members tend to ask the Prime Minister what are his or her official engagements for the day; a supplementary question on virtually any topic can then be put.

PRIVATE BILL – A bill promoted by a body or an individual to give powers additional to, or in conflict with, the general law, and to which a special procedure applies to enable people affected to object.

PRIVATE MEMBERS' BILL – A public bill promoted by a Member who is not a member of the Government.

PRIVATE NOTICE QUESTION – A question adjudged of urgent importance on submission to the Speaker (in the Lords, the Leader of the House), answered at the end of oral questions, usually at 3.30 p.m.

PRIVILEGE – The following are covered by the privilege of Parliament:
(i) freedom from interference in going to, attending at, and going from, Parliament
(ii) freedom of speech in parliamentary proceedings
(iii) the printing and publishing of anything relating to the proceedings of the two Houses is subject to privilege
(iv) each House is the guardian of its dignity and may punish any insult to the House as a whole

PROROGATION – The bringing to an end, by the Sovereign on the advice of the Government, of a session of Parliament. Public bills which have not completed all their stages lapse on prorogation.

QUEEN'S SPEECH – The speech delivered by The Queen at the State Opening of Parliament, in which the Government's programme for the session is set forth. The speech is drafted by civil servants and approved by the Cabinet.

QUESTION TIME – Oral questions are answered by Ministers in the Commons from 2.30 to 3.30 p.m. every day except Friday. They are also taken at the start of the Lords sittings, with a daily limit of four oral questions.

ROYAL ASSENT – The royal assent is signified by letters patent to such bills and measures as have passed both Houses of Parliament (or bills which have been passed under the Parliament Acts 1911 and 1949). The Sovereign has not given royal assent in person since 1854. On occasion, for instance in the prorogation of Parliament, royal assent may be pronounced to the two Houses by Lords Commissioners. More usually royal assent is notified to each House sitting separately in accordance with the Royal Assent Act 1967. The old French formulae for royal assent are then endorsed on the acts by the Clerk of the Parliaments.
The power to withhold assent resides with the Sovereign but has not been exercised in the United Kingdom since 1707, in the reign of Queen Anne.

SELECT COMMITTEES – Consisting usually of ten to 15 members of all parties, select committees are a means used by both Houses in order to investigate certain matters.
Most select committees in the House of Commons are now tied to departments; each committee investigates subjects within a government department's remit. There are other House of Commons select committees dealing with public accounts (i.e. the spending by the Government of money voted by Parliament) and European legislation, and also domestic committees dealing, for example, with privilege and procedure. Major select committees usually take evidence in public; their evidence and reports are published by HMSO.
The principal select committee in the House of Lords is that on the European Communities, which has, at present, six sub-committees dealing with all areas of Community policy. The House of Lords also has a select committee on science and technology, which appoints sub-committees to deal with specific subjects. In addition, *ad hoc* select committees have been set up from time to time to investigate specific subjects, e.g. overseas trade, murder and life imprisonment. There are also some joint com-

mittees of the two Houses, e.g. the Joint Committee on Statutory Instruments.

DEPARTMENTAL COMMITTEES
Agriculture – *Chair*, Sir Jerry Wiggin, MP; *Clerk*, Mr Walker
Defence – *Chair*, Sir Nicholas Bonsor, MP; *Clerks*, Mr Natzler, Mr Shaw
Education – *Chair*, Sir Malcolm Thornton, MP; *Clerk*, Mr Hamlyn
Employment – *Chair*, Hon. Greville Janner, MP; *Clerk*, Dr Seaward
Environment – *Chair*, Andrew Bennett, MP; *Clerks*, Mr Priestley, Miss Adams
Foreign Affairs – *Chair*, Rt. Hon. David Howell, MP; *Clerks*, Dr Ward, Mr Reid
Health – *Chair*, Marion Roe, MP; *Clerks*, Dr James, Mr Healey
Home Affairs – *Chair*, Sir Ivan Lawrence, MP; *Clerks*, Mr Poyser, Mr Fox
National Heritage – *Chair*, Rt. Hon. Gerald Kaufman, MP; *Clerk*, Mrs Sharpe
Northern Ireland – *Chair*, Clive Soley, MP, *Clerk*, Mr Phillips
Science and Technology – *Chair*, Sir Giles Shaw, MP; *Clerk*, Ms Samson
Scottish Affairs – *Chair*, William McKelvey, MP; *Clerk*, Mr Doherty
Social Security – *Chair*, Frank Field, MP; *Clerk*, Mr Lawrence Smyth
Trade and Industry – *Chair*, Richard Caborn, MP; *Clerks*, Mr Gerhold, Ms Gardner
Transport – *Chair*, Rt. Hon. Paul Channon, MP; *Clerk*, Ms Long, Mr Stanton
Treasury and Civil Service – *Chair*, Sir Thomas Arnold, MP; *Clerks*, Mr Proctor, Mr Hensher
Welsh Affairs – *Chair*, Gareth Wardell, MP; *Clerk*, Mr Hutton

NON-DEPARTMENTAL COMMITTEES
Deregulation – *Chair*, Barry Field, MP; *Clerks*, Mr Rogers, Mr Lloyd
European Legislation – *Chair*, James Hood, MP; *Clerk*, Mr Rogers
Members' Interests – *Chair*, Sir Geoffrey Johnson Smith, MP; *Clerk*, Mr Willoughby
Parliamentary Commissioner – *Chair*, James Pawsey, MP; *Clerk*, Mr Azad
Privileges – *Chair*, Rt. Hon. Antony Newton, MP; *Clerk*, Mr Hastings
Procedure – *Chair*, Rt. Hon. Sir Peter Emery, MP; *Clerks*, Mr Kennon, Mrs Mulley
Public Accounts – *Chair*, Rt. Hon. Robert Sheldon, MP; *Clerk*, Mr Brown
Standards in Public Life – *Chair*, Rt. Hon. Antony Newton, MP; *Clerks*, Mr Winnifrith, Mr Doig

THE SPEAKER – The Speaker of the House of Commons is the spokesman and president of the Chamber. He or she is elected by the House at the beginning of each Parliament or when the previous Speaker retires or dies. The Speaker neither speaks in debates nor votes in divisions except when the voting is equal.

STANDING ORDERS – Rules which have from time to time been agreed by each House of Parliament to regulate the conduct of its business. These orders may be amended or repealed, and are from time to time suspended or dispensed with.

STATE OPENING – This marks the start of each new session of Parliament. Parliament is normally opened, in the presence of both Houses, by The Queen in person, who makes the speech from the throne which outlines the Government's policies for the coming session (*see* Queen's Speech). In the absence of The Queen, Parliament is opened by Royal Commission, and The Queen's Speech is read by one of the Lords Commissioners specially appointed by letters patent for the occasion.

STRANGERS – Anyone who is not a Member or Officer of the House is a stranger. Visitors are generally admitted to debates of both Houses but may be excluded if the House so decides; in practice this happens only in time of war. However, the cry of 'I spy strangers' causes the public gallery to be cleared, and occurs often.

TEN MINUTE RULE – A colloquial term for Standing Order No. 19, under which back-benchers have an opportunity on Tuesdays and Wednesdays to state for about ten minutes why a bill on a certain subject should be introduced. Time is also available for a short opposing speech.

VACANT SEATS – When a vacancy occurs in the House of Commons during a session of Parliament, the writ for the by-election is moved by a Whip of the party to which the member whose seat has been vacated belonged. If the House is in recess, the Speaker can issue a warrant for a writ, should two members certify to him that a seat is vacant.

WHIPS – In order to secure the attendance of Members of a particular party in Parliament on all occasions, and particularly on the occasion of an important vote, Whips (originally known as 'Whippers-in') are appointed. The written appeal or circular letter issued by them is also known as a 'whip', its urgency being denoted by the number of times it is underlined. Failure to respond to a three-line whip, headed 'Most important', is tantamount in the Commons to secession (at any rate temporarily) from the party. Whips are officially recognized by Parliament and are provided with office accommodation in both Houses. In both Houses, Government and some Opposition Whips receive salaries from public funds.

PUBLIC INFORMATION SERVICES

HOUSE OF COMMONS – Public Information Office, House of Commons, London SW1A 0AA. Tel: 0171-219 4272
HOUSE OF LORDS – The Journal and Information Office, House of Lords, London SW1A 0PW. Tel: 0171-219 3107

GOVERNMENT OFFICE

The Government is the body of Ministers responsible for the administration of national affairs, determining policy and introducing into Parliament any legislation necessary to give effect to government policy. The majority of Ministers are members of the House of Commons but members of the House of Lords or of neither House may also hold ministerial responsibility. The Lord Chancellor is always a member of the House of Lords. The Prime Minister is, by current convention, always a member of the House of Commons.

THE PRIME MINISTER

The office of Prime Minister, which had been in existence for nearly 200 years, was officially recognized in 1905 and its holder was granted a place in the table of precedence. The Prime Minister, by tradition also First Lord of the Treasury and Minister for the Civil Service, is appointed by the Sovereign and is usually the leader of the party which enjoys, or can secure, a majority in the House of Commons. Other Ministers are appointed by the Sovereign on the recommendation of the Prime Minister, who

also allocates functions amongst Ministers and has the power to obtain their resignation or dismissal individually.

The Prime Minister informs the Sovereign of state and political matters, advises on the dissolution of Parliament, and makes recommendations for important Crown appointments, the award of honours, etc.

As the chairman of Cabinet meetings and leader of a political party, the Prime Minister is responsible for translating party policy into government activity. As leader of the Government, the Prime Minister is responsible to Parliament and to the electorate for the policies and their implementation.

The Prime Minister also represents the nation in international affairs, e.g. summit conferences.

THE CABINET

The Cabinet developed during the eighteenth century as an inner committee of the Privy Council, which was the chief source of executive power until that time. The Cabinet is composed of about twenty Ministers chosen by the Prime Minister, usually the heads of government departments (generally known as Secretaries of State unless they have a special title, e.g. Chancellor of the Exchequer), the leaders of the two Houses of Parliament, and the holders of various traditional offices.

The Cabinet's functions are the final determination of policy, control of government and co-ordination of government departments. The exercise of its functions is dependent upon enjoying majority support in the House of Commons. Cabinet meetings are held in private, taking place once or twice a week during parliamentary sittings and less often during a recess. Proceedings are confidential, the members being bound by their oath as Privy Counsellors not to disclose information about the proceedings.

The convention of collective responsibility means that the Cabinet acts unanimously even when Cabinet Ministers do not all agree on a subject. The policies of departmental Ministers must be consistent with the policies of the Government as a whole, and once the Government's policy has been decided, each Minister is expected to support it or resign.

The convention of ministerial responsibility holds a Minister, as the political head of his or her department, accountable to Parliament for the department's work. Departmental Ministers usually decide all matters within their responsibility, although on matters of political importance they normally consult their colleagues collectively. A decision by a departmental Minister is binding on the Government as a whole.

POLITICAL PARTIES

Before the reign of William and Mary the principal officers of state were chosen by and were responsible to the Sovereign alone and not to Parliament or the nation at large. Such officers acted sometimes in concert with one another but more often independently, and the fall of one did not, of necessity, involve that of others, although all were liable to be dismissed at any moment.

In 1693 the Earl of Sunderland recommended to William III the advisability of selecting a ministry from the political party which enjoyed a majority in the House of Commons and the first united ministry was drawn in 1696 from the Whigs, to which party the King owed his throne. This group became known as the Junto and was regarded with suspicion as a novelty in the political life of the nation, being a small section meeting in secret apart from the main body of Ministers. It may be regarded as the forerunner of the Cabinet and in course of time it led to the establishment of the principle of joint responsibility of Ministers, so that internal disagreement caused a change of personnel or resignation of the whole body of Ministers.

The accession of George I, who was unfamiliar with the English language, led to a disinclination on the part of the Sovereign to preside at meetings of his Ministers and caused the appearance of a Prime Minister, a position first acquired by Robert Walpole in 1721 and retained without interruption for 20 years and 326 days.

DEVELOPMENT OF PARTIES

In 1828 the old party of the Whigs became known as Liberals, a name originally given to it by its opponents to imply laxity of principles, but gradually accepted by the party to indicate its claim to be pioneers and champions of political reform and progressive legislation. In 1861 a Liberal Registration Association was founded and Liberal Associations became widespread. In 1877 a National Liberal Federation was formed, with headquarters in London. The Liberal Party was in power for long periods during the second half of the 19th century and for several years during the first quarter of the 20th century, but after a split in the party the numbers elected were small from 1931. In 1988, a majority of the Liberals agreed on a merger with the Social Democratic Party under the title Social and Liberal Democrats; since 1989 they have been known as the Liberal Democrats. A minority continue separately as the Liberal Party.

Soon after the change from Whig to Liberal the Tory Party became known as Conservative, a name believed to have been invented by John Wilson Croker in 1830 and to have been generally adopted about the time of the passing of the Reform Act of 1832 to indicate that the preservation of national institutions was the leading principle of the party. After the Home Rule crisis of 1886 the dissentient Liberals entered into a compact with the Conservatives, under which the latter undertook not to contest their seats, but a separate Liberal Unionist organization was maintained until 1912, when it was united with the Conservatives.

Labour candidates for Parliament made their first appearance at the general election of 1892, when there were 27 standing as Labour or Liberal-Labour. In 1900 the Labour Representation Committee was set up in order to establish a distinct Labour group in Parliament, with its own whips, its own policy, and a readiness to co-operate with any party which might be engaged in promoting legislation in the direct interest of labour. In 1906 the LRC became known as the Labour Party.

The Council for Social Democracy was announced by four former Labour Cabinet Ministers in January 1981. Subsequently a number of sitting Labour Members of Parliament, together with one Conservative, joined the new group, and on 26 March 1981 the Social Democratic Party was launched. Later that year the SDP and the Liberal Party formed an electoral alliance. In 1988 a majority of the SDP agreed on a merger with the Liberal Party (see above) but a minority continued as a separate party under the SDP title. In 1990 it was decided to wind up the party organization and its three sitting MPs were known as independent social democrats. None were returned at the 1992 general election.

GOVERNMENT AND OPPOSITION

The government of the day is formed by the party which wins the largest number of seats in the House of Commons at a general election, or which has the support of a majority of members in the House of Commons. By tradition, the leader of the majority party is asked by the Sovereign to form a government, while the largest minority party becomes the official Opposition with its own leader and 'Shadow Cabinet'. Leaders of the Government and Opposition sit on the front benches of the Commons with their supporters (the back-benchers) sitting behind them.

FINANCIAL SUPPORT

Financial support to Opposition parties was introduced in 1975 and is commonly known as Short Money, after Edward Short, the Leader of the House at that time, who introduced the scheme. For 1995–6 financial assistance is:

Labour	£1,489,749.12
Liberal Democrats	308,068.16
Plaid Cymru	21,451.92
SNP	35,800.92
SDLP	22,521.84
Democratic Unionists	15,531.96
Ulster Unionsts	45,133.68

PARTIES

The parties included here are those with MPs sitting in the House of Commons in the present Parliament. Addresses of other political parties may be found in the Societies and Institutions section.

CONSERVATIVE AND UNIONIST PARTY
Central Office, 32 Smith Square, London SW1P 3HH
Tel 0171-222 9000
Chairman, The Rt. Hon. Brian Mawhinney, MP
Deputy Chairmen, The Rt. Hon. Dame Angela Rumbold, DBE, MP; M. Trend, MP
Senior Treasurer, The Lord Hambro
Director-General, P. Judge

SCOTTISH CONSERVATIVE AND UNIONIST CENTRAL OFFICE
Suite 1/1, 14 Links Place, Leith, Edinburgh EH6 7EZ
Tel 0131-555 2900
Chairman, Sir Michael Hirst
Vice-Chairmen, Miss A. Goldie; R. Robertson, MP
Hon. Treasurer, W. Y. Hughes, CBE
Director of the Party in Scotland, R. Pratt

LABOUR PARTY
John Smith House, 150 Walworth Road, London SE17 1JT
Tel 0171-701 1234
Parliamentary Party Leader, The Rt. Hon. Tony Blair, MP
Deputy Party Leader, The Rt. Hon. John Prescott, MP
Leader in the Lords, The Lord Richard, PC, QC
Chair, G. Colling
Vice-Chair, Ms D. Jeuda
Treasurer, T. Burlison
General Secretary, T. Sawyer

SHADOW CABINET *as at end July 1995*
Leader of the Opposition, The Rt. Hon. Tony Blair, MP
Deputy Leader, The Rt. Hon. John Prescott, MP
Citizens Charter and Shadow Leader of the House, Ann Taylor, MP
Defence, David Clark, MP
Disabled People's Rights, Tom Clarke, MP
Education, David Blunkett, MP
Employment, Harriet Harman, MP
Environment and London, Frank Dobson, MP
Agriculture, Food and Fisheries, Gavin Strang, MP
Foreign Affairs, Robin Cook, MP
Health, The Rt. Hon. Margaret Beckett, MP
Home Affairs, Jack Straw, MP
National Heritage, Chris Smith, MP
Northern Ireland, Marjorie Mowlam, MP

Overseas Development, Joan Lestor, MP
Scotland, George Robertson, MP
Social Security, Donald Dewar, MP
Trade and Industry, The Rt. Hon. Jack Cunningham, MP
Transport, Michael Meacher, MP
Treasury and Economic Affairs, Gordon Brown, MP
Wales, Ron Davies, MP
Women, Clare Short, MP
Law Officers' Department, The Rt. Hon. John Morris, QC, MP
Lord Chancellor's Department, Paul Boateng, MP

LABOUR CHIEF WHIPS
House of Lords, The Lord Graham of Edmonton
House of Commons, The Rt. Hon. Derek Foster, MP (standing down Oct. 1995)

LIBERAL DEMOCRATS
4 Cowley Street, London SW1P 3NB
Tel 0171-222 7999
President, Robert Maclennan, MP
Hon. Treasurer, T. Razzall
General Secretary, G. Elson
Parliamentary Party Leader, The Rt. Hon. Paddy Ashdown, MP
Leader in the Lords, The Rt. Hon. the Lord Jenkins of Hillhead

LIBERAL DEMOCRAT SPOKESMEN *as at 1 August 1995*
Deputy Leader and Home Affairs, Alan Beith, MP
Treasury, Malcolm Bruce, MP
Foreign Affairs, Defence and Sport, Menzies Campbell, MP
Foreign Affairs and Overseas Development, Sir David Steel, MP
Health and Welfare, and Wales, Alex Carlile, MP
National Heritage and Constitutional Affairs, Robert Maclennan, MP
Community and Urban Affairs, Church of England, Simon Hughes, MP
Environment, Matthew Taylor, MP
Europe, Charles Kennedy, MP
East-West Relations, Sir Russell Johnston, MP
Transport, Agriculture and Rural Affairs, Paul Tyler, MP
Local Government, David Rendel, MP
Scotland and Fishing, Jim Wallace, MP
Scotland, Ray Michie, MP
Northern Ireland, Lord Holme of Cheltenham
Social Security, Liz Lynne, MP
Community Care, Archy Kirkwood, MP
Education, Don Foster, MP
Housing, Family and Women's Issues, Diana Maddock, MP
Trade and Industry, Campaigns, Nick Harvey, MP
Science and Technology, Nigel Jones, MP
Employment and Training, David Chidgey, MP

LIBERAL DEMOCRAT WHIPS
House of Lords, The Lord Harris
House of Commons, Archy Kirkwood, MP (*Chief Whip*); Simon Hughes, MP (*Deputy Whip*)

WELSH LIBERAL DEMOCRATS
57 St Mary Street, Cardiff CF1 1FE
Tel 01222-382210
Party President, M. Thomas, OBE, QC
Party Leader, Alex Carlile, QC, MP
Chairman, P. Black
Treasurer, B. Lopez
Secretary, Mrs P. Badger
Party Manager, Ms J. Lewis, MBE

SCOTTISH LIBERAL DEMOCRATS
4 Clifton Terrace, Edinburgh EH12 5DR
Tel 0131-337 2314
Party President, R. Thomson
Party Leader, Jim Wallace, MP

Chair, Ms M. MacLaren
Hon. Treasurer, N. Stephen
Chief Executive, A. Myles

PLAID CYMRU
51 Cathedral Road, Cardiff CF1 9HD
Tel 01222-231944
Party President, Dafydd Wigley, MP
Chairman, J. Evans
Hon. Treasurer, C. Bryant
Chief Executive/General Secretary, K. Davies

SCOTTISH NATIONAL PARTY
6 North Charlotte Street, Edinburgh EH2 4JH
Tel 0131-226 3661
Parliamentary Party Leader, Margaret Ewing, MP
Chief Whip, Andrew Welsh, MP
National Convener, Alex Salmond, MP
Senior Vice-Convener, Dr A. Macartney
National Treasurer, K. MacAskill
National Secretary, A. Morgan

NORTHERN IRELAND

SOCIAL DEMOCRATIC AND LABOUR PARTY
Cranmore House, 611 Lisburn Road, Belfast BT9 7GT
Tel 01232-668100
Parliamentary Party Leader, John Hume, MP, MEP
Deputy Leader, Seamus Mallon, MP
Chief Whip, Eddie McGrady, MP
Chairman, M. Durkan
Hon. Treasurer, P. O'Hagan
Party Administrator, Mrs G. Cosgrove

ULSTER DEMOCRATIC UNIONIST PARTY
91 Dundela Avenue, Belfast BT4 3BU
Tel 01232-471155
Parliamentary Party Leader, I. Paisley, MP, MEP
Deputy Leader, Peter Robinson, MP
Chairman, W. J. McClure
Hon. Treasurer, D. S. Herron
General Secretary, N. Dodds

ULSTER UNIONIST COUNCIL
3 Glengall Street, Belfast BT12 5AE
Tel 01232-324601
Party Leader, The Rt. Hon. James Molyneaux, MP
Chief Whip, William Ross, MP
President, J. Cunningham
Chairman, J. Nicholson, MEP
Hon. Treasurer, J. Allen
Party Secretary, J. Wilson

MEMBERS OF PARLIAMENT AS AT 31 JULY 1995

For abbreviations, *see* page 241
* Denotes membership of the last Parliament
†Elected at a by-election since the 1992 general election

*Abbott, Ms Diane J. (*b.* 1953) *Lab., Hackney North and Stoke Newington,* maj. 10,727
*Adams, Mrs Irene (*b.* 1948) *Lab., Paisley North,* maj. 9,329
Ainger, Nicholas R. (*b.* 1949) *Lab., Pembroke,* maj. 755
*Ainsworth, Peter M. (*b.* 1956) *C., Surrey East,* maj. 17,656
Ainsworth, Robert W. (*b.* 1952) *Lab., Coventry North East,* maj. 11,676
*Aitken, Jonathan W. P. (*b.* 1942) *C., Thanet South,* maj. 11,513
*Alexander, Richard T. (*b.* 1934) *C., Newark,* maj. 8,229
*Alison, Rt. Hon. Michael J. H. (*b.* 1926) *C., Selby,* maj. 9,508
*Allason, Rupert W. S. (*b.* 1951) *C., Torbay,* maj. 5,787
*Allen, Graham W. (*b.* 1953) *Lab., Nottingham North,* maj. 10,743
*Alton, David P. (*b.* 1951) *LD, Liverpool, Mossley Hill,* maj. 2,606
*Amess, David A. A. (*b.* 1952) *C., Basildon,* maj. 1,480
Ancram, Michael A. F. J. K. (Earl of Ancram) (*b.* 1945) *C., Devizes,* maj. 19,712
*Anderson, Donald (*b.* 1939) *Lab., Swansea East,* maj. 23,482
Anderson, Mrs Janet (*b.* 1949) *Lab., Rossendale and Darwen,* maj. 120
*Arbuthnot, James N. (*b.* 1952) *C., Wanstead and Woodford,* maj. 16,885
*Armstrong, Miss Hilary J. (*b.* 1945) *Lab., Durham North West,* maj. 13,987
*Arnold, Jacques A. (*b.* 1947) *C., Gravesham,* maj. 5,493
*Arnold, Sir Thomas (*b.* 1947) *C., Hazel Grove,* maj. 929
*Ashby, David G. (*b.* 1940) *C., Leicestershire North West,* maj. 979
*Ashdown, Rt. Hon. J. J. D. (Paddy) (*b.* 1941) *LD, Yeovil,* maj. 8,833
*Ashton, Joseph W. (*b.* 1933) *Lab., Bassetlaw,* maj. 9,997
*Aspinwall, Jack H. (*b.* 1933) *C., Wansdyke,* maj. 13,341
*Atkins, Rt. Hon. Robert J. (*b.* 1946) *C., South Ribble,* maj. 5,973
*Atkinson, David A. (*b.* 1940) *C., Bournemouth East,* maj. 14,823
Atkinson, Peter (*b.* 1943) *C., Hexham,* maj. 13,438
Austin-Walker, John E. (*b.* 1944) *Lab., Woolwich,* maj. 2,225
*Baker, Rt. Hon. Kenneth W., CH (*b.* 1934) *C., Mole Valley,* maj. 15,950
*Baker, Nicholas B. (*b.* 1938) *C., Dorset North,* maj. 10,080
*Baldry, Antony B. (*b.* 1950) *C., Banbury,* maj. 16,720
Banks, Matthew (*b.* 1961) *C., Southport,* maj. 3,063
*Banks, Robert G., MBE (*b.* 1937) *C., Harrogate,* maj. 12,589
*Banks, Tony L. (*b.* 1943) *Lab., Newham North West,* maj. 9,171
*Barnes, Harold (*b.* 1936) *Lab., Derbyshire North East,* maj. 6,270
*Barron, Kevin J. (*b.* 1946) *Lab., Rother Valley,* maj. 17,222
Bates, Michael W. (*b.* 1961) *C., Langbaurgh,* maj. 1,564
*Batiste, Spencer L. (*b.* 1945) *C., Elmet,* maj. 3,261
*Battle, John D. (*b.* 1951) *Lab., Leeds West,* maj. 13,828
Bayley, Hugh (*b.* 1952) *Lab., York,* maj. 6,342
*Beckett, Rt. Hon. Margaret M. (*b.* 1953) *Lab., Derby South,* maj. 6,936
*Beggs, Roy (*b.* 1936) *UUP, Antrim East,* maj. 7,422
*Beith, Rt. Hon. Alan J. (*b.* 1943) *LD, Berwick-upon-Tweed,* maj. 5,043
*Bell, Stuart (*b.* 1938) *Lab., Middlesbrough,* maj. 15,784
*Bellingham, Henry C. (*b.* 1955) *C., Norfolk North West,* maj. 11,564

*Bendall, Vivian W. H. (*b.* 1938) *C., Ilford North,* maj. 9,071
*Benn, Rt. Hon. Anthony N. W. (*b.* 1925) *Lab., Chesterfield,* maj. 6,414
*Bennett, Andrew F. (*b.* 1939) *Lab., Denton and Reddish,* maj. 12,084
*Benton, Joseph E. (*b.* 1933) *Lab., Bootle,* maj. 29,442
Beresford, Sir Paul (*b.* 1946) *C., Croydon Central,* maj. 9,650
*Bermingham, Gerald E. (*b.* 1940) *Lab., St Helens South,* maj. 18,209
Berry, Roger L., D.Phil (*b.* 1948) *Lab., Kingswood,* maj. 2,370
Betts, Clive J. C. (*b.* 1950) *Lab., Sheffield, Attercliffe,* maj. 15,480
*Biffen, Rt. Hon. John W. (*b.* 1930) *C., Shropshire North,* maj. 16,211
*Blair, Rt. Hon. Anthony C. L. (*b.* 1953) *Lab., Sedgefield,* maj. 14,859
*Blunkett, David (*b.* 1947) *Lab., Sheffield, Brightside,* maj. 22,681
*Boateng, Paul Y. (*b.* 1951) *Lab., Brent South,* maj. 9,705
*Body, Sir Richard (*b.* 1927) *C., Holland with Boston,* maj. 13,831
*Bonsor, Sir Nicholas, Bt. (*b.* 1942) *C., Upminster,* maj. 13,821
Booth, Hartley, PH.D. (*b.* 1946) *C., Finchley,* maj. 6,388
*Boothroyd, Rt. Hon. Betty (*b.* 1929) *The Speaker, West Bromwich West,* maj. 7,830
*Boswell, Timothy E. (*b.* 1942) *C., Daventry,* maj. 20,274
*Bottomley, Peter J. (*b.* 1944) *C., Eltham,* maj. 1,666
*Bottomley, Rt. Hon. Virginia H. B. M. (*b.* 1948) *C., Surrey South West,* maj. 14,975
*Bowden, Sir Andrew, MBE (*b.* 1930) *C., Brighton, Kemptown,* maj. 3,056
*Bowis, John C., OBE (*b.* 1945) *C., Battersea,* maj. 4,840
*Boyes, Roland (*b.* 1937) *Lab., Houghton and Washington,* maj. 20,808
*Boyson, Rt. Hon. Sir Rhodes (*b.* 1925) *C., Brent North,* maj. 10,131
*Bradley, Keith J. C. (*b.* 1950) *Lab., Manchester, Withington,* maj. 9,735
Brandreth, Gyles D. (*b.* 1948) *C., City of Chester,* maj. 1,101
*Bray, Jeremy W., PH.D. (*b.* 1930) *Lab., Motherwell South,* maj. 14,013
*Brazier, Julian W. H. (*b.* 1953) *C., Canterbury,* maj. 10,805
*Bright, Sir Graham (*b.* 1942) *C., Luton South,* maj. 799
*Brooke, Rt. Hon. Peter L., CH (*b.* 1934) *C., City of London and Westminster South,* maj. 13,369
*Brown, J. Gordon, PH.D. (*b.* 1951) *Lab., Dunfermline East,* maj. 17,444
*Brown, Michael R. (*b.* 1951) *C., Brigg and Cleethorpes,* maj. 9,269
*Brown, Nicholas H. (*b.* 1950) *Lab., Newcastle upon Tyne East,* maj. 13,877
Browning, Mrs Angela F. (*b.* 1946) *C., Tiverton,* maj. 11,089
*Bruce, Ian C. (*b.* 1947) *C., Dorset South,* maj. 13,508
*Bruce, Malcolm G. (*b.* 1944) *LD, Gordon,* maj. 274
*Budgen, Nicholas W. (*b.* 1937) *C., Wolverhampton South West,* maj. 4,966
Burden, Richard (*b.* 1954) *Lab., Birmingham, Northfield,* maj. 630
*Burns, Simon H. M. (*b.* 1952) *C., Chelmsford,* maj. 18,260
*Burt, Alistair J. H. (*b.* 1955) *C., Bury North,* maj. 4,764
*Butcher, John P. (*b.* 1946) *C., Coventry South West,* maj. 1,436
Butler, Peter (*b.* 1951) *C., Milton Keynes North East,* maj. 14,176
*Butterfill, John V. (*b.* 1941) *C., Bournemouth West,* maj. 12,703
Byers, Stephen J. (*b.* 1953) *Lab., Wallsend,* maj. 19,470

*Caborn, Richard G. (*b.* 1943) *Lab., Sheffield Central,* maj. 17,294

*Callaghan, James (*b.* 1927) *Lab., Heywood and Middleton,* maj. 8,074

Campbell, Mrs Anne (*b.* 1940) *Lab., Cambridge,* maj. 580

*Campbell, Ronald (*b.* 1943) *Lab., Blyth Valley,* maj. 8,044

*Campbell, W. Menzies, CBE, QC (*b.* 1941) *LD, Fife North East,* maj. 3,308

*Campbell-Savours, Dale N. (*b.* 1943) *Lab., Workington,* maj. 10,449

*Canavan, Dennis A. (*b.* 1942) *Lab., Falkirk West,* maj. 9,812

Cann, James (*b.* 1946) *Lab., Ipswich,* maj. 265

*Carlile, Alexander C., QC (*b.* 1948) *LD, Montgomery,* maj. 5,209

*Carlisle, John R. (*b.* 1942) *C., Luton North,* maj. 13,094

*Carlisle, Sir Kenneth (*b.* 1941) *C., Lincoln,* maj. 2,049

*Carrington, Matthew H. M. (*b.* 1947) *C., Fulham,* maj. 6,579

*Carttiss, Michael R. H. (*b.* 1938) *C., Great Yarmouth,* maj. 5,309

*Cash, William N. P. (*b.* 1940) *C., Stafford,* maj. 10,900

*Channon, Rt. Hon. H. Paul G. (*b.* 1935) *C., Southend West,* maj. 11,902

*Chapman, Sir Sydney (*b.* 1935) *C., Chipping Barnet,* maj. 13,951

†Chidgey, David W. G. (*b.* 1942) *LD, Eastleigh,* maj. 9,239

Chisholm, Malcolm (*b.* 1949) *Lab., Edinburgh, Leith,* maj. 4,985

†Church, Ms Judith A. (*b.* 1953), *Lab., Dagenham,* maj. 13,344

*Churchill, Winston S. (*b.* 1940) *C., Davyhulme,* maj. 4,426

Clapham, Michael (*b.* 1943) *Lab., Barnsley West and Penistone,* maj. 14,504

Clappison, W. James (*b.* 1956) *C., Hertsmere,* maj. 18,735

*Clark, David G., PH.D. (*b.* 1939) *Lab., South Shields,* maj. 13,477

*Clark, Dr Michael (*b.* 1935) *C., Rochford,* maj. 26,036

Clarke, Eric L. (*b.* 1933) *Lab., Midlothian,* maj. 10,334

*Clarke, Rt. Hon. Kenneth H., QC (*b.* 1940) *C., Rushcliffe,* maj. 19,766

*Clarke, Thomas, CBE (*b.* 1941) *Lab., Monklands West,* maj. 17,065

*Clelland, David G. (*b.* 1943) *Lab., Tyne Bridge,* maj. 15,210

Clifton-Brown, Geoffrey R. (*b.* 1953) *C., Cirencester and Tewkesbury,* maj. 16,058

*Clwyd, Ms Ann (*b.* 1937) *Lab., Cynon Valley,* maj. 21,364

Coe, Sebastian N., OBE (*b.* 1956) *C., Falmouth and Camborne,* maj. 3,267

Coffey, Ms M. Ann (*b.* 1946) *Lab., Stockport,* maj. 1,422

*Cohen, Harry (*b.* 1949) *Lab., Leyton,* maj. 11,484

*Colvin, Michael K. B. (*b.* 1932) *C., Romsey and Waterside,* maj. 15,304

Congdon, David L. (*b.* 1949) *C., Croydon North East,* maj. 7,473

Connarty, Michael (*b.* 1949) *Lab., Falkirk East,* maj. 7,969

*Conway, Derek L. (*b.* 1953) *C., Shrewsbury and Atcham,* maj. 10,965

*Cook, Francis (*b.* 1935) *Lab., Stockton North,* maj. 10,474

*Cook, R. F. (Robin) (*b.* 1946) *Lab., Livingston,* maj. 8,105

*Coombs, Anthony M. V. (*b.* 1952) *C., Wyre Forest,* maj. 10,341

*Coombs, Simon C. (*b.* 1947) *C., Swindon,* maj. 2,826

*Cope, Rt. Hon. Sir John (*b.* 1937) *C., Northavon,* maj. 11,861

*Corbett, Robin (*b.* 1933) *Lab., Birmingham, Erdington,* maj. 4,735

*Corbyn, Jeremy B. (*b.* 1949) *Lab., Islington North,* maj. 12,784

*Cormack, Sir Patrick (*b.* 1939) *C., Staffordshire South,* maj. 22,633

Corston, Ms Jean (*b.* 1942) *Lab., Bristol East,* maj. 2,692

*Couchman, James R. (*b.* 1942) *C., Gillingham,* maj. 16,638

*Cousins, James M. (*b.* 1944) *Lab., Newcastle upon Tyne Central,* maj. 5,288

*Cox, Thomas M. (*b.* 1930) *Lab., Tooting,* maj. 4,107

*Cran, James D. (*b.* 1944) *C., Beverley,* maj. 16,517

*Critchley, Sir Julian (*b.* 1930) *C., Aldershot,* maj. 19,188

*Cummings, John S. (*b.* 1943) *Lab., Easington,* maj. 26,390

*Cunliffe, Lawrence F. (*b.* 1929) *Lab., Leigh,* maj. 18,827

Cunningham, James (*b.* 1941) *Lab., Coventry South East,* maj. 1,311

*Cunningham, Rt. Hon. Dr John A. (Jack) (*b.* 1939) *Lab., Copeland,* maj. 2,439

†Cunningham, Ms Roseanna (*b.* 1951), *SNP, Perth and Kinross,* maj. 7,311

*Currie, Mrs Edwina (*b.* 1946) *C., Derbyshire South,* maj. 4,658

*Curry, David M. (*b.* 1944) *C., Skipton and Ripon,* maj. 19,330

Dafis, Cynog G. (*b.* 1938) *PC, Ceredigion and Pembroke North,* maj. 3,193

*Dalyell, Tam (Sir Thomas Dalyell of the Binns, Bt.) (*b.* 1932) *Lab., Linlithgow,* maj. 7,026

*Darling, Alistair M. (*b.* 1953) *Lab., Edinburgh Central,* maj. 2,126

Davidson, Ian (*b.* 1950) *Lab., Glasgow, Govan,* maj. 4,125

Davies, Bryan (*b.* 1939) *Lab., Oldham Central and Royton,* maj. 8,606

†Davies, Christopher (Chris) (*b.* 1954), *LD, Littleborough and Saddleworth,* maj. 1,993

*Davies, Rt. Hon. D. J. Denzil (*b.* 1938) *Lab., Llanelli,* maj. 19,270

*Davies, J. Quentin (*b.* 1944) *C., Stamford and Spalding,* maj. 22,869

*Davies, Ronald (*b.* 1946) *Lab., Caerphilly,* maj. 22,672

*Davis, David M. (*b.* 1948) *C., Boothferry,* maj. 17,535

*Davis, Terence A. G. (*b.* 1938) *Lab., Birmingham, Hodge Hill,* maj. 7,068

*Day, Stephen R. (*b.* 1948) *C., Cheadle,* maj. 15,778

Denham, John V. (*b.* 1953) *Lab., Southampton, Itchen,* maj. 551

Deva, Niranjan J. A. (*b.* 1948) *C., Brentford and Isleworth,* maj. 2,086

*Devlin, Timothy R. (*b.* 1959) *C., Stockton South,* maj. 3,369

*Dewar, Donald C. (*b.* 1937) *Lab., Glasgow, Garscadden,* maj. 13,340

*Dicks, Terence P. (*b.* 1937) *C., Hayes and Harlington,* maj. 53

*Dixon, Donald (*b.* 1929) *Lab., Jarrow,* maj. 17,907

*Dobson, Frank G. (*b.* 1940) *Lab., Holborn and St Pancras,* maj. 10,824

Donohoe, Brian H. (*b.* 1948) *Lab., Cunninghame South,* maj. 10,680

*Dorrell, Rt. Hon. Stephen J. (*b.* 1952) *C., Loughborough,* maj. 10,883

*Douglas-Hamilton, Lord James (*b.* 1942) *C., Edinburgh West,* maj. 879

*Dover, Densmore (*b.* 1938) *C., Chorley,* maj. 4,246

Dowd, James P. (*b.* 1951) *Lab., Lewisham West,* maj. 1,809

Duncan, Alan J. C. (*b.* 1957) *C., Rutland and Melton,* maj. 25,535

Duncan-Smith, G. Iain (*b.* 1954) *C., Chingford,* maj. 14,938

*Dunn, Robert J. (*b.* 1946) *C., Dartford,* maj. 10,314

*Dunnachie, James F. (*b.* 1930) *Lab., Glasgow, Pollok,* maj. 7,883

*Dunwoody, Hon. Mrs Gwyneth P. (*b.* 1930) *Lab., Crewe and Nantwich,* maj. 2,695

*Durant, Sir Anthony (*b.* 1928) *C., Reading West,* maj. 13,298

*Dykes, Hugh J. (*b.* 1939) *C., Harrow East,* maj. 11,098

Eagle, Ms Angela (*b.* 1961) *Lab., Wallasey,* maj. 3,809

*Eastham, Kenneth (*b.* 1927) *Lab., Manchester, Blackley,* maj. 12,389

*Eggar, Rt. Hon. Timothy J. C. (*b.* 1951) *C., Enfield North,* maj. 9,430

Elletson, Harold D. H. (*b.* 1960) *C., Blackpool North,* maj. 3,040

*Emery, Rt. Hon. Sir Peter (*b.* 1926) *C., Honiton,* maj. 16,511

*Enright, Derek A. (*b.* 1935) *Lab., Hemsworth,* maj. 22,075

Etherington, William (*b.* 1941) *Lab., Sunderland North*, maj. 17,004

*Evans, David J. (*b.* 1935) *C., Welwyn Hatfield*, maj. 8,465

*Evans, John (*b.* 1930) *Lab., St Helens North*, maj. 16,244

Evans, Jonathan P. (*b.* 1950) *C., Brecon and Radnor*, maj. 130

Evans, Nigel M. (*b.* 1957) *C., Ribble Valley*, maj. 6,542

Evans, Roger (*b.* 1947) *C., Monmouth*, maj. 3,204

*Evennett, David A. (*b.* 1939) *C., Erith and Crayford*, maj. 2,339

*Ewing, Mrs Margaret A. (*b.* 1945) *SNP, Moray*, maj. 2,844

Faber, David J. C. (*b.* 1961) *C., Westbury*, maj. 12,606

Fabricant, Michael L. D. (*b.* 1950) *C., Staffordshire Mid*, maj. 6,236

*Fatchett, Derek J. (*b.* 1945) *Lab., Leeds Central*, maj. 15,020

*Faulds, Andrew M. W. (*b.* 1923) *Lab., Warley East*, maj. 7,794

*Fenner, Dame Peggy, DBE (*b.* 1922) *C., Medway*, maj. 8,786

*Field, Barry J. A., TD (*b.* 1946) *C., Isle of Wight*, maj. 1,827

*Field, Frank (*b.* 1942) *Lab., Birkenhead*, maj. 17,613

*Fishburn, J. Dudley (*b.* 1946) *C., Kensington*, maj. 3,548

*Fisher, Mark (*b.* 1944) *Lab., Stoke-on-Trent Central*, maj. 13,420

*Flynn, Paul P. (*b.* 1935) *Lab., Newport West*, maj. 7,779

*Fookes, Dame Janet, DBE (*b.* 1936) *C., Plymouth, Drake*, maj. 2,013

*Forman, F. Nigel (*b.* 1943) *C., Carshalton and Wallington*, maj. 9,943

*Forsyth, Rt. Hon. Michael B. (*b.* 1954) *C., Stirling*, maj. 703

*Forsythe, Clifford (*b.* 1929) *UUP, Antrim South*, maj. 24,559

*Forth, Eric (*b.* 1944) *C., Worcestershire Mid*, maj. 9,870

*Foster, Rt. Hon. Derek (*b.* 1937) *Lab., Bishop Auckland*, maj. 10,087

Foster, Donald M. E. (*b.* 1937) *LD, Bath*, maj. 3,768

*Foulkes, George (*b.* 1942) *Lab., Carrick, Cumnock and Doon Valley*, maj. 16,626

*Fowler, Rt. Hon. Sir Norman (*b.* 1938) *C., Sutton Coldfield*, maj. 26,036

Fox, Dr Liam (*b.* 1961) *C., Woodspring*, maj. 17,509

*Fox, Sir Marcus, MBE (*b.* 1927) *C., Shipley*, maj. 12,382

*Fraser, John D. (*b.* 1934) *Lab., Norwood*, maj. 7,216

*Freeman, Rt. Hon. Roger N. (*b.* 1942) *C., Kettering*, maj. 11,154

*French, Douglas C. (*b.* 1944) *C., Gloucester*, maj. 6,058

*Fry, Sir Peter (*b.* 1931) *C., Wellingborough*, maj. 11,816

*Fyfe, Mrs Maria (*b.* 1938) *Lab., Glasgow, Maryhill*, maj. 13,419

*Galbraith, Samuel L. (*b.* 1945) *Lab., Strathkelvin and Bearsden*, maj. 3,162

*Gale, Roger J. (*b.* 1943) *C., Thanet North*, maj. 18,210

Gallie, Philip (*b.* 1939) *C., Ayr*, maj. 85

*Galloway, George (*b.* 1954) *Lab., Glasgow, Hillhead*, maj. 4,826

Gapes, Michael J. (*b.* 1952) *Lab., Ilford South*, maj. 402

*Gardiner, Sir George (*b.* 1935) *C., Reigate*, maj. 17,664

*Garel-Jones, Rt. Hon. (W. A. T.) Tristan (*b.* 1941) *C., Watford*, maj. 9,590

Garnier, Edward (*b.* 1952) *C., Harborough*, maj. 13,543

*Garrett, John L. (*b.* 1931) *Lab., Norwich South*, maj. 6,181

*George, Bruce T. (*b.* 1942) *Lab., Walsall South*, maj. 3,178

Gerrard, Neil F. (*b.* 1942) *Lab., Walthamstow*, maj. 3,022

*Gilbert, Rt. Hon. Dr John W. (*b.* 1927) *Lab., Dudley East*, maj. 9,200

*Gill, Christopher J. F., RD (*b.* 1936) *C., Ludlow*, maj. 14,152

Gillan, Ms Cheryl E. K. (*b.* 1952) *C., Chesham and Amersham*, maj. 22,220

*Godman, Norman A., PH.D. (*b.* 1938) *Lab., Greenock and Port Glasgow*, maj. 14,979

Godsiff, Roger D. (*b.* 1946) *Lab., Birmingham, Small Heath*, maj. 13,989

*Golding, Mrs Llinos (*b.* 1933) *Lab., Newcastle under Lyme*, maj. 9,839

*Goodlad, Rt. Hon. Alastair R. (*b.* 1943) *C., Eddisbury*, maj. 12,697

*Goodson-Wickes, Dr Charles (*b.* 1945) *C., Wimbledon*, maj. 14,761

*Gordon, Mrs Mildred (*b.* 1923) *Lab., Bow and Poplar*, maj. 8,404

*Gorman, Mrs Teresa E. (*b.* 1931) *C., Billericay*, maj. 22,494

*Gorst, Sir John (*b.* 1928) *C., Hendon North*, maj. 7,122

*Graham, Thomas (*b.* 1944) *Lab., Renfrew West and Inverclyde*, maj. 1,744

*Grant, Sir Anthony (*b.* 1925) *C., Cambridgeshire South West*, maj. 19,637

*Grant, Bernard A. M. (*b.* 1944) *Lab., Tottenham*, maj. 11,968

*Greenway, Harry (*b.* 1934) *C., Ealing North*, maj. 5,966

*Greenway, John R. (*b.* 1946) *C., Ryedale*, maj. 18,439

*Griffiths, Nigel (*b.* 1955) *Lab., Edinburgh South*, maj. 4,176

*Griffiths, Peter H. S. (*b.* 1928) *C., Portsmouth North*, maj. 13,881

*Griffiths, Winston J. (*b.* 1943) *Lab., Bridgend*, maj. 7,326

*Grocott, Bruce J. (*b.* 1940) *Lab., The Wrekin*, maj. 6,648

*Grylls, Sir Michael (*b.* 1934) *C., Surrey North West*, maj. 28,394

*Gummer, Rt. Hon. John S. (*b.* 1939) *C., Suffolk Coastal*, maj. 19,285

Gunnell, W. John (*b.* 1933) *Lab., Leeds South and Morley*, maj. 7,372

*Hague, Rt. Hon. William J. (*b.* 1961) *C., Richmond (Yorks)* maj. 23,504

*Hain, Peter G. (*b.* 1950) *Lab., Neath*, maj. 23,975

Hall, Michael T. (*b.* 1952) *Lab., Warrington South*, maj. 191

*Hamilton, Rt. Hon. Sir Archibald (*b.* 1941) *C., Epsom and Ewell*, maj. 20,021

*Hamilton, M. Neil (*b.* 1949) *C., Tatton*, maj. 15,860

*Hampson, Dr Keith (*b.* 1943) *C., Leeds North West*, maj. 7,671

*Hanley, Rt. Hon. Jeremy J. (*b.* 1945) *C., Richmond and Barnes*, maj. 3,869

*Hannam, Sir John (*b.* 1929) *C., Exeter*, maj. 4,045

Hanson, David G. (*b.* 1957) *Lab., Delyn*, maj. 2,039

*Hardy, Peter (*b.* 1931) *Lab., Wentworth*, maj. 22,449

*Hargreaves, Andrew R. (*b.* 1955) *C., Birmingham, Hall Green*, maj. 3,665

*Harman, Ms Harriet (*b.* 1950) *Lab., Peckham*, maj. 12,005

*Harris, David A. (*b.* 1937) *C., St Ives*, maj. 1,645

Harvey, Nicholas B. (*b.* 1961) *LD, Devon North*, maj. 794

*Haselhurst, Sir Alan (*b.* 1937) *C., Saffron Walden*, maj. 17,424

*Hattersley, Rt. Hon. Roy S. G. (*b.* 1932) *Lab., Birmingham, Sparkbrook*, maj. 13,572

Hawkins, Nicholas J. (*b.* 1957) *C., Blackpool South*, maj. 1,667

Hawksley, P. Warren (*b.* 1943) *C., Halesowen and Stourbridge*, maj. 9,582

*Hayes, Jeremy J. J. (*b.* 1953) *C., Harlow*, maj. 2,940

Heald, Oliver (*b.* 1954) *C., Hertfordshire North*, maj. 16,531

*Heath, Rt. Hon. Sir Edward, KG, MBE (*b.* 1916) *C., Old Bexley and Sidcup*, maj. 15,699

*Heathcoat-Amory, David P. (*b.* 1949) *C., Wells*, maj. 6,649

*Henderson, Douglas J. (*b.* 1949) *Lab., Newcastle upon Tyne North*, maj. 8,946

Hendron, Dr Joseph G. (*b.* 1932) *SDLP, Belfast West*, maj. 589

Hendry, Charles (*b.* 1959) *C., High Peak*, maj. 4,819

Heppell, John B. (*b.* 1948) *Lab., Nottingham East*, maj. 7,680

*Heseltine, Rt. Hon. Michael R. D. (*b.* 1933) *C., Henley*, maj. 18,392

*Hicks, Robert (*b.* 1938) *C., Cornwall South East*, maj. 7,704

*Higgins, Rt. Hon. Sir Terence, KBE (*b.* 1928) *C., Worthing*, maj. 16,533

*Hill, S. James A. (*b.* 1926) *C., Southampton, Test*, maj. 585

Hill, T. Keith (*b.* 1943) *Lab., Streatham*, maj. 2,317

*Hinchliffe, David M. (*b.* 1948) *Lab., Wakefield*, maj. 6,590

†Hodge, Ms Margaret E. (*b.* 1944) *Lab., Barking*, maj. 11,414

*Hoey, Ms Catharine (Kate) L. (b. 1946) Lab., Vauxhall, maj. 10,488

*Hogg, Rt. Hon. Douglas M., QC (b. 1945) C., Grantham, maj. 19,588

*Hogg, Norman (b. 1938) Lab., Cumbernauld and Kilsyth, maj. 9,215

*Home Robertson, John D. (b. 1948) Lab., East Lothian, maj. 10,036

*Hood, James (b. 1948) Lab., Clydesdale, maj. 10,187

Hoon, Geoffrey W. (b. 1953) Lab., Ashfield, maj. 12,987

Horam, John R. (b. 1939) C., Orpington, maj. 12,935

*Hordern, Rt. Hon. Sir Peter (b. 1929) C., Horsham, maj. 25,072

*Howard, Rt. Hon. Michael, QC (b. 1941) C., Folkestone and Hythe, maj. 8,910

*Howarth, Alan T., CBE (b. 1944) C., Stratford-upon-Avon, maj. 22,892

*Howarth, George E. (b. 1949) Lab., Knowsley North, maj. 22,403

*Howell, Rt. Hon. David A. R. (b. 1936) C., Guildford, maj. 13,404

*Howell, Sir Ralph (b. 1923) C., Norfolk North, maj. 12,545

*Howells, Kim S., PH.D. (b. 1946) Lab., Pontypridd, maj. 19,797

*Hoyle, E. Douglas H. (b. 1930) Lab., Warrington North, maj. 12,622

Hughes, Kevin M. (b. 1952) Lab., Doncaster North, maj. 19,813

*Hughes, Robert (b. 1932) Lab., Aberdeen North, maj. 9,237

*Hughes, Robert G. (b. 1951) C., Harrow West, maj. 17,897

*Hughes, Royston J. (b. 1925) Lab., Newport East, maj. 9,899

*Hughes, Simon H. W. (b. 1951) LD, Southwark and Bermondsey, maj. 9,845

*Hume, John, MEP (b. 1937) SDLP, Foyle, maj. 13,005

*Hunt, Rt. Hon. David J. F., MBE (b. 1942) C., Wirral West, maj. 11,064

*Hunt, Sir John (b. 1929) C., Ravensbourne, maj. 19,714

*Hunter, Andrew R. F. (b. 1943) C., Basingstoke, maj. 21,198

*Hurd, Rt. Hon. Douglas R., CBE (b. 1930) C., Witney, maj. 22,568

Hutton, John M. P. (b. 1955) Lab., Barrow and Furness, maj. 3,578

*Illsley, Eric E. (b. 1955) Lab., Barnsley Central, maj. 19,361

*Ingram, Adam P. (b. 1947) Lab., East Kilbride, maj. 11,992

*Jack, J. Michael (b. 1946) C., Fylde, maj. 20,991

Jackson, Ms Glenda, CBE (b. 1936) Lab., Hampstead and Highgate, maj. 1,440

Jackson, Mrs Helen (b. 1939) Lab., Sheffield, Hillsborough, maj. 7,068

*Jackson, Robert V. (b. 1946) C., Wantage, maj. 16,473

Jamieson, David C. (b. 1947) Lab., Plymouth, Devonport, maj. 7,412

*Janner, Hon. Greville E., QC (b. 1928) Lab., Leicester West, maj. 3,978

Jenkin, Hon. Bernard (b. 1959) C., Colchester North, maj. 16,492

*Jessel, Toby F. H. (b. 1934) C., Twickenham, maj. 5,711

*Johnson Smith, Sir Geoffrey (b. 1924) C., Wealden, maj. 20,931

*Johnston, Sir Russell (b. 1932) LD, Inverness, Nairn and Lochaber, maj. 458

*Jones, Gwilym H. (b. 1947) C., Cardiff North, maj. 2,969

*Jones, Ieuan W. (b. 1949) PC, Ynys Môn, maj. 1,106

Jones, Jon O. (b. 1954) Lab., Cardiff Central, maj. 3,465

Jones, Ms Lynne M., PH.D. (b. 1951) Lab., Birmingham, Selly Oak, maj. 2,060

*Jones, Martyn D. (b. 1947) Lab., Clwyd South West, maj. 4,941

Jones, Nigel D. (b. 1948) LD, Cheltenham, maj. 1,668

*Jones, Robert B. (b. 1950) C., Hertfordshire West, maj. 13,940

*Jones, S. Barry (b. 1938) Lab., Alyn and Deeside, maj. 7,851

*Jopling, Rt. Hon. T. Michael (b. 1930) C., Westmorland and Lonsdale, maj. 16,436

Jowell, Ms Tessa (b. 1947) Lab., Dulwich, maj. 2,056

*Kaufman, Rt. Hon. Gerald B. (b. 1930) Lab., Manchester, Gorton, maj. 16,279

Keen, Alan (b. 1937) Lab., Feltham and Heston, maj. 1,995

*Kellett-Bowman, Dame Elaine, DBE (b. 1924) C., Lancaster, maj. 2,953

*Kennedy, Charles P. (b. 1959) LD, Ross, Cromarty and Skye, maj. 7,630

Kennedy, Mrs Jane (b. 1958) Lab., Liverpool, Broadgreen, maj. 7,027

*Key, S. Robert (b. 1945) C., Salisbury, maj. 8,973

Khabra, Piara C. (b. 1924) Lab., Ealing, Southall, maj. 6,866

*Kilfoyle, Peter (b. 1946) Lab., Liverpool, Walton, maj. 28,299

*King, Rt. Hon. Thomas J., CH (b. 1933) C., Bridgwater, maj. 9,716

*Kirkhope, Timothy J. R. (b. 1945) C., Leeds North East, maj. 4,244

*Kirkwood, Archibald J. (b. 1946) LD, Roxburgh and Berwickshire, maj. 4,257

*Knapman, Roger M. (b. 1944) C., Stroud, maj. 13,405

Knight, Mrs Angela A. (b. 1950) C., Erewash, maj. 5,703

*Knight, Rt. Hon. Gregory (b. 1949) C., Derby North, maj. 4,453

*Knight, Dame Jill, DBE (b. 1923) C., Birmingham, Edgbaston, maj. 4,307

*Knox, Sir David (b. 1933) C., Staffordshire Moorlands, maj. 7,410

Kynoch, George A. B. (b. 1946) C., Kincardine and Deeside, maj. 4,495

Lait, Ms Jacqui (b. 1947) C., Hastings and Rye, maj. 6,634

*Lamont, Rt. Hon. Norman S. H. (b. 1942) C., Kingston upon Thames, maj. 10,153

*Lang, Rt. Hon. Ian B. (b. 1940) C., Galloway and Upper Nithsdale, maj. 2,468

*Lawrence, Sir Ivan, QC (b. 1936) C., Burton, maj. 5,996

Legg, Barry (b. 1949) C., Milton Keynes South West, maj. 4,687

*Leigh, Edward J. E. (b. 1950) C., Gainsborough and Horncastle, maj. 16,245

*Lennox-Boyd, Hon. Sir Mark (b. 1943) C., Morecambe and Lunesdale, maj. 11,509

*Lester, James T. (b. 1932) C., Broxtowe, maj. 9,891

*Lestor, Miss Joan (b. 1931) Lab., Eccles, maj. 13,226

*Lewis, Terence (b. 1935) Lab., Worsley, maj. 10,012

†Liddell, Mrs Helen (b. 1950) Lab., Monklands East, maj. 1,640

Lidington, David R., PH.D. (b. 1956) C., Aylesbury, maj. 18,860

*Lightbown, Sir David (b. 1932) C., Staffordshire South East, maj. 7,192

*Lilley, Rt. Hon. Peter B. (b. 1943) C., St Albans, maj. 16,404

*Litherland, Robert K. (b. 1930) Lab., Manchester Central, maj. 18,037

*Livingstone, Ken (b. 1945) Lab., Brent East, maj. 5,971

*Lloyd, Anthony J. (b. 1950) Lab., Stretford, maj. 11,137

*Lloyd, Rt. Hon. Sir Peter (b. 1937) C., Fareham, maj. 24,141

Llwyd, Elfyn (b. 1951) PC, Meirionnydd Nant Conwy, maj. 4,613

*Lofthouse, Sir Geoffrey (b. 1925) Lab., Pontefract and Castleford, maj. 23,495

*Lord, Michael N. (b. 1938) C., Suffolk Central, maj. 16,031

*Loyden, Edward (b. 1923) Lab., Liverpool, Garston, maj. 12,279

Luff, Peter J. (b. 1955) C., Worcester, maj. 6,152

*Lyell, Rt. Hon. Sir Nicholas, QC (b. 1938) C., Bedfordshire Mid, maj. 25,138

Lynne, Ms Elizabeth (b. 1948) LD, Rochdale, maj. 1,839

*McAllion, John (b. 1948) Lab., Dundee East, maj. 4,564

*McAvoy, Thomas M. (b. 1943) Lab., Glasgow, Rutherglen, maj. 15,270

*McCartney, Ian (b. 1951) Lab., Makerfield, maj. 18,118

†McCartney, Robert (b. 1936), *UK Unionist, Down North*, maj. 2,892

*McCrea, Revd Dr R. T. William (b. 1948) *DUP, Ulster Mid*, maj. 6,187

*MacDonald, Calum A. (b. 1956) *Lab., Western Isles*, maj. 1,703

*McFall, John (b. 1944) *Lab., Dumbarton*, maj. 6,129

*McGrady, Edward K. (b. 1935) *SDLP, Down South*, maj. 6,342

*MacGregor, Rt. Hon. John R. R., OBE (b. 1937) *C., Norfolk South*, maj. 17,565

*Mackay, Andrew J. (b. 1949) *C., Berkshire East*, maj. 28,680

*McKelvey, William (b. 1934) *Lab., Kilmarnock and Loudoun*, maj. 6,979

MacKinlay, Andrew S. (b. 1949) *Lab., Thurrock*, maj. 1,172

*Maclean, Rt. Hon. David J. (b. 1953) *C., Penrith and the Border*, maj. 18,449

*McLeish, Henry B. (b. 1948) *Lab., Fife Central*, maj. 10,578

*Maclennan, Robert A. R. (b. 1936) *LD, Caithness and Sutherland*, maj. 5,365

*McLoughlin, Patrick A. (b. 1957) *C., Derbyshire West*, maj. 18,769

*McMaster, Gordon J. (b. 1960) *Lab., Paisley South*, maj. 9,549

*McNair-Wilson, Sir Patrick (b. 1929) *C., New Forest*, maj. 20,405

*McNamara, J. Kevin (b. 1934) *Lab., Hull North*, maj. 15,384

†MacShane, Denis (b. 1948) *Lab., Rotherham*, maj. 6,954

*McWilliam, John D. (b. 1941) *Lab., Blaydon*, maj. 13,343

*Madden, Maxwell F. (b. 1941) *Lab., Bradford West*, maj. 9,502

†Maddock, Mrs Diana (b. 1945) *LD, Christchurch*, maj. 16,427

*Madel, Sir David (b. 1938) *C., Bedfordshire South West*, maj. 21,273

*Maginnis, Kenneth (b. 1938) *UUP, Fermanagh and South Tyrone*, maj. 14,113

*Mahon, Ms Alice (b. 1937) *Lab., Halifax*, maj. 478

Maitland, Lady Olga (b. 1944) *C., Sutton and Cheam*, maj. 10,756

*Major, Rt. Hon. John (b. 1943) *C., Huntingdon*, maj. 36,230

*Mallon, Seamus (b. 1936) *SDLP, Newry and Armagh*, maj. 7,091

Malone, P. Gerald (b. 1950) *C., Winchester*, maj. 8,121

Mandelson, Peter B. (b. 1953) *Lab., Hartlepool*, maj. 8,782

*Mans, Keith D. R. (b. 1946) *C., Wyre*, maj. 11,664

*Marek, John, PH.D. (b. 1940) *Lab., Wrexham*, maj. 6,716

*Marland, Paul (b. 1940) *C., Gloucestershire West*, maj. 4,958

*Marlow, Antony R. (b. 1940) *C., Northampton North*, maj. 3,908

*Marshall, David (b. 1941) *Lab., Glasgow, Shettleston*, maj. 14,834

*Marshall, James (b. 1941) *Lab., Leicester South*, maj. 9,440

*Marshall, John L. (b. 1940) *C., Hendon South*, maj. 12,047

*Marshall, Sir Michael (b. 1930) *C., Arundel*, maj. 19,863

*Martin, David J. P. (b. 1945) *C., Portsmouth South*, maj. 242

*Martin, Michael J. (b. 1945) *Lab., Glasgow, Springburn*, maj. 14,506

*Martlew, Eric A. (b. 1949) *Lab., Carlisle*, maj. 3,108

*Mates, Michael J. (b. 1934) *C., Hampshire East*, maj. 29,165

*Mawhinney, Rt. Hon. Brian S., PH.D. (b. 1940) *C., Peterborough*, maj. 5,376

*Maxton, John A. (b. 1936) *Lab., Glasgow, Cathcart*, maj. 8,001

*Mayhew, Rt. Hon. Sir Patrick, QC (b. 1929) *C., Tunbridge Wells*, maj. 17,132

*Meacher, Michael H. (b. 1939) *Lab., Oldham West*, maj. 8,333

*Meale, J. Alan (b. 1949) *Lab., Mansfield*, maj. 11,724

*Mellor, Rt. Hon. David J., QC (b. 1949) *C., Putney*, maj. 7,526

Merchant, Piers R. G. (b. 1951) *C., Beckenham*, maj. 15,285

*Michael, Alun E. (b. 1943) *Lab., Cardiff South and Penarth*, maj. 10,425

*Michie, Mrs J. Ray (b. 1934) *LD, Argyll and Bute*, maj. 2,622

*Michie, William (b. 1935) *Lab., Sheffield, Heeley*, maj. 14,954

Milburn, Alan (b. 1958) *Lab., Darlington*, maj. 2,798

Miller, Andrew (b. 1949) *Lab., Ellesmere Port and Neston*, maj. 1,989

*Mills, Iain C. (b. 1940) *C., Meriden*, maj. 14,699

*Mitchell, Andrew J. B. (b. 1956) *C., Gedling*, maj. 10,637

*Mitchell, Austin V. (b. 1934) *Lab., Great Grimsby*, maj. 7,504

*Mitchell, Sir David (b. 1928) *C., Hampshire North West*, maj. 17,848

*Moate, Sir Roger (b. 1938) *C., Faversham*, maj. 16,351

*Molyneaux, Rt. Hon. James H. (b. 1920) *UUP, Lagan Valley*, maj. 23,565

*Monro, Rt. Hon. Sir Hector, AE (b. 1922) *C., Dumfries*, maj. 6,415

*Montgomery, Sir Fergus (b. 1927) *C., Altrincham and Sale*, maj. 16,791

*Moonie, Dr Lewis G. (b. 1947) *Lab., Kirkcaldy*, maj. 9,126

*Morgan, H. Rhodri (b. 1939) *Lab., Cardiff West*, maj. 9,291

*Morley, Elliot A. (b. 1952) *Lab., Glanford and Scunthorpe*, maj. 8,412

*Morris, Rt. Hon. Alfred, AO (b. 1928) *Lab., Manchester, Wythenshawe*, maj. 11,996

Morris, Ms Estelle (b. 1952) *Lab., Birmingham, Yardley*, maj. 162

*Morris, Rt. Hon. John, QC (b. 1931) *Lab., Aberavon*, maj. 21,310

*Morris, Rt. Hon. Michael W. L. (b. 1936) *C., Northampton South*, maj. 16,973

*Moss, Malcolm D. (b. 1943) *C., Cambridgeshire North East*, maj. 15,093

*Mowlam, Dr Marjorie (b. 1949) *Lab., Redcar*, maj. 11,577

Mudie, George (b. 1945) *Lab., Leeds East*, maj. 12,697

*Mullin, Christopher J. (b. 1947) *Lab., Sunderland South*, maj. 14,501

*Murphy, Paul P. (b. 1948) *Lab., Torfaen*, maj. 20,754

*Needham, Rt. Hon. Richard F. (The Earl of Kilmorey) (b. 1942) *C., Wiltshire North*, maj. 16,388

*Nelson, R. Anthony (b. 1948) *C., Chichester*, maj. 20,887

*Neubert, Sir Michael (b. 1933) *C., Romford*, maj. 11,420

*Newton, Rt. Hon. Antony H., OBE (b. 1937) *C., Braintree*, maj. 17,494

*Nicholls, Patrick C. M. (b. 1948) *C., Teignbridge*, maj. 8,856

*Nicholson, David J. (b. 1944) *C., Taunton*, maj. 3,336

*Nicholson, Miss Emma H. (b. 1941) *C., Devon West and Torridge*, maj. 3,614

*Norris, Steven J. (b. 1945) *C., Epping Forest*, maj. 20,188

*Oakes, Rt. Hon. Gordon J. (b. 1931) *Lab., Halton*, maj. 18,204

O'Brien, Michael (b. 1954) *Lab., Warwickshire North*, maj. 1,454

*O'Brien, William (b. 1929) *Lab., Normanton*, maj. 8,950

*O'Hara, Edward (b. 1937) *Lab., Knowsley South*, maj. 22,011

Olner, William J. (b. 1942) *Lab., Nuneaton*, maj. 1,631

*O'Neill, Martin J. (b. 1945) *Lab., Clackmannan*, maj. 8,503

*Onslow, Rt. Hon. Sir Cranley, KCMG (b. 1926) *C., Woking*, maj. 19,842

*Oppenheim, Hon. Phillip A. C. L. (b. 1956) *C., Amber Valley*, maj. 712

*Orme, Rt. Hon. Stanley (b. 1923) *Lab., Salford East*, maj. 11,235

Ottaway, Richard G. J. (b. 1945) *C., Croydon South*, maj. 20,425

*Page, Richard L. (b. 1941) *C., Hertfordshire South West*, maj. 20,107

*Paice, James E. T. (b. 1949) *C., Cambridgeshire South East*, maj. 23,810

*Paisley, Revd Ian R. K., MEP (b. 1926) *DUP, Antrim North*, maj. 14,936

*Parry, Robert (b. 1933) *Lab., Liverpool, Riverside*, maj. 17,437

*Patchett, Terry (b. 1940) *Lab., Barnsley East*, maj. 24,777

*Patnick, Sir Irvine, OBE (b. 1929) C., Sheffield, Hallam, maj. 6,741

*Patten, Rt. Hon. John H. C. (b. 1945) C., Oxford West and Abingdon, maj. 3,539

*Pattie, Rt. Hon. Sir Geoffrey (b. 1936) C., Chertsey and Walton, maj. 22,819

*Pawsey, James F. (b. 1933) C., Rugby and Kenilworth, maj. 13,247

*Peacock, Mrs Elizabeth J. (b. 1937) C., Batley and Spen, maj. 1,408

†Pearson, Ian P. (b. 1949) Lab., Dudley West, maj. 20,694

*Pendry, Thomas (b. 1934) Lab., Stalybridge and Hyde, maj. 8,831

Pickles, Eric J. (b. 1952) C., Brentwood and Ongar, maj. 15,145

Pickthall, Colin (b. 1944) Lab., Lancashire West, maj. 2,077

*Pike, Peter L. (b. 1937) Lab., Burnley, maj. 11,491

Pope, Gregory J. (b. 1960) Lab., Hyndburn, maj. 1,960

*Porter, David J. (b. 1948) C., Waveney, maj. 6,702

*Porter, G. B. (Barry) (b. 1939) C., Wirral South, maj. 8,183

*Portillo, Rt. Hon. Michael D. X. (b. 1953) C., Enfield, Southgate, maj. 15,563

*Powell, Raymond (b. 1928) Lab., Ogmore, maj. 23,827

*Powell, William R. (b. 1948) C., Corby, maj. 342

Prentice, Mrs Bridget (b. 1952) Lab., Lewisham East, maj. 1,095

Prentice, Gordon (b. 1951) Lab., Pendle, maj. 2,113

*Prescott, Rt. Hon. John L. (b. 1938) Lab., Hull East, maj. 18,719

*Primarolo, Ms Dawn (b. 1954) Lab., Bristol South, maj. 8,919

Purchase, Kenneth (b. 1939) Lab., Wolverhampton North East, maj. 3,939

*Quin, Miss Joyce G. (b. 1944) Lab., Gateshead East, maj. 18,530

*Radice, Giles H. (b. 1936) Lab., Durham North, maj. 19,637

*Randall, Stuart J. (b. 1938) Lab., Hull West, maj. 10,585

*Rathbone, J. R. (Tim) (b. 1933) C., Lewes, maj. 12,175

Raynsford, W. R. N. (Nick) (b. 1945) Lab., Greenwich, maj. 1,357

*Redmond, Martin (b. 1937) Lab., Don Valley, maj. 13,534

*Redwood, Rt. Hon. John A. (b. 1951) C., Wokingham, maj. 25,709

*Reid, Dr John (b. 1947) Lab., Motherwell North, maj. 18,910

†Rendel, David D. (b. 1949) LD, Newbury, maj. 22,055

*Renton, Rt. Hon. R. Timothy (b. 1932) C., Sussex Mid, maj. 20,528

Richards, Roderick (b. 1947) C., Clwyd North West, maj. 6,050

*Riddick, Graham E. G. (b. 1955) C., Colne Valley, maj. 7,225

*Rifkind, Rt. Hon. Malcolm L., QC (b. 1946) C., Edinburgh, Pentlands, maj. 4,290

Robathan, Andrew R. G. (b. 1951) C., Blaby, maj. 25,347

*Roberts, Rt. Hon. Sir Wyn (b. 1930) C., Conwy, maj. 995

*Robertson, George I. M. (b. 1946) Lab., Hamilton, maj. 16,603

Robertson, Raymond S. (b. 1959) C., Aberdeen South, maj. 1,517

*Robinson, Geoffrey (b. 1938) Lab., Coventry North West, maj. 6,432

Robinson, Mark N. F. (b. 1946) C., Somerton and Frome, maj. 4,341

*Robinson, Peter D. (b. 1948) DUP, Belfast East, maj. 7,787

Roche, Mrs Barbara M. R. (b. 1954) Lab., Hornsey and Wood Green, maj. 5,177

*Roe, Mrs Marion A. (b. 1936) C., Broxbourne, maj. 23,970

†Rogers, Allan R. (b. 1932) Lab., Rhondda, maj. 28,816

*Rooker, Jeffrey W. (b. 1941) Lab., Birmingham, Perry Barr, maj. 8,590

*Rooney, Terence H. (b. 1950) Lab., Bradford North, maj. 7,664

*Ross, Ernest (b. 1942) Lab., Dundee West, maj. 10,604

*Ross, William (b. 1936) UUP, Londonderry East, maj. 18,527

*Rowe, Andrew (b. 1935) C., Kent Mid, maj. 19,649

*Rowlands, Edward (b. 1940) Lab., Merthyr Tydfil and Rhymney, maj. 26,713

*Ruddock, Mrs Joan M. (b. 1943) Lab., Lewisham, Deptford, maj. 12,238

*Rumbold, Rt. Hon. Dame Angela, DBE (b. 1932) C., Mitcham and Morden, maj. 1,734

*Ryder, Rt. Hon. Richard A., OBE (b. 1949) C., Norfolk Mid, maj. 18,948

*Sackville, Hon. Thomas G. (b. 1950) C., Bolton West, maj. 1,079

*Sainsbury, Rt. Hon. Sir Timothy (b. 1932) C., Hove, maj. 12,268

*Salmond, Alexander E. A. (b. 1954) SNP, Banff and Buchan, maj. 4,108

*Scott, Rt. Hon. Sir Nicholas, KBE (b. 1933) C., Chelsea, maj. 12,789

*Sedgemore, Brian C. J. (b. 1937) Lab., Hackney South and Shoreditch, maj. 9,016

*Shaw, David L. (b. 1950) C., Dover, maj. 833

*Shaw, Sir Giles (b. 1931) C., Pudsey, maj. 8,972

*Sheerman, Barry J. (b. 1940) Lab., Huddersfield, maj. 7,258

*Sheldon, Rt. Hon. Robert E. (b. 1923) Lab., Ashton-under-Lyne, maj. 10,935

*Shephard, Rt. Hon. Gillian P. (b. 1940) C., Norfolk South West, maj. 16,931

*Shepherd, Colin (b. 1938) C., Hereford, maj. 3,413

*Shepherd, Richard C. S. (b. 1942) C., Aldridge-Brownhills, maj. 11,024

*Shersby, Sir Michael (b. 1933) C., Uxbridge, maj. 13,179

*Shore, Rt. Hon. Peter D. (b. 1924) Lab., Bethnal Green and Stepney, maj. 12,230

*Short, Ms Clare (b. 1946) Lab., Birmingham, Ladywood, maj. 15,283

Simpson, Alan (b. 1948) Lab., Nottingham South, maj. 3,181

*Sims, Roger E. (b. 1930) C., Chislehurst, maj. 15,276

*Skeet, Sir Trevor (b. 1918) C., Bedfordshire North, maj. 11,618

*Skinner, Dennis E. (b. 1932) Lab., Bolsover, maj. 20,660

*Smith, Andrew D. (b. 1951) Lab., Oxford East, maj. 7,538

*Smith, Christopher R., PH.D. (b. 1951) Lab., Islington South and Finsbury, maj. 10,652

*Smith, Sir Dudley (b. 1926) C., Warwick and Leamington, maj. 8,935

Smith, Llewellyn T. (b. 1944) Lab., Blaenau Gwent, maj. 30,067

*Smith, Timothy J. (b. 1947) C., Beaconsfield, maj. 23,597

*Smyth, Revd W. Martin (b. 1931) UUP, Belfast South, maj. 10,070

*Snape, Peter C. (b. 1942) Lab., West Bromwich East, maj. 2,813

*Soames, Hon. A. Nicholas W. (b. 1948) C., Crawley, maj. 7,765

*Soley, Clive S. (b. 1939) Lab., Hammersmith, maj. 4,754

*Spearing, Nigel J. (b. 1930) Lab., Newham South, maj. 2,502

*Speed, Sir Keith, RD (b. 1934) C., Ashford, maj. 17,359

Spellar, John F. (b. 1947) Lab., Warley West, maj. 5,472

Spencer, Sir Derek, QC (b. 1936) C., Brighton, Pavilion, maj. 3,675

*Spicer, Sir James (b. 1925) C., Dorset West, maj. 8,010

*Spicer, W. Michael H. (b. 1943) C., Worcestershire South, maj. 16,151

Spink, Dr Robert M. (b. 1948) C., Castle Point, maj. 16,830

Spring, Richard J. G. (b. 1946) C., Bury St Edmunds, maj. 18,787

Sproat, Iain M. (b. 1938) C., Harwich, maj. 17,159

*Squire, Ms Rachel (b. 1954) Lab., Dunfermline West, maj. 7,484

*Squire, Robin C. (b. 1944) C., Hornchurch, maj. 9,165

*Stanley, Rt. Hon. Sir John (*b*. 1942) *C., Tonbridge and Malling,* maj. 21,558

*Steel, Rt. Hon. Sir David, KBE (*b*. 1938) *LD, Tweeddale, Ettrick and Lauderdale,* maj. 2,520

*Steen, Anthony D. (*b*. 1939) *C., South Hams,* maj. 13,711

*Steinberg, Gerald N. (*b*. 1945) *Lab., City of Durham,* maj. 15,058

Stephen, B. Michael L. (*b*. 1942) *C., Shoreham,* maj. 14,286

*Stern, Michael C. (*b*. 1942) *C., Bristol North West,* maj. 45

Stevenson, George W. (*b*. 1938) *Lab., Stoke-on-Trent South,* maj. 6,909

*Stewart, J. Allan (*b*. 1942) *C., Eastwood,* maj. 11,688

*Stott, Roger, CBE (*b*. 1943) *Lab., Wigan,* maj. 21,842

*Strang, Gavin S., PH.D. (*b*. 1943) *Lab., Edinburgh East,* maj. 7,211

*Straw, J. W. (Jack) (*b*. 1946) *Lab., Blackburn,* maj. 6,027

Streeter, Gary (*b*. 1955) *C., Plymouth, Sutton,* maj. 11,950

*Sumberg, David A. G. (*b*. 1941) *C., Bury South,* maj. 788

†Sutcliffe, Gerard (*b*. 1953) *Lab., Bradford South,* maj. 9,664

Sweeney, Walter E. (*b*. 1949) *C., Vale of Glamorgan,* maj. 19

Sykes, John D. (*b*. 1956) *C., Scarborough,* maj. 11,734

*Tapsell, Sir Peter (*b*. 1930) *C., Lindsey East,* maj. 11,846

*Taylor, Sir Edward (Teddy) (*b*. 1937) *C., Southend East,* maj. 13,111

*Taylor, Ian C., MBE (*b*. 1945) *C., Esher,* maj. 20,371

*Taylor, Rt. Hon. John D. (*b*. 1937) *UUP, Strangford,* maj. 8,911

*Taylor, John M. (*b*. 1941) *C., Solihull,* maj. 25,146

*Taylor, Matthew O. J. (*b*. 1963) *LD, Truro,* maj. 7,570

*Taylor, Mrs W. Ann (*b*. 1947) *Lab., Dewsbury,* maj. 634

*Temple-Morris, Peter (*b*. 1938) *C., Leominster,* maj. 16,680

Thomason, K. Roy, OBE (*b*. 1944) *C., Bromsgrove,* maj. 13,702

*Thompson, Sir Donald (*b*. 1931) *C., Calder Valley,* maj. 4,878

*Thompson, H. Patrick (*b*. 1935) *C., Norwich North,* maj. 266

*Thompson, John (*b*. 1928) *Lab., Wansbeck,* maj. 18,174

*Thornton, Sir Malcolm (*b*. 1939) *C., Crosby,* maj. 14,806

*Thurnham, Peter G. (*b*. 1938) *C., Bolton North East,* maj. 185

†Timms, Stephen C. (*b*. 1955) *Lab., Newham North East,* maj. 11,818

Tipping, S. Paddy (*b*. 1949) *Lab., Sherwood,* maj. 2,910

†Touhig, J. Donnelly (Don) (*b*. 1959) *Lab., Islwyn,* maj. 13,097

*Townend, John E. (*b*. 1934) *C., Bridlington,* maj. 16,358

*Townsend, Cyril D. (*b*. 1937) *C., Bexleyheath,* maj. 14,086

*Tracey, Richard P. (*b*. 1943) *C., Surbiton,* maj. 9,639

*Tredinnick, David A. S. (*b*. 1950) *C., Bosworth,* maj. 19,094

Trend, Hon. Michael St J. (*b*. 1952) *C., Windsor and Maidenhead,* maj. 12,928

*Trimble, W. David (*b*. 1944) *UUP, Upper Bann,* maj. 16,163

*Trotter, Neville G. (*b*. 1932) *C., Tynemouth,* maj. 597

*Turner, Dennis (*b*. 1942) *Lab., Wolverhampton South East,* maj. 10,240

*Twinn, Dr Ian D. (*b*. 1950) *C., Edmonton,* maj. 593

Tyler, Paul A., CBE (*b*. 1941) *LD, Cornwall North,* maj. 1,921

*Vaughan, Sir Gerard (*b*. 1923) *C., Reading East,* maj. 14,555

*Vaz, N. Keith A. S. (*b*. 1956) *Lab., Leicester East,* maj. 11,316

*Viggers, Peter J. (*b*. 1938) *C., Gosport,* maj. 16,318

*Waldegrave, Rt. Hon. William A. (*b*. 1946) *C., Bristol West,* maj. 6,071

*Walden, George G. H., CMG (*b*. 1939) *C., Buckingham,* maj. 19,791

*Walker, A. Cecil (*b*. 1924) *UUP, Belfast North,* maj. 9,625

*Walker, Rt. Hon. Sir Harold (*b*. 1927) *Lab., Doncaster Central,* maj. 10,682

*Walker, William C. (*b*. 1929) *C., Tayside North,* maj. 3,995

*Wallace, James R. (*b*. 1954) *LD, Orkney and Shetland,* maj. 5,033

*Waller, Gary P. A. (*b*. 1945) *C., Keighley,* maj. 3,596

*Walley, Ms Joan L. (*b*. 1949) *Lab., Stoke-on-Trent North,* maj. 14,777

*Ward, John D., CBE (*b*. 1925) *C., Poole,* maj. 12,831

*Wardell, Gareth L. (*b*. 1944) *Lab., Gower,* maj. 7,018

*Wardle, Charles F. (*b*. 1939) *C., Bexhill and Battle,* maj. 16,307

*Wareing, Robert N. (*b*. 1930) *Lab., Liverpool, West Derby,* maj. 20,425

Waterson, Nigel C. (*b*. 1950) *C., Eastbourne,* maj. 5,481

*Watson, Michael G. (*b*. 1949) *Lab., Glasgow Central,* maj. 11,019

*Watts, John A. (*b*. 1947) *C., Slough,* maj. 514

*Wells, Bowen (*b*. 1935) *C., Hertford and Stortford,* maj. 20,210

*Welsh, Andrew P. (*b*. 1944) *SNP, Angus East,* maj. 954

*Wheeler, Rt. Hon. Sir John (*b*. 1940) *C., Westminster North,* maj. 3,733

*Whitney, Raymond W., OBE (*b*. 1930) *C., Wycombe,* maj. 17,076

Whittingdale, John F. L., OBE (*b*. 1959) *C., Colchester South and Maldon,* maj. 21,821

Wicks, Malcolm H. (*b*. 1947) *Lab., Croydon North West,* maj. 1,526

*Widdecombe, Miss Ann N. (*b*. 1947) *C., Maidstone,* maj. 16,286

*Wiggin, Sir Jerry, TD (*b*. 1937) *C., Weston-super-Mare,* maj. 5,342

*Wigley, Dafydd (*b*. 1943) *PC, Caernarfon,* maj. 14,476

*Wilkinson, John A. D. (*b*. 1940) *C., Ruislip-Northwood,* maj. 19,791

Willetts, David L. (*b*. 1956) *C., Havant,* maj. 17,584

*Williams, Rt. Hon. Alan J. (*b*. 1930) *Lab., Swansea West,* maj. 9,478

*Williams, Dr Alan W. (*b*. 1945) *Lab., Carmarthen,* maj. 2,922

*Wilshire, David (*b*. 1943) *C., Spelthorne,* maj. 19,843

*Wilson, Brian D. H. (*b*. 1948) *Lab., Cunninghame North,* maj. 2,939

*Winnick, David J. (*b*. 1933) *Lab., Walsall North,* maj. 3,824

*Winterton, Mrs J. Ann (*b*. 1941) *C., Congleton,* maj. 11,120

*Winterton, Nicholas R. (*b*. 1938) *C., Macclesfield,* maj. 22,767

*Wise, Mrs Audrey (*b*. 1935) *Lab., Preston,* maj. 12,175

*Wolfson, G. Mark (*b*. 1934) *C., Sevenoaks,* maj. 19,154

*Wood, Timothy J. R. (*b*. 1940) *C., Stevenage,* maj. 4,888

*Worthington, Anthony (*b*. 1941) *Lab., Clydebank and Milngavie,* maj. 12,430

*Wray, James (*b*. 1938) *Lab., Glasgow, Provan,* maj. 10,703

Wright, Anthony W., D.phil. (*b*. 1948) *Lab., Cannock and Burntwood,* maj. 1,506

*Yeo, Timothy S. K. (*b*. 1945) *C., Suffolk South,* maj. 17,289

*Young, David W. (*b*. 1930) *Lab., Bolton South East,* maj. 12,691

*Young, Rt. Hon. Sir George, Bt. (*b*. 1941) *C., Ealing, Acton,* maj. 7,007

BY-ELECTIONS SINCE THE 1992 GENERAL ELECTION

NEWBURY
(6 May 1993)
£81,081　T.71.25%

D. Rendel, *LD*	37,590
J. Davidson, *C.*	15,535
S. Billcliffe, *Lab.*	1,151
A. Sked, *Anti-Maastricht Anti Fed.*	601
A. Bannon, *C. Candidate*	561
S. Martin, *Commoners Party Movement*	435
'Lord' Sutch, *Loony*	432
J. Wallis, *Green*	341
R. Marlar, *Referendum*	338
J. Browne, *C. Rebel*	267
Ms L. St Clair, *Corrective*	170
W. Board, *Maastricht Referendum for Britain*	84
M. Grenville, *NLP*	60
J. Day, *People and Pensioners*	49
C. Palmer, *21st Century*	40
M. Grbin, *Defence of Children's Humanity Bosnia*	33
A. Page, *SDP*	33
Ms A. Murphy, *Comm. GB*	32
M. Stone, *Give Royal Billions to Schools*	21
LD majority	22,055

CHRISTCHURCH
(29 July 1993)
£71,868　T.74.2%

Mrs D. Maddock, *LD*	33,164
R. Hayward, *C.*	16,737
N. Lickley, *Lab.*	1,453
A. Sked, *Anti-Maastricht Anti Fed.*	878
'Lord' Sutch, *Loony Rock-Roll*	404
A. Bannon, *C. Candidate*	357
P. Newman, *Sack Graham Taylor*	80
Ms T. B. Jackson, *Buy Daily Sport*	67
P. Hollyman, *Save NHS*	60
J. Crockard, *Highlander IV Wednesday Promotion Night*	48
M. Griffiths, *NLP*	45
M. Belcher, *Ian for King*	23
K. Fitzhugh, *Alfred Chicken*	18
J. Walley, *Rainbow Alliance Coalition*	16
LD majority	16,427

ROTHERHAM
(5 May 1994)
£60,937　T.44.14%

D. MacShane, *Lab.*	14,912
D. Wildgoose, *LD*	7,958
N. Gibb, *C.*	2,649
'Lord' D. Sutch, *Loony*	1,114
K. Laycock, *NLP*	173
Lab. majority	6,954

BARKING
(9 June 1994)
£50,454　T.38.6%

Ms M. Hodge, *Lab.*	13,704
G. White, *LD*	2,290

Ms T. May, *C.*	1,976
G. Needs, *NF*	551
G. Batten, *UK Ind.*	406
Ms H. Butensky, *NLP*	90
Lab. majority	11,414

BRADFORD SOUTH
(9 June 1994)
£69,914　T.44.0%

G. Sutcliffe, *Lab.*	17,014
Ms H. Wright, *LD*	7,350
R. Farley, *C.*	5,475
'Lord' D. Sutch, *Loony*	727
K. Laycock, *NLP*	187
Lab. majority	9,664

DAGENHAM
(9 June 1994)
£59,645　T.37.2%

Ms J. Church, *Lab.*	15,474
J. Fairrie, *C.*	2,130
P. Dunphy, *LD*	1,804
J. Tyndall, *BNP*	1,511
P. Compobassi, *UK Ind.*	457
M. Leighton, *NLP*	116
Lab. majority	13,344

EASTLEIGH
(9 June 1994)
£91,736　T.58.9%

D. Chidgey, *LD*	24,473
Ms M. Birks, *Lab.*	15,234
S. Reid, *C.*	13,675
N. Farage, *UK Ind.*	952
'Lord' D. Sutch, *Loony*	783
P. Warburton, *NLP*	145
LD majority	9,239

NEWHAM NORTH EAST
(9 June 1994)
£59,555　T.34.5%

S. Timms, *Lab.*	14,668
P. Hammond, *C.*	2,850
A. Kellaway, *LD*	821
A. Scholefield, *UK Ind.*	509
J. Homeless, *House Homeless People*	342
R. Archer, *NLP*	228
Ms V. Garman, *Buy the Daily Sport*	155
Lab. majority	11,818

MONKLANDS EAST
(30 June 1994)
£48,391　T.70.17%

Mrs H. Liddell, *Lab.*	16,960
Ms K. Ullrich, *SNP*	15,320
S. Gallagher, *LD*	878
Ms S. Bell, *C.*	799
A. Bremner, *Network Against Criminal Justice Bill*	69
D. Paterson, *NLP*	58
Lab. majority	1,640

DUDLEY WEST
(15 December 1994)
£87,633　T.46.95%

I. Pearson, *Lab.*	28,400
G. Postles, *C.*	7,706

M. Hadley, *LD*	3,154
M. S. Hyde, *Lib.*	548
M. R. Floyd, *UK Ind.*	590
A. Carmichael, *NF*	561
M. H. Nattrass, *New Britain*	146
Ms M. Nicholson, *FOREST*	77
J. D. Oldbury, *NLP*	70
C. R. Palmer, *21st Century*	55
Lab. majority	20,694

ISLWYN
(16 February 1995)
£50,737　T.45.6%

D. Touhig, *Lab.*	16,030
J. Davies, *PC*	2,933
J. Bushell, *LD*	2,448
R. Buckland, *C.*	913
'Lord' Sutch, *Loony*	506
H. Hughes, *UK Ind.*	289
T. Rees, *NLP*	47
Lab. majority	13,097

PERTH AND KINROSS
(25 May 1995)
£65,410　T.62.0%

Ms R. Cunningham, *SNP*	16,931
D. Alexander, *Lab.*	9,620
J. Godfrey, *C.*	8,990
Ms V. Linklater, *LD*	4,952
'Lord' Sutch, *Loony*	586
V. Linacre, *UK Ind.*	504
R. Harper, *Green*	223
M. Halford, *Scots Conservatory*	88
G. Black, *NLP*	54
SNP majority	7,311

DOWN NORTH
(15 June 1995)
£68,662　T.38.7%

R. McCartney, *UK Unionist*	10,124
A. McFarland, *UUP*	7,232
Sir Oliver Napier, *All.*	6,970
A. Chambers, *Ind. Unionist*	2,170
S. Sexton, *C.*	583
M. Brooks, *Free Para Lee Clegg Now .*	108
C. Carter, *Ulster's Ind. Voice*	101
J. Anderson, *NLP*	100
UK Unionist majority	2,892

LITTLEBOROUGH AND SADDLEWORTH
(27 July 1995)
£65,576　T.63.6%

C. Davies, *LD*	16,231
P. Woolas, *Lab.*	14,238
J. Hudson, *C.*	9,934
'Lord' Sutch, *Loony*	782
J. Whittaker, *UK Ind.*	549
P. Douglas, *C. Party*	193
Mr Blobby, *House Party*	105
A. Pitts, *Soc.*	46
L. D. McLaren, *Old Lab.*	33
C. R. Palmer, *21st Century*	25
LD majority	1,993

RETIRING MPs

The following MPs have announced that they will not be standing at the next general election:

Michael Alison, *C.*, Selby
David Alton, *LD*, Liverpool Mossley Hill
Kenneth Baker, *C.*, Mole Valley
John Biffen, *C.*, Shropshire North
Jeremy Bray, *Lab.*, Motherwell South
John Butcher, *C.*, Coventry South West
Sir Kenneth Carlisle, *C.*, Lincoln
Paul Channon, *C.*, Southend West
Sir Julian Critchley, *C.*, Aldershot
Edwina Currie, *C.*, Derbyshire South
Sir Anthony Durant, *C.*, Reading West
Andrew Faulds, *Lab.*, Warley East
Dudley Fishburn, *C.*, Kensington
Sir Anthony Grant, *C.*, Cambridgeshire South West
Sir John Hannam, *C.*, Exeter
Peter Hardy, *Lab.*, Wentworth
Roy Hattersley, *Lab.*, Birmingham Sparkbrook
Sir Peter Hordern, *C.*, Horsham
Sir John Hunt, *C.*, Ravensbourne
Douglas Hurd, *C.*, Witney
Greville Janner, *Lab.*, Leicester West
Sir Russell Johnston, *LD*, Inverness, Nairn and Lochaber
Dame Jill Knight, *C.*, Birmingham Edgbaston
Max Madden, *Lab.*, Bradford West
Sir Hector Monro, *C.*, Dumfries
Sir Fergus Montgomery, *C.*, Altrincham and Sale
Sir Cranley Onslow, *C.*, Woking
Stan Orme, *Lab.*, Salford East
Bob Parry, *Lab.*, Liverpool Riverside
Terry Patchett, *Lab.*, Barnsley
John Patten, *C.*, Oxford West and Abingdon
Sir Geoffrey Pattie, *C.*, Chertsey and Walton
Tim Renton, *C.*, Sussex Mid
Sir Wyn Roberts, *C.*, Conwy
Peter Shore, *Lab.*, Bethnal Green and Stepney
Sir Keith Speed, *C.*, Ashford
Sir James Spicer, *C.*, Dorset West
Sir David Steel, *LD*, Tweeddale, Ettrick and Lauderdale
Patrick Thompson, *C.*, Norwich North
Peter Thurnham, *C.*, Bolton North East
Neville Trotter, *C.*, Tynemouth
George Walden, *C.*, Buckingham
John Ward, *C.*, Poole
Sir Jerry Wiggin, *C.*, Weston-super-Mare

MEMBERS WITH SMALL MAJORITIES

The following MPs were returned in April 1992 with majorities of fewer than 1,000 votes

*Denotes membership of last Parliament

	Maj.
Walter Sweeney, *C., Vale of Glamorgan*	19
*Michael Stern, *C., Bristol North West*	45
*Terry Dicks, *C., Hayes and Harlington*	53
Phil Gallie, *C., Ayr*	85
Janet Anderson, *Lab., Rossendale and Darwen*	120
Jonathan Evans, *C., Brecon and Radnor*	130
Estelle Morris, *Lab., Birmingham Yardley*	162
*Peter Thurnham, *C., Bolton North East*	185
Mike Hall, *Lab., Warrington South*	191
*David Martin, *C., Portsmouth South*	242
Jamie Cann, *Lab., Ipswich*	265
*Patrick Thompson, *C., Norwich North*	266
*Malcolm Bruce, *LD, Gordon*	274
*William Powell, *C., Corby*	342
Mike Gapes, *Lab., Ilford South*	402
*Sir Russell Johnston, *LD, Inverness, Nairn and Lochaber*	458
*Alice Mahon, *Lab., Halifax*	478
*John Watts, *C., Slough*	514
John Denham, *Lab., Southampton Itchen*	551
Anne Campbell, *Lab., Cambridge*	580
*James Hill, *C., Southampton Test*	585
Dr Joe Hendron, *SDLP, Belfast West*	589
*Dr Ian Twinn, *C., Edmonton*	593
Neville Trotter, *C., Tynemouth*	597
Richard Burden, *Lab., Birmingham Northfield*	630
*Ann Taylor, *Lab., Dewsbury*	634
*Michael Forsyth, *C., Stirling*	703
*Phillip Oppenheim, *C., Amber Valley*	712
Nick Ainger, *Lab., Pembroke*	755
*David Sumberg, *C., Bury South*	788
Nick Harvey, *LD, Devon North*	794
*Graham Bright, *C., Luton South*	799
*David Shaw, *C., Dover*	833
*Lord James Douglas-Hamilton, *C., Edinburgh West*	879
*Sir Tom Arnold, *C., Hazel Grove*	929
*Andrew Welsh, *SNP, Angus East*	954
*David Ashby, *C., Leicestershire North West*	979
*Sir Wyn Roberts, *C., Conwy*	995

General Election statistics

PRINCIPAL PARTIES IN PARLIAMENT SINCE 1970

	1970	1974 Feb.	1974 Oct.	1979	1983	1987	1992
Conservative	330*	296	276	339	397	375	336
Labour	287	301	319	268	209	229	270
Liberal/LD	6	14	13	11	17	17	20
Social Democrat	—	1	—	—	6	5	—
Independent	5†	1	1	2	—	—	—
Plaid Cymru	—	2	3	2	2	3	4
Scottish Nationalist	1	7	11	2	2	3	3
Democratic Unionist	—	—	—	3	3	3	3
SDLP	—	1	1	1	1	3	4
Sinn Fein	—	—	—	—	1	1	—
Ulster Popular Unionist	—	—	—	—	1	1	1
Ulster Unionist‡	*	11	10	6	10	9	9
The Speaker	1	1	1	1	1	1	1
Total	630	635	635	635	650	650	651

* Including 8 Ulster Unionists
† Comprising: Independent Labour 1, Independent Unity 1, Protestant Unity 1, Republican Labour 1, Unity 1
‡ Comprises:
   1974 (February) United Ulster Unionist Council 11
   1974 (October) United Ulster Unionist 10
   1979 Ulster Unionist 5, United Ulster Unionist 1
   1983 Official Unionist 10

PARLIAMENTS SINCE 1970

		Duration		
Assembled	*Dissolved*	*yr*	*m.*	*d.*
29 June 1970	8 February 1974	3	7	10
6 March 1974	20 September 1974	0	6	14
22 October 1974	7 April 1979	4	5	16
9 May 1979	13 May 1983	4	0	4
15 June 1983	18 May 1987	3	11	3
17 June 1987	16 March 1992	4	8	28
27 April 1992				

MAJORITIES IN THE COMMONS SINCE 1970

Year	*Party*	*Maj.*
1970	Conservative	31
1974 Feb.	No majority	
1974 Oct.	Labour	5
1979	Conservative	43
1983	Conservative	144
1987	Conservative	102
1992	Conservative	21

VOTES CAST 1987 AND 1992*

GENERAL ELECTION 1987

Conservative	13,760,525
Labour	10,029,944
Liberal/SDP Alliance	7,341,152
Scottish Nationalist	416,873
Plaid Cymru	123,589
†Green	89,753
Others	37,576

GENERAL ELECTION 1992

Conservative	14,048,283
Labour	11,559,735
Liberal Democrats	5,999,384
Scottish Nationalist	629,552
Plaid Cymru	154,439
Others	436,207

*Excluding Northern Ireland seats
†Excluding Ecology candidate in Northern Ireland

SIZE OF ELECTORATE 1992

	No. of electors	*Average no. of electors per seat*
England and Wales	38,648,000	68,800
Scotland	3,929,000	54,600
Northern Ireland	1,141,000	67,100
Total	43,719,000	67,200

PARLIAMENTARY CONSTITUENCIES AS AT 9 APRIL 1992

The results of voting in each parliamentary division at the general election of 9 April 1992 are given below. The majority in the 1987 general election, and any by-elections between 1987 and 1992, is given below the 1992 result.

Symbols
E. Total number of electors in the constituency at the 1992 general election
T. Turnout of electors at the 1992 general election
* Member of the last Parliament

Abbreviations
All.	Alliance Party (NI)
C.	Conservative
DUP	Democratic Unionist Party
Green	Green Party
Ind.	Independent
Lab.	Labour
L./All.	Liberal Alliance
LD	Liberal Democrat
Lib.	Liberal
PC	Plaid Cymru
SD	Social Democrat
SDLP	Social Democratic and Labour Party
SDP	Social Democrat Party
SF	Sinn Fein
SNP	Scottish National Party
UPUP	Ulster Popular Unionist Party
UUP	Ulster Unionist Party
ADS	After Dinner Speaker
AFE	Anti-Federal Europe
Alt.	Alternative
Anti Fed.	Anti Federalist League
Anti H.	Anti-Heseltine Independent
APAKBI	Anti-Paddy Ashdown Keep Britain Independent

AS	Anglo Saxon
Bastion	Bastion Party
BNP	British National Party
Brewer	Jolly Small Brewers Party
Brit. Ind.	British Independence Party
CD	Christian Democrat
Century	21st Century Party
Choice	People's Choice
CL	Communist League
Comm. GB	Communist Party of Great Britain
CRA	Chauvinist Raving Alliance
CSP	Common Sense Party
C. Thatch.	Conservative Thatcherite
DLC	Democrat Liberal Conservative
DOS	Doctor of Stockwell
EFRA	Epping Forest Residents Association
ERIP	Equal Representation in Parliament
EUVJJ	End Unemployment Vote Justice for the Jobless
FDP	Fancy Dress Party
Fellowship	Fellowship Party
FP	Feudal Party
FTA	Fair Trials Abroad
FTM	Forward to Mars Party
Fun	Funstermentalist
Gremloids	Gremloids
Hardcore	The Altern-8-ive (Hardcore) Party
Homeland	Independent British Homeland Defence
Hove C.	Official Conservative Hove Party
IFM	Irish Freedom Movement
ILP	Independent Labour Party
Ind. U.	Independent Unionist
Int. Comm.	International Communist Party
Islamic	Islamic Party
ISS	Illegal Sunday Shopping
JBR	Justice from British Rail

Loony	Official Monster Raving Loony Party
Loony G.	Loony Green
LP	Lodestar Party
LTU	Labour and Trade Union
MBI	Morecambe Bay Independent
NA	Noise Abatement
Nat.	Nationalist
NF	National Front
NLP	Natural Law Party
Pensioners	Pensioners' Party
PP	People's Party
PPP	Peoples' Peace Party
PR	Proportional Representation
Prog. Soc.	Independent Progressive Socialist
Prot. Ref.	Protestant Reformation
QFI.	Quality for Life Party
RAVA	Rainbow Ark Voters Association
RCC	Revolutionary Christian Communist
Real Bean	Real Bean
Rev. Comm.	Revolutionary Communist
Rizz	Rizz Party – Rainbow
Scallywagg	Scallywagg
SML	Scottish Militant Labour
SOADDA	Struck Off and Die Doctor's Alliance
Soc.	Socialist
Soc. Lab.	Socialist Labour
True Lab.	True Labour
UTCHAP	Up The Creek Have A Party
WAR	Workers Against Racism
Wessex	Save Wessex
Whiplash	Whiplash Corrective
WP	Workers' Party
WRP	Workers' Revolutionary Party
WUWC	Wake Up Wokingham Campaign
YSOR	Young Socialist – Occupy Ravenscraig

ENGLAND

ALDERSHOT (Hants)
*E.*81,754   *T.*78.71%
*J. Critchley, C.	36,974
A. Collett, *LD*	17,786
J. Anthony Smith, *Lab.*	8,552
D. Robinson, Lib.	1,038
C. majority	19,188

(June 1987, C. maj. 17,784)

ALDRIDGE-BROWNHILLS (W. Midlands)
*E.*63,404   *T.*82.55%
*R. Shepherd, C.	28,431
N. Fawcett, *Lab.*	17,407
S. Reynolds, *LD*	6,503
C. majority	11,024

(June 1987, C. maj. 12,396)

ALTRINCHAM AND SALE (Greater Manchester)
*E.*65,897   *T.*80.66%
*Sir F. Montgomery, C.	29,066
Ms M. Atherton, *Lab.*	12,275
J. Mulholland, *LD*	11,601
J. Renwick, *NLP*	212

C. majority 16,791
(June 1987, C. maj. 14,228)

AMBER VALLEY (Derbys)
*E.*70,155   *T.*84.69%
*Hon. P. Oppenheim, C.	27,418
J. Cooper, *Lab.*	26,706
G. Brocklebank, *LD*	5,294
C. majority	712

(June 1987, C. maj. 9,500)

ARUNDEL (W. Sussex)
*E.*79,241   *T.*77.06%
*Sir M. Marshall, C.	35,405
Dr J. Walsh, *LD*	15,542
R. Nash, *Lab.*	8,321
Mrs D. Renson, Lib.	1,103
R. Corbin, *Green*	693
C. majority	19,863

(June 1987, C. maj. 18,880)

ASHFIELD (Notts)
*E.*75,075   *T.*77.70%
G. Hoon, *Lab.*	32,018
L. Robertson, *C.*	19,031

J. Turton, *LD*	7,291
Lab. majority	12,987

(June 1987, Lab. maj. 4,400)

ASHFORD (Kent)
*E.*71,767   *T.*79.20%
*K. Speed, C.	31,031
Ms C. Headley, *LD*	13,672
Ms D. Cameron, *Lab.*	11,365
Dr A. Porter, *Green*	773
C. majority	17,359

(June 1987, C. maj. 15,488)

ASHTON-UNDER-LYNE (Greater Manchester)
*E.*58,701   *T.*73.87%
*Rt. Hon. R. Sheldon, *Lab.*	24,550
J. Pinniger, *C.*	13,615
C. Turner, *LD*	4,005
C. Hall, Lib.	907
J. Brannigan, *NLP*	289
Lab. majority	10,935

(June 1987, Lab. maj. 9,286)

AYLESBURY (Bucks)
E.79,208   T.80.29%
D. Lidington, C.   36,500
Ms S. Bowles, LD   17,640
R. Priest, Lab.   8,517
N. Foster, Green   702
B. D'Arcy, NLP   239
C. majority   18,860
(June 1987, C. maj. 16,558)

BANBURY (Oxon)
E.71,840   T.81.51%
*A. Baldry, C.   32,215
Ms A. Billingham, Lab.   15,495
G. Fisher, LD   10,602
Dr R. Ticiiati, NLP   250
C. majority   16,720
(June 1987, C. maj. 17,330)

BARKING (Greater London)
E.50,454   T.69.99%
*Ms J. Richardson, Lab.   18,224
J. Kennedy, C.   11,956
S. Churchman, LD   5,133
Lab. majority   6,268
(June 1987, Lab. maj. 3,409)
See also page 238

BARNSLEY CENTRAL (S. Yorks)
E.55,373   T.70.53%
*E. Illsley, Lab.   27,048
D. Senior, C.   7,687
S. Cowton, LD   4,321
Lab. majority   19,361
(June 1987, Lab. maj. 19,051)

BARNSLEY EAST (S. Yorks)
E.54,051   T.72.73%
*T. Patchett, Lab.   30,346
J. Procter, C.   5,569
Ms S. Anginotti, LD   3,399
Lab. majority   24,777
(June 1987, Lab. maj. 23,511)

BARNSLEY WEST AND
PENISTONE (S. Yorks)
E.63,374   T.75.75%
M. Clapham, Lab.   27,965
G. Sawyer, C.   13,461
I. Nicolson, LD   5,610
D. Jones, Green   970
Lab. majority   14,504
(June 1987, Lab. maj. 14,191)

BARROW AND FURNESS (Cumbria)
E.67,764   T.82.11%
J. Hutton, Lab.   26,568
*C. Franks, C.   22,990
C. Crane, LD   6,089
Lab. majority   3,578
(June 1987, C. maj. 3,928)

BASILDON (Essex)
E.67,585   T.79.61%
*D. Amess, C.   24,159
J. Potter, Lab.   22,679
G. Williams, LD   6,967
C. majority   1,480
(June 1987, C. maj. 2,649)

BASINGSTOKE (Hants)
E.82,952   T.82.79%
*A. Hunter, C.   37,521
D. Bull, Lab.   16,323

C. Curtis, LD   14,119
Ms V. Oldaker, Green   714
C. majority   21,198
(June 1987, C. maj. 17,893)

BASSETLAW (Notts)
E.58,583   T.92.97%
*J. Ashton, Lab.   29,061
Mrs C. Spelman, C.   19,064
M. Reynolds, LD   6,340
Lab. majority   9,997
(June 1987, Lab. maj. 5,613)

Bath (Avon)
E.63,689   T.82.54%
D. Foster, LD   25,718
*Rt. Hon. C. Patten, C.   21,950
Ms P. Richards, Lab.   4,102
D. McCanlis, Green   433
Ms M. Barker, Lib.   172
Dr A. Sked, Anti Fed.   117
J. Rumming, Ind.   79
LD majority   3,768
(June 1987, C. maj. 1,412)

BATLEY AND SPEN (W. Yorks)
E.76,417   T.79.63%
*Mrs E. Peacock, C.   27,629
Mrs E. Durkin, Lab.   26,221
G. Beever, LD   6,380
C. Lord, Green   628
C. majority   1,408
(June 1987, C. maj. 1,362)

BATTERSEA (Greater London)
E.68,218   T.76.63%
*J. Bowis, C.   26,390
A. Dubs, Lab.   21,550
R. O'Brien, LD   3,659
I. Wingrove, Green   584
W. Stevens, NLP   98
C. majority   4,840
(June 1987, C. maj. 857)

BEACONSFIELD (Bucks)
E.64,268   T.82.27%
*T. Smith, C.   33,817
Ms A. Purse, LD   10,220
G. Smith, Lab.   7,163
W. Foulds, Ind. C.   1,317
A. Foss, NLP   196
Ms J. Martin, ERIP   166
C. majority   23,597
(June 1987, C. maj. 21,339)

BECKENHAM (Greater London)
E.59,440   T.77.86%
P. Merchant, C.   26,323
K. Ritchie, Lab.   11,038
Ms M. Williams, LD   8,038
G. Williams, Lib.   643
P. Shaw, NLP   243
C. majority   15,285
(June 1987, C. maj. 13,464)

BEDFORDSHIRE MID
E.81,864   T.84.45%
*Rt. Hon. Sir N. Lyell, C.   40,230
R. Clayton, Lab.   15,092
N. Hills, LD   11,957
P. Cottier, Lib.   1,582
M. Lorys, NLP   279

C. majority   25,138
(June 1987, C. maj. 22,851)

BEDFORDSHIRE NORTH
E.73,789   T.80.03%
*Sir T. Skeet, C.   29,920
P. Hall, Lab.   18,302
M. Smithson, LD   10,014
Ms L. Smith, Green   643
B. Bench, NLP   178
C. majority   11,618
(June 1987, C. maj. 16,505)

BEDFORDSHIRE SOUTH WEST
E.79,662   T.82.39%
*W. D. Madel, C.   37,498
B. Elliott, Lab.   16,225
M. Freeman, LD   10,988
P. Rollings, Green   689
D. Gilmour, NLP   239
C. majority   21,273
(June 1987, C. maj. 22,305)

BERKSHIRE EAST
E.90,365   T.81.41%
*A. Mackay, C.   43,898
Ms L. Murray, LD   15,218
K. Dibble, Lab.   14,458
C. majority   28,680
(June 1987, C. maj. 22,626)

BERWICK-UPON-TWEED
(Northumberland)
E.54,919   T.79.12%
*A. Beith, LD   19,283
Dr A. Henfrey, C.   14,240
Dr G. Adam, Lab.   9,933
LD majority   5,043
(June 1987, L./All. maj. 13,945)

BETHNAL GREEN AND STEPNEY
(Greater London)
E.55,675   T.65.45%
*Rt. Hon. P. Shore, Lab.   20,350
J. Shaw, LD   8,120
Miss J. Emmerson, C.   6,507
R. Edmonds, BNP   1,310
S. Kelsey, Comm. GB   156
Lab. majority   12,230
(June 1987, Lab. maj. 5,284)

BEVERLEY (Humberside)
E.81,198   T.79.69%
*J. Cran, C.   34,503
A. Collinge, LD   17,986
C. Challen, Lab.   12,026
D. Hetherington, NLP   199
C. majority   16,517
(June 1987, C. maj. 12,595)

BEXHILL AND BATTLE (E. Sussex)
E.65,850   T.78.99%
*C. Wardle, C.   31,330
Ms S. Prochak, LD   15,023
F. Taylor, Lab.   4,883
J. Prus, Green   594
Mrs M. Smith, CSP   190
C. majority   16,307
(June 1987, C. maj. 20,519)

BEXLEYHEATH (Greater London)
E.57,684   T.82.17%
*C. Townsend, C.   25,606
J. Browning, Lab.   11,520

Ms W. Chaplin, *LD*   10,107
R. Cundy, *Ind.*   170
C. majority   14,086
(June 1987, C. maj. 11,687)

BILLERICAY (Essex)
*E.*80,388   *T.*82.34%
Mrs T. Gorman, C.   37,406
F. Bellard, *LD*   14,912
Ms A. Miller, *Lab.*   13,880
C. majority   22,494
(June 1987, C. maj. 18,016)

BIRKENHEAD (Merseyside)
*E.*62,682   *T.*72.96%
*F. Field, *Lab.*   29,098
R. Hughes, *C.*   11,485
P. Williams, *LD*   4,417
Ms T. Fox, *Green*   543
Ms B. Griffiths, *NLP*   190
Lab. majority   17,613
(June 1987, Lab. maj. 15,372)

BIRMINGHAM EDGBASTON
(W. Midlands)
*E.*53,041   *T.*71.29%
Dame J. Knight, C.   18,529
J. Wilton, *Lab.*   14,222
I. Robertson-Steel, *LD*   4,419
P. Simpson, *Green*   643
C. majority   4,307
(June 1987, C. maj. 8,581)

BIRMINGHAM ERDINGTON
(W. Midlands)
*E.*52,398   *T.*70.15%
*R. Corbett, *Lab.*   18,549
S. Hope, *C.*   13,814
Dr J. Campbell, *LD*   4,398
Lab. majority   4,735
(June 1987, Lab. maj. 2,467)

BIRMINGHAM HALL GREEN
(W. Midlands)
*E.*60,091   *T.*78.17%
A. Hargreaves, C.   21,649
Ms J. Slowey, *Lab.*   17,984
D. McGrath, *LD*   7,342
C. majority   3,665
(June 1987, C. maj. 7,621)

BIRMINGHAM HODGE HILL
(W. Midlands)
*E.*57,651   *T.*70.82%
*T. Davis, *Lab.*   21,895
Miss E. Gibson, *C.*   14,827
S. Hagan, *LD*   3,740
E. Whicker, *NF*   370
Lab. majority   7,068
(June 1987, Lab. maj. 4,789)

BIRMINGHAM LADYWOOD
(W. Midlands)
*E.*56,970   *T.*65.92%
*Ms C. Short, *Lab.*   24,887
Mrs B. Ashford, *C.*   9,604
B. Worth, *LD*   3,068
Lab. majority   15,283
(June 1987, Lab. maj. 10,028)

BIRMINGHAM NORTHFIELD
(W. Midlands)
*E.*70,533   *T.*76.08%
R. Burden, *Lab.*   24,433
*R. King, *C.*   23,803
D. Cropp, *LD*   5,431
Lab. majority   630
(June 1987, C. maj. 3,135)

BIRMINGHAM PERRY BARR
(W. Midlands)
*E.*72,161   *T.*71.62%
*J. Rooker, *Lab.*   27,507
G. Green, *C.*   18,917
T. Philpott, *LD*   5,261
Lab. majority   8,590
(June 1987, Lab. maj. 6,933)

BIRMINGHAM SELLY OAK
(W. Midlands)
*E.*72,150   *T.*76.61%
Ms L. Jones, *Lab.*   25,430
A. Beaumont-Dark, C.   23,370
D. Osborne, *LD*   5,679
P. Slatter, *Green*   535
C. Barwood, *NLP*   178
K. Malik, *Rev Comm*   84
Lab. majority   2,060
(June 1987, C. maj. 2,584)

BIRMINGHAM SMALL HEATH
(W. Midlands)
*E.*55,213   *T.*62.95%
R. Godsiff, *Lab.*   22,675
A. Qayyum Chaudhary, *C.*   8,686
H. Thomas, *LD*   2,575
Ms H. Clawley, *Green*   824
Lab. majority   13,989
(June 1987, Lab. maj. 15,521)

BIRMINGHAM SPARKBROOK
(W. Midlands)
*E.*51,677   *T.*66.80%
*Rt. Hon. R. Hattersley, *Lab.*   22,116
M. Khamisa, *C.*   8,544
D. Parry, *LD*   3,028
C. Alldrick, *Green*   833
Lab. majority   13,572
(June 1987, Lab. maj. 11,859)

BIRMINGHAM YARDLEY
(W. Midlands)
*E.*54,749   *T.*77.98%
Ms E. Morris, *Lab.*   14,884
A. D. G. Bevan, C.   14,722
J. Hemming, *LD*   12,899
Miss P. Read, *NF*   192
Lab. majority   162
(June 1987, C. maj. 2,522)

BISHOP AUCKLAND (Durham)
*E.*72,572   *T.*76.52%
*D. Foster, *Lab.*   27,763
D. Williamson, *C.*   17,676
W. Wade, *LD*   10,099
Lab. majority   10,087
(June 1987, Lab. maj. 7,035)

BLABY (Leics)
*E.*81,790   *T.*83.39%
A. Robathan, *C.*   39,498
Ms E. Ranson, *Lab.*   14,151
Ms M. Lewin, *LD*   13,780

J. Peacock, *BNP*   521
Ms S. Lincoln, *NLP*   260
C. majority   25,347
(June 1987, C. maj. 22,176)

BLACKBURN (Lancs)
*E.*73,251   *T.*75.05%
*J. Straw, *Lab.*   26,633
R. Coates, *C.*   20,606
D. Mann, *LD*   6,332
R. Field, *Green*   878
Mrs M. Carmichael-Grimshaw, *LP*
                                      334
W. Ayliffe, *NLP*   195
Lab. majority   6,027
(June 1987, Lab. maj. 5,497)

BLACKPOOL NORTH (Lancs)
*E.*58,087   *T.*77.55%
H. Elletson, *C.*   21,501
E. Kirton, *Lab.*   18,461
A. Lahiff, *LD*   4,786
Sir G. Francis, *Loony*   178
H. Walker, *NLP*   125
C. majority   3,040
(June 1987, C. maj. 7,321)

BLACKPOOL SOUTH (Lancs)
*E.*56,801   *T.*77.35%
N. Hawkins, *C.*   19,880
G. Marsden, *Lab.*   18,213
R. Wynne, *LD*   5,675
D. Henning, *NLP*   173
C. majority   1,667
(June 1987, C. maj. 6,744)

BLAYDON (Tyne & Wear)
*E.*66,044   *T.*77.69%
*J. McWilliam, *Lab.*   27,028
P. Pescod, *C.*   13,685
P. Nunn, *LD*   10,602
Lab. majority   13,343
(June 1987, Lab. maj. 12,488)

BLYTH VALLEY (Northumberland)
*E.*60,913   *T.*80.77%
*R. Campbell, *Lab.*   24,542
P. Tracey, *LD*   16,498
M. Revell, *C.*   7,691
S. Tyley, *Green*   470
Lab. majority   8,044
(June 1987, Lab. maj. 853)

BOLSOVER (Derbys)
*E.*66,693   *T.*78.94%
*D. Skinner, *Lab.*   33,973
T. James, *C.*   13,313
Ms S. Barber, *LD*   5,363
Lab. majority   20,660
(June 1987, Lab. maj. 14,120)

BOLTON NORTH EAST (Greater
Manchester)
*E.*58,659   *T.*82.26%
*P. Thurnham, *C.*   21,644
D. Crausby, *Lab.*   21,459
B. Dunning, *LD*   4,971
P. Tong, *NLP*   181
C. majority   185
(June 1987, C. maj. 813)

BOLTON SOUTH EAST (Greater Manchester)
E.65,600   T.75.53%

*D. Young, *Lab.*	26,906
N. Wood-Dow, *C.*	14,215
D. Lee, *LD*	5,243
W. Hardman, *Ind. Lab.*	2,894
L. Walch, *NLP*	290
Lab. majority	12,691

(June 1987, Lab. maj. 11,381)

BOLTON WEST (Greater Manchester)
E.71,344   T.83.53%

*Hon. T. Sackville, *C.*	26,452
C. Morris, *Lab.*	25,373
Ms B. Ronson, *LD*	7,529
Ms J. Phillips, *NLP*	240
C. majority	1,079

(June 1987, C. maj. 4,593)

BOOTHFERRY (Humberside)
E.80,747   T.79.73%

*D. Davis, *C.*	35,266
Ms L. Coubrough, *Lab.*	17,731
J. Goss, *LD*	11,388
C. majority	17,535

(June 1987, C. maj. 18,970)

BOOTLE (Merseyside)
E.69,308   T.72.46%

*J. Benton, *Lab.*	37,464
C. Varley, *C.*	8,022
J. Cunningham, *LD*	3,301
Ms M. Hall, *Lib.*	1,174
T. Haynes, *NLP*	264
Lab. majority	29,442

(June 1987, Lab. maj. 24,477)
(May 1990, Lab. maj. 23,517)
(November 1990, Lab. maj. 19,465)

BOSWORTH (Leics)
E.80,234   T.84.13%

*D. Tredinnick, *C.*	36,618
D. Everitt, *Lab.*	17,524
G. Drozdz, *LD*	12,643
B. Fewster, *Green*	716
C. majority	19,094

(June 1987, C. maj. 17,016)

BOURNEMOUTH EAST (Dorset)
E.75,089   T.72.82%

*D. Atkinson, *C.*	30,820
N. Russell, *LD*	15,997
P. Brushett, *Lab.*	7,541
Ms S. Holmes, *NLP*	329
C. majority	14,823

(June 1987, C. maj. 14,683)

BOURNEMOUTH WEST (Dorset)
E.74,738   T.75.72%

*J. Butterfill, *C.*	29,820
Ms J. Dover, *LD*	17,178
B. Grower, *Lab.*	9,423
A. Springham, *NLP*	232
C. majority	12,642

(June 1987, C. maj. 12,651)

BOW AND POPLAR (Greater London)
E.56,685   T.65.84%

*Mrs M. Gordon, *Lab.*	18,487
P. Hughes, *LD*	10,083
S. Pearce, *C.*	6,876

J. Tyndall, *BNP*	1,107
S. Petter, *Green*	612
W. Hite, *NLP*	158
Lab. majority	8,404

(June 1987, Lab. maj. 4,631)

BRADFORD NORTH (W. Yorks)
E.66,719   T.73.38%

*T. Rooney, *Lab.*	23,420
M. Riaz, *C.*	15,756
D. Ward, *LD*	9,133
W. Beckett, *Loony*	350
M. Nasr, *Islamic*	304
Lab. majority	7,664

(June 1987, Lab. maj. 1,663)
(November 1990, Lab. maj. 9,514)

BRADFORD SOUTH (W. Yorks)
E.69,914   T.75.61%

*G. R. Cryer, *Lab.*	25,185
A. Popat, *C.*	20,283
B. Boulton, *LD*	7,243
M. Naseem, *Islamic*	156
Lab. majority	4,902

(June 1987, Lab. maj. 309)
See also page 238

BRADFORD WEST (W. Yorks)
E.70,016   T.69.90%

*M. Madden, *Lab.*	26,046
Dr A. Ashworth, *C.*	16,544
Dr. A. Griffiths, *LD*	5,150
P. Braham, *Green*	735
D. Pidcock, *Islamic*	471
Lab. majority	9,502

(June 1987, Lab. maj. 7,551)

BRAINTREE (Essex)
E.78,880   T.83.41%

*Rt. Hon. A. Newton, *C.*	34,415
I. Willmore, *Lab.*	16,921
Ms D. Wallis, *LD*	13,603
J. Abbott, *Green*	855
C. majority	17,494

(June 1987, C. maj. 16,857)

BRENT EAST (Greater London)
E.53,319   T.68.82%

*K. Livingstone, *Lab.*	19,387
D. Green, *C.*	13,416
M. Cummins, *LD*	3,249
Ms T. Dean, *Green*	548
Ms A. Murphy, *Comm. GB*	96
Lab. majority	5,971

(June 1987, Lab. maj. 1,653)

BRENT NORTH (Greater London)
E.58,917   T.70.57%

*Rt. Hon. Sir R. Boyson, *C.*	23,445
J. Moher, *Lab.*	13,314
P. Lorber, *LD*	4,149
T. Vipul, *Ind.*	356
T. Davids, *NLP*	318
C. majority	10,131

(June 1987, C. maj. 15,720)

BRENT SOUTH (Greater London)
E.56,034   T.64.10%

*P. Boateng, *Lab.*	20,662
R. Blackman, *C.*	10,957
M. Harskin, *LD*	3,658
D. Johnson, *Green*	479
C. Jani, *NLP*	166

Lab. majority	9,705

(June 1987, Lab. maj. 7,931)

BRENTFORD AND ISLEWORTH (Greater London)
E.70,880   T.76.22%

N. Deva, *C.*	24,752
Ms A. Keen, *Lab.*	22,666
Ms J. Salmon, *LD*	5,683
J. Bradley, *Green*	927
C. majority	2,086

(June 1987, C. maj. 7,953)

BRENTWOOD AND ONGAR (Greater London)
E.65,830   T.84.70%

E. Pickles, *C.*	32,145
Ms E. Bottomley, *LD*	17,000
F. Keohane, *Lab.*	6,080
Ms C. Bartley, *Green*	535
C. majority	15,145

(June 1987, C. maj. 18,921)

BRIDGWATER (Somerset)
E.71,567   T.79.51%

*Rt. Hon. T. King, *C.*	26,610
W. Revans, *LD*	16,894
P. James, *Lab.*	12,365
G. Dummett, *Green*	746
A. Body, *Ind.*	183
Ms G. Sanson, *NLP*	112
C. majority	9,716

(June 1987, C. maj. 11,195)

BRIDLINGTON (Humberside)
E.84,829   T.77.93%

*J. Townend, *C.*	33,604
J. Leeman, *LD*	17,246
S. Hatfield, *Lab.*	15,263
C. majority	16,358

(June 1987, C. maj. 17,321)

BRIGG AND CLEETHORPES (Humberside)
E.82,377   T.77.98%

*M. Brown, *C.*	31,673
I. Cawsey, *Lab.*	22,404
Ms M. Cockbill, *LD*	9,374
N. Jacques, *Green*	790
C. majority	9,269

(June 1987, C. maj. 12,250)

BRIGHTON KEMPTOWN (E. Sussex)
E.57,646   T.76.14%

*A. Bowden, *C.*	21,129
Ms G. Haynes, *Lab.*	18,073
P. Scott, *LD*	4,461
Ms E. Overall, *NLP*	230
C. majority	3,056

(June 1987, C. maj. 9,260)

BRIGHTON PAVILION (E. Sussex)
E.57,616   T.76.81%

D. Spencer, *C.*	20,630
D. Lepper, *Lab.*	16,955
T. Pearce, *LD*	5,606
I. Brodie, *Green*	963
Ms E. Turner, *NLP*	103
C. majority	3,675

(June 1987, C. maj. 9,142)

BRISTOL EAST (Avon)
E.62,577   T.80.40%
Ms J. Corston, *Lab.*   22,418
*J. Sayeed, *C.*   19,726
J. Kiely, *LD*   7,903
I. Anderson, *NF*   270
Lab. majority   2,692
(June 1987, C. maj. 4,123)

BRISTOL NORTH WEST (Avon)
E.72,726   T.82.35%
*M. Stern, *C.*   25,354
D. Naysmith, *Lab.*   25,309
J. Taylor, *LD*   8,498
H. Long, *SD*   729
C. majority   45
(June 1987, C. maj. 6,952)

BRISTOL SOUTH (Avon)
E.64,309   T.78.04%
*Ms D. Primarolo, *Lab.*   25,164
J. Bercow, *C.*   16,245
P. Crossley, *LD*   7,892
J. Boxall, *Green*   756
N. Phillips, *NLP*   136
Lab. majority   8,919
(June 1987, Lab. maj. 1,404)

BRISTOL WEST (Avon)
E.70,579   T.74.37%
*Rt. Hon. W. Waldegrave, *C.*   22,169
C. Boney, *LD*   16,098
H. Bashforth, *Lab.*   12,992
A. Sawday, *Green*   906
D. Cross, *NLP*   104
B. Brent, *Rev. Comm.*   92
P. Hammond, *SOADDA*   87
T. Hedges, *Anti Fed.*   42
C. majority   6,071
(June 1987, C. maj. 7,703)

BROMSGROVE (H & W)
E.71,111   T.82.49%
K. R. Thomason, *C.*   31,709
Ms C. Mole, *Lab.*   18,007
Ms A. Cassin, *LD*   8,090
J. Churchman, *Green*   856
C. majority   13,702
(June 1987, C. maj. 16,685)

BROXBOURNE (Herts)
E.72,116   T.79.95%
*Mrs M. Roe, *C.*   36,094
M. Hudson, *Lab.*   12,124
Mrs J. Davies, *LD*   9,244
G. Woolhouse, *NLP*   198
C. majority   23,970
(June 1987, C. maj. 22,995)

BROXTOWE (Notts)
E.73,123   T.83.40%
*J. Lester, *C.*   31,096
J. Walker, *Lab.*   21,205
J. Ross, *LD*   8,395
D. Lukehurst, *NLP*   293
C. majority   9,891
(June 1987, C. maj. 16,651)

BUCKINGHAM
E.56,063   T.84.21%
*G. Walden, *C.*   29,496
T. Jones, *LD*   9,705
K. White, *Lab.*   7,662

L. Sheaff, *NLP*   353
C. majority   19,791
(June 1987, C. maj. 18,526)

BURNLEY (Lancs)
E.68,952   T.74.38%
*P. Pike, *Lab.*   27,184
Mrs B. Binge, *C.*   15,693
G. Birtwistle, *LD*   8,414
Lab. majority   11,491
(June 1987, Lab. maj. 7,557)

BURTON (Staffs)
E.75,292   T.82.43%
*I. Lawrence, *C.*   30,845
Ms P. Muddyman, *Lab.*   24,849
R. Renold, *LD*   6,375
C. majority   5,996
(June 1987, C. maj. 9,830)

BURY NORTH (Greater Manchester)
E.69,529   T.84.77%
*A. Burt, *C.*   29,266
J. Dobbin, *Lab.*   24,502
C. McGrath, *LD*   5,010
M. Sullivan, *NLP*   163
C. majority   4,764
(June 1987, C. maj. 6,929)

BURY SOUTH (Greater Manchester)
E.65,793   T.82.10%
*D. Sumberg, *C.*   24,873
Ms H. Blears, *Lab.*   24,085
A. Cruden, *LD*   4,832
Mrs N. Sullivan, *NLP*   228
C. majority   788
(June 1987, C. maj. 2,679)

BURY ST EDMUNDS (Suffolk)
E.79,967   T.78.38%
R. Spring, *C.*   33,554
T. Sheppard, *Lab.*   14,767
J. Williams, *LD*   13,814
Ms J. Lillis, *NLP*   550
C. majority   18,787
(June 1987, C. maj. 21,458)

CALDER VALLEY (W. Yorks)
E.74,417   T.82.09%
*Sir D. Thompson, *C.*   27,753
D. Chaytor, *Lab.*   22,875
S. Pearson, *LD*   9,842
Ms V. Smith, *Green*   622
C. majority   4,878
(June 1987, C. maj. 6,045)

CAMBRIDGE
E.69,022   T.73.18%
Mrs A. Campbell, *Lab.*   20,039
M. Bishop, *C.*   19,459
D. Howarth, *LD*   10,037
T. Cooper, *Green*   720
D. Brettell-Winnington, *Loony*   175
R. Chalmers, *NLP*   83
Lab. majority   580
(June 1987, C. maj. 5,060)

CAMBRIDGESHIRE NORTH EAST
E.79,935   T.79.38%
*M. Moss, *C.*   34,288
M. Leeke, *LD*   19,195
R. Harris, *Lab.*   8,746
C. Ash, *Lib.*   998
Mrs M. Chalmers, *NLP*   227

C. majority   15,093
(June 1987, C. maj. 1,428)

CAMBRIDGESHIRE SOUTH EAST
E.78,600   T.80.57%
*J. Paice, *C.*   36,693
R. Wotherspoon, *LD*   12,883
M. Jones, *Lab.*   12,688
J. Marsh, *Green*   836
Ms B. Langridge, *NLP*   231
C. majority   23,810
(June 1987, C. maj. 17,502)

CAMBRIDGESHIRE SOUTH WEST
E.84,418   T.81.10%
*Sir A. Grant, *C.*   38,902
Ms S. Sutton, *LD*   19,265
K. Price, *Lab.*   9,378
Ms L. Whitebread, *Green*   699
F. Chalmers, *NLP*   225
C. majority   19,637
(June 1987, C. maj. 18,251)

CANNOCK AND BURNTWOOD (Staffs)
E.72,600   T.84.21%
A. Wright, *Lab.*   28,139
*G. Howarth, *C.*   26,633
P. Treasaden, *LD*   5,899
M. Hartshorne, *Loony*   469
Lab. majority   1,506
(June 1987, C. maj. 2,689)

CANTERBURY (Kent)
E.75,181   T.78.12%
*J. Brazier, *C.*   29,827
M. Vye, *LD*   19,022
M. Whitemore, *Lab.*   8,936
Ms W. Arnall, *Green*   747
Ms S. Curphey, *NLP*   203
C. majority   10,805
(June 1987, C. maj. 14,891)

CARLISLE (Cumbria)
E.55,140   T.79.39%
*E. Martlew, *Lab.*   20,479
C. Condie, *C.*   17,371
R. Aldersey, *LD*   5,740
Ms N. Robinson, *NLP*   190
Lab. majority   3,108
(June 1987, Lab. maj. 916)

CARSHALTON AND WALLINGTON
(Surrey)
E.65,179   T.80.94%
*F. N. Forman, *C.*   26,243
T. Brake, *LD*   16,300
Ms M. Moran, *Lab.*   9,333
R. Steel, *Green*   614
D. Bamford, *Loony G.*   266
C. majority   9,943
(June 1987, C. maj. 14,409)

CASTLE POINT (Essex)
E.66,229   T.80.50%
Dr R. Spink, *C.*   29,629
D. Flack, *Lab.*   12,799
A. Petchey, *LD*   10,208
Ms I. Willis, *Green*   683
C. majority   16,830
(June 1987, C. maj. 19,248)

CHEADLE (Greater Manchester)
E.66,131   T.84.43%
*S. Day, C.   32,504
Ms P. Calton, LD   16,726
Ms S. Broadhurst, Lab.   6,442
Ms P. Whittle, NLP   168
C. majority   15,778
(June 1987, C. maj. 10,631)

CHELMSFORD (Essex)
E.83,441   T.84.61%
*S. Burns, C.   39,043
H. Nicholson, LD   20,783
Dr R. Chad, Lab.   10,010
Ms E. Burgess, Green   769
C. majority   18,260
(June 1987, C. maj. 7,761)

CHELSEA (Greater London)
E.42,371   T.63.31%
*Rt. Hon. N. Scott, C.   17,471
Ms R. Horton, Lab.   4,682
Ms S. Broidy, LD   4,101
Ms N. Kortvelyessy, Green   485
D. Armstrong, Anti Fed.   88
C. majority   12,789
(June 1987, C. maj. 13,319)

CHELTENHAM (Glos)
E.79,808   T.80.32%
N. Jones, LD   30,351
J. Taylor, C.   28,683
Ms P. Tatlow, Lab.   4,077
M. Rendall, AFE   665
H. Brighouse, NLP   169
M. Bruce-Smith, Ind.   162
LD majority   1,668
(June 1987, C. maj. 4,896)

CHERTSEY AND WALTON (Surrey)
E.70,465   T.80.52%
*Rt. Hon. Sir G. Pattie, C.   34,163
A. Kremer, LD   11,344
Ms I. Hamilton, Lab.   10,791
Ms S. Bennell, NLP   444
C. majority   22,819
(June 1987, C. maj. 17,469)

CHESHAM AND AMERSHAM (Bucks)
E.69,895   T.81.93%
Ms C. Gillan, C.   36,273
A. Ketteringham, LD   14,053
Ms C. Atherton, Lab.   5,931
Ms C. Strickland, Green   753
T. Griffith-Jones, NLP   255
C. majority   22,220
(June 1987, C. maj. 19,440)

CHESTER, CITY OF
E.63,370   T.83.84%
G. Brandreth, C.   23,411
D. Robinson, Lab.   22,310
G. Smith, LD   6,867
T. Barker, Green   448
S. Cross, NLP   98
C. majority   1,101
(June 1987, C. maj. 4,855)

CHESTERFIELD (Derbys)
E.71,783   T.77.98%
*A. Benn, Lab.   26,461
A. Rogers, LD   20,047
P. Lewis, C.   9,473

Lab. majority   6,414
(June 1987, Lab. maj. 8,577)

CHICHESTER (W. Sussex)
E.82,124   T.77.77%
*R. A. Nelson, C.   37,906
P. Gardiner, LD   17,019
Ms D. Andrewes, Lab.   7,192
E. Paine, Green   876
Ms J. Weights, Lib.   643
Ms J. Jackson, NLP   238
C. majority   20,887
(June 1987, C. maj. 20,177)

CHINGFORD (Greater London)
E.55,401   T.78.41%
G. I. Duncan-Smith, C.   25,730
P. Dawe, Lab.   10,792
S. Banks, LD   5,705
D. Green, Lib.   602
J. Baguley, Green   575
Revd C. John, Ind.   41
C. majority   14,938
(June 1987, C. maj. 17,955)

CHIPPING BARNET (Greater London)
E.57,153   T.78.57%
*S. Chapman, C.   25,589
A. Williams, Lab.   11,638
D. Smith, LD   7,247
Ms D. Derksen, NLP   222
C. Johnson, Fun.   213
C. majority   13,951
(June 1987, C. maj. 14,871)

CHISLEHURST (Greater London)
E.53,782   T.78.89%
*R. Sims, C.   24,761
I. Wingfield, Lab.   9,485
W. Hawthorne, LD   6,683
I. Richmond, Lib.   849
Dr F. Speed, Green   652
C. majority   15,276
(June 1987, C. maj. 14,507)

CHORLEY (Lancs)
E.78,531   T.82.81%
*D. Dover, C.   30,715
R. McManus, Lab.   26,469
Ms J. Ross-Mills, LD   7,452
P. Leadbetter, NLP   402
C. majority   4,246
(June 1987, C. maj. 8,057)

CHRISTCHURCH (Dorset)
E.71,438   T.80.70%
*R. Adley, C.   36,627
Revd D. Bussey, LD   13,612
A. Lloyd, Lab.   6,997
J. Barratt, NLP   243
A. Wareham, CRA   175
C. majority   23,015
(June 1987, C. maj. 22,374)
See also page 238

CIRENCESTER AND TEWKESBURY (Glos)
E.88,299   T.82.05%
G. Clifton-Brown, C.   40,258
E. Weston, LD   24,200
T. Page, Lab.   7,262
R. Clayton, NLP   449

P. Trice-Rolph, Ind.   287
C. majority   16,058
(June 1987, C. maj. 12,662)

CITY OF LONDON AND WESTMINSTER SOUTH
E.55,021   T.63.08%
*Rt. Hon. P. Brooke, C.   20,938
C. Smith, Lab.   7,569
Ms J. Smithard, LD   5,392
G. Herbert, Green   458
P. Stockton, Loony   147
A. Farrell, IFM   107
R. Johnson, NLP   101
C. majority   13,369
(June 1987, C. maj. 12,034)

COLCHESTER NORTH (Essex)
E.86,479   T.79.11%
Hon. B. Jenkin, C.   35,213
Dr J. Raven, LD   18,721
D. Lee, Lab.   13,870
M. Tariq Shabbeer, Green   372
M. Mears, NLP   238
C. majority   16,492
(June 1987, C. maj. 13,623)

COLCHESTER SOUTH AND MALDON (Essex)
E.86,410   T.79.22%
J. Whittingdale, C.   37,548
I. Thorn, LD   15,727
C. Pearson, Lab.   14,158
M. Patterson, Green   1,028
C. majority   21,821
(June 1987, C. maj. 15,483)

COLNE VALLEY (W. Yorks)
E.72,043   T.81.97%
*G. Riddick, C.   24,804
J. Harman, Lab.   17,579
N. Priestley, LD   15,953
R. Stewart, Green   443
Mrs M. Staniforth, Loony   160
J. Hasty, Ind.   73
J. Tattersall, NLP   44
C. majority   7,225
(June 1987, C. maj. 1,677)

CONGLETON (Cheshire)
E.70,477   T.84.47%
*Mrs J. A. Winterton, C.   29,163
I. Brodie-Browne, LD   18,043
M. Finnegan, Lab.   11,927
P. Brown, NLP   399
C. majority   11,120
(June 1987, C. maj. 7,969)

COPELAND (Cumbria)
E.54,911   T.83.54%
*Dr J. Cunningham, Lab.   22,328
P. Davies, C.   19,889
R. Putnam, LD   3,508
J. Sinton, NLP   148
Lab. majority   2,439
(June 1987, Lab. maj. 1,894)

CORBY (Northants)
E.68,333   T.82.88%
*W. Powell, C.   25,203
A. Feather, Lab.   24,861
M. Roffe, LD   5,792
Ms J. Wood, Lib.   784

C. majority	342
(June 1987, C. maj. 1,805)	

CORNWALL NORTH
E.76,844   T.81.51%
P. Tyler, LD	29,696
*Sir G. Neale, C.	27,775
F. Jordan, Lab.	4,103
P. Andrews, Lib.	678
G. Rowe, Ind.	276
Mrs H. Treadwell, NLP	112
LD majority	1,921
(June 1987, C. maj. 5,682)	

CORNWALL SOUTH EAST
E.73,027   T.82.14%
*R. Hicks, C.	30,565
R. Teverson, LD	22,861
Mrs L. Gilroy, Lab.	5,536
Miss M. Cook, Lib.	644
A. Quick, Anti Fed.	227
Miss R. Allen, NLP	155
C. majority	7,704
(June 1987, C. maj. 6,607)	

COVENTRY NORTH EAST
(W. Midlands)
E.64,787   T.73.20%
R. Ainsworth, Lab.	24,896
K. Perrin, C.	13,220
V. McKee, LD	5,306
*J. Hughes, Ind. Lab.	4,008
Lab. majority	11,676
(June 1987, Lab. maj. 11,867)	

COVENTRY NORTH WEST
(W. Midlands)
E.50,670   T.77.63%
*G. Robinson, Lab.	20,349
Mrs A. Hill, C.	13,917
Ms A. Simpson, LD	5,070
Lab. majority	6,432
(June 1987, Lab. maj. 5,663)	

COVENTRY SOUTH EAST
(W. Midlands)
E.48,796   T.74.87%
J. Cunningham, Lab.	11,902
Mrs M. Hyams, C.	10,591
*D. Nellist, Ind. Lab.	10,551
A. Armstrong, LD	3,318
N. Tompkinson, NF	173
Lab. majority	1,311
(June 1987, Lab. maj. 6,653)	

COVENTRY SOUTH WEST
(W. Midlands)
E.63,474   T.80.14%
*J. Butcher, C.	23,225
R. Slater, Lab.	21,789
G. Sewards, LD	4,666
R. Wheway, Lib.	989
D. Morris, NLP	204
C. majority	1,436
(June 1987, C. maj. 3,210)	

CRAWLEY (W. Sussex)
E.78,277   T.79.16%
*Hon. A. N. Soames, C.	30,204
Ms L. Moffatt, Lab.	22,439
G. Seekings, LD	8,558
M. Wilson, Green	766

C. majority	7,765
(June 1987, C. maj. 12,138)	

CREWE AND NANTWICH (Cheshire)
E.74,993   T.81.87%
*Hon. Mrs G. Dunwoody, Lab.	28,065
B. Silvester, C.	25,370
G. Griffiths, LD	7,315
Ms N. Wilkinson, Green	651
Lab. majority	2,695
(June 1987, Lab. maj. 1,092)	

CROSBY (Merseyside)
E.82,537   T.82.45%
*M. Thornton, C.	32,267
Ms M. Eagle, Lab.	17,461
Ms F. Clucas, LD	16,562
J. Marks, Lib.	1,052
S. Brady, Green	559
N. Paterson, NLP	152
C. majority	14,806
(June 1987, C. maj. 6,853)	

CROYDON CENTRAL (Greater
London)
E.55,798   T.71.73%
Sir P. Beresford, C.	22,168
G. Davies, Lab.	12,518
Ms D. Richardson, LD	5,342
C. majority	9,650
(June 1987, C. maj. 12,617)	

CROYDON NORTH EAST (Greater
London)
E.64,405   T.72.01%
D. Congdon, C.	23,835
Ms M. Walker, Lab.	16,362
J. Fraser, LD	6,186
C. majority	7,473
(June 1987, C. maj. 12,519)	

CROYDON NORTH WEST (Greater
London)
E.57,241   T.70.76%
M. Wicks, Lab.	19,152
*H. Malins, C.	17,626
Ms L. Hawkins, LD	3,728
Lab. majority	1,526
(June 1987, C. maj. 3,988)	

CROYDON SOUTH (Greater London)
E.64,768   T.77.57%
R. Ottaway, C.	31,993
P. Billenness, LD	11,568
Miss H. Salmon, Lab	6,444
M. Samuel, Choice	-239
C. majority	20,425
(June 1987, C. maj. 19,063)	

DAGENHAM (Greater London)
E.59,645   T.70.65%
*B. Gould, Lab.	22,027
D. Rossiter, C.	15,294
C. Marquand, LD	4,824
Lab. majority	6,733
(June 1987, Lab. maj. 2,469)	
See also page 238

DARLINGTON (Durham)
E.66,094   T.83.60%
A. Milburn, Lab.	26,556
*M. Fallon, C.	23,758
P. Bergg, LD	4,586
Dr D. Clarke, BNP	355

Lab. majority	2,798
(June 1987, C. maj. 2,661)	

DARTFORD (Kent)
E.72,366   T.83.14%
*B. Dunn, C.	31,194
Dr H. Stoate, Lab.	20,880
Dr P. Bryden, LD	7,584
A. Munro, FDP	262
Ms A. Holland, NLP	247
C. majority	10,314
(June 1987, C. maj. 14,929)	

DAVENTRY (Northants)
E.71,824   T.82.75%
*T. Boswell, C.	34,734
Ms L. Koumi, Lab.	14,460
A. Rounthwaite, LD	9,820
R. France, NLP	422
C. majority	20,274
(June 1987, C. maj. 19,690)	

DAVYHULME (Greater Manchester)
E.61,679   T.81.82%
*W. Churchill, C.	24,216
B. Brotherton, Lab.	19,790
Ms J. Pearcey, LD	5,797
T. Brotheridge, NLP	665
C. majority	4,426
(June 1987, C. maj. 8,199)	

DENTON AND REDDISH (Greater
Manchester)
E.68,463   T.76.77%
*A. Bennett, Lab.	29,021
J. Horswell, C.	16,937
Dr F. Ridley, LD	4,953
M. Powell, Lib.	1,296
J. Fuller, NLP	354
Lab. majority	12,084
(June 1987, Lab. maj. 8,250)	

DERBY NORTH
E.73,176   T.80.65%
*G. Knight, C.	28,574
R. Laxton, Lab.	24,121
R. Charlesworth, LD	5,638
E. Wall, Green	383
P. Hart, NF	245
N. Onley, NLP	58
C. majority	4,453
(June 1987, C. maj. 6,280)	

DERBY SOUTH
E.66,328   T.75.52%
*Mrs M. Beckett, Lab.	25,917
N. Brown, C.	18,981
S. Hartropp, LD	5,198
Lab. majority	6,936
(June 1987, Lab. maj. 1,516)	

DERBYSHIRE NORTH EAST
E.70,707   T.83.61%
*H. Barnes, Lab.	28,860
J. Hayes, C.	22,590
D. Stone, LD	7,675
Lab. majority	6,270
(June 1987, Lab. maj. 3,720)	

DERBYSHIRE SOUTH
E.82,342   T.85.49%
*Mrs E. Currie, C.	34,266
M. Todd, Lab.	29,608
Ms D. Brass, LD	6,236

T. Mercer, *NLP* 291
C. majority 4,658
(June 1987, C. maj. 10,311)

DERBYSHIRE WEST
E.71,201　*T*.84.99%
*P. McLoughlin, *C*. 32,879
R. Fearn, *LD* 14,110
S. Clamp, *Lab*. 13,528
C. majority 18,769
(June 1987, C. maj. 10,527)

DEVIZES (Wilts)
E.89,745　*T*.81.67%
M. Ancram, *C*. 39,090
Ms J. Mactaggart, *LD* 19,378
Ms R. Berry, *Lab*. 13,060
S. Coles, *Lib*. 962
D. Ripley, *Green* 808
C. majority 19,712
(June 1987, C. maj. 17,830)

DEVON NORTH
E.68,998　*T*.84.36%
N. Harvey, *LD* 27,414
*A. Speller, *C*. 26,620
P. Donner, *Lab*. 3,410
Ms C. Simmons, *Green* 658
G. Treadwell, *NLP* 107
LD majority 794
(June 1987, C. maj. 4,469)

DEVON WEST AND TORRIDGE
E.76,933　*T*.81.46%
*Miss E. Nicholson, *C*. 29,627
D. McBride, *LD* 26,013
D. Brenton, *Lab*. 5,997
Dr F. Williamson, *Green* 898
D. Collins, *NLP* 141
C. majority 3,614
(June 1987, C. maj. 6,468)

DEWSBURY (W. Yorks)
E.72,839　*T*.80.18%
*Mrs W. A. Taylor, *Lab*. 25,596
J. Whitfield, *C*. 24,962
R. Meadowcroft, *LD* 6,570
Lady J. Birdwood, *BNP* 660
N. Denby, *Green* 471
Mrs J. Marsden, *NLP* 146
Lab. majority 634
(June 1987, Lab. maj. 445)

DONCASTER CENTRAL (S. Yorks)
E.68,890　*T*.74.24%
*Rt. Hon. H. Walker, *Lab*. 27,795
W. Glossop, *C*. 17,113
C. Hampson, *LD* 6,057
M. Driver, *WRP* 184
Lab. majority 10,682
(June 1987, Lab. maj. 8,196)

DONCASTER NORTH (S. Yorks)
E.74,732　*T*.73.92%
K. Hughes, *Lab*. 34,135
R. Light, *C*. 14,322
S. Whiting, *LD* 6,787
Lab. majority 19,813
(June 1987, Lab. maj. 19,938)

DON VALLEY (S. Yorks)
E.76,327　*T*.76.25%
*M. Redmond, *Lab*. 32,008
N. Paget-Brown, *C*. 18,474

M. Jevons, *LD* 6,920
S. Platt, *Green* 803
Lab. majority 13,534
(June 1987, Lab. maj. 11,467)

DORSET NORTH
E.76,718　*T*.81.79%
*N. Baker, *C*. 34,234
Ms L. Siegle, *LD* 24,154
J. Fitzmaurice, *Lab*. 4,360
C. majority 10,080
(June 1987, C. maj. 11,907)

DORSET SOUTH
E.75,788　*T*.76.91%
*I. Bruce, *C*. 29,319
B. Ellis, *LD* 15,811
Dr A. Chedzoy, *Lab*. 12,298
Mrs J. Nager, *Ind*. 673
M. Griffiths, *NLP* 191
C. majority 13,508
(June 1987, C. maj. 15,067)

DORSET WEST
E.67,256　*T*.81.18%
*Sir J. Spicer, *C*. 27,766
R. Legg, *LD* 19,756
J. Mann, *Lab*. 7,082
C. majority 8,010
(June 1987, C. maj. 12,364)

DOVER (Kent)
E.68,962　*T*.83.50%
*D. Shaw, *C*. 25,395
G. Prosser, *Lab*. 24,562
M. Sole, *LD* 6,212
A. Sullivan, *Green* 637
P. Sherred, *Ind*. 407
B. Philp, *Ind. C*. 250
C. Percy, *NLP* 127
C. majority 833
(June 1987, C. maj. 6,541)

DUDLEY EAST (W. Midlands)
E.75,355　*T*.74.96%
*Dr J. Gilbert, *Lab*. 29.806
J. Holland, *C*. 20,606
I. Jenkins, *LD* 5,400
G. Cartwright, *NF* 675
Lab. majority 9,200
(June 1987, Lab. maj. 3,473)

DUDLEY WEST (W. Midlands)
E.86,632　*T*.82.08%
*J. Blackburn, *C*. 34,729
K. Lomax, *Lab*. 28,940
G. Lewis, *LD* 7,446
C. majority 5,789
(June 1987, C. maj. 10,244)
See also page 238

DULWICH (Greater London)
E.55,141　*T*.67.91%
Ms T. Jowell, *Lab*. 17,714
*G. Bowden, *C*. 15,658
Dr A. Goldie, *LD* 4,078
Lab. majority 2,056
(June 1987, C. maj. 180)

DURHAM, CITY OF
E.68,165　*T*.74.61%
*G. Steinberg, *Lab*. 27,095
M. Woodroofe, *C*. 12,037
N. Martin, *LD* 10,915

Ms S. J. Banks, *Green* 812
Lab. majority 15,058
(June 1987, Lab. maj. 6,125)

DURHAM NORTH
E.73,694　*T*.76.08%
*G. Radice, *Lab*. 33,567
Ms E. Sibley, *C*. 13,930
P. Appleby, *LD* 8,572
Lab. majority 19,637
(June 1987, Lab. maj. 18,433)

DURHAM NORTH WEST
E.61,139　*T*. 75.58%
*Miss H. Armstrong, *Lab*. 26,734
Mrs T. May, *C*. 12,747
T. Farron, *LD* 6,728
Lab. majority 13,987
(June 1987, Lab. maj. 10,162)

EALING ACTON (Greater London)
E.58,687　*T*.76.03%
*Sir G. Young, *C*. 22,579
Ms Y. Johnson, *Lab*. 15,572
L. Rowe, *LD* 5,487
Ms A. Seibe, *Green* 554
T. Pitt-Aikens, *Ind. C*. 432
C. majority 7,007
(June 1987, C. maj. 12,233)

EALING NORTH (Greater London)
E.63,528　*T*.78.84%
*H. Greenway, *C*. 24,898
M. Stears, *Lab*. 18,932
P. Hankinson, *LD* 5,247
D. Earl, *Green* 554
C. Hill, *NF* 277
R. Davis, *CD* 180
C. majority 5,966
(June 1987, C. maj. 15,153)

EALING SOUTHALL (Greater London)
E.65,574　*T*.75.49%
P. Khabra, *Lab*. 23,476
P. Treleaven, *C*. 16,610
*S. Bidwell, *True Lab*. 4,665
Ms P. Nandhra, *LD* 3,790
N. Goodwin, *Green* 964
Lab. majority 6,866
(June 1987, Lab. maj. 7,977)

EASINGTON (Durham)
E.65,061　*T*.72.46%
*J. Cummings, *Lab*. 34,269
W. Perry, *C*. 7,879
P. Freitag, *LD* 5,001
Lab. majority 26,390
(June 1987, Lab. maj. 24,639)

EASTBOURNE (E. Sussex)
E.76,103　*T*.80.97%
N. Waterson, *C*. 31,792
*D. Bellotti, *LD* 26,311
I. Gibbons, *Lab*. 2,834
D. Aherne, *Green* 391
Ms T. Williamson, *Lib*. 296
C. majority 5,481
(June 1987, C. maj 16,923)
(October 1990, LD maj. 4,550)

EASTLEIGH (Hants)
E91,736 T.82.91%
S. Milligan, *C.* 38,998
D. Chidgey, *LD* 21,296
Ms J. Sugrue, *Lab.* 15,768
C. majority 17,702
(June 1987, C. maj. 13,355)
See also page 238

ECCLES (Greater Manchester)
E64,910 T.74.12%
*Miss J. Lestor, *Lab.* 27,357
G. Ling, *C.* 14,131
G. Reid, *LD* 5,835
R. Duriez, *Green* 521
Miss J. Garner, *NLP* 270
Lab. majority 13,226
(June 1987, Lab. maj. 9,699)

EDDISBURY (Cheshire)
E75,089 T.82.55%
*A. Goodlad, *C.* 31,625
Ms N. Edwards, *Lab.* 18,928
D. Lyon, *LD* 10,543
A. Basden, *Green* 783
N. Pollard, *NLP* 107
C. majority 12,697
(June 1987, C. maj. 15,835)

EDMONTON (Greater London)
E63,052 T.75.66%
*Dr I. Twinn, *C.* 22,076
A. Love, *Lab.* 21,483
E. Jones, *LD* 3,940
Ms E. Solley, *NLP* 207
C. majority 593
(June 1987, C. maj. 7,286)

ELLESMERE PORT AND NESTON
(Cheshire)
E71,572 T.84.12%
A. Miller, *Lab.* 27,782
A. Pearce, *C.* 25,793
Ms E. Jewkes, *LD* 5,944
Dr M. Money, *Green* 589
Dr A. Rae, *NLP* 105
Lab. majority 1,989
(June 1987, C. maj. 1,853)

ELMET (W. Yorks)
E70,558 T.82.53%
*S. Batiste, *C.* 27,677
C. Burgon, *Lab.* 24,416
Mrs A. Beck, *LD* 6,144
C. majority 3,261
(June 1987, C. maj. 5,356)

ELTHAM (Greater London)
E51,989 T.78.72%
*P. Bottomley, *C.* 18,813
C. Efford, *Lab.* 17,147
C. McGinty, *LD* 4,804
A. Graham, *Ind. C.* 165
C. majority 1,666
(June 1987, C. maj. 6,460)

ENFIELD NORTH (Greater London)
E67,421 T.77.91%
*T. Eggar, *C.* 27,789
M. Upham, *Lab.* 18,359
Ms S. Tustin, *LD* 5,817
J. Markham, *NLP* 565

C. majority 9,430
(June 1987, C. maj. 14,015)

ENFIELD SOUTHGATE (Greater
London)
E64,311 T.76.28%
*M. Portillo, *C.* 28,422
Ms K. Livney, *Lab.* 12,859
K. Keane, *LD* 7,080
Ms M. Hollands, *Green* 696
C. majority 15,563
(June 1987, C. maj. 18,345)

EPPING FOREST (Essex)
E67,585 T.80.55%
*S. Norris, *C.* 32,407
S. Murray, *Lab.* 12,219
Mrs B. Austen, *LD* 9,265
A. O'Brien, *EFRA* 552
C. majority 20,188
(June 1987, C. maj. 21,513)
(December 1988, C. maj. 4,504)

EPSOM AND EWELL (Surrey)
E68,138 T.80.14%
*Rt. Hon. A. Hamilton, *C.* 32,861
M. Emerson, *LD* 12,840
R. Warren, *Lab.* 8,577
G. Hatchard, *NLP* 334
C. majority 20,021
(June 1987, C. maj. 20,761)

EREWASH (Derbys)
E75,627 T.83.78%
Mrs A. Knight, *C.* 29,907
S. Stafford, *Lab.* 24,204
P. Tuck, *LD* 8,606
L. Johnson, *BNP* 645
C. majority 5,703
(June 1987, C. maj. 9,754)

ERITH AND CRAYFORD (Kent)
E59,213 T.79.66%
*D. Evennett, *C.* 21,926
N. Beard, *Lab.* 19,587
Ms F. Jamieson, *LD* 5,657
C. majority 2,339
(June 1987, C. maj. 6,994)

ESHER (Surrey)
E58,840 T.80.80%
*I. Taylor, *C.* 31,115
J. Richling, *LD* 10,744
Ms J. Reay, *Lab.* 5,685
C. majority 20,371
(June 1987, C. maj. 19,068)

EXETER (Devon)
E76,723 T.82.21%
*Sir J. Hannam, *C.* 26,543
J. Lloyd, *Lab.* 22,498
G. Oakes, *LD* 12,059
Ms A. Micklem, *Lib.* 1,119
T. Brenan, *Green* 764
M. Turnbull, *NLP* 98
C. majority 4,045
(June 1987, C. maj. 7,656)

FALMOUTH AND CAMBORNE
(Cornwall)
E70,702 T.81.10%
S. Coe, *C.* 21,150
Ms T. Jones, *LD* 17,883
J. Cosgrove, *Lab.* 16,732

P. Holmes, *Lib.* 730
K. Saunders, *Green* 466
F. Zapp, *Loony* 327
A. Pringle, *NLP* 56
C. majority 3,267
(June 1987, C. maj. 5,039)

FAREHAM (Hants)
E81,124 T.81.85%
*P. Lloyd, *C.* 40,482
J. Thompson, *LD* 16,341
Ms E. Weston, *Lab.* 8,766
M. Brimecome, *Green* 818
C. majority 24,141
(June 1987, C. maj. 18,795)

FAVERSHAM (Kent)
E81,977 T.79.71%
*R. Moate, *C.* 32,755
Ms H. Brinton, *Lab.* 16,404
R. Truelove, *LD* 15,896
R. Bradshaw, *NLP* 294
C. majority 16,351
(June 1987, C. maj. 13,978)

FELTHAM AND HESTON (Greater
London)
E81,221 T.73.90%
A. Keen, *Lab.* 27,660
*P. Ground, *C.* 25,665
M. Hoban, *LD* 6,700
Lab. majority 1,995
(June 1987, C. maj. 5,430)

FINCHLEY (Greater London)
E52,907 T.77.64%
H. Booth, *C.* 21,039
Ms A. Marjoram, *Lab.* 14,651
Ms H. Leighter, *LD* 4,568
A. Gunstock, *Green* 564
Ms S. Johnson, *Loony* 130
J. Macrae, *NLP* 129
C. majority 6,388
(June 1987, C. maj. 8,913)

FOLKESTONE AND HYTHE (Kent)
E65,856 T.79.61%
*Rt. Hon. M. Howard, *C.* 27,437
Mrs L. Cufley, *LD* 18,527
P. Doherty, *Lab.* 6,347
A. Hobbs, *NLP* 123
C. majority 8,910
(June 1987, C. maj. 9,126)

FULHAM (Greater London)
E52,740 T.76.16%
*M. Carrington, *C.* 21,438
N. Moore, *Lab.* 14,859
P. Crystal, *LD* 3,339
Ms E. Streeter, *Green* 443
J. Darby, *NLP* 91
C. majority 6,579
(June 1987, C. maj. 6,322)

FYLDE (Lancs)
E63,573 T.78.50%
*M. Jack, *C.* 30,639
N. Cryer, *LD* 9,648
Ms C. Hughes, *Lab.* 9,382
P. Leadbetter, *NLP* 239
C. majority 20,991
(June 1987, C. maj. 17,772)

GAINSBOROUGH AND HORNCASTLE
(Lincs)
E.72,038   T.80.87%
*E. Leigh, C.	31,444
N. Taylor, LD	15,199
Ms F. Jones, Lab.	11,619
C. majority	16,245
(June 1987, C. maj. 9,723)

GATESHEAD EAST (Tyne & Wear)
E.64,355   T.73.63%
*Miss J. Quin, Lab.	30,100
M. Callanan, C.	11,570
R. Beadle, LD	5,720
Lab. majority	18,530
(June 1987, Lab. maj. 17,228)

GEDLING (Notts)
E.68,953   T.82.34%
*A. J. B. Mitchell, C.	30,191
V. Coaker, Lab.	19,554
D. George, LD	6,863
Ms A. Miszeweka, NLP	168
C. majority	10,637
(June 1987, C. maj. 16,539)

GILLINGHAM (Kent)
E.71,851   T.80.32%
*J. Couchman, C.	30,201
P. Clark, Lab.	13,563
M. Wallbank, LD	13,509
C. MacKinlay, Ind.	248
D. Jolicoeur, NLP	190
C. majority	16,638
(June 1987, C. maj. 12,549)

GLANFORD AND SCUNTHORPE
(Humberside)
E.73,479   T.78.91%
*E. Morley, Lab.	30,623
Dr A. Saywood, C.	22,211
W. Paxton, LD	4,172
C. Nottingham, SD	982
Lab. majority	8,412
(June 1987, Lab. maj. 512)

GLOUCESTER
E.80,578   T.80.24%
*D. French, C.	29,870
K. Stephens, Lab.	23,812
J. Sewell, LD	10,978
C. majority	6,058
(June 1987, C. maj. 12,035)

GLOUCESTERSHIRE WEST
E.80,007   T.83.89%
*P. Marland, C.	29,232
Ms D. Organ, Lab.	24,274
L. Boait, LD	13,366
A. Reeve, Brit. Ind.	172
C. Palmer, Century	75
C. majority	4,958
(June 1987, C. maj. 11,679)

GOSPORT (Hants)
E.69,638   T.76.79%
*P. Viggers, C.	31,094
M. Russell, LD	14,776
Ms M. Angus, Lab.	7,275
P. Ettie, Pensioners	332
C. majority	16,318
(June 1987, C. maj. 13,723)

GRANTHAM (Lincs)
E.83,463   T.79.29%
*Hon. D. Hogg, C.	37,194
S. Taggart, Lab.	17,606
J. Heppell, LD	9,882
J. Hiley, Lib.	1,500
C. majority	19,588
(June 1987, C. maj. 21,303)

GRAVESHAM (Kent)
E.70,740   T.83.48%
*J. Arnold, C.	29,322
G. Green, Lab.	23,829
D. Deedman, LD	5,269
A. Bunstone, Ind.	273
R. Khilkoff-Boulding, ILP	187
B. Buxton, Soc.	174
C. majority	5,493
(June 1987, C. maj. 8,792)

GREAT GRIMSBY (Humberside)
E.67,427   T.75.28%
*A. V. Mitchell, Lab.	25,895
P. Jackson, C.	18,391
Ms P. Frankish, LD	6,475
Lab. majority	7,504
(June 1987, Lab. maj. 8,784)

GREAT YARMOUTH (Norfolk)
E.68,263   T.77.94%
*M. Carttiss, C.	25,505
Ms B. Baughan, Lab.	20,196
M. Scott, LD	7,225
Ms P. Larkin, NLP	284
C. majority	5,309
(June 1987, C. maj. 10,083)

GREENWICH (Greater London)
E.47,789   T.74.63%
W. R. N. Raynsford, Lab.	14,630
*Mrs R. Barnes, SD	13,273
Mrs A. McNair, C.	6,960
R. McCracken, Green	483
R. Mallone, Fellowship	147
M. Hardee, UTCHAP	103
J. Small, NLP	70
Lab. majority	1,357
(June 1987, SDP/All. maj. 2,141)

GUILDFORD (Surrey)
E.77,265   T.78.48%
*Rt. Hon. D. Howell, C.	33,516
Mrs M. Sharp, LD	20,112
H. Mann, Lab.	6,781
A. Law, NLP	234
C. majority	13,404
(June 1987, C. maj. 12,607)

HACKNEY NORTH AND STOKE
NEWINGTON (Greater London)
E.54,655   T.63.53%
*Ms D. Abbott, Lab.	20,083
C. Manson, C.	9,356
K. Fitchett, LD	3,996
Ms H. Hunt, Green	1,111
J. Windsor, NLP	178
Lab. majority	10,727
(June 1987, Lab. maj. 7,678)

HACKNEY SOUTH AND SHOREDITCH
(Greater London)
E.57,935   T.63.82%
*B. Sedgemore, Lab.	19,730
A. Turner, C.	10,714
G. Wintle, LD	5,533
L. Lucas, Green	772
Ms G. Norman, NLP	226
Lab. majority	9,016
(June 1987, Lab. maj. 7,522)

HALESOWEN AND STOURBRIDGE (W. Midlands)
E.77,644   T.82.28%
P. W. Hawksley, C.	32,312
A. Hankon, Lab.	22,730
V. Sharma, LD	7,941
T. Weller, Green	908
C. majority	9,582
(June 1987, C. maj. 13,808)

HALIFAX (W. Yorks)
E.73,401   T.78.69%
*Ms A. Mahon, Lab.	25,115
T. Martin, C.	24,637
I. Howell, LD	7,364
R. Pearson, Nat.	649
Lab. majority	478
(June 1987, Lab. maj. 1,212)

HALTON (Cheshire)
E.74,906   T.78.34%
*Rt. Hon. G. Oakes, Lab.	35,025
G. Mercer, C.	16,821
D. Reaper, LD	6,104
S. Herley, Loony	398
N. Collins, NLP	338
Lab. majority	18,204
(June 1987, Lab. maj. 14,578)

HAMMERSMITH (Greater London)
E.47,229   T.71.90%
*C. Soley, Lab.	17,329
A. Hennessy, C.	12,575
J. Bates, LD	3,380
R. Crosskey, Green	546
K. Turner, NLP	89
Ms H. Szamuely, Anti Fed.	41
Lab. majority	4,754
(June 1987, Lab. maj. 2,415)

HAMPSHIRE EAST
E.92,139   T.80.35%
*M. Mates, C.	47,541
Ms S. Baring, LD	18,376
J. Phillips, Lab.	6,840
I. Foster, Green	1,113
S. Hale, RCC	165
C. majority	29,165
(June 1987, C. maj. 23,786)

HAMPSHIRE NORTH WEST
E.73,101   T.80.75%
*Sir D. Mitchell, C.	34,310
M. Simpson, LD	16,462
M. Stockwell, Lab.	7,433
Ms D. Ashley, Green	825
C. majority	17,848
(June 1987, C. maj. 13,437)

HAMPSTEAD AND HIGHGATE
(Greater London)
E.58,203   T.73.04%

Ms G. Jackson, *Lab.*	19,193
O. Letwin, *C.*	17,753
D. Wrede, *LD*	4,765
S. Games, *Green*	594
Dr R. Prosser, *NLP*	86
Ms A. Hall, *RAVA*	44
C. Scallywag Wilson, *Scallywag*	44
Captain Rizz, *Rizz*	33
Lab. majority	1,440

(June 1987, C. maj. 2,221)

HARBOROUGH (Leics)
E.76,514   T.82.11%

E. Garnier, *C.*	34,280
M. Cox, *LD*	20,737
Ms C. Mackay, *Lab.*	7,483
A. Irwin, *NLP*	328
C. majority	13,543

(June 1987, C. maj. 18,810)

HARLOW (Essex)
E.68,615   T.82.56%

*J. Hayes, *C.*	26,608
W. Rammell, *Lab.*	23,668
Ms L. Spenceley, *LD*	6,375
C. majority	2,940

(June 1987, C. maj. 5,877)

HARROGATE (N. Yorks)
E.76,250   T.77.98%

*R. Banks, *C.*	32,023
T. Hurren, *LD*	19,434
A. Wright, *Lab.*	7,230
A. Warneken, *Green*	780
C. majority	12,589

(June 1987, C. maj. 11,902)

HARROW EAST (Greater London)
E.74,733   T.77.83%

*H. Dykes, *C.*	30,752
A. McNulty, *Lab.*	19,654
Ms V. Chamberlain, *LD*	6,360
P. Burrows, *Lib.*	1,142
Mrs S. Hamza, *NLP*	212
J. Lester, *Anti Fed.*	49
C. majority	11,098

(June 1987, C. maj. 18,273)

HARROW WEST (Greater London)
E.69,616   T.78.69%

*R. G. Hughes, *C.*	30,240
C. Moraes, *Lab.*	12,343
C. Noyce, *LD*	11,050
G. Aitman, *Lib.*	845
Mrs J. Argyle, *NLP*	306
C. majority	17,897

(June 1987, C. maj. 15,444)

HARTLEPOOL (Cleveland)
E.67,968   T.76.07%

P. Mandelson, *Lab.*	26,816
G. Robb, *C.*	18,034
I. Cameron, *LD*	6,860
Lab. majority	8,782

(June 1987, Lab. maj. 7,289)

HARWICH (Essex)
E.80,260   T.77.70%

I. Sproat, *C.*	32,369
Mrs P. Bevan, *LD*	15,210

R. Knight, *Lab.*	14,511
Mrs E. McGrath, *NLP*	279
C. majority	17,159

(June 1987, C. maj. 12,082)

HASTINGS AND RYE (E. Sussex)
E.71,838   T.74.86%

Ms J. Lait, *C.*	25,573
M. Palmer, *LD*	18,939
R. Stevens, *Lab.*	8,458
Ms S. Phillips, *Green*	640
T. Howell, *Loony*	168
C. majority	6,634

(June 1987, C. maj. 7,347)

HAVANT (Hants)
E.74,217   T.79.01%

D. Willetts, *C.*	32,233
S. van Hagen, *LD*	14,649
G. Morris, *Lab.*	10,968
T. Mitchell, *Green*	793
C. majority	17,584

(June 1987, C. maj. 16,510)

HAYES AND HARLINGTON (Greater
London)
E.54,449   T.79.70%

*T. Dicks, *C.*	19,489
J. McDonnell, *Lab.*	19,436
T. Little, *LD*	4,472
C. majority	53

(June 1987, C. maj. 5,965)

HAZEL GROVE (Greater Manchester)
E.64,302   T.84.94%

*Sir T. Arnold, *C.*	24,479
A. Stunell, *LD*	23,550
C. McAllister, *Lab.*	6,390
M. Penn, *NLP*	204
C. majority	929

(June 1987, C. maj. 1,840)

HEMSWORTH (W. Yorks)
E.55,679   T.75.91%

*D. Enright, *Lab.*	29,942
G. Harrison, *C.*	7,867
Ms V. Megson, *LD*	4,459
Lab. majority	22,075

(June 1987, Lab. maj. 20,700)
(November 1991, Lab. maj. 11,087)

HENDON NORTH (Greater London)
E.51,513   T.75.08%

*J. Gorst, *C.*	20,569
D. Hill, *Lab.*	13,447
P. Kemp, *LD*	4,136
Ms P. Duncan, *Green*	430
Ms P. Orr, *NLP*	95
C. majority	7,122

(June 1987, C. maj. 10,932)

HENDON SOUTH (Greater London)
E.48,401   T.72.38%

*J. Marshall, *C.*	20,593
Ms L. Lloyd, *Lab.*	8,546
J. Cohen, *LD*	5,609
J. Leslie, *NLP*	289
C. majority	12,047

(June 1987, C. maj. 11,124)

HENLEY (Oxon)
E.64,702   T.79.84%

*Rt. Hon. M. Heseltine, *C.*	30,835
D. Turner, *LD*	12,443
I. Russell-Swinnerton, *Lab.*	7,676
A. Plane, *Anti H.*	431
Ms S. Banerji, *NLP*	274
C. majority	18,392

(June 1987, C. maj. 17,082)

HEREFORD
E.69,676   T.81.29%

*C. Shepherd, *C.*	26,727
G. Jones, *LD*	23,314
Ms J. Kelly, *Lab.*	6,005
C. Mattingly, *Green*	596
C. majority	3,413

(June 1987, C. maj. 1,413)

HERTFORD AND STORTFORD
E.76,654   T.81.05%

*B. Wells, *C.*	35,716
C. White, *LD*	15,506
A. Bovaird, *Lab.*	10,125
J. Goth, *Green*	780
C. majority	20,210

(June 1987, C. maj. 17,140)

HERTFORDSHIRE NORTH
E.80,066   T.84.44%

O. Heald, *C.*	33,679
R. Liddle, *LD*	17,148
Ms S. Bissett Johnson, *Lab.*	16,449
B. Irving, *NLP*	339
C. majority	16,531

(June 1987, C. maj. 11,442)

HERTFORDSHIRE SOUTH WEST
E.70,836   T.83.76%

*R. Page, *C.*	33,825
Ms A. Shaw, *LD*	13,718
A. Gale, *Lab.*	11,512
C. Adamson, *NLP*	281
C. majority	20,107

(June 1987, C. maj. 15,784)

HERTFORDSHIRE WEST
E.78,573   T.82.36%

*R. Jones, *C.*	33,340
Mrs E. McNally, *Lab.*	19,400
M. Trevett, *LD*	10,464
J. Hannaway, *Green*	674
J. McAuley, *NF*	665
G. Harvey, *NLP*	175
C. majority	13,940

(June 1987, C. maj. 14,924)

HERTSMERE (Herts)
E.69,951   T.80.89%

W. J. Clappison, *C.*	32,133
Dr D. Souter, *Lab.*	13,398
Mrs Z. Gifford, *LD*	10,681
Ms D. Harding, *NLP*	373
C. majority	18,735

(June 1987, C. maj. 18,106)

HEXHAM (Northumberland)
E.57,812   T.82.37%

P. Atkinson, *C.*	24,967
I. Swithenbank, *Lab.*	11,529
J. Wallace, *LD*	10,344
J. Hartshorne, *Green*	781

C. majority 13,438
(June 1987, C. maj. 8,066)

HEYWOOD AND MIDDLETON
(Greater Manchester)
*E.*57,176   *T.*74.92%
**J. Callaghan, *Lab.* 22,380
E. Ollerenshaw, *C.* 14,306
Dr M. Taylor, *LD* 5,262
P. Burke, *Lib.* 757
Ms A. Scott, *NLP* 134
Lab. majority 8,074
(June 1987, Lab. maj. 6,848)

HIGH PEAK (Derbys)
*E.*70,793   *T.*84.62%
C. Hendry, *C.* 27,538
T. Levitt, *Lab.* 22,719
S. Molloy, *LD* 8,861
R. Floyd, *Green* 794
C. majority 4,819
(June 1987, C. maj. 9,516)

HOLBORN AND ST PANCRAS
(Greater London)
*E.*64,480   *T.*62.99%
**F. Dobson, *Lab.* 22,243
A. McHallam, *C.* 11,419
Ms J. Horne-Roberts, *LD* 5,476
P. Wolf-Light, *Green* 959
M. Hersey, *NLP* 212
R. Headicar, *Soc.* 175
N. Lewis, *WAR* 133
Lab. majority 10,824
(June 1987, Lab. maj. 8,853)

HOLLAND WITH BOSTON (Lincs)
*E.*67,900   *T.*77.93%
**Sir R. Body, *C.* 29,159
J. Hough, *Lab.* 15,328
N. Ley, *LD* 8,434
C. majority 13,831
(June 1987, C. maj. 17,595)

HONITON (Devon)
*E.*79,223   *T.*80.74%
**Sir P. Emery, *C.* 33,533
Ms J. Sharratt, *LD* 17,022
R. Davison, *Lab.* 8,142
D. Owen, *Ind. C.* 2,175
S. Hughes, *Loony G.* 1,442
G. Halliwell, *Lib.* 1,005
A. Tootill, *Green* 650
C. majority 16,511
(June 1987, C. maj. 16,562)

HORNCHURCH (Greater London)
*E.*60,522   *T.*79.78%
**R. Squire, *C.* 25,817
Ms L. Cooper, *Lab.* 16,652
B. Oddy, *LD* 5,366
T. Matthews, *SD* 453
C. majority 9,165
(June 1987, C. maj. 10,694)

HORNSEY AND WOOD GREEN
(Greater London)
*E.*73,491   *T.*75.85%
Mrs B. Roche, *Lab.* 27,020
A. Boff, *C.* 21,843
P. Dunphy, *LD* 5,547
Ms L. Crosbie, *Green* 1,051
P. Davies, *NLP* 197

W. Massey, *Rev. Comm.* 89
Lab. majority 5,177
(June 1987, C. maj. 1,779)

HORSHAM (W. Sussex)
*E.*84,158   *T.*81.27%
**Sir P. Hordern, *C.* 42,210
Ms J. Stainton, *LD* 17,138
S. Uwins, *Lab.* 6,745
Ms J. Elliott, *Lib.* 1,281
T. King, *Green* 692
J. Duggan, *PPP* 332
C. majority 25,072
(June 1987, C. maj. 23,907)

HOUGHTON AND WASHINGTON
(Tyne & Wear)
*E.*79,325   *T.*70.60%
**R. Boyes, *Lab.* 34,733
A. Tyrie, *C.* 13,925
O. Dumpleton, *LD* 7,346
Lab. majority 20,808
(June 1987, Lab. maj. 20,193)

HOVE (E. Sussex)
*E.*67,450   *T.*74.26%
**Hon. T. Sainsbury, *C.* 24,525
D. Turner, *Lab.* 12,257
A. Jones, *LD* 9,709
N. Furness, *Hove C.* 2,658
G. Sinclair, *Green* 814
J. Morilly, *NLP* 126
C. majority 12,268
(June 1987, C. maj. 18,218)

HUDDERSFIELD (W. Yorks)
*E.*67,604   *T.*72.32%
**B. Sheerman, *Lab.* 23,832
Ms J. Kenyon, *C.* 16,574
Ms A. Denham, *LD* 7,777
N. Harvey, *Green* 576
M. Cran, *NLP* 135
Lab. majority 7,258
(June 1987, Lab. maj. 7,278)

HULL EAST
*E.*69,036   *T.*69.29%
**J. Prescott, *Lab.* 30,092
J. Fareham, *C.* 11,373
J. Wastling, *LD* 6,050
C. Kinzell, *NLP* 323
Lab. majority 18,719
(June 1987, Lab. maj. 14,689)

HULL NORTH
*E.*71,363   *T.*66.71%
**J. K. McNamara, *Lab.* 26,619
B. Coleman, *C.* 11,235
A. Meadowcroft, *LD* 9,504
G. Richardson, *NLP* 253
Lab. majority 15,384
(June 1987, Lab. maj. 12,169)

HULL WEST
*E.*56,111   *T.*65.70%
**S. Randall, *Lab.* 21,139
D. Stewart, *C.* 10,554
R. Tress, *LD* 4,867
B. Franklin, *NLP* 308
Lab. majority 10,585
(June 1987, Lab. maj. 8,130)

HUNTINGDON (Cambs)
*E.*92,913   *T.*79.16%
**Rt. Hon. J. Major, *C.* 48,662
H. Seckleman, *Lab.* 12,432
A. Duff, *LD* 9,386
P. Wiggin, *Lib.* 1,045
Miss D. Birkhead, *Green* 846
Lord D. Sutch, *Loony* 728
M. Flanagan, *C. Thatch.* 231
Lord Buckethead, *Gremloids* 107
C. Cockell, *FTM* 91
D. Shepheard, *NLP* 26
C. majority 36,230
(June 1987, C. maj. 27,044)

HYNDBURN (Lancs)
*E.*58,539   *T.*83.97%
G. Pope, *Lab.* 23,042
**K. Hargreaves, *C.* 21,082
Ms Y. Stars, *LD* 4,886
S. Whittle, *NLP* 150
Lab. majority 1,960
(June 1987, C. maj. 2,220)

ILFORD NORTH (Greater London)
*E.*58,670   *T.*77.98%
**V. Bendall, *C.* 24,698
Ms L. Hilton, *Lab.* 15,627
R. Scott, *LD* 5,430
C. majority 9,071
(June 1987, C. maj. 12,090)

ILFORD SOUTH (Greater London)
*E.*55,741   *T.*76.83%
M. Gapes, *Lab.* 19,418
**N. Thorne, *C.* 19,016
G. Hogarth, *LD* 4,126
N. Bramachari, *NLP* 269
Lab. majority 402
(June 1987, C. maj. 4,572)

IPSWICH (Suffolk)
*E.*67,261   *T.*80.32%
J. Cann, *Lab.* 23,680
**M. Irvine, *C.* 23,415
J. White, *LD* 6,159
Ms J. Scott, *Green* 591
E. Kaplan, *NLP* 181
Lab. majority 265
(June 1987, C. maj. 874)

ISLE OF WIGHT
*E.*99,838   *T.*79.76%
**B. Field, *C.* 38,163
Dr P. Brand, *LD* 36,336
K. Pearson, *Lab.* 4,784
C. Daly, *NLP* 350
C. majority 1,827
(June 1987, C. maj. 6,442)

ISLINGTON NORTH (Greater
London)
*E.*56,270   *T.*67.26%
**J. Corbyn, *Lab.* 21,742
Mrs L. Champagnie, *C.* 8,958
Ms S. Ludford, *LD* 5,732
C. Ashby, *Green* 1,420
Lab. majority 12,784
(June 1987, Lab. maj. 9,657)

ISLINGTON SOUTH AND FINSBURY
(Greater London)
*E.*55,541   *T.*72.52%
*C. Smith, *Lab.*   20,586
M. Jones, *C.*   9,934
C. Pryce, *LD*   9,387
Ms R. Hersey, *JBR*   149
Ms M. Avino, *Loony*   142
M. Spinks, *NLP*   83
Lab. majority   10,652
(June 1987, Lab. maj. 805)

JARROW (Tyne & Wear)
*E.*62,611   *T.*74.44%
*D. Dixon, *Lab.*   28,956
T. Ward, *C.*   11,049
K. Orrell, *LD*   6,608
Lab. majority   17,907
(June 1987, Lab. maj. 18,795)

KEIGHLEY (W. Yorks)
*E.*66,358   *T.*82.58%
*G. Waller, *C.*   25,983
T. Flanagan, *Lab.*   22,387
I. Simpson, *LD*   5,793
M. Crowson, *Green*   642
C. majority   3,596
(June 1987, C. maj. 5,606)

KENSINGTON (Greater London)
*E.*42,129   *T.*73.29%
*J. D. Fishburn, *C.*   15,540
Ms A. Holmes, *Lab.*   11,992
C. Shirley, *LD*   2,770
Ms A. Burlingham-Johnson, *Green*
                                              415
A. Hardy, *NLP*   90
Ms A. Bulloch, *Anti Fed.*   71
C. majority   3,548
(June 1987, C. maj. 4,447)
(July 1988, C. maj. 815)

KENT MID
*E.*74,459   *T.*79.66%
*A. Rowe, *C.*   33,633
T. Robson, *Lab.*   13,984
G. Colley, *LD*   11,476
G. Valente, *NLP*   224
C. majority   19,649
(June 1987, C. maj. 14,768)

KETTERING (Northants)
*E.*67,853   *T.*82.58%
*R. Freeman, *C.*   29,115
P. Hope, *Lab.*   17,961
R. Denton-White, *LD*   8,962
C. majority   11,154
(June 1987, C. maj. 11,327)

KINGSTON UPON THAMES (Greater
London)
*E.*51,077   *T.*78.41%
*Rt. Hon. N. Lamont, *C.*   20,675
D. Osbourne, *LD*   10,522
R. Markless, *Lab.*   7,748
A. Amer, *Lib.*   771
D. Beaupre, *Loony*   212
G. Woollcoombe, *NLP*   81
A. Scholefield, *Anti Fed.*   42
C. majority   10,153
(June 1987, C. maj. 11,186)

KINGSWOOD (Avon)
*E.*71,727   *T.*83.85%
R. Berry, *Lab.*   26,774
*R. Hayward, *C.*   24,404
Ms J. Pinkerton, *LD*   8,960
Lab. majority   2,370
(June 1987, C. maj. 4,393)

KNOWSLEY NORTH (Merseyside)
*E.*48,761   *T.*72.81%
*G. Howarth, *Lab.*   27,517
S. Mabey, *C.*   5,114
J. Murray, *LD*   1,515
Mrs K. Lappin, *Lib.*   1,180
V. Ruben, *NLP*   179
Lab. majority   22,403
(June 1987, Lab. maj. 21,098)

KNOWSLEY SOUTH (Merseyside)
*E.*62,260   *T.*74.77%
*E. O'Hara, *Lab.*   31,933
L. Byrom, *C.*   9,922
I. Smith, *LD*   4,480
M. Raiano, *NLP*   217
Lab. majority   22,011
(June 1987, Lab. maj. 20,846)
(September 1990, Lab. maj. 11,367)

LANCASHIRE WEST
*E.*77,462   *T.*82.55%
C. Pickthall, *Lab.*   30,128
*K. Hind, *C.*   28,051
P. Reilly, *LD*   4,884
P. Pawley, *Green*   546
B. Morris, *NLP*   336
Lab. majority   2,077
(June 1987, C. maj. 1,353)

LANCASTER (Lancs)
*E.*58,714   *T.*78.78%
*Dame E. Kellett-Bowman, *C.*   21,084
Ms R. Henig, *Lab.*   18,131
J. Humberstone, *LD*   6,524
Ms G. Dowding, *Green*   433
R. Barcis, *NLP*   83
C. majority   2,953
(June 1987, C. maj. 6,453)

LANGBAURGH (Cleveland)
*E.*79,566   *T.*83.05%
M. Bates, *C.*   30,018
*A. Kumar, *Lab.*   28,454
P. Allen, *LD*   7,615
C. majority   1,564
(June 1987, C. maj. 2,088)
(November 1991, C. maj. 1,975)

LEEDS CENTRAL (W. Yorks)
*E.*62,058   *T.*61.29%
*D. Fatchett, *Lab.*   23,673
Mrs T. Holdroyd, *C.*   8,653
D. Pratt, *LD*   5,713
Lab. majority   15,020
(June 1987, Lab. maj. 11,505)

LEEDS EAST (W. Yorks)
*E.*61,695   *T.*70.02%
G. Mudie, *Lab.*   24,929
N. Carmichael, *C.*   12,232
P. Wrigley, *LD*   6,040
Lab. majority   12,697
(June 1987, Lab. maj. 9,526)

LEEDS NORTH EAST (W. Yorks)
*E.*64,372   *T.*76.89%
*T. Kirkhope, *C.*   22,462
F. Hamilton, *Lab.*   18,218
C. Walmsley, *LD*   8,274
J. Noble, *Green*   546
C. majority   4,244
(June 1987, C. maj. 8,419)

LEEDS NORTH WEST (W. Yorks)
*E.*69,406   *T.*72.84%
*Dr K. Hampson, *C.*   21,750
Ms B. Pearce, *LD*   14,079
Ms S. Egan, *Lab.*   13,782
D. Webb, *Green*   519
N. Nowosielski, *Lib.*   427
C. majority   7,671
(June 1987, C. maj. 5,201)

LEEDS SOUTH AND MORLEY
(W. Yorks)
*E.*63,107   *T.*72.58%
W. J. Gunnell, *Lab.*   23,896
R. Booth, *C.*   16,524
Ms J. Walmsley, *LD*   5,062
R. Thurston, *NLP*   327
Lab. majority   7,372
(June 1987, Lab. maj. 6,711)

LEEDS WEST (W. Yorks)
*E.*67,084   *T.*71.14%
*J. Battle, *Lab.*   26,310
P. Bartlett, *C.*   12,482
G. Howard, *LD*   4,252
M. Meadowcroft, *Lib.*   3,980
Ms A. Mander, *Green*   569
R. Tenny, *NF*   132
Lab. majority   13,828
(June 1987, Lab. maj. 4,692)

LEICESTER EAST
*E.*63,434   *T.*78.40%
*N. K. A. S. Vaz, *Lab.*   28,123
J. Stevens, *C.*   16,807
Ms S. Mitchell, *LD*   4,043
M. Frankland, *Green*   453
D. Taylor, *Homeland*   308
Lab. majority   11,316
(June 1987, Lab. maj. 1,924)

LEICESTER SOUTH
*E.*71,120   *T.*75.09%
*J. Marshall, *Lab.*   27,934
Dr M. Dutt, *C.*   18,494
Ms A. Crumbie, *LD*   6,271
J. McWhirter, *Green*   554
Ms P. Saunders, *NLP*   154
Lab. majority   9,440
(June 1987, Lab. maj. 1,877)

LEICESTER WEST
*E.*65,510   *T.*73.66%
*Hon. G. Janner, *Lab.*   22,574
J. Guthrie, *C.*   18,596
G. Walker, *LD*   6,402
Ms C. Wintram, *Green*   517
Ms J. Rosta, *NLP*   171
Lab. majority   3,978
(June 1987, Lab. maj. 1,201)

LEICESTERSHIRE NORTH WEST
*E.*72,414   *T.*86.11%

D. Ashby, C.	28,379
D. Taylor, *Lab.*	27,400
J. Beckett, *LD*	6,353
J. Fawcett, *NLP*	229
C. majority	979

(June 1987, C. maj. 7,828)

LEIGH (Greater Manchester)
*E.*70,064   *T.*75.02%

L. Cunliffe, Lab.	32,225
J. Egerton, *C.*	13,398
R. Bleakley, *LD*	6,621
A. Tayler, *NLP*	320
Lab. majority	18,827

(June 1987, Lab. maj. 16,606)

LEOMINSTER (H & W)
*E.*70,873   *T.*81.69%

P. Temple-Morris, C.	32,783
D. Short, *LD*	16,103
C. Chappell, *Lab.*	6,874
Ms F. Norman, *Green*	1,503
Capt. E. Carlise, *Anti Fed.*	640
C. majority	16,680

(June 1987, C. maj. 14,075)

LEWES (E. Sussex)
*E.*73,918   *T.*81.81%

J. R. Rathbone, C.	33,042
N. Baker, *LD*	20,867
Ms A. Chapman, *Lab.*	5,758
A. Beaumont, *Green*	719
N. Clinch, *NLP*	87
C. majority	12,175

(June 1987, C. maj. 13,620)

LEWISHAM DEPTFORD (Greater London)
*E.*57,014   *T.*65.05%

Mrs J. Ruddock, Lab.	22,574
Miss T. O'Neill, *C.*	10,336
Ms J. Brightwell, *LD*	4,181
Lab. majority	12,238

(June 1987, Lab. maj. 6,771)

LEWISHAM EAST (Greater London)
*E.*57,674   *T.*74.78%

Mrs B. Prentice, *Lab.*	19,576
Hon. C. Moynihan, C.	18,481
J. Hawkins, *LD*	4,877
Ms G. Mansour, *NLP*	196
Lab. majority	1,095

(June 1987, C. maj. 4,814)

LEWISHAM WEST (Greater London)
*E.*59,317   *T.*73.11%

J. Dowd, *Lab.*	20,378
J. Maples, C.	18,569
Ms E. Neale, *LD*	4,295
P. Coulam, *Anti Fed.*	125
Lab. majority	1,809

(June 1987, C. maj. 3,772)

LEYTON (Greater London)
*E.*57,271   *T.*67.38%

H. Cohen, Lab.	20,334
Miss C. Smith, *C.*	8,850
J. Fryer, *LD*	8,180
L. de Pinna, *Lib.*	561
K. Pervez, *Green*	412
R. Archer, *NLP*	256

Lab. majority	11,484

(June 1987, Lab. maj. 4,641)

LINCOLN
*E.*78,905   *T.*79.15%

K. Carlisle, C.	28,792
N. Butler, *Lab.*	26,743
D. Harding-Price, *LD*	6,316
Ms S. Wiggin, *Lib.*	603
C. majority	2,049

(June 1987, C. maj. 7,483)

LINDSEY EAST (Lincs)
*E.*80,026   *T.*78.07%

Sir P. Tapsell, C.	31,916
J. Dodsworth, *LD*	20,070
D. Shepherd, *Lab.*	9,477
Ms R. Robinson, *Green*	1,018
C. majority	11,846

(June 1987, C. maj. 8,616)

LITTLEBOROUGH AND SADDLEWORTH (Greater Manchester)
*E.*65,576   *T.*81.61%

G. Dickens, C.	23,682
C. Davies, *LD*	19,188
A. Brett, *Lab.*	10,649
C. majority	4,494

(June 1987, C. maj. 6,202)
See also page 238

LIVERPOOL BROADGREEN
*E.*60,080   *T.*69.59%

Mrs J. Kennedy, *Lab.*	18,062
Ms R. Cooper, *LD*	11,035
T. Fields, Soc. Lab.	5,952
Mrs H. Roche, *C.*	5,405
S. Radford, *Lib.*	1,211
Mrs A. Brennan, *NLP*	149
Lab. majority	7,027

(June 1987, Lab. maj. 6,047)

LIVERPOOL GARSTON
*E.*57,538   *T.*70.60%

E. Loyden, Lab.	23,212
J. Backhouse, *C.*	10,933
W. Roberts, *LD*	5,398
A. Conrad, *Lib.*	894
P. Chandler, *NLP*	187
Lab. majority	12,279

(June 1987, Lab. maj. 13,777)

LIVERPOOL MOSSLEY HILL
*E.*60,409   *T.*68.52%

D. Alton, LD	19,809
N. Bann, *Lab.*	17,203
S. Syder, *C.*	4,269
B. Rigby, *NLP*	114
LD majority	2,606

(June 1987, L./All. maj. 2,226)

LIVERPOOL RIVERSIDE
*E.*49,595   *T.*54.57%

R. Parry, Lab.	20,550
Dr A. Zsigmond, *C.*	3,113
M. Akbar Ali, *LD*	2,498
L. Brown, *Green*	738
J. Collins, *NLP*	169
Lab. majority	17,437

(June 1987, Lab. maj. 20,689)

LIVERPOOL WALTON
*E.*70,102   *T.*67.40%

P. Kilfoyle, Lab.	34,214
B. Greenwood, *C.*	5,915
J. Lang, *LD*	5,672
T. Newall, *Lib.*	963
D. Carson, *Prot. Ref.*	393
Ms D. Raiano, *NLP*	98
Lab. majority	28,299

(June 1987, Lab. maj. 23,253)
(July 1991, Lab. maj. 6,860)

LIVERPOOL WEST DERBY
*E.*56,718   *T.*69.84%

R. Wareing, Lab.	27,014
S. Fitzsimmons, *C.*	6,589
Ms G. Bundred, *LD*	4,838
D. Curtis, *Lib.*	1,021
C. Higgins, *NLP*	154
Lab. majority	20,425

(June 1987, Lab. maj. 20,496)

LOUGHBOROUGH (Leics)
*E.*75,450   *T.*78.52%

S. Dorrell, C.	30,064
A. Reed, *Lab.*	19,181
A. Stott, *LD*	8,953
I. Sinclair, *Green*	817
P. Reynolds, *NLP*	233
C. majority	10,883

(June 1987, C. maj. 17,648)

LUDLOW (Salop)
*E.*68,935   *T.*80.87%

C. Gill, C.	28,719
D. Phillips, *LD*	14,567
Ms B. Mason, *Lab.*	11,709
N. Appleton-Fox, *Green*	758
C. majority	14,152

(June 1987, C. maj. 11,699)

LUTON NORTH (Beds)
*E.*76,857   *T.*81.91%

J. Carlisle, C.	33,777
A. McWalter, *Lab.*	20,683
Ms J. Jackson, *LD*	7,570
R. Jones, *Green*	633
K. Buscombe, *NLP*	292
C. majority	13,094

(June 1987, C. maj. 15,573)

LUTON SOUTH (Beds)
*E.*73,016   *T.*79.10%

G. Bright, C.	25,900
W. McKenzie, *Lab.*	25,101
D. Rogers, *LD*	6,020
Ms L. Bliss, *Green*	550
D. Cooke, *NLP*	191
C. majority	799

(June 1987, C. maj. 5,115)

MACCLESFIELD (Cheshire)
*E.*76,548   *T.*82.29%

N. Winterton, C.	36,447
Mrs M. Longworth, *Lab.*	13,680
Dr P. Beatty, *LD*	12,600
Mrs C. Penn, *NLP*	268
C. majority	22,767

(June 1987, C. maj. 19,092)

MAIDSTONE (Kent)
E.72,834   T.80.08%
*Miss A. Widdecombe, C.   31,611
Ms P. Yates, LD   15,325
Ms A. Logan, Lab.   10,517
Ms P. Kemp, Green   707
F. Ingram, NLP   172
C. majority   16,286
(June 1987, C. maj. 10,364)

MAKERFIELD (Greater Manchester)
E.71,425   T.76.09%
*I. McCartney, Lab.   32,832
Mrs D. Dickson, C.   14,714
S. Jeffers, LD   5,097
Ms S. Cairns, Lib.   1,309
C. Davies, NLP   397
Lab. majority   18,118
(June 1987, Lab. maj. 15,558)

MANCHESTER BLACKLEY
E.55,234   T.69.31%
*K. Eastham, Lab.   23,031
W. Hobhouse, C.   10,642
S. Wheale, LD   4,324
M. Kennedy, NLP   288
Lab. majority   12,389
(June 1987, Lab. maj. 10,122)

MANCHESTER CENTRAL
E.56,446   T.56.90%
*R. Litherland, Lab.   23,336
P. Davies, C.   5,299
M. Clayton, LD   3,151
A. Buchanan, CL   167
Ms V. Mitchell, NLP   167
Lab. majority   18,037
(June 1987, Lab. maj. 19,867)

MANCHESTER GORTON
E.62,410   T.60.84%
*Rt. Hon. G. Kaufman, Lab.   23,671
J. Bullock, C.   7,392
P. Harris, LD   5,327
T. Henderson, Lib.   767
M. Daw, Green   595
Ms P. Lawrence, Rev. Comm.   108
P. Mitchell, NLP   84
Ms C. Smith, Int. Comm.   30
Lab. majority   16,279
(June 1987, Lab. maj. 14,065)

MANCHESTER WITHINGTON
E.63,838   T.71.27%
*K. Bradley, Lab.   23,962
E. Farthing, C.   14,227
G. Hennell, LD   6,457
B. Candeland, Green   725
C. Menhinick, NLP   128
Lab. majority   9,735
(June 1987, Lab. maj. 3,391)

MANCHESTER WYTHENSHAWE
E.53,548   T.69.68%
*Rt. Hon. A. Morris, Lab.   22,591
K. McKenna, C.   10,595
S. Fenn, LD   3,633
G. Otten, Green   362
Ms E. Martin, NLP   133
Lab. majority   11,996
(June 1987, Lab. maj. 11,855)

MANSFIELD (Notts)
E.66,964   T.82.23%
*J. A. Meale, Lab.   29,932
G. Mond, C.   18,208
S. Thompstone, LD   6,925
Lab. majority   11,724
(June 1987, Lab. maj. 56)

MEDWAY (Kent)
E.61,736   T.80.22%
*Dame P. Fenner, C.   25,924
R. Marshall-Andrews, Lab.   17,138
C. Trice, LD   4,751
M. Austin, Lib.   1,480
P. Kember, NLP   234
C. majority   8,786
(June 1987, C. maj. 9,929)

MERIDEN (W. Midlands)
E.76,994   T.78.85%
*I. Mills, C.   33,462
N. Stephens, Lab.   18,763
Ms J. Morris, LD   8,489
C. majority   14,699
(June 1987, C. maj. 16,820)

MIDDLESBROUGH (Cleveland)
E.58,844   T.69.85%
*S. Bell, Lab.   26,343
P. Rayner, C.   10,559
Ms R. Jordan, LD   4,201
Lab. majority   15,784
(June 1987, Lab. maj. 14,958)

MILTON KEYNES NORTH EAST
(Bucks)
E.62,748   T.80.95%
P. Butler, C.   26,212
Ms M. Cosin, Lab.   12,036
P. Gaskell, LD   11,693
A. Francis, Green   529
Mrs M. Kavanagh-Dowsett, Ind. C.
                                       249
M. Simson, NLP   79
C. majority   14,176
(New constituency)

MILTON KEYNES SOUTH WEST
(Bucks)
E.66,422   T.77
B. Legg, C.   23,840
K. Wilson, Lab.   19,153
C. Pym, LD   7,429
Dr C. Field, Green   525
H. Kelly, NLP   202
C. majority   4,687
(New constituency)

MITCHAM AND MORDEN (Greater
London)
E.63,723   T.80.32%
*Rt. Hon. A. Rumbold, C.   23,789
Ms S. McDonagh, Lab.   22,055
J. Field, LD   4,687
T. Walsh, Green   655
C. majority   1,734
(June 1987, C. maj. 6,183)

MOLE VALLEY (Surrey)
E.66,949   T.81.97%
*Rt. Hon. K. Baker, C.   32,549
M. Watson, LD   16,599
Dr T. Walsh, Lab.   5,291

Ms J. Thomas, NLP   442
C. majority   15,950
(June 1987, C. maj. 16,076)

MORECAMBE AND LUNESDALE
(Lancs)
E.56,426   T.78.35%
*Hon. M. Lennox-Boyd, C.   22,507
Ms J. Yates, Lab.   10,998
A. Saville, LD   9,584
M. Turner, MBI   916
R. Marriott, NLP   205
C. majority   11,509
(June 1987, C. maj. 11,785)

NEWARK (Notts)
E.68,801   T.82.17%
*R. Alexander, C.   28,494
D. Barton, Lab.   20,265
P. Harris, LD   7,342
Ms P. Wood, Green   435
C. majority   8,229
(June 1987, C. maj. 13,543)

NEWBURY (Berks)
E.80,252   T.82.75%
Mrs J. Chaplin, C.   37,135
D. Rendel, LD   24,778
R. Hall, Lab.   3,962
J. Wallis, Green   539
C. majority   12,357
(June 1987, C. maj. 16,658)
See also page 238

NEWCASTLE UNDER LYME (Staffs)
E.66,595   T.80.34%
*Mrs L. Golding, Lab.   25,652
A. Brierley, C.   15,813
A. Thomas, LD   11,727
R. Lines, NLP   314
Lab. majority   9,839
(June 1987, Lab. maj. 5,132)

NEWCASTLE UPON TYNE CENTRAL
E.59,973   T.71.32%
*J. Cousins, Lab.   21,123
M. Summersby, C.   15,835
L. Opik, LD   5,816
Lab. majority   5,288
(June 1987, Lab. maj. 2,483)

NEWCASTLE UPON TYNE EAST
E.57,165   T.70.73%
*N. Brown, Lab.   24,342
J. Lucas, C.   10,465
A. Thompson, LD   4,883
G. Edwards, Green   744
Lab. majority   13,877
(June 1987, Lab. maj. 12,500)

NEWCASTLE UPON TYNE NORTH
E.66,187   T.76.80%
*D. Henderson, Lab.   25,121
I. Gordon, C.   16,175
P. Maughan, LD   9,542
Lab. majority   8,946
(June 1987, Lab. maj. 5,243)

NEW FOREST (Hants)
E.75,413   T.80.76%
*Sir P. McNair-Wilson, C.   37,986
Ms J. Vernon-Jackson, LD   17,581
M. Shutler, Lab.   4,989
Ms F. Carter, NLP   350

C. *majority* 20,405
(June 1987, C. maj. 21,732)

NEWHAM NORTH EAST (Greater London)
E.59,555　T.60.34%
*R. Leighton, *Lab.* 20,952
J. Galbraith, *C.* 10,966
J. Aves, *LD* 4,020
Lab. majority 9,986
(June 1987, Lab. maj. 8,236)
See also page 238

NEWHAM NORTH WEST (Greater London)
E.46,471　T.56.02%
*T. Banks, *Lab.* 15,911
M. Prisk, *C.* 6,740
A. Sawdon, *LD* 2,445
Ms A. Standford, *Green* 587
T. Jug, *Loony G.* 252
D. O'Sullivan, *Int. Comm.* 100
Lab. majority 9,171
(June 1987, Lab. maj. 8,496)

NEWHAM SOUTH (Greater London)
E.51,143　T.60.19%
*N. Spearing, *Lab.* 14,358
Ms J. Foster, *C.* 11,856
A. Kellaway, *LD* 4,572
Lab. majority 2,502
(June 1987, Lab. maj. 2,766)

NORFOLK MID
E.80,336　T.81.64%
*Rt. Hon. R. Ryder, *C.* 35,620
M. Castle, *Lab.* 16,672
J. Gleed, *LD* 13,072
Ms C. Waite, *NLP* 226
C. majority 18,948
(June 1987, C. maj. 18,008)

NORFOLK NORTH
E.73,780　T.80.84%
*R. Howell, *C.* 28,810
N. Lamb, *LD* 16,265
M. Cullingham, *Lab.* 13,850
Ms A. Zelter, *Green* 559
Ms S. Jackson, *NLP* 167
C. majority 12,545
(June 1987, C. maj. 15,310)

NORFOLK NORTH WEST
E.77,438　T.80.67%
*H. Bellingham, *C.* 32,554
Dr G. Turner, *Lab.* 20,990
A. Waterman, *LD* 8,599
S. Pink, *NLP* 330
C. majority 11,564
(June 1987, C. maj. 10,825)

NORFOLK SOUTH
E.81,647　T.83.99%
*Rt. Hon. J. MacGregor, *C.* 36,081
C. Brocklebank-Fowler, *LD* 18,516
C. Needle, *Lab.* 12,422
Ms S. Ross-Wagenknecht, *Green* 702
N. Clark, *NLP* 320
R. Peacock, *Ind.* 304
R. Watkins, *Ind. C.* 232
C. majority 17,565
(June 1987, C. maj. 12,418)

NORFOLK SOUTH WEST
E.77,652　T.79.30%
*Mrs G. Shephard, *C.* 33,637
Ms M. Page, *Lab.* 16,706
J. Marsh, *LD* 11,237
C. majority 16,931
(June 1987, C. maj. 20,436)

NORMANTON (W. Yorks)
E.65,562　T.76.35%
*W. O'Brien, *Lab.* 25,936
R. Sturdy, *C.* 16,986
M. Galdas, *LD* 7,137
Lab. majority 8,950
(June 1987, Lab. maj. 7,287)

NORTHAMPTON NORTH
E.69,139　T.78.52%
*A. Marlow, *C.* 24,865
Ms J. Thomas, *Lab.* 20,957
R. Church, *LD* 8,236
B. Spivack, *NLP* 232
C. majority 3,908
(June 1987, C. maj. 9,256)

NORTHAMPTON SOUTH
E.83,477　T.79.90%
*M. Morris, *C.* 36,882
J. Dickie, *Lab.* 19,909
G. Mabbutt, *LD* 9,912
C. majority 16,973
(June 1987, C. maj. 17,803)

NORTHAVON (Avon)
E.83,496　T.84.16%
*Rt. Hon. Sir J. Cope, *C.* 35,338
Ms H. Larkins, *LD* 23,477
Ms J. Norris, *Lab.* 10,290
Ms J. Greene, *Green* 789
P. Marx, *Lib.* 380
C. majority 11,861
(June 1987, C. maj. 14,270)

NORWICH NORTH (Norfolk)
E.63,308　T.81.82%
*H. P. Thompson, *C.* 22,419
I. Gibson, *Lab.* 22,153
D. Harrison, *LD* 6,706
L. Betts, *Green* 433
R. Arnold, *NLP* 93
C. majority 266
(June 1987, C. maj. 7,776)

NORWICH SOUTH (Norfolk)
E.63,603　T.80.60%
*J. Garrett, *Lab.* 24,965
D. Baxter, *C.* 18,784
C. Thomas, *LD* 6,609
A. Holmes, *Green* 803
B. Parsons, *NLP* 104
Lab. majority 6,181
(June 1987, Lab. maj. 336)

NORWOOD (Greater London)
E.52,496　T.65.87%
*J. Fraser, *Lab.* 18,391
J. Samways, *C.* 11,175
Ms S. Lawman, *LD* 4,087
S. Collins, *Green* 790
M. Leighton, *NLP* 138
Lab. majority 7,216
(June 1987, Lab. maj. 4,723)

NOTTINGHAM EAST
E.67,939　T.70.08%
J. Heppell, *Lab.* 25,026
*M. Knowles, *C.* 17,346
T. Ball, *LD* 3,695
A. Jones, *Green* 667
C. Roylance, *Lib.* 598
J. Ashforth, *NLP* 283
Lab. majority 7,680
(June 1987, C. maj. 456)

NOTTINGHAM NORTH
E.69,494　T.74.98%
*G. Allen, *Lab.* 29,052
I. Bridge, *C.* 18,309
A. Skelton, *LD* 4,477
A. Cadman, *NLP* 274
Lab. majority 10,743
(June 1987, Lab. maj. 1,665)

NOTTINGHAM SOUTH
E.72,796　T.74.22%
A. Simpson, *Lab.* 25,771
*M. Brandon-Bravo, *C.* 22,590
G. D. Long, *LD* 5,408
Ms J. Christou, *NLP* 263
Lab. majority 3,181
(June 1987, C. maj. 2,234)

NUNEATON (Warwicks)
E.70,906　T.83.70%
W. Olner, *Lab.* 27,157
*L. Stevens, *C.* 25,526
Ms R. Merritt, *LD* 6,671
Lab. majority 1,631
(June 1987, C. maj. 5,655)

OLD BEXLEY AND SIDCUP (Greater London)
E.49,449　T.81.94%
*Rt. Hon. E. Heath, *C.* 24,450
Ms D. Brierly, *Lab.* 8,751
D. Nicolle, *LD* 6,438
B. Rose, *Alt. C.* 733
R. Stephens, *NLP* 148
C. majority 15,699
(June 1987, C. maj. 16,274)

OLDHAM CENTRAL AND ROYTON (Greater Manchester)
E.61,333　T.74.20%
B. Davies, *Lab.* 23,246
Mrs T. Morris, *C.* 14,640
Ms A. Dunn, *LD* 7,224
I. Dalling, *NLP* 403
Lab. majority 8,606
(June 1987, Lab. maj. 6,279)

OLDHAM WEST (Greater Manchester)
E.54,063　T.75.65%
*M. Meacher, *Lab.* 21,580
J. Gillen, *C.* 13,247
J. Smith, *LD* 5,525
Ms S. Dalling, *NLP* 551
Lab. majority 8,333
(June 1987, Lab. maj. 5,967)

ORPINGTON (Greater London)
E.57,318　T.83.67%
J. Horam, *C.* 27,421
C. Maines, *LD* 14,486
S. Cowan, *Lab.* 5,512

R. Almond, *Lib.*	539
C. majority	12,935
(June 1987, C. maj. 12,732)	

OXFORD EAST
E.63,075   T.74.59%

*A. Smith, *Lab.*	23,702
Dr M. Mayall, *C.*	16,164
M. Horwood, *LD*	6,105
Mrs C. Lucas, *Green*	933
Miss A. Wilson, *NLP*	101
K. Thompson, *Rev. Comm.*	48
Lab. majority	7,538
(June 1987, Lab. maj. 1,288)	

OXFORD WEST AND ABINGDON
E.72,328   T.76.68%

*Rt. Hon. J. Patten, *C.*	25,163
Sir W. Goodhart, *LD*	21,624
B. Kent, *Lab.*	7,652
M. Woodin, *Green*	660
R. Jenking, *Lib.*	194
Miss S. Nelson, *Anti Fed.*	98
G. Wells, *NLP*	75
C. majority	3,539
(June 1987, C. maj. 4,878)	

PECKHAM (Greater London)
E.58,269   T.53.87%

*Ms H. Harman, *Lab.*	19,391
C. Frazer, *C.*	7,386
Mrs R. Colley, *LD*	4,331
G. Dacres, *WRP*	146
V. Emmanuel, *Whiplash*	140
Lab. majority	12,005
(June 1987, Lab. maj. 9,489)	

PENDLE (Lancs)
E.64,063   T.82.91%

G. Prentice, *Lab.*	23,497
*J. Lee, *C.*	21,384
A. Davies, *LD*	7,976
Mrs V. Thorne, *Anti Fed.*	263
Lab. majority	2,113
(June 1987, C. maj. 2,639)	

PENRITH AND THE BORDER
(Cumbria)
E.73,769   T.79.67%

*D. Maclean, *C.*	33,808
G. Walker, *LD*	15,359
J. Metcalfe, *Lab.*	8,871
R. Gibson, *Green*	610
I. Docker, *NLP*	129
C. majority	18,449
(June 1987, C. maj. 17,366)	

PETERBOROUGH (Cambs)
E.87,638   T.75.12%

*B. Mawhinney, *C.*	31,827
Ms J. Owens, *Lab.*	26,451
Ms A. Taylor, *LD*	5,208
E. Murat, *Lib.*	1,557
R. Heaton, *BNP*	311
P. Beasley, *PP*	271
C. Brettell, *NLP*	215
C. majority	5,376
(June 1987, C. maj. 9,784)	

PLYMOUTH DEVONPORT (Devon)
E.65,799   T.77.83%

D. Jamieson, *Lab.*	24,953
K. Simpson, *C.*	17,541

M. Mactaggart, *LD*	6,315
H. Luscombe, *SD*	2,152
F. Lyons, *NLP*	255
Lab. majority	7,412
(June 1987, SDP/All. maj. 6,470)	

PLYMOUTH DRAKE (Devon)
E.51,667   T.75.56%

*Dame J. Fookes, *C.*	17,075
P. Telford, *Lab.*	15,062
Ms V. Cox, *LD*	5,893
D. Stanbury, *SD*	476
Ms A. Harrison, *Green*	441
T. Pringle, *NLP*	95
C. majority	2,013
(June 1987, C. maj. 3,125)	

PLYMOUTH SUTTON (Devon)
E.67,430   T.81.17%

G. Streeter, *C.*	27,070
A. Pawley, *Lab.*	15,120
J. Brett-Freeman, *LD*	12,291
J. Bowler, *NLP*	256
C. majority	11,950
(June 1987, C. maj. 4,013)	

PONTEFRACT AND CASTLEFORD
(W. Yorks)
E.64,648   T.74.25%

*G. Lofthouse, *Lab.*	33,546
A. Rockall, *C.*	10,051
D. Ryan, *LD*	4,410
Lab. majority	23,495
(June 1987, Lab. maj. 21,626)	

POOLE (Dorset)
E.79,221   T.79.39%

*J. Ward, *C.*	33,445
B. Clements, *LD*	20,614
H. White, *Lab.*	6,912
M. Steen, *Ind. C.*	1,620
A. Bailey, *NLP*	303
C. majority	12,831
(June 1987, C. maj. 14,808)	

PORTSMOUTH NORTH (Hants)
E.79,592   T.77.05%

*P. Griffiths, *C.*	32,240
A. Burnett, *Lab.*	18,359
A. Bentley, *LD*	10,101
Ms H. Palmer, *Green*	628
C. majority	13,881
(June 1987, C. maj. 18,401)	

PORTSMOUTH SOUTH (Hants)
E.77,645   T.69.09%

*D. Martin, *C.*	22,798
M. Hancock, *LD*	22,556
S. Rapson, *Lab.*	7,857
A. Zivkovic, *Green*	349
W. Trend, *NLP*	91
C. majority	242
(June 1987, C. maj. 205)	

PRESTON (Lancs)
E.64,158   T.71.74%

*Mrs A. Wise, *Lab.*	24,983
S. O'Toole, *C.*	12,808
W. Chadwick, *LD*	7,897
Ms J. Ayliffe, *NLP*	341
Lab. majority	12,175
(June 1987, Lab. maj. 10,645)	

PUDSEY (W. Yorks)
E.70,847   T.80.14%

*Sir G. Shaw, *C.*	25,067
A. Giles, *Lab.*	16,095
D. Shutt, *LD*	15,153
Ms J. Wynne, *Green*	466
C. majority	8,972
(June 1987, C. maj. 6,436)	

PUTNEY (Greater London)
E.61,914   T.77.91%

*Rt. Hon. D. Mellor, *C.*	25,188
Ms J. Chegwidden, *Lab.*	17,662
J. Martyn, *LD*	4,636
K. Hagenbach, *Green*	618
P. Levy, *NLP*	139
C. majority	7,526
(June 1987, C. maj. 6,907)	

RAVENSBOURNE (Greater London)
E.57,259   T.81.24%

*Sir J. Hunt, *C.*	29,506
P. Booth, *LD*	9,792
E. Dyer, *Lab.*	6,182
I. Mouland, *Green*	617
P. White, *Lib.*	318
J. Shepheard, *NLP*	105
C. majority	19,714
(June 1987, C. maj. 16,919)	

READING EAST (Berks)
E.72,151   T.75.02%

*Sir G. Vaughan, *C.*	29,148
Ms G. Parker, *Lab.*	14,593
D. Thair, *LD*	9,528
Ms A. McCubbin, *Green*	861
C. majority	14,555
(June 1987, C. maj. 16,217)	

READING WEST (Berks)
E.67,937   T.77.98%

*Sir A. Durant, *C.*	28,048
P. Ruhemann, *Lab.*	14,750
K. Lock, *LD*	9,572
P. Unsworth, *Green*	613
C. majority	13,298
(June 1987, C. maj. 16,753)	

REDCAR (Cleveland)
E.62,494   T.77.73%

*Dr M. Mowlam, *Lab.*	27,184
R. Goodwill, *C.*	15,607
C. Abbott, *LD*	5,789
Lab. majority	11,577
(June 1987, Lab. maj. 7,735)	

REIGATE (Surrey)
E.71,853   T.78.54%

*Sir G. Gardiner, *C.*	32,220
B. Newsome, *LD*	14,556
Ms H. Young, *Lab.*	9,150
M. Dilcliff, *SD*	513
C. majority	17,664
(June 1987, C. maj. 18,173)	

RIBBLE VALLEY (Lancs)
E.64,996   T.85.73%

N. Evans, *C.*	29,178
*M. Carr, *LD*	22,636
R. Pickup, *Lab.*	3,649
D. Beesley, *Loony G.*	152
Ms N. Holmes, *NLP*	112

C. majority   6,542
(June 1987, C. maj. 19,528)
(March 1991, LD maj. 4,641)

RICHMOND AND BARNES (Greater London)
E.53,081   T.85.01%
*J. Hanley, *C.*   22,894
Dr J. Tonge, *LD*   19,025
D. Touhig, *Lab.*   2,632
Ms J. Maciejowska, *Green*   376
C. Cunningham, *NLP*   89
R. Meacock, *QFL*   62
Ms A. Ellis-Jones, *Anti Fed.*   47
C. majority   3,869
(June 1987, C. maj. 1,766)

RICHMOND (N. Yorks)
E.82,879   T.78.41%
*W. Hague, *C.*   40,202
G. Irwin, *LD*   16,698
R. Cranston, *Lab.*   7,523
M. Barr, *Ind.*   570
C. majority   23,504
(June 1987, C. maj. 19,576)
(Feb 1989, C. maj. 2,634)

ROCHDALE (Greater Manchester)
E.69,522   T.76.47%
Ms E. Lynne, *LD*   22,776
D. Williams, *Lab.*   20,937
D. Goldie-Scott, *C.*   8,626
K. Henderson, *BNP*   620
V. Lucker, *NLP*   211
LD majority   1,839
(June 1987, L./All. maj. 2,779)

ROCHFORD (Essex)
E.76,869   T.82.99%
*Dr M. Clark, *C.*   38,967
N. Harris, *LD*   12,931
D. Quinn, *Lab.*   10,537
Ms L. Farmer, *Lib.*   1,362
C. majority   26,036
(June 1987, C. maj. 19,694)

ROMFORD (Greater London)
E.54,001   T.78%
*Sir M. Neubert, *C.*   23,834
Ms E. Gordon, *Lab.*   12,414
Ms P. Atherton, *LD*   5,329
F. Gibson, *Green*   546
C. majority   11,420
(June 1987, C. maj. 13,471)

ROMSEY AND WATERSIDE (Hants)
E.82,628   T.83.15%
*M. Colvin, *C.*   37,375
G. Dawson, *LD*   22,071
Mrs A. Mawle, *Lab.*   8,688
J. Spottiswood, *Green*   577
C. majority   15,304
(June 1987, C. maj. 15,272)

ROSSENDALE AND DARWEN (Lancs)
E.76,909   T.83.06%
Mrs J. Anderson, *Lab.*   28,028
*D. Trippier, *C.*   27,908
K. Connor, *LD*   7,226
J. Gaffney, *Green*   596
P. Gorrod, *NLP*   125
Lab. majority   120
(June 1987, C. maj. 4,982)

ROTHERHAM (S. Yorks)
E.60,937   T.71.68%
J. Boyce, *Lab.*   27,933
S. Yorke, *C.*   10,372
D. Wildgoose, *LD*   5,375
Lab. majority   17,561
(June 1987, Lab. maj. 16,012)
See also page 238

ROTHER VALLEY (S. Yorks)
E.68,303   T.74.98%
*K. Barron, *Lab.*   30,977
T. Horton, *C.*   13,755
K. Smith, *LD*   6,483
Lab. majority   17,222
(June 1987, Lab. maj. 15,790)

RUGBY AND KENILWORTH (Warwicks)
E.77,766   T.83.72%
*J. Pawsey, *C.*   34,110
J. Airey, *Lab.*   20,863
J. Roodhouse, *LD*   9,934
S. Withers, *NLP*   202
C. majority   13,247
(June 1987, C. maj. 16,264)

RUISLIP-NORTHWOOD (Greater London)
E.54,151   T.81.91%
*J. Wilkinson, *C.*   28,097
Ms R. Brooks, *Lab.*   8,306
H. Davies, *LD*   7,739
M. Sheehan, *NLP*   214
C. majority   19,791
(June 1987, C. maj. 16,971)

RUSHCLIFFE (Notts)
E.76,253   T.83.04%
*Rt. Hon. K. Clarke, *C.*   34,448
A. Chewings, *Lab.*   14,682
Dr A. Wood, *LD*   12,660
S. Anthony, *Green*   775
M. Maelor-Jones, *Ind. C.*   611
D. Richards, *NLP*   150
C. majority   19,766
(June 1987, C. maj. 20,839)

RUTLAND AND MELTON (Leics)
E.80,976   T.80.82%
A. Duncan, *C.*   38,603
Ms J. Taylor, *Lab.*   13,068
R. Lustig, *LD*   12,682
J. Berreen, *Green*   861
R. Grey, *NLP*   237
C. majority   25,535
(June 1987, C. maj. 23,022)

RYEDALE (N. Yorks)
E.87,048   T.81.73%
*J. Greenway, *C.*   39,888
Mrs E. Shields, *LD*   21,449
J. Healey, *Lab.*   9,812
C. majority   18,439
(June 1987, C. maj. 9,740)

SAFFRON WALDEN (Essex)
E.74,878   T.83.21%
*A. Haselhurst, *C.*   35,272
M. Hayes, *LD*   17,848
J. Kotz, *Lab.*   8,933
M. Miller, *NLP*   260

C. majority   17,424
(June 1987, C. maj. 16,602)

ST ALBANS (Herts)
E.74,188   T.83.47%
*Rt. Hon. P. Lilley, *C.*   32,709
Ms M. Howes, *LD*   16,305
K. Pollard, *Lab.*   12,016
C. Simmons, *Green*   734
D. Lucas, *NLP*   161
C. majority   16,404
(June 1987, C. maj. 10,881)

ST HELENS NORTH (Merseyside)
E.71,261   T.77.35%
*J. Evans, *Lab.*   31,930
B. Anderson, *C.*   15,686
J. Beirne, *LD*   7,224
Ms A. Lynch, *NLP*   287
Lab. majority   16,244
(June 1987, Lab. maj. 14,260)

ST HELENS SOUTH (Merseyside)
E.67,507   T.73.77%
*G. Bermingham, *Lab.*   30,391
Mrs P. Buzzard, *C.*   12,182
B. Spencer, *LD*   6,933
Dr H. Jump, *NLP*   295
Lab. majority   18,209
(June 1987, Lab. maj. 13,801)

ST IVES (Cornwall)
E.71,152   T.80.29%
*D. Harris, *C.*   24,528
A. George, *LD*   22,883
S. Warran, *Lab.*   9,144
Dr G. Stephens, *Lib.*   577
C. majority   1,645
(June 1987, C. maj. 7,555)

SALFORD EAST (Greater Manchester)
E.52,616   T.64.36%
*Rt. Hon. S. Orme, *Lab.*   20,327
D. Berens, *C.*   9,092
N. Owen, *LD*   3,836
M. Stanley, *Green*   463
C. Craig, *NLP*   150
Lab. majority   11,235
(June 1987, Lab. maj. 12,056)

SALISBURY (Wilts)
E.75,916   T.79.89%
*S. R. Key, *C.*   31,546
P. Sample, *LD*   22,573
S. Fear, *Lab.*   5,483
Dr S. Elcock, *Green*   609
S. Fletcher, *Ind.*   233
T. Abbott, *Wessex*   117
Ms A. Martell, *NLP*   93
C. majority   8,973
(June 1987, C. maj. 11,443)

SCARBOROUGH (N. Yorks)
E.76,364   T.77.18%
J. Sykes, *C.*   29,334
D. Billing, *Lab.*   17,600
B. Davenport, *LD*   11,133
Dr D. Richardson, *Green*   876
C. majority   11,734
(June 1987, C. maj. 13,626)

SEDGEFIELD (Durham)
E.61,024   T.77.06%
*A. Blair, Lab.	28,453
N. Jopling, C.	13,594
G. Huntington, LD	4,982
Lab. majority	14,859
(June 1987, Lab. maj. 13,058)

SELBY (N. Yorks)
E.77,178   T.80.16%
*Rt. Hon. M. Alison, C.	31,067
J. Grogan, Lab.	21,559
E. Batty, LD	9,244
C. majority	9,508
(June 1987, C. maj. 13,779)

SEVENOAKS (Kent)
E.71,050   T.81.35%
*G. M. Wolfson, C.	33,245
R. Walshe, LD	14,091
Ms J. Evans, Lab.	9,470
Ms M. Lawrence, Green	786
P. Wakeling, NLP	210
C. majority	19,154
(June 1987, C. maj. 17,345)

SHEFFIELD ATTERCLIFFE (S. Yorks)
E.69,177   T.71.81%
C. Betts, Lab.	28,563
G. Millward, C.	13,083
Ms H. Woolley, LD	7,283
G. Ferguson, Green	751
Lab. majority	15,480
(June 1987, Lab. maj. 17,191)

SHEFFIELD BRIGHTSIDE (S. Yorks)
E.63,810   T.66.26%
*D. Blunkett, Lab.	29,771
T. Loughton, C.	7,090
R. Franklin, LD	5,273
D. Hyland, Int. Comm.	150
Lab. majority	22,681
(June 1987, Lab. maj. 24,191)

SHEFFIELD CENTRAL (S. Yorks)
E.59,059   T.56.12%
*R. Caborn, Lab.	22,764
V. Davies, C.	5,470
A. Sangar, LD	3,856
G. Wroe, Green	750
M. Clarke, EUVJJ	212
Ms J. O'Brien, CL	92
Lab. majority	17,294
(June 1987, Lab. maj. 19,342)

SHEFFIELD HALLAM (S. Yorks)
E.76,584   T.70.83%
*C. I. Patnick, C.	24,693
Dr P. Gold, LD	17,952
Ms V. Hardstaff, Lab.	10,930
M. Baker, Green	473
R. Hurford, NLP	101
Ms T. Clifford, Rev. Comm.	99
C. majority	6,741
(June 1987, C. maj. 7,637)

SHEFFIELD HEELEY (S. Yorks)
E.70,953   T.70.89%
*W. Michie, Lab.	28,005
D. Beck, C.	13,051
P. Moore, LD	9,247
Lab. majority	14,954
(June 1987, Lab. maj. 14,440)

SHEFFIELD HILLSBOROUGH
(S. Yorks)
E.77,343   T.77.19%
Mrs H. Jackson, Lab.	27,568
D. Chadwick, LD	20,500
S. Cordle, C.	11,640
Lab. majority	7,068
(June 1987, Lab. maj. 3,286)

SHERWOOD (Notts)
E.73,354   T.85.48%
S. P. Tipping, Lab.	29,788
*A. Stewart, C.	26,878
J. Howard, LD	6,039
Lab. majority	2,910
(June 1987, C. maj. 4,495)

SHIPLEY (W. Yorks)
E.68,816   T.82.12%
*Sir M. Fox, C.	28,463
Ms A. Lockwood, Lab.	16,081
J. Cole, LD	11,288
C. Harris, Green	680
C. majority	12,382
(June 1987, C. maj. 12,630)

SHOREHAM (W. Sussex)
E.71,252   T.81.17%
B. M. L. Stephen, C.	32,670
M. King, LD	18,384
P. Godwin, Lab.	6,123
W. Weights, Lib.	459
J. Dreben, NLP	200
C. majority	14,286
(June 1987, C. maj. 17,070)

SHREWSBURY AND ATCHAM (Salop)
E.70,620   T.82.45%
*D. Conway, C.	26,681
K. Hemsley, LD	15,716
Ms E. Owen, Lab.	15,157
G. Hardy, Green	677
C. majority	10,965
(June 1987, C. maj. 9,064)

SHROPSHIRE NORTH
E.82,675   T.77.68%
*Rt. Hon. J. Biffen, C.	32,443
J. Stevens, LD	16,232
R. Hawkins, Lab.	15,550
C. majority	16,211
(June 1987, C. maj. 14,415)

SKIPTON AND RIPON (N. Yorks)
E.75,628   T.81.34%
*D. Curry, C.	35,937
R. Hall, LD	16,607
Ms K. Allott, Lab.	8,978
C. majority	19,330
(June 1987, C. maj. 17,174)

SLOUGH (Berks)
E.73,889   T.78.24%
*J. Watts, C.	25,793
E. Lopez, Lab.	25,279
P. Mapp, LD	4,041
J. Clark, Lib.	1,426
D. Alford, Ind. Lab.	699
A. Carmichael, NF	290
M. Creese, NLP	153
Ms E. Smith, ERIP	134
C. majority	514
(June 1987, C. maj. 4,090)

SOLIHULL (W. Midlands)
E.77,303   T.81.61%
*J. Taylor, C.	38,385
M. Southcombe, LD	13,239
Ms N. Kutapan, Lab.	10,544
C. Hards, Green	925
C. majority	25,146
(June 1987, C. maj. 21,786)

SOMERTON AND FROME (Somerset)
E.71,354   T.82.75%
M. Robinson, C.	28,052
D. Heath, LD	23,711
R. Ashford, Lab.	6,154
Ms L. Graham, Green	742
Ms J. Pollock, Lib.	388
C. majority	4,341
(June 1987, C. maj. 9,538)

SOUTHAMPTON ITCHEN (Hants)
E.72,104   T.76.93%
J. Denham, Lab.	24,402
*C. Chope, C.	23,851
J. Hodgson, LD	7,221
Lab. majority	551
(June 1987, C. maj. 6,716)

SOUTHAMPTON TEST (Hants)
E.72,932   T.77.40%
*S. J. A. Hill, C.	24,504
A. Whitehead, Lab.	23,919
Ms D. Maddock, LD	7,391
J. Michaelis, Green	535
D. Plummer, NLP	101
C. majority	585
(June 1987, C. maj. 6,954)

SOUTHEND EAST (Essex)
E.56,708   T.73.80%
*Sir E. Taylor, C.	24,591
G. Bramley, Lab.	11,480
Ms J. Horne, LD	5,107
B. Lynch, Lib.	673
C. majority	13,111
(June 1987, C. maj. 13,847)

SOUTHEND WEST (Essex)
E.64,198   T.77.80%
*Rt. Hon. P. Channon, C.	27,319
Ms N. Stimson, LD	15,417
G. Viney, Lab.	6,139
A. Farmer, Lib.	495
C. Keene, Green	451
P. Warburton, NLP	127
C. majority	11,902
(June 1987, C. maj. 8,400)

SOUTH HAMS (Devon)
E.83,061   T.81.09%
*A. Steen, C.	35,951
V. Evans, LD	22,240
Ms E. Cohen, Lab.	8,091
C. Titmuss, Green	846
Mrs L. Summerville, NLP	227
C. majority	13,711
(June 1987, C. maj. 13,146)

SOUTHPORT (Merseyside)
E.71,443   T.77.60%
M. Banks, C.	26,081
*R. Fearn, LD	23,018
J. King, Lab.	5,637
J. Walker, Green	545

G. Clements, *NLP* 159
C. majority 3,063
(June 1987, L./All. maj. 1,849)

SOUTH RIBBLE (Lancs)
*E.*78,173   *T.*82.99%
*R. Atkins, *C.* 30,828
Dr G. Smith, *Lab.* 24,855
S. Jones, *LD* 8,928
Dr R. Decter, *NLP* 269
C. majority 5,973
(June 1987, C. maj. 8,430)

SOUTH SHIELDS (Tyne & Wear)
*E.*59,392   *T.*70.07%
*D. Clark, *Lab.* 24,876
J. Howard, *C.* 11,399
A. Preece, *LD* 5,344
Lab. majority 13,477
(June 1987, Lab. maj. 13,851)

SOUTHWARK AND BERMONDSEY
(Greater London)
*E.*60,251   *T.*62.62%
*S. Hughes, *LD* 21,459
R. Balfe, *Lab.* 11,614
A. Raca, *C.* 3,794
S. Tyler, *BNP* 530
T. Blackham, *NF* 168
Dr G. Barnett, *NLP* 113
J. Grogan, *CL* 56
LD majority 9,845
June 1987, L./All. maj. 2,779

SPELTHORNE (Surrey)
*E.*69,343   *T.*80.36%
*D. Wilshire, *C.* 32,627
Ms A. Leedham, *Lab.* 12,784
R. Roberts, *LD* 9,202
Ms J. Wassell, *Green* 580
D. Rea, *Loony* 338
D. Ellis, *NLP* 195
C. majority 19,843
(June 1987, C. maj. 20,050)

STAFFORD
*E.*74,663   *T.*82.91%
*W. Cash, *C.* 30,876
D. Kidney, *Lab.* 19,976
Mrs J. Calder, *LD* 10,702
C. Peat, *Hardcore* 178
P. Lines, *NLP* 176
C. majority 10,900
(June 1987, C. maj. 13,707)

STAFFORDSHIRE MID
*E.*73,414   *T.*85.66%
M. Fabricant, *C.* 31,227
*Mrs S. Heal, *Lab.* 24,991
B. Stamp, *LD* 6,432
Ms D. Grice, *NLP* 239
C. majority 6,236
(June 1987, C. maj. 14,654)
(March 1990, Lab. maj. 9,449)

STAFFORDSHIRE MOORLANDS
*E.*75,036   *T.*83.66%
*D. Knox, *C.* 29,240
J. Siddelley, *Lab.* 21,830
Ms C. Jebb, *LD* 9,326
M. Howson, *Anti Fed.* 2,121
P. Davies, *NLP* 261

C. majority 7,410
(June 1987, C. maj. 14,427)

STAFFORDSHIRE SOUTH
*E.*82,758   *T.*81.54%
*P. Cormack, *C.* 40,266
B. Wylie, *Lab.* 17,633
I. Sadler, *LD* 9,584
C. majority 22,633
(June 1987, C. maj. 25,268)

STAFFORDSHIRE SOUTH EAST
*E.*70,199   *T.*82.05%
*D. Lightbown, *C.* 29,180
B. Jenkins, *Lab.* 21,988
Dr G. Penlington, *LD* 5,540
Miss J. Taylor, *SD* 895
C. majority 7,192
(June 1987, C. maj. 10,885)

STALYBRIDGE AND HYDE (Greater
Manchester)
*E.*68,189   *T.*73.46%
*T. Pendry, *Lab.* 26,207
S. Mort, *C.* 17,376
I. Kirk, *LD* 4,740
R. Powell, *Lib.* 1,199
D. Poyzer, *Loony* 337
E. Blomfield, *NLP* 238
Lab. majority 8,831
(June 1987, Lab. maj. 5,663)

STAMFORD AND SPALDING (Lincs)
*E.*75,153   *T.*81.16%
*J. Q. Davies, *C.* 35,965
C. Burke, *Lab.* 13,096
B. Lee, *LD* 11,939
C. majority 22,869
(June 1987, C. maj. 14,007)

STEVENAGE (Herts)
*E.*70,233   *T.*83.03%
*T. Wood, *C.* 26,652
Ms J. Church, *Lab.* 21,764
A. Reilly, *LD* 9,668
A. Calcraft, *NLP* 233
C. majority 4,888
(June 1987, C. maj. 5,340)

STOCKPORT (Greater Manchester)
*E.*58,095   *T.*82.27%
Ms M. A. Coffey, *Lab.* 21,096
*A. Favell, *C.* 19,674
Ms A. Corris, *LD* 6,539
Ms J. Filmore, *Green* 436
D. Saunders, *NLP* 50
Lab. majority 1,422
(June 1987, C. maj. 2,853)

STOCKTON NORTH (Cleveland)
*E.*69,451   *T.*76.83%
*F. Cook, *Lab.* 27,918
S. Brocklebank-Fowler, *C.* 17,444
Ms S. Fletcher, *LD* 7,454
K. McGarvey, *Ind. Lab.* 550
Lab. majority 10,474
(June 1987, Lab. maj. 8,801)

STOCKTON SOUTH (Cleveland)
*E.*75,959   *T.*82.77%
*T. Devlin, *C.* 28,418
J. Scott, *Lab.* 25,049
Ms K. Kirkham, *LD* 9,410

C. majority 3,369
(June 1987, C. maj. 774)

STOKE-ON-TRENT CENTRAL (Staffs)
*E.*65,527   *T.*68.12%
*M. Fisher, *Lab.* 25,897
N. Gibb, *C.* 12,477
M. Dent, *LD* 6,073
N. Pullen, *NLP* 196
Lab. majority 13,420
(June 1987, Lab. maj. 9,770)

STOKE-ON-TRENT NORTH (Staffs)
*E.*73,141   *T.*73.42%
*Ms J. Walley, *Lab.* 30,464
L. Harris, *C.* 15,687
J. Redfern, *LD* 7,167
A. Morrison, *NLP* 387
Lab. majority 14,777
(June 1987, Lab. maj. 8,513)

STOKE-ON-TRENT SOUTH (Staffs)
*E.*71,316   *T.*74.33%
G. Stevenson, *Lab.* 26,380
R. Ibbs, *C.* 19,471
F. Jones, *LD* 6,870
Mrs E. Lines, *NLP* 291
Lab. majority 6,909
(June 1987, Lab. maj. 5,053)

STRATFORD-UPON-AVON
(Warwicks)
*E.*82,824   *T.*82.07%
*A. Howarth, *C.* 40,251
N. Fogg, *LD* 17,359
Ms S. Brookes, *Lab.* 8,932
R. Roughan, *Green* 729
A. Saunders, *Ind. C.* 573
M. Twite, *NLP* 130
C. majority 22,892
(June 1987, C. maj. 21,165)

STREATHAM (Greater London)
*E.*56,825   *T.*69.03%
K. Hill, *Lab.* 18,925
*Sir W. Shelton, *C.* 16,608
J. Pindar, *LD* 3,858
R. Baker, *Green* 443
A. Hankin, *Islamic* 154
Mrs C. Payne, *ADS* 145
J. Parsons, *NLP* 97
Lab. majority 2,317
(June 1987, C. maj. 2,407)

STRETFORD (Greater Manchester)
*E.*54,467   *T.*68.76%
*A. Lloyd, *Lab.* 22,300
C. Rae, *C.* 11,163
F. Beswick, *LD* 3,722
A. Boyton, *NLP* 268
Lab. majority 11,137
(June 1987, Lab. maj. 9,402)

STROUD (Glos)
*E.*82,553   *T.*84.49%
*R. Knapman, *C.* 32,201
D. Drew, *Lab.* 18,796
M. Robinson, *LD* 16,751
Ms S. Atkinson, *Green* 2,005
C. majority 13,405
(June 1987, C. maj. 12,375)

SUFFOLK CENTRAL
E.82,735   T.80.26%
*M. Lord, C.   32,917
Ms L. Henniker-Major, LD   16,886
J. Harris, Lab.   15,615
J. Matthissen, Green   800
Ms J. Wilmot, NLP   190
C. majority   16,031
(June 1987, C. maj. 16,290)

SUFFOLK COASTAL
E.79,333   T.81.62%
*Rt. Hon. J. Gummer, C.   34,680
P. Monk, LD   15,395
T. Hodgson, Lab.   13,508
A. Slade, Green   943
Ms F. Kaplan, NLP   232
C. majority   19,285
(June 1987, C. maj. 15,280)

SUFFOLK SOUTH
E.84,833   T.81.73%
*T. Yeo, C.   34,793
Ms K. Pollard, LD   17,504
S. Hesford, Lab.   16,623
T. Aisbitt, NLP   420
C. majority   17,289
(June 1987, C. maj. 16,243)

SUNDERLAND NORTH (Tyne &
Wear)
E.72,874   T.68.86%
W. Etherington, Lab.   30,481
Miss J. Barnes, C.   13,477
V. Halom, LD   5,389
Ms W. Lundgren, Lib.   841
Lab. majority   17,004
(June 1987, Lab. maj. 14,672)

SUNDERLAND SOUTH (Tyne &
Wear)
E.72,607   T.69.87%
*C. Mullin, Lab.   29,399
G. Howe, C.   14,898
J. Lennox, LD   5,844
T. Scouler, Green   596
Lab. majority   14,501
(June 1987, Lab. maj. 12,613)

SURBITON (Greater London)
E.42,421   T.82.44%
*R. Tracey, C.   19,033
Ms B. Janke, LD   9,394
R. Hutchinson, Lab.   6,384
W. Parker, NLP   161
C. majority   9,639
(June 1987, C. maj. 9,741)

SURREY EAST
E.57,878   T.82.53%
P. Ainsworth, C.   29,767
R. Tomlin, LD   12,111
Mrs G. Roles, Lab.   5,075
I. Kilpatrick, Green   819
C. majority   17,656
(June 1987, C. maj. 18,126)

SURREY NORTH WEST
E.83,648   T.78.27%
*Sir M. Grylls, C.   41,772
Mrs C. Clark, LD   13,378
M. Hayhurst, Lab.   8,886
Ms Y. Hockey, Green   1,441

C. majority   28,394
(June 1987, C. maj. 23,575)

SURREY SOUTH WEST
E.72,288   T.82.77%
*Mrs V. Bottomley, C.   35,008
N. Sherlock, LD   20,033
P. Kelly, Lab.   3,840
N. Bedrock, Green   710
K. Campbell, NLP   147
D. Newman, AS   98
C. majority   14,975
(June 1987, C. maj. 14,343)

SUSSEX MID
E.80,827   T.82.85%
*Rt. Hon. T. Renton, C.   39,524
Ms M. Collins, LD   18,996
Ms L. Gregory, Lab.   6,951
H. Stevens, Green   772
P. Berry, Loony   392
P. Hodkin, PR   246
Dr A. Hankey, NLP   89
C. majority   20,528
(June 1987, C. maj. 18,292)

SUTTON AND CHEAM (Greater
London)
E.60,949   T.82.39%
Lady O. Maitland, C.   27,710
P. Burstow, LD   16,954
G. Martin, Lab.   4,980
J. Duffy, Green   444
Ms A. Hatchard, NLP   133
C. majority   10,756
(June 1987, C. maj. 15,718)

SUTTON COLDFIELD (W. Midlands)
E.71,410   T.79.51%
*Rt. Hon. Sir N. Fowler, C.   37,001
J. Whorwood, LD   10,965
Ms J. Bott-Obi, Lab.   8,490
H. Meads, NLP   324
C. majority   26,036
(June 1987, C. maj. 21,183)

SWINDON (Wilts)
E.90,067   T.81.46%
*S. Coombs, C.   31,749
J. D'Avila, Lab.   28,923
S. Cordon, LD   11,737
W. Hughes, Green   647
R. Gillard, Loony G.   236
V. Farrar, Ind.   78
C. majority   2,826
(June 1987, C. maj. 4,857)

TATTON (Cheshire)
E.71,085   T.80.83%
*M. N. Hamilton, C.   31,658
J. Kelly, Lab.   15,798
Ms C. Hancox, LD   9,597
M. Gibson, FP   410
C. majority   15,860
(June 1987, C. maj. 17,094)

TAUNTON (Somerset)
E.78,036   T.82.32%
*D. Nicholson, C.   29,576
Ms J. Ballard, LD   26,240
Ms J. Hole, Lab.   8,151
P. Leavey, NLP   279

C. majority   3,336
(June 1987, C. maj. 10,380)

TEIGNBRIDGE (Devon)
E.74,892   T.83.43%
*P. Nicholls, C.   31,272
R. Younger-Ross, LD   22,416
R. Kennedy, Lab.   8,128
A. Hope, Loony   437
N. Hayes, NLP   234
C. majority   8,856
(June 1987, C. maj. 10,425)

THANET NORTH (Kent)
E.70,978   T.76.02%
*R. Gale, C.   30,867
A. Bretman, Lab.   12,657
Ms J. Phillips, LD   9,563
Ms H. Dawe, Green   873
C. majority   18,210
(June 1987, C. maj. 17,480)

THANET SOUTH (Kent)
E.62,441   T.78.17%
*J. Aitken, C.   25,253
M. James, Lab.   13,740
W. Pitt, LD   8,948
Ms S. Peckham, Green   871
C. majority   11,513
(June 1987, C. maj. 13,683)

THURROCK (Essex)
E.69,171   T.78.15%
A. MacKinlay, Lab.   24,791
*T. Janman, C.   23,619
A. Banton, LD   5,145
C. Rogers, Pensioners   391
P. Compobassi, Anti Fed.   117
Lab. majority   1,172
(June 1987, C. maj. 690)

TIVERTON (Devon)
E.71,024   T.82.98%
Mrs A. Browning, C.   30,376
D. Cox, LD   19,287
Ms S. Gibb, Lab.   5,950
D. Morrish, Lib.   2,225
P. Foggitt, Green   1,007
B. Rhodes, NLP   96
C. majority   11,089
(June 1987, C. maj. 9,212)

TONBRIDGE AND MALLING (Kent)
E.77,292   T.82.66%
*Rt. Hon. Sir J. Stanley, C.   36,542
P. Roberts, LD   14,984
Ms M. O'Neill, Lab.   11,533
J. Tidy, Green   612
Mrs J. Hovarth, NLP   221
C. majority   21,558
(June 1987, C. maj. 16,429)

TOOTING (Greater London)
E.68,306   T.74.79%
*T. Cox, Lab.   24,601
M. Winters, C.   20,494
B. Bunce, LD   3,776
Ms C. Martin, Lib.   1,340
P. Owens, Green   694
F. Anklesalria, NLP   119
M. Whitelaw, CD   64
Lab. majority   4,107
(June 1987, Lab. maj. 1,441)

TORBAY (Devon)
E.71,171   T.80.63%
*R. Allason, C.	28,624
A. Sanders, LD	22,837
P. Truscott, Lab.	5,503
R. Jones, NF	268
Ms A. Thomas, NLP	157
C. majority	5,787

(June 1987, C. maj. 8,820)

TOTTENHAM (Greater London)
E.68,319   T.65.60%
*B. Grant, Lab.	25,309
A. Charalambous, C.	13,341
A. L'Estrange, LD	5,120
P. Budge, Green	903
Ms M. Obomanu, NLP	150
Lab. majority	11,968

(June 1987, Lab. maj. 4,141)

TRURO (Cornwall)
E.75,101   T.82.35%
*M. Taylor, LD	31,230
N. St Aubyn, C.	23,660
J. Geach, Lab.	6,078
L. Keating, Green	569
C. Tankard, Lib.	208
Ms M. Hartley, NLP	108
LD majority	7,570

(June 1987, L./All. maj. 4,753)

TUNBRIDGE WELLS (Kent)
E.76,808   T.78.11%
*Rt. Hon. Sir P. Mayhew, C.	34,162
A. Clayton, LD	17,030
E. Goodman, Lab.	8,300
E. Fenna, NLP	267
R. Edey, ISS	236
C. majority	17,132

(June 1987, C. maj. 16,122)

TWICKENHAM (Greater London)
E.63,072   T.84.27%
*T. Jessel, C.	26,804
Dr V. Cable, LD	21,093
M. Gold, Lab.	4,919
G. Gill, NLP	152
D. Griffith, DLC	103
A. Miners, Lib.	85
C. majority	5,711

(June 1987, C. maj. 7,127)

TYNE BRIDGE (Tyne & Wear)
E.53,079   T.62.64%
*D. Clelland, Lab.	22,328
C. Liddell-Grainger, C.	7,118
J. Burt, LD	3,804
Lab. majority	15,210

(June 1987, Lab. maj. 15,573)

TYNEMOUTH (Tyne & Wear)
E.74,955   T.80.39%
*N. Trotter, C.	27,731
P. Cosgrove, Lab.	27,134
P. Selby, LD	4,855
A. Buchanan-Smith, Green	543
C. majority	597

(June 1987, C. maj. 2,583)

UPMINSTER (Greater London)
E.64,138   T.80.46%
*Sir N. Bonsor, C.	28,791
T. Ward, Lab.	14,970

T. Hurlstone, LD	7,848
C. majority	13,821

(June 1987, C. maj. 16,857)

UXBRIDGE (Greater London)
E.61,744   T.78.87%
*J. M. Shersby, C.	27,487
R. Evans, Lab.	14,308
S. Carey, LD	5,900
I. Flindall, Green	538
M. O'Rourke, BNP	350
A. Deans, NLP	120
C. majority	13,179

(June 1987, C. maj. 15,970)

VAUXHALL (Greater London)
E.62,473   T.62.35%
*Ms C. Hoey, Lab.	21,328
B. Gentry, C.	10,840
M. Tuffrey, LD	5,678
Ms P. Shepherd, Green	803
A. Khan, DOS	156
Ms S. Hill, Rev. Comm.	152
Lab. majority	10,488

(June 1987, Lab. maj. 9,019)
(June 1989, Lab. maj. 9,766)

WAKEFIELD (W. Yorks)
E.69,794   T.76.27%
*D. Hinchliffe, Lab.	26,964
D. Fanthorpe, C.	20,374
T. Wright, LD	5,900
Lab. majority	6,590

(June 1987, Lab. maj. 2,789)

WALLASEY (Merseyside)
E.65,676   T.82.50%
Ms A. Eagle, Lab.	26,531
*Rt. Hon. L. Chalker, C.	22,722
N. Thomas, LD	4,177
Ms S. Davis, Green	650
G. Gay, NLP	105
Lab. majority	3,809

(June 1987, C. maj. 279)

WALLSEND (Tyne & Wear)
E.77,941   T.74.12%
S. Byers, Lab.	33,439
Miss M. Gibbon, C.	13,969
M. Huscroft, LD	10,369
Lab. majority	19,470

(June 1987, Lab. maj. 19,384)

WALSALL NORTH (W. Midlands)
E.69,604   T.74.98%
*D. Winnick, Lab.	24,387
R. Syms, C.	20,563
A. Powis, LD	6,629
K. Reynolds, NF	614
Lab. majority	3,824

(June 1987, Lab. maj. 1,790)

WALSALL SOUTH (W. Midlands)
E.65,642   T.76.26%
*B. George, Lab.	24,133
L. Jones, C.	20,955
G. Williams, LD	4,132
R. Clarke, Green	673
J. Oldbury, NLP	167
Lab. majority	3,178

(June 1987, Lab. maj. 1,116)

WALTHAMSTOW (Greater London)
E.49,140   T.72.35%
N. Gerrard, Lab.	16,251
*H. Summerson, C.	13,229
P. Leighton, LD	5,142
Ms J. Lambert, Green	594
V. Wilkinson, Lib.	241
A. Planton, NLP	94
Lab. majority	3,022

(June 1987, C. maj. 1,512)

WANSBECK (Northumberland)
E.63,457   T.79.29%
*J. Thompson, Lab.	30,046
G. Sanderson, C.	11,872
B. Priestley, LD	7,691
N. Best, Green	710
Lab. majority	18,174

(June 1987, Lab. maj. 16,789)

WANSDYKE (Avon)
E.77,156   T.84.33%
*J. Aspinwall, C.	31,389
D. Norris, Lab.	18,048
Ms D. Darby, LD	14,834
F. Hayden, Green	800
C. majority	13,341

(June 1987, C. maj. 16,144)

WANSTEAD AND WOODFORD
(Greater London)
E.55,821   T.78.28%
*J. Arbuthnot, C.	26,204
Ms L. Brown, Lab.	9,319
G. Staight, LD	7,362
F. Roads, Green	637
A. Brickell, NLP	178
C. majority	16,885

(June 1987, C. maj. 16,412)

WANTAGE (Oxon)
E.68,328   T.82.68%
*R. Jackson, C.	30,575
R. Morgan, LD	14,102
V. Woodell, Lab.	10,955
R. Ely, Green	867
C. majority	16,473

(June 1987, C. maj. 12,156)

WARLEY EAST (W. Midlands)
E.51,717   T.71.72%
*A. Faulds, Lab.	19,891
G. Marshall, C.	12,097
A. Harrod, LD	4,547
A. Groucott, NLP	561
Lab. majority	7,794

(June 1987, Lab. maj. 5,585)

WARLEY WEST (W. Midlands)
E.57,164   T.73.90%
J. Spellar, Lab.	21,386
Mrs S. Whitehouse, C.	15,914
Ms E. Todd, LD	4,945
Lab. majority	5,472

(June 1987, Lab. maj. 5,393)

WARRINGTON NORTH (Cheshire)
E.78,548   T.77.38%
*E. D. H. Hoyle, Lab.	33,019
C. Daniels, C.	20,397
I. Greenhalgh, LD	6,965
B. Davies, NLP	400

Lab. majority 12,622
(June 1987, Lab. maj. 8,013)

WARRINGTON SOUTH (Cheshire)
E.77,694   T.82.04%
M. Hall, Lab.   27,819
*C. Butler, C.   27,628
P. Walker, LD   7,978
S. Benson, NLP   321
Lab. majority   191
(June 1987, C. maj. 3,609)

WARWICK AND LEAMINGTON
E.71,259   T.81.54%
*Sir D. Smith, C.   28,093
M. Taylor, Lab.   19,158
Ms S. Boad, LD   9,645
Ms J. Alty, Green   803
R. Newby, Ind.   251
J. Brewster, NLP   156
C. majority   8,935
(June 1987, C. maj. 13,982)

WARWICKSHIRE NORTH
E.71,473   T.83.82%
M. O'Brien, Lab.   27,599
*Hon. F. Maude, C.   26,145
N. Mitchell, LD   6,167
Lab. majority   1,454
(June 1987, C. maj. 2,829)

WATFORD (Herts)
E.72,291   T.82.34%
*W. A. T. T. Garel-Jones, C.   29,072
M. Jackson, Lab.   19,482
M. Oaten, LD   10,231
J. Hywel-Davies, Green   566
L. Davis, NLP   176
C. majority   9,590
(June 1987, C. maj. 11,736)

WAVENEY (Suffolk)
E.84,181   T.81.81%
*D. Porter, C.   33,174
E. Leverett, Lab.   26,472
A. Rogers, LD   8,925
D. Hook, NLP   302
C. majority   6,702
(June 1987, C. maj. 11,783)

WEALDEN (E. Sussex)
E.74,665   T.80.83%
*Sir G. Johnson Smith, C.   37,263
M. Skinner, LD   16,332
S. Billcliffe, Lab.   5,579
I. Guy-Moore, Green   1,002
Dr R. Graham, NLP   182
C. majority   20,931
(June 1987, C. maj. 20,110)

WELLINGBOROUGH (Northants)
E.73,875   T.81.89%
*P. Fry, C.   32,302
P. Sawford, Lab.   20,486
Ms J. Trevor, LD   7,714
C. majority   11,816
(June 1987, C. maj. 14,070)

WELLS (Somerset)
E.69,833   T.82.71%
*D. Heathcoat-Amory, C.   28,620
H. Temperley, LD   21,971
J. Pilgrim, Lab.   6,126
M. Fenner, Green   1,042

C. majority 6,649
(June 1987, C. maj. 8,541)

WELWYN HATFIELD (Herts)
E.72,146   T.84.39%
*D. Evans, C.   29,447
R. Little, Lab.   20,982
R. Parker, LD   10,196
Ms E. Lucas, NLP   264
C. majority   8,465
(June 1987, C. maj. 10,903)

WENTWORTH (S. Yorks)
E.64,914   T.74.03%
*P. Hardy, Lab.   32,939
M. Brennan, C.   10,490
Ms C. Roderick, LD   4,629
Lab. majority   22,449
(June 1987, Lab. maj. 20,092)

WEST BROMWICH EAST
(W. Midlands)
E.56,940   T.75.25%
*P. Snape, Lab.   19,913
C. Blunt, C.   17,100
M. Smith, LD   5,360
J. Lord, NF   477
Lab. majority   2,813
(June 1987, Lab. maj. 983)

WEST BROMWICH WEST
(W. Midlands)
E.57,655   T.70.41%
*Miss B. Boothroyd, Lab.   22,251
D. Swayne, C.   14,421
Miss S. Broadbent, LD   3,925
Lab. majority   7,830
(June 1987, Lab. maj. 5,253)

WESTBURY (Wilts)
E.87,356   T.82.99%
D. Faber, C.   36,568
Ms V. Rayner, LD   23,962
W. Stallard, Lab.   9,642
P. Macdonald, Lib.   1,440
P. French, Green   888
C. majority   12,606
(June 1987, C. maj. 10,097)

WESTMINSTER NORTH (Greater
London)
E.58,847   T.75.75%
*Sir J. Wheeler, C.   21,828
Ms J. Edwards, Lab.   18,095
J. Wigoder, LD   3,341
Ms A. Burke, Green   1,017
J. Hinde, NLP   159
M. Kelly, Anti Fed.   137
C. majority   3,733
(June 1987, C. maj. 3,310)

WESTMORLAND AND LONSDALE
(Cumbria)
E.71,865   T.77.76%
*Rt. Hon. M. Jopling, C.   31,798
S. Collins, LD   15,362
D. Abbott, Lab.   8,436
R. Johnstone, NLP   287
C. majority   16,436
(June 1987, C. maj. 14,920)

WESTON-SUPER-MARE (Avon)
E.78,839   T.79.75%
*A. W. Wiggin, C.   30,022
B. Cotter, LD   24,680
D. Murray, Lab.   6,913
Dr R. Lawson, Green   1,262
C. majority   5,342
(June 1987, C. maj. 7,998)

WIGAN (Greater Manchester)
E.72,739   T.76.16%
*R. Stott, Lab.   34,910
E. Hess, C.   13,068
G. Davies, LD   6,111
K. White, Lib.   1,116
Ms A. Taylor, NLP   197
Lab. majority   21,842
(June 1987, Lab. maj. 20,462)

WILTSHIRE NORTH
E.85,851   T.81.71%
*R. Needham, C.   39,028
Ms C. Napier, LD   22,640
Ms C. Reid, Lab.   6,945
Ms L. Howitt, Green   850
G. Hawkins, Lib.   622
S. Martienssen, Bastion   66
C. majority   16,388
(June 1987, C. maj. 10,939)

WIMBLEDON (Greater London)
E.61,917   T.80.23%
*Dr C. Goodson-Wickes, C.   26,331
K. Abrams, Lab.   11,570
Ms A. Willott, LD   10,569
V. Flood, Green   860
H. Godfrey, NLP   181
G. Hadley, Ind.   170
C. majority   14,761
(June 1987, C. maj. 11,301)

WINCHESTER (Hants)
E.79,218   T.83.46%
P. G. Malone, C.   33,113
A. Barron, LD   24,992
P. Jenks, Lab.   4,917
*J. Browne, Ind. C.   3,095
C. majority   8,121
(June 1987, C. maj. 7,479)

WINDSOR AND MAIDENHEAD
(Berks)
E.77,327   T.81.68%
Hon. M. Trend, C.   35,075
J. Hyde, LD   22,147
Ms C. Attlee, Lab.   4,975
R. Williams, Green   510
D. Askwith, Loony   236
Miss E. Bigg, Ind.   110
M. Grenville, NLP   108
C. majority   12,928
(June 1987, C. maj. 17,836)

WIRRAL SOUTH (Merseyside)
E.61,116   T.82.37%
*G. B. Porter, C.   25,590
Ms H. Southworth, Lab.   17,407
E. Cunniffe, LD   6,581
N. Birchenough, Green   584
G. Griffiths, NLP   182
C. majority   8,183
(June 1987, C. maj. 10,963)

WIRRAL WEST (Merseyside)
E.62,453   T.81.57%
*Rt. Hon. D. Hunt, C.	26,852
Ms H. Stephenson, Lab.	15,788
J. Thornton, LD	7,420
Ms G. Bowler, Green	700
N. Broome, NLP	188
C. majority	11,064

(June 1987, C. maj. 12,723)

WITNEY (Oxon)
E.78,521   T.81.89%
*Rt. Hon. D. Hurd, C.	36,256
J. Plaskitt, Lab.	13,688
I. Blair, LD	13,393
Ms C. Beckford, Green	716
Ms S. Catling, NLP	134
Miss M. Brown, FTA	119
C. majority	22,568

(June 1987, C. maj. 18,464)

WOKING (Surrey)
E.80,842   T.79.20%
*Rt. Hon. C. Onslow, C.	37,744
Mrs D. Buckrell, LD	17,902
J. Dalgleish, Lab.	8,080
Mrs T. Macintyre, NLP	302
C. majority	19,842

(June 1987, C. maj. 16,544)

WOKINGHAM (Berks)
E.85,914   T.82.41%
*J. Redwood, C.	43,497
P. Simon, LD	17,788
N. Bland, Lab.	8,846
P. Owen, Loony	531
P. Harriss, WUWC	148
C. majority	25,709

(June 1987, C. maj. 20,387)

WOLVERHAMPTON NORTH EAST
(W. Midlands)
E.62,695   T.78%
K. Purchase, Lab.	24,106
*Mrs M. Hicks, C.	20,167
M. Gwinnett, LD	3,546
K. Bullman, Lib.	1,087
Lab. majority	3,939

(June 1987, C. maj. 204)

WOLVERHAMPTON SOUTH EAST
(W. Midlands)
E.56,158   T.72.86%
*D. Turner, Lab.	23,215
P. Bradbourn, C.	12,975
R. Whitehouse, LD	3,881
Ms C. Twelvetrees, Lib.	850
Lab. majority	10,240

(June 1987, Lab. maj. 6,398)

WOLVERHAMPTON SOUTH WEST
(W. Midlands)
E.67,288   T.78.28%
*N. Budgen, C.	25,969
S. Murphy, Lab.	21,003
M. Wiggin, LD	4,470
C. Hallmark, Lib.	1,237
C. majority	4,966

(June 1987, C. maj. 10,318)

WOODSPRING (Avon)
E.77,534   T.83.21%
Dr L. Fox, C.	35,175
Ms N. Kirsen, LD	17,666
R. Stone, Lab.	9,942
N. Brown, Lib.	836
Ms R. Knifton, Green	801
B. Lee, NLP	100
C. majority	17,509

(June 1987, C. maj. 17,852)

WOOLWICH (Greater London)
E.55,977   T.70.91%
J. Austin-Walker, Lab.	17,551
*J. Cartwright, SD	15,326
K. Walmsley, C.	6,598
Ms S. Hayward, NLP	220
Lab. majority	2,225

(June 1987, SDP/All. maj. 1,937)

WORCESTER
E.74,211   T.80.99%
P. Luff, C.	27,883
R. Berry, Lab.	21,731
J. Caiger, LD	9,561
M. Foster, Green	592
M. Soden, Brewer	343
C. majority	6,152

(June 1987, C. maj. 10,453)

WORCESTERSHIRE MID
E.84,269   T.81.07%
*E. Forth, C.	33,964
Ms J. Smith, Lab.	24,094
D. Barwick, LD	9,745
P. Davis, NLP	520
C. majority	9,870

(June 1987, C. maj. 14,911)

WORCESTERSHIRE SOUTH
E.80,423   T.79.99%
*W. M. H. Spicer, C.	34,792
P. Chandler, LD	18,641
N. Knowles, Lab.	9,727
G. Woodford, Green	1,178
C. majority	16,151

(June 1987, C. maj. 13,645)

WORKINGTON (Cumbria)
E.57,597   T.81.52%
*D. Campbell-Savours, Lab.	26,719
S. Sexton, C.	16,270
Ms C. Neale, LD	3,028
D. Langstaff, Loony	755
Ms N. Escott, NLP	183
Lab. majority	10,449

(June 1987, Lab. maj. 7,019)

WORSLEY (Greater Manchester)
E.72,244   T.77.74%
*T. Lewis, Lab.	29,418
N. Cameron, C.	19,406
R. Boyd, LD	6,490
P. Connolly, Green	677
G. Phillips, NLP	176
Lab. majority	10,012

(June 1987, Lab. maj. 7,337)

WORTHING (W. Sussex)
E.77,540   T.77.41%
*Rt. Hon. T. Higgins, C.	34,198
Mrs S. Bucknall, LD	17,665
J. Deen, Lab.	6,679

Mrs P. Beever, Green	806
N. Goble, Lib.	679
C. majority	16,533

(June 1987, C. maj. 18,501)

THE WREKIN (Salop)
E.90,892   T.77.14%
*B. Grocott, Lab.	33,865
Mrs E. Holt, C.	27,217
A. West, LD	8,032
R. Saunders, Green	1,008
Lab. majority	6,648

(June 1987, Lab. maj. 1,456)

WYCOMBE (Bucks)
E.72,564   T.78.01%
*R. Whitney, C.	30,081
T. Andrews, LD	13,005
J. Huddart, Lab.	12,222
J. Laker, Green	686
A. Page, SD	449
T. Anton, NLP	168
C. majority	17,076

(June 1987, C. maj. 13,819)

WYRE (Lancs)
E.67,778   T.79.54%
*K. Mans, C.	29,449
D. Borrow, Lab.	17,785
J. Ault, LD	6,420
R. Perry, NLP	260
C. majority	11,664

(June 1987, C. maj. 14,661)

WYRE FOREST (H & W)
E.73,550   T.82.36%
*A. Coombs, C.	28,983
R. Maden, Lab.	18,642
M. Jones, LD	12,958
C. majority	10,341

(June 1987, C. maj. 7,224)

YEOVIL (Somerset)
E.73,057   T.81.98%
*Rt. Hon. J. J. D. Ashdown, LD	30,958
J. Davidson, C.	22,125
Ms V. Nelson, Lab.	5,765
J. Risbridger, Green	639
D. Sutch, Loony	338
R. Simmerson, APAKBI	70
LD majority	8,833

(June 1987, L./All. maj. 5,700)

YORK (N. Yorks)
E.79,242   T.80.97%
H. Bayley, Lab.	31,525
*C. Gregory, C.	25,183
Ms K. Anderson, LD	6,811
S. Kenwright, Green	594
Ms P. Orr, NLP	54
Lab. majority	6,342

(June 1987, C. maj. 147)

WALES

ABERAVON (W. Glamorgan)
E.51,650   T.77.57%
*Rt. Hon. J. Morris, *Lab.* 26,877
H. Williams, *C.* 5,567
Mrs M. Harris, *LD* 4,999
D. Saunders, *PC* 1,919
Capt. Beany, *Real Bean* 707
Lab. majority 21,310
(June 1987, Lab. maj. 20,609)

ALYN AND DEESIDE (Clwyd)
E.60,477   T.80.08%
*S. B. Jones, *Lab.* 25,206
J. Riley, *C.* 17,355
R. Britton, *LD* 4,687
J. Rogers, *PC* 551
V. Button, *Green* 433
J. Cooksey, *Ind.* 200
Lab. majority 7,851
(June 1987, Lab. maj. 6,383)

BLAENAU GWENT
E.55,638   T.78.13%
L. Smith, *Lab.* 34,333
D. Melding, *C.* 4,266
A. Burns, *LD* 2,774
A. Davies, *PC* 2,099
Lab. majority 30,067
(June 1987, Lab. maj. 27,861)

BRECON AND RADNOR (Powys)
E.51,509   T.85.94%
J. P. Evans, *C.* 15,977
*R. Livsey, *LD* 15,847
C. Mann, *Lab.* 11,634
Ms S. Meredudd, *PC* 418
H. Richards, *Green* 393
C. majority 130
(June 1987, L./All. maj. 56)

BRIDGEND (Mid Glamorgan)
E.58,531   T.80.44%
*W. Griffiths, *Lab.* 24,143
D. Unwin, *C.* 16,817
D. Mills, *LD* 4,827
A. Lloyd Jones, *PC* 1,301
Lab. majority 7,326
(June 1987, Lab. maj. 4,380)

CAERNARFON (Gwynedd)
E.46,468   T.78.15%
*D. Wigley, *PC* 21,439
P. Fowler, *C.* 6,963
Ms S. Mainwaring, *Lab.* 5,641
R. Arwel Williams, *LD* 2,101
G. Evans, *NLP* 173
PC majority 14,476
(June 1987, PC maj. 12,812)

CAERPHILLY (Mid Glamorgan)
E.64,529   T.77.20%
*R. Davies, *Lab.* 31,713
H. Philpott, *C.* 9,041
L. Whittle, *PC* 4,821
S. Wilson, *LD* 4,247
Lab. majority 22,672
(June 1987, Lab. maj. 19,167)

CARDIFF CENTRAL (S. Glamorgan)
E.57,716   T.74.35%
J. O. Jones, *Lab.* 18,014
*I. Grist, *C.* 14,549

Ms J. Randerson, *LD* 9,170
H. Marshall, *PC* 748
C. von Ruhland, *Green* 330
B. Francis, *NLP* 105
Lab. majority 3,465
(June 1987, C. maj. 1,986)

CARDIFF NORTH (S. Glamorgan)
E.56,721   T.84.15%
*G. H. Jones, *C.* 21,547
Ms J. Morgan, *Lab.* 18,578
Ms E. Warlow, *LD* 6,487
Ms E. Bush, *PC* 916
J. Morse, *BNP* 121
D. Palmer, *NLP* 86
C. majority 2,969
(June 1987, C. maj. 8,234)

CARDIFF SOUTH AND PENARTH
(S. Glamorgan)
E.61,484   T.77.25%
*A. Michael, *Lab.* 26,383
T. Hunter Jarvie, *C.* 15,958
P. Verma, *LD* 3,707
Ms B. Anglezarke, *PC* 776
L. Davey, *Green* 676
Lab. majority 10,425
(June 1987, Lab. maj. 4,574)

CARDIFF WEST (S. Glamorgan)
E.58,898   T.77.56%
*H. R. Morgan, *Lab.* 24,306
M. Prior, *C.* 15,015
Ms J. Gasson, *LD* 5,002
Ms P. Bestic, *PC* 1,177
A. Harding, *NLP* 184
Lab. majority 9,291
(June 1987, Lab. maj. 4,045)

CARMARTHEN (Dyfed)
E.68,887 T. 82.70%
*Dr A. W. Williams, *Lab.* 20,879
R. Thomas, *PC* 17,957
S. Cavenagh, *C.* 12,782
Mrs J. Hughes, *LD* 5,353
Lab. majority 2,922
(June 1987, Lab. maj. 4,317)

**CEREDIGION AND PEMBROKE
NORTH** (Dyfed)
E.66,180   T.77.36%
C. Dafis, *PC* 16,020
*G. Howells, *LD* 12,827
J. Williams, *C.* 12,718
J. Davies, *Lab.* 9,637
PC majority 3,193
(June 1987, L./All. maj. 4,700)

CLWYD NORTH WEST
E.67,351   T.78.64%
R. Richards, *C.* 24,488
C. Ruane, *Lab.* 18,438
R. Ingham, *LD* 7,999
T. Neil, *PC* 1,888
Ms M. Swift, *NLP* 158
C. majority 6,050
(June 1987, C. maj. 11,781)

CLWYD SOUTH WEST
E.60,607   T.81.52%
*M. Jones, *Lab.* 21,490
G. Owen, *C.* 16,549

G. Williams, *LD* 6,027
E. Lloyd Jones, *PC* 4,835
N. Worth, *Green* 351
Mrs J. Leadbetter, *NLP* 155
Lab. majority 4,941
(June 1987, Lab. maj. 1,028)

CONWY (Gwynedd)
E.53,576   T.78.85%
*Rt. Hon. Sir W. Roberts, *C.* 14,250
Revd R. Roberts, *LD* 13,255
Ms E. Williams, *Lab.* 10,883
R. Davies, *PC* 3,108
O. Wainwright, *Ind. C.* 637
Ms D. Hughes, *NLP* 114
C. majority 995
(June 1987, C. maj. 3,024)

CYNON VALLEY (Mid Glamorgan)
E.49,695   T.76.46%
*Ms A. Clwyd, *Lab.* 26,254
A. Smith, *C.* 4,890
T. Benney, *PC* 4,186
M. Verma, *LD* 2,667
Lab. majority 21,364
(June 1987, Lab. maj. 21,571)

DELYN (Clwyd)
E.66,591   T.83.40%
D. Hanson, *Lab.* 24,979
M. Whitby, *C.* 22,940
R. Dodd, *LD* 6,208
A. Drake, *PC* 1,414
Lab. majority 2,039
(June 1987, C. maj. 1,224)

GOWER (W. Glamorgan)
E.57,231   T.81.84%
*G. Wardell, *Lab.* 23,455
A. Donnelly, *C.* 16,437
C. Davies, *LD* 4,655
A. Price, *PC* 1,658
B. Kingzett, *Green* 448
G. Egan, *Loony G.* 114
M. Beresford, *NLP* 74
Lab. majority 7,018
(June 1987, Lab. maj. 5,764)

ISLWYN (Gwent)
E.51,079   T.81.48%
*Rt. Hon. N. Kinnock, *Lab.* 30,908
P. Bone, *C.* 6,180
M. Symonds, *LD* 2,352
Ms H. Jones, *PC* 1,636
Lord Sutch, *Loony* 547
Lab. majority 24,728
(June 1987, Lab. maj. 22,947)
See also page 238

LLANELLI (Dyfed)
E.65,058   T.77.80%
*Rt. Hon. D. Davies, *Lab.* 27,802
G. Down, *C.* 8,532
M. Phillips, *PC* 7,878
K. Evans, *LD* 6,404
Lab. majority 19,270
(June 1987, Lab. maj. 20,935)

MEIRIONNYDD NANT CONWY
(Gwynedd)
*E.*32,413   *T.*81.47%

E. Llwyd, *PC*	11,608
G. Lewis, *C.*	6,995
R. Williams, *Lab.*	4,978
Mrs R. Parry, *LD*	2,358
W. Pritchard, *Green*	471
PC majority	4,613

(June 1987, PC maj. 3,026)

MERTHYR TYDFIL AND RHYMNEY
(Mid Glamorgan)
*E.*58,430   *T.*75.84%

*E. Rowlands, *Lab.*	31,710
R. Rowland, *LD*	4,997
M. Hughes, *C.*	4,904
A. Cox, *PC*	2,704
Lab. majority	26,713

(June 1987, Lab. maj. 28,207)

MONMOUTH (Gwent)
*E.*59,147   *T.*86.06%

R. Evans, *C.*	24,059
*H. Edwards, *Lab.*	20,855
Mrs F. David, *LD*	5,562
M. Witherden, *Green/PC*	431
C. majority	3,204

(June 1987, C. maj. 9,350)
(May 1991, Lab. maj. 2,406)

MONTGOMERY (Powys)
*E.*41,386   *T.*79.87%

*A. Carlile, *LD*	16,031
Mrs J. France-Hayhurst, *C.*	10,822
S. Wood, *Lab.*	4,115
H. Parsons, *PC*	1,581
P. Adams, *Green*	508
LD majority	5,209

(June 1987, L./All. maj. 2,558)

NEATH (W. Glamorgan)
*E.*56,392   *T.*80.58%

*P. Hain, *Lab.*	30,903
D. Adams, *C.*	6,928
Dr D. Evans, *PC*	5,145
M. Phillips, *LD*	2,467
Lab. majority	23,975

(June 1987, Lab. maj. 20,578)
(April 1991, Lab. maj. 9,830)

NEWPORT EAST (Gwent)
*E.*51,603   *T.*81.21%

*R. J. Hughes, *Lab.*	23,050
Mrs A. Emmett, *C.*	13,151
W. Oliver, *LD*	4,991
S. Ainley, *Green/PC*	716
Lab. majority	9,899

(June 1987, Lab. maj. 7,064)

NEWPORT WEST (Gwent)
*E.*54,871   *T.*82.82%

*P. Flynn, *Lab.*	24,139
A. Taylor, *C.*	16,360
A. Toye, *LD*	4,296
P. Keelan, *PC*	653
Lab. majority	7,779

(June 1987, Lab. maj. 2,708)

OGMORE (Mid Glamorgan)
*E.*52,195   *T.*80.62%

*R. Powell, *Lab.*	30,186
D. Edwards, *C.*	6,359
J. Warman, *LD*	2,868
Ms L. McAllister, *PC*	2,667
Lab. majority	23,827

(June 1987, Lab. maj. 22,292)

PEMBROKE (Dyfed)
*E.*73,187   *T.*82.86%

N. Ainger, *Lab.*	26,253
*N. Bennett, *C.*	25,498
P. Berry, *LD*	6,625
C. Bryant, *PC*	1,627
R. Coghill, *Green*	484
M. Stoddart, *Anti Fed.*	158
Lab. majority	755

(June 1987, C. maj. 5,700)

PONTYPRIDD (Mid Glamorgan)
*E.*61,685   *T.*79.25%

*K. Howells, *Lab.*	29,722
Dr P. Donnelly, *C.*	9,925
Dr D. Bowen, *PC*	4,448
S. Belzak, *LD*	4,180
Ms E. Jackson, *Green*	615
Lab. majority	19,797

(June 1987, Lab. maj. 17,277)
(Feb. 1989, Lab. maj. 10,794)

RHONDDA (Mid Glamorgan)
*E.*59,955   *T.*76.61%

*A. Rogers, *Lab.*	34,243
G. Davies, *PC*	5,427
J. Richards, *C.*	3,588
P. Nicholls-Jones, *LD*	2,431
M. Fisher, *Comm. GB*	245
Lab. majority	28,816

(June 1987, Lab. maj. 30,596)

SWANSEA EAST (W. Glamorgan)
*E.*59,196   *T.*75.56%

*D. Anderson, *Lab.*	31,179
H. Davies, *C.*	7,697
R. Barton, *LD*	4,248
Ms E. Bonner-Evans, *PC*	1,607
Lab. majority	23,482

(June 1987, Lab. maj. 19,338)

SWANSEA WEST (W. Glamorgan)
*E.*59,785   *T.*73.34%

*Rt. Hon. A. Williams, *Lab.*	23,238
R. Perry, *C.*	13,760
M. Shrewsbury, *LD*	4,620
Dr D. Lloyd, *PC*	1,668
B. Oubridge, *Green*	564
Lab. majority	9,478

(June 1987, Lab. maj. 7,062)

TORFAEN (Gwent)
*E.*61,104   *T.*77.47%

*P. Murphy, *Lab.*	30,352
M. Watkins, *C.*	9,598
M. Hewson, *LD*	6,178
Dr J. Cox, *Green/PC*	1,210
Lab. majority	20,754

(June 1987, Lab. maj. 17,550)

VALE OF GLAMORGAN
(S. Glamorgan)
*E.*66,672   *T.*81.93%

W. Sweeney, *C.*	24,220
*J. Smith, *Lab.*	24,201
K. Davies, *LD*	5,045
D. Haswell, *PC*	1,160
C. majority	19

(June 1987, C. maj 6,251)
(May 1989, Lab. maj. 6,028)

WREXHAM (Clwyd)
*E.*63,720   *T.*80.71%

*J. Marek, *Lab.*	24,830
O. Paterson, *C.*	18,114
A. Thomas, *LD*	7,074
G. Wheatley, *PC*	1,415
Lab. majority	6,716

(June 1987, Lab. maj. 4,152)

YNYS MÔN (Gwynedd)
*E.*53,412   *T.*80.62%

*I. W. Jones, *PC*	15,984
G. Price Rowlands, *C.*	14,878
Dr R. Jones, *Lab.*	10,126
Ms P. Badger, *LD*	1,891
Mrs S. Parry, *NLP*	182
PC majority	1,106

(June 1987, PC maj. 4,298)

SCOTLAND

ABERDEEN NORTH (Grampian)
*E.*60,217   *T.*66.52%

*R. Hughes, *Lab.*	18,845
J. McGugan, *SNP*	9,608
P. Cook, *C.*	6,836
Dr M. Ford, *LD*	4,772
Lab. majority	9,237

(June 1987, Lab. maj. 16,278)

ABERDEEN SOUTH (Grampian)
*E.*58,881   *T.*69.78%

R. Robertson, *C.*	15,808
*F. Doran, *Lab.*	14,291
J. Davidson, *SNP*	6,223
Ms I. Keith, *LD*	4,767
C. majority	1,517

(June 1987, Lab. maj. 1,198)

ANGUS EAST (Tayside)
*E.*63,170   *T.*75.03%

*A. Welsh, *SNP*	19,006
Dr R. Harris, *C.*	18,052
G. Taylor, *Lab.*	5,994
C. McLeod, *LD*	3,897
D. McCabe, *Green*	449
SNP majority	954

(June 1987, SNP maj. 1,544)

ARGYLL AND BUTE (Strathclyde)
E.47,894   T.76.19%
*Mrs J. R. Michie, *LD*   12,739
J. Corrie, *C.*   10,117
Prof. N. MacCormick, *SNP*   8,689
D. Browne, *Lab.*   4,946
LD majority   2,622
(June 1987, L./All. maj. 1,394)

AYR (Strathclyde)
E.65,481   T.83.08%
P. Gallie, *C.*   22,172
A. Osborne, *Lab.*   22,087
Mrs B. Mullin, *SNP*   5,949
J. Boss, *LD*   4,067
R. Scott, *NLP*   132
C. majority   85
(June 1987, C. maj. 182)

BANFF AND BUCHAN (Grampian)
E.64,873   T.71.20%
*A. Salmond, *SNP*   21,954
S. Manson, *C.*   17,846
B. Balcombe, *Lab.*   3,803
Mrs R. Kemp, *LD*   2,588
SNP majority   4,108
(June 1987, SNP maj. 2,441)

CAITHNESS AND SUTHERLAND
(Highland)
E.30,905   T.71.93%
*R. Maclennan, *LD*   10,032
G. Bruce, *C.*   4,667
K. MacGregor, *SNP*   4,049
M. Coyne, *Lab.*   3,483
LD majority   5,365
(June 1987, SDP/All. maj. 8,494)

CARRICK, CUMNOCK AND DOON
VALLEY (Strathclyde)
E.55,330   T.76.94%
*G. Foulkes, *Lab.*   25,142
J. Boswell, *C.*   8,516
C. Douglas, *SNP*   6,910
Ms M. Paris, *LD*   2,005
Lab. majority   16,626
(June 1987, Lab. maj. 16,802)

CLACKMANNAN (Central)
E.48,963   T.78.34%
*M. O'Neill, *Lab.*   18,829
A. Brophy, *SNP*   10,326
J. Mackie, *C.*   6,638
Ms A. Watters, *LD*   2,567
Lab. majority   8,503
(June 1987, Lab. maj. 12,401)

CLYDEBANK AND MILNGAVIE
(Strathclyde)
E.47,337   T.77.79%
*A. Worthington, *Lab.*   19,637
G. Hughes, *SNP*   7,207
W. Harvey, *C.*   6,654
A. Tough, *LD*   3,216
Ms J. Barrie, *NLP*   112
Lab. majority   12,430
(June 1987, Lab. maj. 16,304)

CLYDESDALE (Strathclyde)
E.61,878   T.77.62%
*J. Hood, *Lab.*   21,418
Ms C. Goodwin, *C.*   11,231
I. Gray, *SNP*   11,084

Ms E. Buchanan, *LD*   3,957
S. Cartwright, *BNP*   342
Lab. majority   10,187
(June 1987, Lab. maj. 10,502)

CUMBERNAULD AND KILSYTH
(Strathclyde)
E.46,489   T.79.06%
*N. Hogg, *Lab.*   19,855
T. Johnston, *SNP*   10,640
I. Mitchell, *C.*   4,143
Ms J. Haddow, *LD*   2,118
Lab. majority   9,215
(June 1987, Lab. maj. 14,403)

CUNNINGHAME NORTH
(Strathclyde)
E.54,803   T.78.21%
*B. Wilson, *Lab.*   17,564
Ms E. Clarkson, *C.*   14,625
D. Crossan, *SNP*   7,813
D. Herbison, *LD*   2,864
Lab. majority   2,939
(June 1987, Lab. maj. 4,422)

CUNNINGHAME SOUTH
(Strathclyde)
E.49,010   T.75.88%
B. Donohoe, *Lab.*   19,687
R. Bell, *SNP*   9,007
S. Leslie, *C.*   6,070
B. Ashley, *LD*   2,299
W. Jackson, *NLP*   128
Lab. majority   10,680
(June 1987, Lab. maj. 16,633)

DUMBARTON (Strathclyde)
E.57,222   T.77.11%
*J. McFall, *Lab.*   19,255
T. Begg, *C.*   13,126
W. McKechnie, *SNP*   8,127
J. Morrison, *LD*   3,425
Ms D. Krass, *NLP*   192
Lab. majority   6,129
(June 1987, Lab. maj. 5,222)

DUMFRIES (D & G)
E.61,145   T.79.97%
*Sir H. Monro, *C.*   21,089
P. Rennie, *Lab.*   14,674
A. Morgan, *SNP*   6,971
N. Wallace, *LD*   5,749
G. McLeod, *Ind. Green*   312
T. Barlow, *NLP*   107
C. majority   6,415
(June 1987, C. maj. 7,493)

DUNDEE EAST (Tayside)
E.58,959   T.72.10%
*J. McAllion, *Lab.*   18,761
D. Coutts, *SNP*   14,197
S. Blackwood, *C.*   7,549
I. Yuill, *LD*   1,725
Ms S. Baird, *Green*   205
R. Baxter, *NLP*   77
Lab. majority   4,564
(June 1987, Lab. maj. 1,015)

DUNDEE WEST (Tayside)
E.59,953   T.69.82%
*E. Ross, *Lab.*   20,498
K. Brown, *SNP*   9,894
A. Spearman, *C.*   7,746

Ms E. Dick, *LD*   3,132
Ms E. Hood, *Green*   432
D. Arnold, *NLP*   159
Lab. majority   10,604
(June 1987, Lab. maj. 16,526)

DUNFERMLINE EAST (Fife)
E.50,179   T.75.62%
*J. G. Brown, *Lab.*   23,692
M. Tennant, *C.*   6,248
J. Lloyd, *SNP*   5,746
Ms T. Little, *LD*   2,262
Lab. majority   17,444
(June 1987, Lab. maj. 19,589)

DUNFERMLINE WEST (Fife)
E.50,948   T.76.44%
Ms R. Squire, *Lab.*   16,374
M. Scott-Hayward, *C.*   8,890
J. Smith, *SNP*   7,563
Ms E. Harris, *LD*   6,122
Lab. majority   7,484
(June 1987, Lab. maj. 9,402)

EAST KILBRIDE (Strathclyde)
E.64,080   T.80.01%
*A. Ingram, *Lab.*   24,055
Ms K. McAlorum, *SNP*   12,063
G. Lind, *C.*   9,781
Ms S. Grieve, *LD*   5,377
Lab. majority   11,992
(June 1987, Lab. maj. 12,624)

EAST LOTHIAN
E.66,699   T.82.37%
*J. Home Robertson, *Lab.*   25,537
J. Hepburne Scott, *C.*   15,501
G. Thomson, *SNP*   7,776
T. McKay, *LD*   6,126
Lab. majority   10,036
(June 1987, Lab. maj. 10,105)

EASTWOOD (Strathclyde)
E.63,685   T.80.97%
*J. A. Stewart, *C.*   24,124
P. Grant-Hutchison, *Lab.*   12,436
Miss M. Craig, *LD*   8,493
P. Scott, *SNP*   6,372
Dr L. Fergusson, *NLP*   146
C. majority   11,688
(June 1987, C. maj. 6,014)

EDINBURGH CENTRAL (Lothian)
E.56,527   T.69.26%
*A. Darling, *Lab.*   15,189
P. Martin, *C.*   13,063
Ms L. Devine, *SNP*   5,539
A. Myles, *LD*   4,500
R. Harper, *Green*   630
D. Wilson, *Lib.*   235
Lab. majority   2,126
(June 1987, Lab. maj. 2,262)

EDINBURGH EAST (Lothian)
E.45,687   T.73.89%
*G. Strang, *Lab.*   15,446
K. Ward, *C.*   8,235
D. McKinney, *SNP*   6,225
D. Scobie, *LD*   3,432
G. Farmer, *Green*   424
Lab. majority   7,211
(June 1987, Lab. maj. 9,295)

EDINBURGH LEITH (Lothian)
E.56,520　*T*.71.30%

M. Chisholm, *Lab.*	13,790
Ms F. Hyslop, *SNP*	8,805
M. Bin Ashiq Rizvi, *C.*	8,496
Mrs H. Campbell, *LD*	4,975
*R. Brown, *Ind. Lab.*	4,142
A. Swan, *NLP*	96
Lab. majority	4,985
(June 1987, Lab. maj. 11,327)	

EDINBURGH PENTLANDS (Lothian)
E.55,567　*T*.80.18%

*Rt. Hon. M. Rifkind, *C.*	18,128
M. Lazarowicz, *Lab.*	13,838
Ms K. Caskie, *SNP*	6,882
K. Smith, *LD*	5,597
D. Rae, *NLP*	111
C. majority	4,290
(June 1987, C. maj. 3,745)	

EDINBURGH SOUTH (Lothian)
E.61,355　*T*.72.67%

*N. Griffiths, *Lab.*	18,485
S. Stevenson, *C.*	14,309
B. McCreadie, *LD*	5,961
R. Knox, *SNP*	5,727
G. Manclark, *NLP*	108
Lab. majority	4,176
(June 1987, Lab. maj. 1,859)	

EDINBURGH WEST (Lothian)
E.58,998　*T*.82.67%

*Lord J. Douglas-Hamilton, *C.*	18,071
D. Gorrie, *LD*	17,192
Ms I. Kitson, *Lab.*	8,759
G. Sutherland, *SNP*	4,117
A. Fleming, *Lib.*	272
Ms L. Hendry, *Green*	234
D. Bruce, *BNP*	133
C. majority	879
(June 1987, C. maj. 1,234)	

FALKIRK EAST (Central)
E.51,918　*T*.76.91%

M. Connarty, *Lab.*	18,423
R. Halliday, *SNP*	10,454
K. Harding, *C.*	8,279
Miss D. Storr, *LD*	2,775
Lab. majority	7,969
(June 1987, Lab. maj. 14,023)	

FALKIRK WEST (Central)
E.50,126　*T*.76.77%

*D. Canavan, *Lab.*	19,162
W. Houston, *SNP*	9,350
M. Macdonald, *C.*	7,558
M. Reilly, *LD*	2,414
Lab. majority	9,812
(June 1987, Lab. maj. 13,552)	

FIFE CENTRAL
E.56,152　*T*.74.33%

*H. McLeish, *Lab.*	21,036
Mrs T. Marwick, *SNP*	10,458
Ms C. Cender, *C.*	7,353
C. Harrow, *LD*	2,892
Lab. majority	10,578
(June 1987, Lab. maj. 15,709)	

FIFE NORTH EAST
E.53,747　*T*.77.84%

*W. M. Campbell, *LD*	19,430
Mrs M. Scanlon, *C.*	16,122
D. Roche, *SNP*	3,589
Miss L. Clark, *Lab.*	2,319
T. Flynn, *Green*	294
D. Senior, *Lib.*	85
LD majority	3,308
(June 1987, L./All. maj. 1,447)	

GALLOWAY AND UPPER NITHSDALE
(D & G)
E.54,474　*T*.81.66%

*Rt. Hon. I. Lang, *C.*	18,681
M. Brown, *SNP*	16,213
J. Dowson, *Lab.*	5,766
J. McKerchar, *LD*	3,826
C. majority	2,468
(June 1987, C. maj. 3,673)	

GLASGOW CATHCART (Strathclyde)
E.44,689　*T*.75.38%

*J. Maxton, *Lab.*	16,265
J. Young, *C.*	8,264
W. Steven, *SNP*	6,107
G. Dick, *LD*	2,614
Ms K. Allan, *Green*	441
Lab. majority	8,001
(June 1987, Lab. maj. 11,203)	

GLASGOW CENTRAL (Strathclyde)
E.48,107　*T*.63.05%

*M. Watson, *Lab.*	17,341
B. O'Hara, *SNP*	6,322
E. Stewart, *C.*	4,208
Dr A. Rennie, *LD*	1,921
Ms I. Brandt, *Green*	435
T. Burn, *Comm. GB*	106
Lab. majority	11,019
(June 1987, Lab. maj. 17,253)	
(June 1989, Lab. maj. 6,462)	

GLASGOW GARSCADDEN
(Strathclyde)
E.41,289　*T*.71.13%

*D. Dewar, *Lab.*	18,920
R. Douglas, *SNP*	5,580
J. Scott, *C.*	3,385
C. Brodie, *LD*	1,425
W. Orr, *NLP*	61
Lab. majority	13,340
(June 1987, Lab. maj. 18,977)	

GLASGOW GOVAN (Strathclyde)
E.45,822　*T*.76.03%

I. Davidson, *Lab.*	17,051
*J. Sillars, *SNP*	12,926
J. Donnelly, *C.*	3,458
R. Stewart, *LD*	1,227
D. Spaven, *Green*	181
Lab. majority	4,125
(June 1987, Lab. maj. 19,509)	
(Nov. 1988, SNP maj. 3,554)	

GLASGOW HILLHEAD (Strathclyde)
E.57,223　*T*.68.80%

*G. Galloway, *Lab.*	15,148
C. Mason, *LD*	10,322
Ms A. Bates, *C.*	6,728
Miss S. White, *SNP*	6,484
Ms L. Collie, *Green*	558
Ms H. Gold, *Rev. Comm.*	73

D. Patterson, *NLP*	60
Lab. majority	4,826
(June 1987, Lab. maj. 3,251)	

GLASGOW MARYHILL (Strathclyde)
E.48,426　*T*.65.16%

*Mrs M. Fyfe, *Lab.*	19,452
C. Williamson, *SNP*	6,033
J. Godfrey, *C.*	3,248
J. Alexander, *LD*	2,215
P. O'Brien, *Green*	530
M. Henderson, *NLP*	78
Lab. majority	13,419
(June 1987, Lab. maj. 19,364)	

GLASGOW POLLOK (Strathclyde)
E.46,139　*T*.70.74%

*J. Dunnachie, *Lab.*	14,170
T. Sheridan, *SML*	6,287
R. Gray, *C.*	5,147
G. Leslie, *SNP*	5,107
D. Jago, *LD*	1,932
Lab. majority	7,883
(June 1987, Lab. maj. 17,983)	

GLASGOW PROVAN (Strathclyde)
E.36,560　*T*.65.31%

*J. Wray, *Lab.*	15,885
Ms A. MacRae, *SNP*	5,182
A. Rosindell, *C.*	1,865
C. Bell, *LD*	948
Lab. majority	10,703
(June 1987, Lab. maj. 18,372)	

GLASGOW RUTHERGLEN
(Strathclyde)
E.52,709　*T*.75.23%

*T. McAvoy, *Lab.*	21,962
B. Cooklin, *C.*	6,692
J. Higgins, *SNP*	6,470
D. Baillie, *LD*	4,470
Ms B. Slaughter, *Int. Comm.*	62
Lab. majority	15,270
(June 1987, Lab. maj. 13,995)	

GLASGOW SHETTLESTON
(Strathclyde)
E.51,910　*T*.68.91%

*D. Marshall, *Lab.*	21,665
Ms N. Sturgeon, *SNP*	6,831
N. Mortimer, *C.*	5,396
Ms J. Orskov, *LD*	1,881
Lab. majority	14,834
(June 1987, Lab. maj. 18,981)	

GLASGOW SPRINGBURN
(Strathclyde)
E.45,842　*T*.65.65%

*M. Martin, *Lab.*	20,369
S. Miller, *SNP*	5,863
A. Barnett, *C.*	2,625
R. Ackland, *LD*	1,242
Lab. majority	14,506
(June 1987, Lab. maj. 22,063)	

GORDON (Grampian)
E.80,103　*T*.73.86%

*M. Bruce, *LD*	22,158
J. Porter, *C.*	21,884
B. Adam, *SNP*	8,445
P. Morrell, *Lab.*	6,682
LD majority	274
(June 1987, L./All. maj. 9,519)	

GREENOCK AND PORT GLASGOW
(Strathclyde)
E.52,053   T.73.72%
*N. Godman, *Lab.*	22,258
I. Black, *SNP*	7,279
Dr J. McCullough, *C.*	4,479
C. Lambert, *LD*	4,359
Lab. majority	14,979
(June 1987, Lab. maj. 20,055)

HAMILTON (Strathclyde)
E.61,531   T.76.15%
*G. Robertson, *Lab.*	25,849
W. Morrison, *SNP*	9,246
Ms M. Mitchell, *C.*	8,250
J. Oswald, *LD*	3,515
Lab. majority	16,603
(June 1987, Lab. maj. 21,662)

INVERNESS NAIRN AND LOCHABER
(Highland)
E.69,468   T.73.27%
*Sir R. Johnston, *LD*	13,258
D. Stewart, *Lab.*	12,800
F. Ewing, *SNP*	12,562
J. Scott, *C.*	11,517
J. Martin, *Green*	766
LD majority	458
(June 1987, L./All maj. 5,431)

KILMARNOCK AND LOUDOUN
(Strathclyde)
E.62,002   T.79.99%
*W. McKelvey, *Lab.*	22,210
A. Neil, *SNP*	15,231
R. Wilkinson, *C.*	9,438
Mrs K. Philbrick, *LD*	2,722
Lab. majority	6,979
(June 1987, Lab. maj. 14,127)

KINCARDINE AND DEESIDE
(Grampian)
E.66,617   T.78.74%
G. Kynoch, *C.*	22,924
*N. Stephen, *LD*	18,429
Dr A. Macartney, *SNP*	5,927
M. Savidge, *Lab.*	4,795
S. Campbell, *Green*	381
C. majority	4,495
(June 1987, C. maj. 2,063)
(Nov. 1991, LD maj. 7,824)

KIRKCALDY (Fife)
E.51,762   T.75.06%
*Dr L. Moonie, *Lab.*	17,887
S. Hosie, *SNP*	8,761
S. Wosley, *C.*	8,476
Ms S. Leslie, *LD*	3,729
Lab. majority	9,126
(June 1987, Lab. maj. 11,570)

LINLITHGOW (Lothian)
E.61,082   T.78.66%
*T. Dalyell, *Lab.*	21,603
K. MacAskill, *SNP*	14,577
Ms E. Forbes, *C.*	8,424
M. Falchikov, *LD*	3,446
Lab. majority	7,026
(June 1987, Lab. maj. 10,373)

LIVINGSTON (Lothian)
E.61,092   T.74.62%
*R. Cook, *Lab.*	20,245
P. Johnston, *SNP*	12,140
H. Gordon, *C.*	8,824
F. Mackintosh, *LD*	3,911
A. Ross-Smith, *Green*	469
Lab. majority	8,105
(June 1987, Lab. maj. 11,105)

MIDLOTHIAN
E.60,255   T.77.87%
E. Clarke, *Lab.*	20,588
A. Lumsden, *SNP*	10,254
J. Stoddart, *C.*	9,443
P. Sewell, *LD*	6,164
I. Morrice, *Green*	476
Lab. majority	10,334
(June 1987, Lab. maj. 12,253)

MONKLANDS EAST (Strathclyde)
E.48,391   T.75.07%
*Rt. Hon. J. Smith, *Lab.*	22,266
J. Wright, *SNP*	6,554
S. Walters, *C.*	5,830
P. Ross, *LD*	1,679
Lab. majority	15,712
(June 1987, Lab. maj. 16,389)
See also page 238

MONKLANDS WEST (Strathclyde)
E.49,269   T.77.45%
*T. Clarke, *Lab.*	23,384
K. Bovey, *SNP*	6,319
A. Lownie, *C.*	6,074
Ms S. Hamilton, *LD*	2,382
Lab. majority	17,065
(June 1987, Lab. maj. 18,333)

MORAY (Grampian)
E.63,255   T.72.46%
*Mrs M. Ewing, *SNP*	20,299
Ms R. Hossack, *C.*	17,455
C. Smith, *Lab.*	5,448
B. Sheridan, *LD*	2,634
SNP majority	2,844
(June 1987, SNP maj. 3,685)

MOTHERWELL NORTH
(Strathclyde)
E.57,290   T.76.71%
*Dr J. Reid, *Lab.*	27,852
D. Clark, *SNP*	8,942
R. Hargrave, *C.*	5,011
Miss H. Smith, *LD*	2,145
Lab. majority	18,910
(June 1987, Lab. maj. 23,595)

MOTHERWELL SOUTH
(Strathclyde)
E.50,042   T.76.17%
*J. Bray, *Lab.*	21,771
Mrs K. Ullrich, *SNP*	7,758
G. McIntosh, *C.*	6,097
A. Mackie, *LD*	2,349
D. Lettice, *YSOR*	146
Lab. majority	14,013
(June 1987, Lab. maj. 16,930)

ORKNEY AND SHETLAND
E.31,472   T.65.53%
| *J. Wallace, *LD* | 9,575 |
| Dr P. McCormick, *C.* | 4,542 |

J. Aberdein, *Lab.*	4,093
Mrs F. McKie, *SNP*	2,301
Ms C. Wharton, *NLP*	115
LD majority	5,033
(June 1987, L./All. maj. 3,922)

PAISLEY NORTH (Strathclyde)
E.46,403   T.73.39%
*Mrs I. Adams, *Lab.*	17,269
R. Mullin, *SNP*	7,940
D. Sharpe, *C.*	5,576
Miss E. McCartin, *LD*	2,779
D. Mellor, *Green*	412
N. Brennan, *NLP*	81
Lab. majority	9,329
(June 1987, Lab. maj. 14,442)
(Nov. 1990, Lab. maj. 3,770)

PAISLEY SOUTH (Strathclyde)
E.47,889   T.75.01%
*G. McMaster, *Lab.*	18,202
I. Lawson, *SNP*	8,653
Ms S. Laidlaw, *C.*	5,703
A. Reid, *LD*	3,271
S. Porter, *NLP*	93
Lab. majority	9,549
(June 1987, Lab. maj. 15,785)
(Nov. 1990, Lab. maj. 5,030)

PERTH AND KINROSS (Tayside)
E.65,410   T.76.86%
*Sir N. Fairbairn, *C.*	20,195
Ms R. Cunningham, *SNP*	18,101
M. Rolfe, *Lab.*	6,267
M. Black, *LD*	5,714
C. majority	2,094
(June 1987, C. maj. 5,676)
See also page 238

RENFREW WEST AND INVERCLYDE
(Strathclyde)
E.58,122   T.80.32%
*T. Graham, *Lab.*	17,085
Ms A. Goldie, *C.*	15,341
C. Campbell, *SNP*	9,444
S. Nimmo, *LD*	4,668
D. Maltman, *NLP*	149
Lab. majority	1,744
(June 1987, Lab. maj. 4,063)

ROSS, CROMARTY AND SKYE
(Highland)
E.55,524   T.73.90%
*C. Kennedy, *LD*	17,066
J. Gray, *C.*	9,436
R. Gibson, *SNP*	7,618
J. MacDonald, *Lab.*	6,275
D. Jardine, *Green*	642
LD majority	7,630
(June 1987, SDP/All. maj. 11,319)

ROXBURGH AND BERWICKSHIRE
(Borders)
E.43,485   T.77.71%
*A. Kirkwood, *LD*	15,852
S. Finlay-Maxwell, *C.*	11,595
M. Douglas, *SNP*	3,437
S. Lambert, *Lab.*	2,909
LD majority	4,257
(June 1987, L./All maj. 4,008)

STIRLING (Central)
E.58,266　T.82.29%
*M. Forsyth, *C.*	19,174
Ms K. Phillips, *Lab.*	18,471
G. Fisher, *SNP*	6,558
W. Robertson, *LD*	3,337
W. Thomson, *Green*	342
R. Sharp, *Loony*	68
C. majority	703

(June 1987, C. maj. 548)

STRATHKELVIN AND BEARSDEN
(Strathclyde)
E.61,116　T.82.33%
*S. Galbraith, *Lab.*	21,267
M. Hirst, *C.*	18,105
T. Chalmers, *SNP*	6,275

Ms B. Waterfield, *LD*	4,585
D. Whitley, *NLP*	90
Lab. majority	3,162

(June 1987, Lab. maj. 2,452)

TAYSIDE NORTH
E.55,969　T.77.64%
*W. Walker, *C.*	20,283
J. Swinney, *SNP*	16,288
S. Horner, *LD*	3,791
S. Maclennan, *Lab.*	3,094
C. majority	3,995

(June 1987, C. maj. 5,016)

TWEEDDALE, ETTRICK AND
LAUDERDALE (Borders)
E.39,493　T.78.04%
*Rt. Hon. Sir D. Steel, *LD*	12,296

L. Beat, *C.*	9,776
Mrs C. Creech, *SNP*	5,244
A. Dunton, *Lab.*	3,328
J. Hein, *Lib.*	177
LD majority	2,520

(June 1987, L./All. maj. 5,942)

WESTERN ISLES
E.22,784　T.70.35%
*C. MacDonald, *Lab.*	7,664
Ms F. MacFarlane, *SNP*	5,961
R. Heany, *C.*	1,362
N. Mitchison, *LD*	552
A. Price, *Ind.*	491
Lab. majority	1,703

(June 1987, Lab. maj. 2,340)

NORTHERN IRELAND

ANTRIM EAST
E.62,839　T.62.46%
*R. Beggs, *UUP*	16,966
N. Dodds, *DUP*	9,544
S. Neeson, *All.*	9,132
Miss M. Boal, *C.*	3,359
Ms A. Palmer, *NLP*	250
UUP majority	7,422

(June 1987, UUP maj. 15,360)

ANTRIM NORTH
E.69,124　T.65.82%
*Revd I. Paisley, *DUP*	23,152
J. Gaston, *UUP*	8,216
S. Farren, *SDLP*	6,512
G. Williams, *All.*	3,442
R. Sowler, *C.*	2,263
J. McGarry, *SF*	1,916
DUP majority	14,936

(June 1987, DUP maj. 23,234)

ANTRIM SOUTH
E.68,013　T.62.10%
*C. Forsythe, *UUP*	29,956
D. McClelland, *SDLP*	5,397
J. Blair, *All.*	5,224
H. Cushinan, *SF*	1,220
D. Martin, *Loony G.*	442
UUP majority	24,559

(June 1987, UUP maj. 19,587)

BELFAST EAST
E.52,833　T.67.74%
*P. Robinson, *DUP*	18,437
Dr J. Alderdice, *All.*	10,650
D. Greene, *C.*	3,314
Ms D. Dunlop, *Ind. U.*	2,256
J. O'Donnell, *SF*	679
J. Bell, *WP*	327
G. Redden, *NLP*	128
DUP majority	7,787

(June 1987, DUP maj. 9,798)

BELFAST NORTH
E.55,062　T.65.22%
*A. C. Walker, *UUP*	17,240
A. Maginness, *SDLP*	7,615
P. McManus, *SF*	4,693
T. Campbell, *All.*	2,246
Ms M. Redpath, *C.*	2,107

S. Lynch, *NA*	1,386
Ms M. Smith, *WP*	419
D. O'Leary, *NLP*	208
UUP majority	9,625

(June 1987, UUP maj. 8,560)

BELFAST SOUTH
E.52,032　T.64.54%
*Revd W. M. Smyth, *UUP*	16,336
Dr A. McDonnell, *SDLP*	6,266
J. Montgomery, *All.*	5,054
L. Fee, *C.*	3,356
S. Hayes, *SF*	1,123
P. Hadden, *LTU*	875
P. Lynn, *WP*	362
Ms T. Mullan, *NLP*	212
UUP majority	10,070

(June 1987, UUP maj. 11,954)

BELFAST WEST
E.54,609　T.73.19%
Dr J. Hendron, *SDLP*	17,415
*G. Adams, *SF*	16,826
F. Cobain, *UUP*	4,766
J. Lowry, *WP*	750
M. Kennedy, *NLP*	213
SDLP majority	589

(June 1987, SF maj. 2,221)

DOWN NORTH
E.68,662　T.65.47%
*J. Kilfedder, *UPUP*	19,305
Dr L. Kennedy, *C.*	14,371
Ms A. Morrow, *All.*	6,611
D. Vitty, *DUP*	4,414
A. Wilmot, *NLP*	255
UPUP majority	4,934

(June 1987, UPUP maj. 3,953)
See also page 238

DOWN SOUTH
E.76,093　T.80.92%
*E. McGrady, *SDLP*	31,523
D. Nelson, *UUP*	25,181
S. Fitzpatrick, *SF*	1,843
M. Healey, *All.*	1,542
Mrs S. McKenzie-Hill, *C.*	1,488
SDLP majority	6,342

(June 1987, SDLP maj. 731)

FERMANAGH AND SOUTH TYRONE
E.70,192　T.78.53%
*K. Maginnis, *UUP*	26,923
T. Gallagher, *SDLP*	12,810
F. Molloy, *SF*	12,604
D. Kettyles, *Prog. Soc.*	1,094
E. Bullick, *All.*	950
G. Cullen, *NA*	747
UUP majority	14,113

(June 1987, UUP maj. 12,823)

FOYLE
E.74,585　T.69.57%
*J. Hume, *SDLP*	26,710
G. Campbell, *DUP*	13,705
M. McGuinness, *SF*	9,149
Ms L. McIlroy, *All.*	1,390
G. McKenzie, *WP*	514
J. Burns, *NLP*	422
SDLP majority	13,005

(June 1987, SDLP maj. 9,860)

LAGAN VALLEY
E.72,645　T.67.39%
*Rt. Hon. J. H. Molyneaux, *UUP*	29,772
S. Close, *All.*	6,207
H. Lewsley, *SDLP*	4,626
T. Coleridge, *C.*	4,423
P. Rice, *SF*	3,346
Ms A.-M. Lowry, *WP*	582
UUP majority	23,565

(June 1987, UUP maj. 23,373)

LONDONDERRY EAST
E.75,559　T.69.79%
*W. Ross, *UUP*	30,370
A. Doherty, *SDLP*	11,843
Ms P. Davey-Kennedy, *SF*	5,320
P. McGowan, *All.*	3,613
A. Elder, *C.*	1,589
UUP majority	18,527

(June 1987, UUP maj. 20,157)

NEWRY AND ARMAGH
E.67,508　T.77.87%
*S. Mallon, *SDLP*	26,073
J. Speers, *UUP*	18,982
B. Curran, *SF*	6,547
Mrs E. Bell, *All.*	972

SDLP majority	7,091			

SDLP majority 7,091
(June 1987, SDLP maj. 5,325)

STRANGFORD
*E.*68,870   *T.*65.02%
*Rt. Hon. J. Taylor, *UUP*   19,517
S. Wilson, *DUP*   10,606
K. McCarthy, *All.*   7,585
S. Eyre, *C.*   6,782
D. Shaw, *NLP*   295
UUP majority   8,911
(June 1987, UUP maj. 20,646)

ULSTER MID
*E.*69,071   *T.*79.28%
*Revd Dr R. T. W. McCrea, *DUP*   23,181
D. Haughey, *SDLP*   16,994
B. McElduff, *SF*   10,248
J. McLoughlin, *Ind.*   1,996
Ms A. Gormley, *All.*   1,506
H. Hutchinson, *LTU*   389
T. Owens, *WP*   285
J. Anderson, *NLP*   164
DUP majority   6,187
(June 1987, DUP maj. 9,360)

UPPER BANN
*E.*67,446   *T.*67.43%
*W. D. Trimble, *UUP*   26,824
Mrs B. Rodgers, *SDLP*   10,661
B. Curran, *SF*   2,777
Dr W. Ramsey, *All.*   2,541
Mrs C. Jones, *C.*   1,556
T. French, *WP*   1,120
UUP majority   16,163
(June 1987, OUP maj. 17,361)
(May 1990, OUP maj. 13,849)

COMMONWEALTH PARLIAMENTARY ASSOCIATION (1911)

The Commonwealth Parliamentary Association consists of 126 branches in the national, state, provincial or territorial parliaments in the countries of the Commonwealth. Conferences and general assemblies are held every year in different countries of the Commonwealth.
President (1994–5), Hon. K. B. Ratnayake, MP, Speaker of the Parliament, Sri Lanka
Vice-President (1994–5), Y. B. Tan Sri Dato' Mohamed Zahir Haji Ismail, MP, Speaker of the House of Representatives, Malaysia
Chairman of the Executive Committee (1993–), Colin Shepherd, MP (United Kingdom)
Secretary-General, A. R. Donahoe, QC, Suite 700, Westminster House, 7 Millbank, London SW1P 3JA

UNITED KINGDOM BRANCH
Hon. Presidents, The Lord Chancellor; Madam Speaker
Chairman of Branch, The Rt. Hon. John Major, MP

Chairman of Executive Committee, Sir Ivan Lawrence, QC, MP
Secretary, P. Cobb, OBE, Westminster Hall, Houses of Parliament, London, SW1A 0AA

THE INTER-PARLIAMENTARY UNION (1889)

To facilitate personal contact between members of all Parliaments in the promotion of representative institutions, peace and international co-operation.
Secretary-General, P. Cornillon, Place du Petit-Saconnex. BP 99, 1211 Geneva 19, Switzerland

BRITISH GROUP
Palace of Westminster, London SW1A 0AA

Hon. Presidents, The Lord Chancellor; Madam Speaker
President, The Rt. Hon. John Major, MP
Chairman, Dame Jill Knight, DBE, MP
Secretary, D. Ramsay

European Parliament

European Parliament elections take place at five-yearly intervals. In mainland Britain MEPs are elected in all constituencies on a first-past-the-post basis; in Northern Ireland three MEPs are elected by proportional representation. From 1979 to 1994 the number of seats held by the UK in the European Parliament was 81. At the June 1994 election the number of seats increased to 87 (England 71, Wales 5, Scotland 8, Northern Ireland 3).

Since 1994, nationals of member states of the European Union have the right to vote in elections to the European Parliament in the UK. British subjects and citizens of the Irish Republic can stand in the UK for election to the European Parliament provided they are 21 or over and not subject to disqualification.

MEPs receive a salary from the parliaments or governments of their respective member states, set at the level of the national parliamentary salary and subject to national taxation rules (for salary of British MPs, *see* page 224).

UK MEMBERS AS AT END JULY 1995

*Denotes membership of the last European Parliament

*Adam, Gordon J., PH.D. (*b.* 1934), *Lab., Northumbria,* maj. 66,158

*Balfe, Richard A. (*b.* 1944), *Lab., London South Inner,* maj. 59,220

*Barton, Roger (*b.* 1945), *Lab., Sheffield,* maj. 50,288

Billingham, Mrs Angela T. (*b.* 1939), *Lab., Northamptonshire and Blaby,* maj. 26,085

*Bowe, David R. (*b.* 1955), *Lab., Cleveland and Richmond,* maj. 57,568

*Cassidy, Bryan M. D. (*b.* 1934), *C., Dorset and Devon East,* maj. 2,264

Chichester, Giles B. (*b.* 1946), *C., Devon and Plymouth East,* maj. 700

*Coates, Kenneth S. (*b.* 1930), *Lab., Nottinghamshire North and Chesterfield,* maj. 76,260

*Collins, Kenneth D. (*b.* 1939), *Lab., Strathclyde East,* maj. 52,340

Corrie, John A. (*b.* 1935), *C., Worcestershire and Warwickshire South,* maj. 1,204

*Crampton, Peter D. (*b.* 1932), *Lab., Humberside,* maj. 40,618

*Crawley, Mrs Christine M. (*b.* 1950), *Lab., Birmingham East,* maj. 55,120

Cunningham, Thomas A. (Tony) (*b.* 1952), *Lab., Cumbria and Lancashire North,* maj. 22,988

*David, Wayne (*b.* 1957), *Lab., South Wales Central,* maj. 86,082

*Donnelly, Alan J. (*b.* 1957), *Lab., Tyne and Wear,* maj. 88,380

Donnelly, Brendan P. (*b.* 1950), *C., Sussex South and Crawley,* maj. 1,746

*Elles, James E. M. (*b.* 1949), *C., Buckinghamshire and Oxfordshire East,* maj. 30,665

*Elliott, Michael N. (*b.* 1932), *Lab., London West,* maj. 42,275

Evans, Robert J. E. (*b.* 1956), *Lab., London North West,* maj. 17,442

*Ewing, Mrs Winifred M. (*b.* 1929), *SNP, Highlands and Islands,* maj. 54,916

*Falconer, Alexander (*b.* 1940), *Lab., Scotland Mid and Fife,* maj. 31,413

*Ford, J. Glyn (*b.* 1950), *Lab., Greater Manchester East,* maj. 55,986

*Green, Mrs Pauline (*b.* 1948), *Lab., London North,* maj. 48,348

Hallam, David J. A. (*b.* 1948), *Lab., Herefordshire and Shropshire,* maj. 1,850

Hardstaff, Mrs Veronica M. (*b.* 1941), *Lab., Lincolnshire and Humberside South,* maj. 13,745

*Harrison, Lyndon H. A. (*b.* 1947), *Lab., Cheshire West and Wirral,* maj. 47,176

Hendrick, Mark P. (*b.* 1958), *Lab., Lancashire Central,* maj. 12,191

*Hindley, Michael J. (*b.* 1947), *Lab., Lancashire South,* maj. 41,404

Howitt, Richard (*b.* 1961), *Lab., Essex South,* maj. 21,367

*Hughes, Stephen S. (*b.* 1952), *Lab., Durham,* maj. 111,638

*Hume, John, MP (*b.* 1937), *SDLP, Northern Ireland,* polled 161,992 votes

*Jackson, Mrs Caroline F., D.PHIL. (*b.* 1946), *C., Wiltshire North and Bath,* maj. 8,787

*Kellett-Bowman, Edward T. (*b.* 1931), *C., Itchen, Test and Avon,* maj. 6,903

Kerr, Hugh (*b.* 1944), *Lab., Essex West and Hertfordshire East,* maj. 3,067

Kinnock, Mrs Glenys E. (*b.* 1944), *Lab., South Wales East,* maj. 120,247

*Lomas, Alfred (*b.* 1928), *Lab., London North East,* maj. 57,085

Macartney, W. J. Allan, PH.D. (*b.* 1941), *SNP, Scotland North East,* maj. 31,227

McCarthy, Ms Arlene (*b.* 1960), *Lab., Peak District,* maj. 49,307

*McGowan, Michael (*b.* 1940), *Lab., Leeds,* maj. 53,082

*McIntosh, Ms Anne C. B. (*b.* 1954), *C., Essex North and Suffolk South,* maj. 3,633

*McMahon, Hugh R. (*b.* 1938), *Lab., Strathclyde West,* maj. 25,023

*McMillan-Scott, Edward H. C. (*b.* 1949), *C., Yorkshire North,* maj. 7,072

McNally, Mrs Eryl M. (*b.* 1942), *Lab., Bedfordshire and Milton Keynes,* maj. 33,209

*Martin, David W. (*b.* 1954), *Lab., Lothians,* maj 37,207

Mather, Graham C. S. (*b.* 1954), *C., Hampshire North and Oxford,* maj. 9,194

*Megahy, Thomas (*b.* 1929), *Lab., Yorkshire South West,* maj. 59,562

Miller, Bill (*b.* 1954), *Lab., Glasgow,* maj. 43,158

*Moorhouse, C. James O. (*b.* 1924), *C., London South and Surrey East,* maj. 8,739

Morgan, Ms Eluned (*b.* 1967), *Lab., Wales Mid and West,* maj. 29,234

*Morris, Revd David R. (*b.* 1930), *Lab., South Wales West,* maj. 84,970

Murphy, Simon F., PH.D. (*b.* 1962), *Lab., Midlands West,* maj. 54,823

Needle, Clive (*b.* 1956), *Lab., Norfolk,* maj. 26,287

*Newens, A. Stanley (*b.* 1930), *Lab., London Central,* maj. 25,059

*Newman, Edward (*b.* 1953), *Lab., Greater Manchester Central,* maj. 42,445

*Nicholson, James F. (*b.* 1945), *UUUP, Northern Ireland,* polled 133,459 votes

*Oddy, Ms Christine M. (*b.* 1955), *Lab., Coventry and Warwickshire North,* maj. 43,901

*Paisley, Revd Ian R. K., MP (*b.* 1926), *DUP, Northern Ireland,* polled 163,246 votes

Perry, Roy J. (*b.* 1943), *C., Wight and Hampshire South,* maj. 5,101

*Plumb, The Lord (*b.* 1925), *C., Cotswolds,* maj. 4,268
*Pollack, Ms Anita J. (*b.* 1946), *Lab., London South West,* maj. 30,975
Provan, James L. C. (*b.* 1936), *C., South Downs West,* maj. 21,067
*Read, Ms I. M. (Mel) (*b.* 1939), *Lab., Nottingham and Leicestershire North West,* maj. 39,668
*Seal, Barry H., PH.D. (*b.* 1937), *Lab., Yorkshire West,* maj. 48,197
*Simpson, Brian (*b.* 1953), *Lab., Cheshire East,* maj. 39,279
Skinner, Peter W. (*b.* 1959), *Lab., Kent West,* maj. 16,777
*Smith, Alexander (*b.* 1943), *Lab., Scotland South,* maj. 45,155
*Spencer, Thomas N. B. (*b.* 1948), *C., Surrey,* maj. 27,018
Spiers, Shaun M. (*b.* 1962), *Lab., London South East,* maj. 8,022
*Stevens, John C. C. (*b.* 1955), *C., Thames Valley,* maj. 758
*Stewart, Kenneth A. (*b.* 1925), *Lab., Merseyside West,* maj. 51,811
*Stewart-Clark, Sir John, Bt. (*b.* 1929), *C., Sussex East and Kent South,* maj. 6,212
Sturdy, Robert W. (*b.* 1944), *C., Cambridgeshire,* maj. 3,942
Tappin, Michael (*b.* 1946), *Lab., Staffordshire West and Congleton,* maj. 40,277

Teverson, Robin (*b.* 1952), *LD, Cornwall and Plymouth West,* maj. 29,498
Thomas, David E. (*b.* 1955), *Lab., Suffolk and Norfolk South West,* maj. 12,535
*Titley, Gary (*b.* 1950), *Lab., Greater Manchester West,* maj. 58,635
*Tomlinson, John E. (*b.* 1939), *Lab., Birmingham West,* maj. 39,350
*Tongue, Ms Carole (*b.* 1955), *Lab., London East,* maj. 57,389
Truscott, Peter, PH.D. (*b.* 1959), *Lab., Hertfordshire,* maj. 10,304
Waddington, Mrs Susan A. (*b.* 1944), *Lab., Leicester,* maj. 20,284
Watson, Graham R. (*b.* 1956), *LD, Somerset and Devon North,* maj. 22,509
Watts, Mark F. (*b.* 1964), *Lab., Kent East,* maj. 635
*West, Norman, (*b.* 1935), *Lab., Yorkshire South,* maj. 88,309
*White, Ian (*b.* 1947), *Lab., Bristol,* maj. 29,955
Whitehead, Phillip (*b.* 1937), *Lab., Staffordshire East and Derby,* maj. 72,196
*Wilson, A. Joseph (*b.* 1937), *Lab., Wales North,* maj. 15,242
*Wynn, Terence (*b.* 1946), *Lab., Merseyside East and Wigan,* maj. 74,087

UK CONSTITUENCIES AS AT 9 JUNE 1994

Abbreviations	
Anti Fed.	UK Independence Anti-Federal
Anti Fed. C.	Official Anti-Federalist Conservative
Beanus	Eurobean from Planet Beanus
C. Non Fed.	Conservative Non-Federal Party
Capital P.	Restoration of Capital Punishment
Comm.	Communist
Comm. YBG	Communist Y Blaid Gomiwyddol
Const. NI	Constitutional Independence for N. Ireland
Corr.	Corrective Party
CPP	Christian People's Party
ICP	International Communist Party
ICP4	International Communist Party (4th International)
Ind. AES	Independent Anti-European Superstate
Ind. Out	Independent Out of Europe
Judo	European People's Party Judo Christian Alliance
Loony C	Raving Loony Commonsense
Loony CP	Monster Raving Loony Christian Party
Loony X	Monster Raving Loony Project X Party
MCCARTHY	Make Criminals Concerned About Our Response To Hostility and Yobbishness
MK	Mebyon Kernow
NCSA	Network Against Child Support Agency
Neeps	North East Ethnic Party, The Neeps
Rainbow	Rainbow Connection – Oui-Say-Non-Party
Sportsman	Sportsman Anti-Common Market Bureaucracy
UUUP	United Ulster Unionist Party
For other abbreviations, *see* page 241	

ENGLAND

BEDFORDSHIRE AND MILTON KEYNES
E. 525,524   *T.* 38.74%
E. McNally, *Lab.*   94,837
Mrs E. Currie, *C.*   61,628
Ms M. Howes, *LD*   27,994
A. Sked, *UK Independence*   7,485
A. Francis, *Green*   6,804
A. Howes, *New Britain*   3,878
L. Sheaff, *NLP*   939
Lab. majority   33,209
(Boundary change since June 1989)

BIRMINGHAM EAST
E. 520,782   *T.* 29.77%
*Mrs C. Crawley, *Lab.*   90,291
A. Turner, *C.*   35,171
Ms C. Cane, *LD*   19,455
P. Simpson, *Green*   6,268
R. Cook, *Soc.*   1,969
M. Brierley, *NLP*   1,885
Lab. majority   55,120
(June 1989, Lab. maj. 46,948)

BIRMINGHAM WEST
E. 509,948   *T.* 28.49%
*J. Tomlinson, *Lab.*   77,957
D. Harman, *C.*   38,607
N. McGeorge, *LD*   14,603
Dr B. Juby, *Anti Fed.*   5,237
M. Abbott, *Green*   4,367
A. Carmichael, *NF*   3,727
H. Meads, *NLP*   789
Lab. majority   39,350
(June 1989, Lab. maj. 30,860)

BRISTOL
E. 503,218   *T.* 40.91%
*I. White, *Lab.*   90,790
The Earl of Stockton, *C.*   60,835
J. Barnard, *LD*   40,394

J. Boxall, *Green*   7,163
T. Whittingham, *UK Independence*   5,798
T. Dyball, *NLP*   876
Lab. majority   29,955
(Boundary change since June 1989)

BUCKINGHAMSHIRE AND OXFORDSHIRE EAST
E. 487,692   *T.* 37.31%
*J. Elles, *C.*   77,037
D. Enright, *Lab.*   46,372
Ms S. Bowles, *LD*   42,836
L. Roach, *Green*   8,433
Ms A. Micklem, *Lib.*   5,111
Dr G. Clements, *NLP*   2,156
C. majority   30,665
(Boundary change since June 1989)

CAMBRIDGESHIRE
E. 495,383   *T.* 35.91%
R. Sturdy, *C.*   66,921
Ms M. Johnson, *Lab.*   62,979
A. Duff, *LD*   36,114
Ms M. Wright, *Green*   5,756
P. Wiggin, *Lib.*   4,051
F. Chalmers, *NLP*   2,077
C. majority   3,942
(Boundary change since June 1989)

CHESHIRE EAST
E. 502,726   *T.* 32.46%
*B. Simpson, *Lab.*   87,586
P. Slater, *C.*   48,307
P. Harris, *LD*   20,552
D. Wild, *Green*   3,671
P. Dixon, *Loony CP*   1,600
P. Leadbetter, *NLP*   1,488
Lab. majority   39,279
(Boundary change since June 1989)

CHESHIRE WEST AND WIRRAL
E. 538,571 *T.* 36.78%

*L. Harrison, *Lab.*	106,160
D. Senior, *C.*	58,984
I. Mottershaw, *LD*	20,746
D. Carson, *British Home Rule*	6,167
M. Money, *Green*	5,096
A. Wilmot, *NLP*	929
Lab. majority	47,176

(Boundary change since June 1989)

CLEVELAND AND RICHMOND
E. 499,580 *T.* 35.26%

*D. Bowe, *Lab.*	103,355
R. Goodwill, *C.*	45,787
B. Moore, *LD*	21,574
G. Parr, *Green*	4,375
R. Scott, *NLP*	1,068
Lab. majority	57,568

(Boundary change since June 1989)

CORNWALL AND PLYMOUTH WEST
E. 484,697 *T.* 44.92%

R. Teverson, *LD*	91,113
*C. Beazley, *C.*	61,615
Mrs D. Kirk, *Lab.*	42,907
Mrs P. Garnier, *UK Independence*	
	6,466
P. Holmes, *Lib.*	6,414
Ms K. Westbrook, *Green*	4,372
Dr L. Jenkin, *MK*	3,315
F. Lyons, *NLP*	921
M. Fitzgerald, *Subsidiarity*	606
LD majority	29,498

(Boundary change since June 1989)

COTSWOLDS
E. 497,588 *T.* 39.27%

*The Lord Plumb, *C.*	67,484
Ms T. Kingham, *Lab.*	63,216
J. Thomson, *LD*	44,269
M. Rendell, *New Britain*	11,044
D. McCanlis, *Green*	8,254
H. Brighouse, *NLP*	1,151
C. majority	4,268

(Boundary change since June 1989)

COVENTRY AND WARWICKSHIRE NORTH
E. 523,448 *T.* 32.54%

*Ms C. Oddy, *Lab.*	89,500
Ms J. Crabb, *C.*	45,599
G. Sewards, *LD*	17,453
R. Meacham, *Free Trade*	9,432
P. Baptie, *Green*	4,360
R. Wheway, *Lib.*	2,885
R. France, *NLP*	1,098
Lab. majority	43,901

(Boundary change since June 1989)

CUMBRIA AND LANCASHIRE NORTH
E. 498,557 *T.* 40.78%

A. Cunningham, *Lab.*	97,599
*The Lord Inglewood, *C.*	74,611
R. Putnam, *LD*	24,233
R. Frost, *Green*	5,344
I. Docker, *NLP*	1,500
Lab. majority	22,988

(Boundary change since June 1989)

DEVON AND PLYMOUTH EAST
E. 524,320 *T.* 45.07%

G. Chichester, *C.*	74,953
A. Sanders, *LD*	74,253
Ms L. Gilroy, *Lab.*	47,596
D. Morrish, *Lib.*	14,621
P. Edwards, *Green*	11,172
R. Huggett, *Literal Democrat*	10,203
J. Everard, *Ind.*	2,629
A. Pringle, *NLP*	908
C. majority	700

(Boundary change since June 1989)

DORSET AND DEVON EAST
E. 531,842 *T.* 41.21%

*B. Cassidy, *C.*	81,551
P. Goldenberg, *LD*	79,287
A. Gardner, *Lab.*	34,856
M. Floyd, *UK Independence*	10,548
Mrs K. Bradbury, *Green*	8,642
I. Mortimer, *C. Non-Fed.*	3,229
M. Griffiths, *NLP*	1,048
C. majority	2,264

(Boundary change since June 1989)

DURHAM
E. 532,051 *T.* 35.62%

*S. Hughes, *Lab.*	136,671
P. Bradbourn, *C.*	25,033
Dr N. Martin, *LD*	20,935
S. Hope, *Green*	5,670
C. Adamson, *NLP*	1,198
Lab. majority	111,638

(June 1989, Lab. maj. 86,848)

ESSEX NORTH AND SUFFOLK SOUTH
E. 497,098 *T.* 41.33%

*Ms A. McIntosh, *C.*	68,311
C. Pearson, *Lab.*	64,678
S. Mole, *LD*	52,536
S. de Chair, *Ind. AES*	12,409
J. Abbott, *Green*	6,641
N. Pullen, *NLP*	884
C. majority	3,633

(Boundary change since June 1989)

ESSEX SOUTH
E. 487,221 *T.* 33.08%

R. Howitt, *Lab.*	71,883
L. Stanbrook, *C.*	50,516
G. Williams, *LD*	26,132
B. Lynch, *Lib.*	6,780
G. Rumens, *Green*	4,691
M. Heath, *NLP*	1,177
Lab. majority	21,367

(Boundary change since June 1989)

ESSEX WEST AND HERTFORDSHIRE EAST
E. 504,095 *T.* 36.39%

H. Kerr, *Lab.*	66,379
*Ms P. Rawlings, *C.*	63,312
Ms G. James, *LD*	35,695
B. Smalley, *Britain*	10,277
Ms F. Mawson, *Green*	5,632
P. Carter, *Sportsman*	1,127
L. Davis, *NLP*	1,026
Lab. majority	3,067

(Boundary change since June 1989)

GREATER MANCHESTER CENTRAL
E. 481,779 *T.* 29.11%

*E. Newman, *Lab.*	74,935
Mrs S. Mason, *C.*	32,490
J. Begg, *LD*	22,988
B. Candeland, *Green*	4,952
P. Burke, *Lib.*	3,862
P. Stanley, *NLP*	1,017
Lab. majority	42,445

(Boundary change since June 1989)

GREATER MANCHESTER EAST
E. 501,125 *T.* 27.17%

*G. Ford, *Lab.*	82,289
J. Pinniger, *C.*	26,303
A. Riley, *LD*	20,545
T. Clarke, *Green*	5,823
W. Stevens, *NLP*	1,183
Lab. majority	55,986

(Boundary change since June 1989)

GREATER MANCHESTER WEST
E. 512,618 *T.* 29.70%

*G. Titley, *Lab.*	94,129
D. Newns, *C.*	35,494
F. Harasiwka, *LD*	13,650
R. Jackson, *Green*	3,950
G. Harrison, *MCCARTHY*	3,693
T. Brotheridge, *NLP*	1,316
Lab. majority	58,635

(Boundary change since June 1989)

HAMPSHIRE NORTH AND OXFORD
E. 525,982 *T.* 38.31%

G. Mather, *C.*	72,209
Ms J. Hawkins, *LD*	63,015
J. Tanner, *Lab.*	48,525
D. Wilkinson, *UK Independence*	8,377
Dr M. Woodin, *Green*	7,310
H. Godfrey, *NLP*	1,027
R. Boston, *Boston Tea Party*	1,018
C. majority	9,194

(Boundary change since June 1989)

HEREFORDSHIRE AND SHROPSHIRE
E. 536,470 *T.* 38.69%

D. Hallam, *Lab.*	76,120
*Sir C. Prout, *C.*	74,270
J. Gallagher, *LD*	44,130
Ms F. Norman, *Green*	11,578
T. Mercer, *NLP*	1,480
Lab. majority	1,850

(Boundary change since June 1989)

HERTFORDSHIRE
E. 522,338 *T.* 40.11%

Dr P. Truscott, *Lab.*	81,821
P. Jenkinson, *C.*	71,517
D. Griffiths, *LD*	38,995
Ms L. Howitt, *Green*	7,741
M. Biggs, *New Britain*	6,555
J. McAuley, *NF*	1,755
D. Lucas, *NLP*	734
J. Laine, *Century*	369
Lab. majority	10,304

(Boundary change since June 1989)

HUMBERSIDE
E. 519,013 *T.* 32.38%

*P. Crampton, *Lab.*	87,296
D. Stewart, *C.*	46,678
Ms D. Wallis, *LD*	28,818
Ms S. Mummery, *Green*	4,170

Ms A. Miszewska, *NLP* 1,100
Lab. majority 40,618
(Boundary change since June 1989)

ITCHEN, TEST AND AVON
E. 550,406 *T.* 41.83%
*E. Kellett-Bowman, *C.* 81,456
A. Barron, *LD* 74,553
E. Read, *Lab.* 52,416
N. Farage, *UK Independence* 12,423
Ms F. Hulbert, *Green* 7,998
A. Miller-Smith, *NLP* 1,368
C. majority 6,903
(Boundary change since June 1989)

KENT EAST
E. 499,662 *T.* 40.34%
M. Watts, *Lab.* 69,641
*C. Jackson, *C.* 69,006
J. Macdonald, *LD* 44,549
C. Bullen, *UK Independence* 9,414
S. Dawe, *Green* 7,196
C. Beckley, *NLP* 1,746
Lab. majority 635
(Boundary change since June 1989)

KENT WEST
E. 505,658 *T.* 37.33%
P. Skinner, *Lab.* 77,346
*B. Patterson, *C.* 60,569
J. Daly, *LD* 33,869
C. Mackinlay, *UK Independence* 9,750
Ms P. Kemp, *Green* 5,651
J. Bowler, *NLP* 1,598
Lab. majority 16,777
(Boundary change since June 1989)

LANCASHIRE CENTRAL
E. 505,224 *T.* 33.23%
M. Hendrick, *Lab.* 73,420
*M. Welsh, *C.* 61,229
Ms J. Ross-Mills, *LD* 20,578
D. Hill, *Home Rule* 6,751
C. Maile, *Green* 4,169
Ms J. Ayliffe, *NLP* 1,727
Lab. majority 12,191
(Boundary change since June 1989)

LANCASHIRE SOUTH
E. 514,840 *T.* 33.14%
*M. Hindley, *Lab.* 92,598
R. Topham, *C.* 51,194
J. Ault, *LD* 17,008
J. Gaffney, *Green* 4,774
Mrs E. Rokas, *Ind.* 3,439
J. Renwick, *NLP* 1,605
Lab. majority 41,404
(Boundary change since June 1989)

LEEDS
E. 521,989 *T.* 30.03%
*M. McGowan, *Lab.* 89,160
N. Carmichael, *C.* 36,078
Ms J. Harvey, *LD* 17,575
M. Meadowcroft, *Lib.* 6,617
Ms C. Nash, *Green* 6,283
Ms S. Hayward, *NLP* 1,018
Lab. majority 53,082
(June 1989, Lab. maj. 42,518)

LEICESTER
E. 515,343 *T.* 37.63%
Ms S. Waddington, *Lab.* 87,048
A. Marshall, *C.* 66,764
M. Jones, *LD* 28,890
G. Forse, *Green* 8,941
Ms P. Saunders, *NLP* 2,283
Lab. majority 20,284
(Boundary change since June 1989)

LINCOLNSHIRE AND HUMBERSIDE
SOUTH
E. 539,981 *T.* 36.34%
Mrs V. Hardstaff, *Lab.* 83,172
*W. Newton Dunn, *C.* 69,427
K. Melton, *LD* 27,241
Ms R. Robinson, *Green* 8,563
E. Wheeler, *Lib.* 3,434
I. Selby, *NCSA* 2,973
H. Kelly, *NLP* 1,429
Lab. majority 13,745
(Boundary change since June 1989)

LONDON CENTRAL
E. 494,610 *T.* 32.57%
*S. Newens, *Lab.* 75,711
A. Elliott, *C.* 50,652
Ms S. Ludford, *LD* 20,176
Ms N. Kortvelyessy, *Green* 7,043
H. Le Fanu, *UK Independence* 4,157
C. Slapper, *Soc.* 1,593
Ms S. Hamza, *NLP* 1,215
G. Weiss, *Rainbow* 547
Lab. majority 25,059
(June 1989, Lab. maj. 11,542)

LONDON EAST
E. 511,523 *T.* 33.38%
*Ms C. Tongue, *Lab.* 98,759
Ms V. Taylor, *C.* 41,370
K. Montgomery, *LD* 15,566
G. Batten, *UK Independence* 5,974
J. Baguley, *Green* 4,337
O. Tillett, *Third Way Independence* 3,484
N. Kahn, *NLP* 1,272
Lab. majority 57,389
(June 1989, Lab. maj. 27,385)

LONDON NORTH
E. 541,269 *T.* 34.00%
*Mrs P. Green, *Lab.* 102,059
M. Keegan, *C.* 53,711
I. Mann, *LD* 15,739
Ms H. Jago, *Green* 5,666
I. Booth, *UK Independence* 5,099
G. Sabrizi, *Judo* 880
J. Hinde, *NLP* 856
Lab. majority 48,348
(June 1989, Lab. maj. 5,837)

LONDON NORTH EAST
E. 486,016 *T.* 26.60%
*A. Lomas, *Lab.* 80,256
S. Gordon, *C.* 23,171
K. Appiah, *LD* 10,242
Ms J. Lambert, *Green* 8,386
E. Murat, *Lib.* 2,573
P. Compobassi, *UK Independence* 2,015
R. Archer, *NLP* 1,111
M. Fischer, *Comm. GB* 869
A. Hyland, *ICP4* 679

Lab. majority 57,085
(June 1989, Lab. maj. 47,767)

LONDON NORTH WEST
E. 481,272 *T.* 35.13%
R. Evans, *Lab.* 80,192
*The Lord Bethell, *C.* 62,750
Ms H. Leighter, *LD* 18,998
D. Johnson, *Green* 4,743
Ms A. Murphy, *Comm. GB* 858
Ms T. Sullivan, *NLP* 807
C. Palmer, *Century* 740
Lab. majority 17,442
(June 1989, C. maj. 7,400)

LONDON SOUTH AND SURREY EAST
E. 486,358 *T.* 34.38%
*J. Moorhouse, *C.* 64,813
Ms G. Rolles, *Lab.* 56,074
M. Reinisch, *LD* 32,059
J. Cornford, *Green* 7,046
J. Major, *Loony X* 3,339
A. Reeve, *Capital P.* 2,983
P. Levy, *NLP* 887
C. majority 8,739
(Boundary change since June 1989)

LONDON SOUTH EAST
E. 493,178 *T.* 35.38%
S. Spiers, *Lab.* 71,505
*P. Price, *C.* 63,483
J. Fryer, *LD* 25,271
I. Mouland, *Green* 6,399
R. Almond, *Lib.* 3,881
K. Lowne, *NF* 2,926
J. Small, *NLP* 1,025
Lab. majority 8,022
(Boundary change since June 1989)

LONDON SOUTH INNER
E. 510,609 *T.* 27.30%
*R. Balfe, *Lab.* 85,079
A. Boff, *C.* 25,859
A. Graves, *LD* 20,708
S. Collins, *Green* 6,570
M. Leighton, *NLP* 1,179
Lab. majority 59,220
(Boundary change since June 1989)

LONDON SOUTH WEST
E. 479,246 *T.* 34.35%
*Ms A. Pollack, *Lab.* 81,850
Prof. P. Treleaven, *C.* 50,875
G. Blanchard, *LD* 18,697
T. Walsh, *Green* 5,460
A. Scholefield, *UK Independence* 4,912
C. Hopewell, *Capital P.* 1,840
M. Simson, *NLP* 625
J. Quanjer, *Spirit of Europe* 377
Lab. majority 30,975
(Boundary change since June 1989)

LONDON WEST
E. 505,791 *T.* 36.02%
*M. Elliott, *Lab.* 94,562
R. Guy, *C.* 52,287
W. Mallinson, *LD* 21,561
J. Bradley, *Green* 6,134
G. Roberts, *UK Independence* 4,583
W. Binding, *NF* 1,963
R. Johnson, *NLP* 1,105
Lab. majority 42,275
(June 1989, Lab. maj. 14,808)

MERSEYSIDE EAST AND WIGAN
E. 518,196   T. 24.66%

*T. Wynn, *Lab.*	91,986
C. Manson, *C.*	17,899
Ms F. Clucas, *LD*	8,874
J. Melia, *Lib.*	4,765
L. Brown, *Green*	3,280
G. Hutchard, *NLP*	1,009
Lab. majority	74,087

(June 1989, Lab. maj. 76,867)

MERSEYSIDE WEST
E. 515,909   T. 26.18%

*K. Stewart, *Lab.*	78,819
C. Varley, *C.*	27,008
D. Bamber, *LD*	19,097
S. Radford, *Lib.*	4,714
Ms L. Lever, *Green*	4,573
J. Collins, *NLP*	852
Lab. majority	51,811

(June 1989, Lab. maj. 49,817)

MIDLANDS WEST
E. 533,742   T. 31.28%

S. Murphy, *Lab.*	99,242
M. Simpson, *C.*	44,419
G. Baldauf-Good, *LD*	12,195
M. Hyde, *Lib.*	5,050
C. Mattingly, *Green*	4,390
J. Oldbury, *NLP*	1,641
Lab. majority	54,823

(June 1989, Lab. maj. 42,364)

NORFOLK
E. 513,553   T. 44.25%

C. Needle, *Lab.*	102,711
*P. Howell, *C.*	76,424
P. Burall, *LD*	39,107
A. Holmes, *Green*	7,938
B. Parsons, *NLP*	1,075
Lab. majority	26,287

(Boundary change since June 1989)

NORTHAMPTONSHIRE AND BLABY
E. 524,916   T. 39.37%

Mrs A. Billingham, *Lab.*	95,317
*A. Simpson, *C.*	69,232
K. Scudder, *LD*	27,616
Ms A. Bryant, *Green*	9,121
I. Whitaker, *Ind.*	4,397
B. Spivack, *NLP*	972
Lab. majority	26,085

(Boundary change since June 1989)

NORTHUMBRIA
E. 516,680   T. 33.65%

*G. Adam, *Lab.*	103,087
J. Flack, *C.*	36,929
L. Opik, *LD*	20,195
D. Lott, *UK Independence*	7,210
J. Hartshorne, *Green*	5,714
L. Walch, *NLP*	740
Lab. majority	66,158

(June 1989, Lab. maj. 60,040)

NOTTINGHAM AND LEICESTERSHIRE NORTH WEST
E. 507,915   T. 37.68%

*Ms M. Read, *Lab.*	95,344
M. Brandon-Bravo, *C.*	55,676
A. Wood, *LD*	23,836
Ms S. Blount, *Green*	7,035
J. Downes, *UK Independence*	5,849

P. Walton, *Ind. Out*	2,710
Mrs J. Christou, *NLP*	927
Lab. majority	39,668

(Boundary change since June 1989)

NOTTINGHAMSHIRE NORTH AND CHESTERFIELD
E. 490,330   T. 36.95%

*K. Coates, *Lab.*	114,353
D. Hazell, *C.*	38,093
Ms S. Pearce, *LD*	21,936
G. Jones, *Green*	5,159
Ms S. Lincoln, *NLP*	1,632
Lab. majority	76,260

(Boundary change since June 1989)

PEAK DISTRICT
E. 511,357   T. 39.02%

Ms A. McCarthy, *Lab.*	105,853
R. Fletcher, *C.*	56,546
Ms S. Barber, *LD*	29,979
M. Shipley, *Green*	5,598
D. Collins, *NLP*	1,533
Lab. majority	49,307

(Boundary change since June 1989)

SHEFFIELD
E. 476,530   T. 27.50%

*R. Barton, *Lab.*	76,397
Ms S. Anginotti, *LD*	26,109
Ms K. Twitchen, *C.*	22,374
B. New, *Green*	4,742
M. England, *Comm.*	834
R. Hurford, *NLP*	577
Lab. majority	50,288

(Boundary change since June 1989)

SOMERSET AND DEVON NORTH
E. 517,349   T. 47.09%

G. Watson, *LD*	106,187
*Mrs M. Daly, *C.*	83,678
J. Pilgrim, *Lab.*	34,540
D. Taylor, *Green*	10,870
G. Livings, *New Britain*	7,165
M. Lucas, *NLP*	1,200
LD majority	22,509

(Boundary change since June 1989)

SOUTH DOWNS WEST
E. 486,793   T. 39.45%

J. Provan, *C.*	83,813
Dr J. Walsh, *LD*	62,746
Ms L. Armstrong, *Lab.*	32,344
E. Paine, *Green*	7,703
W. Weights, *Lib.*	3,630
P. Kember, *NLP*	1,794
C. majority	21,067

(Boundary change since June 1989)

STAFFORDSHIRE EAST AND DERBY
E. 519,553   T. 35.46%

P. Whitehead, *Lab.*	102,393
Ms J. Evans, *C.*	50,197
Ms D. Brass, *LD*	17,469
I. Crompton, *UK Independence*	6,993
R. Clarke, *Green*	4,272
R. Jones, *NF*	2,098
Ms D. Grice, *NLP*	793
Lab. majority	72,196

(Boundary change since June 1989)

STAFFORDSHIRE WEST AND CONGLETON
E. 502,395   T. 31.60%

M. Tappin, *Lab.*	84,337
A. Brown, *C.*	44,060
J. Stevens, *LD*	24,430
D. Hoppe, *Green*	4,533
D. Lines, *NLP*	1,403
Lab. majority	40,277

(Boundary change since June 1989)

SUFFOLK AND NORFOLK SOUTH WEST
E. 477,668   T. 38.38%

D. Thomas, *Lab.*	74,304
*A. Turner, *C.*	61,769
R. Atkins, *LD*	37,975
A. Slade, *Green*	7,760
E. Kaplan, *NLP*	1,530
Lab. majority	12,535

(Boundary change since June 1989)

SURREY
E. 514,130   T. 37.51%

*T. Spencer, *C.*	83,405
Mrs S. Thomas, *LD*	56,387
Ms F. Wolf, *Lab.*	30,894
Mrs S. Porter, *UK Independence*	7,717
H. Charlton, *Green*	7,198
J. Walker, *Ind. Britain in Europe*	4,627
Mrs J. Thomas, *NLP*	2,638
C. majority	27,018

(Boundary change since June 1989)

SUSSEX EAST AND KENT SOUTH
E. 513,550   T. 41.90%

*Sir J. Stewart-Clark, *C.*	83,141
D. Bellotti, *LD*	76,929
N. Palmer, *Lab.*	35,273
A. Burgess, *UK Independence*	9,058
Ms R. Addison, *Green*	7,439
Ms T. Williamson, *Lib.*	2,558
P. Cragg, *NLP*	765
C. majority	6,212

(Boundary change since June 1989)

SUSSEX SOUTH AND CRAWLEY
E. 492,413   T. 37.64%

B. Donnelly, *C.*	62,860
Ms J. Edmond Smith, *Lab.*	61,114
J. Williams, *LD*	41,410
Ms P. Beever, *Green*	9,348
D. Horner, *Ind. Euro-Sceptic*	7,106
N. Furness, *Anti-Fed. C.*	2,618
A. Hankey, *NLP*	901
C. majority	1,746

(Boundary change since June 1989)

THAMES VALLEY
E. 543,685   T. 34.80%

*J. Stevens, *C.*	70,485
J. Howarth, *Lab.*	69,727
N. Bathurst, *LD*	33,187
P. Unsworth, *Green*	6,120
J. Clark, *Lib.*	5,381
P. Owen, *Loony C*	2,859
M. Grenville, *NLP*	1,453
C. majority	758

(June 1989, C. maj. 26,491)

TYNE AND WEAR
E. 516,436   T. 28.02%

*A. Donnelly, *Lab.*	107,604
I. Liddell-Grainger, C.	19,224
P. Maughan, LD	8,706
G. Edwards, *Green*	4,375
Ms W. Lundgren, *Lib.*	4,164
A. Fisken, *NLP*	650
Lab. majority	88,380

(June 1989, Lab. maj. 95,780)

WIGHT AND HAMPSHIRE SOUTH
E. 488,398   T. 37.16%

R. Perry, C.	63,306
M. Hancock, LD	58,205
Ms S. Fry, *Lab.*	40,442
J. Browne, *Ind.*	12,140
P. Fuller, *Green*	6,697
W. Treend, *NLP*	722
C. majority	5,101

(Boundary change since June 1989)

WILTSHIRE NORTH AND BATH
E. 496,591   T. 41.46%

*Mrs C. Jackson, C.	71,872
Ms J. Matthew, LD	63,085
Ms J. Norris, *Lab.*	50,489
P. Cullen, *Lib.*	6,760
M. Davidson, *Green*	5,974
T. Hedges, *UK Independence*	5,842
D. Cooke, *NLP*	1,148
Dr J. Day, *CPP*	725
C. majority	8,787

(Boundary change since June 1989)

WORCESTERSHIRE AND WARWICKSHIRE SOUTH
E. 551,162   T. 37.98%

J. Corrie, C.	73,573
Ms G. Gschaider, *Lab.*	72,369
P. Larner, LD	44,168
Ms J. Alty, *Green*	9,273
C. Hards, *National Independence*	8,447
J. Brewster, *NLP*	1,510
C. majority	1,204

(Boundary change since June 1989)

YORKSHIRE NORTH
E. 475,686   T. 38.70%

*E. McMillan-Scott, C.	70,036
B. Regan, *Lab.*	62,964
M. Pitts, LD	43,171
Dr R. Richardson, *Green*	7,036
S. Withers, *NLP*	891
C. majority	7,072

(Boundary change since June 1989)

YORKSHIRE SOUTH
E. 523,401   T. 28.64%

*N. West, *Lab.*	109,004
J. Howard, C.	20,695
Ms C. Roderick, LD	11,794
P. Davies, *UK Independence*	3,948
J. Waters, *Green*	3,775
N. Broome, *NLP*	681
Lab. majority	88,309

(June 1989, Lab. maj. 91,784)

YORKSHIRE SOUTH WEST
E. 547,469   T. 29.03%

*T. Megahy, *Lab.*	94,025
Mrs C. Adamson, C.	34,463
D. Ridgway, LD	21,595

A. Cooper, *Green*	7,163
G. Mead, *NLP*	1,674
Lab. majority	59,562

(Boundary change since June 1989)

YORKSHIRE WEST
E. 490,078   T. 34.61%

*B. Seal, *Lab.*	90,652
R. Booth, C.	42,455
C. Bidwell, LD	20,452
R. Pearson, *New Britain*	8,027
C. Harris, *Green*	7,154
D. Whitley, *NLP*	894
Lab. majority	48,197

(Boundary change since June 1989)

WALES

SOUTH WALES CENTRAL
E. 477,182   T. 39.40%

*W. David, *Lab.*	115,396
Ms L. Verity, C.	29,314
G. Llywelyn, PC	18,857
J. Dixon, LD	18,471
C. von Ruhland, *Green*	4,002
R. Griffiths, *Comm. YBG*	1,073
G. Duguay, *NLP*	889
Lab. majority	86,082

(Boundary change since June 1989)

SOUTH WALES EAST
E. 454,794   T. 43.07%

Mrs G. Kinnock, *Lab.*	144,907
Mrs R. Blomfield-Smith, C.	24,660
C. Woolgrove, LD	9,963
C. Mann, PC	9,550
R. Coghill, *Green*	4,509
Ms S. Williams, *Welsh Soc.*	1,270
Dr R. Brussatis, *NLP*	1,027
Lab. majority	120,247

(Boundary change since June 1989)

SOUTH WALES WEST
E. 395,131   T. 39.92%

*Revd D. Morris, *Lab.*	104,263
R. Buckland, C.	19,293
J. Bushell, LD	15,499
Ms C. Adams, PC	12,364
Ms J. Evans, *Green*	4,114
Ms H. Evans, *NLP*	1,112
Capt. Beany, *Beanus*	1,106
Lab. majority	84,970

(Boundary change since June 1989)

WALES MID AND WEST
E. 401,529   T. 48.00%

Ms E. Morgan, *Lab.*	78,092
M. Phillips, PC	48,858
P. Bone, C.	31,606
Ms J. Hughes, LD	23,719
D. Rowlands, *UK Independence*	5,536
Dr C. Busby, *Green*	3,938
T. Griffith-Jones, *NLP*	988
Lab. majority	29,234

(Boundary change since June 1989)

WALES NORTH
E. 475,829   T. 45.34%

*J. Wilson, *Lab.*	88,091
D. Wigley, PC	72,849
G. Mon Hughes, C.	33,450

Ms R. Parry, LD	14,828
P. Adams, *Green*	2,850
D. Hughes, *NLP*	2,065
M. Cooksey, *Ind.*	1,623
Lab. majority	15,242

(Boundary change since June 1989)

SCOTLAND

GLASGOW
E. 463,364   T. 34.46%

W. Miller, *Lab.*	83,953
T. Chalmers, SNP	40,795
T. Sheridan, SML	12,113
R. Wilkinson, C.	10,888
J. Money, LD	7,291
P. O'Brien, *Green*	2,252
J. Fleming, *Soc.*	1,125
M. Wilkinson, *NLP*	868
C. Marsden, *ICP*	381
Lab. majority	43,158

(June 1989, Lab. maj. 59,232)

HIGHLANDS AND ISLANDS
E. 328,104   T. 39.09%

*Mrs W. Ewing, SNP	74,872
M. Macmillan, *Lab.*	19,956
M. Tennant, C.	15,767
H. Morrison, LD	12,919
Dr E. Scott, *Green*	3,140
M. Carr, *UK Independence*	1,096
Ms M. Gilmour, *NLP*	522
SNP majority	54,916

(June 1989, SNP maj. 44,695)

LOTHIANS
E. 520,943   T. 38.69%

*D. Martin, *Lab.*	90,531
K. Brown, SNP	53,324
Dr P. McNally, C.	33,526
Ms H. Campbell, LD	17,883
R. Harper, *Green*	5,149
J. McGregor, *Soc.*	637
M. Siebert, *NLP*	500
Lab. majority	37,207

(June 1989, Lab. maj. 38,826)

SCOTLAND MID AND FIFE
E. 546,060   T. 38.25%

*A. Falconer, *Lab.*	95,667
R. Douglas, SNP	64,254
P. Page, C.	28,192
Ms H. Lyall, LD	17,192
M. Johnston, *Green*	3,015
T. Pringle, *NLP*	532
Lab. majority	31,413

(June 1989, Lab. maj. 52,157)

SCOTLAND NORTH EAST
E. 575,748   T. 37.72%

A. Macartney, SNP	92,892
*H. McCubbin, *Lab.*	61,665
Dr R. Harris, C.	40,372
S. Horner, LD	18,008
K. Farnsworth, *Green*	2,569
Ms M. Ward, *Comm. GB*	689
L. Mair, *Neeps*	584
D. Paterson, *NLP*	371

SNP majority 31,227
(June 1989, Lab. maj. 2,613)

SCOTLAND SOUTH
E. 500,643   T. 40.14%
*A. Smith, Lab. 90,750
A. Hutton, C. 45,595
Mrs C. Creech, SNP 45,032
D. Millar, LD 13,363
J. Hein, Lib. 3,249
Ms L. Hendry, Green 2,429
G. Gay, NLP 539
Lab. majority 45,155
(June 1989, Lab. maj. 15,693)

STRATHCLYDE EAST
E. 492,618   T. 37.26%
*K. Collins, Lab. 106,476
I. Hamilton, SNP 54,136
B. Cooklin, C. 13,915
R. Stewart, LD 6,383
A. Whitelaw, Green 1,874
D. Gilmour, NLP 787
Lab. majority 52,340
(June 1989, Lab. maj. 60,317)

STRATHCLYDE WEST
E. 489,129   T. 40.05%
*H. McMahon, Lab. 86,957
C. Campbell, SNP 61,934
J. Godfrey, C. 28,414
D. Herbison, LD 14,772
Ms K. Allan, Green 2,886
Ms S. Gilmour, NLP 918
Lab. majority 25,023
(June 1989, Lab. maj. 39,591)

NORTHERN IRELAND

Northern Ireland forms a three-
member seat with a single transferable
vote system
E. 1,150,304 T. 48.67%
*Revd I. Paisley, DUP 163,246
*J. Hume, SDLP 161,992
*J. Nicholson, UUUP 133,459
Mrs M. Clark-Glass, All. 23,157
T. Hartley, SF 21,273
Ms D. McGuinness, SF 17,195
F. Molloy, SF 16,747
Revd H. Ross, Ulster Independence
7,858
Miss M. Boal, C. 5,583
J. Lowry, WP 2,543
N. Cusack, Ind. Lab. 2,464
J. Anderson, NLP 1,418
Mrs J. Campion, Peace Coalition 1,088
D. Kerr, Independence for Ulster 571
Ms S. Thompson, NLP 454
M. Kennedy, NLP 419
R. Mooney, Const. NI 400

Speakers of the Commons since 1708

The date of appointment given is the day on which the Speaker was first elected by the House of Commons. The appointment requires royal approbation before it is confirmed and this is usually given within a few days. The present Speaker is the 155th.

PARLIAMENT OF GREAT BRITAIN

Sir Richard Onslow (Lord Onslow), 16 November 1708
William Bromley, 25 November 1710
Sir Thomas Hanmer, 16 February 1714
Spencer Compton (Earl of Wilmington), 17 March 1715
Arthur Onslow, 23 January 1728
Sir John Cust, 3 November 1761
Sir Fletcher Norton (Lord Grantley), 22 January 1770
Charles Cornwall, 31 October 1780
Hon. William Grenville (Lord Grenville), 5 January 1789
Henry Addington (Viscount Sidmouth), 8 June 1789

PARLIAMENT OF THE UNITED KINGDOM

Sir John Mitford (Lord Redesdale), 11 February 1801

Charles Abbot (Lord Colchester), 10 February 1802
Charles Manners-Sutton (Viscount Canterbury), 2 June 1817
James Abercromby (Lord Dunfermline), 19 February 1835
Charles Shaw-Lefevre (Viscount Eversley), 27 May 1839
J. Evelyn Denison (Viscount Ossington), 30 April 1857
Sir Henry Brand (Viscount Hampden), 9 February 1872
Arthur Wellesley Peel (Viscount Peel), 26 February 1884
William Gully (Viscount Selby), 10 April 1895
James Lowther (Viscount Ullswater), 8 June 1905
John Whitley, 27 April 1921
Hon. Edward Fitzroy, 20 June 1928
Douglas Clifton-Brown (Viscount Ruffside), 9 March 1943
William Morrison (Viscount Dunrossil), 31 October 1951
Sir Harry Hylton-Foster, 20 October 1959
Horace King (Lord Maybray-King), 26 October 1965
Selwyn Lloyd (Lord Selwyn-Lloyd), 12 January 1971
George Thomas (Viscount Tonypandy), 2 February 1976
Bernard Weatherill (Lord Weatherill), 15 June 1983
Betty Boothroyd, 27 April 1992

The Government

THE CABINET AS AT 31 JULY 1995

Prime Minister, First Lord of the Treasury and Minister for the Civil Service
The Rt. Hon. John Major, MP, since November 1990
First Secretary of State and Deputy Prime Minister
The Rt. Hon. Michael Heseltine, MP, since July 1995
Lord High Chancellor
The Lord Mackay of Clashfern, PC, since October 1987
Chancellor of the Exchequer
The Rt. Hon. Kenneth Clarke, QC, MP, since May 1993
Secretary of State for the Home Department
The Rt. Hon. Michael Howard, QC, MP, since May 1993
Secretary of State for Foreign and Commonwealth Affairs
The Rt. Hon. Malcolm Rifkind, QC, MP, since July 1995
Lord President of the Council and Leader of the House of Commons
The Rt. Hon. Antony Newton, OBE, MP, since April 1992
Secretary of State for the Environment
The Rt. Hon. John Gummer, MP, since May 1993
Secretary of State for Social Security
The Rt. Hon. Peter Lilley, MP, since April 1992
Chief Secretary to the Treasury
The Rt. Hon. William Waldegrave, MP, since July 1995
Secretary of State for Trade and Industry and President of the Board of Trade
The Rt. Hon. Ian Lang, MP, since July 1995
Secretary of State for Northern Ireland
The Rt. Hon. Sir Patrick Mayhew, QC, MP, since April 1992
Secretary of State for National Heritage
The Rt. Hon. Virginia Bottomley, MP, since July 1995
Secretary of State for Education and Employment
The Rt. Hon. Gillian Shephard, MP, since July 1994 (Education)/July 1995 (Employment)
Secretary of State for Defence
The Rt. Hon. Michael Portillo, MP, since July 1995
Minister Without Portfolio (Party chairman)
The Rt. Hon. Brian Mawhinney, MP, since July 1995
Secretary of State for Health
The Rt. Hon. Stephen Dorrell, MP, since July 1995
Lord Privy Seal and Leader of the House of Lords
Viscount Cranborne, PC, since July 1994
Secretary of State for Transport
The Rt. Hon. Sir George Young, Bt., MP, since July 1995
Minister of Agriculture, Fisheries and Food
The Rt. Hon. Douglas Hogg, QC, MP, since July 1995
Secretary of State for Scotland
The Rt. Hon. Michael Forsyth, MP, since July 1995
Chancellor of the Duchy of Lancaster
The Rt. Hon. Roger Freeman, MP, since July 1995
Secretary of State for Wales
The Rt. Hon. William Hague, MP, since July 1995

LAW OFFICERS

Attorney-General
The Rt. Hon. Sir Nicholas Lyell, QC, MP, since April 1992
Lord Advocate
The Lord Rodger of Earlsferry, PC, QC, since April 1992
Solicitor-General
Sir Derek Spencer, QC, MP, since April 1992

Solicitor-General for Scotland
Donald Mackay, QC, since May 1995

MINISTERS OF STATE

Agriculture, Fisheries and Food
Anthony Baldry, MP
Defence
The Hon. Nicholas Soames, MP (*Armed Forces*)
James Arbuthnot, MP (*Defence Procurement*)
Education and Employment
Eric Forth, MP
The Lord Henley
Environment
David Curry, MP (*Minister for Local Government, Housing, Urban Regeneration*)
The Earl Ferrars, PC (*Minister for Environment and Countryside*)
Robert Jones, MP (*Minister for Construction and Planning*)
Foreign and Commonwealth Affairs
The Baroness Chalker of Wallasey, PC (*Minister for Overseas Development*)
David Davis, MP (*Minister for European Union*)
The Rt. Hon. Jeremy Hanley, MP (*Minister for Hong Kong and the Middle East*)
Sir Nicholas Bonsor, MP (*Minister for former Yugoslavia, UN and eastern Europe*)
Health
Gerald Malone, MP
Home Office
The Rt. Hon. David Maclean, MP
The Baroness Blatch, PC
Ann Widdecombe, MP
National Heritage
Iain Sproat, MP (*Minister for Sport*)
Northern Ireland Office
The Rt. Hon. Sir John Wheeler, MP
Michael Ancram, MP
Scottish Office
Lord James Douglas-Hamilton, MP
Social Security
The Lord Mackay of Ardbrecknish
Alistair Burt, MP (*Minister for Social Security and Disabled People*)
Trade and Industry
The Rt. Hon. Timothy Eggar, MP
The Lord Fraser of Carmyllie, PC, QC
Anthony Nelson, MP
Transport
John Watts, MP
Treasury
Michael Jack, MP (*Financial Secretary*)
David Heathcoat-Amory, MP (*Paymaster-General*)
Angela Knight, MP (*Economic Secretary*)

UNDER-SECRETARIES OF STATE

Agriculture, Fisheries and Food
Angela Browning, MP
Timothy Boswell, MP

Office of the Minister for the Civil Service
John Horam, MP
Defence
The Earl Howe
Education and Employment
Robin Squire, MP
James Paice, MP
Cheryl Gillan, MP
Environment
Sir Paul Beresford, MP
James Clappison, MP
Health
The Baroness Cumberlege, CBE
The Hon. Thomas Sackville, MP
John Bowis, OBE, MP
Home Office
Nicholas Baker, MP
Lord Chancellor's Department
John Taylor, MP
National Heritage
The Lord Inglewood
Northern Ireland
The Baroness Denton of Wakefield, CBE
Malcolm Moss, MP
Scottish Office
George Kynoch, MP
Raymond Robertson, MP
The Earl of Lindsay
Social Security
Roger Evans, MP
Oliver Heald, MP
Andrew Mitchell, MP
Trade and Industry
Ian Taylor, MBE, MP
Jonathan Evans, MP
Richard Page, MP
Hon. Phillip Oppenheim, MP
Transport
Steven Norris, MP
The Viscount Goschen
Treasury
The Lords Commissioners, *see* Government whips
Welsh Office
Gwilym Jones, MP
Roderick Richards, MP

Comptroller of HM Household
Timothy Wood, MP
Vice-Chamberlain of HM Household
Timothy Kirkhope, MP
Lords Commissioners
Andrew Mackay, MP; Derek Conway, MP; Bowen Wells, MP; Simon Burns, MP; David Willetts, MP
Assistant Whips
Michael Bates, MP; Liam Fox, MP; Patrick McLoughlin, MP; Roger Knapman, MP; Gary Streeter, MP

GOVERNMENT WHIPS

HOUSE OF LORDS

Captain of the Honourable Corps of Gentlemen-at-Arms (Chief Whip)
The Lord Strathclyde, PC
Captain of The Queen's Bodyguard of the Yeomen of the Guard (Deputy Chief Whip)
The Lord Chesham
Lords-in-Waiting
The Viscount Long; The Lord Lucas of Crudwell; The Earl of Courtown
Baronesses-in-Waiting
The Baroness Trumpington, PC; The Baroness Miller of Hendon

HOUSE OF COMMONS

Parliamentary Secretary to the Treasury (Chief Whip)
The Rt. Hon. Alastair Goodlad, MP
Treasurer of HM Household (Deputy Chief Whip)
The Rt. Hon. Gregory Knight, MP

Government Departments and Public Offices

This section covers central government departments, executive agencies, regulatory bodies, other statutory independent organizations, and bodies which are government-financed or whose head is appointed by a government minister.

THE CIVIL SERVICE

Changes are currently being introduced into the civil service with the aim of reducing its functions to a central core and privatizing or contracting out the rest of its work. Many semi-autonomous executive agencies have already been established under the 'Next Steps' programme. Executive agencies operate within a framework set by the responsible minister which specifies policies, objectives and available resources. They are usually headed by a chief executive, who is responsible for the day-to-day operations of the agency and who is accountable to the minister for the use of resources and for the performance of the agency. About 65 per cent of the work of the civil service is now conducted by executive agencies. In April 1995 there were about 516,000 permanent civil servants.

Most of the Home Civil Service's senior grades have been absorbed into an Open pay and grading structure. Executive agencies are responsible for their own pay and grading systems and will therefore not necessarily fit into this structure. Responsibility for pay and grading of staff below senior levels will be delegated to all government departments by April 1996. The Open structure represents the following:

Grade	Title
1	Permanent Secretary
1A	Second Permanent Secretary
2	Deputy Secretary
3	Under-Secretary
4	Chief Scientific Officer B, Professional and Technology Directing A
5	Assistant Secretary, Deputy Chief Scientific Officer, Professional and Technology Directing B
6	Senior Principal, Senior Principal Scientific Officer, Professional and Technology Superintending Grade
7	Principal, Principal Scientific Officer, Principal Professional and Technology Officer

SALARIES

MINISTERIAL SALARIES *as at 1 January 1995*
Ministers who are Members of the House of Commons receive a reduced parliamentary salary (£24,985 in 1995) in addition to their ministerial salary.

Prime Minister	£57,018
Secretary of State	£42,834
Minister of State (Lords)	£48,835
Minister of State (Commons)	£30,307
Parliamentary Under-Secretary (Lords)	£41,065
Parliamentary Under-Secretary (Commons)	£23,002

*CIVIL SERVICE SALARIES 1995–6

Secretary of the Cabinet and Head of the Home Civil Service	£90,000–£150,000
Permanent Secretary to the Treasury	£90,000–£150,000
Head of the Diplomatic Service	£90,000–£150,000
Grade 1	£90,000–£150,000
Grade 1A	£90,000–£150,000
Grade 2	£67,500–£98,000
Grade 3	£55,000–£82,500
†Grade 4	£45,278–£54,815
†Grade 5	£36,739–£54,815
†Grade 6	£28,213–£47,044
†Grade 7	£24,724–£38,290
Senior Executive Officer	£19,215–£25,289
Higher Executive Officer	£15,363–£20,634
Administration Trainee/HEO(D)	£13,396–£24,589
Executive Officer	£11,208–£16,496
Administrative Officer	£8,778–£12,174
Administrative Assistant	£6,928–£10,279

London Rates

†Grade 4	£47,043–£56,953
†Grade 5	£38,341–£56,953
†Grade 6	£29,482–£48,879
†Grade 7	£25,837–£40,012
Senior Executive Officer	£20,013–£26,340
Higher Executive Officer	£16,000–£21,491
Executive Officer	£11,673–£17,182
Administrative Officer	£9,393–£13,025
Administrative Assistant	£7,412–£10,999

*Most grades no longer have an incremental scale; pay is based solely on performance and can be set at any level between the minimum and maximum of the range. A recruitment and retention allowance of up to £3,000 a year was introduced in October 1994, when London weighting of up to £1,776 a year was abolished. The allowance is used to attract and retain staff in any part of the country at each department's discretion
†1994–5 figures

ADJUDICATOR'S OFFICE
Haymarket House, 28 Haymarket, London SW1Y 4SP
Tel 0171-930 2292

The Adjudicator's Office investigates complaints made about the way the Inland Revenue, Customs and Excise and the Contributions Agency have handled an individual's affairs. The Adjudicator's Office opened in July 1993.
The Adjudicator, Ms E. Filkin
Head of Office, D. I. Richardson

ADVISORY, CONCILIATION AND ARBITRATION SERVICE
27 Wilton Street, London SW1X 7AZ
Tel 0171-210 3613

The Advisory, Conciliation and Arbitration Service (ACAS) is an independent organization set up under the

Employment Protection Act 1975 (the provisions now being found in the Trade Union and Labour Relations (Consolidation) Act 1992). ACAS is directed by a Council consisting of a full-time chairman and part-time employer, trade union and independent members, all appointed by the Secretary of State for Trade and Industry. The functions of the Service are to promote the improvement of industrial relations in general, to provide facilities for conciliation, mediation and arbitration as means of avoiding and resolving industrial disputes, and to provide advisory and information services on industrial relations matters to employers, employees and their representatives.

ACAS also has main offices in Birmingham, Bristol, Cardiff, Fleet, Glasgow, Leeds, Liverpool, Manchester, Newcastle upon Tyne and Nottingham.

Chairman, J. Hougham
Chief Conciliation Officer (G4), D. Evans

MINISTRY OF AGRICULTURE, FISHERIES AND FOOD
Whitehall Place, London SW1A 2HH
Tel 0171-238 6000; *enquiries* 0645-335577

The Ministry of Agriculture, Fisheries and Food is responsible for administering government policies on agriculture, horticulture and fisheries in England and policies relating to the safety and quality of food in the UK as a whole. In association with the Agriculture Departments of the Scottish, Welsh and Northern Ireland Offices and with the Intervention Board (*see* page 319), the Ministry is responsible for the negotiation and administration of the EU common agricultural and fisheries policies, for matters relating to the single European market, and for international agricultural and food trade policy. It commissions research to assist in the formulation and assessment of policy.

The Ministry administers policies on the control and eradication of animal, plant and fish diseases, and on assistance to capital investment in farm and horticultural businesses; it also has responsibilities relating to the protection and enhancement of the countryside and the marine environment as well as to flood defence and other rural issues.

The Ministry is responsible for ensuring public health standards in the manufacture, preparation and distribution of basic foods, and for planning to safeguard essential food supplies in times of emergency. It is responsible for government relations with the UK food and drink manufacturing industries and the food and drink importing, distributive and catering trades.

The Food Safety Directorate is responsible for many aspects of food safety and quality. These include pesticide safety approval, biotechnology, meat hygiene, animal health and welfare, and related public health issues.

Minister, The Rt. Hon. Douglas Hogg, QC, MP
  Principal Private Secretary (G7), W. F. G. Strang
  Private Secretary, T. Render
Minister of State, Tony Baldry, QC, MP (*Farming and Fisheries*)
  Private Secretary, Miss R. J. Gower
Parliamentary Secretary, Timothy Boswell, MP (*Countryside*)
Parliamentary Secretary, Angela Browning, MP (*Food*)
  Private Secretary, Mrs E. C. Ratcliffe
Parliamentary Clerk, Miss A. Evans
Permanent Secretary (G1), R. J. Packer
  Private Secretary, R. Campbell

ESTABLISHMENT DEPARTMENT
Director of Establishments (G3), C. J. Barnes

ESTABLISHMENTS (GENERAL) AND OFFICE SERVICES DIVISION
Victory House, 30–34 Kingsway, London WC2B 6TU
Tel 0171-405 4310

Head of Division (G6), Dr J. A. Bailey

WELFARE BRANCH
Victory House, 30–34 Kingsway, London WC2B 6TU
Tel 0171-405 4310

Chief Welfare Officer (SEO), D. J. Jones

PERSONNEL MANAGEMENT AND DEVELOPMENT DIVISION
Victory House, 30–34 Kingsway, London WC2B 6TU
Tel 0171-405 4310

Head of Division (G5), G. P. McLachlan

DEPARTMENTAL HEALTH AND SAFETY UNIT
Head of Unit (G7), C. R. Bradburn

†STAFF TRAINING BRANCH
Principal (G7), J. M. Cowley

BUILDING AND ESTATE MANAGEMENT
Eastbury House, 30–34 Albert Embankment, London SE1 7TL
Tel 0171-238 6000

Head of Division (G5), J. A. S. Nickson

INFORMATION DIVISION
Chief Information Officer (G5), J. Haslam
Chief Press Officer (G7), M. Smith
Chief Publicity Officer (G7), N. Wagstaffe
Principal Librarian (G7), P. McShane

FINANCE DEPARTMENT
19–29 Woburn Place, London WC1H 0LU
Tel 0171-270 8080

Principal Finance Officer (G3), Ms V. K. Timms

FINANCIAL POLICY DIVISION
Head of Division (G5), P. P. Nash

FINANCIAL MANAGEMENT DIVISION
Head of Division (G5), Ms J. Allfrey

PROCUREMENT AND CONTRACTS DIVISION
Director of Audit (G5), D. V. Fisher

MARKET TESTING AND PROCUREMENT ADVICE
Victory House, 30–34 Kingsway, London WC2B 6TU
Tel 0171-405 4310

Director (G5), D. B. Rabey

RESOURCE MANAGEMENT STRATEGY UNIT
Head of Division (G5), J. D. Garnett

LEGAL DEPARTMENT
55 Whitehall, London SW1A 2EY
Tel 0171-238 6000

Legal Adviser and Solicitor (G2), R. Woolman
Principal Assistant Solicitors (G3), B. T. Atwood; D. J. Pearson; (G4), Ms C. A. Crisham

LEGAL DIVISIONS
Assistant Solicitor, Division A1 (G5), L. Gunatilleke
Assistant Solicitor, Division A2 (G5), Mrs C. A. Davis
Assistant Solicitor, Division A3 (G5), T. J. Middleton
Assistant Solicitor, Division A4 (G5), Miss E. A. Stephens

---

†At Nobel/Ergon House, 17 Smith Square, London SW1P 3JR. Tel: 0171-238 6000

Assistant Solicitor, Division B1 (G5), Dr M. R. Parke
Assistant Solicitor, Division B2 (G4), Ms S. B. Spence
Assistant Solicitor, Division B3 (G5), A. I. Corbett
Assistant Solicitor, Division C1 (G5), P. R. Hall
Assistant Solicitor, Division C2 (G5), P. D. Davis
Assistant Solicitor, Division C3 (G5), P. Kent

INVESTIGATION UNIT
Chief Investigation Officer, Miss J. Panting

AGRICULTURAL COMMODITIES, TRADE AND FOOD PRODUCTION
Deputy Secretary (G2), D. A. Hadley, CB

EUROPEAN COMMUNITY
Under-Secretary (G3), vacant

DIVISIONS
Head, European Community I (G5), A. J. Lebrecht
Head, European Community II (G6), L. G. Mitchell

ARABLE CROPS
Under-Secretary (G3), D. H. Griffiths

DIVISIONS
Head, Cereals and Set-Aside (G4), G. M. Trevelyan
Head , Sugar, Tobacco, Oilseeds and Protein (G5), Mrs A. M. Blackburn
†*Head, Horticulture and Potatoes (G5)*, R. A. Saunderson

LIVESTOCK GROUP
Under-Secretary (G3), G. A. Hollis

DIVISIONS
Head, Beef (G5), T. D. Rossington
Head, Sheep and Livestock Subsidies (G5), J. R. Cowan
Head, Pigs, Eggs and Poultry (G5), G. W. Noble
Head, Milk and Milk Products (G5), B. J. Harding

FOOD, DRINK AND MARKETING POLICY
Under-Secretary (G3), J. W. Hepburn

DIVISIONS
Head, Food and Drinks Industry (G5), R. E. Melville
Head, International Relations and Export Promotion (G5), D. V. Orchard
Head, Trade Policy and Tropical Foods (G5), Miss S. E. Brown
†*Head, Market Task Force (G5)*, H. B. Brown

FOOD SAFETY
Deputy Secretary (G2), R. J. D. Carden

†FOOD SAFETY GROUP
Under-Secretary *(G3)*, B. H. B. Dickinson
Chief Scientist (Fisheries and Food) (G3), Dr W. H. B. Denner

DIVISIONS
Head, Consumer Protection (G5), C. A. Cockbill
Head, Food Hygiene (G5), Ms S. Nason
Head, Additives and Novel Foods (G5), Dr J. R. Bell
Head, Food Labelling and Standards (G5), G. Meekings
Head, Food Contaminants (G5), Dr R. Burt
Head, Consumers and Nutrition (G5), Miss E. J. Wordley

†CHIEF SCIENTIST'S GROUP

DIVISIONS
Head, Agriculture and Food Technology (G5), Dr J. C. Sherlock
Head, Veterinary Science and Food Safety (G5), Dr K. J. MacOwan

AGRICULTURAL INPUTS, PLANT PROTECTION AND EMERGENCIES
Under-Secretary (G3), A. R. Cruickshank

DIVISIONS
Head, Emergencies and Food Protection (G5), Dr J. R. Park
Head, Plant Health (G5), A. J. Perrins
Head, Plant Variety, Rights Office and Seeds (G5), D. A. Boreham
Head, Agricultural Resources Policy (G5), A. R. Burne

ANIMAL HEALTH AND VETERINARY GROUP
Government Buildings, Hook Rise South, Tolworth, Surbiton, Surrey KT6 7NF
Tel 0181-330 4411
Under-Secretary (G3), M. T. Haddon
Chief Veterinary Officer (G3), K. C. Meldrum, CB

DIVISIONS
Head, Animal Health (Zoonoses) (G5), R. J. G. Cawthorne
Head, Animal Health (Disease Control) (G5), T. E. D. Eddy
Head, Animal Health (International Trade) (G5), R. A. Bell
Head, Meat Hygiene (G5), Mrs K. J. A. Brown
Head, Resource Management (G6), R. A. Gregg
Head, Animal Welfare (G5), C. J. Ryder

STATE VETERINARY SERVICE
Government Buildings, Hook Rise South, Tolworth, Surbiton, Surrey KT15 3NB
Tel 0181-330 4411
Director of Veterinary Field Services (G3), I. Crawford

LASSWADE VETERINARY LABORATORY
East of Scotland College of Agriculture, The Bush Estate, Penicuik, Midlothian EH26 0SA
Tel 0131-445 5371
Head of Laboratory (G6), Miss G. Mackenzie

COUNTRYSIDE, MARINE ENVIRONMENT AND FISHERIES
Deputy Secretary (G2), C. R. Cann

LAND USE, CONSERVATION AND COUNTRYSIDE
†*Under-Secretary (G3)*, P. W. Murphy

DIVISIONS
†*Head, Countryside (G5)*, R. C. McIvor
†*Head, Land Use and Tenure (G5)*, T. J. Osmond
†*Head, Conservation Policy (G5)*, P. M. Boyling
†*Head, Environmentally-Sensitive Areas (G5)*, C. R. Bodrell
†*Head, Land Use Planning Unit (G5)*, J. R. Mathias
†*Head, Rural White Paper Unit (G5)*, P. Elliott

†FISHERIES DEPARTMENT
Fisheries Secretary (G3), S. Wentworth

DIVISIONS
Head, Fisheries I (G5), A. Kuyk
Head, Fisheries II (G5), P. A. Cocking
Head, Fisheries III (G5), J. E. Robbs
Head, Fisheries IV (G6), B. S. Edwards
Chief Inspector, Sea Fisheries Inspectorate (G6), M. G. Jennings

FISHERIES RESEARCH
Pakefield Road, Lowestoft, Suffolk NR33 0HT
Tel 01502-562244
Director of Fisheries Research and Development for Great Britain (G4), P. W. Greig-Smith

Deputy Directors of Fisheries Research (G5), J. W. Horwood; J. E. Portmann

FISHERIES LABORATORY
Pakefield Road, Lowestoft, Suffolk NR33 OHT
Tel 01502-562244

FISHERIES LABORATORY
Remembrance Avenue, Burnham-on-Crouch, Essex CM0 8HA
Tel 01621-782658

FISHERIES EXPERIMENT STATION
Benarth Road, Conwy, Gwynedd LL32 8UB
Tel 01492-593883

FISH DISEASES LABORATORY
33–33A Albany Road, Granby Industrial Estate, Weymouth, Dorset DT4 9TU
Tel 01305-772137
Officer-in-Charge (Principal Scientific Officer) (G6), B. J. Hill, PH.D.

ENVIRONMENT POLICY
Under-Secretary (G3), M. Madden

DIVISIONS
†*Head, Environmental Protection (G5)*, D. L. Dawson
†*Head, Marine Environmental Protection (G5)*, vacant
†*Head, Salmon, Whaling and Inland Fisheries (G5)*, C. I. Llewelyn

FLOOD AND COASTAL DEFENCE
Eastbury House, 30–34 Albert Embankment, London SE1 7TL
Tel 0171-238 3000
Head of Division (G5), R. A. Hathaway

ECONOMICS AND STATISTICS
Under-Secretary (G3), R. E. Mordue

DIVISIONS
Senior Economic Adviser, Economics and Statistics (Farm Business) (G5), J. P. Muriel
Senior Economic Adviser, Economics (International and Food) (G5), Dr J. M. Slater
Senior Economic Adviser, Economics (Resource Use) (G5), R. W. Irving

STATISTICS DIVISION
Foss House, 1–2 Peasholme Green, King's Pool, York YO1 2PX
Tel 01904-455328

Chief Statistician (Commodities and Food) (G4), Dr P. J. Lund
Chief Statistician (Census and Surveys) (G5), P. F. Helm

†CHIEF SCIENTIST
Chief Scientist (G3), D. W. F. Shannon, PH.D.
Head, Environment Fisheries Services (G5), Dr M. Parker
Scientific Liaison Officer (Fisheries) (G6), Dr J. Lock
Head, Research Policy Co-ordination Division (G5), J. Suich

REGIONAL ORGANIZATION
†*Director of Regional Administration (G3)*, D. J. Coates
Head, Agencies and Citizen's Charter (G5), D. P. Hunter
†*Head, Regional Services Division (G5)*, Miss V. A. Smith

REGIONAL SERVICE CENTRES
ANGLIA REGION, Block B, Government Buildings, Brooklands Avenue, Cambridge CB2 2DR. Tel: 01223-462727. *Regional Director (G5)*, Miss C. J. Rabagliati
EAST MIDLANDS REGION, Government Buildings, Block 7, Chalfont Drive, Nottingham NG8 3SN. Tel: 0115-929 1191. *Regional Director (G5)*, M. J. Finnigan

NORTH-EAST REGION, Government Buildings, Crosby Road, Northallerton, N. Yorks DL6 1AD. Tel: 01609-773751. *Regional Director (G6)*, P. Watson
NORTHERN REGION, Eden Bridge House, Lowther Street, Carlisle, Cumbria CA3 8DX. Tel: 01228-23400. *Regional Director (G5)*, D. E. Jones
NORTH MERCIA REGION, Berkeley Towers, Nantwich Road, Crewe, Cheshire CW2 6PT. Tel: 01270-69211. *Regional Director (G6)*, R. Bettley-Smith
SOUTH-EAST REGION, Block A, Government Buildings, Coley Park, Reading, Berks RG1 6DT. Tel: 01734-581222. *Regional Director (G5)*, R. Anderson
SOUTH MERCIA REGION, Block C, Government Buildings, Whittington Road, Worcester WR5 2LQ. Tel: 01905-763355. *Regional Director (G6)*, P. G. Gething
SOUTH-WEST REGION, Government Buildings, Alphington Road, Exeter EX2 8NQ. Tel: 01392-77951. *Regional Director (G6)*, M. R. W. Highman
WESSEX REGION, Block 3, Government Buildings, Burghill Road, Westbury-on-Trym, Bristol BS10 6NJ. Tel: 01272-591000. *Regional Director (G6)*, Mrs A. J. L. Ould

INFORMATION TECHNOLOGY DIRECTORATE
Government Buildings, Epsom Road, Guildford, Surrey GU1 2LD
Tel 01483-68121
Director (G4), A. G. Matthews

EXECUTIVE AGENCIES

AGRICULTURAL DEVELOPMENT AND ADVISORY SERVICE (ADAS)
ADAS Headquarters, Oxford Spires Business Park, The Boulevard, Kidlington, Oxon OX5 1NZ
Tel 01865-842742

The Agricultural Development and Advisory Service (ADAS) provides a range of consultancy services to the land-based industries. It is a joint executive agency of MAFF and the Welsh Office and carries out research, performs certain statutory functions and provides advice on policy for both departments. The Government has announced its intention of privatizing the commercial parts of ADAS.
Chief Executive (G2) (acting), P. Needham
Director of Operations (G3), vacant
Research Director (G4), Dr A. D. Hughes
Marketing Director (G5), D. N. Hall
Finance Director (G5), Dr C. Herring
Personnel Director (G5), Ms S. Nason
Director for Wales (G5), W. I. C. Davies
Non-Executive Directors, C. Bystram (*Chairman*); P. Christensen, CBE

CENTRAL SCIENCE LABORATORY
London Road, Slough, Berks SL3 7HJ
Tel 01753-534626

The Central Science Laboratory was enlarged in April 1994 by merging with the Food Science Laboratory, Norwich and the Torry Research Station, Aberdeen. The agency provides MAFF with technical support and policy advice on the protection and quality of the food supply and on related environmental issues.
Chief Executive (G3), Prof. P. I. Stanley
Research Director (G5), Prof. A. R. Hardy
Head of Food Science Laboratory (G5), Dr J. Gilbert, Norwich Research Park, Colney Lane, Norwich NR4 7UQ. Tel: 01603-259350

---

†At Nobel/Ergon House, 17 Smith Square, London SW1P 3JR. Tel: 0171-238 6000

Director, Torry Research Station (G5), K. Whittle, PH.D., PO Box 31, 135 Abbey Road, Aberdeen AB9 8DG. Tel: 01224-877071

CENTRAL VETERINARY LABORATORY
Woodham Lane, New Haw, Addlestone, Surrey KT15 3NB
Tel 01932-341111

The Central Veterinary Laboratory provides scientific and technical expertise in animal and public health.
Director and Chief Executive (G3), Dr T. W. A. Little
Director of Research (G4), Dr J. A. Morris
Director of Operations (G5), R. W. Saunders

INTERVENTION BOARD
— *see* page 319

MEAT HYGIENE SERVICE
Foss House, 1–2 Peasholme Green, King's Pool, York
YO1 2PX
Tel 01904-455500

The Agency was launched in April 1995 and is responsible for the fresh meat hygiene enforcement arrangements formerly carried out by local authorities.
Chief Executive (G4), J. McNeill

PESTICIDES SAFETY DIRECTORATE
Mallard House, King's Pool, 3 Peasholme Green, York
YO1 2PX
Tel 01904-640500

The Pesticides Safety Directorate is responsible for the evaluation and approval of pesticides and the development of policies relating to them, in order to protect consumers, users and the environment.
Chief Executive (G4), G. K. Bruce
Director (Policy) (G5), J. A. Bainton
Director (Approvals) (G5), Dr A. D. Martin

VETERINARY MEDICINES DIRECTORATE
Woodham Lane, New Haw, Addlestone, Surrey KT15 3NB
Tel 01932-336911

The Veterinary Medicines Directorate is responsible for all aspects of licensing and control of animal medicines, including the protection of the consumer from hazardous or unacceptable residues.
Chief Executive and Director of Veterinary Medicines (G4), Dr J. M. Rutter
Director (Policy and Finance) (G5), C. J. Lawson
Director (Licensing) (G5), Dr K. N. Woodward
Licensing Manager, Pharmaceuticals and Feed Additives (G6), J. P. O'Brien
Licensing Manager, Immunologicals and Suspected Adverse Reactions (SARS) (G6), Dr A. M. T. Lee

COLLEGE OF ARMS OR HERALDS COLLEGE
Queen Victoria Street, London EC4V 4BT
Tel 0171-248 2762

The Sovereign's Officers of Arms (Kings, Heralds and Pursuivants of Arms) were first incorporated by Richard III. The powers vested by the Crown in the Earl Marshal (the Duke of Norfolk) with regard to state ceremonial are largely exercised through the College. The College is also the official repository of the arms and pedigrees of English, Northern Irish and Commonwealth (except Canadian) families and their descendants, and its records include official copies of the records of Ulster King of Arms, the originals of which remain in Dublin. The 13 officers of the College specialize in genealogical and heraldic work for their respective clients.

Arms have been and still are granted by letters patent from the Kings of Arms. A right to arms can only be established by the registration in the official records of the College of Arms of a pedigree showing direct male line descent from an ancestor already appearing therein as being entitled to arms, or by making application through the College of Arms for a grant of arms.

The College of Arms is open Monday–Friday 10–4.
Earl Marshal, His Grace the Duke of Norfolk, KG, GCVO, CB, CBE, MC

KINGS OF ARMS
Garter, P. L. Gwynn-Jones, LVO
Clarenceux, J. P. B. Brooke-Little, CVO, FSA
Norroy and Ulster (and Registrar), D. H. B. Chesshyre, LVO, FSA

HERALDS
Windsor, T. D. Mathew
Somerset, T. Woodcock, FSA
Richmond, P. L. Dickinson
York, H. E. Paston-Bedingfeld
Chester, T. H. S. Duke
Lancaster, vacant

Earl Marshal's Secretary, Sir Walter Verco, KCVO, Surrey Herald Extraordinary

PURSUIVANTS
Bluemantle, R. J. B. Noel
Portcullis, W. G. Hunt, TD
Rouge Croix, vacant
Rouge Dragon, vacant

COURT OF THE LORD LYON
HM New Register House, Edinburgh EH1 3YT
Tel 0131-556 7255

The Court of the Lord Lyon is the Scottish Court of Chivalry (including the genealogical jurisdiction of the *Ri-Sennachie* of Scotland's Celtic Kings). The Lord Lyon King of Arms has jurisdiction, subject to appeal to the Court of Session and the House of Lords, in questions of heraldry and the right to bear arms. The Court also administers the Scottish Public Register of All Arms and Bearings and the Public Register of All Genealogies. Pedigrees are established by decrees of Lyon Court and by letters patent. As Royal Commissioner in Armory, the Lord Lyon grants patents of arms (which constitute the grantee and heirs noble in the Noblesse of Scotland) to 'virtuous and well-deserving' Scotsmen and to petitioners (personal or corporate) in Her Majesty's overseas realms of Scottish connection, and issues birthbrieves.
Lord Lyon King of Arms, Sir Malcolm Innes of Edingight, KCVO, WS

HERALDS
Albany, J. A. Spens, RD, WS
Rothesay, Sir Crispin Agnew of Lochnaw, Bt.
Ross, C. J. Burnett, FSA SCOT

PURSUIVANTS
Kintyre, J. C. G. George, FSA SCOT
Unicorn, Alastair Campbell of Airds, FSA SCOT
Carrick, Mrs C. G. W. Roads, MVO, FSA SCOT

Lyon Clerk and Keeper of Records, Mrs C. G. W. Roads, MVO, FSA SCOT
Procurator-Fiscal, D. F. Murby, WS
Herald Painter, Mrs J. Phillips
Macer, A. M. Clark

ARTS COUNCILS

The Arts Council of Great Britain was established as an independent body in 1946 to be the principal channel for the Government's support of the arts. In 1994 the Scottish and Welsh Arts Councils became autonomous and the Arts Council of Great Britain became the Arts Council of England.

The Arts Councils are responsible for the distribution of one-fifth of the proceeds of the National Lottery allocated to 'good causes'. They had received about £167 million for distribution as at July 1995 and had made awards to the value of £104.835 million.

ARTS COUNCIL OF ENGLAND
14 Great Peter Street, London SW1P 3NQ
Tel 0171-333 0100

The Arts Council of England funds the major arts organizations in England and the ten Regional Arts Boards. It works closely with the Scottish Arts Council and the Arts Council of Wales.

The Council also provides advice, information and help to artists and arts organizations. Its objectives are to develop and improve the understanding and practice of the arts and to increase their accessibility to the public.

The Council distributes an annual grant from the Department of National Heritage; the grant for 1995–6 is £191.1 million.
Chairman, The Lord Gowrie
Vice-Chairman, Sir Richard Rogers
Members, R. Cork; C. Frayling; Ms M. Guillebaud; P. Gummer; Sir Ernest Hall; G. Henderson; Ms T. Holt; T. Nunn, CBE; S. Phillips; Ms U. Prashar, CBE; D. Reid; Ms S. Robinson; Ms P. Skene; R. Southgate
Secretary-General, Ms M. Allen

REGIONAL ARTS BOARDS

EASTERN ARTS BOARD, Cherry Hinton Hall, Cherry Hinton Road, Cambridge CB1 4DW. Tel: 01223-215355. *Chair,* Dr D. Harrison
EAST MIDLANDS ARTS BOARD, Mountfields House, Forest Road, Loughborough, Leics LE11 3HU. Tel: 01509-218292. *Chair,* Prof. R. Cowell
LONDON ARTS BOARD, Elme House, 133 Long Acre, London WC2E 9AF. Tel: 0171-240 1313. *Chair,* C. Priestley
NORTHERN ARTS BOARD, 9–10 Osborne Terrace, Newcastle upon Tyne NE2 1NZ. Tel: 0191-281 6334. *Chair,* Mrs S. Robinson
NORTH-WEST ARTS BOARD, 12 Harter Street, Manchester M1 6HY. Tel: 0161-228 3062. *Chair,* Prof. B. Cox
SOUTH-EAST ARTS BOARD, 10 Mount Ephraim, Tunbridge Wells, Kent TN4 8AS. Tel: 01892-515210. *Chair,* B. Nicholson
SOUTHERN ARTS BOARD, 13 St Clement Street, Winchester SO23 9DQ. Tel: 01962-855099. *Chair,* D. Reid
SOUTH-WEST ARTS BOARD, Bradninch Place, Gandy Street, Exeter EX4 3LS. Tel: 01392-218188. *Chair,* Ms M. Guillebaud
WEST MIDLANDS ARTS BOARD, 82 Granville Street, Birmingham B1 2LH. Tel: 0121-631 3121. *Chair,* R. Southgate
YORKSHIRE AND HUMBERSIDE ARTS BOARD, 21 Bond Street, Dewsbury, W. Yorks WF13 1AX. Tel: 01924-455555. *Chair,* Sir Ernest Hall

SCOTTISH ARTS COUNCIL
12 Manor Place, Edinburgh EH3 7DD
Tel 0131-226 6051

The Scottish Arts Council funds arts organizations in Scotland and is funded directly by the Scottish Office. The grant for 1995–6 is £24.47 million.
Chairman, Dr W. Brown
Vice-Chairman, Ms F. Walker
Members, Dr Sheila Brock; D. Connell; J. Denholm; P. Dowds; K. Geddes; G. Hallewell; P. Hamilton; R. Love; Dr Rita McAllister; Dr I. McGowan; Ms J. Richardson; Prof. E. Spiller; Ms L. Thomson
Director, Ms S. Reid

ARTS COUNCIL OF WALES
Museum Place, Cardiff CF1 3NX
Tel 01222-394 711

The Arts Council of Wales funds arts organizations in Wales and is funded directly by the Welsh Office. The grant for 1995–6 is £14.189 million.
Chairman, Sir Richard Lloyd Jones, KCB
Members, Ms J. Davidson; M. Edwards; F. Evans; K. Evans; Ms K. Gass; P. Griffiths; G. S. Jones; R. G. Jones; M. Pepper; D. Richards; A. Roberts; E. Thomas; Prof. G. Thomas; Ms M. Vincentelli
Chief Executive, E. Jenkins

ARTS COUNCIL OF NORTHERN IRELAND
185 Stranmillis Road, Belfast BT9 5DU
Tel 01232-381591

The Arts Council of Northern Ireland disburses government funds in support of the arts in Northern Ireland. It is funded by the Department of Education for Northern Ireland, and the grant for 1995–6 is £6.66 million.
Chairman, D. Deeny, QC
Vice-Chairman, Sir Charles Brett
Members, J. Aiken; F. Cobain; P. Donnelly; Ms R. Duffy; Dr Tess Hurson; Ms K. Ingram; Prof. Edna Longley; W. O'Connell; R. Pierce; Ms C. Poulter; Ms I. Sandford; Prof. R. Welch
Chief Executive, B. Ferran

ART GALLERIES, ETC

ROYAL FINE ART COMMISSION
7 St James's Square, London SW1Y 4JU
Tel 0171-839 6537

Established in 1924, the Commission is an autonomous authority on the aesthetic implications of any project or development, primarily but not exclusively architectural, which affects the visual environment.
Chairman, The Lord St John of Fawsley, PC
Commissioners, Prof. R. D. Carter, CBE; Sir Philip Dowson, CBE, RA; D. H. Fraser; M. Girouard, PH.D.; M. J. Hopkins, CBE, RA; S. A. Lipton; Prof. Margaret MacKeith, PH.D.; H. T. Moggridge, OBE; Mrs J. Nutting; T. Osborne, FRICS; I. Ritchie; Prof. J. R. Steer, FSA; J. Sutherland, FENg.; Miss W. Taylor, CBE; Q. Terry, FRIBA; J. Winter, MBE; Dr G. Worsley
Secretary (G6), F. Golding

ROYAL FINE ART COMMISSION FOR SCOTLAND
9 Atholl Crescent, Edinburgh EH3 8HA
Tel 0131-229 1109

The Commission was established in 1927 and advises ministers and local authorities on the visual impact and quality of design of construction projects. It is an independent body and gives its opinions impartially.

Chairman, The Lord Cameron of Lochbroom, PC, FRSE
Commissioners, Prof. G. Benson; Miss K. Borland;
 W. A. Cadell; Mrs K. Dalyell; A. S. Matheson, FRIBA;
 D. Page; Miss B. Rae; Prof. T. Ridley, FRSE;
 R. R. Steedman, RSA; Prof. R. Webster; R. Wedgwood
Secretary, C. Prosser

NATIONAL GALLERY
Trafalgar Square, London WC2N 5DN
Tel 0171-839 3321

The National Gallery, which houses a permanent collection of western painting since the 13th century, was founded in 1824, following a parliamentary grant of £60,000 for the purchase and exhibition of the Angerstein collection of pictures. The present site was first occupied in 1838; a substantial extension to the north of the building with a public entrance in Orange Street was opened in 1975, and the Sainsbury wing was opened in 1991. Total government grant-in-aid for 1995–6 is £18.322 million.

BOARD OF TRUSTEES
Chairman, N. H. Baring
Trustees, B. Gascoigne, FRSL; P. Troughton; Sir Derek
 Oulton, GCB, QC; E. Uglow; Sir Keith Thomas, FBA; The
 Hon. Simon Sainsbury; Lady Bingham; Sir Mark
 Richmond, SC.D., FRS; A. Bennett; Lady Monck; Mrs
 P. Ridley; Sir Ewen Fergusson, GCMG, GCVO; R. Gavron,
 CBE

OFFICERS
Director (G3), R. N. MacGregor
Chief Curator (G5), Dr C. P. H. Brown
Senior Curators (G5), Dr N. Penny; (G7), Dr S. Foister; Dr
 D. Gordon; J. Leighton
Chief Restorer (G5), M. H. Wyld
Head of Exhibitions (G5), M. J. Wilson
Scientific Adviser (G5), Dr A. Roy
Director of Administration (G5), J. MacAuslan
Head of Finance and Personnel (G5), T. Tarkowski
Head of Press and Public Relations (G7), Miss J. Liddiard

NATIONAL PORTRAIT GALLERY
St Martin's Place, London WC2H 0HE
Tel 0171-306 0055

A grant was made in 1856 to form a gallery of the portraits of the most eminent persons in British history. The present building was opened in 1896 and an extension in 1933. There are four outstations displaying portraits in appropriate settings: Montacute House, Gawthorpe Hall, Beningbrough Hall and Bodelwyddan Castle. Total government grant-in-aid for 1995–6 is £5.065 million.

BOARD OF TRUSTEES
Chairman, H. Keswick
Trustees, The Lord President of the Council (ex officio);
 The President of the Royal Academy of Arts (ex
 officio); J. Roberts, D.phil.; The Lord Morris of Castle
 Morris, D.phil.; Prof. N. Lynton; Sir Eduardo Paolozzi;
 J. Tusa; Sir Antony Acland, GCMG, GCVO; Lady Acland;
 Mrs J. E. Benson, LVO, OBE; Mrs W. Tumim; Sir David
 Scholey, CBE; Mrs C. Tomalin; Baroness Willoughby de
 Eresby; M. Hastings; Prof. The Earl Russell
Director (G3), C. Saumarez-Smith, PH.D.

TATE GALLERY
Millbank, London SW1P 4RG
Tel 0171-887 8000

The Tate Gallery comprises the national collections of British painting and 20th-century painting and sculpture.

The Gallery was opened in 1897, the cost of erection (£80,000) being defrayed by Sir Henry Tate, who also contributed the nucleus of the present collection. The Turner wing was opened in 1910, galleries to contain the collection of modern foreign painting in 1926, and a new sculpture hall in 1937. In 1979 a further extension was built, and the Clore Gallery, for the Turner collection, was opened in 1987. The Tate Gallery Liverpool opened in 1988 and the Tate Gallery St Ives in 1993. Total government grant-in-aid for 1995–6 is £18.9 million.

BOARD OF TRUSTEES
Chairman, D. Stevenson, CBE
Trustees, The Lord Attenborough, CBE; The Hon. Mrs
 J. de Botton; Sir Richard Carew Pole; M. Craig-Martin;
 R. Deacon; B. Gascoigne; D. Gordon; Mrs P. Ridley;
 D. Verey; Prof. Dawn Ades

OFFICERS
Director (G3), N. Serota
Director of Public and Regional Services (G5), S. Nairne
Keeper of the British Collection (G5), A. Wilton
Keeper of the Modern Collection (G5), R. Morphet
Curator, Tate Gallery Liverpool (G6), L. Biggs
Curator, Tate Gallery St Ives (G6), M. Tooby

WALLACE COLLECTION
Hertford House, Manchester Square, London W1M 6BN
Tel 0171-935 0687

The Wallace Collection was bequeathed to the nation by the widow of Sir Richard Wallace, Bt. in 1897, and Hertford House was subsequently acquired by the Government. Total government grant-in-aid for 1995–6 is £1.913 million.

Director, Miss R. J. Savill
Head of Administration, A. W. Houldershaw

NATIONAL GALLERIES OF SCOTLAND
The Mound, Edinburgh EH2 2EL
Tel 0131-556 8921

The National Galleries of Scotland comprise the National Gallery of Scotland, the Scottish National Portrait Gallery and the Scottish National Gallery of Modern Art. There are also outstations at Paxton House, Berwickshire, and Duff House, Banffshire. Total government grant-in-aid for 1995–6 is £8.876 million.

TRUSTEES
Chairman of the Trustees, A. M. Grossart, CBE
Trustees, J. Packer, OBE; A. R. Cole-Hamilton; Mrs
 L. W. Gibbs; Lord Macfarlane of Bearsden; Dr
 T. Johnston; Prof. A. A. Tait; E. Hagman; Prof. E. Fernie;
 M. Shea; The Countess of Airlie, CVO

OFFICERS
Director (G4), T. Clifford
Keeper of Conservation (G6), J. P. Dick, OBE
Keeper of Information (G7), vacant
Keeper of Education (G7), M. Cassin
Registrar (G7), Miss A. Buddle
Secretary (G6), Ms S. Edwards
Buildings (G7), R. Galbraith
Keeper, National Gallery of Scotland (G6), M. Clarke
Keeper, Scottish National Portrait Gallery (G6), D. Thomson,
 PH.D.
 Curator of Photography, Miss S. F. Stevenson
Keeper, Scottish National Gallery of Modern Art (G6),
 R. Calvocoressi

UK ATOMIC ENERGY AUTHORITY
Harwell, Oxon OX11 0RA
Tel 01235-821111

The UKAEA was established by the Atomic Energy Authority Act 1954. Since 1986 the UKAEA has been required by the Government to operate on a commercial footing and in 1990 it adopted the trading name AEA Technology. It provides scientific and technical services, products and consultancy in nuclear and non-nuclear fields to governments, utilities and industries world-wide. The UKAEA has six research and engineering centres. Many of the technical staff and activities of the Warren Spring Laboratory merged with the environmental capabilities of AEA Technology in 1994 to create the National Environmental Technology Centre based within AEA Technology. The Government announced in 1994 its intention to privatize the commercial activities of the AEA.
Chairman (part-time), Sir Anthony Cleaver
Deputy Chairman and Chief Executive, AEA Technology, Dr B. L. Eyre, CBE
Chief Executive, UKAEA Government Division, Dr D. Pooley, CBE

AUDIT COMMISSIONS

AUDIT COMMISSION FOR LOCAL AUTHORITIES AND THE NATIONAL HEALTH SERVICE IN ENGLAND AND WALES
1 Vincent Square, London SW1P 2PN
Tel 0171-828 1212

The Audit Commission was set up in 1983 with responsibility for the external audit of local authorities. This remit was extended from 1990 to include the audit of the National Health Service bodies in England and Wales. The Commission appoints the auditors, who may be from the District Audit Service or from a private firm of accountants. The Commission is also responsible for promoting value for money in the services provided by local authorities and health bodies.

The Commission has 15–17 members appointed by the Secretary of State for the Environment in consultation with the Secretaries of State for Wales and for Health. Though appointed by the Secretary of State, the Commissioners are responsible to Parliament.
Chairman, C. Thompson (acting)
Deputy Chairman, C. M. Stuart, CBE
Controller of Audit, A. Foster
Chief Executive of District Audit Service, D. Prince

ACCOUNTS COMMISSION FOR SCOTLAND
18 George Street, Edinburgh EH2 2QU
Tel 0131-477 1234

The Commission was set up in 1975. It is responsible for securing the audit of the accounts of Scottish local authorities and certain joint boards and joint committees. On 1 April 1995 it assumed responsibility for securing the audit of National Health Service bodies in Scotland. Amongst its duties the Commission is required to deal with reports made by the Controller of Audit on items of account contrary to law; on incorrect accounting; and on losses due to misconduct, negligence and failure to carry out statutory duties. Since 1988 the Commission has had responsibility for value-for-money audits of authorities.

Members are appointed by the Secretary of State for Scotland.
Chairman, Prof. J. P. Percy
Controller of Audit, R. W. Black
Secretary, W. F. Magee

THE BANK OF ENGLAND
Threadneedle Street, London EC2R 8AH
Tel 0171-601 4444

The Bank of England was incorporated in 1694 under royal charter. It is the banker of the Government, on whose behalf it executes monetary policy and manages the note issue and the national debt. It is also responsible for promoting the efficiency and competitiveness of financial services. As the central reserve bank of the country, the Bank keeps the accounts of British banks, who maintain with it a proportion of their cash resources, and of most overseas central banks. The Bank is divided into two divisions, Monetary Stability and Financial Stability. (*See also* page 615).
Governor, E. A. J. George
Deputy Governor, H. J. Davies
Directors, Sir David Cooksey; Mrs F. A. Heaton; Sir Christopher Hogg; P. H. Kent; Sir John Keswick; M. A. King; Sir David Lees; Ms S. V. Masters; Sir Christopher Morse, KCMG; I. Plenderleith; B. Quinn; Sir David Scholey, CBE, FRSA; N. I. Simms; D. A. G. Simon; Prof. Sir Roland Smith; Sir Colin Southgate
Advisers to the Governor, Sir Peter Petrie; P. C. Peddie; I. G. Watt
Chief Cashier and Deputy Director, Banking and Market Services, G. E. A. Kentfield
Chief Registrar, D. A. Bridger
General Manager, Printing Works, A. W. Jarvis
Secretary, J. R. E. Footman
The Auditor, M. J. W. Phillips

BOUNDARY COMMISSIONS

The Commissions are constituted under the Parliamentary Constituencies Act 1986. The Speaker of the House of Commons is ex-officio chairman of all four commissions in the UK. Each of the four commissions is required by law to keep the parliamentary constituencies in their part of the UK under review. A review started after the 1992 General Election was completed in April 1995; the final proposals await parliamentary approval. Each of the three commissions in Great Britain is required by law to keep the European parliamentary constituencies in their part of Great Britain under review.

ENGLAND
St Catherine's House, 10 Kingsway, London WC2B 6JP
Tel 0171-396 2105
Deputy Chairman, The Hon. Mr Justice Knox
Joint Secretaries, R. McLeod; S. Limpkin

WALES
St Catherine's House, 10 Kingsway, London WC2B 6JP
Tel 0171-396 2105
Deputy Chairman, vacant
Joint Secretaries, R. McLeod; S. Limpkin

SCOTLAND
St Andrew's House, Edinburgh EH1 3DG
Tel 0131-244 2196/2027

Deputy Chairman, The Hon. Lord Davidson
Secretary, D. K. C. Jeffrey

NORTHERN IRELAND
Frances House, 9–11 Brunswick Street, Belfast BT2 7GE
Tel 01232-321292

Deputy Chairman, The Hon. Mr Justice Pringle
Secretary, J. R. Fisher

BRITISH BROADCASTING CORPORATION
Broadcasting House, Portland Place, London WIA IAA
Tel 0171-580 4468
Television Centre, Wood Lane, London W12 7RJ
Tel 0181-743 8000

The BBC was incorporated under royal charter as successor to the British Broadcasting Company Ltd, whose licence expired in 1926. Its present charter came into force in 1981 and a new charter will come into force on 1 January 1997. The chairman, vice-chairman and other governors are appointed by The Queen-in-Council. The BBC is financed by revenue from receiving licences for the home services and by grant-in-aid from Parliament for the World Service (radio).
For services, *see* Broadcasting section.

BOARD OF GOVERNORS *as at 1 July 1995*
Chairman (£63,670), M. Hussey
Vice-Chairman (£16,340), The Lord Cocks of Hartcliffe, PC
National Governors (*each* £16,340), Sir Kenneth Bloomfield, KCB (*N. Ireland*); Dr G. Jones (*Wales*); Revd N. Drummond (*Scotland*)
Governors (*each* £8,170), W. B. Jordan, CBE; Lord Nicholas Gordon Lennox, KCMG, KCVO; Mrs M. Spurr, OBE; Mrs J. Cohen

BOARD OF MANAGEMENT
Director-General, J. Birt
Deputy Director-General, , R. Phillis
Managing Directors, W. Wyatt (*Network Television*); Ms E. Forgan (*Network Radio*); R. Neil (*Regional Broadcasting*); T. Hall (*News and Current Affairs*); R. Lynch (*Resources*); Dr J. Thomas (*BBC Worldwide TV*); N. Chapman (*Worldwide Publishing*); S. Younger (*World Service*)
Directors, C. Browne (*Corporate Affairs*); Mrs M. Salmon (*Personnel*); Miss P. Hodgson, CBE (*Policy and Planning*); R. Baker-Bates (*Finance and Information Technology*); Ms J. Drabble (*Education*)

OTHER SENIOR STAFF
The Secretary, M. Stevenson
Controller, BBC1, A. Yentob
Controller, BBC2, M. Jackson
Deputy Managing Director, Network Radio and Controller, Radio 4, M. Green
Controller, Radio 1, M. Bannister
Controller, Radio 2, Ms F. Line (*until early 1996*); J. Moir (*from early 1996*)
Controller, Radio 3, N. Kenyon
Controller, Radio 5 Live, Ms J. Abramsky
Controller, BBC Scotland, J. McCormick
Controller, BBC Wales, G. Talfan Davies
Controller, BBC N. Ireland, P.Loughrey
Head of Broadcasting, BBC South, J. Shearer
Head of Broadcasting, BBC North, C. Adams
Head of Broadcasting, BBC Midlands and East, N. Chapman
Director of Broadcasting, World Service, S. Younger
Controller, Editorial Policy, R. Ayre
Legal Adviser, G. Roscoe

BRITISH COAL CORPORATION
Hobart House, Grosvenor Place, London SWIX 7AE
Tel 0171-201 4141

The British Coal Corporation (formerly the National Coal Board) was constituted in 1946 and took over the mines on 1 January 1947. The Coal Industry Act 1994 established the statutory framework for the privatization of British Coal's mining operations. British Coal's ownership of coal reserves and responsibility for licensing other coal producers were transferred to the Coal Authority, a non-departmental public body (*see* page 295). The sale of regional coal companies, into which British Coal's operational mining assets had been transferred, was concluded in December 1994. The Act also charged British Coal with the disposal of its non-mining activities. This process is continuing, and the bulk of the assets are expected to have been disposed of by the end of 1996. The British Coal Corporation will be wound up when the process is completed.
Chairman, J. N. Clarke
Executive Member, P. L. Hutchinson (*Secretary/Legal Adviser*)
Non-Executive Members, A. P. Hichens; Sir Robert Davidson, FEng.; D. B. Vaughan

THE BRITISH COUNCIL
10 Spring Gardens, London SWIA 2BN
Tel 0171-930 8466
Medlock Street, Manchester MI5
Tel 0161-957 7000

The British Council was established in 1934 and incorporated by royal charter in 1940. It is an independent, non-political organization which promotes Britain abroad. It provides access to British ideas, talents and experience in education and training, books and periodicals, the English language, the arts, the sciences and technology.
The Council is represented in 108 countries and runs 187 offices, 116 libraries, 72 English language schools and 29 resource centres around the world.
The Council's annual turnover in 1995–6 is estimated at £439 million. Total sources of funding in 1994–5, including government grants and contracted money, was £426.9 million, of which the Council's own revenue was £115.26 million.
Chairman, Sir Martin Jacomb
Deputy Chairman, The Lord Chorley
Director-General, Sir John Hanson, KCMG, CBE

BRITISH FILM COMMISSION
70 Baker Street, London WIM IDJ
Tel 0171-224 5000

The British Film Commission was established in 1992 and is funded by the Department of National Heritage. The Commission promotes the UK as an international production centre, encourages the use of locations, facilities, services and personnel, and provides a comprehensive computerized information service on all aspects of filming in the UK.
Commissioner, Sir Sydney Samuelson, CBE
Chief Executive, A. Patrick

BRITISH FILM INSTITUTE
21 Stephen Street, London w1p 1pl
Tel 0171-255 1444

The British Film Institute was established in 1933 under royal charter. Its aims are to encourage the development of the art of film and its use as a record of contemporary life in Great Britain, and to foster the study, appreciation and use of films for television. It includes the National Film and Television Archive, the National Film Theatre and the Museum of the Moving Image, and it supports a network of 38 regional film theatres. The BFI Library contains the world's largest collection of material relating to film and television. Total government funding for 1995–6 is £16.973 million.
Chairman, J. Thomas
Director, W. Stevenson

BRITISH PHARMACOPOEIA COMMISSION
Market Towers, 1 Nine Elms Lane, London sw8 5nq
Tel 0171-273 0561

The British Pharmacopoeia Commission sets standards for medicinal products used in human and veterinary medicine. It is responsible for the British Pharmacopoeia (a publicly-available statement of the standard that a product must meet throughout its shelf-life), the British Pharmacopoeia (Veterinary) and the selection of British Approved Names. It also participates in the work of the European Pharmacopoeia on behalf of the UK. It has 15 members who are appointed by the Secretary of State for Health and the Minister for Agriculture, Fisheries and Food.
Chairman, Prof. D. Ganderton, obe
Vice-Chairman, Dr D. H. Calam
Secretary (G6), Dr R. C. Hutton

BRITISH RAILWAYS BOARD
Euston House, 24 Eversholt Street, PO Box 100, London
nw1 1dz
Tel 0171-928 5151

The British Railways Board came into being in 1963 under the terms of the Transport Act 1962. Under the Railways Act 1993, the activities of the Board have been restructured in preparation for privatization. In the meantime, the Board continues as operator of train services in Great Britain. For details of privatization and railway operations, *see* Transport section.
Chairman and Chief Executive (£180,000), J. K. Welsby, cbe
Vice-Chairman, C. J. Campbell, cbe
Finance and Planning, J. J. Jerram, cbe
Personnel, A. P. Watkinson
Part-time non-executive members, P. Allen, cbe; J. Aziz;
   J. Butler; K. H. M. Dixon; Sir William Francis, cbe; Miss
   K. T. Kantor; W. Wilson
Secretary, P. Trewin

BRITISH STANDARDS INSTITUTION (BSI)
389 Chiswick High Road, London w4 4al
Tel 0181-996 9000

The British Standards Institution is the recognized authority in the UK for the preparation and publication of national standards for industrial and consumer products. In consultation with the interests concerned, BSI prepares standards relating to nearly every sector of the nation's industry and trade. It also represents the UK at European and international standards meetings. About 80 per cent of its standards work is now internationally linked. British Standards are issued for voluntary adoption, though in a number of cases compliance with a British Standard is required by legislation. Industrial and consumer products certified as complying with the relevant British Standard may carry the Institution's certification trade mark, known as the 'Kitemark'.
Chief Executive, Sir Neville Purvis, kcb

BRITISH TOURIST AUTHORITY
Thames Tower, Black's Road, London w6 9el
Tel 0181-846 9000

Established under the Development of Tourism Act 1969, the British Tourist Authority has specific responsibility for promoting tourism to Great Britain from overseas. It also has a general responsibility for the promotion and development of tourism and tourist facilities within Great Britain as a whole, and for advising the Government on tourism matters.
Chairman (*part-time*), Ms A. Biss
Chief Executive, A. Sell

BRITISH WATERWAYS
Willow Grange, Church Road, Watford, Herts wd1 3qa
Tel 01923-226422

British Waterways is the navigation authority for over 2,000 miles of canals and river navigations in England, Scotland and Wales. Some 380 miles are maintained and are being developed as commercial waterways for use by freight-carrying vessels. Another 1,200 miles, the cruising waterways, are being developed for boating, fishing and other leisure activities. The remaining 500 miles, the remainder waterways, are maintained with due regard to safety, public health and the preservation of amenities. Of this remaining mileage, nearly two-thirds is navigable or has been restored to navigation over the past twenty years.
Chairman (*part-time*), B. Henderson, cbe
Vice-Chairman (*part-time*), Sir Peter Hutchison, Bt.
Members (*all part-time*), J. Gordon; D. H. R. Yorke;
   M. Cairns; Sir Neil Cossons; Ms J. Elvey; Ms J. Lewis-
   Jones
Chief Executive, B. C. Dice
Secretary and Solicitor, R. J. Duffy

BROADCASTING STANDARDS COUNCIL
7 The Sanctuary, London sw1p 3js
Tel 0171-233 0544

The Council was set up in 1988 but received its statutory powers under the Broadcasting Act 1990. Its role is advisory, not regulatory. It monitors the portrayal of violence, sex and matters of taste and decency in all broadcast programmes and advertisements on television, radio, cable and satellite services. The Council publishes a code of practice, considers complaints and conducts research into audience attitudes. Members of the Council are appointed by the Secretary of State for National Heritage. The appointments are part-time.

The Government has announced plans to merge the BSC with the Broadcasting Complaints Commission.

Chair (£41,660), The Lady Howe of Aberavon
Deputy Chairman (£31,410), The Lord Dubs
Members (*each* £12,530), Ms R. Bevan; Dr Jean Curtis-Raleigh; R. Kernohan, OBE; the Very Revd J. Lang; M. Parris; Ms S. O'Sullivan
Director, C. Shaw, CBE

THE BROADS AUTHORITY
Thomas Harvey House, 18 Colegate, Norwich NR3 1BQ
Tel 01603-610734

The Broads Authority is a special statutory authority set up under the Norfolk and Suffolk Broads Act 1988, with powers and responsibilities similar to those of National Park Authorities. The functions of the Authority are to conserve and enhance the natural beauty of the Broads; to promote the enjoyment of the Broads by the public; and to protect the interests of navigation. The Authority comprises 35 members.
Chairman, J. S. Peel, CBE, MC
Chief Executive, M. A. Clark

THE CABINET OFFICE

The Cabinet Office comprises the Secretariat, who support Ministers collectively in the conduct of Cabinet business; and the Office of Public Service (OPS) which is responsible for the Citizen's Charter initiative, the Next Steps programme, policy on open government, senior Civil Service and public appointments, market testing and efficiency in the Civil Service, and Civil Service recruitment.

The OPS supports the Prime Minister in his capacity as Minister for the Civil Service, with responsibility for day-to-day supervision delegated to the Chancellor of the Duchy of Lancaster.

Prime Minister and Minister for the Civil Service,
The Rt. Hon. John Major, MP

PRIME MINISTER'S OFFICE
10 Downing Street, London SW1A 2AA
Tel 0171-270 3000
Principal Private Secretary (*G3*), A. Allan
Private Secretaries (*G5*), R. Lyne, CMG (*Overseas Affairs*); vacant (*Economic Affairs*); M. Adams (*Parliamentary Affairs*); (*G7*), Ms R. Reynolds (*Home Affairs*)
Assistant Private Secretaries, Miss A. B. Hordern; Miss J. L. Wilkinson
Diary Secretary, Ms A. Warburton
Political Secretary, H. James
Policy Unit, N. Blackwell; Mrs K. Ramsey; D. Morris; J. Rees; D. Soskin; S. Williams; Ms C. Fairbairn; T. Collins
Parliamentary Private Secretary, J. Ward, MP
Chief Press Secretary (*G2*), C. J. R. Meyer, CMG
Deputy Chief Press Secretary (*G5*), A. Marre

Secretary for Appointments, and Ecclesiastical Secretary to the Lord Chancellor (*G2*), J. Holroyd, CB
Parliamentary Clerk, R. Stone
Secretary of the Cabinet and Head of Home Civil Service,
Sir Robin Butler, GCB, CVO
Private Secretary, Miss M. J. Leech

SECRETARIAT
70 Whitehall, London SW1A 2AS
Tel 0171-270 3000

Deputy Secretaries (*G2*), P. Lever, CMG; Sir Gerald Warner, KCMG; B. Bender; K. J. Mackenzie;
Under-Secretaries (*G3*), D. J. Gould; A. Cahn; A. C. Galsworthy, CMG
Grade 5, A. Sandall; M. K. Collins; R. G. Wakeford; Brig. J. A. J. Budd; M. J. Lyall-Grant

OFFICE OF PUBLIC SERVICE (OPS)
Horse Guards Road, London SW1P 3AL
Tel 0171-270 6000
70 Whitehall, London SW1A 2AS
Tel 0171-270 1234
First Secretary of State and Deputy Prime Minister,
The Rt. Hon. Michael Heseltine, MP
Parliamentary Private Secretary, R. Ottaway, MP
Chancellor of the Duchy of Lancaster, The Rt. Hon. Roger Freeman, MP
Principal Private Secretary, J. Buck
Private Secretary, Ms H. Paxman
Parliamentary Private Secretary, S. Coe, MP
Parliamentary Secretary, John Horam, MP
Private Secretary, P. F. Lynch
Second Permanent Secretary (*G1A*), R. Mountfield, CB
Private Secretary, K. T. Roberts
Parliamentary Clerk, Mrs T. N. Oakley
Press Secretary (*G5*), B. Sutlieff

CITIZEN'S CHARTER UNIT
Government Offices, Great George Street, London SW1P 3AL
Tel 0171-270 1826

Director (*G2*), Miss E. C. Turton
Deputy Directors (*G5*), Mrs G. Craig; C. Sanger

EFFICIENCY UNIT
70 Whitehall, London SW1A 2AS
Tel 0171-270 0273

Prime Minister's Adviser on Efficiency and Effectiveness,
Sir Peter Levene, KBE
Head of Unit (*G3*), J. Oughton
Deputy Head of Unit (*G5*), vacant
Grade 5, Ms C. Souter; Ms H. Ghosh; P. Matwijiw; Ms F. Wilson
Head of Next Steps Project Team (*G5*), M. J. Cowper

ADVISORY UNIT ON MINISTERS' AGENCIES
Adviser, C. M. Brendish
Head of Unit (*G6*), D. R. Wood

CIVIL SERVICE EMPLOYER GROUP
Under-Secretary (*G3*), H. H. Taylor
Grade 5, Mrs J. Britton (*Equal Opportunities*); C. J. Parry (*Development*); Mrs N. Tomkinson (*Top Management Programme Course Director*); D. Pain (*Pensions*); I. Strachan (*Personnel Management and Conditions of Service*)
Head of European Staffing Unit (*G6*), Dr J. Fuller

SENIOR CIVIL SERVICE GROUP
Under-Secretary (*G3*), B. Fox
Grade 5, D. Laughrin; Ms A. Clendinning

MACHINERY OF GOVERNMENT AND STANDARDS
Grade 3, A. D. Whetnall
Head of Security (G5), J. K. Barron

OFFICE OF THE CIVIL SERVICE COMMISSIONERS
(OCSC)
Horse Guards Road, London SWIP 3AL
Tel 0171-270 5081
First Commissioner (G2), Sir Michael Bett, CBE
Commissioners (part-time), M. D. Geddes;Ms U. Prashar,
CBE; Mrs J. Rubin; G. Maddrell; K. E. C. Sorensen;
D. J. Burr
Secretary to the Commissioners and Head of the Office (G5), Miss
E. M. Goodison

INFORMATION OFFICER MANAGEMENT UNIT
Director (G5), T. J. Perks

CCTA (THE GOVERNMENT CENTRE FOR
INFORMATION SYSTEMS)
Riverwalk House, 157–161 Millbank, London SWIP 4RT
Tel 0171-217 3000
Gildengate House, Upper Green Lane, Norwich NR3 IDW
Tel 01603-694620
Director (G3), R. Dibble
Deputy Director (G4), W. Houldsworth

CEREMONIAL BRANCH
53 Parliament Street, London SWIA 2NG
Tel 0171-210 5056
Honours Nomination Unit: Tel 0171-210 5071
Ceremonial Officer (G5), A. J. Merifield, CB

ESTABLISHMENT OFFICER'S GROUP
Government Offices, Great George Street, London SWIP
3AL
Tel 0171-270 3000
Principal Establishment and Finance Officer (G3),
R. W. D. Venning
Deputy Establishment Officer (G5), K. Bastin
Senior Finance Officer (G6), K. Tolladay

HISTORICAL AND RECORDS SECTION
Hepburn House, Marsham Street, London SWIP 4HW
Tel 0171-217 6032
Grade 5, Miss P. M. Andrews

EXECUTIVE AGENCIES

CENTRAL OFFICE OF INFORMATION
— *see* below

CHESSINGTON COMPUTER CENTRE
Government Buildings, Leatherhead Road, Chessington,
Surrey KT9 2LT
Tel 0181-391 3800
The Centre provides administrative and financial services
to the public sector.
Chief Executive (G5), R. N. Edwards

CIVIL SERVICE COLLEGE
Sunningdale Park, Ascot, Berks SL5 0QE
Tel 01344-634000
11 Belgrave Road, London SWIV IRB
Tel 0171-834 6644
The College provides training in management and pro-
fessional skills for the public and private sectors.
Chief Executive (G3), Dr S. H. F. Hickey
Director of Studies (G5), D. R. Smith
Business Executives (G5/G6), C. W. H. Aitken; M. N. Barnes;

Mrs M. B. Chapman; Ms E. Chennells;
G. W. Llewellyn; Ms S. J. McCarthy; M. Timmis; Miss
J. A. Topham; Miss M. A. Wood

HMSO
— *see* page 349

OCCUPATIONAL HEALTH AND SAFETY AGENCY
18–20 Hill Street, Edinburgh EH2 3NB
Tel 0131-220 4177
The Occupational Health and Safety Agency provides
services and advice to all government departments and
executive agencies, and to other public bodies, on matters
relating to the health of their employees in their working
environment.
Chief Executive, Dr E. C. McCloy
Director of Medical Services, Dr P. Litchfield

RECRUITMENT AND ASSESSMENT SERVICES (RAS)
Alencon Link, Basingstoke, Hants RG21 7JB
Tel 01256-29222
24 Whitehall, London SWIA 2ED
Tel 0171-210 3000
RAS provides professional recruitment and staff develop-
ment services to the Civil Service and other public sector
bodies.
*Chief Executive and Director of Fast Stream Recruitment
(acting)*, C. Muir
Director of Recruitment, Finance and Administration,
Mrs J. A. Lovegrove
Director of Business Development, F. D. Bedford

CENTRAL ADJUDICATION SERVICES
Quarry House, Quarry Hill, Leeds LS2 7UB
Tel 0113-232 4000
New Court, 48 Carey Street, London WC2A 2LS
Tel 0171-412 1504

The Chief Adjudication Officer and Chief Child Support
Officer are independent statutory authorities under the
Social Security Act 1975 (as amended) and the Child
Support Act 1991. They are appointed by the Secretary of
State for Social Security to give advice to adjudication
officers and child support officers, to keep under review the
operation of the systems of adjudication, and to report
annually to the Secretary of State on adjudication standards.
   Adjudication officers make decisions of first instance on
all claims for social security cash benefits, and child support
officers make decisions of first instance on applications for
child maintenance made to the Child Support Agency.
Officers of the Chief Adjudication Officer also enter
written observations on all appeals made to the Social
Security Commissioners, and officers of the Chief Child
Support Officer make written observations on appeals to
the Child Support Commissioners.
Chief Adjudication Officer and Chief Child Support Officer,
E. W. Hazlewood

CENTRAL OFFICE OF INFORMATION
Hercules Road, London SEI 7DU
Tel 0171-928 2345

The Central Office of Information (COI) is an executive
agency which procures publicity and information services
for government departments, other executive agencies and

public sector bodies. It provides consultancy, design, production, procurement and project management services for a wide range of publicity services in all media. Though the majority of COI's work is for government departments in the UK, it also produces a range of publicity materials for overseas consumption. Administrative responsibility for the COI rests with the Minister of Public Service within the Cabinet Office.
Chief Executive and Head of the Government Information Service (G3), G. M. Devereau
Senior Personal Secretary, Mrs J. Rodrigues

MANAGEMENT BOARD
Members, G. M. Devereau; K. Williamson; R. Windsor; D. A. Low; R. Smith
Secretary, Miss K. Gilding

DIRECTORS
Director, Marketing and Client Services (G6), M. Richardson
Director, Advertising (G6), P. Buchanan
Director, Research (G6), M. Rigg
Director, Direct Marketing (G6), C. Noble
Director, Events (G6), A. Chard
Director, Press and Pictures (G6), V. Rowlands
Director, Publications (G6), J. Murray
Director, Publishing and Translations (G6), D. Beynon
Director, Films, Television and Radio (G6), I. Hamilton
Principal Finance Officer (G5), K. Williamson
Director, Regional Network (G6), R. Haslam

NETWORK OFFICES
EASTERN, Three Crowns House, 72–80 Hills Road, Cambridge CB2 1LL. *Network Director (G7)*, Mrs V. Burdon
MIDLANDS, Five Ways House, Islington Row Middleway, Edgbaston, Birmingham B15 1SH. *Network Director (G6)*, B. Garner
NORTH-EAST, Wellbar House, Gallowgate, Newcastle upon Tyne NE1 4TB. *Network Director (G7)*, H. Cozens
NORTH-WEST, Sunley Tower, Piccadilly Plaza, Manchester M1 4BD. *Network Director (G7)*, Mrs E. Jones
SOUTH-EAST, Hercules Road, London SE1 7DU. *Network Director (G6)*, D. Smith
SOUTH-WEST, The Pithay, Bristol BS1 2NF. *Network Director (G7)*, P. Whitbread
YORKSHIRE AND HUMBERSIDE, City House, New Station Street, Leeds LS1 4JG. *Network Director (G7)*, vacant

CENTRAL STATISTICAL OFFICE
Great George Street, London SW1P 3AQ
Tel 0171-270 6363/6364

The work of the Central Statistical Office (CSO) encompasses data collection from businesses; the preparation and publication of macro-economic statistics and social statistics abstracts; statistics relating to institutional sectors and financial statistics; the retail prices index, employment data and the family expenditure survey; liaison with international statistical bodies; and central management of the Government Statistical Service (GSS). The Central Statistical Office became an executive agency of the Treasury in 1991.
The Government has announced its intention to merge the CSO and the Office of Population Censuses and Surveys (*see* pages 336–7)
Director and Head of the Government Statistical Service (G1A), Dr T. Holt
Private Secretary, S. Beard
Deputy Director (G2), D. C. L. Wroe, CB

Head of Employment Statistics (G3), P. Stibbard
Head of Statistical Methods and Quality (G5), T. Jones
Head of Policy Secretariat (G5), J. Pullinger

GSS AND GENERAL DIVISION
Grade 3, J. R. Calder
Heads of Branches (G5), Miss J. Church (*Social and regional statistics and household expenditure*); Mrs M. Haworth (*Retail Prices*); A. Machin (*Departmental Deregulation Unit*)

BUSINESS STATISTICS DIVISION
Grade 3, Dr M. P. G. Pepper
Heads of Branches (G5), K. Francombe (*Distribution and services*); C. J. Spiller (*Production*); G. D. Walker (*Central initiatives*); J. D. Kinder (*Product prices and sales*); M. R. Brand (*Companies and overseas*)

ECONOMIC ACCOUNTS DIVISION
Grade 3, J. E. Kidgell
Heads of Branches (G5), R. Lynch (*National accounts*); K. Mansell (*Expenditure*); S. Brown (*Balance of payments*); G. Jenkinson (*Company and personal sectors*); Mrs P. Walker (*Public sector and financial accounts*)

CENTRAL SERVICES DIVISION
Grade 3, Dr L. Mayhew
Heads of Branches (G5), M. Pape (*Information systems*); D. R. Lewis (*Personnel and staff development*); H. W. Joiner (*Finance and office services*); (*G6*), I. G. Scott (*Press and public information*); P. Powell (*Marketing and sales*)

CERTIFICATION OFFICE FOR TRADE UNIONS AND EMPLOYERS' ASSOCIATIONS
27 Wilton Street, London SW1X 7AZ
Tel 0171-210 3734/5

The Certification Office is an independent statutory authority. The Certification Officer is appointed by the Secretary of State for Employment and is responsible for receiving and scrutinizing annual returns from trade unions and employers' associations; for reimbursing certain costs of trade unions' postal ballots; for dealing with complaints concerning trade union elections; for ensuring observance of statutory requirements governing political funds and trade union mergers; and for certifying the independence of trade unions.
Certification Officer, E. G. Whybrew
Assistant Certification Officer, G. S. Osborne

SCOTLAND
58 Frederick Street, Edinburgh EH2 1LN
Tel 0131-226 3224
Assistant Certification Officer for Scotland, J. L. J. Craig

CHARITY COMMISSION
St Alban's House, 57–60 Haymarket, London SW1Y 4QX
Tel 0171-210 4556
2nd Floor, 20 King's Parade, Queen's Dock, Liverpool L3 4DQ
Tel 0151-703 1500
Woodfield House, Tangier, Taunton, Somerset TA1 4BL
Tel 01823-345000

The Charity Commission is established under the Charities Act 1993 with the general function of promoting the effective use of charitable resources in England and Wales. The Commission gives information and advice to charity trustees to make the administration of their charity more effective; investigates misconduct and the abuse of charitable assets, and takes or recommends remedial action; and maintains a public register of charities. The Commission does not have at its disposal any funds with which to make grants to organizations or individuals.

At the end of 1994 the total number of registered charities was 178,609.

Chief Commissioner (G3), R. Fries
Commissioners (G3), R. M. C. Venables; *(G4)*, J. Farquharson
Commissioners (part-time) (G4), J. Bonds; Mrs T. Baring
Heads of Legal Sections (G5), J. A. Dutton; G. S. Goodchild; K. M. Dibble; S. Slack
Executive Director (G4), Mrs E. A. Shaw
Director of Operations (G5), V. F. Mitchell
Establishment Officer (G5), Mrs J. Cotton
Information Systems Controller (G5), Ms G. Cruickshank

The offices responsible for charities in Scotland and Northern Ireland are:

SCOTLAND – Scottish Charities Office, Crown Office, 25 Chambers Street, Edinburgh EH1 1LA. Tel: 0131-226 2626

NORTHERN IRELAND – Department of Health and Social Services, Charities Branch, Annexe 3, Castle Buildings, Stormont Estate, Belfast BT4 3RA. Tel: 01232-522 595

CHIEF ADJUDICATION OFFICER AND CHIEF CHILD SUPPORT OFFICER
— *see* Central Adjudication Services

CHILD SUPPORT AGENCY
— *see* page 348

CHURCH COMMISSIONERS
1 Millbank, London SW1P 3JZ
Tel 0171-222 7010

The Church Commissioners were established in 1948 by the amalgamation of Queen Anne's Bounty (established 1704) and the Ecclesiastical Commissioners (established 1836).

The Commissioners are responsible for the management of most of the Church of England's assets, the income from which is predominantly used to pay, house and pension the clergy. The Commissioners own nearly 141,000 acres of agricultural land, a number of residential estates in central London, and commercial property in Great Britain and the USA. They also carry out administrative duties in connection with pastoral reorganization and redundant churches, and have been designated by the General Synod as the central stipends authority of the Church of England.

The Commissioners are: the Archbishops of Canterbury and of York; the 41 diocesan bishops; five deans or provosts, ten other clergy and ten lay persons appointed by the General Synod; four lay persons nominated by The Queen; four persons nominated by the Archbishop of Canterbury; the Lord Chancellor; the Lord President of the Council; the First Lord of the Treasury; the Chancellor of the Exchequer; the Secretary of State for the Home Department; the Speaker of the House of Commons; the Lord Chief Justice; the Master of the Rolls; the Attorney-General; the Solicitor-General; the Lord Mayor and two Aldermen of the City of London; the Lord Mayor of York; and one representative from each of the Universities of Oxford and Cambridge.

INCOME AND EXPENDITURE
for year ended 31 December 1994

	£ million
Total income	161.2
Net income	145.0
Investments	78.8
Property	70.7
Interest from loans, etc.	11.7
Total expenditure	153.4
Clergy stipends	54.1
Clergy and widows' pensions	73.9
Clergy houses	1.8
Episcopal and cathedral housing	2.7
Financial provision for resigning clergy	2.6
Commissioners' administration of central church functions	5.4
Episcopal administration and payments to Chapters	10.1
Church buildings	0.6
Administration costs of other bodies	2.2
Deficit for year	(8.4)

CHURCH ESTATES COMMISSIONERS
First, Sir Michael Colman, Bt.
Second, The Rt. Hon. Michael Alison, MP
Third, Mrs M. H. Laird

OFFICERS
Secretary, P. Locke
Deputy Secretary (Policy and Planning), R. S. Hopgood
Deputy Secretary (Finance and Investment), C. W. Daws
Assistant Secretaries:
  The Accountant, G. C. Baines
  Management Accountant, B. J. Hardy
  Chief Surveyor, A. C. Brown
  Computer Manager, J. W. Ferguson
  Estates, P. H. P. Shaw, LVO
  Investments Manager, A. S. Hardy
  Pastoral, Houses and Redundant Churches, M. D. Elengorn
  Stipends and Allocations, M. G. S. Farrell
  Senior Architect, J. A. Taylor
Official Solicitor, J. P. Guy

CIVIL AVIATION AUTHORITY
CAA House, 45–59 Kingsway, London WC2B 6TE
Tel 0171-379 7311

The CAA is responsible for the economic regulation of UK airlines by licensing air routes and air travel organizers and by approving fares for journeys outside the European Union; for the safety regulation of UK civil aviation by the certification of airlines and aircraft and by licensing aerodromes, flight crew and aircraft engineers; and, through National Air Traffic Services, for the provision of air traffic control and telecommunications services.

The CAA also advises the Government on aviation issues, represents consumer interests, conducts economic and scientific research, produces statistical data and provides specialist services including calibration of navigation aids, fire-fighting and other training, and consultancy services to clients world-wide.

Chairman (part-time) (£67,772), The Rt. Hon.
  Sir Christopher Chataway
Secretary, R. J. Britton

THE COAL AUTHORITY
200 Lichfield Lane, Mansfield, Notts NG22 8ND
Tel 01623–427162

The Coal Authority was established under the Coal Industry Act 1994 to manage certain functions previously undertaken by British Coal, including ownership of unworked coal. It is responsible for licensing coal mining operations and for providing information on coal reserves and past and future coal mining. It settles subsidence claims not falling on coal mining operators. It is also responsible for the management and disposal of property, and for dealing with surface hazards such as abandoned coal mine shafts.
Chairman, Sir David White
Chief Executive, N. Washington, OBE.

COMMONWEALTH DEVELOPMENT CORPORATION
1 Bessborough Gardens, London SW1V 2JQ
Tel 0171-828 4488

The Commonwealth Development Corporation is charged with the task of assisting overseas countries in the development of their economies. Its main activity is providing long-term finance, as loans and risk capital, for projects. The Corporation's area of operations includes British dependent territories and, with ministerial approval, Commonwealth or other developing countries. At present, the Corporation is authorized to operate in more than 60 countries and territories. Its investments and commitments at the end of 1994 were £1,700 million.
Chairman (part-time), The Earl Cairns, CBE
Deputy Chairman (part-time), Sir William Ryrie, KCB
Chief Executive, Dr R. Reynolds

COMMONWEALTH SECRETARIAT
— *see* Index

COMMONWEALTH WAR GRAVES COMMISSION
2 Marlow Road, Maidenhead, Berks SL6 7DX
Tel 01628-34221

The Commonwealth War Graves Commission (formerly Imperial War Graves Commission) was founded by royal charter in 1917. It is responsible for the commemoration of 1,694,930 members of the forces of the Commonwealth who fell in the two world wars. More than one million graves are maintained in 23,071 burial grounds throughout the world. Over three-quarters of a million men and women who have no known grave or who were cremated are commemorated by name on memorials built by the Commission.
The funds of the Commission are derived from the six participating governments, i.e. the UK, Australia, Canada, India, New Zealand and South Africa.
President, HRH The Duke of Kent, KG, GCMG, GCVO, ADC
Chairman, The Secretary of State for Defence in the UK
Vice-Chairman, Air Chief Marshal Sir Joseph Gilbert, KCB, CBE
Members, The Secretary of State for the Environment in the UK; The High Commissioners in London for Australia, Canada, India, New Zealand and South

Africa; Dame Janet Fookes, DBE, MP; Sir Nigel Mobbs; The Viscount Ridley, KG, GCVO, TD; Prof. R. J. O'Neill, AO; Mrs L. Golding, MP; Sir Harold Walker, KCMG; Gen. Sir John Akehurst, KCB, CBE; Adm. Sir John Kerr, GCB
Director-General and Secretary to the Commission, D. Kennedy
Deputy Directors-General, T. F. Penfold (*Administration*); R. J. Dalley (*Operations*)
Directors, P. Noakes (*Finance*); A. Coombe (*Works*); D. C. Parker (*Horticulture*); D. R. Parker (*Personnel*); J. P. D. Gee (*Information and Secretariat*)
Legal Adviser and Solicitor, G. C. Reddie

IMPERIAL WAR GRAVES ENDOWMENT FUND
Trustees, The Lord Remnant, CVO (*Chairman*); Air Chief Marshal Sir Joseph Gilbert, KCB, CBE; A. C. Barker
Secretary to the Trustees, P. Noakes

COUNTRYSIDE COMMISSION
John Dower House, Crescent Place, Cheltenham, Glos.
GL50 3RA
Tel 01242-521381

The Countryside Commission was set up in 1968 and is an independent agency which promotes the conservation and enhancement of landscape beauty in England. It encourages the provision and improvement of facilities in the countryside, and works to secure access for open air recreation. Since 1982 the Commission has been funded by an annual grant from the Department of the Environment. Members of the Commission are appointed by the Secretary of State for the Environment.
In April 1995 the Commission's National Forest initiative was transferred to the National Forest Company, a public company limited by guarantee.
Chairman, R. Simmonds
Director-General (G3), M. Dower
Directors (G5), R. Clarke (*Policy*); M. J. Kirby (*Operations*); M. Taylor (*Resources*)
National Heritage Adviser, P. Walshe
Head of Corporate Planning (G7), N. Holliday
Head of Land Use Branch (G7), Ms A. Ewins
Head of Recreation and Access Branch (G7), T. Robinson
Head of Public Affairs (G7), R. Roberts
Head of Finance and Establishments (G7), V. Ellis
Head of National Parks and Planning Branch (G7), R. Lloyd
Head of Environmental Protection Branch (G7), Ms P. Jones
Regional Officers (G7), K. Buchanan (*Newcastle*); Dr M. Carroll (*Cambridge*); Dr S. A. Bucknall (*Leeds*); E. Holdaway (*Bristol*); Dr Liz Newton (*Manchester*); D. E. Coleman (*London*); F. S. Walmsley (*Birmingham*)
Special Initiatives, Dr M. Rawson (*Community Forests*); T. Allen (*Countryside Stewardship*)

COUNTRYSIDE COUNCIL FOR WALES/ CYNGOR CEFN GWLAD CYMRU
Plas Penrhos, Fford Penrhos, Bangor, Gwynedd LL57 2LQ
Tel 01248-370444

The Countryside Council for Wales is the Government's statutory adviser on wildlife, countryside and maritime conservation matters in Wales, and it is the executive authority for the conservation of habitats and wildlife. It promotes the protection of the Welsh landscape and encourages opportunities for public access and enjoyment of the countryside. It provides grant aid to local authorities, voluntary organizations and individuals to pursue

countryside management. It is funded by the Welsh Office and accountable to the Secretary of State for Wales, who appoints its members.
Chairman, E. M. W. Griffith, CBE
Chief Executive, Prof. I. Mercer (*until end 1995*)
Chief Scientist, Dr M. Smith
Director, Operations, I. R. Bonner

COVENT GARDEN MARKET AUTHORITY
Covent House, New Covent Garden Market, London
SW8 5NX
Tel 0171-720 2211

The Covent Garden Market Authority is constituted under the Covent Garden Market Acts 1961 to 1977, the members being appointed by the Minister of Agriculture, Fisheries and Food. The Authority owns and operates the 56-acre New Covent Garden Markets (fruit, vegetables, flowers) which have been trading since 1974.
Chairman (part-time), W. P. Bowman, CBE
General Manager, Dr P. M. Liggins
Secretary, C. Farey

CRIMINAL INJURIES COMPENSATION BOARD
Tay House, 300 Bath Street, Glasgow G2 4JR
Tel 0141-331 2726
Morley House, 26–30 Holborn Viaduct, London ECIA 2JQ
Tel 0171-842 6800

The Board was constituted in 1964 to administer the government scheme for *ex gratia* payments of compensation to victims of crimes of violence. The Government has proposed changes to the compensation scheme, including the replacement of the Board by a new Criminal Injuries Compensation Authority.
Chairman (part-time) (£34,096), The Lord Carlisle of Bucklow, PC, QC
Director, P. G. Spurgeon

CROFTERS COMMISSION
4–6 Castle Wynd, Inverness IV2 3EQ
Tel 01463-663450

The Crofters Commission is a statutory body established in 1955 which is responsible for reorganizing, developing and regulating crofting in the seven crofting (and former county) areas of Argyll, Caithness, Inverness, Orkney, Ross and Cromarty, Shetland and Sutherland. The Commission keeps under review all matters relating to crofting, advises the Secretary of State for Scotland on crofting matters and liaises with other relevant bodies. The Commission also administers the Crofting Counties Agricultural Grants (Scotland) Scheme 1988.
Chairman, H. A. M. Maclean
Secretary (G6), M. Grantham

CROWN AGENTS FOR OVERSEA GOVERNMENTS AND ADMINISTRATIONS
St Nicholas House, St Nicholas Road, Sutton, Surrey
SM1 1EL
Tel 0181-643 3311

Incorporated under the Crown Agents Act 1979, the Crown Agents are commercial, financial and professional agents for over 130 governments and over 300 public authorities, international bodies and other organizations, primarily in the public sector. The Government has announced its intention to transfer the Crown Agents to an independent foundation.
Chairman, D. H. Probert
Managing Director, P. F. Berry

CROWN ESTATE
16 Carlton House Terrace, London SW1Y 5AH
Tel 0171-210 4377

The land revenues of the Crown in England and Wales have been collected on the public account since 1760, when George III surrendered them to Parliament and received a fixed annual payment or Civil List. At the time of the surrender the gross revenues amounted to about £89,000 and the net return to about £11,000.

The land revenues in Ireland have been carried to the Consolidated Fund since 1820; from 1923, as regards the Republic of Ireland, they have been collected and administered by the Irish Government.

The land revenues in Scotland were transferred to the predecessors of the Crown Estate Commissioners in 1833.

In the year ended 31 March 1995, the gross income from the Crown Estate totalled £133.245 million. The sum of £84.8 million was paid to the Exchequer in 1994–5 as surplus revenue.
First Commissioner and Chairman (part-time), Sir Denys Henderson
Second Commissioner and Chief Executive, C. K. Howes, CB
Commissioners (part-time), R. B. Caws, CBE, FRICS;
    J. N. C. James, CBE; A. S. Macdonald, CBE;
    J. H. M. Norris, CBE; The Lord De Ramsey
Deputy Chief Executives, D. E. Murray (*Property*);
    D. E. G. Griffiths (*Finance and Administration*)
Legal Adviser, M. L. Davies
Crown Estate Surveyor, C. F. Hynes
Urban Estates Managers, M. W. Dillon; A. Bickmore;
    R. Wyatt
Agricultural Estates Manager, R. J. Mulholland
Marine Estates Manager, F. G. Parrish
Information Systems Manager, D. Kingston-Smith
Valuation and Investment Analysis Manager, P. Shearmur
Internal Audit Manager, J. E. Ford
Finance Manager, J. G. Lelliott
Corporate Services Manager, M. E. Beckwith
Personnel Manager, R. J. Blake
Public Relations and Press Officer, Mrs G. Coates

SCOTLAND
10 Charlotte Square, Edinburgh EH2 4BR
Tel 0131-226 2741

Crown Estate Receiver for Scotland, M. J. Gravestock

WINDSOR ESTATE
The Great Park, Windsor, Berks SL4 2HT
Tel 01753-860222

Deputy Ranger and Surveyor, M. J. O'Lone

CROWN PROSECUTION SERVICE
— see page 370

BOARD OF CUSTOMS AND EXCISE
*New King's Beam House, 22 Upper Ground, London
SE1 9PJ
Tel 0171-620 1313

Commissioners of Customs were first appointed in 1671 and housed by the King in London. The Excise Department was formerly under the Inland Revenue Department and was amalgamated with the Customs Department in 1909.

HM Customs and Excise is responsible for collecting and administering customs and excise duties and VAT, and advises the Chancellor of the Exchequer on any matters connected with them. The Department is also responsible for preventing and detecting the evasion of revenue laws and for enforcing a range of prohibitions and restrictions on the importation of certain classes of goods. In addition, the Department undertakes certain agency work on behalf of other departments, including the compilation of UK overseas trade statistics from customs import and export documents.

THE BOARD
Chairman (G1), Mrs V. P. M. Strachan, CB
Private Secretaries, D. Hook; Ms E. Walker
Deputy Chairman (G2), A. W. Russell
Commissioners (G3), D. F. O. Battle; A. C. Sawyer;
L. J. Harris; Mrs L. Woods; M. J. Eland; M. R. Brown;
D. R. Howard; A. Paynter
Head of Board's Secretariat (G5), A. Killikelly

DEPUTY CHAIRMAN'S GROUP
Press and Publicity Office
Tel 0171-865 5665
Principal Information Officer, Ms L. J. Sinclair

INFORMATION SYSTEMS DIRECTORATE
Alexander House, Victoria Avenue, Southend-on-Sea
SS99 1AU
Tel 01702-348944
Director, A. Paynter

CUSTOMS POLICY DIRECTORATE
Director, M. Eland

EXCISE AND CENTRAL POLICY DIRECTORATE
Director, D. Howard

VAT POLICY DIRECTORATE
Director, L. Harris

PERSONNEL AND FINANCE DIRECTORATE
Director, D. Battle

CENTRAL OPERATIONS DIRECTORATE
Alexander House, Victoria Avenue, Southend-on-Sea
SS99 1AU
Tel 01702-348944
Director, M. Brown

Tariff and Statistical Office
Controller, A. Cowley

Accounting Services Division
Accountant and Comptroller-General, D. Hewett

*Unless otherwise stated, this is the address and telephone number of directorates of the Board

COMPLIANCE DIRECTORATE
Director, Mrs L. Woods

PREVENTION DIRECTORATE
Director, A. Sawyer

Investigation Division
Custom House, Lower Thames Street, London EC3R 6EE
Tel 0171-283 5353
Chief Investigation Officer, R. Kellaway

SOLICITOR'S OFFICE
Solicitor (G2), D. E. J. Nissen
Principal Assistant Solicitors (G3), R. D. S. Wylie;
G. Fotherby

COLLECTORS OF HM CUSTOMS AND EXCISE (G5)
Anglia, R. C. Shepherd
Central England, A. Bowen
Eastern England, M. D. Patten
London Airports, F. D. Tweddle
London Central, J. Maclean
Northern England, H. Peden
Northern Ireland, T. W. Logan
North-west England, A. Allen
Scotland, C. Arnott
South-east England, W. I. Stuttle
South London and Thames, R. L. H. Lawrence, CBE
Southern England, C. J. Packman
Thames Valley, J. B. Eaton
Wales, the West and Borders, H. Burnard

OFFICE OF THE DATA PROTECTION REGISTRAR
Wycliffe House, Water Lane, Wilmslow, Cheshire
SK9 5AF
Tel 01625-535711 (administration); 01625-535777 (enquiries)

The Office of the Data Protection Registrar was created by the Data Protection Act 1984. It is the Registrar's duty to compile and maintain the Register of data users and computer bureaux and to provide facilities for members of the public to examine the Register; to promote observance of data protection principles; to consider complaints made by data subjects; to disseminate information about the Act; to encourage the production of codes of practice by trade associations and other bodies; to guide data users in complying with data protection principles; to co-operate with other parties to the Council of Europe Convention and act as UK authority for the purposes of Article 13 of the Convention; and to report annually to Parliament on the performance of his functions.
Registrar, Mrs E. France

MINISTRY OF DEFENCE
— see pages 384–7

DESIGN COUNCIL
1 Oxendon Street, London SW1Y 4EE
Tel 0171-208 2121

The Design Council is incorporated by royal charter and registered as a charity. It is the national authority on the role of design in commercial, economic and social development. Direct advice to industry on design matters is now

provided by a local network, Business Links, run by the Department of Trade and Industry.
Chairman, J. Sorrell
Chief Executive, A. Summers

THE DUCHY OF CORNWALL
10 Buckingham Gate, London SW1E 6LA
Tel 0171-834 7346

The Duchy of Cornwall was created by Edward III in 1337 for the support of his eldest son, Edward, the Black Prince. It is the oldest of the English duchies. Before elevation to a dukedom, it was an earldom from 1227, when Richard, King of the Romans and younger brother of Henry III, was created Earl of Cornwall. Since 1503 the eldest surviving son of the Sovereign has, as heir apparent, succeeded to the dukedom by inheritance. The present Prince of Wales is the 24th Duke of Cornwall, and the estate's primary function is still to provide an income for the Duke of Cornwall and his family. The estate is primarily agricultural, with 130,000 acres in 23 counties but mostly in the south-west of England. The Duchy also has some residential property, a number of shops and offices, and a Stock Exchange portfolio.

THE PRINCE'S COUNCIL
Chairman, HRH The Prince of Wales, KG, KT, GCB
Lord Warden of the Stannaries, The Earl Peel
Receiver-General, The Earl Cairns, CBE
Attorney-General to the Prince of Wales, J. M. Sullivan, QC
Secretary and Keeper of the Records, J. N. C. James, CBE
Other members, Earl of Shelburne; Cdr. R. J. Aylard, CVO, RN; J. E. Pugsley; A. M. J. Galsworthy; C. Howes, CB; W. N. Hood, CBE

OTHER OFFICERS
Auditors, I. Brindle; H. Hughes
Sheriff (1995–6), Mrs E. Bolitho

THE DUCHY OF LANCASTER
Lancaster Place, Strand, London WC2E 7ED
Tel 0171-836 8277

The estates and jurisdiction known as the Duchy of Lancaster have belonged to the reigning monarch since 1399 when John of Gaunt's son came to the throne as Henry IV. As the Lancaster Inheritance it goes back as far as 1265 when Henry III granted his youngest son Edmund lands and possessions following the Baron's war. In 1267 Henry gave Edmund the County, Honor and Castle of Lancaster and created him the first Earl of Lancaster. In 1351 Edward III created Lancaster a County Palatine.

The Chancellor of the Duchy of Lancaster is responsible for the administration of the Duchy, the appointment of justices of the peace in Lancashire, Greater Manchester and Merseyside and ecclesiastical patronage in the Duchy gift. The Chancellorship is also a Cabinet post.
Chancellor of the Duchy of Lancaster, The Rt. Hon. Roger Freeman, MP
Attorney-General, T. A. W. Lloyd, QC
Receiver-General, Maj. Sir Shane Blewitt, KCVO
Clerk of the Council, M. K. Ridley, CVO
Chief Clerk, Col. F. N. J. Davies

DEPARTMENT FOR EDUCATION AND EMPLOYMENT
Sanctuary Buildings, Great Smith Street, London SW1P 3BT
Tel 0171-925 5000

The Government Department of Education was originally a committee of the Privy Council appointed in 1839 to supervise the distribution of certain grants which had been made by Parliament since 1834. The Act of 1899 established the Board of Education, with a President and Parliamentary Secretary, and created a Consultative Committee. The Education Act 1944 established the Ministry of Education. In 1964 the office of the Minister of Science was combined with the Ministry to form the Department of Education and Science. In 1992 responsibility for science was transferred out of the department and it was re-named the Department for Education. In 1995 the Department took over responsibility for the Employment Service, careers and training and was re-named the Department for Education and Employment. The final structure of the merged department had not been confirmed at time of going to press.
Secretary of State for Education, The Rt. Hon. Gillian Shephard, MP
　Private Secretary, Miss P. Laidlaw
　Special Adviser, Dr E. Cottrell
　Parliamentary Private Secretary, A. Coombs, MP
Ministers of State, Eric Forth, MP; The Lord Henley
　Private Secretaries, Ms C. Maye; Ms P. Clarke
　Parliamentary Private Secretary, J. Whittingdale, MP
Parliamentary Under-Secretaries of State, Robin Squire, MP; James Paice, MP; Cheryl Gillan, MP
　Private Secretaries, D. McGrath; Ms A. McNicholl; D. Walsh
Permanent Secretaries (*G1*), Sir Tim Lankester; M. Bichard
　Private Secretaries, C. S. Wormald; Miss K. Driver
Deputy Secretaries (*G2*), R. J. Dawe, CB, OBE (*Further and Higher Education and International*); P. F. Owen, CB (*Schools Curriculum and Teachers*); J. C. Hedger (*Schools*)

PERSONNEL AND ORGANIZATION BRANCH
Director of Services (*G3*), D. Normington
Grade 3, P. A. Shaw
Deputy Director of Services (*G5*), T. B. Jeffery
Head of Resource Management Division (*G5*), Mrs I. Wilde
Controller, Darlington (*G5*), L. B. Webb

INFORMATION SYSTEMS BRANCH
Director of Information Systems (*G5*), A. K. C. Gibson

ANALYTICAL SERVICES BRANCH
Head of Branch (*G3*), D. Allnutt
Chief Statisticians (*G5*), J. W. Gardner; Miss P. Annesley; Miss S. J. Walton
Head of Economics (*G5*), D. J. Thompson
Head of Operations Research Unit (*G5*), R. B. Ladley

SCHOOL ORGANIZATION BRANCH
Head of Branch (*G3*), M. J. Richardson
Grade 5, B. Glickman; M. Hipkins; A. J. Shaw; P. J. Thorpe; J. W. Whitaker
Chief Architect (*G5*), J. J. Wilson
Chief Engineer (*G6*), M. J. Patel

PUPILS AND PARENTS BRANCH
Head of Branch (*G3*), R. L. Smith
Grade 5, R. J. Green; Mrs P. A. Masters; M. D. Phipps; A. J. Sargent

SCHOOL FUNDING BRANCH
Head of Branch (G3), N. Summers
Grade 5, M. C. Stark; A. Clarke; S. A. Marston

SCHOOL CURRICULUM BRANCH
Head of Branch (G3), C. H. Saville
Grade 5, Miss C. A. Bienkowska; R. P. Ritzema;
    M. F. Neale; S. R. Williams

TEACHERS BRANCH
Head of Branch (G3), N. J. Sanders
Grade 5, Ms S. L. Scales; A. J. Wye

HIGHER EDUCATION BRANCH
Head of Branch (G3), C. A. Clark
Grade 5, A. Woollard; Mrs S. J. Trundle; J. Moore

FURTHER EDUCATION BRANCH
Head of Branch (G3), D. M. Forrester
Head of FE Support Unit (G4), B. D. Short, CBE
Grade 5, Miss J. Benham; S. E. Kershaw; C. Barnham

INTERNATIONAL RELATIONS AND YOUTH BRANCH
Head of Branch (G3), E. R. Morgan
Grade 5, Miss C. E. Hodkinson; Miss C. E. Treen

TRAINING, ENTERPRISE AND EDUCATION
DIRECTORATE
Moorfoot, Sheffield SI 4PQ
Tel 0114-275 3275

Director-General (G2), vacant
Director of Operations (G3), S. Loveman
Head of Financial Control Unit (G5), P. Jones
Regional Directors, see pages 306–7

Youth and Education Policy Division
Director (G3), Mrs V. Bayliss
Heads of Branches (G5); J. Robertson (*Schools and Partnerships
    Policy*); R. Wye (*Young People and Work*); T. Fellows
    (*Further and Higher Education*); Ms L. Ammon (*Careers
    Service*)

Training Infrastructure and Employers Division
Director (G3), N. Schofield
Heads of Branches (G5), M. Nicholas (*Employer Investment*);
    J. Fuller (*European Training Policy, Programmes and
    Funding*); E. Galvin (*Qualifications and Industry Training
    Organizations*); T. Down (*Development Strategy Unit*)

Planning Division
Director (G4), Ms F. Everiss
Heads of Branches (G5), H. Sharp (*Operational Policy*); J. West
    (*Resource Planning*); E. Morrey (*Operational Monitoring*)

Adults and Training Strategy Division
Director (G3), B. Heatley
Head of Branches (G5/G6), D. Tansley (*Adult and Training
    Strategy*); J. Smith (*Individual Commitment*); R. Harrison
    (*Training Strategy and Secretariat*)

Quality Assurance Division
Director (G3), P. Thomas
Heads of Branches (G5), N. White (*Analysis and Planning*);
    V. Keddie (*Quality Studies*); K. Franklin (*Quality Policy,
    Good Practice and Dissemination*)

LEGAL BRANCH
Legal Adviser (G3), R. N. Ricks
Assistant Legal Advisers (G5), S. T. Harker, A. D. Preston;
    F. D. W. Clarke

INFORMATION BRANCH
Head of Branch (G4), J. W. Coe
Deputy Head of Branch (G6), K. B. Kerslake
Head of News (G6), M. Paterson
Chief Press Officer (G7), T. R. Cook

Marketing Manager (G7), J. M. Brown

Information Bureau and Library
Chief Librarian, Miss M. Wilson

FINANCE BRANCH
Accountant-General (G3), R. D. Horne
Deputy Accountant-General (G5), D. Sandeman
Head of Internal Audit G5), N. J. Thirtle
Grade 5, J. S. Street
Assistant Accountant-General (G6), T. A. H. Tyler

EXECUTIVE AGENCIES

THE EMPLOYMENT SERVICE
St Vincent House, 30 Orange Street, London WC2H 7HT
Tel 0171-839 5600
The Employment Service is responsible for providing
services and administering programmes to help unem-
ployed people get back to work as quickly as possible and to
make payments to those entitled to benefit.
Chief Executive (G3+), M. E. G. Fogden, CB
Senior Director of Operations (G3), D. Grover
Director of Finance and Resources (G4), A. G. Johnson
Director of Information and Systems (G4), R. Phillips
Director of Business Development (G4), K. White
Director of Human Resources (G4), D. B. Price
Regional Directors (G4), R. Foster (*London and South-east*);
    (*G5*), Mrs A. Le Sage (*East Midlands*); P. Robson
    (*Northern*); J. Roberts (*North-west*); K. Pascoe (*South-
    west*); Miss R Thew (*West Midlands*); G. Humphreys
    (*Yorkshire and Humberside*)
Director for Scotland (G5), A. R. Brown
Director for Wales (G5), E. B. Pearce

TEACHERS PENSION AGENCY
Staindrop Road, Darlington, Co. Durham DL3 9EE
Tel 01325-392929
The Agency administers the teachers' superannuation
scheme in England and Wales.
Chief Executive, Mrs D. Metcalfe
Directors, K. M. Miles; P. M. Bleasdale; A. Allison;
    D. G. Sanders

OFFICE FOR STANDARDS IN EDUCATION
(OFSTED)
Alexandra House, 33 Kingsway, London WC2B 6SE
Tel 0171-421 6800
A non-ministerial government department established in
1992 to keep the Secretary of State informed about the
standards and management of schools in England, and to
establish and monitor an independent inspection system
for maintained schools in England.
HM Chief Inspector (G2), C. Woodhead
Director of Administration (G4), Mrs H. Douglas
Directors of Inspection (G4), A. J. Rose; M. J. Tomlinson

TEAM MANAGERS
Access and Intelligence (G5), D. Singleton
Contracts (G5), B. Townsend
Curriculum and Assessment (G5), T. Wylie
External Relations (G5), P. Singh
Independent, International and Island Schools (G5),
    Mrs B. Fawcett
Management (G5), C. Payne
Monitoring (G5), I. Shelton
Personnel (G5), Miss J. Phillips
Post-Compulsory Education (G5), D. West
Quality Assurance and Development (G5), A. P. Matthews
Registration (G5), J. Grewe
Research and Analysis (G5), Mrs C. Agambar

Resource Planning (G5), D. W. Taylor
School Support and Development (G5), Miss E. Passmore
Special Educational Needs (G5), Miss D. Chorley
Teacher Education (G5), V. Green, CBE
Training and Assessment of Independent Inspectors (G5), Miss E. Pagliacci
Information (G6), J. Lawson
Information Systems (G6), M. Childs
Competition and Compliance (G7), C. Bramley

There are 24 Grade 5 Inspectors and 191 Grade 6 Inspectors

OFFICE OF ELECTRICITY REGULATION
Hagley House, Hagley Road, Birmingham B16 8QG
Tel 0121-456 2100
SCOTLAND: Regent Court, 70 West Regent Street,
Glasgow G2 2QZ
Tel 0141-331 2678

The Office of Electricity Regulation (OFFER) is the regulatory body for the electricity supply industry in England, Scotland and Wales. Its functions are to promote competition in the generation and supply of electricity; to ensure that all reasonable demands for electricity are satisfied; to protect customers' interests in relation to prices, security of supply and quality of services; and to promote the efficient use of electricity. Headed by the Director-General of Electricity Supply, OFFER was set up under the Electricity Act 1989 but is independent of ministerial control.
Director-General of Electricity Supply, Prof. S. C. Littlechild
Deputy Director-General, C. P. Carter
Deputy Director-General for Scotland, G. L. Sims
Directors of Regulation and Business Affairs, vacant;
   T. M. Davis; A. J. Boorman
Director of Consumer Affairs, Dr D. P. Hauser
Technical Director, Dr B. Wharmby
Director of Public Affairs, Miss J. D. Luke
Director of Administration, H. P. Jones
Legal Adviser, D. R. B. Bevan
Chief Examiner, J. D. Cooper

OFFICE OF ELECTRICITY REGULATION NORTHERN IRELAND
Brookmount Buildings, 42 Fountain Street, Belfast BT1 5EE
Tel 01232-311575

OFFER NI is the regulatory body for the electricity supply industry in Northern Ireland.
Director-General of Electricity Supply for Northern Ireland, vacant
Deputy Director-General, C. H. Coulthard

ENGLISH HERITAGE
— *see* Historic Buildings and Monuments Commission for England

ENGLISH NATURE
Northminster House, Peterborough PE1 1UA
Tel 01733-340345

English Nature (the Nature Conservancy Council for England) was established in 1991 and is responsible for advising the Government on nature conservation in England. It promotes, directly and through others, the conservation of England's wildlife and natural features. It selects, establishes and manages National Nature Reserves and identifies and notifies Sites of Special Scientific Interest. It provides advice and information about nature conservation, and supports and conducts research relevant to these functions. Through the Joint Nature Conservation Committee (*see* page 332), it works with its sister organizations in Scotland and Wales on UK and international nature conservation issues.
Chairman, The Earl of Cranbrook
Chief Executive, Dr D. R. Langslow
Directors, Dr K. L. Duff; E. T. Idle; Miss C. E. M. Wood; Ms S. Collins

ENGLISH PARTNERSHIPS
16–18 Old Queen Street, London SW1H 9HP
Tel 0171-976 7070

English Partnerships, in statute the Urban Regeneration Agency, came into full operation in April 1994. Its primary aim is to secure the reclamation and reuse of vacant and derelict land throughout England for employment, green space, housing or any other use that will help to regenerate the area. It works in partnership with the public, private and voluntary sectors.
Chairman, The Lord Walker of Worcester, MBE, PC
Deputy Chairman, Sir Idris Pearce, CBE
Chief Executive, D. Taylor

DEPARTMENT OF THE ENVIRONMENT
2 Marsham Street, London SW1P 3EB
Tel 0171-276 3000

The Department of the Environment is responsible for planning and land use; local government; housing and construction; inner city areas; new towns; environmental protection; conservation areas and countryside affairs; health and safety at work; energy efficiency; and property holdings.
   In July 1995 a review of the senior management of the Department recommended structural and organizational changes; details were not confirmed at time of going to press.
Secretary of State for the Environment, The Rt. Hon. John Gummer, MP
   Private Secretary, A. Davis
   Special Advisers, T. Burke; K. Adams; L. O'Connor; G. Barwell
   Parliamentary Private Secretary, D. French, MP
Minister for Local Government, David Curry, MP
   Private Secretary, B. Hackland
   Parliamentary Private Secretary, J. Hayes, MP
Minister for Planning, Construction and Energy Efficiency, Robert Jones, MP
   Private Secretary, C. T. Wood
Minister for Environment and Countryside, The Earl Ferrers, PC
   Private Secretary, C. T. Wood
Parliamentary Under-Secretaries of State, Sir Paul Beresford, MP; James Clappison, MP
   Private Secretaries, D. Gleave; Miss D. Butler
Lord-in-Waiting, The Lord Lucas
   Private Secretary, Miss A. Hemming
Parliamentary Clerk, T. Teehan
Permanent Secretary (G1), A. Turnbull, CB, CVO
   Private Secretary, Mrs P. Allars

ORGANIZATION AND ESTABLISHMENTS
Principal Establishments Officer (G3), Mrs M. McDonald
Principal Finance Officer (G3), W. F. S. Rickett

PERSONNEL
Grade 5, K. G. Arnold; L. B. Hicks
Chief Welfare Officer (G7), Miss E. T. Haines

FINANCE CENTRAL
Heads of Divisions (G5), B. L. Glicksman; A. C. Allberry;
P. D. Walton

ADMINISTRATION RESOURCES
Grade 5, I. S. Elrick; M. R. Haselip; J. J. O'Callaghan;
Y. M. Yarnall

DIRECTORATE OF COMMUNICATION
Director (G4), S. Dugdale
Grade 5, J. Gee

CITIES AND COUNTRYSIDE GROUP
Deputy Secretary (G2), P. J. Fletcher

CITIES AND COUNTRYSIDE POLICY DIRECTORATE
Director (G3), M. B. Gahagan
Heads of Divisions (G5), J Jacobs; A. Richardson; D. Liston-
Jones; R. O. Shaw

INTEGRATED REGIONAL OFFICES UNIT
Under-Secretary (G3), A. G. Watson
Grade 5, T. Abraham; B. Hopson

WILDLIFE AND COUNTRYSIDE DIRECTORATE
Under-Secretary (G3), J. P. Plowman
Grade 5, R. M. Pritchard; R. W. Bunce; R. Hepworth

CITIES, COUNTRYSIDE AND PRIVATE FINANCE
Director (G3), A. G. Watson
Grade 5, I. H. Nicol; J. McCarthy; G. L. Laufer

HOUSING AND CONSTRUCTION GROUP
Deputy Secretary (G2), Miss D. A. Nichols, CB

SECRETARIAT
Grade 7, P. G. Tobia

HOUSING POLICY AND PRIVATE SECTOR
Under-Secretary (G3), Dr C. P. Evans
Grade 5, J. E. Roberts; Mrs H. Ghosh; C. L. L. Braun

HOUSING AND URBAN MONITORING AND ANALYSIS
Under-Secretary (G3), Dr C. P. Evans
Grade 5, J. E. Turner; Mrs J. Littlewood; M. Hughes;
S. Aldridge

HOUSING RESOURCES AND MANAGEMENT
Under-Secretary (G3), Mrs D. S. Phillips
Grade 5, A. Wells; C. H. Bowden; R. S. Horsman;
L. G. Packer

CONSTRUCTION SPONSORSHIP
Director (G3), P. Ward
Grade 5, J. P. Channing; Dr J. F. A. Moore; J. N. Lithgow;
Dr R. P. Thorogood

PROPERTY AND BUILDINGS
Director (G4), D. O. McCreadie
Grade 5, J. M. Leigh-Pollitt; P. F. Everall

ENERGY EFFICIENCY OFFICE
Grade 3, J. Hobson
Grade 5, R. J. Dinwiddy; Dr J. Miles; A. F. Galloway;
N. Sanders

CENTRAL MANAGEMENT AND ANALYSIS UNIT
Chief Economist (G3), C. Riley
Grade 5, W. C. R. Wilson
Economists (G6), T. M. Davis; E. Evans

PROPERTY HOLDINGS AND CENTRAL SUPPORT SERVICES
Deputy Secretary (G2), A. J. Lane, CB

PRINCIPAL FINANCE OFFICER AND AGENCY SPONSORSHIP
Under-Secretary (G3), J. P. Henry
Grade 5, B. Redfern

PROPERTY HOLDINGS DIRECTORATE
Director (G3), N. E. Borrett
Grade 5, R. W. P. Brice; A. R. Edwards
Heads of Outstations (G6), P. R. Stewart; J. C. Lewis;
A. R. Jones; R. M. Barry; M. J. Hathaway; A. J. Partridge;
C. G. H. Young

LOCAL GOVERNMENT AND PLANNING
Deputy Secretary (G2), C. J. S. Brearley, CB

LOCAL GOVERNMENT FINANCE POLICY
Director, Local Government Finance Policy (G3), P. J. J. Britton
Heads of Divisions (G5), Miss L. F. Bell; R. J. Gibson;
M. J. C. Faulkner; N. Dorling; Mrs P. Peneck, Dr
C. Myerscough

LOCAL GOVERNMENT
Under-Secretary (G3), Mrs L. A. Heath
Heads of Divisions (G5), M. H. Coulshed; P. Rowsell;
J. R. Footit

PLANNING DIRECTORATE
Under-Secretary (G3), J. F. Ballard
Heads of Divisions (G5), D. N. Donaldson; R. Jones;
W. E. Chapman; M. R. Ash; J. Zetter; R. C. Mabey;
A. M. Oliver

LEGAL
Solicitor and Legal Adviser (G2), Mrs M. A. Morgan
Deputy Solicitors (G3), J. A. Catlin; Ms S. D. Unerman;
P. J. Szell
Assistant Solicitors (G5), J. L. Comber; I. D. Day; Mrs
S. Headley; Mrs P. J. Conlon; Mrs G. Hedley-Dent;
D. W. Jordan; Miss D. C. S. Phillips; Ms A. Brett-Holt;
D. J. Noble

DEPARTMENTAL TASK FORCE
Under-Secretary (G3), N. Kinghan
Grade 5, P. N. Bristow

ENVIRONMENT PROTECTION
Deputy Secretary (G2), vacant

HM INSPECTORATE OF POLLUTION
The Inspectorate's functions will be taken over by the proposed new Environment Agency for England and Wales in April 1996.
Director and Chief Inspector (G3), Dr D. H. Slater
Deputy Chief Inspector (G4), Dr A. Duncan
Heads of Divisions (G5), Dr K. Speakman;
Dr J. R. F. Burdett; Dr D. J. Bryce

DIRECTORATE OF AIR, CLIMATE AND TOXIC SUBSTANCES
Under-Secretary (G3), Dr D. J. Fisk
Heads of Divisions (G5), P. Dykins; Dr N. J. King; R. Mills

CHIEF SCIENTIST
Chief Scientist (G3), Dr D. J. Fisk
Head of Division (G5), Dr A. J. Apling

DIRECTORATE OF POLLUTION CONTROL AND WASTES
Under-Secretary (*G3*), R. S. Dudding
Heads of Divisions (*G5*), Mrs L. A. C. Simcock;
A. McBrayne; Dr P. Hinchcliffe; J. Cleary; Dr
N. Williams; Dr S. R. A. Brown

GLOBAL ENVIRONMENT
Director (*G3*), R. Sharp
Heads of Divisions (*G5*), J. S. Stevens; J. W. M. Rogers;
J. Adams; P. F. Unwin

WATER DIRECTORATE
Director (*G3*), N. W. Summerton
Heads of Divisions (*G5*), A. J. C. Simcock; J. Vaughan;
M. Nelson; Mrs H. Chipping

Drinking Water Inspectorate
Grade 5, M. J. Rouse

REGIONAL OFFICES
— *see* pages 306–7

EXECUTIVE AGENCIES

BUILDING RESEARCH ESTABLISHMENT
Garston, Watford, Herts WD2 7JR
Tel 01923-894040

The BRE carries out research and provides advice on the design, construction and performance of buildings, and supports government departments in their related responsibilities.
Chief Executive (*G3*), R. G. Courtney
Deputy Chief Executive (*G4*), N. O. Milbank
Directors of Groups (*G4*), Dr W. D. Woolley; (*G5*), B. O. Hall;
Dr N. J. Cook, Dr V. H. C. Crisp; Dr A. B. Birtles
Finance Director (*G5*), J. Horan
Personnel Director (*G6*), Mrs A. Elkeles

THE BUYING AGENCY
Royal Liver Building, Pier Head, Liverpool L3 1PE
Tel 0151-227 4262

The Agency provides a professional purchasing service to government departments and other public bodies.
Chief Executive (*G5*), S. P. Sage

ORDNANCE SURVEY
— *see* page 334

PLANNING INSPECTORATE
Tollgate House, Houlton Street, Bristol BS2 9DJ
Tel 0117-987 8950

The Inspectorate is responsible for casework involving planning, housing, roads, environmental and related legislation. It is a joint executive agency of the Department of the Environment and the Welsh Office.
Chief Executive and Chief Inspector of Planning (*G3*),
C. Shepley
Deputy Chief Inspector of Planning (*G4*), J. Greenfield
Assistant Chief Planning Inspectors (*G5*), J. Acton;
R. E. Wilson; C. Jenkins; Mrs S. Bruton; J. T. Graham;
D. E. John
Head of Administration (*G5*), Ms S. Carter
Head of Finance, Management Services and Information Systems
(*G5*), M. Brasher

QUEEN ELIZABETH II CONFERENCE CENTRE
Broad Sanctuary, London SWIP 3EE
Tel 0171-798 4010

The Centre provides conference and banqueting facilities for both private sector and government use.
Chief Executive (*G5*), M. C. Buck

SECURITY FACILITIES EXECUTIVE
St Christopher House, Southwark Street, London SEI OTE
Tel 0171-921 4813

The Agency provides a range of security support services, products and systems for central government, the wider public sector and other approved customers.
Chief Executive (*G5*), J. C. King

ROYAL COMMISSION ON
ENVIRONMENTAL POLLUTION
Church House, Great Smith Street, London SWIP 3BZ
Tel 0171-276 2080

The Commission was set up in 1970 to advise on matters, both national and international, concerning the pollution of the environment; on the adequacy of research in this field; and the future possibilities of danger to the environment.
Chairman, Sir John Houghton, CBE, FRS
Members, Sir Geoffrey Allen, FRS; Prof. G.S. Boulton, FRS,
FRSE; Prof. C. E. D. Chilvers; Prof. Dame Barbara
Clayton, DBE; Dr P. Doyle, CBE, FRSE; H. R. Fell, CBE;
Sir Martin Holdgate, CB; Prof. J. H. Lawton, FRS;
Prof. R. Macrory; Prof. J. G. Morris, CBE, FRS; The Earl
of Selborne, KBE, FRS; Prof. Z. A. Silberston, CBE
Secretary, D. R. Lewis

EQUAL OPPORTUNITIES COMMISSION
Overseas House, Quay Street, Manchester M3 3HN
Tel 0161-833 9244

Press Office, 36 Broadway, London SWIH 0XH. Tel: 0171-
222 1110
Other Offices, Stock Exchange House, 7 Nelson Mandela
Place, Glasgow G2 1QW. Tel: 0141-248 5833; Caerwys
House, Windsor Place, Cardiff. Tel: 01222-343552

The Commission was set up by Parliament in 1975 as a result of the passing of the Sex Discrimination Act. It works towards the elimination of discrimination on the grounds of sex or marital status and to promote equality of opportunity between men and women generally. It is responsible to the Department for Education and Employment..
Chairwoman (£45,320), Ms K. Bahl
Deputy Chairwoman (£30,390), Lady (Diana) Brittan, CBE
Members, Ms A. Watts, OBE; Ms N. Bray; Ms A. Gibson;
Ms C. Wells; P. Smith; Ms M. Berg; R. K.Fleeman;
R. Grayson; Dr J. Stringer
Chief Executive, P. Naish

EQUAL OPPORTUNITIES COMMISSION FOR NORTHERN
IRELAND
Chamber of Commerce House, 22 Great Victoria Street,
Belfast BT2 7BA
Tel 01232-242752
Chair and Chief Executive, Mrs J. Smyth

EXCHEQUER AND AUDIT DEPARTMENT
— *see* National Audit Office

ECGD (EXPORT CREDITS GUARANTEE
DEPARTMENT)
PO Box 2200, 2 Exchange Tower, Harbour Exchange
Square, London E14 9GS
Tel 0171-512 7000

ECGD (Export Credits Guarantee Department), the
official export credit insurer, is a separate government
department responsible to the President of the Board of
Trade and functions under the Export and Investment
Guarantees Act 1991. This enables ECGD to facilitate UK
exports by making available export credit insurance to
British firms engaged in selling overseas and to guarantee
repayment to banks in Britain providing finance for export
credit for goods sold on credit terms of two years or more.
The Act also empowers ECGD to insure British private
investment overseas against political risks such as war,
expropriation and restrictions on remittances.
Chief Executive, W. B. Willott
Group Directors (*G3*), M. V. Hawtin (*Underwriting*);
　J. R. Weiss (*Asset Management*); T. M. Jaffray (*Resource
　Management*)

DIVISIONS
Head, Finance (*G5*), J. C. W. Croall
Head, Central Services (*G5*), P. J. Callaghan
Head, Underwriting Divisions (*G5*), S. R. Dodgson
　(*Division 1*); M. D. Pentecost (*Division 3*); Mrs
　M. E. Maddox (*Division 4*); D. C. Cooper (*Division 5*);
　A. P. Fowell (*Division 6*)
Head, Office of the General Counsel (*G5*), R. G. Elden
Head, International Debt (*G5*), R. Gotts
Head, Reinsurance (*G5*), R. F. Lethbridge
Head, Claims (*G5*), V. P. Lunn-Rockliffe
Head, Treasury Management (*G5*), R. A. Ranson
Head, Risk Management (*G5*), R. J. Radford
Head, Chief Executive's Division (*G5*), J. S. Snowdon

EXPORT GUARANTEES ADVISORY COUNCIL
Chairman, R. T. Fox, CBE
Other Members, B. P. Dawe Mathews, TD; T. M. Evans, CBE;
　Sir Frank Lampl; G. W. Lynch; J. W. Melbourn, CBE;
　D. B. Newlands; Sir Derek Thomas, KCMG; The
　Viscount Weir

OFFICE OF FAIR TRADING
Field House, Bream's Buildings, London EC4A 1PR
Tel 0171-242 2858

The Office of Fair Trading is a non-ministerial government department headed by the Director-General of Fair
Trading. It keeps commercial activities in the UK under
review and seeks to protect consumers against unfair
trading practices. The Director-General's consumer protection duties under the Fair Trading Act 1973, together
with his responsibilities under the Consumer Credit Act
1974, the Estate Agents Act 1979, and Control of Misleading Advertisements Regulations 1988, are administered by
the Office's Consumer Affairs Division. The Competition
Policy Division is concerned with monopolies and mergers
(under the Fair Trading Act 1973), and the Director-
General's other responsibilities for competition matters,
including those under the Restrictive Trade Practices Act
1976, the Resale Prices Act 1976, the Competition Act
1980, the Financial Services Act 1986 and the Broadcasting
Act 1990. The Office is the UK competent authority on the
application of the European Commission's competition

rules, and also liaises with the Commission on consumer
protection initiatives.
Director-General, J. Bridgeman

CONSUMER AFFAIRS DIVISION
Director (*G3*), G. Horton
Assistant Directors (*G5*), P. Casey; D. W. Lightfoot;
　J. Chapman; R. Watson

COMPETITION POLICY DIVISION
Director (*G3*), Dr M. Howe, CB
Assistant Directors (*G5*), A. J. White; R. Upson; H. L. Emden;
　C. J. C. Wright; E. L. Whitehorn

LEGAL DIVISION
Director (*G3*), A. M. Inglese
Assistant Directors (*G5*), M. A. Khan; P. T. Rostron
Senior Economic Adviser (*G5*), D. Elliott
Establishment and Finance Officer (*G5*), Miss C. Banks
Chief Information Officer (*G6*), D. Hill

FOREIGN AND COMMONWEALTH
OFFICE
Downing Street, London SW1A 2AL
Tel 0171-270 3000

The Foreign and Commonwealth Office provides, mainly
through diplomatic missions, the means of communication
between the British Government and other governments
and international governmental organizations for the
discussion and negotiation of all matters falling within the
field of international relations. It is responsible for alerting
the British Government to the implications of developments overseas; for protecting British interests overseas;
for protecting British citizens abroad; for explaining
British policies to, and cultivating friendly relations
with, governments overseas; and for the discharge of
British responsibilities to the dependent territories.

DIPLOMATIC SERVICE SALARIES *since 1 April 1995*
Permanent Under-Secretary and
　Head of the Diplomatic Service　£90,000–£150,000
Senior Grade DS1　　　　　　　　£90,000–£150,000
Senior Grade DS2　　　　　　　　£67,500–£98,000
Senior Grade DS3　　　　　　　　£55,000–£82,500
*Diplomatic Service Grade 4 (DS4)　£38,341–£56,953
*1994–5 figure

Secretary of State, The Rt. Hon. Malcolm Rifkind, QC, MP
　Principal Private Secretary, W. G. Ehrman
　Private Secretaries, C. R. V. Stagg; S. J. Sharpe
　Special Adviser, C. Blunt
Minister of State (*Minister for Overseas Development*), The
　Baroness Chalker of Wallasey, PC
　Private Secretary, R. Calvert
　Parliamentary Private Secretary, D. Faber, MP
Ministers of State, David Davis, MP (*Minister for Europe*);
　The Rt. Hon. Jeremy Hanley, MP; Sir Nicholas Bonsor,
　Bt., MP
　Private Secretaries, N. S. Archer; G. J. Dorey; J. Benjamin
Parliamentary Relations Unit, E. Jenkinson (*Head*);
　A. Mehmet, MVO (*Deputy Head and Parliamentary Clerk*)
*Permanent Under-Secretary of State and Head of the Diplomatic
　Service*, Sir John Coles, KCMG
　Private Secretary, J. King
Deputy Under-Secretary and Political Director, Miss
　P. Neville-Jones, CMG
Deputy Under-Secretaries (*DS2*), J. R. Young (*Chief Clerk*);
　M. H. Jay, CMG (*Economic Director*); Sir Timothy Daunt,
　KCMG; D. J. Wright, CMG, LVO; J. Q. Greenstock, CMG

Deputy Political Director and UK Perm. Rep. on the Council of WEU (DS3), T. L. Richardson, CMG
Director of Information Systems (DS3), J. Ling, CMG
Principal Finance Officer and Chief Inspector (DS3), K. R. Tebbit
Assistant Under-Secretaries (DS3), A. M. Goodenough, CMG; C. O. Hum; A. F. Green, CMG; S. J. L. Wright; J. R. de Fonblanque; D. J. M. Dain; C. Battiscombe, CMG; W. Marsden, CMG; P. J. Torry; F. F. Mingay, CMG; R. H. Smith; F. N. Richards, CVO, CMG
HM Vice-Marshal of the Diplomatic Corps, A. St J. H. Figgis, CMG
Legal Adviser (DS2), Sir Franklin Berman, KCMG, QC
Second Legal Adviser, D. H. Anderson, CMG
Deputy Legal Advisers, M. R. Eaton, CMG; K. J. Chamberlain, CMG

HEADS OF DEPARTMENTS (DS4)

*Aid Policy Department, S. Chakrabarti
Aviation and Maritime Department, R. A. Kealy
British Diplomatic Spouses Association, Mrs C. Young
Central European Department, N. J. Thorpe
Commonwealth Co-ordination Department, D. Broad
Commonwealth Foreign and Security Policy Unit, H. J. R. Mortimer
Conference on Security and Co-operation in Europe Unit, C. A. Munro
Consular Department, S. F. Howarth
Cultural Relations Department, A. D. Sprake
Drugs, International Crime and Terrorism Department, R. P. Flowers
Eastern Adriatic Unit, A. Charlton
Eastern Department, R. D. Wilkinson
*Economic Advisers Department, J. Rollo
*Economic Relations Department, D. F. Richmond
Engineering Services, I. Whitehead
Environment Science and Energy Department, G. H. Boyce
Equatorial Africa Department, D. R. MacLennan
European Community Department (External), J. M. MacGregor
European Community Department (Internal), A. J. Cary
Far Eastern and Pacific Department, G. Fry
Home Estate Department, D. Brown, CMG
Hong Kong Department, S. L. Cowper Coles
Honours Unit, D. E. Tarling
Human Rights Policy Unit, P. S. Astley
Information Department, Sir John Ramsden, Bt.
Information Systems Division (Operations), S. I. Soutar
Information Systems Division (Projects), K. Willis
Internal Audit, R. Elias
Joint Assistance Unit (Central Europe), D. Coates
Joint Assistance Unit (Eastern Europe), M. McCulloch
†*Joint Export Promotion Directorate*, Q. M. Quayle
Latin America Department, L. G. Faulkner
Library and Records Department, S. I. Soutar
*Management Review Staff, S. R. H. Pease
Medical and Welfare Unit, Miss D. M. Symes, OBE
Middle East Department, N. W. Browne
Migration and Visa Department, M. E. Frost
National Audit Office, R. Burwood
Nationality, Treaty and Claims Department, R. D. Hart
Near East and North Africa Department, P. W. Ford
News Department, N. E. Sheinwald

Non-Proliferation Department, B. Cleghorn
North America Department, M. E. Pellew, LVO
Overseas Estate Department, M. H. R. Bertram, CBE
Overseas Inspectorate, K. R. Tebbit (*Chief Inspector and Principal Finance Officer*)
Overseas Police Adviser, L. Grundy (*Senior Police Adviser*)
Permanent Under-Secretary's Department, D. G. Martin
Personnel Management Department, P. J. Torry
Personnel Policy Department, J. Poston
Personnel Services Department, G. G. Wetherell
Policy Planning Staff, D. G. Manning, CMG
PROSPER, C. J. Edgerton, OBE
Protocol Department, R. S. Gorham (*First Assistant Marshal of the Diplomatic Corps*)
Republic of Ireland Department, D. A. Lamont
Research and Analysis Department, Director, B. S. Eastwood
Resource and Finance Department, J. W. Thorp
Royal Matters Unit, J. E. Brook
Security Department, D. S. Broucher
Security Policy Department, Ms A. J. K. Bailes
Services Planning and Resources Department, M. Hodge, MBE
South Asian Department, L. B. Smith
South Atlantic and Antarctic Department, A. J. Longrigg
South-East Asian Department, M. R. J. Guest
Southern Africa Department, B. H. Dinwiddy
Southern European Department, H. B. Warren-Gash
Support Services Department, M. Carr
Training Department, I. W. Mackley
United Nations Department, Miss M. G. D. Evans, CMG
Western European Department, M. L. H. Hope
West Indian and Atlantic Department, C. Drace-Francis
Whitley Council, J. P. Girdlestone

EXECUTIVE AGENCY

WILTON PARK CONFERENCE CENTRE
Wiston House, Steyning, W. Sussex BN44 3DZ
Tel 01903-815020

The Centre organizes international affairs conferences and is hired out to government departments and commercial users.
Chief Executive, R. Langhorne

THE SECRET INTELLIGENCE SERVICE (MI6)
Vauxhall Cross, PO Box 1300, London SE1 1BD

The Secret Intelligence Service produces secret intelligence in support of the Government's security, defence, foreign and economic policies. It was placed on a statutory footing by the Intelligence Services Act 1994.
Director-General, D. Spedding, CVO, OBE

GOVERNMENT COMMUNICATIONS HEADQUARTERS (GCHQ)
Priors Road, Cheltenham, Glos GL52 5AJ
Tel 01242-221491

GCHQ produces signal intelligence in support of the Government's security, defence, foreign and economic policies. It was placed on a statutory footing by the Intelligence Services Act 1994. GCHQ also provides advice and assistance to government departments and the armed forces on the security of their communications and information technology systems.
Director, Sir John Adye, KCMG

---

*Joint Foreign and Commonwealth Office/Overseas Development Administration department

†Joint Foreign and Commonwealth Office/Department of Trade and Industry directorate

CORPS OF QUEEN'S MESSENGERS
Support Services Department, Foreign and
Commonwealth Office, London SW1A 2AH
Tel 0171-270 2779

Superintendent of the Corps of Queen's Messengers,
 Maj. I. G. M. Bamber
Queen's Messengers, Maj. J. E. A. Andre;
 Cdr. D. H. Barraclough; Maj. A. N. D. Bols;
 Lt.-Cdr. K. E. Brown; Lt.-Col. W. P. A. Bush;
 Lt.-Col. M. B. de S. Clayton; Capt. G. Courtauld;
 Maj. P. C. H. Dening-Smitherman; Maj. P. T. Dunn;
 Sqn. Ldr. J. S. Frizzell; Capt. N. C. E. Gardner;
 Cdr. P. G. Gregson; Maj. D. A. Griffiths;
 Wg Cdr. J. O. Jewiss; Lt.-Col. P. S. Kerr-Smiley;
 Lt.-Col. J. M. C. Kimmins; Lt.-Col. R. C. Letchworth;
 Maj. D. R. Nevile; Maj. K. J. Rowbottom;
 Maj. M. R. Senior; Cdr. K. M. C. Simmons, AFC;
 Maj. P. M. O. Springfield; Maj. J. S. Steele;
 Col. D. W. F. Taylor

FOREIGN COMPENSATION COMMISSION
3 Central Buildings, Matthew Parker Street, London
SW1H 9NL
Tel 0171-210 8297

The Commission was set up by the Foreign Compensation Act 1950 primarily to distribute, under Orders in
Council, funds received from other governments in
accordance with agreements to pay compensation for
expropriated British property and other losses sustained
by British nationals.
 The Commission also has the duty of registering claims
for British-owned property in contemplation of agreements with other countries, and it has done so in seven
instances since 1950.
Chairman, A. W. E. Wheeler, CBE
Secretary, A. N. Grant

FORESTRY COMMISSION
231 Corstorphine Road, Edinburgh EH12 7AT
Tel 0131-334 0303

The Forestry Commission is the government department
responsible for forestry policy in Great Britain. It reports
directly to forestry ministers (i.e. the Minister of Agriculture, Fisheries and Food, the Secretary of State for Scotland and the Secretary of State for Wales), to whom it is
responsible for advice on forestry policy and for the
implementation of that policy in Great Britain. There is a
statutorily-appointed Chairman and Board of Commissioners (four executive and seven non-executive) with
prescribed duties and powers. In discharging their functions, the Forestry Commissioners have a statutory duty to
endeavour to achieve a reasonable balance between the
needs of forestry and the environment.
 The Commission is organized to distinguish between its
departmental, regulatory and management functions. A
Policy and Resources Group is responsible for the
parliamentary and policy aspects of the Commission's
duties as a government department. As the Forestry
Authority, the Commission provides advice and sets the
standards for the forestry industry, administers the grant-
aid schemes for private woodlands, carries out regulatory
functions for plant health and felling control and undertakes forest research. Forest Enterprise, a trading body
operating as an executive agency of the Commission,
manages its forestry estate on a multi-use basis.

Chairman (part-time) (£36,965), Sir Peter Hutchison, Bt.,
 CBE
Director-General and Deputy Chairman (G2), T. R. Cutler,
 CBE
Commissioner, Policy and Resources (G3), D. S. Grundy
Head of the Forestry Authority (G3), D. L. Foot
Secretary to the Commissioners (G5), T. J. D. Rollinson

FOREST ENTERPRISE, 231 Corstorphine Road, Edinburgh
 EH12 7AT. Tel: 0131-334 0303. *Chief Executive,*
 N. A. H. McKerrow

REGISTRY OF FRIENDLY SOCIETIES
15 Great Marlborough Street, London W1V 2LL
Tel 0171-437 9992

The Registry of Friendly Societies is a government
department serving three statutory bodies, the Building
Societies Commission, the Friendly Societies Commission, and the Central Office of the Registry of Friendly
Societies (together with the Assistant Registrar of Friendly
Societies for Scotland).
 The Building Societies Commission was established by
the Building Societies Act 1986. The Commission is
responsible for the supervision of building societies and
administers the system of regulation. It also advises the
Treasury and other government departments on matters
relating to building societies.
 The Friendly Societies Commission was established by
the Friendly Societies Act 1992. Its responsibilities for the
supervision of friendly societies parallel those of the
Building Societies Commission for building societies.
 The Central Office of the Registry of Friendly Societies
provides a public registry for mutual organizations registered under the Building Societies Act 1986, Friendly
Societies Acts 1974 and 1992, and the Industrial and
Provident Societies Act 1965. It is responsible for the
supervision of friendly societies and credit unions, and
advises the Government on issues affecting those societies.

BUILDING SOCIETIES COMMISSION
Chairman, G. E. Fitchew
Deputy Chairman, H. G. Walsh
Commissioners, J. M. Palmer; *T. F. Mathews, CBE;
 *F. E. Worsley; *F. G. Sunderland; *N. Fox Bassett; *Sir
 James Birrell
* part-time

FRIENDLY SOCIETIES COMMISSION
Chairman, D. W. Lee
Commissioners, F. da Rocha; *A. Wilson; *J. A. Geddes;
 *P. E. Couse; *Dr J. Dine
* part-time

CENTRAL OFFICE
Chief Registrar, G. E. Fitchew
Assistant Registrars (G4), D. W. Lee; A. J. Perrett

THE REGISTRY
First Commissioner and Chief Registrar (G2), G. E. Fitchew

BUILDING SOCIETIES COMMISSION STAFF
Grade 3, H. G. Walsh
Grade 4, J. M. Palmer
Grade 5, D. A. W. Stevens; W. Champion; R. K. Gabbertas;
 E. Engstrom
Grade 6, N. F. Digance

FRIENDLY SOCIETIES COMMISSION STAFF
Grade 4, D. W. Lee
Grade 6, F. da Rocha

CENTRAL SERVICES STAFF
Legal Adviser (G4), A. J. Perrett
Establishment and Finance Officer (G5), J. Stevens
Legal Staff (G6), P. G. Ashcroft; P. Kee; R. Caune;
  C. Stallard

REGISTRY OF FRIENDLY SOCIETIES, SCOTLAND
58 Frederick Street, Edinburgh, EH2 1NB
Tel 0131-226 3224
Assistant Registrar (G5), J. L. J. Craig, WS

GAMING BOARD FOR GREAT BRITAIN
Berkshire House, 168–173 High Holborn, London
WC1V 7AA
Tel 0171-306 6200

The Board was established in 1968 and is responsible to the
Home Secretary. Its functions are to ensure that those
involved in organizing gaming and lotteries are fit to do so;
to ensure that gaming and lotteries are run fairly and in
accordance with the law; and to advise the Home Secretary
on developments in gaming and lotteries so that the law can
respond to change.
Chairman (part-time) (£33,165), Lady Littler
Secretary, T. Kavanagh

OFFICE OF GAS SUPPLY
Stockley House, 130 Wilton Road, London SW1V 1LQ
Tel 0171-828 0898

The Office of Gas Supply (Ofgas) is a regulatory body set
up under the Gas Act 1986. It is headed by the Director-
General of Gas Supply, who is independent of ministerial
control.
  The principal functions of Ofgas are to control British
Gas prices and levels of service; to protect the interests of
the gas consumer; and to facilitate the development of
competition in the gas market. Other functions are to grant
authorizations to gas suppliers; to fix and publish maxi-
mum charges for the resale of gas; and to investigate
complaints.
Director-General, Ms C. Spottiswoode
Chief Economic Adviser, Dr Eileen Marshall
Legal Adviser, D. R. M. Long
Director, Public Affairs, C. Webb
Director, Consumer Affairs, W. Macleod
Director, Network Operations, M. Higson
Director, Administration, R. Field
Director, Legislation and Licensing, A. Ward

GOVERNMENT ACTUARY'S DEPARTMENT
22 Kingsway, London WC2B 6LE
Tel 0171-242 6828

The Government Actuary provides a consulting service to
government departments, the public sector, and overseas
governments. The actuaries advise on social security
schemes and superannuation arrangements in the public
sector at home and abroad, on population and other
statistical studies, and on government supervision of
insurance companies and friendly societies.
Government Actuary, C. D. Daykin, CB
Directing Actuaries, D. G. Ballantine; D. H. Loades;
  M. A. Pickford, CB

Chief Actuaries, E. I. Battersby; Ms W. M. Beaver;
  T. W. Hewitson; A. I. Johnston; J. C. A. Rathbone;
  D. I. Tomlinson; A. G. Young

GOVERNMENT HOSPITALITY FUND
8 Cleveland Row, London SW1A 1DH
Tel 0171-210 3000

The Government Hospitality Fund was instituted in 1908
for the purpose of organizing official hospitality on a
regular basis with a view to the promotion of international
goodwill.
Minister in Charge, Sir Nicholas Bonsor, Bt., MP
Secretary, Col. T. Earl

GOVERNMENT OFFICES FOR THE
REGIONS

In 1994 integrated government offices were set up in the
English regions to bring together the existing regional
offices of the Department of the Environment, the Department of Transport, the Department of Trade and Industry
and the Training, Enterprise and Education Directorate of
the Department of Employment (now part of the Department for Education and Employment). The regional
directors are accountable to the Secretaries of State of all
four Departments. The offices' role is to promote a
coherent approach to competitiveness, sustainable economic development and regeneration using public and
private resources.
Central Unit, Room N12/19, 2 Marsham Street, London
SW1P 3EB
Tel 0171-276 4563
Head of Unit (G5), T. P. Abraham

EASTERN
Secretariat: Enterprise House, Vision Park, Histon,
Cambridge CB4 4DZ
Tel 01223-202065

Regional Director (G3), J. Turner
Directors (G5), C. Dunabin (*Housing*); T. Bird (*Planning and
Transport*); M. Oldham (*Trade and Industry*); Mrs
C. Hunter (*Employment and Training*)

EAST MIDLANDS
Secretariat: Cranbrook House, Cranbrook Street,
Nottingham NG1 7DW
Tel 0115-935 2419

Regional Director (G3), M. Lanyon
Directors (G4), D. Morrison (*Environment and Transport*);
  (*G5*), M. Briggs (*Trade and Industry*); A. Davies
  (*Employment and Training*)

LONDON
Secretariat: Room P2/154b, 2 Marsham Street, London
SW1P 3EB
Tel 0171-276 5833

Regional Director (G2), R. Young
Directors (G3), J. A. Owen (*Regeneration Programmes*);
  M. Lambirth (*Planning and Transport*); (*G5*), Ms
  W. Harris (*Employment, Training and Economic
  Development*); Mrs J. Bridges (*Planning*); S. Whiteley
  (*Transport Policy and Management*); G. Emes (*Transport
  Assessment*); Mrs L. Meek (*Strategy and Co-ordination
  Unit*); Mrs E. Ryle (*Business Competitiveness*)

Heads of Regeneration Programmes (*G5*), R. Compton (*Policy, Finance and Europe*); I. Scotter (*London East*); (*G6*), P. Fiddeman (*London South*); J. Sienkiewicz (*London Development Unit*)

MERSEYSIDE
Secretariat: Room 402, Graeme House, Derby Square, Liverpool L2 7SU
Tel 0151-224 6300

Regional Director (*G3*), J. Stoker
Directors (*G5*), I. Urqhart (*Housing, Europe and Transport*); S. Dunmore (*Urban and Economic Affairs*); Ms P. Jackson (*Trade and Industry*); P. Houton (*Employment, Training and Planning*)

NORTH-EAST
Secretariat: Room 406, Stangate House, 2 Groat Market, Newcastle upon Tyne NE1 1YN
Tel 0191-235 7722

Regional Director (*G3*), Ms P. Denham
Directors (*G5*), J. Darlington (*Environment and Transport*); Miss D. Caudle (*Regeneration and Housing*); A. Dell (*Trade, Industry and Europe*); K. Heslop (*Employment and Training*)

NORTH-WEST
Secretariat: 20th Floor, Sunley Tower, Piccadilly Plaza, Manchester M1 4BE
Tel 0161-952 4000

Regional Director (*G3*), Miss M. Neville-Rolfe
Directors (*G4*), J. K. Chapman (*Trade and Industry*); (*G5*), B. Isherwood (*Regeneration*); P. Styche (*Infrastructure and Planning*); P. Keen (*Employment and Training*); (*G6*), R. Watkinson (*Business Services*); P. Walton (*Overseas Trade, Environment and Technology*); A. Gore (*Careers Education and Quality Assurance*); D. Duff (*TEC Policy and Finance*); J. Brown (*Europe*); D. Stewart (*Corporate Services and Transport*)

SOUTH-EAST
Secretariat: Room 522, Charles House, 375 Kensington High Street, London W14 8QH
Tel 0345-125341

Regional Director (*G3*), Ms G. Ashmore
Directors (*G5*), J. B. Wilson (*Planning*); T. Radice (*Regeneration, Housing and Environment*); Mrs E. A. Baker (*Transport*); E. W. Beston (*Trade and Industry*); D. W. Main (*Employment and Training*)

SOUTH-WEST
Secretariat: 4th Floor, The Pithay, Bristol BS1 2NQ
Tel 0117-945 6992

Regional Director (*G3*), B. H. Leonard
Directors (*G5*), S. McQuillin (*Devon and Cornwall*); M. Quinn (*Environment and Transport*); J. Bowder (*Trade and Industry*); Ms W. Mauger (*Employment and Training*); (*G6*), D. Way (*Resources*)

WEST MIDLANDS
Secretariat: 6th Floor, 77 Paradise Circus, Queensway, Birmingham B1 2DT
Tel 0121-212 5257

Regional Director (*G3*), D. Ritchie
Directors (*G4*), Dr M. Sutton (*Trade and Industry*); (*G5*), Mrs P. Holland (*Single Regeneration Budget*); J. Northover (*Housing and Environment*); P. Longley (*Planning*); H. Tollyfield (*Employment and Training*); (*G6*), Ms L. Eastwood (*Resource Management*); K. Griffiths (*European Division*)

YORKSHIRE AND HUMBERSIDE
Secretariat: City House, New Station Street, Leeds LS1 4JD
Tel 0113-280 0600

Regional Director (*G3*), J. Walker
Directors (*G4*), Ms S. Seymour (*Trade, Industry and Europe*); (*G5*), I. Crowther (*Housing, Planning and Transport*); Mrs L. Kerry (*Regeneration*); G. Dyche (*Employment and Training*); (*G6*), N. Best (*Strategy and Resources*)

DEPARTMENT OF HEALTH
Richmond House, 79 Whitehall, London SW1A 2NS
Tel 0171-210 3000

The Department of Health is responsible for the provision of the National Health Service in England and for social care, including oversight of personal social services run by local authorities in England for children, the elderly, the infirm, the handicapped and other persons in need. It is responsible for health promotion and has functions relating to public and environmental health, food safety and nutrition. The Department is also responsible for the ambulance and emergency first aid services, under the Civil Defence Act 1948. The Department represents the UK at the European Union and other international organizations including the World Health Organization. It also supports UK-based healthcare and pharmaceutical industries.

Secretary of State for Health, The Rt. Hon. Stephen Dorrell, MP
  Principal Private Secretary, Ms C. Moriarty
  Private Secretaries, J. Holden; M. Yates
  Special Adviser, T. Hockley
  Parliamentary Private Secretary, G. Brandreth, MP
Minister of State, Gerald Malone, MP
  Private Secretary, A. Taylor
Parliamentary Under-Secretaries of State, The Baroness Cumberlege, CBE; The Hon. Thomas Sackville, MP; John Bowis, OBE, MP
  Private Secretaries, Ms E. Woodeson;
  Mrs M. Weatherseed; G. Larner
Parliamentary Clerk, Ms T. Fretten
Permanent Secretary (*G1*), G. A. Hart, CB
  Private Secretary, B. Dyson
Chief Medical Officer (*G1A*), Dr K. Calman
Chief Executive, NHS Executive (*G1A*), A. Langlands
Deputy Chief Medical Officer (*G2*), Dr J. S. Metters, CB

NATIONAL HEALTH SERVICE POLICY BOARD
Chairman, The Secretary of State for Health
Members, Gerald Malone, MP (*Minister of State*); The Baroness Cumberlege, CBE; The Hon. T. Sackville, MP; J. Bowis, OBE, MP (*Parliamentary Under-Secretaries*); Dr K. Calman (*Chief Medical Officer*); A. Langlands (*Chief Executive, NHS Executive*); G. A. Hart, CB (*Permanent Secretary*); Prof. C. Chantler; P. Gummer; Mrs Y. Moores; Miss K. Jenkins; Ms S. Masters; B. Baker; Dr S. Burgess, CBE; K. Ackroyd; Ms R. Fritchie; J. Greetham, CBE; Sir William Staveley, GCB; W. Wells; Sir Donald Wilson

PUBLIC HEALTH POLICY GROUP

HEALTH ASPECTS OF ENVIRONMENT AND FOOD DIVISION
Under-Secretary (*G3*), Dr E. Rubery
Grade 4, Dr R. Skinner; Dr E. Smales
Assistant Secretary (*G5*), C. P. Kendall

COMMUNITY SERVICES DIVISION
Under-Secretary (*G3*), T. R. H. Luce

Assistant Secretaries (*G5*), R. M. Orton; N. F. Duncan;
D. P. Walden; Mrs E. Hunter-Johnston; R.Tyrrell

HEALTH PROMOTION DIVISION
Under-Secretary (*G3*), G. J. F. Podger
Principal Medical Officer (*G4*), Dr D. McInnes
Assistant Secretaries (*G5*), J. F. Sharpe, CBE; Miss A. Mithani;
Ms L. Lockyer; K. J. Guinness

NURSING DIVISION
Chief Nursing Officer/Director of Nursing (*G3*), Mrs
Y. Moores
Deputy Chief Nursing Officer (*G4*), J. Tait, OBE
Assistant Chief Nursing Officers (*G4*), Mrs P. Cantrill; (*G5*),
Dr G. Chapman; C. Butler

SOCIAL SERVICES INSPECTORATE
Chief Inspector (*G2*), H. Laming, CBE
Deputy Chief Inspectors (*G4*), D. C. Brand; Miss C. M. Hey
Assistant Chief Inspectors (*HQ*), J. Kennedy; F. Tolan;
J. G. Smith; Mrs W. Rose
Assistant Chief Inspectors (*Regions*), S. Allard; J. K. Corcoran;
J. Cypher; D. Gilroy; B. Riddell; A. Jones;
D. G. Lambert; Miss A. Taylor; Mrs P. K. Hall;
C. P. Brearley; A. Nottage

NHS EXECUTIVE
Quarry House, Quarry Hill, Leeds LS2 7UE
Tel 0113-254 5000

Chief Executive, A. Langlands
Director of Corporate Affairs, J. F. Shaw
Director of Human Resources, K. Jarrold
Director of Finance and Corporate Information, C. Reeves
Medical Director, Dr G. Winyard
Chief Nursing Officer, Mrs Y. Moores
Director of Research and Development,
Prof. Sir Michael Peckham
Director of Planning and Performance Management,
A. D. M. Liddell

PERSONNEL DIRECTORATE
Director of Human Resources (*G2*), K. Jarrold

PERSONNEL DIVISION
Deputy Director (*G3*), J. M. Rogers
Under-Secretary (*G3*), R. M. Drury
Assistant Secretaries (*G5*), M. G. Sturges; B. A. J. Bennett;
Ms C. Langridge; Miss N. Fenton

RESEARCH AND DEVELOPMENT DIVISION
Director of Research and Development,
Prof. Sir Michael Peckham
Deputy Director of Research Management (*G4*), Prof. G. Smith
Assistant Secretaries (*G5*), Mrs J. Griffin; Mrs B. Soper; Dr
P. Greenaway; Dr C. Henshall
Senior Medical Officers (*G5*), Ms J. Ennis; Dr G. Lewis;
Dr J. Toy
Senior Principal Research Officers (*G6*), Ms A. Kauder;
Dr C. Davies
Nursing Officers (*G6*), Dr E. Meerabeau; Miss E. Scott

HEALTH CARE DIRECTORATE
Deputy Chief Medical Officer (*G2*), Dr G. Winyard

PUBLIC HEALTH DIVISION
Grade 4, Dr T. Mann
Assistant Secretary (*G5*), P. Spellman
Senior Medical Officers (*G5*), Dr M. Charny; Dr I. Bowns;
Dr A. Lakhani

MEDICAL EDUCATION, TRAINING AND STAFFING
DIVISION
Senior Principal Medical Officer (*G3*), J. R. W. Hangartner
Senior Medical Officers (*G5*), Dr R. Cairncross; Dr
C. Marvin; Dr S. Horsley; Dr J. Davies
Assistant Secretaries (*G5*), S. D. Catling; T. Ashe; Miss
A. Simkins

PRIMARY CARE AND DENTAL SERVICES
Deputy Secretary (*G2*), A. D. M. Liddell
Assistant Secretary (*G5*), S. Alcock

PRIMARY CARE DIVISION 2
Grade 4, J. A. Thompson
Senior Dental Officers, C. Audrey; K. A. Eaton; I. Cooper
Dental Officer, Dr G. Wilson

OFFICE OF THE CHIEF DENTAL OFFICER
Chief Dental Officer, R. B. Mouatt
Dental Officer, A. J. Hawkes

OFFICE OF THE CHIEF PHARMACIST
Chief Pharmaceutical Officer (*G4*), B. H. Hartley

FINANCE AND PLANNING DIRECTORATE
Director (*G2*), C. Reeves

FINANCE BRANCH
Under-Secretary (*Health*) (*G3*), A. B. Barton
Assistant Secretaries (*G5*), J. M. Brownlee; J. C. Middleton;
K. S. Jacobsen; J. Stopes-Roe

FINANCE AND PLANNING DIRECTORATE A
Deputy Director (*G3*), P. Garland
Heads of Branches (*G5*), H. Gwynn; C. Dobson; M. A. Harris;
A. Angilley; J. Middleton

FINANCE AND PERFORMANCE DIVISION B
Deputy Director (*G3*), B. Marsden
Heads of Branches (*G5*), J. Tomlinson; S. Saunders;
M. Harris

FINANCE DIVISION D
Under-Secretary (*Social Security*) (*G3*), J. Tross
Assistant Secretaries (*G5*), S. Lord; Dr L. Mayhew; G. Foster

DEPARTMENTAL RESOURCES AND
SERVICES GROUP
Deputy Secretary (*G2*), J. Pilling, CB

STATISTICS DIVISION
Director of Statistics (*G3*), Mrs R. J. Butler
Chief Statisticians (*G5*), R. K. Willmer; G. J. O. Phillpotts

DEPARTMENTAL MANAGEMENT
Principal Establishment Officer (*G3*), D. J. Clark
Assistant Secretaries (*G5*), Miss A. Stephenson; P. Allen;
J. E. Knight; Ms P. A. Stewart

INFORMATION SERVICES DIRECTORATE
Director of Information Systems (*G4*), Dr A. A. Holt
Heads of Branches (*G5*), C. M. O'Rourke; J. Bilsby; (*G6*),
Miss S. Blackburn; P. Cobb; Mrs L. Wishart; C. Horsey;
Dr N. Beer

ECONOMICS AND OPERATIONAL RESEARCH DIVISION
(HEALTH)
Chief Economic Adviser (*G3*), C. H. Smee
Senior Economic Advisers (*G5*), Dr S. Harding; J. W. Hurst

INFORMATION DIVISION
Director of Information (*G4*), Miss R. Christopherson
Deputy Directors (*G6*), C. P. Wilson (*news*); Mrs A. Rea
(*publicity*)

SOLICITOR'S OFFICE

Solicitor (G2), P. K. J. Thompson
Principal Assistant Solicitor (G3), A. D. Roberts
Proceedings Operational Director (G4), P. C. Nilsson

ADVISORY COMMITTEES

COMMITTEE ON THE SAFETY OF MEDICINES, Market Towers, 1 Nine Elms Lane, London SW8 5NQ. Tel: 0171-273 0451. *Chairman*, Prof. M. D. Rawlins
ADVISORY COMMITTEE ON THE MICROBIOLOGICAL SAFETY OF FOOD, Room 601A, Skipton House, 80 London Road, London SE1 6LW. Tel: 0171-972 5049. *Chairman*, Prof. H. M. Dick
CLINICAL STANDARDS ADVISORY GROUP, Room LG22, Wellington House, 133–155 Waterloo Road, London SE1 8UG. Tel: 0171-972 4926. *Chairman*, Sir Gordon Higginson

EXECUTIVE AGENCIES

MEDICINES CONTROL AGENCY
Market Towers, 1 Nine Elms Lane, London SW8 5NQ
Tel 0171-273 0000
The Agency controls medicines through licensing, monitoring and inspection, and enforces safety standards.
Chief Executive, Dr K. H. Jones
Head, Licensing Division, Dr D. B. Jefferys
Head, Post Licensing, Dr S. M. Wood
Head, Inspection and Enforcement, B. H. Hartley
Head, Executive Support, R. K. Alder
Finance Director, M. Read

MEDICAL DEVICES AGENCY
Hannibal House, Elephant and Castle, London SE1 6TE
Tel 0171-972 2000
The Agency safeguards the performance, quality and safety of medical devices.
Director (G4), A. Kent
Head, European and Standards Business (G5), vacant
Head, Device Technology and Safety Business (G5), Dr E. Hoxey
Head, Device Evaluation and Publications Business (G6), B. Wignall
Head, Manufacturers' Registration Scheme Business (G6), R. W. B. Allen
Senior Medical Officers, Medical and Nursing Advice (G5), Dr S. M. Ludgate; Dr S. P. Vahl
Head, Corporate Finance Business (G6), K. Cornelius
Head, Corporate Management Business (G6), T. F. Crawley

NHS ESTATES
1 Trevelyan Square, Boar Lane, Leeds LS1 6AE
Tel 0113-254 7000
The agency provides advice and support in the area of healthcare estate functions to the NHS and the healthcare industry.
Chief Executive (G3), J. C. Locke
Estate Policy Director (G5), G. G. Mayers
Director of Business Development (G5), A. R. Tanner
Director of Resources (G5), L. J. Wardle
Chief Engineer (G5), L. W. M. Arrowsmith
Principal Nursing Adviser (G6), Mrs D. Vass

NHS PENSIONS
Hesketh House, 200–220 Broadway, Fleetwood, Lancs. FY7 8LG
Tel 01253-774890
The agency administers the NHS occupational pension scheme.
Chief Executive (G5), A. F. Cowan

NATIONAL HEALTH SERVICE

REGIONAL HEALTH AUTHORITIES
The chairmen and members of Regional Health Authorities are appointed by the Secretary of State for Health. In April 1996 the Regional Health Authorities, District Health Authorities and Family Health Services Authorities will be replaced with all-purpose Health Authorities.

ANGLIA AND OXFORD, 6–12 Capital Drive, Linford Wood, Milton Keynes MK14 6QP. *Chairman*, Sir Stuart Burgess, CBE, PH.D., FRSC; *Regional Director*, Ms B. Stocking
NORTHERN AND YORKSHIRE, Benfield Road, Walker Gate, Newcastle upon Tyne NE6 4PY. *Chairman*, J. Greetham, CBE; *Regional Director*, Prof. L. Donaldson
NORTH THAMES, 40 Eastbourne Terrace, London W2 3QR. *Chairman*, Sir William Staveley, GCB; *Regional Director*, R. Kerr
NORTH WEST, 930–932 Birchwood Boulevard, Millennium Park, Birchwood, Warrington WA3 7QN. *Chairman*, Sir Donald Wilson, KBE; *Regional Director*, R. Tinston
SOUTH AND WEST, Westward House, Lime Kiln Close, Stoke Gifford, Bristol BS12 6SR. *Chairman*, Ms R. Fritchie; *Regional Director*, A. Laurance
SOUTH THAMES, 40 Eastbourne Terrace, London W2 3QR. *Chairman*, W. Wells; *Regional Director*, C. Spry
TRENT, Fulwood House, Old Fulwood Road, Sheffield S10 3TH. *Chairman*, K. Ackroyd, CBE; *Regional Director*, K. McLean
WEST MIDLANDS, Arthur Thompson House, 146 Hagley Road, Birmingham B16 9PA. *Chairman*, B. W. Baker; *Regional Director*, B. Edwards, CBE

SPECIAL HEALTH AUTHORITIES

HEALTH EDUCATION AUTHORITY, Hamilton House, Mabledon Place, London WC1H 9TX. Tel: 0171-383 3833. *Chairman*, A. Close; *Chief Executive*, vacant
NATIONAL BLOOD AUTHORITY, Oak House, Reeds Crescent, Watford, Herts WD1 1QH. Tel: 01923-212121. *Chairman*, Sir Colin Walker, OBE; *Chief Executive*, J. Adey
NHS SUPPLIES AUTHORITY, Apex Plaza, Forbury Road, Reading, Berks RG1 1AX. Tel: 01734-595085. *Chairman*, Sir Robin Buchanan; *National Director of Supplies*, T. Hunt
SPECIAL HOSPITALS SERVICE AUTHORITY, Charles House, Kensington High Street, London W14. Tel: 0171-605 9700. The Special Hospitals Service is provided by three hospitals: Rampton, Broadmoor and Ashworth. *Chairman*, Mrs A. M. Nelson; *Chief Executive*, C. Kaye
CENTRE FOR APPLIED MICROBIOLOGY AND RESEARCH, Porton Down, Salisbury, Wilts SP4 0JG. Tel: 01980-612100. *Director*, Prof. J. Melling, PH.D.

NATIONAL HEALTH SERVICE, SCOTLAND
—*see* Scottish Office entry

HEALTH AND SAFETY COMMISSION
Rose Court, 2 Southwark Bridge, London SE1 9HS
Tel 0171-717 6000

The Health and Safety Commission was created under the Health and Safety at Work etc. Act 1974, with duties to reform health and safety law, to propose new regulations, and generally to promote the protection of people at work and of the public from hazards arising from industrial and commercial activity, including major industrial accidents and the transportation of hazardous materials.

The Commission members are appointed by the Secretary of State for the Environment, although the Commission assists a number of Secretaries of State concerned with aspects of its functions. It is made up of representatives of employers, trades unions and local authorities, and has a full-time chairman.

The Commission can appoint agents, and it works in conjunction with local authorities who enforce the Act in such premises as offices and warehouses.

Chairman, F. J. Davies, CBE
Members, A. D. Tuffin, CBE; R. Symons, CBE; P. Gallagher; E. Carrick, N. J. Pitcher; C. Chope; Dr G. M. Schofield; A. Grant; Ms A. Scully, OBE
Secretary, T. A. Gates

HEALTH AND SAFETY EXECUTIVE
Rose Court, 2 Southwark Bridge, London SE1 9HS
Tel 0171-717 6000

The Health and Safety Executive is the Health and Safety Commission's major instrument. Through its inspectorates it enforces health and safety law in the majority of industrial premises, to protect people at work and the public. The Executive advises the Commission in its major task of laying down safety standards through regulations and practical guidance for many industrial processes, liaising as necessary with government departments and other institutions. The Executive is also the licensing authority for nuclear installations and the reporting officer on the severity of nuclear incidents in Britain. In carrying out its functions the Executive acts independently of the Government, guided only by the Commission as to general health and safety policy.

Director-General (G2), Miss J. H. Bacon, CB *(at G1A)*
Deputy Director-General (G2), D. C. T. Eves, CB *(HM Chief Inspector of Factories)*
Director of Field Operations, HM Factory Inspectorate (G3), Dr J. T. Carter
HM Chief Agricultural Inspector (G3), F. D. Lindsay
HM Chief Inspector of Mines (G3), K. Twist
HM Chief Inspector of Nuclear Installations (G3), Dr S. A. Harbison
HM Chief Inspecting Officer of Railways (G3), S. S. J. Robertson
Director, Strategy and General Division (G3), Dr J. McQuaid
Director, Technology and Health Sciences Division (Includes HM Explosives Inspectorate) (G3), Dr A. F. Ellis
Director, Safety Policy Division (G3), M. Addison
Director, Research and Laboratory Services Division (G4), Dr A. F. Roberts
Director of Medical Services (G3), P. Graham
Solicitor (G4), B. J. Ecclestone
Director, Resources and Planning Division (Including the Accident Prevention Advisory Unit) (G3), R. Hillier
Chief Executive, Offshore Safety Division (G3), R. S. Allison

HIGHLANDS AND ISLANDS ENTERPRISE
Bridge House, 20 Bridge Street, Inverness IV1 1QR
Tel 01463-234171

Highlands and Islands Enterprise (HIE) was set up under the Enterprise and New Towns (Scotland) Act 1991. Its role is to design, direct and deliver enterprise development, training, environmental and social projects and services. HIE is made up of a strategic core body and ten Local Enterprise Companies (LECs) to which many of its individual functions are delegated. The LECs design and develop initiatives at local level covering a wide range of economic and community development, training and environmental improvements.

Chairman, F. Morrison
Chief Executive, I. A. Robertson, CBE

HISTORIC BUILDINGS AND MONUMENTS COMMISSION FOR ENGLAND (ENGLISH HERITAGE)
23 Savile Row, London W1X 1AB
Tel 0171-973 3000

Under the National Heritage Act 1983, the duties of the Commission are to secure the preservation of ancient monuments and historic buildings; to promote the preservation and enhancement of conservation areas; and to promote the public's enjoyment of, and advance their knowledge of, ancient monuments and historic buildings and their preservation. The Commission has advisory committees on historic buildings and areas, ancient monuments, cathedrals and churches, parks and gardens, and London.

Chairman, J. Stevens, CVO
Commissioners, HRH The Duke of Gloucester; C. Green *(Chief Executive);* Dr R. W. Brunskill; The Lord Cavendish of Furness; Ms B. Cherry; Sir Neil Cossons; T. Farrell; Sir David Wilson; Mrs C. Lycett-Green; J. Seymour; G. Wilson; A. Fane; Lady Gass; Prof. E. Fernie, CBE; R. MacCormac; Ms K. McLeod

HISTORIC BUILDINGS COUNCIL FOR WALES
Brunel House, 2 Fitzalan Road, Cardiff CF2 1UY
Tel 01222-465511

The Council's function is to advise the Secretary of State for Wales through Cadw: Welsh Historic Monuments *(see page 359),* which is an executive agency within the Welsh Office.

Chairman, T. Lloyd, FSA
Members, W. Lindsay Evans; R. Haslam; Dr P. Morgan; Mrs S. Furse; Dr S. Unwin; Dr E. Wiliam
Secretary, R. W. Hughes

HISTORIC BUILDINGS COUNCIL FOR SCOTLAND
Longmore House, Salisbury Place, Edinburgh EH9 1SH
Tel 0131-668 8787

The Historic Buildings Council for Scotland is the advisory body to the Secretary of State for Scotland on matters related to buildings of special architectural or historical interest and in particular to proposals for awards by him of grants for the repair of buildings of outstanding architectural or historical interest or lying within outstanding conservation areas.

Chairman, Sir Raymond Johnstone, CBE
Members, Sir Ilay Campbell, Bt.; Mrs P. Chalmers; M. Ellington; Dr J. Frew; Lady Jane Grosvenor; J. Hunter Blair; I. Hutchison, OBE; K. Martin; Miss G. Nayler; Revd C. Robertson; Mrs F. Walker
Secretary, Ms S. Adams

ROYAL COMMISSION ON THE HISTORICAL MONUMENTS OF ENGLAND
National Monuments Record Centre, Kemble Drive, Swindon SN2 2GZ
Tel 01793-414700
London Search Room: 55 Blandford Street, London WIH 3AT.
Tel: 0171-208 8200

The Royal Commission on the Historical Monuments of England was established in 1908. It is the national body of architectural and archaeological survey and record. It manages England's public archive of heritage information, the National Monuments Record.
Chairman, The Lord Faringdon
Commissioners, Prof. R. Bradley, FSA; D. J. Keene, PH.D.; Prof. G. I. Meirion-Jones, PH.D., FSA; Prof. A. C. Thomas, CBE, D.Litt., FSA; Prof. M. Biddle, FBA, FSA; R. D. H. Gem, PH.D., FSA; T. R. M. Longman; R. A. Yorke; Miss A. Riches, FSA; Dr M. Airs, FSA; Prof. M. Fulford, PH.D., FSA; Dr M. Palmer, FSA; Miss A. Arrowsmith
Secretary, T. G. Hassall, FSA

ROYAL COMMISSION ON THE ANCIENT AND HISTORICAL MONUMENTS OF WALES
Crown Building, Plas Crug, Aberystwyth, Dyfed SY23 INJ
Tel 01970-621233

The Royal Commission was established in 1908 to make an inventory of the ancient and historical monuments of Wales and Monmouthshire. It is currently empowered by a royal warrant of 1992 to survey, record, publish and maintain a database of ancient and historical sites, structures and landscapes in Wales. The Commission is also responsible for the National Monuments Record of Wales, which is open daily for public reference.
Chairman, Prof. J. B. Smith
Commissioners, Prof. R. W. Brunskill, OBE, PH.D., FSA; Prof. D. Ellis Evans, D.phil., FBA; Prof. R. A. Griffiths, PH.D.; D. Gruffydd Jones; R. M. Haslam, FSA; Prof. G. B. D. Jones, D.phil., FSA; Mrs A. Nicol; S. B. Smith; Prof. G. J. Wainwright, MBE, PH.D., FSA; E. Wiliam, PH.D., FSA
Secretary, P. R. White, FSA

ROYAL COMMISSION ON THE ANCIENT AND HISTORICAL MONUMENTS OF SCOTLAND
John Sinclair House, 16 Bernard Terrace, Edinburgh EH8 9NX
Tel 0131-662 1446

The Royal Commission was established in 1908 and is appointed to provide for the survey and recording of ancient and historical monuments connected with the culture, civilization and conditions of life of the people in Scotland from the earliest times. It compiles and maintains the National Monuments Record of Scotland as the national record of the archaeological and historical environment. The National Monuments Record is open for reference Monday–Thursday 9.30–4.30, Friday 9.30–4.
Chairman, Sir William Fraser, GCB, FRSE
Commissioners, Prof. J. M. Coles, PH.D., FBA; Prof. J. D. Dunbar-Nasmith, CBE, FRIBA; Prof. Rosemary Cramp, CBE, FSA; Prof. T. C. Smout, CBE, FRSE, FBA; The

Hon. Lord Cullen; Dr Deborah Howard, FSA; Prof. R. A. Paxton, FRSE; Dr Barbara Crawford, FSA, FSA scot.; Miss A. Riches
Secretary, R. J. Mercer, FSA

ANCIENT MONUMENTS BOARD FOR WALES
Brunel House, 2 Fitzalan Road, Cardiff CF2 IUY
Tel 01222-500200

The Ancient Monuments Board for Wales advises the Secretary of State for Wales on his statutory functions in respect of ancient monuments.
Chairman, Prof. R. R. Davies, CBE, D.phil., FBA
Members, Dr S. H. R. Aldhouse-Green, FSA; R. G. Keen; Mrs F. M. Lynch Llewellyn, FSA; Prof. W. H. Manning, PH.D., FSA; Dr P. Smith, FSA; Prof. J. B. Smith; Prof. W. E. Davies, PH.D., FBA; M. J. Garner
Secretary, S. Morris

ANCIENT MONUMENTS BOARD FOR SCOTLAND
Longmore House, Salisbury Place, Edinburgh EH9 ISH
Tel 0131-668 8764

The Ancient Monuments Board for Scotland advises the Secretary of State for Scotland on the exercise of his functions, under the Ancient Monuments and Archaeological Areas Act 1979, of providing protection for monuments of national importance. Protection may be provided by including a monument in a statutory list of protected monuments, by acquisition, or by guardianship in which the Secretary of State assumes responsibility for maintenance.
Chairman, Prof. E. C. Fernie, CBE, FRSE, FSA, FSA scot.
Members, J. Simpson, FSA scot.; Mrs E. V. W. Proudfoot, FSA, FSA scot.; Mrs K. Dalyell, FSA scot.; J. H. A. Gerrard, FRSA, FSA scot.; T. R. H. Godden, CB; L. J. Masters, FSA; Dr Anna Ritchie, FSA, FSA scot.; R. D. Kernohan, OBE; Dr Janet Morgan, FSA; Prof. C. D. Morris, FSA, FSA scot.; R. J. Mercer, FRSE, FSA, FSA scot.; W. D. H. Sellar, FSA scot.; B. Mackie; Miss L. M. Thoms
Secretary, R. A. J. Dalziel
Assessor, D. J. Breeze, PH.D., FRSE, FSA scot.

HOME-GROWN CEREALS AUTHORITY
Hamlyn House, Highgate Hill, London N19 5PR
Tel 0171-263 3391

Set up under the Cereals Marketing Act 1965, the Authority consists of seven members representing UK cereal growers, seven representing dealers in, or processors of, grain and two independent members. The Authority's functions are to improve the production and marketing of UK-grown cereals and oilseeds through a research and development programme, to provide a market information service, to promote UK cereals in export markets and to support work at Food from Britain. The Authority also undertakes agency work for the Intervention Board in connection with the application in the UK of the Common Agricultural Policy for cereals.
Chairman, G. B. Nelson, CBE
Chief Executive, A. J. Williams

HOME OFFICE
50 Queen Anne's Gate, London SW1H 9AT
Tel 0171-273 3000

The Home Office deals with those internal affairs in England and Wales which have not been assigned to other government departments. The Home Secretary is particularly concerned with the administration of justice; criminal law; the treatment of offenders, including probation and the prison service; the police; immigration and nationality; passport policy matters; community relations; certain public safety matters; and fire and civil emergencies services. The Home Secretary personally is the link between The Queen and the public, and exercises certain powers on her behalf, including that of the Royal Pardon.

Other subjects dealt with include electoral arrangements; addresses and petitions to The Queen; ceremonial and formal business connected with honours; requests for extradition of criminals; scrutiny of local authority bye-laws; granting of licences for scientific procedures involving animals; cremations, burials and exhumations; firearms; dangerous drugs and poisons; general policy on laws relating to shops, liquor licensing, gaming and lotteries, charitable collections and marriage; theatre and cinema licensing; co-ordination of government action in relation to the voluntary social services; and race relations policy.

The Home Secretary is also the link between the UK government and the governments of the Channel Islands and the Isle of Man.

In June 1995 a report was published which proposed major changes to the structure of the Home Office by April 1996.

Secretary of State for the Home Department, The Rt. Hon.
    Michael Howard, QC, MP
    Principal Private Secretary (G5), K. D. Sutton
    Private Secretaries, Mrs M. K. Bramwell;
    C. C. R. Hudson; N. Newcomen
    Special Adviser, P. Rock
    Parliamentary Private Secretary, D. Lidington, MP
Ministers of State, The Rt. Hon. David Maclean, MP;
    Ann Widdecombe, MP; The Baroness Blatch, CBE, PC
    Private Secretaries, Miss S. Gooch; A. E. Jones; Mrs
    V. Molloy
    Special Adviser, Miss R. Whetstone
Parliamentary Under-Secretary of State, Nicholas Baker, MP
    Private Secretary, N. Amos
    Parliamentary Clerk, Miss R. McCool
Permanent Under-Secretary of State (G1), R. T. J. Wilson, CB
    Private Secretary, Ms J. L. Hutcheon
Chief Medical Officer (*at Department of Health*), Dr K. Calman

LEGAL ADVISER'S BRANCH
Legal Adviser (G2), M. L. Saunders, CB
Principal Assistant Legal Advisers (G3), Mrs S. A. Evans;
    D. Seymour
Assistant Legal Advisers, R. J. Clayton; Mrs S. A. Evans;
    J. R. O'Meara; C. M. L. Osborne; S. A. Parker

PERSONNEL AND OFFICE SERVICES, FINANCE, FIRE AND EMERGENCY PLANNING DEPARTMENTS
Deputy Under-Secretary (G2), T. C. Platt

PERSONNEL AND OFFICE SERVICES DEPARTMENT
Assistant Under-Secretary of State (G3), Miss P. Drew
    (*Personnel, Organization and Management Services*)
Heads of Divisions (G5), J. F. Acton; M. D. Boyle;
    B. M. Caffarey

Senior Principals (G6), J. G. Daly; A. W. Gillman;
    D. J. Grant; D. C. Houghton; R. Williams

CENTRAL INFORMATION SYSTEMS DIVISION
Head of Division (G5), C. R. Muid
Senior Principals (G6), D. Meakin; S. E. Wharton

ASSESSMENT CONSULTANCY DIVISION
Director (G5), Dr M. Allnutt
Deputy Director (G6), J. G. Jones
Principal Psychologist (G7), D. J. Murray

PUBLIC RELATIONS BRANCH
Director of Information Services (G4), M. Granatt
Deputy Director of Information Services and Head of News (G5),
    J. G. Blakeway
Head of Publicity (G6), C. Skinner
Communications Co-ordinator (G6), A. Underwood
Chief Press Officer (G7), B. R. McBride

FINANCE DEPARTMENT
Assistant Under-Secretary of State (*Principal Finance Officer*)
    (G3), S. G. Norris
Heads of Divisions (G5), R. W. Eagle; J. L. Haugh;
    J. A. Ingman; Miss J. MacNaughton; G. E. Guy
Senior Principals (G6), D. Birleson; K. Cole; P. G. Davies;
    A. K. Holman; R. McBurney; Ms E. A. Sparrow

FIRE AND EMERGENCY PLANNING DEPARTMENT
Assistant Under-Secretary of State (G3), A. P. Wilson
Civil Emergencies Adviser, Rear-Adm. D. K. Bawtree, CB
Heads of Divisions (G5), M. J. Addison; Mrs V. V. R. Harris;
    R. J. Miles; Dr D. M. S. Peace

HM FIRE SERVICE INSPECTORATE
HM Chief Inspector, B. T. A. Collins, OBE
HM Territorial Inspectors, D. McCallum, OBE; P. Morphew,
    QFSM; N. Musselwhite, CBE; G. P. Reid, QFSM; A. Rule,
    QFSM
Lay Inspector, P. Cummings
HM Inspectors, W. Ambalino; D. Berry; G. P. Bowles;
    S. D. Christian; M. T. Franklin; D. Kent; E. G. Pearn,
    QFSM; R. M. Simpson, OBE; A. C. Wells, QFSM; D. Wright
Principal (G7), K. O'Sullivan

EMERGENCY PLANNING COLLEGE
The Hawkhills, Easingwold, Yorks YO6 3EG
Tel 01347-821400
Head of College (G6), A. R. Blackley
College Secretary (G7), A. Richmond

CRIMINAL, RESEARCH AND STATISTICS DEPARTMENTS
Deputy Under-Secretary (G2), J. F. Halliday, CB

CRIMINAL POLICY DEPARTMENT
Assistant Under-Secretary of State (G3), J. Lyon
Heads of Divisions (G5), D. M. Ackland; R. A. Harrington;
    J. M. Potts; P. G. Spurgeon; Miss C. J. Stewart

RESEARCH AND STATISTICS DEPARTMENT
Assistant Under-Secretary of State (G3), C. P. Nuttall

RESEARCH AND PLANNING UNIT
Head of Unit (G5), R. Tarling
Grade 6, D. Butcher; P. J. Jordan; Mrs P. Mayhew;
    A. D. Moxon; Ms J. Vennard

ECONOMICS UNIT
Head of Unit (G6), Dr S. Field

STATISTICS DEPARTMENT
Chief Statisticians (G5), C. G. Lewis; J. L. Walker;
    P. W. Ward
Grade 6, G. C. Barclay; Mrs C. L. Lehmann; M. J. Narey;
    R. M. Taylor

CRIMINAL JUSTICE AND CONSTITUTIONAL
DEPARTMENT
Assistant Under-Secretary of State (G3), R. M. Morris
Heads of Divisions (G5), E. A. Grant; P. J. Honour; Miss
S. Marshall; N. R. Varney
Chief Inspector, Drugs Branch (G6), A. McFarlane
Grade 6, R. G. Evans; Miss A. Fletcher; G. H. Marriage;
A. Norbury, OBE
HM Chief Inspector of Probation (G4), G. W. Smith, CBE
HM Deputy Chief Inspector of Probation (G5), vacant
HM Assistant Chief Inspectors of Probation (G6), L. C. Bridges;
G. W. Childs; J. Eastwood

ANIMALS (SCIENTIFIC PROCEDURE) INSPECTORATE
Chief Inspector, Dr R. M. Watt

POLICE DEPARTMENT
Deputy Under-Secretary (G2), S. Boys Smith

POLICE DEPARTMENT
Assistant Under-Secretaries of State (G3), C. L. Scoble; Miss
C. Sinclair; J. Warne; C. Walters
Heads of Divisions (G5), Mrs P. G. W. Catto; Mrs
F. Clarkson; J. I. Chisholm; Mrs C. Crawford;
J. B. Duke-Evans; Mrs B. Fair; D. A. Hill; A. Holt; Miss
D. Loudon; Ms C. Pelham; N. C. Sanderson;
P. N. Wrench

POLICE SCIENTIFIC DEVELOPMENT BRANCH
Woodcock Hill, Sandridge, St Albans, Herts AL4 9HQ
Tel 01727-865051
Director (G5), Dr D. Bizley
Chief Scientist (G6), Dr P. Young
Langhurst House, Langhurstwood Road, Nr Horsham,
W. Sussex RH12 4WX
Tel 01403-55451
Head of Unit (G6), Dr G. Thomas

POLICE NATIONAL COMPUTER (HENDON DATA
CENTRE)
Aerodrome Road, Colindale, London NW9 5LN
Tel 0181-200 2424
Head of Division (G6), J. Ladley

HM INSPECTORATE OF CONSTABULARY
HM Chief Inspector of Constabulary, T. A. Morris, CBE, QPM
HM Inspectors, D. Crompton, QPM; G. J. Dear, QPM;
D. J. O'Dowd, CBE, QPM; C. Smith, CBE, CVO, QPM;
P. J. Winship, QPM
Lay Inspectors, P. T. G. Hobbs; Dr A. P. Williams

POLICE STAFF COLLEGE
Bramshill House, Basingstoke, Hants RG27 0JW
Tel 0125 126-2931
Commandant, P. J. Ryan, QPM
Deputy Commandant and Director of Courses, Mrs S. Davies

THE SECURITY SERVICE (MI5)
Thames House, PO Box 3255, London SW1P 1AE
The Security Service is responsible for protecting national
security. It took over responsibility for mainland intelligence about Irish terrorism from the anti-terrorist branch
of the Metropolitan Police in 1992. Counter-terrorism
activities account for 70 per cent of its work; 25 per cent
involves counter-espionage and counter-proliferation
activities, and the remaining 5 per cent involves the
monitoring of subversive organizations. The Service is
split into two sections, Operations and Administration. It
was placed on a statutory footing by the Security Service
Act 1989.
Director-General, Mrs S. Rimington

EQUAL OPPORTUNITIES, IMMIGRATION
AND NATIONALITY DEPARTMENTS
Deputy Under-Secretary (G2), T. E. Walker

EQUAL OPPORTUNITIES AND GENERAL DEPARTMENT
Assistant Under-Secretary of State (G3), M. E. Head, CVO
Heads of Divisions (G5), R. Kornicki; A. Harding; E. Soden

Voluntary Services Unit
Assistant Secretary (G5), H. Webber

GAMING BOARD FOR GREAT BRITAIN
— see page 306

IMMIGRATION AND NATIONALITY DEPARTMENT
Lunar House, 40 Wellesley Road, Croydon, Surrey,
CR9 2BY
Tel 0181-686 0688

Assistant Under-Secretaries of State (G3), T. Flesher;
A. R. Rawsthorne
Heads of Divisions (G5), D. A. L. Cooke; Miss V. M. Dews;
E. B. Nicholls; Mrs E. C. L. Pallett; Miss A. Smith;
A. Walmsley; R. M. Whalley; R. G. Yates

Immigration Service
Director (Ports) (G5), T. Farrage
Director (Immigration Service Enforcement) (G5),
C. B. Manchip
Deputy Directors (G6), G. Boiling; V. Hogg;
D. J. McDonough

EUROPEAN COMMUNITIES UNIT
Head of Division (G5), M. J. Gillespie

HM PRISON SERVICE
Cleland House, Page Street, London SW1P 4LN
Tel 0171-217 6000
An executive agency of the Home Office.

SALARIES 1995–6

Assistant Director	£48,835–£52,133
Governor 1	£46,467
Governor 2	£41,959
Governor 3	£36,236
Governor 4	£29,817–£31,163
Governor 5	£25,473–£29,974

THE PRISONS BOARD
Director-General (G2), D. C. Lewis
Director of Personnel (G3), vacant
Director of Finance (G3), B. Landers
Director of Security and Programmes (G3), R. R. Tilt
Directors of Operations (G3), A. J. Pearson (*North*); A. Walker
(*South*)
Director of Services (G3), A. J. Butler
Director of Health Care (G3), Dr Rosemary Wool, CB
Non-Executive Members, Mrs M. Banerjee; F. W. Bentley;
G. Keeys; Sir Duncan Nichol, CBE

PRISON SERVICE HEADQUARTERS
Heads of Groups (Asst. Dir.), P. Wheatley (*custody*);
W. J. Abbott (*security*); I. Boon (*pay and industrial
relations*); (*G5*), K. Heal (*programmes policy*); Miss S. Paul
(*health care policy*); Mrs E. J. Grimsey (*personnel planning*);
T. Wilson (*contracts and competitions*); S. Hickson
(*finance*); J. Le Vay (*planning*); P. Sleightholme (*systems
strategy*); (*G6*), Mrs H. Bayne (*lifer*); Mrs A. Nelson
(*prison service communications*); K. Lockyer (*secretariat*)
Strategic Development Adviser (SMO), Dr L. Joyce
Heads of Services (Gov. 1), J. Dring (*training*); (*Gov. 3*), Mrs
U. McCullom-Gordon (*staff care and welfare*) (*G4*),
R. Haines (*construction*); (*G5*), Miss L. Gill (*prisoner
services*); (*G6*), B. Johnson (*office services*); Mrs Y. Wilmott

(*nursing*); Dr C. McDougall (*personnel*); J. Gunderson (*prisoner escorts and custody*); S. Jenner (*internal audit*); A. Pay (*accounting*); (*G7*), T. Kelly (*personnel finance*); (*PMO*), Dr D. Howells (*healthcare professional development*)
Chaplain-General and Archdeacon of the Prison Service, Ven. D. Fleming
Chief Education Adviser (*G6*), I. G. Benson
Chief Physical Education Adviser (*G6*), M. W. Denton

PRISON ENTERPRISE AND ACTIVITY SERVICES
Block A, Whitgift Centre, Wellesley Road, Croydon, Surrey CR9 3LY
Tel 0181-686 8710
Director (*G5*), P. R. A. Fulton

SUPPLY AND TRANSPORT SERVICES
Crown House, 52 Elizabeth Street, Corby, Northants
Tel 01536-202101
Director (*G5*), D. J. C. Kent

AREA MANAGERS
Directorate of Operations (*North*)
Central (*Asst. Dir.*), J. Blakey
East Midlands (*Gov. 1*), J. C. Mullens
Mercia (*Gov. 1*), D. Curtis
North-East (*Asst. Dir.*), A. H. Papps
North-West (*Gov. 1*), D. I. Lockwood
Trans-Pennine (*Asst. Dir.*), T. Bone
Yorkshire (*Gov. 1*), M. Codd

Directorate of Operations (*South*)
Chilterns (*Gov. 1*), A. de Frisching
East Anglia (*Gov. 1*), T. G. Murtagh, OBE
Kent (*Gov. 1*), J. Hunter
London North (*G5*), Miss A. M. Edwards
London South (*Asst. Dir.*), P. J. Kitteridge
South Coast (*Gov. 1*), A. Rayfield
Wales and the West (*Gov. 1*), J. Wilkinson
Wessex (*Gov. 1*), J. May

PRISONS
ACKLINGTON, Morpeth, Northumberland NE65 9XF. *Governor*, F. P. Masserick
ALBANY, Newport, Isle of Wight PO30 5RS. *Governor*, vacant
ALDINGTON, Ashford, Kent TN25 7BQ. *Governor*, D. A. Bratton
ASHWELL, Oakham, Leics LE15 7LS. *Governor*, H. Reid
*ASKHAM GRANGE, Askham Richard, York YO2 3PT. *Governor*, H. E. Crew
BEDFORD, St Loyes Street, Bedford MK40 1HG. *Governor*, E. Willets
BELMARSH, Western Way, Thamesmead, London SE28 0EB. *Governor*, H. D. Jones
BIRMINGHAM, Winson Green Road, Birmingham B18 4AS. *Governor*, G. Gregory-Smith
BLAKENHURST (private prison), Hewell Lane, Redditch, Worcs B97 6QS. *Monitor*, P. J. Hanglin
BLANTYRE HOUSE, Goudhurst, Cranbrook, Kent TN17 2NH. *Governor*, B . Pollett
BLUNDESTON, Lowestoft, Suffolk NR32 5BG. *Governor*, S. Robinson
BRISTOL, Cambridge Road, Bristol BS7 8PS. *Governor*, R. D. Dixon
BRIXTON, PO Box 369, Jebb Avenue, London SW2 5XF. *Governor*, Dr A. Coyle
BROCKHILL, Redditch, Worcs B97 6RD. *Governor*, K. Naisbitt
BUCKLEY HALL (private prison), Buckley Road, Rochdale, Lancs OL12 9DP. *Monitor*, Miss V. Bird
BULLINGDON, Padrick Haugh Road, Arncott, Bicester, Oxon OX6 0PZ. *Governor*, Ms S. Fielder

*BULLWOOD HALL, High Road, Hockley, Essex SS5 4TE. *Governor*, Mrs E. Butler
CAMP HILL, Newport, Isle of Wight PO30 5PB. *Governor*, S. Moore
CANTERBURY, Longport, Canterbury, Kent CT1 1PJ. *Governor*, G. Davies
CARDIFF, Knox Road, Cardiff CF2 1UG. *Governor*, N. D. Clifford
CHANNINGS WOOD, Denbury, Newton Abbott, Devon TQ12 6DW. *Governor*, R. S. Brandon
CHELMSFORD, Springfield Road, Chelmsford, Essex CM2 6LQ. *Governor*, D. B. Sinclair
COLDINGLEY, Bisley, Woking, Surrey GU24 9EX. *Governor*, J. Smith
*COOKHAM WOOD, Cookham Wood, Rochester, Kent ME1 3LU. *Governor*, I. Smout
DARTMOOR, Princetown, Yelverton, Devon PL20 6RR. *Governor*, J. Lawrence
DONCASTER (private prison), Off North Bridge, Marshgate, Doncaster DN5 8UX. *Director*, K. Rogers
DORCHESTER, North Square, Dorchester, Dorset DT1 1JD. *Governor*, R. Walker
DOWNVIEW, Sutton Lane, Sutton, Surrey SM2 5PD. *Governor*, D. M. Lancaster
*DRAKE HALL, Eccleshall, Staffs ST21 6LQ. *Governor*, G. Hughes
*DURHAM, Old Elvet, Durham DH1 3HU. *Governor*, R. Mitchell
*EAST SUTTON PARK, Sutton Valence, Maidstone, Kent ME17 3DF. *Governor*, Mrs C. J. Galbally
*ELMLEY, Church Road, Eastchurch, Sheerness, Kent ME12 4DZ. *Governor*, A. Smith
ERLESTOKE HOUSE, Devizes, Wilts SN10 5TU. *Governor*, Ms A. J. Gomme
EVERTHORPE, Brough, North Humberside HU15 1RB. *Governor*, R. Smith
EXETER, New North Road, Exeter, Devon EX4 4EX. *Governor*, T. C. H. Newth
FEATHERSTONE, New Road, Featherstone, Wolverhampton WV10 7PU. *Governor*, C. Scott
FORD, Arundel, W. Sussex BN18 0BX. *Governor*, D. A. Godfrey
FRANKLAND, Frankland, Brasside, Durham, DH1 5YD. *Governor*, J. Harrison
FULL SUTTON, Full Sutton, York YO4 1PS. *Governor*, J. W. Staples
GARTH, Ulnes Walton Lane, Leyland, Preston, Lancs PR5 3NE. *Governor*, W. Rose-Quirie
GARTREE, Leicester Road, Market Harborough, Leics LE16 7RP. *Governor*, R. J. Perry
GLOUCESTER, Barrack Square, Gloucester GL1 2JN. *Governor*, P. W. Winkley
GRENDON, Grendon Underwood, Aylesbury, Bucks HP18 0TL. *Governor*, T. C. Newell
HASLAR, Dolphin Way, Gosport, Hants PO12 2AW. *Governor*, I. Truffet
HAVERIGG, Haverigg Camp, Millom, Cumbria LA18 4NA. *Governor*, B. Wilson
HEWELL GRANGE, Redditch, Worcs B97 6QQ. *Governor*, D. W. Bamber
HIGHDOWN, Sutton Lane, Sutton, Surrey SM2 5PJ. *Governor*, S. Pryor
HIGHPOINT, Stradishall, Newmarket, Suffolk CB8 9YG. *Governor*, C. D. Sherwood
HINDLEY, Gibson Street, Bickershaw, Hindley, Wigan, Lancs WN2 5TH. *Governor*, R. Crouch
HOLLESLEY BAY COLONY, Hollesley, Woodbridge, Suffolk IP12 3JS. *Governor*, M. F. Clarke
*HOLLOWAY, Parkhurst Road, London N7 0NU. *Governor*, Miss J. King

HOLME HOUSE, Holme House Road, Stockton-on-Tees, Cleveland TS18 2QU. *Governor,* R. Roberts

HULL, Hedon Road, Hull, N. Humberside HU9 5LS. *Governor,* R. Daly

KINGSTON, Milton Road, Portsmouth PO3 6AS. *Governor,* J. R. Dovell

KIRKHAM, Preston, Lancs PR4 2RA. *Governor,* A. F. Jennings

KIRKLEVINGTON GRANGE, Yarm, Cleveland TS15 9PA. *Governor,* Mrs A. Midgley

LANCASTER, The Castle, Lancaster LA1 1YL. *Governor,* D. G. McNaughton

LATCHMERE HOUSE, Church Road, Ham Common, Richmond, Surrey TW10 5HH. *Governor,* S. O'Neill

LEEDS, Armley, Leeds LS12 2TJ. *Governor,* A. J. Fitzpatrick

LEICESTER, Welford Road, Leicester LE2 7AJ. *Governor,* G. ROSS, OBE

LEWES, Brighton Road, Lewes, E. Sussex BN7 1EA. *Governor,* J. F. Dixon

LEYHILL, Wotton-under-Edge, Glos GL12 8HL. *Governor,* D. T. Williams

LINCOLN, Greetwell Road, Lincoln LN2 4BD. *Governor,* D. Shaw

LINDHOLME, Bawtry Road, Hatfield, Woodhouse, Doncaster DN7 6EE. *Governor,* M. Shann

LITTLEHEY, Perry, Huntingdon, Cambs PE18 0SR. *Governor,* M. L. Knight

LIVERPOOL, 68 Hornby Road, Liverpool L9 3DF. *Governor,* R. H. Jacques

LONG LARTIN, South Littleton, Evesham, Worcs WR11 5TZ. *Governor,* J. Mullen

MAIDSTONE, County Road, Maidstone ME14 1UZ. *Governor,* H. Bagshaw

MANCHESTER, Southall Street, Manchester M60 9AH. *Governor,* R. P. Halward

MOORLAND, Hatfield Woodhouse, Doncaster DN7 6BW. *Governor,* C. R. Griffiths

MORTON HALL, Swinderby, Lincoln LN6 9PS. *Governor,* C. P. A. Bushell

THE MOUNT, Molyneaux Avenue, Bovingdon, Hemel Hempstead HP3 0NZ. *Governor,* Mrs M. Donnelly

*NEW HALL, Dial Wood, Flockton, Wakefield, W. Yorks WF4 4AX. *Governor,* D. England

NORTH SEA CAMP, Freiston, Boston, Lincs PE22 0QX. *Governor,* M. A. Lewis

NORWICH, Mousehold, Norwich NR1 4LU. *Governor,* vacant

NOTTINGHAM, Perry Road, Sherwood, Nottingham NG5 3AG. *Governor,* P. J. Bennett

OXFORD, New Road, Oxford OX1 1LZ. *Governor,* Ms S. Fielder

PARKHURST, Newport, Isle of Wight PO30 5NX. *Governor,* D. M. Morrison

PENTONVILLE, Caledonian Road, London N7 8TT. *Governor,* K. Brewer

PRESTON, 2 Ribbleton Lane, Preston, Lancs OR1 5AB. *Governor,* R. Doughty

RANBY, Ranby, Retford, Notts DN22 8EU. *Governor,* T. J. Williams

*RISLEY, Warrington Road, Risley, Warrington WA3 6BP. *Governor,* F. B. O'Friel.

ROCHESTER, Rochester, Kent ME1 3QS. *Governor,* R. A. Chapman

RUDGATE, Wetherby, W. Yorks LS23 7AZ. *Governor,* H. Jones

SEND, Ripley Road, Send, Woking, Surrey GU23 7LJ. *Governor,* S. Guy-Gibbons

SHEPTON MALLET, Cornhill, Shepton Mallet, Somerset BA4 5LU. *Governor,* P. O'Sullivan

SHREWSBURY, The Dana, Shrewsbury, Salop SY1 2HR. *Governor,* D. J. Bradley

STAFFORD, 54 Gaol Road, Stafford ST16 3AW. *Governor,* R. Feeney

STANDFORD HILL, Church Road, Eastchurch, Sheerness, Kent ME12 4AA. *Governor,* D. M. Twiner

STOCKEN, Stocken Hall Road, Stretton, Nr Oakham, Leics LE15 7RD. *Governor,* D. Hall

STOKE HEATH, Market Drayton, Shropshire TF9 2JL. *Governor,* J. Aldridge

*STYAL, Wilmslow, Cheshire SK9 4HR. *Governor,* M. Goodwin

SUDBURY, Sudbury, Derbys DE6 5HW. *Governor,* P. E. Salter

SWALESIDE, Eastchurch, Isle of Sheppey, Kent ME12 4AX. *Governor,* R. Tasker

SWANSEA, Oystermouth Road, Swansea SA1 2SR. *Governor,* J. Heyes

USK, 29 Maryport Street, Usk, Gwent NP5 1XP. *Governor,* N. J. Evans

THE VERNE, Portland, Dorset DT5 1EQ. *Governor,* T. M. Turner

WAKEFIELD, Love Lane, Wakefield WF2 9AG. *Governor,* R. S. Duncan

WANDSWORTH, PO Box 757, Heathfield Road, London SW18 3HS. *Governor,* C. G. Clarke

WAYLAND, Wayland, Griston, Thetford, Norfolk IP25 6RL. *Governor,* W. S. Duff

WEALSTUN, Wetherby, W. Yorks LS23 7AY. *Governor,* G. Barnard

WELLINGBOROUGH, Millers Park, Doddington Road, Wellingborough, Northants NN8 2NH. *Governor,* J. Whetton

WHATTON, Whatton, Notts NG13 9FQ. *Governor,* J. McCourt

WHITEMOOR, Longhill Road, March, Cambs PE15 0PR. *Governor,* R. B. Clarke

WINCHESTER, Romsey Road, Winchester, Hants SO22 5DF. *Governor,* M. K. Pascoe

WOODHILL, Tattenhoe Street, Milton Keynes MK4 4DA. *Governor,* Ms M. Gorman

WORMWOOD SCRUBBS, PO Box 757, Du Cane Road, London W12 0AE. *Governor,* J. F. Perris

WYMOTT, Moss Lane, Ulnes Walton, Leyland, Preston, Lancs PR5 3LW. *Governor,* G. Brunskill

YOUNG OFFENDER INSTITUTIONS

AYLESBURY, Bierton Road, Aylesbury, Bucks HP20 1EH. *Governor,* M. Sheldrick

BRINSFORD, New Road, Featherstone, Wolverhampton WV10 7PY. *Governor,* B. Payling

*BULLWOOD HALL, High Road, Hockley, Essex SS5 4TE. *Governor,* Mrs E. Butler

CASTINGTON, Morpeth, Northumberland NE65 9XF. *Governor,* C. Harder

DEERBOLT, Bowes Road, Barnard Castle, Co. Durham DL12 9BG. *Governor,* W. J. Ginn

DOVER, The Citadel, Western Heights, Dover, Kent CT17 9DR. *Governor,* B. W. Sutton

*DRAKE HALL, Eccleshall, Staffs ST21 6LQ. *Governor,* G. Hughes

*EAST SUTTON PARK, Sutton Valence, Maidstone, Kent ME17 3DF. *Governor,* Mrs C. J. Galbally

EASTWOOD PARK, Falfield, Wotton-under-Edge, Glos GL12 8DB. *Governor,* Ms S. J. Swift

FELTHAM, Bedfont Road, Feltham, Middx TW13 4ND. *Governor,* I. Ward

GLEN PARVA, Tigers Road, Wigston, Leics LE8 2TN. *Governor,* C. Williams

GUYS MARSH, Shaftesbury, Dorset SP7 0AH. *Governor (acting),* R. Monksummers

HATFIELD, Hatfield, Doncaster DN7 6EL. *Governor,* H. Jones

HOLLESLEY BAY COLONY, Hollesley, Woodbridge, Suffolk IP12 3JS. *Governor,* M. F. Clarke

---

*Women's establishments/establishments with units for women

HUNTERCOMBE, Huntercombe Place, Nuffield, Henley-on-Thames RG9 5SB. *Governor*, D. Strong
LANCASTER FARMS, Stone Row Head, off Quernmore Road, Lancaster LA1 3QZ. *Governor*, D. J. Waplington
*NEW HALL, Dial Wood, Flockton, Wakefield WF4 4AX. *Governor*, D. England
NORTHALLERTON, East Road, Northallerton, N. Yorks DL6 1NW. *Governor*, D. P. G. Appleton
ONLEY, Willoughby, Rugby, Warks CV23 8AP. *Governor*, J. N. Brooke
PORTLAND, Easton, Portland, Dorset DT5 1DL. *Governor*, D. Brisco
PRESCOED, 29 Maryport Street, Usk, Gwent NP4 0TD. *Governor*, N. J. Evans
STOKE HEATH, Market Drayton, Salop TF9 2JL. *Governor*, J. Aldridge
*STYAL, Wilmslow, Cheshire, SK9 4HR. *Governor*, M. Goodwin
SWINFEN HALL, Lichfield, Staffs WS14 9QS. *Governor*, Mrs J. Francis
THORN CROSS, Arley Road, Appleton Thorn, Warrington WA4 4RL. *Governor*, I. Windebank
WERRINGTON, Stoke-on-Trent ST9 0DX. *Governor*, B. Stanhope
WETHERBY, York Road, Wetherby, W. Yorks LS22 5ED. *Governor*, P. J. Atkinson

REMAND CENTRES

BRINSFORD, New Road, Featherstone, Wolverhampton WV10 7PY. *Governor*, B. Payling
CARDIFF, Knox Road, Cardiff CF2 1UG. *Governor*, N. D. Clifford
EXETER, New North Road, Exeter, Devon EX4 4EX. *Governor*, T. C. H. Newth
FELTHAM, Bedfont Road, Feltham, Middx TW13 4ND. *Governor*, I. Ward
GLEN PARVA, Tigers Road, Wigston, Leics LE8 2TN. *Governor*, C. Williams
LANCASTER FARMS, Stone Rowe Head, Off Quernmore Road, Lancaster LA1 3QZ. *Governor*, D. J. Waplington
LOW NEWTON, Brasside, Durham DH1 5SD. *Governor*, Mrs M. Egan
NORWICH, Mousehold, Norwich, Norfolk NR1 4LU. *Governor*, vacant
PUCKLECHURCH, Bristol BS17 3QJ. *Governor*, Ms S. J. Swift
READING, Forbury Road, Reading, Berks RG1 3HY. *Governor*, G. Petherick
THE WOLDS (private remand prison), Everthorpe, Brough, N. Humberside HU15 2JZ. *Director*, J. McDonnell

HM INSPECTORATE OF PRISONS
HM Chief Inspector of Prisons, vacant
HM Deputy Chief Inspector of Prisons (*G5*), C. Allen
HM Inspectors, Mrs G. Bakelmun; P. Clarke; E. Hornblow; J. Phillips; A. Wood
Principal Psychologist, S. Boddis
Press Officer (*G7*), M. Deaves

FIRE SERVICE COLLEGE
Moreton-in-Marsh, Glos GL56 0RH
Tel 01608-650831
An executive agency of the Home Office.
Chief Executive, N. K. Finlayson
Commandant, F. David
Dean, Dr R. Willis-Lee
Director of Development and Services (*G7*), Dr T. Jeans

FORENSIC SCIENCE SERVICE HEADQUARTERS
Priory House, Gooch Street North, Birmingham B5 6QQ
Tel 0121-666 6606
An executive agency of the Home Office.
Director-General (*G3*), Dr J. Thompson
Head of Organization Development (*G5*), Dr P. D. B. Clarke
Chief Scientist (*G5*), Dr A. W. Scaplehorn
Director of Finance (*G5*), K. Cloran
Head of Procurement and Administration (*G6*), Dr R. Totty
Director of Business Development (*G6*), T. H. Howitt

UK PASSPORT AGENCY
Clive House, Petty France, London SW1H 9HD
Tel 0171-799 2728
An executive agency of the Home Office.
Chief Executive (*G5*), D. Gatenby
Deputy Chief Executive and Director of Operations (*G6*), T. Lonsdale
Director of Resources (*G6*), K. J. Sheehan
Director of Systems (*G6*), R. G. Le Marechal

HORSERACE TOTALISATOR BOARD
74 Upper Richmond Road, London SW15 2SU
Tel 0181-874 6411

The Horserace Totalisator Board was established by the Betting, Gaming and Lotteries Act 1963, as successor to the Racecourse Betting Control Board. Its function is to operate totalisators on approved racecourses in Great Britain, and it also provides on- and off-course cash and credit offices. Under the Horserace Totalisator and Betting Levy Board Act 1972, it is further empowered to offer bets at starting price (or other bets at fixed odds) on any sporting event. The chairman and members of the Board are appointed by the Home Secretary.
Chairman (£95,000), The Lord Wyatt of Weeford
Chief Executive, B. McDonnell

HOUSING CORPORATION
149 Tottenham Court Road, London W1P 0BN
Tel 0171-393 2000

Established by Parliament in 1964, the Housing Corporation registers, promotes, funds and supervises housing associations. The Corporation's duties were extended under the provisions of the Housing Act 1988 to cover the payment of capital and revenue grants to housing associations, advice for tenants interested in Tenants' Choice, and the approval and revocation of potential new landlords under this policy.
There are over 2,200 registered associations in England providing more than 600,000 homes for people in need of housing. Housing associations are non-profit making bodies run by voluntary committees.
Chairman, Sir Brian Pearse
Chief Executive, A. Mayer

*Women's establishments/establishments with units for women

HUMAN FERTILIZATION AND EMBRYOLOGY AUTHORITY
Paxton House, 30 Artillery Lane, London EI 7LS
Tel 0171-377 5077

The Authority was established under the Human Fertilization and Embryology Act 1990. Its function is to license persons carrying out any of the following activities: the creation or use of embryos outside the body in the provision of infertility treatment services; the use of donated gametes in infertility treatment; the storage of gametes or embryos; and research on human embryos. The Authority also keeps under review information about embryos and, when requested to do so, gives advice to the Secretary of State for Health.
Chairman, Mrs R. Deech
Deputy Chairman, Lady (Diana) Brittan
Members, Prof. R. J. Berry; Mrs J. Denton; Ms E. Forgan; Ms J. Harbison; Prof. S. Hillier; ph.d.; The Most Revd R. Holloway; Prof. M. Johnson; R. Jones; Ms P. Keith; Dr B. Lieberman; Dr C. Lindsey; Mrs A. Mays; Dr A. McLaren; Dr J. Naish; Rabbi Julia Neuberger; D. Shilson; Prof. A. Templeton; Ms J. Tugendhat; J. Williams
Chief Executive, Mrs F. Goldhill

INDEPENDENT COMMISSION FOR POLICE COMPLAINTS FOR NORTHERN IRELAND
Chamber of Commerce House, 22 Great Victoria Street, Belfast BT2 7LP
Tel 01232-244821

The Independent Commission for Police Complaints was established under the Police (Northern Ireland) Order 1987. It has powers to supervise the investigation of certain categories of serious complaints, can direct that disciplinary charges be brought, and has oversight of the informal resolution procedure for less serious complaints.
Chairman, J. Grew
Chief Executive, B. McClelland

INDEPENDENT REVIEW SERVICE FOR THE SOCIAL FUND
Millbank Tower, 21–24 Millbank, London, SWIP 4QU
Tel 0171-630 9886
4th Floor, Centre City Podium, 5 Hill Street, Birmingham B5 4UB
Tel 0121-606 2100

The Social Fund Commissioner is appointed by the Secretary of State for Social Security. The Commissioner appoints Social Fund Inspectors, who provide an independent review of decisions made by Social Fund Officers in the Benefits Agency of the Department of Social Security.
Social Fund Commissioner, J. Scampion

INDEPENDENT TELEVISION COMMISSION
33 Foley Street, London WIP 7LB
Tel 0171-255 3000

The Independent Television Commission replaced the Independent Broadcasting Authority in 1991. The Commission is responsible for licensing and regulating all commercially funded UK television services. Members are appointed by the Secretary of State for National Heritage.
Chairman (£61,344), Sir George Russell, CBE
Deputy Chairman, J. Stevens, CVO
Members, Earl of Dalkeith; Mrs P. Mathias; R. Goddard; Mrs E. Wynne Jones; Dr J. Beynon, FENg.; Ms J. Goffe; Dr Maria Moloney; J. Ranelagh
Chief Executive, D. Glencross, CBE
Secretary, M. Redley

INDUSTRIAL INJURIES ADVISORY COUNCIL
6th Floor, The Adelphi, 1–11 John Adam Street, London WC2N 6HT
Tel 0171-962 8066

The Industrial Injuries Advisory Council is a statutory body under the Social Security Act 1975 which considers and advises the Secretary of State for Social Security on regulations and other questions relating to industrial injuries benefits or their administration.
Chairman, Prof. J. M. Harrington, CBE
Secretary, R. Heigh

BOARD OF INLAND REVENUE
Somerset House, London WC2R ILB
Tel 0171-438 6622

The Board of Inland Revenue was constituted under the Inland Revenue Board Act 1849, by the consolidation of the Board of Excise and the Board of Stamps and Taxes. In 1909 the administration of excise duties was transferred to the Board of Customs. The Board of Inland Revenue administers and collects direct taxes – mainly income tax, stamp duty, development land tax and petroleum revenue tax – and advises the Chancellor of the Exchequer on policy questions involving them.

The Department is organized into a series of accountable management units under the Next Steps programme and has its own pay structure. The day-to-day operations in assessing and collecting tax and in providing internal support services are carried out by 29 Executive Offices. The Department's Valuation Office is an executive agency responsible for valuing property for tax purposes, for compensation, for compulsory purchase, and (in England and Wales) for local rating purposes. In 1993–4 the Inland Revenue collected over £77,469.5 million in tax.

THE BOARD
Chairman (*G1*), Sir Anthony Battishill, KCB
  Private Secretary, Dr F. Khan
Deputy Chairmen (*G2*), S. C. T. Matheson, CB; C. W. Corlett, CB
Principal Establishments Officer (*G2*), G. H. Bush

DIVISIONS
Directors, Subject Divisions (*G3*), E. McGivern; M. F. Cayley; B. Mace; P. Lewis; I. R. Spence; E. J. Gribbon
Director, Personnel Division (*G3*), J. Gant
Director, Management Services Division (*G4*), N. C. Munro
Head, Change Management Division, D. A. Smith
Principal Finance Officer (*G3*), R. R. Martin
Director, Policy Co-ordination Unit, P. Lewis
Director, Business Operations Division (*G3*), M. A. Johns
Director, Quality Development Division (*G3*), K. V. Deacon

EXECUTIVE OFFICES
ACCOUNTS OFFICE (CUMBERNAULD), Cumbernauld,
Glasgow G70 5TR. *Controller*, A. Geddes, OBE
ACCOUNTS OFFICE (SHIPLEY), Shipley, Bradford, W. Yorks
BD98 8AA. *Controller*, P. Clark

CAPITAL TAXES OFFICE
Ferrers House, PO Box 38, Castle Meadow Road,
Nottingham NG2 1BB
Controller, B. D. Kent

CAPITAL TAXES OFFICE (SCOTLAND)
Mulberry House, 16 Picardy Place, Edinburgh, EH1 3NB
Registrar, I. Fraser

CORPORATE COMMUNICATIONS OFFICE
Controller, R. N. Hooper
Press Secretary, Mrs T. A. Middleton

ENFORCEMENT OFFICE
South Block, Barrington Road, Worthing, W. Sussex
BN12 4SE
Controller, Mrs S. Walsh

FINANCIAL INTERMEDIARIES AND CLAIMS OFFICE
St John's House, Merton Road, Bootle L69 9BB
Fitz Roy House, Castle Meadow Road, Nottingham NG2
1BD
Controller, D. A. Hartnett

FINANCIAL INTERMEDIARIES AND CLAIMS OFFICE
(SCOTLAND)
Trinity Park House, South Trinity Road, Edinburgh
EH5 3SD
Officer in Charge, J. Duguid

FINANCIAL ACCOUNTING OFFICE
Barrington Road, Worthing, W. Sussex BN12 4XH
Controller, J. D. Easey

BUSINESS SERVICES OFFICE
Director (G3), J. E. Yard
Divisional Directors, R. A. Assirati; R. Massingale;
R. H. Wearing

INTERNAL AUDIT OFFICE
22 Kingsway, London WC2B 4PP
Chief Internal Auditor, N. R. Buckley

OIL TAXATION OFFICE
Melbourne House, Aldwych, London WC2B 4LL
Controller, R. C. Mountain

PENSION SCHEMES OFFICE
Yorke House, PO Box 62, Castle Meadow Road,
Nottingham NG2 1BG
Controller, S. J. McManus

SOLICITOR FOR INLAND REVENUE
Solicitor (G2), B. E. Cleave, CB
Principal Assistant Solicitors (G3), J. D. H. Johnston;
J. G. H. Bates; G. F. Butt
Board's Advisory Accountant, T. C. Carne

SOLICITOR OF INLAND REVENUE (SCOTLAND)
80 Lauriston Place, Edinburgh EH3 9SL
Solicitor, I. K. Laing

SPECIAL COMPLIANCE OFFICE
Angel Court, 199 Borough High Street, London SE1 1HZ
Controller, F. J. Brannigan
Board's Investigating Officer, F. B. Dunbar

THE STAMP OFFICE
South-West Wing, Bush House, Strand, London WC2B
4QN
Controller, K. S. Hodgson

THE STAMP OFFICE (SCOTLAND)
Mulberry House, 16 Picardy Place, Edinburgh EH1 3NF
Controller, D. G. Hunter

STATISTICS AND ECONOMICS OFFICE
Director (G3), R. Ward
Chief Statisticians, Dr G. A. Keenay; Dr G. J. Parker;
R. J. Eason; E. Ko
Information Technology, Dr R. James
Senior Economics Adviser, W. M. McNie

TRAINING OFFICE
Inland Revenue Staff College, Lawres Hall, Riseholme
Park, Lincoln LN2 2BJ
Controller, T. Kuczys

REGIONAL EXECUTIVE OFFICES
INLAND REVENUE EAST, Midgate House, Peterborough
PE1 1TD
INLAND REVENUE LONDON, New Court, Carey Street,
London WC2A 2JE
INLAND REVENUE NORTH, 100 Russell Street,
Middlesbrough, Cleveland TS1 2RZ
INLAND REVENUE NORTH-WEST, The Triad, Stanley
Road, Bootle, Merseyside L20 3PD
INLAND REVENUE SOUTH-EAST, Albion House, Chertsey
Road, Woking GU21 1BT
INLAND REVENUE SOUTH-WEST, Longbrook House, New
North Road, Exeter EX4 4UA
INLAND REVENUE SOUTH YORKSHIRE, Sovereign House,
110 Queen Street, Sheffield S1 2EN
INLAND REVENUE WALES AND MIDLANDS, Chadwick
House, Blenheim Court, Solihull, W. Midlands B91 2AA;
Ty Rodfa, Ty Glas Avenue, Llanishen, Cardiff CF4 5TS
INLAND REVENUE SCOTLAND, 80 Lauriston Place,
Edinburgh EH3 9SL
INLAND REVENUE NORTHERN IRELAND, Dorchester House,
52–58 Great Victoria Street, Belfast BT2 7QE
INLAND REVENUE LARGE GROUPS OFFICE, New Court,
Carey Street, London WC2A 2JE

THE VALUATION OFFICE EXECUTIVE AGENCY
New Court, 48 Carey Street, London WC2A 2JE
Tel 0171-324 1183/1057
Meldrum House, 15 Drumsheugh Gardens, Edinburgh
EH3 7UN
Tel 0131-225 8511

Chief Executive (G2), A. J. Langford
Head of Profession (G3), R. J. Pawley
Chief Valuer, Scotland, A. MacLaren

INQUIRY INTO EXPORTS OF DEFENCE
EQUIPMENT AND DUAL-USE GOODS TO
IRAQ
Room 2.2.5, 1 Palace Street, London SW1E 5HE
Tel 0171-238 3799; *Media*: 0171-238 3809

Sir Richard Scott was asked by the President of the Board of
Trade, after the collapse of the Matrix Churchill case in
1992, to examine the facts in relation to the export from the
UK of defence equipment and dual-use goods to Iraq
between 1984 and 1990. The final report of the inquiry is
expected to be published around the end of 1995. From two
months after publication, queries should be directed to the
Secretary to the Inquiry, c/o the Treasury Solicitor's
Department (*see* page 356).
Inquiry headed by The Rt. Hon. Sir Richard Scott, The
Vice-Chancellor
Secretary to the Inquiry (G5), C. P. J. Muttukumaru

Counsel to the Inquiry, Miss P. Baxendale, QC
Media Relations Officer (*G6*), D. Price

INTERCEPTION COMMISSIONER
c/o The Home Office, 50 Queen Anne's Gate, London SW1H 9AT

The Commissioner is appointed by the Prime Minister. He keeps under review the issue by the Home Secretary and the Secretary of State for Scotland of warrants under the Interception of Communications Act 1985 and safeguards made in respect of intercepted material obtained through the use of such warrants. He is also required to give all such assistance as the Interception of Communications Tribunal may require to enable it to carry out its functions, and to submit an annual report to the Prime Minister with respect to the carrying out of his functions. In 1994 the Home Secretary issued 947 warrants, and the Secretary of State for Scotland 100 warrants.
Commissioner, The Rt. Hon. the Lord Nolan

INTERCEPTION OF COMMUNICATIONS TRIBUNAL
PO Box 44, London SE1 0TX
Tel 0171-273 4096

Under the Interception of Communications Act 1985, the Tribunal is required to investigate applications from any person who believes that communications sent to or by them have been intercepted in the course of their transmission by post or by means of a public telecommunications system. The Tribunal comprises senior members of the legal profession, who are appointed by The Queen.
President, The Hon. Mr Justice Macpherson of Cluny
Vice-President, Sir Cecil Clothier, KCB, QC
Members, Sir David Calcutt, QC; I. Guild, CBE; P. Scott, QC

INTERVENTION BOARD
Fountain House, Queen's Walk, Reading RG1 7QW
Tel 01734-583626

The Intervention Board was established as a government department in 1972 and became operational in 1973; it became an executive agency in 1990. The Board is responsible for the implementation of European Union regulations covering the market support arrangements of the Common Agricultural Policy. Members are appointed by and are responsible to the Minister of Agriculture, Fisheries and Food and the Secretaries of State for Scotland, Wales and Northern Ireland.
Chairman, A. Marshall
Chief Executive (*G3*), G. Stapleton, CB

HEADS OF DIVISIONS
External Trade Division (*G5*), G. N. Dixon
Internal Market Division (*G5*), H. MacKinnon
Corporate Services Division (*G5*), J. W. M. Peffers
Finance Division (*G5*), G. R. R. Jenkins
Legal Division (*G5*), J. F. McCleary
Chief Accountant (*G6*), R. Bryant
External Operations (*G6*), J. P. Bradbury
Procurement and Supply (*G6*), P. J. Offer

Information Systems (*G6*), T. T. Simpson
Internal Market Operations (*G6*), J. A. Sutton

LAND AUTHORITY FOR WALES
The Custom House, Customhouse Street, Cardiff CF1 5AP
Tel 01222-223444

The Authority, established under the Local Government Planning and Land Act 1980, is responsible for identifying and acquiring land suitable for development in Wales and making it available for development by others.
Chairman (*part-time*) (£32,495), Sir Geoffrey Inkin, OBE
Chief Executive, B. Ryan, FRICS

LAND REGISTRIES

HM LAND REGISTRY
Lincoln's Inn Fields, London WC2A 3PH
Tel 0171-917 8888

The registration of title to land was first introduced in England and Wales by the Land Registry Act 1862; HM Land Registry operates today under the Land Registration Acts 1925 to 1988. The object of registering title to land is to create and maintain a register of landowners whose title is guaranteed by the state and so to simplify the transfer, mortgage and other dealings with real property. Registration on sale is now compulsory throughout England and Wales. The register has been open to inspection by the public since December 1990.

HM Land Registry is an executive agency administered under the Lord Chancellor by the Chief Land Registrar. The work is decentralized to a number of regional offices. The Chief Land Registrar is also responsible for the Land Charges Department and the Agricultural Credits Department.

HEADQUARTERS OFFICE
Chief Land Registrar and Chief Executive, J. J. Manthorpe, CB
Solicitor to Land Registry (*G3*), C. J. West
Director of Corporate Services (*G4*), E. G. Beardsall
Senior Land Registrar (*G5*), Mrs J. G. Totty
Director of Operations (*G5*), G. N. French
Director of Information Technology (*G5*), P. J. Smith
Director of Management Services (*G6*), P. R. Laker
Land Registrar (*G5*), M. L. Wood
Deputy Establishment Officer (*G6*), J. Hodder
Controller of Operations Development (*G6*), A. W. Howarth

COMPUTER SERVICES DIVISION
Burrington Way, Plymouth PL5 3LP
Tel 01752-779831
Head of Services Division (*G6*), P. A. Maycock
Head of Development Division (*G6*), R. J. Smith

LAND CHARGES AND AGRICULTURAL CREDITS DEPARTMENT
Burrington Way, Plymouth PL5 3LP
Tel 01752-779831
Superintendent of Land Charges (*G7*), J. Hughes

DISTRICT LAND REGISTRIES
BIRKENHEAD – Old Market House, Hamilton Street, Birkenhead L41 5FL. Tel: 0151-473 1110. *District Land Registrar* (*G5*), M. G. Garwood
COVENTRY – Leigh Court, Torrington Avenue, Coventry CV4 9XZ. Tel: 01203-632442. *District Land Registrar* (*G5*), S. P. Kelway

CROYDON – Sunley House, Bedford Park, Croydon CR9 3LE. Tel: 0181-781 9100. *District Land Registrar (G5)*, D. M. J. Moss

DURHAM – Southfield House, Southfield Way, Durham DH1 5TR. Tel: 0191-301 3500. *District Land Registrar (G5)*, C. W. Martin

GLOUCESTER – Twyver House, Bruton Way, Gloucester GL1 1DQ. Tel: 01452-511111. *District Land Registrar (G5)*, W. W. Budden

HARROW – Lyon House, Lyon Road, Harrow, Middx HA1 2EU. Tel: 0181-427 8811. *District Land Registrar (G5)*, J. V. Timothy

KINGSTON UPON HULL – Earle House, Portland Street, Hull HU2 8JN. Tel: 01482-223244. *District Land Registrar (G5)*, S. R. Coveney

LEICESTER – Thames Tower, 99 Burleys Way, Leicester LE1 3UB. Tel: 0116-265 4000. *District Land Registrar (G6)*, Mrs J. A. Goodfellow

LYTHAM – Birkenhead House, Lytham St Annes, Lancs FY8 5AB. Tel: 01253-849849. *District Land Registrar (G5)*, J. G. Cooper

NOTTINGHAM – Chalfont Drive, Nottingham NG8 3RN. Tel: 0115-929 1166. *District Land Registrar (G5)*, P. J. Timothy

PETERBOROUGH – Touthill Close, City Road, Peterborough PE1 1XN. Tel: 01733-288288. *District Land Registrar (G5)*, L. M. Pope

PLYMOUTH – Plumer House, Tailyour Road, Crownhill, Plymouth PL6 5HY. Tel: 01752-701234. *District Land Registrar (G5)*, A. J. Pain

PORTSMOUTH – St Andrews Court, St Michael's Road, Portsmouth PO1 2JH. Tel: 01705-865022. *District Land Registrar (G6)*, S. R. Sehrawat

STEVENAGE – Brickdale House, Swingate, Stevenage, Herts SG1 1XG. Tel: 01438-313003. *District Land Registrar (G5)*, C. Tate

SWANSEA – Tybryn Glas, High Street, Swansea SA1 1PW. Tel: 01792-458877. *District Land Registrar (G5)*, G. A. Hughes.

TELFORD – Parkside Court, Hall Park Way, Telford TF3 4LR. Tel: 01952-290355. *District Land Registrar (G5)*, M. A. Roche

TUNBRIDGE WELLS – Curtis House, Hawkenbury, Tunbridge Wells, Kent TN2 5AQ. Tel: 01892-510015. *District Land Registrar (G5)*, G. R. Tooke

WEYMOUTH – 1 Cumberland Drive, Weymouth, Dorset DT4 9TT. Tel: 01305-776161. *District Land Registrar (G5)*, Mrs P. M. Reeson

YORK – James House, James Street, York YO1 3YZ. Tel: 01904-450000. *District Land Registrar (G6)*, Mrs R. F. Lovel

REGISTERS OF SCOTLAND (EXECUTIVE AGENCY)

Meadowbank House, 153 London Road, Edinburgh EH8 7AU
Tel 0131-659 6111

The Registers of Scotland is an executive agency of the Scottish Office. The Registers consist of: General Register of Sasines and Land Register of Scotland; Register of Deeds in the Books of Council and Session; Register of Protests; Register of Judgments; Register of Service of Heirs; Register of the Great Seal; Register of the Quarter Seal; Register of the Prince's Seal; Register of Crown Grants; Register of Sheriffs' Commissions; Register of the Cachet Seal; Register of Inhibitions and Adjudications; Register of Entails; Register of Hornings.

The General Register of Sasines and the Land Register of Scotland form the chief security in Scotland of the rights of land and other heritable (or real) property.
Chief Executive and Keeper of the Registers of Scotland (G4), A. W. Ramage
Deputy Chief Executive (G5), J. K. Mason
Deputy Keeper (G5), A. G. Rennie
Senior Directors (G6), B. J. Corr; A. M. Falconer
Directors (G7), R. Glen (*Human resources*); Miss M. M. D. Archer (*Land Register*); D. McCallum (*Land Register*); L. J. Mitchell (*Sasines*); A. M. Gardiner (*Land Register*); I. M. Nicol (*Finance*); Ms A. Rooney (*Communications*); T. Wilson (*Commercial*)

LAW COMMISSION

Conquest House, 37–38 John Street, Theobalds Road, London WC1N 2BQ
Tel 0171-453 1220

The Law Commission was set up in 1965, under the Law Commissions Act 1965, to make proposals to the Government for the examination of the law in England and Wales and for its revision where it is unsuited for modern requirements, obscure, or otherwise unsatisfactory. It recommends to the Lord Chancellor programmes for the examination of different branches of the law and suggests whether the examination should be carried out by the Commission itself or by some other body. The Commission is also responsible for the preparation of Consolidation and Statute Law (Repeals) Bills.
Chairman, The Hon. Mr Justice Brooke
Commissioners, C. Harpum; A. S. Burrows; Miss D. Faber; S. Silber, QC
Secretary, M. W. Sayers

SCOTTISH LAW COMMISSION

140 Causewayside, Edinburgh EH9 1PR
Tel 0131-668 2131

The Commission keeps the law in Scotland under review and makes proposals for its development and reform.
Chairman, The Hon. Lord Davidson
Commissioners (full-time), Dr E. M. Clive; N. R. Whitty; (*part-time*) Prof. K. G. C. Reid; W. Nimmo Smith, QC
Secretary, K. F. Barclay

LAW OFFICERS' DEPARTMENTS

Legal Secretariat to the Law Officers, Attorney-General's Chambers, 9 Buckingham Gate, London SW1E 6JP
Tel 0171-828 7155
Attorney-General's Chambers, Royal Courts of Justice, Belfast BT1 3JY
Tel 01232-235111

The Law Officers of the Crown for England and Wales are the Attorney-General and the Solicitor-General. The Attorney-General, assisted by the Solicitor-General, is the chief legal adviser to the Government and is also ultimately responsible for all Crown litigation. He has overall responsibility for the work of the Law Officers' Departments (the Treasury Solicitor's Department, the Crown Prosecution Service, the Serious Fraud Office and the Legal Secretariat to the Law Officers). He has a specific statutory duty to superintend the discharge of their duties by the Director of Public Prosecutions (who is head of the Crown Prosecution Service) and the Director of the Serious Fraud Office. The Director of Public Prosecutions for Northern Ireland is responsible to the Attorney-General for the performance of his functions. The Attorney-General has additional responsibilities in relation to aspects of the civil and criminal law.

Attorney-General (*£45,516), The Rt. Hon. Sir Nicholas Lyell, QC, MP
  Private Secretary, S. A. Moore
Solicitor-General (*£37,321), Sir Derek Spencer, QC, MP
  Private Secretary, S. A. Moore
  Parliamentary Private Secretary, G. Streeter, MP
  Legal Secretary (G2), Miss J. L. Wheldon, CB
  Deputy Legal Secretary (G4), S. J. Wooler
* Excluding reduced parliamentary salary of £24,985

LEGAL AID BOARD
85 Gray's Inn Road, London WC1X 8AA
Tel 0171-813 1000

The Legal Aid Board has the general function of ensuring that advice, assistance and representation are available in accordance with the Legal Aid Act 1988. In 1989 it took over from the Law Society responsibility for administering legal aid. The Board is a non-departmental government body whose members are appointed by the Lord Chancellor.

Chairman, Sir Tim Chessells
Members, S. Orchard (*Chief Executive*); F. Collins; J. Crosby, Ms J. Dunkley; C. George; P. Jones; Ms K. Markus; Ms D. Payne; Ms P. Pearce; G. Pulman, QC; D. Sinker; A. Thomas

---

SCOTTISH LEGAL AID BOARD
44 Drumsheugh Gardens, Edinburgh EH3 7SW
Tel 0131-226 7061

The Scottish Legal Aid Board was set up under the Legal Aid (Scotland) Act 1986. It is responsible for ensuring that advice, assistance and representation are available in accordance with the Act. The Board is a non-departmental government body whose members are appointed by the Secretary of State for Scotland.

Chairman, Ms C. A. M. Davis
Members, G. Barrie; Mrs K. Blair; Mrs P. A. M. Bolton; Mrs P. M. M. Bowman; Mrs S. Campbell; Mrs J. Couper; A. Gilchrist; Prof. P. H. Grinyer; D. A. Leitch; R. J. Livingstone; C. N. McEachran, QC; Sheriff R. G. McEwan, QC; Mrs G. M. Peebles; A. F. Wylie, QC
Chief Executive, R. Scott

OFFICE OF THE LEGAL SERVICES OMBUDSMAN
22 Oxford Court, Oxford Street, Manchester M2 3WQ
Tel 0161-236 9532

The Legal Services Ombudsman is appointed by the Lord Chancellor under the Courts and Legal Services Act 1990 to oversee the handling of complaints against solicitors, barristers and licensed conveyancers by their professional bodies. A complainant must first complain to the relevant professional body before raising the matter with the Ombudsman. The Ombudsman is independent of the legal profession and his services are free of charge.

Legal Services Ombudsman, M. Barnes
  Secretary, S. Murray

OFFICE OF THE SCOTTISH LEGAL SERVICES OMBUDSMAN
2 Greenside Lane, Edinburgh EH1 3AH
Tel 0131-556 5574

Scottish Legal Services Ombudsman, G. S. Watson

LIBRARIES

LIBRARY AND INFORMATION COMMISSION
2 Sheraton Street, London W1V 4BH
Tel 0171-411 0059

The Commission is an independent body set up by the Secretary of State for National Heritage in 1995 to advise the Government and others on library and information matters, notably in the areas of research strategy and international links. It also aims to promote co-operation and co-ordination between different types of information services.

Chairman, M. Evans
Commissioners, D. Adams; E. Arram; Sir Charles Chadwyck-Healey; Dr G. Chambers; Prof. Judith Elkin; Dr B. Lang; D. Law; Dr R. McKee; Rabbi Julia Neuberger; Sir Peter Swinnerton-Dyer; Dr Sandra Ward; M. Wood
Executive Secretary, S. Brewer

THE BRITISH LIBRARY
96 Euston Road, London NW1 2DB
Tel 0171-412 7000

The British Library was established in 1973. It is the UK's national library and occupies the central position in the library and information network. The Library aims to serve scholarship, research, industry, commerce and all other major users of information. Its services are based on collections which include over 18 million volumes, 1 million discs, and 55,000 hours of tape recordings, at 18 buildings in London and one complex in West Yorkshire. The British Library's new purpose-built accommodation at St Pancras, London NW1 is scheduled to open to the public in 1997.

Access to the Humanities and Social Sciences reading rooms is limited to holders of a British Library Reader's Pass; information about eligibility is available from the Reader Admissions Office. The reading rooms of the Science Reference and Information Service are open to the general public without charge or formality.

Opening hours of services vary; most services are closed for one week each year. Specific information should be checked by telephone.

BRITISH LIBRARY BOARD
96 Euston Road, London NW1 2DB
Tel 0171-412 7262

Chairman, Sir Anthony Kenny, D.Phil., D.Litt., FBA
Chief Executive and Deputy Chairman (G2), Dr B. Lang
Deputy Chief Executive (G4), J. M. Smethurst
Director-General (G4), D. Russon
Part-time Members, T. J. Rix; D. Peake; The Hon. E. Adeane, CVO; Sir Matthew Farrer, GCVO; Mrs P. M. Lively, OBE; Prof. M. Anderson, FBA, FRSE

BRITISH LIBRARY, BOSTON SPA
Boston Spa, Wetherby, W. Yorks LS23 7BQ
Tel 01937-546000

DOCUMENT SUPPLY CENTRE, *Director* (G5), D. Bradbury

NATIONAL BIBLIOGRAPHIC SERVICE. Tel: 01937-546585.
Director (G6), S. J. Ede
London Unit, 2 Sheraton Street, London WIV 4BH. Tel:
0171-412 7077
ACQUISITIONS PROCESSING AND CATALOGUING, *Director*
(G5), Mrs J. E. Butcher
COMPUTING AND TELECOMMUNICATIONS. Tel: 01937-
546879. *Director (G5)*, J. R. Mahoney

BRITISH LIBRARY, LONDON
Great Russell Street, London WC1B 3DG
Tel 0171-636 1544

St Pancras Project Director (G4), D. Lyman
Director of Project Services St Pancras Planning (G6), Dr
R. Coman

ADMINISTRATION, 2 Sheraton Street, London WIV 4BH.
Tel: 0171-412 7132. *Director (G5) (acting)*, H.
McCorquodale
PRESS AND PUBLIC RELATIONS, 96 Euston Road, London
NW1 2DB. Tel: 0171-412 7111. *Head (G7)*, M. Jackson
PUBLIC SERVICES. Tel: 0171-412 7626. *Director (G5)*, Ms
J. Carr
Exhibitions and Education Service. Tel: 0171-412 7595
Reader Admissions. Tel: 0171-412 7677

HUMANITIES AND SOCIAL SCIENCES. Tel: 0171-412 7676.
Director (G5), A. Phillips
West European Collections, Slavonic and East European
Collections, English Language Collections. Tel: 0171-412
7676
Information Branch, Official Publications and Social Science
Service. Tel: 0171-412 7536
Information Sciences Service (BLISS), Ridgmount Street,
London WC1E 7AE. Tel: 0171-412 7688
Newspaper Library, Colindale Avenue, London NW9 5HE.
Tel: 0171-412 7353
National Sound Archive, 29 Exhibition Road, London SW7
2AS. Tel: 0171-412 7440

COLLECTIONS AND PRESERVATION. Tel: 0171-412 7676.
Director (G5), Dr M. Foot
Preservation Service (National Preservation Office). Tel: 0171-
412 7612

SPECIAL COLLECTIONS. Tel: 0171-412 7513. *Director (G5)*,
Dr A. Prochaska
Oriental and India Office Collections, 197 Blackfriars Road,
London SE1 8NG. Tel: 0171-412 7873
Western Manuscripts. Tel: 0171-412 7513
Map Library. Tel: 0171-412 7700
Music Library. Tel: 0171-412 7528
Philatelic Collections. Tel: 0171-412 7729

SCIENCE REFERENCE AND INFORMATION SERVICE,
25 Southampton Buildings, London WC2A 1AW. Tel:
0171-412 7494; 9 Kean Street, London WC2B 4AT. Tel:
0171-412 7288. *Director (G5)*, A. Gomersall

RESEARCH AND DEVELOPMENT DEPARTMENT, 2 Sheraton
Street, London WIV 4BH. Tel: 0171-412 7055. *Director*
(G6), N. Macartney

NATIONAL LIBRARY OF SCOTLAND
33 Salisbury Place, Edinburgh EH9 1SL
Tel 0131-226 4531

The Library, which was founded as the Advocates' Library
in 1682, became the National Library of Scotland in 1925. It
contains about six million books and pamphlets, 20,000
current periodicals, 230 newspaper titles and 100,000
manuscripts. It has an unrivalled Scottish collection.

The Reading Room is for reference and research which
cannot conveniently be pursued elsewhere. Admission is
by ticket issued to an approved applicant. Opening hours:
Reading Room, weekdays, 9.30–8.30 (Wednesday,
10–8.30); Saturday 9.30–1. Map Library, weekdays, 9.30–5
(Wednesday, 10–5); Saturday 9.30–1. Exhibition, week-
days, 10–5; Saturday 10–5; Sunday 2–5. Scottish Science
Library, weekdays, 9.30–5 (Wednesday, 10–8.30).
Chairman of the Trustees, The Earl of Crawford and
Balcarres, PC
Librarian and Secretary to the Trustees (G4), I. D. McGowan
Secretary of the Library (G6), M. C. Graham
Keepers of Printed Books (G6), A. M. Marchbank, PH.D.; Ms
A. Matheson, PH.D.
Keeper of Manuscripts (G6), I. C. Cunningham
Director of Computer Services and Research (G6), B. Gallivan
Director of Scottish Science Library (G6), Ms A. J. Bunch

NATIONAL LIBRARY OF WALES/
LLYFRGELL GENEDLAETHOL CYMRU
Aberystwyth, Dyfed SY23 3BU
Tel 01970-623816

The National Library of Wales was founded by Royal
Charter in 1907, and is maintained by annual grant from the
Treasury. It contains about four million printed books,
40,000 manuscripts, four million deeds and documents,
numerous maps, prints and drawings, and a sound and
moving image collection. It specializes in manuscripts and
books relating to Wales and the Celtic peoples. It is the
repository for pre-1858 Welsh probate records, manorial
records and tithe documents, and certain legal records.
Readers' room open weekdays, 9.30–6 (Saturday 9.30–5);
closed first week of October. Admission by Reader's
Ticket.
President, Prof. Emeritus J. Gwynn Williams
Librarian (G4), J. L. Madden
Heads of Departments (G6), M. W. Mainwaring
(*Administration and Technical Services*); G. Jenkins
(*Manuscripts and Records*); W. R. L. Griffiths (*Printed*
Books); D. H. Owen (*Pictures and Maps*)

LIGHTHOUSE AUTHORITIES

CORPORATION OF TRINITY HOUSE
Trinity House, Tower Hill, London EC3N 4DH
Tel 0171-480 6601

Trinity House, the first general lighthouse and pilotage
authority in the kingdom, was granted its first charter by
Henry VIII in 1514. The Corporation is the general
lighthouse authority for England, Wales and the Channel
Islands and maintains 67 lighthouses (of which 11 are
manned), 14 major floating aids to navigation and more
than 400 buoys. It also has statutory jurisdiction over
aids to navigation maintained by local harbour authorities and is responsible for dealing with wrecks
dangerous to navigation, except those occurring within
port limits or wrecks of HM ships.
The Trinity House Lighthouse Service is maintained
out of the General Lighthouse Fund which is provided
from light dues levied on ships calling at ports of the UK
and the Republic of Ireland. The Corporation is also a
deep-sea pilotage authority and a charitable organization.
The affairs of the Corporation are controlled by a board
of Elder Brethren, who are master mariners with long
experience of command in the Royal Navy or merchant
navy, together with figures from the world of commerce,
and the Secretary. The board is assisted by administrative

and technical staff. A separate board, which comprises Elder Brethren, senior staff and outside representatives, currently controls the Lighthouse Service. The Elder Brethren also act as nautical assessors in marine cases in the Admiralty Division of the High Court of Justice.

ELDER BRETHREN
Master, HRH The Duke of Edinburgh, KG, KT
Deputy Master, Rear-Adm. P. B. Rowe, CBE, LVO
Elder Brethren, Capt. D. J. Orr; Capt. N. M. Turner, RD; HRH The Prince of Wales, KG, KT; HRH The Duke of York, CVO, ADC; Capt. R. N. Mayo, CBE; Capt. Sir David Tibbits, DSC, RN; Capt. D. A. G. Dickens; Capt. J. E. Bury; Capt. J. A. N. Bezant, DSC, RD, RNR (retd.); Capt. Sir Miles Wingate, KCVO; The Rt. Hon. Sir Edward Heath, KG, MBE, MP; Capt. I. R. C. Saunders; Capt. P. F. Mason, CBE; Capt. T. Woodfield, OBE; Sir Eric Drake, CBE; The Lord Simon of Glaisdale, PC; Admiral of the Fleet the Lord Lewin, KG, GCB, LVO, DSC; Capt. D. T. Smith, RN; Cdr. Sir Robin Gillett, GBE, RD, RNR; Sir John Cuckney; The Lord Carrington, KG, GCMG, CH, MC, PC; Sir Brian Shaw; The Lord Mackay of Clashfern, PC; Sir Adrian Swire; Capt. P. H. King; The Lord Sterling of Plaistow, CBE, RNR; Cdr. M. J. Rivett-Carnac, RN; Capt. C. M. C. Stewart

OFFICERS
Secretary, R. Dobb
Director of Finance, K. W. Clark
Director of Engineering, M. G. B. Wannell
Director of Administration, D. I. Brewer
General Manager Operations, Capt. J. M. Barnes
Personnel and General Services Manager, Mrs B. C. Heesom
Operations Administration Manager, S. J. W. Dunning
Legal and Insurance Manager, J. D. Price
Navigation Manager, N. J. Cutmore
Deputy Director of Engineering, P. N. Hyde
Senior Inspector of Shipping, J. R. Dunnett
Information Officer, H. L. Cooper

COMMISSIONERS OF NORTHERN LIGHTHOUSES
84 George Street, Edinburgh EH2 3DA
Tel 0131-226 7051

The Commissioners of Northern Lighthouses are the general lighthouse authority for Scotland and the Isle of Man. The present board owes its origin to an Act of Parliament passed in 1786. At present the Commissioners operate under the Merchant Shipping Act 1894 and are 19 in number.

The Commissioners control 11 major manned lighthouses, 73 major automatic lighthouses, 112 minor lights and many lighted and unlighted buoys. They have a fleet of two motor vessels.

COMMISSIONERS
The Lord Advocate; the Solicitor-General for Scotland; the Lord Provosts of Edinburgh, Glasgow and Aberdeen; the Provost of Inverness; the Chairman of Argyll and Bute District Council; the Sheriffs-Principal of North Strathclyde, Tayside, Central and Fife, Grampian, Highlands and Islands, South Strathclyde, Dumfries and Galloway, Lothians and Borders, and Glasgow and Strathkelvin; T. Macgill; A. J. Struthers; W. F. Hay, CBE; J. Hann, CBE; Capt. D. M. Cowell; Adm. Sir Michael Livesay, KCB

OFFICERS
Chief Executive, Capt. J. B. Taylor, RN
Secretary, I. A. Dickson
Director of Engineering, W. Paterson

Director of Operations and Navigational Requirements, P. J. Christmas

LOCAL COMMISSIONERS

COMMISSION FOR LOCAL ADMINISTRATION IN ENGLAND
21 Queen Anne's Gate, London SW1H 9BU
Tel 0171-915 3210

Local Commissioners (local government ombudsmen) are responsible for investigating complaints from members of the public against local authorities (but not town and parish councils); police authorities; the Commission for New Towns and new town development corporations (housing functions); urban development corporations (town and country planning functions) and certain other authorities. The Commissioners are appointed by the Crown on the recommendation of the Secretary of State for the Environment.

Certain types of action are excluded from investigation, including personnel matters and commercial transactions unless they relate to the purchase or sale of land. Complaints can be sent direct to the Local Government Ombudsman or through a councillor, although the Local Government Ombudsman will not consider a complaint unless the council has had an opportunity to investigate and reply to a complainant.

A free booklet *Complaint about the Council? How to complain to the Local Government Ombudsman* is available from the Commission's office.
Chairman of the Commission and Local Commissioner (£95,051), E. B. C. Osmotherly, CB
Vice-Chairman and Local Commissioner (£77,875), Mrs P. A. Thomas
Local Commissioner (£76,875), J. R. White
Member (ex officio), The Parliamentary Commissioner for Administration
Secretary (£48,087), G. D. Adams

COMMISSION FOR LOCAL ADMINISTRATION IN WALES
Derwen House, Court Road, Bridgend CF31 1BN
Tel 01656-661325

The Local Commissioner for Wales has similar powers to the Local Commissioners in England. The Commissioner is appointed by the Crown on the recommendation of the Secretary of State for Wales. A free leaflet *Your Local Ombudsman in Wales* is available from the Commission's office.
Local Commissioner, E. R. Moseley
Secretary, D. Bowen
Member (ex officio), The Parliamentary Commissioner for Administration

COMMISSIONER FOR LOCAL ADMINISTRATION IN SCOTLAND
23 Walker Street, Edinburgh EH3 7HX
Tel 0131-225 5300

The Local Commissioner for Scotland has similar powers to the Local Commissioners in England, and is appointed by the Crown on the recommendation of the Secretary of State for Scotland.
Local Commissioner, F. C. Marks, OBE
Deputy and Secretary, Ms J. H. Renton

LONDON REGIONAL TRANSPORT
55 Broadway, London SW1H 0BD
Tel 0171-222 5600

Subject to the financial objectives and principles approved by the Secretary of State for Transport, London Regional Transport has a general duty to provide or secure the provision of public transport services for Greater London.
Chairman (£150,000), P. Ford
Member (£82,500), A. J. Sheppeck
Member, and Managing Director of London Underground Ltd (£105,500), D. Tunnicliffe

LORD ADVOCATE'S DEPARTMENT
2 Carlton Gardens, London SW1Y 5AA
Tel 0171-210 1010

The Law Officers for Scotland are the Lord Advocate and the Solicitor-General for Scotland. The Lord Advocate's Department is responsible for drafting Scottish legislation, for providing legal advice to other departments on Scottish questions and for assistance to the Law Officers for Scotland in certain of their legal duties.
Lord Advocate (£55,409), The Lord Rodger of Earlsferry, PC, QC
  Private Secretary, A. G. Maxwell
Solicitor-General for Scotland (£47,697), Donald Mackay
  Private Secretary, A. G. Maxwell
Legal Secretary and First Scottish Parliamentary Counsel (G2), J. C. McCluskie, QC
Assistant Legal Secretaries and Scottish Parliamentary Counsel (G3), G. M. Clark; G. Kowalski; P. J. Layden, TD; C. A. M. Wilson
Assistant Legal Secretary and Depute Scottish Parliamentary Counsel (G5), J. D. Harkness

LORD CHANCELLOR'S DEPARTMENT
Trevelyan House, 30 Great Peter Street, London SW1P 2BY
Tel 0171-210 8500

The Lord Chancellor is the principal legal adviser of the Crown, Speaker of the House of Lords, President of the House of Lords as an Appellate Court, of the Court of Appeal, and of the Chancery Division of the High Court of Justice, and acting President of the Judicial Committee of the Privy Council. The Lord Chancellor appoints Justices of the Peace (except in Lancashire) and advises the Crown on the appointment of most members of the higher judiciary. He is responsible for promoting general reforms in the civil law, for the procedure of the civil courts and for legal aid schemes. He is a member of the Cabinet. He also has ministerial responsibility for magistrates' courts, which are administered locally. Administration of the Supreme Court and county courts in England and Wales was taken over by the Court Service, an executive agency of the department, in April 1995.
The Lord Chancellor is also responsible for ensuring that letters patent and other formal documents are passed in the proper form under the Great Seal of the Realm, of which he is the custodian. The work in connection with this is carried out under his direction in the Office of the Clerk of the Crown in Chancery.
Lord Chancellor (£126,138), The Lord Mackay of Clashfern, PC
  Private Secretary, M. Ormerod

Parliamentary Secretary, John Taylor, MP
  Private Secretary, S. Jones
Permanent Secretary (G1), Sir Thomas Legg, KCB, QC
  Private Secretary, D. Willink

CROWN OFFICE
House of Lords, London SW1A 0PW
Clerk of the Crown in Chancery (G1), Sir Thomas Legg, KCB, QC
Deputy Clerk of the Crown in Chancery (G2), M. Huebner, CB
Clerk of the Chamber, C. I. P. Denyer

JUDICIAL APPOINTMENTS GROUP
Southside, 105 Victoria Street, London SW1E 6QT
Tel 0171-210 1630

Head of Group (G3), R. E. K. Holmes
Grade 5, D. E. Staff (*policy and conditions of service*); Mrs M. Pigott (*circuit bench*); Miss J. Killick (*circuit bench*); R. Venne (*district bench and tribunals*); R. V. Grobler (*magistrates' appointments*)

Judicial Studies Board
14 Little St James's Street, London SW1A 1DP
Tel 0171-925 0185
Grade 5, P. G. Taylor

POLICY GROUP
Trevelyan House, 30 Great Peter Street, London SW1P 2BY
Tel 0171-210 8872

Head of Group (G2), I. M. Burns, CB
Heads of Divisions (G5), S. Smith (*legal aid*); Ms J. Rowe (*criminal policy*); D. Gladwell (*civil policy*); R. Sams (*magistrates' courts*); W. Arnold (*family policy*)
Head of Secretariat (G7), Ms A. Jones
Head of Agency Monitoring Unit (G7), Miss M. Burton

LEGAL GROUP
Southside, 105 Victoria Street, London SW1E 6QT
Tel 0171-210 2005

Legal Adviser (G3), R. H. H. White
Grade 4, M. H. Collon (*legal advice and litigation*)
Grade 5, J. Watherston (*international*); M. Kron (*rules of court and regulations*)
Grade 6, K. Garrett (*statutory publications office*)

PERSONNEL, FINANCE AND SERVICES GROUP
Trevelyan House, 30 Great Peter Street, London SW1P 2BY
Tel 0171-210 8519

Head of Group (G3), Mrs N. A. Oppenheimer
Grade 5, Ms H. Tuffs (*personnel management*); A. Cogbill (*finance*); P. G. Harris (*planning and communications*)
Grade 6, K. Cregeen (*accommodation and magistrates' courts building*); A. Rummins (*internal audit*)

ECCLESIASTICAL PATRONAGE
10 Downing Street, London SW1A 2AA
Tel 0171-930 4433

Secretary for Ecclesiastical Patronage, J. H. Holroyd, CB
Assistant Secretary for Ecclesiastical Patronage, N. C. Wheeler

MAGISTRATES' COURTS' SERVICE INSPECTORATE
Southside, 105 Victoria Street, London SW1E 6QJ
Tel 0171-210 1655

Chief Inspector (G5), Mrs R. L. Melling
Senior Inspectors (G6), Ms J. Eeles; D. Gear; C. Monson; Ms S. Steel

LORD CHANCELLOR'S ADVISORY COMMITTEE ON STATUTE LAW
6 Spring Gardens, London SW1A 2BP
Tel 0171-389 3244

The Advisory Committee advises the Lord Chancellor on all matters relating to the revision, modernization and publication of the statute book.

Chairman, The Lord Chancellor
Deputy Chairman, Sir Thomas Legg, KCB, QC
Members, Sir Michael Wheeler-Booth, KCB; Sir Clifford
Boulton, KCB; The Hon. Mr Justice Brooke; The Hon.
Lord Davidson; C. Jenkins, CB, QC; J. C. McCluskie, QC;
G. Hosker, CB, QC; R. Brodie, CB; R. H. H White;
J. Gibson; Dr P. Freeman; (ex officio) First Legislative
Counsel, Northern Ireland
Secretary, C. Carey

EXECUTIVE AGENCIES

THE COURT SERVICE
Southside, 105 Victoria Street, London SW1E 6QT
Tel 0171-210 1775

The Court Service provides administrative support to the
Supreme Court of England and Wales, county courts and a
number of tribunals.
Chief Executive (G2), M. Huebner
Grade 5, P. Handcock (*operational support*)

FINANCE AND ADMINISTRATION GROUP
Director (G3), C. W. V. Everett
Grade 5, K. Pogson (*resources*); Miss B. Kenny (*personnel and
training*); P. Jacob (*major reviews*); A. Shaw
(*accommodation, procurement, libraries and records*); P. White
(*information technology (ISD)*)

ROYAL COURTS OF JUSTICE
Strand, London WC2A 2LL
Tel 0171-936 6000
Administrator, G. E. Calvett

For Supreme Court departments and offices and circuit
administrators, *see* Law Courts and Offices section

HM LAND REGISTRY
— *see* pages 319–20

PUBLIC RECORD OFFICE
— *see* pages 339–40

PUBLIC TRUST OFFICE
— *see* pages 338–9

LORD GREAT CHAMBERLAIN'S OFFICE
House of Lords, London SW1A 0PW
Tel 0171-219 3100

The Lord Great Chamberlain is a Great Officer of State,
the office being hereditary since the grant of Henry I to the
family of De Vere, Earls of Oxford. The Lord Great
Chamberlain is responsible for the Royal Apartments of
the Palace of Westminster, i.e. The Queen's Robing Room,
the Royal Gallery and, in conjunction with the Lord
Chancellor and Madam Speaker, Westminster · Hall. The
Lord Great Chamberlain has particular responsibility for
the internal administrative arrangements within the House
of Lords for State Openings of Parliament.
Lord Great Chamberlain, The Marquess of Cholmondeley
Secretary to the Lord Great Chamberlain, Gen. Sir Edward
Jones, KCB, CBE
Clerks to the Lord Great Chamberlain, Mrs S. E. Douglas;
Miss R. M. Wilkinson

LORD PRIVY SEAL'S OFFICE
Privy Council Office, 68 Whitehall, London SW1A 2AT
Tel 0171-270 3000

As leader of the House of Lords, the Lord Privy Seal is
responsible to the Prime Minister for the organization of
government business in the House. He also has a respon-
sibility to the House itself to advise it on procedural
matters and other difficulties which arise. The Lord Privy
Seal has no departmental portfolio, but is a member of a
number of domestic and economic Cabinet committees.
Lord Privy Seal, and Leader of the House of Lords, Viscount
Cranborne, PC
Principal Private Secretary, Mrs J. M. Bailey
Private Secretary (House of Lords), Mrs M. Ollard
Special Adviser, Ms S. McEwen

LOTTERY, OFFICE OF THE NATIONAL
— *see* page 331

OFFICE OF MANPOWER ECONOMICS
Oxford House, 76 Oxford Street, London W1N 9FD
Tel 0171-636 1742

The Office of Manpower Economics was set up in 1971. It
is an independent non-statutory organization which is
responsible for servicing independent review bodies which
advise on the pay of various public service groups (*see*
Review Bodies, page 341), the Pharmacists Review Panel
and the Police Negotiating Board. The Office is also
responsible for servicing *ad hoc* bodies of inquiry and for
undertaking research into pay and associated matters as
requested by the Government.
Director, M. J. Horsman
Deputy Director (G4), M. Emmott
Assistant Directors (G5), P. J. H. Edwards; G. S. Charles; Mrs
S. Webber

MENTAL HEALTH ACT COMMISSION
Maid Marian House, 56 Hounds Gate, Nottingham
NG1 6BG
Tel 0115-950 4040

The Mental Health Act Commission was established in
1983. Its functions are to keep under review the operation
of the Mental Health Act 1983; to visit and interview
patients detained under the Act; to investigate complaints
falling within the Commission's remit; to operate the
consent to treatment safeguards in the Mental Health Act;
to publish a biennial report on its activities; to monitor the
implementation of the Code of Practice; and to advise
ministers. Commissioners are appointed by the Secretary
of State for Health in the following categories: lay; legal;
medical; nursing; psychology; social worker; and specialist.
Chairman, The Viscountess Runciman of Doxford, OBE
Vice-Chairman, N. Pleming
Chief Executive (G6), W. Bingley

MILLENNIUM COMMISSION
2 Little Smith Street, London SW1P 3DH
Tel 0171-416 8070

The Millennium Commission was established in February 1994. It is an independent body which will distribute 20 per cent of the money allocated to 'good causes' from National Lottery proceeds to projects to mark the millennium. The Commission had received about £167 million for distribution as at July 1995. The first grants were made in September 1995.
Chairman, The Rt. Hon. Virginia Bottomley, MP
Members, Prof. Heather Couper, FRAS; Earl of Dalkeith; The Lord Glentoran, CBE; Sir John Hall; The Rt. Hon. M. Heseltine, MP; S. Jenkins; M. Montague, CBE; Miss P. Scotland, QC
Chief Executive, Miss J. A. Page, CBE

MONOPOLIES AND MERGERS COMMISSION
New Court, 48 Carey Street, London WC2A 2JT
Tel 0171-324 1407

The Commission was established in 1949 as the Monopolies and Restrictive Practices Commission and became the Monopolies and Mergers Commission under the Fair Trading Act 1973. Its role is to investigate and report on matters which are referred to it by the Secretary of State for Trade and Industry or the Director-General of Fair Trading or, in the case of privatized industries, by the appropriate regulator. Its decisions are determined by the criteria set out in the legislation covering the different types of reference. The main types of reference which can be made are: monopolies; mergers; newspaper mergers; general, involving general practices in an industry; restrictive labour practices; competition, involving anti-competitive practices of individual firms; public sector audits; privatized industries; and Channel 3 (ITV) networking arrangements between holders of regional Channel 3 licences. References may be made under the Fair Trading Act 1973, the Competition Act 1980, the Broadcasting Act or other relevant statutes.

The Commission consists of about 35 members, including a full-time chairman and three part-time deputy chairmen, all appointed by the Secretary of State for Trade and Industry. Each inquiry is conducted on behalf of the Commission by a group of four to six members who are appointed by the chairman.
Chairman (£97,440), G. D. W. Odgers
Deputy Chairmen (£47,855), D. Morris, PH.D.; P. H. Dean, CBE; D. G. Goyder
Members (£13,765/*£9,175 each), A. G. Armstrong; I. Barter; Mrs C. Blight; P. Brenan; J. S. Bridgeman; R. H. F. Croft, CB; R. Davies; Prof. S. Eilon; J. Evans; *N. H. Finney, OBE; Sir Archibald Forster; *Sir Ronald Halstead, CBE; D. B. Hammond; *Ms P. A. Hodgson; D. J. Jenkins, MBE; *A. L. Kingshott; R. Lyons; *N. F. Matthews; Prof. J. S. Metcalfe, CBE; Prof. P. Minford; J. D. Montgomery; *Dr D. J. Morris; *Mrs K. Mortimer; *Prof. J. Pickering; *L. Priestley; M. R. Prosser; Dr A. Robinson; *J. K. Roe; *Dr L. M. Rouse; Mrs C. Tritton, QC; Prof. G. Whittington
Secretary, A. J. Nieduszynski
* Reserve members

MUSEUMS

MUSEUMS AND GALLERIES COMMISSION
16 Queen Anne's Gate, London SW1H 9AA
Tel 0171-233 4200

Established in 1931 as the Standing Commission on Museums and Galleries, the Commission was renamed and took up new functions in 1981. Its sponsor department is the Department of National Heritage. The Commission advises the Government, including the Department of Education for Northern Ireland, the Scottish Education Department and the Welsh Office, on museum affairs. There are 15 Commissioners, appointed by the Prime Minister.

The Commission's executive functions include providing the services of the Museums Security Adviser; allocating grants to the seven Area Museum Councils in England; funding and monitoring the work of the Museum Documentation Association; and administering grant schemes for non-national museums. The Commission administers the arrangements for government indemnities and the acceptance of works of art in lieu of inheritance tax, and its Conservation Unit advises on conservation and environmental standards. A registration scheme for museums in the UK is operated by the Commission.
Chairman, G. Greene, CBE
Members, The Marchioness of Anglesey, DBE; J. Baer; Prof. P. Bateson, FRS; The Baroness Brigstocke; Prof. R. Buchanan; The Viscountess Cobham; R. Foster; Adm. Sir John Kerr, GCB; J. Last, CBE; Prof. D. Michie; The Lord Rees, PC, QC; R. H. Smith; A. Warhurst, CBE; Dame Margaret Weston, DBE
Director and Secretary, T. Mason

THE BRITISH MUSEUM
Great Russell Street, London WC1B 3DG
Tel 0171-636 1555

The British Museum houses the national collection of antiquities, coins and paper money, medals, and prints and drawings. The ethnographical collections are displayed at the Museum of Mankind. The British Museum may be said to date from 1753, when Parliament approved the holding of a public lottery to raise funds for the purchase of the collections of Sir Hans Sloane and the Harleian manuscripts, and for their proper housing and maintenance. The building (Montagu House) was opened in 1759. The present buildings were erected between 1823 and the present day, and the original collection has increased to its present dimensions by gifts and purchases. Total government grant-in-aid for 1995–6 is £33.405 million.

BOARD OF TRUSTEES
Appointed by the Sovereign, HRH The Duke of Gloucester, GCVO
Appointed by the Prime Minister, The Lord Windlesham, CVO, PC (*Chairman*); N. Barber; Prof. Gillian Beer, FBA; J. Browne, FEng.; Sir Matthew Farrer, KCVO; Sir Peter Harrop, KCB; M. Hopkins, CBE, RA, RIBA; Sir Joseph Hotung; S. Keswick; Hon. Mrs Marten, OBE; Sir John Morgan, KCMG; The Rt. Hon. Sir Timothy Raison; Prof. G. H. Treitel, DCL, FBA, QC
Nominated by the Learned Societies, Prof. Jean Thomas, CBE (*Royal Society*); A. Jones, RA (*Royal Academy*); Sir Claus Moser, KCB, CBE, FBA (*British Academy*); The Lord Renfrew of Kaimsthorn, FBA, FSA (*Society of Antiquaries*)
Appointed by the Trustees of the British Museum, Sir David

Attenborough, CVO, CBE, FRS; Prof. Rosemary Cramp, CBE, FSA; The Lord Egremont; G. C. Greene, CBE; Dr Jennifer Montagu, FBA

OFFICERS
Director (G2), Dr R. G. W. Anderson, FRSC, FSA
Deputy Director (G4), Miss J. M. Rankine
Secretary (G6), Mrs C. Nihoul Parker
Head of Public Services (G6), G. A. L. House
Head of Press and Public Relations (SIO), A. E. Hamilton
Head of Design (G6), Miss M. Hall, OBE
Head of Education (G7), J. F. Reeve
Head of Administration (G5), C. E. I. Jones
Head of Building and Security Services (G6), K. T. Stannard
Head of Architectural and Building Services (G6), C. J. Walker
Head of Finance (G7), D. E. Williams
Head of Security (G7), I. Slessor
Head of Personnel and Office Services (G7), Miss B. A. Hughes

KEEPERS
Keeper of Prints and Drawings (G5), A. V. Griffiths
Keeper of Coins and Medals (G5), Dr A. M. Burnett
Keeper of Egyptian Antiquities (G5), W. V. Davies
Keeper of Western Asiatic Antiquities (G5), Dr J. E. Curtis
Keeper of Greek and Roman Antiquities (G5), Dr D. J. R. Williams
Keeper of Medieval and Later Antiquities (G5), N. M. Stratford
Keeper of Prehistoric and Romano-British Antiquities (G5), Dr I. H. Longworth, CBE
Keeper of Japanese Antiquities (G5), L. R. H. Smith
Keeper of Oriental Antiquities (G5), R. J. Knox
Keeper of Ethnography (G5), B. J. Mack
Keeper of Scientific Research (G5), Dr S. G. E. Bowman
Keeper of Conservation (G5), W. A. Oddy

NATURAL HISTORY MUSEUM
Cromwell Road and Exhibition Road, London SW7 5BD
Tel 0171-938 9123

The Natural History Museum originates from the natural history departments of the British Museum, which grew extensively during the 19th century and in 1881 were moved to South Kensington. In 1963 the Natural History Museum became completely independent with its own body of trustees. The Zoological Museum, Tring, bequeathed by the second Lord Rothschild, has formed part of the Museum since 1938. The Geological Museum merged with the Natural History Museum in 1985. Total government grant-in-aid for 1995–6 is £28.790 million.

BOARD OF TRUSTEES
Appointed by the Prime Minister: Prof. R. May, FRS (*Chairman*); Sir Owen Green; The Baroness Blackstone, PH.D.; E. N. K. Clarkson, FRS; Mrs J. M. d'Abo; Sir Denys Henderson; Sir Crispin Tickell, GCMG, KCVO; Dame Anne McLaren, DBE, FRS
Nominated by the Royal Society, Prof. J. L. Harper, FRS
Appointed by the Trustees of the Natural History Museum, R. J. Carter; Prof. B. K. Follett, FRS; Sir Anthony Laughton, FRS

OFFICERS
Director (G3), N. R. Chalmers, PH.D.
Director of Science (G5), Prof. P. Henderson, D.phil.
Secretary (G5), C. J. E. Legg
Head of Development and Marketing Department (G6), Mrs T. Burman
Marketing Manager (G6), Ms J. Batchelor
Science Marketing (G6), Dr R. Lincoln
Public Relations Manager (G6), Miss J. Bevan
Keeper of Zoology (G5), C. R. Curds, D.sc
Director, Tring Zoological Museum (G6), I. R. Bishop, OBE
Keeper of Entomology (G5), Dr R. P. Lane

Keeper of Botany (G5), S. Blackmore, PH.D.
Keeper of Palaeontology (G5), L. R. M. Cocks, D.sc
Keeper of Mineralogy (G5), R. Symes
Head of Finance (G6), J. Card
Personnel Officer (G7), Mrs P. H. I. Orchard
Head of Library Services (G6), R. E. R. Banks
Head of Education and Exhibitions (G5), Dr G. Clarke
Head of Exhibition and Design (G7), R. M. Bloomfield, PH.D.

THE SCIENCE MUSEUM
South Kensington, London SW7 2DD
Tel 0171-938 8000

The Science Museum, part of the National Museum of Science and Industry, houses the national collections of science, technology, industry and medicine. The Museum began as the science collection of the South Kensington Museum and first opened in 1857. In 1883 it acquired the collections of the Patent Museum and in 1909 the science collections were transferred to the new Science Museum, leaving the art collections with the Victoria and Albert Museum.

Some of the Museum's commercial aircraft, agricultural machinery, and road and rail transport collections are at Wroughton, Wilts. The Museum is also responsible for the National Railway Museum, York; the National Museum of Photography, Film and Television, Bradford; and the Concorde Exhibition at the Fleet Air Arm Museum, Yeovilton.

Total government grant-in-aid for 1995–6 is £21.20 million.

BOARD OF TRUSTEES
Chairman, Dr P. Williams, CBE (*from Jan. 1996*)
Members, HRH The Duke of Kent, KG, GCMG, GCVO, ADC; Dr Mary Archer; The Viscount Downe; Miss M. S. Goldring, OBE; Mrs A. Higham; Mrs J. Kennedy, OBE; Dr Bridget Ogilvie; Sir Michael Quinlan, GCB; L. de Rothschild, CBE; Sir Christopher Wates

OFFICERS
Director, Sir Neil Cossons, OBE, FSA
Assistant Director and Head of Resource Management Division, J. J. Defries
Head of Personnel and Training, C. Gosling
Head of Finance, Ms A. Caine
Assistant Director and Head of Collections Division, Dr T. Wright
Head of Physical Sciences and Engineering Group, Dr D. A. Robinson
Head of Life and Communications Technologies Group, Dr R. F. Bud
Head of Collections Management Group, Dr S. Keene
Assistant Director and Head of Public Affairs Division, C. M. Pemberton
Assistant Director and Head of Science Communication Division, Prof. J. R. Durant
Head of Education, Dr R. Jackson
Head of Programmes, Dr G. Farmelo
Assistant Director and Head of Project Development Division, Mrs G. M. Thomas
Head of Design, T. Molloy
Head of National Railway Museum, A. Scott
Head of National Museum of Photography, Film and Television, Ms A. Nevill

VICTORIA AND ALBERT MUSEUM
South Kensington, London SW7 2RL
Tel 0171-938 8500

The national museum of all branches of fine and applied art and design, the Victoria and Albert Museum descends directly from the Museum of Manufactures, which opened in Marlborough House in 1852 after the Great Exhibition of 1851. The Museum was moved in 1857 to become part of the South Kensington Museum. It was renamed the Victoria and Albert Museum in 1899. It also houses the National Art Library and Print Room.

The branch museum at Bethnal Green, which houses the Museum of Childhood, was opened in 1872 and the building is the most important surviving example of the type of glass and iron construction used by Paxton for the Great Exhibition. The Museum is also responsible for the Wellington Museum (Apsley House), and the Theatre Museum. Total government grant-in-aid for 1995–6 is £31.554 million.

BOARD OF TRUSTEES
Chairman, The Lord Armstrong of Ilminster, GCB, CVO
Deputy Chairman, Sir Michael Butler, GCMG
Members, The Lord Barnett, PC; Miss N. Campbell; Sir Clifford Chetwood; The Viscountess Cobham; E. Dawe; R. Fitch, CBE; Prof. C. Frayling, PH.D.; R. Gorlin; Pamela, Lady Harlech; Sir Terence Heiser, GCB; Sir Nevil Macready, Bt., CBE; Miss A. Plowden; Prof. M. Podro, PH.D., FBA; M. Saatchi; Prof. J. Steer, FSA
Secretary to the Board of Trustees (G7), P. A. Wilson

OFFICERS
Director (G3), A. C. N. Borg, CBE, PH.D.
Assistant Directors (G5), T. Stevens (*Collections*); J. W. Close (*Administration*)
Head of Buildings and Estate (G5), J. G. Charlesworth
Surveyor of Collections (G5), Mrs G. F. Miles
Head of Conservation Department (G5), Dr J. Ashley-Smith
Head of Finance and Central Services (G5), Miss R. M. Sykes
Development Director, D. Charlton
Head of Education (G6), D. Anderson
Curator, Ceramics Collection (G6), Dr O. Watson
Curator, Far Eastern Collection (G6), Miss R. Kerr
Curator, Furniture and Woodwork Collection (G6), C. Wilk
Curator, Indian and South-East Asian Collection (G6), Dr D. Swallow
Curator, Metalwork Collection (G6), Mrs P. Glanville
Head of Personnel (G6), Mrs G. Henchley
Curator, Prints, Drawings and Paintings Collection (G6), Miss S. B. Lambert
Head of Public Affairs (G5), R. Cole-Hamilton
Head of Marketing and Public Relations (G7), Miss R. Griffith-Jones
Head of Research (G5), P. Greenhalgh
Curator, Sculpture Collection (G6), P. E. D. Williamson
Curator, Textiles and Dress Collection (G6), Mrs V. D. Mendes
Managing Director, V. and A. Enterprises Ltd, M. Cass
Curator and Chief Librarian, National Art Library (G5), J. F. van den Wateren
Head of Bethnal Green Museum of Childhood (G6), A. P. Burton
Head of Theatre Museum (G6), Ms M. Benton
Curator of Wellington Museum (*Apsley House*), J. R. S. Voak

MUSEUM OF LONDON
London Wall, London EC2Y 5HN
Tel 0171-600 3699

The Museum of London illustrates the history of London from prehistoric times to the present day. It opened in 1976 and is based on the amalgamation of the former Guildhall Museum and London Museum. The Museum is controlled by a Board of Governors, appointed (nine each) by the Government and the Corporation of London. The Museum is funded jointly by the Department of National Heritage and the Corporation of London, each contributing £4.446 million in 1995–6.

Chairman of Board of Governors, P. Revell-Smith, CBE
Director, M. G. Hebditch, CBE, FSA

COMMONWEALTH INSTITUTE
Kensington High Street, London W8 6NQ
Tel 0171-603 4535

The Commonwealth Institute has permanent exhibitions on all Commonwealth nations, special exhibitions, a Resource Centre and a Conference Centre. It is an independent statutory body funded by the British government with contributions from other Commonwealth governments. The Institute is controlled by a Board of Governors which includes the High Commissioners of all Commonwealth countries represented in London. It comprises the centre in London and the autonomous Scottish Institute in Edinburgh. Total government grant-in-aid for 1995–6 is £2.7 million.

Director-General, S. Cox
Administrative and Commercial Director, P. Kennedy
Projects Director, J. Stevenson

IMPERIAL WAR MUSEUM
Lambeth Road, London SE1 6HZ
Tel 0171-416 5000

The Museum, founded in 1917, illustrates and records all aspects of the two world wars and other military operations involving Britain and the Commonwealth since 1914. It was opened in its present home, formerly Bethlem Hospital or Bedlam, in 1936. The Museum also administers HMS *Belfast* in the Pool of London, Duxford Airfield near Cambridge and the Cabinet War Rooms in Westminster.

Total government grant-in-aid for 1995–6 is £11.107 million.

Director-General (G4), vacant
Deputy Director-General (G5), R. W. K. Crawford
Secretary (G6), J. J. Chadwick
Personnel Officer (G7), P. L. Cracknell
Finance Officer (G7), Mrs P. A. Whitfield
Museum Superintendent (G6), D. A. Needham
Information Systems Officer (G7), J. C. Barrett
Director of Duxford Airfield (G5), E. O. Inman
Director of HMS Belfast (G6), E. J. Wenzel

KEEPERS
Department of Museum Services (G6), C. Dowling, D.PHIL
Department of Documents (G6), R. W. A. Suddaby
Department of Exhibits and Firearms (G6), D. J. Penn
Department of Printed Books (G6), G. M. Bayliss, PH.D.
Department of Art (G6), Miss A. H. Weight
Department of Film (G6), R. B. N. Smither
Department of Photographs (G6), Miss K. J. Carmichael
Department of Sound Records (G6), Mrs M. A. Brooks
Department of Marketing and Training (G6), Miss A. Godwin
Curator of the Cabinet War Rooms (G7), P. Reed

NATIONAL MARITIME MUSEUM
Greenwich, London SE10 9NF
Tel 0181-858 4422

Established by Act of Parliament in 1934, the National Maritime Museum illustrates the maritime history of Great Britain in the widest sense, underlining the importance of the sea and its influence on the nation's power, wealth, culture, technology and institutions. The Museum is in three groups of buildings in Greenwich Park – the main building, the Queen's House (built by Inigo Jones, 1616–35) and the Old Royal Observatory (including Wren's Flamsteed House). Total government grant-in-aid for 1995–6 is £10.8 million.

Director, R. L. Ormond

NATIONAL ARMY MUSEUM
Royal Hospital Road, London sw3 4ht
Tel 0171-730 0717

The National Army Museum covers the history of five
centuries of the British Army. It was established by royal
charter in 1960. Total government grant-in-aid for 1995–6
is £3.189 million.
Director, I. G. Robertson
Assistant Directors, D. K. Smurthwaite; A. J. Guy;
Maj. P. R. Bateman

ROYAL AIR FORCE MUSEUM
Grahame Park Way, London nw9 5ll
Tel 0181-205 2266

Situated on the former airfield at Hendon, the Museum
illustrates the development of aviation from before the
Wright brothers to the present-day RAF. Total govern-
ment grant-in-aid for 1995–6 is £2.957 million.
Director, Dr M. A. Fopp
Deputy Director, J. D. Freeborn
Keepers, D. C. R. Elliott; P. Elliott; D. F. Lawrence

NATIONAL MUSEUMS AND GALLERIES ON MERSEYSIDE
William Brown Street, Liverpool l3 8en
Tel 0151-207 0001

The Board of Trustees of the National Museums and
Galleries on Merseyside was established in 1986 to take
over responsibility for the museums and galleries pre-
viously administered by Merseyside County Council. The
Board is responsible for the Liverpool Museum, the
Merseyside Martime Museum (incorporating HM
Customs and Excise National Museum), the Museum of
Liverpool Life, the Lady Lever Art Gallery, the Walker
Art Gallery and Sudley House. Total government grant-
in-aid for 1995–6 is £13.025 million.
Chairman of the Board of Trustees, D. McDonnell
Director, R. Foster
Head of Central Services, P. Sudbury, ph.d.
Keeper of Art Galleries, J. Treuherz
Keeper of Conservation (acting), J. Larson
Keeper, Liverpool Museum, E. Greenwood
*Keeper, Merseyside Maritime Museum and Museum of Liverpool
Life,* M. Stammers

NATIONAL MUSEUMS AND GALLERIES OF WALES/AMGUEDDFEYDD AC ORIELAU CENEDLAETHOL CYMRU
Cathays Park, Cardiff cf1 3np
Tel 01222-397951

The National Museums and Galleries of Wales comprise
the National Museum and Gallery, the Museum of Welsh
Life, the Roman Legionary Museum, Turner House Art
Gallery, the Snowdonia Museum, the Welsh Slate
Museum, the Segontium Roman Museum, the Museum
of the Welsh Woollen Industry, the Welsh Industrial and
Maritime Museum, and the Graham Sutherland Gallery.
Total government grant-in-aid for 1995–6 is £12 million.
President, C. R. T. Edwards
Vice-President, M. C. T. Pritchard, cbe
Director, C. Ford, cbe
Assitant Directors, T. Arnold (*resource management*);
C. Thomas (*public services*); E. Wiliam, ph.d. (*museums
development*); I. Fell (*education and interpretation*);
D. Alston (*collections and research*) (*acting*)
Keepers, M. G. Bassett, ph.d. (*geology*); B. A. Thomas, ph.d.
(*botany*); P. M. Morgan (*zoology*); S. H. R. Aldhouse-
Green, ph.d. (*archaeology*); D. Alston (*art*)

Curator, Museum of Welsh Life, Dr E. Williams
Keepers, E. Scourfield, ph.d.; J. Williams-Davies
Officer in Charge, Roman Legionary Museum, P. Guest, ph.d.
Keeper in Charge, Turner House Art Gallery, D. Alston
Keeper, Snowdonia Museum, D. Roberts, ph.d.
Keeper in Charge, Welsh Slate Museum, D. Roberts, ph.d.
Officer in Charge, Segontium Roman Museum, R. J. Brewer
Officer in Charge, Museum of the Welsh Woollen Industry,
E. Scourfield, ph.d.
Keeper, Welsh Industrial and Maritime Museum, E. S. Owen-
Jones, ph.d.
Officer in Charge, Graham Sutherland Gallery, T. Egan

NATIONAL MUSEUMS OF SCOTLAND
Chambers Street, Edinburgh eh1 1jf
Tel 0131-225 7534

The National Museums of Scotland comprise the Royal
Museum of Scotland, the Museum of Antiquities, the
Scottish United Services Museum, the Scottish Agricul-
tural Museum, the Museum of Flight, the Biggar Gasworks
Museum and Shambellie House Museum of Costume.
Total government grant-in-aid for 1995–6 is £19.9 million.

BOARD OF TRUSTEES
Chairman, R. Smith, fsa scot.
Members, Prof. L. Bown, obe; R. D. Cramond, cbe, fsa scot.;
Countess of Dalkeith; Prof. T. Devine; S. G. Gordon,
cbe; Sir Alistair Grant; Prof. P. H. Jones; A. Massie;
D. H. Pringle, cbe; Dr Anna Ritchie; The Countess of
Rosebery; Sir John Thomson; Dr Veronica Van
Heyingen

OFFICERS
Director, M. Jones, fsa, fsa scot., frsa
*Depute Director (Resources) and Project Director, Museum of
Scotland,* I. Hooper, fsa scot.
*Depute Director (Collections) and Keeper of History and Applied
Art* (G5), Miss D. Idiens, frsa, fsa scot.
Keeper of Archaeology, D. V. Clarke, ph.d., fsa, fsa scot.
Keeper of Geology (G5), W. D. I. Rolfe, ph.d., frse, frsa
Keeper of Natural History (G5), M. Shaw, d.phil.
Keeper of Science, Technology and Working Life (G5),
D. J. Bryden, ph.d., fsa
Head of Public Affairs (G6), Ms M. Bryden
Head of Museum Services (G6), S. R. Elson, fsa scot.
Head of Administration (G6), A. G. Young
Campaign Director, Museum of Scotland, Ms S. Brock, ph.d.,
frsa
Keeper, Scottish United Services Museum, S. C. Wood
Curator, Scottish Agricultural Museum, G. Sprott
Curator, Museum of Flight, Sqn. Ldr. R. Major
Curator, Biggar Gasworks Museum, J. Wood
Keeper, Shambellie House Museum of Costume, Miss D. Idiens,
frsa, fsa scot.

NATIONAL AUDIT OFFICE
157–197 Buckingham Palace Road, London sw1w 9sp
Tel 0171–798 7000

The National Audit Office came into existence under the
National Audit Act 1983 to replace and continue the work
of the former Exchequer and Audit Department. The Act
reinforced the Office's total financial and operational
independence from the Government and brought its head,
the Comptroller and Auditor-General, into a closer
relationship with Parliament as an officer of the House of
Commons.

The National Audit Office provides independent information, advice and assurance to Parliament and the

public about all aspects of the financial operations of government departments and many other bodies receiving public funds. It does this by examining and certifying the accounts of these organizations and by regularly publishing reports to Parliament on the results of its value for money investigations of the economy, efficiency and effectiveness with which public resources have been used. The National Audit Office is also the auditor by agreement of the accounts of certain international and other organizations. In addition, the Office authorizes the issue of public funds to government departments.

Comptroller and Auditor-General, Sir John Bourn, KCB
   Private Secretary, F. Grogan
Deputy Comptroller and Auditor-General, R. N. Le Marechal, CB
Assistant Auditors-General, T. Burr; J. A. Higgins;
   L. H. Hughes; J. Marshall; M. C. Pfleger
Directors, A. G. Brown; C. L. Press; C. K. Beauchamp;
   B. Hogg; J. Parsons; J. M. Pearce; A. G. Roberts;
   R. A. Skeen; R. E. Spurgeon; A. Fiander; M. Daynes;
   Miss C. Mawhood; R. J. Eales; J. Colman; B. Payne;
   R. Douglas; N. Sloan; D. Woodward; Ms W. Kenway-
   Smith; R. Frith; J. Cavanagh; R. Maggs; M. Sinclair

NATIONAL CONSUMER COUNCIL
20 Grosvenor Gardens, London SW1W ODH
Tel 0171-730 3469

The National Consumer Council was set up by the Government in 1975 to give an independent voice to consumers in the UK. Its job is to advocate the consumer interest to decision-makers in national and local government, industry and regulatory bodies, business and the professions. It does this through a combination of research and campaigning. It is funded by a grant-in-aid from the Department of Trade and Industry.
Chairman, Lady Wilcox
Vice-Chairman, Mrs A. Scully, OBE
Director, R. Evans

NATIONAL DEBT OFFICE
— *see* National Investment and Loans Office

DEPARTMENT OF NATIONAL HERITAGE
2–4 Cockspur Street, London SW1Y 5DH
Tel 0171-270 3000

The Department of National Heritage was established in 1992 and is responsible for government policy relating to the arts, broadcasting, the press, museums and galleries, libraries, sport and recreation, heritage and tourism. It funds the Arts Councils and other arts bodies, including the National Heritage Memorial Fund. It also funds the Museums and Galleries Commission, the national museums and galleries in England, the British Library, the Sports Council, the British Tourist Authority and the English Tourist Board, and the British Film Institute. It is responsible for the issue of export licences on works of art, antiques and collector's items; the Government Art Collection; the built heritage, including the Royal Parks and Historic Royal Palaces executive agencies; and statistical services including the International Passenger Survey and broadcasting statistics. The Department is also responsible for policy and implementation of the National Lottery.
Secretary of State for National Heritage, The Rt. Hon. Virginia Bottomley, MP
   Private Secretary, J. Kingman

Minister of State, Iain Sproat, MP
   Private Secretary, N. Mackenzie
Parliamentary Under-Secretary, The Lord Inglewood
Lady-in-Waiting, The Baroness Trumpington
Parliamentary Clerk, C. Hutson
Permanent Secretary (*G1*), G. H. Phillips, CB
   Private Secretary, Ms C. Pillmen

LIBRARIES, GALLERIES AND MUSEUMS GROUP
Head of Group (*G3*), Miss M. O'Mara
Head of Libraries and Information Services Division (*G5*),
   D. Wilson
Head of Museums and Galleries Division (*G5*), P. Gregory
Director, Government Art Collection (*G6*), Dr Wendy Baron, OBE
Head of Cultural Property Unit (*G7*), M. Helston

ARTS, SPORTS AND LOTTERY GROUP
Head of Group (*G3*), A. Ramsay
Head of Arts Division (*G5*), N. Kroll
Head of National Lottery Division (*G5*), S. MacDonald
Head of Sport and Recreation Division (*G5*), Miss A. Stewart

BROADCASTING AND MEDIA GROUP
Head of Group (*G3*), P. Wright
Head of Broadcasting Policy Division (*G5*), Ms S. Booth, CBE
Head of Media Division (*G5*), P. Edwards

HERITAGE AND TOURISM GROUP
Head of Group (*G3*), D. Chesterton
Head of Heritage Division (*G5*), A. Corner
Head of Royal Estate Division (*G5*), Dr K. Gray
Head of Tourism Division (*G5*), Ms J. Evans

RESOURCES AND SERVICES GROUP
Director (*G4*), N. Pittman
Director of Finance and Corporate Planning (*G5*),
   R. MacLachlan
Director of Implementation and Review (*G5*), S. Broadley
Director of Personnel (*G5*), G. Jones

INFORMATION
Head of Information (*G5*), Miss A. MacLean

EXECUTIVE AGENCIES

HISTORIC ROYAL PALACES
The Birdwood Annexe, Hampton Court Palace, East Molesey, Surrey KT8 9AU
Tel 0181-781 9750

The Historic Royal Palaces agency manages the Tower of London, Hampton Court Palace, Kensington Palace, Kew Palace with Queen Charlotte's Cottage, and the Banqueting House, Whitehall.
Chief Executive (*G3*), D. C. Beeton
Director of Finance and Resources (*G5*), A. Cornwell
Surveyor of the Fabric (*G5*), S. Bond
Director of Marketing (*G6*), P. D. Hammond
Curator, Historic Royal Palaces (*G5*), Dr S. J. Thurley
Commercial Director, Hampton Court Palace (*G5*), R. Evans
Resident Governor, HM Tower of London (*G5*), Maj.-Gen. M. G. Field
Administrator, Kensington Palace (*G7*), N. J. Arch

ROYAL PARKS
The Royal Parks Headquarters, Hyde Park, London W2 2UH
Tel 0171-298 2000

The agency is responsible for maintaining and developing the royal parks.
Chief Executive (*G5*), D. Welch

NATIONAL HERITAGE MEMORIAL FUND
10 St James's Street, London SWIA IEF
Tel 0171-930 0963

The National Heritage Memorial Fund is an independent body established in 1980 as a memorial to those who have died for the UK. The Fund is empowered by the National Heritage Act 1980 to give financial assistance towards the cost of acquiring, maintaining or preserving land, buildings, works of art and other objects of outstanding interest which are also of importance to the national heritage. The Fund is administered by 13 trustees who are appointed by the Prime Minister.

The National Lottery Act 1993 designated the Fund as distributor of the heritage share of proceeds from the National Lottery (one fifth of the proceeds to the 'good causes'). In effect, this positioned the Fund as an umbrella organization operating two funds: the Heritage Memorial Fund and the Heritage Lottery Fund. The Heritage Memorial Fund receives on annual grant from the Government (£8.8 million in 1995–6). The Heritage Lottery Fund had received about £167 million for distribution as at July 1995 and had made awards to the value of £48.254 million.

TRUSTEES
Chairman, The Lord Rothschild
Members, Sir Richard Carew Pole, Bt.; The Lord Crathorne; W. L. Evans; Sir Nicholas Goodison; Sir Martin Holdgate; Mrs C. Hubbard; Sir Martin Jacomb; J. Keegan; The Lord Macfarlane of Bearsden; Prof. P. J. Newbould; Mrs J. Nutting; Mrs C. Porteous; Cdr. L. M. M. Saunders Watson
Director (acting), F. Carnwath

NATIONAL INSURANCE JOINT AUTHORITY
The Adelphi, 1–11 John Adam Street, London WC2N 6HT
Tel 0171-962 8523

The Authority's function is to co-ordinate the operation of social security legislation in Great Britain and Northern Ireland, including the necessary financial adjustments between the two National Insurance Funds.
Members, The Secretary of State for Social Security; the Head of the Department of Health and Social Services for Northern Ireland.
Secretary, Ms G. E. Taylor

NATIONAL INVESTMENT AND LOANS OFFICE
1 King Charles Street, London SWIA 2AP
Tel 0171-270 3861

The National Investment and Loans Office was set up in 1980 by the merger of the National Debt Office and the Public Works Loan Board. The Office provides staff and services for the National Debt Commissioners and the Public Works Loan Commissioners. The National Debt Office is responsible for the investment and management of statutory funds relating to the surplus monies of certain government bodies; the management of some residual operations relating to the national debt; and the facilitation of raising funds by central government following Article 104 of the Maastricht Treaty, in pursuance of section 211 of the Finance Act 1993. The function of the Public Works Loan Board is to make loans for capital purposes from central government funds to local authorities and to collect repayments.
Director, I. H. Peattie
Establishment Officer, A. G. Ladd

NATIONAL DEBT OFFICE
Comptroller-General, I. H. Peattie

PUBLIC WORKS LOAN BOARD
Chairman, Sir Robin Dent, KCVO
Deputy Chairman, Miss F. M. Cook, CBE
Other Commissioners, Miss V. J. Di Palma, OBE; D. H. Adams; R. A. Chapman; A. Morton; G. G. Williams; J. E. Scotford, CBE; A. Gillespie; A. D. Loehnis, CMG; L. B. Woodhall; Ms S. V. Masters
Secretary, I. H. Peattie
Assistant Secretary, Miss L. M. Ashcroft

OFFICE OF THE NATIONAL LOTTERY
2 Monck Street, London SWIP 2BQ
Tel 0345-125596

The Office of the National Lottery (OFLOT) was established as a non-ministerial government department under the National Lottery Act 1993. It regulates the National Lottery operations and licenses games promoted as part of the Lottery.

About 27 per cent of national lottery proceeds is currently allocated equally to five 'good causes': the arts, charities, heritage, sport and the Millennium Fund. More than £830 million had been allocated to the good causes as at July 1995.
Director-General (G2), P. Davis
Deputy Director-General (G5), Ms D. Kahn
Head of Compliance Regulation (G5), K. Dunn

NATIONAL LOTTERY CHARITIES BOARD
7th Floor, St Vincent House, 30 Orange Street, London WC2H 7HH
Tel 0171-839 5371

The Board was established under the National Lottery Act 1993 to distribute the lottery proceeds allocated for charitable expenditure (one-fifth of the 27 per cent allocated to 'good causes'). The Board consists of a chairman and 16 members, all appointed by the Home Secretary. The Board had received about £167 million for distribution as at July 1995. The first grants will be made in October 1995.
Chairman, The Hon. D. Sieff
Members, Mrs T. Baring; A. Bhatia; Ms J. Kauffman; Sir Adam Ridley; Ms A. Jordan; A. Phillips; C. Woodcock; Mrs A. McGinley; W. McStay; J. Simpson; G. Bowie; Ms P. de Lima; W. Kirkpatrick; Mrs J. Churchman; T. Jones; Ms L. Quinn

NATIONAL PHYSICAL LABORATORY
Queen's Road, Teddington, Middx TW11 0LW
Tel 0181-977 3222

The Laboratory is government-owned but contractor-operated. It develops and disseminates national measurement standards.
Chief Executive and Director, vacant

NATIONAL RADIOLOGICAL PROTECTION BOARD

Chilton, Didcot, Oxon OX11 ORQ
Tel 01235-831600

The National Radiological Protection Board is an independent statutory body created by the Radiological Protection Act 1970. It is the national point of authoritative reference on radiological protection for both ionizing and non-ionizing radiations, and has issued recommendations on limiting human exposure to electromagnetic fields and radiation from a range of sources, including X-rays, the sun and power generators.

Chairman, Prof. Sir Keith Peters
Director, Prof. R. H. Clarke

NATIONAL RIVERS AUTHORITY

Rivers House, Waterside Drive, Aztec West,
Almondsbury, Bristol BS12 4UD
Tel 0117-962 4400
Eastbury House, 30–34 Albert Embankment, London
SE1 7TL
Tel 0171-820 0101

The National Rivers Authority (NRA) is an independent body set up under the Water Act 1989, now the Water Resources Act 1991. Its responsibilities include monitoring the quality of water, controlling pollution, and the management of water resources, flood defence and fisheries. It has head offices in Bristol and London and eight regional units. The NRA has a board of 14 members, two of whom are appointed by the Minister of Agriculture, Fisheries and Food, one by the Secretary of State for Wales, and the rest by the Secretary of State for the Environment. The functions of the NRA will be taken over by the proposed new Environment Agency for England and Wales in April 1996.

Chairman, The Lord Crickhowell, PC
Chief Executive, E. Gallagher
Director, Water Management, Dr C. Swinnerton
Finance Director, N. Reader
Personnel Director, P. Humphreys
Director of Public Affairs, M. Wilson
Director, Operations, K. Bond
Director, Market Testing, G. Mance
Secretary and Director, Legal Services, C. Martin

DEPARTMENT FOR NATIONAL SAVINGS

Charles House, 375 Kensington High Street, London
W14 8SD
Tel 0171-605 9300

The Department for National Savings was established as a government department in 1969. The Department is responsible for the administration of a wide range of schemes for personal savers.

Director of Savings (*G2*), vacant
Director of Corporate Resources (*G3*), K. Chivers
Head of Information Systems (*G5*), A. S. McGill
Head of Personnel (*G5*), D. S. Speedie
Head of Finance (*G5*), M. A. Nicholls
Head of Marketing (*G5*), Miss A. Nash
Head of Policy and Product Development (*G5*),
    P. N. S. Hickman-Robertson

Director of Operations (*G5*), D. H. Monaghan
For details of schemes, *see* National Savings section

JOINT NATURE CONSERVATION COMMITTEE

Monkstone House, City Road, Peterborough PE1 1JY
Tel 01733-62626

The Committee was established under the Environmental Protection Act 1990 and began work in 1991. It advises the Government and others on UK and international nature conservation issues and disseminates knowledge on these subjects. It establishes common standards for the monitoring of nature conservation and research, and analyses the resulting information. It commissions research relevant to these roles, and provides guidance to English Nature, Scottish Natural Heritage, the Countryside Council for Wales and the Department of the Environment for Northern Ireland.

Chairman, The Earl of Selborne, KBE, FRS
Chief Officer, C. R. Walker, CB
Director, Life Sciences and Resources, vacant
Director, Aquatic and Earth Sciences, Dr M. A. Vincent

NORTHERN IRELAND OFFICE

Whitehall, London SW1A 2AZ
Tel 0171-210 3000
Stormont Castle, Belfast BT4 3ST
Tel 01232-520700

The Northern Ireland Office was established in 1972, when the Northern Ireland (Temporary Provisions) Act transferred the legislative and executive powers of the Northern Ireland Parliament and Government to the UK Parliament and a Secretary of State.

The Northern Ireland Office is responsible primarily for security issues, law and order and prisons, and for matters relating to the political and constitutional future of the province. It also deals with international issues as they affect Northern Ireland, including the Anglo-Irish Agreement. The Northern Ireland departments are responsible for the administration of social, industrial and economic policies.

The names of most civil servants are not listed for security reasons.

Secretary of State for Northern Ireland, The Rt. Hon. Sir
    Patrick Mayhew, QC, MP
    Special Adviser, J. Caine
    Parliamentary Private Secretary, J. Cran, MP
Ministers of State, Michael Ancram, MP; The Rt. Hon. Sir
    John Wheeler, MP
    Parliamentary Private Secretary to Michael Ancram,
    R. Robertson, MP
Parliamentary Under-Secretaries of State, The Baroness
    Denton of Wakefield, CBE; Malcolm Moss, MP
Permanent Under-Secretary of State (*G1*), Sir John Chilcot,
    KCB
*Second Permanent Under-Secretary of State, Head of the
    Northern Ireland Civil Service* (*G1A*), Sir David. Fell, KCB

LONDON
Deputy Secretary (*G2*)
Under-Secretaries (*G3*), (Security and International;
    Constitutional and Political; Economic and Social);
    (Establishment and Finance)
Grade 4, (Information Services)

BELFAST
Deputy Secretary (*G2*)
Under-Secretaries (*G3*), (Security); (Criminal Justice);
(Political); (Establishment and Finance)

EXECUTIVE AGENCIES
COMPENSATION AGENCY, Royston House, Upper Queen
Street, Belfast BT1 6FD. Tel: 01232-2499444
PRISON SERVICE AGENCY, Dundonald House, Upper
Newtownards Road, Belfast B4 3SU. Tel: 01232 520700

DEPARTMENT OF AGRICULTURE FOR NORTHERN IRELAND
Dundonald House, Upper Newtownards Road, Belfast
BT4 3SB
Tel 01232-520100

Parliamentary Under-Secretary of State, The Baroness
Denton of Wakefield, CBE
Permanent Secretary (*G2*)
Under-Secretaries (*G3*), (Central Services and Rural
Development); (Food and Farm Policy); (Agri-
Environment Policy, Forestry and Fisheries);
(Veterinary); (Science); (Agri-Food Development)

EXECUTIVE AGENCY
INTERVENTION BOARD
— *see* page 319

DEPARTMENT OF ECONOMIC DEVELOPMENT NORTHERN IRELAND
Netherleigh, Massey Avenue, Belfast BT4 2JP
Tel 01232-529900

Parliamentary Under-Secretary of State, The Baroness
Denton of Wakefield, CBE
Permanent Secretary (*G2*)
Under-Secretaries (*G3*), (Resources Group); (Regulatory
Services Group)
INDUSTRIAL DEVELOPMENT BOARD, IDB House, 64
Chichester Street, Belfast BT1 4JX. Tel: 01232-233233

EXECUTIVE AGENCIES
INDUSTRIAL RESEARCH AND TECHNOLOGY UNIT,
Netherleigh, Massey Avenue, Belfast BT4 2JP. Tel:
01232-529900
TRAINING AND EMPLOYMENT AGENCY (NORTHERN
IRELAND), Clarendon House, 9–21 Adelaide Street,
Belfast BT2 8DJ. Tel: 01232-541541

DEPARTMENT OF EDUCATION FOR NORTHERN IRELAND
Rathgael House, Balloo Road, Bangor, Co. Down BT19 7PR
Tel 01247-279279

Minister of State, Michael Ancram, MP
Permanent Secretary (*G2*)
Under-Secretaries (*G3*), (Educational Services);
(Establishment and Finance); (Education and Training
Inspectorate)

DEPARTMENT OF THE ENVIRONMENT FOR NORTHERN IRELAND
Clarence Court, 10–18 Adelaide Street, Belfast BT2 8GB
Tel 01232-540540

Parliamentary Under-Secretary of State, Malcolm Moss, MP
Permanent Secretary (*G2*)
Under-Secretaries (*G3*), (Personnel, Finance, Housing and
Local Government); (Rural and Urban Affairs); (Roads,
Water and Transport); (Planning, Works and
Environment)

EXECUTIVE AGENCIES
DRIVER AND VEHICLE LICENSING AGENCY (NORTHERN
IRELAND), County Hall, Castlerock Road, Coleraine,
Co. Londonderry BT51 3HS. Tel: 01265-41200
DRIVER AND VEHICLE TESTING AGENCY (NORTHERN
IRELAND), Balmoral Road, Belfast BT12 6QL. Tel: 01232-
681831
ORDNANCE SURVEY OF NORTHERN IRELAND, Colby House,
Stranmillis Court, Belfast BT9 5BJ. Tel: 01232-661244
PUBLIC RECORD OFFICE (NORTHERN IRELAND) – *see* page
340
RATE COLLECTION AGENCY (NORTHERN IRELAND), Oxford
House, 49–55 Chichester Street, Belfast BT1 4HH. Tel:
01232-231936

ADVISORY BODIES
HISTORIC BUILDINGS COUNCIL FOR NORTHERN IRELAND,
c/o Environment Service, Historic Monuments and
Buildings, 5–33 Hill Street, Belfast BT1 2LA. Tel: 01232-
235000
HISTORIC MONUMENTS COUNCIL FOR NORTHERN IRELAND,
c/o Environment Service, Historic Monuments and
Buildings, 5–33 Hill Street, Belfast BT1 2LA. Tel: 01232-
235000
COUNCIL FOR NATURE CONSERVATION AND THE
COUNTRYSIDE, c/o Environment Service, 5–33 Hill
Street, Belfast BT1 2LA. Tel: 01232-235000

DEPARTMENT OF FINANCE AND PERSONNEL
Parliament Buildings, Stormont, Belfast BT4 3SW
Tel 01232-520400

Minister of State, The Rt. Hon. Sir John Wheeler, MP
Permanent Secretary (*G2*)
Under-Secretaries (*G3*), (Supply Group); (Resources
Control and Professional Services Group); (Central
Personnel Group); (Government Purchasing Service)

NORTHERN IRELAND CIVIL SERVICE (NICS)
Stormont Castle, Belfast BT4 3TT
Tel 01232-520700

Head of Civil Service (*G1A*), Sir David Fell, KCB
Under-Secretaries (*G3*), (Central Secretariat); (Legal
Services); (Office of the Legislative Council)

GENERAL REGISTER OFFICE (NORTHERN IRELAND)
Oxford House, 49–65 Chichester Street, Belfast BT1 4HL
Tel 01232-252000

Registrar-General (*G6*)

EXECUTIVE AGENCY
VALUATION AND LANDS AGENCY, Queen's Court, 56–66
Upper Queen Street, Belfast BT4 6FD. Tel: 01232-
439303

DEPARTMENT OF HEALTH AND SOCIAL SERVICES NORTHERN IRELAND
Dundonald House, Upper Newtownards Road, Belfast
BT4 3SF
Tel 01232-520500

Parliamentary Under-Secretary of State, Malcolm Moss, MP
Permanent Secretary (*G2*)
Chief Medical Officer (*G2A*)
Under-Secretaries (*G3*), (Health and Personal Social
Services Management Executive); (Health and
Personal Social Services Policy); (Medical and Allied
Services); (Central Services)

NORTHERN IRELAND CHILD SUPPORT AGENCY, Great
Northern Tower, 17 Great Victoria Street, Belfast
BT2 7AD. Tel: 01232-339000
NORTHERN IRELAND SOCIAL SECURITY AGENCY, Castle
Buildings, Stormont, Belfast BT4 3SJ. Tel: 01232-520520

OCCUPATIONAL PENSIONS BOARD
PO Box 2EE, Newcastle upon Tyne NE99 2EE
Tel 0191-225 6414

The Occupational Pensions Board (OPB) is an independent statutory body set up under the Social Security Act
1973 to administer the contracting-out of occupational
pensions from the State Earnings Related Pension Scheme
(SERPS), and to advise the Secretary of State. Its functions
have been extended by subsequent legislation and it is now
also responsible for administering equal access, preservation and modification requirements and appropriate
personal pension schemes. Following the Social Security
Act 1990, the OPB was appointed as Registrar of Occupational and Personal Pension Schemes and granted powers
to make grants to approved bodies in the field. The OPB
now funds the operation of the Occupational Pensions
Advisory Service (OPAS).
In 1994 the Government published a White Paper
including proposals to replace the OPB with a statutory
regulator.

Chairman, P. D. Carr, CBE
Deputy Chairman, Miss C. H. Dawes, OBE
Secretary to the Board and General Manager of Executive Office
(G6), M. McLean

OMBUDSMEN
— see Local Commissioners *and* Parliamentary
Commissioner. For non-statutory Ombudsmen, *see* Index

ORDNANCE SURVEY
Romsey Road, Maybush, Southampton SO16 4GU
Tel 01703-792000

The Ordnance Survey is the national mapping agency for
Britain. It became an executive agency in 1990 and reports
to the Secretary of State for the Environment.
The Ordnance Survey has military origins. It produces
over 220,000 large scale maps of the country at three basic
scales. These are 1:1,250 (50 inches to 1 mile) for urban
areas; 1:2,500 (25 inches to 1 mile) for rural areas; and
1:10,000 (6 inches to 1 mile) for mountain and moorland.
Ordnance Survey also produces a range of small scale maps
and other products for general use.
Director-General and Chief Executive, Prof. D. Rhind

OVERSEAS DEVELOPMENT
ADMINISTRATION
94 Victoria Street, London SW1E 5JL
Tel 0171-917 7000
Abercrombie House, Eaglesham Road, East Kilbride,
Glasgow G75 8EA
Tel 01355-844000

The Overseas Development Administration deals with
British development assistance to overseas countries. This
includes both capital aid on concessional terms and

technical assistance (mainly in the form of specialist staff
abroad and training facilities in the UK), whether provided
directly to developing countries or through the various
multilateral aid organizations, including the United
Nations and its specialized agencies.
Minister for Overseas Development, The Baroness Chalker of
Wallasey, PC
  Private Secretary (G7), R. Calvert
Permanent Secretary (G1A), J. M. M. Vereker
  Private Secretary, M. J. Winsley
Deputy Secretary (G2), R. M. Ainscow, CB
Under-Secretaries (G3), N. B. Hudson; B. R. Ireton;
  J. V. Kerby; R. G. Manning; A. J. Bennett;
  J. B. Wilmshurst; J. L. Faint; P. D. M. Freeman

ECONOMIC AND SOCIAL DIVISION
Head of the Economic Service (G3), J. B. Wilmshurst
Senior Economic Advisers (G5), J. C. H. Morris;
  B. P. Thomson; J. Roberts; M. Foster; P. J. Ackroyd
Senior Small Enterprise Development Adviser (G6),
  D. L. Wright
Small Business Adviser (G7), D. M. Spence
Chief Statistician (G5), A. B. Williams
Principal Finance Management and Administration Adviser
  (G5), K. L. Sparkhall
Senior Police Adviser (G6), L. Grundy
Chief Social Development Adviser (G5), Dr R. J. Eyben
Chief Health and Population Adviser (G5), Dr D. Nabarro
Forestry Adviser (G7), Dr J. Clark
Purchasing Adviser (G7), R. H. Marriott

INFORMATION DEPARTMENT
Head of Information (G6), P. Aylett
Principal Information Officer (G7), R. W. Fosker

ADMINISTRATIVE STAFF
Grade 5, Miss A. M. Archbold; M. Bawden; A. Bearpark,
  CBE; S. Chakrabarti; J. H. S. Chard; Ms M. Cund;
  A. D. Davis; M. J. Dinham; J. R. Drummond; R. Elias;
  D. S. Fish; R. M. Graham-Harrison; B. W. Hammond;
  Mrs P. J. Hilton; Mrs S. Jay; Mrs B. M. Kelly, CBE;
  M. C. McCulloch; J. C. Machin; V. J. McClean;
  C. Myhill; M. A. Power; C. P. Raleigh; S. Ray; D. Sands-
  Smith; D. L. Stanton; G. M. Stegmann; D. P. Turner;
  Ms S. E. Unsworth; Miss M. Vowles; M. Wickstead;
  Mrs P. M. Wilkinson; R. J. Wilson

ADVISORY AND SPECIALIST STAFF
Chief Education Adviser (G5), Ms M. Harrison
Chief Engineering Adviser (G5), J. W. Hodges
Senior Electrical and Mechanical Engineering Adviser (G6),
  R. P. Jones
Senior Architectural and Physical Planning Advisers (G6),
  M. W. Parkes; W. M. Housego-Woolgar
Chief Health and Population Advisers (G6), Dr P. Key, OBE;
  Miss J. Isard; Dr M. Kapila; Ms S. Simmonds; J. Lambert
Chief Natural Resources Adviser (G3), A. J. Bennett
Deputy Chief Natural Resources Advisers (G5), J. M. Scott
  (*Agriculture*); Dr I. Haines (*Research*)
Animal Health Advisers (G6), G. G. Freeland; Dr A. D. Irvin;
  Ms L. Bell
Senior Fisheries Advisers (G6), Dr J. Tarbit; R. W. Beales
Senior Forestry Advisers (G6), J. Hudson; I. Napier
Senior Procurement Adviser (G6), R. Davidson
Senior Technical Education Advisers (G6), C. Lewis;
  Dr G. R. H. Jones
Industrial Training Advisers (G7), A. Wray; D. G. Marr
Agricultural Education and Training Adviser (G7), A. Hall

NATURAL RESOURCES INSTITUTE
Central Avenue, Chatham Maritime, Chatham, Kent
ME4 4TB
Tel 01634-880088

An executive agency of the ODA, the NRI provides scientific and technical expertise in renewable natural resources for the overseas aid programme.
Director and Chief Executive (G3), G. A. Beattie

OFFICE OF THE PARLIAMENTARY COMMISSIONER FOR ADMINISTRATION AND HEALTH SERVICE COMMISSIONER
Church House, Great Smith Street, London SW1P 3BW
Tel 0171-276 2130 (*Parliamentary Commissioner*); 0171-276 2035 (*Health Service Commissioner*)

The Parliamentary Commissioner for Administration (the Parliamentary Ombudsman) is independent of Government and is an officer of Parliament. He is responsible for investigating complaints referred to him by MPs from members of the public who claim to have sustained injustice in consequence of maladministration by or on behalf of government departments and certain non-departmental public bodies. Certain types of action by government departments or bodies are excluded from investigation. The Parliamentary Commissioner is also responsible for investigating complaints, referred by MPs, alleging that access to official information has been wrongly refused under the Code of Practice on Access to Government Information 1994.

The Health Service Commissioners (the Health Service Ombudsmen) for England, for Scotland and for Wales are responsible for investigating complaints against National Health Service authorities and trusts that are not dealt with by those authorities to the satisfaction of the complainant. Complaints can be referred direct by the member of the public who claims to have sustained injustice or hardship in consequence of the failure in a service provided by a relevant body, failure of that body to provide a service or in consequence of any other action by that body. Certain types of action are excluded, in particular, action taken solely in consequence of the exercise of clinical judgment. (The Government has announced its intention to introduce legislation, expected to come into effect in spring 1996, to extend the Ombudsmens' jurisdiction to cover complaints about family doctors, dentists, pharmacists and opticians, and complaints about matters of clinical judgment.) The Health Service Ombudsmen are also responsible for investigating complaints that information has been wrongly refused under the Code of Practice on Openness in the National Health Service 1995. The three offices are presently held by the Parliamentary Commissioner.
Parliamentary Commissioner and Health Service Commissioner (G1), W. K. Reid, CB
Deputy Parliamentary Commissioners (G3), J. E. Avery; Miss P. A. Edwards
Deputy Health Service Commissioners (G3), R. A. Oswald; Miss M. I. Nisbet
Directors, Parliamentary Commissioner (G5), Mrs A. H. P. Bates; Mrs A. M. Boulton; D. J. Coffey; Mrs S. P. Maunsell; J. L. Railton; A. Watson
Directors, Health Service Commissioners (G5), Miss H. Bainbridge; D. P. Flaherty; N. J. Jordan; R. H. Keynes; D. R. G. Pinchin; P. Pugh; C. H. Wilson
Finance and Establishment Officer (G6), T. G. Hull

NORTHERN IRELAND PARLIAMENTARY COMMISSIONER FOR ADMINISTRATION AND NORTHERN IRELAND COMMISSIONER FOR COMPLAINTS
Progressive House, 33 Wellington Place, Belfast BT1 6HN
Tel 01232-233821

The Commissioner is appointed under legislation with powers to investigate complaints by people claiming to have sustained injustice in consequence of maladministration arising from action taken by a Northern Ireland government department, or any other public body within the Commissioner's remit. Staff are presently seconded from the Northern Ireland Civil Service.
Commissioner, Mrs J. McIvor, CBE, QSM
Deputy Commissioner, G. R. Dawson
Directors, C. O'Hare; R. Doherty

PARLIAMENTARY COUNSEL
36 Whitehall, London SW1A 2AY
Tel 0171-210 6633

Parliamentary Counsel draft all government bills (i.e. primary legislation) except those relating exclusively to Scotland, the latter being drafted by the Lord Advocate's Department. They also advise on all aspects of parliamentary procedure in connection with such bills and draft government amendments to them as well as any motions (including financial resolutions) necessary to secure their introduction into, and passage through, Parliament.
First Counsel (£90,000–£150,000), J. C. Jenkins, CB, QC
Second Counsel (£85,450), D. W. Saunders, CB
Counsel (£67,500–£98,000), E. G. Caldwell, CB; E. G. Bowman, CB; G. B. Sellers, CB; E. R. Sutherland, CB; P. F. A. Knowles; S. C. Laws; R. S. Parker; Miss C. E. Johnston; P. J. Davies

PAROLE BOARD FOR ENGLAND AND WALES
Abell House, John Islip Street, London SW1P 4LH
Tel 0171-217 5314

The Board was constituted under the Criminal Justice Act 1967 and continued under the Criminal Justice Act 1991. Its duty is to advise the Secretary of State for the Home Department with respect to matters referred to it by him which are connected with the early release or recall of prisoners. Its functions include giving directions concerning the release on licence of prisoners serving discretionary life sentences and of certain prisoners serving long-term determinate sentences; and making recommendations to the Secretary of State concerning the early release on licence of other prisoners, the conditions of parole and licences and the variation and cancellation of such conditions, and the recall of long-term and life prisoners while on licence.
Chairman, The Lord Belstead, PC
Vice-Chairman, The Hon. Mr Justice Potts
Secretary, T. E. Russell

PAROLE BOARD FOR SCOTLAND
Calton House, 5 Redheughs Rigg, Edinburgh EH12 9HW
Tel 0131-244 8755

The Board directs and advises the Secretary of State for Scotland on the release of prisoners on licence, and related matters.
Chairman, I. McNee
Vice-Chairman, Sheriff G. Shiach
Secretary, H. P. Boyle

PATENT OFFICE
Cardiff Road, Newport, Gwent NP9 1RH
Tel 01633-814000

The Patent Office is an executive agency of the Department of Trade and Industry. The duties of the Patent Office are to administer the Patent Acts, the Registered Designs Act and the Trade Marks Act, and to deal with questions relating to the Copyright, Designs and Patents Act 1988. The Search and Advisory Service carries out commercial searches through patent information. In 1994 the Office granted 9,530 patents and registered 8,261 designs and 28,768 trade and service marks.
Comptroller-General (G3), P. R. S. Hartnack
Assistant Comptroller, Industrial Property and Copyright Department (G4), A. Sugden
Assistant Comptroller, Patents and Designs (G4), R. J. Marchant
Assistant Registrar, Trade Marks (G4), Miss A. Brimelow
Head of Marketing and Information (Supt. Examiner), E. F. Blake
Head of Administration and Resources (G5), T. Cassidy
Head of ADP Unit (G6), G. Bennett

PAYMASTER
The Office of HM Paymaster-General
HM Treasury, Parliament Street, London SW1P 3AG
Tel 0171-270 4349
Sutherland House, Russell Way, Crawley, W. Sussex RH10 1UH
Tel 01293-560999

PAYMASTER, the Office of HM Paymaster-General, was formed by the consolidation in 1835 of various separate pay departments. Its function is that of paying agent for government departments other than the revenue departments. Most of its payments are made through banks, to whose accounts the necessary transfers are made at the Bank of England. The calculation and payment of over 1.5 million public service pensions is an important feature of its work. The Office became an executive agency of the Treasury in 1993.
Paymaster-General, David Heathcoat-Amory, MP
Assistant Paymaster-General/Chief Executive (G5), K. Sullens
Grade 6, M. D. West

OFFICE OF THE PENSIONS OMBUDSMAN
11 Belgrave Road, London SW1V 1RB
Tel 0171-834 9144

The Pensions Ombudsman is appointed by the Secretary of State for Social Security under the Pension Schemes Act 1993 to deal with complaints against, and disputes with, occupational and personal pension schemes. He is completely independent.
Pensions Ombudsman, Dr J. T. Farrand

POLICE COMPLAINTS AUTHORITY
10 Great George Street, London SW1P 3AE
Tel 0171-273 6450

The Police Complaints Authority was established under the Police and Criminal Evidence Act 1984 to provide an independent system for dealing with serious complaints by members of the public against police officers in England and Wales. The authority has powers to supervise the investigation of certain categories of serious complaints and certain statutory functions in relation to the disciplinary aspects of complaints. It does not deal with police operational matters; these are usually dealt with by the Chief Constable of the relevant force.
Chairman, Sir Leonard Peach
Deputy Chairman (Investigations), J. Cartwright
Deputy Chairman (Discipline), P. W. Moorhouse
Members, Mrs L. Cawsey; M. Chapman; N. Dholakia, OBE; J. Elliott; Miss L. Haye; A. Kelly; Mrs M. Meacher; Mrs C. Mitchell; E. Wignall; A. Williams

INDEPENDENT COMMISSION FOR POLICE COMPLAINTS FOR NORTHERN IRELAND
— *see* page 317

POLITICAL HONOURS SCRUTINY COMMITTEE
Cabinet Office, 53 Parliament Street, London SW1A 2NG
Tel 0171-210 5058

The function of the Political Honours Scrutiny Committee was set out in an Order of Council in 1991 and amended by Orders in Council in 1992 and 1994. The Prime Minister submits certain particulars to the Committee about persons proposed to be recommended for honour for their political services. The Committee, after such enquiry as they think fit, report to the Prime Minister whether, so far as they believe, the persons whose names are submitted to them are fit and proper persons to be recommended.
Chairman, The Lord Pym, MC, PC
Members, The Lord Cledwyn of Penrhos, CH, PC; The Lord Thomson of Monifieth, KT, PC
Secretary, A. J. Merifield, CB

OFFICE OF POPULATION CENSUSES AND SURVEYS
St Catherine's House, 10 Kingsway, London WC2B 6JP
Tel 0171-242 0262

The Office of Population Censuses and Surveys (OPCS) was created by the merger in 1970 of the General Register Office and the Government Social Survey Department. The Registrar-General controls the local registration service in England and Wales in the exercise of its registration and marriage duties. Copies of the original registrations of births, still births, marriages and deaths and a register of adopted children are kept at Smedley Hydro, Southport PR8 2HH. Central indexes are compiled annually and certified copies of entries may be obtained, on payment of certain fees, either by personal application from St Catherine's House or by post from Southport.

Since 1841 the Registrar-General has been responsible for taking the census of population. He also prepares and publishes a wide range of statistics and appropriate commentary relating to population, fertility, births, still births, marriages, deaths and cause of death and infectious diseases. The Registrar-General is also responsible for conducting surveys on a range of subjects for other government departments. He maintains, at Southport, the National Health Service Register.

Hours of access to Public Search Room, St Catherine's House, Monday–Friday, 8.30–4.30.

The Government has announced its intention to merge the OPCS and the Central Statistical Office (*see* page 293).
Director and Registrar-General for England and Wales (*G2*), P. J. Wormald, CB
Deputy Director and Director of Statistics (*G3*), D. L. H. Roberts
Deputy Director and Chief Medical Statistician (*G3*), A. J. Fox, PH.D.
Deputy Registrar-General (*G5*), Mrs I. Macdonald-Davies
Principal Establishment and Finance Officer (*G5*), B. S. Smith
Principal Information Officer (*G7*), Miss S. Wallace
Heads of Divisions (*G5*), I. K. G. Arnold (*Information Technology*); Prof. M. P. Coleman (*Deputy Chief Medical Statistician*); R. Barnes (*Social Survey Division*); J. Craig (*Census*); B. H. Mahon (*Population Statistics*); Ms K. Dunnell (*Health Statistics*); Dr N. Wood (*Marketing*)
Heads of Divisions (*G6*), W. Jenkins (*Deputy Head of Registration*); B. W. Meakings (*Data Services*)

PORT OF LONDON AUTHORITY
Devon House, 58–60 St Katharine's Way, London E1 9LB
Tel 0171-265 2656

The Port of London Authority is a public trust constituted under the Port of London Act 1908 and subsequent legislation. It is the governing body for the Port of London, covering the tidal portion of the River Thames from Teddington to the seaward limit. The Board comprises a chairman and up to seven but not less than four non-executive members appointed by the Secretary of State for Transport, and up to four but not less than one executive members appointed by the Board.
Chairman, Sir Brian Shaw
Vice-Chairman, J. H. Kelly, CBE
Chief Executive, D. Jeffery
Secretary, G. E. Ennals

THE POST OFFICE
148 Old Street, London EC1V 9HQ
Tel 0171-490 2888

Crown services for the carriage of government dispatches were set up in about 1516. The conveyance of public correspondence began in 1635 and the mail service was made a parliamentary responsibility with the setting up of a Post Office in 1657. Telegraphs came under Post Office control in 1870 and the Post Office Telephone Service began in 1880. The National Girobank service of the Post Office began in 1968. The Post Office ceased to be a government department in 1969 when responsibility for the running of the postal, telecommunications, giro and

remittance services was transferred to a public authority called the Post Office. The 1981 British Telecommunications Act separated the functions of the Post Office, making it solely responsible for postal services and Girobank. Girobank was privatized in 1990.

The chairman, chief executive and members of the Post Office Board are appointed by the Secretary of State for Trade and Industry but responsibility for the running of the Post Office as a whole rests with the Board in its corporate capacity.

FINANCIAL RESULTS £m	1993–4	1994–5
Post Office Group		
Turnover	5,568	5,878
Trading profit before tax	306	472
Royal Mail		
Turnover	4,223	4,540
Trading profit before tax and		
interest on long-term loans	276	430
Parcelforce		
Turnover	498	481
Trading loss before tax and		
interest on long-term loans	17	30
Post Office Counters		
Turnover	1,089	1,118
Trading profit before tax and		
interest on long-term loans	34	30

POST OFFICE BOARD
Chairman, M. Heron
Chief Executive, W. Cockburn, CBE, TD
Members, P. Howarth, CBE (*Managing Director, Royal Mail*); K. Williams (*Managing Director, Parcelforce*); R. Dykes (*Managing Director, Post Office Counters Ltd*); R. Close (*Managing Director, Finance*)
Secretary, D. Savill
For postal services, *see* pages 510–2

PRIME MINISTER'S OFFICE
— *see* page 291

PRISONS OMBUDSMAN FOR ENGLAND AND WALES
St Vincent House, 30 Orange Street, London WC2H 7HH
Tel 0171-389 1527

The Prisons Ombudsman is an independent point of appeal for prisoners' grievances about their lives in prison, including disciplinary issues. The Ombudsman cannot investigate grievances relating to issues which are the subject of litigation or criminal proceedings, decisions taken by ministers on the release of life sentence prisoners, or actions of bodies outside the prison service. The Ombudsman was appointed in May 1994.
Prisons Ombudsman, Sir Peter Woodhead, KCB

For Scotland, *see* Scottish Prisons Complaints Commission

PRIVY COUNCIL OFFICE
Whitehall, London SW1A 2AT
Tel 0171-270 3000

The Office is responsible for the arrangements leading to the making of all royal proclamations and Orders in Council; for certain formalities connected with ministerial changes; for considering applications for the granting (or amendment) of royal charters; for the scrutiny and approval of by-laws and statutes of chartered bodies; and for the appointment of High Sheriffs and many Crown and Privy Council appointments to governing bodies.

Lord President of the Council (and Leader of the House of Commons), The Rt. Hon. Antony Newton, OBE, MP
  Private Secretary, P. Cohen
  Special Adviser, P. Moman
Clerk of the Council (G3), N. H. Nicholls, CBE
Deputy Clerk of the Council (G5), R. P. Bulling
Senior Clerk, Miss M. A. McCullagh

PROCURATOR FISCAL SERVICE
— *see* pages 373–4

PUBLIC HEALTH LABORATORY SERVICE
61 Colindale Avenue, London NW9 5DF
Tel 0181-200 1295

The Public Health Laboratory Service comprises ten groups of laboratories on a number of sites in England and Wales, the Central Public Health Laboratory and the Communicable Disease Surveillance Centre. The PHLS provides diagnostic microbiological services to hospitals, and has reference facilities that are available nationally. It collates information on the incidence of infection, and when necessary it institutes special inquiries into outbreaks and the epidemiology of infectious disease. It also undertakes bacteriological surveillance of the quality of food and water for local authorities and others. The PHLS is often called upon to advise central and local government and the hospital service on many aspects of infectious disease. It maintains close contact with veterinary and other scientific organizations in areas of mutual interest, and collaborates with the World Health Organization and with national laboratory and epidemiological services overseas.

Chairman, Dr M. P. W. Godfrey, CBE, FRCP
Deputy Chairman, A. Graham-Dixon, QC
Director, Dr Diana Walford, FRCP, FRCPath.
Deputy Directors, Prof. B. I. Duerden, MD, FRCPath.
  (*Programmes*); K. M. Saunders (*Corporate Planning and Resources*)
Board Secretary, K. M. Saunders

CENTRAL PUBLIC HEALTH LABORATORY
Colindale Avenue, London NW9 5HT
Director, Dr Morag C. Timbury

COMMUNICABLE DISEASES SURVEILLANCE CENTRE
Colindale Avenue, NW9 5EQ
Director, Dr C. L. R. Bartlett

OTHER SPECIAL LABORATORIES AND UNITS
ANAEROBE REFERENCE UNIT, Public Health Laboratory, Cardiff. *Director*, Prof. B. I. Duerden, MD, FRCPath.
CRYPTOSPROIDIUM REFERENCE UNIT, Public Health Laboratory, Rhyl. *Director*, D. N. Looker
GONOCOCCUS REFERENCE UNIT, Public Health Laboratory, Bristol. *Director*, A. E. Jephcott, MD
LEPTOSPIRA REFERENCE LABORATORY, Public Health Laboratory, Hereford. *Director*, Dr T. J. Coleman
MALARIA REFERENCE LABORATORY, London School of Hygiene and Tropical Medicine, London WC1. *Directors*, Prof. D. J. Bradley, DM; D. C. Warhurst, PH.D., FRCPath.
MENINGOCOCCAL REFERENCE LABORATORY, Public Health Laboratory, Manchester. *Director*, Dr B. A. Oppenheim
MYCOBACTERIUM REFERENCE UNIT, Public Health Laboratory, Cardiff. *Director*, Dr T. Jenkins

MYCOLOGY REFERENCE LABORATORY, Public Health Laboratory, Bristol. *Director*, Dr D. Warnock; Public Health Laboratory, Leeds. *Director*, Prof. E. G. V. Evans
PARASITOLOGY REFERENCE LABORATORY, Hospital for Tropical Diseases, London. *Director*, Dr P. L. Chiodini
TOXOPLASMA REFERENCE LABORATORIES, Public Health Laboratory, Swansea. *Director*, D. H. M. Joynson; Public Health Laboratory, Tooting, London. *Director*, Prof. A. R. M. Coates

PHLS GROUPS OF LABORATORIES AND GROUP DIRECTORS
Anglia and North-East Thames, Dr Philippa M. B. White
Mid South, Dr S. A. Rousseau
Northern and Yorkshire, Dr N. F. Lightfoot
North-West, Dr P. Morgan-Capner
North-West Thames and Oxford, Dr A. G. Hellyar
South Thames, Prof. R. Y. Cartwright
South-West, Dr K. A. V. Cartwright
Trent, Dr P. J. Wilkinson
West Midlands, Dr R. E. Warren
Wales, Dr A. J. Howard

REGISTRAR OF PUBLIC LENDING RIGHT
Bayheath House, Prince Regent Street,
Stockton-on-Tees, TS18 1DF
Tel 01642-604699

Under the Public Lending Right system, in operation since 1983, payment is made from public funds to authors whose books are lent out from public libraries. Payment is made once a year and the amount each author receives is proportionate to the number of times (established from a sample) that each registered book has been lent out during the previous year.

The Registrar of PLR, who is appointed by the Secretary of State for National Heritage, compiles the register of authors and books. Only living authors resident in the UK or Germany are eligible to apply. (The term 'author' covers writers, illustrators, translators, and some editors/compilers.)

A payment of two pence was made in 1994–5 for each estimated loan of a registered book, up to a top limit of £6,000 for the books of any one registered author; the money for loans above this level is used to augment the remaining PLR payments. In February 1995, the sum of £4.337 million was made available for distribution to 19,388 registered authors and assignees as the annual payment of PLR.

The PLR Advisory Committee advises the Secretary of State for National Heritage and the Registrar of Public Lending Right. Its members are appointed by the Secretary of State.

Chairman of Advisory Committee, P. S. Ziegler, CVO
Registrar, Dr J. G. Parker

PUBLIC RECORD OFFICE
— *see* pages 339–40

PUBLIC TRUST OFFICE
Stewart House, 24 Kingsway, London WC2B 6JX
Tel 0171-269 7000
COURT FUNDS OFFICE, 22 Kingsway, London WC2B 6LE
Tel 0171-936 6000

The Public Trust Office became an executive agency of the Lord Chancellor's Department in 1994. The chief executive of the agency holds the statutory titles of Public Trustee and Accountant-General of the Supreme Court.

The Public Trustee is a trust corporation created to undertake the business of executorship and trusteeship; she can act as executor or administrator of the estate of a deceased person, or as trustee of a will or settlement. The Public Trustee is also responsible for the performance of all the administrative, but not the judicial, tasks required of the Court of Protection under Part VII of the Mental Health Act 1983, relating to the management and administration of the property and affairs of persons suffering from mental disorder. The Public Trustee also acts as Receiver when so directed by the Court, usually where there is no other person willing or able so to act.

The Accountant-General of the Supreme Court, through the Court Funds Office, is responsible for the investment and accounting of funds in court for persons under a disability, monies in court subject to litigation and statutory deposits.

Chief Executive (Public Trustee and Accountant-General), Ms J. C. Lomas
Assistant Public Trustee, H. N. Mather
Investment Manager, H. Stevenson
Chief Property Adviser, A. Nightingale

MENTAL HEALTH SECTOR
Head, Mrs H. M. Bratton
Receivership Activity, Miss G. Bradshaw
Protection Activity, P. L. Hales

TRUSTS AND FUNDS SECTOR
Head, F. J. Eddy
Court Funds Activity, I. S. Price
Trust Activity, M. Munt

ESTABLISHMENTS AND FINANCE SECTOR
Head, E. A. Bloomfield
Finance, M. Guntrip
Planning, Mrs N. M. Hunt

PUBLIC WORKS LOAN BOARD
— *see* National Investment and Loans Office

COMMISSION FOR RACIAL EQUALITY
Elliot House, 10–12 Allington Street, London SW1E 5EH
Tel 0171-828 7022

The Commission was established in 1977, under the Race Relations Act 1976, to work towards the elimination of discrimination and promote equality of opportunity and good relations between different racial groups.
Chairman, H. Ouseley
Deputy Chairs, R. Sondhi; A. Rose
Members, Dr M. C. K. Chan, MBE; A. Rose, OBE; R. Purkiss; Dr D. Neil; Ms M. Cunningham; Dr R. Chandran; Dr Z. Khan; M. Hastings; H. Harris; M. Jogee; Mrs Z. Manzoor; Dr J. Singh
Executive Director, D. Sharma

THE RADIO AUTHORITY
Holbrook House, 14 Great Queen Street, London WC2B 5DG
Tel 0171-430 2724

The Radio Authority was established in 1991 under the Broadcasting Act 1990. It is the regulator and licensing authority for all independent radio services. Members of the Authority are appointed by the Secretary of State for

National Heritage; senior executive staff are appointed by the Authority.
Chairman, Sir Peter Gibbings
Deputy Chairman, M. Moriarty, CB
Members, Ms J. Francis; M. Reupke; Lady Sheil; A. Reid
Chief Executive, A. Stoller
Deputy Chief Executive, D. Vick
Secretary to the Authority, J. Norrington

OFFICE OF THE RAIL REGULATOR
1 Waterhouse Square, 138–142 Holborn, London ECIN 2ST
Tel 0171-282 2000

The Office of the Rail Regulator was set up under the Railways Act 1993. It is headed by the Rail Regulator, who is independent of ministerial control. The Regulator's function is to protect the public interest. The main activities that enable him to do so are licensing train operators and approving the terms and conditions by which these operators gain access to the track, stations and depots in order to run services; and exercising responsibilities for competition law which he shares with the Director-General of Fair Trading. He also decides on the closure of railway facilities, and sponsors a network of Rail Users' Consultative Committees, which represent the interests of passengers.
Rail Regulator, J. A. Swift, QC
Director, Personnel, Finance and Administration, P. D. Murphy
Director, Network Regulation, C. J. F. Brown
Director, Passenger Services Regulation, J. A. Rhodes
Chief Legal Adviser, M. R. Brocklehurst

RECORD OFFICES

ADVISORY COUNCIL ON PUBLIC RECORDS
Secretariat: Trevelyan House, Great Peter Street, London SW1P 2BY
Tel 0171-210 8810

Council members are appointed by the Lord Chancellor, under the Public Records Act 1958, to advise him on matters concerning public records in general and, in particular, on those aspects of the work of the Public Record Office which affect members of the public who make use of it. The Council meets quarterly and produces an annual report which is published alongside the Report of the Keeper of Public Records as a House of Commons sessional paper.
Chairman, The Master of the Rolls
Assessor, Mrs S. Tyacke
Secretary, R. Wright

THE PUBLIC RECORD OFFICE
Ruskin Avenue, Kew, Richmond, Surrey TW9 4DU
Chancery Lane, London WC2A 1LR
Tel 0181-876 3444

The Public Record Office, originally established in 1838 under the Master of the Rolls, was placed under the direction of the Lord Chancellor in 1958. It became an executive agency in 1992. The Lord Chancellor appoints a Keeper of Public Records, whose duties are to co-ordinate and supervise the selection of records of government departments and the law courts for permanent preservation, to safeguard the records and to make them available to the public. There is a separate record office for Scotland (*see* page 340).

The Office holds records of central government dating from the *Domesday Book* (1086) to the present. Under the Public Records Act 1967 they are normally open to inspection when 30 years old, and are then available, without charge, in the reading rooms, Monday–Friday, 9.30–5. The museum at Chancery Lane is open Monday–Friday, 10–5 and the census rooms are open Monday–Saturday, 9.30–5.

Keeper of Public Records (G3), Mrs S. Tyacke
Director, Public Services Division (G5), Dr E. Hallam Smith
Director, Archival Services Division (G5), Dr N. G. Cox
Director, Corporate Services Division (G5), Dr D. Simpson

HOUSE OF LORDS RECORD OFFICE
House of Lords, London SW1A 0PW
Tel 0171-219 3074

Since 1497, the records of Parliament have been kept within the Palace of Westminster. They are in the custody of the Clerk of the Parliaments. In 1946 a record department was established to supervise their preservation and their availability to the public. The search room of the office is open to the public Monday–Friday, 9.30–5 (Tuesday to 8, by appointment).

Some three million documents are preserved, including Acts of Parliament from 1497, journals of the House of Lords from 1510, minutes and committee proceedings from 1610, and papers laid before Parliament from 1531. Amongst the records are the Petition of Right, the Death Warrant of Charles I, the Declaration of Breda, and the Bill of Rights. The House of Lords Record Office also has charge of the journals of the House of Commons (from 1547), and other surviving records of the Commons (from 1572), including documents relating to private bill legislation from 1818. Among other documents are the records of the Lord Great Chamberlain, the political papers of certain members of the two Houses, and documents relating to Parliament acquired on behalf of the nation. A permanent exhibition was established in the Royal Gallery in 1979.

Clerk of the Records (£40,117–£58,729), D. J. Johnson, FSA
Deputy Clerk of the Records (£31,258–£50,655), S. K. Ellison
Assistant Clerk of the Records (£18,611–£32,731), D. L. Prior

ROYAL COMMISSION ON HISTORICAL MANUSCRIPTS
Quality House, Quality Court, Chancery Lane, London WC2A 1HP
Tel 0171-242 1198

The Commission was set up by royal warrant in 1869 to enquire and report on collections of papers of value for the study of history which were in private hands. In 1959 a new warrant enlarged these terms of reference to include all historical records, wherever situated, outside the Public Records and gave it added responsibilities as a central co-ordinating body to promote, assist and advise on their proper preservation and storage. The Commission has published over 200 volumes of reports.

It also maintains the National Register of Archives, which contains over 38,000 unpublished lists and catalogues of manuscript collections describing the holdings of local record offices, national and university libraries, specialist repositories and others in the UK and overseas. The NRA can be searched using computerised indices which are available in the Commission's search room.

The Commission also administers the Manorial and Tithe Documents Rules on behalf of the Master of the Rolls.

Chairman, The Rt. Hon. Sir Thomas Bingham
Commissioners, The Lord Blake, FBA; Prof. S. F. C. Milsom, FBA; P. T. Cormack, FSA, MP; D. G. Vaisey, FSA; The Lord Egremont and Leconfield; Mrs J. Thirsk, CBE, ph.D., FBA;

Sir Matthew Farrer, GCVO; Miss B. Harvey, FBA, FSA; Sir John Sainty, KCB, FSA; Prof. R. H. Campbell, OBE, ph.D.; Very Revd H. E. C. Stapleton, FSA; Sir Keith Thomas, PBA; Mrs C. M. Short; The Earl of Scarbrough; Mrs A. Dundas-Bekker; G. E. Aylmer, D.phil, FBA; Mrs S. J. Davies, ph.D.

Secretary, C. J. Kitching, ph.D., FSA

SCOTTISH RECORDS ADVISORY COUNCIL
HM General Register House, Edinburgh EH1 3YY
Tel 0131-556 6585

The Council was established under the Public Records (Scotland) Act 1937. Its members are appointed by the Secretary of State for Scotland and it may submit proposals or make representations to the Secretary of State, the Lord Justice General or the Lord President of the Court of Session on questions relating to the public records of Scotland.

Chairman, Prof. M. Anne Crowther
Secretary, D. M. Abbott

SCOTTISH RECORD OFFICE
HM General Register House, Edinburgh EH1 3YY
Tel 0131-535 1314

The history of the national archives of Scotland can be traced back to the 13th century. The Scottish Record Office keeps the administrative records of pre-Union Scotland, the registers of central and local courts of law, the public registers of property rights and legal documents, and many collections of local and church records and private archives. Certain groups of records, mainly the modern records of government departments in Scotland, the Scottish railway records, the plans collection, and private archives of an industrial or commercial nature, are preserved in the branch repository at the West Register House in Charlotte Square. The search rooms in both buildings are open Monday–Friday, 9–4.45. A permanent exhibition at the West Register House and changing exhibitions at the General Register House are open to the public on weekdays, 10–4. The National Register of Archives (Scotland), which is a branch of the Scottish Record Office, is based in the West Register House.

The Scottish Record Office became an executive agency of the Scottish Office in 1993.

Keeper of the Records of Scotland, P. M. Cadell
Deputy Keeper, Dr P. D. Anderson

PUBLIC RECORD OFFICE (NORTHERN IRELAND)
66 Balmoral Avenue, Belfast BT9 6NY
Tel 01232-251318

The Public Record Office (Northern Ireland) is responsible for identifying and preserving Northern Ireland's archival heritage and making it available to the public. It is an executive agency of the Department of the Environment for Northern Ireland. The search room is open on weekdays, 9.15–4.15.

Chief Executive (G5), Dr A. P. Malcomson

CORPORATION OF LONDON RECORDS OFFICE
Guildhall, London EC2P 2EJ
Tel 0171-332 1251

The Corporation of London Records Office contains the municipal archives of the City of London which are regarded as the most complete collection of ancient municipal records in existence. The collection includes charters of William the Conqueror, Henry II, and later kings and queens to 1957; ancient custumals: Liber Horn,

Dunthorne, Custumarum, Ordinacionum, Memorandorum and Albus, Liber de Antiquis Legibus, and collections of Statutes; continuous series of judicial rolls and books from 1252 and Council minutes from 1275; records of the Old Bailey and Guildhall Sessions from 1603; financial records from the 16th century; the records of London Bridge from the 12th century; and numerous subsidiary series and miscellanea of historical interest. Readers' Room open Monday–Friday, 9.30–4.45.
Keeper of the City Records, The Town Clerk
City Archivist, J. R. Sewell
Deputy City Archivist, Mrs J. M. Bankes

RED DEER COMMISSION
Knowsley, 82 Fairfield Road, Inverness IV3 5LH
Tel 01463-231751

The Red Deer Commission has the general functions of furthering the conservation and control of red and sika deer in Scotland and of keeping under review all matters relating to roe deer. It has the statutory duty, with powers, to prevent damage to agriculture and forestry by red and sika deer. The Commission also has the power to advise in the interest of conservation any owner of land on questions relating to the carrying of stocks of red deer, sika deer and roe deer on that land, and to carry out research into matters of scientific importance relating to deer.
Chairman (part-time), P. Gordon-Duff-Pennington, OBE
Chief Executive and Secretary, A. Rinning
Technical Director, R. W. Youngson

RESEARCH COUNCILS
— see pages 707–11

REVIEW BODIES

The secretariat for these bodies is provided by the Office of Manpower Economics (*see* page 325)

ARMED FORCES PAY
The Review Body on Armed Forces Pay was appointed in 1971 to advise the Prime Minister on the pay and allowances of members of naval, military and air forces of the Crown and of any women's service administered by the Defence Council.
Chairman, G. M. Hourston
Members, C. M. Bolton; J. C. L. Cox, CBE; J. Crosby; Sir Gavin Laird; Air Chief Marshal Sir Roger Palin, KCB, OBE; Mrs D. Venables

DOCTORS' AND DENTISTS' REMUNERATION
The Review Body on Doctors' and Dentists' Remuneration was set up in 1971 to advise the Prime Minister on the remuneration of doctors and dentists taking any part in the National Health Service.
Chairman, C. B. Gough
Members, J. Benningsen; Ms T. Boyden; Mrs B. Brewer; Miss S. Field; M. Innes; Dr E. Nelson; D. Penton

NURSING STAFF, MIDWIVES, HEALTH VISITORS AND PROFESSIONS ALLIED TO MEDICINE
The Review Body for nursing staff, midwives, health visitors and professions allied to medicine was set up in 1983 to advise the Prime Minister on the remuneration of nursing staff, midwives and health visitors employed in the National Health Service; and also of physiotherapists, radiographers, remedial gymnasts, occupational therapists, orthoptists, chiropodists, dietitians and related grades employed in the National Health Service.
Chairman, Sir Michael Bett, CBE
Members, Mrs A. Dean; Mrs S. Gleig; L. Haddon; Ms R. Lea; Miss A. Mackie, OBE; Prof. Gillian Raab

SCHOOL TEACHERS
The School Teachers' Review Body (STRB) is a statutory body, set up under the School Teachers' Pay and Conditions Act 1991. It is required to examine and report on such matters relating to the statutory conditions of employment of school teachers in England and Wales as may be referred to it by the Secretary of State for Education. The STRB's reports are submitted to the Prime Minister and the Secretary of State and the latter is required to publish them.
Chairman, J. Gardiner
Members, Mrs B. Amey; Mrs J. Cuthbertson; Mrs E. Drummond; P. Halsey, CB, LVO; M. Harding; Mrs G. Rostron; Mrs A. Vinton

SENIOR SALARIES
A Top Salaries Review Body was set up in 1971 to advise the Prime Minister on the remuneration of the higher judiciary and other judicial appointments, senior civil servants, and senior officers of the armed forces. In 1993 its name was changed to the Senior Salaries Review Body, and its remit was officially extended to cover the pay, pensions and allowances of MPs, ministers and others whose pay is determined by a Ministerial and Other Salaries Order, and the allowances of peers. It is also required to reward performance where appropriate, and to take into account equal opportunities policy.
Chairman, Sir Michael Perry, CBE
Members, Prof. G. Bain; Mrs R. Day; G. M. Hourston; Sir Sydney Lipworth, QC; Miss P. Mann; Mrs Y. Newbold; M. Sheldon; Sir Anthony Wilson

ROYAL BOTANIC GARDEN EDINBURGH
Inverleith Row, Edinburgh EH3 5LR
Tel 0131-552 7171

The Royal Botanic Garden Edinburgh (RBGE) originated as the Physic Garden, established in 1670 beside the Palace of Holyroodhouse. Since 1986, RBGE has been administered by a Board of Trustees established under the National Heritage (Scotland) Act 1985. It receives an annual grant from the Scottish Office.

RBG Edinburgh is an international centre for scientific research on plant diversity, maintaining collections of living plants and reference resources, including a herbarium of some two million specimens of preserved plants. Other statutory functions of RBGE include the provision of education and information on botany and horticulture, and the provision of public access to the living plant collections.

The Garden moved to its present site at Inverleith, Edinburgh in 1821. There are also three specialist gardens: Younger Botanic Garden Benmore, near Dunoon, Argyllshire; Logan Botanic Garden, near Stranraer, Wigtownshire; and Dawyck Botanic Garden, near Stobo, Peeblesshire. Public opening hours: RBGE, daily (except Christmas Day and New Year's Day) November–

February 10–4; March–April and September–October 10–6; May–August 10–8; specialist gardens, 15 March–October 10–6. Admission free.
Chairman of the Board of Trustees, Prof. M. Wilkins, FRSE
Regius Keeper, Prof. D. S. Ingram, SC.D., FRSE
Deputy Keeper, Dr D. J. Mann

ROYAL BOTANIC GARDENS KEW
Richmond, Surrey TW9 3AB
Tel 0181-940 1171
Wakehurst Place, Ardingly, nr Haywards Heath,
W. Sussex RH17 6TN
Tel 01444-892701

The Royal Botanic Gardens (RBG) Kew were originally laid out as a private garden for Kew House for George III's mother, HRH Princess Augusta, in 1759. They were much enlarged in the 19th century, notably by the inclusion of the grounds of the former Richmond Lodge. In 1965 the garden at Wakehurst Place was acquired; it is owned by the National Trust and managed by RBG Kew. Under the National Heritage Act 1983 a Board of Trustees was set up to administer the Gardens which in 1984 became an independent body supported by a grant-in-aid from the Ministry of Agriculture, Fisheries and Food.

The functions of RBG Kew are to carry out research into plant sciences, to disseminate knowledge about plants and to provide the public with the opportunity to gain knowledge and enjoyment from the Gardens' collections. There are extensive national reference collections of living and preserved plants and a comprehensive library and archive. The main emphasis is on plant conservation and biodiversity.

Open daily (except Christmas Day and New Year's Day) from 9.30 a.m. The closing hour varies from 4 p.m. in midwinter to 6 p.m. on weekdays and 7.30 p.m. on Sundays and Bank Holidays in mid-summer. Admission (1995), £4.00. Concessionary schemes available. Glasshouses, 9.30–4.30 (winter); 9.30–5.30 (summer). No dogs except guide-dogs for the blind.

BOARD OF TRUSTEES
Chairman, R. A. E. Herbert
Members, R. P. Bauman; The Viscount Blakenham;
   C. D. Brickell, CBE; Prof. W. G. Chaloner, FRS; Sir Philip
   M. Dowson, CBE, PRA; Mrs A. Lennox-Boyd;
   Prof. R. May, FRS; J. Pettifer; The Lady Renfrew of
   Kaimsthorn, PH.D.; The Earl of Selbourne, KBE, FRS
   (*Queen's Trustee*); Mrs V. R. Wakefield
Director, Prof. Sir Ghillean Prance, FRS

ROYAL COMMISSION FOR THE EXHIBITION OF 1851
Sherfield Building, Imperial College of Science, Technology and Medicine, London SW7 2AZ
Tel 0171-594 8790

The Royal Commission was incorporated by supplemental charter as a permanent Commission after winding up the affairs of the Great Exhibition of 1851. Its object is to promote scientific and artistic education by means of funds derived from its Kensington estate, purchased with the surplus left over from the Great Exhibition.
President, HRH The Duke of Edinburgh, KG, KT, PC
Chairman, Board of Management, Sir Denis Rooke, CBE, FRS, FEng.
Secretary to Commissioners, J. P. W. Middleton, CB

THE ROYAL MINT
Llantrisant, nr Pontyclun, Mid Glamorgan CF7 8YT
Tel 01443-222111

The prime responsibility of the Royal Mint is the provision of United Kingdom coinage, but it actively competes in world markets for a share of the available circulating coin business and, based on the last ten years, two-thirds of the 15,000 tonnes of coins produced annually is exported to more than 100 countries. The Mint also manufactures special proof and uncirculated quality coins in gold, silver and other metals; military and civil decorations and medals; commemorative and prize medals; and royal and official seals.

The Royal Mint became an executive agency of the Treasury in 1990.
Master of the Mint, The Chancellor of the Exchequer (ex officio)
Deputy Master and Comptroller, R. de L. Holmes

ROYAL NATIONAL THEATRE BOARD
South Bank, London, SE1 9PX
Tel 0171-928 2033

The chairman and members of the Board of the Royal National Theatre are appointed by the Secretary of State for National Heritage.
Chairman, Sir Christopher Hogg
Members, The Hon. P. Benson; The Hon. Lady Cazalet;
   M. Codron, CBE; Lady Greenbury; Ms S. Hall; S. Lipton;
   Sir Derek Mitchell, KCB, CVO; D. Nandy; M. Oliver; The
   Rt. Hon. Sir Michael Palliser, GCMG; L. Sieff, OBE; T.
   Stoppard, CBE; S. Yassukovich, CBE
Company Secretary and Head of Finance, A. Blackstock
Board and Committee Secretary, M. McGregor

RURAL DEVELOPMENT COMMISSION
141 Castle Street, Salisbury, Wilts. SP1 3TP
Tel 01722-336255

The Rural Development Commission is the government agency set up to assist the economic and social development of the English countryside. It ensures that the needs of rural communities and businesses are taken into account when government policy is made. It has a local advisory role (particularly on planning matters), provides support for voluntary activity and assists selected activities, such as housing, transport and village shops.
Chairman, The Lord Shuttleworth
Deputy Chairman, R. Thompson
Chief Executive, R. Butt

SCOTT INQUIRY
— *see* pages 318–19

SCOTTISH COURTS ADMINISTRATION
— *see* page 372

SCOTTISH ENTERPRISE
120 Bothwell Street, Glasgow G2 7JP
Tel 0141-248 2700

In 1991 Scottish Enterprise took over the economic development and environmental improvement functions of the Scottish Development Agency and the training functions of the Training Agency in lowland Scotland. Its remit is to further the development of Scotland's economy, to enhance the skills of the Scottish workforce, to promote Scotland's international competitiveness and to improve the environment. Many of its functions are contracted out to a network of local enterprise companies. Through Locate in Scotland (*see* page 347), Scottish Enterprise is also concerned with attracting firms to Scotland.
Chairman, Prof. D. MacKay
Chief Executive, C. Beveridge, CBE

SCOTTISH HOMES
Thistle House, 91 Haymarket Terrace, Edinburgh EH12 5HE
Tel 0131-313 0044

Scottish Homes, the national housing agency for Scotland, aims to improve the quality and variety of housing available in Scotland by working in partnership with the public and private sectors. The agency is a major funder of new and improved housing provided by housing associations and private developers. It is currently transferring its own 40,000 rented houses to alternative landlords. It is also involved in housing research and in piloting innovative housing solutions. Board members are appointed by the Secretary of State for Scotland.
Chairman, Sir James Mellon
Chief Executive, P. McKinlay

SCOTTISH NATURAL HERITAGE
12 Hope Terrace, Edinburgh EH9 2AS
Tel 0131-447 4784

Scottish Natural Heritage came into existence in 1992 under the Natural Heritage (Scotland) Act 1991. It provides advice on nature conservation to all those whose activities affect wildlife, landforms and features of geological interest in Scotland, and seeks to develop and improve facilities for the enjoyment of the Scottish countryside.
Chairman, M. Magnusson, KBE
Chief Executive, R. Crofts
Chief Scientific Adviser, M. B. Usher
Director of Policy, J. Thomson
Director of Communications, D. Campbell
Director of Resources, L. Montgomery

SCOTTISH OFFICE

The Secretary of State for Scotland is responsible in Scotland for a wide range of statutory functions which in England and Wales are the responsibility of a number of departmental ministers. He also works closely with ministers in charge of Great Britain departments on topics of special significance to Scotland within their fields of responsibility. His statutory functions are administered by five main departments which, together with a central services department, are collectively known as the Scottish Office. The Scottish Office is to be restructured in October 1995, when five new departments will be created: the Scottish Office Agriculture, Environment and Fisheries Department; the Scottish Office Development Department; the Scottish Office Education and Industry Department; the Scottish Office Department of Health; and the Scottish Office Home Department.

In addition there are a number of other Scottish departments for which the Secretary of State has some degree of responsibility; these include the Scottish Courts Administration, the General Register Office, the Scottish Record Office and the Department of the Registers of Scotland. The Secretary of State also bears ministerial responsibility for the activities in Scotland of several statutory bodies, such as the Forestry Commission, whose functions extend throughout Great Britain.

Dover House, Whitehall, London, SW1A 2AU
Tel 0171-270 3000
Secretary of State for Scotland, The Rt. Hon. Michael Forsyth, MP
　Private Secretary (G5), M. B. Foulis
　Special Adviser, G. Warner
Minister of State, Lord James Douglas-Hamilton, MP (*Home Affairs and Health*)
　Private Secretary, Ms J. Macbeth
Parliamentary Under-Secretaries of State, Raymond Robertson, MP (*Education, Housing and Fisheries*); George Kynoch, MP (*Industry and Local Government*); The Earl of Lindsay (*Agriculture, Forestry and the Environment*)
　Private Secretaries, Ms S. J. Morrell; D. McLaren; D. Milne
Parliamentary Clerk, Mrs L. J. Stirling
Permanent Under-Secretary of State (G1), Sir Russell Hillhouse, KCB
　Private Secretary, Miss S. C. Gartside

LIAISON DIVISION
Assistant Secretary (G5), E. W. Ferguson

MANAGEMENT GROUP SUPPORT STAFF
Principal (G7), M. Grant

St Andrew's House, Edinburgh EH1 3DG
Tel 0131-556 8400

CENTRAL SERVICES
Grade 2, G. R. Wilson, CB

PERSONNEL GROUP
16 Waterloo Place Edinburgh, EH1 3DN
Tel 0131-556 8400
Principal Establishment Officer (G3), C. C. MacDonald
Assistant Secretaries (G5), G. D. Calder; W. R. J. McQueen

ADMINISTRATIVE SERVICES
James Craig Walk, Edinburgh EH1 3BA
Tel 0131-556 8400
Director of Administrative Services (G3), R. S. B. Gordon
Head of Information Technology (G5), A. M. Brown
Director of Purchasing and Supplies (G5), D. Ramsay
Head of IT Services (G6), I. W. Goodwin
Director of Efficiency Unit (G6), I. McEwan
Director of Telecommunications (G6), K. Henderson, OBE
Chief Estates Officer (G6), R. I. K. White, FRICS

FINANCE DIVISION
New St Andrew's House, Edinburgh EH1 3TG
Tel 0131-556 8400

Principal Finance Officer (G3), Miss E. A Mackay
Assistant Secretaries (G5), Dr P. S. Collings; D. Crawley; Ms
   I. M. Low; D. G. N. Reid; W. T. Tait
Director of Financial Systems Unit (G6), R. Smith
Head of Accountancy Services Unit (G6), I. M. Smith
Assistant Director of Finance Strategy (G6), I. A. McLeod

SOLICITOR'S OFFICE
For the Scottish departments and certain UK services,
including HM Treasury, in Scotland
Solicitor (G2), R. Brodie, CB
Deputy Solicitor (G3), N. W. Boe
Divisional Solicitors (G4), J. L. Jamieson; (G5), K. F. Barclay;
   R. Bland *(seconded to Scottish Law Commission)*;
   G. C. Duke; I. H. Harvie; R. M. Henderson;
   H. F. Macdiarmid; J. G. S. Maclean; N. Raven; Mrs
   L. A. Wallace

SCOTTISH OFFICE INFORMATION DIRECTORATE
For the Scottish departments and certain UK services
Director (G5), Ms E. S. B. Drummond
Deputy Director (G6), W. A. McNeill

SCOTTISH OFFICE AGRICULTURE AND FISHERIES DEPARTMENT

Pentland House, 47 Robb's Loan, Edinburgh EH14 1TY
Tel 0131-556 8400

Secretary (G2), A. M. Russell
Under-Secretary (G3), T. A. Cameron
Fisheries Secretary (G3), I. W. Gordon
Assistant Secretaries (G5), D. R. Dickson; J. Duffy;
   I. W. Gordon; R. A. Grant; C. K. McIntosh;
   A. J. Matheson; K. W. Moore; A. J. Rushworth;
   I. M. Whitelaw
Chief Agricultural Officer (G4), W. A. Macgregor
Deputy Chief Agricultural Officer (G5), J. I. Woodrow
Assistant Chief Agricultural Officers (G6), J. A. Hardie;
   J. G. Muir; A. Robb; A. J. Robertson
Chief Agricultural Economist (G6), J. R. Wildgoose, D.phil.
Chief Food and Dairy Officer (G7), D. J. MacDonald
Chief Surveyor (G6), N. Taylor, FRICS
Scientific Adviser (G5), T. W. Hegarty, ph.D.
Senior Principal Scientific Officers (G6), Dr D. Jenkinson; Mrs
   L. A. D. Turl

FISHERIES RESEARCH SERVICES
Marine Laboratory, PO Box 101, Victoria Road, Torry,
Aberdeen AB9 8DB
Tel 01224-876544

Director of Fisheries Research for Scotland (G4),
   Prof. A. D. Hawkins, ph.D., FRSE
Deputy Director (G5), J. Davies

Freshwater Fisheries Laboratory
Faskally, Pitlochry, Perthshire PH16 5LB
Tel 01796-472060

Senior Principal Scientific Officers (G6), R. G. J. Shelton,
   ph.D.; J. E. Thorpe, ph.D.
Inspector of Salmon and Freshwater Fisheries for Scotland (G7),
   R. B. Williamson, OBE

EXECUTIVE AGENCIES
INTERVENTION BOARD
— *see* page 319

SCOTTISH AGRICULTURAL SCIENCE AGENCY
East Craigs, Edinburgh EH12 8NJ
Tel 0131-556 8400

The Agency provides scientific information and advice on
agricultural and horticultural crops and the environment,
and has various statutory and regulatory functions.
Director (G5), Dr R. K. M. Hay
Deputy Director (G6), S. R. Cooper
Senior Principal Scientific Officers (G6), A. D. Ruthven;
   W. J. Rennie

SCOTTISH FISHERIES PROTECTION AGENCY
Pentland House, 47 Robb's Loan, Edinburgh EH14 1TW
Tel 0131-556 8400

The Agency enforces fisheries law and regulations in
Scottish waters and ports.
Chief Executive (G5), Capt. P. Du Vivier, RN
Director of Policy and Resources (G6), J. B. Roddin
Director of Operations (G6), R. J. Walker
Marine Superintendent, Capt. R. M. Mill-Irving

SCOTTISH OFFICE EDUCATION DEPARTMENT

New St Andrew's House, Edinburgh EH1 3TG
Tel 0131-556 8400

Secretary (G2), G. R. Wilson, CB
Under-Secretaries (G3), W. A. P. Weatherston, CB;
   J. S. B. Martin
Assistant Secretaries (G5), D. S. Henderson; R. D. Jackson;
   T. J. Kelly; G. McHugh; Miss M. MacLean; Mrs
   V. MacNiven; Mrs N. S. Munro
Chief Statistician (G5), G. C. Jones

HM INSPECTORS OF SCHOOLS
Senior Chief Inspector (G3), T. N. Gallacher
Deputy Senior Chief Inspectors (G4), W. T. Beveridge;
   D. A. Osler
Chief Inspectors (G5), J. Boyes; G. H. C. Donaldson; Miss
   K. M. Fairweather; G. P. D. Gordon; D. E. Kelso;
   J. J. McDonald; A. S. McGlynn; M. Roebuck;
   H. M. Stalker; R. M. S. Tuck
There are 90 Grade 6 Inspectors.

EXECUTIVE AGENCY
STUDENT AWARDS AGENCY FOR SCOTLAND
Gyleview House, 3 Redheughs Rigg, Edinburgh EH12 9HH
Tel 0131-244 5715
Chief Executive, K. MacRae

SCOTTISH OFFICE ENVIRONMENT DEPARTMENT

New St Andrew's House, Edinburgh EH1 3TG
Tel 0131-556 8400
Secretary (G2), H. H. Mills, CB
Under-Secretaries (G3), J. S. Graham; S. F. Hampson;
   D. F. Middleton *(acting)*
Assistant Secretaries (G5), M. T. Affolter; J. A. Ewing; Dr
   J. M. Francis; J. W. L. Lonie; J. N. Randall; E. C. Reavley;
   J. A. Rennie

PROFESSIONAL STAFF
Chief Engineer (G3), A. C. Paton
Deputy Chief Engineer (G5), T. D. Macdonald
Director of Building and Chief Architect (G3), J. E. Gibbons,
   ph.D., FSA scot.
Deputy Director of Building and Deputy Chief Architect (G5),
   C. Gray
Deputy Director (G6), A. J. Wyllie
Chief Planner (G4), A. Mackenzie
Deputy Chief Planner (G5), D. R. Dare
HM Chief Industrial Pollution Inspector (G5), I. W. W. Wright

LOCAL GOVERNMENT DIVISION
Victoria Quay, Edinburgh EH6 6QQ
Tel 0131-556 8400

Assistant Secretary (G5), G. M. D. Thomson

LOCAL GOVERNMENT FINANCE GROUP
New St Andrew's House, Edinburgh EH1 3TB
Tel 0131-556 8400

Assistant Secretaries (G5), A. G. Beattie; K. W. McKay

INQUIRY REPORTERS
Robert Stevenson House, 2 Greenside Lane, Edinburgh
EH1 3AG
Tel 0131-244 5680

Chief Reporter (G3), Miss G. Pain
Deputy Chief Reporter (G5), R. M. Hickman

EXECUTIVE AGENCY
HISTORIC SCOTLAND
Longmore House, Salisbury Place, Edinburgh EH9 1SH
Tel 0131-668 8600

The agency's role is to protect Scotland's historic monuments, buildings and lands, and to promote public understanding and enjoyment of them.
Chief Executive (G3), G. N. Munro
Directors (G5), F. J. Lawrie; I. Maxwell; B. Naylor; *(G6)*,
  S. Rosie
Chief Inspector of Ancient Monuments, Dr D. J. Breeze
Chief Inspector, Building Division, J. R. Hume

SCOTTISH OFFICE HOME AND HEALTH DEPARTMENT
St Andrew's House, Edinburgh EH1 3DG
Tel 0131-556 8400

Secretary (G2), J. Hamill
Under-Secretaries (G3), D. Belfall; N. G. Campbell;
  D. J. Essery; Mrs G. M. Stewart
Assistant Secretaries (G5), C. Baxter; Mrs M. H. Brannan;
  J. T. Brown; Mrs M. B. Gunn; C. M. A. Lugton;
  R. S. T. MacEwen; C. K. McIntosh; D. Macniven, TD;
  R. H. Scott

NATIONAL HEALTH SERVICE IN SCOTLAND
MANAGEMENT EXECUTIVE
Chief Executive, G. Scaife
Director of Purchasing (G4), Dr K. J. Woods
Director of NHS Trusts (G4), P. Wilson
Director of Strategic Development (G6), I. Snedden
Director of Finance (G5), S. Featherstone
Director of Corporate Affairs (G5), Dr D. Steel
Director of Information Services, NHS, C. B. Knox
Director of Human Resources (G5), M. Sibbald
Director of Primary Care (G5), Mrs A. Robson
Director of Estates (G6), H. R. McCallum

MEDICAL SERVICES
Chief Medical Officer (G2), Prof. R. E. Kendell, CBE, MD
Deputy Chief Medical Officer (G3), Dr A. B. Young, FRCPE
Principal Medical Officers, Dr J. V. Basson; Dr C. F. Fleming;
  Dr Margaret Hennigan; Dr Rosalind Skinner; Dr
  Elizabeth Sowler
Senior Medical Officers, R. E. G. Aitken, TD; Dr Angela
  Anderson; I. R. Bashford; P. W. Brooks; Dr
  K. Brotherston; S. Capewell; Dr D. J. Ewing;
  Dr A. Findlay; Dr D. Jolliffe; Ms E. Keel; Dr Patricia
  Madden; Dr R. Simmons; Dr O. A. Thores
Chief Scientist, Prof. I. A. D. Bouchier, CBE, FRCP
Chief Dental Officer, J. R. Wild
Deputy Chief Dental Officer, M. Yewe-Dyer

Regional Dental Officers, K. J. McKenzie; M. G. Platt; Miss
  A. J. Power; G. A. Reid
Chief Nursing Officer, Miss A. Jarvie
Chief Pharmacist (G5), W. Scott
Chief Research Officer, Dr C. P. A. Levein
Senior Principal Research Officers (G6), Mrs A. Millar; Dr
  Jacqueline Tombs

SOCIAL WORK SERVICES GROUP
43 Jeffrey Street, Edinburgh EH1 1DN
Tel 0131-556 8400

Under Secretary (G3), N. G. Campbell
Assistant Secretaries (G5), G. A. Anderson; Ms L. J. Clare;
  J. W. Sinclair
Chief Inspector of Social Work Services, A. Skinner
Assistant Chief Inspectors, Mrs H. Dempster; Ms M. L. Hunt;
  F. A. O'Leary; D. Pia; I. C. Robertson; A. Sabine

OTHER APPOINTMENTS
HM Chief Inspector of Constabulary, J. Boyd, CBE, QPM
HM Chief Inspector of Prisons, C. Fairweather, OBE
Commandant, Scottish Police College, H. I. Watson, QPM
HM Chief Inspector of Fire Services, N. Morrison
Commandant, Scottish Fire Service Training School, D. Grant,
  QFSM
Secretary, Clinical Resources and Audit Group, NHS,
  W. J. Farquhar

MENTAL WELFARE COMMISSION FOR SCOTLAND
25 Drumsheugh Gardens, Edinburgh EH3 7NS
Tel 0131-225 7034

Chairman, Sheriff H. J. Aronson, QC
Commissioners, Mrs A. Baxter; Mrs N. Bennie; P. H. Brodie;
  Mrs F. Cotier; R. G. Davis; Ms A. M. Green; Mrs
  M. Jeffcoat; Dr M. Livingston; Dr D. McCall-Smith; Dr
  M. McCreadie; D. J. Macdonald; J. Murray; Ms
  L. M. Noble; I. Ross; J. G. Sutherland
Medical Commissioners, J. A. T. Dyer; A. Jacques
Social Work Commissioner, C. E. McGregor
Secretary, D. Hogg

COUNSEL TO THE SECRETARY OF STATE FOR SCOTLAND UNDER THE PRIVATE LEGISLATION PROCEDURE (SCOTLAND) ACT 1936
50 Frederick Street, Edinburgh EH2 1EX
Tel 0131-226 6499

Senior Counsel, G. S. Douglas, QC
Junior Counsel, N. M. P. Morrison

NATIONAL HEALTH SERVICE, SCOTLAND
HEALTH BOARDS

ARGYLL AND CLYDE, Ross House, Hawkhead Road,
  Paisley. *Chairman*, R. R. Reid; *General Manager*,
  I. C. Smith
AYRSHIRE AND ARRAN, PO Box 13, Seafield House,
  Doonfoot Road, Ayr. *Chairman*, J. W. G. Donaldson, CBE;
  General Manager, J. M. Eckford, OBE
BORDERS, Huntlyburn, Melrose, Roxburghshire. *Chairman*,
  D. A. C. Kilshaw; *General Manager*, D. A. Peters, OBE
DUMFRIES AND GALLOWAY, Nithbank, Dumfries. *Chairman*,
  J. A. M. McIntyre, CBE; *General Manager*, D. Banks
FIFE, Springfield House, Cupar. *Chairman*, R. Baker, OBE;
  General Manager, Miss P. Frost
FORTH VALLEY, 33 Spittal Street, Stirling. *Chairman*,
  Mrs J. D. Isbister; *General Manager*, D. Hird
GRAMPIAN, Summerfield House, 2 Eday Road, Aberdeen.
  Chairman, C. MacLeod, CBE; *General Manager*,
  F. E. L. Hartnett, OBE

GREATER GLASGOW, 112 Ingram Street, Glasgow. *Chairman*, Sir Robert Calderwood; *General Manager* (*acting*), T. A. Divers
HIGHLAND, Reay House, 17 Old Edinburgh Road, Inverness. *Chairman*, J. D. M. Robertson, CBE; *General Manager*, Dr G. V. Stone
LANARKSHIRE, 14 Beckford Street, Hamilton, Lanarkshire. *Chairman*, I. Livingstone, OBE; *General Manager*, Prof. F. Clark, CBE
LOTHIAN, 148 The Pleasance, Edinburgh. *Chairman*, Dr J. W. Baynham, CBE; *General Manager*, J. Lusby
ORKNEY, Balfour Hospital, New Scapa Road, Kirkwall, Orkney. *Chairman*, J. Leslie; *General Manager*, E. Jackson
SHETLAND, Brevik House, South Road, Lerwick. *Chairman*, Mrs F. Grains, OBE; *General Manager*, B. J. Atherton
TAYSIDE, PO Box 75, Vernonholme, Riverside Drive, Dundee. *Chairman*, J. C. MacFarlane, OBE; *General Manager*, Miss L. Barrie
WESTERN ISLES, 37 South Beach Street, Stornoway, Isle of Lewis. *Chairman*, A. Matheson; *General Manager*, R. Mullan

HEALTH EDUCATION BOARD FOR SCOTLAND
Woodburn House, Canaan Lane, Edinburgh EH10 4SG
Tel 0131-447 8044

Chairman, D. Campbell
General Manager, Dr A. Tannahill

STATE HOSPITAL
Carstairs Junction, Lanark ML11 8RP
Tel 01555-840293

Chairman, P. Hamilton-Grierson
General Manager, R. Manson

COMMON SERVICES AGENCY
Trinity Park House, South Trinity Road, Edinburgh EH5 3SE
Tel 0131-552 6255

Chairman, G. Scaife
General Manager (*acting*), Dr F. Gibb

EXECUTIVE AGENCIES

REGISTERS OF SCOTLAND
— *see* page 320

SCOTTISH OFFICE PENSIONS AGENCY
St Margaret's House, 151 London Road, Edinburgh EH8 7TG
Tel 0131-244 3217

The Agency is responsible for the pension arrangements of some 300,000 people, mainly NHS and teaching services employees and pensioners.
Chief Executive, N. MacLeod
Directors (*G7*), G. Mowat (*Policy*); A. M. Small (*Operations*); J. Edgar (*Resources and Customer Services*)

SCOTTISH PRISON SERVICE
Calton House, 5 Redheughs Rigg, Edinburgh EH12 9HW
Tel 0131-244 8745

Chief Executive of Scottish Prison Service (*G3*), E. W. Frizzell
Director of Custody (*G4*), P. Withers
Director, Human Resources (*G5*), J. D. Gallagher
Director, Finance and Information Systems (*G5*), W. Pretswell
Director, Strategy and Corporate Affairs (*G5*), D. A. Stewart
Deputy Director, Regime Services and Supplies (*G6*), N. Harvey
Deputy Director, Estates and Buildings (*G6*), D. D. Sutherland
Area Director, South and West (*G5*), J. Pearce
Area Director, North and East (*G5*), P. Russell
Governor, Scottish Prison Service College, vacant

PRISONS
ABERDEEN, Craiginches, Aberdeen AB9 2HN. *Governor*, W. A. R. Rattray
BARLINNIE, Barlinnie, Glasgow G33 2QX. *Governor*, R. L. Houchain
CASTLE HUNTLY YOUNG OFFENDERS INSTITUTION, Castle Huntly, Longforgan, nr Dundee DD2 5HL. *Governor*, K. Rennie
CORNTON VALE, Cornton Road, Stirling FK9 5NY. *Governor*, R. R. H. Glen
DUMFRIES YOUNG OFFENDERS INSTITUTION, Terregles Street, Dumfries DG2 9AX. *Governor*, G. Taylor
DUNGAVEL, Dungavel House, Strathaven, Lanarkshire ML10 6RF. *Governor*, Ms M. Wood
EDINBURGH, 33 Stenhouse Road, Edinburgh EH1 3LN. *Governor*, J. Durno
FRIARTON, Friarton, Perth PH2 8DW. *Governor*, E. A. Gordon
GLENOCHIL PRISON AND YOUNG OFFENDERS INSTITUTION, King O'Muir Road, Tullibody, Clackmannanshire FK10 3AD. *Governor*, L. McBain
GREENOCK, Gateside, Greenock PA16 9AH. *Governor*, D. E. Gunn
INVERNESS, Porterfield, Inverness IV2 3HH. *Governor*, W. M. Weir
LONGRIGGEND REMAND INSTITUTION, Longriggend, nr Airdrie, Lanarkshire ML6 7TL. *Governor*, A. F. King
LOW MOSS, Low Moss, Bishopbriggs, Glasgow G64 2QB. *Governor*, W. Middleton
NORANSIDE, Noranside, Fern, by Forfar, Angus DD8 3QY. *Governor*, E. Brownsmith
PENNINGHAME, Penninghame, Newton Stewart DG8 6RG. *Governor*, H. Ross
PERTH, 3 Edinburgh Road, Perth PH2 8AT. *Governor*, M. Duffy
PETERHEAD, Salthouse Head, Peterhead, Aberdeenshire AB4 6YY. *Governor*, A. P. Spencer
POLMONT YOUNG OFFENDERS INSTITUTION, Brightons, Falkirk, Stirlingshire FK2 0AB. *Governor*, W. McKinlay
SHOTTS, Shotts ML7 4LF. *Governor*, G. M. Shearer, OBE
SHOTTS ALTERNATIVE UNIT, Shotts ML7 4LF. *Governor*, A. McVicar
SHOTTS NATIONAL INDUCTION UNIT, Shotts ML7 4LE. *Governor*, Ms S. Brookes

SCOTTISH RECORD OFFICE
— *see* page 340

SCOTTISH OFFICE INDUSTRY DEPARTMENT
New St Andrew's House, Edinburgh EH1 3TG
Tel 0131-556 8400

Secretary (*G2*), vacant
Under-Secretaries (*G3*), J. W. Elvidge; E. J. Weeple
Assistant Secretaries (*G5*), D. A. Brew; A. W. Fraser; I. F. Gray; D. Hart; P. Hetherington; R. N. Irvine; Mrs R. Menlowe; R. Tait; G. M. D. Thomson
Senior Economic Advisers (*G5*), Dr J. A. Rigg; C. L. Wood

NATIONAL ROADS DIRECTORATE
New St Andrews's House, Edinburgh EH1 3TG
Tel 0131-556 8400

Director of Roads (*G3*), J. Innes
Deputy Chief Engineer (*Roads*) (*G5*), J. A. Howison
Deputy Chief Engineer (*Bridges*) (*G5*), B. MacKenzie

INDUSTRIAL EXPANSION
Alhambra House, 45 Waterloo Street, Glasgow G2 6AT
Tel 0141-248 2855

Under-Secretary (*G3*), G. Robson
Industrial Adviser, Dr C. K. Benington
Scientific Adviser, I. McGhee

Assistant Secretaries (G5), M. T. S. Batho; W. Malone; Ms
J. Morgan

LOCATE IN SCOTLAND
120 Bothwell Street, Glasgow G2 7JP
Tel 0141-248 2700

Director (G4), M. Togneri

SCOTTISH TRADE INTERNATIONAL
120 Bothwell Street, Glasgow G2 7JP
Tel 0141-248 2700

Director, D. Taylor

GENERAL REGISTER OFFICE
New Register House, Edinburgh EH1 3YT
Tel 0131-334 0380

The General Register Office for Scotland is an associated
department of the Scottish Office. It is the office of the
Registrar-General for Scotland, who has responsibility for
civil registration and the taking of censuses in Scotland and
has in his custody the following records: the statutory
registers of births, deaths, still births, adoptions, marriages
and divorces; the old parish registers (recording births,
deaths and marriages, etc., before civil registration began in
1855); and records of censuses of the population in Scotland. Hours of public access: Monday–Friday 9–4.30.
Registrar-General (G4), J. Meldrum
Deputy Registrar-General (G5), B. V. Philp
Senior Principal (G6), D. A. Orr
Principals (G7), D. B. L. Brownlee; R. C. Lawson;
F. D. Garvie
Statisticians (G7), J. Arrundale; G. W. L. Jackson;
F. G. Thomas

SCOTTISH PRISONS COMPLAINTS
COMMISSION
Government Buildings, Broomhouse Drive, Edinburgh
EH11 3XD
Tel 0131-244 8423

The Commission was established in December 1994. It is
an independent body to which prisoners in Scottish prisons
can make application in relation to any matter where they
have failed to obtain satisfaction from the Prison Service's
internal grievance procedures. Clinical judgments made
by medical officers, matters which are the subject of legal
proceedings and matters relating to sentence, conviction
and parole decision-making are excluded from the Commission's jurisdiction.
Commissioner, Dr J. McManus
Deputy Commissioner, A. Quinn

SEA FISH INDUSTRY AUTHORITY
18 Logie Mill, Logie Green Road, Edinburgh EH7 4HG
Tel 0131-558 3331

Established under the Fisheries Act 1981, the Authority is
required to promote the efficiency of the sea fish industry.
It carries out research relating to the industry and gives
advice on related matters. It provides training, promotes
the marketing, consumption and export of sea fish and sea
fish products, and may provide financial assistance for the
improvement of fishing vessels in respect of essential safety
equipment.
Chairman, B. Skipper, CBE
Chief Executive, P. D. Chaplin

THE SECURITY SERVICE COMMISSIONER
c/o The Home Office, 50 Queen Anne's Gate,
London SW1H 9AT

The Commissioner is appointed by the Prime Minister.
He keeps under review the issue of warrants by the
Home Secretary under the Security Service Act 1989,
and is required to help the Security Service Tribunal by
investigating complaints which allege interference with
property and by offering all such assistance in discharging its functions as it may require. He is also
required to submit an annual report on the discharge of
his functions to the Prime Minister.
Commissioner, The Rt. Hon. Lord Justice Stuart-Smith

SECURITY SERVICE TRIBUNAL
PO Box 18, London SE1 0TZ

The Security Service Act 1989 established a tribunal of
three to five senior members of the legal profession,
independent of the Government and appointed by The
Queen, to investigate complaints from any person about
anything which they believe the Security Service has done
to them or to their property.
President, The Rt. Hon. Lord Justice Simon Brown
Vice-President, Sheriff J. McInnes, QC
Member, Sir Richard Gaskell

SERIOUS FRAUD OFFICE
Elm House, 10–16 Elm Street, London, WC1X 0BJ
Tel 0171-239 7272

The Serious Fraud Office is an autonomous department
under the superintendence of the Attorney-General. Its
remit is to investigate and prosecute serious and complex
fraud. (Other fraud cases are currently handled by the fraud
investigation unit of the Crown Prosecution Service.) The
scope of its powers covers England, Wales and Northern
Ireland. The staff includes lawyers, accountants and other
support staff; investigating teams work closely with the
police.
Director, G. Staple
Deputy Director, J. Knox

DEPARTMENT OF SOCIAL SECURITY
Richmond House, 79 Whitehall, London, SW1A 2NS
Tel 0171-210 3000

The Department of Social Security is responsible for the
payment of benefits and the collection of contributions
under the National Insurance and Industrial Injuries
schemes, and for the payment of child benefit, one-parent
benefit, Income Support and Family Credit. It administers
the Social Fund, and is responsible for assessing the means
of applicants for legal aid. It is also responsible for the
payment of war pensions.
Secretary of State for Social Security, The Rt. Hon. Peter
Lilley, MP
Private Secretary, S. Czerniawski
Special Adviser, P. Barnes
Parliamentary Private Secretary, P. Merchant, MP

Minister of State, Alistair Burt, MP (*Social Security and Disabled People*)
  Private Secretary, G. Tempest-Hay
Minister of State, The Lord Mackay of Ardbrecknish
  Private Secretary, Ms C. Payne
Parliamentary Under-Secretaries of State, Roger Evans, MP; Andrew Mitchell, MP; Oliver Heald, MP
  Private Secretaries, M. Baldeck; T. Saunders; Ms L. Linaker
  Parliamentary Private Secretary, Mrs J. Lait, MP
Permanent Secretary (G1), Mrs A. E. Bowtell, CB
  Private Secretary, Ms L. Makinson

RESOURCE MANAGEMENT AND PLANNING GROUP
Deputy Secretary (G2), J. Tross

CORPORATE STRATEGY AND PERSONNEL DIVISION
Grade 3, S. Hewitt
Assistant Secretaries (G5), M. Street; Mrs M. Walmsley; G. Fiegehen

*ANALYTICAL SERVICES DIVISION
Director (G3), D. Stanton
Chief Statisticians (G5), N. Dyson; M. McDowall
Senior Economic Advisers (G5), J. Ball; G. Harris
Deputy Chief Scientific Officer (G5), D. Barnbrook
Chief Research Officer (G5), Ms S. Duncan

FINANCE DIVISION
Grade 3, S. Lord

SOCIAL SECURITY POLICY GROUP
Deputy Secretary (G2), vacant

*SOCIAL SECURITY DIVISION A
Under-Secretary (G3), R. Allen
Assistant Secretaries (G5), N. Ward; K. Limm; G. Bowen; Mrs C. Rookes; Mrs A. Lingwood

*SOCIAL SECURITY DIVISION B
Under-Secretary (G3), M. Whippman
Assistant Secretaries (G5), J. Groombridge; Miss G. Moore; C. B. Evans; Mrs L. Richards; P. Cleasby

*SOCIAL SECURITY DIVISION C
Under Secretary (G3), Miss M. Peirson
Assistant Secretaries (G5), Miss J. Liebling; D. Hill; Ms J. Clayton; C. B. Evans

*SOCIAL SECURITY DIVISION D
Under-Secretary (G3), R. Brown
Assistant Secretaries (G5), D. Jackson; O. C. L. Thorpe; R. H. Layton; I. Williams

*SOCIAL SECURITY DIVISION E
Under-Secretary (G3), D. Brereton
Assistant Secretaries (G5), S. Wilcox; D. Allsop

INFORMATION DIVISION
Head of Information (G5), S. Reardon
Deputy Head of Information (G6), T. Grace
Principal Information Officer (G7), J. Bretherton
Chief Publicity Officer (G7), Ms H. Midlane

SOLICITOR'S OFFICE
Solicitor (G2), P. K. J. Thompson

SOLICITOR'S DIVISION A
New Court, 48 Carey Street, London WC2A 2LS
Tel 0171-412 1342

Principal Assistant Solicitor (G3), Mrs G. S. Kerrigan

Assistant Solicitors (G5), D. P. Dunleavy; J. M. Swainson; Mrs G. Massiah; K. K. Baublys; J. P. Canlin; Mrs F. A. Logan

SOLICITOR'S DIVISION B
New Court, 48 Carey Street, London WC2A 2LS
Tel 0171-412 1370

Proceedings Operational Director (G4), P. C. Nilsson
Assistant Solicitors (G5), S. M. Cooper; R. G. S. Aitken; R. S. Powell; C. G. Blake

SOLICITOR'S DIVISION C
New Court, 48 Carey Street, London WC2A 2LS
Tel 0171-412 1466

Principal Assistant Solicitor (G3), A. D. Roberts
Assistant Solicitors (G5), Miss R. Lester; P. Milledge; R. J. Dormer; Mrs M. Astbury; Miss M. E. Trefgarne

MAXWELL PENSIONS UNIT
7 St James's Square, London SW1Y 4JU
Tel 0171-839 3599

Director (G5), R. P. Cleasby

EXECUTIVE AGENCIES

BENEFITS AGENCY
Quarry House, Quarry Hill, Leeds LS2 7UA
Tel 0113-232 4000

The Agency administers claims for and payments of social security benefits.
Chief Executive (G2), P. Mathison
  Private Secretary (G7), Ms E. Clayton
Directors (G3), D. Riggs (*finance*); P. Murray (*personnel*)
Directors of Territories (G3), Ms U. Brennan (*Scotland/Northern England*); (*G4*), A. Cleveland (*Southern England*); I. Stewart (*Wales/Central England*)

Benefits Agency Medical Services
Director (G3), Dr P. Castaldi
Principal Medical Officers, Dr M. Aylward; Dr P. Dewis; Dr C. Hudson; Dr P. Doughty

CHILD SUPPORT AGENCY
Millbank Tower, 21–24 Millbank, London SW1P 4QU
Tel 0171-210 3000

The Agency was set up in April 1993. It is responsible for the administration of the Child Support Act and for the assessment, collection and enforcement of maintenance payments for all new cases; it is currently re-assessing existing cases where the parent with care is claiming benefit, but the take-up of existing non-benefit cases has been indefinitely postponed. In 1994–5 the Agency took on 398,584 new cases and completed 568,149 assessments. It saved £479 million in benefit payments against a target of £460 million.
Chief Executive (G4), Miss A. Chant
Directors, S. Heminsley; C. Francis; A. Ward; S. Hughes; M. Davison

CONTRIBUTIONS AGENCY
DSS Longbenton, Benton Park Road, Newcastle upon Tyne NE98 1YX
Tel 0191-225 7665

The Agency collects and records National Insurance contributions, maintains individual records, and provides an advisory service.
Chief Executive (G3), Mrs F. Boardman
Deputy Chief Executive (G5), G. Bertram
Management Board, K. Wilson; R. Roberts, OBE; T. Lord; vacant
Non-Executive Member, J. Wilson

---

*At the Adelphi, 1–11 John Adam Street, London WC2N 6HT. Tel: 0171-962 8000

INFORMATION TECHNOLOGY SERVICES AGENCY
4th Floor, Verulam Point, Station Way, St Albans, Herts
AL1 5HE
Tel 01727-815838

The Agency maintains and oversees policies on information technology strategy, procurement, technical standards and security.
Chief Executive (acting), K. Caldwell
Directors, G. McCorkell; S. Williams; J. Thomas;
  N. Haighton; G. Hextall; J. Brewood; P. Crahan;
  G. Kemp; T. Perl; P. Sharkey
Non-Executive Director, T. Drury

RESETTLEMENT AGENCY
Euston Tower, 286 Euston Road, London, NW1 3DN
Tel 0171-388 1188

The Agency operates hostels for single homeless people, provides incentives for voluntary organizations or local authorities to purchase the hostels, and undertakes related activities.
Chief Executive (G6), P. Winstanley

WAR PENSIONS AGENCY
Norcross, Blackpool, Lancs. FY5 3WP
Tel 01253-858858

The Agency administers the payment of war disablement pensions and provides welfare services and support to war disablement pensioners, war widows and their dependants and carers. It became an executive agency in April 1994.
Chief Executive, vacant

Central Advisory Committee on War Pensions
Room 1138, The Adelphi, 1–11 John Adam Street,
London WC2N 6HT
Tel 0171-962 8028
Secretary, S. Adams

SOCIAL SECURITY ADVISORY
COMMITTEE
New Court, Carey Street, London, WC2A 2LS
Tel 0171-412 1507

The Social Security Advisory Committee (SSAC) was established by the Social Security Act 1980 to advise the Secretary of State for Social Security and the Department of Health and Social Services for Northern Ireland on all social security matters except those relating to benefits for industrial injuries and diseases and occupational pensions. The Social Security Housing Benefit Act 1982 added housing benefit to the Committee's responsibilities.
Chairman, vacant
Secretary, L. C. Smith

SPORTS COUNCIL
16 Upper Woburn Place, London WC1H 0QP
Tel 0171-388 1277

The Sports Council is an independent body established in 1972 by royal charter. It promotes the development of sport and fosters the provision of facilities for sport and recreation in Great Britain. Government funding for 1995–6 is £49 million.
  The Council is also responsible, with the other Sports Councils, for administering the National Lottery Sports Fund. The Councils had received about £167 million as at

July 1995 and had made awards to the value of £75.019 million.
  In January 1996 the Council will be replaced by a United Kingdom Sports Council and an English Sports Council.
Chairman, R. Walker
Director-General, D. Casey

For Sports Councils for Scotland, Wales and N. Ireland, *see* page 713.

HMSO (HER MAJESTY'S STATIONERY
OFFICE)
St Crispins, Duke Street, Norwich NR3 1PD
Tel 01603-622211

HMSO (Her Majesty's Stationery Office) was established in 1786. It provides printing, binding and business supplies to government departments and publicly funded organizations. It is an executive agency accountable to the Chancellor of the Duchy of Lancaster (the Minister of Public Service) within the Cabinet Office. HMSO is also the Government's publisher, and has bookshops for the sale of government publications in seven cities as well as appointed agents in other UK cities and throughout the world. HMSO obtains most of its supplies and printing from commercial sources, but about 20 per cent of its printing requirement, such as Hansard and Bills and Acts of Parliament, is produced in its own printing works.
Controller and Chief Executive (acting), M. D. Lynn
Director-General of Corporate Services, P. J. Macdonald

DIRECTORS
Publications, C. N. Southgate
Office Supplies, A. M. Cole
Print, E. Hendry
Finance and Planning, C. J. Penn
Business Systems, D. C. Kerry
Engineering and Estates, W. E. Scott
Human Resources, J. McDonald
Copiers, V. G. Bell
Furniture, G. A. H. Turner
HMSO Scotland, G. W. Bedford
HMSO N. Ireland, D. M. Connor

BIRMINGHAM – *Bookshop*, 258 Broad Street, Birmingham
  B1 2HE
BRISTOL, Distribution Park, Hawkley Drive, Woodlands
  Lane, Bradley Stoke, Bristol BS12 0BF. *Bookshop*, 33 Wine
  Street, Bristol BS1 2BH
LONDON – *Publications Centre*, 51 Nine Elms Lane,
  London SW8 5DR. *Bookshop*, 49 High Holborn, London
  WC1V 6HB
MANCHESTER, Broadway, Chadderton, Oldham, Lancs
  OL9 9QH. *Bookshop*, 9–21 Princess Street, Manchester
  M60 8AS
SCOTLAND, South Gyle Crescent, Edinburgh EH12 9EB.
  Bookshop, 71 Lothian Road, Edinburgh EH3 9AZ
WALES – *Bookshop*, The Friary, Cardiff CF1 4AA
NORTHERN IRELAND, IDB House, Chichester Street,
  Belfast BT1 4PS. *Bookshop*, 16 Arthur Street, Belfast
  BT1 4GD

OFFICE OF TELECOMMUNICATIONS
50 Ludgate Hill, London EC4M 7JJ
Tel 0171-634 8700

The Office of Telecommunications (Oftel) is a non-ministerial government department which is responsible for supervising telecommunications activities in the UK. Its principal functions are to ensure that holders of telecommunications licences comply with their licence conditions; to maintain and promote effective competition in telecommunications; and to promote the interests of purchasers and other users of telecommunication services and apparatus in respect of prices, quality and variety.

The Director-General has powers to deal with anti-competitive practices and monopoly situations. He also has a duty to consider all reasonable complaints and representations about telecommunication apparatus and services.

Director-General, D. G. Cruickshank
Deputy Director-General, Mrs A. Walker
Director of Competition, Mrs A. Taylor
Director of Consumer Affairs, Ms C. Farnish
Director of Licensing, Ms S. Chambers
Director of Licence Compliance, M. Owen
Technical Director, P. Walker
Economic Director, A. Bell
Legal Director, D. H. M. Ingham
Director of Information, D. Redding

TOURIST BOARDS
(For British Tourist Authority, *see* page 290)

The English Tourist Board, the Scottish Tourist Board, the Wales Tourist Board and the Northern Ireland Tourist Board are responsible for developing and marketing the tourist industry in their respective countries. The Boards' main objectives are to promote holidays and to encourage the provision and improvement of tourist amenities.

ENGLISH TOURIST BOARD, Thames Tower, Black's Road, London W6 9EL. Tel: 0181-846 9000. *Chief Executive*, J. East
SCOTTISH TOURIST BOARD, 23 Ravelston Terrace, Edinburgh EH4 3EU. Tel: 0131-332 2433. *Chief Executive*, D. D. Reid
WALES TOURIST BOARD, Brunel House, 2 Fitzalan Road, Cardiff CF2 1UY. Tel: 01222-499909. *Chief Executive*, P. Loveluck, CBE
NORTHERN IRELAND TOURIST BOARD, St Anne's Court, 59 North Street, Belfast BT1 1NB. Tel: 01232-231221. *Chief Executive*, I. Henderson

DEPARTMENT OF TRADE AND INDUSTRY
1 Victoria Street, London SW1H 0ET
Tel 0171-215 5000

Enterprise Initiative: Tel 0800-500200
Business in Europe: Tel 01272-444888
Innovation Enquiry Line: Tel 0800-442001

The Department is responsible for international trade policy, including the promotion of UK trade interests in the European Union, GATT, OECD, UNCTAD and other international organizations; the promotion of UK exports and assistance to exporters; policy in relation to industry and commerce, including industrial relations policy and legislation and policy in relation to the Post Office; competition policy, consumer protection and co-ordination of policy on deregulation; the development of national policies in relation to all forms of energy and the development of new sources of energy, including international aspects of energy policy; policy on science and technology research and development; space policy; stan-dards, quality and design; and company legislation and the regulation of insurance industries.

President of the Board of Trade and Secretary of State for Trade and Industry, The Rt. Hon. Ian Lang, MP
Principal Private Secretary, J. Alty
Private Secretaries, R. Jenkinson; M. Hilton
Minister for Industry and Energy, The Rt. Hon. Timothy Eggar, MP
Private Secretary, M. Baldwin
Parliamentary Private Secretary, P. Luff, MP
Minister for Trade, Anthony Nelson, MP
Private Secretary, U. Marthaler
Minister of State, The Rt. Hon. The Lord Fraser of Carmyllie, QC
Private Secretary, I. Gibbons
Parliamentary Under-Secretary of State for Science and Technology, Ian Taylor, MBE, MP
Private Secretary, J. Walker
Parliamentary Under-Secretary of State for Small Business, Industry and Energy, Richard Page, MP
Private Secretary, I. McKenzie
Parliamentary Under-Secretary of State for Competition and Consumer Affairs, Jonathan Evans, MP
Private Secretary, P. Hadley
Parliamentary Under-Secretary of State for Trade and Industry, The Rt. Hon. Phillip Oppenheim, MP
British Overseas Trade Board Chairman, Sir Derek Hornby
Private Secretary, R. Pringle
Parliamentary Clerk, T. Williams
Permanent Secretary (G1), Sir Peter Gregson, KCB
Private Secretary, C. Parker
Deputy Secretaries (G2), C. W. Roberts, CB (*Trade Policy and Export Promotion*); D. Durie (*Regional and Small Firms*); B. Hilton, CB (*Laboratories and Corporate and Consumer Affairs*); A. Hammond, CB (*The Solicitor*); C. Henderson, CB (*Energy*); A. C. Hutton, CB (*Principal Establishment and Finance Officer*); A. Macdonald, CB (*Industry*)

DIVISIONAL ORGANIZATION

‡AEROSPACE DIVISION
Head of Division (G3), R. Foster
Heads of Branches (G5), Ms R. J. Anderson; M. Ralph; S. I. Charik; Miss V. Evans

ATOMIC ENERGY
Head of Division (G3), N. Hirst
Heads of Branches (G5), Mrs H. Haddon; Dr D. Lumley; S. D. Spivey

BRITISH NATIONAL SPACE CENTRE
Bridge Place, 88–89 Eccleston Square, London SW1V 1PT
Director-General (G3), D. R. Davis
Deputy Director-General (G4), D. Leadbeater
Heads of Branches (G5), Dr R. Jude; H. Evans; (*G6*), Dr D. Williams; J. Thomas; Dr P. Murdin

CHEMICALS AND BIOTECHNOLOGY DIVISION
Head of Division (G3), Dr E. G. Finer
Heads of Branches (G5), Ms G. Alliston; Dr E. A. M. Baker; N. Owen

COAL DIVISION
Head of Division (G3), W. I. MacIntyre, CB
Heads of Branches (G5), J. A. V. Collett; A. Berry

COAL PRIVATIZATION UNIT
Head of Division (G3), P. Loughead
Grade 5, Ms F. S. Price

COMPANIES DIVISION
Head of Division (G3), Mrs S. Brown

Heads of Branches (*G5*), N. D. Peace; J. Healey; F. C. Jenkins;
D. E. Love

COMPETITION POLICY DIVISION
Head of Division (*G3*), A. J. Pryor
Heads of Branches (*G5*), A. Cooper; C. C. Bridge

CONSUMER AFFAIRS DIVISION
Head of Division (*G3*), J. Dorken
Heads of Branches (*G5*), D. Jones; P. D. Atkinson;
M. Oldham; D. Gane

ECONOMICS AND STATISTICS DIVISION
Chief Economic Adviser (*G3*), D. R. Coates
Heads of Branches (*G5*), Dr D. S. Higham; S. Penneck;
M. S. Bradbury

ELECTRICITY AND NUCLEAR FUELS DIVISION
Head of Division (*G3*), C. C. Wilcock
Heads of Branches (*G5*), S. F. D. Powell; J. H. T. Green; Dr
P. Fenwick; Miss S. Haird

‡ELECTRONICS AND ENGINEERING DIVISION
Head of Division (*G3*), R. M. Rumbelow
Heads of Branches (*G5*), T. J. Soane; S. C. Pride; Dr
I. Eddison; Miss C. Bradley; P. Rothwell

ENERGY POLICY AND ANALYSIS UNIT
Head of Division (*G4*), N. Hartley
Heads of Branches (*G5*), H. Charman; D. Hodgson;
S. A. Price; G. C. White; Dr R. Van Slooten

‡ENVIRONMENT AND ENERGY TECHNOLOGIES
DIVISION
Head of Division (*G3*), Dr C. Hicks
Heads of Branches (*G5*), C. Brewer; Dr A. Eggington;
A. Steele; G. Bevan

EUROPEAN COMMUNITY AND TRADE RELATIONS
DIVISION
Head of Division (*G3*), W. L. Stow
Grade 4, S. Fremantle
Heads of Branches (*G5*), J. Rhodes; D. I. Richardson;
M. D. C. Johnson

EXPORT CONTROL AND NON-PROLIFERATION
DIVISION
Kingsgate House, 66–74 Victoria Street, London SW1E 6SW
Head of Division (*G3*), R. J. Meadway
Heads of Branches (*G5*), P. H. Agrell; A. J. Mantle

EXPORTS TO ASIA, AFRICA AND AUSTRALASIA DIVISION
Kingsgate House, 66–74 Victoria Street, London SW1E 6SW
Head of Division (*G3*), M. M. Baker
Heads of Branches (*G5*), M. Cohen; I. Cliff; (*G6*),
A. E. Reynolds; N. McInnes

EXPORTS TO EUROPE AND THE AMERICAS DIVISION
Head of Division (*G3*), N. Thornton
Heads of Branches (*G5*), K. D. Levinson; B. Hampton; S. Lyle
Smythe; K. Timmins; (*G6*), L. Rabstaff

FINANCE AND RESOURCE MANAGEMENT DIVISION
Head of Division (*G3*), M. K. O'Shea
Heads of Branches (*G5*), D. T. Smith; Mrs M. Bloom;
J. Hobday; J. P. Clayton

INDUSTRIAL RELATIONS DIVISION
Caxton House, Tothill Street, London SW1H 9NF
Tel 0171-273 3000
Head of Division (*G3*), Ms H. Leiser
Heads of Branches (*G5*), P. Parker; K. Masson; R. Niblett;
A. Wright

INFORMATION DIVISION
Head of Information (*G4*), Ms J. M. Caines

Head of News (*G6*), M. Ricketts
Publicity
Bridge Place, 88–89 Eccleston Square, London SW1V 1PT
Head of Branch (*G5*), Miss P. R. A. Freedman

INSURANCE DIVISION
Head of Division (*G3*), J. Spencer
Heads of Branches (*G5*), R. Allen; R. Hobbs; K. Long

INTERNAL AUDIT
Head of Internal Audit (*G5*), A. C. Elkington

INTERNATIONAL TRADE POLICY DIVISION
Head of Division (*G3*), J. Cooke
Heads of Branches (*G5*), J. Hunt; J. Startup; S. J. Bowen;
C. B. Moir

INVESTIGATIONS DIVISION
Head of Division (*G3*), M. G. Roberts
Grade 4, Mrs T. J. Dunstan
Inspector of Companies (*G4*), G. Harp
Heads of Branches (*G5*), S. L. Parkinson; A. Mier; Miss
H. Pottle; H. Bradshaw; Mrs B. Chase; A. Robertshaw

INVEST IN BRITAIN BUREAU
Kingsgate House, 66–74 Victoria Street, London SW1E 6SW
Chief Executive (*G3*), A. Fraser
Head of Branch (*G5*), H. A. Gestadt

JOINT EXPORT PROMOTION DIRECTORATE
(FCO/DTI)
Kingsgate House, 66–74 Victoria Street, London SW1E 6SW
Director-General of Export Promotion (*G3*), F. R. Mingay, CMG
Directors (*G5*), D. Saunders; (*DS4*), M. Dougal

‡MANAGEMENT AND TECHNOLOGY SERVICES
DIVISION
Head of Division (*G3*), Dr K. C. Shotton
Heads of Branches (*G5*), C. W. Johnston; Dr K. Poulter; Dr
R. Hinder; Dr M. S. Draper

OIL AND GAS DIVISION
Head of Division (*G3*), M. J. Michell
Heads of Branches (*G5*), M. H. Atkinson; (*RES2*),
J. R. V. Brooks; B. Coleman; (*PS2*), G. N. Marriott
Director of Oil and Gas Royalties Office (*G6*), A. Wilson

Gas and Oil Measurement Branch
3 Tigers Road, Wigston, Leicester LE18 4UX
Tel 0116-278 5354
Director (*G5*), J. Plant

Oil and Gas Office (Aberdeen)
Atholl House, 86–88 Guild Street, Aberdeen AB9 1DR
Tel 01224-213557
Grade 5, A. S. Wilson

OIL AND GAS PROJECTS AND SUPPLIES OFFICE
Tay House, 300 Bath Street, Glasgow G2 4DX
Tel 0141-228 3646
1 Victoria Street, London SW1E 0ET
Tel 0171-215 5000
Chief Executive (*G3*), D. Watson
Heads of Branches (*G5*), A. E. Maule; Mrs R. E. Ebbers;
H. M. Whiteside; (*G6*), J. Roddie

PERSONNEL DIVISION
Head of Division (*G3*), Miss P. Boys
Heads of Branches (*G5*), J. Thompson; R. Rogers

PROJECTS EXPORT PROMOTION DIVISION
Head of Division (*G3*), D. J. Hall

‡At 151 Buckingham Palace Road, London SW1W 9SS

Heads of Branches (G5), A. G. Atkinson; D. Marsh;
N. M. S. Armour

REGIONAL DEVELOPMENT DIVISION
Kingsgate House, 66–74 Victoria Street, London SW1E 6SW
Head of Division (G3), vacant
Director, IDU (G3), A. Dunnett
Heads of Branches (G5), R. H. S. Wells, CBE; K. Holt; Mrs
M. A. Wilks; D. A. Miner

SERVICES MANAGEMENT DIVISION
Kingsgate House, 66–74 Victoria Street, London SW1E 6SW
Head of Division (G3), Dr R. Heathcote
Grade 4, R. J. Wheeler
Heads of Branches (G5), R. Nicklen; Mrs E. Drage; B. Avery

SMALL FIRMS AND BUSINESS LINK DIVISION
St Mary's House, Level 2, Moorfoot, Sheffield S1 4PQ
Tel 0114-270 1356
Kingsgate House, 66–74 Victoria Street, London SW1E 6SW
Tel 0171-215 5000
Head of Division (G3), H. V. Brown
Heads of Branches (G5), J. M. Reid; R. M. Anderson;
M. Garrod

SOLICITOR'S OFFICE
The Solicitor (G2), A. Hammond, CB
Grade 3, P. H. Bovey; Miss K. Morton; J. M. Stanley;
C. Kerse
Assistant Solicitors (G5), M. Bucknill; J. Burnett; Mrs
J. Darvell; Miss P. A. E. Granados; R. D. B. Green;
A. S. W. Hyett; D. S. Mangat; I. K. Mathers;
S. G. Milligan; R. Nicklen; Miss E. N. O'Flynn;
R. C. Perkins; Miss G. Richmond; J. W. Roberts;
A. M. Susman; B. Welch; A. J. Woods

‡TECHNOLOGY AND INNOVATION POLICY DIVISION
Head of Division (G3), Dr D. Evans
Heads of Branches (G5), R. T. King; I. C. Downing;
P. E. Mason; P. L. Bunn; J. M. Barber; G. C. Riggs; Dr
A. Keddie; C. M. Cruickshank

‡TELECOMMUNICATIONS AND POSTS DIVISION
Head of Division (G3), P. Salvidge
Grade 4, S. R. Temple
Heads of Branches (G5), D. D. Sibbick; P. Waller;
N. McMillan; J. S. Neilson; D. A. Hendon; N. Worman;
Dr D. Walker

‡TEXTILES AND RETAILING DIVISION
Head of Division (G3), I. M. Jones
Heads of Branches (G5), T. L. Roberts; C. L. Jackson

‡VEHICLES, METALS AND MINERALS DIVISION
Head of Division (G3), M. Stanley
Heads of Branches (G5), T. M. H. Shearer; H. P. Brown;
B. F. Harding; (*G6*), R. Poole

OFFICE OF SCIENCE AND TECHNOLOGY
Albany House, 84–86 Petty France, London SW1H 9ST
Tel 0171-270 1234

Chief Scientific Adviser and Head of Office (G1A),
Prof. R. M. May, FRS
Private Secretary, C. Forster
Director-General of Research Councils, Sir John Cadogan
Grade 3, Mrs H. Williams (*Transdepartmental Science and Technology Group*); A. L. C. Quigley (*Science and Engineering Base Group*)

‡At 151 Buckingham Palace Road, London SW1W 9SS

Grade 5, A. A. Carter (*Research Councils*); R. D. J. Wright
(*International Science*); C. G. L. de Grouchy
(*Transdepartmental Division*); D. Barker (*Research Manpower*)

BRITISH OVERSEAS TRADE BOARD
Kingsgate House, 66–74 Victoria Street, London SW1E 6SW
Tel 0171-215 5000

President, The President of the Board of Trade
Chairman, Sir Derek Hornby
Vice-Chairman, HRH The Duke of Kent, KG, GCMG, GCVO
Members, Dr D. Baldwin, CBE; G. J. Bull; Sir Colin
Chandler; Sir Alan Cockshaw; Mrs H. M. Cropper;
I. L. Dale, OBE; H. Davies; Mrs J. Hall; Dr A. Hayes, CB;
D. Lanigan, CBE; R. Mingay, CMG; The Rt. Hon. Sir
Michael Palliser, GCMG; D. Peake; C. W. Roberts, CB;
B. D. Taylor, CBE; B. W. Willott; D. Wright, CMG, LVO
Secretary (G5), D. Saunders

REGIONAL OFFICES
— *see* pages 306–7

EXECUTIVE AGENCIES
COMPANIES HOUSE
Companies House, Crown Way, Cardiff CF4 3UZ
Tel 01222-388588
London Search Room, 55–71 City Road, London EC1Y 1BB
Tel 0171-253 9393
37 Castle Terrace, Edinburgh EH1 2EB
Tel 0131-535 5800

Companies House incorporates companies, registers
company documents and provides company information.
Registrar of Companies for England and Wales (G4),
D. Durham
Registrar for Scotland, J. Henderson

THE INSOLVENCY SERVICE
PO Box 203, 5th Floor, 21 Bloomsbury Street, London
WC1B 3QW
Tel 0171-323 3090
The Service administers and investigates the affairs of
bankrupts and companies in compulsory liquidation; deals
with the disqualification of directors in all corporate
failures; regulates insolvency practitioners and their pro-
fessional bodies; provides banking and investment services
for bankruptcy and liquidation estates; and advises
ministers on insolvency policy issues.
Inspector-General and Chief Executive, P. R. Joyce
Deputy Inspectors-General (G4), D. J. Flynn;
M. C. A. Osborne

LABORATORY OF THE GOVERNMENT CHEMIST
Queens Road, Teddington, Middx TW11 0LY
Tel 0181-943 7000
The Laboratory provides chemical analytical services,
method development, contract research, special studies
and consultancy to both government organizations and the
private sector. It is scheduled to be privatized by April
1996.
Government Chemist and Chief Executive (G3), Dr
R. D. Worswick

NATIONAL ENGINEERING LABORATORY
East Kilbride, Glasgow G75 0QU
Tel 013552-20222
The National Engineering Laboratory is expected to be
privatized by the end of 1995.
Chief Executive (G3), W. Edgar

NATIONAL WEIGHTS AND MEASURES LABORATORY
Stanton Avenue, Teddington, Middx TW11 0JZ
Tel 0181-943 7272
The Laboratory administers weights and measures legislation.
Chief Executive (G5), Dr S. Bennett

PATENT OFFICE
— *see* page 336

RADIOCOMMUNICATIONS AGENCY
South Quay Three, 189 Marsh Wall, London E14 9SX
Tel 0171-211 0211
The Agency is responsible for most civil radio matters other than telecommunications broadcasting policy and the radio equipment market.
Chief Executive (G3), J. Norton

DEPARTMENT OF TRANSPORT
Great Minster House, 76 Marsham Street, London
SW1P 4DR
Tel 0171-271 5000

The Department of Transport is responsible for land, sea and air transport, including sponsorship of the rail and bus industries; airports; domestic and international civil aviation; shipping and the ports industry; navigational lights, pilotage, HM Coastguard and marine pollution; motorways and other trunk roads; oversight of road transport including vehicle standards, registration and licensing, driver testing and licensing, bus and road freight licensing, regulation of taxis and private hire cars and road safety; and oversight of local authorities' transport planning, including payment of Transport Supplementary Grant.
Secretary of State for Transport, The Rt. Hon. Sir George Young, Bt., MP
  Private Secretary, Miss B. Hill
  Parliamentary Private Secretary, Dr C. Goodson-Wickes, MP
Minister of State, John Watts, MP
  Private Secretary, vacant
  Parliamentary Private Secretary, T. Dicks, MP
Parliamentary Under-Secretaries, The Viscount Goschen (*Roads and Traffic*); Steven Norris, MP (*Transport in London*)
  Private Secretaries, M. Scammell; S. Heard
  Parliamentary Clerk, Miss P. Gaunt
Permanent Under-Secretary of State (G1), Sir Patrick Brown, KCB
  Private Secretary, vacant

INFORMATION
Head of Information (G5), M. J. Helm

CENTRAL SERVICES
Principal Establishment and Finance Officer (G2), D. J. Rowlands, CB

PERSONNEL
Director of Personnel (G3), R. Bird
Grade 5, R. D. Bayly; D. L. McMillan
Grade 6, B. Meakins; E. M. Gibbons
Chief Welfare Officer (G7), Miss E. T. Haines

FINANCE
Under-Secretary (G3), B. Wadsworth
Accounting Adviser (G4), A. R. Allum

Heads of Divisions (G5), S. K. Reeves (*Finance Transport Programmes*); D. M. Smith (*Financial Information Requirements Review*)

EXECUTIVE AGENCIES DIRECTORATE
Under-Secretary (G3), J. Phillips
Grade 5, S. P. Connolly; A. C. Melville; P. A. A. Sanders

INTERNAL AUDIT
Ashdown House, Sedlescombe Road North, Hastings, E. Sussex TN37 7GA
Tel 01424-458306
Head of Branch (G5), M. J. Reece

CENTRAL SERVICES UNIT
Ashdown House, Sedlescombe Road North, Hastings, E. Sussex TN37 7GA
Tel 01424-458306
Grade 4, M. R. Newey
Heads of Divisions (G5), D. E. Bridge (*Management Support Services*); G. L. Jones (*Departmental Procurement Unit*); I. R. Heawood (*HQ Relocation Division*)
Grade 6, I. Harris (*Accommodation and Office Services*)

STATISTICAL SERVICES
Romney House, 43 Marsham Street, London SW1P 3PY
Tel 0171-276 8513
Under-Secretary (G3), D. W. Flaxen
Grade 5, Miss B. J. Wood; Dr R. L. Butchart; P. J. Capell; R. P. Donachie

CHIEF SCIENTIST
Chief Scientist (G4), Dr D. H. Metz

TRANSPORT SECURITY
Portland House, Stag Place, London SW1E 5BH
Tel 0171-460 3016
Director and Co-ordinator (G5), R. D. Lord
Grade 5, Mrs A. M. Moss

MOBILITY UNIT
Head of Unit (G5), Miss E. A. Frye

RAILWAYS
Deputy Secretary (G2), N. L. J. Montagu, CB

RAILWAY INFRASTRUCTURE
Under-Secretary (G3), C. R. Grimsey
Heads of Divisions (G4), Dr J. H. Denning (*Railways 1A*); A. Burchell (*Railways Economics*); R. J. Griffins (*Rail Link Bill*); (*G5*), M. R. Fawcett (*International Railways 1*); Miss P. M. Williams (*International Railways 2*); A. P. Moss (*Channel Tunnel*)

RAILWAY PRIVATIZATION
Under-Secretary (G3), Mrs J. M. Williams
Grade 4, P. J. Coby
Heads of Divisions (G5), P. H. McCarthy; R. C. Bennett; R. Linnard; D. B. Cooke; R. S. Peal; M. J. Fuhr; J. E. Wakeling

CHANNEL TUNNEL SAFETY UNIT
Grade 3, E. A. Ryder, CB

ROADS, LOCAL TRANSPORT AND TRANSPORT POLICY
Deputy Secretary (G2), P. Wood

NATIONAL ROADS POLICY DIRECTORATE
Grade 3, H. C. S. Derwent
Heads of Divisions (G5), M. A. Walsh (*Highways Economic and Traffic Appraisal*); Dr C. M. Woodman (*Highways Policy and Programmes*); Mrs C. M. Dixon (*Tolled Roads and Crossings*)

URBAN AND LOCAL TRANSPORT
Under-Secretary (*G3*), R. A. Allan
Heads of Divisions (*G5*), A. B. Murray (*Public Transport London A*); E. C. Neve (*Public Transport London B*); M. R. Pitwood (*London Transport Policy*); T. E. Worsley (*Economics, Local Transport and General*); A. S. D. Whybrow (*Traffic Policy*); M. F. Talbot (*Driver Information and Traffic Management*)

ROAD AND VEHICLE SAFETY
Under-Secretary (*G3*), Miss S. J. Lambert
Heads of Divisions (*G5*), I. R. Jordan (*Vehicle Standards and Engineering*); Dr R. M. Kimber (*Road Safety*); J. L. Gansler (*Driver Vehicle Licensing Policy*); J. R. Fells (*Freight and Road Haulage*); (*G6*), J. Winder (*Traffic Area Co-ordinating*)

TRANSPORT POLICY UNIT
Head of Unit (*G5*), D. R. Instone

CHIEF MECHANICAL ENGINEER'S OFFICE
Director and Chief Mechanical Engineer (*G5*), M. St J. Fendick

DEPARTMENTAL MEDICAL ADVISER
Grade 5, Dr P. A. M. Diamond, OBE

AVIATION AND SHIPPING
Deputy Secretary (*G2*), J. W. S. Dempster, CB

CIVIL AVIATION DIRECTORATE
Under-Secretary (*G3*), J. Henes
Grade 5, Ms A. Munro (*Airport Policy*); Ms M. J. Clare (*CAA and Safety Policy*); M. C. Mann (*Economics Aviation Maritime International*); Ms E. A. Duthie (*Noise and Pollution*); J. C. Neve (*European*)

INTERNATIONAL AVIATION DIRECTORATE
Under-Secretary (*G3*), A. J. Goldman, CB
Grade 4, D. S. Evans
Heads of Divisions (*G4*), A. T. Baker; (*G5*), N. J. Starling; Dr P. H. Martin

AIR ACCIDENTS INVESTIGATION BRANCH
Royal Aerospace Establishment, Farnborough, Hants GU14 6TD
Tel 01252-510300
Chief Inspector of Air Accidents (*G4*), K. P. R. Smart
Deputy Chief Inspector of Air Accidents (*G5*), R. C. McKinlay

MARINE ACCIDENTS INVESTIGATION BRANCH
5–7 Brunswick Place, Southampton SO1 2AN
Tel 01703-232424
Chief Inspector of Marine Accidents (*G5*), Capt. P. B. Marriott

SHIPPING POLICY DIRECTORATE
Under-Secretary (*G3*), R. E. Clarke
Heads of Divisions (*G5*), L. S. Moyle; J. F. Wall; R. T. Bishop; G. D. Rowe

REGIONAL OFFICES
— see pages 306–7

EXECUTIVE AGENCIES

COASTGUARD AGENCY
Spring Place, 105 Commercial Road, Southampton SO1 0ZD
Tel 01703-329100
The Agency's role is to minimize loss of life among seafarers and coastal users, and to minimize pollution from ships to sea and coastline.
Chief Executive (*G4*), C. J. Harris
Chief Coastguard (*G5*), Cdr D. T. Ancona, RN (retd)

DRIVER AND VEHICLE LICENSING AGENCY
Longview Road, Morriston, Swansea SA6 7JL
Tel 01792-782318
The Agency issues driving licences, registers and licenses vehicles, and collects excise duty.
Chief Executive (*G3*), Dr S. J. Ford
Heads of Divisions (*G5*), R. J. Verge; T. J. Horton; J. C. Betts

DRIVING STANDARDS AGENCY
Stanley House, Talbot Street, Nottingham NG1 5GU
Tel 0115-947 4222
The Agency's role is to carry out driving tests and approve driving instructors.
Chief Executive (*G5*), B. L. Herdan

HIGHWAYS AGENCY
St Christopher House, Southwark Street, London SE1 0TE
Tel 0171-928 3666
The Agency is responsible for the management and maintenance of the motorway and trunk road network and for road construction and improvement.
Chief Executive (*G2*), L. J. Haynes

Finance Directorate
Director (*G4*), J. Seddon
Heads of Divisions (*G5*), P. A. Houston (*Finance and Procurement*); Ms E. A. Bostock (*Lands, Claims and Graphics*); D. Kershaw (*Computing*)

Private Finance Directorate
Director (*G4*), P. G. Collis

Human Resources Directorate
Director (*G4*), K. A. Wyatt

Engineering and Environmental Policy Directorate
Director (*G3*), T. A. Rochester
Deputy Director (*G4*), J. A. Kerman
Head of Divisions (*G5*), Mrs V. A. Bodnar (*Agency Environmental Policy*); N. S. Organ (*Road Engineering and Environmental*); A. J. Pickett (*Bridges Engineering*)

Road Programme Directorate
Director (*G3*), J. W. Fellows
Deputy Director (*G4*), D. York
Heads of Divisions (*G4*), D. A. Holland (*Technical Services*); (*G5*), K. McKenzie (*Administrative Services*); D. E. Oddy (*Motorways Operations*); R. R. Bineham (*Northern Operations*); D. Ward (*Southern Operations*); J. P. Boud (*Construction Operations*); J. M. Bradley (*Administrative Operations*)

Network Management and Maintenance Directorate
Director (*G3*), B. J. Billington
Deputy Director (*G4*), P. E. Nutt
Heads of Divisions (*G5*), R. Eastman (*Network General and Maintenance*); M. G. Quinn (*Network Communications*); K. A. Lasbury (*Northern Network Management*); W. S. C. Wadrup (*Midland Network Management*); A. D. Rowland (*Southern Network Management*); R. T. Thorndike (*London Network Management*)

MARINE SAFETY AGENCY
Spring Place, 105 Commercial Road, Southampton SO1 0ZD
Tel 01703-329100
The Agency's role is to develop, promote and enforce high standards of marine safety and to minimize the risk of pollution of the marine environment from ships.
Chief Executive (*G4*), R. M. Bradley
Directors (*G5*), W. A. Graham (*Ship Construction and Navigation*); Capt. D. Bell (*Marine Safety Operations and Seafarers Standards*); (*G6*), R. Padgett (*Finance, Personnel and Corporate Services*)

TRANSPORT RESEARCH LABORATORY
Crowthorne, Berks RG11 6AU
Tel 01344-773131

The Agency conducts and manages transport research and provides advice. It is due to be privatized by the end of 1995.
Chief Executive (G3), H. J. Wootton
Directors (G5), Dr P. H. Bly (*Research*); D. H. Goody (*Finance*); E. D. Gould (*Resource*); G. M. Clarke (*Business Development*); J. Porter (*Civil Engineering Programme*); P. B. Hunt (*Traffic and Transport Programme*); D. A. Lynam (*Vehicles and Safety Programme*)

VEHICLE CERTIFICATION AGENCY
1 Eastgate Office Centre, Eastgate Road, Bristol BS5 6XX
Tel 0117-951 5151

The Agency tests and certificates vehicles to UK and international standards.
Chief Executive (G5), D. W. Harvey

VEHICLE INSPECTORATE
Berkeley House, Croydon Street, Bristol BS5 0DA
Tel 0117-954 3274

The Agency carries out annual testing and inspection of heavy goods and other vehicles and administers the MOT testing scheme.
Chief Executive (G4), R. J. Oliver
Deputy Chief Executive (G5), J. A. T. David

TRAFFIC DIRECTOR FOR LONDON
College House, Great Peter Street, London SW1P 3LN
Tel 0171-222 4545

The Traffic Director for London is a non-departmental public body which is independent from the Department of Transport but responsible to the Secretary of State for Transport and to Parliament. Its role is to co-ordinate the introduction of the Priority (Red) Route Network in London and monitor its operation.
Traffic Director for London, D. Turner

TRAFFIC AREA OFFICES

LICENSING AUTHORITIES AND TRAFFIC COMMISSIONERS
EASTERN (Nottingham and Cambridge), Brig. C. M. Boyd
NORTH-EASTERN (Newcastle upon Tyne and Leeds), K. R. Waterworth
NORTH-WESTERN (Manchester), M. S. Albu
SCOTTISH (Edinburgh), Brig. M. W. Betts
SOUTH-EASTERN AND METROPOLITAN (Eastbourne), Brig. M. H. Turner
SOUTH WALES (Cardiff), J. M. C. Pugh
WESTERN (Bristol), Air Vice-Marshal R. G. Ashford, CBE
WEST MIDLANDS (Birmingham), J. M. C. Pugh

THE TREASURY
Parliament Street, London SW1P 3AG
Tel 0171-270 3000

The Office of the Lord High Treasurer has been continuously in commission for well over 200 years. The Lord High Commissioners of HM Treasury are the First Lord of the Treasury (who is also the Prime Minister), the Chancellor of the Exchequer and five junior Lords (who are government whips in the House of Commons). This Board of Commissioners is assisted at present by the Chief Secretary, a Parliamentary Secretary who is also the government Chief Whip, a Financial Secretary, an Economic Secretary, the Paymaster-General, and the Permanent Secretary.

The Prime Minister is not primarily concerned in the day-to-day aspects of Treasury business; the management of the Treasury devolves upon the Chancellor of the Exchequer and the other Treasury ministers.

The Chief Secretary is responsible for the planning and control of public expenditure; pay and efficiency in the public sector, excluding the Civil Service; parliamentary pay; and export credit.

The Financial Secretary discharges the traditional responsibility of the Treasury for the largely formal procedure for the voting of funds by Parliament. He also has responsibility for other parliamentary financial business; the legislative programme; oversight of the Inland Revenue; Inland Revenue taxes (excluding stamp duties); privatization, competition and deregulation policy; and Civil Service pay, management and industrial relations.

The Economic Secretary has responsibility for monetary policy; the financial system (including financial institutions); the Government Actuary's Department; the Central Statistical Office; international financial business; Economic and Monetary Union; stamp duties; the Valuation Office; the Royal Mint; the Department for National Savings; the Registry of Friendly Societies; the National Investment and Loans Office; wider share-ownership; Treasury interest in small firms' policy; procurement policy; and economic briefing.

The Paymaster-General is responsible for general oversight of Customs and Excise; Customs and Excise duties and taxes; assisting the Chief Secretary on public expenditure planning and control; Treasury interest in women's issues; charities; the environment (including energy efficiency); the EC budget; general accounting issues; PAYMASTER (*see* page 336) and ministerial correspondence.

All Treasury ministers are concerned in tax matters.
Prime Minister and First Lord of the Treasury,
The Rt. Hon. John Major, MP
Chancellor of the Exchequer (*£42,834),
The Rt. Hon. Kenneth Clarke, QC, MP
Principal Private Secretary, N. I. MacPherson
Private Secretary, I. Rogers
Special Adviser, D. Ruffley
Chief Secretary to the Treasury (*£42,834), The
Rt. Hon. William Waldegrave, MP
Private Secretary, P. T. Wanless
Special Adviser, D. Rutley
Financial Secretary to the Treasury (*£30,307), Michael Jack, MP
Private Secretary, Ms S. Cook
Economic Secretary (*£30,307), Angela Knight, MP
Private Secretary, S. G. Meck
Paymaster-General (*£30,307), David Heathcoat-Amory, MP
Private Secretary, M. Young
Special Adviser to the Treasury Ministers, E. Troup
Parliamentary Secretary to the Treasury and Government Chief Whip (*£34,037), The Rt. Hon. Alastair Goodlad, MP
Private Secretary, M. Maclean
Treasurer of HM Household and Deputy Chief Whip (*£30,307), The Rt. Hon. Gregory Knight, MP
Comptroller of HM Household (*£19,502), Timothy Wood, MP
Vice-Chamberlain of HM Household (*£19,502), Timothy Kirkhope, MP

*In addition to a reduced parliamentary salary of £24,985

Lord Commissioners of the Treasury (*£19,502), A. J. MacKay,
MP; D. Conway, MP; B. Wells, MP; D. Willetts, MP;
S. Burns, MP
Assistant Whips (*£19,502), M. Bates, MP; Dr L. Fox, MP;
P. McLoughlin, MP; R. Knapman, MP; G. Streeter, MP
Parliamentary Clerk, D. S. Martin
Panel of Independent Forecasters to the Treasury, W. Godley;
G. Davies; T. Congdon; A. Britton; D. Currie;
P. Minford
Permanent Secretary to the Treasury (*G1*), Sir Terence Burns,
GCB
   Private Secretary, Miss S. M. A. James
Second Permanent Secretaries (*G1A*), Sir Nigel Wicks, KCB,
CVO, CBE (*International Finance*); R. P. Culpin, CB, CVO
(*Spending*); Prof. A. Budd (*Macroeconomic Policy and
Prospects*)
*Head of Government Accountancy Service and Chief Accountancy
Adviser to the Treasury*, A. Likierman

DIRECTORATES

Leader, Ministerial Support Team (*G5*), N. Macpherson
Leader, Communications Team (*G5*), A. Hudson
Leader, Strategy Team (*G5*), N. Holgate

MACROECONOMIC POLICY AND PROSPECTS
Director (*G1A*), Prof. A. Budd
Deputy Directors (*G3*), C. J. Mowl; A. O'Donnell, CB
Team Leaders (*G5*), M. Bradbury; J. S. Cunliffe; C. M. Kelly;
S. W. Matthews; S. Pickford; D. Savage

INTERNATIONAL FINANCE
Director (*G1A*), Sir Nigel Wicks, KCB, CVO, CBE
Deputy Directors (*G3*), P. McIntyre; D. L. C. Peretz
Team Leaders (*G5*), S. Brooks; N. J. Ilett; Ms S. Owen;
D. Roe; Ms J. Rutter

BUDGET AND PUBLIC FINANCES
Director (*G2*), P. R. C. Gray
Deputy Directors (*G3*), S. W. Boys-Smith; Mrs A. F. Case;
E. J. W. Gieve
Team Leaders (*G5*), Mrs S. D. Brown; D. Deaton; J. Dixon;
Ms R. Kosmin; N. M. Hansford; D. W. Rayson;
A. W. Ritchie; A. Sharples; P. Short; S. N. Wood; (*G6*),
M. Parkinson

SPENDING
Director (*G1A*), R. P. Culpin, CB, CVO
Deputy Directors (*G3*), N. Glass; Miss G. M. Noble;
Ms A. Perkins; P. N. Sedgwick
Team Leaders (*G5*), R. Bent; P. Brook; J. W. Grice;
J. Halligan; M. C. Mercer; M. Neale; I. Rogers;
T. J. Sutton; I. V. W. Taylor; Ms R. Thompson;
Ms S. Walker; Ms M. Wallace

FINANCIAL MANAGEMENT, REPORTING AND AUDIT
Director (*Chief Accountancy Adviser*), A. Likierman
Deputy Director (*G3*), J. E. Mortimer
Team Leaders (*G5*), K. Bradley; Mrs R. M. Dunn;
N. Holgate; (*G6*), C. Butler; P. Holden; P. Tickner

FINANCE, REGULATION AND INDUSTRY
Director (*G2*), S. Robson
Deputy Directors (*G3*), N. Deverell; A. Whiting;
M. L. Williams
Team Leaders (*G5*), H. J. Bush; J. Colling; Mrs P. C. Diggle;
C. Farthing; J. J. Heywood; C. R. Pickering; R. Saunders;
Ms J. Simpson; P. Wynn Owen; Ms E. Young; (*G6*),
J. May

PERSONNEL AND SUPPORT
Director (*G3*), vacant
Team Leaders (*G5*), D. Batt; I. Cooper; S. Judge;
Ms C. Slocock; D. Truman

EXECUTIVE AGENCIES

CENTRAL STATISTICAL OFFICE
— *see* page 293

PAYMASTER
— *see* page 336

ROYAL MINT
— *see* page 342

THE TREASURY SOLICITOR
DEPARTMENT OF HM PROCURATOR-GENERAL AND
TREASURY SOLICITOR
Queen Anne's Chambers, 28 Broadway, London
SW1H 9JS
Tel 0171-210 3000

The Treasury Solicitor's Department provides legal
services for many government departments. Those without their own lawyers are provided with legal advice, and
both they and other departments are provided with
litigation services. The Treasury Solicitor is also the
Queen's Proctor, and is responsible for collecting Bona
Vacantia on behalf of the Crown.
HM Procurator-General and Treasury Solicitor (*G1*), vacant
Deputy Treasury Solicitor (*G2*), D. A. Hogg

CENTRAL ADVISORY DIVISION
Grade 5, Mrs I. G. Letwin

LITIGATION DIVISION
Grade 3, D. Brummell
Grade 4, F. L. Croft
Grade 5, Mrs D. Babar; Miss P. J. Carroll; A. D. Lawton;
A. Leithead; P. R. Messer; Mrs J. B. C. Oliver; D. Palmer;
R. J. Phillips; A. J. Sandal; P. F. O. Whitehurst

QUEEN'S PROCTOR DIVISION
Queen's Proctor, vacant
Assistant Queen's Proctor, Mrs D. Babar

RESOURCES AND SERVICES DIVISION
Principal Establishment and Finance Officer and Security Officer
(*G5*), A. J. E. Hollis
*Departmental Services Manager and Deputy Establishment and
Security Officer* (*G7*), R. B. M. Smith
Personnel Officer (*G7*), Ms H. Donnelly
Finance Officer (*G7*), C. A. Woolley
Information Systems Manager (*G7*), G. N. Younger
Business Support Manager (*G7*), J. Hoadly

BONA VACANTIA DIVISION
Grade 5, vacant

EUROPEAN DIVISION
Grade 3, J. E. G. Vaux
Grade 5, J. E. Collins; D. Macrae

NATIONAL HERITAGE DIVISION
Grade 5, P. C. Jenkins

OFFICE OF PUBLIC SERVICE DIVISION
Grade 5, M. C. L. Carpenter

MINISTRY OF DEFENCE DIVISION
Metropole Building, Northumberland Avenue, London
WC2N 5BL
Tel 0171-218 4691
Grade 3, D. F. W. Pickup

Grade 5, J. R. J. Braggins; Miss V. F. Dewhurst

DEPARTMENT FOR EDUCATION AND EMPLOYMENT DIVISION
Caxton House, Tothill Street, London SW1H 9NF
Tel 0171-273 3000

Grade 3, H. R. L. Purse; R. N. Ricks
Grade 5, R. J. Baker; C. House; Miss R. Jeffreys;
N. A. D. Lambert; F. D. W. Clarke; A. D. Preston;
S. T. Harker

DEPARTMENT OF TRANSPORT DIVISION
2 Marsham Street, London SW1P 3EB
Tel 0171-276 3000

Grade 3, M. C. P. Thomas
Grade 5, D. J. Aries; R. G. Bellis; P. D. Coopman;
C. W. M. Ingram; A. G. Jones; R. Lines; N. C. Thomas

HM TREASURY ADVISORY DIVISION
Treasury Chambers, Parliament Street, London SW1P 3AG
Tel 0171-270 3000

Grade 2, M. A. Blythe
Grade 5, Mrs P. A. Dayer; M. J. Hemming; Mrs V. Collett;
Miss J. V. Stokes

GOVERNMENT PROPERTY LAWYERS
Riverside Chambers, Castle Street, Taunton, Somerset
TA1 4AP
Tel 01823-345200
An executive agency of the Treasury Solicitor's Department.

Chief Executive (G3), P. Horner
Group Directors (G5), M. Benmayor; I. P. Parker;
M. F. Rawlins; A. M. Scarfe
Director of Lands Advisory (G5), R. C. Paddock
Assistant Directors of Lands Advisory (G7), T. P. Baker;
S. R. Bould
Finance and Personnel Director (G7), M. J. Robbins

COUNCIL ON TRIBUNALS
7th Floor, 22 Kingsway, London WC2B 6LE
Tel 0171-936 7045

The Council on Tribunals is an independent statutory body. It keeps under review the constitution and working of the various tribunals which have been placed under its general supervision, and considers and reports on administrative procedures relating to statutory inquiries. It is consulted by government departments on proposals for legislation affecting tribunals and inquiries, and on proposals where the need for an appeals procedure may arise. It also offers advice on draft primary legislation. Some 70 tribunals are currently under the Council's supervision.

The Scottish Committee of the Council generally considers Scottish tribunals and matters relating only to Scotland.

Members of the Council are appointed by the Lord Chancellor and the Lord Advocate. The Scottish Committee is composed partly of members of the Council designated by the Lord Advocate and partly of others appointed by him. The Parliamentary Commissioner for Administration is ex officio a member of both the Council and the Scottish Committee.

Chairman, The Lord Archer of Sandwell, PC, QC
Members, The Parliamentary Commissioner for
Administration; Mrs A. Anderson; G. A. Anderson;
T. N. Biggart, CBE, WS (*Chairman of the Scottish Committee*);
M. B. Dempsey; Mrs S. Friend, MBE; C. Heaps; B. Hill,

CBE; Prof. M. J. Hill; W. N. Hyde; R. H. Jones, CVO; Dr
C. A. Kaplan; L. F. Read, QC; I. D. Penman, CB; Prof.
M. Partington
Secretary, J. D. Saunders

SCOTTISH COMMITTEE OF THE COUNCIL ON TRIBUNALS
44 Palmerston Place, Edinburgh EH12 5BJ
Tel 0131-220 1236

Chairman, T. N. Biggart, CBE, WS
Members, The Parliamentary Commissioner for
Administration; G. A. Anderson; Mrs H. Sheerin, OBE;
Ms M. Burns; Mrs A. Middleton; I. D. Penman, CB;
Mrs P. Y. Berry
Secretary, Mrs E. MacRae

TRIBUNALS
— *see* pages 376–9

UNRELATED LIVE TRANSPLANT REGULATORY AUTHORITY
Department of Health, Room 520, Eileen House,
80–94 Newington Causeway, London SE1 6EF
Tel 0171-972 2739

The Unrelated Live Transplant Regulatory Authority (ULTRA) is a statutory body established in 1990. In every case where the transplant of an organ within the definition of the Human Organ Transplants Act 1989 is proposed between a living donor and a recipient who are not genetically related, the proposal must be referred to ULTRA. Applications must be made by registered medical practitioners.

The Authority comprises a chairman and ten members appointed by the Secretary of State for Health. The secretariat is provided by Department of Health officials.
Chairman, Prof. M. Bobrow, CBE
Members, Revd Prof. G. R. Dunstan, CBE; Dr P. A. Dyer;
Mrs D. Eccles; Prof. M. G. McGeown, CBE;
S. G. Macpherson; Prof. N. P. Mallick;
Prof. J. R. Salaman; Miss F. Smithers; Miss S. M. Taber;
J. Wellbeloved
Administrative Secretary, J. R. Walden
Medical Secretary, Dr P. Doyle

WALES YOUTH AGENCY
Leslie Court, Lon-y-Llyn, Caerphilly, Mid Glamorgan
CF8 1BQ
Tel 01222-880088

The Wales Youth Agency is a non-departmental public body funded by the Welsh Office. Its functions include the encouragement and development of the partnership between statutory and voluntary agencies relating to young people; the promotion of staff development and training; and the extension of marketing and information services in the relevant fields. The board of directors is appointed by the Secretary of State for Wales; directors do not receive a salary.
Chairman of the Board of Directors, G. Davies
Vice-Chairman of the Board of Directors, Dr H. Williamson
Executive Director, B. Williams

OFFICE OF WATER SERVICES
Centre City Tower, 7 Hill Street, Birmingham B5 4UA
Tel 0121-625 1300

The Office of Water Services (Ofwat) was set up under the Water Act 1989 to support the Director-General of Water Services, who regulates the economic framework of the water industry in England and Wales. His main duties are to ensure that water and sewerage companies (*see* page 496) can carry out and finance the functions specified in the Water Act, and to protect the interests of water consumers. The Director-General has established ten regional customer service committees which investigate complaints and identify customer concerns. The Ofwat National Customer Council is a non-statutory body set up by the Director-General in 1993 to represent the views of water customers nationally.

The Director-General is independent of ministerial control and directly accountable to Parliament.
Director-General of Water Services, I. C. R. Byatt

WELSH DEVELOPMENT AGENCY
Pearl House, Greyfriars Road, Cardiff CF1 3XX
Tel 01433-845500

The Welsh Development Agency was established under the Welsh Development Agency Act 1975 and came into existence in 1976. Its remit is to help further the regeneration of the economy and improve the environment in Wales. The Agency's main activities include helping to boost the growth, profitability and competitiveness of indigenous Welsh companies; encouraging investment by the private sector in site development; grant-aiding land reclamation; and stimulating quality urban and rural regeneration and development. Through its International Division it also promotes inward investment into Wales.
Chairman, D. Rowe-Beddoe
Deputy Chairman, vacant
Chief Executive, B. Hartop

WELSH OFFICE

The Welsh Office has responsibility in Wales for ministerial functions relating to health and personal social services; education, except for terms and conditions of service and student awards; training; the Welsh language, arts and culture; the implementation of the Citizen's Charter in Wales; local government; housing; water and sewerage; environmental protection; sport; agriculture and fisheries; forestry; land use, including town and country planning and countryside and nature conservation; new towns; non-departmental public bodies and appointments in Wales; ancient monuments and historic buildings and the Welsh Arts Council; roads; tourism; financial assistance to industry; the Strategic Development Scheme in Wales and the Programme for the Valleys; the operation of the European Regional Development Fund in Wales and other European Community matters; civil emergencies; and all financial aspects of these matters, including Welsh rate support grant.

Gwydyr House, Whitehall, London SW1A 2ER
Tel 0171-270 3000

Secretary of State for Wales, The Rt. Hon. William Hague, MP
Private Secretary, Miss K. Jennings
Parliamentary Under-Secretaries, Gwilym Jones, MP; Roderick Richards, MP
Private Secretaries, V. R. Watkin; M. Parkinson
Special Adviser, H. Williams
Parliamentary Clerk, A. Green
Permanent Secretary (*G1*), M. C. Scholar, CB
Private Secretary, R. Shearer

Cathays Park, Cardiff CF1 3NQ
Tel 01222-825111

LEGAL GROUP
Legal Adviser (*G3*), D. G. Lambert
Assistant Solicitors (*G5*), P. J. Murrin; J. H. Turnbull

INFORMATION DIVISION
Director of Information (*G5*), H. G. Roberts
Chief Press Officer (*G7*), R. Lehnert
Principal Publicity Officer (*G7*), W. J. Edwards

ESTABLISHMENT GROUP
Principal Establishment Officer (*G3*), C. D. Stevens
Heads of Divisions (*G5*), R. M. Abel; G. A. Thomas; Ms H. Angus
Chief Statistician (*G5*), W. R. L. Alldritt
Head of Health Statistics and Analysis Unit (*G6*), M. R. Brand
Head of Training and Education Intelligence Unit (*G6*), P. J. Fullerton
Medical Director of Cancer Registry, Dr M. Cotter

FINANCE GROUP
Principal Finance Officer (*G3*), R. A. Wallace
Heads of Divisions (*G5*), D. T. Richards; L. A. Pavelin
Senior Economic Adviser (*G5*), M. G. Phelps
Grade 6, M. G. Horlock
Head of Internal Audit (*G6*), D. Howarth

AGRICULTURE, ECONOMIC DEVELOPMENT AND INDUSTRY AND TRAINING
Deputy Secretary (*G2*), J. F. Craig, CB

AGRICULTURE DEPARTMENT
Head of Department (*G3*), L. K. Walford
Heads of Divisions (*G5*), G. Podmore; D. R. Thomas
Divisional Executive Officers (*G7*), W. K. Griffiths (*Carmarthen*); E. Hughes (*Caernarfon*); J. C. Alexander (*Llandrindod Wells*)

ECONOMIC DEVELOPMENT GROUP
Head of Group (*G3*), M. J. Cochlin
Heads of Divisions (*G5*), B. J. Mitchell; Miss E. N. M. Davies; M. L. Evans

INDUSTRY AND TRAINING DEPARTMENT
Director (*G3*), D. W. Jones
Industrial Director (*G4*), J. Cameron
Heads of Divisions (*G5*), G. T. Evans; H. Brodie; N. E. Thomas; (*G6*), Dr R. J. Loveland

EDUCATION, HOUSING, HEALTH AND SOCIAL SERVICES, TRANSPORT, LOCAL GOVERNMENT, PLANNING AND ENVIRONMENT
Deputy Secretary (*G2*), J. W. Lloyd, CB

EDUCATION DEPARTMENT
Head of Department (*G3*), S. H. Martin
Heads of Divisions (*G5*)°, W. G. Davies; H. Evans; R. J. Davies; Dr H. F. Rawlings

OFFICE OF HM CHIEF INSPECTOR FOR SCHOOLS IN WALES

Chief Inspector (*G4*)°, R. L. James
Staff Inspectors (*G5*)°, S. J. Adams; J. R. N. Evans; T. E. Parry; G. Thomas; P. Thomas
There are 45 Grade 6 Inspectors.
Head of Administration (*G7*), J. Roberts

LOCAL GOVERNMENT FINANCE, HOUSING AND SOCIAL SERVICES GROUP

Head of Group (*G3*), R. W. Jarman
Heads of Divisions (*G5*), D. Adams; M. J. Clancy; Mrs B. J. M. Wilson; Mrs E. A. Taylor
Chief Inspector, Social Services Inspectorate (*Wales*) (*G5*), D. G. Evans
Deputy Chief Inspectors, J. F. Mooney; R. C. Woodward
Social Services Inspectors (*G7*), D, Barker; D. A. Brushett; G. H. Davies; Miss R. E. Evans; I. Forster; Mrs J. Jenkins; C. D. Vyvyan; Mrs P. White

HEALTH DEPARTMENT

Director (*G3*), P. R. Gregory
Heads of Divisions (*G5*), D. H. Jones; D. A. Pritchard; C. L. Jones; B. Wilcox; R. C. Williams; A. G. Thornton

HEALTH PROFESSIONAL GROUP

Chief Medical Officer (*G3*), Dr D. J. Hine

Public Health Sub Group (*HPG M1*)
Deputy Chief Medical Officer (*G4*), Dr A. M. George
Senior Medical Officers (*G5*), Dr J. Ludlow; Dr J. G. Avery

Hospital Services Sub Group (*HPG M2*)
Principal Medical Officer (*G4*), Dr B. Fuge
Senior Medical Officers (*G5*), Dr D. Salter; Dr P. Lyne

Community and Primary Care Services Sub Group (*HPG M3*)
Principal Medical Officer (*G4*), Dr J. K. Richmond
Senior Medical Officers (*G5*), D. E. Davies; Dr R. Owen; Dr H. N. Williams
Medical Adviser (*part time*), Dr J. Andrew
Chief Dental Officer (*G5*), D. M. Heap
Senior Dental Officer (*G5*), P. Langmaid
Chief Scientific Adviser (*G5*), Dr J. A. V. Pritchard
Deputy Scientific Adviser (*G6*), Dr E. O. Crawley
Chief Pharmaceutical Adviser (*G5*), Dr G. B. A. Veitch
Deputy Pharmaceutical Adviser (*G6*), Mrs D. Kay Roberts
Chief Environmental Health Adviser (*G5*), R. Alexander
Deputy Environmental Health Adviser (*G6*), D. Worthington

NURSING DIVISION

Chief Nursing Officer, Miss M. Bull
Deputy Chief Nursing Officer, Mrs B. Melvin
Nursing Officers, Mrs S. M. Drayton; P. Johnson; Mrs J. Sait; M. F. Tonkin

TRANSPORT, PLANNING AND ENVIRONMENT GROUP

Head of Group (*G3*), G. C. G. Craig
Director of Highways (*G4*), K. J. Thomas°
Deputy Director of Highways (*G5*), J. G. Evans*
Heads of Divisions (*G5*), A. H. H. Jones; D. I. Westlake°
Chief Planning Adviser (*G5*), W. P. Roderick
Superintending Engineers (*G6*), J. R. Rees*; B. H. Hawker, OBE*
Chief Estates Adviser (*G6*), G. K. Hoad
Senior Principal (*G6*), P. R. Marsden
Scientific Adviser (*G6*), Dr H. Prosser
Principal Planning Officers (*G7*), L. Owen; J. V. Spear

Principal Research Officers (*G7*), A. S. Dredge; Ms L. J. Roberts
Principal Estates Officer (*G7*), R. W. Wilson
Principal Professional and Technology Officers, Highways Directorate° (*G7*), M. J. Gilbert*; I. A. Grindulais; A. P. Howcroft; A. L. Perry; R. H. Powell; S. C. Shouler; J. Collins; K. J. Alexander; R. H. Hooper*; R. K. Cone; J. Dawkins; T. Dorken; R. Shaw; M. J. A. Parker; V. S. Pownall*

LOCAL GOVERNMENT REORGANIZATION GROUP

Head of Group (*G3*), J. D. Shortridge

HM INSPECTORATE OF POLLUTION FOR WALES
11th Floor, Brunel House, 2 Fitzalan Road, Cardiff CF2 ITT
Tel 01222-49558

The Inspectorate's functions will be taken over by the proposed new Environment Agency for England and Wales in April 1996.

Inspector, Hazardous Wastes (*G7*), G. Taylor
Inspector, Radiation and Chemicals (*G7*) (*acting*), Dr C. Hardman
Inspector, Water (*G7*), A. A. Houlden

HEALTH AUTHORITIES

CLWYD, Preswylfa, Hendy Road, Mold, Clwyd CH7 1PZ. *Chief Executive Director*, B. F. Jones
DYFED, St David's Hospital, Jobswell Road, Carmarthen, Dyfed SA31 3HB. *Managing Director*, M. Ponton
GWENT, Mamhilad Park Estate, Pontypool, Gwent NP4 0YP. *Chief Executive*, J. Hallett
GWYNEDD, Coed Mawr, Bangor, Gwynedd LL57 4TP. *District General Manager*, C. H. Thomas
MID GLAMORGAN, District Headquarters, Albert Road, Pontypridd CF37 1LA. *District General Manager*, E. J. Thomas
POWYS, Mansion House, Bronllys, Brecon, Powys LD3 0LS. *Chief Executive*, Mrs P. A. Archer-Jones
SOUTH GLAMORGAN, Temple of Peace and Health, Cathays Park, Cardiff CF1 3NW. *Chief Executive*, Dr G. B. Todd
WEST GLAMORGAN, The Oldway Centre, 36 Orchard Street, Swansea SA1 5AQ. *Chief Executive Director*, A. Beddow

EXECUTIVE AGENCIES

AGRICULTURAL DEVELOPMENT AND ADVISORY SERVICE (ADAS)
— *see* page 284

CADW: WELSH HISTORIC MONUMENTS
Brunel House, Fitzalan Road, Cardiff CF2 1UY
Tel 01222-465511

Cadw supports the preservation, conservation, appreciation and enjoyment of the built heritage in Wales.
Chief Executive, T. Cassidy
Director of Policy and Administration, R. W. Hughes
Conservation Architect (*G6*), J. D. Hogg
Principal Inspector of Ancient Monuments and Historic Buildings, J. R. Avent
Inspectors of Ancient Monuments and Historic Buildings, J. K. Knight; A. D. McLees; Dr S. E. Rees; R. C. Turner; M. J. Yates

INTERVENTION BOARD
— *see* page 319

Based at:
° Ty Glas Road, Llanishen, Cardiff CF4 5LE. Tel: 01222-761456
* Government Buildings, Dinerth Road, Rhos-on-Sea, Colwyn Bay LL28 4UL. Tel: 01492-44261

PLANNING INSPECTORATE
Cathays Park, Cardiff CF1 3NQ
Tel 01222-823892

A joint executive agency of the Department of the Environment and the Welsh Office (*see* page 302).
Chief Executive and Chief Inspector of Planning (*G3*),
    C. Shepley
Assistant Chief Planning Inspector (*G5*), Mrs S. Bruton

WOMEN'S NATIONAL COMMISSION
Level 4, Caxton House, Tothill Street, London SW1H 9NF
Tel 0171-273 5486

The Women's National Commission is an independent advisory committee to the Government. Its remit is to ensure by all possible means that the informed opinions of women are given their due weight in the deliberations of the Government. The Commission's 50 members are all women who are elected or appointed by national organizations with a large and active membership of women. The organizations include the women's sections of the major political parties, trade unions and religious groups, professional women's organizations and other bodies broadly representative of women.
Government Co-Chairman, Mrs A. Browning, MP
Elected Co-Chairman, Mrs E. Bavidge
Joint Secretaries, Ms J. Bailey; Ms W. Brown

Law Courts and Offices

THE JUDICIAL COMMITTEE OF THE PRIVY COUNCIL

The Judicial Committee of the Privy Council is the final court of appeal from courts of the United Kingdom dependencies and courts of independent Commonwealth countries which have retained the right of appeal (Antigua and Barbuda, the Bahamas, Barbados, Belize, Brunei, Dominica, The Gambia, Jamaica, Kiribati, Mauritius, New Zealand, St Christopher and Nevis, St Lucia, St Vincent and the Grenadines, Trinidad and Tobago, and Tuvalu). The Committee also hears appeals from courts of the Channel Islands and the Isle of Man, the disciplinary and health committees of the medical and allied professions, and some ecclesiastical appeals under the Pastoral Measure 1983.

The Judicial Committee includes the Lord Chancellor, the Lords of Appeal in Ordinary (*see* page 362) and other members of the Privy Council who hold or have held high judicial office, and certain judges from the Commonwealth. Commonwealth appeals are usually heard by a board of five judges.

PRIVY COUNCIL OFFICE (JUDICIAL COMMITTEE), Downing Street, London SW1A 2AJ. Tel: 0171-270 0483

Registrar of the Privy Council, D. H. O. Owen

Chief Clerk, K. N. Stringer

The Judicature of England and Wales

The legal system of England and Wales is separate from those of Scotland and Northern Ireland and differs between them in law, judicial procedure and court structure, although there is a common distinction between civil law (disputes between individuals) and criminal law (acts harmful to the community).

The supreme judicial authority for England and Wales is the House of Lords, which is the ultimate Court of Appeal from all courts in Great Britain and Northern Ireland (except criminal courts in Scotland) for all cases except those concerning the interpretation and application of European Community law, including preliminary rulings requested by British courts and tribunals, which are decided by the European Court of Justice (*see* pages 780–1). As a Court of Appeal the House of Lords consists of the Lord Chancellor and the Lords of Appeal in Ordinary (law lords).

The Supreme Court of Judicature comprises the Court of Appeal, the High Court of Justice and the Crown Court. The High Court of Justice is the superior civil court and is divided into three divisions. The Chancery Division is concerned mainly with equity, bankruptcy and contentious probate business. The Queen's Bench Division deals with commercial and maritime law, serious personal injury and medical negligence cases, cases involving a breach of contract and professional negligence actions. The Family Division deals with matters relating to family law. Sittings are held at the Royal Courts of Justice in London or at 126 District Registries outside the capital. High Court judges sit alone to hear cases at first instance. Appeals from lower courts are heard by two or three judges, or by single judges of the appropriate division. The Restrictive Practices Court, set up under the Restrictive Trade Practices Act 1956, and the Official Referees' Courts, which deal almost exclusively with cases concerning the construction industry, are also part of the High Court. Appeals from the High Court are heard in the Court of Appeal (Civil Division), presided over by the Master of the Rolls, and may go on to the House of Lords.

In criminal matters the decision to prosecute in the majority of cases rests with the Crown Prosecution Service, the independent prosecuting body in England and Wales (*see* page 370). At the head of the service is the Director of Public Prosecutions, who discharges her duties under the superintendence of the Attorney-General. Certain categories of offence continue to require the Attorney-General's consent for prosecution.

The Crown Court sits in about 90 centres, divided into six circuits, and is presided over by High Court judges, full-time circuit judges, and part-time recorders and assistant recorders, sitting with a jury in all trials which are contested. There were 338 assistant recorders at 22 June 1995. The Crown Court deals with trials of the more serious criminal offences, the sentencing of offenders committed for sentence by magistrates' courts (when the magistrates consider their own power of sentence inadequate), and appeals from magistrates' courts. Magistrates usually sit with a circuit judge or recorder to deal with appeals and committals for sentence. Appeals from the Crown Court, either against sentence or conviction, are made to the Court of Appeal (Criminal Division), presided over by the Lord Chief Justice. A further appeal from the Court of Appeal to the House of Lords can be brought if a point of law of general public importance is considered to be involved.

Minor criminal offences (summary offences) are dealt with in magistrates' courts, which usually consist of three unpaid lay magistrates (justices of the peace) sitting without a jury, who are advised on points of law and procedure by a legally-qualified clerk to the justices. There were 30,088 justices of the peace at 1 January 1995. In busier courts a full-time, salaried and legally-qualified stipendiary magistrate presides alone. Cases involving people under 18 are heard in youth courts, specially constituted magistrates' courts which sit apart from other courts. Preliminary proceedings in a serious case to decide whether there is evidence to justify committal for trial in the Crown Court are also dealt with in the magistrates' courts. Appeals from magistrates' courts against sentence or conviction are made to the Crown Court. Appeals upon a point of law are made to the High Court, and may go on to the House of Lords.

Most minor civil cases are dealt with by the county courts, of which there are about 270 (details may be found in the local telephone directory). Cases are heard by circuit judges or district judges. There were 315 district judges at 30 June 1995. For cases involving small claims there are special simplified procedures. Where there are financial limits on county court jurisdiction, claims which exceed those limits may be tried in the county courts with the consent of the parties, or in certain circumstances on transfer from the High Court. Outside London, bankruptcy proceedings can be heard in designated county courts. Magistrates' courts can deal with certain classes of civil case and committees of magistrates license public houses, clubs and betting shops. For the implementation of the Children Act 1989, a new structure of hearing centres was set up in 1991 for family proceedings cases, involving magistrates' courts (family proceedings courts), divorce county courts, family hearing centres and care centres. Appeals in family matters heard in the family proceedings courts go to the Family Division of the High Court; affiliation appeals and appeals from decisions of the licensing committees of magistrates go to the Crown Court. Appeals from county courts are heard in the Court of Appeal (Civil Division), and may go on to the House of Lords.

Coroners' courts investigate violent and unnatural deaths or sudden deaths where the cause is unknown. Cases may be brought before a local coroner (a senior lawyer or doctor) by doctors, the police, various public authorities or members of the public. Where a death is sudden and the cause is unknown, the coroner may order a post-mortem examination to determine the cause of death rather than hold an inquest in court.

Judicial appointments are made by The Queen; the most senior appointments are made on the advice of the Prime Minister and other appointments on the advice of the Lord Chancellor.

Under the provisions of the Criminal Appeal Act 1995, a Commission will be set up to direct and supervise investigations into possible miscarriages of justice and to refer cases to the courts on the grounds of conviction and sentence; these functions were formerly the responsibility of the Home Secretary.

THE HOUSE OF LORDS
AS FINAL COURT OF APPEAL

The Lord High Chancellor
The Rt. Hon. the Lord Mackay of Clashfern, *born* 1927, *apptd* 1987

LORDS OF APPEAL IN ORDINARY (each £114,874)
Style, The Rt. Hon. Lord —

Rt. Hon. Lord Keith of Kinkel, *born* 1922, *apptd* 1977
Rt. Hon. Lord Goff of Chieveley, *born* 1926, *apptd* 1986
Rt. Hon. Lord Jauncey of Tullichettle, *born* 1925, *apptd* 1988
Rt. Hon. Lord Browne-Wilkinson, *born* 1930, *apptd* 1991
Rt. Hon. Lord Mustill, *born* 1931, *apptd* 1992
Rt. Hon. Lord Slynn of Hadley, *born* 1930, *apptd* 1992
Rt. Hon. Lord Woolf, *born* 1933, *apptd* 1992
Rt. Hon. Lord Lloyd of Berwick, *born* 1929, *apptd* 1993
Rt. Hon. Lord Nolan, *born* 1928, *apptd* 1994
Rt. Hon. Lord Nicholls of Birkenhead, *born* 1933, *apptd* 1994
Rt. Hon. Lord Steyn, *born* 1932, *apptd* 1995
Rt. Hon. Lord Hoffman, *born* 1934, *apptd* 1995
Registrar, The Clerk of the Parliaments (*see* page 223)

SUPREME COURT OF JUDICATURE

COURT OF APPEAL

The Master of the Rolls (£114,874), The Rt. Hon. Sir Thomas Bingham, *born* 1933, *apptd* 1992
Secretary, Miss V. Seymour
Clerk, D. G. Grimmett

LORDS JUSTICES OF APPEAL (each £110,137)
Style, The Rt. Hon. Lord/Lady Justice [surname]

Rt. Hon. Sir Brian Neill, *born* 1923, *apptd* 1985
Rt. Hon. Sir Martin Nourse, *born* 1932, *apptd* 1985
Rt. Hon. Sir Patrick Russell, *born* 1926, *apptd* 1987
Rt. Hon. Dame Elizabeth Butler-Sloss, DBE, *born* 1933, *apptd* 1988
Rt. Hon. Sir Murray Stuart-Smith, *born* 1927, *apptd* 1988
Rt. Hon. Sir Christopher Staughton, *born* 1933, *apptd* 1988
Rt. Hon. Sir Anthony McCowan, *born* 1928, *apptd* 1989
Rt. Hon. Sir Roy Beldam, *born* 1925, *apptd* 1989
Rt. Hon. Sir Andrew Leggatt, *born* 1930, *apptd* 1990
Rt. Hon. Sir Paul Kennedy, *born* 1935, *apptd* 1992
Rt. Hon. Sir David Hirst, *born* 1925, *apptd* 1992
Rt. Hon. Sir Simon Brown, *born* 1937, *apptd* 1992
Rt. Hon. Sir Anthony Evans, *born* 1934, *apptd* 1992
Rt. Hon. Sir Christopher Rose, *born* 1937, *apptd* 1992
Rt. Hon. Sir John Waite, *born* 1932, *apptd* 1993
Rt. Hon. Sir John Roch, *born* 1934, *apptd* 1993
Rt. Hon. Sir Peter Gibson, *born* 1934, *apptd* 1993
Rt. Hon. Sir John Hobhouse, *born* 1932, *apptd* 1993
Rt. Hon. Sir Denis Henry, *born* 1931, *apptd* 1993
Rt. Hon. Sir Mark Saville, *born* 1936, *apptd* 1994
Rt. Hon. Sir Peter Millett, *born* 1932, *apptd* 1994
Rt. Hon. Sir Swinton Thomas, *born* 1931, *apptd* 1994
Rt. Hon. Sir Andrew Morritt, CVO, *born* 1938, *apptd* 1994
Rt. Hon. Sir Philip Otton, *born* 1933, *apptd* 1995
Rt. Hon. Sir Robin Auld, *born* 1937, *apptd* 1995
Rt. Hon. Sir Malcolm Pill, *born* 1938, *apptd* 1995
Rt. Hon. Sir William Aldous, *born* 1936, *apptd* 1995
Rt. Hon. Sir Alan Ward, *born* 1938, *apptd* 1995
Rt. Hon. Sir Michael Hutchison, *born* 1933, *apptd* 1995
Rt. Hon. Sir Konrad Schiemann, *born* 1937, *apptd* 1995
Rt. Hon. Sir Nicholas Phillips, *born* 1938, *apptd* 1995
Rt. Hon. Sir Mathew Thorpe, *born* 1938, *apptd* 1995

Ex officio Judges, The Lord High Chancellor; the Lord Chief Justice of England; the Master of the Rolls; the President of the Family Division; and the Vice-Chancellor

COURT OF APPEAL (CRIMINAL DIVISION)
Judges, The Lord Chief Justice of England; the Master of the Rolls; Lords Justices of Appeal; and Judges of the High Court of Justice

COURTS-MARTIAL APPEAL COURT
Judges, The Lord Chief Justice of England; the Master of the Rolls; Lords Justices of Appeal; and Judges of the High Court of Justice

HIGH COURT OF JUSTICE
CHANCERY DIVISION

President, The Lord High Chancellor
The Vice-Chancellor (£110,137), The Rt. Hon. Sir Richard Scott, *born* 1934, *apptd* 1994
Clerk, W. Northfield, BEM

JUDGES (each £98,957)
Style, The Hon. Mr/Mrs Justice [surname]

Hon. Sir Jeremiah Harman, *born* 1930, *apptd* 1982
Hon. Sir John Knox, *born* 1925, *apptd* 1985
Hon. Sir Donald Rattee, *born* 1937, *apptd* 1989
Hon. Sir John Mummery, *born* 1938, *apptd* 1989
Hon. Sir Francis Ferris, TD, *born* 1932, *apptd* 1990
Hon. Sir John Chadwick, ED, *born* 1941, *apptd* 1991
Hon. Sir Jonathan Parker, *born* 1937, *apptd* 1991
Hon. Sir John Lindsay, *born* 1935, *apptd* 1992
Hon. Dame Mary Arden, DBE, *born* 1947, *apptd* 1993

Hon. Sir Edward Evans-Lombe, *born* 1937, *apptd* 1993
Hon. Sir Robin Jacob, *born* 1941, *apptd* 1993
Hon. Sir William Blackburne, *born* 1944, *apptd* 1993
Hon. Sir Gavin Lightman, *born* 1939, *apptd* 1994
Hon. Sir Robert Walker, *born* 1938, *apptd* 1994
Hon. Sir Robert Carnwath, *born* 1945, *apptd* 1994
Hon. Sir Colin Rimer, *born* 1944, *apptd* 1994
Hon. Sir Hugh Laddie, *born* 1946, *apptd* 1995

HIGH COURT OF JUSTICE IN BANKRUPTCY

Judges, The Vice-Chancellor and judges of the Chancery Division of the High Court

COMPANIES COURT

Judges, The Vice Chancellor and judges of the Chancery Division of the High Court

PATENT COURT (APPELLATE SECTION)

Judge, The Hon. Mr Justice Jacob

QUEEN'S BENCH DIVISION

The Lord Chief Justice of England (£124,138) The Rt. Hon. the Lord Taylor of Gosforth, *born* 1930, *apptd* 1992
Private Secretary, E. Adams
Clerk, J. Bond

JUDGES (each £98,957)
Style, The Hon. Mr/Mrs Justice [surname]

Hon. Sir Ronald Waterhouse, *born* 1926, *apptd* 1978
Hon. Sir Christopher French, *born* 1925, *apptd* 1979
Hon. Sir Charles McCullough, *born* 1931, *apptd* 1981
Hon. Sir Oliver Popplewell, *born* 1927, *apptd* 1983
Hon. Sir William Macpherson of Cluny, TD, *born* 1926, *apptd* 1983
Hon. Sir Richard Tucker, *born* 1930, *apptd* 1985
Hon. Sir Robert Gatehouse, *born* 1924, *apptd* 1985
Hon. Sir Patrick Garland, *born* 1929, *apptd* 1985
Hon. Sir Michael Turner, *born* 1931, *apptd* 1985
Hon. Sir John Alliott, *born* 1932, *apptd* 1986
Hon. Sir Harry Ognall, *born* 1934, *apptd* 1986
Hon. Sir John Owen, *born* 1925, *apptd* 1986
Hon. Sir Humphrey Potts, *born* 1931, *apptd* 1986
Hon. Sir Richard Rougier, *born* 1932, *apptd* 1986
Hon. Sir Ian Kennedy, *born* 1930, *apptd* 1986
Hon. Sir Stuart McKinnon, *born* 1938, *apptd* 1988
Hon. Sir Mark Potter, *born* 1937, *apptd* 1988
Hon. Sir Scott Baker, *born* 1937, *apptd* 1988
Hon. Sir Henry Brooke, *born* 1936, *apptd* 1988
Hon. Sir Igor Judge, *born* 1941, *apptd* 1988
Hon. Sir Edwin Jowitt, *born* 1929, *apptd* 1988
Hon. Sir Michael Morland, *born* 1929, *apptd* 1989
Hon. Sir Mark Waller, *born* 1940, *apptd* 1989
Hon. Sir Roger Buckley, *born* 1939, *apptd* 1989
Hon. Sir Anthony Hidden, *born* 1936, *apptd* 1989
Hon. Sir Michael Wright, *born* 1932, *apptd* 1990
Hon. Sir Charles Mantell, *born* 1937, *apptd* 1990
Hon. Sir John Blofeld, *born* 1932, *apptd* 1990
Hon. Sir Peter Cresswell, *born* 1944, *apptd* 1991
Hon. Sir Anthony May, *born* 1940, *apptd* 1991
Hon. Sir John Laws, *born* 1945, *apptd* 1992
Hon. Dame Ann Ebsworth, DBE, *born* 1937, *apptd* 1992
Hon. Sir Simon Tuckey, *born* 1941, *apptd* 1992
Hon. Sir David Latham, *born* 1942, *apptd* 1992
Hon. Sir Christopher Holland, *born* 1937, *apptd* 1992
Hon. Sir John Kay, *born* 1943, *apptd* 1992
Hon. Sir Richard Curtis, *born* 1933, *apptd* 1992
Hon. Sir Stephen Sedley, *born* 1939, *apptd* 1992
Hon. Dame Janet Smith, DBE, *born* 1940, *apptd* 1992
Hon. Sir Anthony Colman, *born* 1938, *apptd* 1992

Hon. Sir Anthony Clarke, *born* 1943, *apptd* 1993
Hon. Sir John Dyson, *born* 1943, *apptd* 1993
Hon. Sir Thayne Forbes, *born* 1938, *apptd* 1993
Hon. Sir Michael Sachs, *born* 1932, *apptd* 1993
Hon. Sir Stephen Mitchell, *born* 1941, *apptd* 1993
Hon. Sir Rodger Bell, *born* 1939, *apptd* 1993
Hon. Sir Michael Harrison, *born* 1939, *apptd* 1993
Hon. Sir Bernard Rix, *born* 1944, *apptd* 1993
Hon. Dame Heather Steel, DBE, *born* 1940, *apptd* 1993
Hon. Sir William Gage, *born* 1938, *apptd* 1993
Hon. Sir Jonathan Mance, *born* 1943, *apptd* 1993
Hon. Sir Andrew Longmore, *born* 1944, *apptd* 1993
Hon. Sir Thomas Morison, *born* 1939, *apptd* 1993
Hon. Sir Richard Buxton, *born* 1938, *apptd* 1993
Hon. Sir David Keene, *born* 1941, *apptd* 1994
Hon. Sir Andrew Collins, *born* 1942, *apptd* 1994
Hon. Sir Maurice Kay, *born* 1942, *apptd* 1995
Hon. Sir Brian Smedley, *born* 1934, *apptd* 1995
Hon. Sir Anthony Hooper, *born* 1937, *apptd* 1995
Hon. Sir Alexander Butterfield, *born* 1942, *apptd* 1995
Hon. Sir George Newman, *born* 1941, *apptd* 1995
Hon. Sir David Poole, *born* 1938, *apptd* 1995

FAMILY DIVISION

President (£110,137) Rt. Hon. Sir Stephen Brown, *born* 1929, *apptd* 1988
Secretary, Mrs S. Leung
Clerk, Mrs S. Bell

JUDGES (each £98,957)
Style, The Hon. Mr/Mrs Justice [surname]

Hon. Sir Anthony Hollis, *born* 1927, *apptd* 1982
Hon. Sir Edward Cazalet, *born* 1936, *apptd* 1988
Hon. Sir Robert Johnson, *born* 1933, *apptd* 1989
Hon. Sir Douglas Brown, *born* 1931, *apptd* 1989
Hon. Dame Joyanne Bracewell, DBE, *born* 1934, *apptd* 1990
Hon. Sir Michael Connell, *born* 1939, *apptd* 1991
Hon. Sir Peter Singer, *born* 1944, *apptd* 1993
Hon. Sir Nicholas Wilson, *born* 1945, *apptd* 1993
Hon. Sir Nicholas Wall, *born* 1945, *apptd* 1993
Hon. Sir Andrew Kirkwood, *born* 1944, *apptd* 1993
Hon. Sir Christopher Stuart-White, *born* 1933, *apptd* 1993
Hon. Dame Brenda Hale, DBE, *born* 1945, *apptd* 1994
Hon. Sir Hugh Bennett, *born* 1943, *apptd* 1995
Hon. Sir Edward Holman, *born* 1947, *apptd* 1995

RESTRICTIVE PRACTICES COURT

Room 410, Thomas More Building, Royal Courts of Justice, Strand, London WC2A 2LL
Tel 0171-936 6727

President, The Hon. Mr Justice Buckley
Judges, The Hon. Mr Justice Ferris; The Hon. Mr Justice Buxton
Lay Members, B. M. Currie; Sir Lewis Robertson, CBE; R. Garrick, CBE; S. J. Ahearne; J. A. Graham; Mrs D. H. Hatfield; S. McDowall; J. A. Scott; B. D. Colgate; J. A. C. King
Clerk of the Court, M. Buckley

OFFICIAL REFEREES' COURTS

St Dunstan's House, 133–137 Fetter Lane, London EC4A 1HD
Tel 0171-936 7429

JUDGES (each £85,241)
His Hon. Judge Lewis, QC (*Senior Official Referee*)
His Hon. Judge Bowsher, QC
His Hon. Judge Loyd, QC
His Hon. Judge Hicks, QC

His Hon. Judge Havery, QC
His Hon. Judge Lloyd, QC
His Hon. Judge Newman, QC
His Hon. Judge Thornton, QC
Chief Clerk, Miss B. Joy

LORD CHANCELLOR'S DEPARTMENT
— *see* Government Departments and Public Offices

SUPREME COURT DEPARTMENTS AND OFFICES
Royal Courts of Justice, London WC2A 2LL
Tel 0171-936 6000

ADMINISTRATOR'S OFFICE
Administrator (G5), G. E. Calvett
Deputy Administrator (G6), I. Hyams
Secretary to the Family Division (G6), R. P. Knight

ADMIRALTY AND COMMERCIAL REGISTRY AND MARSHAL'S OFFICE
Registrar (£59,327), P. Miller
Marshal and Chief Clerk (G7), A. Ferrigno

BANKRUPTCY DEPARTMENT
Chief Registrar (£72,524), G. L. Pimm
Bankruptcy Registrars (£59,327), W. S. James;
   J. A. Simmonds; D. G. Scott; P. J. S. Rawson
Chief Clerk (SEO), M. Brown

CENTRAL OFFICE OF THE SUPREME COURT
Senior Master of the Supreme Court (QBD), *and Queen's Remembrancer* (£72,524), W. K. Topley
Masters of the Supreme Court (QBD) (£59,327), P. B.
   Creightmore; D. L. Prebble; G. H. Hodgson; R. L.
   Turner; J. Trench; M. Tennant; P. Miller; N. O. G.
   Murray; I. H. Foster; G. H. Rose; P. G. A. Eyre
Chief Clerk (*Central Office*) (G7), C. F. Jones

CHANCERY DIVISION
Chief Clerk (G7), P. Emery

CHANCERY CHAMBERS
Chief Master of the Supreme Court (£72,524), J. M. Dyson
Masters of the Supreme Court (£59,327), J. S. Gowers; G. A.
   Barratt; J. I. Winegarten; J. A. Moncaster
Chief Clerk (SEO), G. Robinson
Conveyancing Counsel of the Supreme Court, W. D. Ainger;
   H. M. Harrod; A. C. Taussig

COMPANIES COURT
Registrar (£59,327), M. Buckley
Chief Clerk (SEO), M. Brown

COURT OF APPEAL CIVIL DIVISION
Registrar (£72,524), J. D. R. Adams
Chief Clerk (SEO), Miss H. M. Goddard

COURT OF APPEAL CRIMINAL DIVISION
Registrar (£72,524), M. McKenzie, QC
Deputy Registrar (G5), M. N. Farmer
Chief Clerk (G7), M. Bishop

COURTS-MARTIAL APPEALS OFFICE
Registrar (£72,524), M. McKenzie, QC
Chief Clerk (G7), M. Bishop

CROWN OFFICE OF THE SUPREME COURT
Master of the Crown Office, and Queen's Coroner and Attorney
   (£72,524), M. McKenzie, QC
Head of Crown Office (G5), Mrs L. Knapman
Chief Clerk (G7), M. Bishop

EXAMINERS OF THE COURT
Empowered to take examination of witnesses in all Divisions of the High Court
R. G. Wood; Mrs G. M. Kenne; Miss L. Driscoll;
   R. M. Planterose; Miss V. E. I. Selvaratnam

RESTRICTIVE PRACTICES COURT
Clerk of the Court, M. Buckley
Chief Clerk (SEO), M. Brown

SUPREME COURT TAXING OFFICE
Chief Master (£72,524), P. T. Hurst
Masters of the Supreme Court (£59,327), C. R. N. Martyn;
   M. Ellis; T. H. Seager Berry; C. C. Wright; P. A. Rogers;
   G. N. Pollard
Chief Clerk (*Administration*) (G7), R. Cuthbert
Chief Taxing Officer (G7), T. J. Ryan

COURT OF PROTECTION
Stewart House, 24 Kingsway, London WC2B 6HD
Tel 0171-269 7000
Master (£72,524), Mrs A. B. Macfarlane

ELECTION PETITIONS OFFICE
Room E218, Royal Courts of Justice, Strand, London
WC2A 2LL
Tel 0171-936 6131
The office accepts petitions and deals with all matters relating to the questioning of parliamentary, European Parliament and local government elections, and with applications for relief under the Representation of the People legislation.
Prescribed Officer, W. K. Topley
Chief Clerk, Miss J. L. Waine

OFFICE OF THE LORD CHANCELLOR'S VISITORS
Rochester House, 33 Greycoat Street, London SW1P 2QF
Tel 0171-210 1389
Legal Visitor, A. R. Tyrrell
Medical Visitors, A. G. Fullerton; K. Khan; D. Parr;
   J. Roberts; W. B. Spry; E. Mateu

OFFICIAL RECEIVERS' DEPARTMENT
21 Bloomsbury Street, London WC1B 3SS
Tel 0171-323 3090
Senior Official Receiver, M. C. A. Osborne
Official Receivers, M. J. Pugh; L. T. Cramp; J. Norris

OFFICIAL SOLICITOR'S DEPARTMENT
81 Chancery Lane, London WC2B 6HD
Tel 0171-911 7105
Official Solicitor to the Supreme Court, P. M. Harris
Deputy Official Solicitor, H. J. Baker
Chief Clerk (G7), R. Lancaster

PRINCIPAL REGISTRY (FAMILY DIVISION)
Somerset House, London WC2R 1LP
Tel 0171-936 6000
Senior District Judge (£72,524), G. B. N. A. Angel
District Judges (£59,327), T. G. Guest; J. E. Artro-Morris;
   R. B. Rowe; B. P. F. Kenworthy-Browne; Mrs K. T.
   Moorhouse; M. J. Segal; R. Conn;
   Miss I. M. Plumstead; G. J. Maple; Miss H. C. Bradley;

K. J. White; A. R. S. Bassett-Cross; N. A. Grove;
M. C. Berry; Miss S. M. Bowman; C. Million;
P. Waller; Miss P. Cushing; R. Harper
Secretary (G6), R. P. Knight

District Probate Registrars
Birmingham and Stoke-on-Trent, C. Marsh
Brighton and Maidstone, M. N. Emery
Bristol, Exeter and Bodmin, P. L. Speyer
Ipswich, Norwich and Peterborough, E. R. Alexander
Leeds, Lincoln and Sheffield, A. P. Dawson
Liverpool, Lancaster and Chester, B. J. Thomas
Llandaff, Bangor, Carmarthen and Gloucester, R. F. Yeldam
Manchester and Nottingham, M. A. Moran
Newcastle, Carlisle, York and Middlesbrough, P. Sanderson
Oxford, R. R. Da Costa
Winchester, A. K. Biggs

OFFICE OF THE JUDGE ADVOCATE OF THE FLEET
The Law Courts, Barker Road, Maidstone ME16 8EQ
Tel 01622-754966

Judge Advocate of the Fleet (£72,524), His Hon. Judge Sessions

OFFICE OF THE JUDGE ADVOCATE-GENERAL OF THE FORCES
(Joint Service for the Army and the Royal Air Force)
22 Kingsway, London WC2B 6LE
Tel 0171-305 7910

Judge Advocate-General (£85,241), His Hon. Judge J. W. Rant, CB, QC
Vice-Judge Advocate-General (£72,524), E. G. Moelwyn-Hughes
Assistant Judge Advocates-General (£47,150–£54,400), D. M. Berkson; M. A. Hunter; T. G. Pontius; J. P. Camp; Miss S. E. Woollam; R. C. C. Seymour
Deputy Judge Advocates (£33,000–£46,250), I. H. Pearson; R. G. Chapple

HIGH COURT AND CROWN COURT CENTRES

First-tier centres deal with both civil and criminal cases and are served by High Court and circuit judges. Second-tier centres deal with criminal cases only and are served by High Court and circuit judges. Third-tier centres deal with criminal cases only and are served only by circuit judges.

MIDLAND AND OXFORD CIRCUIT
First-tier – Birmingham, Lincoln, Nottingham, Oxford, Stafford, Warwick
Second-tier – Leicester, Northampton, Shrewsbury, Worcester
Third-tier – Coventry, Derby, Grimsby, Hereford, Peterborough, Stoke-on-Trent, Wolverhampton
Circuit Administrator, R. Stoate, The Priory Courts, 6th Floor, 33 Bull Street, Birmingham B4 6DW. Tel: 0121-681 3000

Courts Administrators: Birmingham Group, P. Barton;
Nottingham Group, Mrs E. A. Folman; *Stafford Group*, A. F. Parker

NORTH-EASTERN CIRCUIT
First-tier – Leeds, Newcastle upon Tyne, Sheffield, Teesside
Second-tier – Bradford, York
Third-tier – Doncaster, Durham
Circuit Administrator, P. J. Farmer, 17th Floor, West Riding House, Albion Street, Leeds LS1 5AA. Tel: 0113-251 1200
Courts Administrators: Leeds Group, P. Delany, OBE; *Newcastle upon Tyne Group*, K. Budgen; *Sheffield Group*, G. Bingham

NORTHERN CIRCUIT
First-tier – Carlisle, Liverpool, Manchester, Preston
Third-tier – Barrow-in-Furness, Bolton, Burnley, Lancaster
Circuit Administrator, R. A. Vincent, 15 Quay Street, Manchester M60 9FD. Tel: 0161-833 1005
Courts Administrators: Manchester Group, Mrs A. Prior; *Liverpool Group*, D. A. Beaumont; *Preston Group*, Mrs C. A. Mayer

SOUTH-EASTERN CIRCUIT
First-tier – Chelmsford, Lewes, London (Isleworth), Norwich
Second-tier – Ipswich, London (Central Criminal Court), Luton, Maidstone, Reading, St Albans
Third-tier – Aylesbury, Brighton, Bury St Edmunds, Cambridge, Canterbury, Chichester, Guildford, King's Lynn, London (Croydon, Harrow, Inner London Sessions House, Kingston upon Thames, Knightsbridge, Middlesex Guildhall, Snaresbrook, Southwark, Wood Green), Southend
Circuit Administrator, J. Brindley, New Cavendish House, 18 Maltravers Street, London WC2R 3EU. Tel: 0171-936 7235
Deputy Circuit Administrator, P. Stockton
Courts Administrators: Chelmsford Group, M. Littlewood; *Maidstone Group*, Mrs H. Hartwell; *Kingston Group*, J. L. Powell; *London Group (Civil)*, P. Risk; *London Group (Crime)*, G. F. Addicott

The High Court in Greater London sits at the Royal Courts of Justice.

WALES AND CHESTER CIRCUIT
First-tier – Caernarfon, Cardiff, Chester, Mold, Swansea
Second-tier – Carmarthen, Merthyr Tydfil, Newport, Welshpool
Third-tier – Dolgellau, Haverfordwest, Knutsford, Warrington
Circuit Administrator, V. Grove, Churchill House, Churchill Way, Cardiff CF1 4HH. Tel: 01222-396925
Courts Administrators: Cardiff Group, A. M. Eshelby; *Chester Group*, T. D. Beckett

WESTERN CIRCUIT
First-tier – Bristol, Exeter, Truro, Winchester
Second-tier – Dorchester, Gloucester, Plymouth, Weymouth
Third-tier – Barnstaple, Bournemouth, Newport (IOW), Portsmouth, Salisbury, Southampton, Swindon, Taunton
Circuit Administrator, R. J. Clark, Bridge House, Sion Place, Clifton, Bristol BS8 4BN. Tel: 0117-974 3763
Courts Administrators: Bristol Group, A. C. Butler; *Exeter Group*, J. Ardern; *Winchester Group*, D. Ryan

CIRCUIT JUDGES

Senior Circuit Judges, each £85,241
Circuit Judges, each £72,524
Style, His/Her Hon. Judge [surname]
Senior Presiding Judge, The Rt. Hon. Lord Justice
    McCowan

MIDLAND AND OXFORD CIRCUIT

Presiding Judges, Hon. Mr Justice Judge; Hon. Mr Justice
    Latham

W. A. L. Allardice; F. A. Allen; Miss C. Alton;
B. J. Appleby, QC; M. J. Astill; D. P. Bennett;
R. S. A. Benson; I. J. Black, QC; R. W. A. Bray;
D. W. Brunning; J. J. Cavell; F. A. Chapman;
P. N. R. Clark; R. R. B. Cole; T. G. E. Corrie; P. F. Crane;
*P. J. Crawford, QC (*Recorder of Birmingham*);
I. T. R. Davidson, QC; P. N. de Mille; T. M. Dillon, QC;
C. H. Durman; B. A. Farrer, QC; Miss E. N. Fisher;
J. E. Fletcher; A. C. Geddes; R. J. H. Gibbs, QC; V. E. Hall;
J. Hall; D. R. D. Hamilton; S. T. Hammond;
G. C. W. Harris, QC; M. K. Harrison-Hall; M. J. Heath;
C. R. Hodson; J. R. Hopkin; R. H. Hutchinson;
J. E. M. Irvine; R. P. V. Jenkins; J. G. Jones; A. W. P. King;
M. K. Lee, QC; D. L. McCarthy; M. H. Mander;
K. Matthewman, QC; W. D. Matthews; R. G. May;
H. R. Mayor, QC; P. R. Morrell; J. I. Morris;
A. J. H. Morrison; M. D. Mott; A. J. D. Nicholl;
R. T. N. Orme; R. C. C. O'Rorke; J. F. F. Orrell;
D. S. Perrett, QC; C. J. Pitchers; R. F. D. Pollard;
F. M. Potter; D. P. Pugsley; J. R. Pyke; R. J. Rubery;
J. A. O. Shand; J. R. S. Smyth; D. P. Stanley; P. J. Stretton;
G. C. Styler; H. C. Tayler, QC; A. B. Taylor; M. B. Ward;
D. J. R. Wilcox; H. Wilson; J. W. Wilson;
K. S. W. Wilson Mellor, QC; C. G. Young

NORTH-EASTERN CIRCUIT

Presiding Judges, Hon. Mr Justice Holland; Hon.
    Mrs Justice Smith

J. Altman; T. G. F. Atkinson; T. W. Barber; J. E. Barry;
G. N. Barr Young; D. R. Bentley, QC; A. N. J. Briggs;
D. M. A. Bryant; J. W. M. Bullimore; B. Bush; M. C. Carr;
M. L. Cartlidge; P. J. Charlesworth; P. J. Cockroft;
G. J. K. Coles, QC; J. Crabtree; M. T. Cracknell;
W. H. R. Crawford, QC; Mrs J. Davies; I. J. Dobkin;
E. J. Faulks; P. J. Fox, QC; A. N. Fricker, QC; M. S. Garner;
A. R. Goldsack, QC; R. A. Grant; S. P. Grenfell;
W. Hannah; G. F. R. Harkins; D. Herrod, QC;
P. M. L. Hoffman; R. Hunt; A. E. Hutchinson, QC;
N. H. Jones, QC; G. H. Kamil; T. D. Kent-Jones, TD;
C. F. Kolbert; G. M. Lightfoot; R. P. Lowden;
A. G. McCallum; A. C. Macdonald;
Miss M. B. M. MacMurray, QC; M. K. Mettyear;
R. J. Moore; A. L. Myerson, QC; R. A. Orde;
Miss H. E. Paling; P. E. Robertshaw; *D. M. Savill, QC;
R. M. Scott; J. Stephenson; *R. A. R. Stroyan, QC (*Recorder
of Newcastle upon Tyne*); Mrs L. Sutcliffe; R. C. Taylor;
J. D. G. Walford; M. Walker; P. H. C. Walker;
J. S. Wolstenholme; D. R. Wood

NORTHERN CIRCUIT

Presiding Judge, Hon. Mr Justice Forbes

M. P. Allweis; H. H. Andrew, QC; J. F. Appleton;
A. W. Bell; R. C. W. Bennett; Miss I. Bernstein;
M. S. Blackburn; R. Brown; J. K. Burke, QC;
I. B. Campbell; F. B. Carter, QC; B. I. Caulfield; D. Clark;
D. C. Clarke, QC; G. M. Clifton; I. W. Crompton;
G. P. Crowe, QC; *R. E. Davies, QC (*Recorder of Manchester*);
M. Dean, QC; Miss A. E. Downey; B. R. Duckworth;

S. B. Duncan; Miss D. B. Eaglestone; T. K. Earnshaw;
D. M. Evans, QC; S. J. D. Fawcus; P. S. Fish;
J. R. B. Geake; D. S. Gee; J. A. D. Gilliland, QC;
R. G. Hamilton; J. A. Hammond; F. D. Hart, QC;
M. Hedley; T. D. T. Hodson; F. R. B. Holloway;
R. C. Holman; Miss M. Holt; N. J. G. Howarth;
G. W. Humphries; C. E. F. James; P. M. Kershaw, QC
(*Commercial Circuit Judge*); H. L. Lachs; P. M. Lakin;
C. N. Lees; J. M. Lever, QC; R. J. D. Livesey, QC;
R. Lockett; D. Lynch; D. I. Mackay; J. B. Macmillan;
D. G. Maddison; B. C. Maddocks; C. J. Mahon;
J. A. Morgan; W. P. Morris; F. D. Owen, TD;
R. E. I. Pickering; D. A. Pirie; A. J. Proctor; J. H. Roberts;
Miss G. D. Ruaux; M. H. S. Singer; E. Slinger; W. P. Smith;
Miss E. M. Steel; C. B. Tetlow; J. P. Townend;
I. J. C. Trigger; P. W. G. Urquhart; W. R. Wickham
(*Recorder of Liverpool*); B. Woodward

SOUTH-EASTERN CIRCUIT

Presiding Judges, Hon. Mr Justice Blofeld; Hon. Mr
    Justice Wright

J. R. S. Adams; M. F. Addison; F. J. Aglionby;
S. A. Anwyl, QC; J. A. Baker; J. B. Baker, QC;
M. F. Baker, QC; M. J. D. Baker; P. V. Baker, QC;
A. F. Balston; G. S. Barham; C. J. A. Barnett, QC;
W. E. Barnett, QC; K. Bassingthwaighte; G. A. Bathurst
Norman; P. J. L. Beaumont, QC; N. E. Beddard;
M. G. Binning; G. J. Binns; J. E. Bishop; B. M. B. Black;
P. C. Bowsher, QC; A. V. Bradbury; P. N. Brandt;
L. J. Bromley, QC; A. E. Brooks; R. G. Brown;
J. M. Bull, QC; G. N. Butler, QC; *N. M. Butter, QC;
H. J. Byrt, QC; C. V. Callman; B. E. Capstick, QC;
B. E. F. Catlin; B. L. Charles, QC; D. J. Clarkson, QC;
P. C. Clegg; M. Cohen, QC; S. H. Colgan; P. H. Collins;
C. C. Colston, QC; S. S. Coltart; Viscount Colville of
Culross, QC; J. S. Colyer, QC; C. D. Compston;
T. A. C. Coningsby, QC; R. D. Connor; M. J. Cook;
R. A. Cooke; G. H. Coombe; M. R. Coombe; A. Cooray;
P. E. Copley; Dr E. Cotran; R. C. Cox; J. F. Crocker;
D. L. Croft, QC; H. M. Crush; G. L. Davies;
I. H. Davies, TD; W. L. M. Davies, QC; W. N. Denison, QC
(*Common Serjeant*); J. E. Devaux; M. N. Devonshire, TD;
A. E. J. Diamond, QC; W. H. Dunn, QC; A. H. Durrant;
C. M. Edwards; Q. T. Edwards, QC; C. Elwen;
F. P. L. Evans; S. J. Evans; J. D. Farnworth; P. Fingret;
J. J. Finney; P. Ford; J. J. Fordham; G. C. F. Forrester;
Ms D. A. Freedman; R. Gee; L. Gerber;
Miss A. F. Goddard, QC; S. A. Goldstein;
P. W. Goldstone; M. B. Goodman; C. G. M. Gordon;
J. B. Gosschalk; J. H. Gower, QC; M. Graham, QC;
B. S. Green, QC; P. B. Greenwood; D. J. Griffiths;
G. D. Grigson; R. B. Groves, TD, VRD; N. T. Hague, QC;
A. B. R. Hallgarten, QC; Miss G. Hallon; P. J. Halnan;
J. Hamilton; C. R. H. Hardy; B. Hargrove, OBE, QC;
M. F. Harris; R. O. Havery, QC; R. G. Hawkins, QC;
R. J. Haworth; A. H. Head; J. C. Hicks, QC;
A. N. Hitching; D. Holden; A. C. W. Hordern, QC;
K. A. D. Hornby; R. W. Howe; M. Hucker; Sir David
Hughes-Morgan, Bt., CB, CBE; J. G. Hull, QC; M. J. Hyam;
D. A. Inman; Dr P. J. E. Jackson; C. P. James;
T. J. C. Jospeh; M. Kennedy, QC; A. M. Kenny;
T. R. King; L. G. Krikler; L. H. C. Lait;
P. St J. H. Langan, QC; Capt. J. B. R. Langdon, RN;
G. F. B. Laughland, QC; R. Laurie; T. Lawrence;
D. M. Levy, QC; E. A. G. Lewis, QC; H. J. Lloyd, QC;
F. R. Lockhart; D. B. D. Lowe; Mrs N. M. Lowry;
R. J. Lowry, QC; J. A. T. Loyd, QC; Capt. S. Lyons;
K. M. McHale; K. A. Machin, QC; M. B. McMullan;
K. C. Macrae; T. Maher; J. R. Main, QC; B. A. Marder, QC;

F. J. M. Marr-Johnson; L. A. Marshall;
D. N. N. Martineau; N. A. Medawar, QC; D. B. Meier;
D. J. Mellor; G. D. Mercer; A. L. Mildon, QC;
D. Q. Miller; H. M. Morgan; D. Morton Jack; R. T. Moss;
J. I. Murchie; T. M. E. Nash; Mrs N. F. Negus;
M. H. D. Neligan; C. W. F. Newman, QC;
Mrs M. F. Norrie; Brig. A. P. Norris, OBE; P. W. O'Brien;
M. A. Oppenheimer; D. A. Paiba; Mrs N. Pearce;
Prof. D. S. Pearl; Miss V. A. Pearlman; J. R. Peppitt, QC;
F. H. L. Petre; N. A. J. Philpot; D. C. Pitman; J. R. Platt;
P. B. Pollock; W. D. C. Poulton; H. C. Pownall, QC;
R. J. C. V. Prendergast; J. E. Previté, QC; B. H. Pryor, QC;
J. E. Pullinger; J. W. Rant, QC; E. V. P. Reece;
M. P. Reynolds; G. K. Rice; M. S. Rich, QC; G. Rivlin, QC;
S. D. Robbins; D. A. H. Rodwell, QC; J. W. Rogers, QC;
G. H. Rooke, TD, QC; P. C. R. Rountree; J. H. Rucker;
T. R. G. Ryland; R. B. Sanders; J. S. Sennitt; J. L. Sessions;
J. D. Sheerin; D. R. A. Sich; A. G. Simmons; A. Simpson;
K. T. Simpson; P. R. Simpson; M. Singh, QC;
J. K. E. Slack, TD; S. P. Sleeman; P. M. J. Slot;
C. M. Smith, QC; S. A. R. Smith; R. J. Southan;
S. B. Spence; C. J. Sumner; W. F. C. Thomas;
A. C. L. Thornton, QC; A. G. Y. Thorpe; A. H. Tibber;
C. H. Tilling; A. M. Troup; S. Tumim; J. T. Turner;
C. J. M. Tyrer; Mrs A. P. Uziell-Hamilton; J. E. van der
Werff; Sir Lawrence Verney, TD (*Recorder of London*);
A. O. R. Vick, QC; T. L. Viljoen; Miss M. S. Viner, CBE,
QC; R. Walker; D. B. Watling, QC; V. B. Watts;
*F. J. White; S. R. Wilkinson; E. G. Wrintmore;
K. H. Zucker, QC

WALES AND CHESTER CIRCUIT

Presiding Judges, Hon. Mr Justice Curtis; Hon. Mr
Justice Kay (*from 1 Jan. 1996*)
M. R. Burr; S. P. Clarke; T. R. Crowther, QC; Miss
J. M. P. Daley; G. H. M. Daniel; Sir Robin David, QC;
D. T. A. Davies; J. B. S. Diehl, QC; D. E. H. Edwards;
G. O. Edwards, QC; Lord Elystan-Morgan;
D. R. Evans, QC; T. M. Evans, QC; *M. Gibbon, QC;
D. R. Halbert; D. J. Hale; D. M. Hughes; G. J. Jones;
H. D. H. Jones; G. E. Kilfoil; T. E. I. Lewis-Bowen;
C. G. Masterman; D. G. Morgan; D. G. Morris;
D. C. Morton; T. H. Moseley; P. J. Price, QC;
E. J. Prosser, QC; H. E. P. Roberts, QC; S. M. Stephens, QC;
H. V. Williams, QC

WESTERN CIRCUIT

Presiding Judges, Hon. Mr Justice Mantell; Hon. Mr
Justice Tuckey
P. T. S. Batterbury; J. F. Beashel; J. A. M. Bonvin;
C. L. Boothman; M. J. L. Brodrick; J. M. J. Burford, QC;
R. D. H. Bursell; J. R. Chalkley; M. G. Cotterill;
G. W. A. Cottle; Ms H. Counsell; S. C. Darwall Smith;
Mrs S. P. Darwall Smith; Mrs L. H. Davies; M. Dyer;
*P. Fallon, QC; J. D. Foley; D. L. Griffiths; J. D. Griggs;
Mrs C. M. A. Hagen; P. J. C. R. Hooton; G. B. Hutton;
R. E. Jack, QC; A. G. H. Jones; T. N. Mackean;
Miss S. M. D. McKinney; I. S. McKintosh; I. G. McLean;
J. G. McNaught; T. J. Milligan; G. E. Neville;
S. K. O'Malley; S. K. Overend; R. C. Pryor, QC;
J. N. P. Rudd; A. Rutherford; D. H. D. Selwood;
R. M. Shawcross; D. A. Smith, QC; W. E. M. Taylor;
P. M. Thomas; A. A. R. Thompson, QC;
H. J. M. Tucker, QC; D. M. Webster, QC; J. H. Weeks, QC;
J. R. Whitley; J. A. J. Wigmore; J. C. Willis; J. H. Wroath

RECORDERS (each £346 per day)

F. A. Abbott; R. D. I. Adam; J. D. R. Adams; P. C. Ader;
R. J. P. Aikens, QC; J. F. Akast; D. J. Ake; R. Akenhead, QC;

I. D. G. Alexander, QC; C. D. Allan; C. J. Alldis;
J. H. Allen; D. M. Altaras; A. J. Anderson, QC;
W. P. Andreae-Jones, QC; P. J. Andrews, QC;
R. A. Anelay, QC; A. R. L. Ansell; M. G. Anthony;
Miss L. E. Appleby, QC; J. F. A. Archer, QC;
Lord Archer of Sandwell, PC, QC; A. J. Arlidge, QC;
E. K. Armitage, QC; P. J. B. Armstrong; G. K. Arran;
R. Ashton; J. M. Aspinall; E. G. Aspley; B. Atchley;
N. J. Atkinson, QC; M. G. Austin-Smith, QC;
M. J. S. Axtell; W. S. Aylen, QC; J. F. Badenoch, QC;
A. B. Baillie; N. R. J. Baker, QC; S. W. Baker;
C. G. Ball, QC; A. Barker, QC; B. J. Barker, QC;
D. Barker, QC; G. E. Barling, QC; R. O. Barlow;
D. N. Barnard; D. M. W. Barnes, QC; H. J. Barnes;
T. P. Barnes, QC; K. E. Barnett; R. A. Barratt, QC;
R. Bartfield; D. A. Bartlett; G. R. Bartlett, QC;
J. C. T. Barton, QC; D. C. Bate, QC; S. D. Batten, QC;
P. D. Batty, QC; J. J. Baughan, QC; R. A. Bayliss; J. Beatson;
C. H. Beaumont; C. O. M. Bedingfield, TD, QC;
R. V. M. E. Behar; C. O. J. Behrens; R. W. Belben; The
Hon. M. J. Beloff, QC; J. M. Bennett; P. Bennett, QC;
P. C. Benson; R. A. Benson, QC; H. L. Bentham;
D. M. Berkson; C. R. Berry; M. Bethel, QC; J. P. V. Bevan;
J. C. Beveridge, QC; Mrs C. V. Bevington; N. Bidder;
P. V. Birkett, QC; M. I. Birnbaum; W. J. Birtles;
P. W. Birts, QC; H. O. Blacksell, QC; B. G. D. Blair, QC
J. A. Blair-Gould; A. N. H. Blake; C. Bloom, QC;
D. J. Blunt, QC; O. S. P. Blunt, QC; J. G. Boal, QC;
D. R. L. Bodey, QC; J. G. Boggis, QC; R. H. Bond;
G. T. K. Boney, QC; D. J. Boulton; S. N. Bourne-
Arton, QC; P. H. Bowers; S. C. Boyd, QC; J. J. Boyle;
D. L. Bradshaw; W. T. S. Braithwaite, QC;
N. D. Bratza, QC; G. B. Breen; D. J. Brennan, QC;
M. L. Brent, QC; G. J. B. G. Brice, QC; J. N. W. Bridges-
Adams; A. J. Brigden; P. J. Briggs; R. P. Brittain;
J. Bromley-Davenport; S. C. Brown, QC; D. J. M. Browne,
QC; J. N. Browne, QC; A. N. Brunner, QC; R. V. Bryan;
A. Bueno, QC; D. L. Bulmer; J. P. Burgess; J. P. Burke, QC;
H. W. Burnett, QC; R. H. Burns; S. J. Burnton, QC;
M. J. Burton, QC; K. Bush; A. J. Butcher, QC; Miss J. Butler;
C. W. Byers; M. D. Byrne; Mrs B. A. Calvert, QC;
D. Calvert-Smith; R. Camden Pratt, QC;
Miss S. M. C. Cameron, QC; A. N. Campbell, QC;
J. Q. Campbell; J. M. Caplan; G. M. C. Carey, QC;
A. C. Carlile, QC, MP; The Lord Carlisle of
Bucklow, PC, QC; H. B. H. Carlisle, QC; M. J. Carroll;
J. J. Carter-Manning, QC; R. Carus, QC; J. A. Chadwin, QC;
N. M. Chambers, QC; D. C. Champion; V. R. Chapman;
J. M. Cherry, QC; J. R. Cherryman, QC;
C. F. Chruszcz, QC; C. H. Clark, QC; P. C. L. Clark;
C. S. C. S. Clarke, QC; P. W. Clarke; A. S. L. Cleary;
W. Clegg, QC; T. A. Clover; M. F. Coates; W. P. Coates;
D. J. Cocks, QC; J. J. Coffey; T. A. Coghlan, QC;
W. J. Coker, QC; J. R. Cole; A. J. S. Coleman;
N. J. Coleman; N. B. C. Coles, QC; A. R. Collender, QC;
P. N. Collier, QC; J. M. Collins; Ms M. Colton;
Mrs J. R. Comyns; G. D. Conlin; J. G. Connor;
C. S. Cook; A. E. M. Cooper; Miss B. P. Cooper, QC;
P. J. Cooper, QC; Miss S. M. Corkhill; C. J. Cornwall;
P. J. Cosgrove, QC; Miss D. R. Cotton, QC;
J. S. Coward, QC; P. R. Cowell; B. R. E. Cox, QC;
Mrs L. M. Cox, QC; P. Crampin, QC; N. Crichton;
D. I. Crigman; M. L. S. Cripps; A. A. Critchlow;
D. R. Crome; J. D. Crowley, QC; E. J. R. Crowther, OBE;
W. R. H. Crowther, QC; D. M. Cryan; T. S. Culver;
Miss E. A. M. Curnow, QC; T. Curran; P. D. Curran;
J. W. O. Curtis, QC; M. J. Curwen; K. C. Cutler;
A. J. G. Dalziel; P. M. Darlow; A. M. Darroch;
G. W. Davey; C. P. M. Davidson; A. R. M. Davies;
J. T. L. Davies; R. L. Davies, QC; W. E. Davis;

A. W. Dawson; D. H. Day, QC; J. J. Deave; J. B. Deby, QC;
P. G. Dedman; Mrs P. A. Deeley; C. F. Dehn, QC; P. A. de
la Piquerie; M. A. de Navarro, QC; R. L. Denyer, QC;
S. C. Desch, QC; H. A. D. de Silva; T. Deva Pillay;
P. N. Digney; C. E. Dines; A. D. Dinkin, QC;
D. R. Dobbin; R. A. M. Doggett; Ms B. Dohmann, QC;
D. T. Donaldson, QC; A. M. Donne, QC; A. K. Dooley;
P. H. Downes; J. Dowse; S. M. Duffield;
P. R. Dunkels, QC; J. D. Durham Hall, QC; R. T. Dutton;
J. M. Dyson; D. Eady, QC; H. W. P. Eccles, QC;
Miss S. M. Edwards, QC; D. F. Elfer, QC; G. Elias, QC;
E. A. Elliott; D. R. Ellis; R. C. Elly; J. A. Elvidge;
R. M. Englehart, QC; T. M. English; G. A. Ensor;
D. A. Evans, QC; D. H. Evans, QC; F. W. H. Evans, QC;
G. W. R. Evans, QC; M. J. Evans; Sir Graham Eyre, QC;
T. M. Faber; W. D. Fairclough; R. B. Farley, QC;
D. J. Farrer, QC; K. J. Farrow; P. E. Feinberg, QC;
R. Fernyhough, QC; M. C. Field; J. E. P. Finnigan;
D. T. Fish; D. P. Fisher; G. D. Flather, QC;
P. E. J. Focke, QC; R. A. Fordham, QC; A. J. Forrest;
M. D. P. Fortune; D. R. Foskett, QC; J. R. Foster, QC;
Miss R. M. Foster; J. H. Fryer-Spedding, OBE;
M. T. Fugard, CB; M. Gale, QC; J. E. Gardner, QC;
C. R. Garside, QC; J. W. Gaskell; R. C. Gaskell;
S. A. G. L. Gault; A. H. Gee, QC; I. W. Geering, QC;
D. S. Geey; W. George; D. C. Gerrey; J. S. Gibbons, QC;
C. A. H. Gibson; F. H. S. Gilbert, QC; K. Gillance;
N. B. D. Gilmour, QC; L. Giovene; A. T. Glass, QC;
H. B. Globe, QC; Miss E. Gloster, QC; H. K. Goddard, QC;
H. A. Godfrey, QC; Ms L. S. Godfrey, QC;
J. J. Goldberg, QC; J. B. Goldring, QC;
P. H. Goldsmith, QC; L. C. Goldstone, QC;
I. F. Goldsworthy, QC; A. J. J. Gompertz, QC;
A. A. Gordon; J. P. Gorman, QC; J. R. W. Goss;
T. J. C. Goudie, QC; C. O. G. Gould; A. A. Goymer;
G. Gozem; A. S. Grabiner, QC; C. A. St J. Gray, QC;
G. Gray, QC; R. M. K. Gray, QC; H. Green, QC; Miss
J. E. G. Greenberg, QC; J. C. Greenwood;
J. G. Grenfell, QC; R. D. Grey, QC; R. H. Griffith-Jones;
J. C. Griffiths, CMG, QC; J. P. G. Griffiths, QC; M. G. Grills;
M. S. E. Grime, QC; P. Grobel; P. H. Gross, QC;
M. A. W. Grundy; S. J. Gullick; A. S. Hacking, QC;
M. F. Haigh; J. W. Haines; N. J. Hall; S. J. Hall;
J. P. N. Hallam; D. T. Hallchurch; Miss H. C. Hallett, QC;
D. W. Halton; G. M. Hamilton, TD, QC; P. L. Hamlin;
J. Hampton; J. L. Hand; Miss R. S. A. Hare, QC;
R. D. Harman, QC; G. T. Harrap; P. J. Harrington, QC;
D. M. Harris, QC; R. D. Harrison; R. M. Harrison, QC;
H. M. Harrod; J. M. Harrow; C. P. Hart-Leverton, QC;
B. Harvey; C. S. Harvey, MBE, TD; M. L. T. Harvey, QC;
T. S. A. Hawkesworth, QC; J. M. Haworth; R. W. P. Hay;
Prof. D. J. Hayton; R. M. Hayward; R. Hayward-
Smith, QC; A. J. Healey; A. T. Hedworth;
T. B. Hegarty, QC; G. E. Heggs; R. A. Henderson, QC;
R. H. Q. Henriques, QC; M. J. Henshell;
P. J. M. Heppel, QC; R. C. Herman; M. S. Heslop QC;
R. B. Hickman; B. J. Higgs, QC; E. M. Hill, QC;
J. W. Hillyer, QC; J. H. Hilton, QC; Ms E. J. Hindley, QC;
W. T. J. Hirst; J. D. Hitchen; S. A. Hockman, QC; The
Hon. Mary Hogg, QC; A. J. C. Hoggett, QC;
D. A. Hollis, VRD, QC; C. J. Holmes; J. F. Holt;
R. M. Hone; A. T. Hoolahan, QC; S. Hopkins;
M. A. P. Hopmeier; M. Horowitz, QC; E. T. Horridge;
Miss R. Horwood-Smart; C. P. Hotten, QC;
B. F. Houlder, QC; M. N. Howard, QC; C. I. Howells;
M. J. Hubbard, QC; A. P. G. Hughes, QC; Mrs
H. M. Hughes; Miss J. C. A. Hughes, QC;
P. T. Hughes, QC; R. P. Hughes; T. M. Hughes, QC;
J. Hugill, QC; L. D. Hull; W. G. B. Hungerford;
D. P. Hunt; D. R. N. Hunt, QC; P. J. Hunt, QC;

I. G. A. Hunter, QC; M. Hussain, QC; B. A. Hytner, QC;
R. A. G. Inglis; P. R. Isaacs; A. B. Issard-Davies;
D. G. A. Jackson; M. R. Jackson; R. M. Jackson, QC;
I. E. Jacob; P. J. Jacobs; N. F. B. Jarman, QC;
J. M. Jarvis, QC; A. H. Jeffreys; D. A. Jeffreys, QC;
J. Jeffs, QC; J. D. Jenkins, QC; D. B. Johnson, QC;
D. A. F. Jones; D. L. Jones; N. G. Jones; R. A. Jones, QC;
S. E. Jones, QC; T. G. Jones; W. H. Joss; H. M. Joy;
P. S. L. Joyce, QC; R. W. S. Juckes; M. D. L. Kalisher, QC;
M. L. Kallipetis, QC; I. G. F. Karsten, QC; S. S. Katkhuda;
R. G. Kaye, QC; M. L. Keane; D. N. Keating, QC;
K. R. Keen, QC; B. R. Keith, QC; C. L. Kelly;
C. J. B. Kemp; D. Kennett Brown; L. D. Kershen, QC;
G. M. Khayat, QC; R. I. Kidwell, QC; T. R. A. King, QC;
W. M. Kingston, QC; R. C. Klevan, QC; B. J. Knight, QC;
M. S. Knott; Miss P. E. Knowles; Miss J. C. M. Korner, QC;
S. E. Kramer; Miss L. J. Kushner, QC; P. E. Kyte;
L. P. Laity; C. A. Lamb; D. G. Lane, QC;
G. J. H. Langley; B. F. J. Langstaff, QC;
R. B. Latham, QC; S. W. Lawler, QC;
Sir Ivan Lawrence, QC, MP; M. H. Lawson, QC;
G. S. Lawson-Rogers, QC; P. L. O. Leaver, QC;
D. Lederman, QC; B. W. T. Leech; I. Leeming, QC;
C. H. de V. Leigh, QC; Sir Godfrey Le Quesne, QC;
H. B. G. Lett; B. H. Leveson, QC; S. Levine;
A. E. Levy, QC; M. E. Lewer, QC; A. K. Lewis, QC;
B. W. Lewis; M. ap G. Lewis, QC; R. S. Lewis;
C. C. D. Lindsay, QC; S. J. Linehan, QC; J. S. Lipton;
B. J. E. Livesey, QC; C. G. Llewellyn-Jones, QC;
S. H. Lloyd; J. Lloyd-Eley, QC; C. J. Lockhart-
Mummery, QC; A. J. C. Lodge, QC; T. Longbotham;
D. C. Lovell-Pank, QC; G. W. Lowe; N. H. Lowe;
J. A. M. Lowen; G. W. Lowther; F. D. L. Loy; Mrs
C. M. Ludlow; E. Lyons, QC; A. W. McCreath;
A. G. McDowall; A. G. MacDuff, QC; D. D. McEvoy, QC;
K. M. P. Macgill; C. I. McGonigal; R. J. McGregor-
Johnson; R. D. Machell, QC; J. V. Machin; B. M. McIntyre;
C. C. Mackay, QC; D. L. Mackie; W. N. McKinnon;
I. McLeod; N. R. B. Macleod, QC; N. J. C. McLusky;
A. R. Malcolm; M. E. Mann, QC;
The Hon. G. R. J. Mansfield; A. C. B. Markham-David;
R. L. Marks; A. S. Marron, QC; P. Marsh; R. G. Marshall-
Andrews, QC; G. C. Marson; H. R. A. Martineau;
D. Matheson, QC; P. R. Matthews; Mrs S. P. Matthews,
QC; P. B. Mauleverer, QC; R. B. Mawrey, QC;
J. F. M. Maxwell; R. Maxwell, QC; Mrs P. R. May;
M. Meggeson; N. F. Merriman, QC; C. S. J. Metcalf;
J. T. Milford, QC; R. A. Miller; S. M. Miller, QC;
J. B. M. Milmo, QC; D. C. Milne, QC; Miss A. E. Mitchell;
C. R. Mitchell; D. C. Mitchell; F. I. Mitchell;
N. J. Mitchell; J. E. Mitting, QC; F. R. Moat;
E. G. Moelwyn-Hughes; C. R. D. Moger, QC;
D. R. P. Mole, QC; H. J. Montlake; M. J. Moore-Bick, QC;
M. G. C. Moorhouse; G. E. Moriarty, QC;
A. P. Morris, QC; The Rt. Hon. J. Morris, QC, MP;
C. Morris-Coole; T. J. Mort; A. G. Moses, QC;
C. J. Moss, QC; P. C. Mott, QC; Miss M. J. S. Mowat;
R. W. Moxon-Browne, QC; J. H. Muir; F. J. Muller, QC;
G. S. Murdoch, QC; I. P. Murphy, QC;
M. J. A. Murphy, QC; N. O. G. Murray; N. J. Mylne, QC;
H. G. Narayan; J. O. Neligan; R. F. Nelson, QC;
D. E. Neuberger, QC; R. E. Newbold;
A. R. H. Newman, QC; G. Nice, QC; C. A. A. Nicholls, QC;
C. V. Nicholls, QC; M. C. Nicholson; A. S. T. E. Nicol;
B. Nolan, QC; M. C. Norman; J. M. Norris; P. H. Norris;
J. G. Nutting, QC; D. P. O'Brien, QC; E. M. Ogden, QC;
Mrs F. M. Oldham, QC; S. Oliver-Jones; R. W. Onions;
C. P. L. Openshaw, QC; M. N. O'Sullivan;
D. B. W. Ouseley, QC; G. V. Owen, QC; R. M. Owen, QC;
T. W. Owen; N. D. Padfield, QC; S. R. Page;

D. C. J. Paget, QC; A. O. Palmer, QC; A. W. Palmer, QC;
D. P. Pannich, QC; A. D. W. Pardoe, QC; S. A. B. Parish;
G. C. Parkins, QC; G. E. Parkinson; M. P. Parroy, QC;
D. J. Parry; D. J. T. Parry; E. O. Parry; M. A. Parry Evans;
N. S. K. Pascoe, QC; A. Patience, QC; J. G. Paulusz;
W. E. Pawlak; R. J. Pearse Wheatley; B. P. Pearson;
D. H. Penry-Davey, QC; J. Perry, QC; M. Pert, QC;
B. J. Phelvin; J. A. Phillips; W. B. Phillips; J. C. Phipps;
M. A. Pickering, QC; C. J. Pitchford, QC;
The Hon. B. M. D. Pitt; A. P. Pitts; Miss E. F. Platt, QC;
R. Platts; J. R. Playford, QC; A. G. S. Pollock, QC;
T. G. Pontius; A. R. Porten, QC; L. R. Portnoy; Mrs
R. M. Poulet, QC; S. Pratt; T. W. Preston, QC;
G. A. L. Price, QC; J. A. Price, QC; N. P. L. Price, QC;
R. N. M. Price; A. C. Pugh, QC; G. V. Pugh, QC;
C. P. B. Purchas, QC; R. M. Purchas, QC;
N. R. Purnell, QC; P. O. Purnell, QC; Q. C. W. Querelle;
D. A. Radcliffe; D. W. Radford; Mrs N. P. Radford, QC;
Ms A. J. Rafferty, QC; T. W. H. Raggatt, QC;
A. Rankin, QC; A. D. Rawley, QC; P. R. Raynor, QC;
L. F. Read, QC; J. H. Reddihough; A. R. F. Redgrave, QC;
J. Reeder, QC; P. Rees; C. E. Reese, QC; J. R. Reid, QC;
P. C. Reid; P. C. Rhodes; R. E. Rhodes, QC; D. G. Rice;
D. W. Richards; H. A. Richardson; N. P. Riddell;
S. V. Riordan, QC; G. Risius; Miss J. H. Ritchie, QC;
M. W. Roach; J. A. Roberts, QC; J. D. Roberts;
J. M. Roberts; J. M. G. Roberts, QC; A. J. Robertson;
V. Robinson, QC; D. E. H. Robson, QC;
G. W. Roddick, QC; Miss D. J. Rodgers;
J. M. T. Rogers, QC; P. F. G. Rook, QC; W. M. Rose;
J. G. Ross; J. G. Ross Martyn; P. C. Rouch; J. J. Rowe, QC;
R. J. Royce, QC; A. A. Rumbelow, QC; N. J. Rumfitt, QC;
A. P. Russell; R. R. Russell; G. C. Ryan, QC;
J. R. T. Rylance; C. N. Salmon; D. A. Salter;
J. E. A. Samuels, QC; A. T. Sander; G. R. Sankey, QC;
N. L. Sarony; J. H. B. Saunders, QC; M. P. Sayers, QC;
R. J. Scholes, QC; A. R. G. Scott-Gall; R. J. Seabrook, QC;
C. Seagroatt, QC; M. R. Selfe; W. P. L. Sellick;
O. M. Sells, QC; D. Serota, QC; R. W. Seymour, QC;
A. J. Seys-Llewellyn; A. R. F. Sharp; P. P. Shears;
S. J. Sher, QC; Miss J. Shipley; J. M. Shorrock, QC;
S. R. Silber, QC; P. F. Singer, QC; J. C. N. Slater, QC;
A. C. Smith; A. T. Smith, QC; R. D. H. Smith, QC;
R. S. Smith, QC; Ms Z. P. Smith; S. M. Solley, QC;
R. F. Solman; E. Somerset Jones, QC; R. C. Southwell, QC,
R. C. E. Southwell; M. H. Spence, QC; J. Spencer, QC;
M. G. Spencer, QC; S. M. Spencer, QC;
R. V. Spencer Bernard; D. P. Spens, QC; L. Spittle;
R. W. Spon-Smith; D. W. Steel, QC; D. Steer, QC;
M. T. Steiger, QC; D. H. Stembridge, QC;
Mrs L. J. Stern, QC; A. W. Stevenson, TD;
J. S. H. Stewart, QC; R. M. Stewart, QC; W. R. Stewart
Smith; G. J. C. Still; D. A. Stockdale, QC;
D. M. A. Stokes, QC; M. G. T. Stokes, QC;
E. D. R. Stone, QC; J. B. Storey, QC; P. L. Storr;
T. M. F. Stow, QC; D. M. A. Strachan, QC; M. Stuart-
Moore, QC; F. R. C. Such; A. B. Suckling, QC;
J. M. Sullivan, QC; Ms L. E. Sullivan, QC; D. M. Sumner;
J. P. C. Sumption, QC; P. J. Susman; R. P. Sutton, QC;
J. A. Swanson; D. R. Swift; L. Swift, QC; M. R. Swift, QC;
Miss H. H. Swindells, QC; C. J. M. Symons, QC;
J. P. Tabor, QC; J. A. Tackaberry, QC; R. K. K. Talbot;
R. B. Tansey; G. F. Tattersall, QC; E. Taylor;
M. J. Taylor; J. J. Teare; R. H. Tedd, QC;
A. D. Temple, QC; V. B. A. Temple, QC; M. H. Tennant;
M. I. Tennant; D. M. Thomas, OBE, QC;
D. O. Thomas, QC; R. J. L. Thomas, QC;
R. L. Thomas, QC; R. U. Thomas, QC; P. J. Thompson;
D. K. Ticehurst, QC; J. Tiley; M. B. Tillett; J. W. Tinnion;
R. N. Titheridge, QC; S. M. Tomlinson, QC;

R. S. W. Tonking; J. K. Toulmin, CMG, QC;
R. G. Toulson, QC; J. B. S. Townend, QC;
C. M. Treacy, QC; H. B. Trethowan;
A. D. H. Trollope, QC; M. G. Tugendhat, QC;
H. W. Turcan; D. A. Turner, QC; P. A. Twigg, QC;
A. R. Tyrrell, QC; N. E. Underhill, QC; J. G. G. Ungley;
N. P. Valios, QC; A. R. Vandermeer, QC;
D. A. J. Vaughan, QC; M. J. D. Vere-Hodge, QC;
J. P. Wadsworth, QC; S. P. Waine; J. J. Wait; Miss
A. P. Wakefield; R. Wakefield; R. M. Wakerley, QC;
W. H. Waldron, QC; Mrs E. A. Walker; R. A. Walker, QC;
R. J. Walker, QC; T. E. Walker, QC; Sir Jonah Walker-
Smith, Bt.; S. P. Waller; B. Walsh, QC; T. M. Walsh;
C. T. Walton; J. J. Wardlow; J. C. Warner; J. Warren, QC;
D. E. B. Waters; Sir James Watson, Bt.; C. D. G. Waud;
B. J. Waylen; A. R. Webb; R. S. Webb, QC; M. Weisman;
P. Weitzman, QC; C. S. Welchman; C. P. C. Whelon;
G. Whitburn, QC; C. H. Whitby, QC; W. J. M. White;
D. R. B. Whitehouse, QC; P. G. Whiteman, QC;
P. J. M. Whiteman, TD; A. Whitfield, QC;
D. G. Widdicombe, QC; C. T. Wide, QC;
R. Wigglesworth; A. D. F. Wilcken; A. F. Wilkie, QC;
K. H. P. Wilkinson; N. V. M. Wilkinson; D. B. Williams;
G. H. G. Williams, QC; Lord Williams of Mostyn, QC;
Miss J. A. Williams; J. G. Williams, QC; J. L. Williams, QC;
M. J. Williams; W. L. Williams, QC;
S. W. Williamson, QC; A. M. Wilson, QC; C. Wilson-
Smith, QC; G. W. Wingate-Saul, QC; R. J. Winstanley;
M. E. Wolff; H. Wolton, QC; D. A. Wood, QC;
N. A. Wood; W. R. Wood; L. G. Woodley, QC; Miss
S. Woodley; J. T. Woods; W. C. Woodward, QC;
M. E. Woolf; N. G. Wootton; T. H. Workman;
Miss A. M. Worrall, QC; D. Worsley; P. F. Worsley, QC;
J. J. Wright; D. E. M. Young, QC

STIPENDIARY MAGISTRATES

PROVINCIAL (each £59,327)

Cheshire, P. K. Dodd, OBE, *apptd* 1991
Devon, P. H. Wassall, *apptd* 1994
East and West Sussex, P. C. Tain, *apptd* 1992
Essex, K. A. Gray, *apptd* 1995
Greater Manchester, W. D. Fairclough, *apptd* 1982;
    Miss J. E. Hayward, *apptd* 1991; A. Berg, *apptd* 1994;
    C. R. Darnton, *apptd* 1994
Hampshire, T. G. Cowling, *apptd* 1989
Humberside, N. H. White, *apptd* 1985
Lancashire/Merseyside, J. Finestein, *apptd* 1992
Leicestershire, vacant
Merseyside, D. R. G. Tapp, *apptd* 1992; P. S. Ward, *apptd*
    1994; P. J. Firth, *apptd* 1994
Middlesex, N. A. McKittrick, *apptd* 1989; S. Somjee, *apptd*
    1991; S. N. Day, *apptd* 1991
Mid Glamorgan, B. R. Oliver, *apptd* 1983; J. T. Curran, *apptd*
    1990; Miss P. J. Watkins, *apptd* 1995
Norfolk, N. P. Heley, *apptd* 1994
North-East London, G. E. Cawdron, *apptd* 1993
Nottinghamshire, P. F. Nuttall, *apptd* 1991; M. L. R. Harris,
    apptd 1991
Shropshire, P. H. R. Browning, *apptd* 1994
South Glamorgan, G. R. Watkins, *apptd* 1993
South Yorkshire, J. A. Browne, *apptd* 1992; W. D. Thomas,
    apptd 1989; M. A. Rosenberg, *apptd* 1993
Staffordshire, P. G. G. Richards, *apptd* 1991
West Midlands, W. M. Probert, *apptd* 1983; B. Morgan,
    apptd 1989; I. Gillespie, *apptd* 1991; M. F. James, *apptd*
    1991; C. M. McColl, *apptd* 1994

West Yorkshire, F. D. L. Loy, *apptd* 1972; Mrs P. A. Hewitt, *apptd* 1990; G. A. K. Hodgson, *apptd* 1993

METROPOLITAN

Chief Metropolitan Stipendiary Magistrate and Chairman of Committee of Magistrates for Inner London Area (*£74,524), P. G. N. Badge, *apptd* 1992 (*Bow Street*)

Magistrates (each *£63,327)

Bow Street, The Chief Magistrate; R. D. Bartle, *apptd* 1972; J. G. Connor, *apptd* 1979; Mrs E. Rees, *apptd* 1994; R. House, *apptd* 1995
Camberwell Green, C. P. M. Davidson, *apptd* 1984; T. H. Workman, *apptd* 1986; H. Gott, *apptd* 1992; Miss E. Roscoe, *apptd* 1994
Clerkenwell, M. L. R. Romer, *apptd* 1972; C. J. Bourke, *apptd* 1972; B. Loosley, *apptd* 1989
Family Proceedings and Youth Courts, London NW1, G. Wicks, *apptd* 1987; N. Crichton, *apptd* 1987
Greenwich and Woolwich, D. A. Cooper, *apptd* 1991; P. S. Wallis, *apptd* 1993; H. Riddle, *apptd* 1995
Highbury Corner, D. Barr, *apptd* 1976; Miss D. Quick, *apptd* 1986; A. T. Evans, *apptd* 1990; D. Simpson, *apptd* 1993
Horseferry Road, G. Parkinson, *apptd* 1982; A. R. Davies, *apptd* 1985; G. Breen, *apptd* 1986; Mrs K. R. Keating, *apptd* 1987
Marlborough Street, J. Q. Campbell, *apptd* 1981; Miss D. Wickham, *apptd* 1989
Marylebone, D. Kennett-Brown, *apptd* 1982; A. C. Baldwin, *apptd* 1990; T. English, *apptd* 1986; K. Maitland-Davies, *apptd* 1984
Old Street, M. A. Johnstone, *apptd* 1980; C. Pratt, *apptd* 1990
South-Western, S. G. Clixby, *apptd* 1981; C. D. Voelcker, *apptd* 1982; A. Ormerod, *apptd* 1988
Thames, I. Bing, *apptd* 1989; W. A. Kennedy, *apptd* 1991; M. J. Read, *apptd* 1993; S. Dawson, *apptd* 1994
Tower Bridge, Mrs J. R. Comyns, *apptd* 1982; R. D. Philips, *apptd* 1989; M. Kelly, *apptd* 1992
Wells Street, Miss A. M. Jennings, *apptd* 1972; I. M. Baker, *apptd* 1990; Ms G. Babington-Browne, *apptd* 1991
West London, H. J. Cook, *apptd* 1975; D. Thomas, *apptd* 1990
Unattached Magistrates, C. S. F. Black, *apptd* 1993; H. N. Evans, *apptd* 1990; Mrs L. Morgan, *apptd* 1995

MAGISTRATES' COURTS COMMITTEE FOR THE INNER LONDON AREA
65 Romney Street, London SW1P 3RD
Tel 0171-799 3332

Justices' Chief Executive and Clerk to the Committee (*£80,000), vacant
Justices' Clerk (*Training*) (£*48,971), vacant

* 1994–5 figure

CROWN PROSECUTION SERVICE
50 Ludgate Hill, London EC4M 7EX
Tel 0171-273 8000

The Crown Prosecution Service (CPS) is responsible for the independent review and conduct of criminal proceedings instituted by police forces in England and Wales, with the exception of cases conducted by the Serious Fraud Office (*see* page 347) and certain minor offences.

The Director of Public Prosecutions is the head of the Service and discharges her statutory functions under the superintendence of the Attorney-General.

The Service comprises a headquarters office and 13 Areas covering England and Wales. Each of the CPS Areas is supervised by a Chief Crown Prosecutor.

For salaries, *see* page 281

Director of Public Prosecutions (*G1*), Mrs B. Mills, QC
Principal Establishment and Finance Officer (*G3*), D. Nooney
Director (*Casework*) (*G3*), C. Newell
Director (*Operations*) (*G3*), G. Duff
Director (*Policy*) (*G3*), K. Ashken

CPS AREAS

CPS ANGLIA, Queen's House, 58 Victoria Street, St Albans AL1 3HZ. Tel: 01727-818100. *Chief Crown Prosecutor* (*G4*), R. J. Chronnell
CPS EAST MIDLANDS, 2 King Edward Court, King Edward Street, Nottingham NG1 1EL. Tel: 0115-948 0480. *Chief Crown Prosecutor* (*G4*), B. T. McArdle
CPS HUMBER, Belgrave House, 47 Bank Street, Sheffield S1 2EH. Tel: 0114-273 1261. *Chief Crown Prosecutor* (*G4*), D. Adams, CBE
CPS LONDON, Portland House, Stag Place, London SW1E 5BH. Tel: 0171-915 5700. *Chief Crown Prosecutor* (*G3*), G. D. Etheringdon
CPS MERSEY/LANCASHIRE, 7th Floor (South), Royal Liver Building, Pier Head, Liverpool L3 1HN. Tel: 0151-236 7575. *Chief Crown Prosecutor* (*G4*), C. Woodcock
CPS MIDLANDS, 14th Floor, Colmore Gate, 2 Colmore Row, Birmingham B3 2QA. Tel: 0121-629 7202. *Chief Crown Prosecutor* (*G4*), T. M. McGowran
CPS NORTH, Benton House, 136 Sandyford Road, Newcastle upon Tyne NE2 1QE. Tel: 0191-201 2390. *Chief Crown Prosecutor* (*G4*) (*acting*), M. Graham
CPS NORTH-WEST, PO Box 377, 8th Floor, Sunlight House, Quay Street, Manchester M60 3LU. Tel: 0161-837 7402. *Chief Crown Prosecutor* (*G4*), A. R. Taylor
CPS SEVERN/THAMES, Artillery House, Heritage Way, Droitwich, Worcester WR9 8YB. Tel: 01905-793763. *Chief Crown Prosecutor* (*G4*), A. S. R. Clarke
CPS SOUTH-EAST, Stoke Mill, Woking Road, Guildford, Surrey GU1 1AQ. Tel: 01483-573255. *Chief Crown Prosecutor* (*G4*), D. E. J. Dracup
CPS SOUTH-WEST, 8 Kew Court, Pynes Hill, Rydon Lane, Exeter EX2 5SS. Tel: 01392-445422. *Chief Crown Prosecutor* (*G4*), P. Boeuf
CPS WALES, Tudor House, 16 Cathedral Road, Cardiff CF1 9LJ. Tel: 01222-783000. *Chief Crown Prosecutor* (*G4*), R. A. Prickett
CPS YORKSHIRE, 6th Floor, Ryedale Building, 60 Piccadilly, York YO1 1NS. Tel: 01904-610726. *Chief Crown Prosecutor* (*G4*), D. V. Dickenson

The Scottish Judicature

Scotland has a legal system separate from and differing greatly from the English legal system in enacted law, judicial procedure and the structure of courts.

In Scotland the system of public prosecution is headed by the Lord Advocate and is independent of the police, who have no say in the decision to prosecute. The Lord Advocate, discharging his functions through the Crown Office in Edinburgh, is responsible for prosecutions in the High Court, sheriff courts and district courts. Prosecutions in the High Court are prepared by the Crown Office and conducted in court by one of the law officers, by an advocate-depute, or by a solicitor advocate. In the inferior courts the decision to prosecute is made and prosecution is preferred by procurators fiscal, who are lawyers and full-time civil servants subject to the directions of the Crown Office. A permanent legally-qualified civil servant known as the Crown Agent is responsible for the running of the Crown Office and the organization of the Procurator Fiscal Service, of which he is the head.

Scotland is divided into six sheriffdoms, each with a full-time Sheriff Principal. The sheriffdoms are further divided into sheriff court districts, each of which has a legally-qualified, resident sheriff or sheriffs, who are the judges of the court.

In criminal cases sheriffs principal and sheriffs have the same powers; sitting with a jury of 15 members, they may try more serious cases on indictment, or, sitting alone, may try lesser cases under summary procedure. Minor summary offences are dealt with in district courts which are administered by the district and the islands local government authorities and presided over by lay justices of the peace (of whom there are about 4,200) and, in Glasgow only, by stipendiary magistrates. Juvenile offenders (children under 16) may be brought before an informal children's hearing comprising three local lay people. The superior criminal court is the High Court of Justiciary which is both a trial and an appeal court. Cases on indictment are tried by a High Court judge, sitting with a jury of 15, in Edinburgh and on circuit in other towns. Appeals from the lower courts against conviction or sentence are heard also by the High Court, which sits as an appeal court only in Edinburgh. There is no further appeal to the House of Lords in criminal cases.

In civil cases the jurisdiction of the sheriff court extends to most kinds of action. Appeal against decisions of the sheriff may be made to the Sheriff Principal and thence to the Court of Session, or direct to the Court of Session, which sits only in Edinburgh. The Court of Session is divided into the Inner and the Outer House. The Outer House is a court of first instance in which cases are heard by judges sitting singly, sometimes with a jury of 12. The Inner House, itself subdivided into two divisions of equal status, is mainly an appeal court. Appeals may be made to the Inner House from the Outer House as well as from the sheriff court. An appeal may be made from the Inner House to the House of Lords.

The judges of the Court of Session are the same as those of the High Court of Justiciary, the Lord President of the Court of Session also holding the office of Lord Justice General in the High Court. Senators of the College of Justice are Lords Commissioners of Justiciary as well as judges of the Court of Session. On appointment, a Senator takes a judicial title, which is retained for life. Although styled 'The Hon./Rt. Hon. Lord —', the Senator is not a peer.

The office of coroner does not exist in Scotland. The local procurator fiscal inquires privately into sudden and suspicious deaths and may report findings to the Crown Agent. In some cases a fatal accident inquiry may be held before the sheriff.

COURT OF SESSION AND HIGH COURT OF JUSTICIARY

The Lord President and Lord Justice General (£114,874)
  The Lord Hope of Craighead, PC, *born* 1938, *apptd* 1989

INNER HOUSE

Lords of Session (each £110,137)

FIRST DIVISION

The Lord President
Hon. Lord Allanbridge (William Stewart), *born* 1925, *apptd* 1977
Hon. Lord Sutherland (Ranald Sutherland), *born* 1932, *apptd* 1985
Hon. Lord Clyde (James Clyde), *born* 1932, *apptd* 1985

SECOND DIVISION

Lord Justice Clerk (£114,137), The Rt. Hon. Lord Ross (Donald Ross), *born* 1927, *apptd* 1985
Hon. The Lord McCluskey, *born* 1929, *apptd* 1984
Hon. Lord Morison (Alastair Morison), *born* 1931, *apptd* 1985
Hon. Lord Weir (David Weir), *born* 1931, *apptd* 1985

OUTER HOUSE

Lords of Session (each £98,957)

Hon. Lord Davidson (Charles Davidson) (*seconded to Scottish Law Commission*), *born* 1929, *apptd* 1983
Hon. Lord Cullen (Douglas Cullen), *born* 1935, *apptd* 1986
Hon. Lord Prosser (William Prosser), *born* 1934, *apptd* 1986
Hon. Lord Kirkwood (Ian Kirkwood), *born* 1932, *apptd* 1987
Hon. Lord Coulsfield (John Cameron), *born* 1934, *apptd* 1987
Hon. Lord Milligan (James Milligan), *born* 1934, *apptd* 1988
Hon. Lord Caplan (Philip Caplan), *born* 1929, *apptd* 1989
Rt. Hon. The Lord Cameron of Lochbroom, *born* 1931, *apptd* 1989
Hon. Lord Marnoch (Michael Bruce), *born* 1938, *apptd* 1990
Hon. Lord MacLean (Ranald MacLean), *born* 1938, *apptd* 1990
Hon. Lord Penrose (George Penrose), *born* 1938, *apptd* 1990
Hon. Lord Osborne (Kenneth Osborne), *born* 1937, *apptd* 1990
Hon. Lord Abernethy (John Cameron), *born* 1938, *apptd* 1992
Hon. Lord Johnston (Alan Macpherson), *born* 1942, *apptd* 1994
Hon. Lord Gill (Brian Gill), *born* 1942, *apptd* 1994

Hon. Lord Hamilton (Arthur Hamilton), *born* 1942, *apptd* 1995

Hon. Lord Dawson (Thomas Dawson), *born* 1948, *apptd* 1995

Hon. Lord Macfadyen (Donald Macfadyen), *born* 1945, *apptd* 1995

COURT OF SESSION AND HIGH COURT OF JUSTICIARY
Parliament House, Parliament Square, Edinburgh EH1 1RQ
Tel 0131-225 2595

Principal Clerk of Session and Justiciary (£36,739–£54,815), H. S. Foley
Deputy Principal Clerk of Justiciary and Administration (£24,724–£38,290), T. Fyffe
Deputy Principal Clerk of Session and Principal Extractor (£24,724–£38,290), G. McKeand
Deputy Principal Clerk (Keeper of the Rolls) (£24,724–£38,290), T. M. Thomson
Depute Clerks of Session and Justiciary (£19,215–£25,289), N. J. Dowie; I. Smith; T. Higgins; T. B. Cruickshank; Q. Oliver; F. Shannly; A. S. Moffat; D. J. Shand; G. Ellis; D. G. Lynn; R. Cockburn; W. Dunn; A. Finlayson; C. Armstrong; S. Hindes; P. Crow; R. McMillan; G. Prentice; C. Cockburn; S. F. Bain; S. Walker; R. Jenkins; J. O. McLean; M. Weir

SCOTTISH COURTS ADMINISTRATION
Hayweight House, 23 Lauriston Street, Edinburgh EH3 9DQ
Tel 0131-229 9200

The Scottish Courts Administration is responsible to the Secretary of State for Scotland for the performance of the Scottish Court Service and central administration pertaining to the judiciary in the Supreme and Sheriff Courts; and to the Lord Advocate for certain aspects of court procedures, jurisdiction and legislation, law reform and other matters.
Director (G2), J. Hamill
Deputy Director (Legal Policy) (Assistant Solicitor) (G5), P. M. Beaton
Deputy Director (Resources and Liaison) (G6), D. Stewart

SCOTTISH COURT SERVICE
Hayweight House, 23 Lauriston Street, Edinburgh EH3 9DQ
Tel 0131-229 9200

The Scottish Court Service became an executive agency within the Scottish Courts Administration in April 1995. It is responsible to the Secretary of State for Scotland for the provision of staff, court houses and associated services for the Supreme and Sheriff Courts.
Chief Executive, M. Ewart

SHERIFF COURT OF CHANCERY
27 Chambers Street, Edinburgh EH1 1LB
Tel 0131-225 2525

The Court deals with service of heirs and completion of title in relation to heritable property.
Sheriff of Chancery, C. G. B. Nicholson, QC

HM COMMISSARY OFFICE
27 Chambers Street, Edinburgh EH1 1LB
Tel 0131-225 2525

The Office is responsible for issuing confirmation, a legal document entitling a person to execute a deceased person's will, and other related matters.
Commissary Clerk, J. L. Anderson

SCOTTISH LAND COURT
1 Grosvenor Crescent, Edinburgh EH12 5ER
Tel 0131-225 3595

The court deals with disputes relating to agricultural and crofting land in Scotland.
Chairman (£85,241), The Hon. Lord Philip (Alexander Philip), QC
Members, D. D. McDiarmid; D. M. Macdonald; J. Kinloch *(part-time)*
Principal Clerk, K. H. R. Graham, WS

SHERIFFDOMS

SALARIES

Sheriff Principal	£85,241
Sheriff	£72,524
Regional Sheriff Clerk	£28,213–£54,815
Sheriff Clerk	£11,208–£38,290

*Floating Sheriff

GRAMPIAN, HIGHLANDS AND ISLANDS
Sheriff Principal, D. J. Risk
Regional Sheriff Clerk, J. Robertson

SHERIFFS AND SHERIFF CLERKS
Aberdeen and Stonehaven, D. W. Bogie; G. C. Warner; D. Kelbie; L. A. S. Jessop; A. Pollock; *Sheriff Clerks*, D. Nicoll (*Aberdeen*); I. Smith (*Stonehaven*)
Peterhead and Banff, K. A. McLernan; *Sheriff Clerk*, A. Hempseed (*Peterhead*); *Sheriff Clerk Depute*, Mrs F. L. MacPherson (*Banff*)
Elgin, N. McPartlin; *Sheriff Clerk*, M. McBey
Inverness, Lochmaddy, Portree, Stornoway, Dingwall, Tain, Wick and Dornoch, W. J. Fulton; D. Booker-Milburn; J. O. A. Fraser; I. A. Cameron; *Sheriff Clerks*, J. Robertson (*Inverness*); W. Cochrane (*Dingwall*); *Sheriff Clerks Depute*, Miss M. Campbell (*Lochmaddy and Portree*); Mrs M. Macdonald (*Stornoway*); L. MacLachlan (*Tain*); Mrs J. McEwan (*Wick*); Miss R. MacSween (*Dornoch*)
Kirkwall and Lerwick, G. S. Mackenzie; *Sheriff Clerks Depute*, R. Cantwell (*Kirkwall*); A. C. Norris (*Lerwick*)
Fort William, vacant (also *Oban*); *Sheriff Clerk Depute*, D. Hood

TAYSIDE, CENTRAL AND FIFE
Sheriff Principal, J. J. Maguire, QC
Regional Sheriff Clerk, J. S. Doig

SHERIFFS AND SHERIFF CLERKS
Arbroath and Forfar, K. A. Veal; *C. N. R. Stein; *Sheriff Clerks*, M. Herbertson (*Arbroath*); S. Munro (*Forfar*)
Dundee, R. A. Davidson; A. L. Stewart; *J. N. Young; C. Smith (also *Cupar*); *Sheriff Clerk*, J. S. Doig
Perth, J. F. Wheatley; J. C. McInnes, QC; *Sheriff Clerk*, W. Jones
Falkirk, A. V. Sheehan; A. J. Murphy; *Sheriff Clerk*, D. Forrester
Stirling, The Hon. R. E. G. Younger; *Mrs A. M. Cowan; *Sheriff Clerk*, J. Clark
Alloa, W. M. Reid; *Sheriff Clerk*, G. McKeand
Cupar, C. Smith (also *Dundee*); *Sheriff Clerk*, R. Hughes
Dunfermline, J. S. Forbes; C. W. Palmer; *Sheriff Clerk*, W. McCulloch
Kirkcaldy, W. J. Christie; Mrs L. G. Patrick; *Sheriff Clerk*, I. Hay

LOTHIAN AND BORDERS

Sheriff Principal, C. G. B. Nicholson, QC
Regional Sheriff Clerk, J. Anderson

SHERIFFS AND SHERIFF CLERKS

Edinburgh, N. E. D. Thomson (also *Peebles*);
P. G. B. McNeill, PH.D., QC; Miss H. J. Aronson, QC;
R. G. Craik, QC; G. I. W. Shiach; Miss I. A. Poole;
R. J. D. Scott; A. M. Bell; J. M. S. Horsburgh, QC;
G. W. S. Presslie (also *Haddington*); J. A. Farrell;
*A. Lothian; *F. J. Keane; I. D. Macphail, QC; *Sheriff Clerk*, J. Anderson
Peebles, N. E. D. Thomson, CBE (also *Edinburgh*); *Sheriff Clerk Depute*, R. McArthur
Linlithgow, H. R. MacLean; G. R. Fleming; *Sheriff Clerk*, R. Sinclair
Haddington, G. W. S. Presslie (also *Edinburgh*); *Sheriff Clerk*, J. O'Donnell
Jedburgh and Duns, J. V. Paterson; *Sheriff Clerk*, J. W. Williamson
Selkirk, J. V. Paterson; *Sheriff Clerk Depute*, L. McFarlane

NORTH STRATHCLYDE

Sheriff Principal, R. C. Hay, CBE
Regional Sheriff Clerk, A. A. Brown

SHERIFFS AND SHERIFF CLERKS

Oban, vacant (also *Fort William*); *Sheriff Clerk Depute*, G. Whitelaw
Dumbarton, J. T. Fitzsimons; T. Scott; S. W. H. Fraser; *Sheriff Clerk*, N. R. Weir
Paisley, R. G. Smith; C. N. Stoddart; J. Spy; C. K. Higgins; *C. G. McKay; *N. Douglas; *D. J. Pender; *Sheriff Clerk*, A. A. Brown
Greenock, J. Herald (also *Rothesay*); Sir Stephen Young; *Sheriff Clerk*, J. Tannahill
Kilmarnock, T. M. Croan; D. B. Smith; T. F. Russell; *Sheriff Clerk*, J. Shaw
Dunoon, A. W. Noble; *Sheriff Clerk Depute*, Mrs C. Carson
Campbeltown, vacant; *Sheriff Clerk Depute*, P. G. Hay
Rothesay, J. Herald (also *Greenock*); *Sheriff Clerk Depute*, Mrs J. O'Donnell

GLASGOW AND STRATHKELVIN

Sheriff Principal, N. D. MacLeod, QC
Regional Sheriff Clerk, C. McLay

SHERIFFS AND SHERIFF CLERKS

Glasgow, A. C. Horsfall, QC (*seconded to Scottish Lands Tribunal*); B. Kearney; G. H. Gordon, CBE, PH.D., QC;
Mrs D. J. B. Robertson; B. A. Lockhart; I. G. Pirie;
Mrs A. L. A. Duncan; G. J. Evans; E. H. Galt;
A. C. Henry; J. K. Mitchell; A. G. Johnston;
J. P. Murphy; M. Sischy; Miss S. A. O. Raeburn, QC;
A. B. Wilkinson; D. Convery; J. McGowan;
B. A. Kerr, QC; Mrs C. M. A. F. Gimblett;
I. A. S. Peebles, QC; *Sheriff Clerk*, C. McLay

SOUTH STRATHCLYDE, DUMFRIES AND GALLOWAY

Sheriff Principal, G. L. Cox, QC
Regional Sheriff Clerk, M. Bonar

SHERIFFS AND SHERIFF CLERKS

Hamilton, L. Cameron; A. C. MacPherson; W. F. Lunny;
D. C. Russell; V. J. Canavan (also *Airdrie*);
W. E. Gibson; H. Stirling; *Sheriff Clerk*, P. Feeney
Lanark, J. D. Allan; *Sheriff Clerk*, J. Lynn

Ayr, N. Gow, QC; R. G. McEwan, QC; *Sheriff Clerk*, G. W. Waddell
Stranraer and Kirkcudbright, J. R. Smith (also *Dumfries*); *Sheriff Clerks*, W. McIntosh (*Stranraer*); B. Lindsay (*Kirkcudbright*)
Dumfries, K. G. Barr; M. J. Fletcher; J. R.Smith (also *Stranraer and Kirkcudbright*); *Sheriff Clerk*, P. McGonigle
Airdrie, J. H. Stewart; V. J. Canavan (also *Hamilton*);
R. H. Dickson; I. C. Simpson; *Sheriff Clerk*, M. Bonar

STIPENDIARY MAGISTRATES

GLASGOW

R. Hamilton, *apptd* 1984; J. B. C. Nisbet, *apptd* 1984;
R. B. Christie, *apptd* 1985; Mrs J. A. M. MacLean, *apptd* 1990

PROCURATOR FISCAL SERVICE

CROWN OFFICE
25 Chambers Street, Edinburgh EH1 1LA
Tel 0131-226 2626

Crown Agent (£65,990–£79,396), J. D. Lowe, CB
Deputy Crown Agent (£45,278–£54,815), N. McFadyen

PROCURATORS FISCAL

SALARIES 1994–5

Regional Procurator Fiscal–grade 3	£52,704–£62,817
Regional Procurator Fiscal–grade 4	£45,278–£54,815
Procurator Fiscal–upper level	£36,739–£54,815
Procurator Fiscal–lower level	£26,418–£45,078

GRAMPIAN, HIGHLANDS AND ISLANDS REGION

Regional Procurator Fiscal, A. D. Vannett (*Aberdeen*)
Procurators Fiscal, E. K. Barbour (*Stonehaven*);
A. J. M. Colley (*Banff*); I. S. McNaughton (*Peterhead*);
J. F. MacKay (*Elgin*); A. N. MacDonald (*Wick*);
C. B. McClory (*Portree and Lochmaddy*); Mrs D. Wilson (*Stornoway*); H. T. Westwater (*Dornoch* and *Tain*);
G. K. Buchanan (*Inverness*); D. K. Adam (*Kirkwall* and *Lerwick*); Mrs A. Neizer (*Fort William*); D. R. Hingston (*Dingwall*)

TAYSIDE, CENTRAL AND FIFE REGION

Regional Procurator Fiscal, B. K. Heywood (*Dundee*)
Procurators Fiscal, Mrs B. Bott (*Arbroath*); I. C. Walker (*Forfar*); I. A. McLeod (*Perth*); G. E. Scott (*Falkirk*);
J. J. Miller (*Stirling*); I. D. Douglas (*Alloa*); E. B. Russell (*Cupar*); R. T. Hamilton (*Dunfermline*); F. R. Crowe (*Kirkcaldy*)

LOTHIAN AND BORDERS REGION

Regional Procurator Fiscal, R. F. Lees (*Edinburgh*)
Procurators Fiscal, R. F. Lees (*Peebles*); Miss L. M. Ruxton (*Linlithgow*); A. J. P. Reith (*Haddington*); A. R. G. Fraser (*Duns* and *Jedburgh*); D. McNeill (*Selkirk*)

NORTH STRATHCLYDE REGION

Regional Procurator Fiscal, J. D. Friel (*Paisley*)
Procurators Fiscal, I. Henderson (*Campbeltown*);
C. C. Donnelly (*Dumbarton*); J. Macdonald (*Greenock* and *Rothesay*); D. L. Webster (*Dunoon*); J. G. MacGlennan (*Kilmarnock*); B. R. Maguire (*Oban*)

GLASGOW AND STRATHKELVIN REGION
Regional Procurator Fiscal, A. C. Normand (*Glasgow*)

SOUTH STRATHCLYDE, DUMFRIES AND GALLOWAY
REGION
Regional Procurator Fiscal, W. G. Carmichael (*Hamilton*)

Procurators Fiscal, S. R. Houston (*Lanark*); D. A. Brown
(*Ayr*); F. Walkingshaw (*Stranraer*); D. J. Howdle
(*Dumfries* and *Stranraer* and *Kirkcudbright*); A. T. Wilson
(*Airdrie*)

Northern Ireland Judicature

In Northern Ireland the legal system and the structure of courts closely resemble those of England and Wales; there are, however, often differences in enacted law.

The Supreme Court of Judicature of Northern Ireland comprises the Court of Appeal, the High Court of Justice and the Crown Court. The practice and procedure of these courts is similar to that in England. The superior civil court is the High Court of Justice, from which an appeal lies to the Northern Ireland Court of Appeal; the House of Lords is the final civil appeal court.

The Crown Court, served by High Court and county court judges, deals with criminal trials on indictment. Cases are heard before a judge and, except those involving offences specified under emergency legislation, a jury. Appeals from the Crown Court against conviction or sentence are heard by the Northern Ireland Court of Appeal; the House of Lords is the final court of appeal.

The decision to prosecute in cases tried on indictment and in summary cases of a serious nature rests in Northern Ireland with the Director of Public Prosecutions, who is responsible to the Attorney-General. Minor summary offences are prosecuted by the police.

Minor criminal offences are dealt with in magistrates' courts by a legally qualified resident magistrate and, where an offender is under 17, by juvenile courts each consisting of a resident magistrate and two lay members specially qualified to deal with juveniles (at least one of whom must be a woman). In June 1995 there were 987 justices of the peace in Northern Ireland. Appeals from magistrates' courts are heard by the county court, or by the Court of Appeal on a point of law or an issue as to jurisdiction.

Magistrates' courts in Northern Ireland can deal with certain classes of civil case but most minor civil cases are dealt with in county courts. Judgments of all civil courts are enforceable through a centralized procedure administered by the Enforcement of Judgments Office.

SUPREME COURT OF JUDICATURE
The Royal Courts of Justice, Belfast BT1 3JF
Tel 01232-235111

Lord Chief Justice of Northern Ireland (£114,874), The Rt.
Hon. Sir Brian Hutton, *born* 1931, *apptd* 1988
Principal Secretary, D. A. Lavery

LORDS JUSTICES OF APPEAL (each £110,137)
Style, The Rt. Hon. Lord Justice [surname]

Rt. Hon. Sir John MacDermott, *born* 1927, *apptd* 1987
Rt. Hon. Sir Robert Carswell, *born* 1934, *apptd* 1993
Rt. Hon. Sir Michael Nicholson, *born* 1933, *apptd* 1995

PUISNE JUDGES (EACH £98,957)
Style, The Hon. Mr Justice [surname]

Hon. Sir William McCollum, *born* 1933, *apptd* 1987

Hon. Sir Anthony Campbell, *born* 1936, *apptd* 1988
Hon. Sir John Sheil, *born* 1938, *apptd* 1989
Hon. Sir Brian Kerr, *born* 1948, *apptd* 1993
Hon. Sir John Pringle, *born* 1929, *apptd* 1993
Hon. Sir Malachy Higgins, *born* 1944, *apptd* 1993
Hon. Sir Frederick Girvan, *born* 1948, *apptd* 1995

MASTERS OF THE SUPREME COURT (each £59,327)
Master, Queen's Bench and Appeals and Clerk of the Crown,
J. W. Wilson, QC
Master, High Court, Mrs D. M. Kennedy
Master, Office of Care and Protection, F. B. Hall
Master, Chancery Office, R. A. Ellison
Master, Bankruptcy and Companies Office, J. B. C. Glass
Master, Probate and Matrimonial Office, R. T. Millar
Master, Taxing Office, J. C. Napier

COUNTY COURTS

JUDGES (each £85,241)
Style, His Hon. Judge [surname]

Judge Curran, QC; Judge McKee, QC; Judge Gibson, QC;
Judge Hart, QC; Judge Petrie, QC; Judge Smyth, QC; Judge
Markey, QC; Judge McKay, QC; Judge Chambers, QC
(*Chief Social Security and Child Support Commissioner*); Judge
Martin, QC; one vacancy

RECORDERS (each £82,641)
Belfast, Judge Russell, QC
Londonderry, Judge Burgess

MAGISTRATES' COURTS

RESIDENT MAGISTRATES (each £59,327)
There are 17 resident magistrates in Northern Ireland.

CROWN SOLICITOR'S OFFICE
PO Box 410, Royal Courts of Justice, Belfast BT1 3JY
Tel 01232-235111

Crown Solicitor, N. P. Roberts

DEPARTMENT OF THE DIRECTOR OF
PUBLIC PROSECUTIONS
Royal Courts of Justice, Belfast BT1 3NX
Tel 01232-235111

Director of Public Prosecutions, A. Fraser, CB, QC
Deputy Director of Public Prosecutions, D. Magill

NORTHERN IRELAND COURT SERVICE
Windsor House, Bedford Street, Belfast BT2 7LT
Tel 01232-328594

Director (G3)

Ecclesiastical Courts

Original jurisdiction is exercised by the consistory court of each diocese in England, presided over by the Chancellor of that diocese. Appellate jurisdiction is exercised by the provincial courts detailed below, by the Court for Ecclesiastical Causes Reserved, and by commissions of review (the membership of these being newly constituted for each case).

COURT OF ARCHES (PROVINCE OF CANTERBURY)
Registry, 16 Beaumont Street, Oxford OXI 2LZ
Tel 01865-241974

Dean of the Arches, The Rt. Worshipful Sir John Owen

COURT OF THE VICAR-GENERAL OF THE PROVINCE OF CANTERBURY
Registry, 16 Beaumont Street, Oxford OXI 2LZ
Tel 01865-241974

Vicar-General, The Rt. Worshipful Miss S. Cameron, QC

CHANCERY COURT OF YORK
Registry, 1 Peckitt Street, York YOI ISG
Tel 01904-623487

Auditor, The Rt. Worshipful Sir John Owen

THE VICAR-GENERAL OF THE PROVINCE OF YORK
Registry, 1 Peckitt Street, York YOI ISG
Tel 01904-623487

Vicar-General, His Honour the Worshipful Judge T. A. C. Coningsby, QC

COURT OF FACULTIES
Registry, 1 The Sanctuary, London SWIP 3JT
Tel 0171-222 5381

Office for the issue of special and common marriage licences, appointment of notaries public, etc. Office hours, Monday–Friday, 10–4.

Master of the Faculties, The Rt. Worshipful Sir John Owen

The Probation Service

ENGLAND AND WALES

The Probation Service is employed in each area (55 in total) by an independent committee of justices and it provides a professional social work agency in the courts, with responsibility for a wide range of duties which include:
(a) a pre-sentence report service for the criminal courts
(b) provision of a range of non-custodial measures involving the supervision of offenders in the community
(c) supervisory aftercare for offenders released from custody, together with social work in penal establishments and help for the families of those serving sentences
(d) an enquiry, conciliation and supervision service in the divorce and domestic courts
(e) support for and promotion of preventive and containment measures in the community designed to reduce the level of crime and domestic breakdown
It is a direct grant service funded 80 per cent from the Home Office and 20 per cent from the relevant local authority.

Its national representative bodies are:
THE CENTRAL PROBATION COUNCIL, 38 Belgrave Square, London SWIX 8NT. Tel: 0171-245 9364. *Director*, I. Miles
THE ASSOCIATION OF CHIEF OFFICERS OF PROBATION, 20–30 Lawefield Lane, Wakefield WF2 8SP. Tel: 01924–361156. *General Secretary*, Ms M. Honeyball
THE NATIONAL ASSOCIATION OF PROBATION OFFICERS, 3 Chivalry Road, London SWII IHT. Tel: 0171-223 4887. *General Secretary*, Ms J. McKnight

SCOTLAND

The probation service in Scotland is a statutory duty of local authorities under section 27 of the Social Work (Scotland) Act 1968. Social workers have to supervise and provide advice, guidance and assistance to those persons living in their area who are subject to a court's supervision order. This is done by social workers as part of their normal duties and not by a separate probation staff.

Tribunals

AGRICULTURAL LAND TRIBUNALS
c/o Land Use and Tenure Division, Ministry of
Agriculture, Fisheries and Food, Nobel House, 17 Smith
Square, London SW1P 3JR
Tel 0171-238 3000

Agricultural Land Tribunals were set up under the
Agriculture Act 1947 and settle disputes and other issues
between agricultural landlords and tenants. They also
settle drainage disputes between neighbours.

There are seven tribunals covering England and one
covering Wales. For each tribunal the Lord Chancellor
appoints a chairman and one or more deputies, who must
be barristers or solicitors of at least seven years standing.
The Lord Chancellor also appoints lay members to three
statutory panels of members: the 'landowners' panel, the
'farmers' panel and the 'drainage' panel.

Each of the eight tribunals is an independent statutory
body with jurisdiction only within its own area. A separate
tribunal is constituted for each case, and consists of a chairman (who may be the chairman or one of the deputy chairmen) and two lay members nominated by the chairman.
Chairmen (England) (£243 a day), W. D. Greenwood;
K. J. Fisher; P. A. de la Piquerie; C. H. Beaumont;
M. K. Lee; G. L. Newsom; His Hon. Judge Robert Taylor
Chairman (Wales) (£243 a day), W. J. Owen

COMMONS COMMISSIONERS
Golden Cross House, Duncannon Street, London
WC2N 4JF
Tel 0171-210 4584

The Commons Commissioners are responsible for de-
ciding disputes arising under the Commons Registration
Act 1965 and the Common Land (Rectification of
Registers) Act 1989. They also enquire into the ownership
of unclaimed common land. Commissioners are appointed
by the Lord Chancellor.
Chief Commons Commissioner (part-time) (£33,056), M. Roth
Commissioners, I. L. R. Romer; D. M. Burton
Clerk, Miss F. A. A. Buchan

COPYRIGHT TRIBUNAL
Room 4/6, Hazlitt House, 45 Southampton Buildings,
London WC2A 1AR
Tel 0171- 438 4776

The Copyright Tribunal is the successor to the Performing
Right Tribunal which was established by the Copyright
Act 1956 to resolve various classes of copyright dispute,
principally in the field of collective licensing. Its juris-
diction was extended by the Copyright, Designs and
Patents Act 1988 and the Broadcasting Act 1990.

The chairman and two deputy chairmen are appointed
by the Lord Chancellor. Up to eight ordinary members are
appointed by the Secretary of State for Trade and Industry.
Chairman (£316 a day), J. M. Bowers
Secretary, Miss J. E. M. Durdin

DATA PROTECTION TRIBUNAL
c/o The Home Office, Queen Anne's Gate, London
SW1H 9AT
Tel 0171-273 3386

The Data Protection Tribunal was established under the
Data Protection Act 1984 to determine appeals against
decisions of the Data Protection Registrar (*see* page 297).
The chairman and two deputy chairmen are appointed by
the Lord Chancellor and must be legally qualified. Lay
members are appointed by the Home Secretary to represent the interests of data users or data subjects.

A tribunal consists of a legally-qualified chairman sitting
with equal numbers of the lay members appointed to
represent the interests of data users and data subjects.
Chairman (£332 a day), J. A. C. Spokes, QC
Secretary, M. Jones

EMPLOYMENT APPEAL TRIBUNAL
Central Office, Audit House, 58 Victoria Embankment,
London EC4Y 0DS
Tel 0171-273 1041
Divisional Office, 52 Melville Street, Edinburgh EH3 7HF
Tel 0131-225 3963

The Employment Appeal Tribunal was established as a
superior court of record under the provisions of the
Employment Protection Act 1975, hearing appeals on a
question of law arising from any decision of an industrial
tribunal.

A tribunal consists of a legally-qualified chairman and
two lay members, one from each side of industry. They are
appointed by The Queen on the recommendation of the
Lord Chancellor and the Secretary of State for Trade and
Industry.
President, The Hon. Mr Justice Mummery
Scottish Chairman, The Hon. Lord Coulsfield
Registrar, Miss V. J. Selio

IMMIGRATION APPELLATE AUTHORITIES
Thanet House, 231 Strand, London WC2R 1DA
Tel 0171-353 8060

The Immigration Appeal Adjudicators hear appeals from
immigration decisions concerning the need for, and refusal
of, leave to enter or remain in the UK, refusals to grant
asylum, decisions to make deportation orders and directions to remove persons subject to immigration control
from the UK. The Immigration Appeal Tribunal hears
appeals direct from decisions to make deportation orders in
matters concerning conduct contrary to the public good
and refusals to grant asylum. Its principal jurisdiction is,
however, the hearing of appeals from adjudicators by the
party (Home Office or individual) who is aggrieved by the
decision. Appeals are subject to leave being granted by the
tribunal.

An adjudicator sits alone. The tribunal sits in divisions of
three, normally a legally qualified member and two lay

members. Members of the tribunal and adjudicators are appointed by the Lord Chancellor.

IMMIGRATION APPEAL TRIBUNAL
President (£72,524), G. W. Farmer
Vice-Presidents, Prof. D. C. Jackson; Mrs J. Chatwani

IMMIGRATION APPEAL ADJUDICATORS
Chief Adjudicator, His Hon. Judge Pearl
Deputy Chief Adjudicator, R. G. Care

INDEPENDENT TRIBUNAL SERVICE
City Gate House, 39–45 Finsbury Square, London
EC2A 1PX
Tel 0171-814 6500

The service is the judicial authority which exercises judicial and administrative control over the independent social security and child support appeal tribunals, medical and disability appeal tribunals and vaccine damage tribunals.
President, His Hon. Judge Bassingthwaighte
Chief Executive, S. Williams

INDUSTRIAL TRIBUNALS

CENTRAL OFFICE (ENGLAND AND WALES)
19–29 Woburn Place, London WC1H 0LU
Tel 0171-273 8659

Industrial Tribunals for England and Wales sit in 11 regions. The tribunals deal with matters of employment law, redundancy, dismissal, contract disputes, sexual and racial discrimination and related areas of dispute which may arise in the workplace. A central registration unit records all applications and maintains a public register at Southgate Street, Bury St Edmunds, Suffolk IP33 2AQ. The tribunals are funded by the Department of Trade and Industry.

Chairmen, who may be full-time or part-time, are legally qualified. They are appointed by the Lord Chancellor. Tribunal members are nominated by specified employer and employee groups and appointed by the Secretary of State for Trade and Industry.
President, His Hon. Judge Timothy Lawrence

CENTRAL OFFICE (SCOTLAND)
Eagle Building, 215 Bothwell Street, Glasgow G2 7TS
Tel 0141-204 0730

Tribunals in Scotland have the same remit as those in England and Wales. Chairmen are appointed by the Lord President of the Court of Session and lay members by the Secretary of State for Trade and Industry.
President (£85,241), Mrs D. Littlejohn

INDUSTRIAL TRIBUNALS AND THE FAIR EMPLOYMENT TRIBUNAL (NORTHERN IRELAND)
Long Bridge House, 20–24 Waring Street, Belfast BT1 2EB
Tel 01232-327666

The industrial tribunal system in Northern Ireland was set up in 1965 and is similar to the system operating in the rest of the UK. The main legislation in Northern Ireland giving jurisdiction to industrial tribunals to hear complaints relating to employment matters corresponds to legislation enacted in Great Britain, except that there is no equivalent legislation to the Race Relations Act.

Since 1990 there has been a separate Fair Employment Tribunal in Northern Ireland. The Fair Employment Tribunal hears and determines individual cases of alleged religious or political discrimination in employment. Employers can also appeal to the Fair Employment Tribunal if they consider the directions of the Fair Employment Commission to be unreasonable, inappropriate or unnecessary, and the Fair Employment Commission can make application to the Tribunal for the enforcement of undertakings or directions with which an employer has not complied.

The president, vice-president and part-time chairmen of the Fair Employment Tribunal are appointed by the Lord Chancellor. The full-time chairman and the part-time chairmen of the industrial tribunals and the panel members to both the industrial tribunals and the Fair Employment Tribunal are appointed by the Department of Economic Development Northern Ireland.
President of the Industrial Tribunals and the Fair Employment Tribunal (£85,241), J. Maguire
Vice-President of the Industrial Tribunals and the Fair Employment Tribunal, Mrs M. Perceval-Price
Secretary, J. Murphy

LANDS TRIBUNAL
48–49 Chancery Lane, London WC2A 1JR
Tel 0171-936 7200

The Lands Tribunal is an independent judicial body constituted by the Lands Tribunal Act 1949 for the purpose of determining a wide range of questions relating to the valuation of land, rating appeals from valuation tribunals and the discharge or modification of restrictive covenants. The Act also empowers the tribunal to accept the function of arbitration under references by consent. The tribunal consists of a president and a number of other members, who are appointed by the Lord Chancellor.
President, His Hon. Judge Marder, QC
Members (£72,524), Dr T. Hoyes, FRICS; M. St J. Hopper, FRICS
Members (part-time) (£330 a day), J. C. Hill, TD; His Hon. Judge Rich, QC; A. P. Musto, FRICS; P. H. Clarke, FRICS
Registrar, C. A. McMullan

LANDS TRIBUNAL FOR SCOTLAND
1 Grosvenor Crescent, Edinburgh EH12 5ER
Tel 0131-225 7996

The Lands Tribunal for Scotland was constituted by the Lands Tribunal Act 1949. Its remit is the same as the tribunal for England and Wales but also covers questions relating to tenants rights. The president is appointed by the Lord President of the Court of Session.
President, The Hon. Lord Philip, QC
Members (£72,524), Sheriff A. C. Horsfall, QC; A. R. MacLeary; J. Devine (*full-time*); R. A. Edwards, CBE, WS (*part-time*)
Clerk, D. Pentland

MENTAL HEALTH REVIEW TRIBUNALS

The Mental Health Review Tribunals are independent judicial bodies established under the Mental Health Act 1959 and which now operate under the Mental Health Act 1983. They are responsible for reviewing the cases of patients compulsorily detained under the Act's provisions. They have the power to discharge the patient, to recommend leave of absence, delayed discharge, transfer to another hospital or that a guardianship order be made, and to reclassify both restricted and unrestricted patients. There are eight tribunals in England, each headed by a regional chairman who is appointed by the Lord Chancellor's Department on a part-time basis. Each tribunal is made up of at least three members, and must include a lawyer, who acts as president (£221 a day), a medical member (£226 a day) and a lay member (£91 a day).

The Mental Health Review Tribunals' secretariat is based in five regional offices:

LIVERPOOL, 3rd Floor, Cressington House, 249 St Mary's Road, Garston, Liverpool L19 0NF. Tel: 0151-494 0095. *Clerk*, Mrs B. Foot

LONDON (NORTH), Spur 3, Block 1, Government Buildings, Honeypot Lane, Stanmore, Middx HA7 1AY. Tel: 0171-972 3738. *Clerk*, P. Barnett

LONDON (SOUTH), Block 3, Crown Offices, Kingston Bypass Road, Surbiton, Surrey KT6 5QN. Tel: 0181-398 4166. *Clerk*, Mrs J. Innes

NOTTINGHAM, Spur A, Block 5, Government Buildings, Chalfont Drive, Western Boulevard, Nottingham NG8 3RZ. Tel: 0115-929 4222. *Clerk*, M. Chapman

WALES, 1st Floor, New Crown Buildings, Cathays Park, Cardiff CF1 3NQ. Tel: 01222-823036. *Clerk*, Mrs C. Thomas

NATIONAL HEALTH SERVICE TRIBUNAL

The NHS Tribunal was set up under the National Health Service Act 1977. It inquires into representations that the continued inclusion of a family practitioner (doctor, dentist, pharmacist or optician) on a Family Practitioner Committee's list would be prejudicial to the efficiency of the services concerned. The tribunal sits when required, about eight times a year, and usually in London. The chairman is appointed by the Lord Chancellor and members are appointed by the Secretary of State for Health.
Chairman (£246 a day), A. Whitfield, QC
Deputy Chairmen, Miss E. Platt, QC; Dr R. N. Ough
Clerk, I. D. Keith, East Hookers, Twineham, nr Haywards Heath, W. Sussex RH17 5NN. Tel: 01444-881345

NATIONAL HEALTH SERVICE TRIBUNAL (SCOTLAND)
Erskine House, 68 Queen Street, Edinburgh EH2 4NN
Tel 0131-226 6541

The tribunal was set up under the National Health Service (Scotland) Act 1978, and exists to consider representations that the continued inclusion of a registered doctor, dentist, optometrist or pharmacist on a health board's list would be prejudicial to the continuing efficiency of the service in question.

The tribunal meets when required and is composed of a chairman, one lay member, and one practitioner member drawn from a representative professional panel. The chairman is appointed by the Lord President of the Court of Session, and the lay member and the members of the professional panel are appointed by the Secretary of State for Scotland.
Chairman (£246 a day), W. C. Galbraith, QC
Lay member, J. D. M. Robertson
Clerk to the Tribunal, D. G. Brash, WS

PENSIONS APPEAL TRIBUNALS

CENTRAL OFFICE (ENGLAND AND WALES)
48–49 Chancery Lane, London WC2A 1JR
Tel 0171-936 7034

The Pensions Appeal Tribunals are responsible for hearing appeals from ex-servicemen or women and widows who have had their claims for a war pension rejected by the Secretary of State for Social Security. The Entitlement Appeal Tribunals hear appeals in cases where the Secretary of State has refused to grant a war pension. The Assessment Appeal Tribunals hear appeals against the Secretary of State's assessment of the degree of disablement caused by an accepted condition.

The tribunal members are appointed by the Lord Chancellor.
President (£59,327), J. R. T. Holt
Secretary, W. Thomas

PENSIONS APPEAL TRIBUNALS FOR SCOTLAND
20 Walker Street, Edinburgh EH3 7HS
Tel 0131-220 1404
President (£270 a day), C. N. McEachran, QC

OFFICE OF THE SOCIAL SECURITY AND CHILD SUPPORT COMMISSIONERS
Harp House, 83–86 Farringdon Street, London EC4A 4DH
Tel 0171-353 5145
23 Melville Street, Edinburgh EH3 7PW
Tel 0131-225 2201

The Social Security Commissioners are the final statutory authority to decide appeals relating to entitlement to social security benefits. The Child Support Commissioners are the final statutory authority to decide appeals relating to child support. Appeals may be made in relation to both matters only on a point of law. The Commissioners' jurisdiction covers England, Wales and Scotland. There are 17 commissioners; they are all qualified lawyers.
Chief Social Security Commissioner and Chief Child Support Commissioner, His Hon. Judge Machin, QC
Secretary, S. Hill (*London*); R. Lindsay (*Edinburgh*)

OFFICE OF THE SOCIAL SECURITY AND CHILD SUPPORT COMMISSIONERS FOR NORTHERN IRELAND
Lancashire House, 5 Linenhall Street, Belfast BT2 8AA
Tel 01232-332344

The role of Northern Ireland Social Security and Child Support Commissioners is similar to that of the Commissioners in Great Britain. There are two commissioners for Northern Ireland.
Chief Commissioner, His Hon. Judge Chambers, QC
Registrar of Appeals, W. D. Pollock

THE SOLICITORS' DISCIPLINARY TRIBUNAL
227–228 Strand, London WC2A 1BA
Tel 0171-242 0219

The Solicitors' Disciplinary Tribunal was constituted under the provisions of the Solicitors Act 1974. It is an independent statutory body whose members are appointed by the Master of the Rolls. The tribunal considers applications made to it alleging either professional misconduct and/or a breach of the statutory rules by which solicitors are bound against an individually named solicitor, former solicitor, or registered foreign lawyer. The tribunal's jurisdiction extends to solicitor's clerks, in respect of whom they may make an order restricting that clerk's employment by solicitors. The president and members do not receive remuneration.
President, G. B. Marsh
Clerk, Mrs S. C. Elson

SPECIAL COMMISSIONERS OF INCOME TAX
15–19 Bedford Avenue, London WC1B 3AS
Tel 0171-631 4242

The Special Commissioners are an independent body appointed by the Lord Chancellor to hear complex appeals against decisions of the Board of Inland Revenue and its officials. There are three full-time and 11 part-time commissioners; all are legally qualified.
Presiding Special Commissioner, His Hon. Stephen Oliver, QC
Special Commissioners (£59,327), T. H. K. Everett;
    D. A. Shirley
Clerk, R. P. Lester

TRAFFIC COMMISSIONERS
c/o Western Traffic Area, The Gaunt's House, Denmark Street, Bristol BS1 5DR
Tel 0117-975 5065

The Traffic Commissioners are responsible for the licensing of operators of heavy goods and public service vehicles, and they also have responsibility for appeals relating to the licensing of operators and for disciplinary cases involving the conduct of drivers of these vehicles. There are seven Commissioners in the eight traffic areas covering Great Britain. Each Traffic Commissioner constitutes a tribunal for the purposes of the Tribunals and Inquiries Act 1971. For Traffic Area Offices and Commissioners, *see* page 355.
Senior Traffic Commissioner (£50,335), Air Vice-Marshal
    R. G. Ashford, CBE

TRANSPORT TRIBUNAL
48–49 Chancery Lane, London, WC2A 1JR
Tel 0171-936 7493

The Transport Tribunal was set up in 1947 and hears appeals against decisions made by Traffic Commissioners at public inquiries. The tribunal consists of a legally-qualified president, two legal members who may sit as chairmen, and five lay members. The president and legal members are appointed by the Lord Chancellor and the lay members are appointed by the Secretary of State for Transport.
President (part-time), His Hon. Judge Harold Wilson
Legal members (£243 a day), His Hon. Judge Brodrick (*part-time*); R. Owen, QC
Lay members (£194 a day), T. W. Hall; J. W. Whitworth;
    G. Simms; Miss E. B. Haran; P. Rogers
Secretary, W. Thomas

VALUATION TRIBUNALS
c/o Warwickshire Valuation Tribunal, 2nd Floor, Walton House, 11 Parade, Leamington Spa, Warks CV32 4DG
Tel 01926-421875

The Valuation Tribunals hear appeals concerning the council tax, non-domestic rating and land drainage rates in England and Wales. They also have residual jurisdiction to hear appeals concerning the community charge, the pre-1990 rating list, disabled rating and mixed hereditaments. There are 56 tribunals in England, and eight in Wales. Each tribunal is a separate independent body; those in England are funded by the Department of the Environment and those in Wales by the Welsh Office. A separate tribunal is constituted for each hearing, and normally consists of a chairman and two other members. Members are appointed by the local authority/authorities, and serve on a voluntary basis. A National Committee of Valuation Tribunals considers all matters affecting valuations tribunals in England, and the Council of Wales, Valuation Tribunal Presidents, performs the same function in Wales.
President, National Committee of Valuation Tribunals,
    A. H. W. Kennard
Secretary, National Committee of Valuation Tribunals,
    B. P. Massen
Chairman, Council of Wales, Valuation Tribunal Presidents,
    T. D. M. John

VAT AND DUTIES TRIBUNALS
15–19 Bedford Avenue, London WC1B 3AS
Tel 0171-631 4242

VAT and Duties Tribunals are administered by the Lord Chancellor's Department in England and Wales, and by the Secretary of State in Scotland. They are independent, and decide disputes between taxpayers and the Commissioners of Customs and Excise. In England and Wales, the president and chairmen are appointed by the Lord Chancellor and members are appointed by the Treasury. Chairmen in Scotland are appointed by the Lord President of the Court of Session.
President, His Hon. Stephen Oliver, QC
Vice-President, England and Wales (£59,327), A. W. Simpson
Vice-President, Scotland (£59,327), R. A. Bennett, CBE, QC
Vice-President, Northern Ireland (£59,327), D. C. Morgan, QC
Registrar, R. P. Lester

TRIBUNAL CENTRES
EDINBURGH, 44 Palmerston Place, Edinburgh EH12 5BJ.
    Tel: 0131–226 3551
LONDON (including Belfast), 15–19 Bedford Avenue,
    London WC1B 3AS. Tel: 0171-631 4242
MANCHESTER, Warwickgate House, Warwick Road, Old
    Trafford, Manchester M16 0GP. Tel: 0161-872 6471

The Police Service

There are 52 police forces in the United Kingdom, each responsible for law enforcement in its area. Most forces' area is conterminous with an English county or Welsh or Scottish local authority area, though there are several combined forces. Law enforcement in London is carried out by the Metropolitan Police and the City of London Police; in Northern Ireland by the Royal Ulster Constabulary; and by the Isle of Man, States of Jersey, and Guernsey forces in their respective islands and bailiwicks. National services include the National Criminal Intelligence Service and the National Missing Persons Bureau (*see* below).

Each police force is maintained by a police authority. The authorities of English and Welsh forces comprise local councillors, magistrates and independent members. In Scotland, the region and islands councils are the authorities at present but from April 1996 will be replaced by four joint police boards made up of local councillors. In London the authority for the Metropolitan Police is the Home Secretary, advised by the Metropolitan Police Committee; for the City of London Police the authority is a committee of the Corporation of London and includes councillors and magistrates. In Northern Ireland the Secretary of State appoints the police authority.

Police authorities are financed by central and local government grants and a precept on the council tax. Subject to the approval of the Home Secretary and to regulations, they appoint the chief constable. In England and Wales they are responsible for publishing annual policing plans and annual reports, setting local objectives and a budget, and levying the precept. The police authorities in Scotland are responsible for setting a budget, providing the resources necessary to police the area adequately, appointing officers of the rank of Assistant Chief Constable and above, and determining the number of officers and civilian staff in the force. The structure and responsibilities of the police authority in Northern Ireland are under review.

The Home Secretary and the Secretaries of State for Scotland and Northern Ireland are responsible for the organization, administration and operation of the police service. They make regulations covering matters such as police ranks, discipline, hours of duty, and pay and allowances. All police forces are subject to inspection by HM Inspectors of Constabulary, who report to the respective Secretary of State.

The investigation and resolution of a serious complaint against a police officer in England and Wales is subject to the scrutiny of the Police Complaints Authority. An officer who is dismissed or reduced in rank may appeal to the Police Appeal Tribunal, consisting of a legally qualified chairman, a member of the police authority, and two police representatives. In Scotland, chief constables are obliged to investigate a complaint against one of their officers; if there is a suggestion of criminal activity, the complaint is investigated by an independent public prosecutor. In Northern Ireland complaints are investigated by the Independent Commission for Police Complaints.

BASIC RATES OF PAY *from 1 September 1995**

Chief Constable	
No fixed term	£59,742–£85,431
Fixed term appointment	£62,730–£89,598
Deputy Chief Constable	80% of their
	Chief Constable's pay
Assistant Chief Constable	
No fixed term	£50,769–£58,278
Fixed term appointment	£53,310–£61,191
Superintendent	£38,724–£46,362
Chief Inspector	£30,984–£34,386
Inspector	£28,470–£30,147
Sergeant	£22,014–£25,674
Constable	£14,412–£22,809

Metropolitan Police
(excluding London weighting and London allowance)

Metropolitan Commissioner	£90,148
Deputy Commissioner	£83,712–£94,593
Assistant Commissioner	£75,699–£83,343
Commander	£50,769–£61,191
Superintendent	£38,724–£46,362
Chief Inspector	£32,286–£35,691
Inspector	£29,775–£31,449
Sergeant	£22,014–£25,674
Constable	£14,412–£22,809

The rank of Chief Superintendent was abolished in April 1995. Existing appointments continue and receive the higher ranges of the pay scale for Superintendents
*To be confirmed

THE SPECIAL CONSTABULARY

The Special Constabulary is the part-time volunteer branch of the police force. Special Constables have full police powers within their force and adjoining force areas, and undertake regular officers' routine policing duties when required, thus freeing regulars at times of emergency for those tasks which only they can perform. There were 20,096 Special Constables in England and Wales at the end of 1994.

NATIONAL CRIMINAL INTELLIGENCE SERVICE

The function of the National Criminal Intelligence Service (NCIS) is to gather, collate and disseminate information and intelligence on serious crime of a regional, national and international nature. It is independent of any other police organization.
Headquarters: Spring Gardens, 2 Citadel Place, London
  SE11 5EF. Tel: 0171-238 8000
Strength, 500
Director-General, A. H. Pacey, CBE, QPM
Deputy Director-General (Director (Intelligence)),
  J. P. Hamilton
Director, International Division, P. J. Byrne, MBE
Director, UK Division, P. L. Clay
Director, Resources Division, R. Creedon

NATIONAL MISSING PERSONS BUREAU

The Police National Missing Persons Bureau (PNMPB) acts as a central clearing house of information, receiving reports about vulnerable missing persons that are still outstanding after 28 days and details of unidentified persons or remains within 48 hours of being found from all forces in England and Wales. Reports are also received from Scottish police forces, the RUC, and foreign police forces via Interpol.
Headquarters: New Scotland Yard, Broadway, London
  SW1H 0BG. Tel: 0171-230 1212
Director, C. J. Coombes

POLICE AUTHORITIES

Strength: actual strength of force as at mid June 1995
Chair: chairman/convener of the police authority/police
committee

ENGLAND

AVON AND SOMERSET CONSTABULARY, *HQ,* PO Box 37,
Valley Road, Portishead, Bristol BS20 8QJ. Tel: 01275-
818181. *Strength,* 3,066; *Chief Constable,* D. J. Shattock, CBE,
QPM; *Chair,* D. Heath, CBE
BEDFORDSHIRE POLICE, *HQ,* Woburn Road, Kempston,
Bedford MK43 9AX. Tel: 01234-841212. *Strength,* 1,125;
Chief Constable, A. Dyer, QPM; *Chair,* A. P. Hendry
CAMBRIDGESHIRE CONSTABULARY, *HQ,* Hinchingbrooke
Park, Huntingdon, Cambs PE18 8NP. Tel: 01480-456111.
Strength, 1,252; *Chief Constable,* D. G. Gunn, QPM; *Chair,*
J. Reynolds
CHESHIRE CONSTABULARY, *HQ,* Nuns Road, Chester,
CH1 2PP. Tel: 01244-350000. *Strength,* 1,935; *Chief
Constable,* J. M. Jones, QPM; *Chair,* R. Tilling
CLEVELAND CONSTABULARY, *HQ,* PO Box 70, Ladgate
Lane, Middlesbrough, Cleveland TS8 9EH. Tel: 01642-
326326. *Strength,* 1,436; *Chief Constable,* B. B. D. Shaw,
QPM; *Chair,* A. Gwenlan
CUMBRIA CONSTABULARY, *HQ,* Carleton Hall, Penrith,
Cumbria CA10 2AU. Tel: 01768-891999. *Strength,* 1,159;
Chief Constable, A. G. Elliott, QPM; *Chair,* R. Watson
DERBYSHIRE CONSTABULARY, *HQ,* Butterley Hall, Ripley,
Derbyshire DE5 3RS. Tel: 01773-570100. *Strength,* 1,786;
Chief Constable, J. F. Newing, QPM; *Chair,* K. Wilkinson
DEVON AND CORNWALL CONSTABULARY, *HQ,*
Middlemoor, Exeter EX2 7HQ. Tel: 01392-52101.
Strength, 2,800; *Chief Constable,* J. S. Evans, QPM; *Chair,* B.
Homer
DORSET POLICE FORCE, *HQ,* Winfrith, Dorchester, Dorset
DT2 8DZ. Tel: 01929-462727. *Strength,* 1,284; *Chief
Constable,* D. W. Aldous, QPM; *Chair,* Sir Stephen
Hammick, Bt.
DURHAM CONSTABULARY, *HQ,* Aykley Heads, Durham
DH1 5TT. Tel: 0191-386 4929. *Strength,* 1,389; *Chief
Constable,* F. W. Taylor, QPM; *Chair,* J. Knox
ESSEX POLICE, *HQ,* PO Box 2, Springfield, Chelmsford
CM2 6DA. Tel: 01245-491491. *Strength,* 2,910; *Chief
Constable,* J. H. Burrow, CBE; *Chair,* R. H. Boyd
GLOUCESTERSHIRE CONSTABULARY, *HQ,* Holland House,
Lansdown Road, Cheltenham, Glos GL51 6QH. Tel:
01242-521321. *Strength,* 1,115; *Chief Constable,*
A. J. P. Butler, QPM; *Chair,* R. Somers, PH.D.
GREATER MANCHESTER POLICE, *HQ,* PO Box 22 (S. West
PDO), Chester House, Boyer Street, Manchester
M16 0RE. Tel: 0161-872 5050. *Strength,* 7,047; *Chief
Constable,* D. Wilmot, QPM; *Chair,* S. Murphy
HAMPSHIRE CONSTABULARY, *HQ,* West Hill, Winchester,
Hants SO22 5DB. Tel: 01962-868133. *Strength,* 3,253; *Chief
Constable,* J. C. Hoddinott, CBE, QPM; *Chair,* M. J. Clark
HERTFORDSHIRE CONSTABULARY, *HQ,* Stanborough
Road, Welwyn Garden City, Herts AL8 6XF. Tel: 01707-
354200. *Strength,* 1,702; *Chief Constable,* P. Sharpe, QPM;
Chair, R. Gordon
HUMBERSIDE POLICE, *HQ,* Queens Gardens, Kingston
upon Hull, N. Humberside HU1 3DJ. Tel: 01482-210031.
Strength, 2,029; *Chief Constable,* D. A. Leonard, QPM; *Chair,*
I. A. Cawsey
KENT CONSTABULARY, *HQ,* Sutton Road, Maidstone,
Kent ME15 9BZ. Tel: 01622-690690. *Strength,* 3,106; *Chief
Constable,* J. D. Phillips, QPM; *Chair,* Sir John Grugeon

LANCASHIRE CONSTABULARY, *HQ,* PO Box 77, Hutton, Nr
Preston, Lancs PR4 5SB. Tel: 01772-614444. *Strength,*
3,212; *Chief Constable,* Mrs P. A. Clare; *Chair,* Mrs R. B.
Henig
LEICESTERSHIRE CONSTABULARY, *HQ,* PO Box 999,
Leicester LE99 1AZ. Tel: 0116-253 0066. *Strength,* 1,847;
Chief Constable, K. Povey, QPM; *Chair,* R. A. Wann
LINCOLNSHIRE POLICE, *HQ,* PO Box 999, Lincoln LN5 7PH.
Tel: 01522-532222. *Strength,* 1,209; *Chief Constable,*
J. P. Bensley, QPM; *Chair,* R. Staples
MERSEYSIDE POLICE, *HQ,* PO Box 59, Canning Place,
Liverpool L69 1JD. Tel: 0151-709 6010. *Strength,* 4,611;
Chief Constable, J. Sharples, QPM; *Chair,* Ms C. Gustafason
NORFOLK CONSTABULARY, *HQ,* Martineau Lane,
Norwich NR1 2DJ. Tel: 01603-768769. *Strength,* 1,396;
Chief Constable, K. R. Williams, QPM; *Chair,* B. J. Landale
NORTHAMPTONSHIRE POLICE, *HQ,* Wootton Hall,
Northampton NN4 0JQ. Tel: 01604-700700. *Strength,*
1,185; *Chief Constable,* E. Crew, QPM; *Chair,* Dr M. Dickie
NORTHUMBRIA POLICE, *HQ,* Ponteland, Newcastle upon
Tyne NE20 0BL. Tel: 01661-872555. *Strength,* 3,600; *Chief
Constable,* J. A. Stevens, QPM; *Chair,* G. Gill
NORTH YORKSHIRE POLICE, *HQ,* Newby Wiske Hall,
Newby Wiske, Northallerton, N. Yorks DL7 9HA. Tel:
01609-783131. *Strength,* 1,315; *Chief Constable,* D. M.
Burke, QPM; *Chair,* Mrs A. F. Harris
NOTTINGHAMSHIRE CONSTABULARY, *HQ,* Sherwood
Lodge, Arnold, Nottingham NG5 8PP. Tel: 0115-967
0999. *Strength,* 2,376; *Chief Constable,* C. F. Bailey, QPM;
Chair, C. P. Winterton
SOUTH YORKSHIRE POLICE, *HQ,* Snig Hill, Sheffield
S3 8LY. Tel: 0114-276 8522. *Strength,* 3,032; *Chief Constable,*
R. Wells, QPM; *Chair,* Sir John Layden
STAFFORDSHIRE POLICE, *HQ,* Cannock Road, Stafford
ST17 0QG. Tel: 01785-57717. *Strength,* 2,209; *Chief
Constable,* C. H. Kelly, CBE, QPM; *Chair,* J. T. Meir
SUFFOLK CONSTABULARY, *HQ,* Martlesham Heath,
Ipswich IP5 7QS. Tel: 01473-613500. *Strength,* 1,182; *Chief
Constable,* A. T. Coe, QPM; *Chair,* M. N. Smith
SURREY POLICE, *HQ,* Mount Browne, Sandy Lane,
Guildford, Surrey GU3 1HG. Tel: 01483-571212. *Strength,*
1,697; *Chief Constable,* D. J. Williams, QPM; *Chair,*
A. C. Tisdall
SUSSEX POLICE, *HQ,* Malling House, Church Lane, Lewes,
E. Sussex BN7 2DZ. Tel: 01273-475432. *Strength,* 2,945;
Chief Constable, P. Whitehouse, QPM; *Chair,* Dr J. M. M.
Walsh, RD
THAMES VALLEY POLICE, *HQ,* Oxford Road, Kidlington,
Oxon. OX5 2NX. Tel: 01865-846000. *Strength,* 3,883; *Chief
Constable,* C. Pollard, QPM; *Chair,* Mrs D. J. Priestley
WARWICKSHIRE CONSTABULARY, *HQ,* PO Box 4, Leek
Wootton, Warwick CV35 7QB. Tel: 01926-415000.
Strength, 999; *Chief Constable,* P. D. Joslin, QPM; *Chair,* F.
Pithie
WEST MERCIA CONSTABULARY, *HQ,* PO Box 55, Hindlip
Hall, Hindlip, Worcester WR3 8SP. Tel: 01905-723000.
Strength, 2,046; *Chief Constable,* D. C. Blakey, QPM; *Chair,*
P. H. Fallows, TD
WEST MIDLANDS POLICE, *HQ,* PO Box 52, Lloyd House,
Colmore Circus, Queensway, Birmingham B4 6NQ. Tel:
0121-626 5000. *Strength,* 7,050; *Chief Constable,* Sir Ronald
Hadfield, QPM; *Chair,* M. Bromley
WEST YORKSHIRE POLICE, *HQ,* PO Box 9, Laburnum
Road, Wakefield, W. Yorks WF1 3QP. Tel: 01924-375222.
Strength, 5,041; *Chief Constable,* K. Hellawell, QPM; *Chair,*
T. Brennan
WILTSHIRE CONSTABULARY, *HQ,* London Road, Devizes,
Wilts SN10 2DN. Tel: 01380-722341. *Strength,* 1,161; *Chief
Constable,* W. R. Girven, QPM; *Chair,* Mrs J. M. Wood

WALES

DYFED–POWYS POLICE, *HQ*, PO Box 99, Llangunnor, Carmarthen, Dyfed SA31 2PF. Tel: 01267-222020. *Strength*, 974; *Chief Constable*, R. White, QPM; *Chair*, W. J. W. Evans

GWENT CONSTABULARY, *HQ*, Croesyceiliog, Cwmbran, Gwent NP44 2XJ. Tel: 01633-838111. *Strength*, 1,010; *Chief Constable*, A. T. Burden, QPM; *Chair*, B. Sutton

NORTH WALES POLICE, *HQ*, Glan-y-Don, Colwyn Bay, Clwyd LL29 8AW. Tel: 01492-517171. *Strength*, 1,369; *Chief Constable*, M. J. Argent, QPM; *Chair*, A. Jones

SOUTH WALES CONSTABULARY, *HQ*, Cowbridge Road, Bridgend, Mid Glamorgan CF31 3SU. Tel: 01656-655555. *Strength*, 3,014; *Chief Constable*, W. R. Lawrence, QPM; *Chair*, B. P. Murray

SCOTLAND

CENTRAL SCOTLAND POLICE, *HQ*, Randolphfield, Stirling FK8 2HD. Tel: 01786-456000. *Strength*, 656; *Chief Constable*, W. J. M. Wilson, QPM; *Convener*, J. Anderson, CBE

DUMFRIES AND GALLOWAY CONSTABULARY, *HQ*, Cornwall Mount, Dumfries DG1 1PZ. Tel: 01387-252112. *Strength*, 384; *Chief Constable*, H. R. Cameron, QPM; *Chair*, K. Cameron

FIFE CONSTABULARY, *HQ*, Detroit Road, Glenrothes, Fife KY6 2RJ. Tel: 01592-418888. *Strength*, 788; *Chief Constable*, W. M. Moodie, CBE, QPM; *Chair*, G. Bird

GRAMPIAN POLICE, *HQ*, Queen Street, Aberdeen AB9 1BA. Tel: 01224-639111. *Strength*, 1,173; *Chief Constable*, I. T. Oliver, QPM, PH.D.; *Chair*, G. Macdonald/Ms R. Kemp

LOTHIAN AND BORDERS POLICE, *HQ*, Fettes Avenue, Edinburgh EH4 1RB. Tel: 0131-311 3131. *Strength*, 2,507; *Chief Constable*, Sir William Sutherland, QPM; *Chair*, R. B. Martin

NORTHERN CONSTABULARY, *HQ*, Perth Road, Inverness IV2 3SY. Tel: 01463-715555. *Strength*, 658; *Chief Constable*, H. C. MacMillan, CBE, QPM; *Chair*, N. Graham

STRATHCLYDE POLICE, *HQ*, 173 Pitt Street, Glasgow G2 4JS. Tel: 0141-204 2626. *Strength*, 7,073; *Chief Constable*, L. Sharp, QPM; *Chair*, J. Jennings

TAYSIDE POLICE, *HQ*, PO Box 59, West Bell Street, Dundee DD1 9JU. Tel: 01382-223200. *Strength*, 1,087; *Chief Constable*, W. A. Spence, QPM; *Chair*, A. Shand

NORTHERN IRELAND

ROYAL ULSTER CONSTABULARY, *HQ*, Brooklyn, Knock Road, Belfast BT5 6LE. Tel: 01232-650222. *Strength*, 8,465; *Chief Constable*, Sir Hugh Annesley, QPM; *Chair*, D. Cooke

ISLANDS

ISLAND POLICE FORCE, *HQ*, Hospital Lane, St Peter Port, Guernsey GY1 2QN. Tel: 01481-725111. *Strength*, 148; *Chief Officer*, M. Le Moignan, QPM; *President, States Committee for Home Affairs*, M. Torode

STATES OF JERSEY POLICE, *HQ*, Rouge Bouillon, PO Box 789, St Helier, Jersey JE2 3ZA. Tel: 01534-612612. *Strength*, 232; *Chief Officer*, R. H. Le Breton; *Chair*, M. Wavell

ISLE OF MAN CONSTABULARY, *HQ*, Glencrutchery Road, Douglas, Isle of Man IM2 4RG. Tel: 01624-631212. *Strength*, 213; *Chief Constable*, R. E. N. Oake; *Chairman, Police Committee*, Hon. R. K. Corkill

METROPOLITAN POLICE SERVICE

New Scotland Yard, Broadway, London SW1H 0BG
Tel 0171-230 1212

Establishment, 27,994

Commissioner, Sir Paul Condon, QPM
Deputy Commissioner, B. Hayes, CBE, QPM
Receiver, vacant

OPERATIONAL AREAS
Assistant Commissioners, A. J. Speed, QPM (*Central*);
  B. H. Skitt, BEM, QPM (*North-West*); A. Dunn, QPM (*North-East*); W. I. R. Johnston, QPM (*South-East*); P. Manning (*South-West*)
Deputy Assistant Commissioners, A. G. Fry, QPM; L. T. Roach, QPM; D. Flanders, QPM; M. J. Sullivan, QPM
Commanders, D. M. T. Kendrick, QPM; J. F. Purnell, GM;
  B. J. Luckhurst; T. D. Laidlaw, QPM; H. N. L. Blenkin, QPM; C. R. Pearman; A. L. Rowe; M. Briggs; M. R. Campbell; W. I. Griffiths; S. C. Pilkington; D. A. Ray, QPM; T. M. Williamson

SPECIALIST OPERATIONS DEPARTMENT
Assistant Commissioner, D. C. Veness, QPM
Deputy Assistant Commissioners, J. A. Howley, QPM; D. N. Meynell, OBE
Commanders, K. G. Churchill-Coleman, OBE, QPM;
  R. C. Marsh, QPM; D. M. Tucker; B. G. Moss;
  J. G. D. Grieve; R. A. C. Ramm

Metropolitan Police Forensic Science Laboratory
Director, Dr B. Sheard
Deputy Directors, G. J. O. Lee; M. R. Loveland; P. D. Martin; Dr W. D. C. Wilson

COMPLAINTS INVESTIGATION BUREAU
Commander, I. G. Quinn

INSPECTORATE
Commander, J. D. Gibson

STRATEGIC CO-ORDINATION
Director, Mrs B. Reeves
Commander, J. Townsend

PERSONNEL DEPARTMENT
Director of Personnel, H. Maslen
Commanders, B. F. Aitchison (*Training*); C. A. Couch (*Director, Career Management*)

OTHER DEPARTMENTS
Director, Consultancy and Information Services,
  Mrs S. Merchant
Director, Public Affairs, Mrs S. Cullum
Solicitor, D. Hamilton
Director, Finance, J. A. Crutchlow
Director, Technology, N. Boothman
Director, Property Services, T. G. Lawrence

CITY OF LONDON POLICE

26 Old Jewry, London EC2R 8DJ
Tel 0171-601 2222

Strength (June 1995), 901

The City of London Police is responsible for policing the City of London. Though small, the area includes one of the most important financial centres in the world and the force has particular expertise in areas such as fraud investigation as well as the areas required of any police force.

The force has a wholly elected police authority, the police committee of the Corporation of London, which appoints the Commissioner.

Commissioner (£78,138), W. Taylor, QPM
Assistant Commissioner (£59,424), P. Nove
Commander (£48,657), J. Davison
Chairman of Police Committee, Maj.-Gen. P. Maclellan, CB, CVO, MBE

BRITISH TRANSPORT POLICE
15 Tavistock Place, London WC1H 9SJ
Tel 0171-388 7541

Strength (March 1995), 2,147

British Transport Police is the national police force for the railways in England, Wales and Scotland, including the London Underground system and the Docklands Light Railway. The Chief Constable reports to the British Transport Police Committee, a statutory body set up under the British Transport Police Force Scheme 1963. The members of the Committee are appointed by the British Railways Board, Railtrack and London Underground Ltd.

Chief Constable, D. O'Brien, OBE, QPM
Deputy Chief Constable, A. Parker, QPM

MINISTRY OF DEFENCE POLICE
MDP Wethersfield, Braintree, Essex CM7 4AZ
Tel 01371-854000

Strength (April 1995), 4,930

The Ministry of Defence Police is a statutory police force directly responsible to the Secretary of State for Defence for the policing of all military land, stations and establishments in the United Kingdom. There are plans for the force to become a defence agency at some point in the future.

Chief Constable, W. E. E. Boreham, OBE
Deputy Chief Constable, A. V. Comben
Head of Secretariat, J. A. Smallwood

ROYAL PARKS CONSTABULARY
The Old Police House, Hyde Park, London W2 2UH
Tel 0171-298 2000

Strength (June 1995), 190

The Royal Parks Constabulary is maintained by the Royal Parks Agency, an executive agency of the Department of National Heritage, and is responsible for the policing of eight royal parks in and around London. These comprise an area in excess of 6,300 acres. Officers of the Force are appointed under the Parks Regulations Act 1872 as amended.

Chief Officer, W. Ross
Deputy Chief Officer, A. McLean

UNITED KINGDOM ATOMIC ENERGY AUTHORITY CONSTABULARY
Building E6, Culham Laboratory, Abingdon, Oxon. OX14 3DB
Tel 01235-463760

Strength (July 1995), 479

The Constabulary is responsible for policing United Kingdom Atomic Energy Authority and British Nuclear Fuels PLC establishments and for escorting nuclear material between establishments. The Chief Constable is responsible, through the Atomic Energy Authority Police Committee, to the President of the Board of Trade.

Chief Constable, H. J. McMorris, QPM
Assistant Chief Constable, A. J. Pointer, QPM

STAFF ASSOCIATIONS

ASSOCIATION OF CHIEF POLICE OFFICERS OF ENGLAND, WALES AND NORTHERN IRELAND, Room 311, Wellington House, 67–73 Buckingham Gate, London SW1E 6BE. Tel: 0171-230 7184. Represents the Chief Constables, Deputy and Assistant Chief Constables of England, Wales and Northern Ireland, and officers of the rank of Commander and above in the Metropolitan and City of London Police. *General Secretary*, Miss M. C. E. Barton

THE POLICE SUPERINTENDENTS' ASSOCIATION OF ENGLAND AND WALES, 67A Reading Road, Pangbourne, Reading RG8 7JD. Tel: 01734-844005. Represents officers of the rank of Superintendent. *Secretary*, Chief Supt. D. A. Clark

THE POLICE FEDERATION OF ENGLAND AND WALES, 15–17 Langley Road, Surbiton, Surrey KT6 6LP. Tel: 0181-399 2224. Represents officers up to and including the rank of Chief Inspector. *General Secretary*, L. Williams; *Chairman*, F. H. J. Broughton

ASSOCIATION OF CHIEF POLICE OFFICERS IN SCOTLAND, Police Headquarters, Fettes Avenue, Edinburgh EH4 1RB. Tel: 0131-311 3051. Represents the Chief Constables, Deputy and Assistant Chief Constables of the Scottish police forces. *Hon. Secretary*, Sir William Sutherland, QPM

THE ASSOCIATION OF SCOTTISH POLICE SUPERINTENDENTS, Secretariat, 173 Pitt Street, Glasgow G2 4JS. Tel: 0141-221 5796. Represents officers of the rank of Superintendent. *Hon. Secretary*, Chief Supt. A. Forrest

THE SCOTTISH POLICE FEDERATION, 5 Woodside Place, Glasgow G3 7QF. Tel: 0141-332 5234. Represents officers up to and including the rank of Chief Inspector. *General Secretary*, D. J. Keil, QPM

THE SUPERINTENDENTS' ASSOCIATION OF NORTHERN IRELAND, MSU RUC Station, Musgrave Street, Belfast BT1 3HX. Tel: 01232-700507. Represents Superintendents and Chief Superintendents in the RUC. *Hon. Secretary*, Supt. W. T. Brown

THE POLICE FEDERATION FOR NORTHERN IRELAND, Royal Ulster Constabulary, Garnerville, Garnerville Road, Belfast BT4 2NX. Tel: 01232-760831. Represents officers up to and including the rank of Chief Inspector. *Secretary*, D. A. McClurg

Defence

The armed forces of the United Kingdom comprise the Royal Navy, the Army and the Royal Air Force. The Queen is commander-in-chief of all the armed forces. The Ministry of Defence, headed by a Secretary of State, provides the support structure for the armed forces. Within the Ministry of Defence, the Defence Council has overall responsibility for running the armed forces. The Chief of Staff of each service reports through the Chief of the Defence Staff to the Secretary of State on matters relating to the running of his service. The Chief of Staff also chairs the executive committee of the appropriate service board, which manages the service in accordance with centrally-determined objectives and budgets. The military-civilian Central Staffs, headed by the Vice-Chief of the Defence Staff and the Second Permanent Under-Secretary of State, are responsible for policy, operational requirements, commitments, financial management, resource planning and civilian personnel management. The Procurement Executive is responsible for purchasing equipment. The Defence Intelligence Staff and the Defence Scientific Staff also form part of the Ministry of Defence.

As a result of the 1994 'Front Line First' defence costs study the Ministry of Defence has been restructured, and a permanent Joint Headquarters for the conduct of joint operations will be set up at Northwood in April 1996. The Joint Headquarters will connect the policy and strategic functions of the MoD Head Office with the conduct of operations and strengthen the policy/executive division. A new executive agency, the Defence Evaluation and Research Agency, has brought together all the major MoD non-nuclear science and technology organizations, including the Defence Research Agency, the Defence Operational Analysis Centre, the Chemical and Biological Defence Establishment and the Directorate-General of Test and Evaluation.

ARMED FORCES STRENGTHS *as at 1 July 1995*

All Services	230,356
Men	213,976
Women	16,380
Royal Naval Services	50,307
Men	46,448
Women	3,859
Army	109,921
Men	103,477
Women	6,444
Royal Air Force	70,128
Men	64,051
Women	6,077

DEFENCE CUTS

*DEFENCE SPENDING PLANS

	£ million
1995–6	21,723
1996–7	21,924
1997–8	22,317

*Including provision for the military redundancy and other costs arising from the implementation of the 1994 'Front Line First' defence costs study

SERVICE PERSONNEL

	Royal Navy	Army	RAF
1990 strength	63,200	152,800	89,700
1991 target for 1995	55,000	116,000	75,000
July 1994 target for 2000	49,100	117,800	62,500
May 1995 plans for 1996	48,000	117,000	66,500

MoD CIVILIAN PERSONNEL

1990–1 level	170,642
February 1994 level	144,010
April 1994 target for 1996	128,700
July 1994 target for 2000	121,600
May 1995 plans for 1998	120,700

DEPLOYMENT AS AT APRIL 1995

Outside Great Britain, army units were stationed in Antarctica, Belize, Brunei, Cyprus, the Falkland Islands, Germany, Gibraltar, the Gulf, Hong Kong (the Brigade of Gurkhas), and Northern Ireland. Royal Air Force units were stationed in the central Atlantic, the Channel, Cyprus, the eastern Atlantic and North Sea, the Falkland Islands, Germany, Gibraltar, the Gulf, Hong Kong, Italy, Northern Ireland, Turkey and the former Yugoslavia.

Members of the British armed forces were also deployed with the United Nations Force in Cyprus (UNFICYP), the United Nations Iraq-Kuwait Observer Mission (UNIKOM), and the United Nations Protection Force in the former Yugoslavia (UNPROFOR).

MINISTRY OF DEFENCE
Main Building, Whitehall, London SWIA 2HB
Tel 0171-218 6645

For ministerial and civil service salaries, *see* page 281
For Services salaries, *see* pages 393–5
Secretary of State for Defence, The Rt. Hon. Michael Portillo, MP
  Private Secretary, Ms M. Aldred
  Special Adviser, Ms A. Broom
  Parliamentary Private Secretary, D. Ames, MP
Minister of State for the Armed Forces, The Hon. Nicholas Soames, MP
  Private Secretary, D. King
Minister of State for Defence Procurement, The Rt. Hon. James Arbuthnot, MP
  Private Secretary, J. Wright
Parliamentary Under-Secretary of State, The Earl Howe
  Private Secretary, G. Dean
Permanent Under-Secretary of State (G1), R. C. Mottram
  Private Secretary, D. Stephens
Chief of the Defence Staff, Field Marshal Sir Peter Inge, GCB

THE DEFENCE COUNCIL

The Defence Council is responsible for running the Armed Forces. It is chaired by the Secretary of State for Defence and consists of: the Ministers of State; the Parliamentary Under-Secretary of State; the Permanent Under-Secretary of State; the Chief of the Defence Staff; the Vice-Chief of the Defence Staff; the Chief Scientific Adviser; the Chief of

Defence Procurement; the Second Permanent Under-Secretary of State; the Chief of the Naval Staff; the Chief of the General Staff; and the Chief of the Air Staff.

CHIEFS OF STAFF

CHIEF OF THE NAVAL STAFF

Chief of the Naval Staff and First Sea Lord, Adm. Sir Jock Slater, GCB, LVO, ADC
Asst Chief of the Naval Staff, Rear-Adm. J. J. Blackham

CHIEF OF THE GENERAL STAFF

Chief of the General Staff, Gen. Sir Charles Guthrie, GCB, LVO, OBE, ADC (*Gen.*)
Asst Chief of the General Staff, Maj.-Gen. T. J. Granville-Chapman, CBE

CHIEF OF THE AIR STAFF

Chief of the Air Staff, Air Chief Marshal Sir Michael Graydon, GCB, CBE, ADC
Asst Chief of the Air Staff, Air Vice-Marshal P. T. Squire, DFC, AFC
British-American Community Relations, Air Marshal Sir John Kemball (retd)
Chief Executive, National Air Traffic Services (*G2*), D. J. McLauchlan
Director-General, Policy and Plans, Air Vice-Marshal J. D. L. Feesey
Director-General, Projects and Engineering (*G3*), C. G. Davies

CENTRAL STAFFS

Vice-Chief of the Defence Staff, Air Chief Marshal Sir John Willis, KCB, CBE
Second Permanent Under-Secretary of State (*G1A*), Sir Moray Stewart, KCB
Defence Services Secretary, Air Vice-Marshal P. J. Harding, CB, CBE, AFC
Leader, Joint Headquarters Implementation Team, Maj.-Gen. C. B. Q. Wallace, OBE

DEFENCE COMMITMENTS STAFF

Deputy CDS (*Commitments*), Lt.-Gen. A. G. H. Harley, CB, OBE
Asst Under-Secretary (*Commitments*) (*G3*), B. R. Hawtin
Asst CDS (*Overseas*), Air Vice-Marshal N. B. Baldwin, CBE
Asst CDS (*Operations and Security*), Air Vice-Marshal A. J. Harrison

DEFENCE LOGISTICS STAFF

Asst CDS (*Logistics*), Rear-Adm. F. B. Goodson, OBE
Deputy CDS (*Systems*), Vice-Adm. J. H. Dunt
Asst CDS, Operational Requirements (*Sea Systems*), Rear-Adm. J. A. Trewby
Asst CDS, Operational Requirements (*Land Systems*), Maj.-Gen. E. F. G. Burton, OBE
Asst CDS, Operational Requirements (*Air Systems*), Air Vice-Marshal C. C. C. Coville, CB
Director-General, Information and Communications Services, Maj.-Gen. W. J. P. Robins, OBE

DEFENCE PROGRAMMES AND PERSONNEL STAFF

Deputy CDS (*Programmes and Personnel*), Lt.-Gen. the Hon. Sir Thomas Boyd-Carpenter, KBE
Asst CDS (*Programmes*), Air Vice-Marshal G. A. Robertson, CBE

DEFENCE MEDICAL SERVICES DIRECTORATE

Surgeon-General, Surgeon Vice-Adm. A. L. Revell, QHS

Director, Defence Dental Services, Air Vice-Marshal J. Mackey, QHDS
Director, Defence Nursing Services, Air Cdre V. M. Hand

POLICY

Deputy Under-Secretary (*Policy*) (*G2*), D. B. Omand
Asst Under-Secretary (*Policy*) (*G3*), G. W. Hopkinson
Asst CDS (*Policy and Nuclear*), Air Vice-Marshal D. F. A. Henderson

DEFENCE INFORMATION STAFF

Press Secretary and Chief of Information (*G4*), Ms G. Samuel
Deputy Press Secretary and Director of Information (*Policy and Procurement*) (*G5*), I. Lee
Director, Public Relations (*Navy*), Capt. C. Beagley, RN
Director, Public Relations (*Army*), Brig. P. Trousdell
Director, Public Relations (*RAF*), Air Cdre G. McRobbie

MANAGEMENT AND FINANCE

Deputy Under-Secretaries (*G2*), J. F. Howe, OBE (*Civilian Management*); J. K. Ledlie, CB, OBE (*Personnel and Logistics*); R. T. Jackling, CB, CBE (*Resources, Finance and Programmes*)
Chief Executive, Housing Trust (*G2*), J. H. Robinson
Asst Under-Secretaries (*G3*), D. C. R. Heyhoe (*General Finance*); I. D. Fauset (*Civilian Personnel Management*); B. A. E. Taylor (*Civilian Policy Management*); C. V. Balmer (*Management Strategy*); Miss A. Walker (*Service Personnel*); R. P. Hatfield (*Director-General of Management and Organization*); D. J. Seammen (*Programmes*); D. Fisher (*Systems*); T. F. W. B. Knapp (*Infrastructure and Logistics*); D. F. W. Pickup (*Legal Adviser*)
Head, Competing for Quality Organization, Dr D. Lees
Chief Statistical Adviser and Chief Executive of Defence Analytical Services Agency (*G4*), P. Altobell
Chief Executive, Defence Accounts Agency (*G4*), M. J. Dymond
Grade 4, P. L. Combes (*Defence Land Services*)

DEFENCE INTELLIGENCE STAFF

Chief of Defence Intelligence, Lt.-Gen. Sir John Foley, KCB, OBE, MC
Director-General, Intelligence (*Assessments*)
Director-General, Scientific and Technical Intelligence
Director-General, Management and Support of Intelligence
Director-General, Intelligence Geographic Resources, Maj.-Gen. M. P. B. G. Wilson
Director, Defence Intelligence (*Secretariat*) (*G5*), P. I. Bailey

DEFENCE SCIENTIFIC STAFF

Chief Scientific Adviser (*G1A*), Prof. Sir David Davies, KBE
Chief Scientist (*G2*), P. D. Ewins, CB
Nuclear Weapon Safety Adviser (*G2*), Dr A. Ferguson
Deputy Chief Scientists (*G3*), P. M. Sutcliffe (*Research and Technology*); G. H. B. Jordan (*Scrutiny and Analysis*)
Asst Chief Scientific Advisers, (*G3*) Dr G. S. Pearson, CB (*Non-Proliferation*); (*G4*) A. L. C. Quigley (*Nuclear*)
Chief Executive, Defence Evaluation and Research Agency (*G2*), J. A. R. Chisholm

SECOND SEA LORD/COMMANDER-IN-CHIEF NAVAL HOME COMMAND

Second Sea Lord and C.-in-C. Naval Home Command, Adm. Sir Michael Boyce, KCB, OBE
Director-General, Naval Personnel (*Strategy and Plans*) *and Chief of Staff to Second Sea Lord*, Rear-Adm. R. B. Lees
Asst Under-Secretary (*Naval Personnel*) (*G3*), J. M. Moss

Naval Secretary and Director-General, Naval Manning, Rear-Adm. A. W. J. West, DSC
Director-General, Naval Medical Services, Surgeon Rear-Adm. A. Craig, QHP
Director-General, Naval Chaplaincy Services, Ven.
M. W. Bucks, QHC

NAVAL SUPPORT COMMAND

Chief of Fleet Support, Vice-Adm. Sir Richard Frere, KCB
Asst Under-Secretary (Fleet Support) (G3), A. J. D. Pawson
Director-General, Fleet Support (Ships) (G3), R. V. Babbington
Director-General, Supplies and Transport (N) (G3),
D. G. Jones
Director-General, Fleet Support (Operations and Plans), Rear-Adm. P. Spencer
Director-General, Aircraft (Navy), Rear-Adm. D. J. Wood
Hydrographer of the Royal Navy and Chief Executive, Hydrographic Office, Rear-Adm. N. R. Essenhigh

COMMANDER-IN-CHIEF FLEET

C.-in-C. Fleet, Adm. Sir Peter Abbott, KCB
Deputy Commander Fleet and Chief of Staff, Vice-Adm.
J. J. R. Tod, CBE
Chief of Staff (Operations) and Flag Officer Submarines, Rear-Adm. R. C. Lane-Nott
Flag Officer Surface Flotilla, Vice-Adm. J. R. Brigstocke
Flag Officer Sea Training, Rear-Adm. J. G. Tolhurst, CB
Flag Officer Naval Aviation, Rear-Adm. T. W. Loughran
Commandant-General, Royal Marines, Lt.-Gen. Sir Robert Ross, KCB, OBE

QUARTERMASTER-GENERAL'S DEPARTMENT

Quartermaster-General, Lt.-Gen. the Hon. Sir William Rous, KCB, OBE
Chief of Staff, Maj.-Gen. P. J. Sheppard, CB, CBE
Asst Under-Secretary (Quartermaster) (G3), Dr A. M. Fox
Director-General, Communications and Information Systems (Army) and Signals Officer in Chief (Army), Maj.-Gen.
A. H. Boyle
Director-General, Logistic Support (Army), Maj.-Gen.
M. S. White, CBE
Director-General, Equipment (Army), Maj.-Gen. P. J. G. Corp
Chief Executive, Logistics Information Systems Agency, Brig.
A. W. Pollard
Chief Executive, Defence Postal and Courier Service, Brig.
T. M. Brown, OBE
Chief Executive, Defence Transport and Movements Executive, Brig. M. Hodson, CBE
Chief Executive, Defence Clothing and Textiles Agency, Col.
J. Robertson

ADJUTANT-GENERAL'S DEPARTMENT

Adjutant-General, Gen. Sir Michael Rose, KCB, CBE, DSO, QGM
Director-General, HQ Directorate Adjutant-General's Corps, Maj.-Gen. M. D. Regan, OBE
Director-General, Army Manning and Recruiting, Maj.-Gen.
D. L. Burden, CBE
Chaplain-General, Revd Dr V. Dobbins
Director, Army Legal Services, Maj.-Gen. A. P. V. Rogers, OBE
Head, Command Secretariat (G4), W. A. Perry
Military Secretary, Maj.-Gen. M. I. E. Scott, CBE, DSO
Director-General, Army Medical Services, Maj.-Gen. F. B. Mayes, CB, QHS, FRCS

INSPECTOR-GENERAL, DOCTRINE AND TRAINING

Inspector-General, Doctrine and Training, Lt.-Gen. S. Cowan, CBE
Director-General, Army Training, Maj.-Gen.
R. W. M. McAfee
Director-General, Land Warfare, Maj.-Gen. T. J. Sulivan, CBE
Director, Royal Armoured Corps, Brig. A. C. I. Gadsby
Director, Royal Artillery, Maj.-Gen. I. G. C. Durie, CBE
Director, Infantry, Maj.-Gen. R. A. Pett, CB, MBE
Director, Army Aviation, Maj.-Gen. S. W. St J. Lytle, CB
Engineer-in-Chief (Army), vacant

HQ STRIKE COMMAND

Air Officer Commanding-in-Chief, Air Chief Marshal Sir William Wratten, KBE, CB, AFC
Chief of Staff and Deputy Commander-in-Chief, Air Marshal Sir John Allison, KCB, CBE
Senior Air Staff Officer, Air Vice-Marshal D. A. Hurrell
Air Officer Administration, Air Vice-Marshal T. B. Sherrington, OBE
Air Officer Engineering and Supply, Air Vice-Marshal
D. J. Saunders, CBE
Head, Command Secretariat (G4) A. J. H. Ward

HQ LOGISTIC COMMAND

Air Officer Commanding-in-Chief and Air Member for Logistics, Air Chief Marshal Sir Michael Alcock, KBE, CB
Chief of Staff and Deputy Air Officer Commanding-in-Chief, Air Vice-Marshal C. G. Terry, CB, OBE
Air Officer Communications Information Systems and Air Officer Commanding Signals Units, Air Vice-Marshal J. B. Main, OBE
Director-General, Support Management (RAF), Air Vice-Marshal P. D. Markey
Command Secretary (G3), H. Griffiths
Chief Executive, RAF Maintenance Group Agency, Air Vice-Marshal R. H. Kyle, MBE

HQ PERSONNEL AND TRAINING COMMAND

Air Member for Personnel and Air Officer Commanding-in-Chief, Air Marshal D. Cousins, CB, AFC
Chief of Staff and Director-General, Strategic Policy and Plans, Air Vice-Marshal P. G. Beer, CB, CBE, LVO
Air Officer Training, Air Vice-Marshal J. A. G. May, CB, CBE
Air Secretary, Air Vice-Marshal R. P. O'Brien, OBE
Commandant, RAF Staff College, Bracknell, Air Vice-Marshal M. P. Donaldson, MBE
Commandant, RAF Staff College, Cranwell, Air Vice-Marshal A. J. Stables
Director-General, Medical Services (RAF), Air Vice-Marshal J. A. Baird, QHP
Director, Legal Services (RAF), Air Vice-Marshal
G. W. Carleton
Chaplain-in-Chief (RAF), Ven. P. R. Turner, QHC

PROCUREMENT EXECUTIVE

Chief of Defence Procurement (G1), Dr M. K. McIntosh
Deputy Chief of Defence Procurement (South of England) and Controller of the Navy, Vice-Adm. Sir Robert Walmsley, KCB
Deputy Chief of Defence Procurement (London) and Master-General of the Ordnance, Lt.-Gen. R. J. Hayman Joyce, CBE
Deputy Chief of Defence Procurement (Operations) and Controller, Aircraft, Air Marshal Sir Roger Austin, KCB, AFC

Deputy Chief of Defence Procurement (Support) (*G3*),
M. J. V. Bell
Director-General (Business Strategy) (*G3*), J. A. Gulvin
Director-General (Finance) (*G3*), B. Miller
Director-General, Technical Services, Rear-Adm.
M. R. Thomas
Director-General, Commercial Directorate (*G3*), G. E. Roe
Principal Director, Pricing and Quality Services (*G4*),
J. V. A. Crawford
Director-General, Submarines (*G3*), C. V. Betts
Director-General, Surface Ships, Rear-Adm. F. P. Scourse,
MBE
Director-General, Surface Weapons (Naval) (*G3*), A. M. Stagg
Chief, Strategic Systems Executive, Rear-Adm.
P. A. M. Thomas (*from Dec. 1995*)
Director-General, Strategic Weapons Systems (*G3*),
Dr J. P. Catchpole
Director-General (Nuclear), Dr D. R. Glue
Director, Nuclear Projects (*G4*), R. E. Jones
Director-General, Land Fighting Systems, Maj.-Gen.
G. Sharman
Director-General, Air Systems 1 (*G3*), J. A. Gordon
Director-General, Air Systems 2, Air Vice-Marshal
P. C. Norriss, AFC
Director-General, Weapons and Information Systems (*G3*),
G. N. Beaven
Chief Executive, Atomic Weapons Establishment (*G2*),
A. Glasgow

DEFENCE EXPORT SERVICES ORGANIZATION
Head of Defence Export Services (*G2*), C. B. G. Masefield
Military Deputy to Head of DES, Rear-Adm. J. F. T. G. Salt
(retd)
Director-General, Marketing (*G3*), D. J. Bowen
Asst Under-Secretary (Export Policy and Finance) (*G3*),
C. T. Sandars
Director-General, Saudi Armed Forces Project, Air Marshal
I. D. Macfadyen, CB, OBE

DEFENCE AGENCIES

ARMY BASE REPAIR ORGANIZATION, Monxton Road,
Andover, Hants SP11 8HT. Tel: 01264-383148. *Chief
Executive*, Brig. J. R. Drew, CBE, ADC
ARMY BASE STORAGE AND DISTRIBUTION AGENCY,
Monxton Road, Andover, Hants SP11 8HT. Tel: 01264-
383355. *Chief Executive*, Brig. K. Goad
DEFENCE ACCOUNTS AGENCY, Warminster Road, Bath
BA1 5AA. Tel: 01225-828105. *Chief Executive* (*G4*),
P. J. Trevelyan
DEFENCE ANALYTICAL SERVICES AGENCY,
Northumberland House, Northumberland Avenue,
London WC2N 5BP. Tel: 0171-218 0729. *Chief Executive*
(*G4*), P. Altobell
DEFENCE ANIMAL CENTRE, Welby Lane, Melton
Mowbray, Leics LE13 0SL. Tel: 01664-411811. *Chief
Executive*, Col. A. Roache
DEFENCE CLOTHING AND TEXTILES AGENCY, Monxton
Road, Andover, Hants SP11 8HT. Tel: 01264-382265.
Chief Executive, Col. J. Robertson
DEFENCE EVALUATION AND RESEARCH AGENCY,
Farnborough, Hants GU14 6TD. Tel: 01252-392000. *Chief
Executive* (*G2*), J. A. R. Chisholm
DEFENCE POSTAL AND COURIER SERVICE, Inglis
Barracks, Mill Hill, London NW7 1PX. Tel: 0181-818
6300. *Director and Chief Executive*, Brig. T. M. Brown, OBE
DEFENCE TRANSPORT AND MOVEMENTS EXECUTIVE,
Monxton Road, Andover, Hants SP11 8HT. Tel: 01264-
382139. *Chief Executive*, Brig. M. Hodson, CBE

DISPOSAL SALES AGENCY, St Christopher House,
Southwark Street, London SE1 OTD. Tel: 0171-921 1707.
Chief Executive, K. Ellender
HQ SERVICE CHILDREN'S SCHOOLS (NORTH-WEST
EUROPE), HQ UKSC(G), BFPO 140. Tel: 00-49 2161
473296. *Chief Executive*, I. S. Mitchelson
HYDROGRAPHIC OFFICE, Taunton, Somerset TA1 2DN.
Tel: 01823-337900. *Chief Executive, and Hydrographer of
the Royal Navy*, Rear-Adm. N. R. Essenhigh
LOGISTICS INFORMATION SYSTEMS AGENCY, Monxton
Road, Andover, Hants SP11 8HT. Tel: 01264-382815.
Chief Executive, Brig. A. W. Pollard
METEOROLOGICAL OFFICE, London Road, Bracknell,
Berks RG12 2SZ. Tel: 01344-854600. *Chief Executive* (*G3*),
Prof. J. C. R. Hunt, FRS
MILITARY SURVEY, Elmwood Avenue, Feltham, Middx
TW13 7AH. Tel: 0181-818 2193. *Chief Executive* (*acting*),
Brig. A. J. Hoon
NAVAL AIRCRAFT REPAIR ORGANIZATION, Royal Naval
Yard, Fleetlands, Gosport, Hants PO13 0AW. Tel: 01705-
544910. *Chief Executive*, Capt. W. S. Graham, RN
NAVAL RECRUITING AND TRAINING AGENCY, Victory
Building, HM Naval Base, Portsmouth, Hants PO1 3LS.
Tel: 01705-727641. *Chief Executive*, Rear-Adm.
J. Clarke, LVO, MBE
RAF MAINTENANCE GROUP AGENCY, RAF Brampton,
Huntingdon, Cambs PE18 8QL. Tel: 01480-52151. *Chief
Executive*, Air Vice-Marshal R. H. Kyle, MBE
RAF SIGNALS ENGINEERING ESTABLISHMENT, RAF
Henlow, Beds SG16 6DN. Tel: 01462-851515. *Chief
Executive*, Air Cdre P. C. Ayee
RAF TRAINING GROUP AGENCY, RAF Innsworth,
Gloucester GL3 1EZ. Tel: 01452-712612. *Chief Executive*,
Air Vice-Marshal J. A. G. May, CB, CBE

The Royal Navy

LORD HIGH ADMIRAL OF THE UNITED KINGDOM
HM The Queen

ADMIRALS OF THE FLEET
HRH The Prince Philip, Duke of Edinburgh, KG, KT, OM,
GBE, AC, QSO, PC, *apptd* 1953
The Lord Hill-Norton, GCB, *apptd* 1971
Sir Michael Pollock, GCB, LVO, DSC, *apptd* 1974
Sir Edward Ashmore, GCB, DSC, *apptd* 1977
The Lord Lewin, KG, GCB, LVO, DSC, *apptd* 1979
Sir Henry Leach, GCB, *apptd* 1982
Sir William Staveley, GCB, *apptd* 1989
Sir Julian Oswald, GCB, *apptd* 1993
Sir Benjamin Bathurst, GCB, *apptd* 1995

ADMIRALS
Slater, Sir Jock, GCB, LVO, ADC (*Chief of the Naval Staff and
First Sea Lord*)
White, Sir Hugo, GCB, CBE (*Governor and C.-in-C. Gibraltar*)
Boyce, Sir Michael, KCB, OBE, ADC (*C.-in-C. Naval Home
Command and Second Sea Lord*)
Abbott, Sir Peter, KCB (*C.-in-C. Fleet*)

VICE-ADMIRALS
Newman, Sir Roy, KCB (*Flag Officer South and Naval Base
Comd. Devonport*)
Morgan, C. C. (*Flag Officer Scotland, N. England and N.
Ireland*)
Frere, Sir Richard, KCB (*Chief of Fleet Support*)

Moore, M. A. C., LVO (*Chief of Staff to Commander, Allied Naval Forces Southern Europe*)
Walmsley, Sir Robert, KCB (*Deputy Chief of Defence Procurement (South of England) and Controller of the Navy*)
Revell, A. L., QHS (*Surgeon-General*)
Tod, J. J. R., CBE (*Deputy Comd. Fleet and Chief of Staff*)
Gretton, M. P. (*Supreme Allied Commander Atlantic's Representative in Europe*)
Dunt, J. H. (*Deputy CDS (Systems)*)
Brigstocke, J. R. (*Flag Officer Surface Flotilla*)
Garnett, I. D. G. (*Deputy Supreme Allied Commander Atlantic*)

REAR-ADMIRALS

Wilkinson, N. J., CB (*Commandant, Joint Services Defence College, Greenwich*)
Rankin, N. E., CB, CBE
Tolhurst, J. G., CB (*Flag Officer Sea Training*)
Goodson, F. B., OBE (*Asst CDS (Logistics)*)
Blackham, J. J. (*Asst Chief of Naval Staff*)
Lane-Nott, R. C. (*Chief of Staff (Operations) and Flag Officer Submarines*)
Essenhigh, N. R. (*Hydrographer of the Navy and Chief Executive, Hydrographic Office Defence Support Agency*)
Craig, A., QHP (*Director-General, Naval Medical Services*)
Haddacks, P. K. (*Asst CDS (Policy and Requirements) to Supreme Allied Commander Europe*)
West, A. W. J., DSC (*Naval Secretary and Director-General, Naval Manning*)
Trewby, J. A. (*Asst CDS Operational Requirements (Sea Systems)*)
Clarke, J. P., LVO, MBE (*Flag Officer Training and Recruiting*)
Blackburn, D. A. J. (*Head of British Defence Staff Washington*)
Scourse, F. P., MBE (*Director-General, Surface Ships*)
Thomas, M. R. (*Director-General, Technical Services*)
Franklyn, P. M. (*Commander, UK Task Group*)
Perowne, J. F. (*Senior Naval Member, Royal College of Defence Studies*)
Wood, D. J. (*Director-General, Aircraft (Navy)*)
Lees, R. B. (*Director-General, Naval Personnel (Strategy and Plans) and Chief of Staff to Second Sea Lord*)
Spencer, P. (*Director-General, Fleet Support (Operations and Plans)*)
Loughran, T. W. (*Flag Officer Naval Aviation*)
Thomas, P. A. M. (*Chief, Strategic Systems Executive, from Dec. 1995*)

HM FLEET AS AT 1 APRIL 1995

SUBMARINES

TRIDENT
Operational: Vanguard, Victorious†

POLARIS
Operational: Renown, Repulse

FLEET
Operational: Sceptre, Sovereign, Spartan, Splendid, Talent, Tireless, Torbay, Trafalgar, Trenchant, Triumph
Refitting/standby: Superb, Turbulent

ANTI-SUBMARINE WARFARE (ASW) CARRIERS

Operational: Illustrious, Invincible
Refitting/standby: Ark Royal

ASSAULT SHIPS

Operational: Fearless
Refitting/standby: Intrepid

DESTROYERS

TYPE 42
Operational: Cardiff, Exeter, Glasgow, Gloucester, Liverpool, Manchester, Newcastle, Nottingham, Southampton, York
Refitting/standby: Birmingham, Edinburgh

FRIGATES

TYPE 23
Operational: Iron Duke, Marlborough, Monmouth, Montrose†, Norfolk, Northumberland†, Richmond†, Somerset*, Westminster
Refitting/standby: Argyll, Lancaster

TYPE 22
Operational: Battleaxe, Beaver, Boxer, Brave, Brazen, Brilliant, Campbeltown, Chatham, Coventry, Cumberland, London, Sheffield
Refitting/standby: Cornwall

OFFSHORE PATROL

CASTLE CLASS
Operational: Dumbarton Castle, Leeds Castle

ISLAND CLASS
Operational: Alderney, Anglesey, Guernsey, Lindisfarne, Orkney, Shetland

MINEHUNTERS

HUNT CLASS
Operational: Atherstone, Berkeley, Bicester, Brecon, Brocklesby, Cattistock, Chiddingfold, Cottesmore, Dulverton, Hurworth, Ledbury, Middleton, Quorn

SANDOWN CLASS
Operational: Bridport, Cromer, Inverness, Sandown, Walney

PATROL CRAFT

PEACOCK CLASS
Operational: Peacock, Plover, Starling

RIVER CLASS
Operational: Arun, Blackwater, Itchen, Orwell, Spey

COASTAL TRAINING CRAFT‡
Operational: Archer, Biter, Blazer, Charger, Dasher, Example, Exploit, Explorer, Express, Loyal Chancellor, Loyal Watcher, Puncher, Pursuer, Smiter

GIBRALTAR SEARCH AND RESCUE CRAFT
Operational: Ranger, Trumpeter

ROYAL YACHT
Operational: Britannia

ICE PATROL SHIP
Operational: Endurance

---

* Under construction at 1 April 1995 and planned to enter service 1995–6
† Engaged in trials or training at 1 April 1995
‡ Coastal training craft are operated by the University Royal Naval Units

SURVEY SHIPS

Operational: Beagle, Gleaner, Hecla, Herald, Roebuck
Refitting/standby: Bulldog

SOLD/DECOMMISSIONED 1994–5

Active, Andromeda, Avenger, Broadsword, Cygnet,
Kingfisher, Redpole, Resolution, Unicorn, Unseen,
Upholder, Ursula, Valiant, Wilton

ROYAL FLEET AUXILIARY (RFA)

The Royal Fleet Auxiliary supplies ships of the fleet with
fuel, food, water, spares and ammunition while at sea. Its
ships are manned by merchant seamen. In April 1995 there
were 21 ships in the RFA.

FLEET AIR ARM

The Fleet Air Arm was established in 1937 and operates
aircraft (including helicopters) for the Royal Navy. In April
1995 there were 207 aircraft in the Fleet Air Arm.

ROYAL NAVAL RESERVE (RNR)

The Royal Naval Reserve is a totally integrated part of the
Royal Navy. It comprises about 3,500 men and women
nationwide who volunteer to train in their spare time for a
variety of sea and shore tasks which they would carry out in
time of tension or war.
Director, Naval Reserves, Capt. T. J. Norman-Walker

ROYAL MARINES

The Royal Marines were formed in 1664 and are part of the
Naval Service. Their primary purpose is to conduct
military operations from the sea. The principal operational
elements are 3 Commando Brigade Royal Marines, an
amphibious all-arms commando brigade trained to operate
in arduous environments; Commacchio Group, Royal
Marines, which is responsible for the security of nuclear
facilities; and Special Boat Service Royal Marines, the
maritime special forces. The Royal Marines also provide
detachments for some warships and land-based naval
parties. The Royal Marines Band Service provides military
musical support for the Naval Service. The principal Royal
Marines bases are Portsmouth, Plymouth, Arbroath, Poole,
Taunton and Deal (which is scheduled to close). The
Corps of Royal Marines is about 6,500 strong.
Commandant-General, Royal Marines, Lt.-Gen. Sir Robert
Ross, KCB, OBE
Major-General, S. J. Pack, CBE (*Commander British Forces
Gibralter*)

ROYAL MARINES RESERVE (RMR)

The Royal Marines Reserve is a commando-trained
volunteer force with the principal role, when mobilized,
of supporting the Royal Marines. There are RMR centres
in London, Glasgow, Bristol, Liverpool and Newcastle.
The current strength of the RMR is about 1,000.
Director, Col. B. L. Carter, OBE

QUEEN ALEXANDRA'S ROYAL NAVAL NURSING SERVICE

The first nursing sisters were appointed to naval hospitals
in 1884 and the Queen Alexandra's Royal Naval Nursing
Service (QARNNS) gained its current title in 1902.
Nursing ratings were introduced in 1960 and men were
integrated into the Service in 1982; both men and women
serve as officers and ratings. Female medical assistants
were introduced in 1987. Qualified staff and learners are
mainly based at the UK Royal Naval Hospitals, and
continue their responsibility for the health and fitness of
naval personnel. The strength is about 600.
Patron, HRH Princess Alexandra, the Hon. Lady Ogilvy
Matron-in-Chief, Principal Nursing Officer Miss
C. M. Taylor

The Army

THE QUEEN

FIELD MARSHALS

HRH The Prince Philip, Duke of Edinburgh, KG, KT, OM,
GBE, AC, QSO, PC, *apptd* 1953 (*see also* page 131)
Sir James Cassels, GCB, KBE, DSO, *apptd* 1968
The Lord Carver, GCB, CBE, DSO, MC, *apptd* 1973
Sir Roland Gibbs, GCB, CBE, DSO, MC, *apptd* 1979
The Lord Bramall, KG, GCB, OBE, MC, *apptd* 1982
Sir John Stanier, GCB, MBE, *apptd* 1985
Sir Nigel Bagnall, GCB, CVO, MC, *apptd* 1988
Sir Richard Vincent, GBE, KCB, DSO, Col. Cmdt. RA
(*Chairman of NATO's Military Committee*), *apptd* 1991
Sir John Chapple, GCB, CBE, *apptd* 1992
HRH The Duke of Kent, KG, GCMG, GCVO, ADC, *apptd* 1993
(*see also* page 133)
Sir Peter Inge, GCB, Col. Green Howards, Col. Cmdt.
APTC (*Chief of the Defence Staff*), *apptd* 1994

GENERALS

Guthrie, Sir Charles, GCB, LVO, OBE, ADC (*Gen.*), Col. Cmdt.
Int. Corps (*Chief of the General Staff*)
Wilsey, Sir John, KCB, CBE, ADC (*Gen.*), Col. D and D, Col.
Cmdt. Royal Logistic Corps (*C.-in-C., Land*)
Mackenzie, Sir Jeremy, KCB, OBE, Col. Cmdt. AG Corps,
Col. The Highlanders (*D. SACEUR*)
Rose, Sir Michael, KCB, CBE, DSO, QGM (*Adjutant-General*)

LIEUTENANT-GENERALS

Rous, The Hon. Sir William, KCB, OBE, Col. Coldstream
Guards (*Quartermaster-General*)
Boyd-Carpenter, the Hon. Sir Thomas, KBE (*Deputy CDS
(Programmes and Personnel)*)
Wheeler, Sir Roger, KCB, CBE (*GOC Northern Ireland*)
Denison-Smith, Sir Anthony, KBE, Col. PWRR (*GOC 4
Divn*)
Foley, Sir John, KCB, OBE, MC, Col. Cmdt. The Light
Division (*Chief of Defence Intelligence*)
Walker, Sir Michael, KCB, CBE, Col. Cmdt. The Queen's
Division, Col. Cmdt. AAC (*Cmdt. NATO Rapid Reaction
Corps*)
Cowan, S., CBE, Col. QGS (*Inspector-General, Doctrine and
Training*)

Hayman-Joyce, R. J., CBE, Col. Cmdt. RAC (*Deputy Chief of Defence Procurement (London) and Master-General of the Ordnance*)

Smith, R. A., DSO, OBE, QGM, Col. Cmdt. Parachute Regiment, Col. Cmdt. Corps of REME (*Comd. Bosnia-Hercegovina Command*)

Harley, A. G. H., CB, OBE (*Deputy CDS (Commitments)*)

Pike, H. W. R., DSO, MBE, Col. Cmdt. SASC (*Deputy C.-in-C., Land*)

MAJOR-GENERALS

Wallace, C. B. Q., OBE, Col. Cmdt. 2 RGJ (*Joint Headquarters Implementation Team*)

Courage, W. J., CB, MBE (*Director-General, TA*)

Pett, R. A., CB, MBE, Col. Cmdt. The King's Division (*Director, Infantry*)

Boyle, A. H. (*Director-General, CIS (Army) and Signals Officer-in-Chief (Army)*)

Burton, E. F. G., OBE (*Asst CDS, Operational Requirements (Land Systems)*)

Freer, I. L., CB, CBE, Col. Cmdt. POW Division, Col. Staffords (*GOC 5 Divn*)

Regan, M. D., OBE, Col. LI (*Director-General, HQ Directorate AG Corps*)

Mayes, F. B., CB, QHS, FRCS (*Director-General, Army Medical Services*)

Dutton, B. H., CBE (*Comd. British Forces Hong Kong*)

Grant, S. C., CB, Col. QLR (*Chief of Staff UKSC(G)*)

Lytle, S. W. St J., CB (*Director, Army Aviation*)

Sheppard, P. J., CB, CBE (*Chief of Staff (Quartermaster)*)

Robins, W. J. P., OBE (*Director-General, Information and Communications Services*)

Jackson, M. D., CBE (*GOC 3 (UK) Divisional HQ*)

Kennedy, A. I. G., CBE (*Senior Army Member, Royal College of Defence Studies*)

Mackay-Dick, I. C., MBE (*GOC London District*)

Scott, M. I. E., CBE, DSO (*Military Secretary*)

Burden, D. L., CBE (*Director-General, Army Manning and Recruiting*)

Cordingley, P. A. J., DSO (*GOC 2 Divn*)

Willcocks, M. A. (*Chief of Staff HQ ACE Rapid Reaction Corps*)

Deverell, J. F., OBE (*Cmdt. RMAS*)

Leask, A. de C. L., CBE (*Comd. Land Forces and DD Ops. N. Ireland*)

Pigott, A. D., CBE (*Comdt. Staff College*)

Wilson, M. P. B. G. (*Director-General, Intelligence Geographic Resources*)

Durie, I. G. C., CBE (*Director, Royal Artillery*)

Hall, J. M. F. C., OBE, Col. Cmdt. The Scottish Division, Col. Cmdt. RAVC (*GOC Scotland*)

McAfee, R. W. M., Col. Cmdt. RTR (*Director-General, Army Training*)

Richards, N. W. F., OBE (*Chief Combat Support ACE Rapid Reaction Corps*)

Vyvyan, C. G. C., Col. Comdt. 1 RGJ (*Chief of Staff, HQ Land*)

White, M. S., CBE (*Director-General, Logistic Support (Army)*)

Rogers, A. P. V., OBE (*Director, Army Legal Services*)

Cowan, G. O., CBE (*Cmdt. Royal Army Medical College*)

Cordy-Simpson, R. A. (*GOC 1 Armd Division*)

Corp, P. J. G. (*Director-General, Equipment (Army)*)

Pack, S. J. (*Comd. British Forces Gibraltar*)

Sulivan, T. J., CBE (*Director-General, Land Warfare*)

Granville-Chapman, T. J., CBE (*Asst Chief of the General Staff*)

Jenkins, D. J. M., CBE, (*Cmdt. RMCS*)

Drewienkiewicz, K. J. (*Director of Support LANDCENT*)

Oliver, R. A., OBE (*Deputy Chief of Staff, HQ Land*)

Pennefather, D. A. S. (*Comd. Reaction Force Operating Staff, Bosnia*)

Sharman, G. (*Director-General, Land Fighting Systems*)

Elliott, C. L., MBE (*UK Military Adviser to the Co-Chairman of the International Conference on the former Yugoslavia*)

CONSTITUTION OF THE ARMY

The regular forces include the following arms, branches and corps. Soldiers' record offices are shown at the end of each group; records of officers are maintained at the Ministry of Defence.

THE ARMS

HOUSEHOLD CAVALRY – The Household Cavalry Regiment (The Life Guards and The Blues and Royals). *Records*, Queen's Park, Chester

ROYAL ARMOURED CORPS – Cavalry Regiments: 1st The Queen's Dragoon Guards; The Royal Scots Dragoon Guards (Carabiniers and Greys); The Royal Dragoon Guards; The Queen's Royal Hussars (The Queen's Own and Royal Irish); 9th/12th Royal Lancers (Prince of Wales's); The King's Royal Hussars; The Light Dragoons; The Queen's Royal Lancers; Royal Tank Regiment comprising two regular regiments. *Records*, Queen's Park, Chester

ARTILLERY – Royal Regiment of Artillery. *Records*, Imphal Barracks, Fulford Road, York

ENGINEERS – Corps of Royal Engineers. *Records*, Kentigern House, Brown Street, Glasgow

SIGNALS – Royal Corps of Signals. *Records*, Kentigern House, Brown Street, Glasgow

THE INFANTRY

The Foot Guards and regiments of Infantry of the Line are grouped in divisions as follows:

GUARDS DIVISION – Grenadier, Coldstream, Scots, Irish and Welsh Guards. *Divisional HQ*, HQ Foot Guards, Wellington Barracks, London SW1. *Depot*, Infantry Training Centre, Vimy Barracks, Catterick, N. Yorks. *Records*, Imphal Barracks, Fulford Road, York

SCOTTISH DIVISION – The Royal Scots (The Royal Regiment); The Royal Highland Fusiliers (Princess Margaret's Own Glasgow and Ayrshire Regiment); The King's Own Scottish Borderers; The Black Watch (Royal Highland Regiment); The Highlanders (Seaforth, Gordons and Camerons); The Argyll and Sutherland Highlanders (Princess Louise's). *Divisional HQ*, The Castle, Edinburgh. *Depot*, Infantry Training Centre, Vimy Barracks, Catterick, N. Yorks. *Records*, Imphal Barracks, Fulford Road, York.

QUEEN'S DIVISION – The Princess of Wales's Royal Regiment (Queen's and Royal Hampshire's); The Royal Regiment of Fusiliers; The Royal Anglian Regiment. *Divisional HQ*, Bassingbourn Barracks, Royston, Herts. *Depot*, Infantry Training Centre, Vimy Barracks, Catterick, N. Yorks. *Records*, Higher Barracks, Exeter

KING'S DIVISION – The King's Own Royal Border Regiment; The King's Regiment; The Prince of Wales's Own Regiment of Yorkshire; The Green Howards (Alexandra, Princess of Wales's Own Yorkshire Regiment); The Queen's Lancashire Regiment; The Duke of Wellington's Regiment (West Riding). *Divisional HQ*, Imphal Barracks, Fulford Road, York. *Depot*, Infantry Training Centre, Vimy Barracks, Catterick, N. Yorks. *Records*, Imphal Barracks, Fulford Road, York

THE ROYAL IRISH REGIMENT (one general service and six home service battalions) – 27th (Inniskilling), 83rd, 87th and the Ulster Defence Regiment. *Regimental HQ* and *Depot*, St Patrick's Barracks, BFPO 808. *Records*, Imphal Barracks, Fulford Road, York

PRINCE OF WALES'S DIVISION – The Devonshire and Dorset Regiment; The Cheshire Regiment; The Royal Welch Fusiliers; The Royal Regiment of Wales (24th/41st Foot); The Royal Gloucestershire, Berkshire and Wiltshire Regiment; The Worcestershire and Sherwood Foresters Regiment (29th/45th Foot); The Staffordshire Regiment (The Prince of Wales's). *Divisional HQ*, Whittington Barracks, Lichfield, Staffs. *Depot*, Infantry Training Centre, Vimy Barracks, Catterick, N. Yorks. *Records*, Imphal Barracks, Fulford, York

LIGHT DIVISION – The Light Infantry; The Royal Green Jackets. *Divisional HQ*, Sir John Moore Barracks, Andover Road North, Winchester, Hants. *Depot*, Infantry Training Centre, Vimy Barracks, Catterick, N. Yorks. *Records*, Higher Barracks, Exeter

BRIGADE OF GURKHAS – The Royal Gurkha Rifles; The Queen's Gurkha Engineers; Queen's Gurkha Signals; The Queen's Own Gurkha Transport Regiment. *Regimental HQ*, *Depot* and *Records*, Queen Elizabeth Barracks, Church Crookham, Fleet, Aldershot, Hants

THE PARACHUTE REGIMENT (three regular battalions) – *Regimental HQ*, Browning Barracks, Aldershot, Hants. *Depot*, Infantry Training Centre, Vimy Barracks, Catterick, N. Yorks. *Records*, Higher Barracks, Exeter

SPECIAL AIR SERVICE REGIMENT – *Regimental HQ* and *Depot*, Stirling Lines, Hereford. *Records*, Higher Barracks, Exeter

ARMY AIR CORPS – *Regimental HQ* and *Depot*, Middle Wallop, Stockbridge, Hants. *Records*, Higher Barracks, Exeter

THE SERVICES

Royal Army Chaplain's Department – *Regimental HQ* and *Depot*, Bagshot Park, Surrey

The Royal Logistic Corps – *Regimental HQ*, Blackdown Barracks, Deepcut, Camberley, Surrey. *Depot*, Princess Royal Barracks, Deepcut, Camberley, Surrey. *Records*, Kentigern House, Brown Street, Glasgow; South Wigston, Leicester; Higher Barracks, Exeter

Royal Army Medical Corps – *Regimental HQ* and *Depot*, Keogh Barracks, Ashvale, Aldershot, Hants. *Records*, Queen's Park, Chester

Corps of Royal Electrical and Mechanical Engineers – *Regimental HQ* and *Depot*, Hazebrouck Barracks, Isaac Newton Road, Arborfield, Reading, Berks. *Records*, Glen Parva Barracks, Saffron Road, Wigston, Leicester

Adjutant-General's Corps – *Corps HQ* and *Depot*, Worthy Down, Winchester, Hants. *Records*, Queen's Park, Chester

Royal Army Veterinary Corps – *Corps HQ*, Gallowey Road, Aldershot, Hants. *Depot*, Welby Lane Camp, Elmhurst Avenue, Melton Mowbray, Leics. *Records*, Higher Barracks, Exeter

Small Arms School Corps – *Corps HQ* and *Depot*, School of Infantry, Imber Road, Warminster, Wilts. *Records*, Higher Barracks, Exeter

Royal Army Dental Corps – *Regimental HQ*, Evelyn Woods Road, Aldershot, Hants. *Depot*, Keogh Barracks, Ashvale, Aldershot, Hants. *Records*, Queen's Park, Chester

Intelligence Corps – *Corps HQ* and *Depot*, Templer Barracks, Ashford, Kent. *Records*, Higher Barracks, Exeter

Army Physical Training Corps – *Regimental HQ* and *Depot*, Queen's Avenue, Aldershot, Hants. *Records*, Higher Barracks, Exeter

General Service Corps – *Records*, Imphal Barracks, Fulford Road, York

Queen Alexander's Royal Army Nursing Corps – *Regimental HQ* and *Depot*, Keogh Barracks, Ashvale, Aldershot, Hants. *Records*, Queen's Park Chester

Corps of Army Music – *Corps HQ* and *Depot*, Army School of Music, Netherhall, Kneller Road, Twickenham, Middx. *Records*, Higher Barracks, Exeter

ARMY EQUIPMENT HOLDINGS

The Army is equipped (as at 1 January 1995) with 905 tanks, 4,050 armoured combat vehicles or ACV lookalikes, 510 artillery pieces, 41 landing craft and 269 helicopters.

THE TERRITORIAL ARMY (TA)

The Territorial Army is designed to be a General Reserve to the Army. It exists to reinforce the regular Army as and when required, with individuals, sub-units or units either in the UK or overseas, and to provide the framework and basis for regeneration and reconstitution in times of national emergency. The TA also provides an essential link between the military and civilian communities. Its structure has recently been reviewed. Its peacetime establishment is 59,000.

Director-General, Maj.-Gen. W. J. Courage, CB, MBE

QUEEN ALEXANDRA'S ROYAL ARMY NURSING CORPS

The Queen Alexandra's Royal Army Nursing Corps (QARANC) was founded in 1902 as Queen Alexandra's Imperial Military Nursing Service (QAIMNS) and gained its present title in 1949. The QARANC has trained nurses for the register since 1950 and has many other nursing employments. Since 1992 men have been eligible to join the QARANC. The Corps provides service in military hospitals in the UK (including Northern Ireland), Germany, Hong Kong, Cyprus, Falkland Islands, Belize and wherever they may be needed world-wide.

Colonel-in-Chief, HRH The Princess Margaret, Countess of Snowdon, GCVO, CI

Matron-in-Chief (Army) and Director, Army Nursing Services, Col. J. Arigho

---

The Royal Air Force

THE QUEEN

MARSHALS OF THE ROYAL AIR FORCE

HRH The Prince Philip, Duke of Edinburgh, KG, KT, OM, GBE, AC, QSO, PC, *apptd* 1953
Sir John Grandy, GCB, GCVO, KBE, DSO, *apptd* 1971
Sir Denis Spotswood, GCB, CBE, DSO, DFC, *apptd* 1974
Sir Michael Beetham, GCB, CBE, DFC, AFC, *apptd* 1982
Sir Keith Williamson, GCB, AFC, *apptd* 1985
The Lord Craig of Radley, GCB, OBE, *apptd* 1988

AIR CHIEF MARSHALS

Graydon, Sir Michael, GCB, CBE, ADC (*Chief of the Air Staff*)

Stear, Sir Michael, KCB, CBE (*Deputy C.-in-C. Allied Forces Central Europe*)

Alcock, Sir Michael, KBE, CB (*Air Officer Commanding-in-Chief and Air Member for Logistics*)

Johns, Sir Richard, KCB, CBE, LVO (*C.-in-C. Allied Forces North-Western Europe*)

Wratten, Sir William, KBE, CB, AFC, ADC (*AOC.-in-C. Strike Command and Comd. Allied Air Forces North-Western Europe*)

Willis, Sir John, KCB, CBE (*Vice-Chief of the Defence Staff*)

AIR MARSHALS

Austin, Sir Roger, KCB, AFC (*Deputy Chief of Defence Procurement (Operations) and Controller, Aircraft*)

Harris, Sir John, KCB, CBE (*AOC No. 18 Group*)

Garden, Sir Timothy, KCB (*Commandant, Royal College of Defence Studies*)

Allison, Sir John, KCB, CBE (*Chief of Staff and Deputy C.-in-C. Strike Command*)

Macfadyen, I. D., CB, OBE (*Director-General, Saudi Armed Forces Project*)

Cheshire, Sir John, KBE, CB (*UK Military Representative to NATO Military Committee, Brussels*)

Cousins, D., CB, AFC (*Air Member for Personnel and Air Officer Commanding-in-Chief*)

AIR VICE-MARSHALS

Harding, P. J., CB, CBE, AFC (*Defence Services Secretary*)

Dodworth, P., CB, OBE, AFC (*Senior Director of Studies (Air), Royal College of Defence Studies*)

Baird, J. A., QHP (*Director-General, Medical Services (RAF)*)

Beer, P. G., CB, CBE, LVO (*Chief of Staff and Director-General, Strategic Policy and Plans*)

Robertson, G. A., CBE (*Asst CDS (Programmes)*)

Squire, P. T., DFC, AFC (*Asst Chief of the Air Staff*)

French, D. R., CB, MBE

Saunders, D. J., CBE (*Air Officer Engineering and Supply*)

Chapple, R., QHP (*Principal Medical Officer, RAF Support Command*)

Norriss, P. C., AFC (*Director-General, Air Systems 2*)

Kyle, R. H., MBE (*Chief Executive, RAF Maintenance Group Agency*)

Mackey, J., QHDS (*Director, Defence Dental Services*)

Sherrington, T. B., OBE (*Air Officer Admin., Strike Command*)

Carleton, G. W. (*Director, Legal Services (RAF)*)

Coville, C. C. C., CB (*Asst CDS Operational Requirements (Air Systems)*)

O'Brien, R. P., OBE (*Air Secretary*)

Bagnall, A. J. C., CB, OBE (*AOC No. 11 Group*)

May, J. A. G., CB, CBE (*Air Officer Training*)

Baldwin, N. B., CBE (*Asst CDS (Overseas)*)

Donaldson, M. P., MBE (*Cmdt. RAF Staff College, Bracknell*)

Terry, C. G., CB, OBE (*Chief of Staff and Deputy Air Officer Commanding-in-Chief, Logistics Command)*)

Feesey, J. D. L. (*Director-General, Policy and Plans*)

Goddard, P. J. (*Deputy Comd., Intermediate Command and Control Centre, Messtetten, Germany*)

Goodall, R. H., CBE, AFC (*AOC No. 2 Group*)

Main, J. B., OBE (*Air Officer Communications Information Systems and Air Officer Commanding Signals Units*)

Henderson, D. F. A., CBE (*Asst CDS (Policy and Nuclear*))

Jenner, T. I.

Day, J. R. (*AOC No. 1 Group*)

Hull, D. H., QHS (*Dean of Air Force Music*)

Stables, A. J. (*Cmdt. RAF Staff College, Cranwell*)

Harrison, A. J. (*Asst CDS (Operations and Security)*))

Markey, P. D. (*Director-General, Support Management (RAF)*)

Millar, P. (*Comd. British Forces Cyprus*)

Hurrell, D. A. (*Senior Air Staff Officer*)

CONSTITUTION OF THE ROYAL AIR FORCE

The RAF consists of three commands. Strike Command is the RAF's operational command for the UK and designated locations abroad (including Germany); its roles include strike/attack, air defence, control and reporting, maritime surveillance, air reconnaissance, air-to-air refuelling, offensive support, air transport, aero-medical facilities, and search and rescue. Logistics Command is responsible for all logistics, engineering support, and maintenance. Personnel and Training Command is responsible for air and ground training, hospitals, and personnel administration.

RAF EQUIPMENT *as at 1 April 1995*
Aircraft– 249 Tornado, 57 Harrier, 54 Jaguar, 9 Canberra, 29 Nimrod, 24 VC10, 9 Tristar, 60 Hercules, 25 Hawk, 11 BAe, 7 AEW
Helicopters– 37 Puma, 46 Wessex, 20 Sea King, 23 Chinook, 1 Gazelle
Miscellaneous training aircraft, etc.
Rapier missiles

ROYAL AUXILIARY AIR FORCE (RAUXAF)

Formed in 1924, the Auxiliary Air Force received the prefix 'Royal' in 1947 in recognition of its war record. The RAUXAF supports the RAF in maritime air operations, air and ground defence of airfields, air movements and aeromedical evacuation. Plans have been announced for the merger of the RAUXAF and the RAFVR.
Air Commodore-in-Chief, HM The Queen
Director of Personnel Management (Airmen) and Controller of Reserve Forces (RAF), Air Cdre M. L. Jackson, OBE

ROYAL AIR FORCE VOLUNTEER RESERVE (RAFVR)

The Royal Air Force Volunteer Reserve was created in 1936 to train the increased number of aircrew who were seen as necessary for the forthcoming conflict. The RAFVR was reconstituted in 1947 following war service. It provides specialist personnel who fill specific wartime intelligence support, photo interpretation and public relations appointments. A small number of RAFVR aircrew augment regular crews on Nimrod (Maritime Reconnaissance) aircraft in wartime. Plans have been announced for the merger of the RAFVR and the RAUXAF.
Director of Personnel Management (Airmen) and Controller of Reserve Forces (RAF), Air Cdre M. L. Jackson, OBE

PRINCESS MARY'S ROYAL AIR FORCE NURSING SERVICE

The Princess Mary's Royal Air Force Nursing Service (PMRAFNS) offers commissions to Registered General Nurses (RGN) with a minimum of two years experience after obtaining RGN and normally with a second qualification. RGNs with no additional experience or qualification are recruited as non-commissioned officers in the grade of Staff Nurse.
Air Chief Commandant, HRH Princess Alexandra, the Hon. Lady Ogilvy, GCVO
Matron-in-Chief, Gp Capt. R. H. Williams

SERVICE SALARIES

The following rates of pay apply from 1 April 1995 to 1 April 1996. The increasing integration of women in the armed services is reflected in equal pay for equal work and the X factor addition is now the same for men and women (11.5 per cent).

Annual salaries are derived from daily rates in whole pence and rounded to the nearest £.

The pay rates shown are for Army personnel. The rates apply also to personnel of equivalent rank and pay band in the other services.

OFFICERS' SALARIES

MAIN SCALE

Rank	Daily	Annual
Second Lieutenant	£36.48	£13,352
Lieutenant		
On appointment	48.22	17,649
After 1 year in the rank	49.49	18,113
After 2 years in the rank	50.76	18,578
After 3 years in the rank	52.03	19,043
After 4 years in the rank	53.30	19,508
Captain		
On appointment	61.67	22,571
After 1 year in the rank	63.34	23,182
After 2 years in the rank	65.01	23,794
After 3 years in the rank	66.68	24,405
After 4 years in the rank	68.35	25,016
After 5 years in the rank	70.02	25,627
After 6 years in the rank	71.69	26,239
Major		
On appointment	78.26	28,643
After 1 year in the rank	80.20	29,353
After 2 years in the rank	82.14	30,063
After 3 years in the rank	84.08	30,773
After 4 years in the rank	86.02	31,483
After 5 years in the rank	87.96	32,193
After 6 years in the rank	89.90	32,903
After 7 years in the rank	91.84	33,613
After 8 years in the rank	93.78	34,323

Rank	Daily	Annual
Special List Lieutenant-Colonel	£108.19	£39,598
Lieutenant-Colonel		
On appointment with less than 19 years service	110.33	40,381
After 2 years in the rank or with 19 years service	113.23	41,442
After 4 years in the rank or with 21 years service	116.13	42,504
After 6 years in the rank or with 23 years service	119.03	43,565
After 8 years in the rank or with 25 years service	121.93	46,626
Colonel		
On appointment	128.47	47,020
After 2 years in the rank	131.85	48,257
After 4 years in the rank	135.23	49,494
After 6 years in the rank	138.61	50,731
After 8 years in the rank	141.99	51,968
Brigadier	157.75	57,737
Major-General	173.50	63,501
Lieutenant-General	193.99	71,000
General	266.20	97,429
Field Marshal	330.96	121,131

SALARIES OF OFFICERS COMMISSIONED FROM THE RANKS (LIEUTENANTS AND CAPTAINS ONLY)

YEARS OF COMMISSIONED SERVICE	YEARS OF NON-COMMISSIONED SERVICE FROM AGE 18					
	Less than 12 years		12 years but less than 15 years		15 years or more	
	Daily	Annual	Daily	Annual	Daily	Annual
On appointment	£68.32	£25,005	£71.79	£26,275	£75.26	£27,545
After 1 year service	70.05	25,638	73.52	26,908	76.35	27,944
After 2 years service	71.79	26,275	75.26	27,545	77.47	28,354
After 3 years service	73.52	26,908	76.35	27,944	78.59	28,764
After 4 years service	75.26	27,545	77.47	28,354	79.71	29,174
After 5 years service	76.35	27,944	78.59	28,763	80.83	29,584
After 6 years service	77.47	28,354	79.71	29,174	81.95	29,994
After 8 years service	78.59	28,764	80.83	29,584	83.07	30,404
After 10 years service	79.71	29,174	81.95	29,994	83.07	30,404
After 12 years service	80.83	29,584	83.07	30,404	83.07	30,404
After 14 years service	81.95	29,994	83.07	30,404	83.07	30,404
After 16 years service	83.07	30,404	83.07	30,404	83.07	30,404

The pay structure below officer level is divided into pay bands. Jobs at each rank are allocated to bands according to their score in the job evaluation system.

Scale A: committed to serve/have completed less than 6 years

Scale B: committed to serve/have completed 6 years but less than 9 years

Scale C: committed to serve/have completed more than 9 years

Daily rates of pay effective from 1 April 1995 are:

SALARIES OF WARRANT OFFICERS AND SENIOR NCOs

Rank	Scale A				Scale B				Scale C			
	Band 4	Band 5	Band 6	Band 7	Band 4	Band 5	Band 6	Band 7	Band 4	Band 5	Band 6	Band 7
Sergeant	£45.51	£50.04	£54.98	£ —	£45.81	£50.34	£55.28	£ —	£46.26	£50.79	£55.73	£ —
Staff Sergeant	48.18	52.64	57.61	63.58	48.43	52.94	57.91	63.88	48.88	53.39	58.36	64.33
Warrant Officer												
Class 2	51.46	55.99	62.09	68.19	51.76	56.29	62.39	68.49	52.21	56.74	62.84	68.94
Class 1	54.88	59.39	65.58	71.67	55.18	59.69	65.88	71.97	55.63	60.14	66.33	72.42

SALARIES OF ADULT PERSONNEL OF THE RANK OF CORPORAL AND BELOW

Rank	Scale A			Scale B			Scale C		
	Band 1	Band 2	Band 3	Band 1	Band 2	Band 3	Band 1	Band 2	Band 3
Private									
Class 4	£22.84	£ —	£ —	£23.14	£ —	£ —	£23.59	£ —	£ —
Class 3	25.59	29.71	34.28	25.89	30.01	34.58	26.34	30.46	35.03
Class 2	28.61	32.76	37.34	28.91	33.06	37.64	29.36	33.51	38.09
Class 1	31.12	35.26	39.83	31.42	35.56	40.13	31.87	36.01	40.58
Lance-Corporal									
Class 3	31.12	35.26	39.83	31.42	35.56	40.13	31.87	36.01	40.58
Class 2	33.24	37.39	42.34	33.54	37.69	42.64	33.99	38.14	43.09
Class 1	35.76	39.91	44.86	36.06	40.21	45.16	36.51	40.66	45.61
Corporal									
Class 2	38.40	42.55	47.51	38.70	42.85	47.81	39.15	43.30	48.26
Class 1	41.22	45.36	50.32	41.52	45.66	50.62	41.97	46.11	51.07

RELATIVE RANK – ARMED FORCES

	Royal Navy		*Army*		*Royal Air Force*
1	Admiral of the Fleet	1	Field Marshal	1	Marshal of the RAF
2	Admiral (Adm.)	2	General (Gen.)	2	Air Chief Marshal
3	Vice-Admiral (Vice-Adm.)	3	Lieutenant-General (Lt.-Gen.)	3	Air Marshal
4	Rear-Admiral (Rear-Adm.)	4	Major-General (Maj.-Gen.)	4	Air Vice-Marshal
5	Commodore (1st & 2nd class) (Cdre)	5	Brigadier (Brig.)	5	Air Commodore (Air Cdre)
6	Captain (Capt.)	6	Colonel (Col.)	6	Group Captain (Gp Capt.)
7	Commander (Cdr.)	7	Lieutenant-Colonel (Lt.-Col.)	7	Wing Commander (Wg Cdr.)
8	Lieutenant-Commander (Lt.-Cdr.)	8	Major (Maj.)	8	Squadron Leader (Sqn. Ldr.)
9	Lieutenant (Lt.)	9	Captain (Capt.)	9	Flight Lieutenant (Flt. Lt.)
10	Sub-Lieutenant (Sub-Lt.)	10	Lieutenant (Lt.)	10	Flying Officer (FO)
11	Acting Sub-Lieutenant (Acting Sub-Lt.)	11	Second Lieutenant (2nd Lt.)	11	Pilot Officer (PO)

SERVICE RETIRED PAY on compulsory retirement

Those who leave the services having served at least five years, but not long enough to qualify for the appropriate immediate pension, now qualify for a preserved pension and terminal grant, both of which are payable at age 60. The tax-free resettlement grants shown below are payable on release to those who qualify for a preserved pension and who have completed nine years service from age 21 (officers) or 12 years from age 18 (other ranks).

The annual rates for army personnel are given. The rates apply also to personnel of equivalent rank in the other services, including the nursing services.

OFFICERS
Applicable to officers who give full pay service on the active list on or after 31 March 1995

No. of years reckonable service over age 21	Capt. and below	Major	Lt.-Col.	Colonel	Brigadier	Major-General	Lieutenant-General	General
16	£ 7,548	£ 8,948	£11,779	£ —	£ —	£ —	£ —	£ —
17	7,805	9,373	12,324	—	—	—	—	—
18	8,151	9,798	12,869	14,985	—	—	—	—
19	8,498	10,224	13,413	15,619	—	—	—	—
20	8,845	10,649	13,958	16,254	—	—	—	—
21	9,191	11,074	14,503	16,888	—	—	—	—
22	9,538	11,499	15,048	17,523	20,249	—	—	—
23	9,885	11,924	15,592	18,157	20,888	—	—	—
24	10,231	12,349	16,137	18,792	21,528	23,742	—	—
25	10,578	12,775	16,682	19,426	22,168	24,448	—	—
26	10,925	13,200	17,227	20,060	22,808	25,153	—	—
27	11,271	13,625	17,772	20,695	23,448	25,859	28,913	—
28	11,618	14,050	18,316	21,329	24,087	26,564	29,702	—
29	11,965	14,475	18,861	21,964	24,727	27,270	30,491	—
30	12,311	14,900	19,406	22,598	25,367	27,976	31,280	42,924
31	12,658	15,326	19,951	23,233	26,007	28,681	32,068	44,007
32	13,005	15,751	20,495	23,867	26,646	29,387	32,857	45,089
33	13,351	16,176	21,040	24,502	27,286	30,092	33,648	46,172
34	13,698	16,601	21,585	25,136	27,926	30,798	34,435	47,254

Field Marshal – active list retired pay at the rate of £58,748 a year

WARRANT OFFICERS, NCOS AND PRIVATES
Applicable to soldiers who give full pay service on or after 31 March 1995

No. of years reckonable service	Below Corporal	Corporal	Sergeant	Staff Sergeant	Warrant Officer Class II	Warrant Officer Class I
22	£4,314	£5,516	£6,133	£ 6,981	£ 7,215	£ 7,975
23	4,465	5,708	6,347	7,225	7,471	8,262
24	4,615	5,901	6,561	7,468	7,727	8,549
25	4,766	6,093	6,775	7,712	7,982	8,836
26	4,916	6,286	6,989	7,956	8,238	9,122
27	5,067	6,478	7,203	8,199	8,494	9,409
28	5,218	6,671	7,417	8,443	8,750	9,696
29	5,368	6,863	7,631	8,687	9,006	9,983
30	5,519	7,056	7,845	8,930	9,261	10,270
31	5,669	7,248	8,059	9,174	9,517	10,557
32	5,820	7,441	8,273	9,418	9,773	10,844
33	5,971	7,633	8,487	9,661	10,029	11,131
34	6,121	7,826	8,701	9,905	10,285	11,417
35	6,272	8,018	8,915	10,149	10,540	11,704
36	6,422	8,211	9,129	10,392	10,796	11,991
37	6,573	8,403	9,343	10,636	11,052	12,278

RESETTLEMENT GRANTS
Terminal grants are in each case three times the rate of retired pay or pension. There are special rates of retired pay for certain other ranks not shown above. Lower rates are payable in cases of voluntary retirement.

A gratuity of £2,535 is payable for officers with short service commissions for each year completed. Resettlement grants are: officers £8,722; non-commissioned ranks £5,746.

The Christian Churches

The Church of England

The Church of England is the established (i.e. state) church in England and the mother church of the Anglican Communion. It originated in the conflicts between church and state throughout the Middle Ages, culminating in the Act of Supremacy issued by Henry VIII in 1534. This repudiated papal supremacy and declared the King to be the supreme head of the Church in England. Since 1559 the English monarch has been termed the Supreme Governor of the Church of England. The Thirty-Nine Articles, a set of doctrinal statements which, together with the Book of Common Prayer of 1662 and the Ordinal, define the position of the Church of England, were adopted in their final form in 1571 and include the emphasis on personal faith and the authority of the scriptures common to the Protestant Reformation throughout Europe.

The Church of England is divided into the two provinces of Canterbury and York, each under an archbishop. The two provinces are subdivided into 44 dioceses. Decisions on matters concerning the Church of England are made by the General Synod, established in 1970. It also discusses and expresses opinion on any other matter of religious or public interest. The General Synod has 574 members in total, divided between three houses: the House of Bishops, the House of Clergy and the House of Laity. It is presided over jointly by the Archbishops of Canterbury and York and normally meets twice a year. The Synod has the power, delegated by Parliament, to frame statute law (known as a Measure) on any matter concerning the Church of England. A Measure must be laid before both Houses of Parliament, who may accept or reject it but cannot amend it. Once accepted the Measure is submitted for royal assent and then has the full force of law. The Synod appoints a number of committees, boards and councils which deal with, or advise on, a wide range of matters. In addition to the General Synod, there are synods of clergy and laity at diocesan level.

A commission headed by the Bishop of Durham is examining the structure and organization of the Church of England. It will report in September 1995 and its conclusions will be debated at the General Synod in November 1995.

In 1993 the Church of England had an electoral roll membership of 1.5 million, of whom about 1.1 million regularly attended Sunday services. There are (1994 figures) two archbishops, 111 diocesan, suffragan and (stipendiary) assistant bishops, 9,666 male and 783 female full-time stipendiary clergy, and over 16,000 churches and places of worship. (The Diocese in Europe is not included in these figures.)

The Ordination of Women

On 11 November 1992, the General Synod of the Church of England voted to permit the ordination of women as priests. In the House of Bishops there were 39 votes (75 per cent) in favour of the legislation and 13 (25 per cent) against; in the House of Clergy, 176 (70.4 per cent) in favour and 74 (29.6 per cent) against; and in the House of Laity, 169 (67.3 per cent) in favour and 82 (32.7 per cent) against. After receiving parliamentary approval and royal assent, the canon was promulged in the General Synod in February 1994 and the first 32 women priests were ordained on 12 March 1994 by the Bishop of Bristol.

The Priests (Ordination of Women) Measure 1993 contains provisions safeguarding the position of bishops and parishes who are opposed to the priestly ministry of women. In November 1993 the General Synod agreed to the appointment of up to three 'provincial visitors' to work with those who are unable to accept the ministry of bishops ordaining women priests. The provincial visitors, who are suffragan bishops in the newly created sees of Ebbsfleet (Province of Canterbury), Beverley (Province of York) and Richborough (Province of Canterbury), are allowed to carry out confirmations and ordinations in parishes opposed to women priests, as long as they have the permission of the diocesan bishop. Clergy who feel compelled to leave the ministry are entitled to financial assistance.

Porvoo Common Statement

The Porvoo Common Statement was drawn up by the British and Irish Anglican churches and the Nordic and Baltic Lutheran churches and was approved by the General Synod of the Church of England in July 1995. In the House of Bishops the motion was approved by 34 votes to 0, in the House of Clergy by 176 votes to 8, and in the House of Laity by 169 votes to 15.

Churches that agree the statement regard baptized members of each other's churches as members of their own, and allow free interchange of episcopally ordained ministers within the rules of each church.

General Synod of the Church of England, Church House, Dean's Yard, London SW1P 3NZ. Tel: 0171-222 9011. *Secretary-General*, P. Mawer

House of Bishops: *Chairman*, The Archbishop of Canterbury; *Vice-Chairman*, The Archbishop of York

House of Clergy: *Joint Chairmen*, Revd Dr J. Sentamu; Canon J. Stanley

House of Laity: *Chairman*, Prof. J. D. McClean, CBE, QC; *Vice-Chairman*, Dr Christina Baxter

Stipends 1995–6

Archbishop of Canterbury	£45,350
Archbishop of York	£39,730
Bishop of London	£37,030
Other diocesan bishops	£24,590
Suffragan bishops	£20,210
Deans and provosts	£20,210
Residentiary canons	£16,530
Incumbents and clergy of similar status	£13,420*

*national average

Stipendiary Clergy *as at 31 December 1994*

	Male	Female
Bath and Wells	237	19
Birmingham	200	24
Blackburn	269	8
Bradford	124	9
Bristol	148	25
Canterbury	178	13
Carlisle	160	12
Chelmsford	428	31
Chester	296	13
Chichester	337	8

	Male	Female
Coventry	158	16
Derby	196	13
Durham	238	20
Ely	152	14
Exeter	281	10
Gloucester	171	13
Guildford	194	25
Hereford	121	12
Leicester	162	10
Lichfield	352	36
Lincoln	204	24
Liverpool	257	31
London	525	50
Manchester	324	21
Newcastle	167	9
Norwich	204	10
Oxford	427	42
Peterborough	161	7
Portsmouth	124	7
Ripon	155	24
Rochester	227	17
St Albans	284	31
St Edmundsbury and Ipswich	175	15
Salisbury	227	13
Sheffield	199	20
Sodor and Man	21	0
Southwark	365	43
Southwell	195	20
Truro	123	5
Wakefield	188	15
Winchester	249	10
Worcester	158	15
York	305	23
Total	9,666	783

Province of Canterbury

CANTERBURY

103rd Archbishop and Primate of All England
Most Revd and Rt. Hon. George L. Carey, ph.d., *cons.* 1987, *trans.* 1991, *apptd* 1991; Lambeth Palace, London sei 7ju. *Signs* George Cantuar:

Bishops Suffragan
Dover, Rt. Revd J. Richard A. Llewellin, *cons.* 1985, *apptd* 1992; Upway, St Martin's Hill, Canterbury, cti ipr
Maidstone, Rt. Revd Gavin H. Reid, *cons.* 1992, *apptd* 1992; Bishop's House, Pett Lane, Charing, Ashford tn27 odl
Ebbsfleet, Rt. Revd John Richards, *cons.* 1994, *apptd* 1994 (provincial episcopal visitor); The Rectory, Church Leigh, Stoke-on-Trent, Staffs sti0 4pt
Richborough, Rt. Revd Edwin Barnes, *cons.* 1995, *apptd* 1995 (provincial episcopal visitor); St Stephen's House, Marston Street, Oxford ox4 ijx

Dean
Very Revd John Arthur Simpson, *apptd* 1986

Canons Residentiary
P. Brett, *apptd* 1983; Ven. M. Till, *apptd* 1986; R. H. C. Symon, *apptd* 1994; Dr M. Chandler, *apptd* 1995

Organist, D. Flood, frco, *apptd* 1988

Archdeacons
Canterbury, Ven. M. Till, *apptd* 1986

Maidstone, Ven. P. Evans, *apptd* 1989
Vicar-General of Province and Diocese, Chancellor S. Cameron, qc
Commissary-General, His Hon. Judge Richard Walker
Joint Registrars of the Province, F. E. Robson, obe; B. J. T. Hanson
Registrar of the Diocese, A. O. E. Davies
Diocesan Secretary, D. Kemp, Diocesan House, Lady Wootton's Green, Canterbury cti inq. Tel: 01227-459401

LONDON

132nd Bishop
Rt. Revd Richard C. Chartres; 8 Barton Street, London swip 3ne. *Signs* Richard Londin:

Area Bishops
Edmonton, Rt. Revd Brian J. Masters, *cons.* 1982, *apptd* 1984; 1 Regent's Park Terrace, London nw1 7ee
Kensington, vacant; 19 Campden Hill Square, London w8 7jy
Stepney, vacant; 63 Coborn Road, London e3 2db
Willesden, Rt. Revd Graham G. Dow; 173 Willesden Lane, London nw6 7yn

Bishop Suffragan
Fulham, Rt. Revd C. John Klyberg, *cons.* 1985, *apptd* 1985; 4 Cambridge Place, London w8 5pb

Dean of St Paul's
Very Revd T. Eric Evans, *apptd* 1988

Canons Residentiary
Ven. G. Cassidy, *apptd* 1987; C. J. Hill, *apptd* 1989; R. J. Halliburton, *apptd* 1990; M. J. Saward, *apptd* 1991

Registrar and Receiver of St Paul's, Brig. R. W. Acworth, cbe
Organist, J. Scott, frco, *apptd* 1990

Archdeacons
Charing Cross, Rt. Revd C. J. Klyberg, *apptd* 1989
Hackney, Ven. C. Young, *apptd* 1992
Hampstead, Ven. P. Wheatley, *apptd* 1995
London, Ven. G. Cassidy, *apptd* 1987
Middlesex, Ven. T. J. Raphael, *apptd* 1983
Northolt, Ven. P. Broadbent, *apptd* 1995

Chancellor, Miss S. Cameron, qc, *apptd* 1992
Registrar, D. W. Faull, obe
Diocesan Secretary, C. J. A. Smith, 36 Causton Street, London swip 4au. Tel: 0171-932 1100

WINCHESTER

96th Bishop
Rt. Revd Michael C. Scott-Joynt, *cons.* 1987, *trans.* 1995, *apptd* 1995 (*from end 1995*); Wolvesey, Winchester so23 9nd. *Signs* Michael Winton:

Bishops Suffragan
Basingstoke, Rt. Revd D. Geoffrey Rowell, *cons.* 1994, *apptd* 1994; Little Acorns, Boynes Wood Road, Medstead gu34 5ea
Southampton, Rt. Revd John F. Perry, *cons.* 1989, *apptd* 1989; Ham House, The Crescent, Romsey so51 7ng

Dean
Very Revd Trevor R. Beeson, *apptd* 1987 (*until Feb. 1996*)

Dean of Jersey (A Peculiar), Very Revd John Seaford, *apptd* 1993

Dean of Guernsey (*A Peculiar*), Very Revd Marc Trickey, *apptd* 1995

CANONS RESIDENTIARY
A. K. Walker, *apptd* 1987; Ven. A. F. Knight, *apptd* 1991; P. B. Morgan, *apptd* 1994

Organist, D. Hill, FRCO, *apptd* 1988

ARCHDEACONS
Basingstoke, Ven. A. F. Knight, *apptd* 1990
Winchester, Ven. A. G. Clarkson, *apptd* 1984

Chancellor, C. Clark, *apptd* 1993
Registrar and Legal Secretary, P. M. White
Diocesan Secretary, R. Anderton, Church House, 9 The Close, Winchester, Hants SO23 9LS. Tel: 01962-844644

BATH AND WELLS

76TH BISHOP
Rt. Revd James L. Thompson, *cons.* 1978, *apptd* 1991; The Palace, Wells BA5 2PD. *Signs* James Bath & Wells

BISHOP SUFFRAGAN
Taunton, Rt. Revd J. H. Richard Lewis, *cons.* 1992, *apptd* 1992; Sherford Farm House, Sherford, Taunton TA1 3RF

DEAN
Very Revd Richard Lewis, *apptd* 1990

CANONS RESIDENTIARY
P. de N. Lucas, *apptd* 1988; G. O. Farran, *apptd* 1985; R. Acworth, *apptd* 1993; P. G. Walker, *apptd* 1994

Organist, A. Crossland, FRCO, *apptd* 1970

ARCHDEACONS
Bath, Ven. J. E. Burgess, *apptd* 1975
Taunton, Ven. R. M. C. Frith, *apptd* 1992
Wells, Ven. R. Ackworth, *apptd* 1993

Chancellor, T. Briden, *apptd* 1993
Registrar, Secretary and Chapter Clerk, T. Berry
Diocesan Secretary, N. Denison, The Old Deanery, Wells, Somerset BA5 2UG. Tel: 01749-670777

BIRMINGHAM

7TH BISHOP
Rt. Revd Mark Santer, *cons.* 1981, *apptd* 1987; Bishop's Croft, Harborne, Birmingham B17 0BG. *Signs* Mark Birmingham

BISHOP SUFFRAGAN
Aston, Rt. Revd John Austin, *cons.* 1992, *apptd* 1992; Strensham House, 8 Strensham Hill, Moseley, Birmingham B13 8AG

PROVOST
Very Revd Peter A. Berry, *apptd* 1986

CANONS RESIDENTIARY
Ven. C. J. G. Barton, *apptd* 1990; A. H. F. Luff, *apptd* 1992

Organist, M. Huxley, FRCO, *apptd* 1986

ARCHDEACONS
Aston, Ven. C. J. G. Barton, *apptd* 1990
Birmingham, Ven. J. F. Duncan, *apptd* 1985

Chancellor, His Honour Judge Aglionby, *apptd* 1970
Registrar and Legal Secretary, H. Carslake

Diocesan Secretary, Canon J. Pendorf, 175 Harborne Park Road, Harborne, Birmingham B17 0BH. Tel: 0121-427 5141

BRISTOL

54TH BISHOP
Rt. Revd Barry Rogerson, *cons.* 1979, *apptd* 1985; Bishop's House, Clifton Hill, Bristol BS8 1BW. *Signs* Barry Bristol

BISHOP SUFFRAGAN
Swindon, Rt. Revd Michael Doe, *cons.* 1994, *apptd* 1994; Mark House, Field Rise, Old Town, Swindon SN1 4HP

DEAN
Very Revd Dr A. Wesley Carr, *apptd* 1987

CANONS RESIDENTIARY
A. L. J. Redfern, *apptd* 1987; J. L. Simpson, *apptd* 1989; P. F. Johnson, *apptd* 1990

Organist, C. Brayne, *apptd* 1990

ARCHDEACONS
Bristol, Ven. D. J. Banfield, *apptd* 1990
Swindon, Ven. M. Middleton, *apptd* 1992

Chancellor, Sir David Calcutt, QC, *apptd* 1971
Registrar and Secretary, D. Ratcliffe
Diocesan Secretary, Mrs L. Farrall, Diocesan Church House, 23 Great George Street, Bristol, Avon BS1 5QZ. Tel: 0117-921 4411

CHELMSFORD

7TH BISHOP
Rt. Revd John Waine, *cons.* 1975, *apptd* 1986 (*until April 1996*); Bishopscourt, Margaretting, Ingatestone CM4 0HD. *Signs* John Chelmsford

BISHOPS SUFFRAGAN
Barking, Rt. Revd Roger F. Sainsbury, *cons.* 1991, *apptd* 1991; 110 Capel Road, Forest Gate, London E7 0JS
Bradwell, Rt. Revd Laurence Green, *cons.* 1993, *apptd* 1993; The Vicarage, Orsett Road, Horndon-on-the-Hill, Stanford-le-Hope, Essex SS17 8NS
Colchester, Rt. Revd Edward Holland, *cons.* 1986, *apptd* 1995; 1 Fitzwalter Road, Lexden, Colchester CO3 3SS

PROVOST
Very Revd John H. Moses, PH.D., *apptd* 1982

CANONS RESIDENTIARY
T. Thompson, *apptd* 1988; B. P. Thompson, *apptd* 1988; D. Knight, *apptd* 1991

Organist, Dr G. Elliott, PH.D., FRCO, *apptd* 1981

ARCHDEACONS
Colchester, Ven. E. C. F. Stroud, *apptd* 1983
Harlow, Ven. M. J. Fox, *apptd* 1993
Southend, Ven. D. Jennings, *apptd* 1992
West Ham, Ven. T. J. Stevens, *apptd* 1991

Chancellor, Miss S. M. Cameron, QC, *apptd* 1970
Diocesan Registrar, B. Hood
Diocesan Secretary, D. Phillips, 53 New Street, Chelmsford, Essex CM1 1AT. Tel: 01245-266731

CHICHESTER

102ND BISHOP
Rt. Revd Eric W. Kemp, DD, *cons.* 1974, *apptd* 1974; The Palace, Chichester PO19 1PY. *Signs* Eric Cicestr:

BISHOPS SUFFRAGAN
Horsham, Rt. Revd Lindsay G. Urwin, *cons.* 1993, *apptd* 1993; Bishop's House, 21 Guildford Road, Horsham, W. Sussex RH12 1LU
Lewes, Rt. Revd Ian P. M. Cundy, *cons.* 1992, *apptd* 1992; Beacon House, Berwick, Polegate BN26 6ST

DEAN
Very Revd John D. Treadgold, LVO, *apptd* 1989

CANONS RESIDENTIARY
R. T. Greenacre, *apptd* 1975; F. J. Hawkins, *apptd* 1981; J. F. Hester, *apptd* 1985

Organist, A. J. Thurlow, FRCO, *apptd* 1980

ARCHDEACONS
Chichester, Ven. M. Brotherton, *apptd* 1991
Horsham, Ven. W. C. L. Filby, *apptd* 1983
Lewes and Hastings, Ven. H. Glaisyer, *apptd* 1991

Chancellor, His Honour Judge Q. T. Edwards, QC, *apptd* 1978
Legal Secretary and Registrar, C. L. Hodgetts
Diocesan Secretary, J. Prichard, Diocesan Church House, 211 New Church Road, Hove, E. Sussex BN3 4ED. Tel: 01273-421021

COVENTRY

7TH BISHOP
Rt. Revd Simon Barrington-Ward, *cons.* 1985, *apptd* 1985; The Bishop's House, 23 Davenport Road, Coventry CV5 6PW. *Signs* Simon Coventry

BISHOP SUFFRAGAN
Warwick, Rt. Revd George C. Handford, *cons.* 1990, *apptd* 1990; 139 Kenilworth Road, Coventry CV4 7AF

PROVOST
Very Revd John F. Petty, *apptd* 1987

CANONS RESIDENTIARY
P. Oestreicher, *apptd* 1986; V. Faull, *apptd* 1994; J. C. Burch, *apptd* 1995

Organist, A. P. Leddington Wright, *apptd* 1984

ARCHDEACONS
Coventry, Ven. H. I. L. Russell, *apptd* 1989
Warwick, Ven. M. J. J. Paget-Wilkes, *apptd* 1990

Chancellor, Sir William Gage, *apptd* 1980
Registrar, D. J. Dumbleton
Diocesan Secretary, J. Allen, Church House, Palmerston Road, Coventry CV5 6FJ. Tel: 01203-674328

DERBY

6TH BISHOP
Rt. Revd Jonathan S. Bailey, *cons.* 1992, *apptd* 1995; The Bishop's Office, Derby Church House, Full Street, Derby DE1 3DR. *Signs* Jonathan Derby

BISHOP SUFFRAGAN
Repton, Rt. Revd F. Henry A. Richmond, *cons.* 1986, *apptd* 1986; Repton House, Lea, Matlock DE4 5JP

PROVOST
Very Revd Benjamin H. Lewers, *apptd* 1981

CANONS RESIDENTIARY
G. A. Chesterman, *apptd* 1989; Ven. I. Gatford, *apptd* 1992; G. O. Marshall, *apptd* 1992; R. M. Parsons, *apptd* 1993
Organist, P. Gould, *apptd* 1982

ARCHDEACONS
Chesterfield, Ven. G. R. Phizackerley, *apptd* 1978
Derby, Ven. I. Gatford, *apptd* 1992

Chancellor, J. W. M. Bullimore, *apptd* 1981
Registrar, J. S. Battie
Diocesan Secretary, R. Carey, Derby Church House, Full Street, Derby DE1 3DR. Tel: 01332-382233

ELY

67TH BISHOP
Rt. Revd Stephen W. Sykes, *cons.* 1990, *apptd* 1990; The Bishop's House, Ely, Cambs CB7 4DW. *Signs* Stephen Ely

BISHOP SUFFRAGAN
Huntingdon, Rt. Revd William G. Roe, D.phil., *cons.* 1980, *apptd* 1980; 14 Lynn Road, Ely, Cambs CB6 1DA

DEAN
Very Revd Michael Higgins, *apptd* 1991

CANON RESIDENTIARY
D. J. Green, *apptd* 1980
Organist, P. Trepte, FRCO, *apptd* 1991

ARCHDEACONS
Ely, Ven. J. Watson, *apptd* 1993
Huntingdon, Ven. R. K. Sledge, *apptd* 1978
Wisbech, Ven. J. Rone, *apptd* 1995

Chancellor, W. Gage, QC
Joint Registrars, W. H. Godfrey; P. F. B. Beesley (*Legal Secretary*)
Diocesan Secretary, Dr M. Lavis, Bishop Woodford House, Barton Road, Ely, Cambs CB7 4DX. Tel: 01353-663579

EXETER

69TH BISHOP
Rt. Revd G. Hewlett Thompson, *cons.* 1974, *apptd* 1985; The Palace, Exeter EX1 1HY. *Signs* Hewlett Exon:

BISHOPS SUFFRAGAN
Crediton, Rt. Revd Peter E. Coleman, *cons.* 1984, *apptd* 1984; 10 The Close, Exeter EX1 1EZ
Plymouth, Rt. Revd Richard S. Hawkins, *cons.* 1988, *apptd* 1988; 31 Riverside Walk, Tamerton Foliot, Plymouth PL5 4AQ

DEAN
vacant

CANONS RESIDENTIARY
A. C. Mawson, *apptd* 1979; K. C. Parry, *apptd* 1991
Organist, L. A. Nethsingha, FRCO, *apptd* 1973

ARCHDEACONS
Barnstaple, Ven. T. Lloyd, *apptd* 1989
Exeter, Ven. A. F. Tremlett, *apptd* 1994

Plymouth, Ven. R. G. Ellis, *apptd* 1982
Totnes (*acting*), Preb. C. T. Pidsley, *apptd* 1994

Chancellor, Sir David Calcutt, QC, *apptd* 1971
Registrar, R. K. Wheeler
Diocesan Secretary, Revd R. Huddleson, Diocesan House, Palace Gate, Exeter, Devon EX1 1HX. Tel: 01392-72686

GIBRALTAR IN EUROPE

BISHOP
Rt. Revd John Hind, *cons.* 1991, *apptd* 1993; 14 Tufton Street, London SW1P 3QZ. *Signs* John Gibraltar

BISHOP SUFFRAGAN
In Europe Rt. Revd Henry Scriven, *cons.* 1995, *apptd* 1994; 14 Tufton Street, London SW1P 3QZ

Vicar-General, Canon W. G. Reid
Dean, Cathedral Church of the Holy Trinity, Gibraltar, Very Revd B. W. Horlock, OBE
Chancellor, Pro-Cathedral of St Paul, Valletta, Malta, vacant
Chancellor, Pro-Cathedral of the Holy Trinity, Brussels, Belgium, Canon N. Walker

ARCHDEACONS
Aegean, Ven. S. J. B. Peake
North-West Europe, Ven. G. G. Allen
France, Ven. M. Draper
Gibraltar, Ven. K. Robinson
Italy, Rt. Revd E. Devenport
Scandinavia, Ven. G. A. C. Brown
Switzerland, Ven. P. J. Hawker

Chancellor, Sir David Calcutt, QC
Diocesan Registrar and Legal Secretary, J. G. Underwood
Diocesan Secretary, Revd W. G. Reid, 14 Tufton Street, London SW1P 3QZ. Tel: 0171-976 8001

GLOUCESTER

39TH BISHOP
Rt. Revd David Bentley, *cons.* 1986, *apptd* 1993; Bishopscourt, Gloucester GL1 2BQ. *Signs* David Gloucestr

BISHOP SUFFRAGAN
Tewkesbury, Rt. Revd John S. Went, *cons.* 1995, *apptd* 1995; Green Acre, Hempsted, Gloucester GL2 6LG

DEAN
Very Revd Kenneth N. Jennings, *apptd* 1982

CANONS RESIDENTIARY
R. D. M. Grey, *apptd* 1982; N. Chatfield, *apptd* 1992; N. Heavisides, *apptd* 1993; C. H. Morgan, *apptd* 1996 (*from 1996*)

Organist, D. Briggs, FRCO, *apptd* 1994

ARCHDEACONS
Cheltenham, Ven. J. A. Lewis, *apptd* 1988
Gloucester, Ven. C. J. H. Wagstaff, *apptd* 1982

Chancellor and Vicar-General, Ms D. J. Rogers, *apptd* 1990
Registrar, C. G. Peak
Diocesan Secretary, M. Williams, Church House, College Green, Gloucester GL1 2LY. Tel: 01452-410022

GUILDFORD

8TH BISHOP
Rt. Revd John W. Gladwin, *cons.* 1994, *apptd* 1994; Willow Grange, Woking Road, Guildford GU4 7QS. *Signs* John Guildford

BISHOP SUFFRAGAN
Dorking, vacant; 13 Pilgrims Way, Guildford GU4 8AD

DEAN
Very Revd Alexander G. Wedderspoon, *apptd* 1987

CANONS RESIDENTIARY
R. D. Fenwick, *apptd* 1990; J. Schofield, *apptd* 1995

Organist, A. Millington, FRCO, *apptd* 1982

ARCHDEACONS
Dorking, vacant
Surrey, vacant

Chancellor, His Hon. Judge Goodman
Legal Secretary and Registrar, P. F. B. Beesley
Diocesan Secretary, Mrs K. Ingate, Diocesan House, Quarry Street, Guildford GU1 3XG. Tel: 01483-571826

HEREFORD

103RD BISHOP
Rt. Revd John Oliver, *cons.* 1990, *apptd* 1990; The Palace, Hereford HR4 9BN. *Signs* John Hereford

BISHOP SUFFRAGAN
Ludlow, Rt. Revd Dr John Saxbee, *cons.* 1994, *apptd* 1994; Bishop's House, Halford, Craven Arms, Shropshire SY7 9BT

DEAN
Very Revd Robert A. Willis, *apptd* 1992

CANONS RESIDENTIARY
P. Iles, *apptd* 1983; J. Tiller, *apptd* 1984; J. Butterworth, *apptd* 1994

Organist, Dr R. Massey, FRCO, *apptd* 1974

ARCHDEACONS
Hereford, Ven. L. G. Moss, *apptd* 1992
Ludlow, Rt. Revd J. C. Saxbee, *apptd* 1992

Chancellor, J. M. Henty
Joint Registrars, V. T. Jordan; P. F. B. Beesley
Diocesan Secretary, Miss S. Green, The Palace, Hereford HR4 9BL. Tel: 01432-353863

LEICESTER

5TH BISHOP
Rt. Revd Thomas F. Butler, PH.D., LL D, *cons.* 1985, *apptd* 1991; Bishop's Lodge, 10 Springfield Road, Leicester LE2 3BD. *Signs* Thomas Leicester

STIPENDIARY ASSISTANT BISHOP
Rt. Revd William Down, *cons.* 1990, *apptd* 1995

PROVOST
Very Revd Derek Hole, *apptd* 1992

CANONS RESIDENTIARY
M. T. H. Banks, *apptd* 1988; M. Wilson, *apptd* 1988

Organist, J. T. Gregory, *apptd* 1994

ARCHDEACONS
Leicester, Ven. M. Edson, *apptd* 1994
Loughborough, Ven. I. Stanes, *apptd* 1992

Chancellor, N. Seed, *apptd* 1989
Registrars, P. C. E. Morris; R. H. Bloor
Diocesan Secretary, J. Cryer, Church House, 3–5 St Martin's East, Leicester LEI 5FX. Tel: 0116-262 7445

LICHFIELD

97TH BISHOP
Rt. Revd Keith N. Sutton, *cons.* 1978, *apptd* 1984; Bishop's House, The Close, Lichfield WS13 7LG. *Signs* Keith Lichfield

BISHOPS SUFFRAGAN
Shrewsbury, Rt. Revd David M. Hallatt, *cons.* 1994, *apptd* 1994; 68 London Road, Shrewsbury SY2 6PG
Stafford, vacant; Ash Garth, Broughton Crescent, Barlaston, Staffs ST12 9DD
Wolverhampton, Rt. Revd Michael G. Bourke, *cons.* 1993, *apptd* 1993; 61 Richmond Road, Wolverhampton WV3 9JH

DEAN
Very Revd Tom Wright, *apptd* 1993

CANONS RESIDENTIARY
Ven. R. B. Ninis, *apptd* 1974; A. N. Barnard, *apptd* 1977; J. Howe, *apptd* 1988; C. W. Taylor, *apptd* 1995
Organist, A. Lumsden, *apptd* 1992

ARCHDEACONS
Lichfield, Ven. R. B. Ninis, *apptd* 1974
Salop, Ven. G. Frost, *apptd* 1987
Stoke-on-Trent, Ven. D. Ede, *apptd* 1989

Chancellor, His Honour Judge Shand
Diocesan Registrar, J. P. Thorneycroft
Diocesan Secretary, D. R. Taylor, St Mary's House, The Close, Lichfield, Staffs WS13 7LD. Tel: 01543-414551

LINCOLN

70TH BISHOP
Rt. Revd Robert M. Hardy, *cons.* 1980, *apptd* 1987; Bishop's House, Eastgate, Lincoln LN2 1QQ. *Signs* Robert Lincoln

BISHOPS SUFFRAGAN
Grantham, Rt. Revd William Ind, *cons.* 1987, *apptd* 1987; Fairacre, Barrowby High Road, Grantham NG31 8NP
Grimsby, Rt. Revd David Tustin, *cons.* 1979, *apptd* 1979; Bishop's House, Church Lane, Irby-upon-Humber, Grimsby DN37 7JR

DEAN
Very Revd Brandon D. Jackson, *apptd* 1989

CANONS RESIDENTIARY
B. R. Davis, *apptd* 1977; A. J. Stokes, *apptd* 1992; V. White, *apptd* 1994
Organist, C. S. Walsh, FRCO, *apptd* 1988

ARCHDEACONS
Lincoln, Ven. A. Hawes, *apptd* 1995
Lindsey, vacant
Stow, Ven. R. J. Wells, *apptd* 1989

Chancellor, His Honour Judge Goodman, *apptd* 1971
Registrar and Legal Secretary, D. M. Wellman

Diocesan Secretary, Capt. D. Williamson, RN, The Old Palace, Lincoln LN2 1PU. Tel: 01522-529241

NORWICH

70TH BISHOP
Rt. Revd Peter J. Nott, *cons.* 1977, *apptd* 1985; Bishop's House, Norwich NR3 1SB. *Signs* Peter Norvic:

BISHOPS SUFFRAGAN
Lynn, Rt. Revd David Conner, *cons.* 1994, *apptd* 1994; The Old Vicarage, Castle Acre, King's Lynn PE32 2AA
Thetford, Rt. Revd Hugo F. de Waal, *cons.* 1992, *apptd* 1992; Rectory Meadow, Bramerton, Norwich NR14 7DW

DEAN
Very Revd Stephen Platten, *apptd* 1995

CANONS RESIDENTIARY
M. F. Perham, *apptd* 1992; Ven. C. J. Offer, *apptd* 1994; R. J. Hammer, *apptd* 1994
Organist, D. Cooper, *apptd* 1994

ARCHDEACONS
Lynn, Ven. A. C. Foottit, *apptd* 1987
Norfolk, Ven. A. M. Handley, *apptd* 1993
Norwich, Ven. C. J. Offer, *apptd* 1994

Chancellor, His Honour J. H. Ellison, VRD, *apptd* 1955
Registrar and Secretary, J. W. F. Herring
Diocesan Secretary, D. Adeney, Diocesan House, 109 Dereham Road, Easton, Norwich, Norfolk NR9 5ES. Tel: 01603-880853

OXFORD

41ST BISHOP
Rt. Revd Richard D. Harries, *cons.* 1987, *apptd* 1987; Diocesan Church House, North Hinksey, Oxford OX2 0NB. *Signs* Richard Oxon:

AREA BISHOPS
Buckingham, Rt. Revd Colin J. Bennetts, *cons.* 1994, *apptd* 1994; Sheridan, Grimms Hill, Great Missenden HP16 9BD
Dorchester, Rt. Revd Anthony J. Russell, *cons.* 1988, *apptd* 1988; Holmby House, Sibford Ferris, Banbury, Oxon OX15 5RG
Reading, Rt. Revd John F. E. Bone, *cons.* 1989, *apptd* 1989; Greenbanks, Old Bath Road, Sonning, Reading RG4 0SY

DEAN OF CHRIST CHURCH
Very Revd John H. Drury, *apptd* 1991

CANONS RESIDENTIARY
Ven. F. V. Weston, *apptd* 1982; O. M. T. O'Donovan, D.Phil., *apptd* 1982; J. M. Pierce, *apptd* 1987; J. S. K. Ward, *apptd* 1991; Rt. Revd A. R. M. Gordon, *apptd* 1991; Prof. P. Hinchcliff, *apptd* 1991
Organist, S. Darlington, FRCO, *apptd* 1985

ARCHDEACONS
Berkshire, Ven. M. A. Hill, *apptd* 1992
Buckingham, Ven. J. A. Morrison, *apptd* 1989
Oxford, Ven. F. V. Weston, *apptd* 1982

Chancellor, P. T. S. Boydell, QC, *apptd* 1958
Registrar and Legal Secretary, Dr F. E. Robson
Secretary to the Diocesan Board of Finance, T. Landsbert, Diocesan Church House, North Hinksey, Oxford OX2 0NB. Tel: 01865-244566

PETERBOROUGH

BISHOP
vacant; The Palace, Peterborough PE1 1YA. *Signs* –
Petriburg:

BISHOP SUFFRAGAN
Brixworth, Rt. Revd Paul E. Barber, *cons*. 1989, *apptd* 1989;
4 The Avenue, Dallington, Northampton NN1 4RZ

DEAN
Very Revd Michael Bunker, *apptd* 1992

CANONS RESIDENTIARY
T. R. Christie, *apptd* 1980; J. Higham, *apptd* 1983;
T. Willmott, *apptd* 1989
Organist, C. S. Gower, FRCO, *apptd* 1977

ARCHDEACONS
Northampton, Ven. M. R. Chapman, *apptd* 1991
Oakham, Ven. B. Fernyhough, *apptd* 1977

Chancellor, T. A. C. Coningsby, QC, *apptd* 1989
Registrar and Legal Secretary, R. Hemingray
Diocesan Secretary, P. Haines, The Palace, Peterborough,
Cambs PE1 1YB. Tel: 01733-64448

PORTSMOUTH

8TH BISHOP
Rt. Revd Dr Kenneth W. Stevenson, *cons*. 1995, *apptd* 1995;
Bishopswood, Fareham, Hants PO14 1NT. *Signs* Kenneth
Portsmouth

PROVOST
Very Revd Michael Yorke, *apptd* 1994

CANONS RESIDENTIARY
C. J. Bradley, *apptd* 1990; D. T. Isaac, *apptd* 1990; Jane
Hedges, *apptd* 1993
Organist, A. Lucas, FRCO, *apptd* 1990

ARCHDEACONS
Isle of Wight, Ven. A. H. M. Turner, *apptd* 1986
Portsmouth, Ven. G. P. Knowles, *apptd* 1993

Chancellor, His Honour Judge Aglionby, *apptd* 1978
Registrar, Miss H. A. G. Tyler
Diocesan Secretary, M. Jordan, Cathedral House, St
Thomas's Street, Portsmouth, Hants PO1 2HA. Tel:
01705-825731

ROCHESTER

106TH BISHOP
Rt. Revd Dr Michael Nazir-Ali, *cons*. 1984, *apptd* 1994;
Bishopscourt, Rochester ME1 1TS. *Signs* Michael Roffen:

BISHOP SUFFRAGAN
Tonbridge, Rt. Revd Brian A. Smith, *cons*. 1993, *apptd* 1993;
Bishop's Lodge, St Botolph's Road, Sevenoaks TN13 3AG

DEAN
Very Revd Edward F. Shotter, *apptd* 1990

CANONS RESIDENTIARY
E. R. Turner, *apptd* 1981; R. J. R. Lea, *apptd* 1988; J. Armson,
apptd 1989; N. Warren, *apptd* 1989
Organist, R. Sayer, FRCO, *apptd* 1995

ARCHDEACONS
Bromley, Ven. G. Norman, *apptd* 1994
Rochester, Ven. N. L. Warren, *apptd* 1989
Tonbridge (acting), Canon Judith Rose

Chancellor, His Honour Judge M. B. Goodman, *apptd* 1971
Registrar, O. R. Woodfield
Diocesan Secretary, P. Law, St Nicholas Church, Boley Hill,
Rochester ME1 1SL. Tel: 01634-830333

ST ALBANS

9TH BISHOP
Rt. Revd Christopher W. Herbert, *cons*. 1995, *apptd* 1995;
Abbey Gate House, St Albans AL3 4HD. *Signs* Christopher
St Albans

BISHOPS SUFFRAGAN
Bedford, Rt. Revd John H. Richardson, *cons*. 1994, *apptd* 1994;
168 Kimbolton Road, Bedford MK41 8DN
Hertford, Rt. Revd Robin J. N. Smith, *cons*. 1990, *apptd* 1990;
Hertford House, Abbey Mill Lane, St Albans AL3 4HE

DEAN
Very Revd Christopher Lewis, *apptd* 1993

CANONS RESIDENTIARY
C. Garner, *apptd* 1984; G. R. S. Ritson, *apptd* 1987;
M. Sansom, *apptd* 1988; C. R. J. Foster, *apptd* 1994
Organist, Dr B. Rose, *apptd* 1988

ARCHDEACONS
Bedford, Ven. M. L. Lesiter, *apptd* 1993
St Albans, Ven. P. B. Davies, *apptd* 1987

Chancellor, His Honour Judge Bursell, QC, *apptd* 1992
Registrar and Legal Secretary, D. N. Cheetham
Diocesan Secretary, L. Nicholls, Holywell Lodge, 41
Holywell Hill, St Albans AL1 1HE. Tel: 01727-854532

ST EDMUNDSBURY AND IPSWICH

8TH BISHOP
Rt. Revd John Dennis, *cons*. 1979, *apptd* 1986; Bishop's
House, 4 Park Road, Ipswich IP1 3ST. *Signs* John St
Edmundsbury and Ipswich

BISHOP SUFFRAGAN
Dunwich, vacant; The Old Vicarage, Stowupland,
Stowmarket IP14 4BQ

PROVOST
Very Revd J. Atwell, *apptd* 1995

CANONS RESIDENTIARY
A. M. Shaw, *apptd* 1989; M. E. Mingins, *apptd* 1993
Organist, M. Cousins, *apptd* 1993

ARCHDEACONS
Ipswich, Ven. T. A. Gibson, *apptd* 1987
Sudbury, Ven. J. Cox, *apptd* 1995
Suffolk, Ven. G. Arrand, *apptd* 1994

Chancellor, His Honour Sir John Blofeld, QC, *apptd* 1974
Registrar, Revd J. D. Mitson
Diocesan Secretary, I. Dodd, 13–15 Tower Street, Ipswich
IP1 3BG. Tel: 01473-211028

SALISBURY

77TH BISHOP
Rt. Revd David S. Stancliffe, *cons.* 1993, *apptd* 1993; South Canonry, The Close, Salisbury SP1 2ER. *Signs* David Sarum

BISHOPS SUFFRAGAN
Ramsbury, Rt. Revd Peter St G. Vaughan, *cons.* 1989, *apptd* 1989; Bishop's House, Urchfont, Devizes, Wilts SN10 4QH
Sherborne, Rt. Revd John D. G. Kirkham, *cons.* 1976, *apptd* 1976; Little Bailie, Sturminster Marshall, Wimborne BH21 4AD

DEAN
Very Revd the Hon. Hugh G. Dickinson, *apptd* 1986

CANONS RESIDENTIARY
D. J. C. Davies, *apptd* 1985; D. M. K. Durston, *apptd* 1992; June Osborne, *apptd* 1995

Organist, R. G. Seal, FRCO, *apptd* 1968

ARCHDEACONS
Dorset, Ven. G. E. Walton, *apptd* 1982
Sarum, Ven. B. J. Hopkinson, *apptd* 1986
Sherborne, Ven. P. C. Wheatley, *apptd* 1991
Wilts, Ven. B. J. Smith, *apptd* 1980

Chancellor, His Honour J. H. Ellison, VRD, *apptd* 1955
Registrar and Legal Secretary, F. M. Broadbent
Diocesan Secretary, Lt.-Col. C. C. G. Ross, Church House, Crane Street, Salisbury SP1 2QB. Tel: 01722-411922

SOUTHWARK

8TH BISHOP
Rt. Revd Robert K. Williamson, *cons.* 1984, *trans.* 1991, *apptd* 1991; Bishop's House, 38 Tooting Bec Gardens, London SW16 1QZ. *Signs* Robert Southwark

AREA BISHOPS
Croydon, Rt. Revd Dr Wilfred D. Wood, DD, *cons.* 1985, *apptd* 1985; St Matthew's House, George Street, Croydon CRO 1PE
Kingston upon Thames, Rt Revd Martin Wharton, *cons.* 1992, *apptd* 1992; *Kingston Episcopal Area Office,* Whitelands College, West Hill, London SW15 3SN
Woolwich, Rt. Revd A. Peter Hall, *cons.* 1984, *apptd* 1984; 8B Hilly Fields Crescent, London SE4 1QA

PROVOST
Very Revd Colin B. Slee, *apptd* 1994

CANONS RESIDENTIARY
Dr M. Kitchen, *apptd* 1988; D. Painter, *apptd* 1991; Helen Cunliffe, *apptd* 1995

Organist, P. Wright, FRCO, *apptd* 1989

ARCHDEACONS
Croydon, Ven. V. A. Davies, *apptd* 1994
Lambeth, Ven. C. R. B. Bird, *apptd* 1988
Lewisham, Ven. G. Kuhrt, *apptd* 1989
Reigate, vacant
Southwark, Ven. D. L. Bartles-Smith, *apptd* 1985
Wandsworth, Ven. D. Gerrard, *apptd* 1989

Chancellor, R. M. K. Gray, QC, *apptd* 1990
Registrar, P. Morris

Diocesan Secretary, M. Cawte, Trinity House, 4 Chapel Court, Borough High Street, London SE1 1HW. Tel: 0171-403 8686

TRURO

13TH BISHOP
Rt. Revd Michael T. Ball, *cons.* 1980, *apptd* 1990; Lis Escop, Truro TR3 6QQ. *Signs* Michael Truro

BISHOP SUFFRAGAN
St Germans, Rt. Revd Graham R. James, *cons.* 1993, *apptd* 1993; 32 Falmouth Road, Truro TR1 2HX

DEAN
Very Revd David J. Shearlock, *apptd* 1982

CANONS RESIDENTIARY
Ven. R. L. Ravenscroft, *apptd* 1988; P. R. Gay, *apptd* 1994; K. P. Mellor, *apptd* 1994

Organist, A. Nethsingha, FRCO, *apptd* 1994

ARCHDEACONS
Cornwall, Ven. R. L. Ravenscroft, *apptd* 1988
Bodmin, Ven. R. D. C. Whiteman, *apptd* 1989

Chancellor, P. T. S. Boydell, QC, *apptd* 1957
Registrar and Secretary, M. J. Follett
Diocesan Secretary, C. B. Gorton, Diocesan House, Kenwyn, Truro TR1 3DU. Tel: 01872-74351

WORCESTER

111TH BISHOP
Rt. Revd Philip H. E. Goodrich, *cons.* 1973, *apptd* 1982; The Bishop's House, Hartlebury Castle, Kidderminster DY11 7XX. *Signs* Philip Worcester

BISHOP SUFFRAGAN
Dudley, Rt. Revd Dr Rupert Hoare, *cons.* 1993, *apptd* 1993; The Bishop's House, Brooklands, Halesowen Road, Cradley Heath B64 7JF

DEAN
Very Revd Robert M. C. Jeffery, *apptd* 1987

CANONS RESIDENTIARY
Ven. F. Bentley, *apptd* 1984; D. G. Thomas, *apptd* 1987; I. M. MacKenzie, *apptd* 1989

Organist, Dr D. Hunt, FRCO, *apptd* 1975

ARCHDEACONS
Dudley, Ven. J. Gathercole, *apptd* 1987
Worcester, Ven. F. Bentley, *apptd* 1984

Chancellor, P. T. S. Boydell, QC, *apptd* 1959
Registrar, M. Huskinson
Diocesan Secretary, J. Stanbury, The Old Palace, Deansway, Worcester WR1 2JE. Tel: 01905-20537

ROYAL PECULIARS

WESTMINSTER
The Collegiate Church of St Peter
Dean, Very Revd Michael Mayne, *apptd* 1986
Sub Dean and Archdeacon, A. E. Harvey, *apptd* 1987

Canons of Westminster, A. E. Harvey, *apptd* 1982; D. C. Gray, *apptd* 1987; C. D. Semper, *apptd* 1987; D. H. Hutt, *apptd* 1995
Chapter Clerk and Receiver-General, Rear-Adm. K. A. Snow, CB, *apptd* 1987
Organist, M. Neary, FRCO, *apptd* 1988
Registrar, S. J. Holmes, MVO, *apptd* 1984, 20 Dean's Yard, London SW1P 3PA

WINDSOR

The Queen's Free Chapel of St George within Her Castle of Windsor
Dean, Very Revd Patrick R. Mitchell, FSA, *apptd* 1989
Canons Residentiary, J. A. White, *apptd* 1982; D. M. Stanesby, PH.D., *apptd* 1985; M. A. Moxon, *apptd* 1990
Chapter Clerk, Lt.-Col. N. J. Newman, *apptd* 1990
Organist, J. Rees-Williams, FRCO, *apptd* 1991

Province of York

YORK

96TH ARCHBISHOP AND PRIMATE OF ENGLAND
Most Revd and Rt. Hon. David M. Hope, D.phil., LL D, *cons.* 1985, *trans.* 1995, *apptd* 1995 *(from late 1995)*; Bishopthorpe, York YO2 1QE. *Signs* David Ebor:

BISHOPS SUFFRAGAN
Hull, Rt. Revd James S. Jones, *cons.* 1994, *apptd* 1994; Hullen House, Woodfield Lane, Hessle, Hull HU13 0ES
Selby, Rt. Revd Humphrey V. Taylor, *cons.* 1991, *apptd* 1991; 10 Precentor's Court, York YO1 2ES
Whitby, Rt. Revd Gordon Bates, *cons.* 1983, *apptd* 1983; 60 West Green, Stokesley, Middlesbrough TS9 5BD
Beverley, Rt. Revd John Gaisford, *cons.* 1994, *apptd* 1994 (provincial episcopal visitor); 3 North Lane, Roundhay, Leeds LS8 2QJ

DEAN
Very Revd Raymond Furnell, *apptd* 1994

CANONS RESIDENTIARY
J. Toy, PH.D., *apptd* 1983; R. Metcalfe, *apptd* 1988; P. J. Ferguson, *apptd* 1995; E. R. Norman, PH.D., DD, *apptd* 1995
Organist, P. Moore, FRCO, *apptd* 1983

ARCHDEACONS
Cleveland, Ven. C. J. Hawthorn, *apptd* 1991
East Riding, Ven. H. F. Buckingham, *apptd* 1988
York, Ven. G. B. Austin, *apptd* 1988

Official Principal and Auditor of the Chancery Court, J. A. D. Owen, QC
Chancellor of the Diocese, His Honour Judge Coningsby, QC, *apptd* 1977
Vicar-General of the Province and Official Principal of the Consistory Court, His Honour Judge Coningsby, QC
Registrar and Legal Secretary, L. P. M. Lennox
Diocesan Secretary, K. W. Dodgson, Church House, Ogleforth, York YO1 2JE. Tel: 01904-611696

DURHAM

92ND BISHOP
Rt. Revd A. Michael A. Turnbull, *cons.* 1988, *apptd* 1994; Auckland Castle, Bishop Auckland DL14 7NR. *Signs* Michael Dunelm:

BISHOP SUFFRAGAN
Jarrow, Rt. Revd Alan Smithson, *cons.* 1990, *apptd* 1990; The Old Vicarage, Hallgarth, Pittington, Durham DH6 1AB

DEAN
Very Revd John R. Arnold, *apptd* 1989

CANONS RESIDENTIARY
M. C. Perry, *apptd* 1970; R. L. Coppin, *apptd* 1974; Ven. J. D. Hodgson, *apptd* 1983; D. W. Brown, *apptd* 1990; G. S. Pedley, *apptd* 1993
Organist, J. B. Lancelot, FRCO, *apptd* 1985

ARCHDEACONS
Auckland, Ven. G. G. Gibson, *apptd* 1993
Durham, Ven. J. D. Hodgson, *apptd* 1993

Chancellor, His Honour Judge Bursell, QC, *apptd* 1989
Registrar and Legal Secretary, D. M. Robertson
Diocesan Secretary, W. Hurworth, Auckland Castle, Bishop Auckland, Co. Durham DL14 7QJ. Tel: 01388-604515

BLACKBURN

7TH BISHOP
Rt. Revd Alan D. Chesters, *cons.* 1989, *apptd* 1989; Bishop's House, Ribchester Road, Blackburn BB1 9EF. *Signs* Alan Blackburn

BISHOPS SUFFRAGAN
Burnley, Rt. Revd Martyn W. Jarrett, *cons.* 1994, *apptd* 1994; Dean House, 449 Padiham Road, Burnley BB12 6TE
Lancaster, Rt. Revd John Nicholls, *cons.* 1990, *apptd* 1990; Wheatfields, 7 Dallas Road, Lancaster LA1 1TN

PROVOST
Very Revd David Frayne, *apptd* 1992

CANONS RESIDENTIARY
J. M. Taylor, *apptd* 1976; K. J. Parfitt, *apptd* 1994; J. M. Hall, *apptd* 1994; D. M. Galilee, *apptd* 1995
Organist, G. Stewart, *apptd* 1995

ARCHDEACONS
Blackburn, Ven. W. D. Robinson, *apptd* 1986
Lancaster, Ven. K. H. Gibbons, *apptd* 1981

Chancellor, J. W. M. Bullimore, *apptd* 1990
Registrar, T. A. Hoyle
Diocesan Secretary, Revd M. J. Wedgeworth, Diocesan Office, Cathedral Close, Blackburn BB1 5AA. Tel: 01254-54421

BRADFORD

8TH BISHOP
Rt. Revd David J. Smith, *cons.* 1987, *apptd* 1992; Bishopscroft, Ashwell Road, Heaton, Bradford BD9 4AU. *Signs* David Bradford

PROVOST
Very Revd John S. Richardson, *apptd* 1990

CANON RESIDENTIARY
C. G. Lewis, *apptd* 1993
Organist, A. Horsey, FRCO, *apptd* 1986

ARCHDEACONS
Bradford, Ven. D. H. Shreeve, *apptd* 1984
Craven, Ven. M. L. Grundy, *apptd* 1994

Chancellor, D. M. Savill, QC, *apptd* 1976

Registrar and Secretary, J. G. H. Mackrell
Diocesan Secretary, M. Halliday, Cathedral Hall, Stott Hill,
Bradford BD1 4ET. Tel: 01274-725958

CARLISLE

65TH BISHOP
Rt. Revd Ian Harland, *cons.* 1985, *apptd* 1989; Rose Castle,
Dalston, Carlisle CA5 7BZ. *Signs* Ian Carliol:

BISHOP SUFFRAGAN
Penrith, Rt. Revd Richard Garrard, *cons.* 1994, *apptd* 1994;
Holm Croft, Castle Road, Kendal, Cumbria LA9 7AU

DEAN
Very Revd Henry E. C. Stapleton, *apptd* 1988

CANONS RESIDENTIARY
R. A. Chapman, *apptd* 1978; Ven. D. C. Turnbull, *apptd* 1993;
D. W. V. Weston, *apptd* 1994

Organist, J. Suter, FRCO, *apptd* 1991

ARCHDEACONS
Carlisle, Ven. D. C. Turnbull, *apptd* 1993
West Cumberland, Ven. J. R. Packer, *apptd* 1991
Westmorland and Furness, Ven. D. T. I. Jenkins, *apptd* 1995

Chancellor, His Honour Judge Aglionby, *apptd* 1991
Registrar and Secretary, Mrs S. Holmes
Diocesan Secretary, vacant; Church House, West Walls,
Carlisle CA3 8UE. Tel: 01228-22573

CHESTER

39TH BISHOP
Rt. Revd Michael A. Baughen, *cons.* 1982, *apptd* 1982;
Bishop's House, Chester CH1 2JD. *Signs* Michael Cestr:

BISHOPS SUFFRAGAN
Birkenhead, Rt. Revd Michael L. Langrish, *cons.* 1993, *apptd*
1993; 67 Bidston Road, Oxton, Birkenhead L43 6TR
Stockport, Rt. Revd Geoffrey M. Turner, *cons.* 1994, *apptd*
1994; Bishop's Lodge, Back Lane, Dunham Town,
Altrincham, Cheshire WA14 4SG

DEAN
Very Revd Dr Stephen S. Smalley, *apptd* 1986

CANONS RESIDENTIARY
R. M. Rees, *apptd* 1990; O. A. Conway, *apptd* 1991; Dr
T. J. Dennis, *apptd* 1994; J. W. S. Newcome, *apptd* 1994

Organist, R. Fisher, FRCO, *apptd* 1968

ARCHDEACONS
Chester, Ven. C. Hewetson, *apptd* 1994
Macclesfield, Ven. R. J. Gillings, *apptd* 1994

Chancellor, H. H. Lomas, *apptd* 1977
Registrar and Legal Secretary, A. K. McAllester
Diocesan Secretary, P. J. Mills, Diocesan House, Raymond
Street, Chester CH1 4PN. Tel: 01244-379222

LIVERPOOL

6TH BISHOP
Rt. Revd David S. Sheppard, *cons.* 1969, *apptd* 1975; Bishop's
Lodge, Woolton Park, Liverpool L25 6DT. *Signs* David
Liverpool

BISHOP SUFFRAGAN
Warrington, Rt. Revd Michael Henshall, *cons.* 1976, *apptd*
1976; Martinsfield, Elm Avenue, Great Crosby,
Liverpool L23 2SX   •

DEAN
Very Revd Rhys D. C. Walters, OBE, *apptd* 1983

CANONS RESIDENTIARY
M. M. Wolfe, *apptd* 1982; D. J. Hutton, *apptd* 1983;
M. C. Boyling, *apptd* 1994

Organist, Prof. I. Tracey, *apptd* 1980

ARCHDEACONS
Liverpool, Ven. R. L. Metcalf, *apptd* 1994
Warrington, Ven. C. D. S. Woodhouse, *apptd* 1981

Chancellor, R. G. Hamilton
Registrar and Cathedral Chapter Clerk, R. H. Arden
Diocesan Secretary, K. Cawdron, Church House, 1 Hanover
Street, Liverpool L1 3DW. Tel: 0151-709 9722

MANCHESTER

10TH BISHOP
Rt. Revd Christopher J. Mayfield, *cons.* 1985, *apptd* 1993;
Bishopscourt, Bury New Road, Manchester M7 0LE.
Signs Christopher Manchester

BISHOPS SUFFRAGAN
Bolton, Rt. Revd David Bonser, *cons.* 1991, *apptd* 1991;
4 Sandfield Drive, Lostock, Bolton BL6 4DU
Hulme, Rt. Revd Colin J. F. Scott, *cons.* 1984, *apptd* 1984;
1 Raynham Avenue, Didsbury, Manchester M20 0BW
Middleton, Rt. Revd Stephen Venner, *cons.* 1994, *apptd* 1994;
The Hollies, Manchester Road, Rochdale OL11 3QY

DEAN
Very Revd Kenneth Riley, *apptd* 1993

CANONS RESIDENTIARY
Ven. R. B. Harris, *apptd* 1980; J. R. Atherton, PH.D., *apptd* 1984;
A. E. Radcliffe, *apptd* 1991

Organist, C. Stokes, *apptd* 1992

ARCHDEACONS
Bolton, Ven. L. M. Davies, *apptd* 1992
Manchester, Ven. R. B. Harris, *apptd* 1980
Rochdale, Ven. J. M. M. Dalby, *apptd* 1991

Chancellor, G. C. H. Spafford, *apptd* 1976
Registrar, M. Darlington
Diocesan Secretary, Mrs J. Park, Diocesan Church House,
90 Deansgate, Manchester M3 2GH. Tel: 0161-833 9521

NEWCASTLE

10TH BISHOP
Rt. Revd Andrew A. K. Graham, *cons.* 1977, *apptd* 1981;
Bishop's House, 29 Moor Road South, Gosforth,
Newcastle upon Tyne NE3 1PA. *Signs* A. Newcastle

STIPENDIARY ASSISTANT BISHOP
Rt. Revd Kenneth Gill, *cons.* 1972, *apptd* 1980

PROVOST
Very Revd Nicholas G. Coulton, *apptd* 1990

CANONS RESIDENTIARY
R. Langley, *apptd* 1985; P. R. Strange, *apptd* 1986;
I. F. Bennett, *apptd* 1988; Ven. P. Elliott, *apptd* 1993

Organist, T. G. Hone, FRCO, *apptd* 1987

ARCHDEACONS
Lindisfarne, Ven. M. E. Bowering, *apptd* 1987
Northumberland, Ven. P. Elliott, *apptd* 1993

Chancellor, His Honour A. J. Blackett-Ord, CVO, *apptd* 1971
Registrar and Secretary, Mrs B. J. Lowdon
Diocesan Secretary, J. M. Craster, Church House, Grainger Park Road, Newcastle upon Tyne NE4 8SX. Tel: 0191-226 0622

RIPON

11TH BISHOP
Rt. Revd David N. de L. Young, *cons.* 1977, *apptd* 1977; Bishop Mount, Ripon HG4 5DP. *Signs* David Ripon

BISHOP SUFFRAGAN
Knaresborough, Rt. Revd Malcolm J. Menin, *cons.* 1986, *apptd* 1986; 16 Shaftesbury Avenue, Roundhay, Leeds LS8 1DT

DEAN
Very Revd John Methuen, *apptd* 1995

CANONS RESIDENTIARY
P. J. Marshall, *apptd* 1985; M. R. Glanville-Smith, *apptd* 1990
Organist, K. Beaumont, FRCO, *apptd* 1994

ARCHDEACONS
Leeds, Ven. J. M. Oliver, *apptd* 1992
Richmond, Ven. K. Good, *apptd* 1993

Chancellor, His Honour Judge Grenfell, *apptd* 1992
Registrar and Legal Secretary, J. R. Balmforth
Diocesan Secretary, G. M. Royal, Diocesan Office, St Mary's Street, Leeds LS9 7DP. Tel: 0113-248 7487

SHEFFIELD

5TH BISHOP
Rt. Revd David R. Lunn, *cons.* 1980, *apptd* 1980; Bishopscroft, Snaithing Lane, Sheffield S10 3LG. *Signs* David Sheffield

BISHOP SUFFRAGAN
Doncaster, Rt. Revd. Michael F. Gear, *cons.* 1993, *apptd* 1993; Bishops Lodge, Hooton Roberts, Rotherham S65 4PF

PROVOST
Very Revd Michael Sadgrove, *apptd* 1995

CANONS RESIDENTIARY
T. M. Page, *apptd* 1982; Ven. S. R. Lowe, *apptd* 1988; C. M. Smith, *apptd* 1991; Jane E. M. Sinclair, *apptd* 1993
Organist, S. Lole, *apptd* 1994

ARCHDEACONS
Doncaster, Ven. B. L. Holdridge, *apptd* 1994
Sheffield, Ven. S. R. Lowe, *apptd* 1988

Chancellor, Prof. J. D. McClean, *apptd* 1992
Registrar and Legal Secretary, C. P. Rothwell
Diocesan Secretary, C. A. Beck, FCIS, Diocesan Church House, 95–99 Effingham Street, Rotherham S65 1BL. Tel: 0114-283 7547

SODOR AND MAN

79TH BISHOP
Rt. Revd Noel D. Jones, CB, *cons.* 1989, *apptd* 1989; The Bishop's House, Quarterbridge Road, Douglas, Isle of Man IM2 3RF. *Signs* Noel Sodor and Man

CANONS
B. H. Kelly, *apptd* 1980; B. H. Partington, *apptd* 1985; J. Sheen, *apptd* 1991; F. H. Bird, *apptd* 1993

ARCHDEACON
Isle of Man, Ven. D. A. Willoughby, *apptd* 1982

Vicar-General and Chancellor, P. W. S. Farrant
Registrar, C. J. Callow
Diocesan Secretary, The Hon. C. Murphy, c/o Cooil Voorath, The Cronk, Ballaugh, Isle of Man IM7 5AX. Tel: 01624-897880

SOUTHWELL

9TH BISHOP
Rt. Revd Patrick B. Harris, *cons.* 1973, *apptd* 1988; Bishop's Manor, Southwell NG25 0JR. *Signs* Patrick Southwell

BISHOP SUFFRAGAN
Sherwood, Rt. Revd Alan W. Morgan, *cons.* 1989, *apptd* 1989; Sherwood House, High Oakham Road, Mansfield NG18 5AJ

PROVOST
Very Revd David Leaning, *apptd* 1991

CANONS RESIDENTIARY
D. P. Keene, *apptd* 1981; I. G. Collins, *apptd* 1985; M. R. Austin, *apptd* 1988
Organist, P. Hale, *apptd* 1989

ARCHDEACONS
Newark, Ven. D. C. Hawtin, *apptd* 1992
Nottingham, Ven. T. O. Walker, *apptd* 1991

Chancellor, J. Shand, *apptd* 1981
Registrar, C. C. Hodson
Diocesan Secretary, B. Noake, Dunham House, Westgate, Southwell, Notts NG25 0JL. Tel: 01636-814331

WAKEFIELD

11TH BISHOP
Rt. Revd Nigel S. McCulloch, *cons.* 1986, *apptd* 1992; Bishop's Lodge, Woodthorpe Lane, Wakefield WF2 6JL. *Signs* Nigel Wakefield

BISHOP SUFFRAGAN
Pontefract, Rt. Revd John Finney, *cons.* 1993, *apptd* 1993; Pontefract House, 181A Manygates Lane, Wakefield WF2 7DR

PROVOST
Very Revd John E. Allen, *apptd* 1982

CANONS RESIDENTIARY
R. D. Baxter, *apptd* 1986; I. C. Knox, *apptd* 1989; D. O'Connor, *apptd* 1992; G. Nairn-Briggs, *apptd* 1992
Organist, J. Bielby, FRCO, *apptd* 1972

ARCHDEACONS
Halifax, Ven. R. Inwood, *apptd* 1995
Pontefract, Ven. J. Flack, *apptd* 1992

Chancellor, P. Collier, QC, *apptd* 1992
Registrar and Secretary, L. Box
Diocesan Secretary, J. Clark, Church House, 1 South Parade,
Wakefield WF1 ILP. Tel: 01924-371802

The Anglican Communion

The Anglican Communion consists of 37 independent
provincial or national Christian churches throughout the
world, many of which are in Commonwealth countries and
originated from missionary activity by the Church of
England. There is no single world authority linking the
Communion, but all recognize the leadership of the
Archbishop of Canterbury and have strong ecclesiastical
and historical links with the Church of England. Every ten
years all the bishops in the Communion meet at the
Lambeth Conference, convened by the Archbishop of
Canterbury. The Conference has no policy-making
authority but is an important forum for the discussion of
issues of common concern. The Anglican Consultative
Council was set up in 1968 to function between conferences and the meeting of the Primates every two years.

There are about 70 million Anglicans and 800 archbishops and bishops world-wide.

THE CHURCH IN WALES

The Anglican Church was the established church in Wales
from the 16th century until 1920, when the estrangement of
the majority of Welsh people from Anglicanism resulted in
disestablishment. Since then the Church in Wales has been
an autonomous province consisting of six sees, with one of
the diocesan bishops being elected Archbishop of Wales by
an electoral college comprising elected lay and clerical
members.

The legislative body of the Church in Wales is the
Governing Body, which has 349 members in total, divided
between the three orders of bishops, clergy and laity. It is
presided over by the Archbishop of Wales and meets twice
annually. Its decisions are binding upon all members of the
Church. There are about 100,000 members of the Church
in Wales, with six bishops, about 700 stipendiary clergy and
1,142 parishes.

THE GOVERNING BODY OF THE CHURCH IN WALES,
39 Cathedral Road, Cardiff CF1 9XF. Tel: 01222–231638.
Secretary-General, J. W. D. McIntyre

10TH ARCHBISHOP OF WALES, Most Revd Alwyn R. Jones
(Bishop of St Asaph), *elected* 1991

THE RT. REVD BISHOPS
Bangor (79th), Rt. Revd Dr Barry C. Morgan, *b.* 1947, *cons.*
1993, *apptd* 1992; Tŷ'r Esgob, Bangor LL57 2SS. *Signs* Barry
Bangor. *Stipendiary clergy,* 70
Llandaff (101st), Rt. Revd Roy T. Davies, *b.* 1934, *cons.* 1985,
apptd 1985; Llys Esgob, The Cathedral Green, Llandaff,
Cardiff CF5 2YE. *Signs* Roy Landav. *Stipendiary clergy,* 158
Monmouth (8th), Rt. Revd Rowan D. Williams, *b* 1950, *cons.*
1992, *apptd* 1992; Bishopstow, Stow Hill, Newport NP9
4EA. *Signs* Rowan Monmouth. *Stipendiary clergy,* 120
St Asaph (74th), Most Revd Alwyn R. Jones, *b.* 1934, *cons.*
1982, *apptd* 1982; Esgobty, St Asaph, Clwyd LL17 0TW.
Signs Alwyn Cambrensis. *Stipendiary clergy,* 112
St David's (125th), vacant; Llys Esgob, Abergwili, Dyfed SA31
2JG. *Signs* – St Davids. *Stipendiary clergy,* 132

Swansea and Brecon (7th), Rt. Revd Dewi M. Bridges, *b.* 1933,
cons. 1988, *apptd* 1988; Ely Tower, Brecon, Powys LD3
9DE. *Signs* Dewi Swansea & Brecon. *Stipendiary clergy,* 100

The stipend of a diocesan bishop of the Church in Wales is
£24,198 a year from 1995

THE SCOTTISH EPISCOPAL CHURCH

The Scottish Episcopal Church was founded after the Act
of Settlement (1690) established the presbyterian nature of
the Church of Scotland. The Scottish Episcopal Church is
in full communion with the Church of England but is
autonomous. The governing authority is the General
Synod, an elected body of 180 members which meets once
a year. The diocesan bishop who convenes and presides at
meetings of the General Synod is called the Primus and is
elected by his fellow bishops.

There are 54,495 members of the Scottish Episcopal
Church, of whom 34,266 are communicants. There are
seven bishops, 188 stipendiary clergy, and 323 churches
and places of worship.

THE GENERAL SYNOD OF THE SCOTTISH EPISCOPAL
CHURCH, 21 Grosvenor Crescent, Edinburgh EH12 5EE.
Tel: 0131-225 6357. *Secretary-General,* J. W. Simpson

PRIMUS OF THE SCOTTISH EPISCOPAL CHURCH, Most
Revd Richard F. Holloway (Bishop of Edinburgh),
elected 1992

THE RT. REVD BISHOPS
Aberdeen and Orkney, A. Bruce Cameron, *b.* 1941, *cons.* 1992,
apptd 1992. *Clergy* 19
Argyll and the Isles, Douglas M. Cameron, *b.* 1935, *cons.* 1993,
apptd 1992. *Clergy* 9
Brechin, Robert T. Halliday, *b.* 1932, *cons.* 1990, *apptd* 1990.
Clergy 16
Edinburgh, Richard F. Holloway, *b.* 1933, *cons.* 1986, *apptd*
1986. *Clergy* 53
Glasgow and Galloway, John M. Taylor, *b.* 1932, *cons.* 1991,
apptd 1991. *Clergy* 48
Moray, Ross and Caithness, Gregor Macgregor, *b.* 1933, *cons.*
1994, *apptd* 1994. *Clergy* 13
St Andrews, Dunkeld and Dunblane, Michael H. G. Henley, *b.*
1938, *cons.* 1995, *apptd* 1995. *Clergy* 30

The minimum stipend of a diocesan bishop of the Scottish
Episcopal Church was £18,000 in 1995

THE CHURCH OF IRELAND

The Anglican Church was the established church in
Ireland from the 16th century but never secured the
allegiance of a majority of the Irish and was disestablished
in 1871. The Church in Ireland is divided into the
provinces of Armagh and Dublin, each under an archbishop. The provinces are subdivided into 12 dioceses.

The legislative body is the General Synod, which has
660 members in total, divided between the House of
Bishops and the House of Representatives. The Archbishop of Armagh is elected by the House of Bishops; other
episcopal elections are made by an electoral college.

There are about 375,000 members of the Church of
Ireland, with two archbishops, ten bishops, about 600
clergy and about 1,000 churches and places of worship.

CENTRAL OFFICE, Church of Ireland House, Church
Avenue, Rathmines, Dublin 6. Tel: 00-353-1-4978422.

Chief Officer and Secretary of the Representative Church Body,
R. H. Sherwood; *Assistant Secretary of the General Synod,*
D. G. Meredith

PROVINCE OF ARMAGH

ARCHBISHOP OF ARMAGH AND PRIMATE OF ALL IRELAND,
Most Revd Robert H. A. Eames, PH.D., *b.* 1937, *cons.* 1975,
trans. 1986. *Clergy* 52

THE RT. REVD BISHOPS
Clogher, Brian D. A. Hannon, *b.* 1936, *cons.* 1986, *apptd* 1986.
Clergy 32
Connor, James E. Moore, *b.* 1933, *cons.* 1995, *apptd.* 1995.
Clergy 112
Derry and Raphoe, James Mehaffey, PH.D., *b.* 1931, *cons.* 1980,
apptd 1980. *Clergy* 57
Down and Dromore, Gordon McMullan, PH.D., TH.D., *b.* 1934,
cons. 1980, *trans.* 1986. *Clergy* 110
Kilmore, Elphin and Ardagh, Michael H. G. Mayes, *b.* 1941,
cons. 1993, *apptd* 1993. *Clergy* 29
Tuam, Killala and Achonry, John R. W. Neill, *b.* 1945, *cons.*
1986, *apptd* 1986. *Clergy* 12

PROVINCE OF DUBLIN

ARCHBISHOP OF DUBLIN, BISHOP OF GLENDALOUGH,
AND PRIMATE OF IRELAND, Most Revd Donald A. Caird,
DD, *b.* 1925, *cons.* 1970, *trans.* 1976, 1985. *Clergy* 88

THE RT. REVD BISHOPS
Cashel and Ossory, Noel V. Willoughby, *b.* 1926, *cons.* 1980,
apptd 1980. *Clergy* 37
Cork, Cloyne and Ross, Robert A. Warke, *b.* 1930, *cons.* 1988,
apptd 1988. *Clergy* 29
Limerick and Killaloe, Edward F. Darling, *b.* 1933, *cons.* 1985,
apptd 1985. *Clergy* 23
Meath and Kildare, Most Revd Walton N. F. Empey, *b.* 1934,
cons. 1981, *trans.* 1985. *Clergy* 24

Anglican Communion Overseas

ANGLICAN CHURCH OF AOTEAROA, NEW ZEALAND AND POLYNESIA

PRIMATE AND ARCHBISHOP OF AOTEAROA, NEW
ZEALAND AND POLYNESIA, The Most Revd Brian
N. Davis (Bishop of Wellington), *cons.* 1980, *apptd* 1986

THE RT. REVD BISHOPS
Aotearoa, Whakahuhui Vercoe, *cons.* 1981, *apptd* 1981
Auckland, John Paterson, *cons.* 1995, *apptd* 1995
Christchurch, David Coles, *cons.* 1990, *apptd* 1990
Dunedin, Penelope Jamieson, *cons.* 1990, *apptd* 1990
Nelson, Derek Eaton, *cons.* 1990, *apptd* 1990
Polynesia, Jabez Bryce, *cons.* 1975, *apptd* 1975
Waiapu, Murray Mills, *cons.* 1991, *apptd* 1991
Waikato, David Moxon, *cons.* 1993, *apptd* 1993
Wellington, see above

ANGLICAN CHURCH OF AUSTRALIA

PRIMATE OF AUSTRALIA, The Most Revd Keith Rayner
(Archbishop of Melbourne), *cons.* 1969, *apptd* 1991

PROVINCE OF NEW SOUTH WALES

METROPOLITAN
Archbishop of Sydney, The Most Revd R. Harry Goodhew,
cons. 1982, *apptd* 1993

THE RT. REVD BISHOPS
Armidale, Peter Chiswell, *cons.* 1976, *apptd* 1976
Bathurst, Bruce W. Wilson, *cons.* 1984, *apptd* 1989
Canberra and Goulburn, George V. Browning, *apptd* 1993
Grafton, Bruce A. Schultz, *cons.* 1985, *apptd* 1985
Newcastle, Roger A. Herft, *apptd* 1993
Riverina, Bruce Q. Clark, *apptd* 1993

PROVINCE OF QUEENSLAND

METROPOLITAN
Archbishop of Brisbane, The Most Revd Peter Hollingworth,
cons. 1985, *apptd* 1990

THE RT. REVD BISHOPS
Carpentaria, Anthony F. B. Hall-Matthews, *cons.* 1984, *apptd*
1984
North Queensland, John Lewis, *cons.* 1971, *apptd* 1971
Northern Territory, Richard F. Appleby, *cons.* 1992, *apptd*
1992
Rockhampton, George A. Hearn, *cons.* 1981, *apptd* 1981

PROVINCE OF SOUTH AUSTRALIA

METROPOLITAN
Archbishop of Adelaide, The Most Revd Ian G. C. George,
cons. 1989, *apptd* 1991

THE RT. REVD BISHOPS
The Murray, Graham H. Walden, *cons.* 1981, *apptd* 1989
Willochra, W. David H. McCall, *cons.* 1987, *apptd* 1987

PROVINCE OF VICTORIA

METROPOLITAN
Archbishop of Melbourne, The Most Revd Keith Rayner, *cons.*
1969, *apptd* 1990 (*see* above)

THE RT. REVD BISHOPS
Ballarat, R. David Silk, *cons.* 1994, *apptd* 1994
Bendigo, vacant
Gippsland, Arthur L. V. Jones, *cons.* 1994, *apptd* 1994
Wangaratta, Paul Richardson, *cons.* 1987, *apptd* 1995

PROVINCE OF WESTERN AUSTRALIA

METROPOLITAN
Archbishop of Perth, The Most Revd Peter F. Carnley, PH.D.,
cons. 1981, *apptd* 1981

THE RT. REVD BISHOPS
Bunbury, Hamish J. U. Jamieson, *cons.* 1974, *apptd* 1984
North-West Australia, Anthony Nicholls, *cons.* 1992, *apptd*
1992

EXTRA-PROVINCIAL DIOCESE

Bishop of Tasmania, Rt. Revd Phillip K. Newell, AO, *cons.*
1982, *apptd* 1982

EPISCOPAL ANGLICAN CHURCH OF BRAZIL
Igreja Episcopal Anglicana Do Brasil

PRIMATE, The Most Revd Glauco Soares de Lima (Bishop
of South Central Brazil), *cons.* 1989, *apptd* 1994

THE RT. REVD BISHOPS
Brasilia, Almir dos Santos, *cons.* 1989, *apptd* 1989
Central Brazil, Sydney A. Ruiz, *cons.* 1985, *apptd* 1985
Northern Brazil, Clovis E. Rodrigues, *cons.* 1985, *apptd* 1986
Pelotas, Luiz O. P. Prado, *cons.* 1987, *apptd* 1989
South Central Brazil, *see* above, *apptd* 1989
Southern Brazil, Claudio V. S. Gastal, *cons.* 1984, *apptd* 1984
South-Western Brazil, Jubal P. Neves, *cons.* 1993, *apptd* 1993

CHURCH OF THE PROVINCE OF BURUNDI

ARCHBISHOP OF PROVINCE, The Most Revd Samuel
  Sindamuka (Bishop of Matana), *cons.* 1975, *apptd* 1989

THE RT. REVD BISHOPS
Bujumbura, Pie Ntukamazina, *cons.* 1990, *apptd* 1990
Buye, Samuel Ndayisenga, *apptd* 1979
Gitega, Jean Nduwayo, *apptd* 1985
Matana, *see* above

ANGLICAN CHURCH OF CANADA

ARCHBISHOP AND PRIMATE, The Most Revd Michael
  G. Peers, *cons.* 1977, *elected* 1986

PROVINCE OF BRITISH COLUMBIA
METROPOLITAN
Archbishop of Kootenay, The Most Revd David Crawley, *cons.*
  1990, *elected* 1994

THE RT. REVD BISHOPS
British Columbia, Barry Jenks, *cons.* 1992, *elected* 1992
Caledonia, John Hannen, *cons.* 1981, *elected* 1981
Cariboo, James Cruickshank, *cons.* 1992, *elected* 1992
Kootenay, *see* above, *elected* 1990
New Westminster, Michael Ingham, *cons.* 1994, *elected* 1993
Yukon, Terrence O. Buckle, *cons.* 1993, *elected* 1995

PROVINCE OF CANADA
METROPOLITAN
Archbishop of Western Newfoundland, The Most Revd Stewart
  S. Payne, *cons.* 1978, *elected* 1990

THE RT. REVD BISHOPS
Central Newfoundland, Edward Marsh, *cons.* 1990, *elected* 1990
Eastern Newfoundland and Labrador, Donald Harvey, *cons.*
  1993, *elected* 1992
Fredericton, George Lemon, *cons.* 1989, *elected* 1989
Montreal, Andrew Hutchison, *cons.* 1990, *elected* 1990
Nova Scotia, Arthur Peters, *cons.* 1982, *elected* 1982
Quebec, Bruce Stavert, *cons.* 1991, *elected* 1991
Western Newfoundland, *see* above

PROVINCE OF ONTARIO

METROPOLITAN
Archbishop of Huron, The Most Revd Percival O'Driscoll,
  cons. 1987, *elected* 1993

THE RT. REVD BISHOPS
Algoma, Ronald Ferris, *cons.* 1981, *elected* 1995
Huron, *see* above
Moosonee, Caleb Lawrence, *cons.* 1980, *elected* 1980
Niagara, Walter Asbil, *cons.* 1990, *elected* 1990
Ontario, Peter Mason, *cons.* 1992, *elected* 1992
Ottawa, John Baycroft, *cons.* 1985, *elected* 1993
Toronto, Terence Finlay, *cons.* 1986, *elected* 1990

PROVINCE OF RUPERT'S LAND

METROPOLITAN
Archbishop of Calgary, The Most Revd Barry Curtis, *cons.*
  1983, *elected* 1994

THE RT. REVD BISHOPS
Arctic, J. Christopher Williams, *cons.* 1987, *elected* 1991
Athabasca, John Clarke, *cons.* 1992, *elected* 1992
Brandon, Malcolm Harding, *cons.* 1992, *elected* 1992
Calgary, *see* above, *elected* 1983
Edmonton, Kenneth Genge, *cons.* 1988, *elected* 1988
Keewatin, Thomas Collings, *cons.* 1991, *elected* 1991
Qu' Appelle, Eric Bays, *cons.* 1986, *elected* 1986
Rupert's Land, Patrick Lee, *cons.* 1994, *elected* 1994
Saskatchewan, Anthony Burton, *cons.* 1993, *elected* 1993
Saskatoon, Thomas Morgan, *cons.* 1985, *elected* 1993

CHURCH OF THE PROVINCE OF CENTRAL AFRICA

ARCHBISHOP OF PROVINCE, The Most Revd Walter
  P. K. Makhulu (Bishop of Botswana), *cons.* 1979, *apptd*
  1980

THE RT. REVD BISHOPS
Botswana, *see* above
Central Zambia, Clement Shaba, *cons.* 1984, *apptd* 1984
Harare, vacant
Lake Malawi, Peter Nyanja, *cons.* 1978, *apptd* 1978
The Lundi, Jonathan Siyachitema, *cons.* 1981, *apptd* 1981
Lusaka, Stephen Mumba, *cons.* 1981, *apptd* 1981
Manicaland, Elijah Masuko, *cons.* 1981, *apptd* 1981
Matabeleland, Theophilus Naledi, *cons.* 1987, *apptd* 1987
Northern Zambia, Bernard Malango, *cons.* 1988, *apptd* 1988
Southern Malawi, Nathaniel Aipa, *cons.* 1987, *apptd* 1987

CHURCH OF THE PROVINCE OF THE INDIAN OCEAN

ARCHBISHOP OF PROVINCE, The Most Revd Remi
  Rabenirina (Bishop of Atananarivo), *cons.* 1984, *apptd*
  1995

THE RT. REVD BISHOPS
Antananarivo, *see* above, *apptd* 1984
Antsiranana, Keith Benzies, OBE, *cons.* 1982, *apptd* 1982
Mahajanga, vacant
Mauritius, Rex Donat, *cons.* 1984, *apptd* 1984
Seychelles, French Chang-Him, *cons.* 1979, *apptd* 1979
Toamasina, Donald Smith, *cons.* 1990, *apptd* 1990

HOLY CATHOLIC CHURCH IN JAPAN
Nippon Sei Ko Kai

PRIMATE, The Most Revd James T. Yashiro (Bishop of
  Kita Kanto), *cons.* 1985, *apptd* 1994

THE RT. REVD BISHOPS
Chubu, Samuel W. Hoyo, *cons.* 1987, *apptd* 1987
Hokkaido, Augustine H. Amagi, *cons.* 1987, *apptd* 1987
Kita Kanto, *see* above, *apptd* 1985
Kobe, John J. Furumoto, *cons.* 1992, *apptd* 1992
Kyoto, Barnabas M. Muto, *cons.* 1995, *apptd* 1995
Kyushu, Joseph N. Iida, *cons.* 1982, *apptd* 1982
Okinawa, Paul S. Nakamura, *cons.* 1972, *apptd* 1972
Osaka, Augustine K. Takano, *cons.* 1995, *apptd* 1995

Tohoku, William T. Murakami, *cons.* 1993, *apptd* 1993
Tokyo, John M. Takeda, *cons.* 1988, *apptd* 1988
Yokohama, Raphael S. Kajiwara, *cons.* 1984, *apptd* 1984

EPISCOPAL CHURCH IN JERUSALEM AND THE MIDDLE EAST

PRESIDENT-BISHOP, Rt. Revd Samir Kafity, *apptd* 1986

THE RT. REVD BISHOPS
Jerusalem, Samir Kafity, *cons.* 1984, *apptd* 1986
Iran, Iraj Mottahedeh, *cons.* 1990, *apptd* 1990
Egypt, Ghais A. Malik, *cons.* 1984, *apptd* 1984
Cyprus and the Gulf, vacant

CHURCH OF THE PROVINCE OF KENYA

ARCHBISHOP OF PROVINCE *(acting),* Rt Revd David Gitari (Bishop of Kirinyaga), *cons.* 1975, *apptd* 1994

THE RT. REVD BISHOPS
Butere, Horace Etemesi, *cons.* 1993, *apptd* 1993
Eldoret, Stephen Kewasis, *cons.* 1992, *apptd* 1992
Embu, Moses Njue, *cons.* 1990, *apptd* 1990
Kajiado, vacant
Katakwa, Eliud Okiring, *cons.* 1991, *apptd* 1991
Kirinyaga, see above, *apptd* 1975
Kitui, Benjamin Nzimbi, *cons.* 1985, *apptd* 1995
Machakos, vacant
Maseno North, vacant
Maseno South, Francis M. Abiero, *cons.* 1994, *apptd* 1994
Maseno West, Joseph Wesonga, *cons.* 1991, *apptd* 1991
Mombasa, Julius Kalu, *cons.* 1994, *apptd* 1994
Mount Kenya Central, Julius G. Gachuche, *cons.* 1993, *apptd* 1993
Mount Kenya South, vacant
Mount Kenya West, Alfred Chipman, *cons.* 1993, *apptd* 1993
Mumias, William C. W. Shikukule, *cons.* 1993, *apptd* 1993
Nairobi, vacant
Nakuru, Stephen M. Njihia, *cons.* 1990, *apptd* 1990
Nambale, Josiah M. Were, *cons.* 1993, *apptd* 1993
Southern Nyanza, Haggai Nyang', *cons.* 1990, *apptd* 1993
Taita/Taveta, Samson M. Mwaluda, *cons.* 1993, *apptd* 1993

CHURCH OF THE PROVINCE OF KOREA

ARCHBISHOP OF PROVINCE, The Most Revd Simon S. Kim (Bishop of Seoul), *apptd* 1993

THE RT. REVD BISHOPS
Pusan, Bundo C. H. Kim, *apptd* 1988
Seoul, see above
Taejon, Paul Hwan Yoon, *apptd* 1988

CHURCH OF THE PROVINCE OF MELANESIA

ARCHBISHOP OF PROVINCE, The Most Revd Ellison L. Pogo (Bishop of Central Melanesia), *cons.* 1981, *apptd* 1994

THE RT. REVD BISHOPS
Central Melanesia, see above
Hanuato'o, James Mason, *cons.* 1991, *apptd* 1991

Malaita, Raymond Aumae, *cons.* 1990, *apptd* 1990
Temotu, Lazarus Munamua, *cons.* 1987, *apptd* 1987
Vanuatu, Michael Tavoa, *cons.* 1990, *apptd* 1990
Ysabel, Walter Siba, *cons.* 1990, *apptd* 1994

EPISCOPAL CHURCH OF MEXICO

ARCHBISHOP OF PROVINCE, The Most Revd José G. Saucedo (Bishop of Cuernavaca), *cons.* 1958, *elected* 1995

THE RT. REVD BISHOPS
Cuernavaca, see above, *apptd* 1989
Mexico, Sergio Carrauza-Gomez, *cons.* 1989, *apptd* 1989
Northern Mexico, German Martinez, *cons.* 1987, *apptd* 1987
South-East Mexico, Claro H. Rames, *cons.* 1980, *apptd* 1989
Western Mexico, Samuel Espinoza-Venegas, *cons.* 1981, *apptd* 1983

CHURCH OF THE PROVINCE OF MYANMAR

ARCHBISHOP OF PROVINCE, The Most Revd Andrew Mya Han (Bishop of Yangon), *cons.* 1988, *apptd* 1988

THE RT. REVD BISHOPS
Hpa'an, Daniel Hoi Kyin, *cons.* 1992, *apptd* 1992
Mandalay, Andrew Hla Aung, *cons.* 1988, *apptd* 1988
Myitkyina, John Shan Lum, *cons.* 1994, *apptd* 1994
Sittwe, Barnabas Theaung Hawi, *cons.* 1978, *apptd* 1980
Toungoo, John Wilme, *cons.* 1994, *apptd* 1994
Yangon (Rangoon), see above

CHURCH OF THE PROVINCE OF NIGERIA

ARCHBISHOP OF PROVINCE, The Most Revd Joseph Adetiloye (Bishop of Lagos), *apptd* 1991

THE RT. REVD BISHOPS
Aba, A. O. Iwuagwu, *apptd* 1985
Abuja, Peter Akinole, *apptd* 1989
Akoko, J. O. K. Olowokure, *apptd* 1986
Akure, Emmanuel Gbonigi, *apptd* 1983
Asaba, Roland Nwosu, *apptd* 1977
Awka, Maxwell Anikwenwa, *apptd* 1987
Bauchi, Emmanuel O. Chukwuma, *apptd* 1990
Benin, John George, *apptd* 1985
Calabar, W. G. Ekprikpo
Egba-Abeokuta, T. I. Akintayo, *apptd* 1977
Egbado, Timothy Bolaji
Ekiti, C. A. Akinbola, *apptd* 1986
Enugu, Gideon Otubelu, *apptd* 1969
Ibadan, Gideon Olajide, *apptd* 1988
Ife, Gabriel Oloniyo
Ijebu, Abraham Olowoyo, *apptd* 1990
Ijebu Remo, E. O. I. Ogundana, *apptd* 1984
Ilesha, E. A. Ademowo, *apptd* 1989
Jos, B. A. Kwashi
Kaduna, Titus Ogbonyomi, *apptd* 1975
Kafanchan, William Diya, *apptd* 1990
Kano, B. O. Omosebi, *apptd* 1990
Katsina, J. S. Kwasu, *apptd* 1990
Kwara, Herbert Haruna, *apptd* 1974
Lagos, see above, *apptd* 1985
Maiduguri, E. K. Mani, *apptd* 1990
Makurdi, Nathan Nyom
Mbaise, Cyril Chukwka

Minna, Nathaniel Yisa, *apptd* 1990
The Niger, Jonathan Onyemelukwe, *apptd* 1975
Niger Delta, Samuel Elenwo, *apptd* 1981
Nsukka, Jonah Ilonuba
Oke-Osun, Abraham O. Awoson
Okigwe North, Alfred Nwaizuzu
Okigwe South, Bennett Okoro
Orlu, Samuel Ebo, *apptd* 1984
Ondo, Samuel Aderin, *apptd* 1981
Osun, Seth Fagbemi, *apptd* 1987
Owerri, Benjamin Nwankiti, *apptd* 1968
Owo, Peter A. Adebiyi
Sabongida Ora, Albert A. Agbaje
Sokoto, J. A. Idowu-Fearon, *apptd* 1990
Ukwa, Uju Obinya
Umuahia, Ngochukwe U. Ezuoke
Uyo, Ebenezar Nglass
Warri, Nathaniel Enuku
Yola, Chris O. Efobi, *apptd* 1990

ANGLICAN CHURCH OF PAPUA NEW GUINEA

Archbishop of Province, vacant

The Rt. Revd Bishops
Aipo Rongo, James Ayong, *cons.* 1995, *elected* 1995
Dogura, Tevita Talanoa, *cons.* 1992, *elected* 1992
New Guinea Islands, vacant
Popondota, Reuben Tariambari, *cons.* 1995, *elected* 1994
Port Moresby, Isaac Gadebo, *cons.* 1983, *elected* 1983

EPISCOPAL CHURCH IN THE PHILIPPINES

Prime Bishop, The Most Revd Narciso V. Ticobay, *cons.* 1986, *apptd* 1993

The Rt. Revd Bishops
Central Philippines, Manuel C. Lumpias, *cons.* 1977, *apptd* 1978
North Central Philippines, Joel A. Pachao, *cons.* 1993, *apptd* 1993
Northern Luzon, Ignacio C. Soliba, *cons.* 1990, *apptd* 1990
Northern Philippines, Robert L. Longid, *cons.* 1983, *apptd* 1986
Southern Philippines, James B. Manguramas, *cons.* 1993, *apptd* 1993

CHURCH OF THE PROVINCE OF RWANDA

Archbishop of Province, The Most Revd Augustin Nshamihigo (Bishop of Shyira), *apptd* 1992

The Rt. Revd Bishops
Butare, Justin Ndandali, *apptd* 1992
Byunba, Onesphore Rwaje
Cyangugu, Daniel Nduhura
Kibungo, Augustin Mvunabandi
Kigali, Adonia Sebununguri, *cons.* 1965
Kigeme, Norman Kayumba
Shyira, *see* above, *apptd* 1984
Shyogwe, Samuel Musubyimana

CHURCH OF THE PROVINCE OF SOUTHERN AFRICA

Metropolitan
Archbishop of Cape Town, The Most Revd Desmond M. B. Tutu, *cons.* 1976, *trans.* 1986

The Rt. Revd Bishops
Bloemfontein, Thomas Stanage, *cons.* 1978, *trans.* 1982
Christ the King, Peter Lee, *cons.* 1990, *elected* 1990
George, Derek Damant, *cons.* 1985, *elected* 1985
Grahamstown, David Russell, *cons.* 1986, *trans.* 1987
Johannesburg, Duncan Buchanan, *cons.* 1986, *elected* 1986
Kimberley and Kuruman, W. N. Ndungane, *cons.* 1991, *elected* 1991
Klerksdorp, David Nkwe, *cons.* 1990, *elected* 1990
Lebombo, Dinis Sengulane, *cons.* 1976, *elected* 1976
Lesotho, Philip Mokuku, *cons.* 1978, *elected* 1978
Namibia, James Kauluma, *cons.* 1978, *elected* 1981
Natal, Michael Nuttall, *cons.* 1975, *trans.* 1982
Niassa, Paulino Manhique, *cons.* 1986, *elected* 1986
Port Elizabeth, Eric Pike, *cons.* 1989, *trans.* 1993
Pretoria, Richard Kraft, *cons.* 1982, *elected* 1982
St Helena, John Ruston, *cons.* 1985, *trans.* 1991
St John's, Jacob Dlamini, *cons.* 1980, *elected* 1985
St Mark the Evangelist, Rollo Le Feuvre, *cons.* 1987, *elected* 1987
South-Eastern Transvaal, David Beetge, *cons.* 1990, *elected* 1990
Swaziland, Lawrence Zulu, *cons.* 1975, *trans.* 1993
Umzimvubu, Geoffrey Davies, *cons.* 1987, *elected* 1991
Zululand, Peter Harker, *cons.* 1993, *elected* 1993

Order of Ethiopia, Sigqibo Dwane, *cons.* 1983, *apptd* 1983

ANGLICAN CHURCH OF THE SOUTHERN CONE OF AMERICA

Presiding Bishop, Rt. Revd Colin Bazley (Bishop of Chile), *cons.* 1969

The Rt. Revd Bishops
Argentina, David Leake, *cons.* 1969, *apptd* 1990
Chile, see above, *apptd* 1977
Northern Argentina, Maurice Sinclair, *cons.* 1990, *apptd* 1990
Paraguay, John Ellison, *cons.* 1988, *apptd* 1988
Peru and Bolivia, vacant
Uruguay, Harold Godfrey, *cons.* 1986, *apptd* 1986

PROVINCE OF THE EPISCOPAL CHURCH OF THE SUDAN

Archbishop of Province, The Most Revd Benjamin W. Yugusuk (Bishop of Juba)

The Rt. Revd Bishops
Bor, Nathaniel Garang
Juba, see above
Kajokeji, Manaseh B. Dawidi
Khartoum, Bulus Idris Tia
Malakal, Kedekia Mabier
Maridi, Joseph Marona
Mundri, Eluzai Munda
Rumbek, Gabriel R. Jur
Wau (*acting*), Gabriel R. Jur
Western Sudan, Kurkeil M. Khamis

Yambio, Daniel Zindo, *cons.* 1984, *apptd* 1984
Yei, Seme L. Solomona

CHURCH OF THE PROVINCE OF TANZANIA

ARCHBISHOP OF PROVINCE, The Most Revd John
A. Ramadhani (Bishop of Zanzibar and Tanga), *cons.*
1980, *apptd* 1984

THE RT. REVD BISHOPS
Central Tanganyika, Godfrey Mhogolo, *cons.* 1989, *apptd*
1989
Dar es Salaam, Basil Sambano, *cons.* 1992, *apptd* 1992
Kagera, Edwin Nyamubi, *cons.* 1993, *apptd* 1993
Mara, vacant
Masasi, Christopher Sadiki, *cons.* 1992, *apptd* 1992
Morogoro, Dudley Mageni, *cons.* 1987, *apptd* 1987
Mount Kilimanjaro, Simon Makundi, *cons.* 1991, *apptd* 1991
Mpwapwa, Simon Chiwanga, *cons.* 1991, *apptd* 1991
Rift Valley, Alpha Mohamed, *cons.* 1982, *apptd* 1991
Ruaha, Donald Mtetemela, *cons.* 1982, *apptd* 1990
Ruvuma, Stanford Shauri, *cons.* 1989, *apptd* 1989
South-West Tanganyika, Charles Mwaigoga, *cons.* 1983, *apptd*
1983
Tabora, Francis Ntiruka, *cons.* 1989, *apptd* 1989
Victoria Nyanza, John Changae, *cons.* 1993, *apptd* 1993
Western Tanganyika, Gerard Mpango, *cons.* 1983, *apptd* 1983
Zanzibar and Tanga, see above

CHURCH OF THE PROVINCE OF UGANDA

ARCHBISHOP OF PROVINCE, vacant

THE RT. REVD BISHOPS
Bukedi, Nicodemus Okille, *apptd* 1984
Bunyoro-Kitara, Yonasani Rwakaikara
Busoga, Cyprian Bamwoze, *apptd* 1972
East Ankole, Elisha Kyamugambi, *cons.* 1992, *apptd* 1992
Kampala, vacant
Karamoja, Peter Lomongin, *apptd* 1987
Kigezi, William Rukirande
Lango, Melchizedek Otim, *apptd* 1976
Luwero, M. Bugimbi, *cons.* 1990, *apptd* 1990
Madi and West Nile, vacant
Mbale, Israel Koboyi, *cons.* 1992, *apptd* 1992
Mityana, Wilson Mutebi, *apptd* 1977
Muhabura, Ernest M. Shalita, *cons.* 1990, *apptd* 1990
Mukono, Livingstone Mpalanyi-Nkoyoyo, *apptd* 1985
Namirembe, Samuel Ssekkadde
Nebbi, Henry L. Orombi, *cons.* 1993, *apptd* 1993
North Kigezi, vacant
North Mbale, Peter Mudonyi, *cons.* 1992, *apptd* 1992
Northern Uganda, Gideon Oboma
Ruwenzori, Eustace Kamanyire, *apptd* 1981
Soroti, Geresom Ilukor, *apptd* 1976
South Kigezi, vacant
South Ruwenzori, Zebidee Masereka
West Ankole, Yorumu Bamunoba, *apptd* 1977
West Buganda, Christopher Senyonjo, *apptd* 1974

EPISCOPAL CHURCH IN THE USA

PRESIDING BISHOP AND PRIMATE, Most Revd Edmond
Lee Browning, DD, *cons.* 1968, *apptd* 1986

RT. REVD BISHOPS
Province I
Connecticut, Clarence Coleridge, *cons.* 1981, *apptd* 1994
Maine, Edward C. Chalfant, *cons.* 1984, *apptd* 1986
Massachusetts, M. Thomas Shaw, *cons.* 1994, *apptd* 1995
New Hampshire, Douglas E. Theuner, *cons.* 1986, *apptd* 1986
Rhode Island, vacant
Vermont, Mary A. Mcleod, *cons.* 1993, *apptd* 1993
Western Massachusetts, vacant

Province II
Albany, David S. Ball, *cons.* 1984, *apptd* 1984
Central New York, David B. Joslin, *cons.* 1991, *apptd* 1992
Europe, Convocation of American Churches in, Jeffery
Rowthorn, *cons.* 1987
*Haiti, Zaché Duracin, *cons.* 1993, *apptd* 1994
Long Island, Orris Walker, *cons.* 1988, *apptd* 1991
New Jersey, Joe M. Doss, *cons.* 1993, *apptd* 1993
New York, Richard Grein, *cons.* 1981, *apptd* 1989
Newark, John S. Spong, *cons.* 1976, *apptd* 1979
Rochester, William G. Burrill, *cons.* 1984, *apptd* 1984
*Virgin Islands, vacant
Western New York, David C. Bowman, *cons.* 1986, *apptd* 1987

Province III
Bethlehem, J. Mark Dyer, *cons.* 1982, *apptd* 1983
Central Pennsylvania, Charlie F. McNutt jun., *cons.* 1982,
apptd 1982
Delaware, C. Cabell Tennis, *cons.* 1986, *apptd* 1986
Easton, Martin G. Townsend, *cons.* 1992, *apptd* 1993
Maryland, Charles Longest (*Bishop-in-charge*), *cons.* 1989
North-Western Pennsylvania, Robert D. Rowley jun., *cons.*
1989, *apptd* 1991
Pennsylvania, Allen L. Bartlett, *cons.* 1986, *apptd* 1987
Pittsburgh, Alden M. Hathaway, *cons.* 1981, *apptd* 1983
Southern Virginia, Frank Vest, *cons.* 1985, *apptd* 1991
South-Western Virginia, A. Heath Light, *cons.* 1979, *apptd*
1979
Virginia, Peter J. Lee, *cons.* 1984, *apptd* 1985
Washington, Ronald Haines, *cons.* 1986, *apptd* 1990
West Virginia, John H. Smith, *cons.* 1989, *apptd* 1989

Province IV
Alabama, Robert O. Miller, *cons.* 1988, *apptd* 1988
Atlanta, Frank K. Allan, *cons.* 1988, *apptd* 1989
Central Florida, John Howe, *cons.* 1989, *apptd* 1990
Central Gulf Coast, Charles F. Duvall, *cons.* 1981, *apptd* 1981
East Carolina, Sidney Saunders, *cons.* 1979, *apptd* 1983
East Tennessee, Robert G. Tharp, *cons.* 1991, *apptd* 1992
Florida, Stephen Jecko, *cons.* 1994, *apptd* 1994
Georgia, Henry Louttit, *cons.* 1994, *apptd* 1994
Kentucky, Ted Gulick, *cons.* 1964
Lexington, Don A. Wimberley, *cons.* 1984, *apptd* 1985
Louisiana, James B. Brown, *cons.* 1976, *apptd* 1976
Mississippi, Alfred C. Marble jun., *cons.* 1991, *apptd* 1993
North Carolina, Robert Johnson, *cons.* 1994, *apptd* 1994
South Carolina, Edward Salmon jun., *cons.* 1990, *apptd* 1990
South-East Florida, Calvin O. Schofield jun., *cons.* 1979, *apptd*
1980
South-West Florida, Rogers Harris, *cons.* 1989, *apptd* 1989
Tennessee, Bertram N. Herlong, *cons.* 1993, *apptd* 1993
Upper South Carolina, William A. Beckham, *cons.* 1979, *apptd*
1979
West Tennessee, James Coleman, *cons.* 1993
Western North Carolina, Robert Johnson, *cons* 1989, *apptd*
1990

---

*missionary diocese

Province V
Chicago, Frank T. Griswold III, *cons.* 1985, *apptd* 1987
Eau Claire, William C. Wantland, *cons.* 1980, *apptd* 1980
Fond Du Lac, Russell Jacobus, *cons.* 1994, *apptd* 1994
Indianapolis, Edward W. Jones, *cons.* 1977, *apptd* 1977
Michigan, R. Stewart Wood, *cons.* 1990, *apptd* 1990
Milwaukee, Roger J. White, *cons.* 1984, *apptd* 1985
Missouri, Hays Rockwell, *cons.* 1991, *apptd* 1993
Northern Indiana, Francis C. Gray, *cons.* 1986, *apptd* 1987
Northern Michigan, Thomas K. Ray, *cons.* 1982, *apptd* 1982
Ohio, J. Clark Grew, *cons.* 1994, *apptd* 1994
Quincy, Keith L. Ackerman, *cons.* 1994, *apptd* 1994
Southern Ohio, Herbert Thompson jun., *cons.* 1988, *apptd* 1992
Springfield, Peter H. Beckwith, *cons.* 1991
Western Michigan, Edward L. Lee jun., *cons.* 1989, *apptd* 1989

Province VI
Colorado, William Winterrowd, *cons.* 1991, *apptd* 1991
Iowa, C. Christopher Epting, *cons.* 1988, *apptd* 1988
Minnesota, James Jelinek, *cons.* 1993, *apptd* 1993
Montana, Charles I. Jones, *cons.* 1986, *apptd* 1986
Nebraska, James E. Krotz, *cons.* 1989, *apptd* 1989
North Dakota, Andrew H. Fairfield, *cons.* 1990, *apptd* 1990
South Dakota, Creighton Robertson, *cons.* 1994, *apptd* 1994
Wyoming, Bob G. Jones, *cons.* 1977, *apptd* 1977

Province VII
Arkansas, Larry Maze, *cons.* 1994, *apptd* 1994
Dallas, James Stanton, *cons.* 1993, *apptd* 1993
Fort Worth, Jack Iker, *cons.* 1993, *apptd* 1994
Kansas, William E. Smalley, *cons.* 1989, *apptd* 1989
North-West Texas, Sam B. Hulsey, *cons.* 1980, *apptd* 1980
Oklahoma, Robert M. Moodey, *cons.* 1988, *apptd* 1989
Rio Grande, Terence Kelshaw, *cons.* 1989, *apptd* 1989
Texas, Claude Payne, *cons.* 1994
West Missouri, John C. Buchanan, *cons.* 1989, *apptd* 1989
West Texas, John H. MacNaughton, *cons.* 1986, *apptd* 1987
Western Kansas, Vernon Strickland, *cons.* 1995
Western Louisiana, Robert Hargrove, *cons.* 1989, *apptd* 1990

Province VIII
Alaska, Stephen Charleston, *cons.* 1991, *apptd* 1991
Arizona, Robert R. Shahan, *cons.* 1992, *apptd* 1993
California, William E. Swing, *cons.* 1979, *apptd* 1980
El Camino Real, Richard L. Skimpfky, *cons.* 1990, *apptd* 1990
Eastern Oregon, Rustin R. Kimsey, *cons.* 1980, *apptd* 1980
Hawaii (acting), George Hunt
Idaho, John Thornton, *cons.* 1990, *apptd* 1990
Los Angeles, Frederick L. Borsch, *cons.* 1988, *apptd* 1988
Navajoland Area Mission, Steven T. Plummer, *cons.* 1989, *apptd* 1989
Nevada, Stewart C. Zabriskie, *cons.* 1986, *apptd* 1986
Northern California, Jerry A. Lamb, *cons.* 1991, *apptd* 1992
Olympia, Vincent W. Warner, *cons.* 1989, *apptd* 1990
Oregon, Robert L. Ladehoff, *cons.* 1985, *apptd* 1986
San Diego, Gethin B. Hughes, *cons.* 1992, *apptd* 1992
San Joaquin, John-David Schofield, *cons.* 1988, *apptd* 1989
Spokane, Frank Terry, *cons.* 1990, *apptd* 1991
Taiwan, John C. T. Chien, *cons.* 1988, *apptd* 1988
Utah, George E. Bates, *cons.* 1986, *apptd* 1986

Province IX
Central Ecuador, Neptali L. Moreno, *cons.* 1990, *apptd* 1990
Colombia, Bernardo Merino-Botero, *cons.* 1979, *apptd* 1979
Dominican Republic, Julio C. Holguin, *apptd* 1991
Guatemala, Armando Guerra-Soria, *cons.* 1982, *apptd* 1982
Honduras, Leopold Frade, *cons.* 1984, *apptd* 1984
Nicaragua, Sturdie W. Downs, *cons.* 1985, *apptd* 1985

Panama, vacant
El Salvador, Martin Barahona, *cons.* 1992, *apptd* 1992

Extra-Provincial
Costa Rica, Cornelius J. Wilson, *cons.* 1978, *apptd* 1978
Puerto Rico, David Alvarez, *cons.* 1987, *apptd* 1987
Venezuela, Orlando Guerrero, *cons.* 1995

CHURCH OF THE PROVINCE OF WEST AFRICA

ARCHBISHOP OF PROVINCE, The Most Revd Robert Okine (Bishop of Koforidua), *cons.* 1981, *apptd* 1993

THE RT. REVD BISHOPS
Accra, Francis Thompson, *cons.* 1983, *apptd* 1983
Bo, Samuel Gbonda, *cons.* 1994, *apptd* 1994
Cape Coast, Kobina Quashie, *apptd* 1992
Freetown, vacant
Gambia, Solomon Johnson, *cons.* 1990, *apptd* 1990
Guinea, vacant
Koforidua, see above, *apptd* 1981
Kumasi, Edmund Yeboah, *cons.* 1985, *apptd* 1985
Liberia, vacant
Sekondi, Theophilus Annobil, *cons.* 1981, *apptd* 1981
Sunyani/Tamale, Joseph Dadson, *cons.* 1981, *apptd* 1981
The Anglican Church of Cameroon is a missionary area of the Province

CHURCH IN THE PROVINCE OF THE WEST INDIES

ARCHBISHOP OF PROVINCE, The Most Revd Orland Lindsay (Bishop of North-Eastern Caribbean and Aruba), *cons.* 1970, *apptd* 1986

THE RT. REVD BISHOPS
Barbados, Drexel Gomez, CMG, *cons.* 1972, *apptd* 1972
Belize, Sylvestre D. Romero-Palma
Guyana, Randolph George, *cons.* 1976, *apptd* 1980
Jamaica, Neville de Souza, *cons.* 1973, *apptd* 1979
Nassau and the Bahamas, Michael Eldon, CMG, *cons.* 1971, *apptd* 1972
North-Eastern Caribbean and Aruba, see above
Trinidad and Tobago, Clive Abdulah, *cons.* 1970, *apptd* 1970
Windward Islands, Sehon Goodridge

CHURCH OF THE PROVINCE OF ZAÏRE

ARCHBISHOP OF PROVINCE, The Most Revd Byankya Njojo (Bishop of Boga-Zaïre), *cons.* 1980, *apptd* 1992

THE RT. REVD BISHOPS
Boga-Zaïre, see above, *apptd* 1980
Bukavu, Balafuga Dirokpa, *cons.* 1982, *apptd* 1982
Kisangani, Sylvestre Tibafa, *cons.* 1980, *apptd* 1980
Nord-Kivu, Methusela Munzenda, *cons.* 1992, *apptd* 1992
Shaba, Emmanuel Kolini, *cons.* 1980, *apptd* 1980

OTHER CHURCHES AND EXTRA-PROVINCIAL DIOCESES

ANGLICAN CHURCH OF BERMUDA, vacant

EPISCOPAL CHURCH OF CUBA, The Rt. Revd Jorge Perera Hurtado, *apptd* 1995
HONG KONG AND MACAO, The Rt. Revd Peter Kwong
KUCHING, The Rt. Revd Datuk John Leong Chee Yun
SABAH, The Rt. Revd Datuk Yong Ping Chung, *apptd* 1991
SINGAPORE, The Rt. Revd Moses Leng Kong Tay, *apptd* 1982
WEST MALAYSIA, The Rt. Revd Cheng Ean Lim, *apptd* 1995
LUSITANIAN CHURCH (*Portuguese Episcopal Church*), The Rt. Revd Fernando da Luz Soares, *apptd* 1971
SPANISH REFORMED CHURCH, vacant

The Church of Scotland

The Church of Scotland is the established (i.e. state) church of Scotland. The Church is Reformed and evangelical in doctrine, and presbyterian in constitution. In 1560 the jurisdiction of the Roman Catholic Church in Scotland was abolished and the first assembly of the Church of Scotland ratified the Confession of Faith, drawn up by a committee including John Knox. In 1592 Parliament passed an Act guaranteeing the liberties of the Church and its presbyterian government. James VI (James I of England) and later Stuart monarchs attempted to restore episcopacy, but a presbyterian church was finally restored in 1690 and secured by the Act of Settlement (1690) and the Act of Union (1707). The Free Church of Scotland was formed in 1843 in a dispute over patronage and state interference; in 1900 most of its ministers joined with the United Presbyterian Church (formed in 1847) to form the United Free Church of Scotland. In 1929 most of this body rejoined the Church of Scotland to form the united Church of Scotland.

The Church of Scotland is presbyterian in its organization, i.e. based on a hierarchy of councils of ministers and elders and, since 1990, of members of a diaconate. At local level the kirk session consists of the parish minister and ruling elders. At district level the presbyteries, of which there are 47, consist of all the ministers in the district, one ruling elder from each congregation, and those members of the diaconate who qualify for membership. The General Assembly is the supreme authority, and is presided over by a Moderator chosen annually by the Assembly. The Sovereign, if not present in person, is represented by a Lord High Commissioner who is appointed each year by the Crown.

The Church of Scotland has about 753,000 members, 1,260 ministers and 1,700 churches. There are about 100 ministers and other personnel working overseas.

Lord High Commissioner (1995), Lady Fraser
Moderator of the General Assembly (1995), The Rt. Revd J. Harkness
Principal Clerk, The Very Revd J. L. Weatherhead, DD
Deputy Clerk, Revd F. A. J. MacDonald
Procurator, A. Dunlop, QC
Law Agent and Solicitor of the Church, Mrs J. S. Wilson
Parliamentary Agent, I. McCulloch (*London*)
General Treasurer, D. F. Ross
CHURCH OFFICE, 121 George Street, Edinburgh EH2 4YN. Tel: 0131-225 5722

PRESBYTERIES AND CLERKS

Edinburgh, Revd W. P. Graham
West Lothian, Revd D. Shaw
Lothian, J. D. McCulloch
Melrose and Peebles, Revd C. A. Duncan

Duns, Revd A. C. D. Cartwright
Jedburgh, Revd N. R. Combe
Annandale and Eskdale, Revd C. B. Haston
Dumfries and Kirkcudbright, Revd G. M. A. Savage
Wigtown and Stranraer, Revd D. Dutton
Ayr, Revd J. Crichton
Irvine and Kilmarnock, Revd C. G. F. Brockie
Ardrossan, Revd D. Broster
Lanark, Revd I. D. Cunningham
Paisley, Revd J. P. Cubie
Greenock, Revd D. Mill
Glasgow, Revd A. Cunningham
Hamilton, Revd J. H. Wilson
Dumbarton, Revd D. P. Munro
South Argyll, Revd R. H. McNidder
Dunoon, Revd R. Samuel
Lorn and Mull, Revd W. Hogg
Falkirk, Revd D. E. McClements
Stirling, Revd B. W. Dunsmore
Dunfermline, Revd W. E. Farquhar
Kirkcaldy, Revd B. L. Tomlinson
St Andrews, Revd J. W. Patterson
Dunkeld and Meigle, Revd A. F. Chisholm
Perth, Revd D. Main
Dundee, Revd J. A. Roy
Angus, Revd R. J. Ramsay
Aberdeen, Revd H. C. Sefton
Kincardine and Deeside, Revd J. W. S. Brown
Gordon, Revd I. U. Thomson
Buchan, Revd R. Neilson
Moray, Revd J. T. Stuart
Abernethy, Revd J. A. I. MacEwan
Inverness, Revd R. J. V. Logan
Lochaber, Revd A. Ramsay
Ross, Revd R. M. MacKinnon
Sutherland, Revd J. L. Goskirk
Caithness, Revd M. G. Mappin
Lochcarron / Skye, Revd A. I. Macarthur
Uist, Revd G. J. Elliot
Lewis, Revd T. S. Sinclair
Orkney (*Finstown*), Revd T. Hunt
Shetland (*Lerwick*), Revd M. Cheyne
England (*London*), Revd W. A. Cairns
Europe (*Portugal*), Revd R. Hill

The minimum stipend of a minister in the Church of Scotland in 1995 was £14,844

The Roman Catholic Church

The Roman Catholic Church is one world-wide Christian Church acknowledging as its head the Bishop of Rome, known as the Pope (Father). The Pope is held to be the successor of St Peter and thus invested with the power which was entrusted to St Peter by Jesus Christ. A direct line of succession is therefore claimed from the earliest Christian communities. Papal authority over the doctrine and jurisdiction of the Church in western Europe developed early and was unrivalled after the split with the Eastern Orthodox Church until the Protestant Reformation in the 16th century. With the fall of the Roman Empire the Pope also became an important political leader. His temporal power is now limited to the 107 acres of the Vatican City State.

The Pope exercises spiritual authority over the Church with the advice and assistance of the Sacred College of Cardinals, the supreme council of the Church. He is also advised about the concerns of the Church locally by his ambassadors, who liaise with the Bishops' Conference in each country.

In addition to advising the Pope, those members of the Sacred College of Cardinals who are under the age of 80 also elect a successor following the death of a Pope. The assembly of the Cardinals at the Vatican for the election of a new Pope is known as the Conclave in which, in complete seclusion, the Cardinals elect by a secret ballot; a two-thirds majority is necessary before the vote can be accepted as final. When a Cardinal receives the necessary votes, the Dean of the Sacred College formally asks him if he will accept election and the name by which he wishes to be known. On his acceptance of the office the Conclave is dissolved and the First Cardinal Deacon announces the election to the assembled crowd in St Peter's Square. On the first Sunday or Holyday following the election, the new Pope assumes the pontificate at High Mass in St Peter's Square. A new pontificate is dated from the assumption of the pontificate.

The number of cardinals was fixed at 70 by Pope Sixtus V in 1586, but has been steadily increased since the pontificate of John XXIII and now stands at 165 (as at end June 1995).

The Roman Catholic Church universally and the Vatican City State are run by the Curia, which is made up of the Secretariat of State, the Sacred Council for the Public Affairs of the Church, and various congregations, secretariats and tribunals assisted by commissions and offices. The congregations are permanent commissions for conducting the affairs of the Church and are made up of cardinals, one of whom occupies the office of prefect. Below the Secretariat of State and the congregations are the secretariats and tribunals, all of which are headed by cardinals. (The Curial cardinals are analogous to ministers in charge of government departments.)

The Vatican State has its own diplomatic service, with representatives known as nuncios. Papal nuncios with full diplomatic recognition are given precedence over all other ambassadors to the country to which they are appointed; where precedence is not recognized the Papal representative is known as a pro-nuncio. Where the representation is only to the local churches and not to the government of a country, the Papal representative is known as an apostolic delegate. The Roman Catholic Church has an estimated 890.9 million adherents world-wide.

SOVEREIGN PONTIFF

His Holiness Pope John Paul II (Karol Wojtyla), *born* Wadowice, Poland, 18 May 1920; *ordained priest* 1946; *appointed Archbishop* of Krakow 1964; *created Cardinal* 1967; *assumed pontificate* 16 October 1978

SECRETARIAT OF STATE

Secretary of State, HE Cardinal Angelo Sodano
First Section (General Affairs), Mgr G. Re (Archbishop of Vescovio)
Second Section (Relations with other states), Mgr J. L. Tauran (Archbishop of Telepte)

BISHOPS' CONFERENCE

The Roman Catholic Church in England and Wales is governed by the Bishops' Conference, membership of which includes the Diocesan Bishops, the Apostolic Exarch of the Ukrainians, the Bishop of the Forces and the Auxiliary Bishops. The Conference is headed by the President (Cardinal Basil Hume, Archbishop of West-

minster) and Vice-President (the Archbishop of Liverpool). There are five departments, each with an episcopal chairman: the Department for Christian Life and Worship (the Archbishop of Southwark), the Department for Mission and Unity (Bishop Alan Clark), the Department for Catholic Education and Formation (the Bishop of Leeds), the Department for Christian Responsibility and Citizenship (the Bishop of Middlesbrough), and the Department for International Affairs (the Bishop of Salford).

The Bishops' Standing Committee, made up of all the Archbishops and the chairman of each of the above departments, has general responsibility for continuity and policy between the plenary sessions of the Conference. It prepares the Conference agenda and implements its decisions. It is serviced by a General Secretariat. There are also agencies and consultative bodies affiliated to the Conference.

The Bishops' Conference of Scotland has as its president Archbishop Winning of Glasgow and is the permanently constituted assembly of the Bishops of Scotland. To promote its work, the Conference establishes various agencies which have an advisory function in relation to the Conference. The more important of these agencies are called Commissions and each one has a Bishop President who, with the other members of the Commissions, are appointed by the Conference.

The Irish Episcopal Conference has as its acting president Archbishop Connell of Dublin. Its membership comprises all the Archbishops and Bishops of Ireland and it appoints various Commissions to assist it in its work. There are three types of Commissions: (a) those made up of lay and clerical members chosen for their skills and experience, and staffed by full-time expert secretariats; (b) Commissions whose members are selected from existing institutions and whose services are supplied on a part-time basis; and (c) Commissions of Bishops only.

The Roman Catholic Church in Britain and Ireland has an estimated 8,992,092 members, 11 archbishops, 67 bishops, 11,260 priests, and 8,588 churches and chapels open to the public.

Bishops' Conferences secretariats:

ENGLAND AND WALES, 39 Eccleston Square, London SW1V 1PD. Tel: 0171-630 8220. *General Secretary*, The Rt. Revd Philip Carroll

SCOTLAND, Candida Casa, 8 Corsehill Road, Ayr, Scotland KA7 2ST. Tel: 01292-256750. *General Secretary*, The Rt. Revd Maurice Taylor, Bishop of Galloway

IRELAND, Iona, 65 Newry Road, Dundalk, Co. Louth. *Executive Secretary*, Revd Hugh G. Connelly

---

GREAT BRITAIN

APOSTOLIC NUNCIO TO THE UNITED KINGDOM OF GREAT BRITAIN AND NORTHERN IRELAND
The Most Revd Luigi Barbarito, 54 Parkside, London SW19 5NE. Tel: 0181-946 1410

ENGLAND AND WALES

THE MOST REVD ARCHBISHOPS
Westminster, HE Cardinal Basil Hume, *cons.* 1976
 Auxiliaries, Victor Guazzelli, *cons.* 1970; Vincent Nichols, *cons.* 1992; James J. O'Brien, *cons.* 1977; Patrick O'Donoghue, *cons.* 1993
 Clergy, 814
 Archbishop's Residence, Archbishop's House, Ambrosden Avenue, London SW1P 1QJ. Tel: 0171-834 4717

Birmingham, Maurice Couve de Murville, *cons*. 1982, *apptd* 1982
  Auxiliaries, Terence Brain, *cons*. 1991; Philip Pargeter, *cons*. 1989
  Clergy, 475
  Diocesan Curia, Cathedral House, St Chad's Queensway, Birmingham B4 6EX. Tel: 0121-236 5535
Cardiff, John A. Ward, *cons*. 1981, *apptd* 1983
  Clergy, 147
  Diocesan Curia, Archbishop's House, 41–43 Cathedral Road, Cardiff CF1 9HD. Tel: 01222-220411
Liverpool, Derek Worlock, *cons*. 1965, *apptd* 1976 (has retired, but continuing until successor appointed)
  Auxiliaries, John Rawsthorne, *cons*. 1981; Vincent Malone, *cons*. 1989
  Clergy, 493
  Diocesan Curia, 152 Brownlow Hill, Liverpool L3 5RQ. Tel: 0151-709 4801
Southwark, Michael Bowen, *cons*. 1970, *apptd* 1977
  Auxiliaries, Charles Henderson, *cons*. 1972; Howard Tripp, *cons*. 1980; John Jukes, *cons*. 1980
  Clergy, 465
  Diocesan Curia, Archbishop's House, 150 St George's Road, London SE1 6HX. Tel: 0171-928 5592

THE RT. REVD BISHOPS
Arundel and Brighton, Cormac Murphy-O'Connor, *cons*. 1977. *Clergy*, 289. *Diocesan Curia*, Bishop's House, The Upper Drive, Hove, E. Sussex BN3 6NE. Tel: 01273-506387
Brentwood, Thomas McMahon, *cons*. 1980, *apptd* 1980. *Clergy*, 170. *Bishop's Office*, Cathedral House, Ingrave Road, Brentwood, Essex CM15 8AT. Tel: 01277-232266
Clifton, Mervyn Alexander, *cons*. 1972, *apptd* 1975. *Clergy*, 219. *Diocesan Curia*, Egerton Road, Bishopston, Bristol BS7 8HU. Tel: 0117-924 1378
East Anglia, Peter Smith, *cons*. 1995, *apptd* 1995. *Clergy*, 111. *Diocesan Curia*, The White House, 21 Upgate, Poringland, Norwich NR14 7SH. Tel: 01508-492202
Hallam, Gerald Moverley, *cons*. 1968, *apptd* 1980. *Clergy*, 98. *Bishop's Residence*, 'Quarters', Carsick Hill Way, Sheffield S10 3LT. Tel: 0114-230 9101
Hexham and Newcastle, Michael Ambrose Griffiths, *cons*. 1992. *Clergy*, 310. *Diocesan Curia*, Bishop's House, East Denton Hall, 800 West Road, Newcastle upon Tyne NE5 2BJ. Tel: 0191-228 0003
  Auxiliary, Owen Swindelhurst, *cons*. 1977
Lancaster, John Brewer, *cons*. 1971, *apptd* 1985. *Clergy*, 246. *Bishop's Residence*, Bishop's House, Cannon Hill, Lancaster LA1 5NG. Tel: 01524-32231
Leeds, David Konstant, *cons*. 1977, *apptd* 1985. *Clergy*, 263. *Diocesan Curia*, 7 St Marks Avenue, Leeds LS2 9BN. Tel: 0113-244 4788
Menevia (*Wales*), Daniel Mullins, *cons*. 1970, *apptd* 1987. *Clergy*, 61. *Diocesan Curia*, 115 Walter Road, Swansea SA1 5RE. Tel: 01792-644017
Middlesbrough, John Crowley, *cons*. 1986, *apptd* 1992. *Clergy*, 198. *Diocesan Curia*, 50A The Avenue, Linthorpe, Middlesbrough, Cleveland TS5 6QT. Tel: 01642-850505
  Auxiliary, Thomas O'Brien, *cons*. 1981
Northampton, Patrick Leo McCartie, *cons*. 1977, *apptd* 1990. *Clergy*, 136. *Diocesan Curia*, Bishop's House, Marriott Street, Northampton NN2 6AW. Tel: 01604-715635
Nottingham, James McGuinness, *cons*. 1972, *apptd* 1975. *Clergy*, 218. *Diocesan Curia*, Willson House, Derby Road, Nottingham NG1 5AW. Tel: 0115-953 9800
Plymouth, Christopher Budd, *cons*. 1986. *Clergy*, 199. *Diocesan Curia*, Vescourt, Hartley Road, Plymouth PL3 5LR. Tel: 01752-772950

Portsmouth, F. Crispian Hollis, *cons*. 1987, *apptd* 1989. *Clergy*, 260. *Bishop's Residence*, Bishop's House, Edinburgh Road, Portsmouth, Hants PO1 3HG. Tel: 01705-820894
Salford, Patrick Kelly, *cons*. 1984. *Clergy*, 403. *Diocesan Curia*, Cathedral House, 250 Chapel Street, Salford M3 5LL. Tel: 0161-834 9052
Shrewsbury, Brian Noble, *cons*. 1995, *apptd* 1995. *Clergy*, 204. *Diocesan Curia*, 2 Park Road South, Birkenhead, Merseyside L43 4UX. Tel: 0151-652 9855
Wrexham (*Wales*), Edwin Regan, *apptd* 1994. *Clergy*, 85. *Diocesan Curia*, Bishop's House, Sontley Road, Wrexham, Clwyd LL13 7EW. Tel: 01978-262726

SCOTLAND

THE MOST REVD ARCHBISHOPS
St Andrews and Edinburgh, Keith Patrick O'Brian, *cons*. 1985
  Auxiliary, Kevin Rafferty, *cons*. 1990
  Clergy, 201
  Diocesan Curia, 106 Whitehouse Loan, Edinburgh EH9 1BD. Tel: 0131-452 8244
Glasgow, HE Cardinal Thomas Winning, *cons*. 1971, *apptd* 1974
  Clergy, 303
  Diocesan Curia, 196 Clyde Street, Glasgow G1 4JY. Tel: 0141-226 5898

THE RT. REVD BISHOPS
Aberdeen, Mario Conti, *cons*. 1977. *Clergy*, 58. *Bishop's Residence*, 156 King's Gate, Aberdeen AB2 6BR. Tel: 01224-319154
Argyll and the Isles, Roderick Wright, *cons*. 1990. *Clergy*, 32. *Diocesan Curia*, St Mary's, Belford Road, Fort William, Inverness-shire PH33 6BT. Tel: 01397-706046
Dunkeld, Vincent Logan, *cons*. 1981. *Clergy*, 55. *Diocesan Curia*, 26 Roseangle, Dundee DD1 4LR. Tel: 01382-25453
Galloway, Maurice Taylor, *cons*. 1981. *Clergy*, 66. *Diocesan Curia*, 8 Corsehill Road, Ayr KA7 2ST. Tel: 01292-266750
Motherwell, Joseph Devine, *cons*. 1977, *apptd* 1983. *Clergy*, 180. *Diocesan Curia*, Coursington Road, Motherwell ML1 1PW. Tel: 01698-269114
Paisley, John A. Mone, *cons*. 1984, *apptd* 1988. *Clergy*, 95. *Diocesan Curia*, Cathedral House, 8 East Buchanan Street, Paisley, Renfrewshire PA1 1HS. Tel: 0141-889 3601

IRELAND

There is one hierarchy for the whole of Ireland. Several of the dioceses have territory partly in the Republic of Ireland and partly in Northern Ireland.

APOSTOLIC NUNCIO TO IRELAND
  The Most Revd Emanuele Gerada (titular Archbishop of Nomenta), 183 Navan Road, Dublin 7. Tel: 00 353 1-380577

THE MOST REVD ARCHBISHOPS
Armagh, HE Cardinal Cahal B. Daly, *cons*. 1990
  Coadjutor, Sean Brady
  Auxiliary, Gerard Clifford, *cons*. 1991
  Clergy, 183
  Diocesan Curia, Ara Coeli, Armagh BT61 7QY. Tel: 01861-522045
Cashel, Dermot Clifford, *cons*. 1986
  Clergy, 136
  Archbishop's Residence, Archbishop's House, Thurles, Co. Tipperary. Tel: 00 353 504-21512
Dublin, Desmond Connell, *cons*. 1988, *apptd* 1988
  Auxiliaries, Donal Murray, *cons*. 1982; Dermot O'Mahony, *cons*. 1975; James Moriarty, *cons*. 1992;

Eamonn Walsh, *cons.* 1990; Desmond Williams, *cons.*
1985; Fiachra O'Ceallaigh, *cons* 1994
Clergy, 994
Archbishop's Residence, Archbishop's House, Drumcondra,
Dublin 9. Tel: 00 353 1-8373732
Tuam, Michael Neary, *cons.* 1992
Clergy, 180
Archbishop's Residence, Archbishop's House, Tuam, Co.
Galway. Tel: 00 353 93-24166

THE MOST REVD BISHOPS
Achonry, Thomas Flynn, *cons.* 1975. *Clergy*, 62. *Bishop's
Residence*, Bishop's House, Ballaghadaderreen, Co.
Roscommon. Tel: 00 353 907-60021
Ardagh and Clonmacnois, Colm O'Reilly, *cons.* 1983.
Clergy, 100. *Diocesan Office*, Bishop's House, St Michael's,
Longford, Co. Longford. Tel: 00 353 43-46432
Clogher, Joseph Duffy, *cons.* 1979. *Clergy*, 108. *Bishop's
Residence*, Bishop's House, Monaghan. Tel: 00 353 47-
81019
Clonfert, Joseph Kirby, *cons.* 1988. *Clergy*, 71. *Bishop's
Residence*, St Brendan's, Coorheen, Loughrea, Co.
Galway. Tel: 00 353 91-41560
Cloyne, John Magee, *cons.* 1987. *Clergy*, 158. *Diocesan Centre*,
Cobh, Co. Cork. Tel: 00 353 21-811430
Cork and Ross, Michael Murphy, *cons.* 1976. *Clergy*, 338.
Diocesan Office, Bishop's House, Redemption Road,
Cork. Tel: 00 353 21-301717
Auxiliary, John Buckley, *cons.* 1984
Derry, Seamus Hegarty, *cons.* 1984, *apptd* 1994. *Clergy*, 157.
Bishop's Residence, Bishop's House, St Eugene's
Cathedral, Derry BT48 9AP. Tel: 01504-262302
Auxiliary, Francis Lagan, *cons.* 1988
Down and Connor, Patrick J. Walsh, *cons.* 1991. *Clergy*, 248.
Bishop's Residence, Lisbreen, 73 Somerton Road, Belfast,
Co. Antrim DT15 4DE. Tel: 01232-776185
Auxiliaries, Anthony Farquhar, *cons.* 1983; William
Philbin, *cons.* 1991; Michael Dallat, *cons.* 1994
Dromore, Francis Brooks, *cons.* 1976. *Clergy*, 78. *Bishop's
Residence*, Bishop's House, Violet Hill, Newry, Co. Down
BT35 6PN. Tel: 01693-62444
Elphin, Christopher Jones, *cons.* 1994. *Clergy*, 101. *Bishop's
Residence*, St Mary's, Sligo. Tel: 00 353 71-62670
Ferns, Brendon Comiskey, *cons.* 1980. *Clergy*, 161. *Bishop's
Office*, Bishop's House, Summerhill, Wexford. Tel:
00 353 53-22177
Galway and Kilmacduagh, James McLoughlin, *cons.* 1993.
Clergy, 90. *Diocesan Office*, The Cathedral, Galway. Tel:
00 353 91-63566
Kerry, William Murphy, *cons.* 1995. *Clergy*, 149. *Bishop's
Residence*, Bishop's House, Killarney, Co. Kerry. Tel:
00 353 64-31168
Kildare and Leighlin, Laurence Ryan, *cons.* 1984. *Clergy*, 136.
Bishop's Residence, Bishop's House, Carlow. Tel:
00 353 503-31102
Killala, Thomas Finnegan, *cons.* 1970. *Clergy*, 62. *Bishop's
Residence*, Bishop's House, Ballina, Co. Mayo. Tel:
00 353 96-21518
Killaloe, William Walsh, *cons.* 1994. *Clergy*, 149. *Bishop's
Residence*, Westbourne, Ennis, Co. Clare. Tel: 00 353 65-
28638
Kilmore, Francis McKiernan, *cons.* 1972. *Clergy*, 115. *Bishop's
Residence*, Bishop's House, Cullies, Co. Cavan. Tel:
00 353 49-31496
Limerick, Jeremiah Newman, *cons.* 1974. *Clergy*, 152. *Diocesan
Offices*, 66 O'Connell Street, Limerick. Tel: 00 353 61-
315856
Meath, Michael Smith, *cons.* 1984, *apptd* 1990. *Clergy*, 141.
Bishop's Residence, Bishop's House, Dublin Road,
Mullingar, Co. Westmeath. Tel: 00 353 44-48841

Ossory, Laurence Forristal, *cons.* 1980. *Clergy*, 111. *Bishop's
Residence*, Sion House, Kilkenny. Tel: 00 353 56-62448
Raphoe, Philip Boyce, *cons.* 1994. *Clergy*, 96. *Bishop's Residence*,
Ard Adhamhnáin, Letterkenny, Co. Donegal. Tel:
00 353 74-21208
Waterford and Lismore, William Lee, *cons.* 1993. *Clergy*, 130.
Bishop's Residence, Woodleigh, Summerville Avenue,
Waterford. Tel: 00 353 51-71432

RESIDENTIAL ARCHBISHOPRICS THROUGHOUT THE WORLD

ALBANIA
Durrës-Tirana, Brok K. Mirdita
Shkodër, Frano Illia

ALGERIA
Algiers, Henri Teissier

ANGOLA
Huambo, Francisco Viti
Luanda, HE Cardinal Alexandre do Nascimento
Lubango, Manuel Franklin da Costa
  Coadjutor, Zacarias Kamwenho

ARGENTINA
Bahia Blanca, Romulo Garcia
Buenos Aires, HE Cardinal Antonio Quarracino
Córdoba, HE Cardinal Raúl Francisco Primatesta
Corrientes, Domingo S. Castagna
La Plata, Carlos Galán
Mendoza, Candido Genaro Rubiolo
  Coadjutor, Jose M. Arancibia
Paraná, Estanislao Esteban Karlic
Resistencia, Carmelo J. Giaquinta
Rosario, Eduardo Vicente Miras
Salta, Moises J. Blanchoud
San Juan de Cuyo, Italo Severino Di Stefano
Santa Fe, Edgardo Gabriel Storni
Tucumán, Arsenio R. Casado

AUSTRALIA
Adelaide, Leonard Anthony Faulkner
Brisbane, John A. Bathersby
Canberra, Francis P. Carroll
Hobart, Joseph E. D'Arcy
Melbourne, Thomas Francis Little
Perth, Barry J. Hickey
Sydney, HE Cardinal Edward B. Clancy

AUSTRIA
Salzburg, Georg Eder
Vienna, Christoph Schoenborn

BANGLADESH
Dhaka, Michael Rozario

BELARUS
Minsk-Mohilev Archdiocese, HE Cardinal Kazimierz Swiatek

BELGIUM
Malines-Bruxelles, HE Cardinal Godfried Danneels

BENIN
Cotonou, Isidore de Souzá

BOLIVIA
Cochabamba, Rene Fernandez Apaza
La Paz, Luis Sainz Hinojosa
Santa Cruz de la Sierra, Julio T. Sandoval
Sucre, Jesus G. Pérez Rodriguez

BOSNIA HERCEGOVINA
Vrhbosna, Sarajevo, HE Cardinal Vinko Puljić

BRAZIL
Aparacida, Geraldo Maria de Morais Penido
Aracaju, Luciano José Cabral Duarte
Bélem do Pará, Vicente Joaquim Zico
Belo Horizonte, Serafim Fernandes de Araújo
Botucatu, Antonio M. Mucciolo
Brasilia, HE Cardinal Jose Freire Falcao
Campinas, Gilberto Pereira Lopes
Campo Grande, Vitorio Pavanello
Cascavel, Armando Cirio
Cuiaba, Bonifacio Piccinini
Curitiba, Pedro Antonio Fedalto
Diamantina, Geraldo Majelo Reis
Florianópolis, Eusebio Oscar Scheid
Fortaleza, HE Cardinal Aloisio Lorscheider
Goiania, Antonio Ribeiro de Oliveira
Juiz de Fora, Clovis Frainer
Londrina, Albano Bortoletto Cavallin
Maceió, Edvaldo G. Amaral
Manaus, Luiz S. Vieira
Mariana, Luciano Mendes de Almeida
Maringá, Jaime Luis Coelho
Natal, Heitor de Araujo Sales
Niteroi, Carlos A. Navarro
Olinda and Recife, José Cardoso Sobrinho
Paraiba, José M. Pires
Porto Alegre, Altamiro Rossato
Porto Velho, José Martins da Silva
Pouso Alegre, João Bergese
Ribeirão Preto, Arnaldo Ribeiro
São Luis do Maranhão, Paulo Eduardo de Andrade Ponte
São Paulo, HE Cardinal Paulo Evaristo Arns
São Salvador da Bahia, HE Cardinal Lucas Moreira Neves
São Sebastião do Rio de Janeiro, HE Cardinal Eugenio de Araújo Sales
Sorocaba, José Lambert
Teresina, Miguel F. Camara Filho
Uberaba, Benedito de Ulhôa Vieira
Vitória, Silvestre L. Scandian

BURKINA
Ouagadougou, HE Cardinal Paul Zoungrana

BURUNDI
Gitega, Joachim Ruhuna

CAMEROON
Bamenda, Paul Verdzekov
Douala, HE Cardinal Christian W. Tumi
Garoua, Antoine Ntalou
Yaoundé, Jean Zoa

CANADA
Edmonton, Joseph N. MacNeil
Gatineau-Hull, Roger Ebacher
Grouard-McLennon, Henri Légaré
Halifax, Austin-Emile Burke
Keewatin-Le Pas, Peter Alfred Sutton
Kingston, Francis John Spence
Moncton, Donat Chiasson
Montreal, HE Cardinal Jean-Claude Turcotte
Ottawa, Marcel A. Gervais
Quebec, Maurice Couture
Regina, Peter Mallon
Rimouski, Bertrand Blanchet
St Boniface, Antoine Hacault
St Johns, Newfoundland, James H. MacDonald
Sherbrooke, Jean Marie Fortier
  Coadjutor, Andre Gaumond

Toronto, Aloysius Matthew Ambrosic
Vancouver, Adam J. Exner
Winnipeg, Leonard J. Wall; (Ukrainian rite), Michael Bzdel

CAUCASIA
Caucasia Apostolic Administrator, Jean-Paul Gobel

CENTRAL AFRICAN REPUBLIC
Bangui, Joachim N'Dayen

CHAD
Ndjamena, Charles Vandame

CHILE
Antofagasta, Patricio Infante Alfonso
Concepción, Antonio M. Casamitjana
La Serena, Francisco J. Cox Huneeus
Puerto Montt, Savino B. Cazzaro Bertollo
Santiago de Chile, HE Cardinal Carlos Oviedo Cavada

CHINA
Anking, Huai-Ning, vacant
Canton, vacant
Changsha, vacant
Chungking, vacant
Foochow, Min-Hou, vacant
Hangchow, vacant
Hankow, vacant
Kaifeng, vacant
Kunming, vacant
Kweyang, vacant
Lanchow, vacant
Mukden, vacant
Nanchang, vacant
Nanking, vacant
Nanning, vacant
Peking (Beijing), vacant
Sian, vacant
Suiyüan, Francis Wang Hsueh-Ming
Taiyuan, vacant
Tsinan, vacant

COLOMBIA
Barranquilla, Felix Maria Torres Parra
Bogotá, Pedro Rubiano Sáenz
Bucaramanga, Dario Castrillon Hoyos
Cali, vacant
Cartagena, Carlos José Ruiseco Vieira
Ibague, Juan S. Jaramillo
Manizales, José de Jesús Pimiento Rodriguez
Medellin, Hector Rueda Hernández
Nueva Pamplona, Victor M. Lopez Forero
Popayán, Alberto G. Jaramillo
Santa Fe de Antioquia, Ignacio Gomez Afistizabal
Tunja, Augusto Trujillo Arango

CONGO
Brazzaville, Barthélémy Batantu

COSTA RICA
San José, Román Arrieta Villalobos

CÔTE D'IVOIRE
Abidjan, Bernard Agre
Bouake, Vital Komenan Yao
Gagnoa, Noel Kokora-Tekry
Kornogo, Auguste Nobou

CROATIA
Rijeka-Senj, Anton Tamarut
Split-Makarska, Ante Juric
Zadar, Marijan Oblak
Zagreb, HE Cardinal Franjo Kuharić

CUBA
San Cristóbal de la Habana, HE Cardinal Jaime Lucas Ortega
  y Alamino
Santiago de Cuba, Pedro Meurice Estiu

CYPRUS
Cyprus (Maronite seat at Nicosia), Boutros Gemayel

CZECH REPUBLIC
Olomouc, Jan Graubner
Prague, HE Cardinal Miloslav Vlk

DOMINICAN REPUBLIC
Santiago de los Caballeros, Juan A. F. Santana
Santo Domingo, HE Cardinal Nicolás de Jesús López
  Rodriguez

ECUADOR
Cuenca, Alberto Luna Tobar
Guayaquil, Ignacio Larrea Holguin
Quito, Antonio J. González Zumárraga

EQUATORIAL GUINEA
Malabo, Idlefonso Obama Obono

ETHIOPIA
Addis Ababa, HE Cardinal Paul Tzadua

FRANCE
Aix, Louis-Marie Bille
Albi, Roger Meindre
Auch, Gabriel Vanel
Avignon, Raymond Bouchex
Besançon, Lucien Daloz
Bordeaux, Pierre Eyt
Bourges, Pierre Plateau
Cambrai, Jacques Delaporte
Chambéry, Claude Feidt
Lyon, Jean Balland
Marseilles, Bernard Panafieu
Paris, HE Cardinal J. M. Lustiger
Reims, vacant
Rennes, Jacques Jullien
Rouen, Joseph Duval
Sens, Gérard Defois
Strasbourg, Charles Amarin Brand
Toulouse, André Collini
Tours, Jean Honoré

FRENCH POLYNESIA
Papeete, Michel Coppenrath

GABON
Libreville, André Fernand Anguilé

GERMANY
Bamberg, Karl Braun
Berlin, HE Cardinal George M. Sterzinsky
Cologne, HE Cardinal Joachim Meisner
Freiburg im Breisgau, Oskar Saier
Munich and Freising, HE Cardinal Friedrich Wetter
Paderborn, Johannes Joachim Degenhardt

GHANA
Accra, Dominic K. Andoh
Cape Coast, Peter Kodwo A. Turkson
Tamale, Gregory E. Kpiebaya

GREECE
Athens, Nicholaos Foscolos
Corfu, Antonio Varthalitis
Naxos, Nicolaos Printesis
Rhodes, vacant (Apostolic Administrator, Nicholaos
  Foscolos)

GUATEMALA
Guatemala, Prospero Penados del Barrio

GUINEA
Conakry, Robert Sarah

HAITI
Cap-Haitien, François Gayot
Port au Prince, François-Wolff Ligondé

HONDURAS
Tegucigalpa, Oscar A. Maradiaga

HONG KONG
Hong Kong, HE Cardinal J. B. Wu Cheng Chung

HUNGARY
Eger, Istvan Seregely
Esztergom, HE Cardinal Laslo Paskai
Kalocsa, Laszlo Danko

INDIA
Agra, Cecil de Sa
Bangalore, Alphonsus Mathias
Bhopal, Paschal Topno
Bombay, HE Cardinal I. Pimenta
Calcutta, Henry Sebastian D'Souza
Changanacherry, Joseph Powathil
Cuttack-Bhubaneswar, Raphael Cheenath
Delhi, Alan de Lastic
Ernakulam, HE Cardinal Anthony Padiyara
Goa and Daman, Raul Nicolau Gonsalves
Hyderabad, Saminini Arulappa
Madras and Mylapore, James M. Arul Das
Madurai, Marianus Arokiasamy
Nagpur, Leobard D'Souza
Pondicherry and Cuddalore, Michael Augustine
Ranchi, Telesphore P. Toppo
Shillong-Gauhati, vacant
Trivandrum (Syrian Melekite rite), vacant
Verapoly, Cornelius Elanjikal

INDONESIA
Ende, Donatus Djagom
Jakarta, Leo Soekoto
Kupang, Gregorius Manteiro
Medan, Alfred Gonti Pius Datubara
Merauke, Jacobus Duivenvoorde
Pontianak, Hieronymus Herculanus Bumbun
Semarang, HE Cardinal Julius R. Darmaatmadja
Ujung Pandang, Johannes Liku Ada'

IRAN
Ahváz, Hanna Zora
Tehran, Youhannan Semaan Issayi
Urmyã, Thomas Meram

IRAQ
Arbil, Hanna Markho
Baghdad (Latin rite), Paul Dahdah; (Syrian rite), Athanase
  M. S. Matoka; (Armenian rite), Paul Coussa
Basra, Yousif Thomas
Kirkuk, André Sana
Mosul (Chaldean rite), Georges Garmo; (Syrian rite),
  Cyrille E. Benni

ISRAEL (*see also* Patriarchs, page 423)
Akka (Greek Melekite Catholic rite), Maximos Salloum

ITALY
Acerenza, Michele Scandiffio
Amalfi, Beniamino De Palma
Ancona, Franco Festorazzi
Bari, Mariano Magrassi
Benevento, Serafino Sprovieri

Bologna, HE Cardinal Giacomo Biffi
Brindisi, Settimio Todisco
Cagliari, Otterino Pietro Alberti
Camerino, Piergiorgio Nesti
Campobasso-Boiano, Ettore Di Filippo
Capua, Luigi Diligenza
Catania, Luigi Bommarito
Catanzaro, Antonio Cantisani
Chieti, Edoardo Menichelli
Conza, Mario Milano
Cosenza, Dino Trabalzini
Crotone-Santa Severina, Giuseppe Agostino
Fermo, Cleto Bellucci
Ferrara, Luigi Maverna
Florence, HE Cardinal Silvano Piovanelli
Foggia, Giuseppe Casale
Gaeta, Vincenzo Farano
Genoa, Dionigi Tettamanzi
Gorizia and Gradisca, Antonio Vitale Bommarco
Lanciano, Enzio d'Antonio
L'Aquila, Mario Peressin
Lecce, Cosmo F. Ruppi
Lucca, Bruno Tommasi
Manfredonia, Vincenzo D'Addario
Matera, Antonio Ciliberti
Messina, Ignazio Cannavó
Milan, HE Cardinal Carlo Maria Martini
Modena, Santo B. Quadri
Monreale, Salvatore Cassisa
Naples, HE Cardinal Michele Giordano
Oristano, Pier Luigi Tiddia
Otranto, Francesco Cacucci
Palermo, HE Cardinal Salvatore Pappalardo
Perugia, Ennio Antonelli
Pescara-Penne, Francesco Cuccarese
Pisa, Alessandro Plotti
Potenza, Ennio Appignanesi
Ravenna, Luigi Amaducci
Reggio Calabria, Vittorio L. Mondello
Rossano-Cariati, Andrea Cassone
Salerno, Gerardo Pierro
Sassari, Salvatore Isgrò
Siena, Gaetano Bonicelli
Siracusa, Giuseppe Costanzo
Sorrento, Felice Cece
Spoleto, vacant
Taranto, Luigi Papa
Trani and Barletta, Carmelo Cassati
Trento, Giovanni Sartori
Turin, HE Cardinal Giovanni Saldarini
Udine, Alfredo Battisti
Urbino, Donato U. Bianchi
Vercelli, Tarcisio Bertone

JAMAICA
Kingston, Edgerton R. Clarke

JAPAN
Nagasaki, Francis Xavier Shimamoto
Osaka, Paul Hisao Yasuda
Tokyo, HE Cardinal Peter Seiichi Shirayanagi

JORDAN
Petra and Filadelfia (Greek Melekite Catholic rite), George
  El-Murr

KAZAKHSTAN
Karaganda Apostolic Administration (Latin rite), Apostolic
  Administrator, Mgr Jan Lenga (titular Bishop of Arba)

KENYA
Kisumu, Zaccharus Okoth

Mombasa, John Njenga
Nairobi, HE Cardinal Maurice Otunga
Nyeri, Nicodemus Kirima

KOREA
Kwangju, Victorinus Kong-Hi Youn
Seoul, HE Cardinal Stephen Sou Hwan Kim
Taegu, Paul Moun-Hi Ri

LATVIA
Riga, Jānis Pujats

LEBANON
Antelias (Maronite rite), Joseph Mohsen Bechara
Baalbek, Eliopoli (Greek Melekite Catholic rite), Salim
  Bustros
Baniyas (Greek Melekite Catholic rite), Antoine Hayek
Beirut (Greek Melekite Catholic rite), Habib Bacha;
  (Maronite rite), Khalil Abinader
Saida (Greek Melekite Catholic rite), Georges Kwaiter
Tripoli (Maronite rite), Gabriel Toubia; (Greek Melekite
  Catholic rite), Elias Nijmé
Tyre (Greek Melekite Catholic rite), Jean A. Haddad;
  (Maronite rite), Maroun Sader
Zahle and Furzol (Greek Melekite Catholic rite), Andre
  Haddad

LESOTHO
Maseru, Bernard Mohlalisi

LIBERIA
Monrovia, Michael Kpakala Francis

LITHUANIA
Kaunas, HE Cardinal Vincentas Sladkevicius
Vilnius, Audris J. Bačkis

LUXEMBOURG
Luxembourg, Fernand Franck

MADAGASCAR
Antananarive, HE Cardinal Armand G. Razafindratandra
Antsiranana, Albert Joseph Tsiahoana
Fianarantsoa, Philibert Randriambololona

MALAWI
Blantyre, James Chiona

MALAYSIA
Kuala Lumpur, Anthony S. Fernandez
Kuching, Peter Chung Hoan Ting

MALI
Bamako, Luc Auguste Sangaré

MALTA
Malta, Joseph Mercieca

MARTINIQUE
Fort de France, Maurice Marie-Sainte

MEXICO
Acapulco, Rafael Bello Ruiz
Antequera, Hector G. Martinez
Chihuahua, José Fernández Arteaga
Durango, José M. Perez
Guadalajara, HE Cardinal Juan Sandoval Iniguez
Hermosillo, Carlos Quintero Arce
Jalapa, Sergio Obeso Rivera
Mexico City, Norberto R. Carrera
Monterrey, HE Cardinal Adolfo Suarez Rivera
Morelia, Alberto S. Inda
Puebla de los Angeles, Rosendo Huesca Pacheco
San Luis Potosi, Arturo A. Szymanski Ramirez
Tlalnepantla, Manuel P. Gil Gonzalez
Yucatán, Emilio C. B. Belaunzaran

MONACO
Monaco, Joseph-Marie Sardou

MOROCCO
Rabat, Hubert Michon
Tangier, Antonio J. Peteiro Freire

MOZAMBIQUE
Beira, Jaime P. Goncalves
Maputo, HE Cardinal Alexandre José Maria dos Santos
Nampula, Manuel Vieira Pinto

MYANMAR (BURMA)
Mandalay, Alphonse U. Than Aung
Yangon (Rangoon), Gabriel Thohey Mahn Gaby

NAMIBIA
Windhoek, Bonifatius Haushiku

NETHERLANDS
Utrecht, HE Cardinal Adrianus J. Simonis

NEW ZEALAND
Wellington, HE Cardinal Thomas Stafford Williams

NICARAGUA
Managua, HE Cardinal Miguel Obando Bravo

NIGERIA
Jos, Gabriel G. Ganaka
Kaduna, Peter Yariyok Jatau
Lagos, Anthony Okogie
Onitsha, Albert K. Obiefuna

OCEANIA
Agaña, Anthony Sablan Apuron
Honiara, Adrian Thomas Smith
Nouméa, Michel-Marie-Bernard Calvet
Papeete, Michel-Gaspard Copenrath
Samoa, Apia and Tokelau, HE Cardinal Pio Taofino'u
Suva, Petero Mataca

PAKISTAN
Karachi, Simeon Pereira

PANAMA
Panama, Jose Dimas C. Delgado

PAPUA NEW GUINEA
Madang, Benedict To Varpin
Mount Hagen, Michael Meier
Port Moresby, Peter Kurongku
Rabaul, Karl Hesse

PARAGUAY
Asuncion, Felipe Santiago B. Avalos

PERU
Arequipa, Fernando Vargas Ruiz de Somocurcio
Ayacucho o Huamanga, Juan L. C. Thorne
Cuzco, Alcides Mendoza Castro
Huancayo, vacant
Lima, Augusto Vargas Alzamora
Piura, Oscar Rolando Cantuarias Pastor
Trujillo, Manuel Prado Pérez-Rosas

PHILIPPINES
Caceres, Leonardo Legazpi
Cagayan de Oro, Jesus B. Tuquib
Capiz, Onesimo C. Gordoncillo
Cebu, HE Cardinal Ricardo Vidal
Cotabato, Philip Frances Smith
Davao, Antonio Mabutas
Jaro, Alberto J. Piamonte
Lingayen-Dagupan, Oscar V. Cruz
Lipa, Gaudencio B. Rosales
Manila, HE Cardinal Jaime L. Sin

Nueva Segovia, Orlando Quevedo
Ozamiz, Jesus Dosado
Palo, Pedro R. Dean
San Fernando, Paciano Aniceto
Tuguegarao, Diosdado A. Talamayan
Zamboanga, Carmelo D. F. Morelos

POLAND
Bialystok, Stanislaw Szymecki
Czestochowa, Stanislaw Nowak
Gdańsk, Tadeusz Goclowski
Gniezno, Henryk Muszyński
Katowice, Damian Zimoń
Kraków, HE Cardinal Franciszek Macharski
Lodz, Wladyslaw Ziolek
Lublin, Boleslaw Pylak
Poznań, Jerzy Stroba
Przemyśl of the Latins, Jozef Michalik
Szczecin-Kamień, Marian Przykucki
Warmia, Edmund Piszcz
Warsaw, HE Cardinal Józef Glemp
Wroclaw, HE Cardinal Henryk Roman Gulbinowicz

PORTUGAL
Braga, Eurico Dias Nogueira
Evora, Maurilio Jorge Quintal de Gouveia

PUERTO RICO
San Juan, HE Cardinal Luis Aponte Martinez

ROMANIA
Alba Julia (Latin rite), Gyorgy-Miklos Jakubinyi
Bucaręsti, Ioan Robu
Fagaras and Alba Julia (Romanian Byzantine rite), Lucian Muresan

RUSSIA
Moscow Apostolic Administration (covering European Russia), Apostolic Administrator, Archbishop Tadeusz Kondrusiewicz
Novosibirsk Apostolic Administration (covering Siberia), Apostolic Administrator, Mgr Joseph Werth, SJ (titular Bishop of Bulna)

RWANDA
Kigali, vacant

ST LUCIA
Castries, Kelvin E. Felix

EL SALVADOR
San Salvador, Fernando S. Lacalle

SENEGAL
Dakar, HE Cardinal Hyacinthe Thiandoum

SIERRA LEONE
Freetown and Bo, Joseph Ganda

SINGAPORE
Singapore, Gregory Yong Sooi Ngean

SLOVAK REPUBLIC
Trnava, Jan Sokol

SLOVENIA
Ljubljana, Alojzij Suštar

SOUTH AFRICA
Bloemfontein, Peter John Butelezi
Cape Town, Lawrence Patrick Henry
Durban, Wilfrid Fox Napier
Pretoria, George Francis Daniel

SPAIN
Barcelona, Ricardo Maria Carles Gordó
Burgos, Santiago Martinez Acebes

Granada, José Méndez Asensio
Madrid, Antonio M. Rouco Varela
Oviedo, Gabino Diaz Merchán
Pamplona, Fernando S. Aquilar
Santiago de Compostela, vacant
Sevilla, Carlos Amigo Vallejo
Tarragona, Ramon Torrella Cascante
Toledo, Francisco A. Martinez
Valencia, Agustin Garcia-Gasco Vicente
Valladolid, José Delicado Baeza
Zaragoza, Eliaz Yanez Alvarez

SRI LANKA
Colombo, Nicholas Marcus Fernando

SUDAN
Juba, Paulino Lukudu Loro
Khartoum, Gabriel Zubeir Wako

SYRIA
Alep, Beroea, Halab (Greek Melekite Catholic rite), vacant;
    (Syrian rite), Raboula A. Beylouni; (Maronite rite),
    Pierre Callaos; (Armenian rite), Boutros Marayati
Baniyas (Greek Melekite Catholic rite), Antoine Hayek
Bosra, Bostra, Boulos Nassif Borkhoche
Damascus (Greek Melekite Catholic rite), S. B. Maximos
    V. Hakim; (Syrian rite), Eustache J. Mounayer;
    (Maronite rite), Hamid A. Mourany
Hassaké-Nisibi, Georges Habib Hafouri
Homs, Emesa (Greek Melekite Catholic rite), Abraham
    Nehmé; (Syrian Catholic rite), Basile Daoud
Laodicea (Greek Melekite Catholic rite), Michel Yatim

TAIWAN
Taipei, Joseph Ti-Kang

TANZANIA
Dar es Salaam, Polycarp Pengo
Mwanza, Antony Mayala
Songea, Norbert W. Mtega
Tabora, Mario E. A. Mgulunde

THAILAND
Bangkok, HE Cardinal Michael Michai Kitbunchu
Tharé and Nonseng, Lawrence Khai Saen-Phon-On

TOGO
Lomé, Philippe F. K. Kpodzro

TRINIDAD
Port of Spain, Gordon Anthony Pantin

TURKEY
Diarbekir, Paul Karatas
Istanbul (Constantinople), Jean Tcholakian
Izmir, Giuseppe G. Bernardini

UGANDA
Kampala, HE Cardinal Emmanuel Wamala

UKRAINE
Lvov (Latin rite), Marian Jaworski (Archbishop of Lvov of
    the Latins); (Ukrainian rite), HE Cardinal Myroslav
    I. Lubachivsky (Major Archbishop of Lvov of the
    Ukrainians)

URUGUAY
Montevideo, José Gottardi Cristelli

USA
Anchorage, Francis Thomas Hurley
Atlanta, John F. Donoghue
Baltimore, HE Cardinal William Henry Keeler
Boston, HE Cardinal Bernard F. Law
Chicago, HE Cardinal Joseph L. Bernardin
Cincinnati, Daniel E. Pilarczyk

Denver, James Francis Stafford
Detroit, Adam J. Maida
Dubuque, Daniel W. Kucera
Hartford, Daniel A. Cronin
Indianapolis, Daniel Mark Buechlein
Kansas City, James P. Keleher
Los Angeles, HE Cardinal Roger M. Mahony
Louisville, Thomas C. Kelly
Miami, John C. Favalora
Milwaukee, Rembert G. Weakland
Mobile, Oscar H. Lipscomb
Newark, Theodore E. McCarrick
New Orleans, Francis B. Schulte
New York, HE Cardinal John J. O'Connor
Oklahoma City, Eusebius Joseph Beltran
Omaha, Elden Curtiss
Philadelphia, HE Cardinal Anthony J. Bevilacqua;
    (Ukrainian rite), Stephen Sulyk
Pittsburgh (Byzantine rite), Judson M. Procyk
Portland (Oregon), William J. Levada
St Louis (Missouri), Justin F. Rigali
St Paul and Minneapolis, John Robert Roach
San Antonio, Patrick F. Flores
San Francisco, John R. Quinn
Santa Fe, Michael Sheehan
Seattle, Thomas J. Murphy
Washington, HE Cardinal James A. Hickey

VENEZUELA
Barquisimeto, Julio Manuel Chirivella Varela
Calabozo, Helimenas de J. R. Paredes
Caracas, Ignacio A. V. Garcia
Ciudad Bolivar, Medardo Luzardo Romero
Cumana, Alfredo J. R. Figueroa
Maracaibo, Ramon O. Perez Morales
Mérida, Baltazar P. Cardozo
Valencia, Jorge Liberato Urosa Savino

VIETNAM
Hanoi, HE Cardinal Paul Joseph Pham Dinh Tung
Hue Apostolic Administrator, Etienne N. N. Thê
Thanh-Phô Hôchiminh, vacant

WEST INDIES
Castries, Kelvin Edward Felix, OBE

YUGOSLAV FEDERAL REPUBLIC
Bar, Petar Perkolić
Belgrade, Franc Perko

ZAÏRE
Bukavu, Christophe Munzihirwa Mwene Ngabo
Kananga, Bakole wa Ilunga
Kinshasa, HE Cardinal Frederick Etsou-Nzabi-
    Bamungwabi
Kisangani, Laurent Monsengwo Pasinya
Lubumbashi, Kabanga Songasonga
Mbandaka-Bikoro, Joseph Kumuondala Mbimba

ZAMBIA
Kasama, James Spaita
Lusaka, Adrian Mungandu

ZIMBABWE
Harare, Patrick Chakaipa

PATRIARCHS IN COMMUNION WITH THE ROMAN CATHOLIC CHURCH

Alexandria, HB Stephanos II Ghattas (Patriarch for Catholic
    Copts); HB Parthenios III (Greek Orthodox Patriarch of
    Alexandria and All Africa)
Antioch, HB Ignace Antoine II Hayek (Patriarch for Syrian
    rite Catholics); HB Maximos V. Hakim (Patriarch for

Greek Melekite rite Catholics); HB Nasrallah Pierre
Sfeir (Patriarch for Maronite rite Catholics)
Jerusalem, HB Michel Sabbah (Patriarch for Latin rite
Catholics); HB Maximos V. Hakim (Patriarch for Greek
Melekite rite Catholics)
Babilonia of the Chaldeans, HB Raphael I Bidawid
Cilicia of the Armenians, HB Jean Pierre XVIII Kasparian
(Patriarch for Armenian rite Catholics)
Oriental India, Archbishop Raul Nicolau Gonsalves
Lisbon, HE Cardinal Antonio Ribeiro
Venice, HE Cardinal Marco Ce

Other Churches in the UK

AFRICAN AND AFRO-CARIBBEAN CHURCHES

There are more than 160 Christian churches or groups of
African or Afro-Caribbean origin in the UK. These include
the Apostolic Faith Church, the Cherubim and Seraphim
Church, the New Testament Church Assembly, the New
Testament Church of God and the Wesleyan Holiness
Church.

The Afro-West Indian United Council of Churches and
the Council of African and Afro-Caribbean Churches UK
(which was initiated as the Council of African and Allied
Churches in 1979 to give one voice to the various Christian
churches of African origin in the UK) are the media
through which the member churches can work jointly to
provide services they cannot easily provide individually.

There are about 70,000 adherents of African and Afro-
Caribbean churches in the UK, and about 1,000 congregations. The Afro-West Indian United Council of
Churches has about 30,000 individual members, 135
ministers and 65 places of worship. The Council of African
and Afro-Caribbean Churches UK has about 15,000
members, 250 ministers and 75 congregations.

AFRO-WEST INDIAN UNITED COUNCIL OF CHURCHES,
Overstone Hall Conference Centre, Main House,
Overstone Park, Overstone, Northampton NN6 0AD. Tel:
01604-645944. *Chairman,* Revd E. Brown

COUNCIL OF AFRICAN AND AFRO-CARIBBEAN CHURCHES
UK, 31 Norton House, Sidney Road, London SW9 0UJ.
Tel: 0171-274 5589. *Chairman,* His Grace The Most
Revd Father Olu A. Abiola

ASSOCIATED PRESBYTERIAN CHURCHES OF SCOTLAND

The Associated Presbyterian Churches came into being in
1989 as a result of a division within the Free Presbyterian
Church of Scotland. Following two controversial disciplinary cases, the culmination of deepening differences
within the Church, a presbytery was formed calling itself
the Associated Presbyterian Churches (APC). The Associated Presbyterian Churches has about 1,000 members, 15
ministers and 20 churches.
Clerk of the Scottish Presbytery, D. K. Laing, 1 Golden Square,
Aberdeen AB9 1HA. Tel: 01862-87541

THE BAPTIST CHURCH

Baptists trace their origins to John Smyth, who in 1609 in
Amsterdam reinstituted the baptism of conscious believers
as the basis of the fellowship of a gathered church. Members
of Smyth's church established the first Baptist church in
England in 1612. They came to be known as 'General'
Baptists and their theology was Arminian, whereas a later
group of Calvinists who adopted the baptism of believers
came to be known as 'Particular' Baptists. The two sections
of the Baptists were united into one body, the Baptist Union
of Great Britain and Ireland, in 1891. In 1988 the title was
changed to the Baptist Union of Great Britain.

Baptists emphasize the complete independence of the
local church, although individual churches are linked in
various kinds of associations. There are international
bodies (such as the Baptist World Alliance) and national
bodies, but many Baptist churches belong to neither.
However, in Great Britain the majority of churches and
associations belong to the Baptist Union of Great Britain.
There are also Baptist Unions in Wales, Scotland and
Ireland which are much smaller than the Baptist Union of
Great Britain, and there is some overlap of membership.

There are over 38 million Baptist church members
world-wide; in the Baptist Union of Great Britain there are
157,000 members, 1,864 pastors and 2,130 churches. In the
Baptist Union of Scotland there are 14,328 members, 140
pastors and 171 churches. In the Baptist Union of Wales
there are 24,178 members, 118 pastors and 537 churches. In
the Baptist Union of Ireland there are 8,448 members, 101
pastors and 108 churches.
President of the Baptist Union of Great Britain (1995–6), Revd
P. H. K. Tongeman
General Secretary, Revd D. R. Coffey, Baptist House, PO Box
44, 129 Broadway, Didcot, Oxon OX11 8RT. Tel: 01235-
512077

THE CHURCH OF CHRIST, SCIENTIST

The Church of Christ, Scientist was founded by Mary
Baker Eddy in the USA in 1879 to 'reinstate primitive
Christianity and its lost element of healing'. Christian
Science teaches the need for spiritual regeneration and
salvation from sin, but is best known for its reliance on
prayer alone in the healing of sickness. Adherents believe
that such healing is a law, or Science, and is in direct line
with that practised by Jesus Christ (revered, not as God, but
as the Son of God) and by the early Christian Church.

The denomination consists of The First Church of
Christ, Scientist, in Boston, Massachusetts, USA (the
Mother Church) and its branch churches in over 60
countries world-wide. Branch churches are democratically
governed by their members, while a five-member Board of
Directors, based in Boston, is authorized to transact the
business of the Mother Church. The Bible and Mary Baker
Eddy's book, *Science and Health with Key to the Scriptures,* are
used at services; there are no clergy. Those engaged in full-
time healing are called practitioners, of whom there are
3,500 world-wide.

No membership figures are available, since Mary Baker
Eddy felt that numbers are no measure of spiritual vitality
and ruled that such statistics should not be published.
There are over 2,400 branch churches world-wide, including nearly 200 in the UK.
CHRISTIAN SCIENCE COMMITTEE ON PUBLICATION,
2 Elysium Gate, 126 New Kings Road, London SW6 4LZ.

Tel: 0171-371 0600. *District Manager for Great Britain and Ireland*, A. Grayson

THE CHURCH OF JESUS CHRIST OF LATTER-DAY SAINTS

The Church (often referred to as 'the Mormons') was founded in New York State, USA, in 1830, and came to Britain in 1837. The oldest continuous branch in the world is to be found in Preston, Lancs. Mormons are Christians who claim to belong to the Restored Church of Jesus Christ. They believe that true Christianity died when the last original apostle died, but that it was given back to the world by God and Christ through Joseph Smith, the Church's founder and first president. They accept and use the Bible as scripture, but believe in continuing revelation from God and use additional scriptures, including *The Book of Mormon: Another Testament of Jesus Christ*. The importance of the family is central to the Church's beliefs and practices. Church members set aside Monday evenings as Family Home Evenings when Christian family values are taught. Polygamy was formally discontinued in 1890.

The Church has no paid ministry; local congregations are headed by a leader chosen from amongst their number. The world governing body, based in Utah, USA, is the three-man First Presidency, assisted by the Quorum of the Twelve Apostles.

There are about 9 million members world-wide, with about 170,000 adherents in Britain in over 350 congregations.

President of the Europe North Area (including Britain), Elder G. W. Doxey

BRITISH HEADQUARTERS, Church Offices, 751 Warwick Road, Solihull, W. Midlands B91 3DQ. Tel: 0121-711 2244

THE CONGREGATIONAL FEDERATION

The Congregational Federation was founded by members of Congregational churches in England and Wales who did not join the United Reformed Church (q.v.) in 1972. There are also churches in Scotland and Australia affiliated to the Federation. The Federation exists to encourage congregations of believers to worship in free assembly, but it has no authority over them and emphasizes their right to independence and self-government.

The Federation has 11,923 members, 71 recognized ministers and 313 churches.

President of the Federation (1995–6), Revd B. Pavis

General Secretary, G. M. Adams, The Congregational Centre, 4 Castle Gate, Nottingham NG1 7AS. Tel: 0115–941 3801

THE FREE CHURCH OF ENGLAND

The Free Church of England is a union of two bodies in the Anglican tradition, the Free Church of England, founded in 1844 as a protest against the Oxford Movement in the established Church, and the Reformed Episcopal Church, founded in America in 1873 but which also had congregations in England. As both Churches sought to maintain the historic faith, tradition and practice of the Anglican Church since the Reformation, they decided to unite as one body in England in 1927. The historic episcopate was conferred on the English Church in 1876 through the line

of the American bishops, who had pioneered an open table Communion policy towards members of other denominations.

The Free Church of England has 1,550 members, 42 ministers and 26 churches in England. It also has three house churches and three ministers in New Zealand, and one church and one minister in St Petersburg, Russia.

General Secretary, Revd W. J. Lawler, 45 Broughton Road, Wallasey, Merseyside L44 4DT. Tel: 0151-638 2564

THE FREE CHURCH OF SCOTLAND

The Free Church of Scotland was formed in 1843 when over 400 ministers withdrew from the Church of Scotland as a result of interference in the internal affairs of the church by the civil authorities. In 1900, all but 26 ministers joined with others to form the United Free Church (most of which rejoined the Church of Scotland in 1929). In 1904 the remaining 26 ministers were recognized by the House of Lords as continuing the Free Church of Scotland.

The Church maintains strict adherence to the Westminster Confession of Faith (1648) and accepts the Bible as the sole rule of faith and conduct. Its General Assembly meets annually. It also has links with Reformed Churches overseas. The Free Church of Scotland has about 20,000 members, 110 ministers and 140 churches.

General Treasurer, I. D. Gill, The Mound, Edinburgh EH1 2LS. Tel: 0131-226 5286

THE FREE PRESBYTERIAN CHURCH OF SCOTLAND

The Free Presbyterian Church of Scotland was formed in 1893 by two ministers of the Free Church of Scotland who refused to accept a Declaratory Act passed by the Free Church General Assembly in 1892. The Free Presbyterian Church of Scotland is Calvinistic in doctrine and emphasizes observance of the Sabbath. It adheres strictly to the Westminster Confession of Faith of 1648.

The Church has about 3,000 members in Scotland and about 7,000 in overseas congregations. It has 26 ministers and 50 churches.

Moderator, Revd A. McPherson, 11 Mavisbank Gardens, Burghmuir, Perth PH1 1HY. Tel: 01738-442992

Clerk of Synod, Revd J. MacLeod, 16 Matheson Road, Stornoway, Isle of Lewis HS1 2LA. Tel: 01851-702755

THE INDEPENDENT METHODIST CHURCHES

The Independent Methodist Churches seceded from the Wesleyan Methodist Church in 1805 and remained independent when the Methodist Church in Great Britain was formed in 1932. They are mainly concentrated in the industrial areas of the north of England.

The churches are Methodist in doctrine but their organization is congregational. All the churches are members of the Independent Methodist Connexion of Churches. The controlling body of the Connexion is the Annual Meeting, to which churches send delegates. The Connexional President is elected annually. Between annual meetings the affairs of the Connexion are handled by departmental committees. Ministers are appointed by

the churches and trained through the Connexion. The ministry is open to both men and women and is unpaid. There are 3,250 members, 113 ministers and 101 churches in Great Britain.
Connexional President (1995–6), Mrs N. Hobson
General Secretary, J. M. Day, The Old Police House, Croxton, Stafford ST21 6PE. Tel: 0163-062 0671

JEHOVAH'S WITNESSES

The movement now known as Jehovah's Witnesses grew from a Bible study group formed by Charles Taze Russell in 1872 in Pennsylvania, USA. In 1896 it adopted the name of the Watch Tower Bible and Tract Society, and in 1931 its members became known as Jehovah's Witnesses. Jehovah's (God's) Witnesses believe in the Bible as the word of God, and consider it to be inspired and historically accurate. They take the scriptures literally, except where there are obvious indications that they are figurative or symbolic, and reject the doctrine of the Trinity. Witnesses believe that the earth will remain for ever and that all those approved of by Jehovah will have eternal life on a cleansed and beautified earth; only 144,000 will go to heaven to rule with Christ. They believe that the second coming of Christ and his thousand-year reign on earth have been imminent since 1914, and that Armageddon (a final battle in which evil will be defeated) will precede Christ's rule of peace. They refuse to take part in military service, and do not accept stimulants or blood transfusions. They publish a magazine, *The Watchtower.*

The 12-member world governing body is based in New York, USA. Witnesses world-wide are divided into branches, countries or areas, districts, circuits and congregations. There are overseers at each level, and two assemblies are held annually for each circuit. There is no paid ministry, but each congregation has elders assigned to look after various duties and every Witness is assigned homes to visit in their congregation.

There are about 5 million Jehovah's Witnesses world-wide, with 125,000 Witnesses in the UK organized into about 1,400 congregations.
BRITISH ISLES HEADQUARTERS, Watch Tower House, The Ridgeway, London NW7 1RN. Tel: 0181-906 2211

THE LUTHERAN CHURCH

Lutheranism is based on the teachings of Martin Luther, the German leader of the Protestant Reformation. The authority of the scriptures is held to be supreme over Church tradition and creeds, and the key doctrine is that of justification by faith alone.

Lutheranism is one of the largest Protestant denominations and it is particularly strong in northern Europe and the USA. Some Lutheran churches are episcopal, while others have a synodal form of organization; unity is based on doctrine rather than structure. Most Lutheran churches are members of the Lutheran World Federation, based in Geneva.

Lutheran services in Great Britain are held in many languages to serve members of different nationalities. English-language congregations are members either of the Lutheran Church in Great Britain–United Synod, or of the Evangelical Lutheran Church of England. The United Synod and most of the various national congregations are members of the Lutheran Council of Great Britain.

There are over 70 million Lutherans world-wide; in Great Britain there are 27,000 members, 45 ministers and 100 churches.
Chairman of the Lutheran Council of Great Britain, Very Revd R. J. Patkai, 8 Collingham Gardens, London SW5 0HW. Tel: 0171-373 1141

THE METHODIST CHURCH

The Methodist movement started in England in 1729 when the Revd John Wesley, an Anglican priest, and his brother Charles met with others in Oxford and resolved to conduct their lives and study by 'rule and method'. In 1739 the Wesleys began evangelistic preaching and the first Methodist chapel was founded in Bristol in the same year. In 1744 the first annual conference was held, at which the Articles of Religion were drawn up. Doctrinal emphases included repentance, faith, the assurance of salvation, social concern and the priesthood of all believers. After John Wesley's death in 1791 the Methodists withdrew from the established Church to form the Methodist Church. Methodists gradually drifted into many groups, but in 1932 the Wesleyan Methodist Church, the United Methodist Church and the Primitive Methodist Church united to form the Methodist Church in Great Britain as it now exists.

The governing body and supreme authority of the Methodist Church is the Conference, but there are also 33 district synods, consisting of all the ministers and selected lay people in each district, and circuit meetings of the ministers and lay people of each circuit.

There are over 60 million Methodists world-wide; in Great Britain (1992 figures) there are 408,107 members, 3,601 ministers, 10,414 lay preachers and 6,950 churches.
President of the Conference in Great Britain (1995–6), Revd B. R. Hoare
Vice-President of the Conference (1995–6), Mrs S. Bristow
Secretary of the Conference, Revd B. E. Beck, Methodist Church, Conference Office, 25 Marylebone Road, London NW1 5JR. Tel: 0171-486 5502

THE METHODIST CHURCH IN IRELAND

The Methodist Church in Ireland is closely linked to British Methodism but is autonomous. It has 18,326 members, 197 ministers, 315 lay preachers and 234 churches.
President of the Conference in Ireland (1995–6), Revd C. G. Walpole, Aldersgate, Lisnaskea, Co. Fermanagh BT92 0DX. Tel 013657-22144
Secretary of the Conference in Ireland, Revd E. T. I. Mawhinney, 1 Fountainville Avenue, Belfast BT9 6AN. Tel: 01232-324554

THE ORTHODOX CHURCH

The Orthodox Church (or Eastern Orthodox Church) is a communion of self-governing Christian churches recognizing the honorary primacy of the Oecumenical Patriarch of Constantinople.

In the first millennium of the Christian era the faith was slowly formulated. Between AD 325 and 787 there were seven Oecumenical Councils at which bishops from the entire Christian world assembled to resolve various doctrinal disputes which had arisen. The estrangement between East and West began after Constantine moved the centre of the Roman Empire from Rome to Constantinople, and it gained momentum after the temporal administration was divided. Linguistic and cultural differences between Greek East and Latin West served to encourage separate ecclesiastical developments which became pronounced in the tenth and early 11th centuries.

The administration of the church was divided between five ancient patriarchates: Rome and all the West, Constantinople (the imperial city – the 'New Rome'), Jerusalem and all Palestine, Antioch and all the East, and Alexandria and all Africa. Of these, only Rome was in the Latin West and after the Great Schism in 1054, Rome developed a structure of authority centralized on one source, the Papacy, while the Orthodox East maintained the style of localized administration.

To the older patriarchates were later added the Patriarchates of Russia, Georgia, Serbia, Bulgaria and Romania. The Orthodox Church also includes autocephalous (self-governing) national churches in Greece, Cyprus, Poland, Albania, Czechoslovakia and Sinai, and autonomous national churches in Finland and Japan. The Estonian and Latvian Orthodox Churches are in practice part of the Moscow Patriarchate. The Belorussians and Ukrainians have recently been given greater autonomy by Moscow, but some Ukrainians have broken away to establish an independent Ukrainian Patriarchate. In Macedonia the local hierarchy has declared itself independent of the Serbian Patriarchate. The Russian dioceses in the diaspora fall into four groups: those under the direct control of the Moscow Patriarchate; the Russian Orthodox Church Outside Russia, sometimes known as the Synod in Exile; the Russian Archdiocese centred at the cathedral in rue Daru, Paris, which is part of the Patriarchate in Constantinople; and the Orthodox Church in America, which was granted autocephalous status in 1970.

The position of Orthodox Christians is that the faith was fully defined during the period of the Oecumenical Councils. In doctrine it is strongly trinitarian, and stresses the mystery and importance of the sacraments. It is episcopal in government. The structure of the Orthodox Christian year differs from that of western Churches (*see* page 82).

Orthodox Christians throughout the world are estimated to number about 150 million.

PATRIARCHS

Archbishop of Constantinople, New Rome and Oecumenical Patriarch, Bartholomew, *elected* 1991
Pope and Patriarch of Alexandria and All Africa, Parthenios III, *elected* 1987
Patriarch of Antioch and All the East, Ignatios IV, *elected* 1979
Patriarch of Jerusalem and All Palestine, Diodoros, *elected* 1981
Patriarch of Moscow and All Russia, Alexei II, *elected* 1990
Archbishop of Tbilisi and Mtskheta, Catholicos-Patriarch of All Georgia, Ilia II, *elected* 1977
Archbishop of Pec, Metropolitan of Belgrade and Karlovci, Patriarch of Serbia, Paul, *elected* 1990
Archbishop of Bucharest and Patriarch of Romania, Teoctist, *elected* 1986
Metropolitan of Sofia and Patriarch of Bulgaria, Maxim, *elected* 1971
Patriarch of Kiev and All Ukraine, no Patriarch agreed upon owing to division among the Ukrainian Orthodox

ORTHODOX CHURCHES IN THE UK

THE GREEK ORTHODOX CHURCH (PATRIARCHATE OF CONSTANTINOPLE)

The presence of Greek Orthodox Christians in Britain dates back to 1677 when Archbishop Joseph Geogirenes of Samos fled from Turkish persecution and came to London, where a church was built for him in Soho. The present Greek cathedral in Moscow Road, Bayswater, was opened for public worship in 1879 and the Diocese of Thyateira and Great Britain was established in 1922. There are now 87 parishes in Great Britain, served by eight bishops and 87 churches.

In Great Britain the Patriarchate of Constantinople is represented by Archbishop Gregorios of Thyateira and Great Britain, 5 Craven Hill, London W2 3EN. Tel: 0171–723 4787.

THE RUSSIAN ORTHODOX CHURCH (PATRIARCHATE OF MOSCOW) AND THE RUSSIAN ORTHODOX CHURCH OUTSIDE RUSSIA

The earliest records of Russian Orthodox Church activities in Britain date from the visit to England of Tsar Peter I at the beginning of the 18th century. Clergy were sent from Russia to serve the chapel established to minister to the staff of the Imperial Russian Embassy in London.

After 1917 the Church of Russia was persecuted. The Patriarch of Moscow, St Tikhon the New Martyr, anathematized both the atheistic persecutors of the Church and all who collaborated with them. Because of the civil war normal administrative contact with Russian Orthodox Christians outside the country was impossible, and he therefore authorized the establishment of a higher church administration, i.e. a synod in exile, by Russian bishops who were then outside Russia. This is the origin of the Russian Orthodox Church Outside Russia. The attitude of the Church of Russia to the former Soviet regime was always a source of contention between the two hierarchies; tensions are now lessening but remain unresolved.

In Britain the Patriarchate of Moscow is represented by Metropolitan Anthony of Sourozh, 67 Ennismore Gardens, London SW7 1NH. Tel: 0171-584 0096. He is assisted by one archbishop, one bishop and about 13 priests. There are 15 parishes.

The Russian Orthodox Church Outside Russia is represented by Archbishop Mark of Richmond and Great Britain (also Archbishop of Berlin and Germany), 14 St Dunstan's Road, London W6 8RB. Tel: 0181-748 4232. There are eight parishes and two monasteries, served by six priests.

THE SERBIAN ORTHODOX CHURCH (PATRIARCHATE OF SERBIA)

There was a small congregation of Orthodox Christian Serbs in London before the Second World War, but most Serbian parishes in Britain have been established since 1945. There is no resident bishop as the parishes are part of the Serbian Orthodox Diocese of Western Europe, which has its centre in Germany. There are five main parishes in Britain and several smaller communities served by seven priests.

In Britain the Patriarchate of Serbia is represented by the Episcopal Vicar, the Very Revd Milun Kostic, 89 Lancaster Road, London W11 1QQ. Tel: 0171-727 8367.

OTHER NATIONALITIES

Latvian, Polish and some Belorussian Orthodox parishes in Britain are under the care of the Patriarchate of Constantinople. The Patriarchates of Antioch, Bulgaria and Romania are represented by one priest each. Both the Ukrainian Autocephalous Orthodox Church and the Belorussian Autocephalic Orthodox Church have a few parishes in Britain.

ORTHODOX CHURCH PUBLIC RELATIONS OFFICE, St George Orthodox Information Service, 64 Prebend

Gardens, London w6 oxu. Tel: 0181-741 9624. *Secretary,* A. Bond

PENTECOSTAL CHURCHES

Pentecostalism is inspired by the descent of the Holy Spirit upon the apostles at Pentecost. The movement began in Los Angeles, USA, in 1906 and is characterized by baptism with the Holy Spirit, divine healing, speaking in tongues (glossolalia), and a literal interpretation of the scriptures. The Pentecostal movement in Britain dates from 1907. Initially, groups of Pentecostalists were led by laymen and did not organize formally. However, in 1915 the Elim Foursquare Gospel Alliance (more usually called the Elim Pentecostal Church) was founded in Ireland by George Jeffreys and in 1924 about 70 independent assemblies formed a fellowship, the Assemblies of God in Great Britain and Ireland. The Apostolic Church grew out of the 1904–5 revivals in South Wales and was established in 1916, and the New Testament Church of God was established in England in 1953. In recent years many aspects of Pentecostalism have been adopted by the growing charismatic movement within the Roman Catholic, Protestant and Eastern Orthodox churches.

There are about 22 million Pentecostalists world-wide, with about 130,000 adult adherents in Great Britain and Ireland.

THE APOSTOLIC CHURCH, International Administration Offices, PO Box 389, 24–27 St Helens Road, Swansea, West Glamorgan sa1 1zh. Tel: 01792-473992. *President,* Pastor P. Cawthorne; *Administrator,* Pastor M. Davies. The Apostolic Church has about 130 churches, 5,500 adherents and 83 ministers

THE ASSEMBLIES OF GOD IN GREAT BRITAIN AND IRELAND, General Offices, 106–114 Talbot Street, Nottingham ng1 5gh. Tel: 0115-947 4525. *General Superintendent,* W. Shenton; *General Administrator,* B. D. Varnam. The Assemblies of God has 645 churches, about 75,000 adherents (including children) and 678 accredited ministers

THE ELIM PENTECOSTAL CHURCH, PO Box 38, Cheltenham, Glos gl50 3hn. Tel: 01242-519904. *General Superintendent,* Pastor I. W. Lewis; *Administrator,* Pastor B. Hunter. The Elim Pentecostal Church has about 470 churches, 50,000 adherents and 475 accredited ministers

THE NEW TESTAMENT CHURCH OF GOD, Main House, Overstone Park, Overstone, Northampton nn6 oad. Tel: 01604-645944. *National Overseer,* Revd Dr S. E. Arnold. The New Testament Church of God has 110 organized congregations, 7,500 baptized members, about 20,000 adherents and 242 accredited ministers

THE PRESBYTERIAN CHURCH IN IRELAND

The Presbyterian Church in Ireland is Calvinistic in doctrine and presbyterian in constitution. Presbyterianism was established in Ireland as a result of the Ulster plantation in the early 17th century, when English and Scottish Protestants settled in the north of Ireland.

There are 21 presbyteries and five regional synods under the chief court known as the General Assembly. The General Assembly meets annually and is presided over by a Moderator who is elected for one year. The ongoing work of the Church is undertaken by 18 boards under which there are a number of specialist committees.

There are about 330,000 Presbyterians in Ireland, mainly in the north, in 562 congregations and with 400 ministers.

Moderator (1995–6), Rt. Revd Dr J. Ross
Clerk of Assembly and General Secretary, Revd S. Hutchinson, Church House, Belfast bt1 6dw. Tel: 01232-322284

THE PRESBYTERIAN CHURCH OF WALES

The Presbyterian Church of Wales or Calvinistic Methodist Church of Wales is Calvinistic in doctrine and presbyterian in constitution. It was formed in 1811 when Welsh Calvinists severed the relationship with the established church by ordaining their own ministers. It secured its own confession of faith in 1823 and a Constitutional Deed in 1826, and since 1864 the General Assembly has met annually, presided over by a Moderator elected for a year. The doctrine and constitutional structure of the Presbyterian Church of Wales was confirmed by Act of Parliament in 1931–2.

The Church has 53,870 members, 141 ministers and 964 churches.

Moderator (1995–6), Revd W. H. Whomsley
General Secretary, Revd D. H. Owen, 53 Richmond Road, Cardiff cf2 3up. Tel: 01222-494913

THE RELIGIOUS SOCIETY OF FRIENDS (QUAKERS)

Quakerism is a movement, not a church, which was founded in the 17th century by George Fox and others in an attempt to revive what they saw as 'primitive Christianity'. The movement was based originally in the Midlands, Yorkshire and north-west England, but there are now Quakers in 36 countries around the world. The colony of Pennsylvania, founded by William Penn, was originally Quaker.

Emphasis is placed on the experience of God in daily life rather than on sacraments or religious occasions. There is no church calendar. Worship is largely silent and there are no appointed ministers; the responsibility for conducting a meeting is shared equally among those present. Social reform and religious tolerance have always been important to Quakers, together with a commitment to non-violence in resolving disputes.

There are 213,800 Quakers world-wide, with over 19,000 in Great Britain and Ireland. There are about 460 meeting houses in Great Britain.

CENTRAL OFFICES: (GREAT BRITAIN) Friends House, Euston Road, London nw1 2bj. Tel: 0171-387 3601; (IRELAND) Swanbrook House, Morehampton Road, Dublin 4. Tel: 00 353 1-683684

THE SALVATION ARMY

The Salvation Army was founded by a Methodist minister, William Booth, in the east end of London in 1865, and has since become established in 98 countries world-wide. It was first known as the Christian Mission, and took its present name in 1878 when it adopted a quasi-military command structure intended to inspire and regulate its endeavours and to reflect its view that the Church was engaged in spiritual warfare. Salvationists emphasize evangelism, social work and the relief of poverty.

The world leader, known as the General, is elected by a High Council composed of the Chief of the Staff and senior ranking officers known as commissioners.

There are 1,087,826 members, 17,286 active officers (full-time ordained ministers) and 14,558 corps (churches) and outposts world-wide. In Great Britain and Ireland there are 58,052 members, 1,776 active officers and 993 worship centres.

General, P. Rader

UK Territorial Commander, Commissioner D. Pender
TERRITORIAL HEADQUARTERS, PO Box 249, 101 Queen
   Victoria Street, London EC4P 4EP. Tel: 0171-236 5222

THE SEVENTH-DAY ADVENTIST CHURCH

The Seventh-day Adventist Church was founded in 1863 in the USA. Its members look forward to the second coming of Christ and observe the Sabbath (the seventh day) as a day of rest, worship and ministry. The Church bases its faith and practice wholly on the Bible and has developed 27 fundamental beliefs.

The World Church is divided into 12 divisions, each made up of unions of churches. The Seventh-day Adventist Church in the British Isles is known as the British Union of Seventh-day Adventists and is a member of the Trans-European Division. In the British Isles the administrative organization of the church is arranged in three tiers: the local churches; the regional conferences for south England, north England, Wales, Scotland and Ireland, which are held every three years; and the national 'union' conference which is held every five years.

There are over 7 million Adventists and 36,032 churches in 204 countries world-wide. In the UK and Ireland there are 18,486 members, 152 ministers and 252 churches.

President of the British Union Conference (1991–6), Pastor
   C. R. Perry
BRITISH ISLES HEADQUARTERS, Stanborough Park,
   Watford WD2 6JP. Tel: 01923-672251

UNDEB YR ANNIBYNWYR CYMRAEG
The Union of Welsh Independents

The Union of Welsh Independents was formed in 1872 and is a voluntary association of Welsh Congregational Churches and personal members. It is entirely Welsh-speaking. Congregationalism in Wales dates back to 1639 when the first Welsh Congregational Church was opened in Gwent. Member Churches are Calvinistic in doctrine and congregationalist in organization. Each church has complete independence in the government and adminis-tration of its affairs.

The Union has 45,462 members, 115 ministers and 605 chapels.

President of the Union (1995–6), Revd J. G. E. Watkin
General Secretary, Revd D. Morris Jones, Tŷ John Penry, 11
   Heol Sant Helen, Swansea SA1 4AL. Tel: 01792-652542

UNITARIAN AND FREE CHRISTIAN CHURCHES

Unitarianism has its historical roots in the Judaeo-Christian tradition but denies the deity of Christ and the doctrine of the trinity. It allows the individual to embrace insights from all the world's faiths and philosophies, as there is no formal creed. It is accepted that beliefs may evolve in the light of personal experience.

Unitarian communities first became established in Poland and Transylvania in the 16th century. The first avowedly Unitarian place of worship in the British Isles opened in London in 1774. The General Assembly of Unitarian and Free Christian Churches came into exis-tence in 1928 as the result of the amalgamation of two earlier organizations.

There are about 10,000 Unitarians in Great Britain and Ireland, and 150 Unitarian ministers. About 250 self-governing congregations and fellowship groups, including a small number overseas, are members of the General Assembly.

GENERAL ASSEMBLY OF UNITARIAN AND FREE
   CHRISTIAN CHURCHES, Essex Hall, 1–6 Essex Street,
   Strand, London WC2R 3HY. Tel: 0171-240 2384. *General
   Secretary*, J. J. Teagle

THE UNITED REFORMED CHURCH

The United Reformed Church was formed by the union of most of the Congregational churches in England and Wales with the Presbyterian Church of England in 1972.

Congregationalism dates from the mid 16th century. It is Calvinistic in doctrine, and its followers form independent self-governing congregations bound under God by cove-nant, a principle laid down in the writings of Robert Browne (1550–1633). From the late 16th century the movement was driven underground by persecution, but the cause was defended at the Westminster Assembly in 1643 and the Savoy Declaration of 1658 laid down its principles. Congregational churches formed county asso-ciations for mutual support and in 1832 these associations merged to form the Congregational Union of England and Wales.

The Presbyterian Church in England also dates from the mid 16th century, and was Calvinistic and evangelical in its doctrine. It was governed by a hierarchy of courts.

In the 1960s there was close co-operation locally and nationally between Congregational and Presbyterian Churches. This led to union negotiations and a Scheme of Union, supported by Act of Parliament in 1972. In 1981 a further unification took place, with the Reformed Associ-ation of Churches of Christ becoming part of the URC. In its basis the United Reformed Church reflects local church initiative and responsibility with a conciliar pattern of oversight. The General Assembly is the central body, and is made up of equal numbers of ministers and lay members.

The United Reformed Church is divided into 12 Provinces, each with a Provincial Moderator who chairs the Synod, and 75 Districts. There are 106,537 members, 813 full-time stipendiary ministers, 207 non-stipendiary ministers and 1,784 local churches.

General Secretary, Revd A. G. Burnham, 86 Tavistock Place,
   London WC1H 9RT. Tel: 0171-916 2020

THE WESLEYAN REFORM UNION

The Wesleyan Reform Union was founded by Methodists who left or were expelled from Wesleyan Methodism in 1849 following a period of internal conflict. Its doctrine is conservative evangelical and its organization is congre-gational, each church having complete independence in

the government and administration of its affairs. The main
concentration of churches is in Yorkshire.

The Union has 2,516 members, 20 ministers, 143 lay
preachers and 122 churches.

President (1995–6) *and General Secretary*, Revd E. W.
Downing, Wesleyan Reform Church House, 123 Queen
Street, Sheffield si 2DU. Tel: 0114-272 1938

Archbishops of Canterbury since 1414

Henry Chichele (1362–1443), translated 1414
John Stafford (?–1452), translated 1443
John Kemp (*c.*1380–1454), translated 1452
Thomas Bourchier (*c.*1410–86), translated 1454
John Morton (*c.*1420–1500), translated 1486
Henry Deane (?–1503), translated 1501
William Warham (1450–1532), translated 1503
Thomas Cranmer (1489–1556), translated 1533
Reginald Pole (1500–58), translated 1556
Matthew Parker (1504–75), translated 1559
Edmund Grindal (*c.* 1519–83), translated 1576
John Whitgift (*c.*1530–1604), translated 1583
Richard Bancroft (1544–1610), translated 1604
George Abbot (1562–1633), translated 1611
William Laud (1573–1645), translated 1633
William Juxon (1582–1663), translated 1660
Gilbert Sheldon (1598–1677), translated 1663
William Sancroft (1617–93), translated 1678
John Tillotson (1630–94), translated 1691
Thomas Tenison (1636–1715), translated 1695
William Wake (1657–1737), translated 1716

John Potter (*c.*1674–1747), translated 1737
Thomas Herring (1693–1757), translated 1747
Matthew Hutton (1693–1758), translated 1757
Thomas Secker (1693–1768), translated 1758
Hon. Frederick Cornwallis (1713–83), translated 1768
John Moore (1730–1805), translated 1783
Charles Manners-Sutton (1755–1828), translated 1805
William Howley (1766–1848), translated 1828
John Bird Sumner (1780–1862), translated 1848
Charles Longley (1794–1868), translated 1862
Archibald Campbell Tait (1811–82), translated 1868
Edward White Benson (1829–96), translated 1883
Frederick Temple (1821–1902), translated 1896
Randall Davidson (1848–1930), translated 1903
Cosmo Lang (1864–1945), translated 1928
William Temple (1881–1944), translated 1942
Geoffrey Fisher (1887–1972), translated 1945
Michael Ramsey (1904–88), translated 1961
Donald Coggan (1909–), translated 1974
Robert Runcie (1921–), translated 1980
George Carey (1935–), translated 1991

Archbishops of York since 1606

Tobias Matthew (1546–1628), translated 1606
George Montaigne (1569–1628), translated 1628
Samuel Harsnett (1561–1631), translated 1629
Richard Neile (1562–1640), translated 1632
John Williams (1582–1650), translated 1641
Accepted Frewen (1588–1664), translated 1660
Richard Sterne (1596–1683), translated 1664
John Dolben (1625–86), translated 1683
Thomas Lamplugh (1615–91), translated 1688
John Sharp (1645–1714), translated 1691
William Dawes (1671–1724), translated 1714
Launcelot Blackburn (1658–1743), translated 1724
Thomas Herring (1693–1757), translated 1743
Matthew Hutton (1693–1758), translated 1747
John Gilbert (1693–1761), translated 1757
Robert Hay Drummond (1711–76), translated 1761

William Markham (1719–1807), translated 1777
Edward Vernon Harcourt (1757–1847), translated 1808
Thomas Musgrave (1788–1860), translated 1847
Charles Longley (1794–1868), translated 1860
William Thomson (1819–90), translated 1862
William Connor Magee (1821–91), translated 1891
William Maclagan (1826–1910), translated 1891
Cosmo Lang (1864–1945), translated 1909
William Temple (1881–1944), translated 1929
Cyril Garbett (1875–1955), translated 1942
Michael Ramsey (1904–88), translated 1956
Donald Coggan (1909–), translated 1961
Stuart Blanch (1918–94), translated 1975
John Habgood (1927–), translated 1983
David Hope (1940–), translated 1995

Non-Christian Faiths

BUDDHISM

Buddhism originated in northern India, in the teachings of Siddharta Gautama, who was born near Kapilavastu about 560 BC. After a long spiritual quest he experienced enlightenment beneath a tree at the place now known as Bodhgaya, and began missionary work.

Fundamental to Buddhism is the concept that there is no such thing as a permanent soul or self; when someone dies, consciousness is the only one of the elements of which they were composed which is lost. All the other elements regroup in a new body and carry with them the consequences of the conduct of the earlier life (known as the law of *karma*). This cycle of death and rebirth is broken only when the state of *nirvana* has been reached. Buddhism steers a middle path between belief in personal immortality and belief in death as the final end.

The Four Noble Truths of Buddhism (*dukkha*, suffering; *tanha*, a thirst or desire for continued existence which causes dukkha; *nirvana*, the final liberation from desire and ignorance; and *ariya*, the path to nirvana) are all held to be universal and to sum up the *dhamma* or true nature of life. Necessary qualities to promote spiritual development are *sila* (morality), *samadhi* (meditation) and *panna* (wisdom).

There are two main schools of Buddhism: *Theravada* Buddhism, the earliest extant school, which is more traditional, and *Mahayana* Buddhism, which began to develop about 100 years after the Buddha's death and is more liberal; it teaches that all people may attain Buddahood. Important schools which have developed within Mahayana Buddhism are *Zen* Buddhism, *Nichiren* Buddhism and Pure Land Buddhism or *Amidism*. There are also distinctive Tibetan forms of Buddhism. Buddhism began to establish itself in the West at the beginning of the 20th century.

The scripture of Theravada Buddhism is the *Pali Canon*, which dates from the first century BC. Mahayana Buddhism uses a Sanskrit version of the Pali Canon but also has many other works of scripture.

There is no set time for Buddhist worship, which may take place in a temple or in the home. Worship centres around *paritta* (chanting), acts of devotion centring on the image of the Buddha, and, where possible, offerings to a relic of the Buddha. Buddhist festivals vary according to local traditions and within Theravada and Mahayana Buddhism. For religious purposes Buddhists use solar and lunar calendars, the New Year being celebrated in April. Other festivals mark events in the life of the Buddha.

There is no supreme governing authority in Buddhism. In the United Kingdom communities representing all schools of Buddhism have developed and operate independently. The Buddhist Society was established in 1924; it runs courses and lectures, and publishes books about Buddhism. It represents no one school of Buddhism.

There are estimated to be at least 300 million Buddhists world-wide, and about 275 organizations and groups, an estimated 25,000 adherents and 15 temples or monasteries in the United Kingdom.

THE BUDDHIST SOCIETY, 58 Eccleston Square, London SW1V 1PH. Tel: 0171-834 5858. *General Secretary*, R. C. Maddox

HINDUISM

Hinduism has no historical founder but is known to have been highly developed in India by about 1200 BC. Its adherents originally called themselves Aryans; Muslim invaders first called the Aryans 'Hindus' (derived from the word 'Sindhu', the name of the river Indus) in the eighth century.

Hinduism's evolution has been complex and it embraces many different religious beliefs, mythologies and practices. Most Hindus hold that *satya* (truthfulness), *ahimsa* (non-violence), honesty, physical labour and tolerance of other faiths are essential for good living. They believe in one supreme spirit (*Brahman*), and in the transmigration of *atman* (the soul). Most Hindus accept the doctrine of *karma* (consequences of actions), the concept of *samsara* (successive lives) and the possibility of all atmans achieving *moksha* (liberation from samsara) through *jnana* (knowledge), *yoga* (meditation), *karma* (work or action) and *bhakti* (devotion).

Most Hindus offer worship to *murtis* (images or statues) representing different aspects of Brahman, and follow their *dharma* (religious and social duty) according to the traditions of their *varna* (social class), *ashrama* (stage in life), *jati* (caste) and *kula* (family).

Hinduism's sacred texts are divided into *shruti* ('heard' or divinely inspired), including the *Vedas*, or *smriti* ('remembered' tradition), including the *Ramayana*, the *Mahabharata*, the *Puranas* (ancient myths), and the sacred law books. Most Hindus recognize the authority of the *Vedas*, the oldest holy books, and accept the philosophical teachings of the *Upanishads*, the *Vedanta Sutras* and the *Bhagavad-Gita*.

Brahman is formless, limitless and all-pervading, and is represented in worship by murtis which may be male or female and in the form of a human, animal or bird. Brahma, Vishnu and Shiva are the most important gods worshipped by Hindus; their respective consorts are Saraswati, Lakshmi and Durga or Parvati, also known as Shakti. There are held to have been ten *avatars* (incarnations) of Vishnu, of whom the most important are Rama and Krishna. Other popular gods are Ganesha, Hanuman and Subrahmanyam. All gods are seen as aspects of the supreme God, not as competing deities.

Orthodox Hindus revere all gods and goddesses equally, but there are many sects, including the Hare-Krishna movement (ISKCon), the Arya Samaj, the Swami Narayan Hindu mission and the Satya Sai-Baba movement. Worship in the sects is concentrated on one deity to the exclusion of others. In some sects a human *guru* (spiritual teacher), usually the head of the organization, is revered more than the deity, while in other sects the guru is seen as the source of spiritual guidance.

Hinduism does not have a centrally-trained and ordained priesthood. The pronouncements of the *shankaracharyas* (heads of monasteries) of Shringeri, Puri, Dwarka and Badrinath are heeded by the orthodox but may be ignored by the various sects.

The commonest form of worship is a *puja*, in which offerings of red and yellow powders, rice grains, water, flowers, food, fruit, incense and light are made to the image of a deity. Puja may be done either in a home shrine or a *mandir* (temple). Many British Hindus celebrate life-cycle rituals with Sanskrit mantras for naming a baby, the sacred thread (an initiation ceremony), marriage and cremation. For details of the Hindu calendar, main festivals etc, *see* pages 84–5.

The largest communities of Hindus in Britain are in Leicester, London, Birmingham and Bradford, and developed as a result of immigration from India, east Africa and Sri Lanka. Many Hindus now are British by birth, with English as their first language; the main ethnic languages are Gujarati, Hindi, Punjabi, Tamil, Bengali and Marathi.

There are an estimated 800 million Hindus world-wide; there are about 360,000 adherents and over 150 temples in the UK.

ARYA PRATINIDHI SABHA (UK), 69A Argyle Road, London WI3 OLY

BHARATIYA VIDYA BHAVAN, Old Church Building, 4A Castletown Road, London WI4 9HQ. Tel: 0171-381 3086. *Executive Director*, Dr M. Nandakumara

INTERNATIONAL SOCIETY FOR KRISHNA CONSCIOUSNESS (ISKCon), Bhaktivedanta Manor, Letchmore Heath, nr Watford, Herts WD2 8EP. Tel: 01923-857244. *Governing Body Commissioner*, H. H. Sivarama Swami

NATIONAL COUNCIL OF HINDU TEMPLES, c/o Shree Sanatan Mandir, Weymouth Street, off Catherine Street, Leicester LE4 6FP. Tel: 0116-266 1402. *Secretary*, R. C. Barber

SWAMINARAYAN HINDU MISSION, 54–62 Meadow Garth, London NW10 8HD. Tel: 0181-965 2651

VISHWA HINDU PARISHAD (UK), 48 Wharfedale Gardens, Thornton Heath, Surrey CR7 6LB. Tel: 0181-679 7505. *General Secretary*, K. Ruparelia

ISLAM

Islam (which means 'peace arising from submission to the will of Allah' in Arabic) is a monotheistic religion which originated in Arabia through the Prophet Muhammad, who was born in Mecca (Makkah) in AD 570. Islam spread to Egypt, North Africa, Spain and the borders of China in the century following the prophet's death, and is now the predominant religion in Indonesia, the Near and Middle East, North and parts of West Africa, Pakistan, Bangladesh, Malaysia and some of the republics of the former Soviet Union. There are also large Muslim communities in many other countries.

For Muslims (adherents of Islam), God (*Allah*) is one and holds absolute power. His commands were revealed to mankind through the prophets, who include Abraham, Moses and Jesus, but his message was gradually corrupted until revealed finally and in perfect form to Muhammad through the angel *Jibril* (Gabriel) over a period of 23 years. This last, incorruptible message has been recorded in the *Qur'an* (Koran), which contains 114 divisions called *surahs*, each made up of *ayahs*, and is held to be the essence of all previous scriptures. The *Ahadith* are the records of the Prophet Muhammad's deeds and sayings (the *Sunnah*) as recounted by his immediate followers. A culture and a system of law and theology gradually developed to form a distinctive Islamic civilization. Islam makes no distinction between sacred and worldly affairs and provides rules for every aspect of human life. The *Shari'ah* is the sacred law of Islam based upon prescriptions derived from the Qur'an and the Sunnah of the Prophet.

The 'five pillars of Islam' are *shahadah* (a declaration of faith in the oneness and supremacy of Allah and the messengership of Muhammad); *salat* (formal prayer, to be performed five times a day facing the *Ka'bah* (sacred house) in the holy city of Mecca); *zakat* (welfare due); *saum* (fasting

during the month of Ramadan); and *hajj* (pilgrimage to Mecca); some Muslims would add *jihad* (striving for the cause of good and resistance to evil).

Two main groups developed among Muslims. *Sunni* Muslims accept the legitimacy of Muhammad's first four *caliphs* (successors as head of the Muslim community) and of the authority of the Muslim community as a whole. About 90 per cent of Muslims are *Sunni* Muslims. *Shi'ites* recognize only Muhammad's son-in-law Ali as his rightful successor and the *Imams* (descendants of Ali, not to be confused with *imams* (prayer leaders or religious teachers)) as the principal legitimate religious authority. The largest group within *Shi'ism* is *Twelver Shi'ism*, which has been the official school of law and theology in Iran since the 16th century; other subsects include the *Ismailis* and the *Druze*, the latter being an offshoot of the Ismailis and differing considerably from the main body of Muslims.

There is no organized priesthood, but learned men such as *ulama*, *imams* and *ayatollahs* are accorded great respect. The *Sufis* are the mystics of Islam. Mosques are centres for worship and teaching and also for social and welfare activities. For details of the Muslim calendar and festivals, *see* page 86.

Islam was first known in western Europe in the eighth century AD when 800 years of Muslim rule began in Spain. Later, Islam spread to eastern Europe. More recently, Muslims came to Europe from Africa, the Middle East and Asia in the late 19th century. Both the Sunni and Shi'ah traditions are represented in Britain, but the majority of Muslims in Britain adhere to Sunni Islam.

The largest communities are in London, Liverpool, Manchester, Birmingham, Bradford, Cardiff, Edinburgh and Glasgow. There is no central organization, but the Islamic Cultural Centre, which is the London Central Mosque, and the Imams and Mosques Council are influential bodies; there are many other Muslim organizations in Britain.

There are about 1,000 million Muslims world-wide, with more than one million adherents and over 350 mosques in Britain.

IMAMS AND MOSQUES COUNCIL, 20–22 Creffield Road, London W5 3RP. Tel: 0181-992 6636. *Director of the Council and Principal of the Muslim College*, Dr M. A. Z. Badawi

ISLAMIC CULTURAL CENTRE, 146 Park Road, London NW8 7RG. Tel: 0171-724 3363. *Director*, Dr M. A. al-Ghamdi

MUSLIM WORLD LEAGUE, 46 Goodge Street, London WIP IFJ. Tel: 0171-636 7568. *Director*, Dr V. Alim

UNION OF MUSLIM ORGANIZATIONS OF THE UK AND EIRE, 109 Campden Hill Road, London W8 7TL. Tel: 0171-229 0538. *Geneal Secretary*, Dr S. A. Pasha

JUDAISM

Judaism is the oldest monotheistic faith. The primary authority of Judaism is the Hebrew Bible or *Tanakh*, which records how the descendants of Abraham were led by Moses out of their slavery in Egypt to Mount Sinai where God's law (*Torah*) was revealed to them as the chosen people. The *Talmud*, which consists of commentaries on the *Mishnah* (the first text of rabbinical Judaism), is also held to be authoritative, and may be divided into two main categories: the *halakah* (dealing with legal and ritual matters) and the *Aggadah* (dealing with theological and ethical matters not directly concerned with the regulation of conduct). The *Midrash* comprises rabbinic writings containing biblical interpretations in the spirit of the

Aggadah. The *halakah* has become a source of division; Orthodox Jews regard Jewish law as derived from God and therefore unalterable; Reform and Liberal Jews seek to interpret it in the light of contemporary considerations; and Conservative Jews aim to maintain most of the traditional rituals but to allow changes in accordance with that tradition. Reconstructionist Judaism, a 20th-century movement, regards Judaism as a culture rather than a theological system and therefore accepts all forms of Jewish practice.

The family is the basic unit of Jewish ritual, with the synagogue playing an important role as the centre for public worship and religious study. A synagogue is led by a group of laymen who are elected to office. The Rabbi is primarily a teacher and spiritual guide. The Sabbath is the central religious observance. For details of the Jewish calendar, fasts and festivals, *see* page 85. Most British Jews are descendants of either the *Ashkenazim* of central and eastern Europe or the *Sephardim* of Spain and Portugal.

The Chief Rabbi of the United Hebrew Congregations of the Commonwealth is appointed by a Chief Rabbinate Conference, and is the rabbinical authority of the Orthodox sector of the Ashkenazi Jewish community. His authority is not recognized by the Reform Synagogues of Great Britain (the largest progressive group), the Union of Liberal and Progressive Synagogues, the Union of Orthodox Hebrew Congregations, the Federation of Synagogues, the Sephardi community, or the Assembly of Masorti Synagogues. He is, however, generally recognized both outside the Jewish community and within it as the public religious representative of the totality of British Jewry.

The *Beth Din* (Court of Judgment) is the rabbinic court. The *Dayanim* (Assessors) adjudicate in disputes or on matters of Jewish law and tradition; they also oversee dietary law administration. The Chief Rabbi is President of the *Beth Din* of the United Synagogue.

The Board of Deputies of British Jews was established in 1760 and is the representative body of British Jewry. The basis of representation is mainly synagogal, but communal organizations are also represented. It watches over the interests of British Jewry and seeks to counter anti-Jewish discrimination.

There are over 12.5 million Jews world-wide; in Great Britain and Ireland there are an estimated 300,000 adherents and about 350 synagogues. Of these, 185 congregations and about 150 rabbis and ministers are under the jurisdiction of the Chief Rabbi; 99 orthodox congregations have a more independent status; and 72 congregations do not recognize the authority of the Chief Rabbi.

CHIEF RABBINATE, Adler House, Tavistock Square, London WC1H 9HN. Tel: 0171-387 1066. *Chief Rabbi,* Dr Jonathan Sacks; *Executive Director,* J. Kestenbaum

BETH DIN (COURT OF THE CHIEF RABBI), Adler House, Tavistock Square, London WC1H OEP. Tel: 0171-387 5772. *Registrar,* J. Phillips; *Dayanim,* Rabbi C. Ehrentreu; Rabbi I. Binstock; Rabbi C. D. Kaplin; Rabbi M. Gelley

BOARD OF DEPUTIES OF BRITISH JEWS, Woburn House, Tavistock Square, London WC1H OEZ. Tel: 0171-387 3952. *President,* E. Tabachnik, QC; *Chief Executive,* N. A. Nagler

ASSEMBLY OF MASORTI SYNAGOGUES, 766 Finchley Road, London NW11 7TH. Tel: 0181-201 8772. *Development Director,* H. Freedman

FEDERATION OF SYNAGOGUES, 65 Watford Way, London NW4 3AQ. Tel: 0181-202 2263. *Administrator,* G. Kushner

REFORM SYNAGOGUES OF GREAT BRITAIN, The Sternberg Centre for Judaism, Manor House, 80 East End Road, London N3 2SY. Tel: 0181-349 4731. *Chief Executive,* Rabbi T. Bayfield

SPANISH AND PORTUGUESE JEWS' CONGREGATION, 2 Ashworth Road, London W9 1JY. Tel: 0171-289 2573. *Chief Executive,* Mrs J. Velleman

UNION OF LIBERAL AND PROGRESSIVE SYNAGOGUES, The Montagu Centre, 21 Maple Street, London W1P 6DS. Tel: 0171-580 1663. *Director,* Mrs R. Rosenberg

UNION OF ORTHODOX HEBREW CONGREGATIONS, 40 Queen Elizabeth's Walk, London N16 0HH. Tel: 0181-802 6226. *Executive Director,* Rabbi A. Klein

UNITED SYNAGOGUE HEAD OFFICE, Woburn House, Tavistock Square, London WC1H OEZ. Tel: 0171-387 4300. *Chief Executive,* J. M. Lew

SIKHISM

The Sikh religion dates from the birth of Guru Nanak in the Punjab in 1469. The word 'guru' means teacher, but in Sikh tradition it has come to represent the divine presence of God giving inner spiritual guidance. Nanak's role as the human vessel of the divine guru was passed on to nine successors, the last of whom (Guru Gobind Singh) died in 1708. The immortal guru is now held to reside in the sacred scripture, *Guru Granth Sahib,* and so to be present in all Sikh gatherings.

Guru Nanak taught that there is one God and that different religions are like different roads leading to the same destination. He condemned religious conflict, ritualism and caste prejudices. The fifth Guru, Guru Arjan, compiled the Sikh Holy Book, a collection of hymns (*gurbani*) known as the *Adi Granth.* It includes the writings of the first five Gurus and selected writings of Hindu and Muslim saints whose views are in accord with the Guru's teachings. Guru Arjan also built the Golden Temple at Amritsar, the centre of Sikhism. The tenth Guru, Guru Gobind Singh, passed on the guruship to the sacred scripture, Guru Granth Sahib. He also founded the *Khalsa,* an order intended to fight against tyranny and injustice. Male initiates to the order added 'Singh' to their given names and women added 'Kaur'. Guru Gobind Singh also made five symbols obligatory: *kaccha* (a special undergarment), *kara* (a steel bangle), *kirpan* (a small sword), *kesh* (long unshorn hair, and consequently the wearing of a turban), and *kangha* (a comb). These practices are still compulsory for those Sikhs who are initiated into the *Khalsa* (the *Amritdharis*). Those who do not seek initiation are known as *Sahajdharis.*

There are no professional priests in Sikhism; anyone with a reasonable proficiency in the Punjabi language can conduct a service. Worship can be offered individually or communally, and in a private house or a *gurdwara* (temple). Sikhs are forbidden to eat meat prepared by ritual slaughter; they are also asked to abstain from smoking, alcohol and other intoxicants. For details of the Sikh calendar and main celebrations, *see* page 86.

There are about 12.5 million Sikhs world-wide and an estimated 400,000 adherents and 250 gurdwaras in Great Britain. The largest communities are in London, Bradford, Leeds, Huddersfield, Birmingham, Nottingham, Coventry and Wolverhampton. Every gurdwara manages its own affairs and there is no central body in the UK. The Sikh Missionary Society provides an information service.

SIKH CULTURAL SOCIETY OF GREAT BRITAIN, 88 Mollison Way, Edgware, Middx HA8 5QW. Tel: 0181-952 1215. *General Secretary,* A. S. Chhatwal

SIKH MISSIONARY SOCIETY UK, 10 Featherstone Road, Southall, Middx UB2 5AA. Tel: 0181-574 1902. *Hon. Secretary,* T. S. Manget

Education

For addresses of national education departments, *see* Government Departments and Public Offices. For other addresses, *see* Education Directory

Responsibility for education in the United Kingdom is largely decentralized. Overall responsibility for all aspects of education in England lies with the Secretary of State for Education and Employment; in Wales with the Secretary of State for Wales; in Scotland with the Secretary of State for Scotland acting through the Scottish Office Education and Industry Department; and in Northern Ireland with the Secretary of State for Northern Ireland.

The main concerns of the education departments (the Department for Education and Employment (DFEE), the Welsh Office, the Scottish Office Education and Industry Department (SOEID), and the Department of Education for Northern Ireland (DENI)) are the formulation of national policies for education, and the maintenance of consistency in educational standards. They are responsible for the broad allocation of resources for education, for the rate and distribution of educational building and for the supply, training and superannuation of teachers. The Welsh Office and the Scottish Office Education and Industry Department fund individual schools which have opted out of local education authority control and applied for direct funding from the Secretaries of State; those in England are funded by the Funding Agency for Schools (FAS). In addition, the Department for Education and Employment, in association with sponsors from industry, funds the City Technology Colleges (CTCs), the City College for the Technology of the Arts and pays grants to Technology Colleges. Technology Academies are proposed on a similar basis in Scotland.

Schools in Northern Ireland providing integrated education are able to apply for grant-maintained status from the Department of Education for Northern Ireland.

EXPENDITURE

The Department for Education and Employment, the Welsh Office, the Scottish Office and the Northern Ireland Office act within a framework of estimates approved by Parliament.

In real terms expenditure on education by central government departments was (£ million):

	1994–5 estimated outturn	1995–6 planned
DFEE	10,417	10,851
Welsh Office	487.7	510.7
SOEID	1,320	1,369
DENI	1,260	1,319

In the United Kingdom in 1992–3, central government provisional expenditure on education was (£million):

Schools	18,896.9
Further and higher education	8,017.2
Other education and related expenditure	2,971.3

Most of this expenditure is incurred by local authorities, which make their own expenditure decisions according to their local situations and needs. The bulk of direct expenditure by the DFEE, the Welsh Office and SOEID is directed towards supporting higher education in universities and colleges through the Higher Education Funding Councils (HEFCs) and further education and

sixth form colleges through the Further Education Funding Councils (FEFCs) in England and Wales and directly from central government in Scotland. In addition, the DFEE funds grant-maintained schools through the Funding Agency for Schools and CTCs in the schools sector.

The Welsh Office also funds grants for higher and further education, grant-maintained schools, educational services and research, and supports bilingual education and the Welsh language.

In Scotland the bulk of expenditure on education is at a local level by the regional and islands councils. In addition to those outlined above, the main elements of central government expenditure are grant-aided special schools, self-governing schools, student awards, curriculum development, special educational needs and community education.

The Department of Education for Northern Ireland finances higher education, teacher education, teacher salaries and superannuation, student awards, grant-maintained integrated schools, and voluntary grammar schools. Remaining expenditure is by education and library boards at local level.

Current net expenditure on education by local education authorities in England and Wales, regional and islands councils in Scotland, and education and library boards in Northern Ireland is as follows (£million):

	1994–5 estimated outturn	1995–6 planned
England	19,956	17,204
Wales	1,233.5	1,235.5
Scotland	2,476	2,501
Northern Ireland	905	916

LOCAL EDUCATION ADMINISTRATION

The education service at present is a national service in which the provision of most school education is locally administered; its administration is still largely decentralized.

In England and Wales the education service is administered by local education authorities (LEAs), which carry the day-to-day responsibility for providing most state primary and secondary education in their areas, although the planning and supply of school places is to be shared with the Funding Agency for Schools as the number of pupils in grant-maintained schools grows. They also share with the Further Education Funding Councils the duty to provide adult education to meet the needs of their areas.

The LEAs own and maintain schools and colleges, build new ones and provide equipment. Most of the public money spent on education is disbursed by the local authorities. LEAs are financed largely from the council tax and aggregate external finance (AEF) from the Department of the Environment in England and the Welsh Office in Wales.

The powers of local education authorities as regards the control of schools have been modified in recent years and schools can choose to opt out of local authority control. These grant-maintained (GM) schools are funded by the Funding Agency for Schools in England. Those in Wales are funded by the Welsh Office at present but the Schools Funding Council for Wales will take over when the number of grant-maintained schools is sufficient to warrant the change. Primary schools can apply for grant-maintained status as a group as well as individually. An Education Association can be set up to take over the management of failing schools where both the LEA and the governing body have not brought about the improvements identified as necessary.

The duty of providing education locally in Scotland rests at present with the nine regional and three islands councils. They are responsible for the construction of buildings, the employment of teachers and other staff, and the provision of equipment and materials. Management is to be devolved to all primary and secondary schools by April 1996, although the deadline has been extended to April 1998 in primary schools with headteachers who teach full-time and to April 1997 in all special schools. The councils' responsibility for the curricula taught in schools is shared with headteachers under the guidance of the Secretary of State for Scotland advised by the Scottish Consultative Council on the Curriculum.

The powers of local authorities over educational institutions under their control have been reduced also in Scotland. Education authorities are required to establish school boards consisting of parents and teachers as well as co-opted members, responsible among other things for the appointment of staff. Schools can choose to withdraw from local authority control and become self-governing; the institution of Technology Academies directly funded by central government has been provided for; at least half the members of further education college councils must be drawn from employers, and substantial functions have been delegated to these new councils.

Education is administered locally in Northern Ireland by five education and library boards, whose costs are met in full by DENI. A review of educational administration is taking place but no major changes will be introduced before 1997. All grant-aided schools include elected parents and teachers on their boards of governors. Provision has been made for schools wishing to provide integrated education to have grant-maintained integrated status from the outset. All schools and colleges of further education have full responsibility for their own budgets, including staffing costs.

The Council for Catholic Maintained Schools forms an upper tier of management for Catholic schools and provides advice on matters relating to management and administration.

THE INSPECTORATE

The Office for Standards in Education (OFSTED) is a non-ministerial government department headed by HM Chief Inspector of Schools in England (HMCI). Its counterpart in Wales is the Office of HM Chief Inspector of Schools in Wales (OHMCI Wales). OFSTED's remit is to inspect, report on and improve standards of achievement and quality of education through regular independent inspection, public reporting and informed advice. All state schools are inspected by teams of independent inspectors, including educationalists and lay people and headed by registered inspectors, on a four-year cycle starting from September 1993 for secondary schools and September 1994 for primary and special schools. OFSTED selects the teams of independent inspectors following bids for the contracts. A summary of the inspection report must be sent to parents of each pupil, followed by a copy of the governors' action plan thereon. The inspection of further and higher education in England and Wales is the responsibility of inspectors appointed to the respective funding councils. HM Inspectorate in Scotland carries out the inspection of schools and further education institutions in that country, using teams which include lay people, and

in addition requires schools to produce a document setting out their educational targets for the two years ahead and a report on progress over the previous two years. The inspection of higher education is the responsibility of inspectors appointed to the Higher Education Funding Council for Scotland. Inspection is carried out in Northern Ireland by the Department of Education's Education and Training Inspectorate, which also performs an advisory function to the Secretary of State for Northern Ireland. From September 1992 a five-year cycle of inspection was introduced.

There were, in 1995–6, 215 HMIs who act as special advisers to OFSTED, 1,295 registered inspectors and 6,839 independent inspectors in England, 48 HMIs and about 755 independent inspectors in Wales, 99 HMIs in Scotland and 60 members of the Inspectorate in Northern Ireland.

SCHOOLS AND PUPILS

Schooling is compulsory in Great Britain for all children between five and 16 years and between four and 16 years in Northern Ireland. Some provision is made for children under five and many pupils remain at school after the minimum leaving age. No fees are charged in any publicly maintained school in England, Wales and Scotland. In Northern Ireland, fees are paid by pupils in preparatory departments of grammar schools, but pupils admitted to the secondary departments of grammar schools do not pay fees.

In the UK, parents have a right to express a preference for a particular school and have a right to appeal if dissatisfied. The policy known as more open enrolment requires schools to admit children up to the limit of their capacity if there is a demand for places, and to publish their criteria for selection if they are over-subscribed, in which case parents have a right of appeal.

The 'Parents' Charter', available free from education departments, is a booklet which tells parents about the education system. Schools are now required to make available information about themselves, their public examination results, truancy rates, and destination of leavers. Corporal punishment is no longer legal in publicly maintained schools in the UK.

FALL AND RISE IN NUMBERS

In primary education, and increasingly in secondary education, pupil numbers in the UK declined through the 1980s. In nursery and primary schools pupil numbers reached their lowest figure of 4.5 million in 1990. Numbers are expected to increase gradually year by year until by 2000 they reach about 5.3 million. In secondary schools pupil numbers peaked at 4.6 million in 1981. They stood at 3.6 million in 1993 and are projected to rise to about 4 million in 2005.

ENGLAND AND WALES

There are two main categories of school in England and Wales: publicly maintained schools, which charge no fees; and independent schools, which charge fees (see pages 437–8). Publicly maintained schools are maintained by local education authorities except for: grant-maintained schools, which are funded through the Funding Agency for Schools in England and by the Welsh Office in Wales and comprise primary and secondary schools which, although still providing free education, have applied to opt out of local education authority control in favour of grant-maintained status; and City Technology Colleges (see below). There are 26,528 schools in the maintained sector and 2,328 independent schools.

Maintained schools are of two types: (i) county schools (16,128 in 1994) which are owned by LEAs and wholly funded by them. They are non-denominational and provide primary and secondary education; and (ii) voluntary schools (7,260 in 1994) which also provide primary and secondary education. Although the buildings are in many cases provided by the voluntary bodies (mainly religious denominations), they are financially maintained by an LEA.

Voluntary schools are of three kinds: controlled (3,031), aided (4,175) and special agreement (54). In controlled schools the LEA bears all costs. In aided schools the building is usually provided by the voluntary body. The managers or governors are responsible for repairs to the school building and for improvements and alterations to it, though the Department for Education and Employment may reimburse part of approved capital expenditure, while the LEA pays for internal maintenance and other running costs. Special agreement schools are those where the LEA may, by special agreement, pay between one-half and three-quarters of the cost of building a new, or extending an existing, voluntary school, almost always a secondary school. There are no special agreement schools in Wales.

All publicly maintained schools have a governing body, usually made up of a number of parent representatives, governors appointed by the LEA if the school is LEA maintained, the headteacher (unless he or she chooses otherwise), and serving teachers. Schools can appoint up to four sponsor governors from business who will be expected to provide financial and managerial assistance. Parental involvement in the running of schools has increased considerably in recent years, and parents have also been given the power to decide by ballot whether their child's school should opt out of local authority control and become grant-maintained. Governors are responsible for the overall policies of schools and their academic aims and objectives; they also control matters of school discipline and the appointment and dismissal of staff. Governing bodies select inspectors for their schools, are responsible for action as a result of inspection reports and are required to make those reports and their action plans thereon available to parents. Under the Local Management of Schools (LMS) initiative LEAs are required to delegate 85 per cent of school budgets, including staffing costs, directly to schools. LEAs continue to retain responsibility for various services, including transport and school meals.

Technology Colleges and Language Colleges – The Technology College programme was launched in September 1993 and is open to all state secondary schools wishing to specialize in the teaching of technology, mathematics and science. The programme has been broadened to include support for schools wishing to develop a special strength in language teaching as Language Colleges. In addition to the normal funding arrangements, the colleges receive business sponsorship (up to four sponsor governors may sit on governing bodies) and complementary capital grants from central government, together with annual grants to assist the delivery of an enhanced curriculum. By September 1995, there were 85 technology colleges and two language colleges. In Wales the Technology Schools Initiative provides grants to enhance technology teaching to those schools successful in attracting funding through open competition.

Grant-maintained (GM) schools – All secondary and primary schools are eligible to apply for grant-maintained status, subject to a ballot of parents. GM schools are maintained directly by the Secretary of State and the Welsh Office, not the LEA, and are wholly run by their own governing body. The Funding Agency for Schools was set up in April 1994 to take over the payment of grants to grant-maintained schools in England. The Schools Funding Council for Wales will be instituted when the number of GM schools, 16 in September 1995, justifies the change in funding arrangements. In September 1995 there were about 1,075 schools operating under grant-maintained status, about 60 per cent of them secondary schools.

City Technology Colleges (CTCs) and *City Colleges for the Technology of the Arts (CCTAs)* are state-aided but independent of LEAs. Their aim is to widen the choice of secondary education in disadvantaged urban areas and to teach a broad curriculum with an emphasis on science, technology, business understanding and arts technologies. Capital costs are shared by government and sponsors from industry and commerce, and running costs are covered by a per capita grant from the DFEE in line with comparable costs in an LEA maintained school. The first city technology college opened in 1988 in Solihull. By September 1995 there were 14. The first CCTA, known as Britschool, opened in Croydon in 1991.

SCOTLAND

Schools in Scotland fall into three main categories: education authority schools (3,798) (known as public schools), which are managed by the regional and islands councils and financed jointly by the councils and central government; grant-aided schools (10), conducted by voluntary managers who receive grants direct from the Scottish Office Education and Industry Department; and independent schools (116), which receive no direct grant and charge fees, but are subject to inspection and registration. An additional category is that of self-governing schools opting to be managed entirely by a board of management consisting of the headmaster, parent and staff representatives and co-opted members. The change of status requires a ballot of parents and the publication of proposals by the board, and the achievement of self-government is subject to a final decision by the Secretary of State. These schools remain in the public sector and are funded by direct government grant set to match the resources the school would have received under education authority management. One has so far been established.

Education authorities are required to establish school boards to participate in the administration and management of schools. These boards consist of elected parents and staff members as well as co-opted members.

Technology Academies (TAs) – The Self-Governing Schools etc. (Scotland) Act 1989 provides for setting up technology academies in areas of urban deprivation. These secondary schools are intended to be so placed as to draw on a wide catchment, and to offer a broad curriculum with an emphasis on science and technology. They are to be founded and managed in partnership with industrial sponsors, with central government meeting the running costs by grant-aid thereafter. None has yet been set up.

NORTHERN IRELAND

There are three main categories of grant-aided school in Northern Ireland: controlled schools (683), which are controlled by the education and library boards with all costs paid from public funds; voluntary maintained schools (561), mainly under Roman Catholic management, which receive grants towards capital costs and running costs in whole or in part; and voluntary grammar schools (53), which may be under Roman Catholic or non-denominational management and receive grants from the Department of Education for Northern Ireland. All grant-aided schools include elected parents and teachers on their boards of governors, whose responsibilities also include financial management under the Local Management of Schools (LMS) initiative. About 85 per cent of the potential funds available to schools are now delegated to them. Voluntary maintained and voluntary grammar schools can apply for designation as a new category of voluntary school, which is eligible for a 100 per cent as opposed to 85 per cent grant. Such schools are managed by a board of governors on which no single interest group has a majority of nominees. There are also 21 independent schools in Northern Ireland.

The majority of children in Northern Ireland are educated in schools which in practice are segregated on religious lines. Integrated schools exist to educate Protestant and Roman Catholic children together. There are two types: grant-maintained integrated schools which are funded by DENI; and controlled integrated schools funded by the education and library boards. Procedures are also in place for balloting parents in existing segregated schools to determine whether they want instead to have integrated schools. By September 1995, 28 integrated schools had been established, nine of them secondary.

THE STATE SYSTEM

NURSERY EDUCATION – Nursery education is for children from two to five years and is not compulsory. It takes place in nursery schools or nursery classes in primary schools. In 1992–3, 847,600 pupils under five years of age were receiving education in maintained nursery and primary schools, an increase of 30,000 on the previous year. Of the total, 85,000 were in nursery schools, 705,300 in primary schools, and 50,200 in non-maintained nursery schools. Expressed as a percentage of the population aged three and four years, the 847,600 represented 55 per cent, compared to 53 per cent in the previous year. Many children also attend pre-school playgroups organized by parents and voluntary bodies such as the Pre-School Learning Alliance. In order to increase participation in nursery education, every parent of a four-year-old is to be given a voucher worth £1,100 exchangeable for up to three terms of pre-school education. The scheme is being piloted in 1996 and will be fully operational by April 1997.

PRIMARY EDUCATION – Primary education begins at five years in Great Britain and four years in Northern Ireland, and is almost always co-educational. In England, Wales and Northern Ireland the transfer to secondary school is generally made at 11 years. In Scotland, the primary school course lasts for seven years and pupils transfer to secondary courses at about the age of 12.

Primary schools consist mainly of infants' schools for children aged five to seven, junior schools for those aged seven to 11, and combined junior and infant schools for both age groups. First schools in some parts of England cater for ages five to ten as the first stage of a three-tier system: first, middle and secondary. Many primary schools provide nursery classes for children under five (see above).

The number of primary schools in the UK in 1992–3 was 23,904, which was 54 fewer than in 1991–2, with 5,099,900 full- and part-time pupils, of which 847,600 were under five. Between 1993 and 2000 primary school pupil numbers are projected to rise by about 4.2 per cent.

Pupil-teacher ratios in maintained primary schools were:

	1991–2	1992–3
England	22.0	22.2
Wales	22.3	22.1
Scotland	19.5	19.3
Northern Ireland	22.6	22.3
UK	21.6	21.9

The average size of classes 'as taught' fell to 23.8 in 1991 but rose to 25.8 in 1994.

MIDDLE SCHOOLS – Middle schools (which take children from first schools), mostly in England, cover varying age ranges between eight and 14 and usually lead on to comprehensive upper schools.

SECONDARY EDUCATION – Secondary schools are for children aged 11 to 16 and for those who choose to stay on to 18. At 16, many students prefer to move on to tertiary or sixth form colleges (see page 441). Most secondary schools in England, Wales and Scotland are co-educational. The largest secondary schools have over 2,000 pupils but only 24 per cent of the schools take over 1,000 pupils.

In England and Wales the main types of secondary schools are: comprehensive schools (86.1 per cent of pupils in England, 99.1 in Wales), whose admission arrangements are without reference to ability or aptitude; middle deemed secondary schools for children aged variously between eight and 14 years who then move on to senior comprehensive schools at 12, 13 or 14 (5.6 per cent of pupils in England); secondary modern schools (3.5 per cent of pupils in England) providing a general education with a practical bias; secondary grammar schools (3.8 per cent of pupils in England) with selective intake providing an academic course from 11 to 16–18 years; and technical schools (0.1 per cent in England), providing an integrated academic and technical education.

In January 1993 there were in England and Wales 3,065,400 pupils in maintained secondary schools, including 10.3 per cent in England and 12.3 per cent in Wales who were 16 or over. After falling by 16 per cent between 1987 and 1991, numbers are projected to rise 14.8 per cent by 2000.

Pupil-teacher ratios improved steadily from 15.7 in 1987 to 15.3 in 1990 in England and Wales, then rose to 16.1 in 1994. The average class size in England and Wales in 1994 was 20.9.

In Scotland all pupils in education authority secondary schools attend schools with a comprehensive intake. Most of these schools provide a full range of courses appropriate to all levels of ability from first to sixth year. In 1993–4 there were 311,320 pupils in education authority schools, of whom 24.6 per cent were 16 or over. Numbers are projected to increase to 328,000 in 2001. Pupil-teacher ratios worsened from 12.4 in 1993 to 12.8 in 1994. The average class size in 1994 remained at 19.4.

In most areas of Northern Ireland there is a selective system of secondary education with pupils transferring either to grammar schools or secondary schools at 11–12 years of age. Parents can choose the school they would like their children to attend and all those who apply must be admitted if they meet the criteria. If a school is over-subscribed beyond its statutory admissions number, selection is on the basis of published criteria, which, for most grammar schools, place emphasis on performance in the transfer procedure tests which are set and administered by the Northern Ireland Council for the Curriculum, Examinations and Assessment. When parents consider that a school has not applied its criteria fairly they have access to independent appeals tribunals. Grammar schools provide an academic type of secondary education with A-levels at the end of the seventh year, while secondary non-grammar schools follow a curriculum suited to a wider range of aptitudes and abilities.

In 1994 there were 148,264 pupils in public sector secondary schools, of whom 89,167 (59.3 per cent) attended non-grammar secondary and 59,097 (39.8 per cent) attended grammar schools. Of all pupils 15.5 per cent were 16 or over. Pupil-teacher ratios in Northern Ireland were 15.4 in 1993.

SPECIAL EDUCATION – Special education is provided for children with special educational needs, usually because they have a disability which either prevents or hinders them from making use of educational facilities of a kind generally provided for children of their age in schools within the area of the local authority concerned. Wherever possible, such children are educated in ordinary schools, taking the parents' wishes into account and schools are required to publish their policy for pupils with special educational needs. LEAs are required to identify and secure provision for the needs of children with learning difficulties, to involve the parents in any decision and draw up a formal statement of the child's special educational needs and how they intend to meet them, all within statutory time limits. Parents have a right to appeal to a Special Educational Needs (SEN) Tribunal if they disagree with the statement.

Maintained special schools are run by education authorities which pay all the costs of maintenance, but under the terms of Local Management of Schools (LMS), those able and wishing to manage their own budgets may choose to do so. These schools are also able to apply to become grant-maintained. Non-maintained special schools are run by voluntary bodies; they may receive some grant from central government for capital expenditure and for equipment, but their current expenditure is met primarily from the fees charged to education authorities for pupils placed in the schools. Some independent schools provide education wholly or mainly for children with special educational needs and are required to meet similar standards to those for maintained and non-maintained special schools. It is intended that pupils with special education needs should have access to as much of the national curriculum as possible, but there is provision for them to be exempt from it or for it to be modified to suit their capabilities.

In January 1993 in the UK there was a total of 111,700 full-time pupils in special schools and 500 in hospital schools in England, Wales and Northern Ireland. Of the 111,700, 95,100 were in England, 3,600 in Wales, 8,800 in Scotland and 4,200 in Northern Ireland. Numbers have decreased since 1975–6 as education authorities in England, Wales and Northern Ireland must now ensure that children with special needs are educated as far as possible in ordinary schools with support teaching.

In Scotland, school placing is a matter of agreement between education authorities and parents. Parents have the right to say which school they want their child to attend, and a right of appeal where their wishes are not being met. Whenever possible, children with special needs are integrated into ordinary schools. However, for those who require a different environment or specialized facilities, there are special schools, both grant-aided by central government and independent, and special classes within ordinary schools. Education authorities are required to respond to reasonable requests for independent special schools and to send children with special needs to schools outside Scotland if appropriate provision is not available within the country. A new centre has been opened which practises conductive education methods for children with motor impairments.

ALTERNATIVE PROVISION

There is no legal obligation on parents in the UK to educate their children at school provided that the local education authority is satisfied that the child is receiving full-time education suited to its age, abilities and aptitudes. The education authority need not be informed that a child is being educated at home unless the child is already registered at a state school. In this case the parents must arrange for the child's name to be removed from the school's register (by writing to the headteacher) before education at home can begin. Failure to do so leaves the parents liable to prosecution for condoning non-attendance.

In most cases an initial visit is made by an education adviser or education welfare officer, and sometimes subsequent inspections are made, but practice varies according to the individual education authority. There is no requirement for parents educating their children at home to be in possession of a teaching qualification.

Further advice on educating children other than at school can be obtained from Education Otherwise (see page 450).

INDEPENDENT SCHOOLS

Independent schools receive no grants from public funds. They charge fees, and are owned and managed under special trusts, with profits being used for the benefit of the schools concerned. There is a wide variety of provision, from kindergartens to large day and boarding schools, and from experimental schools to traditional institutions. A number of independent schools have been instituted by religious and ethnic minorities.

All independent schools in the UK are open to inspection by approved inspectors (see page 434) and must register with the appropriate government education department. The education departments lay down certain minimum standards and can make schools remedy any unacceptable features of their building or instruction and exclude any unsuitable teacher or proprietor. Most independent schools offer a similar range of courses to state schools and enter pupils for the same public examinations. Introduction of the national curriculum and the associated education targets and assessment procedures is not obligatory in the independent sector.

The term public schools is often applied to those independent schools in membership of the Headmasters' Conference, the Governing Bodies Association or the Governing Bodies of Girls' Schools Association. Most public schools are single-sex but there are some mixed schools and an increasing number of schools have mixed sixth forms.

Preparatory schools are so-called because they prepare children for the common entrance examination to senior independent schools. Most cater for boys from about seven to 13 years, some are for girls, and an increasing number are co-educational. The common entrance examination is set by the Common Entrance Examination Board, but marked by the independent school to which the pupil intends to go. It is taken at 13 by boys, and from 11 to 13 by girls.

In January 1994 there were 2,266 independent schools in England with 555,900 full-time and part-time pupils and a pupil-teacher ratio of 10.3.

In Wales in 1993–4 there were 64 independent schools, with 10,672 pupils and a pupil-teacher ratio of 9.6.

In Scotland in 1993–4 there were 116 registered independent schools with 32,900 pupils and a pupil-teacher ratio of 10.2. Most independent schools in Scotland follow the English examination system, i.e. GCSE followed by A-levels, although some take the Scottish Education Certificate at Standard grade followed by Highers or Advanced Highers.

There are 21 independent schools in Northern Ireland with 939 pupils and a pupil-teacher ratio of 11.3.

ASSISTED PLACES SCHEME

The Assisted Places Scheme enables children to attend independent secondary schools which their parents could not otherwise afford. The scheme provides help with tuition fees and other expenses, except boarding costs, on a sliding scale depending on the family's income. The take-up rate for places available at age 11 to 13 at the 303 participating schools in England and Wales is around 99.5 per cent, and the proportion of pupils receiving full fee remission is about 37 per cent. In the 1994–5 academic year, 34,996 places were offered in England and Wales. The 55 participating schools in Scotland admitted about 3,000 pupils on the scheme in 1994–5, which, unlike that in England and Wales, is cash-limited. The proportion of pupils receiving full fee remission was about 43 per cent.

The scheme is administered and funded in England by the Department for Education and Employment, in Wales by the Welsh Office, and in Scotland by the Scottish Office Education and Industry Department. The scheme does not operate in Northern Ireland as the independent sector admits non-fee-paying pupils. There is, however, a similar scheme known as the Talented Children's Scheme to help pupils gifted in music and dance.

Further information can be obtained from the Independent Schools Information Service (*see* page 450).

THE CURRICULUM

ENGLAND AND WALES

The Education Reform Act 1988 legislated for the progressive introduction of a national curriculum in primary and secondary schools between autumn 1989 and autumn 1997, for the period of compulsory schooling from five to 16. The national curriculum as originally proposed was widely criticized for being too prescriptive and time-consuming. It was revised in 1994 and its requirements were substantially reduced; the revisions were implemented in August 1995 for key stages 1 to 3 and will be introduced from August 1996 and August 1997 for key stage 4. The statutory subjects for 5- to 11-year-olds (key stages 1 and 2) are English (and Welsh in Wales), mathematics, science (which form the core subjects), technology (including information technology), history, geography, art and music (foundation subjects).

For 11- to 14-year-olds (key stage 3) a modern foreign language is added. From August 1996 for 14- to 16-year-olds (key stage 4) art, music, history and geography will be optional subjects, but pupils will be required to take full courses in English, mathematics and science and at least a short course in a modern foreign language and technology. Pupils at all key stages are required to do physical education. Religious education, although not prescribed by the national curriculum, is a requirement across all key stages; the syllabus is devised locally and parents have the right to remove their children if they wish. National tests and tasks in English and mathematics at key stage 1, with the addition of science at key stages 2 and 3, are in place. Teachers make their own assessments of their pupils' progress to set alongside the test results. At key stage 4 the GCSE and vocational equivalents will be the main form of assessment. Plans to use the test results at seven and 14 in compiling publicly available comparative tables of schools have been abandoned as a result of resistance from schools and only A, AS, GCSE and GNVQ results have featured for 1995. However, it is planned that the results of tests on 11-year-olds will be published when the tests are fully established. Teachers have expressed dissatisfaction with the tests since their inception on account of excessive workload and the denial of teachers' own professional accountability. In response to their concerns the government review of the manageability of the national curriculum and testing system announced that there would be fewer and shorter tests for seven- and 14-year-olds and that teachers would have discretion over making and recording

their assessments which would be given equal weighting with test results in all forms of public reporting. The burden on teachers has been reduced by the introduction of external marking for tests of 11- and 14-year-olds; assistance has been provided for teachers of seven-year-olds administering tests and for teachers of other age groups in certain circumstances; mandatory external auditing of teachers' own assessment of classroom work has been discontinued. In 1995 approximately two million pupils took the tests or tasks, about 650,000 at key stages 1–3, the remainder at key stage 4.

In Wales in 1993–4 the Welsh language was in use as the main or secondary medium of instruction or taught as a second language in 96.8 per cent of primary schools. In secondary schools Welsh was taught as a first or second language in 96.5 per cent of schools. It constitutes a core subject of the national curriculum in Welsh-speaking schools and a foundation subject in the others, although there is provision for exemptions to be made; by September 1999 all pupils will be taught Welsh throughout the period of compulsory schooling.

In England the School Curriculum and Assessment Authority (SCAA), funded by the Department for Education and Employment, is responsible for the promotion and support of curriculum development, in addition to advising the Secretary of State on the school curriculum and school tests/examinations. In Wales its functions are performed by the Curriculum and Assessment Authority for Wales, funded by the Welsh Office.

SCOTLAND

The content and management of the curriculum in Scotland are not prescribed by statute, but are the responsibility of education authorities and individual headteachers. Advice and guidance is provided by the Scottish Office Education and Industry Department and the Scottish Consultative Council on the Curriculum. SOEID has produced guidelines for each of the curriculum areas for the age group 5 to 14, to be implemented by 1999. There are also guidelines for assessment across the whole curriculum and standardized national tests for English language and mathematics at five levels for this age group. A major programme to extend modern language teaching to primary schools is in progress. The curriculum for 14- to 16-year-olds includes study within each of eight modes: language and communication, mathematical studies, science, technology, social studies, creative activities, physical education and religious and moral education. There is a recommended percentage of class time to be devoted to each area over the two years. Provision is made for teaching in Gaelic in Gaelic-speaking areas.

For 16- to 18-year-olds, there is available a modular system of vocational courses, certificated by the Scottish Vocational Education Council, in addition to academic courses and a new unified framework of courses and awards is to be introduced in 1997–8.

The Scottish Consultative Council on the Curriculum is responsible for development and advisory work on the curriculum in Scotland.

NORTHERN IRELAND

A curriculum common to all grant-aided schools exists. Pupils are required to study religious education and, depending on which key stage they have reached, certain subjects from six broad areas of study: English, science and technology; the environment and society; creative and expressive studies and, in key stages 3 and 4, languages. The statutory curriculum requirements at key stages 1 to 3 are being revised and new programmes of study will be introduced in September 1996. Six cross-curricular educational themes, which include information technology and education for mutual understanding, are woven through the main subjects of the curriculum. Irish is a foundation subject in schools that use it as a medium of instruction. Arrangements for the assessment of pupils for all compulsory subjects, broadly in line with those in England and Wales, are proposed at the ages of eight, 11, 14 and 16. Voluntary pilot assessments have been carried out since June 1993 for 11- and 14-year-olds and since May 1994 for eight-year-olds. It is proposed to introduce statutory assessment in 1996–7. The GCSE will be used to assess 16-year-olds. In Northern Ireland, as in England and Wales, teachers were dissatisfied with the assessment arrangements which have as a result been simplified.

The Northern Ireland Council for the Curriculum, Examinations and Assessment (NICCEA) monitors and advises the department and teachers on all matters relating to the curriculum and assessment arrangements in grant-aided schools in Northern Ireland. It conducts GCSE, A- and AS-level examinations, pupil assessment at key stages and sets and administers the transfer procedure tests.

RECORDS OF ACHIEVEMENT

The National Record of Achievement (NRA) sets down the range of a school-leaver's achievements and activities both inside and outside the classroom, including those not tested by examination. It is issued to all those leaving school in England, Wales and Northern Ireland. It is not compulsory in Scotland but is available to all education authorities for issue to school leavers. Parents in England and Wales must receive a written yearly progress report on all aspects of their children's achievements. There is a similar commitment for Northern Ireland. In Scotland the school report card gives parents information on their children's progress.

THE PUBLIC EXAMINATION SYSTEM

ENGLAND, WALES AND NORTHERN IRELAND

Until the end of 1987, secondary school pupils at the end of compulsory schooling around the age of 16, and others, took the General Certificate of Education (GCE) Ordinary-level or the Certificate of Secondary Education (CSE). From 1988 these were replaced by a single system of examinations, the General Certificate of Secondary Education (GCSE), which is usually taken after five years of secondary education. The GCSE is the main method of assessing the performance of pupils at age 16 in all national curriculum subjects required to be assessed at the end of compulsory schooling. The structure of the exam is being adapted in accordance with national curriculum requirements; new subject criteria were published in 1995 to govern GCSE syllabuses introduced in 1996 for first examination in 1998. From September 1996 GCSE short course qualifications will be introduced in modern foreign languages, information technology, and design and technology. The syllabus will take half the time typically of a GCSE course.

The GCSE differs from its predecessors in that there are syllabuses based on national criteria covering course objectives, content and assessment methods; differentiated assessment (i.e. different papers or questions for different ranges of ability); and grade-related criteria (i.e. grades awarded on absolute rather than relative performance). The GCSE certificates are awarded on a seven-point scale, A to G. From 1994 there has been an additional 'starred' A grade (A*), to recognize the achievement of the highest attainers at GCSE. Grades A to C are the equivalent of the corresponding O-level grades A to C or CSE grade 1. Grades D, E, F and G record achievement at least as high as

that represented by CSE grades 2 to 5. All GCSE syllabuses, assessments and grading procedures are monitored by the School Curriculum and Assessment Authority (see page 438) to ensure that they conform to the national criteria. GCSE examinations are offered to schools/exam centres by Examining Groups.

In the UK in 1992–3, 85.5 per cent of all 15-year-olds achieved one or more graded GCSE, SCE Standard grade, or equivalent, results.

From September 1991, many maintained schools have offered BTEC Firsts (see page 442) and it is hoped that more schools will offer BTEC Nationals. National Vocational Qualifications in the form of General NVQs have been available to students in schools from September 1992 (see pages 442–3). The Part 1 GNVQ was piloted from September 1995. It is a two-year course available at foundation and intermediate levels, broadly equivalent to two GCSEs.

The General Diploma was introduced in 1995 for 16- to 18-year-olds achieving GCSE at grades A* to C in English, mathematics and science, plus two other GCSEs at the same grades or their vocational equivalent.

Advanced (A-level) examinations are taken by those who choose to continue their education after GCSE. A-level courses last two years and have traditionally provided the foundation for entry to higher education. A-levels are marked on a seven-point scale, from A to E, N (narrow failure) and U (unclassified), which latter grade will not be certificated.

Advanced Supplementary level (AS-level) examinations were introduced in September 1987, as an alternative to, and to complement, A-level examinations. AS-levels are for full-time A-level students but are also open to other students. An AS-level syllabus covers not less than half the amount of ground covered by the corresponding A-level syllabus and, where possible, is related to it. An AS-level course lasts two years and requires not less than half the teaching time of the corresponding A-level course, and two AS-levels are equivalent to one A-level. AS-level passes are graded A to E, with grade standards related to the A-level grades.

A mixture of A-level courses in the subjects to be specialized in and AS-levels form the standard for admission to higher education.

In the UK in 1992–3, 31.3 per cent of all 17-year-olds achieved one or more A-level or SCE H-grade results, an increase of 1 per cent on the previous year. This figure includes those continuing their education in maintained further education establishments including tertiary colleges, as well as school leavers.

Of these, 585,000 achieved at least one A-level or SCE H-grade (46 per cent were boys). Of those in Great Britain who entered for at least one A-level, or at least two SCE H-grades, 33 per cent studied sciences (56 per cent of boys, 44 per cent of girls) and 67 per cent studied arts/social studies (26.5 per cent of boys, 73.5 per cent of girls).

Most examining boards allow the option of an additional paper of greater difficulty to be taken by A-level candidates to obtain what is known as a Special-level or Scholarship-level qualification. S-level papers are available in most of the traditional academic subjects and are marked on a three-point scale.

The C & G (City and Guilds) Diploma of Vocational Education superseded the Certificate of Pre-Vocational Education (CPVE) in schools and colleges in England, Wales and Northern Ireland from September 1992. It is intended for a wide ability range, including pupils who might not go on to A-levels but would like to continue their education on completion of compulsory secondary schooling.

The Diploma of Vocational Education provides recognition of achievement at three levels: foundation, intermediate and national; the two latter broadly corresponding to the GNVQ (*see* page 443) at intermediate and advanced levels. The intermediate and national levels are being phased out in favour of the corresponding GNVQs. The Diploma at Foundation level continues to be available. Within guidelines schools and colleges design their own courses, which stress activity-based learning, core skills which include application of numbers, communication and information technology, and work experience. The Diploma of Vocational Education is mainly for those who want to find out what aptitudes they may have and to prepare themselves for work, but who are not yet committed to a particular occupation. According to level, it can be taken alongside other courses such as GCSEs, A- or AS-levels.

SCOTLAND

Scotland has its own system of public examinations. At the end of the fourth year of secondary education, at about the age of 16, pupils take the Standard grade of the Scottish Certificate of Education Examination which progressively replaced the Ordinary grade by 1995. Standard grade courses and examinations have been designed to suit every level of ability, with assessment against nationally determined standards of performance.

For most courses there are three separate examination papers at the end of the two-year Standard grade course. They are set at Credit (leading to awards at grade 1 or 2), General (leading to awards at grade 3 or 4) and Foundation (leading to awards at grade 5 or 6) levels. Grade 7 is available to those who, although they have completed the course, have shown no significant level of attainment. Normally pupils will take examinations covering two pairs of grades, either grades 1–4 or grades 3–6. Most candidates take eight Standard grade examinations.

The Higher grade of the Scottish Certificate of Education is normally taken one year after Standard grade, at the age of 17 or thereabouts. It is common for pupils to be presented for four or more Higher grades at a single diet of the examination.

The Certificate of Sixth Year Studies (CSYS) is designed to give direction and purpose to sixth-year work by encouraging pupils who have completed their main subjects at Higher grade to study a maximum of three of these subjects in depth. Pupils may also use the sixth year to gain improved or additional Higher grades or Standard grades. A major programme of reform is afoot which will draw all upper secondary qualifications into a single framework by 1998–9. There will be five levels of attainment, the first three corresponding to Standard grade levels, plus Higher and Advanced Higher (which will replace CSYS). Students will study individual units (of 40 or 80 hours) which will be internally assessed and may combine these into courses (with internal assessment) or group awards.

The examining body for the Scottish Certificate of Education and the Certificate of Sixth Year Studies is the Scottish Examination Board.

National Certificates provide an alternative to, and complement Highers and CSYS. They are awarded to pupils normally over the age of 16 who have successfully completed a programme of vocational courses based on modular study units, and the assessment system is based on national criteria. National Certificates are awarded by the Scottish Vocational Education Council (*see also* page 442).

THE INTERNATIONAL BACCALAUREATE

The International Baccalaureate is an internationally recognized two-year pre-university course and examination designed to facilitate the mobility of students and to promote international understanding. Candidates must offer one subject from each of six subject groups, at least three at higher level and the remainder at subsidiary level. Single subjects can be offered, for which a certificate is received. There are 29 schools and colleges in the UK which offer the International Baccalaureate diploma.

TEACHERS

ENGLAND AND WALES

Teachers are appointed by local education authorities, school governing bodies, or school managers. Those in publicly maintained schools must be approved as qualified. Approval is given by the Teacher Training Agency, subject to criteria published by the Secretaries of State. To become a qualified teacher it is necessary to have successfully completed a course of initial teacher training, usually either a Bachelor of Education (B.Ed.) degree or the Postgraduate Certificate of Education (PGCE), but a one-year course is being considered which will qualify certain non-graduates to teach at nursery and infant level. Teacher training was formerly largely integrated with the rest of higher education, with training places concentrated in universities and institutes or colleges of education, but it has now become largely school-based, with student teachers on secondary PGCE courses spending two-thirds of their training in the classroom. Changes have also been made to primary phase teacher training to make it more school-based and to give schools a role in course design and delivery. Since September 1993 individual schools or consortia of schools and CTCs have been able to bid for funds from the DFEE to carry out their own teacher training, including recruitment of students, subject to approval of their proposed training programme by the TTA and monitoring and evaluation by the Office for Standards in Education (OFSTED). Funds are given to schools to meet the costs of designing and delivering the courses, and students receive flat-rate bursaries.

The Teacher Training Agency (TTA) began operations in September 1994. The TTA accredits those institutions which meet the standards set by the Secretaries of State for their courses and will also be a central source of advice and information on teacher training. It funds all types of teacher training, whether run by schools, universities or colleges, and some educational research in England. These provisions were formerly funded by the Higher Education Funding Council in respect of education institutions, and for schools by LEAs. The TTA will exercise only non-funding functions for Wales, where the institutions will be accredited and funded by the HEFCW.

With certain exceptions the profession at present has an all-graduate entry. Teachers in further education are not required to have qualified teacher status, though roughly half have a teaching qualification and most have industrial, commercial or professional experience.

The TTA has responsibility for the Licensed Teacher Scheme, which is designed to attract into the teaching profession entrants over 24 years of age without formal teaching qualifications but with relevant training and experience. All licensees are required to have the equivalent of two years' higher education in the UK and the equivalent of grade C in GCSE maths and English. Each school is responsible for devising a suitable two-year training programme for any licensed teachers they may appoint to their schools. A licensee with at least two years' experience as an instructor may be eligible for qualified teacher status after one year.

The Specialist Teacher Assistant (STA) scheme was introduced in September 1994 to provide trained support to qualified teachers in the teaching of reading, writing and arithmetic to young pupils. Training will be part-time over one year and results in a Specialist Teacher Assistant Record (STAR), which will count towards entry to teacher training.

SCOTLAND

All teachers in maintained schools must be registered with the General Teaching Council for Scotland. They are registered provisionally for a two-year probationary period which can be extended if necessary. Only graduates are accepted as entrants to the teaching profession in Scotland. As a result of a review of initial teacher training instituted in 1992 a greater proportion of training is now classroom-based. The mentor teacher scheme, which will operate in secondary schools from 1996–7, is designed to provide students with support from designated experienced teachers on classroom management and performance. The colleges of education provide both in-service and pre-service training for teachers and are funded by the Scottish Higher Education Funding Council.

NORTHERN IRELAND

Teacher training in Northern Ireland is provided by the two universities and two colleges of education. The colleges are concerned with teacher education mainly for the primary school sector. They also provide B.Ed. courses for intending secondary school teachers of religious education, commercial studies, and craft, design and technology. With these exceptions, the training of teachers for secondary schools is provided in the education departments of the universities. A professional qualification is not mandatory to teach in secondary schools. The Licensed Teacher route is not accepted for qualified teacher status in Northern Ireland. A review of primary and secondary teacher training has taken place as a result of which from 1996–7 all student teachers will spend more time in the classroom and will have the support of a mentoring arrangement with an experienced teacher. The current probationary year is to be replaced by a two-year induction period by 1996–7.

The Northern Ireland Teacher Education Committee advises DENI on the design and implementation of a co-ordinated approach to teacher training.

ACCREDITATION OF TRAINING INSTITUTIONS

Advice to central government on the accreditation, content and quality of initial teacher training courses is given in England by the TTA, in Wales by the HEFCW and in Northern Ireland by validating bodies. These bodies also monitor and disseminate good practice, assisted in Northern Ireland by the Teacher Education Committee..

In Scotland all training courses in colleges of education must be approved by the Scottish Office Education Department and a validating body.

NEWLY-TRAINED TEACHERS

Of teachers who in 1992 had successfully completed initial training courses in the UK, 15,400 had completed a postgraduate course and 8,300 a course for non-graduates.

Because of a shortage of teachers in a number of secondary subjects, a tax-free bursary scheme for trainee teachers on one- or two-year full-time courses has been introduced. The scheme is administered by the TTA. The subjects are: physics or chemistry, or a combination of the two; mathematics; modern languages (including Welsh in

Wales); technology; and craft, design and technology (CDT). The bursary is £1,000 a year.

SERVING TEACHERS

In 1992–3 there were 605,000 teachers (full-time and full-time equivalent) in public sector schools and establishments of further and higher education in the UK, excluding universities. Of these, 491,000 were in maintained schools and 114,000 in further education. There were 210,000 full-time teachers in public sector primary schools, 229,000 in public sector secondary schools and 19,000 in special schools.

SALARIES

Qualified teachers in England, Wales and Northern Ireland, other than heads and deputy heads, are paid on an 18-point scale ranging from £11,883 to £32,169 (April 1995 figures). Entry points and placement depend on qualifications, experience, responsibilities, excellence, and recruitment and retention factors as calculated by the relevant body, i.e. in grant-maintained schools and LEA schools with delegated budgets, the governing body; otherwise the LEA. Headteachers' salaries range from £24,453 to £53,559 and deputy headteachers' salaries range from £23,676 to £38,946. There is a statutory superannuation scheme in maintained schools.

Teachers in Scotland are paid (April 1995 figures) on a ten-point scale from £12,147 to £20,190. The entry point depends on type of qualification, and additional allowances are payable under certain circumstances. Headteachers are paid on a scale from £29,739 to £47,436 and deputy headteachers from £29,190 to £35,493, depending on whether the school is primary or secondary and the size of school roll.

FURTHER EDUCATION

The Education Reform Act 1988 defines further education as all provision outside schools to people aged over 16 of education up to and including A-level and its equivalent. The Further Education Funding Councils for England and Wales, the Scottish Office Education and Industry Department and the Education and Library Boards in Northern Ireland have a duty to secure provision of adequate facilities for further education in their areas.

ENGLAND AND WALES

Further education and sixth form colleges are funded directly by central government through the Further Education Funding Council for England (FEFCE) and the Further Education Funding Council for Wales (FEFCW). These councils are also responsible for the assessment of quality, in which the Councils' inspectorates play a key role. The colleges are controlled by autonomous further education corporations, which include substantial representation from industry and commerce, and which own their own assets and employ their own staff. Their funding is determined in part by the number of students recruited.

In England and Wales further education courses are taught at a variety of institutions. These range from universities which were formerly polytechnics, colleges of higher education and colleges of further education (some of which also offer higher education courses) to tertiary colleges and sixth form colleges, which concentrate on the provision of normal sixth form school courses as well as a range of vocational courses. A number of institutions specific to a particular form of training, e.g. the Royal College of Music, are also involved.

Teaching staff in further education establishments are not necessarily required to have teaching qualifications although many do so, but they are subject to regular appraisal of teaching performance.

Much of the post-school provision outside the higher education sector is broadly vocational in purpose and employers are often involved in designing courses. It ranges from lower-level technical and commercial courses through courses for those aiming at higher-level posts in industry, commerce and administration, to professional courses. Facilities for GCSE courses, the Diploma of Vocational Education, AS-levels and A-level courses are also provided (*see* pages 439–40). These courses can form the foundation for progress to higher education qualifications.

The main courses and examinations in the vocational field, all of which link in with the National Vocational Qualification (NVQ) framework (*see* below), are offered by the following bodies, but there are also many others:

The Business and Technology Education Council (BTEC) provides programmes of study across a wide range of subject areas. The main qualifications are the BTEC First Certificate and the BTEC First Diploma; the BTEC National Certificate and the BTEC National Diploma; the BTEC Higher National Diploma; BTEC NVQs; and BTEC foundation, intermediate and advanced GNVQs in some vocational areas. BTEC First and National diplomas are to be phased out gradually as GNVQs are introduced.

City and Guilds (C&G) is the UK's largest assessment and awarding body. It specializes in developing qualifications and assessments for work-related, general education and leisure qualifications. It awards nationally recognized certificates in over 500 subjects, many of which are NVQs or GNVQs. Its progressive structure of awards spans seven levels, from foundation to the highest level of professional competence.

RSA Examinations Board schemes cover a wide range of vocational qualifications, including accounting, business administration, customer service, management, language schemes, information technology and teaching qualifications. A wide range of NVQs and GNVQs are offered and a policy operates of credit accumulation, so that candidates can take a single unit or complete qualifications.

There are 378 further education establishments in England and Wales and 1,538 adult education centres. In 1993–4 there were 681,719 full-time and sandwich-course students and 712,861 part-time students on further education courses.

SCOTLAND

Further education comprises non-advanced courses up to SCE Highers grade, GCE A-level and SCOTVEC vocational courses. Further education colleges are funded by central government but a further education funding council is proposed at a later stage. Courses are taught mainly at colleges of further education, including technical colleges, and in some schools.

Further education colleges are self-governing, with boards of management which run the colleges and employ staff. The boards include the principal and staff and student representatives among their ten to 16 members, and at least half the members must have experience of commerce, industry or the practice of a profession.

The Scottish Vocational Education Council (SCOTVEC) awards qualifications for most occupations (paralleling the work of the Business and Technology Education Council, City and Guilds, the RSA and other bodies in England, Wales and Northern Ireland). It awards

at non-advanced level the National Certificate which is available in over 3,000 individual modules and covers the whole range of non-advanced further education provision in Scotland. Students may study for the National Certificate on a full-time, part-time, open learning or work-based learning basis. National Certificate modules can be taken in further education colleges, secondary schools and other centres, normally from the age of 16 onwards. SCOTVEC also offers modular advanced-level HNC/HND qualifications and a few post-graduate or post-experience qualifications which are available in further education colleges and higher education institutions. SCOTVEC accredits and awards Scottish Vocational Qualifications (SVQs) which are analogous with the system of NVQs which operates in the rest of the UK. SVQs are essentially work-based but are also available in further education colleges and other centres.

The Record of Education and Training (RET) has been introduced to provide a single certificate recording SCOTVEC achievements; an updated version is provided as and when necessary. SCOTVEC also administers the National Record of Achievement in Scotland on behalf of the Scottish Office.

In 1992–3 there were 36,750 full-time and sandwich-course students and 84,324 part-time students on non-advanced vocational courses of further education in the 43 further education colleges and five colleges of education.

NORTHERN IRELAND

The Education and Library Boards are obliged to submit for approval to the Department of Education for Northern Ireland, schemes setting out the principles to be applied by the boards in planning the further education provision to be made by colleges under their management.

The colleges of further education are maintained by the Education and Library Boards, but financial powers and responsibilities are delegated to the boards of governors of the colleges. The boards of governors must include at least 50 per cent membership from the professions, local business or industry, or other fields of employment relevant to the activities of the college. The review of further education provision which took place during 1991–2 recommended that college and course provision should be rationalized by the amalgamation of some colleges. From September 1994 the mergers reduced the number of free-standing institutions from 24 to 17. No decisions have yet been taken regarding the central funding of colleges in Northern Ireland, either through a funding council or directly by DENI.

On reaching school-leaving age, pupils may attend colleges of further education to pursue the same type of vocational courses as are provided in colleges in England and Wales, administered by the same examining bodies.

In 1994–5 Northern Ireland had 17 institutions of further education. In 1994–5 there were 21,304 full-time students and 51,813 part-time students on non-advanced vocational courses of further education.

COURSE INFORMATION

Applications for further education courses are generally made directly to the colleges concerned. Information on further education courses in the UK and addresses of colleges can be found in the *Directory of Further Education* published annually by the Careers Research and Advisory Centre.

NATIONAL VOCATIONAL QUALIFICATIONS

The National Council for Vocational Qualifications (NCVQ) was set up by the Government in 1986 to achieve a coherent national framework for vocational qualifications in England, Wales and Northern Ireland. The Council does not award qualifications but accredits National Vocational Qualifications (NVQs), General National Vocational Qualifications (GNVQs) and core skills. Candidates are assessed through awarding bodies who bestow the qualifications where candidates reach the required standards. SCOTVEC (*see* page 442) performs similar functions in Scotland, but its role includes the awarding of qualifications.

The NVQ framework is currently based on five levels. From September 1992 General National Vocational Qualifications (GNVQs) were introduced into colleges and schools as a vocational alternative to academic qualifications. They cover broad categories in the NVQ framework and are aimed at those wishing to familiarize themselves with a range of opportunities. Advanced GNVQ or the vocational A-level (formerly level 3) is designed to be equivalent to two A-levels; intermediate (formerly level 2) is equivalent to four or five good GCSEs. Foundation GNVQs (formerly level 1) became available in September 1994.

HIGHER EDUCATION

The term higher education is used to describe education above A-level, Advanced Higher grade and their equivalent, which is provided mainly in universities and colleges of higher education.

The Further and Higher Education Act 1992 and parallel legislation in Scotland removed the distinction between higher education provided by the universities, which were funded by the Universities Funding Council (UFC), and that provided in England and Wales by the former polytechnics and colleges of higher education, funded by the Polytechnics and Colleges Funding Council (PCFC), and in Scotland by the former central institutions and other institutions funded by central government. All are now funded by the Higher Education Funding Councils for England, Wales and Scotland. The Acts also provided for other changes to bring the non-university sector in line with the universities, including the right for all polytechnics, and other higher education institutions which satisfy the necessary criteria, to award their own taught course and research degrees and to adopt the title of university. All the polytechnics and art colleges have since adopted the title of university. The change of name does not affect the legal constitution of the institutions.

In 1992–3, there were 957,600 full-time and sandwich-course students in higher education in the UK, of whom 95,900 were from overseas. The number of part-time students in the UK, including the Open University, was 486,000. The proportion of 16- to 20-year-olds entering full-time higher education in Great Britain rose from 16.1 per cent in 1985–6 to 26.9 per cent in 1992–3. The number of mature entrants (those aged 21 and over when starting an undergraduate course and 25 and over when starting a postgraduate course) to higher education in Great Britain in 1992 (excluding those at the Open University) was 319,400, up by 128 per cent on 1982. The number of full-time students on science courses in 1992–3 was 153,300, of whom 54,300 were female.

UNIVERSITIES AND COLLEGES

The universities are self-governing institutions established by royal charter or Act of Parliament. They have academic freedom and are responsible for their own academic appointments, curricula and student admissions and award their own degrees.

Responsibility for universities in England rests with the Secretary of State for Education and Employment, and in their territories with the Secretaries of State for Scotland, Wales and Northern Ireland. Advice to the Government on matters relating to the universities is provided by the Higher Education Funding Councils for England, Wales and Scotland, and by the Northern Ireland Higher Education Council. The HEFCs receive a block grant from central government which they allocate to the universities and colleges. The grant is allocated directly by central government in Northern Ireland.

There are now 86 universities in the UK, where only 47 existed prior to the Further and Higher Education Acts 1992. Of these 86, 70 are in England (including one federal university), two (one a federal institution) in Wales, 12 in Scotland and two in Northern Ireland.

The pre-1992 universities each have their own system of internal government but broad similarities exist. Most are run by two main bodies: the senate, which deals primarily with academic issues and consists of members elected from within the university; and the council, which is the supreme body and is responsible for all appointments and promotions, and bidding for and allocation of financial resources. At least half the members of the council are drawn from outside the university. Joint committees of senate and council are becoming increasingly common.

In 1993–4, at the 45 universities which were funded through the UFC (eight in Scotland, a single federal university in Wales, and the remainder in England) and the two centrally funded universities in Northern Ireland, there were 470,565 full-time students (27,042 from EU countries; 48,474 from other overseas countries) and 83,311 part-time students. Women formed 45.8 per cent of the full-time total and 47.3 per cent of the part-time total.

Those universities which were formerly polytechnics and the colleges of higher education are run by higher education corporations (HECs), which are controlled by boards of governors whose members were initially appointed by the Secretaries of State but which will subsequently make their own appointments. At least half the members of each board must be drawn from industry, business, commerce and the professions.

In England in 1993, there were 510,530 students in the 35 former polytechnics. Of these, 498,212 were on higher education courses, of whom 358,185 were full-time or sandwich-course students. In the 47 colleges of higher education in England in 1993 there were 144,439 students, 133,159 of those on higher education courses and of whom 99,401 were full-time or sandwich-course students.

In 1993 there were 349 major establishments in higher education in England (maintained, assisted by LEAs, in receipt of direct central government grant, or voluntary) outside the PCFC sector. In England in 1993 they catered for 133,477 students on higher education courses funded by the PCFC, including 44,241 on full-time or sandwich courses. In Wales in 1993 there were 137,924 students in 36 publicly funded institutions, 37,133 of those on higher education courses of whom 25,873 were full-time or sandwich students. The higher education courses in these establishments are now funded by the HEFCs for England and Wales, and their further education courses are funded through the FEFCs.

The non-residential Open University provides courses nationally leading to degrees. Teaching is through a combination of television and radio programmes, correspondence, tutorials, short residential courses and local audio-visual centres. No qualifications are needed for entry. The Open University offers a modular programme of undergraduate courses by credit accumulation and post-experience and postgraduate courses, including a programme of higher degrees which comprises B.Phil., M.Phil. and Ph.D. through research, and MA, MBA and M.Sc. through taught courses. The Open University throughout the UK is funded by the Higher Education Funding Council for England. In 1995, about 95,000 undergraduates were registered at the Open University, of whom about 50 per cent were women. Estimated cost (year 1995) of a six-credit degree was around £1,670.

The independent University of Buckingham provides a two-year course leading to a bachelor's degree and its tuition fees were £9,140 for 1995. It receives no capital or recurrent income from the Government but its students are eligible for mandatory awards from local education authorities. Its academic year consists of four terms of ten weeks each.

ACADEMIC STAFF

Each university and college appoints its own academic staff on its own conditions. However, there is a common salary structure and, except for Oxford and Cambridge, a common career structure in those universities formerly funded by the UFC; and a common salary structure for the former PCFC sector. Staff can be dismissed for good cause and for redundancy.

The Education Reform Act 1988 took polytechnics and higher education colleges in England and Wales out of local education authority control, turning them into employers on their own account. The Universities and Colleges Employers Association (UCEA) acts as a pay agency for universities and colleges.

Teaching staff in higher education require no formal teaching qualification, but teacher trainers are required to spend a certain amount of time in schools to ensure that they have sufficient recent practical experience.

In 1993–4, there were 60,858 full-time and part-time academic staff in universities funded by the UFC and 43,162 teaching higher education courses in institutions formerly in the PCFC sector in England and Wales or centrally funded in Scotland and Northern Ireland.

Salary scales for staff in the former UFC sector differ from those in the former polytechnics and colleges; it is hoped eventually to amalgamate them. The 1995–6 salary scales for non-clinical academic staff in universities formerly funded by the UFC are:

Lecturer grade A	£15,154–£19,848
Lecturer grade B	£20,677–£26,430
Senior lecturer	£27,747–£31,357
Professor from	£31,999

The salaries of clinical academic staff are kept broadly comparable to those of doctors and dentists in the National Health Service.

Salary scales for lecturers in the former polytechnics, now universities, and colleges of further and higher education in England, Wales and Northern Ireland are (September 1994):

Lecturer	£12,756–£21,264
Senior lecturer	£20,553–£26,223
Principal lecturer	£24,804–£31,118
Head of Department from	£26,304

The salary scales for staff in Scotland are (April 1995):

Lecturer	£14,607–£26,216
Senior lecturer	£24,044–£31,081
Head of department/professor from	£32,058

FINANCE

Although universities and colleges are expected to look to a much wider range of funding sources than before, and to generate additional revenue in collaboration with industry, they are still largely financed, directly or indirectly, from government resources.

In the academic year 1993–4, the final year for which these figures are available, the total recurrent income of the 47 pre-1992 universities funded by the UFC was £5,888 million (£5,406 million in 1992–3). The exchequer grant was £1,780 million (£1,621 million in 1992–3), forming 30 per cent of total income, compared to 1985–6 when it formed 58 per cent. Income from research grants and contracts in 1993–4 was £1,239 million, an increase of 12 per cent on the previous year.

In the academic year 1993–4 the HEFC's recurrent grant to institutions outside its sector and LEAs for the provision of higher education courses was £230.6 million.

COURSES

In the UK all universities, including the Open University, and some colleges award their own degrees and other qualifications and can act as awarding and validating bodies for neighbouring colleges which are not yet accredited. The Higher Education Quality Council (HEQC), funded by institutional contributions, advises the Secretaries of State on applications for degree-awarding powers.

Higher education courses last full-time for at least four weeks or, if part-time, involve more than 60 hours of instruction. Facilities exist for full-time and part-time study, day release, sandwich or block release. Credit accumulation and transfer (CATS) is a system of study which is now becoming widely available. It allows a student to achieve a final qualification by accumulating credits for courses of study successfully achieved, or even professional experience, over a period. Credit transfer information and values are carried on an electronic database called ECCTIS 2000, which is available in most careers offices and many schools and colleges.

Higher education courses include: first degree and postgraduate (including research); Diploma in Higher Education (Dip.HE); Higher National Diploma (HND) and Higher National Certificate (HNC); and preparation for professional examinations. The in-service training of teachers is also included, but from September 1994 has been funded in England by the TTA (*see* page 440), not the HEFC.

The Diploma of Higher Education (Dip.HE) is a two-year diploma usually intended to serve as a stepping-stone to a degree course or other further study. The Dip.HE is awarded by the institution itself if it is accredited; by an accredited institution of its choice if not. The BTEC Higher National Certificate (HNC) is awarded after two years part-time study. The BTEC Higher National Diploma (HND) is awarded after two years full-time, or three years sandwich-course or part-time study.

With the exception of certain Scottish universities where master is sometimes used for a first degree in arts subjects, undergraduate courses lead to the title of Bachelor, Bachelor of Arts (BA) and Bachelor of Science (B.Sc.) being the most common. For a higher degree the titles are, Master of Arts (MA), Master of Science (M.Sc.) (usually taught courses) and the research degrees of Master of Philosophy (M.Phil.) and Doctor of Philosophy (Ph.D. or, at a few universities, D.Phil.).

Most undergraduate courses at British universities and colleges of higher education run for three years, except in Scotland and at the University of Keele where they may take four years. Professional courses in subjects such as medicine, dentistry and veterinary science take longer. Details of courses on offer and of predicted entry requirements for the following year's intake are provided in *University and College Entrance: Official Guide* published annually by the Universities and Colleges Admissions Service (UCAS), which includes degree, Dip.HE and HND courses at all universities (excluding the Open

University) and most colleges of HE (for address, see page 452).

Postgraduate studies vary in length. Taught courses which lead to certificates, diplomas or master's degrees usually take one year full-time or two years part-time. Research degrees take from two to three years full-time and much longer if completed on a part-time basis. Details of taught courses and research degree opportunities can be found in *Graduate Studies* published annually for the Careers Research and Advisory Centre (CRAC) by Hobsons Publishing PLC (for address, see page 452).

Post-experience short courses are forming an increasing part of higher education provision, reflecting the need to update professional and technical training. Most of these courses fund themselves.

ADMISSIONS

The number of students entering higher education has been set at 30 per cent of the 18- to 19-year-old age group. Apart from quotas for medical, dental and veterinary students, there are no limits set for other subjects and the individual university or college decides which students to accept. The formal entry requirements to most degree courses are two A-levels at grade E or above (or equivalent), and to HND courses one A-level (or equivalent). In practice, most offers of places require qualifications in excess of this, higher requirements usually reflecting the popularity of a course. These requirements do not, however, exclude applications from students with a variety of non-GCSE qualifications or unquantified experience and skills.

For admission to a degree, Dip.HE or HND, potential students apply through a central clearing house. All universities and most colleges providing higher education courses in the UK are members of the Universities and Colleges Admission Service (UCAS). Applicants are supplied with an application form and a *UCAS Handbook*, available from schools, colleges and careers offices or direct from UCAS, and may apply to a maximum of eight institutions/courses on the UCAS form. The only exception among universities is the Open University, which conducts its own admissions.

There are a number of studio-based art and design courses for which applications are made through the Art and Design Admissions Registry (ADAR). Applications for undergraduate teacher training courses are made through UCAS.

For admission as a postgraduate student, universities and colleges normally require a good first degree in a subject related to the proposed course of study or research, but other experience and qualifications will be considered on merit. Most applications are made to individual institutions but there are two clearing houses of relevance. Postgraduate teacher training courses in England and Wales utilize the Graduate Teacher Training Registry (*see* page 452). Postgraduate teacher training courses in Scotland are applied to through the Teacher Education Admissions Clearing House (TEACH) (*see* page 452). For social work the Social Work Admissions System operates (*see* page 452).

SCOTLAND

The Scottish Higher Education Funding Council (SHEFC) funds 22 institutions of higher education, including 13 universities. The universities are broadly managed as described above and each institution of higher education is managed by an independent governing body which includes representatives of industrial, commercial, professional and educational interests. Most of the courses

outside the universities have a vocational orientation and a substantial number are sandwich courses.

In 1992–3, there was a total of 169,268 students enrolled on courses of higher education, of which number 42,880 were on higher education courses in further education colleges. Of the total number, 75 per cent were on full-time or sandwich courses.

Applications to institutions of higher education in Scotland are made through UCAS, except for applications for postgraduate teacher training courses which are made through TEACH (*see* page 452). Details of initial teacher training courses can be obtained from colleges of education and those universities offering such courses, and from the Committee of Scottish Higher Education Principals (COSHEP).

NORTHERN IRELAND

In Northern Ireland advanced courses are provided by 17 institutions of further education and by the two universities. As well as offering first and postgraduate degrees, the University of Ulster offers courses leading to the BTEC Higher National Diploma and professional qualifications. Applications to undertake courses of higher education other than degree courses are made to the institutions direct. Applications for degree courses are made through UCAS. Applications for PGCE courses at institutions in Northern Ireland are made to the Department of Education for Northern Irelalnd.

In 1994–5, 6,136 students were enrolled on advanced courses of higher education in the institutions of further education, 48.5 per cent of whom were women. There were 2,371 students on full-time or sandwich courses.

FEES

The tuition fees for students with mandatory awards (*see* below) are paid by the grant-awarding body. Students from member states of the European Union pay fees at home student rates. Since 1980–1 students from outside the EU have paid fees that are meant to cover the cost of their education, but financial help is available under a number of schemes. Information about these schemes is available from British Council offices world-wide.

Universities and colleges are free to set their own charges for students from non-EU countries. Undergraduate fees for the academic year 1995–6 for home and EU students are £750 for arts courses (band 1), £1,600 for laboratory or workshop based courses, mainly science (band 2), and £2,800 for clinical courses (band 3).

For postgraduate students, the maximum tuition fee that will be reimbursed through the awards system is £2,430 in 1995–6.

GRANTS FOR STUDENTS

Students in the UK who plan to take a full-time or sandwich course of further study after leaving school may be eligible for a grant. A parental contribution is deductible on a sliding scale dependent on income. For married students this may be deducted from their spouse's income instead. However, parental contribution is not deducted from the grant to students over 25 years of age who have been self-supporting for at least three years. The main rates of mandatory grant have been frozen since 1991–2 as it is envisaged that students will increasingly support themselves by loans. Tuition fees are paid in full for all students in receipt of a grant, regardless of parental income, and they are usually paid direct to the university or college by the education authority.

Grants are paid by local education authorities in England, Wales and Northern Ireland, of which 100 per cent of the cost is reimbursed by central government, and by the Scottish Office Education and Industry Department in Scotland through the Students Award Agency. Applications are made to the authority in the area in which the student normally lives. Applications should not, however, be made earlier than the January preceding the start of the course.

TYPES OF GRANT

Grants are of two kinds: mandatory and discretionary. Mandatory grants are those which awarding authorities must pay to students who are attending designated courses and who can satisfy certain other conditions. Such a grant is awarded normally to enable the student to attend only one designated course and there is no general entitlement to an award for any particular number of years. Discretionary grants are those for which each awarding authority has discretion to decide its own policy.

Designated courses are those full-time or sandwich courses leading to: a degree; the Diploma of Higher Education; the BTEC Higher National Diploma; initial teacher-training courses, including those for the postgraduate certificate of education and the art teachers' certificate or diploma; a university certificate or diploma course lasting at least three years; other qualifications which are specifically designated as being comparable to first degree courses; and the SCOTVEC Higher National Diploma. The local education authority should be consulted for advice about eligibility for a grant.

A means-tested maintenance grant, usually paid once a term, covers periods of attendance during term as well as the Christmas and Easter vacations, but not the summer vacation. It is subject to deduction on account of the student's own income and her/his parents' or spouse's income. The basic grant rates for 1995–6 are: £2,340 if living in a hall of residence or lodgings and studying within the London area (£2,270 for students from Scotland); £1,885 as above but outside the London area (£1,820 for students from Scotland); £1,530 if living at the parental home (£1,390 for students in Scotland). Additional allowances are available if, for example, the course requires a period of study abroad.

LEA and Scottish Office Education Department expenditure on student fees and maintenance in 1993–4 was £3,095.4 million; 868,344 mandatory awards were made.

STUDENT LOANS

The Education (Student Loans) Act 1990 legislated for interest-free but indexed top-up loans of up to £1,695 in 1995–6 to be made available to eligible students in the UK. The Government expects that at least £644 million will be taken up in loans in 1995–6.

Students apply direct to the Student Loans Company Ltd (see page 452), which will require a certificate of eligibility from their place of study. Loans are available to students on designated courses within the scope of mandatory awards and the same residency conditions apply. Repayment is normally over five to seven years, although it can be deferred if income is at or below 85 per cent of national average earnings, about £14,000 a year.

ACCESS FUNDS

Access funds are allocated by education departments to the appropriate funding councils in England, Wales and Scotland and administered by further and higher education institutions. In Northern Ireland they are allocated by central government to the institutions direct. They are available to students whose access to higher education might otherwise be inhibited by financial considerations or where real financial difficulties are faced. For the academic year 1995–6, provision in the UK will be £34.9 million.

POSTGRADUATE AWARDS

Unlike funding for undergraduates, which is mandatory for most degree and equivalent level courses, grants for postgraduate study are usually discretionary. Grants are also often dependent on the class of first degree, especially for research degrees.

An increasing number of scholarships are available from research charities, endowments and particular industries or companies. For residents in England and Wales, several schemes of postgraduate bursaries or studentships are funded by the Department for Education and Employment, the government research councils, the Ministry of Agriculture, Fisheries and Food, and the British Academy, which awards grants for study in the humanities.

In Scotland postgraduate funding is provided by the Scottish Office Education and Industry Department, the Scottish Office Agriculture and Fisheries Department, and the research councils as in England and Wales.

Awards in Northern Ireland are made by the Department of Education for Northern Ireland, the Department of Agriculture for Northern Ireland, and the Medical Research Council.

In 1992–3 in the UK 21,200 awards were made. The national rates for twelve-month studentships in 1995–6 are: £5,695 in college or lodgings in London; £4,525 in college or lodgings outside London; £3,335 for those living with parents or spouse's parents. The rates for 30-week bursaries for 1995–6 are: £3,375 in college or lodgings in London; £2,665 in college or lodgings outside London; £2,015 if living with parents or spouse's parents.

ADULT AND CONTINUING EDUCATION

The term adult education covers a broad spectrum of educational activities ranging from non-vocational courses of general interest, through the acquiring of special vocational skills needed in industry or commerce, to study for a degree at the Open University.

The responsibility for securing adult and continuing education in England and Wales is statutory and shared between: the Further Education Funding Councils, which are responsible for and fund those courses which take place in their sector and lead to academic and vocational qualifications, prepare students to undertake further or higher education courses, or confer basic skills; the Higher Education Funding Councils, which fund advanced courses of continuing education; and LEAs, which are responsible for those courses which do not fall within the remit of the funding councils. Funding in Northern Ireland is through the education and library boards and in Scotland by the Scottish Office Education and Industry Department.

PROVIDERS

Courses specifically for adults are provided by many bodies. They include, in the statutory sector: local education authorities in England and Wales; the regional and islands education authorities in Scotland and the Scottish Office Education and Industry Department; education and library boards in Northern Ireland; further education colleges; higher education colleges; universities, especially the Open University and Birkbeck College of the University of London; residential colleges; the BBC, independent television and local radio stations. There are also a number of voluntary bodies.

The local education authorities in England and Wales operate through 'area' adult education centres (1,538 in 1993), institutes or colleges, and the adult studies departments of colleges of further education. The Scottish Office Education and Industry Department funds adult education, including that provided by the universities and the Workers' Educational Association, at vocational further education colleges (46 in 1993) and evening centres (129 in 1993). In addition, SOEID provides grants to a number of voluntary organizations. Provision in the statutory sector in Northern Ireland is the responsibility of the universities and the education and library boards, which operate 17 further education colleges and a number of community schools.

The involvement of universities in adult education and continuing education has diversified considerably and is supported by a variety of administrative structures ranging from dedicated departments to a devolved approach. Birkbeck College in the University of London caters solely for part-time students. Those institutions and colleges formerly in the PCFC sector in England and Wales, because of their range of courses and flexible patterns of student attendance, provide opportunities in the field of adult and continuing education. The Forum for the Advancement of Continuing Education (FACE) promotes collaboration between institutions of higher education active in this area. The Open University, in partnership with the BBC, provides distance teaching leading to first degrees, and also offers post-experience and higher degree courses (*see* page 460–1).

Of the voluntary bodies, the biggest is the Workers' Educational Association (WEA) which operates throughout the UK, reaching about 180,000 adult students annually. The FEFCs for England and Wales, the Scottish Office Education and Industry Department, the Department of Education for Northern Ireland and local education authorities make grants towards provision.

The National Institute of Adult Continuing Education (England and Wales) (NIACE) provides information and advice to organizations and providers on all aspects of adult continuing education. NIACE conducts research, project and development work, and is funded by the DFEE, the LEAs and other funding bodies. The Welsh committee, NIACE Cymru, receives financial support from the Welsh Office, support in kind from the Welsh Joint Education Committee, and advises government, voluntary bodies and education providers on adult continuing education and training matters in Wales. In Scotland advice on adult and community education, and promotion thereof, is provided by the Scottish Community Education Council. The Northern Ireland Council for Adult Education has an advisory role. Its membership includes representatives of the education and library boards and of most organizations involved in the field, together with an assessor appointed by DENI.

Membership of the Universities Association for Continuing Education is open to any university or university college in the UK. It promotes university continuing education, facilitates the interchange of information, and supports research and development work in continuing education.

COURSES

Although lengths vary, most courses are part-time. Long-term residential colleges in England and Wales are grant-aided by the Further Education Funding Councils and provide full-time courses lasting one or two years. Some colleges and centres offer short-term residential courses, lasting from a few days to a few weeks, in a wide range of subjects. Local education authorities directly sponsor many of the colleges, while others are sponsored by universities or voluntary organizations. A list of courses, *Time to Learn*, is published by NIACE.

GRANTS

Although full-time courses at degree level attract mandatory awards, for courses below that level all students over the age of 19 must pay a fee. However, discretionary grants may be available. Adult education bursaries for students at the long-term residential colleges of adult education are the responsibility of the colleges themselves. The awards are administered for the colleges by the Awards Officer of the Residential Colleges Committee for students resident in England and are funded by the FEFC for England in English colleges; for colleges in Wales they are funded and administered by the FEFC for Wales; and for colleges in Scotland and Northern Ireland they are funded by central government and administered by the education authorities. A booklet, *Adult Education Bursaries*, can be obtained from the Awards Officer, Adult Education Bursaries, c/o Ruskin College (*see* page 463).

NUMBERS

There are no comprehensive statistics covering all aspects of adult education. However, enrolments on evening courses in the UK numbered 1,640,000 in 1992–3 (65.9 per cent women). This number included 629,000 students at adult education centres. In 1993–4, liberal adult education and professional updating short courses organized by former UFC institutions were attended by 967,839 students, an increase of 1.6 per cent on 1992–3.

Education Directory

LOCAL EDUCATION AUTHORITIES

ENGLAND

COUNTY COUNCILS

AVON, PO Box 57, Avon House North, St James Barton, Bristol BS99 7EB. Tel: 0117-987 4055. *Director,* G. Badman

BEDFORDSHIRE, County Hall, Cauldwell Street, Bedford MK42 9AP. Tel: 01234-363222. *Director,* D. G. Wadsworth

BERKSHIRE, PO Box 902, Shire Hall, Shinfield Park, Reading RG2 9XE. Tel: 01734-233401. *Chief Education Officer,* S. R. Goodchild

BUCKINGHAMSHIRE, County Hall, Aylesbury HP20 IUA. Tel: 01296-382641. *Chief Education Officer,* S. Sharp

CAMBRIDGESHIRE, Castle Court, Shire Hall, Castle Hill, Cambridge CB3 0AP. Tel: 01223-317990. *Director,* J. Ferguson

CHESHIRE, County Hall, Chester CH1 1SQ. Tel: 01244-602201. *Director,* D. Cracknell

CLEVELAND, Woodlands Road, Middlesbrough TS1 3BN. Tel: 01642-248155. *County Education Officer,* B. Worthy

CORNWALL, County Hall, Truro TR1 3AY. Tel: 01872-322000. *Secretary of Education,* J. Harris

CUMBRIA, 5 Portland Square, Carlisle CA1 IPU. Tel: 01228-23456. *Director,* J. Nellist

DERBYSHIRE, County Offices, Matlock DE4 3AG. Tel: 01629-580000. *Chief Education Officer,* Mrs V. Hannon

DEVON, County Hall, Topsham Road, Exeter EX2 4QG. Tel: 01392-382000. *Chief Education Officer,* S. W. Jenkin

DORSET, County Hall, Dorchester DT1 IXJ. Tel: 01305-251000. *Director,* R. H. Ely

DURHAM, County Hall, Durham DH1 5UJ. Tel: 0191-386 4411. *Director,* K. Mitchell

EAST SUSSEX, PO Box 4, County Hall, St Anne's Crescent, Lewes BN7 1SG. Tel: 01273-481000. *County Education Officer,* D. Mallen

ESSEX, PO Box 47, A Block, County Hall, Victoria Road South, Chelmsford CM1 ILD. Tel: 01245-492211. *Director,* P. Lincoln

GLOUCESTERSHIRE, Shire Hall, Westgate Street, Gloucester GL1 2TP. Tel: 01452-425302. *Director,* K. D. Anderson, CBE

HAMPSHIRE, The Castle, Winchester SO23 8UG. Tel: 01962-841841. *County Education Officer,* P. J. Coles

HEREFORD AND WORCESTER, County Hall, Spetchley Road, Worcester WR5 2NP. Tel: 01905-763763. *County Education Officer,* D. A. J. Stanley

HERTFORDSHIRE, County Hall, Hertford SG13 8DF. Tel: 01992-555701. *County Education Officer,* Mrs H. du Quesnay

HUMBERSIDE, County Hall, Beverley HU17 9BA. Tel: 01482-867131. *Director,* Prof. M. W. Garnett

ISLE OF WIGHT, County Hall, Newport PO30 IUD. Tel: 01983-823400. *Director,* A. Kaye

KENT, Springfield, Maidstone ME14 2LJ. Tel: 01622-671411. *Director,* R. Pryke

LANCASHIRE, PO Box 61, County Hall, Preston PR1 8RJ. Tel: 01772-254868. *Chief Education Officer,* J. A. Collier, CBE

LEICESTERSHIRE, County Hall, Glenfield, Leicester LE3 8RF. Tel: 0116-232 3232. *Director,* Mrs J. Strong

LINCOLNSHIRE, County Offices, Newland, Lincoln LN1 IYQ. Tel: 01522-552222. *Director,* N. J. Riches

NORFOLK, County Hall, Martineau Lane, Norwich NR1 2DH. Tel: 01603-222300. *Director,* M. H. Edwards

NORTHAMPTONSHIRE, PO Box 149, County Hall, Northampton NN1 1AU. Tel: 01604-236236. *Director,* R. Atkinson

NORTHUMBERLAND, County Hall, Morpeth NE61 2EF. Tel: 01670-533000. *Director,* C. C. Tipple

NORTH YORKSHIRE, County Hall, Northallerton DL7 8AD. Tel: 01609-780780. *Director,* F. F. Evans

NOTTINGHAMSHIRE, County Hall, West Bridgford, Nottingham NG2 7QP. Tel: 0115-982 3823. *Director,* R. Valentine

OXFORDSHIRE, Macclesfield House, New Road, Oxford OX1 1NA. Tel: 01865-815449. *Chief Education Officer,* Mrs J. Stephens

SHROPSHIRE, The Shirehall, Abbey Foregate, Shrewsbury SY2 6ND. Tel: 01743-251000. *County Education Officer,* Ms C. Adams

SOMERSET, County Hall, Taunton TA1 4DY. Tel: 01823-333451. *Chief Education Officer,* N. Henwood

STAFFORDSHIRE, Tipping Street, Stafford ST16 2DH. Tel: 01785-223121. *Chief Education Officer,* P. J. Hunter, PH.D.

SUFFOLK, St Andrew House, County Hall, Ipswich IP4 ILJ. Tel: 01473-264627. *County Education Officer,* D. J. Peachey

SURREY, County Hall, Penrhyn Road, Kingston upon Thames KT1 2DJ. Tel: 0181-541 9501. *County Education Officer,* Ms J. H. Barrows

WARWICKSHIRE, PO Box 24, 22 Northgate Street, Warwick CV34 4SR. Tel: 01926-410410. *Director,* E. Wood

WEST SUSSEX, County Hall, West Street, Chichester PO19 1RF. Tel: 01243-777100. *Director,* R. D. C. Bunker

WILTSHIRE, County Hall, Trowbridge BA14 8JH. Tel: 01225-713000. *Director,* K. Robinson, PH.D.

METROPOLITAN DISTRICT COUNCILS

BARNSLEY, Berneslai Close, S70 2HS. Tel: 01226-770770. *Director,* D. Dalton

BIRMINGHAM, Council House, Margaret Street, B3 3BU. Tel: 0121-235 2550. *Chief Education Officer,* T. Brighouse

BOLTON, Paderborn House, Civic Centre, BL1 IJW. Tel: 01204-522311. *Director,* B. Hughes

BRADFORD, Flockton House, Flockton Road, BD4 7RY. Tel: 01274-751840. *Education Officer (acting),* K. Sutcliffe

BURY, Athenaeum House, Market Street, BL9 0BN. Tel: 0161-705 5652. *Chief Education Officer,* J. Beech

CALDERDALE, Northgate House, Northgate, Halifax HX1 IUN. Tel: 01422-357257. *Director,* I. Jennings

COVENTRY, Council House, Earl Street, CV1 5RR. Tel: 01203-833333. *Chief Education Officer,* Ms. C. Goodwin

DONCASTER, PO Box 266, The Council House, DN1 3AD. Tel: 01302-734444. *Director,* A. M. Taylor

DUDLEY, Westox House, 1 Trinity Road, DY1 IJB. Tel: 01384-452200. *Chief Education Officer (acting),* R. Colligan

GATESHEAD, Civic Centre, Regent Street, NE8 IHH. Tel: 0191-477 1011. *Director,* J. D. Arbon

KIRKLEES, Oldgate House, 2 Oldgate, Huddersfield HD1 6QW. Tel: 01484-446742. *Chief Education Officer,* R. Vincent

KNOWSLEY, Huyton Hey Road, Huyton, Merseyside L36 5YH. Tel: 0151-489 6000. *Director of Educataion,* P. Wylie

LEEDS, Merrion House, 110 Merrion Centre, LS2 8DT. Tel: 0113-247 5575. *Chief Education Officer,* J. Rawlinson

LIVERPOOL, 14 Sir Thomas Street, LI 6BJ. Tel: 0151-225 2799. *Director,* M. F. Cogley

MANCHESTER, Cumberland House, Crown Square, M60 3BB. Tel: 0161-234 7121. *Chief Education Officer,* R. Jobson

NEWCASTLE UPON TYNE, Civic Centre, NEI 8PU. Tel: 0191-232 8520. *Education Officer,* N. Purser

NORTH TYNESIDE, Stephenson House, Stephenson Street, North Shields NE30 1QA. Tel: 0191-257 5544. *Education Officer,* J. C. Benneworth

OLDHAM, Town Hall, Middleton Road, Chadderton, OL9 6PP. Tel: 0161-911 4260. *Director (acting),* Mrs H. Holmes

ROCHDALE, PO Box 70, Municipal Offices, Smith Street, OL16 1YD. Tel: 01706-47474. *Director,* Mrs D. Cavanagh

ROTHERHAM, Norfolk House, Walker Place, Rotherham, S60 1QT. Tel: 01709-822500. *Education Officer,* B. H. Yemm

ST HELENS, Rivington Centre, Rivington Road, WAIO 4ND. Tel: 01744-456000. *Director,* B. M. Mainwaring

SALFORD, Chapel Street, M3 5LT. Tel: 0161-832 9751. *Chief Education Officer,* D. Johnston

SANDWELL, PO Box 41, Shaftesbury House, 402 High Street, West Bromwich B70 9LT. Tel: 0121-525 7366. *Director,* S. Gallacher

SEFTON, Town Hall, Oriel Road, Bootle, Merseyside L20 7AE. Tel: 0151-933 6003. *Education Officer,* J. A. Marsden

SHEFFIELD, Leopold Street, SI 1RJ. Tel: 0114-272 6341. *Director,* vacant

SOLIHULL, PO Box 20, Council House, B91 3QU. Tel: 0121-704 6000. *Director,* C. J. Trinick

SOUTH TYNESIDE, Town Hall and Civic Offices, Westoe Road, South Shields NE32 2RL. Tel: 0191-427 1717. *Director,* I. L. Reid

STOCKPORT, Stopford House, Piccadilly, SKI 3XE. Tel: 0161-474 3808. *Director,* M. K. J. Hunt

SUNDERLAND, PO Box 101, Civic Centre, Burdon Road, SR2 7DN. Tel: 0191-567 6161. *Director,* J. Williams

TAMESIDE, Council Offices, Wellington Road, Ashton-under-Lyne OL6 6DL. Tel: 0161-342 8355. *Director,* A. M. Webster

TRAFFORD, PO Box 19, Sale Town Hall, Tatton Road, Sale M33 1YR. Tel: 0161-912 1212. *Director,* A. Lee

WAKEFIELD, County Hall, Bond Street, WFI 2QL. Tel: 01924-306090. *Education Officer,* J. McLeod

WALSALL, Civic Centre, Darwall Street, WSI 1DQ. Tel: 01922-650000. *Education Officer,* M. J. Quinn

WIGAN, Gateway House, Standishgate, WNI 1AE. Tel: 01942-828880. *Education Officer,* R. Clark

WIRRAL, Hamilton Building, Conway Street, Birkenhead L41 4FD. Tel: 0151-666 2121. *Director,* D. Rigby

WOLVERHAMPTON, Civic Centre, St Peter's Square, WVI 1RR. Tel: 01902-27811. *Director,* R. Lockwood

LONDON

*Inner London borough

BARKING AND DAGENHAM, Town Hall, Barking, Essex IGII 7LU. Tel: 0181-592 4500. *Education Officer,* A. Larbalastier

BARNET, Old Town Hall, Friern Barnet Lane, NII 3DL. Tel: 0181-359 2000. *Education Officer,* J. Bailey

BEXLEY, Hill View, Hill View Drive, Welling, Kent DAI4 6BT. Tel: 0181-303 7777. *Director,* P. McGee

BRENT, Chesterfield House, 9 Park Lane, Wembley, Middx HA9 7RW. Tel: 0181-937 3020. *Chief Education Officer (acting),* P. Doherty

BROMLEY, Civic Centre, Stockwell Close, BRI 3UH. Tel: 0181-464 3333. *Director,* A. Baxter

*CAMDEN, Crowndale Centre, 218–220 Eversholt Street, NWI 1BD. Tel: 0171-911 1525. *Education Officer,* R. Litchfield

*CITY OF LONDON, Education Department, Corporation of London, PO Box 270, Guildhall, EC2P 2EJ. Tel: 0171-332 1750. *City Education Officer,* D. Smith

*CITY OF WESTMINSTER, PO Box 240, City Hall, 64 Victoria Street, SWIE 6QP. Tel: 0171-798 2771. *Education Officer (acting),* Mrs D. McGrath

CROYDON, Taberner House, Park Lane, CR9 1TP. Tel: 0181-760 5555. *Director,* P. Benians

EALING, Perceval House, 14–16 Uxbridge Road, W5 2HL. Tel: 0181-758 5484. *Director,* M. Herrman

ENFIELD, PO Box 56, Civic Centre, Silver Street, ENI 3XQ. Tel: 0181-967 9423. *Director,* Ms L. Graham

*GREENWICH, Riverside House, Woolwich High Street, Woolwich, SEI8 6DN. Tel: 0181-854 8888. *Director,* J. Kramer

*HACKNEY, Edith Cavell Building, Enfield Road, NI 5AZ. Tel: 0171-214 8400. *Director,* G. John

*HAMMERSMITH AND FULHAM, Cambridge House, Cambridge Grove, W6 4LE. Tel: 0181-748 3020. *Director,* Ms C. Whatford

HARINGEY, 48 Station Road, Wood Green, N22 4TY. Tel: 0181-975 9700. *Director,* Miss J. Tonge

HARROW, PO Box 22, Civic Centre, Harrow HAI 2UW. Tel: 0181-863 5611. *Director,* Mrs C. Gilbert

HAVERING, Broxhill Centre, Broxhill Road, Harold Hill, Romford RM4 1XN. Tel: 01708-772222. *Director,* C. Hardy

HILLINGDON, Civic Centre, High Street, Uxbridge, Middx UB8 1UW. Tel: 01895-250111. *Education Officer,* Mrs G. Andrews

HOUNSLOW, Civic Centre, Lampton Road, TW3 4DN. Tel: 0181-862 5301. *Director,* J. D. Trickett

*ISLINGTON, Laycock Street, NI 1TH. Tel: 0171-457 5753. *Education Officer,* H. Nicole

*KENSINGTON AND CHELSEA, Town Hall, Hornton Street, W8 7NX. Tel: 0171-937 5464. *Director,* M. Stoten

KINGSTON UPON THAMES, Guildhall 2, High Street, KTI 1EU. Tel: 0181-547 5220. *Director,* W. Dickinson

*LAMBETH, Blue Star House, 234–244 Stockwell Road, SW9 9SP. Tel: 0171-926 2248. *Chief Education Officer,* Mrs J. Stansfield

*LEWISHAM, Laurence House, 1 Catford Road, SE6 4SW. Tel: 0181-695 6000. *Director,* L. Fullick

MERTON, Civic Centre, London Road, Morden, Surrey SM4 5DX. Tel: 0181-563 2222. *Director (acting),* Ms J. Cairns

NEWHAM, Broadway House, 322 High Street, E15 1AJ. Tel: 0181-555 5552. *Director,* I. Harrison

REDBRIDGE, Lynton House, 255–259 High Road, Ilford IGI 1NN. Tel: 0181-478 3020. *Director,* D. Capper

RICHMOND UPON THAMES, Regal House, London Road, Twickenham TWI 3QS. Tel: 0181-891 7500. *Director,* G. Alexander

*SOUTHWARK, 1 Bradenham Close, SE17 2BA. Tel: 0171-525 5000. *Director,* G. Mott

SUTTON, The Grove, Carshalton, Surrey SM5 3AL. Tel: 0181-770 6500. *Director,* C. Blurton

*TOWER HAMLETS, Mulberry Place, 5 Clove Crescent, E14 2BG. Tel: 0171-364 5000. *Education Officer,* Mrs A. Sofer

WALTHAM FOREST, Municipal Offices, High Road, Leyton, EIO 5QJ. Tel: 0181-527 5544. *Director,* A. Lockhart

*WANDSWORTH, Town Hall, Wandsworth High Street, SW18 2PU. Tel: 0181-871 6000. *Director,* P. Robinson

WALES

COUNTY COUNCILS†

CLWYD, Shire Hall, Mold CH7 6NB. Tel: 01352-702500. *Director,* K. McDonogh

DYFED, Pibwrlwyd, Carmarthen SA31 2NH. Tel: 01267-233333. *Director,* J. G. Ellis

GWENT, County Hall, Cwmbran NP44 2XG. Tel: 01633-838838. *Director,* J. D. Griffiths

GWYNEDD, County Offices, Shirehall Street, Caernarfon LL55 1SH. Tel: 01286-672255. *Director,* G. Jarvis

MID GLAMORGAN, County Hall, Cathays Park, Cardiff CF1 3NF. Tel: 01222-820820. *Director,* K. Davies

POWYS, County Hall, Llandrindod Wells LD1 5LG. Tel: 01597-826000. *Director,* M. R. J. Barker

SOUTH GLAMORGAN, County Hall, Atlantic Wharf, Cardiff CF1 5UW. Tel: 01222-872000. *Director,* T. P. Davies

WEST GLAMORGAN, County Hall, Swansea SA1 3SN. Tel: 01792-471111. *Director,* H. G. Roberts

SCOTLAND

REGIONAL AND ISLANDS COUNCILS†

BORDERS, Regional Headquarters, Newtown St Boswells, Melrose TD6 0SA. Tel: 01895-823301. *Director,* I. Dutton

CENTRAL, Regional Council Offices, Viewforth, Stirling FK8 2ET. Tel: 01786-442000. *Director,* Mrs M. Allan

DUMFRIES AND GALLOWAY, 30 Edinburgh Road, Dumfries DG1 1JQ. Tel: 01387-261234. *Director (acting),* K. A. Macleod

FIFE, Fife House, North Street, Glenrothes KY7 5LT. Tel: 01592-414141. *Director,* B. Welsh

GRAMPIAN, Woodhill House, Westburn Road, Aberdeen AB9 2LU. Tel: 01224-664600. *Director,* Mrs N. Webster

HIGHLAND, Regional Buildings, Glenurquhart Road, Inverness IV3 5NX. Tel: 01463-702801. *Director,* A. C. Gilchrist

LOTHIAN, 40 Torphichen Street, Edinburgh EH3 8JJ. Tel: 0131-229 9166. *Director,* Mrs E. Reid

ORKNEY, Council Offices, Kirkwall KW15 1NY. Tel: 01856-873535. *Director,* J. Anderson

SHETLAND, Schlumberger, Gremista Industrial Estate, Lerwick ZE1 0PX. Tel: 01595-3535. *Director,* J. Halcrow

STRATHCLYDE, 20 India Street, Glasgow G2 4PF. Tel: 0141-204 2900. *Director,* F. Pignatelli

TAYSIDE, Tayside House, 28 Crichton Street, Dundee DD1 3RJ. Tel: 01382-23281. *Director,* J. Anderson

WESTERN ISLES, Council Offices, Sandwick Road, Stornoway, Isle of Lewis PA87 2BW. Tel: 01851-703773. *Director,* N. R. Galbraith, OBE

NORTHERN IRELAND

EDUCATION AND LIBRARY BOARDS

BELFAST, 40 Academy Street, Belfast BT1 2NQ. Tel: 01232-564000. *Chief Executive,* T. G. J. Moag

---

†These are the local education authorities in Wales and Scotland until April 1996, when local government reorganization takes place. Each new council will set up a LEA, which will operate in much the same way as the present LEAs

NORTH EASTERN, County Hall, 182 Galgorm Road, Ballymena, Co. Antrim BT42 1HN. Tel: 01266-653333. *Chief Executive,* G. Topping

SOUTH EASTERN, 18 Windsor Avenue, Belfast BT9 6EF. Tel: 01232-381188. *Chief Executive,* T. Nolan, OBE

SOUTHERN, 3 Charlemont Place, The Mall, Armagh BT61 9AX. Tel: 01861-512200. *Chief Executive,* J. G. Kelly

WESTERN, 1 Hospital Road, Omagh, Co. Tyrone BT79 0AW. Tel: 01662-240240. *Chief Executive,* J. Martin

ISLANDS

GUERNSEY, Grange Road, St Peter Port GY1 1RQ. Tel: 01481-710821. *Director,* J. D. Stephenson

JERSEY, PO Box 142, St Saviour JE4 8QJ. Tel: 01534-509500. *Director,* B. Grady

ISLE OF MAN, Department of Education, Murray House, Mount Havelock, Douglas IM1 2SG. Tel: 01624-685685. *Director,* G. Baker

ISLES OF SCILLY, Town Hall, St Mary's TR21 0LW. Tel: 01720-422537. *Secretary for Education,* P. S. Hygate

---

ADVISORY BODIES

SCHOOLS

EDUCATION OTHERWISE, PO Box 7420, London N9 9SG. *Helpline,* tel: 0891-518303

INTERNATIONAL BACCALAUREATE, Examinations Office, Pascal Close, St Mellons, Cardiff CF3 0YP. Tel: 01222-770770. *Director of Examinations,* C. Carthew

NATIONAL ADVISORY COUNCIL FOR EDUCATION TRAINING AND TARGETS, 7th Floor, 222 Grays Inn Road, London WC1X 8HL. Tel: 0171-211 5012. *Chairman,* P. Davis; *Director,* M. Waring

NATIONAL COUNCIL FOR EDUCATIONAL TECHNOLOGY, Milburn Hill Road, Science Park, Coventry CV4 7JJ. Tel: 01203-416994. *Chief Executive,* Mrs M. Bell

SPECIAL EDUCATIONAL NEEDS TRIBUNAL, 71 Victoria Street, London SW1H 0HW. Tel: 0171-925 6925. *President,* T. Aldridge; *Secretary,* Ms J. Saraga

INDEPENDENT SCHOOLS

ASSISTED PLACES COMMITTEE, 26 Queen Anne's Gate, London SW1H 9AN. Tel: 0171-222 9595. *Secretary,* P. F. V. Waters

GOVERNING BODIES ASSOCIATION, The Coach House, Pickforde Lane, Ticehurst, E. Sussex TN5 7BJ. Tel: 01580-200855. *Secretary,* D. G. Banwell

GOVERNING BODIES OF GIRLS' SCHOOLS ASSOCIATION, The Coach House, Pickforde Lane, Ticehurst, E. Sussex TN5 7BJ. Tel: 01580-200855. *Secretary,* D. G. Banwell

INDEPENDENT SCHOOLS EXAMINATIONS BOARD, Jordan House, Christchurch Road, New Milton, Hants BH25 6QJ. Tel: 01425-621111. *Administrator,* Mrs J. Williams

INDEPENDENT SCHOOLS INFORMATION SERVICE, 56 Buckingham Gate, London SW1E 6AG. Tel: 0171-630 8793. *National Director,* D. J. Woodhead

FURTHER EDUCATION

FURTHER EDUCATION DEVELOPMENT AGENCY, Vauxhall Unit, Citadel Place, Tinworth Street, London SE11 5EH. Tel: 0171-962 1280. *Chief Executive,* S. Crown

NATIONAL COUNCIL FOR VOCATIONAL QUALIFICATIONS, 222 Euston Road, London NW1 2BZ. Tel: 0171-387 9898. *Chief Executive,* J. Hillier

Regional Advisory Councils

ASSOCIATION OF COLLEGES IN THE EASTERN REGION, Merlin Place, Milton Road, Cambridge CB4 4DP. Tel: 01223-424022. *Chief Executive,* J. Graystone

CENTRA (NORTH WEST EDUCATION AND TRAINING SERVICES) LTD, Duxbury Park, Duxbury Hall Road, Chorley, Lancs PR7 4AT. Tel: 01257-241428. *Chief Executive,* R. S. Welsh

EMFEC (EAST MIDLAND FURTHER EDUCATION COUNCIL), Robins Wood House, Robins Wood Road, Aspley, Nottingham NG8 3NH. Tel: 0115-929 3291. *Chief Executive,* R. Ainscough

LASER ADVISORY COUNCIL (LONDON AND SOUTH EAST), Chenies House, 21 Bedford Square, London WC1B 3HH. Tel: 0171-637 3073. *Director,* L. South

NCFE (NORTHERN COUNCIL FOR FURTHER EDUCATION), 5 Grosvenor Villas, Grosvenor Road, Newcastle upon Tyne NE2 2RU. Tel: 0191-281 3242. *Chief Executive,* J. F. Pearce

SOUTHERN REGIONAL COUNCIL FOR FURTHER EDUCATION AND TRAINING, The Mezzanine Suite, PO Box 2055, Civic Centre, Reading RG1 7ET. Tel: 01734-390592. *Chief Executive,* B. J. Knowles

SOUTH WEST ASSOCIATION FOR FURTHER EDUCATION AND TRAINING, Bishops Hull House, Bishops Hull, Taunton, Somerset TA1 5RA. Tel: 01823-335491. *Chief Executive,* F. S. Fisher

WELSH JOINT EDUCATION COMMITTEE, 245 Western Avenue, Cardiff CF5 2YX. Tel: 01222-265000. *Secretary,* C. Heycock

YORKSHIRE AND HUMBERSIDE ASSOCIATION FOR FURTHER AND HIGHER EDUCATION, 13 Wellington Road East, Dewsbury, W. Yorks WF13 1XG. Tel: 01924-450900. *Chief Executive,* Prof. N. Woodhead

HIGHER EDUCATION

ASSOCIATION OF COMMONWEALTH UNIVERSITIES, John Foster House, 36 Gordon Square, London WC1H 0PF. Tel: 0171-387 8572. *Secretary-General,* Dr A. Christodoulou, CBE

COMMITTEE OF VICE-CHANCELLORS AND PRINCIPALS OF THE UNIVERSITIES OF THE UNITED KINGDOM, 29 Tavistock Square, London WC1H 9EZ. Tel: 0171-387 9231. *Chairman,* Prof. G. Roberts, FRS; *Chief Executive* Ms D. Warwick

HIGHER EDUCATION QUALITY COUNCIL, 344–354 Gray's Inn Road, London WC1X 8BP. Tel: 0171-837 2223. *Company Secretary,* G. L. Middleton

NORTHERN IRELAND HIGHER EDUCATION COUNCIL, Rathgael House, Balloo Road, Bangor BT19 7PR. Tel: 01247-279333. *Chairman,* Sir Kenneth Bloomfield, KCB; *Secretary,* J. Coote

CURRICULUM COUNCILS, ETC

CURRICULUM AND ASSESSMENT AUTHORITY FOR WALES, Castle Buildings, Womanby Street, Cardiff CF1 9SX. Tel: 01222-344946. *Chief Executive,* J. V. Williams

NORTHERN IRELAND COUNCIL FOR THE CURRICULUM, EXAMINATIONS AND ASSESSMENT, Stranmillis College, Stranmillis Road, Belfast BT9 5DY. Tel: 01232-381414. *Chief Executive,* Mrs C. Coxhead

SCHOOL CURRICULUM AND ASSESSMENT AUTHORITY, Newcombe House, 45 Notting Hill Gate, London W11 3JB. Tel: 0171-229 1234. *Chairman,* Sir Ron Dearing, CB; *Chief Executive,* N. Tate, PH.D.

SCOTTISH CONSULTATIVE COUNCIL ON THE CURRICULUM, Gardyne Road, Broughty Ferry,

Dundee DD5 1NY. Tel: 01382-455053. *Chief Executive,* C. E. Harrison

TVEI UNIT, Schools Policy Branch (Yepa 1), Department for Education and Employment, Room E435, Moorfoot, Sheffield S1 4PQ. Tel: 0114-259 3857

EXAMINING BODIES

GCSE

MIDLAND EXAMINING GROUP, 1 Hills Road, Cambridge CB1 2EU. Tel: 01223-553311. *Chief Executive,* R. R. McLone, PH.D.

NORTHERN EXAMINATIONS AND ASSESSMENT BOARD, Devas Street, Manchester M15 6EX. Tel: 0161-953 1180. *Chief Executive,* Mrs K. Tattersall

NORTHERN IRELAND COUNCIL FOR THE CURRICULUM, EXAMINATIONS AND ASSESSMENT, Beechill House, 42 Beechill Road, Belfast BT8 4RS. Tel: 01232-704666. *Chief Executive,* Mrs C. Coxhead

SEG (SOUTHERN EXAMINING GROUP), Stag Hill House, Guildford, Surrey GU2 5XJ. Tel: 01483-506506. *Secretary-General,* J. A. Day

UNIVERSITY OF LONDON EXAMINATIONS AND ASSESSMENT COUNCIL, Stewart House, 32 Russell Square, London WC1B 5DN. Tel: 0171-331 4000. *Chief Executive,* A. Smith

WELSH JOINT EDUCATION COMMITTEE, 245 Western Avenue, Cardiff CF5 2YX. Tel: 01222-265000. *Secretary,* C. Heycock

A-LEVEL

ASSOCIATED EXAMINING BOARD, Stag Hill House, Guildford, Surrey GU2 5XJ. Tel: 01483-506506. *Secretary-General,* J. A. Day

NORTHERN EXAMINATIONS AND ASSESSMENT BOARD, Devas Street, Manchester M15 6EX. Tel: 0161-953 1180. *Chief Executive,* Mrs K. Tattersall

NORTHERN IRELAND COUNCIL FOR THE CURRICULUM, EXAMINATIONS AND ASSESSMENT, Beechill House, 42 Beechill Road, Belfast BT8 4RS. Tel: 01232-704666. *Chief Executive,* Mrs C. Coxhead

OXFORD AND CAMBRIDGE SCHOOLS EXAMINATION BOARD, Purbeck House, Purbeck Road, Cambridge CB2 2PU. Tel: 01223-411211. (Part of UCLES)

OXFORD AND CAMBRIDGE SCHOOLS EXAMINATION BOARD, Elsfield Way, Oxford OX2 8EP. Tel: 01865-54421. (Part of UCLES)

UNIVERSITY OF CAMBRIDGE LOCAL EXAMINATIONS SYNDICATE (UCLES), Syndicate Buildings, 1 Hills Road, Cambridge CB1 2EU. Tel: 01223-553311. *Chief Executive,* M. P. Halstead, PH.D. Also the OXFORD AND CAMBRIDGE EXAMINATIONS AND ASSESSMENT COUNCIL

UNIVERSITY OF LONDON EXAMINATIONS AND ASSESSMENT COUNCIL, Stewart House, 32 Russell Square, London WC1B 5DN. Tel: 0171-331 4000. *Chief Executive,* A. Smith

UNIVERSITY OF OXFORD DELEGACY OF LOCAL EXAMINATIONS, Ewert House, Ewert Place, Summertown, Oxford OX2 7BZ. Tel: 01865-54291. (Part of UCLES)

WELSH JOINT EDUCATION COMMITTEE, 245 Western Avenue, Cardiff CF5 2YX. Tel: 01222-265000. *Secretary,* C. Heycock

SCOTLAND

SCOTTISH EXAMINATION BOARD, Ironmills Road,
Dalkeith, Midlothian EH22 ILE. Tel: 0131-663 6601.
Chief Executive, H. A. Long, PH.D.

SCOTTISH VOCATIONAL EDUCATION COUNCIL,
Hanover House, 24 Douglas Street, Glasgow G2 7NQ.
Tel: 0141-248 7900. *Chief Executive,* T. J. McCool, CBE

FURTHER EDUCATION

BUSINESS AND TECHNOLOGY EDUCATION COUNCIL,
Central House, Upper Woburn Place, London
WC1H OHH. Tel: 0171-413 8400. *Chief Executive,* Ms
C. Townsend, PH.D.

CITY AND GUILDS OF LONDON INSTITUTE, 1 Giltspur
Street, London EC1A 9DD. Tel: 0171-294 2468. *Director-
General,* N. Carey, PH.D.

RSA EXAMINATIONS BOARD, Westwood Way, Coventry
CV4 8HS. Tel: 01203-470033. *Chief Executive,* M. F. Cross

FUNDING COUNCILS

SCHOOLS

FUNDING AGENCY FOR SCHOOLS, Albion Wharf,
25 Skeldergate, York YO1 2XL. Tel: 01904-661604.
Chairman, Sir Christopher Benson; *Chief Executive,*
M. Collier

FURTHER EDUCATION

FURTHER EDUCATION FUNDING COUNCIL FOR
ENGLAND, Cheylesmore House, Quinton Road,
Coventry CV1 2WT. Tel: 01203-863000. *Chief Executive,*
Sir William Stubbs

FURTHER EDUCATION FUNDING COUNCIL FOR WALES,
Lambourne House, Cardiff Business Park, Llanishen,
Cardiff CF4 5GL. Tel: 01222-761861. *Chief Executive,*
Prof. J. A. Andrews

SCOTTISH FURTHER EDUCATION FUNDING UNIT,
Scottish Office Education Department, 43 Jeffrey
Street, Edinburgh EH1 1DN. Tel: 0131-244 0278. *Director,*
R. D. Jackson

HIGHER EDUCATION

HIGHER EDUCATION FUNDING COUNCIL FOR
ENGLAND, Northavon House, Coldharbour Lane,
Bristol BS16 1QD. Tel: 0117-931 7317. *Chief Executive,*
Prof. B. Fender

HIGHER EDUCATION FUNDING COUNCIL FOR WALES,
Lambourne House, Cardiff Business Park, Llanishen,
Cardiff CF4 5GL. Tel: 01222-761861. *Chief Executive,*
Prof. J. A. Andrews

SCOTTISH HIGHER EDUCATION FUNDING COUNCIL,
Donaldson House, 97 Haymarket Terrace, Edinburgh
EH12 5HD. Tel: 0131-313 6500. *Chief Executive,*
Prof. J. Sizer, CBE

STUDENT LOANS COMPANY LTD, 100 Bothwell Street,
Glasgow G2 7JD. Tel: 0141-306 2000. *Chief Executive*
(acting), Sir Eric Ash

TEACHER TRAINING AGENCY, Portland House, Stag
Place, London SW1E 5TT. Tel: 0171-925 3700. *Chairman,*
G. Parker; *Chief Executive,* Ms A. Millett

ADMISSIONS AND COURSE INFORMATION

ART AND DESIGN ADMISSIONS REGISTRY, Penn House, 9
Broad Street, Hereford HR4 9AP. Tel: 01432-266653.
Registrar, T. W. M. Gourdie

CAREERS RESEARCH AND ADVISORY CENTRE (CRAC),
Sheraton House, Castle Park, Cambridge CB3 OAX. Tel:
01223-460277. *Director,* D. Blandford. *Publishers,*
Hobsons Publishing PLC, Bateman Street, Cambridge
CB2 1LZ

COMMITTEE OF SCOTTISH HIGHER EDUCATION
PRINCIPALS (COSHEP), St Andrew House, 141 West
Nile Street, Glasgow G1 2RN. Tel: 0141-353 1880.
Secretary, Dr R. L. Crawford

GRADUATE TEACHER TRAINING REGISTRY, Fulton
House, Jessop Avenue, Cheltenham, Glos GL50 3SH.
Tel: 01242-225868. *Registrar,* Mrs M. Griffiths

SOCIAL WORK ADMISSIONS SYSTEM, Fulton House,
Jessop Avenue, Cheltenham, Glos GL50 3SH. Tel:
01242-225977. *Admissions Officer,* Mrs M. Griffiths

TEACHER EDUCATION ADMISSIONS CLEARING HOUSE
(TEACH) (Scottish postgraduate only), PO Box 165,
Holyrood Road, Edinburgh EH8 8AT. *Registrar,* Miss
R. C. Williamson

UNIVERSITIES AND COLLEGES ADMISSIONS SERVICE,
Fulton House, Jessop Avenue, Cheltenham, Glos
GL50 3SH. Tel: 01242-222444. *Chief Executive,*
M. A. Higgins, PH.D.

UNIVERSITIES

THE UNIVERSITY OF ABERDEEN (1495)
Regent Walk, Aberdeen AB9 1FX
Tel 01224-272000
Full-time students (1993–4), 9,500
Chancellor, Sir Kenneth Alexander, FRSE (1987)
Principal, Prof. J. Maxwell Irvine, PH.D.
Registrar, Dr P. J. Murray
Secretary, N. R. D. Begg
Rector, I. Hamilton, QC (1994–6)

THE UNIVERSITY OF ABERTAY (1994)
Bell Street, Dundee DD1 1HG
Tel: 01382-308000
Full-time students (1994–5), 4,000
Chancellor, The Earl of Airlie, KT, GCVO, PC
Vice-Chancellor and Principal, Prof. B. King
Vice-Principal, Prof. W. J. Emond

ANGLIA POLYTECHNIC UNIVERSITY (1992)
Bishop Hall Lane, Chelmsford, Essex CM1 1SQ
Tel 01245-493131
Full-time students (1994–5), 10,000
Chancellor, The Lord Prior, PC (1992)
Vice-Chancellor, M. Malone-Lee
Head of Student Administration, D. Davies
Secretary, S. G. Bennett

ASTON UNIVERSITY (1966)
Aston Triangle, Birmingham B4 7ET
Tel 0121-359 3611
Full-time students (1994–5), 4,388
Chancellor, Sir Adrian Cadbury (1979)

Vice-Chancellor, Prof. Sir Frederick Crawford, ph.d., d.eng., d.sc., feng.
Registrar and Secretary, R. D. A. Packham

THE UNIVERSITY OF BATH (1966)
Claverton Down, Bath ba2 7ay
Tel 01225-826826
Full-time students (1994–5), 6,450
Chancellor, Sir Denys Henderson (1993)
Vice-Chancellor, Prof. V. D. Vandelinde
Registrar, J. Bursey

THE UNIVERSITY OF BIRMINGHAM (1900)
Edgbaston, Birmingham b15 2tt
Tel 0121-414 3344
Full-time students (1994–5), 16,026
Chancellor, Sir Alexander Jarratt, cb (1983)
Vice-Chancellor, Prof. Sir Michael Thompson, d.sc.
Registrar and Secretary, D. R. Holmes

BOURNEMOUTH UNIVERSITY (1992)
Poole House, Talbot Campus, Fern Barrow,
Dorset bh12 5bb
Tel 01202-524111
Full-time students (1994–5), 8,200
Chancellor, The Baroness Cox (1992)
Vice-Chancellor, Prof. G. Slater
Registrar, N. Richardson
Secretary, R. Allen

THE UNIVERSITY OF BRADFORD (1966)
Bradford bd7 1dp
Tel 01274-733466
Full-time students (1994–5), 6,733
Chancellor, Sir Trevor Holdsworth (1992)
Vice-Chancellor, Prof. D. J. Johns, ph.d., d.sc. (1989)
Registrar and Secretary, N. Andrew

THE UNIVERSITY OF BRIGHTON (1992)
Mithras House, Lewes Road, Brighton bn2 4at
Tel 01273-600900
Full-time students (1994–5), 9,300
Chairman of the Board, M. J. Aldrich
Director, Prof. D. J. Watson
Deputy Director, D. E. House

THE UNIVERSITY OF BRISTOL (1909)
Senate House, Tyndall Avenue, Bristol bs8 1th
Tel 0117-928 9000
Full-time students (1994–5), 10,627
Chancellor, Sir Jeremy Morse, kcmg (1989)
Vice-Chancellor, Sir John Kingman, frs
Registrar, J. H. M. Parry
Secretary, Ms K. McKenzie, d.phil.

BRUNEL UNIVERSITY (1966)
Uxbridge, Middx ub8 3ph
Tel 01895-274000
Full-time students (1994–5), 11,335
Chancellor, The Earl of Halsbury, frs (1966)
Vice-Chancellor, Prof. M. J. H. Sterling
Secretary-General and Registrar, D. Neave

THE UNIVERSITY OF BUCKINGHAM (1983)
Founded 1976 as University College at Buckingham
Buckingham mk18 1eg
Tel 01280-814080
Full-time students (1994–5), 1,006
Chancellor, The Baroness Thatcher, om, pc, frs (1992)

Vice-Chancellor, The Rt. Hon. Sir Richard Luce
Director of Administration, J. Elder

THE UNIVERSITY OF CAMBRIDGE
University Offices, The Old Schools, Cambridge cb2 1tn
Tel 01223-337733
Undergraduates in residence (1995–6), 10,836

University Officers, etc.

Chancellor, HRH The Duke of Edinburgh, kg, kt, om, gbe, pc (1977)
Vice-Chancellor, Prof. Sir David Williams (*Wolfson*) (1989)
High Steward, The Lord Runcie, pc, dd (1991)
Deputy High Steward, The Lord Richardson of Duntisbourne, pc, mbe, td (1983)
Commissary, The Lord Oliver of Aylmerton, pc (*Trinity Hall*) (1989)
Proctors, A. M. Tettenborn (*Pembroke*); C. K. Hadley (*Girton*) (1995)
Orator, A. J. Bowen (*Jesus*) (1993)
Registrary, S. G. Fleet, ph.d. (*Downing*) (1983)
Deputy Registrary, N. J. B. A. Branson, ph.d. (*Darwin*) (1993)
Librarian, P. K. Fox (*Selwyn*) (1994)
Treasurer, Ms J. Womack (*Trinity*) (1993)
Secretary-General of the Faculties, D. A. Livesey, ph.d. (*Emmanuel*) (1992)
Director of the Fitzwilliam Museum, D. D. Robinson (*Clare*) (1995)

Colleges and Halls, etc.
with dates of foundation

Christ's (1505), *Master,* A. J. Munro, ph.d. (1995)
Churchill (1960), *Master,* Prof. A. N. Broers, ph.d., frs (1990)
Clare (1326), *Master,* Prof. B. A. Hepple, ll d (1993)
Clare Hall (1966), *President,* Prof. G. P. K. Beer, litt.d., fba (1994)
Corpus Christi (1352), *Master,* Prof. E. A. Wrigley, ph.d. (1994)
Darwin (1964), *Master,* Prof. G. E. R. Lloyd, ph.d., fba (1989)
Downing (1800), *Master,* Prof. D. A. King, frs (1995)
Emmanuel (1584), *Master,* The Lord St John of Fawsley, pc, litt.d. (1991)
Fitzwilliam (1966), *Master,* Prof. A. W. Cuthbert, ph.d., frs (1991)
Girton (1869), *Mistress,* Mrs J. J. d'A. Campbell, cmg (1992)
Gonville and Caius (1348), *Master,* Prof. P. Gray, sc.d., frs (1988)
Homerton (1824) (for B.Ed. students), *Principal,* Mrs K. B. Pretty, ph.d. (1991)
Hughes Hall (1885) (for post-graduate students), *President,* J. T. Dingle, d.sc. (1993)
Jesus (1496), *Master,* Prof. the Lord Renfrew of Kaimsthorn, sc.d. (1986)
King's (1441), *Provost,* Prof. P. P. G. Bateson, sc.d., frs (1987)
*Lucy Cavendish College (1965) (for women research students and mature and affiliated undergraduates), *President,* The Baroness Perry of Southwark (1994)
Magdalene (1542), *Master,* Prof. Sir John Gurdon, d.phil., frs (1995)
*New Hall (1954), *President,* Mrs A. Lonsdale (1996)
*Newnham (1871), *Principal,* Ms O. S. O'Neill, cbe (1992)
Pembroke (1347), *Master,* Sir Roger Tomkys, kcmg (1992)
Peterhouse (1284), *Master,* Prof. Sir John Meurig Thomas, frs (1993)

QUEENS' (1448), *President*, Revd J. C. Polkinghorne, SC.D., FRS (1989)
ROBINSON (1977), *Warden*, Prof. the Lord Lewis of Newnham, SC.D., FRS (1977)
ST CATHARINE'S (1473), *Master*, Prof. Sir Terence English (1993)
ST EDMUND'S (1896), *Master*, R. M. Laws, CBE, PH.D. (1986)
ST JOHN'S (1511), *Master*, Prof. P. Goddard, PH.D., FRS (1994)
SELWYN (1882), *Master*, D. Harrison, CBE, SC.D., F.Eng. (1993)
SIDNEY SUSSEX (1596), *Master*, Prof. G. Horn, SC.D., FRS (1992)
TRINITY (1546), *Master*, Sir Michael Atiyah, PH.D., FRS, FRSE (1990)
TRINITY HALL (1350), *Master*, Sir John Lyons, PH.D. (1984)
WOLFSON (1965), *President*, G. Johnson PH.D. (1994)
*College for women only

THE UNIVERSITY OF CENTRAL ENGLAND IN BIRMINGHAM (1992)
Perry Barr, Birmingham B42 2SU
Tel 0121-331 5000
Full-time students (1994–5), 12,996
Chancellor, The Lord Mayor of Birmingham
Vice-Chancellor, Dr P. C. Knight, CBE
Secretary and Registrar, Ms M. Penlington

THE UNIVERSITY OF CENTRAL LANCASHIRE (1992)
Preston PRI 2HE
Tel 01772-201201
Full-time students (1994–5), 12,487
Chancellor, Sir Francis Kennedy, KCMG, CBE
Vice-Chancellor, B. G. Booth
Secretary, Ms P. M. Ackroyd

THE CITY UNIVERSITY (1966)
Northampton Square, London ECIV OHB
Tel 0171-477 8000
Full-time students (1994–5), 6,373
Chancellor, The Rt. Hon. the Lord Mayor of London
Vice-Chancellor and Principal, Prof. R. N. Franklin, CBE, D.phil., D.SC.
Academic Registrar, A. H. Seville, PH.D.
Secretary, M. M. O'Hara

COVENTRY UNIVERSITY (1992)
Priory Street, Coventry CVI 5FB
Tel 01203-631313
Full-time students (1994–5), 14,676
Chancellor, The Lord Plumb, MEP
Vice-Chancellor, M. Goldstein, PH.D., D.SC.
Registrar, J. Gledhill, PH.D.
Secretary, Ms L. Arlidge

DE MONTFORT UNIVERSITY (1992)
The Gateway, Leicester LEI 9BH
Tel 0116-255 1551
Full-time students (1994–5), 19,464
Chancellor, Sir Clive Whitmore
Vice-Chancellor, Prof. K. Barker, CBE
Registrar, V. E. Critchlow

THE UNIVERSITY OF DERBY (1993)
(formerly Derbyshire College of Higher Education)
Kedleston Road, Derby DE22 1GB
Tel 01332-622222
Full-time students (1994–5), 8,500
Patron, HRH Princess Alice, Duchess of Gloucester
Vice-Chancellor, Prof. R. Waterhouse
Registrar and Secretary, Mrs J. Fry

THE UNIVERSITY OF DUNDEE (1967)
Dundee DDI 4HN
Tel 01382-223181
Full-time students (1993–4), 6,700
Chancellor, Sir James Black, FRCP, FRS (1992)
Principal and Vice-Chancellor, Dr I. J. Graham-Bryce
Secretary, R. Seaton
Rector, S. Fry (1992–8)

THE UNIVERSITY OF DURHAM
Founded 1832; re-organized 1908, 1937 and 1963
Old Shire Hall, Durham DHI 3HP
Tel 0191-374 2000
Full-time students (1994–5), 8,645
Chancellor, Sir Peter Ustinov, CBE, FRSL
Vice-Chancellor and Warden, Prof. E. A. V. Ebsworth, PH.D., SC.D., FRSE
Registrar and Secretary, J. C. F. Hayward

COLLEGES
COLLINGWOOD, *Principal*, G. H. Blake, PH.D.
GRADUATE SOCIETY, *Principal*, M. Richardson, PH.D.
GREY, *Master*, V. E. Watts
HATFIELD, *Master*, Prof. J. P. Barber, PH.D.
ST AIDAN'S, *Principal*, R. J. Williams
ST CHAD'S, *Principal*, The Revd Dr D. Arnold
ST CUTHBERT'S SOCIETY, *Principal*, S. G. C. Stoker
ST HILD AND ST BEDE, *Principal*, J. V. Armitage, PH.D.
ST JOHN'S, *Principal*, D. V. Day
ST MARY'S, *Principal*, Miss J. M. Kenworthy
TREVELYAN, *Principal (acting)*, G. Marshall, PH.D.
UNIVERSITY (DURHAM), *Master*, E. C. Salthouse, PH.D.
UNIVERSITY (STOCKTON), *Principal*, J. C. F. Hayward
USHAW, *President*, Rt. Revd Mgr R. Atherton, OBE
VAN MILDERT, *Principal*, Dr J. Turner

THE UNIVERSITY OF EAST ANGLIA (1963)
Norwich NR4 7TJ
Tel 01603-456161
Full-time students (1994–5), 7,431
Chancellor, Sir Geoffrey Allen, FENG, FRS (1994)
Vice-Chancellor, Dame Elizabeth Esteve-Coll, DBE
Registrar and Secretary, M. G. E. Paulson-Ellis, OBE

THE UNIVERSITY OF EAST LONDON (1992)
Longbridge Road, Dagenham, Essex RM8 2AS
Tel 0181-590 7000
Full-time students (1994–5), 10,100
Vice-Chancellor, Prof. F. Gould
Secretary and Registrar, A. Ingle

THE UNIVERSITY OF EDINBURGH (1583)
Old College, South Bridge, Edinburgh EH8 9YL
Tel 0131-650 1000
Full-time students (1994–5), 16,173
Chancellor, HRH The Prince Philip, Duke of Edinburgh, KG, KT, OM, GBE, PC, FRS (1952)
Vice-Chancellor and Principal, Prof. Sir Stewart Sutherland, FBA, FRSE
Secretary, M. J. B. Lowe, PH.D.
Rector, Dr. M. Macleod (1994–7)

THE UNIVERSITY OF ESSEX (1964)
Wivenhoe Park, Colchester CO4 3SQ
Tel 01206-873333
Full-time students (1994–5), 5,107
Chancellor, The Rt. Hon. Sir Patrick Nairne, GCB, MC, LL D (1983)
Vice-Chancellor (acting), I. Crewe
Registrar and Secretary, A. F. Woodburn

THE UNIVERSITY OF EXETER (1955)
Northcote House, The Queen's Drive, Exeter EX4 4QJ
Tel 01392-263263
Full-time students (1994–5), 8,583
Chancellor, Sir Rex Richards, D.SC., FRS (1981)
Vice-Chancellor, Sir Geoffrey Holland, KCB
Academic Registrar and Secretary, I. H. C. Powell

GLAMORGAN UNIVERSITY (1992)
Pontypridd, Mid Glamorgan CF37 1DL
Tel 01443-480480
Full-time students (1994–5), 9,735
Chancellor, The Lord Rees, PC, QC
Vice-Chancellor, Prof. A. L. Webb
Academic Registrar, J. O'Shea
Secretary, J. L. Bracegirdle

THE UNIVERSITY OF GLASGOW (1451)
Glasgow G12 8QQ
Tel 0141-339 8855
Full-time students (1994–5), 16,000
Chancellor, Sir Alexander Cairncross, KCMG, FBA, ph.D., LL D (1972)
Vice-Chancellor and Principal, Prof. G. Davies, ph.D., FEng.
Registrar, J. M. Black
Rector, J. Ball (1993–6)

GLASGOW CALEDONIAN UNIVERSITY (1993)
Cowcaddens Road, Glasgow G4 0BA
Tel 0141-331 3000
Full-time students (1993–4), 11,500
Chancellor, The Lord Nickson, KBE
Vice-Chancellor, Prof. J. S. Mason, ph.D.
Head of Academic Administration, B. Ferguson

THE UNIVERSITY OF GREENWICH (1992)
Wellington Street, Woolwich, London SE18 6PF
Tel 0181-316 8000
Full-time students (1993–4), 13,539
Chancellor, The Baroness Young
Vice-Chancellor, Dr D. Fussey
Academic Registrar, A. I. Mayfield
Secretary, J. Charles

HERIOT-WATT UNIVERSITY (1966)
Riccarton, Edinburgh EH14 4AS
Tel 0131-449 5111
Full-time students (1994–5), 8,960
Chancellor, The Lord Mackay of Clashfern, PC, QC, FRSE (1979)
Principal and Vice-Chancellor, Prof. A. G. J. MacFarlane, CBE, ph.D., FRS, FRSE, FEng. (1989)
Registrar, D. Sturgeon
Secretary, P. L. Wilson

THE UNIVERSITY OF HERTFORDSHIRE (1992)
College Lane, Hatfield, Herts AL10 9AB
Tel 01707-284000
Full-time students (1994–5), 11,336

Chancellor, Sir Brian Corby
Vice-Chancellor, Prof. N. K. Buxton
Registrar and Secretary, P. G. Jeffreys

THE UNIVERSITY OF HUDDERSFIELD (1992)
Queensgate, Huddersfield HD1 3DH
Tel 01484-422288
Full-time students (1994–5), 10,070
Chancellor, vacant
Vice-Chancellor and Principal, Prof. J. R. Tarrant, ph.D.
Secretary, D. J. Lock
Academic Registrar, M. E. Bond

THE UNIVERSITY OF HULL (1954)
Cottingham Road, Hull HU6 7RX
Tel 01482-46311
Full-time students (1993–4), 9,000
Chancellor, The Lord Armstrong of Ilminster, GCB, CVO
Vice-Chancellor, Prof. D. Dilks, FRSL
Registrar and Secretary, P. A. Bolton

THE UNIVERSITY OF HUMBERSIDE (1992)
Cottingham Road, Hull HU6 7RT
Tel 01482-440550
Full-time students (1993–4), 8,989
Pro-Chancellor, Dr Harry Hooper, CBE
Vice-Chancellor, Prof. R. King
Registrar, F. Marks
Secretary, Miss M. Harries-Jenkins

THE UNIVERSITY OF KEELE (1962)
Keele, Newcastle under Lyme, Staffs ST5 5BG
Tel 01782-621111
Full-time students (1995–6), 5,339
Chancellor, Sir Claus Moser, KCB, CBE, FBA (1986)
Vice-Chancellor, Prof. B. E. Fender, CMG, ph.D.
Registrar, D. Cohen, ph.D.

THE UNIVERSITY OF KENT AT CANTERBURY (1965)
Canterbury CT2 7NZ
Tel 01227-764000
Full-time students (1994–5), 6,774
Chancellor, vacant
Vice-Chancellor, Prof. R. Sibson, ph.D.
Registrar, T. Mead, ph.D.

KINGSTON UNIVERSITY (1992)
Penrhyn Road, Kingston upon Thames, Surrey KT1 2EE
Tel 0181-547 2000
Full-time students (1994-5), 10,987
Chancellor, Sir Frank Lampl
Vice-Chancellor, R. C. Smith, CBE, ph.D.
Secretary, E. Lang

THE UNIVERSITY OF LANCASTER (1964)
Bailrigg, Lancaster LA1 4YW
Tel 01524-65201
Full-time students (1994–5), 9,315
Chancellor, HRH Princess Alexandra, the Hon. Lady Ogilvy, GCVO (1964)
Vice-Chancellor, Prof. W. Ritchie
Academic Registrar, Mrs M. E. McClintock
Secretary, S. A. C. Lamley

THE UNIVERSITY OF LEEDS (1904)
Leeds LS2 9JT
Tel 0113-243 1751
Full-time students (1994–5), 19,479
Chancellor, HRH The Duchess of Kent, GCVO (1966)
Vice-Chancellor, Prof. A. G. Wilson
Registrar (acting), D. Robinson, PH.D.

LEEDS METROPOLITAN UNIVERSITY (1992)
Calverley Street, Leeds LS1 3HE
Tel 0113-283 2600
Full-time students (1994–5), 16,000
Principal and Chief Executive, Prof. L. Wagner
Secretary, M. Wilkinson

THE UNIVERSITY OF LEICESTER (1957)
University Road, Leicester LE1 7RH
Tel 0116-252 2522
Full-time students (1994–5), 8,466
Chancellor, Sir Michael Atiyah (1995)
Vice-Chancellor, K. J. R. Edwards, PH.D.
Registrar and Secretary, K. J. Julian

THE UNIVERSITY OF LIVERPOOL (1903)
PO Box 147, Liverpool L69 3BX
Tel 0151-794 2000
Full-time students (1994–5), 12,710
Chancellor, vacant
Vice-Chancellor, Prof. P. N. Love, CBE
Registrar and Secretary, M. D. Carr

LIVERPOOL JOHN MOORES UNIVERSITY
(1992)
Rodney House, 70 Mount Pleasant, Liverpool L3 5UX
Tel 0151-231 2121
Full-time students (1992–3), 19,000
Chancellor, J. Moores, CBE
Vice-Chancellor, Prof. P. Toyne
Registrar, Ms A. Richardson
Secretary, P. Blackburn

THE UNIVERSITY OF LONDON (1836)
Senate House, Malet Street, London WC1E 7HU
Tel 0171-636 8000
Internal students (1994–5), 75,873, External students,
   21,057
Visitor, HM The Queen in Council
Chancellor, HRH The Princess Royal, GCVO, FRS (1981)
Vice-Chancellor, Prof. A. Rutherford, CBE
Chairman of the Council, The Lord Woolf, PC
Chairman of Convocation, Prof. Sir William Taylor, CBE
Principal, P. Holwell

COLLEGES OF THE UNIVERSITY
BIRKBECK COLLEGE, Malet Street, London
   WC1E 7HX. *Master,* The Baroness Blackstone, PH.D.
BRITISH POSTGRADUATE MEDICAL FEDERATION, 33
   Millman Street, London WC1N 3EJ. *Director,*
   Dr M. Green, DM, FRCP
   Comprises:
   Eastman Dental Institute, 256 Gray's Inn Road, London
   WC1X 8LD. *Dean,* Prof. C. Scully, MD, PH.D., FRCPath.
   Institute of Cancer Research, Royal Cancer Hospital,
   Chester Beatty Laboratories, 17A Onslow Gardens,
   London SW7 3AL. *Chief Executive,* Prof. P. B. Garland,
   PH.D., FRSE
   Institute of Child Health, 30 Guilford Street, London
   WC1N 1EH. *Dean,* Prof. R. J. Levinsky, MD, FRCP
   Institute of Neurology, The National Hospital, Queen
   Square, London WC1N 3BG. *Dean,* Prof. D. N. Landon

   Institute of Ophthalmology, 11–43 Bath Street, London
   EC1V 9EL. *Dean,* Prof. A. M. Sillito
   National Heart and Lung Institute, Dovehouse Street,
   London SW3 6LY. *Dean,* Prof. T. Clark, MD, FRCP
CHARING CROSS AND WESTMINSTER MEDICAL SCHOOL,
   The Reynolds Building, St Dunstan's Road, London
   W6 8RP. *Dean,* Prof. R. M. Greenhalgh, FRCS
GOLDSMITHS COLLEGE, Lewisham Way, New Cross,
   London SE14 6NW. *Warden,* Prof. K. J. Gregory, PH.D.
HEYTHROP COLLEGE, Kensington Square, London
   W8 5HQ. *Principal,* Revd B. A. Callaghan, SJ
IMPERIAL COLLEGE OF SCIENCE, TECHNOLOGY AND
   MEDICINE (includes St Mary's Hospital Medical
   School), South Kensington, London SW7 2AZ. *Rector,*
   Prof. Sir Ronald Oxburgh, KBE, FRS
INSTITUTE OF EDUCATION, 20 Bedford Way, London
   WC1H 0AL. *Director,* Prof. P. Mortimore
KING'S COLLEGE LONDON (includes King's College
   School of Medicine and Dentistry), Strand, London
   WC2R 2LS. *Principal,* Prof. A. Lucas, PH.D.
   Associated Institute:
   Institute of Psychiatry, De Crespigny Park, Denmark Hill,
   London SE5 8AF. *Dean,* Prof. S. Checkley
THE LONDON HOSPITAL MEDICAL COLLEGE, Turner
   Street, London E1 2AD. *Dean,* Prof. Sir Colin Berry,
   FRCPath.
LONDON SCHOOL OF ECONOMICS AND POLITICAL
   SCIENCE, Houghton Street, London WC2A 2AE. *Director,*
   J. M. Ashworth, PH.D., D.SC.
LONDON SCHOOL OF HYGIENE AND TROPICAL
   MEDICINE, Keppel Street, London WC1E 7HT. *Dean,*
   Prof. H. Spencer
QUEEN MARY AND WESTFIELD COLLEGE, Mile End
   Road, London E1 4NS. *Principal,* Prof. G. Zellick, PH.D.
ROYAL FREE HOSPITAL SCHOOL OF MEDICINE, Rowland
   Hill Street, London NW3 2PF. *Dean,* Prof. A. J.
   Zuckerman, MD, FRCP
ROYAL HOLLOWAY, Egham Hill, Egham, Surrey TW20
   0EX. *Principal,* Prof. N. Gowar, M.PHIL.
ROYAL POSTGRADUATE MEDICAL SCHOOL,
   Hammersmith Hospital, Du Cane Road, London
   W12 7HT. *Dean,* Prof. Sir Colin Dollery, FRCP
ROYAL VETERINARY COLLEGE, Royal College Street,
   London NW1 0TU. *Principal and Dean,*
   Prof. L. E. Lanyon, PH.D.
ST BARTHOLOMEW'S HOSPITAL MEDICAL COLLEGE,
   West Smithfield, London EC1A 7BE. *Dean,* Prof.
   L. H. Rees, MD, FRCP
ST GEORGE'S HOSPITAL MEDICAL SCHOOL, Cranmer
   Terrace, London SW17 0RE. *Dean,* Prof. Sir
   William Asscher, MD, FRCP, FRCPath.
SCHOOL OF ORIENTAL AND AFRICAN STUDIES,
   Thornhaugh Street, Russell Square, London
   WC1H 0XG. *Director,* M. D. McWilliam
SCHOOL OF PHARMACY, 29–39 Brunswick Square,
   London WC1N 1AX. *Dean,* Prof. A. T. Florence, PH.D.,
   FRSE
UNITED MEDICAL AND DENTAL SCHOOLS OF GUY'S AND
   ST THOMAS' HOSPITALS, Guy's, London Bridge,
   London SE1 9RT; St Thomas', Lambeth Palace Road,
   London SE1 7EH. *Principal,* Prof. C. Chantler, FRCP
UNIVERSITY COLLEGE LONDON (including UCL
   Medical School), Gower Street, London
   WC1E 6BT. *Provost,* Sir Derek Roberts, CBE, FRS
WYE COLLEGE, Wye, Near Ashford, Kent
   TN25 5AH. *Principal,* Prof. J. H. D. Prescott, PH.D.

SCHOOL OF ADVANCED STUDY
Senate House, Malet Street, London WC1E 7HU. *Dean,* Prof.
T. C. Daintith

Comprises:

INSTITUTE OF ADVANCED LEGAL STUDIES, Charles Clore House, 17 Russell Square, London WC1B 5DR. *Director,* Prof. B. A. K. Rider

INSTITUTE OF CLASSICAL STUDIES, 31–34 Gordon Square, London WC1H 0PY. *Director,* Prof. R. R. K. Sorabji, FBA

INSTITUTE OF COMMONWEALTH STUDIES, 27–28 Russell Square, London WC1B 5DS. *Director,* Prof. J. Manor

INSTITUTE OF GERMANIC STUDIES, 29 Russell Square, London WC1B 5DP. *Hon. Director,* E. M. Batley

INSTITUTE OF HISTORICAL RESEARCH, Senate House, Malet Street, London WC1E 7HU. *Director,* Prof. P. K. O'Brien, D.Phil.

INSTITUTE OF LATIN AMERICAN STUDIES, 31 Tavistock Square, London WC1H 9HA. *Director,* Prof. V. G. Bulmer-Thomas, D.Phil.

INSTITUTE OF ROMANCE STUDIES, Senate House, Malet Street, London WC1E 7HU. *Hon. Director,* Prof. A. Lavers, Ph.D.

INSTITUTE OF UNITED STATES STUDIES, Senate House, Malet Street, London WC1E 7HU. *Director,* Prof. G. L. McDowell, Ph.D.

WARBURG INSTITUTE, Woburn Square, London WC1H 0AB. *Director,* Prof. C. N. J. Mann, Ph.D.

INSTITUTES AND ASSOCIATE INSTITUTIONS
BRITISH INSTITUTE IN PARIS, 9–11 rue de Constantine, 75340, Paris, Cedex 07, France. *Director,* Prof. C. L. Campos, Ph.D. *London office:* Senate House, Malet Street, London WC1E 7HU

CENTRE FOR DEFENCE STUDIES, King's College London, Strand, London WC2R 2LS. *Director,* Prof. L. Freedman

CENTRE FOR ENGLISH STUDIES, Senate House, Malet Street, London WC1E 7HU. *Director,* Dr W. L. Chernaik

COURTAULD INSTITUTE OF ART, North Block, Somerset House, Strand, London WC2R 0RN. *Director,* Prof. E. C. Fernie

INSTITUTE OF ZOOLOGY, Royal Zoological Society, Regent's Park, London NW1 4RY. *Director,* Prof. M. Gosling.

JEWS' COLLEGE, 44A Albert Road, London NW4 2SJ. *Principal,* Rabbi Dr D. Sinclair

LONDON BUSINESS SCHOOL, Sussex Place, Regent's Park, London NW1 4SA. *Principal,* Prof. G. S. Bain, D.Phil.

ROYAL ACADEMY OF MUSIC, Marylebone Road, London NW1 5HT. *Principal,* Prof. C. Price

ROYAL COLLEGE OF MUSIC, Prince Consort Road, London SW7 2BS. *Director,* Ms J. Ritterman, Ph.D.

SCHOOL OF SLAVONIC AND EAST EUROPEAN STUDIES, Senate House, Malet Street, London WC1E 7HU. *Director,* Prof. M. A. Branch, Ph.D.

TRINITY COLLEGE OF MUSIC, 11–13 Mandeville Place, London W1M 6AQ. *Principal,* G. Henderson

UNIVERSITY MARINE BIOLOGICAL STATION MILLPORT, Isle of Cumbrae, Scotland KA28 0EG. *Director,* Prof. J. Davenport, Ph.D., D.SC., FRSE

LONDON GUILDHALL UNIVERSITY (1993)
133 Whitechapel High Street, London E1 7QA
Tel 0171-320 1000
Full-time students (1994–5), 7,017
Principal, HRH The Prince Philip, Duke of Edinburgh, KG, KT, OM, GBE, PC, FRS
Provost, Prof. R. Floud, D.Phil.
Academic Registrar, Ms J. Grinstead

LOUGHBOROUGH UNIVERSITY OF TECHNOLOGY (1966)
Loughborough, Leics LE11 3TU
Tel 01509-263171
Full-time students (1994–5), 9,963
Chancellor, Sir Denis Rooke, CBE, FRS, FEng (1989)
Vice-Chancellor, Prof. D.Wallace, Ph.D., FRS, FRSE
Registrar, D. E. Fletcher, Ph.D.
Academic Secretary, N. A. McHard

UNIVERSITY OF LUTON (1993)
(formerly Luton College of Higher Education)
Park Square, Luton LU1 3JU
Tel 01582-34111
Full-time students (1994–5), 14,000
Chancellor, Sir David Plastow
Vice-Chancellor, Dr A. Wood
Academic Registrar, R. M. Driver

THE UNIVERSITY OF MANCHESTER
(Founded 1851; re-organized 1880 and 1903)
Oxford Road, Manchester M13 9PL
Tel: 0161-275 2000
Full-time students (1994–5), 17,000
Chancellor, The Lord Flowers, FRS
Vice-Chancellor, Prof. M. B. Harris, CBE, Ph.D.
Registrar and Secretary, E. Newcomb

UNIVERSITY OF MANCHESTER INSTITUTE OF SCIENCE AND TECHNOLOGY (1824)
PO Box 88, Manchester M60 1QD
Tel 0161-236 3311
Full-time students (1994–5), 6,000
Chancellor, Prof. Sir Rowland Smith, Ph.D. (1995)
Vice-Chancellor, Prof. R. F. Boucher, FEng.
Registrar and Secretary, P. C. C. Stephenson

MANCHESTER METROPOLITAN UNIVERSITY (1992)
All Saints, Manchester M15 6BH
Tel 0161-247 2000
Full-time students (1994–5), 23,734
Chancellor, The Duke of Westminster
Vice-Chancellor, Sir Kenneth Green
Registrar, J. Karczewski-Slowikowski
Secretary, vacant

MIDDLESEX UNIVERSITY (1992)
White Hart Lane, London N17 8HR
Tel 0181-362 5000
Full-time students (1994–5), 16,084
Chancellor, The Baroness Platt of Writtle
Vice-Chancellor, Prof. D. Melville, Ph.D.
Registrar and Secretary, G. Jones

NAPIER UNIVERSITY (1992)
219 Colinton Road, Edinburgh EH14 1DJ
Tel 0131-444 2266
Full-time students (1993–4), 7,685
Chancellor, The Lord Younger of Prestwick, KCVO, TD, PC, FRSE
Vice-Chancellor and Principal, Prof. J. Mavor
Secretary and Registrar, I. J. Miller

THE UNIVERSITY OF NEWCASTLE UPON TYNE

(Founded 1852; re-organized 1908, 1937 and 1963)
6 Kensington Terrace, Newcastle upon Tyne NE1 7RU
Tel 0191-222 6000
Full-time students (1994–5), 11,209
Chancellor, The Viscount Ridley, KG, GCVO, TD (1989)
Vice-Chancellor, J. R. G. Wright
Registrar, D. E. T. Nicholson

THE UNIVERSITY OF NORTH LONDON
(1992)
166–220 Holloway Road, London N7 8DB
Tel 0171-607 2789
Full-time students (1994–5), 7,000
Vice-Chancellor and Chief Executive, B. Roper
Academic Registrar, Dr M. Storey
Secretary, C. Wragg

THE UNIVERSITY OF NORTHUMBRIA AT NEWCASTLE (1992)
Ellison Place, Newcastle upon Tyne NE1 8ST
Tel 0191-232 6002
Full-time students (1993–4), 11,295
Chancellor, The Lord Glenamara, CH, PC (1984)
Vice-Chancellor, Prof. L. Barden, CBE, PH.D., D.SC.
Registrar and Secretary, R. A. Bott

THE UNIVERSITY OF NOTTINGHAM (1948)
University Park, Nottingham NG7 2RD
Tel 0115-951 5151
Full-time students (1994–5), 11,270
Chancellor, Sir Ron Dearing, CB (1993)
Vice-Chancellor, Prof. Sir Colin Campbell
Registrar, D. Allen

NOTTINGHAM TRENT UNIVERSITY (1992)
Burton Street, Nottingham NG1 4BU
Tel 0115-941 8418
Full-time students (1994–5), 15,300
Vice-Chancellor, Prof. R. Cowell, PH.D.
Academic Registrar, D. Samson

THE UNIVERSITY OF OXFORD
University Offices, Wellington Square, Oxford OX1 2JD
Tel 01865-270001
Students in residence (1994–5), 14,957

UNIVERSITY OFFICERS, ETC.
Chancellor, The Lord Jenkins of Hillhead, OM, PC (*Balliol*), elected 1987
High Steward, The Lord Goff of Chieveley, PC (*Lincoln* and *New College*), elected 1990
Vice-Chancellor, Dr P. M. North, CBE, QC, FBA (*Jesus*), elected 1993
Proctors, Dr J. Black (*Wolfson*); Dr W. Macmillan (*Hertford*), elected 1995
Assessor, Dr P. A. W. Bullock (*All Souls*), elected 1995
Public Orator, J. Griffin (*Balliol*), elected 1992
Bodley's Librarian, D. G. Vaisey (*Exeter*), elected 1986
Keeper of Archives, D. G. Vaisey (*Exeter*), elected 1995
Director of the Ashmolean Museum, C. J. White (*Worcester*), elected 1985
Registrar of the University, A. J. Dorey, D.phil. (*Linacre*), elected 1979
Surveyor to the University, P. M. R. Hill, elected 1993
Secretary of Faculties, A. P. Weale (*Worcester*), elected 1984
Secretary of the Chest, vacant
Deputy Registrar (Administration), P. W. Jones (*Green*), elected 1991

OXFORD COLLEGES AND HALLS
with dates of foundation

ALL SOULS (1438), *Warden,* Prof. J. Davis (1994)
BALLIOL (1263), *Master,* C. R. Lucas, D.phil. (1994)
BRASENOSE (1509), *Principal,* The Lord Windlesham, CVO, PC (1989)
CHRIST CHURCH (1546), *Dean,* Very Revd J. H. Drury (1991)
CORPUS CHRISTI (1517), *President,* Prof. Sir Keith Thomas, FBA (1986)
EXETER (1314), *Rector,* Prof. M. Butler (1994)
GREEN (1979), *Warden,* Sir Crispin Tickell, GCMG, KCVO (1990)
HERTFORD (1874), *Principal,* Prof. Sir Christopher Zeeman, FRS (1988)
JESUS (1571), *Principal,* Dr P. M. North, CBE, FBA (1984)
KEBLE (1868), *Warden,* A. Cameron, FBA, FSA (1994)
KELLOG (1990) (formerly Rewley House), *President,* G. P. Thomas, PH.D. (1990)
LADY MARGARET HALL (1878), *Principal,* D. M. Stewart (1979)
LINACRE (1962), *Principal,* Sir Bryan Cartledge, KCMG (1988)
LINCOLN (1427), *Rector,* E. K. Anderson, FRSE (1994)
MAGDALEN (1458), *President,* A. D. Smith, CBE (1988)
MANSFIELD (1886), *Principal,* D. J. Trevelyan, CB (1989)
MERTON (1264), *Warden,* Dr. J Rawson, FBA (1994)
NEW COLLEGE (1379), *Warden,* H. McGregor, QC, DCL (1985)
NUFFIELD (1937), *Warden,* Prof. A. Atkinson, FBA (1994)
ORIEL (1326), *Provost,* E. W. Nicholson, DD, FBA (1990)
PEMBROKE (1624), *Master,* Prof. R. Stevens, DCL (1993)
QUEEN'S (1340), *Provost,* G. Marshall (1993)
ST ANNE'S (1952) (originally Society of Oxford Home-Students (1879)), *Principal,* Mrs R. L. Deech (1991)
ST ANTONY'S (1950), *Warden,* The Lord Dahrendorf, KBE, PH.D., FBA (1987)
ST CATHERINE'S (1962), *Master,* The Lord Plant of Highfield (1994)
ST CROSS (1965), *Master,* R. C. Repp, D.phil. (1987)
ST EDMUND HALL (c.1278), *Principal,* J. C. B. Gosling (1983)
*ST HILDA'S (1893), *Principal,* Miss E. Llewellyn-Smith, CB (1990)
ST HUGH'S (1886), *Principal,* D. Wood, QC (1991)
ST JOHN'S (1555), *President,* W. Hayes, D.phil. (1987)
ST PETER'S (1929), *Master,* J. P. Barron, D.phil. (1991)
SOMERVILLE (1879), *Principal,* Mrs C. E. Hughes, CMG (1989)
TEMPLETON (1965), *President,* C. L. Brundin
TRINITY (1554), *President,* Sir John Burgh, KCMG, CB (1987)
UNIVERSITY (1249), *Master,* W. J. Albery, D.phil., FRS (1989)
WADHAM (1612), *Warden,* J. S. Flemming (1993)
WOLFSON (1966), *President,* Sir David Smith, D.phil. (1994)
WORCESTER (1714), *Provost,* R. G. Smethurst (1991)
BLACKFRIARS (1921), *Regent,* Revd B. E. A. Davies (1994)
CAMPION HALL (1896), *Master,* Revd J. A. Munitiz (1989)
GREYFRIARS (1910), *Warden,* Revd M. W. Sheehan, D.phil. (1990)
MANCHESTER (1786), *Principal,* Revd R. Waller, PH.D. (1990)
REGENT'S PARK (1810), *Principal,* Revd P. S. Fiddes, D.phil. (1989)
ST BENET'S HALL (1897), *Master,* Revd H. Wansbrough, OSB (1991)

---

* College for women only

OXFORD BROOKES UNIVERSITY (1993)
Headington, Oxford OX3 OBP
Tel 01865-741111
Full-time students (1994–5), 7,668
Chancellor, Ms H. Kennedy, QC
Vice-Chancellor, Dr C. Booth
Deputy Vice-Chancellor, Corporate Services, B. Summers

THE UNIVERSITY OF PAISLEY (1992)
(formerly Paisley College of Technology)
High Street, Paisley PAI 2BE
Tel 0141-848 3000
Full-time students (1993–4), 6,162
Chancellor, Sir Robert Easton, CBE
Vice-Chancellor and Principal, Prof. R. W. Shaw
Registrar, D. Rigg
Secretary, J. Fraser

UNIVERSITY OF PLYMOUTH (1992)
Drake Circus, Plymouth PL4 8AA
Tel 01752-600600
Full-time students (1994–5), 11,345
Vice-Chancellor, Prof. J. Bull
Registrar, Dr C. J. Sparrow

UNIVERSITY OF PORTSMOUTH (1992)
University House, Winston Churchill Avenue,
Portsmouth POI 2UP
Tel 01705-876543
Full-time students (1994–5), 12,468
Chancellor, The Lord Palumbo
Vice-Chancellor (acting), Dr M. Bateman
Secretary, R. Moore

THE QUEEN'S UNIVERSITY OF BELFAST
(1908)
Belfast BT7 INN
Tel 01232-245133
Full-time students (1994–5), 13,600
Chancellor, Sir David Orr
Vice-Chancellor, Sir Gordon Beveridge, PH.D., FRSE
Academic Secretary, Dr G. Baird
Administrative Secretary, D. Wilson

THE UNIVERSITY OF READING (1926)
Whiteknights, PO Box 217, Reading RG6 2AH
Tel 01734-875123
Full-time students (1994–5), 9,668
Chancellor, The Lord Carrington, KG, GCMG, CH, MC, PC
    (1992)
Vice-Chancellor, Prof. R. Williams
Registrar, D. C. R. Frampton

THE ROBERT GORDON UNIVERSITY (1992)
Schoolhill, Aberdeen AB9 IFR
Tel 01224-262000
Full-time students (1994–5), 6,211
Chancellor, Sir Bob Reid (1993)
Vice-Chancellor and Principal, Dr D. A. Kennedy
Secretary, D. Caldwell

THE UNIVERSITY OF ST ANDREWS (1411)
College Gate, St Andrews KYI6 9AJ
Tel 01334-476161
Full-time students (1994–5), 5,038
Chancellor, Sir Kenneth Dover, D.LItt., FRSE, FBA (1981)
Vice-Chancellor and Principal, Prof. S. Arnott, SC.D., FRS, FRSE
Secretary of Court, D. J. Corner
Rector, D. Findlay, QC (1993–6)

THE UNIVERSITY OF SALFORD (1967)
Salford M5 4WT
Tel 0161-745 5000
Full-time students (1993–4), 6,995
Chancellor, Sir Walter Bodmer, PH.D., FRS
Vice-Chancellor, Prof. T. M. Husband, PH.D., FEng.
Registrar, M. D. Winton, PH.D.

THE UNIVERSITY OF SHEFFIELD (1905)
8 Palmerston Road, Sheffield SIO 2TE
Tel 0114-276 8555
Full-time students (1994–5), 18,000
Chancellor, The Lord Dainton, PH.D., SC.D., FRS (1979)
Vice-Chancellor, Prof. G. G. Roberts, PH.D., FRS
Registrar and Secretary, J. S. Padley, PH.D.

SHEFFIELD HALLAM UNIVERSITY (1992)
Pond Street, Sheffield SI IWB
Tel 0114-272 0911
Full-time students (1993–4), 16,856
Chancellor, Sir Bryan Nicholson
Vice-Chancellor, J. Stoddart, CBE
Registrar, Ms J. Tory
Secretary, Ms S. Neocosmos

THE UNIVERSITY OF SOUTHAMPTON
(1952)
Highfield, Southampton SOI7 IBJ
Tel 01703-595000
Full-time students (1994–5), 9,908
Chancellor, The Earl Jellicoe, KBE, DSO, MC, PC, FRS (1984)
Vice-Chancellor, Prof. H. Newby, CBE, PH.D.
Secretary and Registrar, J. F. D. Lauwerys
Academic Registrar, R. Knight

SOUTH BANK UNIVERSITY (1992)
103 Borough Road, London SEI OAA
Tel 0171-898 8989
Full-time students (1994–5), 15,000
Chancellor, C. McLaren
Vice-Chancellor, Prof. G. Bernbaum
Registrar, R. Phillips
Secretary, Mrs L. Gander

STAFFORDSHIRE UNIVERSITY (1992)
College Road, Stoke-on-Trent ST4 2DE
Tel 01782-294000
Full-time students (1994–5), 12,302
Chancellor, The Lord Ashley of Stoke, CH, PC
Vice-Chancellor, Prof. C. E. King, PH.D.
Academic Registrar, Miss F. Francis
Secretary, K. Sproston

THE UNIVERSITY OF STIRLING (1967)
Stirling FK9 4LA
Tel 01786-73171
Full-time students (1994–5), 5,020
Chancellor, The Lord Balfour of Burleigh, FRSE (1988)
Principal and Vice-Chancellor, Prof. A. Miller, PH.D., FRSE
Registrar, D. J. Farrington, D.Phil.
Secretary, K. J. Clarke

THE UNIVERSITY OF STRATHCLYDE (1964)
16 Richmond Street, Glasgow GI IXQ
Tel 0141-552 4400
Full-time students (1994–5), 13,700
Chancellor, The Lord Tombs, LL D, D.SC., FEng. (1990)
Principal and Vice-Chancellor, Prof. J. P. Arbuthnott, FRSE
Secretary, P. W. A. West

THE UNIVERSITY OF SUNDERLAND (1992)
Langham Tower, Ryhope Road, Sunderland sr2 7ee
Tel 0191-515 2000
Full-time students (1994–5), 12,588
Vice-Chancellor, Ms A. Wright, ph.d.
Academic Registrar, S. Porteous
Secretary, J. D. Pacey

THE UNIVERSITY OF SURREY (1966)
Guildford, Surrey gu2 5xh
Tel 01483-300800
Full-time students (1994–5), 6,559
Chancellor, HRH The Duke of Kent, kg, gcmg, gcvo (1977)
Vice-Chancellor, Prof. R. J. Dowling, ph.d., feng.
Secretary and Registrar, H. W. B. Davies

THE UNIVERSITY OF SUSSEX (1961)
Falmer, Brighton bn1 9rh
Tel 01273-606755
Full-time students (1994–5), 8,905
Chancellor, The Duke of Richmond and Gordon (1985)
Vice-Chancellor, Prof. G. Conway, ph.d.
Registrar and Secretary, G. Lockwood, d.phil.

THE UNIVERSITY OF TEESSIDE (1992)
Middlesbrough, Cleveland ts1 3ba
Tel 01642-218121
Full-time students (1994–5), 9,700
Chancellor, Sir Leon Brittan
Vice-Chancellor, Prof. D. Fraser
University Secretary, J. M. McClintock

THAMES VALLEY UNIVERSITY (1992)
St Mary's Road, Ealing, London w5 5rf
Tel 0181-579 5000
Full-time students (1994–5), 13,730
Chancellor, P. Hamlyn, cbe
Vice-Chancellor, Dr M. Fitzgerald
Academic Registrar, Ms A. Denton
Secretary, Ms M. Joyce

THE UNIVERSITY OF ULSTER (1984)
(Amalgamation of New University of Ulster and Ulster Polytechnic)
Cromore Road, Coleraine bt52 1sa
Tel 01265-44141
Full-time students (1993–4), 11,700
Chancellor, Rabbi J. Neuberger
Vice-Chancellor, Prof. T. A. Smith
Academic Registrar, K. Millar, ph.d.

THE UNIVERSITY OF WALES (1893)
King Edward VII Avenue, Cathays Park, Cardiff cf1 3ns
Tel 01222-382656
Full-time students (1994–5), 36,567
Chancellor, HRH The Prince of Wales, kg, kt, gcb, pc (1976)
Senior Vice-Chancellor, Prof. K. Robbins, d.litt., d.phil., frse
Secretary-General, J. D. Pritchard

COLLEGES

St David's University College, Lampeter, Dyfed sa48 7ed. Tel: 01570-422351. *Principal*, Prof. K. Robbins, d.litt., d.phil., frse (1992)
University College of North Wales, Bangor, Gwynedd ll57 2dg. Tel: 01248-351151. *Vice-Chancellor and Principal*, Prof. H. R. Evans, ph.d., feng. (1995)
University College of Swansea, Singleton Park, Swansea sa2 8pp. Tel: 01792-205678. *Vice-Chancellor and Principal*, Prof. R. H. Williams, ph.d., frs (1994)

University College of Wales, Old College, King Street, Aberystwyth, Dyfed sy23 2ax. Tel: 01970-623111. *Vice-Chancellor and Principal*, Prof. D. Llwyd Morgan, d.phil. (1995)
University of Wales College of Cardiff, PO Box 920, Cardiff cf1 3xp. Tel: 01222-874000. *Vice-Chancellor and Principal*, Prof. E. B. Smith, ph.d., d.sc. (1993)
University of Wales College of Medicine, Heath Park, Cardiff cf4 4xn. Tel: 01222-747747. *Provost and Vice-Chancellor*, Prof. I. R. Cameron, frcp (1994)

THE UNIVERSITY OF WARWICK (1965)
Coventry cv4 7al
Tel 01203-523523
Full-time students (1994–5), 10,700
Chancellor, Sir Shridath Surendranath Ramphal, gcmg, qc (1989)
Vice-Chancellor, Prof. Sir Brian Follett, frs, d.sc.
Registrar, M. L. Shattock, obe

THE UNIVERSITY OF WESTMINSTER (1992)
309 Regent Street, London w1r 8al
Tel 0171-911 5000
Full-time students (1994–5), 8,974
Rector, Prof. T. E. Burlin
Deputy-Rector, Dr G. M. Copland
Registrar, Ms J. Hopkinson

THE UNIVERSITY OF THE WEST OF ENGLAND, BRISTOL (BRISTOL UWE) (1992)
Coldharbour Lane, Bristol bs16 1qy
Tel 0117-965 6261
Full-time students (1994–5), 13,180
Chancellor, Dame Elizabeth Butler-Sloss, dbe
Vice-Chancellor, A. C. Morris
Academic Registrar, Ms M. J. Carter
Secretary, W. Evans

THE UNIVERSITY OF WOLVERHAMPTON (1992)
Wulfruna Street, Wolverhampton wv1 1sb
Tel 01902-321000
Full-time students (1994–5), 16,863
Chancellor, The Earl of Shrewsbury and Talbot
Vice-Chancellor / Director, Prof. M. J. Harrison
Pro-Vice-Chancellor / Assistant Director, G. R. Brooks

THE UNIVERSITY OF YORK (1963)
Heslington, York yo1 5dd
Tel 01904-430000
Full-time students (1994–5), 5,000
Chancellor, Dame Janet Baker, dbe
Vice-Chancellor, Prof. R. U. Cooke, ph.d.
Registrar, D. J. Foster

CRANFIELD UNIVERSITY (1969)
Cranfield, Beds mk43 0al
Tel 01234-750111
Cranfield University (formerly the Cranfield Institute of Technology) grants degrees in applied science, engineering, technology and management.
Full-time students (1994–5), 2,438
Chancellor, The Lord Kings Norton, ph.d., feng. (1969)
Vice-Chancellor, Prof. F. R. Hartley, d.sc.
Secretary and Registrar, J. K. Pettifer

THE OPEN UNIVERSITY (1969)
Walton Hall, Milton Keynes mk7 6aa
Tel 01908-274066
Students and clients (1995), c.200,000

Tuition by correspondence linked with special radio and television programmes, video and audio cassettes, computing, residential schools and a locally-based tutorial and counselling service. The University awards degrees of BA, B.SC., B.Phil., MA, MBA, MBA (Technology), M.SC., M.Phil., Ph.D., D.Ed., D.SC. and D.Litt. There are eight faculties: arts; education; health, welfare and community education; management; mathematics and computing; science; social sciences; technology; and a wide range of qualification courses and study packs.

Chancellor, The Rt. Hon. Betty Boothroyd, MP
Vice-Chancellor, Sir John Daniel
Secretary, D. J. Clinch

THE ROYAL COLLEGE OF ART (1837)

Kensington Gore, London SW7 2EU
Tel 0171-584 5020
Under royal charter (1967) the Royal College of Art grants the degrees of Doctor, Doctor of Philosophy, Master of Philosophy, Master of Arts and Master of Design.
Students (1994–5), 750 (all postgraduate)
Provost, The Earl of Snowdon, GCVO (1995)
Rector and Vice-Provost, Prof. A. Jones
Registrar, A. Selby

COLLEGES

It is not possible to name here all the colleges offering courses of higher or further education. The list does not include colleges forming part of a polytechnic or a university. The English colleges that follow are confined to those in the Higher Education Funding Council for England sector; there are many more colleges in England providing higher education courses, some with HEFCFE funding.

The list of colleges in Wales, Scotland and Northern Ireland includes institutions providing at least one full-time course leading to a first degree granted by an accredited validating body.

ENGLAND

BATH COLLEGE OF HIGHER EDUCATION, Newton Park, Newton St Loe, Bath BA2 9BN. Tel: 01225-873701. *Director,* Prof. B. L. Gomes da Costa

BISHOP GROSSETESTE COLLEGE, Lincoln LN1 3DY. Tel: 01522-527347. *Principal,* Prof. L. Marsh, OBE, D.Phil.

BOLTON INSTITUTE OF HIGHER EDUCATION, Deane Road, Bolton BL3 5AB. Tel: 01204-528851. *Principal,* R. Oxtoby, Ph.D.

BRETTON HALL, West Bretton, Wakefield, W. Yorks WF4 4LG. Tel: 01924-830261. *Principal,* Prof. G.H. Bell

BUCKINGHAMSHIRE COLLEGE, Queen Alexandra Road, High Wycombe, Bucks HP11 2JZ. Tel: 01494-522141. *Director,* Prof. P. B. Mogford

CANTERBURY CHRIST CHURCH COLLEGE, North Holmes Road, Canterbury, Kent CT1 1QU. Tel: 01227-767700. *Principal,* M. H. A. Berry, TD

THE CENTRAL SCHOOL OF SPEECH AND DRAMA, Embassy Theatre, Eton Avenue, London NW3 3HY. Tel: 0171-722 8183. *Principal,* Prof. R. S. Fowler, FRSA

CHELTENHAM AND GLOUCESTER COLLEGE OF HIGHER EDUCATION, PO Box 220, The Park, Cheltenham, Glos GL50 2QF. Tel: 01242-532700. *Director,* Miss J. O. Trotter, OBE

CHESTER COLLEGE, Cheyney Road, Chester CH1 4BJ. Tel: 01244-375444. *Principal,* Revd E. V. Binks

CHICHESTER INSTITUTE OF HIGHER EDUCATION, College Lane, Chichester, West Sussex PO19 4PE. Tel: 01243-787911. *Director,* Dr J. F. Wyatt

COLLEGE OF ST MARK AND ST JOHN, Derriford Road, Plymouth PL6 8BH. Tel: 01752-777188. *Principal,* Dr W. J. Rea

DARTINGTON COLLEGE OF ARTS, Totnes, Devon TQ9 6EJ. Tel: 01803-862224. *Principal,* Prof. K. Thompson

EDGE HILL COLLEGE OF HIGHER EDUCATION, St Helens Road, Ormskirk, Lancs L39 4QP. Tel: 01695-575171. *Director,* Dr. J. Cater

FALMOUTH COLLEGE OF ARTS, Woodlane, Falmouth, Cornwall TR11 4RA. Tel: 01326-211077. *Principal,* Prof. A. G. Livingston

HARPER ADAMS AGRICULTURAL COLLEGE, Newport, Shropshire TF10 8NB. Tel: 01952-820280. *Principal,* G. R. McConnell

HOMERTON COLLEGE, Cambridge CB2 2PH. Tel: 01223-411141. *Principal,* Mrs K. Pretty, Ph.D.

INSTITUTE OF ADVANCED NURSING, Royal College of Nursing, 20 Cavendish Square, London W1M 0AB. Tel: 0171-355 1396. *Principal,* J. C. A. Wells

KENT INSTITUTE OF ART AND DESIGN, Oakwood Park, Maidstone ME16 8AG (*also* New Dover Road, Canterbury CT1 3AN; and Fort Pitt, Rochester ME1 1DZ). Tel: 01622-691471/757286. *Director,* P. I. Williams

KING ALFRED'S COLLEGE OF HIGHER EDUCATION, Sparkford Road, Winchester SO22 4NR. Tel: 01962-841515. *Principal,* Prof. J. P. Dickinson

LIVERPOOL INSTITUTE OF HIGHER EDUCATION, PO Box 6, Stand Park Road, Liverpool L16 9JD. Tel: 0151-737 3477. *Rector,* Prof. S. Lee

THE LONDON INSTITUTE, 65 Davies Street, London W1Y 2DA. Tel: 0171-514 6000. *Rector,* Prof. J. C. McKenzie
Comprising:
Camberwell College of Arts, Peckham Road, London SE5 8UF
Central St Martins College of Art and Design, Southampton Row, London WC1B 4AP
Chelsea College of Art and Design, Manresa Road, London SW3 6LS
London College of Fashion, 20 John Prince's Street, London W1M 0BJ
London College of Printing and Distributive Trades, Elephant and Castle, London SE1 6SB

LOUGHBOROUGH COLLEGE OF ART AND DESIGN, Radmoor, Loughborough, Leics LE11 3BT. Tel: 01509-261515. *Principal,* I. Pugh

LSU COLLEGE OF HIGHER EDUCATION, The Avenue, Southampton SO17 1BG. Tel: 01703-228761. *Principal,* Dr A. C. Chitnis

NENE COLLEGE, Park Campus, Boughton Green Road, Northampton NN2 7AL. Tel: 01604-735500. *Director,* S. M. Gaskell, Ph.D.

NEWMAN COLLEGE, Genners Lane, Bartley Green, Birmingham B32 3NT. Tel: 0121-476 1181. *Principal,* Prof. B. Ray

RAVENSBOURNE COLLEGE OF DESIGN AND COMMUNICATION, Walden Road, Chislehurst, Kent BR7 5SN. Tel: 0181-295 8105. *Director,* Prof. R. Baker

ROEHAMPTON INSTITUTE, Senate House, Roehampton Lane, London SW15 5PU. Comprises Digby Stuart College, Froebel Institute College, Southlands College and Whitelands College. Tel: 0181-392 3000. *Rector,* Prof. S. C. Holt, Ph.D.

ROSE BRUFORD COLLEGE, Lamorbey Park, Sidcup, Kent DA15 9DF. Tel: 0181-300 3024. *Principal,* R. Ely

ROYAL ACADEMY OF MUSIC, Marylebone Road, London NW1 5HT. Tel: 0171-873 7373. *Principal,* Prof. C. Price

ROYAL COLLEGE OF MUSIC, Prince Consort Road, London SW7 2BS. Tel: 0171-589 3643. *Director,* Ms J. Ritterman, PH.D.

ROYAL NORTHERN COLLEGE OF MUSIC, 124 Oxford Road, Manchester M13 9RD. Tel: 0161-273 6283. *Principal,* Sir John Manduell, CBE

SOUTHAMPTON INSTITUTE, East Park Terrace, Southampton SO14 0YN. Tel: 01703-319000. *Director,* Prof. D. G. Leyland

SURREY INSTITUTE OF ART AND DESIGN, Falkner Road, The Hart, Farnham, Surrey GU9 7DS. Tel: 01252-722441. *Director,* N. J. Taylor

TRINITY AND ALL SAINTS' COLLEGE, Brownberrie Lane, Horsforth, Leeds LS18 5HD. Tel: 0113-283 7100. *Principal,* Dr G. L. Turnbull

TRINITY COLLEGE OF MUSIC, 11–13 Mandeville Place, London W1M 6AQ. Tel: 0171-935 5773. *Principal,* G. Henderson

UNIVERSITY COLLEGE OF RIPON AND YORK ST JOHN, Lord Mayor's Walk, York YO3 7EX. Tel: 01904-656771. *Principal,* Prof. R. Butlin

UNIVERSITY COLLEGE OF S. MARTIN, Lancaster LA1 3JD. Tel: 01524-63446. *Principal,* D. Edynbry, PH.D.

UNIVERSITY COLLEGE SCARBOROUGH, THE NORTH RIDING COLLEGE, Filey Road, Scarborough, N. Yorks YO11 3AZ. Tel: 01723-362392. *Principal,* R. A. Withers, PH.D.

WESTHILL COLLEGE, Hamilton Building, Weoley Park Road, Selly Oak, Birmingham B29 6LL. Tel: 0121-472 7245. *Principal,* Dr J. G. Priestley

WESTMINSTER COLLEGE, Oxford OX2 9AT. Tel: 01865-247644. *Principal,* Revd Dr K. B. Wilson, OBE

WINCHESTER SCHOOL OF ART, Park Avenue, Winchester, Hants SO23 8DL. Tel: 01962-842500. *Principal,* M. Sadler-Forster

WORCESTER COLLEGE OF HIGHER EDUCATION, Henwick Grove, Worcester WR2 6AJ. Tel: 01905-855000. *Principal,* Ms D. Urwin

WALES

CARDIFF INSTITUTE OF HIGHER EDUCATION, Western Avenue, Llandaff, Cardiff CF5 2SG. Tel: 01222-551111. *Director,* J. D. Winslow

GWENT COLLEGE OF HIGHER EDUCATION, College Crescent, Caerleon, Newport, Gwent NP6 1XJ. Tel: 01633-430088. *Principal,* Dr K. J. Overshott

NORMAL COLLEGE, Bangor, Gwynedd LL57 2PX. Tel: 01248-370171. *Principal,* H. G. Roberts, PH.D.

THE NORTH-EAST WALES INSTITUTE OF HIGHER EDUCATION, Plas Coch, Mold Road, Wrexham, Clwyd LL11 2AW. Tel: 01978-290666. *Principal,* Prof. J. O. Williams, PH.D, D.SC.

SWANSEA INSTITUTE OF HIGHER EDUCATION, Townhill Road, Swansea SA2 0UT. Tel: 01792-481000. *Principal,* G. Stockdale, PH.D.

TRINITY COLLEGE, Carmarthen, Dyfed, SA31 3EP. Tel: 01267-237971. *Principal,* D. C. Jones-Davies, OBE

WELSH COLLEGE OF MUSIC AND DRAMA, Castle Grounds, Cathays Park, Cardiff CF1 3ER. Tel: 01222-342854. *Principal,* E. Fivet

SCOTLAND

BELL COLLEGE OF TECHNOLOGY, Almada Street, Hamilton, Lanarkshire ML3 0JB. Tel: 01698-283100. *Principal,* J. Reid

GLASGOW SCHOOL OF ART, 167 Renfrew Street, Glasgow G3 6RQ. Tel: 0141-353 4500. *Director,* Prof. D. Cameron

NORTHERN COLLEGE OF EDUCATION, Hilton Place, Aberdeen AB9 1FA. Tel: 01224-283500; Gardyne Road, Dundee DD5 1NY. Tel: 01382-464000. *Principal,* D. A. Adams

QUEEN MARGARET COLLEGE, Clerwood Terrace, Edinburgh EH12 8TS. Tel: 0131-317 3000; Duke Street, Edinburgh EH6 8HF. Tel: 0131-317 3355. *Principal,* Prof. D. F. Leach

ROYAL SCOTTISH ACADEMY OF MUSIC AND DRAMA, 100 Renfrew Street, Glasgow G2 3DB. Tel: 0141-332 4101. *Principal,* Dr P. Ledger, CBE, FRSE

SAC (SCOTTISH AGRICULTURAL COLLEGE), Central Office, West Mains Road, Edinburgh EH9 3JG. Tel: 0131-662 1303. Campuses at Aberdeen, Auchincruive, Ayr, and Edinburgh. *Principal and Chief Executive,* Prof. P. C. Thomas

ST ANDREW'S COLLEGE OF EDUCATION, Duntocher Road, Bearsden, Glasgow G61 4QA. Tel: 0141-943 1424. *Principal,* Prof. B. J. McGettrick, OBE

NORTHERN IRELAND

DOWN COLLEGE OF FURTHER EDUCATION, Market Street, Downpatrick, Co. Down BT30 6ND. Tel: 01396-615815. *Principal,* T. L. Place

ST MARY'S COLLEGE, 191 Falls Road, Belfast BT12 6FE. Tel: 01232-327678. *Principal,* Revd M. O'Callaghan

STRANMILLIS COLLEGE, Stranmillis Road, Belfast BT9 5DY. Tel: 01232-381271. *Principal,* Dr J. R. McMinn

ADULT AND CONTINUING EDUCATION

FORUM FOR THE ADVANCEMENT OF CONTINUING EDUCATION, Department of Continuing Education, Westminster College, Oxford OX2 9AT. Tel: 01865-247644. *Secretary,* Dr. P. Percy

NATIONAL INSTITUTE OF ADULT CONTINUING EDUCATION, 21 De Montfort Street, Leicester LE1 7GE. Tel: 0116-255 1451. *Director,* A. Tuckett

NIACE CYMRU, 245 Western Avenue, Cardiff CF5 2YX. Tel: 01222-571201. *Associate Director,* Ms A. Poole

NORTHERN IRELAND COUNCIL FOR ADULT EDUCATION, c/o Western Education and Library Board, 1 Hospital Road, Omagh, Co. Tyrone BT79 0AW. Tel: 01662-240240. *Chairman,* J. Martin; *Education Officer,* Ms T. Devine

THE RESIDENTIAL COLLEGES COMMITTEE, c/o Ruskin College, Oxford OX1 2HE. Tel: 01865-56360. *Awards Officer,* Mrs F. A. Bagchi

SCOTTISH COMMUNITY EDUCATION COUNCIL, Rosebery House, 9 Haymarket Terrace, Edinburgh EH12 5EZ. Tel: 0131-313 2488. *Executive Director,* C. McConnell

THE UNIVERSITIES ASSOCIATION FOR CONTINUING EDUCATION, Department of Adult Continuing Education, University of Leeds, Leeds LS2 9JT. Tel: 0113-233 3222. *Secretary,* Prof. R. Taylor

THE WORKER'S EDUCATIONAL ASSOCIATION, Temple House, 17 Victoria Park Square, London E2 9PB. Tel: 0181-983 1515. *General Secretary,* R. Lochrie

LONG-TERM RESIDENTIAL COLLEGES FOR ADULT EDUCATION

COLEG HARLECH, Harlech, Gwynedd LL46 2PU. Tel: 01766-780363. *Warden,* J. W. England

CO-OPERATIVE COLLEGE, Stanford Hall, Loughborough, Leics LE12 5QR. Tel: 01509-852333. *Principal,* R. Wildgusp

FIRCROFT COLLEGE, 1018 Bristol Road, Selly Oak, Birmingham B29 6LH. Tel: 0121-472 0116. *Principal,* K. Jackson

HILLCROFT COLLEGE, South Bank, Surbiton, Surrey KT6 6DF. Tel: 0181-399 2688. For women only. *Principal,* Ms E. Aird

NEWBATTLE ABBEY COLLEGE, Dalkeith, Midlothian EH22 3LL. Tel: 0131-663 1921. *Principal,* W. M. Conboy

NORTHERN COLLEGE, Wentworth Castle, Stainborough, Barnsley, S. Yorks S75 3ET. Tel: 01226-285426. *Principal,* Prof. R. H. Fryer

PLATER COLLEGE, Pullens Lane, Oxford OX3 ODT. Tel: 01865-741676. *Principal,* M. Blades

RUSKIN COLLEGE, Walton Street, Oxford OX1 2HE. Tel: 01865-58376. *Principal,* S. Yeo, D.Phil.

PROFESSIONAL EDUCATION
Excluding postgraduate study

The organizations listed below are those which, by providing specialist training or conducting examinations, control entry into a profession, or organizations responsible for maintaining a register of those with professional qualifications in their sector.

Many professions now have a largely graduate entry, and possession of a first degree can exempt entrants from certain of the professional examinations. Enquiries about obtaining professional qualifications should be made to the relevant professional organization(s). Details of higher education providers of first degrees may be found in *University and College Entrance: Official Guide* (available from UCAS, *see* page 452).

ACCOUNTANCY

The main bodies granting membership on examination after a period of practical work are:

INSTITUTE OF CHARTERED ACCOUNTANTS IN ENGLAND AND WALES, Chartered Accountants' Hall, PO Box 433, Moorgate Place, London EC2P 2BJ. Tel: 0171-920 8100. *Secretary and Chief Executive,* A. J. Colquhoun

INSTITUTE OF CHARTERED ACCOUNTANTS OF SCOTLAND, 27 Queen Street, Edinburgh EH2 1LA. Tel: 0131-225 5673. *Chief Executive,* P. W. Johnston

CHARTERED ASSOCIATION OF CERTIFIED ACCOUNTANTS, 29 Lincoln's Inn Fields, London WC2A 3EE. Tel: 0171-242 6855. *Chief Executive,* Mrs A. L. Rose

CHARTERED INSTITUTE OF MANAGEMENT ACCOUNTANTS, 63 Portland Place, London WIN 4AB. Tel: 0171-637 2311. *Secretary,* J. S. Chester, OBE

CHARTERED INSTITUTE OF PUBLIC FINANCE AND ACCOUNTANCY, 3 Robert Street, London WC2N 6BH. Tel: 0171-895 8823. *Secretary,* N. P. Hepworth, OBE

ACTUARIAL SCIENCE

Two professional organizations grant qualifications after examination:

INSTITUTE OF ACTUARIES, Staple Inn Hall, High Holborn, London WCIV 7QJ. Tel: 0171-242 0106. *Secretary-General,* A. G. Tait. Enquiries to Actuarial Education Service, Napier House, 4 Worcester Street, Oxford OX1 2AW. Tel: 01865-794144

FACULTY OF ACTUARIES IN SCOTLAND, 40–44 Thistle Street, Edinburgh EH2 1EN. Tel: 0131-220 4555. *Secretary,* W. W. Mair

ARCHITECTURE

The Education and Professional Development Committee of the Royal Institute of British Architects sets standards and guides the whole system of architectural education throughout the UK. The RIBA recognizes courses at 38 schools of architecture in the UK for exemption from their own examinations.

THE ROYAL INSTITUTE OF BRITISH ARCHITECTS, 66 Portland Place, London 4AD. Tel: 0171-580 5533. *President,* Dr F. Duffy; *Director-General,* A. Reid, PH.D.

Schools of architecture outside the universities include:

THE ARCHITECTURAL ASSOCIATION, 34–36 Bedford Square, London WCIB 3ES. *Secretary,* E. A. Le Maistre

PRINCE OF WALES'S INSTITUTE OF ARCHITECTURE, 14–15 Gloucester Gate, London NWI 4HG. Tel: 0171-916 7380. *Director,* Dr R. John

BANKING

Professional organizations granting qualifications after examination are:

CHARTERED INSTITUTE OF BANKERS, 10 Lombard Street, London EC3V 9AS. Tel: 0171-623 3531. *Chief Executive,* G. Shreeve

CHARTERED INSTITUTE OF BANKERS IN SCOTLAND, 19 Rutland Square, Edinburgh EHI 2DE. Tel: 0131-229 9869. *Chief Executive,* Dr C. W. Munn

BIOLOGY, CHEMISTRY, PHYSICS

Professional qualifications are awarded by:

INSTITUTE OF BIOLOGY, 20–22 Queensberry Place, London SW7 2DZ. Tel: 0171-581 8333. *President,* Prof. F. A. Hibbert; *General Secretary,* Dr R. H. Priestley

ROYAL SOCIETY OF CHEMISTRY, Burlington House, Piccadilly, London WIV OBN. Tel: 0171-437 8656. *President,* Prof. J. H. Purnell; *Secretary-General,* Dr T. Inch

INSTITUTE OF PHYSICS, 47 Belgrave Square, London SWIX 8QX. Tel: 0171-235 6111. *Chief Executive,* Dr A. Jones

BUILDING

Examinations are conducted by:

CHARTERED INSTITUTE OF BUILDING, Englemere, King's Ride, Ascot, Berks SL5 8BJ. Tel: 01344-23355. *Chief Executive,* K. Banbury

INSTITUTE OF BUILDING CONTROL, 21 High Street, Ewell, Epsom, Surrey KTI7 ISB. Tel: 0181-393 6860. *Director,* Ms R. Raywood

INSTITUTE OF CLERKS OF WORKS OF GREAT BRITAIN, 41 The Mall, London W5 3TJ. Tel: 0181-579 2917/8. *Secretary,* A. P. Macnamara

BUSINESS, MANAGEMENT AND ADMINISTRATION

Professional bodies conducting training and/or examinations in business, administration, management or commerce include:

AMETS (ASSOCIATION FOR MANAGEMENT EDUCATION AND TRAINING IN SCOTLAND), c/o University of Stirling, Stirling FK9 4LA. Tel: 01786-450906. *Vice-Chairman,* M. Makower

CAM Foundation (Communications, Advertising and Marketing Education Foundation), Abford House, 15 Wilton Road, London swiv inj. Tel: 0171-828 7506. *General Secretary,* J. Knight

Chartered Institute of Housing, Octavia House, Westwood Business Park, Westwood Way, Coventry cv4 8jp. Tel: 01203-694433. *Chief Executive,* Ms C. Laird

Chartered Institute of Marketing, Moor Hall, Cookham, Maidenhead, Berks sl6 9qh. Tel: 01628-524922. *Director-General,* S. Cuthbert

Chartered Institute of Purchasing and Supply, Easton House, Easton on the Hill, Stamford, Lincs pe9 3nz. Tel: 01780-56777. *Director-General,* P. Thomson

Chartered Institute of Transport, 80 Portland Place, London win 4dp. Tel: 0171-636 9952. *Director,* Mrs S. Gross

Faculty of Secretaries and Administrators, Brightstowe, Catteshall Lane, Godalming, Surrey gu7 ilt. Tel: 01483-454213. *Secretary,* Mrs D. M. Rummery

Henley Management College, Greenlands, Henley-on-Thames, Oxon rg9 3au. Tel: 01491-571454. *Principal,* Prof. R. Wild

Institute of Administrative Management, 40 Chatsworth Parade, Petts Wood, Orpington, Kent br5 irw. Tel: 01689-875555. *Chief Executive,* Prof. G. Robinson

Institute of Chartered Secretaries and Administrators, 16 Park Crescent, London win 4ah. Tel: 0171-580 4741. *Chief Executive,* M. J. Ainsworth

Institute of Chartered Shipbrokers, 3 Gracechurch Street, London ec3v oat. Tel: 0171-283 1361. *Secretary,* Mrs B. Fletcher

Institute of Export, Export House, 64 Clifton Street, London ec2a 4hb. Tel: 0171-247 9812. *Director-General,* I. J. Campbell

Institute of Health Services Management, 39 Chalton Street, London nwi ijd. Tel: 0171-388 2626. *Director,* R. Rowden

Institute of Management, Management House, Cottingham Road, Corby, Northants nni7 itt. Tel: 01536-204222. *Director-General,* R. Young

Institute of Personnel and Development, IPD House, Camp Road, London swi9 4ux. Tel: 0181-971 9000. *Director-General,* G. Armstrong

Institute of Practitioners in Advertising, 44 Belgrave Square, London swix 8qs. Tel: 0171-235 7020. *Secretary,* J. Raad

London Business School, Sussex Place, Regent's Park, London nwi 4sa. Tel: 0171-262 5050. *Principal,* Prof. G. Bain, ph.d.

London Chamber of Commerce and Industry Examinations Board, Marlowe House, Station Road, Sidcup, Kent da15 7bj. Tel: 0181-302 0261. *Chief Executive,* W. J. Swords

Manchester Business School, Booth Street West, Manchester m15 6pb. Tel: 0161-275 6413. *Director,* Prof. J. A. Arnold

DANCE

Royal Academy of Dancing, 36 Battersea Square, London swii 3ra. Tel: 0171-223 0091. *Chief Executive,* D. Watchman; *Artistic Director,* Miss L. Wallis

Royal Ballet School, 155 Talgarth Road, London wi4 9de. Tel: 0181-748 6335. Also at White Lodge, Richmond Park, Surrey twio 5hr. Tel: 0181-876 5547. *Director,* Dame Merle Park, dbe

Imperial Society of Teachers of Dancing, Euston Hall, Birkenhead Street, London wcih 8be. Tel: 0171-837 9967. *General Secretary,* M. J. Browne

DEFENCE

Royal College of Defence Studies, Seaford House, 27 Belgrave Square, London swix 8ns. Tel: 0171-915 4800. Prepares selected senior officers and officials for responsibilities in the direction and management of defence and security. *Commandant,* Air Marshal Sir Timothy Garden, kcb

Royal Naval Colleges

Royal Naval College, Greenwich, London seio 9nn. Tel: 0181-858 2154. *Admiral President,* Rear-Adm. J. B. Blackham; *Dean of the College,* Prof. G. Till, ph.d.

Britannia Royal Naval College, Dartmouth, Devon tq6 ohj. Tel: 01803-832141. Provides general and academic officer training. *Captain,* Capt. A. P. Masterton-Smith

Military Colleges

Staff College, Camberley, Surrey gu15 4np. Tel: 01276-412632. *Commandant,* Maj.-Gen. A. D. Piggott, cbe

Royal Military Academy Sandhurst, Camberley, Surrey gu15 4pq. Tel: 01276-63344. *Commandant,* Maj.-Gen. H. W. R. Pike, dso, mbe

Royal Military College of Science, Shrivenham, Swindon, Wilts sn6 8la. Tel: 01793-785435. Students from UK and overseas study from degree to postgraduate levels in management, science and technology. The College is a faculty of Cranfield University. *Commandant,* Maj.-Gen. D. J. M. Jenkins, cbe; *Principal,* Prof. A. C. Baynham, ph.d.

Directorate of Educational and Training Services, Director-General Adjutant General's Corp, Worthydown, Winchester, Hants so21 2rg. Tel: 01962-887665. *Director,* Brig. A. D. Thompson

Royal Air Force Colleges

Royal Air Force Staff College, Bracknell, Berks rgi2 9dd. Prepares selected senior officers for high-grade command and staff appointments. Two-thirds of the students are RAF officers; the others are officers from the other UK Services and overseas air forces. *Air Officer Commanding and Commandant,* Air Vice-Marshal M. P. Donaldson

Royal Air Force College, Cranwell, Sleaford, Lincs. ng34 8hb. Provides initial training for all officer entrants to the RAF. Also provides specialist training for junior officers of some ground branches and supervision of elementary flying training, general service training for University Air Squadrons, and supervision of the Air Cadet Organization. *Air Officer Commanding and Commandant,* Air Vice-Marshal A. J. Stables, cbe

Royal Air Force School of Education and Training Support, RAF Newton, Nottingham ngi3 8hl. Tel: 01949-20771. *Commanding Officer,* Gp Capt J. Rennie

DENTISTRY

To be entitled to be registered in the Dentists Register, a person must hold the degree or diploma in dental surgery of a university in the UK or the diploma of any of the licensing authorities (the Royal Colleges of Surgeons of England and of Edinburgh, and the Royal College of Physicians and Surgeons of Glasgow). Nationals of an EU

member state holding an appropriate European diploma, and holders of certain overseas diplomas, may also be registered. The Dentists Register is maintained by:
THE GENERAL DENTAL COUNCIL, 37 Wimpole Street, London WIM 8DQ. Tel: 0171-486 2171. *Registrar,* N. T. Davies, MBE

DIETETICS
See also FOOD AND NUTRITION SCIENCE

The professional association is the British Dietetic Association. Full membership is open to dietitians holding a recognized qualification, who may also become State Registered Dietitians through the Council for Professions Supplementary to Medicine (*see* Medicine)
THE BRITISH DIETETIC ASSOCIATION, 7th Floor, Elizabeth House, 22 Suffolk Street, Queensway, Birmingham BI ILS. Tel: 0121-643 5483

DRAMA

The national validating body for courses providing training in drama for the professional theatre is the National Council for Drama Training. It currently has accredited courses at the following: Academy of Live and Recorded Arts; Arts Educational Schools; Birmingham School of Speech Training and Dramatic Art; Bristol Old Vic Theatre School; Central School of Speech and Drama; Drama Centre, London; Drama Studio, London; Guildford School of Acting; Guildhall School of Music and Drama, London; London Academy of Music and Dramatic Art; Manchester Metropolitan University School of Theatre; Mountview Theatre School; Queen Margaret College, Edinburgh; Rose Bruford College, Sidcup; Royal Academy of Dramatic Art, London; Royal Scottish Academy of Music and Drama; Webber Douglas Academy of Dramatic Art; Welsh College of Music and Drama.
The accreditation of a course in a school does not necessarily imply that other courses of different type or duration in the same school are also accredited
THE NATIONAL COUNCIL FOR DRAMA TRAINING, 5 Tavistock Place, London WCIH 9SN. *Secretary,* Ms A. Bailey

ENGINEERING

The Engineering Council supervises the engineering profession through the 41 nominated engineering institutions who are represented on its Board for Engineers' Registration. Working with and through the institutions, the Council sets the standards for the registration of individuals, and also the accreditation for academic courses in universities and colleges and the practical training in industry.
THE ENGINEERING COUNCIL, 10 Maltravers Street, London WC2R 3ER. Tel: 0171-240 7891. *Director-General,* M. Heath
The principal qualifying bodies are:
BRITISH COMPUTER SOCIETY, 1 Sanford Street, Swindon SNI IHJ. Tel: 01793-417417. *Chief Executive,* J. Scott
CHARTERED INSTITUTION OF BUILDING SERVICES ENGINEERS, Delta House, 222 Balham High Road, London SWI2 9BS. Tel: 0181-675 5211. *Secretary,* A. V. Ramsay
INSTITUTION OF CHEMICAL ENGINEERS, The Davis Building, 165–171 Railway Terrace, Rugby, Warks CV2I 3HQ. Tel: 01788-578214. *Chief Executive,* Dr T. J. Evans
INSTITUTION OF CIVIL ENGINEERS, Great George Street, London SWIP 3AA. Tel: 0171-222 7722. *Director-General,* R. Dobson

INSTITUTION OF ELECTRICAL ENGINEERS, Savoy Place, London WC2R OBL. Tel: 0171-240 1871. *Secretary,* Dr J. C. Williams, FENG.
INSTITUTE OF ENERGY, 18 Devonshire Street, London WIN 2AU. Tel: 0171-580 7124. *Secretary,* J. E. H. Leach
INSTITUTION OF GAS ENGINEERS, 21 Portland Place, London WIN 3AF. Tel: 0171-636 6603. *Secretary,* Mrs S. M. Raine
INSTITUTE OF MARINE ENGINEERS, The Memorial Building, 76 Mark Lane, London EC3R 7JN. Tel: 0171-481 8493. *Secretary,* J. E. Sloggett, OBE
INSTITUTE OF MATERIALS, 1 Carlton House Terrace, London SWIY 5DB. Tel: 0171-839 4071. *Secretary,* Dr J. A. Catterall
INSTITUTE OF MEASUREMENT AND CONTROL, 87 Gower Street, London WCIE 6AA. Tel: 0171-387 4949. *Secretary,* M. J. Yates
INSTITUTION OF MECHANICAL ENGINEERS, 1 Birdcage Walk, London 9JJ. Tel: 0171-222 7899. *Director-General,* Dr R. Pike
INSTITUTION OF MINING ENGINEERS, Danum House, 6A South Parade, Doncaster DNI 2DY. Tel: 01302-320486. *Secretary,* G. J. M. Woodrow
INSTITUTION OF MINING AND METALLURGY, 44 Portland Place, London WIN 4BR. Tel: 0171-580 3802. *Secretary,* M. J. Jones
INSTITUTE OF PHYSICS, 47 Belgrave Square, London SWIX 8QX. Tel: 0171-235 6111. *Chief Executive,* Dr A. Jones
ROYAL AERONAUTICAL SOCIETY, 4 Hamilton Place, London WIV OBQ. Tel: 0171-499 3515. *Director,* R. J. Kennett
ROYAL INSTITUTION OF NAVAL ARCHITECTS, 10 Upper Belgrave Street, London SWIX 8BQ. Tel: 0171-235 4622. *Secretary,* J. Rosewarn
INSTITUTION OF STRUCTURAL ENGINEERS, 11 Upper Belgrave Street, London SWIX 8BH. Tel: 0171-235 4535. *Chief Executive,* Dr J. W. Dougill

FOOD AND NUTRITION SCIENCE
See also DIETETICS

Scientific and professional bodies include:
INSTITUTE OF FOOD SCIENCE & TECHNOLOGY, 10 Cambridge Court, 210 Shepherd's Bush Road, London W6 7NL. Tel: 0171-603 6316. *Executive Secretary,* Ms H. G. Wild
NUTRITION SOCIETY, 10 Cambridge Court, 210 Shepherds Bush Road, London W6 7NJ. Tel: 0171-602 0228. *Hon. Secretary,* Prof. J. Mathers

FORESTRY AND TIMBER STUDIES

Professional organizations include:
ROYAL FORESTRY SOCIETY OF ENGLAND, WALES AND NORTHERN IRELAND, 102 High Street, Tring, Herts HP23 4AF. Tel: 01442-822028. *Director,* J. E. Jackson, PH.D.
ROYAL SCOTTISH FORESTRY SOCIETY, 62 Queen Street, Edinburgh EH2 4NA. Tel: 0131-225 8142. *Director,* M. Osborne
INSTITUTE OF CHARTERED FORESTERS, 7A St Colme Street, Edinburgh EH3 6AA. Tel: 0131-225 2705. *Secretary,* Mrs M. W. Dick
COMMONWEALTH FORESTRY ASSOCIATION, c/o Oxford Forestry Institute, South Parks Road, Oxford OXI 3RB. Tel: 01865-275072. *Chairman,* P. J. Wood

FUEL AND ENERGY SCIENCE

The principal professional bodies are:
INSTITUTE OF ENERGY, 18 Devonshire Street, London WIN 2AU. Tel: 0171-580 7124. *Secretary,* J. Leach

INSTITUTION OF GAS ENGINEERS, 21 Portland Place, London WIN 3AF. Tel: 0171-636 6603. *Secretary,* Mrs S. M. Raine

INSTITUTE OF PETROLEUM, 61 New Cavendish Street, London WIM 8AR. Tel: 0171-467 7100. *Director-General,* I. Ward

HOTELKEEPING, CATERING AND INSTITUTIONAL MANAGEMENT

See also DIETETICS, and FOOD AND NUTRITION SCIENCE

The qualifying professional body in these areas is:
HOTEL AND CATERING INTERNATIONAL MANAGEMENT ASSOCIATION, 191 Trinity Road, London SW17 7HN. Tel: 0181-672 4251. *Chief Executive,* J. Logie

INDUSTRIAL AND VOCATIONAL TRAINING

There are 120 industry training organizations, employer-led independent organizations whose role includes setting the standards of National and Scottish Vocational Qualifications.
NATIONAL COUNCIL OF INDUSTRY TRAINING ORGANIZATIONS, 10 Meadowcourt, Amos Road, Sheffield S9 1BX. Tel: 0114-261 9926. *Chair,* Ms L. Millington; *Administrator,* Miss J. Maisari

INSURANCE

Organizations conducting examinations and awarding diplomas are:
ASSOCIATION OF AVERAGE ADJUSTERS, 200 Aldersgate Street, London EC1A 4JJ. Tel: 0171-956 0066. *Hon. Secretary,* D. W. Taylor

CHARTERED INSTITUTE OF LOSS ADJUSTERS, Manfield House, 376 Strand, London WC2R 0LR. Tel: 0171-240 1496. *Director,* A. F. Clack

CHARTERED INSURANCE INSTITUTE, 20 Aldermanbury, London EC2V 7HY. Tel: 0171-606 3835. *Director-General,* Prof. D. E. Bland

JOURNALISM

Courses for trainee newspaper journalists are available at 20 centres. One-year full-time courses are available for selected students and 18-week courses for graduates. Particulars of all these courses are available from the National Council for the Training of Journalists. Short courses for mid-career development can be arranged, as can various distance learning courses. The NCTJ also offers Assessor, Internal Verifier (IV) and Accreditation of Prior Achievement (APA) training, and NVQs.

For periodical journalists, there are eight centres running courses approved by the Periodicals Training Council.
THE NATIONAL COUNCIL FOR TRAINING OF JOURNALISTS, Latton Bush Centre, Southern Way, Harlow, Essex CM18 7BL. Tel: 01279-430009. *Chief Executive,* R. Selwood

THE PERIODICALS TRAINING COUNCIL, Imperial House, 15–19 Kingsway, London WC2B 6UN. Tel: 0171-836 8798. *Executive Director,* Ms J. Butcher

LAW

THE BAR

Admission to the Bar of England and Wales is controlled by the Inns of Court, admission to the Bar of Northern Ireland by the Honorable Society of the Inn of Court of Northern Ireland and admission as an Advocate of the Scottish Bar is controlled by the Faculty of Advocates. The governing body of the barristers' branch of the legal profession in England and Wales is the General Council of the Bar. The governing body in Northern Ireland is the Honorable Society of the Inn of Court of Northern Ireland, and the Faculty of Advocates is the governing body of the Scottish Bar. The education and examination of students for the Bar of England and Wales is currently provided by the Council of Legal Education but the regulation of education and training will be covered by the General Council of the Bar from 1996. The Inns of Court School of Law is the sole provider of the Bar's vocational course, which must be taken by those who intend to practise at the Bar of England and Wales.

THE GENERAL COUNCIL OF THE BAR, 3 Bedford Row, London WC1R 4DB. Tel: 0171-242 0082. *Chairman,* P. Goldsmith, QC; *Chief Executive,* N. Morison

The Inns of Court

THE INNER TEMPLE, London EC4Y 7HL. Tel: 0171-797 8250. *Treasurer,* The Rt. Hon. Lord Justice Hirst; *Sub-Treasurer,* Brig. P. Little

THE MIDDLE TEMPLE, London EC4Y 9AT. *Treasurer,* D. A. Hollis, QC; *Deputy Treasurer,* Brig. C. T. J. Wright

GRAY'S INN, 8 South Square, London WC1R 5EU. Tel: 0171-405 8164. *Treasurer,* C, Dehn, QC; *Under-Treasurer,* D. Machin

LINCOLN'S INN, London WC2A 3TL. Tel: 0171-405 1393. *Treasurer,* The Rt. Hon. Lord Justice Gibson; *Under-Treasurer,* Capt. P. M. Carver, RN

INNS OF COURT SCHOOL OF LAW, 39 Eagle Street, London WC1R 4AJ. Tel: 0171-404 5787. *Chairman,* The Hon. Mr Justice Phillips; *Dean, Inns of Court School of Law,* Mrs M. A. Phillips

FACULTY OF ADVOCATES, Advocates Library, Parliament House, Edinburgh EH1 1RF. Tel: 0131-226 5071. *Dean,* A. R. Hardie, QC; *Clerk,* J. R. Doherty

THE HONORABLE SOCIETY OF THE INN OF COURT OF NORTHERN IRELAND, Royal Courts of Justice, Belfast BT1 3JF. Tel: 01232-235111. *Treasurer* (1995), His Hon. Judge Chambers, QC; *Under-Treasurer,* J. A. L. McLean, QC

SOLICITORS

Qualifications for solicitor are obtainable only from one of the Law Societies, which control the education and examination of trainee solicitors, and the admission of solicitors.
LAW SOCIETY OF ENGLAND AND WALES, 113 Chancery Lane, London WC2A 1PL. Tel: 0171-242 1222. *President* (1995–6), M. J. P. Mears; *Vice-President* (1995–6), R. Sayer; *Secretary-General,* J. W. Hayes, CBE

THE COLLEGE OF LAW provides courses for the Common Professional Examination and Legal Practice Course at Braboeuf Manor, St Catherines, Guildford, Surrey GU3 1HA; 14 Store Street, London WC1E 7DE; Christleton Hall, Chester CH3 7AB; Bishopthorpe Road, York YO2 1QA

THE SOLICITORS COMPLAINTS BUREAU, Victoria Court, 8 Dormer Place, Leamington Spa, Warks CV32 5AE. Tel: 01926-820082. The Bureau is an establishment of the Law Society set up to handle complaints about solicitors.

LAW SOCIETY OF SCOTLAND, Law Society's Hall, 26 Drumsheugh Gardens, Edinburgh EH3 7YR. Tel: 0131-226 7411. *President* (1995–6), A. R. Boyd; *Secretary,* K. W. Pritchard, OBE

LAW SOCIETY OF NORTHERN IRELAND, Law Society House, 98 Victoria Street, Belfast BT1 3JZ. Tel: 01232-231614. *Secretary,* M. C. Davey

LIBRARIANSHIP AND INFORMATION SCIENCE/MANAGEMENT

The Library Association accredits degree and postgraduate courses in library and information science which are offered by 18 universities in the UK. A full list of accredited degree and postgraduate courses is available from its Information Service. The Association also maintains a professional register of Chartered Members open to graduate ordinary members of the Association.
THE LIBRARY ASSOCIATION, 7 Ridgmount Street, London WC1E 7AE. Tel: 0171-636 7543. *Chief Executive*, R. Shimmon

MATERIALS STUDIES

The qualifying body is:
INSTITUTE OF MATERIALS, 1 Carlton House Terrace, London SW1Y 5DB. Tel: 0171-839 4071. *Secretary*, Dr J. A. Catterall

MEDICINE

EXAMINING BODY FOR DIPLOMAS
UNITED EXAMINING BOARD, Apothecaries Hall, Black Friars Lane, London EC4V 6EJ. Tel: 0171-236 1180. *Chairman*, P. Edmond, CBE; *Registrar*, A. M. Wallington-Smith

COLLEGES/SOCIETIES HOLDING POSTGRADUATE MEMBERSHIP AND DIPLOMA EXAMINATIONS
ROYAL COLLEGE OF ANAESTHETISTS, 48–49 Russell Square, London WC1B 4JY. Tel: 0171-813 1900. *President*, Prof. C. Prys-Roberts; *Chief Executive*, Sir Geoffrey de Deney, KCVO
ROYAL COLLEGE OF GENERAL PRACTITIONERS, 14 Princes Gate, London SW7 1PU. Tel: 0171-581 3232. *Hon. President*, Dr L. Newman, OBE; *Hon. Secretary*, Dr W. Reith
ROYAL COLLEGE OF OBSTETRICIANS AND GYNAECOLOGISTS, 27 Sussex Place, London NW1 4RG. Tel: 0171-262 5425. *President*, Dr N. Patel; *Secretary*, P. A. Barnett
ROYAL COLLEGE OF PATHOLOGISTS, 2 Carlton House Terrace, London SW1Y 5AF. Tel: 0171-930 5861. *President*, Prof. A. J. Bellingham, FRCP, FRCPath.; *Secretary*, K. Lockyer
ROYAL COLLEGE OF PHYSICIANS, 11 St Andrews Place, London NW1 4LE. Tel: 0171-935 1174. *President*, Prof. Sir Leslie Turnberg; *Secretary*, D. B. Lloyd
ROYAL COLLEGE OF PHYSICIANS OF EDINBURGH, 9 Queen Street, Edinburgh EH2 1JQ. Tel: 0131-225 7324. *President*, Dr J. D. Cash; *Secretary*, Dr J. St J. Thomas
ROYAL COLLEGE OF PHYSICIANS AND SURGEONS OF GLASGOW, 234–242 St Vincent Street, Glasgow G2 5RJ. Tel: 0141-221 6072. *President*, N. McKay; *Hon. Secretary*, Dr S. Slater
ROYAL COLLEGE OF PSYCHIATRISTS, 17 Belgrave Square, London SW1X 8PG. Tel: 0171-235 2351. *President*, Dr F. Caldicott; *Secretary*, Mrs V. Cameron
ROYAL COLLEGE OF RADIOLOGISTS, 38 Portland Place, London W1N 4QJ. Tel: 0171-636 4432. *President*, Dr M. J. Brindle; *Secretary*, A. J. Cowles
ROYAL COLLEGE OF SURGEONS OF ENGLAND, 35–43 Lincoln's Inn Fields, London WC2A 3PN. Tel: 0171-405 3474. *President*, Sir Rodney Sweetnam; *Secretary*, R. H. E. Duffett
ROYAL COLLEGE OF SURGEONS OF EDINBURGH, Nicolson Street, Edinburgh EH8 9DW. Tel: 0131-556 6206. *President*, Prof. Sir Robert Shields; *Secretary*, I. B. Macleod, FRCSED.

SOCIETY OF APOTHECARIES OF LONDON, 14 Black Friars Lane, London EC4V 6EJ. Tel: 0171-236 1189. *Clerk*, R. J. Stringer

PROFESSIONS SUPPLEMENTARY TO MEDICINE

The standard of professional education in biomedical sciences, chiropody, dietetics, occupational therapy, orthoptics, physiotherapy and radiography is the responsibility of seven professional boards, which also publish an annual register of qualified practitioners. The work of the boards is co-ordinated by the Council for Professions Supplementary to Medicine.
THE COUNCIL FOR PROFESSIONS SUPPLEMENTARY TO MEDICINE, Park House, 184 Kennington Park Road, London SE11 4BU. Tel: 0171-582 0866. *Registrar (acting)*, Dr P. Burley

BIOMEDICAL SCIENCES
Qualifications from higher or further education establishments and training in medical laboratories are required for progress to the professional examinations and qualifications of the INSTITUTE OF BIOMEDICAL SCIENCE, 12 Coldbath Square, London EC1R 5HL. Tel: 0171-636 8192. *Chief Executive*, A. Potter

CHIROPODY
Professional recognition is granted by the Society of Chiropodists and Podiatrists to students who are awarded B.Sc. degrees in Podiatry or Podiatric Medicine after attending a course of full-time training for three or four years at one of the 14 recognized schools in the UK (11 in England and Wales, two in Scotland and one in Northern Ireland). Qualifications granted and degrees recognized by the Society are approved by the Chiropodists Board for the purpose of State Registration, which is a condition of employment within the National Health Service.
THE SOCIETY OF CHIROPODISTS AND PODIATRISTS, 53 Welbeck Street, London W1M 7HE. Tel: 0171-486 3381. *General Secretary*, J. G. C. Trouncer

See also DIETETICS

OCCUPATIONAL THERAPY
Professional qualifications are awarded by the College of Occupational Therapists upon completion of one of the 31 training courses approved by the College.
COLLEGE OF OCCUPATIONAL THERAPISTS, 6–8 Marshalsea Road, London SE1 1HL. Tel: 0171-357 6480. *Secretary*, M. D. Hall, OBE, GM

See also OPHTHALMIC AND DISPENSING OPTICS

ORTHOPTICS
Orthoptists undertake the diagnosis and treatment of all types of squint and other anomalies of binocular vision, working in close collaboration with ophthalmologists. The training and maintenance of professional standards are the responsibility of the Orthoptists Board of the Council for the Professions Supplementary to Medicine. The professional body is the British Orthoptic Society. Training is at degree level.
THE BRITISH ORTHOPTIC SOCIETY, Tavistock House North, Tavistock Square, London WC1H 9HX. *Hon. Secretary*, Mrs A. Charnock

OSTEOPATHY
Osteopathy is accorded statutory regulation by the Osteopaths Act 1993. There are currently five bodies that accredit courses leading to a qualification in Osteopathy

but these are due to be replaced by a General Osteopathic Council when it opens a new register, expected to be in 1996. Osteopathy is becoming an all-graduate profession. Courses vary in length from three to five years, granting various qualifications from diploma to honours degree. Shorter courses are available for qualified doctors. Details of accrediting institutions and courses can be obtained from the Osteopathic Information Service.

OSTEOPATHIC INFORMATION SERVICE, PO Box 2074, Reading, Berks RG1 4YR. Tel: 01734-512051. *Public Relations Manager*, B. Daniels

PHYSIOTHERAPY

Full-time three- or four-year degree courses are available at 31 recognized schools in the UK. Information about courses leading to eligibility for Membership of the Chartered Society of Physiotherapy and to State Registration is available from the Chartered Society of Physiotherapy.

THE CHARTERED SOCIETY OF PHYSIOTHERAPY, 14 Bedford Row, London WC1R 4ED. Tel: 0171-306 6600. *Secretary*, T. Simon

RADIOGRAPHY AND RADIOTHERAPY

In order to practise both diagnostic and therapeutic radiography in the UK, it is necessary to have successfully completed a course of education and training recognized by the Privy Council. Such courses are offered by universities and colleges throughout the UK and lead to the award of a degree in radiography. Further information is available from the college.

THE COLLEGE OF RADIOGRAPHERS, 14 Upper Wimpole Street, London WIM 8BN. Tel: 0171-935 5726. *Chief Executive*, S. Evans

COMPLEMENTARY MEDICINE

Professional courses are validated by:
INSTITUTE FOR COMPLEMENTARY MEDICINE, PO Box 194, London SE16 1QZ. Tel: 0171-237 5165. *Director*, A. Baird

MERCHANT NAVY TRAINING SCHOOLS

OFFICERS

WARSASH MARITIME CENTRE, Southampton Institute, Newtown Road, Warsash, Southampton SO3 9ZL. Tel: 01489-576161. *Dean*, Capt. G. B. Angas

SEAFARERS

INDEFATIGABLE SCHOOL, Plas Llanfair, Llanfairpwll, Anglesey LL61 6NT. Tel: 01248-714338. *Headmaster*, Capt. P. White

NATIONAL SEA TRAINING COLLEGE, Denton, Gravesend, Kent DA12 2HR. Tel: 01474-363656. *Principal*, R. Brown

MUSIC

ASSOCIATED BOARD OF THE ROYAL SCHOOLS OF MUSIC, 14 Bedford Square, London WC1B 3JG. The Board conducts music examinations throughout the world and provides other services to music education. It is connected to the Royal Academy of Music and the Royal College of Music in London, the Royal Northern College of Music, Manchester and the Royal Scottish Academy of Music and Drama, Glasgow. *Chief Executive*, R. Morris

GUILDHALL SCHOOL OF MUSIC AND DRAMA, Silk Street, London EC2Y 8DT. Tel: 0171-628 2571. *Principal*, I. Horsbrugh

LONDON COLLEGE OF MUSIC, Thames Valley University, St Mary's Road, London W5 5RF. Tel: 0181-231 2304. *Director*, A. Creamer

ROYAL ACADEMY OF MUSIC, Marylebone Road, London NW1 5HT. Tel: 0171-873 7373. *Principal*, Prof. C. Price

ROYAL COLLEGE OF MUSIC, Prince Consort Road, London SW7 2BS. Tel: 0171-589 3643. *Director*, Ms J. Ritterman, PH.D.

ROYAL NORTHERN COLLEGE OF MUSIC, 124 Oxford Road, Manchester M13 9RD. Tel: 0161-273 6283. *Principal*, Sir John Manduell, CBE

ROYAL SCOTTISH ACADEMY OF MUSIC AND DRAMA, 100 Renfrew Street, Glasgow G2 3DB. Tel: 0141-332 4101. *Principal*, Dr P. Ledger, CBE, FRSE

ROYAL COLLEGE OF ORGANISTS, 7 St Andrew Street, London EC4A 3LQ. Tel: 0171-936 3606. *Chief Executive*, Dr M. Nicholas

TRINITY COLLEGE OF MUSIC, 11–13 Mandeville Place, London W1M 6AQ. Tel: 0171-935 5773. *Principal*, G. Henderson

NURSING

Courses leading to registration as a nurse are at least three years in length. There are also some programmes which are combined with degrees. Students study in colleges of nursing or in institutions of higher education. Courses offer a combination of theoretical and practical experience in a wide variety of settings. Depending on the type of course, students will register in adult, child, mental health or mental handicap (learning disabilities) nursing. A wide variety of specialist programmes are available after registration, for example in district nursing or occupational health nursing.

The Royal College of Nursing, within its Institute of Advanced Nursing Education, provides education at post-basic level in hospital, occupational health and community health fields. Advanced courses are held in preparation for senior posts in management and teaching; and other short and special courses.

THE ROYAL COLLEGE OF NURSING OF THE UNITED KINGDOM, 20 Cavendish Square, London W1M 0AB. Tel: 0171-409 3333. *General Secretary*, Miss C. Hancock; *Principal of the Institute of Advanced Nursing Education (acting)*, Prof. A. Kitson

UK CENTRAL COUNCIL FOR NURSING, MIDWIFERY AND HEALTH VISITING, 23 Portland Place, London W1N 4JT. Tel: 0171-637 7181. *Registrar and Chief Executive*, Ms S. Norman

ENGLISH NATIONAL BOARD FOR NURSING, MIDWIFERY AND HEALTH VISITING, Victory House, 170 Tottenham Court Road, London W1P 0HA. Tel: 0171-388 3131. *Chief Executive Officer*, A. P. Smith

WELSH NATIONAL BOARD FOR NURSING, MIDWIFERY AND HEALTH VISITING, Floor 13, Pearl Assurance House, Greyfriars Road, Cardiff CF1 3AG. Tel: 01222-395535. *Chief Executive Officer*, D. A. Ravey

NATIONAL BOARD FOR NURSING, MIDWIFERY AND HEALTH VISITING FOR SCOTLAND, 22 Queen Street, Edinburgh EH2 1NT. Tel: 0131-226 7371. *Chief Executive Officer*, Mrs L. Mitchell

NATIONAL BOARD FOR NURSING, MIDWIFERY AND HEALTH VISITING FOR NORTHERN IRELAND, Centre House, 79 Chichester Street, Belfast BT1 4JE. Tel: 01232-238152. *Chief Executive Officer*, Dr O. D'A. Slevin

OPHTHALMIC AND DISPENSING OPTICS

Professional bodies are:
THE COLLEGE OF OPTOMETRISTS, 10 Knaresborough
Place, London SW5 OTG. Tel: 0171-373 7765. Grants
qualifications as an optometrist. *General Secretary*,
P. D. Leigh
THE ASSOCIATION OF BRITISH DISPENSING OPTICIANS,
6 Hurlingham Business Park, Sulivan Road, London
SW6 3DU. Tel: 0171-736 0088. Grants qualifications as a
dispensing optician. *Registrar*, D. G. Baker

PHARMACY

Information may be obtained from the Secretary and
Registrar of the Royal Pharmaceutical Society of Great
Britain.
ROYAL PHARMACEUTICAL SOCIETY OF GREAT BRITAIN,
1 Lambeth High Street, London SE1 7JN. Tel: 0171-735
9141. *Secretary and Registrar*, J. Ferguson, OBE

PHOTOGRAPHY

The professional body is:
BRITISH INSTITUTE OF PROFESSIONAL PHOTOGRAPHY,
Fox Talbot House, Amwell End, Ware, Herts SG12 9HN.
Tel: 01920-464011. *Chief Executive*, A. Mair

PRINTING

Details of training courses in printing can be obtained from
the Institute of Printing and the British Printing Industries
Federation. In addition to these examining and organizing
bodies, examinations are held by various independent
regional examining boards in further education.
BRITISH PRINTING INDUSTRIES FEDERATION, 11
Bedford Row, London WC1R 4DX. Tel: 0171-242 6904.
Director-General, T. P. E. Machin
INSTITUTE OF PRINTING, 8 Lonsdale Gardens,
Tunbridge Wells, Kent TN1 1NU. Tel: 01892-538118.
Secretary-General, D. Freeland

SOCIAL WORK

The Central Council for Education and Training in Social
Work promotes education and training for social work and
social care in the UK. It approves education and training
programmes, including those leading to its qualifying
award, the Diploma in Social Work.
THE CENTRAL COUNCIL FOR EDUCATION AND
TRAINING IN SOCIAL WORK, Derbyshire House, St
Chad's Street, London WC1H 8AD. Tel: 0171-278 2455.
Chairman, J. Greenwood; *Director*, T. Hall

SPEECH THERAPY

The Royal College of Speech and Language Therapists
provides details of courses leading to qualification as a
speech and language therapist. Other professionals may
become Associates of the College. A directory of registered
members is published annually.
THE ROYAL COLLEGE OF SPEECH AND LANGUAGE
THERAPISTS, 7 Bath Place, London EC2A 3DR. Tel:
0171-613 3855. *Director*, Mrs P. Evans

SURVEYING

The qualifying professional bodies include:
ROYAL INSTITUTION OF CHARTERED SURVEYORS
(incorporating The Institute of Quantity Surveyors), 12
Great George Street, London SW1P 3AD. Tel: 0171-222
7000. *Chief Executive*, Ms C. Makin

ARCHITECTS AND SURVEYORS INSTITUTE, St Mary
House, 15 St Mary Street, Chippenham,
Wilts SN15 3WD. Tel: 01249-444505. *Chief Executive*,
C. G. A. Nash, OBE
ASSOCIATION OF BUILDING ENGINEERS, Jubilee House,
Billing Brook Road, Weston Favell, Northampton
NN3 8NW. Tel: 01604-404121. *Chief Executive*,
B. D. Hughes
INSTITUTE OF REVENUES, RATING AND VALUATION, 41
Doughty Street, London WC1N 2LF. Tel: 0171-831 3505.
Director, C. Farrington
INCORPORATED SOCIETY OF VALUERS AND
AUCTIONEERS (1968), 3 Cadogan Gate, London
SW1X 0AS. Tel: 0171-235 2282. *Chief Executive*, H. Whitty

TEACHING

To become a qualified teacher it is necessary to have
successfully completed a course of initial teacher training.
Non-graduates usually qualify by way of a three- or four-
year course leading to a Bachelor of Education (B.Ed.)
honours degree, but some universities offer first degree
courses (BA, B.Sc.) taken concurrently with a certificate of
education. Graduates take a one-year postgraduate certificate of education (PGCE).
Details of courses in England and Wales are contained in
the *Handbook of Degree and Advanced Courses* published
annually by the National Association of Teachers in
Further and Higher Education. Details of courses in
Scotland can be obtained from the colleges of education,
from COSHEP, and from TEACH (*see* page 452). Details
of courses in Northern Ireland can be obtained from the
Department of Education for Northern Ireland. Applications for teacher training courses in Northern Ireland are
made to the institutions direct. For applications, *see* page
445.
Teacher training is increasingly school-based and
schools, or consortia of schools, carry out their own
teacher-training, subject to approval of their training
scheme. State-run school-based schemes include the
licensed teacher scheme in England and Wales, and the
mentor teacher scheme in Scotland (*see also* pages 440–1).

TEXTILES

THE TEXTILE INSTITUTE, International Headquarters, 10
Blackfriars Street, Manchester M3 5DR. Tel: 0161-834
8457. *Chief Executive*, R. G. Denyer

THEOLOGICAL COLLEGES

The number of students training for the ministry in the
academic year 1994–5 is shown in parenthesis. Those
marked * show figures for 1993–4.

ANGLICAN

COLLEGE OF THE RESURRECTION, Mirfield, W. Yorks
WF14 0BW. Tel: 01924-490441. (31). *Principal*, Revd
Dr D. J. Lane
CRANMER HALL, St John's College, Durham DH1 3RJ. Tel:
0191-374 3579. (70). *Principal*, D. V. Day
OAK HILL COLLEGE, Chase Side, London N14 4PS. Tel:
0181-449 0467. (45). *Principal*, Revd Canon G. Bridger
RIDLEY HALL, Cambridge CB3 9HG. Tel: 01223-353040.
(60). *Principal*, Revd G. A. Cray
RIPON COLLEGE, Cuddesdon, Oxford OX44 9EX. Tel:
01865-874404. (70). *Principal*, Revd Canon J. H. Garton
ST JOHN'S COLLEGE, Chilwell Lane, Bramcote,
Nottingham NG9 3DS. Tel: 0115-925 1114. (75).
Principal, Revd Dr J. Goldingay

St Michael's Theological College, Llandaff, Cardiff CF5 2YJ. Tel: 01222-563379/116. (39). *Warden*, Revd Canon J. H. L. Rowlands

St Stephen's House, 16 Marston Street, Oxford OX4 1JX. Tel: 01865-247874. (40). *Principal (acting)*, Revd A. Burnham

Theological Institute of the Scottish Episcopal Church, 21 Inverleith Terrace, Edinburgh EH3 5NS. Tel: 0131-343 2038. (24). *Principal*, Revd R. Nixon

Trinity College, Stoke Hill, Bristol BS9 1JP. Tel: 0117-968 2803. (120). *Principal*, Revd Canon D. Gillett

Westcott House, Jesus Lane, Cambridge CB5 8BP. Tel: 01223-350074. (55). *Principal*, Revd M. G. V. Roberts

Wycliffe Hall, 54 Banbury Road, Oxford OX2 6PW. Tel: 01865-274200. (68). *Principal*, Revd Dr A. McGrath

Baptist

Bristol Baptist College, Woodland Road, Bristol BS8 1UN. Tel: 0117-926 0248. (24). *Principal*, Revd Dr B. Haymes

Northern Baptist College, Luther King House, Brighton Grove, Rusholme, Manchester M14 5JP. Tel: 0161-224 2214. (30). *Principal*, Revd Dr R. L. Kidd

North Wales Baptist College, Ffordd Ffriddoedd, Bangor, Gwynedd LL57 2EH. Tel: 01248-362608. (1). *Warden*, Revd Dr D. D. Morgan

Regent's Park College, Oxford OX1 2LB. Tel: 01865-288120. (25). *Principal*, Revd Dr P. S. Fiddes

The Scottish Baptist College, 12 Aytoun Road, Glasgow G41 5RN. Tel: 0141-424 0747. (19). *Principal*, Revd K. B. E. Roxburgh

South Wales Baptist College, 54 Richmond Road, Cardiff CF2 3UR. Tel: 01222-496060. (28). *Principal*, Revd D. H. Matthews

Spurgeon's College, South Norwood Hill, London SE25 6DJ. Tel: 0181-653 0850. (120). *Principal*, Revd M. Quicke

Church of Scotland

Christ's College, 25 High Street, Old Aberdeen AB2 3EE. Tel: 01224-272138. (30). *Master*, Revd Prof. A. Main, TD, PH.D.

New College, Mound Place, Edinburgh EH1 2LU. Tel: 0131-650 8900. (50). *Principal*, Revd Prof. D. B. Forrester

Trinity College, 4 The Square, University of Glasgow, Glasgow G12 8QQ. Tel: 0141-339 8855. (60). *Principal*, Revd Prof. G. M. Newlands

Congregational

College of the Welsh Independents, 38 Pier Street, Aberystwyth, Dyfed. *Principal*, Revd Dr E. S. John

Scottish Congregational College, 20 Inverleith Terrace, Edinburgh EH3 5NS. Tel: 0131-315 3595. (9). *Principal*, Revd Dr J. W. S. Clark

Ecumenical

Queen's College, Somerset Road, Edgbaston, Birmingham B15 2QH. Tel: 0121-454 1527. (70). *Principal*, Revd P. Fisher

Methodist

Edghill Theological College, 9 Lennoxvale, Belfast BT9 5BY. Tel: 01232-665870. (18). *Principal*, Revd D. Cooke, PH.D.

Hartley Victoria College, Northern Federation for Training in Ministry, Luther King House, Brighton Grove, Manchester M14 5JP. Tel: 0161-224 2215. (23). *Principal*, Revd G. Slater

Wesley College, College Park Drive, Henbury Road, Bristol BS10 7QD. Tel: 0117-959 1200. (65). *Principal*, Revd Dr N. Richardson

Wesley House, Jesus Lane, Cambridge CB5 8BJ. (*34). *Principal*, Revd Dr I. H. Jones

Wesley Study Centre, 55 The Avenue, Durham DH1 4EB. Tel: 0191-386 1833. (23). *Director*, Revd P. Luscombe, PH.D.

Non-Denominational

St Mary's College, The University, St Andrews, Fife KY16 9JU. Tel: 01334-462851. (179). *Principal*, Dr R. A. Piper

Presbyterian

Union Theological College, Belfast BT7 1JT. Tel: 01232-325374. (41). *Principal*, Revd Prof. T. S. Reid

Presbyterian Church of Wales

United Theological College, Aberystwyth SY23 2LT. Tel: 01970-624574. (20). *Principal*, Revd Prof. E. ap N. Roberts

Roman Catholic

Allen Hall College, 28 Beaufort Street, London SW3 5AA. Tel: 0171-351 1296. (35). *Principal*, Revd K. Barltrop, STL

Campion House College, 112 Thornbury Road, Isleworth, Middx TW7 4NN. Tel: 0181-560 1924. (25). *Principal*, Revd C. C. Dykehoff, SJ

Oscott College, Chester Road, Sutton Coldfield, W. Midlands B73 5AA. Tel: 0121-354 7117. (65). *Rector*, Rt. Revd Mgr P. McKinney, STL

Scotus College, 2 Chesters Road, Bearsden, Glasgow G61 4AG. Tel: 0141-942 8384. (50). *Rector*, Rt Revd Mgr M. J. Conway

St John's Seminary, Wonersh, Guildford, Surrey GU5 0QX. Tel: 01483-892217. (70). *Rector*, Fr K. Haggerty

Ushaw College, Durham DH7 9RH. Tel: 0191-373 1366. (70). *Principal*, Rt. Revd Mgr R. Atherton, OBE

Unitarian

Unitarian College, Northern Federation for Training in Ministry, Luther King House, Brighton Grove, Rusholme, Manchester M14 5JP. Tel: 0161-224 2849. (6). *Principal*, Revd L. Smith, PH.D.

United Reformed

Bala-Bangor Independent College, Bangor LL57 2EH. (*15). *Principal*, R. T. Jones, D.phil., DD

Mansfield College, Mansfield Road, Oxford OX1 3TF. Tel: 01865-270999. (25). *Principal*, D. J. Trevelyan, CB

Northern College, Northern Federation for Training in Ministry, Luther King House, Brighton Grove, Rusholme, Manchester M14 5JP. Tel: 0161-224 4381. (29). *Principal*, Revd Dr D. R. Peel

Westminster College, Madingley Road, Cambridge CB3 0AA. Tel: 01223-353997. (28). *Principal*, Revd M. H. Cressey

Jewish

Jews' College, Albert Road, London NW4 2SJ. (*12). *Principal*, Rabbi Dr D. Sinclair

Leo Baeck College, Sternberg Centre for Judaism, 80 East End Road, London N3 2SY. Tel: 0181-349 4525. (15). *Principal*, Rabbi Dr J. Magonet

TOWN AND COUNTRY PLANNING

Degree and diploma courses in town planning are accredited by the Royal Town Planning Institute.

THE ROYAL TOWN PLANNING INSTITUTE, 26 Portland Place, London WIN 4BE. Tel: 0171-636 9107. *Secretary-General,* D. Fryer, OBE

TRANSPORT

Qualifying examinations in transport management and logistics leading to chartered professional status are conducted by the Chartered Institute of Transport.

THE CHARTERED INSTITUTE OF TRANSPORT, 80 Portland Place, London WIN 4DP. Tel: 0171-636 9952. *Director,* Mrs S. Gross

Independent Schools

The following pages list those independent schools whose Head is a member of the Headmasters' Conference, the Society of Headmasters and Headmistresses of Independent Schools or the Girls' Schools Association

THE HEADMASTERS' CONFERENCE

Chairman (1996), A. C. V. Evans (Portsmouth Grammer School)
Secretary, V. S. Anthony, 130 Regent Road, Leicester LEI 7PG. Tel: 0116-285 4810
Membership Secretary, R. N. P. Griffiths, 1 Russell House, Bepton Road, Midhurst, W. Sussex GU29 9NB. Tel: 01730-815635. The annual meeting is, as a rule, held at the end of September or early in October

* Woodard Corporation School, 1 The Sanctuary, London SWIP 3JT. Tel: 0171-222 5381
† Girls in VI form
‡ Co-educational
° 1994 figures

Name of School	Foun-ded	No. of pupils	Annual fees £		Head (with date of appointment)
			Boarding	Day	
ENGLAND AND WALES					
Abbotsholme School, Staffs.	1889	250‡	11,391	7,614	D. J. Farrant (1984)
Abingdon School, Oxon.	1256	760	9,849	5,262	M. St J. Parker (1975)
Ackworth School, W. Yorks.	1779	400‡	9,333	5,316	M. J. Dickinson (1995)
Aldenham School, Herts.	1597	365†	11,460	7,860	S. Borthwick (1994)
Alleyn's School, London SE22	1619	915‡	—	5,640	Dr C. H. R. Niven (1992)
Ampleforth College (*RC*), Yorks.	1802	556	12,015	6,195	Revd G. F. L. Chamberlain, OSB (1993)
*Ardingly College, W. Sussex	1858	450‡	11,640	9,195	J. W. Flecker (1980)
Arnold School, Blackpool	1896	838‡	—	3,735	W. T. Gillen (1993)
Ashville College, Harrogate	1877	556‡	8,382	4,500	M. H. Crosby (1987)
Bablake School, Coventry	1560	860‡	—	3,750	Dr S. Nuttall (1991)
Bancroft's School, Essex	1727	739‡	—	5,694	Dr P. C. D. Southern (1985)
Barnard Castle School, Co. Durham	1883	524†	8,358	4,947	F. S. McNamara (1980)
Batley Grammar School, W. Yorks.	1612	550†	—	3,627	W. M. Duggan (1995)
Bedales School, Hants.	1893	404‡	12,996	9,567	Mrs A. A. Willcocks (1995)
Bedford School	1552	720	11,145	7,005	Dr I. P. Evans (1990)
Bedford Modern School	1566	962	8,640	4,491	P. J. Squire (1977)
Berkhamsted School, Herts.	1541	726†	11,034	6,774	Revd K. H. Wilkinson (1989)
Birkenhead School, Merseyside	1860	702	—	3,663	S. J. Haggett (1988)
Bishop's Stortford College, Herts.	1868	337†	10,320	7,440	S. G. G. Benson (1984)
*Bloxham School, Oxon.	1860	330†	12,105	9,510	D. K. Exham (1991)
Blundell's School, Devon	1604	476‡	11,550	7,050	J. Leigh (1991)
Bolton School	1524	850	—	4,476	A. W. Wright (1983)
Bootham School, York	1823	336‡	9,924	6,429	I. M. Small (1986)
Bradfield College, Berks.	1850	580†	12,225	9,168	P. B. Smith (1985)
Bradford Grammar School	1662	928†	—	3,957	D. A. G. Smith (1973)
Brentwood School, Essex	1557	1,040‡	10,095	5,771	J. A. B. Kelsall (1993)
Brighton College, E. Sussex	1845	474‡	11,940	7,854	J. D. Leach (1987)
Bristol Grammar School	1532	1,013‡	—	3,888	C. E. Martin (1986)
Bromsgrove School, Worcs.	1553	640‡	9,825	6,150	T. M. Taylor (1986)
Bryanston School, Dorset	1928	650‡	12,720	8,480	T. D. Wheare (1983)
Bury Grammar School, Lancs.	1634	690	—	3,702	K. Richards (1990)
Canford School, Dorset	1923	500‡	12,380	9,285	J. D. Lever (1992)
Caterham School, Surrey	1811	850‡	11,196	5,796	R. Davey (1995)
Charterhouse, Surrey	1611	700†	12,765	10,548	C. Carter (1995)
Cheadle Hulme School, Cheshire	1855	954‡	—	4,086	D. J. Wilkinson (1990)
Cheltenham College, Glos.	1841	570†	12,120	9,225	P. D. V. Wilkes (1990)
Chetham's School of Music, Manchester	1653	268‡	15,600	12,075	Revd P. F. Hullah (1992)
Chigwell School, Essex	1629	370†	9,471	6,231	A. R. M. Little (1989)
Christ College, Brecon	1541	342‡	9,405	7,290	S. W. Hockey (1982)
Christ's Hospital, W. Sussex	1553	450‡	varies	—	R. C. Poulton (1987)
Churcher's College, Hants.	1722	579‡	—	4,995	G. W. Buttle (1988)
City of London, London EC4	1442	880	—	5,832	R. Dancey (1995)

Name of School	Foun-ded	No. of pupils	Annual fees £ Boarding	Day	Head (with date of appointment)
City of London Freemen's School, Surrey	1854	400‡	9,090	5,823	D. C. Haywood (1987)
Clifton College, Bristol	1862	630‡	12,050	8,430	H. Monro (1990)
Colfe's School, London SE12	1652	723†	—	5,037	Dr D. Richardson (1990)
Colston's Collegiate School, Bristol	1710	430‡	10,080	5,475	D. Crawford (1995)
Cranleigh School, Surrey	1863	520†	12,420	9,330	A. Hart (1984)
Culford School, Suffolk	1881	390‡	10,401	6,771	J. Richardson (1992)
Dame Allan's School, Newcastle upon Tyne	1705	418†	—	3,570	T. A. Willcocks (*Principal*) (1988)
Dauntsey's School, Wilts.	1543	620‡	10,542	6,494	C. R. Evans (1985)
Dean Close School, Cheltenham	1884	450‡	12,225	8,535	C. J. Bacon (1979)
*Denstone College, Staffs.	1873	302‡	10,890	7,770	H. C. K. Carson (1990)
Douai School (*RC*), Berks.	1903	200‡	10,125	6,525	Revd E. Power (1993)
Dover College, Kent	1871	250‡	11,100	5,970	M. P. G. Wright (1991)
Downside School (*RC*), Somerset	1607	350	11,130	7,134	Dom. A. Sutch (1995)
Dulwich College, London SE21	1619	1,240	12,270	6,135	C. Field (*Master*) (*acting*)
Durham School	1414	321†	11,406	7,419	M. A. Lang (1982)
Eastbourne College, E. Sussex	1867	476†	11,619	8,592	C. M. P. Bush (1993)
*Ellesmere College, Shropshire	1884	290‡	10,500	6,900	D. R. du Croz (1988)
Eltham College, London SE9	1842	580†	11,505	5,451	D. M. Green (1990)
Emanuel School, London SW11	1594	720‡	—	4,587	T. Jones-Parry (1994)
Epsom College, Surrey	1855	652†	11,595	8,616	A. H. Beadles (1993)
Eton College, Berks.	1440	1,270	12,888	—	J. E. Lewis (1994)
Exeter School	1633	730†	7,950	5,200	N. W. Gamble (1992)
Felsted School, Essex	1564	350‡	12,360	9,750	S. C. Robert (1993)
Forest School, London E17	1834	834†	8,610	5,484	A. Boggis (*Warden*) (1992)
Framlingham College, Suffolk	1864	432‡	9,687	6,216	Mrs. G. M. Randall (1994)
Frensham Heights, Surrey	1925	290‡	11,670	7,470	P. de Voil (1993)
Giggleswick School, N. Yorks.	1512	301‡	11,544	7,656	A. P. Millard (1993)
Gresham's School, Norfolk	1555	505‡	11,180	8,250	J. H. Arkell (1991)
Haberdashers' Aske's School, Herts.	1690	1,100	—	5,610	K. Dawson (1987)
Haileybury, Herts.	1862	610†	12,720	9,225	D. J. Jewell (1987)
Hampton School, Middx.	1557	945	—	4,920	G. G. Able (1988)
Harrow School, Middx.	1571	785	13,425	—	N. R. Bomford (1991)
Hereford Cathedral School	1384	179‡	7,980	4,530	Dr H. C. Tomlinson (1987)
Highgate School, London N6	1565	615	—	7,125	R. P. Kennedy (1989)
Hulme Grammar School, Oldham	1611	700	—	3,546	G. F. Dunkin (1987)
*Hurstpierpoint College, W. Sussex	1849	345‡	11,370	9,060	S. Meek (1995)
Hymers College, Hull	1889	722‡	—	3,555	J. C. Morris (1990)
Ipswich School, Suffolk	1390	603†	8,652	5,062	I. G. Galbraith (1993)
John Lyon School, Middx.	1876	510	—	5,355	Revd T. J. Wright (1986)
Kelly College, Devon	1877	320‡	11,385	7,155	M. Turner (1995)
Kent College, Canterbury	1885	504‡	10,098	5,664	E. B. Halse (1995)
Kimbolton School, Cambs.	1600	560‡	8,985	5,235	R. V. Peel (1987)
King Edward VI School, Southampton	1553	939‡	—	4,710	T. R. Cookson (1990)
King Edward VII School, Lytham	1908	500	—	3,690	P. J. Wilde (1993)
King Edward's School, Bath	1552	686†	—	4,293	P. J. Winter (1993)
King Edward's School, Birmingham	1552	875	—	4,440	H. R. Wright (*Chief Master*) (1991)
King Edward's School, Witley, Surrey	1553	436‡	8,970	6,240	R. J. Fox (1988)
King Henry VIII School, Coventry	1545	820‡	—	3,750	T. J. Vardon (1994)
*King's College, Taunton	1880	460	11,490	7,530	R. S. Funnell (1988)
King's College School, London SW19	1829	720	—	6,270	R. M. Reeve (1980)
King's School, Bruton, Somerset	1519	312†	10,965	7,770	R. I. Smyth (1993)
King's School, Canterbury	600	710‡	12,795	8,835	Revd Canon A. C. J. Phillips (1986)
King's School, Chester	1541	511	—	4,032	A. R. D. Wickson (1981)
King's School, Ely, Cambs.	970	400‡	11,487	7,326	R. H. Youdale (1992)
King's School, Gloucester	1541	328‡	9,420	5,670	P. Lacey (1992)
King's School, Macclesfield	1502	1,070‡	—	4,122	A. G. Silcock (1987)
King's School, Rochester, Kent	604	323‡	11,682	6,702	Dr I. R. Walker (1986)
*King's School, Tynemouth	1860	660‡	—	3,720	Dr D. Younger (1993)
King's School, Worcester	1541	802‡	8,793	5,091	Dr J. M. Moore (1983)
Kingston Grammar School, Surrey	1561	600‡	—	5,285	C. D. Baxter (1991)
Kingswood School, Bath	1748	450‡	11,160	6,999	G. M. Best (1987)
*Lancing College, W. Sussex	1848	520†	12,030	9,045	C. J. Saunders (1993)

Name of School	Foun-ded	No. of pupils	Annual fees £ Boarding	Day	Head (with date of appointment)
Latymer Upper School, London w6	1624	950	—	5,802	C. Diggory (1991)
Leeds Grammar School	1552	1,174	—	4,395	B. W. Collins (1986)
Leicester Grammar School	1981	585‡	—	4,080	J. B. Sugden (1989)
Leighton Park School, Reading	1890	375‡	11,196	8,397	J. A. Chapman (1986)
The Leys School, Cambridge	1875	420‡	11,940	8,700	Revd J. C. A. Barrett (1990)
Liverpool College	1840	640‡	—	4,080	B. R. Martin (1992)
Llandovery College, Dyfed	1848	240‡	9,510	6,204	Dr C. E. Evans (Warden) (1988)
Lord Wandsworth College, Hants.	1912	373†	9,492	7,380	G. de W. Waller (1993)
Loughborough Grammar School	1495	940	8,208	4,428	D. N. Ireland (1984)
Magdalen College School, Oxford	1480	509	9,126	4,809	P. M. Tinniswood (Master) (1991)
Malvern College, Worcs.	1865	660‡	12,210	8,880	R. de C. Chapman (1983)
Manchester Grammar School	1515	1,425	—	4,140	G. M. Stephen, ph.d (High Master) (1994)
Marlborough College, Wilts.	1843	800‡	12,750	8,985	E. J. H. Gould (1993)
Merchant Taylors' School, Liverpool	1620	720	—	3,744	S. J. R. Dawkins (1986)
Merchant Taylors' School, Middx.	1561	748	11,050	6,650	J. R. Gabitass (1991)
Millfield, Street, Somerset	1935	1,247‡	13,320	8,310	C. S. Martin (1990)
Mill Hill School, London nw7	1807	550†	11,640	7,530	W. Winfield (acting)
Monkton Combe School, Bath	1868	310‡	11,685	8,085	M. J. Cuthbertson (1990)
Monmouth School, Gwent	1614	558	8,175	4,908	T. H. P. Haynes (1995)
Mount St Mary's College (RC), Sheffield	1842	298‡	8,970	6,063	P. Fisher (1991)
Newcastle under Lyme School	1874	1,144‡	—	3,540	Dr R. M. Reynolds (Principal) (1990)
Norwich School	1250	616†	—	4,530	C. D. Brown (1984)
Nottingham High School	1513	830	—	4,644	C. S. Parker (1995)
Oakham School, Rutland	1584	1,020‡	11,670	6,450	G. Smallbone (1985)
The Oratory School (RC), Berks.	1859	400-	11,760	8,220	S. W. Barrow (1992)
Oundle School, Northants.	1556	854‡	12,800	—	D. B. McMurray (1984)
Pangbourne College, Berks.	1917	345‡	11,310	7,920	A. B. E. Hudson (1988)
Perse School, Cambridge	1615	500†	—	4,524	N. Richardson (1994)
Plymouth College	1877	600‡	8,910	4,650	A. J. Morsley (1992)
Pocklington School, York	1514	604‡	8,688	4,842	J. N. D. Gray (1992)
Portsmouth Grammar School	1732	810‡	—	4,485	A. C. V. Evans (1983)
Prior Park College (RC), Bath	1830	490‡	10,074	5,571	J. W. R. Goulding (1989)
Queen Elizabeth GS, Wakefield	1591	750†	—	4,122	R. P. Mardling (1985)
Queen Elizabeth's GS, Blackburn	1567	990†	—	3,942	D. S. Hempsall (1995)
Queen Elizabeth's Hospital, Bristol	1590	500	6,957	3,915	Dr R. Gliddon (1985)
Queen's College, Taunton	1843	442‡	9,270	6,075	C. T. Bradnock (1991)
Radley College, Oxon.	1847	620	12,300	—	R. M. Morgan (Warden) (1991)
Ratcliffe College (RC), Leicester	1844	475‡	9,096	6,066	Revd K. A. Tomlinson (1993)
Reading Blue Coat School	1646	550†	9,570	5,250	Revd A. Sanders (1974)
Reed's School, Surrey	1813	320†	10,239	7,740	D. E. Prince (1983)
Reigate Grammar School, Surrey	1675	773‡	—	4,872	J. G. Hamlin (1982)
Rendcomb College, Glos.	1920	245‡	10,329	8,178	J. Tolputt (1987)
Repton School, Derby	1557	570‡	11,604	8,730	G. E. Jones (1987)
RNIB New College, Worcester	1987	121‡	21,977	14,651	Mrs H. Williams (1995)
Rossall School, Lancs.	1844	420‡	11,400	4,200	R. D. W. Rhodes (1987)
Royal Grammar School, Guildford	1552	836	—	5,985	T. M. S. Young (1991)
Royal Grammar School, Newcastle upon Tyne	1545	940	—	3,609	J. F. X. Miller (1994)
Royal Grammar School, Worcester	1291	780	—	4,338	W. A. Jones (1993)
Rugby School, Warwicks.	1567	700‡	12,720	7,545	M. B. Mavor, cvo (1990)
Rydal Penrhos School, Clwyd (Boys)	1880	320‡	9,849	7,104	N. W. Thorne (1991)
Ryde School (with Upper Chine), Isle of Wight	1921	490‡	8,871	4,182	M. D. Featherstone (1990)
St Albans School, Herts.	1570	650†	—	5,460	A. R. Grant (1993)
St Ambrose College, Cheshire	1946	720	—	3,460	G. E. Hester (1991)
St Anselm's College (RC), Birkenhead	1933	609	—	3,150	C. Cleugh (1993)
St Bede's College (RC), Manchester	1876	974‡	—	3,870	J. Byrne (1983)
St Bees School, Cumbria	1583	288‡	10,491	7,218	P. A. Chamberlain (1988)
St Benedict's School (RC), London w5	1902	595†	—	4,860	Dr A. J. Dachs (1987)
St Dunstan's College, London se6	1888	622‡	—	5,370	J. D. Moore (1993)

Name of School	Foun-ded	No. of pupils	Annual fees £		Head (with date of appointment)
			Boarding	Day	
St Edmund's College (RC), Herts.	1568	534‡	9,555	6,120	D. J. J. McEwen (1984)
St Edmund's School, Canterbury	1749	277‡	12,030	7,860	A. N. Ridley (1994)
St Edward's College (RC), Liverpool	1853	760‡	—	3,498	J. E. Waszek (1992)
St Edward's School, Oxford	1863	575†	12,000	9,000	D. Christie (Warden) (1988)
St George's College (RC), Surrey	1869	530†	—	6,495	J. Peake (1995)
St John's School, Surrey	1851	400†	10,500	7,200	C. H. Tongue (1993)
St Lawrence College in Thanet, Kent	1879	370‡	11,160	7,455	J. H. Binfield (1983)
St Mary's College (RC), Merseyside	1919	597‡	—	3,600	W. Hammond (1991)
St Paul's School, London SW13	1509	775	12,357	8,082	R. S. Baldock (High Master) (1992)
St Peter's School, York	627	480‡	10,386	6,534	A. F. Trotman (1995)
Sedbergh School, Cumbria	1525	375	11,640	8,145	C. H. Hirst (1995)
Sevenoaks School, Kent	1418	937‡	11,619	7,074	R. P. Barker (1981)
Sherborne School, Dorset	1550	630	12,555	9,570	P. H. Lapping (1988)
Shrewsbury School	1552	695	12,375	8,700	F. E. Maidment (1988)
Silcoates School, W. Yorks.	1820	412‡	—	5,244	A. P. Spillane (1991)
Solihull School, W. Midlands	1560	830†	—	4,285	A. Lee (1983)
Stamford School, Lincs.	1532	566	8,130	4,065	G. J. Timm (1978)
Stockport Grammar School	1487	1,013‡	—	3,897	D. R. J. Bird (1985)
Stonyhurst College (RC), Lancs.	1593	400†	11,472	7,125	Dr R. G. G. Mercer (1985)
Stowe School, Bucks.	1923	550†	12,780	8,970	J. G. L. Nichols (1989)
Sutton Valence School, Kent	1576	350‡	11,073	7,389	N. A. Sampson (1994)
Taunton School	1847	500‡	11,355	7,260	B. B. Sutton (1987)
Tettenhall College, Staffs.	1863	240‡	9,012	5,556	Dr P. Bodkin (1994)
Tonbridge School, Kent	1553	660	12,969	9,153	J. M. Hammond (1990)
Trent College, Derbys.	1868	699‡	10,425	6,375	J. S. Lee (1988)
Trinity School, Surrey	1596	850	—	5,304	B. J. Lennon (1995)
Truro School	1879	790‡	8,580	4,608	G. A. G. Dodd (1993)
University College School, London NW3	1830	700	—	6,825	G. D. Slaughter (1983)
Uppingham School, Leics.	1584	600†	12,750	7,650	S. C. Winkley (1991)
Warwick School	914	797	9,840	4,590	P. J. Cheshire (1988)
Wellingborough School, Northants.	1595	380‡	9,300	5,175	F. R. Ullmann (1993)
Wellington College, Berks.	1856	812†	12,270	8,955	C. J. Driver (1989)
Wellington School, Somerset	1837	560‡	8,040	4,398	A. J. Rogers (1990)
Wells Cathedral School, Somerset	1180	617‡	9,114	5,352	J. S. Baxter (1986)
West Buckland School, Devon	1858	455‡	8,970	4,866	M. Downward (1979)
Westminster School, London SW1	1560	670†	12,900	8,850	D. M. Summerscale (1986)
Whitgift School, Surrey	1596	700	—	5,497	C. A. Barnett, D.Phil. (1991)
William Hulme's GS, Manchester	1887	790‡	—	4,287	P. A. Briggs (1987)
Winchester College, Hants.	1382	667	13,290	9,966	J. P. Sabben-Clare (1985)
Wisbech Grammar School, Cambs.	1379	640‡	—	4,650	R. S. Repper (1988)
Wolverhampton Grammar School	1512	692‡	—	4,800	B. St J. Trafford (1990)
Woodbridge School, Suffolk	1662	540‡	8,796	5,252	S. H. Cole (1994)
Woodhouse Grove School, Bradford	1812	550‡	8,940	5,265	D. W. Welsh (1991)
*Worksop College, Notts.	1895	330‡	10,785	7,440	R. A. Collard (1994)
Worth School (RC), W. Sussex	1959	292	11,490	7,665	Fr C. Jamison (1994)
Wrekin College, Shropshire	1880	250‡	11,310	6,180	P. Johnson (1991)
Wycliffe College, Glos.	1882	345‡	11,985	8,190	D. C. M. Prichard (1994)
Yarm School, Cleveland	1978	490†	—	4,734	R. Neville Tate (1978)

SCOTLAND

Name of School	Foun-ded	No. of pupils	Annual fees £		Head (with date of appointment)
Daniel Stewart's and Melville College, Edinburgh	1832	760	8,550	4,410	P. J. F. Tobin (Principal) (1989)
Dollar Academy, Clackmannanshire	1818	720‡	9,195	4,149	J. S. Robertson (Rector) (1994)
The Edinburgh Academy	1824	507†	10,842	5,085	J. V. Light (Rector) (1995)
Fettes College, Edinburgh	1870	377‡	12,255	8,235	M. T. Thyne, FRSE (1988)
George Heriot's School, Edinburgh	1659	980‡	—	3,750	K. P. Pearson (1983)
George Watson's College, Edinburgh	1741	1,271‡	8,280	4,140	F. E. Gerstenberg (Principal) (1985)
Glasgow Academy	1845	589‡	—	4,290	D. Comins (Rector) (1994)
Glenalmond College, Perthshire	1841	280‡	11,475	7,650	I. G. Templeton (Warden) (1992)
Gordonstoun School, Moray	1934	460‡	12,105	7,809	M. C. S.-R. Pyper (1990)
High School of Dundee	1239	1,150‡	—	3,909	R. Nimmo, OBE (Rector) (1977)
High School of Glasgow	1124	619‡	—	4,266	R. G. Easton (1983)

Name of School	Foun-ded	No. of pupils	Annual fees £		Head (with date of appointment)
			Boarding	Day	
Hutchesons' Grammar School, Glasgow	1641	1,178‡	—	3,834	D. R. Ward (*Rector*) (1987)
Kelvinside Academy, Glasgow	1878	430	—	4,400	J. H. Duff (*Rector*) (1980)
Loretto School, E. Lothian	1827	307‡	11,510	7,740	K. J. Budge (1995)
Merchiston Castle School, Edinburgh	1833	350	11,505	7,440	D. M. Spawforth (1981)
Morrison's Academy, Crieff	1860	490‡	10,590	3,645	H. A. Ashmall (*Rector*) (1979)
Robert Gordon's College, Aberdeen	1729	960‡	—	3,900	G. A. Allan (1978)
St Aloysius' College, Glasgow	1859	800‡	—	3,160	Revd Dr J. W. Hanvey (1991)
Strathallan School, Perthshire	1913	500‡	11,055	7,710	A. McPhail (1993)

NORTHERN IRELAND

Bangor Grammar School, Co. Down	1856	920	—	400	T. W. Patton (1979)
Belfast Royal Academy	1785	1,369‡	—	varies	W. M. Sillery (1980)
Campbell College, Belfast	1894	680	4,300	993	Dr R. J. I. Pollock (1987)
Coleraine Academical Institution	1856	850	3,222	65	R. S. Forsythe (1984)
Methodist College, Belfast	1868	1,825‡	5,738	155	T. W. Mulryne (1988)
Portora Royal School, Enniskillen	1618	440	—	nil	R. L. Bennett (1983)
Royal Belfast Academical Institution	1810	1,040	—	395	R. M. Ridley (1990)

CHANNEL ISLANDS AND ISLE OF MAN

Elizabeth College, Guernsey	1563	570†	6,135	2,460	J. H. F. Doulton (1988)
King William's College, Isle of Man	1668	325‡	11,160	7,950	S. A. Westley (*Principal*) (1989)

EUROPE

Aiglon College, Switzerland	1949	285‡	Fr.50,220	Fr.34,275	R. McDonald (1994)
British School in the Netherlands	1935	500‡	—	Gld.19,530	M. J. Cooper (*Principal*) (1990)
British School of Brussels	1970	514‡	—	Fr.603,000	Ms J. M. Bray (*Principal*) (1992)
The English School, Nicosia, Cyprus	1900	834‡	—	C£1,700	A. M. Hudspeth (1988)
The International School of Geneva	1924	1,083‡	Fr.41,885	Fr.18,670	G. Walker, OBE (*Director-General*) (1991)
The International School of Paris	1964	230‡	—	Fr.80,500	N. M. Prentki (1988)
St Columba's College, Dublin	1843	300‡	Ir£5,895	Ir£3,375	T. E. Macey (*Warden*) (1988)
St George's English School, Rome	1958	370‡	—	L.19m	B. Gardner (1994)
Sir James Henderson British School, Milan	1969	170‡	—	L.15m	C. T. G. Leech (*Principal*) (1986)

OTHER OVERSEAS MEMBERS

AFRICA

FALCON COLLEGE, PO Esigodini, Zimbabwe. *Head*, P. N. Todd

HILTON COLLEGE, Natal 3245, SA. *Head*, P. Marsh

MICHAELHOUSE, Balgowan, Natal 3275, SA. *Head*, J. H. Pluke

PETERHOUSE, Marondera, Zimbabwe. *Head*, Revd Dr A. J. Megahey

ST GEORGE'S COLLEGE, Harare, Zimbabwe. *Head*, K. F. Brennan

DIOCESAN COLLEGE, Rondebosch, SA. *Head*, C. Watson

ST JOHN'S COLLEGE, Johannesburg, SA. *Head*, W. Macfarlane

ST STITHIAN'S COLLEGE, Randburg, SA. *Head*, D. B. Wylde

AUSTRALIA

ANGLICAN CHURCH GRAMMAR SCHOOL, Brisbane. *Head*, C. V. Ellis

BRIGHTON GRAMMAR SCHOOL, Brighton, Victoria. *Head*, R. L. Rofe

BRISBANE BOYS' COLLEGE, Brisbane. *Head*, G. M. Cujes

CAMBERWELL GRAMMAR SCHOOL, Canterbury, Victoria 3101. *Head*, C. F. Black

CANBERRA GS, Redhill, ACT 2603. *Head*, T. C. Murray

CAULFIELD GRAMMAR SCHOOL, East St Kilda, Victoria. *Head*, S. H. Newton

CHRIST CHURCH GRAMMAR SCHOOL, Claremont 6010, W. Australia. *Head*, J. J. S. Madin

CHURCH OF ENGLAND GRAMMAR SCHOOL, Melbourne. *Head*, A. J. de V. Hill

CHURCH OF ENGLAND GRAMMAR SCHOOL, Sydney, NSW. *Head*, R. A. I. Grant

CRANBROOK SCHOOL, Sydney, NSW. *Head*, Dr B. N. Carter

GEELONG CHURCH OF ENGLAND GRAMMAR SCHOOL, Corio. *Head*, J. E. Lewis

THE GEELONG COLLEGE, Geelong, Victoria. *Head*, A. P. Sheahan

GUILDFORD GRAMMAR SCHOOL, W. Australia. *Head*, J. M. Moody

HAILEYBURY COLLEGE, Keysborough, Victoria 3175. *Head*, A. H. M. Aikman

HALE SCHOOL, Wembley Downs, W. Australia. *Head*, R. J. Inverarity

KING'S SCHOOL, Parramatta, NSW. *Head,* J. A. Wickham
KINROSS WOLAROI SCHOOL, NSW. *Head,*
A. E. S. Anderson
KNOX GS, Wahroonga 2076, NSW. *Head,* Dr I. Paterson
ST PETER'S COLLEGE, St Peter's, S. Australia. *Head,*
R. L. Burchnall
SCOTCH COLLEGE, Adelaide, S. Australia. *Head,* K. Webb
SCOTCH COLLEGE, Hawthorn, Melbourne, Victoria. *Head,*
Dr F. G. Donaldson
SCOTCH COLLEGE, Swanbourne, W. Australia. *Head,*
W. R. Dickinson
SCOTS COLLEGE, Sydney, NSW. *Head,* G. A. W. Renney
THE SOUTHPORT SCHOOL, Southport, Queensland. *Head,*
B. A. Cook
SYDNEY GRAMMAR SCHOOL, NSW. *Head,*
Dr R. D. Townsend
WESLEY COLLEGE, Melbourne. *Head,* D. G. McArthur

CANADA

BRENTWOOD COLLEGE SCHOOL, Vancouver, BC. *Head,*
W. T. Ross
GLENLYON-NORFOLK SCHOOL, Victoria, BC. *Head,*
D. Brooks
HILLFIELD-STRATHALLAN COLLEGE, Hamilton, Ontario.
Head, M. B. Wansbrough
PICKERING COLLEGE, Newmarket, Ontario. *Head,*
S. H. Clark
ST ANDREW'S COLLEGE, Aurora, Ontario. *Head,*
R. P. Bedard
TRINITY COLLEGE SCHOOL, Port Hope, Ontario. *Head,*
R. C. N. Wright
UPPER CANADA COLLEGE, Toronto. *Head,* J. D. Blakey

HONG KONG

ISLAND SCHOOL, Borrett Road. *Head,* D. J. James
KING GEORGE V SCHOOL, Kowloon. *Head,* M. J. Behennah

INDIA

CATHEDRAL AND JOHN CONNON SCHOOL, Bombay. *Head,*
D. E. W. Shaw
LAWRENCE SCHOOL, Sanawar. *Head,* S. Singh
THE SCINDIA SCHOOL, Gwalior. *Head,* Dr S. D. Singh

NEW ZEALAND

CHRIST'S COLLEGE, Christchurch. *Head,* Dr M. J. Rosser
KING'S COLLEGE, Auckland. *Head,* J. S. Taylor
ST ANDREW'S COLLEGE, Christchurch. *Head,*
Dr A. J. Rentoul
THE COLLEGIATE SCHOOL, Wanganui. *Head,*
T. S. McKinley
WAITAKI BOYS' HIGH SCHOOL, Oamaru. *Head,*
B. R. Gollop

PHILIPPINES

BRENT SCHOOL, Baguio City. *Head,* P. Gysin

SOUTH AMERICA

ACADEMIA BRITANICA CUSCATLECA, El Salvador. *Head,*
R. Braund
MARKHAM COLLEGE, Lima, Peru. *Head,* W. J. Baker
ST ANDREW'S SCOTS SCHOOL, Buenos Aires, Argentina.
Head, K. Prior
ST GEORGE'S COLLEGE, Quilmes, Argentina. *Head,*
N. P. O. Green
ST PAULS' SCHOOL, São Paulo, Brazil. *Head,*
M. T. M. C. McCann
THE BRITISH SCHOOLS, Montevideo, Uruguay. *Head,*
C. D. T. Smith

ADDITIONAL MEMBERS

The headteachers of some maintained schools are by
invitation Additional Members of the HMC. They include
the following:

BISHOP WORDSWORTH SCHOOL, Salisbury. *Head,*
C. Barnett
DURHAM JOHNSTONE SCHOOL, Durham. *Head,* J. Dunford
EGGBUCKLAND COMMUNITY COLLEGE, Plymouth. *Head,*
H. Green
HAYWARDS HEATH SIXTH FORM COLLEGE, W. Sussex.
Head, B. W. Derbyshire
THE JUDD SCHOOL, Tonbridge, Kent. *Head,* K. A. Starling
KING EDWARD VI CAMP HILL SCHOOL FOR BOYS,
Birmingham. *Head,* R. Dancey
LISKEARD SCHOOL, Cornwall. *Head,* A. D. Wood
THE LONDON ORATORY SCHOOL, London SW6. *Head,*
J. C. McIntosh
PRESCOT SCHOOL, Merseyside. *Head,* P. A. Barlow
PRINCE HENRY'S GRAMMAR SCHOOL, Otley, W Yorks.
Head, M. Franklin
PRINCE WILLIAM SCHOOL, Oundle, Cambs. *Head,*
C. J. Lowe
THE ROYAL GRAMMAR SCHOOL, Lancaster. *Head,*
P. J. Mawby
ST JOHN'S SCHOOL, Marlborough, Wilts. *Head,* J. Price
WESTMINSTER CITY SCHOOL, London SW1. *Head,*
M. Billingham

SOCIETY OF HEADMASTERS AND HEADMISTRESSES OF INDEPENDENT SCHOOLS

The Society was founded in 1961 and, in general, represents smaller boarding schools.

Hon. Secretary, I. D. Cleland, The Coach House, 34A Heath Road, Upton-by-Chester, Cheshire CH2 1HX. Tel: 01244-379649

Headmasters of the following schools are members of both HMC and SHMIS; details of these schools appear in the HMC list: Abbotsholme School, Ackworth School, Bedales School, Churcher's College, City of London Freemen's School, Colston's Collegiate School, King's School, Gloucester, King's School, Tynemouth, Lord Wandsworth College, Pangbourne College, Reading Blue Coat School, Reed's School, Rendcomb College, Ryde School, St George's College, Silcoates School, Tettenhall College, Wisbech Grammar School, Woodbridge School, Yarm School

* Woodard Corporation School
† Girls in VI form
‡ Co-educational
° Entry into SHMIS subject to confirmation

Name of School	Foun-ded	No. of pupils	Annual fees £ Boarding	Day	Head (with date of appointment)
Austin Friars School (*RC*), Carlisle	1951	304‡	7,578	4,338	M. G. Taylor (1994)
°Battle Abbey School, E. Sussex	1912	120‡	9,090	5,625	D. J. A. Teall (1982)
Bearwood College, Berks.	1827	204‡	10,050	5,550	Dr R. J. Belcher (1993)
Bedstone College, Shropshire	1948	155‡	9,639	6,006	M. S. Symonds (1990)
Bembridge School, Isle of Wight	1919	200‡	9,270	4,620	J. High (1986)
Bentham School, N. Yorks	1726	250‡	8,985	4,476	T. Halliwell (1995)
Bethany School, Kent	1866	265‡	9,441	6,039	W. M. Harvey (1988)
Birkdale School, Sheffield	1904	475†	—	4,425	Revd M. D. A. Hepworth (1983)
Box Hill School, Surrey	1959	286‡	10,200	6,150	Dr R. A. S. Atwood (1987)
Carmel College (*Jewish*), Oxon.	1948	216‡	13,065	7,305	P. D. Skelker (1984)
Claremont Fan Court School, Surrey	1932	375‡	8,985	5,685	Mrs P. B. Farrar (*Principal*) (1994)
Claysmore School, Dorset	1896	283‡	11,190	7,830	D. J. Beeby (1986)
Cokethorpe School, Oxon.	1957	150‡	11,940	7,860	P. J. S. Cantwell (1995)
Duke of York's Royal Military School, Dover	1803	338‡	750	—	Col. G. H. Wilson (1992)
Elmhurst Ballet School, Surrey	1903	233‡	9,120	6,690	J. McNamara (1994)
Embley Park School, Romsey, Hants.	1946	230‡	9,670	5,835	D. F. Chapman (1987)
Ewell Castle School, Surrey	1926	320†	—	4,425	R. A. Fewtrell (1983)
Friends' School, Essex	1702	250‡	10,014	6,066	Miss S. H. Evans (1989)
Fulneck School (Boys), W. Yorks.	1753	425‡	8,655	4,620	Mrs B. A. Heppell (1994)
*Grenville College, Devon	1954	383‡	9,954	4,881	M. C. V. Cane, PH.D. (1992)
Halliford School, Middx.	1956	273‡	—	4,440	J. R. Crook (1984)
Hipperholme Grammar School, Halifax	1648	350‡	—	3,504	C. C. Robinson (1988)
Keil School, Dumbarton	1915	210‡	8,900	5,000	J. A. Cummings (1993)
Kingham Hill School, Oxon.	1886	200‡	9,477	5,685	M. Payne (*Warden*) (1990)
Kirkham Grammar School, Lancs.	1549	540‡	6,975	3,675	B. Stacey (1991)
Langley School, Norfolk	1910	266‡	9,810	5,160	S. J. W. McArthur (1989)
Lord Mayor Treloar College, Hants.	1908	130‡	39,465	29,601	N. Clark (1989)
Milton Abbey School, Dorset	1954	210	11,604	7,746	W. J. Hughes-D'Aeth (1995)
Oswestry School, Shropshire	1407	289‡	9,090	5,316	P. K. Smith (1995)
The Purcell School (music), Middx.	1962	150‡	14,400	8,514	K. J. Bain (1983)
Rannoch School, Perthshire	1959	250‡	10,350	5,490	M. Barratt (1982)
Rishworth School, W. Yorks.	1724	420‡	9,288	4,800	M. J. Elford (1992)
Rougemont School, Gwent	1919	166‡	—	4,350	I. Brown (1995)
Royal Hospital School, Ipswich	1712	600‡	7,500	—	N. K. D. Ward (1995)
Royal Russell School, Surrey	1853	430‡	10,035	5,295	R. D. Balaam (1981)
Royal School, Dungannon, N. Ireland	1614	700‡	5,726	85	P. D. Hewitt (1984)
Royal Wolverhampton School	1850	310‡	9,045	5,175	Mrs B. A. Evans (1995)
Ruthin School, Clwyd	1574	163‡	9,885	6,225	J. S. Rowlands (1993)
St Bede's School, E. Sussex	1979	413‡	11,400	7,050	R. A. Perrin (1978)
St David's College, Gwynedd	1965	230	9,642	6,270	W. Seymour (1991)
Scarborough College, N. Yorks.	1898	382‡	9,420	5,106	T. Kirkup (1996)
Seaford College, W. Sussex	1884	330†	9,630	5,925	R. C. Hannaford (1990)
Shebbear College, Devon	1841	240‡	9,330	5,010	R. J. Buley (1983)
Shiplake College, Oxon.	1959	310	11,175	7,530	N. V. Bevan (1988)
Sibford School, Oxon.	1842	277‡	9,600	5,085	J. Dunston (1990)
Sidcot School, Avon	1808	395‡	9,561	5,718	C. J. Greenfield (1986)
Stafford Grammar School, Staffs.	1982	295‡	—	3,945	M. James (1992)
Stanbridge Earls School, Hants.	1952	185‡	11,655	8,745	H. Moxon (1984)
Warminster School, Wilts.	1707	307‡	9,270	5,370	T. D. Holgate (1990)
Yehudi Menuhin School (music), Surrey	1963	47‡	varies	varies	N. Chisholm (1988)

GIRLS' SCHOOLS ASSOCIATION

THE GIRLS' SCHOOLS ASSOCIATION, 130 Regent Road, Leicester LE1 7PG. Tel: 0116-254 1619
President (1995–6), Miss M. Rudland
Secretary, Ms S. Cooper

CSC Church Schools Company, 1A Doughty Street, London WCIN 2PH. Tel: 0171-404 3134
§ Girls Public Day School Trust, 26 Queen Anne's Gate, London SW1H 9AN. Tel: 0171-222 9595
* Woodard Corporation School
† Boys in VI form
‡ Co-educational
° 1994 figures

Name of School	Founded	No. of pupils	Annual fees £		Head (with date of appointment)
			Boarding	Day	
ENGLAND AND WALES					
Abbey School, Reading	1887	720	—	4,140	Miss B. C. L. Sheldon (1991)
Abbot's Hill, Herts.	1912	150	10,275	6,060	Mrs J. Kingsley (1979)
Adcote School, Shropshire	1907	106	9,195	5,100	Mrs S. B. Cecchet (1979)
Alice Ottley School, Worcester	1883	576	—	4,785	Miss C. Sibbit (1986)
Amberfield School, Ipswich	1952	162	—	3,810	Mrs L. A. Lewis (1992)
Ashford School, Kent	1910	377	10,479	5,850	Mrs P. Metham (1992)
Atherley School, Southampton (*CSC*)	1926	300	—	4,254	Mrs C. Madina (1995)
Badminton School, Bristol	1858	300	11,250	6,225	C. J. T. Gould (1981)
Ballard College, Hants	1890	110‡	7,890	5,310	Revd A. J. Folks (1985)
§Bath High School	1875	418	—	3,984	Miss M. A. Winfield (1985)
Bedford High School	1882	748	9,042	4,749	Mrs B. Stanley (1995)
Bedgebury School, Kent	1860	229	10,788	6,678	Mrs L. J. Griffin (1995)
Beechwood School (*RC*), Kent	1915	138	10,605	6,330	T. Hodkinson (1994)
§Belvedere School, Liverpool	1880	486	—	3,984	Mrs C. H. Evans (1992)
Benenden School, Kent	1923	440	12,630	—	Mrs G. D. duCharme (1985)
Berkhamsted School, Herts.	1888	410	11,327	5,487	Miss V. E. M. Shepherd (1980)
§Birkenhead High School	1901	690	—	3,984	Mrs K. R. Irving (1986)
§Blackheath High School, London SE3	1880	369	—	4,644	Miss R. K. Musgrave (1989)
*The Bolitho School, Penzance	1889	40	8,361	4,416	I. Halford (1986)
Bolton School, Lancs.	1877	805	—	4,476	Miss E. J. Panton (1993)
Bradford Girls' Grammar School	1875	690	—	3,996	Mrs L. J. Warrington (1987)
§Brighton and Hove High School	1876	521	—	3,984	Miss R. A. Woodbridge (1989)
Brigidine School, Windsor	1948	230	—	4,425	Mrs M. B. Cairns (1986)
§Bromley High School, Kent	1883	545	—	4,644	Mrs E. J. Hancock (1989)
Bruton School, Somerset	1900	478‡	6,990	3,786	Mrs J. M. Wade (1987)
Burgess Hill School, W. Sussex	1906	370	9,285	5,520	Mrs R. F. Lewis (1993)
Bury Grammar School, Lancs.	1884	827	—	3,702	Miss J. M. Lawley (1987)
Casterton School, Cumbria	1823	305	9,030	5,664	A. F. Thomas (1990)
§Central Newcastle High School	1895	597	—	3,984	Mrs A. M. Chapman (1985)
Channing School, London N6	1885	323	—	5,700	Mrs I. R. Raphael (1984)
Cheltenham Ladies' College, Glos.	1853	850	12,285	7,800	Miss E. Castle (*Principal*) (1987)
City of London School for Girls, London EC2	1894	550	—	5,094	Mrs Y. A. Burne, PH.D. (1995)
Clifton High School, Bristol	1877	443	8,160	4,275	Mrs Y. Graham (1996)
Cobham Hall, Kent	1962	165	12,855	8,250	Mrs R. J. McCarthy (1989)
Colston's Girls' School, Bristol	1891	500	—	3,582	Mrs J. P. Franklin (1989)
Combe Bank School, Kent	1868	220	—	5,190	Miss N. Spurr (1993)
Commonweal Lodge School, Surrey	1916	120	—	4,515	Mrs S. Law (1995)
Cranford House School, Oxon.	1931	74	—	4,920	Mrs A. B. Gray (1992)
Croft House School, Dorset	1941	120	9,750	6,885	M. P. Hawkins (1993)
Croham Hurst School, Surrey	1899	310	—	4,590	Miss S. C. Budgen (1994)
§Croydon High School, Surrey	1874	716	—	4,644	Mrs P. E. Davies (1990)
Dame Allan's Girls' School, Newcastle upon Tyne	1705	388†	—	3,570	T. A. Willcocks (*Principal*) (1988)
Derby High School	1892	314	—	4,350	G. H. Goddard, PH.D. (1983)
Downe House, Berks.	1907	617	12,420	9,000	Miss S. Cameron (1989)
Dunottar School, Surrey	1926	305	—	4,530	Miss J. Burnell (1985)
Durham High School	1884	423	—	4,377	Miss M. L. Walters (1992)
Edgbaston Church of England College	1886	350	—	4,275	Mrs A. Varley-Tipton (1992)

Name of School	Founded	No. of pupils	Annual fees £ Boarding	Day	Head (with date of appointment)
Edgbaston High School	1876	485	—	4,215	Mrs S. J. Horsman (1987)
Edgehill College, Devon	1884	355‡	9,480	5,175	Mrs E. M. Burton (1987)
Elmslie Girls' School, Lancs.	1918	300	—	3,885	Miss E. M. Smithies (1978)
Farlington School, W. Sussex	1896	250	9,360	5,790	Mrs P. Mawer (1992)
Farnborough Hill, Hants.	1889	530	—	4,428	Sr E. McCormack (1988)
Farringtons and Stratford House, Kent	1911	360	9,561	4,962	Mrs B. J. Stock (1987)
Francis Holland School, London NW1	1878	370	—	5,295	Mrs P. H. Parsonson (1988)
Francis Holland School, London SW1	1881	181	—	5,940	Mrs J. A. Anderson (1982)
Gateways School, Leeds	1941	170	—	3,540	Mrs J. E. Stephen (1995)
Godolphin School, Wilts.	1726	387	10,779	6,456	Mrs H. Fender (1989)
Godolphin and Latymer School, London w6	1905	700	—	5,625	Miss M. Rudland (1986)
Greenacre School, Surrey	1933	205	—	4,800	Mrs P. M. Wood (1990)
Guildford High School (CSC)	1888	765	—	5,100	Mrs S. H. Singer (1991)
Haberdashers' Aske's School for Girls, Herts.	1873	836	—	4,140	Mrs P. Penney (1991)
Haberdashers' Monmouth School, Gwent	1891	551	7,992	4,221	Mrs D. L. Newman (1992)
Harrogate Ladies' College	1893	340	8,985	5,985	G. F. Hazell (acting)
Headington School, Oxford	1915	570	9,030	4,524	Miss E. M. Tucker (1982)
Heathfield School, Ascot, Berks.	1900	210	12,525	—	Mrs J. Benammar (1992)
§Heathfield School, Pinner, Middx.	1900	294	—	4,644	Mrs J. Merritt (1988)
Hethersett Old Hall School, Norwich	1928	194	8,550	4,350	Mrs V. M. Redington (1983)
Highclare School, W. Midlands	1932	153†	—	4,155	Mrs C. A. Hanson (1974)
Hollygirt School, Nottingham	1877	230	—	3,636	Mrs M. R. Banks (1985)
Holy Child School, Birmingham	1933	150	—	4,500	Mrs J. Hill (1993)
Holy Trinity College, Bromley	1886	280	—	4,140	Mrs D. Bradshaw (1994)
Holy Trinity School, Kidderminster	1903	182	—	3,549	Mrs S. M. Bell (1990)
Howell's School, Denbigh, Clwyd	1859	211	9,846	6,435	Mrs M. Steel (1991)
§Howell's School, Llandaff, Cardiff	1860	554	—	3,984	Mrs C. J. Fitz (1991)
Hull High School (CSC)	1890	149	—	3,957	Mrs M. A. Benson (1994)
Hulme Grammar School, Oldham	1895	519	—	3,549	Miss M. S. Smolenski (1992)
Ilford Ursuline High School, Essex	1903	370	—	4,329	Miss J. Reddington (1990)
§Ipswich High School	1878	471	—	3,984	Miss V. MacCuish (1993)
James Allen's Girls' School, London SE22	1741	750	—	5,505	Mrs M. Gibbs (1994)
Kent College	1885	247	10,584	6,330	Miss B. Crompton (1990)
King Edward VI High School for Girls, Birmingham	1883	550	—	4,230	Miss E. W. Evans (1977)
King's HS for Girls, Warwick	1879	560	—	4,095	Mrs J. M. Anderson (1987)
Kingsley School, Warwicks.	1884	455	—	4,245	Mrs M. A. Webster (1988)
Lady Eleanor Holles School, Middx.	1711	681	—	5,040	Miss E. M. Candy (1981)
La Retraite School, Wilts.	1953	130	—	4,575	Mrs R. A. Simmons (1994)
La Sagesse Convent High School, Newcastle upon Tyne	1906	350	—	3,720	Miss L. Clark (1994)
Lavant House-Rosemead School, W. Sussex	1919	140	9,870	5,550	Mrs H. A. Kingham (1995)
Leeds Girls' High School	1876	610	—	4,236	Miss P. A. Randall (1977)
Leicester High School	1906	275	—	4,275	Mrs P. A. Watson (1992)
Loughborough High School	1850	533	—	3,969	Miss J. E. L. Harvatt (1978)
Luckley-Oakfield School, Berks.	1895	275	7,950	4,929	R. C. Blake (1984)
Malvern Girls' College, Worcs.	1893	460	11,700	7,800	Dr A. Lee (1994)
Manchester High School	1874	715	—	3,915	Miss E. M. Diggory (1994)
Manor House School, Little Bookham, Surrey	1927	129	7,845	5,400	Mrs L. Mendes (1989)
Maynard School, Exeter	1877	470	—	4,173	Miss F. Murdin (1980)
Merchant Taylors' School, Liverpool	1888	656	—	3,744	Mrs J. Mills (1994)
Micklefield Wadhurst School, E. Sussex	1910	180	10,110	6,420	E. Reynolds (1994)
Moira House School, E. Sussex	1875	280	10,710	6,900	A. R. Underwood (1975)
More House School, London SW1	1953	230	—	5,460	Miss M. Connell (1991)
Moreton Hall, Shropshire	1913	280	10,950	7,590	J. Forster (1992)
Mount School, York	1831	250	9,690	5,995	Miss B. J. Windle (1986)
Newcastle upon Tyne Church HS	1885	386	—	3,735	Miss P. E. Davies (1974)
New Hall School, Essex	1642	430	10,314	6,603	Sr Margaret Mary Horton (1986)
Northampton High School	1878	580	—	4,110	Mrs L. A. Mayne (1988)
North Foreland Lodge, Hants.	1909	170	10,275	6,600	Miss D. L. Matthews (1983)
North London Collegiate School	1850	970	—	4,848	Mrs J. L. Clanchy (1986)
Northwood College, Middx.	1878	301	—	4,836	Mrs J. A. Mayou (1991)
§Norwich High School	1875	652	—	3,984	Mrs V. C. Bidwell (1985)
§Nottingham High School	1875	823	—	3,984	Mrs C. Bowering (1984)

Name of School	Foun-ded	No. of pupils	Annual fees £		Head (with date of appointment)
			Boarding	Day	
§Notting Hill and Ealing High School	1873	565	—	4,644	Mrs S. M. Whitfield (1991)
Ockbrook School, Derby	1799	176	6,906	3,723	Miss D. P. Bolland (1995)
Old Palace School, Surrey	1887	612	—	3,978	Miss K. L. Hilton (1974)
§Oxford High School	1875	556	—	3,984	Mrs J. Townsend (1981)
Palmers Green High School, London N21	1905	140	—	4,020	Mrs S. Grant (1989)
Parsons Mead, Surrey	1897	250	8,829	5,025	Miss E. B. Plant (1990)
Perse School for Girls, Cambridge	1881	540	—	4,656	Miss H. S. Smith (1989)
*Peterborough High School	1939	200	8,259	4,113	Mrs A. Storey (1977)
Pipers Corner School, Bucks.	1930	300	9,330	5,580	Dr M. M. Wilson (1986)
Polam Hall, Co. Durham	1848	300	8,724	4,266	Mrs H. C. Hamilton (1987)
§Portsmouth High School	1882	534	—	3,984	Mrs J. M. Dawtrey (1984)
Princess Helena College, Herts.	1820	155	9,990	6,960	J. Jarvis (1995)
Prior's Field, Surrey	1902	210	9,810	6,555	Mrs J. M. McCallum (1987)
§Putney High School, London SW15	1893	575	—	4,644	Mrs E. Merchant (1991)
Queen Anne's School, Berks.	1698	324	11,250	7,380	Mrs D. Forbes (1993)
Queen Ethelburga's College, York	1912	173	10,197	6,477	Mrs G. L. Richardson (Principal) (1993)
Queen Margaret's School, York	1901	368	10,218	6,474	Dr G. A. H. Chapman (1993)
Queen Mary School, Lytham, Lancs.	1930	600	—	3,690	Miss M. C. Ritchie (1981)
Queen's College, London W1	1848	370	—	5,820	Lady Goodhart (1991)
Queen's Gate School, London SW7	1891	250	—	5,400	Mrs A. M. Holyoak (Principal) (1988)
Queen's School, Chester	1878	485	—	4,320	Miss D. M. Skilbeck (1989)
Queenswood, Herts.	1894	390	11,442	6,768	Mrs A. M. B. Butler (1981)
Redland High School, Bristol	1882	640	—	3,966	Mrs C. Lear (1989)
Red Maids' School, Bristol	1634	503	7,440	3,720	Miss S. Hampton (1987)
Rickmansworth Masonic School, Herts.	1788	548	8,391	5,106	Mrs I. M. Andrews (1992)
Roedean School, Brighton	1885	440	12,975	—	Mrs A. R. Longley (1984)
Royal School, Bath	1864	270	11,001	5,886	Mrs E. McKendrick (1994)
The Royal School, Surrey	1840	400	9,507	6,057	C. Brooks (1984)
Rydal Penrhos Senior School, Clwyd (Girls)	1880	225	9,345	6,405	C. M. J. Allen (1993)
Rye St Antony School (RC), Oxford	1930	314	8,250	5,085	Miss A. M. Jones (1990)
St Albans High School, Herts.	1889	528	—	4,710	Mrs C. Y. Daly (1994)
St Andrew's School, Bedford	1897	180	—	3,555	Mrs J. M. Mark (1995)
St Anne's School, Cumbria	1863	250	9,126	6,051	R. Hunter (1996)
St Antony's-Leweston School (RC), Dorset	1891	285	10,515	6,861	Miss C. Denley Lloyd (1993)
St Catherine's School, Surrey	1885	462	9,255	5,655	Mrs C. Oulton (1994)
St David's School, Middx.	1716	240†	8,985	5,175	Mrs J. G. Osborne (1985)
St Dunstan's Abbey, Devon	1850	200	8,010	4,500	R. A. Bye (1990)
St Elphin's School, Derbys.	1844	170	9,711	5,658	Mrs V. E. Fisher (1994)
St Felix School, Suffolk	1897	235	10,700	6,970	Mrs S. R. Campion (1991)
St Francis' College (RC), Herts.	1933	196	9,810	5,025	Miss M. Hegarty (1993)
St Gabriel's School, Berks.	1929	156	—	4,971	D. Cobb (1990)
St George's School, Ascot, Berks.	1923	280	11,625	6,825	Mrs A. M. Griggs (1989)
School of S. Helen and S. Katharine, Oxon.	1903	520	—	4,500	Mrs C. L. Hall (1993)
St Helen's School, Middx.	1899	940	8,994	4,773	Mrs D. Jefkins (1995)
*S. Hilary's School, Cheshire	1880	115	—	4,041	Ms G. M. Case (1995)
St James's and the Abbey, Worcs.	1896	188	10,962	7,308	Miss E. M. Mullenger (1986)
St Joseph's Convent School (RC), Berks.	1909	378	—	3,795	Mrs V. Brookes (1990)
St Joseph's School, Lincoln	1905	220	8,670	4,245	Mrs M. Bradley (1994)
St Leonards-Mayfield School, E. Sussex	1850	525	9,855	6,570	Sr J. Sinclair (1980)
St Margaret's School, Bushey, Herts.	1749	430	8,760	5,475	Miss M. de Villiers (1992)
*St Margaret's School, Exeter	1904	340†	6,705	4,080	Mrs M. D'Albertanson (1993)
St Martin's School, Solihull, W. Midlands	1941	250	—	4,419	Mrs S. J. Williams (1988)
*School of S. Mary and S. Anne, Abbots Bromley, Staffs.	1874	280	10,665	7,110	A. Grigg (1989)
St Mary's Convent School, Worcester	1934	200	—	3,600	Miss G. Morrissey (1995)
St Mary's Hall, Brighton	1836	264	8,955	5,940	Mrs P. J. James (1992)
St Mary's School (RC), Ascot, Berks.	1885	335	11,433	6,861	Sr M. M. Orchard (1982)
St Mary's School, Calne, Wilts.	1872	307	11,550	6,825	Miss D. H. Burns (1985)
St Mary's School, Cambridge	1898	580	6,930	3,870	Miss M. Conway (1989)
St Mary's School, Colchester	1908	240	—	3,690	Mrs G. M. G. Mouser (1981)
St Mary's School, Gerrards Cross	1872	190	—	4,995	Mrs F. Balcombe (1995)
St Mary's School (RC), Shaftesbury	1945	287	9,600	6,150	Sr M. Campion Livesey (1985)

Name of School	Foun-ded	No. of pupils	Annual fees £		Head (with date of appointment)
			Boarding	Day	
St Mary's School, Wantage, Oxon.	1873	240	10,860	7,200	Mrs S. Bodinham (1994)
St Maur's Senior School, Weybridge	1898	379	—	4,725	Mrs M. E. Dodds (1991)
St Michael's, Limpsfield, Surrey	1850	111	10,500	5,985	Ms M. J. Hustler, PH.D. (1989)
St Paul's Girls' School, London w6	1904	605	—	6,282	Miss J. Gough (*High Mistress*) (1992)
St Swithun's School, Winchester	1884	458	11,130	6,720	Ms H. Harvey, PH.D. (1995)
St Teresa's School, Dorking	1928	340	10,785	5,070	L. Allan (1987)
Selwyn School, Glos.	—	175	8,430	4,800	Miss L. M. Brown (1994)
§Sheffield High School	1878	530	—	3,984	Mrs M. A. Houston (1989)
Sherborne School for Girls, Dorset	1899	420	11,550	7,950	Miss J. M. Taylor (1985)
§Shrewsbury High School	1885	408	—	3,984	Miss S. Gardner (1990)
Sir William Perkins's School, Surrey	1725	592	—	3,945	Miss S. Ross (1994)
§South Hampstead High School, London NW3	1876	625	—	4,644	Mrs J. G. Scott (1993)
Stamford High School, Lincs.	1876	710	8,178	4,089	Miss G. K. Bland (1978)
Stonar School, Wilts.	1921	403	9,546	5,289	Mrs S. Hopkinson (1985)
Stover School, Devon	1932	186	8,475	4,425	P. Bujak (1995)
§Streatham Hill and Clapham High School, London SW2	1887	421	—	4,644	Miss G. M. Ellis (1979)
Sunderland High School (*CSC*)	1884	220‡	—	3,915	Miss C. Rendle-Short (1993)
Surbiton High School (*CSC*), Surrey	1884	538	—	4,839	Miss G. Perry (1993)
§Sutton High School, Surrey	1884	504	—	4,644	Mrs A. J. Coutts (1995)
§Sydenham High School, London SE26	1887	466	—	4,644	Mrs G. Baker (1988)
Talbot Heath, Dorset	1886	418	8,640	4,950	Mrs C. Dipple (1991)
Teesside High School, Cleveland	1970	388	—	3,705	Miss J. F. Hamilton (1995)
Tormead School, Surrey	1905	492	—	5,100	Mrs H. E. M. Alleyne (1992)
Truro High School	1880	320	7,995	4,380	J. Graham-Brown (1992)
Tudor Hall School, Oxon.	1850	266	10,140	6,318	Miss N. Godfrey (1984)
Ursuline Convent School, Kent	1904	400	10,563	5,355	Sr A. Montgomery (1995)
Wakefield Girls' High School	1878	756	—	4,122	Mrs P. A. Langham (1987)
Walthamstow Hall, Kent	1838	347	11,775	6,345	Mrs J. S. Lang (1984)
Wentworth Milton Mount, Dorset	1871	250	8,835	5,541	Miss S. Coe (1991)
Westfield School, Newcastle upon Tyne	1962	210	—	4,140	Mrs M. Farndale (1990)
West Heath, Kent	1867	102	11,040	7,755	Mrs A. Williamson (1994)
Westholme School, Lancs.	1923	650	—	3,525	Mrs L. Croston (*Principal*) (1988)
Westonbirt, Glos.	1928	245	10,785	6,936	Mrs G. Hylson-Smith (1986)
§Wimbledon High School, London SW19	1880	561	—	4,644	Dr J. L. Clough (1995)
Wispers School, Surrey	1946	130	9,135	5,880	L. H. Beltran (1979)
Withington Girls' School, Manchester	1890	505	—	3,750	Mrs M. Kenyon (1986)
Woldingham School, Surrey	1842	530	11,436	6,927	Ms P. Dineen, PH.D. (1985)
Wroxall Abbey School, Warwick	1872	70	9,660	4,935	Mrs J. M. Gowen (1993)
Wychwood School, Oxford	1897	160	6,885	4,350	Mrs M. L. Duffill (1981)
Wycombe Abbey School, Bucks.	1896	485	12,240	9,180	Mrs J. M. Goodland (1989)
Wykeham House School, Fareham, Hants.	1913	174	—	3,870	Mrs R. Kamaryc (1995)
York College for Girls (*CSC*)	1908	113	—	5,250	Mrs E. Taylor (1995)
SCOTLAND					
Kilgraston School, Perthshire	1930	220	9,825	5,655	Mrs J. L. Austin (1993)
Laurel Bank School, Glasgow	1903	236	—	4,032	Mrs E. Surber (1995)
Mary Erskine School, Edinburgh	1694	657	8,280	4,140	P. F. J. Tobin (*Principal*) (1989)
Park School, Glasgow	1880	250	—	3,969	Mrs M. E. Myatt (1986)
St Denis and Cranley School, Edinburgh	1858	130	9,150	4,485	Mrs J. M. Munro (1984)
St George's School, Edinburgh	1888	550	8,655	4,485	J. McClure, D.PHIL. (1994)
St Leonards School, St Andrews	1877	280	11,775	6,225	Mrs M. James (1988)
St Margaret's School, Aberdeen	1846	235	—	3,702	Miss L. M. Ogilvie (1989)
St Margaret's School, Edinburgh	1890	°369	°8,010	°3,960	Miss A. Mitchell (1994)
CHANNEL ISLANDS					
The Ladies' College, Guernsey	1872	340	—	2,055	Miss M. Macdonald (1993)

Social Welfare

National Health Service

and Local Authority Personal Social Services

The National Health Service came into being on 5 July 1948 as a result of the National Health Service Act 1946, covering England and Wales, and separate legislation for Scotland and Northern Ireland. The Acts placed a duty on the relevant Secretaries of State to promote the establishment of a comprehensive health service designed to secure improvement in the mental and physical health of the people and the prevention, diagnosis and treatment of illness. The National Health Service is administered in England by the Secretary of State for Health, and in Wales, Scotland and Northern Ireland by the Secretaries of State for Wales, Scotland and Northern Ireland.

The National Health Service covers a comprehensive range of hospital, specialist, family practitioner (medical, dental, ophthalmic and pharmaceutical), artificial limb and appliance, ambulance, and community health services. Everyone normally resident in the UK is entitled to use any of these services without charge, except where charges are specifically provided for by statute, e.g. prescriptions.

In addition, the Secretary of State for Health is responsible under the Local Authority Social Services Act 1970 for the provision by local authorities of social services for the elderly, the disabled, those with mental disorders and for families and children.

The NHS is financed mainly from taxation and the cost met from moneys voted by Parliament. The present level of expenditure is £41,000 million a year.

STRUCTURE

The National Health Service and Community Care Act 1990 reformed management and patient care. The Act provided for more streamlined Regional and District Health Authorities and Family Health Services Authorities, and for the establishment of NHS Trusts, which operate as self-governing health care providers. One result of the Act is that health care is provided through NHS contracts, where one body (the purchaser) is responsible for obtaining the appropriate health care for its population from another body (the provider). From 1 April 1993, the Community Care Reforms introduced changes in the way care is administered for the elderly, the mentally ill, the physically handicapped and people with learning disabilities.

From 1 April 1996 the eight Regional Health Authorities (RHAs) in England will be replaced by eight NHS Executive regional offices which will take on the functions of the RHAs. They are responsible for regional planning, the allocation of resources to District Health Authorities (DHAs), Family Health Services Authorities (FHSAs) and general practitioner fundholders, and the promotion of national policies and priorities, and are directly accountable to the Secretary of State for Health. From 1 April 1996 the DHAs and FHSAs will be replaced by single health authorities which will have the combined duties and responsibilities of both DHAs and FHSAs.

The 105 District Health Authorities (DHAs) are responsible for purchasing health care for the people who live within their area, and for the operational management of health services and planning within regional and national strategic guidelines. DHAs' resources are allocated by RHAs, to which they are also accountable for their performance

---

HEALTH SERVICES

FAMILY DOCTOR SERVICE

In England and Wales the Family Doctor Service (or General Medical Services) is managed by 98 Family Health Services Authorities (FHSAs) which also organize the general dental, pharmaceutical and ophthalmic services for their areas. From 1 April 1996 the FHSAs will be replaced by single health authorities who will have the combined duties and responsibilities of both DHAs and FHSAs. In England the chairman is appointed by the Secretary of State and the non-executive members by the RHA (NHS Executive regional office from 1 April 1996). In Wales the chairman and non-executive members are appointed by the Secretary of State.

Any doctor may take part in the Family Doctor Service (provided the area in which he/she wishes to practise has not already an adequate number of doctors) and about 28,000 general practitioners in England and Wales do so. They may at the same time have private fee-paying patients. Family doctors are paid for their NHS work in accordance with a scheme of remuneration which includes a basic practice allowance, capitation fees, reimbursement of certain practice expenses and payments for out-of-hours work.

The National Health Service and Community Care Act 1990 enables general practitioner practices to apply for fundholding status. This makes the practice responsible for its own NHS budget for a specified range of goods and services. From 1 April 1996 there will be two types of general practitioner fundholding: Standard fundholders, for practices with at least 5,000 patients, who will purchase a full range of in- and out-patient services; and Community fundholders, for smaller practices of at least 3,000 patients, who will purchase only community nursing services and diagnostic tests. There are currently 2,007 fundholding units, comprising 2,603 practices. Fundholding practices are monitored by the FHSAs on behalf of the RHAs.

Everyone aged 16 or over can choose their doctor (parents or guardians choose for children under 16) and the doctor is also free to accept a person or not as he or she chooses. A person may change their doctor if they wish, by going to the surgery of a general practioner of their choice who is willing to accept them, and either handing in their medical card to register or filling in a form. When people are away from home they can still use the Family Doctor Service if they ask to be treated as temporary residents, and in an emergency, if a person's own doctor is not available, any doctor in the service will give treatment and advice.

Patients are treated either in the doctor's surgery or, when necessary, at home. Doctors may prescribe for their patients all drugs and medicines which are medically necessary for their treatment and also a certain number of surgical appliances (the more elaborate being provided through hospitals).

Dental Service

Dentists, like doctors, may take part in the NHS and also have private patients. About 16,000 of the dentists available for general practice in England provide NHS general dental services. They are responsible to the FHSAs in whose areas they provide services.

Patients are free to go to any dentist who is taking part in the NHS and willing to accept them. Dentists are paid a capitation fee for patients registered with them who are under 18 years of age. They receive payment for items of treatment for individual adult patients and, in addition, a continuing care payment for those registered with them.

Patients are asked to pay 80 per cent of the cost of NHS dental treatment. The maximum charge for a course of treatment is £300. There is no charge for arrest of bleeding, repairs to dentures, home visits by the dentist or re-opening a surgery in an emergency (in these two cases, payment will be for treatment given in the normal way). The following are exempt from dental charges/have charges remitted:

(i)   young people under 18
(ii)   full-time students under 19
(iii)   expectant mothers who were pregnant when accepted for treatment
(iv)   women who have had a child in the previous 12 months
(v)   people who receive income support or family credit and their dependants

Leaflet AB11 available from post offices and leaflet D11 available from local social security offices explain how other people on a low income can, depending on their financial circumstances, get free treatment or help with charges.

Pharmaceutical Service

Patients may obtain medicines, appliances and oral contraceptives prescribed under the NHS from any pharmacy whose owner has entered into arrangements with the FHSA (unitary health authority after 1 April 1996) to provide this service. Almost all pharmacy owners have done so and display notices that they dispense under the NHS; the number of these pharmacies in England and Wales in March 1995 was about 10,500. There are also some appliance suppliers who only provide special appliances. In country areas where access to a pharmacy may be difficult, patients may be able to obtain medicines, etc., from their doctor.

Except for contraceptives (for which there is no charge), a charge of £5.25 is payable for each item supplied unless the patient is exempt and the declaration on the back of the prescription form is completed. Exemptions cover:

(i)   children under 16
(ii)   full-time students under 19
(iii)   men aged 65 and over
(iv)   women aged 60 and over
(v)   pregnant women
(vi)   women who have had a baby within the last 12 months
(vii)   people suffering from certain medical conditions
(viii) people who receive income support or family credit and their dependants
(ix)   people who receive disability working allowance with personal capital of £8,000 or less, and their partners
(x)   people who hold an AG2 certificate issued by the Health Benefits Unit, and their dependants
(xi)   war pensioners (for their accepted disablements)

Prepayment certificates (£27.20 valid for four months, £74.80 valid for a year) may be purchased by those patients not entitled to exemption who require frequent prescriptions. Further information about the exemption and prepayment arrangements is given in leaflet P11.

General Ophthalmic Services

General Ophthalmic Services, which are administered by FHSAs (unitary health authorities after 1 March 1996), form part of the ophthalmic services available under the NHS. The NHS sight test is available free to:

(i)   children under 16
(ii)   full-time students under the age of 19
(iii)   people in receipt of income support or family credit, and their partners
(iv)   people in receipt of disability working allowance with personal capital of £8,000 or less, and their partners
(v)   people prescribed complex lenses
(vi)   the registered blind and partially sighted
(vii)   diagnosed diabetic and glaucoma patients
(viii) close relatives aged 40 or over of diagnosed glaucoma patients

Those on a low income may qualify for help with the cost.

Certain groups are automatically entitled to help with the purchase of glasses under an NHS voucher scheme:

(i)   children under 16
(ii)   full-time students under 19
(iii)   people in receipt of income support or family credit, and their partners
(iv)   people in receipt of disability working allowance with personal capital of £8,000 or less, and their partners
(v)   people wearing certain complex lenses
(vi)   people whose spectacles are lost or damaged as a result of their disability, injury or illness

The value of the voucher depends on the lenses required. Vouchers may be used to help pay for the glasses or contact lenses of the patient's choice. People with a low income may claim help on form AG1. Glasses or contact lenses should not be purchased until the result of a claim is known as no refunds can be given. Booklet G11 gives further details.

Diagnosis and specialist treatment of eye conditions is available through the Hospital Eye Service as well as the provision of glasses of a special type.

Testing of sight may be carried out by any ophthalmic medical practitioner or ophthalmic optician. The optician must give the prescription, and a voucher if eligible, to the patient who can take this to any supplier of glasses of his/her choice to have dispensed. However, only registered opticians can supply glasses to children and to people registered as blind or partially sighted.

Primary Health Care Services

Primary health care services include the general medical, dental, ophthalmic and pharmaceutical services. They also include community services run by DHAs, health centres and clinics, family planning outside the hospital service, and preventive activities in the community including vaccination, immunization and fluoridation.

The district nursing and health visiting services include community psychiatric nursing for mentally ill people living outside hospital, and school nursing for the health surveillance of schoolchildren of all ages. Ante- and post-natal care and chiropody are also an integral part of the primary health care service.

COMMUNITY CHILD HEALTH SERVICES

Pre-school services at GP surgeries or child health clinics provide regular surveillance of children's physical, mental and emotional health and development, and advice to parents on their children's health and welfare.

The School Health Service provides for the medical and dental examination of schoolchildren, and advises the local education authority, the school, the parents and the pupil of any health factors which may require special consideration during the pupil's school life. GPs are increasingly undertaking child health surveillance to improve the preventive health care of children.

HOSPITALS AND OTHER SERVICES

The Secretary of State for Health has a duty to provide, to such extent as he/she considers necessary to meet all reasonable requirements, hospital and other accommodation; medical, dental, nursing and ambulance services; other facilities for the care of expectant and nursing mothers and young children; facilities for the prevention of illness and the care and after-care of persons suffering from illness; and such other services as are required for the diagnosis and treatment of illness. Rehabilitation services (occupational therapy, physiotherapy and speech therapy) may also be provided for those who need it and surgical and medical appliances are supplied in appropriate cases. NHS services and equipment should be free of charge unless current legislation on prescriptions states otherwise.

Specialists and consultants who work in the NHS can engage in private practice, including the treatment of their private patients in NHS hospitals. Any private work a consultant does is additional to NHS duties.

Trusts

The National Health Service and Community Care Act 1990 enables hospitals and other providers of health care to become independent of health authority control as self-governing NHS Trusts run by boards of directors. The Trusts derive their income principally from contracts to provide health services to health authorities and fund-holding general practitioners. As at April 1995 there were 433 trusts, representing the majority of hospitals in England.

Charges

In a number of hospitals, accommodation is available for the treatment of private in-patients who undertake to pay the full costs of hospital accommodation and services and (usually) separate medical fees to a specialist as well. The amount of the medical fees is a matter for agreement between doctor and patient. Hospital charges for private in-patients are set locally at a commercial rate.

Certain hospitals have accommodation in single rooms or small wards which, if not required for patients who need privacy for medical reasons, may be made available to patients who desire it as an amenity for a small charge. These patients are still NHS patients and are treated as such.

There is no charge for drugs supplied to NHS hospital in-patients but out-patients pay £5.25 an item unless they are exempt.

With certain exceptions, hospital out-patients have to pay fixed charges for dentures, contact lenses and certain appliances. Glasses may be obtained either from the hospital or an optician and the charge will be related to the type of lens prescribed and the choice of frame.

PERSONAL SOCIAL SERVICES

Local authorities are responsible for personal social services within their area. Each authority has a Director of Social Services and a Social Services Committee responsible for the social services functions placed upon them by the Local Authority Social Services Act 1970.

National Insurance and Related Cash Benefits

The state insurance and assistance schemes, comprising schemes of national insurance and industrial injuries insurance, national assistance, and non-contributory old age pensions came into force from 5 July 1948. The Ministry of Social Security Act 1966 replaced national assistance and non-contributory old age pensions with a scheme of non-contributory benefits. These and subsequent measures relating to social security provision in Great Britain were consolidated by the Social Security Act 1975; the Social Security (Consequential Provisions) Act 1975; and the Industrial Injuries and Diseases (Old Cases) Act 1975. Corresponding measures were passed for Northern Ireland. The Social Security Pensions Act 1975 introduced a new state pensions scheme in 1978, and the graduated pension scheme 1961 to 1975 has been wound up, existing rights being preserved. Under the Pensions Act 1995 the age of retirement is to be 65 for both men and women, this being phased in between 2010 and 6 April 2020. The Pensioners' Payments and Social Security Act 1979 provided for a £10 Christmas bonus for pensioners in 1979 and for the payment of a bonus in succeeding years at levels then to be determined. The Child Benefit Act 1975 replaced family allowances (introduced 1946) with child benefit and one parent benefit. Some of this legislation has been superseded by the provisions of the Social Security Acts 1968 to 1992.

NATIONAL INSURANCE SCHEME

The National Insurance (NI) scheme operates under the Social Security Contributions and Benefits Act 1992 and the Social Security Administration Act 1992, and orders and regulations made thereunder. The scheme is financed by contributions payable by earners, employers and others (such as non-employed persons paying voluntary contributions). It provides the funds required for paying the benefits payable under the Social Security Acts out of the National Insurance Fund and not out of other public money, and for the making of payments towards the cost of the National Health Service. In 1991 the Redundancy Fund was absorbed into the National Insurance Fund. The yearly Treasury supplement to the National Insurance Fund was abolished in 1989. A Treasury grant was introduced from 1993.

CONTRIBUTIONS

National Insurance contributions are of four classes:

CLASS 1 CONTRIBUTIONS

These are earnings-related, based on a percentage of the employee's earnings.

Primary Class 1 contributions are payable by employed earners and office-holders over age 16 with gross earnings at or above the lower earnings limit of £58.00 per week. Employees earning less than the lower earnings limit do not pay any contributions. For those with gross earnings at or above this level, contributions are payable on all earnings up to an upper limit of £440.00 per week. 'Gross earnings' include overtime pay, commission, bonus, etc., without deduction of any superannuation contributions. Contributions are paid at 2 per cent of earnings up to the lower earnings limit, plus contributions at a higher percentage on earnings between the lower earning limit and the employees' upper earnings limit. Employees contributing at the reduced rate continue to pay at that rate on earnings up to and including the employees' upper earnings limit.

Secondary Class 1 contributions are payable by employers of employed earners, and by the appropriate authorities in the case of office-holders. In 1985 the upper earnings limit for employers' contributions was abolished and secondary contributions are payable on all the employee's earnings if they reach or exceed £58.00 per week.

Women who marry for the first time no longer have a right to elect not to pay the full contribution rate. Married women and widows who before 12 May 1977 elected not to pay contributions at the full rate retain the right to pay a reduced rate over the same earnings range, which includes a contribution to the National Health Service. They lose this right if, after 5 April 1978, there are two consecutive tax years in which they receive no earnings on which primary Class 1 contributions are payable and in which they have not been at any time self-employed earners. No primary contributions are due on earnings paid for a period on or after the employee's pension age, even when retirement is deferred.

Primary contributions are deducted from earnings by the employer and are paid, together with the employer's contributions, to the Inland Revenue along with income tax collected under the PAYE system.

For the period 6 April 1995 to 5 April 1996 the earnings brackets determining Class 1 contributions are:

Earnings bracket	Weekly earnings
1	£58.00–104.99
2	105.00–149.99
3	150.00–204.99
4	205.00–440.00
5	over 440.00

CLASS 2 CONTRIBUTIONS

These are flat-rate, paid weekly by self-employed earners over age 16. Those with earnings below £3,260 a year for the tax year 1995–6 can apply for exemption from liability to pay Class 2 contributions. People who while self-employed are exempted from liability to pay contributions on the grounds of small earnings may pay either Class 2 or Class 3 contributions voluntarily. Self-employed earners (whether or not they pay Class 2 contributions) may also be liable to pay Class 4 contributions based on profits or gains within certain limits. There are special rules for those who are concurrently employed and self-employed.

Married women and widows can no longer choose not to pay Class 2 contributions. Those who elected not to pay Class 2 contributions before 12 May 1977 retain the right until there is a period of two consecutive tax years after 5 April 1978 in which they were not at any time either self-employed earners or had earnings on which primary Class 1 contributions were payable.

CLASS 3 CONTRIBUTIONS

These are voluntary flat-rate contributions payable by persons over age 16 who would otherwise be unable to qualify for retirement pension and certain other benefits because they have an insufficient record of Class 1 or Class 2 contributions. Married women and widows who on or before 11 May 1977 elected not to pay Class 1 (full rate) or Class 2 contributions cannot pay Class 3 contributions while they retain this right.

CLASS 4 CONTRIBUTIONS

These are payable by self-employed earners, whether or not they pay Class 2 contributions, on annual profits or gains from a trade, profession or vocation chargeable to income tax under Schedule D, where these fall between £6,640 and £22,880 a year. The maximum Class 4 contribution, payable on profits or gains of £22,880 or more, is £1,185.52.

Class 4 contributions are generally assessed and collected by the Inland Revenue along with Schedule D income tax. Self-employed persons under 16 or who at the beginning of a tax year are over pension age even where retirement is deferred, are not liable to pay Class 4 contributions. There are special rules for people who have more than one job or who pay Class 1 contributions on earnings which are chargeable to income tax under Schedule D.

Regulations state the cases in which earners may be exempted from liability to pay contributions, and the conditions upon which contributions are credited to persons who are exempted. Leaflet NI 208 is obtainable from local social security offices.

CONTRIBUTION RATES *from 6 April 1995 to 5 April 1996*
CLASS 1 CONTRIBUTIONS – EMPLOYEE'S RATES
Not Contracted Out

Earnings bracket	Percentage of reckonable income			
	On first £58.00		On earnings from £58.00–£440.00	
	standard	reduced	standard	reduced
1	2	3.85	10	3.85
2	2	3.85	10	3.85
3	2	3.85	10	3.85
4	2	3.85	10	3.85
5	*2	*3.85	*10	*3.85

*To a maximum of £440.00 per week

CLASS 1 CONTRIBUTIONS – EMPLOYEE'S RATES
Contracted Out (see also page 488)

Earnings bracket	On first £58.00		On earnings from £58.00–£440.00	
	standard	reduced	standard	reduced
1	2	3.85	8.2	3.85
2	2	3.85	8.2	3.85
3, 4, 5	2	3.85	8.2	3.85

CLASS 1 CONTRIBUTIONS – EMPLOYER'S RATES

Earnings bracket	On first £58.00	On earnings from £58.00–£440.00	On any earnings over £440.00
1	3.0	0.0	0
2	5.0	2.0	0
3	7.0	4.0	0
4	10.2	7.2	0
5	10.2	7.2	10.2

CLASS 2 CONTRIBUTIONS, £5.75 weekly flat rate

CLASS 3 CONTRIBUTIONS, £5.65

CLASS 4 CONTRIBUTIONS, 7.3% of profits or gains

The Social Security (Contributions) Act 1991 added a new class of contributions: 1A, payable in respect of car fuel by persons liable to pay secondary Class 1 contributions. It was effective from the 1991–2 tax year.

THE STATE EARNINGS RELATED PENSION SCHEME (SERPS)

The Social Security Pensions Act 1975, which came into force in 1978, aims to reduce reliance upon means-tested benefit in old age, in widowhood and in chronic ill-health by providing better pensions; to ensure that occupational pension schemes which are contracted out of part of the state scheme fulfil the conditions of a good scheme; that pensions are adequately protected against inflation; and that in both the state and occupational schemes men and women are treated equally.

Under the state earnings-related pension scheme, retirement, invalidity and widow's pensions for employees are related to the earnings on which NI contributions have been paid. For employees of either sex with a complete insurance record, the scheme provides a category A retirement pension in two parts, a basic and an additional pension. The basic pension corresponds to the old personal flat-rate national insurance pension. The additional pension is 1.25 per cent of average earnings between the lower weekly earnings limit for Class 1 contribution liability and the upper earnings limit for each year of such earnings under the scheme, and will thus build up to 25 per cent in twenty years. Retirement, widow's and invalidity pensions under the new scheme started to be paid in 1979. Since 1979 the basic retirement pension has been augmented for employed earners by the additional pension related to earnings, but it will be twenty years before these additional pensions become payable at the full rate.

The additional pension will be calculated in a different way for individuals who reach pension age after 6 April 1999. The changes are to be phased in over ten years. From 2010 a lifetime's earnings will be included in the calculation and for years from 1988–9 onwards the accrual rate on these surplus earnings will be 20 per cent. The accrual rate on surplus earnings for the years from 1978–9 to 1987–8 will remain at 25 per cent.

Actual earnings are to be revalued in terms of the earnings level current in the last complete tax year before pension age (or death or incapacity). Both components of pensions in payment will be uprated annually in line with the movement of prices. Graduated retirement pensions in payment, and rights to such pensions earned by people who are still working, will be brought into the annual review of benefits.

Self-employed persons pay contributions towards the basic pension. Employees with earnings below the lower limit and people not in employment may contribute voluntarily for basic pension. Although no primary Class 1 contributions or Class 2 or Class 4 contributions are payable by persons who work beyond pension age (65 for men, 60 for women), the employer's liability for secondary Class 1 contributions continues if earnings are at or above the lower earnings limit. Class 4 contributions are still payable up to the end of the tax year during which pension age is reached.

Widows will get the whole of any additional pensions earned by their husbands with their widowed mother's allowances or widow's pensions; and can add to the retirement pensions earned by their own contributions any additional pensions earned by their husbands up to the maximum payable on one person's contributions. Men whose wives die when they are both over pension age can add together their own and their wives' pension rights in the same way.

The scheme permits years of home responsibilities to reduce the number of qualifying years (since 1978) needed by women for retirement pension. The range of short-term social security benefits and industrial injury benefits under the Social Security Act 1975 continues with only minor changes.

CONTRACTED-OUT AND PERSONAL PENSION SCHEMES

Members of occupational pension schemes which meet the standards laid down in the Social Security Pensions Act 1975 or the Social Security Act 1986 can be contracted-out of the earnings-related part of the state scheme relating to retirement and widows' benefits.

Until 1988 occupational pension schemes could contract out only if they promised a pension that was related to earnings (a contracted-out salary-related scheme). They must provide a pension that is not less than the guaranteed minimum pension (GMP), which is broadly equivalent to the state earnings-related pension. Since 6 April 1988 occupational pension schemes which promise a minimum level of contributions (a contracted-out money purchase scheme) have also been able to contract out. They provide a pension based on the fund built up in the scheme over the years plus the results of the way they have been invested.

Since July 1988 employees whose employers do not provide a pension scheme have been able to start their own personal pension instead of staying in SERPS. Since 6 April 1988, this choice has been open to all employees even if their employer does have a pension scheme. A personal pension, like a contracted-out money purchase scheme, provides a pension based on the fund built up in the scheme over the years plus the results of the way they have been invested.

The decision on whether or not an occupational pension scheme may become contracted-out lies with the Occupational Pension Board, an independent statutory body which has a general responsibility for supervising contracting-out. They also consider and approve personal pension schemes which can be used instead of state additional pension.

The state earnings-related pension payable to a member of a contracted-out salary-related scheme, or his widow, will be reduced by the amount of GMP payable (which in the case of a widow must be at least half of the late husband's GMP entitlement). Members of contracted-out money purchase schemes and personal pension schemes, or their widows, have no GMP entitlement as such. But the state earnings-related pension payable will be reduced by an amount equivalent to a GMP (or widow's GMP).

Since 1988 contracted-out salary-related schemes must also provide a widower's GMP which must be at least half of the late wife's GMP entitlement built up from 6 April 1988. (A scheme need not provide entitlement to a GMP for widowers of earners dying before April 1989.) Contracted-out money purchase schemes and personal pension schemes must provide half-rate widower's benefit.

In contracted-out schemes, both the employee and the employer pay the full ordinary rate of contribution on the first £58.00 (1995–6 figure) of earnings but earnings above that amount attract a lower rate of contribution from the employee, and from the employer where the employee's earnings are under £440.00; where the employee's earnings exceed this amount, the full ordinary rate of contribution is payable only by the employer and the employee has no liability for contributions on these earnings (*see also* page 487).

An employee who chooses a personal pension in place of SERPS or their employer's pension scheme must pay NI contributions at the full ordinary rate (the employer's share must also be paid at the same rate). The DSS pays the difference between the lower contracted-out rate and the full ordinary rate directly into the personal pension scheme.

NATIONAL INSURANCE FUND

The National Insurance Fund receives all social security contributions (less only the National Health Service) and it bears the cost of all contributory benefits provided by the Social Security Acts and the cost of administration.

Approximate receipts and payments of the National Insurance Fund for the year ended 31 March 1994, were:

Receipts	£'000
Balance, 1 April 1993	3,436,244
Contributions under the Social Security Acts (net of SSP/SMP)	35,089,751
Treasury Grant	7,589,000
Compensation from Consolidated Fund for SSP/SMP recoveries	1,122,000
Income from investments	469,809
Other receipts	64,576
	47,771,380

Payments	£'000	£'000
Unemployment benefit	1,651,764	
Sickness benefit	365,000	
Invalidity benefit	7,067,828	
Maternity allowance	33,000	
Widow's benefit	1,040,000	
Guardian's allowance and child's special allowance	1,000	
Retirement pension	28,183,114	
Pensioners' lump sum payments	122,089	38,463,795
Personal pensions		2,859,527
Transfers to Northern Ireland		40,000
Administration		1,555,387
Other payments		35,045
Redundancy payments		268,974
Balance, 31 March 1994		4,548,652
		47,771,380

BENEFITS

The benefits payable under the Social Security Acts are as follows:

CONTRIBUTORY BENEFITS
Unemployment benefit
Incapacity benefit
Maternity allowance
Widow's benefit, comprising widow's payment, widowed mother's allowance and widow's pension
Retirement pensions, categories A and B

NON-CONTRIBUTORY BENEFITS
Child benefit
One parent benefit
Guardian's allowance
Invalid care allowance
Mobility allowance
Severe disablement allowance
Attendance allowance
Disability living allowance
Disability working allowance

Retirement pensions, categories C and D
Income support
Family credit
Social Fund

BENEFITS FOR INDUSTRIAL INJURIES, DISABLEMENT
AND DEATH

OTHER
Statutory sick pay
Statutory maternity pay

Leaflets relating to the various benefits and payments are obtainable from local social security offices.

The latest increases in benefit rates took effect from the week commencing 10 April 1995. It did not apply to all benefits.

CONTRIBUTORY BENEFITS

Entitlement to contributory benefits depends on contribution conditions being satisfied either by the claimant or by some other person (depending on the kind of benefit). The class or classes of contribution which for this purpose are relevant to each benefit are:

Unemployment benefit	Class 1
Incapacity benefit	Class 1 or 2
Maternity allowance	Class 1 or 2
Widow's benefits	Class 1, 2 or 3
Retirement pensions categories A and B	Class 1, 2 or 3

The system of contribution conditions relates to yearly levels of earnings on which contributions have been paid. The contribution conditions for different benefits are set out in leaflets available at local social security offices.

UNEMPLOYMENT BENEFIT

Benefit is payable in a period of interruption of employment for up to 312 days a year, excluding Sundays. Spells of unemployment and sickness not separated by more than eight weeks count as one period of interruption of employment. A person who has exhausted benefit requalifies when he/she has again worked as an employed earner for at least 16 hours a week for 13 weeks. These weeks need not be consecutive but must generally fall within 26 weeks prior to the date of the claim.

There are disqualifications from receiving benefit, e.g. for a period not exceeding 26 weeks if a person has lost their employment through misconduct, or has voluntarily left employment without just cause, or has, without good cause, refused an offer of employment or training.

INCAPACITY BENEFIT

Incapacity benefit replaced state sickness benefit and invalidity benefit on 13 April 1995. The new benefit has short-term and long-term elements. Short-term benefit consists of a lower rate payable for the first 28 weeks of sickness, and a higher rate payable after 28 weeks. Long-term benefit is payable after 52 weeks and is not payable after pension age. The terminally ill and those entitled to the highest rate care component of disability living allowance are able to get the long-term rate after 28 weeks rather than 52 weeks. Incapacity benefit is taxable after 28 weeks of incapacity. Sickness and invalidity benefit claimants were transferred to incapacity benefit on equivalent rates and special transitional arrangements apply.

Two rates of age addition are paid with long-term benefit based on the claimant's age when incapacity started. The higher rate is payable where incapacity for work commenced before the age of 35; and the lower rate where

incapacity commenced before the age of 45. Increases for dependents are also payable with short and long-term incapacity benefit.

A new medical test of incapacity for all work was introduced for incapacity benefit as well as other benefits paid on the basis of incapacity for work. The medical test normally applies after 28 weeks of incapacity for work and assesses ability to perform a range of work-related activities rather than the ability to perform a specific job. The new test applies to former sickness and invalidity benefit claimants.

MATERNITY BENEFIT

Statutory maternity pay (SMP) is administered by employers (*see* page 494). The state maternity allowance scheme covers women who are self-employed or otherwise do not qualify for SMP. The Maternity (Compulsory Leave) Regulations 1994 apply to both schemes and effectively prohibit women from working for two weeks after the date of childbirth.

A woman may qualify for maternity allowance (MA) if she has been working and paying contributions at the full rate for at least 26 weeks in the 66-week period which ends one week before the week the baby is due. She also has an element of choice in deciding when to stop work and receive MA, which is not payable for any period she works. Women employed at the 15th week before the baby is due will receive £52.50 per week for up to 18 weeks, and self-employed and unemployed women will receive £45.55 for up to 18 weeks.

WIDOW'S BENEFITS

Only the late husband's contributions of any class count for widow's benefit in any of its three forms:

Widow's payment – may be received by a woman who at her husband's death is under 60, or whose husband was not entitled to a Category A retirement pension when he died

Widowed mother's allowance – payable to a widow if she is entitled or treated as entitled to child benefit, or if she is expecting her husband's baby

Widow's pension – a widow may receive this pension if aged 45 or over at the time of her husband's death (40 or over if widowed before 11 April 1988) or when her widowed mother's allowance ends. If aged 55 or over (50 or over if widowed before 11 April 1988) she will receive the full widow's pension rate

Widow's benefit of any form ceases upon remarriage or during a period in which she lives with a man as his wife.

RETIREMENT PENSION: CATEGORIES A AND B

A Category A pension is payable for life to men or women on their own contributions if they are over pension age (65 for a man and 60 for a woman).

Where a person defers making a claim at 65 (60 for a woman) or later opts to be treated as if he/she had not made a claim, and does not draw a Category A pension, the weekly rate of pension is increased when he or she finally makes a claim or reaches the age of 70 (65 for a woman), in respect of weeks when pension is forgone during the five years after reaching minimum pension age. Details of the increase in the rate of pension due to deferred retirement are given in leaflet NP46, available at social security offices. If a married man defers his own Category A pension, his wife may defer receiving her Category B pension based on his contribution record. During this time she earns increments to the Category B pension, provided she does not claim retirement pension or graduated retirement benefit in her own right; increments are payable to her (and not her husband) when they both claim their pensions.

A Category B pension is normally payable for life to a woman on her husband's contributions when he has claimed, or is over 70, and has qualified for his own Category A pension, and she has reached 60. It is also payable on widowhood after 60 whether or not the late husband had retired and qualified for his own pension. The pension is payable at the rate of the increase for a wife while the husband is alive, and at the single person's rate on widowhood after 60. Where a woman is widowed before she reaches 60, a Category B pension is paid to her on reaching 60 at the same rate as her widow's pension if she claims. If a woman qualifies for a pension of each category she receives whichever pension is the larger.

The earnings rule, which stated that anyone who had qualified for pension would have it reduced if he or she earned more than a certain amount, was abolished in 1989. Where an adult dependant is living with the claimant, an adult dependants increase (£35.25) will only be payable if the dependant's earnings do not exceed the standard rate of unemployment benefit for a single person under pension-able age (see below). For the purpose of the dependency rule only, earnings will include payments by way of occupational or personal pension. The earnings of a separated spouse affect the increase of retirement pension if they exceed £35.25 a week.

Unemployment benefit is payable to men between 65 and 70, and women between 60 and 65 (65 and 70 from 2010) who have not claimed their retirement pension and who would have been entitled to a retirement pension if they had claimed at pension age. This applies in the case of incapacity benefit if incapacity for work is the result of an industrial accident or prescribed disease. These rates of benefit for people over pension age are shown in leaflet NI 196. A retirement pension will be increased by the amount of any invalidity allowance the pensioner was getting within the period of eight weeks and one day before reaching minimum pension age but this will be offset against any additional pension or GMP. An age addition of 25p per week is payable if a retirement pensioner is aged 80 or over.

GRADUATED RETIREMENT BENEFIT

Graduated NI contributions were first payable from 1961 and were calculated as a percentage of earnings between certain bands. They were discontinued in 1975. Any graduated pension which an employed person over 18 and under 70 (65 for a woman) had earned by paying graduated contributions will be paid when the contributor claims retirement pension or at 70 (65 for a woman), in addition to any retirement pension for which he or she qualifies.

Graduated retirement benefit is at the rate of 7.64p a week (April 1995) for each 'unit' of graduated contributions paid by the employee (half a unit or more counts as a whole unit). A unit of contributions is £7.50 for men and £9.00 for women of graduated contributions paid.

A wife can get a graduated pension in return for her own graduated contributions, but not for her husband's. A widow, or a widower whose wife died after 5 April 1979 when they were both over pensionable age, gets a graduated addition to his/her retirement pension equal to half of any graduated additions earned by his/her late spouse, plus any additions earned by his/her own gradu-ated contributions. If a person defers making a claim beyond 65 (60 for a woman) entitlement may be increased by one seventh of a penny per £1 of its weekly rate for each complete week of deferred retirement, as long as the retirement is deferred for a minimum of seven weeks.

WEEKLY RATES OF BENEFIT
from week commencing 10 April 1995

Unemployment benefit: standard rate

Person under pension age	£46.45
Increase for adult dependant	22.65
*Person over pension age	52.35
Increase for adult dependant	35.25

Short-term incapacity benefit

Person under pension age – lower-rate	44.40
*Person under pension age – higher rate	52.50
Increase for wife/other adult dependant	28.05
*Person over pension age	56.45
Increase for wife/other adult dependant	33.85

Long-term incapacity benefit

Person (under or over pension age)	58.85
Increase for wife/other adult dependant	35.25

Invalidity allowance: maximum amount payable

Higher rate	12.40
Middle rate	7.80
Lower rate	3.90

Maternity allowance

Employed	52.50
Self-employed or unemployed	45.55

Widow's benefits

Widow's payment (lump sum)	1,000.00
*Widowed mother's allowance	58.85
*Widow's pension	58.85

Retirement pension: categories A and B

Single person	58.85
Increase for wife/other adult dependant	35.25

*These benefits attract an increase for each dependent child (in addition to child benefit) of £9.85 for the first or only child and £11.05 for each subsequent child

NON-CONTRIBUTORY BENEFITS

CHILD BENEFIT

Child benefit is payable for virtually all children aged under 16, and for those aged 16 to 18 who are studying full-time up to and including A-level or equivalent standard. It is also payable for a short period if the child has left school recently and is registered for work or youth training at a careers office.

ONE PARENT BENEFIT

This benefit may be paid to a person in receipt of child benefit who is responsible for bringing up one or more children on his/her own. It is a flat rate non-means tested, non-contributory benefit payable for the eldest child.

GUARDIAN'S ALLOWANCE

Where the parents of a child are dead, the person who has the child in his/her family may claim a guardian's allowance in addition to child benefit. The allowance, in exceptional circumstances, is payable on the death of only one parent.

INVALID CARE ALLOWANCE

Invalid care allowance is payable to persons of working age who are not gainfully employed because they are regularly and substantially engaged in caring for a severely disabled person who is receiving attendance allowance, the middle or highest rate of disability living allowance or constant attendance allowance, paid at not less than the normal maximum rate, under the industrial injuries or war pensions schemes.

SEVERE DISABLEMENT ALLOWANCE

Persons of working age who have been continuously incapable of work for a period of at least 28 weeks but who do not qualify for contributory incapacity benefit may be entitled to severe disablement allowance. People who first become incapable of work after their 20th birthday must be at least 80 per cent disabled.

ATTENDANCE ALLOWANCE

This is payable to disabled people over 65 who need a lot of care or supervision because of physical or mental disability for a period of at least six months. People not expected to live for six months because of an illness do not have to wait six months. The allowance has two rates: the lower rate is for day or night care, and the higher rate is for day and night care.

DISABILITY LIVING ALLOWANCE

This is payable to disabled people under 65 who have personal care and mobility needs because of an illness or disability for a period of at least three months and are likely to need care for a further six months or more. People not expected to live for six months because of an illness do not have to wait three months. The allowance has two components: the care component, which has three rates, and the mobility component, which has two rates. The rates depend on the care and mobility needs of the claimant. The mobility component is payable only to those aged five or over.

DISABILITY WORKING ALLOWANCE

This is a tax-free, income-related benefit for people who are working 16 hours a week or more but have an illness or disability which puts them at a disadvantage in getting a job. To qualify a person must be aged 16 or over and must, at the date of the claim, have one of the 'qualifying benefits', such as disability living allowance. The amount payable depends on the size of the family and weekly income. The allowance is not payable if any savings exceed £16,000.

RETIREMENT PENSION: CATEGORIES C AND D

A Category C pension is provided, subject to a residence test, for persons who were over pensionable age on 5 July 1948, and for women whose husbands are so entitled if they are over pension age, with increases for adult and child dependants. A Category D pension is provided for others when they reach 80 if they are not already getting a retirement pension of any category or if they are getting that pension at less than these rates. An age addition of 25p per week is payable if persons entitled to retirement pension are aged 80 or over.

WEEKLY RATES OF BENEFIT
from week commencing 5 April 1995

Child benefit (first child)	£10.40
Each subsequent child	8.45
One-parent benefit	
First or only child of certain lone parents	6.30
Guardian's allowance (eldest child)	9.85
Each subsequent child	11.05
* Severe disablement allowance	
†Basic rate	35.55
Under 40	12.40
40–49	7.80
50–59	3.90
Increase for wife/other adult dependant	21.15
*Invalid care allowance	35.25
Increase for wife/other adult dependant	21.10

Attendance allowance	
Higher rate	£46.70
Lower rate	31.20
Disability living allowance	
Care component	
Higher rate	46.70
Middle rate	31.20
Lower rate	12.40
Mobility component	
Higher rate	32.65
Lower rate	12.40
Disability working allowance	
Single person	46.85
Couple or single parent	73.40
Child aged under 11	11.40
aged 11–15	18.90
aged 16–17	23.45
aged 18	32.80
‡Applicable amount (income threshold)	
Single person	54.75
Couple or single parent	73.00
Retirement pension: categories *C and D	
Single person	35.25
Increase for wife/other adult dependant	21.10
(not payable with Category D pension)	

*These benefits attract an increase for each dependent child (in addition to child benefit) of £9.85 for the first or only child and £11.05 for each subsequent child
†The age addition applies to the age when incapacity began
‡70 pence is deducted from the maximum DWA payable (this is obtained by adding up the appropriate allowance for each person in the family) for every pound coming in each week over the appropriate applicable amount. Where weekly income is below the applicable amount, maximum DWA is payable

INCOME SUPPORT

Income support is a benefit for those aged 18 and over (although certain vulnerable 16- and 17-year-olds may be eligible) whose income falls below set levels. Others who may be eligible include people who are over 60, bringing up children alone, unable to work through sickness or disability, caring for a disabled person, or unemployed or working part-time. Except in special cases income support is not available to those who work for more than 16 hours per week or who have a partner who works for more than 16 hours per week.

Income support is not payable if the claimant, or claimant and partner, have capital or savings in excess of £8,000. For capital or savings in excess of £3,000 a deduction of £1 is made for every £250, or part of £250, held.

Sums payable depend on fixed allowances laid down by law for people in different circumstances. If both partners are entitled to income support, either may claim it for the couple. People receiving income support may be able to receive housing benefit, help with mortgage or home loan interest and help with health care. They may also be eligible for help with exceptional expenses from the Social Fund. Leaflet IS20 gives a detailed explanation of income support.

Special rates may apply to some people living in residential care or nursing homes. Details are available from local social security offices.

INCOME SUPPORT PREMIUMS

Income support premiums are additional weekly payments for those with special needs. People qualifying for more than one premium will normally only receive the highest single premium for which they qualify. However, family premium, disabled child's premium, severe disability premium and carer premium are payable in addition to other premiums.

People with children qualify for a family premium if they have at least one child; a disabled child's premium if they have a child who receives disability living allowance or is registered blind; or a lone parent premium if they are bringing up one or more children alone. If someone receives invalid care allowance, they qualify for the carer premium.

Long-term sick or disabled people qualify for a disability premium if they or their partner are receiving certain benefits because they are disabled or cannot work; are registered blind; or if the claimant, but not their partner, is incapable of work or receiving statutory sick pay for at least 364 days (not broken by any period longer than 56 days), or 196 days if terminally ill. If someone is living alone and they are in receipt of attendance allowance, or disability living allowance at the middle or higher rate, without anyone receiving invalid care allowance for looking after them, they may qualify for a severe disability premium in addition to a disability premium.

People qualify for a pensioner premium if they or their partner are aged between 60 and 74, an enhanced pensioner premium if they or their partner are aged between 75 and 79, and a higher pensioner premium if they or their partner are aged 80 or over. A higher pensioner premium is also payable to people aged between 60 and 79 who receive attendance allowance, disability living allowance, long-term incapacity benefit or severe disablement allowance, or who are registered blind.

WEEKLY RATES OF BENEFIT
from week commencing 6 April 1995

Income support
Single people
aged 16–17	£28.00
aged 16–17 (certain circumstances)	36.80
aged 18–24	36.80
aged 25 and over	46.50
aged 18 and over and a single parent	46.50

Couples*
both under 18	55.55
both aged 18 or over	73.00

For each child in a family
under 11	15.95
aged 11–15	23.40
†aged 16–17	28.00
†aged 18 and over	36.80

Premiums
Family premium	10.25
Disabled child's premium	19.80
Lone parent premium	5.20
Disability premium	
Single	19.80
Couple	28.30
Severe disability premium	
Single	35.05
Couple (one person qualified)	35.05
Couple (both qualified)	70.10
Pensioner premium	
Single	18.60
Couple	28.05
Higher pensioner premium	
Single	25.15
Couple	35.95

Enhanced pensioner premium
Single	£20.70
Couple	30.95

*Where one or both partners are aged under 18, their personal allowance will depend on their situation
†If in full-time education up to A-level or equivalent standard

FAMILY CREDIT

Family credit is a tax-free benefit for working families with children. To qualify, a family must include at least one child under 16 (under 19 if in full-time education up to A-level or equivalent standard) and the claimant, or partner if there is one, must be working for at least 16 hours per week. It does not matter which partner is working and they may be employed or self-employed. The right to family credit does not depend on NI contributions and the same rates of benefit are paid to one- and two-parent families. Family credit is not payable if the claimant, or claimant and partner, have capital or savings in excess of £8,000. The rate of benefit is affected if capital or savings in excess of £3,000 are held. The rate of benefit payable depends upon the claimant's (and partner's) net income (excluding child benefit), number of children, and children's ages. Family credit, one parent benefit, and the first £15.00 of any maintenance in payment are paid for 26 weeks and the amount payable will usually remain the same throughout this period, regardless of change of circumstances. In certain cases where there are formal childcare arrangements for children under 11, costs of up to £40 per week will be taken into account. Up to £10 a week is paid to parents working 30 hours or more a week. Payment is made weekly via post offices or every four weeks directly into a bank or building society account. Family credit is claimed by post. A claim pack FC1 which includes a claim form can be obtained at a post office or social security office or call the Family Credit Helpline on 01253-500050. In two-parent families the woman should claim.

WEEKLY RATES OF BENEFIT
from week commencing 4 April 1995

The maximum amount will be payable where net income is no more than £73.00 a week. Where net income exceeds that amount, the maximum credit is reduced by 70 per cent of the excess and the result is the family credit payable. The maximum rate consists of:
Adult credit (for one or two parents)	£45.10
plus for each child	
aged under 11	11.40
aged 11–15	18.90
aged 16–17	23.45
aged 18	32.80

CLAIMS AND QUESTIONS

With a few exceptions, claims and questions relating to social security benefits are decided by statutory authorities who act independently of the Department of Social Security and Department of Employment.

The first of the statutory authorities, the Adjudication Officer, determines entitlement to benefit. A client who is dissatisfied with that decision has the right of appeal to an independent social security appeal tribunal. There is a further right of appeal to a Social Security Commissioner against the tribunal's decision but leave to appeal must first be obtained. Appeals to the Commissioner must be on a point of law. Provision is also made for the determination of certain questions by the Secretary of State for Social Services.

Disablement questions are decided by adjudicating medical authorities or medical appeal tribunals. Appeal to the Commissioner against a tribunal's decision is with leave and on a point of law only.

Leaflet NI246, which is available from social security offices, explains how to appeal, and leaflet NI260 is a guide to reviews and appeals.

THE SOCIAL FUND

The Social Fund helps people with expenses which are difficult to meet from regular income. Regulated maternity, funeral and cold weather payments are decided by Adjudication Officers and are cash-limited. Discretionary community care grants, and budgeting and crisis loans are decided by Social Fund Officers and come out of a yearly budget which is allocated to each district (1995–6, grants £97 million; loans £309 million).

REGULATED PAYMENTS

Maternity Payments

A payment of up to £100 for each baby expected, born or adopted. It is payable to people on income support, disability working allowance and family credit and is non-repayable.

Funeral Payments

Payable for reasonable funeral expenses incurred by people receiving income support, disability working allowance, family credit or housing benefit. It is recoverable from the estate of the deceased.

Cold Weather Payments

£8.50 for any consecutive seven days when the average temperature is 0°C or below. Paid to people on income support who are pensioners, disabled or parents with a child under the age of five. It is non-repayable.

DISCRETIONARY PAYMENTS

Community Care Grants

They are intended to help people on income support to move into the community or avoid institutional or residential care; ease exceptional pressures on families; and/or meet certain essential travelling expenses. They are usually non-repayable.

Budgeting Loans

These are interest-free loans to people who have been receiving income support for at least six months, for intermittent expenses that may be difficult to budget for.

Crisis Loans

These are interest-free loans to anyone, whether receiving benefit or not, who is without resources in an emergency, where there is no other means of preventing serious risk or damage to health or safety.

Loans are normally repaid over a period of up to 78 weeks at 15, 10 or 5 per cent of income support (less housing costs), depending on other commitments.

SAVINGS

Savings over £500 (£1,000 for people aged 60 or over) are taken into account for maternity and funeral payments,

community care grants and budgeting loans. All savings are taken into account for crisis loans.

APPEALS AND REVIEWS

For regulated payment there is a right of appeal to an independent Social Security Appeal Tribunal and thereafter to a Social Security Commissioner. For discretionary payments there is a review system where persons can ask for a review at the local office with a further right of review to an independent Social Fund Inspector.

INDUSTRIAL INJURIES, DISABLEMENT AND DEATH BENEFITS

The industrial injuries scheme, administered under the Social Security Contributions and Benefits Act 1992, provides a range of benefits designed to compensate for disablement resulting from an industrial accident (i.e. an accident arising out of and in the course of an employed earner's employment) or from a prescribed disease due to the nature of a person's employment. Rates of benefit are increased annually.

BENEFITS

Disablement benefit is normally payable 15 weeks (90 days) after the date of accident or onset of disease if the employed earner suffers from loss of physical or mental faculty such that the resulting disablement is assessed at not less than 14 per cent. The amount of disablement benefit payable varies according to the degree of disablement (in the form of a percentage) assessed by an adjudicating medical authority or medical appeal tribunal.

Disablement assessed at less than 14 per cent does not normally attract basic benefit except for certain chest diseases. A weekly pension is payable where the assessment of disablement is between 14 and 100 per cent (assessments of 14 to 19 per cent are payable at the 20 per cent rate). Payment can be made for a limited period or for life. The basic rates are applicable to adults and to juveniles entitled to an increase for a child or adult dependant; other juveniles receive lower rates.

Basic rates of pension are not related to the pensioner's loss of earning power, and are payable whether he/she is in work or not. There is provision for increases of pension if the pensioner requires constant attendance or if his/her disablement is exceptionally severe. A pensioner may draw statutory sick pay or incapacity benefit as appropriate, in addition to disablement pension, during spells of incapacity for work.

Regulations impose certain obligations on claimants and beneficiaries and on employers, including, in the case of claimants for disablement benefit, that of submitting themselves for medical examination.

SUPPLEMENTARY ALLOWANCES

Special schemes under the Industrial Injuries and Diseases (Old Cases) Act 1975 provide supplementary allowances to those entitled to receive weekly payments of workmen's compensation for loss of earnings due to injury at work, or disease contracted during employment before 5 July 1948 when the industrial injuries scheme was introduced. Other schemes under the Act provide allowances to those who contracted slowly-developing diseases during employment before July 1948 where neither workmen's compensation nor industrial injuries benefits are payable. A lump sum death benefit of up to £300 may also be payable to a dependant of such a person. Leaflet NI196 provides details relating to these allowances.

WEEKLY RATES OF BENEFIT
from 6 April 1995

*Disablement benefit/pension
Degree of disablement

100 per cent	£95.30
90	85.77
80	76.24
70	66.71
60	57.15
50	47.65
40	38.12
30	28.59
20	19.06
†Unemployability supplement	58.85
Addition for adult dependant (subject to earnings rule)	35.25
Reduced earnings allowance (maximum)	38.12
Constant attendance allowance (normal maximum rate)	38.20
Exceptionally severe disablement allowance	38.20

*There is a weekly benefit for those under 18 with no dependants which is set at a lower rate
†This benefit attracts an increase for each dependent child (in addition to child benefit) of £9.85 for the first child and £11.05 for each subsequent child

CLAIMS AND QUESTIONS

Provision is made for the determination of certain questions by the Secretary of State for Social Security, and of 'disablement questions' by a medical board (or a single doctor) or, on appeal, by a medical appeal tribunal. An appeal on a point of law against a medical appeal tribunal decision is determined by the Social Security Commissioner.

Claims for benefit and certain questions arising in connection with a claim for or award of benefit (e.g. whether the accident arose out of and in the course of the employment) are determined by an adjudication officer appointed by the Secretary of State, or a social security appeal tribunal, or in certain circumstances, on further appeal, by the Commissioners.

OTHER BENEFITS

STATUTORY SICK PAY

Employers usually pay statutory sick pay (SSP) to their employees for up to 28 weeks of sickness in any period of incapacity for work. SSP is paid at £52.50 a week and is subject to PAYE tax and NI deductions. Employees who cannot get SSP may be able to claim incapacity benefit. Employers can recover some SSP costs under the percentage threshold scheme where a large part of the workforce is off sick at the same time. Where SSP payments exceed 13 per cent of the employer's total NI liability for any tax month the employer can recover excess SSP paid above the 13 per cent threshold. Leaflet NI 244 is obtainable from local Social Security offices.

STATUTORY MATERNITY PAY

In general, employers pay statutory maternity pay to pregnant women who have been employed by them full or part-time for at least 26 weeks, and whose earnings are on average at least at the lower earnings limit for the payment of NI contributions. All women who meet these conditions receive payment of 90 per cent of their average earnings for six weeks, followed by a maximum of 12 weeks at £52.50. Women have some choice in deciding when to begin

maternity leave but SMP is not payable for any week in which work is done. Employers are reimbursed for 92 per cent of the SMP they pay (105 per cent for those whose annual NI liability is £20,000 or less).

War Pensions

The War Pensions Agency, an executive agency of the Department of Social Security (DSS), awards war pensions under The Naval, Military and Air Forces, Etc. (Disablement and Death) Service Pensions Order 1983 to members of the armed forces in respect of the periods 4 August 1914 to 30 September 1921 and subsequent to 3 September 1939 (including present members of the armed forces). There is also a scheme for civilians and civil defence workers in respect of the 1939–45 war, and other schemes for groups such as merchant seamen and Polish armed forces who served under British command.

War pensions for the period 1 October 1921 to 2 September 1939 are dealt with by the Ministry of Defence, which is also responsible for the Armed Forces Pension Scheme.

PENSIONS

War disablement pension is awarded for the disabling effects of any injury, wound or disease which is attributable to, or has been aggravated by, conditions of service in the armed forces. It cannot be paid until the serviceman or woman has left the armed forces.

Disablement is assessed by comparison of the disabled person's health with that of a normal, healthy person of the same age and sex, without taking into account the disabled person's earning capacity or occupation, and is expressed on a percentage scale up to 100 per cent. Disablement of 20 per cent and above, for which a pension is awarded, is assessed in steps of 10 per cent. Maximum assessment does not necessarily imply total incapacity. For assessment of less than 20 per cent a lump sum is usually payable. No award is made where disablement in respect of noise-induced sensorineural hearing loss is assessed at less than 20 per cent.

The dependency allowance in respect of a wife or child was abolished in 1992 and an equivalent amount incorporated into the basic war disablement pension.

War widow's pension is awarded where death occurs as a result of service or where a war disablement pensioner was receiving constant attendance allowance at the time of his death, or would have been receiving it if he were not in hospital, in which case his widow has automatic entitlement to a war widow's pension, regardless of the cause of death. Additional allowances are payable for dependent children, in addition to child benefit.

A lower weekly rate is payable to war widows of men below the rank of Lieutenant-Colonel who are under the age of 40, without children and capable of maintaining themselves. This is increased to the standard rate at age 40.

Rank additions to both disablement gratuities and widow's pensions may be paid where the rank held was above that of private (or equivalent).

SUPPLEMENTARY ALLOWANCES

A number of supplementary allowances may be awarded to a war pensioner which are intended to meet various needs, such as mobility, unemployability, constant nursing care, which may result from disablement or death and take account of its particular effect on the pensioner or spouse.

The principal supplementary allowances are:

Unemployability supplement – paid to a war pensioner whose pensioned disablement is so serious as to make him unemployable. An invalidity allowance may also be payable if the incapacity for work began more than five years before normal retirement age.

Allowance for lowered standard of occupation – awarded to a partially disabled pensioner whose pensioned disablement permanently prevents him from following his regular occupation. The allowance, together with the basic war disablement pension, must not exceed pension at the 100 per cent rate.

Constant attendance allowance – awarded if the pensioner is receiving a pension at the 80 per cent rate or more and needs care and attendance because of the disability. It is paid at one of four rates depending on how much care is needed.

Widow's child's allowance – paid in addition to child benefit.

Other supplementary allowances include exceptionally severe disablement allowance, severe disablement occupational allowance, treatment allowance, mobility supplement, comforts allowance, clothing allowance, age allowance, widow's age allowance, and education allowance. There is a rent allowance available on a war widow's pension.

Decisions on supplementary allowances are made on a discretionary basis and there is no provision for a statutory right of appeal against them. However, war pensioners may discuss any aspect of their pension position with their local war pensions committee, which may be able to arrange help or make representations to the DSS.

WAR PENSIONERS ABROAD

The DSS is responsible for the payment of war pensions, and, where necessary, meeting the cost of treatment for accepted disablement, to pensioners who reside overseas. They receive the same pension rates and annual upratings as war pensioners in this country.

SOCIAL SECURITY BENEFITS

Most social security benefits are paid in addition to the basic war disablement pension or war widow's pension. Any retirement pension for which a war widow qualifies on her own contributions, and any graduated retirement benefit or additional earnings-related pension inherited from her husband, can be paid in addition to her war widow's pension.

A war pensioner or war widow who claims income support, family credit or disability working allowance has the first £10 of pension disregarded. A similar provision operates for housing benefit and council tax benefit; but the local authority may, at its discretion, disregard any or all of the balance.

CLAIMS AND QUESTIONS

Where a claim in respect of death or disablement is made no later than seven years after the termination of service, the claimant does not have to prove that the disablement or death on which the claim is based is related to service and receives the benefit of any reasonable doubt. Where a claim in respect of death or disablement is made more than seven years after the termination of service the claimant has to show that disablement or death is related to service. However, the claim succeeds if reliable evidence is produced which raises a reasonable doubt whether or not disablement or death is related to service. There is no time limit for making a claim for war pension.

Independent pensions appeal tribunals hear appeals against the decisions of the DSS on entitlement and assessment of disablement in respect of the 1939–45 war

and subsequent service cases. There are no time limits within which an entitlement appeal must be made but there are time limits within which an assessment appeal should be made. However, there are now no rights of appeal in the 1914–21 war disablement cases, the great majority of which were given final assessment in the 1920s with a 12 months' right of appeal at the time. An appeal by a 1914 war widow must be made within twelve months of the date on which the rejection of the claim is notified.

WAR PENSIONERS WELFARE SERVICE

The DSS operates a war pensioners welfare service to advise and assist war pensioners and their widows on any matters affecting their welfare. Welfare officers are attached to war pensioners' welfare offices located in the major towns, and the service is available to any war pensioner or war widow who needs it.

The current rates of all war pensions and allowances are listed in WPA leaflet 9, *Rates of War Pensions and Allowances*, obtainable from war pensioners welfare service office, the Leaflets Unit, PO Box 21, Stanmore, Middx HA7 1AY, or by phoning the War Pension Helpline on 01253-858858.

WEEKLY RATES OF PENSIONS AND ALLOWANCES
from week commencing 10 April 1995

War disablement pension
Degree of disablement:

100 per cent	£101.10
90 per cent	90.99
80 per cent	80.88
70 per cent	70.77
60 per cent	60.66
50 per cent	50.55
40 per cent	40.44
30 per cent	30.33
20 per cent	20.22

Unemployability supplement

Personal allowance	62.45
Increase for wife/other adult dependant	35.25
Increase for first child	9.85
Increase for other children	11.05

Allowance for lowered standard of occupation

(maximum)	38.12

Widow's pension
(widow of Private or equivalent rank)

Standard rate	76.35
Increase for first child	14.00
Increase for other children	15.20
Childless widow under 40	17.66

Widow's age allowance

aged 65–69	8.70
aged 70–79	16.75
aged 80 and over	24.95

The Water Industry

ENGLAND AND WALES

In England and Wales the Secretaries of State for the Environment and for Wales have overall responsibility for water policy and set the environmental and health and safety standards for the water industry. The Director-General of Water Services, as the independent economic regulator, is responsible for ensuring that the private water companies are able to fulfil their statutory obligation to provide water supply and sewerage services, and for protecting the interests of consumers.

The Minister of Agriculture, Fisheries and Food and the Secretary of State for Wales are responsible for policy relating to land drainage, flood protection, sea defences and the protection and development of fisheries.

The National Rivers Authority is responsible for water quality and the control of pollution, the management of water resources and nature conservation. The Drinking Water Inspectorate and local authorities are responsible for the quality of drinking water.

THE WATER COMPANIES

Until 1989 nine regional water authorities in England and the Welsh Water Authority in Wales were responsible for water supply and the development of water resources, sewerage and sewage disposal, pollution control, freshwater fisheries, flood protection, water recreation, and environmental conservation. The Water Act 1989 provided for the creation of a privatized water industry under public regulation, and the functions of the regional water authorities were taken over by ten holding companies and the regulatory bodies.

Of the 99 per cent of the population of England and Wales who are connected to a public water supply, 75 per cent are supplied by the water companies (through their principal operating subsidiaries, the water service companies). The remaining 25 per cent are supplied by statutory water companies which were already in the private sector. Most of these have now converted to public limited company (PLC) status. The ten water service companies are also responsible for sewerage and sewage disposal in England and Wales.

Water Service Companies

ANGLIAN WATER SERVICES LTD, Compass House, Chivers Way, Histon, Cambs CB4 4ZY

DWR CYMRU (WELSH WATER), Cambrian Way, Brecon, Powys LD3 7HP

NORTHUMBRIAN WATER LTD, Abbey Road, Pity Me, Durham DHI 5FS

NORTH WEST WATER LTD, Dawson House, Liverpool Road, Great Sankey, Warrington WA5 3LW

SEVERN TRENT WATER LTD, 2297 Coventry Road, Sheldon, Birmingham B26 3PU

SOUTHERN WATER SERVICES LTD, Southern House, Yeoman Road, Worthing, W. Sussex BNI3 3NX

SOUTH WEST WATER SERVICES LTD, Peninsula House, Rydon Lane, Exeter EX2 7HR

THAMES WATER UTILITIES LTD, Nugent House, Vastern Road, Reading RGI 8DB

WESSEX WATER SERVICES LTD, Wessex House, Passage Street, Bristol BS2 0JQ

YORKSHIRE WATER SERVICES LTD, West Riding House, 67 Albion Street, Leeds LSI 5AA

REGULATORY BODIES

The Director-General of Water Services is appointed by the Secretaries of State for the Environment and for Wales. Independent of ministers and directly accountable to Parliament, his main duties are to ensure that the water companies can carry out and finance their statutory obligations and to protect the interests of water consumers. All the water companies are subject to a system of price control which sets a limit on the average increase in their prices each year. The Office of Water Services (*see* page 358) was set up to support the director-general's activities.

An independent national body, the National Rivers Authority (*see* page 332) took over the regulatory and river management functions of the regional water authorities. It has statutory duties and powers in relation to water resources, pollution control, flood defence, fisheries, recreation, conservation and navigation in England and Wales. The National Rivers Authority will be absorbed into the new Environment Agency which is to be set up in April 1996.

The Drinking Water Inspectorate (*see* page 302) is responsible for assessing the quality of the drinking water supplied by the water companies, inspecting the companies themselves and investigating any accidents affecting drinking water quality. The Chief Inspector presents an annual report to the Secretaries of State for the Environment and for Wales.

METHODS OF CHARGING

In England and Wales, most householders still pay for domestic water supply and sewerage services through charges based on the assessed value of their property under the old domestic rating system. Industrial and most commercial users are charged according to consumption, which is recorded by meter.

The Water Industry Act 1991 gives the water companies until 2000 to decide on and introduce a suitable method of charging. The main options under consideration are a flat-rate licence fee, property banding, and metering. The Government believes metering to be the best basis for payment. However, extension of the use of meters to all households will take considerable time to achieve. The Government has therefore decided to allow water companies to continue to use the old domestic rating system as a basis for their unmeasured charges after 2000.

SCOTLAND

Overall responsibility for national water policy in Scotland rests with the Secretary of State for Scotland. Most aspects of water policy are administered through the Scottish Office Environment Department, but fisheries and certain aspects of land drainage are the responsibility of the Scottish Office Agriculture and Fisheries Department.

Water supply and sewerage services are at present local authority responsibilities and are provided by the nine regional councils and the three islands councils.

The Central Scotland Water Development Board currently has the function of developing new sources of water supply for the purpose of providing water in bulk to water authorities whose limits of supply are within the board's area, i.e. Central, Fife, Lothian, Strathclyde and Tayside Regional Councils. The Local Government etc. (Scotland) Act 1994 provides for three new public water authorities, covering the north, east and west of Scotland respectively, to be established to take over the provision of water and sewerage services from 1 April 1996. From that date, the Central Scotland Water Development Board will be abolished. The Act also provides for a Scottish Water and Sewerage Customers Council to be established to represent consumer interests.

Seven river purification boards and the Islands Councils of Orkney, Shetland and the Western Isles have the specific duty of promoting the cleanliness of Scotland's rivers, lochs and coastal waters and conserving water resources. They are responsible for the prevention and control of pollution within their own areas. These responsibilities are expected to be transferred to the new Scottish Environment Protection Agency which is to be set up in April 1996.

CENTRAL SCOTLAND WATER DEVELOPMENT BOARD,
Balmore, Torrance, Glasgow G64 4AJ. *Director*,
W. G. Mitchell

METHODS OF CHARGING

Domestic consumers pay a council water charge or pay by water metering; sewerage services are paid for through the council tax. Non-domestic consumers pay non-domestic water rates or metered charges, and non-domestic sewerage rates. Charges and rates are currently set by each regional and islands council.

From 1 April 1996 the new water and sewerage authorities will set charges for their services in a charges scheme, or by agreement with the person using the service. Charges schemes will be subject to approval by the Scottish Water and Sewerage Customers Council. The new water and sewerage authorities will be required to publish a summary of their charges schemes.

NORTHERN IRELAND

In Northern Ireland ministerial responsibility for water services lies with the Secretary of State for Northern Ireland. The Department of the Environment for Northern Ireland, operating through the Water Executive, is responsible for policy and co-ordination with regard to supply, distribution and cleanliness of water, and the provision and maintenance of sewerage services.

The Water Executive is divided into four regions, the Eastern, Northern, Western and Southern Divisions. These are based in Belfast, Ballymena, Londonderry and Craigavon respectively. The Water Executive will become an executive agency in April 1996.

On major issues the Department of the Environment for Northern Ireland seeks the views of the Northern Ireland Water Council, a body appointed to advise the Department on the exercise of its water and sewerage functions. The Council includes representatives from agriculture, angling, industry, commerce, tourism, trade unions and local government.

METHODS OF CHARGING

Usually householders do not pay separately for water and sewerage services; the costs of these services are allowed for in the Northern Ireland regional rate. Water consumed by industry, commerce and agriculture in excess of 100 cubic metres (22,000 gallons) per half year is charged through meters. Traders operating from industrially derated premises are required to pay for the treatment and disposal of the trade effluent which they discharge into the public sewerage system.

Energy

THE COAL INDUSTRY

Coal has been mined in Britain for centuries and the availability of coal was crucial to the industrial revolution of the 18th and 19th centuries. Mines were in private ownership until 1947 when they were nationalized and came under the management of the National Coal Board (latterly the British Coal Corporation). In addition to producing coal at its own deep-mine and opencast sites, British Coal was responsible for licensing private operators.

Privatization

Under the Coal Industry Act 1994, a new body, the Coal Authority, was established to take over ownership of coal reserves and to issue licences to private mining companies as part of the privatization of British Coal. The Coal Authority will also deal with the physical legacy of mining, e.g. subsidence damage claims, and is responsible for holding and making available all existing records.

The Government offered the mines for sale in five businesses based in the separate regions of Scotland, Wales and the North-East and two based on the central areas of the Midlands and Yorkshire. All five businesses have been sold, the three businesses in England being sold to a single purchaser as one company. Coal production in the UK is now undertaken entirely in the private sector.

Supply and Demand

The main domestic customer for coal is the electricity supply industry, but the latter's demand for coal has declined as it has turned increasingly to alternative fuels. In the first ten months of 1993, the amount of coal consumed at power stations was 15.7 per cent less than during the corresponding period in 1992. National Power has announced that it expects to close ten of its 18 coal-fired power stations by 2000.

Supply 1993	million tonnes
Production of deep-mined coal	50.5
Production of opencast coal	17.0
Recovered slurry, fines, etc.	0.7
Imports	18.4
Change in colliery stocks	+1.3
Change in stocks at opencast sites	+0.5
Total supply	84.8

Home consumption 1993	
Electricity supply industry	66.2
Coke ovens	8.5
Low temperature carbonization plants	0.5
Manufactured fuel plants	0.8
Railways	—
Collieries	—
Industry	5.3
Domestic	4.6
Public services	0.6
Miscellaneous	0.2
Total home consumption	86.8
Overseas shipments and bunkers	0.7
Total consumption and shipments	87.5
*Change in distributed stocks	−3.6
†Balance	0.9

*Stock change excludes industrial and domestic stocks
†This is the balance between supply and consumption, shipments and changes in known distributed stocks
Source: HMSO – Annual Abstract of Statistics 1995

THE GAS INDUSTRY

The gas industry in the United Kingdom was nationalized in 1949 under the Gas Act 1948, and operated as the Gas Council. The Gas Act 1972 replaced the Gas Council with the British Gas Corporation and led to greater centralization of the industry. The British Gas Corporation was privatized in 1986 as British Gas PLC and is currently the main supplier of gas in Great Britain. The Office of Gas Supply (see page 306) is the regulatory body for the gas industry.

In 1993 the Monopolies and Mergers Commission found that British Gas's integrated business in Great Britain as a gas trader and the owner of the gas transportation system was against the public interest, and it recommended that the company divest itself of its gas supply business in Great Britain. The President of the Board of Trade announced that competition would be introduced into the domestic gas supply market in April 1996, and that British Gas should separate fully its supply and transportation operations; it would not be required to divest itself of its supply business. The Government plans a phased introduction of competition into the domestic gas market. The first tranche of liberalization will take place in April 1996 when a pilot project involving 500,000 customers in Cornwall, Devon and Wales will be implemented. The second tranche will commence in April 1997, when competition will be extended to cover two million customers. In April 1998 competition will be extended to cover all customers.

Fuel Input and Gas Output: Gas Sales 1993

Fuel input to gas industry	GWh
Petroleum (million tonnes)	—
*Petroleum gases	50
Natural gas	—
Coke oven gas	—
Total to gas works	50
Natural gas for direct supply	701,272
Total fuel input	701,322

Gas output and sales	
Gas output:	
Town gas	32
Natural gas supplied direct	701,272
Gross total available	701,304
Own use	−2,930
†Statistical difference	−30,104
Total sales	668,270

*Butane, propane, ethane and refinery tail gases
†Supply greater than recorded demand (−). Includes losses in distribution
Source: HMSO – Annual Abstract of Statistics 1995

NATURAL GAS CONSUMPTION 1994

	GWh
Domestic	329,541
Electricity generators	116,016
Iron and steel industry	16,570
Other industries	153,595
Other	95,407
Total	711,129

Source: Department of Trade and Industry

BRITISH GAS PLC

The principal business of British Gas is the purchase, transmission and sale of natural gas to domestic, industrial and commercial customers in Great Britain. It is increasingly seeking to exploit overseas markets. British Gas has hydrocarbon exploration and production operations offshore and onshore, both in Great Britain and overseas, and it has an interest in gas-related activities world-wide.

British Gas is divided into three parts: the UK Gas Business, Exploration and Production, and International Downstream. In 1994 it restructured its UK operations to separate its gas supply business from its gas transportation business. Its regional structure was abolished and replaced by five business units: TransCo, which provides transportation and storage services to shippers; Public Gas Supply, which sells gas to domestic and other customers using less than 2,500 therms per year; Business Gas, which sells gas to industrial and commercial customers using more than 2,500 therms per year; Retail, which markets gas appliances through a national chain of shops; and Service, which handles the servicing and installation of gas central heating and other equipment.

BRITISH GAS PLC, Rivermill House, 152 Grosvenor Road, London SW1V 3JL. Tel: 0171-821 1444. *Chairman,* R. V. Giordano; *Chief Executive,* C. H. Brown, FEng.

SUPPLY AND TRANSMISSION

British Gas obtains natural gas from fields on mainland Britain, in coastal waters and in the North Sea. It also imports gas from other countries. In 1993 total production of gas from UK continental shelf fields was 352.2 billion cubic feet; in 1994 total production was 350.3 billion cubic feet.

The mainland national transmission system is operated by British Gas, with other gas suppliers entering contracts to use the system. British Gas operates five reception terminals; a sixth is to be commissioned in 1996. The length of mains in use in 1994 was 267,300 km: 249,300 km of distribution mains and 18,000 km of transmission mains.

CHARGES FOR DOMESTIC USE *from 1 January 1995*

Standing charge per day	pence
Standard	10.39
Paid by direct debit	10.10
Unit charges	pence per kilowatt hour
Annual consumption	
First 73,200 KWh (standard)	1.520
First 73,200 KWh (paid by direct debit)	1.433
73,201–146,536 KWh	1.420
146,537–293,071 KWh	1.380
293,072–732,678 KWh	1.340

BRITISH GAS FINANCE
£ million

	1993	1994
Turnover		
UK gas supply	8,055	7,623
*Overseas gas supply	965	669
Exploration and production	1,219	1,161
UK marketing activities	763	733
Other activities	238	342
Less: intra-group sales	(854)	(830)
Total	10,386	9,698
Operating costs include:		
Raw materials and consumables	3,601	3,397
Employee costs	1,701	1,675
Exceptional costs	1,683	195
Current cost depreciation	1,078	1,146
Total	10,701	8,711
Current cost operating profit (loss)	(366)	1,020
Gearing adjustment	65	67
Net interest payable	(298)	(184)
Current cost profit (loss) before tax	(569)	918
Current cost profit (loss) after tax	(537)	414
Minority shareholders' interest	3	(4)
Current cost profit (loss) attributable to British Gas shareholders	(534)	410
Dividends	(628)	(631)
Transfer from reserves	(1,162)	(221)

* Discontinued June 1994

THE ELECTRICITY SUPPLY INDUSTRY

Under the Electricity Act 1989 twelve public electricity supply companies were formed from the twelve area electricity boards in England and Wales; the companies were floated on the stock market in 1990. Four companies were formed from the Central Electricity Generating Board: three generating companies (National Power PLC, Nuclear Electric PLC and PowerGen PLC) and the National Grid Company PLC. National Power PLC and PowerGen PLC were floated on the stock market in 1991, the Government retaining a 40 per cent holding in both companies. In 1995 a second flotation took place when the Government sold its remaining 40 per cent holding in the two companies.

In Scotland, three new companies were formed: Scottish Power PLC, Scottish Hydro-Electric PLC and Scottish Nuclear Ltd. Flotation of Scottish Power PLC and Scottish Hydro-Electric PLC on the stock market took place in 1991.

In Northern Ireland, Northern Ireland Electricity PLC was set up in 1993 under a 1991 Order in Council. It has been floated on the stock market.

A trade and representational organization, the Electricity Association, was created by the newly formed electricity companies; its principal subsidiaries were Electricity Association Services Ltd (for representational and professional services) and Electricity Association Technology Ltd (for distribution and utilization research, development and technology transfer). Electricity Association Technology Ltd (now renamed EA Technology Ltd) left the Electricity Association group of companies in 1993.

The Offices of Electricity Regulation (*see* page 300) are the regulatory bodies for the industry.

ELECTRICITY ASSOCIATION SERVICES LTD, 30 Millbank, London SW1P 4RD. Tel: 0171-344 5700. *Chief Executive,* P. E. G. Daubeney
EA TECHNOLOGY LTD, Capenhurst, Chester CH1 6ES. Tel: 0151-339 4181. *Managing Director,* Dr S. F. Exell

SUPPLY COMPANIES

THE NATIONAL GRID COMPANY PLC, National Grid House, Kirby Corner Road, Coventry CV4 8JY. Tel: 01203-537777. *Chief Executive,* D. Jones
NATIONAL POWER PLC, Windmill Hill Business Park, Whitehill Way, Swindon, Wilts SN5 9NX. Tel: 01793-877777. *Chief Executive,* K. Henry
NUCLEAR ELECTRIC PLC, Barnett Way, Barnwood, Glos GL4 7RS. Tel: 01452-652222. *Chairman,* J. Collier
POWERGEN PLC, 53 New Broad Street, London EC2M 1JJ. Tel: 0171-638 5742. *Chief Executive,* E. Wallis

REGIONAL ELECTRICITY COMPANIES

EASTERN ELECTRICITY PLC, PO Box 40, Wherstead, Ipswich IP2 9AQ
EAST MIDLANDS ELECTRICITY PLC, PO Box 4 North PDO, 398 Coppice Road, Arnold, Nottingham NG5 7HX
LONDON ELECTRICITY PLC, Templar House, 8187 High Holborn, London WC1V 6NU
MANWEB PLC, Sealand Road, Chester CH1 4LR
MIDLANDS ELECTRICITY PLC, Mucklow Hill, Halesowen, W. Midlands B62 8BP
NORTHERN ELECTRIC PLC, Carliol House, Newcastle upon Tyne NE99 1SE
NORWEB PLC, Talbot Road, Manchester M16 0MQ
SEEBOARD PLC, Forest Gate, Brighton Road, Crawley, W. Sussex RH11 9BH
SOUTHERN ELECTRIC PLC, Littlewick Green, Maidenhead, Berks SL6 3QB
SWALEC PLC, St Mellons, Cardiff CF3 9XW
SOUTH WESTERN ELECTRICITY PLC, 800 Park Avenue, Aztec West, Almondsbury, Avon BS12 4SE
YORKSHIRE ELECTRICITY GROUP PLC, Scarcroft, Leeds LS14 3HS

SCOTTISH COMPANIES

SCOTTISH HYDRO-ELECTRIC PLC, 16 Rothesay Terrace, Edinburgh EH3 7SE. Tel: 0131-225 1361. *Chief Executive,* R. Young
SCOTTISH NUCLEAR LTD, 3 Redwood Crescent, Peel Park, East Kilbride G74 5PR. Tel: 0135 52-66266. *Chief Executive,* Dr R. C. Jeffrey
SCOTTISH POWER PLC, 1 Atlantic Quay, Glasgow G2 8SP. Tel: 0141-248 8200. *Chief Executive,* I. Robinson

NORTHERN IRELAND

NORTHERN IRELAND ELECTRICITY PLC, PO Box 2, Danesfort, 120 Malone Road, Belfast BT9 5HT. Tel: 01232–661100. *Chief Executive,* Dr P. Haren

GENERATION, SUPPLY AND CONSUMPTION
gigawatt-hours

	1992	1993
Electricity generated		
All generating companies: total	320,961	323,030
Conventional steam stations	232,277	202,651
Nuclear stations	76,807	89,353
Gas turbines and oil engines	358	359
Combined cycle gas turbine stations	3,400	23,418
Hydro-electric stations:		
Natural flow	5,383	4,249
Pumped storage	1,697	1,437
Renewables other than hydro	1,041	1,562

Electricity used on works: total	20,235	19,289
Major generating companies	18,485	17,391
Other generators	1,750	1,898
Electricity supplied (gross)		
All generating companies: total	300,726	303,741
Conventional steam stations	219,930	192,148
Nuclear stations	69,135	80,979
Gas turbines and oil engines	311	324
Combined cycle gas turbine stations	3,358	23,195
Hydro-electric stations:		
Natural flow	5,364	4,236
Pumped storage	1,635	1,388
Renewables other than hydro	993	1,470
Electricity used in pumping		
Major power producers	2,257	1,948
Electricity supplied (net): total	298,469	301,793
Major power producers	279,435	281,175
Other generators	19,034	20,618
Net imports	16,694	16,716
Electricity available	315,163	318,509
Losses in transmission, etc	23,710	23,366
Electricity consumption: total	291,453	295,143
Fuel industries	9,984	9,397
Final users: total	281,468	285,746
Industrial sector	95,277	96,246
Domestic sector	99,482	100,405
Other sectors	86,711	89,095

Source: HMSO – *Annual Abstract of Statistics 1995*

Transport

TOTAL TONNE KILOMETRES (*millions*)	210,930
Road	134,500
Rail (British Rail only)	13,730
Water: coastwise oil products*p	28,800
Water: other*p	22,300
Pipelines (except gases)	11,600
TOTAL (*million tonnes*)	1,984
Road	1,615
Rail (British Rail only)	109
Water: coastwise oil products*p	42
Water: other*p	93
Pipelines (except gases)	125

p provisional
*'Coastwise' includes all sea traffic within the UK, Isle of Man and Channel Islands. 'Other' means other coastwise plus inland waterway traffic and one-port traffic
Source: HMSO – *Annual Abstract of Statistics 1995*

PASSENGER TRANSPORT 1993p
Million passenger kilometres (estimated)

TOTAL	671,000
Air	5,000
Rail*	37,000
Road: Public service vehicles	42,000
Cars, vans and taxis	577,000
Motorcycles	5,000
Pedal cycles	5,000

p provisional
*Including London Regional Transport and Passenger Transport Executive railway systems
Source: HMSO – *Annual Abstract of Statistics 1995*

AIR PASSENGERS 1994*

ALL UK AIRPORTS: TOTAL	123,942,573
LONDON AREA AIRPORTS: TOTAL	78,522,255
Battersea Heliport	4,942
Gatwick	21,208,398
Heathrow	51,720,996
London City	479,020
Luton	1,824,463
Southend	834
Stansted	3,288,544
OTHER UK AIRPORTS: TOTAL	45,415,376
Aberdeen	2,185,582
Barra	5,193
Barrow-in-Furness	473
Belfast International	2,057,791
Belfast City	1,229,508
Benbecula	37,966
Biggin Hill	11,026
Birmingham	4,943,189
Blackpool	80,397
Bournemouth	118,411

Bristol	1,297,448
Cambridge	32,139
Cardiff	1,032,276
Carlisle	1,109
Coventry	3,371
Dundee	22,225
East Midlands	1,622,636
Edinburgh	3,116,559
Exeter	203,360
Glasgow	5,595,977
Gloucestershire	4,574
Hawarden	139
Humberside	262,893
Inverness	280,274
Islay	20,919
Isle of Man	532,526
Isles of Scilly–St Mary's	110,011
–Tresco	22,941
Kent International	6,510
Kirkwall	105,800
Leeds/Bradford	815,468
Lerwick (Tingwall)	4,481
Liverpool	442,318
Londonderry	33,671
Lydd	212
Manchester	14,569,740
Newcastle	2,458,969
Norwich	215,835
Penzance Heliport	88,855
Plymouth	94,253
Prestwick	137,787
Scatsta	12,270
Shoreham	2,774
Southampton	483,723
Stornoway	94,053
Sumburgh	476,194
Teesside	408,552
Tiree	7,896
Unst	86,963
Wick	38,139
CHANNEL IS. AIRPORTS: TOTAL	2,578,830
Alderney	84,126
Guernsey	822,918
Jersey	1,671,786

*Total terminal, transit, scheduled and charter passengers
Source: Civil Aviation Authority

AERODROMES/AIRPORTS

The following aerodromes in the UK, the Isle of Man and the Channel Islands are either state owned or licensed for use by civil aircraft. A number of unlicensed aerodromes not included in this list are also available for private use by special permission. Aerodromes designated as Customs airports are printed in small capitals. Customs facilities are available at certain other aerodromes by special arrangement.

BAA   Owned by BAA PLC
H   Licensed for helicopters
HIAL   Operated by Highland and
       Islands Airports Ltd
L   Owned by municipal
       authority
M   Military aerodromes – civil
       availability by prior
       permission
P   Private ownership
S   Government owned and
       operated

ENGLAND AND WALES

Aberporth, Dyfed   M
Andrewsfield, Essex
Barrow (Walney Island), Cumbria
Bembridge, IOW
Benson, Oxon   M
Beverley/Linley Hill,
   N. Humberside
BIGGIN HILL, Kent   P
BIRMINGHAM   P
Blackbushe, Hants
BLACKPOOL, Lancs   P
Bodmin, Cornwall
Boscombe Down, Wilts   M
Bourn, Cambridge
BOURNEMOUTH, Dorset   P
BRISTOL   P
Brize Norton, Oxford   M
Brough, N. Humberside
Caernarfon, Gwynedd
CAMBRIDGE   P
CARDIFF   P
Carlisle, Cumbria   L
Chichester (Goodwood), Sussex
Chivenor, Devon   M
Church Fenton, N. Yorks   M
Clacton, Essex
Compton Abbas, Dorset
Cosford, Wolverhampton   M
COVENTRY, W. Midlands   L
Cranfield, Beds
Cranwell, Lincs   M
Crowfield, Suffolk
Culdrose, Cornwall   M
Deenethorpe, Northants
Denham, Bucks
Derby
Dishforth, N. Yorks   M
Dunkeswell, Devon
Dunsfold, Surrey   L
Duxford, Cambs   L
Eaglescott, Devon
Earls Colne, Halstead

EAST MIDLANDS, Derbys   P
Elstree, Herts
EXETER, Devon
Fairoaks, Surrey
Farnborough, Hants   S
Fenland, Lincs
Filton, Bristol
Finningley, S. Yorks   M
Fowlmere, Cambs
Full Sutton, N. Yorks
Gloucestershire (Staverton)   P
Great Yarmouth (North Denes),
   Norfolk   H
Halfpenny Green, Staffs
Halton, Bucks   M
Haverfordwest, Dyfed   L
Hawarden, Clwyd
Hucknall, Notts
HUMBERSIDE   P
Ipswich, Suffolk
Isle of Wight/Sandown
Land's End (St Just), Cornwall
Lashenden, Headcorn, Kent
LEEDS/BRADFORD   P
Lee-on-Solent, Hants   M
Leicester
Linton-on-Ouse, Yorks   M
Little Gransden, Beds
LIVERPOOL   P
Llanbedr, Gwynedd   M
LONDON/CITY
LONDON/GATWICK   BAA
LONDON/HEATHROW   BAA
LONDON/LUTON   P
LONDON/STANSTED   BAA
London/Westland Heliport   H
LYDD, Kent
Lyneham, Wilts   M
MANCHESTER   P
Manchester (Barton)
MANSTON/KENT
   INTERNATIONAL   M
Marston Moor, York
Mona, Gwynedd   M
Netherthorpe, S. Yorks
NEWCASTLE UPON TYNE   P
Newton, Notts   M
Northampton (Sywell)
Northolt, Middx   M
NORWICH, Norfolk   L
Nottingham
Old Sarum, Wilts
Oxford (Kidlington)
Penzance, Cornwall   H
Perranporth, Cornwall
Peterborough (Conington)
Peterborough (Sibson)
PLYMOUTH (ROBOROUGH), Devon
Portland Naval, Dorset   MH
Redhill, Surrey
Retford/Gamston, Notts
Rochester, Kent
St Mawgan, Cornwall   M
Sandtoft, Humberside
Scilly Isles (St Mary's)   L
Seething, Norfolk
Shawbury, Shropshire   M
Sherburn-in-Elmet, N. Yorks
Shipdham, Norfolk
Shobdon, Herefordshire
SHOREHAM, W. Sussex   P
Silverstone, Northants

Sleap, Shropshire
SOUTHAMPTON   P
SOUTHEND, Essex   P
Stapleford, Essex
Sturgate, Lincs
Swansea, W. Glam   L
TEESSIDE, Cleveland   P
Thruxton, Hants
Tresco, Isles of Scilly   H
Turweston, Northants
Valley, Gwynedd   M
Warton, Lancs
Wattisham, Suffolk   M
Wellesbourne Mountford, Warwick
Welshpool, Powys
Weston, Avon   H
White Waltham, Berks
Wickenby, Lincs
Woodford, Gtr Manchester
Woodvale, Merseyside   M
Wycombe Air Park (Booker), Bucks
Yeovil, Somerset
Yeovilton, Somerset   M

SCOTLAND

ABERDEEN (DYCE)   BAA
Barra, Hebrides
Benbecula, Hebrides   HIAL
Cumbernauld, Strathclyde
Dundee   L
Eday, Orkneys   L
EDINBURGH   BAA
Fair Isle, Shetlands
Fife   L
Flotta, Orkneys
GLASGOW   BAA
Inverness (Dalcross)   HIAL
Islay (Port Ellen), Hebrides   HIAL
Kirkwall, Orkneys   HIAL
Lerwick (Tingwall), Shetlands   L
Leuchars, Fife   M
Machrihanish, Kintyre   M
North Ronaldsay, Orkneys   L
Papa Westray, Orkneys   L
Perth (Scone)
PRESTWICK, Ayrshire   BAA
Sanday, Orkneys   L
Scatsta, Shetlands
Stornoway, Hebrides   HIAL
Stronsay, Orkneys   L
SUMBURGH, Shetlands   HIAL
Tiree, Hebrides   HIAL
Unst, Shetlands   L
West Freugh, Dumfries   S
Westray, Orkneys   L
Whalsay, Shetlands
Wick, Caithness   HIAL

NORTHERN IRELAND

BELFAST (ALDERGROVE)
Belfast (City)
Enniskillen (St Angelo), Co.
   Fermanagh   P
Londonderry (Eglinton)   L
Newtownards, Co. Down

ISLANDS

ALDERNEY, CI   S
GUERNSEY, CI   S
ISLE OF MAN   S
JERSEY, CI   S

RAILWAYS

Britain pioneered railways and a railway network was developed across Britain by private companies in the course of the 19th century. In 1948 the main railway companies were nationalized and were run by a public authority, the British Transport Commission. The Commission was replaced by the British Railways Board in 1963. On 1 April 1994 the British Railways Board ceased to be responsible for the provision of rail services in Britain but continues as operator (under the operating name British Rail) of all train services until they are sold or franchised to the private sector.

Prior to privatization, management of the railways had been organized into the business sectors of InterCity, Network SouthEast, Regional Railways, Trainload Freight and Railfreight Distribution. These businesses have ceased to exist corporately but the names will continue to be used for trading purposes in the short term. European Passenger Services Ltd was set up to manage international passenger rail services through the Channel Tunnel and ownership was transferred to the Government in May 1994.

PRIVATIZATION

Since 1 April 1994, ownership of track and land has been vested in Railtrack, a government-owned company. Railtrack manages the track and charges for access to it and is responsible for signalling and timetabling. It does not operate train services. It owns the freehold of stations, but station management is being privatized under management contract or lease arrangements. Initially, Railtrack's infrastructure support functions are being provided by 30 British Rail service companies; these companies will be restructured and privatized. Railtrack will invest in infrastructure principally using finance raised by track charges, and will take investment decisions in consultation with rail operators. Railtrack itself will eventually be privatized.

Passenger services have been divided into 25 train-operating units, which will be run by British Rail as 'shadow' franchises before gradually being franchised to private sector operators. The private sector will also be able to run completely new services with a right of open access to the track. The Government will continue to subsidize loss-making but socially necessary rail services. The new franchising director is responsible for awarding franchises by competitive tendering, monitoring the performance of the franchisees, and allocating and administering government subsidy payments.

The first three franchises (Great Western, South West Trains, and London, Tilbury and Southend (LTS) Rail) were offered for sale in 1995. The Government's aim is for half the services to be franchised by April 1996.

British Rail's passenger rolling stock has been divided between three subsidiary companies which will lease rolling stock to franchisees, open-access operators and, pending franchising, to British Rail's 25 operating units. The three companies were transferred to government ownership in July 1995 in preparation for sale to the private sector. Trainload Freight and the contract services business of Railfreight Distribution have been merged and split into three geographically-based companies which were offered for sale in June 1995. The European business of Railfreight Distribution will be privatized when the Channel Tunnel freight services have been established. The domestic and deep-sea container business of Railfreight Distribution (Freightliner) is being restructured for sale during 1995. Rail Express Systems, which carries

Royal Mail letters for the Post Office has also been put on the market.

The new independent Rail Regulator will be responsible for the licensing of new railway operators, approving access agreements, promoting the use and development of the network, and protecting the interests of rail users.

BRITISH RAILWAYS BOARD, *see* page 290
RAILTRACK, 40 Bernard Street, London WC1N 1BY. Tel: 0171-344 7100. *Chairman*, R. Horton. *Chief Executive*, J. Edmonds, CBE
OFFICE OF PASSENGER RAIL FRANCHISING (OPRAF), Golding's House, 2 Hay's Lane, London SE1 2HB. Tel: 0171-940 4200. *Franchising Director*, R. Salmon
OFFICE OF THE RAIL REGULATOR (ORR), 1 Waterhouse Square, Holborn Bars, 138–142 Holborn, London EC1N 2SU. Tel: 0171-282 2000. *Rail Regulator*, J. Swift

RAIL OPERATIONS

At 31 March 1995, Railtrack had 23,452 miles of standard gauge lines and sidings in use, representing 10,275 miles of route of which 3,087 miles were electrified. Standard rail on main line has a weight of 110 lb per yard. British Rail had 1,877 locomotives (1,619 diesel-electric and 258 electric); 1,794 diesel multiple-unit vehicles, 6,403 electric multiple-unit vehicles and 2,468 locomotive-hauled vehicles.

Loaded train miles run in passenger service totalled 221.9 million. Passenger journeys made during the year totalled 702.2 million, including 326.9 million made by holders of season tickets. The average distance of each passenger journey on ordinary fare was 34.2 miles; and on season ticket, 15.2 miles. Passenger stations in use in 1995 numbered 2,506 and freight terminals 59.

There were 13,379 freight vehicles and 818 other vehicles in the non-passenger-carrying stock. Train miles run in freight service totalled 29 million.

On 31 March 1995 British Rail employed 94,344 staff (115,546 at 31 March 1994). Including subsidiaries, the group total at 31 March 1995 was 100,264 (121,025 at 31 March 1994).

FINANCIAL RESULTS

British Rail's profit and loss account for 1994–5 showed a profit of £362 million after interest and extraordinary items, compared with a deficit of £108.4 million in 1993–4. The railway operating surplus was £571 million compared with a surplus of £23 million for the previous year. However, the figures are not directly comparable owing to the new financial arrangements in place. Railtrack's financial results for 1994–5 were not available at the time of going to press.

	£ million 1994–5
Income	
Passenger	2,247
Freight and Parcels	472
Railfreight Distribution	120
Others	105
Income from Railtrack	1,238
Revenue grant	2,060
Total	6,242
Operating expenditure	
Staff costs	2,149
Railtrack access charges	2,169
Materials, supplies and services	1,157
Depreciation	168
Amortization of deferred grant	(91)
Own work capitalized	(22)
Exceptional items	141
Total	5,671

Operating profit		571
Loss on disposals		(41)
Restructuring costs		(62)
Profit before interest		468
Interest		(106)
Group profit		362

The costs of restructuring the operations of British Rail in 1993–5 prior to privatization were £177.2 million, of which £67.3 million was offset by government grants. A further £141 million was spent on voluntary severance schemes for 7,600 employees.

ACCIDENTS ON RAILWAYS

	1992–3	1993–4
Train accidents: total	1,152	977
Persons killed: total	5	6
Passengers	0	0
Railway staff	1	0
Others	4	6
Persons injured: total	153	246
Passengers	66	134
Railway staff	74	95
Others	13	17
Other accidents through movement of railway vehicles		
Persons killed	38	26
Persons injured	2,558	2,373
Other accidents on railway premises		
Persons killed	7	9
Persons injured	7,524	8,244
Trespassers and suicides		
Persons killed	244	253
Persons injured	89	97

THE CHANNEL TUNNEL

The earliest recorded scheme for a submarine transport connection between Britain and France was in 1802. Tunnelling has begun simultaneously on both sides of the Channel three times: in 1881, in the early 1970s, and on 1 December 1987, when construction workers began to bore the first of the three tunnels which form the current project. They 'holed through' the first tunnel (the service tunnel) on 1 December 1990 and tunnelling was completed in June 1991. The tunnel was officially opened by The Queen and President Mitterrand of France on 6 May 1994.

In January 1986 the concession for construction and operation of the tunnel and its services was awarded to a paired Anglo-French private-sector company, CTG-FM, wholly owned by Eurotunnel. Eurotunnel's costs from establishment in 1986 to the first commercial service in 1994 were £8,602 million. The funds available to Eurotunnel amount to £10,535 million, raised through equity and loans. Eurotunnel expect to achieve cash-flow break-even in 1998, and the projected costs until that time are estimated at £10,116 million.

Passenger services (Eurostar) run from Waterloo station, London to Paris and Brussels. Connecting services from Edinburgh and Manchester via London began in 1995 and through services from these cities, not stopping in London, are scheduled to begin in 1996. Vehicle shuttle services (Le Shuttle) operate between Folkestone and Calais.

The submarine link comprises three tunnels. There are two rail tunnels, each carrying trains in one direction, which measure 24.93 ft (7.6 m) in diameter. Between them lies a smaller service tunnel, measuring 15.75 ft (4.8 m) in diameter. The service tunnel is linked to the rail tunnels by 130 cross-passages for maintenance and safety purposes. The tunnels are 31 miles (50 km) long, 24 miles (38 km) of which is under the sea-bed at an average depth of 132 ft (40 m). The rail terminals are situated at Folkestone and Calais, and the tunnels go underground at Shakespeare Cliff, Dover, and Sangatte, west of Calais.

RAIL LINKS

The route for the British rail link was confirmed by the Secretary of State for Transport (John MacGregor) on 24 January and 28 April 1994. The rail link will run from Folkestone to a proposed new terminal at St Pancras station, London, but at present services run into the new terminal at Waterloo station, London. A hybrid bill concerning the route was introduced into Parliament in November 1994.

Construction of the rail link is expected to cost £2,700 million, to be financed jointly with the private sector. A private sector company will be responsible for design, construction and ownership of the rail link, and will take over Union Railways and European Passenger Services Ltd, who will operate international services from London through the Channel tunnel. A final decision on the appointment of a Channel tunnel rail link promoter is expected by the end of 1995. Construction is expected to be completed by 2002.

Infrastructure developments in France have been completed and high-speed trains run from Calais to Paris, linking the Channel tunnel with the high-speed European network.

ROADS

HIGHWAY AUTHORITIES

The powers and responsibilities of highway authorities in England and Wales are set out in the Highways Acts 1980; for Scotland there is separate legislation.

Responsibility for trunk road motorways and other trunk roads in Great Britain rests in England with the Secretary of State for Transport, in Scotland with the Secretary of State for Scotland, and in Wales with the Secretary of State for Wales. The costs of construction, improvement and maintenance are paid for by central government. The highway authority for non-trunk roads in England and Wales is, in general, the county council, metropolitan district council or London borough council in whose area the roads lie, and in Scotland the regional or islands council. This function will be taken over by the new unitary authorities to be established in Wales, Scotland and parts of England. In Northern Ireland the Department of the Environment (Northern Ireland) is responsible for public roads and their maintenance and construction.

FINANCE

The Government contributes towards capital expenditure through Transport Supplementary Grant (TSG) in England and Transport Grant (TG) in Wales. Grant rates are determined by the respective Secretaries of State; at present, grant is paid at 50 per cent of expenditure accepted for grant in England and Wales.

In England TSG is paid towards capital spending on highways and the regulation of traffic; current expenditure is funded by revenue support grant (i.e. central government grants to local authorities for non-specific services). TSG is also paid towards capital spending on bridge assessment and strengthening; towards structural maintenance on the primary route network; and towards all principal 'A' roads. In Wales TG is paid towards capital expenditure only; current expenditure is funded by revenue support grant.

For the financial year 1995–6 local authorities in England will receive £278 million in TSG. Total estimated expenditure on building and maintaining motorways and trunk roads in England in 1993–4 was £1,970 million; estimated outturn for 1994–5 is £2,050 million.

For the financial year 1995–6 local authorities in Wales will receive up to £45 million in TG. Total expenditure on roads in Wales in 1993–4 was £313 million.

Total expenditure on building and maintaining trunk roads in Scotland was £244 million in 1994–5.

In Northern Ireland expenditure on roads in 1994–5 was £151 million, and estimated expenditure for 1995–6 is £150 million.

PRIVATE FINANCE

The Government is seeking to encourage greater involvement by the private sector in the design, finance, construction and operation of roads. A research programme is under way to assess the technology necessary for the introduction of electronic motorway tolls.

ROAD BUILDING PROGRAMME

In 1993–4 the Government conducted a review of its programme of improving the motorway and trunk road network, resulting in the withdrawal in March 1994 of 49 schemes deemed unnecessary or environmentally unacceptable and the suspension of preparation work on 67 other schemes. In spring 1995, 53 schemes were under construction and a further 271 schemes were in preparation. There were also 269 major local authority schemes under construction or in preparation.

ROAD LENGTHS (in miles) as at April 1994

	Total roads	Trunk roads (including motorways)	Motorways*
England	173,278	6,439	1,674
Wales	20,933	1,056	76
Scotland	32,432	1,946	170
N. Ireland	14,971	1,403†	73
UK	241,615	10,843	1,994

*There were in addition 27.6 miles of local authority motorway in England and 19.5 miles in Scotland
†'A' roads; there are no designated trunk roads in N. Ireland

MOTORWAYS

England and Wales:

M1	London to Yorkshire
M2	London to Faversham
M3	London to Southampton
M4	London to South Wales
M5	Birmingham to Exeter
M6	Catthorpe to Carlisle
M10	St Albans spur
M11	London to Cambridge
M18	Rotherham to Goole
M20	London to Folkestone
M23	London to Gatwick
M25	London orbital
M26	M20 to M25 spur
M27	Southampton bypass
M32	M4 to Bristol spur
M40	London to Birmingham
M41	London to West Cross
M42	South-west of Birmingham to Measham
M45	Dunchurch spur
M50	Ross spur
M53	Chester to Birkenhead
M54	M6 to Telford
M55	Preston to Blackpool
M56	Manchester to Chester
M57	Liverpool outer ring
M58	Liverpool to Wigan
M61	Manchester to Preston
M62	Liverpool to Hull
M63	Manchester southern ring road
M65	Calder Valley
M66	Manchester eastern ring road to Rochdale
M67	Manchester Hyde to Denton
M69	Coventry to Leicester
M180	South Humberside

Scotland:

M8	Edinburgh, Glasgow, Greenock
M9	Edinburgh to Stirling
M73	Maryville to Mollisburn
M74	Nether Abington to Millbank
M77	Ayr Road Route
M80	Stirling to Haggs/Glasgow (M8) to Stepps
M85	Friarton Bridge to Perth
M90	Inverkeithing to Perth
M876	Dennyloanhead (M80) to Kincardine Bridge

Northern Ireland:

M1	Belfast to Dungannon
M2	Belfast to Antrim
M5	M2 to Greencastle
M12	M1 to Craigavon
M22	Antrim to Randalstown

DRIVING LICENCES

It is necessary to hold a valid full licence in order to drive on public roads in the UK. Learner drivers obtain a provisional driving licence before starting to learn to drive and must then pass a test to obtain a full driving licence. There are separate tests for driving motor cycles, cars, passenger-carrying vehicles (PCVs) and large goods vehicles (LGVs). Drivers must hold full car entitlement before they can apply for PCV or LGV entitlements. In 1995, 35 million people in the UK held a valid driving licence (full or provisional). The minimum age for driving motor cars, light goods vehicles up to 3.5 tonnes and motor cycles is 17 (moped, 16).

The Driver and Vehicle Licensing Agency is responsible for issuing driving licences, registering and licensing vehicles, and collecting excise duty in Great Britain. In Northern Ireland the Driver and Vehicle Licensing Agency (Northern Ireland) has similar responsibilities.

DRIVING LICENCE FEES *since October 1994*

First provisional licence	£21.00
Changing a provisional to a full licence after passing a driving test	free
Renewal of licence	£6.00
Renewal of licence including PCV or LGV entitlements	£21
Medical renewal	free
Medical renewal (over 70)	£6.00
Duplicate Licence	£6.00
Exchange Licence	£6.00
Removing endorsements	£6.00
New licence after a period of disqualification	£12.00
New licence after disqualification for some drinking and driving offences	£20

DRIVING TESTS

The Driving Standards Agency is responsible for carrying out driving tests and approving driving instructors in Great Britain. In Northern Ireland the Driver and Vehicle Testing Agency (Northern Ireland) is responsible for testing drivers and vehicles.

The number of car driving tests conducted in Great Britain in 1994 was 1,494,713, of which 47 per cent resulted in a pass. In addition a total of 70,247 LGV/PCV tests were undertaken, of which 48 per cent were successful. A total of 84,278 motorcycle tests were undertaken, of which 70.46 per cent were successful.

DRIVING TEST FEES (weekday rate/evening and Saturday rate)

*For cars	£28.50/£38.50
†For motor cycles	£36/£47.50
For lorries, buses	£62/£80
For invalid carriages	free

*In July 1996 a written test will replace the theory element at the end of the present test. A separate fee will be charged
†The first part of the motor cycle test, now known as Compulsory Basic Training, is no longer conducted by the Department of Transport but by appointed motor cycle training organizations, who conduct the majority of basic training tests within the framework of their own training courses and are free to set their own fee. The fee for a certificate of completion of a Compulsory Basic Training course is £5

An extended driving test was introduced in 1992 for those convicted of dangerous driving. The fee is £57/£77.50 (car) or £72/£92 (motorcycle)

MOTOR VEHICLES

Vehicles must be licensed before they can be driven on public roads. They must also be approved as roadworthy by the Vehicle Certification Agency. The Vehicle Inspectorate carries out annual testing and inspection of goods vehicles, buses and coaches.

The number of vehicles with current licences in 1994 was:

	GB	N. Ireland
Private and light goods	22,671,000	515,000
Motor cycles, scooters, mopeds	630,000	9,000
Public transport vehicles	107,000	3,000
Heavy goods vehicles	434,000	15,000
Agricultural tractors	309,000	7,000
Others	50,000	6,000
Total	25,231,000	596,000

This total includes 1,071,000 vehicles exempt from licensing.

VEHICLE LICENCES

Since 1974 registration and first licensing of vehicles has been through local offices (known as Vehicle Registration Offices) of the Department of Transport's Driver and Vehicle Licensing Centre in Swansea. The records of existing vehicles are held at Swansea. Local facilities for relicensing are available as follows:

(i) with a licence reminder (form V11) in person at any post office which deals with vehicle licensing, or post it to the post office shown on the form
(ii) with a vehicle licence renewal (form V10). You may normally apply in person at any licensing post office. You will need to take your vehicle registration document with you; if this is not available you must complete form V62 which is held at post offices. Postal applications can be made to the post offices shown on form V100, available at any post office. This form also provides guidance on registering and licensing vehicles.

Details of the present duties chargeable on motor vehicles are available at post offices and Vehicle Registration Offices. The Vehicle Excise and Registration Act 1994 provides *inter alia* that any vehicle kept on a public road but not used on roads is chargeable to excise duty as if it were in use.

VEHICLE EXCISE DUTY RATES *since 1 July 1995*

	12 months £	6 months £
Motor Cars		
Those first constructed before		
1 January 1947	70.00	38.50
Others	135.00	74.25
Motor Cycles		
With or without sidecar, not exceeding 150 cc	15.00	—
With or without sidecar, 150–250 cc	35.00	—
Others	55.00	30.25
Tricycles (not over 450 kg)		
Not over 150 cc	15.00	—
Others	55.00	30.25
Buses		
Seating less than 16 persons	150.00	82.50
Seating 17–35 persons	200.00	110.00
Seating 36–60 persons	300.00	165.00
Seating over 60 persons	450.00	247.50

MoT TESTING

Cars, motor cycles, motor caravans, light goods and dual-purpose vehicles more than three years old must be covered by a current MoT test certificate. The certificate must be renewed annually. Copies of the legislation governing MoT testing can be obtained from any bookshop which stocks HMSO publications. The legislation comprises the Road Traffic Act 1988 (Sections 45 and 46), the Motor Vehicles (Test) Regulations 1981, and subsequent amendments. The MoT testing scheme is administered by the Vehicle Inspectorate.

A fee is payable to MoT testing stations, which must be authorized to carry out tests. The maximum fees, which are prescribed by regulations, are:

For cars and light vans	£26.10
For solo motor cycles	£11.14
For motor cycle combinations	£18.78
For three-wheeled vehicles	£21.98
For non-public service vehicle buses	£33.04
For light goods vehicles	£28.84

Killed*	3,650
Pedestrians	1,102
Pedal cycles	172
All two-wheeled motor vehicles	435
Cars and taxis	1,655
Others	286

*Died within 30 days of accident

	Killed	Injured
1965	7,952	389,986
1970	7,499	355,869
1975	6,366	318,584
1980	6,010	323,000
1985	5,165	312,359
1990	5,217	335,924
1992	4,229	306,444
1993	3,814	302,206
1994	3,650	311,539

ROAD USE

ESTIMATED TRAFFIC ON ALL ROADS (GREAT BRITAIN) 1994

Million vehicle kilometres

All motor vehicles	421,900
Cars and taxis	345,100
Two-wheeled motor vehicles	4,100
Buses and coaches	4,700
Light vans	38,300
Other goods vehicles	29,600
Total goods vehicles	67,900
Pedal cycles	4,400

Source: Department of Transport

BUSES AND COACHES 1993–4 (GREAT BRITAIN)

Number of vehicles (31 March 1994)	74,900
Vehicle kilometres (millions)	4,024
Local bus passenger journeys (millions)	4,375
Passenger receipts (£ million)	3,219

ROAD GOODS TRANSPORT (GREAT BRITAIN) 1994
Analysis by mode of working and by gross weight of vehicle

Estimated tonne kilometres (thousand million)	137.8
Own account	37.0
Public haulage	100.8
By gross weight of vehicle (billion tonne kilometres)	
Not over 25 tonnes	26.6
Over 25 tonnes	111.2
Estimated tonnes carried (millions)	1,597.0
Own account	618.0
Public haulage	980.0
By gross weight of vehicle (million tonnes)	
Not over 25 tonnes	527.0
Over 25 tonnes	1,070.0

Source: Department of Transport

ROAD ACCIDENTS 1994

Road accidents	234,101
Vehicles involved:	
Pedal cycles	23,387
Motor vehicles	396,519
Total casualties	315,189
Pedestrians	48,541
Vehicle users	266,648

SHIPPING

PRINCIPAL MERCHANT FLEETS 1994

Flag	No	Gross tonnage
Panama	5,799	64,170,219
Liberia	1,621	57,647,708
Greece	1,923	30,161,758
Cyprus	1,619	23,292,954
Bahamas	1,159	22,915,349
Japan	9,706	22,101,606
Norway (NIS)	749	19,976,489
Russia	5,285	16,503,871
China	2,701	15,826,688
Malta	1,086	15,455,370
*United States of America	5,270	13,655,438
Singapore	1,239	11,894,846
Philippines	1,518	9,413,228
Hong Kong	358	7,703,410
Korea (South)	2,121	7,004,199
Italy	1,434	6,818,178
India	881	6,485,374
Taiwan	642	5,996,103
Germany	1,200	5,696,088
Turkey	1,000	5,452,798
St Vincent	1,013	5,420,484
Brazil	565	5,282,869
Ukraine	1,153	5,279,112
Denmark (DIS)	470	5,125,947
United Kingdom	1,481	4,430,158
Iran	429	3,803,342
Netherlands	1,031	3,349,292
Australia	628	3,012,177
Bermuda	82	2,904,490
Sweden	597	2,796,519
Malaysia	632	2,727,572
Romania	432	2,689,180
Indonesia	2,136	2,678,333
Poland	561	2,609,678
Canada	896	2,489,520
Norway	1,510	2,411,447
Marshall Islands	56	2,149,430
France	746	2,132,299
French Antarctic Territory	73	2,110,611
Isle of Man	123	2,093,278

NIS   Norwegian International Ship Register – offshore registry
*Excluding ships of United States Reserve Fleet
DIS   Danish International Register of Shipping – offshore registry
Source: Lloyd's Register of Shipping

MERCHANT SHIPS COMPLETED 1994

	No.	Gross tonnage
COUNTRY OF BUILD		
Japan	597	8,603,600
Korea (South)	118	4,085,798
Germany	93	1,003,127
*China	48	699,740
Denmark	29	653,185
Taiwan	21	611,848
Poland	32	525,662
Italy	23	524,133
Brazil	10	304,427
Croatia	8	262,777
United Kingdom	22	226,643
*Ukraine	17	216,709
Spain	36	201,481
Netherlands	70	188,286
Norway	34	146,372
France	8	119,513
Finland	3	90,611
*Russia	14	75,993
Bulgaria	8	70,300
Singapore	39	66,483
Belgium	7	41,025
Malaysia	56	37,434
Turkey	14	34,828
Slovakia	12	27,304
United States of America	17	25,090
Other countries	101	123,800
FOR REGISTRATION IN		
Panama	176	4,710,579
Liberia	76	3,801,640
Japan	350	857,320
Philippines	32	824,195
Germany	62	810,579
Hong Kong	23	695,737
China	41	666,206
Norway (NIS)	17	641,021
Bahamas	20	534,003
Denmark (DIS)	25	460,734
Italy	22	457,591
Singapore	80	457,263
Cyprus	36	449,911
Taiwan	19	425,520
Greece	12	404,706
Malaysia	36	298,383
Netherlands	45	219,533
India	12	216,082
French Antarctic Territory	1	153,778
Malta	6	142,856
Brazil	8	134,594
United Kingdom	15	129,928
France	9	127,108
Mexico	4	126,913
Russia	42	123,844
Other countries	268	1,096,145
WORLD TOTAL	1,437	18,966,169

*Information incomplete
NIS   Norwegian International Ship Register – offshore registry
DIS   Danish International Register of Shipping – offshore registry
Source: Lloyd's Register of Shipping

BRITISH-REGISTERED* TRADING VESSELS
Of 500 Gross Tons and Over *as at end 1993*

Type of vessel	No.	Gross tonnage
Tankers[1]	106	2,161,000
Bulk carriers[2]	22	293,000
Specialized carriers[3]	13	124,000
Container (fully cellular)	26	1,017,000
Ro-Ro[4]	86	657,000
Other general cargo	82	145,000
Passenger[5]	9	272,000
Total	344	4,670,000

* Registered in the UK and British Crown dependencies
1 Includes oil, gas, chemical and other specialized tankers
2 Includes combination bulk carriers: ore/oil and ore bulk/oil carriers
3 Includes livestock, car and chemical carriers
4 Roll-on, roll-off passenger and cargo vessels
5 Cruise liner and other passenger vessels
Source: HMSO – *Annual Abstract of Statistics 1995*

SEAPORT TRAFFIC OF GREAT BRITAIN 1993
By Mode of Appearance

	Million gross tonnes
Foreign Traffic: *Imports*	183.9
Bulk fuel traffic	78.5
Other bulk traffic	43.4
Container and roll-on traffic	45.2
Semi-bulk traffic	14.7
Conventional traffic	1.9
Foreign Traffic: *Exports*	157.1
Bulk fuel traffic	94.1
Other bulk traffic	20.8
Container and roll-on traffic	35.9
Semi-bulk traffic	5.2
Conventional traffic	1.1
Domestic Traffic*	146.4
Bulk fuel traffic	96.1
Other bulk traffic	35.1
Container and roll-on traffic	9.6
Semi-bulk traffic	0.5
Conventional traffic	0.3
Non-oil traffic with UK offshore installations	4.9
Total Foreign and Domestic Traffic	487.4

* Domestic traffic refers to traffic through the ports of Great Britain only, to all parts of the UK, Isle of Man and the Channel Islands. Traffic to and from offshore installations, landing of sea-dredged aggregates and material shipped for dumping at sea included
Source: HMSO – *Annual Abstract of Statistics 1995*

SEABORNE TRADE OF THE UK 1992
Exports (Including Re-exports) Plus Imports by Sea

	Million tonnes	% carried by UK-registered vessels
By weight		
All cargo	311.2	19
Dry bulk cargo	82.2	21
Other dry cargo	91.8	24
Tanker cargo	137.1	14
	£ million	
By value		
All cargo	1,781,100	36
Dry bulk cargo	69,400	16
Other dry cargo	1,593,400	38
Tanker cargo	118,200	15

Source: HMSO – *Annual Abstract of Statistics 1995*

PASSENGER MOVEMENT BY SEA 1993
*Arrivals plus departures at UK seaports by place of embarkation or landing**

All passenger movements	34,943,000
Irish Republic	3,407,000
Belgium	2,958,000
France†	24,643,000
Netherlands	2,550,000
Other EC countries	801,000
Other European and Mediterranean countries‡	354,000
USA	33,700
Rest of the world	3,300
Pleasure cruises beginning and/or ending at UK seaports	193,000

* Passengers are included at both departure and arrival if their journeys begin and end at a UK seaport
† Includes hovercraft passengers
‡ Includes North Africa and Middle East Mediterranean countries
Source: HMSO – *Annual Abstract of Statistics 1995*

Communications

Postal Services

Responsibility for running postal services rests in the UK with a public authority, the Post Office (*see* page 337). The Secretary of State for Trade and Industry has powers to suspend the monopoly of the Post Office in certain areas and to issue licences to other bodies to provide an alternative service. Non-Post Office bodies are permitted to transfer mail between document exchanges and to deliver letters, provided that a minimum fee of £1 per letter is charged. Charitable organizations are allowed to carry and deliver Christmas and New Year cards.

INLAND POSTAL SERVICES AND REGULATIONS

INLAND LETTER POST RATES*

Not over	1st class†	2nd class†
60 g	25p	19p
100 g	38p	29p
150 g	47p	36p
200 g	57p	43p
250 g	67p	52p
300 g	77p	61p
350 g	88p	70p
400 g	£1.00	79p
450 g	£1.13	89p
500 g	£1.25	98p
600 g	£1.55	£1.20
700 g	£1.90	£1.40
750 g	£2.05	£1.45 (not
800 g	£2.15	admissible
900 g	£2.35	over 750 g)
1,000 g	£2.50	
Each extra 250 g or part thereof	65p	

UK PARCEL RATES

Not over		Not over	
1 kg	£2.70	8 kg	£6.10
2 kg	£3.30	10 kg	£7.10
4 kg	£4.70	30 kg	£8.40
6 kg	£5.25		

*Postcards travel at the same rates as letter post
†There is a two-tier postal delivery system in the UK with first class letters normally being delivered the following day and second class post within three days

OVERSEAS POSTAL SERVICES AND REGULATIONS

OVERSEAS SURFACE MAIL RATES

Letters

Not over		Not over	
20 g	30p	450 g	£2.75
60 g	50p	500 g	£3.04
100 g	72p	750 g	£4.49
150 g	£1.01	1,000 g	£5.94
200 g	£1.30	1,250 g	£7.39
250 g	£1.59	1,500 g	£8.84
300 g	£1.88	1,750 g	£10.29
350 g	£2.17	2,000 g	£11.74
400 g	£2.46		

AIRMAIL LETTER RATES

Europe: Letters

Not over		Not over	
20 g	25p	260 g	£1.74
20 g non EC	30p	280 g	£1.86
40 g	42p	300 g	£1.98
60 g	54p	320 g	£2.10
80 g	66p	340 g	£2.22
100 g	78p	360 g	£2.34
120 g	90p	380 g	£2.46
140 g	£1.02	400 g	£2.58
160 g	£1.14	420 g	£2.70
180 g	£1.26	440 g	£2.82
200 g	£1.38	460 g	£2.94
220 g	£1.50	480 g	£3.06
240 g	£1.62	*500 g	£3.18

* Max. 2 kg

Outside Europe: Letters

	Not over 10 g	Not over 20 g	Each extra 20 g
Zone 1	41p	60p	32p
Zone 2	41p	60p	42p

For airmail letter zones outside Europe, *see* pages 516–7

STAMPS

Postage stamps are sold in values of 1p, 2p, 4p, 5p, 6p, 10p, 19p, 20p, 25p, 29p, 30p, 35p, 36p, 38p, 41p, 50p, £1, £1.50, £2.00, £5.00, and £10.00. Books or rolls of first and second class stamps are also avaiable. Stamps are sold at Post Offices and some other outlets, including stationers and newsagents.

PREPAID STATIONERY

Aerogrammes to all destinations are 36p. Forces Aerogrammes are free to certain destinations. Other mail is charged at a concessionary rate.

Prepaid envelopes:

Size	Small	Medium	Large
Postage paid to	100g	350g	500g
Registered Envelopes	£3.30	£3.80	£4.20

Printed postage stamps cut from envelopes, postcards, newspaper wrappers, etc., may be used as stamps in payment of postage, provided that they are not imperfect or defaced.

POSTAL ORDERS

Postal orders (British pattern) are issued and paid at nearly all post offices in the UK and in many other countries.

Postal orders are printed with a counterfoil for denominations of 50p and £1, followed by £1 steps to £10, £15 and £20. Postage stamps may be affixed in the space provided to increase the value of the postal order by up to 49p. Charges (in addition to the value of the postal order): Up to £1, 25p; £2–£4, 42p; £5–£7, 58p; £8–£10, 66p; £15, 80p; £20, 85p.

The name of the payee must be inserted on the postal order. If not presented within six months of the last day of the month of issue, orders must be sent to the local customer services manager of Post Office Counters Ltd (listed in the telephone directory) to ascertain whether the order may still be paid. If the counterfoil has been retained postal orders not more than four years out of date may be paid when presented with the counterfoil at a post office.

RESTRICTIONS

Articles which may not be sent in the post include offensive or dangerous articles, packets likely to impede Post Office sorters, and certain kinds of advertisement.

Under Department of Trade and Industry regulations the exportation of some goods by post is prohibited except under Department of Trade licence. Enquiries should be addressed to the Export Data Branch, Overseas Trade Divisions, Department of Trade and Industry, 1 Victoria Street, London SW1H 0ET. Tel: 0171-215 5000.

SPECIAL DELIVERY SERVICES

DATAPOST

A guaranteed service for the delivery of documents and packages: (i) Datapost Sameday offers same working day collection and delivery in many areas; (ii) Datapost 10 (for delivery before 10 a.m.) and Datapost 12 (for delivery before noon) offer next working day delivery nationwide and are available only to certain destinations. Items may be collected or handed in at post offices. There are also Datapost links with a number of overseas countries. Parcelforce 24 (next working day delivery) and 48 (delivery in two working days) offer a similar guaranteed service to Datapost.

ROYAL MAIL SPECIAL DELIVERY

A guaranteed next-day delivery service by 12.30 p.m. to most UK destinations for first class letters and packets. The fee of £2.70 is refunded if next working day delivery is not achieved, provided that items are posted before latest recommended posting times.

SWIFTAIR

Express delivery of airmail letters and packets up to 2 kg anywhere in the world. Items normally arrive at least one day in advance of normal air mail. Charge (in addition to postage), £2.70.

OTHER SERVICES

ADVICE OF DELIVERY (INTERNATIONAL)

Written confirmation of delivery from the post office at the stated destination. Charge: 40p plus postage.

CASH ON DELIVERY (INLAND AND INTERNATIONAL)

Inland: an amount up to £500 can, under certain conditions, be collected and remitted to the sender of a parcel containing an invoice. Invoice values of over £100 are only collectable at Post Office premises. Charge per parcel (exclusive of postage and registration): customers under contract, £1.70; other customers, £2.00; COD enquiry, £1.70.

Overseas: this service is only available with Parcelforce International Standard or Economy service. The following fee is added to postage charges, based on the value of the item to be delivered:

Value	Fee
Up to £200	£5.20
£200–£400	£9.85
£400–£600	£15.00
£600–£1,000	£19.15
£1,000–£1,500	£23.30

CERTIFICATE OF POSTING

Issued free on request at time of posting.

COMPENSATION (INLAND AND INTERNATIONAL)

Inland: compensation up to a maximum of £25 may be paid where it can be shown that a letter was damaged or lost in the post due to the fault of the Post Office, its employees or agents. The Post Office does not accept responsibility for loss or damage arising from faulty packing. Charges: Parcelforce – compensation up to £20 per parcel for loss or damage if a certificate of posting has been obtained. Compensation Fee Certificate of Posting – 70p, up to £150 compensation; £1.25, up to £500 compensation.

International: if a certificate of posting is produced, compensation may be given for loss or damage in the UK to uninsured parcels to or from most overseas countries. No compensation will be paid for any loss or damage due to the action of the Queen's Enemies.

INTERNATIONAL REPLY COUPONS

Coupons used to prepay replies to letters, exchangeable abroad for stamps representing the minimum surface mail letter rate from the country concerned to the UK. Charge: 60p each.

NEWSPAPER POST

Copies of newspapers registered at the Post Office may be posted only by the publisher or their agents in open-ended wrappers or unsealed envelopes approved by the Post Office, or tied with string removable without cutting. Wrappers and envelopes must be prominently marked 'newspaper post' in the top left-hand corner. The only additional writing or printing permitted is 'with compliments', the name and address of sender, request for return if undeliverable, and a page reference. Items receive first class letter service.

POSTE RESTANTE

Poste Restante is solely for travellers and is for three months in any one town. A packet may be addressed to any post office, except town sub-offices, and should state 'Poste Restante' or 'to be called for' in the address. Redirection from a Poste Restante is undertaken for up to three months. Letters for an expected ship at a port are kept for two months, otherwise letters are kept for two weeks, or one month if from abroad. At the end of this period mail is treated as undeliverable or is returned.

RECORDED DELIVERY (INLAND)

Provides a record of posting and delivery of letters and ensures a signature on delivery. This service is recommended for items of little or no monetary value. Charge: 55p plus postage.

REDIRECTION

By agent of addressee: mail other than parcels, business reply and freepost items may be reposted free not later than the day after delivery (not counting Sundays and public holidays) if unopened and if original addressee's name is unobscured. Parcels may be redirected free within the same time limits only if the original and substituted address are in the same local parcel delivery area (or the London postal area). Registred packets must be taken to a post office and are re-registered free up to the day after delivery.

By the Post Office: a printed form obtainable from the Post Office must be signed by the person to whom the letters are to be addressed. A fee is payable for each different surname on the application form. Charges: up to 1 calendar month, £6.00; up to 3 calendar months, £13.00; up to 12 calendar months, £30.00.

REGISTERED MAIL (INLAND AND INTERNATIONAL)

Inland: all packets must be handed to the post office and a certificate of posting obtained. Charges (plus postage): up to £500 compensation, £3.00; Registered Plus for compensation between £500 and £1,500, £3.30; up to £2,200 compensation, £3.60. Consequential Loss Insurance provides cover up to £10,000:

Compensation up to	Standard fee in addition to registered fee and postage
£1,000	45p
£2,500	60p
£5,000	85p
£7,500	£1.10
£10,000	£1.35

Compensation in respect of currency or other forms of monetary worth is given only if money is sent by registered letter post. Compensation cannot be paid in the case of any packet containing prohibited articles (*see* Restrictions). Compensation is only paid for well-packed fragile articles and not for exceptionally fragile or perishable articles.

International: packets containing valuable papers, documents or articles can be insured as letters, or as parcels if the country of destination does not accept dutiable goods in the letter post. For HM ships abroad and also members of the Army and RAF overseas using BFPO numbers, parcels only are insurable up to £140 at a fee of £1.20. Charges (plus airmail postage): compensation up to £500, £3.00; up to £1,000, £4.00.

SMALL PACKETS POST (INTERNATIONAL)

Permits the transmission of goods up to 2 kg to all countries, in the same mails as printed papers (NB: to Myanmar (Burma) and Papua New Guinea there is a limit of 500 g). Packets can be sealed and can contain personal correspondence relating to the contents. Registration is allowed as insurance as long as the item is packed in a way complying with any insurance regulations. A customs declaration is required and the packet must be marked with 'small packet' and a return address. Instructions for the disposal of undelivered packets must be given at the time of posting. An undeliverable packet will be returned to the sender at his/her expense.

Surface Mail: World-wide

Not over		Not over	
100 g	48p	450 g	£1.60
150 g	64p	500 g	£1.76
200 g	80p	750 g	£2.56
250 g	96p	1,000 g	£3.36
300 g	£1.12	1,500 g	£4.96
350 g	£1.28	2,000 g	£6.56
400 g	£1.44		

SPECIAL DELIVERY

See above

UNDELIVERED AND UNPAID MAIL

Undelivered mail is returned to the sender provided the return address is indicated either on the outside of the envelope or inside. If the sender's address is not available items not containing property are destroyed. If the packet contains something of value it is retained for up to three months. Undeliverable second class mail containing newspapers, magazines or commercial advertising is destroyed.

All unpaid or underpaid letters are treated as second class mail. The recipient is charged the amount of under-payment plus 15p per item. Parcels over 750 g are charged at first class rates plus 15p.

Public Telecommunications Services

Under the British Telecommunications Act 1981 British Telecom (now BT) was created to provide a national public telecommunications service. The Telecommunications Act 1984 removed BT's monopoly on running the public telecommunications system and BT was privatized in 1984.

The Telecommunications Act 1984 also established the Office of Telecommunications (Oftel) as the independent regulatory body for the telecommunications industry (*see also* Government Departments and Public Offices).

PUBLIC TELECOMMUNICATIONS OPERATORS

Until 1991 the three licensed fixed-link public telecommunications operators (PTOs) in the UK were BT, Mercury Communications Ltd, and Kingston Communications (Hull) PLC. In March 1991 the Government announced that it was opening up the existing duopoly of the two major fixed-link operators and would be encouraging applications for telecommunications licences. Since then there have been 22 recipients of major licences

included in the 77 licences issued by the Department of Trade and Industry. There are 37 applications under consideration.

BT's obligations under its operating licence continue to include the provision of a universal telecommunications service; a service in rural areas; and essential services, such as public call boxes and emergency services.

Mercury Communications is licensed to provide national and international public telecommunications services for residential and business customers. These services utilize the digital network created by Mercury. Mercury can also provide the following services: public and private telephone services; national and international switched voice and data services; electronic messaging (private circuits and networks (national and international), integrated voice and data); data network services; customer equipment; mobile communications services; and Mercury paging.

PRIVATE TELEPHONE SERVICES

There are over 260 private telephone companies which offer information on a variety of subjects such as the weather, stock market analysis, horoscopes, etc., on the BT network. Other services are available on Mercury's network.

The lines and equipment are provided by BT under condition that services adhere to the codes of practice of the Independent Committee for the Supervision of Standards of Telephone Information Services. All services are charged at 48p per minute (peak and standard rate) or 36p per minute (cheap rate).

MOBILE TELEPHONE SYSTEMS

Cellular telephone network systems allow calls to be made to and from mobile telephones. The four companies licensed by the Department of Trade and Industry to provide competing cellular telephone systems are Cellnet, jointly owned by BT and Securicor; Mercury One-2-One; Orange, owned by Hutchison Telecom UK Ltd; and Racal Vodafone Ltd, owned by the Racal Electronics Group. Calls to cellular phones are charged at the 'm' rate.

INLAND TELEPHONES

An individual customer can install an extension telephone socket or apparatus in their own home without the need to buy the items from any of the licensed public telecommunications operators. However, it is necessary to possess a special style of master-socket which must be supplied by the public network operator. Although an individual need not buy or rent an apparatus from a PTO, a telephone bought from a retail outlet must be of an approved standard compatible with the public network (indicated by a green disc on the label).

BT EXCHANGE LINE RENTALS (*including VAT*)

	Per quarter
Residential, exclusive	£24.79
Light user scheme	£24.79
Business, exclusive	£40.15

BT TELEPHONE APPARATUS RENTAL

Residential	from £4.47
Business	from £4.70
Private payphone	from £35.00

EXCHANGE LINE CONNECTION AND TAKE-OVER CHARGES (*including VAT*)

BT

New line	£116.33
Removing customer	£0.00
Take-over of existing lines:	
Simultaneous (same day)	£0.00
Non-simultaneous	£9.99

Mercury

Initial and annual administration charge	£23.50

RATES

BT local and dialled national calls are charged by the second when made from ordinary lines and in 10p units when made from payphones. There is a 5p minimum charge on all BT calls. Mercury charges are calculated to the nearest 100th of a second. All charges are subject to VAT, except those from payphones which are VAT inclusive. VAT charges on ordinary lines are calculated as a percentage of the total quarterly (BT)/monthly (Mercury) bill.

The charge per second depends on the time of day and the distance of the call:

BT	Mercury	
Daytime	Standard	Monday to Friday 8 a.m. to 6 p.m.
Cheap	Economy	Monday to Friday 6 p.m. to 8 a.m.*
Weekend	Weekend	Midnight Friday to midnight Sunday

*also Christmas Day, Boxing Day and New Year's Day

Local rate
Regional rate – up to 35 miles (56 km)
National rate – over 35 miles (56 km) (including Channel Islands and Isle of Man)
'm' rate – dialled calls to mobile phones

DIALLED CALL TIME pence per minute charges (*including VAT*)

	BT	Mercury
Local		
Daytime	4.00	*
Cheap	1.70	*
Weekend	1.00	*
Regional rate		
Daytime/Standard	8.30	7.52
Cheap/Economy	4.00	2.94
Weekend	3.30	2.94
National rate		
Daytime/Standard	9.80	7.52
Cheap/Economy	5.80	2.94
Weekend	3.30	2.94
'm' rate		
Daytime	41.05	32.90†
Cheap	28.32	21.90†

*Mercury advises customers to use BT or cable for local calls

†Calls to Mercury One-2-One mobile phones are charged at the following pence per minute rates:

Mon.–Fri.	0900–1300	15.25p
Mon.–Fri.	0800–0900	11.15p
	1300–1800	
All other times		7.15p

OPERATOR-CONNECTED CALLS

Operator-connected calls from ordinary lines are generally subject to a three-minute minimum charge (and thereafter by the minute) which varies with distance and time of day. Operator-connected calls from payphones are charged in three-minute periods at the payphone tariff. For calls that have to be placed through the operator because a dialled call has failed, the charge is equivalent to the dialled rate, subject normally to the three-minute minimum.

Higher charges apply to other operator-connected calls, including special services calls and those to mobile phones, the Irish Republic and the Channel Islands.

PHONECARDS

BT phonecards to the value of £2, £5, £10 and £20 are available from post offices and other outlets for use in specially designated public telephone boxes. Each phonecard unit is equivalent to a 10p coin in a payphone. Special public payphones at major railway stations and airports also accept commercial credit cards.

INTERNATIONAL TELEPHONES

All UK customers have access to International Direct Dialling (IDD) and can dial direct to numbers on most exchanges in over 200 countries world-wide. Details about how to make calls are given in dialling code information and in the International Telephone Guide.

For countries without IDD, calls have to be made through the International Operator. All operator-connected calls are subject to a three-minute minimum charge. Thereafter the call is charged by the minute.

Countries which can be called on IDD fall into one of 13 international charge bands depending on location. Charges in each band also vary according to the time of day; cheap rate dialled calls are available to all countries at certain times, but there is no reduced rate for operator-connected calls. Details of current international telephone charges can be obtained from the International Operator.

For International Dialling Codes, *see* pages 516–7

OTHER TELECOMMUNICATIONS SERVICES

TELEX SERVICE

There are now 208 countries that can be reached by the BT telex service from the UK, over 200 of them by direct dialling. For most customers, direct dialled calls to international destinations are charged by the second. Calls via the BT operator are charged in one-minute steps with a three-minute minimum, plus a surcharge of £1.30 a call. Operator-connected calls are charged at between 39p and £1.60 a minute depending upon the country called.

Calls made via BT's Telex Plus store and forward facility attract normal telex charges and a handling charge of 13p for inland delivered messages and 30p for international delivered messages.

TELEMESSAGE

Telemessages can be sent by telephone or telex within the UK for 'hard copy' delivery the next working day, including Saturdays. To achieve this, a telemessage must be telephoned/telexed before 10 p.m. Monday to Saturday (7 p.m. Sundays and Bank Holidays). Dial 100 (190 in London, Birmingham and Glasgow) and ask for the Telemessage Service or see the telex directory for codes.

A telemessage costs £5 for the first 50 words and £2.75 for each subsequent group of 50 words – the name and address are free. A sender's copy costs 85p. A selection of cards is available for special occasions at 80p per card. All prices are subject to VAT.

INTERNATIONAL TELEMESSAGE

Telemessage is also available to the USA. For next working day delivery a telemessage must be filed by 10 p.m. UK time Monday to Saturday (7 p.m. Sundays and Bank Holidays). US addresses must include the ZIP code. Charges are £7.25 for the first 50 words and £3.60 for each subsequent group of 50 words. The name and address are free but all charges are subject to VAT.

BT SERVICES

OPERATOR SERVICES – 100
 For difficulties
 For the following call services: alarm calls (booking charge £2.70); advice of duration and charge (charge £1.80); charge card calls (charge £1.50); freephone calls; international personal calls (charge £2.15–£4.30); transferred charge calls (charge £1.80); subscriber controlled transfer (All charges exclude VAT)
INTERNATIONAL OPERATOR – 155
DIRECTORY ENQUIRIES – 192 (25p charge per call)
INTERNATIONAL DIRECTORY ENQUIRIES – 153
EMERGENCY SERVICES – 999
 Services include fire service; police service; ambulance service; coastguard; lifeboat; cave rescue; mountain rescue
FAULTS – 151
TELEMESSAGE – 100 (190 in London, Birmingham and Glasgow)
INTERNATIONAL TELEMESSAGE – 100 (190 in London, Birmingham and Glasgow). The service is only available to the USA
INTERNATIONAL TELEGRAMS – 100 (190 in London, Birmingham and Glasgow). The service is available world-wide
MARITIME SERVICES – 100
 Includes Ship's Telegram Service and Ship's Telephone Service
BT INMARSAT SATELLITE SERVICE – 155
ALL OTHER CALL ENQUIRIES – 191

Forecast Services

WEATHERCALL SERVICE

To obtain local weather forecasts by telephone or fax, dial the prefix code followed by the appropriate regional code. The prefix for telephone calls is 0891-500 4; the prefix for faxes is 0891-44 99. A helpdesk can be faxed on 0171-613 5000

Greater London	01
Kent, Surrey and Sussex	02
Dorset, Hampshire and IOW	03
Devon and Cornwall	04
Wiltshire, Glos, Avon and Somerset	05
Berks, Bucks and Oxfordshire	06
Beds, Herts and Essex	07
Norfolk, Suffolk and Cambridgeshire	08
West, Mid and South Glamorgan and Gwent	09
Shropshire, Hereford and Worcester	10
Central Midlands and Staffs	11
East Midlands	12
Lincolnshire and Humberside	13
Dyfed and Powys	14
Gwynedd and Clwyd	15
North-west England	16
West and South Yorkshire	17
North-east England	18
Cumbria and the Lake District	19
South-west Scotland	20
West Central Scotland	21
Edinburgh, South Fife, Lothian and Borders	22
East Central Scotland and Tayside	23
Grampian and East Highlands	24
North-west Scotland	25
Caithness, Orkney and Shetland	26
Northern Ireland	27

Calls are charged at 39p per minute cheap rate, 49p at all other times (subject to change)

MARINECALL SERVICE

To obtain information about weather conditions up to twelve miles off the coast, dial the prefix code 0891 500, followed by the appropriate area code

Scotland North	451
Scotland East	452
North-east	453
East	454
Anglia	455
Channel East	456
Mid-Channel	457
South-west	458
Bristol Channel	459
Wales	460
North-west	461
Clyde	462
Caledonia	463
Minch	464
Ulster	465
English Channel	992

Calls are charged at 39p per minute cheap rate, 49p at all other times (subject to change)

Inland Letter Post

Year	Basic rate	Year	Basic rate
1840	1d	1979	10p
1918	1½d	1980	12p
1940	2½d	1981	14p
1957	3d	1982	15½p
1965	4d	1983	16p
*1968	5d	1984	17p
1971	3p	1986	18p
1973	3½p	1988	19p
1974	4½p	1989	20p
1975	7p	1990	22p
1975 Sept	8½p	1991	24p
1977	9p	1993	25p

*Two-tier postal system introduced – subsequent figures are for 1st class letter post

Airmail and IDD Codes

AIRMAIL ZONES (AZ)
The table includes airmail letter zones for countries outside Europe, and destinations to which European and European Union airmail letter rates apply (*see also* page 510).
(*Source: Post Office*)

1   airmail zone 1
2   airmail zone 2
e   Europe
eu European Union

INTERNATIONAL DIRECT DIALLING (IDD)
International dialling codes are composed of four elements which are dialled in sequence:

(i)   the international code
(ii) the country code (*see* below)
(iii) the area code
(iv) the customer's telephone number

Calls to some countries must be made via the international operator. (*Source: BT*)

†   Calls must be made via the international operator
p   A pause in dialling is necessary whilst waiting for a second tone
°   Second tone may not always be audible
*   Varies in some areas

Country	AZ	IDD from UK	IDD to UK
Afghanistan	1	00 93	†
Albania	e	00 355	†
Algeria	1	00 213	00p44
Andorra	eu	00 33 628	0p44
Angola	1	00 244	†
Anguilla	1	00 1 809	001 44
Antigua and Barbuda	1	00 1 809	011 44
Argentina	1	00 54	00 44
Armenia	e	00 374	810 44
Aruba	1	00 297	†
Ascension Island	1	00 247	01 44
Australia	2	00 61	00 11 44
Austria	eu	00 43	00 44
Azerbaijan	e	00 994	810 44
Azores	eu	00 351	00 44
Bahamas	1	00 1 809	011 44
Bahrain	1	00 973	0 44
Bangladesh	1	00 880	00 44
Barbados	1	00 1 809	011 44
Belarus	e	00 375	810 44
Belgium	eu	00 32	00 44
Belize	1	00 501	†
Benin	1	00 229	00p44
Bermuda	1	00 1 809	1 44
Bhutan	1	00 975	00 44
Bolivia	1	00 591	00 44
Bosnia-Hercegovina	e	00 387	99 44
Botswana	1	00 267	00 44
Brazil	1	00 55	00 44
British Virgin Islands	1	00 1 809 49	011 44
Brunei	1	00 673	00 44
Bulgaria	e	00 359	00 44
Burkina Faso	1	00 226	00 44
Burundi	1	00 257	90 44
Cambodia	1	00 855	†
Cameroon	1	00 237	00 44
Canada	1	00 1	011 44

Country	AZ	IDD from UK	IDD to UK
Canary Islands	eu	00 34	07p44
Cape Verde	e	00 238	00 44
Cayman Islands	1	00 1 809	0 44
Central African Republic	1	00 236	00p44
Chad	1	00 235	†
Chile	1	00 56	00 44
China	1	00 86	00 44
Colombia	1	00 57	90 44
Comoros	1	00 269	†
Congo	1	00 242	00 44
Cook Islands	2	00 682	00 44
Costa Rica	1	00 506	00 44
Côte d'Ivoire	1	00 225	00 44
Croatia	e	00 385	99 44
Cuba	1	00 53	†
Cyprus	e	00 357	00 44
Czech Republic	e	00 42	00 44
Denmark	eu	00 45	009 44
Djibouti	1	00 253	00 44
Dominica	1	00 1 809	011 44
Dominican Republic	1	00 1 809	†
Ecuador	1	00 593	00 44
Egypt	1	00 20	00 44
Equatorial Guinea	1	00 240	19 44
Eritrea	1	00 291	†
Estonia	e	00 372	810 44
Ethiopia	1	00 251	00 44
Falkland Islands	1	00 500	01 44
Faroe Islands	e	00 298	009 44
Fiji	2	00 679	05 44
Finland	eu	00 358	990 44
France	eu	00 33	19p44°
French Guiana	1	00 594	†
French Polynesia	2	00 689	00 44
Gabon	1	00 241	00 44
The Gambia	1	00 220	00 44
Georgia	e	00 7	810 44
Germany	eu	00 49	00 44
Ghana	1	00 233	00 44
Gibraltar	eu	00 350	00 44
Greece	eu	00 30	00 44
Greenland	e	00 299	009 44
Grenada	1	00 1 809	011 44
Guadeloupe	1	00 590	00 44
Guam	2	00 671	00 44
Guatemala	1	00 502	00 44
Guinea	1	00 224	†
Guinea-Bissau	1	00 245	†
Guyana	1	00 592	011 44
Haiti	1	00 509	†
Honduras	1	00 504	00 44
Hong Kong	1	00 852	001 44
Hungary	e	00 36	00 44
Iceland	e	00 354	00 44
India	1	00 91	00 44
Indonesia	1	00 62	00 44
Iran	1	00 98	00 44
Iraq	1	00 964	00 44
Ireland, Republic of	eu	00 353	00 44
Israel	1	00 972	00 44
Italy	eu	00 39	00 44
Jamaica	1	00 1 809	†
Japan	2	00 81	001 44
Jordan	1	00 962	00 44*
Kazakhstan	e	00 7	810 44
Kenya	1	00 254	00 44
Kiribati	2	00 686	09 44

Country	AZ	IDD from UK	IDD to UK	Country	AZ	IDD from UK	IDD to UK
Korea, North	2	00 850	010 44	Russia	*e*	00 7	810 44
Korea, South	2	00 82	001 44	Rwanda	1	00 250	00 44
Kuwait	1	00 965	00 44	St Helena	1	00 290	01 44
Kyrgystan	*e*	00 7	810 44	St Kitts and Nevis	1	00 1 809	†
Laos	1	00 856	†	St Lucia	1	00 1 809	0 44
Latvia	*e*	00 371	810 44	St Pierre and			
Lebanon	1	00 961	00 44	Miquelon	1	00 508	19*p*44
Lesotho	1	00 266	00 44	St Vincent and the			
Liberia	1	00 231	00 44	Grenadines	1	00 1 809	00 44
Libya	1	00 218	00 44	El Salvador	1	00 503	00 44
Liechtenstein	*e*	00 41 75	00 44	Samoa, American	2	00 684	144
Lithuania	*e*	00 370	810 44	San Marino	*eu*	00 378	00 44
Luxembourg	*eu*	00 352	00 44	São Tomé and			
Macao	1	00 853	00 44	Príncipe	1	00 239	00 44
Macedonia	*e*	00 389	99 44	Saudi Arabia	1	00 966	00 44
Madagascar	1	00 261	16*p*44	Senegal	1	00 221	00*p*44
Madeira	*eu*	00 351 91	00 44*	Serbia	*e*	00 381	99 44
Malawi	1	00 265	101 44	Seychelles	1	00 248	0 44
Malaysia	1	00 60	00 44	Sierra Leone	1	00 232	†
Maldives	1	00 960	00 44	Singapore	1	00 65	005 44
Mali	1	00 223	00 44	Slovak Republic	*e*	00 42	00 44
Malta	1	00 356	00 44	Slovenia	*e*	00 386	99 44
Mariana Islands,				Solomon Islands	2	00 677	00 44
Northern	2	00 670	010 44	Somalia	1	00 252	†
Marshall Islands	2	00 692	012 44	South Africa	1	00 27	09 44
Martinique	1	00 596	19*p*44	Spain	*eu*	00 34	07*p*44
Mauritania	1	00 222	00 44	Sri Lanka	1	00 94	00 44
Mauritius	1	00 230	00 44	Sudan	1	00 249	†
Mayotte	1	00 269	19*p*44	Suriname	1	00 597	00 44
Mexico	1	00 52	98 44	Swaziland	1	00 268	00 44
Micronesia, Federated				Sweden	*eu*	00 46	009 44*p*
States of	2	00 691	†	Switzerland	*e*	00 41	00 44
Moldova	*e*	00 373	810 44	Syria	1	00 963	00 44
Monaco	*eu*	00 33 93	19*p*44	Taiwan	2	00 886	002 44
Mongolia	2	00 976	†	Tajikistan	*e*	00 7	810 44
Montenegro	*e*	00 381	99 44	Tanzania	1	00 255	00 44
Montserrat	1	00 1 809	†	Thailand	1	00 66	001 44
Morocco	1	00 212	00*p*44	Tibet	1	00 86	00 44
Mozambique	1	00 258	00 44	Togo	1	00 228	00 44
Myanmar	1	00 95	0 44	Tonga	2	00 676	00 44
Namibia	1	00 264	09 44	Trinidad and Tobago	1	00 1 809	01 44
Nauru	2	00 674	00 44	Tristan da Cunha	1	†	†
Nepal	1	00 977	00 44	Tunisia	1	00 216	00 44
Netherlands	*eu*	00 31	00 44	Turkey	*e*	00 90	9*p*944
Netherlands Antilles	1	00 599	00 44	Turkmenistan	*e*	00 7	810 44
New Caledonia	2	00 687	00 44	Turks and Caicos			
New Zealand	2	00 64	00 44	Islands	1	00 1 809	0 44
Nicaragua	1	00 505	00 44	Tuvalu	2	00 688	†
Niger	1	00 227	00 44	Uganda	1	00 256	00 44
Nigeria	1	00 234	009 44	Ukraine	*e*	00 380	810 44
Niue	2	00 683	†	United Arab Emirates	1	00 971	00 44
Norfolk Island	2	00 672	00 44	Uruguay	1	00 598	00 44
Norway	*e*	00 47	095 44	USA	1	00 1	011 44
Oman	1	00 968	00 44	Alaska		00 1 907	011 44
Pakistan	1	00 92	00 44	Hawaii		00 1 808	011 44
Palau	2	00 6809	†	Uzbekistan	*e*	00 7	810 44
Panama	1	00 507	00 44	Vanuatu	2	00 678	00 44
Papua New Guinea	2	00 675	05 44	Vatican City State	*eu*	00 39 66982	00 44
Paraguay	1	00 595	002 44	Venezuela	1	00 58	00 44
			003 44	Vietnam	1	00 84	†
Peru	1	00 51	00 44	Virgin Islands (US)	1	00 1 809	011 44
Philippines	2	00 63	00 44	Western Samoa	2	00 685	†
Poland	*e*	00 48	0*p*044	Yemen			
Portugal	*eu*	00 351	00 44	north	1	00 967	00 44
Puerto Rico	1	00 1 809	135 44	south	1	00 965	00 44
Qatar	1	00 974	044	Yugoslav Fed. Rep.	*e*	00 381	99 44
Réunion	1	00 262	19*p*44	Zaïre	1	00 243	00 44
Romania	*e*	00 40	00 44	Zambia	1	00 260	00 44
				Zimbabwe	1	00 263	00 44

Weights and Measures

The Système International d'Unités (SI) is an international and coherent system of units devised to meet all known needs for measurement in science and technology. The system was adopted by the eleventh Conférence Générale des Poids et Mesures (CGPM) in 1960. A comprehensive description of the system is given in *SI The International System of Units*, HMSO. The British Standards describing the essential features of the International System of Units are *Specifications for SI units and recommendations for the use of their multiples and certain other units* (BS 5555:1993) and *Conversion Factors and Tables* (BS 350, Part 1:1974).

The system consists of seven base units and the derived units formed as products or quotients of various powers of the base units. Together the base units and the derived units make up the coherent system of units. In the UK the SI base units, and almost all important derived units, are realized at the National Physical Laboratory and disseminated through the National Measurement System.

BASE UNITS

metre (m) = unit of length
kilogram (kg) = unit of mass
second (s) = unit of time
Ampere (A) = unit of electric current
Kelvin (K) = unit of thermodynamic temperature
mole (mol) = unit of amount of substance
candela (cd) = unit of luminous intensity

DERIVED UNITS

For some of the derived SI units, special names and symbols exist; those approved by the CGPM are as follows:

Hertz (Hz) = unit of frequency
Newton (N) = unit of force
Pascal (Pa) = unit of pressure, stress
Joule (J) = unit of energy, work, quantity of heat
Watt (W) = unit of power, radiant flux
Coulomb (C) = unit of electric charge, quantity of electricity
Volt (V) = unit of electric potential, potential difference, electromotive force
Farad (F) = unit of electric capacitance
Ohm (Ω) = unit of electric resistance
Siemens (S) = unit of electric conductance
Weber (Wb) = unit of magnetic flux
Tesla (T) = unit of magnetic flux density
Henry (H) = unit of inductance
Degree Celsius (°C) = unit of Celsius temperature
Lumen (lm) = unit of luminous flux
Lux (lx) = unit of illuminance
Becquerel (Bq) = unit of activity (of a radionuclide)
Gray (Gy) = unit of absorbed dose, specific energy imparted, kerma, absorbed dose index
Sievert (Sv) = unit of dose equivalent, dose equivalent index

SUPPLEMENTARY UNITS

The derived units include, as a special case, the supplementary units which may be treated as dimensionless within the SI.

Radian (rad) = unit of plane angle
Steradian (sr) = unit of solid angle

Other derived units are expressed in terms of base units and/or supplementary units. Some of the more commonly-used derived units are the following:

Unit of area = square metre (m^2)
Unit of volume = cubic metre (m^3)
Unit of velocity = metre per second ($m\ s^{-1}$)
Unit of acceleration = metre per second squared ($m\ s^{-2}$)
Unit of density = kilogram per cubic metre ($kg\ m^{-3}$)
Unit of momentum = kilogram metre per second ($kg\ m\ s^{-1}$)
Unit of magnetic field strength = ampere per metre ($A\ m^{-1}$)
Unit of surface tension = newton per metre ($N\ m^{-1}$)
Unit of dynamic viscosity = pascal second (Pa s)
Unit of heat capacity = joule per kelvin ($J\ K^{-1}$)
Unit of specific heat capacity = joule per kilogram kelvin ($J\ kg^{-1}\ K^{-1}$)
Unit of heat flux density, irradiance = watt per square metre ($W\ m^{-2}$)
Unit of thermal conductivity = watt per metre kelvin ($W\ m^{-1}\ K^{-1}$)
Unit of electric field strength = volt per metre ($V\ m^{-1}$)
Unit of luminance = candela per square metre ($cd\ m^{-2}$)

SI PREFIXES

Decimal multiples and submultiples of the SI units are indicated by SI prefixes. These are as follows:

multiples	submultiples
yotta (Y) $\times 10^{24}$	deci (d) $\times 10^{-1}$
zetta (Z) $\times 10^{21}$	centi (c) $\times 10^{-2}$
exa (E) $\times 10^{18}$	milli (m) $\times 10^{-3}$
peta (P) $\times 10^{15}$	micro (μ) $\times 10^{-6}$
tera (T) $\times 10^{12}$	nano (n) $\times 10^{-9}$
giga (G) $\times 10^{9}$	pico (p) $\times 10^{-12}$
mega (M) $\times 10^{6}$	femto (f) $\times 10^{-15}$
kilo (k) $\times 10^{3}$	atto (a) $\times 10^{-18}$
hecto (h) $\times 10^{2}$	zepto (z) $\times 10^{-21}$
deca (da) $\times 10$	yocto (y) $\times 10^{-24}$

METRIC UNITS

The metric primary standards are the metre as the unit of measurement of length, and the kilogram as the unit of measurement of mass. Other units of measurement are defined by reference to the primary standards.

MEASUREMENT OF LENGTH

Kilometre (km) = 1000 metres
Metre (m) is the length of the path travelled by light in vacuum during a time interval of 1/299 792 458 of a second
Decimetre (dm) = 1/10 metre
Centimetre (cm) = 1/100 metre
Millimetre (mm) = 1/1000 metre

MEASUREMENT OF AREA

Hectare (ha) = 100 ares
Decare = 10 ares

Are (a) = 100 square metres
Square metre = a superficial area equal to that of a square
   each side of which measures one metre
Square decimetre = 1/100 square metre
Square centimetre = 1/100 square decimetre
Square millimetre = 1/100 square centimetre

MEASUREMENT OF VOLUME

Cubic metre (m³) = a volume equal to that of a cube each
   edge of which measures one metre
Cubic decimetre = 1/1000 cubic metre
Cubic centimetre (cc) = 1/1000 cubic decimetre
Hectolitre = 100 litres
Litre = a cubic decimetre
Decilitre = 1/10 litre
Centilitre = 1/100 litre
Millilitre = 1/1000 litre

MEASUREMENT OF CAPACITY

Hectolitre (hl) = 100 litres
Litre (l or L) = a cubic decimetre
Decilitre (dl) = 1/10 litre
Centilitre (cl) = 1/100 litre
Millilitre (ml) = 1/1000 litre

MEASUREMENT OF MASS OR WEIGHT

Tonne, metric tonne (t) = 1000 kilograms
Kilogram (kg) is equal to the mass of the international
   prototype of the kilogram
Hectogram (hg) = 1/10 kilogram
Gram (g) = 1/1000 kilogram
*Carat (metric) = 1/5 gram
Milligram (mg) = 1/1000 gram

*Used only for transactions in precious stones or pearls

METRICATION IN THE UK

The European Council Directive 80/181/EEC, as
amended by Council Directive 89/617/EEC, relates to
the use of units of measurement for economic, public
health, public safety or administrative purposes in the
member states of the European Union. The provisions of
the directives were incorporated into British law by the
Weights and Measures Act 1985 (Metrication) (Amendment) Order 1994 and the Units of Measurement Regulations 1994; these instruments amended the Weights and
Measures Act 1985. Parallel statutory rules amending
Northern Ireland weights and measures legislation were
made in May 1995.
   The general effect of the 1994 and 1995 legislation is to
end the use of imperial units of measurement for trade,
replacing them with metric units – see below for timetable
for UK metrication. Imperial units can, however, be used in
addition to metric units, as supplementary indications.

IMPERIAL UNITS

The imperial primary standards are the yard as the unit of
measurement of length and the pound as the unit of
measurement of mass. Other units of measurement are
defined by reference to the primary standards. Most of
these units are no longer authorized for use in trade in the
UK – see below.

MEASUREMENT OF LENGTH

*Mile = 1760 yards
Furlong = 220 yards
Chain = 22 yards

*Yard (yd) = 0.9144 metre
*Foot (ft) = 1/3 yard
*Inch (in) = 1/36 yard

MEASUREMENT OF AREA

Square mile = 640 acres
*Acre = 4840 square yards
Rood = 1210 square yards
Square yard (sq. yd) = a superficial area equal to that of a
   square each side of which measures one yard
Square foot (sq. ft) = 1/9 square yard
Square inch (sq. in) = 1/144 square foot

MEASUREMENT OF VOLUME

Cubic yard = a volume equal to that of a cube each edge of
   which measures one yard
Cubic foot = 1/27 cubic yard
Cubic inch = 1/1728 cubic foot

MEASUREMENT OF CAPACITY

Bushel = 8 gallons
Peck = 2 gallons
Gallon (gal) = 4.546 09 cubic decimetres
Quart (qt) = 1/4 gallon
*Pint (pt) = 1/2 quart
Gill = 1/4 pint
*Fluid ounce (fl oz) = 1/20 pint
Fluid drachm = 1/8 fluid ounce
Minim (min) = 1/60 fluid drachm

MEASUREMENT OF MASS OR WEIGHT

Ton = 2240 pounds
Hundredweight (cwt) = 112 pounds
Cental = 100 pounds
Quarter = 28 pounds
Stone = 14 pounds
*Pound (lb) = 0.453 592 37 kilogram
*Ounce (oz) = 1/16 pound
*†Ounce troy (oz tr) = 12/175 pound
Dram (dr) = 1/16 ounce
Grain (gr) = 1/7000 pound
Pennyweight (dwt) = 24 grains
Ounce apothecaries = 480 grains
Drachm (ʒ1) = 1/8 ounce apothecaries
Scruple (Ә1) = 1/3 drachm

*Units of measurement still authorized for use in trade, etc., in the UK
†Used only for transactions in gold, silver or other precious metals, and
articles made therefrom

PHASING-OUT OF IMPERIAL UNITS IN THE UK

The Weights and Measures Act 1985 enacted the legal
units for the United Kingdom. It was amended to
implement the provisions of European Council Directive
80/181/EEC, as amended by Directive 89/617/EEC, by
the Weights and Measures Act 1985 (Metrication)
(Amendment) Order 1994 and the Units of Measurement
Regulations 1994, and by parallel statutory rules in
Northern Ireland in May 1995.
   The effect of the amended legislation is to phase out the
use of imperial units for trade, replacing them with metric
units. With effect from 30 September 1995 imperial units
ceased to be authorized for use in the UK for economic,
public health, public safety and administrative purposes,
with the following exceptions:

520   Weights and Measures

1 Units of measurement authorized for use in specialized fields between 1 October 1995 and 31 December 1999

Unit	Field of application
fathom	Marine navigation
fluid ounce } pint }	Beer, cider, water, lemonade, fruit juice in returnable containers
ounce } pound }	Goods for sale loose from bulk
therm	Gas supply

2 Units of measurement authorized for use in specialized fields from 1 October 1995, without time limit

Unit	Field of application
inch foot yard mile }	Road traffic signs, distance and speed measurement
pint {	Dispense of draught beer or cider Milk in returnable containers
acre	Land registration
troy ounce	Transactions in precious metals

MEASUREMENT OF ELECTRICITY

Units of measurement of electricity are defined by the Weights and Measures Act 1985 as follows:

Ampere (A) = that constant current which, if maintained in two straight parallel conductors of infinite length, of negligible circular cross-section and placed 1 metre apart in vacuum, would produce between these conductors a force equal to 2×10^{-7} newton per metre of length

Ohm (Ω) = the electric resistance between two points of a conductor when a constant potential difference of 1 volt, applied between the two points, produces in the conductor a current of 1 ampere, the conductor not being the seat of any electromotive force

Volt (V) = the difference of electric potential between two points of a conducting wire carrying a constant current of 1 ampere when the power dissipated between these points is equal to 1 watt

Watt (W) = the power which in one second gives rise to energy of 1 joule

Kilowatt (kW) = 1000 watts

Megawatt (MW) = one million watts

WATER AND LIQUOR MEASURES

1 cubic foot = 62.32 lb
1 gallon = 10 lb
1 cubic cm = 1 gram
1000 cubic cm = 1 litre; 1 kilogram
1 cubic metre = 1000 litres; 1000 kg; 1 tonne
An inch of rain on the surface of an acre (43560 sq. ft) = 3630 cubic ft = 100.992 tons

Cisterns: A cistern 4 × 2½ feet and 3 feet deep will hold brimful 186.963 gallons, weighing 1869.63 lb in addition to its own weight

WATER FOR SHIPS

Kilderkin = 18 gallons
Barrel = 36 gallons
Puncheon = 72 gallons
Butt = 110 gallons
Tun = 210 gallons

BOTTLES OF WINE

Traditional equivalents in standard champagne bottles:
Magnum = 2 bottles
Jeroboam = 4 bottles
Rehoboam = 6 bottles
Methuselah = 8 bottles
Salmanazar = 12 bottles
Balthazar = 16 bottles
Nebuchadnezzar = 20 bottles

A quarter of a bottle is known as a *nip*
An eighth of a bottle is known as a *baby*

ANGULAR AND CIRCULAR MEASURES

60 seconds (″) = 1 minute (′)
60 minutes = 1 degree (°)
90 degrees = 1 right angle or quadrant
Diameter of circle × 3.141 6 = circumference
Diameter squared × 0.7854 = area of circle
Diameter squared × 3.141 6 = surface of sphere
Diameter cubed × 0.523 = solidity of sphere
One degree of circumference × 57.3 = radius*
Diameter of cylinder × 3.141 6; product by length or height, gives the surface
Diameter squared × 0.7854; product by length or height, gives solid content

*Or, one radian (the angle subtended at the centre of a circle by an arc of the circumference equal in length to the radius) = 57.3 degrees

MILLION, BILLION, ETC.

Value in the United Kingdom

Million	thousand × thousand	10^6
Billion	million × million	10^{12}
Trillion	million × billion	10^{18}
Quadrillion	million × trillion	10^{24}

Value in USA

Million	thousand × thousand	10^6
Billion	thousand × million	10^9
Trillion	million × million	10^{12}
Quadrillion	million × billion US	10^{15}

The American usage of billion (i.e. 10^9) is increasingly common, and is now universally used by statisticians

NAUTICAL MEASURES

DISTANCE

Distance at sea is measured in nautical miles. The British standard nautical mile was 6080 feet (the length of a minute of an arc of a great circle of the earth, rounded off to a mean value to allow for the length varying at different latitudes). This measure has been obsolete since 1970 when the international nautical mile of 1852 metres was adopted by the Hydrographic Department of the Ministry of Defence as a result of a recommendation by the International Hydrographic Bureau.

The cable (600 feet or 100 fathoms) was a measure approximately one-tenth of a nautical mile. Such distances are now expressed in decimal parts of a sea mile or in metres.

Soundings at sea were recorded in fathoms (6 feet). Depths are now expressed in metres on Admiralty charts.

SPEED

Speed is measured in nautical miles per hour, called knots. A ship moving at the rate of 30 nautical miles per hour is said to be doing 30 knots.

knots	m.p.h.	knots	m.p.h.
1	1.1515	9	10.3636
2	2.3030	10	11.5151
3	3.4545	15	17.2727
4	4.6060	20	23.0303
5	5.7575	25	28.7878
6	6.9090	30	34.5454
7	8.0606	35	40.3030
8	9.2121	40	46.0606

TONNAGE

The tonnage of a vessel is measured in tons of 100 cubic feet.

Gross tonnage = the total volume of all the enclosed spaces of a vessel

Net tonnage = gross tonnage less deductions for crew space, engine room, water ballast and other spaces not used for passengers or cargo

---

DISTANCE OF THE HORIZON

The limit of distance to which one can see varies with the height of the spectator. The greatest distance at which an object on the surface of the sea, or of a level plain, can be seen by a person whose eyes are at a height of five feet from the same level is nearly three miles. At a height of 20 feet the range is increased to nearly six miles, and an approximate rule for finding the range of vision for small heights is to increase the square root of the number of feet that the eye is above the level surface by a third of itself. The result is the distance of the horizon in miles, but is slightly in excess of that in the table below, which is computed by a more precise formula. The table may be used conversely to show the distance of an object of given height that is just visible from a point on the surface of the earth or sea. Refraction is taken into account both in the approximate rule and in the table.

Height in feet	range in miles
5	2.9
20	5.9
50	9.3
100	13.2
500	29.5
1,000	41.6
2,000	58.9
3,000	72.1
4,000	83.3
5,000	93.1
20,000	186.2

TEMPERATURE SCALES

The SI (International System) unit of temperature is the Kelvin, which is defined as the fraction 1/273.16 of the temperature of the triple point of water (i.e. where ice, water and water vapour are in equilibrium). The zero of the Kelvin scale is the absolute zero of temperature. The freezing point of water is 273.15 K and the boiling point (as adopted in the International Temperature Scale of 1990) is 373.124 K.

The Celsius scale (formerly centigrade) is defined by subtracting 273.15 from the Kelvin temperature. The Fahrenheit scale is related to the Celsius scale by the relationships:

$$\text{temperature }°F = (\text{temperature }°C \times 1.8) + 32$$
$$\text{temperature }°C = (\text{temperature }°F - 32) \div 1.8$$

It follows from these definitions that the freezing point of water is 0°C and 32°F. The boiling point is 99.974°C and 211.953°F.

The temperature of the human body varies from person to person and in the same person can be affected by a variety of factors. In most people body temperature varies between 36.5°C and 37.2°C (97.7–98.9°F).

Conversion between scales

°C	°F	°C	°F	°C	°F
100	212	60	140	20	68
99	210.2	59	138.2	19	66.2
98	208.4	58	136.4	18	64.4
97	206.6	57	134.6	17	62.6
96	204.8	56	132.8	16	60.8
95	203	55	131	15	59
94	201.2	54	129.2	14	57.2
93	199.4	53	127.4	13	55.4
92	197.6	52	125.6	12	53.6
91	195.8	51	123.8	11	51.8
90	194	50	122	10	50
89	192.2	49	120.2	9	48.2
88	190.4	48	118.4	8	46.4
87	188.6	47	116.6	7	44.6
86	186.8	46	114.8	6	42.8
85	185	45	113	5	41
84	183.2	44	111.2	4	39.2
83	181.4	43	109.4	3	37.4
82	179.6	42	107.6	2	35.6
81	177.8	41	105.8	1	33.8
80	176	40	104	zero	32
79	174.2	39	102.2	− 1	30.2
78	172.4	38	100.4	− 2	28.4
77	170.6	37	98.6	− 3	26.6
76	168.8	36	96.8	− 4	24.8
75	167	35	95	− 5	23
74	165.2	34	93.2	− 6	21.2
73	163.4	33	91.4	− 7	19.4
72	161.6	32	89.6	− 8	17.6
71	159.8	31	87.8	− 9	15.8
70	158	30	86	−10	14
69	156.2	29	84.2	−11	12.2
68	154.4	28	82.4	−12	10.4
67	152.6	27	80.6	−13	8.6
66	150.8	26	78.8	−14	6.8
65	149	25	77	−15	5
64	147.2	24	75.2	−16	3.2
63	145.4	23	73.4	−17	1.4
62	143.6	22	71.6	−18	0.4
61	141.8	21	69.8	−19	−2.2

PAPER MEASURES

Printing Paper		Writing Paper	
516 sheets = 1 ream		480 sheets = 1 ream	
2 reams = 1 bundle		20 quires = 1 ream	
5 bundles = 1 bale		24 sheets = 1 quire	

BROWN PAPERS

	inches		inches
Casing	46 × 36	Imperial Cap	29 × 22
Double Imperial	45 × 29	Haven Cap	26 × 21
Elephant	34 × 24	Bag Cap	24 × 19½
Double Four		Kent Cap	21 × 18
Pound	31 × 21		

PRINTING PAPERS

	inches		inches
Foolscap	17 × 13½	Double Large	
Double Foolscap	27 × 17	Post	33 × 21
Quad Foolscap	34 × 27	Demy	22½ × 17½
Crown	20 × 15	Double Demy	35 × 22½
Double Crown	30 × 20	Quad Demy	45 × 35
Quad Crown	40 × 30	Music Demy	20 × 15½
Double Quad		Medium	23 × 18
Crown	60 × 40	Royal	25 × 20
Post	19½×15½	Super Royal	27½×20½
Double Post	31½×19½	Elephant	28 × 23
		Imperial	30 × 22

WRITING AND DRAWING PAPERS

	inches		inches
Emperor	72 × 48	Copy or Draft	20 × 16
Antiquarian	53 × 31	Demy	20 × 15½
Double Elephant	40 × 27	Post	19 × 15¼
Grand Eagle	42 × 28¾	Pinched Post	18½×14¾
Atlas	34 × 26	Foolscap	17 × 13½
Colombier	34½ × 23½	Double Foolscap	26½× 16½
Imperial	30 × 22	Double Post	30½× 19
Elephant	28 × 23	Double Large	
Cartridge	26 × 21	Post	33 × 21
Super Royal	27 × 19	Double Demy	31 × 20
Royal	24 × 19	Brief	16½×13½
Medium	22 × 17½	Pott	15 × 12½
Large Post	21 × 16½		

INTERNATIONAL PAPER SIZES

The basis of the international series of paper sizes is a rectangle having an area of one square metre, the sides of which are in the proportion of $1:\sqrt{2}$. The proportions $1:\sqrt{2}$ have a geometrical relationship, the side and diagonal of any square being in this proportion. The effect of this arrangement is that if the area of the sheet of paper is doubled or halved, the shorter side and the longer side of the new sheet are still in the same proportion $1:\sqrt{2}$. This feature is useful where photographic enlargement or reduction is used, as the proportions remain the same.

Description of the A series is by capital A followed by a figure. The basic size has the description A0 and the higher the figure following the letter, the greater is the number of sub-divisions and therefore the smaller the sheet. Half A0 is A1 and half A1 is A2. Where larger dimensions are required the A is preceded by a figure. Thus 2A means twice the size A0; 4A is four times the size of A0.

SUBSIDIARY SERIES

B sizes are sizes intermediate between any two adjacent sizes of the A series. There is a series of C sizes which is used much less. A is for magazines and books, B for posters,

wall charts and other large items, C for envelopes particularly where it is necessary for an envelope (in C series) to fit into another envelope. The size recommended for business correspondence is A4.

Long sizes (DL) are obtainable by dividing any appropriate sizes from the two series above into three, four or eight equal parts parallel with the shorter side in such a manner that the proportion of $1:\sqrt{2}$ is not maintained, the ratio between the longer and the shorter sides being greater than $\sqrt{2}:1$. In practice long sizes should be produced from the A series only.

It is an essential feature of these series that the dimensions are of the trimmed or finished size.

A SERIES

	mm		mm
A0	841 × 1189	A6	105 × 148
A1	594 × 841	A7	74 × 105
A2	420 × 594	A8	52 × 74
A3	297 × 420	A9	37 × 52
A4	210 × 297	A10	26 × 37
A5	148 × 210		

B SERIES

	mm		mm
B0	1000 × 1414	B6	125 × 176
B1	707 × 1000	B7	88 × 125
B2	500 × 707	B8	62 × 88
B3	353 × 500	B9	44 × 62
B4	250 × 353	B10	31 × 44
B5	176 × 250		

C SERIES   DL

	mm		mm
C4	324 × 229	DL	110 × 220
C5	229 × 162		
C6	114 × 162		

BOUND BOOKS

The book sizes most commonly used are listed below. Approximate centimetre equivalents are also shown. International sizes are converted to their nearest imperial size, e.g. A4 = D4; A5 = D8.

		inches	cm
Crown 32mo	C32	2⅛ × 3⅜	6 × 9
Crown 16mo	C16	3⅜ × 5	9 × 13
Foolscap 8vo	F8	4¼ × 6¾	11 × 17
Demy 16mo	D16	4⅜ × 5⅝	11 × 14
Crown 8vo	C8	5 × 7½	13 × 19
Demy 8vo	D8	5⅝ × 8¾	14 × 22
Medium 8vo	M8	5¾ × 9	15 × 23
Royal 8vo	R8	6¼ × 10	16 × 25
Super Royal 8vo	suR8	6⅞ × 10	17 × 25
Foolscap 4to	F4	6¾ × 8½	17 × 22
Crown 4to	C4	7½ × 10	19 × 25
Imperial 8vo	Imp8	7½ × 11	19 × 28
Demy 4to	D4	8¾ × 11¼	22 × 29
Royal 4to	R4	10 × 12½	25 × 31
Super Royal 4to	suR4	10 × 13½	25 × 34
Crown Folio	Cfol	10 × 15	25 × 38
Imperial Folio	Impfol	11 × 15	28 × 38

Folio = a sheet folded in half
Quarto (4to) = a sheet folded into four
Octavo (8vo) = a sheet folded into eight
Books are usually bound up in sheets of 16, 32 or 64 pages. Octavo books are generally printed 64 pages at a time, 32 pages on each side of a sheet of quad.

CONVERSION TABLES FOR WEIGHTS AND MEASURES

Bold figures equal units of either of the columns beside them; thus: 1 cm = 0.394 inches and 1 inch = 2.540 cm

LENGTH			AREA			VOLUME			WEIGHT (MASS)		
Centimetres		*Inches*	*Square cm*		*Square in*	*Cubic cm*		*Cubic in*	*Kilograms*		*Pounds*
2.540	1	0.394	6.452	1	0.155	16.387	1	0.061	0.454	1	2.205
5.080	2	0.787	12.903	2	0.310	32.774	2	0.122	0.907	2	4.409
7.620	3	1.181	19.355	3	0.465	49.161	3	0.183	1.361	3	6.614
10.160	4	1.575	25.806	4	0.620	65.548	4	0.244	1.814	4	8.819
12.700	5	1.969	32.258	5	0.775	81.936	5	0.305	2.268	5	11.023
15.240	6	2.362	38.710	6	0.930	98.323	6	0.366	2.722	6	13.228
17.780	7	2.756	45.161	7	1.085	114.710	7	0.427	3.175	7	15.432
20.320	8	3.150	51.613	8	1.240	131.097	8	0.488	3.629	8	17.637
22.860	9	3.543	58.064	9	1.395	147.484	9	0.549	4.082	9	19.842
25.400	10	3.937	64.516	10	1.550	163.871	10	0.610	4.536	10	22.046
50.800	20	7.874	129.032	20	3.100	327.742	20	1.220	9.072	20	44.092
76.200	30	11.811	193.548	30	4.650	491.613	30	1.831	13.608	30	66.139
101.600	40	15.748	258.064	40	6.200	655.484	40	2.441	18.144	40	88.185
127.000	50	19.685	322.580	50	7.750	819.355	50	3.051	22.680	50	110.231
152.400	60	23.622	387.096	60	9.300	983.226	60	3.661	27.216	60	132.277
177.800	70	27.559	451.612	70	10.850	1147.097	70	4.272	31.752	70	154.324
203.200	80	31.496	516.128	80	12.400	1310.968	80	4.882	36.287	80	176.370
228.600	90	35.433	580.644	90	13.950	1474.839	90	5.492	40.823	90	198.416
254.000	100	39.370	645.160	100	15.500	1638.710	100	6.102	45.359	100	220.464

Metres		*Yards*	*Square m*		*Square yd*	*Cubic m*		*Cubic yd*	*Metric tonnes*		*Tons (UK)*
0.914	1	1.094	0.836	1	1.196	0.765	1	1.308	1.016	1	0.984
1.829	2	2.187	1.672	2	2.392	1.529	2	2.616	2.032	2	1.968
2.743	3	3.281	2.508	3	3.588	2.294	3	3.924	3.048	3	2.953
3.658	4	4.374	3.345	4	4.784	3.058	4	5.232	4.064	4	3.937
4.572	5	5.468	4.181	5	5.980	3.823	5	6.540	5.080	5	4.921
5.486	6	6.562	5.017	6	7.176	4.587	6	7.848	6.096	6	5.905
6.401	7	7.655	5.853	7	8.372	5.352	7	9.156	7.112	7	6.889
7.315	8	8.749	6.689	8	9.568	6.116	8	10.464	8.128	8	7.874
8.230	9	9.843	7.525	9	10.764	6.881	9	11.772	9.144	9	8.858
9.144	10	10.936	8.361	10	11.960	7.646	10	13.080	10.161	10	9.842
18.288	20	21.872	16.723	20	23.920	15.291	20	26.159	20.321	20	19.684
27.432	30	32.808	25.084	30	35.880	22.937	30	39.239	30.481	30	29.526
36.576	40	43.745	33.445	40	47.840	30.582	40	52.318	40.642	40	39.368
45.720	50	54.681	41.806	50	59.799	38.228	50	65.398	50.802	50	49.210
54.864	60	65.617	50.168	60	71.759	45.873	60	78.477	60.963	60	59.052
64.008	70	76.553	58.529	70	83.719	53.519	70	91.557	71.123	70	68.894
73.152	80	87.489	66.890	80	95.679	61.164	80	104.636	81.284	80	78.737
82.296	90	98.425	75.251	90	107.639	68.810	90	117.716	91.444	90	88.579
91.440	100	109.361	83.613	100	119.599	76.455	100	130.795	101.605	100	98.421

Kilometres		*Miles*	*Hectares*		*Acres*	*Litres*		*Gallons*	*Metric tonnes*		*Tons (US)*
1.609	1	0.621	0.405	1	2.471	4.546	1	0.220	0.907	1	1.102
3.219	2	1.243	0.809	2	4.942	9.092	2	0.440	1.814	2	2.205
4.828	3	1.864	1.214	3	7.413	13.638	3	0.660	2.722	3	3.305
6.437	4	2.485	1.619	4	9.844	18.184	4	0.880	3.629	4	4.409
8.047	5	3.107	2.023	5	12.355	22.730	5	1.100	4.536	5	5.521
9.656	6	3.728	2.428	6	14.826	27.276	6	1.320	5.443	6	6.614
11.265	7	4.350	2.833	7	17.297	31.822	7	1.540	6.350	7	7.716
12.875	8	4.971	3.327	8	19.769	36.368	8	1.760	7.257	8	8.818
14.484	9	5.592	3.642	9	22.240	40.914	9	1.980	8.165	9	9.921
16.093	10	6.214	4.047	10	24.711	45.460	10	2.200	9.072	10	11.023
32.187	20	12.427	8.094	20	49.421	90.919	20	4.400	18.144	20	22.046
48.280	30	18.641	12.140	30	74.132	136.379	30	6.599	27.216	30	33.069
64.374	40	24.855	16.187	40	98.842	181.839	40	8.799	36.287	40	44.092
80.467	50	31.069	20.234	50	123.555	227.298	50	10.999	45.359	50	55.116
96.561	60	37.282	24.281	60	148.263	272.758	60	13.199	54.431	60	66.139
112.654	70	43.496	28.328	70	172.974	318.217	70	15.398	63.503	70	77.162
128.748	80	49.710	32.375	80	197.684	363.677	80	17.598	72.575	80	88.185
144.841	90	55.923	36.422	90	222.395	409.137	90	19.798	81.647	90	99.208
160.934	100	62.137	40.469	100	247.105	454.596	100	21.998	90.719	100	110.231

Development Corporations

NEW TOWNS

COMMISSION FOR THE NEW TOWNS
Glen House, Stag Place, London SW1E 5AJ
Tel 0171-828 7722

The Commission was established under the New Towns Act 1959. Its remit is to hold, manage and turn to account the property of development corporations transferred to the Commission; and to dispose of property so transferred and any other property held by it, as soon as it considers it expedient to do so. In carrying out its remit the Commission must have due regard to the convenience and welfare of persons residing, working or carrying on business there and, until disposal, the maintenance and enhancement of the value of the land held and return obtained from it.

The Commission has such responsibilities in Basildon, Bracknell, Central Lancashire, Corby, Crawley, Harlow, Hatfield, Hemel Hempstead, Milton Keynes, Northampton, Peterborough, Redditch, Skelmersdale, Stevenage, Telford, Warrington and Runcorn, Washington, and Welwyn Garden City. The Commission has minimal responsibilities (principally financial and litigation) in Aycliffe and Peterlee, and Cwmbran following the wind-up of their development corporations in 1988.
Chairman, Dr J. R. G. Bradfield, CBE
Members, R. B. Caws, CBE; F. C. Graves, OBE; Sir Brian Jenkins, GBE; M. H. Mallinson; Lady Marsh; J. Trustram Eve
Chief Executive, N. J. Walker

REGIONAL OFFICES
NORTH (Central Lancashire, Skelmersdale, Warrington and Runcorn, Washington, Aycliffe and Peterlee), New Town House, Buttermarket Street, Warrington WA1 2LF. Tel: 01925-651144. *Director,* J. Leigh
CENTRAL (Milton Keynes, Corby, Northampton), Saxon Court, 502 Avebury Boulevard, Central Milton Keynes MK9 3HS. Tel: 01908-692692. *Director,* J. Napleton
WEST MIDLANDS (Redditch, Telford), Jordan House West, Hall Court, Hall Park Way, Telford TF3 4NN. Tel: 01952-293131. *Director,* C. Mackrell
SOUTH (Basildon, Bracknell, Crawley, Harlow, Hatfield, Hemel Hempstead, Stevenage, Welwyn Garden City), Glen House, Stag Place, London SW1E 5AJ. Tel: 0171-828 7722. *Director,* G. D. Johnston

DEVELOPMENT CORPORATIONS
WALES
DEVELOPMENT BOARD FOR RURAL WALES (1977), Ladywell House, Newtown, Powys SY16 1JB. Tel: 01686-626965. *Chairman,* D. Rowe-Beddoe

SCOTLAND
CUMBERNAULD (1956), Cumbernauld House, Cumbernauld G67 3JH. *Chairman,* D. W. Mitchell, CBE. *General Manager,* D. R. Lind. Area, 7,788 acres. Population, 52,060. To be wound up December 1996
EAST KILBRIDE (1947), Atholl House, East Kilbride, Glasgow G74 1LU. *Chairman,* H. H. Marshall, OBE. *Managing Director,* J. C. Shaw. Area, 10,250 acres. Population, 71,940. To be wound up 31 December 1995

GLENROTHES (1948), Balgonie Road, Markinch, Glenrothes KY7 6AH. *Chairman,* Prof. C. Blake, CBE. *General Manager,* J. A. F. McCombie. Area, 5,780 acres. Population, 39,700. To be wound up 31 December 1995
IRVINE (1966), Perceton House, Irvine, Ayrshire KA11 2AL. *Chairman,* M. Crichton, CBE. *Managing Director,* J. Murdoch. Area, 16,000 acres. Population, 56,000. To be wound up March 1997
LIVINGSTON (1962), Sidlaw House, Almondvale North, Livingston, West Lothian EH54 6QA. *Chairman,* R. S. Watt, CBE. *Chief Executive,* J. A. Pollock. Area, 6,868 acres. Population, 43,800. To be wound up December 1996

URBAN DEVELOPMENT CORPORATIONS

Urban development corporations were established under the Local Government, Planning and Land Act 1980. Their remit is to bring land and buildings in selected areas back into effective use by developing infrastructure, housing, employment and the environment. The corporations encourage business, especially from overseas, to invest in the area and can provide grants to assist commercial and industrial development.

ENGLAND
BIRMINGHAM HEARTLANDS (1992), Waterlinks House, Richard Street, Birmingham, B7 4AA. Tel: 0121–333 3060. *Chairman,* Sir Reginald Eyre; *Chief Executive,* J. Beeston. Area, 1,000 hectares. To be wound up March 1998
BLACK COUNTRY (1987), Black Country House, Rounds Green Road, Oldbury B69 2RD. Tel: 0121–511 2000. *Chairman,* G. Carter, CBE; *Chief Executive,* D. Morgan. Area, 2,600 hectares. To be wound up March 1998
BRISTOL (1989), 2nd Floor, Techno House, Redcliffe Way, Bristol BS1 6NX. Tel: 0117–925 5222. *Chairman,* C. Thomas, CBE; *Chief Executive,* G. M. Collinge. Area, 360 hectares. To be wound up 31 December 1995
CENTRAL MANCHESTER (1988), Churchgate House, 56 Oxford Street, Manchester M1 6EU. Tel: 0161–236 1166. *Chairman,* Dr J. Grigor, OBE; *Chief Executive,* J. Glester. Area, 187 hectares. To be wound up 31 March 1996
LEEDS, wound up 31 March 1995
LONDON DOCKLANDS (1981), Thames Quay, 191 Marsh Wall, London E14 9TJ. Tel: 0171–512 3000. *Chairman,* M. Pickard; *Chief Executive,* E. Sorenson. Area, 2,226 hectares. To be wound up March 1998
MERSEYSIDE (1981), Royal Liver Buildings, Pier Head, Liverpool L3 1JH. Tel: 0151–236 6090. *Chairman,* Sir Desmond Pitcher; *Chief Executive,* C. Farrow. Area, 960 hectares. To be wound up March 1998
PLYMOUTH (1993), Royal William Yard, Plymouth PL1 3RP. Tel: 01752–256132. *Chairman,* Sir Robert Gerken, KCB, CBE; *Chief Executive,* J. Collinson. Area, 67 hectares. To be wound up March 1998
SHEFFIELD (1988), Don Valley House, Saville Street East, Sheffield S4 7UQ. Tel: 0114–272 0100. *Chairman,* H. Sykes; *Chief Executive,* G. Kendall. Area, 800 hectares. To be wound up March 1997
TEESSIDE (1987), Dunedin House, Riverside Quay, Stockton-on-Tees TS17 6BJ. Tel: 01642–677123. *Chairman,* Sir Ronald Norman, OBE; *Chief Executive,*

D. Hall. Area, 4,600 hectares. To be wound up March 1998
TRAFFORD PARK (1987), Waterside, Trafford Wharf Road, Trafford Park, Manchester M17 1EX. Tel: 0161–848 8000. *Chairman*, W. Morgan; *Chief Executive*, M. Shields. Area, 1,270 hectares. To be wound up March 1998
TYNE AND WEAR (1987), Scotswood House, Newcastle Business Park, Newcastle upon Tyne NE4 7YL. Tel: 0191–226 1234. *Chairman*, Sir Paul Nicholson; *Chief Executive*, A. Balls, CB. Area, 2,400 hectares. To be wound up March 1998

WALES
CARDIFF BAY (1987), Baltic House, Mount Stuart Square, Cardiff CF1 6DH. Tel: 01222–823958. *Chairman*, Sir Geoffrey Inkin, OBE; *Chief Executive*, M. Boyce. Area, 1,094 hectares

NORTHERN IRELAND
LAGANSIDE (1989), Clarendon Building, 15 Clarendon Road, Belfast BT1 3BG. Tel: 01232–328507. *Chairman*, The Duke of Abercorn; *Chief Executive*, G. Mackey. Area, 122 hectares

HM Coastguard

Founded in 1822, originally to guard the coasts against smuggling, HM Coastguard's role today is the very different one of guarding and saving life at sea. The Service is responsible for co-ordinating all civil maritime search and rescue operations around the 10,500 mile coastline of Great Britain and Northern Ireland and 1,000 miles into the Atlantic. In addition, it co-operates with search and rescue organizations of neighbouring countries in western Europe and around the Atlantic seaboard. The Service maintains a 24-hour radar watch on the Dover Strait, providing a Channel navigation information service for all shipping in one of the busiest sea lanes in the world. It also liaises very closely with the off-shore oil and gas industry and with merchant shipping companies.

Since 1978 HM Coastguard has been organized into six regions, each with a Regional Controller. Each region is subdivided into districts under District Controllers, operating from Maritime Rescue Co-ordination Centres or Sub-Centres. In all there are 21 of these centres. They are on 24-hour watch and are fitted with a comprehensive range of communications equipment. They are supported by some 3,500 smaller stations staffed by part-time Auxiliary Coastguards under the direction of Regulars, each of which keeps its parent centre fully informed of day-to-day casualty risk, particularly on the more remote danger spots around the coast.

Between 1 January and 31 December 1994, the 450 Regular and 3,500 Auxiliary Coastguards co-ordinated 10,409 incidents requiring search and rescue facilities,

resulting in assistance being given to 16,627 persons. All distress telephone and radio calls are centralized on the 21 centres, which are on the alert for people or vessels in distress, shipping hazards and pollution incidents. Using modern telecommunications equipment, including satellite, they can alert and co-ordinate the most appropriate rescue facilities; RNLI lifeboats, Royal Navy, RAF or Coastguard helicopters, fixed-wing aircraft, vessels in the vicinity, or Coastguard shore and cliff rescue teams.

For those who regularly sail in local waters or make longer passages, the Coastguard Yacht and Boat Safety Scheme provides a valuable free service. Its aim is to give the Coastguard a record of the details of craft, their equipment fit and normal operating areas. Yacht and Boat Safety Scheme cards are available from all Coastguard stations, harbourmasters' offices, and most yacht clubs and marinas as well as Coastguard Headquarters.

Members of the public who see an accident or a potentially dangerous incident on or around the coast should dial 999 and ask for the Coastguard.

On 1 April 1994 HM Coastguard and the Marine Pollution Control Unit together formed the Coastguard Agency, an executive agency of the Department of Transport.

Coastguard Headquarters and Office of the Chief Coastguard, Spring Place, 105 Commercial Road, Southampton SO15 1EG. Tel: 01703 – 329100

Local Government

The Local Government Acts of 1972 and 1985, the Local Government (Scotland) Act 1973 and the London Government Act 1963 are the main Acts which have brought about the present structure of local government in Great Britain. This structure has been in effect in England and Wales since 1974, with alterations in 1986 with the abolition of the metropolitan counties and the Greater London Council; and in Scotland since 1975.

The structure is based on two tiers of local authorities (county or regional councils and district councils) in the non-metropolitan areas; and a single tier of metropolitan and London borough councils in the six metropolitan areas of England and in London respectively.

Following recent reviews of the structure of local government in England by the Local Government Commission, the Government proposes to create 38 unitary (all-purpose) authorities to cover certain areas in the non-metropolitan counties. The remaining county areas will continue to have two tiers of local authorities. The county and district councils in the Isle of Wight were replaced by a single unitary authority on 1 April 1995; changes in other areas should take effect in either April 1996 or April 1997.

Legislation passed in 1994 abolishes the two-tier structure in Wales and Scotland with effect from 1 April 1996 and replaces it with a single tier of unitary authorities.

Local authorities are empowered or required by various Acts of Parliament to carry out functions in their areas. The legislation concerned comprises public general Acts and 'local' Acts which local authorities have promoted as private bills.

Elections

Local elections are normally held on the first Thursday in May. Generally, all British subjects or citizens of the Republic of Ireland of 18 years or over who are resident on the qualifying date in the area for which the election is being held, are entitled to vote at local government elections. A register of electors is prepared and published annually by local electoral registration officers.

A returning officer has the overall responsibility for an election. Voting takes place at polling stations, arranged by the local authority and under the supervision of a presiding officer specially appointed for the purpose. Candidates, who are subject to various statutory qualifications and disqualifications designed to ensure that they are suitable persons to hold office, must be nominated by electors for the electoral area concerned.

In England, the Local Government Commission is responsible for carrying out periodic reviews of electoral arrangements and making proposals to the Secretary of State for changes found necessary. In Wales and Scotland these matters are the responsibility of the Local Boundary Commission for Wales and the Local Boundary Commission for Scotland respectively.

Local Government Commission for England, Dolphyn Court, 10–11 Great Turnstile, Lincoln's Inn Fields, London WC1V 7JU. Tel: 0171-430 8400

Internal Organization

The council as a whole is the final decision-making body within any authority. Councils are free to a great extent to make their own internal organizational arrangements.

Normally, questions of policy are settled by the full council, while the administration of the various services is the responsibility of committees of councillors. Day-to-day decisions are delegated to the council's officers, who act within the policies laid down by the councillors.

FINANCE

Local government in England, Wales and Scotland is financed from four sources: the council tax, non-domestic rates, government grants, and income from fees and charges for services. (For arrangements in Northern Ireland, *see* page 530.)

Council Tax

Under the Local Government Finance Act 1992, from 1 April 1993 the council tax replaced the community charge (which had been introduced in April 1989 in Scotland and April 1990 in England and Wales in place of domestic rates).

The council tax is a local tax levied by each local council. Liability for the council tax bill usually falls on the owner-occupier or tenant of a dwelling which is their sole or main residence. Council tax bills may be reduced because of the personal circumstances of people resident in a property, and there are discounts in the case of dwellings occupied by fewer than two adults.

In England and Wales, each county council and each district council (and, from 1 April 1996, each police authority) sets its own council tax rate. The district councils collect the combined council tax and the county councils (and, from 1 April 1996, the police authorities) claim their share from the district councils' collection funds. In Scotland each regional, island and district council sets its own rate of council tax.

The tax relates to the value of the dwelling. Each dwelling is placed in one of eight valuation bands, ranging from A to H, based on the property's estimated market value as at 1 April 1991.

The valuation bands and ranges of values in England, Wales and Scotland are:

England

A	Up to £40,000	E	£88,001–£120,000
B	£40,001–£52,000	F	£120,001–£160,000
C	£52,001–£68,000	G	£160,001–£320,000
D	£68,001–£88,000	H	Over £320,000

Wales

A	Up to £30,000	E	£66,001–£90,000
B	£30,001–£39,000	F	£90,001–£120,000
C	£39,001–£51,000	G	£120,001–£240,000
D	£51,001–£66,000	H	Over £240,000

Scotland

A	Up to £27,000	E	£58,001–£80,000
B	£27,001–£35,000	F	£80,001–£106,000
C	£35,001–£45,000	G	£106,001–£212,000
D	£45,001–£58,000	H	Over £212,000

The council tax within a local area varies between the different bands according to proportions laid down by law. The charge attributable to each band as a proportion of the Band D charge set by the council is approximately:

A	67%	E	122%
B	78%	F	144%
C	89%	G	167%
D	100%	H	200%

The band D rate is given in the tables on pages 548–54 (England), 560 (London), 563 (Wales), and 568–9 (Scotland). There may be variations from the given figure within each district council area because of different parish or community precepts being levied.

NON-DOMESTIC RATES

Non-domestic (business) rates have been collected since 1 April 1990 by billing authorities, i.e. district councils in England and Wales, and regional and islands councils in Scotland. In respect of England and Wales, the Local Government Finance Act 1988 provides for liability for rates to be assessed on the basis of a poundage (multiplier) tax on the rateable value of property (hereditaments). The multiplier is set by central government and rates are collected by the billing authority for the area where a property is located. Rate income collected by billing authorities is paid into a national non-domestic rating (NNDR) pool and redistributed to individual authorities on the basis of the adult population figure as prescribed by the Secretary of State. For the years 1995–6 to 2000–1 actual payment of rates in certain cases are subject to transitional arrangements, to phase in the larger increases and reductions in rates resulting from the effects of the 1995 revaluation.

Rates are levied in Scotland in accordance with the Local Government (Scotland) Act 1975. For 1995–6, the Secretary of State for Scotland has prescribed a single non-domestic rates poundage to apply throughout the country at the same level as the uniform business rate (UBR) in England. Rate income is pooled and redistributed to local authorities on a per capita basis. For the year 1995–6 payment of rates is subject to transitional arrangements to phase in the effect of the 1995 revaluation.

Rateable values for the rating lists came into force on 1 April 1995. They are derived from the rental value of property as at 1 April 1993 and determined on certain statutory assumptions by valuation officers of the Valuation Office Agency in England and Wales, and by Regional Assessors in Scotland. New property which is added to the list, and significant changes to existing property, necessitate amendments to the rateable value on the same basis. Rating lists (valuation rolls in Scotland) remain in force until the next general revaluation. Such revaluations take place every five years, the next being in 2000.

Certain types of property are exempt from rates, e.g. agricultural land and buildings, and places of public religious worship. Charities and other non-profit-making organizations may receive full or partial relief. Empty property is liable to pay rates at 50 per cent, except for certain specified classes which are exempt entirely.

GOVERNMENT GRANTS

In addition to specific grants in support of revenue expenditure on particular services, central government pays revenue support grant to local authorities. This grant is paid to each local authority so that if each authority spends at a level sufficient to provide a standard level of service, all authorities in the same class can set broadly the same council tax.

COMPLAINTS

Commissioners for Local Administration in England, Wales and Scotland (*see* page 323) are responsible for investigating complaints from members of the public who claim to have suffered injustice as a consequence of maladministration in local government or in certain local bodies.

The Northern Ireland Commissioner for Complaints fulfils a similar function in Northern Ireland, investigating complaints about local authorities and certain public bodies.

THE QUEEN'S REPRESENTATIVES

The Lord Lieutenant of a county is the permanent local representative of the Crown in that county. The appointment of Lord Lieutenants is now regulated by the Reserve Forces Act 1980. They are appointed by the Sovereign on the recommendation of the Prime Minister. The retirement age is 75. The office of Lord Lieutenant dates from 1557, and its holder was originally responsible for the maintenance of order and for local defence in the county. The duties of the post include attending on royalty during official visits to the county, performing certain duties in connection with armed forces of the Crown (and in particular the reserve forces), and making presentations of honours and awards on behalf of the Crown. In England, Wales and Northern Ireland, the Lord Lieutenant usually also holds the office of *Custos Rotulorum*. As such, he acts as head of the county's commission of the peace (which recommends the appointment of magistrates).

The office of Sheriff (from the Old English shire-reeve) of a county was created in the tenth century. The Sheriff was the special nominee of the Sovereign, and the office reached the peak of its influence under the Norman kings. The Provisions of Oxford (1258) laid down a yearly tenure of office. Since the mid-16th century the office has been purely civil, with military duties taken over by the Lord Lieutenant of the county. The Sheriff (commonly known as 'High Sheriff') attends on royalty during official visits to the county, acts as the returning officer during parliamentary elections in county constituencies, attends the opening ceremony when a High Court judge goes on circuit, executes High Court writs, and appoints under-sheriffs to act as deputies. The appointments and duties of the High Sheriffs in England and Wales are laid down by the Sheriffs Act 1887.

The serving High Sheriff submits a list of names of possible future sheriffs to a tribunal which chooses three names to put to the Sovereign. The tribunal nominates the High Sheriff annually on 12 November and the Sovereign pricks the name of the Sheriff to succeed in the following year. The term of office runs from 25 March to the following 24 March (the civil and legal year before 1752). No person may be chosen twice in three years if there is any other suitable person in the county.

CIVIC DIGNITIES

District councils may petition for a royal charter granting borough or 'City' status to the district.

In England and Wales the chairman of a borough or county borough council may be called a mayor, and the chairman of a city council a Lord Mayor. Parish councils in England and Wales may call themselves 'town councils', in which case their chairman is the town mayor.

In Scotland the chairman of a district council may be known as a convenor; a provost is the equivalent of a mayor. The chairmen of the councils for the cities of Aberdeen, Dundee, Edinburgh and Glasgow are Lord Provosts.

ENGLAND
(For London, *see* below)

There are currently 39 non-metropolitan counties; all (apart from the Isle of Wight) are divided into non-metropolitan districts, of which there are 294. From 1 April 1996, 13 unitary authorities will be created, in effect replacing three county councils and 20 shire districts; the county areas of Avon, Cleveland and Humberside will be abolished. Subject to parliamentary approval, a further 24 unitary authorities will be effective from 1 April 1997. The populations of most of the new unitary authorities are in the range of 120,000–230,000. The non-metropolitan districts have populations broadly in the range of 60,000 to 100,000; some, however, have larger populations, because of the need to avoid dividing large towns, and some in mainly rural areas have smaller populations.

Six metropolitan counties cover the main conurbations outside Greater London: Tyne and Wear, West Midlands, Merseyside, Greater Manchester, West Yorkshire and South Yorkshire. They are divided into 36 metropolitan districts, most of which have a population of over 200,000.

There are also about 10,000 parishes, in 219 of the non-metropolitan and 18 of the metropolitan districts.

ELECTIONS

For districts, non-metropolitan counties, and for about 8,000 parishes, there are elected councils, consisting of directly elected councillors. The councillors elect annually one of their number as chairman.

Generally, councillors serve four years and there are no elections of district and parish councillors in county election years. In metropolitan districts, one-third of the councillors for each ward are elected each year except in the year when county elections take place elsewhere. Non-metropolitan districts can choose whether to have elections by thirds or whole council elections. In the former case, one-third of the council, as nearly as may be, is elected in each year of metropolitan district elections. If whole council elections are chosen, these are held in the year midway between county elections.

FUNCTIONS

In non-metropolitan areas, functions are divided between the districts and counties, those requiring the larger area or population for their efficient performance going to the county. The metropolitan district councils, with the larger population in their areas, already had wider functions than non-metropolitan councils, and following abolition of the metropolitan county councils were given most of their functions also. A few functions continue to be exercised over the larger area by joint bodies, made up of councillors from each district.

The allocation of functions is as follows:

County councils: education; strategic planning; traffic, transport and highways; fire service; consumer protection; refuse disposal; smallholdings; social services; libraries

Non-metropolitan district councils: local planning; housing; highways (maintenance of certain urban roads and off-street car parks); building regulations; environmental health; refuse collection; cemeteries and crematoria

Metropolitan district councils: their functions are all those listed above, except that fire, civil defence and passenger transport (and in some cases, refuse disposal) are exercised by joint bodies

Concurrently by county and district councils: recreation (parks, playing fields, swimming pools); museums; encouragement of the arts, tourism and industry

The Police and Magistrates Court Act 1994 set up police authorities in England and Wales separate from the local authorities.

PARISH COUNCILS

Parishes with 200 or more electors must generally have parish councils, which means that over three-quarters of the parishes have councils. A parish council comprises at least five members, the number being fixed by the district council. Elections are held every four years, at the time of the election of the district councillor for the ward including the parish. All parishes have parish meetings, comprising the electors of the parish. Where there is no council, the meeting must be held at least twice a year.

Parish council functions include: allotments; encouragement of arts and crafts; community halls, recreational facilities (e.g. open spaces, swimming pools), cemeteries and crematoria; and many minor functions. They must also be given an opportunity to comment on planning applications. They may, like county and district councils, spend limited sums for the general benefit of the parish. They levy a precept on the district councils for their funds.

FINANCE

Aggregate external finance for 1995–6 was originally determined at £34,686 million. Of this, specific and special grants were estimated at £5,018 million. £18,314 million was in respect of revenue support grant and £11,354 million was support from the national non-domestic rate pool. Total standard spending by local authorities considered for grant purposes was £43,507 million.

The average council taxes, expressed in terms of Band C, two-adult properties for 1995–6, were: inner London boroughs £509; outer London boroughs £513; London £512; metropolitan districts £605; non-metropolitan districts £532. The average for England was £543.

National non-domestic rate (or uniform business rate) for 1995–6 is 47.2p. The amount estimated to be raised from central, local and Crown lists is £11.7 billion. Total rateable value held on draft local authority lists at 31 December 1994 was £29.7 billion. The amount to be redistributed to authorities from the pool in 1995–6 is £11.4 billion.

Under the Local Government and Housing Act 1989, local authorities have four main ways of paying for capital expenditure: borrowing and other forms of extended credit; capital grants from central government towards some types of capital expenditure; 'usable' capital receipts from the sale of land, houses and other assets; and revenue.

The amount of capital expenditure which a local authority can finance by borrowing (or other forms of credit) is effectively limited by the credit approvals issued to it by central government. Most credit approvals can be used for any local authority service; these are known as basic credit approvals. Others are for particular projects or services; these are known as supplementary credit approvals.

Generally, the 'usable' part of a local authority's capital receipts consists of 25 per cent of receipts from the sale of council houses and 50 per cent of most other receipts. The balance has to be set aside as provision for repaying debt and meeting other credit liabilities.

EXPENDITURE

Local authority budgeted net revenue expenditure for 1995–6 was (1995–6 cash prices):

Service	£m
Education	18,368
School catering	369
Libraries, museums and art galleries	746
Personal social services	7,322
Police	6,033
Fire	1,238
Other Home Office services	831
Local transport	2,477
Local environmental services	5,491

Agricultural services	38
Consumer protection and trading standards	139
Employment	122
Non-housing revenue account housing	343
Housing benefits	4,979
Parish precepts	121
New net current expenditure	48,617
Capital charges	2,449
Capital charged to revenue	681
Other non-current expenditure	3,415
Interest receipts	−694
Gross revenue expenditure	54,468
Specific and special grants outside AEF*	−8,812
Other income	−56
Revenue expenditure	45,600
Specific and special grants inside AEF*	−1,722
Net revenue expenditure	43,878

AEF = aggregate external finance
*Includes only those grants in support of budgeted revenue expenditure

LONDON

Since the abolition of the Greater London Council in 1986, the Greater London area has not had a single local government body. The area is divided into 32 borough councils, which have a status similar to the metropolitan district councils in the rest of England, and the Corporation of the City of London.

LONDON BOROUGH COUNCILS

The London boroughs have whole council elections every four years, in the year immediately following the county council election year. The next elections will be held in 1998.

The borough councils have responsibility for the following functions: building regulations; cemeteries and crematoria; consumer protection; education; youth employment; environmental health; electoral registration; food; drugs; housing; leisure services; libraries; local planning; local roads; museums; parking; recreation (parks, playing fields, swimming pools); refuse collection and street cleansing; social services; town planning; and traffic management.

THE CORPORATION OF THE CITY OF LONDON
(*see also* pages 555–7)
The Corporation of the City of London is the local authority for the City of London. Its legal definition is 'The Mayor and Commonalty and Citizens of the City of London'. It is governed by the Court of Common Council, which consists of the Lord Mayor, 24 other aldermen, and 130 common councilmen. The Lord Mayor and two sheriffs are nominated annually by the City guilds (the livery companies) and elected by the Court of Aldermen. Aldermen and councilmen are elected by businesses in the 25 wards into which the City is divided; councilmen must stand for re-election annually. The Council is a legislative assembly, and there are no political parties.

The Corporation has the same functions as the London borough councils. In addition, it runs the City of London Police; is the health authority for the Port of London; has health control of animal imports throughout Greater London, including at Heathrow airport; owns and manages public open spaces throughout Greater London; runs the

Central Criminal Court; and runs Billingsgate, Smithfield and Spitalfields markets.

THE CITY GUILDS (LIVERY COMPANIES)
The livery companies of the City of London grew out of early medieval religious fraternities and began to emerge as trade and craft guilds, retaining their religious aspect, in the 12th century. From the early 14th century, only members of the trade and craft guilds could call themselves citizens of the City of London. The guilds began to be called livery companies, because of the distinctive livery worn by the most prosperous guild members on ceremonial occasions, in the late 15th century.

By the early 19th century the power of the companies within their trades had begun to wane, but those wearing the livery of a company continued to play an important role in the government of the City of London. Liverymen still have the right to nominate the Lord Mayor and sheriffs, and most members of the Court of Common Council are liverymen (*see also* page 557).

GREATER LONDON SERVICES
After the abolition of the Greater London Council (GLC) in 1986, the London boroughs took over most of its functions. Successor bodies have also been set up for certain functions.

The London Residuary Body (LRB) was set up in 1986 to deal with residual matters of the GLC which could not easily be transferred elsewhere and in 1990 became responsible for residual matters relating to the Inner London Education Authority. The LRB completed its work and was wound up in 1995, having transferred most residual Greater London matters to the London Borough of Bromley and inner London matters to the Royal Borough of Kensington and Chelsea.

WALES

Since 1974 Wales, including the former Monmouthshire, has been divided into eight counties. Each county is divided into districts, of which there are 37. Under the Local Government (Wales) Act 1994, all county and district councils will be abolished and replaced by a single tier of 22 county and county borough councils with effect from 1 April 1996. The new authorities were elected in May 1995. Each will inherit all the functions of the existing county and district councils, except fire services (which will be provided by three combined fire authorities) and National Parks (which will become the responsibility of three independent boards).

The Police and Magistrates Courts Act 1994 set up four police authorities with effect from 1 April 1995: Dyfed-Powys, Gwent, North Wales, and South Wales.

COMMUNITY COUNCILS

In Wales parishes have been replaced by communities. Unlike England, where many areas are not in any parish, communities have been established for the whole of Wales, approximately 865 communities in all. Community meetings may be convened as and when desired.

Community councils exist in 735 communities and further councils may be established at the request of a community meeting. Community councils have broadly the same range of powers as English parish councils. Community councillors are elected en bloc at the same time as a district council election and for a term of four years.

FINANCE

Aggregate external finance for 1995–6 is £2,466.0 million. This comprises revenue support grant of £1,718.3 million, specific grants of £227.7 million, and support from the national non-domestic rate pool of £520 million. Total standard spending by local authorities considered for grant purposes is £2,782.1 million.

The average council tax levied in Wales for 1995–6 is £392, comprising county councils £287, district councils £66 and police authorities £38.

National non-domestic rates (or uniform business rate) in Wales for 1995–6 is 39.0p. The amount estimated to be raised is £520 million. Total rateable value held on local authority lists at 31 December 1994 was £1,287 million.

SCOTLAND

Since 1975, mainland Scotland has been divided for local government purposes into nine regions within which there are 53 districts. The Local Government etc. (Scotland) Act abolishes the existing two-tier system and replaces it with 29 unitary authorities on the mainland; the three islands councils remain. The new authorities were elected in April 1995. Each will inherit all the functions of the existing regional and district councils, except water and sewerage (which will be provided by three public bodies whose members will be appointed by the Secretary of State for Scotland) and reporters panels (which will become a national agency).

In the three islands areas, Orkney, Shetland and the Western Isles, there are single-tier islands councils responsible for most local authority functions.

ELECTIONS

For the regional, islands and district councils, there are councils consisting of directly elected councillors. The councillors serve for four years, elections to district councils taking place midway between regional council elections. Elections to the unitary authorities (including the islands) will take place every three years; the next elections are in 1999.

In 1995 the register showed 3,960,657 electors in Scotland.

FUNCTIONS

Regional councils: education; social work; strategic planning; the provision of infrastructure such as roads, water and sewerage; consumer protection; flood prevention; coast protection; valuation and rating; the police and fire services; civil defence; electoral registration; public transport; registration of births, deaths and marriages

District councils: housing; leisure and recreation, including tourism, parks, libraries, museums and galleries; development control and building control; environmental health, including cleansing, refuse collection and disposal; food hygiene, inspection of shops, offices and factories, clean air, markets and slaughterhouses, burial and cremation; licensing, including liquor, cinemas and theatres, taxis, street traders, betting and gaming, and charitable collections; allotments; public conveniences; the administration of district courts

COMMUNITY COUNCILS

Unlike the parish councils of England or community councils of Wales, Scottish community councils are not local authorities. Their purpose as defined in statute is to ascertain and express the views of the communities which they represent, and to take in the interests of their communities such action as appears to be expedient or practicable. Over 1,000 community councils have been established under schemes drawn up by district and islands councils in Scotland.

After April 1996 community councils will have an enhanced role, becoming statutory consultees on local planning issues and on the decentralization schemes which the new councils have to draw up for delivery of services.

FINANCE

Figures for 1994–5 show total receipts from non-domestic rates of £1,132.2 million and £985.48 million from the council tax. The average non-domestic rate per £ levied for 1994–5 was 48p and the average Band D council tax payable was £590. The average Band D council water charge payable was £78.

NORTHERN IRELAND

For the purpose of local government Northern Ireland has a system of 26 single-tier district councils.

ELECTIONS

There are 582 members of the councils, elected for periods of four years at a time on the principle of proportional representation.

FUNCTIONS

The district councils have three main roles. These are:

Executive: responsibility for a wide range of local services including building regulations; community services; consumer protection; cultural facilities; environmental health; miscellaneous licensing and registration provisions, including dog control; litter prevention; recreational and social facilities; refuse collection and disposal; street cleansing; and tourist development

Representative: nominating representatives to sit as members of the various statutory bodies responsible for the administration of regional services such as drainage, education, fire, health and personal social services, housing, and libraries

Consultative: acting as the medium through which the views of local people are expressed on the operation in their area of other regional services, notably conservation (including water supply and sewerage services), planning, and roads, provided by those departments of central government which have an obligation, statutory or otherwise, to consult the district councils about proposals affecting their areas

FINANCE

Local government in Northern Ireland is funded by a system of rates (a local property tax calculated by using the rateable value of a property multiplied by an amount per pound of rateable value). Rates are collected by the Department of the Environment for Northern Ireland and consist of a regional rate made by the Department of Finance and Personnel and a district rate made by individual district councils.

In 1995–6 approximately £335 million was raised in rates in Northern Ireland and the total rateable value was £224.7 million. The average domestic poundage levied was 167.27p and the average non-domestic rate poundage was 241.27p.

Political Composition of Local Councils

AS AT END MAY 1995

Abbreviations:

C.	Conservative
Com.	Communist
Dem.	Democrat
Green	Green
Ind.	Independent
Lab.	Labour
Lib.	Liberal
LD	Liberal Democrat
MK	Mebyon Kernow
NP	Non-political/Non-party
PC	Plaid Cymru
RA	Ratepayers'/Residents' Associations
SD	Social Democrat
SNP	Scottish National Party

ENGLAND

COUNTY COUNCILS

*Unitary council
†Abolished from April 1996

†Avon	Lab. 33, C. 25, LD 18
Bedfordshire	Lab. 31, C. 27, LD 14, Ind. 1
Berkshire	LD 34, Lab. 25, C. 14, Ind. 2, Lib. 1
Buckinghamshire	C. 38, LD 16, Lab. 13, Ind. 3, Ind. C. 1
Cambridgeshire	C. 33, Lab. 21, LD 21, Ind. 1, Lib. 1
Cheshire	Lab. 35, C. 22, LD 14
†Cleveland	Lab. 52, C. 14, LD 11
Cornwall	LD 42, Ind. 23, C. 6, Lab. 6, Lib.1, MK 1
Cumbria	Lab. 39, C. 28, LD 14, Ind. 2
Derbyshire	Lab. 54, C. 21, LD 8, Ind. 1
Devon	LD 39, Lab. 21, C. 18, Ind. 4, Lib. 2, vacant 1
Dorset	LD 39, C. 27, Lab. 6, Ind. 5
Durham	Lab. 56, C. 6, LD 6, Ind. 4
East Sussex	LD 30, C. 22, Lab. 18
Essex	Lab. 34, LD 32, C. 30, Ind. 1, vacant 1
Gloucestershire	LD 30, Lab. 20, Ind. C. 12, Others 1
Hampshire	LD 48, C. 28, Lab. 24, Ind. 2
Hereford and Worcester	C. 25, Lab. 24, LD 22, Ind. 5
Hertfordshire	Lab. 31, C. 25, LD 19, Ind. 2
†Humberside	Lab. 43, C. 21, LD 11
*Isle of Wight	LD 34, C. 5, Ind. 5, Lab 3, Others 1
Kent	C. 40, Lab. 31, LD 28
Lancashire	Lab. 54, C. 34, LD 11
Leicestershire	Lab. 37, C. 31, LD 17
Lincolnshire	C. 31, Lab. 25, LD 15, Ind. 5
Norfolk	C. 33, Lab. 32, LD 17, Ind. 2
Northamptonshire	Lab. 34, C. 27, LD 5, Ind. 1, vacant 1
Northumberland	Lab. 39, C. 13, LD 12, Ind. 1, vacant 1
North Yorkshire	LD 36, C. 27, Lab. 23, Ind. 9, vacant 1
Nottinghamshire	Lab. 58, C. 24, LD 6
Oxfordshire	C. 24, Lab. 24, LD 20, Green 1, Ind. C. 1
Shropshire	C. 26, Lab. 24, LD 15, Ind. Lab. 1
Somerset	LD 41, C. 13, Lab. 2, Ind. 1
Staffordshire	Lab. 52, C. 21, LD 5, Ind. 2, RA 2
Suffolk	Lab. 32, C. 25, LD 19, Ind. 4
Surrey	C. 34, LD 29, Lab. 8, RA 3, Ind. 2
Warwickshire	Lab. 30, C. 19, LD 10, Ind. 3
West Sussex	LD 34, C. 26, Lab. 10, Ind. 1
Wiltshire	LD 34, C. 17, Lab. 17

METROPOLITAN DISTRICT COUNCILS

GREATER MANCHESTER

Bolton	Lab. 43, C. 11, LD 6
Bury	Lab. 34, C. 11, LD 3
Manchester	Lab. 82, LD 14, C. 3
Oldham	Lab. 30, LD 23, C. 5, Ind. 1, vacant 1
Rochdale	Lab. 26, LD 22, C. 11, Ind. 1
Salford	Lab. 55, C. 3, LD 2
Stockport	LD 27, Lab. 23, C. 10, Ind. RA 3
Tameside	Lab. 50, C. 5, Others 2
Trafford	C. 29, Lab. 29, LD 5
Wigan	Lab. 67, LD 3, C. 1, Ind. Lab. 1

MERSEYSIDE

Knowsley	Lab. 62, Others 2, C. 1, Ind. Lab. 1
Liverpool	Lab. 49, LD 43, Lib. 3, C. 2, Ind. Lab. 2
St Helens	Lab. 40, LD 10, C. 3, Lib. 1
Sefton	Lab. 29, C. 21, LD 19
Wirral	Lab. 36, C. 22, LD 8

SOUTH YORKSHIRE

Barnsley	Lab. 64, C. 1, Ind. 1
Doncaster	Lab. 56, C. 6, LD 1
Rotherham	Lab. 64, C. 2
Sheffield	Lab. 58, LD 25, C. 4

TYNE AND WEAR

Gateshead	Lab. 50, LD 13, C. 1, Ind. Lab. 1, Lib. 1
Newcastle upon Tyne	Lab. 62, LD 13, C. 2, vacant 1
North Tyneside	Lab. 42, C. 12, LD 6
South Tyneside	Lab. 53, LD 6, Others 1
Sunderland	Lab. 68, C. 4, LD 2, Lib. 1

WEST MIDLANDS

Birmingham	Lab. 75, C. 28, LD 14
Coventry	Lab. 43, C. 11
Dudley	Lab. 50, C. 20, LD 2
Sandwell	Lab. 47, C. 17, Lib. 7, Ind. Lab. 1
Solihull	C. 21, Lab. 15, Lib. 9, Ind. RA 5, Ind. 1
Walsall	Lab. 34, C. 18, LD 6, Ind. 2
Wolverhampton	Lab. 39, C. 19, LD 2

WEST YORKSHIRE

Bradford	Lab. 59, C. 27, LD 4
Calderdale	Lab. 28, C. 16, LD 7, Ind. 2, vacant 1
Kirklees	Lab. 40, C. 16, LD 14, Ind. 2
Leeds	Lab. 75, C. 15, LD 8, Ind. 1
Wakefield	Lab. 57, C. 4, Ind. 1, vacant 1

NON-METROPOLITAN DISTRICT COUNCILS

*Denotes councils where one-third of councillors retire each year except in the year of county council elections
†Becomes part of unitary authority in April 1996

*Adur	*LD* 29, *C.* 5, *Lab.* 3, *RA* 2
Allerdale	*Lab.* 37, *C.* 7, *Ind.* 7, *LD* 4
Alnwick	*LD* 11, *Lab.* 7, *Ind.* 3, *C.* 2, *Others* 6
*Amber Valley	*Lab.* 30, *C.* 10, *Ind.* 3
Arun	*C.* 29, *LD* 14, *Lab.* 10, *Ind.* 3
Ashfield	*Lab.* 33
Ashford	*C.* 18, *LD* 15, *Lab.* 13, *Ind.* 2, *Ind. C.* 1
Aylesbury Vale	*LD* 33, *C.* 12, *Ind.* 8, *Lab.* 5
Babergh	*Ind.* 12, *Lab.* 12, *C.* 9, *LD* 7, *Others* 2
*Barrow-in-Furness	*Lab.* 30, *C.* 8
*Basildon	*Lab.* 16, *C.* 14, *LD* 12
*Basingstoke and Deane	*C.* 25, *LD* 15, *Lab.* 13, *Ind.* 4
*Bassetlaw	*Lab.* 33, *C.* 11, *Ind.* 3, *LD* 2, *vacant* 1
*†Bath	*LD* 29, *C.* 17, *Lab.* 2
*Bedford	*Lab.* 20, *C.* 16, *LD* 12, *Ind.* 5
Berwick-upon-Tweed	*LD* 12, *Ind.* 10, *C.* 2, *Lab.* 2, *Others* 2
†Beverley	*C.* 31, *LD* 19, *Lab.* 2, *Ind.* 1
Blaby	*Lab.* 16, *C.* 12, *LD* 8, *Ind.* 2, *vacant* 1
*Blackburn	*Lab.* 42, *C.* 15, *LD* 2, *vacant* 1
Blackpool	*Lab.* 39, *LD* 3, *C.* 2
Blyth Valley	*Lab.* 40, *LD* 7
Bolsover	*Lab.* 35, *Ind.* 1, *RA* 1
†Boothferry	*C.* 16, *Lab.* 11, *Ind.* 8
Boston	*Lab.* 15, *Ind.* 7, *LD* 7, *C.* 5
Bournemouth	*LD* 26, *C.* 21, *Lab.* 6, *Ind.* 4
Bracknell Forest	*Lab.* 22, *C.* 12, *LD* 6
Braintree	*Lab.* 37, *C.* 10, *Ind.* 7, *LD* 6
Breckland	*Lab.* 25, *C.* 18, *Ind.* 7, *LD* 2, *Green* 1
*Brentwood	*LD* 25, *C.* 12, *Lab.* 1, *vacant* 1
Bridgnorth	*Ind.* 10, *Lab.* 6, *Ind. C.* 5, *LD* 4, *C.* 3, *Ind. Lab.* 1, *NP* 1, *Others* 3
*Brighton	*Lab.* 29, *C.* 19
*†Bristol	*Lab.* 53, *LD* 9, *C.* 6
*Broadland	*C.* 16, *Lab.* 13, *LD* 13, *Ind.* 6, *vacant* 1
Bromsgrove	*Lab.* 24, *C.* 12, *LD* 3
*Broxbourne	*C.* 27, *Lab.* 11, *LD* 4
Broxtowe	*Lab.* 36, *C.* 7, *LD* 5, *Ind.* 1
*Burnley	*Lab.* 34, *LD* 10, *C.* 3, *Ind.* 1
*Cambridge	*Lab.* 20, *LD* 18, *C.* 4
*Cannock Chase	*Lab.* 35, *C.* 5, *LD* 1, *vacant* 1
Canterbury	*LD* 24, *Lab.* 15, *C.* 10
Caradon	*Ind.* 18, *LD* 18, *Lab.* 2, *RA* 2, *C.* 1
*Carlisle	*Lab.* 30, *C.* 17, *LD* 3, *Ind.* 1
Carrick	*LD* 21, *Ind.* 8, *Lab.* 8, *C.* 7, *MK* 1
Castle Morpeth	*Lab.* 12, *Ind.* 9, *C.* 6, *LD* 6, *Others* 1
Castle Point	*Lab.* 34, *C.* 5
Charnwood	*Lab.* 30, *C.* 15, *LD* 5, *Ind.* 2
Chelmsford	*LD* 32, *C.* 13, *Lab.* 7, *Ind.* 4
*Cheltenham	*LD* 29, *C.* 7, *Ind.* 3, *Lab.* 2
*Cherwell	*C.* 23, *Lab.* 22, *LD* 7
*Chester	*Lab.* 23, *C.* 19, *LD* 16, *Ind.* 2
Chesterfield	*Lab.* 37, *LD* 10
Chester-le-Street	*Lab.* 30, *C.* 1, *Ind.* 1, *LD* 1
Chichester	*LD* 25, *C.* 20, *Ind.* 4, *Lab.* 1
Chiltern	*LD* 24, *C.* 22, *RA* 2, *Ind.* 1, *Lab.* 1
*Chorley	*Lab.* 28, *C.* 13, *LD* 6, *Ind.* 1
Christchurch	*LD* 11, *C.* 8, *Ind.* 6
†Cleethorpes	*Lab.* 16, *LD* 12, *C.* 9, *Ind.* 4
*Colchester	*LD* 34, *C.* 13, *Lab.* 12, *Ind.* 1
*Congleton	*LD* 26, *C.* 9, *Lab.* 9, *vacant* 1
Copeland	*Lab.* 37, *C.* 12, *Ind.* 2
Corby	*Lab.* 24, *LD* 2, *C.* 1
Cotswold	*Ind.* 16, *LD* 9, *Lab.* 4, *C.* 3, *Others* 13
*Craven	*LD* 17, *C.* 6, *Ind.* 6, *Lab.* 5
*Crawley	*Lab.* 26, *C.* 2, *Ind.* 2, *LD* 2
*Crewe and Nantwich	*Lab.* 33, *C.* 21, *LD* 3
Dacorum	*Lab.* 33, *C.* 19, *LD* 4, *Ind.* 2
Darlington	*Lab.* 35, *C.* 14, *LD* 2, *Ind.* 1
Dartford	*Lab.* 35, *C.* 10, *Ind. Lab.* 1, *RA* 1
*Daventry	*C.* 15, *Lab.* 15, *Ind.* 3, *LD* 2
*Derby	*Lab.* 30, *C.* 12, *LD* 2
Derbyshire Dales	*LD* 16, *C.* 12, *Lab.* 7, *Ind. C.* 3, *Ind. Lab.* 1
Derwentside	*Lab.* 50, *NP* 5
Dover	*Lab.* 39, *C.* 13, *LD* 4
Durham	*Lab.* 38, *LD* 7, *Ind.* 4
Easington	*Lab.* 44, *Lib.* 3, *Ind.* 2, *Ind. Lab.* 2
*Eastbourne	*LD* 21, *C.* 9
East Cambridgeshire	*Ind.* 13, *LD* 13, *NP* 7, *Lab.* 3, *Ind. C.* 1
East Devon	*C.* 30, *LD* 20, *Ind.* 9, *Others* 1
East Dorset	*LD* 23, *C.* 13
East Hampshire	*LD* 26, *C.* 12, *Ind.* 4
East Hertfordshire	*C.* 23, *LD* 16, *Lab.* 8, *Ind.* 2, *RA* 1
*Eastleigh	*LD* 28, *C.* 13, *Lab.* 3
East Lindsey	*NP* 35, *Lab.* 15, *LD* 6, *Green* 3, *Others* 1
East Northamptonshire	*Lab.* 25, *C.* 9, *LD* 2
East Staffordshire	*Lab.* 36, *C.* 4, *Ind. C.* 3, *LD* 3
†East Yorkshire	*C.* 19, *Ind.* 10, *LD* 6, *Lab.* 5, *SD* 3
Eden	*Ind.* 30, *LD* 4, *Lab.* 2, *vacant* 1
*Ellesmere Port and Neston	*Lab.* 33, *C.* 8
*Elmbridge	*RA* 22, *C.* 20, *LD* 9, *Lab.* 8, *Ind.* 1
*Epping Forest	*C.* 20, *Lab.* 16, *LD* 10, *RA* 10, *Ind* 2, *SD* 1
Epsom and Ewell	*RA* 32, *Lab.* 3, *LD* 3, *vacant* 1
Erewash	*Lab.* 40, *C.* 9, *LD* 2, *Ind.* 1
*Exeter	*Lab.* 19, *C.* 9, *LD* 6, *Lib.* 2
*Fareham	*LD* 19, *C.* 9, *Lab.* 5, *Others* 8, *vacant* 1
Fenland	*Lab.* 21, *C.* 14, *NP* 3, *LD* 2
Forest Heath	*C.* 10, *LD* 6, *Ind.* 5, *Lab.* 4
Forest of Dean	*Lab.* 30, *Ind.* 7, *LD* 5, *C.* 1, *Others* 6
Fylde	*C.* 17, *RA* 10, *Lab.* 6, *LD* 4, *Others* 12
Gedling	*Lab.* 29, *C.* 20, *LD* 7, *Ind.* 1
*Gillingham	*LD* 24, *Lab.* 9, *C.* 8, *Ind. LD* 1
†Glanford	*C.* 18, *Ind.* 10, *Lab.* 8, *Green* 3, *Others* 2
*Gloucester	*Lab.* 20, *LD* 8, *C.* 6, *Ind.* 1
*Gosport	*LD* 18, *C.* 5, *Lab.* 5, *Ind.* 2, *vacant* 1
Gravesham	*Lab.* 34, *C.* 10
*†Great Grimsby	*Lab.* 28, *C.* 9, *LD* 5, *Ind.* 3

*Great Yarmouth	*Lab.* 33, *C.* 14, *LD* 1
Guildford	*LD* 23, *C.* 13, *Lab.* 6, *Ind.* 1, Others 2
*Halton	*Lab.* 45, *LD* 7, *C.* 1
Hambleton	*C.* 25, *Ind.* 15, *Lab.* 4, *LD* 3
Harborough	*LD* 13, *C.* 12, *Lab.* 8, *Ind.* 4
*Harlow	*Lab.* 37, *LD* 3, *C.* 2
*Harrogate	*LD* 40, *C.* 13, *Ind.* 3, *Lab.* 2, *vacant* 2
*Hart	*LD* 14, *C.* 11, *Ind.* 10
*†Hartlepool	*Lab.* 39, *LD* 5, *C.* 2, *Ind. C.* 1
*Hastings	*LD* 14, *Lab.* 12, *C.* 5, *Ind.* 1
*Havant	*LD* 15, *C.* 12, *Lab.* 12, *Ind.* 3
*Hereford	*LD* 22, *Lab.* 4, *C.* 1
*Hertsmere	*Lab.* 19, *C.* 14, *LD* 5, *Ind.* 1
High Peak	*Lab.* 30, *C.* 5, *LD* 5, *Ind.* 4
Hinckley and Bosworth	*LD* 16, *Lab.* 13, *C.* 5
†Holderness	*Ind.* 24, *LD* 7
Horsham	*LD* 24, *C.* 17, *Ind.* 2
Hove	*Lab.* 16, *C.* 11, *LD* 3
*Huntingdonshire	*C.* 31, *LD* 12, *Lab.* 7, *Ind.* 3
*Hyndburn	*Lab.* 36, *C.* 10, *LD* 1
*Ipswich	*Lab.* 36, *C.* 10, *Ind. C.* 1, *LD* 1
Kennet	*Ind.* 14, *Lab.* 9, *LD* 9, *C.* 8
Kerrier	*Ind.* 16, *Lab.* 14, *LD* 13, *C.* 1
Kettering	*Lab.* 33, *C.* 6, *Ind.* 3, *LD* 3
King's Lynn and West Norfolk	*Lab.* 37, *C.* 16, *LD* 6, *Ind.* 1
*†Kingston upon Hull	*Lab.* 59, *LD* 1
†Kingswood	*Lab.* 28, *C.* 15, *LD* 4, *Ind.* 3
Lancaster	*Lab.* 34, *C.* 11, *Ind.* 9, *LD* 5, Others 1
†Langbaurgh on Tees	*Lab.* 49, *LD* 7, *Ind. Lab.* 2, *C.* 1
Leicester	*Lab.* 45, *LD* 7, *C.* 4
*Leominster	*Ind.* 16, *LD* 9, *C.* 4, *Ind. C.* 3, *Lab.* 3, *Green* 1
Lewes	*LD* 28, *C.* 16, *Ind.* 2, *Lab.* 2
Lichfield	*Lab.* 33, *C.* 19, *LD* 2, *Ind.* 1, *Ind. Lab.* 1
*Lincoln	*Lab.* 31, *C.* 2
Luton	*Lab.* 37, *LD* 9, *C.* 2
*Macclesfield	*C.* 33, *LD* 13, *Lab.* 11, *RA* 3
*Maidstone	*C.* 17, *LD* 17, *Lab.* 15, *Ind.* 5, Others 1
Maldon	*C.* 12, *Ind.* 9, *Lab.* 7, *Ind. C.* 1, *LD* 1
Malvern Hills	*Ind.* 19, *LD* 19, *C.* 6, *Green* 3, *Ind. C.* 2, *Lab.* 2
Mansfield	*Lab.* 45, *C.* 1
Melton	*LD* 9, *C.* 8, *Lab.* 5, *Ind.* 4
Mendip	*LD* 21, *Lab.* 9, *C.* 8, *Ind.* 3, *RA* 2
Mid Bedfordshire	*C.* 22, *Lab.* 20, *LD* 5, *Ind.* 4, Others 2
Mid Devon	*LD* 21, *Ind.* 17, *Lab.* 1, *Lib.* 1
†Middlesbrough	*Lab.* 45, *LD* 4, *C.* 2, *Ind.* 1, Others 1
Mid Suffolk	*Lab.* 16, *LD* 12, *C.* 6, *Ind.* 5, *vacant* 1
*Mid Sussex	*LD* 28, *C.* 18, *Ind.* 4, *Lab.* 4
*Milton Keynes	*Lab.* 21, *LD* 12, *C.* 10, *Ind.* 2, Others 1
*Mole Valley	*LD* 20, *C.* 11, *Ind.* 8, *Lab.* 2
Newark and Sherwood	*Lab.* 37, *C.* 10, *LD* 5, *Ind.* 2
Newbury	*LD* 37, *C.* 7, *Ind.* 1
*Newcastle under Lyme	*Lab.* 37, *LD* 12, *C.* 6, *Ind. C.* 1
New Forest	*LD* 32, *C.* 23, *Ind.* 3
Northampton	*Lab.* 34, *LD* 8, *C.* 1
†Northavon	*LD* 28, *C.* 18, *Lab.* 10, Others 1
North Cornwall	*Ind.* 25, *LD* 12, *C.* 1
North Devon	*LD* 30, *Ind.* 12, *C.* 1, *NP* 1
North Dorset	*LD* 19, *Ind.* 12, *C.* 1, *Lab.* 1
North East Derbyshire	*Lab.* 43, *C.* 4, *LD* 3, *Ind. Lab.* 2, *Ind.* 1
*North Hertfordshire	*C.* 22, *Lab.* 21, *LD* 6, *Ind.* 1
North Kesteven	*Lab.* 15, *Ind.* 12, *LD* 8, *C.* 4
North Norfolk	*Lab.* 19, *LD* 12, *NP* 8, *Ind. C.* 7
North Shropshire	*NP* 34, *Lab.* 6
North Warwickshire	*Lab.* 29, *C.* 4, *Ind.* 1
North West Leicestershire	*Lab.* 35, *C.* 3, *Ind.* 2
North Wiltshire	*LD* 30, *C.* 12, *Lab.* 6, *Ind.* 4
*Norwich	*Lab.* 37, *LD* 10, *C.* 1
Nottingham	*Lab.* 51, *LD* 2, *C.* 1, *Green* 1
*Nuneaton and Bedworth	*Lab.* 39, *C.* 6
*Oadby and Wigston	*LD* 25, *C.* 1
Oswestry	*Lab.* 10, *Ind.* 9, *C.* 5, *LD* 5
*Oxford	*Lab.* 38, *LD* 8, *C.* 4, *Green* 1
*Pendle	*LD* 26, *Lab.* 19, *C.* 5, *vacant* 1
*Penwith	*Ind.* 9, *C.* 8, *LD* 8, *Lab.* 5, *MK* 1, Others 3
*Peterborough	*Lab.* 22, *C.* 20, *Ind.* 1, Others 5
Plymouth	*Lab.* 55, *C.* 5
Poole	*LD* 19, *C.* 13, *Lab.* 4
*Portsmouth	*Lab.* 20, *C.* 10, *LD* 9
*Preston	*Lab.* 31, *C.* 18, *LD* 8
*Purbeck	*LD* 10, *Ind.* 5, *C.* 4, *Lab.* 3
*Reading	*Lab.* 32, *C.* 8, *LD* 5
*Redditch	*Lab.* 23, *C.* 5, *LD* 1
*Reigate and Banstead	*C.* 18, *LD* 14, *Lab.* 12, *RA* 3, *Ind.* 2
Restormel	*LD* 29, *Ind.* 9, *Lab.* 2, *C.* 1, *vacant* 3
Ribble Valley	*C.* 19, *LD* 19, *Lab.* 1
Richmondshire	*Ind.* 22, *LD* 9, *C.* 1, *Ind. C.* 1, *SD* 1
Rochester upon Medway	*Lab.* 44, *LD* 5, *C.* 1
*Rochford	*LD* 22, *Lab.* 8, *C.* 7, *RA* 2, *Ind.* 1
*Rossendale	*Lab.* 25, *C.* 11
Rother	*LD* 21, *C.* 14, *Ind.* 5, *Lab.* 5
*Rugby	*Lab.* 19, *C.* 13, *Ind. RA* 7, *LD* 5, *Ind. C.* 2, Others 2
*Runnymede	*C.* 23, *Lab.* 12, *Ind.* 6, *LD* 1
Rushcliffe	*C.* 26, *Lab.* 17, *LD* 10, *Ind.* 1
*Rushmoor	*C.* 18, *LD* 16, *Lab.* 11
Rutland	*Ind.* 12, *C.* 4, *LD* 4
Ryedale	*LD* 25, *Ind.* 10, *C.* 5, *Lab.* 2
*St Albans	*LD* 34, *C.* 13, *Lab.* 10
St Edmundsbury	*Lab.* 23, *C.* 14, *LD* 5, *Ind.* 2
Salisbury	*LD.* 31, *Lab.* 11, *C.* 8, *Ind.* 6, Others 2
Scarborough	*Lab.* 24, *C.* 13, *Ind.* 8, *LD* 4
*†Scunthorpe	*Lab.* 34, *C.* 5, *SD* 1
Sedgefield	*Lab.* 47, *Ind.* 2
Sedgemoor	*C.* 21, *Lab.* 13, *LD* 12, *Ind.* 3
Selby	*Lab.* 28, *C.* 12, *Ind.* 9, *LD* 1
Sevenoaks	*LD* 20, *C.* 17, *Lab.* 11, *Ind.* 5
Shepway	*LD* 21, *C.* 19, *Lab.* 13, *Ind.* 3
*Shrewsbury and Atcham	*Lab.* 19, *LD* 13, *C.* 11, *Ind.* 5
*Slough	*Lab.* 32, *Lib.* 4, *C.* 2, *Ind.* 1, *LD* 1
*Southampton	*Lab.* 26, *LD* 13, *C.* 6
*South Bedfordshire	*C.* 24, *Lab.* 15, *LD* 10, *Ind.* 3, *vacant* 1
South Bucks	*C.* 19, *Ind.* 17, *LD* 4
*South Cambridgeshire	*Ind.* 21, *C.* 16, *LD* 10, *Lab.* 8
South Derbyshire	*Lab.* 27, *C.* 6, *Ind.* 1
*Southend-on-Sea	*LD* 16, *C.* 14, *Lab.* 9

South Hams	*C.* 17, *Ind.* 15, *LD* 10, *Lab.* 1, Others 1
*South Herefordshire	*Ind.* 26, *LD* 9, *C.* 2, *NP* 2
South Holland	*Ind.* 20, *Lab.* 11, *C.* 7
South Kesteven	*Lab.* 17, *Ind.* 14, *C.* 13, *LD* 7, *Ind. Lab.* 3, *Lib.* 2, *Ind. C.* 1
*South Lakeland	*LD* 21, *Ind.* 14, *C.* 11, *Lab.* 6
South Norfolk	*LD* 30, *C.* 12, *Lab.* 3, *Ind.* 2
South Northamptonshire	*C.* 15, *Lab.* 10, *Ind.* 8, *LD* 7
South Oxfordshire	*LD* 21, *Lab.* 13, *C.* 9, *Ind.* 5, *RA* 2
South Ribble	*Lab.* 29, *C.* 16, *LD* 9
South Shropshire	*NP* 9, *LD* 8, *Ind.* 7, Green 2, *Lab.* 1, Others 13
South Somerset	*LD* 46, *C.* 8, *Ind.* 5, *Lab* 1
South Staffordshire	*C.* 26, *Lab.* 15, *LD* 4, *RA* 3, *Ind. C.* 1, *Ind.* 1
Spelthorne	*C.* 21, *Lab.* 16, *LD* 3
Stafford	*Lab.* 33, *C.* 16, *LD* 10, *Ind.* 1
Staffordshire Moorlands	*Lab.* 27, *C.* 10, *LD* 7, *RA* 7, *Ind.* 3, Others 2
*Stevenage	*Lab.* 36, *C.* 2, *LD* 1
†Stockton-on-Tees	*Lab.* 44, *C.* 7, *LD* 4
*Stoke-on-Trent	*Lab.* 50, *C.* 10
*Stratford-upon-Avon	*LD* 24, *C.* 19, *Ind.* 9, *Lab.* 3
*Stroud	*Lab.* 19, *C.* 14, *LD* 12, *Ind.* 6, Green 4
Suffolk Coastal	*C.* 18, *Lab.* 17, *LD* 15, *Ind.* 5
Surrey Heath	*C.* 22, *LD* 7, *Lab.* 5, vacant 2
*Swale	*LD* 20, *C.* 14, *Lab.* 14, *Ind.* 1
*Tamworth	*Lab.* 23, *C.* 4, *Ind.* 3
*Tandridge	*C.* 20, *LD* 18, *Lab.* 4
Taunton Deane	*LD* 29, *C.* 14, *Lab.* 7, *Ind.* 3
Teesdale	*Lab.* 12, *Ind.* 11, *NP* 6, *C.* 2
Teignbridge	*LD* 25, *Ind.* 21, *Lab.* 7, *C.* 5
Tendring	*Lab.* 37, *C.* 8, *LD* 8, *Ind.* 7
Test Valley	*C.* 22, *LD* 22
Tewkesbury	*Ind.* 20, *LD* 8, *Lab.* 5, *C.* 3
*Thamesdown	*Lab.* 37, *C.* 8, *LD* 8, *Ind.* 1
Thanet	*Lab.* 45, *LD* 4, *C.* 3, *Ind.* 2
*Three Rivers	*C.* 21, *LD* 20, *Lab.* 7
*Thurrock	*Lab.* 32, *C.* 4, *Ind.* 3
*Tonbridge and Malling	*C.* 23, *LD* 21, *Lab.* 11
*Torbay	*LD* 28, *C.* 5, *Lab.* 3
Torridge	*Ind.* 15, *LD* 13, *Lab.* 5, *C.* 2, Green 1
*Tunbridge Wells	*LD* 23, *C.* 19, *Lab.* 5, *Ind.* 1
Tynedale	*Lab.* 19, *LD.* 13, *C.* 11, *Ind.* 4
Uttlesford	*LD* 19, *C.* 12, *Ind.* 7, *Lab.* 4
Vale of White Horse	*LD* 34, *C.* 11, *Lab.* 5, *Ind.* 1
Vale Royal	*Lab.* 42, *C.* 15, *Ind.* 3
Wansbeck	*Lab.* 46
†Wansdyke	*C.* 22, *Lab.* 19, *Ind.* 3, *LD* 2, vacant 1
Warrington	*Lab.* 48, *LD* 11, *C.* 1
Warwick	*Lab.* 17, *C.* 13, *LD* 11, *RA* 4
*Watford	*Lab.* 21, *C.* 8, *LD* 7
*Waveney	*Lab.* 36, *C.* 9, *LD* 2, vacant 1
Waverley	*LD* 37, *C.* 17, *Lab.* 2, *Ind.* 1
Wealden	*C.* 29, *LD* 24, *Ind.* 5
Wear Valley	*Lab.* 35, *Ind.* 3, *LD* 2
Wellingborough	*Lab.* 16, *C.* 15, *Ind.* 3
*Welwyn Hatfield	*Lab.* 27, *C.* 20
West Devon	*LD* 15, *Ind.* 14, *Lab.* 1
West Dorset	*C.* 18, *Ind.* 18, *LD* 13, *Lab.* 5, *SD* 1
*West Lancashire	*Lab.* 32, *C.* 23
*West Lindsey	*LD* 15, *Ind.* 8, *C.* 5, *Lab.* 4, Others 5

*West Oxfordshire	*Ind.* 15, *LD* 13, *C.* 12, *Lab.* 9
West Somerset	*NP* 12, *C.* 9, *Lab.* 8, *LD* 2, *Ind. C.* 1
West Wiltshire	*LD* 28, *C.* 8, *Lab.* 4, *Ind.* 3
*Weymouth and Portland	*LD* 14, *Lab.* 10, *C.* 5, *Ind.* 3, *RA* 3
*Winchester	*LD* 33, *C.* 12, *Lab.* 6, *Ind.* 4
Windsor and Maidenhead	*LD* 32, *C.* 17, *Ind.* 7, *Lab.* 2
*Woking	*C.* 14, *LD* 14, *Lab.* 6, *Ind. C.* 1
*Wokingham	*C.* 27, *LD* 26, *Ind.* 1
†Woodspring	*LD.* 29, *C.* 18, *Lab.* 6, *Ind.* 4, Green 1, Lib. 1
*Worcester	*Lab.* 22, *C.* 10, *LD* 3, *Ind.* 1
*Worthing	*LD* 23, *C.* 13
Wrekin	*Lab.* 38, *C.* 3, *Ind. Lab.* 2, *LD* 2, *Ind.* 1
Wychavon	*C.* 18, *LD* 16, *Lab.* 10, *Ind.* 5
Wycombe	*C.* 24, *LD* 18, *Lab.* 15, *Ind.* 2, *RA* 1
Wyre	*Lab.* 31, *C.* 18, *LD* 4, *RA* 2, *Ind. C.* 1
*Wyre Forest	*Lab.* 20, *LD* 15, *C.* 6, *Ind.* 1
*†York	*Lab.* 33, *C.* 7, *LD* 5

GREATER LONDON BOROUGHS

Barking and Dagenham	*Lab.* 47, *RA* 3, Lib. 1
Barnet	*C.* 29, *Lab.* 25, *LD* 6
Bexley	*C.* 24, *Lab.* 24, *LD* 14
Brent	*C.* 33, *Lab.* 28, Lib. 5
Bromley	*C.* 32, *LD* 21, *Lab.* 7
Camden	*Lab.* 47, *C.* 7, *LD* 5
City of Westminster	*C.* 45, *Lab.* 15
Croydon	*Lab.* 40, *C.* 30
Ealing	*Lab.* 49, *C.* 19. *LD* 3
Enfield	*Lab.* 41, *C.* 24, *Ind. C.* 1
Greenwich	*Lab.* 45, *C.* 8, *SD* 4, *LD* 3, *Ind.* 1, vacant 1
Hackney	*Lab.* 42, *LD* 10, *C.* 7, *Ind.* 1
Hammersmith and Fulham	*Lab.* 33, *C.* 15, *LD* 2
Haringey	*Lab.* 57, *C.* 2
Harrow	*LD* 29, *C.* 16, *Lab.* 14, *Ind.* 3, vacant 1
Havering	*Lab.* 31, *RA* 17, *C.* 11, *LD* 4
Hillingdon	*Lab.* 43, *C.* 25, Others 1
Hounslow	*Lab.* 49, *C.* 6, *LD* 5
Islington	*Lab.* 39, *LD* 12, *C.* 1
Kensington and Chelsea	*Ind. C.* 39, *Lab.* 15
Kingston upon Thames	*LD* 27, *C.* 17, *Lab.* 6
Lambeth	*Lab.* 24, *LD* 24, *C.* 16
Lewisham	*Lab.* 63, *LD* 2, *C.* 1, vacant 1
Merton	*Lab.* 39, *C.* 10, *Ind.* 4, *LD* 3, vacant 1
Newham	*Lab.* 60
Redbridge	*Lab.* 29, *C.* 24, *LD* 9
Richmond upon Thames	*LD* 44, *C.* 6, *Lab.* 2
Southwark	*Lab.* 35, *LD* 25, *C.* 3, Lib. 1
Sutton	*LD* 47, *Lab.* 5, *C.* 4
Tower Hamlets	*Lab.* 43, Lib. 7
Waltham Forest	*Lab.* 26, *C.* 16, *LD* 14, *Ind.* 1
Wandsworth	*C.* 45, *Lab.* 16

WALES UNTIL 1 APRIL 1996

COUNTY COUNCILS

Clwyd	*Lab.* 33, *PC* 15, *C.* 8, *Others* 8
Dyfed	*Ind.* 31, *Lab.* 22, *LD* 8, *PC* 7, *C.* 1, *RA* 1
Gwent	*Lab.* 54, *C.* 5, *LD* 1, *PC* 1, *vacant* 2
Gwynedd	*Ind.* 26, *PC* 17, *Lab.* 9, *LD* 7, *Others* 2, *vacant* 1
Mid Glamorgan	*Lab.* 57, *PC* 10, *Ind.* 3, *C.* 1, *vacant* 3
Powys	*Ind.* 36, *Lab.* 6, *LD* 4
South Glamorgan	*Lab.* 38, *C.* 12, *LD* 8, *Ind. Lab.* 1, *PC* 1, *vacant* 2
West Glamorgan	*Lab.* 47, *Ind.* 6, *LD* 4, *C.* 3, *PC* 1

DISTRICT COUNCILS

Aberconwy	*LD* 11, *Lab.* 9, *C.* 8, *Ind.* 4, *NP* 4, *PC* 1, vacant 4
Alyn and Deeside	*Lab.* 28, *C.* 5, *Ind.* 5, *Ind. C.* 2, *LD* 2, *Ind. Lab.* 1
Arfon	*PC* 14, *Ind.* 13, *Lab.* 8, *LD* 2, *Others* 1, *vacant* 1
Blaenau Gwent	*Lab.* 32, *RA* 5, *Ind.* 3, *PC* 2, *C.* 1, *Lib.* 1
Brecknock	*Ind.* 30, *Lab.* 11, *LD* 2, *vacant* 1
Cardiff	*Lab.* 35, *C.* 21, *LD* 9
Carmarthen	*Ind.* 27, *Lab.* 6, *PC* 2, *LD* 1, *RA* 1
Ceredigion	*Ind.* 30, *LD* 9, *PC* 4, *Lab.* 1
Colwyn	*LD* 13, *Ind.* 12, *C.* 7, *Lab.* 2
Cynon Valley	*Lab.* 23, *PC* 12, *Ind.* 3
Delyn	*Ind.* 19, *Lab.* 13, *LD* 3, *C.* 2, *PC* 2, *Others* 2
Dinefwr	*Lab.* 15, *Ind.* 11, *PC* 3, *NP* 1, *vacant* 2
Dwyfor	*PC* 6, *Ind.* 5, *Others* 18
Glyndŵr	*Ind.* 26, *Lab.* 4, *Ind. Lab.* 2, *LD* 2, *PC* 1
Islwyn	*Lab.* 30, *PC* 5
Llanelli	*Lab.* 17, *LD* 5, *Ind.* 4, *Green* 3, *PC* 2, *Others* 4
Lliw Valley	*Lab.* 22, *Ind.* 6, *PC* 4, *C.* 1
Meirionnydd	*PC* 13, *Lab.* 5, *Ind.* 1, *Others* 22
Merthyr Tydfil	*Lab.* 21, *RA* 7, *Ind.* 2, *PC* 1, *Others* 2
Monmouth	*C.* 21, *Lab.* 13, *Ind.* 4, *LD* 1, *vacant* 1
Montgomeryshire	*Ind.* 37, *LD* 5, *Lab.* 2, *C.* 1, *PC* 1
Neath	*Lab.* 24, *PC* 5, *LD* 2, *Ind.* 1, *Ind. Lab.* 1, *Others* 1
Newport	*Lab.* 46, *C.* 1
Ogwr	*Lab.* 36, *C.* 8, *Ind. Lab.* 1, *LD* 1, *vacant* 3
Port Talbot	*Lab.* 21, *RA* 5, *SD* 2, *Ind.* 1, *LD* 1, *vacant* 1
Preseli Pembrokeshire	*Ind.* 36, *Lab.* 2, *C.* 1, *LD* 1
Radnorshire	*Ind.* 25, *Lab.* 4, *LD* 2, *C.* 1, *Green* 1
Rhondda	*Lab.* 23, *PC* 7, *RA* 3
Rhuddlan	*Ind.* 21, *Lab.* 10, *vacant* 1
Rhymney Valley	*Lab.* 28, *PC* 12, *Ind.* 6
South Pembrokeshire	*Ind.* 26, *PC* 2, *Lab.* 1, *vacant* 1
Swansea	*Lab.* 32, *LD* 8, *C.* 6, *Ind.* 6
Taff-Ely	*Lab.* 20, *PC* 14, *Ind.* 4, *LD* 2, *C.* 1, *RA* 1, *SD* 1

Torfaen	*Lab.* 36, *Ind.* 3, *LD* 3, *C.* 1, *Others* 1
Vale of Glamorgan	*Lab.* 20, *C.* 19, *PC* 3, *Others* 4
Wrexham Maelor	*Lab.* 29, *Ind.* 6, *LD* 5, *C.* 4, *Lib.* 1, *PC* 1
Ynys Môn	*Ind.* 25, *PC* 8, *Lab.* 5, *C.* 1

SCOTLAND UNTIL 1 APRIL 1996

REGIONAL AND ISLANDS COUNCILS

Borders	*Ind.* 11, *LD* 8, *SNP* 6, *C.* 2
Central	*Lab.* 23, *SNP* 6, *C.* 4, *Ind.* 2
Dumfries and Galloway	*Lab.* 11, *Ind.* 8, *LD* 6, *C.* 3, *NP* 3, *SNP* 3, *vacant* 1
Fife	*Lab.* 28, *LD* 12, *SNP* 3, *Ind.* 2, *Com.* 1
Grampian	*LD* 18, *SNP* 17, *Lab.* 12, *C.* 8, *Ind.* 2
Highland	*Ind.* 31, *Lab.* 10, *SNP* 4, *LD* 3, *C.* 2, *Lib.* 2, *Others* 2
Lothian	*Lab.* 36, *C.* 5, *LD* 4, *SNP* 4
Orkney	*Ind.* 28
Shetland	*NP* 10, *Ind.* 5, *Lab.* 2, *LD* 2, *Ind. Lab.* 1, *Others* 6
Strathclyde	*Lab.* 86, *SNP* 7, *LD* 6, *C.* 3, *Ind.* 2
Tayside	*SNP* 22, *Lab.* 16, *C.* 4, *LD* 2, *Ind.* 1, *Ind. Lab.* 1
Western Isles	*Ind.* 25, *Lab.* 5

DISTRICT COUNCILS

Aberdeen	*Lab.* 27, *LD* 13, *C.* 10, *SNP* 2
Angus	*SNP* 11, *C.* 7, *Ind.* 2, *Others* 1
Annandale and Eskdale	*LD* 9, *Ind.* 6, *Lab.* 1
Argyll and Bute	*Ind.* 10, *C.* 4, *LD* 3, *SNP* 2, *Lab.* 1, *Others* 6
Badenoch and Strathspey	*Ind.* 11
Banff and Buchan	*Ind.* 10, *SNP* 7, *LD* 1
Bearsden and Milngavie	*C.* 5, *LD* 5
Berwickshire	*C.* 7, *Ind.* 4, *LD* 1
Caithness	*Ind.* 15, *Lib.* 1
Clackmannan	*Lab.* 8, *SNP* 3, *C.* 1
Clydebank	*Lab.* 6, *SNP* 3, *Ind.* 1, *C.* 1
Clydesdale	*Lab.* 8, *C.* 3, *SNP* 3, *Ind.* 2
Cumbernauld and Kilsyth	*Lab.* 7, *SNP* 5
Cumnock and Doon Valley	*Lab.* 10
Cunninghame	*Lab.* 20, *C.* 6, *SNP* 3, *Ind.* 1
Dumbarton	*Lab.* 7, *C.* 5, *SNP* 3, *Ind.* 1
Dundee	*Lab.* 28, *C.* 4, *SNP* 3, *Ind. Lab.* 1
Dunfermline	*Lab.* 22, *LD* 5, *SNP* 4, *C.* 2, *Others* 1
East Kilbride	*Lab.* 12, *C.* 2, *SNP* 2
East Lothian	*Lab.* 9, *C.* 7, *SNP* 1
Eastwood	*C.* 8, *RA* 2, *Lab.* 1, *SLD* 1
Edinburgh	*Lab.* 30, *C.* 23, *LD* 7, *SNP* 2
Ettrick and Lauderdale	*Ind.* 15, *SNP* 1
Falkirk	*Lab.* 16, *SNP* 12, *Ind.* 5, *C.* 3
Glasgow	*Lab.* 55, *C.* 4, *Ind. Lab.* 2, *SNP* 2, *LD* 1, *Others* 2
Gordon	*Ind.* 9, *LD* 5, *C.* 2
Hamilton	*Lab.* 15, *C.* 2, *LD* 2, *Ind. Lab.* 1
Inverclyde	*Lab.* 11, *LD* 8, *C.* 1
Inverness	*Ind.* 13, *Lab.* 8, *LD* 5, *Lib.* 1, *SNP* 1
Kilmarnock and Loudoun	*Lab.* 8, *SNP* 7, *C.* 3

Kincardine and Deeside	*C.* 5, *Ind.* 5, *LD* 1, *SNP* 1
Kirkcaldy	*Lab.* 23, *SNP* 7, *Ind.* 4, *C.* 2, *LD* 2, *Others* 2
Kyle and Carrick	*C.* 16, *Lab.* 9
Lochaber	*Ind.* 4, *NP* 4, *SNP* 4, *Lab.* 2, *Ind. Lab.* 1
Midlothian	*Lab.* 12, *C.* 2, *SNP* 1
Monklands	*Lab.* 17, *SNP* 3
Moray	*Ind.* 8, *SNP* 6, *Lab.* 3, *C.* 1
Motherwell	*Lab.* 22, *SNP* 4, *C.* 2, *Ind.* 2
Nairn	*Ind.* 8, *C.* 1, *SNP* 1
Nithsdale	*Lab.* 9, *Ind.* 8, *C.* 5, *SNP* 5, *LD* 1
North East Fife	*LD* 13, *C.* 4, *Ind.* 1
Perth and Kinross	*C.* 16, *SNP* 5, *Ind.* 3, *Lab.* 3, *LD* 2
Renfrew	*Lab.* 22, *SNP* 12, *C.* 7, *LD* 3, *Ind.* 1
Ross and Cromarty	*Ind.* 17, *SNP* 4, *C.* 1
Roxburgh	*Ind.* 7, *LD* 4, *C.* 1, *NP* 1, *SNP* 1, *Others* 1, *vacant* 1
Skye and Lochalsh	*Ind.* 9, *LD* 1, *SNP* 1
Stewartry	*Ind.* 11, *C.* 1
Stirling	*C.* 10, *Lab.* 10
Strathkelvin	*Lab.* 9, *C.* 6
Sutherland	*Ind.* 14
Tweeddale	*Ind.* 7, *Lab.* 1, *LD* 1, *SNP* 1
West Lothian	*SNP* 11, *Lab.* 10, *C.* 1, *Ind. C.* 1, *Ind.* 1
Wigtown	*Ind.* 11, *C.* 1, *Lab.* 1, *SNP* 1

THE ISLES OF SCILLY

The islands of the Scillies group are administered by the Council of the Isles of Scilly, a 21-member non-political body, which combines the powers and duties of a county council and a district council under the Local Government Act 1972 and the Isles of Scilly Orders 1978. Legislation is specifically applied to the Isles of Scilly by Special Order. The Council is responsible for education, fire services, highways, planning, social services, water, and the airport. The police service is administered by the Devon and Cornwall Police Authority, of which the Council is a member. The Isles are part of the St Ives electoral division.

Administrative Headquarters, Town Hall, St Mary's, Isles of Scilly TR21 0LW

Chairman of the Council, J. P. Greenlaw

Clerk and Chief Executive, P. S. Hygate

Chief Technical Officer, B. M. Lowen

England

The Kingdom of England lies between 55° 46' and 49° 57' 30" N. latitude (from a few miles north of the mouth of the Tweed to the Lizard), and between 1° 46' E. and 5° 43' W. (from Lowestoft to Land's End). England is bounded on the north by the Cheviot Hills; on the south by the English Channel; on the east by the Straits of Dover (Pas de Calais) and the North Sea; and on the west by the Atlantic Ocean, Wales and the Irish Sea. It has a total area of 50,351 sq. miles (130,410 sq. km): land 50,058 sq. miles (129,652 sq. km); inland water 293 sq. miles (758 sq. km).

POPULATION

The population at the 1991 Census was 46,382,050 (males 22,469,707; females 23,912,343). The average density of the population in 1991 was 3.6 persons per hectare.

FLAG

The flag of England is the cross of St George, a red cross on a white field (cross gules in a field argent). The cross of St George, the patron saint of England, has been used since the 13th century.

RELIEF

There is a marked division between the upland and lowland areas of England. In the extreme north the Cheviot Hills (highest point, The Cheviot, 2,674 ft) form a natural boundary with Scotland. Running south from the Cheviots, though divided from them by the Tyne Gap, is the Pennine range (highest point, Cross Fell, 2,930 ft), the main orological feature of the country. The Pennines culminate in the Peak District of Derbyshire (Kinder Scout, 2,088 ft). West of the Pennines are the Cumbrian mountains, which include Scafell Pike (3,210 ft), the highest peak in England, and to the east are the Yorkshire Moors, their highest point being Urra Moor (1,490 ft).

In the west, the foothills of the Welsh mountains extend into the bordering English counties of Shropshire (the Wrekin, 1,334 ft; Long Mynd, 1,694 ft) and Hereford and Worcester (the Malvern Hills – Worcestershire Beacon, 1,394 ft). Extensive areas of high land and moorland are also to be found in the south-western peninsula formed by Somerset, Devon and Cornwall: principally Exmoor (Dunkery Beacon, 1,704 ft), Dartmoor (High Willhays, 2,038 ft) and Bodmin Moor (Brown Willy, 1,377 ft). Ranges of low, undulating hills run across the south of the country, including the Cotswolds in the Midlands and south-west, the Chilterns to the north of London, and the North (Kent) and South (Sussex) Downs of the south-east coastal areas.

The lowlands of England lie in the Vale of York, East Anglia and the area around the Wash. The lowest-lying are the Cambridgeshire Fens in the valleys of the Great Ouse and the River Nene, which are below sea-level in places. Since the 17th century extensive drainage has brought much of the Fens under cultivation. The North Sea coast between the Thames and the Humber, low-lying and formed of sand and shingle for the most part, is subject to erosion and defences against further incursion have been built along many stretches.

HYDROGRAPHY

The Severn is the longest river in Great Britain, rising in the north-eastern slopes of Plynlimon (Wales) and entering England in Shropshire with a total length of 220 miles (354 km) from its source to its outflow into the Bristol Channel, where it receives on the east the Bristol Avon, on the west the Wye, its other tributaries being the

Vyrnwy, Tern, Stour, Teme and Upper (or Warwickshire) Avon. The Severn is tidal below Gloucester, and a high bore or tidal wave sometimes reverses the flow as high as Tewkesbury (13½ miles above Gloucester). The scenery of the greater part of the river is very picturesque and beautiful, and the Severn is a noted salmon river, some of its tributaries being famous for trout. Navigation is assisted by the Gloucester and Berkeley Ship Canal (16¾ miles), which admits vessels of 350 tons to Gloucester. The Severn Tunnel was begun in 1873 and completed in 1886 at a cost of £2 million and after many difficulties from flooding. It is 4 miles 628 yards in length (of which 2¼ miles are under the river). The Severn road bridge between Haysgate, Gwent, and Almondsbury, Glos., with a centre span of 3,240 ft, was opened in 1966.

The longest river wholly in England is the Thames, with a total length of 215 miles (346 km) from its source in the Cotswold hills to the Nore, and is navigable by ocean-going ships to London Bridge. The Thames is tidal to Teddington (69 miles from its mouth) and forms county boundaries almost throughout its course; on its banks are situated London, Windsor Castle, the oldest royal residence still in regular use, Eton College, the first of the public schools, and Oxford, the oldest university in the kingdom.

Of the remaining English rivers those flowing into the North Sea are the Tyne, Wear, Tees, Ouse and Trent from the Pennine Range, the Great Ouse (160 miles), which rises in Northamptonshire, and the Orwell and Stour from the hills of East Anglia. Flowing into the English Channel are the Sussex Ouse from the Weald, the Itchen from the Hampshire Hills, and the Axe, Teign, Dart, Tamar and Exe from the Devonian hills. Flowing into the Irish Sea are the Mersey, Ribble and Eden from the western slopes of the Pennines and the Derwent from the Cumbrian mountains.

The English Lakes, noteworthy for their picturesque scenery and poetic associations, lie in Cumbria, the largest being Windermere (10 miles long), Ullswater and Derwent Water.

ISLANDS

The Isle of Wight is separated from Hampshire by the Solent. The capital, Newport, stands at the head of the estuary of the Medina, Cowes (at the mouth) being the chief port. Other centres are Ryde, Sandown, Shanklin, Ventnor, Freshwater, Yarmouth, Totland Bay, Seaview and Bembridge.

Lundy (the name means Puffin Island), 11 miles north-west of Hartland Point, Devon, is about two miles long and about half a mile broad (average), with a total area of about 1,116 acres, and a population of about 20. It became the property of the National Trust in 1969 and is now principally a bird sanctuary.

The Isles of Scilly consist of about 140 islands and skerries (total area, 6 sq. miles/10 sq. km) situated 28 miles south-west of Land's End. Only five are inhabited: St Mary's, St Agnes, Bryher, Tresco and St Martin's. The population is 1,978. The entire group has been designated a Conservation Area, a Heritage Coast, and an Area of Outstanding Natural Beauty, and has been given National Nature Reserve status by the Nature Conservancy Council because of its unique flora and fauna. Tourism and the winter/spring flower trade for the home market form the basis of the economy of the Isles. The island group is a recognized rural development area.

EARLY HISTORY

Archaeological evidence suggests that England has been inhabited since at least the Palaeolithic period, though the extent of the various Palaeolithic cultures was dependent upon the degree of glaciation. The succeeding Neolithic and Bronze Age cultures have left abundant remains throughout the country, the best-known of these being the henges and stone circles of Stonehenge (ten miles north of Salisbury, Wilts.) and Avebury (Wilts.), both of which are believed to have been of religious significance. In the latter part of the Bronze Age the Goidels, a people of Celtic race, and in the Iron Age other Celtic races of Brythons and Belgae, invaded the country and brought with them Celtic civilization and dialects, place names in England bearing witness to the spread of the invasion over the whole kingdom.

THE ROMAN CONQUEST

The Roman conquest of Gaul (57–50 BC) brought Britain into close contact with Roman civilization, but although Julius Caesar raided the south of Britain in 55 BC and 54 BC, conquest was not undertaken until nearly 100 years later. In AD 43 the Emperor Claudius dispatched Aulus Plautius, with a well-equipped force of 40,000, and himself followed with reinforcements in the same year. Success was delayed by the resistance of Caratacus (Caractacus), the British leader from AD 48–51, who was finally captured and sent to Rome, and by a great revolt in AD 61 led by Boudicca (Boadicea), Queen of the Iceni; but the south of Britain was secured by AD 70, and Wales and the area north to the Tyne by about AD 80.

In AD 122, the Emperor Hadrian visited Britain and built a continuous rampart, since known as Hadrian's Wall, from Wallsend to Bowness (Tyne to Solway). The work was entrusted by the Emperor Hadrian to Aulus Platorius Nepos, legate of Britain from AD 122 to 126, and it was intended to form the northern frontier of the Roman Empire.

The Romans administered Britain as a province under a Governor, with a well-defined system of local government, each Roman municipality ruling itself and its surrounding territory, while London was the centre of the road system and the seat of the financial officials of the Province of Britain. Colchester, Lincoln, York, Gloucester and St Albans stand on the sites of five Roman municipalities, and Wroxeter, Caerleon, Chester, Lincoln and York were at various times the sites of legionary fortresses. Well-preserved Roman towns have been uncovered at (or near) Silchester (*Calleva Atrebatum*), ten miles south of Reading, Wroxeter (*Viroconium Cornoviorum*), near Shrewsbury, and St Albans (*Verulamium*) in Hertfordshire.

Four main groups of roads radiated from London, and a fifth (the Fosse) ran obliquely from Lincoln through Leicester, Cirencester and Bath to Exeter. Of the four groups radiating from London, one ran south-east to Canterbury and the coast of Kent, a second to Silchester and thence to parts of western Britain and south Wales, a third (later known as Watling Street) ran through Verulamium to Chester, with various branches, and the fourth reached Colchester, Lincoln, York and the eastern counties.

In the fourth century Britain was subject to raids along the east coast by Saxon pirates, which led to the establishment of a system of coast defence from the Wash to Southampton Water, with forts at Brancaster, Burgh Castle (Yarmouth), Walton (Felixstowe), Bradwell, Reculver, Richborough, Dover, Lympne, Pevensey and Porchester (Portsmouth). The Irish (Scoti) and Picts in the north were also becoming more aggressive; from about AD 350 incursions became more frequent and more formidable. As the Roman Empire came under attack increasingly towards the end of the fourth century, many troops were removed from Britain for service in other parts of the empire. The island was eventually cut off from Rome by the Teutonic conquest of Gaul, and with the withdrawal of the last Roman garrison early in the fifth century, the Romano-British were left to themselves.

SAXON SETTLEMENT

According to legend, the British King Vortigern called in the Saxons to defend him against the Picts, the Saxon chieftains being Hengist and Horsa, who landed at Ebbsfleet, Kent, and established themselves in the Isle of Thanet; but the events during the one and a half centuries between the final break with Rome and the re-establishment of Christianity are unclear. However, it would appear that in the course of this period the raids turned into large-scale settlement by invaders traditionally known as Angles (England north of the Wash and East Anglia), Saxons (Essex and southern England) and Jutes (Kent and the Weald), which pushed the Romano-British into the mountainous areas of the north and west, Celtic culture outside Wales and Cornwall surviving only in topo-graphical names. Various kingdoms were established at this time which attempted to claim overlordship of the whole country, hegemony finally being achieved by Wessex (capital, Winchester) in the ninth century. This century also saw the beginning of raids by the Vikings (Danes), which were resisted by Alfred the Great (871–899), who fixed a limit to the advance of Danish settlement by the Treaty of Wedmore (878), giving them the area north and east of Watling Street, on condition that they adopt Christianity.

In the tenth century the kings of Wessex recovered the whole of England from the Danes, but subsequent rulers were unable to resist a second wave of invaders. England paid tribute (*Danegeld*) for many years, and was invaded in 1013 by the Danes and ruled by Danish kings from 1016 until 1042, when Edward the Confessor was recalled from exile in Normandy. On Edward's death in 1066 Harold Godwinson (brother-in-law of Edward and son of Earl Godwin of Wessex) was chosen King of England. After defeating (at Stamford Bridge, Yorkshire, 25 September) an invading army under Harald Hadraada, King of Norway (aided by the outlawed Earl Tostig of Northumbria, Harold's brother), Harold was himself defeated at the Battle of Hastings on 14 October 1066, and the Norman conquest secured the throne of England for Duke William of Normandy, a cousin of Edward the Confessor.

CHRISTIANITY

Christianity reached the Roman province of Britain from Gaul in the third century (or possibly earlier); Alban, traditionally Britain's first martyr, was put to death as a Christian during the persecution of Diocletian (22 June 303), at his native town Verulamium; and the Bishops of Londinium, Eboracum (York), and Lindum (Lincoln) attended the Council of Arles in 314. However, the Anglo-Saxon invasions submerged the Christian religion in England until the sixth century when conversion was undertaken in the north from 563 by Celtic missionaries from Ireland led by St Columba, and in the south by a mission sent from Rome in 597 which was led by St Augustine, who became the first archbishop of Canterbury. England appears to have been converted again by the end of the seventh century and followed, after the Council of Whitby in 663, the practices of the Roman Church, which brought the kingdom into the mainstream of European thought and culture.

PRINCIPAL CITIES

BIRMINGHAM

Birmingham (West Midlands) is Britain's second city. It is a focal point in national communications networks with a rapidly expanding International Airport. The generally accepted derivation of 'Birmingham' is the *ham* (dwelling-place) of the *ing* (family) of *Beorma*, presumed to have been Saxon. During the Industrial Revolution the town grew into a major manufacturing centre. In 1889 Birmingham was granted City status.

Despite the decline in manufacturing, Birmingham is still a major hardware trade and motor component industry centre. As well as the National Exhibition Centre and the Aston Science Park, recent developments include the International Convention Centre and the National Indoor Arena.

The principal buildings are the Town Hall (1832–4); the Council House (1879); Victoria Law Courts (1891); the University (1909); the 13th-century Church of St Martin-in-the-Bullring (rebuilt 1873); the Cathedral (formerly St Philip's Church) (1711) and the Roman Catholic Cathedral of St Chad (1839–41).

BRADFORD

Bradford (West Yorkshire) lies on the southern edge of the Yorkshire Dales National Park, including within its boundaries the village of Haworth, home of the Brontë sisters, and Ilkley Moor.

Originally a Saxon township, Bradford received a market charter in 1251 but developed only slowly until the industrialization of the textile industry brought rapid growth during the 19th century; it was granted its city charter in 1897. The prosperity of that period is reflected in much of the city's architecture, particularly the public buildings: City Hall (1873), Wool Exchange (1867), St George's Hall (Concert Hall, 1853), Cartwright Hall (Art Gallery, 1904) and the Technical College (1882). Other chief buildings are the Cathedral (15th century) and Bolling Hall (14th century).

Textiles still play an important part in the city's economy but industry is now more broadly based, including engineering, micro-electronics, printing and chemicals. The city has a strong financial services sector, and a growing tourism industry.

BRISTOL

Bristol (Avon) was a Royal Borough before the Norman Conquest. The earliest form of the name is *Bricgstow*. In 1373 it received from Edward III a charter granting it county status.

The chief buildings include the 12th-century Cathedral (with later additions), with Norman chapter house and gateway, the 14th-century Church of St Mary Redcliffe, Wesley's Chapel, Broadmead, the Merchant Venturers' Almshouses, the Council House (1956), Guildhall, Exchange (erected from the designs of John Wood in 1743), Cabot Tower, the University and Clifton College. The Roman Catholic Cathedral at Clifton was opened in 1973.

The Clifton Suspension Bridge, with a span of 702 feet over the Avon, was projected by Brunel in 1836 but was not completed until 1864. Brunel's SS *Great Britain*, the first ocean-going propeller-driven ship, is now being restored in the City Docks from where she was launched in 1843. The docks themselves have been extensively restored and redeveloped.

CAMBRIDGE

Cambridge, a settlement far older than its ancient University, lies on the River Cam or Granta. The city is a county town and regional headquarters. Its industries include electronics, flour milling, cement making, the manufacture of scientific instruments, and biotechnology. Among its open spaces are Jesus Green, Sheep's Green, Coe Fen, Parker's Piece, Christ's Pieces, the University Botanic Garden, and the Backs, or lawns and gardens through which the Cam winds behind the principal line of college buildings. East of the Cam, King's Parade, upon which stand Great St Mary's Church, Gibbs' Senate House and King's College Chapel with Wilkins' screen, joins Trumpington Street to form one of the most beautiful throughfares in Europe.

University and college buildings provide the outstanding features of Cambridge architecture but several churches (especially St Benet's, the oldest building in the City, and St Sepulchre's, the Round Church) are also notable. The modern Guildhall (1939) stands on a site of which at least part has held municipal buildings since 1224.

CANTERBURY

Canterbury, the Metropolitan City of the Anglican Communion, has a history going back to prehistoric times. It was the Roman *Durovernum Cantiacorum* and the Saxon *Cant-wara-byrig* (stronghold of the men of Kent). Here in 597 St Augustine began the conversion of the English to Christianity, when Ethelbert, King of Kent, was baptized.

Of the Benedictine St Augustine's Abbey, burial place of the Jutish Kings of Kent (whose capital Canterbury was), only ruins remain. St Martin's Church, on the eastern outskirts of the city, is stated by Bede to have been the place of worship of Queen Bertha, the Christian wife of King Ethelbert, before the advent of St Augustine.

In 1170 the rivalry of Church and State culminated in the murder in Canterbury Cathedral, by Henry II's knights, of Archbishop Thomas Becket, whose shrine became a great centre of pilgrimage, as described by Chaucer in his *Canterbury Tales*. After the Reformation pilgrimages ceased, but the prosperity of the city was strengthened by an influx of Huguenot refugees, who introduced weaving. The poet and playwright Christopher Marlowe was born and reared in Canterbury, and there are also literary associations with Defoe, Dickens, Joseph Conrad and Somerset Maugham.

The Cathedral, with architecture ranging from the 11th to the 15th centuries, is world famous. Modern pilgrims are attracted particularly to the Martyrdom, the Black Prince's Tomb, the Warriors' Chapel and the many examples of medieval stained glass.

The medieval city walls are built on Roman foundations and the 14th-century West Gate is one of the finest buildings of its kind in the country.

The 1,000 seat Marlowe Theatre is the base for the Canterbury Arts Festival each autumn.

CARLISLE

Carlisle is situated at the confluence of the River Eden and River Caldew, 309 miles north-west of London and about ten miles from the Scottish border. It was granted a charter in 1158.

The city stands at the western end of Hadrian's Wall and dates from the original Roman settlement of *Luguvalium*. Granted to Scotland in the tenth century, Carlisle is not included in the Domesday Book. William Rufus reclaimed the area in 1092 and the castle and city walls were built to guard Carlisle and the western border; the citadel is a

Tudor addition to protect the south of the city. Until the Union of the Crowns in 1603, Carlisle changed hands several times and was frequently besieged. During the Civil War the city remained Royalist; in 1745 it supported the Young Pretender.

The Cathedral, originally a 12th-century Augustinian priory, was enlarged in the 13th and 14th centuries after the diocese was created in 1133. To the south is a restored Tithe Barn and nearby the 18th-century church of St Cuthbert, the third to stand on a site dating from the seventh century.

Carlisle is the major shopping, commercial and agricultural centre for the area, and industries include the manufacture of metal goods, biscuits and textiles. However, the largest employer is the services sector, notably in central and local government, retailing and transport. The city has an important communications position at the centre of a network of major roads, as an important stage on the main west coast rail services, and with its own airport at Crosby.

CHESTER

Chester is situated on the River Dee, and was granted Borough and City status in 1974. Its recorded history dates from the first century when the Romans founded the fortress of *Deva*. The city's name is derived from the Latin *castra* (a camp or encampment). During the Middle Ages, Chester was the principal port of north-west England but declined with the silting of the Dee estuary and competition from Liverpool. The city was also an important military centre, notably during Edward I's Welsh campaigns and the Elizabethan Irish campaigns. During the Civil War, Chester supported the King and was besieged from 1643 to 1646. Chester's first charter was granted c.1175 and the city was incorporated in 1506. The office of Sheriff is the earliest created in the country (c.1120s), and in 1992 the Mayor was granted the title of Lord Mayor. He/ she also enjoys the title 'Admiral of the Dee'.

The city's architectural features include the city walls (an almost complete two-mile circuit), the unique Rows (covered galleries above the street-level shops), the Victorian Gothic Town Hall (1869), the Castle (rebuilt 1788 and 1822) and numerous half-timbered buildings. The Cathedral was a Benedictine abbey until the Dissolution. Remaining monastic buildings include the chapter house, refectory and cloisters and there is a modern free-standing bell tower. The Norman church of St John the Baptist was a cathedral church in the early Middle Ages.

Chester is a thriving retail, business and tourist centre.

COVENTRY

Coventry (West Midlands) is an important industrial centre, producing vehicles, machine tools, agricultural machinery, man-made fibres, aerospace components and telecommunications equipment. New investment has come from financial services, power transmission, professional services and education.

The city owes its beginning to Leofric, Earl of Mercia, and his wife Godiva who, in 1043, founded a Benedictine monastery. The guildhall of St Mary dates from the 14th century, three of the city's churches date from the 14th and 15th centuries, and 16th-century almshouses may still be seen. Coventry's first cathedral was destroyed at the Reformation, its second in the 1940 blitz (the walls and spire remain) and the new cathedral designed by Sir Basil Spence, consecrated in 1962, now draws innumerable visitors.

Coventry is the home of the University of Warwick and its Science Park, Coventry University, the Westwood

Business Park, the Cable and Wireless College, and the Museum of British Road Transport.

DERBY

Derby stands on the banks of the River Derwent, and its name dates back to 880 when the Danes settled in the locality and changed the original Saxon name of *Northworthy* to *Deoraby*.

Derby has a wide range of industries: its products include aero engines, pipework, specialized mechanical engineering equipment, textiles, chemicals, plastics and the Royal Crown Derby porcelain. The city is an established railway centre, the site of British Rail's Technical Centre with its research laboratories.

Buildings of interest include St Peter's Church and the Old Abbey Building (14th century), the Cathedral (1525), St Mary's Roman Catholic Church (1839) and the Industrial Museum, formerly the Old Silk Mill (1721). The traditional city centre is complemented by the Eagle Centre and 'out-of-centre' retail developments. In addition to the Derby Playhouse, the Assembly Rooms are a multi-purpose venue.

The first charter granting a Mayor and Aldermen was that of Charles I in 1637. Previous charters date back to 1154. It was granted City status in 1977.

DURHAM

The city of Durham is a district in the county of Durham and a major tourist attraction because of its prominent Norman Cathedral and Castle set high on a wooded peninsula overlooking the River Wear. The Cathedral was founded as a shrine for the body of St Cuthbert in 995. The present building dates from 1093 and among its many treasures is the tomb of the Venerable Bede (673–735). Durham's Prince Bishops had unique powers up to 1836, being lay rulers as well as religious leaders. As a palatinate Durham could have its own army, nobility, coinage and courts. The Castle was the main seat of the Prince Bishops for nearly 800 years; it is now used as a college by the University. The University, founded on the initiative of Bishop William Van Mildert, is England's third oldest.

Among other buildings of interest is the Guildhall in the Market Place which dates originally from the 14th century. Much work has been carried out to conserve this area, forming part of the city's major contribution to the Council of Europe's Urban Renaissance Campaign. Annual events include Durham's Regatta in June (claimed to be the oldest rowing event in Britain) and the Annual Gala (formerly Durham Miners' Gala) in July.

The economy of Durham has undergone a significant change with the replacement of mining as the dominant industry by 'white collar' employment. Although still a predominantly rural area, the industrial and commercial sector is growing and a wide range of manufacturing and service industries are based on industrial estates in and around the city.

EXETER

Exeter lies on the River Exe ten miles from the sea. It was granted a Royal Charter by Henry II. The Romans founded *Isca Dumnoniorum* in the first century AD, and in the third century a stone wall (much of which remains) was built, providing protection against Saxon, and then Danish invasions. After the Conquest, the city led resistance to William in the west until reduced by siege. The Normans built the ringwork castle of Rougemont, the gatehouse and one tower of which remain, although the rest was pulled down in 1784. The first bridge across the Exe was built in the early 13th century. The city's main port was situated downstream at Topsham until the construction in the 1560s of the first true canal in England, the redevelopment of which in 1700 brought seaborne trade direct to the city. Exeter was the Royalist headquarters in the west during the Civil War.

The diocese of Exeter was established by Edward the Confessor in 1050, although a minster existed near the Cathedral site from the late seventh century. A new cathedral was built in the 12th century but the present building was begun *c*.1275, although incorporating the Norman towers, and completed about a century later. The Guildhall dates from the 12th century and there are many other medieval buildings in the city, as well as architecture in the Georgian and Regency styles, and the Custom House (1680). Damage suffered by bombing in 1942 led to the redevelopment of the city centre.

Exeter's prosperity from medieval times was based on trade in wool and woollen cloth (commemorated by Tuckers Hall), which remained at its height until the late 18th century when export trade was hit by the French wars. Subsequently Exeter has developed as an administrative and commercial centre, notably in the distributive trades, light manufacturing industries and tourism.

KINGSTON UPON HULL

Hull (officially Kingston upon Hull) lies in the mostly rural county of Humberside, at the junction of the River Hull with the Humber, 22 miles from the North Sea. It is one of the major seaports of the United Kingdom. It has docks covering a water area of 172 acres, equipped to handle cargoes by unit-load techniques, and is a departure point for car ferry services to continental Europe. There is a variety of industry and service industries, as well as increasing tourism and conference business.

The city, restored after heavy air raid damage during the Second World War, has good office and administrative buildings, its municipal centre being the Guildhall, its educational centres the University of Hull and Humberside University and its religious centre the Parish Church of the Holy Trinity. The old town area is being renovated and includes a marina and shopping complex. Just west of the city is the Humber Bridge, the world's longest single-span suspension bridge.

Kingston upon Hull was so named by Edward I. City status was accorded in 1897 and the office of Mayor raised to the dignity of Lord Mayor in 1914.

LEEDS

Leeds (West Yorkshire), situated in the lower Aire Valley, is a junction for road, rail, canal and air services and an important commercial centre. Seventy-three per cent of employment is in services, notably the distributive trades, public administration, medical services and business services. The main manufacturing industries are mechanical engineering, printing and publishing, metal goods and furniture.

The principal buildings are the Civic Hall (1933), the Town Hall (1858), the Municipal Buildings and Art Gallery (1884) with the Henry Moore Gallery (1982), the Corn Exchange (1863) and the University. The Parish Church (St Peter's) was rebuilt in 1841; the 17th-century St John's Church has a fine interior with a famous English Renaissance screen; the last remaining 18th-century church in the city is Holy Trinity in Boar Lane (1727). Kirkstall Abbey (about three miles from the centre of the city), founded by Henry de Lacy in 1152, is one of the most complete examples of Cistercian houses now remaining. Temple Newsam, birthplace of Lord Darnley, was

acquired by the Council in 1922. The present house was largely rebuilt by Sir Arthur Ingram in about 1620. Adel Church, about five miles from the centre of the city, is a fine Norman structure.

Leeds was first incorporated by Charles I in 1626. The earliest forms of the name are *Loidis* or *Ledes*, the origins of which are obscure.

LEICESTER

Leicester is situated geographically in the centre of England. It dates back to pre-Roman times and was one of the five Danish *Burghs*. In 1589 Queen Elizabeth I granted a Charter to the City and the ancient title was confirmed by letters patent in 1919.

The principal industries are hosiery, knitwear, footwear manufacturing and engineering. The growth of Leicester as a hosiery centre increased rapidly from the introduction there of the first stocking frame in 1670 and today it has some of the largest hosiery factories in the world.

The principal buildings are the Town Hall, the New Walk Centre, the University of Leicester, De Montfort University, De Montfort Hall, one of the finest concert halls in the provinces seating over 2,750 people, and the Granby Halls, an indoor sports facility. The ancient churches of St Martin (now Leicester Cathedral), St Nicholas, St Margaret, All Saints, St Mary de Castro, and buildings such as the Guildhall, the 14th-century Newarke Gate, the Castle and the Jewry Wall Roman site still exist. The Haymarket Theatre was opened in 1973 and The Shires shopping centre in 1992.

LINCOLN

Situated 40 miles inland on the River Witham, Lincoln derives its name from a contraction of *Lindum Colonia*, the settlement founded in AD 48 by the Romans to command the crossing of Ermine Street and Fosse Way. Sections of the third-century Roman city wall can be seen, including an extant gateway (Newport Arch), and excavations have discovered traces of a sewerage system unique in Britain. The Romans also drained the surrounding fenland and created a canal system, laying the foundations of Lincoln's agricultural prosperity and also of the city's importance in the medieval wool trade as a port and Staple town.

As one of the Five Boroughs of the Danelaw, Lincoln was an important trading centre in the ninth and tenth centuries and medieval prosperity from the wool trade lasted until the 14th century, enabling local merchants to build parish churches (of which three survive) and attracting in the 12th century a Jewish community (Jew's House and Court, Aaron's House). However, the removal of the Staple to Boston in 1369 heralded a decline from which the city only recovered fully in the 19th century when improved fen drainage made Lincoln agriculturally important and improved canal and rail links led to industrial development, mainly in the manufacture of machinery, components and engineering products.

The castle was built shortly after the Conquest and is unusual in having two mounds; on one motte stands a Keep (Lucy's Tower) added in the 12th century. It currently houses one of the four surviving copies of the Magna Carta. The Cathedral was begun *c*.1073 when the first Norman bishop moved the see of Lindsey to Lincoln, but was mostly destroyed by fire and earthquake in the 12th century. Rebuilding was begun by St Hugh and completed over a century later. Other notable architectural features are the 12th-century High Bridge, the oldest in Britain still to carry buildings, and the Guildhall situated above the 15th–16th century Stonebow gateway.

LIVERPOOL

Liverpool (Merseyside) on the right bank of the River Mersey, three miles from the Irish Sea, is the United Kingdom's foremost port for the Atlantic trade. Tunnels link Liverpool with Birkenhead and Wallasey.

There are 2,100 acres of dockland on both sides of the river and the Gladstone and Royal Seaforth Docks can accommodate the largest vessels afloat. Annual tonnage of cargo handled is approximately 27.8 million tonnes. The main imports are crude oil, grain, ores, edible oils, timber, containers and break-bulk cargo. Liverpool Free Port, Britain's largest, was opened in 1984.

Liverpool was created a free borough in 1207 and a city in 1880. From the early 18th century it expanded rapidly with the growth of industrialization and the Atlantic trade. Surviving buildings from this date include the Bluecoat Chambers (1717, formerly the Bluecoat School), the Town Hall (1754, rebuilt to the original design 1795), and buildings in Rodney Street, Canning Street and the suburbs. Notable from the 19th and 20th centuries are the Anglican Cathedral, built from the designs of Sir Giles Gilbert Scott (the foundation stone was laid in 1904, and the building was completed only in 1980), the Catholic Metropolitan Cathedral (designed by Sir Frederick Gibberd, consecrated 1967) and St George's Hall (1838–54), regarded as one of the finest modern examples of classical architecture. The refurbished Albert Dock (designed by Jesse Hartley) contains the Merseyside Maritime Museum and Tate Gallery, Liverpool.

In 1852 an Act was obtained for establishing a public library, museum and art gallery; as a result Liverpool had one of the first public libraries in the country. The Brown, Picton and Hornby libraries now form one of the country's major libraries. The Victoria Building of Liverpool University, the Royal Liver, Cunard and Mersey Docks & Harbour Company buildings at the Pier Head, the Municipal Buildings and the Philharmonic Hall are other examples of the City's fine buildings.

MANCHESTER

Manchester (the *Mamucium* of the Romans, who occupied it in AD 79) is a commercial and industrial centre with a population engaged in the engineering, chemical, clothing, food processing and textile industries and in education. Banking, insurance and a growing leisure industry are among the prime commercial activities. The city is connected with the sea by the Manchester Ship Canal, opened in 1894, 35½ miles long, and accommodating ships up to 15,000 tons. Manchester Airport handles 15 million passengers yearly.

The principal buildings are the Town Hall, erected in 1877 from the designs of Alfred Waterhouse, together with a large extension of 1938; the Royal Exchange (1869, enlarged 1921); the Central Library (1934); Heaton Hall; the 17th-century Chetham Library; the Rylands Library (1900), which includes the Althorp collection; the University precinct; the 15th-century Cathedral (formerly the parish church); G-MEX exhibition centre and the Free Trade Hall. Recent developments include the Manchester Arena, the largest indoor arena in Europe. Manchester is the home of the Hallé Orchestra, the Royal Northern College of Music, the Royal Exchange Theatre and seven public art galleries. Metrolink, the new light rail system, opened in 1992.

The town received its first charter of incorporation in 1838 and was created a city in 1853. The title of City was retained under local government reorganization.

NEWCASTLE UPON TYNE

Newcastle upon Tyne (Tyne and Wear), on the north bank of the River Tyne, is eight miles from the North Sea. A Cathedral and University city, it is the administrative, commercial and cultural centre for north-east England and the principal port. It is an important manufacturing centre with a wide variety of industries.

The principal buildings include the Castle Keep (12th century), Black Gate (13th century), Blackfriars (13th century), West Walls (13th century), St Nicholas's Cathedral (15th century, fine lantern tower), St Andrew's Church (12th–14th century), St John's (14th–15th century), All Saints (1786 by Stephenson), St Mary's Roman Catholic Cathedral (1844), Trinity House (17th century), Sandhill (16th-century houses), Guildhall (Georgian), Grey Street (1834–9), Central Station (1846–50), Laing Art Gallery (1904), University of Newcastle Physics Building (1962) and Medical Building (1985), Civic Centre (1963), Central Library (1969) and Eldon Square Shopping Development (1976). Open spaces include the Town Moor (927 acres) and Jesmond Dene. Nine bridges span the Tyne at Newcastle.

The city derives its name from the 'new castle' (1080) erected as a defence against the Scots. In 1400 it was made a county, and in 1882 a city.

NORWICH

Norwich (Norfolk) grew from an early Anglo-Saxon settlement near the confluence of the Rivers Yare and Wensum, and now serves as provincial capital for the predominantly agricultural region of East Anglia. The name is thought to relate to the most northerly of a group of Anglo-Saxon villages or *wics*. The city's first known Charter was granted in 1158 by Henry II.

Norwich serves its surrounding area as a market town and commercial centre, banking and insurance being prominent among the city's businesses. From the 14th century until the Industrial Revolution, Norwich was the regional centre of the woollen industry, but now the biggest single industry is financial services and principal trades are engineering, printing, shoemaking, double glazing, and the production of chemicals, clothing, confectionery and other foodstuffs. Norwich is accessible to seagoing vessels by means of the River Yare, entered at Great Yarmouth, 20 miles to the east.

Among many historic buildings are the Cathedral (completed in the 12th century and surmounted by a 15th-century spire 315 feet in height), the keep of the Norman castle (now a museum and art gallery), the 15th-century flint-walled Guildhall (now a tourist information centre), some thirty medieval parish churches, St Andrew's and Blackfriars' Halls, the Tudor houses preserved in Elm Hill and the Georgian Assembly House. The University of East Anglia is located on a site at Earlham on the city's western boundary.

NOTTINGHAM

Nottingham stands on the River Trent and is connected by canal with the Atlantic Ocean and the North Sea. *Snotingaham* or *Notingeham*, literally the homestead of the people of Snot, is the Anglo-Saxon name for the Celtic settlement of *Tigguocobauc*, or the house of caves. In 878, Nottingham became one of the Five Boroughs of the Danelaw. William the Conqueror ordered the construction of Nottingham Castle, while the town itself developed rapidly under Norman rule. Its laws and rights were later formally recognized by Henry II's Charter in 1155. The Castle became a favoured residence of King John. In 1642 King

Charles I raised his personal standard at Nottingham Castle at the start of the Civil War.

Nottingham is a major sporting centre, home to Nottingham Forest FC, Notts County FC (the world's oldest Football league side), Nottingham Racecourse and the National Watersports Centre. The principal industries include textiles, pharmaceuticals, food manufacturing, engineering and telecommunications. There are two universities within the city boundaries.

Architecturally, Nottingham has a wealth of notable buildings, particularly those designed in the Victorian era by T. C. Hine and Watson Fothergill. The City Council owns the Castle, of Norman origin but restored in 1878, Wollaton Hall (1580–8), Newstead Abbey (home of Lord Byron), the Guildhall (1888) and Council House (1929). St Mary's, St Peter's and St Nicholas's Churches are of interest, as is the Roman Catholic Cathedral (Pugin, 1842–4).

Nottingham was granted City status in 1897.

OXFORD

Oxford is a University city, an important industrial centre, and a market town. Industry played a minor part in Oxford until the motor industry was established in 1912.

It is for its architecture that Oxford is of most interest to the visitor, its oldest specimens being the reputedly Saxon tower of St Michael's church, the remains of the Norman castle and city walls, and the Norman church at Iffley. It is chiefly famous, however, for its Gothic buildings, such as the Divinity Schools, the Old Library at Merton College, William of Wykeham's New College, Magdalen College and Christ Church and many other college buildings. Later centuries are represented by the Laudian quadrangle at St John's College, the Renaissance Sheldonian Theatre by Wren, Trinity College Chapel, and All Saints Church; Hawksmoor's mock-Gothic at All Souls College, and the 18th-century Queen's College. In addition to individual buildings, High Street and Radcliffe Square, just off it, both form architectural compositions of great beauty. Most of the Colleges have gardens, those of Magdalen, New College, St John's and Worcester being the largest.

PLYMOUTH

Plymouth is situated on the borders of Devon and Cornwall at the confluence of the Rivers Tamar and Plym. The city has a long maritime history; it was the home port of Sir Francis Drake and the starting point for his circumnavigation of the world, as well as the last port of call for the *Mayflower* when the Pilgrim Fathers sailed for the New World in 1620. Today Plymouth is host to many international yacht races. The Barbican harbour area has many Elizabethan buildings and on Plymouth Hoe stands Smeaton's lighthouse, the third to be built on the Eddystone Rocks 13 miles offshore.

The city centre was rebuilt following extensive war damage, and comprises a large shopping centre, municipal offices, law courts and public buildings. The main employment is provided at the naval base, though many industrial firms and service industries have become established in the post-war period and the city is a growing tourism centre. In 1982 the Theatre Royal was opened. In conjunction with the Cornwall County Council, the Tamar Bridge was constructed linking the city by road with Cornwall.

PORTSMOUTH

Portsmouth occupies Portsea Island, Hampshire, with boundaries extending to the mainland. It is a centre of industry and commerce, including many high technology and manufacturing industries. It is the British headquarters of several major international companies. The Royal Navy base still has a substantial work force, although this has decreased in recent years. The commercial port and continental ferry port is owned and run by the City Council, and carries passengers and vehicles to France and northern Spain.

A major port since the 16th century, Portsmouth is also a thriving seaside resort catering for thousands of visitors annually. Among many historic attractions are Lord Nelson's flagship, HMS *Victory*, the Tudor warship *Mary Rose*, Britain's first 'ironclad' warship, HMS *Warrior*, the D-Day Museum, Charles Dickens' birthplace at 393 Old Commercial Road, the Royal Naval and Royal Marine museums, Southsea Castle (built by Henry VIII), the Round Tower and Point Battery, which for hundreds of years have guarded the entrance to Portsmouth Harbour, Fort Nelson on Portsdown Hill and the Sealife Centre.

ST ALBANS

The origins of St Albans, situated on the River Ver, stem from the Roman town of *Verulamium*. Named after the first Christian martyr in Britain, who was executed here, St Albans has developed around the Norman Abbey and Cathedral Church (consecrated 1115), built partly of materials from the old Roman city. The museums house Iron Age and Roman artefacts and the Roman Theatre, unique in Britain, has a stage as opposed to an amphitheatre. Archaeological excavations in the city centre have revealed evidence of pre-Roman, Saxon and medieval occupation.

The town's significance grew to the extent that it was a signatory and venue for the drafting of the Magna Carta. It was also the scene of riots during the Peasants' Revolt, the French King John was imprisoned there after the Battle of Poitiers, and heavy fighting took place there during the Wars of the Roses.

Previously controlled by the Abbot, the town achieved a Royal Charter in 1553 and City status in 1877. The street market, first established in 1553, is still an important feature of the city, as are many hotels and inns which survive from the days when St Albans was an important coach stop. Tourist attractions include historic churches and houses, and a 15th-century clock tower.

The city now contains a wide range of firms, with special emphasis on micro-technology and electronics, particularly in the medical field. In addition, it is the home of the Royal National Rose Society, and of Rothamsted Park, the agricultural research centre.

SHEFFIELD

Sheffield (South Yorkshire), the centre of the special steel and cutlery trades, is situated at the junction of the Sheaf, Porter, Rivelin and Loxley valleys with the River Don. Though its cutlery, silverware and plate have long been famous, Sheffield has other and now more important industries: special and alloy steels, engineering, toolmaking and medical equipment. Sheffield has two universities and is an important research centre.

The parish church of St Peter and St Paul, founded in the 12th century, became the Cathedral Church of the Diocese of Sheffield in 1914. The Roman Catholic Cathedral Church of St Marie (founded 1847) was created Cathedral for the new diocese of Hallam in 1980. Parts of the present building date from c.1435. The principal buildings are the Town Hall (1897), the Cutlers' Hall (1832), City Hall (1932), Graves Art Gallery (1934), Mappin Art Gallery and the Crucible Theatre. The restored 19th-century Lyceum theatre dates from 1897 and reopened in 1990.

Sheffield was created a city in 1893 and in 1974 retained its city status.

Master Cutler of the Company of Cutlers in Hallamshire 1995–6, D. R. Stone

SOUTHAMPTON

Southampton is the leading British deep-sea port on the Channel and is situated on one of the finest natural harbours in the world. The first Charter was granted by Henry II and Southampton was created a county of itself in 1447. In 1964 it was granted city status by Royal Charter.

There were Roman and Saxon settlements on the site of the city, which has been an important port since the time of the Conquest due to its natural deep-water harbour. The oldest church is St Michael's (1070) which has an unusually tall spire built in the 18th century as a landmark for navigators of Southampton Water. Other buildings and monuments within the city walls are the Tudor House, God's House Tower, the Bargate museum, the Tudor Merchants Hall, the Weigh-house, West Gate, King John's House, Long House, Wool House, the ruins of Holy Rood Church, St Julien's Church and the Mayflower Memorial. The medieval town walls, built for artillery, are among the most complete in Europe. Public open spaces total over 1,000 acres and comprise 9 per cent of the city's area. The Common covers an area of 328 acres in the central district of the city and is mostly natural parkland. Two recent additions to work in marine technology in Southampton are Europe's leading oceanographic research centre (part of the University) and the marine science and technology business park.

STOKE-ON-TRENT

Stoke-on-Trent (Staffordshire), standing on the River Trent and familiarly known as The Potteries, is the main centre of employment for the population of North Staffordshire. The city is the largest clayware producer in the world (china, earthenware, sanitary goods, refractories, bricks and tiles) and also has a wide range of other manufacturing industry, including steel, chemicals, engineering and tyres. Extensive reconstruction has been carried on in recent years.

The city was formed by the federation in 1910 of the separate municipal authorities of Tunstall, Burslem, Hanley, Stoke, Fenton, and Longton, all of which are now combined in the present City of Stoke-on-Trent.

WINCHESTER

Winchester, the ancient capital of England, is situated on the River Itchen. The city is rich in architecture of all types but the Cathedral takes pride of place. The longest Gothic cathedral in the world, it was built in 1079–93 and exhibits examples of Norman, Early English and Perpendicular styles. Winchester College, founded in 1382, is one of the most famous public schools, the original building (1393) remaining largely unaltered. St Cross Hospital, another great medieval foundation, lies one mile south of the city. The almshouses were founded in 1136 by Bishop Henry de Blois, and Cardinal Henry Beaufort added a new almshouse of 'Noble Poverty' in 1446. The chapel and dwellings are of great architectural interest, and visitors may still receive the 'Wayfarer's Dole' of bread and ale.

Excavations have done much to clarify the origins and development of Winchester. Part of the forum and several of the streets of the Roman town have been discovered; excavations in the Cathedral Close have uncovered the entire site of the Anglo-Saxon cathedral (known as the Old Minster) and parts of the New Minster which was built by Alfred's son Edward the Elder and is the burial place of the Alfredian dynasty. The original burial place of St Swithun, before his remains were translated to a site in the present cathedral, was also uncovered.

Excavations in other parts of the city have thrown much light on Norman Winchester, notably on the site of the Royal Castle (adjacent to which the new Law Courts have been built) and in the grounds of Wolvesey Castle, where the great house built by Bishops Giffard and Henry de Blois in the 12th century has been uncovered. The Great Hall, built by Henry III between 1222 and 1236 survives and houses the Arthurian Round Table.

YORK

The city of York (North Yorkshire) is an archiepiscopal seat. Its recorded history dates from AD 71, when the Roman Ninth Legion established a base under Petilius Cerealis which later became the fortress of *Eburacum.* In Anglo-Saxon times the city was the royal and ecclesiastical centre of Northumbria, and after capture by a Viking army in AD 866 it became the capital of the Viking kingdom of Jorvik. By the 14th century the city had become a great mercantile centre, mainly because of its control of the wool trade, and was used as the chief base against the Scots. Under the Tudors its fortunes declined, though Henry VIII made it the headquarters of the Council of the North. Excavations on many sites, including Coppergate, have greatly expanded knowledge of Roman, Viking and medieval urban life.

With its development as a railway centre in the 19th century the commercial life of York expanded. The principal industries are the manufacture of chocolate, scientific instruments and sugar. It is the location of several government departments.

The city is rich in examples of architecture of all periods. The earliest church was built in AD 627 and, in the 12th to 15th centuries, the present Minster was built in a succession of styles. Other examples within the city are the medieval city walls and gateways, churches and guildhalls. Domestic architecture includes the Georgian mansions of The Mount, Micklegate and Bootham.

English Counties and Shires

LORD LIEUTENANTS AND HIGH SHERIFFS

County/Shire	Lord Lieutenant	High Sheriff, 1995–6
Avon	Sir John Wills, Bt., TD	J. Tidmarsh, MBE
Bedfordshire	S. C. Whitbread	B. Woodrow
Berkshire	P. L. Wroughton,	Sir William Benyon
Buckinghamshire	Cdr. the Lord Cottesloe	Sir Henry Aubrey-Fletcher, Bt.
Cambridgeshire	J. G. P. Crowden	Mrs M. E. Thomas
Cheshire	W. Bromley Davenport	J. M. Pickering
Cleveland	The Lord Gisborough	The Hon. D. J. Dugdale
Cornwall	Lady Holborow	Mrs E. M. Bolitho
Cumbria	J. Cropper	H. W. Lawson
Derbyshire	J. K. Bather	J. M. Morgan-Owen
Devon	Lt.-Col. the Earl of Morley	J. H. G. Woollcombe
Dorset	The Lord Digby	J. D. Wrighton
Durham	D. J. Grant, CBE	R. Sale
East Sussex	Adm. Sir Lindsay Bryson, KCB	A. A. M. Mays-Smith
Essex	The Lord Braybrooke	C. F. Pertwee
Gloucestershire	H. W. G. Elwes	F. H. P. H. Wills
Greater London	Field Marshal the Lord Bramall, GCB, OBE, MC	G. J. Hearne, CBE
Greater Manchester	Col. J. B. Timmins, OBE, TD	Maj. E. T. Gartside
Hampshire	Mrs F. M. Fagan	Cdr. M. J. Rivett-Carnac (rtd)
Hereford and Worcester	Capt. Sir Thomas Dunne, KCVO	H. B. Derbyshire
Hertfordshire	S. A. Bowes Lyon	N. G. Halsey, TD
Humberside	R. A. Bethell	F. A. Flear
Isle of Wight	*The Lord Mottistone, CBE	J. J. W. Attrill
Kent	The Lord Kingsdown, PC	R. J. B. White
Lancashire	Sir Simon Towneley, KCVO	R. W. Goodall
Leicestershire	T. G. M. Brooks	J. Cowen
Lincolnshire	Mrs B. K. Cracroft-Eley	D. K. Baker
Merseyside	A. W. Waterworth	A. W. Shone
Norfolk	T. J. Colman	J. O. C. Birkbeck
Northamptonshire	J. L. Lowther, CBE	J. Mackaness
Northumberland	The Viscount Ridley, KG, TD	A. R. Wood
North Yorkshire	Sir Marcus Worsley, Bt.	The Hon. S. B. G. Howard
Nottinghamshire	Sir Andrew Buchanan, Bt.	G. E. P. Thornhill
Oxfordshire	Sir Ashley Ponsonby, Bt., KCVO, MC	J. S. Bridgeman
Shropshire	The Viscount Boyne	N. E. E. Stephens
Somerset	Sir John Vernon Wills, Bt., TD	R. S. G. Hewett
South Yorkshire	J. H. Neill, CBE, TD	P. W. Lee, CBE
Staffordshire	J. A. Hawley, TD	Mrs J. M. Monckton
Suffolk	The Lord Belstead	Sir Richard Parker, Bt.
Surrey	R. E. Thornton, OBE	The Lady Hamilton
Tyne and Wear	Sir Ralph Carr-Ellison, TD	Dr A. W. Lillington
Warwickshire	Capt. the Viscount Daventry	S. G. Evans
West Midlands	R. R. Taylor, OBE	Prof. Sir Frederick Crawford
West Sussex	Maj.-Gen. Sir Philip Ward, KCVO, CBE	H. R. Wyatt
West Yorkshire	J. Lyles	E. N. Pullan
Wiltshire	Field Marshal Sir Roland Gibbs, GCB, CBE, DSO, MC	D. J. Randolph

* Lord Lieutenant and Governor

COUNTY COUNCILS: AREA, POPULATION, FINANCE

Council	Administrative headquarters	Area (hectares)	Population 1993	Total demand upon collection fund 1995–6
*Avon	Avon House North, St James Barton, Bristol	134,628	973,300	£169,500,000
Bedfordshire	County Hall, Bedford	123,468	539,400	83,322,000
Berkshire	Shire Hall, Shinfield Park, Reading	125,901	763,700	125,587,000
Buckinghamshire	County Hall, Aylesbury	188,279	651,700	109,500,000
Cambridgeshire	Shire Hall, Cambridge	340,181	682,600	96,412,455
Cheshire	County Hall, Chester	233,325	971,900	170,409,107
*Cleveland	Municipal Buildings, Middlesbrough	59,079	559,500	86,627,831
Cornwall	County Hall, Truro	356,442†	477,000	72,386,250
Cumbria	The Courts, Carlisle	682,451	490,200	83,975,000
Derbyshire	County Offices, Matlock	263,098	950,900	153,700,000
Devon	County Hall, Exeter	671,096	1,049,200	157,116,000
Dorset	County Hall, Dorchester	265,433	667,500	111,100,100
Durham	County Hall, Durham	243,369	607,500	78,044,850
East Sussex	Pelham House, St Andrew's Lane, Lewes	179,530	722,200	118,409,000
Essex	County Hall, Chelmsford	367,167	1,560,300	240,948,000
Gloucestershire	Shire Hall, Gloucester	264,270	543,900	83,166,000
Hampshire	The Castle, Winchester	378,022	1,593,700	241,000,000
Hereford and Worcester	County Hall, Worcester	392,650	694,800	104,326,590
Hertfordshire	County Hall, Hertford	163,601	999,700	168,000,000
*Humberside	County Hall, Beverley, N. Humberside	351,256	884,400	141,500,000
§Isle of Wight	County Hall, Newport, IOW	38,063	124,800	92,956,900
Kent	County Hall, Maidstone	373,063	1,539,700	241,200,000
Lancashire	County Hall, Preston	306,957	1,420,700	239,228,000
Leicestershire	County Hall, Glenfield, Leicester	255,297	910,300	127,135,000
Lincolnshire	County Offices, Newland, Lincoln	591,791	601,400	86,370,000
Norfolk	County Hall, Norwich	537,482	765,100	114,400,000
Northamptonshire	County Hall, Northampton	236,721	591,900	83,979,000
Northumberland	County Hall, Morpeth	503,165	307,200	49,156,470
North Yorkshire	County Hall, Northallerton	821,236	721,800	111,150,000
Nottinghamshire	County Hall, Nottingham	216,090	1,028,400	167,337,000
Oxfordshire	County Hall, Oxford	260,798	585,800	95,000,000
Shropshire	The Shirehall, Shrewsbury	349,013	413,900	60,000,000
Somerset	County Hall, Taunton	345,233	474,100	77,234,803
Staffordshire	County Buildings, Stafford	271,616	1,053,600	137,389,575
Suffolk	County Hall, Ipswich	379,664	646,200	96,445,785
Surrey	County Hall, Kingston upon Thames	167,924	1,037,900	192,995,000
Warwickshire	Shire Hall, Warwick	198,052	493,600	85,218,476
West Sussex	County Hall, Chichester	198,935	717,700	124,638,000
Wiltshire	County Hall, Trowbridge	347,883	583,000	91,477,000

Source for population figures: OPCS Monitor PP1 94/2, 26 July 1994
* Abolished April 1996. Replaced by unitary authorities
† Including Isles of Scilly
§ Unitary authority, since April 1995

UNITARY AUTHORITIES

Single unitary authorities are replacing the two-tier structure of county and district councils in the following areas:

Avon county council and the six existing district councils to be replaced in April 1996 by four unitary authorities: Bath and North-East Somerset, Bristol, North-West Somerset, South Gloucestershire

Cleveland county council and the four existing district councils to be replaced in April 1996 by four unitary authorities: Hartlepool, Middlesbrough, Redcar and Cleveland, Stockton-on-Tees

Humberside county council and the nine existing district councils to be replaced in April 1996 by four unitary authorities: East Riding of Yorkshire, Kingston-upon-Hull, North-East Lincolnshire, North Lincolnshire

The Isle of Wight county council and Medina and South Wight district councils were replaced in May 1995 by the Isle of Wight unitary authority

In North Yorkshire, the York City Council area is extended and the council becomes a unitary authority in April 1996. The remainder of the county retains the two-tier structure of councils.

COUNTY COUNCILS: Officers and Chairman

Council	*Chief Executive*	*County Treasurer*	*Chairman of County Council*
Avon	R. Jarrett	M. Reynell	Mrs R. Walker
Bedfordshire	D. Cleggett	*B. Phelps	A. R. Sollars
Berkshire	°G. B. Scotford, OBE	†I. Thompson	C. C. Trembath
Buckinghamshire	I. Crookall (*acting*)	*J. Beckerlegg	K. I. Ross
Cambridgeshire	A. G. Lister	*D. Earle	J. L. Gluza
Cheshire	M. E. Pitt	‡‡J. E. H. Whiteoak	Mrs D. McConnell
Cleveland	B. Stevenson	†P. Riley	E. Wood
Cornwall	J. Mills	*S. Nicol	A. R. J. Horn
Cumbria	J. E. Burnet	*R. F. Mather	C. T. Liversedge
Derbyshire	‡J. S. Raine	P. Swaby	H. Lowe
Devon	P. Jenkinson (*acting*)	J. Glasby	K. J. Watson
Dorset	P. K. Harvey	A. P. Peel	Mrs P. A. Hymers
Durham	K. W. Smith	J. Kirkby	J. Walker
East Sussex	††Mrs C. Miller	J. Davies	L. Hamilton
Essex	K. W. S. Ashurst	K. D. Neale	J. J. Gordon
Gloucestershire	M. Honey	**J. R. Cockroft	F. R. Thompson
Hampshire	A. R. Hodgson	J. E. Scotford, CBE	G. J. Smith
Hereford and Worcester	J. W. Turnbull	P. Middleborough	J. W. Wardle, MBE
Hertfordshire	B. Briscoe	**C. Sweeney	Mrs I. Tarry
Humberside	J. A. Parkes	*G. T. Southern	A. Fee
Isle of Wight	F. Hetherington	J. Pulsford	Mrs M. Stolworthy
Kent	P. R. Sabin	*P. Martin	D. A. Molock
Lancashire	G. A. Johnson	B. G. Aldred	G. Davies
Leicestershire	J. B. Sinnott	R. Hale	E. F. White
Lincolnshire	M. Spink (*acting*)	M. Spink	Mrs E. Davies
Norfolk	B. J. Capon, CBE	R. D. Summers	P. Baldwin
Northamptonshire	A. J. Greenwell, CBE	*R. Paver	R. Cross
Northumberland	°°K. Morris	*K. Morris	Mrs B. M. S. Trobe
North Yorkshire	J. A. Ransford	†L. Cornfield	J. E. Clout
Nottinghamshire	P. Housden	R. Latham	R. Strauther
Oxfordshire	J. Harwood	C. Gray	G. Fowler
Shropshire	A. Barnish	N. Pursey	G. Raxster
Somerset	B. M. Tanner	C. N. Bilsland	R. B. Clark
Staffordshire	B. A. Price	R. G. Tettenborn, OBE	J. O'Leary
Suffolk	P. F. Bye	P. B. Atkinson	Mrs A. K. Pollard
Surrey	P. Coen	‡‡P. Derrick	Mrs C. Gerard
Warwickshire	I. G. Caulfield	S. R. Freer	S. R. Tooth
West Sussex	D. P. Rigg	Mrs H. Kilpatrick	C. Robinson
Wiltshire	I. A. Browning	*D. Chalker	Mrs D. J. Main

* Director of Finance
° County Manager
† County Finance Officer
‡ County Director
** Director of Corporate Services
°° Managing Director
†† Head of Paid Service
‡‡ Director of Resources

Metropolitan Councils

SMALL CAPITALS denote CITY status

Council	Population 1993*	Band D charge 1995*	Chief Executive	Mayor (a) Lord Mayor 1995–6
Greater Manchester	2,578,900			
Bolton	264,900	£682.37	B. Collinge	F. A. Rushton
Bury	181,400	622.27	D. J. Burton	N. Singer
MANCHESTER	432,000	789.47	A. Sandford	(a) Ms J. Keller
Oldham	220,500	898.33	C. Smith	J. Farquhar
Rochdale	206,800	684.41	J. F. D. Pierce	R. H. Stott
SALFORD	229,300	785.26	J. C. Willis	M. McDermott
Stockport	291,400	766.83	J. R. Schultz	N. Fields
Tameside	221,600	707.40	M. Greenwood	A. Whitehead
Trafford	217,800	562.95	W. A. Lewis	R. Godwin
Wigan	313,200	619.64	S. M. Jones	B. Holt
Merseyside	1,440,900			
Knowsley	155,300	699.00	D. G. Henshaw	Ms M. Flaherty
LIVERPOOL	477,000	962.68	P. Bounds	(a) M. Black
St Helens	180,200	744.81	Mrs C. A. Hudson	K. Deakin
Sefton	294,300	709.88	G. J. Haywood	T. R. Lewis
Wirral	334,100	747.35	A. White	W. Smith
South Yorkshire	1,306,200			
Barnsley	225,900	591.66	J. A. Edwards, OBE	C. Cawthrow
Doncaster	292,700	575.69	J. D. Hale	A. Lanaghan
Rotherham	255,700	607.05	J. Bell	W. Winder
SHEFFIELD	531,900	674.37	Mrs P. Gordon	(a) D. Hesslop
Tyne and Wear	1,137,900			
Gateshead	202,900	715.50	L. N. Elton	A. S. Brown
NEWCASTLE UPON TYNE	285,300	696.10	G. N. Cook	(a) B. Rice
North Tyneside	194,800	743.17	†C. A. Roberts	T. Cruickshank
South Tyneside	157,200	639.90	†P. J. Haigh	Mrs M. Stewart
SUNDERLAND	297,800	591.99	C. Sinclair	E. Bramfitt
West Midlands	2,633,700			
BIRMINGHAM	1,012,400	673.02	M. T. Lyons	(a) D. Roy
COVENTRY	304,100	793.24	I. Roxburgh	(a) J. Clifford
Dudley	311,500	610.67	A. V. Astling	Mrs S. Portman
Sandwell	294,200	650.72	F. N. Summers	R. Horton
Solihull	200,400	585.88	J. Scampion	L. W. P. Kyles
Walsall	264,700	541.16	D. C. Winchurch	C. G. Leaker
Wolverhampton	246,400	629.28	N. H. Perry, PH.D.	M. M. Benton
West Yorkshire	2,101,600			
BRADFORD	480,000	592.69	R. Penn	(a) Ms M. Beeley
Calderdale	193,700	622.62	M. Ellison	G. Reason
Kirklees	385,800	727.22	R. V. Hughes	K. Sims
LEEDS	724,500	611.00	J. P. Smith	(a) Mrs J. M. White, CBE
WAKEFIELD	317,500	548.67	R. Mather	N. Hartshorne

Source for population figures: OPCS Monitor PP1 94/2, 26 July 1994
* For explanation of council tax, see page 526
† Head of Paid Service

Non-Metropolitan Councils

SMALL CAPITALS denote CITY status
§ Denotes Borough status
† Replaced by unitary authority, April 1996
Source of population figures: OPCS Monitor PP1 94/2, 26 July 1994
For explanation of council tax, *see* page 526

Council	Population 1993	Band D charge 1995	Chief Executive	Chairman 1995–6 (a) Mayor (b) Lord Mayor
Adur, West Sussex	57,800	£627.20	F. M. G. Staden	D. S. Hancock
§Allerdale, Cumbria	96,200	664.62	C. J. Hart	(a) J. Hully
Alnwick, Northumberland	30,300	642.65	L. St Ruth	I. McArthur
§Amber Valley, Derbyshire	113,700	655.00	P. M. Carney	(a) G. Beardsley
Arun, West Sussex	133,400	610.32	I. Sumnall	B. Redman
Ashfield, Nottinghamshire	109,800	690.00	S. Beedham	Mrs Y. White
§Ashford, Kent	93,900	543.33	D. Lambert	(a) Mrs P. Laughton
Aylesbury Vale, Bucks	151,600	562.30	B. J. Quoroll	Mrs A. Davies
Babergh, Suffolk	79,600	545.18	D. C. Bishop	Mrs J. Law
§Barrow-in-Furness, Cumbria	73,300	724.73	*T. O. Campbell	(a) Mrs F. Proudfoot
Basildon, Essex	161,700	624.15	J. Robb	Mrs A. Bruce
§Basingstoke and Deane, Hants	146,500	546.70	Ms K. Sporle	(a) J. W. Greenwood
Bassetlaw, Notts	105,500	687.88	M. S. Havenhand	I. Atkinson
†BATH, Avon	83,100	580.20	*R. F. S. Mimmack	(a) J. Manning
§Bedford	137,300	591.47	L. W. Gould	(a) M. Evans
§Berwick-upon-Tweed, Northumberland	26,700	641.04	E. O. Cawthorn	(a) I. Harris
§†Beverley, Humberside	115,800	662.58	M. Rice	(a) R. Crosby
Blaby, Leics	85,000	551.53	‡E. Hemsley	F. E. Spence
§Blackburn, Lancs	139,500	667.15	G. L. Davies	(a) M. Bateson
§Blackpool, Lancs	153,600	651.60	G. E. Essex-Crosby	(a) D. Owen
§Blyth Valley, Northumberland	80,700	649.86	D. Crawford	(a) J. Clough
Bolsover, Derbyshire	71,200	667.98	J. R. Fotherby	H. McCreadie
§†Boothferry, Humberside	65,300	657.72	J. W. Barber	(a) D. H. Haynes
§Boston, Lincs	54,200	593.78	I. Ward	(a) Ms J. Cammack
§Bournemouth, Dorset	159,900	560.00	D. Newell	(a) Mrs P. Harris
§Bracknell Forest, Berks	101,900	522.75	A. J. Targett	(a) T. Wheaton
Braintree, Essex	121,800	554.31	Ms A. Ralph	Mrs J. Lyon
Breckland, Norfolk	110,800	559.23	R. Garnett	C. W. Armes
Brentwood, Essex	71,200	542.97	C. P. Sivell	(a) Ms V. Fletcher
Bridgnorth, Shropshire	50,000	623.40	Mrs T. M. Elliott	R. Lane
§Brighton, East Sussex	154,400	565.74	G. Jones	(a) Ms S. Schaffer
†BRISTOL, Avon	397,600	769.88	Ms L. de Groot (*acting*)	(b) J. McLaren
Broadland, Norfolk	108,500	524.00	J. H. Bryant	D. Dewgarde
Bromsgrove, Hereford and Worcs	92,800	542.97	R. P. Bradshaw	Ms C. M. V. Mole
§Broxbourne, Herts	82,500	538.80	M. J. Walker	(a) Mrs E. Lazarri
§Broxtowe, Notts	110,600	695.75	M. Brown	(a) T. Martin
§Burnley, Lancs	91,400	701.33	R. Ellis	(a) A. Park
CAMBRIDGE	113,800	587.76	R. Hammond	(a) Ms S. Froggett
Cannock Chase, Staffs	90,700	587.15	M. G. Kemp	M. J. Davey
CANTERBURY, Kent	132,400	588.82	C. Gay	(b) D. Pentin
Caradon, Cornwall	77,800	580.00	J. Neal	E. G. Lewis
CARLISLE, Cumbria	102,900	689.77	R. S. Brackley	(a) A. Brumwell
Carrick, Cornwall	84,500	601.03	P. M. Kidwell-Talbot	Mrs A. J. Carlyon
§Castle Morpeth, Northumberland	50,100	651.10	P. Wilson	(a) T. Simpson
§Castle Point, Essex	86,000	606.33	B. Rollinson	Mrs J. Howlett
§Charnwood, Leics	152,500	565.72	S. M. Peatfield	J. E. Hawkes
§Chelmsford, Essex	155,700	562.07	R. M. C. Hartley	(a) A. R. Willsher
§Cheltenham, Glos	106,700	584.54	C. Nye	(a) L. Freeman
Cherwell, Oxon	125,100	505.00	G. J. Handley	R. E. Groves, MBE
CHESTER, Cheshire	120,800	633.38	P. F. Durham	(b) R. Short
§Chesterfield, Derbyshire	101,200	642.64	D. R. Shaw	(a) D. Stone

* Head of Paid Services
‡ Finance and General Manager

Council	Population 1993	Band D charge 1995	Chief Executive	Chairman 1995–6 (a) Mayor (b) Lord Mayor
Chester-le-Street, Co. Durham	53,900	£589.08	J. A. Greensmith	R. Trotter
Chichester, West Sussex	102,500	552.10	C. E. Evans	A. J. French, TD
Chiltern, Bucks	90,800	568.90	B. R. Catchpole	Miss P. A. Appleby, MBE
§Chorley, Lancs	97,100	642.90	J. W. Davies	(a) G. Birtill, OBE
§Christchurch, Dorset	42,000	537.92	M. A. Turvey	(a) M. J. Peirce
§†Cleethorpes, Humberside	70,500	743.04	P. Daniel	(a) Mrs M. Cracknell
§Colchester, Essex	149,100	569.14	J. Cobley	(a) Mrs M. L. Fairhead, OBE
§Congleton, Cheshire	85,000	626.40	‡A. White (acting)	(a) J. A. Turner
§Copeland, Cumbria	71,400	653.70	*R. G. Smith	(a) H. C. Hanlon
Corby, Northants	52,800	565.15	T. Simmons	(a) T. McConnachie
Cotswold, Glos	79,200	552.21	N. Howells	Mrs S. M. H. Herdman
Craven, North Yorkshire	50,900	554.89	Ms G. Taylor, PH.D	Ms J. Ibbotson
§Crawley, W. Sussex	89,300	577.44	M. D. Sander	(a) C. J. Redmayne
§Crewe and Nantwich, Cheshire	109,500	650.32	A. Wenham	(a) R. Salmon
§Dacorum, Herts	134,300	538.01	K. Hunt	(a) L. H. Taber
§Darlington, Co. Durham	100,200	630.05	H. R. C. Owen	(a) F. S. Robson
§Dartford, Kent	82,600	561.23	C. R. Shepherd	(a) L. Eaton
Daventry, Northants	63,700	568.93	R. J. Symons, RD	R. Atterbury
DERBY	228,600	632.30	R. H. Cowlishaw	(a) J. F. McGiven
Derbyshire Dales	68,600	641.01	D. Wheatcroft	D. R. Burton
Derwentside, Co. Durham	86,900	657.88	N. F. Johnson	G. F. Johnson
Dover, Kent	106,100	584.64	J. P. Moir, TD	P. T. Wilson
DURHAM	88,300	580.27	C. G. Firmin	(a) S. T. McDonnell
Easington, Co. Durham	98,700	660.00	*P. Innes	M. Curry
§Eastbourne, East Sussex	86,800	607.20	Dr M. Blanch	R. A. Parsons
East Cambridgeshire	62,100	526.12	R. C. Carr	J. E. Seaman
East Devon	120,300	565.00	F. J. Vallender	B. Willoughby
East Dorset	79,800	554.16	A. Breakwell	D. J. Wallace
East Hampshire	106,400	569.75	B. P. Roynon	M. C. Johnson, MBE
East Hertfordshire	119,600	536.55	R. J. Bailey	N. Poulton
§Eastleigh, Hants	109,600	548.78	C. Tapp	(a) Mrs J. Watson
East Lindsey, Lincs	120,800	561.54	P. Haigh	P. M. Harness
East Northamptonshire	69,300	574.12	R. K. Heath	E. C. Sampson
East Staffordshire	98,300	572.98	F. W. Saunders	P. Haynes
§†East Yorkshire, Humberside	87,800	670.32	J. H. Gibson	(a) Mrs C. M. Chadwick
Eden, Cumbria	46,800	662.31	I. W. Bruce	J. B. Thornborrow
§Ellesmere Port and Neston, Cheshire	81,500	655.87	S. Ewbank	(a) R. S. Hayward
§Elmbridge, Surrey	117,300	581.07	D. W. L. Jenkins	(a) F. R. Awcock
Epping Forest, Essex	118,200	559.73	J. Burgess	Mrs K. Ellis
§Epsom and Ewell, Surrey	68,800	536.70	D. J. Smith	(a) C. Frazer
§Erewash, Derbyshire	107,200	654.94	G. A. Pook	(a) E. Bevan
EXETER, Devon	105,100	570.51	B. Frowd	(a) Ms M. Midgley
§Fareham, Hants	101,000	561.24	A. A. Davies	(a) M. Godrich
Fenland, Cambs	78,000	555.29	N. R. Topliss	B. E. A. Diggle
Forest Heath, Suffolk	62,500	517.98	S. W. Catchpole	K. Marshall
Forest of Dean, Glos	75,600	577.84	‡R. A. Willis	B. W. Hobman
§Fylde, Lancs	73,700	606.32	J. R. Wilkinson	(a) G. Caldwell
§Gedling, Notts	112,000	695.00	W. Brown	(a) P. Barnes
§Gillingham, Kent	96,000	552.73	J. A. McBride	(a) G. W. Payne
§†Glanford, Humberside	72,700	663.21	D. D. H. Cameron	(a) J. Wardle
GLOUCESTER	104,800	529.09	G. Garbutt	(a) Mrs R. Workman
§Gosport, Hants	75,900	578.83	M. S. Friend	(a) Mrs M. V. Bailey
§Gravesham, Kent	93,000	534.56	E. V. J. Seager	(a) The Lady Murray
§†Great Grimsby, Humberside	91,500	740.00	R. S. G. Bennett	(a) J. Colebrook
§Great Yarmouth, Norfolk	88,800	553.18	R. Packham	(a) Mrs C. Batley
§Guildford, Surrey	126,200	574.10	D. T. Watts	(a) Mrs C. Cobley
§Halton, Cheshire	124,100	637.93	M. Cuff	(a) S. J. Hill
Hambleton, North Yorkshire	81,600	461.10	C. Spencer	L. H. Groves
Harborough, Leics	70,000	584.96	M. C. Wilson	E. V. Hubbard
Harlow, Essex	73,500	673.92	*D. Byrne	T. Kent

‡ Head of Paid Service
* General Manager

Council	Population 1993	Band D charge 1995	Chief Executive	Chairman 1995–6 (a) Mayor (b) Lord Mayor
§Harrogate, North Yorkshire	146,500	£600.44	P. M. Walsh	(a) B. L. Haxby
Hart, Hants	82,900	567.85	G. R. Jelbart	P. Shoesmith
†Hartlepool, Cleveland	92,000	674.12	B. J. Dinsdale	(a) Mrs G. Worthy
§Hastings, East Sussex	82,900	456.82	R. A. Carrier	(a) R. Stevens
§Havant, Hants	117,500	599.45	J. E. Palmer (acting)	(a) Mrs R. Hyson
HEREFORD	50,700	547.86	C. E. S. Willis	(a) G. V. Hyde
§Hertsmere, Hertfordshire	92,700	554.73	**P. Copland	(a) M. Colne
§High Peak, Derbyshire	87,000	672.22	R. P. H. Brady	(a) D. Bond
§Hinckley and Bosworth, Leics	97,600	540.93	‡I. G. Davis (acting)	(a) Mrs M. J. Crooks
†Holderness, Humberside	52,200	689.64	A. Johnson	(a) D. Snowley
Horsham, West Sussex	112,300	542.47	M. J. Pearson	Mrs J. D. Campbell
§Hove, East Sussex	91,000	577.08	J. P. Teasdale	(a) B. A. Jordan
Huntingdonshire, Cambs	148,800	511.31	D. Monks	G. J. Dodson
§Hyndburn, Lancs	79,000	699.75	M. Chambers	(a) Mrs J. Battle
§Ipswich, Suffolk	114,800	680.40	J. D. Hehir	(a) A. Grant
Kennet, Wilts	72,400	559.89	P. L. Owens	D. Parker
Kerrier, Cornwall	89,100	580.00	G. G. Cox	C. Lawrence
§Kettering, Northants	78,500	578.52	P. Walker	(a) Mrs M. Malin
§King's Lynn and West Norfolk	131,600	567.79	A. E. Pask	(a) F. W. S. Juniper
†KINGSTON UPON HULL, Humberside	267,900	733.05	D. Stephenson	(b) J. A. Black
†Kingswood, Avon	92,000	658.25	R. B. Knight	(a) E. N. Payne
LANCASTER, Lancs	133,600	647.00	W. Pearson	(a) Mrs S. Burns
†Langbaurgh-on-Tees, Cleveland	143,900	742.80	A. W. Kilburn	(a) P. Todd
LEICESTER	289,300	652.62	I. Farookhi	(b) M. Johnson
Leominster, Hereford and Worcs	40,500	549.67	G. R. Chilton	F. D. Reading
Lewes, East Sussex	88,600	574.77	J. N. Crawford	Ms C. A. Tester
Lichfield, Staffs	94,000	553.60	J. T. Thompson	J. T. Walker
LINCOLN	85,500	596.79	A. Sparke	(a) G. Ellis
§Luton, Beds	178,600	610.62	J. C. Southwell	(a) M. Ashraf
§Macclesfield, Cheshire	151,400	644.13	B. W. Longden	(a) E. R. Cutler
§Maidstone, Kent	138,500	598.11	J. D. Makepeace	(a) R. Sterry
Maldon, Essex	53,100	539.10	E. A. P. Plumridge	R. G. Boyce
Malvern Hills, Hereford and Worcs	89,300	510.03	M. J. Jones	M. Jolly
Mansfield, Notts	102,100	700.60	R. P. Goad	S. E. Taylor
§Melton, Leics	46,200	593.94	*P. J. G. Herrick	(a) T. E. Metherton
Mendip, Somerset	98,100	593.91	G. Jeffs	C. F. Lockey
Mid Bedfordshire	113,500	550.98	C. A. Tucker	D. Harrowell
Mid Devon	65,600	577.45	M. I. R. Bull	D. J. Allen
‡†Middlesbrough, Cleveland	145,800	727.94	D. Ashton	(a) K. J. Hall
Mid Suffolk	78,400	560.57	H. McFarlane	E. Jones
Mid Sussex	125,000	579.34	B. J. Grimshaw	Mrs R. Burns
§Milton Keynes, Bucks	184,400	620.78	M. J. Murray	(a) B. C. Hardwick
Mole Valley, Surrey	79,100	533.63	H. Kerswell	M. A. J. Anderson
Newark and Sherwood, Notts	104,400	733.62	**R. G. Dix	Mrs D. Westmoreland
Newbury, Berks	141,000	575.26	P. E. McMahon	R. B. Judge
§Newcastle under Lyme, Staffs	123,000	566.88	J. Dunn	(a) Mrs B. Sumnall
New Forest, Hants	164,500	576.00	P. A. D. Hyde	S. S. Wade
§Northampton	187,200	641.90	R. J. B. Morris	(a) L. T. Patterson
†Northavon, Avon	138,100	609.70	F. Maude	A. Gray
North Cornwall	75,600	588.22	D. Brown	K. F. White
North Devon	86,700	578.95	D. T. Cunliffe	E. J. Kingston
North Dorset	54,700	510.00	A. J. Bridgeman	Mrs L. G. Dolan
North East Derbyshire	99,100	678.29	°Mrs C. A. Gilbey	G. Glasby
North Hertfordshire	113,700	537.07	J. S. Philp	Mrs A. Carss
North Kesteven, Lincs	81,200	588.88	S. Lamb	P. Haysom
North Norfolk	93,700	537.48	B. A. Barrell	R. C. Broughton

** Managing Director
‡ Head of Technical Service
* Borough Secretary and Clerk
° Head of Paid Service

Council	Population 1993	Band D charge 1995	Chief Executive	Chairman 1995–6 (a) Mayor (b) Lord Mayor
North Shropshire	53,900	£608.95	D. Pearce	E. J. Dodd
§North Warwickshire	61,800	652.16	D. Monks	(a) A. J. Smith
North West Leicestershire	82,800	607.38	M. J. Diaper	T. A. Smith
North Wiltshire	116,700	612.09	H. Miles	A. S. R. Jackson
NORWICH, Norfolk	128,100	693.44	J. R. Packer	(b) Ms L. Cooper
NOTTINGHAM	282,600	739.78	E. F. Cantle	(b) Ms S. Parsons
§Nuneaton and Bedworth, Warwickshire	118,500	665.08	‡‡J. Walton	(a) D. T. Jacques
§Oadby and Wigston, Leics	53,500	614.26	Mrs R. E. Hyde	(a) Mrs S. A. Spence
§Oswestry, Shropshire	34,200	593.68	D. A. Towers	(a) Mrs H. M. Williams
OXFORD	132,000	650.01	R. S. Block	(b) J. C. Blewitt
§Pendle, Lancs	85,900	710.53	S. Barnes	(a) G. Gilhespy
Penwith, Cornwall	59,700	591.44	‡F. H. Murton	Mrs S. M. Menadue
PETERBOROUGH, Cambs	156,400	537.77	W. E. Samuel	(a) J. Holdich
PLYMOUTH, Devon	259,000	608.05	Mrs A. Stone	(b) P. N. Wood
§Poole, Dorset	137,200	553.50	J. W. Brooks	(a) B. J. Ewart
PORTSMOUTH, Hants	189,100	547.11	*N. Gurney	(b) M. K. G. Chewter
§Preston, Lancs	132,200	703.89	G. Driver	(a) T. Cartwright
Purbeck, Dorset	43,800	522.86	P. B. Croft	D. A. Budd
§Reading, Berks	137,700	610.23	D. Bligh	(a) D. Geary
§Redditch, Hereford and Worcs	78,500	594.26	**Ms S. Manzie	(a) Mrs A. V. Davis
§Reigate and Banstead, Surrey	118,800	562.30	M. Bacon	(a) Mrs P. S. Horsfall
§Restormel, Cornwall	88,300	573.65	D. Brown	(a) Mrs O. R. Irons
§Ribble Valley, Lancs	51,800	647.53	O. Hopkins	(a) Mrs D. Pearson
Richmondshire, N. Yorkshire	45,800	563.71	H. Tabiner	N. J. Watson
ROCHESTER UPON MEDWAY, Kent	146,200	436.23	R. I. Gregory	(a) T. G. Mason
Rochford, Essex	75,900	557.63	P. W. Hughes	Mrs H. L. A. Glynn
§Rossendale, Lancs	65,800	717.80	J. S. Hartley	(a) A. Fishwick
Rother, East Sussex	84,800	581.10	D. F. Powell	F. D. Cheese
§Rugby, Warwickshire	86,200	615.48	J. S. R. Lawton	(a) W. E. Smith
§Runnymede, Surrey	75,100	496.56	T. N. Williams	(a) G. Gleeson
§Rushcliffe, Notts	101,500	661.29	J. Saxton	(a) R. Cook
§Rushmoor, Hants	85,600	566.60	R. Upton	(a) Mrs P. M. Devereux
Rutland, Leics	33,400	609.74	F. A. Dobson	B. A. Montgomery
Ryedale, North Yorkshire	92,600	559.82	M. Walker	A. C. Hall
ST ALBANS, Herts	127,700	551.48	E. A. Hackford	(a) K. Clegg
§St Edmundsbury, Suffolk	92,700	558.27	R. N. T. Toft	(a) C. C. Jones
Salisbury, Wilts	109,800	545.13	D. R. J. Rawlinson	A. J. F. Haywood
§Scarborough, N. Yorkshire	108,700	541.98	J. M. Trebble	(a) I. Stubbs
§†Scunthorpe, Humberside	60,800	665.66	I. M. Hutchinson	(a) J. B. Vessey
Sedgefield, Co. Durham	91,400	686.84	A. J. Roberts	Mrs B. Graham
Sedgemoor, Somerset	100,700	598.25	A. G. Lovell	K. W. W. Dyer
Selby, North Yorkshire	91,800	552.20	J. C. Edwards	D. Howson
Sevenoaks, Kent	109,400	553.25	B. C. Cova, MBE	Dr D. H. Sharp, OBE
Shepway, Kent	95,100	611.59	R. J. Thompson	K. D. Hudson
§Shrewsbury and Atcham	93,700	632.06	D. Bradbury	(a) G. Adams
§Slough, Berks	103,500	452.86	Mrs C. Coppell	(a) M. Mann
SOUTHAMPTON, Hants	209,200	587.29	E. A. Urquhart	(a) Mrs M. J. Singerman
South Bedfordshire	110,000	622.62	T. D. Rix	P. T. Jones
South Buckinghamshire	63,400	527.46	C. Furness	Mrs P. Burry
South Cambridgeshire	123,600	485.72	J. S. Ballantyne	C. W. Tulitt
South Derbyshire	73,600	645.95	T. Day	P. J. Wilkins
§Southend-on-Sea, Essex	167,500	544.93	°D. Moulson	(a) R. F. Copley
South Hams, Devon	78,500	574.87	M. S. Carpenter	Mrs J. I. Roskruge
South Herefordshire	53,600	547.25	A. Hughes	J. W. Edwards
South Holland, Lincs	69,300	601.49	C. J. Simpkins	J. R. Pearl
South Kesteven, Lincs	112,700	578.11	K. R. Cann	J. R. Thompson
South Lakeland, Cumbria	99,600	670.04	A. F. Winstanley	M. C. Bentley
South Norfolk	103,700	562.65	A. G. T. Kellett	S. A. Taylor

‡‡ Borough Manager
‡ Head of Paid Service
* City Manager
** Borough Director
° Clerk

Council	Population 1993	Band D charge 1995	Chief Executive	Chairman 1995–6 (a) Mayor (b) Lord Mayor
South Northamptonshire	71,900	£609.39	K. Whitehead	J. Curtis
South Oxfordshire	121,800	572.01	R. Watson	T. Horton
§South Ribble, Lancs	103,500	642.89	J. B. R. Leadbetter	(a) Mrs D. A. Stewart
South Shropshire	39,400	586.85	G. C. Biggs, MBE	J. McCormick
South Somerset	146,300	608.28	M. Usher	Mrs G. M. Coleshill
South Staffordshire	105,900	508.77	L. Barnfild	N. E. Buxton
§Spelthorne, Surrey	91,600	554.21	M. B. Taylor	(a) D. N. J. White
§Stafford	121,500	531.96	J. K. M. Krawiec	(a) E. A. J. Bevan
Staffordshire Moorlands	95,700	583.36	A. W. Law	M. Ward
§Stevenage, Herts	75,700	596.65	H. L. Miller	(a) D. G. Weston
§†Stockton-on-Tees, Cleveland	177,800	662.70	G. Garlick	(a) Mrs D. Redican
STOKE-ON-TRENT, Staffs	252,900	624.51	B. Smith	(b) J. E. Dunn
Stratford-on-Avon, Warwicks	108,600	599.79	I. B. Prosser	J. H. Davis
Stroud, Glos	105,400	634.96	R. M. Ollin	Mrs M. E. A. Nolder
Suffolk Coastal	110,500	577.24	T. K. Griffin	G. S. Bull
§Surrey Heath	81,300	563.33	N. M. Pughe	(a) G. J. Parris
§Swale, Kent	117,200	529.69	W. Croydon, CBE	(a) D. Jordan
§Tamworth, Staffs	71,600	551.39	C. Moore	(a) Mrs J. M. Jenkins
Tandridge, Surrey	76,600	553.89	P. J. D. Thomas	A. J. Dalrymple
§Taunton Deane, Somerset	97,500	530.00	*Mrs S. Douglas	(a) Mrs L. J. Hole
Teesdale, Co. Durham	24,300	511.47	B. F. Atherton	D. Peart
Teignbridge, Devon	112,100	558.27	B. T. Jones	Mrs R. J. Parker
Tendring, Essex	128,700	565.23	D. Mitchell-Gears	D. Robson
§Test Valley, Hants	105,000	551.00	G. Blythe	(a) I. Carr
§Tewkesbury, Glos	72,200	490.94	**R. A. Wheeler	(a) M. J. Beresford
§Thamesdown, Wilts	173,800	600.80	°R. Clegg	(a) B. Smith
Thanet, Kent	125,500	615.74	D. Ralls, CBE, DFC	Mrs M. Davies
Three Rivers, Herts	82,600	565.87	A. Robertson	A. Littlejohn
§Thurrock, Essex	131,200	563.67	K. Barnes	(a) R. Lee
§Tonbridge and Malling, Kent	102,100	569.58	T. Thompson	(a) Mrs P. Barnes
§Torbay, Devon	121,100	562.96	D. P. Hudson	(a) Mrs A. P. Williams
Torridge, Devon	54,100	523.00	R. K. Brasington	D. A. Poole
§Tunbridge Wells, Kent	101,800	553.89	R. J. Stone	(a) W. Stone
Tynedale, Northumberland	57,500	630.00	A. Baty	Mrs M. J. Howard
Uttlesford, Essex	66,600	555.52	K. Ivory	N. G. Prowse
Vale of White Horse, Oxon	113,200	517.61	‡D. J. Heavens	R. J. Johnston
§Vale Royal, Cheshire	114,600	645.44	W. R. T. Woods	(a) Mrs P. Booher
Wansbeck, Northumberland	61,900	632.88	A. G. White	G. D. H. Cole
†Wansdyke, Avon	80,400	670.00	*P. May	B. S. Organ
§Warrington, Cheshire	185,000	636.27	M. I. M. Sanders	(a) H. Lawson
Warwick	118,600	615.86	J. V. Picking	P. R. Wooller
§Watford, Herts	75,600	625.38	°R. Bedford (acting)	N. Tyrwhitt
Waveney, Suffolk	107,700	575.16	M. Berridge	B. D. Hunter
§Waverley, Surrey	115,100	563.75	Miss C. L. Pointer	(a) M. Blower
Wealden, East Sussex	133,700	598.41	D. R. Holness	Mrs V. Chidson
Wear Valley, Co. Durham	63,800	670.88	°P. J. Worsnop	T. Judd
§Wellingborough, Northants	68,300	315.45	J. E. Thewlass	(a) J. T. L. Watts
Welwyn Hatfield, Herts	95,300	568.66	D. Riddle	Mrs I. McDonald
§West Devon	46,700	588.33	J. S. Ligo	(a) R. Ware
West Dorset	87,700	528.78	R. C. Rennison	Mrs J. D. Cockerill
West Lancashire	109,700	669.19	B. A. Knight	A. Maguire
West Lindsey, Lincs	77,600	585.04	R. W. Nelsey	J. Turner
West Oxfordshire	93,700	523.27	N. J. B. Robson	J. Lever
West Somerset	31,500	606.73	C. Rockall	S. J. Pugsley
West Wiltshire	110,300	592.84	R. S. While	T. P. Chivers
§Weymouth and Portland, Dorset	62,400	568.79	M. N. Ashby	(a) A. Sheppard
WINCHESTER, Hants	100,500	573.95	D. H. Cowan	(a) Mrs P. Norris
§Windsor and Maidenhead, Berks	136,700	540.24	G. B. Blacker	(a) B. Hedley
§Woking, Surrey	88,200	542.88	P. Russell	(a) N. Hinks

* General Manager
** Borough Secretary
° Head of Paid Service
‡ Director of Administration

Council	Population 1993	Band D charge 1995	Chief Executive	Chairman 1995–6 (a) Mayor (b) Lord Mayor
Wokingham, Berks	142,900	£566.42	Mrs G. C. Norton	J. P. Green
†Woodspring, Avon	182,100	656.13	P. May	Mrs S. O. L. Haysom
WORCESTER	87,600	558.95	††D. Wareing	(a) Mrs E. Smith
§Worthing, West Sussex	97,500	573.03	M. J. Ball	(a) C. H. Golds
Wrekin, Shropshire	142,700	656.79	D. G. Hutchison	J. S. Uppal
Wychavon, Hereford and Worcs	104,900	487.53	A. V. Du Sautoy	Mrs V. M. Isaacs
Wycombe, Bucks	161,400	563.92	R. J. Cummins	(a) Mrs J. Gabbitas
§Wyre, Lancs	103,900	652.89	M. Brown	(a) Miss P. Catlow
Wyre Forest, Hereford and Worcs	96,800	569.00	W. S. Baldwin	M. M. G. Oborski
†YORK, North Yorkshire	104,000	583.13	J. Cairns	(b) J. Boardman

†† Head of Paid Service

Roman Names of English Towns and Cities

Bath	*Aquae Sulis*	Leicester	*Ratae Corieltauvorum*
Canterbury	*Durovernum Cantiacorum*	Lincoln	*Lindum*
Carlisle	*Luguvalium*	London	*Londinium*
Chelmsford	*Caesaromagus*	Manchester	*Mamucium*
Chester	*Deva*	Newcastle upon Tyne	*Pons Aelius*
Chichester	*Noviomagus Regnensium*	Pevensey	*Anderetium*
Cirencester	*Corinium Dobunnorum*	Rochester	*Durobrivae*
Colchester	*Camulodunum*	St Albans	*Verulamium*
Doncaster	*Danum*	Salisbury (Old Sarum)	*Sorviodunum*
Dorchester	*Durnovaria*	Silchester	*Calleva Atrebatum*
Dover	*Dubris*	Winchester	*Venta Belgarum*
Exeter	*Isca Dumnoniorum*	Wroxeter	*Viroconium Cornoviorum*
Gloucester	*Glevum*	York	*Eburacum*

London

THE CORPORATION OF LONDON
(see also page 529)

The City of London is the historic centre at the heart of London known as 'the square mile' around which the vast metropolis has grown over the centuries. The City's residential population is 5,400. The civic government is carried on by the Corporation of the City of London through the Court of Common Council.

The City is the financial and business centre of London and includes the head offices of the principal banks, insurance companies and mercantile houses, in addition to buildings ranging from the historic interest of the Roman Wall and the 15th-century Guildhall, to the massive splendour of St Paul's Cathedral and the architectural beauty of Wren's spires.

The City of London was described by Tacitus in AD 62 as 'a busy emporium for trade and traders'. Under the Romans it became an important administration centre and hub of the road system. Little is known of London in Saxon times, when it formed part of the kingdom of the East Saxons. In 886 Alfred recovered London from the Danes and reconstituted it a burgh under his son-in-law. In 1066 the citizens submitted to William the Conqueror who in 1067 granted them a charter, which is still preserved, establishing them in the rights and privileges they had hitherto enjoyed.

THE MAYORALTY
The Mayoralty was probably established about 1189, the first Mayor being Henry Fitz Ailwyn who filled the office for 23 years and was succeeded by Fitz Alan (1212–14). A new charter was granted by King John in 1215, directing the Mayor to be chosen annually, which has ever since been done, though in early times the same individual often held the office more than once. A familiar instance is that of 'Whittington, thrice Lord Mayor of London' (in reality four times, 1397, 1398, 1406, 1419); and many modern cases have occurred. The earliest instance of the phrase 'Lord Mayor' in English is in 1414. It was used more generally in the latter part of the 15th century and became invariable from 1535 onwards. At Michaelmas the liverymen in Common Hall choose two Aldermen who have served the office of Sheriff for presentation to the Court of Aldermen, and one is chosen to be Lord Mayor for the following mayoral year.

LORD MAYOR'S DAY
The Lord Mayor of London was previously elected on the feast of St Simon and St Jude (28 October), and from the time of Edward I, at least, was presented to the King or to the Barons of the Exchequer on the following day, unless that day was a Sunday. The day of election was altered to 16 October in 1346, and after some further changes was fixed for Michaelmas Day in 1546, but the ceremonies of admittance and swearing-in of the Lord Mayor continued to take place on 28 and 29 October respectively until 1751. In 1752, at the reform of the calendar, the Lord Mayor was continued in office until 8 November, the 'New Style' equivalent of 28 October. The Lord Mayor is now presented to the Lord Chief Justice at the Royal Courts of Justice on the second Saturday in November to make the final declaration of office, having been sworn in at Guildhall on the preceding day. The procession to the Royal Courts of Justice is popularly known as the Lord Mayor's Show.

REPRESENTATIVES
Aldermen are mentioned in the 11th century and their office is of Saxon origin. They were elected annually between 1377 and 1394, when an Act of Parliament of Richard II directed them to be chosen for life.

The Common Council, elected annually on the first Friday in December, was, at an early date, substituted for a popular assembly called the *Folkmote*. At first only two representatives were sent from each ward, but the number has since been greatly increased.

OFFICERS
Sheriffs were Saxon officers; their predecessors were the *wic-reeves* and *portreeves* of London and Middlesex. At first they were officers of the Crown, and were named by the Barons of the Exchequer; but Henry I (in 1132) gave the citizens permission to choose their own Sheriffs, and the annual election of Sheriffs became fully operative under King John's charter of 1199. The citizens lost this privilege, as far as the election of the Sheriff of Middlesex was concerned, by the Local Government Act 1888; but the liverymen continue to choose two Sheriffs of the City of London, who are appointed on Midsummer Day and take office at Michaelmas.

The office of Chamberlain is an ancient one, the first contemporary record of which is 1237. The Town Clerk (or Common Clerk) is mentioned in 1274.

ACTIVITIES
The work of the Corporation is assigned to a number of committees which present reports to the Court of Common Council. These Committees are: City Lands and Bridge House Estates, Policy and Resources, Finance, Planning and Transportation, Central Markets, Billingsgate and Leadenhall Markets, Spitalfields Market, Police, Port and City of London Health and Social Services, Libraries, Art Galleries and Records, Boards of Governors of Schools, Music and Drama (Guildhall School of Music and Drama), Establishment, Housing, Gresham (City side), Hampstead Heath Management, Epping Forest and Open Spaces, West Ham Park, Privileges, Barbican Residential and Barbican Centre (Barbican Arts and Conference Centre).

The City's estate, in the possession of which the Corporation of London differs from other municipalities, is managed by the City Lands and Bridge House Estates Committee, the chairmanship of which carries with it the title of Chief Commoner. *Chairman* (1995), J. L. Bird.

The Honourable the Irish Society (The Irish Chamber, St Dunstan's House, 2–4 Carey Lane, London EC2V 8AA. *Clerk*, S. Waley), which manages the Corporation's estates in Ulster, consists of a Governor and five other Aldermen, the Recorder, and 19 Common Councilmen, of whom one is elected Deputy Governor.

THE LORD MAYOR 1994–5*
The Rt. Hon. the Lord Mayor, Sir Christopher Walford
Secretary, Air Vice-Marshal M. Dicken, CB

THE SHERIFFS 1995–6
Sir Peter Levene, KBE (*Alderman, Portsoken*) and K. E. Ayers; *elected*, 26 June 1995; *assumed office*, 28 September 1995

OFFICERS
Town Clerk, S. Jones, apptd 1991
Chamberlain, B. P. Harty, apptd 1983

* The Lord Mayor for 1995–6 was elected on Michaelmas Day *See* Stop-press

The Aldermen

Name and Ward	CC	Ald.	Shff.	Lord Mayor
Cdr. Sir Robin Gillett, Bt., GBE, RD, *Bassishaw*	1965	1969	1973	1976
Sir Peter Gadsden, GBE, *Farringdon Wt.*	1969	1971	1970	1979
Sir Christopher Leaver, GBE, *Dowgate*	1973	1974	1979	1981
Sir Alan Traill, GBE, *Langbourn*	1970	1975	1982	1984
Sir David Rowe-Ham, GBE, *Bridge*	—	1976	1984	1986
Sir Greville Spratt, GBE, TD, *Castle Baynard*	—	1978	1984	1987
Sir Christopher Collett, GBE, *Broad Street*	1973	1979	1985	1988
Sir Hugh Bidwell, GBE, *Billingsgate*	—	1979	1986	1989
Sir Alexander Graham, GBE, *Queenhithe*	1978	1979	1986	1990
Sir Brian Jenkins, GBE, *Cordwainer*	—	1980	1987	1991
Sir Francis McWilliams, GBE, *Aldersgate*	1978	1980	1988	1992
Sir Paul Newall, TD, *Walbrook*	1980	1981	1989	1993
Sir Christopher Walford, *Farringdon Wn.*	—	1982	1990	1994

All the above have passed the Civic Chair

	CC	Ald.	Shff.
Vacant, *Bread Street*	—	—	—
Roger Cork, *Tower*	1978	1983	1992
Leonard Chalstrey, *Vintry*	1981	1984	1993
Richard Nichols, *Candlewick*	1983	1984	1994
Bryan Toye, *Lime Street*	—	1983	
Peter Bull, *Cheap*	1968	1984	
Sir Peter Levene, KBE, *Portsoken*	1983	1984	
Clive Martin, OBE, TD, *Aldgate*	—	1985	
David Howard, *Cornhill*	1972	1986	
James Oliver, *Bishopsgate*	1980	1987	
Gavyn Arthur, *Cripplegate*	1988	1991	
Robert Finch, *Coleman Street*	—	1992	

The Common Council of London

Deputy: Each Common Councilman so described serves as deputy to the Alderman of her/his ward

Absalom, J. D. (1994) — *Farringdon Wt.*
Angell, E. H. (1991) — *Cripplegate Wt.*
Anstee, N. J. (1987) — *Aldersgate*
Archibald, *Deputy* W. W. (1986) — *Cornhill*
Bailey, J. (1993) — *Cripplegate Wt.*
Ballard, K. A., MC (1969) — *Castle Baynard*
Balls, H. D. (1970) — *Castle Baynard*
Barker, *Deputy* J. A. (1981) — *Cripplegate Wt.*
Barnes-Yallowley, H. M. F. (1986) — *Coleman Street*
Beale, *Deputy* M. J. (1979) — *Lime Street*
Bird, J. L. (1977) — *Bridge*
Biroum-Smith, P. L. (1988) — *Dowgate*
Block, S. A. A. (1983) — *Cheap*
Bradshaw, D. J. (1991) — *Cripplegate Wn.*
Bramwell, F. M. (1983) — *Langbourn*
Brewer, D. W. (1992) — *Bassishaw*
Brewster, J. W., OBE (1994) — *Bassishaw*
Brighton, R. L. (1984) — *Portsoken*
Brooks, W. I. B. (1988) — *Billingsgate*
Brown, *Deputy* D. T. (1971) — *Walbrook*
Caspi, D. (1994) — *Bridge*
Cassidy, *Deputy* M. J. (1989) — *Coleman Street*

Catt, B. F. (1982) — *Farringdon Wn.*
Chadwick, R. A. H. (1994) — *Tower*
Challis, G. H., CBE (1978) — *Langbourn*
Cohen, Mrs C. M. (1986) — *Lime Street*
Cole, Lt.-Col. Sir Colin, KCB, KCVO, TD (1964) — *Castle Baynard*
Collinson, Miss A. H. (1991) — *Farringdon Wt.*
Cotgrove, D. (1991) — *Lime Street*
Coven, *Deputy* Mrs E. O., CBE (1972) — *Dowgate*
Currie, Miss S. E. M. (1985) — *Cripplegate Wt.*
Daily-Hunt, R. B. (1989) — *Cripplegate Wt.*
David, C. P. (1984) — *Aldgate*
Davis, C. B. (1991) — *Bread Street*
de Silva, D., QC (1980) — *Farringdon Wt.*
Dove, W. H., MBE (1993) — *Bishopsgate*
Dunitz, A. A. (1984) — *Portsoken*
Edwards, *Deputy* R. D. K. (1978) — *Bassishaw*
Eskenzi, A. N. (1970) — *Farringdon Wn.*
Evans, *Deputy* Mrs J. (1975) — *Farringdon Wt.*
Eve, R. A. (1980) — *Cheap*
Everett, K. M. (1984) — *Candlewick*
Falk, F. A., TD (1984) — *Farringdon Wt.*
Farthing, R. B. C. (1981) — *Aldgate*
Fell, J. A. (1982) — *Queenhithe*
FitzGerald, *Deputy* R. C. A. (1981) — *Bread Street*
Forbes, G. B. (1993) — *Bishopsgate*
Frankenberg, P. B. (1989) — *Cordwainer*
Fraser, S. J. (1993) — *Coleman Street*
Fraser, W. B. (1981) — *Vintry*
Frazer, C. M. (1986) — *Farringdon Wt.*
Galloway, A. D. (1981) — *Broad Street*
Ginsburg, S. (1990) — *Bishopsgate*
Gowman, Miss A. (1991) — *Dowgate*
Graves, A. C. (1985) — *Bishopsgate*
Green, C. (1994) — *Aldersgate*
Halliday, Mrs P. (1992) — *Walbrook*
Harding, N. H., OBE (1970) — *Farringdon Wn.*
Hardwick, Dr P. B. (1987) — *Aldgate*
Hart, *Deputy* M. G. (1970) — *Bridge*
Haynes, J. E. H. (1986) — *Cornhill*
Henderson, *Deputy* J. S., OBE (1975) — *Langbourn*
Henderson-Begg, M. (1977) — *Coleman Street*
Hilliard, N. R. M. (1994) — *Farringdon Wt.*
Holland, *Deputy* J., CBE (1972) — *Aldgate*
Horlock, *Deputy* H. W. S. (1969) — *Farringdon Wn.*
Hughesdon, J. S. (1991) — *Broad Street*
Jackson, L. St J. T. (1978) — *Bread Street*
Keep, Mrs B. (1987) — *Cripplegate Wn.*
Kellett, Mrs M. W. F. (1986) — *Tower*
Kemp, D. L. (1984) — *Coleman Street*
Knowles, S. K. (1984) — *Candlewick*
Langton Way, J. H. (1992) — *Cripplegate Wt.*
Lawrence, G. A. (1994) — *Farringdon Wt.*
Lawson, G. C. H. (1971) — *Portsoken*
Littlestone, N. (1993) — *Aldersgate*
MacLellan, A. P. W. (1989) — *Walbrook*
McNeil, I. D. (1977) — *Lime Street*
Malins, J. H., QC (1981) — *Farringdon Wt.*
Martin, R. C. (1986) — *Queenhithe*
Martinelli, P. J. (1994) — *Bassishaw*
Mayhew, Miss J. (1986) — *Queenhithe*
Mitchell, *Deputy* C. R. (1971) — *Castle Baynard*
Mizen, *Deputy* D. H. (1979) — *Broad Street*
Mobsby, *Deputy* D. J. L. (1985) — *Billingsgate*
Morgan, *Deputy* B. L., CBE (1963) — *Bishopsgate*
Moss, A. D. (1989) — *Tower*
Nash, *Deputy* Mrs J. C. (1983) — *Aldersgate*
Neary, J. E. (1982) — *Aldgate*
Newman, Mrs P. B. (1989) — *Aldersgate*

Northall-Laurie, P. D. (1975)	*Walbrook*
Owen, Mrs J. (1975)	*Langbourn*
Owen-Ward, J. R. (1983)	*Bridge*
Parmley, A. C. (1992)	*Vintry*
Pembroke, *Deputy* Mrs A. M. F. (1978)	*Cheap*
Ponsonby of Shulbrede, *Deputy* Lady (1981)	*Farringdon Wt.*
Pulman, *Deputy* G. A. G. (1983)	*Tower*
Punter, C. (1993)	*Cripplegate Wn.*
Reed, *Deputy* J. L., MBE (1967)	*Farringdon Wn.*
Revell-Smith, *Deputy* P. A., CBE (1959)	*Vintry*
Rigby, P. P., CBE (1972)	*Farringdon Wn.*
Robinson, Mrs D. C. (1989)	*Bishopsgate*
Rodgers, Miss E. H. L. (1987)	*Vintry*
Roney, *Deputy* E. P. T., CBE (1974)	*Bishopsgate*
Samuel, *Deputy* Mrs I., MBE (1971)	*Portsoken*
Sargant, K. A. (1991)	*Cornhill*
Saunders, *Deputy* R. (1975)	*Candlewick*
Savory, M. B. (1980)	*Broad Street*
Scriven, R. G. (1984)	*Candlewick*
Sellon, S. A., OBE, TD (1990)	*Cordwainer*
Shalit, D. M. (1972)	*Farringdon Wn.*
Sharp, *Deputy* Mrs I. M. (1974)	*Queenhithe*
Sherlock, M. R. C. (1992)	*Dowgate*
Simpson, A. S. J. (1987)	*Aldersgate*
Snyder, *Deputy* M. J. (1986)	*Cordwainer*
Spanner, J. H., TD (1984)	*Broad Street*
Stevenson, F. P. (1994)	*Cripplegate Wn.*
Stone, H. V. (1993)	*Billingsgate*
Taylor, J. A. F., TD (1991)	*Bread Street*
Trotter, J. (1993)	*Billingsgate*
Walsh, S. (1989)	*Farringdon Wt.*
Warner, D. W. (1994)	*Cripplegate Wn.*
White, Dr J. W. (1986)	*Cornhill*
Willoughby, P. J. (1985)	*Bishopsgate*
Wilmot, R. T. D. (1973)	*Cordwainer*
Wilson, A. B., CBE (1984)	*Cheap*
Wixley, G. R. A., CBE, TD (1964)	*Coleman Street*
Woods, A. J. A. (1994)	*Farringdon Wt.*
Woodward, *Deputy* C. D., CBE (1971)	*Cripplegate Wn.*
Wooldridge, F. D. (1988)	*Farringdon Wn.*

The City Guilds (Livery Companies)

The constitution of the livery companies has been unchanged for centuries. There are three ranks of membership: freemen, liverymen and assistants. A person can become a freeman by patrimony (through a parent having been a freeman); by servitude (through having served an apprenticeship to a freeman); or by redemption (by purchase).

Election to the livery is the prerogative of the company, who can elect any of its freemen as liverymen. Assistants are usually elected from the livery and form a Court of Assistants which is the governing body of the company. The Master (in some companies called the Prime Warden) is elected annually from the assistants.

As at June 1995, 23,660 liverymen of the guilds were entitled to vote at elections at Common Hall.

The order of precedence, omitting extinct companies, is given in parenthesis after the name of each company in the list below. In certain companies the election of Master or Prime Warden for the year does not take place till the autumn. In such cases the Master or Prime Warden for 1994–5 is given.

THE TWELVE GREAT COMPANIES
In order of civic precedence

MERCERS (*1*). *Hall*, Ironmonger Lane, London EC2V 8HE. *Livery*, 226. *Clerk*, G. M. M. Wakeford, OBE. *Master*, W. O. Clarke

GROCERS (*2*). *Hall*, Princes Street, London EC2R 8AD. *Livery*, 313. *Clerk*, C. G. Mattingley, CBE. *Master*, J. M. Pickard

DRAPERS (*3*). *Hall*, Throgmorton Avenue, London EC2N 2DQ. *Livery*, 239. *Clerk*, A. L. Lang, MBE. *Master*, Revd P. Taylor

FISHMONGERS (*4*). *Hall*, London Bridge, London EC4R 9EL. *Livery*, 370. *Clerk*, K. S. Waters. *Prime Warden*, The Earl of Antrim

GOLDSMITHS (*5*). *Hall*, Foster Lane, London EC2V 6BN. *Livery*, 300. *Clerk*, R. D. Buchanan-Dunlop, CBE. *Prime Warden*, Sir Paul Girolami

MERCHANT TAYLORS (*6/7*). *Hall*, 30 Threadneedle Street, London EC2R 8AY. *Livery* 312. *Clerk*, D. A. Peck. *Master*, J. M. S. Whitehead, CBE

SKINNERS (*6/7*). *Hall*, 8 Dowgate Hill, London EC4R 2SP. *Livery*, 370. *Clerk*, Capt. D. Hart-Dyke, CBE, LVO, RN. *Master*, J. A. C. Haviland

HABERDASHERS (*8*). *Hall*, Staining Lane, London EC2V 7DD. *Livery*, 320. *Clerk*, Capt. R. J. Fisher, RN. *Master*, P. W. Bedford

SALTERS (*9*). *Hall*, 4 Fore Street, London EC2Y 5DE. *Livery*, 175. *Clerk*, Col. M. P. Barneby. *Master*, The Lord Remnant, CVO

IRONMONGERS (*10*). *Hall*, Shaftesbury Place, Barbican, London EC2Y 8AA. *Livery*, 223. *Clerk*, J. A. Oliver. *Master*, Sir Greville Spratt, GBE, TD

VINTNERS (*11*). *Hall*, Upper Thames Street, London EC4V 3BJ. *Livery*, 310. *Clerk*, Brig. G. Read, CBE. *Master*, Q. Morgan Edwards

CLOTHWORKERS (*12*). *Hall*, Dunster Court, Mincing Lane, London EC3R 7AH. *Livery*, 200. *Clerk*, M. G. T. Harris. *Master*, The Viscount Slim, OBE

OTHER CITY GUILDS
In alphabetical order

ACTUARIES (*91*). *Livery*, 180. *Clerk*, P. D. Esslemont, 16A Cadogan Square, London SW1X 0JU. *Master*, C. W. F. Low

AIR PILOTS AND AIR NAVIGATORS, GUILD OF (*81*). *Livery*, 400. *Grand Master*, HRH The Prince Philip, Duke of Edinburgh, KG, KT. *Clerk* (*acting*), Capt C. L. Hodgkinson, Cobham House, 291 Gray's Inn Road, London WC1X 8QF. *Master*, Capt. G. Fowkes

APOTHECARIES, SOCIETY OF (*58*). *Hall*, 14 Black Friars Lane, London EC4V 6EJ. *Livery*, 1,750. *Clerk*, Lt.-Col. R. J. Stringer. *Master*, Prof. B. S. Jay

ARBITRATORS (*93*). *Livery*, 250. *Clerk*, Lt.-Col. I. R. P. Green, 2 Bolts Hill, Castle Camps, Cambs CB1 6GL. *Master*, F. C. Goodall

ARMOURERS AND BRASIERS (*22*). *Hall*, 81 Coleman Street, London EC2R 5BJ. *Livery*, 123. *Clerk*, Cdr. T. J. K. Sloane, OBE. *Master*, G. C. Honnywill

BAKERS (*19*). *Hall*, Harp Lane, London EC3R 6DP. *Livery*, 415. *Clerk* (*acting*), J. W. Tompkins. *Master*, D. Springett

BARBERS (*17*). *Hall*, Monkwell Square, Wood Street, London EC2Y 5BL. *Livery*, 224. *Clerk*, Col. A. B. Harfield, CBE. *Master*, Prof. D. Barltrop, FRCP

BASKETMAKERS (*52*). *Livery*, 363. *Clerk*, Maj. G. J. Flint-Shipman, TD, 48 Seymour Walk, London SW10 9NF. *Prime Warden*, D. L. Kemp

BLACKSMITHS (*40*). *Livery*, 225. *Clerk*, R. C. Jorden, 27 Cheyne Walk, Grange Park, London N21 1DB. *Prime Warden*, C. S. B. Champion

BOWYERS (*38*). *Livery*, 103. *Clerk*, J. R. Owen-Ward, 261 Green Lanes, London N13 4XE. *Master*, J. F. G. James-Crook

BREWERS (*14*). *Hall*, Aldermanbury Square, London EC2V 7HR. *Livery*, 129. *Clerk*, C. W. Dallmeyer. *Master*, R. I. Turner

BRODERERS (*48*). *Livery*, 164. *Clerk*, P. J. C. Crouch, 11 Bridge Road, East Molesey, Surrey KT8 9EU. *Master*, J. M. Wheeler

BUILDERS MERCHANTS (*88*). *Livery*, 215. *Clerk*, Miss S. Robinson, TD, 14 Charterhouse Square, London EC1M 6AX. *Master*, M. Pares

BUTCHERS (*24*). *Hall*, 87 Bartholomew Close, London EC1A 7EB. *Livery*, 782. *Clerk*, A. H. Emus. *Master*, R. E. Seeman

CARMEN (*77*). *Livery*, 435. *Clerk*, Lt.-Col. G. T. Pearce, MBE, 35–37 Ludgate Hill, London EC4M 7JN. *Master*, G. Golder

CARPENTERS (*26*). *Hall*, 1 Throgmorton Avenue, London EC2N 2JJ. *Livery*, 150. *Clerk*, Maj.-Gen. P. T. Stevenson, OBE. *Master*, M. R. Francis

CHARTERED ACCOUNTANTS (*86*). *Livery*, 347. *Clerk*, G. H. Kingsmill, The Grove, Hinton Parva, Swindon SN4 0DH. *Master*, J. M. Renshall, CBE

CHARTERED ARCHITECTS (*98*). *Livery*, 122. *Clerk*, L. W. Groome, OBE, Bourlet House, 4 Bourlet Close, London W1P 7PJ. *Master*, D. Cole-Adams

CHARTERED SECRETARIES AND ADMINISTRATORS (*87*). *Livery*, 225. *Hon. Clerk*, W. C. Hammond, MBE, St Dunstan's House, Carey Lane, London EC2V 8AA. *Master*, C. H. Grinsted

CHARTERED SURVEYORS (*85*). *Livery*, 350. *Clerk*, Mrs A. L. Jackson, 16 St Mary-at-Hill, London EC3R 8EE. *Master*, M. O. Coates

CLOCKMAKERS (*61*). *Livery*, 216. *Hall*, St Dunstan's House, Carey Lane, London EC2V 8AA. *Clerk*, Gp Capt P. H. Gibson, MBE. *Master*, S. J. Thornton

COACHMAKERS AND COACH-HARNESS MAKERS (*72*). *Livery*, 400. *Clerk*, Maj. W. H. Wharfe, 149 Banstead Road, Ewell, Epsom, Surrey KT17 3HL. *Master*, P. G. Sparks

CONSTRUCTORS (*99*). *Livery*, 116. *Clerk*, L. L. Brace, 181 Fentiman Road, London SW8 1JY. *Master*, A. W. J. Appleton

COOKS (*35*). *Livery*, 75. *Clerk*, M. C. Thatcher, 35 Great Peter Street, London SW1P 3LR. *Master*, J. H. Balls

COOPERS (*36*). *Hall*, 13 Devonshire Square, London EC2M 4TH. *Livery*, 260. *Clerk*, J. A. Newton. *Master*, M. J. V. Housley

CORDWAINERS (*27*). *Livery* 149. *Clerk*, Lt.-Col. J. R. Blundell, RM, Eldon Chambers, 30 Fleet Street, London EC4Y 1AA. *Master*, C. J. O. King

CURRIERS (*29*). *Livery*, 96. *Clerk*, Gp Capt F. J. Hamilton, Kestrel Cottage, East Knowle, Salisbury SP3 6AD. *Master*, R. J. Seabrook

CUTLERS (*18*). *Hall*, Warwick Lane, London EC4M 7BR. *Livery*, 115. *Clerk*, K. S. G. Hinde, TD. *Master*, P. J. Butler, CBE

DISTILLERS (*69*). *Livery*, 270. *Clerk*, C. V. Hughes, 71 Lincoln's Inn Fields, London WC2A 3JF. *Master*, P. Hallgarten

DYERS (*13*). *Hall*, 10 Dowgate Hill, London EC4R 2ST. *Livery*, 120. *Clerk*, J. R. Chambers. *Prime Warden*, F. A. Onians

ENGINEERS (*94*). *Livery*, 280. *Clerk*, Cdr. B. D. Gibson, Kiln Bank, Bodle Street Green, Nr Hailsham, E. Sussex BN27 4UA. *Master*, L. F. Turner, OBE

ENVIRONMENTAL CLEANERS (*97*). *Livery*, 180. *Clerk*, S. J. Holt, Whitethorns, Rannoch Road, Crowborough, E. Sussex TN6 1RA. *Master*, T. S. Louis

FAN MAKERS (*76*). *Livery*, 200. *Clerk*, Lt.-Col. I. R. P. Green, 2 Bolts Hill, Castle Camps, Cambs CB1 6GL. *Master*, M. J. Crispin

FARMERS (*80*). *Livery*, 300. *Clerk*, Miss M. L. Winter, Pel House, 35 Station Square, Petts Wood, Kent BR5 1LZ. *Master*, Mrs E. R. Wheatley-Hubbard, OBE

FARRIERS (*55*). *Livery*, 375. *Clerk*, H. W. H. Ellis, 37 The Uplands, Loughton, Essex IG10 1NQ. *Master*, R. Johnson

FELTMAKERS (*63*). *Livery*, 170. *Clerk*, Lt.-Col. C. J. Holroyd, Providence Cottage, Chute Cadley, Andover, Hants SP11 9EB. *Master*, Capt. P. Cobb, OBE, RN

FLETCHERS (*39*). *Hall*, 3 Cloth Street, London EC1A 7LD. *Livery*, 105. *Clerk*, J. R. Owen-Ward. *Master*, J. R. Garnett

FOUNDERS (*33*). *Hall*, 1 Cloth Fair, London EC1A 7HT. *Livery*, 175. *Clerk*, A. J. Gillett. *Master*, R. J. W. L. Stevens

FRAMEWORK KNITTERS (*64*). *Livery*, 218. *Clerk*, D. A. Tate, Parkville House, Bridge Street, Pinner, Middx HA5 3JD. *Master*, A. J. W. Lewis, OBE

FRUITERERS (*45*). *Livery*, 275. *Clerk*, Cdr. M. T. H. Styles, Denmead Cottage, Chawton, Alton, Hants GU34 1SB. *Master*, Sir Rowland Whitehead

FUELLERS (*95*). *Livery*, 85. *Clerk*, Wg Cdr. H. F. C. Squire, OBE, 4 Maycross Avenue, Morden, Surrey SM4 4DA. *Master*, W. M. Pybus

FURNITURE MAKERS (*83*). *Livery*, 258. *Clerk*, Mrs J. A. Wright, 30 Harcourt Street, London W1H 2AA. *Master*, A. F. P. Alston

GARDENERS (*66*). *Livery*, 243. *Clerk*, Col. N. G. S. Gray, 25 Luke Street, London EC2A 4AR. *Master*, D. E. F. Gollin

GIRDLERS (*23*). *Hall*, Basinghall Avenue, London EC2V 5DD. *Livery*, 80. *Clerk*, N. Wyldbore-Smith. *Master*, C. E. Crace

GLASS-SELLERS (*71*). *Livery*, 180. *Hon. Clerk*, B. J. Rawles, 43 Aragon Avenue, Thames Ditton, Surrey KT7 0PY. *Master*, J. G. Thorpe

GLAZIERS AND PAINTERS OF GLASS (*53*). *Hall*, 9 Montague Close, London SE1 9DD. *Livery*, 270. *Clerk*, P. R. Batchelor. *Master*, P. G. Lowe

GLOVERS (*62*). *Livery*, 275. *Clerk*, Mrs M. Hood, 71 Ifield Road, London SW10 9AU. *Master*, J. J. Gardner

GOLD AND SILVER WYRE DRAWERS (*74*). *Livery*, 328. *Clerk*, J. R. Williams, 50 Cheyne Avenue, London E18 2DR. *Master*, G. B. Brunning

GUNMAKERS (*73*). *Livery*, 275. *Clerk*, J. M. Riches, The Proof House, 48–50 Commercial Road, London E1 1LP. *Master*, S. Carroll

HORNERS (*54*). *Livery*, 190. *Clerk*, S. J. Holt, Whitethorns, Rannoch Road, Crowborough, E. Sussex TN6 1RA. *Master* J. V. Webb

INFORMATION TECHNOLOGISTS (*100*). *Livery*, 260. *Clerk*, Mrs G. Davies, 30 Aylesbury Street, London EC1R 0ER. *Master*, C. C. G. Foot, OBE

INNHOLDERS (*32*). *Hall*, College Street, London EC4R 2RH. *Livery*, 107. *Clerk*, J. R. Edwardes Jones. *Master*, R. G. Ames

INSURERS (*92*). *Hall*, 20 Aldermanbury, London EC2V 7HY. *Livery*, 374. *Clerk*, V. D. Webb. *Master*, W. J. Briggs

JOINERS AND CEILERS (*41*). *Livery*, 145. *Clerk*, Mrs A. L. Jackson, 75 Meadway Drive, Horsell, Woking, Surrey GU21 4TF. *Master*, R. L. Hogarth

LAUNDERERS (*89*). *Hall*, 9 Montague Close, London SE1 9DD. *Livery*, 205. *Clerk*, R. C. Jorden. *Master*, J. I. S. Fox

LEATHERSELLERS (*15*). *Hall*, 15 St Helen's Place, London EC3A 6DQ. *Livery*, 150. *Clerk*, Rear-Adm. P. B. Rowe, CBE, LVO. *Master*, D. B. Daniels

LIGHTMONGERS (*96*). *Livery*, 132. *Clerk*, S. H. Birch, 53 Leithcote Gardens, London SW16 2UX. *Master*, M. P. Lippold

LORINERS (*57*). *Livery*, 398. *Clerk*, J. R. Williams, 50 Cheyne Avenue, London E18 2DR. *Master*, J. F. S. Northcott

MAKERS OF PLAYING CARDS (75). *Livery,* 150. *Clerk,* M. J. Smyth, 6 The Priory, Godstone, Surrey RH9 8NL. *Master,* R. A. Howells

MARKETORS (90). *Livery,* 190. *Clerk,* N. Boakes, Europower House, Lower Road, Cookham, Berks SL6 9EH. *Master,* J. B. Scanlon

MASONS (30). *Livery,* 125. *Clerk,* T. F. Ackland, 261 Green Lanes, London N13 4XE. *Master,* R. J. French, OBE

MASTER MARINERS, HONOURABLE COMPANY OF (78). HQS *Wellington,* Temple Stairs, Victoria Embankment, London WC2R 2PN. *Livery,* 260. *Clerk,* J. A. V. Maddock. *Admiral,* HRH The Duke of Edinburgh, KG, KT. *Master,* Capt. J. M. Gray

MUSICIANS (50). *Livery,* 320. *Clerk,* S. F. N. Waley, St Dunstan's House, 2–4 Carey Lane, London EC2V 8AA. *Master,* F. A. A. Carnwath

NEEDLEMAKERS (65). *Livery,* 230. *Clerk,* M. G. Cook, 9 Staple Inn, London WC1V 7QH. *Master,* S. V. C. Flintham

PAINTER-STAINERS (28). *Hall,* 9 Little Trinity Lane, London EC4V 2AD. *Livery,* 312. *Clerk,* Wg Cdr. B. C. Pratt. *Master,* B. E. Edwards, CBE

PATTENMAKERS (70). *Livery,* 188. *Clerk,* C. L. K. Ledger, 17 Orchard Close, The Rutts, Bushey Heath, Herts WD2 1LW. *Master,* D. E. Miller

PAVIORS (56). *Livery,* 240. *Clerk,* R. F. Coe, 154 Dukes Avenue, New Malden, Surrey KT3 4HR. *Master,* J. M. K. Laing

PEWTERERS (16). *Hall,* Oat Lane, London EC2V 7DE. *Livery,* 110. *Clerk,* Maj.-Gen. J. St J. Grey, CB. *Master,* Dr J. D. Campling

PLAISTERERS (46). *Hall,* 1 London Wall, London EC4V 5JU. *Livery,* 208. *Clerk,* R. Vickers. *Master,* R. L. Wakeham

PLUMBERS (31). *Livery,* 349. *Clerk,* Lt.-Col. R. J. A. Paterson-Fox, 49 Queen Victoria Street, London EC4N 4SA. *Master,* J. Jeffery

POULTERS (34). *Livery,* 166. *Clerk,* A. W. Scott, 23 Orchard Drive, Chorleywood, Herts WD3 5QN. *Master,* J. G. Butcher

SADDLERS (25). *Hall,* 40 Gutter Lane, London EC2V 6BR. *Livery,* 69. *Clerk,* Gp Capt W. S. Brereton Martin, CBE. *Master,* R. Ling

SCIENTIFIC INSTRUMENT MAKERS (84). *Hall,* 9 Montague Close, London SE1 9DD. *Livery,* 235. *Clerk,* F. G. Everard. *Master,* D. A. Wallis

SCRIVENERS (44). *Livery,* 162. *Clerk,* P. C. Stevens, HQS *Wellington,* Temple Stairs, Victoria Embankment, London WC2R 2PN. *Master,* A. H. Hamilton-Hopkins

SHIPWRIGHTS (59). *Livery,* 400. *Clerk,* Capt. R. F. Channon, RN, Ironmongers' Hall, Barbican, London EC2Y 8AA. *Permanent Master,* HRH The Duke of Edinburgh, KG, KT. *Prime Warden,* O. S. Kverndal

SOLICITORS (79). *Livery,* 340. *Clerk,* Miss S. M. Robinson, TD, 14 Charterhouse Square, London EC1M 6AX. *Master,* S. N. Beare

SPECTACLE MAKERS (60). *Livery,* 361. *Clerk,* C. J. Eldridge, Apothecaries' Hall, Black Friars Lane, London EC4V 6EL. *Master,* R. Ingham

STATIONERS AND NEWSPAPER MAKERS (47). *Hall,* Ave Maria Lane, London EC4M 7DD. *Livery,* 439. *Clerk,* Capt. P. Hames, RN. *Master,* A. B. Brooker

TALLOW CHANDLERS (21). *Hall,* 4 Dowgate Hill, London EC4R 2SH. *Livery,* 180. *Clerk,* Brig. W. K. L. Prosser, CBE, MC. *Master,* M. M. L. Sutcliffe

TIN PLATE WORKERS alias Wire Workers (67). *Livery,* 174. *Clerk,* S. J. Holt, Whitethorns, Rannoch Road, Crowborough, E. Sussex TN6 1RA. *Master,* B. Marsh

TOBACCO PIPE MAKERS AND TOBACCO BLENDERS (82). *Livery,* 170. *Clerk,* I. J. Kimmins, Penwood, Penwood End, Hook Heath, Woking, Surrey GU22 0JU. *Master,* S. L. Preedy

TURNERS (51). *Livery,* 165. *Clerk,* R. G. Woodwark, DSC, 33A Hill Avenue, Amersham, Bucks HP6 5BX. *Master,* G. M. Sloan

TYLERS AND BRICKLAYERS (37). *Livery,* 129. *Clerk,* F. A. G. Rider, 6 Martin Lane, Cannon Street, London EC4R 0DP. *Master,* P. V. Dickins

UPHOLDERS (49). *Livery,* 200. *Clerk,* G. J. K. Darby, Kirkston, Beckenham Place Park, Beckenham, Kent BR3 2BN. *Master,* Judge R. Cole

WAX CHANDLERS (20). *Hall,* Gresham Street, London EC2V 7AD. *Livery,* 123. *Clerk,* Cdr J. Stevens. *Master,* H. R. C. Riches

WEAVERS (42). *Livery,* 128. *Clerk,* J. G. Ouvry, Saddlers' House, Gutter Lane, London EC2V 6BR. *Upper Bailiff,* J. G. Y. Radcliffe

WHEELWRIGHTS (68). *Livery,* 250. *Clerk,* M. G. Cook, 9 Staple Inn, London WC1V 7QH. *Master,* B. P. Boreham

WOOLMEN (43). *Livery,* 126. *Clerk,* F. Allen, Hollands, Hedsor Road, Bourne End, Bucks SL8 5EC. *Master,* C. S. Dennis

PARISH CLERKS (*No livery*). *Members,* 100. *Clerk,* Lt.-Col. B. J. N. Coombes, 1 Dean Trench Street, London SW1P 3HB. *Master,* J. C. B. Wittich

WATER CONSERVATORS (*No livery*). *Freemen,* 151. *Clerk,* G. M. A. Handhaugh, 20 Aldermanbury, London EC2V 7GF. *Master,* W. S. Smith.

WATERMEN AND LIGHTERMEN (*No livery*). *Craft Owning Freemen,* 250. *Hall,* 18 St Mary-at-Hill, London EC3R 8EE. *Clerk,* R. G. Crouch. *Master,* D. Allen

WORLD TRADERS (*No livery*). *Freemen,* 97. *Clerk,* J. Norman, 13 Pinewood Road, Branksome Park, Poole, Dorset BH13 6JP. *Master,* H. B. G. Montgomery

LONDON BOROUGH COUNCILS

Council	Municipal offices	Population 1993	Band D charge 1995	Chief Executive (*Managing Director)	Mayor (a) Lord Mayor 1995–6
Barking and Dagenham	°Dagenham, RM10 7BN	145,500	£531.00	W. C. Smith	L. E. Bunn
Barnet	†The Burroughs, Hendon, NW4 4BG	304,700	596.44	M. M. Caller	Ms S. Palmer
Bexley	‡Bexleyheath, Kent DA6 7LB	219,900	560.15	C. Duffield	C. E. Wright
Brent	†Forty Lane, Wembley, HA9 9EZ	247,600	465.50	G. Benham	Mrs G. Tookey
Bromley	°Bromley, BR1 3UH	291,800	496.00	D. Bartlett (acting)	C. G. Priest
§Camden	†Euston Road, NW1 2RU	181,400	687.53	J. Smith	S. Deshmukh
§City of Westminster	City Hall, Victoria Street, SW1E 6QP	189,000	275.00	*W. C. Roots	(a) A. Bradley
Croydon	Taberner House, Park Lane, Croydon CR9 3JS	323,300	508.16	D. Wechsler	C. McKenzie
Ealing	°Uxbridge Road, W5 2HL	285,600	517.00	Ms G. Guy	S. Pound
Enfield	°Enfield, EN1 3XA	261,800	585.51	D. Plank	G. Savva
§Greenwich	†Wellington Street, SE18 6PW	214,800	649.17	C. Roberts	A. M. Moon
§Hackney	†Mare Street, E8 1EA	190,900	778.34	A. Elliston	M. Saleem Siddiqui
§Hammersmith and Fulham	†King Street, W6 9JU	155,500	620.00	*N. Newton	J. Abbott
Haringey	°Wood Green, N22 4LE	211,900	756.19	G. Singh	A. Dobbie
Harrow	°Harrow, HA1 2UH	206,600	559.17	A. G. Redmond	S. Giles-Medhurst
Havering	†Romford, RM1 3BD	232,200	550.00	D. R. Bradley	J. Hoepelman
Hillingdon	°Uxbridge, UB8 1UW	239,600	570.58	C. Rippingale	M. Craxton
Hounslow	°Lampton Road, Hounslow, TW3 4DN	206,500	615.93	R. Kerslake	A. Dhillon
§Islington	†Upper Street, N1 2UD	175,500	744.46	E. W. Dear	J. Burke
§Kensington and Chelsea (RB)	†Hornton Street, W8 7NX	148,800	495.24	R. A. Taylor	P. Warrick
Kingston upon Thames (RB)	Guildhall, Kingston upon Thames KT1 1EU	138,100	569.48	B. Quoroll	D. Twigg
§Lambeth	†Brixton Hill, SW2 1RW	259,200	667.00	Ms H. Rabbatts	J. Denny
§Lewisham	†Catford, SE6 4RU	240,400	593.79	B. Quirk	A. Till
Merton	°London Road, Morden, SM4 5DX	175,100	609.51	Ms S. Charteris	Ms B. Smith
Newham	†East Ham, E6 2RP	226,300	576.00	vacant	W. Brown
Redbridge	†Ilford, IG1 1DD	232,700	557.00	M. J. Frater	R. Barden
Richmond upon Thames	°York Street, Twickenham, TW1 3AA	166,600	683.00	R. L. Harbord	R. King
§Southwark	†Peckham Road, SE5 8UB	229,400	589.73	W. Coomber	A. Graham
Sutton	‡St Nicholas Way, Sutton, SM1 1EA	173,300	572.85	Mrs P. Hughes	R. Gleeson
§Tower Hamlets	107 Commercial Street, E1 6BG	169,600	533.31	Ms S. Pierce	G. Mortuza
Waltham Forest	†Forest Road, Walthamstow, E17 4JF	219,800	671.11	A. Tobias	D. Norman
§Wandsworth	†Wandsworth, SW18 2PU	265,700	259.76	G. K. Jones	Mrs V. Graham

§   Inner London Borough
RB Royal Borough
°   Civic Centre
†   Town Hall
‡   Civic Offices
Source of population statistics: OPCS Monitor PP1 94/2, 26 July 1994
For explanation of council tax, *see* page 526

Wales

The Principality of Wales (Cymru) occupies the extreme west of the central southern portion of the island of Great Britain, with a total area of 8,015 sq. miles (20,758 sq. km): land 7,965 sq. miles (20,628 sq. km); inland water 50 sq. miles (130 sq. km). It is bounded on the north by the Irish Sea, on the south by the Bristol Channel, on the east by the English counties of Cheshire, Shropshire, Hereford and Worcester, and Gloucestershire, and on the west by St George's Channel.

Across the Menai Straits is the island of Ynys Môn (Anglesey) (276 sq. miles), communication with which is facilitated by the Menai Suspension Bridge (1,000 ft long) built by Telford in 1826, and by the tubular railway bridge (1,100 ft long) built by Stephenson in 1850. Holyhead harbour, on Holy Isle (north-west of Anglesey), provides accommodation for ferry services to Dublin (70 miles).

POPULATION

The population at the 1991 Census was 2,811,865 (males 1,356,886; females 1,454,979). The average density of population in 1991 was 1.36 persons per hectare.

RELIEF

Wales is a country of extensive tracts of high plateau and shorter stretches of mountain ranges deeply dissected by river valleys. Lower-lying ground is largely confined to the coastal belt and the lower parts of the valleys. The highest mountains are those of Snowdonia in the north-west (Snowdon, 3,559 ft), Berwyn (Aran Fawddwy, 2,971 ft), Cader Idris (Pen y Gadair, 2,928 ft), Dyfed (Plynlimon, 2,467 ft), and the Black Mountain, Brecon Beacons and Black Forest ranges in the south-east (Carmarthen Van, 2,630 ft, Pen y Fan, 2,906 ft, Waun Fâch, 2,660 ft).

HYDROGRAPHY

The principal river rising in Wales is the Severn (*see* page 537), which flows from the slopes of Plynlimon to the English border. The Wye (130 miles) also rises in the slopes of Plynlimon. The Usk (56 miles) flows into the Bristol Channel, through Gwent. The Dee (70 miles) rises in Bala Lake and flows through the Vale of Llangollen, where an aqueduct (built by Telford in 1805) carries the Pontcysyllte branch of the Shropshire Union Canal across the valley. The estuary of the Dee is the navigable portion, 14 miles in length and about five miles in breadth, and the tide rushes in with dangerous speed over the 'Sands of Dee'. The Towy (68 miles), Teifi (50 miles), Taff (40 miles), Dovey (30 miles), Taf (25 miles) and Conway (24 miles), the last named broad and navigable, are wholly Welsh rivers.

The largest natural lake is Bala (Llyn Tegid) in Gwynedd, nearly four miles long and about one mile wide. Lake Vyrnwy is an artificial reservoir, about the size of Bala, and forms the water supply of Liverpool; Birmingham is supplied from reservoirs in the Elan and Claerwen valleys.

WELSH LANGUAGE

According to the 1991 Census results, the percentage of persons of three years and over able to speak Welsh was:

Clwyd	18.2	Powys	20.2
Dyfed	43.7	S. Glamorgan	6.5
Gwent	2.4	W. Glamorgan	15.0
Gwynedd	61.0		
Mid Glamorgan	8.5	Wales	18.7

The 1991 figure represents a slight decline from 18.9 per cent in 1981 (1971, 20.8 per cent; 1961, 26 per cent).

FLAG

The flag of Wales, the Red Dragon (Y Ddraig Goch), is a red dragon on a field divided white over green (per fess argent and vert a dragon passant gules). The flag was augmented in 1953 by a royal badge on a shield encircled with a riband bearing the words *Ddraig Goch Ddyry Cychwyn* and imperially crowned, but this augmented flag is rarely used.

EARLY HISTORY

The earliest inhabitants of whom there is any record appear to have been subdued or exterminated by the Goidels (a people of Celtic race) in the Bronze Age. A further invasion of Celtic Brythons and Belgae followed in the ensuing Iron Age. The Roman conquest of southern Britain and Wales was for some time successfully opposed by Caratacus (Caractacus or Caradog), chieftain of the Catuvellauni and son of Cunobelinus (Cymbeline). South-east Wales was subjugated and the legionary fortress at Caerleon-on-Usk established by about AD 75–77; the conquest of Wales was completed by Agricola about AD 78. Communications were opened up by the construction of military roads from Chester to Caerleon-on-Usk and Caerwent, and from Chester to Conwy (and thence to Carmarthen and Neath). Christianity was introduced during the Roman occupation, in the fourth century.

ANGLO-SAXON ATTACKS

The Anglo-Saxon invaders of southern Britain drove the Celts into the mountain stronghold of Wales, and into Strathclyde (Cumberland and south-west Scotland) and Cornwall, giving them the name of *Waelisc* (Welsh), meaning 'foreign'. The West Saxons' victory of Deorham (AD 577) isolated Wales from Cornwall and the battle of Chester (AD 613) cut off communication with Strathclyde and northern Britain. In the eighth century the boundaries of the Welsh were further restricted by the annexations of Offa, King of Mercia, and counter-attacks were largely prevented by the construction of an artificial boundary from the Dee to the Wye (Offa's Dyke).

In the ninth century Rhodri Mawr (844–878) united the country and successfully resisted further incursions of the Saxons by land and raids of Norse and Danish pirates by sea, but at his death his three provinces of Gwynedd (north), Powys (mid) and Deheubarth (south) were divided among his three sons, Anarawd, Mervyn and Cadell. Cadell's son Hywel Dda ruled a large part of Wales and codified its laws but the provinces were not united again until the rule of Llewelyn ap Seisyllt (husband of the heiress of Gwynedd) from 1018 to 1023.

THE NORMAN CONQUEST

After the Norman conquest of England, William I created palatine counties along the Welsh frontier, and the Norman barons began to make encroachments into Welsh territory. The Welsh princes recovered many of their losses during the civil wars of Stephen's reign and in the early 13th century Owen Gruffydd, prince of Gwynedd, was the dominant figure in Wales. Under Llywelyn ap Iorwerth (1194–1240) the Welsh united in powerful resistance to English incursions and Llywelyn's privileges and *de facto* independence were recognized in Magna Carta. His grandson, Llywelyn ap Gruffydd, was the last native prince; he was killed in 1282 during hostilities between the Welsh and English, allowing Edward I of England to establish his authority over the country. On 7 February

1301, Edward of Caernarvon, son of Edward I, was created Prince of Wales, a title which has subsequently been borne by the eldest son of the sovereign.

Strong Welsh national feeling continued, expressed in the early 15th century in the rising led by Owain Glyndŵr, but the situation was altered by the accession to the English throne in 1485 of Henry VII of the Welsh House of Tudor. Wales was politically assimilated to England under the Act of Union of 1535, which extended English laws to the Principality and gave it parliamentary representation for the first time.

EISTEDDFOD

The Welsh are a distinct nation, with a language and literature of their own, and the national bardic festival (Eisteddfod), instituted by Prince Rhys ap Griffith in 1176, is still held annually (for date, *see* page 12). These *Eisteddfodau* (sessions) form part of the *Gorsedd* (assembly), which is believed to date from the time of *Prydian*, a ruling prince in an age many centuries before the Christian era.

PRINCIPAL CITIES

CARDIFF

Cardiff (South Glamorgan), at the mouth of the Rivers Taff, Rhymney and Ely, is the capital city of Wales and a major administrative, commercial and business centre. It has many industries, including steel and cigars, and its flourishing port is within the Cardiff Bay area, subject of a major redevelopment until the year 2000.

The many fine buildings include the City Hall, the National Museum of Wales, University Buildings, Law Courts, Welsh Office, County Hall, Police Headquarters, the Temple of Peace and Health, Llandaff Cathedral, the Welsh National Folk Museum at St Fagans, Cardiff Castle, the New Theatre, the Sherman Theatre and the Cardiff College of Music and Drama. More recent buildings include St David's Hall, Cardiff International Arena and World Trade Centre, and the Welsh National Ice Rink.

SWANSEA

Swansea (*Abertawe*) is a city and a seaport of West Glamorgan. The Gower peninsula was brought within the city boundary under local government reform in 1974. The trade of the port includes coal, steel products, containerized goods and the import and export of petroleum products and petrochemicals.

The principal buildings are the Norman Castle (rebuilt *c.*1330), the Royal Institution of South Wales, founded in 1835 (including Library), the University College at Singleton, and the Guildhall, containing the Brangwyn panels. More recent buildings include the Industrial and Maritime Museum, the new Maritime Quarter and Marina and the leisure centre.

Swansea was chartered by the Earl of Warwick, *c.*1158–84, and further charters were granted by King John, Henry III, Edward II, Edward III and James II, Cromwell (two) and the Marcher Lord William de Breos.

Welsh Counties

LORD LIEUTENANTS AND HIGH SHERIFFS

County	Lord Lieutenant	High Sheriff, 1995–6
Clwyd	Sir William Gladstone, Bt.	W. F. Glazebrook
Dyfed	Sir David Mansel Lewis, KCVO	I. W. Jones
Gwent	Sir Richard Hanbury-Tenison, KCVO	R. J. Cleeve
Gwynedd	R. E. Meuric Rees, CBE	W. W. Roberts
Mid Glamorgan	M. A. McLaggan	B. S. Butler
Powys	M. L. Bourdillon	P. English
South Glamorgan	Capt. N. Lloyd-Edwards	J. Wynford Evans
West Glamorgan	R. C. Hastie, OBE	J. D. W. Maclean

COUNTY COUNCILS: AREA, POPULATION, FINANCE

Council	Administrative headquarters	Area (hectares)	*Population 1993	Total demand upon collection fund 1995
Clwyd	Shire Hall, Mold	243,015	415,900	£43,167,000
Dyfed	County Hall, Carmarthen	576,575	351,500	42,213,697
Gwent	County Hall, Cwmbran	137,652	450,300	35,043,000
Gwynedd	County Offices, Caernarfon	386,331	240,200	25,332,000
Mid Glamorgan	County Hall, Cathays Park, Cardiff	101,749	544,300	48,888,683
Powys	County Hall, Llandrindod Wells	507,716	119,900	13,010,068
South Glamorgan	County Hall, Atlantic Wharf, Cardiff	41,622	413,200	33,747,000
West Glamorgan	County Hall, Swansea	81,960	371,200	38,648,000

* *Source:* OPCS Monitor PP1 94/2, 26 July 1994

COUNTY COUNCILS: Officers and Chairman

Council	Chief Executive	County Treasurer	Chairman of County Council
Clwyd	E. R. Davies	A. Bell	R. Davies
Dyfed	W. J. Phillips	H. Morse	W. G. Bennett
Gwent	M. J. Perry	J. P. Walsh	J. T. Kirkwood
Gwynedd	H. V. Thomas	T. D. Heald	L. Edwards
Mid Glamorgan	D. H. Thomas, CBE	L. M. James	L. Lodwig
Powys	N. M. Pringle	†J. McNeil	Mrs M. Roberts
South Glamorgan	B. Davies	°K. Bray	C. V. Watkins
West Glamorgan	A. G. Corless	°S. G. Dunster, OBE	C. J. Crowley

† County Finance Officer
° Director of Finance

District Councils

Small capitals denote City status
§ Denotes Borough status

Council	*Population 1993	Band D charge 1995	Chief Executive	Chairman 1995–6 (a) Mayor (b) Lord Mayor
§Aberconwy, Gwynedd	54,400	£399.83	A. G. Carr	(a) P. C. Evans
Alyn and Deeside, Clwyd	74,700	383.07	D. Salisbury	T. Middlehurst
§Arfon, Gwynedd	56,600	383.38	D. L. Jones	(a) R. M. Roberts
§Blaenau Gwent, Gwent	77,000	345.00	R. Leadbeter, OBE	(a) R. Rowlands
§Brecknock, Powys	41,500	387.50	R. O. Doylend	(a) L. Macho
CARDIFF, South Glamorgan	298,700	336.85	R. L. Knight	(b) T. H. Davies
Carmarthen, Dyfed	56,400	439.03	R. R. Morgan	T. K. Davies
Ceredigion, Dyfed	68,900	450.00	D. Morgan	P. Eklund
§Colwyn, Clwyd	56,800	388.60	C. D. Barker	(a) Mrs S. C. Jones
§Cynon Valley, Mid Glamorgan	65,500	388.62	T. B. Roberts, OBE	(a) D. Barnsley
§Delyn, Clwyd	70,100	397.50	P. J. McGreevy	(a) T. Howarth
§Dinefwr, Dyfed	38,500	444.12	E. W. Harries	(a) Dr D. Owen
Dwyfor, Gwynedd	27,100	383.98	E. M. Royles	M. Parry
Glyndŵr, Clwyd	42,200	370.00	J. H. Parry	A. E. Roberts
§Islwyn, Gwent	67,200	334.07	B. Bird	(a) D. M. Gray
§Llanelli, Dyfed	74,000	494.98	D. B. Parry-Jones	(a) D. T. James
§Lliw Valley, West Glamorgan	64,600	420.00	B. J. Preedy	(a) W. D. Morgan
Meirionnydd, Gwynedd	32,800	390.66	G. W. Hughes	E. Williams
§Merthyr Tydfil, Mid Glamorgan	59,700	395.23	R. V. Morris	(a) R. Thomas
§Monmouth, Gwent	78,400	348.76	G. Cummings	(a) R. W. H. Jones
Montgomeryshire, Powys	54,100	373.96	N. J. Bardsley	H. B. Williams
§Neath, West Glamorgan	65,900	456.66	S. Penny	(a) G. L. Rowlands
§Newport, Gwent	137,000	353.15	R. D. Blair	(a) L. R. Turnbull, CBE
§Ogwr, Mid Glamorgan	134,900	401.32	J. G. Cole	(a) E. M. Evans
§Port Talbot, West Glamorgan	51,400	418.80	P. G. Collins	(a) C. T. Wright
Preseli Pembrokeshire, Dyfed	70,900	427.45	I. W. R. David	J. L. Davies
Radnorshire, Powys	24,200	375.20	G. C. Read	F. Barker
§Rhondda, Mid Glamorgan	78,500	400.06	M. Bradley	(a) D. M. Rees
§Rhuddlan, Clwyd	55,000	392.89	E. O. Lake	(a) J. E. Ainsworth
Rhymney Valley, Mid Glamorgan	104,300	401.33	M. T. Benyon	G. Evans
South Pembrokeshire, Dyfed	42,900	413.03	G. H. James	D. G. Williams
SWANSEA, West Glamorgan	189,300	431.61	A. K. B. Boatswain	(b) G. Phillips
§Taff-Ely, Mid Glamorgan	101,400	268.17	D. Gethin	(a) Mrs J. Davies
§Torfaen, Gwent	90,700	348.57	M. B. Mehta	(a) D. Miller
§Vale of Glamorgan, South Glamorgan	114,500	347.50	M. P. A. Smith	(a) C. B. Dunkley
§Wrexham Maelor, Clwyd	117,100	406.07	R. J. Dutton, CBE	(a) M. G. Morris
§Ynys Môn (Isle of Anglesey), Gwynedd	69,300	394.13	E. L. Gibson	(a) R. Madoc-Jones

* Source: OPCS Monitor PP1 94/2, 26 July 1994
For explanation of council tax, see page 526

New unitary authorities FROM 1 APRIL 1996

Key to map	New county (†county borough)	Current district council (DC)/city council (CC)
1	†Aberconwy and Colwyn	Aberconwy DC Colwyn DC, except Cefnmeiriadog and Trefnant communities
2	Anglesey	Ynys Môn DC
3	†Blaenau Gwent	Blaenau Gwent DC, except Llannelly community
4	†Bridgend	Ogwr DC, except Ewenny, St Bride's Major and Wick communities
5	Caernarfonshire and Merionethshire	Arfon DC Dwyfor DC Meirionnydd DC
6	†Caerphilly	Islwyn DC Rhymney Valley DC
7	Cardiff	Cardiff CC Pentyrch community (Taff-Ely DC)
8	Cardiganshire	Ceredigion DC
9	Carmarthenshire	Carmarthen DC Dinefwr DC Llanelli DC
10	Denbighshire	Rhuddlan DC Communities of Aberwheeler, Betws Gwerfil Goch, Bryneglwys, Clocaenog, Corwen, Cyffylliog, Cynwyd, Denbigh, Derwen, Efenechtyd, Gwyddelwern, Henllan, Llanarmon-yn-Iâl, Llanbedr Dyffryn Clwyd, Llandegla, Llandrillo, Llandyrnog, Llanelidan, Llanfair Dyffryn Clwyd, Llanferres, Llangollen, Llangollen Rural, Llangynhafal, Llanrhaeadr-yng-Nghinmeirch, Llantysilio, Llanynys, Nantglyn, Ruthin (Glyndŵr DC) Communities of Cefnmeiriadog, Trefnant (Colwyn DC)
11	Flintshire	Alyn and Deeside DC Delyn DC
12	†Merthyr Tydfil	Merthyr Tydfil DC
13	Monmouthshire	Monmouth DC Llanelly community (Blaenau Gwent DC)
14	†Neath and Port Talbot	Neath DC Port Talbot DC Communities of Cilybebyll, Cwmllynfell, Gwaun-Cae-Gurwen, Pontardawe, Ystalyfera (Lliw Valley DC)
15	†Newport	Newport DC
16	Pembrokeshire	Preseli Pembrokeshire DC South Pembrokeshire DC Caldey Island and St Margaret's Island
17	Powys	Brecknock DC Montgomeryshire DC Radnorshire DC Communities of Llangedwyn, Llanrhaeadr-ym-Mochnant, Llansilin (Glyndŵr DC)
18	†Rhondda, Cynon, Taff	Cynon Valley DC Rhondda DC Taff-Ely DC, except Pentyrch community
19	Swansea	Swansea CC Communities of Clydach, Gorseinon, Gowerton, Grovesend, Llangyfelach, Llwchwr, Mawr, Penllergaer, Pontardulais, Pont-Lliw (Lliw Valley DC)
20	†Torfaen	Torfaen DC
21	†The Vale of Glamorgan	Vale of Glamorgan DC Communities of Ewenny, St Bride's Major, Wick (Ogwr DC)
22	†Wrexham	Wrexham Maelor DC Communities of Ceiriog Ucha, Chirk, Glyntraian, Llansantffraid Glyn Ceiriog (Glyndŵr DC)

Scotland

The Kingdom of Scotland occupies the northern portion of the main island of Great Britain and includes the Inner and Outer Hebrides, and the Orkney, Shetland, and many other islands. It lies between 60° 51′ 30″ and 54° 38′ N. latitude and between 1° 45′ 32″ and 6° 14′ W. longitude, with England to the south, the Atlantic Ocean on the north and west, and the North Sea on the east.

The greatest length of the mainland (Cape Wrath to the Mull of Galloway) is 274 miles, and the greatest breadth (Buchan Ness to Applecross) is 154 miles. The customary measurement of the island of Great Britain is from the site of John o' Groats house, near Duncansby Head, Caithness, to Land's End, Cornwall, a total distance of 603 miles in a straight line and approximately 900 miles by road.

The total area of Scotland is 30,420 sq. miles (78,789 sq. km); land 29,767 sq. miles (77,097 sq. km), inland water 653 sq. miles (1,692 sq. km).

POPULATION

The population at the 1991 Census was 4,998,567 (males 2,391,961; females 2,606,606). The average density of the population in 1991 was 0.65 persons per hectare.

RELIEF

There are three natural orographic divisions of Scotland. The southern uplands have their highest points in Merrick (2,766 ft), Rhinns of Kells (2,669 ft), and Cairnsmuir of Carsphairn (2,614 ft), in the west; and the Tweedsmuir Hills in the east (Hartfell 2,651 ft, Dollar Law 2,682 ft, Broad Law 2,756 ft).

The central lowlands, formed by the valleys of the Clyde, Forth and Tay, divide the southern uplands from the northern Highlands, which extend almost from the extreme north of the mainland to the central lowlands, and are divided into a northern and a southern system by the Great Glen.

The Grampian Mountains, which entirely cover the southern Highland area, include in the west Ben Nevis (4,406 ft), the highest point in the British Isles, and in the east the Cairngorm Mountains (Cairn Gorm 4,084 ft, Braeriach 4,248 ft, Ben Macdui 4,296 ft). The north-western Highland area contains the mountains of Wester and Easter Ross (Carn Eige 3,880 ft, Sgurr na Lapaich 3,775 ft).

Created, like the central lowlands, by a major geological fault, the Great Glen (60 miles long) runs between Inverness and Fort William, and contains Loch Ness, Loch Oich and Loch Lochy. These are linked to each other and to the north-east and south-west coasts of Scotland by the Caledonian Canal, providing a navigable passage between the Moray Firth and the Inner Hebrides.

HYDROGRAPHY

The western coast is fragmented by peninsulas and islands, and indented by fjords (sea-lochs), the longest of which is Loch Fyne (42 miles long) in Argyll. Although the east coast tends to be less fractured and lower, there are several great drowned inlets (firths), e.g. Firth of Forth, Firth of Tay, Moray Firth, as well as the Firth of Clyde in the west.

The lochs are the principal hydrographic feature. The largest in Scotland and in Britain is Loch Lomond (27 sq. miles), in the Grampian valleys; the longest and deepest is Loch Ness (24 miles long and 800 feet deep), in the Great Glen; and Loch Shin (20 miles long) and Loch Maree in the Highlands.

The longest river is the Tay (117 miles), noted for its salmon. It flows into the North Sea, with Dundee on the

estuary, which is spanned by the Tay Bridge (10,289 ft) opened in 1887 and the Tay Road Bridge (7,365 ft) opened in 1966. Other noted salmon rivers are the Dee (90 miles) which flows into the North Sea at Aberdeen, and the Spey (110 miles), the swiftest flowing river in the British Isles, which flows into Moray Firth. The Tweed, which gave its name to the woollen cloth produced along its banks, marks in the lower stretches of its 96-mile course the border between Scotland and England.

The most important river commercially is the Clyde (106 miles), formed by the junction of the Daer and Portrail water, which flows through the city of Glasgow to the Firth of Clyde. During its course it passes over the picturesque Falls of Clyde, Bonnington Linn (30 ft), Corra Linn (84 ft), Dundaff Linn (10 ft) and Stonebyres Linn (80 ft), above and below Lanark. The Forth (66 miles), upon which stands Edinburgh, the capital, is spanned by the Forth (Railway) Bridge (1890), which is 5,330 feet long, and the Forth (Road) Bridge (1964), which has a total length of 6,156 feet (over water) and a single span of 3,000 feet.

The highest waterfall in Scotland, and the British Isles, is Eas a'Chùal Aluinn with a total height of 658 feet (200 m), which falls from Glas Bheinn in Sutherland. The Falls of Glomach, on a head-stream of the Elchaig in Wester Ross, have a drop of 370 feet.

GAELIC LANGUAGE

According to the 1991 Census, 1.4 per cent of the population of Scotland, mainly in the Highlands and western coastal regions, were able to speak the Scottish form of Gaelic.

FLAG

The flag of Scotland is known as the Saltire. It is a white diagonal cross on a blue field (saltire argent in a field azure) and represents St Andrew, the patron saint of Scotland.

THE SCOTTISH ISLANDS

The Hebrides did not become part of the Kingdom of Scotland until 1266, when they were ceded to Alexander III by Magnus of Norway. Orkney and Shetland fell to the Scottish Crown as a pledge for the unpaid dowry of Margaret of Denmark, wife of James III, in 1468, the Danish claims to suzerainty being relinquished in 1590 when James VI married Anne of Denmark.

ORKNEY

The Orkney Islands (total area 375½ sq. miles) lie about six miles north of the mainland, separated from it by the Pentland Firth. Of the 90 islands and islets (holms and skerries) in the group, about one-third are inhabited.

The total population at the 1991 Census was 19,612; the 1991 populations of the islands shown here include those of smaller islands forming part of the same civil parish.

Mainland, 15,128	Rousay, 291
Burray, 363	Sanday, 533
Eday, 166	Shapinsay, 322
Flotta and Fara, 126	South Ronaldsay, 943
Graemsay and Hoy, 477	Stronsay, 382
North Ronaldsay, 92	Westray, 704
Papa Westray, 85	

The islands are rich in Pictish and Scandinavian remains, the most notable being the Stone Age village of Skara Brae, the burial chamber of Maeshowe, the many brochs (Pictish towers) and St Magnus Cathedral. Scapa Flow, between the Mainland and Hoy, was the war station of the British Grand Fleet from 1914 to 1919 and the scene of the scuttling of the surrendered German High Seas Fleet (21 June, 1919).

Most of the islands are low-lying and fertile, and farming (principally beef cattle) is the main industry. Flotta, to the south of Scapa Flow, is now the site of the oil terminal for the Piper, Claymore and Tartan fields in the North Sea. The capital is Kirkwall (population 6,881) on Mainland.

SHETLAND

The Shetland Islands have a total area of 551 sq. miles and a population at the 1991 Census of 22,522. They lie about 50 miles north of the Orkneys, with Fair Isle about half-way between the two groups. Out Stack, off Muckle Flugga, one mile north of Unst, is the most northerly part of the British Isles (60° 51′ 30″ N. lat.).

There are over 100 islands, of which 16 are inhabited. Populations at the 1991 census were:

Mainland, 17,596	Muckle Roe, 115
Bressay, 352	Trondra, 117
East Burra, 72	Unst, 1,055
Fair Isle, 67	West Burra, 857
Fetlar, 90	Whalsay, 1,041
Housay, 85	Yell, 1,075

Shetland's many archaeological sites include Jarlshof, Mousa and Clickhimin, and its long connection with Scandinavia has resulted in a strong Norse influence on its place-names and dialect.

Industries include fishing, knitwear and farming. In addition to the fishing fleet there are fish processing factories, while the traditional handknitting of Fair Isle and Unst is supplemented now with machine-knitted garments. Farming is mainly crofting, with sheep being raised on the moorland and hills of the islands. Latterly the islands have become an important centre of the North Sea oil industry, with pipelines from the Brent and Ninian fields running to the terminal at Sullom Voe, the largest of its kind in Europe. Lerwick is the main centre for supply services for offshore oil exploration and development.

The capital is Lerwick (population 7,901) on Mainland.

THE HEBRIDES

Until the closing years of the 13th century the Hebrides included other Scottish islands in the Firth of Clyde, the peninsula of Kintyre (Argyllshire), the Isle of Man, and the (Irish) Isle of Rathlin. The origin of the name is stated to be the Greek *Eboudai*, latinized as *Hebudes* by Pliny, and corrupted to its present form. The Norwegian name *Sudreyjar* (Southern Islands) was latinized as *Sodorenses*, a name that survives in the Anglican bishopric of Sodor and Man.

There are over 500 islands and islets, of which about 100 are inhabited, though mountainous terrain and extensive peat bogs mean that only a fraction of the total area is under cultivation. Stone, Bronze and Iron Age settlement has left many remains, including those at Callanish on Lewis, and Norse colonization has influenced language, customs and place-names. Occupations include farming (mostly crofting and stock-raising), fishing and the manufacture of tweeds and other woollens. Tourism is also an important factor in the economy.

The Inner Hebrides lie off the west coast of Scotland and relatively close to the mainland. The largest and best-known is Skye (area 643 sq. miles; pop. 8,868; chief town, Portree), which contains the Cuillin Hills (Sgurr Alasdair 3,257 ft), the Red Hills (Beinn na Caillich 2,403 ft), Bla Bheinn (3,046 ft) and The Storr (2,358 ft). Skye is also famous as the refuge of the Young Pretender in 1746. Other islands in the Highland Region include Raasay (pop. 163), Rum, Eigg and Muck.

Islands in the Strathclyde Region include Arran (pop. 4,474) containing Goat Fell (2,868 ft); Coll and Tiree (pop.

940); Colonsay and Oronsay (pop. 106); Islay (area 235 sq. miles; pop. 3,538); Jura (area 160 sq. miles; pop. 196) with a range of hills culminating in the Paps of Jura (Beinn-an-Oir, 2,576 ft, and Beinn Chaolais, 2,477 ft); and Mull (area 367 sq. miles; pop. 2,708; chief town Tobermory) containing Ben More (3,171 ft).

The Outer Hebrides, separated from the mainland by the Minch, now form the Western Isles Islands Council area (area 1,119 sq. miles; population at the 1991 Census 29,600). The main islands are Lewis with Harris (area 770 sq. miles, pop. 21,737), whose chief town, Stornoway, is the administrative headquarters; North Uist (pop. 1,404); South Uist (pop. 2,106); Baleshare (55); Benbecula (pop. 1,803) and Barra (pop. 1,244). Other inhabited islands include Bernera (262), Berneray (141), Eriskay (179), Grimsay (215), Scalpay (382) and Vatersay (72).

EARLY HISTORY

The Picts, believed to be of non-Aryan origin, seem to have inhabited the whole of northern Britain and to have spread over the north of Ireland. Remains are most frequent in Caithness and Sutherland and the Orkney Islands.

Celts arrived from Belgic Gaul during the latter part of the Bronze Age and in the early Iron Age and, except in the extreme north of the mainland and in the islands, the civilization and speech of the people were definitely Celtic at the time of the Roman invasion of Britain.

THE ROMAN INVASION

In AD 79–80 Julius Agricola extended the Roman conquests in Britain by advancing into Caledonia and building a line of fortifications across the isthmus between the Forth and Clyde, but after a victory at Mons Graupius he was recalled. Hadrian's Wall, mostly complete by AD 130, marked the frontier until about AD 143 when the frontier moved north to the Forth–Clyde isthmus and was secured by the Antonine Wall. From about AD 155 the Antonine Wall was damaged by frequent attacks and by the end of the second century the northern limit of Roman Britain had receded to Hadrian's Wall.

THE SCOTS

After the withdrawal or absorption of the Roman garrison of Britain there were many years of tribal warfare between the Picts and Scots (the Gaelic tribe then dominant in Ireland), the Brythonic Waelisc (Welsh) of Strathclyde (south-west Scotland and Cumberland), and the Anglo-Saxons of Lothian. The Waelisc were isolated from their kinsmen in Wales by the victory of the West Saxons at Chester (613), and towards the close of the ninth century the Scots under Kenneth Mac Alpin became the dominant power in Caledonia. In the reign of Malcolm I (943–954) Strathclyde was brought into subjection, the English lowland kingdom (Lothian) being conquered by Malcolm II (1005–1034).

From the late 11th century until the mid 16th century there were constant wars between Scotland and England, the outstanding figures in the struggle being William Wallace, who defeated the English at Stirling Bridge (1297) and Robert Bruce, who won the battle of Bannockburn (1314). James IV and many of his nobles fell at the disastrous battle of Flodden (1513).

THE JACOBITE REVOLTS

In 1603 James VI of Scotland succeeded Elizabeth I on the throne of England (his mother, Mary Queen of Scots, was the great-granddaughter of Henry VII), his successors reigning as sovereigns of Great Britain, although political union of the two countries did not occur until 1707. After the abdication (by flight) in 1688 of James VII and II, the crown devolved upon William III (grandson of Charles I) and Mary (elder daughter of James VII and II). In 1689 Graham of Claverhouse roused the Highlands on behalf of James VII and II, but died after a military success at Killiecrankie.

After the death of Anne (younger daughter of James VII and II), the throne devolved upon George I (great-grandson of James VI and I). In 1715, armed risings on behalf of James Stuart (the Old Pretender) led to the indecisive battle of Sheriffmuir, and the Jacobite movement died down until 1745, when Charles Stuart (the Young Pretender) defeated the Royalist troops at Prestonpans and advanced to Derby (1746). From Derby, the adherents of 'James VIII and III' (the title claimed for his father by Charles Stuart) fell back on the defensive, and the movement was finally crushed at Culloden (16 April 1746).

PRINCIPAL CITIES

ABERDEEN

Aberdeen, 130 miles north-east of Edinburgh, received its charter as a Royal Burgh in 1179. Scotland's third largest city, Aberdeen is the second largest Scottish fishing port and the main centre for offshore oil exploration and production. It is also an ancient university town and distinguished research centre. Other industries include engineering, food processing, textiles, paper manufacturing and chemicals.

Places of interest include King's College, St Machar's Cathedral, Brig o' Balgownie, Duthie Park and Winter Gardens, Hazlehead Park, the Kirk of St Nicholas, Mercat Cross, Marischal College and Marischal Museum, Provost Skene's House, Art Gallery, James Dun's House, Satrosphere Hands-On Discovery Centre, and Aberdeen Maritime Museum in Provost Ross's House.

DUNDEE

Dundee, a Royal Burgh, is situated on the north bank of the Tay estuary. The city's port and dock installations are important to the offshore oil industry and the airport also provides servicing facilities. Principal industries include textiles, computers and other electronic industries, lasers,

printing, tyre manufacture, food processing, carpets, engineering and clothing manufacture.

The unique City Churches – three churches under one roof, together with the 15th-century St Mary's Tower – are the most prominent architectural feature. Dundee has two historic ships; the Dundee-built RRS *Discovery* which took Capt. Scott to the Antarctic lies alongside Discovery Quay, and the frigate *Unicorn*, the only British-built wooden warship still afloat, is moored in Victoria Dock. Places of interest include Mills Public Observatory and the Tay road and rail bridges.

EDINBURGH

Edinburgh is the capital of and seat of government in Scotland. The city is built on a group of hills and contains in Princes Street one of the most beautiful thoroughfares in the world.

The principal buildings are the Castle, which includes St Margaret's Chapel, the oldest building in Edinburgh, and near it, the Scottish National War Memorial; the Palace of Holyroodhouse; Parliament House, the present seat of the judicature; three universities (Edinburgh, Heriot-Watt, Napier); St Giles' Cathedral (restored 1879–83); St Mary's (Scottish Episcopal) Cathedral (Sir Gilbert Scott); the General Register House (Robert Adam); the National and the Signet Libraries; the National Gallery; the Royal Scottish Academy; the National Portrait Gallery; and the Edinburgh International Conference centre, opened in 1995.

GLASGOW

Glasgow, a Royal Burgh, is the principal commercial and industrial centre in Scotland. The city occupies the north and south banks of the Clyde, formerly one of the chief commercial estuaries in the world. The principal industries include engineering, electronics, finance, chemicals and printing. The city has also developed recently as a tourism and conference centre.

The chief buildings are the 13th-century Gothic Cathedral, the University (Sir Gilbert Scott), the City Chambers, the Royal Concert Hall, St Mungo Museum of Religious Life and Art, Pollok House, the School of Art (Mackintosh), Kelvingrove Art Galleries, the Burrell Collection museum and the Mitchell Library. The city is home to the Scottish National Orchestra, Scottish Opera and Scottish Ballet.

LORD LIEUTENANTS

Region	Title	Name
Borders	Berwickshire	Maj.-Gen. Sir John Swinton, KCVO, OBE
	Roxburgh, Ettrick and Lauderdale	The Duke of Buccleuch and Queensberry, KT, VRD
	Tweeddale	Capt. J. D. B. Younger
Central	Clackmannan	Lt.-Col. R. C. Stewart, CBE, TD
	Stirling and Falkirk	Lt.-Col. J. Stirling of Garden, CBE, TD
Dumfries and Galloway	Dumfries	Capt. R. C. Cunningham-Jardine
	The Stewartry of Kirkcudbright	vacant
	Wigtown	Maj. E. S. Orr Ewing
Fife	Fife	The Earl of Elgin and Kincardine, KT
Grampian	Aberdeenshire	Capt. C. A. Farquharson
	Banffshire	J. A. S. McPherson, CBE
	Kincardineshire	The Viscount of Arbuthnott, CBE, DSC, FRSE
	Morayshire	Air Vice-Marshal G. A. Chesworth, CB, OBE, DFC

Region	Title	Name
Highland	Caithness	vacant
	Inverness	Lt.-Cdr. L. R. D. Mackintosh of Mackintosh, OBE
	Nairn	The Earl of Leven and Melville
	Ross and Cromarty	Capt. R. W. K. Stirling of Fairburn, TD
	Sutherland	Maj.-Gen. D. Houston, CBE
Lothian	East Lothian	Sir Hew Hamilton-Dalrymple, Bt., KCVO
	Midlothian	Capt. G. W. Burnett, LVO
	West Lothian	The Earl of Morton
Strathclyde	Argyll and Bute	vacant
	Ayrshire and Arran	Maj. R. Y. Henderson, TD
	Dumbartonshire	Brig. D. D. G. Hardie, TD
	Lanarkshire	H. B. Sneddon, CBE
	Renfrewshire	The Lord Goold
Tayside	Angus	The Earl of Airlie, KT, GCVO, PC
	Perth and Kinross	Sir David Montgomery, Bt.
Orkney	Orkney	Brig. M. G. Dennison
Shetland	Shetland	J. H. Scott
Western Isles	Western Isles	The Viscount Dunrossil, CMG

The Lord Provosts of the four city districts of Aberdeen, Dundee, Edinburgh and Glasgow are Lord Lieutenants for those districts *ex officio*

Scottish Regions and Islands

REGIONAL AND ISLANDS COUNCILS: Area, Population, Finance

Council	Administrative headquarters	Area (hectares)	Population (latest estimate)	Band D charge 1995	Band D water charge per household 1995
Borders	Newtown St Boswells	471,253	103,881	£413.00	£95.00
Central	Stirling	263,455	273,923	444.00	46.00
Dumfries and Galloway	Dumfries	639,561	147,900	406.00	83.25
Fife	Glenrothes	131,201	352,100	381.89	64.00
Grampian	Aberdeen	869,772	532,500	409.00	89.00
Highland	Inverness	2,539,759	206,900	542.12	91.10
Lothian	Edinburgh	171,595	753,900	490.00	92.00
Orkney	Kirkwall	97,581	20,619	440.00	123.00
Shetland	Lerwick	143,268	22,522	428.22	118.36
Strathclyde	Glasgow	1,350,283	2,287,000	451.00	87.00
Tayside	Dundee	749,165	395,000	475.00	74.00
Western Isles	Stornoway, Lewis	289,798	29,400	524.00	186.00

REGIONAL AND ISLAND COUNCILS: Officers and Conveners

Council	Chief Executive	Director of Finance	Convener
Borders	K. J. Clark, CBE	P. Jeary	The Earl of Minto, OBE
Central	D. Sinclair	S. C. Craig	Mrs A. Wallace
Dumfries and Galloway	I. F. Smith	J. C. Stewart	A. Baldwick
Fife	Dr J. A. Markland	A. E. Taylor	R. Gough, CBE
Grampian	J. C. Liddell	R. Dingwall	Ms R. Kemp
Highland	R. H. Stevenson	A. M. Jamieson	D. J. McPherson, CBE
Lothian	T. Aitchison	J. Clark	E. Milligan
Orkney	R. H. Gilbert	D. A. Robertson	H. Halcro-Johnston
Shetland	M. E. Green	A. Matthews	L. S. Smith
Strathclyde	N. McIntosh, CBE	A. Gillespie	W. Perry
Tayside	J. Jenkins	I. B. McIver	Mrs F. E. Duncan
Western Isles	B. W. Stewart	R. Bennie	D. M. Mackay

District Councils

Council	Administrative headquarters	Population (latest estimate)	Band D charge 1995	Chief Executive	Chairman (a) Convener (b) Provost (c) Lord Provost
Aberdeen City (5)	Aberdeen	218,220	£190.00	A. Mearns	(c) J. Wyness
Angus (9)	Forfar	97,420	99.00	P. B. Regan	(b) B. M. C. Milne
Annandale and Eskdale (3)	Annan	37,000	124.00	§W. J. Davidson	(a) D. T. R. Wilson
Argyll and Bute (8)	Lochgilphead	63,260	188.00	M. A. J. Gossip, CBE	G. McMillan
Badenoch and Strathspey (6)	Kingussie	11,000	99.00	Mrs J. M. Fraser	A. Gordon
Banff and Buchan (5)	Banff	88,460	99.00	R. M. Blackburn	(a) W. R. Cruickshank, OBE
Bearsden and Milngavie (8)	Bearsden	41,000	130.00	I. C. Laurie	(b) I. J. Miller
Berwickshire (1)	Duns	19,420	58.50	R. A. Christie	Capt. J. Evans
Caithness (6)	Wick	26,080	86.00	A. Beattie	(a) J. M. Young, OBE
Clackmannan (2)	Alloa	47,679	186.00	R. Allan	(a) J. Watson
Clydebank (8)	Clydebank	46,580	167.00	J. T. McNally	(b) J. McAllister
Clydesdale (8)	Lanark	58,290	147.78	R. Russell	(a) Mrs E. Logan
Cumbernauld and Kilsyth (8)	Cumbernauld	63,980	186.00	J. Hutton	(b) C. Combe
Cumnock and Doon Valley (8)	Cumnock	42,594	200.00	K. W. Inch	(a) E. Ross
Cunninghame (8)	Irvine	137,000	165.00	B. Devine	(a) S. Dewar
Dumbarton (8)	Dumbarton	77,222	199.00	‡W. Connelly (acting)	(b) P. O'Neill
Dundee City (9)	Dundee	155,000	233.00	A. Stephen	(c) vacant
Dunfermline (4)	Dunfermline	130,060	124.00	K. Drennan	(b) Ms M. Millar
East Kilbride (8)	East Kilbride	85,180	169.00	J. Jarvie	(b) S. Crawford
East Lothian (7)	Haddington	85,500	156.00	M. Duncan	G. M. Wanless
Eastwood (8)	Giffnock	61,000	99.00	M. D. Henry	(b) L. M. Rosin
Edinburgh City (7)	Edinburgh	443,600	245.36	W. M. Blythe	(c) Rt. Hon. N. Irons, CBE
Ettrick and Lauderdale (1)	Galashiels	35,490	108.00	C. M. Anderson	(b) W. Hardie
Falkirk (2)	Falkirk	142,800	104.00	W. Weir	(b) J. Constable
Glasgow City (8)	Glasgow	681,470	225.00	T. J. Monaghan	(c) T. Dingwall
Gordon (5)	Inverurie	81,768	90.00	P. Donaldson	(b) R. G. Bisset
Hamilton (8)	Hamilton	105,202	194.00	M. Docherty	(b) R. Newberry
Inverclyde (8)	Greenock	89,990	167.00	R. McPherson	(b) A. Robertson
Inverness (6)	Inverness	63,400	118.00	B. Wilson	(b) W. A. E. Fraser
Kilmarnock and Loudoun (8)	Kilmarnock	79,861	151.00	R. W. Jenner	(b) D. Coffey
Kincardine and Deeside (5)	Stonehaven	55,960	64.00	T. Hyder	(a) Mrs D. Ewing
Kirkcaldy (4)	Kirkcaldy	148,630	163.00	§D. A. Watt	(a) R. King, OBE
Kyle and Carrick (8)	Ayr	112,658	220.00	I. R. D. Smillie	(b) G. T. Macdonald
Lochaber (6)	Fort William	19,400	142.00	N. A. Mackenzie	N. M. Clark
Midlothian (7)	Dalkeith	79,910	150.00	T. Muir	(a) D. Molloy
Monklands (8)	Coatbridge	102,590	233.00	M. V. P. Hart	(b) E. Burns
Moray (5)	Elgin	83,616	99.00	J. P. Summers	(a) E. Aldridge
Motherwell (8)	Motherwell	143,730	179.00	J. Bonomy	(b) W. Wilson
Nairn (6)	Nairn	10,940	114.00	†A. M. Kerr	(b) J. Cattanach
Nithsdale (3)	Dumfries	57,310	129.00	T. Orr	(b) Mrs J. McMurdo
North-East Fife (4)	Cupar	66,888	158.00	D. M. Abbott	Mrs I. M. Cater
Perth and Kinross (9)	Perth	130,490	110.00	H. Robertson	(b) Mrs J. McCormack
Renfrew (8)	Paisley	201,690	186.00	*A. I. Cowe	(b) W. Orr
Ross and Cromarty (6)	Dingwall	50,000	149.00	R. Mair	(a) Maj. A. Cameron, MBE
Roxburgh (1)	Hawick	35,230	107.00	†W. R. Millan	Mrs M. S. Turnbull
Skye and Lochalsh (6)	Portree	11,970	115.00	D. H. Noble	J. F. Munro
Stewartry (3)	Kirkcudbright	23,690	89.00	J. C. Howie	(a) J. Nelson, MBE, TD
Stirling (2)	Stirling	81,630	133.00	G. Bonner	(a) Mrs P. Greenhill
Strathkelvin (8)	Kirkintilloch	85,670	240.00	C. Mallon	(b) R. M. Coyle
Sutherland (6)	Golspie	13,096	102.00	†J. Allison	(a) Mrs A. Magee
Tweeddale (1)	Peebles	15,560	90.00	G. H. T. Garvie	D. Suckling
West Lothian (7)	Bathgate	147,870	91.00	A. M. Linkston	(a) J. McGinley
Wigtown (3)	Stranraer	30,077	123.00	A. Geddes	W. Service

Regions
(1) Borders
(2) Central
(3) Dumfries and Galloway
(4) Fife
(5) Grampian
(6) Highland
(7) Lothian
(8) Strathclyde
(9) Tayside

§ General Manager
‡ District Secretary
† Director of Administration
* Managing Director

For explanation of council tax, *see* page 526

New unitary authorities FROM 1 APRIL 1996

Key to map	New council (*extant council)	Current district council (DC)/city council (CC)
1	Aberdeenshire	Banff and Buchan DC
		Gordon DC
		Kincardine and Deeside DC
2	Angus	Angus DC
		Monifieth and most of area around City of Dundee formerly in county of Angus (City of Dundee CC)
3	Argyll and Bute	Argyll and Bute DC
		Cardross, Helensburgh, Luss and Arden areas (Dumbarton DC)
4	Borders	Berwickshire DC
		Ettrick and Lauderdale DC
		Roxburgh DC
		Tweeddale DC
5	City of Aberdeen	City of Aberdeen CC
6	City of Dundee	City of Dundee CC, except Invergowrie/Longforgan, Monifieth and most of area around City
7	City of Edinburgh	City of Edinburgh CC
8	City of Glasgow	City of Glasgow CC, except Cambuslang, Rutherglen areas
9	Clackmannan	Clackmannan DC
10	Dumbarton and Clydebank	Clydebank DC
		Dumbarton DC, except Cardross, Helensburgh, Luss and Arden areas
11	Dumfries and Galloway	Annandale and Eskdale DC
		Nithsdale DC
		Stewartry DC
		Wigtown DC
12	East Ayrshire	Cumnock and Doon Valley DC
		Kilmarnock and Loudoun DC
13	East Dunbartonshire	Bearsden and Milngavie DC
		Strathkelvin DC, except Auchinleck, Chryston, Moodiesburn, Muirhead, Stepps areas
14	East Lothian	East Lothian DC
15	East Renfrewshire	Eastwood DC
		Barrhead, Neilston, Uplawmoor areas (Renfrew DC)
16	Falkirk	Falkirk DC
17	Fife	Dunfermline DC
		Kirkcaldy DC
		North East Fife DC
18	Highland	Badenoch and Strathspey DC
		Caithness DC
		Inverness DC
		Lochaber DC
		Nairn DC
		Ross and Cromarty DC
		Skye and Lochalsh DC
		Sutherland DC
19	Inverclyde	Inverclyde DC
20	Midlothian	Midlothian DC
21	Moray	Moray DC
22	North Ayrshire	Cunninghame DC
23	North Lanarkshire	Cumbernauld and Kilsyth DC
		Monklands DC
		Motherwell DC
		Auchinleck, Chryston, Moodiesburn, Muirhead, Stepps areas (Strathkelvin DC)
24	*Orkney Islands Council	Orkney Islands Council
25	Perthshire and Kinross	Perth and Kinross DC
		Invergowrie/Longforgan area formerly in the county of Perth (City of Dundee CC)
26	Renfrewshire	Renfrew DC, except Barrhead, Neilston, Uplawmoor areas
27	*Shetland Islands Council	Shetland Islands Council
28	South Ayrshire	Kyle and Carrick DC
29	South Lanarkshire	Clydesdale DC
		East Kilbride DC
		Hamilton DC
		Cambuslang, Rutherglen areas (City of Glasgow CC)
30	Stirling	Stirling DC
31	*Western Isles Islands Council	Western Isles Islands Council
32	West Lothian	West Lothian DC

Northern Ireland

Northern Ireland has a total area of 5,461 sq. miles (14,144 sq. km): land, 5,215 sq. miles (13,506 sq. km); inland water and tideways, 246 sq. miles (638 sq. km).

The population of Northern Ireland at the 1991 Census was 1,577,836 (males, 769,071; females, 808,765). The average density of population in 1991 was 1.11 persons per hectare.

In 1991 the number of persons in the various religious denominations (expressed as percentages of the total population) were: Roman Catholic, 38.4; Presbyterian, 21.4; Church of Ireland, 17.7; Methodist, 3.8; others 7.7; none, 3.7; not stated, 7.3.

PRINCIPAL CITIES

BELFAST

Belfast, the administrative centre of Northern Ireland, is situated at the mouth of the River Lagan at its entrance to Belfast Lough. The city grew, owing to its easy access by sea to Scottish coal and iron, to be a great industrial centre.

The principal buildings are of a relatively recent date and include the Parliament Buildings at Stormont, the City Hall, the Law Courts, the Public Library and the Museum and Art Gallery.

Belfast received its first charter of incorporation in 1613 and was created a city in 1888; the title of Lord Mayor was conferred in 1892.

LONDONDERRY

Londonderry (originally Derry) is situated on the River Foyle, and has important associations with the City of London. The Irish Society was created by the City of London in 1610, and under its royal charter of 1613 it fortified the city and was for long closely associated with its administration. Because of this connection the city was incorporated in 1613 under the new name of Londonderry.

The city is famous for the great siege of 1688–9, when for 105 days the town held out against the forces of James II until relieved by sea. The city walls are still intact and form a circuit of almost a mile around the old city.

Interesting buildings are the Protestant Cathedral of St Columb's (1633) and the Guildhall, reconstructed in 1912 and containing a number of beautiful stained glass windows, many of which were presented by the livery companies of London.

CONSTITUTION AND GOVERNMENT

As part of the United Kingdom, Northern Ireland is subject to the same fundamental constitutional provisions which apply to the rest of the United Kingdom. It had its own parliament and government from 1921 to 1972, but after increasing civil unrest the Northern Ireland (Temporary Provisions) Act 1972 transferred the legislative and executive powers of the Northern Ireland parliament and government to the UK Parliament and a Secretary of State. The Northern Ireland Constitution Act 1973 provided for devolution in Northern Ireland through an assembly and executive, and in January 1974 a power-sharing executive was formed by the Northern Ireland political parties. This arrangement collapsed in May 1974 and since then Northern Ireland has been governed by direct rule under the provisions of the Northern Ireland Act 1974. This allows Parliament to approve all laws for Northern Ireland and places the Northern Ireland department under the direction and control of the Secretary of State for Northern Ireland.

Attempts have been made by successive governments to find a means of restoring a widely acceptable form of devolved government to Northern Ireland. A 78-member Assembly was elected by proportional representation in 1982. However, it was dissolved four years later after it failed to discharge its responsibilities of making proposals for the resumption of devolved government and of monitoring the work of the Northern Ireland departments.

In 1985 the governments of the United Kingdom and the Republic of Ireland signed the Anglo-Irish Agreement, establishing an intergovernmental conference in which the Irish government may put forward views and proposals on certain aspects of Northern Ireland affairs.

Discussions between the British and Irish governments and the four main Northern Ireland parties began in 1991. It was agreed that any political settlement would need to address three key relationships: those within Northern Ireland; those within the island of Ireland (north/south); and those between the British and Irish governments (east/west). Although round table talks ended in November 1992 the process has continued since September 1993 as separate bilateral discussions with three of the Northern Ireland parties (the DUP have declined to participate).

On 15 December 1993 the British and Irish governments published the Joint Declaration complementing the political talks, and making clear that any settlement would need to be founded on principles of democracy and consent. The declaration also stated that all democratically mandated parties could be involved in political talks as long as they permanently renounce paramilitary violence.

The provisional IRA and loyalist paramilitary groups announced cease-fires on 31 August and 13 October 1994 respectively. The Government subsequently initiated a series of separate exploratory meetings with Sinn Fein and loyalist representatives in December 1994. The purposes of these are: to explore the basis upon which Sinn Fein and the loyalist representatives would come to be admitted to an inclusive political talks process; to exchange views on how they would be able to play the same role as the current constitutional parties in the public life of Northern Ireland; and to examine the practical consequences of the ending of violence.

On 22 February 1995 the Prime Minister launched *A Framework for Accountable Government in Northern Ireland* and, with the Irish Prime Minister, *A New Framework for Agreement*. These outline what a comprehensive political settlement might look like. The ideas are not intended to be imposed, but to facilitate multilateral dialogue involving the Northern Ireland parties and the British Government. To this end the Secretary of State for Northern Ireland (Sir Patrick Mayhew) has initiated separate bilateral meetings with the leaders of the four main parties to discuss issues on which agreement must be reached if there is to be a widely acceptable settlement.

The Government had previously given an undertaking to submit the final outcome of the political talks to the electorate of Northern Ireland for approval in a referendum.

FLAG

The official national flag of Northern Ireland is now the Union Flag. The flag formerly in use (a white, six-pointed star in the centre of a red cross on a white field, enclosing a red hand and surmounted by a crown) has not been used since the imposition of direct rule.

ECONOMY

FINANCE

Taxation in Northern Ireland is largely imposed and collected by the United Kingdom government. After deducting the cost of collection and of Northern Ireland's contributions to the European Community the balance, known as the Attributed Share of Taxation, is paid over to the Northern Ireland Consolidated Fund. Northern Ireland's revenue is insufficient to meet its expenditure and is supplemented by a grant-in-aid.

	1994–5*	1995–6**
Public income	£6,234,820,965	£6,656,360,000
Public expenditure	6,234,369,648	6,656,360,000

* Outturn
** Estimate

PRODUCTION

The products of the engineering, shipbuilding and aircraft industries, which employed 31,000 persons in 1992, were valued at £1,632 million. The textile industries, employing about 9,700 persons, produced products valued at approxi-mately £430 million. The food and drink industry, employing about 22,200 persons, produced goods valued at £3,680 million.

In 1994 1,455 persons were employed in mining and quarrying operations in Northern Ireland and the minerals raised (21,746,172 tonnes) were valued at £48,821,155.

COMMUNICATIONS

The total tonnage handled by Northern Ireland ports in 1994 was 20 million. Regular ferry, freight and container services operate to ports in Great Britain and Europe from 18 ports, including Belfast, Coleraine, Larne, Londonderry and Warrenpoint.

The Northern Ireland Transport Holding Company is largely responsible for the supervision of the subsidiary companies, Ulsterbus and Citybus (which operate the public road passenger services) and Northern Ireland Railways. Road freight services are also provided by a large number of hauliers operating competitively under licence.

Belfast International Airport was privatized in July 1994. It has substantial passenger and freight handling facilities and provides scheduled and chartered services on domestic and international routes.

Scheduled services also operate from Belfast City Airport to 21 UK destinations and from Eglinton Airport (Londonderry) to Glasgow, Manchester and to Belfast, providing links to many of the locations serviced by BCA.

Northern Ireland Counties

County	Area* (sq. miles)	Lord Lieutenant	High Sheriff, 1995
Antrim	1,093	The Lord O'Neill, TD	Dr J. H. H. Stewart
‡Belfast City	25	Col. J. E. Wilson, OBE	J. A. Coggle
Armagh	484	The Earl of Caledon	J. C. K. McGowan
Down	945	Col. W. S. Brownlow	The Hon. David Faulkner
Fermanagh	647	The Earl of Erne	The Viscount Brookeborough
†Londonderry	798	Sir Michael McCorkell, KCVO, OBE, TD	Dr J. W. Moore
‡Londonderry City	3.4	J. T. Eaton, CBE, TD	M. G. A. Black
Tyrone	1,211	The Duke of Abercorn	W. R. C. Butler

* Excluding inland waters and tideways
‡ Denotes County Borough
† Excluding the City of Londonderry

District Councils

SMALL CAPITALS denotes CITY status
§ Denotes Borough Council

Council	Population (30 June 1993)	Net Annual Value	Council Clerk	Chairman †Mayor 1995
§Antrim, Co. Antrim	45,600	£7,215,582	S. J. Magee	†T. E. Wallace
§Ards, Co. Down	66,200	8,207,468	D. J. Fallows	†J. Shields
ARMAGH, Co. Armagh	51,700	5,462,737	D. R. D. Mitchell	†Mrs M. H. Black
§Ballymena, Co. Antrim	56,900	8,800,487	M. G. Rankin	†Revd R. Coulter
§Ballymoney, Co. Antrim	24,400	2,739,958	J. C. Alderdice	†C. J. Cousley
Banbridge, Co. Down	36,600	4,230,875	R. Gilmore	W. M. McFadden
Belfast, Co. Antrim and Co. Down	287,200	57,741,003	B. Hanna	Revd E. Smyth (Lord Mayor)
§Carrickfergus, Co. Antrim	34,500	4,758,471	R. Boyd	†W. Hamilton

Council	Population (30 June 1993)	Net Annual Value	Council Clerk	Chairman †Mayor 1995
§Castlereagh, Co. Down	63,000	£8,517,328	J. White	†G. T. A. Dillon
§Coleraine, Co. Londonderry	53,600	7,987,226	W. E. Andrews	†Mrs P. E. A. Armitage
Cookstown, Co. Tyrone	30,900	3,268,255	M. McGuckin	S. A. Glasgow
§Craigavon, Co. Armagh	76,600	11,042,817	E. A. McKinley	†Mrs M. E. Crozier
Derry, Co. Londonderry	99,500	13,072,434	T. J. Keanie	†J. Kerr
Down, Co. Down	59,300	6,420,479	O. O'Connor	J. A. Doris
Dungannon, Co. Tyrone	45,500	4,943,234	W. J. Beattie	J. I. Cavanagh N. R. D. Mulligan
Fermanagh, Co. Fermanagh	54,200	6,189,320	G. Burns, MBE	S. Foster
§Larne, Co. Antrim	29,800	4,086,514	G. McKinley	†S. C. McAllister
§Limavady, Co. Londonderry	29,500	3,030,208	J. K. Stevenson	†B. Doherty
§Lisburn, Co. Antrim and Co. Down	101,900	14,291,448	M. S. Fielding	†W. H. Lewis
Magherafelt, Co. Londonderry	36,300	3,784,870	J. A. McLaughlin	J. J. Hurl
Moyle, Co. Antrim	14,700	1,592,031	R. G. Lewis	M. McSparran
Newry and Mourne, Co. Down and Co. Armagh	81,700	8,608,632	K. O'Neill	P. R. McElroy
§Newtownabbey, Co. Antrim	77,700	11,713,053	J. Campbell	†A. Beattie
§North Down, Co. Down	72,800	10,192,551	A. McDowell	†Mrs S. K. O'Brien
Omagh, Co. Tyrone	45,500	4,822,144	J. P. McKinney	Mrs A. Gormley
Strabane, Co. Tyrone	35,700	3,271,817	Dr V. R. Eakin	E. Turner

Patron Saints

ST GEORGE
Patron Saint of England

St George is believed to have been born in Cappadocia, of Christian parents, in the latter part of the third century and to have served with distinction as a soldier under the Emperor Diocletian, including a visit to England on a military mission. When the persecution of Christians was ordered, St George sought a personal interview to remonstrate with the Emperor and after a profession of faith resigned his military commission. Arrest and torture followed and he was martyred at Nicomedia on 23 April 303, a day ordered to be kept in remembrance as a national festival by the Council of Oxford in 1222, although it was not until the reign of Edward III that he was made patron saint of England.

St George's connection with a dragon seems to date from the close of the sixth century and to be due to the transfer of his remains from Nicomedia to Lydda, close to the scene of the legendary exploit of Perseus in rescuing Andromeda and slaying the sea monster, credit for which became attached to the Christian martyr.

ST DAVID
Patron Saint of Wales

St David is believed to have been born towards the beginning and to have died towards the end of the sixth century. St David was an eloquent preacher, who founded the monastery at Menevia, now St David's. He became the patron of Wales, but there is no record of any papal canonization before 1181. His annual festival is observed on 1 March.

ST ANDREW
Patron Saint of Scotland

St Andrew, one of the Christian Apostles and brother of Simon Peter, was born at Bethsaida on the Sea of Galilee and lived at Capernaum. He preached the Gospel in Asia Minor and in Scythia along the shores of the Black Sea and became the patron saint of Russia. It is believed that he suffered crucifixion at Patras in Achaea, on a *crux decussata* (now known as St Andrew's Cross) and that his relics were removed from Patras to Constantinople and thence to St Andrews, probably in the eighth century, since which time he has been the patron saint of Scotland. The festival of St Andrew is held on 30 November.

ST PATRICK
Patron Saint of Ireland

St Patrick was born, probably in England, about 389 and was carried off to Ireland as a slave about 16 years later, escaping to Gaul at the age of 22. He was ordained deacon at Auxerre and having been consecrated Bishop in 432 was dispatched to Wicklow to reorganize the Christian communities in Ireland. He founded the see of Armagh and introduced Latin into Ireland as the language of the Church. He died *c.*461 and his festival is celebrated on 17 March.

The Isle of Man

Ellan Vannin

The Isle of Man is an island situated in the Irish Sea, in latitude 54° 3'–54° 25' N. and longitude 4° 18'–4° 47' W., nearly equidistant from England, Scotland and Ireland. Although the early inhabitants were of Celtic origin, the Isle of Man was part of the Norwegian Kingdom of the Hebrides until 1266, when this was ceded to Scotland. Subsequently granted to the Stanleys (Earls of Derby) in the 15th century and later to the Dukes of Atholl, it was brought under the administration of the Crown in 1765. The island forms the bishopric of Sodor and Man.

The total land area is 221 sq. miles (572 sq. km). The report on the 1991 Census showed a resident population of 69,788 (males, 33,693; females, 36,095). The main language in use is English. There are no remaining native speakers of Manx Gaelic but 643 people are able to speak the language.

CAPITAL – ΨDouglas; population (1991), 22,214. ΨCastletown (3,152) is the ancient capital; the other towns are ΨPeel (3,829) and ΨRamsey (6,496)

FLAG – A red flag charged with three conjoined armoured legs in white and gold

TYNWALD DAY – 5 July.

GOVERNMENT

The Isle of Man is a self-governing Crown dependency, having its own parliamentary, legal and administrative system. The British Government is responsible for international relations and defence. Under the UK Act of Accession, Protocol 3, the island's relationship with the European Community is limited to trade alone and does not extend to financial aid. The Lieutenant-Governor is The Queen's personal representative in the island.

The legislature, Tynwald, is the oldest parliament in the world in continuous existence. It has two branches: the Legislative Council and the House of Keys. The Council consists of the President of Tynwald, the Bishop of Sodor and Man, the Attorney-General (who does not have a vote) and eight members elected by the House of Keys. The House of Keys has 24 members, elected by universal adult suffrage. The branches sit separately to consider legislation and sit together, as Tynwald Court, for most other parliamentary purposes.

The presiding officer in Tynwald Court is the President of Tynwald, elected by the members, who also presides over sittings of the Legislative Council. The presiding officer of the House of Keys is Mr Speaker, who is elected by members of the House.

The principal members of the Manx Government are the Chief Minister and nine departmental ministers, who comprise the Council of Ministers.

Lieutenant-Governor, His Excellency Sir Timothy Daunt, KCMG
   ADC to the Lieutenant-Governor, M. M. Wood
President of Tynwald, The Hon. Sir Charles Kerruish, OBE
Speaker, House of Keys, The Hon. J. C. Cain
The First Deemster and Clerk of the Rolls, His Honour J. W. Corrin, CBE
Clerk of Tynwald, Secretary to the House of Keys and Counsel to the Speaker, Prof. T. St J. N. Bates
Clerk of Legislative Council and Clerk Assistant of Tynwald, T. A. Bawden
Attorney-General, J. M. Kerruish, QC
Chief Minister, The Hon. M. R. Walker, CBE
Chief Secretary, J. F. Kissack
Chief Financial Officer, J. A. Cashen

ECONOMY

Most of the income generated in the island is earned in the services sector with financial and business services being considerably larger than the traditional industry of tourism. Manufacturing industry is also a major generator of income whilst the island's other traditional industries of agriculture and fishing now play a smaller role in the economy.

Under the terms of Protocol 3, the island has free access to EC markets for its products.

A 20-acre freeport has been developed adjacent to the main airport at Ronaldsway.

The island's unemployment rate is approximately 4 per cent and price inflation is around 3 per cent per annum.

FINANCE

The island's Budget for 1995–6 provided for net expenditure of £211,348,000. The principal sources of government revenue are taxes on income and expenditure. Income tax is payable at a rate of 15 per cent on the first £17,500 of taxable income of resident individuals and 20 per cent on the balance, after personal allowances. The rate of income tax is 20 per cent on the whole taxable income of non-residents and companies. By agreement with the British Government, the island keeps most of its rates of indirect taxation (VAT and duties) the same as those in the United Kingdom, but this agreement may be terminated by either party. However, VAT on tourist accommodation is charged at 5 per cent. A reciprocal agreement on national insurance benefits and pensions exists between the Governments of the Isle of Man and the United Kingdom. Taxes are also charged on property (rates), but these are comparatively low.

The major government expenditure items are health, social security and education, which account for 60 per cent of the government budget. The island makes a voluntary annual contribution to the United Kingdom for defence and other external services.

Although the island has a limited relationship with the European Community, it neither contributes money to nor receives funds from the EC budget.

The Channel Islands

The Channel Islands, situated off the north-west coast of France (at distances of from ten to 30 miles), are the only portions of the Dukedom of Normandy still belonging to the Crown, to which they have been attached since the Conquest. They were the only British territory to come under German occupation during the Second World War, following invasion on 30 June to 1 July 1940. The islands were relieved by British forces on 9 May 1945, and 9 May (Liberation Day) is now observed as a bank and public holiday.

The islands consist of Jersey (28,717 acres/11,630 ha), Guernsey (15,654 acres/6,340 ha), and the dependencies of Guernsey: Alderney (1,962 acres/795 ha), Brechou (74/30), Great Sark (1,035/419), Little Sark (239/97), Herm (320/130), Jethou (44/18) and Lihou (38/15) – a total of 48,083 acres/19,474 ha, or 75 sq. miles/194 sq. km. In 1991 the population of Jersey was 84,082; and of Guernsey, 58,867; Alderney, 2,297 and Sark, 575. The official languages are English and French but French is being supplanted by English, which is the language in daily use. In country districts of Jersey and Guernsey and throughout Sark a Norman-French *patois* is also in use, though to a declining extent.

GOVERNMENT

The islands are Crown dependencies with their own legislative assemblies (the States in Jersey, Guernsey and Alderney, and the Court of Chief Pleas in Sark), and systems of local administration and of law, and their own courts. Acts passed by the States require the sanction of The Queen-in-Council. The British Government is responsible for defence and international relations. The Channel Islands have trading rights alone within the European Community; these rights do not include financial aid.

In both Bailiwicks the Lieutenant-Governor and Commander-in-Chief, who is appointed by the Crown, is the personal representative of The Queen and the channel of communication between the Crown (via the Privy Council) and the island's government.

The government of each Bailiwick is conducted by committees appointed by the States. Justice is administered by the Royal Courts of Jersey and Guernsey, each consisting of the Bailiff and 12 elected Jurats. The Bailiffs of Jersey and Guernsey, appointed by the Crown, are President of the States and of the Royal Courts of their respective islands.

Each Bailiwick constitutes a deanery under the jurisdiction of the Bishop of Winchester (*see* Index).

ECONOMY

A mild climate and good soil have led to the development of intensive systems of agriculture and horticulture, which form a significant part of the economy. Equally important are invisible earnings, principally from tourism and banking and finance, the low rate of income tax (20p in the £ in Jersey and Guernsey; no tax of any kind in Sark) and the absence of super-tax and death duties making the islands a popular tax-haven.

Principal exports are agricultural produce and flowers; imports are chiefly machinery, manufactured goods, food, fuel and chemicals. Trade with the UK is regarded as internal.

British currency is legal tender in the Channel Islands but each Bailiwick issues its own coins and notes (*see* page 612). They also issue their own postage stamps; UK stamps are not valid.

JERSEY

Lieutenant-Governor and Commander-in-Chief of Jersey, His Excellency Gen. Sir Michael Wilkes, KCB, CBE, *apptd* 1995
  Secretary and ADC, Col. A. J. C. Woodrow, OBE
Bailiff of Jersey, P. M. Bailhache
Deputy Bailiff, F. C. Hamon
Attorney-General, M. C. St J. Burt, QC
Receiver-General, Gp Capt R. Green, OBE
Solicitor-General, Miss S. C. Nicolle, QC
Greffier of the States, G. H. C. Coppock
States Treasurer, G. M. Baird

FINANCE

Year to 31 Dec.	1993	1994
Revenue income	£383,743,650	£393,418,443
Revenue expenditure	338,598,976	356,827,170
Capital expenditure	48,304,889	74,762,593
Public debt	0	0

CHIEF TOWN – ΨSt Helier, on the south coast of Jersey
FLAG – A white field charged with a red saltire cross, and the arms of Jersey in the upper centre

GUERNSEY AND DEPENDENCIES

Lieutenant-Governor and Commander-in-Chief of the Bailiwick of Guernsey and its Dependencies, His Excellency Vice-Adm. Sir John Coward, KCB, DSO, *apptd* 1994
  Secretary and ADC, Capt. D. P. L. Hodgetts
Bailiff of Guernsey, Sir Graham Dorey
Deputy Bailiff, de V. G. Carey
HM Procureur and Receiver-General, A. C. K. Day, QC
HM Comptroller, G. R. Rowland, QC
States Supervisor, M. J. Brown

FINANCE

Year to 31 Dec.	1993	1994
Revenue	£158,659,600	£164,719,000
Expenditure	148,953,206	143,957,000

CHIEF TOWNS – ΨSt Peter Port, on the east coast of Guernsey; St Anne on Alderney
FLAG – White, bearing a red cross of St George, with a gold cross overall in the centre

ALDERNEY
President of the States, G. W. Baron
Clerk of the States, D. V. Jenkins
Clerk of the Court, A. Johnson

SARK
Seigneur of Sark, J. M. Beaumont
The Seneschal, L. P. de Carteret
The Greffier, J. P. Hamon

OTHER DEPENDENCIES
Brechou, Lihou and Jethou are leased by the Crown. Herm is leased by the States of Guernsey.

Precedence

ENGLAND AND WALES

The Sovereign
The Prince Philip, Duke of Edinburgh
The Prince of Wales
The Sovereign's younger sons
The Sovereign's grandsons
The Sovereign's cousins
Archbishop of Canterbury
Lord High Chancellor
Archbishop of York
The Prime Minister
Lord President of the Council
Speaker of the House of Commons
Lord Privy Seal
Ambassadors and High Commissioners
Lord Great Chamberlain
Earl Marshal
Lord Steward of the Household
Lord Chamberlain of the Household
Master of the Horse
Dukes, according to their patent of creation:
(1) of England
(2) of Scotland
(3) of Great Britain
(4) of Ireland
(5) those created since the Union
Ministers and Envoys
Eldest sons of Dukes of Blood Royal
Marquesses, according to their patent of creation:
(1) of England
(2) of Scotland
(3) of Great Britain
(4) of Ireland
(5) those created since the Union
Dukes' eldest sons
Earls, according to their patent of creation:
(1) of England
(2) of Scotland
(3) of Great Britain
(4) of Ireland
(5) those created since the Union
Younger sons of Dukes of Blood Royal
Marquesses' eldest sons
Dukes' younger sons
Viscounts, according to their patent of creation:
(1) of England
(2) of Scotland
(3) of Great Britain
(4) of Ireland
(5) those created since the Union
Earls' eldest sons
Marquesses' younger sons
Bishops of London, Durham and Winchester

Other English Diocesan Bishops, according to seniority of consecration
Suffragan Bishops, according to seniority of consecration
Secretaries of State, if of the degree of a Baron
Barons, according to their patent of creation:
(1) of England
(2) of Scotland
(3) of Great Britain
(4) of Ireland
(5) those created since the Union
Treasurer of the Household
Comptroller of the Household
Vice-Chamberlain of the Household
Secretaries of State under the degree of Baron
Viscounts' eldest sons
Earls' younger sons
Barons' eldest sons
Knights of the Garter
Privy Counsellors
Chancellor of the Exchequer
Chancellor of the Duchy of Lancaster
Lord Chief Justice of England
Master of the Rolls
President of the Family Division
Vice-Chancellor
Lords Justices of Appeal
Judges of the High Court
Viscounts' younger sons
Barons' younger sons
Sons of Life Peers
Baronets, according to date of patent
Knights of the Thistle
Knights Grand Cross of the Bath
Members of the Order of Merit
Knights Grand Commanders of the Star of India
Knights Grand Cross of St Michael and St George
Knights Grand Commanders of the Indian Empire
Knights Grand Cross of the Royal Victorian Order
Knights Grand Cross of the British Empire
Companions of Honour
Knights Commanders of the Bath
Knights Commanders of the Star of India
Knights Commanders of St Michael and St George
Knights Commanders of the Indian Empire
Knights Commanders of the Royal Victorian Order
Knights Commanders of the British Empire
Knights Bachelor
Vice-Chancellor of the County Palatine of Lancaster

Official Referees of the Supreme Court
Circuit judges and judges of the Mayor's and City of London Court
Companions of the Bath
Companions of the Star of India
Companions of St Michael and St George
Companions of the Indian Empire
Commanders of the Royal Victorian Order
Commanders of the British Empire
Companions of the Distinguished Service Order
Lieutenants of the Royal Victorian Order
Officers of the British Empire
Companions of the Imperial Service Order
Eldest sons of younger sons of Peers
Baronets' eldest sons
Eldest sons of Knights, in the same order as their fathers
Members of the Royal Victorian Order
Members of the British Empire
Younger sons of the younger sons of Peers
Baronets' younger sons
Younger sons of Knights, in the same order as their fathers
Naval, Military, Air, and other Esquires by office

SCOTLAND

The Sovereign
The Prince Philip, Duke of Edinburgh
The Lord High Commissioner to the General Assembly (while that Assembly is sitting)
The Duke of Rothesay (eldest son of the Sovereign)
The Sovereign's younger sons
The Sovereign's cousins
Lords Lieutenant of Counties
Lord Provosts of Counties of Cities
Sheriffs Principal, successively, within their own localities and during holding of office
Lord Chancellor of Great Britain
Moderator of the General Assembly of the Church of Scotland
The Prime Minister
Keepers of the Great Seal and of the Privy Seal, successively if Peers
Hereditary Lord High Constable of Scotland
Hereditary Master of the Household
Dukes, in same order as in England

Eldest sons of Dukes of the Blood
  Royal
Marquesses, as in England
Dukes' eldest sons
Earls, as in England
Younger sons of Dukes of Blood
  Royal
Marquesses' eldest sons
Dukes' younger sons
Keepers of the Great Seal and of the
  Privy Seal, successively if not
  Peers
Lord Justice General
Lord Clerk Register
Lord Advocate
Lord Justice Clerk
Viscounts, as in England
Earls' eldest sons
Marquesses' younger sons
Lord-Barons, as in England
Viscounts' eldest sons
Earls' younger sons
Lord-Barons' eldest sons
Knights of the Garter
Privy Counsellors
Senators of College of Justice (Lords
  of Session)
Viscounts' younger sons
Lord-Barons' younger sons
Sons of Life Peers
Baronets
Knights of the Thistle
Knights Grand Cross, Grand
  Commander, and Knight
  Commanders, as in England
Solicitor-General for Scotland
Lord Lyon King of Arms
Sheriffs Principal, except as shown
  above
Knights Bachelor
Sheriffs
Companions of Orders, as in England
Commanders of the Royal Victorian
  Order
Commanders of the British Empire
Eldest sons of younger sons of Peers
Companions of the Distinguished
  Service Order
Lieutenants of the Royal Victorian
  Order
Officers of the British Empire
Baronets' eldest sons
Knights' eldest sons, as in England
Members of the Royal Victorian
  Order
Members of the British Empire
Baronets' younger sons
Knights' younger sons
Queen's Counsel
Barons-feudal
Esquires
Gentlemen

WOMEN

Women take the same rank as their husbands or as their brothers; but the daughter of a peer marrying a commoner retains her title as Lady or Honourable. Daughters of peers rank next immediately after the wives of their elder brothers, and before their younger brothers' wives. Daughters of peers marrying peers of lower degree take the same order of precedence as that of their husbands; thus the daughter of a Duke marrying a Baron becomes of the rank of Baroness only, while her sisters married to commoners retain their rank and take precedence of the Baroness. Merely official rank on the husband's part does not give any similar precedence to the wife.

Peeresses in their own right take the same precedence as peers of the same rank, i.e. from their date of creation.

LOCAL PRECEDENCE

England and Wales – No written code of county or city order of precedence has been promulgated, but in counties the Lord Lieutenant stands first, and secondly (normally) the Sheriff, and therefore in cities and boroughs the Lord Lieutenant has social precedence over the Mayor; but at city or borough functions the Lord Mayor or Mayor will preside. At Oxford and Cambridge the High Sheriff takes precedence of the Vice-Chancellor.

Scotland – The Lord Provosts of the city districts of Aberdeen, Dundee, Edinburgh and Glasgow are Lord Lieutenants for those districts ex officio and take precedence as such.

Conservation and Heritage

Countryside Conservation

NATIONAL PARKS

ENGLAND AND WALES

The ten National Parks of England and Wales were set up under the provisions of the National Parks and Access to the Countryside Act 1949 to conserve and protect scenic landscapes from inappropriate development and to provide access to the land for public enjoyment.

The Countryside Commission is the statutory body which has the power to designate National Parks in England, and the Countryside Council for Wales is responsible for National Parks in Wales. Designations in England are confirmed by the Secretary of State for the Environment, and those in Wales by the Secretary of State for Wales. The designation of a National Park does not affect the ownership of the land or remove the rights of the local community. Although the parks are administered through local government, the majority of the land is owned by private landowners (74 per cent) or by bodies such as the National Trust (7 per cent) and the Forestry Commission (7 per cent). The National Park Authorities own only 2.3 per cent of the land in the National Parks.

Under the Local Government Act 1972, National Park Authorities (NPAs) are the authorities responsible for park administration. They also influence land use and development, and deal with planning applications. Two-thirds of the members of each authority are appointed by the county and district councils within whose boundaries the parks lie. One-third of the members are appointed by the relevant Secretary of State with advice from the Countryside Commission or the Countryside Council for Wales. The NPAs appoint the National Park Officer for the National Park they administer.

In the Peak District and the Lake District the NPAs are special boards: the Peak Park Joint Planning Board and the Lake District Special Planning Board. These are autonomous authorities which are financially independent, unlike the authorities in the other eight parks which are county council committees.

Central government provides 75 per cent of the funding for the parks through the National Park Supplementary Grant. The remaining 25 per cent is supplied by the local authorities concerned. Approved net expenditure for all National Parks in England and Wales in 1995–6 was £28,573,831.

The Countryside Commission has stated that other areas are regarded as being worthy of National Parks status. Two areas considered as having equivalent status are the Broads and the New Forest (see page 579).

The National Parks (with date designation confirmed) are:

BRECON BEACONS (1957), 1,351 sq. km/522 sq. miles – The park lies in Powys (66 per cent), Dyfed, Gwent and Mid Glamorgan. The park is centred on the Beacons, Pen y Fan, Corn Du and Cribyn, but also includes the valley of the Usk, the Black Mountains to the east and the Black Mountain to the west. There are information centres at Brecon, Craig-y-nos Country Park, Abergavenny and Llandovery, a study centre at Danywenallt and a day visitor centre near Libanus.

Information Office, 7 Glamorgan Street, Brecon, Powys LD3 7DP. Tel: 01874-624437. *National Park Officer,* M. Fitton

DARTMOOR (1951 and 1994), 954 sq. km/368 sq. miles – The park lies wholly in Devon. It consists of moorland and rocky granite tors, and is rich in prehistoric remains. There are information centres at Newbridge, Tavistock, Bovey Tracey, Steps Bridge, Princetown and Postbridge.

Information Office, Parke, Haytor Road, Bovey Tracey, Devon TQ13 9JQ. Tel: 01626-832093. *National Park Officer,* N. Atkinson

EXMOOR (1954), 693 sq. km/268 sq. miles – The park lies in Somerset (71 per cent) and Devon. Exmoor is a moorland plateau inhabited by wild ponies and red deer. There are many ancient remains and burial mounds. There are information centres at Lynmouth, County Gate, Dulverton and Combe Martin.

Information Office, Exmoor House, Dulverton, Somerset TA22 9HL. Tel: 01398-23665. *National Park Officer,* K. Bungay

LAKE DISTRICT (1951), 2,292 sq. km/885 sq. miles – The park lies wholly in Cumbria. The Lake District includes England's highest mountains (Scafell Pike, Helvellyn and Skiddaw) but it is most famous for its glaciated lakes. There are information centres at Keswick, Waterhead, Hawkshead, Seatoller, Bowness, Grasmere, Coniston, Glenridding and Pooley Bridge, an information van at Gosforth and a park centre at Brockhole, Windermere.

Information Office, Brockhole, Windermere, Cumbria LA23 1LJ. Tel: 01539-446601. *National Park Officer,* J. Toothill

NORTHUMBERLAND (1956), 1,049 sq. km/405 sq. miles – The park lies wholly in Northumberland. It is an area of hill country stretching from Hadrian's Wall to the Scottish Border. There are information centres at Ingram, Once Brewed, Rothbury, Housesteads, Harbottle and Kielder, and an information caravan at Cawfields.

Information Office, Eastburn, South Park, Hexham, Northumberland NE46 1BS. Tel: 01434-605555. *National Park Officer,* G. Taylor

NORTH YORK MOORS (1952), 1,436 sq. km/554 sq. miles – The park lies in North Yorkshire (96 per cent) and Cleveland. It consists of woodland and moorland, and includes the Hambleton Hills and the Cleveland Way. There are information centres at Danby, Pickering, Sutton Bank, Ravenscar, Helmsley and Hutton-le-Hole, and a day study centre at Danby.

Information Office, The Old Vicarage, Bondgate, Helmsley, York YO6 5BP. Tel: 01439-70657. *National Park Officer,* D. Arnold-Forster

PEAK DISTRICT (1951), 1,438 sq. km/555 sq. miles – The park lies in Derbyshire (64 per cent), Staffordshire, South Yorkshire, Cheshire, West Yorkshire and Greater Manchester. The Peak District includes the gritstone moors of the 'dark peak' and the limestone dales of the 'white peak'. There are information centres at Bakewell, Edale, Fairholmes and Castleton, and information points at Torside (in the Longdendale Valley) and at Hartington (former station).

Information Office, Aldern House, Baslow Road, Bakewell, Derbyshire DE45 1AE. Tel: 01629-814321. *National Park Officer,* C. Harrison

PEMBROKESHIRE COAST (1952), 584 sq. km/225 sq. miles – The park lies wholly in Dyfed. It consists of cliffs, moorland and Skomer Island. There are information centres at Tenby, St David's, Pembroke, Newport, Kilgetty, Haverfordwest and Broad Haven. *Information Office,* County Offices, Haverfordwest, Dyfed SA61 1QZ. Tel: 01437-764591. *National Park Officer,* N. Wheeler

SNOWDONIA (1951), 2,142 sq. km/827 sq. miles – Snowdonia lies wholly in Gwynedd. It is an area of deep valleys and rugged mountains. There are information centres at Aberdovey, Bala, Betws y Coed, Blaenau Ffestiniog, Conwy, Harlech, Dolgellau and Llanberis. *Information Office,* Penrhyndeudraeth, Gwynedd LL48 6LS. Tel: 01766-770274. *National Park Officer,* A. Jones

YORKSHIRE DALES (1954), 1,769 sq. km/683 sq. miles – The park lies in North Yorkshire (88 per cent) and Cumbria. The Yorkshire Dales are composed primarily of limestone overlaid in places by millstone grit. The three peaks of Ingleborough, Whernside and Pen-y-Ghent are within the park. There are information centres at Clapham, Grassington, Hawes, Aysgarth Falls, Malham and Sedbergh. *Information Office,* Yorebridge House, Bainbridge, Leyburn, N. Yorks DL8 3BP. Tel: 01969-50456. *National Park Officer,* R. Harvey

Two other areas considered to have equivalent status to national parks are the Broads and the New Forest. The Broads Authority, a special statutory authority, was established in 1989 to develop, conserve and manage the Norfolk and Suffolk Broads (*see also* Government Departments and Public Offices). The Government declared in 1992 its intention of giving the New Forest a status equivalent to that of a National Park by declaring it an 'area of national significance'.

THE BROADS (1989), 303 sq. km/117 sq. miles – The Broads are located between Norwich and Great Yarmouth on the flood plains of the five rivers flowing through the area to the sea. The area is one of fens, winding waterways, woodland and marsh. The forty or so broads are man-made, and are connected to the rivers by dykes, providing over 200 km of navigable waterways. There are information centres at Beccles, Hoveton, North-west Tower (Yarmouth), Ranworth and Toad Hole. *Broads Authority,* Thomas Harvey House, 18 Colegate, Norwich NR3 1BQ. Tel: 01603-610734. *Chief Executive,* A. Clark

THE NEW FOREST, 376 sq. km/145 sq. miles – The forest has been protected since 1079 when it was declared a royal hunting forest. The area consists of forest, ancient woodland and heathland. Much of the Forest is managed by the Forestry Commission, which provides several camp-sites. The main villages are Brockenhurst, Burley and Lyndhurst, which has a visitor centre. *The Forestry Commission,* Office of the Deputy Surveyor of the New Forest and the New Forest Committee, The Queen's House, Lyndhurst, Hants SO43 7NH. Tel: 01703-284149

SCOTLAND AND NORTHERN IRELAND

The National Parks and Access to the Countryside Act 1949 dealt only with England and Wales and made no provision for Scotland or Northern Ireland. Although there are no national parks in these two countries, there is power to designate them in Northern Ireland under the Amenity Lands Act 1965 and the Nature Conservation and Amenity Lands Order (Northern Ireland) 1985. In 1989 the Scottish Office asked Scottish Natural Heritage to report on whether national parks should be designated in Scotland.

AREAS OF OUTSTANDING NATURAL BEAUTY

ENGLAND AND WALES

Under the National Parks and Access to the Countryside Act 1949, provision was made for the designation of Areas of Outstanding Natural Beauty (AONBs) by the Countryside Commission. The Countryside Act 1968 further defines the role of AONBs, suggesting that they should show due regard for the interests of other land users, such as agriculture and forestry groups. The Countryside Commission continues to be responsible for AONBs in England but since April 1991 the Countryside Council for Wales has been responsible for the Welsh AONBs. Designations in England are confirmed by the Secretary of State for the Environment and those in Wales by the Secretary of State for Wales.

Although less emphasis is placed upon the provision of open-air enjoyment for the public than in the national parks, AONBs are areas which are no less beautiful and require the same degree of protection to conserve and enhance the natural beauty of the countryside. This includes protecting flora and fauna, geological and other landscape features. In AONBs planning and management responsibilities are split between county and district councils (there are 17 which cross county boundaries). Finance for the AONBs is provided by grant-aid.

The forty Areas of Outstanding Natural Beauty (with date designation confirmed) are:

ANGLESEY (1967), 221 sq. km/86 sq. miles – The area extends along the entire coastline of the island, except for breaks around the urban areas and in the vicinity of Wylfa

ARNSIDE AND SILVERDALE (1972), 75 sq. km/29 sq. miles – The area embraces the upper half of Morecambe Bay, the Kent estuary, and includes extensive tidal flats in the Bay

BLACKDOWN HILLS (1991), 370 sq. km/143 sq. miles – An area of greensand ridges in Devon and Somerset extending from Cullompton in the west to Chard in the east, south of Taunton to north of Honiton

CANNOCK CHASE (1958), 68 sq. km/26 sq. miles – An area of high heathland in Staffordshire. Deer continue to roam over the Chase

CHICHESTER HARBOUR (1964), 74 sq. km/29 sq. miles – The area extends from Hayling Island to Apuldram and includes Thorney Island

CHILTERNS (1965; extended 1990), 833 sq. km/322 sq. miles – Chalk downlands running from South Oxfordshire north-eastwards to Bedfordshire, including the outlying group of hills beyond Luton

CLWYDIAN RANGE (1985), 157 sq. km/61 sq. miles – A prominent ridge extending southwards from Prestatyn on the north Wales coast. Offa's Dyke runs along the crest of the range

CORNWALL (1959; Camel estuary 1983), 958 sq. km/370 sq. miles – A number of separate areas including Bodmin Moor, most of the Land's End peninsula, the coast between St Michael's Mount and St Austell (with Falmouth omitted), the Fowey estuary; in north

Cornwall most of the coast to Bedruthan Steps and between Perranporth and Godrevy Towans, and the Camel estuary

COTSWOLDS (1966; extended 1990), 2,038 sq. km/787 sq. miles – The area of limestone hills above the Vales of Gloucester and Evesham

CRANBORNE CHASE AND WEST WILTSHIRE DOWNS (1983), 983 sq. km/379 sq. miles – A mainly chalkland and greensand area covering parts of Wiltshire, Dorset, Hampshire and Somerset, including the wooded remnants of the ancient Chase

DEDHAM VALE (1970; extended 1978, 1991), 90 sq. km/35 sq. miles – The area on the Essex/Suffolk border where John Constable painted

EAST DEVON (1963), 268 sq. km/103 sq. miles – The coastline between Exmouth and Lyme Regis, with Sidmouth, Beer and Seaton omitted. Inland, Gittisham Hill, East Hill and Woodbury and Aylebeare Commons are included

NORTH DEVON (1960), 171 sq. km/66 sq. miles – Includes most of the North Devon coastline, from just north of Bude to the boundary of the Exmoor National Park

SOUTH DEVON (1960), 337 sq. km/130 sq. miles – Includes the coast between Bolt Head and Bolt Tail, Salcombe, Slapton Sands and Dartmouth, and the estuaries and valleys of the Yealm, Erme, Avon and Dart

DORSET (1959), 1,129 sq. km/436 sq. miles – The coastline between Lyme Regis and Poole, with the Isle of Portland and Weymouth omitted, stretching inland to include the Purbeck Hills and the downs of Hardy country

FOREST OF BOWLAND (1964), 802 sq. km/310 sq. miles – A moorland area mostly in Lancashire running westward from the River Ribble, with a small outlying area east of the Ribble which includes Pendle Hill

GOWER (1956), 188 sq. km/73 sq. miles – A peninsula in West Glamorgan, known for its coastline

EAST HAMPSHIRE (1962), 383 sq. km/148 sq. miles – A chalkland area stretching from the outskirts of Winchester to the Sussex border about 10 miles inland

SOUTH HAMPSHIRE COAST (1967), 77 sq. km/30 sq. miles – The coastline between Hurst Castle and Calshot Castle, extending inland up the River Beaulieu for about six miles

HIGH WEALD (1983), 1,460 sq. km/564 sq. miles – The area covers parts of East and West Sussex, Kent and Surrey. It is predominantly wooded, and includes larger heathland areas like Ashdown Forest, the remnants of the old Wealden forests

HOWARDIAN HILLS (1987), 204 sq. km/79 sq. miles – Wooded hills which rise above the Vales of York and Pickering

KENT DOWNS (1968), 878 sq. km/339 sq. miles – Running east and south-east from the Surrey border near Westerham to the coast near Dover and Folkestone, with a coastal outlier at South Foreland and a narrow strip of the old sea cliff escarpment west of Hythe overlooking Romney Marsh

LINCOLNSHIRE WOLDS (1973), 558 sq. km/215 sq. miles – The area extends in a south-easterly direction from Laceby and Caistor in the north to the region of Spilsby, about ten miles west of the coast

LLEYN (1957), 161 sq. km/63 sq. miles – The peninsula forming the westernmost part of the county of Gwynedd

MALVERN HILLS (1959), 105 sq. km/40 sq. miles – The whole range of the Malvern Hills in the county of Hereford and Worcester, just touching Gloucestershire

MENDIP HILLS (1972; extended 1989), 198 sq. km/76 sq. miles – Comprising over half of the Mendip Hills, the area stretches from Bleadon Hill to the A39 road north of Wells and includes Cheddar Gorge and Wookey Hole

NIDDERDALE (1994), 603 sq. km/233 sq. miles – The eastern fringe of the Yorkshire Pennines, containing moorland and dales such as the Skell, Washburn, and Nidderdale itself

NORFOLK COAST (1968), 451 sq. km/174 sq. miles – An almost continuous coastal strip three to five miles in depth from Hunstanton to Bacton, with a further small strip between Sea Palling and Winterton-on-Sea. The area includes part of the Sandringham estate

NORTH PENNINES (1988), 1,998 sq. km/766 sq. miles – The northern limit of the Pennine chain, covering parts of Cumbria, Co. Durham and Northumberland

NORTHUMBERLAND COAST (1958), 135 sq. km/52 sq. miles – Stretches from just south of Berwick to Amble and includes Holy Island and the Farne Islands

QUANTOCK HILLS (1957), 99 sq. km/38 sq. miles – A range of sandstone hills in Somerset

ISLES OF SCILLY (1976), 16 sq. km/6 sq. miles – About 140 islands and skerries in the Scillies group of which only five are inhabited. There are a number of Sites of Special Scientific Interest

SHROPSHIRE HILLS (1959), 804 sq. km/310 sq. miles – Most of south-west Shropshire between the Welsh border and the boundary with Hereford and Worcester, including the region around Clun, the area of the Stiperstones, the Long Mynd and Wenlock Edge, with the tongues of land running north-east to the Wrekin and south towards Ludlow

SOLWAY COAST (1964), 115 sq. km/44 sq. miles – A stretch of coastline in Cumbria from Maryport to the estuaries of the Rivers Eden and Esk (with Silloth omitted) backed by the Solway Plain

SUFFOLK COAST AND HEATHS (1970), 403 sq. km/156 sq. miles – The area includes 38 miles of coastline and parts of the Stour and Orwell estuaries, while the Rivers Deben, Alde and Blyth flow through it

SURREY HILLS (1958), 419 sq. km/162 sq. miles – An area to the east and south of Guildford, including the Hog's Back and the ridge of the North Downs

SUSSEX DOWNS (1966), 983 sq. km/379 sq. miles – The area includes the chalk escarpment of the South Downs from Beachy Head to the Hampshire border, and stretches down to the coast between Eastbourne and Seaford

NORTH WESSEX DOWNS (1972), 1,730 sq. km/668 sq. miles – An upland area in Hampshire, Wiltshire, Oxfordshire and Berkshire, bounded by the Marlborough and Lambourn Downs in the west, the Chiltern Hills in the east and Salisbury Plain in the south

ISLE OF WIGHT (1963), 189 sq. km/73 sq. miles – A number of separate areas comprising stretches of coastline, the Yar Valley, the high downland behind Ventnor and the chalk ridge which runs from Newport to Culver Cliff and Foreland

WYE VALLEY (1971), 326 sq. km/126 sq. miles – The deep, wooded river valley running through the counties of Gwent, Gloucestershire, and Hereford and Worcester

The Tamar valley (298 sq. km) in Devon/Cornwall was designated in August 1995. No further designations are planned.

NORTHERN IRELAND

The Department of the Environment for Northern Ireland, with advice from the Council for Nature Conservation and the Countryside, designates Areas of Outstanding Natural Beauty in Northern Ireland. At present there are nine and these cover a total area of approximately 284,948 hectares (704,121 acres).

ANTRIM COAST AND GLENS, Co. Antrim, 70,600 ha/ 174,452 acres
CAUSEWAY COAST, Co. Antrim, 4,200 ha/10,378 acres
LAGAN VALLEY, Co. Down, 2,072 ha/5,119 acres
LECALE COAST, Co. Down, 3,108 ha/7,679 acres
MOURNE, Co. Down, 57,012 ha/140,876 acres
NORTH DERRY, Co. Londonderry, 12,950 ha/31,999 acres
RING OF GULLION, Co. Armagh, 15,353 ha/37,938 acres
SPERRIN, Co. Tyrone/Co. Londonderry, 101,006 ha/ 249,585 acres
STRANGFORD LOUGH, Co. Down, 18,647 ha/46,077 acres

NATIONAL SCENIC AREAS

No Areas of Outstanding Natural Beauty are designated in Scotland. However, National Scenic Areas have a broadly equivalent status. Scottish Natural Heritage recognizes areas of national scenic significance. At present there are 40, covering a total area of 1,001,800 hectares (2,475,448 acres).

Development within National Scenic Areas is dealt with by the local planning authority, who are required to consult Scottish Natural Heritage concerning certain categories of development. Land management uses can also be modified in the interest of scenic conservation. The Secretary of State for Scotland has limited powers of intervention should a planning authority and Scottish Natural Heritage disagree.

	hectares	acres
BORDER		
Eildon and Leaderfoot	3,600	8,896
Upper Tweeddale	10,500	25,945
CENTRAL		
*Loch Lomond	11,200	27,675
*Loch Rannoch and Glen Lyon	1,300	3,212
The Trossachs	4,600	11,367
DUMFRIES AND GALLOWAY		
East Stewartry Coast	4,500	11,119
Fleet Valley	5,300	13,096
Nith Estuary	9,300	22,980
GRAMPIAN		
*The Cairngorm Mountains	29,800	73,636
*Deeside and Lochnagar	32,200	79,566
HIGHLAND		
Assynt-Coigach	90,200	222,884
*Ben Nevis and Glen Coe	79,600	196,692
*The Cairngorm Mountains	37,400	92,415
The Cuillin Hills	21,900	54,115
Dornoch Firth	7,500	18,532
Glen Affric	19,300	47,690
Glen Strathfarrar	3,800	9,390
Kintail	15,500	38,300
Knoydart	39,500	97,604
Kyle of Tongue	18,500	45,713
Loch Shiel	13,400	33,111
Morar, Moidart and Ardnamurchan	13,500	33,358
North-west Sutherland	20,500	50,655
The Small Isles	15,500	38,300
Trotternish	5,000	12,355
Wester Ross	145,300	359,036
ORKNEY ISLANDS		
Hoy and West Mainland	14,800	36,571
SHETLAND ISLANDS		
Shetland	11,600	28,664
STRATHCLYDE		
*Ben Nevis and Glen Coe	17,500	43,242
Jura	21,800	53,868
Knapdale	19,800	48,926
Kyles of Bute	4,400	10,872
*Loch Lomond	16,200	40,030
Loch na Keal, Isle of Mull	12,700	31,382
Lynn of Lorn	4,800	11,861
North Arran	23,800	58,810
Scarba, Lunga and the Garvellachs	1,900	4,695
TAYSIDE		
*Ben Nevis and Glen Coe	4,500	11,119
*Deeside and Lochnagar	7,800	19,274
*Loch Rannoch and Glen Lyon	47,100	116,384
Loch Tummel	9,200	22,733
River Earn	3,000	7,413
River Tay	5,600	13,838
WESTERN ISLES		
St Kilda	900	2,224
South Lewis, Harris and North Uist	109,600	270,822
South Uist Machair	6,100	15,073
TOTAL	1,001,800	2,475,448

*National Scenic Areas in more than one region

Nature Conservation Areas

SITES OF SPECIAL SCIENTIFIC INTEREST

Site of Special Scientific Interest (SSSI) is a legal designation applied to land in England, Scotland or Wales which English Nature (EN), Scottish Natural Heritage (SNH), or the Countryside Council for Wales (CCW) identifies as being of special interest because of its flora, fauna, geological or physiographical features. In some cases, SSSI are managed as nature reserves.

EN, SNH and CCW must notify the designation of a SSSI to the local planning authority, every owner/ occupier of the land, and the Secretary of State for the Environment (or Secretary of State for Scotland or for Wales where applicable). Forestry and agricultural departments and a number of other bodies are also informed of this designation.

Objections to the designation of a SSSI can be made and ultimately considered at a full meeting of the Council of EN or the Statutory Protection Committee of CCW. In Scotland an objection will be dealt with by the appropriate regional board or the main board of SNH, depending on the nature of the objection. Unresolved objections on scientific grounds must be referred to the Advisory Committee for SSSI.

The protection of these sites depends on the co-operation of individual landowners and occupiers. Owner/occupiers must consult EN, SNH or CCW and gain written consent before they can undertake certain listed activities on the site. Funds are available through management agreements and grants to assist owners and occupiers in conserving sites' interests. As a last resort a site can be purchased.

As at 31 March 1995 there were 6,105 SSSI in Britain, covering 1,965,905 hectares (4,857,751 acres).

	no.	hectares	acres
England	3,825	893,335	2,207,477
Scotland	1,381	865,582	2,138,853
Wales	899	206,988	511,260

NORTHERN IRELAND

In Northern Ireland 73 Areas of Special Scientific Interest (ASSIs) have been established by the Department of the Environment for Northern Ireland. These cover a total area of 75,065 hectares (185,487 acres).

NATIONAL NATURE RESERVES

National Nature Reserves are defined in the National Parks and Access to the Countryside Act 1949 as land designated for the study and preservation of flora and fauna, or of geological or physiographical features.

English Nature (EN), Scottish Natural Heritage (SNH) or the Countryside Council for Wales (CCW) can designate as a National Nature Reserve land which is being managed as a nature reserve under an agreement with one of the statutory nature conservation agencies; land held and managed by EN, SNH or CCW; or land held and managed as a nature reserve by another approved body. EN, SNH or CCW can turn to the appropriate Secretary of State to impose by-laws for the protection of the reserves from undesirable development.

As at 31 March 1995 there were 288 National Nature Reserves in Britain, covering 195,879 hectares (484,017 acres).

	no.	hectares	acres
England	164	65,071	160,793
Scotland	71	113,320	280,013
Wales	53	17,488	43,195

NORTHERN IRELAND

National Nature Reserves are established and managed by the Department of the Environment for Northern Ireland, with advice from the Council for Nature Conservation and the Countryside. There are 45 National Nature Reserves covering 4,574 hectares (11,297 acres).

LOCAL NATURE RESERVES

Local Nature Reserves are defined in the National Parks and Access to the Countryside Act 1949 as land designated for the study and preservation of flora and fauna, or of geological or physiographical features. The Act gives local authorities in England and Wales and district councils in Scotland the power to acquire, declare and manage local nature reserves in consultation with English Nature, Scottish Natural Heritage and the Countryside Council for Wales. Conservation trusts can also own and manage non-statutory local nature reserves.

As at 31 March 1995 there were 487 designated Local Nature Reserve areas in Britain, covering 25,076 hectares (61,962 acres).

	no.	hectares	acres
England	444	17,681	43,690
Scotland	17	3,385	8,364
Wales	26	4,010	9,905

An additional 33 km of linear trails are designated as Local Nature Reserves.

FOREST NATURE RESERVES

Forest Enterprise (an executive agency of the Forestry Commission) is responsible for the management of the Commission's forests. With the aim of protecting and conserving special forms of natural habitat, flora and fauna it has created 46 Forest Nature Reserves. There are about 400 SSSI on the estates, some of which are also Nature Reserves.

Forest Nature Reserves extend in size from under 50 hectares (124 acres) to 500 hectares (1,236 acres). The largest include the Black Wood of Rannoch, by Loch Rannoch; Cannop Valley Oakwoods, Forest of Dean; Culbin Forest, near Forres; Glen Affric, near Fort Augustus; Kylerhea, Skye; Pembrey, Carmarthen Bay; Starr Forest, in Galloway Forest Park; and Wyre Forest, near Kidderminster.

NORTHERN IRELAND

There are 36 Forest Nature Reserves in Northern Ireland, covering 1,759 hectares (4,346 acres). They are designated and administered by the Forest Service, a division of the Department of Agriculture for Northern Ireland. There are also 15 National Nature Reserves on Forest Service-owned property.

MARINE NATURE RESERVES

The Wildlife and Countryside Act 1981 gives the Secretary of State for the Environment (and the Secretaries of State for Wales and for Scotland where appropriate) power to designate Marine Nature Reserves, and English Nature, Scottish Natural Heritage and the Countryside Council for Wales powers to select and manage these reserves.

Marine Nature Reserves provide protection for marine flora and fauna, and geological and physiographical features on land covered by tidal waters or parts of the sea in or adjacent to Great Britain. Reserves also provide opportunities for study and research.

The three statutory Marine Nature Reserves are:

LUNDY (1986), Bristol Channel
SKOMER (1990), Dyfed
STRANGFORD LOUGH (1995), Northern Ireland

Two other areas proposed for designation as reserves are: the Menai Strait, and Bardsey Island and part of the Lleyn peninsula, both in Gwynedd.

A number of non-statutory marine reserves have been set up by conservation groups.

Wildlife Conservation

PROTECTED SPECIES

The Wildlife and Countryside Act 1981 gives legal protection to a wide range of wild animals and plants. Subject to parliamentary approval, the Secretary of State for the Environment may vary the animals and plants given legal protection. The most recent variation of Schedules 5 and 8 came into effect in October 1992.

ANIMALS, ETC.

Under Section 9 and Schedule 5 of the Act it is illegal without a licence to kill, injure, take, possess or sell any of the animals mentioned below (whether alive or dead) and to disturb its place of shelter and protection or to destroy that place.

‡Adder (*Vipera berus*)
§Allis shad (*alosa alosa*)
  Anemone, Ivell's Sea (*Edwardsia ivelli*)
  Anemone, Startlet Sea (*Nematostella vectensis*)
  Apus (*Triops cancriformis*)
  Bat, Horseshoe (*Rhinolophidae*, all species)
  Bat, Typical (*Vespertilionidae*, all species)
  Beetle (*Hypebaeus flavipes*)
  Beetle, Lesser Silver Water (*Hydrochara caraboides*)
§§Beetle, Mire Pill (*Curimopsis nigrita*)
  Beetle, Rainbow Leaf (*Chrysolina cerealis*)
  Beetle, Violet Click (*Limoniscus violaceus*)
  Beetle, Water (*Graphoderus zonatus*)
  Beetle, Water (*Paracymus aeneus*)
  Burbot (*Lota lota*)
*Butterfly, Adonis Blue (*Lysandra bellargus*)
*Butterfly, Black Hairstreak (*Strymonidia pruni*)
*Butterfly, Brown Hairstreak (*Thecla betulae*)
*Butterfly, Chalkhill Blue (*Lysandra coridon*)
*Butterfly, Chequered Skipper (*Carterocephalus palaemon*)
*Butterfly, Duke of Burgundy Fritillary (*Hamearis lucina*)
*Butterfly, Glanville Fritillary (*Melitaea cinxia*)
  Butterfly, Heath Fritillary (*Mellicta athalia* (or *Melitaea athalia*))
  Butterfly, High Brown Fritillary (*Argynnis adippe*)
  Butterfly, Large Blue (*Maculinea arion*)
*Butterfly, Large Copper (*Lycaena dispar*)
*Butterfly, Large Heath (*Coenonympha tullia*)
*Butterfly, Large Tortoiseshell (*Nymphalis polychloros*)
*Butterfly, Lulworth Skipper (*Thymelicus acteon*)
*Butterfly, Marsh Fritillary (*Eurodryas aurinia*)
*Butterfly, Mountain Ringlet (*Erebia epiphron*)
*Butterfly, Northern Brown Argus (*Aricia artaxerxes*)
*Butterfly, Pearl-bordered Fritillary (*Boloria euphrosyne*)
*Butterfly, Purple Emperor (*Apatura iris*)
*Butterfly, Silver Spotted Skipper (*Hesperia comma*)
*Butterfly, Silver-studded Blue (*Plebejus argus*)
*Butterfly, Small Blue (*Cupido minimus*)
  Butterfly, Swallowtail (*Papilio machaon*)

---

*the offence relates to 'sale' only
**the offence relates to 'taking' and 'sale' only
†the offence relates to 'killing and injuring' only
‡the offence relates to 'killing, injuring and sale'
§the offence relates to 'killing, injuring and taking'
§§the offence relates only to damaging, destroying or obstructing access to a shelter or protection
††the offence relates to killing, injuring, taking, possession and sale

*Butterfly, White Letter Hairstreak (*Stymonida w-album*)
*Butterfly, Wood White (*Leptidea sinapis*)
  Cat, Wild (*Felis silvestris*)
  Cicada, New Forest (*Cicadetta montana*)
**Crayfish, Atlantic Stream (*Austropotamobius pallipes*)
  Cricket, Field (*Gryllus campestris*)
  Cricket, Mole (*Gryllotalpa gryllotalpa*)
  Dolphin (*Cetacea*)
  Dormouse (*Muscardinus avellanarius*)
  Dragonfly, Norfolk Aeshna (*Aeshna isosceles*)
*Frog, Common (*Rana temporaria*)
  Grasshopper, Wart-biter (*Decticus verrucivorus*)
  Hatchet Shell, Northern (*Thyasira gouldi*)
  Lagoon Snail (*Paludinella littorina*)
  Lagoon Snail, De Folin's (*Caecum armoricum*)
  Lagoon Worm, Tentacled (*Alkmaria romijni*)
  Leech, Medicinal (*Hirudo medicinalis*)
  Lizard, Sand (*Lacerta agilis*)
‡Lizard, Viviparous(*Lacerta vivipara*)
  Marten, Pine (*Martes martes*)
  Moth, Barberry Carpet (*Pareulype berberata*)
  Moth, Black-veined (*Siona lineata* (or *Idaea lineata*))
  Moth, Essex Emerald (*Thetidia smaragdaria*)
  Moth, New Forest Burnet (*Zygaena viciae*)
  Moth, Reddish Buff (*Acosmetia caliginosa*)
  Moth, Sussex Emerald (*Thalera fimbrialis*)
  Moth, Viper's Bugloss (*Hadena irregularis*)
†Mussel, Freshwater Pearl (*Margaritifera margaritifera*)
  Newt, Great Crested (or Warty) (*Triturus cristatus*)
*Newt, Palmate (*Triturus helveticus*)
*Newt, Smooth (*Triturus vulgaris*)
  Otter, Common (*Lutra lutra*)
  Porpoise (*Cetacea*)
  Sandworm, Lagoon (*Armandia cirrhosa*)
††Sea Fan, Pink (*Eunicella verrucosa*)
  Sea-Mat, Trembling (*Victorella pavida*)
  Sea Slug, Lagoon (*Tenellia adspersa*)
  Shrimp, Fairy (*Chirocephalus diaphanus*)
  Shrimp, Lagoon Sand (*Gammarus insensibilis*)
‡Slow-worm (*Anguis fragilis*)
  Snail, Glutinous (*Myxas glutinosa*)
  Snail, Sandbowl (*Catinella arenaria*)
‡Snake, Grass (*Natrix natrix* (*Natrix helvetica*))
  Snake, Smooth (*Coronella austriaca*)
  Spider, Fen Raft (*Dolomedes plantarius*)
  Spider, Ladybird (*Eresus niger*)
  Squirrel, Red (*Sciurus vulgaris*)
  Sturgeon (*Acipenser sturio*)
*Toad, Common (*Bufo bufo*)
  Toad, Natterjack (*Bufo calamita*)
  Turtle, Marine (*Dermochelyidae* and *Cheloniidae*, all species)
  Vendace (*Coregonus albula*)
  Walrus (*Odobenus rosmarus*)
  Whale (*Cetacea*)
  Whitefish (*Coregonus lavaretus*)

PLANTS

Under Section 13 and Schedule 8 of the Wildlife and Countryside Act 1981, it is illegal without a licence to pick, uproot, sell or destroy any of the plants mentioned below and, unless authorized, to uproot any wild plant.

Adder's tongue, Least (*Ophioglossum lusitanicum*)
Alison, Small (*Alyssum alyssoides*)
Blackwort (*Southbya nigrella*)
Broomrape, Bedstraw (*Orobanche caryophyllacea*)

Broomrape, Oxtongue (*Orobanche loricata*)
Broomrape, Thistle (*Orobanche reticulata*)
Cabbage, Lundy (*Rhynchosinapis wrightii*)
Calamint, Wood (*Calamintha sylvatica*)
Caloplaca, Snow (*Caloplaca nivalis*)
Catapyrenium, Tree (*Catapyrenium psoromoides*)
Catchfly, Alpine (*Lychnis alpina*)
Catillaria, Laurer's (*Catellaria laureri*)
Centaury, Slender (*Centaurium tenuiflorum*)
Cinquefoil, Rock (*Potentilla rupestris*)
Cladonia, Upright Mountain (*Cladonia stricta*)
Clary, Meadow (*Salvia pratensis*)
Club-rush, Triangular (*Scirpus triquetrus*)
Colt's-foot, Purple (*Homogyne alpina*)
Cotoneaster, Wild (*Cotoneaster integerrimus*)
Cottongrass, Slender (*Eriophorum gracile*)
Cow-wheat, Field (*Melampyrum arvense*)
Crocus, Sand (*Romulea columnae*)
Crystalwort, Lizard (*Riccia bifurca*)
Cudweed, Broad-leaved (*Filago pyramidata*)
Cudweed, Jersey (*Gnaphalium luteoalbum*)
Cudweed, Red-tipped (*Filago lutescens*)
Diapensia (*Diapensia lapponica*)
Dock, Shore (*Rumex rupestris*)
Earwort, Marsh (*Jamesoniella undulifolia*)
Eryngo, Field (*Eryngium campestre*)
Fern, Dickie's bladder (*Cystopteris dickieana*)
Fern, Killarney (*Trichomanes speciosum*)
Flapwort, Norfolk (*Leiocolea rutheana*)
Fleabane, Alpine (*Erigeron borealis*)
Fleabane, Small (*Pulicaria vulgaris*)
Frostwort, Pointed (*Gymnomitrion apiculatum*)
Galingale, Brown (*Cyperus fuscus*)
Gentian, Alpine (*Gentiana nivalis*)
Gentian, Dune (*Gentianella uliginosa*)
Gentian, Early (*Gentianella anglica*)
Gentian, Fringed (*Gentianella ciliata*)
Gentian, Spring (*Gentiana verna*)
Germander, Cut-leaved (*Teucrium botrys*)
Germander, Water (*Teucrium scordium*)
Gladiolus, Wild (*Gladiolus illyricus*)
Goosefoot, Stinking (*Chenopodium vulvaria*)
Grass-poly (*Lythrum hyssopifolia*)
Grimmia, Blunt-leaved (*Grimmia unicolor*)
Gyalecta, Elm (*Gyalecta ulmi*)
Hare's-ear, Sickle-leaved (*Bupleurum falcatum*)
Hare's-ear, Small (*Bupleurum baldense*)
Hawk's-beard, Stinking (*Crepis foetida*)
Hawkweed, Northroe (*Hieracium northroense*)
Hawkweed, Shetland (*Hieracium zetlandicum*)
Hawkweed, Weak-leaved (*Hieracium attenuatifolium*)
Heath, Blue (*Phyllodoce caerulea*)
Helleborine, Red (*Cephalanthera rubra*)
Helleborine, Young's (*Epipactis youngiana*)
Horsetail, Branched (*Equisetum ramosissimum*)
Hound's-tongue, Green (*Cynoglossum germanicum*)
Knawel, Perennial (*Scleranthus perennis*)
Knotgrass, Sea (*Polygonum maritimum*)
Lady's-slipper (*Cypripedium calceolus*)
Lecanactis, Churchyard (*Lecanactis hemisphaerica*)
Lecanora, Tarn (*Lecanora archariana*)
Lecidea, Copper (*Lecidea inops*)
Leek, Round-headed (*Allium sphaerocephalon*)
Lettuce, Least (*Lactuca saligna*)
Lichen, Arctic Kidney (*Nephroma arcticum*)
Lichen, Ciliate Strap (*Heterodermia leucomelos*)
Lichen, Coralloid Rosette (*Heterodermia propagulifera*)
Lichen, Ear-lobed Dog (*Peltigera lepidophora*)
Lichen, Forked Hair (*Bryoria furcellata*)
Lichen, Golden Hair (*Teloschistes flavicans*)

Lichen, Orange Fruited Elm (*Caloplaca luteoalba*)
Lichen, River Jelly (*Collema dichotomum*)
Lichen, Scaly Breck (*Squamarina lentigera*)
Lichen, Stary Breck (*Buellia asterella*)
Lily, Snowdon (*Lloydia serotina*)
Liverwort (*Petallophyllum ralfsi*)
Liverwort, Lindenberg's Leafy (*Adelanthus lindenbergianus*)
Marsh-mallow, Rough (*Althaea hirsuta*)
Marshwort, Creeping (*Apium repens*)
Milk-parsley, Cambridge (*Selinum carvifolia*)
Moss (*Drepanocladius vernicosus*)
Moss, Alpine Copper (*Mielichoferia mielichoferi*)
Moss, Baltic Bog (*Sphagnum balticum*)
Moss, Blue Dew (*Saelania glaucescens*)
Moss, Blunt-leaved Bristle (*Orthotrichum obtusifolium*)
Moss, Bright Green Cave (*Cyclodictyon laetevirens*)
Moss, Cordate Beard (*Barbula cordata*)
Moss, Cornish Path (*Ditrichum cornubicum*)
Moss, Derbyshire Feather (*Thamnobryum angustifolium*)
Moss, Dune Thread (*Bryum mamillatum*)
Moss, Glaucous Beard (*Barbula glauca*)
Moss, Green Shield (*Buxbaumia viridis*)
Moss, Hair Silk (*Plagiothecium piliferum*)
Moss, Knothole (*Zygodon forsteri*)
Moss, Large Yellow Feather (*Scorpidium turgescens*)
Moss, Millimetre (*Micromitrium tenerum*)
Moss, Multifruited River (*Cryphaea lamyana*)
Moss, Nowell's Limestone (*Zygodon gracilis*)
Moss, Rigid Apple (*Bartramia stricta*)
Moss, Round-leaved Feather (*Rhyncostegium rotundifolium*)
Moss, Schleicher's Thread (*Bryum schleicheri*)
Moss, Triangular Pygmy (*Acaulon triquetrum*)
Moss, Vaucher's Feather (*Hypnum vaucheri*)
Mudwort, Welsh (*Limosella australis*)
Naiad, Holly-leaved (*Najas marina*)
Naiad, Slender (*Najas flexilis*)
Orache, Stalked (*Halimione pedunculata*)
Orchid, Early Spider (*Ophrys sphegodes*)
Orchid, Fen (*Liparis loeselii*)
Orchid, Ghost (*Epipogium aphyllum*)
Orchid, Lapland Marsh (*Dactylorhiza lapponica*)
Orchid, Late Spider (*Ophrys fuciflora*)
Orchid, Lizard (*Himantoglossum hircinum*)
Orchid, Military (*Orchis militaris*)
Orchid, Monkey (*Orchis simia*)
Pannaria, Caledonia (*Pannaria ignobilis*)
Parmelia, New Forest (*Parmelia minarum*)
Parmentaria, Oil Stain (*Parmentaria chilensis*)
Pear, Plymouth (*Pyrus cordata*)
Penny-cress, Perfoliate (*Thlaspi perfoliatum*)
Pennyroyal (*Mentha pulegium*)
Pertusaria, Alpine Moss (*Pertusaria bryontha*)
Physcia, Southern Grey (*Physcia tribacioides*)
Pigmyweed (*Crassula aquatica*)
Pine, Ground (*Ajuga chamaepitys*)
Pink, Cheddar (*Dianthus gratianopolitanus*)
Pink, Childling (*Petroraghia nanteuilii*)
Plantain, Floating Water (*Luronium natans*)
Pseudocyphellaria, Ragged (*Pseudocyphellaria lacerata*)
Psora, Rusty Alpine (*Psora rubiformis*)
Ragwort, Fen (*Senecio paludosus*)
Ramping-fumitory, Martin's (*Fumaria martinii*)
Rampion, Spiked (*Phyteuma spicatum*)
Restharrow, Small (*Ononis reclinata*)
Rock-cress, Alpine (*Arabis alpina*)
Rock-cress, Bristol (*Arabis stricta*)
Rustworth, Western (*Marsupella profunda*)
Sandwort, Norwegian (*Arenaria norvegica*)
Sandwort, Teesdale (*Minuartia stricta*)
Saxifrage, Drooping (*Saxifraga cernua*)

Saxifrage, Marsh (*Saxifrage hirulus*)
Saxifrage, Tufted (*Saxifraga cespitosa*)
Solenopsora, Serpentine (*Solenopsora liparina*)
Solomon's-seal, Whorled (*Polygonatum verticillatum*)
Sow-thistle, Alpine (*Cicerbita alpina*)
Spearwort, Adder's-tongue (*Ranunculus ophioglossifolius*)
Speedwell, Fingered (*Veronica triphyllos*)
Speedwell, Spiked (*Veronica spicata*)
Star-of-Bethlehem, Early (*Gagea bohemica*)
Starfruit (*Damasonium alisma*)
Stonewort, Bearded (*Chara canescens*)
Stonewort, Foxtail (*Lamprothamnium papulosum*)
Strapwort (*Corrigiola litoralis*)
Turpswort (*Geocalyx graveolens*)
Violet, Fen (*Viola persicifolia*)
Viper's-grass (*Scorzonera humilis*)
Water-plantain, Ribbon-leaved (*Alisma gramineum*)
Wood-sedge, Starved (*Carex depauperata*)
Woodsia, Alpine (*Woodsia alpina*)
Woodsia, Oblong (*Woodsia ilvensis*)
Wormwood, Field (*Artemisia campestris*)
Woundwort, Downy (*Stachys germanica*)
Woundwort, Limestone (*Stachys alpina*)
Yellow-rattle, Greater (*Rhinanthus serotinus*)

WILD BIRDS

The Wildlife and Countryside Act 1981 lays down a close season for wild birds (other than game birds) from 1 February to 31 August inclusive, each year. Exceptions to these dates are made for:

Capercaillie and (except Scotland) *Woodcock* – 1 February to 30 September
Snipe – 1 February to 11 August
Wild Duck and *Wild Goose* (below high water mark) – 21 February to 31 August

Birds which may be killed or taken outside the close season (except on Sundays and on Christmas Day in Scotland, and on Sundays in prescribed areas of England and Wales) are the above-named, plus coot, certain wild duck (gadwall, goldeneye, mallard, pintail, pochard, shoveler, teal, tufted duck, wigeon), certain wild geese (Canada, greylag, pink-footed, white-fronted (in England and Wales only)), moorhen, golden plover and woodcock.

Certain wild birds may be killed or taken subject to the conditions of a general licence at any time by authorized persons: crow, collared dove, gull (great and lesser black-backed or herring), jackdaw, jay, magpie, pigeon (feral or wood), rook, sparrow (house), and starling. Conditions usually apply where the birds pose a threat to agriculture, public health, air safety, other bird species, and to prevent the spread of disease.

All other British birds are fully protected by law throughout the year.

CLOSE SEASONS AND TIMES

GAME BIRDS

In each case the dates are inclusive:

Black game – 11 December to 19 August (31 August in Somerset, Devon and New Forest)
*Grouse – 11 December to 11 August
*Partridge – 2 February to 31 August
*Pheasant – 2 February to 30 September
*Ptarmigan – (Scotland only) 11 December to 11 August

*It is also unlawful in England and Wales to kill this game on a Sunday or Christmas Day

HUNTING AND GROUND GAME

There is no statutory close time for fox-hunting or rabbit-shooting, nor for hares. However, by an Act passed in 1892 the sale of hares or leverets in Great Britain is prohibited from 1 March to 31 July inclusive. The recognized date for the opening of the fox-hunting season is 1 November, and it continues till the following April.

DEER

The statutory close seasons for deer (all dates inclusive) are:

	England and Wales	Scotland
Fallow deer		
Male	1 May–31 July	1 May–31 July
Female	1 Mar.–31 Oct.	16 Feb.–20 Oct.
Red deer		
Male	1 May–31 July	21 Oct.–30 June
Female	1 Mar.–31 Oct.	16 Feb.–20 Oct.
Roe deer		
Male	1 Nov.–31 Mar.	21 Oct.–31 Mar.
Female	1 Mar.–31 Oct.	1 April–20 Oct.
Sika deer		
Male	1 May–31 July	21 Oct.–30 June
Female	1 Mar.–31 Oct.	16 Feb.–20 Oct.
Red/Sika hybrids		
Male	—	21 Oct.–30 June
Female	—	16 Feb.–20 Oct.

ANGLING

Game Fishing

Where local by-laws neither specify nor dispense with an annual close season, the statutory close times for game fishing are: Trout, 1 October to end February; Salmon, 1 November to 31 January.

Coarse Fishing

On 13 March 1995 the Government confirmed National Rivers Authority by-laws which make some changes to the close season for coarse fish in England and Wales. The statutory close season runs from 15 March to 15 June on all rivers, streams and drains. Close season arrangements for canals vary from region to region as previously. The close season on all lakes, ponds and reservoirs is at the discretion of the fishery owner, except on the Norfolk Broads and certain Sites of Special Scientific Interest where the statutory close season still applies. It is necessary in all cases to check with the NRA regional office concerning the area (details can be found in the local telephone directory).

Licences

Purchase of a national rod fishing licence is legally required of anglers wishing to fish with rod and line in all waters within the area of the NRA.

	Salmon and sea trout	Non-migratory trout and coarse fish
Full annual	£45.00	£15.00
Concessionary annual	22.50	7.50
Eight-day	13.50	4.50
One-day	4.50	1.50

Concessionary licences are available for juniors (12–16 years), for senior citizens (65 years and over), and disabled who are in receipt of invalidity benefit or severe disability allowance. Those in receipt of a war pension which includes unemployability supplements are also eligible.

Historic Buildings and Monuments

LISTING

Under the Planning (Listed Buildings and Conservation Areas) Act 1990, the Secretary of State for National Heritage has a statutory duty to compile lists of buildings or groups of buildings in England which are of special architectural or historic interest. Under the Ancient Monuments and Archaeological Areas Act 1979 as amended by the National Heritage Act 1983, the Secretary of State is also responsible for compiling a schedule of ancient monuments. Decisions are taken on the advice of English Heritage (*see* page 310).

Listed buildings are classified into Grade I, Grade II* and Grade II. There are currently about 500,000 individual listed buildings in England, of which about 95 per cent are Grade II listed. Almost all pre-1700 buildings are listed, and most buildings of 1700 to 1840. English Heritage is carrying out thematic surveys of particular types of buildings with a view to making recommendations for listing, and members of the public may propose a building for consideration. The main purpose of listing is to ensure that care is taken in deciding the future of a building. No changes which affect the architectural or historic character of a listed building can be made without listed building consent (in addition to planning permission where relevant). Applications for listed building consent are normally dealt with by the local planning authority, although English Heritage is always consulted about proposals affecting Grade I and Grade II* properties. It is a criminal offence to demolish a listed building, or alter it in such a way as to affect its character, without consent.

There are currently about 15,000 scheduled monuments in England. English Heritage is carrying out a Monuments Protection Programme assessing archaeological sites with a view to making recommendations for scheduling, and members of the public may propose a monument for consideration. All monuments proposed for scheduling are considered to be of national importance. Where buildings are both scheduled and listed, ancient monuments legislation takes precedence. The main purpose of scheduling a monument is to preserve it for the future and to protect it from damage, destruction or any unnecessary interference. Once a monument has been scheduled, scheduled monument consent is required before any works are carried out which would damage or alter the monument in any way. The scope of the control is more extensive and more detailed than that applied to listed buildings, but certain minor works, as detailed in the Ancient Monuments Class Consents Order 1994, may be carried out without consent. It is a criminal offence to carry out unauthorized work to scheduled monuments.

Under the Planning (Listed Buildings and Conservation Areas) Act 1990 and the Ancient Monuments and Archaeological Areas Act 1979, the Secretary of State for Wales is responsible for listing buildings and scheduling monuments in Wales on the advice of Cadw (*see* page 359), the Historic Buildings Council for Wales (*see* page 310) and the Ancient Monuments Board for Wales (*see* page 311). The criteria for evaluating buildings are similar to those in England and the same listing system is used. There are about 17,000 listed buildings and about 2,800 scheduled monuments in Wales.

Under the Town and County Planning (Scotland) Act 1972 and the Ancient Monuments and Archaeological Areas Act 1979, the Secretary of State for Scotland is responsible for listing buildings and scheduling monuments in Scotland on the advice of Historic Scotland (*see* page 345), the Historic Buildings Council for Scotland (*see* page 310) and the Ancient Monuments Board for Scotland (*see* page 311). The criteria for evaluating buildings are similar to those in England but an A, B, C grading system is used. There are about 40,000 listed buildings and about 6,000 scheduled monuments in Scotland.

Under the Planning (Northern Ireland) Order 1991 and the Historic Monuments and Archaeological Objects (Northern Ireland) Order 1995, the Department of the Environment for Northern Ireland (*see* page 333) is responsible for listing buildings and scheduling monuments in Northern Ireland on the advice of the Historic Buildings Council for Northern Ireland and the Historic Monuments Council for Northern Ireland. The criteria for evaluating buildings are similar to those in England but no official grading system is used. There are about 8,550 listed buildings and 1,120 scheduled monuments in Northern Ireland.

The Government proposes to reform the system for protecting the built heritage in Great Britain. In March 1995 public consultation was introduced on all listing recommendations arising from English Heritage's thematic surveys of particular building types, and a Green Paper is planned for autumn 1995.

OPENING TO THE PUBLIC

The following is a selection of the many historic buildings and monuments open to the public. The admission charges given are the standard charges for 1995–6; many properties have concessionary rates for children, etc. Opening hours vary. Many properties are closed in winter and some are also closed in the mornings. Most properties are closed on Christmas Eve, Christmas Day, Boxing Day and New Year's Day, and many are closed on Good Friday. During the winter season, most English Heritage monuments are closed on Mondays and monuments in the care of Cadw are closed on Sunday mornings. Information about a specific property should be checked by telephone.

*Closed in winter (usually November-March)
†Closed in winter, and in mornings in summer

ENGLAND

EH English Heritage property
NT National Trust property

*A LA RONDE (NT), Exmouth, Devon. Tel: 01395-265514. Closed Fri. and Sat. Adm. £3.10. Unique 16-sided house built in 1796

*ALNWICK CASTLE, Northumberland. Tel: 01665-510777. Adm. charge. Seat of the Dukes of Northumberland since 1309; Italian Renaissance-style interior

ALTHORP, Northants. Tel: 01604-770107. Opening times and prices subject to change. House originally built in early 16th century. Fine art collection

†ANGLESEY ABBEY (NT), Cambs. Tel: 01223-811200. Closed Mon. (except Bank Holidays) and Tues. Adm. £4.80; gardens only, £3.00. House built *c*.1600; bought by Lord Fairhaven in early 20th century. Outstanding grounds with unique statuary

APSLEY HOUSE, London W1. Tel: 0171-499 5676. Closed Mon. Adm £3.00. Built by Robert Adam 1771-8, home

of the Dukes of Wellington since 1817 and known as
'No. 1 London'. Collection of fine and decorative arts
†ARUNDEL CASTLE, W. Sussex. Tel: 01903-883136.
Closed Sat. and Good Fri. Adm. charge. Castle dating
from the Norman Conquest. Seat of the Dukes of Norfolk
AVERBURY (NT), Wilts. Adm. free. Remains of stone circles
constructed 4,000 years ago surrounding the later
village of Avebury. Also *Avebury Museum*. Tel: 01672-
539250. Adm. £1.35
BANQUETING HOUSE, Whitehall, London SW1. Tel: 0171-
839 8919. Closed Sun. and Bank Holidays. Adm. £2.90.
Designed by Inigo Jones; ceiling paintings by Rubens.
Site of the execution of Charles I
*BASILDON PARK (NT), Berks. Tel: 01734-843040. Closed
Mon. (except Bank Holidays) and Tues. Adm. £3.60;
grounds only, £1.50. Palladian house built in 1776;
unusual octagonal room
BATTLE ABBEY (EH), E. Sussex. Tel: 01424-773792. Adm.
£3.50. Remains of the abbey founded by William the
Conqueror on the site of the Battle of Hastings
BEAULIEU, Hants. Tel: 01590-612345. Adm. charge.
House and gardens, Beaulieu Abbey and exhibition of
monastic life, National Motor Museum (*see also* page
593)
BEESTON CASTLE (EH), Cheshire. Tel: 01829-260464.
Adm. £2.20. Thirteenth-century inner ward with
gatehouse and towers, and remains of large outer ward
†BELTON HOUSE (NT), Grantham, Lincs. Tel: 01476-
66116. Closed Mon. (except Bank Holidays) and Tues.
Adm. £4.30. Fine 17th-century house in landscaped park
*BELVOIR CASTLE, nr Grantham, Lincs. Tel: 01476-
870262. Closed Mon. and Fri. except Bank Holidays.
Adm. £4.25. Seat of the Dukes of Rutland; 19th-century
Gothic-style castle
*BERKELEY CASTLE, Glos. Tel: 01453-810332. Opening
times vary. Adm. £4.00. Completed 1153; site of the
murder of Edward II (1327). Elizabethan terraced
gardens
*BLENHEIM PALACE, Woodstock, Oxon. Tel: 01993-
811325. Adm. charge. Seat of the Dukes of Marlborough
and Winston Churchill's birthplace; designed by
Vanbrugh
†BLICKLING HALL (NT), Norfolk. Tel: 01263-733084.
Closed Mon. (except Bank Holidays) and Thurs. Adm.
£4.90; garden only, £2.50. Jacobean house with state
rooms, Long Gallery, formal gardens, temple and 18th-
century orangery
BODIAM CASTLE (NT), E. Sussex. Tel: 01580-830436.
Closed Mon. in winter. Adm. £2.50. Well-preserved
medieval moated castle
BOLSOVER CASTLE (EH), Derbys. Tel: 01246-823349.
Closed Mon. and Tues. in winter. Adm. £2.50. Notable
for its 17th-century buildings
BOSCOBEL HOUSE (EH), Shropshire. Tel: 01902-850244.
Closed Mon. and Tues. in winter. Adm. £3.30. Timber-
framed 17th-century hunting lodge, refuge of fugitive
Charles II
†BOUGHTON HOUSE, Northants. Tel: 01536-515731.
House open Aug. only; grounds May to Sept. except
Fri. State rooms by prior booking. Adm. £4.00; grounds
£1.50. A 17th-century house with French-style additions
*BOWOOD HOUSE, Wilts. Tel: 01249-812102. Adm. £4.50.
An 18th-century house in Capability Brown park, with
lake, temple and arboretum
†BROADLANDS, Hants. Tel: 01794-516878. Open July-
Sept. Adm. £5.00. Palladian mansion in Capability
Brown parkland. Mountbatten exhibition
BRONTË PARSONAGE, Haworth, W. Yorks. Tel: 01535-
642323. Closed Jan.- Feb. Adm. £3.60. Home of the
Brontë sisters; museum and memorabilia

BUCKFAST ABBEY, Devon. Tel: 01364-642519. Adm. free.
Medieval monastery rebuilt 1907-1938
*BUCKINGHAM PALACE, London SW1. Tel: 0171-799 2331.
Open daily for eight weeks from early Aug. each year.
Adm. £8.50. Purchased by George III in 1762, it has
been the Sovereign's official London residence since
1837. Eighteen state rooms, including the Throne
Room; also the picture gallery
BUCKLAND ABBEY (NT), Devon. Tel: 01822-853607.
Closed Thurs. In winter open only weekend afternoons.
Adm. £4.00. A 13th-century Cistercian monastery.
Home of Sir Francis Drake
*BURGHLEY HOUSE, Stamford, Lincs. Tel: 01780-52451.
Adm. £5.10. Late Elizabethan house; vast state
apartments
†CALKE ABBEY (NT), Derbys. Tel: 01332-863822. Closed
Thurs. and Fri. Adm. £4.50, by timed ticket. Baroque
18th-century mansion
CARISBROOKE CASTLE (EH), Isle of Wight. Tel: 01983-
522107. Adm. £3.20. Norman castle; prison of Charles I
1647-8
CARLISLE CASTLE (EH), Cumbria. Tel: 01228-591922.
Adm. £2.00. Medieval castle, prison of Mary Queen of
Scots
*CARLYLE'S HOUSE (NT), Cheyne Row, London SW3. Tel:
0171-352 7087. Home of Thomas Carlyle
CASTLE ACRE PRIORY (EH), Norfolk. Tel: 01760-755394.
Adm. £2.10. Remains include 12th-century church and
prior's lodgings
*CASTLE DROGO (NT), Devon. Tel: 01647-433306. Closed
Fri. Adm. £4.60; grounds only, £2.00. Granite castle
designed by Lutyens
*CASTLE HOWARD, N. Yorks. Tel: 01653-684333. Adm.
£6.00. Designed by Vanbrugh 1699-1726; mausoleum
designed by Hawksmoor
CASTLE RISING CASTLE (EH), Norfolk. Tel: 01553-
631330. Adm. £1.25. A 12th-century keep in a massive
earthwork with gatehouse and bridge
†CHARTWELL (NT), Kent. Tel: 01732-866368. Closed Fri.
and Mon. (except Bank Holidays). Adm. £4.20; grounds
only, £2.00. Home of Sir Winston Churchill
*CHATSWORTH, Derbys. Tel: 01246-582204. Adm. charge.
Tudor mansion with later additions in magnificent
parkland
CHESTERS ROMAN FORT (EH), Northumberland. Tel:
01434-681379. Adm. £2.00. Fine example of a Roman
cavalry fort
*CHYSAUSTER ANCIENT VILLAGE (EH), Cornwall. Tel:
01736-61889. Adm. £1.30. Romano-Cornish village,
2nd and 3rd century AD, on a probably late Iron Age site
CLIFFORD'S TOWER (EH), York. Tel: 01904-646940. Adm.
£1.50. A 13th-century tower built on a mound
†CLIVEDEN (NT), Berks. Tel: 01628-605069. House open
Thurs. and Sun. only, gardens daily. Adm. £3.80, £1.00
extra for house. Former home of the Astors, now an
hotel set in garden and woodland
CORBRIDGE ROMAN SITE (EH), Northumberland. Tel:
01434-632349. Adm. £2.00. Excavated central area of a
Roman town and successive military bases
CORFE CASTLE (NT), Dorset. Tel: 01929-481294. Nov.-
Jan. open weekend afternoons only. Adm. £2.90. Ruined
former royal castle dating from 11th century
†CROFT CASTLE (NT), Herefordshire. Tel: 01568-780246.
Closed Mon. (except Bank Holidays) and Tues.; April
and Oct. open weekends only. Adm. £3.00. Pre-
Conquest border castle with Georgian-Gothic interior
DEAL CASTLE (EH), Kent. Tel: 01304-372762. Adm. £2.00.
Largest and most complete of the coastal defence forts
built by Henry VIII

DICKENS HOUSE, Doughty Street, London wc1. Tel: 0171-405 2127. Closed Sun. Adm. £3.00. House occupied by Dickens 1837-9; manuscripts, furniture and portraits

DR JOHNSON'S HOUSE, 17 Gough Square, London EC4. Tel: 0171-353 3745. Closed Sun. and Bank Holidays. Adm. £3.00. Home of Samuel Johnson

DOVE COTTAGE, Grasmere, Cumbria. Tel: 015394-35544. Closed Jan. and early Feb. Adm. £3.70. Wordsworth's home 1799-1808; museum and memorabilia

DOVER CASTLE (EH), Kent. Tel: 01304-201628. Adm. £5.25. Castle with Roman, Saxon and Norman features; wartime operations rooms

DUNSTANBURGH CASTLE (EH), Northumberland. Tel: 01665-576231. Adm. £1.25. A 14th-century castle on a cliff, with a substantial gatehouse-keep

FARLEIGH HUNGERFORD CASTLE (EH), Somerset. Tel: 01225-754026. Adm. £1.25. Late 14th-century castle with two courts and chapel with tomb of Sir Thomas Hungerford

*FARNHAM CASTLE KEEP (EH), Surrey. Tel: 01252-713393. Adm. £1.80. Large 12th-century shell-keep on motte

FOUNTAINS ABBEY (NT), nr Ripon, N. Yorks. Tel: 01765-608888. Closed Fri. Nov.-Jan. Adm. £4.00. Ruined Cistercian monastery; 18th-century landscaped gardens of Studley Royal estate

FRAMLINGHAM CASTLE (EH), Suffolk. Tel: 01728-724189. Adm. £1.80. Castle (c.1200) with high curtain walls enclosing an almshouse (1639)

FURNESS ABBEY (EH), Cumbria. Tel: 01229-823420. Adm. £2.00. Remains of church and conventual buildings founded in 1123

GLASTONBURY ABBEY, Somerset. Tel: 01458-832267. Adm. £2.00. Ruins of a 12th-century abbey rebuilt after fire. Site of an early Christian settlement

GOODRICH CASTLE (EH), Herefordshire. Tel: 01600-890538. Adm. £2.00. Remains of 13th- and 14th-century castle with 12th-century keep

GREENWICH, London SE10. *Royal Observatory.* Closed Sun. mornings. Adm. charge. Former Royal Observatory (founded 1675) where the time ball and zero meridian of longitude can be seen. *The Queen's House.* Tel: 0181-858 4422. Closed Sun. mornings. Adm. charge. Designed for Queen Anne, wife of James I, by Inigo Jones. *Painted Hall and Chapel* (Royal Naval College). Closed mornings and Thurs. Visitors are admitted to Sunday service in the chapel at 11 a.m. except during college vacations

GRIMES GRAVES (EH), Norfolk. Tel: 01842-810656. Adm. £1.30. Neolithic flint mines. One shaft can be descended

*GUILDHALL, London EC2. Tel: 0171-606 3030. Closed Sat. Adm. free. Centre of civic government of the City. Built c.1440; facade built 1788-9

*HADDON HALL, Derbys. Tel: 01629-812855. Closed Sun. in July and Aug. except Bank Holiday weekend. Adm. £4.50. Well-preserved 12th-century manor house

HAILES ABBEY (EH), Glos. Tel: 01242-602398. Closed Mon. and Tues. in winter. Adm. £2.00. Ruins of a 13th-century Cistercian monastery

†HAM HOUSE (NT), Richmond, Surrey. Tel: 0181-940 1950. Closed Thurs. and Fri., also Sat. and Sun. mornings Nov.-Dec. Adm. £4.00; garden open all year except Mon., adm. free. Stuart house with fine interiors

HAMPTON COURT PALACE, East Molesey, Surrey. Tel: 0181-781 9500. Adm. £7.50. A 16th-century palace with additions by Wren. Gardens with maze; Tudor tennis court (summer only)

†HARDWICK HALL (NT), Derbys. Tel: 01246-850430. Closed Mon. (except Bank Holidays), Tues. and Fri. Adm. £5.50; garden open daily, adm. £2.00. Built 1591-7 by Bess of Hardwick; notable furnishings

*HARDY'S COTTAGE (NT), Higher Bockhampton, Dorset. Tel: 01305-262366. Interior open only by appointment. Adm. £2.50. Garden open daily, adm. free. Birthplace of Thomas Hardy

*HAREWOOD HOUSE, W. Yorks. Tel: 0113-288 6331. Adm. charge. An 18th-century house designed by John Carr and Robert Adam; park by Capability Brown

†HATFIELD HOUSE, Herts. Tel: 01707-262823. Closed Mon. (except Bank Holidays). Adm. charge. Jacobean house built by Robert Cecil, and family home of the Cecils. Surviving wing of royal Palace of Hatfield (1497)

HELMSLEY CASTLE (EH), N. Yorks. Tel: 01439-770442. Closed Mon. and Tues. in winter. Adm. £2.00. A 12th-century keep and curtain wall with 16th-century buildings. Spectacular earthwork defences

†HEVER CASTLE, Kent. Tel: 01732-865224. Adm. charge. A 13th-century double-moated castle, childhood home of Anne Boleyn

*HOLKER HALL, Cumbria. Tel: 015395-58328. Adm. charge. Former home of the Dukes of Devonshire; award-winning gardens

†HOLKHAM HALL, Norfolk. Tel: 01328-710227. Closed Fri. and Sat. Adm. £3.00. Fine Palladian mansion

HOUSESTEADS ROMAN FORT (EH), Northumberland. Tel: 01434-344363. Adm. £2.30. Excavated infantry fort on Hadrian's Wall with extra-mural civilian settlement

†HUGHENDEN MANOR (NT), High Wycombe. Tel: 01494-532580. Closed Mon. (except Bank Holidays) and Tues.; open weekends only in March. Adm. £3.60. Home of Disraeli; small formal garden

JANE AUSTEN'S HOUSE, Chawton, Hants. Tel: 01420-83262. Open daily April-Oct., opening times vary in winter. Adm. £2.00. Jane Austen's home 1809-17

KEATS HOUSE, Keats Grove, London NW3. Tel: 0171-435 2062. Closed Sun. mornings in summer, mornings except Sat. in winter. Adm. free. Home of John Keats 1818-20

*KELMSCOTT MANOR, nr Lechlade, Glos. Tel: 01367-252486. Open Wed. only (Thurs. and Fri. by written application). Adm. £6.00. Summer home of William Morris, with products of Morris and Co.

KENILWORTH CASTLE (EH), Warks. Tel: 01926-52078. Adm. £2.00. Castle showing many styles of building from 1155 to 1649

KENWOOD (EH), Hampstead Lane, London NW3. Tel: 0181-348 1286. Adm. free. Adam villa housing the Iveagh bequest of paintings and furniture. Open-air concerts in summer

*KEW PALACE, Surrey. Tel: 0181-332 5189. Adm. £1.00 (plus £4.00 adm. to Kew Gardens). Built in 1631 as the Dutch House; residence of George III. Also *Queen Charlotte's Cottage*, weekends and Bank Holidays only. Adm. 70p. Joint ticket £1.00

†KINGSTON LACY HOUSE (NT), Dorset. Tel: 01202-883402. Closed Thurs. and Fri. Adm. £5.50; grounds only, £2.20. A 17th-century house with 19th-century alterations; important collection of paintings

†KNEBWORTH HOUSE, Herts. Tel: 01438-812661. Adm. £4.50; grounds only, £3.00. Tudor manor house concealed by 19th-century Gothic decoration; Lutyens gardens

*KNOLE (NT), Kent. Tel: 01732-450608. Closed Mon. (except Bank Holidays), Tues. and Thurs. morning. Adm. £4.00; park free to pedestrians. House dating from 1456 set in parkland; fine art treasures

LAMBETH PALACE, London SE1. Tel: 0171-928 8282. Visits by written application a year in advance. Official residence of the Archbishop of Canterbury. A 19th-century house with parts dating from the 12th century

*LANERCOST PRIORY (EH), Cumbria. Tel: 016977-3030. Adm. £1.00. The nave of the Augustinian priory church, c.1166, is still used; remains of other claustral buildings

*LANHYDROCK (NT), Cornwall. Tel: 01208-73320. Closed Mon. (except Bank Holidays). Garden open daily including in winter. Adm. £5.40; gardens only, £2.50. House dating from the 17th century; 45 rooms, including kitchen and nursery

LEEDS CASTLE, Kent. Tel: 01622-765400. Adm. £7.30; park only, £5.50. Castle dating from the 9th century, on two islands in a lake

*LEVENS HALL, Cumbria. Tel: 015395-60321. Closed Fri. and Sat. Adm. charge. Elizabethan house with unique topiary garden (1694). Steam engine collection

LINCOLN CASTLE. Tel: 01522-511068. Adm. £2.00. Built by William the Conqueror in 1068

LINDISFARNE PRIORY (EH), Northumberland. Tel: 01289-89200. Open all year, subject to tide times. Adm. £2.30. Bishopric of the Northumbrian kingdom destroyed by the Danes; re-established in the 11th century as a Benedictine priory, now ruined

†LITTLE MORETON HALL (NT), Cheshire. Tel: 01260-272018. Closed Mon. (except Bank Holidays) and Tues. Adm. £3.50. Timber-framed moated manor house with knot garden

LONGLEAT HOUSE, Warminster. Tel: 01985-844400. Open daily; safari park closed winter. Adm. charge. Elizabethan house in Italian Renaissance style

LULLINGSTONE ROMAN VILLA (EH), Kent. Tel: 01322-863467. Adm. £2.00. Large villa occupied for much of the Roman period; fine mosaics

†LUTON HOO, Beds. Tel: 01582-22955. Open Fri.-Sun. and Bank Holiday Mon. Adm. £5.50. Houses the Wernher collection of china, glass, pictures and other *objets d'art*

MANSION HOUSE, London EC4. Tel: 0171-626 2500. Group visits only, by prior arrangement. The official residence of the Lord Mayor of London

MARBLE HILL HOUSE (EH), Twickenham, Middx. Tel: 0181-892 5115. Closed Mon. and Tues. in winter. Adm. £2.00. English Palladian villa with Georgian paintings and furniture

*MICHELHAM PRIORY, E. Sussex. Tel: 01323-844224. Adm. £3.60. Tudor house built onto an Augustinian priory

MIDDLEHAM CASTLE (EH), N. Yorks. Tel: 01969-623899. Adm. £1.50. A 12th-century keep within later fortifications. Childhood home of Richard III

†MONTACUTE HOUSE (NT), Somerset. Tel: 01935-823289. Closed Tues; grounds open all year. Adm. £4.80; grounds only, £2.70. Elizabethan house with National Portrait Gallery portraits from period

*MOUNT GRACE PRIORY (EH), N. Yorks. Tel: 01609-883494. Adm. £2.20. Carthusian monastery, with remains of monastic buildings

NETLEY ABBEY (EH), Hants. Tel: 01705-527667. Adm. free. Remains of Cistercian abbey, used as house in Tudor period

OLD SARUM (EH), Wilts. Tel: 01722-335398. Adm. £1.50. Earthworks enclosing remains of the castle and the 11th-century cathedral

ORFORD CASTLE (EH), Suffolk. Tel: 013944-50472. Adm. £2.00. Circular keep of c.1170 and remains of coastal defence castle built by Henry II

*OSBORNE HOUSE (EH), Isle of Wight. Tel: 01983-200022. Adm. £5.80. Queen Victoria's seaside residence

†OSTERLEY PARK HOUSE (NT), Isleworth, Middx. Tel: 0181-560 3918. Closed Mon. (except Bank Holidays) and Tues; grounds open all year. Adm. £3.60; grounds free. Elizabethan mansion set in parkland

PENDENNIS CASTLE (EH), Cornwall. Tel: 01326-316594. Adm. £2.20. Well-preserved coastal defence castle built by Henry VIII

†PENSHURST PLACE, Kent. Tel: 01892-870307. Adm. £4.95; grounds only, £3.50. House with medieval Baron's Hall and 14th-century gardens

†PETWORTH (NT), W. Sussex. Tel: 01798-342207. Closed Mon. (except Bank Holidays) and Fri. Adm. £4.00. Late 17th-century house set in deer park

PEVENSEY CASTLE (EH), E. Sussex. Tel: 01323-762604. Closed Mon. and Tues. in winter. Adm. charge. Walls of a 4th-century Roman fort enclosing remains of an 11th-century castle

PEVERIL CASTLE (EH), Derbys. Tel: 01433-620613. Adm. £1.30. A 12th-century castle defended on two sides by precipitous rocks

†POLESDEN LACY (NT), Surrey. Tel: 01372-458203. Closed Mon. (except Bank Holidays) and Tues., open weekends only in March. Grounds open daily all year. Adm. £5.50; grounds only £2.50. Regency villa remodelled in the Edwardian era. Fine paintings and furnishings

PORTCHESTER CASTLE (EH), Hants. Tel: 01705-378291. Adm. £2.50. Walls of a late Roman fort enclosing a Norman keep and an Augustinian priory church

*POWDERHAM CASTLE, Devon. Tel: 01626-890243. Closed Sat. Adm. charge. Medieval castle with 18th- and 19th-century alterations

†RABY CASTLE, Co. Durham. Tel: 01833-660202. Closed Sat. (except Bank Holiday weekends). Limited opening in May and June. Adm. £3.50; grounds only, £1.00. A 14th-century castle with walled gardens

*RAGLEY HALL, Warks. Tel: 01789-762090. Closed Mon. (except Bank Holidays) and Fri.; grounds open daily. Adm. £4.50. A 17th-century house with gardens, park and lake

RICHBOROUGH CASTLE (EH), Kent. Tel: 01304-612013. Adm. £2.00. Landing-site of the Claudian invasion in AD 43, with 3rd-century stone walls

RICHMOND CASTLE (EH), N. Yorks. Tel: 01748-822493. Adm. £1.80. A 12th-century keep with 11th-century curtain wall and domestic buildings

RIEVAULX ABBEY (EH), N. Yorks. Tel: 01439-798228. Adm. £2.40. Remains of a Cistercian abbey founded c.1131

ROCHESTER CASTLE (EH), Kent. Tel: 01634-402276. Adm. £2.50. An 11th-century castle partly on the Roman city wall, with a square keep of c.1130

†ROCKINGHAM CASTLE, Northants. Tel: 01536-770240. Open Sun. and Thurs. only (and Bank Holiday Mon. and Tues., and Tues. in Aug.). Adm. £3.80; gardens only, £2.30. Built by William the Conqueror

ROYAL PAVILION, Brighton. Tel: 01273-603005. Adm. charge. Palace of George IV, in Chinese style with Indian exterior and Regency gardens

†RUFFORD OLD HALL (NT), Lancs. Tel: 01704-821254. Closed Thurs. and Fri. Adm. £3.00; garden only, £1.60. A 16th-century hall with unique screen

ST AUGUSTINE'S ABBEY (EH), Canterbury, Kent. Tel: 01227-767345. Adm. £1.50. Remains of Benedictine monastery, with Norman church, on site of abbey founded AD 598 by St Augustine

ST MAWES CASTLE (EH), Cornwall. Tel: 01326-270526. Adm. £1.50. Coastal defence castle built by Henry VIII comprising central tower and three bastions

ST MICHAEL'S MOUNT (NT), Cornwall. Tel: 01736-710507. Closed Sat. and Sun., also Tues. and Thurs. in winter. No regular ferry service in winter; castle open as tide, weather, etc., permit. Adm. £3.50. A 14th-century castle with later additions and alterations, off the coast at Marazion

*SANDRINGHAM, Norfolk. Tel: 01553-772675. Closed for three weeks in summer and when the Royal Family is in residence. Adm. £4.00; grounds only, £3.00. The Queen's private residence; a neo-Jacobean house built in 1870

SCARBOROUGH CASTLE (EH), N. Yorks. Tel: 01723-372451. Adm. £1.50. Remains of 12th-century keep and curtain walls

†SHERBORNE CASTLE, Dorset. Tel: 01935-813182. Open Thurs., Sat., Sun. and Bank Holiday Mon. Adm. charge. Early 12th-century castle owned by Sir Walter Raleigh

*SHUGBOROUGH (NT), Staffs. Tel: 01889-881388. Adm. house, servants' quarters and farm, £7.50; each site alone, £3.50. House set in 18th-century park with monuments, temples and pavilions in the Greek Revival style

SKIPTON CASTLE, N. Yorks. Tel: 01756-792442. Closed Sun. mornings. Adm. £3.20. D-shaped castle with six round towers and beautiful inner courtyard

†SMALLHYTHE PLACE (NT), Kent. Tel: 01580-762334. Closed Thurs.-Fri. (open Good Friday). Adm. £2.50. Half-timbered 16th-century house; home of Ellen Terry 1899-1928

†STANFORD HALL, Leics. Tel: 01788-860250. Open Sat.-Sun.; also Bank Holiday Mon. and Tues. Adm. £3.20; grounds only, £1.80. William and Mary house with Stuart portraits. Motorcycle museum

STONEHENGE (EH), Wilts. Tel: 01980-624715. Adm. £3.00. Prehistoric monument consisting of a series of concentric stone circles surrounded by a ditch and bank

STONELEIGH ABBEY, Warks. Tel: 01926-52116. Open by appointment only; closed weekends. Early 18th-century Georgian mansion on the site of a Cistercian abbey

†STONOR PARK, Oxon. Tel: 01491-638587. Opening days vary. Adm. £4.00. Medieval house with Georgian facade. Centre of Roman Catholicism after the Reformation

†STOURHEAD (NT), Wilts. Tel: 01985-844785. Closed Thurs.-Fri. Gardens open daily all year. Adm. £4.30; gardens, £4.20. English Palladian mansion with famous gardens

*STRATFIELD SAYE HOUSE, Hants. Tel: 01256-882882. Closed Fri. Wellington Country Park, open daily. Adm. charge. House built 1630-40; home of the Dukes of Wellington since 1817

STRAFORD-UPON-AVON, Warks. *Shakespeare's Birthplace* with Shakespeare Centre; *Anne Hathaway's Cottage*, home of Shakespeare's wife; *Mary Arden's House*, home of Shakespeare's mother; *New Place*, where Shakespeare died; and *Hall's Croft*, home of Shakespeare's daughter. Tel: 01789-204016. Adm. charges. Also *Grammar School* attended by Shakespeare, *Royal Shakespeare Theatre* (burnt down 1926, rebuilt 1932) and *Swan Theatre* (opened 1986)

*SUDELEY CASTLE, Glos. Tel: 01242-602308. Adm. £4.95. Castle built in 1442; restored in the 19th century

*SYON HOUSE, Brentford, Middx. Tel: 0181-560 0881. Opening times vary. Adm. charge. Built on the site of a former monastery; Adam interior

TILBURY FORT (EH), Essex. Tel: 01375-858489. Adm. £1.80. A 17th-century coastal fort

TINTAGEL CASTLE (EH), Cornwall. Tel: 01840-770328. Adm. £2.20. A 12th-century cliff-top castle and Dark Age settlement site

TOWER OF LONDON, London EC3. Tel: 0171-709 0765. Adm. charge. Royal palace and fortress begun by William the Conqueror in 1078. Houses the Crown Jewels and the national collection of arms and armour

*TRERICE (NT), Cornwall. Tel: 01637-875404. Closed Tues. Adm. £3.60. Elizabethan manor house

TYNEMOUTH PRIORY AND CASTLE (EH), Tyne and Wear. Tel: 0191-257 1090. Adm. £1.30. Remains of a Benedictine priory, founded 1090, on Saxon monastic site. First World War gun battery open Fri.-Mon. afternoons

†UPPARK (NT), Hants. Tel: 01730-825317. Closed Fri. and Sat. Adm. £5.00 by timed ticket. Late 17th-century house, completely restored after fire. Fetherstonhaugh art collection

WALMER CASTLE (EH), Kent. Tel: 01304-364288. Closed Jan.-Feb. and when the Lord Warden is in residence. Adm. £3.50. One of Henry VIII's coastal defence castles, now the residence of the Lord Warden of the Cinque Ports

WALTHAM ABBEY (EH), Essex. Adm. free. Ruined abbey including the nave of the abbey church, 'Harold's Bridge' and late 14th-century gatehouse. Traditionally the burial place of Harold II (1066)

WARKWORTH CASTLE (EH), Northumberland. Tel: 01665-711423. Adm. £2.00. A 15th-century keep amidst earlier ruins, with 14th-century hermitage (open Wed. and Sun. in summer only) upstream

WARWICK CASTLE. Tel: 01926-408000. Adm. £8.25. Medieval castle with Madam Tussaud's waxworks, in Capability Brown parkland

WHITBY ABBEY (EH), N. Yorks. Tel: 01947-603568. Adm. £1.50. Remains of Norman church on the site of a monastery founded in AD 657

*WILTON HOUSE, Wilts. Tel: 01722-743115. Adm. £5.75. A 17th-century house on the site of a Tudor house and Saxon abbey. Notable art collection

WINDSOR CASTLE, Berks. Tel: 01753-831118 for recorded information on opening times. Adm. £9.00, including the Castle precincts. Official residence of The Queen; oldest royal residence still in regular use. State apartments, Queen Mary's Dolls' House, Exhibition of The Queen's Presents and Royal Carriages. Restoration work in progress on fire-damaged state rooms (which may still be viewed). Also *St George's Chapel* and *Royal Mausoleum*, Frogmore Gardens

WOBURN ABBEY, Beds. Tel: 01525-290666. Closed Nov.-Dec., also Mon.-Fri. Jan.-March. Adm. £6.50. Built on the site of a Cistercian abbey; seat of the Dukes of Bedford. Important art collection; unusual antiques centre

WROXETER ROMAN CITY (EH), Shropshire. Tel: 01743-761330. Closed Mon. and Tues. in winter. Adm. £2.30. Second-century public baths and part of the forum of the Roman town of Viroconium

---

WALES

c Property of Cadw: Welsh Historic Monuments
NT National Trust property

BEAUMARIS CASTLE (C), Anglesey. Tel: 01248-810361. Adm. £1.70. Fine concentrically-planned castle, still almost intact

CAERLEON ROMAN BATHS AND AMPHITHEATRE (C), Gwent. Tel: 01633-422518. Adm. £1.70, joint ticket with Legionary Museum £2.50. Rare example of a legionary bath-house and late 1st-century arena surrounded by bank for spectators

CAERNARFON CASTLE (C), Gwynedd. Tel: 01286-677617. Adm. £3.80. Important Edwardian castle built, with the town wall, between 1283 and 1330

CAERPHILLY CASTLE (C), Mid Glamorgan. Tel: 01222-883143. Adm. £2.20. Concentrically-planned castle (c.1270) notable for its scale and use of water defences

CARDIFF CASTLE, S. Glamorgan. Tel: 01222-822083. Adm. charge. Castle built on the site of a Roman fort; spectacular towers and rich interior

CASTELL COCH (C), S. Glamorgan. Tel: 01222-810101. Adm. £2.20. Rebuilt 1875-90 on medieval foundations

CHEPSTOW CASTLE (C), Gwent. Tel: 01291-624065. Adm. £2.50. Rectangular keep amid extensive fortifications

CONWY CASTLE (C), Gwynedd. Tel: 01492-592358. Adm. £3.00. Built by Edward I, 1283-7

CRICCIETH CASTLE (C), Gwynedd. Tel: 01766-522227. Adm. £2.20. Native Welsh 13th-century castle, altered by Edward I

*DENBIGH CASTLE (C), Clwyd. Tel: 01745-813979. Adm. £1.70. Remains of the castle (begun 1282), including triple-towered gatehouse

HARLECH CASTLE (C), Gwynedd. Tel: 01766-780552. Adm. £3.00. Well-preserved Edwardian castle, constructed 1283-90, on an outcrop above the former shore-line

PEMBROKE CASTLE, Dyfed. Tel: 01646-681510. Adm. £2.20. Castle founded in 1093, with a Great Tower 75 feet tall; birthplace of King Henry VII

†PENRHYN CASTLE (NT), Bangor. Tel: 01248-353084. Closed Tues. Adm. £4.40; garden only, £2.00. Neo-Norman castle built in the 19th century. Industrial railway museum

PORTMEIRION, Gwynedd. Tel: 01766-770228. Adm. £3.00 (April-Oct.), £1.50 (Nov.-March). Village in Italianate style

†POWIS CASTLE (NT), Powys. Tel: 01938-554336. Closed Mon. (except Bank Holidays) and Tues. (except July and Aug.). Adm. £5.80; garden only, £3.80. Medieval castle with interior in variety of styles; 17th-century gardens and Clive of India museum

RAGLAN CASTLE (C), Gwent. Tel: 01291-690228. Adm. £2.20. Remains of 15th-century castle with moated hexagonal keep

ST DAVIDS BISHOP'S PALACE (C), Dyfed. Tel: 01437-720517. Adm. £1.70. Remains of residence of Bishops of St Davids built 1328-47

TINTERN ABBEY (C), Gwent. Tel: 01291-689251. Adm. £2.20. Remains of 13th-century church and conventual buildings of a Cistercian monastery

TRETOWER COURT AND CASTLE (C), Powys. Tel: 01874-730279. Adm. £2.20. Medieval house with remains of 12th-century castle nearby

---

SCOTLAND

HS Historic Scotland property
NTS National Trust for Scotland property

ANTONINE WALL (HS), Central and Strathclyde regions. Adm. free. Built about AD 142, consists of ditch, turf rampart and road, with forts every two miles

BALMORAL CASTLE, Grampian. Tel: 013397-42334. Open May-July. Closed Sun. Adm. £2.50. Mid 19th-century Baronial-style castle built for Victoria and Albert. The Queen's private residence

BLACK HOUSE, ARNOL (HS), Lewis, Western Isles. Tel: 01851-710395. Closed Sun.; also Fri. in winter. Adm. £1.50. Traditional Lewis thatched house

*BLAIR CASTLE, Tayside. Tel: 01796-481207. Adm. £5.00. Mid 18th-century mansion with 13th-century tower; seat of the Dukes of Atholl

*BONAWE IRON FURNACE (HS), Strathclyde. Tel: 018662-432. Closed Sun. mornings. Adm. £2.00. Charcoal-fuelled ironworks founded in 1753

†BOWHILL, Selkirk. Tel: 01750-20732. House open July only; grounds early May to late summer except Fri. Adm. £4.00; grounds only, £1.00. Seat of the Dukes of Buccleuch and Queensberry. Fine collection of paintings, including portrait miniatures

BROUGH OF BIRSAY (HS), Orkney. Adm. free. Remains of Norse church and village on the tidal island of Birsay

CAERLAVEROCK CASTLE (HS), nr Dumfries. Tel: 01387-770244. Closed Sun. mornings. Adm. £2.00. Fine early classical Renaissance building

CALLANISH STANDING STONES (HS), Lewis, Western Isles. Adm. free. Standing stones in a cross-shaped setting, dating from 3000 BC

CATHERTUNS (BROWN AND WHITE) (HS), Tayside. Adm. free. Two large Iron Age hill forts

*CAWDOR CASTLE, Inverness. Tel: 01667-404615. Adm. £4.50; grounds only, £2.50. A 14th-century keep with 15th- and 17th-century additions

CLAVA CAIRNS (HS), Highland. Adm. free. Late Neolithic or early Bronze Age cairns

*CRATHES CASTLE (NTS), Grampian. Tel: 01330-844525. Gardens and grounds open all year. Adm. £4.00; gardens and grounds only, £1.50. A 16th-century baronial castle in woodland, fields and gardens

*CULZEAN CASTLE (NTS), Strathclyde. Tel: 01655-760274. Country park open all year. Adm. £5.50; country park only, £3.00. An 18th-century Adam castle with oval staircase and circular saloon

*DRUMLANRIG CASTLE, nr Dumfries. Tel: 01848-331682. Closed Thurs. and mornings April-mid June. Adm. charge. Castle with baroque decorative features and notable art and furniture collections

DRYBURGH ABBEY (HS), Borders. Tel: 01835-822381. Closed Sun. mornings. Adm. £2.00. A 12th-century abbey containing tomb of Sir Walter Scott

*DUNVEGAN CASTLE, Skye. Tel: 01470-521310. Closed Sun. mornings. Adm. £4.00; gardens only, £2.50. A 13th-century castle with later additions; the home of the chiefs of the Clan MacLeod. Boat trips to seal colony

EDINBURGH CASTLE (HS), Lothian. Tel: 0131-225 9846. Adm. £5.50; war memorial free. Includes the Scottish National War Memorial, Scottish United Services Museum and historic apartments

EDZELL CASTLE (HS), Tayside. Tel: 01356-648631. Closed Sun. mornings; also Thurs. afternoons and Fri. in winter. Adm. £2.00. Medieval tower house; unique walled garden

*EILEAN DONAN CASTLE, Wester Ross. Tel: 0159985-202. Adm. £1.50. A 13th-century castle with Jacobite relics

ELGIN CATHEDRAL (HS), Grampian. Tel: 01343-547171. Closed Sun. mornings; also Thurs. afternoons and Fri. in winter. Adm. £1.20. A 13th-century cathedral with fine chapterhouse

*FLOORS CASTLE, Kelso. Tel: 01573-223333. Closed Fri. and Sat. (except July-Aug.). Adm. £3.80. Largest

inhabited castle in Scotland; seat of the Dukes of Roxburghe

FORT GEORGE (HS), Highland. Tel: 01667-462777. Closed Sun. mornings. Adm. £2.50. An 18th-century fort

*GLAMIS CASTLE, Tayside. Tel: 01307-840242. Adm. £4.50; grounds only, £2.20. Seat of the Lyon family (later Earls of Strathmore and Kinghorne) since 1372

GLASGOW CATHEDRAL (HS), Strathclyde. Tel: 0141-552 6891. Closed Sun. mornings. Adm. free. Medieval cathedral with elaborately vaulted crypt

GLENELG BROCH (HS), Highland. Adm. free. Two broch towers with well-preserved structural features

*HOPETOUN HOUSE, nr Edinburgh. Tel: 0131-331 2451. Adm. £4.00. House designed by Sir William Bruce, enlarged by William Adam

HUNTLY CASTLE (HS), Grampian. Tel: 01466-793191. Closed Sun. mornings; also Thurs. afternoons and Fri. in winter. Adm. £2.00. Ruin of a 16th- and 17th-century house

*INVERARY CASTLE, Argyll. Tel: 01499-2203. Closed Fri. (except July-Aug.) and Sun. morning. Woods open all year. Adm. charge. Gothic-style 18th-century castle; seat of the Dukes of Argyll

IONA ABBEY, Inner Hebrides. Tel: 01681-700404. Adm. £2.00. Monastery founded by St Columba in AD 563

*JARLSHOF (HS), Shetland. Tel: 01950-460112. Closed Sun. mornings. Adm. £2.00. Remains from Stone Age

JEDBURGH ABBEY (HS), Borders. Tel: 01835-863925. Closed Sun. mornings. Adm. £2.50. Romanesque and early Gothic church founded about 1138

KELSO ABBEY (HS), Borders. Closed Sun. mornings. Adm. free. Remains of great abbey church founded 1128

LINLITHGOW PALACE (HS), Lothian. Tel: 01506-842896. Closed Sun. mornings. Adm. £2.00. Ruin of royal palace in park setting. Birthplace of Mary, Queen of Scots

MAES HOWE CHAMBERED CAIRN (HS), Orkney. Tel: 01856-761606. Closed Sun. mornings. Adm. £2.00. Neolithic tomb plundered by Vikings

*MEIGLE SCULPTURED STONE (HS), Tayside. Closed Sun. mornings. Adm. £1.20. Celtic Christian stones

MELROSE ABBEY (HS), Borders. Tel: 01896-822562. Closed Sun. mornings. Adm. £2.50. Ruin of Cistercian abbey founded c.1136

MOUSA BROCH (HS), Shetland. Adm. free. Finest surviving Iron Age broch tower

NETHER LARGIE CAIRNS (HS), Argyll and Bute. Adm. free. Bronze Age and Neolithic cairns

NEW ABBEY CORNMILL (HS), nr Dumfries. Tel: 01387-850260. Closed Sun. mornings; also Thurs. afternoons and Fri. in winter. Adm. £1.50. Water-powered mill

PALACE OF HOLYROODHOUSE, Edinburgh. Tel: 0131-556 7371. Closed when The Queen is in residence. Adm. charge. The Queen's official Scottish residence. Main part of the palace built 1671-9

RING OF BROGAR (HS), Orkney. Adm. free. Neolithic circle of upright stones with an enclosing ditch

RUTHWELL CROSS (HS), Dumfries and Galloway. Adm. free. Seventh-century Anglian cross

ST ANDREWS CASTLE AND CATHEDRAL (HS), Fife. Tel: 01334-477196 (castle); 01334-472563 (cathedral). Adm. £2.00 (castle); £1.50 (cathedral). Closed Sun. mornings. Ruins of 13th-century castle and remains of the largest cathedral in Scotland

*SCONE PALACE, Perth. Tel: 01738-52300. Adm. £4.50. House built 1802-13 on the site of a medieval palace

SKARA BRAE (HS), Orkney. Tel: 01856-841815. Closed Sun. mornings. Adm. £2.50. Stone-Age village

*SMAILHOLM TOWER (HS), Borders. Closed Sun. mornings. Adm. £1.50. Well-preserved tower-house

STIRLING CASTLE (HS), Central. Tel: 01786-450000. Adm. £3.50. Great Hall and gatehouse of James IV, palace of James V, Chapel Royal remodelled by James VI

TANTALLON CASTLE (HS), Lothian. Tel: 01620-892727. Closed Sun. mornings; also Thurs. afternoons and Fri. in winter. Adm. £2.00. Fortification with earthwork defences and a 14th-century curtain wall with towers

*THREAVE CASTLE (HS), Dumfries and Galloway. Tel: 01831-168512. Closed Sun. mornings. Adm. £1.50, including ferry trip. Late 14th-century tower on an island; reached by boat, long walk to castle

URQUHART CASTLE (HS), Loch Ness. Tel: 01456-450551. Adm. £3.00. Closed Sun. morning in winter. Castle remains with well-preserved tower on shore of loch

---

NORTHERN IRELAND

DE Property in the care of the Northern Ireland Department of the Environment

NT National Trust property

CARRICKFERGUS CASTLE (DE), Co. Antrim. Tel: 01960-351273. Closed Sun. mornings. Adm. £2.70. Castle begun in 1180 and garrisoned until 1928

†CASTLE COOLE (NT), Enniskillen. Tel: 01365-322690. Closed Thurs. June-Aug., also Mon.-Fri. April, May and Sept. Adm. £2.50. An 18th-century mansion by James Wyatt in parkland

†CASTLE WARD (NT), Co. Down. Tel: 01396-881204. Closed Thurs. May-Aug., also Mon.-Fri. April and Sept.-Oct; grounds open all year. Adm. £2.60. An 18th-century house with Classical west and Gothic east fronts

*DEVENISH ISLAND (DE), Co. Fermanagh. Closed Sun. mornings and Mon. Adm. £2.25. Island monastery founded in the 6th century by St Molaise

†DOWNHILL CASTLE (NT), Co. Londonderry. Tel: 01265-848728. Closed Mon.-Fri. (except Bank Holidays) in April-June and Sept.; grounds open all year. Adm. free. Ruins of palatial house in landscaped estate including Mussenden Temple

DUNLUCE CASTLE (DE), Co. Antrim. Tel: 012657-31938. Closed Sun. morning and Mon. Adm. £1.50. Ruins of 16th-century stronghold of the MacDonnells

†FORENCE COURT (NT), Co. Fermanagh. Tel: 01365-348249. Closed Tues.; also Mon.-Fri. (except Bank Holidays) in April, May and Sept. Grounds open all year. Adm. £2.50. Mid 18th-century house with rococo plasterwork

*GREY ABBEY (DE), Co. Down. Tel: 01247-788585. Closed Sun. morning and Mon. Adm £1.00. Substantial remains of a Cistercian abbey founded in 1193

HILLSBOROUGH FORT (DE), Co. Down. Closed Sun. mornings and Mon. Adm. free. Built in 1650

†MOUNT STEWART (NT), Co. Down. Tel: 012477-88387. Closed Tues.; also Mon.-Fri. April and Oct. Adm. £3.30; garden and temple only, £2.70. An 18th-century house, childhood home of Lord Castlereagh

NENDRUM MONASTERY (DE), Mahee Island, Co. Down. Closed Sun. mornings and Mon., also Mon.-Fri. in winter. Adm 75p. Founded in the 5th century by St Machaoi

*TULLY CASTLE (DE), Co. Fermanagh. Closed Sun. mornings and Mon. Adm. £1.00. Fortified house and bawn built in 1613

*WHITE ISLAND (DE), Co. Fermanagh. Closed Sun. mornings and Mon. Adm. £2.25. Tenth-century monastery and 12th-century church. Access by ferry

Museums and Galleries

There are more than 2,000 museums and galleries in the United Kingdom. About 1,600 are registered with the Museums and Galleries Commission (*see* page 326), which indicates that they have an appropriate constitution, are soundly financed, have adequate collection management standards and public services, and have access to professional curatorial advice. Museums must achieve full or provisional registration status in order to be eligible for grants from the Museums and Galleries Commission and from Area Museums Councils. Over 700 of the registered museums are run by a local authority.

The national museums and galleries (i.e. the British Museum, the Imperial War Museum, the National Army Museum, the National Galleries of Scotland, the National Gallery, the National Maritime Museum, the National Museums and Galleries on Merseyside, the National Museum of Wales, the National Museums of Scotland, the National Portrait Gallery, the Natural History Museum, the RAF Museum, the Royal Armouries, the Science Museum, the Tate Gallery, the Ulster Folk and Transport Museum, the Ulster Museum, the Victoria and Albert Museum, and the Wallace Collection) receive direct government grant-in-aid. Local authority museums are funded by the local authority and may also receive grants from the Museums and Galleries Commission. Independent museums and galleries mainly rely on their own resources but are also eligible for grants from the Museums and Galleries Commission.

Ten Area Museum Councils in the United Kingdom, which are independent charities that receive an annual grant from the Museums and Galleries Commission, give advice and support to the museums in their area and may offer improvement grants. They also circulate exhibitions and assist with training and marketing.

OPENING TO THE PUBLIC

The following is a selection of the museums and art galleries in the United Kingdom. The admission charges given are the standard charges for 1995-6, where a charge is made; many museums have concessionary rates for children, etc. Opening hours vary. Most museums are closed on Christmas Eve, Christmas Day, Boxing Day and New Year's Day; many are closed on Good Friday, and some are closed on May Day Bank Holiday. Some smaller museums close at lunchtimes. Information about a specific museum or gallery should be checked by telephone.

* Local authority museum/gallery

ENGLAND

BARNARD CASTLE, Co. Durham – *The Bowes Museum*, Westwick Road. Tel: 01833-690606. Closed Sun. mornings. Adm. charge. European art from the late medieval period to the 19th century; music and costume galleries; English period rooms from Elizabeth I to Victoria; local archaeology

BATH – *American Museum in Britain*, Claverton Manor. Tel: 01225-460503. Closed mornings and Mon. (except Bank Holidays); also closed in winter (except on application). Adm. charge. American decorative arts from the 17th to 19th centuries

Museum of Costume, Bennett Street. Tel: 01225-477752. Adm. 3.20. Fashion from the 16th century to the present day

Roman Baths Museum, Abbey Church Yard. Tel: 01225-477774. Adm. (including 18th-century Pump Room) £5.00. Museum adjoins the remains of a Roman baths and temple complex

Victoria Art Gallery, Bridge Street. Tel: 01225-477772. Closed Sun. and Bank Holidays. Adm. free. European Old Masters and British art since the 18th century

BEAMISH, Co. Durham – *The North of England Open Air Museum*. Tel: 01207-231811. Closed Mon. and Fri. in winter. Adm. charge. Recreated northern town *c*.1900, with rebuilt and furnished local buildings, colliery village, farm, railway station, tramway, and horse-yard (set *c*.1800)

BEAULIEU, Hants – *National Motor Museum*. Tel: 01590-612345. Adm. charge. Displays of over 250 vehicles dating from 1895 to the present day

BEVERLEY, N. Humberside – *Museum of Army Transport*, Flemingate. Tel: 01482-860445. Adm. charge. Field workshop, amphibious assault landing, railway section and aircraft

BIRMINGHAM – *Aston Hall*, Albert Road. Tel: 0121-327 0062. Closed mornings and in winter. Adm. free. Jacobean house containing paintings, furniture and tapestries from 17th to 19th centuries

Birmingham Nature Centre, Edgbaston. Tel: 0121-472 7775. Closed Mon.-Fri. in winter. Adm. free. Indoor and outdoor enclosures displaying British wildlife

City Museum and Art Gallery, Chamberlain Square. Tel: 0121-235 2834. Closed Sun. mornings. Adm. free. Includes notable collection of Pre-Raphaelites

Museum of Science and Industry, Newhall Street. Tel: 0121-235 1661. Closed Sun. mornings. Adm. free. Vehicles and industrial machinery from the Industrial Revolution to the present; interactive science centre and mechanical musical instrument collection

BRADFORD – *Cartwright Hall Art Gallery*, Lister Park. Tel: 01274-493313. Closed Mon. (except Bank Holidays). Adm. free. British 19th- and 20th-century fine art

Industrial Museum and Horses at Work, Moorside Road. Tel: 01274-631756. Closed Mon. (except Bank Holidays). Adm. free. Engineering, textiles, transport and social history exhibits, including recreated back-to-back cottages

National Museum of Photography, Film and Television, Pictureville. Tel: 01274-727488. Closed Mon. Adm. free. Photography, film and television equipment and materials, including the only IMAX cinema in the UK and the only public Cinerama theatre in the world

BRIGHTON – *Brighton Museum and Art Gallery*, Church Street. Tel: 01273-603005. Closed Sun. mornings and Wed. Adm. free. Includes fine art, design, fashion, archaeology, Brighton history

BRISTOL – *Blaise Castle House Museum*, Henbury. Tel: 0117-950 6789. Closed Mon. Adm. free. Agricultural and social history collections in an 18th-century mansion

Bristol Industrial Museum, Prince Street. Tel: 0117-925 1470. Closed Mon. Adm. £1.00. Industrial, maritime and transport collections

City Museum and Art Gallery, Queen's Road. Tel: 0117-922 3571. Adm. £2.00. Includes fine and decorative art, oriental art, and Bristol ceramics and paintings

CAMBRIDGE – *Duxford Airfield,* Duxford. Tel: 01223-835000. Adm. £5.95. Displays of military and civil aircraft, tanks, guns and naval exhibits

Fitzwilliam Museum, Trumpington Street. Tel: 01223-332900. Closed Mon. (except Bank Holidays) and Sun. mornings. Some galleries may be closed according to staff availability. Adm. free. Antiquities, fine and applied arts, clocks, ceramics, manuscripts, furniture, sculpture, coins and medals, temporary exhibitions

CARLISLE – *Tullie House Museum and Art Gallery,* Castle Street. Tel: 01228-34781. Closed Sun. mornings. Adm. charge to Border galleries only; ground floor, Old Tullie House and Jacobean galleries, adm. free. Prehistoric archaeology, Hadrian's Wall, Viking and medieval Cumbria, and the social history of Carlisle; also British 19th- and 20th-century art and English porcelain

CHESTER – *Grosvenor Museum,* Grosvenor Street. Tel: 01244-321616. Closed Sun. mornings. Adm. free. Roman collections, natural history, art, Chester silver, local history and costume

CHICHESTER – *Weald and Downland Open Air Museum,* Singleton. Tel: 01243-811348. Open March-Oct. daily. Adm. £4.20. Rebuilt vernacular buildings from south-east England; includes medieval houses, agricultural and rural craft buildings and a working watermill

COLCHESTER – *Colchester Castle Museum,* Castle Park. Tel: 01206-282939. Closed Sun. mornings. Adm. £2.80. Local archaeological antiquities and displays on Roman Colchester; tours of the Roman vaults, castle walls and chapel with medieval and prison displays

COVENTRY – *Herbert Art Gallery and Museum,* Jordan Well. Tel: 01203-832381. Closed Sun. mornings. Local history, archaeology and industry, natural history, oriental ceramics, and fine and decorative art

Museum of British Road Transport, Hales Street. Tel: 01203-832425. Adm. charge. Hundreds of motor vehicles and bicycles

CRICH, nr Matlock, Derbys – *National Tramway Museum.* Tel: 01773-852565. Closed in winter. Open weekends and Bank Holidays, Mon.-Thurs. April-Sept., and some Fridays. Adm. charge. Open-air working museum with tram rides

DERBY – *Derby Museum and Art Gallery,* The Strand. Tel: 01332-255586. Closed Sun. mornings and Bank Holiday mornings. Adm. free. Includes paintings by Joseph Wright of Derby and Derby porcelain

Industrial Museum, off Full Street. Tel: 01332-255308. Closed Sun. mornings and Bank Holiday mornings. Adm. free. Rolls-Royce aero engine collection and a railway engineering gallery

DORCHESTER – *Dorset County Museum,* High West Street. Tel: 01305-262735. Closed Sun. except July and Aug. Adm. £2.35. Includes a collection of Thomas Hardy's manuscripts, books, notebooks and drawings

EXETER – *Exeter Maritime Museum,* The Haven. Tel: 01392-58075. Adm. £4.25. Collection of working boats from around the world

Royal Albert Memorial Museum, Queen Street. Tel: 01392-265858. Closed Sun. Adm. free. Natural history, archaeology, ethnography, and fine and decorative art including Exeter silver

HALIFAX – *Eureka! The Museum for Children,* Discovery Road. Tel: 01426-983191. Open daily. Adm. £4.50 (over age 12), £3.50 (ages 3-12), free (under age 3). Saver ticket £14.50. Museum designed for children up to age 12

HULL – *Ferens Art Gallery,* Queen Victoria Square. Tel: 01482-593902. Closed Sun. mornings. Adm. free. European art, especially Dutch 17th-century paintings, British portraits from 17th to 20th centuries, and marine paintings

Town Docks Museum, Queen Victoria Square. Tel: 01482-593902. Closed Sun. mornings. Adm. free. Whaling, fishing and navigation exhibits

HUNTINGDON – *Cromwell Museum,* Grammar School Walk. Tel: 01480-425830. Closed Mon., and mornings (except Sat. and Sun.) in winter. Adm. free. Portraits and memorabilia relating to Oliver Cromwell

IPSWICH – *Christchurch Mansion and Wolsey Art Gallery,* Christchurch Park. Tel: 01473-253246. Closed Sun. mornings and Mon. Adm. £2.50. Tudor house with paintings by Gainsborough, Constable and other Suffolk artists; furniture and 18th-century ceramics. Art gallery for temporary exhibitions

LEEDS – *Abbey House Museum,* Kirkstall. Tel: 0113-275 5821. Closed Sun. mornings. Adm. charge. Toys, games, dolls, and three full-sized period streets

City Art Gallery, The Headrow. Tel: 0113-247 8248. Closed Sun. and Bank Holidays. Adm. free. British and European paintings including English watercolours, modern sculpture, Henry Moore gallery, print room

City Museum, Calverley Street. Tel: 0113-246 2632. Closed Sun. and Mon. Adm. free. Natural history, archaeology, ethnography and coin collections

LEICESTER – *Jewry Wall Museum of Archaeology,* St Nicholas Circle. Tel: 0116-247 3021. Closed Sun. mornings. Adm. free. Archaeology, Roman Jewry Wall and baths, and mosaics

Leicestershire Museum and Art Gallery, New Walk. Tel: 0116-255 4100. Closed Sun. mornings. Adm. free. Includes notable collection of German Expressionist paintings

Snibston Discovery Park, Coalville. Tel: 01530-510851. Adm. charge. Open-air science and industry museum on site of a coal mine; country park with nature trail

LINCOLN – *Museum of Lincolnshire Life,* Burton Road. Tel: 01522-528448. Closed Sun. mornings in winter. Adm. charge. Social history and agricultural collection

National Cycle Museum, Union Road. Tel: 01522-545091. Adm. charge. Cycles from the early 19th century to the present

Usher Gallery, Lindum Road. Tel: 01522-527980. Closed Sun. mornings. Adm. charge. Watches, miniatures, porcelain, silver; collection of Peter de Wint works; Lincolnshire topography; Tennyson memorabilia

LIVERPOOL – *Lady Lever Art Gallery,* Wirral. Tel: 0151-645 3623. Closed Sun. mornings. Adm. free. Paintings, furniture and porcelain

Liverpool Museum, William Brown Street. Tel: 0151-207 0001. Closed Sun. mornings. Adm. free (except to the Planetarium). Includes Egyptian mummies, weapons and classical sculpture; planetarium, aquarium, vivarium and natural history centre

Merseyside Maritime Museum, Albert Dock. Tel: 0151-207 0001. Joint adm. charge with the Museum of Liverpool Life. Floating exhibits, working displays and craft demonstrations; incorporates *HM Customs and Excise National Museum*

Museum of Liverpool Life, Mann Island. Tel: 0151-207 0001. Joint adm. charge with the Merseyside Maritime Museum. The history of Liverpool

Sudley House, Mossley Hill Road. Tel: 0151-724 3245. Closed Sun. mornings. Adm. free. Late 18th- and 19th-century British paintings in former shipowner's home

Tate Gallery Liverpool, Albert Dock. Tel: 0151-709 3223. Closed Mon. (except Bank Holidays). Adm. free. Twentieth-century painting and sculpture

Walker Art Gallery, William Brown Street. Tel: 0151-207 0001. Closed Sun. mornings. Adm. free. Paintings from the 14th to 20th centuries

LONDON: GALLERIES – *Barbican Art Gallery*, Barbican Centre, EC2. Tel: 0171-638 4141. Temporary exhibitions
Courtauld Institute Galleries, Somerset House, Strand, WC2. Tel: 0171-873 2526. Closed Sun. mornings. Adm. £3.00. The University of London galleries
Dulwich Picture Gallery, College Road, SE21. Tel: 0181-693 5254. Closed Sun. mornings and Mon. Adm. £2.00 (free on Fri.). Built by Sir John Soane to house 17th- and 18th-century collection
Hayward Gallery, South Bank Centre, SE1. Tel: 0171-928 3144. Adm. £5.00. Temporary exhibitions
National Gallery, Trafalgar Square, WC2. Tel: 0171-839 3321. Closed Sun. mornings. Adm. free. Western painting from the 13th to 20th centuries; early Renaissance collection in the Sainsbury wing
National Portrait Gallery, St Martin's Place, WC2. Tel: 0171-306 0055. Closed Sun. mornings and some Bank Holidays. Adm. free. Portraits of eminent people in British history
Percival David Foundation of Chinese Art, Gordon Square, WC1. Tel: 0171-387 3909. Closed weekends and Bank Holidays. Adm free. Chinese ceramics; charge for use of reference library
Photographers Gallery, Great Newport Street, WC2. Tel: 0171-831 1772. Closed Sun. Adm. free. Temporary exhibitions
The Queen's Gallery, Buckingham Palace, SW1. Tel: 0171-799 2331. Adm. £3.50. Art from the Royal Collection
Royal Academy of Arts, Piccadilly, W1. Tel: 0171-439 7438. Adm. charge. British art since 1750 and temporary exhibitions; annual Summer Exhibition
Serpentine Gallery, Kensington Gardens, W2. Tel: 0171-723 9072. Adm. free. Temporary exhibitions
Tate Gallery, Millbank, SW1. Tel: 0171-887 8000. Closed Sun. mornings. Adm. free (charge for special exhibitions). British painting and 20th-century painting and sculpture
Wallace Collection, Manchester Square, W1. Tel: 0171-935 0687. Closed Sun. mornings. Adm. free. Paintings and drawings, French 18th-century furniture, armour, porcelain and clocks
Whitechapel Art Gallery, Whitechapel High Street, E1. Tel: 0171-522 7878. Closed Mon. Adm. free to most exhibitions. Temporary exhibitions of modern art
LONDON: MUSEUMS – *Bank of England Museum*, Threadneedle Street, EC2. Tel: 0171-601 5545. Closed weekends and Bank Holidays. Adm. free. History of the Bank since 1694
Bethnal Green Museum of Childhood, Cambridge Heath Road, E2. Tel: 0181-980 3204. Closed Sun. mornings and Fri. Adm. free but donations invited. Toys, games and exhibits relating to the social history of childhood
British Museum, Great Russell Street, WC1. Tel: 0171-636 1555. Closed Sun. mornings. Adm. free. Antiquities, coins, medals, prints and drawings, European history galleries
Cabinet War Rooms, King Charles Street, SW1. Tel: 0171-930 6961. Adm. £4.00. Underground rooms used by Churchill and the Government during the Second World War
Commonwealth Institute, Kensington High Street, W8. Tel: 0171-603 4535. Closed Sun. mornings. Adm. £1.00. Exhibitions on Commonwealth nations, visual arts and crafts
Cutty Sark, Greenwich, SE10. Tel: 0181-858 3445. Adm. £3.25. Restored and rerigged tea clipper with exhibits on board. Sir Francis Chichester's round-the-world yacht, *Gipsy Moth IV*, can also be seen (separate adm. charge)

Design Museum, Shad Thames, SE1. Tel: 0891-715944. Adm. £4.50. The development of design and the mass-production of consumer objects
Geffrye Museum, Kingsland Road, E2. Tel: 0171-739 9893. Closed Mon.; also Sun. and Bank Holiday mornings. Adm. free. English urban domestic interiors from 1600-1950s; also paintings, furniture, decorative arts, walled herb garden and knot garden
HMS Belfast, Morgans Lane, Tooley Street, SE1. Tel: 0171-407 6434. Adm £4.00. Life on a warship, illustrated on World War II warship
Horniman Museum and Gardens, London Road, SE23. Tel: 0181-699 1872. Closed Sun. mornings. Adm. free. Museum of ethnography, musical instruments, natural history and aquarium. Reference library (by appointment)
Imperial War Museum, Lambeth Road, SE1. Tel: 0171-416 5000. Reference departments closed Sat. (except by appointment) and Sun. Adm. £4.10 (free after 4.30 p.m. daily). All aspects of the two world wars and other military operations involving Britain and the Commonwealth since 1914
Jewish Museum, Albert Street, NW1. Tel: 0171-284 1997. Closed Fri., Sat., public and Jewish holidays. Adm. charge. Jewish life, history and religion
London Transport Museum, Covent Garden, WC2. Tel: 0171-379 6344. Adm. charge. Vehicles, photographs and graphic art relating to the history of London public transport
MCC Museum, Lord's, NW8. Tel: 0171-289 1611. Open match days (closed Sun. mornings); also conducted tours by appointment with Tours Manager. Adm. charge. Cricket museum
Museum of Garden History, Lambeth Palace Road SE1. Tel: 0171-401 8865. Open 11-3 daily except Sat. Closed Dec.-Feb. Adm free but donations invited. Exhibition of aspects of garden history
Museum of London, London Wall, EC2. Tel: 0171-600 3699. Closed Sun. mornings and Mon. Adm. £3.50 (free after 4.30 p.m. daily). History of London from prehistoric times to present day
Museum of Mankind, Burlington Gardens, W1. Tel: 0171-636 1555. Closed Sun. mornings. Adm. free. The ethnographical collections of the British Museum
Museum of the Moving Image, South Bank, SE1. Tel: 0171-401 2636. Adm. £5.50. History of the moving image in cinema and television
National Army Museum, Royal Hospital Road, SW3. Tel: 0171-730 0717. Adm. free. History of the British soldier; the Indian Army room at the Royal Military Academy, Sandhurst, may be viewed by appointment
National Maritime Museum, Greenwich, SE10. Tel: 0181-858 4422. Reference library closed Sat. (except by appointment) and Sun. Comprises the main building, the Old Royal Observatory and the Queen's House (*see page 588*). Adm. charge. Maritime history of Britain
Natural History Museum, Cromwell Road, SW7. Tel: 0171-938 9123. Adm. £5.50. Natural history collections
Royal Air Force Museum, Hendon, NW9. Tel: 0181-205 2266. Adm. charge. Aviation from before the Wright brothers to the present-day RAF; historic aircraft
Royal Mews, Buckingham Palace, SW1. Tel: 0171-799 2331. Open Tues.-Thurs. afternoons in summer, Wed. only in winter. Adm. £3.50. Carriages, coaches, stables and horses
Science Museum, Exhibition Road, SW7. Tel: 0171-938 8000. Closed Sun. and Bank Holiday weekends. Adm. charge. Science, technology, industry and medicine collections

Shakespeare Globe Exhibition, Bankside, SE1. Tel: 0171-928 6406. Adm. £4.00. Recreation of Elizabethan theatre using 16th-century techniques

Sherlock Holmes Museum, Baker Street, NW1. Tel: 0171-935 8866. Adm. £5.00. Recreated rooms of the fictional detective

Sir John Soane's Museum, Lincoln's Inn Fields, WC2. Tel: 0171-405 2107. Closed Sun. and Mon. Adm. free. Art and antiques, temporary exhibitions

Theatre Museum, Russell Street, WC2. Tel: 0171-836 7891. Closed Mon. Adm. £3.00. History of the performing arts

Tower Bridge Walkway and Museum, SE1. Tel: 0171-378 1928. Adm. £5.00. History of the bridge and display of Victorian steam machinery; panoramic views from walkways

Victoria and Albert Museum, Cromwell Road, SW7. Tel: 0171-938 8500. Closed Mon. mornings. Includes National Art Library and Print Room (closed Sun. and Mon.) Adm. free but donations invited. Fine and applied art and design, including furniture, glass, textiles, dress collections

Wimbledon Lawn Tennis Museum, Church Road, SW19. Tel: 0181-946 6131. Closed Sun. mornings and Mon. Adm. £2.50. Tennis trophies, fashion and memorabilia

MANCHESTER – *City Art Galleries*, Mosley Street and Princess Street. Tel: 0161-236 5244. Closed Sun. mornings. Adm. free. Includes Old Masters, Turner, Gainsborough, Stubbs, the Pre-Raphaelites and 20th century art

Gallery of English Costume, Rusholme. Tel: 0161-224 5217. Closed Sun. mornings and Tues. (weekend opening subject to change). Adm. free. Exhibits from the 16th to 20th centuries

Manchester Museum, Oxford Road. Tel: 0161-275 2634. Closed Sun. Adm. free. Archaeology, archery, botany, Egyptology, entomology, ethnography, geology, natural history, numismatics, oriental and zoology collections

Museum of Science and Industry, Castlefield. Tel: 0161-832 1830. Adm. £4.00. On site of world's oldest passenger railway station; galleries relating to space, energy, power, transport, aviation and social history; interactive science centre

Whitworth Art Gallery, Oxford Road. Tel: 0161-273 4865. Closed Sun. Adm. free. Watercolours, drawings, prints, textiles, wallpapers and 20th-century British art

NEWCASTLE UPON TYNE – *Laing Art Gallery*, Higham Place. Tel: 0191-232 7734. Closed Sun. mornings. Adm. free. British and European art, ceramics, glass, silver, textiles and costume; local arts and crafts

Newcastle Discovery Museum, West Blandford Square. Tel: 0191-232 6789. Closed Sun. Adm. free. Local history, fashion, power, and Tyneside's maritime history; hands-on science centre

NEWMARKET – *National Horseracing Museum*, High Street. Tel: 01638-667333. Closed Mon. (except Bank Holidays, July and Aug.), Sun. mornings and Jan.–March. Adm. £3.30. Paintings, trophies and exhibits relating to horseracing

NORWICH – *Castle Museum*. Tel: 01603-223624. Closed Sun. mornings. Adm. charge. Art (including Norwich school), archaeology, natural history, teapot collection; guided tours of battlements and dungeons

NOTTINGHAM – *Brewhouse Yard Museum*, Castle Boulevard. Tel: 0115-948 3504. Adm. free. Daily life from the 17th to 20th centuries

Castle Museum. Tel: 0115-948 3504. Adm. free (except weekends). Paintings, archaeology, ceramics, ethnography, silver and glass; history of Nottingham

Industrial Museum, Wollaton Park. Tel: 0115-928 4602. Closed Sun. mornings, and Mon.–Wed. in winter. Adm. free (except Sat., Sun. and Bank Holidays). Lacemaking machinery, steam engines and transport exhibits

Natural History Museum, Wollaton Park. Tel: 0115-928 1333. Closed Sun. mornings. Adm. free (except Sat., Sun. and Bank Holidays) Local natural history and wildlife dioramas

OXFORD – *Ashmolean Museum*, Beaumont Street. Tel: 01865-278000. Closed Mon. (except Bank Holidays) and Sun. mornings. Adm. free. European and Oriental fine and applied arts, archaeology, Egyptology and numismatics

Museum of Modern Art, Pembroke Street. Tel: 01865-722733. Closed Sun. mornings and Mon. Adm. £2.50. Temporary exhibitions

Oxford University Museum, Parks Road. Tel: 01865-272950. Closed mornings (except for school parties by appointment) and Sun. Adm. free. Entomology, geology, mineralogy and zoology

PLYMOUTH – *City Museum and Art Gallery*, Drake Circus. Tel: 01752-264878. Closed Mon. (except Bank Holidays) and Sun. Adm. free. Local and natural history, ceramics, silver, Old Masters, temporary exhibitions

The Dome, The Hoe. Tel: 01752-603300. Adm. charge. Maritime history museum

PORTSMOUTH – *Charles Dickens Birthplace Museum*, Old Commercial Road. Tel: 01705-827261. Closed in winter. Adm. charge. Dickens memorabilia

D-Day Museum, Clarence Esplanade. Tel: 01705-827261. Adm. charge. Includes the Overlord Embroidery

Naval Heritage Area, HM Naval Base. Story of the Royal Navy using HMS *Victory* (tel: 01705-819604), HMS *Warrior* (tel: 01705-291379), and the *Mary Rose* (tel: 01705-750521). Separate adm. charge to each, combined tickets available

Royal Naval Museum, HM Naval Base. Tel: 01705-733060. Adm. charge. History of the Royal Navy

PRESTON – *Harris Museum and Art Gallery*, Market Square. Tel: 01772-258248. Closed Sun. and Bank Holidays. Adm. free. British art since the 18th century, ceramics, glass, costume and local history

ST ALBANS – *Verulamium Museum*, St Michael's. Tel: 01727-819339. Closed Sun. mornings. Adm. £2.50. Iron Age and Roman Verulamium, including wall plasters, jewellery, mosaics and room reconstructions

ST IVES, Cornwall – *Tate Gallery St Ives*, Porthmeor Beach. Tel: 01736-796226. Closed Mon. Oct.–March. Adm. £2.50. Painting and sculpture by artists associated with St Ives

SHEFFIELD – *City Museum and Mappin Art Gallery*, Weston Park. Tel: 0114-276 8588. Closed Mon. Adm. free. Includes applied arts, natural history, archaeology and ethnography, 19th- and 20th-century art

Graves Art Gallery, Surrey Street. Tel: 0114-273 5858. Closed Sun. Adm. free. British art from the 16th to 20th centuries. Old Masters and non-European art

Kelham Island Industrial Museum, off Alma Street. Tel: 0114-272 2106. Closed Fri. and Sat. Adm. charge. Local industrial and social history

Shepherd Wheel, off Hangingwater Road. Tel: 0114-236 7731. Closed Mon. and Tues. Adm. free. Water-powered cutlery-grinding wheel and workshops

STOKE-ON-TRENT – *Etruria Industrial Museum*, Etruria. Tel: 01782-287557. Closed Mon. and Tues. Adm. free. Britain's sole surviving steam-powered potter's mill

City Museum and Art Gallery, Hanley. Tel: 01782-202173. Closed Sun. mornings. Adm. free. Pottery, china and porcelain collections

Gladstone Pottery Museum, Longton. Tel: 01782-319232. Adm. charge. A working Victorian pottery. Pottery factory tours are available by arrangement Mon.-Fri., except during factory holidays, at the following: *Royal Doulton*, Nile Street, Burslem; *Spode*, Church Street, Stoke; *John Beswick*, Barford Street, Longton; *Royal Grafton China*, Marlborough Road, Longton; *Wedgewood*, Barlaston
STYAL, Cheshire – *Quarry Bank Mill.* Tel: 01625-527468. Closed Mon. in winter. Adm. charge. Working mill illustrating history of cotton industry; costumed display at restored Apprentice House
TRING, Herts – *Tring Zoological Museum*, Akeman Street. Tel: 01442-824181. Closed Sun. mornings. Adm. £2.20. Display of more than 4,000 animal species
WAKEFIELD – *Yorkshire Sculpture Park*, West Bretton. Tel: 01924-830302. Adm. free. Open-air sculpture gallery including works by Moore, Hepworth, Frink and others
WORCESTER – *City Museum and Art Gallery*, Foregate Street. Tel: 01905-25371. Closed Thurs. and Sun. Adm. free. Includes a military museum, 19th-century chemist's shop and changing art exhibitions
Dyson Perrins Museum and Royal Worcester Porcelain Works, Severn Street. Tel: 01905-23221. Closed Sun. Adm. £1.50. Worcester porcelain collection; factory tours on weekdays
WROUGHTON, nr Swindon, Wilts – *Science Museum*, Wroughton Airfield. Tel: 01793-814466. Open selected summer weekends only. Adm. charge. Air displays and some of the Science Museum's transport and agricultural collection
YEOVIL, Somerset – *Fleet Air Arm Museum*, Royal Naval Air Station, Yeovilton. Tel: 01935-840565. Adm. charge. History of naval aviation; historic aircraft, including Concorde 002
Montacute House, Montacute. Tel: 01935-823289. Closed mornings and Tues.; also closed in winter. Adm. £4.80. Elizabethan and Jacobean portraits from the National Portrait Gallery
YORK – *Beningbrough Hall*, Shipton-by-Beningbrough. Tel: 01904-470666. Closed Thurs. and Fri. (except Good Friday and July-Aug.); also closed in winter. Adm. £4.50. Portraits from the National Portrait Gallery
Castle Museum. Tel: 01904-653611. Adm. £4.20. Reconstructed streets; costume and military collections
City Art Gallery, Exhibition Square. Tel: 01904-623839. Closed Sun. mornings. Adm. free. European and British painting spanning seven centuries; modern pottery
Jorvik Viking Centre, Coppergate. Tel: 01904-643211. Adm. £3.95. Reconstruction of Viking York
National Railway Museum, Leeman Road. Tel: 01904-621261. Adm. £4.20. Includes locomotives, rolling stock and carriages
Yorkshire Museum, Museum Gardens. Tel: 01904-629745. Closed Sun. mornings in winter. Adm. £3.00. Yorkshire life from Roman to medieval times; geology gallery

WALES

CAERLEON, Gwent – *Roman Legionary Museum.* Tel: 01633-423134. Closed Sun. mornings. Adm. charge. Material from the site of the Roman fortress of Isca and its suburbs
CARDIFF – *National Museum of Wales*, Cathays Park. Tel: 01222-397951. Closed Sun. mornings and Mon. (except Bank Holidays). Adm. charge. Includes natural sciences, archaeology and Impressionist paintings

Museum of Welsh Life, St Fagans. Tel: 01222-569441. Adm. charge. Open-air museum with re-erected buildings, agricultural equipment and costume
Welsh Industrial and Maritime Museum, Bute Street. Tel: 01222-481919. Closed Sun. mornings and Mon. (except Bank Holidays). Adm. charge. Power, railways, locomotives and shipping exhibitions; miniature railway
DRE-FACH FELINDRE, Dyfed – *Museum of the Welsh Woollen Industry.* Tel: 01559-370929. Closed Sun., and Sat. in winter. Adm. charge. Exhibitions, a working woollen mill and craft workshops
LLANBERIS, Gwynedd – *Museum of the North.* Tel: 01286-870636. Closed Nov.-April (except by appointment). Adm. charge. Multi-media presentation of Welsh history, including the electricity supply industry
Welsh Slate Museum. Tel: 01286-870630. Closed in winter (except by appointment). Adm. charge. Former slate quarry with original machinery and plant; slate crafts demonstrations
ST ASAPH, Clwyd – *Bodelwyddan Castle*, Bodelwyddan. Tel: 01745-583539. Opening times vary. Adm. charge. Portraits from the National Portrait Gallery, furniture from the Victoria and Albert Museum and sculptures from the Royal Academy
SWANSEA – *Glyn Vivian Art Gallery and Museum*, Alexandra Road. Tel: 01792-655006. Closed Mon. (except Bank Holidays). Adm. free. Paintings, ceramics, Swansea pottery and porcelain, clocks, glass and Welsh art
Swansea Maritime and Industrial Museum, Museum Square. Tel: 01792-650351. Closed Mon. (except Bank Holidays). Adm. free. Includes a working woollen mill and historic boats

SCOTLAND

ABERDEEN – *Aberdeen Art Gallery*, Schoolhill. Tel: 01224-646333. Closed Sun. mornings. Adm. free. Art from the 18th to 20th centuries
Aberdeen Maritime Museum, Shiprow. Tel: 01224-585788. Closed Sun. Adm. free. Maritime history, including shipbuilding and North Sea oil
EDINBURGH – *City Art Centre*, Market Street. Tel: 0131-529 3541. Closed Sun. Adm. free. Late 19th- and 20th-century art and temporary exhibitions
Commonwealth Institute Scotland, Rutland Square. Tel: 0131-229 6668. Closed weekends. Adm. free. Exhibitions relating to countries of the Commonwealth
Huntly House Museum, Canongate. Tel: 0131-529 4143. Closed Sun. Adm. free. Local history, silver, glass and Scottish pottery
Museum of Antiquities, Queen Street. Tel: 0131-255 7534. Closed Sun. mornings. Adm. free. Scotland since the Stone Age
Museum of Childhood, High Street. Tel: 0131-529 4142. Closed Sun. Adm. free. Toys, games, clothes and exhibits relating to the social history of childhood
Museum of Flight, East Fortune Airfield, nr North Berwick. Tel: 01620-880308. Closed in winter. Adm. charge. Display of more than 30 aircraft
National Gallery of Scotland, The Mound. Tel: 0131-556 8921. Closed Sun. mornings. Adm. free. Paintings, drawings and prints from the 16th to 20th centuries, and the national collection of Scottish art
The People's Story, Canongate. Tel: 0131-529 4057. Closed Sun. Adm. free. Edinburgh life since the 18th century
Royal Museum of Scotland, Chambers Street. Tel: 0131-225 7534. Closed Sun. mornings. Adm. free. Scottish and

international collections from prehistoric times to the
present
Scottish Agricultural Museum, Ingliston. Tel: 0131-225
7534. Closed in winter and on Sun., also on Sat. in May
and Sept. Adm. free. History of agriculture in Scotland
Scottish National Portrait Gallery, Queen Street. Tel: 0131-
556 8921. Closed Sun. mornings. Adm. free. Portraits of
eminent people in Scottish history, and the national
collection of photography
Scottish National Gallery of Modern Art, Belford Road. Tel:
0131-556 8921. Closed Sun. mornings. Adm. free.
Twentieth-century painting, sculpture and graphic art
Scottish United Services Museum, Edinburgh Castle. Tel:
0131-225 7534. Closed Sun. mornings in winter. Adm.
free. History of the armed forces of Scotland
*The Writer's Museum, Lawnmarket. Tel: 0131-529 4901.
Closed Sun. Adm. free. Robert Louis Stevenson, Walter
Scott and Robert Burns exhibits
FORT WILLIAM – *West Highland Museum*, Cameron Square.
Tel: 01397-702169. Closed to end March 1996. Includes
tartan collections and exhibits relating to 1745 uprising
GLASGOW – **Burrell Collection*, Pollokshaws Road. Tel:
0141-649 7151. Adm. free. Nineteenth-century
paintings, textiles, furniture, ceramics, stained glass and
silver
*Glasgow Art Gallery and Museum, Kelvingrove. Tel: 0141-
221 9600. Adm. free. Includes Old Masters, 19th-century
French paintings and armour collection
Hunterian Art Gallery, Hillhead Street. Tel: 0141-330
5431. Closed Sun. Adm. free. Rennie Mackintosh and
Whistler collections; also Old Masters and modern
prints
*McLellan Galleries, Sauchiehall Street. Tel: 0141-331
1854. Adm. charge. Temporary exhibitions
*Museum of Transport, Bunhouse Road. Tel: 0141-221
9600. Adm. free. Includes a reproduction of a 1938
Glasgow street, cars since the 1930s, trams and a
Glasgow subway station
*People's Palace Museum, Glasgow Green. Tel: 0141-554
0223. Adm. free. History of Glasgow since 1175
*Pollok House, Pollokshaws Road. Tel: 0141-632 0274.
Closed to March 1996. Adm. free. Spanish paintings,
furniture, silver and ceramics
*St Mungo Museum of Religious Life and Art, Castle Street.
Tel: 0141-553 2557. Adm. free. Explores universal
themes through objects of all the main world religions

NORTHERN IRELAND

BELFAST – *Ulster Museum*, Botanic Gardens. Tel: 01232-
381251. Closed weekend mornings. Adm. free. Irish
antiquities, natural and local history, fine and applied
arts
HOLYWOOD, Co. Down – *Ulster Folk and Transport Museum*,
Cultra. Tel: 01232-428428. Closed Sun. mornings, also
Sat. mornings in winter. Adm. £3.30. Indoor galleries and
reconstructed buildings in the open air, Irish National
Railway and Titanic exhibitions
LONDONDERRY – *The Tower Museum*, Union Hall Place.
Tel: 01504-372411. Closed Sun. morning July-Aug.;
Sun. and Mon. (except Bank Holidays) Sep.-June. Adm.
£2.75. Tells the story of Ireland through the history of
Londonderry
OMAGH, Co. Tyrone – *Ulster American Folk Park*,
Castletown. Tel: 01662-243292. Closed weekends in
winter. Adm. £3.50. Open-air museum telling the story
of Ulster's emigrants to America; restored or recreated
dwellings and workshops; ship and dockside gallery

Sights of London

For historic buildings, museums and galleries in London, see pages 586–598

ALEXANDRA PALACE, Wood Green, London N22 4AY. Tel: 0181-365 2121. The Victorian Palace was severely damaged by fire in 1980 but was restored, and reopened in 1988. Alexandra Palace now provides modern facilities for exhibitions, sports, conferences and leisure activities. There is an ice rink, open daily.

BARBICAN CENTRE, Silk Street, London EC2Y 8DS. Tel: 0171-638 4141 ext. 7537/8. Owned, funded and managed by the Corporation of London, the Barbican Centre opened in 1982 and houses the 1,166-seat Barbican Theatre, a 200-seat studio theatre (The Pit), and the 2,026-seat Barbican Hall. There are also three cinemas, two art galleries, a sculpture court, a lending library, trade exhibition and conference facilities, and shops.

BRIDGES. The bridges over the Thames (from east to west) are:

The Queen Elizabeth II Bridge, opened 1991, from Dartford to Thurrock

Tower Bridge, opened 1894 (*see also* page 596)

London Bridge, opened after rebuilding by Rennie, 1831; the new London Bridge opened 1973

Alexandra Bridge (railway bridge), built 1863–6

Southwark Bridge (Rennie), built 1814–19; rebuilt 1912–21

Blackfriars Railway Bridge, completed 1864

Blackfriars Bridge, built 1760–9; rebuilt 1860–9; widened 1907–10

Waterloo Bridge (Rennie), opened 1817; rebuilt 1937–42

Hungerford Railway Bridge (Brunel), suspension bridge built 1841–5; replaced by present railway and footbridge 1863

Westminster Bridge (width 84 ft), opened 1750; rebuilt 1854–62

Lambeth Bridge, built 1862; rebuilt 1929–32

Vauxhall Bridge, built 1811–16; rebuilt 1895–1906

Grosvenor Bridge (railway bridge), built 1859–60; rebuilt 1963–7

Chelsea Bridge, built 1851–8; replaced by suspension bridge 1934; widened 1937

Albert Bridge, opened 1873; restructured (Bazalgette) 1884; strengthened 1971–3

Battersea Bridge (Holland), opened 1772; rebuilt (Bazalgette) 1890

Battersea Railway Bridge, opened 1863

Wandsworth Bridge, opened 1873; rebuilt 1940

Putney Railway Bridge, opened 1889

Putney Bridge, built 1727–9; rebuilt (Bazalgette) 1882–6; starting point of Oxford and Cambridge Boat Race

Hammersmith Bridge, built 1824–7; rebuilt (Bazalgette) 1883–7

Barnes Railway Bridge (also pedestrian), built 1846–9; restructured 1893

Chiswick Bridge, opened 1933

Kew Railway Bridge, opened 1869

Kew Bridge, built 1758–9; rebuilt and renamed King Edward VII Bridge 1903

Richmond Lock; lock, weir and footbridge opened 1894

Twickenham Bridge, opened 1933

Richmond Railway Bridge, opened 1848; restructured 1906–8

Richmond Bridge, built 1774–7; widened 1937

Teddington Lock, footbridge opened 1889; marks the end of the tidal reach of the Thames

Kingston Bridge, built 1825–8; widened 1914

Hampton Court Bridge, built 1753; replaced by iron bridge 1865; present bridge built 1933

CEMETERIES. *Abney Park*, Stamford Hill, N16 (35 acres), tomb of General Booth, founder of the Salvation Army, and memorials to many Nonconformist divines. *Brompton*, Old Brompton Road, SW10 (40 acres), graves of Sir Henry Cole, Emmeline Pankhurst, John Wisden. *City of London Cemetery and Crematorium*, Aldersbrook Road, E12 (200 acres). *Golders Green Crematorium*, Hoop Lane, NW11 (12 acres), with Garden of Rest and memorials to many famous men and women. *Hampstead*, Fortune Green Road, NW6 (36 acres), graves of Kate Greenaway, Lord Lister, Marie Lloyd. *Highgate*, Swains Lane, N6 (38 acres), tombs of George Eliot, Faraday and Marx; guided tours only, west side, £3.00. *Kensal Green*, Harrow Road, W10 (70 acres), tombs of Thackeray, Trollope, Sydney Smith, Wilkie Collins, Tom Hood, George Cruikshank, Leigh Hunt, I. K. Brunel and Charles Kemble. Churchyard of the former *Marylebone Chapel*, Marylebone High Street, W1 (Charles Wesley and his son Samuel Wesley buried; chapel demolished in 1949, now Garden of Rest. *Nunhead*, Linden Grove, SE15 (26 acres), closed in 1969, recently restored and opened for burials. *St Marylebone Cemetery and Crematorium*, East End Road, N2 (47 acres). *West Norwood Cemetery and Crematorium*, Norwood High Street, SE27 (42 acres), tombs of Sir Henry Bessemer, Mrs Beeton, Sir Henry Tate and Joseph Whitaker (*Whitaker's Almanack*).

CENOTAPH, Whitehall, London SW1. The word 'cenotaph' means 'empty tomb'. The monument, erected 'To the Glorious Dead', is a memorial to all ranks of the sea, land and air forces who gave their lives in the service of the Empire during the First World War. Designed by Sir Edwin Lutyens and erected as a temporary memorial in 1919, it was replaced by a permanent structure unveiled by George V on Armistice Day 1920. An additional inscription was made after the Second World War to commemorate those who gave their lives in that conflict.

CHARTERHOUSE, Sutton's Hospital, Charterhouse Square, London EC1M 6AN. Tel: 0171-253 9503. A Carthusian monastery from 1371 to 1537, purchased in 1611 by Thomas Sutton, who endowed it as a hospital for aged men 'of gentle birth' and a school for poor scholars (removed to Godalming in 1872). Open to visitors on Wednesdays at 2.15 (April–July). Admission £2.00. *Registrar and Clerk to the Governors*, Lt.-Col. I. Macdonald.

CHELSEA PHYSIC GARDEN, 66 Royal Hospital Road, London SW3 4HS. Tel: 0171-352 5646. A garden of general botanical research, maintaining a wide range of rare and unusual plants. The garden was established in 1673 by the Society of Apothecaries. Open Wednesday and Sunday p.m. during summer months. All enquiries to the Curator.

DOWNING STREET, London SW1. Number 10 Downing Street is the official town residence of the Prime Minister, No. 11 of the Chancellor of the Exchequer and No. 12 is the office of the Government Whips. The street was named after Sir George Downing, Bt., soldier and diplomatist, who was MP for Morpeth from 1660 to 1684.

Chequers, a Tudor mansion in the Chilterns near Princes Risborough, was presented by Lord and Lady Lee of Fareham in 1917 to serve, from 1921, as a country residence for the Prime Minister of the day.

GEORGE INN, Borough High Street, London SE1. The last galleried inn in London, built in 1677. Now run as an ordinary public house.

GREENWICH, London SE10. *The Royal Naval College* was until 1873 the Greenwich Hospital. It was built by Charles II, largely from designs by John Webb, and by Queen Anne and William III, from designs by Wren. It stands on the site of an ancient royal palace and of the more recent Palace of Placentia constructed by Humphrey, Duke of Gloucester (1391–1447), son of Henry IV. Henry VIII, Mary I and Elizabeth I were born in the royal palace (which reverted to the Crown in 1447) and Edward VI died there. *Greenwich Park* (196½ acres) was enclosed by Humphrey, Duke of Gloucester, and laid out by Charles II from the designs of Le Nôtre. On a hill in Greenwich Park is the former Royal Observatory (founded 1675). Its buildings are now managed by the National Maritime Museum (*see* page 595) and the first observatory is named Flamsteed House, after John Flamsteed (1646–1719), the first Astronomer Royal. *The Cutty Sark*, the last of the famous tea clippers, has been preserved as a memorial to ships and men of a past era (*see* page 595). The yacht *Gipsy Moth IV* is preserved alongside the *Cutty Sark*.

HORSE GUARDS, Whitehall, London SW1. Archway and offices built about 1753. The mounting of the guard takes place at 11 a.m. (10 a.m. on Sundays) and the dismounted inspection at 4 p.m. Only those on the Lord Chamberlain's list may drive through the gates and archway into *Horse Guards' Parade* (230,000 sq. ft), where the Colour is 'trooped' on The Queen's official birthday.

THE HOUSES OF PARLIAMENT, Westminster, London SW1. The royal palace of Westminster, originally built by Edward the Confessor, was the normal meeting place of Parliament from about 1340. St Stephen's Chapel was used from about 1550 for the meetings of the House of Commons, which had previously been held in the Chapter House or Refectory of Westminster Abbey. The House of Lords met in an apartment of the royal palace.

The fire of 1834 destroyed much of the palace and the present Houses of Parliament were erected on the site from the designs of Sir Charles Barry and Augustus Welby Pugin between 1840 and 1867. The chamber of the House of Commons was destroyed by bombing in 1941 and a new Chamber designed by Sir Giles Gilbert Scott was used for the first time in 1950.

Westminster Hall was the only part of the old palace of Westminster to survive the fire of 1834. It was built by William Rufus (1097–9) and altered by Richard II (1394–9). The hammerbeam roof of carved oak dates from 1396–8. The Hall was the scene of the trial of Charles I.

The Victoria Tower of the House of Lords is about 330 ft high, and when Parliament is sitting the Union flag flies by day from its flagstaff. *The Clock Tower* of the House of Commons is about 320 ft high and contains 'Big Ben', the hour bell said to be named after Sir Benjamin Hall, First Commissioner of Works when the original bell was cast in 1856. This bell, which weighed 16 tons 11 cwt, was found to be cracked in 1857. The present bell (13½ tons) is a recasting of the original and was first brought into use in 1859. The dials of the clock are 23 ft in diameter, the hands being 9 ft and 14 ft long (including balance piece). A light is displayed from the Clock Tower at night when Parliament is sitting.

For security reasons tours of the Houses of Parliament are available only to those who have made advance arrangements through an MP or peer.

Admission to the Strangers' Gallery of the House of Lords is arranged by a peer or by queue via St Stephen's Entrance. Admission to the Strangers' Gallery of the House of Commons is by Members' order (Members' orders should be sought several weeks in advance), or by queue via St Stephen's Entrance. Queues are usually shorter after 6 p.m., Monday–Thursday. Overseas visitors may write to the Public Information Office to obtain a permit to tour the Houses of Parliament, or obtain cards of introduction from their Embassy or High Commission to attend the public gallery.

INNS OF COURT. The *Inner* and *Middle Temple*, Fleet Street/Victoria Embankment, London EC4, have occupied since the early 14th century the site of the buildings of the Order of Knights Templars. *Inner Temple Hall* is open by appointment on application to the Treasurer's Office. *Middle Temple Hall* (1562–70) is open when not in use, Monday–Friday 10–11.30 and 3–4; closed on public holidays. In Middle Temple Gardens (not open to the public) Shakespeare (Henry VI, Part I) places the incident which led to the 'Wars of the Roses' (1455–85).

Temple Church, London EC4, has a nave which forms one of five remaining round churches in England. Open Wednesday–Friday 10–4. Services: 8.30 and 11.15 a.m. except in August and September. *Master of the Temple*, Revd Canon J. Robinson.

Lincoln's Inn, Chancery Lane/Lincoln's Inn Fields, London WC2, occupies the site of the palace of a former Bishop of Chichester and of a Black Friars monastery. The hall and library buildings are of 1845, although the library is first mentioned in 1474; the old hall (late 15th century) and the chapel were rebuilt c.1619–23. Halls open by appointment, chapel and gardens, Monday–Friday 12–2.30. Chapel services Sunday 11.30 a.m. during law terms. *Lincoln's Inn Fields* (7 acres). The square was laid out by Inigo Jones.

Gray's Inn, Holborn/Gray's Inn Road, London WC1. Early 14th century; hall 1556–8. Chapel services 11.15 a.m. (during law dining terms only). Holy Communion first Sunday in every month except August–September. Gardens open Monday–Friday 12–2.30. Tel: 0171-405 8164.

No other 'Inns' are active, but there are remains of *Staple Inn*, a gabled front on Holborn (opposite Gray's Inn Road). *Clement's Inn* (near St Clement Danes Church), *Clifford's Inn*, Fleet Street, and *Thavies Inn*, Holborn Circus, are all rebuilt. *Serjeants' Inn*, Fleet Street, and another (demolished 1910) of the same name in Chancery Lane, were composed of Serjeants-at-Law, the last of whom died in 1922.

KEW GARDENS, Surrey – *see* index.

LLOYD'S, Lime Street, London EC3M 7HA. Society of private underwriters which evolved during the 18th century from Lloyds Coffee House. The present building was opened for business in May 1986, and houses the Lutine Bell. Underwriting is on four floors with a total area of 114,000 sq. feet. A visitors' gallery is open Monday–Friday for pre-booked groups.

LONDON PARKS, ETC.

Maintained by the Crown

Bushy Park (1,099 acres), Surrey. Adjoining Hampton Court, contains avenue of horse-chestnuts enclosed in a fourfold avenue of limes planted by William III. 'Chestnut Sunday' (when the trees are in full bloom with their 'candles') is usually about 1 to 15 May

Green Park (49 acres), London W1. Between Piccadilly and St James's Park, with Constitution Hill leading to Hyde Park Corner

Greenwich Park (196½ acres), London SE10

Hampton Court Gardens (54 acres), Surrey

Hampton Court Green (17 acres), Surrey
Hampton Court Park (622 acres), Surrey
Hyde Park (341 acres), London W1/W2. From Park Lane to Kensington Gardens, containing the Serpentine. Fine gateway at Hyde Park Corner, with Apsley House, the Achilles Statue, Rotten Row and the Ladies' Mile. To the north-east is the Marble Arch, originally erected by George IV at the entrance to Buckingham Palace and re-erected in the present position in 1851
Kensington Gardens (275 acres), London W2/W8. From the western boundary of Hyde Park to Kensington Palace, containing the Albert Memorial
Kew, Royal Botanic Gardens, see Index
Regent's Park and *Primrose Hill* (464 acres), London NW1. From Marylebone Road to Primrose Hill surrounded by the Outer Circle and divided by the Broad Walk leading to the Zoological Gardens
Richmond Park (2,469 acres), Surrey
St James's Park (93 acres), London SW1. From Whitehall to Buckingham Palace. Ornamental lake of 12 acres. The original suspension bridge built in 1857 was replaced in 1957. The Mall leads from the Admiralty Arch to Buckingham Palace, Birdcage Walk from Storey's Gate to Buckingham Palace
Maintained by the Corporation of London
Ashtead Common (500 acres), Surrey
Burnham Beeches and *Fleet Wood* (540 acres), Bucks. Purchased by the Corporation for the benefit of the public in 1880, Fleet Wood (65 acres) being presented in 1921
Coulsdon Common (133 acres), Surrey
Epping Forest (6,000 acres), Essex. Purchased by the Corporation and opened to the public in 1882. The present forest is 12 miles long by 1 to 2 miles wide, about one-tenth of its original area
Farthing Downs (121 acres), Surrey
Hampstead Heath (789 acres), London NW3. Including Golders Hill (36 acres) and Parliament Hill (271 acres)
Highgate Wood (70 acres), London N6/N10
Kenley Common (138 acres), Surrey
Queen's Park (30 acres), London NW6
Riddlesdown (90 acres), Surrey
Spring Park (51 acres), Kent
West Ham Park (77 acres), London E15
West Wickham Common (25 acres), Kent
Woodredon and Warlies Park Estate (740 acres), Waltham Abbey
Also smaller open spaces within the City of London, including *Finsbury Circus Gardens*
LONDON PLANETARIUM, Marylebone Road, London NW1 5LR. Tel: 0171-935 6861. Open daily (except Christmas Day), star show and interactive exhibits 12.20–4.40. Admission charge.
MADAME TUSSAUD's, Marylebone Road, London NW1 5LR. Tel: 0171-935 6861. Waxwork exhibition. Open daily (except Christmas Day) 10–5.30. Admission charge.
MARKETS. The London markets are mostly administered by the Corporation of the City of London. *Billingsgate* (fish), Thames Street site dating from 1875, a market site for over 1,000 years, moved to the Isle of Dogs in 1982. *Borough*, SE1 (vegetables, fruit, flowers, etc.), established on present site 1756, privately owned and run. *Covent Garden* (vegetables, fruit, flowers, etc.), established in 1661 under a charter of Charles II, moved in 1973 to Nine Elms. *Leadenhall*, EC3 (meat, poultry, fish, etc.), built 1881, part recently demolished. *London Fruit Exchange*, Brushfield Street, built by Corporation of London 1928–9 as buildings for Spitalfields market; not connected with the market since it moved in 1991. *Petticoat Lane*, Middlesex Street, E1, a market has existed on the site for over 500 years, now a Sunday morning market

selling almost anything. *Portobello Road*, W11, originally for herbs and horse-trading from 1870; became famous for antiques after the closure of the Caledonian Market in 1948; Saturdays. *Smithfield, Central Meat, Fish, Fruit, Vegetable and Poultry Markets*, built 1851–66, the site of St Bartholomew's Fair from 12th to 19th century, new hall built 1963, market refurbished 1993–4. *Spitalfields*, E1 (vegetables, fruit, etc.), established 1682, modernized 1928, moved to Leyton in 1991.
MARLBOROUGH HOUSE, Pall Mall, London SW1A 5HX. Built by Wren for the first Duke of Marlborough and completed in 1711, the house reverted to the Crown in 1835. In 1863 it became the London house of the Prince of Wales and was the London home of Queen Mary until her death in 1953. In 1959 Marlborough House was given by The Queen as a centre for Commonwealth government conferences and it was opened as such in 1962. The Queen's Chapel, Marlborough Gate, begun in 1623 from the designs of Inigo Jones for the Infanta Maria of Spain, and completed for Queen Henrietta Maria, is open to the public for services on Sundays at 8.30 a.m. and 11.15 a.m. between Easter Day and end July (*see* St James's Palace for winter services in The Chapel Royal).
LONDON MONUMENT (commonly called The Monument), Monument Street, London EC3. Built from designs of Wren, 1671–7, to commemorate the Great Fire of London, which broke out in Pudding Lane on 2 September 1666. The fluted Doric column is 120 ft high; the moulded cylinder above the balcony supporting a flaming vase of gilt bronze is an additional 42 ft; and the column is based on a square plinth 40 ft high (with fine carvings on the west face) making a total height of 202 ft. Splendid views of London from gallery at top of column (311 steps). As total refurbishment planned from autumn 1995, check with Public Relations office for access. Tel: 0171-606 3030.
MONUMENTS (sculptor's name in parenthesis). *Albert Memorial* (Durham), Kensington Gore; *Royal Air Force* (Blomfield), Victoria Embankment; *Viscount Alanbrooke*, Whitehall; *Beaconsfield*, Parliament Square; *Beatty* (Macmillan), Trafalgar Square; *Belgian Gratitude* (setting by Blomfield, statue by Rousseau), Victoria Embankment; *Boadicea* (or Boudicca), Queen of the Iceni (Thornycroft), Westminster Bridge; *Brunel* (Marochetti), Victoria Embankment; *Burghers of Calais* (Rodin), Victoria Tower Gardens, Westminster; *Burns* (Steel), Embankment Gardens; *Carlyle* (Boehm), Chelsea Embankment; *Cavalry* (Jones), Hyde Park; *Edith Cavell* (Frampton), St Martin's Place; *Cenotaph* (Lutyens), Whitehall; *Charles I* (Le Sueur), Trafalgar Square; *Charles II* (Gibbons), South Court, Chelsea Hospital; *Churchill* (Roberts-Jones), Parliament Square; *Cleopatra's Needle* (68½ ft high, c.1500 BC, erected on the Thames Embankment in 1877–8; the sphinxes are Victorian); *Clive* (Tweed), King Charles Street; *Captain Cook* (Brock), The Mall; *Crimean*, Broad Sanctuary; *Oliver Cromwell* (Thornycroft), outside Westminster Hall; *Cunningham* (Belsky), Trafalgar Square; *Gen. Charles de Gaulle*, Carlton Gardens; *Lord Dowding* (Faith Winter), Strand; *Duke of Cambridge* (Jones), Whitehall; *Duke of York* (124 ft), Carlton House Terrace; *Edward VII* (Mackennal), Waterloo Place; *Elizabeth I* (1586, oldest outdoor statue in London; from Ludgate), Fleet Street; *Eros* (Shaftesbury Memorial) (Gilbert), Piccadilly Circus; *Marechal Foch* (Mallisard), copy of one in Cassel, France), Grosvenor Gardens; *Charles James Fox* (Westmacott), Bloomsbury Square; *George III* (Cotes Wyatt), Cockspur Street; *George IV* (Chantrey), riding without stirrups, Trafalgar Square; *George V* (Reid Dick), Old Palace Yard;

George VI (Macmillan), Carlton Gardens; *Gladstone* (Thornycroft), Strand; *Guards'* (Crimea) (Bell), Waterloo Place; (Great War) (Ledward, figures, Bradshaw, cenotaph), Horse Guards' Parade; *Haig* (Hardiman), Whitehall; *Sir Arthur (Bomber) Harris* (Faith Winter), Strand; *Irving* (Brock), north side of National Portrait Gallery; *James II* (Gibbons and/or pupils), Trafalgar Square; *Jellicoe* (Wheeler), Trafalgar Square; *Samuel Johnson* (Fitzgerald), opposite St Clement Danes; *Kitchener* (Tweed), Horse Guards' Parade; *Abraham Lincoln* (Saint-Gaudens, copy of one in Chicago), Parliament Square; *Milton* (Montford), St Giles, Cripplegate; *The Monument* (*see* above); *Mountbatten*, Foreign Office Green; *Nelson* (170 ft 2 in), Trafalgar Square, with Landseer's lions (cast from guns recovered from the wreck of the *Royal George*); *Florence Nightingale* (Walker), Waterloo Place; *Palmerston* (Woolner), Parliament Square; *Peel* (Noble), Parliament Square; *Pitt* (Chantrey), Hanover Square; *Portal* (Nemon), Embankment Gardens; *Prince Consort* (Bacon), Holborn Circus; *Queen Elizabeth Gate*, Hyde Park Corner; *Raleigh* (Macmillan), Whitehall; *Richard I (Coeur de Lion)* (Marochetti), Old Palace Yard; *Roberts* (Bates), Horse Guards' Parade; *Franklin D. Roosevelt* (Reid Dick), Grosvenor Square; *Royal Artillery* (South Africa) (Colton), The Mall; (Great War), Hyde Park Corner; *Captain Scott* (Lady Scott), Waterloo Place; *Shackleton* (Sarjeant Jagger), Kensington Gore; *Shakespeare* (Fontana, copy of one by Scheemakers in Westminster Abbey), Leicester Square; *Smuts* (Epstein), Parliament Square; *Sullivan* (Goscombe John), Victoria Embankment; *Trenchard* (Macmillan), Victoria Embankment; *Victoria Memorial*, in front of Buckingham Palace; *George Washington* (Houdon copy), Trafalgar Square; *Wellington* (Boehm), Hyde Park Corner; (Chantrey) riding without stirrups, outside Royal Exchange; *John Wesley* (Adams Acton), City Road; *William III* (Bacon), St James's Square; *Wolseley* (Goscombe John), Horse Guards' Parade.

PORT OF LONDON. The Port of London covers the tidal section of the River Thames from Teddington to the seaward limit (Tongue light vessel), a distance of 150 km. The governing body is the Port of London Authority (PLA). Eighty-eight per cent of the total port traffic is handled at privately operated riverside terminals between Fulham and Canvey Island, the rest at the enclosed dock at Tilbury, 40 km below London Bridge. Passenger vessels and cruise liners can be handled at moorings at Greenwich, Tower Bridge and Tilbury.

ROMAN REMAINS. The city wall of Roman *Londinium* was largely rebuilt during the medieval period but sections may be seen near the White Tower in the Tower of London; at Tower Hill; at Coopers' Row; at All Hallows, London Wall, its vestry being built on the remains of a semi-circular Roman bastion; at St Alphage, London Wall, showing a succession of building repairs from the Roman until the late medieval period; and at St Giles, Cripplegate. Sections of the great forum and basilica, more than 165 metres square, have been encountered during excavations in the area of Leadenhall, Gracechurch Street and Lombard Street. Traces of Roman activity along the river include a massive riverside wall built in the late Roman period, and a succession of Roman timber quays along Lower and Upper Thames Street.

Other major buildings are the Provincial Governor's Palace in Cannon Street; the amphitheatre at Guildhall; remains of a bath-building, preserved in Lower Thames Street; and the Temple of Mithras in Walbrook.

ROYAL ALBERT HALL, Kensington Gore, London sw7 2sr. Tel: 0171-589 3203. The elliptical hall, one of the largest

in the world, was completed in 1871, and since 1941 has been the venue each summer for the Promenade Concerts founded in 1895 by Sir Henry Wood. Other events include pop and classical music concerts, dance, opera, sporting events, conferences and banquets.

ROYAL HOSPITAL, CHELSEA, Royal Hospital Road, London sw3 4sr. Tel: 0171-730 0161. Founded by Charles II in 1682, and built by Wren; opened in 1692 for old and disabled soldiers. Open Monday–Saturday 10–12, daily 2–4. The extensive grounds include the former Ranelagh Gardens and are the venue for the Chelsea Flower Show each May. *Governor*, Gen. Sir Brian Kenny, GCB, CBE; *Lt.-Governor and Secretary*, Maj.-Gen. F. G. Sugden, CB, CBE.

ROYAL OPERA HOUSE, Covent Garden, London wc2e 9dd. Home of The Royal Ballet (1931) and The Royal Opera (1946). The Royal Opera House is the third theatre to be built on the site, opening 1858; the first was opened in 1732.

ST JAMES'S PALACE, Pall Mall, London sw1. Built by Henry VIII; the Gatehouse and Presence Chamber remain; later alterations were made by Wren and Kent. The Chapel Royal is open for services on Sundays at 8.30 a.m. and 11.15 a.m. between the beginning of October and Good Friday (*see* Marlborough House for summer services in The Queen's Chapel). Representatives of foreign powers are still accredited 'to the Court of St James's'. *Clarence House* (1825) in the palace precinct is the home of The Queen Mother.

ST PAUL'S CATHEDRAL, London ec4m 8ad. Built 1675–1710, cost £747,660. The cross on the dome is 365 ft above the ground level, the inner cupola 218 ft above the floor. 'Great Paul' in the south-west tower weighs nearly 17 tons. The organ by Father Smith (enlarged by Willis and rebuilt by Mander) is in a case carved by Grinling Gibbons, who also carved the choir stalls. Open for sightseeing Monday–Saturday 8.30–4.00. Admission to cathedral and crypt: £3.00, children £2.00; Galleries £2.50/£1.50. Services: Sundays, 8, 11 and 3.15. Weekdays, 7.30, 8, 12.30 and 5 (Saturday Mattins 10 a.m.).

SOMERSET HOUSE, Strand and Victoria Embankment, London wc2. The river façade (600 ft. long) was built in 1776–86 from the designs of Sir William Chambers; the eastern extension, which houses part of King's College, was built by Smirke in 1829. Somerset House was the property of Lord Protector Somerset, at whose attainder in 1552 the palace passed to the Crown, and it was a royal residence until 1692.

SOUTH BANK, London se1. The arts complex on the south bank of the River Thames includes the South Bank Centre, owned and managed by the South Bank Board, which consists of the 2,903-seat *Royal Festival Hall* (opened in 1951 for the Festival of Britain), the adjacent 1,056-seat *Queen Elizabeth Hall*, the 368-seat *Purcell Room*, and the 77-seat Voice Box. Tel: 0171-928 8800.

The *National Film Theatre* (opened 1952), administered by the British Film Institute, has three auditoria showing almost 2,000 films a year. The London Film Festival is held here every November. Tel: 0171-928 3232.

The *Royal National Theatre* opened in 1976 and stages classical, modern, new and neglected plays in its three auditoria: the 1,160-seat Olivier theatre, the 890-seat Lyttelton theatre and the Cottesloe theatre which seats up to 400. Tel: 0171-928 2252.

SOUTHWARK CATHEDRAL, London se1 9da. Mainly 13th century, but the nave is largely rebuilt. The tomb of John Gower (1330–1408) is between the Bunyan and Chaucer memorial windows in the north aisle; Shakespeare's effigy backed by a view of Southwark and the Globe Theatre in the south aisle; the tomb of Bishop Andrews

(died 1626) is near the screen. The lady chapel was the scene of the consistory courts of the reign of Mary (Gardiner and Bonner) and is still used as a consistory court. John Harvard, after whom Harvard University is named, was baptized here in 1607, and the chapel by the north choir aisle is his memorial chapel. Open 8.30–6, admission free. Services: Sundays, 11, 3. Weekdays, 12.45, 5.30 (sung on Tuesdays and Fridays), Saturdays, 12 noon.

THAMES EMBANKMENTS. The *Victoria Embankment*, on the north side from Westminster to Blackfriars, was constructed by Sir Joseph Bazalgette (1819–91) for the Metropolitan Board of Works, 1864–70; the seats, of which the supports of some are a kneeling camel, laden with spicery, and of others a winged sphinx, were presented by the Grocers' Company and by W. H. Smith, MP, in 1874; the *Albert Embankment*, on the south side from Westminster Bridge to Vauxhall, 1866–9; the *Chelsea Embankment*, 1871–4. The total cost exceeded £2,000,000. Bazalgette also inaugurated the London main drainage system, 1858–65. A medallion (*Flumini vincula posuit*) has been placed on a pier of the Victoria Embankment to commemorate the engineer.

THAMES FLOOD BARRIER. Officially opened in May 1984, though first used in February 1983, the barrier consists of ten rising sector gates which span 570 yards from bank to bank of the Thames at Woolwich Reach. When not in use the gates lie horizontally, allowing shipping to navigate the river normally; when the barrier is closed, the gates turn through 90 degrees to stand vertically more than 50 feet above the river bed. The barrier took eight years to complete and can be raised within about 30 minutes.

THAMES TUNNELS. The *Rotherhithe Tunnel*, opened 1908, connects Commercial Road, London E14, with Lower Road, Rotherhithe; it is 1 mile 332 yards long, of which 525 yards are under the river. The first *Blackwall Tunnel* (northbound vehicles only), opened 1897, connects East India Dock Road, Poplar, with Blackwall Lane, East Greenwich. The height restriction on the northbound tunnel is 13ft 4in. A second tunnel (for southbound vehicles only) opened 1967. The lengths of the tunnels measured from East India Dock Road to the Gate House on the south side are 6,215 ft (old tunnel) and 6,152 ft. *Greenwich Tunnel* (pedestrians only), opened 1902, connects the Isle of Dogs, Poplar, with Greenwich; it is 406 yards long. The *Woolwich Tunnel* (pedestrians only), opened 1912, connects North and South Woolwich below the passenger and vehicular ferry from North Woolwich Station, London E16, to High Street, Woolwich, London SE18; it is 552 yards long.

WALTHAM CROSS, Herts. At Waltham Cross is one of the crosses (partly restored) erected by Edward I to mark a resting place of the corpse of Queen Eleanor on its way to Westminster Abbey. Ten crosses were erected, but only those at Geddington, Northampton and Waltham survive; 'Charing' Cross originally stood near the spot now occupied by the statue of Charles I at Whitehall.

WESTMINSTER ABBEY, London SW1. Built between 1050 and 1745; contains the chapel of Henry VII, chapter house and cloisters, Edward the Confessor's shrine, tombs of kings and queens and many other monuments, including the grave of 'The Unknown Warrior' and Poets' Corner. The Coronation Chair encloses the Stone of Scone, removed from Scotland by Edward I in 1296. Open on weekdays 9.20–6 (9.20–7.45 Wednesday). Admission to the Royal Chapels, Poets' Corner, Quire and Statesmen's Aisle £4.00, con. £2.00/£1.00. Last admission Monday–Friday 4 p.m., Saturday 5 p.m. Nave open on Sundays between services. Services: Sundays, 8,

10, 11.15, 3, 6.30 (generally preceded by an organ recital). Monday–Friday, 7.30, 8, 12.30, 5. Saturdays, 8, 9.20, 3.

WESTMINSTER CATHEDRAL, Ashley Place, London SW1P 1QW. Roman Catholic cathedral built 1895–1903 from the designs of J. F. Bentley. The campanile is 283 feet high. Cathedral open 6.45 a.m.–8 p.m. Masses: Sundays, 7, 8, 9, 10.30 (sung), 12, 5.30 and 7; Solemn Vespers and Benediction 3.30. Monday–Friday, 7, 8, 8.30, 9, 10.30, 12.30, 1.05 and 5.30 (sung). Morning Prayer 7.40, Vespers 5. Saturdays 7, 8, 8.30, 9, 10.30 (sung), 12.30 and 6, Morning Prayer 7.40, Vespers 5.30. Holy days of obligation, Low Masses 7, 8, 8.30, 9, 10.30, 12.30, 1.05, 5.30 (sung) and 7.

ZOOLOGICAL GARDENS (London Zoo), Regent's Park, London NW1. Tel: 0171-722 3333. Opened in 1828. Open daily (except Christmas Day) 10–5.30 March–September, 10–4 in winter. Admission £7.00

LONDON TOURISM BOARD AND CONVENTION BUREAU, Tourist Information Centre, Victoria Station Forecourt, London SW1V 1JU. Tel: 0171–730 3488

Hallmarks

Hallmarks are the symbols stamped on gold, silver or platinum articles to indicate that they have been tested at an official Assay Office and that they conform to one of the legal standards. With certain exceptions, all gold, silver, or platinum articles are required by law to be hallmarked before they are offered for sale. Hallmarking was instituted in England in 1300 under a statute of Edward I.

MODERN HALLMARKS

Normally a complete modern hallmark consists of four symbols – the sponsor's mark, the assay office mark, the standard mark and the date letter. Additional marks have been authorized from time to time.

SPONSOR'S MARK

Instituted in England in 1363, the sponsor's mark was originally a device such as a bird or fleur-de-lis. Now it consists of the initial letters of the name or names of the manufacturer or firm. Where two or more sponsors have the same initials, there is a variation in the surrounding shield or style of letters.

STANDARD MARK

The standard mark indicates that the content of the precious metal in the alloy from which the article is made, is not less than the legal standard. The legal standard is the minimum content of precious metal by weight in parts per thousand, and the standards are:

Gold	916.6	(22 carat)
	750	(18 carat)
	585	(14 carat)
	375	(9 carat)
Silver	958.4	(Britannia)
	925	(sterling)
Platinum	950	

The metals are marked as follows, if they are manufactured in the United Kingdom:

GOLD – a crown followed by the millesimal figure for the standard, e.g. 916 for 22 carat (see table above)

SILVER – Britannia silver: a full-length figure of Britannia. Sterling silver: a lion passant (England) or a lion rampant (Scotland)

 Britannia Silver

 Sterling Silver (England)

 Sterling Silver (Scotland)

PLATINUM – an orb

ASSAY OFFICE MARK

This mark identifies the particular assay office at which the article was tested and marked. The existing assay offices in Britain are:

LONDON, Goldsmiths' Hall, London EC2V 8AQ. Tel: 0171-606 8975

BIRMINGHAM, Newhall Street, Birmingham B3 1SB. Tel: 0121-236 6951

 Gold and platinum

 Silver

SHEFFIELD, 137 Portobello Street, Sheffield S1 4DS. Tel: 0114–275 5111

EDINBURGH, 9 Granton Road, Edinburgh EH5 3QJ. Tel: 0131-551 2189

Assay offices formerly existed in other towns, e.g. Chester, Exeter, Glasgow, Newcastle, Norwich and York, each having its own distinguishing mark.

DATE LETTER

The date letter shows the year in which an article was assayed and hallmarked. Each alphabetical cycle has a distinctive style of lettering or shape of shield. The date letters were different at the various assay offices and the particular office must be established from the assay office mark before reference is made to tables of date letters.

The table on page 605 shows specimen shields and letters used by the London Assay Office on silver articles in each period from 1498. The same letters are found on gold articles but the surrounding shield may differ. Since 1 January 1975, each office has used the same style of date letter and shield for all articles.

OTHER MARKS

FOREIGN GOODS

Since 1842 foreign goods imported into Britain have been required to be hallmarked before sale. The marks consist of the importer's mark, a special assay office mark, the figure denoting fineness (fineness mark) and the annual date letter.

The following are the assay office marks for gold imported articles. For silver and platinum the symbols remain the same but the shields differ in shape.

 London

 Birmingham

 Sheffield

 Edinburgh

Convention Hallmarks

Special marks at authorized assay offices of the signatory countries of the International Convention (Austria, Denmark, Finland, Ireland, Norway, Portugal, Sweden, Switzerland and the UK) are legally recognized in the United Kingdom as approved hallmarks. These consist of a sponsor's mark, a common control mark, a fineness mark (arabic numerals showing the standard in parts per thousand), and an assay office mark. There is no date letter.

The fineness marks are:

Gold	750	(18 carat)
	585	(14 carat)
	375	(9 carat)
Silver	925	(sterling)
Platinum	950	

The common control marks are:

 Gold (18 carat)

 Silver

 Platinum

Duty Marks

In 1784 an additional mark of the reigning sovereign's head was introduced to signify that the excise duty had been paid. The mark became obsolete on the abolition of the duty in 1890.

Commemorative Marks

There are three other marks to commemorate special events, the Silver Jubilee of King George V and Queen Mary in 1935, the Coronation of Queen Elizabeth II in 1953, and her Silver Jubilee in 1977.

LONDON (GOLDSMITHS' HALL) DATE LETTERS from 1498

		from	to
	Black letter, small	1498–9	1517–8
	Lombardic	1518–9	1537–8
	Roman and other capitals	1538–9	1557–8
	Black letter, small	1558–9	1577–8
	Roman letter, capitals	1578–9	1597–8
	Lombardic, external cusps	1598–9	1617–8
	Italic letter, small	1618–9	1637–8
	Court hand	1638–9	1657–8

		from	to
	Black letter, capitals	1658–9	1677–8
	Black letter, small	1678–9	1696–7
	Court hand	1697	1715–6
	Roman letter, capitals	1716–7	1735–6
	Roman letter, small	1736–7	1738–9
	Roman letter, small	1739–40	1755–6
	Old English, capitals	1756–7	1775–6
	Roman letter, small	1776–7	1795–6
	Roman letter, capitals	1796–7	1815–6
	Roman letter, small	1816–7	1835–6
	Old English, capitals	1836–7	1855–6
	Old English, small	1856–7	1875–6
	Roman letter, capitals [A to M square shield N to Z as shown]	1876–7	1895–6
	Roman letter, small	1896–7	1915–6
	Black letter, small	1916–7	1935–6
	Roman letter, capitals	1936–7	1955–6
	Italic letter, small	1956–7	1974
	Italic letter, capitals	1975	

Economic Statistics

GENERAL GOVERNMENT RECEIPTS *£ billion*

	Outturn 1993–4	Forecast 1994–5	Forecast 1995–6
Income tax	58.4	64.2	70.1
Corporation tax	14.9	20.1	26.4
Value added tax	38.9	43.3	49.0
Excise duties	24.2	26.3	28.0
Other taxes and royalties	38.6	39.7	43.0
Social security receipts	38.7	42.5	44.5
Other receipts	17.1	16.3	17.8
Total general government receipts	230.8	252.5	278.9

Source: HM Treasury – *Financial Statement and Budget Report 1995–6*

THE CONTROL TOTAL AND GENERAL GOVERNMENT EXPENDITURE
(EXCLUDING PRIVATIZATION PROCEEDS) *£ million*

	Estimated outturn 1994–5	Plans/ projections 1995–6
Central government expenditure	175,700	179,600
Local authority expenditure	73,400	73,400
Financing requirements of nationalized industries	1,520	−370
Reserve	—	3,000
Allowance for short-fall	−1,000	—
Control total	249,600	255,700
Cyclical social security	14,100	14,100
Central government debt interest	22,100	24,500
Accounting adjustments	9,500	10,700
General government expenditure excluding privatization proceeds	295,200	305,000
GGE excluding privatization proceeds as a percentage of GDP	43.5%	42.5%

Source: HM Treasury – *Financial Statement and Budget Report 1995–6*

CONTROL TOTAL EXPENDITURE BY DEPARTMENT *£ million*

	Estimated outturn 1994–5	New plans 1995–6
Defence	22,510	21,720
Foreign Office	1,440	1,160
Overseas Development	2,400	2,360
Agriculture, Fisheries and Food	2,660	3,020
Trade and Industry	1,860	1,380
ECGD	−70	−20
Employment	3,720	3,460
Transport	6,100	4,390
DoE – Housing	7,350	6,900
DoE – Environment	2,170	1,980
DoE – PH, PSA, etc.	−130	−210
DoE – Local government	29,900	30,290
Home Office	6,260	6,410
Legal departments	2,650	2,800
Education	10,530	10,960
National Heritage	980	1,000
Health	31,750	32,960
Social security	70,360	72,970
Scotland	14,200	14,410
Wales	6,580	6,770
Northern Ireland	7,490	7,720
Chancellor of the Exchequer's departments	3,390	3,220
Cabinet Office – OPSS	1,320	1,340
Cabinet Office – other, etc.	1,200	1,120
European Communities	2,040	2,820
Local authority self-financed expenditure	11,900	11,800
Reserve	—	3,000
Allowance for shortfall	−1,000	—
Control total	249,600	255,700

Source: HM Treasury – *Financial Statement and Budget Report 1995–6*

FINANCING REQUIREMENTS OF NATIONALIZED INDUSTRIES *£ million*

	Estimated outturn 1994–5	Plans 1995–6
Trade and Industry	1,000	440
British Coal	740	380
British Shipbuilders	10	0
Nuclear Electric	480	270
Post Office	−230	−210
Transport	2,460	1,130
Railways*	1,500	200
Civil Aviation Authority	60	35
London Transport	900	890
DoE – Environment	50	50
British Waterways Board	50	50
Scotland	−30	−30
Caledonian MacBrayne Ltd	10	10
Scottish Nuclear	−40	−40
Scottish Transport Group	0	—
Total	3,480	1,580

* Includes British Rail, Railtrack, Union Railways and European Passenger Services
Source: HM Treasury – *Financial Statement and Budget Report 1995–6*

LOCAL AUTHORITY EXPENDITURE   *£ million*

	Estimated outturn 1994–5	Plans 1995–6
CURRENT		
Aggregate External Finance		
England	34,330	34,670
Scotland	5,310	5,310
Wales	2,420	2,450
TOTAL	42,070	42,440
Other current grants	13,750	13,800
TOTAL CURRENT	55,820	56,230
CAPITAL		
Capital grants	1,600	1,510
Credit approvals	4,010	3,940
TOTAL CAPITAL SUPPORT	5,610	5,450
TOTAL CENTRAL GOVERNMENT SUPPORT TO LOCAL AUTHORITIES	61,400	61,700
LOCAL AUTHORITY SELF-FINANCED EXPENDITURE	11,900	11,800
TOTAL LOCAL AUTHORITY EXPENDITURE	73,400	73,400

Source: HM Treasury – *Financial Statement and Budget Report 1995–6*

PUBLIC SECTOR BORROWING REQUIREMENT

	Outturn 1993–4	Forecast 1994–5	Forecast 1995–6
PSBR (£ billion)	45.4	34.4	21.5
As % of GDP	7	5	3

Source: HM Treasury – *Financial Statement and Budget Report 1995–6*

GDP BY INDUSTRY 1993 BEFORE DEPRECIATION BUT AFTER STOCK APPRECIATION

£ million

Agriculture, hunting, forestry and fishing	10,373
Mining and quarrying, including gas and oil extraction	12,147
Manufacturing	118,294
Electricity, gas and water supply	13,944
Construction	29,221
Wholesale and retail trade; repairs; hotels and restaurants	78,348
Transport, storage and communication	46,263
Financial intermediation; real estate; renting and business activities	133,956
Public administration, national defence and compulsory social security	38,199
Education; health; social work	57,457
Other services, including sewerage and refuse disposal	31,292
TOTAL	569,544
less adjustment for financial services	23,741
Statistical discrepancy (income adjustment)	317
GROSS DOMESTIC PRODUCT	546,120

Source: HMSO – *Annual Abstract of Statistics 1995*

UNEMPLOYMENT BY STANDARD REGIONS
SEASONALLY ADJUSTED, AT MID APRIL 1995*

	Total	% of workforce
United Kingdom	2,327,900	8.3
England:		
North	148,700	10.6
Yorkshire and Humberside	208,300	8.9
East Midlands	148,600	7.7
East Anglia	65,200	6.4
South East	726,000	8.0
South West	166,600	7.3
West Midlands	211,500	8.4
North West	254,800	8.8
Wales	106,900	8.3
Scotland	202,600	8.1
Northern Ireland	88,700	11.8

Note: Percentages calculated using mid-1994 estimates of total employees in employment, unemployed, self-employed and HM Forces, and participants in work-related government training schemes
* provisional
Source: Department of Employment

BALANCE OF PAYMENTS 1993   *£ million*

CURRENT ACCOUNT
Visible trade

Exports (fob)	121,414
Imports (fob)	134,623
Visible balance	−13,209
Invisibles	
Credits	116,000
Debits	113,102
Invisibles balance	2,898
of which:	
Services balance	4,942
Investment income	3,062
Transfers balance	−5,106
CURRENT BALANCE	−10,311

*TRANSACTIONS IN EXTERNAL ASSETS AND
LIABILITIES
Investment overseas by UK residents

Direct	−17,292
Portfolio	−85,603
Total UK investment overseas	−102,895
Investment in the UK by overseas residents	
Direct	9,502
Portfolio	40,009
Total overseas investment in UK	49,511
Foreign currency lending abroad by UK banks	12,688
Foreign currency borrowing abroad by UK banks	23,706
Net foreign currency transactions of UK banks	36,394
Sterling lending abroad by UK banks	−8,260
Sterling borrowing and deposit liabilities abroad of UK banks	712
Net sterling transactions of UK banks	−7,548
Deposits with and lending to banks abroad by UK non-bank private sector	−10,142
Borrowing from banks abroad by:	
UK non-bank private sector	15,628
Public corporations	−24
General government	−2,944
Official reserves (additions to −, drawings on +)	−702
Other external assets of:	
UK non-bank private sector and public corporations	−48,529
General government	−610
Other external liabilities of:	
UK non-bank private sector and public corporations	80,278
General government	−101
NET TRANSACTIONS IN ASSETS AND LIABILITIES	8,313
BALANCING ITEM	1,998

* Assets: increase − /decrease ; +
Liabilities: increase + /decrease −
Source: HMSO – *Annual Abstract of Statistics 1995*

VISIBLE TRADE OF THE UK
ON A BALANCE OF PAYMENTS BASIS   *£ million*

	Exports	Imports	Visible balance
1984	70,265	75,601	−5,336
1985	77,991	81,336	−3,345
1986	72,627	82,186	−9,559
1987	79,153	90,735	−11,582
1988	80,346	101,826	−21,480
1989	92,154	116,837	−24,683
1990	101,718	120,527	−18,809
1991	103,413	113,697	−10,284
1992	107,343	120,447	−13,104
1993	121,414	134,623	−13,209

Source: HMSO – *Annual Abstract of Statistics 1995*

VALUE OF UK EXPORTS 1994
BY DESTINATION   *£ million*

European Community	70,353.8
Other western Europe	11,388.7
Eastern Europe	2,820.1
North America	19,010.8
Other America	2,789.7
Middle East and North Africa	6,649.0
Sub-Saharan Africa	3,121.5
Asia and Oceania	17,188.6
Low-value exports	538.5
Total non-EC exports	63,506.9
Total exports	133,580.5

Source: HM Customs and Excise

VALUE OF UK IMPORTS 1994
BY SOURCE   *£ million*

European Community	74,780.3
Other western Europe	16,974.1
Eastern Europe	2,829.0
North America	19,697.2
Other America	2,713.8
Middle East and North Africa	3,209.5
Sub-Saharan Africa	2,261.2
Asia and Oceania	25,484.0
Low-value imports	421.4
Total non-EC imports	73,580.1
Total imports	145,350.3

Source: HM Customs and Excise

HOUSEHOLDS AND THEIR EXPENDITURE 1993[1]

NUMBER OF HOUSEHOLDS
SUPPLYING DATA	6,979
Total number of persons	17,291
Total number of adults[2]	12,792

HOUSEHOLD PERCENTAGE
DISTRIBUTION BY TENURE
Rented unfurnished	27.9%
Rented furnished	3.7%
Rent-free	1.5%
Owner-occupied	66.9%

AVERAGE NUMBER OF PERSONS
PER HOUSEHOLD
All persons	2.478
Males	1.201
Females	1.276
Adults[2]	1.833
Persons under 65	1.466
Persons 65 and over	0.367
Children[2]	0.645
Children under 2	0.076
Children 2 and under 5	0.123
Children 5 and under 18	0.446
Persons economically active	1.153
Persons not economically active	1.324
Men 65 and over, women 60 and over	0.400
Others	0.925

AVERAGE WEEKLY HOUSEHOLD EXPENDITURE ON
COMMODITIES AND SERVICES

	Weekly average £	As % of total
Housing[3]	44.85	16.2
Fuel, light and power	13.24	4.8
Food	49.96	18.1
Alcoholic drink	11.95	4.3
Tobacco	5.59	2.0
Clothing and footwear	17.40	6.3
Household goods	23.05	8.3
Household services	15.44	5.6
Personal goods and services	11.04	4.0
Motoring expenditure	36.28	13.1
Fares and other travel costs	6.95	2.5
Leisure goods	13.26	4.8
Leisure services	25.56	9.2
Miscellaneous	2.10	0.8
Total	276.68	100.0

[1] Information derived from the Family Expenditure Survey; relates to the UK
[2] Adults = all persons 18 and over and married persons under 18
Children = all unmarried persons under 18
[3] Excludes mortgage payments but includes imputed expenditure (i.e. the weekly equivalent of rateable value)
Source: HMSO – *Annual Abstract of Statistics 1995*

SOURCES OF HOUSEHOLD INCOME 1993*

AVERAGE WEEKLY INCOME BY SOURCE (£)
Wages and salaries	228.30
Self-employment	29.23
Investments	18.00
Annuities and pensions (other than social security benefits	21.89
Social security benefits	48.91
Other sources	6.70
Total	353.03

SOURCES AS A PERCENTAGE OF TOTAL HOUSEHOLD
INCOME (%)
Wages and salaries	64.7
Self-employment	8.3
Investments	5.1
Annuities and pensions (other than social security benefits	6.2
Social security benefits	13.9
Other sources	1.9
Total	100.0

* Information derived from the Family Expenditure Survey; relates to the UK. Number of households supplying data, 6,979
Source: HMSO – *Annual Abstract of Statistics 1995*

AVAILABILITY OF CERTAIN DURABLE GOODS 1993*
PERCENTAGE OF HOUSEHOLDS

Car	68.6
One	45.6
Two	19.1
Three or more	3.9
Central heating, full or partial	82.5
Washing machine	89.3
Refrigerator or fridge/freezer	99.1
Freezer or fridge/freezer	86.6
Television	98.3†
Telephone	89.6
Home computer	19.1†
Video recorder	73.4

* Information derived from the Family Expenditure Survey; relates to the UK. Number of households supplying data, 6,979
† 1992 figure
Source: HMSO – *Annual Abstract of Statistics 1995*

Cost of Living and Inflation Rates

The first cost of living index to be calculated took July 1914 as 100 and was based on the pattern of expenditure of working-class families in 1914. The cost of living index was superseded in 1947 by the general index of retail prices (RPI), although the older term is still popularly applied to it.

GENERAL INDEX OF RETAIL PRICES

The general index of retail prices measures the changes month by month in the average level of prices of goods and services purchased by most households in the United Kingdom. The spending pattern on which the index is based is revised each year, mainly using information from the Family Expenditure Survey. The expenditure of certain higher income households and of households mainly dependent on state pensions is excluded.

The index is compiled using a selection of over 600 goods and services and the prices charged for these items are collected at regular intervals in about 180 locations throughout the country. For the index, the price changes are weighted in accordance with the pattern of consumption of the average family.

INFLATION RATE

The twelve-monthly percentage change in the 'all items' index of the RPI is usually referred to as the rate of inflation. The percentage change in prices between any two months/years can be obtained using the following formula:

$$\frac{\text{Later date RPI} - \text{Earlier date RPI}}{\text{Earlier date RPI}} \times 100$$

e.g. to find the rate of inflation for 1988, using the annual averages for 1987 and 1988:

$$\frac{106.9 - 101.9}{101.9} \times 100 = 4.9\%$$

PURCHASING POWER OF THE POUND

Changes in the internal purchasing power of the pound may be defined as the 'inverse' of changes in the level of prices; when prices go up, the amount which can be purchased with a given sum of money goes down. To find the purchasing power of the pound in one month or year, given that it was 100p in a previous month or year, the calculation would be:

$$100p \times \frac{\text{Earlier month/year RPI}}{\text{Later month/year RPI}}$$

Thus, if the purchasing power of the pound is taken to be 100p in 1975, the comparable purchasing power in 1993 would be:

$$100p \times \frac{34.2}{140.7} = 24.31p$$

For longer term comparisons, it has been the practice to use an index which has been constructed by linking together the RPI for the period 1962 to date; an index derived from the consumers expenditure deflator for the period from 1938 to 1962; and the prewar 'Cost of Living' index for the period 1914 to 1938. This long-term index enables the internal purchasing power of the pound to be calculated for any year from 1914 onwards. It should be noted that these figures can only be approximate.

	Long-term index of consumer goods and services (Jan. 1987 = 100)	Comparable purchasing power of £1 in 1994	Rate of inflation (annual average)
1914	2.8	51.46	
1915	3.5	41.17	
1920	7.0	20.59	
1925	5.0	28.82	
1930	4.5	32.02	
1935	4.0	36.03	
1938	4.4	32.75	
There are no official figures for 1939–45			
1946	7.4	19.47	
1950	9.0	16.01	
1955	11.2	12.87	
1960	12.6	11.44	
1965	14.8	9.74	
1970	18.5	7.79	
1975	34.2	4.21	
1980	66.8	2.16	18.0
1981	74.8	1.93	11.9
1982	81.2	1.77	8.6
1983	84.9	1.70	4.6
1984	89.2	1.62	5.0
1985	94.6	1.52	6.1
1986	97.8	1.47	3.4
1987	101.9	1.41	4.2
1988	106.9	1.35	4.9
1989	115.2	1.25	7.8
1990	126.1	1.14	9.5
1991	133.5	1.08	5.9
1992	138.5	1.04	3.7
1993	140.7	1.02	1.6
1994	144.1	1.00	2.4

Finance

British Currency

COIN

Gold Coins	*Nickel-Brass Coins*
*One hundred pounds	Two pounds £2
£100	One pound £1
*Fifty pounds £50	
*Twenty-five pounds £25	*Cupro-Nickel Coins*
*Ten pounds £10	Crown £5 (since 1990)
Five pounds £5	50 pence 50p
Two pounds £2	Crown 25p (pre-1990)
Sovereign £1	20 pence 20p
Half-Sovereign 50p	‡10 pence 10p
	§5 pence 5p
†*Silver Coins*	
(Maundy Money)	*Bronze Coins*
Fourpence 4p	2 pence 2p
Threepence 3p	1 penny 1p
Twopence 2p	
Penny 1p	*Copper-plated Steel Coins*
	2 pence 2p
	1 penny 1p

*Britannia gold bullion coins, introduced in October 1987
†Gifts of special money distributed by the Sovereign annually on Maundy Thursday to the number of aged poor men and women corresponding to the Sovereign's own age
‡New 10 pence coin introduced on 30 September 1992
§New 5 pence coin introduced on 27 June 1990

GOLD COIN

Gold ceased to circulate during the First World War. Since then controls on buying, selling and holding gold coin have been imposed at various times but subsequently have been revoked. Under the Exchange Control (Gold Coins Exemption) Order 1979 gold coins may now be imported and exported without restriction, except gold coins which are more than fifty years old and valued at a sum in excess of £8,000; these cannot be exported without specific authorization from the Department of Trade and Industry.

On 1 April 1982 the Government introduced VAT (currently 17.5 per cent) on sales of all gold coin.

SILVER COIN

Prior to 1920 silver coins were struck from sterling silver, an alloy of which 925 parts in 1,000 were silver. In 1920 the proportion of silver was reduced to 500 parts. From 1 January 1947 all 'silver' coins, except Maundy money, have been struck from cupro-nickel, an alloy of copper 75 parts and nickel 25 parts, except for the 20p, composed of copper 84 parts, nickel 16 parts. Maundy coins continue to be struck from sterling silver.

BRONZE COIN

Bronze, introduced in 1860 to replace copper, is an alloy of copper 97 parts, zinc 2.5 parts and tin 0.5 part. These proportions have been subject to slight variations in the past. Bronze has been replaced by copper-plated steel in September 1992.

LEGAL TENDER

Gold, dated 1838 onwards, if not below least current weight, is legal tender to any amount. £5 (Crown since 1990), £2 and £1 coins are legal tender to any amount; 50p, 25p (Crown pre-1990) and 20p coins are legal tender up to £10; 10p and 5p coins are legal tender up to £5, and 2p and 1p coins are legal tender for amounts up to 20p.

Farthings ceased to be legal tender on 31 December 1960, the halfpenny on 1 August 1969, the halfcrown on 1 January 1970, the threepence and penny on 31 August 1971, the sixpence on 30 June 1980, the decimal halfpenny on 31 December 1984, the old 5p on 31 December 1990, and the old 10p on 30 June 1993.

The decimal system was introduced on 15 February 1971. Since 1982 the word 'new' in 'new pence' displayed on decimal coins has been dropped.

The Channel Islands and the Isle of Man issue their own coinage, which are legal tender only in the island of issue. For denominations, *see* page 612.

Metal		Standard weight (g)	Standard diameter (cm)
Penny	bronze	3.564	2.032
Penny	copper-plated steel	3.564	2.032
2 pence	bronze	7.128	2.591
2 pence	copper-plated steel	7.128	2.591
5p	cupro-nickel	3.25	1.80
10p	cupro-nickel	6.5	2.45
20p	cupro-nickel	5.0	2.14
25p Crown	cupro-nickel	28.276	3.861
50p	cupro-nickel	13.5	3.0
£1	nickel-brass	9.5	2.25
£2	nickel-brass	15.98	2.84
£5 Crown	cupro-nickel	28.28	3.861

The 'remedy' is the amount of variation from standard permitted in weight and fineness of coins when first issued from the Mint.

The Trial of the Pyx is the examination by a jury to ascertain that coins made by the Royal Mint, which have been set aside in the pyx (or box), are of the proper weight, diameter and composition required by law. The trial is held annually, presided over by the Queen's Remembrancer (the Senior Master of the Supreme Court), with a jury of freemen of the Company of Goldsmiths.

BANKNOTES

Bank of England notes are currently issued in denominations of £5, £10, £20 and £50 for the amount of the fiduciary note issue, and are legal tender in England and Wales. Banknotes which are no longer legal tender are payable when presented at the head office of the Bank of England in London.

The old white notes for £10, £20, £50, £100, £500 and £1,000, which were issued until April 1943, ceased to be legal tender in May 1945, and the old white £5 note in March 1946.

The white £5 note issued between October 1945 and September 1956, the £5 notes issued between 1957 and 1963, (bearing a portrait of Britannia) and the first series to bear a portrait of The Queen, issued between 1963 and 1971, ceased to be legal tender in March 1961, June 1967 and September 1973 respectively.

The series of £1 notes issued during the years 1928 to 1960 and the 10 shilling notes issued from 1928 to 1961 (those without the royal portrait) ceased to be legal tender in May and October 1962 respectively. The £1 note first issued in March 1960 (bearing on the back a representation of Britannia) and the £10 note first issued in February 1964 (bearing a lion on the back), both bearing a portrait of The Queen on the front, ceased to be legal tender in June 1979. The £1 note first issued in 1978 ceased to be legal tender on 11 March 1988. The 10 shilling note was replaced by the 50p coin in October 1969, and ceased to be legal tender on 21 November 1970.

The D series of banknotes was introduced in 1970 and ceased to be legal tender from 1991 onwards. The predominant identifying feature of each note was the portrayal on the back of a prominent figure from Britain's history:

£1	Feb. 1978–March 1988	Sir Isaac Newton
£5	Nov. 1971–Nov. 1991	The Duke of Wellington
£10	Feb. 1975–May 1994	Florence Nightingale
£20	July 1970–March 1993	William Shakespeare
£50	March 1981–	Sir Christopher Wren

The £1 coin was introduced on 21 April 1983 to replace the £1 note. The £50 note is still legal tender.

The E series of notes was introduced in June 1990 replacing the D series. The historical figures portrayed in this series are:

£5	June 1990–	George Stephenson
£10	April 1992–	Charles Dickens
£20	June 1991–	Michael Faraday
£50	April 1994–	Sir John Houblon

NOTE CIRCULATION

Note circulation is highest at the two peak spending periods of the year, around Christmas and during the summer holiday period. The total value of notes in circulation at 21 December 1994 was £20,060 million, compared to £19,280 million at 22 December 1993.

The value of notes in circulation at end February 1994 and 1995 was:

	1994	1995
£1*	£57m	£57m
£5	£1,135m	£1,072m
£10	£5,245m	£5,348m

£20	£6,817m	£7,723m
£50	£2,883m	£2,852m
Other notes†	—	£1,004m
Total	—	£18,056m

* No £1 notes have been issued since 1984

† Includes higher value notes used internally in the Bank of England, e.g. as cover for the note issues of banks of issue in Scotland and Northern Ireland in excess of their permitted issue

OTHER BANKNOTES

SCOTLAND – Banknotes are issued by three Scottish banks. The Royal Bank of Scotland and the Bank of Scotland issue notes for £5, £10, £20 and £100. The Royal Bank of Scotland also issues £1 notes. The Clydesdale Bank issues notes for £5, £10, £20, £50, £100. Scottish notes are not legal tender in Scotland but they are an authorized currency and enjoy there a status comparable to that of the Bank of England note.

NORTHERN IRELAND – Banknotes are issued by four banks in Northern Ireland. The Northern Bank and the Ulster Bank issue notes for £5, £10, £20, £50 and £100. First Trust Bank issues notes for £10, £20, £50 and £100, and the Bank of Ireland issues notes for £5, £10, £20 and £100. Northern Ireland notes are not legal tender in Northern Ireland but they circulate widely and enjoy a status comparable to that of Bank of England notes.

CHANNEL ISLANDS – The States of Guernsey issues its own currency notes and coinage. The notes are for £1, £5, £10, £20 and £50, and the coins are for 1p, 2p, 5p, 10p, 20p, 50p, £1 and £2. The States of Jersey issues its own currency notes and coinage. The notes are for £1, £5, £10, £20 and £50, and the coins are for 1p, 2p, 5p, 10p, 20p, 50p and £1.

THE ISLE OF MAN – The Isle of Man Government issues notes for £1, £5, £10, £20 and £50. Although these notes are only legal tender in the Isle of Man, they are accepted at face value in branches of the clearing banks in the United Kingdom. The Isle of Man issues coins for 1p, 2p, 5p, 10p, 20p, 50p, £1, £2 and £5.

Although none of the series of notes specified above is legal tender in the United Kingdom, they are generally accepted by the banks irrespective of their place of issue. At one time the banks made a commission charge for handling Scottish and Irish notes but this was abolished some years ago.

Slang Terms for Money

(Reproduced from *Whitaker's Almanack* 1891)

In addition to the ordinary terms there are others which, although puzzling to a foreigner, are tolerably well understood in this country. In Scotland, a man who flies 'kites' may not be worth a 'bodle', and in England not worth a 'mag' – coins which no one ever saw. Such a man will toss you for a 'bob'. He, of course, would be shunned by the lady who lost a 'pony' on last year's Oaks, and by her husband who lost a 'monkey' on the Derby at Epsom a day or two previously. A gentleman who is worth a 'plum' (£100,000) need never be short of 'tin'; while the outcast who begs a few 'coppers' in order to procure a bed generally has no 'blunt'. The following words are commonly in use:

A Joey = 4d.	A Pony = £25
A Tanner = 6d.	A Monkey = £500
A Bob = 1s.	A Kite = An accommodation Bill
Half a Bull = 2s. 6d.	Browns = Copper or bronze
A Bull = 5s.	Tin = Money generally
A Quid = £1	Blunt = Silver, or money in general

Investment Business Regulation

The growth of Britain's financial services industry in the 1970s and 1980s left the regulatory structure existing at that time inadequate to deal with the new competitive climate or to provide the necessary safeguards for the investing public. Under the Financial Services Act 1986, a new supervisory framework was set up to regulate companies conducting investment business and new criminal offences were created. The Act came into force on 29 April 1988, when it became a criminal offence to conduct investment business without authorization, unless specifically exempt from the authorization requirement.

The Securities and Investments Board (SIB) is the designated agency under the Financial Services Act 1986 for regulating the activities of investment businesses in the UK. Although not a statutory body, the SIB has statutory powers under the Act to recognize self-regulating organizations, professional bodies, investment exchanges and clearing houses, and directly to authorize firms to undertake investment business in the UK.

The SIB oversees the regulation of all investment business in the UK. It is not responsible for areas involving public issues, takeovers and mergers, and insider dealing investigation. Its area of authority overlaps with that of the Bank of England, the Department of Trade and Industry (for insurance companies) and the Building Societies Commission where their respective member bodies are carrying out investment business.

The regulatory sanctions of the SIB are as follows:

1 It may issue public or private reprimands
2 It may restrict business
3 It may suspend authorization
4 It may withdraw authorization
5 In certain cases it may take out a civil injunction
6 It may petition the courts for the winding up of companies
7 It may ban persons from the industry for life

CENTRAL REGISTER
Checkline 0171-929 3652

The SIB maintains a register (the Central Register) of all firms who are authorized to carry on investment business. The entry for each firm gives its name, address and telephone number; an SIB reference number; its authorization status; its appropriate regulatory body; and whether it can handle client money.

INVESTORS COMPENSATION SCHEME
The Investors Compensation Scheme, run by a management company as part of the overall investor protection offered by the SIB, comes into play when authorized firms become insolvent owing money to private investors. It is funded by means of a levy on all member firms, according to their size and category. The maximum compensation that the scheme can pay to an investor is £48,000.

SECURITIES AND INVESTMENTS BOARD LTD, Gavrelle House, 2–14 Bunhill Row, London EC1Y 8RA. Tel: 0171-638 1240. *Chief Executive*, J. Young, CBE.

SELF-REGULATING ORGANIZATIONS

The SIB recognizes self-regulating organizations (SROs), which are responsible to the SIB for ensuring financial supervision in their respective sectors of investment business. Most members of the financial services industry obtain their authorization by being members of an SRO.

The following are recognized by the SIB as being able to provide proper regulation of the investment business carried out by their members, and the necessary standard of investor protection:

*IMRO (Investment Management Regulatory Organization), Broadwalk House, Appold Street, London EC2A 2LL. Tel: 0171-628 6022
†PIA (Personal Investment Authority), 1 Canada Square, Canary Wharf, London E14 5AZ. Tel: 0171-538 8860
SFA (Securities and Futures Authority Ltd), Cottons Centre, Cottons Lane, London SE1 2QB. TEL: 0171-378 9000

* IMRO, also regulates the activities of friendly societies.
† The PIA replaced FIMBRA and LAUTRO as the main SRO for the retail sector with effect from 18 July 1994. FIMBRA and LAUTRO were wound up when their existing business was completed in autumn 1995.

RECOGNIZED PROFESSIONAL BODIES

The SIB is empowered to recognize professional bodies (RPBs) who, as a result, can authorize their members for investment business. Such business must not form the whole or main part of the total business undertaken by the firm.

INSTITUTE OF CHARTERED ACCOUNTANTS IN ENGLAND AND WALES, Chartered Accountants Hall, PO Box 433, Moorgate Place, London EC2P 2BJ. Tel: 0171-920 8100
INSTITUTE OF CHARTERED ACCOUNTANTS OF SCOTLAND, 27 Queen Street, Edinburgh EH2 1LA. Tel: 0131-225 5673
INSTITUTE OF CHARTERED ACCOUNTANTS IN IRELAND, 11 Donegall Square South, Belfast BT1 5JE. Tel: 01232-321600
CHARTERED ASSOCIATION OF CERTIFIED ACCOUNTANTS, 29 Lincoln's Inn Fields, London WC2A 3EE. Tel: 0171-242 6855
THE LAW SOCIETY, 113 Chancery Lane, London WC2A 1PL. Tel: 0171-242 1222
LAW SOCIETY OF SCOTLAND, Law Society's Hall, 26 Drumsheugh Gardens, Edinburgh EH3 7YR. Tel: 0131-226 7411
LAW SOCIETY OF NORTHERN IRELAND, Law Society's House, 98 Victoria Street, Belfast BT1 3JZ. Tel: 01232-231614
INSTITUTE OF ACTUARIES, Staple Inn Hall, High Holborn, London WC1V 7QJ. Tel: 0171-242 0106
INSURANCE BROKERS REGISTRATION COUNCIL, 15 St Helen's Place, London EC3A 6DS. Tel: 0171-588 4387

RECOGNIZED INVESTMENT EXCHANGES

Investment exchanges are exempt from needing authorization from the SIB as an investment business. However, to be a recognized investment exchange (RIE), each must fulfil the following requirements: adequate financial resources; proper conduct of business rules; a proper market in its products; procedures for recording transactions; effective monitoring and enforcement of rules; proper arrangements for the clearing and performance of contracts.

INTERNATIONAL PETROLEUM EXCHANGE (IPE), International House, 1 St Katharine's Way, London E1 9UN. Tel: 0171-481 0643

LONDON COMMODITY EXCHANGE LTD, 1 Commodity Quay, St Katharine Docks, London EI 9AX. Tel: 0171-481 2080

LONDON INTERNATIONAL FINANCIAL FUTURES EXCHANGE (LIFFE), Royal Exchange, London EC3V 3PJ. Tel: 0171-623 0444

LONDON METAL EXCHANGE LTD (LME), 56 Leadenhall Street, London EC3A 2BJ. Tel: 0171-264 5555

THE LONDON SECURITIES AND DERIVATIVES EXCHANGE LTD (OMLX), 107 Cannon Street, London EC4N 5AD. Tel: 0171-283 0678

TRADEPOINT FINANCIAL NETWORKS PLC, 35 King Street, London WC2E 8JD. Tel: 0171-240 8000

The following exchanges are recognized by the Treasury as offering adequate investor protection:

INTERNATIONAL STOCK EXCHANGE OF THE UNITED KINGDOM AND THE REPUBLIC OF IRELAND (LSE), Old Broad Street, London EC2N 1HP. Tel: 0171-588 2355

CHICAGO BOARD OF TRADE (CBOT), European Office, 52–54 Gracechurch Street, London EC3V 0EH. Tel: 0171-929 0021

CHICAGO MERCANTILE EXCHANGE (CME), Pinnacle House, 23–26 St Dunstan's Hill, London EC3R 8HL. Tel: 0171-623 2550

MATIF, 176 rue Montmatre, 75083 Paris, Cedex 02, France. Tel: 00 331-4028 8282

MEFF RF, Via Laietana, 58-08003 Barcelona, Spain. Tel: 00-34 3 412 1128

MEFF RV, Torre Picasso, Planta 26, 28020 Madrid, Spain. Tel: 00-34 1 585 0800

NATIONAL ASSOCIATION OF SECURITIES DEALERS AUTOMATED QUOTATIONS SYSTEM (NASDAQ), 43 London Wall, London EC2M 5TB. Tel: 0171-374 6969

NEW YORK MERCANTILE EXCHANGE (NYMEX), 35 Piccadilly, London W1V 9PB. Tel: 0171-734 1280

PARIS BOURSE, London Representative, 199 Bishopsgate, London EC2M 3TT. Tel: 0171-814 6624

SCMC–MONEP, London Representative, 199 Bishopsgate, London EC2M 3TT. Tel: 0171-814 6624

SYDNEY FUTURES EXCHANGE LTD, 30–32 Grosvenor Street, Sydney, NSW 2000, Australia. Tel: 00–612 256 0555

RECOGNIZED CLEARING HOUSES

A recognized clearing house (RCH) must satisfy the same kind of criteria to obtain recognition as the RIEs. There is one RCH which acts as a clearing house for some of the above RIEs:

LONDON CLEARING HOUSE LTD (LCH), Roman Wall House, 1–2 Crutched Friars, London EC3N 2AN. Tel: 0171-265 2000

DESIGNATED INVESTMENT EXCHANGES

The SIB has drawn up a list of 51 overseas exchanges (known as DIEs) whose operations are set in a regulatory context which provides investor protection equivalent to that available from RIEs. Designation does not allow an overseas investment exchange to do business in the UK and, while showing that an exchange meets certain basic criteria, it carries no guarantee for the investor.

OMBUDSMAN SCHEMES

Independent ombudsman schemes have been set up for banks, building societies, and insurance companies. They provide an independent and impartial method of resolving disputes that arise between a company and its customer. In each ombudsman scheme there is a council which appoints and supervises the Ombudsman. The Ombudsman Council is composed of people representing public and consumer interests and member companies. The schemes are funded in various ways: annual subscription from member companies, a levy on member companies according to the size of their assets, a charge for each complaint handled against a particular company, or a combination of these.

The Investment Ombudsman is responsible for resolving disputes that arise between a customer and a member company of IMRO. The Personal Investment Authority (PIA) Ombudsman is responsible for resolving complaints against PIA members about personal investments.

The Pensions Ombudsman is appointed by the Secretary of State for Social Security under the Pension Schemes Act 1993, and is responsible to Parliament. He can resolve grievances between an individual and his/her pension scheme (but not National Insurance benefits). His decisions are binding on both parties. A statutory levy on pension schemes, based on the number of members therein, contributes to the funding of the scheme.

THE OFFICE OF THE BANKING OMBUDSMAN, 70 Gray's Inn Road, London WC1X 8NB. Tel: 0171-404 9944. *Banking Ombudsman*, L. Shurman

THE OFFICE OF THE BUILDING SOCIETIES OMBUDSMAN, Grosvenor Gardens House, 35–37 Grosvenor Gardens, London SW1X 7AW. Tel: 0171-931 0044. *Building Societies Ombudsman*, B. Murphy

THE INSURANCE OMBUDSMAN BUREAU, City Gate One, 135 Park Street, London SE1 9EA. Tel: 0171-928 4488. *Insurance Ombudsman*, L. Slade

THE OFFICE OF THE INVESTMENT OMBUDSMAN, 6 Frederick's Place, London EC2R 8BT. Tel: 0171-796 3065. *Investment Ombudsman*, R. Youard

THE PENSIONS OMBUDSMAN, 11 Belgrave Road, London SW1V 1RB. Tel: 0171-834 9144. *Pensions Ombudsman*, Dr J. T. Farrand

THE PIA OMBUDSMAN BUREAU, 3rd Floor, Centre Point, 103 New Oxford Street, London WC1A 1QH. Tel: 0171-240 3838. *Principle Ombudsman*, S. Edell; *Ombudsman*, A. Samuel

THE TAKEOVER PANEL

The Takeover Panel was set up in 1968 in response to concern about practices unfair to shareholders in take-over bids for public and certain private companies. Its principal objective is to ensure equality of treatment, and fair opportunity for all shareholders to consider on its merits an offer that would result in the change of control of a company. It is a non-statutory body that operates the City code on take-overs and mergers.

The chairman, deputy chairmen and three lay members of the panel are appointed by the Bank of England. The remainder are representatives of the banking, insurance, investment, pension fund and accountancy professional bodies, the CBI, IMRO and the Stock Exchange.

THE TAKEOVER PANEL, PO Box 226, The Stock Exchange Building, London, EC2P 2JX. Tel: 0171-382 9026. *Chairman*, Sir David Calcutt, QC

Banking

Deposit-taking institutions may be broadly divided into two sectors: the monetary sector, which is predominantly banks and is supervised by the Bank of England; and those institutions outside the monetary sector, of which the most important are the building societies and the National Savings Bank.

The main institutions within the British banking system are the Bank of England (the central bank), the retail banks, the merchant banks, the overseas banks, and the discount houses.

The Banking Act 1987 established a single category of authorized institutions eligible to carry out banking business. Under the 1987 Act, the Bank of England exercises a regulatory role over the banking system, and ensures the efficient functioning of payment and settlement systems and efficient services. In its role as the central bank, the Bank of England also acts as banker to the Government and as a note-issuing authority. It is responsible for executing monetary policy and therefore sets the base rates.

BANK BASE RATES 1994–5

12 September 1994	5.75%
7 December 1994	6.25%
2 February 1995	6.75%

RETAIL BANKS

The major retail banks (sometimes referred to as clearing banks) are Abbey National, Bank of Scotland, Barclays, Lloyds, Midland, National Westminster, the Royal Bank of Scotland Group, and the TSB.

Retail banks offer a wide variety of financial services to companies and individuals, including current and deposit accounts, loan facilities, automated teller (cashpoint) machines, cheque guarantee cards, credit cards and debit cards.

The Banking Ombudsman scheme provides independent and impartial arbitration in disputes between a bank and its customer (see also page 614).

Banking hours differ throughout Great Britain. Many banks in England and Wales are experimenting with longer hours and Saturday morning opening, and hours vary from branch to branch. Current minimum opening hours are:
ENGLAND AND WALES: Monday–Friday 9.30–3.30 (City of London town clearers 9.30–3)
SCOTLAND: Monday–Wednesday, Friday, 9.15–4.45; Thursday 9.15–5.30

NORTHERN IRELAND: Open four days a week 10–3; open one day a week 9.30–5

PAYMENT CLEARINGS

The Association for Payment Clearing Services (APACS) is an umbrella organization for payment clearings in the UK. It operates three clearing companies:
– BACS Ltd is the UK's automated clearing house for bulk clearing of electronic debits and credits (e.g. direct debits and salary credits)
– the Cheque and Credit Clearing Company Ltd operates bulk clearing systems for inter-bank cheques and paper credit items in England and Wales
– CHAPS Clearing Company Ltd provides same-day clearing for high-value electronic funds transfers throughout the UK
Membership of APACS and the clearing companies is open to any appropriately regulated financial institution providing payment services and meeting the relevant membership criteria. As at June 1995, APACS had 22 members, comprising the major banks and building societies.
ASSOCIATION FOR PAYMENT CLEARING SERVICES (APACS), Mercury House, Triton Court, 14 Finsbury Square, London EC2A 1BR. Tel: 0171-711 6200. Head of Public Affairs, R. Tyson-Davies
BACS LTD, De Havilland Road, Edgware, Middlesex HA8 5QA. Chief Executive, G. Younger
CHEQUE AND CREDIT CLEARING COMPANY LTD, Mercury House, Triton Court, 14 Finsbury Square, London EC2A 1BR
CHAPS CLEARING COMPANY LTD, Mercury House, Triton Court, 14 Finsbury Square, London EC2A 1BR

AUTHORIZED INSTITUTIONS

Banking in the United Kingdom is regulated by the Banking Act 1987 as amended by the European Community's Second Banking Co-ordination Directive, which came into effect on 1 January 1993.

The Directive permits banks incorporated in one EU member state to carry on certain banking activities in another member state without the need for authorization by that state. Consequently, the Bank of England no longer authorizes banks incorporated in other EU states with branches in the UK so that they may accept deposits in the

MAJOR RETAIL BANKS: FINANCIAL RESULTS 1994

Bank Group	P/L before taxation £m	P/L after taxation £m	Total assets £m	Number of UK branches
Abbey National	1,006	610	94,319	675
*Bank of Scotland	449.7	282.3	34,103.8	420
Barclays	1,859	1,251	162,403	2,067
Lloyds	1,034	879	73,200	1,860
Midland	905	616	80,375	1,736
National Westminster	1,592	1,133	158,046	2,416
The Royal Bank of Scotland Group PLC	532	386	45,320	750

*For year ended 28 February 1995

UK; the authorization of their home state supervisor is sufficient provided that certain notification requirements are met. However, UK-incorporated subsidiaries of banks incorporated in other EU states which wish to accept deposits in the UK continue to need authorization by the Bank of England. As at end February, there were 146 institutions recognized under the Second Banking Co-ordination Directive as European authorized institutions (EAIs).

As at 28 February 1995, a total of 525 institutions were authorized to carry out business in the UK:

Authorized under the Banking Act 1987	379
UK-incorporated	224
Incorporated outside the UK	301
Of which:	
Incorporated outside the EEA	155
EAIs with UK branches entitled	
to accept deposits in UK	102
Other EAIs	44

The following lists show the institutions authorized or entitled to accept deposits in the UK and covered by the UK's deposit protection scheme, as at 1 September 1995.

AUTHORIZED BY THE BANK OF ENGLAND

UK-INCORPORATED
(Including partnerships formed under the law of any part of the UK)

*In administration

ABC International Bank PLC
ANZ Grindlays Bank PLC
AY Bank Ltd
Abbey National PLC
Abbey National Treasury Services PLC
Adam & Company PLC
Afghan National Credit & Finance Ltd
Airdrie Savings Bank
Alexanders Discount PLC
Alliance Trust (Finance) Ltd
Allied Bank Philippines (UK) PLC
Allied Trust Bank Ltd
Alpha Bank London Ltd
Anglo-Romanian Bank Ltd
Henry Ansbacher & Co. Ltd
Arbuthnot Latham & Co. Ltd
Assemblies of God Property Trust
Associates Capital Corporation Ltd
Avco Trust PLC

Banamex Investment Bank PLC
Bankgesellschaft Berlin (UK) PLC
Bank Leumi (UK) PLC
Bank of America International Ltd
Bank of Cyprus (London) Ltd
Bank of Montreal Europe Ltd
Bank of Scotland
Bank of Scotland Treasury Services PLC
Bank of Tokyo International Ltd
Bank of Wales PLC
Bankers Trust International PLC
Banque Nationale de Paris PLC
The Baptist Union Corporation Ltd
Barclays Bank PLC
Barclays Bank Trust Company Ltd
Barclays de Zoete Wedd Ltd
Baring Brothers Ltd
Belmont Bank Ltd
Beneficial Bank PLC
*Bishopscourt (BB & Co.) Ltd

The British Bank of the Middle East
The British Linen Bank Ltd
British Railways Savings Company Ltd
Brown, Shipley & Co. Ltd

CIBC Bank PLC
CLF Municipal Bank PLC
Caledonian Bank PLC
Cater Allen Ltd
Central Hispano Bank (UK) Ltd
The Charities Aid Foundation Money Management Company Ltd
Chartered Trust PLC
Charterhouse Bank Ltd
Chase Investment Bank Ltd
Cheltenham and Gloucester PLC
Chemical Investment Bank Ltd
Citibank International PLC
Clive Discount Company Ltd
Close Brothers Ltd
Clydesdale Bank PLC
Consolidated Credits Bank Ltd
The Co-operative Bank PLC
County NatWest Ltd
Coutts & Co.
Crédit Agricole Lazard Financial Products Bank
Credit Suisse Financial Products
Cyprus Credit Bank (UK) Ltd

Daiwa Europe Bank PLC
Dalbeattie Finance Co. Ltd
Dao Heng Bank (London) PLC
Davenham Trust PLC
Direct Line Financial Services Ltd
The Dorset, Somerset & Wilts Investment Society Ltd
Dryfield Trust PLC
Dunbar Bank PLC
Duncan Lawrie Ltd

Eccles Savings and Loans Ltd
Exeter Bank Ltd

FIBI Bank (UK) PLC
Fairmount Capital Management Ltd
Financial & General Bank PLC
James Finlay Bank Ltd
First National Bank PLC
First National Commercial Bank PLC
The First Personal Bank PLC
First Trust Bank (AIB Group Northern Ireland PLC)
Robert Fleming & Co. Ltd
Ford Credit Europe PLC
Foreign & Colonial Management Ltd
Forward Trust Ltd
Forward Trust Personal Finance Ltd
Frizzell Bank Ltd

Gartmore Money Management Ltd
Gerrard & National Ltd
Girobank PLC
Goldman Sachs Ltd
Granville Bank Ltd
Gresham Trust PLC
Guinness Mahon & Co. Ltd

HFC Bank PLC
HSBC Investment Bank Ltd
Habibsons Bank Ltd
Hambros Bank Ltd
Hampshire Trust PLC
The Hardware Federation Finance Co. Ltd
Harrods Bank Ltd
Harton Securities Ltd

Havana International Bank Ltd
The Heritable & General Investment Bank Ltd
Hill Samuel Bank Ltd
C. Hoare & Co.
Julian Hodge Bank Ltd
Humberclyde Finance Group Ltd
Hungarian International Bank Ltd

3i PLC
3i Group PLC
IBJ International PLC
Iran Overseas Investment Bank Ltd
Italian International Bank PLC

Jordan International Bank PLC
Leopold Joseph & Sons Ltd

KDB Bank (UK) Ltd
KEXIM Bank (UK) Ltd
King & Shaxson Ltd
Kleinwort Benson Ltd
Kleinwort Benson Investment Management Ltd
Korea Long Term Credit Bank International Ltd

LTCB International Ltd
Lazard Brothers & Co. Ltd
Lloyds Bank PLC
Lloyds Bank (BLSA) Ltd
Lloyds Bowmaker Ltd
Lloyds Private Banking Ltd
Lombard & Ulster Ltd
Lombard Bank Ltd
Lombard North Central PLC
London Scottish Bank PLC
London Trust Bank PLC
Lordsvale Finance PLC

MBNA International Bank Ltd
W. M. Mann & Co. (Investments) Ltd
Marks and Spencer Financial Services Ltd
Matheson Bank Ltd
Matlock Bank Ltd
Meghraj Bank Ltd
Mellon Europe Ltd
Merrill Lynch International Bank Ltd
The Methodist Chapel Aid Association Ltd
Midland Bank PLC
Midland Bank Trust Company Ltd
Minories Finance Ltd
Minster Trust Ltd
Samuel Montagu & Co. Ltd
Morgan Grenfell & Co. Ltd
Moscow Narodny Bank Ltd
Mutual Trust and Savings Ltd

NIIB Group Ltd
NWS Bank PLC
National Bank of Egypt International Ltd
National Bank of Kuwait (International) PLC
The National Mortgage Bank PLC
National Westminster Bank PLC
NationsBank Europe Ltd
The Nikko Bank (UK) PLC
Noble Grossart Ltd
Nomura Bank International PLC
Northern Bank Ltd
Northern Bank Executor & Trustee Company Ltd

Omega Trust Co. Ltd

Paine Webber International Bank Ltd
Pointon York Ltd
The Private Bank and Trust Company Ltd

Ralli Investment Company Ltd
R. Raphael & Sons PLC
Rathbone Bros & Co. Ltd
Rea Brothers Ltd
Reliance Bank Ltd
Riggs AP Bank Ltd
Riyad Bank Europe Ltd
N. M. Rothschild & Sons Ltd
Royal Bank of Canada Europe Ltd
The Royal Bank of Scotland PLC
RoyScot Trust PLC

SBI European Bank Ltd
Sabanci Bank PLC
Sanwa International PLC
Saudi American Bank (UK) Ltd
Saudi International Bank (Al-Bank Al-Saudi Al-Alami
    Ltd)
Schroder Leasing Ltd
J. Henry Schroder & Co. Ltd
Scotiabank (UK) Ltd
Scottish Amicable Money Managers Ltd
Scottish Widows Bank PLC
Seccombe Marshall & Campion PLC
Secure Trust Bank PLC
Singer & Friedlander Ltd
Smith & Williamson Securities
Southsea Mortgage & Investment Co. Ltd
Standard Bank London Ltd
Standard Chartered Bank
Sun Banking Corporation Ltd

TSB Bank PLC
TSB Bank Scotland PLC
Tokai Bank Europe PLC
Toronto Dominion Bank Europe Ltd
Turkish Bank (UK) Ltd

UBAF Bank Ltd
UCB Bank PLC
Ulster Bank Ltd
Union Discount Company Ltd
The United Bank of Kuwait PLC
United Dominions Trust Ltd
United Trust Bank Ltd
Unity Trust Bank PLC

Wagon Finance Ltd
S. G. Warburg & Co. Ltd
Weatherbys & Co. Ltd
Wesleyan Savings Bank Ltd
Western Trust & Savings Ltd
West Merchant Bank Ltd
Whiteaway Laidlaw Bank Ltd
*Wimbledon & South West Finance PLC
Wintrust Securities Ltd
Woodchester Credit Lyonnais PLC

Yamaichi Bank (UK) PLC
Yorkshire Bank PLC

INCORPORATED OUTSIDE THE EUROPEAN ECONOMIC
AREA
(Including partnerships or other unincorporated associa-
tions formed under the law of any member state of the
European Union other than the UK)

†Provisional liquidator appointed

ABSA Bank Ltd
Allied Bank of Pakistan Ltd
American Express Bank Ltd
Arab African International Bank

Arab Bank PLC
Arab Banking Corporation BSC
Arab National Bank
Asahi Bank Ltd
Ashikaga Bank Ltd
Australia & New Zealand Banking Group Ltd

BSI – Banca della Svizzera Italiana
Banca Serfin SA
Banco de la Nación Argentina
Banco do Brasil SA
Banco do Estado de São Paulo SA
Banco Inverlat SA
Banco Mercantil de São Paulo SA
Banco Nacional de Mexico SNC
Banco Real SA
Bancomer SA
Bangkok Bank Public Company Ltd
Bank Julius Baer & Co. Ltd
Bank Bumiputra Malaysia Berhad
PT Bank Ekspor Impor Indonesia (Persero)
Bank Handlowy w Warszawie SA
Bank Hapoalim BM
Bank Mellat
Bank Melli Iran
PT Bank Negara Indonesia (Persero)
Bank of America Illinois
Bank of America NT & SA
Bank of Baroda
The Bank of N. T. Butterfield & Son Ltd
Bank of Ceylon
Bank of China
The Bank of East Asia Ltd
The Bank of Fukuoka Ltd
Bank of India
Bank of Montreal
The Bank of New York
The Bank of Nova Scotia
The Bank of Tokyo Ltd
The Bank of Yokohama Ltd
Bank Saderat Iran
Bank Sepah-Iran
Bank Tejarat
Bank von Ernst & Co. Ltd
Bankers Trust Company
Beirut Riyad Bank SAL

Canadian Imperial Bank of Commerce
Canara Bank
Chang Hwa Commercial Bank Ltd
The Chase Manhattan Bank NA
Chemical Bank
The Chiba Bank Ltd
Cho Hung Bank
The Chuo Trust & Banking Co. Ltd
Citibank NA
Commercial Bank of Korea Ltd
Commonwealth Bank of Australia
CoreStates Bank NA
Crédit Suisse
The Cyprus Popular Bank Ltd

The Dai-Ichi Kangyo Bank Ltd
The Daiwa Bank Ltd
The Development Bank of Singapore Ltd
Discount Bank and Trust Company

Emirates Bank International Ltd

First Bank of Nigeria PLC
First Commercial Bank
First Fidelity Bank NA

The First National Bank of Boston
The First National Bank of Chicago
Fleet Bank of Massachusetts, NA
French Bank of Southern Africa Ltd
The Fuji Bank Ltd

Ghana Commercial Bank
Gulf International Bank BSC

Habib Bank AG Zurich
Habib Bank Ltd
Hanil Bank
Harris Trust and Savings Bank
The Hiroshima Bank Ltd
The Hokkaido Takushoku Bank Ltd
The Hokuriku Bank Ltd
The Hongkong and Shanghai Banking Corporation Ltd

The Industrial Bank of Japan Ltd

The Joyo Bank Ltd

Korea Exchange Bank
Korea First Bank

The Long-Term Credit Bank of Japan Ltd

Macquarie Bank Ltd
Malayan Banking Berhad
Mashreq Bank PSC
Mellon Bank NA
Merchants National Bank & Trust Company of
    Indianapolis (National City Bank, Indiana)
The Mitsubishi Bank Ltd
The Mitsubishi Trust and Banking Corporation
The Mitsui Trust & Banking Co. Ltd
Morgan Guaranty Trust Company of New York

NBD Bank
Nacional Financiera SNC
National Australia Bank Ltd
National Bank of Abu Dhabi
National Bank of Canada
The National Bank of Dubai Public Joint Stock Company
National Bank of Pakistan
NationsBank NA (Carolinas)
Nedcor Bank Ltd
The Nippon Credit Bank Ltd
The Norinchukin Bank
The Northern Trust Company

Oversea-Chinese Banking Corporation Ltd
Overseas Trust Bank Ltd
Overseas Union Bank Ltd

Philippine National Bank

Qatar National Bank SAQ

†Rafidain Bank
Republic National Bank of New York
The Riggs National Bank of Washington DC
Riyad Bank
Royal Bank of Canada

The Sakura Bank Ltd
The Sanwa Bank Ltd
Saudi American Bank
The Saudi British Bank
Seoulbank
Shanghai Commercial Bank Ltd
Shinhan Bank
The Siam Commercial Bank Public Company Ltd
Sonali Bank
State Bank of India
State Street Bank and Trust Company

The Sumitomo Bank Ltd
The Sumitomo Trust & Banking Co. Ltd
Swiss Bank Corporation
Syndicate Bank

TC Ziraat Bankasi
The Thai Farmers Bank Public Company Ltd
The Tokai Bank Ltd
The Toronto-Dominion Bank
The Toyo Trust & Banking Company Ltd
Türkiye Iş Bankasi AŞ

Uco Bank
Union Bancaire Privée CBI-TDB
Union Bank of Nigeria PLC
Union Bank of Switzerland
United Bank Ltd
United Mizrahi Bank Ltd
United Overseas Bank Ltd

Westpac Banking Corporation

The Yasuda Trust & Banking Co. Ltd

Zambia National Commercial Bank Ltd
Zivnostenská Banka AS

EUROPEAN AUTHORIZED INSTITUTIONS ENTITLED TO ESTABLISH UK BRANCHES

The following are entitled to establish branches in the UK for the purpose of accepting deposits in the UK. The country of the home state supervisory authority is in parenthesis.

ABN AMRO Bank NV (Netherlands)
AIB Capital Markets PLC (Republic of Ireland)
AIB Finance Ltd (Republic of Ireland)
ASLK-CGER Bank NV-SA (Belgium)
Allied Irish Banks PLC (Republic of Ireland)
Alpha Credit Bank AE (Greece)
Anglo Irish Bank Corporation PLC (Republic of Ireland)

BfG Bank AG (Germany)
Banca Cassa di Risparmio di Torino SpA (Italy)
Banca Commerciale Italiana (Italy)
Banca di Roma SpA (Italy)
Banca March SA (Spain)
Banca Nazionale dell'Agricoltura SpA (Italy)
Banca Nazionale del Lavoro SpA (Italy)
Banca Popolare di Milano (Italy)
Banca Popolare di Novara (Italy)
Banco Ambrosiano Veneto SpA (Italy)
Banco Bilbao-Vizcaya (Spain)
Banco Central Hispanoamericano SA (Spain)
Banco de Sabadell (Spain)
Banco di Napoli SpA (Italy)
Banco di Sicilia SpA (Italy)
Banco Español de Crédito SA (Spain)
Banco Espirito Santo e Comercial de Lisboa (Portugal)
Banco Exterior de España SA (Spain)
Banco Nacional Ultramarino SA (Portugal)
Banco Português do Atlântico (Portugal)
Banco Santander (Spain)
Banco Santander de Negocious SA (Spain)
Banco Totta & Açores SA (Portugal)
Bank Austria AG (Austria)
Bank Brussels Lambert (Belgium)
Bankgesellschaft Berlin AG (Germany)
The Bank of Ireland (Republic of Ireland)
Banque Arabe et Internationale d'Investissement (France)
Banque Banorabe (France)
Banque Française de l'Orient (France)

Banque Française du Commerce Extérieur (France)
Banque Indosuez (France)
Banque Internationale à Luxembourg SA (Luxembourg)
Banque Nationale de Paris (France)
Banque Paribas (France)
Bayerische Hypotheken-und Wechsel-Bank AG (Germany)
Bayerische Landesbank Girozentrale (Germany)
Bayerische Vereinsbank AG (Germany)
Belgolaise SA (Belgium)
Berliner Bank AG (Germany)
Berliner Handels-und Frankfurter Bank (Germany)
Byblos Bank Belgium SA (Belgium)

CARIPLO (Cassa di Risparmio delle Provincie Lombarde SpA) (Italy)
Caisse Nationale de Crédit Agricole (France)
Cassa di Risparmio di Verona Vicenza Belluno e Ancona SpA (Italy)
Christiania Bank og Kreditkasse (Norway)
Commerzbank AG (Germany)
Compagnie Financière de CIC et de l'Union Européenne (France)
Confederacion Española de Cajas de Ahorros (Spain)
Creditanstalt-Bankverein (Austria)
Crédit Commercial de France (France)
Crédit du Nord (France)
Crédit Lyonnais (France)
Crédit Lyonnais Bank Nederland NV (Netherlands)
Credito Italiano (Italy)

De Nationale Investeringsbank NV (Netherlands)
Den Danske Bank Aktieselskab (Denmark)
Den norske Bank AS (Norway)
Deutsche Bank AG (Germany)
Deutsche Genossenschaftsbank (Germany)
Dresdner Bank AG (Germany)

Ergobank SA (Greece)

First National Building Society (Republic of Ireland)

Generale Bank (Belgium)
GiroCredit Bank Aktiengesellschaft der Sparkassen (Austria)

Hamburgische Landesbank Girozentrale (Germany)

ICS Building Society (Republic of Ireland)
Indosuez Carr Futures SNC (France)
Internationale Nederlanden Bank NV (Netherlands)
Ionian and Popular Bank of Greece SA (Greece)
Irish Nationwide Building Society (Republic of Ireland)
Irish Permanent PLC (Republic of Ireland)
Istituto Bancario San Paolo di Torino SpA (Italy)

Jyske Bank (Denmark)

Kas-Associatie NV (Netherlands)
Kredietbank NV (Belgium)

Landesbank Berlin Girozentrale (Germany)
Landesbank Hessen-Thüringen Girozentrale (Germany)

MeesPierson NV (Netherlands)
Merita Bank Ltd (Finland)
Monte dei Paschi di Siena (Italy)

National Bank of Greece SA (Greece)
Nordbanken AB (publ) (Sweden)
Norddeutsche Landesbank Girozentrale (Germany)

Postipankki Ltd (Finland)

Rabobank (Coöperatieve Centrale Raiffeisen-Boerenleenbank BA) (Netherlands)
Raiffeisen Zentralbank Osterreich AG (Austria)

Skandinaviska Enskilda Banken AB (publ) (Sweden)
Société Générale (France)
Südwestdeutsche Landesbank Girozentrale (Germany)
Svenska Handelsbanken AB (publ) (Sweden)
SwedBank (Sweden)

Triodosbank NV (Netherlands)
Ulster Investment Bank Ltd (Republic of Ireland)
Unibank AS (Denmark)

Westdeutsche Landesbank Girozentrale (Germany)

The National Debt

Net central government borrowing each year represents an addition to the National Debt. At the end of March 1994 the National Debt amounted to some £306,900 million of which about £18,300 million was in currencies other than sterling. Of the £288,600 million sterling debt, £210,800 million consisted of gilt-edged stock; of this, 27 per cent had a maturity of up to five years, 46 per cent a maturity of over five years and up to 15 years, and 27 per cent a maturity of over 15 years or undated. The remaining sterling debt was made up mainly of national savings (£43,300 million), certificates of tax deposits, Treasury bills, and Ways and Means advances (very short-term internal government borrowing).

Sizeable trust funds have been established over the past 50 years for the purpose of reducing the National Debt. The National Fund was established in 1927 with an original gift of £499,878. At 31 March 1995 it was valued at approximately £114 million; it is administered by Baring Brothers & Co. Ltd. The Elsie Mackay Fund was established in 1929 with an original gift of £527,809 to run for 45–50 years. It was wound up in 1979, when it was valued at £4,902,864. The John Buchanan Fund was established in 1932 with gifts totalling £36,702 to run for 50 years. It was wound up in 1982, when it was valued at £204,138.

Mutual Societies

FRIENDLY SOCIETIES IN BRITAIN

Friendly societies are voluntary mutual organizations, the main purposes of which are the provision of relief or maintenance during sickness, unemployment or retirement, and the provision of life assurance. Many of the older traditional societies complement their business activities by social activity and a general care for individual members in ways normally outside the scope of a purely commercial organization. There are three main categories of friendly societies: societies with separately registered branches, commonly called orders; centralized societies, which conduct business directly with members (having no separately registered branches); and collecting societies. Collecting societies conduct industrial assurance business and are subject to the requirements of the Industrial Assurance Acts in addition to the Friendly Societies Acts. Industrial assurance is life assurance for which the premiums are payable at intervals of less than two months and are received by means of collectors who make house-to-house visits for the purpose.

The Friendly Societies Act 1974 allows three other main classes of society to be registered: benevolent societies, working men's clubs and specially authorized societies. Benevolent societies are established for any charitable or benevolent purpose, to provide the same type of benefits as would be permissible for a friendly society, but in contrast the benefits must be for persons who are not members instead of, or in addition to, members. Working men's clubs provide social and recreational facilities for members. Specially authorized societies are registered for any purpose authorized by the Treasury as a purpose to which some or all of the provisions of the 1974 Act ought to be extended. Examples are societies for the promotion of science, literature and the fine arts, or to enable members to pursue an interest in sports and games.

The most recent legislation, the Friendly Societies Act 1992, created a new legislative framework for friendly societies, enabling them to provide a wider range of services to their members and allowing them to compete on more equal terms with other financial institutions. At the same time it provided for more flexible prudential supervision to safeguard members of societies.

The Act enables friendly societies to incorporate and establish subsidiaries to provide various financial and other services to their members and the public. By 31 March 1995, 23 societies had incorporated and ten of these had set up one or more subsidiaries. The activities which subsidiaries are able to conduct include those to establish and manage unit trust schemes and personal equity plans; to arrange for the provision of credit, whether as agents or providers; to carry on long-term or general insurance business; to provide insurance intermediary services; to provide fund management services for trustees of pension funds; to administer estates and execute trusts of wills; and to establish and manage sheltered housing, residential homes for the elderly, hospitals and nursing homes.

The Act established a new framework to oversee friendly societies, including a Friendly Societies Commission, whose principal functions are to regulate the activities of friendly societies, promote their financial stability and protect members' funds. All friendly societies carrying on insurance or non-insurance business require authorization by the Commission, which has a broad range of prudential powers. Friendly societies were also to be brought within the scope of the Policyholders Protection Act 1975, the statutory investor protection scheme covering insurance policyholders.

In April 1995 the Treasury, with the assistance of the Commission, issued a consultation document as required by the Deregulation and Contracting Out Act 1994. This sets out proposals to amend the Friendly Societies Act 1992 in ways which will ease the administrative burden for friendly societies without removing any necessary protection for their members. Following the end of the consultation period a draft order is to be laid before Parliament to give effect to amendments to the 1992 Act, and a working party has been established to explore other areas where administrative burdens on societies might be eliminated or reduced.

As part of the Deregulation Initiative the Government agreed to review the Industrial Assurance Acts and the Treasury published a consultation document seeking views on proposals either to repeal or amend the Acts. The definition of industrial assurance given in the opening paragraph above derives from the Industrial Assurance Act 1923. The 1923 Act was intended to curb abuses which were widespread at the time, specifically in relation to overselling; obtaining signatures to proposal forms without regard to full disclosure of medical history (which led to insurers refusing to pay on subsequent death on the ground of non-disclosure of material fact); various forms of misrepresentation on the canvass of new policies; and restrictive practices by the collectors. The Act was successful as an early form of consumer protection, but has now been superseded by the Financial Services Act 1986.

The principal statistics at the end of 1993 are given in the table below.

	No. of societies	No. of members 000s	Benefits paid £000s	Total funds £000s
Orders and branches	1,191*	337†	9,297†	186,782†
Collecting societies	24	12,448‡	283,384	4,878,010
Other centralized societies	334	2,858	444,740	3,324,809
Benevolent societies	76	329	5,231	37,394
Working men's clubs	2,326	1,274°	n/a	162,793°
Specially authorized societies				
Loans	6	16	n/a	282
Others	132	95	1,147	24,304

* 16 orders, 1,175 branches
† 1992 figure
° 1990 figure
‡ Assurances

INDUSTRIAL AND PROVIDENT SOCIETIES IN BRITAIN

The familiar 'Co-op' societies are amongst the wide variety which are registered under the Industrial and Provident Societies Act 1965. This consolidating Act, which is administered by the Chief Registrar of Friendly Societies, provides for the registration of societies and lays down the broad framework within which they must operate. Internal relations of societies are governed by their registered rules.

Registration under the Act confers upon a society corporate status by its registered name with perpetual succession and a common seal, and limited liability. A society qualifies for registration if it is carrying on an industry, business or trade, and it satisfies the Registrar either (a) that it is a bona fide co-operative society, or (b) that in view of the fact that its business is being, or is intended to be, conducted for the benefit of the community, there are special reasons why it should be registered under the Act rather than as a company under the Companies Act.

The Credit Unions Act 1979 added a new class of society registerable under the 1965 Act. It also made provision for the supervision of these savings and loan bodies. Unlike other classes, where the role of the Registry is solely that of a registration authority, it is for credit unions the prudential supervisor, seeking to encourage the prudent safekeeping of investors' money.

During 1993 the number of registered societies of all classes decreased by 344 to 11,004 but the number of credit unions increased by 44 to 427. Assets of industrial and provident societies increased by almost 18 per cent during 1993 to £42 billion, most of which is held in the 4,232 housing societies. The principal statistics at the end of 1993 are given in the table below.

	No. of socie-ties	No. of mem-bers 000s	Funds of members £000s	Total assets £000s
Retail	148	6,471	1,374,590	2,657,727
Wholesale and productive	178	181	512,024	1,390,411
Agricultural	1,029	295	213,430	472,831
Fishing	94	7	6,540	19,450
Clubs	3,766	2,377	301,475	521,320
General service	1,130	354	8,452,981	9,229,641
Housing	4,232	194	20,519,990	27,686,631
Credit unions	427	110	42,599	44,671
TOTAL	11,004	9,989	31,423,629	42,022,682

BUILDING SOCIETIES IN THE UK

The Building Societies Act 1986 gave building societies a completely new legal framework, the first since the initial comprehensive building society legislation in 1874. It made provision for a Building Societies Commission to promote the protection of shareholders and depositors, the financial stability of societies, and to administer the system of regulation of building societies provided under the Act. The Chairman of the Commission is also Chief Registrar of Friendly Societies (see Index). Much of the Act is concerned with the powers of control of the Commission and provision in relation to the management of societies, accounts, audit and so on. But the greatest impact flowed from the new powers which societies could adopt, leading to an increased range of services which they might provide. There were also some significant changes in relation to members' rights.

In 1994 the Government announced a review of the Act and the outcome of the first stage of the review included a package of measures designed to give societies opportunities to develop and introduce extra competition into matters where they had not previously been able to operate directly, e.g. owning an insurance company offering buildings contents and mortgage protection insurance policies. Following extensive consultations, the Government announced the outcome of the second stage of the review on 24 February 1995, outlining its intention to replace the current prescriptive legislative framework governing building societies' powers by a more permissive regime. In future, with a few exceptions, a society will be able to pursue any activities set out in its memorandum, subject to a statutory principal purpose requirement and to overall limits on the composition of assets and liabilities. Following the announcement, Commission and Treasury staff developed a new policy framework to carry forward this proposal, in consultation with the Building Societies Association.

In May 1995 the Government announced that draft legislation to implement this new framework would be published for consultation early in the next session of Parliament and put forward a 15-point package of measures on accountability, the most important of which will:

- improve the information given to members about their rights
- remove the distinction between shareholders and retail depositors
- make various changes to the procedures for the election of directors which would make it easier for society members to be nominated for election to society boards
- make the summary financial statements more user-friendly

This package also is under discussion with the Building Societies Association. A number of these proposals will require primary legislation.

The second major development of 1994–5 was that the size and stature of the building society sector might change significantly as major societies seek to convert to public limited company status. This led to a good deal of speculation about the future of mutuality.

In April 1994 the Cheltenham and Gloucester Building Society announced its intention of accepting an offer to transfer its business to a wholly-owned subsidiary company of Lloyds Bank Financial Services (Holdings) Ltd, which is itself a wholly-owned subsidiary of Lloyds Bank. The arrangements included proposals to distribute funds to members (and others) which proved to be controversial and attracted a good deal of publicity. The 1986 Act allows a society or its successor company to make a distribution of funds to members of the society in connection with a transfer of the society's business to an existing company but only to such members as have held shares in the society continously for two years up to the qualifying day. The society, however, originally proposed that a distribution of funds would be made, not by the society or the successor company, but by Lloyds Bank Financial Services (Holdings) Ltd. They also proposed that it should be made to all shareholders (whether or not of two years' standing) and borrowing members, and also to depositors, employees and pensioners. The Commision's view was that the proposed cash payments scheme did not comply with the 1986 Act. The Cheltenham and Gloucester applied to the High Court for a declaration that its proposed scheme was lawful.

The High Court held that cash distributions to members could be made only by the society or its successor and only to shareholders of two or more years' standing. The Court also held, however, that there was nothing in the 1986 Act to prevent a third party (in this case, the successor's immediate parent) from making payments to non-members, that is to depositors, employees and pensioners, provided the terms of the transfer were approved by the members. The society subsequently announced a revised scheme, designed to conform with the High Court declaration. This scheme was set out in a statutory transfer statement which was approved by the Commission in February 1995.

The necessary resolutions to approve the transfer of business were passed in March 1995 by the investing and borrowing members of the society and, following a confirmation hearing, the Commission announced on 30 June 1995 that it had confirmed the proposed transfer.

An outstanding problem which had arisen in connection with joint accounts in these and similar circumstances was resolved during the year. On 17 January 1995, Douglas French, MP, introduced a bill under the ten minute rule to enable second-named holders of building society joint accounts to receive any benefits in connection with the transfer of the business of a building society to a company which would have accrued to a first-named holder who had died, or where a sole account was transferred into a joint account on marriage, or where a joint account was ended on divorce. The Government supported the bill and it came into force on 1 May 1995.

On 25 November 1994 the Halifax and Leeds Permanent building societies announced that they had reached agreement on a proposal to merge the two societies and subsequently to convert the combined society to a public company authorized under the Banking Act 1987 and listed on the London Stock Exchange. The merger will be effected by a transfer of the engagements of the Leeds Permanent to the Halifax. The Commission announced on 11 July 1995 that it had confirmed the proposed transfer.

On 10 July 1995 the National and Provincial Building Society announce that it had accepted a takeover proposal from Abbey National (the first building society to convert to company status).

OMBUDSMAN SCHEME

Societies must belong to an ombudsman scheme for the investigation of complaints. Matters to be covered by the scheme include operation of share and deposit accounts, loans (but not the making of new loans), money transmission services, foreign exchange services, agency payments and receipts, and the provision of credit. Grounds for complaint include breach of the Act or contract, unfair treatment or maladministration, and where the complainant has suffered pecuniary loss or expense or inconvenience. A society must agree to be bound by decisions of the adjudicator unless it agrees to give notice to its members and the public of its reasons for not doing so. For address of the Building Societies Ombudsman scheme, *see* page 614.

BUILDING SOCIETIES 1993–4

	1993	1994
No. of societies – total	101	96
– authorized	84	82
No. of shareholders (000s)	37,809	38,150
No. of depositors (000s)	5,486	5,509
No. of borrowers (000s)	7,229	7,370
Share balances (£m)	194,975	201,812
Deposit balances (£m)	64,861	71,900
Mortgage balances (£m)	224,168	236,658
Total assets (£m)	281,152	301,011
Advances during year		
No. (000s)	1,011	1,093
Amount (£m)	33,183	36,792

MORTGAGE ARREARS AND REPOSSESSIONS

The economic recession resulted in a sharp rise in mortgage arrears and repossessions, with more than 75,000 properties repossessed in 1991. That total fell by 7,000 in 1992 as a result of a greater willingness by societies to enter into arrangements with borrowers. The number continued to decline in the following two years. In 1994 repossessions fell to less than 50,000 for the first time since 1990. Details of loans outstanding and properties repossessed for recent years are shown below.

	1987	1988	1989	1990	1991	1992	1993	1994
No. of loans at end year (000s)	8,283	8,564	9,125	9,415	9,815	9,922	10,137	10,410
Properties repossessed in year								
Number	26,390	18,510	15,810	43,890	75,540	68,540	58,540	49,190
%	0.32	0.22	0.17	0.47	0.77	0.70	0.58	0.47

INTEREST RATES: MORTGAGE AND SHARE 1990–5

The interest rates prevailing on mortgage lending and share investment vary from society to society and in relation to the type or amount of loan or investment.

The interval between the payments or compounding of interest is crucial in determining the competitiveness of particular societies' accounts. In order to make a true comparison of interest rates, the annual percentage rate or APR, which should appear in all advertisements and leaflets, must be used.

	1990	1991	1992	1993	1994	1995 1st quarter
Average bank base rate	14.77	11.70	9.56	6.01	5.46	6.58
Building societies average mortgage rate	14.99	12.72	10.65	8.09	7.68	7.94
Building societies average share rate	13.49	10.88	8.45	5.78	5.36	5.72

SOCIETIES WITH TOTAL ASSETS EXCEEDING £1 MILLION at end of financial year 1994

Name of Society* and head office address	Share investors	Total assets £'000
Alliance and Leicester, 49 Park Lane, London WIY 4EQ	3,076,926	21,949,200
Barnsley, Regent Street, Barnsley, South Yorks S70 2EH	33,336	180,923
Bath Investment, 20 Charles Street, Bath BAI IHY	13,293	51,563
Beverley, 57 Market Place, Beverley, N. Humberside HUI7 8AA	5,793	38,375
Birmingham Midshires, PO Box 81, 35–49 Lichfield Street, Wolverhampton WVI IEL	702,057	5,127,470
Bradford and Bingley, Crossflatts, Bingley, West Yorks BDI6 2UA	1,352,549	14,562,504
Bristol and West, Broad Quay, Bristol BS99 7AX	1,080,426	8,149,800
Britannia, Britannia House, Cheadle Road, Leek, Staffs STI3 5RG	1,168,735	13,464,300
Buckinghamshire, High Street, Chalfont St Giles, Bucks HP8 4QB	7,000	59,806
Cambridge, 32 St Andrew's Street, Cambridge CB2 3AR	48,225	340,915
Catholic, 7 Strutton Ground, London SWIP 2HY	3,581	23,784
Century, 21 Albany Street, Edinburgh EHI 3QW	1,619	11,661
Chelsea, Thirlestaine Hall, Thirlestaine Road, Cheltenham, Glos GL53 7AL	175,732	2,427,123
Cheltenham and Gloucester, Barnett Way, Gloucester GL4 7RL	889,000	19,403,400
Chesham, 12 Market Square, Chesham, Bucks HP5 IER	14,715	93,152
Cheshire, Castle Street, Macclesfield, Cheshire SKII 6AH	223,478	1,419,811
Chorley and District, Key House, Foxhole Road, Chorley, Lancs PR7 INZ	10,513	64,748
City and Metropolitan, 219 High Street, Bromley, Kent BRI IPR	9,682	96,817
Clay Cross Benefit, Eyre Street, Clay Cross, Chesterfield S45 9NS	3,250	15,866
Coventry, PO Box 9, High Street, Coventry CVI 5QN	505,597	3,210,344
Cumberland, Cumberland House, Castle Street, Carlisle CA3 8RX	145,878	528,308
Darlington, Sentinel House, Lingfield Way, Darlington, Co. Durham DLI 4PR	43,552	281,429
Derbyshire, Duffield Hall, Duffield, Derby DE56 IAG	301,782	1,765,108
Dudley, Dudley House, Stone Street, Dudley DYI INP	20,690	82,503
Dunfermline, Caledonia House, Carnegie Avenue, Dunfermline, Fife KYII 5PJ	150,569	906,049
Earl Shilton, 22 The Hollow, Earl Shilton, Leicester LE9 7NB	10,430	56,415
Ecology, 18 Station Road, Cross Hills, Keighley, West Yorks BD20 7EH	3,708	15,619
Furness, 51–55 Duke Street, Barrow-in-Furness LAI4 4JX	61,558	345,397
Gainsborough, 9 Lord Street, Gainsborough, Lincs DN2I 2DD	5,490	26,635
Greenwich, 279–283 Greenwich High Road, London SEI0 8NL	22,102	155,539
Halifax, Trinity Road, Halifax, West Yorks HXI 2RG	7,253,100	72,150,800
Hanley Economic, Granville House, Festival Park, Hanley, Stoke-on-Trent, Staffs STI 5TB	28,493	172,202
Harpenden, 14 Station Road, Harpenden, Herts AL5 4SE	9,422	44,154
Hinckley and Rugby, Upper Bond Street, Hinckley, Leics LEI0 IDG	45,644	264,001
Holmesdale, 43 Church Street, Reigate, Surrey RH2 0AE	6,287	66,251
Ilkeston Permanent, 24–26 South Street, Ilkeston, Derby DE7 5HQ	3,682	16,045
Ipswich, 44 Upper Brook Street, Ipswich IP4 IDP	32,588	173,927
Kent Reliance, Reliance House, Manor Road, Chatham, Kent ME4 6AF	42,147	244,135
Lambeth, 118–120 Westminster Bridge Road, London SEI 7XE	44,787	513,325
Leeds and Holbeck, 105 Albion Street, Leeds LSI 5AS	295,916	2,537,153
Leeds Permanent, Permanent House, 1 Lovell Park Road, Leeds LSI INS	3,584,285	20,619,700
Leek United, 50 St Edward Street, Leek, Staffs STI3 5DH	51,236	341,452
Londonderry Provident, 31A Carlisle Road, Londonderry BT48 6JJ	1,046	7,668
Loughborough, 6 High Street, Loughborough, Leics LEII 2QB	13,287	101,791
Manchester, 18–20 Bridge Street, Manchester M3 3BU	10,690	98,937
Mansfield, Regent House, Regent Street, Mansfield, Notts NGI8 ISS	19,110	107,147
Market Harborough, Welland House, The Square, Market Harborough, Leics LEI6 7PD	32,746	202,429
Marsden, 6–20 Russell Street, Nelson, Lancs BB9 7NJ	58,900	259,895
Melton Mowbray, 39 Nottingham Street, Melton Mowbray, Leics LEI3 INR	31,501	196,332
Mercantile, Mercantile House, The Silverlink Business Park, Wallsend, Tyne and Wear NE28 9NY	23,608	132,560
Monmouthshire, John Frost Square, Newport, Gwent NP9 IPX	26,342	168,145
National and Provincial, Provincial House, Bradford BDI INL	2,307,270	13,256,200
National Counties, National Counties House, Church Street, Epsom, Surrey KTI7 4NL	15,567	378,431
Nationwide, Nationwide House, Pipers Way, Swindon SN38 INW	6,086,629	35,742,231
Newbury, 17–20 Bartholomew Street, Newbury, Berks RGI4 5LY	30,202	227,315
Newcastle, Portland House, New Bridge Street, Newcastle upon Tyne NEI 8AL	157,881	1,277,413
Northern Rock, Northern Rock House, Gosforth, Newcastle upon Tyne NE3 4PL	1,299,739	10,030,500
Norwich and Peterborough, Peterborough Business Park, Lynchwood, Peterborough PE2 6WZ	184,391	1,411,507
Nottingham, 5–13 Upper Parliament Street, Nottingham NGI 2BX	137,014	867,269
Nottingham Imperial, Imperial Building, 29 Bridgford Road, West Bridgford, Nottingham NG2 6AU	6,522	39,822
Penrith, 7 King Street, Penrith, Cumbria CAII 7AR	6,087	47,435
Portman, Portman House, Richmond Hill, Bournemouth, Dorset BH2 6EP	548,797	3,244,443
Principality, PO Box 89, Principality Buildings, Queen Street, Cardiff CFI IUA	232,502	1,304,635

Name of Society* and head office address	Share investors	Total assets £'000
Progressive, 33–37 Wellington Place, Belfast BT1 6HH	46,879	344,946
Saffron Walden, Herts and Essex, 1A Market Street, Saffron Walden, Essex CB10 1HX	43,124	235,919
Scarborough, Prospect House, 442/444 Scalby Road, Scarborough, North Yorks YO12 6EQ	79,943	455,515
Scottish, 23 Manor Place, Edinburgh EH3 7XE	17,928	108,351
Shepshed, Bull Ring, Shepshed, Loughborough, Leics LE12 9QD	6,745	33,957
Skipton, The Bailey, Skipton, North Yorks BD23 1DN	240,269	2,907,024
Stafford Railway, 4 Market Square, Stafford ST16 2JH	8,658	47,731
Staffordshire, Jubilee House, PO Box 66, 84 Salop Street, Wolverhampton WV3 0SA	197,935	977,987
Standard, 64 Church Way, North Shields, Tyne and Wear NE29 0AF	2,126	15,176
Stroud and Swindon, Rowcroft, Stroud, Glos GL5 3BG	105,306	639,281
Swansea, 11 Cradock Street, Swansea SA1 3EW	3,410	30,535
Teachers, Allenview House, Hanham Road, Wimborne, Dorset BH21 1AG	11,553	122,597
Tipton and Coseley, 70 Owen Street, Tipton, West Midlands DY4 8HG	19,602	101,024
Universal, Universal House, Kings Manor, Newcastle upon Tyne NE1 6PA	31,900	233,204
Vernon, 19 St Petersgate, Stockport, Cheshire SK1 1HF	28,272	120,720
West Bromwich, 374 High Street, West Bromwich, West Midlands B70 8LR	292,787	1,509,251
West Cumbria, Cumbria House, Murray Road, Workington CA14 2AD	6,899	36,995
Woolwich, Watling Street, Bexleyheath, Kent DA6 7RR	3,250,000	26,882,800
Yorkshire, Yorkshire House, Yorkshire Drive, Bradford BD5 8LJ	735,567	5,831,283

* 'Building Society' are the last words in every society's name

National Savings

NATIONAL SAVINGS BANK

On 31 May 1995, there were about 15,971,344 active accounts with the sum of approximately £1,420.9 million due to depositors in ordinary accounts and about 4,667,013 active accounts with the sum of approximately £8,707.2 million due to depositors in investment accounts.

Interest is earned at 3.25 per cent per year on each ordinary account for every complete calendar month in which the balance is £500 or more, provided the account is kept open for the whole of 1995 (31 December 1994 to 1 January 1996); and at 2.0 per cent per year for other months or for accounts opened or closed during 1995. The minimum deposit is £10; maximum balance £10,000 plus interest credited. On 31 May 1995 the average amount held in ordinary accounts was approximately £89.

The investment account pays a higher rate of interest depending on the account balance (the current rate can be found at any post office). The minimum deposit is £20; maximum balance £100,000 plus interest credited. On 31 May 1995 the average amount held in investment accounts was approximately £1,865.

PREMIUM BONDS

Premium Bonds are a government security which were first introduced in 1956. Premium Bonds enable savers to enter a regular draw for tax-free prizes, while retaining the right to get their money back. A sum equivalent to interest on each bond is put into a prize fund and distributed by monthly prize draws. (The rate of interest is 5.2 per cent a year from 1 April 1994.) The prizes are drawn by ERNIE (electronic random number indicator equipment) and are free of all UK income tax and capital gains tax.

Bonds are in units of £1, with a minimum purchase of £100; above this, purchases must be in multiples of £10, up to a maximum holding limit of £20,000 per person. Winners of £50 and £100 prize warrants will be invited to return their prize warrants to National Savings, Blackpool, if they wish to reinvest. This transaction cannot be made through the Post Office. Bonds can only be held in the name of an individual and not by organizations.

Bonds become eligible for prizes once they have been held for one clear calendar month following the month of purchase. Each £1 unit can win only one prize per draw, but it will be awarded the highest for which it is drawn. Bonds remain eligible for prizes until they are repaid. When a holder dies, bonds remain eligible for prizes up to and including the twelfth monthly draw after the month in which the holder dies.

By April 1995 bonds to the value of £8,529 million had been sold. Of these £3,464 million had been cashed, leaving £5,065 million still invested. By the April 1995 prize draw, 47.9 million prizes totalling £2,843 million had been distributed since the first prize draw in June 1957.

INCOME BONDS

National Savings Income Bonds were introduced in 1982. They are suitable for those who want to receive regular monthly payments of interest while preserving the full cash value of their capital. The bonds are sold in multiples of £1,000. The minimum holding is £2,000 and the maximum £250,000 (sole or joint holding).

Interest is calculated on a day-to-day basis and paid monthly. Interest is taxable but is paid without deduction of tax at source. The bonds have a guaranteed life of ten years, but may be repaid at par before maturity on giving three months' notice. If repayment of a bond is made within the

first year of purchase, interest from the date of purchase to the date of repayment is earned at half rate. If the sole or sole surviving holder dies, however, no fixed period of notice is required and there is no loss of interest for repayment made within the first year.

Net investment in National Savings Income Bonds was £10,836 million at the end of April 1995.

PENSIONERS GUARANTEED INCOME BONDS

Pensioners Guaranteed Income Bonds were introduced in January 1994 and are designed for people aged 65 and over who wish to receive regular monthly payments with a rate of interest that is fixed for a five-year period whilst preserving the full cash value of their investment.

The minimum limit for each purchase is £500. The maximum holding is £20,000 (£40,000 for a joint holding); within those limits bonds can be bought for any amount in pounds and pence. The rate of interest is fixed and guaranteed for the first five years. Interest is taxable but is paid without deduction of tax at source.

Holders can apply for repayment (or part repayment of a bond subject to the minimum holding limits) by giving 60 days notice (if repayment is before the fifth anniversary date). No interest is earned during the notice period. If repayment is requested within two weeks of any fifth anniversary of purchase, there is no formal period of notice. On the death of a holder or sole surviving investor in a joint holding repayment will be made without notice. Interest will be paid in full up to the date of repayment.

Net investment in Pensioners Guaranteed Income Bonds was £1,950 million at the end of March 1995.

CHILDREN'S BONUS BONDS

Children's Bonus Bonds were introduced in 1991. The latest issue, Issue G, was introduced in September 1994. They can be bought for any child under 16 and will go on growing in value until he or she is 21. The bonds are sold in multiples of £25. The minimum holding is £25, the maximum holding in Issue G is £1,000 per child. This is in addition to holdings of earlier issues of the bond (excluding interest and bonuses). Bonds for children under 16 must be held by a parent or guardian.

Children's Bonus Bonds (Issue G) earn 5 per cent a year over five years. A bonus (18.28 per cent) of the purchase price is added at the fifth anniversary. This is equal to 7.85 per cent a year compound. All returns are totally exempt from UK income tax. No interest is earned on bonds cashed in before the first anniversary of purchase. Bonuses are only payable if the bond is held until the next bonus date. Bonds over five years old continue to earn interest and bonuses until the holder is 21, when they should be cashed in. If bonds are not cashed in on the holder's 21st birthday, they earn no interest after that birthday.

FIRST OPTION BONDS

FIRST (Fixed Interest Rate Savings Tax-paid) Option Bonds were introduced in 1992. They offer guaranteed rates without the need for long-term commitment for personal savers over 16. They can be held indefinitely and will continue to grow in value at rates of interest fixed for 12 months at a time. Tax is deducted from the interest at source. The minimum purchase is £1,000 and the maximum holding is £250,000. Withdrawals can be made without penalty at any anniversary date and there is no formal notice period for repayment. No interest is earned on repayments before the first anniversary.

CAPITAL BONDS

National Savings Capital Bonds were introduced in 1989. The latest series, Series I, was introduced in September 1994. Capital Bonds offer capital growth over five years with guaranteed returns at fixed rates. The interest is taxable each year (for those who pay income tax) but is not deducted at source. The minimum purchase is £100. There is a maximum holding limit of £250,000 from Series B onwards.

Capital Bonds will be repaid in full with all interest gained at the end of five years. No interest is earned on bonds repaid in the first year. Reinvestment or extension terms may also be available.

GILTS ON THE NATIONAL SAVINGS STOCK REGISTER

Government stock or 'gilts' are Stock Exchange securities issued by the Government. They usually have a life of between five and 20 years and most pay a guaranteed fixed rate of interest twice a year throughout this period. When they reach the end of this period they are 'redeemed' (which means repaid) at their face value.

The National Savings Stock Register (NSSR) enables investors to buy and sell gilts by post. It is now possible to have most new issues of gilts registered on the NSSR. Interest on gilts held on the NSSR, although taxable, is paid in full without deduction of tax at source.

NATIONAL SAVINGS CERTIFICATES

RECENT ISSUES

The amount, including accrued interest, index-linked increase or bonus remaining to the credit of investors in National Savings Certificates on 30 April 1995 was approximately £18,604.8 million. In 1994–5, approximately £2,166.8 million was subscribed and £1,604.7 million (excluding interest, index-linked increase or bonus) was repaid. Interest, index-linked increase, bonus or other sum payable is free of UK income tax (including investment income surcharge) and capital gains tax.

From June 1982, savings certificates of the 7th to 35th Issues will be extended on general extension rates as they reach the end of their existing extension periods. The percentage interest rate is determined by the Treasury and any change in this general extension rate will be applicable from the first of the month following its announcement. Under the system, a certificate earns interest for each complete period of three months beyond the expiry of the previous extension terms. Within each three-month period, interest is calculated separately for each month at the rate applicable from the beginning of that month. The interest for each month is one-twelfth of the annual rate (i.e. it does not vary with the number of days in the month) and is capitalized annually on the anniversary of the date of purchase. The current rate of interest under the general extension rate is given in leaflets available at post offices.

FOURTH INDEX-LINKED ISSUE
1 August 1986–30 June 1990
Maximum holding: 200 units
Unit cost: £25
Interest per unit: the repayment value, subject to their being held for one year, is related to the movement of the UK General Index of Retail Prices. In addition, there is guaranteed extra interest of 3 per cent for the first year; 3.25 per cent for the second year; 3.5 per cent for the third year; 4.5 per cent for the fourth year, and 6 per cent for the fifth year. This interest is worth 4.04 per cent compound over a full five years. Certificates held beyond the fifth anniversary earn index-linking plus half a per cent interest on each following anniversary*

THIRTY-FOURTH ISSUE
22 July 1988–16 June 1990
Maximum holding: 40 units, plus facilities to hold up to a further 400 units
Unit cost: £25
Value after five years: £35.89
Interest per unit: after one year the repayment value increases by 6 per cent for ordinarily held 34th Issue. However, reinvestment certificates earn interest during the first year at a rate of 6 per cent a year for each three-month period. Thereafter, all 34th Issue earn 6.25 per cent after two years; 6.5 per cent after three years; 7 per cent after four years; and 7.5 per cent after five years*

THIRTY-FIFTH ISSUE
18 June 1990–14 March 1991
Maximum holding: 40 units, plus special facilities to hold up to a further 400 units
Unit cost: £25
Value after five years: £39.36
Interest per unit: after one year the repayment value increases by 6.5 per cent for ordinarily held 35th Issue. However, reinvestment certificates earn interest during the first year at a rate of 6.5 per cent a year. Thereafter, all 35th Issue earn 7 per cent after two years; 7.75 per cent after three years; 8.5 per cent after four years; and 9.5 per cent after five years

FIFTH INDEX-LINKED ISSUE
2 July 1990–12 November 1992
Maximum holding: 400 units, plus special facilities to hold up to a further 400 units
Unit cost: £25
Interest per unit: the repayment value, subject to their being held for one year, is related to the movement of the UK General Index of Retail Prices. In addition, there is guaranteed extra interest which is paid from the date of purchase for each full year the certificates are held. After the first year the return is the Retail Price Index (RPI) only. Certificates repaid before the first anniversary date earn RPI for each complete month held from the purchase date. For the second year, the RPI plus 0.5 per cent; for the third, the RPI plus 1 per cent; for the fourth, the RPI plus 2 per cent; and at the fifth anniversary, RPI plus 4.5 per cent

THIRTY-SIXTH ISSUE
2 April 1991–2 May 1992
Maximum holding: 400 units, plus special facilities to hold up to a further 400
Unit cost: £25
Value after five years: £37.59
Interest per unit: after one year the repayment value increases by 5.5 per cent for ordinarily held 36th Issue. However, reinvestment certificates earn interest during the first year at a rate of 5.5 per cent a year. Thereafter, all 36th Issue earn 6 per cent after two years; 6.75 per cent after three years; 7.5 per cent after four years; and 8.5 per cent after five years

THIRTY-SEVENTH ISSUE
13 May 1992–5 August 1992
Maximum holding: 300 units, plus special facilities to hold up to a further 400
Unit cost: £25
Value after five years: £36.74
Interest per unit: after one year the repayment value increases by 5.5 per cent for ordinarily held 37th Issue. However, reinvestment certificates earn interest during the first year at a rate of 5.5 per cent a year. After one year, £1.38 is added; during the second year, 41 pence per completed three months; during the third year, 56 pence per completed three months; during the fourth year, 71 pence per completed three months; and during the fifth year, 91 pence per completed three months

THIRTY-EIGHTH ISSUE
24 August 1992–22 September 1992
Maximum holding: 200 units, plus special facilities to hold up to a further 400
Unit cost: £25
Value after five years: £35.89
Interest per unit: after one year the repayment value increases by 5.25 per cent for ordinarily held 38th Issue. However, reinvestment certificates earn interest during the first year at a rate of 5.25 per cent a year. After one year, £1.31 is added; during the second year, 41 pence per completed three months; during the third year, 50 pence per completed three months; during the fourth year, 63

pence per completed three months; and during the fifth year, 86 pence per completed three months

Thirty-ninth Issue
5 October 1992–12 November 1992
Maximum holding: 50 units, plus special facilities to hold up to a further 100
Unit cost: £100
Value after five years: £138.63
Interest per unit: after one year the repayment value increases by 4.6 per cent for ordinarily held 39th Issue. However, reinvestment certificates earn interest during the first year at a rate of 4.6 per cent a year. After one year, £4.60 is added; during the second year, £1.37 per completed three months; during the third year, £1.86 per completed three months; during the fourth year, £2.32 per completed three months; and during the fifth year, £2.96 per completed three months

Fortieth Issue
7 December 1992–16 December 1993
Maximum holding: 400 units, plus special facilities to hold up to a further 800
Unit cost: £100; reinvestment certificates £25
Value after five years: £132.25
Interest per unit: after one year the repayment value increases by 4 per cent for ordinarily held 40th Issue. However, reinvestment certificates earn interest during the first year at a rate of 4 per cent a year. On a £100 unit after one year, £4 is added; during the second year, £1.15 per completed three months; during the third year, £1.56 per completed three months; during the fourth year, £1.54 per completed three months; and during the fifth year, £2.42 per completed three months

Sixth Index-linked Issue
7 December 1992–16 December 1993
Maximum holding: 400 units, plus special facilities to hold up to a further 800
Unit cost: £100; reinvestment certificates £25
Interest per unit: the repayment value, subject to their being held for one year, is related to the movement of the UK General Index of Retail Prices. In addition, there is a guaranteed extra interest of 1.5 per cent for the first year; 2 per cent for the second year; 2.75 per cent for the third year; 3.75 per cent for the fourth year; and 6.32 per cent for the fifth year. This is worth 3.25 per cent compound over the full five years. Reinvestment certificates repaid before the first anniversary date earn RPI plus extra interest of 1.5 per cent a year for each complete month

Seventh Index-linked Issue
17 December 1993–19 September 1994
Maximum holding: 400 units, plus special facilities to hold up to a further 800
Unit cost: £100; reinvestment certificates £25
Interest per unit: the repayment value, subject to their being held for one year, is related to the movement of the UK General Index of Retail Prices. In addition, there is a guaranteed extra interest of 1.25 per cent for the first year; 1.75 per cent for the second year; 2.5 per cent for the third year; 3.5 per cent for the fourth year and 6.07 per cent for the fifth year. This is worth 3 per cent compound over the full five years. Reinvestment certificates repaid before the first anniversary date will earn RPI plus extra interest of 1.25 per cent a year for each complete month

Forty-first Issue
17 December 1993–19 December 1994
Maximum holding: 400 units, plus special facilities to hold up to a further 800
Unit cost: £100; reinvestment certificates £25
Value after five years: £130.08
Interest per unit: after one year the repayment value increased by 3.65 per cent for ordinarily held 41st Issue. However, reinvestment certificates if encashed before the first anniversary earn interest at 3.65 per cent for each complete period of three months. On a £100 unit after one year, £3.65 is added; during the second year, £1.05 per completed three months; during the third year, £1.45 per completed three months; during the fourth year, £1.82 per completed three months; and during the fifth year, £2.28 per completed three months

Forty-second Issue
20 September 1994–
Maximum holding: £10,000, plus special facilities to hold up to a further £20,000

Unit cost: certificates may be purchased for any amount, subject to a minimum purchase at any time of £100; reinvestment certificates are available for any amount and are not subject to a minimum purchase requirement
Value after five years: £132.88
Interest: after one year the repayment value increases by 4 per cent for ordinarily held 42nd Issue. However, reinvestment certificates if encashed before the first anniversary earn interest at 4 per cent for each complete period of three months. On a £100 certificate after one year £4.00 is added; during the second year £1.19 per completed three months; during the third year, £1.49 per completed three months; during the fourth year, £1.93 per completed three months; and during the fifth year, £2.59 per completed three months

Eighth Index-linked Issue
20 September 1994–
Maximum holding: £10,000, plus special facilities to hold up to a further £20,000
Unit cost: certificates may be purchased for any amount, subject to a minimum purchase at any time of £100; reinvestment certificates are available for any amount and are not subject to a minimum purchase requirement
Interest: The repayment value, subject to their being held for one year, is related to the movement of the UK General Index of Retail Prices. In addition, there is a guaranteed extra interest of 1.25 per cent for the first year, 1.75 per cent for the second year, 2.5 per cent for the third year, 3.5 per cent for the fourth year and 6.07 per cent for the fifth year. This is worth 3 per cent compound over the full five years. Reinvestment certificates repaid before the first anniversary date will earn RPI plus extra interest of 1.25 per cent a year for each complete month

*As announced by the Treasury

Insurance

AUTHORIZATION AND REGULATION

The Insurance Companies Act 1982 empowers the Department of Trade and Industry to authorize corporate bodies to transact insurance in the United Kingdom provided they comply with the financial and other regulations detailed in the Act. At the end of 1994 there were 828 insurance companies with authorization from the DTI to transact one or more classes of insurance business. However, with the establishment of the single European insurance market on 1 July 1994 an insurer authorized by a national regulator in any of the European Union (EU) countries can now transact insurance in the UK without further formality; this creates a potential market of about 4,133 insurance companies.

Under the Financial Services Act 1986, the Securities and Investments Board (SIB) is empowered to make, monitor and enforce rules about the conduct of investment business. Insurance companies offering investment contracts like life insurance, pensions, unit trusts and annuities can either obtain authorization direct from SIB or from the Personal Investment Authority (PIA) (*see* page 636).

Disputes between a company and a customer may be referred to the Insurance Ombudsman or the PIA Ombudsman (*see* page 614).

THE EUROPEAN UNION

On 1 July 1994 the single market for insurance in the European Union officially came into existence. In 1993 the total premium income of EU insurers amounted to ECU 383 billion, of which UK premiums comprised 27 per cent. Cross-border cover is now possible for anyone seeking insurance although only a small number of people or organizations have taken advantage of this freedom because of language difficulties or fear of having to deal with an unfamiliar legal system if problems occur.

Most insurers have, to date, opted for selling on an establishment basis (establishing a branch in the country concerned) rather than a services basis (selling from a base outside the country).

The work towards total harmonization continues and experts agree that taxation will continue to be the main barrier for some time to come.

ASSOCIATION OF BRITISH INSURERS

Ninety per cent of the world-wide business of insurance companies is transacted by the 450 members of the Association of British Insurers (51 Gresham Street, London EC2V 7HQ), a trade association which represents both life and general insurers. On general insurance (motor, household, holiday, etc.), ABI acts as a regulatory organization for insurance intermediaries who do not qualify to be registered brokers.

INSURANCE BROKERS

The Insurance Brokers Registration Act 1977 empowers the Insurance Brokers Registration Council (15 St Helen's Place, London EC3A 6DS) as the statutory body responsible for the registration of insurance brokers. The Council is responsible for the registration and training of insurance brokers, conduct of business, and discipline, and it lays down rules relating to such matters as accounting practice, staff qualifications, advertising, etc.

It is possible to act as an insurance intermediary without being registered with the IBRC but unregistered intermediaries are forbidden to use the words 'Insurance Broker' as a title.

IBRC Registered Brokers 1994

Registered individuals	14,618
Limited companies registered	2,456
Sole traders and partnerships	1,217
(containing 2,053 partners and directors)	

CONTRIBUTION TO THE BALANCE OF PAYMENTS

	1992	1993
Insurance	£4,271m	£4,623m

GENERAL INSURANCE

General insurance had a good year in 1994; claims costs were reduced with the result that premiums, on average, were stable or reduced. Unfortunately, the benefit was not as marked as it might have been as all general insurance premiums had to rise by 2.5 per cent following the imposition of insurance premium tax at 2.5 per cent from 1 October 1994.

The world-wide general business trading result was a profit of 11.5 per cent of premium income, the best figure since 1988. Although insurers can claim that loss prevention measures are now bearing fruit, the main cause of the improved results was probably the absence of any major weather incidents like the storms of 1987 or 1990, subsidence, or hurricanes and earthquakes overseas.

In the UK, the motor sector's small profit of 1993 (1 per cent of premiums) grew to £295 million (4.6 per cent of premiums). Non-motor business was also better, turning around a loss of 1 per cent of premiums to a profit of £916 million (7.7 per cent of premiums). One of the causes of this increased profitability can be attributed to insurers responding to consumer pressure. For many years consumers and the media have pressed for the introduction of premium discounts on homes with good security and latterly for better-protected vehicles. During 1994 these became more common, with a consequent reduction of motor and non-motor theft claims.

In commercial insurance, the decision by insurers to impose a claims limit on employers' liability policies (previously unlimited) prompted the Government to hold a review of all aspects of employers' liability cover, which is compulsory. The results are expected in the autumn of 1995.

Overseas general business again recorded a loss but this was down on 1993. US motor insurance losses were reduced from 6.8 per cent of premiums to 3 per cent but elsewhere the figure worsened slightly from 8 per cent to 8.7 per cent. Non-motor figures for the USA went from 13.1 per cent of premiums to 16 per cent but elsewhere the losses were halved from 10.2 per cent to just over 4 per cent.

WORLD-WIDE GENERAL BUSINESS UNDERWRITING RESULT

	1993				1994			
	UK	USA	Other	Total	UK	USA	Other	Total
Motor								
Premiums: £m	6,424	1,662	2,868	10,955	6,378	1,633	3,032	11,042
Profit (loss): £m	72	(112)	(250)	(290)	295	(50)	(244)	1
% of premiums	1.1	(6.8)	(8.7)	(2.6)	4.6	(3.0)	(8.0)	(0.0)
Non-motor								
Premiums: £m	11,410	2,418	4,130	17,958	11,955	2,188	4,262	18,405
Profit (loss): £m	(113)	(316)	(419)	(849)	916	(351)	(184)	382
% of premiums	(1.0)	(13.1)	(10.2)	(4.7)	7.7	(16.0)	(4.3)	2.1

NET PREMIUM INCOME BY TERRITORY 1994

	UK £m	Other EU countries £m	USA £m	Other £m	Total £m	Change on 1993 %
Motor	6,378	1,481	1,633	1,551	11,042	0.8
Non-motor	11,955	1,755	2,188	2,507	18,405	—
Marine, aviation and transport	1,581	208	258	199	2,247	—
Reinsurance	913	331	61	838	2,142	—
Other three-year business	490	20	6	140	656	9.7
Total general business	21,317	3,795	4,146	5,234	34,492	2.6
Ordinary long-term	41,821	3,878	2,864	4,077	52,641	(3.0)
Industrial long-term	1,291	—	—	—	1,291	(3.9)
Total long-term business	43,112	3,878	2,864	4,077	53,932	(3.1)

BRITISH INSURANCE COMPANIES

The following insurance company figures refer to members of the Association of British Insurers, and also to certain non-members.

CLAIMS STATISTICS (£ million)

	1993	1994
Fire claims		
Commercial fires	423	415
Domestic fires	224	191
Theft claims		
Commercial theft (inc. money)	426	207
Domestic theft	744	633
Weather damage		
Commercial damage	137	109
Domestic damage	423	281

WORLD-WIDE GENERAL BUSINESS TRADING RESULT

	1993 £m	1994 £m
Net written premiums	33,629	34,492
Underwriting profit (loss) for one year account business	(1,223)	311
Transfer to profit and loss account for other business		
Marine, Aviation, Transport	(434)	(256)
Other	(549)	(220)
Total underwriting result	(2,205)	(164)
Net investment income	4,051	4,118
Overall trading profit	1,846	3,953
Profit as % of premium income	5.5	11.5

LLOYD'S OF LONDON

Lloyd's of London is an incorporated society of private underwriters who provide an international market for almost all types of insurance. Lloyd's currently earns a gross premium income of around £9,000 million for underwriters each year. Much of this business comes from outside Great Britain and makes a valuable contribution to the balance of payments.

Today, a policy is underwritten at Lloyd's by private individuals with unlimited liability and the newly included corporate members admitted for the first time in 1992. Specialist underwriters accept insurance risks at Lloyd's on behalf of members (often referred to as 'names') grouped in syndicates. There are currently around 279 syndicates of varying sizes, some with over 2,000 names, each managed by an underwriting agent approved by the Council of Lloyd's.

Lloyd's membership is drawn from many sources. Industry, commerce and the professions are strongly represented, while many members work at Lloyd's either for brokerage firms or for underwriting agencies. Underwriting membership of Lloyd's is open to anyone provided they meet the stringent financial requirements of the Corporation of Lloyd's. Substantial financial assets have to be shown and a deposit lodged with the Corporation as security for underwriting liabilities. This deposit, which must be in the form of approved securities, is determined at 30 per cent of the member's annual premium income and showing nominal means.

Lloyd's is incorporated by an Act of Parliament (Lloyd's Acts 1871–1982) and is governed by a council of 18 members. Market management is handled by a Market Board of 19 members (comprising six working members of the Council, the chief executive officer, six further working members, three external members and three Corporation executives). Regulation is supervised by a Board of 16 members (comprising six nominated members of the

Council, five external members of the Council, four working members and the Solicitor to the Corporation).

The Corporation is a non-profit making body chiefly financed by its members' subscriptions. It provides the premises, administrative staff and services enabling Lloyd's underwriting syndicates to conduct their business. It does not, however, assume corporate liability for the risks accepted by its members, who remain responsible to the full extent of their personal means for their underwriting affairs.

Lloyd's syndicates have no direct contact with the public. All business is transacted through insurance brokers accredited by the Corporation of Lloyd's. In addition, non-Lloyd's brokers in the United Kingdom, when guaranteed by Lloyd's brokers, are able to deal directly with Lloyd's motor syndicates, a facility which has made the Lloyd's market more accessible to the insuring public.

Lloyd's also provides the most comprehensive shipping intelligence service in the world. The shipping and other information received from Lloyd's agents, shipowners, news agencies and other sources throughout the world is collated and distributed to the media as well as to the maritime and commercial sectors in general. *Lloyd's List* is London's oldest daily newspaper and contains news of general commercial interest as well as shipping information. *Lloyd's Shipping Index*, also published daily, lists some 25,000 ocean-going vessels in alphabetical order and gives the latest known report of each.

Developments in 1994

Lloyd's three-year accounting period meant that, although the 1994 general insurance results were an improvement on 1992 and 1993, the Lloyd's results for the 1992 year, announced in the same week, were still in the red. The overall trading loss was reduced from £2,048 million in 1991 to £1,193 million; this brings cumulative global losses to £8,000 million since 1988. The losses continue to put pressure on names, the debt rising to £732 million from £630 million in 1993.

The market still has serious problems and stories of hardship and litigation appear regularly in the media. The Council of Lloyd's believe that the proposals in their business plan, published in 1993, will begin to solve some of these problems. The proposals include the reinsuring of pre-1992 losses. This will enable names who wish to resign from Lloyd's to know precisely the extent of their losses. It will also reassure newcomers to the market that they will not be asked to contribute to pre-1992 liabilities. Other proposals include a move to an annual accounting basis and provision of £2,800 million to settle disputes and end litigation.

Lloyd's Membership

	1992	1993	1994
Total no. of underwriting members participating
Individuals	22,259	19,537	17,526
Corporate	—	—	95

Gross Market Capacity

	1992	1993	1994
Average market capacity per member
Individual	£451,000	£454,000	£534,000
Corporate	—	—	16,947

Lloyd's Global Accounts *as at 31 December 1994*

	1991 £m	1992 £m
Gross premiums	9,675	9,130
Premiums in respect of reinsurance ceded	3,661	2,799
Net premiums	6,014	6,331
Reinsurance premiums received from closed year of account	3,955	3,897
Reserves brought forward in respect of run-off years of account	7,014	8,413
Total premiums	16,983	18,641
Gross claims	13,340	11,284
Reinsurance recoveries	7,119	5,283
Net claims	6,221	6,001
Reinsurance premiums paid to close the account	4,010	3,573
Reserves retained in respect of run-off years of account	8,745	9,891
Total claims	18,976	19,465
Underwriting result	(1,993)	(824)
Adjustment in respect of double count	533	240
Result after adjusting for double count	(1,460)	(584)
Profit (loss) on currency exchange	(83)	39
Syndicate expenses	(748)	(667)
Net underwriting result/balance	(2,291)	(1,212)
Gross investment income	579	655
Gross investment appreciation	136	(193)
Gross investment return	715	462
Loss before personal expenses and tax	(1,576)	(750)
Members' personal expenses	(472)	(443)
Loss before tax and after personal expenses	(2,048)	(1,193)

Lloyd's Results 1992

	Marine 1991 £m	Marine 1992 £m	Non-marine 1991 £m	Non-marine 1992 £m
Net premiums	1,439.2	1,376.9	3,415.9	3,508.8
Pure year result	(452.0)	148.5	(62.3)	(201.1)

	Aviation 1991 £m	Aviation 1992 £m	Motor 1991 £m	Motor 1992 £m
Net premiums	434.9	446.1	753.1	977.0
Pure year result	(106.6)	13.7	5.9	124.7

LIFE INSURANCE AND PENSIONS

At the end of 1993 the Securities and Investment Board published the result of the investigation by KPMG into the quality of advice given on transfers out of company pension schemes into personal pensions. This found that in only 9 per cent of cases was there satisfactory documentary evidence that good advice had been given. This did not automatically mean that the advice was inappropriate for all the remaining 91 per cent but a major investigation conducted during 1994 has revealed widespread problems either in the advice that was given or the documentary evidence that was kept to corroborate the validity of such advice. The result has been large fines by the regulators against life companies, their sales staff and independent financial advisers. The investigation is not over but the publicity it has received has undoubtedly dented the credibility of life insurance and particularly pension products. The result was a UK net premium income for life insurance and pensions of £43,112 million, an unprecedented 9 per cent fall on 1993.

Payments to policyholders were at a record high of £47,518 million. Outside the UK premiums rose by 16 per cent to £10,820 million, with payments to policyholders of £7,079 million.

PREMIUM INCOME FOR WORLD-WIDE LONG-TERM INSURANCE BUSINESS

	1993 £m	1994 £m
Ordinary Branch		
Business written in UK		
Annual premiums		
Life	10,644	11,133
Annuities	65	62
Pensions	9,183	9,767
Single premiums		
Life	9,863	8,566
Annuities	874	592
Pensions	13,857	11,216
Other	438	485
Business written overseas		
Annual premiums	4,847	4,849
Single premiums	4,518	5,971
Industrial Business	1,344	1,291
Total	55,633	53,932

PAYMENTS TO POLICYHOLDERS

	1993 £m	1994 £m
Ordinary Branch		
Payments to UK policyholders	28,531	28,850
Payments to overseas policyholders	5,585	7,079
Industrial Branch		
Payments to UK policyholders	2,169	2,168
Total	36,285	38,098

INDIVIDUAL PENSIONS: NEW BUSINESS 1993–4

	Annual premium policies		Single policy premiums		Renewed single premiums £m
	No. new policies	New premiums £m	No. new policies	New premiums £m	
1993					
1st quarter	335,000	268	165,000	1,021	248
2nd quarter	352,000	309	198,000	1,113	258
3rd quarter	291,000	259	214,000	1,024	188
4th quarter	305,000	298	189,000	1,161	280
1994					
1st quarter	275,000	272	120,000	929	262
2nd quarter	287,000	275	117,000	933	281
3rd quarter	258,000	224	69,000	657	199
4th quarter	260,000	244	73,000	622	234

INVESTMENTS OF INSURANCE COMPANIES 1994

Investment of funds	Long-term business £m	General business £m
Index-linked British Government securities	7,199	878
British Government authority securities (excluding those above)	57,819	12,018
Other government, provincial and municipal stocks	29,576	12,743
Debentures, loan stocks, preference and guaranteed stocks and shares	46,697	10,053
Ordinary stocks and shares	246,410	17,102
Mortgages	14,423	1,590
Real property and ground rents	39,379	4,343
Other invested assets	22,038	10,034
Net current assets	4,600	8,827
Total net assets	468,142	77,589
Gross income for year on investment holdings (gross of tax and interest paid)	23,819	4,356
Interest payable in year	325	238

DIRECTORY OF INSURANCE COMPANIES

Classes of insurance undertaken
G   General
L   Life
M   Marine
Re Reinsurance

Group membership
(CU)   Commercial Union
(ES)   Eagle Star
(GA)   General Accident
(GRE) Guardian Royal Exchange
(NU)   Norwich Union
(R)   Royal
(SA)   Sun Alliance & London

Nature of business	Name of company	Head Office address
GLM Re	AGF	41 Botolph Lane, London EC3R 8DL
L	AIG Life (UK)	Alico House, 22 Addiscombe Road, Croydon CR0 5AZ
GM Re	Albion	9–13 Fenchurch Buildings, London EC3M 5HR
L	Alico	Alico House, 22 Addiscombe Road, Croydon CR0 5AZ
GLM	Alliance Assurance (SA)	1 Bartholomew Lane, London EC2N 2AB
L	Allied Dunbar	Allied Dunbar Centre, Swindon SN1 1EL
L	American Life	2–8 Altyre Road, Croydon CR9 2LG
G	Ansvar	31 St Leonards Road, Eastbourne BN21 3UR
GM	Atlas (GRE)	Royal Exchange, London EC3V 3LS
L	Australian Mutual Provident	100 Temple Street, Bristol BS1 6EA
L	Axa Equity and Law	Amersham Road, High Wycombe HP13 5AL
G	Baptist	1 Merchant Street, London E3 4LY
L	Barclays Life	94 St Paul's Churchyard, London EC4M 8EH
GLM Re	Black Sea and Baltic	65 Fenchurch Street, London EC3M 4EV
GLM	Bradford (SA)	North Park, Halifax HX1 2TU
L	Britannia Life	Britannia Court, 50 Bothwell Street, Glasgow G2 6HR
GL	Britannic	Moor Green, Moseley, Birmingham B13 8QF
M	British & Foreign Marine (R)	New Hall Place, Liverpool
Engineering	British Engine (R)	Longridge House, Manchester M60 4DT
GLM	British Equitable (GRE)	Royal Exchange, London EC3V 3LS
L	British Life Office	Reliance House, Mount Ephraim, Tunbridge Wells, Kent TN4 8BL
G	British Oak (GRE)	Royal Exchange, London EC3V 3LS
L	Caledonian (GRE)	Royal Exchange, London EC3V 3LS
GM	Cambrian (GRE)	Royal Exchange, London EC3V 3LS
L	Canada Life	Canada Life House, Potters Bar, Herts EN6 5BA
GM	Car & General (GRE)	Royal Exchange, London EC3V 3LS
L	Century Life	Century House, 5 Old Bailey, London EC4M 7BA
GL	Cigna	PO Box 42, Greenock, Renfrewshire PA15 1AB
L	Citibank Life	21–23 Perrymount Road, Haywards Heath, W. Sussex RH16 3TP
L	City of Glasgow Friendly	200 Bath Street, Glasgow G2 4HJ
L	Clerical, Medical Group	15 St James Square, London SW1Y 4LQ
L	Colonial Mutual	Colonial Mutual House, Chatham Maritime, Kent ME14 4YY
GLM Re	Commercial Union	St Helen's, 1 Undershaft, London EC3P 3DQ
L	Commercial Union Life	St Helen's, 1 Undershaft, London EC3P 3DQ
L	Confederation Life	Lytton Way, Stevenage, Herts SG1 2NN
G	Congregational and General	Currer House, Currer Street, Bradford BD1 5BA
GLM Re	Co-operative	Miller Street, Manchester M60 0AL
GLM Re	Cornhill	57 Ladymead, Guildford GU1 1DB

Nature of business	Name of company	Head Office address
L	Crown Financial Management	Crown House, Crown Square, Woking GU21 1XW
GL	Direct Line Insurance	3 Edridge Road, Croydon CR9 1AG
GM	Dominion	52–54 Leadenhall Street, London EC3A 2AQ
GLM Re	Eagle Star	60 St Mary Axe, London EC3A 8JQ
GL	Ecclesiastical	Beaufort House, Brunswick Road, Gloucester GL1 1JZ
GL	Economic	Economic House, 25 London Road, Sittingbourne ME10 1PE
Animal Ins.	Equine and Livestock	PO Box 100, Ouseburn, York YO5 9SZ
L	Equitable Life	Walton Street, Aylesbury HP21 7QW
G	Federation General	PO Box 196, Redhill, Surrey RH1 1FG
L	Friends' Provident	United Kingdom House, Castle Street, Salisbury SP1 3SH
G	Gan	12 Arthur Street, London EC4R 9BT
GM Re	General Accident	Pitheavlis, Perth, Scotland PH2 0NH
L	General Accident Life	2 Rougier Street, York YO1 1HR
GLM Re	GRE	Royal Exchange, London EC3V 3LS
G	Gresham Fire & Accident	11 Queen Victoria Street, London EC4N 4XP
GM	Guarantee Society (GA)	42–47 Minories, London EC3N 1BX
L	Guardian Assurance (GRE)	Royal Exchange, London EC3V 3LS
GLM Re	Hibernian	Haddington Road, Dublin 4
L	Hill Samuel	NLA Tower, Addiscombe Road, Croydon CR9 6BP
GL	Ideal	Pitmaston, Birmingham B13 8NG
L	Irish Life	Irish Life Centre, Victoria Street, St Albans AL1 5TS
GF	Iron Trades	Iron Trades House, 21–24 Grosvenor Place, London SW1X 7JA
L	LAS Group	Britannia Court, 50 Bothwell Street, Glasgow G2 6HR
GLM Re	Legal and General	Temple Court, 11 Queen Victoria Street, London EC4N 4TP
L	Liberty Life	Liberty House, Station Road, New Barnet EN5 1PA
GF	Licenses & General (GRE)	Royal Exchange, London EC3V 3LS
L	Lincoln National (UK) PLC	The Quays, 101–105 Oxford Road, Uxbridge, UB8 1LZ
GM	Liverpool Marine & General (SA)	1 Bartholomew Lane, London EC2N 2AB
L	Liverpool Victoria Friendly	Victoria House, Southampton Row, London WC1B 4DB
GM	Local Government Guarantee (GRE)	Royal Exchange, London EC3V 3LS
GM Re	Lombard General	Lombard House, 182 High Street, Tonbridge TN9 1BY
GM	London & Edinburgh	The Warren, Worthing, W. Sussex BN14 9QD
L	London & Manchester	Winslade Park, Exeter, Devon EX5 1DS
GM	London & Scottish (CU)	St Helen's, 1 Undershaft, London EC3
L	M & G Assurance	Three Quays. Tower Hill, London EC3R 6BQ
L	Manulife	St George's Way, Stevenage SG1 1HP
M	Marine (R)	34–36 Lime Street, London EC3M 7JE
M	Maritime (NU)	Surrey Street, Norwich NR1 3NS
L	Medical, Sickness, Annuity and Life	Pynes Hill House, Rydon Lane, Exeter EX2 5SP
Re	Mercantile & General	Moorfields House, Moorfields, London EC4R 9BJ
L	Merchant Investors (MI Group)	St Bartholomew's House, Lewins Mead, Bristol BS1 2NH
GF	Methodist	Brazennose House, Brazennose Street, Manchester M2 5AS
L	MGM Assurance	MGM House, Heene Road, Worthing BN11 2DY
G	Motor Union (GRE)	Royal Exchange, London EC3V 3LS
L	NPI	NPI House, Tunbridge Wells, Kent TN1 2UE
GL	Nalgo Insurance Association	137 Euston Road, London NW1 2AU
G	National Guarantee & Suretyship (CU)	St Helen's, 1 Undershaft, London EC3P 3DQ
L	National Mutual Life	The Priory, Hitchin, Herts SG5 2DW
Engineering	National Vulcan Eng. Ins. Group (SA)	St Mary's Parsonage, Manchester M60 9AP
G	Navigators & General (ES)	113 Queens Road, Brighton BN1 3XN
GL Re	NFU Avon	Tiddington Road, Stratford-upon-Avon CV37 7BJ
G	NIG Skandia	Crown House, 145 City Road, London EC1V 1LP
L	NM Financial Management	Enterprise House, Isambard Brunel Road, Portsmouth PO1 2AW
GM Re	Norwich Union Fire	PO Box 6, Surrey Street, Norwich NR1 3NS
L	Norwich Union Life	PO Box 4, Surrey Street, Norwich NR1 3NG
Re	NRG Victory Reinsurance	Castle Hill Avenue, Folkestone CT20 2TF
GLM Re	Pearl	The Pearl Centre, Lynchwood, Peterborough PE2 6FY
GL Sickness	Permanent	Pynes Hill House, Pynes Hill, Rydon Lane, Exeter EX2 5SP
GLM	Phoenix (SA)	1 Bartholomew Lane, London EC2N 2AB
L	Property Growth	Leon House, High Street, Croydon CR9 1LU
L	Provident Life Association	Provident Way, Basingstoke, Hants RG21 2SZ
L	Provident Mutual Life	Six Hills Way, Stevenage, Herts SG1 2ST
F	Provincial	Stramongate, Kendal, Cumbria LA9 4BE
GLM Re	Prudential	142 Holborn Bars, London EC1N 2NH
GL	Refuge	Refuge House, Alderley Road, Wilmslow, Cheshire SK9 1PF

Nature of business	Name of company	Head Office address
GM	Reliance Marine (GRE)	Royal Exchange, London EC3V 3LS
L	Reliance Mutual	Reliance House, Mount Ephraim, Tunbridge Wells, Kent TN4 8BL
G	Road Transport & General (GA)	Pitheavlis, Perth PH2 0NH
G	Royal Exchange	Royal Exchange, London EC3V 3LS
L	Royal Heritage Life	Royal Insurance House, Business Park, Peterborough PE2 6GG
G	Royal Insurance	New Hall Place, Liverpool L69 3EN
L	Royal Life	PO Box 30, New Hall Place, Liverpool L69 3HS
L	Royal Liver	Royal Liver Building, Pier Head, Liverpool L3 1HT
GL	Royal London	Royal London House, Middleborough, Colchester CO1 1RA
L	Royal National Pension Fund for Nurses	Burdett House, 15 Buckingham Street, Strand, London WC2N 6ED
F	Salvation Army	117–121 Judd Street, London WC1H 9NN
L	Save & Prosper	1 Finsbury Avenue, London EC2M 2QY
L	Scottish Amicable	150 St Vincent Street, Glasgow G2 5NQ
Engineering	Scottish Boiler (GA)	Pitheavlis, Perth, Scotland PH2 0NH
L	Scottish Equitable	28 St Andrew Square, Edinburgh EH2 1YF
L	Scottish Friendly	16 Blythswood Square, Glasgow G2 6HJ
M	Scottish General (GA)	PO Box 896, 103 Westerhill Road, Bishopbriggs, Glasgow G64 2QX
L	Scottish Legal Life	95 Bothwell Street, Glasgow G2 7HY
L	Scottish Life	19 St Andrew Square, Edinburgh EH2 2YA
L	Scottish Mutual	109 St Vincent Street, Glasgow G2 5HN
L	Scottish Provident Institution	6 St Andrew Square, Edinburgh EH2 2YA
GLM	Scottish Union & National (NU)	Surrey Street, Norwich NR1 3NS
L	Scottish Widows'	15 Dalkeith Road, Edinburgh EH16 5BU
GM	Sea (SA)	1 Bartholomew Lane, London EC2N 2AB
L	Stalwart Assurance	Stalwart House, 142 South Street, Dorking RH4 2EV
L	Standard Life	3 George Street, Edinburgh EH2 2XZ
GM	State Assurance (GRE)	Royal Exchange, London EC3V 3LS
GLM	Sun Alliance and London	1 Bartholomew Lane, London EC2N 2AB
GM	Sun Insurance Office (SA)	1 Bartholomew Lane, London EC2N 2AB
L	Sun Life Assurance	107 Cheapside, London EC2N 6DU
L Re	Sun Life of Canada	Basing View, Basingstoke, Hants RG21 2DZ
L	Swiss Life	PO Box 127, Swiss Life House, 101 London Road, Sevenoaks, Kent TN13 1BG
L	Swiss Pioneer Life	16 Crosby Road North, Waterloo, Liverpool L22 0NY
GL	Teacher's Assurance	Tringham House, Wessex Fields, Deansleigh Road, Bournemouth BH7 7DT
L	Tunstall & District	Station Chambers, Tunstall, Stoke-on-Trent ST6 6DU
M	Ulster Marine (GA)	Pitheavlis, Perth PH2 0NH
L	UIA Insurance Ltd	137–139 Euston Road, London NW1 2AZ
GM	Union Insurance Society of Canton (GRE)	Royal Exchange, London EC3V 3LS
GL	United Friendly	42 Southwark Bridge Road, London SE1 9HE
GL Re	Wesleyan Assurance	Colmore Circus, Birmingham B4 6AR
L	Windsor Life	Windsor House, Telford, Salop TF3 4NB
GM Re	Zurich	Zurich House, Stanhope Road, Portsmouth PO1 1DU
L	Zurich Life	Hippodrome House, 11 Guildhall Walk, Portsmouth PO1 2RL

The London Stock Exchange

The International Stock Exchange of the United Kingdom and Republic of Ireland Ltd serves the needs of government, industry and investors by providing facilities for raising capital and a central market-place for securities trading. This central market-place covers government stocks (called gilts), UK and overseas company shares (called equities and fixed interest stocks), and traditiional options.

At the end of 1994 there were 2,070 British and Irish companies listed on the London Stock Exchange; their equity capital had a total market value of £775,000 million. The Unlisted Securities Market listed 207 companies, with a total equity market value of £4,900 million. In addition, 464 foreign companies were listed, with a total equity market value of £1,983,000 million. UK and Irish equity turnover in 1994 was £606,000 million, a 7.5 per cent increase on 1993, with an average of 37,247 transactions a day. Turnover in non-UK equities was £719,000 million, a 24 per cent increase on 1993, with an average of 11,986 transactions a day. Trading in European equities was £429,000 million but Japan was the largest single non-UK sector with trading of £165,000 million.

BIG BANG

During 1986 the London Stock Exchange went through the greatest period of change in its 200-year history. In March 1986 it opened its doors for the first time to overseas and corporate membership of the Exchange, allowing banks, insurance companies and overseas securities houses to become members of the Exchange and to buy existing member firms. On 27 October 1986, three major reforms took place, changes which became known as 'Big Bang'.

- abolition of scales of minimum commissions, allowing clients to negotiate freely with their brokers about the charge for their services
- abolition of the separation of member firms into brokers and jobbers: firms are now broker/dealers, able to act as agents on behalf of clients; to act as principals buying and selling shares for their own account; and to become registered market makers, making continuous buying and selling prices in specific secuties.
- the introduction of the Stock Exchange automated quotations (SEAQ) system.

Of all these changes, the implementation of SEAQ has had the most visible effect. Dealing in stocks and shares now takes place via the telephone in the firms' own dealing rooms, rather than face to face on the floor of the Exchange. The new systems also provide increased investor protection. All deals taking place via the Exchange's SEAQ system are recorded on a database which can be used to resolve disputes or to carry out investigations.

Members of the London Stock Exchange buy and sell shares on behalf of the public, as well as institutions such as pension funds or insurance companies. In return for transacting the deal, the broker will charge a commission, which is usuallly based upon the value of the transaction. The market makers, or wholesalers, in each security do not charge a commission for their services, but will quote the broker two prices, a price at which they will buy and a price at which they will sell. It is the middle of these two prices which is published in lists of Stock Exchange prices in newspapers.

REGULATORY BODIES

Since 1986 the International Stock Exchange of the United Kingdom and Republic of Ireland Ltd and the Securities and Futures Authority have been the two regulatory bodies. They were formed under the provisions of the Financial Services Act 1986, which requires investment businesses to be authorized and regulated by a self-regulating organization (SRO), of which the Securities and Futures Authority is one. The Act also requires business to be conducted through a recognized investment exchange (RIE). The London Stock Exchange is an RIE, regulating three main markets: UK equities, international equities and gilts.

PRIMARY MARKETS

The Exchange serves the needs of industry by providing a mechanism where companies can raise capital for development and growth through the issue of securities. For a company entering the market for the first time there is a choice of possible Stock Exchange markets, depending upon the size, history and requirements of the company. The first is the listed market, which exists for well-established companies, which must comply with stringent criteria relating to all aspects of their operations. At present, companies coming to this market require a three-year trading record with a minimum of 25 per cent of the shares held in public hands. The Unlisted Securities Market was established in 1980 with the smaller and newer company in mind but will be closed at the end of 1996 and no longer accepts listings. The Alternative Investment Market (AIM) began trading in June 1995. It enables small, young and growing companies to raise capital, widen their investor base and have their shares traded on a regulated market without the expense of a full Stock Exchange listing.

Once admitted to the Exchange, all companies are obliged to keep their shareholdes informed of their progress, making announcements of a price-sensitive nature through the Exchange's company announcements department.

THE GOVERNING BOARD

The International Stock Exchange has its headquarters in London, and representative offices around the UK and the Republic of Ireland. At present there are about 380 member firms.

The governing board is responsible for overall policy and the strategic direction of the Exchange. The board consists of representatives drawn from listed companies, investors and other major users, elected at the annual general meeting, and the Government Broker, the Chief Executive and up to five senior executives of the Stock Exchange.

LONDON STOCK EXCHANGE, Old Broad Street, London EC2N 1HP. Tel: 0171-797 1000
Chairman, J. Kemp-Welch
Chief Executive, M. Lawrence
Government Broker, I. Plenderleith
Other Board members, G. Allen, CBE; J. Bond; D. Brydon, OBE; S. Cooke; Ms C. Dann; M. Kaneko; M. Marks; R. Metzler; R. Mueller; H. Post; M. Radcliffe; M. Rivett-Carnac; I. Salter; B. Solomons; G. Vardey; N. Verey; Ms F. Wicker-Miurin

Stamp Duties

Stamp duty is a tax on documents. There are a number of separate duties, under different heads of charge. The Finance Act 1990 included provisions abolishing all the stamp duty charges on transactions in shares from a date to be fixed by Treasury order (which has not yet been made). The Finance Act 1991 removed the stamp duty charges on documents relating to all other types of property except land and buildings, again from a date to be specified (no date yet specified). The Chancellor has indicated that these provisions are unlikely to be brought into force for two to three years. In the list of documents which follows, those which will be affected by the above provisions are indicated with an asterisk*.

AGREEMENT FOR LEASE, *see* LEASES

AGREEMENT FOR SALE OF PROPERTY

Charged with *ad valorem* duty as if an actual conveyance on sale, with certain exceptions, e.g. agreements for the sale of land, stocks and shares, goods, wares or merchandise, or a ship (*see* S. 59 (1), Stamp Act 1891). If *ad valorem* duty is paid on an agreement in accordance with this provision, the subsequent conveyance or transfer is not chargeable with any *ad valorem* duty and the Commissioners will upon application either place a denoting stamp on such conveyance or transfer or will transfer the *ad valorem* duty thereto. Further, if such an agreement is rescinded, not performed, etc., the Commissioners will return the *ad valorem* duty paid.

ASSIGNMENT

By way of sale, *see* CONVEYANCE
By way of gift, *see* VOLUNTARY DISPOSITION

*BEARER INSTRUMENT

Inland bearer instrument, i.e. share warrant, stock certificate to bearer or any other instrument to bearer by which stock can be transferred, issued by a company or body formed or established in the UK, 1.5 per cent

Overseas bearer instrument, i.e. such an instrument issued in Great Britain by a company formed out of the UK, 1.5 per cent

BILL OF SALE, ABSOLUTE, *see* CONVEYANCE ON SALE

CONTRACT, *see* AGREEMENT

*CONTRACT OR GRANT FOR PAYMENT OF A SUPERANNUATION ANNUITY

For every £10 or fractional part of £10, 5p

CONVEYANCE OR TRANSFER ON SALE
(In the case of a Voluntary Disposition, *see* below)

Conveyance or transfer on sale of any property (except stock or marketable securities), where the conveyance or transfer contains a certificate of value certifying that the transaction does not form part of a larger transaction or a series of transactions in respect of which the aggregate amount or value of the consideration exceeds £60,000, *nil*

Exceeds £60,000 (for every £100 or fraction of £100), £1

If the conveyance or transfer on sale does not contain the appropriate statement, duty at the full rate of £1 for every £100 or fraction of £100 will be payable whatever the amount of the consideration.

Conveyances to charities are exempt from duty under this head provided the instrument is stamped with a denoting stamp.

CONVEYANCE OR TRANSFER OF ANY OTHER KIND

Fixed duty, 50p

However, under the Stamp Duty (Exempt Instruments) Regulations 1987, instruments which would otherwise fall under this head are exempt from stamp duty provided that the document is duly certified. The certificate must contain a sufficient description of the category into which the instrument falls, and must be signed by the transferor, his solicitor or agent: 'I/We hereby certify that this instrument falls within category ... in the Schedule to the Stamp Duty (Exempt Instruments) Regulations 1987.'

COVENANT, for original creation and sale of any annuity, *see* CONVEYANCE

DECLARATION OF TRUST

Not being a will or settlement, 50p

DEMISE, *see* LEASES

DUPLICATE OR COUNTERPART

Same duty as original, but not to exceed 50p

GIFT, *see* VOLUNTARY DISPOSITION

LEASES (INCLUDING AGREEMENTS FOR LEASES)

Lease or tack for any definite term less than a year of any furnished dwelling-house or apartments where the rent for such term exceeds £500, £1

Of any lands, tenements, etc., in consideration of any rent, according to the following:

Annual rent not exceeding	†Term not exceeding			Exceeding
	7 yrs	35 yrs	100 yrs	100 yrs
£	£ p	£ p	£ p	£ p
5	nil	0.10	0.60	1.20
10	nil	0.20	1.20	2.40
15	nil	0.30	1.80	3.60
20	nil	0.40	2.40	4.80
25	nil	0.50	3.00	6.00
50	nil	1.00	6.00	12.00
75	nil	1.50	9.00	18.00
100	nil	2.00	12.00	24.00
150	nil	3.00	18.00	36.00
200	nil	4.00	24.00	48.00
250	nil	5.00	30.00	60.00
300	nil	6.00	36.00	72.00
350	nil	7.00	42.00	84.00
400	nil	8.00	48.00	96.00
450	nil	9.00	54.00	108.00
500	nil	10.00	60.00	120.00

Exceeding £500, *for every* £50 *or fraction thereof*

	0.50	1.00	6.00	12.00

†If the term is indefinite the same duty is payable as if the term did not exceed seven years.

Where a consideration other than rent is payable, the same rule applies where the consideration does not exceed £60,000 as under conveyance or transfer on sale (except stock or marketable securities), provided that any rent payable does not exceed £600 a year and a certificate of value is included in the conveyance or transfer.

Where a lease is granted pursuant to a prior agreement for lease, the agreement itself is liable to duty. Credit for any duty paid on the agreement will be given against the duty payable on the lease and the Commissioners will place a denoting stamp on the lease. Where there is no prior agreement for lease, the lease must contain a certificate that it has not been made in pursuance of an agreement.

Leases to charities are exempt from duty under this head provided the instrument is stamped with a denoting stamp.

MORTGAGES, exempt

*TRANSFER OF STOCK AND SHARES BY SALE, 0.5 per cent

*UNIT TRUST INSTRUMENT

Any trust instrument of a unit trust scheme, for every £100 or fraction of £100 of the amount or value of the property subject to the trusts created or recorded by the instrument, 25p

By the Finance Act 1989, the transfer of units in certain authorized unit trusts is no longer subject to duty.

VOLUNTARY DISPOSITION, *inter vivos*

Fixed duty, 50p

However, under the Stamp Duty (Exempt Intruments) Regulations 1987, instruments which would otherwise fall under this head are exempt from stamp duty provided that the document is certified as falling within category L in the schedule to the Regulations. *See* Conveyance or Transfer of Any Other Kind, above.

TIME FOR STAMPING

A stampable instrument may, subject to exceptions, be stamped without penalty if presented for stamping within 30 days after its date of first execution. Where wholly executed abroad, the period begins to run from the date of arrival in the UK.

Instruments presented after the proper time (subject to special provisions in some cases and subject to the Commissioner's power to mitigate), a penalty equal to the unpaid duty (and interest thereon if duty exceeds £10) plus £10

Taxation

INCOME TAX

Income tax is charged on the total income of individuals for a year of assessment commencing on 6 April and ending on the following 5 April. The rates of tax and the calculation of liability will frequently differ, sometimes substantially, as between one year of assessment and another. The following information is confined to the year of assessment 1995–6 ending on 5 April 1996.

Liability to income tax is determined by establishing the taxable income for a year of assessment. The income will be reduced by an individual's personal allowance and some other reliefs. The first £3,200 of taxable income remaining is assessable to income tax at the lower rate of 20 per cent and the next £21,100 at the basic rate of 25 per cent. Should any excess remain over £24,300 (£3,200 plus £21,100) this will be taxable at the higher rate of 40 per cent.

The three rates apply to the assessment of both earned and investment income. There is little distinction between the two classes, although the receipt of earned income may produce an entitlement to some allowances not available against investment income. Special rules apply to tax on company dividends. Certain allowances and reliefs are given at the rate of 15 or 20 per cent as a deduction from tax payable. These adjustments can only be made once the full amount of tax otherwise payable has been calculated.

The tables below show the income tax payable for 1995–6 by an individual on the amount of income specified, after deducting the personal allowance and providing relief for the married couple's allowance, where appropriate. Elderly persons over the age of 74 years may pay rather less tax. Some taxpayers may be entitled to transitional allowances and other reliefs which reduce the tax payable below the amount shown by the tables.

Trustees administering settled property are chargeable to income tax at the basic rate of 25 per cent. Where the trustees retain discretionary powers or income is accumulated, there will also be liability to the additional rate of 10 per cent. Companies residing in the United Kingdom are not liable to income tax but suffer corporation tax on income, profits and gains.

The charge to income tax arises on all taxable income accruing from sources in the United Kingdom. Individuals who are resident in this territory may also become liable on income arising overseas. An individual is resident in the UK if he or she normally resides here. Persons not normally residing in the UK may become resident if they visit this territory for periods which average three months or more throughout a period of years, or are present for at least 183 days in a particular year.

Income arising overseas will often incur liability to foreign taxation. If that income is also chargeable to United Kingdom income tax, excessive liability could arise. The UK has concluded double taxation agreements with many overseas territories and these ensure that the same slice of income is not doubly taxed. In the absence of such an agreement, foreign tax suffered can usually be relieved under the domestic code when calculating liability to UK income tax.

Independent Taxation

Since the introduction of independent taxation on 6 April 1990, a husband and wife have been separately taxed, with each entitled to a personal allowance. In most situations any unused personal allowance available to one spouse cannot be transferred to the other. A married man 'living with' his wife can obtain a married couple's allowance. In the absence of any claim, this allowance must be used by the husband but where any balance remains the surplus may be transferred to the wife. It is possible for a married

Single Persons and Married Women					Married Men				
Income	Persons under 65		Persons 65 or over*		Income	Couples under 65		Couples 65 or over†	
£	Income tax £	Average rate %	Income tax £	Average rate %	£	Income tax £	Average rate %	Income tax £	Average rate %
4,000	95	2.4	—	—	4,000	—	—	—	—
5,000	295	5.9	74	1.5	5,000	—	—	—	—
6,000	495	8.3	274	4.6	6,000	237	4.0	—	—
7,000	709	10.1	474	6.8	7,000	451	6.4	25	0.4
8,000	959	12.0	683	8.5	8,000	701	8.8	233	2.9
9,000	1,209	13.4	933	10.4	9,000	951	10.6	483	5.4
10,000	1,459	14.6	1,183	11.8	10,000	1,201	12.0	733	7.3
12,000	1,959	16.3	1,683	14.0	12,000	1,701	14.2	1,233	10.3
14,000	2,459	17.6	2,183	15.6	14,000	2,201	15.7	1,733	12.4
16,000	2,959	18.5	2,858	17.9	16,000	2,701	16.9	2,408	15.1
18,000	3,459	19.2	3,459	19.2	18,000	3,161	17.6	3,099	17.2
20,000	3,959	19.8	3,959	19.8	20,000	3,701	18.5	3,701	18.5
25,000	5,209	20.8	5,209	20.8	25,000	4,951	19.8	4,951	19.8
30,000	6,785	22.6	6,785	22.6	30,000	6,527	21.8	6,527	21.8
40,000	10,785	27.0	10,785	27.0	40,000	10,527	26.3	10,527	26.3
50,000	14,785	29.6	14,785	29.6	50,000	14,527	29.1	14,527	29.1
60,000	18,785	31.3	18,785	31.3	60,000	18,527	30.9	18,527	30.9
100,000	34,785	34.8	34,785	34.8	100,000	34,527	34.5	34,527	34.5

* Persons aged 75 or over suffer less tax on income falling below £16,000 on this table

† Persons aged 75 or over suffer less tax on income falling below £18,000 on this table

woman to claim half the basic married couple's allowance as of right. In addition, the entire basic allowance may be claimed by the wife, if her husband so agrees.

Each spouse may obtain other allowances and reliefs where the underlying conditions are satisfied. Income must be accurately allocated between a husband and wife by reference to the individual beneficially entitled to that income. Where income arises from jointly-held assets, this must be apportioned equally between husband and wife. However, in those cases where the beneficial interests in jointly-held assets are not equal, a special declaration can be made to apportion income by reference to the actual interests in that income.

INCOME TAXABLE

Income tax is assessed and collected under several Schedules. Each Schedule determines the extent of liability and establishes the amount to be included in taxable income. In some instances the actual income arising in a year of assessment will be charged to income tax for that year.

A different basis of assessment may be used for income taxable under Cases I to V of Schedule D. Throughout a period of many years income has been assessed under these Cases on a 'preceding year' basis. This involves measuring income for the year by reference to that arising in a previous year or period but there are special rules where a new source is acquired or an existing source discontinued. The 'preceding year' basis is being replaced by a 'current year' basis of assessment. This requires that business profits assessable under Case I or Case II of Schedule D will be those for the accounting period ending in the year of assessment, with special adjustments for the opening and closing years of a business. Other income assessable under Schedule D will be that which arises in the actual year of assessment.

The new 'current year' basis will apply at the outset for new sources commenced on and after 6 April 1994. Sources existing before that date will become subject to the current year basis in 1997–8, although special rules will apply to achieve a smooth transition from the old basis to the new.

Following the withdrawal of income tax liability for most commercial woodlands in the United Kingdom, Schedule B no longer applies. The contents of the remaining schedules are shown below.

Schedule A

Tax is charged under Schedule A on the annual profits or gains arising from any business carried on for the exploitation of land in the United Kingdom. Whilst the broad scope of this Schedule has remained unchanged for many years, substantial amendments have been made to the calculation of profits and gains for 1995–6 and future years. The calculation of liability for a Schedule A business, as it is now described, adopts principles identical to those used when establishing the profits or gains of a trade, profession or vocation. Rents and other income from the exploitation of land will be included in the calculation, and outgoings incurred wholly and exclusively for the purposes of the Schedule A business may be deducted from income.

Schedule A does not extend to profits from farming, market gardening or woodlands, nor does it apply to mineral rents and royalties. Premiums arising on the grant of a lease for a period not exceeding 50 years in duration are treated as rents. However, the amount of the taxable premium may be reduced by 2 per cent for each complete year, after the first twelve months, of the leasing period. The previous ability to exercise an option to assess income from furnished lettings under Case VI of Schedule D or

Schedule A no longer applies. However, income arising from the provision of certain furnished holiday accommodation attracts a number of tax advantages not otherwise available to most income chargeable under Schedule A.

Receipts not exceeding £3,250 annually and accruing to an individual from letting property furnished in his or her own home are not chargeable to income tax.

Schedule C

This Schedule is confined to interest or dividends on government or public authority funds and certain payments made out of the public revenues of overseas countries.

Schedule D

This Schedule is divided into six Cases:

Cases I and II – profits arising from trades, professions and vocations, including farming and market gardening. Capital expenditure incurred on assets used for business purposes will often produce an entitlement to capital allowances which reduce the profits chargeable. These profits may also be reduced by claims for loss relief and other matters.

Case III – interest on government stocks not taxed at source (e.g. war loan and British savings bonds), interest on National Savings Bank deposits and discounts. Interest up to £70 on ordinary National Savings Bank deposits is exempt from income tax. The exemption applies to both husband and wife separately. Interest on National Savings Bank special investment accounts is not exempt.

Cases IV and V – interest from overseas securities, rents, dividends and all other income accruing outside the UK. Assessment is based on the full amount of income arising, whether remitted to the UK or retained overseas, but individuals who are either not domiciled in the UK or who are ordinarily resident overseas may be taxed on a remittance basis. Overseas pensions are taxable but the amount arising may be reduced by 10 per cent for assessment purposes. Dividends on overseas investments are chargeable at the lower rate of 20 per cent and the higher rate of 40 per cent.

Case VI – sundry profits and annual receipts not assessed under any other Case or Schedule. These may include insurance commissions, post-cessation receipts and numerous other receipts specifically charged under Case VI.

Schedule E

All emoluments from an office or employment are assessable under this Schedule. There are three Cases:

Case I – applies to all emoluments of an individual resident and ordinarily resident in the UK.

Case II – of application where the individual is not resident or not ordinarily resident and extends to emoluments for duties undertaken in the UK.

Case III – applies in rare situations to other emoluments remitted to the UK.

Although earnings for duties performed overseas may be assessable under Case I where the employee is resident and ordinarily resident in the UK, a foreign earnings deduction of 100 per cent may be available, which reduces the overseas assessable earnings to nil. This deduction can be obtained where duties are performed overseas for a continuous period reaching or exceeding 365 days and is confined to earnings from the overseas activity.

A 'receipts basis' applies for determining the year of assessment in which earnings must be taxed. Where emoluments are assessable under Case I or Case II, the date of receipt will comprise the earlier of the date of payment, or the date entitlement arises. In the case of company directors it is the earliest of the two dates with the addition of the following three which establish the time of receipt: the date emoluments are credited in the company's books; where emoluments for a period are determined after the end of that period, the date of determination; where emoluments for a period are determined in that period, the last day of that period.

The emoluments assessable under Schedule E include all salaries, wages, director's fees and other money sums. In addition, there is a wide range of benefits which must be added to taxable emoluments. These include the provision of living accommodation on advantageous terms and advantages arising from the use of vouchers.

Further taxable benefits accrue to directors and also to employees receiving emoluments of £8,500 or more in the year of assessment. These benefits include the reimbursement of expenses, the availability of motor cars for private motoring, the provision of petrol or other fuel for private motoring, the use of vans, the provision of interest-free loans, and other benefits provided at the employer's expense. The cost of providing a limited range of child care facilities may be excluded.

In arriving at the amount to be assessed under Schedule E, all expenses incurred wholly, exclusively and necessarily in the performance of the duties may be deducted. This includes fees and subscriptions paid to certain professional bodies and learned societies. Fees paid to managers by entertainers, actors and others assessable under Schedule E may be deducted, up to a maximum of 17.5 per cent of earnings.

Compensation for loss of office and other sums received on the termination of an office or employment are assessable to tax. However, the first £30,000 may be excluded with only the balance remaining chargeable, unless the compensatory payment is linked with the retirement of the recipient.

Earnings received from an approved profit-related pay scheme are exempt from income tax.

Schedule F

This Schedule is concerned with company dividends and distributions. A UK resident company paying a dividend or making a distribution must account to the Inland Revenue for advance corporation tax. A shareholder residing in the UK obtains the dividend or distribution together with a tax credit equal to one-quarter of the sum received for 1995–6. The dividend or distribution is regarded as having suffered income tax, equal to the tax credit, at the lower rate of 20 per cent. Where the shareholder is not liable, or not fully liable, at that rate a repayment can be obtained. Dividends or distributions are not liable to tax at the difference between the lower rate of 20 per cent and the basic rate of 25 per cent. However, shareholders liable at the higher rate of 40 per cent will incur further liability on the grossed-up equivalent of the sum received at the rate of 40 per cent, less the tax credit of 20 per cent.

Some payments made by an unquoted trading company to redeem or purchase its own shares are not treated as distributions.

Building society and bank interest

Many payments of interest by building societies and banks are received after the deduction of income tax at the basic rate of 25 per cent. However, investors not liable to income tax may arrange to receive interest gross, with no tax being deducted on payment. Others who suffer income tax by deduction can obtain a repayment in whole or in part if they are not fully liable at the basic rate.

INCOME NOT TAXABLE

This includes interest on National Savings certificates, most scholarship income, bounty payments to members of the armed services and annuities payable to the holders of certain awards. Dividend income arising from investments in personal equity plans and venture capital trusts may be exempt from tax. Income received under most maintenance agreements and court orders made after 30 June 1988 will not be liable to tax. Nor will payments made under many deeds of covenant executed after 14 March 1988 be recognized for tax purposes, unless the recipient is a charity. Interest arising on a tax exempt special savings account (TESSA) opened with a building society or bank will be exempt from tax if the account is maintained throughout a five-year period.

SOCIAL SECURITY BENEFITS

Many social security benefits are not liable to income tax. These include income support, family credit, maternity allowance, child benefit, war widow's pension and disability living allowance, among others. Among the limited range of benefits which are taxable is the retirement pension, widow's pension, widowed mother's allowance, and unemployment benefits. Short-term sick pay and maternity pay payable by an employer are also chargeable to tax. Incapacity benefit, introduced on 6 April 1995 to replace invalidity benefit and sickness benefit, is chargeable to tax. However, no liability arises for the first 28 weeks of receiving benefit.

PAY AS YOU EARN

The Pay As You Earn system is not an independent form of taxation but is designed to collect income tax by deduction from most emoluments. When paying emoluments to employees, an employer is usually required to deduct income tax and account for that tax to the Inland Revenue. In many cases this deduction procedure will fully exhaust the individual's liability to income tax, unless there is other income. The date of 'receipt' used for assessment purposes (*see* above) also identifies the date of 'payment' when establishing liability for PAYE.

The PAYE system is also used to collect tax on certain payments made 'in kind'. This includes payment in the form of gold bullion, diamonds and marketable securities, among others.

ALLOWANCES

The allowances available to individuals for 1995–6 are outlined below.

Personal allowance

Each individual receives a basic personal allowance of £3,525. This is increased to £4,630 for individuals over the age of 64 on 5 April 1996, and further increased to £4,800 for those over the age of 74 on the same date. The increased allowance is available for those who died during the year of assessment but who would otherwise have achieved the appropriate age not later than 5 April 1996.

The amount of the increased personal allowance for older taxpayers will be reduced by one-half of total income in excess of £14,600. This reduction in the allowance will continue until it has been reduced to the basic personal allowance of £3,525.

Apart from limited transitional matters mentioned below, any unused part of the personal allowance of one spouse cannot be transferred to the other.

The personal allowance is given as a deduction in calculating taxable income and may therefore produce relief at the rate of 20, 25 or 40 per cent, as appropriate.

Married couple's allowance

A married man who was 'living with' his wife at any time in the year ending on 5 April 1996 is entitled to a married couple's allowance. The basic allowance is £1,720. This may be increased to £2,995 if either the husband or the wife is 65 years or over at any time in the year ending on 5 April 1996. A further increase to £3,035 can be obtained where either party to the marriage was 75 or over on 5 April 1996. Where an individual would otherwise have reached either age by 5 April 1996, but who died earlier in the year, the increased allowance is given.

The amount of the increased married couple's allowance may be reduced where the income of the husband (excluding the income of the wife) exceeds £14,600. The reduction will comprise:

(a) one-half of the husband's total income in excess of £14,600, less
(b) the amount of any reduction made when calculating the husband's increased personal allowance

This reduction in the married couple's allowance cannot reduce that allowance below the basic amount of £1,720.

If husband and wife were married during 1995–6 the married couple's allowance of £1,720, or any increased sum, must be reduced by one-twelfth for each complete month commencing on 6 April 1995, and preceding the date of marriage.

Unlike the personal allowance, the married couple's allowance does not reduce taxable income. Relief is granted by reducing the tax payable by 15 per cent of the allowance. Should the allowance exceed taxable income, no tax will be due.

In the absence of any further action the married couple's allowance will be given to the husband. If he is unable to utilize all or any part of that allowance due to an absence of income, the husband may transfer the unused portion to his wife. The decision whether or not to transfer remains at the discretion of the husband.

However, a wife may file an election to obtain one-half of the basic married couple's allowance as of right, leaving the husband with the balance of that allowance. Alternatively, the couple may jointly elect that the entire basic allowance should be allocated to the wife only. Except in the year of marriage, the election must be made before the commencement of the year of assessment to which it is to apply. Should either spouse be unable to utilize his or her share of the married couple's allowance the unused part may be transferred to the other spouse.

Additional personal allowance

An allowance of £1,720 is available to a single person who has a qualifying child resident with him or her in 1995–6. The allowance can also be obtained by a married man whose wife is totally incapacitated by physical or mental infirmity throughout the year.

A 'qualifying child' for 1995–6 must be born during the year, be under the age of 16 years at the commencement of the year, or be over the age of 16 at the commencement of the year and either receiving full-time instruction at a university, college, school or other educational establishment or undergoing training for a trade, profession or vocation throughout a minimum period of two years. It is also necessary that the child is the claimant's own, a stepchild, an illegitimate child if the parents married after the child's birth, or an adopted child under the age of 18 at the time of adoption. Alternatively it must be shown that the child was either born during 1995–6 or under the age of 18 at the commencement of the year and maintained by the claimant at his or her own expense during the whole of the succeeding 12-month period.

Only one additional personal allowance of £1,720 can be obtained by an individual notwithstanding the number of children involved. Where an unmarried couple are living together as husband and wife, it is not possible for both to obtain the additional personal allowance. The allowance is given by reducing tax payable at the rate of 15 per cent of £1,720.

Widow's bereavement allowance

For the year of assessment in which a husband dies his surviving widow may obtain a widow's bereavement allowance, which is £1,720 for 1995–6. It is a requirement that the parties were 'living together' immediately before the husband's death. A similar allowance will be available in the year following death, unless the widow remarried in the year of death. No widow's bereavement allowance can be obtained for future years. Relief is granted by reducing tax payable at the rate of 15 per cent of £1,720.

Blind person's allowance

An allowance of £1,200 is available to an individual if at any time during the year ending on 5 April 1996, he or she was registered as blind on a register maintained by a local authority. If the individual is 'living with' a wife or husband, any unused part of the blind person's allowance can be transferred to the other spouse. The allowance reduces taxable income and may therefore give rise to relief at the taxpayer's highest rate of tax suffered.

Transitional allowances

There are three limited transitional allowances which are intended to ensure that the introduction of independent taxation on 6 April 1990 did not increase liability to income tax for subsequent years. These allowances comprise:

(a) an increased personal allowance available to a wife where the husband cannot fully use that allowance in 1995–6
(b) a special personal allowance available to a husband where his wife falls into a higher age group, namely over 64 or over 74
(c) a married couple's allowance available to a separated husband not 'living with' his wife if the separation occurred before 6 April 1990

LIFE ASSURANCE RELIEF

Life assurance deduction relief is limited to premiums paid on policies made before 14 March 1984. No relief is available for policies issued after this date. Where the terms of a policy made before 14 March 1984 are subsequently varied or extended to produce increased benefits, future premiums paid may no longer qualify for relief.

When paying premiums under a qualifying policy made before 14 March 1984, the payer will deduct and retain income tax at the rate of 12.5 per cent. The ability to retain deductions made in this manner is not affected by the payer's liability to income tax on taxable income. No restriction to the deduction procedure arises if aggregate premiums paid during a year of assessment do not exceed £1,500 (calculated before deducting tax). Should premiums exceed this amount, relief will be confined to £1,500 or one-sixth of total income, whichever is the greater. Where sums deducted exceed the maximum limit, the excess must be accounted for to the Inland Revenue.

INTEREST

In addition to personal and blind person's allowances, which reduce taxable income, and other allowances which reduce tax payable, further reliefs may be available to an individual. These include payments of interest.

In some instances, interest paid by a business proprietor may be included when calculating profits chargeable to income tax under Case I or Case II of Schedule D. In addition, relief for interest paid on a loan applied to acquire or develop land may be obtained for 1995–6 and future years by including the outlay in the calculation of income chargeable under Schedule A. However, many private individuals cannot obtain relief in this manner and must satisfy stringent requirements before relief will be forthcoming. In general terms it is a requirement that before interest can qualify for relief it must be paid for a qualifying purpose. Relief will not be available to the extent that interest exceeds a reasonable commercial rate and no relief is forthcoming for interest on an overdraft.

For 1995–6 relief will be available on the following payments:

(a) Interest on a loan to purchase, develop or improve an interest in land owned by the individual and used as the only or main residence of that individual. 'Land' includes large houseboats and also caravans used for residential purposes. No relief is available for interest on loans applied after 5 April 1988 for the development or improvement of land, unless the work involves the construction of a new building. Relief is available for interest paid on a loan applied to acquire a property which is the only or main residence of a dependent relative, a separated spouse or a divorced former spouse, but only where that person occupied the property before 6 April 1988. Relief may also be forthcoming for interest on a loan used to acquire some other property, perhaps to be used as the only or main residence on retirement, by an individual who is compelled to occupy property by reason of his or her work. If the loan, or aggregate of several loans, exceeds £30,000, relief is restricted to interest on that amount. Where two or more persons apply loans after 31 July 1988 to acquire interests in a single building, these persons cannot, collectively, obtain relief for interest on more than £30,000 in relation to that building. Relief is given by reducing tax payable at the rate of 15 per cent. There can be no relief at the increased rates of 25 or 40 per cent.

(b) Interest on a loan made to acquire an interest in a close company or in a partnership, or to advance money to such a person

(c) Interest on a loan to a member of a partnership to acquire machinery or plant for use in the partnership business

(d) Interest on a loan to an employed person to acquire machinery or plant for the purposes of his/her employment

(e) Interest on a loan made for the purpose of contributing capital to an industrial co-operative

(f) Interest on a loan applied for investment in an employee-controlled company

(g) Interest on a loan made to elderly persons for the purchase of an annuity where the loan is secured on land. If the loan exceeds £30,000, relief is limited to interest on this amount. This relief is restricted to income tax at the basic rate of 25 per cent.

(h) Interest on a loan to personal representatives to provide funds for the payment of capital transfer tax or inheritance tax

Relief for many payments of mortgage interest is obtained through a special scheme known as MIRAS (mortgage interest relief at source). This applies to interest paid to a building society, bank, insurance company and certain other approved persons. When making payments of this nature in 1995–6 the payer will deduct and retain income tax at the rate of 15 per cent. This will provide the payer with full relief at that rate and no other relief will be necessary. Qualifying payments of interest outside the MIRAS scheme continue to produce relief by reducing tax payable at the rate of 15 per cent.

Other relief under headings (b) to (h) (but not (g)) are given by deducting interest from taxable income. This enables the taxpayer to obtain relief at his or her top rate suffered.

OTHER OUTGOINGS

Many employees pay contributions to an approved occupational pension scheme. The amount of their contributions may be deducted when calculating emoluments assessable under Schedule E. Relief should also be available for any additional voluntary contributions paid.

Self-employed individuals and those receiving earnings not covered by an occupational pension scheme may contribute under personal pension scheme arrangements. These individuals may also pay premiums under retirement annuity schemes if the arrangements were concluded before 1 July 1988. Contributions paid under both headings may obtain income tax relief by deduction from taxable income, subject to maximum limits.

Subject to a maximum of £100,000 in any one year, the cost of subscribing for shares in an unquoted company may qualify for relief under the Enterprise Investment Scheme. Many requirements must be satisfied before this relief can be obtained, but husband and wife may each take advantage of the £100,000 annual maximum. Relief is given by reducing tax payable at the rate of 20 per cent of the share subscription cost. Further relief, also to a maximum of £100,000 and given at the rate of 20 per cent, is available for a subscription of shares in a venture capital trust.

SELF-ASSESSMENT

The UK tax system is on the threshold of substantial change which will apply for 1996–7 and future years. This change is because of the introduction of self-assessment, whereby many taxpayers must calculate the amount of income tax they must pay.

Under the new system, income tax returns must normally be submitted by 31 January following the end of the year of assessment to which the return relates. In addition to completing the return, the taxpayer must calculate the amount of income tax due. If this calculation procedure is to be avoided the return must be forwarded to the Inland Revenue not later than the previous 30 September. An Inland Revenue representative will then calculate the amount of tax and advise the taxpayer. This is the only advantage of providing a completed return not later than 30 September as it remains the responsibility of the taxpayer to submit payments of tax on time.

There may be three different payment dates when discharging income tax for a year of assessment, namely:

(a) an instalment due on 31 January in the year of assessment

(b) a second instalment due on the following 31 July

(c) a balancing payment, or perhaps a repayment, on the following 31 January

The two payments on account will be based on tax payable for the previous year of assessment, but liability may be avoided where the amounts are small.

Taxpayers affected by self-assessment will broadly comprise self-employed individuals, those receiving income from the exploitation of land in the UK and others with investment income liable to higher rate income tax. The majority of individuals receiving only earnings from an employment where the PAYE system applies will be largely unaffected.

Failure to submit completed tax returns by 31 January or to discharge payments of income tax on time will incur liability to interest, surcharges and perhaps penalties.

The self-assessment procedure is not limited to income tax but extends also to capital gains tax. However, there will be no requirement to make payments on account of capital gains tax as the entire amount due for disposals taking place in a year of assessment must be paid on the following 31 January.

CAPITAL GAINS TAX

An individual is chargeable to capital gains tax on chargeable gains which accrue to him or her during a year of assessment ending on 5 April. The application of the tax has been amended substantially in recent years and the following information is confined to the year of assessment 1995–6, ending on 5 April 1996.

Liability extends to individuals who are either resident or ordinarily resident for the year but special rules apply where a person permanently leaves the UK or comes to this territory for the purpose of acquiring residence. Non-residents are not liable to capital gains tax unless, exceptionally, they carry on a business in the UK through a branch or agency.

Trustees residing in the United Kingdom are chargeable to capital gains tax but chargeable gains accruing to companies are assessable to corporation tax.

Capital gains tax is chargeable on the total of chargeable gains which accrue to a person in a year of assessment, after subtracting allowable losses arising in the same year. Unused allowable losses brought forward from some earlier year may be offset against current chargeable gains but in the case of individuals this must not reduce the net chargeable gains for 1995–6 below £6,000. It is possible to utilize trading losses against chargeable gains where those losses have not been offset against income.

RATE OF TAX

Where the net chargeable gains accruing to an individual during 1995–6 do not exceed £6,000 there will be no liability to capital gains tax. If the net gains exceed £6,000 the excess is chargeable at the taxpayer's marginal rate of income tax. This is achieved by adding the excess net chargeable gains to the amount of income chargeable to income tax. The rate attributable to this top slice will disclose the rate of capital gains tax payable, which may be at 20 per cent, 25 per cent, 40 per cent or a combination of the three. Although income tax rates are used, capital gains tax remains a separate tax.

Capital gains tax for 1995–6 normally falls due for payment on or before 1 December 1996. If the return or other information recording chargeable gains is delayed, interest may become chargeable.

HUSBAND AND WIFE

Following the introduction of independent taxation a husband and wife 'living together' are separately assessed to capital gains tax. Each spouse must independently calculate his or her gains and losses, with each entitled to the annual exemption of £6,000. No liability to capital gains tax arises from the transfer of assets between husband and wife 'living together'.

DISPOSAL OF ASSETS

Before liability to capital gains tax can arise a disposal, or deemed disposal, of an asset must take place. This occurs not only where assets are sold or exchanged but applies on the making of a gift. There is also a disposal of assets where any capital sum is derived from assets, for example, where compensation is received for loss or damage to an asset.

The date on which a disposal must be treated as having taken place will determine the year of assessment into which the chargeable gain or allowable loss falls. In those cases where a disposal is made under an unconditional contract, the time of disposal will be that when the contract was entered into and not the subsequent date of conveyance or transfer. A disposal under a conditional contract or option is treated as taking place when the contract becomes unconditional or the option is exercised. Disposals by way of gift are undertaken when the gift becomes effective.

VALUATION OF ASSETS

The amount actually received as consideration for the disposal of an asset will be the sum from which very limited outgoings must be deducted for the purpose of establishing the gain or loss. In some cases, however, the consideration passing will not accurately reflect the value of the asset and a different basis must be used. This applies, in particular, where an asset is transferred by way of gift or otherwise than by a bargain made at arm's length. Such transactions are deemed to take place for a consideration representing market value, which will determine both the disposal proceeds accruing to the transferor and the cost of acquisition to the transferee.

Market value represents the price which an asset might reasonably be expected to fetch on a sale in the open market. In the case of unquoted shares or securities, it is to be assumed that the hypothetical purchaser in the open market would have available all the information which a prudent prospective purchaser of shares or securities might reasonably require if he were proposing to purchase them from a willing vendor by private treaty and at arm's length. This is an important consideration as the amount of information deemed to be available to a hypothetical purchaser may materially affect the price 'reasonably' offered in an open market situation. The market value of unquoted shares or securities will usually be established following negotiations with the Shares Valuation Division of the Capital Taxes Office. The valuation of land and interests in land in the UK will be dealt with by the District Valuer.

Special rules apply to determine the market value of shares quoted on the Stock Exchange.

DEDUCTION FOR OUTGOINGS

Once the actual or notional disposal proceeds have been determined, it only remains to subtract eligible outgoings for the purpose of computing the gain or loss. There is the general rule that any outgoings deducted, or which are available to be deducted, when calculating income tax liability must be ignored. Subject to this, deductions will usually be limited to:

(a) the cost of acquiring the asset, together with incidental costs wholly and exclusively incurred in connection with the acquisition

(b) expenditure incurred wholly and exclusively on the asset in enhancing its value, being expenditure reflected in the state or nature of the asset at the time of the disposal, and any other expenditure wholly and exclusively incurred in establishing, preserving or defending title to, or a right over, the asset

(c) the incidental costs of making the disposal

Where the disposal concerns a leasehold interest having less than 50 years to run, any expenditure falling under (a) and (b) must be written off throughout the duration of the lease. This recognizes that a lease is a wasting asset which, at the termination of the leasing period, will retain no value.

Assets held on 31 March 1982

Where the disposal relates to assets held on 31 March 1982, the actual cost of acquisition will not usually enter into the calculation of gain. It is to be assumed that such assets were acquired on 31 March 1982 for a consideration representing market value on that date. The increase in value, if any, occurring before 31 March 1982 will not be assessable to capital gains tax.

Indexation Allowance

An indexation allowance may be available on the disposal of an asset. This allowance is based on percentage increases in the retail prices index between the month of March 1982 or the month in which expenditure is incurred, if later, and the month of disposal. The increase is applied to the items of expenditure in (a) and (b) above to determine the amount of the indexation allowance. However, if the asset was acquired before 31 March 1982, the allowance will be based on market value at 31 March 1982.

Previously the indexation allowance could be subtracted from the gain, added to the loss or used to convert a gain into a loss. However, where the disposal has taken place after 29 November 1993 the indexation allowance may only be applied to reduce a gain. It cannot increase the amount of a loss, and where the allowance exceeds the amount of a gain it only remains necessary to reduce the gain to nil.

As a transitional measure some limited relief was available to individuals undertaking the disposal of assets between 30 November 1993 and 5 April 1995. If that relief was not utilized by 5 April 1995, it cannot be carried forward and used in 1995–6.

Exemptions

There is a general exemption from liability to capital gains tax where the net gains of an individual for 1995–6 do not exceed £6,000. This general exemption applies separately to a husband and to his wife where the parties are 'living together'.

The disposal of many assets will not give rise to chargeable gains or allowable losses and these assets include:

(a) private motor cars
(b) government securities
(c) loan stock and other securities (but not shares)
(d) options and contracts relating to securities within (b) and (c)
(e) National Savings Certificates, Premium Bonds, Defence Bonds and National Development Bonds
(f) currency of any description acquired for personal expenditure outside the UK
(g) decorations awarded for valour
(h) betting wins and pools, lottery or games prizes
(i) compensation or damages for any wrong or injury suffered by an individual in his/her person or in his/her profession or vocation
(j) life assurance and deferred annuity contracts where the person making the disposal is the original beneficial owner
(k) dwelling-houses and land enjoyed with the residence which is an individual's only or main residence
(l) tangible movable property, the consideration for the disposal of which does not exceed £6,000
(m) certain tangible movable property which is a wasting asset having a life not exceeding 50 years
(n) assets transferred to charities and other bodies
(o) works of art, historic buildings and similar assets
(p) assets used to provide maintenance funds for historic buildings
(q) assets transferred to trustees for the benefit of employees

Dwelling-Houses

Exemption from capital gains tax will usually be available for any gain which accrues to an individual from the disposal of, or of an interest in, a dwelling-house or part of a dwelling-house which has been his/her only or main residence. The exemption extends to land which has been occupied and enjoyed with the residence as its garden or grounds. Some restriction may be necessary where the land exceeds half a hectare.

The gain will not be chargeable to capital gains tax if the dwelling-house, or part, has been the individual's only or main residence throughout the period of ownership, or throughout the entire period except for all or any part of the last three years. A proportionate part of the gain will be exempt in other cases if the dwelling-house has been the individual's only or main residence for part only of the period of ownership. In the case of property acquired before 31 March 1982, the period of ownership is treated as commencing on this date.

Where part of the dwelling-house has been used exclusively for business purposes, that part of the gain attributable to business use will not be exempt. It will be comparatively unusual for any part to be used exclusively for such a purpose, except perhaps in the case of doctors' or dentists' surgeries.

In those cases where part of a qualifying dwelling-house has been used to provide rented residential accommodation this non-personal use may frequently be ignored when calculating exemption from capital gains tax, unless relatively substantial sums are involved.

Dwellings occupied by dependent relatives or separated or divorced former spouses, may also qualify for the exemption, but only where occupation commenced before 6 April 1988.

Roll-over Relief – Business Assets

Persons carrying on business will often undertake the disposal of an asset and use the proceeds to finance the acquisition of a replacement asset. Where this situation arises a claim for roll-over relief may be available. The broad effect of such a claim is that all or part of the gain arising on the disposal of the old asset may be disregarded. The gain or part is then subtracted from the cost of acquiring the replacement asset. As this cost is reduced, any gain arising from the future disposal of the replacement asset will be correspondingly increased, unless of course a further roll-over situation then develops.

It remains a requirement that both the old and the replacement asset must be used for the purpose of the taxpayer's business. Relief will only be available if the acquisition of the replacement asset takes place within a period commencing twelve months before, and ending three years after, the disposal of the old asset, although the Inland Revenue retain a discretion to extend this period where the circumstances were such that it was impossible for the taxpayer to acquire the replacement asset before the expiration of the normal time limit.

Whilst many business assets qualify for roll-over relief there are exceptions.

Roll-over Relief – Shares

An additional form of roll-over relief was introduced for disposals taking place after 15 March 1993 and matched with the acquisition of shares in unquoted companies. The conditions governing this relief have been relaxed on several occasions but from 29 November 1994, gains arising on the disposal of virtually any asset will enable an individual, and some trustees, to contemplate the availability of roll-over relief. It is a necessary requirement that the individual or trustee making the disposal acquires shares in a qualifying unquoted trading company. Most shareholdings in trading companies will qualify unless the company also undertakes non-trading activities. An unusual feature of roll-over relief on the reinvestment in shares is that, subject to upper limits, the individual or trustee can roll over any part of the chargeable gain arising on the disposal of assets. The ability to select the amount to be rolled over enables the claimant to leave undisturbed the remaining gain, which can be offset against available losses or perhaps used to absorb the annual exemption of £6,000.

Deferral Relief

A novel form of roll-over relief was introduced for disposals taking place after 28 November 1994. Gains arising from disposals of this nature may be matched, in whole or in part, with an investment in shares under the enterprise investment scheme. To the extent that the investment qualifies for income tax relief, any part of the gain arising on disposal, not exceeding the investment qualifying for relief, may become the subject of a claim. Unlike the more usual form of roll-over relief, this claim does not eliminate or reduce the chargeable gain. It has the effect of deferring that gain until the time of some future event, which will usually be identified by the disposal of shares.

A similar form of deferral relief is available for gains arising on disposals taking place after 5 April 1995. It is a necessary requirement that the individual undertaking the disposal makes a qualifying investment in a venture capital trust. To the extent of the gain arising, which must not exceed the amount of the investment qualifying for income tax relief, that gain is deferred until the time of a future event, which will normally comprise the disposal of shares in the venture capital trust.

Hold-over Relief – Gifts

The gift of an asset is treated as a disposal made for a consideration equal to market value, with a corresponding acquisition by the transferee at an identical value. In the case of gifts made by individuals and a limited range of trustees to a transferee resident in the UK, a form of hold-over relief may be available. Relief is limited to the transfer of certain assets, including the following:

(a) assets used for the purposes of a trade or similar activity carried on by the transferor or his/her personal company

(b) shares or securities of a trading company which is neither quoted on a stock exchange nor dealt in on the Unlisted Securities Market

(c) shares or securities of a trading company which is quoted or listed but which is the transferor's personal company

(d) many interests in agricultural property qualifying for business property relief or agricultural property relief for inheritance tax purposes

(e) assets involved in transactions which are lifetime transfers for inheritance tax purposes, other than potentially exempt transfers

The effect of the claim is similar to that following a claim for roll-over relief on the disposal of business assets, but adjustments will be necessary where some consideration is given for the transfer, the asset has not been used for business purposes throughout the period of ownership, or not all assets of a company are used for business purposes.

Retirement Relief

Retirement relief is available to an individual who disposes by way of sale or gift of the whole or part of a business. It does not necessarily follow that the isolated disposal of assets will represent the disposal of the whole or part of a business. The main condition for granting this relief is that throughout a period of at least one year the business has been owned either by the individual or by a trading company in which the individual retained a sufficient shareholding interest. The relief extends also to cases where an individual disposes by way of sale or gift of shares or securities of a company. It must be demonstrated that the company was a trading company, that the individual retained a sufficient shareholding interest, and that he/she was engaged as a full-time working officer or employee.

An individual who has attained the age of 55 years at the time of a disposal taking place after 29 November 1993 may obtain retirement relief up to a maximum of £625,000. The amount of this relief must be reduced if the underlying conditions have not been satisfied throughout a ten-year period. With a single exception no retirement relief can be obtained if the disposal occurs before the individual's 55th birthday. This exception arises where an individual is compelled to retire early on the grounds of ill-health. The normal retirement relief may then be obtained. Any retirement relief must be subtracted from the net gains arising on disposal, leaving the balance remaining, if any, chargeable to capital gains tax in the normal manner.

Death

No capital gains tax is chargeable on the value of assets retained at the time of death. However, the personal representatives administering the deceased's estate are deemed to acquire those assets for a consideration representing market value on death. This ensures that any increase in value occurring before the date of death will not be chargeable to capital gains tax. If a legatee or other person acquires an asset under a will or intestacy no chargeable gain will accrue to the personal representatives, and the person taking the asset will also be treated as having acquired it at the time of death for its then market value.

INHERITANCE TAX

Liability to inheritance tax may arise on a limited range of lifetime gifts and other dispositions and also on the value of assets retained, or deemed to be retained, at the time of death. An individual's domicile at the time of any gift or on death is an important matter. Domicile will generally be determined by applying normal rules, although special considerations may be necessary where an individual was previously domiciled in the UK but subsequently acquired a domicile of choice overseas. Where a person was domiciled in the UK at the time of a disposition on death the location of assets is immaterial and full liability to inheritance tax arises. Individuals domiciled outside the UK are, however, chargeable to inheritance tax only on transactions affecting assets located in the UK.

The assets of husband and wife are not merged for inheritance tax purposes. Each spouse is treated as a separate individual entitled to receive the benefit of his or her exemptions, reliefs and rates of tax. Where husband and wife retain similar assets, e.g. shares in the same family company, special 'related property' provisions may require the merger of those assets for valuation purposes only.

LIFETIME GIFTS AND DISPOSITIONS

Gifts and dispositions made during lifetime fall under four broad headings, namely:
(a) dispositions which are not transfers of value
(b) exempt transfers
(c) potentially exempt transfers
(d) chargeable transfers

Dispositions which are not transfers of value

Several lifetime transactions are not treated as transfers of value and may be entirely disregarded for inheritance tax purposes. These include transactions not intended to confer gratuitous benefit, the provision of family maintenance, the waiver of the right to receive remuneration or dividends, and the grant of agricultural tenancies for full consideration.

Exempt transfers

Certain transfers are treated as exempt transfers and incur no liability to inheritance tax. The main exempt transfers are listed below:

Transfers between spouses – Transfers between husband and wife are usually exempt. However, if the transferor is, but the transferee spouse is not, domiciled in the UK, transfers will be exempt only to the extent that the total does not exceed £55,000. Unlike the requirement used for income tax and capital gains tax purposes, it is immaterial whether husband and wife are living together.

Annual exemption – The first £3,000 of gifts and other dispositions made in a year ending on 5 April is exempt. If the exemption is not used, or not wholly used, in any year the balance may be carried forward to the following year only. The annual exemption will only be available for a potentially exempt transfer if that transfer subsequently becomes chargeable by reason of the donor's death.

Small gifts – Outright gifts of £250 or less to any person in one year ending 5 April are exempt.

Normal expenditure – A transfer made during lifetime and comprising normal expenditure is exempt. To obtain this exemption it must be shown that:
(a) the transfer was made as part of the normal expenditure of the transferor
(b) taking one year with another, the transfer was made out of income
(c) after allowing for all transfers of value forming part of normal expenditure the transferor was left with sufficient income to maintain his or her usual standard of living

Gifts in consideration of marriage – These are exempt if they satisfy certain requirements. The amount allowed will be governed by the relationship between the donor and a party to the marriage. The allowable amounts comprise:
(a) gifts by a parent, £5,000
(b) gifts by a grandparent, £2,500
(c) gifts by a party to the marriage, £2,500
(d) gifts by other persons, £1,000

Gifts to charities – These are exempt from liability.

Gifts to political parties – Gifts which satisfy certain requirements are generally exempt.

Gifts for national purposes – Gifts made to an extensive list of bodies are exempt from liability. These include, among others, the National Gallery, the British Museum, the National Trust, the National Art Collections Fund, the National Heritage Memorial Fund, the Historic Buildings and Monuments Commission for England (English Heritage), any local authority, any university or university college in the UK.

A number of other gifts made for the public benefit are also exempt.

Potentially exempt transfers

Lifetime gifts and dispositions which are neither to be ignored nor comprise exempt transfers incur possible liability to inheritance tax. However, relief is available for a range of potentially exempt transfers. These comprise gifts made by an individual to:
(a) a second individual
(b) trustees administering an accumulation and maintenance trust
(c) trustees administering a disabled person's trust

The accumulation and maintenance trust mentioned in (b) must provide that on reaching a specified age, not exceeding 25 years, a beneficiary will become absolutely entitled to trust assets or obtain an interest in possession in the income from those assets.

Additions to the above list affect settled property administered by trustees where an individual, or individuals, retain an interest in possession. The transfer of assets to, the removal of assets from, or the rearrangement of interests in such property comprise potentially exempt transfers if the person transferring an interest and the person benefiting from the transfer are both individuals.

No immediate liability to inheritance tax will arise on the making of a potentially exempt transfer. Should the donor survive for a period of seven years, immunity from liability will be confirmed. However, the donor's death within the seven-year *inter vivos* period produces liability if the amounts involved are sufficiently substantial (*see* below).

Chargeable transfers

Any remaining lifetime gifts or dispositions which are neither to be ignored nor represent exempt transfers or potentially exempt transfers, incur liability to inheritance tax. The range of such chargeable transfers is severely limited and is broadly confined to transfers made to or affecting discretionary trusts, transfers to non-individuals and transfers involving companies.

GIFTS WITH RESERVATION

A lifetime gift of assets made at any time after 17 March 1986 may incur additional liability to inheritance tax if the donor retains some interest in the subject matter of the gift. This may arise, for example, where a parent transfers a dwelling-house to a son or daughter and continues to occupy the property or to enjoy some benefit from that property. The retention of a benefit may be ignored where it is enjoyed in return for full consideration, perhaps a commercial rent, or where the benefit arises from changed circumstances which could not have been foreseen at the time of the original gift. The gift with reservation provisions will not usually apply to most exempt transfers.

There are three possibilities which may arise where the donor reserves or enjoys some benefit from the subject matter of a previous gift and subsequently dies, namely:
(a) if no benefit is enjoyed within a period of seven years before death there can be no further liability
(b) if the benefit ceased to be enjoyed within a period of seven years before the date of death, the original donor is deemed to have made a potentially exempt transfer representing the value of the asset at the time of cessation
(c) if the benefit is enjoyed at the time of death, the value of the asset must be included in the value of the deceased's estate on death

It must be emphasized that the existence of a benefit enjoyed at any time within a period of seven years before death will establish liability to tax on gifts with reservation, notwithstanding that the gift may have been made many years earlier, providing it was undertaken after 17 March 1986.

Death

Immediately before the time of death an individual is deemed to make a transfer of value. This transfer will comprise the value of assets forming part of the deceased's estate after subtracting most liabilities. Any exempt transfers may, however, be excluded. These include transfers for the benefit of a surviving spouse, a charity and a qualifying political party, together with bequests to approved bodies and for national purposes.

Death may also trigger three additional liabilities, namely:

(a) A potentially exempt transfer made within the period of seven years ending on death loses its potential status and becomes chargeable to inheritance tax

(b) The value of gifts made with reservation may incur liability if any benefit was enjoyed within a period of seven years preceding death

(c) Additional tax may become payable for chargeable lifetime transfers made within seven years before death

Valuations

The valuation of assets is an important matter as this will establish the value transferred for lifetime dispositions and also the value of a person's estate at the time of death. The value of property will represent the price which might reasonably be expected from a sale in the open market. This price cannot be reduced on the grounds that, should the whole property be placed on the market simultaneously, values would be depressed.

In some cases it may be necessary to incorporate the value of 'related property'. This will include property comprised in the estate of the transferor's spouse and certain property previously transferred to charities. The purpose of the related property valuation rule is not to add the value of the property to the estate of the transferor. Related property must be merged to establish the aggregate value of the respective interests and this value is then apportioned, usually on a *pro rata* basis, to the separate interests.

The value of shares and securities quoted on the Stock Exchange will be determined by extracting figures from the daily list of official prices.

Where quoted shares and securities are sold or the quotation is suspended within a period of 12 months following the date of death, a claim may be made to substitute the proceeds or subsequent value for the value on death. This claim will only be beneficial if the gross proceeds realized are lower or the value has fallen below market value at the time of death. A similar claim may be available for interests in land sold within a period of four years following death.

Relief for Assets

Special relief is made available for certain assets, notably:

Woodlands

Where woodlands pass on death the value will usually be included in the deceased's estate. However, an election may be made in respect of land in the UK on which trees or underwood is growing to delete the value of those assets. Relief is confined to the value of trees or underwood and does not extend to the land on which they are growing. Liability to inheritance tax will arise if and when the trees or underwood are sold on a future occasion.

Agricultural property

Relief is available for the agricultural value of agricultural property. Such property must be occupied and used for agricultural purposes and relief is confined to the agricultural value.

The value transferred, either on a lifetime gift or on death, must be determined. This value may then be reduced by a percentage. The percentage has changed from time to time but for events taking place after 9 March 1992 a 100 per cent deduction will be available if the transferor retained vacant possession or could have obtained that possession within a period of 12 months following the transfer. In other cases, notably including land let to tenants, a lower deduction of 50 per cent is usually available. However, this lower deduction may be increased to 100 per cent if the letting was made after 31 August 1995.

It remains a requirement that the agricultural property was either occupied by the transferor for the purposes of agriculture throughout a two-year period ending on the date of the transfer, or was owned by him/her throughout a period of seven years ending on that date and also occupied for agricultural purposes.

Business property

Where the value transferred is attributable to relevant business property, that value may be reduced by a percentage. The reduction in value applies to:

(a) property consisting of a business or an interest in a business

(b) shares or securities of an unquoted company which provided the transferor with control

(c) unquoted shares or securities not falling within (b) which provided the transferor with more than 25 per cent of voting rights

(d) other unquoted shares or securities not falling within (c)

(e) shares or securities of a quoted company which provided the transferor with control

(f) any land, building, machinery or plant which, immediately before the transfer, was used wholly or mainly for the purposes of a business carried on by a company of which the transferor had control

(g) any land, building, machinery or plant which, immediately before the transfer, was used wholly or mainly for the purposes of a business carried on by a partnership of which the transferor was a partner

(h) any land, building, machinery or plant which, immediately before the transfer, was used wholly or mainly for the purposes of a business carried on by the transferor and was then settled property in which he retained an interest in possession

Here also the percentage deductions have changed, but for events occurring after 9 March 1992 a deduction of 100 per cent is available for assets falling within (a), (b) or (c). A reduced deduction of 50 per cent can be obtained for assets within (d) to (h).

It is a general requirement that the property must have been retained for a period of two years before the transfer or death and restrictions may be necessary if the property has not been used wholly for business purposes. The same property cannot obtain both business property relief and the relief available for agricultural property.

Calculation of Tax Payable

The calculation of inheritance tax payable adopts the use of a cumulative total. Each chargeable lifetime transfer is added to the total with a final addition made on death. The top slice added to the total for the current event determines the rate at which inheritance tax must be paid. However, the cumulative total will only include transfers made within a period of seven years before the current event and those undertaken outside this period must be excluded.

Lifetime chargeable transfers

The value transferred by the limited range of lifetime chargeable transfers must be added to the seven-year cumulative total to calculate whether any inheritance tax is due. Should the nil rate band be exceeded, tax will be imposed on the excess at one-half of the rate shown below. However, if the donor dies within a period of seven years from the date of the chargeable lifetime transfer, additional tax may be due. This is calculated by applying tax at the full rate (in substitution for the one-half previously used). The amount of tax is then reduced to a percentage by applying tapering relief. This percentage is governed by the number of years from the date of the lifetime gift to the date of death and is as follows:

Period of years before death
Not more than 3   100%
More than 3 but not more than 4   80%
More than 4 but not more than 5   60%
More than 5 but not more than 6   40%
More than 6 but not more than 7   20%
Should this exercise produce liability greater than that previously paid at the one-half rate on the lifetime transfer, additional tax, representing the difference, must be discharged. Where the calculation shows an amount falling below tax paid on the lifetime transfer, no additional liability can arise nor will the deficiency become repayable.

Tapering relief will, of course, only be available if the calculation discloses a liability to inheritance tax. There can be no liability to the extent that the lifetime transfer falls within the nil rate band.

Potentially exempt transfers

Where a potentially exempt transfer loses immunity from liability due to the donor's death within the seven-year *inter vivos* period, the value transferred by that transfer enters into the cumulative total. Any liability to inheritance tax will be calculated by applying the full rate shown below, reduced to the percentage governed by tapering relief if the original transfer occurred more than three years before death. Liability can only arise to the extent, if any, that the nil rate band is exceeded.

Death

The final addition to the seven-year cumulative total will comprise the value of an estate on death. Inheritance tax will be calculated by applying the full rate shown below to the extent the nil rate band is exceeded. No tapering relief can be obtained.

RATES OF TAX

In earlier times there were several rates of inheritance tax which progressively increased as the value transferred grew in size. However, for events taking place after 5 April 1995, a nil rate applies to the first £154,000. Any excess is charged at the single positive rate of 40 per cent.

Only one-half of the 40 per cent rate (namely 20 per cent) will be applicable for chargeable lifetime transfers.

PAYMENT OF TAX

Inheritance tax usually falls due for payment six months after the end of the month in which the chargeable transaction takes place. Where a transfer other than that made on death occurs after 5 April and before the following 1 October, tax falls due on the following 30 April, although there are some exceptions to this general rule.

Inheritance tax attributable to the transfer of certain land, controlling shareholding interests, unquoted shares, businesses and interests in businesses, together with agricultural property, may usually be satisfied by instalments spread over ten years. Except in the case of non-agricultural land, where interest is charged on outstanding instalments, no liability to interest arises where tax is paid on the due date. In all cases, delay in the payment of tax may incur liability to interest.

SETTLED PROPERTY

Complex rules apply to establish inheritance tax liability on settled property. Where a person is beneficially entitled to an interest in possession, that person is effectively deemed to own the property in which the interest subsists. It follows that where the interest comes to an end during the beneficiary's lifetime and some other person becomes entitled to the property or interest, the beneficiary is treated as having made a transfer of value. However, this will usually comprise a potentially exempt transfer. In addition, no liability will arise where the property vests in the absolute ownership of the previous beneficiary. The death of a person entitled to an interest in possession will require the value of the underlying property to be added to the value of the deceased's estate.

In the case of other settled property where there is no interest in possession (e.g. discretionary trusts), liability to tax will arise on each ten-year anniversary of the trust. There will also be liability if property ceases to be held on discretionary trusts before the first ten-year anniversary date is reached or between anniversaries. The rate of tax suffered will be governed by several considerations, including previous dispositions made by the settlor, transactions concluded by the trustees, and the period throughout which property has been held in trust.

Accumulation and maintenance settlements which require assets to be distributed, or interests in income to be created, not later than a beneficiary's 25th birthday may be exempt from any liability to inheritance tax.

CORPORATION TAX

Profits, gains and income accruing to companies resident in the UK incur liability to corporation tax. Non-resident companies are immune from this tax unless they carry on a trade in the UK through a permanent establishment, branch or office. Companies residing outside the UK may be liable to income tax at the basic rate on other income arising in the UK, perhaps from letting property. The following comments are confined to companies resident in the UK and have little application to those residing overseas.

Liability to corporation tax is governed by the profits, gains or income for an accounting period. This is usually the period for which financial accounts are made up, and in the case of companies preparing accounts to the same accounting date annually will comprise successive periods of 12 months.

RATE OF TAX

The amount of profits or income for an accounting period must be determined on normal taxation principles. The special rules which apply to individuals where a source of income is acquired or discontinued are ignored and consideration is confined to the actual profits or income for an accounting period.

The rate of corporation tax is fixed for a financial year ending on 31 March. Where the accounting period of a company overlaps this date and there is a change in the rate of corporation tax, profits and income must be apportioned.

In recent years the rate of corporation tax has been as follows:

Financial year

Ending 31 March 1990	35%
31 March 1991	34%
31 March 1992, 1993, 1994, 1995, 1996	33%

SMALL COMPANIES RATE

Where the profits of a company do not exceed stated limits, corporation tax becomes payable at the small companies rate. It is the amount of profits and not the size of the company which governs the application of this rate.

Financial year

Ending 31 March 1990, 1991, 1992, 1993, 1994, 1995, 1996	25%

The level of profits which a company may derive without losing the benefit of the small companies rate is frequently changed. For each year ending on 31 March 1995 and 31 March 1996 the limit is £300,000. However, if profits exceed £300,000 but fall below £1,500,000 marginal small companies rate applies. The effect of marginal relief is that the first £300,000 of profits is taxed at the small companies rate of 25 per cent. Profits falling in the margin then incur liability at the marginal rate of 35 per cent. Different upper limits and marginal rates applied for earlier years. Where the accounting period of a company overlaps 31 March, profits must be apportioned to establish the appropriate rate for each part of those profits.

The lower limit of £300,000 and the upper limit of £1,500,000 apply for a period of 12 months and must be proportionally reduced for shorter periods. Some restriction in the small companies rate and the marginal rate may be necessary if there are two or more associated companies, namely companies under common control.

The small companies rate is not available for close investment-holding companies. These are mainly investment companies, other than those receiving most of their income from letting land and property.

CAPITAL GAINS

Chargeable gains arising to a company are calculated in a manner similar to that used for individuals. However, companies cannot obtain the annual exemption of £6,000 or the special indexation allowance for loss-making disposals made before 6 April 1995. Nor are they assessed to capital gains tax. In place of this tax companies suffer liability to corporation tax on chargeable gains. Tax is suffered on the full chargeable gain, after subtracting relief for losses, if any.

DISTRIBUTIONS

Dividends and other qualifying distributions made by a UK resident company are not satisfied after deduction of income tax. However, when making a distribution a company is required to account to the Inland Revenue for advance corporation tax. The amount of this tax is based on the distribution and changes in the rate have been introduced in recent years as follows:

Distribution	Rate
Year ending 5 April 1993	one third
Year ending 5 April 1994	nine thirty-firsts
Year ending 5 April 1995	one quarter
Year ending 5 April 1996	one quarter

Advance corporation tax accounted for in this manner in relation to distributions made in an accounting period may usually be set against a company's corporation tax liability for the same period. Some restrictions are imposed on the amount which can be offset but any surplus may be carried forward, or perhaps carried backwards, and set against corporation tax paid or due for other accounting periods.

A UK resident shareholder receiving a qualifying distribution also obtains a tax credit based on the distribution made. Over the same four-year period the tax credit will be calculated as follows:

Distribution	Rate
Year ending 5 April 1993	one third
Year ending 5 April 1994	one quarter
Year ending 5 April 1995	one quarter
Year ending 5 April 1996	one quarter

The total income of the individual therefore comprises the aggregate of the distribution and the tax credit. It will be noted that whilst the rate of advance corporation tax and the amount of the tax credit are identical for three of these years, the amounts differed in 1993–4.

For 1993–4 and later years a distribution is treated as having suffered income tax at the lower rate of 20 per cent. If the individual is not liable or not fully liable to income tax at this rate, all or part of the tax credit can be refunded by the Inland Revenue. There is no liability on distributions at the basic rate of 25 per cent. However, individuals with substantial income incur liability to income tax at the higher rate of 40 per cent on the aggregate of the distribution and the tax credit. With tax deemed to have been suffered at the lower rate of 20 per cent the additional liability will be limited to the excess over this rate, which is also 20 per cent.

INTEREST

On making many payments of interest a company is required to deduct income tax at the basic rate and account for the tax deducted to the Inland Revenue. The gross amount of interest paid will usually comprise a charge on income to be offset against profits on which corporation tax becomes payable.

GROUPS OF COMPANIES

Each company within a group is separately charged to corporation tax on profits, gains and income. However, where one group member realizes a loss, other than a capital loss, a claim may be made to offset the deficiency against profits of some other member of the same group.

Claims are also available to avoid the payment of advance corporation tax on distributions, or the deduction of income tax on the payment of interest, for transactions between members of a group of companies. The transfer of capital assets from one member of a group to a fellow member will incur no liability to tax on chargeable gains.

PAY AND FILE

For accounting periods ending after 30 September 1993 a 'pay and file' system now affects all companies. Under this system tax is payable on a self-assessment basis nine months following the end of the accounting period involved, with accounts and returns being submitted three months later. Failure to satisfy corporation tax or to submit documents within these time limits will result in a liability to discharge interest and penalties.

VALUE ADDED TAX

Value added tax (VAT) is charged on the value of the supplies made by a registered trader and extends to both the supply of goods and the supply of services. It is administered by Customs and Excise.

Liability to account for VAT arises on the value of goods imported into the UK from sources outside the European Community. Since 1 January 1993 goods imported by a trader from a second trader in a member state of the European Community attract no VAT on importation. Instead there is an acquisition tax whereby a trader who acquires goods must include the acquisition in his normal VAT return and account for the tax due. A UK trader who exports goods to a member state will not be required to account for VAT on the supply, if that trader observes the requirements laid down by regulations.

REGISTRATION

All traders, including professional men and women and companies, making taxable supplies of a value exceeding stated limits are required to register for VAT purposes. Taxable supplies represent the supply of goods and services potentially chargeable with VAT. The limits which govern mandatory registration are amended annually but from 30 November 1994 an unregistered trader must register:
(a) at any time, if there are reasonable grounds for believing that the value of taxable supplies in the next 30 days will exceed £46,000
(b) at the end of any month if the value of taxable supplies in the 12 months then ending has exceeded £46,000.

Liability to register under (b) may be avoided if it can be shown that the value of supplies in the period of 12 months then beginning will not exceed £44,000. There may, however, be liability to register immediately where a business is taken over from another trader as a 'going concern'.

Where the limits governing mandatory registration have been exceeded, it is necessary for the trader to notify Customs and Excise. In the event of failure to provide prompt notification, the person concerned will be required to account for VAT from the proper registration date.

A trader whose taxable supplies do not reach the mandatory registration limits may apply for voluntary registration. This step may be thought advisable to recover input tax or to compete with other registered traders.

A registered trader may submit an application for deregistration if the value of taxable supplies subsequently falls. From 30 November 1994, an application for de-registration can be made if the value of taxable supplies for the year beginning on the application date is not expected to exceed £44,000.

INPUT TAX

A registered trader will both suffer tax (input tax) when obtaining goods or services for the purposes of his business and also become liable to account for tax (output tax) on the value of goods and services which he supplies. Relief can usually be obtained for input tax suffered, either by setting that tax against output tax due or by repayment. Most items of input tax can be relieved in this manner but there are exceptions, including the prohibition of relief for the cost of business entertaining. Where a registered trader makes both exempt supplies and also taxable supplies to his customers or clients, there may be some restriction in the amount of input tax which can be recovered.

OUTPUT TAX

When making a taxable supply of goods or services a registered trader must account for output tax, if any, on the value of the supply. Usually the price charged by the registered trader will be increased by adding VAT but failure to make the required addition will not remove liability to account for output tax.

The application of output tax, and also input tax, may be affected where a trader is using the special second-hand goods scheme.

EXEMPT SUPPLIES

No VAT is chargeable on the supply of goods or services which are treated as exempt supplies. These include the provision of burial and cremation facilities, insurance, finance and education. The granting of a lease to occupy land or the sale of land will usually comprise an exempt supply, but there are numerous exceptions. In particular, the sale of new non-domestic buildings or certain buildings used by charities cannot be treated as exempt supplies.

A taxable person may elect to tax rents and other supplies of buildings and agricultural land not used for residential or charitable purposes.

Exempt supplies do not enter into the calculation of taxable supplies which governs liability to mandatory registration. Such supplies made by a registered trader may, however, limit the amount of input tax which can be relieved. It is for this reason that the election may be useful.

RATES OF TAX

Two rates of VAT have applied since 1 April 1991, namely:
(a) a zero, or nil, rate
(b) a standard rate of 17.5 per cent
In addition, a special reduced rate of 8 per cent has applied to supplies of domestic fuel since March 1994. Although no tax is due on a zero-rated supply, this does comprise a taxable supply which must be included in the calculation governing liability to register.

ZERO-RATING

A large number of supplies are zero-rated; the following list is not exhaustive but indicates the wide range of supplies which may be zero-rated:
(a) the supply of many items of food and drink for human consumption. This does not include ice creams, chocolates, sweets, potato crisps and alcoholic drinks. Nor does it extend to supplies made in the course of catering or to items supplied for consumption in a restaurant or café. Whilst the supply of cold items, e.g. sandwiches, for consumption away from the supplier's premises, is zero-rated, the supply of hot food, for example fish and chips, is not
(b) animal feeding stuffs
(c) sewerage and water, unless supplied for industrial purposes
(d) books, brochures, pamphlets, leaflets, newspapers, maps and charts
(e) talking books for the blind and handicapped, and wireless sets for the blind
(f) supplies of services, other than professional services, when constructing a new domestic building or a building to be used by a charity. The supply of materials for such a building is also zero-rated, together with the sale or the grant of a long lease for these buildings. Alterations to some protected buildings are also zero-rated

(g) the transportation of persons in a vehicle, ship or aircraft designed to carry not less than twelve persons
(h) supplies of drugs, medicines and other aids for the handicapped
(i) supplies of clothing and footwear for young persons
(j) exports

COLLECTION OF TAX

Registered traders submit VAT returns for accounting periods usually of three months duration but arrangements can be made to submit returns on a monthly basis. Very large traders must account for tax on a monthly basis but this does not affect the three-monthly return. The return will show both the output tax due for supplies made by the trader in the accounting period and also the input tax for which relief is claimed. If the output tax exceeds input tax the balance must be remitted with the VAT return. Where input tax suffered exceeds the output tax due the registered trader may claim recovery of the excess from Customs and Excise.

This basis for collecting tax explains the structure of VAT. Where supplies are made between registered traders the supplier will account for an amount of tax which will usually be identical to the tax recovered by the person to whom the supply is made. However, where the supply is made to a person who is not a registered trader there can be no recovery of input tax and it is on this person that the final burden of VAT eventually falls.

In those cases where goods are acquired by a UK trader from a supplier within a member state of the European Community the trader must also account for the tax due on acquisition.

An optional scheme is available for registered traders having an annual turnover of taxable supplies not exceeding £350,000. Such traders may, if they wish, render returns annually. Nine equal payments of VAT will be paid on account, with a final balancing payment accompanying submission of the return.

BAD DEBTS

Many retailers operate special retail schemes for calculating the amount of VAT due. These schemes are, broadly, based on the volume of consideration received in an accounting period. Should a customer fail to pay for goods or services supplied, there will be no consideration on which VAT falls to be calculated.

To avoid the problem of bad debts incurred by traders not operating a special retail scheme, an optional system of cash accounting is available. This scheme, confined to traders with annual taxable supplies not exceeding £350,000, enables returns to be made on a cash basis, in substitution for the normal supply basis. Traders using such a scheme will not, of course, include bad debts in the calculation of cash receipts.

Where neither the cash accounting arrangements nor the special retail scheme applies, output tax falls due on the value of the supply and liability is not affected by failure to receive consideration. However, where a debt is more than six months old and is written off in the supplier's books, relief for bad debts will be forthcoming.

OTHER SPECIAL SCHEMES

In addition to the schemes for retailers, there are several special schemes applied to calculate the amount of VAT due and which also limit the ability to recover input tax. Before 1 January 1995 these schemes were confined to a limited range of goods, but on and after this date virtually all second-hand goods have been brought within special margin schemes.

FARMERS

Farmers may elect to apply a special flat rate scheme. This scheme is available to farmers who are not registered traders. Under the scheme a flat-rate addition of 4 per cent may be made on sales, with the amount of the addition being retained by the farmer. Registered traders to whom such a supply is made may treat the 4 per cent addition as recoverable input tax.

Legal Notes

IMPORTANT

The purpose of these notes is to outline some of the more common parts of the law as they may affect the average person. They are believed to be correct at the time of going to press. However, the law is constantly developing and changing, and it is always best to take expert advice. Anyone who does not have a solicitor already and is unable to find one through the recommendation of a friend, can contact the Citizens' Advice Bureau (addresses from the telephone directory or any post office or town hall). Each CAB has a list of solicitors in the area who deal with particular types of problem. Alternatively, assistance can be sought from The Law Society, 113 Chancery Lane, London WC2A 1PL or The Law Society of Scotland, 26 Drumsheugh Gardens, Edinburgh EH3 7YR.

The legal aid and legal advice and assistance schemes exist to make the help of the trained lawyer available to those who would not otherwise be able to afford legal advice. The best policy is to go to a solicitor without delay; timely advice will set your mind at rest but sitting on your rights can mean that you lose them.

It is not necessary for a dispute to have arisen before advice is sought from a solicitor; the legal advice and assistance scheme enables a solicitor to advise you on your rights, for instance under a tenancy agreement, the estate of a deceased person or in connection with matrimonial and consumer matters, and to write letters or take other steps on your behalf. Entitlement to take advantage of the scheme depends on your means (*see* pages 673–5) but a solicitor or Citizens' Advice Bureau will be able to advise about entitlement.

BRITISH CITIZENSHIP

There are three types of citizenship: British Citizenship; Citizenship of the British Dependent Territories; and British Overseas Citizenship.

Acquisition of citizenship on change of law

The British Nationality Act 1981 which came into force on 1 January 1983 made substantial changes to the law of citizenship, which before that date did not distinguish between the three types of citizenship referred to above. Almost all persons who were then both citizens of the UK and colonies and who had a right of abode in the UK became British citizens when the Act came into force. Most UK and colonies citizens who did not have a right of abode in the UK became Citizens of the British Dependent Territories. This type of citizenship was, broadly speaking, conferred on citizens of the UK and colonies by birth, naturalization or registration in dependent territories. Dependent territories include Bermuda, Gibraltar, St Helena and its dependencies, and the British Virgin Islands. Any UK and colonies citizen who, on 1 January 1983, did not acquire either British or British Dependent Territories Citizenship became a British Overseas Citizen. In 1985 citizens of the Falklands Islands became British citizens.

Hong Kong ceases to be a British Dependent Territory when it passes to China on 1 July 1997. A person at that date who but for a connection with Hong Kong would not be a British Dependent Territories Citizen will lose his/her citizenship. Such people may apply to register as British Nationals (Overseas). This does not carry the right of abode in the UK. However, the British Nationality (Hong Kong) Act 1990 provides a scheme which operates by way of a points system whereby those who qualify may register as British citizens.

Later acquisition of British citizenship

British citizenship is acquired automatically by those born in the UK (including, for this purpose, the Channel Islands and the Isle of Man) who have a parent who is a British citizen or a parent who is settled in the UK. Certain other categories of children born in the UK also acquire this type of citizenship, i.e. foundlings, those whose parents subsequently settle in the UK, those who live in the UK for ten years from birth and those adopted in the UK.

A person born outside the UK may acquire British citizenship in the following ways:

(a) if one of his/her parents is a British citizen otherwise than by descent, e.g. parent was born in the UK

(b) if one of his/her parents is a British citizen serving the Crown overseas

(c) if the Secretary of State consents to his/her registration while he/she is a minor

(d) if he/she is a Citizen of the British Dependent Territories, a British Overseas Citizen, a British subject or a British Protected Person (these last two are residual categories of people who have not acquired one of the three types of citizenship) and has been lawfully resident in the UK for five years without any time restriction

(e) if he/she is a British Dependent Territories Citizen who is a national of the UK for the purposes of the EU (i.e. a Gibraltarian)

(f) if he/she is naturalized. Naturalization may be applied for only by adults and the Secretary of State has a discretion whether to permit it. The basic requirements are five years' residence, good character, sufficient knowledge of the English or Welsh language, and an intention to reside in the UK permanently. The requirements are somewhat less restrictive in the case of an applicant who is married to a British citizen

Where parents are married the status of either may confer citizenship on their child. If a child is illegitimate, the status of the mother only determines the child's citizenship.

Acquisition of British Dependent Territories and British Overseas Citizenship after the Act

These citizenships are intended for persons connected with certain Commonwealth countries other than the UK. In the case of dependent territories the rules are very similar to those for acquiring British citizenship, except that the connection is with the dependent territory rather than with the UK. British Overseas Citizenship may be acquired by the wife and minor children of a British Overseas Citizen in certain circumstances.

Retention of nationality by persons born in or who are citizens of the Republic of Ireland

By the Ireland Act 1949, a person who was born before 6 December 1922 in what is now the Republic of Ireland (Eire) and was a British subject immediately before 1 January 1949, is not deemed to have ceased to be a British subject unless either he/she (a) was domiciled in the Irish Free State on 6 December 1922, (b) was on or after 10 April 1935 and before 1 January 1949 permanently resident there, or (c) had before 1 January 1949 been registered as a citizen of Eire under the laws of that country.

In addition, by the British Nationality Act 1948, any citizen of Eire who immediately before 1 January 1949 was also a British subject can retain that status by submitting at any time a claim to the Home Secretary on any of the following grounds:

(a) he/she has been in the service of the UK government
(b) he/she holds a British passport issued in the UK or in any colony, protectorate, UK mandated or trust territory
(c) he/she has associations by way of descent, residence or otherwise with any such place
(d) on complying with similar legislation in any of the 'dominions'

The British Nationality Act 1981 provides that persons who have made a claim may continue to be British subjects. Any citizen of Eire who was a British subject before 1 January 1949 and who has not yet made a claim may do so provided that:

(a) he/she is or has been in Crown service under the UK government
(b) he/she has associations by way of descent, residence or otherwise with the UK or any dependent territory

Renunciation and resumption

A person may cease to be a British citizen by renouncing his/her citizenship (with the consent of the Secretary of State in wartime). The renunciation is required to be registered with the Secretary of State and will be revoked if no new citizenship or nationality is acquired within six months. If renounced, citizenship may be reacquired once if the renunciation was necessary to retain or acquire some other citizenship or nationality. Similar rules as to renunciation and reacquisition apply in the case of British Dependent Territories Citizenships and of renunciation (but not reacquisition) in the case of British Overseas Citizenship.

Status of aliens

Property may be held by an alien in the same manner as by a natural-born British subject, but he/she may not hold public office, exercise the franchise or own a British ship or aircraft. The Republic of Ireland Act 1949 declares that the Republic, though not part of HM Dominions, is not a foreign country, and any reference in an Act of Parliament to foreigners, aliens, foreign countries, etc., shall be construed accordingly.

European Union Nationals

As a member of the European Union, UK citizens are also EU citizens and entitled to travel freely to other Eu countries to work, study, reside and become established in self-employment.

CONSUMER LAW

THE SUPPLY OF GOODS AND SERVICES

(1) The Sale of Goods Act 1979 provides protection to the purchaser of goods, by implying certain terms into every contract for the sale of goods. These implied terms are:

(a) A condition that the seller will pass good title to the buyer (unless the seller agrees to transfer only such title as he or his principal has) and warranties that the goods will be free from undisclosed encumbrances, and that the buyer will enjoy quiet possession of the goods.
(b) Where there is a sale of goods by description, a condition that the goods will correspond with that description, and where the sale is by sample and description, a condition that the bulk of the goods shall correspond with both sample and description.
(c) Where the seller sells goods in the course of a business, a condition that the goods will be of satisfactory quality, unless before the contract is made, the buyer has examined the goods and ought to have noticed the defect, bearing in mind the purchaser's knowledge of the goods and the extent of the examination, or unless the seller has specifically drawn the attention of the buyer to the defect. Goods are of satisfactory quality if they meet the standard that a reasonable person would regard as satisfactory taking account of any description of the goods, the price if relevant, and all the other relevant circumstances. The quality of the goods includes their state and condition, relevant aspects being whether the goods are fit for all the purposes for which goods of the kind in question are commonly supplied, their appearance and finish, their freedom from minor defects, their safety, and their durability.
(d) A condition that where the seller sells goods in the course of a business, the goods are reasonably fit for any purpose made known to the seller by the buyer, unless the buyer does not rely on the seller's skill and judgment, or it would be unreasonable for him to do so.
(e) Where there is a sale of goods by sample, conditions that the bulk of the goods shall correspond with the sample in quality, that the buyer will have a reasonable opportunity of comparing the bulk with the sample, and that the goods are free from any defect rendering them unmerchantable, which would not be apparent from the sample.

For these purposes, the broad difference between a condition and a warranty is that the remedy for a breach of an implied condition may enable the buyer to reject the goods and recover damages if he has suffered loss, whereas the remedy for a breach of warranty will only enable the buyer to recover damages.

It is possible for a seller to exclude some of the above terms from a contract, subject to restrictions imposed by the Unfair Contract Terms Act 1977 as given below. These restrictions give more protection where the buyer 'deals as consumer'. In a contract of sale of goods, a buyer 'deals as consumer' where there is a sale by a seller in the course of a business, where the goods are of a type ordinarily bought for private use or consumption, and where the goods are sold to a person who does not buy or hold himself out as buying them in the course of a business. A buyer in a sale by auction or competitive tender never 'deals as consumer'.

The 1977 Act prohibits the exclusion of the implied terms given in (b) to (e) above, where the buyer 'deals as consumer'. In sales where the buyer does not 'deal as consumer', terms purporting to exclude these implied terms may be relied upon only to the extent that it would be reasonable to allow reliance. The Act provides guidelines for determining whether it would be reasonable to allow reliance. The implied terms in (a) above cannot be excluded whether the buyer 'deals as consumer' or not.

(2) Similar terms to those implied in contracts of sale of goods are implied into contracts of hire-purchase by the Supply of Goods (Implied Terms) Act 1973, and the 1977 Act limits the exclusion of these implied terms in a similar manner.

(3) Under the Supply of Goods and Services Act 1982, terms similar to those in the Sale of Goods Act relating to quiet possession, compliance with description, satisfactory quality, fitness for purpose and correspondence with sample are implied into other types of contract under which ownership of goods passes (e.g. a contract for 'work and materials' such as a supply of new parts during the servicing of a motor car) and also into contracts for the hire of goods. In the case of contracts under which ownership of goods is to pass, there is also an implied condition as to title.

The 1977 Act limits the exclusion of these implied terms in a similar manner to the implied terms in the Sale of Goods Act.

(4) The Supply of Goods and Services Act 1982 also implies into a contract for the supply of services terms that the supplier will use reasonable care and skill, carry out the service within a reasonable time (unless the time is agreed) and make a reasonable charge (unless the charge is agreed).

(5) The Unfair Terms in Consumer Contracts Regulations 1994 apply to contracts between business sellers or suppliers of goods or services and consumers, where any term has not been individually negotiated, i.e. where the term has been drafted in advance and the consumer has not been able to influence its substance.

An unfair term is one which, contrary to the requirement of good faith, causes a significant imbalance in the parties' rights and obligations under the contract to the detriment of the consumer. This is assessed taking into account the nature of the goods or services, the surrounding circumstances and all the other terms of the contract. An unfair term does not bind the consumer, but the contract continues to bind the parties if it is capable of existing without the unfair term. In assessing 'good faith', regard is had to the bargaining strength of the parties, whether the consumer had an inducement to agree to the term, whether goods were sold or supplied to the consumer's special order, and the extent to which the dealings were fair and equitable. Fairness of certain terms is disregarded, provided they are in plain intelligible language, namely terms defining the main subject matter of the contract or the adequacy of the price or remuneration.

The Regulations contain a non-exhaustive list of terms which are regarded as unfair, e.g. where the agreement inappropriately limits the consumer's legal rights in the event of total or partial non-performance or inadequate performance, or where the agreement irrevocably binds the consumer to terms with which he had no real opportunity to become acquainted before the contract was made.

(6) The Trade Descriptions Act 1968 provides that it is a criminal offence for a trader or businessman to apply a false trade description to any goods, or to supply or offer to supply any goods to which a false trade description has been applied. A trade description includes a description as to quantity, size, method, place and date of manufacture, other history, composition, other physical characteristics, fitness for purpose, behaviour or accuracy, testing or approval. It is also an offence to give a false indication as to the price of goods. Prosecutions are brought by trading standards inspectors.

(7) The Fair Trading Act 1973 is also designed to protect the consumer. It provides for the appointment of a Director-General of Fair Trading, whose duties include keeping under review commercial activities in the UK relating to the supply of goods or services to consumers, and collecting information to discover practices that may adversely affect the economic interests of the consumer. He may refer certain consumer trade practices to the Consumer Protection Advisory Committee, or of his own initiative take proceedings against firms that are trading unfairly. He may also publish information and advice to consumers. Examples of practices which have been prohibited by virtue of references made under this Act include the use of certain void exclusion clauses in contracts for the sale of goods and hire-purchase, and advertisements by traders appearing to sell as private persons.

(8) The Consumer Protection Act 1987 makes the producer of a product liable for any damage exceeding £275 caused by a defect in that product, subject to certain defences.

(9) The Consumer Protection (Cancellation of Contracts Concluded Away from Business Premises) Regulations 1987 allow consumers a seven-day period in which to cancel most contracts for supply of goods or services exceeding £35 in cost, where these contracts have been made following an unsolicited visit to the consumer's home or workplace.

Scotland

The Sale of Goods Act 1979 applies with some modification to Scotland. It has been amended by the Sale and Supply of Goods Act 1994. For example, it is not necessary in Scotland to distinguish between the words condition and warranty. The remedies for the buyer in both cases are the same, i.e. the buyer can either within a reasonable time reject the goods and treat the contract as repudiated, or retain the goods and treat the failure to perform such material part as a breach which may give rise to a claim for compensation or damages. The 1994 Act introduces the concept of an implied term of 'satisfactory quality', replacing the former 'merchantable quality' test.

The Trade Descriptions Act 1968 applies with minor modifications to Scotland. Although the Supply of Goods and Services Act 1982 does not extend to Scotland, certain of its provisions are introduced by virtue of the Sale and Supply of Goods Act 1994.

CONSUMER CREDIT

The Consumer Credit Act 1974 provides a system for the protection of the consumer, of licensing and control of all matters relating to the provision of credit or to the supply of goods on hire or hire-purchase, administered by the Director-General of Fair Trading. A licence is required to carry on a consumer credit or consumer hire business, or to deal in credit brokerage, debt adjusting, counselling or collecting, for which group licences are available. Any 'fit' person may apply to the Director-General of Fair Trading for a licence, which is normally renewable after ten years. A licence is not necessary if such types of business are only transacted 'occasionally' or if exempt agreements only are involved.

For the Act's provisions to apply, the agreement must be 'regulated', i.e. be to individuals or partnerships only; must not be exempt, e.g. certain loans by local authorities or building societies; and the total credit must not exceed £15,000. The terms of a regulated agreement can be varied by the creditor, but only if the agreement gives him the right to do so and the debtor receives notice in the prescribed form.

To be enforceable the agreement must be properly executed, and the specified information must be given during the antecedent negotiations for the contract. These are conducted by the creditor, credit broker or supplier (these being the creditor's agents) and begin when the parties first begin discussions.

The agreement must state certain information such as the amount of credit, the annual percentage rate of interest, and the amount and timing of repayments.

An agreement is cancellable under the Act if oral representations were made in the debtor's presence during antecedent negotiations and the debtor signed the agreement other than at the creditor's (or credit-broker's or negotiator's) place of business. Time for cancellation expires five clear days after the debtor receives a second copy of the agreement. The agreement must inform the debtor of his right to cancel and how to cancel.

Where there are arrangements or connections between the creditor and supplier, the former is generally liable for any misrepresentation or breach of contract by the latter, and will thus be liable to indemnify the debtor.

If the debtor is in arrears or is otherwise in breach of the agreement, the creditor may not enforce the agreement, e.g. by repossessing goods, without serving a default notice on the debtor. This notice will give the debtor a chance to remedy the default. Even if the default is not remedied by the debtor, if the agreement is a hire-purchase or conditional sale agreement, the creditor cannot repossess the goods without an order of the court if the debtor has paid one-third of the total price of the goods.

Where the agreement requires the debtor to make grossly exorbitant payments or grossly contravenes the ordinary principles of fair dealing, the court can reopen it either at the debtor's request or during enforcement proceedings and (*inter alia*) alter the terms of the contract or set aside any obligations it imposes so as to do justice between the parties. Whether an agreement is such an extortionate credit bargain is decided by reference (*inter alia*) to interest rates prevailing at the date of agreement, the pressure for finance the debtor was under, etc.

If a credit reference agency was used to check the debtor's financial standing the creditor must give the agency's name to the debtor, who is entitled to see the agency's file on him/her on payment of a fee of £1.

Scotland

The Consumer Credit Act also extends to Scotland and goes far in assimilating the Scots law on this topic with English law. The Supply of Goods (Implied Terms) Act 1973 also applies to Scotland. Parts II and III only of the Unfair Contract Terms Act 1977 apply to Scotland.

RECEIPTS

The law on receipts in Scotland is governed by the Prescription and Limitations (Scotland) Act 1973, which for this purpose came into force on 25 July 1976. Receipts need only be kept for a period of five years and if a creditor does not make a relevant claim within that period no action can be raised.

THE CROWN – PROCEEDINGS AGAINST

Before 1947, proceedings against the Crown were generally possible only by a procedure known as a petition of right, which placed the litigant at a considerable disadvantage. However, the Crown Proceedings Act 1947, which came into operation on 1 January 1948, places the Crown, in its public capacity, largely in the same position as a subject, although some procedural disadvantages remain, e.g. the enforcement of judgments against the Crown.

Scotland

The 1947 Act as amended extends to Scotland and has the effect of bringing the practice of the two countries as closely together as the different legal systems will permit. While formerly actions against the Crown, when permissible, were confined to the Court of Session, proceedings may now be brought in the Sheriff Court.

The Act lays down that arrestment of money in the hands of the Crown or of a government department is competent in any case where arrestment in the hands of a subject would have been competent, but an exception is made in respect of National Savings Bank deposits. Section 2 (1) of the Law Reform (Miscellaneous Provisions) (Scotland) Act 1966 removes the privilege whereby the wages of Crown servants, other than serving members of the armed forces, are exempt from arrestment in execution.

DEATHS

REGISTRATION
(For Certificates, *see* page 663)

England and Wales

When a death takes place, information of it must be given in person to the local Registrar of Births and Deaths, and the register signed in his/her presence by a relative of the deceased present at the death or in attendance during the last illness; or by some other relative of the deceased; in default of any relatives by (a) a person present at the death, or the occupier of the house in which the death happened, or (b) an inmate of the house, or (c) the person arranging the disposal of the body.

The registration must be made within five days of the death, or within the same time written notice of the death must be sent to the Registrar. If the deceased was attended during his/her last illness by a registered medical practitioner, a certificate of cause of death must be sent by the doctor to the Registrar. The doctor must give to the informant of the death a written notice of the signing of the certificate, which must be delivered to the Registrar.

If the death is not registered within five days (or 14 days if written notice of the occurrence of the death is sent to him/her), the Registrar may require any one of the above-mentioned persons to attend to register at a stated time and place. Failure to comply involves a penalty. The registration of a death is free of charge. After 12 months no death can be registered without the Registrar-General's consent.

Whenever the death of a child is registered, particulars of the name and occupation of the mother are to be entered in the register.

It is essential that a certificate for disposal should be obtained from the Registrar before the funeral or cremation. No fee is chargeable for this certificate. A body must not be disposed of until either the Registrar has given a certificate to the effect that he/she has registered or received notice of the death, or until the Coroner has made a disposal order.

A person disposing of a body must within 96 hours deliver to the Registrar a notification as to the date, place, and means of the disposal of the body.

Still births: see page 663.

Death at sea: the master of a British ship must record any death on board and send particulars to the Registrar-General of Shipping.

Death abroad: consular officers are authorized to register deaths of British subjects occurring abroad. Certificates are obtainable at the Registrar-General's Office, London. If the deceased was of Scottish domicile, particulars are sent to the Registrar-General for Scotland.

With regard to the registration of deaths of members of the armed forces and deaths occurring on HM ships and aircraft, *see* the Registration of Births, etc. Act 1957.

Scotland

The Registration of Births, Deaths and Marriages (Scotland) Act 1965 supersedes provisions in former Acts.

Personal notification within eight days must be given to the Registrar of either the registration district in which the death took place, or any registration district in which the deceased was ordinarily resident immediately before his/her death. When a body is found and the place of death is not known, notification must be given to the Registrar of either the registration district in which the body was found or any other registration district appropriate by virtue of the preceding sentence. When a person dies (in or out of Scotland) in a ship, aircraft or land vehicle during a journey and the body is conveyed therein to any place in Scotland the death shall, unless the Registrar-General otherwise directs, be deemed to have occurred at that place.

The register must be signed in the presence of the Registrar by one of the following: (a) any relative of the deceased; (b) any person present at the death; (c) the deceased's executor or other legal representative; (d) the occupier, at the time of the death, of the premises where the death took place; (e) if these fail, any other person having knowledge of the particulars to be registered. Failure to comply involves a penalty.

The medical practitioner who attended the deceased during the last illness must sign a certificate of the cause of death within seven days. If there is no such medical practitioner, any medical practitioner who is able to do so may sign the certificate. At the time of registering the death the Registrar shall, without charge, give the informant a certificate of registration, and the person to whom the certificate is given must hand it to the undertaker before cremation. A body may, however, be interred before the death is registered, in which case the undertaker must deliver a certificate of burial to the Registrar within three days.

BURIAL

The duty of burial is placed on the deceased person's executors (if any appointed); it is also a recognized obligation of the parent of a child, and of a householder where the body lies. Funeral expenses of a reasonable amount will be repayable out of the deceased's estate in priority to any other claims. Directions as to place and mode of burial are frequently contained in the deceased's will, in some memorandum placed with private papers, or may have been communicated verbally to a relative. Consequently, steps should immediately be taken to ascertain the deceased's wishes from the above sources. If the wishes are considered objectionable, they are not necessarily enforceable; legal advice should be taken. A person may legally leave directions for the anatomical examination of his/her body. As to the place of burial, the parish churchyard is the normal burying place for parishioners or any person dying in the parish, but nowadays this will apply only in villages and smaller towns. In populous districts cemeteries and crematoria have been established and burials will take place there in accordance with the regulations. For an exclusive right to a burial space in the churchyard, a faculty is required from the Ecclesiastical Court. Poor persons may be buried at the public expense by the local authority. As to the necessity for obtaining a Registrar's certificate or authority from the Coroner for disposal, *see* above.

CREMATION

Under the Cremation Acts 1902 and 1952, regulations are made by the Home Secretary dealing fully with the cremation of a body, disposal of ashes, etc., and containing numerous safeguards.

If cremation is desired it is advisable for instructions to be left in writing to that effect. However, in Scotland, even if the deceased wished his/her body to be cremated or anatomically dissected, relatives can still veto his/her wishes.

To arrange for cremation, the executor or near relative should instruct the undertaker to that effect and obtain from him the forms required by statute.

INTESTACY

Where a person dies intestate on or after 15 March 1977, the position is governed by the Administration of Estates Act 1925, as amended by the Intestates' Estates Act 1952, the Family Provision Act 1966 and Orders made thereunder. If the intestate leaves a spouse and issue, the spouse takes:

(a) the 'personal chattels'
(b) £125,000 with interest at 6 per cent from death until payment
(c) a life interest in half of the rest of the estate

This life interest can be capitalized at the option of the spouse. Personal chattels are articles of household use or ornament (including motor cars), not used for business purposes. The rest of the estate goes to the issue.

If the intestate leaves a spouse and no issue, but leaves a parent or brother or sister of the whole blood or issue of such brothers and sisters the spouse takes

(a) the 'personal chattels'
(b) £200,000 with interest at 6 per cent from death until payment
(c) half of the rest of the estate absolutely

The other half of the rest of the estate goes to the parents, equally if more than one, or, if none, to the brothers and sisters of the whole blood or issue of such brothers and sisters.

If the intestate leaves a spouse, but no issue, no parents and no brothers or sisters of the whole blood or their issue, the spouse takes the whole estate absolutely.

If resident therein at the intestate's death, the surviving spouse may generally require the personal representatives to appropriate the interest of the intestate in the matrimonial home in or towards satisfaction of any absolute interest of the spouse, including the capitalized value of a life interest. In certain cases, leave of court is required. On a partial intestacy any benefit (other than personal chattels specifically bequeathed) received by the surviving spouse under the will must be brought into account against the statutory legacy of £125,000 or £200,000, as the case may be. If there is no surviving spouse, the estate is distributed among those who survive the intestate in the following order (those entitled under earlier numbers taking to the exclusion of those entitled under later numbers):

(1) children
(2) father or mother (equally, if both alive)
(3) brothers and sisters of the whole blood
(4) brothers and sisters of the half blood
(5) grandparents (equally, if more than one alive)
(6) uncles and aunts of the whole blood
(7) uncles and aunts of the half blood
(8) the Crown, Duchy of Lancaster or the Duke of Cornwall

In cases (1), (3), (4), (6) and (7), the persons entitled lose their interests unless they not only survive the intestate but also attain 18 or marry under that age, their shares going to the persons (if any) within the same group who do attain 18 or marry. Moreover, in the same cases, succession is not per capita, but *per stirpes*, i.e. by stocks or families. Thus, if the intestate leaves one child and two grandchildren, being the children of a child of the intestate who predeceased the intestate, the two grandchildren represent their deceased parent and take between them one-half of the issue's share, the remaining half going to the surviving child. Similarly, nephews and nieces represent a deceased brother, and so on.

When the deceased died partially intestate (i.e. leaving a will which disposed of only part of his/her property), the above rules apply to the intestate part.

Children must bring into account (hotchpot) any substantial advances received from the intestate during his/her lifetime before claiming any further share under the intestacy. Special hotchpot provisions apply to partial intestacy.

In respect of deaths occurring on or after 4 April 1988, Section 18 of the Family Law Reform Act 1987 provides that references to any relationship between two persons shall, unless the contrary intention appears, be construed without regard to whether or not the father and mother of either of them, or the father and mother of any person through whom the relationship is deduced, have or had been married to each other at any time.

In respect of deaths after March 1976 the provisions of the Inheritance (Provision for Family and Dependants) Act 1975 may allow other persons to claim provision out of the estate. *See* page 659.

Significant changes to the above provisions may occur in 1996 if the Law Reform (Succession) Bill is passed.

For personal application for probate or letters of administration, *see* page 660.

Scotland

The Succession (Scotland) Act 1964, provides that the whole estate of any person dying intestate shall devolve without distinction between heritable and moveable property. By that Act the surviving spouse of an intestate may, as a prior right (in addition to legal rights, *see* below), claim the matrimonial home to a maximum of £110,000, or a choice of one matrimonial home if more than one (or in certain circumstances the value thereof), with its furniture and plenishings not exceeding £20,000 in value, plus the sum of £30,000 if the deceased left issue or, if no issue, the sum of £50,000. These figures have applied since 26 November 1993 and may be increased from time to time by order of the Secretary of State.

The fact that a person was born illegitimate no longer has any effect in their rights of succession as against a legitimate child, by virtue of the Law Reform (Parent and Child) (Scotland) Act 1986.

Legal rights, referred to above, are:

Jus relicti(ae) – the right of a surviving spouse to one half of the deceased's net moveable estate after satisfaction of prior rights if there are no surviving children, or to one-third if there are any surviving children

Legitim – the right of surviving children to one-half of the net moveable estate of deceased parents if no surviving spouse, or one-third of the net moveable estate of deceased parents after satisfaction of prior rights where there is a surviving spouse.

There are no legal rights in heritage.

In general, the lines of succession are:
(1) descendants
(2) collaterals

(3) ascendants and their collaterals, and so on in the ascending scale

The Crown is *ultimus haeres*

The right of representation, i.e. the right of the issue of a person who would have succeeded if he/she had survived the intestate, is open to any line of succession where previously it was limited to apply only when there were next of kin or the issue of predeceasing next of kin. The surviving mother of an intestate now has equal rights of succession with the surviving father, where formerly these were restricted. The intestate's maternal relations, who prior to the Act had no rights of succession, are now on an equal footing with the paternal relations. Where the intestate is survived only by parents and by brothers and sisters (collaterals), half of the estate is taken by the parents and the other half by the brothers and sisters, those of the whole blood being preferred to those of the half blood. Where, however, succession opens to collaterals (which expression can include the brothers and sisters of an ancestor of the intestate) of the half blood, they shall rank equally amongst themselves, whether related to the intestate (or his/her ancestor) through their father or their mother.

WILLS

The following notes and those on intestacy must be read subject to the provisions of the Inheritance (Provision for Family and Dependants) Act 1975, which can affect the estate of anyone dying domiciled in England and Wales after March 1976. Very broadly, a spouse, former spouse who has not remarried, a child of the deceased or one treated by the deceased as a child of his/her family, or any person maintained by him/her at his/her death may apply to the Court under the Act. If the Court thinks that the will or the law of intestacy or both do not make reasonable provision for the applicant, it may order payment out of the net estate of maintenance or a lump sum. It may also order the transfer of property or vary certain trusts, and the powers can affect property disposed of by the deceased in his/her lifetime intending to defeat the Act. It is up to the applicant to take the initiative, and the application must generally be made within six months of the grant of probate or letters of administration.

MAKING A WILL

Every person over the age of 18 should make a will. However small the estate, the rules of intestacy (*see* above) may not reflect a person's wishes as to his/her property. In any case a will can do more than just deal with property. It can in particular appoint executors, give directions as to the disposal of the body and appoint guardians to take care of children in the event of the parents' death. For the wealthier person an appropriately drawn will can operate to reduce the burden of inheritance tax.

It is considered desirable for a will to be properly drawn up by a solicitor. Although normally the making of a will is not one of the services which can be provided under the legal advice and assistance scheme, it can be provided for certain special categories of person such as the aged and infirm.

In no circumstances should one person prepare a will for another person where the former is to take any benefit under it. This can easily lead to a suggestion of undue influence, which may cause the will to be held bad.

Assuming a lawyer is not employed, a person having resolved to make a will must remember that it is only after a person is dead and cannot explain his/her meaning that his/her will can be open to dispute. It is the more necessary, therefore, to express what is meant in language of the utmost clarity, avoiding the use of any word or expression that admits of another meaning than the one intended. Avoid the use of legal terms, such as heirs and issue, when the same thing may be expressed in plain language. If in writing the will a mistake is made, it is better to rewrite the whole. Before a will is executed (*see* below), an alteration may be made by striking through the words with a pen, but opposite to such alteration the testator and witnesses should write their names or place their initials. Never scratch out a word with a knife or other instrument; no alteration of any kind whatever must be made after the will is executed. If the testator afterwards wishes to change the disposition of his/her estate, it is best to make a new will, revoking the old one. The use of codicils should be left to a lawyer.

A will should be written in ink and very legibly, on a single sheet of paper. Although forms of wills must vary to suit different cases, the following forms may be found useful to those who, in cases of emergency, are called upon to draw up wills, either for themselves or others. Nothing more complicated should be attempted. The forms should be studied in conjunction with the following notes:

This is the last will and testament of me [*Thomas Smith*] of [*Vine Cottage, Silver Street, Reading, Berks*] which I make this [*thirteenth*] day of [*February* 1996] and whereby I revoke all previous wills and testamentary dispositions.

1. I hereby appoint [*John Green of* _____ *and Richard Brown of* _____] to be the executor(s) of this my will.

2. I give all my property real and personal to [*my wife Mary* or *my sons John and David equally* or as the case may be].

Signed by the testator in the presence of us both present at the same time who, at his request, in his presence and in the presence of each other have hereunto set our names as witnesses.

Thomas Smith
Signature of Testator;

William Jones (*signed*)
of Green Gables, South Street, Reading, tailor.

Henry Morgan (*signed*)
of 16 North Street, Reading, butcher.

Should it be desired to give legacies and/or gifts of specific property, instead of giving the whole estate to one or more persons, the form above should be used with the substitution for clause 2 of the following clauses:

2. I give to _____ of _____ the sum of £_____ and to _____ of _____ the sum of £_____ and to _____ of _____ all my books [*or as the case may require*].

3. All the residue of my property real and personal I give to _____ of _____ .

Terms

Real property includes freehold land and houses, while personal property includes debts due, arrears of rents, money, leasehold property, house furniture, goods, assurance policies, stocks and shares in companies, and the like. The words 'my money', apart from the context, will normally only include actual real money. The expression 'goods and chattels' should not be used. In giving particular property, ordinary language is sufficient, e.g. my house, Vine Cottage, Silver Street, Reading, Berks. Such specific gifts fail if the property is not owned by the testator at his/her death.

Residuary legatees

It is well in all cases where legacies or specific gifts are made, to leave to some person or persons 'the residue of my property', although it may be thought that the whole of the property has been disposed of in legacies, etc., already mentioned in the will. It should be remembered that a will can only take effect with regard to property owned at the date of death and that any gift of property not owned at the date of death will fail.

Execution of a will, and witnesses

The testator should sign his/her name at the foot or end of the will, in the presence of two witnesses, who will immediately afterwards sign their names in the testator's and in each other's presence. A person who has been left any gift or share of residue in the will, or whose wife or husband has been left such a gift, should not be an attesting witness. Their attestation would be good, but they would forfeit the gift. It is better that a person named as executor should not be a witness. Husband and wife may both be witnesses, provided neither is a legatee. If a solicitor be appointed executor, it is lawful to direct that his/her ordinary fees and charges shall be paid; but in this case the solicitor (as an interested party) must not be a witness to the will.

It is desirable that the witnesses should be fully described, as they may possibly be wanted at some future time. If the testator should be too ill to sign, even by a mark, another person may sign the testator's name to the will for him/her, in his/her presence and by his/her direction, and in this case it should be shown that the testator knew the contents of the document. The attestation clause should therefore be worded:

Signed by Thomas Brown, by the direction and in the presence of the testator, Thomas Smith, in the joint presence of us, who thereupon signed our names in his presence and in the presence of each other, the will having been first read over to the testator, who appeared fully to understand the same.

Where there is any suspicion that the testator is not, by reason of age or infirmity, fully in command of his/her faculties it is desirable to ask his/her doctor to act as a witness (*see* Testamentary capacity, page 660).

A blind person may make a will in braille. If the testator is blind the will should be read aloud to him/her in the presence of the witnesses, and the fact mentioned in the attestation clause. A blind person cannot witness a will.

If by inadvertence the testator should have signed his/her will without the witnesses being present, then the attestation should be: 'The testator acknowledged his signature already made as his signature to his last will and testament, in the joint presence,' etc. Any omission in the observance of these details may invalidate the will. The stringency of the law as to signature and witnessing of a will is only relaxed in favour of soldiers, sailors and airmen in certain circumstances.

Executors

There is no restriction on the number of executors who can be appointed; it is usual to appoint two executors, although one is sufficient. The name and address of each executor should be given in full. An executor may be a legatee. Thus a child of full age or wife to whom the whole or a portion of the estate is left may be appointed sole executor, or one of two executors. The addresses of the executors are not essential, but it is desirable here as elsewhere, to avoid ambiguity or vagueness.

Lapsed legacies

If a legatee dies in the lifetime of the testator, the legacy generally lapses and falls into the residue. Where a residuary legatee predeceases the testator, his/her share of the residuary estate will not generally pass to the other residuary legatees, but will pass to the persons entitled on the deceased's intestacy. In all such cases it is desirable to make a new will.

An important exception to the general rule of lapse stated above is contained in section 33 of the Wills Act as amended, where there is a gift to a child or remoter issue of the testator who dies before the testator leaving issue who survive the testator. In such a case the gift will pass to the issue of the deceased child.

Testamentary capacity

A person under the age of 18 cannot make a will (except for soldiers, sailors and airmen in exceptional circumstances).

So far as mental capacity is concerned the testator must be able to understand and appreciate the nature and effect of making a will, the property of which he/she can dispose and the claims to which he/she ought to give effect. If a person is not mentally able to make a will, provision exists (under the Mental Health Act 1983) for the Court to do this for him/her.

REVOCATION

A later will revokes an earlier will if it expressly says so, or is completely inconsistent with it. Otherwise the earlier one is revoked only in so far as it is inconsistent with the later one. A will may also be revoked by burning, tearing or otherwise destroying the will with the intention of revoking it. Such destruction must either be by the testator or by some other person in the testator's presence and at his/her direction. It is not sufficient to obliterate the will with a pen. Marriage in every case acts as the revocation of a will, except that under the Administration of Justice Act 1982, there is a provision to the effect that if it appears from a will that at the time it was made the testator was expecting to be married to a particular person and that he/she intended that the will (or a disposition in the will) should not be revoked by the marriage to that person, the will will not be revoked by marriage to that person. The Act also provides that where after a testator has made a will the testator's marriage is terminated by a decree of divorce or nullity, any gift to a spouse shall lapse and any appointment of the spouse as executor shall be omitted from the will unless the will shows a contrary intention.

PROBATE OR LETTERS OF ADMINISTRATION

Application for probate or for letters of administration may be made in person at the Personal Application Department of the Principal Registry of the Family Division, a district probate registry or sub-registry, or a probate office, by the executors or persons entitled to a grant of administration. Applicants should bring (a) the will, if any; (b) a certificate of death; (c) particulars of all property and assets left by the deceased; and (d) a list of debts and funeral expenses.

Intending applicants, before attending at a registry or probate office, should write or telephone to the nearest probate registry or sub-registry for the necessary forms. Postal or telephone applications cannot be dealt with at the local probate offices, which are part-time only.

Certain property can be disposed of on death without a grant of probate or administration, or in pursuance of a nomination made by the deceased, provided the amount involved does not exceed £5,000. (See The Administration of Estates (Small Payments) Act 1965.)

WHERE TO FIND A PROVED WILL

A will proved since 1858 must have been proved either at the Principal Registry at Somerset House, or a district registry. In the former case the original will itself is preserved at Somerset House, the copy of which probate has been granted is in the hands of the executors who proved the will, and another copy for Parliament is bound up in a folio volume of wills made by testators of that initial and date. The indices to these volumes may be examined at Somerset House and a copy of any will read. In the latter case, the original will proved in the district registry is kept there and may be seen or a copy obtained, but a copy is sent to and filed at Somerset House, where also it may be seen. A general index of grants, both probates and administrations, is prepared and printed annually in lexicographical form, and may be seen at either the Principal Registry or a district registry. This index is usually ready by about October of the following year.

Recent deaths

A system introduced in 1975 enables a person to discover when a grant of probate or letters of administration is made which may be invaluable to a creditor of the deceased or applicant under the Inheritance (Provision for Family and Dependants) Act 1975 (*see* page 658). A standing search may be made by sending a request in the form set out below with a small fee by post to any district probate registry. The searcher will receive particulars of any grant made in the previous 12 months or the following six months, including names and addresses of the executors or administrators and the registry in which the grant was made.

Form of search

> In the High Court of Justice
> Family Division
> The Principal Registry (Probate)
> I/We apply for the entry of a standing search so that there shall be sent to me/us an office copy of every grant of representation in England and Wales in the estate of:
> Full name of deceased:
> Alternative or alias name
> Full address
> Exact date of death
>
> Which either has issued not more than twelve months before the entry of this application or issues within six months hereafter
> Signed _____ (full address).

SCOTLAND

A domiciled Scotsman cannot in certain circumstances dispose effectively of the entirety of his estate. If he leaves a widow and children, the widow is entitled to a one-third share in the whole of the moveable estate (her *jus relictae*), and the children are entitled to another one-third share equally between them (their *legitim*). If he leaves a widow but no children, or children but no widow, the *jus relictae* or *legitim* is increased to a one-half share of the net moveable estate. The remaining portion is known as the dead's part. A surviving husband and children have comparable rights (*jus relicti* and *legitim*) in the wife's estate. The dead's part is the only portion of which the testator can freely dispose. Legacies and bequests are payable only out of the dead's part. All debts are payable out of the whole estate before any division.

Pupils, i.e. a girl up to the age of 12 or a boy up to the age of 14, cannot make wills. Formerly a minor could dispose only of moveables but since the passing of the Succession

(Scotland) Act 1964, a minor has a like capacity to test on heritable property.

The Requirements of Writing (Scotland) Act 1995 which came into force on 1 August 1995 regulates the writing requirement of documents executed after 1 August 1995. A will no longer need be 'holographed' as the status of 'privileged' documents has been abolished. Previously a will was attested by two witnesses with the grantor signing each page of the document. From 1 August 1995, the grantor still requires to sign each page but only one witness is required.

If the testator writer is blind, or cannot write, the will may be authenticated by a law agent, notary public, justice of the peace, advocate or a Sheriff Clerk and one witness. It is better that the will is not witnessed by a beneficiary thereunder although this circumstance will not invalidate the attestation of the will or (as it would be in England) the gift.

A Scottish will is not revoked by the subsequent marriage of the testator. The subsequent birth of a child for whom no testamentary provision has been made may revoke a will. A will may be revoked by a subsequent will, either expressly or by implication; but in so far as the two can be read together, both wills will have effect. If a subsequent will is revoked, the earlier will is revived.

Wills may be registered in the Books of the Sheriffdom in which the deceased died domiciled, or in the Books of Council and Session at HM General Register House, Edinburgh. The original deed may be inspected on payment of a small fee and a certified official copy may be obtained.

Confirmation

Confirmation (probate) is obtained in the sheriff court of the sheriffdom in which the deceased was domiciled at the date of his/her death or, where the deceased had no fixed domicile or died abroad, in the Commissariat of Edinburgh. Executors are either 'nominate' or 'dative'. An executor nominate is one nominated by the deceased in the will or, where such person has predeceased the testator, by the residuary beneficiary. An executor dative is one appointed by the court in the case of intestacy or where the deceased had failed to name an executor in the will and there is no residuary beneficiary. In the former case the deceased's next-of-kin are all entitled to be declared executors dative. An inventory of the deceased's estate and a schedule of debts, together with an affidavit, must first be given up. In estates under £17,000 gross, confirmation can be obtained under a simplified procedure at reduced fees.

Presumption of Survivorship

The Succession (Scotland) Act 1964 provides, by s. 31, that where two persons die in circumstances indicating that they died simultaneously or if it is uncertain which was the survivor, the younger will be deemed to have survived the elder unless the elder person left testamentary provision in favour of the younger, whom failing in favour of a third person, the younger person having died intestate (partially or wholly); but if the persons so dying were husband and wife, neither shall be presumed to have survived the other.

EMPLOYMENT

Wages and Sick Pay

Under the Wages Act 1986, subject to certain exceptions, employers may not make deductions from an employee's wages unless authorized by statute or contract or with the employee's prior written consent. There is an upper limit of one-tenth of gross pay for deductions from retail workers' wages on account of cash or stock shortages.

Under the Social Security Contributions and Benefits Act 1992, an employee absent from work because of illness or injury is entitled to receive Statutory Sick Pay (SSP) from the employer for a maximum period of 28 weeks in any period of three years. No payment is made for the first three days of any period of illness.

Under the Statutory Sick Pay Act 1994, employers no longer receive any state reimbursement of SSP (except for small employers whose contributions do not exceed £20,000 in any year). The 1994 Act also provides that women employees between the ages of 60 and 65 are now entitled to SSP.

The Equal Pay Act 1970, which extends to Scotland, prevents discrimination as regards terms and conditions of employment between men and women employed on like work in the same employment.

The Employment Protection (Part-time Employees) Regulations 1995 substantially extends the right of part-time workers and in most circumstances brings into line the treatment of part-time and full-time workers.

Particulars of Terms of Employment

Under the Employment Protection (Consolidation) Act 1978 (as amended), an employer must give each employee working more than eight hours a week and based in Great Britain, within two months of the beginning of the employment a written statement containing the following particulars of the contract between them:

(a) the date when the employment began (when continuous employment began if previous work counts as continuous with this job)
(b) the rate of remuneration (or how it is calculated)
(c) the intervals at which wages are paid
(d) the hours of work
(e) the employee's entitlement to holidays (including public holidays) and holiday pay
(f) the title of the employee's job
(g) the place or places of work
(h) terms relating to sickness, injury and sick pay
(i) details of any pension scheme
(j) the length of notice which the employee should give and receive in order to terminate the contract, or when it is to end if it is a fixed term contract.
(k) particulars of any collective agreement which directly affects the terms of employment
(l) if the employee is required to work outside the UK for more than one month, the period of such work and the currency in which payment is made.

In addition, the written particulars must specify any disciplinary rules; and also must identify the person to whom the employee can apply if dissatisfied with any disciplinary decision or to seek redress of any grievance, and what further steps may ensue.

Termination of Employment

An employee may be dismissed without notice if guilty of gross breach of contract, such as disobedience to a lawful order or dishonesty. The employee is then entitled only to wages accrued due at the date of dismissal.

In other cases, the employee is entitled to reasonable notice which, under the Employment Protection (Consolidation) Act 1978, must not be less than one week if he/she has been continuously employed for four weeks but less than two years; after two years it is two weeks' notice, increasing by one week's notice for each further full year worked up to a maximum of 12 weeks' notice after 12 years' service.

An employer who wrongfully dismisses an employee (i.e. with less than the length of notice to which he/she is entitled) is generally liable to pay wages for the period of proper notice.

An employee who has a fixed term contract has no claim against his/her employer for breach of contract (wrongful dismissal) if the contract is not renewed when it expires. If he/she is wrongfully dismissed before the contract expires, he/she is generally entitled to remuneration payable over the full period of the contract.

An employee may be entitled to a redundancy payment or to compensation for unfair dismissal if the employment has been terminated by the employer (with or without proper notice) or he/she has a fixed term contract which expires without being renewed or the employment has been terminated by the employee by reason of the employer's breach of contract.

Under the Employment Protection (Consolidation) Act 1978, an employee who satisfies the foregoing conditions and has been continuously employed for two years and who is dismissed by reason of redundancy may be entitled to a redundancy payment calculated by reference to his/her age, pay and length of service.

The 1978 Act also enables an employee who is unfairly dismissed to complain to an industrial tribunal (generally within three months of dismissal). The onus will then be on the employer to prove that the dismissal was due to capability, conduct, redundancy, illegality or some other substantial reason justifying dismissal. The tribunal must decide whether the employer acted reasonably in dismissing the employee. If the employer fails to prove that the dismissal was due to one or more of the above five reasons, or the tribunal decides that the employer did not act reasonably in dismissing the employee, the dismissal will be unfair, in which case the tribunal can:
(a) order re-engagement or reinstatement
(b) award compensation consisting of a basic and a compensatory award
For an employee to bring himself/herself within the unfair dismissal provisions, usually he/she must have been continuously employed for a period of two years.

All complaints of unfair dismissal are referred to a conciliation officer or the Department of Employment and a high proportion of complaints are disposed of in this way.

DISCRIMINATION

Discrimination on the grounds of sex or marital status is made unlawful by the Sex Discrimination Act 1975. The provisions of the Sex Discrimination Act are similar to those of the Race Relations Act 1976 which make discrimination on 'racial grounds' unlawful. 'Racial grounds' include colour, race, nationality, or ethnic or national origins. The Equal Opportunities Commission and the Commission for Racial Equality have the function of eliminating such discriminations and may provide assistance in pursuing allegations of discrimination. Awards by industrial tribunals are not capped in discrimination cases.

FAMILY LAW

ADOPTION OF CHILDREN

In England and Wales the adoption of children is mainly governed by the Adoption Act 1976, as amended by the Children Act 1989. A court order is necessary to legalize the adoption, which, when completed, has the effect of making the adopted child the child of the adopter as if he or she had been born to the adopter in lawful wedlock, and the original responsibilities of the natural parents are thereby cut. The adopter is able to decide all issues relating to the child, such as residence, education, etc., and the child is treated as his/hers for the purpose of any devolution of property on an intestacy occurring or under any disposition made after the adoption order. The application may be made to the High Court (Family Division) or to a county court or family proceedings court.

Orders may be made in favour of married couples, single, widowed or divorced persons, but not of one party to a marriage alone unless the other spouse cannot be found, is physically or mentally incapable of making an application, or they are separated in circumstances likely to be permanent. A person aged under 21 cannot adopt.

The child's parents or guardians must consent unconditionally to the making of the order unless the court dispenses with the consent, which it may do if the parent cannot be found or is incapable of giving consent, is withholding consent unreasonably, or has neglected or ill-treated the child.

Restrictions are placed on societies which may arrange adoptions.

An adopted person aged over 18 may apply to the Registrar-General for information to enable him/her to obtain a full certificate of his/her birth, but before being supplied with the information he/she will be informed that counselling services are available to him/her. The 1989 Act provides for the creation of a new register (the Adoption Contact Register) in which details of those who have had their children adopted, and of adopted persons themselves, may be recorded.

An adopter and the adopted child are within the prohibited degrees for the purposes of marriage to one another.

All adoptions in Great Britain are registered in the Registers of Adopted Children kept by the Registrars-General in London and Edinburgh respectively. Certificates from these registers, including short certificates which contain no reference to adoptions, can be obtained on conditions similar to those relating to birth certificates (*see* page 663).

Scotland

The law is consolidated in the Adoption (Scotland) Act 1978 as amended by the Children Act 1989. The law relating to fostering is consolidated in the Foster Children (Scotland) Act 1984. A petition for adoption is presented either to the Sheriff Court or the Court of Session. As in England, the petitioner(s) must be 21 or over and may be a married couple or one person who, if married, is living apart permanently from his or her spouse. The consent of the child's natural parents/guardians is required unless dispensed with, or the child is already free for adoption.

The Succession (Scotland) Act 1964 gives the adopted child the same rights of succession as a child born to the adopter in wedlock but deprives him/her of any such rights in the estates of his natural parents.

BIRTHS (REGISTRATION)

When a birth takes place, personal information of it must be given to the Registrar of Births and Deaths for the sub-district in which the birth occurred, and the register signed in his/her presence by the father or mother of the child; or, if they fail, by (a) the occupier of the house in which the birth happened; (b) a person present at the birth; or (c) the person having charge of the child. The duty of attending to the registration therefore rests firstly on the parents. The mother is responsible for the registration of the birth of an illegitimate child.

The registration is required to be made within 42 days of the birth. Failure to do this without reasonable cause involves liability to a penalty. The registration of a birth is free. In England or Wales, the informant, instead of attending before the registrar of the sub-district where the birth occurred, may make a declaration of the particulars required to be registered in the presence of any registrar. Under the National Health Service Act 1977, notice of every birth must be given by the father, or person in attendance on the mother, to the district medical officer of health by post within 36 hours of the birth. This is in addition to the registration already mentioned.

Still birth: a still birth must be registered, and a certificate signed by the doctor or midwife who was present at the birth or who has examined the body of the child must be produced to the registrar. The certificate must, where possible, state the cause of death and the estimated duration of the pregnancy. A still birth may only be registered within three months of the birth.

Re-registration: the re-registration of the birth of a person legitimated by the subsequent marriage of the parents is provided for in the Births and Deaths Registration Act 1953, as amended by the Family Law Reform Act 1987. Special provisions apply to the registration and re-registration of births of abandoned children, and the re-registration of births of illegitimate children showing the father's name; the mother must normally be party to the latter application.

Birth at sea: the master of a British ship must record any birth on board and send particulars to the Registrar-General of Shipping.

Birth abroad: consular officers are authorized to register births of British subjects occurring abroad. Certificates are obtainable in due course at the Registrar-General's Office, London.

The registration of births occurring out of the UK among members of the armed forces or occurring on board HM ships and aircraft, is provided for by the Registration of Births, Deaths and Marriages (Special Provisions) Act 1957, applicable also to Scotland.

Scotland

The Registration of Births, Deaths and Marriages (Scotland) Act 1965 supersedes former Acts. Personal notification within 21 days of any birth must be given to the registrar of either the registration district in which the birth took place, or any registration district in which the mother of the child was ordinarily resident at the time of the birth. In the case of a foundling child, dead or alive, when the place of birth is not known, notification must be given to the registrar of the registration district in which the child or the body was found, within two months from the date on which the child was found. When a child is born (in or out of Scotland) in a ship, aircraft or land vehicle during a journey and the child is conveyed therein to any place in Scotland, the birth shall, unless the Registrar-General otherwise directs, be deemed to have occurred at that place.

The register must be signed in the presence of the registrar by the father or mother of the child; or, if they fail, by (a) any relative of either parent who has knowledge of the birth; (b) the occupier of the premises in which the child was, to the knowledge of that occupier, born; (c) any person present at the birth; (d) any person having charge of the child. Failure without reasonable cause involves a penalty.

The name of the father of a child born out of wedlock may be entered in the register of births at the time of registration if jointly requested by the mother and father,

and the latter's name may also be recorded at a later date on declaration by both parents. A free abbreviated certificate of birth will be issued to the informant at the time of registration.

Still birth: a still birth must be registered, and a certificate, signed by the doctor or certified midwife present at the birth or who has examined the body of the child must be produced.

Re-registration: provision is made for the re-registration of the birth of a person made legitimate by the subsequent marriage of the parents or whose birth entry is affected by any matter respecting status or paternity, or has been so made as to imply that he/she is a foundling.

CERTIFICATES OF BIRTHS, DEATHS OR MARRIAGES

Records of births, deaths and marriages registered in England and Wales since 1837 are kept at the Office of Population Censuses and Surveys (OPCS), St Catherine's House, 10 Kingsway, London WC2B 6JP. Certificates of births, deaths or marriages in England and Wales can be obtained from the OPCS, or from the Superintendent Registrar having the legal custody of the register containing the entry of which a certificate is required. Certificates of marriage can also be obtained from the incumbent of the church in which the marriage took place, or from the Nonconformist minister (or other authorized person) where the marriage takes place in a registered building.

When a certificate is required, the nearest register office will be able to advise on the best way of obtaining it and any fees payable. As a rule, copies of entries in the registers may be obtained by a personal visit to OPCS at St Catherine's House, London, or by postal application (provided sufficient information is given to identify the certificate required) from Smedley Hydro, Trafalgar Road, Birkdale, Southport PR8 2HH.

One short birth certificate is issued free of charge at registration. Fees for other certificates (from 1 April 1995) are:

Obtained from Superintendent Registrar

Standard certificate of birth, death or marriage, £5.50
Copy of an entry of birth, death of marriage, £5.50
Certificate of birth, death or marriage for certain statutory purposes, £2.00
Short certificate of birth, £3.00

Obtained from Registrar

Standard certificate of birth, death or marriage, £2.50
Copy of an entry of birth, death or marriage, £2.50
Certificate of birth, death or marriage for certain statutory purposes, £2.00
Short certificate of birth (other than the one issued at time of registration of birth), £2.00
Certificate of death issued to certain professional bodies, £2.50

General Search (Superintendent Registrar)

For general search in indexes not exceeding six successive hours, £16.00
For each verification exceeding the eight covered by the general search fee, £2.50

No fee is payable for a search in the indexes when a particular entry in the register is specified.

The Society of Genealogists, 14 Charterhouse Buildings, Goswell Road, London ECIM 7BA, possesses many records of baptisms, marriages and deaths prior to 1837, including copies in whole or in part of about 4,000 parish registers.

Scotland

Certificates of births, deaths or marriages registered from 1855 (when compulsory registration commenced in Scotland) can be obtained personally at the General Register Office, New Register House, Edinburgh EH1 3YT, or from the appropriate local registrar, on payment of the fee of £10 for an entry (full or abbreviated) of birth, death or marriage (£12 by post). An abbreviated certificate of registration of death is issued free of charge for National Insurance purposes in certain cases. A Register of Divorces (which includes decrees of declaration of nullity of marriage) is kept by the Registrar-General at the General Register Office. The fee for an extract decree is £10 (£12 by post). The fees for searches of the registers vary according to the nature of the search and/or of the application; rates are available from the General Register Office.

There are also available at the General Register Office old parish registers of the date prior to 1855, which were formerly kept under the administration of the established Church of Scotland. An extract of an entry in these registers may be obtained for a fee of £12.00 (which includes the search fee).

The Registration of Presumed Deaths (Prescription of Particulars) (Scotland) Regulations 1978 as read with Presumption of Death (Scotland) Act 1977 prescribe the particulars to be notified by the clerk of court to the Registrar-General after a decree or variation order has been granted in an action of declarator of death of a missing person.

DIVORCE, SEPARATION AND ANCILLARY MATTERS

Matrimonial suits may be conveniently divided into two classes: those in which it is sought to annul the marriage because of some defect; and those in which, the marriage being admitted, it is sought to end the marriage or the duties arising from it. By virtue of the Matrimonial and Family Proceedings Act 1984, all matrimonial causes are commenced in one of the divorce county courts designated by the Lord Chancellor or in the Divorce Registry in London. If the suit becomes defended, it may be transferred to the High Court.

NULLITY OF MARRIAGE

Nullity of marriage is now mainly governed as to England and Wales by the Matrimonial Causes Act 1973. A marriage is void *ab initio* if the parties were within the prohibited degrees of affinity; or were not male and female; if it was bigamous; if one of the parties was under the age of consent, i.e. 16; or, in the case of a polygamous marriage entered into outside England and Wales, if either party was at the time of the marriage domiciled in England or Wales. Where the formalities of the marriage were defective, the marriage is generally void if both parties knew of the defect (e.g. where marriage took place otherwise than in an authorized building). However, absence of the consent of parents or guardians (or of the court or other authority, in lieu thereof) in the case of minors does not invalidate the marriage.

A marriage is voidable (i.e. a decree of nullity may be obtained but until such time the marriage remains valid) on the following grounds:

(a) incapacity of either party to consummate
(b) respondent's wilful refusal to consummate

(c) that either party did not validly consent to the marriage, whether in consequence of duress, mistake, unsoundness of mind or otherwise
(d) that either party at the time of marriage was a mentally disordered person
(e) that at the time of marriage the respondent was suffering from communicable venereal disease
(f) that at the time of the marriage the respondent was pregnant by another man

In cases (e) and (f), the petitioner must have been ignorant of the grounds at the date of the marriage. In cases (c), (d), (e) and (f) proceedings must be instituted within three years of the marriage, although leave may be obtained to petition outside this period in the case of certain persons suffering from mental illness. In all cases the court shall not grant a decree where the petitioner has led the respondent to believe that he/she would not seek a decree and it would be unjust for it to be granted.

The 1973 Act provides that a decree of nullity in a voidable marriage only annuls the marriage from the date of the decree. The marriage remains valid until the decree, and any children of the marriage are legitimate. Children of a void marriage are illegitimate unless the father was domiciled in England or Wales at the child's birth (or father's death, if earlier), and at the time of conception (or marriage if later) both or either of the parents reasonably believed the marriage was valid.

A spouse's insistence upon the use of contraceptives will not constitute wilful refusal to consummate within (b) above, even though there has been no normal intercourse, but it may in certain circumstances constitute unreasonable behaviour for the purpose of divorce. Further, it has been allowed as a defence to a charge of desertion against the aggrieved party.

JUDICIAL SEPARATION AND DIVORCE

The second class of suit includes a suit for judicial separation (which does not dissolve a marriage) and a suit for divorce (which, if successful, dissolves the marriage altogether and leaves the parties at liberty to marry again). Either spouse may petition for judicial separation. It is not necessary to prove that the marriage has broken down irretrievably and the facts listed below are grounds for judicial separation.

DIVORCE

The sole ground on which a divorce is obtained by either husband or wife is the irretrievable breakdown of the marriage. However, the court is precluded from holding that a marriage has irretrievably broken down unless it is satisfied of one or more of the following facts:

(a) that the respondent has committed adultery since the marriage and the petitioner finds it intolerable to live with the respondent
(b) that the respondent has behaved in such a way that the petitioner cannot reasonably be expected to continue cohabitation
(c) desertion by the respondent for two years immediately before the petition
(d) five years' separation immediately before the petition (but only two years where the respondent consents to the decree). Matrimonial Causes Act 1973

The foregoing is subject to a clause prohibiting any petition for divorce (but not for judicial separation) before the lapse of one year from the date of the marriage.

Desertion may be defined as a voluntary withdrawal from cohabitation by one spouse without just cause and against the wishes of the other. Where one spouse is guilty of conduct of a serious nature which forces the other to leave, the party at fault is said to be guilty of constructive desertion.

Encouragement of reconciliation

The 1973 Act requires the solicitor for the petitioner in certain cases to certify whether the possibility of a reconciliation has been discussed with the petitioner and whether or not the solicitor has given the petitioner the names and addresses of persons qualified to help effect a reconciliation.

A total period of less than six months during which the parties have resumed living together is to be disregarded in determining whether the prescribed period of desertion or separation has been continuous (but cannot be included as part of the period of separation). Similar provision for effecting a reconciliation exists in relation to the other proofs of breakdown, but a petitioner cannot rely on an act of adultery by the other party if they have lived together for more than six months after discovery of that act of adultery.

Obtaining the decree nisi

Where the suit is defended, i.e. the respondent opposes the dissolution or the fact/ground on which the petitioner seeks it, the petition will be heard by a judge in open court, the parties giving oral evidence. Where the suit is undefended, the evidence will normally take the form of a sworn written statement made by the petitioner which will be sent to the court and read over by a district judge. If the district judge is satisfied that the petitioner has proved the contents of the petition, he/she will simply fix a date for the pronouncement of the decree nisi in open court, it being unnecessary for either party to attend. Only if the district judge is not satisfied as above will he/she order that the petition be heard formally by the judge.

Children

After giving his/her certificate in relation to the decree nisi, the district judge must consider whether he/she should exercise any of his/her powers under the Children Act 1989. If the district judge thinks it may be necessary to exercise those powers, he/she can in exceptional circumstances delay the grant of the decree absolute.

Decree absolute

Every decree of divorce or nullity is in the first instance a decree nisi, and the marriage subsists until the decree is made absolute, usually six weeks after decree nisi on the petitioner's application. After the decree absolute either party is free to remarry.

Maintenance, etc

The court has wide powers to order either party to the marriage to make financial provision (e.g. periodical payments, a lump sum, the transfer of property) for the other party or, in certain circumstances, any child of the family, having regard to the party's means, the recipient's needs and all the important aspects of the case. These so-called ancillary matters often present more difficulty than the divorce itself, especially where they affect the home, and may go on long after the marriage is dissolved. There is, however, nothing to stop financial matters being negotiated by the parties through their solicitors before the divorce goes through.

The jurisdiction of the court to make child maintenance orders has been restricted by the Child Support Act 1991. Under this Act, the Child Support Agency has become responsible for assessing the maintenance that absent parents should pay for their natural children.

The court may, where the husband has neglected to provide reasonable maintenance for the wife or children, order the husband to make provision for the wife and, in certain circumstances, the children, even though no matrimonial suit is pending between the parties to the marriage, and while such an order is in force the court may also make orders relating to the children.

Orders Regarding Children

The Court may make orders in respect of children in connection with a suit for divorce, nullity or judicial separation (see above), or with an application to the family proceedings court (see below) whether the suit succeeds or not. In addition, if there is no other matrimonial suit involved, a parent may apply for orders under the Children Act 1989, and any person interested may apply to the High Court for the child to be made a ward of court.

In all cases the welfare of the child is the paramount consideration. The categories of child who may be covered by any particular type of proceedings differ according to the nature of those proceedings and to the nature of the particular relief sought, but it should be borne in mind that in connection with divorce, nullity and judicial separation a child which has been treated by the spouses as a child of the family may be included as a 'child of the family' as well as the children of the spouses themselves. This also applies to most maintenance cases in the family proceedings court (see below). It should be borne in mind that where there is financial need (because of continuing education or disability, for instance), maintenance may be ordered for children even beyond the age of majority.

Any dispute relating to the above matters should be placed in the hands of a solicitor without delay.

Separation by Agreement

Husband and wife may enter into an agreement to separate and live apart but the agreement, to be valid, must be followed by an immediate separation. It is desirable to consult a solicitor in every such case, who will often advise obtaining a court order by consent.

Family Proceedings Court

For many years the law relating to domestic proceedings in magistrates' courts (now family proceedings courts) was out of line with the divorce law which was reformed in 1969. The Domestic Proceedings and Magistrates' Courts Act 1978 took effect in early 1981 and now contains the relevant law.

A husband or wife can apply to a family proceedings court for a matrimonial order on the grounds that the other spouse: (a) has failed to pay reasonable maintenance for the applicant; (b) has failed to make a proper contribution towards the reasonable maintenance of a child of the family; (c) has deserted the applicant; or (d) has behaved in such a way that the applicant cannot reasonably be expected to live with the respondent.

If the case is proved the court can order: (a) periodical payments for the applicant; (b) periodical payments for a child of the family (except where the court's jurisdiction has been superseded by the Child Support Agency, see above); or (c) a lump sum (not exceeding £1,000) for the benefit of the applicant and/or for any child of the family.

In deciding what orders (if any) to make, the court must consider a number of guidelines which are similar to those governing financial orders on divorce. There are also special provisions relating to consent orders and separation by agreement. The court also has powers to make orders relating to a child of the family and these orders together with orders for child maintenance can be made even though the court makes no order for spouse maintenance. Other provisions of the Act relate to interim orders, and variation, discharge and revival of orders. An order may be enforceable even though the parties are living together, but in some cases it will cease to have effect if they continue to do so for six months. The hearing of matrimonial disputes is separate from ordinary court business, and the public are not admitted.

DOMESTIC VIOLENCE

The Domestic Violence and Matrimonial Proceedings Act 1976, the Domestic Proceedings and Magistrates' Courts Act 1978 and the Matrimonial Homes Act 1983 have made it easier for one spouse who has been subjected to violence by the other to obtain an order to restrain further violence and if need be to have the other excluded from the home. Such orders can be obtained very quickly, and a person disobeying them is liable to be imprisoned for contempt of court. There are some differences of detail between the three Acts; in particular the 1976 Act also applies to unmarried couples. Such orders may also be obtained in the course of suits for divorce and judicial separation.

The Family Homes and Domestic Violence Bill will, when enacted, consolidate the present law relating to domestic violence and provide for greater protection for a wider category of applicant.

SCOTLAND

NULLITY OF MARRIAGE

A declaration of nullity of marriage may be obtained on the ground of any impediment, such as consanguinity and affinity, subsistence of a previous marriage, nonage of one of the parties, incapacity or insanity of one of the parties, or by the absence of genuine consent. The financial provisions on divorce contained in the Family Law (Scotland) Act 1985 also apply to an action for declaration of nullity of marriage.

JUDICIAL SEPARATION

Under the Divorce (Scotland) Act 1976, a decree of judicial separation can be obtained by proof of the same facts necessary to obtain decree of divorce, except that for the principle of irretrievable breakdown there is substituted that of grounds justifying separation. This type of action is competent in both the Court of Session and the Sheriff Court.

DIVORCE

Actions of divorce could formerly only be raised in the Court of Session, having jurisdiction to entertain such actions only if either of the parties to the marriage in question is domiciled in Scotland on the date when the action is begun, or was habitually resident in Scotland throughout the period of one year ending with that date. As from 1 May 1984, however, when the Divorce Jurisdiction, Court Fees and Legal Aid (Scotland) Act 1983 came into force, actions of divorce may also be raised in the Sheriff Courts provided the above conditions are complied with, and provided either party to the marriage was resident in the sheriffdom for a period of 40 days ending with the date the action was begun, or was resident in the sheriffdom for a period of not less than 40 days ending not more than 40 days before the date the action was begun.

Under the Divorce (Scotland) Act 1976, which for the purposes of divorce came into force on 1 January 1977, the sole ground of divorce is irretrievable breakdown of the marriage. This can be established only in one of the following ways:

(a) The defending spouse has committed adultery since the date of the marriage. It is not necessary for the pursuing spouse to prove that the fact of adultery made it intolerable to live with the defending spouse

(b) The defending spouse has behaved in such a way that the pursuing spouse cannot reasonably be expected to cohabit with him or her. It is immaterial whether or not the conduct founded upon is active or passive

(c) The defending spouse has deserted the pursuing spouse for a continuous period of two years. There must be no question of the pursuing spouse having refused a genuine and reasonable offer to adhere. Nor is irretrievable breakdown established if cohabitation is resumed for a period of more than three months after the two-year period has expired

(d) There has been no cohabitation at any time during a continuous period of two years immediately preceding the action between the parties to the action, and the defending spouse consents to the divorce being granted

(e) There has been no cohabitation at any time during a continuous period of five years, as in (d), except that on the expiry of the five-year period, the consent of the defending spouse is not required

The facts of desertion and separation are not interrupted by the parties cohabiting for a period or periods not exceeding six months. However, such a period or periods of cohabitation would not be included in the calculation of the two-year or five-year periods.

Encouragement of reconciliation

The burden of promoting a reconciliation between spouses in a divorce action falls upon the court by virtue of the 1976 Act. Where an action of divorce has been raised, it may be postponed by the court to enable the parties to seek to effect a reconciliation if the court feels that there may be a reasonable prospect of such reconciliation. If the parties do cohabit during such postponement, no account shall be taken of such cohabitation if the action later proceeds.

Maintenance, etc.

The 1976 Act also provides that either party to a marriage can apply to the court at any time prior to decree being granted for: (a) an order for interim custody of all or some of the children of the marriage under 16 years of age; (b) an order for access to all or some of the children of the marriage under 16 years of age in the custody of the other party.

The financial provisions on divorce in the 1976 Act have been superseded by the Family Law (Scotland) Act 1985, which allows either party to the marriage to apply to the court for an order for payment of a capital sum or for a periodical allowance or for an incidental order. The Act sets out principles to be applied by the court, one of these being that the financial provisions awarded to a party who has been dependent for financial support on the other party should be given over a period of not more than three years.

The Act also defines the rights and obligations of aliment between parents and children, thereby excluding aliment between grandparents and grandchildren and of children to parents, and provides that a child is entitled to aliment up to the age of 18 or to 25 if in full-time further education, and for the claiming of aliment whether in connection with an action of divorce, etc., or independently.

Procedure

Appearance in court at a proof in an undefended divorce action has been unnecessary since 1978. A full proof is still necessary if the action is defended in any respect. In place of court appearance, affidavits (statements sworn before a notary public) by the pursuer and any witnesses are lodged in the court together with a Minute by the solicitor craving decree.

A simplified procedure for 'do-it-yourself' divorce was introduced in 1983 for certain divorces. Thus, if the action is based on (d) or (e) above and will not be opposed, and if there are no children under 16 and no financial claims, then the applicant can write directly to the local sheriff court or to the Court of Session, Divorce Section (SP), Parliament House, Edinburgh, for the appropriate forms to enable him or her to proceed. The fee is £55 unless the applicant receives income support, family credit or legal advice and assistance, in which case there is no fee.

CUSTODY OF CHILDREN

In actions for divorce and separation, the court has a discretion in awarding the custody of the children of the parties. The welfare of the children is the paramount consideration, and the mere fact that a spouse, by reason of his or her behaviour, brought about the breakdown of the marriage does not of itself preclude him or her from being awarded custody. The Children Act 1975, as amended, also applies to Scotland.

DOMESTIC VIOLENCE

The Matrimonial Homes (Family Protection) (Scotland) Act 1981, as amended, provides that one spouse, whether or not he or she has title to the matrimonial home, can obtain an exclusion order suspending the other spouse's occupancy rights in the matrimonial home. The court (either Court of Session or Sheriff Court) is empowered to make such an order if satisfied that it is necessary to protect the applicant or any child of the family from any conduct, actual or threatened or reasonably apprehended, of the other spouse which would be injurious to the physical or mental health of the applicant or child. In making the order the court may include a warrant for the summary ejection of the non-applicant spouse from the matrimonial home and for an interdict prohibiting him/her from entering it.

ILLEGITIMACY AND LEGITIMATION

The Children Act 1989 gives the mother parental responsibility for her child when not married to the father. The father can acquire parental responsibility by agreement with her (in prescribed form) or by court order.

Prima facie every child born of a married woman during a marriage is legitimate; and this presumption can only be rebutted by strong evidence. However, under the Family Law Reform Act 1969, any presumption of law as to the legitimacy (or illegitimacy) of any person may in civil proceedings be rebutted by evidence showing that it is more probable than not that the person is illegitimate (or legitimate) and in any proceedings where paternity is in question, blood tests may be ordered. If, however, the husband and wife are separated under an order of the court, a child conceived by the wife during such separation is presumed not to be the husband's child.

LEGITIMATION

The Legitimacy Act 1976 consolidates earlier legislation dating back to 1 January 1927. Where the parents of an illegitimate person marry, or have married, whether before or after that date, the marriage, if the father is at the date thereof domiciled in England or Wales, renders that person, if living, legitimate as from 1 January 1927, or from the date of the marriage, whichever last happens. Marriage legitimates a person even though the father or mother was married to a third person at the time when the illegitimate person was born. It is the duty of the parents to supply to the Registrar-General information for re-registration of the birth of a legitimate child.

Declarations of legitimacy

A person claiming that he/she, his/her parents, or any remoter ancestor has become legitimated, may petition the High Court or the county court for the necessary declaration.

Rights and duties of legitimated persons

A legitimated person, his/her spouse or children may take property under an intestacy occurring after the date of legitimation, or under any disposition (e.g. a will) coming into operation after such date, as if he/she had been legitimate. He/she must maintain all persons whom he/she would be bound to maintain had he/she been born legitimate, and he/she is entitled to the benefit of any Act of Parliament which confers rights on legitimate persons to recover damages or compensation. The Act specially provides that nothing therein contained is to render any person capable of succeeding to or transmitting a right to any dignity or title.

PROPERTY RIGHTS OF ILLEGITIMATE CHILDREN

By the Family Law Reform Act 1969 the rights of an illegitimate child on an intestacy were broadly equated with those of a legitimate child, and in any disposition made after 31 December 1969, any reference to children or other relatives was, unless the contrary intention appears, to be construed as including any person who is illegitimate or who is related through another person who is illegitimate. However, these provisions of the 1969 Act have been replaced by the general provision of the Family Law Reform Act 1987 (*see* page 658).

SCOTLAND

The Law Reform (Parent and Child) Scotland Act 1986 contains a general provision granting equal status to all persons whatever the marital status of their parents. The mother of an illegitimate child may raise an action of affiliation and aliment against the father, either in the Court of Session or, more usually, in the Sheriff Court. Where in any such action the court finds that the defender is the father of the child, the court shall, in awarding expenses, or aliment, have regard to the means of the parties and the whole circumstances of the case. The court may, upon application by the mother or by the father of any illegitimate child, or in any action for aliment for an illegitimate child, make such order as it may think fit regarding the custody of such child and the right of access thereto of either parent, having regard to the welfare of the child and to the conduct of the parents and to the wishes as well of the mother as of the father and may on the application of either parent recall or vary such order. The obligation of the mother and of the father of an illegitimate child to provide aliment for such child shall (without prejudice to any obligation attaching at common law) endure until the child attains the age of 16.

LEGITIMATION

By Scottish law an illegitimate child is legitimated by and on the date of the subsequent marriage of its parents and there is no objection to there having been an impediment to the marriage of the parents at the time of the child's conception; see the Legitimation (Scotland) Act 1968, which came into operation on 8 June 1968, on which date thousands of existing illegitimate children were regarded as legitimated. By the Registration of Births, Deaths and Marriages (Scotland) Act 1965, a child so legitimated who has already been registered as illegitimate may be re-registered as legitimate. The consent of the father of an illegitimate child to its adoption is not required unless he has been awarded parental rights by the court.

MARRIAGE

Marriage According to Rites of the Church of England

Marriage by banns

The Marriage Act 1949 prescribes audible publication according to the rubric, on three Sundays preceding the ceremony during morning service or, if there is no morning service on a Sunday on which the banns are to be published, during evening service. Where the parties reside in different parishes, the banns must be published in both. Under the Act, banns may be published and the marriage solemnized in the parish church which is the usual place of worship of the persons to be married or either of them, although neither of such persons dwells in such parish; but this publication of banns is in addition to any other publication required by law and does not apply if the church or the residence of either party is in Wales. The Act provides specially for the case where one of the parties resides in Scotland and the other in England, the publication being then in the parish in England in which one party resides, and according to the law and custom in Scotland in the place where the other party resides. After the lapse of three months from the last time of publication, the banns become useless, and the parties must either obtain a licence (*see* below), or submit to the republication of banns.

Marriage by licence

(i) *Common Licence:* a common licence, dispensing with the necessity for banns, is granted by the archbishops and bishops through their surrogates (parochial clergyman), for marriages in any church or chapel duly licensed for marriages. A common licence can be obtained at the offices of the bishop's registrars; licences obtained at the bishop's diocesan registry only enable the parties to be married in the diocese in which they are issued. No instructions, either verbal or in writing, can be received, except from one of the parties. Affidavits are prepared from the personal instructions of one of the parties about to be married, and the licence is delivered to the party upon payment of a fee (*see* pages 669–70). Before a licence can be granted one of the parties must make an affidavit that there is no legal impediment to the intended marriage; and also that one of such parties has had his or her usual place of abode for the space of fifteen days immediately preceding the issuing of the licence within the parish or ecclesiastical district of the church in which the marriage is to be solemnized, or that the church in which the marriage is to be solemnized is the usual place of worship of the parties or one of them. The affidavit may be taken before a parochial clergyman (surrogate), and it is his/her office to deliver the licence personally to the applicant. (In some dioceses it is necessary for the surrogate to procure the licence from the bishop's registry.) The licence continues in force for three months from its date.

(ii) *Special Licence:* a special licence is granted by the Archbishop of Canterbury in special circumstances for marriage at any place with or without previous residence in the district, or at any time, etc.; but the reasons assigned must meet with the archbishop's approval. Application must be made to the Faculty Office. For fee, *see* page 670.

Marriage under Superintendent Registrar's certificate

A marriage may be performed in church on the Superintendent Registrar's certificate (*see* below) without banns, provided that the incumbent's consent is obtained. One of the parties must be resident within the ecclesiastical parish of the church in which the marriage is to take place unless the church is the usual place of worship of the parties or one of them.

Marriage under Superintendent Registrar's Certificate

The following marriages may be solemnized on the authority of a Superintendent Registrar's certificate (either with or without a licence):

(a) a marriage in a registered building, e.g. a Nonconformist church registered for the solemnization of marriages therein
(b) a marriage in a register office
(c) a marriage on approved premises (*see* page 669)
(d) a marriage according to the usages of the Society of Friends (commonly called Quakers)
(e) a marriage between two persons professing the Jewish religion according to the usages of the Jews
(f) a marriage according to the rites of the Church of England (*see* above; in this case the marriage can only be without licence)
(g) a marriage of a person who is housebound or is detained at the place where he or she normally resides (*see* page 669)

Notice of the intended marriage must be given as follows: *Marriage by certificate (without licence):* if both parties reside in the same registration district, they must both have resided there for seven days before the notice can be given. It may then be given by either party. If the parties reside in different registration districts, notice must be given by each to the Superintendent Registrar of the district in which he or she resides, and the preliminary residential qualification of seven days must be fulfilled by each before either notice can be given.

Marriage by certificate (with licence): one notice only is necessary, whether the parties live in the same or in different registration districts. Either party may give the notice, which must be given to the Superintendent Registrar of any registration district in which one of the parties has resided for the period of 15 days immediately preceding the giving of notice, but both parties must be resident in England or Wales on the day notice is given.

The notice (in either case) must be in the prescribed form and must contain particulars as to names, marital status, occupation, residence, length of residence, and the building in which the marriage is to take place. The notice must also contain or have added at the foot thereof a solemn declaration that there is no legal impediment to the marriage, and, in the case of minors, that the consent of the person whose consent to the marriage is required by law (*see* Minors, page 670) has been duly given, and that the residential qualifications mentioned above have been complied with. A person making a false declaration renders himself or herself liable to prosecution for perjury. The notice is entered in the marriage notice book.

Issue of certificate

Without licence: the notice (or an exact copy thereof) is affixed in some conspicuous place in the Superintendent Registrar's office for 21 days after the notice was entered in the marriage notice book. After the lapse of this period the Superintendent Registrar may, provided no impediment is shown, issue his certificate for the marriage which can then take place at any time within three months from the date of the entry of the notice.

With licence: the notice in this case is not affixed in the office of the Superintendent Registrar. After the lapse of one whole day (other than a Sunday, Christmas Day or Good Friday) from the date of entry of the notice, the Superintendent Registrar may, provided no impediment is shown, issue his certificate and licence for the marriage, which can then take place on any day within three months from the date of entry of the notice.

SOLEMNIZATION OF THE MARRIAGE

In a registered building

The marriage may take place at any building whether or not either party resides in that district.

The presence of a Registrar of Marriages is not necessary at marriages at registered buildings which have adopted the provisions of section 43 of the Marriage Act 1949. This section provides for the appointment of an authorized person (a person, usually the minister or an official of the building, certified by the trustees or governing body as having been duly authorized for the purpose) who must be present and must register the marriage.

The marriage must be solemnized between the hours of 8 a.m. and 6 p.m., in the presence of two or more witnesses. The parties must at some time during the ceremony make the following declaration: 'I do solemnly declare that I know not of any lawful impediment why I, A. B., may not be joined in matrimony to C. D.' Also each of the parties must say to the other: 'I call upon these persons here present to witness that I, A. B., do take thee, C. D., to be my lawful wedded wife [or husband],' or, if the marriage is solemnized in the presence of an authorized person without the presence of a registrar, each party may say in lieu thereof: 'I, A. B., do take thee, C. D., to be my wedded wife [or husband].'

In a register office

The marriage may be solemnized in the office of the Superintendent Registrar to whom notice of the marriage has been given. The marriage must be solemnized between the hours of 8 a.m. and 6 p.m., with open doors, in the presence of the Superintendent Registrar or a registrar of the registration district of that Superintendent Registrar, and in the presence of two witnesses. The parties must make the following declaration: 'I do solemnly declare that I know not of any lawful impediment why I, A. B., may not be joined in matrimony to C. D.,' and each party must say to the other: 'I call upon these persons here present to witness that I, A. B., do take thee, C. D., to be my lawful wedded wife [or husband].'

No religious ceremony may take place in the register office, though the parties may, on production of their marriage certificate, go through a subsequent religious ceremony in any church or persuasion of which they are members.

On approved premises

The marriage must be solemnized in the presence of the Superintendent Registrar and a registrar of the registration district in which the premises are situated, and in the presence of two witnesses. The parties make the same declaration as in a register office.

No religious ceremony may take place on approved premises, as is the case for a marriage solemnized in a register office.

Other cases

If both parties are members of the Society of Friends (Quakers), or if, not being in membership, they have been authorized by the Society of Friends to solemnize their marriage in accordance with its usages, they may be married in a Friends' meeting-house. The marriage must be registered by the registering officer of the Society

appointed to act for the district in which the meeting-house is situated. The presence of a Registrar of Marriages is not necessary.

If both parties are Jews they may marry according to their usages in a synagogue which has a certified marriage secretary, or in a private dwelling-house at any hour; the building may be situated within or without the district of residence. The marriage must be registered by the secretary of the synagogue of which the man is a member. The presence of a Registrar of Marriages is not necessary.

MARRIAGE UNDER REGISTRAR-GENERAL'S LICENCE

The main purpose of the Marriage (Registrar-General's Licence) Act 1970, which came into force on 1 January 1971, is to enable non-Anglicans to be married in unregistered premises where one of the persons to be married is seriously ill, is not expected to recover, and cannot be moved to registered premises.

DETAINED AND HOUSEBOUND PERSONS

The Marriage Act 1983 (which does not extend to Scotland) enables marriages of detained persons and housebound persons to be solemnized at their place of residence. The Act came into operation on 1 May 1984.

MARRIAGE IN ENGLAND OR WALES WHEN ONE PARTY LIVES IN SCOTLAND OR NORTHERN IRELAND

Notice for a marriage by a Superintendent Registrar's certificate in a register office or registered building may be given in the usual way by the party resident in England. As regards Scotland, the party there should give notice of intention to marry to the Registrar. As regards Northern Ireland, the party there, after a residence of seven days, must give notice to the District Registrar of Marriages. Notice cannot be given for such marriages to take place by certificate with licence of the Superintendent Registrar.

Marriage of such parties may take place in a church of the Church of England after the publication of banns, or by ecclesiastical licence.

CIVIL FEES from 1 April 1995

Marriage at the register office

By Superintendent Registrar's certificate
– where both parties live in the same district, £42.00
– where the parties live in different districts, £61.00
By Superintendent Registrar's licence, £87.00
Fees include the fee of £23.00 for the registrar's attendance on the day of the wedding

Marriage on approved premises

By Superintendent Registrar's certificate
– where both parties live in the same district, £19.00
– where the parties live in different districts, £38.00
By Superintendent Registrar's licence, £64.00
In addition to these fees, a fee must be paid for the Superintendent Registrar's and registrar's attendence at the marriage; this fee is set locally by the responsible local authority. A further charge is likely to be made by the owners of the building for the use of the premises

Marriage in a religious building

(other than in the Church of England or the Church in Wales)
By Superintendent Registrar's certificate
– where both parties live in the same district, £19.00
– where the parties live in different districts, £38.00
By Superintendent Registrar's licence, £64.00
In addition to these fees, a fee of £33.00 must be paid for the registrar's attendance at the marriage unless an 'authorized person' appointed by the trustees of the building is to register the marriage. Additional fees may

also be charged by the trustees of the building used for the wedding, and by the person who performs the ceremony

For Superintendent Registrar to attend outside his/her office to attest a notice of marriage or for a marriage ceremony, £35.00

For registrar to attend a marriage outside a register office, £33.00

Fee for entry in the marriage notice book, £19.00

Total fees for the preliminaries to marriage by Registrar-General's licence, £15.00

For marriage certificate on day of marriage, £2.50

ECCLESIASTICAL FEES from 1 January 1995

Marriage after banns
For publication of banns, £12.00
For certificate of banns issued at time of publication, £7.00
For marriage service, £110.00

Marriages by common licence
Fee for licence varies, but usually £45.00

Marriage by special licence
Fee payable at Faculty Office, £90.00

Further fees may be payable for additional facilities at the marriage, e.g. the organist's fee
Some of the above fees may not apply to the Church in Wales

MISCELLANEOUS NOTES

Consanguinity and affinity

A marriage between persons within the prohibited degrees of consanguinity or affinity is void. Relaxations have, however, been made by various statutes which have now been replaced by the Marriage Act 1949 (see 1st Schedule to the Act) and the Marriage (Enabling) Act 1960. It is now permitted for a man to contract a marriage with:

(a) the sister, aunt or niece of a former wife (whether she is living or not)

(b) the former wife of a brother, uncle or nephew (whether he is living or not)

No member of the clergy can be compelled to solemnize any of the foregoing marriages, but he/she may allow his church to be used for the purpose by another minister.

The Marriage (Prohibited Degrees of Relationship) Act 1986 makes further provision with regard to the marriage of persons related by affinity, e.g. after section 1 of the Act came into force, a marriage between a man and the daughter or granddaughter of his former wife will not be void by reason only of that relationship if both parties have attained 21 at the time of the marriage and the younger party has not at any time before attaining 18 been a child of the family in relation to the other party.

Minors

Persons under 18 years of age are generally required to obtain the consent of certain persons (Marriage Act 1949, section 3 and 2nd Schedule as amended by the Children Act 1989). Where both parents are living, both must consent. Where one is dead, the survivor, or, if there is a guardian appointed by the deceased parent, the guardian and the survivor must consent. (For the position where the parents of the child were not married to each other at the time of the birth, see Schedule 12, paragraph 5 to the Children Act 1989.) No consent is required in the case of a minor's second marriage. In certain exceptional cases consent may be dispensed with, e.g. the insanity of a parent.

If consent is refused the court may, on application being made, consent to the marriage; application can be made for this purpose to the High Court, the county court, or a court of summary jurisdiction. The Act prohibits any marriage where either party is under 16 years of age.

SCOTLAND

According to the law of Scotland, marriage is a contract which is completed by the mutual consent of the parties. The Marriage (Scotland) Act 1977, which came into force on 1 January 1978, states or restates the law in convenient form. References in this section are to that Act.

IMPEDIMENTS TO MARRIAGE

These are: (a) nonage, i.e. where either party is under the age of 16; (b) forbidden degrees of relationship (Section 2) as amended by the Marriage Prohibited Degrees of Relationship Act 1986; (c) subsisting previous marriage; (d) incapacity to understand the nature of the contract; (e) both parties of the same sex; (f) non-residence, i.e. if the requirements of prior residence of one or other of the parties in Scotland have not been complied with.

The Act also states the grounds on which certain marriages may be declared void, but this is amended by the Law Reform (Miscellaneous Provisions) (Scotland) Act 1980 which prevents a marriage being rendered void solely due to the failure to comply with certain formalities, provided the particulars of that marriage are entered in a register of marriages by or at the behest of an appropriate registrar.

REGULAR AND IRREGULAR MARRIAGES

Regular marriages

A regular marriage is one which is celebrated by a minister of religion or authorized registrar or other celebrant specified in the Act. The parties must submit to the district registrar a statutory notice of intention to marry, the fee for which is £10.00 each. The registrar will then enter the parties' names and particulars in the marriage notice book which must also show the intended date of the marriage. The registrar must then display the notice of intention to marry in a prominent public place until the intended date, and any person claiming an interest may lodge written objections thereto with the registrar (Section 5). The registrar, after 14 clear days of receipt of the marriage notice and on being satisfied that there are no legal impediments to the marriage, will issue to either or both parties a marriage schedule. The 14-day period may be shortened in exceptional circumstances. The marriage schedule must be produced to the celebrant of the marriage. The fee for the solemnization ceremony in a register office is £40.00. After the ceremony the marriage must be registered within three days with the Registrar-General for inclusion in the Register of Births, Deaths and Marriages. Within one month of the ceremony, the fee for an extract marriage certificate is £7; thereafter it is £10.

Irregular marriages

Since the Marriage (Scotland) Act 1939 the only form of irregular marriage to be recognized by law, marriage by habit and repute, remains competent under the 1977 Act. If the parties live together constantly as husband and wife and are held to be such by the general repute of the neighbourhood and among their friends and relations, then there may arise a presumption from which marriage can be inferred. Before such a marriage can be registered, however, a decree of declarator of marriage must be obtained from the Deputy Principal Clerk of the Court of Session. It is the duty of the Deputy Principal Clerk to register the decree as soon as it is granted.

JURY SERVICE

Every parliamentary or local elector between the ages of 18 and 70 who has resided in the UK, Channel Islands or Isle of Man for at least five years since he/she attained the age of 13 will be qualified to serve on a jury unless he/she is ineligible or disqualified.

Ineligible persons include those who have at any time been judges, magistrates and certain senior court officials, those who within the previous ten years have been concerned with the law (such as barristers and solicitors and their clerks, court officers, coroners, police, prison and probation officers); priests of any religion and vowed members of religious communities; and certain sufferers from mental illness.

Disqualified persons are those who have at any time been sentenced by a court in the UK, Channel Islands or Isle of Man, to a term of imprisonment or custody for life or five years or more, or a person who in the last ten years has (a) served any part of a sentence of imprisonment, youth custody or detention; (b) been detained in a young offender institution; (c) had passed on him/her or made in respect of him/her a suspended sentence of imprisonment or order for detention; or (d) had made in respect of him/her a community service order. A person who at any time in the last five years has been placed on probation is also disqualified.

Some others are excusable as of right. These include persons over 65, members and officers of the Houses of Parliament, full-time serving members of the armed forces, registered and practising members of the medical, dental, nursing, veterinary and pharmaceutical professions, and any person who has served on a jury in the two years before he/she is summoned. In other cases the court may excuse a juror at its discretion, e.g. where the service would be a hardship to the juror, or defer the date of attendance.

If a person serves on a jury knowing himself/herself to be disqualified or ineligible, he/she is liable to be fined up to £5,000 or £500 respectively.

A juror is entitled to subsistence and travelling expenses, compensation for other expenses incurred in consequence of attendance for jury service, loss of earnings and loss of national insurance benefits, but certain maximum figures (which are revised from time to time) are laid down.

A verdict of a jury must normally be unanimous but after two hours' consideration (or such longer period as the court thinks reasonable), a majority verdict is acceptable if ten jurors agree to it (or nine if the size of the jury has been reduced to ten, e.g. by illness during the trial).

Jury trial is now very unusual in civil cases but a person charged with any but the least serious crimes is entitled to be tried by a jury. The defendant may object to any juror if he/she can show that that juror ought not to be on the jury, e.g. because he/she is ineligible or is biased against him/her.

The Coroners Act 1988 (which does not extend to Scotland) makes provision in relation to qualification to serve on coroners' juries.

Scotland

It is the duty of the sheriff principal of each sheriffdom, in respect of each sheriff court district in the sheriffdom, to maintain a book (the general jury book) containing the names and designations of persons within the district who are qualified and liable to serve as jurors. The book, which is compiled from information which every householder is required to provide, is kept open for the inspection by any person, upon payment of a nominal fee, at the sheriff clerk's office for the district.

Under section 1 of the Law Reform (Miscellaneous Provisions) (Scotland) Act 1980, every man or woman between the ages of 18 and 65 who is for the time being registered as a parliamentary or local government elector and who has been ordinarily resident in the UK, the Channel Islands or the Isle of Man for any period of at least five years since attaining the age of 13 years, is qualified to serve on a jury.

Ineligible persons include those who at any time within the past ten years have been judges of the supreme courts, sheriffs and certain other senior court officials, those who at any time within the past five years have been concerned with the administration of justice (such as advocates and their clerks, solicitors, court staff, police officers, prison officers, sheriff officers, procurator fiscals, and members of parole boards and children's panels), and certain sufferers from mental illness.

The same rules for disqualified persons operate in Scotland as in England.

Those excusable as of right are members and officers of the Houses of Parliament, full-time serving members of the armed forces, registered and practising members of the medical, dental, nursing, veterinary and pharmaceutical professions, ministers of religion and other persons in holy orders, and any person who has attended for jury service in the past five years.

If a person serves on a jury knowing himself/herself to be disqualified or ineligible, he/she is liable to be fined up to £5,000 or £1,000 respectively. Jurors failing to attend without good cause are liable to a maximum fine of £200.

Part II of the Juries Act 1949 (amended by regulations following thereon and by the Law Reform (Miscellaneous Provisions) (Scotland) Act 1980) applies only to Scotland and provides, *inter alia*, for the payment of travelling expenses and subsistence allowances to jurors and for loss of earnings.

The number of a jury in a civil cause in the Court of Session is 12 and in the Sheriff Court seven. In a criminal trial the number is 15.

LANDLORD AND TENANT

Although basically the relationship between the parties to a lease is governed by the lease itself, the position is complicated by numerous statutory provisions. The few points dealt with may show the desirability of seeking professional assistance in these matters. Important provisions include the following:

(1) The Agricultural Holdings Act 1986, among other things, regulates the length of notice necessary to determine an agricultural tenancy, the tenant's right to remove fixtures on the land, his right to compensation for damage done by game, for improvements and for disturbance, and his right to require the consent of the Agricultural Land Tribunal to the operation of a notice to quit.

(2) The Landlord and Tenant Acts 1927 and 1954, as amended: Part II of the 1954 Act gives security of tenure to the tenant of most business premises, and in effect the tenant can only be ousted on one or more of the seven grounds set out in the Act. In some cases, where the landlord can resume possession, the tenant is entitled to compensation.

(3) The complicated mass of legislation regarding dwelling-houses is embodied in the Rent Act 1977 and the Housing Act 1988.

If a tenancy of a house is within the Rent Act, the tenant has a personal right to reside there, and may only be ousted on certain grounds. Tenancies with full Rent Act protection are known as regulated tenancies. The maximum rent recoverable under such a tenancy is the rent agreed between the landlord and tenant, unless a fair rent has been registered, in which case that is the maximum. Application for the registration of a fair rent may be made by either the landlord or tenant, to the local rent officer, and appeal against his decision lies to the rent assessment committee.

Since the Housing Act 1988 came into force on 15 January 1989, it has not generally been possible to create a new regulated tenancy, although the above protection remains for existing regulated tenancies. Tenancies granted on or after 15 January 1989 are known as assured tenancies provided they satisfy certain conditions, which are broadly the same as those for regulated tenancies under the 1977 Act. However, the rent payable by an assured tenant is either that agreed with the landlord or the open market rent fixed by the rent assessment committee.

(4) The Protection from Eviction Act 1977, as amended by the Housing Act 1988, provides that if any person with intent to cause the residential occupier of any premises to give up the occupation thereof does any act calculated to interfere with the peace or comfort of the residential occupier or members of the household, that person shall be guilty of an offence. A further provision prevents a landlord enforcing without a court order a right to possession against a tenant who is not protected by any security of tenure legislation, and there are special rules in such cases relating to agricultural employees.

(5) A notice to quit any dwelling-house must be given at least four weeks before it is to take effect, and must be in writing and in the prescribed statutory form.

(6) Part I of the Landlord and Tenant Act 1954 applies to most tenancies of houses for over 21 years at a ground rent. Where it applies, the contractual tenancy is continued until brought to an end in the manner prescribed by the Act, and in effect the landlord can only get possession on limited grounds.

Further, under the Leasehold Reform Act 1967, tenants of houses under leases for over 21 years at a low rent are in most cases given a right to purchase the freehold or to take an extended lease for a term of fifty years, provided the tenant at the time when he/she seeks to exercise the right has been occupying the house as his/her residence for the last three years or for periods amounting to three years in the last ten years.

(7) Full Rent Act or Housing Act protection is available only if a dwelling-house is let on a tenancy. If the occupier of a dwelling-house has a mere licence to occupy, he/she does not have protection. Even if he/she has a tenancy, he/she will not be protected if a low rent is payable. For these reasons, many occupants of houses owned by farmers and occupied by farm workers did not enjoy full security of tenure. The Rent (Agriculture) Act 1976 contains detailed provisions conferring security of tenure on certain agricultural workers housed by their employers and on their successors on death.

(8) Under the Landlord and Tenant Act 1985, in a lease of a dwelling-house granted for a term of less than seven years, there is implied a covenant by the landlord (a) to keep in repair the structure and exterior of the house and (b) to keep in repair and proper working order the installations in the house for the supply of water, gas and electricity, for sanitation, and for space heating or heating water.

(9) The Housing Act 1985 gives security of tenure to many tenants of local authorities and certain other bodies. Subject to certain conditions, such tenants may have the right to purchase their houses or to take a long lease of their flats.

(10) Tenants of flats and other dwellings are given a number of special rights by the Landlord and Tenant Act 1987 as amended, and the Leasehold Reform, Housing and Urban Development Act 1993.

Scotland

A lease is a contract, the relationship of the parties being governed by the terms thereof. As is also the case in England, legislation has played an important part in regulating that relationship. Thus, what at common law was an agreement binding only the parties to the deed, becomes in virtue of the Leases Act 1449, a contract binding the landlord's successors, as purchasers or creditors, provided the following four conditions are observed: (a) the lease, if for more than one year, must be in writing; (b) there must be a rent; (c) there must be a term of expiry; and (d) the tenant must have entered into possession.

It would be impracticable to enter here upon a general discussion of this branch of the law. A few important provisions include:

(1) The Agricultural Holdings (Scotland) Act 1991 is a consolidating Act applicable to Scotland. It contains provisions similar to those in the English Act alluded to in the preceding section.

The Scottish Land Court, which is now regulated by the Scottish Land Court Act 1993, has jurisdiction over a large proportion of agricultural and pastoral land in Scotland.

(2) In Scotland business premises are not controlled by statute to so great an extent as in England, but the Tenancy of Shops (Scotland) Act 1949 gives a measure of security to tenants of shops. This Act enables the tenant of a shop who is threatened with eviction to apply to the sheriff for a renewal of the tenancy. If the landlord has offered to sell the property to the tenant at an agreed price the application for a renewal of the tenancy may be dismissed. Reference should be made to section 1 (3) of the 1949 Act for particulars of other circumstances in which the sheriff has a discretion to dismiss an application. The Act extends to premises held by the Crown or government departments, either as landlord or tenant.

(3) Many leases contain references to the term and quarter days in connection with the expiry of the lease payment dates or for rent reviews. At common law these days and dates are respectively Candlemas (2 February), Whitsunday (15 May), Lammas (1 August) and Martinmas (11 November). The Term and Quarter Days (Scotland) Act 1990 amended these dates to 28 February, 28 May, 28 August and 28 November respectively, with effect from 13 July 1991, unless, in the case of a deed executed before that date an application had been made to a sheriff for a declaration that a date other than the statutory date should apply. Where a pre-existing deed contains a reference to a specific date instead of or in addition to a day, then it is that date which shall apply.

(4) The Housing (Scotland) Act 1987 consolidates previous legislation in regard to the extensive powers and duties to local authorities in relation to housing. Included therein is the general provision regarding the rights of

public sector tenants to purchase the houses which they occupy and the restrictions regarding this right in certain circumstances where the house has been designed or adapted for occupation by the elderly. This Act also makes provision for secure tenancies for public sector tenants.

(5) The Housing (Scotland) Act 1988 creates, with certain exceptions, two new forms of tenancy for tenancies created after 2 January 1989: assured tenancies, and short assured tenancies. The assured tenancy significantly reduces the concept of security of tenure and abolishes any method of regulating rent other than market forces. The short assured tenancy lasts for at least six months and if properly constituted will allow the landlord to recover possession on its expiry. Provision is made for a tenant to apply to the rent assessment committee to fix a rent based on the rent a landlord might reasonably expect for a short assured tenancy of the property.

(6) For most tenancies created before 2 January 1989, the Rent (Scotland) Act 1984 will continue to apply. It defines regulated tenancies, which may be either furnished or unfurnished, and lays down the system by which a landlord or tenant may obtain from the Rent Office registration of a fair rent. The Act gives to tenants of either furnished or unfurnished lets a substantial degree of security of tenure. There are, however, certain exceptions; they do not apply to tenancies where the interest belongs to the Crown or to a government department or to a local authority, a development corporation of a new town or a housing corporation. There must be a true tenancy for the Act to apply. It does not apply to licencees such as lodgers or persons allowed to occupy houses on a grace and favour basis or to services occupiers.

The Act regulates the short tenancy, a category of let under which, on compliance with certain conditions, the landlord can be assured of recovering possession on the expiry of the stipulated period of let. The Act defines the circumstances in which generally a landlord may apply for increased rent as a consequence of having carried out improvements to the property, and also lays down the system of phasing such rent increases. On the death of a statutory successor to a tenancy, the tenancy may pass for a second time to a member of the family or a relative who has been in residence in the house for a period of at least six months. The Act further lays down the duties and functions of rent officers and rent assessment committees with regard to unfurnished accommodation and of rent tribunals for furnished accommodation.

The Secretary of State for Scotland is given power in the 1988 Act to repeal or amend those sections of the 1984 Act relating to the phasing of rent increases. The other major features of the 1988 Act are to establish Scottish Homes, and to permit public sector properties to be transferred to Scottish Homes or a landlord approved by Scottish Homes.

LEGAL AID

The Legal Aid Act 1988 (as amended) is designed to make legal aid and advice more readily available for persons of small and moderate means. The main structure of the service is contained in the Act itself and the regulations made thereunder, administered by the Legal Aid Board.

CIVIL PROCEEDINGS

Legal aid is available for proceedings (including matrimonial causes) in the House of Lords, Court of Appeal, High Court, county courts, Lands Tribunal, Employment Appeal Tribunal, Restrictive Practices Court, before the Commons Commissioners, and civil proceedings in magistrates' courts. In any event, an application for legal aid will not be approved if it appears that the applicant would gain only a trivial advantage from the proceedings. Further, proceedings wholly or partly in respect of defamation are excepted from the scheme, as are also relator actions and election petitions. Legal aid is not available for proceedings before tribunals other than those mentioned above. It is generally not available for obtaining the decree in undefended divorce and judicial separation, although the legal advice and assistance scheme (see below) is, and legal aid is still available to deal with property, disputes over children, etc., arising in the suit.

Where a person is concerned in proceedings only in a representative, fiduciary or official capacity, his/her personal resources are not to be taken into account in considering eligibility for legal aid. In certain public law proceedings under the Children Act 1989, non-means tested legal aid is available. Apart from this, eligibility in civil proceedings depends upon an applicant's disposable income and disposable capital; particulars can be obtained from a solicitor, the Law Society or a Citizens' Advice Bureau. Except in cases where they are living apart or have a contrary interest, any resources of a person's spouse or cohabitee are to be treated as that person's resources. These figures will be assessed by the Department of Social Security and will be referred to the Legal Aid Board, who will determine whether reasonable grounds exist for the grant of a civil aid certificate. Appeal from refusal of a certificate lies to an area committee.

A person resident in England or Wales desiring legal aid should apply for a certificate to the appropriate area director for the area in which he or she resides; if resident elsewhere, application should be made to an area director in London. If a certificate is granted, the applicant may select his/her solicitor, and, if necessary, counsel from a panel. The costs of the assisted person's solicitor and counsel will be paid out of the legal aid fund. When, however, damages or property are recovered or preserved by the assisted person, the legal aid fund has a charge over them in respect of these costs less any contribution towards costs recovered from the unsuccessful party. In matrimonial cases, maintenance is exempt, as is the first £2,500 of any property settlement. The court may order that the costs of a successful unassisted party shall be paid out of the legal aid fund.

In an urgent case, e.g. domestic violence or to restrain the kidnapping abroad of a child, legal aid may be granted without the applicant's means being fully investigated beforehand. If on a full examination later he/she is found financially ineligible, he/she is liable to pay all the costs incurred on his/her behalf.

LEGAL ADVICE AND ASSISTANCE

The scheme is governed by the Legal Aid Act 1988. Under the legal advice and assistance scheme a client may obtain such advice or assistance as is normally provided by a solicitor. If necessary, the advice of a barrister may be obtained but, with the exception of domestic proceedings in a family proceedings court and certain other proceedings (see page 674), the scheme does not extend to taking any step in any proceedings before any court or tribunal. Where legal aid is available for civil proceedings (see above) or in criminal cases (see page 674), the scheme covers work done in making application for such legal aid.

A person (other than one receiving advice and assistance at a police station or from a duty solicitor) is eligible for advice or assistance under the scheme provided his/her disposable capital and his/her disposable income do not exceed the limits in force or if he/she is eligible for income support or family credit. In calculating disposable income, income tax and National Insurance contributions are deducted. For a married man or person with children or other dependants, further deductions will be made from both income and capital. It is intended that the financial limits shall approximate to those applying for legal aid in civil proceedings. Except when they are separated or have conflicting interests, the means of husband and wife or cohabiting couple will be aggregated for the purpose of determining financial eligibility. Particulars may be obtained from a solicitor, the Law Society or a Citizens' Advice Bureau.

Unless the solicitor's firm holds a franchise, a solicitor cannot do more than two hours' work, or three hours' in the case of divorce (where acting for the petitioner and drafting the petition), without leave of the area legal aid committee. The solicitor's costs are paid out of any monies recovered in respect of costs or damages from another party (although this may be waived by leave of the area committee in cases of hardship) and the balance will be paid by the legal aid fund.

The Act also extends the scheme to cover the costs of a solicitor who is present within the precincts of a family proceedings court or county court and is requested by the court to advise or represent a person who is in need of help.

In 1980 the scheme was enlarged to cover the cost of representation in domestic proceedings in a magistrates' court. It has since been extended to cover the representation of patients before Mental Health Review Tribunals. Cover for representation before Mental Health Review Tribunals is available regardless of means. Otherwise, representation is subject to financial eligibility limits. Application is made to the area or local committee for 'approval of assistance by way of representation' which will replace legal aid for such proceedings. The two-hour limit referred to above will not apply. An applicant who is outside the financial limits but eligible for legal aid will still have to apply for a legal aid certificate as before. Free advice and assistance, and assistance by way of representation from a duty solicitor, are also available in limited circumstances to persons appearing before a magistrates' court charged with a criminal offence.

In 1986 the scheme was further extended to provide free advice and assistance to all suspects detained at a police station, whether arrested or merely helping police with their enquiries, and free representation for all arrested persons who are the subject of an application for a warrant of further detention under the Police and Criminal Evidence Act 1984. Such persons may instruct a solicitor of their choice or take advantage of the duty solicitor scheme which has now been extended to cover police stations.

CRIMINAL PROCEEDINGS

The Legal Aid Act 1988 provides for legal aid in criminal proceedings. A criminal court (e.g. magistrates' court, Crown Court) has power to order legal aid to be granted where it appears desirable to do so in the interests of justice. The court shall make an order in certain cases, e.g. where a person is committed for trial on a charge of murder. However, the court may not make an order unless it appears to the court that the person's disposable income and capital are such that he/she requires assistance in meeting the costs of the particular proceedings in question. Application should be made to the appropriate court where proceedings are to take place.

An applicant shall be required to make a contribution towards the costs of his/her case if his/her disposable income and capital exceed certain prescribed limits.

Persons in receipt of income support are automatically exempt. In order to ascertain the amount of this contribution an applicant will have to produce written evidence of his/her means. Investigation of means will be carried out by the court. Any person who falls into arrears with the payment of contribution is liable to have the order revoked.

Any practising barrister or solicitor may act for a legally aided person in criminal proceedings unless excluded by reason of misconduct. In general, where legal aid is given it will normally include representation by both counsel and solicitor. However, in connection with magistrates' courts, representation will be by solicitor alone unless the offence is a serious one.

Where any doubt arises about the grant of a legal aid order, that doubt is to be resolved in favour of the applicant. The court also has power to amend or revoke a legal aid order. Legal aid may also be granted in connection with appellate proceedings, e.g. on appeal to the Criminal Division of the Court of Appeal under the Criminal Appeal Act 1968.

SCOTLAND

Legal aid in Scotland is governed by the Legal Aid (Scotland) Act 1986 and the regulations made thereunder. This Act established the Scottish Legal Aid Board, which has the general function of securing that legal aid and legal advice and assistance are available in accordance with the Act, and of administering the Scottish Legal Aid Fund.

CIVIL PROCEEDINGS

Civil legal aid is available in relation to civil proceedings in the House of Lords in appeals from the Court of Session, in the Court of Session, the Lands Valuation Appeal Court, the Scottish Land Court, the Sheriff Court, the Lands Tribunal for Scotland, the Employment Appeals Tribunal and to the European Court of Human Rights. Civil legal aid is granted if, on application to the Board, the Board is satisfied that there is *probabilis causa litigandi* and that it is reasonable in the particular circumstances of the case that legal aid should be awarded. Eligibility and any contribution required from an applicant is dependent on their disposable income and disposable capital. Information on current financial limits can be obtained from the Scottish Legal Aid Board, a solicitor, or a Citizens' Advice Bureau.

A person believing himself/herself to be eligible may instruct any solicitor of his/her own choice. If a court action is not immediately contemplated, application will be made for legal advice and assistance, which operates in a similar manner to the legal advice and assistance scheme in England. If proceedings are contemplated then a formal application for civil legal aid will be made and there are special provisions for emergency applications in appropriate circumstances.

If proceedings are decided against a person in receipt of legal aid the court shall determine a reasonable sum in the circumstances as an appropriate award of expenses to be made against the applicant. The court may make an award out of the fund only if proceedings were instituted by the legally assisted person and the court is satisfied that the resisting party would suffer severe financial hardship unless the order is made, and if the court is satisfied that in all the circumstances it is just and equitable that an award be made. If monies are recovered by a legally assisted person these fall to be paid to the Scottish Legal Aid Board who will then determine the appropriate level of contribution from the sums received which should be made to the expenses of their litigation.

CRIMINAL PROCEEDINGS

Legal aid in criminal causes is also administered under the Legal Aid (Scotland) Act 1986. The procedure for application for criminal legal aid is dependent on the circumstances of each case. In serious cases heard before a jury under solemn procedure it is for the court to decide whether to grant legal aid. Applications for legal aid must normally be made on the prescribed forms to the clerk of the court in question and an applicant is required to provide therein particulars of the merits of his/her case and his/her financial circumstances. In summary criminal causes, however, the procedure is dependent on whether the applicant is in custody; if so he/she is entitled to automatic free legal aid from the duty solicitor. If the applicant is not in custody and wishes to plead guilty, he/she is ineligible for full legal aid but may be entitled to criminal legal advice and assistance, and in some circumstances may qualify for assistance by way of representation which will enable his/her solicitor to appear and make a plea in mitigation on his/her behalf. If he/she is not in custody and wishes to plead not guilty, he/she can apply to the Scottish Legal Aid Board for criminal legal aid on the prescribed form not later than 14 days after the first court appearance at which he/she made the plea, and legal aid shall be granted only if the Board is satisfied that the accused cannot meet the expenses of the case without undue hardship and that it is in the interest of justice as defined by the 1986 Act.

TOWN AND COUNTRY PLANNING

The Town and Country Planning Act 1990 (consolidating earlier Acts) as amended by the Planning and Compensation Act 1991, contains provisions affecting the liberty of an owner of land to develop and use it at will. A person has generally to get planning permission from the local planning authority before carrying out any development on the land.

Development includes:

(a) carrying out of building, engineering, mining or other operations
(b) making a material change in use

It is expressly provided that if one dwelling-house is converted into two or more dwelling-houses, this involves a material change in use.

The following do not constitute 'development':

(a) maintaining, improving or altering the interior of a building, provided there is no material change to the exterior, with the exception that any expansion, or works begun for the expansion, of a building below ground level constitutes development
(b) changing the use of property within the curtilage of a dwelling-house for a purpose incidental to the use of the dwelling-house as such. (It will, however, be development if building operations are carried out)

Application can be made to the local planning authority to determine whether or not an operation or change of use constitutes development.

PLANNING PERMISSION

Application for planning permission is not always necessary, as the Secretary of State may make development orders giving general permission for a specified type of development, e.g. enlargement of a dwelling-house (including erection of a garage), so long as the cubic content of the original dwelling (external measurement) is not exceeded by more than 70 cubic metres or 15 per cent, whichever is greater, subject to a maximum of 115 cubic metres. However, in the case of a terraced house, the limitation is 50 cubic metres or 10 per cent, whichever is the greater, subject to the maximum of 115 cubic metres.

Appeal against refusal of permission lies to the Secretary of State and from his decision, in limited circumstances, to the High Court. If the result of the appeal is unsatisfactory, an applicant may in certain circumstances require the local authority to purchase the land.

SCOTLAND

The Town and Country Planning (Scotland) Act 1972 consolidates the statute law relating to town and country planning in Scotland.

The uses of buildings are classified by the Town and Country Planning (Use Classes) (Scotland) Order 1988 (as amended). Changes in use prior to 31 December 1984 are immune from enforcement proceedings.

Development normally requires to be commenced within five years from the date of granting permission.

The 1972 Act contains provisions for an appeal to the Secretary of State against the refusal of planning permission. The decision of the Secretary of State is final.

Sections 87 and 92 of the Local Government, Planning and Land Act 1980 contain important provisions on planning applications and, unlike certain parts of this Act, extend to Scotland.

VOTERS' QUALIFICATIONS

The franchise is governed by the Representation of the People Acts 1983 and 1985 (as amended by the Representation of the People Acts 1989, 1990, 1991 and 1993). Those entitled to vote as electors at a parliamentary election in any constituency are all persons resident there on the qualifying date who, at that date and on the date of the poll, are Commonwealth citizens or citizens of the Republic of Ireland and who are not subject to any legal incapacity to vote and who on the date of the poll are at least 18 years of age. However, a person is not entitled to vote at a parliamentary election in any constituency in Northern Ireland unless he/she was resident in Northern Ireland during the whole of the period of three months ending on the qualifying date for that election. Also, no person can use his/her vote unless he/she is on the register of electors kept for the constituency. A person who is of voting age on the date of the poll at a parliamentary or local government election is entitled to vote, whether or not he/she was of voting age on the qualifying date. Accordingly, a qualified person will be entitled to be registered in a register of parliamentary electors or a register of local government electors if he/she will attain voting age within 12 months from the date on which the register is required to be published. Subject to certain conditions, the 1985 Act extends the franchise to British citizens overseas.

The register is prepared by the registration officer in each constituency in Great Britain. It is the registration officer's duty to have a house-to-house or other sufficient inquiry made as to the persons entitled to be registered and to publish preliminary electors' lists showing the persons appearing to him/her to be entitled to be registered. Any person whose name is omitted may claim registration, and any person on the list may object to the inclusion therein of other persons' names; the registration officer determines the claims and objections.

Voters at a parliamentary or local government election must generally vote in person at the allotted polling station, except for those entitled to vote by post or at any polling station, and those for whom proxies have been appointed. Certain people can apply to be treated as absent voters at a parliamentary election and thus able to vote by post; among these are registered service voters, those unable by reason of blindness or other physical incapacity or by reason of the general nature of their occupation, service or employment to go in person to the polling station, and those no longer at their qualifying address or unable to go in person from their qualifying address to the polling station without making a journey by air or sea.

Unless entitled to vote by post, a person registered as a service voter may vote by proxy at a parliamentary or local government election. A proxy may also be appointed by a registered elector, where the registration officer is satisfied that the applicant's circumstances on the date of the poll are likely to be such that he/she cannot reasonably be expected to vote in person at the allotted polling station. The appointment of a person to vote as proxy at parliamentary elections has effect also for the purposes of local government elections.

The Cinque Ports

As their name implies, the Cinque Ports were originally five in number: Hastings, New Romney, Hythe, Dover and Sandwich. They were formed during the eleventh century to defend the Channel coast and, after the Norman Conquest, were recognized as a Confederation by a charter of 1278. The 'antient towns' of Winchelsea and Rye were added at some time after the Conquest. The other members of the Confederation, known as Limbs, are Lydd, Faversham, Folkestone, Deal, Tenterden, Margate and Ramsgate.

Until 1855 the duty of the Cinque Ports was to provide ships and men for the defence of the state in return for considerable privileges, such as tax exemptions and the framing of by-laws. Of these privileges only jurisdiction in Admiralty remains.

The Barons of the Cinque Ports have the ancient privilege of attending the Coronation ceremony and are allotted special places in Westminster Abbey.

Lord Warden of the Cinque Ports, HM Queen Elizabeth the Queen Mother
Judge, Court of Admiralty, G. Darling, RD, QC
Registrar, I. G. Gill, LVO, 3 Waterloo Crescent, Dover, Kent CT16 ILA. Tel: 01304-225225

LORD WARDENS OF THE CINQUE PORTS *since* 1904

The Marquess Curzon	1904
The Prince of Wales	1905
The Earl Brassey	1908
The Earl Beauchamp	1913
The Marquess of Reading	1934
The Marquess of Willingdon	1936
Winston Churchill	1941
Sir Robert Menzies	1965
HM Queen Elizabeth the Queen Mother	1978

Intellectual Property

COPYRIGHT

Copyright protects all original literary, dramatic, musical and artistic works, published editions of works, computer programs, sound recordings, films (including video) and broadcasts (including cable and satellite broadcasts). Under copyright the creators of these works can control the various ways in which their material may be exploited, the rights broadly covering copying, adapting, issuing copies to the public, performing in public, and broadcasting the material.

Copyright protection in the United Kingdom is automatic and there is no registration system. The term of copyright protection in literary, dramatic, musical and artistic works is currently the life of the author plus 50 years. This was increased to 70 years in the member states of the European Union from July 1995; legislation to bring the longer term into effect in the UK had not been passed at the time of going to press but was expected to be introduced in Parliament in autumn 1995. Other forms of copyright usually last for 50 years or less.

The main international treaties protecting copyright are the Berne Convention for the Protection of Literary and Artistic Works, the Rome Convention for the Protection of Performers, Producers of Phonograms and Broadcasting Organizations, and the Universal Copyright Convention (UCC); the UK is a signatory to these conventions. Copyright material created by UK nationals or residents is protected in each country which is a member of the conventions by the national law of that country. A full list of participating countries may be obtained from the Patent Office.

LICENSING

Reproduction of copyright material without seeking permission in each instance may be permitted under licence. In the UK the Copyright Licensing Agency licenses the reprographic copying of literary works. The International Federation of Reproduction Rights Organizations facilitates agreements between its member licensing agencies and on behalf of its members with organizations such as the World Intellectual Property Organization, UNESCO, the European Union and the Council of Europe.

LEGAL DEPOSIT

Publishers are legally obliged to send one copy of a new publication to each of the copyright deposit libraries within one month of publication. The aim of legal deposit is to keep a complete national archive of published works as a current reference and information source. The copyright deposit libraries are the British Library, the Bodleian Library in Oxford, Cambridge University Library, the National Library of Scotland, the National Library of Wales, and Trinity College Library in Dublin.

The duties of the British Library's Legal Deposit Office are split between two locations. Books and other publications are deposited at Boston Spa, and newspapers and periodicals at the Newspaper Legal Deposit Office in London. All publications for the other four copyright libraries in the UK are dealt with by the Agent for Copyright Libraries.

PATENTS

A patent is a document issued by the Patent Office relating to an invention and giving the proprietor monopoly rights, effective within the United Kingdom (including the Isle of Man). In return the patentee pays a fee to cover the costs of processing the patent and publicly discloses details of the invention.

To qualify for a patent an invention must be new, must exhibit an inventive step, and must be capable of industrial application. The patent is valid for a maximum of 20 years from the date on which the application was filed, subject to payment of annual fees from the end of the fourth year.

The Patent Office, established in 1852, is responsible for ensuring that all stages of an application comply with the Patents Act 1977, and that the invention meets the criteria for a patent. Patent Office Examiners check that the invention is new and innovative by searching previously published documents on the Patent Office databank, which contains details of some two million British patents, together with published international and European applications. The contents of the databank and of the Science Reference Library, which developed from the library established at the Patent Office, are available to the public.

The World Intellectual Property Organization (WIPO), a United Nations body, is responsible for administering many of the international conventions on intellectual property. The Patent Co-operation Treaty allows inventors to file a single application for patent rights in some or all of the 79 contracting states. This application is searched by an International Searching Authority and published by the International Bureau of WIPO. It may also be the subject of an (optional) international preliminary examination. Applicants must then deal directly with the patent offices in the countries where they are seeking patent rights.

The European Patent Convention, linked to the Patent Co-operation Treaty, allows inventors to obtain patent rights in all 17 contracting states by filing a single European patent application which is processed by the European Patent Office (EPO). Once granted, the patent is subject to national laws in each signatory country. To comply with security requirements, an applicant resident in the UK must file a European patent application with the UK Patent Office unless the Patent Office gives permission for it to be filed directly with the EPO. The EPO office for international patent documentation acts as an information, collection and reference centre for patent offices around the world.

TRADE MARKS

Trade marks are a means of identification, whether a word or device or a combination of both, a logo, or the shape of goods or their packaging, which enable traders to make their goods or services readily distinguishable from those supplied by other traders. Registration prevents other traders using the same or a similar trade mark for similar products or services for which the mark is registered.

In the UK trade marks are registered at the Trade Marks Registry in the Patent Office. In order to qualify for registration a mark must be capable of distinguishing its proprietor's goods or services from those of other undertakings. It should be non-deceptive and not easily confused with a mark that has already been registered for the same or similar goods or services. The relevant current legislation is the Trade Marks Act 1994.

It is possible to obtain an international trade mark registration, effective in over 30 countries, under the Madrid Agreement. UK companies cannot take advantage of this because the UK is not a party to this agreement. Following revision of UK trade marks law, however, the UK has ratified the protocol to the Madrid Agreement. Once the protocol has come into effect, British companies will be able to obtain international trade mark registration through a single application to WIPO in those countries party to the protocol.

EC trade mark regulation is now in force and will be administered by the Office for Harmonization in the Internal Market (trade marks and designs) in Alicante, Spain. The office, due to open in 1996, will register EC trade marks, which will be a unitary right valid throughout the European Union. The national registration of trade marks in member states will continue in parallel with the EC trade mark.

DESIGN PROTECTION

Design protection covers the outward appearance of an article and takes two forms in the UK, registered design and design right, which are not mutually exclusive. Registered design protects the aesthetic appearance of an article, including shape, configuration, pattern or ornament, although artistic works such as sculptures are excluded, being generally protected by copyright. In order to qualify for protection, a design must be new and materially different from earlier UK published designs. The owner of the design must apply to the Designs Registry at the Patent Office. Initial registration lasts for five years and is extendible in five-yearly steps to a maximum of 25 years. The current legislation is the Registered Designs Act 1949 (as amended).

There is no international design registry currently available to UK applicants; in general, separate applications must be made in each country in which protection is sought. Proposals for an EC design regulation are being discussed. If adopted, these would result in a unitary design right valid throughout the European Union, obtainable via a single application.

Design right is an automatic right which applies to the shape or configuration of articles and does not require registration. Unlike registered design, two-dimensional designs do not qualify for protection but designs of semiconductor chips (topographies) are protected by design right. Designs must be original and non-commonplace. The term of design right is ten years from first marketing of the design and the right is effective only in the UK. The current legislation is Part 3 of the Copyright, Designs and Patents Act 1988.

ORGANIZATIONS

AGENT FOR THE COPYRIGHT LIBRARIES, 100 Euston Street, London NW1 2HQ. Tel: 0171-380 0240. *Agent*, A. T. Smail
AUTHORS' LICENSING AND COLLECTING SOCIETY, 74 New Oxford Street, London WC1A 1EF. Tel: 0171-255 2034
CHARTERED INSTITUTE OF PATENT AGENTS, Staple Inn Buildings, London WC1V 7PZ. Tel: 0171-405 9450
COPYRIGHT LICENSING AGENCY LTD, 90 Tottenham Court Road, London W1P 9HE. Tel: 0171-436 5931
DESIGNS REGISTRY, The Patent Office, Cardiff Road, Newport, Gwent NP9 1RH. Tel: 01633-814000
EUROPEAN PATENT OFFICE, *Headquarters*, Erhardstrasse 27, D-80331 Munich, Germany
INTERNATIONAL FEDERATION OF REPRODUCTION RIGHTS ORGANIZATIONS (IFRRO), Goethestrasse 49, D-80336 Munich 2, Germany
LEGAL DEPOSIT OFFICE, The British Library, Boston Spa, Wetherby, West Yorkshire LS23 7BY. Tel: 01937-546267
NEWSPAPER LEGAL DEPOSIT OFFICE, The British Library Newspaper Library, 120 Colindale Avenue, London NW9 5LF. Tel: 0171-412 7378
OFFICE FOR HARMONIZATION IN THE INTERNAL MARKET (TRADE MARKS AND DESIGNS) (CTMO), 20 Avenida de la Aguilera, 03007 Alicante, Spain
THE PATENT OFFICE, Cardiff Road, Newport, Gwent NP9 1RH. Tel: 01633-814000
PUBLISHERS LICENSING SOCIETY, 90 Tottenham Court Road, London W1P 9HE. Tel: 0171-436 5931
SCIENCE REFERENCE LIBRARY, 25 Southampton Buildings, London WC2A 1AW. Tel: 0171-323 7494
TRADE MARKS REGISTRY, The Patent Office, Cardiff Road, Newport, Gwent NP9 1RH. Tel: 01633-814000
WORLD INTELLECTUAL PROPERTY ORGANIZATION (WIPO), 34 chemin des Colombettes, 1211 Geneva 20, Switzerland

The Media

Broadcasting

The British Broadcasting Corporation (*see* page 289) is responsible for public service broadcasting in the UK. Its role is to provide high-quality programmes with wide-ranging appeal that educate, inform and entertain. Its constitution and finances are governed by royal charter and by a licence and agreement.

The Independent Television Commission (*see* page 317) and the Radio Authority (*see* page 339) were set up under the terms of the Broadcasting Act 1990. The ITC is the regulator and licensing authority for all commercially-funded television services, including cable and satellite services. The Radio Authority is the regulator and licensing authority for all independent radio services.

There are rules on cross-media ownership to prevent undue concentration of ownership. These might change as a result of government proposals published in May 1995 (*see* page 1176).

FUTURE OF THE BBC

The BBC's present charter expires at the end of 1996. In July 1994 the Government published a White Paper which set out plans for the structure and operation of the BBC under a new charter and agreement to operate for ten years from 1 January 1997. A draft charter will be published in the autumn of 1995 and will be debated in both Houses of Parliament.

COMPLAINTS

The Broadcasting Complaints Commission (BCC) was set up in 1981. It considers and adjudicates upon complaints of unfair treatment or unwarranted infringement of privacy in all broadcast programmes and advertisements on television, radio, cable and satellite services. The Broadcasting Standards Council (BSC) was set up under the Broadcasting Act 1990. It is an advisory body which monitors the portrayal of violence, sex and matters of taste and decency in all broadcast programmes and advertisements on television, radio, cable and satellite services. The Government has announced plans to merge the BCC and BSC.

BROADCASTING COMPLAINTS COMMISSION, Grosvenor Gardens House, 35–37 Grosvenor Gardens, London SW1W 0BS. Tel: 0171-630 1966. *Chairman,* Canon P. Pilkington; *Secretary,* R. M. Hargreaves
BROADCASTING STANDARDS COUNCIL, 7 The Sanctuary, London SW1P 3JS. Tel: 0171-233 0544. *Chair,* The Lady Howe of Aberavon; *Director,* C. Shaw, CBE

TELEVISION

All channels are broadcast in colour on 625 lines UHF from a network of transmitting stations which are owned and operated by the BBC and by National Transcommunications Ltd. Transmissions are available to more than 99 per cent of the population.

The total number of receiving television licences in the UK at end June 1995 was 20,834,304, of which 753,748 were for monochrome receivers and 20,080,556 for colour receivers. Annual television licence fees are: monochrome £28.50; colour £86.50.

BBC TELEVISION

Television Centre, Wood Lane, London W12 7RJ
Tel 0181-743 8000

The BBC's experiments in television broadcasting started in 1929 and in 1936 the BBC began the world's first public service of high-definition television from Alexandra Palace. The BBC broadcasts two national television services, BBC 1 and BBC 2; outside England these services are designated BBC Scotland on 1, BBC Scotland on 2, BBC 1 Northern Ireland, BBC 2 Northern Ireland, BBC Wales on 1 and BBC Wales on 2.

BBC WORLDWIDE TELEVISION

80 Wood Lane, London W12 0TT
Tel 0181-576 2783

BBC Worldwide Television (formerly BBC World Service Television) was set up in 1991 to assume responsibility for the BBC's satellite television interests. It has a global alliance with Pearson PLC and now produces three satellite channels. Its core service is a 24-hour news and information channel, BBC World, which is now broadcast in Europe, Asia, Africa, Canada, Japan and New Zealand. An Arabic language channel for the Middle East, North Africa and Europe is broadcast for eight hours a day. BBC Prime is a subscription entertainment channel available across Europe.

INDEPENDENT TELEVISION

The ITV franchises for the 15 regional companies and for breakfast television were allocated new ten-year licences from January 1993. A new independent national television channel was due to be established by autumn 1993, but the ITC decided not to award the licence to Channel Five Holdings Ltd, the only applicant. The ITC received a further four bids for the licence in May 1995. The winner will be announced in autumn 1995 and the new channel is due to be on air by January 1997.

ITV NETWORK CENTRE/ITV ASSOCIATION

200 Gray's Inn Road, London WC1X 8HF
Tel 0171-843 8000

The ITV Network Centre is wholly owned by the ITV companies and undertakes the commissioning and scheduling of those television programmes which are shown across the ITV network. Through its sister organization, the ITV Association, it also provides a range of services to the ITV companies where a common approach is required.
Network Director, M. Plantin
Director, ITV Association, B. Cox

INDEPENDENT TELEVISION NETWORK COMPANIES

ANGLIA TELEVISION (owned by MAI) (*eastern England*), Anglia House, Norwich NR1 3JG. Tel: 01603-615151
BORDER TELEVISION PLC (*the Borders*), Television Centre, Carlisle CA1 3NT. Tel: 01228-25101
CARLTON TELEVISION LTD (*London (weekdays)*), 101 St Martin's Lane, London WC2N 4AZ. Tel: 0171-240 4000
CENTRAL INDEPENDENT TELEVISION PLC (owned by Carlton Communications) (*the Midlands*), Central House, Broad Street, Birmingham B1 2JP. Tel: 0121-643 9898
CHANNEL TELEVISION LTD (*Channel Islands*), The Television Centre, St Helier, Jersey JE2 3ZD. Tel: 01534-68999
GRAMPIAN TELEVISION PLC (*northern Scotland*), Queen's Cross, Aberdeen AB9 2XJ. Tel: 01224-646464

GRANADA TELEVISION LTD (*north-west England*), Granada TV Centre, Quay Street, Manchester M60 9EA. Tel: 0161-832 7211

HTV GROUP (*Wales and western England*), HTV Wales, Television Centre, Culverhouse Cross, Cardiff CF5 6XJ. Tel: 01222-590590; HTV Ltd, Television Centre, Bath Road, Bristol BS4 3HG. Tel: 0117-977 8366

LONDON WEEKEND TELEVISION (owned by Granada Group) (*London (weekends)*), London Television Centre, Upper Ground, London SE1 9LT. Tel: 0171-620 1620

MERIDIAN BROADCASTING LTD (owned by MAI) (*south and south-east England*), Television Centre, Southampton SO9 5HZ. Tel: 01703-222555

SCOTTISH TELEVISION PLC (*central Scotland*), Cowcaddens, Glasgow G2 3PR. Tel: 0141-332 9999

TYNE TEES TELEVISION LTD (*north-east England*), The Television Centre, City Road, Newcastle upon Tyne NE1 2AL. Tel: 0191-261 0181

ULSTER TELEVISION PLC (*Northern Ireland*), Havelock House, Ormeau Road, Belfast BT7 1EB. Tel: 01232-328122

WESTCOUNTRY TELEVISION LTD (*south-west England*), Western Wood Way, Langage Science Park, Plymouth PL7 5BG. Tel: 01752-333333

YORKSHIRE TELEVISION LTD (*Yorkshire*), The Television Centre, Leeds LS3 1JS. Tel: 0113-243 8283

OTHER INDEPENDENT TELEVISION COMPANIES

CHANNEL FOUR TELEVISION CORPORATION, 124 Horseferry Road, London SW1P 2TX. Tel: 0171-396 4444. Provides a service to the UK except Wales, and is charged to cater for interests under-represented by the ITV network companies. Channel 4 sells its own advertising. The ITV companies are committed to providing financial support for Channel 4 if Channel 4's income falls below a certain point. They also benefit financially if Channel 4's revenues are higher; in 1994 Channel 4 gave the ITV companies £38.2 million. In return ITV promotes Channel 4 programmes.

GMTV LTD (*breakfast television*), The London Television Centre, Upper Ground, London SE1 9TT. Tel: 0171-827 7000

INDEPENDENT TELEVISION NEWS LTD, 200 Gray's Inn Road, London WC1X 8XZ. Tel: 0171-833 3000

TELETEXT LTD, 101 Farm Lane, London SW6 1QJ. Tel: 0171-386 5000. Provides teletext services for the ITV companies and Channel 4

WELSH FOURTH CHANNEL AUTHORITY (Sianel Pedwar Cymru), Parc Ty Glas, Llanishen, Cardiff CF4 5DU. Tel: 01222-747444. S4C schedules Welsh language programmes and relays most Channel 4 programmes

DIRECT BROADCASTING BY SATELLITE TELEVISION

BRITISH SKY BROADCASTING LTD, 6 Centaurs Business Park, Isleworth, Middx TW7 5QD. Tel: 0171-705 3000. Broadcasts nine channels which are wholly owned by Sky (Sky One, Sky News, Sky Sports, Sky Sports 2, Sky Movies, The Movie Channel, Sky Movies Gold, Sky Soap and Sky Travel). Twelve channels are available in the multi-channel package which is broadcast, but not owned, by Sky.

RADIO

BBC RADIO
Broadcasting House, Portland Place, London W1A 1AA
Tel 0171-580 4468

BBC Radio broadcasts five national services to the UK, Isle of Man and the Channel Islands. There is also a tier of national regional services in Wales, Scotland and Northern Ireland and 38 local radio stations in England and the Channel Islands. In Wales there are two regional services based on the Welsh and English languages respectively.

BBC NATIONAL SERVICES

RADIO 1 (Pop and rock music, social action campaigns and comedy) – 24 hours a day. *Frequencies:* FM 97.6–99.8 MHz, coverage 99%

RADIO 2 (Popular music, entertainment, comedy and the arts) – 24 hours a day. *Frequencies:* FM 88–90.2 MHz, coverage 99%

RADIO 3 (Classical music, drama, documentaries, poetry, and schools programmes) – 6.55 a.m.–12.30 a.m. daily. *Frequencies:* FM 90.2–92.4 MHz, coverage 99%

RADIO 4 (News, documentaries, drama, entertainment, and cricket on long wave in season) – 5.55 a.m.–12.45 a.m. daily, with BBC World Service overnight. *Frequencies:* FM in England 92.4–94.6 MHz, elsewhere 92.4–96.1 and 103.5–105 MHz, coverage 99%; LW 198kHz/1515m, plus eight local fillers on MW

RADIO 5 LIVE (News and sport) – 24 hours a day. *Frequencies:* MW 693 kHz and 909 kHz, plus one local filler

BBC NATIONAL REGIONAL SERVICES

RADIO SCOTLAND *Frequencies:* MW 810 kHz plus two local fillers; FM 92.4–96.1 MHz, coverage 94%. Local programmes on FM as above: HIGHLANDS; NORTH-EAST (also MW 990 kHz); BORDERS; SOUTH-WEST (also MW 585 kHz); ORKNEY; SHETLAND. RADIO NAN GAIDHEAL (Gaelic service) (FM 103.5–105 MHz) available in Western Highlands and Islands and Moray Firth areas. Programmes also available throughout Scotland on MW 810 kHz every weekday 9–10 p.m.

RADIO ULSTER *Frequencies:* MW 1341 kHz, plus two local fillers; FM 92.4–96.1 MHz, coverage 96%. Local programmes on RADIO FOYLE *Frequencies:* MW 792 kHz; FM 93.1 MHz

RADIO WALES *Frequencies:* MW 882 kHz plus two local fillers, coverage 96%. Local news for CLWYD on MW 657 kHz

RADIO CYMRU (Welsh-language) *Frequencies:* FM 92.4–96.1 and 103.5–105 MHz, coverage 96%

BBC LOCAL RADIO STATIONS

There are 38 local stations serving England and the Channel Islands:

BBC 3 COUNTIES RADIO, PO Box 3CR, Luton, Beds LU1 5XL. Tel: 01582-441000. *Frequencies:* MW 1161/630 kHz, 95.5/103.8 FM

BERKSHIRE, Broadcasting House, 42A Portman Road, Reading, Berks RG3 1NB. Tel: 01734-567056. *Frequencies:* 94.6/95.4/104.1/104.4 FM

BRISTOL, 3 Tyndalls Park Road, Bristol BS8 1PP. Tel: 0117-974 1111. *Frequencies:* MW 1548 kHz, 94.9/95.5/104.6 FM

CAMBRIDGESHIRE, Broadcasting House, 104 Hills Road, Cambridge CB2 1LD. Tel: 01223-259696. *Frequencies:* MW 1026 kHz, 95.7 FM

CLEVELAND, PO Box 95 FM, Newport Road, Middlesbrough, Cleveland TS1 5DG. Tel: 01642-225211. *Frequencies:* MW 1548 kHz, 95.0/95.8 FM

CORNWALL, Phoenix Wharf, Truro, Cornwall TR1 1UA. Tel: 01872-75421. *Frequencies:* MW 630/657 kHz, 95.2/96.0/103.9 FM

CUMBRIA, Annetwell Street, Carlisle CA3 8BB. Tel: 01228-592444. *Frequencies:* MW 756/1458/837 kHz, 95.2/95.6/96.1/104.2 FM

CWR (COVENTRY AND WARWICKSHIRE RADIO), 25 Warwick Road, Coventry CVI 2WR. Tel: 01203-559911. *Frequencies:* 94.8/103.7 FM

DERBY, 56 St Helen's Street, Derby DEI 3HL. Tel: 01332-361111. *Frequencies:* MW 1116 kHz, 94.2/95.3/104.5 FM

DEVON, PO Box 5, Broadcasting House, Seymour Road, Plymouth PL3 5BD. Tel: 01752-260323. *Frequencies:* MW 801/990/1458/801 kHz, 103.4/96.0/95.8/94.8 FM

ESSEX, PO Box 765, 198 New London Road, Chelmsford CM2 9AB. Tel: 01245-262393. *Frequencies:* MW 765/729/1530 kHz, 103.5/95.3 FM

GLOUCESTERSHIRE, London Road, Gloucester GLI ISW. Tel: 01452-308585. *Frequencies:* 95.0/104.7 FM

GLR (GREATER LONDON RADIO), 35A Marylebone High Street, London WIA 4LG. Tel: 0171-224 2424. *Frequencies:* MW 1458 kHz, 94.9 FM

GMR (GREATER MANCHESTER RADIO), New Broadcasting House, Oxford Road, Manchester M60 ISJ. Tel: 0161-200 2000. *Frequencies:* MW 1458 kHz, 95.1 FM

GUERNSEY, Commerce House, Les Banques, St Peter Port, Guernsey. Tel: 01481-728977. *Frequencies:* MW 1116 kHz, 93.2 FM

HEREFORD AND WORCESTER, 43 Broad Street, Hereford HR4 9HH. Tel: 01432-355252; Hylton Road, Worcester WR2 5WW. Tel: 01905-748485. *Frequencies:* MW 738/819 kHz, 104.6/104.0/94.7 FM

HUMBERSIDE, 9 Chapel Street, Hull HUI 3NU. Tel: 01482-323232. *Frequencies:* MW 1485 kHz, 95.9 FM

JERSEY, 18 Parade Road, St Helier, Jersey. Tel: 01534-870000. *Frequencies:* MW 1026 kHz, 88.8 FM

KENT, Sun Pier, Chatham, Kent ME4 4EZ. Tel: 01634-830555. *Frequencies:* MW 1035/774/1602 kHz, 96.7/104.2 FM

LANCASHIRE, 20–26 Darwen Street, Blackburn BB2 2EA. Tel: 01254-262411. *Frequencies:* MW 855/1557 kHz, 95.5/104.5/103.9 FM

LEEDS, Broadcasting House, Woodhouse Lane, Leeds LS2 9PN. Tel: 0113-244 2131. *Frequencies:* MW 774 kHz, 92.4/95.3 FM

LEICESTER, Epic House, Charles Street, Leicester LEI 3SH. Tel: 0116-251 6688. *Frequencies:* MW 837 kHz, 104.9 FM

LINCOLNSHIRE, Radio Buildings, Newport, Lincoln LNI 3XY. Tel: 01522-511411. *Frequencies:* MW 837 kHz, 104.9 FM

MERSEYSIDE, 55 Paradise Street, Liverpool LI 3BP. Tel: 0151-708 5500. *Frequencies:* MW 1485 kHz, 95.8 FM

NEWCASTLE, Broadcasting Centre, Barrack Road, Fenham, Newcastle upon Tyne NE99 IRN. Tel: 0191-232 4141. *Frequencies:* MW 1458 kHz, 95.4/104.4/96.0 FM

NORFOLK, Norfolk Tower, Surrey Street, Norwich NRI 3PA. Tel: 01603-617411. *Frequencies:* MW 855/873 kHz, 95.1/104.4 FM

NORTHAMPTON, Broadcasting House, Abington Street, Northampton NNI 2BE. Tel: 01604-239100. *Frequencies:* 104.2/106.3 FM

NOTTINGHAM, York House, Mansfield Road, Nottingham NGI 3JB. Tel: 0115-941 5161. *Frequencies:* MW 1584/1521 kHz, 103.8/95.5 FM

OXFORD, 269 Banbury Road, Oxford OX2 7DW. Tel: 01865-311444. *Frequency:* 95.2 FM

SHEFFIELD, Ashdell Grove, 60 Westbourne Road, Sheffield SIO 2QU. Tel: 0114-268 6185. *Frequencies:* MW 1035 kHz, 94.7/104.1/88.6 FM

SHROPSHIRE, 2–4 Boscobel Drive, Shrewsbury SYI 3TT. Tel: 01743-248484. *Frequencies:* MW 1584 kHz, 95.0/96.0 FM

SOLENT, Broadcasting House, Havelock Road, Southampton SOI OXR. Tel: 01703-631311. *Frequencies:* MW 999/1359 kHz, 96.1 FM

SOUTHERN COUNTIES, Broadcasting House, Guildford, Surrey GU2 5AP. Tel: 01483-306306; Marlborough Place, Brighton BNI ITU. Tel: 01273-680231. *Frequencies:* MW 1485/1161/1368 kHz, 95.0/95.1/95.3/104.5/104.6/104.0 FM

STOKE, Conway House, Cheapside, Hanley, Stoke-on-Trent STI IJJ. Tel: 01782-208080. *Frequencies:* MW 1503 kHz, 94.6 FM

SUFFOLK, Broadcasting House, St Matthew's Street, Ipswich IPI 3EP. Tel: 01473-250000. *Frequencies:* 95.5/103.9/104.6 FM

WILTSHIRE SOUND, Broadcasting House, 56–58 Prospect Place, Swindon SNI 3RW. Tel: 01793-513626. *Frequencies:* MW 1332/1368 kHz, 103.6/103.4/103.5 FM

WM (WEST MIDLANDS), Pebble Mill Road, Birmingham B5 7SD. Tel: 0121-414 8484. *Frequencies:* MW 828/1458 kHz, 95.6 FM

YORK, 20 Bootham Row, York YO3 7BR. Tel: 01904-641351. *Frequencies:* MW 666/1260 kHz, 103.7/104.3/95.5 FM

BBC WORLD SERVICE

Bush House, Strand, London WC2B 4PH
Tel 0171-240 3456

The BBC World Service broadcasts 918 hours of programmes a week in 41 languages including English. Eighty-six transmitters are used, 40 of them in the UK and 46 at relay stations overseas. In addition the World Service supplies 432 hours of programmes a week for other radio stations.

In 1995 the World Service was reorganized into six regions, each responsible for programmes in English as well as regional languages.

AFRICA AND THE MIDDLE EAST, Arabic, French, Hausa, Somali and Swahili; English programmes including *Network Africa* and *Focus on Africa*.

ASIA PACIFIC, Burmese, Cantonese, Indonesian, Mandarin, Thai and Vietnamese; English programmes including *East Asia Today*.

EUROPE, Albanian, Bulgarian, Croatian, Czech, Finnish, German, Greek, Hungarian, Polish, Romanian, Serbian, Slovak, Slovene and Turkish; English programmes including *Europe Today*.

FORMER SOVIET UNION AND SOUTH-WEST ASIA, Russian, Ukrainian, Pashto, Persian, Azeri and Uzbek.

SOUTH ASIA, Bengali, Hindi, Nepali, Sinhala, Tamil and Urdu; English programmes including *South Asia Report*.

THE AMERICAS, Portuguese for Brazil, Spanish; English programmes including *Caribbean Report* and *Calling the Falklands*.

BBC ENGLISH teaches English world-wide through radio, television and a wide range of published courses

BBC MONITORING provides regional summaries and a teleprinted news service from the output of overseas radio and television stations

BBC RADIO INTERNATIONAL sells a wide range of BBC radio programmes on CD to broadcasters in over 100 countries

BBC TRAINING runs journalism, management and skills training courses for overseas broadcasters

BBC MARSHALL PLAN OF THE MIND TRUST produces business skills radio courses for Russia and Ukraine.

BBC INTERNATIONAL BROADCASTING AND AUDIENCE RESEARCH carries out audience research and sells printed publications and data

INDEPENDENT RADIO

Three independent national radio stations have been licensed since 1991. Five independent regional local radio stations began broadcasting in February 1995. Since January 1991 the Authority has awarded 48 other new local radio licences, has readvertised 114 local licences, and has a further 11 to be readvertised by the autumn of 1995. A further 35 new licences will be advertised by early 1997.

ASSOCIATION OF INDEPENDENT RADIO COMPANIES, 46 Westbourne Grove, London W2 5SH. Tel: 0171-727 2646. *Director,* P. Brown

INDEPENDENT NATIONAL RADIO STATIONS

CLASSIC FM, Academic House, 24–28 Oval Road, London NW1 7DQ. Tel: 0171-284 3000. 24 hours a day. *Frequencies:* FM 99.9–101.9 MHz

TALK RADIO UK, 76 Oxford Street, London WIN 0TR. Tel: 0171-636 1089. 24 hours a day. *Frequencies:* MW 1053/1089 kHz

VIRGIN RADIO, 1 Golden Square, London WIR 4DJ. Tel: 0171-434 1215. 24 hours a day. *Frequencies:* MW 1215/1197/1233/1242/1260 kHz

INDEPENDENT REGIONAL LOCAL RADIO STATIONS

CENTURY RADIO (*North-east*), PO Box 100, Gateshead NE8 2YY. Tel: 0191-477 6666. *Frequencies:* 100.7/101.8/96.2 FM

GALAXY RADIO (*Severn Estuary*), Broadcast Centre, Portland Square, Bristol BS1 8RZ. Tel: 0117-924 0111. *Frequencies:* 101 FM; 97.2 FM (Bristol)

HEART FM (*West Midlands*), 1 The Square, 111 Broad Street, Birmingham B115 1AS. Tel: 0121-626 1007. *Frequency:* 100.7 FM

JFM (*North-west*), The World Trade Centre, Exchange Quay, Manchester M5 3EJ. Tel: 0161-877 1004. *Frequency,* 100.4 FM

SCOT FM (*Central Scotland*), Number 1 Shed, Albert Quay, Leith Docks, Edinburgh EH6 7DN. Tel: 0131-554 6677. *Frequencies:* 100.3/101.1 FM

INDEPENDENT LOCAL RADIO STATIONS

A1 FM LTD, The Lindens, 34 Carmel Road, Darlington DL3 8DJ. Tel: 01325-467558. *Frequency:* 103.2 FM

THE BAY, PO Box 969, St George's Quay, Lancaster LA1 3LD. Tel: 01524-848747. *Frequencies:* 96.9/102.3/103.2 FM

BEACON RADIO, 267 Tettenhall Road, Wolverhampton WV6 0DQ. Tel: 01902-757211. *Frequencies:* 97.2/103.1 FM

BOSS 603 RADIO, Churchill Studios, Churchill Road, Cheltenham, Glos GL53 7EP. Tel: 01242-255023. *Frequency:* MW 603 kHz

BREEZE, Radio House, Clifftown Road, Southend-on-Sea, Essex SS1 1SX. Tel: 01702-333711. *Frequency:* MW 1359/1431 kHz

BRUNEL CLASSIC GOLD, PO Box 2020, Swindon SN4 7EX. Tel: 01793-440301; PO Box 2020, Bristol BS99 7SN. Tel: 0117-983 3201. *Frequencies:* MW 1260 kHz (Bristol); 1161 kHz (Swindon); 936 kHz (West Wilts)

CAPITAL FM AND GOLD, Euston Tower, London NW1 3DR. Tel: 0171-608 6080. *Frequencies:* MW 1548 kHz (*Gold*), 95.8 FM

CENTRAL FM, Stirling Enterprise Park, Kerse Road, Stirling FK7 7XJ. Tel: 01786-451188. *Frequency:* 103.1 FM

CFM, PO Box 964, Carlisle, Cumbria CA1 3NG. Tel: 01228-818964. *Frequencies:* 96.4 FM; 102.5 FM (Penrith)

CHANNEL 103 FM, 6 Tunnel Street, St Helier, Jersey JE2 4LU. Tel: 01543-888103. *Frequency:* 103.7 FM

CHILTERN RADIO PLC, Broadcast Centre, Chiltern Road, Dunstable, Beds LU6 1HQ. Tel: 01582-666001. *Frequencies:* MW 828 kHz, 97.6 FM(Luton), 792 kHz, 96.9 FM (Bedford)

CHOICE FM, 16–18 Trinity Gardens, London SW9 8DP. Tel: 0171-738 7969. *Frequency:* 96.9 FM

CHOICE FM – BIRMINGHAM, 95 Broad Street, Birmingham B15 1AU. Tel: 0121-616 1000. *Frequency:* 102.4 FM

CITY FM, 8–10 Stanley Street, Liverpool L1 6AF. Tel: 0151-227 5100. *Frequency:* 96.7 FM

CLASSIC GOLD 828, 5 Southcote Road, Bournemouth, Dorset BH1 3LR. Tel: 01202-294881. *Frequency:* MW 828 kHz

CLASSIC GOLD 1332, PO Box 2020, Queensgate Centre, Peterborough PE1 1LL. Tel: 01733-460460. *Frequency:* MW 1332 kHz

CLASSIC GOLD 1431 AM, PO Box 210, Reading, Berks RG31 7RZ. Tel: 01734-254400. *Frequency:* MW 1431 kHz

CLYDE 1 AND 2, Clydebank Business Park, Clydebank, Glasgow G81 2RX. Tel: 0141-306 2200. *Frequencies:* MW 1152 kHz, 102.5 FM; 97.0 FM (Vale of Leven); 103.3 FM (Firth of Clyde)

COAST FM, The Studios, 41 Conwy Road, Colwyn Bay, Clwyd. Tel: 01492-534555. *Frequency:* 96.3 FM

COOL FM, PO Box 974, Belfast BT1 1RT. Tel: 01247-817181. *Frequency:* 97.4 FM

COUNTRY 1035, Unit 7, Hurlingham Business Park, Sullivan Road, London SW6 3DU. Tel: 0171-384 1175. *Frequency:* 1035 kHz

ELEVEN SEVENTY AM, PO Box 1170, High Wycombe, Bucks HP13 6YT. Tel: 01494-446611. *Frequency:* MW 1170 kHz

ESSEX FM, Radio House, Clifftown Road, Southend-on-Sea, Essex SS1 1SX. Tel: 01702-333711. *Frequencies:* 96.3 FM (Southend), 102.6 FM (Chelmsford)

FORTH FM, Forth House, Forth Street, Edinburgh EH1 3LF. Tel: 0131-556 9255. *Frequencies:* 97.3/97.6 FM

FORTUNE 1458, PO Box 1458, Quay West, Trafford Park, Manchester M17 1FL. Tel: 0161-877 1458. *Frequency:* 1458 kHz

FOX FM, Brush House, Pony Road, Cowley, Oxford OX4 2XR. Tel: 01865-748787. *Frequencies:* 102.6/97.4 FM

GEM-AM, 29–31 Castle Gate, Nottingham NG1 7AP. Tel: 0115-952 7000. *Frequencies:* MW 999/945 kHz

GEMINI AM, Hawthorn House, Exeter Business Park, Exeter EX1 3QS. Tel: 01392-444444. *Frequencies:* MW 666/954 kHz

GEMINI FM, Hawthorn House, Exeter Business Park, Exeter EX1 3QS. Tel: 01392-444444. *Frequencies:* 97.0/96.4/103.0 FM

GOLD RADIO, Longmead, Shaftesbury, Dorset SP7 8QQ. Tel: 01747-855711. *Frequency:* 97.4 FM

GREAT NORTH RADIO, Newcastle upon Tyne NE99 1BB. Tel: 0191-420 3040. *Frequencies:* MW 1152/1170 kHz

GREAT YORKSHIRE GOLD, 900 Herries Road, Sheffield S6 1RH. Tel: 0114-285 2121; Forster Square, Bradford BD1 5NE. Tel: 01274-731521; Commercial Road, Hull HU1 2SG. Tel: 01482-25141. *Frequencies:* MW 1548/1305/990 kHz (S. Yorks, N. Midlands); 1278/1530 kHz (W. Yorks); 1161 kHz (Humberside)

GWR FM (BRISTOL AND BATH), PO Box 2000, Bristol BS99 7SN. Tel: 0117-984 3200. *Frequencies:* 96.3/103.0 FM

GWR FM (WILTSHIRE), PO Box 2000, Swindon SN4 7EX. Tel: 01793-440300. *Frequencies:* 96.5 FM (Marlborough); 97.2 FM (Swindon); 102.2 FM (West Wilts)

HALLAM FM, Radio House, 900 Herries Road, Hillsborough, Sheffield S6 1RH. Tel: 0114-285 3333. *Frequencies:* 97.4 FM (Sheffield); 96.1 FM (Rotherham); 102.9 FM (Barnsley); 103.4 FM (Doncaster)

HEART 106.2, The Chrysalis Building, Bramley Road, London W10 6SP. Tel: 0171-468 1062. *Frequency:* 106.2 FM

HEARTLAND FM, Atholl Curling Rink, Lower Oakfield, Pitlochry, Perthshire PH16 5DS. Tel: 01796-474040. *Frequency:* 97.5 FM

HORIZON RADIO, Broadcast Centre, Crownhill, Milton Keynes, Bucks MK8 0AB. Tel: 01908-269111. *Frequency:* 103.3 FM

INVICTA FM AND SUPERGOLD, Radio House, John Wilson Business Park, Whitstable, Kent CT5 3QX. Tel: 01227-772004. *Frequencies:* MW 1242/603 kHz, 102.8/95.9/97.0/96.1/103.1 FM

ISLAND FM, 12 Westerbrook, St Sampson, Guernsey, Channel Islands. Tel: 01481-42000. *Frequencies:* 93.7/104.7 FM

ISLE OF WIGHT RADIO, Dodnor Park, Newport, Isle of Wight PO30 5XE. Tel: 01983-822557. *Frequency:* MW 1242 kHz

JFM 102.2, 26–27 Castlereagh Street, London W1H 5YR. Tel: 0171-706 4100. *Frequency:* 102.2 FM

KCBC, PO Box 1548, Robinson Close, Telford Industrial Estate, Kettering, Northants NN16 8PU. Tel: 01536-412413. *Frequency:* MW 1548 kHz

KFM, 1 East Street, Tonbridge, Kent TN9 1AR. Tel: 01732-369200. *Frequencies:* 96.2/101.6 FM

KISS 100 FM, Kiss House, 80 Holloway Road, London N7 8JG. Tel: 0171-700 6100. *Frequency:* 100.0 FM

KISS 102, Kiss House, PO Box 102, Manchester M60 1GJ. Tel: 0161-228 0102. *Frequency:* 102 FM

KIX 96, Ringway House, Hill Street, Coventry CV1 4AN. Tel: 01203-525656. *Frequency:* 96.2 FM

KL.FM, 18 Blackfriars Street, King's Lynn, Norfolk PE30 1NN. Tel: 01553-772777. *Frequency:* 96.7 FM

LANTERN RADIO, The Light House, 17 Market Place, Bideford, N. Devon EX39 2DR. Tel: 01237-424444. *Frequency:* 96.2 FM

LEICESTER SOUND, Granville House, Granville Road, Leicester LE1 7RW. Tel: 0116-256 1300. *Frequency:* 103.2 FM

LINCS FM, Witham Park, Waterside South, Lincoln LN5 7JN. Tel: 01522-549900. *Frequency:* 102.2 FM

LONDON GREEK RADIO, Florentia Village, Vale Road, London N4 1TD. Tel: 0181-800 8001. *Frequency:* 103.3 FM

LONDON NEWS 97.3 FM, 72 Hammersmith Road, London W14 8YE. Tel: 0171-973 1152. *Frequency:* 97.3 FM

LONDON NEWS TALK 1152 AM, 72 Hammersmith Road, London W14 8YE. Tel: 0171-973 1152. *Frequency:* 1152 kHz

LONDON TURKISH RADIO LTR, 185B High Road, Wood Green, London N22 6BA. Tel: 0181-881 0606. *Frequency:* MW 1584 kHz

MAGIC 828, PO Box 2000, Leeds LS3 1LR. Tel: 0113-245 2299. *Frequency:* MW 828 kHz

MARCHER GOLD, The Studios, Mold Road, Wrexham, Clwyd LL11 4AF. Tel: 01978-752202. *Frequency:* MW 1260 kHz

MAX AM, Forth House, Forth Street, Edinburgh EH1 3LF. Tel: 0131-556 9255. *Frequency:* MW 1548 kHz

MELLOW 1557, 21–23 Walton Road, Frinton-on-Sea, Essex CO13 0AA. Tel: 01253-675303. *Frequency:* MW 1557 kHz

MELODY FM, 180 Brompton Road, London SW3 1HF. Tel: 0171-581 1054. *Frequency:* 105.4 FM

MERCIA FM AND MERCIA CLASSIC GOLD, Hertford Place, Coventry CV1 3TT. Tel: 01203-868200. *Frequencies:* MW 1359 kHz; 97.0/102.9 FM

MERCURY EXTRA AM, Broadfield House, Brighton Road, Crawley, W. Sussex RH11 9TT. Tel: 01293-519161. *Frequencies:* MW 1476/1521 kHz

METRO FM, Newcastle upon Tyne NE99 1BB. Tel: 0191-420 0971. *Frequencies:* 97.1/103.0 FM

MFM, The Studios, Mold Road, Wrexham, Clwyd LL11 4AF. Tel: 01978-752202. *Frequencies:* 103.4/97.1 FM

MINSTER FM, PO Box 123, Dunnington, York YO1 5ZX. Tel: 01904-488888. *Frequency:* 104.7 FM

MIX 96, Friars Square Studios, 11 Bourbon Street, Aylesbury, Bucks HP20 2PZ. Tel: 01296-399396. *Frequency:* 96.2 FM

MORAY FIRTH RADIO, PO Box 271, Inverness IV3 6SF. Tel: 01463-224433. *Frequencies:* MW 1107 kHz, 97.4/96.6 FM

NEVIS RADIO, Inverlochy, Fort William, Inverness-shire PH33 6LU. Tel: 01397-700007. *Frequency:* 96.6 FM

NEW 102.7 HEREWARD FM, Queensgate Centre, Peterborough PE1 1XJ. Tel: 01733-460460. *Frequency:* 102.7 FM

96.4 FM BRMB, Aston Road North, Birmingham B6 4BX. Tel: 0121-359 4481 *Frequency:* 96.4 FM

96.7 BCR, Russell Court Building, Claremont Street, Lisburn Road, Belfast BT9 6JX. Tel: 01232-438500. *Frequency:* 96.7 FM

NORTHANTS RADIO, The Enterprise Park, Boughton Green Road, Northampton NN2 7AH. Tel: 01604-792411. *Frequencies:* MW 1557 kHz, 96.6 FM

NORTH-EAST COMMUNITY RADIO, Inverurie, Town House, Kintore, Aberdeenshire AB51 0US. Tel: 01467-632878. *Frequency:* 102.1 FM

NORTHSOUND ONE AND TWO, 45 Kings Gate, Aberdeen AB2 6BL. Tel: 01224-632234. *Frequencies:* MW 1035 kHz, 96.9/97.6/103 FM

OASIS, The Broadcast Centre, 7 Hatfield Road, St Albans, Herts AL1 3RS. Tel: 01727-831966. *Frequency:* 96.6 FM

OCEAN FM, Radio House, Whittle Avenue, Segensworth West, Fareham, Hants PO15 5SH. Tel: 01489-589911. *Frequencies:* 97.5/96.7 FM

ORCHARD FM, Haygrove House, Shoreditch, Taunton TA3 7BT. Tel: 01823-338448. *Frequencies:* 102.6/97.1 FM

PICCADILLY RADIO LTD, 127-131 The Piazza, Piccadilly Plaza, Manchester M1 4AW. Tel: 0161-236 9913. *Frequencies:* MW 1152 kHz (*Piccadilly Gold*), 103.0 FM (*Piccadilly Key 103 FM*)

PIRATE FM 102, Carn Brea Studios, Wilson Way, Redruth, Cornwall TR15 3XX. Tel: 01209-314400. *Frequencies:* 102.2/102.8 FM

PLYMOUTH SOUND LTD, Earl's Acre, Plymouth PL3 4HX. Tel: 01752-227272. *Frequencies:* MW 1152 kHz, 97.0/96.6 FM

POWERFM, Radio House, Whittle Avenue, Segensworth West, Fareham, Hants PO15 5SH. Tel: 01489-589911. *Frequency:* 103.2 FM

PREMIER RADIO, Glen House, Stag Place, London SW1E 5AG. Tel: 0171-233 6705. *Frequencies:* MW 1305/1332/1413 kHz

THE PULSE, Forster Square, Bradford BD1 5NE. Tel: 01274-731521. *Frequencies:* 97.5/102.5 FM

Q102.9, The Riverside Suite, The Old Waterside Railway Station, Duke Street, Waterside, Londonderry BT47 1DH. Tel: 01504-44449. *Frequency:* 102.9 FM

Q103 FM, Enterprise House, The Vision Park, Chivers Way, Histon, Cambridge CB4 4WW. Tel: 01223-235255. *Frequencies:* 103.0/97.4 FM

Q96, 21 Lady Lane, Paisley PA1 2LG. Tel: 0141-887 9630. *Frequency:* 96.3 FM

RADIO AIRE FM, 51 Burley Road, PO Box 2000, Leeds LS3 1LR. Tel: 0113-245 2299. *Frequency:* 96.3 FM

RADIO BORDERS, Tweedside Park, Galashiels TD1 3TD. Tel: 01896-759444. *Frequencies:* 96.8/97.5/103.4 FM

RADIO BROADLAND, St George's Plain, 47–49 Colegate, Norwich NR3 1DB. Tel: 01603-630621. *Frequencies:* MW 1152 kHz, 102.4 FM

RADIO CEREDIGION, Yr Hen Ysgol Gymraeg, Ffordd Alexandra, Aberystwyth, Dyfed SY23 ILF. Tel: 01970-627999. *Frequencies:* 103.3/96.6 FM

RADIO CITY GOLD, 8–10 Stanley Street, Liverpool L1 6AF. Tel: 0151-227 5100. *Frequency:* MW 1548 kHz

RADIO MALDWYN, The Studios, The Park, Newtown, Powys SY16 2NZ. Tel: 01686-623555. *Frequency:* MW 756 kHz

RADIO MERCURY FM (EAST), Broadfield House, Brighton Road, Crawley, W. Sussex. Tel: 01293-519161. *Frequency:* 102.7 FM

RADIO MERCURY FM (WEST), The Friary, PO Box 964, Guildford, Surrey GU1 4YX. Tel: 01483-451964. *Frequencies:* 96.4/97.1 FM

RADIO TAY, 6 North Isla Street, Dundee DD3 7JQ. Tel: 01382-200800. *Frequencies:* MW 1161 kHz, 102.8 FM (Dundee); 1584 kHz, 96.4 FM (Perth)

RADIOWAVE, 965 Mowbray Drive, Blackpool, Lancs FY3 7JR. Tel: 01253-304965. *Frequency:* 96.5 FM

RADIO WYVERN, 5 Barbourne Terrace, Worcester WR1 3JZ. Tel: 01905-612212. *Frequencies:* MW 954 kHz, 97.6 FM (Hereford); 1530 kHz, 102.8 FM (Worcester)

RADIO XL 1296 AM, KMS House, Bradford Street, Birmingham B12 0JD. Tel: 0121-753 5353. *Frequency:* MW 1296 kHz

RAM FM, The Market Place, Derby DE1 3AA. Tel: 01332-292945. *Frequency:* 102.8 FM

RED DRAGON FM, Radio House, West Canal Wharf, Cardiff CF1 5XJ. Tel: 01222-384041. *Frequencies:* 97.4/103.2 FM

RED ROSE GOLD AND RED ROSE ROCK FM, PO Box 999, St Paul's Square, Preston, Lancs PR1 1XS. Tel: 01772-556301. *Frequencies:* MW 999 kHz (*Gold*), 97.4 FM (*Rock FM*)

RTM, Harrow Manor Way, Thamesmead South, London SE2 9XH. Tel: 0181-311 3112. *Frequency:* 103.8 FM

SABRAS SOUND, Radio House, 63 Melton Road, Leicester LE4 6PN. Tel: 0116-261 0666. *Frequency:* MW 1260 kHz

SEVERN SOUND AND SEVERN SOUND SUPERGOLD, Broadcast Centre, 67 Southgate Street, Gloucester GL1 2DQ. Tel: 01452-423791. *Frequencies:* MW 774 kHz (*SuperGold*), 103.0/102.4 FM

SGR COLCHESTER, Abbeygate Two, 9 Whitewell Road, Colchester CO2 7DE. Tel: 01206-575859. *Frequency:* 96.1 FM

SGR-FM BURY, PO Box 250, Bury St Edmunds, Suffolk IP33 1AD. Tel: 01284-702622. *Frequencies:* MW 1251 kHz, 96.4 FM

SGR-FM IPSWICH, Radio House, Alpha Business Park, Whitehouse Road, Ipswich IP1 5LT. Tel: 01473-461000. *Frequencies:* MW 1170 kHz, 97.1 FM

SIBC, Market Street, Lerwick, Shetland ZE1 0JN. Tel: 01595-695299. *Frequency:* 96.2 FM

SIGNAL CHESHIRE, Regent House, Heaton Lane, Stockport SK4 1BX. Tel: 0161-480 5445. *Frequencies:* 104.9/96.4 FM

SIGNAL ONE AND SIGNAL GOLD, Stoke Road, Stoke-on-Trent ST4 2SR. Tel: 01782-747047. *Frequencies:* MW 1170 kHz, 102.6/96.9 FM

SOUTH COAST RADIO, Radio House, Whittle Avenue, Segensworth West, Fareham, Hants PO15 5PA. Tel: 01489-589911; Radio House, PO Box 2000, Brighton BN14 2SS. Tel: 01273-430111. *Frequencies:* MW 1170/1557/1323 kHz

SOUTHERN FM, Radio House, PO Box 2000, Brighton BN41 2SS. Tel: 01273-430111. *Frequencies:* 103.5 FM (Brighton); 96.9 FM (Newhaven); 102.4 FM (Eastbourne); 102.0 FM (Hastings)

SOUTH WEST SOUND, Campbell House, Bankend Road, Dumfries DG1 4TH. Tel: 01387-250999. *Frequency:* 97.2 FM

SOUTH WEST SUSSEX RADIO, 1 Argyle Road, Bognor Regis, W. Sussex PO21 IDY. Tel: 01243-828488. *Frequencies:* 96.6/102.3 FM

SPECTRUM INTERNATIONAL RADIO, Endeavour House, Brent Cross, London NW2 1JT. Tel: 0181-905 5000. *Frequency:* MW 558 kHz

SPIRE FM, City Hall Studios, Malthouse Lane, Salisbury, Wilts SP2 7QQ. Tel: 01722-416644. *Frequency:* 102.0 FM

STAR FM, Tristar Broadcasting Ltd, The Observatory Shopping Centre, Slough, Berks SL1 ILH. Tel: 01753-551016. *Frequency:* 106.6 FM

STRAY FM, Stray Studios, PO Box 972, Station Parade, Harrogate HG1 5YF. Tel: 01423-522972. *Frequency:* 97.2 FM

SUN CITY 103.4 FM, PO Box 1034, Sunderland SR1 3YZ. Tel: 0191-567 3333. *Frequency:* 103.4 FM

SUNRISE FM, Sunrise House, 30 Chapel Street, Little Germany, Bradford BD1 5DN. Tel: 01274-735043. *Frequency:* 103.2 FM

SUNRISE RADIO, Sunrise House, Sunrise Road, Southall, Middx UB2 4AU. Tel: 0181-574 6666. *Frequency:* MW 1458 kHz

SUNSHINE 855, Sunshine House, Waterside, Ludlow, Shropshire SY8 1GS. Tel: 01584-873795. *Frequency:* MW 855 kHz

SWANSEA SOUND, Victoria Road, Gowerton, Swansea SA4 3AB. Tel: 01792-893751. *Frequencies:* MW 1170 kHz, 96.4 FM

TEN 17, Latton Bush Centre, Southern Way, Harlow, Essex CM18 7BU. Tel: 01279-432415. *Frequency:* 101.7 FM

TFM RADIO, Yale Crescent, Thornaby, Stockton-on-Tees, Cleveland TS17 6AA. Tel: 01642-615111. *Frequencies:* 96.6 FM

1152 XTRA AM, Radio House, Aston Road North, Birmingham B6 4BX. Tel: 0121-359 4481. *Frequency:* MW 1152 kHz

TOUCH AM, PO Box 99, Cardiff CF1 5YJ. Tel: 01222-237878. *Frequencies:* MW 1359 kHz (Cardiff); 1305 kHz (Newport)

TOWNLAND RADIO 828 AM, PO Box 828, Cookstown, Co. Tyrone BT80 9LQ. Tel: 016487-64828. *Frequency:* MW 828 kHz

TRENT-FM, 29–31 Castle Gate, Nottingham NG1 7AP. Tel: 0115-952 7000. *Frequency:* 96.2/96.5 FM

2CR FM, 5 Southcote Road, Bournemouth BH1 3LR. Tel: 01202-294881. *Frequency:* 102.3 FM

2-TEN FM, PO Box 210, Reading, Berks RG31 7RZ. Tel: 01734-254400. *Frequencies:* 97.0/102.9 FM

VIKING FM, Commercial Road, Hull HU1 2SG. Tel: 01482-325141. *Frequency:* 96.9 FM

VIRGIN RADIO LONDON, 1 Golden Square, London W1R 4DJ. Tel: 0171-434 1215. *Frequency:* 105.8 FM

VIVA! 963 AM, Golden Rose House, 26–27 Castlereagh Street, London W1H 6DJ. Tel: 0171-706 9963. *Frequency:* MW 963 kHz

WABC, 267 Tettenhall Road, Wolverhampton WV6 0DQ. Tel: 01902-757211. *Frequencies:* MW 990/1017 kHz (Wolverhampton); 1017 kHz (Shrewsbury and Telford)

WESSEX FM, Radio House, Trinity Street, Dorchester, Dorset DT1 1DJ. Tel: 01305-250333. *Frequencies:* 97.2/96.0 FM

WEST SOUND RADIO, Radio House, Holmston Road, Ayr KA7 3BE. Tel: 01292-283662. *Frequencies:* MW 1035 kHz, 96.7/97.5 FM

WEY VALLEY RADIO, Prospect Place, Mill Lane, Alton, Hants GU34 2SY. Tel: 01420-544444. *Frequencies:* 102/101.6 FM

YORKSHIRE COAST RADIO, PO Box 962, Scarborough, N. Yorks YO12 5YX. Tel: 01723-500962. *Frequencies:* 96.2/103.1 FM

The Press

The newspaper and periodical press in the UK is large and diverse, catering for a wide variety of views and interests. There is no state control or censorship of the press, though it is subject to the laws on publication and the Press Complaints Commission (*see* below) was set up by the industry as a means of self-regulation.

The press is not state-subsidized and receives few tax concessions. The income of most newspapers and periodicals is derived largely from sales and from advertising; the press is the largest advertising medium in Britain.

SELF-REGULATION

When the report of the Committee on Privacy and Related Matters, chaired by David Calcutt, QC, was published in June 1990, the then Home Secretary (David Waddington) said that the Government would review the performance of a non-statutory Press Complaints Commission after 18 months of operation to determine whether statutory measures were required. The Press Complaints Commission began work on 1 January 1991, and in July 1992 the then Secretary of State for National Heritage (David Mellor) asked Sir David Calcutt, QC, to conduct the review. The *Calcutt Review of Press Self-Regulation* was presented to Parliament by the then Secretary of State for National Heritage (Peter Brooke) in January 1993 (for summary, *see* Whitaker's Almanack 1994).

COMPLAINTS

The Press Complaints Commission was founded by the newspaper and magazine industry in January 1991 to replace the Press Council (established in 1953). It is a voluntary, non-statutory body set up to operate the press's self-regulation system, and funded by the industry through the Press Standards Board of Finance.

The Commission's objects are to consider, adjudicate, conciliate, and resolve complaints of unfair treatment by the press; and to ensure that the press maintains the highest professional standards with respect to generally recognized freedoms, including freedom of expression, the public's right to know, and the right of the press to operate free from improper pressure. The Commission judges newspaper and magazine conduct by a code of practice drafted by editors, agreed by the industry and ratified by the Commission.

Seven of the Commission's members are editors of national, regional and local newspapers and magazines, and nine, including the chairman, are drawn from other fields. One member has been appointed Privacy Commissioner with special powers to investigate complaints about invasion of privacy.

THE PRESS COMPLAINTS COMMISSION, 1 Salisbury Square, London EC3Y 8AE. Tel: 0171-353 1248.
Chairman, Lord Wakeham, PC; *Director*, M. Bolland

NEWSPAPERS

Newspapers are usually financially independent of any political party, though most adopt a political stance in their editorial comments, usually reflecting proprietorial influence. Ownership of the national and regional daily newspapers is concentrated in the hands of large corporations whose interests cover publishing and communications.

There are rules on cross-media ownership to prevent undue concentration of newspaper ownership.

There are about 15 daily and ten Sunday national papers, about 80 regional daily papers, and several hundred local papers that are published weekly or twice-weekly. Scotland, Wales and Northern Ireland all have at least one daily and one Sunday national paper.

Newspapers are usually published in either broadsheet or tabloid format. The 'quality' daily papers, i.e. those providing detailed coverage of a wide range of public matters, have a broadsheet format. The tabloid papers take a more popular approach and are more illustrated.

NATIONAL DAILY NEWSPAPERS

DAILY EXPRESS, Ludgate House, 245 Blackfriars Road, London SE1 9UX. Tel: 0171-928 8000
DAILY MAIL, Northcliffe House, 2 Derry Street, London W8 5TT. Tel: 0171-938 6000
DAILY MIRROR, 1 Canada Square, Canary Wharf, London E14 5AP. Tel: 0171-293 3000
DAILY SPORT, 19 Great Ancoats Street, Manchester M60 4BT. Tel: 0161-236 4466
DAILY STAR, Ludgate House, 245 Blackfriars Road, London SE1 9UX. Tel: 0171-928 8000
DAILY TELEGRAPH, 1 Canada Square, Canary Wharf, London E14 5DT. Tel: 0171-538 5000
THE EUROPEAN, Orbit House, 5 New Fetter Lane, London EC4A 1AP. Tel: 0171-418 7777
FINANCIAL TIMES, 1 Southwark Bridge, London SE1 9HL. Tel: 0171-873 3000
THE GUARDIAN, 119 Farringdon Road, London EC1R 3ER. Tel: 0171-278 2332
THE INDEPENDENT, 40 City Road, London EC1Y 2DB. Tel: 0171-253 1222
MORNING STAR, 1–3 Ardleigh Road, London N1 4HS. Tel: 0171-254 0033
RACING POST, 112–120 Coombe Lane, London SW20 0BA. Tel: 0181-879 3377
THE SCOTSMAN, 20 North Bridge, Edinburgh EH1 1YT. Tel: 0131-225 2468
THE SPORTING LIFE, Orbit House, 1 New Fetter Lane, London EC4A 1AR. Tel: 0171-822 2119
THE SUN, 1 Virginia Street, London E1 9XP. Tel: 0171-782 4000
THE TIMES, 1 Pennington Street, London E1 9XN. Tel: 0171-782 5000
TODAY, 1 Virginia Street, London E1 9BS. Tel: 0171-782 4600

REGIONAL DAILY NEWSPAPERS

Aberdeen: PRESS AND JOURNAL, and EVENING EXPRESS, PO Box 43, Lang Stracht, Mastrick, AB9 8AF
Aylesford: KENT TODAY, Messenger House, New Hythe Lane, Larkfield, ME20 6SG
Barrow-in-Furness: NORTH-WEST EVENING MAIL, Newspaper House, Abbey Road, LA14 5QS
Basildon: EVENING ECHO, Newspaper House, Chester Hall Lane, SS14 3BL
Belfast: BELFAST TELEGRAPH, 124 Royal Avenue, BT1 1EB; IRISH NEWS AND BELFAST MORNING NEWS, 113–117 Donegall Street, BT1 2GE; NEWS LETTER, 46–56 Boucher Crescent, BT12 6QY

Birmingham: THE BIRMINGHAM POST, and BIRMINGHAM EVENING MAIL, 28 Colmore Circus, Queensway, B4 6AX

Blackburn: LANCASHIRE EVENING TELEGRAPH, Newspaper House, High Street, BB1 1HT

Blackpool: WEST LANCASHIRE EVENING GAZETTE, PO Box 20, Preston New Road, FY4 4AU

Bolton: BOLTON EVENING NEWS, Churchgate, BL1 1DE

Bournemouth: EVENING ECHO, Richmond Hill, BH2 6HH

Bradford: TELEGRAPH AND ARGUS, Hall Ings, BD1 1JR

Brighton: EVENING ARGUS, Argus House, Crowhurst Road, Hollingbury, BN1 8AR; *also* 1 Grand Parade, Crawley, RH10 1BU; 47–49 Warwick Street, Worthing, BN11 3DH

Bristol: BRISTOL EVENING POST, and WESTERN DAILY PRESS, Temple Way, BS99 7HD

Burton-on-Trent: BURTON MAIL, 65–68 High Street, DE14 1LE

Cambridge: CAMBRIDGE EVENING NEWS, 51 Newmarket Road, CB5 8EJ

Cardiff: SOUTH WALES ECHO, and WESTERN MAIL, Thomson House, Havelock Street, CF1 1WR

Carlisle: NEWS AND STAR, Newspaper House, Dalston Road, CA2 5UA

Cheltenham: GLOUCESTERSHIRE ECHO, 1 Clarence Parade, GL50 3NZ

Colchester: EVENING GAZETTE, Oriel House, 43–44 North Hill, CO1 1TZ

Coventry: COVENTRY EVENING TELEGRAPH, Corporation Street, CV1 1FP

Darlington: NORTHERN ECHO, Priestgate, DL1 1NF

Derby: DERBY EVENING TELEGRAPH, Northcliffe House, Meadow Road, DE1 2DW

Dundee: COURIER AND ADVERTISER, and EVENING TELEGRAPH AND POST, 2 Albert Square, DD1 9QJ

Edinburgh: EVENING NEWS, 20 North Bridge, EH1 1YT

Exeter: EXPRESS AND ECHO, Heron Road, Sowton, EX2 7NF

Glasgow: DAILY RECORD, 40 Anderston Quay, G3 8DA; EVENING TIMES, 195 Albion Street, G1 1QP; SCOTTISH DAILY EXPRESS, Park House, Park Circus Place, G3 6AF

Gloucester: THE GLOUCESTERSHIRE CITIZEN, St John's Lane, GL1 2AY

Greenock: GREENOCK TELEGRAPH, 2 Crawford Street, PA15 1LH

Grimsby: GRIMSBY EVENING TELEGRAPH, 80 Cleethorpe Road, DN31 3EH

Guernsey: GUERNSEY EVENING PRESS AND STAR, PO Box 57, Braye Road, Vale

Halifax: EVENING COURIER, PO Box 19, Courier Buildings, King Cross Street, HX1 2SF

Hartlepool: HARTLEPOOL MAIL, Clarence Road, TS24 8BU

Huddersfield: HUDDERSFIELD DAILY EXAMINER, PO Box A26, Queen Street South, HD1 2TD

Hull: HULL DAILY MAIL, Blundell's Corner, Beverley Road, HU3 1XS

Ipswich: EAST ANGLIAN DAILY TIMES, and EVENING STAR, 30 Lower Brook Street, IP4 1AN

Jersey: JERSEY EVENING POST, PO Box 582, Five Oaks, St Saviour, JE4 8XQ

Kettering: NORTHAMPTONSHIRE EVENING TELEGRAPH, Northfield Avenue, NN16 9TT

Leeds: YORKSHIRE EVENING POST, and YORKSHIRE POST, PO Box 168, Wellington Street, LS1 1RF

Leicester: LEICESTER MERCURY, St George Street, LE1 9FQ

Lincoln: LINCOLNSHIRE ECHO, Brayford Wharf East, LN5 7AT

Liverpool: DAILY POST, and LIVERPOOL ECHO, PO Box 48, Old Hall Street, L69 3EB

London: THE EVENING STANDARD, Northcliffe House, 2 Derry Street, W8 5TT

Manchester: MANCHESTER EVENING NEWS, 164 Deansgate, M60 2RR

Middlesbrough: EVENING GAZETTE, Gazette Buildings, Borough Road, TS1 3AZ

Mold: EVENING LEADER, Mold Business Park, Wrexham Road, CH7 1XY

Newcastle upon Tyne: EVENING CHRONICLE, and THE JOURNAL, Thomson House, Groat Market, NE1 1ED

Newport: SOUTH WALES ARGUS, Cardiff Road, Maesglas, NP9 1QW

Northampton: CHRONICLE AND ECHO, Upper Mounts, NN1 3HR

Norwich: EASTERN DAILY PRESS, and EASTERN EVENING NEWS, Prospect House, Rouen Road, NR1 1RE

Nottingham: EVENING POST, PO Box 99, Forman Street, NG1 4AB

Nuneaton: HEARTLAND EVENING NEWS, Newspaper House, 11–15 Newtown Road, CV11 4HR

Oldham: EVENING CHRONICLE, 172 Union Street, OL1 1EQ

Oxford: OXFORD MAIL, Newspaper House, Osney Mead, OX2 0EJ

Paisley: PAISLEY DAILY EXPRESS, 195 Albion Street, Glasgow G1 1QP

Peterborough: PETERBOROUGH EVENING TELEGRAPH, New Priestgate House, 57 Priestgate, PE1 1JW

Plymouth: WESTERN MORNING NEWS, and EVENING HERALD, 17 Brest Road, Derriford Business Park, PL6 5AA

Portsmouth: THE NEWS, The News Centre, Hilsea, PO2 9SX

Preston: LANCASHIRE EVENING POST, Oliver's Place, Fulwood, PR2 4ZA

Reading: EVENING POST, 8 Tessa Road, RG1 8NS

Scarborough: SCARBOROUGH EVENING NEWS, 17–23 Aberdeen Walk, YO11 1BB

Scunthorpe: SCUNTHORPE EVENING TELEGRAPH, Telegraph House, Doncaster Road, DN15 7RE

Sheffield: THE STAR; DONCASTER STAR; ROTHERHAM STAR; BARNSLEY STAR, York Street, S1 1PU

South Shields: SHIELDS GAZETTE and SUNDERLAND ECHO, Chapter Row, NE33 1BL

Southampton: SOUTHERN DAILY ECHO, 45 Above Bar, SO14 7AA

Stoke-on-Trent: EVENING SENTINEL, Sentinel House, Etruria, ST1 5SS

Swansea: SOUTH WALES EVENING POST, Adelaide Street, SA1 1QT

Swindon: EVENING ADVERTISER and EVENING CHRONICLE, Newspaper House, 100 Victoria Road, SN1 3BE

Telford: SHROPSHIRE STAR, Ketley, TF1 4HU

Torquay: HERALD EXPRESS, Harmsworth House, Barton Hill Road, TQ2 8JN

Weymouth: DORSET EVENING ECHO, 57 St Thomas Street, DT4 8EU

Wigan: WIGAN EVENING POST, Martland Mill, Martland Mill Lane, WN5 0LX

Wolverhampton: EXPRESS AND STAR, 51–53 Queen Street, WV1 3BU

Worcester: EVENING NEWS, Hylton Road, WR2 5JX

York: YORKSHIRE EVENING PRESS, PO Box 29, 76–86 Walmgate, YO1 1YN

WEEKLY NEWSPAPERS

AL MAJALLA, Arab Press House, 184 High Holborn, London WC1V 7AP. Tel: 0171-831 8181

ASIAN TIMES, 3rd Floor, Tower House, 141–149 Fonthill Road, London N4 3HF. Tel: 0171-281 1191

CARIBBEAN TIMES, 3rd Floor, Tower House, 141–149 Fonthill Road, London N4 3HF. Tel: 0171-281 1191
THE GUARDIAN WEEKLY, 119 Farringdon Road, London EC1R 3ER. Tel: 0171-278 2332
THE INDEPENDENT ON SUNDAY, 40 City Road, London EC1Y 2DB. Tel: 0171-253 1222
INDIA TIMES, Suites F and G, 2nd Floor, Liberty Shopping Centre, 14 South Road, Southall, Middx UB1 1RT. Tel: 0181-843 1605
THE MAIL ON SUNDAY, Northcliffe House, 2 Derry Street, London W8 5TS. Tel: 0171-938 6000
NEWS OF THE WORLD, 1 Virginia Street, London E1 9XR. Tel: 0171-782 4000
THE OBSERVER, 119 Farringdon Road, London EC1R 3ER. Tel: 0171-278 2332
THE PEOPLE, 1 Canada Square, Canary Wharf, London E14 5AP. Tel: 0171-293 3000
SCOTLAND ON SUNDAY, 20 North Bridge, Edinburgh EH1 1YT. Tel: 0131-225 2468
SUNDAY EXPRESS, Ludgate House, 245 Blackfriars Road, London SE1 9UX. Tel: 0171-928 8000
SUNDAY MAIL, 40 Anderston Quay, Glasgow G3 8DA. Tel: 0141-248 7000
SUNDAY MIRROR, 1 Canada Square, Canary Wharf, London E14 5AP. Tel: 0171-293 3000
SUNDAY NEWS, 46–56 Boucher Crescent, Belfast BT12 6QY. Tel: 01232-680000
SUNDAY POST, Courier Place, Dundee DD1 9QJ. Tel: 01382-23131
SUNDAY SPORT, Marten House, 39–47 East Road, London N1 6AH. Tel: 0171-251 2544
SUNDAY TELEGRAPH, 1 Canada Square, Canary Wharf, London E14 5AR. Tel: 0171-538 5000
THE SUNDAY TIMES, 1 Pennington Street, London E1 9XN. Tel: 0171-782 5000
THE VOICE, 370 Coldharbour Lane, London SW9 8PL. Tel: 0171-737 7377
WALES ON SUNDAY, Thomson House, Havelock Street, Cardiff CF1 1WR. Tel: 01222-583583
WEEKLY NEWS, Courier Place, Dundee, Angus DD1 9QJ. Tel: 01382-23131
WEEKLY TELEGRAPH, 1 Canada Square, Canary Wharf, London E14 5DT. Tel: 0171-538 6298

RELIGIOUS PAPERS

Alt. = Alternate; *M.* = Monthly; *Q.* = Quarterly; *W.* = Weekly

BAPTIST TIMES, PO Box 54, 129 The Broadway, Didcot, Oxon OX11 8XB. *W.*
CATHOLIC HERALD, Herald House, Lamb's Passage, Bunhill Row, London EC1Y 8TQ. *W.*
CHALLENGE – THE GOOD NEWS PAPER, Revenue Buildings, Chapel Road, Worthing, W. Sussex BN11 1BQ. *M.*
CHRISTIAN HERALD, Herald House, 96 Dominion Road, Worthing, W. Sussex BN14 8JP. *W.*
CHRISTIAN SCIENCE MONITOR, Monitor House, 20 Beulah Road, London SW19 3SU. *W.*
CHURCH OF ENGLAND NEWSPAPER, 10 Little College Street, London SW1P 3SH. *W.*
CHURCH OF IRELAND GAZETTE, 36 Bachelor's Walk, Lisburn, Co. Antrim, BT28 1XN. *W.*
CHURCH TIMES, 33 Upper Street, London N1 6PN. *W.*
ENGLISH CHURCHMAN, 22 Lesley Avenue, Canterbury, Kent CT1 3LF. *Alt. W.*
THE FRIEND, Drayton House, 30 Gordon Street, London WC1H 0BQ. *W.*

THE INQUIRER, Essex Hall, 1–6 Essex Street, London WC2R 3HY. *Alt. W.*
JEWISH CHRONICLE, 25 Furnival Street, London EC4A 1JT. *W.*
JEWISH GAZETTE, 27 Bury Old Road, Prestwich, Manchester M25 8EY. *W.*
JEWISH TELEGRAPH, Telegraph House, 11 Park Hill, Bury Old Road, Prestwich, Manchester M25 0HH. *W.*
LIFE AND WORK, Church of Scotland, 121 George Street, Edinburgh EH2 4YN. *M.*
METHODIST RECORDER, 122 Golden Lane, London EC1Y 0TL. *W.*
MIDDLE WAY, Buddhist Society, 58 Eccleston Square, London SW1V 1PH. *Q.*
ORTHODOX OUTLOOK, 37 Salop Road, Welshpool, Powys SY21 7GA. *Alt. M.*
PRESBYTERIAN HERALD, Church House, Fisherwick Place, Belfast BT1 6DW. *Ten times a year*
QUAKER MONTHLY, Friends House, Euston Road, London NW1 2BJ. *M.*
REFORM, United Reformed Church, 86 Tavistock Place, London WC1H 9RT. *Eleven times a year*
SIKH MESSENGER, 43 Dorset Road, London SW19 3EZ. *Q.*
THE TABLET, 1 King Street Cloisters, Clifton Walk, London W6 0QZ. *W.*
THE UNIVERSE, 1st Floor, St James Building, Oxford Street, Manchester M1 6FP. *W.*
THE WAR CRY, 101 Queen Victoria Street, London EC4P 4EP. *W.*

PERIODICALS

There are about 6,700 periodicals published in Britain. These are classified as consumer, i.e. general interest, or as trade, professional or academic.

CONSUMER PERIODICALS

Alt. = Alternate; *M.* = Monthly; *Q.* = Quarterly; *W.* = Weekly

AMATEUR PHOTOGRAPHER, King's Reach Tower, Stamford Street, London SE1 9LS. *W.*
ANGLING TIMES, Bretton Court, Bretton, Peterborough PE3 8DZ. *W.*
ANNABEL, 80 Kingsway East, Dundee, Angus DD4 8SL. *M.*
THE ANTIQUE COLLECTOR, 7 St John's Road, Harrow, Middx HA1 2EE. *Ten times a year*
APOLLO, 29 Chesham Place, London SW1X 8HB. *M.*
ARENA, 3rd Floor, Block A, Exmouth House, Pine Street, London EC1R 0JL. *Alt. M.*
THE ARTIST, Caxton House, 63–65 High Street, Tenterden, Kent TN30 6BD. *M.*
ASTRONOMY NOW, Douglas House, 32–34 Simpson Road, Bletchley, Milton Keynes, Bucks MK1 1BA. *M.*
ATHLETICS WEEKLY, Bretton Court, Bretton, Peterborough PE3 8DZ. *W.*
AUTOCAR AND MOTOR, 38–42 Hampton Road, Teddington, Middx TW11 0JE. *W.*
BBC GARDENER'S WORLD, 101 Bayham Street, London NW1 0AG. *M.*
BBC GOOD FOOD, 101 Bayham Street, London NW1 0AG. *M.*
BBC WILDLIFE MAGAZINE, Woodlands, 80 Wood Lane, London W12 0TT. *M.*
BELFAST GAZETTE (*Official*), 64 Chichester Street, Belfast BT1 4PS. *W.*

BELLA, 2nd Floor, Shirley House, 25–27 Camden Road, London NW1 9LL. *W.*

BEST, 10th Floor, Portland House, Stag Place, London SW1E 5AU. *W.*

BIRDS, RSPB, The Lodge, Sandy, Beds SG19 2DL. *Q.*

BIRD WATCHING, Bretton Court, Bretton, Peterborough PE3 8DZ. *M.*

BOXING NEWS, PO Box 300, London SW15 5QF. *W.*

BRIDES & SETTING UP HOME, Vogue House, Hanover Square, London W1R 0AD. *Alt. M.*

THE BURLINGTON MAGAZINE, 6 Bloomsbury Square, London WC1A 2LP. *M.*

CAMPING & CARAVANNING, Greenfields House, Westwood Way, Coventry CV4 8JH. *M.*

CAR, Bushfield House, Orton Centre, Peterborough PE2 5UW. *M.*

CAT WORLD, 10 Western Road, Shoreham-by-Sea, W. Sussex BN43 5WD. *M.*

CD-ROM NEWSLETTER, PO Box 3, Omega Park, Alton, Hants GU34 2PG. *Alt. M.*

CHAT, King's Reach Tower, Stamford Street, London SE1 9LS. *W.*

CITY LIMITS, 3rd Floor, 115 Shaftesbury Avenue, London WC2H 8ED. *W.*

CLASSIC AND SPORTSCAR, 60 Waldegrave Road, Teddington, Middx TW11 8LG. *M.*

CLASSIC CD, Beauford Court, 30 Monmouth Street, Bath BA1 2BW. *M.*

CLOTHES SHOW MAGAZINE, 80 Wood Lane, London W12 0TT. *M.*

COARSE ANGLING, King's Reach Tower, Stamford Street, London SE1 9LS. *M.*

COIN NEWS, 105 High Street, Honiton, Devon EX14 8PE. *M.*

COMPANY, 72 Broadwick Street, London W1V 2BP. *M.*

COMPETITORS JOURNAL, PO Box 300, London SW15 5QF. *Alt. M.*

COMPUTER AND VIDEO GAMES, Priory Court, 30–32 Farringdon Road, London EC1R 3AU. *M.*

COSMOPOLITAN, National Magazine House, 72 Broadwick Street, London W1V 2BP. *M.*

COUNTRY HOMES AND INTERIORS, King's Reach Tower, Stamford Street, London SE1 9LS. *M.*

COUNTRY LIFE, King's Reach Tower, Stamford Street, London SE1 9LS. *W.*

COUNTRY LIVING, National Magazine House, 72 Broadwick Street, London W1V 2BP. *M.*

THE COUNTRYMAN, Sheep Street, Burford, Oxon OX18 4LH. *Alt. M.*

CRICKETER INTERNATIONAL, Beech Hanger, Ashurst, Tunbridge Wells, Kent TN3 9ST. *M.*

CYCLING WEEKLY, King's Reach Tower, Stamford Street, London SE1 9LS. *W.*

THE DALESMAN, Stable Courtyard, Broughton Hall, Skipton, N. Yorks BD23 3AE. *M.*

DALTONS WEEKLY, CI Tower, St George's Square, New Malden, Surrey KT3 4JA. *W.*

DANCE AND DANCERS, 214 Panther House, 38 Mount Pleasant, London WC1X 0AP. *M.*

DANCING TIMES, Clerkenwell House, 45–47 Clerkenwell Green, London EC1R 0EB. *M.*

DOGS TODAY, 6 Station Parade, Sunningdale, Ascot, Berks SL5 0EP. *M.*

DOG WORLD, 9 Tufton Street, Ashford, Kent TN23 1QN. *W.*

THE ECOLOGIST, Agriculture House, Bath Road, Sturminster Newton, Dorset DT10 1DU. *Alt. M.*

THE ECONOMIST, 25 St James's Street, London SW1A 1HG. *W.*

EDINBURGH GAZETTE (*Official*), HMSO, PO Box 276, London SW8 5DT. *Alt. W.*

ELLE, 20 Orange Street, London WC2H 7ED. *M.*

EMPIRE, 42–48 Great Portland Street, London W1N 5AH. *M.*

ESQUIRE, National Magazine House, 72 Broadwick Street, London W1V 2BP. *M.*

ESSENTIALS, 57–59 Long Acre, London WC2E 9JL. *M.*

EVERYWOMAN, 34 Islington Green, London N1 8DU. *M.*

EXCHANGE AND MART, Link House, West Street, Poole, Dorset BH15 1LL. *W.*

THE FACE, 3rd Floor, Block A, Exmouth House, Pine Street, London EC1R 0JL. *M.*

FAMILY CIRCLE, King's Reach Tower, Stamford Street, London SE1 9LS. *M.*

FHM, 9–11 Curtain Road, London EC2A 3LT. *M.*

THE FIELD, Astley House, 33 Notting Hill Gate, London W11 3JQ. *M.*

FILM REVIEW, 9 Blades Court, Deodar Road, London SW15 2NU. *M.*

FORE!, Bretton Court, Bretton, Peterborough PE3 8DZ. *M.*

GARDEN NEWS, Apex House, Oundle Road, Peterborough PE2 9NP. *W.*

GAY TIMES, Ground Floor, Worldwide House, 116–134 Bayham Street, London NW1 0BA. *M.*

GEOGRAPHICAL MAGAZINE, 52 George Street, London W1H 5RF. *M.*

GIBBONS STAMP MONTHLY, 5 Parkside, Christchurch Road, Ringwood, Hants BH24 3SH. *M.*

GOLF WORLD, Advance House, 37–39 Millharbour, London E14 9TX. *M.*

GOOD HOLIDAY MAGAZINE, 1–2 Dawes Court, 93 High Street, Esher, Surrey KT10 9QD. *Q.*

GOOD HOUSEKEEPING, National Magazine House, 72 Broadwick Street, London W1V 2BP. *M.*

GQ, Vogue House, Hanover Square, London W1R 0AD. *M.*

GRAMOPHONE, 177–179 Kenton Road, Harrow, Middx HA3 0HA. *M.*

GRANTA, 2–3 Hanover Yard, Noel Road, London N1 8BE. *Q.*

GUIDING, 17–19 Buckingham Palace Road, London SW1W 0PT. *M.*

HANSARD, *see* Parliamentary Debates

HARPERS AND QUEEN, National Magazine House, 72 Broadwick Street, London W1V 2BP. *M.*

HELLO!, 69–71 Upper Ground, London SE1 9PQ. *W.*

HOMES AND GARDENS, King's Reach Tower, Stamford Street, London SE1 9LS. *M.*

HORSE AND HOUND, King's Reach Tower, Stamford Street, London SE1 9LS. *W.*

HOUSE AND GARDEN, Vogue House, Hanover Square, London W1R 0AD. *M.*

HOUSE BEAUTIFUL, National Magazine House, 72 Broadwick Street, London W1V 2BP. *Ten times a year*

i–D MAGAZINE, 44 Earlham Street, London WC2H 9LA. *M.*

IDEAL HOME, King's Reach Tower, Stamford Street, London SE1 9LS. *M.*

ILLUSTRATED LONDON NEWS, 20 Upper Ground, London SE1 9PF. *Twice a year*

IN BRITAIN, Haymarket House, 1 Oxendon Street, London SW1Y 4EE. *M.*

IRISH POST, Uxbridge House, 464 Uxbridge Road, Hayes, Middx UB4 0SP. *W.*

JAZZ JOURNAL INTERNATIONAL, 1–5 Clerkenwell Road, London EC1M 5PA. *M.*

JUST SEVENTEEN, 20 Orange Street, London WC2H 7ED. *W.*

LABOUR RESEARCH, 78 Blackfriars Road, London SE1 8HF. *M.*

THE LADY, 39–40 Bedford Street, London WC2E 9ER. *W.*

LAND AND LIBERTY, 177 Vauxhall Bridge Road, London SW1V 1EU. *Alt. M.*

LITERARY REVIEW, 51 Beak Street, London W1R 3LF. *M.*

LIVING, King's Reach Tower, Stamford Street, London SE1 9LS. *M.*

LONDON GAZETTE (*Official*) PO Box 7923, London SE1 5ZH. *Five times a week*

LONDON REVIEW OF BOOKS, Tavistock House South, Tavistock Square, London WC1H 9JZ. *Alt. W.*

LONDON WEEKLY ADVERTISER, 137 George Lane, London E18 1AJ. *W.*

MAJESTY, 26–28 Hallam Street, London W1N 5LF. *M.*

MARIE CLAIRE, 2 Hatfields, London SE1 9PG. *M.*

ME, 57–59 Long Acre, London WC2E 9JL. *W.*

MELODY MAKER (MM), King's Reach Tower, Stamford Street, London 9LS. *W.*

METEOROLOGICAL MAGAZINE, HMSO, PO Box 276, London SW8 5DT. *M.*

MIZZ, King's Reach Tower, Stamford Street, London SE1 9LS. *Alt. W.*

MODEL BOATS, Argus House, Boundary Way, Hemel Hempstead, Herts HP2 7ST. *M.*

MONEYWISE, Berkeley Square House, Berkeley Square, London W1X 6AB. *M.*

MORE!, 20 Orange Street, London WC2H 7ED. *Alt. W.*

MOTHER AND BABY, Victory House, 14 Leicester Place, London WC2H 7BP. *M.*

MOTOR CYCLE NEWS, 20–22 Station Road, Kettering, Northants NN15 7HH. *W.*

MOTORING NEWS, Standard House, Bonhill Street, London EC2A 4DA. *W.*

MOTOR SPORT, Standard House, Bonhill Street, London EC2A 4DA. *M.*

MY WEEKLY, 80 Kingsway East, Dundee DD4 8SL. *W.*

NATIONAL STUDENT EXTRA, PO Box 5, Glossop, Derbys SK13 8PT. *Alt. M.*

NATURE, 4 Little Essex Street, London WC2R 3LF. *W.*

NEEDLECRAFT, Beauford Court, 30 Monmouth Street, Bath BA1 2BW. *M.*

NEW DIY, Link House, Dingwall Avenue, Croydon, Surrey CR9 2TA. *M.*

NEW INTERNATIONALIST, 55 Rectory Road, Oxford OX4 1BW. *M.*

NEW MUSICAL EXPRESS (NME), King's Reach Tower, Stamford Street, London SE1 9LS. *W.*

NEW SCIENTIST, King's Reach Tower, Stamford Street, London SE1 9LS. *W.*

NEW STATESMAN AND SOCIETY, Foundation House, Perseverance Works, 38 Kingsland Road, London E2 8DQ. *W.*

NEWSWEEK (British Isles edition), 18 Park Street, London W1Y 4HH. *W.*

NEW WOMAN, 20 Orange Street, London WC2H 7ED. *M.*

19, King's Reach Tower, Stamford Street, London SE1 9LS. *M.*

OK!, Swan House, 52–53 Poland Street, London W1V 3DF. *M.*

THE OLDIE, 26 Charlotte Street, London W1P 1HJ. *Alt. W.*

OPERA, 1A Mountgrove Road, London N5 2LU. *M.*

OPERA NOW, 241 Shaftesbury Avenue, London WC2H 8EH. *M.*

OPTIONS, King's Reach Tower, Stamford Street, London SE1 9LS. *M.*

OUR DOGS, 5 Oxford Road, Station Approach, Manchester M60 1SX. *W.*

PARENTS, Victory House, 14 Leicester Place, London WC2H 7BP. *M.*

PARLIAMENTARY DEBATES (COMMONS) (Hansard), HMSO, PO Box 276, London SW8 5DT. *Daily or weekly during parliamentary session*

PARLIAMENTARY DEBATES (LORDS) (Hansard), HMSO, PO Box 276, London SW8 5DT. *Daily or weekly during parliamentary session*

PC USER, 33–39 Bowling Green Lane, London EC1R 0DA. *Alt. W.*

PEOPLE'S FRIEND, 80 Kingsway East, Dundee DD4 8SL. *W.*

PLAYS AND PLAYERS, Northway House, 1379 High Road, Whetstone, London N20 9LP. *M.*

POETRY REVIEW, 22 Betterton Street, London WC2H 9BU. *Q.*

PONY, 296 Ewell Road, Surbiton, Surrey KT6 7AQ. *M.*

PRACTICAL BOAT OWNER, Westover House, West Quay Road, Poole, Dorset BH15 1JG. *M.*

PRACTICAL CARAVAN, 38–42 Hampton Road, Teddington, Middx TW11 0JE. *M.*

PRACTICAL GARDENING, Apex House, Oundle Road, Peterborough PE2 9NP. *M.*

PRACTICAL PARENTING, King's Reach Tower, Stamford Street, London SE1 9LS. *M.*

PRACTICAL PHOTOGRAPHY, Apex House, Oundle Road, Peterborough PE2 9NP. *M.*

PRIMA, 9th Floor, Portland House, Stag Place, London SW1E 5AU. *M.*

PRIVATE EYE, 6 Carlisle Street, London W1V 5RG. *Alt. W.*

PROGRESS (*Braille type*), RNIB, Technical Consumer Services Division, Orton, Southgate, Peterborough PE2 0XU. *M.*

THE PUZZLER, Glenthorne House, Hammersmith Grove, London W6 0LG. *M.*

Q, Mappin House, 4 Winsley Street, London W1M 7AR. *M.*

RACING CALENDAR, The Jockey Club, Weatherbys, Sanders Road, Wellingborough, Northants NN8 4BX. *W.*

RADIO TIMES, 80 Wood Lane, London W12 0TT. *W.*

RAILWAY MAGAZINE, King's Reach Tower, Stamford Street, London SE1 9LS. *M.*

RAILWAY MODELLER, Peco Publications, Beer, Seaton, Devon EX12 3NA. *M.*

READER'S DIGEST, Berkeley Square House, Berkeley Square, London W1X 6AB. *M.*

RIDING, Corner House, Foston, Grantham, Lincs NG32 2JU. *M.*

RUGBY LEAGUER, Martland Mill, Martland Mill Lane, Wigan, Lancs WN5 0LX. *W.*

RUGBY WORLD AND POST, Weirbank, Bray on Thames, Maidenhead, Berks SL6 2ED. *M.*

SCOTS MAGAZINE, 2 Albert Square, Dundee DD1 9QJ. *M.*

SCOTTISH FIELD, 7th Floor, The Plaza Tower, East Kilbride, Glasgow G74 1LW. *M.*

SCOUTING, Baden-Powell House, Queen's Gate, London SW7 5JS. *M.*

SEA ANGLER, Bretton Court, Bretton, Peterborough PE3 8DZ. *M.*

SHE, National Magazine House, 72 Broadwick Street, London W1V 2BP. *M.*

SHOOT, King's Reach Tower, Stamford Street, London SE1 9LS. *W.*

SHOOTING TIMES AND COUNTRY MAGAZINE, Astley House, 33 Notting Hill Gate, London W11 3JQ. *W.*

SKY MAGAZINE, 5th Floor, Mappin House, 4 Winsley Street, London W1N 7AR. *M.*

SLIMMING MAGAZINE, Victory House, 14 Leicester Place, London WC2H 7BP. *Ten times a year*

SMASH HITS, Mappin House, 4 Winsley Street, London W1M 7AR. *Alt. W.*

THE SPECTATOR, 56 Doughty Street, London WC1N 2LL. *W.*

THE STRAD, 7 St John's Road, Harrow, Middx HA1 2EE. *M.*

TATLER, Vogue House, Hanover Square, London WIR OAD. *Ten times a year*

TENNIS WORLD, The Spendlove Centre, Enstone Road, Charlbury, Chipping Norton, Oxon OX7 3PQ. *M.*

THIS ENGLAND, Alma House, 73 Rodney Road, Cheltenham, Glos GL50 1HT. *Q.*

TIME INTERNATIONAL, Time Life Building, 153 New Bond Street, London W1Y 0AA. *W.*

TIME OUT, Universal House, 251 Tottenham Court Road, London W1P 0AB. *W.*

THE TIMES EDUCATIONAL SUPPLEMENT, Admiral House, 66–68 East Smithfield, London E1 9XY. *W.*

THE TIMES HIGHER EDUCATION SUPPLEMENT, Admiral House, 66–68 East Smithfield, London E1 9XY. *W.*

THE TIMES LITERARY SUPPLEMENT, Admiral House, 66–68 East Smithfield, London E1 9XY. *W.*

TRIBUNE, 308 Gray's Inn Road, London WC1X 8DY. *W.*

TROUT AND SALMON, Bretton Court, Bretton, Peterborough PE3 8DZ. *M.*

TV TIMES, King's Reach Tower, Stamford Street, London SE1 9LS. *W.*

VACHER'S PARLIAMENTARY COMPANION, 113 High Street, Berkhamsted, Herts HP4 2DJ. *Q.*

VANITY FAIR, Vogue House, Hanover Square, London WIR OAD. *M.*

VIZ COMIC, The Boat House, Crabtree Lane, London SW6 6LU. *Alt. M.*

VOGUE, Vogue House, Hanover Square, London WIR OAD. *M.*

VOX, King's Reach Tower, Stamford Street, London SE1 9LS. *M.*

WEATHER, 104 Oxford Road, Reading RG1 7LJ. *M.*

WELSH NATION, 51 Cathedral Road, Cardiff CF1 9HD. *Alt. M.*

WHICH?, 2 Marylebone Road, London NW1 4DX. *M.*

WOMAN, King's Reach Tower, Stamford Street, London SE1 9LS. *W.*

WOMAN AND HOME, King's Reach Tower, Stamford Street, London SE1 9LS. *M.*

WOMAN'S JOURNAL, King's Reach Tower, Stamford Street, London SE1 9LS. *M.*

WOMAN'S OWN, King's Reach Tower, Stamford Street, London SE1 9LS. *W.*

WOMAN'S REALM, King's Reach Tower, Stamford Street, London SE1 9LS. *W.*

WOMAN'S WEEKLY, King's Reach Tower, Stamford Street, London SE1 9LS. *W.*

WORLD OF INTERIORS, Vogue House, Hanover Square, London WIR OAD. *Eleven times a year*

YACHTING MONTHLY, King's Reach Tower, Stamford Street, London SE1 9LS. *M.*

TRADE, PROFESSIONAL AND ACADEMIC PERIODICALS

Alt. = Alternate; *M.* = Monthly; *Q.* = Quarterly; *W.* = Weekly

ACCOUNTANCY, Institute of Chartered Accountants, 40 Bernard Street, London WC1N 1LD. *W.*

ACCOUNTANCY AGE, VNU House, 32–34 Broadwick Street, London W1A 2HG. *W.*

ACCOUNTANTS' MAGAZINE, Institute of Chartered Accountants of Scotland, 27 Queen Street, Edinburgh EH2 1LA. *Alt. M.*

THE ACTUARY, Aura House, 53 Oldridge Road, London NW3 2PL. *M.*

AGRICULTURE AND EQUIPMENT INTERNATIONAL, Yew Tree House, Horne, Horley, Surrey RH6 9JP. *Alt. M.*

ANTIQUARIES JOURNAL, Oxford University Press, Medical and Journals Division, Walton Street, Oxford OX2 6DP. *Annual*

ANTIQUE DEALER AND COLLECTORS' GUIDE, PO Box 805, London SE10 8TD. *M.*

ANTIQUES TRADE GAZETTE, 17 Whitcomb Street, London WC2H 7PL. *W.*

ARCHITECTS' JOURNAL, 33–39 Bowling Green Lane, London EC1R 0DA. *W.*

ARCHITECTURAL REVIEW, 33–39 Bowling Green Lane, London EC1R 0DA. *M.*

ARMED FORCES DEFENCE INTERNATIONAL, 21 Hawley Road, London NW1 8RP. *Q.*

THE AUTHOR, Society of Authors, 84 Drayton Gardens, London SW10 9SB. *Q.*

THE BANKER, 1st Floor, Maple House, 149 Tottenham Court Road, London W1P 9LL. *M.*

BANKING WORLD (Chartered Institute of Bankers), Haymarket House, 1 Oxendon Street, London SW1Y 4EE. *M.*

THE BIOCHEMIST, The Biochemical Society, 59 Portland Place, London W1N 3AJ. *Alt. M.*

BIOLOGIST, Institute of Biology, 20–22 Queensberry Place, London SW7 2DZ. *Five times a year*

THE BOOKSELLER, 12 Dyott Street, London WC1A 1DF. *W.*

BRAIN, Oxford University Press, Medical and Journals Division, Walton Street, Oxford OX2 6DP. *Alt. M.*

BREWING AND DISTILLING INTERNATIONAL, Southbound House, 163 Burton Road, Burton-on-Trent, Staffs DE14 3DP. *M.*

BRITISH BAKER, Maclaren House, 19 Scarbrook Road, Croydon CR9 1QH. *W.*

BRITISH DENTAL JOURNAL, BMA House, Tavistock Square, London WC1H 9JR. *Alt. W.*

BRITISH FOOD JOURNAL, 60–62 Toller Lane, Bradford, W. Yorks BD8 9BY. *Ten times a year*

BRITISH JEWELLER, 2nd Floor, 67 Clerkenwell Road, London EC1R 5BH. *M.*

BRITISH JOURNAL FOR THE PHILOSOPHY OF SCIENCE, Oxford University Press, Medical and Journals Division, Walton Street, Oxford OX2 6DP. *Q.*

BRITISH JOURNAL OF PHOTOGRAPHY, 58 Fleet Street, London EC4Y 1JU. *W.*

BRITISH JOURNAL OF PSYCHIATRY, Royal College of Psychiatrists, 17 Belgrave Square, London SW1X 8PG. *M.*

BRITISH JOURNAL OF PSYCHOLOGY, British Psychological Society, 13A Church Lane, London N2 8DX. *Q.*

BRITISH JOURNAL OF SOCIAL WORK, Oxford University Press, Medical and Journals Division, Walton Street, Oxford OX2 6DP. *Alt. M.*

BRITISH MEDICAL JOURNAL, British Medical Association, BMA House, Tavistock Square, London WC1H 9JR. *W.*

BRITISH PRINTER, Maclean Hunter House, Chalk Lane, Cockfosters Road, Barnet, Herts EN4 0BU. *M.*

BRITISH TAX REVIEW, South Quay Plaza, 183 Marsh Wall, London E14 9FT. *Alt. M.*

BRITISH VETERINARY JOURNAL, 24–28 Oval Road, London NW1 7DX. *Alt. M.*

BUILDING, Builder House, 1 Millharbour, London E14 9RA. *W.*

BUILDING TRADE & INDUSTRY, 131–133 Duckmoor Road, Ashton Gate, Bristol BS3 2BH. *M.*

BUSINESS CONNECTIONS, Node Court, Drivers End, Codicote, Hitchin, Herts SG4 8TR. *Q.*

BUSINESS EDUCATION TODAY, 128 Long Acre, London WC2E 9AN. *Alt. M.*

CABINET MAKER, PO Box 20, Sovereign Way, Tonbridge, Kent TN9 1RW. *W.*

CAMPAIGN, 22 Lancaster Gate, London W2 3LY. *W.*

CARPET AND FLOORCOVERINGS REVIEW, PO Box 20, Sovereign Way, Tonbridge, Kent TN9 1RW. *Alt. W.*

CATERER AND HOTELKEEPER, Quadrant House, The Quadrant, Sutton, Surrey SM2 5AS. *W.*

CHEMIST AND DRUGGIST, PO Box 20, Sovereign Way, Tonbridge, Kent TN9 1RW. *W.*

CHEMISTRY AND INDUSTRY, 14 Belgrave Square, London SW1X 8PS. *Alt. W.*

CHEMISTRY IN BRITAIN, Royal Society of Chemistry, Burlington House, Piccadilly, London W1V 0BN. *M.*

CHILD EDUCATION, Villiers House, Clarendon Avenue, Leamington Spa, Warks CV32 5PR. *M.*

CLASSICAL MUSIC, 241 Shaftesbury Avenue, London WC2H 8EH. *Alt. W.*

CLASSICAL QUARTERLY, Oxford University Press, Medical and Journals Division, Walton Street, Oxford OX2 6DP. *Twice a year.*

CLASSICAL REVIEW, Oxford University Press, Medical and Journals Division, Walton Street, Oxford OX2 6DP. *Twice a year*

COMPUTER SHOPPER, 19 Bolsover Street, London W1P 7HJ. *M.*

COMPUTER WEEKLY, Quadrant House, The Quadrant, Sutton, Surrey SM2 5AS. *W.*

COMPUTING, VNU House, 32–34 Broadwick Street, London W1A 2HG. *W.*

CONSTRUCTION NEWS, 2–6 Boundary Row, London SE1 8HN. *W.*

CONTAINERISATION INTERNATIONAL, Scriptor Court, 155 Farringdon Road, London EC1R 3AD. *M.*

CONTRACT JOURNAL, Quadrant House, The Quadrant, Sutton, Surrey SM2 5AS. *W.*

CONTROL AND INSTRUMENTATION, Morgan-Grampian House, 30 Calderwood Street, London SE18 6QH. *M.*

CRAFTS MAGAZINE, Crafts Council, 44A Pentonville Road, London N1 9BY. *Alt. M.*

CRIMINOLOGIST, East Row, Little London, Chichester, W. Sussex PO19 1PG. *Q.*

DAIRY FARMER AND DAIRY BEEF PRODUCER, Fenton House, Wharfedale Road, Ipswich IP1 4LG. *M.*

DAIRY INDUSTRIES INTERNATIONAL, Wilmington House, Church Hill, Wilmington, Dartford, Kent DA2 7EF. *M.*

THE DENTIST, Warman House, 20 Leas Road, Guildford, Surrey GU1 4QT. *M.*

DESIGN WEEK, St Giles House, 49–50 Poland Street, London W1V 4AX. *W.*

THE DIRECTOR, Institute of Directors, Mountbarrow House, 6–20 Elizabeth Street, London SW1W 9RB. *M.*

ECONOMIC JOURNAL, 108 Cowley Road, Oxford OX4 1JF. *Alt. M.*

EDUCATION, 21–27 Lamb's Conduit Street, London WC1N 3NJ. *W.*

ELECTRICAL AND RADIO TRADING, Quadrant House, The Quadrant, Sutton, Surrey SM2 5AS. *W.*

ELECTRICAL REVIEW, Quadrant House, The Quadrant, Sutton, Surrey SM2 5AS. *Alt. W.*

ELECTRICAL TIMES, Quadrant House, The Quadrant, Sutton, Surrey SM2 5AS. *Ten times a year*

ELECTRONIC ENGINEERING, Morgan-Grampian House, 30 Calderwood Street, London SE18 6QH. *M.*

ENERGY MANAGEMENT, Maclean Hunter House, Chalk Lane, Cockfosters Road, Barnet, Herts EN4 0BU. *Alt. M.*

THE ENGINEER, Morgan-Grampian House, 30 Calderwood Street, London SE18 6QH. *W.*

ENGINEERING, Chester Court, High Street, Knowle, Solihull, W. Midlands B93 0LL. *Eleven times a year*

ENGLISH HISTORICAL REVIEW, Longman House, Burnt Mill, Harlow, Essex CM20 2JE. *Five times a year*

ENGLISH TODAY, Cambridge University Press, The Edinburgh Building, Shaftesbury Road, Cambridge CB2 2RU. *Q.*

THE ENVIRONMENTALIST, 2–6 Boundary Row, London SE1 8HN. *Q.*

EQUITY JOURNAL, Guild House, Upper St Martin's Lane, London WC2H 9EG. *Q.*

ESTATES GAZETTE, 151 Wardour Street, London W1V 4BN. *W.*

FAIRPLAY INTERNATIONAL SHIPPING WEEKLY, 20 Ullswater Crescent, Ullswater Business Park, Coulsdon, Surrey CR5 2HR. *W.*

FARMERS WEEKLY, Quadrant House, The Quadrant, Sutton, Surrey SM2 5AS. *W.*

FASHION WEEKLY, 67 Clerkenwell Road, London EC1R 5BH. *W.*

FIRE, Queensway House, 2 Queensway, Redhill, Surrey RH1 1QS. *M.*

FIRE PREVENTION, 140 Aldersgate Street, London EC1A 4HX. *Ten times a year*

FISH, Institute of Fisheries Management, 151 Cove Road, Farnborough, Hants GU14 0HQ. *Q.*

FISH TRADER, Queensway House, 2 Queensway, Redhill, Surrey RH1 1QS. *M.*

FLIGHT INTERNATIONAL, Quadrant House, The Quadrant, Sutton, Surrey SM2 5AS. *W.*

FOOD TRADE REVIEW, Station House, Hortons Way, Westerham, Kent TN16 1BZ. *M.*

FORESTRY AND BRITISH TIMBER, PO Box 20, Sovereign Way, Tonbridge, Kent TN9 1RW. *M.*

FOUNDRY TRADE JOURNAL, Queensway House, 2 Queensway, Redhill, Surrey RH1 1QS. *Alt. W.*

FROZEN AND CHILLED FOODS, Queensway House, 2 Queensway, Redhill, Surrey RH1 1QS. *M.*

FUEL, Linacre House, Jordan Hill, Oxford OX2 8DP. *M.*

GARDEN TRADE NEWS, Apex House, Oundle Road, Peterborough PE2 9NP. *M.*

GAS WORLD INTERNATIONAL, PO Box 105, 25–31 Ironmonger Row, London EC1V 3PN. *Q.*

GEOGRAPHY, Geographical Association, 343 Fulwood Road, Sheffield S10 3BP. *Q.*

GEOLOGICAL MAGAZINE, Cambridge University Press, The Edinburgh Building, Shaftesbury Road, Cambridge CB2 2RU. *Alt. M.*

GLASS AND GLAZING PRODUCTS, Maclaren House, 19 Scarbrook Road, Croydon CR9 1QH. *M.*

GREECE AND ROME, Oxford University Press, Medical and Journals Division, Walton Street, Oxford OX2 6DP. *Twice a year*

THE GROCER, Broadfield Park, Crawley, W. Sussex RH11 9RT. *W.*

GROWER, Warwick House, Azalea Drive, Swanley, Kent BR8 8HY. *W.*

HAIRDRESSERS' JOURNAL INTERNATIONAL, Quadrant House, The Quadrant, Sutton, Surrey SM2 5AS. *W.*

THE HEALTH SERVICE JOURNAL, 4 Little Essex Street, London WC2R 3LF. *W.*

HEALTH VISITOR, BMA House, Tavistock Square, London WC1H 9JR. *M.*

HEATING, VENTILATING AND PLUMBING, PO Box 13, Hereford House, Bridle Path, Croydon, Surrey CR9 4NL. *M.*

HISTORY TODAY, 20 Old Compton Street, London W1V 5PE. *M.*

INDEPENDENT RETAILER, Alliance House, 14 Pierpoint Street, Worcester WR1 1TA. *M.*

INDUSTRIAL EXCHANGE AND MART, Link House, West Street, Poole, Dorset BH15 1LL. *W.*

INDUSTRIAL RELATIONS JOURNAL, 108 Cowley Road, Oxford OX4 1JF. *Q.*

INTERNATIONAL AFFAIRS, Cambridge University Press, The Edinburgh Building, Shaftesbury Road, Cambridge CB2 2RU. *Q.*

JANE'S INFORMATION WEEKLY, Sentinel House, 163 Brighton Road, Coulsdon, Surrey CR5 2NH. *W.*

THE JOURNALIST, National Union of Journalists, Acorn House, 314 Gray's Inn Road, London WC1X 8DP. *Alt. M.*

JOURNAL OF ALTERNATIVE AND COMPLEMENTARY MEDICINE, Mariner House, 53A High Street, Bagshot, Surrey GU19 5AH. *M.*

JOURNAL OF THE BRITISH ASTRONOMICAL ASSOCIATION, Burlington House, Piccadilly, London W1V 9AG. *Alt. M.*

JOURNAL OF THE CHEMICAL SOCIETY, Thomas Graham House, Science Park, Milton Road, Cambridge CB4 4WF. *Irregular*

JUSTICE OF THE PEACE REPORTS, East Row, Little London, Chichester, W. Sussex PO19 1PG. *Alt. W.*

THE LANCET, 42 Bedford Square, London WC1B 3SL. *W.*

LAW QUARTERLY REVIEW, South Quay Plaza, 183 Marsh Wall, London E14 9FT. *Q.*

THE LAW REPORTS, 3 Stone Buildings, Lincoln's Inn, London WC2A 3XN. *M.*

LAW SOCIETY'S GAZETTE, 50 Chancery Lane, London WC2A 1SX. *W.*

LEATHER, PO Box 20, Sovereign Way, Tonbridge, Kent TN9 1RW. *M.*

LIBRARY ASSOCIATION RECORD, 7 Ridgmount Street, London WC1E 7AE. *M.*

LLOYD'S LOADING LIST, Collwyn House, Sheepen Place, Colchester, Essex CO3 3LP. *W.*

LLOYD'S SHIPPING INDEX, Collwyn House, Sheepen Place, Colchester, Essex CO3 3LP. *W.*

LOCAL GOVERNMENT CHRONICLE, 33–39 Bowling Green Lane, London EC1R 0DA. *W.*

MACHINERY AND PRODUCTION ENGINEERING, Franks Hall, Franks Lane, Horton Kirby, Dartford, Kent DA4 9LL. *Alt. W.*

MACHINERY MARKET, 6 Blyth Road, Bromley, Kent BR1 3RX. *W.*

MANAGEMENT ACCOUNTING, Chartered Institute of Management Accountants, 63 Portland Place, London W1N 4AB. *M.*

MANAGEMENT TODAY, 22 Lancaster Gate, London W2 3LY. *M.*

MANUFACTURING CHEMIST, Morgan-Grampian House, 30 Calderwood Street, London SE18 6QH. *M.*

MARKETING, 30 Lancaster Gate, London W2 3LY. *W.*

MARKETING WEEK, St Giles House, 49–50 Poland Street, London W1V 4AX. *W.*

MATERIALS RECYCLING WEEKLY, Maclaren House, 19 Scarbrook Road, Croydon, Surrey CR9 1QH. *W.*

MATERIALS WORLD, Institute of Materials, 1 Carlton House Terrace, London SW1Y 5DB. *M.*

MEAT TRADES' JOURNAL, Maclaren House, 19 Scarbrook Road, Croydon, Surrey CR9 1QH. *W.*

MEDIA WEEK, 33–39 Bowling Green Lane, London EC1R 0DA. *W.*

METALS INDUSTRY NEWS, Queensway House, 2 Queensway, Redhill, Surrey RH1 1QS. *Q.*

MIND, Oxford University Press, Medical and Journals Division, Walton Street, Oxford OX2 6DP. *Q.*

MINING JOURNAL, 60 Worship Street, London EC2A 2HD. *W.*

MOTOR TRANSPORT, Quadrant House, The Quadrant, Sutton, Surrey SM2 5AS. *W.*

MUNICIPAL JOURNAL, 32 Vauxhall Bridge Road, London SW1V 2SS. *W.*

MUNICIPAL REVIEW AND AMA NEWS, 35 Great Smith Street, London SW1P 3BJ. *Ten times a year*

MUSEUMS JOURNAL, Museums Association, 42 Clerkenwell Close, London EC1R 0PA. *M.*

THE MUSICAL TIMES, 7 St John's Road, Harrow, Middx HA1 2EE. *M.*

MUSIC AND LETTERS, Oxford University Press, Medical and Journals Division, Walton Street, Oxford OX2 6DP. *Q.*

MUSIC WEEK, 8th Floor, Ludgate House, 245 Blackfriars Road, London SE1 9UR. *W.*

NOTES AND QUERIES, Oxford University Press, Medical and Journals Division, Walton Street, Oxford OX2 6DP. *Q.*

NUCLEAR ENGINEERING INTERNATIONAL, Quadrant House, The Quadrant, Sutton, Surrey SM2 5AS. *M.*

NURSING TIMES & NURSING MIRROR, 4 Little Essex Street, London WC2R 3LF. *W.*

OFF-LICENCE NEWS, Broadfield Park, Crawley, W. Sussex RH11 9RT. *W.*

OPTICIAN, Quadrant House, The Quadrant, Sutton, Surrey SM2 5AS. *W.*

OPTOMETRY TODAY, 233–234 Blackfriars Road, London SE1 8NW. *Alt. W.*

PACKAGING WEEK, PO Box 20, Sovereign Way, Tonbridge, Kent TN9 1RW. *W.*

PC PLUS, Beauford Court, 30 Monmouth Street, Bath, Avon BA1 2BW. *M.*

PERSONAL COMPUTER WORLD, 32–34 Broadwick Street, London W1A 2HG. *M.*

PERSONNEL MANAGEMENT (Institute of Personnel Management), 17 Britton Street, London EC1M 5NQ. *M.*

PHARMACEUTICAL JOURNAL, 1 Lambeth High Street, London SE1 7JN. *W.*

PHILOSOPHY, Cambridge University Press, The Edinburgh Building, Shaftesbury Road, Cambridge CB2 2RU. *Q.*

THE PHOTOGRAPHER, Fox Talbot House, Amwell End, Ware, Herts SG12 9HN. *M.*

PHYSICS WORLD, Techno House, Redcliffe Way, Bristol BS1 6NX. *M.*

PLUMBING AND HEATING NEWS, Peterson House, Northbank, Berryhill Industrial Estate, Droitwich, Worcs WR9 9BL. *M.*

POLICE REVIEW, South Quay Plaza 2, 183 Marsh Wall, London E14 9FS. *W.*

THE PRACTITIONER, Morgan-Grampian House, 30 Calderwood Street, London SE18 6QH. *M.*

PRINTING WORLD, PO Box 20, Sovereign Way, Tonbridge, Kent TN9 1RW. *W.*

PROBATION JOURNAL, 3–4 Chivalry Road, London SW11 1HT. *Q.*

PROFESSIONAL CARE OF MOTHER AND CHILD, PO Box 100, Chichester, W. Sussex PO19 1XR. *Ten times a year*

THE PSYCHOLOGIST, The British Psychological Society, St Andrews House, 48 Princess Road East, Leicester LE1 7DR. *M.*

QUARRY MANAGEMENT, 7 Regent Street, Nottingham NG1 5BY. *M.*

RAILWAY GAZETTE INTERNATIONAL, Quadrant House, The Quadrant, Sutton, Surrey SM2 5AS. *M.*

RATING & VALUATION REPORTER, 4 Breams Buildings, London EC4A 1AQ. *M.*

RETAIL NEWSAGENT, Robert Taylor House, 11 Angel Gate, City Road, London EC1V 2PT. *W.*

RETAIL WEEK, Maclaren House, PO Box 109, Croydon CR9 1QH. *W.*

REVIEW OF ENGLISH STUDIES, Oxford University Press, Medical and Journal Division, Walton Street, Oxford OX2 6DP. *Q.*

RUSI JOURNAL, Royal United Services Institute for Defence Studies, Whitehall, London SW1A 2ET. *Alt. M.*

SHIPPING WORLD & SHIPBUILDER, 4 Hubbard Road, Houndsmill, Basingstoke, Hants RG21 2UH. *M.*

SHOE & LEATHER NEWS, 19 Scarbrook Road, Croydon, Surrey CR9 1QH. *M.*

SMALLHOLDER, High Street, Stoke Ferry, King's Lynn, Norfolk PE33 9SF. *M.*

SOCIOLOGICAL REVIEW, 108 Cowley Road, Oxford OX4 1JF. *Q.*

SOLICITORS' JOURNAL, 21–27 Lamb's Conduit Street, London WC1N 3NJ. *W.*

SPORTS RETAILING, 147 Temple Chambers, Temple Avenue, London EC4Y 0DT. *M.*

THE STAGE AND TELEVISION TODAY, Stage House, 47 Bermondsey Street, London SE1 3XT. *W.*

THE STRUCTURAL ENGINEER, 11 Upper Belgrave Street, London SW1X 8BH. *Alt. W.*

SURVEYOR, 32 Vauxhall Bridge Road, London SW1V 2SS. *W.*

TAXATION PRACTITIONER, Tolley House, 2 Addiscombe Road, Croydon, Surrey CR9 5AF. *M.*

TAXI, Taxi House, 7–11 Woodfield Road, London W9 2BA. *Alt. W.*

THE TEACHER, National Union of Teachers, Hamilton House, Mabledon Place, London WC1H 9BD. *Eight times a year*

TEACHING HISTORY, 59A Kennington Park Road, London SE11 4JH. *Q.*

TELEVISION, Royal Television Society, Holborn Hall, 100 Gray's Inn Road, London WC1X 8AL. *Eight times a year*

TEXTILE HORIZONS, 33 Bedford Place, London WC1B 5JX. *M.*

TEXTILE MONTH, 76 Kirkgate, Bradford, W. Yorks BD1 1TB. *M.*

TOBACCO, Queensway House, 2 Queensway, Redhill, Surrey RH1 1QS. *Alt. M.*

TOWN AND COUNTRY PLANNING, 17 Carlton House Terrace, London SW1Y 5AS. *M.*

TOWN PLANNING REVIEW, PO Box 147, Liverpool L69 3BX. *Q.*

TOY TRADER, Turret House, 171–173 High Street, Rickmansworth, Herts WD3 1SN. *M.*

TRADE MARKS JOURNAL, Patent Office, 25 Southampton Buildings, London WC2A 1AY. *W.*

THE TRADER, Link House, West Street, Poole, Dorset BH15 1LL. *M.*

TRAVEL TRADE GAZETTE (UK & IRELAND), Morgan-Grampian House, 30 Calderwood Street, London SE18 6QH. *W.*

TTJ-TIMBER TRADES JOURNAL, PO Box 20, Sovereign Way, Tonbridge, Kent TN9 1RW. *W.*

UK PRESS GAZETTE, Maclean Hunter House, Chalk Lane, Cockfosters Road, Barnet, Herts EN4 0BU. *W.*

WEEKLY LAW REPORTS, 3 Stone Buildings, Lincoln's Inn, London WC2A 3XN. *W.*

WOODCARVING, 166 High Street, Lewes, E. Sussex BN7 1XU. *Alt. M.*

WORLD PAPER, PO Box 20, Sovereign Way, Tonbridge, Kent TN9 1RW. *M.*

WORLD'S FAIR, 2 Daltry Street, Oldham, Lancs OL1 4BB. *W.*

NEWS AGENCIES IN LONDON

News agencies provide general, business, sport and television news to a variety of subscribers including the press, other media, and industrial, commercial, financial and business users.

THE ASSOCIATED PRESS LTD (AP), 12 Norwich Street, London EC4A 4BP. Tel: 0171-353 1515

CENTRAL PRESS FEATURES LTD, 20 Spectrum House, 32–34 Gordon House Road, London NW5 1LP. Tel: 0171-284 1433

EXTEL FINANCIAL LTD, Fitzroy House, 13–17 Epworth Street, London EC2A 4DL. Tel: 0171-253 3333

HAYTERS, 146–148 Clerkenwell Road, London EC1R 5DP. Tel. 0171-837 2420

PARLIAMENTARY AND EU NEWS SERVICE, 19 Douglas Street, London SW1P 4PA. Tel: 0171-233 8283

PRESS ASSOCIATION, 85 Fleet Street, London EC4P 4BE. Tel: 0171-353 7440

REUTERS LTD, 85 Fleet Street, London EC4P 4AJ. Tel: 0171-510 7921

TWO-TEN COMMUNICATIONS LTD, 210 Old Street, London EC1V 9UN. Tel: 0171-490 8111

UNITED PRESS INTERNATIONAL (UK) LTD, 2 Greenwich View, Millharbour, London E14 9NN. Tel: 0171-538 0932

Book Publishers

More than 15,000 firms, individuals and societies have published one or more books in recent years. The list which follows is a selective one comprising those firms whose names are most familiar to the general public. A fuller list, *Publishers in the United Kingdom and Their Addresses*, containing some 2,500 names and addresses is published annually in March by the publishers of *Whitaker's Almanack*.

ADDISON-WESLEY PUBLISHERS, Finchampstead Road, Wokingham, Berks RG11 2NZ. Tel: 01734-794000

ALLAN (IAN), Coombelands House, Coombelands Lane, Addlestone, Surrey KT15 1HY. Tel: 01932-855909

ALLEN (J. A.), 1 Lower Grosvenor Place, London SW1W 0EL. Tel: 0171-834 0090

APPLE PRESS, 6 Blundell Street, London N7 9BH. Tel: 0171-700 2001

ARMADA BOOKS, 77 Fulham Palace Road, London W6 8JB. Tel: 0181-741 7070

ARMS & ARMOUR PRESS, 125 Strand, London WC2R 0BB. Tel: 0171-420 5555

ARNOLD (EDWARD), 338 Euston Road, London NW1 3BH. Tel: 0171-873 6000

ARROW BOOKS, 20 Vauxhall Bridge Road, London SW1V 2SA. Tel: 0171-973 9700

ATHLONE PRESS, 1 Park Drive, London NW11 7SG. Tel: 0181-458 0888

AURUM PRESS, 25 Bedford Avenue, London WC1B 3AT. Tel: 0171-637 3225

AUTOMOBILE ASSOCIATION, Norfolk House, Priestly Road, Basingstoke, Hants RG24 9NY. Tel: 01256-491524

BAILLIÈRE TINDALL, 24 Oval Road, London NW1 7DX. Tel: 0171-267 4466

BANTAM BOOKS, 61 Uxbridge Road, London W5 5SA. Tel: 0181-579 2652

BARRIE & JENKINS, 20 Vauxhall Bridge Road, London SW1V 2SA. Tel: 0171-973 9690

BARTHOLOMEW, 77 Fulham Palace Road, London W6 8JB. Tel: 0181-741 7070

BATSFORD (B. T.), 4 Fitzhardinge Street, London W1H 0AH. Tel: 0171-486 8484

BBC BOOKS, 80 Wood Lane, London W12 0TT. Tel: 0181-576 2570

BLACK (A. & C.), 35 Bedford Row, London WC1R 4JH. Tel: 0171-242 0946

BLACKIE CHILDREN'S BOOKS, 27 Wrights Lane, London W8 5TZ. Tel: 0171-416 3000

BLACKWELL PUBLISHERS, 108 Cowley Road, Oxford OX4 1JF. Tel: 01865-791100

BLANDFORD PRESS, 125 Strand, London WC2R 0BB. Tel: 0171-420 5555

BLOOMSBURY PUBLISHING, 2 Soho Square, London W1V 5DE. Tel: 0171-494 2111

BODLEY HEAD, 20 Vauxhall Bridge Road, London SW1V 2SA. Tel: 0171-973 9730

BOXTREE, 21 Broadwall, London SE1 9PL. Tel: 0171-928 9696

BOYARS (MARION), 24 Lacy Road, London SW15 1NL. Tel: 0181-788 9522

BRIMAX BOOKS, 4 Studlands Park Industrial Estate, Exning Road, Newmarket, Suffolk CB8 7AU. Tel: 01638-664611

BRITISH MUSEUM PRESS, 46 Bloomsbury Street, London WC1B 3QQ. Tel: 0171-323 1234

BUTTERWORTH & Co., 35 Chancery Lane, London WC2A 1ER. Tel: 0171-400 2500

CADOGAN BOOKS, London House, Parkgate Road, London SW11 4NQ. Tel: 0171-738 1961

CALDER PUBLICATIONS, 179 King's Cross Road, London WC1X 9BZ. Tel: 0171-833 1300

CAMBRIDGE UNIVERSITY PRESS, The Edinburgh Building, Cambridge CB2 2RU. Tel: 01223-312393

CANONGATE BOOKS, 14 High Street, Edinburgh EH1 1TE. Tel: 0131-557 5111

CAPE (JONATHAN), 20 Vauxhall Bridge Road, London SW1V 2SA. Tel: 0171-973 9730

CASSELL, 125 Strand, London WC2R 0BB. Tel: 0171-420 5555

CAVENDISH PUBLISHING, The Glass House, Wharton Street, London WC1X 9PX. Tel: 0171-278 8000

CENTURY PUBLISHING Co., *see* Random House UK

CHAMBERS, 24 Great Titchfield Street, London, W1P 7AD. Tel: 0171-631 0878

CHANCELLOR PRESS, 81 Fulham Road, London SW3 6RB. Tel: 0171-581 9393

CHAPMAN & HALL, 2 Boundary Row, London SE1 8HN. Tel: 0171-865 0066

CHAPMAN (GEOFFREY), 125 Strand, London WC2R 0BB. Tel: 0171-420 5555

CHAPMANS PUBLISHERS, 5 Upper St Martin's Lane, London WC2H 9EA. Tel: 0171-240 3444

CHATTO & WINDUS, 20 Vauxhall Bridge Road, London SW1V 2SA. Tel: 0171-973 9740

CHIVERS PRESS, Windsor Bridge Road, Bath BA2 3AX. Tel: 01225-335336

CHURCH HOUSE PUBLISHING, Church House, Great Smith Street, London SW1P 3NZ. Tel: 0171-222 9011

CHURCHILL LIVINGSTONE, 1–3 Baxter's Place, Leith Walk, Edinburgh EH1 3AF. Tel: 0131-556 2424

COLLINS (WILLIAM), *see* HarperCollins Publishers

CONSTABLE & Co., 3 The Lanchesters, 162 Fulham Palace Road, London W6 9ER. Tel: 0181-741 3663

CONSUMERS' ASSOCIATION, 2 Marylebone Road, London NW1 4DF. Tel: 0171-830 6000

CORGI BOOKS, 61 Uxbridge Road, London W5 5SA. Tel: 0181-579 2652

DARTON, LONGMAN & TODD, 1 Spencer Court, 140 Wandsworth High Street, London SW18 4JJ. Tel: 0181-875 0155

DAVID & CHARLES, Brunel House, Newton Abbot, Devon TQ12 4PU. Tel: 01626-61121

DEAN & SON, 81 Fulham Road, London SW3 6RB. Tel: 0171-581 9393

DENT (J. M.) & SONS, 5 Upper St Martin's Lane, London WC2H 9EA. Tel: 0171-240 3444

DEUTSCH (ANDRE), 106 Great Russell Street, London WC1B 3LJ. Tel: 0171-580 2746

DORLING KINDERSLEY, 9 Henrietta Street, London WC2E 8PS. Tel: 0171-836 5411

DOUBLEDAY, 61 Uxbridge Road, London W5 5SA. Tel: 0181-579 2652

DUCKWORTH & Co., 48 Hoxton Square, London N1 6PB. Tel: 0171-729 5986

EBURY PRESS, 20 Vauxhall Bridge Road, London SW1V 2SA. Tel: 0171-973 9690

ELEMENT BOOKS, The Old School House, The Courtyard, Bell Street, Shaftesbury, Dorset SP7 8BP. Tel: 01747-851448

ELLIOT RIGHT WAY BOOKS, Kingswood Building, Kingswood, Tadworth, Surrey KT20 6TD. Tel: 01737-832202

ELSEVIER SCIENCE, The Boulevard, Langford Lane, Kidlington, Oxon OX5 1GB. Tel: 01865-843000

ENCYCLOPAEDIA BRITANNICA INTERNATIONAL, Carew House, Station Approach, Wallington, Surrey SM6 0DA. Tel: 0181-669 4355

EPWORTH PRESS, c/o SCM Press, 26 Tottenham Road, London NI 4BZ. Tel: 0171-249 7262

EVANS BROS, 2A Portman Mansions, Chiltern Street, London WIM 1LE. Tel: 0171-935 7160

EVERYMAN, see Orion Publishing Group

EVERYMAN'S LIBRARY, 79 Berwick Street, London WIV 3PF. Tel: 0171-287 0035

FABER & FABER, 3 Queen Square, London WC1N 3AU. Tel: 0171-465 0045

FLAMINGO, see HarperCollins Publishers

FONTANA, 77 Fulham Palace Road, London W6 8JB. Tel: 0181-741 7070

FOULIS (G. T.), Sparkford, Yeovil, Somerset BA22 7JJ. Tel: 01963-440635

FOULSHAM (W.) & Co., Bennetts Close, Cippenham, Slough SL1 5AP. Tel: 01753-526769

FOURTH ESTATE, 6 Salem Road, London W2 4BU. Tel: 0171-727 8993

FRENCH (SAMUEL), 52 Fitzroy Street, London WIP 6JR. Tel: 0171-387 9373

GAIA BOOKS, 20 High Street, Stroud GL5 1AS. Tel: 01453-752985

GIBBONS (STANLEY), 5 Parkside, Christchurch Road, Ringwood, Hants BH24 3SH. Tel: 01425-472363

GINN & Co., Prebendal House, Parson's Fee, Aylesbury, Bucks HP20 2QZ. Tel: 01296-394442

GOLLANCZ (VICTOR), 125 Strand, London WC2R 0BB. Tel: 0171-420 5555

GOWER PUBLISHING Co., Croft Road, Aldershot, Hants GU11 3HR. Tel: 01252-331551

GRAFTON BOOKS, 77 Fulham Palace Road, London W6 8JB. Tel: 0181-741 7070

GRANTA BOOKS, 2 Hanover Yard, London NI 8BE. Tel: 0171-704 9776

GUINNESS PUBLISHING, 33 London Road, Enfield, Middx EN2 6DJ. Tel: 0181-367 4567

HALE (ROBERT), 45 Clerkenwell Green, London EC1R 0HT. Tel: 0171-251 2661

HAMILTON (HAMISH), 27 Wrights Lane, London W8 5TZ. Tel: 0171-416 3000

HAMLYN (PAUL), 81 Fulham Road, London SW3 6RB. Tel: 0171-581 9393

HARCOURT BRACE, 24 Oval Road, London NWI 7DX. Tel: 0171-267 4466

HARPERCOLLINS PUBLISHERS, 77 Fulham Palace Road, London W6 8JB. Tel: 0181-741 7070

HARRAP, 24 Great Titchfield Street, London WIP 7AD. Tel: 0171-631 0878

HAYNES (J. H.), Sparkford, Yeovil, Somerset BA22 7JJ. Tel: 01963-440635

HEADLINE BOOK PUBLISHING, see Hodder Headline

HEINEMANN (WILLIAM), 81 Fulham Road, London SW3 6RB. Tel: 0171-581 9393

HERBERT PRESS, 46 Northchurch Road, London NI 4EJ. Tel: 0171-254 4379

HIPPO BOOKS, 7 Pratt Street, London NWI 0AE. Tel: 0171-284 4474

HMSO, PO Box 276, London SW8 5DT. Tel: 0171-873 0011

HODDER & STOUGHTON, see Hodder Headline

HODDER HEADLINE, 338 Euston Road, London NWI 3BH. Tel: 0171-873 6000

HOGARTH PRESS, 20 Vauxhall Bridge Road, London SWIV 2SA. Tel: 0171-973 9740

HUTCHINSON, see Random House UK

JARROLD PUBLISHING, Whitefriars, Norwich NR3 1TR. Tel: 01603-763300

JORDAN PUBLISHING, 21 St Thomas Street, Bristol BS1 6JS. Tel: 0117-923 0600

JOSEPH (MICHAEL), 27 Wrights Lane, London W8 5TZ. Tel: 0171-416 3000

KEGAN PAUL INTERNATIONAL, PO Box 256, London WC1B 3SW. Tel: 0171-580 5511

KINGFISHER BOOKS, 24 Great Titchfield Street, London WIP 7AD. Tel: 0171-631 0878

KINGSWAY PUBLICATIONS, Lottbridge Drove, Eastbourne BN23 6NT. Tel: 01323-410930

KOGAN PAGE, 120 Pentonville Road, London NI 9JN. Tel: 0171-278 0433

LADYBIRD BOOKS, Beeches Road, Loughborough LE11 2NQ. Tel: 01509-268021

LAROUSSE, 24 Great Titchfield Street, London WIP 7AD. Tel: 0171-631 0878

LASCELLES (ROGER), 47 York Road, Brentford, Middx TW8 0QP. Tel: 0181-847 0935

LAWRENCE & WISHART, 144A Old South Lambeth Road, London SW8 1XX. Tel: 0171-820 9281

LENNARD PUBLISHING, Windmill Cottage, Mackerye End, Harpenden, Herts AL5 5DR. Tel: 01582-715866

LETTS OF LONDON, 24 Nutford Place, London WIH 6AE. Tel: 0171-724 7773

LINCOLN (FRANCES), 4 Torriano Mews, Torriano Avenue, London NW5 2RZ. Tel: 0171-284 4009

LION PUBLISHING, Sandy Lane West, Oxford OX4 5HG. Tel: 01865-747550

LITTLE, BROWN & Co., Brettenham House, Lancaster Place, London WC2E 7EN. Tel: 0171-911 8000

LONGMAN GROUP, Burnt Mill, Harlow, Essex CM20 2JE. Tel: 01279-426721

LUND HUMPHRIES, 1 Russell Gardens, London NWII 9NN. Tel: 0181-458 6314

LUTTERWORTH PRESS, PO Box 60, Cambridge CB1 2NT. Tel: 01223-350865

MACDONALD & EVANS, 128 Long Acre, London WC2E 9AN. Tel: 0171-379 7383

MACDONALD YOUNG BOOKS, 61 Western Road, Hove, E. Sussex BN3 1JD. Tel: 01273-722561

McGRAW-HILL, Shoppenhangers Road, Maidenhead, Berks SL6 2QL. Tel: 01628-23432

MACMILLAN PUBLISHERS, 4 Little Essex Street, London WC2R 3LF. Tel: 0171-836 6633

MACRAE (JULIA), 20 Vauxhall Bridge Road, London SWIV 2SA. Tel: 0171-973 9750

MAMMOTH, 38 Hans Crescent, London SWIX 0LZ. Tel: 0171-581 9393

MANDALA, see HarperCollins Publishers

MANDARIN, 81 Fulham Road, London SW3 6RB. Tel: 0171-581 9393

METHUEN LONDON, 81 Fulham Road, London SW3 6RB. Tel: 0171-581 9393

MILLS & BOON, 18 Paradise Road, Richmond, Surrey TW9 1SR. Tel: 0181-948 0444

MINERVA PRESS, 10 Cromwell Place, London SW7 2JE. Tel: 0171-225 3113

MITCHELL BEAZLEY, 81 Fulham Road, London SW3 6RB. Tel: 0171-581 9393

MOWBRAY, 125 Strand, London WC2R 0BB. Tel: 0171-420 5555

MURRAY (JOHN), 50 Albemarle Street, London WIX 4BD. Tel: 0171-493 4361

NATIONAL CHRISTIAN EDUCATION COUNCIL, 1020 Bristol Road, Selly Oak, Birmingham B29 6LB. Tel: 0121-472 4242

NELSON (THOMAS), Mayfield Road, Walton-on-Thames KT12 5PL. Tel: 01932-252211

NEW ENGLISH LIBRARY, see Hodder Headline

NEXUS SPECIAL INTEREST, Nexus House, Boundary Way, Hemel Hempstead, Herts HP2 7ST. Tel: 01442-66551

NISBET & CO., 78 Tilehouse Street, Hitchin, Herts SG5 2DY. Tel: 01462-438331

NOVELLO & CO., 8 Frith Street, London W1V 5TZ. Tel: 0171-434 0066

OCTOPUS BOOKS, 81 Fulham Road, London SW3 6RB. Tel: 0171-581 9393

OLIVER & BOYD, Longman House, Burnt Mill, Harlow, Essex CM20 2JE. Tel: 01279-426721

O'MARA (MICHAEL) BOOKS, 9 Lion Yard, Tremadoc Road, London SW4 7NQ. Tel: 0171-720 8643

ORCHARD BOOKS, 96 Leonard Street, London EC2A 4RH. Tel: 0171-739 2929

ORION PUBLISHING GROUP, 5 Upper St Martin's Lane, London WC2H 9EA. Tel: 0171-240 3444

OWEN (PETER), 73 Kenway Road, London SW5 0RE. Tel: 0171-373 5628

OXFORD UNIVERSITY PRESS, Walton Street, Oxford OX2 6DP. Tel: 01865-56767

PAN BOOKS, Cavaye Place, London SW10 9PG. Tel: 0171-373 6070

PELHAM BOOKS, 27 Wrights Lane, London W8 5TZ. Tel: 0171-416 3000

PENGUIN BOOKS, 27 Wrights Lane, London W8 5TZ. Tel: 0171-416 3000

PERGAMON PRESS, The Boulevard, Langford Lane, Kidlington, Oxon OX5 1GB. Tel: 01865-843000

PHAIDON PRESS, Regent's Wharf, All Saints Street, London N1 9PA. Tel: 0171-843 1000

PHARMACEUTICAL PRESS, 1 Lambeth High Street, London SE1 7JN. Tel: 0171-735 9141

PHILIP (GEORGE), 81 Fulham Road, London SW3 6RB. Tel: 0171-581 9393

PIATKUS BOOKS, 5 Windmill Street, London W1P 1HF. Tel: 0171-631 0710

PICADOR, see Pan Books

PICCADILLY PRESS, 5 Castle Road, London NW1 8PR. Tel: 0171-267 4492

PINTER PUBLISHERS, 125 Strand, London WC2R 0BB. Tel: 0171-420 5555

PITKIN PICTORIALS, Healey House, Dene Road, Andover, Hants SP10 2AA. Tel: 01264-334303

PITMAN PUBLISHING, 128 Long Acre, London WC2E 9AN. Tel: 0171-379 7383

QUARTET BOOKS, 27 Goodge Street, London W1P 1FD. Tel: 0171-636 3992

QUILLER BOOKS, 46 Lillie Road, London SW6 1TN. Tel: 0171-499 6529

RANDOM HOUSE UK, 20 Vauxhall Bridge Road, London SW1V 2SA. Tel: 0171-973 9000

READER'S DIGEST, 25 Berkeley Square, London W1X 6AB. Tel: 0171-629 8144

RELIGIOUS & MORAL EDUCATION PRESS, St Mary's Works, St Mary's Plain, Norwich NR3 3BH. Tel: 01603-615995

ROUGH GUIDES, 1 Mercer Street, London WC2H 9QJ. Tel: 0171-379 3329

ROUTLEDGE, 11 New Fetter Lane, London EC4P 4EE. Tel: 0171-583 9855

ST ANDREW PRESS, 121 George Street, Edinburgh EH2 4YN. Tel: 0131-225 5722

SCM PRESS, 26 Tottenham Road, London N1 4BZ. Tel: 0171-249 7262

SCRIPTURE UNION, 130 City Road, London EC1V 2NJ. Tel: 0171-782 0013

SECKER & WARBURG, 81 Fulham Road, London SW3 6RB. Tel: 0171-581 9393

SERPENT'S TAIL PUBLISHING, 4 Blackstock Mews, London N4 2BT. Tel: 0171-354 1949

SEVERN HOUSE, 9 Sutton High Street, Sutton SM1 1DF. Tel: 0181-770 3930

SHELDON PRESS, Holy Trinity Church, Marylebone Road, London NW1 4DU. Tel: 0171-387 5282

SIDGWICK & JACKSON, Cavaye Place, London SW10 9PG. Tel: 0171-373 6070

SIMON & SCHUSTER, Campus 400, Maylands Avenue, Hemel Hempstead, Herts HP2 7EZ. Tel: 01442-881900

SINCLAIR-STEVENSON, 81 Fulham Road, London SW3 6RB. Tel: 0171-581 9393

SOUVENIR PRESS, 43 Great Russell Street, London WC1B 3PA. Tel: 0171-580 9307

SPCK, Holy Trinity Church, Marylebone Road, London NW1 4DU. Tel: 0171-387 5282

SPON (E. & F. N.), 2 Boundary Row, London SE1 8HN. Tel: 0171-865 0066

STEPHENS (PATRICK), Sparkford, Yeovil BA22 7JJ. Tel: 01963-440635

SUTTON (ALAN) PUBLISHING, Phoenix Mill, Far Thrupp, Stroud, Glos GL5 2BU. Tel: 01453-731114

SWEET & MAXWELL, 183 Marsh Wall, London E14 9FT. Tel: 0171-538 8686

THAMES & HUDSON, 30 Bloomsbury Street, London WC1B 3QP. Tel: 0171-636 5488

THORSONS, 77 Fulham Palace Road, London W6 8JB. Tel: 0181-741 7070

TIMES BOOKS, 77 Fulham Palace Road, London W6 8JB. Tel: 0181-741 7070

UNIVERSITY OF WALES PRESS, 6 Gwennyth Street, Cardiff CF2 4YD. Tel: 01222-231919

VIKING, 27 Wrights Lane, London W8 5TZ. Tel: 0171-416 3000

VIRAGO PRESS, 20 Vauxhall Bridge Road, London SW1V 2SA. Tel: 0171-973 9750

VIRGIN PUBLISHING, 33–34 Grand Union Centre, 332 Ladbroke Grove, London W10 5AH. Tel: 0181-968 7554

WALKER BOOKS, 87 Vauxhall Walk, London SE11 5HJ. Tel: 0171-793 0909

WARD LOCK, 125 Strand, London WC2R 0BB. Tel: 0171-420 5555

WARD LOCK EDUCATIONAL CO., 1 Christopher Road, East Grinstead, W. Sussex RH19 3BT. Tel: 01342-318980

WARNE (FREDERICK), see Penguin Books

WATTS BOOKS, 96 Leonard Street, London EC2A 4RH. Tel: 0171-739 2929

WEIDENFELD & NICOLSON, 5 Upper St Martin's Lane, London WC2H 9EA. Tel: 0171-240 3444

WHICH? BOOKS, see Consumer's Association

WHITAKER (J.), 12 Dyott Street, London WC1A 1DF. Tel: 0171-836 8911

WILEY (JOHN) & SONS, Baffins Lane, Chichester, W. Sussex PO19 1UD. Tel: 01243-779777

WISDEN (JOHN), 25 Down Road, Merrow, Guildford GU1 2PY. Tel: 01483-570358

Annual Reference Books

If the address of the editorial office of a publication differs from the address to which orders should be sent, the address given is usually the one for orders

ADVERTISER'S ANNUAL, East Grinstead House, East Grinstead, W. Sussex RH19 1XA. 3 vol. £180.00

ALLIED DUNBAR INVESTMENT AND SAVINGS HANDBOOK, PO Box 88, Harlow, Essex CM19 5SR. £21.00

ALLIED DUNBAR TAX HANDBOOK, PO Box 88, Harlow, Essex CM19 5SR. £21.00

ANNUAL ABSTRACT OF STATISTICS, PO Box 276, London SW8 5DT. (Feb.) £37.50

ANNUAL REGISTER: A RECORD OF WORLD EVENTS, 12–14 Slaidburn Crescent, Southport, Merseyside PR9 9YF. £97.50

ANTIQUE SHOPS OF BRITAIN, GUIDE TO THE, 5 Church Street, Woodbridge, Suffolk IP12 1DS. £14.95

ART SALES INDEX, 1 Thames Street, Weybridge, Surrey KT13 8JG. 2 vol. £95.00

ART WORLD DIRECTORY, 39 Milton Park, Abingdon, Oxon OX14 4TD. (Jan.) £19.50

ASSOCIATION OF CONSULTING ENGINEERS DIRECTORY OF MEMBERS FIRMS, Alliance House, 12 Caxton Street, London SW1H 0QL. £10.00

ASTRONOMICAL ALMANAC, HMSO, PO Box 276, London SW8 5DT. (Dec.) £19.00

ATHLETICS: INTERNATIONAL TRACK AND FIELD ANNUAL, Waldenbury, North Common, North Chailey, Lewes, E. Sussex BN8 4DR. (May) £13.95

AUTOMOBILE YEAR, Waldenbury, North Common, North Chailey, Lewes, E. Sussex BN8 4DR. £29.95

BAILY'S HUNTING DIRECTORY, Chesterton Mill, French's Road, Cambridge CB4 3NP. (Nov.) £29.95

BANKER'S ALMANAC, East Grinstead House, East Grinstead, W. Sussex RH19 1XE. (Feb.) 3 vol. £295.00

BENEDICTINE AND CISTERCIAN MONASTIC YEAR Book, Ampleforth Abbey, York YO6 4EN. (Dec.) £1.75

BENN'S MEDIA, Riverbank House, Angel Lane, Tonbridge, Kent TN9 1SE. 3 vol. £312.00

BIRMINGHAM POST AND MAIL YEAR BOOK AND WHO'S WHO, 137 Newhall Street, Birmingham B3 1SF. (Sept.) £29.90

BPIF SERVICES AND LIST OF MEMBERS, 11 Bedford Row, London WC1R 4DX. £90.00

BRASSEY'S DEFENCE YEAR BOOK, PO Box 87, Osney Mead, Oxford OX2 0DT. £36.00

BRITAIN: AN OFFICIAL HANDBOOK, HMSO, PO Box 276, London SW8 5DT. (Jan.) £25.00

BRITANNICA BOOK OF THE YEAR, Carew House, Station Approach, Wallington, Surrey SM6 0DA. (May) £76.00

BRITISH CLOTHING INDUSTRY YEAR BOOK, 11 The Swan Courtyard, Charles Edward Road, Yardley, Birmingham B26 1BU. £65.00

BRITISH EXPORTS, East Grinstead House, East Grinstead, W. Sussex RH19 1XA. £150.00

BRITISH MUSIC YEARBOOK, 241 Shaftesbury Avenue, London WC2H 8EH. £17.95

BRITISH PERFORMING ARTS YEAR BOOK, 241 Shaftesbury Avenue, London WC2H 8EH. (Jan.) £18.95

BRITISH PLASTICS AND RUBBER DIRECTORY, Catalyst House, 159 Clapham High Street, London SW4 7SS. £10.00

BROWN'S NAUTICAL ALMANACK DAILY TIDE TABLES, 4–10 Darnley Street, Glasgow G41 2SD. (Sept.) £34.50

BUILDING AND CONSTRUCTION INDEX, Riverbank House, Angel Lane, Tonbridge, Kent TN9 1SE. (Jan.) £62.00

BUILDING SOCIETIES YEAR BOOK, South Quay Plaza, 183 Marsh Wall, London E14 9FS. £63.00

BUSES YEARBOOK, 39 Milton Park, Abingdon, Oxon OX14 4TD. £10.99

BUTTERWORTHS LAW DIRECTORY AND LEGAL SERVICES DIRECTORY, Maypole House, Maypole Road, East Grinstead, W. Sussex RH19 1HH. (Feb.) 2 vol. £49.00

CATERING BUYERS GUIDE, Riverbank House, Angel Lane, Tonbridge, Kent TN9 1SE. (Jan.) £65.00

CATHOLIC DIRECTORY OF ENGLAND AND WALES, St James's Buildings, Oxford Street, Manchester M1 6FP. £23.50

CHARITIES DIGEST, 501–505 Kingsland Road, London E8 4AU. £16.95

CHEMICAL INDUSTRY EUROPE, Riverbank House, Angel Lane, Tonbridge, Kent TN9 1SE. £83.00

CHEMIST AND DRUGGIST DIRECTORY, Riverbank House, Angel Lane, Tonbridge, Kent TN9 1SE. £95.00

CHRISTIES' REVIEW OF THE SEASON, 1 Stewart's Court, 220 Stewart's Road, London SW8 4UD. (Nov.) £30.00

CHURCH OF ENGLAND YEAR BOOK, Church House, Great Smith Street, London SW1P 3NZ. (Jan.) £19.50

CHURCH OF SCOTLAND YEAR BOOK, 121 George Street, Edinburgh EH2 4YN. (Sept.) £10.00

CITY OF LONDON DIRECTORY AND LIVERY COMPANIES GUIDE, Seatrade House, 42–48 North Station Road, Colchester, Essex CO1 1RB. £20.00, £18.00

CIVIL SERVICE YEAR BOOK, HMSO, PO Box 276, London SW8 5DT. (Feb.) £21.00

COMMONWEALTH UNIVERSITIES YEAR BOOK, 36 Gordon Square, London WCIH 0PF. (July) 2 vol. £120.00

COMMONWEALTH YEAR BOOK, HMSO, PO Box 276, London SW8 5DT. (May) £25.00

COMPUTER USERS' YEAR BOOK, 32–34 Broadwick Street, London W1A 2HG. 3 vol. £235.00

CONCRETE YEAR BOOK, Thomas Telford House, 1 Heron Quay, London E14 4JD. £55.00

CURRENT LAW YEAR BOOK, Cheriton House, North Way, Andover, Hants SP10 5BE. £115.00

DEBRETT'S PEOPLE OF TODAY, 73–77 Britannia Road, PO Box 357, London SW6 2JY. (April) £97.50

DIPLOMATIC SERVICE LIST, HMSO, PO Box 276, London SW8 5DT. (April) £19.50

DIRECTORY OF DIRECTORS, East Grinstead House, East Grinstead, W. Sussex RH19 1XA. (April) 2 vol. £189.00

DIRECTORY OF FURTHER EDUCATION, Bateman Street, Cambridge CB2 1LZ. (June) £56.95, £46.95

DIRECTORY OF HIGHER EDUCATION, Bateman Street, Cambridge CB2 1LZ. (June) £56.95, £46.95

DIRECTORY OF OFFICIAL ARCHITECTURE AND PLANNING, PO Box 88, Harlow, Essex CM19 5SR. £72.00

DIY TRADE BUYERS GUIDE, Riverbank House, Angel Lane, Tonbridge, Kent TN9 1SE. £69.00

DOD'S PARLIAMENTARY COMPANION, Hurst Green, Etchingham, E. Sussex TN19 7PX. £75.00

EDUCATION AUTHORITIES' DIRECTORY AND ANNUAL, Derby House, Bletchingley Road, Merstham, Surrey RH1 3DN. (Jan.) £62.00, £50.00

EDUCATION YEAR BOOK, PO Box 88, Harlow, Essex CM19 5SR. £76.00

ELECTRICAL AND ELECTRONIC TRADES DIRECTORY, Michael Faraday House, Six Hills Way, Stevenage, Herts SG1 2AY. (Feb.) £75.00

ELECTRICITY SUPPLY HANDBOOK, PO Box 935, Finchingfield, Braintree, Essex CM7 4LN. (Feb.) £40.00

EUROPA WORLD YEAR BOOK, 18 Bedford Square, London WC1B 3JN. 2 vol. £325.00

EUROPEAN FOOD TRADES DIRECTORY, 32 Vauxhall Bridge Road, London SW1V 2SS. 2 vol. £140.00

EUROPEAN GLASS DIRECTORY AND BUYER'S GUIDE, 2 Queensway, Redhill, Surrey RH1 1QS. £98.60

FLIGHT INTERNATIONAL DIRECTORY, PO Box 1315, Potters Bar, Herts EN6 1PU. 2 vol. £48.00, £45.00

FROZEN AND CHILLED FOODS YEAR BOOK, 2 Queensway, Redhill, Surrey RH1 1QS. £69.20

FURNITURE AND FURNISHINGS INDUSTRY, DIRECTORY OF THE, Riverbank House, Angel Lane, Tonbridge, Kent TN9 1SE. £79.00

GAS INDUSTRY DIRECTORY, Riverbank House, Angel Lane, Tonbridge, Kent TN9 1SE. (Oct.) £86.00

GIBBONS' STAMPS OF THE WORLD CATALOGUE, 5 Parkside, Christchurch Road, Ringwood, Hants BH24 3SH. (Oct.) 3 vol. £22.95, £22.95, £19.95

GOOD FOOD GUIDE, Bath Road, Harmondsworth, West Drayton, Middx UB7 0DA. £14.99

GOOD HOTEL GUIDE, Brunel Road, Houndmills, Basingstoke, Hants RG21 2XS. £13.99

GOVERNMENT AND MUNICIPAL BUYERS GUIDE, Riverbank House, Angel Lane, Tonbridge, Kent TN9 1SE. (Jan.) £62.00

GRADUATE STUDIES, Bateman Street, Cambridge CB2 1LZ. (July) £99.95

GUINNESS BOOK OF ANSWERS, 33 London Road, Enfield EN2 6DJ. £14.99

GUINNESS BOOK OF RECORDS, 33 London Road, Enfield EN2 6DJ. (Oct.) £14.99

HEALTH CARE BUYERS GUIDE, Riverbank House, Angel Lane, Tonbridge, Kent TN9 1SE. £76.00

HISTORIC HOUSES, CASTLES AND GARDENS, East Grinstead House, East Grinstead, W. Sussex RH19 1XA. (March) £8.20

HOLLIS UK PRESS AND PR ANNUAL, Contact House, Lower Hampton Road, Sunbury-on-Thames TW16 5HG. (Oct.) £70.00

HOSPITALS AND HEALTH SERVICES YEARBOOK AND DIRECTORY OF HOSPITAL SUPPLIERS, 39 Chalton Street, London NW1 1JD. £99.00

HUTCHINS' PRICED SCHEDULES, PO Box 5, Rushden, Northants NN10 6XJ. £49.95

INDEPENDENT SCHOOLS YEAR BOOK, PO Box 19, Huntingdon, Cambs PE19 3SF. £24.00

INSURANCE DIRECTORY AND YEAR BOOK, Garrard House, 2–6 Homesdale Road, Bromley, Kent BR2 9WL. (Jan.) 4 vol. £320.00

INTERNATIONAL PAPER DIRECTORY, PHILLIPS', Riverbank House, Angel Lane, Tonbridge, Kent TN9 1SE. £115.00

INTERNATIONAL WHO'S WHO, 18 Bedford Square, London WC1R 4JH. (Sept.) £140.00

INTERNATIONAL YEARBOOK AND STATESMEN'S WHO'S WHO, East Grinstead House, East Grinstead, W. Sussex RH19 1XA. (April) £162.00

JANE'S ALL THE WORLD'S AIRCRAFT, Sentinel House, 163 Brighton Road, Coulsdon, Surrey CR5 2NH. (Oct.) £185.00

JANE'S ARMOUR AND ARTILLERY, Sentinel House, 163 Brighton Road, Coulsdon, Surrey CR5 2NH. (Nov.) £185.00

JANE'S FIGHTING SHIPS, Sentinel House, 163 Brighton Road, Coulsdon, Surrey CR5 2NH. £185.00

JANE'S HIGH SPEED MARINE CRAFT, Sentinel House, 163 Brighton Road, Coulsdon, Surrey CR5 2NH. £190.00

JANE'S INFANTRY WEAPONS, Sentinel House, 163 Brighton Road, Coulsdon, Surrey CR5 2NH. (Aug.) £175.00

JANE'S INTERMODAL TRANSPORTATION, Sentinel House, 163 Brighton Road, Coulsdon, Surrey CR5 2NH. (Nov.) £190.00

JANE'S NAVAL WEAPON SYSTEMS, Sentinel House, 163 Brighton Road, Coulsdon, Surrey CR5 2NH. £290.00

JANE'S WORLD RAILWAYS, Sentinel House, 163 Brighton Road, Coulsdon, Surrey CR5 2NH. £195.00

JEWISH YEAR BOOK, Star Road, Partridge Green, Horsham, W. Sussex RH13 8LD. (Feb.) £22.50

KELLY'S BUSINESS DIRECTORY, East Grinstead House, East Grinstead, W. Sussex RH19 1XA. £164.00

KEMPE'S ENGINEERS YEAR BOOK, Riverbank House, Angel Lane, Tonbridge, Kent TN9 1SE. £102.00

KIME'S INTERNATIONAL LAW DIRECTORY, PO Box 88, Harlow, Essex CM19 5SR. (Dec.) £70.00

LAXTON'S BUILDING PRICE BOOK, East Grinstead House, East Grinstead, W. Sussex RH19 1XA. 2 vol. £89.50

LIBRARY ASSOCIATION YEARBOOK, 7 Ridgmount Street, London WC1E 7AE. (June) £26.00

LLOYD'S LIST OF SHIPOWNERS, 71 Fenchurch Street, London EC3M 4BS. (Sept.) £115.00

LLOYD'S MARITIME DIRECTORY, Sheepen Place, Colchester CO3 3LP. (Jan.) £150.00

LLOYD'S NAUTICAL YEAR BOOK, Sheepen Place, Colchester CO3 3LP. (Sept.) £45.00

LLOYD'S REGISTER OF SHIPS, 71 Fenchurch Street, London EC3M 4BS. (July). 3 vol. £425.00

LYLE'S OFFICIAL ANTIQUES PRICE GUIDE, Glenmayne, Galashiels TD1 3NR. £17.95

MACMILLAN AND SILK CUT NAUTICAL ALMANACK, Brunel Road, Houndmills, Basingstoke, Hants RG21 2XS. £25.99

MAGISTRATES' COURT GUIDE, Halsbury House, 35 Chancery Lane, London WC2A 1EL. £20.00

MEDICAL ANNUAL, Falcon House, Queen Square, Lancaster LA1 1RN. £29.50

MEDICAL DIRECTORY, PO Box 88, Harlow, Essex CM19 5SR. (June) 3 vol. £165.00

MEDICAL REGISTER, 44 Hallam Street, London W1N 6AE. (March) 3 vol. £90.00

MIDDLE EAST AND NORTH AFRICA, 18 Bedford Square, London WC1B 3JN. (Oct.) £160.00

MILLER'S ANTIQUES PRICE GUIDE, The Cellars, 5 High Street, Tenterden, Kent TN30 6BN. £21.99

MINING ANNUAL REVIEW, PO Box 10, Edenbridge, Kent TN8 5NE. £63.00

MINING INTERNATIONAL YEAR BOOK, PO Box 88, Harlow, Essex CM19 5SR. (June) £160.00

MOTOR INDUSTRY OF GREAT BRITAIN WORLD AUTOMOTIVE STATISTICS, Forbes House, Halkin Street, London SW1X 7DS. (Oct.) £75.00

MOTOR SHIP DIRECTORY, PO Box 935, Finchingfield, Braintree, Essex CM7 4LN. £95.00

MUNICIPAL YEARBOOK AND PUBLIC SERVICES DIRECTORY, 32 Vauxhall Bridge Road, London SW1V 2SS. (Dec.) 2 vol. £155.00

MUSEUMS AND GALLERIES IN GREAT BRITAIN AND IRELAND, East Grinstead House, East Grinstead, W. Sussex RH19 1XA. (Oct.) £7.45

NAUTICAL ALMANAC, HMSO, PO Box 276, London SW8 5DT. (Oct.) £18.50

PACKAGING INDUSTRY DIRECTORY, Riverbank House, Angel Lane, Tonbridge, Kent TN9 1SE. £83.00

PEARS CYCLOPEDIA, 27 Wright's Lane, London W8 5TZ. £14.99

PHOTOGRAPHY YEAR BOOK, Fountain House, 2 Gladstone Road, Kingston upon Thames, Surrey KT1 3HD. £24.95

POLYMERS, PAINT AND COLOUR YEAR BOOK, 2 Queensway, Redhill, Surrey RH1 1QS. £106.30

PORTS OF THE WORLD, Sheepen Place, Colchester, Essex CO3 3LP. £160.00

PRINTING TRADES DIRECTORY, Riverbank House, Angel Lane, Tonbridge, Kent TN9 1SE. £97.00

PUBLIC AUTHORITIES DIRECTORY, Lansdowne Mews, 196 High Street, Tonbridge, Kent TN9 1EF. (Jan.) £84.00

PUBLIC SERVICES YEARBOOK, Cheriton House, North Way, Andover, Hants SP10 5BE. (April) £29.95

PUBLISHERS IN THE UNITED KINGDOM AND THEIR ADDRESSES, 12 Dyott Street, London WC1A 1DF. (March) £9.95

PUBLISHING, DIRECTORY OF, Artillery House, Artillery Row, London SW1P 1RT. (Oct.) £55.00

RAC EUROPEAN HOTEL GUIDE, 39 Milton Park, Abingdon, Oxon OX14 4TD. £8.99

RAC HOTEL GUIDE, 39 Milton Park, Abingdon, Oxon OX14 4TD. £9.99

RAILWAY DIRECTORY, PO Box 935, Finchingfield, Braintree, Essex CM7 4LN. (Dec.) £80.00

REGIONAL TRENDS, PO Box 276, London SW8 5DT. (July) £34.95

RETAIL DIRECTORY OF THE UNITED KINGDOM, 32 Vauxhall Bridge Road, London SW1V 2SS. £155.00

RIBA DIRECTORY OF PRACTICES, 39 Moreland Street, London EC1V 8BB. (Oct.) £57.75

ROTHMANS FOOTBALL YEAR BOOK, 39 Milton Park, Abingdon, Oxon OX14 4TD. (Aug.) £30.00, £16.99

ROTHMAN'S RUGBY LEAGUE YEAR BOOK, 39 Milton Park, Abingdon, Oxon OX14 4TD. (Sept.) £16.99

ROTHMAN'S RUGBY UNION YEAR BOOK, 39 Milton Park, Abingdon, Oxon OX14 4TD. (Sept.) £16.99

ROYAL AND ANCIENT GOLFER'S HANDBOOK, Brunel Road, Houndmills, Basingstoke, Hants RG21 2XS. (April) £42.50, £18.50

ROYAL SOCIETY YEAR BOOK, 6 Carlton House Terrace, London SW1Y 5AG. (Feb.) £17.75

RUFF'S GUIDE TO THE TURF AND SPORTING LIFE ANNUAL, Orbit House, 1 New Fetter Lane, London EC4A 1AR. (Jan.) £55.00

SALVATION ARMY YEAR BOOK, 117–121 Judd Street, London WC1H 9NN. (April) £10.75, £5.50

SCOTTISH CURRENT LAW YEAR BOOK, 21 Alva Street, Edinburgh EH2 4PS. 2 vol. £115.00

SCOTTISH LAW DIRECTORY, 59 George Street, Edinburgh EH2 2LQ. £32.00

SELL'S PRODUCTS AND SERVICES DIRECTORY, Riverbank House, Angel Lane, Tonbridge, Kent TN9 1SE. (June) £82.00

SHEET METAL INDUSTRIES YEAR BOOK, 2 Queensway, Redhill, Surrey RH1 1QS. £69.00

SHOWCASE INTERNATIONAL MUSIC BOOK, 12 Felix Avenue, London N8 9TL. £30.00

SOCIAL SERVICES YEAR BOOK, PO Box 88, Harlow, Essex CM19 5SR. (April) £80.00

SOCIAL TRENDS, PO Box 276, London SW8 5DT. (Jan.) £37.50

SOLICITORS AND BARRISTERS, DIRECTORY OF, 50 Chancery Lane, London WC2A 1SX. £50.00

SPON'S ARCHITECTS' AND BUILDERS' PRICE BOOK, Cheriton House, North Way, Andover, Hants SP10 5BE. £69.50

SPON'S MECHANICAL AND ELECTRICAL SERVICES PRICE BOOK, Cheriton House, North Way, Andover, Hants SP10 5BE. £70.00

STATESMAN'S YEARBOOK, Brunel House, Houndmills, Basingstoke, Hants RG21 2XS. (Aug.) £44.00

STOCK EXCHANGE OFFICIAL YEAR BOOK, Brunel House, Houndmills, Basingstoke, Hants RG21 2XS. £210.00

STONE'S JUSTICES' MANUAL, Halsbury House, 35 Chancery Lane, London WC2A 1EL. 3 vol. (May) £200.00

TANKER REGISTER, 12 Camomile Street, London EC3A 7BP. (April) £150.00

TIMBER TRADES ADDRESS BOOK, Riverbank House, Angel Lane, Tonbridge, Kent TN9 1SE. £63.00

TRAINING AND ENTERPRISE DIRECTORY, 120 Pentonville Road, London N1 9JN. £25.00

TRAVEL TRADE GAZETTE DIRECTORY, Riverbank House, Angel Lane, Tonbridge, Kent TN9 1SE. (April) £67.00

UK KOMPASS REGISTER, East Grinstead House, East Grinstead, W. Sussex RH19 1XD. 5 vol. £880.00

UNITED KINGDOM MINERALS YEARBOOK, British Geological Survey, Keyworth, Nottingham NG12 5GG. £30.00

UNITED REFORMED CHURCH YEAR BOOK, 86 Tavistock Place, London WC1H 9RT. (Sept.) £13.50

UNIT TRUST YEAR BOOK, Maple House, 149 Tottenham Court Road, London W1P 9LL. £250.00

UNIVERSITY AND COLLEGE ENTRANCE, 14 Cooper's Row, London EC3N 2BH. (June) £12.00

VETERINARY ANNUAL, Osney Mead, Oxford OX2 0EL. £70.00

WATER SERVICES YEAR BOOK, 2 Queensway, Redhill, Surrey RH1 1QS. (Oct.) £70.00

WHITAKER'S ALMANACK, 12 Dyott Street, London WC1A 1DF. (Nov.) £30.00

WHITAKER'S BOOKS IN PRINT, 12 Dyott Street, London WC1A 1DF. (Jan.) 5 vol. £263.00

WHITAKER'S CONCISE ALMANACK, 12 Dyott Street, London WC1A 1DF. (Nov.) £9.95

WHO OWNS WHOM?, Holmers Farm Way, High Wycombe, Bucks HP12 4UL. 2 vol. £338.00

WHO'S WHO, 35 Bedford Row, London WC1R 4JH. £95.00

WILLING'S PRESS GUIDE, East Grinstead House, East Grinstead, W. Sussex RH19 1XA. (Feb.) 2 vol. £152.00

WISDEN CRICKETERS' ALMANACK, 13–14 Eldon Way, Lineside Estate, Littlehampton, W. Sussex BN17 7HE. (April) £23.50

WORLD HOTEL DIRECTORY, PO Box 88, Harlow, Essex CM19 5SR. £98.00

WORLD INSURANCE, PO Box 88, Harlow, Essex CM19 5SR. £150.00

WORLD MINERAL STATISTICS, British Geological Survey, Keyworth, Notts NG12 5GG. (Sept.) 2 vol. £70.00

WORLD OF LEARNING, 18 Bedford Square, London WC1B 3JN. (Jan.) 2 vol. £200.00

WORLD SHIPPING DIRECTORY, PO Box 96, Coulsdon, Surrey CR5 2TE. £99.00

WRITERS' AND ARTISTS' YEAR BOOK, 35 Bedford Row, London WC1R 4JH. (Sept.) £10.99

Employers' and Trade Associations

At 31 December 1994 there were 117 employers' associations listed by the Certification Officer (*see* page 293). Most national employers' associations are members of the Confederation of British Industry (CBI). For ACAS, the Certification Office, the Commission for Racial Equality, the Equal Opportunities Commission, the Health and Safety Commission, the Industrial Tribunals and Review Bodies, *see* Index.

CONFEDERATION OF BRITISH INDUSTRY
Centre Point, 103 New Oxford Street, London WC1A 1DU
Tel 0171-379 7400

The Confederation of British Industry was founded in 1965 and is an independent non-party political body financed by industry and commerce. It exists primarily to ensure that the Government understands the intentions, needs and problems of British business. It is the recognized spokesman for the business viewpoint and is consulted as such by the Government.

The CBI represents, directly and indirectly, some 250,000 companies, large and small, from all sectors.

The governing body of the CBI is the 400-strong Council, which meets monthly in London under the chairmanship of the President. It is assisted by some 27 expert standing committees which advise on the main aspects of policy. There are 13 regional councils and offices covering the administrative regions of England, Wales, Scotland and Northern Ireland. There is also an office in Brussels.

President, Sir Bryan Nicholson
Director-General, A. Turner
Secretary, M. W. Hunt

ASSOCIATIONS

ADVERTISING ASSOCIATION, Abford House, 15 Wilton Road, London SW1V 1NJ. Tel: 0171-828 2771. *Director-General,* A. Brown

AEROSPACE COMPANIES LTD, SOCIETY OF BRITISH, 29 King Street, London SW1Y 6RD. Tel: 0171-839 3231. *Director,* Sir Barry Duxbury, KCB, CBE

APPAREL AND TEXTILE CONFEDERATION, BRITISH, 5 Portland Place, London W1N 3AA. Tel: 0171-636 7788. *Director-General,* J. R. Wilson

BAKERS, FEDERATION OF, 20 Bedford Square, London WC1B 3HF. Tel: 0171-580 4252. *Director,* A. Casdagli, CBE

BANKERS' ASSOCIATION, BRITISH, 10 Lombard Street, London EC3V 9EL. Tel: 0171-623 4001. *Director-General,* T. P. Sweeney

BLC (BRITISH LEATHER CONFEDERATION) – THE LEATHER TECHNOLOGY CENTRE, Leather Trade House, Kings Park Road, Moulton Park, Northampton NN3 6JD. Tel: 01604-494131. *Chief Executive,* K. T. W. Alexander, PH.D.

BREWERS' AND LICENSED RETAILERS' ASSOCIATION, 42 Portman Square, London W1H 0BB. Tel: 0171-486 4831. *Director,* R. W. Simpson

BRUSH MANUFACTURERS' ASSOCIATION, BRITISH, Brooke House, 4 The Lakes, Bedford Road,

Northampton NN4 7YD. Tel: 01604-22023. *Secretary,* A. N. Nisbet

BUILDING EMPLOYERS' CONFEDERATION, 82 New Cavendish Street, London W1M 8AD. Tel: 0171-580 5588. *Director-General,* I. A. Deslandes

BUILDING MATERIAL PRODUCERS, NATIONAL COUNCIL OF, 26 Store Street, London WC1E 7BT. Tel: 0171-323 3770. *Director-General,* N. M. Chaldecott, OBE

CHAMBER OF SHIPPING LTD, Carthusian Court, 12 Carthusian Street, London EC1M 6EB. Tel: 0171-417 8400. *Director-General,* Adm. Sir Nicholas Hunt, GCB, LVO

CHEMICAL INDUSTRIES ASSOCIATION LTD, Kings Buildings, Smith Square, London SW1P 3JJ. Tel: 0171-834 3399. *Director-General,* J. C. L. Cox, CBE

CLOTHING INDUSTRY ASSOCIATION LTD, BRITISH, 5 Portland Place, London W1N 3AA. Tel: 0171-636 7788. *Director-General,* J. R. Wilson

DAIRY INDUSTRY FEDERATION, 19 Cornwall Terrace, London NW1 4QP. Tel: 0171-486 7244. *Director-General,* J. P. Price

ELECTROTECHNICAL AND ALLIED MANUFACTURERS' ASSOCIATIONS, FEDERATION OF BRITISH (BEAMA), Westminster Tower, 3 Albert Embankment, London SE1 7SL. Tel: 0171-793 3000. *Director-General,* J. G. Gaddes

ENGINEERING EMPLOYERS' FEDERATION, Broadway House, Tothill Street, London SW1H 9NQ. Tel: 0171-222 7777. *Director-General,* G. R. Mackenzie, F.ENG.

FARMERS' UNION, NATIONAL (NFU), 22 Long Acre, London WC2E 9LY. Tel: 0171-235 5077. *Director-General,* D. Evans, CBE

FARMERS' UNION OF SCOTLAND, NATIONAL, Rural Centre-West Mains, Ingliston, Newbridge, Midlothian EH28 8LT. Tel: 0131-335 3111. *Chief Executive,* T. J. Brady

FARMERS' UNION, ULSTER, Dunedin, 475–477 Antrim Road, Belfast BT15 3DA. Tel: 01232-370222. *Director-General,* A. MacLaughlin

FINANCE AND LEASING ASSOCIATION, 18 Upper Grosvenor Street, London W1X 9PB. Tel: 0171-491 2783. *Director,* N. A. D. Grant, CBE

FOOD AND DRINK FEDERATION, 6 Catherine Street, London WC2B 5JJ. Tel: 0171-836 2460. *Director-General,* M. P. Mackenzie

FREIGHT TRANSPORT ASSOCIATION LTD, Hermes House, 157 St John's Road, Tunbridge Wells, Kent TN4 9UZ. Tel: 01892-526171. *Director-General,* D. C. Green

INSURERS, ASSOCIATION OF BRITISH, 51 Gresham Street, London EC2V 7HQ. Tel: 0171-600 3333. *Director-General,* M. Boléat

KNITTING INDUSTRIES' FEDERATION LTD, 53 Oxford Street, Leicester LE1 5XY. Tel: 0116-254 1609. *Director,* J. P. Harrison

LEATHER PRODUCERS' ASSOCIATION, Leather Trade House, Kings Park Road, Moulton Park, Northampton NN3 6JD. Tel: 01604-494131. *National Secretary,* J. Purvis

MANAGEMENT CONSULTANCIES ASSOCIATION, 11 West Halkin Street, London SW1X 8JL. Tel: 0171-235 3897. *Executive Director,* B. O'Rorke

MARINE INDUSTRIES FEDERATION, BRITISH, Meadlake Place, Thorpe Lea Road, Egham, Surrey TW20 8HE. Tel: 01784-473377. *Executive Chairman,* A. V. Beechey

MARKET TRADERS' FEDERATION, NATIONAL, Hampton House, Hawshaw Lane, Hoyland, Barnsley s74 0HA. Tel: 01226-749021. *General Secretary*, D. E. Feeny

MASTER BUILDERS, FEDERATION OF, Gordon Fisher House, 14–15 Great James Street, London wc1n 3dp. Tel: 0171-242 7583. *Director-General*, J. D. Maiden

MOTOR MANUFACTURERS AND TRADERS LTD, SOCIETY OF, Forbes House, Halkin Street, London sw1x 7ds. Tel: 0171-235 7000. *Chief Executive*, R. E. Thompson

NEWSPAPER PUBLISHERS ASSOCIATION LTD, 34 Southwark Bridge Road, London se1 9eu. Tel: 0171-928 6928. *Director*, D. Pollock

NEWSPAPER SOCIETY, Bloomsbury House, 74–77 Great Russell Street, London wc1b 3da. Tel: 0171-636 7014. *Director*, D. Nisbet-Smith

OFFICE SYSTEMS AND STATIONERY FEDERATION, BRITISH, 6 Wimpole Street, London w1m 8as. Tel: 0171-637 7692. *Chief Executive*, P. H. Carlisle

PAPER FEDERATION OF GREAT BRITAIN LTD, THE, Papermakers House, Rivenhall Road, Swindon sn5 7bd. Tel: 01793-886086. *Director-General*, W. J. Bartlett

PASSENGER TRANSPORT UK, CONFEDERATION OF, Sardinia House, 52 Lincoln's Inn Fields, London wc2a 3lz. Tel: 0171-831 7546. *Director-General*, Mrs V. Palmer, OBE

PLASTICS FEDERATION, BRITISH, 6 Bath Place, London ec2a 3je. Tel: 0171-457 5000. *Director-General*, D. R. Jones

PORTS ASSOCIATION, BRITISH, Africa House, 64–78 Kingsway, London wc2b 6ah. Tel: 0171-242 1200. *Director*, D. Whitehead

PRINTING INDUSTRIES FEDERATION, BRITISH, 11 Bedford Row, London wc1r 4dx. Tel: 0171-242 6904. *Director-General*, T. P. E. Machin

PRIVATE MARKET OPERATORS, ASSOCIATION OF, 4 Worrygoose Lane, Rotherham s60 4ad. Tel: 01709-700072. *Secretary*, D. J. Glasby

PROPERTY FEDERATION, BRITISH, 35 Catherine Place, London sw1e 6dy. Tel: 0171-828 0111. *Director-General*, W. A McKee

PUBLISHERS ASSOCIATION, THE, 19 Bedford Square, London wc1b 3hj. Tel: 0171-580 6321. *Chief Executive*, C. Bradley

RADIO COMPANIES LTD, ASSOCIATION OF INDEPENDENT, Radio House, 46 Westbourne Grove, London w2 5sh. Tel: 0171-727 2646. *Chief Executive*, P. Brown

RETAIL CONSORTIUM, BRITISH, Bedford House, 69–79 Fulham High Street, London sw6 3jw. Tel: 0171-371 5185. *Director-General*, J. N. W. May

RETAIL NEWSAGENTS, NATIONAL FEDERATION OF, Yeoman House, Sekforde Street, London ec1r 0hd. Tel: 0171-253 4225. *Chief Executive*, R. P. Frost

ROAD FEDERATION, BRITISH, Pillar House, 194–202 Old Kent Road, London se1 5tg. Tel: 0171-703 9769. *Director*, R. Diment

ROAD HAULAGE ASSOCIATION LTD, Roadway House, 35 Monument Hill, Weybridge, Surrey kt13 8rn. Tel: 01932-841515. *Director-General*, D. B. H. Colley, cb, cbe

RUBBER MANUFACTURERS' ASSOCIATION LTD, BRITISH, 90 Tottenham Court Road, London w1p 0br. Tel: 0171-580 2794. *Director*, W. R. Pollock

SPORT AND ALLIED INDUSTRIES FEDERATION LTD, BRITISH, Federation House, National Agricultural Centre, Stoneleigh Park, Warks cv8 2rf. Tel: 01203-414999. *Chief Executive*, J. Hooper

TIMBER GROWERS ASSOCIATION, 5 Dublin Street Lane South, Edinburgh eh1 3px. Tel: 0131-538 7111. *Chief Executive*, P. H. Wilson

TIMBER MERCHANTS' ASSOCIATION, BRITISH, Stocking Lane, Hughenden Valley, High Wycombe, Bucks hp14 4jz. Tel: 01494-563602. *Secretary*, N. Moore

TIMBER TRADE FEDERATION, Clareville House, 26–27 Oxendon Street, London sw1y 4el. Tel: 0171-839 1891. *Director-General*, P. G. Harris

UK OFFSHORE OPERATORS ASSOCIATION LTD, 3 Hans Crescent, London sw1x 0ln. Tel: 0171-589 5255. *Director-General*, Dr H. W. D. Hughes, OBE

UK PETROLEUM INDUSTRY ASSOCIATION LTD, 9 Kingsway, London wc2b 6xf. Tel: 0171-240 0289. *Director-General*, D. Parker

Trade Unions

At 31 December 1994 there were 267 trade unions listed by the Certification Officer (*see* page 293). In 1993 8,661,293 people were members of listed trade unions, compared with 8,928,902 in 1992. Over 80 per cent of trade union members belong to unions affiliated to the TUC (*see* below).

The Central Arbitration Committee arbitrates in industrial disputes between trade unions and employers, and determines disclosure of information complaints. The Commissioner for the Rights of Trade Union Members provides assistance to individuals taking action against their trade union when they have not been afforded their statutory rights or when specific union rules have been breached. The Commissioner for Protection Against Unlawful Industrial Action assists individuals who have been, or are likely to be, deprived of goods or services because of industrial action unlawfully organized by a trade union.

For ACAS, the Certification Office, the Commission for Racial Equality, the Equal Opportunities Commission, the Health and Safety Commission, the Industrial Tribunals and Review Bodies, *see* Index.

THE CENTRAL ARBITRATION COMMITTEE, 39 Grosvenor Place, London SW1X 7BD. Tel: 0171-210 3737/8. *Chairman*, Prof. Sir John Wood, CBE; *Secretary*, S. Gouldstone

THE COMMISSIONER FOR THE RIGHTS OF TRADE UNION MEMBERS, 1st Floor, Bank Chambers, 2A Rylands Street, Warrington, Cheshire WA1 1EN. Tel: 01925-415771. *Commissioner*, Mrs G. Rowlands

THE COMMISSIONER FOR PROTECTION AGAINST UNLAWFUL INDUSTRIAL ACTION, 2nd Floor, Bank Chambers, 2A Rylands Street, Warrington, Cheshire WA1 1EN. Tel: 01925-414128. *Commissioner*, Mrs G. Rowlands

---

TUC-AFFILIATED TRADE UNIONS

TRADES UNION CONGRESS (TUC)
Congress House, 23–28 Great Russell Street, London WC1B 3LS
Tel 0171-636 4030

The Trades Union Congress, founded in 1868, is an independent association of trade unions. Its main job is to help unions achieve together things which they could not do alone. It draws up common policies and promotes and publicizes them. It makes representations to government, to employers and, increasingly, to international bodies such as the European Union. The TUC also carries out research, campaigns and a programme of trade union education. Resolving disputes between unions is another task it undertakes. TUC representatives sit on many public bodies at national and international level.

The governing body of the TUC is the annual Congress. Between Congresses, business is conducted by a General Council, which meets five times a year, and an Executive Committee, which meets monthly. The full-time staff is headed by the General Secretary who is elected by Congress and is a permanent member of the General Council.

Affiliated unions (in 1994–5) totalled 67 with an aggregate membership of 6,894,604.
President (1995–6), A. Dubbins (GPMU)
General Secretary, J. Monks, *elected* 1993

SCOTTISH TRADES UNION CONGRESS
16 Woodlands Terrace, Glasgow G3 6DF
Tel 0141-332 4946

The Congress was formed in 1897 and acts as a national centre for the trade union movement in Scotland. In 1995 it consisted of 49 unions with a membership of 689,365 and 27 directly affiliated Trades Councils.

The Annual Congress in April elects a 36-member General Council on the basis of eight industrial sections.
Chairperson, P. McCormick
General Secretary, C. Christie

AFFILIATED UNIONS *as at 1 September 1995*
(Number of members in parenthesis)

AMALGAMATED ENGINEERING AND ELECTRICAL UNION (AEEU) (781,137), Hayes Court, West Common Road, Bromley, Kent BR2 7AU. Tel: 0181-462 7755. *General Secretary*, P. Gallagher

ASSOCIATED METALWORKERS' UNION (AMU) (928), 92 Worsley Road North, Worsley, Manchester M28 5QW. Tel: 01204-793245. *General Secretary*, R. Marron

ASSOCIATED SOCIETY OF LOCOMOTIVE ENGINEERS AND FIREMEN, (ASLEF) (17,000), 9 Arkwright Road, London NW3 6AB. Tel: 0171-431 0275. *General Secretary*, L. Adams

ASSOCIATION OF FIRST DIVISION CIVIL SERVANTS (10,459), 2 Caxton Street, London SW1H 0QH. Tel: 0171-222 6242. *General Secretary*, Ms E. Symons

ASSOCIATION OF MAGISTERIAL OFFICERS (4,555), 35 High Street, Crawley, W. Sussex RH10 1BQ. Tel: 01293-547515. *General Secretary*, Ms R. Eagleson

ASSOCIATION OF UNIVERSITY TEACHERS (35,000), United House, 9 Pembridge Road, London W11 3JY. Tel: 0171-221 4370. *General Secretary*, D. Triesman

BAKERS, FOOD AND ALLIED WORKERS' UNION (30,250), Stanborough House, Great North Road, Stanborough, Welwyn Garden City, Herts AL8 7TA. Tel: 01707-260150. *General Secretary*, J. R. Marino

BANKING, INSURANCE AND FINANCE UNION (131,434), Sheffield House, 1B Amity Grove, London SW20 0LG. Tel: 0181-946 9151. *General Secretary*, L. A. Mills, CBE

BRITISH ACTORS' EQUITY ASSOCIATION (43,000), Guild House, Upper St Martin's Lane, London WC2H 9EG. Tel: 0171-379 6000. *General Secretary*, I. McGarry

BRITISH AIR LINE PILOTS ASSOCIATION, THE (8,000), 81 New Road, Harlington, Hayes, Middx UB3 5BG. Tel: 0181-476 4000. *General Secretary*, C. Darke

BRITISH ASSOCIATION OF COLLIERY MANAGEMENT, THE (5,000), 17 South Parade, Doncaster, S. Yorks DN1 2DN. Tel: 01302-349152. *General Secretary*, M. Gillespie

BROADCASTING, ENTERTAINMENT, CINEMATOGRAPH AND THEATRE UNION (BECTU) (30,000), 111 Wardour Street, London W1V 4AY. Tel: 0171-437 8506. *General Secretary*, R. Bolton

CARD SETTING MACHINE TENTERS' SOCIETY (88), 48 Scar End Lane, Staincliffe, Dewsbury, W. Yorks WF12 4NY. Tel: 01924-400206. *Secretary*, A. Moorhouse

CERAMIC AND ALLIED TRADES UNION, THE (22,500), Hillcrest House, Garth Street, Hanley, Stoke-on-Trent STI 2AB. Tel: 01782-272755. *General Secretary*, G. Bagnall

CHARTERED SOCIETY OF PHYSIOTHERAPY, THE (26,000), 14 Bedford Row, London WC1R 4ED. Tel: 0171-306 6666. *Secretary*, T. Simon

CIVIL AND PUBLIC SERVICES ASSOCIATION, THE (124,500), 160 Falcon Road, London SW11 2LN. Tel: 0171-924 2727. *General Secretary*, B. Reamsbottom

COMMUNICATION MANAGERS' ASSOCIATION (15,000), CMA House, Ruscombe Road, Twyford, Reading RG10 9JD. Tel: 01734-342300. *General Secretary*, T. L. Deegan

COMMUNICATION WORKERS' UNION (280,000), Greystoke House, 150 Brunswick Road, London W5 1AW. Tel: 0181-998 2981. *Joint General Secretaries*, A. I. Young; A. Johnson

EDUCATIONAL INSTITUTE OF SCOTLAND, THE (49,371), 46 Moray Place, Edinburgh EH3 6BH. Tel: 0131-225 6244. *General Secretary*, R. A. Smith

ENGINEERING AND FASTENER TRADE UNION (268), 42 Galton Road, Warley, West Midlands, B67 5JU. Tel: 0121-429 2594. *General Secretary*, J. Burdis

ENGINEERS' AND MANAGERS' ASSOCIATION (35,000), Flaxman House, Gogmore Lane, Chertsey, Surrey KT16 9JS. Tel: 01932-577007. *General Secretary*, D. A. Cooper

FIRE BRIGADES UNION, THE (50,706), Bradley House, 68 Coombe Road, Kingston upon Thames, Surrey KT2 7AE. Tel: 0181-541 1765. *General Secretary*, K. Cameron

GENERAL UNION OF ASSOCIATIONS OF LOOM OVERLOOKERS, THE (490), 9 Wellington Street, St Johns, Blackburn, Lancs BB1 8AF. Tel: 01254-51760. *President*, D. J. Rishton

GMB (FORMERLY GENERAL, MUNICIPAL, BOILERMAKERS AND ALLIED TRADES UNION) (830,000), 22–24 Worple Road, London SW19 4DD. Tel: 0181-947 3131. *General Secretary*, J. Edmonds

GRAPHICAL, PAPER AND MEDIA UNION (225,000), 63–67 Bromham Road, Bedford MK40 2AG. Tel: 01234-351521. *General Secretary*, A. D. Dubbins

HOSPITAL CONSULTANTS AND SPECIALISTS ASSOCIATION, THE (2,340), 1 Kingsclere Road, Overton, Basingstoke, Hants RG25 3JA. Tel: 01256-771777. *Chief Executive*, S. J. Charkham

INLAND REVENUE STAFF FEDERATION (55,000), Douglas Houghton House, 231 Vauxhall Bridge Road, London SW1V 1EH. Tel: 0171-834 8254. *General Secretary*, C. Brooke

INSTITUTION OF PROFESSIONALS, MANAGERS AND SPECIALISTS (81,015), 75–79 York Road, London SE1 7AQ. Tel: 0171-928 9951. *General Secretary*, W. Brett

IRON AND STEEL TRADES CONFEDERATION, THE (50,000), Swinton House, 324 Gray's Inn Road, London WC1X 8DD. Tel: 0171-837 6691. *General Secretary*, D. K. Brookman

MANUFACTURING, SCIENCE AND FINANCE UNION (MSF) (452,000), MSF Centre, 33–37 Moreland Street, London EC1V 8BB. Tel: 0171-505 3000. *General Secretary*, R. Lyons

MILITARY AND ORCHESTRAL MUSICAL INSTRUMENT MAKERS' TRADE SOCIETY (52), 2 Whitehouse Avenue, Borehamwood, Herts WD6 1HD. Tel: 0181-952 7711. *General Secretary*, F. McKenzie

MUSICIANS' UNION (32,534), 60–62 Clapham Road, London SW9 0JJ. Tel: 0171-582 5566. *General Secretary*, D. Scard

NATFHE (THE UNIVERSITY AND COLLEGE LECTURERS UNION), (71,430), 27 Britannia Street, London WC1X 9JP. Tel: 0171-837 3636. *General Secretary*, J. Akker

NATIONAL ASSOCIATION OF COLLIERY OVERMEN, DEPUTIES AND SHOTFIRERS (1,500), Simpson House, 48 Nether Hall Road, Doncaster DN1 2PZ. Tel: 01302-368015. *Secretary*, P. McNestry

NATIONAL ASSOCIATION OF CO-OPERATIVE OFFICIALS (3,697), Coronation House, Arndale Centre, Manchester M4 2HW. Tel: 0161-834 6029. *General Secretary*, L. W. Ewing

NATIONAL ASSOCIATION OF LICENSED HOUSE MANAGERS (8,500), 9 Coombe Lane, London SW20 8NE. Tel: 0181-947 3080. *General Secretary*, P. Love

NATIONAL ASSOCIATION OF PROBATION OFFICERS (7,381), 3–4 Chivalry Road, London SW11 1HT. Tel: 0171-223 4887. *Secretary*, Ms J. McKnight

NATIONAL ASSOCIATION OF SCHOOLMASTERS AND UNION OF WOMEN TEACHERS (NAS/UWT) (146,266), 5 King Street, London WC2E 8HN. Tel: 0171-379 9499. *General Secretary*, N. de Gruchy

NATIONAL LEAGUE OF THE BLIND AND DISABLED, THE (1,700), 2 Tenterden Road, London N17 8BE. Tel: 0181-808 6030. *General Secretary*, M. A. Barrett (*until end Sept. 1995*)

NATIONAL UNION OF CIVIL AND PUBLIC SERVANTS (NUCPS) (110,076), New Bridgewater House, 5–13 Great Suffolk Street, London SE1 0NS. Tel: 0171-928 9671. *General Secretary*, J. Sheldon

NATIONAL UNION OF DOMESTIC APPLIANCES AND GENERAL OPERATIVES THE (2,504), 6–8 Imperial Buildings, Corporation Street, Rotherham, S. Yorks S60 1PB. Tel: 01709-382820. *General Secretary*, A. McCarthy

NATIONAL UNION OF INSURANCE WORKERS (10,686), 27 Old Gloucester Street, London WC1N 3AF. Tel: 0171-405 6798. *General Secretary*, K. Perry

NATIONAL UNION OF JOURNALISTS (NUJ) (25,000), Acorn House, 314–320 Gray's Inn Road, London WC1X 8DP. Tel: 0171-278 7916. *General Secretary*, J. Foster

NATIONAL UNION OF KNITWEAR, FOOTWEAR AND APPAREL TRADES (49,910), The Grange, 108 Northampton Road, Earls Barton, Northampton NN6 0JH. Tel: 01604-810326. *General Secretary*, Mrs H. McGrath

NATIONAL UNION OF LOCK AND METAL WORKERS (4,900), Bellamy House, Wilkes Street, Willenhall, W. Midlands WV13 2BS. Tel: 01902-366651. *General Secretary*, R. Ward

NATIONAL UNION OF MARINE, AVIATION AND SHIPPING TRANSPORT OFFICERS, THE (18,350), Oceanair House, 750–760 High Road, London E11 3BB. Tel: 0181-989 6677. *General Secretary*, B. Orrell

NATIONAL UNION OF MINEWORKERS (NUM) (18,227), Miners' Offices, 2 Huddersfield Road, Barnsley, S. Yorks S70 2LS. Tel: 01226-284006. *President*, A. Scargill

NATIONAL UNION OF RAIL, MARITIME AND TRANSPORT WORKERS (RMT) (78,000), Unity House, Euston Road, London NW1 2BL. Tel: 0171-387 4771. *General Secretary*, J. Knapp

NATIONAL UNION OF TEACHERS (NUT) (189,192), Hamilton House, Mabledon Place, London WC1H 9BD. Tel: 0171-388 6191. *General Secretary*, D. McAvoy

NORTHERN CARPET TRADES' UNION (750), 22 Clare Road, Halifax, W. Yorks HX1 2HX. Tel: 01422-360492. *General Secretary*, K. Edmondson

POWER LOOM CARPET WEAVERS' AND TEXTILE WORKERS' UNION, THE (1,670), 148 Hurcott Road, Kidderminster, Worcs DY10 2RL. Tel: 01562-823192. *General Secretary*, R. White

PRISON OFFICERS' ASSOCIATION, THE (28,000), Cronin House, 245 Church Street, London N9 9HW. Tel: 0181-803 0255. *General Secretary*, D. Evans

PROFESSIONAL FOOTBALLERS ASSOCIATION (1,814), 2 Oxford Court, Bishopsgate, Manchester M2 3WQ. Tel: 0161-236 0575. *General Secretary*, G. Taylor

ROSSENDALE UNION OF BOOT, SHOE AND SLIPPER OPERATIVES, THE (1,384), Taylor House, 7 Tenterfield Street, Waterfoot, Rossendale, Lancs BB4 7BA. Tel: 01706-215657. *General Secretary*, M. Murray, MBE

SCOTTISH PRISON OFFICERS' ASSOCIATION (3,375), 21 Calder Road, Edinburgh EH11 3PF. Tel: 0131-443 8105. *General Secretary*, D. Turner

SCOTTISH UNION OF POWER-LOOM OVERLOOKERS (62), 3 Napier Terrace, Dundee DD2 2SL. Tel: 01382-612196. *Secretary*, J. D. Reilly

SHEFFIELD WOOL SHEAR WORKERS' UNION (12), 50 Bankfield Road, Malin Bridge, Sheffield S6 4RD. Tel: 0114-233 3688. *Secretary*, J. H. R. Cutler

SOCIETY OF RADIOGRAPHERS (14,000), 14 Upper Wimpole Street, London WIM 8BN. Tel: 0171-935 5726. *General Secretary*, S. Evans

SOCIETY OF TELECOM EXECUTIVES (20,000), 1 Park Road, Teddington, Middx TW11 0AR. Tel: 0181-943 5181. *General Secretary*, S. Petch

TRANSPORT AND GENERAL WORKERS' UNION (TGWU) (907,000), 16 Palace Street, London SW1E 5JD. Tel: 0171-828 7788. *General Secretary*, W. Morris

TRANSPORT SALARIED STAFFS' ASSOCIATION (36,780), Walkden House, 10 Melton Street, London NW1 2EJ. Tel: 0171-387 2101. *General Secretary*, R. A. Rosser

UNION OF CONSTRUCTION, ALLIED TRADES AND TECHNICIANS (UCATT) (135,878), UCATT House, 177 Abbeville Road, London SW4 9RL. Tel: 0171-622 2442. *Secretary*, G. Brumwell

UNION OF SHOP, DISTRIBUTIVE AND ALLIED WORKERS (USDAW) (296,000), Oakley, 188 Wilmslow Road, Fallowfield, Manchester M14 6LJ. Tel: 0161-224 2804. *Secretary*, D. G. Davies

UNION OF TEXTILE WORKERS (1,567), Foxlowe, Market Place, Leek, Staffs ST13 6AD. Tel: 01538-382068. *General Secretary*, A. Hitchmough

UNISON (1,300,000), 1 Mabledon Place, London WC1H 9AJ. Tel: 0171-388 2366. *General Secretary*, A. Jinkinson

UNITED ROAD TRANSPORT UNION (18,000), 76 High Lane, Chorlton-cum-Hardy, Manchester M21 9EF. Tel: 0161-881 6245. *General Secretary*, D. Higginbottom

WRITERS' GUILD OF GREAT BRITAIN, THE (1,800), 430 Edgware Road, London W2 1EH. Tel: 0171-723 8074. *General Secretary*, Ms A. Gray

MERGERS, ETC, 1994–5

The National Communications Union and the Union of Communication Workers merged in January 1995 to form the Communication Workers Union.

The Electrical and Plumbing Industries Union merged with the TGWU in June 1995.

The National Union of Civil and Public Servants and the Inland Revenue Staff Federation plan to merge, to form the Public Services, Tax and Commerce Union from January 1996.

NON-AFFILIATED TRADE UNIONS

THE ASSOCIATION OF TEACHERS AND LECTURERS, (150,000), 7 Northumberland Street, London WC2N 5DA. Tel: 0171-930 6441. *General Secretary*, P. Smith

BRITISH DENTAL ASSOCIATION (15,000), 64 Wimpole Street, London W1M 8AL. Tel: 0171-935 0875. *Chief Executive*, J. M. G. Hunt

CHARTERED INSTITUTE OF JOURNALISTS, (2,000), 2 Dock Offices, Surrey Quays, Lower Road, London SE16 2XU. Tel: 0171-252 1187. *General Secretary*, C. Underwood

NATIONAL ASSOCIATION OF HEAD TEACHERS (NAHT) (39,078), 1 Heath Square, Boltro Road, Haywards Heath, W. Sussex RH16 1BL. Tel: 01444-458133. *General Secretary*, D. Hart, OBE

NATIONAL SOCIETY FOR EDUCATION IN ART AND DESIGN (2,300), The Gatehouse, Corsham Court, Corsham, Wilts SN13 0BZ. Tel: 01249-714825. *General Secretary*, J. H. M. Steers

PATTERN WEAVERS SOCIETY(58), 20 Hayfield Avenue, Oakes, Huddersfield HD3 4FZ. Tel: 01484-656886. *Treasurer/Secretary*, D. Mellor

RETAIL BOOK, STATIONERY AND ALLIED TRADES EMPLOYEES' ASSOCIATION (6,000), 8–9 Commercial Road, Swindon SN1 5RB. Tel: 01793-615811. *President*, A. Willmott

ROYAL COLLEGE OF MIDWIVES (36,000), 15 Mansfield Street, London W1M 0BE. Tel: 0171-872 8100. *General Secretary*, Mrs J. Allison

SCOTTISH SECONDARY TEACHERS' ASSOCIATION (7,200), 15 Dundas Street, Edinburgh EH3 6QG. Tel: 0131-556 5919. *General Secretary*, A. M. Lamont

SECONDARY HEADS ASSOCIATION (8,500), 130 Regent Road, Leicester LE1 7PG. Tel: 0116-247 1797. *General Secretary*, J. Sutton

SOCIETY OF AUTHORS (5,800), 84 Drayton Gardens, London SW10 9SB. Tel: 0171-373 6642. *General Secretary*, M. Le Fanu

SOCIETY OF CHIROPODISTS AND PODIATRISTS (5,880), 53 Welbeck Street, London W1M 7HE. Tel: 0171-486 3381. *General Secretary*, J. G. C. Trouncer

National Academies of Scholarship

The British Academy is an independent, self-governing learned society for the promotion of historical, philosophical and philological studies. It supports advanced academic research in the humanities and social sciences, and is a channel for the Government's support of research in those disciplines. The Humanities Research Board is responsible for the administration of the majority of the Academy's grant programmes.

The Fellows are scholars who have attained distinction in one of the branches of study that the Academy exists to promote. Candidates must be nominated by existing Fellows. At 1 June 1995 there were 621 Fellows, 14 Honorary Fellows, and 310 Corresponding Fellows overseas.

President, Sir Keith Thomas, PBA
Vice-Presidents, J. S. Flemming, FBA; Prof. G. P. K. Beer, FBA
Treasurer, Dr E. A. Wrigley, FBA
Foreign Secretary, Prof. J. B. Trapp, FBA
Publications Officer, Prof. D. E. Luscombe, FBA
Chairman, Humanities Research Board, Prof. J. D. Laver, FBA
Secretary, P. W. H. Brown

The Royal Academy of Arts is an independent, self-governing society devoted to the encouragement and promotion of the fine arts.

Membership of the Academy is limited to 80 Royal Academicians, all being painters, engravers, sculptors or architects. Candidates are nominated and elected by the existing Academicians. There is also a limited class of honorary membership and there were 11 honorary members as at mid-1995.

President, Sir Philip Dowson, CBE, PRA
Treasurer, Sir Philip Powell, CH, OBE, RA
Keeper, L. McComb, RA
Secretary, P. Rodgers

The Royal Academy of Engineering was established as the Fellowship of Engineering in 1976. It was granted a Royal Charter in 1983 and its present title in 1992. It is an independent, self-governing body whose object is the pursuit, encouragement and maintenance of excellence in the whole field of engineering, in order to promote the advancement of the science, art and practice of engineering for the benefit of the public.

Election to the Fellowship is by invitation only from nominations supported by the body of Fellows. Fellows are chosen from among chartered engineers of all disciplines. At July 1995 there were 1,011 Fellows, 14 Honorary Fellows and 62 Foreign Members. The Duke of Edinburgh is the Senior Fellow and the Duke of Kent is a Royal Fellow.

President, Sir William Barlow, FEng
Senior Vice-President, B. W. Manley, CBE, FEng
Vice-Presidents, Sir David Davies, CBE, FEng, FRSE; R. J. Margetts, FEng; S. N. Mustow, CBE, FEng
Hon. Treasurer, D. Hanson
Hon. Secretaries, P. N. Paul, FEng (*Civil Engineering*); Dr J. R. Forrest, FEng (*Electrical Engineering*); P. C. Ruffles, FEng (*Mechanical Engineering*); G. Clerehugh, OBE, FEng (*Process Engineering*); B. R. R. Butler, OBE, FEng (*International Activities*); Sir Gordon Higginson, FEng (*Education, Training and Competence to Practise*)
Executive Secretary, J. R. Appleton

The Scottish Academy was founded in 1826 to arrange exhibitions for contemporary paintings and to establish a society of fine art in Scotland. The Academy was granted a Royal Charter in 1838.

Members are elected from the disciplines of painting, sculpture, architecture and printmaking. Elections are from nominations put forward by the existing membership. At mid-1995 there were 9 Senior Academicians, 36 Academicians, 43 Associates, three non-resident Associates and 21 Honorary Members.

President, W. J. L. Baillie, PRSA
Secretary, I. McKenzie Smith, RSA
Treasurer, J. Morris, RSA
Librarian, P. Collins, RSA
Administrative Secretary, B. Laidlaw

The Royal Society is the United Kingdom's national academy of science. It is an independent, self-governing body under a Royal Charter, promoting and advancing all fields of physical and biological sciences, of mathematics and engineering, medical and agricultural sciences, their applications and place in society.

Election to Fellowship of the Royal Society is limited to those distinguished for original scientific work. Each year up to 40 new Fellows and six Foreign Members are elected from the most distinguished scientists. In addition, the Council can recommend for election members of the Royal family and, on average, one person each year for conspicuous service to the cause of science. At March 1995, there were 1,164 Fellows and 107 Foreign Members.

President, Sir Aaron Klug, FRS
Treasurer, Prof. J. H. Horlock, F.Eng, FRS

Biological Secretary, Prof. P. J. Lachmann, FRS
Physical Secretary, Prof. J. S. Rowlinson, FRS
Foreign Secretary, Dr A. L. McLaren, DBE, FRS
Executive Secretary, Dr P. T. Warren

THE ROYAL SOCIETY OF EDINBURGH
(1783)
22–24 George Street, Edinburgh EH2 2PQ
Tel 0131-225 6057

The Royal Society of Edinburgh is Scotland's premier learned society. The Society was founded by Royal Charter in 1783 for 'the advancement of Learning and Useful Knowledge', and its principal role is the promotion of scholarship in all its branches. It provides a forum for broadly-based interdisciplinary activity in Scotland, including organizing public lectures, conferences and specialist research seminars; providing advice to Parliament and government; administering a range of research fellowships held in Scotland; and publishing learned journals.

Fellows are elected by ballot after being nominated by at least four existing Fellows. At 31 May 1995 there were 1,091 Ordinary Fellows and 69 Honorary Fellows.

President, Dr T. L. Johnston
Treasurer, Sir Lewis Robertson, CBE, FRSE
General Secretary, Prof. V. B. Proudfoot
Executive Secretary, Dr W. Duncan

Royal Academicians

*Senior Academician

1991	Abrahams, Ivor
1991	Ackroyd, Prof. Norman
1972	Adams, Norman
1988	Aitchison, Craigie
1991	Armfield, Diana
1994	*Armitage, Kenneth
1991	Ayres, Gillian, OBE
1991	Bellany, John, CBE
1992	Berg, Adrian
1976	Blackadder, Elizabeth, OBE
1981	Blake, Peter, CBE
1975	*Blamey, Norman
1978	Blow, Sandra
1975	Bowey, Olwyn
1981	Bowyer, William
1972	Brown, Ralph
1972	Butler, James
1975	*Cadbury-Brown, Prof. H. T., OBE
1984	Camp, Jeffery
1970	*Casson, Sir Hugh, CH, KCVO
1993	Caulfield, Patrick
1989	Christopher, Ann
1976	Clarke, Geoffrey
1973	Clatworthy, Robert
1972	Coker, Peter
1972	Cooke, Jean
1994	Cragg, Prof. Tony
1993	Craxton, John
1991	Cullinan, Edward, CBE
1974	Cuming, Frederick
1992	Cummins, Gus
1983	Dannatt, Prof. Trevor
1976	Dickson, Jennifer

1985	Dowson, Sir Philip, CBE
1991	Draper, Kenneth
1968	Dunstan, Bernard
1994	Durrant, Jennifer
1986	Eyton, Anthony
1992	*Fedden, Mary
1991	Flanagan, Barry, OBE
1991	Foster, Sir Norman
1985	Fraser, Donald Hamilton
1991	Freeth, Peter
1992	*Frost, Terry
1995	Gear, William
1972	*Gore, Frederick, CBE
1977	Green, Anthony
1994	Grimshaw, Nicholas
1970	Hayes, Colin
1990	*Herman, Josef, OBE
1991	Hockney, David
1984	*Hogarth, Paul, OBE
1992	Hopkins, Sir Michael, CBE
1991	Howard, Ken
1991	Hoyland, John
1991	Huxley, Prof. Paul
1991	Jacklin, Bill
1991	*Jellicoe, Sir Geoffrey
1986	Jones, Allen
1986	Kenny, Michael
1991	Kiff, Ken
1988	King, Prof. Phillip, CBE
1991	Kitaj, R. B.
1974	Kneale, Bryan
1991	Koralek, Paul, CBE
1991	*Lasdun, Sir Dennis, CBE
1991	Lawson, Sonia
1986	Levene, Ben

1987	McComb, Leonard
1993	MacCormac, Richard, CBE
1956	*Machin, Arnold, OBE
1995	Maine, John
1979	*Manasseh, Leonard, OBE
1994	Manser, Michael
1985	*Martin, Sir Leslie
1991	Mistry, Dhruva
1994	Moon, Mick
1992	Neiland, Brendan
1995	Orr, Christopher
1979	Paolozzi, Sir Eduardo, CBE
1988	Partridge, John, CBE
1983	*Pasmore, Victor, CH, CBE
1989	Phillips, Tom
1977	Powell, Sir Philip, CH, OBE
1973	*Roberts-Jones, Ivor, CBE
1984	Rogers, Sir Richard
1991	Rooney, Michael
1969	*Rosoman, Leonard, OBE
1989	Sandle, Prof. Michael
1986	Stephenson, Ian
1988	Sutton, Philip
1991	Tilson, Joe
1979	Tindle, David
1991	Titchell, John
1992	Tucker, William
1965	*Ward, John, CBE
1965	*Weight, Prof. Carel, CBE
1989	Whishaw, Anthony
1974	*Williams, Kyffin, OBE
1991	Wilson, Colin St J.
1991	Wragg, John

The Research Councils

The Government funds basic and applied civil science research, mostly through the six research councils, which are supported by the Department of Trade and Industry. The councils conduct research through their own establishments and by supporting selected research, study and training in universities and other higher education establishments. They also receive income for research commissioned by government departments and the private sector.

BIOTECHNOLOGY AND BIOLOGICAL SCIENCES RESEARCH COUNCIL (BBSRC)
Polaris House, North Star Avenue, Swindon, Wilts SN2 1UH
Tel 01793-413200

The purpose of the BBSRC is to promote and support research and postgraduate training relating to the understanding and exploitation of biological systems; to advance knowledge and technology, and provide trained scientists to meet the needs of biotechnological-related industries; and to provide advice, disseminate knowledge, and promote public understanding of biotechnology and the biological sciences. Government funding for 1995–6 is £172.3 million.
Chairman, Sir Alistair Grant
Chief Executive, Prof. T. L. Blundell, FRS

INSTITUTES

BABRAHAM INSTITUTE
Director, Dr R. G. Dyer, Babraham Hall, Babraham, Cambridge CB2 4AT. Tel: 01223-832312

INSTITUTE FOR ANIMAL HEALTH
Director, Prof. F. J. Bourne, CBE., Compton, Newbury, Berks RG20 7NN. Tel: 01635-577238

BBSRC AND MRC NEUROPATHOGENESIS UNIT, Ogston Building, West Mains Road, Edinburgh EH9 3JF. Tel: 0131-667 5204/5. *Head*, vacant
COMPTON LABORATORY, Compton, Newbury, Berks RG20 7NN. Tel: 01635-578411. *Head of Division in Charge*, Dr P. Jones
PIRBRIGHT LABORATORY, Ash Road, Pirbright, Woking, Surrey GU24 0NF. Tel: 01483-232441. *Head*, Dr A. I. Donaldson

INSTITUTE OF ARABLE CROPS RESEARCH
Director, Prof. B. Miflin, Rothamsted, Harpenden, Herts AL5 2JQ. Tel: 01582-763133
IACR – BROOM'S BARN, Higham, Bury St Edmunds, Suffolk IP28 6NP. Tel: 01284-810363. *Head*, Prof. T. H. Thomas
IACR – LONG ASHTON RESEARCH STATION, Department of Agricultural Sciences, University of Bristol, Long Ashton, Bristol BS18 9AF. Tel: 01275-392181. *Head*, Prof. P. R. Shewry
IACR – ROTHAMSTED, Harpenden, Herts AL5 2JQ. Tel: 01582-763133. *Head*, Prof. B. Miflin.

INSTITUTE OF FOOD RESEARCH
Director, Prof. A. D. B. Malcolm, Earley Gate, Whiteknights Road, Reading RG6 6BZ. Tel: 01734-357055

NORWICH LABORATORY, Norwich Research Park, Colney Lane, Norwich NR4 7UA. Tel: 01603-255000. *Deputy Director and Head of Laboratory*, Prof. P. S. Belton
READING LABORATORY, Earley Gate, Whiteknights Road, Reading RG6 6BZ. Tel: 01734-357000. *Deputy Director and Head of Laboratory*, Dr H. J. H. MacFie

INSTITUTE OF GRASSLAND AND ENVIRONMENTAL RESEARCH
Director, Prof. C. J. Pollock, Plas Gogerddan, Aberystwyth, Dyfed SY23 3EB. Tel: 01970-828255
ABERYSTWYTH RESEARCH CENTRE, Plas Gogerddan, Aberystwyth, Dyfed SY23 3EB. Tel: 01970-828255. *Head*, Prof. D. Wilson
NORTH WYKE RESEARCH STATION, Okehampton, Devon EX20 2SB. Tel: 01837-82558. *Head*, Prof. R. J. Wilkins

JOHN INNES CENTRE
Director, Prof. R. B. Flavell, John Innes Institute, Colney Lane, Norwich NR4 7UH. Tel: 01603-452571
NITROGEN FIXATION LABORATORY, University of Sussex, Brighton BN1 9RQ. Tel: 01273-678252. *Head*, Prof. B. E. Smith

ROSLIN INSTITUTE
Director, Prof. G. Bulfield, Roslin, Midlothian EH25 9PS. Tel: 0131-440 2726

SILSOE RESEARCH INSTITUTE
Director, Prof. B. J. Legg, Wrest Park, Silsoe, Bedford MK45 4HS. Tel: 01525-860000

INTERDISCIPLINARY RESEARCH CENTRES

ADVANCED CENTRE FOR BIOCHEMICAL ENGINEERING
Director, Prof. P. Dunnill, FEng., University College London, Torrington Place, London WC1E 7JE. Tel: 0171-380 7031
CENTRE FOR GENOME RESEARCH
Director (acting), Dr M. Hooper, University of Edinburgh, King's Buildings, West Mains Road, Edinburgh EH9 3JQ. Tel: 0131-650 5890
OXFORD CENTRE FOR MOLECULAR SCIENCES
Director, Prof. J. E. Baldwin, FRS, New Chemistry Laboratory, University of Oxford, South Parks Road, Oxford OX1 3QT. Tel: 01865-275654
SUSSEX CENTRE FOR NEUROSCIENCE
Director, Prof. M. O'Shea, School of Biological Sciences, University of Sussex, Brighton BN1 9QG. Tel: 01273-678055

SCOTTISH AGRICULTURAL AND BIOLOGICAL RESEARCH INSTITUTES

BIOMATHEMATICS AND STATISTICS SCOTLAND (BioSS), University of Edinburgh, James Clerk Maxwell Building, The King's Buildings, Mayfield Road, Edinburgh EH9 3JZ. Tel: 0131-650 4900. *Director*, R. A. Kempton
HANNAH RESEARCH INSTITUTE, Ayr KA6 5HL. Tel: 01292-476013. *Director*, Prof. M. Peaker
MACAULAY LAND USE RESEARCH INSTITUTE, Craigiebuckler, Aberdeen AB9 2QJ. Tel: 01224-318611. *Director*, Prof. T. J. Maxwell

MOREDUN RESEARCH INSTITUTE, 408 Gilmerton Road, Edinburgh EH17 7JH. Tel: 0131-664 3262. *Director,* Prof. I. D. Aitken

ROWETT RESEARCH INSTITUTE, Greenburn Road, Bucksburn, Aberdeen AB2 9SB. Tel: 01224-712751. *Director,* Prof. W. P. T. James, CBE

SCOTTISH CROP RESEARCH INSTITUTE, Invergowrie, Dundee DD2 5DA. Tel: 01382-562731. *Director,* Prof. J. Hillman, FRSE

COUNCIL FOR THE CENTRAL LABORATORY OF THE RESEARCH COUNCILS (CCLRC)
Chilton, Didcot, Oxon OX11 0QX
Tel 01235-821900

The CCLRC was set up in April 1995 and is responsible for the Daresbury and Rutherford Appleton Laboratories previously administered by the Engineering and Physical Sciences Research Council. Funding for 1995–6 is £1.5 million.

Chairman and Chief Executive, Dr P. R. Williams

DARESBURY LABORATORY, Daresbury, Warrington, Cheshire WA4 4AD. Tel: 01925-603000. *Head,* Dr R. W. Newport

RUTHERFORD APPLETON LABORATORY, Chilton, Didcot, Oxon OX11 0QX. Tel: 01235-821900. *Head,* Dr T. G. Walker

ECONOMIC AND SOCIAL RESEARCH COUNCIL (ESRC)
Polaris House, North Star Avenue, Swindon, Wilts SN2 1UJ
Tel 01793-413000

The purpose of the ESRC is to promote and support research and postgraduate training in the social sciences; to advance knowledge and provide trained social scientists; to provide advice on, and disseminate knowledge and promote public understanding of, the social sciences. Government funding for 1995–6 is £61.2 million

Chairman, Dr B. Smith, OBE

Chief Executive, Prof. R. Amann

RESEARCH CENTRES

CAMBRIDGE GROUP FOR THE HISTORY OF POPULATION AND SOCIAL STRUCTURE, 27 Trumpington Street, Cambridge CB2 1QA. Tel: 01223-333186. *Director,* Dr R. Smith

CENTRE FOR BUSINESS RESEARCH, Department of Applied Economy, University of Cambridge, Sidgwick Avenue, Cambridge CB3 9DE. Tel: 01223-335248. *Director,* A. Hughes

CENTRE FOR ECONOMIC PERFORMANCE, London School of Economics, Houghton Street, London WC2A 2AE. Tel: 0171-955 7048. *Director,* Prof. R. Layard

CENTRE FOR HOUSING RESEARCH, University of Glasgow, 25 Bute Gardens, Hillhead, Glasgow G12 8LE. Tel: 0141-339 8855. *Director,* Prof. D. MacLennan, PH.D.

CENTRE FOR MICRO-ECONOMIC ANALYSIS OF FISCAL POLICY, Institute for Fiscal Studies, 7 Ridgmount Street, London WC1E 7AE. Tel: 0171-636 3784. *Director,* Prof. R. Blundell

CENTRE FOR RESEARCH IN DEVELOPMENT INSTRUCTION AND TRAINING, Department of Psychology, University of Nottingham, Nottingham NG7 2RD. Tel: 0115-951 5312. *Director,* Prof. D. J. Wood

CENTRE FOR RESEARCH IN ETHNIC RELATIONS, University of Warwick, Gibbet Hill Road, Coventry CV4 7AL. Tel: 01203-523523. *Director,* Prof. Z. Layton-Henry

CENTRE FOR RESEARCH INTO ELECTIONS AND SOCIAL TRENDS, Social and Community Planning Research, 35 Northampton Square, London EC1V 0AX. Tel: 0171-250 1866. *Director,* Prof. R. Jowell

CENTRE FOR SCIENCE TECHNOLOGY, ENERGY AND ENVIRONMENTAL POLICY, Science Policy Research Unit, University of Sussex, Mentell Building, Falmer, Brighton BN1 9RF. Tel: 01273-686758. *Director,* Prof. M. Gibbons

CENTRE FOR SOCIAL AND ECONOMIC RESEARCH ON THE GLOBAL ENVIRONMENT, School of Environmental Sciences, University of East Anglia, Norwich NR4 7TJ. Tel: 01603-593176; University College London, Gower Street, London WC1E 6BT. Tel: 0171-387 7050. *Director,* Prof. D. Pearce

CENTRE FOR SOCIAL WORK RESEARCH, University of Stirling, Stirling FK9 4LA. Tel: 01786-467724. *Director,* Prof. J. Cheetham

CENTRE FOR THE STUDY OF AFRICAN ECONOMIES, St Cross Building, Manor Road, Oxford OX1 3UL. Tel: 01865-271084. *Director,* Prof. P. Collier

CENTRE OF EDUCATIONAL SOCIOLOGY, University of Edinburgh, 7 Buccleuch Place, Edinburgh EH8 9LW. Tel: 0131-650 4190. *Director,* Prof. D. Raffe

FINANCIAL MARKETS GROUP, London School of Economics, Houghton Street, London WC2A 2AE. Tel: 0171-955 7002. *Director,* Prof. D. Webb

HUMAN COMMUNICATION RESEARCH CENTRE, University of Edinburgh, 2 Buccleuch Place, Edinburgh EH8 9LW. Tel: 0131-650 2335. *Director,* Prof. K. Stenning

INDUSTRIAL RELATIONS RESEARCH UNIT, School of Industrial and Business Studies, University of Warwick, Gibbet Hill Road, Coventry CV4 7AL. Tel: 01203-523523. *Director,* Prof. K. Sisson

MRC/ESRC SOCIAL AND APPLIED PSYCHOLOGY UNIT, Department of Psychology, University of Sheffield, Sheffield S10 2TN. Tel: 0114-275 6600. *Director,* Prof. P. Warr

RESEARCH CENTRE IN MICRO-SOCIAL CHANGE, University of Essex, Wivenhoe Park, Colchester, Essex CO4 3SQ. Tel: 01206-872957. *Director,* Prof. J. Gershuny

TRANSPORT STUDIES UNIT, University of Oxford, 11 Bevington Road, Oxford OX2 6NB. Tel: 01865-274715. *Director,* Dr P. Goodwin

RESOURCE CENTRES

CENTRE FOR APPLIED SOCIAL SURVEYS, Social and Community Planning Research, 35 Northampton Square, London EC1V 0AX. *Director,* R. Thomas

CENTRE FOR ECONOMIC POLICY RESEARCH, 25–28 Old Burlington Street, London W1X 1LB. Tel: 0171-734 9110. *Director,* Prof. R. Portes

ESRC DATA ARCHIVE, University of Essex, Wivenhoe Park, Colchester, Essex CO4 3SQ. Tel: 01206-872001. *Director,* Prof. D. Lievesley

INTERNATIONAL BIBLIOGRAPHY OF SOCIAL SCIENCES, British Library of Political and Economic Science, London School of Economics, Houghton Street, London WC2A 2AE. Tel: 0171-405 7686. *Director,* Ms L. Brindley

QUALITATIVE DATA ARCHIVAL RESOURCE CENTRE, Department of Sociology, University of Essex, Wivenhoe Park, Colchester, Essex CO4 3SQ. Tel: 01206-873333. *Director*, Prof. P. Thompson
RESOURCE CENTRE FOR ACCESS TO DATA IN EUROPE, Department of Geography, University of Durham, Old Shire Hall, Durham DH1 3HP. *Director*, Prof. R. Hudson

---

ENGINEERING AND PHYSICAL SCIENCES RESEARCH COUNCIL (EPSRC)
Polaris House, North Star Avenue, Swindon, Wilts SN2 1ET
Tel 01793-444000

The purpose of the EPSRC is to encourage and support all basic and strategic research and training in UK higher education institutions in the natural and physical sciences and engineering. It no longer has any research institutions. Government funding for 1995–6 is £365.7 million.
Chairman, Dr A. Rudge, OBE, FRS, FEng.
Chief Executive, Dr R. Brook, OBE

MEDICAL RESEARCH COUNCIL (MRC)
20 Park Crescent, London W1N 4AL
Tel 0171-636 5422

The purpose of the MRC is to promote medical and related biological research. The council employs its own research staff and funds research by other institutions and individuals, complementing the research resources of the universities and hospitals. Government funding for 1995–6 is £277.8 million.
Chairman, Sir David Plastow
Cheif Executive, Sir Dai Rees, D.SC., FRS
Chairman, Neurosciences and Mental Health Board, Prof. Sir Michael Rutter, CBE, MD, FRCP, FRCPsych., FRS
Chairman, Molecular and Cellular Medicine Board, Prof. T. M. Dexter, D.SC., FRS
Chairman, Physiological Medicine and Infections Board, Prof. J. R. Pattison, DM, FRCpath.
Chairman, Health Services and Public Health Research Board, Prof. M. Roland, DM
NATIONAL INSTITUTE FOR MEDICAL RESEARCH, The Ridgeway, Mill Hill, London NW7 1AA. Tel: 0181-959 3666. *Director*, J. Skehel, PH.D., FRS
CLINICAL SCIENCES CENTRE, Royal Postgraduate Medical School, Du Cane Road, London W12 0NN. Tel: 0181-743 7117. *Director*, Prof. A. McNeish
LABORATORY OF MOLECULAR BIOLOGY, Hills Road, Cambridge CB2 2QH. Tel: 01223-248011. *Director*, Prof. Sir Aaron Klug, SC.D., FRS

RESEARCH UNITS

ANATOMICAL NEUROPHARMACOLOGY UNIT, Mansfield Road, Oxford OX1 3TH. Tel: 01865-271865. *Hon. Director*, Prof. A. D. Smith, D.phil.
APPLIED PSYCHOLOGY UNIT, 15 Chaucer Road, Cambridge CB2 2EF. Tel: 01223-355294. *Director*, A. D. Baddeley, PH.D., FRS
BBSRC/MRC NEUROPATHOGENESIS UNIT, Ogston Building, West Mains Road, Edinburgh EH9 3JF. Tel: 0131-667 5204. *Director*, vacant
BIOCHEMICAL AND CLINICAL MAGNETIC RESONANCE UNIT, University Department of Biochemistry, South

Parks Road, Oxford OX1 3QU. Tel: 01865-275274. *Hon. Director*, Prof. G. K. Radda, CBE, D.phil., FRS
BIOSTATISTICS UNIT, Institute of Public Health, University Forvie Site, Robinson Way, Cambridge CB2 2SR. Tel: 01223-330366. *Hon. Director*, Prof. N. E. Day, PH.D.
BLOOD GROUP UNIT, University College, London, Wolfson House, 4 Stephenson Way, London NW1 2HE. Tel: 0171-388 7752. *Director*, P. Tippett, OBE, PH.D.
BRAIN METABOLISM UNIT, University Department of Pharmacology, 1 George Square, Edinburgh EH8 9JZ. Tel: 0131-650 3543. *Director*, Prof. G. Fink, MD, D.phil., FRSE
CELL MUTATION UNIT, University of Sussex, Falmer, Brighton BN1 9RR. Tel: 01273-678123. *Director*, Prof. B. A. Bridges, PH.D., FIBiol.
CELLULAR IMMUNOLOGY UNIT, Sir William Dunn School of Pathology, Oxford OX1 3RE. Tel: 01865-275594. *Director* (*acting*), D. W. Mason
CHILD PSYCHIATRY UNIT, Institute of Psychiatry, De Crespigny Park, Denmark Hill, London SE5 8AF. Tel: 0171-703 5411. *Hon. Director*, Prof. Sir Michael Rutter, CBE, MD, FRCP, FRCPsych, FRS
CLINICAL ONCOLOGY AND RADIOTHERAPEUTICS UNIT, MRC Centre, Hills Road, Cambridge CB2 2QH. Tel: 01223-245133. *Hon. Director*, Prof. N. M. Bleehen, CBE, FRCP, FRCR
COGNITIVE DEVELOPMENT UNIT, 4 Taviton Street, London WC1H 0BT. Tel: 0171-387 4692. *Director*, Prof. J. Morton, PH.D.
COLLABORATIVE CENTRE, 1–3 Burtonhole Lane, Mill Hill, London NW7 1AD. Tel: 0181-906 3811. *Director*, C. C. G. Hentschel, PH.D.
CYCLOTRON UNIT, MRC Clinical Sciences Centre, RPMS Hammersmith Hospital, Du Cane Road, London W12 0NN. Tel: 0181-740 3162. *Director* (*acting*), T. Jones, D.SC., MD
DUNN NUTRITION UNIT, Downhams Lane, Milton Road, Cambridge CB4 1XJ. Tel: 01223-426356. *Director*, R. G. Whitehead, CBE, PH.D.
ENVIRONMENTAL EPIDEMIOLOGY UNIT, Southampton General Hospital, Southampton SO9 4XY. Tel: 01703-777624. *Director*, Prof. D. J. P. Barker, MD, PH.D, FRCP, FRCOG
EPIDEMIOLOGY AND MEDICAL CARE UNIT, Wolfson Institute of Preventive Medicine, St Bartholomew's Medical College, Charterhouse Square, London EC1M 6BQ. Tel: 0171-982 6000. *Director*, Prof. T. W. Meade, CBE, DM, FRCP
EPIDEMIOLOGY UNIT (SOUTH WALES), Llandough Hospital, Penarth, South Glamorgan CF64 2XW. Tel: 01222-711404. *Director*, P. C. Elwood, MD, FRCP
EXPERIMENTAL EMBRYOLOGY AND TERATOLOGY UNIT, St George's Hospital Medical School, Cranmer Terrace, London SW17 0RE. Tel: 0181-672 9944 ext. 56309. *Director*, Prof. D. G. Whittingham, D.SC., FRCVS, FIBiol.
HUMAN BIOCHEMICAL GENETICS UNIT, The Galton Laboratory, University College London, Wolfson House, 4 Stephenson Way, London NW1 2HE. Tel: 0171-387 7050. *Director*, Prof. D. A. Hopkinson, MD
HUMAN GENETICS UNIT, Western General Hospital, Crewe Road, Edinburgh EH4 2XU. Tel: 0131-332 2471. *Director*, Prof. H. J. Evans, PH.D., FIBiol., FRCPE, FRCSE, FRSE
HUMAN MOVEMENT AND BALANCE UNIT, Institute of Neurology, National Hospital for Neurology and Neuro-surgery, Queen Square, London WC1 3BG. Tel: 0171-837 3611. *Hon. Director*. Prof. C. D. Marsden, D.SC., FRCP, FRS

IMMUNOCHEMISTRY UNIT, University Department of Biochemistry, South Parks Road, Oxford OX1 3QU. Tel: 01865-275354. *Director*, K. B. M. Reid, PH.D.

INSTITUTE OF HEARING RESEARCH, University of Nottingham, Nottingham NG7 2RD. Tel: 0115-922 3431. *Director*, Prof. M. P. Haggard, PH.D.

MEDICAL SOCIOLOGY UNIT, 6 Lilybank Gardens, Glasgow G12 8QQ. Tel: 0141-357 3949. *Director*, Prof. S. Macintyre, PH.D.

MOLECULAR HAEMATOLOGY UNIT, Institute of Molecular Medicine, John Radcliffe Hospital, Headington, Oxford OX3 9DU. Tel: 01865-222359. *Hon. Director*, Prof. Sir David Weatherall, MD, FRCP, FRCPath., FRS

MOLECULAR IMMUNOPATHOLOGY UNIT, MRC Centre, University Medical School, Hills Road, Cambridge CB2 2QH. Tel: 01223-245133. *Hon. Director*, Prof. P. J. Lachmann, PH.D., SC.D., FRCP, FRCPath., FRS

MRC/ESRC SOCIAL AND APPLIED PSYCHOLOGY UNIT, Dept. of Psychology, University of Sheffield, Sheffield S10 2TN. Tel: 0114-275 6600. *Director*, Prof. P. B. Warr, PH.D.

MRC LABORATORIES, THE GAMBIA, PO Box 273, Banjul, The Gambia, W. Africa. *Director*, B. M. Greenwood, CBE, MD, FRCP

MRC LABORATORIES, JAMAICA, University of the West Indies, Mona, Kingston 7, Jamaica. *Director*, Prof. G. R. Serjeant, CMG, MD, FRCP

MUSCLE AND CELL MOTILITY UNIT, Division of Biomedical Sciences, King's College London, 26–29 Drury Lane, London WC2B 5RL. Tel: 0171-836 8851. *Hon. Director*, Prof. R. M. Simmons, PH.D.

NEUROCHEMICAL PATHOLOGY UNIT, Newcastle General Hospital, Westgate Road, Newcastle upon Tyne NE4 6BE. Tel: 0191-273 5251. *Director*, Prof. J. A. Edwardson, PH.D.

PROTEIN FUNCTION AND DESIGN UNIT, Department of Chemistry, University of Cambridge, Lensfield Road, Cambridge CB2 1EW. Tel: 01223-336341. *Hon. Director*, Prof. A. R. Fersht, PH.D., FRS

PROTEIN PHOSPHORYLATION UNIT, Department of Biochemistry, Medical Sciences Institute, University of Dundee, Dundee DD1 4HN. Tel: 01382-307238. *Hon. Director*, Prof. P. Cohen, PH.D., FRS, FRSE

RADIOBIOLOGY UNIT, Chilton, Didcot, Oxon OX11 ORD. Tel: 01235-834393. *Director*, Prof. G. E. Adams, D.SC.

REPRODUCTIVE BIOLOGY UNIT, Centre for Reproductive Biology, 37 Chalmers Street, Edinburgh EH3 9EW. Tel: 0131-229 2575. *Director*, Prof. D. W. Lincoln, D.SC., FRSE

SOCIAL AND COMMUNITY PSYCHIATRY UNIT, Institute of Psychiatry, De Crespigny Park, Denmark Hill, London SE5 8AF. Tel: 0171-703 5411. *Director*, Prof. J. P. Leff, MD, FRCPsych.

TOXICOLOGY UNIT, Hodgkin Building, University of Leicester, PO Box 138, Lancaster Road, Leicester LE1 9HN. Tel: 0116-252 5600. *Director*, L. Smith, PH.D.

TUBERCULOSIS AND RELATED INFECTIONS UNIT, MRC Clinical Sciences Centre, RPMS, Hammersmith Hospital, Du Cane Road, London W12 0NN. Tel: 0181-740 3161. *Director*, Prof. J. Ivanyi, MD, PH.D.

UK HUMAN GENOME MAPPING PROJECT RESOURCE CENTRE, Sanger Centre, Hinxton Hall, Hinxton, Cambridge CB10 1RQ. *Manager*, K. Gibson, PH.D.

VIROLOGY UNIT, Institute of Virology, Church Street, Glasgow G11 5JR. Tel: 0141-330 4017. *Director*, Dr D. J. McGeoch

NATURAL ENVIRONMENT RESEARCH COUNCIL (NERC)

Polaris House, North Star Avenue, Swindon, Wilts SN2 1EU

Tel 01793-411500

The purpose of the NERC is to promote and support research, survey, long-term environmental monitoring and related postgraduate training in terrestrial, marine and freshwater biology, and Earth, atmospheric, hydrological, oceanographic and polar sciences and Earth observation; to advance knowledge and technology, and provide services and trained scientists and engineers; to provide advice, disseminate knowledge and promote understanding in these fields. Government funding for 1995–6 is £155.5 million.

Chairman, R. Malpas, CBE, FEng.
Chief Executive, Prof. J. R. Krebs, FRS
Director, NERC Scientific Services, B. J. Hinde, OBE

BRITISH ANTARCTIC SURVEY, Madingley Road, Cambridge CB3 0ET. Tel: 01223-61188. *Director*, Dr B. Heywood

BRITISH GEOLOGICAL SURVEY, Nicker Hill, Keyworth, Nottingham NG12 5GG. Tel: 0115-936 3100. *Director*, Dr P. Cook

CENTRE FOR ECOLOGY AND HYDROLOGY
Director, Prof. W. B. Wilkinson (based at Institute of Hydrology)

INSTITUTE OF FRESHWATER ECOLOGY, The Ferry House, Far Sawrey, Ambleside, Cumbria LA22 0LP. Tel: 015394-42468. *Director*, Prof. A. D. Pickering

INSTITUTE OF HYDROLOGY, Maclean Building, Crowmarsh Gifford, Wallingford, Oxon OX10 8BB. Tel: 01491-838800. *Director*, A. Debney

INSTITUTE OF TERRESTRIAL ECOLOGY, Monks Wood, Abbots Ripton, Huntingdon PE17 2LS. Tel: 014873-773381. *Director*, Dr T. M. Roberts

INSTITUTE OF VIROLOGY AND ENVIRONMENTAL MICROBIOLOGY, Mansfield Road, Oxford OX1 3SR. Tel: 01865-512361. *Director*, Dr P. Nuttall

CENTRE FOR COASTAL AND MARINE SCIENCE
Director, Dr B. Bayne (based at Plymouth Marine Laboratory)

PLYMOUTH MARINE LABORATORY, Prospect Place, The Hoe, Plymouth PL1 3PB. Tel: 01752-222772. *Director*, vacant

PROUDMAN OCEANOGRAPHIC LABORATORY, Bidston, Birkenhead L43 7RA. Tel: 0151-653 8633. *Director*, Dr B. S. McCartney

DUNSTAFFNAGE MARINE LABORATORY, PO Box 3, Oban, Argyll PA34 4AD. Tel: 01631-62244. *Director*, vacant

SOUTHAMPTON OCEANOGRAPHY CENTRE
University of Southampton, Empress Dock, Southampton SO14 3XH
Tel 01703-595105/6
Director, Dr J. Shepherd

INSTITUTE OF OCEANOGRAPHIC SCIENCES

JAMES RENNELL CENTRE FOR OCEAN CIRCULATION

RESEARCH VESSEL SERVICES

UNIVERSITY UNITS

SEA MAMMAL RESEARCH UNIT, c/o British Antarctic Survey (*see* above). Tel: 01223-311354. *Head*, J. Harwood, PH.D.

UNIT OF AQUATIC BIOCHEMISTRY, Stirling University, Stirling FK9 4LA. Tel: 01789-473171. *Director*, Prof. J. R. Sargent

UNIT OF COMPARATIVE PLANT ECOLOGY, Department of Animal and Plant Biology and Ecology, University of Sheffield, Sheffield S10 2TN. Tel: 0114-276 8555. *Director*, Prof. J. P. Grime

ENVIRONMENTAL SYSTEMS SCIENCE CENTRE, Department of Geography, Reading University, Whiteknights, Reading RG6 2AB. Tel: 01734-318741. *Director*, Prof. R. Gurney

CENTRE FOR POPULATION BIOLOGY, Imperial College, Silwood Park, Ascot, Berks SL5 7PY. Tel: 01344-294354. *Director*, Prof. J. Lawton

---

PARTICLE PHYSICS AND ASTRONOMY RESEARCH COUNCIL (PPARC)
Polaris House, North Star Avenue, Swindon, Wilts SN2 1EU
Tel 01793-442000

The purpose of the PPARC is to support research into elementary particles and the fundamental forces of nature, planetary and solar research, including space physics, and astronomy, astrophysics and cosmology. It funds research in the universities and is responsible for funding both national and international facilities, including the European Laboratory for Particle Physics (CERN) and the European Space Agency. Government funding for 1995–6 is £196.4 million.
Chairman, Dr P. Williams, CBE
Chief Executive, Prof. K. Pounds, CBE, FRS

THE ROYAL OBSERVATORIES
Director, Prof. A. Boksenberg, FRS

ROYAL GREENWICH OBSERVATORY, Madingley Road, Cambridge CB3 0EZ. Tel: 01223-374000
ROYAL OBSERVATORY, EDINBURGH, Blackford Hill, Edinburgh EH9 3HJ. Tel: 0131-668 8100

ISAAC NEWTON GROUP OF TELESCOPES
Apartado de Coreos 321, Santa Cruz de la Palma, Tenerife 38780, Canary Islands. Tel: 00 3422-411048. *Head*, Dr S. Unger

JOINT ASTRONOMY CENTRE
660 N A'ohoku Place, University Park, Hilo, Hawaii 96720. Tel: 00 808-961 3756. *Head*, Prof. I. Robson

---

Research Associations

The following industrial and technological research bodies are members of the Association of Independent Research and Technology Organizations (AIRTO). Its members include research associations associated with a specific product, industry or technology, and contract research organizations which specialize in certain areas of a technology but are not associated with a specific product or industry. They provide consultancy advice in design in science and engineering, and undertake research and development programmes under contract. AIRTO publishes a directory to help clients identify the organizations which might be able to assist them.
AIRTO, PO Box 330, Cambridge CB5 8DU. Tel: 01223-467831. *Secretary-General*, J. Bennett

ADVANCED MANUFACTURING TECHNOLOGY RESEARCH INSTITUTE, Hulley Road, Macclesfield, Cheshire SK10 2NE. Tel: 01625-425421. *Managing Director*, D. Palethorpe

AIRCRAFT RESEARCH ASSOCIATION LTD, Manton Lane, Bedford MK41 7PF. Tel: 01234-350681. *Chief Executive*, Dr J. E. Green

BHR GROUP LTD (*Fluid mechanics and process technology*), Cranfield, Bedford MK43 0AJ. Tel: 01234-750422. *Chief Executive*, I. Cooper

BIBRA INTERNATIONAL (*Assessment of toxicity of food and chemicals to humans*), Woodmansterne Road, Carshalton, Surrey SM5 4DS. Tel: 0181-652 1000. *Director*, Dr S. E. Jaggers

BLC (THE LEATHER TECHNOLOGY CENTRE), Leather Trade House, Kings Park Road, Moulton Park, Northants NN3 6JD. Tel: 01604-494131. *Chief Executive*, Dr K. Alexander

BRITISH GLASS, Northumberland Road, Sheffield S10 2UA. Tel: 0114-268 6201. *Director-General*, Dr W. Cook

BRITISH MARITIME TECHNOLOGY LTD, Orlando House, 1 Waldegrave Road, Teddington, Middx TW11 8LZ. Tel: 0181-943 5544. *Chief Executive*, D. Goodrich

BRITISH TEXTILE TECHNOLOGY GROUP, Wira House, West Park Ring Road, Leeds LS16 6QL. Tel: 0113-259 1999; Shirley House, Didsbury, Manchester M20 8RX. Tel: 0161-445 8141. *Chief Executive*, A. King

BUILDING SERVICES RESEARCH AND INFORMATION ASSOCIATION, Old Bracknell Lane West, Bracknell, Berks RG12 7AH. Tel: 01344-426511. *Chief Executive*, G. J. Baker

CAMBRIDGE CONSULTANTS LTD (*Product and process development of technology applications in business*), Science Park, Milton Road, Cambridge CB4 4DW. Tel: 01223-420024. *Chief Executive*, Dr J. P. Auton

CAMBRIDGE REFRIGERATION TECHNOLOGY (CRT), 140 Newmarket Road, Cambridge CB5 8HE. Tel: 01223-65101. *Technical Director*, R. D. Heap

CAMPDEN AND CHORLEYWOOD FOOD RESEARCH ASSOCIATION, Chipping Campden, Glos GL55 6LD. Tel: 01386-840319; Chorleywood, Herts WD3 5SH. Tel: 01923-284111. *Director-General*, Prof. C. Dennis

CERAM (BRITISH CERAMIC RESEARCH LTD), Queen's Road, Penkhull, Stoke-on-Trent ST4 7LQ. Tel: 01782-45431. *Chief Executive*, Dr N. E. Sanderson

CIRIA (CONSTRUCTION INDUSTRY RESEARCH AND INFORMATION ASSOCIATION), 6 Storey's Gate, London SW1P 3AU. Tel: 0171-222 8891. *Director-General*, Dr P. L. Bransby

CUTLERY AND ALLIED TRADES RESEARCH ASSOCIATION, Henry Street, Sheffield S3 7EQ. Tel: 0114-276 9736. *Director of Research*, R. C. Hamby

EA TECHNOLOGY (*Use and distribution of electricity*), Capenhurst, Chester CH1 6ES. Tel: 0151-339 4181. *Chief Executive*, Dr S. F. Exell

ERA TECHNOLOGY LTD (*Electronic, electrical, materials and structural engineering*), Cleeve Road, Leatherhead, Surrey KT22 7SA. Tel: 01372-367000. *Chief Executive*, M. J. Withers

FABRIC CARE RESEARCH ASSOCIATION, Forest House Laboratories, Knaresborough Road, Harrogate, N. Yorks HG2 7LZ. Tel: 01423-885977. *Managing Director*, C. Tebbs

FURNITURE INDUSTRY RESEARCH ASSOCIATION, Maxwell Road, Stevenage, Herts SG1 2EW. Tel: 01438-313433. *Chief Executive*, Dr C. A. Aitkenhead

INTERNATIONAL RESEARCH AND DEVELOPMENT LTD
(*Mechanical and electrical engineering, electronics and control
engineering, applied sciences, materials technology*), Fossway,
Newcastle upon Tyne NE6 2YD. Tel: 0191-265 0451.
General Manager, R. Potts

LEATHERHEAD FOOD RESEARCH ASSOCIATION, Randalls
Road, Leatherhead, Surrey KT22 7RY. Tel: 01372-376761.
Director, Dr M. P. J. Kierstan

MOTOR INDUSTRY RESEARCH ASSOCIATION, Watling
Street, Nuneaton, Warks CV10 0TU. Tel: 01203-348541.
Managing Director, J. R. Wood

THE NATIONAL COMPUTING CENTRE LTD, Oxford
House, Oxford Road, Manchester MI 7ED. Tel: 0161-228
6333. *Chief Executive*, N. Banister

PAINT RESEARCH ASSOCIATION, 8 Waldegrave Road,
Teddington, Middx TW11 8LD. Tel: 0181-977 4427.
Managing Director, J. A. Bernie

PERA INTERNATIONAL (*Multi-disciplinary research, design,
development and consultancy*), Melton Mowbray, Leics LE13
0PB. Tel: 01664-501501. *Chief Executive*, R. A. Armstrong

PIRA INTERNATIONAL (*Paper and board, printing, publishing
and packaging*), Randalls Road, Leatherhead, Surrey KT22
7RU. Tel: 01372-376161. *Managing Director*, B. W.
Blunden, OBE

RAPRA TECHNOLOGY LTD (*Rubber and plastics*),
Shawbury, Shrewsbury SY4 4NR. Tel: 01939-250383;
North East Centre, 18 Belasis Court, Belasis
Technology Park, Billingham, Cleveland TS23 4AZ. Tel:
01642-370406. *Chief Executive*, Dr M. Copley

SATRA FOOTWEAR TECHNOLOGY CENTRE, Satra
House, Rockingham Road, Kettering, Northants NN16
9JH. Tel: 01536-410000. *Chief Executive*, Dr R. E.
Whittaker

SIRA LTD (*Measurement, instrumentation, control and optical
systems technology*), South Hill, Chislehurst, Kent BR7 5EH.
Tel: 0181-467 2636. *Managing Director*, R. A. Brook

SMITH SYSTEM ENGINEERING LTD, Surrey Research
Park, Guildford, Surrey GU2 5YP. Tel: 01483-442000.
Chairman, Dr B. G. Smith, OBE

SPRING RESEARCH AND MANUFACTURERS' ASSOCIATION,
Henry Street, Sheffield S3 7EQ. Tel: 0114-276 0771.
Director, D. Saynor

THE WELDING INSTITUTE (TWI), Abington Hall,
Abington, Cambridge CB1 6AL. Tel: 01223-891162. *Chief
Executive*, A. B. M. Braithwaite, OBE

WRC PLC, (*Water, waste water and environmental
management*), PO Box 16, Marlow, Bucks SL7 2HD. Tel:
01491-571531. *Managing Director*, Dr J. Moss

Sports Bodies

* Governing body for the sport

Sports Councils

†THE SPORTS COUNCIL, 16 Upper Woburn Place, London WC1H 0QP. Tel: 0171-388 1277. *Chief Executive*, D. Casey

SCOTTISH SPORTS COUNCIL, Caledonia House, South Gyle, Edinburgh EH12 9DQ. Tel: 0131-317 7200. *Chief Executive*, F. A. L. Alstead, CBE

SPORTS COUNCIL FOR WALES, Sophia Gardens, Cardiff CF1 9SW. Tel: 01222-397571. *Chief Executive*, L. Tatham

SPORTS COUNCIL FOR NORTHERN IRELAND, House of Sport, Upper Malone Road, Belfast BT9 5LA. Tel: 01232 381222. *Chief Executive*, E. McCartan

CENTRAL COUNCIL OF PHYSICAL RECREATION, Francis House, Francis Street, London SW1P 1DE. Tel: 0171-828 3163. *General Secretary*, P. Lawson

Alpine Skiing

*BRITISH SKI FEDERATION, 258 Main Street, East Calder, Livingston, West Lothian EH53 0EE. Tel: 01506-884343. *Chief Executive*, M. Jardine

Angling

*NATIONAL FEDERATION OF ANGLERS, Halliday House, Egginton Junction, Derbys DE65 6GU. Tel: 01283-734735. *Chief Administration Officer*, K. E. Watkins

Archery

*GRAND NATIONAL ARCHERY SOCIETY, 7th Street, National Agricultural Centre, Stoneleigh, Kenilworth, Warks CV8 2LG. Tel: 01203-696631. *Chief Executive*, J. S. Middleton

Association Football

*THE FOOTBALL ASSOCIATION, 16 Lancaster Gate, London W2 3LW. Tel: 0171-262 4542. *Chief Executive*, R. H. G. Kelly

FOOTBALL LEAGUE LTD, 319 Clifton Drive South, Lytham St Annes, Lancs FY8 1JG. Tel: 01253-729421. *Secretary*, J. D. Dent

*SCOTTISH FOOTBALL ASSOCIATION, 6 Park Gardens, Glasgow G3 7YF. Tel: 0141-332 6372. *Chief Executive* J. Farry

SCOTTISH FOOTBALL LEAGUE, 188 West Regent Street, Glasgow G2 4RY. Tel: 0141-248 3844. *Secretary*, P. Donald

*FOOTBALL ASSOCIATION OF WALES, Plymouth Chambers, 3 Westgate Street, Cardiff CF1 1DD. Tel: 01222-372325. *Secretary*, D. Collins

*IRISH FOOTBALL ASSOCIATION, 20 Windsor Avenue, Belfast BT9 6EE. Tel: 01232-669458. *General Secretary*, D. I. Bowen

IRISH FOOTBALL LEAGUE, 96 University Street, Belfast BT7 1HE. Tel: 01232-242888. *Secretary*, H. Wallace

Athletics

*BRITISH ATHLETIC FEDERATION, 225A Bristol Road, Edgbaston, Birmingham B5 7UB. Tel: 0121-440 5000. *Executive Chairman*, Prof. P. F. Radford

AMATEUR ATHLETIC ASSOCIATION OF ENGLAND, 225A Bristol Road, Edgbaston, Birmingham B5 7UB. Tel: 0121-440 5000. *Executive Chairman*, Prof. P. F. Radford

SCOTTISH ATHLETICS FEDERATION, Caledonia House, South Gyle, Edinburgh EH12 9DQ. Tel: 0131-317 7320. *Administrator*, N. F. Park

ATHLETICS ASSOCIATION OF WALES, Morfa Athletics Stadium, Upper Bank, Landore, Swansea, W. Glamorgan SA1 7DF. Tel: 01792-456237. *National Administrator*, Mrs B. Currie

NORTHERN IRELAND AMATEUR ATHLETIC FEDERATION, House of Sport, Upper Malone Road, Belfast BT9 5LA. Tel: 01232-381222. *Secretary*, J. Allen

Badminton

*BADMINTON ASSOCIATION OF ENGLAND LTD, National Badminton Centre, Bradwell Road, Loughton Lodge, Milton Keynes MK8 9LA. Tel: 01908-568822. *Chief Executive*, G. Snowdon

*SCOTTISH BADMINTON UNION, Cockburn Centre, 40 Bogmoor Place, Glasgow G51 4TQ. Tel: 0141-445 1218. *Chief Executive*, Miss A. Smillie

*WELSH BADMINTON UNION, Fourth Floor, 3 Westgate Street, Cardiff CF1 1DD. Tel: 01222-222082. *Coaching Development Manager*, L. Williams

Baseball

*BRITISH BASEBALL FEDERATION, 66 Belvedere Road, Hessle, N. Humberside HU13 9JJ. Tel: 01482-643551. *Secretary*, K. Macadam

Basketball

*ENGLISH BASKETBALL ASSOCIATION, 48 Bradford Road, Stanningley, Leeds LS28 6DF. Tel: 0113-236 1166. *Chief Executive*, D. Ransom

*SCOTTISH BASKETBALL ASSOCIATION, Caledonia House, South Gyle, Edinburgh EH12 9DQ. Tel: 0131-317 7260. *President*, W. D. McInnes

*BASKETBALL ASSOCIATION OF WALES, Connies House, Rhymney River Bridge Road, Cardiff CF3 7YZ. Tel: 01222-454395. *Administrator*, F. M. Daw

Billiards

*WORLD PROFESSIONAL BILLIARDS AND SNOOKER ASSOCIATION, 27 Oakfield Road, Clifton, Bristol BS8 2AT. Tel: 0117-974 4491. *Company Secretary*, M. Hulley

*WORLD LADIES BILLIARDS AND SNOOKER ASSOCIATION, 3 Felsted Avenue, Wisbech, Cambs PE13 3SL. Tel: 01945-589589. *Secretary*, Ms M. Fisher

Bobsleigh

*BRITISH BOBSLEIGH ASSOCIATION, The Chestnuts, 85 High Street, Codford, Warminster, Wilts BA12 0ND. Tel: 01895-850064. *Secretary*, Ms H. Alderman

Bowls

*BRITISH ISLES BOWLING COUNCIL, 28 Woodford Park, Lurgan, Co. Armagh BT66 7HA. Tel: 01762-322036. *Hon. Secretary*, W. A. Gracey

*BRITISH ISLES INDOOR BOWLS COUNCIL, 9 Highlights Lane, Barry, S. Glamorgan CF62 8AA. Tel: 01446-733978. *Secretary*, J. R. Thomas, MBE

*BRITISH ISLES WOMEN'S BOWLING COUNCIL, 2 Case Gardens, Seaton, Devon EX12 2AP. Tel: 01297-21317. *Hon. Secretary*, Mrs N. Colling

*BRITISH ISLES WOMEN'S INDOOR BOWLS COUNCIL, 16 Windsor Crescent, Radyr, Cardiff CF4 8AE. Tel: 01222-842391. *Hon. Secretary*, Mrs J. Johns

---

† To be replaced by a UK Sports Council and an English Sports Council in January 1996

*English Bowling Association, Lyndhurst Road, Worthing, W. Sussex BN11 2AZ. Tel: 01903-820222. Secretary, D. Johnson

*English Women's Bowling Association, 2 Case Gardens, Seaton, Devon EX12 2AP. Tel: 01297-21317. Hon. Secretary, Mrs N. Colling

Boxing

*Amateur Boxing Association of England Ltd, Crystal Palace National Sports Centre, London SE19 2BB. Tel: 0181-778 0251. Secretary, C. Brown

*British Boxing Board of Control Ltd, Jack Petersen House, 52A Borough High Street, London SE1 1XW. Tel: 0171-403 5879. General Secretary, J. Morris

*British Amateur Boxing Association, 96 High Street, Lochee, Dundee DD2 3AY. Tel: 01382-611412. Chief Executive, F. Hendry

Canoeing

*British Canoe Union, Adbolton Lane, West Bridgford, Nottingham NG2 5AS. Tel: 0115-982 1100. Chief Executive, P. Owen

Chess

*British Chess Federation, 9A Grand Parade, St Leonard's-on-Sea, E. Sussex TN38 0DD. Tel: 01424-442500. General Manager, Mrs G. White

Clay Pigeon Shooting

*Clay Pigeon Shooting Association, 107 Epping New Road, Buckhurst Hill, Essex IG9 5TQ. Tel: 0181-505 6221. Director, E. Orduna

Cricket

*‡Cricket Council, Lord's, London NW8 8QZ. Tel: 0171-286 4405. Chairman, W. R. S. Chamberlain; Secretary, A. C. Smith

MCC, Lords, London NW8 8QN. Tel: 0171-289 1611. President, The Hon. Sir Oliver Popplewell; Secretary, R. Knight

‡Test and County Cricket Board, Lord's, London NW8 8QZ. Tel: 0171-286 4405. Chairman (1995–6), D. R. W. Silk; Chief Executive, A. C. Smith

Croquet

*Croquet Association, c/o The Hurlingham Club, Ranelagh Gardens, London SW6 3PR. Tel: 0171-736 3148. Secretary, L. W. D. Antenen

Cycling

*British Cycling Federation, National Cycling Centre, Stuart Street, Manchester. M11 4DQ. Tel: 0161-230 2301. Chief Executive, J. Hendry

*Road Time Trials Council, 77 Arlington Drive, Pennington, Leigh, Lancs WN7 3QP. Tel: 01942-603976. National Secretary, P. Heaton

Diving

*Great Britain Diving Federation, PO Box 222, Batley, W. Yorks WF17 8XD. Tel: 01924-422322. Director of Administration, J. Cryer

Equestrianism

*British Equestrian Federation, British Equestrian Centre, Stoneleigh Park, Kenilworth, Warks CV8 2LR. Tel: 01203-696697. Director-General, Col. J. D. Smith-Bingham

Eton Fives

*Eton Fives Association, Welches, Bentley, Farnham, Surrey GU10 5HZ. Tel: 01420-22107. Hon. Secretary, M. P. Powell

Fencing

*Amateur Fencing Association, 1 Barons Gate, 33–35 Rothschild Road, London W4 5HT. Tel: 0181-742 3032. Secretary, Miss G. Kenneally

Gliding

*British Gliding Association, Kimberley House, Vaughan Way, Leicester LE1 4SE. Tel: 0116-253 1051. Secretary, B. Rolfe

Golf

*Royal and Ancient Golf Club, St Andrews, Fife KY16 9JD. Tel: 01334-472112. Secretary, M. F. Bonallack, OBE

*Ladies' Golf Union, The Scores, St Andrews, Fife KY16 9AT. Tel: 01334-475811. Administrator, Mrs E. A. Mackie

Greyhound Racing

*National Greyhound Racing Club Ltd, 24–28 Oval Road, London NW1 7DA. Tel: 0171-267 9256. Chief Executive, F. Melville

Gymnastics

*British Amateur Gymnastics Association, Ford Hall, Lilleshall National Sports Centre, nr. Newport, Shropshire TF10 9NB. Tel: 01952-820330. General Secretary, D. Minnery

Hockey

*Hockey Association, Norfolk House, 102 Saxon Gate West, Milton Keynes MK9 2EP. Tel: 01908-241100. Chief Executive, S. P. Baines

*All England Women's Hockey Association, 51 High Street, Shrewsbury SY1 1ST. Tel: 01743-233572. Executive Director, Miss T. Morris

*Scottish Hockey Union, 48 The Pleasance, Edinburgh EH8 9TJ. Tel: 0131-650 8170. Chairman, Mrs E. Raistrick

*Welsh Hockey Union, Welsh Hockey Office, Deeside Leisure Centre, Chester Road West, Deeside, Clwyd CH5 1SA. Tel: 01244-811825. Executive Secretary, J. G. Williams

Horseracing

*British Horseracing Board, 42 Portman Square, London W1H 0EN. Tel: 0171-396 0011. Chief Executive, R. T. Ricketts

The Jockey Club, 42 Portman Square, London W1H 0EN. Tel: 0171-486 4921. Senior Steward, Sir Thomas Pilkington, Bt.

Ice Hockey

*British Ice Hockey Association, Second Floor Offices, 517 Christchurch Road, Boscombe, Bournemouth BH1 4AG. Tel: 01202-303946. Chief Executive, D. Frame

Ice Skating

*National Ice Skating Association of the United Kingdom Ltd, 15–27 Gee Street, London EC1V 3RE. Tel: 0171-253 3824. Chief Executive, Ms C. Godsall

Judo

*British Judo Association, 7A Rutland Street, Leicester LE1 1RB. Tel: 0116-255 9669. Office Manager, Ms S. Startin

Lacrosse

*English Lacrosse Union, 70 High Road, Rayleigh, Essex SS6 7AD. Tel: 01268-770758. Hon. Secretary, R. Balls

*All England Women's Lacrosse Association, 4 Western Court, Bromley Street, Digbeth, Birmingham B9 4AN. Tel: 0121-773 4422. Administrator, Ms A. Chesses

Lawn Tennis

*Lawn Tennis Association, The Queen's Club, London W14 9EG. Tel: 0171-381 7000. Secretary, J. C. U. James

---

‡ To be replaced by an English Cricket Board in 1996

Lugeing
*GREAT BRITAIN LUGE ASSOCIATION, Mortimer House, Holmer Road, Hereford HR4 9SB. Tel: 01432-353539. *General Secretary*, J. G. Evans

Martial Arts
MARTIAL ARTS DEVELOPMENT COMMISSION, PO Box 381, Erith, Kent DA8 1TF. Tel: 01322-431440. *Office Administrator*, Mrs E. Jewell

Motor Sports
*AUTO-CYCLE UNION, ACU House, Wood Street, Rugby, Warks CV21 2YX. Tel: 01788-540519. *Chief Executive*, M. Mardle
BRITISH MOTOR CYCLE RACING CONTROL BOARD, PO Box 72, Castle Donington, Derby DE74 2ZQ. Tel: 01332-853822. *Manager*, D. R. Barnfield
*RAC MOTOR SPORTS ASSOCIATION LTD, Motor Sports House, Riverside Park, Colnbrook, Slough SL3 0HG. Tel: 01753-681736. *Chief Executive*, J. R. Quenby
*SCOTTISH AUTO CYCLE UNION LTD, Block 2, Unit 6, Whiteside Industrial Estate, Bathgate, West Lothian EH48 2RX. Tel: 01506-630262. *Secretary*, A. M. Brownlie

Mountaineering
*BRITISH MOUNTAINEERING COUNCIL, 177-179 Burton Road, West Didsbury, Manchester M20 2BB. Tel: 0161-445 4747. *General Secretary*, R. Payne

Multi-Sport Bodies
BRITISH OLYMPIC ASSOCIATION, 1 Wandsworth Plain, London SW18 1EH. Tel: 0181-871 2677. *General Secretary*, R. Palmer, OBE
COMMONWEALTH GAMES COUNCIL FOR ENGLAND, Tavistock House South, Tavistock Square, London WC1H 9JZ. Tel: 0171-388 6643. *General Secretary*, Ms A. Hogbin
COMMONWEALTH GAMES FEDERATION, Walkden House, 3-10 Melton Street, London NW1 2EB. Tel: 0171-383 5596. *Hon. Secretary*, D. Dixon, CVO
BRITISH UNIVERSITIES SPORTS ASSOCIATION, 8 Union Street, London SE1 1SZ. Tel: 0171-357 8555. *Chief Executive*, G. Gregory-Jones

Netball
*ALL ENGLAND NETBALL ASSOCIATION, Netball House, 9 Paynes Park, Hitchin, Herts SG5 1EH. Tel: 01462-442344. *Chief Executive*, Mrs E. M. Nicholl
*SCOTTISH NETBALL ASSOCIATION, Kelvin Hall Sports Complex, Argyle Street, Glasgow G3 8AW. Tel: 0141-334 3650. *Administrator*, Ms L. Wilson
*WELSH NETBALL ASSOCIATION, 82 Cathedral Road, Cardiff CF1 9LN. Tel: 01222-237048. *Chairman*, Mrs A. Lloyd

Orienteering
*BRITISH ORIENTEERING FEDERATION, Riversdale, Dale Road North, Darley Dale, Matlock, Derbyshire DE4 2HX. Tel: 01629-734042. *Office Manager*, vacant

Polo
*HURLINGHAM POLO ASSOCIATION, Winterlake, Kirtlington, Kidlington, Oxon OX5 3HG. Tel: 01869-350044. *Secretary*, J. W. M. Crisp

Rackets and Real Tennis
*TENNIS AND RACKETS ASSOCIATION, c/o The Queen's Club, Palliser Road, London W14 9EQ. Tel: 0171-386 3447. *Chief Executive*, Brig. A. D. Myrtle, CB, CBE

Rifle Shooting
*NATIONAL RIFLE ASSOCIATION, Bisley Camp, Brookwood, Woking GU24 0PB. Tel: 01483-797777. *Chief Executive*, Lt.-Col. C. C. C. Cheshire, OBE

*NATIONAL SMALL-BORE RIFLE ASSOCIATION, Lord Roberts House, Bisley Camp, Brookwood, Woking GU24 0NP. Tel: 01483-476969. *Secretary*, Lt.-Col. J. D. Hoare

Rowing
*AMATEUR ROWING ASSOCIATION LTD, The Priory, 6 Lower Mall, London W6 9DJ. Tel: 0181-748 3632. *Senior Administrative Officer*, Mrs R. Napp
HENLEY ROYAL REGATTA, Regatta Headquarters, Henley-on-Thames, Oxon RG9 2LY. Tel: 01491-572153. *Secretary*, R. S. Goddard
SCOTTISH AMATEUR ROWING ASSOCIATION, 134 Newton Street, Greenock PA16 8SJ. Tel: 01475-722996. *Secretary*, Mrs M. Pow
*WELSH AMATEUR ROWING ASSOCIATION, 15 Kingfisher Close, St Mellons, Cardiff CF3 0DD. Tel: 01222-777398. *Hon. Secretary*, M. Nhatiw

Rugby Fives
*RUGBY FIVES ASSOCIATION, The Old Forge, Sutton Valence, Maidstone, Kent ME17 3AW. Tel: 01622-842278. *General Secretary*, M. F. Beaman

Rugby League
*RUGBY FOOTBALL LEAGUE, Red Hall House, Red Hall Lane, Leeds LS17 8NB. Tel: 01132-624637. *Chief Executive*, M. P. Lindsay
*BRITISH AMATEUR RUGBY LEAGUE ASSOCIATION, West Yorkshire House, 4 New North Parade, Huddersfield HD1 5JP. Tel: 01484-544131. *Chief Executive*, M. F. Oldroyd

Rugby Union
*RUGBY FOOTBALL UNION, Twickenham TW1 1DZ. Tel: 0181-892 8161. *Secretary*, A. P. Hallett
*SCOTTISH RUGBY UNION, Murrayfield, Edinburgh EH12 5PJ. Tel: 0131-346 5000. *Chief Executive*, I. A. L. Hogg
*WELSH RUGBY UNION, Cardiff Arms Park, PO Box 22, Westgate Street, Cardiff CF1 1JL. Tel: 01222-390111. *Secretary*, E. H. Jones.
*IRISH RUGBY FOOTBALL UNION, 62 Lansdowne Road, Dublin 4, Republic of Ireland. Tel: 00 353-16-684601. *Secretary*, P. Browne
RUGBY FOOTBALL UNION FOR WOMEN (ENGLAND), 33 Rice Mews, St Thomas, Exeter EX2 9AY. Tel: 01635-278177. *Secretary*, Ms S. Eakers
SCOTTISH WOMEN'S RUGBY UNION, 11 Bavelaw Crescent, Penicuik, Midlothian EH26 9AX. Tel: 01968-673355. *Secretary*, Ms M. Sharp
WELSH WOMEN'S RUGBY UNION, 40 Wolseley Street, Pillwenlly, Gwent NP9 2HP. Tel: 01633-220249. *Secretary*, Ms F. Margerison
IRISH WOMEN'S RUGBY UNION, 31 Ashley Drive, Belfast BT9 7BE. Tel: 01232-664363. *Secretary*, Ms J. Hall

Snooker
*WORLD PROFESSIONAL BILLIARDS AND SNOOKER ASSOCIATION, 27 Oakfield Road, Clifton, Bristol BS8 2AT. Tel: 0117-974 4491. *Company Secretary*, M. Hulley
*WORLD LADIES BILLIARDS AND SNOOKER ASSOCIATION, 3 Felsted Avenue, Wisbech, Cambs PE13 3SL. Tel: 01945-589589. *Secretary*, Ms M. Fisher

Speedway
*SPEEDWAY CONTROL BOARD, ACU Headquarters, Wood Street, Rugby, Warks CV21 2YX. Tel: 01788-540096. *Manager*, G. Reeve

Squash Rackets
*SQUASH RACKETS ASSOCIATION, Westpoint, 33-34 Warple Way, London W3 0RG. Tel: 0181-746 1616. *General Secretary*, N. Moore

*SCOTTISH SQUASH, Caledonia House, South Gyle, Edinburgh EH12 9DQ. Tel: 0131-317 7343. *Secretary,* N. Brydon

*WELSH SQUASH RACKETS FEDERATION, 7 Kymin Terrace, Penarth, South Glamorgan CF6 IAP. Tel: 01222-704096. *Chairman,* S. Osborne

BRITISH SQUASH PROFESSIONALS' ASSOCIATION, 16 Station Road, Chingford, London E4 7BE. Tel: 0181-523 7019. *Chief Executive,* C. Walker

Swimming

*AMATEUR SWIMMING ASSOCIATION, Harold Fern House, Derby Square, Loughborough, Leics LE11 0AL. Tel: 01509-230431. *Chief Executive,* D. Sparkes

*SCOTTISH AMATEUR SWIMMING ASSOCIATION, Holmhills Farm, Greenlees Road, Cambuslang, Glasgow G72 8DT. Tel: 0141-641 8818. *Administration Manager,* Mrs E. Mackenzie

*WELSH AMATEUR SWIMMING ASSOCIATION, Wales Empire Pool, Wood Street, Cardiff CF1 1PP. Tel: 01222-342201. *Hon. General Secretary,* P. Rees

*BRITISH SUB-AQUA CLUB, Telfords Quay, Ellesmere Port, South Wirral, Cheshire L65 4FY. Tel: 0151-357 1951. *Chairman,* H. Painter

Table Tennis

*ENGLISH TABLE TENNIS ASSOCIATION, Queensbury House, Havelock Road, Hastings TN34 1HF. Tel: 01424-722525. *Chief Executive,* R. Yule

Volleyball

*ENGLISH VOLLEYBALL ASSOCIATION, 27 South Road, West Bridgford, Nottingham NG2 7AG. Tel: 0115-981 6324. *National Director,* G. Bulman

*SCOTTISH VOLLEYBALL ASSOCIATION, 48 The Pleasance, Edinburgh EH8 9TJ. Tel: 0131-556 4633. *Director,* N. S. Moody

*WELSH VOLLEYBALL ASSOCIATION, 70 Swakeleys Road, Ickenham, Uxbridge, Middx UB10 8BD. Tel: 01895-673369. *Secretary,* B. Goodman

Walking

*RACE WALKING ASSOCIATION, Hufflers, Heard's Lane, Shenfield, Brentwood, Essex CM15 0SF. Tel: 01277-220687. *Hon. Secretary,* P. J. Cassidy

Water Skiing

*BRITISH WATER SKI FEDERATION, 390 City Road, London EC1V 2QA. Tel: 0171-833 2855. *Executive Officer,* Ms G. Hill

Weightlifting

*BRITISH AMATEUR WEIGHTLIFTERS ASSOCIATION, 3 Iffley Turn, Oxford OX4 4DU. Tel: 01865-778319. *Hon. Secretary,* W. Holland, OBE

Wrestling

*BRITISH AMATEUR WRESTLING ASSOCIATION, 41 Great Clowes Street, Salford, Manchester M7 9RQ. Tel: 0161-832 9209. *National Development Officer,* R. Tomlinson

Yachting

*ROYAL YACHTING ASSOCIATION, RYA House, Romsey Road, Eastleigh, Hants SO50 9YA. Tel: 01703-627400. *Secretary-General,* R. Duchesne, OBE

The Olympic Games

Venues of the modern Olympic Games

I	Athens, Greece	1896
II	Paris, France	1900
III	St Louis, USA	1904
*	Athens	1906
IV	London, Britain	1908
V	Stockholm, Sweden	1912
†VI	Berlin, Germany	1916
VII	Antwerp, Belgium	1920
VIII	Paris, France	1924
IX	Amsterdam, Netherlands	1928
X	Los Angeles, USA	1932
XI	Berlin, Germany	1936
†XII	Tokyo, Japan, then Helsinki, Finland	1940
†XIII	London, Britain	1944
XIV	London, Britain	1948
XV	Helsinki, Finland	1952
§XVI	Melbourne, Australia	1956
XVII	Rome, Italy	1960
XVIII	Tokyo, Japan	1964
XIX	Mexico City, Mexico	1968
XX	Munich, West Germany	1972
XXI	Montreal, Canada	1976
XXII	Moscow, USSR	1980
XXIII	Los Angeles, USA	1984
XXIV	Seoul, South Korea	1988
XXV	Barcelona, Spain	1992
XXVI	Atlanta, USA	1996
XXVII	Sydney, Australia	2000

WINTER OLYMPIC GAMES

I	Chamonix, France	1924
II	St Moritz, Switzerland	1928
III	Lake Placid, USA	1932
IV	Garmisch-Partenkirchen, Germany	1936
V	St Moritz, Switzerland	1948
VI	Oslo, Norway	1952
VII	Cortina d'Ampezzo, Italy	1956
VIII	Squaw Valley, USA	1960
IX	Innsbruck, Austria	1964
X	Grenoble, France	1968
XI	Sapporo, Japan	1972
XII	Innsbruck, Austria	1976
XIII	Lake Placid, USA	1980
XIV	Sarajevo, Yugoslavia	1984
XV	Calgary, Canada	1988
XVI	Albertville, France	1992
XVII	Lillehammer, Norway	1994
XVIII	Nagano, Japan	1998
XIX	Salt Lake City, USA	2002

* The 'Intercalated' Games
† These Games were scheduled but did not take place owing to World Wars
§ Equestrian events were held in Stockholm, Sweden

Clubs

ALPINE CLUB (1857), 55 Charlotte Road, London EC2A 3QT. Tel: 0171-613 0755. *Hon. Secretary*, G. D. Hughes

AMERICAN WOMEN'S CLUB (1899), 68 Old Brompton Road, London SW7 3LQ. Tel: 0171-589 8292. *Secretary*, Ms M. Pratt

ANGLO-BELGIAN CLUB (1955), 60 Knightsbridge, London SWIX 7LF. Tel: 0171-235 2121. *Secretary*, Baronne van Havre

ARMY AND NAVY CLUB (1837), 36–39 Pall Mall, London SWIY 5JN. Tel: 0171-930 9721. *Secretary*, Maj. D. B. Taylor

ARTS CLUB (1863), 40 Dover Street, London WIX 3RB. Tel: 0171-499 8581. *Secretary*, Ms J. Downing

ARTS THEATRE CLUB (1927), 50 Frith Street, London WIV 5TE. Tel: 0171-287 9236. *Hon. Secretary*, S. Labisko

THE ATHENAEUM (1824), 107 Pall Mall, London SWIY 5ER. Tel: 0171-930 4843. *Hon. Secretary*, R. T. Smith

AUTHORS' CLUB (1892), 40 Dover Street, London WIX 3RB. Tel: 0171-499 8581. *Secretary*, Mrs A. Carter

BEEFSTEAK CLUB (1876), 9 Irving Street, London WC2H 7AT. Tel: 0171-930 5722. *Secretary*, Sir John Lucas-Tooth, Bt.

BOODLE'S (1762), 28 St James's Street, London SWIA 1HJ. Tel: 0171-930 7166. *Secretary*, R. J. Edmonds

BROOKS'S (1764), St James's Street, London SWIA 1LN. Tel: 0171-493 4411. *Secretary*, G. Snell

BUCK'S CLUB (1919), 18 Clifford Street, London WIX 1RG. Tel: 0171-734 6896. *Secretary*, Capt. P. Murison, RN

CALEDONIAN CLUB (1891), 9 Halkin Street, London SWIX 7DR. Tel: 0171-235 5162. *Secretary*, P. J. Varney

CANNING CLUB (1910), 94 Piccadilly, London WIV OBP. Tel: 0171-499 5163. *Secretary*, T. M. Harrington

CARLTON CLUB (1832), 69 St James's Street, London SWIA 1PJ. Tel: 0171-493 1164. *Secretary*, R. N. Linsley

CAVALRY AND GUARDS CLUB (1893), 127 Piccadilly, London WIV OPX. Tel: 0171-499 1261. *Secretary*, N. J. Walford

CHELSEA ARTS CLUB (1891), 143 Old Church Street, London SW3 6EB. Tel: 0171-376 3311. *Secretary*, D. Winterbottom

CITY LIVERY CLUB (1914), Sion College, Victoria Embankment, London EC4Y ODN. Tel: 0171-353 2431. *Hon. Secretary*, B. L. Morgan, CBE

CITY OF LONDON CLUB (1832), 19 Old Broad Street, London EC2N 1DS. Tel: 0171-588 7991. *Secretary*, G. S. Jones

CITY UNIVERSITY CLUB (1895), 50 Cornhill, London EC3V 3PD. Tel: 0171-626 8571. *Secretary*, Miss R. C. Graham

EAST INDIA CLUB (1849), 16 St James's Square, London SWIY 4LH. Tel: 0171-930 1000. *Secretary*, J. G. F. Stoy

FARMERS CLUB (1842), 3 Whitehall Court, London SWIA 2EL. Tel: 0171-930 3751. *Secretary*, Gp Capt. G. P. Carson

FLYFISHERS' CLUB (1884), 69 Brook Street, London WIY 2ER. Tel: 0171-629 5958. *Secretary*, Cdr. N. T. Fuller (retd)

GARRICK CLUB (1831), 15 Garrick Street, London WC2E 9AY. Tel: 0171-379 6478. *Secretary*, M. J. Harvey

GREEN ROOM CLUB (1877), 9 Adam Street, London WC2N 6AA. Tel: 0171-836 7453. *Secretary*, Ms J. McCarron

GROUCHO CLUB (1985), 45 Dean Street, London WIV 5AP. Tel: 0171-439 4685. *Company Secretary*, Miss Z. Noordin

HURLINGHAM CLUB (1869), Ranelagh Gardens, London SW6 3PR. Tel: 0171-736 8411. *Secretary*, P. H. Covell

KEMPTON PARK CLUB (1878), Kempton Park Racecourse, Sunbury-on-Thames, Middx TW16 5AQ. Tel: 01932-782292. *Secretary*, Mrs C. Milburn-Lee

KENNEL CLUB (1873), 1–5 Clarges Street, London WIY 8AB. Tel: 0171-493 6651. *Secretary*, Mrs B. E. Ormerod

LANSDOWNE CLUB (1934), 9 Fitzmaurice Place, London WIX 6JD. Tel: 0171-629 7200. *Secretary*, Lt.-Cdr. T. P. Havers (retd)

LONDON ROWING CLUB (1856), Embankment, Putney, London SW15 1LB. Tel: 0181-788 1400. *Hon. Secretary*, N. A. Smith

MCC (MARYLEBONE CRICKET CLUB) (1787), Lord's Cricket Ground, London NW8 8QN. Tel: 0171-289 1611. *Secretary*, R. D. V. Knight

NATIONAL CLUB (1845), c/o The Carlton Club, 69 St James's Street, London SWIA 1PJ. Tel: 0171-493 1164. *Hon. Secretary*, I. Nash

NATIONAL LIBERAL CLUB (1882), Whitehall Place, London SWIA 2HE. Tel: 0171-930 9871. *Secretary*, S. J. Roberts

NAVAL AND MILITARY CLUB (1862), 94 Piccadilly, London WIV OBP. Tel: 0171-499 5163. *Secretary*, Cdr. J. A. Holt, MBE

NAVAL CLUB (1946), 38 Hill Street, London WIX 8DP. Tel: 0171-493 7672. *Secretary*, Capt. R. J. Husk, CBE, RN (retd)

NEW CAVENDISH CLUB (1984), 44 Great Cumberland Place, London WIH 8BS. Tel: 0171-723 0391. *Secretary*, J. Malone-Lee

DEN NORSKE KLUB (1924), Norway House, 21–24 Cockspur Street, London SWIY 5BN. Tel: 0171-930 4084. *Secretary*, Ms J. P. Okkenhaug

ORIENTAL CLUB (1824), Stratford House, Stratford Place, London WIN OES. Tel: 0171-629 5126. *Secretary*, S. C. Doble

PORTLAND CLUB (1816), 42 Half Moon Street, London WIY 7RD. Tel: 0171-499 1523. *Secretary*, J. Burns, CBE

PRATT'S CLUB (1841), 14 Park Place, London SWIA 1LP. Tel: 0171-493 0397. *Secretary*, G. Snell

QUEEN'S CLUB, THE (1886), Palliser Road, London W14 9EQ. Tel: 0171-385 3421. *Secretary*, J. A. S. Edwardes

RAILWAY CLUB (1899), Room 208, 25 Marylebone Road, London NWI 5JS. Tel: 0173-7812175. *Hon. Secretary*, A. G. Wells

REFORM CLUB (1836), 104–105 Pall Mall, London SWIY 5EW. Tel: 0171-930 9374. *Secretary*, R. A. M. Forrest

ROEHAMPTON CLUB (1901), Roehampton Lane, London SW15 5LR. Tel: 0181-876 5505. *Chief Executive*, M. Yates

ROYAL AIR FORCE CLUB (1918), 128 Piccadilly, London WIV OPY. Tel: 0171-499 3456. *Secretary*, P. N. Owen

ROYAL AUTOMOBILE CLUB (1897), 89–91 Pall Mall, London SWIY 5HS. Tel: 0171-930 2345. *General Secretary*, Col. N. A. Johnson, OBE, TD

ROYAL OCEAN RACING CLUB (1925), 20 St James's Place, London SWIA INN. Tel: 0171-493 2248. *General Manager*, D. J. Minords, OBE

ROYAL OVER-SEAS LEAGUE (1910), Over-Seas House, Park Place, St James's Street, London SWIA 1LR. Tel: 0171-408 0214. *Director-General*, R. F. Newell

ROYAL THAMES YACHT CLUB (1775), 60 Knightsbridge, London SW1X 7LF. Tel: 0171-235 2121. *Secretary*, Capt. D. Goldson, RN (retd)

ST STEPHEN'S CONSTITUTIONAL CLUB (1870), 34 Queen Anne's Gate, London SW1H 9AB. Tel: 0171-222 1382. *Secretary*, L. D. Mawby

SAVAGE CLUB (1857), 1 Whitehall Place, London SW1A 2HD. Tel: 0171-930 8118. *Hon. Secretary*, D. Stirling

SAVILE CLUB (1868), 69 Brook Street, London W1Y 2ER. Tel: 0171-629 5462. *Secretary*, N. Storey

SKI CLUB OF GREAT BRITAIN (1903), 118 Eaton Square, London SW1W 9AF. Tel: 0171-245 1033. *Chief Executive*, Ms I. Grimsey

THAMES ROWING CLUB (1860), Embankment, Putney, London SW15 ILB. Tel: 0181-788 0798. *Hon. Secretary*, Mrs N. S. Powell

TRAVELLERS CLUB (1819), 106 Pall Mall, London SW1Y 5EP. Tel: 0171-930 8688. *Secretary*, M. S. Allcock

TURF CLUB (1868), 5 Carlton House Terrace, London SW1Y 5AQ. Tel: 0171-930 8555. *Secretary*, J. Rigby, OBE

UNITED OXFORD AND CAMBRIDGE UNIVERSITY CLUB (1972), 71 Pall Mall, London SW1Y 5HD. Tel: 0171-930 5151. *Secretary*, G. R. Buchanan

UNIVERSITY WOMEN'S CLUB (1886), 2 Audley Square, South Audley Street, London W1Y 6DB. Tel: 0171-499 2268. *Secretary*, J. Robson

VICTORIA CLUB (1863), 1 North Court, Great Peter Street, London SW1P 3LL. Tel: 0171-222 2357. *Secretary*, Ms S. David

VICTORY SERVICES CLUB (1907), 63–79 Seymour Street, London W2 2HF. Tel: 0171-723 4474. *General Manager*, G. F. Taylor

WHITE'S CLUB (1693), 37–38 St James's Street, London SW1A 1JG. Tel: 0171-493 6671. *Secretary*, D. C. Ward

WIG AND PEN CLUB (1908), 229–230 Strand, London WC2R 1BA. Tel: 0171-583 7255. *Administrator*, J. Reynolds

CLUBS OUTSIDE LONDON

Bath: BATH AND COUNTY CLUB (1865), Queens Parade, Bath BA1 2NJ. Tel: 01225-423732. *Secretary*, Mrs G. M. Jones

Birmingham: BIRMINGHAM CLUB (1872), Winston Churchill House, 8 Ethel Street, Birmingham B2 4BG. Tel: 0121-643 3357. *Hon. Secretary*, T. R. Pepper

ST PAUL'S CLUB (1859), 34 St Paul's Square, Birmingham B3 1QZ. Tel: 0121-236 1950. *Hon. Secretary*, E. A. Fellowes

Bishop Auckland: THE CLUB (1868), 1 Victoria Avenue, Bishop Auckland, Co. Durham DL14 7JH. Tel: 01388-603219. *Hon. Secretary*, R. Kellett

Blackburn: DISTRICT AND UNION CLUB (1849), Northwood, 1 West Park Road, Blackburn BB2 6DE. Tel: 01254-51474. *Hon. Secretary*, B. Haydock

Bristol: CLIFTON CLUB (1882), 22 The Mall, Clifton, Bristol BS8 4DS. Tel: 0117-973 5527. *Secretary*, M. G. Henry

Cambridge: AMATEUR DRAMATIC CLUB (1855), ADC Theatre, Park Street, Cambridge CB5 8AS. Tel: 01223-359547. *Secretary*, M. Mitchell

THE UNION (1815), Bridge Street, Cambridge CB2 1UB. Tel: 01223-361521. *Chief Clerk*, B. Thoday

Canterbury: KENT AND CANTERBURY CLUB (1868), The Elms, 17 Old Dover Road, Canterbury CT1 3JB. Tel: 01227-462181. *Secretary*, H. V. Brown, LVO, QPM, CPM

Cheltenham: NEW CLUB (1874), Montpellier Parade, Cheltenham GL50 1UD. Tel: 01242-523285. *Hon. Secretary*, N. S. Parrack

Chichester: THE REGNUM CLUB (1862), 45A South Street, Chichester, W. Sussex PO19 1DS. Tel: 01243-780219. *Chairman*, M. Pearson

Durham: COUNTY CLUB (1890), 52 Old Elvet, Durham DH1 3HJ. Tel: 0191-384 8156. *Secretary*, Mrs C. Arnot

DURHAM UNION SOCIETY (1842), 24 North Bailey, Durham DH1 3EP. Tel: 0191-384 3724. *Secretary*, Mrs E. M. Hardcastle

Guildford: COUNTY CLUB, 158 High Street, Guildford GU1 3HJ. Tel: 01483-575370. *Hon. Secretary*, R. W. D. Hemingway

Henley-on-Thames: LEANDER CLUB (1818), Henley-on-Thames, Oxon RG9 2LP. Tel: 01491-575782. *Hon. Secretary*, J. Beveridge

PHYLLIS COURT CLUB (1906), Marlow Road, Henley, Oxon RG9 2HT. Tel: 01491-574366. *Secretary*, R. Edwards

Hove: HOVE CLUB (1882), 28 Fourth Avenue, Hove, E. Sussex BN3 2PJ. Tel: 01273-730872. *Secretary*, J. C. Ager, RD

Leamington: TENNIS COURT CLUB (1846), 50 Bedford Street, Leamington, Warks CV32 5DT. Tel: 01926-424977. *Hon. Secretary*, O. D. R. Dixon

Leeds: LEEDS CLUB (1850), 3 Albion Place, Leeds LS1 6JL. Tel: 0113-242 1591. *Manager*, Mrs C. Myers

Leicester: LEICESTERSHIRE CLUB (1873), 9 Welford Place, Leicester LE1 6ZH. Tel: 0116-254 0399. *Hon. Secretary*, G. C. Jones

Liverpool: THE ATHENAEUM (1797), Church Alley, Liverpool L1 3DD. Tel: 0151-709 7770. *Secretary*, B. B. P. Kinsman

Macclesfield: OLD BOYS' AND PARK GREEN CLUB, 7 Churchside, Macclesfield, Cheshire SK10 1HG. Tel: 01625-423292. *Hon. Secretary*, M. J. Garrity

Manchester: ST JAMES'S CLUB, St James's House, Charlotte Street, Manchester M1 4DZ. Tel: 0161-236 2235. *Hon. Secretary*, H. J. J. Rylands

Newcastle upon Tyne: NORTHERN CONSTITUTIONAL CLUB (1882), 37 Pilgrim Street, Newcastle upon Tyne NE1 6QE. Tel: 0191-232 0884. *Hon. Secretary*, J. L. Browne

Northampton: NORTHAMPTON AND COUNTY CLUB (1873), George Row, Northampton NN1 1DF. Tel: 01604-32962. *Secretary*, J. Green

Norwich: NORFOLK CLUB (1770), 17 Upper King Street, Norwich NR3 1RB. Tel: 01603-610652. *Secretary*, A. J. M. Williamson

Nottingham: NOTTINGHAM AND NOTTS UNITED SERVICES CLUB (1920), Newdigate House, Castle Gate, Nottingham NG1 6AF. Tel: 0115-947 2138. *Hon. Secretary*, A. C. Ready

Oxford: FREWEN CLUB (1869), 98 St Aldate's, Oxford OX1 1BT. Tel: 01865-243816. *Hon. Secretary*, B. R. Boyt

VINCENT'S CLUB (1863), 1A King Edward Street, Oxford OX1 4HS. Tel: 01865-722984. *Steward*, H. Dean

Paignton: PAIGNTON CLUB (1882), The Esplanade, Paignton, Devon TQ4 6ED. Tel: 01803-559682. *Hon. Secretary*, P. Grafton

Shrewsbury: SALOP CLUB (1974), The Old House, Dogpole, Shrewsbury SY1 1EP. Tel: 01743-362182. *Secretary*, J. W. Rouse

Stourbridge: STOURBRIDGE OLD EDWARDIAN CLUB (1898), Drury Lane, Stourbridge, West Midlands DY8 1BL. Tel: 01384-395635. *Hon. Secretary*, D. J. Lucas

Teddington: ROYAL CANOE CLUB (1866), Trowlock Island, Teddington, Middx TW11 9QZ. Tel: 0181-977 5269. *Hon. Secretary*, Mrs J. S. Evans

WALES

Cardiff: CARDIFF AND COUNTY CLUB (1866), Westgate Street, Cardiff CF1 1DA. Tel: 01222-220846. *Hon. Secretary,* Cdr. J. E. Payn, RD

SCOTLAND

Aberdeen: ROYAL NORTHERN AND UNIVERSITY CLUB (1854/1889, amal. 1979), 9 Albyn Place, Aberdeen AB1 1YE. Tel: 01224-583292. *Secretary,* Miss R. A. Black
Ayr: AYR COUNTY CLUB (1872), Savoy Park Hotel, Ayr KA7 2UT. Tel: 01292-266112. *Hon. Secretary,* G. Hay
Edinburgh: NEW CLUB (1787), 86 Princes Street, Edinburgh EH2 2BB. Tel: 0131-226 4881. *Secretary,* A. D. Orr Ewing
Glasgow: GLASGOW ART CLUB (1867), 135 Wellington Street, Glasgow G2 2XE. Tel: 0141-248 3904. *Secretary,* L. J. McIntyre
   ROYAL SCOTTISH AUTOMOBILE CLUB (1899), 11 Blythswood Square, Glasgow G2 4AG. Tel: 0141-221 3850. *Secretary,* J. C. Lord
   WESTERN CLUB (1825), 32 Royal Exchange Square, Glasgow G1 3AB. Tel: 0141-221 2016. *Secretary,* D. H. Gifford

NORTHERN IRELAND

Belfast: ULSTER REFORM CLUB (1885), 4 Royal Avenue, Belfast BT1 1DA. Tel: 01232-323411. *Secretary,* Miss M. P. Mackintosh
Londonderry: NORTHERN COUNTIES CLUB (1880), 24 Bishop Street, Londonderry BT48 6PP. Tel: 01504-262012. *Hon. Secretary,* N. Dykes

CHANNEL ISLANDS

Guernsey: UNITED CLUB (1870), Pier Steps, St Peter Port, Guernsey GY1 2LF. Tel: 01481-725722. *Hon. Secretary,* G. D. E. Chaloner
Jersey: VICTORIA CLUB (1853), Beresford Street, St Helier, Jersey JE2 4WN. Tel: 01534-23381. *Secretary,* Miss C. Rynd

YACHT CLUBS

Bembridge: BEMBRIDGE SAILING CLUB (1886), Embankment Road, Bembridge, IOW, PO35 5NR. Tel: 01983-872237. *Hon. Secretary,* vacant
Birkenhead: ROYAL MERSEY YACHT CLUB (1844), Bedford Road East, Rock Ferry, Birkenhead, Merseyside L42 1LS. Tel: 0151-645 3204. *Hon. Secretary,* P. Bastow
Bridlington: ROYAL YORKSHIRE YACHT CLUB (1847), 1 Windsor Crescent, Bridlington, N. Humberside YO15 3HX. Tel: 01262-672041. *Secretary,* J. H. Evans
Burnham-on-Crouch: ROYAL CORINTHIAN YACHT CLUB (1872), Burnham-on-Crouch, Essex CM0 8AX. Tel: 01621-782105. *Hon. Secretary,* K. W. Bushell
Chichester: CHICHESTER YACHT CLUB (1965), Chichester Yacht Basin, Birdham, Chichester, W. Sussex PO20 7EJ. Tel: 01243-512918. *Secretary,* Mrs V. A. Allan
Cowes: ROYAL YACHT SQUADRON (1815), The Castle, Cowes, IOW, PO31 7QT. Tel: 01983-292191. *Secretary,* Maj. R. P. Rising, RM
   ROYAL LONDON YACHT CLUB (1838), The Parade, Cowes, IOW, PO31 7QS. Tel: 01983-299727. *Secretary,* Lt.-Col. R. J. Freeman-Wallace (retd)
Dover: ROYAL CINQUE PORTS YACHT CLUB (1872), 5 Waterloo Crescent, Dover, Kent CT16 1LA. Tel: 01304-206262. *Secretary,* Mrs C. A. Partridge

Fowey: ROYAL FOWEY YACHT CLUB (1881), Whitford Yard, Fowey, Cornwall PL23 1BH. Tel: 01726-833573. *Hon. Secretary,* E. P. Warren
Harwich: ROYAL HARWICH YACHT CLUB (1843), Woolverstone, Ipswich IP9 1AT. Tel: 01473-780319. *Secretary,* I. A. Murdoch
Kingswear: ROYAL DART YACHT CLUB (1866), Priory Street, Kingswear, Dartmouth, Devon TQ6 0AB. Tel: 01803-752496. *Hon. Secretary,* N. Baxter
Leigh-on-Sea: ESSEX YACHT CLUB (1890), HQS Bembridge, Foreshore, Leigh-on-Sea, Essex SS9 1BD. Tel: 01702-78404. *Hon. Secretary,* A. Manning
London: THE CRUISING ASSOCIATION (1908), CA House, 1 Northey Street, Limehouse Basin, London E14 8BT. Tel: 0171-537 2828. *General Secretary,* Mrs L. Hammett
   ROYAL CRUISING CLUB (1880), c/o Royal Thames Yacht Club, 60 Knightsbridge, London SW1X 7LF. Tel: 01276-65946. *Hon. Secretary,* P. Price
   ROYAL THAMES YACHT CLUB (1775), 60 Knightsbridge, London SW1X 7LF. Tel: 0171-235 2121. *Secretary,* Capt. D. Goldson, RN (retd)
Lowestoft: ROYAL NORFOLK AND SUFFOLK YACHT CLUB (1859), Royal Plain, Lowestoft, Suffolk NR33 0AQ. Tel: 01502-566726. *Hon. Secretary,* P. J. Hardiman
Lymington: ROYAL LYMINGTON YACHT CLUB (1922), Bath Road, Lymington, Hants SO41 3SE. Tel: 01590-672677. *Secretary,* Gp Capt J. D. Hutchinson (retd)
Plymouth: ROYAL WESTERN YACHT CLUB OF ENGLAND (1827), Queen Anne's Battery, Plymouth PL4 0TW. Tel: 01752-660077. *Secretary,* Maj. J. Lewis, RM
   ROYAL PLYMOUTH CORINTHIAN YACHT CLUB (1877), Madeira Road, Plymouth PL1 2NY. Tel: 01752-664327. *Hon. Secretary,* V. J. De Boo
Poole: EAST DORSET SAILING CLUB (1875), 352 Sandbanks Road, Poole, Dorset BH14 8HY. Tel: 01202-848948. *Hon. Secretary,* Ms H. Knott
   PARKSTONE YACHT CLUB (1895), Pearce Avenue, Poole, Dorset BH14 8EH. Tel: 01202-743610. *Secretary,* D. E. Norman
   POOLE HARBOUR YACHT CLUB (1949), 38 Salterns Way, Lilliput, Poole, Dorset BH14 8JR. Tel: 01202-707321. *Secretary,* J. N. J. Smith
   POOLE YACHT CLUB (1865), New Harbour Road West, Hamworthy, Poole, Dorset BH15 4AQ. Tel: 01202-672687. *Secretary/Manager,* Miss L. Clark
Portsmouth: ROYAL NAVAL CLUB AND ROYAL ALBERT YACHT CLUB (1867), 17 Pembroke Road, Portsmouth PO1 2NT. Tel: 01705-824491. *Secretary,* Cdr. N. J. Stone, OBE
Ramsgate: ROYAL TEMPLE YACHT CLUB (1857), 6 Westcliff Mansions, Ramsgate, Kent CT11 9HY. Tel: 01843-591766. *Hon. Secretary,* G. F. Randell
Southampton: ROYAL AIR FORCE YACHT CLUB (1932), Riverside House, Rope Walk, Hamble, Southampton SO31 4HD. Tel: 01703-452208. *Secretary,* Mrs S. E. Fullwood
   ROYAL SOUTHAMPTON YACHT CLUB, 1 Channel Way, Ocean Village, Southampton SO14 3QF. Tel: 01703-223352. *Secretary,* A. D. H. Porter
   ROYAL SOUTHERN YACHT CLUB (1837), Rope Walk, Hamble, Southampton SO31 4HB. Tel: 01703-453271. *Secretary,* Mrs J. A. Atkins
Torquay: ROYAL TORBAY YACHT CLUB (1863), Beacon Hill, Torquay, Devon TQ1 2BQ. Tel: 01803-292006. *Hon. Secretary,* J. N. Carleton-Stiff, TD
Westcliff-on-Sea: THAMES ESTUARY YACHT CLUB (1895), 3 The Leas, Westcliff-on-Sea, Essex SS0 7ST. Tel: 01702-345967. *Hon. Secretary,* D. Howard

Weymouth: ROYAL DORSET YACHT CLUB (1875),
11 Custom House Quay, Weymouth, Dorset DT4 8BG.
Tel: 01305-786258. *Secretary,* Mrs K. Mead

Windermere: ROYAL WINDERMERE YACHT CLUB (1860),
Fallbarrow Road, Bowness-on-Windermere,
Windermere, Cumbria LA23 3DJ. Tel: 015394-43106. *Hon.
Secretary,* P. V. Barraclough

Yarmouth: ROYAL SOLENT YACHT CLUB (1878), Yarmouth,
IOW, PO41 0NS. Tel: 01983-760256. *Secretary,* Mrs S.
Tribe

WALES

Beaumaris: ROYAL ANGLESEY YACHT CLUB (1802),
6–7 Green Edge, Beaumaris, Gwynedd LL58 8BY. Tel:
01248-810295. *Hon. Secretary,* V. G. Keep

Caernarfon: ROYAL WELSH YACHT CLUB (1847), Porth-Yr-
Aur, Caernarfon, Gwynedd LL55 1SW. Tel: 01286-
672599. *Hon. Secretary,* G. Tecwyn Evans

Penarth: PENARTH YACHT CLUB (1880). The Esplanade,
Penarth, S. Glamorgan CF64 3AU. Tel: 01222-708196.
Hon. Secretary, R. S. McGregor

Swansea: BRISTOL CHANNEL YACHT CLUB (1875),
744 Mumbles Road, Mumbles, Swansea SA3 4EL. Tel:
01792-366000. *Hon. Secretary,* B. G. T. Rees

SCOTLAND

Dundee: ROYAL TAY YACHT CLUB (1885), 34 Dundee
Road, Broughty Ferry, Dundee DD5 1LX. Tel: 01382-
477516. *Hon. Secretary,* S. Buchanan

Edinburgh: ROYAL FORTH YACHT CLUB (1868), Middle
Pier, Granton Harbour, Edinburgh EH5 1HF. Tel: 0131-
552 8560. *Hon. Secretary,* A. R. Woods

Glasgow: ROYAL WESTERN YACHT CLUB (1875), Lochaber,
20 Barclay Drive, Helensburgh, Dunbartonshire G84
9RB. Tel: 01436-672088. *Hon. Secretary,* D. G. M. Watson

Oban: ROYAL HIGHLAND YACHT CLUB (1881), Ythan,
Ferryfield Road, Connel, Argyll PA37 1SR. Tel: 01631-
710738. *Secretary,* Mrs A. Wood

Rhu: ROYAL NORTHERN AND CLYDE YACHT CLUB (1824,
amal. 1978), Rhu, Helensburgh, Dunbartonshire G84
8NG. Tel: 01436-820322. *Hon. Secretary,* B. C. Staig

NORTHERN IRELAND

Bangor: ROYAL ULSTER YACHT CLUB (1866), 101 Clifton
Road, Bangor, Co. Down BT20 5HY. Tel: 01247-270568.
Hon. Secretary, N. D. Brookes

CHANNEL ISLANDS

Jersey: ROYAL CHANNEL ISLANDS YACHT CLUB (1862), Le
Boulevard, Bulwarks, St Aubin, Jersey. Tel: 01534-
45783. *Hon. Secretary,* D. C. Dale

Societies and Institutions

Although this section is arranged in alphabetical order, organizations are usually listed by the keyword in their title. The date in parenthesis after the organization's title is the year of its foundation.

ABBEYFIELD SOCIETY, Abbeyfield House, 53 Victoria Street, St Albans, Herts ALI 3UW. Tel: 01727-857536. Housing for elderly people. *Chief Executive*, F. Murphy

ACCOUNTANTS, CHARTERED ASSOCIATION OF CERTIFIED (1904), 29 Lincoln's Inn Fields, London WC2A 3EE. Tel: 0171-242 6855. *Secretary*, Mrs A. L. Rose

ACCOUNTANTS, INSTITUTE OF COMPANY (1974), 40 Tyndalls Park Road, Bristol BS8 1PL. Tel: 0117-973 8261. *Director-General*, B. T. Banks

ACCOUNTANTS, INSTITUTE OF FINANCIAL (1916), Burford House, 44 London Road, Sevenoaks, Kent TN13 1AS. Tel: 01732-458080. *Chief Executive*, J. M. Dean

ACCOUNTANTS IN ENGLAND AND WALES, INSTITUTE OF CHARTERED (1880), Chartered Accountants' Hall, PO Box 433, Moorgate Place, London EC2P 2BJ. Tel: 0171-920 8100. *Secretary*, A. J. Colquhoun

ACCOUNTANTS IN IRELAND, INSTITUTE OF CHARTERED (1888), Chartered Accountants House, 87–89 Pembroke Road, Dublin 4. Tel: 00 353-1-6680400/01232-321600. *Director*, R. F. Hussey

ACCOUNTANTS OF SCOTLAND, THE INSTITUTE OF CHARTERED (1854), 27 Queen Street, Edinburgh EH2 1LA. Tel: 0131-225 5673. *Chief Executive*, P. W. Johnston

ACCOUNTING TECHNICIANS, ASSOCIATION OF (1980), 154 Clerkenwell Road, London ECIR 5AD. Tel: 0171-837 8600. *Secretary*, J. Hanson

ACE STUDY TOURS (formerly Association for Cultural Exchange), Babraham, Cambridge CB2 4AP. Tel: 01223-835055. *General Secretary*, P. B. Barnes

ACTION RESEARCH (1952), Vincent House, North Parade, Horsham, W. Sussex RHI2 2DP. Tel: 01403-210406. *Director*, Mrs A. Luther

ACTORS' BENEVOLENT FUND (1882), 6 Adam Street, London WC2N 6AA. Tel: 0171-836 6378. *General Secretary*, Mrs R. Stevens

ACTORS' CHARITABLE TRUST (1896), 365 Euston Road, London NWI 3AR. Tel: 0171-735 6955. *Chief Executive*, J. Dunn

ACTORS' CHURCH UNION (1899), St Paul's Church, Bedford Street, London WC2E 9ED. Tel: 0171-836 5221. *Senior Chaplain*, Canon W. Hall

ACTUARIES, INSTITUTE OF (1848), Staple Inn Hall, High Holborn, London WCIV 7QJ. Tel: 0171-242 0106. *Secretary-General*, A. G. Tait

ACTUARIES IN SCOTLAND, THE FACULTY OF (1856), 40–44 Thistle Street, Edinburgh EH2 1EN. Tel: 0131-220 4555. *Secretary*, W. W. Mair

ADMINISTRATIVE MANAGEMENT, INSTITUTE OF (1915), 40 Chatsworth Parade, Petts Wood, Orpington, Kent BR5 1RW. Tel: 01689-875555. *Chief Executive*, Prof. G. Robinson

ADULT SCHOOL ORGANIZATION, NATIONAL (1899), MASU Centre, Gaywood Croft, Cregoe Street, Birmingham BI5 2ED. Tel: 0121-622 3400. *General Secretary*, W. J. Scarle

ADVERTISING BENEVOLENT SOCIETY, NATIONAL (1913), 199–205 Old Marylebone Road, London NWI 5QP. Tel: 0171-723 8028. *Director*, Mrs D. Larkin

ADVERTISING, INSTITUTE OF PRACTITIONERS IN (1927), 44 Belgrave Square, London SWIX 8QS. Tel: 0171-235 7020. *Director-General*, N. Phillips

ADVERTISING STANDARDS AUTHORITY (1962), Brook House, 2 Torrington Place, London WCIE 7HW. Tel: 0171-580 5555. *Director-General*, Mrs M. Alderson

AERONAUTICAL SOCIETY, ROYAL (1866), 4 Hamilton Place, London WIV 0BQ. Tel: 0171-499 3515. *Director*, R. J. Kennett

AFRICAN INSTITUTE, INTERNATIONAL (1926), SOAS, Thornhaugh Street, Russell Square, London WCIH 0XG. Tel: 0171-323 6035. *Hon. Director*, Prof. D. Parkin

AFRICAN MEDICAL AND RESEARCH FOUNDATION, 11 Old Queen Street, London SWIH 9JA. Tel: 0171-233 0066. *Director*, A. Heroys

AGE CONCERN CYMRU, 4th Floor, 1 Cathedral Road, Cardiff CFI 9SD. Tel: 01222-371566. *Director*, R. W. Taylor

AGE CONCERN ENGLAND (1940), Astral House, 1268 London Road, London SWI6 4ER. Tel: 0181-679 8000. *Director-General*, Ms S. Greengross

AGE CONCERN NORTHERN IRELAND (1976), 3 Lower Crescent, Belfast BT7 1NR. Tel: 01232-245729. *Director*, C. J. Common

AGE CONCERN SCOTLAND (1943), 113 Rose Street, Edinburgh EH2 3DT. Tel: 0131-220 3345. *Director*, Ms M. O'Neill

AGED POOR SOCIETY, *see* ST JOSEPH'S SOCIETY FOR THE RELIEF OF THE AGED POOR

AGEING, CENTRE FOR POLICY ON (1947), 25–31 Ironmonger Row, London ECIV 3QP. Tel: 0171-253 1787. *Director*, Dr G. Dalley

AGEING, RESEARCH INTO (1978), Baird House, 15–17 St Cross Street, London ECIN 8UN. Tel: 0171-404 6878. *Director*, Mrs. E. Mills

AGRICULTURAL BENEVOLENT INSTITUTION, ROYAL (1860), Shaw House, 27 West Way, Oxford OX2 0QH. Tel: 01865-724931. *Chief Executive*, Brig. A. G. Staniforth, CBE

AGRICULTURAL BENEVOLENT INSTITUTION, ROYAL SCOTTISH (1897), Ingliston, Edinburgh, EH28 8NB. Tel: 0131-333 1023. *Director*, I. C. Purves-Hume

AGRICULTURAL ENGINEERS ASSOCIATION (1875), Samuelson House, Paxton Road, Orton Centre, Peterborough PE2 5LT. Tel: 01733-371381. *Director-General*, J. Vowles

AGRICULTURAL SOCIETY, EAST OF ENGLAND, East of England Showground, Peterborough PE2 6XE. Tel: 01733-234451. *Chief Executive*, T. Gibson, OBE

AGRICULTURAL SOCIETY OF ENGLAND, ROYAL (1838), National Agricultural Centre, Stoneleigh Park, Warks CV8 2LZ. Tel: 01203-696969. *Chief Executive*, C. Runge

AGRICULTURAL SOCIETY OF THE COMMONWEALTH, ROYAL (1957), 55 Sleaford Street, London SW8 5AB. Tel: 0171-978 1301. *Hon. Secretary*, F. R. Francis, CVO, MBE

AGRICULTURAL SOCIETY, ROYAL ULSTER (1826), The King's Hall, Balmoral, Belfast BT9 6GW. Tel: 01232-665225. *Chief Executive*, W. H. Yarr, OBE

AIR LEAGUE, THE (1909), 4 Hamilton Place, London WIV 0BQ. Tel: 0171-491 0470. *Director*, Gp Capt. E. R. Cox

ALCOHOLICS ANONYMOUS (1947), PO Box 1, Stonebow House, Stonebow, York YO1 2NJ. Tel: 01904-644026. *General Secretary*, J. Keeney

ALEXANDRA ROSE DAY (1912), 1 Castelnau, Barnes, London SW13 9RP. Tel: 0181-748 4824. *National Director*, Mrs G. Greenwood

ALLOTMENT AND LEISURE GARDENERS LIMITED, NATIONAL SOCIETY OF (1930), Hunters Road, Corby, Northants NN17 5JE. Tel: 01536-266576. *National Secretary*, G. W. Stokes

ALMSHOUSES, NATIONAL ASSOCIATION OF (1946), Billingbear Lodge, Wokingham, Berks RG11 5RU. Tel: 01344-52922. *Director*, D. M. Scott

ALZHEIMER'S DISEASE SOCIETY (1979), Gordon House, 10 Greencoat Place, London SW1P 1PH. Tel: 0171-306 0606. *Executive Director*, H. Cayton

AMNESTY INTERNATIONAL (1961), 99–119 Rosebery Avenue, London EC1R 4RE. Tel: 0171-814 6200. *Director*, D. Bull

ANAESTHETISTS OF GREAT BRITAIN AND IRELAND, ASSOCIATION OF (1932), 9 Bedford Square, London WC1B 3RA. Tel: 0171-631 1650. *Hon. Secretary*, Dr D. A. Saunders

ANCIENT BUILDINGS, SOCIETY FOR THE PROTECTION OF (1877), 37 Spital Square, London E1 6DY. Tel: 0171-377 1644. *Secretary*, P. Venning, FSA

ANCIENT MONUMENTS SOCIETY (1924), St Ann's Vestry Hall, 2 Church Entry, London EC4V 5HB. Tel: 0171-236 3934. *Secretary*, M. J. Saunders

ANGLO-ARAB ASSOCIATION (1961), The Arab British Centre, 21 Collingham Road, London SW5 0NU. Tel: 0171-373 8414. *Executive Director*, A. Lee

ANGLO-BELGIAN SOCIETY (1982), 45 West Common, Haywards Heath, W. Sussex RH16 2AJ. *Hon. Secretary*, Mrs A. M. Woodhead

ANGLO-BRAZILIAN SOCIETY (1943), 32 Green Street, London WIY 3FD. Tel: 0171-493 8493. *Secretary*, Mrs J. Byers

ANGLO-DANISH SOCIETY (1924), 25 New Street Square, London EC4A 3LN Tel: 01753-884846. *Chairman*, Sir Andrew Stark, KCMG, CVO

ANGLO-NORSE SOCIETY (1918), 25 Belgrave Square, London SW1X 8QD. Tel: 0171-235 7151. *Chairman*, Dame Gillian Brown, DCVO, CMG

ANIMAL CONCERN (SCOTLAND) (1988), 62 Old Dumbarton Road, Glasgow G3 8RE. Tel: 0141-334 6014. *Organizing Secretary*, J. F. Robins

ANIMAL HEALTH TRUST (1942), PO Box 5, Newmarket, Suffolk CB8 7DW. Tel: 01638-661111. *Director*, A. J. Higgins, PH.D.

ANTHROPOLOGICAL INSTITUTE, ROYAL (1843), 50 Fitzroy Street, London W1P 5HS. Tel: 0171-387 0455. *Director*, J. C. M. Benthall

ANTHROPOSOPHICAL SOCIETY IN GREAT BRITAIN (1923), Rudolf Steiner House, 35 Park Road, London NW1 6XT. Tel: 0171-723 4400. *General Secretary*, N. C. Thomas

ANTIQUARIES OF LONDON, SOCIETY OF (1717), Burlington House, Piccadilly, London W1V 0HS. Tel: 0171-734 0193. *General Secretary*, D. M. Evans, FSA

ANTIQUARIES OF SCOTLAND, SOCIETY OF (1780), National Museums of Scotland, York Buildings, Queen Street, Edinburgh EH2 1JD. Tel: 0131-225 7534, ext. 327. *Director*, Mrs F. Ashmore

ANTIQUE DEALERS' ASSOCIATION, BRITISH (1918), 20 Rutland Gate, London SW7 1BD. Tel: 0171-589 4128. *Secretary-General*, Mrs E. J. Dean

ANTI-SLAVERY INTERNATIONAL FOR THE PROTECTION OF HUMAN RIGHTS (1839), Unit 4, Stableyard, Broomgrove Road, London SW9 9TL. Tel: 0171-924 9555. *Director*, Miss L. Roberts

ANTI-VIVISECTION: BRITISH UNION FOR THE ABOLITION OF VIVISECTION (1898), 16A Crane Grove, London N7 8LB. Tel: 0171-700 4888. *Director (acting)*, Dr M. Eames

ANTI-VIVISECTION SOCIETY, NATIONAL (1875), 261 Goldhawk Road, London W12 9PE. Tel: 0181-846 9777. *Director*, Ms J. Creamer

APOSTLESHIP OF THE SEA (1920), Stella Maris, 66 Dock Road, Tilbury, Essex RM18 7BX. Tel: 01375-845641. *National Director*, Revd J. Maguire

APOTHECARIES OF LONDON, SOCIETY OF (1617), 14 Black Friars Lane, London EC4V 6EJ. Tel: 0171-236 1189. *Clerk*, R. J. Stringer

ARBITRATORS, CHARTERED INSTITUTE OF (1915), 24 Angel Gate, City Road, London EC1V 2RS. Tel: 0171-837 4483. *Secretary-General*, K. R. K. Harding

ARCHAEOLOGICAL ASSOCIATION, CAMBRIAN (1846), The Laurels, Westfield Road, Newport, Gwent NP9 4ND. Tel: 01633-262449. *General Secretary*, Dr J. M. Hughes

ARCHAEOLOGICAL INSTITUTE, ROYAL (1843), c/o Society of Antiquaries of London, Burlington House, Piccadilly, London W1V 0HS. *Secretary*, J. G. Coad, FSA

ARCHAEOLOGY, COUNCIL FOR BRITISH (1944), Bowes Morrell House, 111 Walmgate, York YO1 2UA. Tel: 01904-671417. *Director*, R. K. Morris

ARCHITECTS, ROYAL INSTITUTE OF BRITISH (1834), 66 Portland Place, London W1N 4AD. Tel: 0171-580 5533. *President*, Dr F. Duffy; *Director-General*, A. Reid, PH.D.

ARCHITECTS AND SURVEYORS INSTITUTE (1926), St Mary House, 15 St Mary Street, Chippenham, Wilts SN15 3WD. Tel: 01249-444505. *Chief Executive*, C. G. A. Nash, OBE

ARCHITECTS BENEVOLENT SOCIETY (1850), 66 Portland Place, London W1N 4AD. Tel: 0171-580 2823. *Hon. Secretary*, R. J. Double

ARCHITECTS IN SCOTLAND, ROYAL INCORPORATION OF (1922), 15 Rutland Square, Edinburgh EH1 2BE. Tel: 0131-229 7545. *Secretary*, S. Tombs

ARCHITECTS REGISTRATION COUNCIL OF THE UNITED KINGDOM (1931), 73 Hallam Street, London W1N 6EE. Tel: 0171-580 5861. *Registrar*, D. W. Smart

ARCHITECTURAL ASSOCIATION INC. (1847), 34–36 Bedford Square, London WC1B 3ES. Tel: 0171-636 0974. *Secretary*, E. Le Maistre

ARCHITECTURAL HERITAGE FUND, THE (1976), 27 John Adam Street, London WC2N 6HX. Tel: 0171-925 0199. *Secretary*, Lady Weir

ARCHIVISTS, SOCIETY OF (1947), Information House, 20–24 Old Street, London EC1V 9AP. Tel: 0171-253 5087. *Executive Secretary*, P. S. Cleary

ARK ENVIRONMENTAL FOUNDATION, THE (1988), Suite 640-3, Linen Hall, 162-8 Regent Street, London W1R 5TB. Tel: 0171-439 4567. *Co-ordinator*, Ms J. Vaus

ARLIS/UK AND IRELAND, THE ART LIBRARIES SOCIETY (1969). *Administrator*, Ms S. French, 18 College Road, Bromsgrove, Worcs B60 2NE. Tel: 01527-579298

ARMY BENEVOLENT FUND (1944), 41 Queen's Gate, London SW7 5HR. Tel: 0171-584 5232. *Controller*, Maj.-Gen. G. M. G. Swindells, CB

ARMY CADET FORCE ASSOCIATION (1930), E Block, Duke of York's HQ, London SW3 4RR. Tel: 0171-730 9733/4. *General Secretary*, Brig. R. B. MacGregor-Oakford, CBE, MC

ART, ROYAL CAMBRIAN ACADEMY OF (1882), Crown Lane, Conwy, Gwynedd LL32 8BH. Tel: 01492-593413. *Curator and Secretary*, Ms V. Macdonald

ART COLLECTIONS FUND, NATIONAL (1903), Millais House, 7 Cromwell Place, London SW7 2JN. Tel: 0171-225 4800. *Director*, D. Barrie

ARTHRITIS AND RHEUMATISM COUNCIL FOR RESEARCH (1936), Copeman House, St Mary's Court, St Mary's Gate, Chesterfield, Derbys S41 7TD. Tel: 01246-558033. *Chief Executive*, J. Norton

ARTHRITIS CARE (1949), 18 Stephenson Way, London NW1 2HD. Tel: 0171-916 1500. *Secretary*, J. R. Collins

ARTISTS' GENERAL BENEVOLENT INSTITUTION (1814) AND ARTISTS' ORPHAN FUND (1871), Burlington House, Piccadilly, London W1V 0DJ. Tel: 0171-734 1193. *Secretary*, Ms A. Connett-Dance

ARTISTS, FEDERATION OF BRITISH, 17 Carlton House Terrace, London SW1Y 5BD. Tel: 0171-930 6844. *Chairman*, J. Walton

ARTS, NATIONAL CAMPAIGN FOR THE (1984), Francis House, Francis Street, London SW1P 1DE. Tel: 0171-828 4448. *Director*, Ms J. Edwards

ASIAN FAMILY COUNSELLING SERVICE (1985), 74 The Avenue, London W13 8LB. Tel: 0181-997 5749. *National Director*, Mrs R. Atma

ASLIB, The Association for Information Management (1924), Information House, 20–24 Old Street, London EC1V 9AP. Tel: 0171-253 4488. *Chief Executive*, R. Bowes

ASTHMA CAMPAIGN, NATIONAL (1927), Providence House, Providence Place, London N1 0NT. Tel: 0171-226 2260. *Chief Executive*, Ms M. Letts

ASTRONOMICAL ASSOCIATION, BRITISH (1890), Burlington House, Piccadilly, London W1V 9AG. Meetings at the Scientific Societies Lecture Theatre, 23 Savile Row, London W1X 1AB. *Assistant Secretary*, Miss P. M. Barber

ASTRONOMICAL SOCIETY, ROYAL (1820), Burlington House, Piccadilly, London W1V 0NL. Tel: 0171-734 3307. *President*, Prof. Sir Martin Rees, FRS; *Executive Secretary*, J. E. Lane

ATS/WRAC BENEVOLENT FUNDS (1964), Block 10, AGC Centre, Worthy Down, Winchester, Hants SO21 2RG. Tel: 01962-887612/478. *Secretaries*, Mrs A. H. S. Matthews; Lt.-Col. D. Dunn

AUDIT BUREAU OF CIRCULATIONS LTD (1931), Black Prince Yard, 207–209 High Street, Berkhamsted, Herts HP4 1AD. Tel: 01442-870800. *Secretary*, J. Beadell

AUTHORS, SOCIETY OF (1884), 84 Drayton Gardens, London SW10 9SB. Tel: 0171-373 6642. *General Secretary*, M. Le Fanu, OBE

AUTOMOBILE ASSOCIATION (1905), Norfolk House, Priestley Road, Basingstoke, Hants RG24 9NY. Tel: 01256-20123. *Director-General*, S. Dyer, CBE

AVICULTURAL SOCIETY (1894), c/o Bristol Zoological Gardens, Clifton, Bristol BS8 3HA. *Hon. Secretary*, G. R. Greed

AYRSHIRE CATTLE SOCIETY OF GREAT BRITAIN AND IRELAND (1877), 1 Racecourse Road, Ayr KA7 2DE. Tel: 01292-267123. *General Secretary*, S. J. Thomson

BACK PAIN ASSOCIATION, NATIONAL (1968), 16 Elm Tree Road, Teddington, Middx TW11 8ST. Tel: 0181-977 5474. *Executive Director*, G. Thomas

BALTIC AIR CHARTER ASSOCIATION (1949), 6 The Office Village, Romford Road, London E15 4EA. Tel: 0181-519 3909. *Hon. Executive*, D. Shepherd

BALTIC EXCHANGE, THE (1903), St Mary Axe, London EC3A 8BH. Tel: 0171-623 5501. *Chief Executive*, J. Buckley

BALTIC EXCHANGE CHARITABLE SOCIETY (1978), 38 St Mary Axe, London EC3A 8BH. Tel: 0171-369 1643/4. *Secretary*, D. A. Painter

BALZAN FOUNDATION – PRIZE, INTERNATIONAL (1956), Piazzetta U. Giordano 4, Milan 20122, Italy. Awards prizes for literature; moral sciences and the arts; physical, mathematical and natural sciences; medicine; humanity, peace and brotherhood. *Secretary-General*, Dr F. M. Tedeschi

BANKERS, CHARTERED INSTITUTE OF (1879), 10 Lombard Street, London EC3V 9AS. Tel: 0171-623 3531. *Chief Executive*, G. Shreeve

BANKERS IN SCOTLAND, CHARTERED INSTITUTE OF (1875), 19 Rutland Square, Edinburgh EH1 2DE. Tel: 0131-229 9869. *Chief Executive*, Dr C. W. Munn

BAPTIST MISSIONARY SOCIETY (1792), Baptist House, PO Box 49, 129 Broadway, Didcot, Oxon OX11 8XA. Tel: 01235-512077. *General Secretary*, Revd R. G. S. Harvey

BAR ASSOCIATION FOR LOCAL GOVERNMENT AND THE PUBLIC SERVICE (1945), c/o Milton Keynes Borough Council, Civic Offices, 1 Saxon Gate East, Milton Keynes MK9 3HG. Tel: 01908-682205. *Chairman*, P. G. Stivadoros

BARNARDO'S (1866), Tanners Lane, Barkingside, Ilford, Essex IG6 1QG. Tel: 0181-550 8822. *Senior Director*, R. Singleton

BARONETAGE, STANDING COUNCIL OF THE (1898), The Church House, Bibury, Cirencester, Glos GL7 5NR. Tel: 0171-938 2955. *Chairman*, Sir Tobias Clarke, Bt.

BARRISTERS' BENEVOLENT ASSOCIATION (1873), 14 Gray's Inn Square, London WC1R 5JP. Tel: 0171-242 4761. *Secretary*, Mrs A. Ashley

BEECHAM TRUST, SIR THOMAS (1946), Denton House, Denton, Harleston, Norfolk IP20 0AA. Tel: 01986-788780. *Secretary*, Shirley, Lady Beecham

BEE-KEEPERS' ASSOCIATION, BRITISH (1874), National Agricultural Centre, Stoneleigh Park, Kenilworth, Warks CV8 2LZ. Tel: 01203-696679. *General Secretary*, A. C. Waring

BIBLE SOCIETY, BRITISH AND FOREIGN (1804), Stonehill Green, Westlea, Swindon SN5 7DG. Tel: 01793-418100. *Executive Director*, N. Crosbie

BIBLIOGRAPHICAL SOCIETY (1892), National Art Library, Victoria and Albert Museum, London SW7 2RL. Tel: 0171-938 8312. *Hon. Secretary,* D. Pearson

BIBLIOGRAPHICAL SOCIETY, EDINBURGH (1890), c/o New College Library, Mound Place, Edinburgh EH1 2LU. Tel: 0131-650 8956. *Hon. Secretary,* Dr M. C. T. Simpson

BIOCHEMICAL SOCIETY (1911), 59 Portland Place, London WIN 3AJ. Tel: 0171-580 5530. *Executive Secretary,* G. D. Jones

BIOLOGICAL ENGINEERING SOCIETY (1960), Royal College of Surgeons, Lincoln's Inn Fields, London WC2A 3PN. Tel: 0171-242 7750. *Hon. Secretary,* Dr R. E. Trotman

BIOLOGY, INSTITUTE OF (1950), 20–22 Queensberry Place, London SW7 2DZ. Tel: 0171-581 8333. *General Secretary,* Dr. R. H. Priestley

BIRMINGHAM AND MIDLAND INSTITUTE (1854) and PRIESTLEY LIBRARY (1779), Margaret Street, Birmingham B3 3BS. Tel: 0121-236 3591. *Administrator,* P. A. Fisher

BIRTHDAY TRUST FUND, NATIONAL (1928), 27 Sussex Place, London NW1 4RG.Tel: 0171-706 3903. For extension of maternity services

BLIND, GUIDE DOGS FOR THE, *see* GUIDE DOGS FOR THE BLIND ASSOCIATION

BLIND, NATIONAL LIBRARY FOR THE (1882), Cromwell Road, Bredbury, Stockport, Cheshire SK6 2SG. Tel: 0161-494 0217. *Chief Executive,* Mrs P. M. Lynn

BLIND PEOPLE, ACTION FOR (1857), 14–16 Verney Road, London SE16 3DZ. Tel: 0171-732 8771. *Director,* S. Remington

BLIND, ROYAL LONDON SOCIETY FOR THE (1838), 105 Salusbury Road, London NW6 6RH. Tel: 0171-624 8844. *Chief Executive,* P. Talbot

BLIND, ROYAL NATIONAL COLLEGE FOR THE (1872), College Road, Hereford HR1 1EB. Tel: 01432-265725. *Principal,* C. Housby-Smith, PH.D.

BLIND, ROYAL NATIONAL INSTITUTE FOR THE, *see* ROYAL NATIONAL INSTITUTE FOR THE BLIND

BLIND, ROYAL SCHOOL FOR THE, *see* SeeAbility

BLOOD TRANSFUSION ASSOCIATION, SCOTTISH NATIONAL (1940), Totleywells House, Winchburgh, Broxburn, West Lothian EH52 6QJ. Tel: 0131-319 2155. *Secretary,* P. C. Taylor

BLOOD TRANSFUSION SERVICE, NATIONAL (1948), National Blood Authority, Oak House, Reeds Crescent, Watford, Herts WD1 1QH. Tel: 01923-212121. *Chief Executive,* J. Adey

BLUE CROSS (1897), Shilton Road, Burford, Oxon OX18 4PF. Tel: 01993-822651. *Secretary,* A. Kennard, MBE

BODLEIAN, FRIENDS OF THE (1925), Bodleian Library, Oxford OX1 3BG. Tel: 01865-277022/234. *Secretary,* G. Groom

BOOK AID INTERNATIONAL (1954), 39–41 Coldharbour Lane, London SE5 9NR. Tel: 0171-733 3577. *Director,* Mrs S. Harrity

BOOKSELLERS ASSOCIATION OF GREAT BRITAIN AND IRELAND (1895), Minister House, 272 Vauxhall Bridge Road, London SW1V 1BA. Tel: 0171-834 5477. *Chief Executive,* T. E. Godfray

BOOK TRADE BENEVOLENT SOCIETY (1967), Dillon Lodge, The Retreat, Kings Langley, Herts WD4 8LT. Tel: 01923-263128. *Executive Secretary,* Mrs A. R. Brown

BOOK TRUST (1986), Book House, 45 East Hill, London SW18 2QZ. Tel: 0181-870 9055. *Executive Director,* B. Perman

BORN FREE FOUNDATION, THE (1984), Cherry Tree Cottage, Coldharbour, Dorking, Surrey RH5 6HA. Tel: 01306-712091. *Director,* W. Travers

BOTANICAL SOCIETY OF THE BRITISH ISLES (1836), The Natural History Museum, Cromwell Road, London SW7 5BD. Tel: 0171-938 8701. *Hon. General Secretary,* Mrs M. Briggs, MBE

BOTANICAL SOCIETY OF SCOTLAND, c/o Royal Botanic Garden, Inverleith Row, Edinburgh EH3 5LR. Tel: 0131-552 7171. *Hon. General Secretary,* R. Galt

BOY SCOUTS ASSOCIATION, *see* SCOUT ASSOCIATION

BOYS' BRIGADE (1883), Felden Lodge, Hemel Hempstead, Herts HP3 0BL. Tel: 01442-231681. *Brigade Secretary,* S. Jones, OBE

BOYS' AND GIRLS' CLUBS OF NORTHERN IRELAND (1940), 2nd Floor, 38 Dublin Road, Belfast BT2 7HN. Tel: 01232-241924. *General Secretary,* K. Culbert

BREWING, INSTITUTE OF (1886), 33 Clarges Street, London W1Y 8EE. Tel: 0171-499 8144. *Chief Executive,* P. W. E. Istead

BRIDEWELL ROYAL HOSPITAL (1553), Witley, Godalming, Surrey GU8 5SG. Tel: 01428-682371. *Registrar,* Mrs J. Benyon

BRITAIN-NEPAL SOCIETY (1960), 3c Gunnersbury Avenue, London W5 3NH. Tel: 0181-992 0173. *Hon. Secretary,* Mrs P. Mellor

BRITAIN-RUSSIA CENTRE (1959), 14 Grosvenor Place, London SW1X 7HW. Tel: 0171-235 2116. *Director,* Dr I. Elliot

BRITISH AND FOREIGN SCHOOL SOCIETY (1808), Richard Mayo Hall, Eden Street, Kingston upon Thames, Surrey KT1 1HZ. Tel: 0181-546 2379. *Secretary,* S. M. A. Banister

BRITISH INSTITUTE IN EASTERN AFRICA (1959), 20–22 Queensberry Place, London SW7 2DZ. Tel: 0171-584 4653. *London Secretary,* Mrs J. Moyo

BRITISH INSTITUTE OF ARCHAEOLOGY AT ANKARA (1948), 31–34 Gordon Square, London WC1H 0PY. Tel: 0171-388 2361. *London Secretary,* Ms G. Coulthard

BRITISH INSTITUTE OF PERSIAN STUDIES (1961), 63 Old Street, London EC1V 9HX. Tel: 0171-490 4404. *Assistant Secretary,* Ms J. Dryden

BRITISH INTERPLANETARY SOCIETY (1933), 27–29 South Lambeth Road, London SW8 1SZ. Tel: 0171-735 3160. *Executive Secretary,* Ms S. A. Jones

BRITISH ISRAEL WORLD FEDERATION (1919), 8 Blades Court, Deodar Road, London SW15 2NU. Tel: 0181-877 9010. *Secretary,* A. E. Gibb

BRITISH LEGION, ROYAL (1921), 48 Pall Mall, London SW1Y 5JY. Tel: 0171-973 0633. *General Secretary,* Lt.-Col. P. C. E. Creasy, OBE, FCIS

BRITISH LEGION SCOTLAND, ROYAL (1921), New Haig House, Logie Green Road, Edinburgh EH7 4HR. Tel: 0131-557 2782. *General Secretary,* Maj.-Gen. J. D. MacDonald, CB, CBE

BRITISH MEDICAL ASSOCIATION (1832), BMA House, Tavistock Square, London WC1H 9JP. Tel: 0171-387 4499. *Chairman,* Dr A. Macara; *Secretary,* Dr E. M. Armstrong

BRITISH NATIONAL PARTY (1982), PO Box 117, Welling, Kent DA16 3DW. Tel: 0181-316 4721. *Chairman,* J. Tyndall

BRITISH RED CROSS (1870), 9 Grosvenor Crescent, London SW1X 7EJ. Tel: 0171-235 5454. *Director-General*, M. R. Whitlam

BRITISH SCHOOL OF ARCHAEOLOGY IN JERUSALEM (1919), 21 Buccleuch Place (Top Flat), University of Edinburgh, Edinburgh EH8 9LN. Tel: 0131-650 3975. *President*, P. R. S. Moorey, PH.D., FBA

BTCV (BRITISH TRUST FOR CONSERVATION VOLUNTEERS) (1970), 36 St Mary's Street, Wallingford, Oxon OX10 OEU. Tel: 01491-839766. *Chief Executive*, T. Flood

BTG (BRITISH TECHNOLOGY GROUP INTERNATIONAL) PLC, 101 Newington Causeway, London SE1 6BU. Tel: 0171-403 6666. *Chief Executive*, I. A. Harvey

BUDDHIST SOCIETY, THE (1924), 58 Eccleston Square, London SW1V 1PH. Tel: 0171-834 5858. *General Secretary*, R. C. Maddox

BUDGERIGAR SOCIETY, THE (1925), 49–53 Hazelwood Road, Northampton NN1 1LG. Tel: 01604-24549. *General Secretary*, D. Whittaker

BUILDING, CHARTERED INSTITUTE OF (1834), Englemere, Kings Ride, Ascot, Berks SL5 8BJ. Tel: 01344-23355. *Chief Executive*, K. Banbury

BUILDING ENGINEERS, ASSOCIATION OF (1925), Jubilee House, Billing Brook Road, Weston Favell, Northampton NN3 8NW. Tel: 01604-404121. *Chief Executive*, B. D. Hughes

BUILDING SERVICES ENGINEERS, CHARTERED INSTITUTION OF (1897), Delta House, 222 Balham High Road, London SW12 9BS. Tel: 0181-675 5211. *Secretary*, A. V. Ramsay

BUILDING SOCIETIES ASSOCIATION (1936), 3 Savile Row, London W1X 1AF. Tel: 0171-437 0655. *Director-General*, A. Coles

BUSINESS AND PROFESSIONAL WOMEN UK LTD (1938), 23 Ansdell Street, London W8 5BN. Tel: 0171-938 1729. *General Secretary*, Mrs R. Bangle

BUSINESS ARCHIVES COUNCIL (1934), 4 Maguire Street, London SE1 2NQ. Tel: 0171-407 6110. *Secretary-General*, Ms W. S. Quinn

CADET FORCE ASSOCIATION, COMBINED (1952), 'E' Block, The Duke of York's HQ, London SW3 4RR. Tel: 0171-730 9733. *Secretary*, Brig. R. B. MacGregor-Oakford, CBE, MC

CAFOD (CATHOLIC FUND FOR OVERSEAS DEVELOPMENT) (1962), Romero Close, Stockwell Road, London SW9 9TY. Tel: 0171-733 7900. *Director*, J. Filochowski

CALOUSTE GULBENKIAN FOUNDATION (1956), 98 Portland Place, London W1N 4ET. Tel: 0171-636 5313. *Director*, B. Whitaker

CAMBRIDGE PRESERVATION SOCIETY (1929), Wandlebury Ring, Gog Magog Hills, Babraham, Cambridge CB2 4AE. Tel: 01223-243830. *Secretary*, G. Brewster

CAMERON FUND, THE (1971), Tavistock House North, Tavistock Square, London WC1H 9HR. Tel: 0171-388 0796. *Secretary*, Mrs J. Martin

CAMPAIGN FOR NUCLEAR DISARMAMENT (CND) (1958), 162 Holloway Road, London N7 8DQ. Tel: 0171-700 2393. *Chair*, Ms J. Bloomfield

CANCER RELIEF MACMILLAN FUND (1911), Anchor House, 15–19 Britten Street, London SW3 3TZ. Tel: 0171-351 7811. *Chief Executive*, D. Scott, OBE

CANCER RESEARCH CAMPAIGN, 10 Cambridge Terrace, London NW1 4JL. Tel: 0171-224 1333. *Director-General*, D. de Peyer

CANCER RESEARCH FUND, IMPERIAL (1902), PO Box 123, Lincoln's Inn Fields, London WC2A 3PX. Tel: 0171-269 3032. *Secretary*, Miss M. J. Craggs

CANCER RESEARCH, INSTITUTE OF, Royal Cancer Hospital, 17A Onslow Gardens, London SW7 3AL. Tel: 0171-352 8133. *Chief Executive*, Prof. P. Garland

CANCER UNITED PATIENTS, BRITISH ASSOCIATION OF (BACUP) (1985), 3 Bath Place, Rivington Street, London EC2A 3JR. Tel: 0171-696 9003. *Chief Executive*, Ms J. Mossman

CARERS NATIONAL ASSOCIATION (1988), Ruth Pitter House, 20–25 Glasshouse Yard, London EC1A 4JS. Tel: 0171-490 8818. *Director*, Ms J. Pitkeathley, OBE

CARNEGIE DUNFERMLINE TRUST (1903), Abbey Park House, Dunfermline, Fife KY12 7PB. Tel: 01383-723638. *Secretary*, W. C. Runciman

CARNEGIE HERO FUND TRUST (1908), Abbey Park House, Dunfermline, Fife KY12 7PB. Tel: 01383-723638. *Secretary*, W. C. Runciman

CARNEGIE UNITED KINGDOM TRUST (1913), Comely Park House, Dunfermline, Fife KY12 7EJ. Tel: 01383-721445. *Secretary*, C. J. Naylor, OBE

CATHEDRALS FABRIC COMMISSION FOR ENGLAND (1949), Fielden House, Little College Street, London SW1P 3SH. Tel: 0171-222 3793. *Secretary*, Dr. R. Gem

CATHOLIC CENTRAL LIBRARY (1914), St Francis Friary, 47 Francis Street, London SW1P 1QR. Tel: 0171-834 6128

CATHOLIC ENQUIRY CENTRE (1954), 120 West Heath Road, London NW3 7TY. Tel: 0181-455 9871. *Director*, Revd P. Billington

CATHOLIC RECORD SOCIETY (1904), c/o 114 Mount Street, London W1Y 6AH. *Hon. Secretary*, Dr L. Gooch

CATHOLIC TRUTH SOCIETY (1868), 192 Vauxhall Bridge Road, London SW1V 1PD. Tel: 0171-834 4392. *General Secretary*, D. Murphy

CATHOLIC UNION OF GREAT BRITAIN (1872), St Maximilian Kolbe House, 63 Jeddo Road, London W12 9EE. Tel: 0181-749 1321. *President*, The Lord Craigmyle; *Secretary*, P. H. Higgs

CATTLE BREEDERS' ASSOCIATION, NATIONAL, Lawford Grange, Lawford Heath, Rugby, Warks CV23 9HG. Tel: 01788-565264. *Secretary*, R. W. Kershaw-Dalby

CATTLE BREEDER'S CLUB LTD, BRITISH (1945), 16A Swan Street, Loughborough, Leics LE11 0BL. Tel: 01509-261810. *Secretary*, M. J. Peasnall

CENTRAL AND CECIL HOUSING TRUST (1926), 2 Priory Road, Kew, Richmond, Surrey TW9 3DG. Tel: 0181-940 9828. *Secretary*, G. Brighton

CENTRAL BUREAU FOR EDUCATIONAL VISITS AND EXCHANGES (1948), Seymour Mews House, Seymour Mews, London W1H 9PE. Tel: 0171-486 5101. *Director* A. H. Male

CHADWICK TRUST (1895), Department of Civil and Environmental Engineering, University College London, Gower Street, London WC1E 6BT. Tel: 0171-380 7327. For the promotion of health and prevention of disease. *Secretary to the Trustees*, I. K. Orchardson PH.D.

CHANTREY BEQUEST (1875), Royal Academy of Arts, Burlington House, Piccadilly, London W1V 0DS. Tel: 0171-439 7438. *Secretary*, P. Rodgers

CHARITIES AID FOUNDATION (1974), 48 Pembury Road, Tonbridge, Kent TN9 2JD. Tel: 01732-771333. *Executive Director*, M. Brophy

CHEMICAL ENGINEERS, INSTITUTION OF (1922), The Davis Building, 165–171 Railway Terrace, Rugby, Warks CV21 3HQ. Tel: 01788-578214. *Chief Executive and Secretary*, Dr T. J. Evans

CHEMISTRY, ROYAL SOCIETY OF, Burlington House, Piccadilly, London W1V 0BN. Tel: 0171-437 8656. *Secretary-General*, Dr T. D. Inch

CHESHIRE (LEONARD) FOUNDATION, *see* LEONARD CHESHIRE FOUNDATION

CHESS FEDERATION, BRITISH (1904), 9A Grand Parade, St Leonards-on-Sea, E. Sussex TN38 0DD. Tel: 01424-442500. *General Manager*, Mrs G. White

CHEST, HEART AND STROKE ASSOCIATION, *see* STROKE ASSOCIATION, THE

CHILDBIRTH TRUST, NATIONAL (1956), Alexandra House, Oldham Terrace, London W3 6NH. Tel: 0181-992 8637. *Director*, Ms C. Swarbrick

CHILDREN 1ST (Royal Scottish Society for Prevention of Cruelty to Children) (1884), Melville House, 41 Polwarth Terrace, Edinburgh EH11 1NU. Tel: 0131-337 8539. *Chief Executive*, A. M. M. Wood, OBE

CHILDREN'S SOCIETY, THE (1881), Edward Rudolf House, Margery Street, London WC1X 0JL. Tel: 0171-837 4299. *Chief Executive*, I. Sparks

CHINA ASSOCIATION, THE (1889), Swire House, 59 Buckingham Gate, London SW1E 6AJ. Tel: 0171-821 3220. *Executive Director*, Brig. B. G. Hickey, OBE, MC

CHIROPODISTS AND PODIATRISTS, SOCIETY OF (1945), 53 Welbeck Street, London W1M 7HE. Tel: 0171-486 3381. *General Secretary*, J. G. C. Trouncer

CHIROPRACTIC ASSOCIATION, BRITISH (1925), 29 Whitley Street, Reading, Berks RG2 0EG. Tel: 01734-757557. *Executive Director*, Miss S. Wakefield

CHOIRS SCHOOLS ASSOCIATION (1921), The Minster School, Deangate, York YO1 2JA. Tel: 01904-625217. *Administrator*

CHRISTIAN ACTION, 125 Kennington Road, London SE11 6SF. Tel: 0171-735 2372. *Hon. Director*, Revd Canon E. James

CHRISTIAN AID (1945), PO Box 100, London SE1 7RT. Tel: 0171-620 4444. *Director*, Revd M. H. Taylor

CHRISTIAN EDUCATION COUNCIL, NATIONAL (1809), 1020 Bristol Road, Selly Oak, Birmingham B29 6LB. Tel: 0121-472 4242. *Executive Officer*, Revd J. Gear

CHRISTIAN EDUCATION MOVEMENT (1965), Royal Buildings, Victoria Street, Derby DE1 1GW. Tel: 01332-296655. *General Secretary*, Revd Dr S. Orchard

CHRISTIAN EVIDENCE SOCIETY (1870), St Stephen's House, St Stephen's Crescent, Brentwood, Essex CM13 2AT. Tel: 01277-214623. *Administrator*, Mrs G. M. Ryeland

CHRISTIAN KNOWLEDGE, SOCIETY FOR PROMOTING (SPCK) (1698), Holy Trinity Church, Marylebone Road, London NW1 4DU. Tel: 0171-387 5282. *General Secretary*, P. Chandler

CHRISTIANS AND JEWS, COUNCIL OF (1942), 1 Dennington Park Road, London NW6 1AX. Tel: 0171-794 8178. *Executive Director*, M. Latham

CHURCH ARMY (1882), Independents Road, London SE3 9LG. Tel: 0181-318 1226. *Chief Secretary*, Capt. P. Johanson

CHURCH BUILDING SOCIETY, INCORPORATED (1818), Fulham Palace, London SW6 6EA. Tel: 0171-736 3054. *Secretary*, M. W. Tippen

CHURCH EDUCATION CORPORATION, Bedgebury School, Goudhurst, Cranbrook, Kent TN17 2SH. Tel: 01580-211630. *Secretary*, Col. C. G. Champion

CHURCH HOUSE, THE CORPORATION OF (1888), Dean's Yard, London SW1P 3NZ. Tel: 0171-222 5261. *Secretary*, C. D. L. Menzies

CHURCH LADS' AND CHURCH GIRLS' BRIGADE (1891), 2 Barnsley Road, Wath upon Dearne, Rotherham, S. Yorkshire S63 6PY. Tel: 01709-876535. *General Secretary*, J. S. Cresswell

CHURCH MISSION SOCIETY (1799), Partnership House, 157 Waterloo Road, London SE1 8UU. Tel: 0171-928 8681. *General Secretary*, Ms D. K. Witts

CHURCH MUSIC, ROYAL SCHOOL OF (1927), Addington Palace, Croydon CR9 5AD. Tel: 0181-654 7676. *Chief Executive*, C. King

CHURCH OF ENGLAND PENSIONS BOARD (1926), 7 Little College Street, London SW1P 3SF. Tel: 0171-222 2091. *Secretary*, R. G. Radford

CHURCH UNION (1859), Faith House, 7 Tufton Street, London SW1P 3QN. Tel: 0171-222 6952. *General Secretary*, A. Leggatt

CHURCHES, COUNCIL FOR THE CARE OF (1921), Fielden House, Little College Street, London SW1P 3SH. Tel: 0171-222 3793. *Secretary*, Dr. T. Cocke

CHURCHES FOR BRITAIN AND IRELAND, COUNCIL OF (1942), Inter-Church House, 35–41 Lower Marsh, London SE1 7RL. Tel: 0171-620 4444. *General Secretary*, Revd J. P. Reardon

CHURCHES, FRIENDS OF FRIENDLESS (1957), St Ann's Vestry Hall, 2 Church Entry, London EC4V 5HB. Tel: 0171-236 3934. *Hon. Director*, M. Saunders

CHURCHES MAIN COMMITTEE (1941), Fielden House, Little College Street, London SW1P 3JZ. Tel: 0171-222 4984. *Secretary*, D. Taylor Thompson, CB

CHURCHES TOGETHER IN ENGLAND (1990), Inter-Church House, 35–41 Lower Marsh, London SE1 7RL. Tel: 0171-620 4444. *General Secretary*, Revd Canon M. Reardon

CHURCHES TOGETHER IN SCOTLAND, ACTION OF (1990), Scottish Churches House, Kirk Street, Dunblane FK15 0AJ. Tel: 01786-823588. *General Secretary*, Revd M. Craig

CHURCHILL SOCIETY (1990), 18 Grove Lane, Ipswich IP4 1NR. Tel: 01473-221607. *Founder*, N. H. Rogers

CITIZENS' ADVICE BUREAUX, NATIONAL ASSOCIATION OF (1931), Myddelton House, 115–123 Pentonville Road, London N1 9LZ. Tel: 0171-833 2181. *Chief Executive*, Ms A. Abraham

CITY BUSINESS LIBRARY, Brewers Hall Garden, London EC2V 5BX. Tel: 0171-638 8215

CITY PAROCHIAL FOUNDATION (1891), 6 Middle Street, London EC1A 7PH. Tel: 0171-606 6145. *Clerk*, T. Cook

CIVIC TRUST, THE (1957), 17 Carlton House Terrace, London SW1Y 5AW. Tel: 0171-930 0914. *Director*, M. C. Bradshaw

CIVIL DEFENCE AND DISASTER STUDIES, INSTITUTE OF (1938), Bell Court House, 11 Blomfield Street, London EC2M 7AY. Tel: 0181-592 6975. *Hon. General Secretary*, C. Lloyd

CIVIL ENGINEERS, INSTITUTION OF (1818), Great George Street, London SW1P 3AA. Tel: 0171-222 7722. *Secretary,* R. S. Dobson, OBE

CIVIL LIBERTIES, NATIONAL COUNCIL FOR, *see* LIBERTY

CLASSICAL ASSOCIATION (1903), Department of Classics, University of Keele, Keele, Newcastle under Lyme, Staffs ST5 5BG. Tel: 01782-583048. *Hon. Treasurer,* R. Wallace

CLEAN AIR AND ENVIRONMENTAL PROTECTION, NATIONAL SOCIETY FOR (1899), 136 North Street, Brighton BN1 1RG. Tel: 01273-326313. *Secretary-General,* Dr T. Crossett

CLERGY ORPHAN CORPORATION (1749), 57B Tufton Street, London SW1P 3QL. Tel: 0171-222 1812. *Secretary,* Miss J. Buncher

CLERKS OF WORKS OF GREAT BRITAIN INC., INSTITUTE OF (1882), 41 The Mall, London W5 3TJ. Tel: 0181-579 2917/8. *Secretary,* A. P. Macnamara

COACHING CLUB (1871), West Compton House, West Compton, Shepton Mallet, Somerset BA4 4PD. Tel: 01749-890633. *Secretary,* D. H. Clarke

COLITIS AND CROHN'S DISEASE, NATIONAL ASSOCIATION FOR (1979), PO Box 205, St Albans, Herts AL1 1NX. Tel: 01727-844296. *Director,* R. Driscoll

COMMERCE, BRITISH CHAMBERS OF (1860), 9 Tufton Street, London SW1P 3QB. Tel: 0171-222 1555. *Director-General,* R. G. Taylor, CBE

COMMERCE, ASSOCIATION OF SCOTTISH CHAMBERS OF, 3 Randolph Crescent, Edinburgh EH3 7UD. Tel: 0131-225 5851. *Director-General,* C. Winter

COMMERCE AND INDUSTRY, LONDON CHAMBER OF (1881), Swan House, 33 Queen Street, London EC4R 1AP. Tel: 0171-248 4444. *Chief Executive,* S. G. Sperryn

COMMERCE AND MANUFACTURERS, EDINBURGH CHAMBER OF (1786), 3 Randolph Crescent, Edinburgh EH3 7UD. Tel: 0131-225 5851. *Chief Executive,* D. I. Brown

COMMERCE AND MANUFACTURES, GLASGOW CHAMBER OF (1783), 30 George Square, Glasgow G2 1EQ. Tel: 0141-204 2121. *Chief Executive,* G. Runcie

COMMERCE, CANADA–UNITED KINGDOM CHAMBER OF (1921), 3 Regent Street, London SW1Y 4NZ. Tel: 0171-930 7711. *Executive Director,* G. F. Bacon

COMMERCIAL TRAVELLERS' BENEVOLENT INSTITUTION (1849), Gable End, Mill Hill Road, Arnesby, Leics LE8 3WG. Tel: 0116-247 8647. *Secretary,* M. N. Bown

COMMISSIONAIRES, THE CORPS OF (1859), Market House, 85 Cowcross Street, London EC1M 6BP. Tel: 0171-490 1125. *Managing Director,* C. J. Salt

COMMONWEALTH TRUST (linking the Royal Commonwealth Society and the Victoria League for Commonwealth Friendship), Commonwealth House, 18 Northumberland Avenue, London WC2N 5BJ. Tel: 0171-930 6733. *Director-General,* Sir David Thorne, KBE, CVO

COMMUNICATORS IN BUSINESS, BRITISH ASSOCIATION OF (1949), 3 Locks Yard, High Street, Sevenoaks, Kent TN13 1LT. Tel: 01732-459331. *Director,* A. F. Brobyn

COMPLEMENTARY AND ALTERNATIVE MEDICINE, COUNCIL FOR (1985), 179 Gloucester Place, London NW1 6DX. Tel: 0171-724 9103. *Secretary,* Ms C. Daglish

COMPLEMENTARY MEDICINE, INSTITUTE FOR (1856), PO Box 194, London SE16 1QZ. Tel: 0171-237 5165. *Director,* A. Baird

COMPOSERS' GUILD OF GREAT BRITAIN (1945), 34 Hanway Street, London W1P 9DE. Tel: 0171-436 0007. *General Secretary,* Ms H. Rosenblatt

COMPUTER SOCIETY, BRITISH (1957), 1 Sanford Street, Swindon SN1 1HJ. Tel: 01793-417417. *Chief Executive,* G. Kirkpatrick

CONSERVATION OF HISTORIC AND ARTISTIC WORKS, INTERNATIONAL INSTITUTE FOR (1950), 6 Buckingham Street, London WC2N 6BA. Tel: 0171-839 5975. *Secretary-General,* D. Bomford

CONSULTANTS BUREAU, BRITISH (1965), 1 Westminster Palace Gardens, 1–7 Artillery Row, London SW1P 1RJ. Tel: 0171-222 3651. *Director,* C. Adams, CBE

CONSULTING ECONOMISTS' ASSOCIATION, INTERNATIONAL (1986), 1C Barnes High Street, London SW13 9LB. Tel: 0181-875 9960. *Chairman,* Ms H. Acton

CONSULTING ENGINEERS, ASSOCIATION OF (1913), Alliance House, 12 Caxton Street, London SW1H 0QL. Tel: 0171-222 6557. *Chief Executive,* H. C. Woodrow

CONSULTING SCIENTISTS, ASSOCIATION OF (1958), Westgate House, 39-41 Romsey Road, Winchester, Hants SO22 5BE. Tel: 01962-869128. *Hon. Secretary,* B. A. Richardson

CONSUMERS' ASSOCIATION (1957), c/o The Association for Consumer Research, 2 Marylebone Road, London NW1 4DF. Tel: 0171-830 6000. *Director,* Dr J. Beishon

CONTEMPORARY APPLIED ARTS (1948), 43 Earlham Street, London WC2H 9LD. Tel: 0171-836 6993. *Director,* Ms M. La Trabe-Bateman

CONVENIENCE STORES, ASSOCIATION OF (1890), Federation House, 17 Farnborough Street, Farnborough, Hants GU14 8AG. Tel: 01252-515001. *National Secretary,* T. Dixon

CONVEYANCERS, COUNCIL FOR LICENSED (1986), 16 Glebe Road, Chelmsford, Essex CM1 1QG. Tel: 01245-349599. *Director,* Mrs V. Eden

CO-OPERATIVE PARTY, Victory House, 10–14 Leicester Square, London WC2H 7QH. Tel: 0171-439 0123. *Secretary,* P. Clarke

CO-OPERATIVE UNION LTD (1869), Holyoake House, Hanover Street, Manchester M60 0AS. Tel: 0161-832 4300. *Chief Executive,* D. L. Wilkinson

CO-OPERATIVE WHOLESALE SOCIETY LTD (CWS) (1863), PO Box 53, New Century House, Manchester M60 4ES. Tel: 0161-834 1212. *Chief Executive,* D. Skinner

COPYRIGHT COUNCIL, BRITISH (1953), 29–33 Berners Street, London W1P 4AA. *Secretary,* G. V. Adams

CORONERS' SOCIETY OF ENGLAND AND WALES (1846), 44 Ormond Avenue, Hampton, Middx TW12 2RX. *Hon. Secretary,* M. J. G. Burgess

CORPORATE TREASURERS, ASSOCIATION OF (1979), 12 Devereux Court, London WC2R 3JJ. Tel: 0171-936 2354. *Secretary,* Ms R. Robinson

CORPORATE TRUSTEES, ASSOCIATION OF (1974), The Glen House, 43 Surrey Road, Westbourne, Bournemouth, Dorset BH4 9HR. Tel: 01202-761112. *Secretary,* R. J. Payne

CORRESPONDENCE COLLEGES, ASSOCIATION OF BRITISH (1955), 6 Francis Grove, London SW19 4DT. Tel: 0181-544 9559. *Secretary,* Mrs H. Owen

CORRYMEELA COMMUNITY (1965), Corrymeela House, 8 Upper Crescent, Belfast BT7 1NT. Tel: 01232-325008. *Director,* Revd T. Williams

COTTON GROWING ASSOCIATION, BRITISH (1904), Knowle Hill Park, Fairmile Lane, Cobham, Surrey KT11 2PD. Tel: 01932-861000. *Managing Director,* P. R. Walters

COUNCIL FOR THE PROTECTION OF RURAL ENGLAND, *see* RURAL

COUNSEL AND CARE (1954), Twyman House, 16 Bonny Street, London NW1 9PG. Tel: 0171-485 1550. Advice Line: 0171- 485 1566. *General Manager,* J. Smith

COUNTRY HOUSES ASSOCIATION (1955), 41 Kingsway, London WC2B 6UB. Tel: 0171-836 1624. *Chief Executive,* R. D. Bratby

COUNTRY LANDOWNERS ASSOCIATION (1907), 16 Belgrave Square, London SW1X 8PQ. Tel: 0171-235 0511. *Director-General,* J. Anderson

COUNTY CHIEF EXECUTIVES, ASSOCIATION OF (1974), PO Box 9, Shire Hall, Warwick CV34 4RR. Tel: 01926-412559. *Hon. Secretary,* I. G. Caulfield

COUNTY COUNCILS, ASSOCIATION OF (1890), Eaton House, 66A Eaton Square, London SW1W 9BH. Tel: 0171-201 1500. *Secretary,* R. G. Wendt

COUNTY EMERGENCY PLANNING OFFICERS' SOCIETY, *see* EMERGENCY PLANNING

COUNTY SECRETARIES, SOCIETY OF (1974), 9 Holme Close, Scotby, Carlisle CA4 8BN. Tel: 01228-513480. *Hon. Secretary,* A. Fraser

COUNTY SURVEYORS' SOCIETY (1884), Director of Planning and Highways, Wiltshire County Council, County Hall, Trowbridge BA14 8JD. Tel: 01225-713318. *Hon. Secretary,* D. T. Gardner

COUNTY TREASURERS, SOCIETY OF (1903), PO Box 4, County Hall, Chelmsford, Essex CM1 1JZ. Tel: 01245-431000. *Hon. Secretary,* K. D. Neale

CRAFTS COUNCIL (1971), 44A Pentonville Road, London N1 9BY. Tel: 0171-278 7700. *Director,* T. Ford

CRISIS (1967), 7 Whitechapel Road, London E1 1DU. Tel: 0171-377 0489. *Director,* M. Scothern

CROSSLINKS (1922), 251 Lewisham Way, London SE4 1XF. Tel: 0181-691 6111. *General Secretary,* vacant

CRUEL SPORTS, THE LEAGUE AGAINST (1924), 83 Union Street, London SE1 1SG. Tel: 0171-403 6155. *Executive Director,* J. Barrington

CRUELTY TO ANIMALS, SOCIETY FOR THE PREVENTION OF, *see* ROYAL and SCOTTISH

CRUELTY TO CHILDREN, SOCIETY FOR THE PREVENTION OF, *see* NATIONAL and ROYAL SCOTTISH

CRUSE – BEREAVEMENT CARE (1959), 126 Sheen Road, Richmond, Surrey TW9 1UR. Tel: 0181-940 4818. Bereavement Line: 0181-332 7227. *Director,* R. Pearce

CURWEN INSTITUTE (1875), 5 Bigbury Close, Styvechale, Coventry CV3 5AJ. Tel: 01203-413010. *Director,* J. Dowding

CWMNI URDD GOBAITH CYMRU (1922), Swyddfa'r Urdd, Aberystwyth, Dyfed SY23 1EN. Tel: 01970-623744. *Director,* J. E. Williams

CYCLISTS' TOURING CLUB (1878), Cotterell House, 69 Meadrow, Godalming, Surrey GU7 3HS. Tel: 01483-417217. *Director,* A. Harlow

CYMMRODORION, THE HONOURABLE SOCIETY OF (1751), 30 Eastcastle Street, London W1N 7PD. Tel: 0171-631 0502. *Hon. Secretary,* D. L. Jones

CYSTIC FIBROSIS TRUST (1964), Alexandra House, 5 Blyth Road, Bromley BR1 3RS. Tel: 0181-464 7211. *Executive Director,* G. J. Edkins

CYTUN (CHURCHES TOGETHER IN WALES) (1990), 21 St Helen's Road, Swansea SA1 4AP. Tel: 01792-460876. *General Secretary,* Revd N. A. Davies

DAIRY FARMERS, ROYAL ASSOCIATION OF BRITISH (1876), 55 Sleaford Street, London SW8 5AB. Tel: 0171-627 2111. *Chief Executive,* P. M. Gilbert

DAIRY TECHNOLOGY, SOCIETY OF (1943), 72 Ermine Street, Huntingdon, Cambs PE18 6EZ. Tel: 01480-450741. *National Secretary,* Mrs R. Gale

DATA (DESIGN AND TECHNOLOGY ASSOCIATION), 16 Wellesbourne House, Walton Road, Wellesbourne, Warks CV35 9JB. Tel: 01789-470007. *Chairman,* R. V. Peacock, OBE, Ph.D

D-DAY AND NORMANDY FELLOWSHIP (1968), 9 South Parade, Southsea, Hants PO5 2JB. Tel: 01705-812180. *Hon. Secretary,* Mrs L. R. Reed

DEAF, COMMONWEALTH SOCIETY FOR THE (1959), Dilke House, Malet Street, London WC1E 7JA. *Chairman,* F. R. Rutter

DEAF ASSOCIATION, BRITISH (1890 *formerly* BRITISH DEAF AND DUMB ASSOCIATION), 38 Victoria Place, Carlisle CA1 1HU. Tel: 01228-48844. *Chief Executive,* J. McWhinney

DEAF CHILDREN, ROYAL SCHOOL FOR (1792), Victoria Road, Margate, Kent CT9 1NB. Tel: 01843-227561. *Secretary,* D. E. Downs

DEAF PEOPLE, FOLEY HOUSE RESIDENTIAL HOME FOR (1851), Foley House, 115 High Garrett, Braintree, Essex CM7 5NU. Tel: 01376-326652. *Director,* Mrs N. Hartard

DEAF PEOPLE, ROYAL ASSOCIATION IN AID OF (1841), 27 Old Oak Road, London W3 7HN. Tel: 0181-743 6187. *General Secretary,* B. Edmond

DEAF PEOPLE, ROYAL NATIONAL INSTITUTE FOR (1911), 105 Gower Street, London WC1E 6AH. Tel: 0171-387 8033. *Chief Executive,* D. Alker

DEFENCE STUDIES, ROYAL UNITED SERVICES INSTITUTE FOR (1831), Whitehall, London SW1A 2ET. Tel: 0171-930 5854. *Director,* Rear-Adm. R. Cobbold, CB

DEMOCRATIC LEFT (1991), 6 Cynthia Street, London N1 9JF. Tel: 0171-278 4443. *Secretary,* Ms N. Temple.

DENTAL ASSOCIATION, BRITISH (1880), 64 Wimpole Street, London W1M 8AL. Tel: 0171-935 0875. *Chief Executive,* J. M. G. Hunt

DENTAL COUNCIL, GENERAL (1956), 37 Wimpole Street, London W1M 8DQ. Tel: 0171-486 2171. *Registrar,* N. T. Davies, MBE

DENTAL HOSPITALS OF THE UNITED KINGDOM, ASSOCIATION OF (1942), Birmingham Dental Hospital, St Chad's Queensway, Birmingham B4 6NN. Tel: 0121-236 8611, ext. 5732. *Hon. Secretary,* Mrs P. Harrington

DESIGN AND INDUSTRIES ASSOCIATION (1915), Suite 104, Business Design Centre, 52 Upper Street, London N1 0QH. Tel: 0171-288 6212. *Chairman,* G. Adams

DESIGNERS FOR INDUSTRY, FACULTY OF ROYAL (1936), RSA, 8 John Adam Street, London WC2N 6EZ. Tel: 0171-930 5115. *Secretary,* C. Lucas

DESIGNERS, CHARTERED SOCIETY OF (1930), 29 Bedford Square, London WC1B 3EG. Tel: 0171-631 1510. *Director,* B. Lymbery

DIABETIC ASSOCIATION, BRITISH (1934), 10 Queen Anne Street, London W1M 0BD. Tel: 0171-323 1531. *Director-General,* M. Cooper

DICKENS FELLOWSHIP (1902), Dickens House,
48 Doughty Street, London WCIN 2LF. Tel: 0171-405
2127. *Hon. General Secretary,* E. Preston

DIRECTORS, INSTITUTE OF (1903), 116 Pall Mall, London
SWIY 5ED. Tel: 0171-839 1233. *Director-General,*
T. Melville Ross

DIRECTORS OF PUBLIC HEALTH, ASSOCIATION OF (1982),
Walsall Health Authority, Litchfield House, 27–31
Litchfield Street, Walsall, West Midlands WSI ITE. Tel:
01922-720255. *Hon. Secretary,* Dr S. Ramaiah

DIRECTORY PUBLISHERS ASSOCIATION (1970), 93A
Blenheim Crescent, London WII 2EQ. Tel: 0171-221
9089. *Secretary,* Ms R. Pettit

DISPENSING OPTICIANS, ASSOCIATION OF BRITISH
(1925), 6 Hurlingham Business Park, Sulivan Road,
London SW6 3DU. Tel: 0171-736 0088. *Registrar,*
D. S. Baker

DISTRICT COUNCILS, ASSOCIATION OF (1974),
26 Chapter Street, London SWIP 4ND. Tel: 0171-233
6868. *Secretary,* G. Filkin

DISTRICT SECRETARIES, ASSOCIATION OF (1974),
9 Margaret Road, Bishopsworth, Bristol BSI3 9DQ. Tel:
0117-964 7299. *Hon. Secretary,* E. Richards

DITCHLEY FOUNDATION, Ditchley Park, Enstone,
Chipping Norton, Oxon OX7 4ER. Tel: 01608-677346.
Director, Sir Michael Quinlan, GCB

DOWNS SYNDROME ASSOCIATION (1970), 155 Mitcham
Road, London SWI7 9PG. Tel: 0181-682 4001. *Director,*
Ms A. Khan

DOWSERS, BRITISH SOCIETY OF (1933), Sycamore Barn,
Hastingleigh, Ashford, Kent TN25 5HW. Tel: 01233-
750253. *Secretary,* M. D. Rust

DRAINAGE AUTHORITIES, ASSOCIATION OF (1937), The
Mews, 3 Royal Oak Passage, High Street, Huntingdon,
Cambs PEI8 6EA. Tel: 01480-411123. *Secretary,* D. Noble

DRINKING FOUNTAIN AND CATTLE TROUGH
ASSOCIATION, METROPOLITAN (1859), Oaklands, 5
Queensborough Gardens, Chislehurst, Kent BR7 6NP.
Secretary

DRIVING SOCIETY, BRITISH (1957), 27 Dugard Place,
Barford, Warwick CV35 8DX. Tel: 01926-624420.
Secretary, Mrs J. M. Dillon

DRUG DEPENDENCE, INSTITUTE FOR THE STUDY OF
(ISDD) (1968), 32 Loman Street, London SEI OEE. Tel:
0171-928 1211. *Director,* Ms A. Bradley

DUKE OF EDINBURGH'S AWARD SCHEME (1956), Gulliver
House, Madeira Walk, Windsor, Berks SL4 IEU. Tel:
01753-810753. *Director,* Maj.-Gen. M. F. Hobbs, CBE

DYERS AND COLOURISTS, SOCIETY OF (1884), Perkin
House, 82 Grattan Road, Bradford BDI 2JB. Tel: 01274-
725138. *General Secretary,* J. D. Watson

DYSLEXIA INSTITUTE (1972), 133 Gresham Road, Staines,
Middx TWI8 2AJ. Tel: 01784-463851. *Executive Director,*
Mrs E. J. Brooks

EARLY CHILDHOOD EDUCATION, BRITISH ASSOCIATION
FOR (1923), 111 City View House, 463 Bethnal Green
Road, London E2 9QY. Tel: 0171-739 7594. *Secretary,*
Mrs B. Boon

ECCLESIASTICAL HISTORY SOCIETY (1961), Department
of Medieval History, University of Glasgow, Glasgow
GI2 8QQ. Tel: 0141-339 8855. *Secretary,* M. J. Kennedy

ECCLESIOLOGICAL SOCIETY (1839), Underedge, Back
Lane, Hathersage, Derbys S30 IAR. Tel: 01742-768555
ext. 4719/01433-650833. *Hon. Secretary,*
Prof. K. H. Murta

EDITH CAVELL AND NATION'S FUND FOR NURSES (1917),
Flints, Petersfield Road, Winchester, Hants SO23 OJD.
Tel: 01962-860900. *Administrator,* Mrs M. A. Rich

EDITORS, GUILD OF (1946), Bloomsbury House,
74–77 Great Russell Street, London WCIB 3DA. Tel:
0171-636 7014. *Secretary,* Ms V. L. Hird

EDUCATION OFFICERS, SOCIETY OF (1971), Boulton
House, 17–21 Chorlton Street, Manchester MI 3HY. Tel:
0161-236 5766. *General Secretary,* J. Hendy

EDUCATION OFFICERS' SOCIETY, COUNTY (1889),
Education Department, Northamptonshire County
Council, PO Box 149, County Hall, Northampton
NNI IAU. Tel: 01604-236250. *Hon. Secretary,*
J. R. Atkinson

EDUCATIONAL RESEARCH IN ENGLAND AND WALES,
NATIONAL FOUNDATION FOR (1946), The Mere, Upton
Park, Slough SLI 2DQ. Tel: 01753-574123. *Director,*
Dr S. Hegarty

EGYPT EXPLORATION SOCIETY (1882), 3 Doughty Mews,
London WCIN 2PG. Tel: 0171-242 1880. *Secretary,*
Dr P. A. Spencer

ELECTORAL REFORM SOCIETY, 6 Chancel Street, London
SEI OUU. Tel: 0171-928 1622. *President,* Baroness Seear,
PC; *Office Manager,* P. Stock

ELECTRICAL ENGINEERS, INSTITUTION OF (1871), Savoy
Place, London WC2R OBL. Tel: 0171-240 1871. *Secretary,*
J. C. Williams, PH.D., FENG.

ELGAR FOUNDATION (1973), 23 Meadow Hill Road,
King's Norton, Birmingham B38 8DE. Tel: 0121-458
2747. *Secretary to the Trustees,* J. G. Hughes

ELGAR SOCIETY (1951), Huntingdon, Orchard Road,
Malvern, Worcs WRI4 3PA. Tel: 01684-568822. *Secretary,*
Mrs C. Holt

EMERGENCY PLANNING SOCIETY (1966), Emergency
Planning Officer, London Borough of Brent, Pyramid
House, Forthway, Wembley HA9 OLJ. Tel: 0181-908
7035. *Hon. Secretary,* K. D. Gosling

ENERGY ASSOCIATION, BRITISH (1924), 34 St James's
Street, London SWIA IHD. Tel: 0171-930 1211. *Director,*
M. Jefferson

ENERGY, INSTITUTE OF (1927), 18 Devonshire Street,
London WIN 2AU. Tel: 0171-580 7124. *Secretary,*
J. E. H. Leach

ENERGY SAVING TRUST (1992), 11–12 Buckingham Gate,
London SWIE 6LB. Tel: 0171-931 8401. *Chief Executive,* Dr
E. Lees

ENGINEERING COUNCIL, THE (1981), 10 Maltravers
Street, London WC2R 3ER. Tel: 0171-240 7891. *Public
Affairs Director,* T. Miller

ENGINEERING DESIGNERS, INSTITUTION OF (1945),
Courtleigh, Westbury Leigh, Westbury, Wilts BAI3 3HB.
Tel: 01373-822801. *Secretary,* M. J. Osborne

ENGINEERING INDUSTRIES ASSOCIATION (1941),
16 Dartmouth Street, London SWIH 9BL. Tel: 0171-222
2367. *Director-General,* N. J. Harvey

ENGINEERS, INSTITUTION OF BRITISH (1928), Royal
Liver Building, 6 Hampton Place, Brighton BNI 3DD.
Tel: 01273-734274. *Secretary,* Mrs D. Henry

ENGINEERS, THE SOCIETY OF (INCORPORATED) (1854),
Guinea Wiggs, Nayland, Colchester, Essex CO6 4NF.
Tel: 01206-263332. *Secretary,* Mrs L. C. A. Wright

ENGLISH ASSOCIATION, THE (1906), University of
Leicester, Leicester LEI 7RH. Tel: 0116-252 5927.
Secretary, Ms H. Lucas

ENGLISH FOLK DANCE AND SONG SOCIETY (1932), Cecil Sharp House, 2 Regent's Park Road, London NW1 7AY. Tel: 0171-485 2206. *Chief Officer,* J. Ripley

ENGLISH PLACE-NAME SURVEY (1923), Grey College, Durham DH1 3LG. Tel: 0191-374 2960. *Hon. Director,* V. Watts

ENGLISH-SPEAKING UNION OF THE COMMONWEALTH, THE (1918), Dartmouth House, 37 Charles Street, London W1X 8AB. Tel: 0171-493 3328. *Director-General,* Mrs V. Mitchell

ENTOMOLOGICAL SOCIETY OF LONDON, ROYAL (1833), 41 Queen's Gate, London SW7 5HR. Tel: 0171-584 8361. *Registrar,* G. G. Bentley

ENVIRONMENTAL HEALTH, CHARTERED INSTITUTE OF (1883), Chadwick Court, 15 Hatfields, London SE1 8DJ. Tel: 0171-928 6006. *Secretary,* M. Cooke

ENVIRONMENT COUNCIL (1969), 21 Elizabeth Street, London SW1W 9RP. Tel: 0171-824 8411. *Chief Executive,* S. Robinson

EPILEPSY ASSOCIATION, BRITISH (1949), Anstey House, 40 Hanover Square, Leeds LS3 1BE. Tel: 0113-243 9393. *Chief Executive,* T. J. O'Leary

EPILEPSY, NATIONAL SOCIETY FOR (1892), Chalfont St Peter, Gerrards Cross, Bucks SL9 0RJ. Tel: 01494-873991. *Chief Executive,* Col. D. W. Eking

EQUESTRIAN FEDERATION, BRITISH (1972), British Equestrian Centre, Stoneleigh Park, Kenilworth, Warks CV8 2LR. Tel: 01203-696697. *Director-General,* Col. J. D. Smith-Bingham

ESPERANTO ASSOCIATION OF BRITAIN (1977), 140 Holland Park Avenue, London W11 4UF. Tel: 0171-727 7821. *General Secretary,* vacant

ESTATE AGENTS, NATIONAL ASSOCIATION OF (1962), Arbon House, 21 Jury Street, Warwick CV34 4EH. Tel: 01926-496800. *Chief Executive,* H. Dunsmore-Hardy

ESTATE AGENTS, OMBUDSMAN FOR CORPORATE (1990), Beckett House, 4 Bridge Street, Salisbury, Wilts SP1 2LX. Tel: 01722-332296. *Ombudsman,* T. D. Quayle, CB

EUGENICS SOCIETY, *see* GALTON INSTITUTE

EVANGELICAL ALLIANCE (1846), Whitefield House, 186 Kennington Park Road, London SE11 4BT. Tel: 0171-582 0228. *General Director,* Revd C. R. Calver

EVANGELICAL LIBRARY, THE (1928), 78A Chiltern Street, London W1M 2HB. Tel: 0171-935 6997. *Librarian,* S. J. Taylor

EXPORT, INSTITUTE OF (1935), Export House, 64 Clifton Street, London EC2A 4HB. Tel: 0171-247 9812. *Director-General,* I. J. Campbell

EX-SERVICES LEAGUE, BRITISH COMMONWEALTH (1921), 48 Pall Mall, London SW1Y 5JG. Tel: 0171-973 0633. *Secretary-General,* Brig. M. J. Doyle, MBE

EX-SERVICES MENTAL WELFARE SOCIETY (1919), Broadway House, The Broadway, London SW19 1RL. Tel: 0181-543 6333. *Director,* Brig. A. K. Dixon

FABIAN SOCIETY (1884), 11 Dartmouth Street, London SW1H 9BN. Tel: 0171-222 8877. *General Secretary,* S. Crine

FAIR ISLE BIRD OBSERVATORY TRUST (1948), Burkle, Fair Isle, Shetland ZE2 9JU. Tel: 0135-12284. *Secretary,* Ms C. Ross-Smith

FAMILY HISTORY SOCIETIES, FEDERATION OF (1974), The Benson Room, Birmingham and Midland Institute, Margaret Street, Birmingham B3 3BS. *Administrator,* Mrs P. A. Saul

FAMILY MEDIATION AND CONCILIATION SERVICES, THE NATIONAL ASSOCIATION OF (1982), 9 Tavistock Place, London WC1H 9SN. Tel: 0171-383 5993. *Director,* Ms T. Fisher

FAMILY PLANNING ASSOCIATION (1939), 27–35 Mortimer Street, London W1N 7RJ. Tel: 0171-636 7866. *Director,* T. O'Brien

FAMILY WELFARE ASSOCIATION (1869), 501–505 Kingsland Road, London E8 4AU. Tel: 0181-254 6251. *Director,* Ms L. Berry

FAUNA AND FLORA INTERNATIONAL (1903), Great Eastern House, Tenison Road, Cambridge CB1 2DU. Tel: 01223-461471. *Director,* M. Rose

FELLOWSHIP HOUSES TRUST (1937), Clock House, 192 High Road, Byfleet, Surrey KT14 7RN. Tel: 01932-343172. *Secretary,* Mrs A. J. Elliot

FIELD ARCHAEOLOGISTS, INSTITUTE OF (1982), University of Manchester, Oxford Road, Manchester M13 9PL. Tel: 0161-275 2304. *General Secretary,* F. M. Walls

FIELD SPORTS SOCIETY, BRITISH (1930), 59 Kennington Road, London SE1 7PZ. Tel: 0171-928 4742. *Director,* R. Hanbury-Tenison, OBE

FIELD STUDIES COUNCIL (1943), Preston Montford, Montford Bridge, Shrewsbury SY4 1HW. Tel: 01743-850674. *Director,* A. D. Thomas

FILM CLASSIFICATION, BRITISH BOARD OF (1912), 3 Soho Square, London W1V 6HD. Tel: 0171-439 7961. *Director,* J. Ferman

FIRE ENGINEERS, INSTITUTION OF (1918), 148 New Walk, Leicester LE1 7QB. Tel: 0116-255 3654. *General Secretary,* D. Evans

FIRE PROTECTION ASSOCIATION (1946), Melrose Avenue, Borehamwood, Herts WD6 2BJ. Tel: 0181-207 2345. *Director,* A. S. Kidd

FIRE SERVICES ASSOCIATION, BRITISH (1949), 86 London Road, Leicester LE2 0QR. Tel: 0116-254 2879. *General Secretary,* D. Stevens

FIRE SERVICES NATIONAL BENEVOLENT FUND (1943), Marine Court, Fitzalan Road, Littlehampton, W. Sussex BN17 5NF. Tel: 01903-717185. *General Manager,* C. W. Pile

FLAG INSTITUTE, THE (1971), 10 Vicarage Road, Chester CH2 3HZ. Tel: 01244-351335. *Director,* Dr W. G. Crampton

FLEET AIR ARM OFFICERS ASSOCIATION (1957), 94 Piccadilly, London W1V 0BP. Tel: 0171-499 0360. *Chairman,* Capt. A. A. Hensher, MBE, RN

FOLKLORE SOCIETY, c/o University College, Gower Street, London WC1E 6BT. Tel: 0171-387 5894. *Hon. Secretary,* Dr J. Wood

FOOD FROM BRITAIN (1983), 301–344 Market Towers, New Covent Garden Market, London SW8 5NQ. Tel: 0171-720 2144. *Chairman,* G. John, OBE

FOOD SCIENCE AND TECHNOLOGY, INSTITUTE OF (1964), 10 Cambridge Court, 210 Shepherd's Bush Road, London W6 7NL. Tel: 0171-603 6316. *Executive Secretary,* Ms H. G. Wild

FORCES HELP SOCIETY AND LORD ROBERTS WORKSHOPS (1899), 122 Brompton Road, London SW3 1JE. Tel: 0171-589 3243. *Comptroller and Secretary,* Col. A. W. Davis, OBE

FOREIGN PRESS ASSOCIATION IN LONDON (1888), 11 Carlton House Terrace, London SW1Y 5AJ. Tel: 0171-930 0445. *Secretary,* Ms D. Crole

FORENSIC SCIENCE SOCIETY, THE (1959), Clarke House, 18A Mount Parade, Harrogate, N. Yorks HGI 1BX. Tel: 01423-506068. *Hon. Secretary,* Dr A. R. W. Forrest

FORENSIC SCIENCES, BRITISH ACADEMY OF (1959), Anaesthetic Unit, The London Hospital Medical College, Turner Street, London EI 2AD. Tel: 0171-377 9201. *Secretary-General,* Dr P. J. Flynn

FORESTERS, INSTITUTE OF CHARTERED (1982), 7A St Colme Street, Edinburgh EH3 6AA. Tel: 0131-225 2705. *Secretary,* Mrs M. W. Dick

FORESTRY ASSOCIATION, COMMONWEALTH (1921), c/o Oxford Forestry Institute, South Parks Road, Oxford OXI 3RB. Tel: 01865-275072. *Chairman,* P. J. Wood

FORESTRY SOCIETY OF ENGLAND, WALES AND NORTHERN IRELAND, ROYAL (1882), 102 High Street, Tring, Herts HP23 4AF. Tel: 01442-822028. *Director,* J. E. Jackson, PH.D.

FORESTRY SOCIETY, ROYAL SCOTTISH (1854), 62 Queen Street, Edinburgh EH2 4NA. Tel: 0131-225 8142. *Director,* M. Osborne

FOUNDRYMEN, INSTITUTE OF BRITISH (1904), Bordesley Hall, The Holloway, Alvechurch, Birmingham B48 7QA. Tel: 01527-596100. *Secretary,* G. A. Schofield

FRANCO-BRITISH SOCIETY (1924), Room 623, Linen Hall, 162–168 Regent Street, London WIR 5TB. Tel: 0171-734 0815. *Executive Secretary,* Mrs M. Clarke

FREE CHURCH FEDERAL COUNCIL (1940), 27 Tavistock Square, London WCIH 9HH. Tel: 0171-387 8413. *General Secretary,* Revd D. Staple, OBE

FREEDOM ASSOCIATION (1975), 35 Westminster Bridge Road, London SEI 7JB. Tel: 0171-928 9925. *Office Manager,* Mrs P. North

FREEMASONS, GRAND LODGE OF ANTIENT FREE AND ACCEPTED MASONS OF SCOTLAND (1736), Freemasons' Hall, 96 George Street, Edinburgh EH2 3DH. Tel: 0131-225 5304. *Grand Master Mason of Scotland,* The Lord Burton; *Grand Secretary,* C. M. McGibbon

FREEMASONS, UNITED GRAND LODGE OF ENGLAND (1717), Freemasons' Hall, Great Queen Street, London WC2B 5AZ. Tel: 0171-831 9811. *Grand Master,* HRH The Duke of Kent, KG, GCMG, GCVO; *Grand Secretary,* Cdr. M. B. S. Higham

FREEMEN OF ENGLAND AND WALES (1966), Glenrise, Churchfields, Stonesfield, Witney, Oxon OX8 8PP. Tel: 01993-891414. *Deputy President,* R. J. M. Bishop

FREEMEN'S GUILDS:

City of Coventry Freemen's Guild (1946), 5 Adare Drive, Styvechale, Coventry CV3 6AD. *Hon. Clerk,* J. H. Bradbury

Guild of Freemen of the City of London (1908), PO Box 153, 40A Ludgate Hill, London EC4M 7DE. Tel: 0171-223 7638. *Clerk,* Col. D. Ivy

Gild of Freemen of the City of York (1953), 29 Albemarle Road, York YO2 1EW. Tel: 01904-653698. *Hon. Clerk,* R. Lee

FRIENDLY SOCIETIES, THE ASSOCIATION OF (1887), Royex House, Aldermanbury Square, London EC2V 7HR. Tel: 0171-606 1881. *General Secretary,* Miss M. Poole

FRIENDS OF CATHEDRAL MUSIC (1956), 26 Dumbrells Court, North End, Ditchling, W. Sussex BN6 8TG. *Secretary,* V. Waterhouse

FRIENDS OF THE CLERGY CORPORATION, THE (1972), 27 Medway Street, London SWIP 2BD. Tel: 0171-222 2288. *Secretary,* J. M. Greany

FRIENDS OF THE EARTH (1971), 26–28 Underwood Street, London NI 7JQ. Tel: 0171-490 1555. *Director,* C. Secrett

FRIENDS OF THE ELDERLY AND GENTLEFOLK'S HELP (1905), 42 Ebury Street, London SWIW 0LZ. Tel: 0171-730 8263. *Chief Executive,* Mrs S. Levett

FRIENDS OF THE NATIONAL LIBRARIES (1931), c/o The British Library, London WCIB 3DG. Tel: 0171-412 7559. *Hon. Secretary,* M. Borrie, OBE, FSA

FURNITURE HISTORY SOCIETY (1964), 1 Mercedes Cottages, St John's Road, Haywards Heath, W. Sussex RHI6 4EH. Tel: 01444-413845. *Membership Secretary,* Dr B. Austen

GALLIPOLI ASSOCIATION (1915), Earlydene Orchard, Earlydene, Ascot, Berks SL5 9JY. Tel: 01344-26523. *Hon. Secretary,* J. C. Watson Smith

GALTON INSTITUTE, THE (formerly The Eugenics Society) (1907), 19 Northfields Prospect, London SW18 1PE. Tel: 0181-874 7257. *General Secretary,* Mrs L. Brooks

GAMBLERS ANONYMOUS (1954), PO Box 88, London SWIO 0EU. Tel: 0181-741 4181

GAME CONSERVANCY TRUST, THE (1969), Fordingbridge, Hants SP6 1EF. Tel: 01425-652381. *Director-General,* G. R. Potts, PH.D., D.SC.

GARDEN HISTORY SOCIETY (1965), 5 The Knoll, Hereford HRI 1RU. Tel: 01432-354479. *Hon. Membership Secretary,* Mrs A. Richards

GARDENERS' ASSOCIATION, THE GOOD (1968), Pinetum, Churcham, Glos GL2 8AD. Tel: 01452-750402. *Hon. Director,* D. Wilkin

GARDENERS' ROYAL BENEVOLENT SOCIETY, THE (1839), Bridge House, 139 Kingston Road, Leatherhead, Surrey KT22 7NT. Tel: 01372-373962. *Chief Executive,* C. R. C. Bunce

GARDENS SCHEME CHARITABLE TRUST, NATIONAL (1927), Hatchlands Park, East Clandon, Guildford, Surrey GU4 7RT. Tel: 01483-211535. *Director,* Lt.-Col. T. A. Marsh

GAS CONSUMERS COUNCIL (1986), 6th Floor, Abford House, 15 Wilton Road, London SWIV 1LT. Tel: 0171-931 0977. *Director,* I. W. Powe

GAS ENGINEERS, INSTITUTION OF (1863), 21 Portland Place, London WIN 3AF. Tel: 0171-636 6603. *Secretary,* Mrs S. M. Raine

GEMMOLOGICAL ASSOCIATION AND GEM TESTING LABORATORY OF GREAT BRITAIN (1931), 27 Greville Street, Saffron Hill Entrance, London ECIN 8SU. Tel: 0171-404 3334. *Director,* Dr R. R. Harding

GENEALOGICAL RESEARCH SOCIETY, IRISH (1936), c/o The Irish Club, 82 Eaton Square, London SWIW 9AJ. Tel: 0171-235 4164. *Hon. Secretary*

GENEALOGISTS AND RECORD AGENTS, ASSOCIATION OF (1968), 29 Badgers Close, Horsham, W. Sussex RHI2 5RU. *Secretaries*

GENEALOGISTS, SOCIETY OF (1911), 14 Charterhouse Buildings, Goswell Road, London ECIM 7BA. Tel: 0171-251 8799. *Director,* A. J. Camp

GENERAL PRACTITIONERS, ROYAL COLLEGE OF (1952), 14 Princes Gate, London SW7 1PU. Tel: 0171-581 3232. *Secretary,* Dr W. Reith

GENTLEPEOPLE, GUILD OF AID FOR (1904), 10 St Christopher's Place, London WIM 6HY. Tel: 0171-935 0641. *Secretary*

GEOGRAPHICAL ASSOCIATION, 343 Fulwood Road, Sheffield S10 3BP. Tel: 0114-267 0666. *Senior Administrator*, Miss F. Soar

GEOGRAPHICAL SOCIETY, ROYAL (1830), 1 Kensington Gore, London SW7 2AR. Tel: 0171-589 5466. *President,* The Earl Jellicoe, KBE, DSO, MC, FRS, PC; *Director*, Dr J. Hemming, CMG

GEOGRAPHICAL SOCIETY, ROYAL SCOTTISH (1884), Graham Hills Building, 40 George Street, Glasgow G1 1QE. Tel: 0141-552 3330. *Director*, A. B. Cruickshank

GEOLOGICAL SOCIETY (1807), Burlington House, Piccadilly, London W1V 0JU. Tel: 0171-434 9944. *Executive Secretary*, R. M. Bateman

GEOLOGISTS' ASSOCIATION (1858), Burlington House, Piccadilly, London W1V 9AG. Tel: 0171-434 9298. *Executive Secretary*, Ms S. Stafford

GEORGIAN GROUP (1937), 6 Fitzroy Square, London W1P 6DX. Tel: 0171-387 1720. *Secretary*, N. Burton

GIFTED CHILDREN, NATIONAL ASSOCIATION FOR (1966), Park Campus, Boughton Green Road, Northampton NN2 7AL. Tel: 01604-792300. *Executive Director*, P. Carey

GILBERT AND SULLIVAN SOCIETY (1924), 1A Tower Lane, Bearsted, Maidstone, Kent ME14 4JJ. Tel: 01622-738249. *Hon. Secretary*, Miss B. Dove

GINGERBREAD, AN ASSOCIATION FOR ONE PARENT FAMILIES (1970), 49 Wellington Street, London WC2E 7BN. Tel: 0171-240 0953. *Chief Executive,* K. Murphy

GIRL GUIDES, *see* GUIDE ASSOCIATION

GIRLS' BRIGADE, THE, Girls' Brigade House, 62 Foxhall Road, Didcot, Oxon OX11 7BQ. Tel: 01235-510425. *Brigade Secretary*, Mrs S. Bunting

GIRLS' FRIENDLY SOCIETY AND TOWNSEND FELLOWSHIP (1875), 126 Queens Gate, London SW7 5LQ. Tel: 0171-589 9628. *General Secretary,* Mrs H. Crompton

GIRLS' VENTURE CORPS AIR CADETS (1964), Redhill Aerodrome, Kings Mill Lane, South Nutfield, Redhill RH1 5JY. Tel: 01737-823345. *Corps Director*, Mrs M. Rowland

GLASS ENGRAVERS, GUILD OF (1975), 19 Wildwood Road, London NW11 6UL. Tel: 0181-731 9352. *Secretary*

GLASS TECHNOLOGY, SOCIETY OF (1916), Thornton, 20 Hallam Gate Road, Sheffield S10 5BT. Tel: 0114-266 3168. *Administration Manager*, Miss J. Costello

GLIDING ASSOCIATION, BRITISH (1930), Kimberley House, Vaughan Way, Leicester LE1 4SE. Tel: 0116-253 1051. *Secretary*, B. Rolfe

GOAT SOCIETY, BRITISH (1879), 34–36 Fore Street, Bovey Tracey, Newton Abbot, Devon TQ13 9AD. Tel: 01626-833168. *Secretary*, Ms S. Knowles

GRAPHIC FINE ART, SOCIETY OF (1919), 9 Newburgh Street, London W1V 1LH. *Secretary*, Ms J. Caesar

GRAPHOLOGISTS, BRITISH INSTITUTE OF (1983), 24–26 High Street, Hampton Hill, Middx TW12 1PD. *Chairman*, Dr C. Molander

GREEK INSTITUTE (1969), 34 Bush Hill Road, London N21 2DS. Tel: 0181-360 7968. *Director*, Dr K. Tofallis

GREEN PARTY, THE (1973), 1A Waterlow Road, London N19 5NJ. Tel: 0171-272 4474. *Office Manager,* Ms V. Olliver

GREENPEACE UK (1971), Canonbury Villas, London N1 2PN. Tel: 0171-354 5100. *Executive Director,* The Lord Melchett

GUIDE ASSOCIATION, THE (1910), 17–19 Buckingham Palace Road, London SW1W 0PT. Tel: 0171-834 6242. *Chief Commissioner,* Mrs M. Wright; *Chief Executive,* Ms H. Williams

GUIDE DOGS FOR THE BLIND ASSOCIATION (1931), Hillfields, Burghfield, Reading RG7 3YG. Tel: 01734-835555. *Director-General,* J. C. Oxley

GULBENKIAN FOUNDATION, *see* CALOUSTE GULBENKIAN FOUNDATION

HAEMOPHILIA SOCIETY, THE (1950), 123 Westminster Bridge Road, London SE1 7HR. Tel: 0171-928 2020. *Director of Services and Development*, G. Barker

HAIG HOMES (1928), Alban Dobson House, Green Lane, Morden, Surrey SM4 5NS. Tel: 0181-648 0335. *General Secretary*, J. B. Holt

HAKLUYT SOCIETY (1846), c/o Map Library, The British Library, Great Russell Street, London WC1B 3DG. Tel: 01986-788359. *Hon. Secretary*, A. P. Payne

HANSARD SOCIETY FOR PARLIAMENTARY GOVERNMENT, THE (1944), St Philips Building North, Sheffield Street, London WC2A 2EX. Tel: 0171-955 7478. *Director,* D. Harris

HARD OF HEARING, BRITISH ASSOCIATION OF THE (1948), 7–11 Armstrong Road, London W3 7JL. Tel: 0181-743 1110. *Director*, C. J. Meyer, OBE

HARVEIAN SOCIETY OF EDINBURGH (1782), Department of Medicine, The Royal Infirmary, Edinburgh EH3 9YW. Tel: 0131-536 2351. *Joint Secretaries*, A. B. MacGregor; Dr N. J. Douglas

HARVEIAN SOCIETY OF LONDON (1831), Lettson House, 11 Chandos Street, London W1M 0EB. Tel: 0171-580 1043. *Executive Secretary*, M. Griffiths, TD

HEALTH AUTHORITIES AND TRUSTS, NATIONAL ASSOCIATION OF (1974), Birmingham Research Park, Vincent Drive, Birmingham B15 2SQ. Tel: 0121-471 4444. *Director*, P. Hunt, OBE

HEALTH CARE ASSOCIATION, BRITISH (1931), 24A Main Street, Garforth, Leeds LS25 1AA. Tel: 0113-232 0903. *Chief Executive*, Mrs C. Bell

HEALTH EDUCATION, INSTITUTE OF (1962), 14 High Elm Road, Hale Barns, Altrincham, Cheshire WA15 0HS. Tel: 0161-980 8276. *Hon. Secretary*, Prof. L. Baric, PH.D.

HEALTH, GUILD OF (1904), Edward Wilson House, 26 Queen Anne Street, London W1M 9LB. Tel: 0171-580 2492. *General Secretary*, Revd A. Lynn

HEALTH SERVICES MANAGEMENT, INSTITUTE OF (1902), 39 Chalton Street, London NW1 1JD. Tel: 0171-388 2626. *Director*, R. Rowden

HEART FOUNDATION, BRITISH (1963), 14 Fitzhardinge Street, London W1H 4DH. Tel: 0171-935 0185. *Director-General*, Maj.-Gen. L. F. H. Busk, CB

HEDGEHOG PRESERVATION SOCIETY, BRITISH (1982), Knowbury House, Knowbury, Ludlow, Shropshire SY8 3LQ. Tel: 01584-890287. *Founder*, Maj. A. H. Coles

HELLENIC STUDIES, SOCIETY FOR THE PROMOTION OF (1879), 31–34 Gordon Square, London WC1H 0PP. Tel: 0171-387 7495. *Secretary*, Miss F. J. Fisher

HELP THE AGED (1960), St James's Walk, Clerkenwell Green, London EC1R 0BE. Tel: 0171-253 0253. *Director-General*, J. Mayo, OBE

HERALDIC AND GENEALOGICAL STUDIES, INSTITUTE OF (1961), 79–82 Northgate, Canterbury, Kent CT1 1BA. Tel: 01227-768664. *Registrar*, J. Palmer

HERALDRY SOCIETY, THE (1947), 44–45 Museum Street, London WC1A 1LY. Tel: 0171-430 2172. *Secretary*, Mrs M. Miles, MBE

HERPETOLOGICAL SOCIETY, BRITISH (1947), c/o Zoological Society of London, Regent's Park, London NW1 4RY. Tel: 0181-452 9578. *Secretary*, Mrs M. Green

HISPANIC AND LUSO BRAZILIAN COUNCIL (1943), Canning House, 2 Belgrave Square, London SW1X 8PJ. Tel: 0171-235 2303. *Director-General*, Sir Michael Simpson-Orlebar, KCMG

HISTORICAL ASSOCIATION, THE (1906), 59A Kennington Park Road, London SE11 4JH. Tel: 0171-735 3901. *Secretary*, Mrs M. Stiles

HISTORICAL SOCIETY, ROYAL (1868), University College London, Gower Street, London WC1E 6BT. Tel: 0171-387 7532. *Executive Secretary*, Mrs J. N. McCarthy

HOMOEOPATHIC ASSOCIATION, BRITISH (1902), 27A Devonshire Street, London W1N 1RJ. Tel: 0171-935 2163. *General Secretary*, Mrs E. Segall

HONG KONG ASSOCIATION (1961), Swire House, 59 Buckingham Gate, London SW1E 6AJ. *Executive Director*, Brig. B. G. Hickey, OBE, MC

HOROLOGICAL INSTITUTE, BRITISH (1858), Upton Hall, Upton, Newark, Notts NG23 5TE. Tel: 01636-813795/6. *Secretary*, Ms H. Bartlett

HOROLOGICAL SOCIETY, ANTIQUARIAN (1953), New House, High Street, Ticehurst, Wadhurst, E. Sussex TN5 7AL. Tel: 01580-200155. *Secretary*, Mrs M. A. Collins

HORSE SOCIETY, BRITISH (1947) (incorporating The Pony Club), British Equestrian Centre, Stoneleigh Park, Kenilworth, Warks CV8 2LR. Tel: 01203-696697. *Chief Executive*, Col. T. Eastwood

HOSPITAL FEDERATION, INTERNATIONAL (1947), 4 Abbot's Place, London NW6 4NP. Tel: 0171-372 7181. *Director-General*, Dr E. N. Pickering

HOSPITAL SATURDAY FUND, THE (1873), 24 Upper Ground, London SE1 9PQ. Tel: 0171-928 6662. *Chief Executive*, K. R. Bradley

HOSPITAL SAVING ASSOCIATION, THE, Hambleden House, Andover, Hants SP10 1LQ. Tel: 01264-353211. *General Secretary*, J. A. Young

HOSPITALITY ASSOCIATION, BRITISH (1907), Queen's House, 55–56 Lincoln's Inn Fields, London WC2A 3BH. Tel: 0171-404 7744. *Chief Executive*, R. Lees, CB, MBE

HOTEL AND CATERING INTERNATIONAL MANAGEMENT ASSOCIATION (1971), 191 Trinity Road, London SW17 7HN. Tel: 0181-672 4251. *Chief Executive*, J. Logie

HOUSE OF ST BARNABAS-IN-SOHO (1846), 1 Greek Street, London W1V 6NQ. Tel: 0171-437 1894. For homeless women in London. *Director*, D. G. Saunders

HOUSING, CHARTERED INSTITUTE OF, Octavia House, Westwood Business Park, Westwood Way, Coventry CV4 8JP. Tel: 01203-694433. *Director*, Ms C. Laird

HOUSING AID SOCIETY, CATHOLIC (1956), 209 Old Marylebone Road, London NW1 5QT. Tel: 0171-723 7273. *Director*, Ms R. Rafferty

HOUSING AND TOWN PLANNING COUNCIL, NATIONAL (1900), 14–18 Old Street, London EC1V 9AB. Tel: 0171-251 2363. *Director*, Ms A. Holmes

HOVERCRAFT SOCIETY, THE (1971), 24 Jellicoe Avenue, Alverstoke, Gosport, Hants PO12 2PE. Tel: 01705-601310. *Chairman*, M. J. Cox

HOWARD LEAGUE FOR PENAL REFORM (1866), 708 Holloway Road, London N19 3NL. Tel: 0171-281 7722. *Director*, Ms F. Crook

HUGUENOT SOCIETY OF GREAT BRITAIN AND IRELAND (1885), The Huguenot Library, University College, Gower Street, London WC1E 6BT. Tel: 0171-380 7094. *Hon. Secretary*, Mrs M. Bayliss

HUMANE RESEARCH TRUST (1974), Brook House, 29 Bramhall Lane South, Bramhall, Stockport, Cheshire SK7 2DN. Tel: 0161-439 8041. *Chairman*, K. Cholerton

HUMANIST ASSOCIATION, BRITISH (1963), 47 Theobald's Road, London WC1X 8SP. Tel: 0171-430 0908. *Administrator*, Ms A. Todd

HYDROGRAPHIC SOCIETY (1972), c/o University of East London, Longbridge Road, Dagenham, Essex RM8 2AS. Tel: 0181-597 1946. *Hon. Secretary*, V. J. Abbott

HYMN SOCIETY OF GREAT BRITAIN AND IRELAND (1936), St Nicholas Rectory, Glebe Fields, Curdworth, Sutton Coldfield, W. Midlands B76 9ES. Tel: 01675-470384. *Secretary*, Revd M. Garland

IMMIGRATION ADVISORY SERVICE (1970), County House, 190 Great Dover Street, London SE1 4YB. Tel: 0171-357 7511/24 hour line: 0181-814 1559. *Chief Executive*, K. Best

INDEPENDENT BRITAIN, CAMPAIGN FOR AN (1976), 81 Ashmole Street, London SW8 1NF. Tel: 0181-340 0314. *Hon. Secretary*, Sir Robin Williams, Bt.

INDEPENDENT SCHOOL BURSARS' ASSOCIATION (1933), Woodlands, Closewood Road, Denmead, Waterlooville, Hants PO7 6JD. Tel: 01705-264506. *Secretary*, D. J. Bird

INDEPENDENT SCHOOLS CAREERS ORGANIZATION (1942), 12A Princess Way, Camberley, Surrey GU15 3SP. Tel: 01276-21188. *National Director*, G. W. Searle

INDEPENDENT SCHOOLS INFORMATION SERVICE (ISIS) (1972), 56 Buckingham Gate, London SW1E 6AG. Tel: 0171-630 8793. *Director*, D. J. Woodhead

INDEPENDENT SCHOOLS JOINT COUNCIL (1974), Grosvenor Gardens House, 35–37 Grosvenor Gardens, London SW1W 0BS. Tel: 0171-630 0144. *General Secretary*, Dr A. G. Hearnden, OBE

INDEXERS, SOCIETY OF (1957), 38 Rochester Road, London NW1 9JJ. Tel: 0171-916 7809. *Secretary*, Mrs C. Troughton

INDUSTRIAL SOCIETY, THE (1918), Robert Hyde House, 48 Bryanston Square, London W1H 7LN. Tel: 0171-262 2401. *Chief Executive*, T. Morgan

INDUSTRY AND PARLIAMENT TRUST, 1 Buckingham Place, London SW1E 6HR. Tel: 0171-976 5311. *Director*, F. R. Hyde-Chambers

INDUSTRY CHURCHES FORUM (formerly Industrial Christian Fellowship) (1877), 86 Leadenhall Street, London EC3A 3DH. Tel: 0171-283 6120. *Director*, Revd R. Holloway

INDUSTRY TRAINING ORGANIZATIONS, NATIONAL COUNCIL OF (1988), 10 Meadowcourt, Amos Road, Sheffield S9 1BX. Tel: 0114-261 9926. *Administrator*, J. Maisari

INFANT DEATHS, FOUNDATION FOR THE STUDY OF (1971), 35 Belgrave Square, London SW1X 8QB. Tel: 0171-235 0965/1721 (Cot death helpline). *Secretary-General*, Mrs J. Epstein

INFORMATION SCIENTISTS, INSTITUTE OF (1958), 44–45 Museum Street, London WC1A 1LY. Tel: 0171-831 8003. *Director*, E. Hyams

INNER WHEEL CLUBS IN GREAT BRITAIN AND IRELAND, ASSOCIATION OF (1934), 51 Warwick Square, London SW1V 2AT. Tel: 0171-834 4600. *General Secretary,* Miss J. Dobson

INSOLVENCY, SOCIETY OF PRACTITIONERS OF (1990), 18–19 Long Lane, London EC1A 9HE. Tel: 0171-600 3375. *General Secretary,* R. M. Stancombe

INSURANCE AND INVESTMENT BROKERS' ASSOCIATION, BRITISH, BIIBA House, 14 Bevis Marks, London EC3A 7NT. Tel: 0171-623 9043. *Chairman,* S. R. Arnold

INSURANCE BROKERS REGISTRATION COUNCIL, 15 St Helen's Place, London EC3A 6DS. Tel: 0171-588 4387. *Registrar,* Miss E. J. Rees

INSURANCE INSTITUTE, CHARTERED (1897), 20 Aldermanbury, London EC2V 7HY. Tel: 0171-606 3835. *Director-General,* Prof. D. E. Bland

INSURERS, ASSOCIATION OF BRITISH (1985), 51 Gresham Street, London EC2V 7HQ. Tel: 0171-600 3333. *Director-General,* M. Boléat

INTERCON (INTERCONTINENTAL CHURCH SOCIETY) (1823), 175 Tower Bridge Road, London SE1 2AQ. Tel: 0171-407 4588. *General Secretary,* Deaconess P. K. L. Schmiegelow

INTERNATIONAL AFFAIRS, ROYAL INSTITUTE OF (1920), Chatham House, 10 St James's Square, London SW1Y 4LE. Tel: 0171-957 5700. *Director,* Sir Laurence Martin

INTERNATIONAL FRIENDSHIP LEAGUE (1931), 3 Creswick Road, London W3 9HE. Tel: 0181-992 0221. *Secretary,* Mrs B. Macdonald

INTERNATIONAL POLICE ASSOCIATION (British Section) (1950), 1 Fox Road, West Bridgford, Nottingham NG2 6AJ. Tel: 0115-981 3638. *Chief Executive Officer,* A. F. Carter

INTERNATIONAL STUDENTS HOUSE (1962), 229 Great Portland Street, London W1N 5HD. Tel: 0171-631 8300. *Executive Director,* P. Anwyl

INTERNATIONAL TIN RESEARCH INSTITUTE (1932), Kingston Lane, Uxbridge, Middx UB8 3PJ. Tel: 01895-272406. *Director,* R. Bedder

INTERSERVE (1852), 325 Kennington Road, London SE11 4QH. Tel: 0171-735 8227. *National Director,* R. Clark

INTER VARSITY CLUBS, ASSOCIATION OF (1946), 2nd Floor, Grosvenor House, 94–96 Grosvenor Street, Manchester M1 7HL. Tel: 0161-273 2316. *Secretary,* D. Bousfield

INVALID CHILDREN'S AID NATIONWIDE (I CAN) (1888), 10 Bowling Green Lane, London EC1R 0BD. Tel: 0171-253 9111. *Director,* B. J. Jones

INVALIDS-AT-HOME (1966), 17 Lapstone Gardens, Kenton, Harrow HA3 0EB. Tel: 0181-907 1706. *Executive Officer,* Mrs S. Lomas

INVISIBLES, BRITISH (1983), 6th Floor, Windsor House, 39 King Street, London EC2V 8DQ. Tel: 0171-600 1198. *Director-General,* Mrs A. Wright

INVOLVEMENT AND PARTICIPATION ASSOCIATION (1884), 42 Colebrooke Row, London N1 8AF. Tel: 0171-354 8040. *Director,* B. C. Stevens

IRAN SOCIETY (1936), 2 Belgrave Square, London SW1X 8PJ. Tel: 0171-235 5122. *Hon. Secretary,* A. D. Ashmole

JACQUELINE DU PRÉ MUSIC BUILDING APPEAL (1988), The Development and Alumnae Office, St Hilda's College, Oxford OX4 1DY. Tel: 01865-276803. *Chairman,* Dr J. H. Mellanby

JAPAN ASSOCIATION, THE (1950), Swire House, 59 Buckingham Gate, London SW1E 6AJ. *Executive Director,* Brig. B. G. Hickey, OBE, MC

JERUSALEM AND THE MIDDLE EAST CHURCH ASSOCIATION, THE (1887), 1 Hart House, The Hart, Farnham, Surrey GU9 7HA. Tel: 01252-726994. *Secretary,* Mrs V. Wells

JEWISH HISTORICAL SOCIETY OF ENGLAND (1893), 33 Seymour Place, London W1H 5AP. Tel: 0171-723 5852. *Hon. Secretary,* C. M. Drukker

JEWISH YOUTH, ASSOCIATION FOR (1899), 128 East Lane, Wembley, Middx HA0 3NL. Tel: 0181-908 4747. *Executive Director,* M. Shaw

JEWS, CHURCH'S MINISTRY AMONG THE (1809), 30c Clarence Road, St Albans, Herts AL1 4JJ. Tel: 01727-833114. *General Director,* Revd Dr W. Riggans

JOURNALISTS, THE CHARTERED INSTITUTE OF (1883), 2 Dock Offices, Surrey Quays, Lower Road, London SE16 2XU. Tel: 0171-252 1187. *General Secretary,* C. J. Underwood

JUSTICE (British Section of the International Commission of Jurists) (1957), 59 Carter Lane, London EC4V 5AQ. Tel: 0171-329 5100. *Director,* Ms A. Owers

JUSTICES' CLERKS' SOCIETY (1839), The Law Courts, Petters Way, Yeovil, Somerset BA20 1SW. Tel: 01935-21912. *Hon. Secretary,* L. G. C. Cramp

KING EDWARD'S HOSPITAL FUND FOR LONDON (THE KING'S FUND) (1897), 11–13 Cavendish Square, London W1M 0AN. Tel: 0171-307 2400. *Director,* Dr R. J. Maxwell, CBE

KING GEORGE'S FUND FOR SAILORS (1917), 8 Hatherley Street, London SW1P 2YY. Tel: 0171-932 0000. *Director-General,* Capt. M. J. Appleton, RN

KIPLING SOCIETY, THE (1927), PO Box 68, Haslemere, Surrey GU27 2YR. Tel: 01428-652709. *Hon. Secretary,* N. Entract

LADIES IN REDUCED CIRCUMSTANCES, SOCIETY FOR THE ASSISTANCE OF (1886), Lancaster House, 25 Hornyold Road, Malvern, Worcs WR14 1QQ. Tel: 01684-574645. *Secretary*

LANDSCAPE INSTITUTE (1929), 6–7 Barnard Mews, London SW11 1QU. Tel: 0171-738 9166. *Registrar,* S. Royston

LAND-VALUE TAXATION AND FREE TRADE, INTERNATIONAL UNION FOR, 177 Vauxhall Bridge Road, London SW1V 1EU. Tel: 0171-834 4266. *Hon. Secretary,* Mrs B. P. Sobrielo

LANGUAGE LEARNING, ASSOCIATION FOR (1990), 150 Railway Terrace, Rugby CV21 3HN. Tel: 01788-546443. *Secretary-General,* Mrs C. Wilding

LAW REPORTING FOR ENGLAND AND WALES, INCORPORATED COUNCIL OF (1865), 3 Stone Buildings, Lincoln's Inn, London WC2A 3XN. Tel: 0171-242 6471. *Secretary,* B. Symondson

LEAGUE OF THE HELPING HAND (1908), Petersham Hollow, 226 Petersham Road, Petersham, Richmond, Surrey TW10 7AL. Tel: 0181-940 7303. *Secretary,* Mrs I. Goodlad

LEAGUE OF WELLDOERS (1893), 119–133 Limekiln Lane, Liverpool L5 8SN. Tel: 0151-207 1984. *Warden and Secretary,* K. H. Stanton

LEATHER AND HIDE TRADES' BENEVOLENT INSTITUTION (1860), 60 Wickham Hill, Hurstpierpoint, Hassocks, W. Sussex BN6 9NP. Tel: 01273-843488. *Secretary*, Mrs G. M. Stapleton, MBE

LEGAL EXECUTIVES, INSTITUTE OF (1892), Kempston Manor, Kempston, Bedford MK42 7AB. Tel: 01234-841000. *Secretary-General*, R. Ball

LEONARD CHESHIRE FOUNDATION (1955), 26–29 Maunsel Street, London SW1P 2QN. Tel: 0171-828 1822. *Director-General*, J. Stanford

LEPROSY MISSION, THE (England and Wales) (1874), Goldhay Way, Orton Goldhay, Peterborough PE2 5GZ. Tel: 01733-370505. *Executive Director*, Revd J. A. Lloyd, PH.D.

LEUKAEMIA RESEARCH FUND (1962), 43 Great Ormond Street, London WC1N 3JJ. Tel: 0171-405 0101. *Executive Director*, D. L. Osborne

LIBERAL PARTY (1877; relaunched 1989), Gayfere House, 22 Gayfere Street, London SW1 3HP. Tel: 0171-233 2124. *Secretary-General*, N. Ashton

LIBERTY (NATIONAL COUNCIL FOR CIVIL LIBERTIES) (1934), 21 Tabard Street, London SE1 4LA. Tel: 0171-403 3888. *General Secretary*, A. Puddephatt

LIBRARY ASSOCIATION (1877), 7 Ridgmount Street, London WC1E 7AE. Tel: 0171-636 7543. *Chief Executive*, R. Shimmon

LIFEBOATS, *see* ROYAL NATIONAL LIFEBOAT INSTITUTION

LIGHT HORSE BREEDING SOCIETY, NATIONAL (1885), 96 High Street, Edenbridge, Kent TN8 5AR. Tel: 01732-866277. *Secretary*, G. W. Evans

LINGUISTS, INSTITUTE OF (1910), 24A Highbury Grove, London N5 2EA. Tel: 0171-359 7445. *Director*, Ms E. H. F. Ostarhild

LINNEAN SOCIETY OF LONDON, THE (1788), Burlington House, Piccadilly, London W1V 0LQ. Tel: 0171-434 4479. *President*, Prof. B. G. Gardiner; *Executive Secretary*, Dr J. C. Marsden

LIONS CLUBS INTERNATIONAL (British Isles and Ireland) (1949), 257 Alcester Road South, Kings Heath, Birmingham B14 6BT. Tel: 0121-441 4544. *Office Manager*, Mrs J. Davis

LLOYD'S OF LONDON, 1 Lime Street, London EC3M 7HA. Tel: 0171-623 7100. *Chief Executive*, P. J. Middleton

LLOYD'S PATRIOTIC FUND (1803), Lloyd's, Lime Street, London EC3M 7HA. Tel: 0171-327 5925. *Secretary*, Mrs L. Harper

LLOYD'S REGISTER, 71 Fenchurch Street, London EC3M 4BS. Tel: 0171-709 9166

LOCAL AUTHORITY CHIEF EXECUTIVES, SOCIETY OF (1974), PO Box 21, Archway Road, Huyton, Knowsley, Merseyside L36 9YU. Tel: 0151-443 3931. *Executive Officer*, Ms S. Rheinlander

LOCAL COUNCILS, NATIONAL ASSOCIATION OF (1947), 109 Great Russell Street, London WC1B 3LD. Tel: 0171-637 1865. *Secretary*, J. Clark, OBE

LOCAL GOVERNMENT INTERNATIONAL BUREAU (1913), *also* Council of European Municipalities and Regions (British Section) and International Union of Local Authorities (British Section) (1951), 35 Great Smith Street, London SW1P 3BJ. Tel: 0171-222 1636. *Secretary-General*, vacant

LOCAL HISTORY, BRITISH ASSOCIATION FOR (1843), 24 Lower Street, Harnham, Salisbury, Wilts SP2 8EY. Tel: 01722-320115. *Administrator*, M. Cowan

LONDON APPRECIATION SOCIETY (1932), 14 Hillview, 24 Primrose Hill Road, London NW3 3AX. *Hon. Secretary*, Miss V. Colin-Russ

LONDON CITY MISSION (1835), 175 Tower Bridge Road, London SE1 2AH. Tel: 0171-407 7585. *General Secretary*, Revd J. McAllen

LONDON COURT OF INTERNATIONAL ARBITRATION (1892), 12 Carthusian Street, London EC1M 6EB. Tel: 0171-417 8228. *Registrar*, B. W. Vigrass, OBE, VRD

LONDON FLOTILLA (1937), Marden Rise, 81 Lower Road, Fetcham, Leatherhead, Surrey KT22 9HG. Tel: 01372-453059. *Hon. Secretary*, Lt. Cdr. P. A. G. Norman, RD, RNR

LONDON GOVERNMENT, ASSOCIATION OF (1964), 32 Old Queen Street, London SW1H 9JF. Tel: 0171-222 7799. *Secretary*, J. McDonnell

LONDON LIBRARY, THE (1841), 14 St James's Square, London SW1Y 4LG. Tel: 0171-930 7705. *Librarian*, A. S. Bell

LONDON MAGISTRATES' CLERKS' ASSOCIATION (1889), c/o Thames Magistrates' Court, 58 Bow Road, London E3 4DJ. Tel: 0181-980 1000, ext. 3708. *Hon. Secretary*, J. Mulreany

LONDON PLAYING FIELDS SOCIETY, THE (1890), Boston Manor Playing Field, Boston Gardens, Brentford, Middx TW8 9LR. Tel: 0181-560 3667. *Secretary*, D. Northwood

LONDON SOCIETY, THE (1912), 4th Floor, Senate House, Malet Street, London WC1E 7HU. Tel: 0171-580 5537. *Hon. Secretary*, Mrs B. Jones

LORD'S DAY OBSERVANCE SOCIETY, THE (1831), 6 Sherman Road, Bromley, Kent BR1 3JH. Tel: 0181-313 0456. *General Secretary*, J. G. Roberts

LOTTERIES COUNCIL, THE (1979), c/o Community Publishing (Avon) Ltd, PO Box 215, Pamwell House, Pennywell Road, Bristol BS99 7QX. Tel: 0117-954 1111. *Hon. Secretary*, P. Broderick

LUNG FOUNDATION, BRITISH (1985), 8 Peterborough Mews, London SW6 3BL. Tel: 0171-371 7704. *Director*, I. J. Govendir

MAGISTRATES' ASSOCIATION, THE (1920), 28 Fitzroy Square, London W1P 6DD. Tel: 0171-387 2353. *Secretary*, Ms S. Dickson

MAILING PREFERENCE SERVICE (1983). To limit direct mail: Freepost 22, London W1E 7EZ. Business: 5 Reef House, London SW11 3UF. Tel: 0171-738 1625. *Chief Executive*, Ms K. Beckett

MAIL USERS' ASSOCIATION (1976), Pharos House, Wye Valley Business Park, Hay-on-Wye, Hereford HR3 5PG. Tel: 01497-821357. *President*, L. K. Morelli

MALAYSIAN RUBBER PRODUCERS' RESEARCH ASSOCIATION (1938), Tun Abdul Razak Laboratory, Brickendonbury, Hertford SG13 8NL. Tel: 01992-584966. *Director*, Dr C. S. L. Baker

MALCOLM SARGENT CANCER FUND FOR CHILDREN (1968), 14 Abingdon Road, London W8 6AF. Tel: 0171-937 4548. *Chief Executive*, Ms S. Darley, OBE

MANAGEMENT, INSTITUTE OF (1992), 3rd Floor, 2 Savoy Court, Strand, London WC2R 0EZ. Tel: 0171-497 0580. *Director-General*, R. Young

MANAGEMENT AND PROFESSIONAL STAFFS, ASSOCIATION OF (1972), Parkgates, Bury New Road, Prestwich, Manchester M25 8JX. Tel: 0161-773 8621. *Executive Secretary*, A. J. Casey

MANAGEMENT SERVICES, INSTITUTE OF, 1 Cecil Court, London Road, Enfield, Middx EN2 6DD. Tel: 0181-366 1261. *Secretary*

MANIC DEPRESSION FELLOWSHIP (1983), 8–10 High Street, Kingston upon Thames, Surrey KT1 1EY. Tel: 0181-974 6550. *Director*, Ms M. Fulford

MANORIAL SOCIETY OF GREAT BRITAIN (1906), 104 Kennington Road, London SE11 6RE. Tel: 0171-735 6633. *Hon. Chairman*, R. A. Smith

MANPOWER SOCIETY (1969), 39 Apple Tree Walk, Climping, Littlehampton, W. Sussex BN17 5QN. Tel: 01903-731728. *Administrator*, Mrs H. Gale

MARIE CURIE CANCER CARE (1948), 28 Belgrave Square, London SW1X 8QG. Tel: 0171-235 3325. *Scottish Office*, 21 Rutland Street, Edinburgh EH1 2AH. Tel: 0131-229 8332. *Director-General*, Maj.-Gen. M. E. Carleton-Smith, CBE

MARINE ARTISTS, ROYAL SOCIETY OF (1939), 17 Carlton House Terrace, London SW1Y 5BD. Tel: 0171-930 6844. *Secretary*, Ms S. Robinson

MARINE BIOLOGICAL ASSOCIATION OF THE UK (1884), Citadel Hill, Plymouth PL1 2PB. Tel: 01752-669762. *Secretary*, Dr M. Whitfield

MARINE ENGINEERS, INSTITUTE OF (1889), The Memorial Building, 76 Mark Lane, London EC3R 7JN. Tel: 0171-481 8493. *Secretary*, J. E. Sloggett, OBE

MARINE SCIENCE, THE SCOTTISH ASSOCIATION FOR (1914), PO Box 3, Oban, Argyll PA34 4AD. Tel: 01631-562244. *Secretary*, Prof. J. B. L. Matthews, FRSE

MARINE SOCIETY, THE (1756), 202 Lambeth Road, London SE1 7JW. Tel: 0171-261 9535. *General Secretary*, Lt. Cdr. R. M. Frampton

MARIO LANZA EDUCATIONAL FOUNDATION (1976), 7 Lionsfield Avenue, Allesley Village, Coventry CV5 9GN. *Hon. Secretary*, Miss P. Barron

MARKET AUTHORITIES, NATIONAL ASSOCIATION OF BRITISH (1948), 21 Tarnside Road, Orrell, Wigan WN5 8RN. Tel: 01695-623860. *Secretary*, J. Edwards

MARKETING, CHARTERED INSTITUTE OF (1911), Moor Hall, Cookham, Maidenhead, Berks SL6 9QH. Tel: 01628-524922. *Director-General*, S. Cuthbert

MARK MASTER MASONS, GRAND LODGE OF (1856), Mark Masons' Hall, 86 St James's Street, London SW1A 1PL. Tel: 0171-839 5274. *Grand Master*, HRH Prince Michael of Kent, KCVO; *Grand Secretary*, P. G. Williams

MARRIAGE CARE (formerly the Catholic Marriage Advisory Council) (1946), Clitherow House, 1 Blythe Mews, Blythe Road, London W14 0NW. Tel: 0171-371 1341. *Chief Executive*, Mrs M. Corbett

MASONIC BENEVOLENT INSTITUTION, ROYAL (1842), 20 Great Queen Street, London WC2B 5BG. Tel: 0171-405 8341. *Chief Executive*, Ms J. Reynolds

MASONIC BENEVOLENT INSTITUTIONS IN IRELAND, 17–19 Molesworth Street, Dublin 2. Tel: 00 353-1-679 6799. *Secretary*, M. R. McWilliam

MASONIC TRUST FOR GIRLS AND BOYS (1985), 31 Great Queen Street, London WC2B 5AG. Tel: 0171-405 2644. *Secretary*, Lt.-Col. J. C. Chambers

MASTERS OF WINE, INSTITUTE OF (1955), Five Kings House, 1 Queen Street Place, London EC4R 1QS. Tel: 0171-236 4427. *Executive Director*, J. F. Casson

MATERNAL AND CHILD WELFARE, NATIONAL ASSOCIATION FOR (1911), 40–42 Osnaburgh Street, London NW1 3ND. Tel: 0171-383 4117. *Administrator*, Mrs V. A. Farebrother

MATERIALS, INSTITUTE OF (1985), 1 Carlton House Terrace, London SW1Y 5DB. Tel: 0171-839 4071. *Secretary*, Dr J. A. Catterall

MATERNITY ALLIANCE, THE (1980), 15 Britannia Street, London WC1X 9JP. Tel: 0171-837 1265. *Chair*, A. Phillips

MATHEMATICAL ASSOCIATION (1871), 259 London Road, Leicester LE2 3BE. Tel: 0116-270 3877. *Executive Secretary*, Ms H. Whitby

MATHEMATICS AND ITS APPLICATIONS, INSTITUTE OF (1964), Catherine Richards House, 16 Nelson Street, Southend-on-Sea, Essex SS1 1EF. Tel: 01702-354020. *Executive Secretary*, Dr A. M. Lepper

ME ASSOCIATION (1976), Stanhope House, High Street, Stanford-le-Hope, Essex SS17 0HA. Tel: 01375-642466. *Chief Executive*, vacant

MEASUREMENT AND CONTROL, INSTITUTE OF, 87 Gower Street, London WC1E 6AA. Tel: 0171-387 4949. *Secretary*, M. Yates

MECHANICAL ENGINEERS, INSTITUTION OF (1847), 1 Birdcage Walk, London SW1H 9JJ. Tel: 0171-222 7899. *Director-General*, Dr R. Pike

MEDIC-ALERT FOUNDATION, 12 Bridge Wharf, 156 Caledonian Road, London N1 9UU. Tel: 0171-833 3034. *Chief Executive*, Miss J. Friend

MEDICAL COUNCIL, GENERAL (1858), 178–202 Great Portland Street, London W1N 6JE. Tel: 0171-580 7642. *Registrar*, F. Scott, TD

MEDICAL SOCIETY OF LONDON (1773), Lettsom House, 11 Chandos Street, London W1M 0EB. Tel: 0171-580 1043. *Registrar*, M. Griffiths, TD

MEDICAL WOMEN'S FEDERATION (1917), Tavistock House North, Tavistock Square, London WC1H 9HX. *Hon. Secretary*, Dr I. Weinreb

MEMORIAL FUND FOR DISASTER RELIEF, Europa House, 13–17 Ironmonger Row, London EC1V 3QN. Tel: 0171-250 1700. *Director*, D. Childs

MENCAP (THE ROYAL SOCIETY FOR MENTALLY HANDICAPPED CHILDREN AND ADULTS) (1946), 123 Golden Lane, London EC1Y 0RT. Tel: 0171-454 0454. *Chief Executive*, F. Heddell

MENTAL AFTER CARE ASSOCIATION (1879), 25 Bedford Square, London WC1B 3HW. Tel: 0171-436 6194. *Director*, B. G. Garner

MENTAL HEALTH FOUNDATION, THE (1949), 37 Mortimer Street, London W1N 8JU. Tel: 0171-580 0145. *Director-General*, Ms J. McKerrow

MERCHANT NAVY WELFARE BOARD (1948), 19–21 Lancaster Gate, London W2 3LN. Tel: 0171-723 3642. *General Secretary*, Capt. D. A. Parsons

METAL TRADES BENEVOLENT SOCIETY, ROYAL (1843), Brooke House, 4 The Lakes, Bedford Road, Northampton NN4 7YD. Tel: 01604-22023. *General Secretary*, A. N. Nisbet

METEOROLOGICAL SOCIETY, ROYAL (1850), 104 Oxford Road, Reading, Berks RG1 7LJ. Tel: 01734-568500. *Executive Secretary*, R. P. C. Swash

METROPOLITAN AND CITY POLICE ORPHANS FUND (1870), 30 Hazlewell Road, London SW15 6LH. Tel: 0181-788 5140. *Secretary,* R. Duff-Cole, BEM

METROPOLITAN AUTHORITIES, ASSOCIATION OF (1974), 35 Great Smith Street, London SW1P 3BJ. Tel: 0171-222 8100. *Secretar,* R. Brooke

METROPOLITAN HOSPITAL-SUNDAY FUND (1872), 40 High Street, Teddington, Middx TW11 8EW. Tel: 0181-977 4154. *Secretary,* D. A. B. Lynch

MIDDLE EAST ASSOCIATION, THE (1961), Bury House, 33 Bury Street, London SW1Y 6AX. Tel: 0171-839 2137. *Director-General,* J. R. Grundon

MIDWIVES, ROYAL COLLEGE OF (1881), 15 Mansfield Street, London WIM 0BE. Tel: 0171-872 8100. *General Secretary,* Mrs J. Allison

MIGRAINE ASSOCIATION, BRITISH (1958), 178A High Road, Byfleet, West Byfleet, Surrey KT14 7ED. Tel: 01932-352468. *Director,* Mrs J. Liddell

MIGRAINE TRUST (1965), 45 Great Ormond Street, London WC1N 3HZ. Tel: 0171-278 2676. *Director,* Ms A. Rush

MILITARY HISTORICAL SOCIETY, National Army Museum, Royal Hospital Road, London SW3 4HT. Tel: 0181-460 7341. *Hon. Secretary,* J. Gaylor

MIND (NATIONAL ASSOCIATION FOR MENTAL HEALTH), Granta House, 15–19 Broadway, Stratford, London E15 4BQ. Tel: 0181-519 2122. Information Line: 0181-522 1728. *National Director,* Ms J. Clements

MINERALOGICAL SOCIETY (1876), 41 Queen's Gate, London SW7 5HR. Tel: 0171-584 7516. *Hon. General Secretary,* Dr B. A. Cressey

MINES OF GREAT BRITAIN, FEDERATION OF SMALL, 29 King Street, Newcastle under Lyme, Staffs ST5 1ER. Tel: 01782-614618. *Secretary,* R. W. Bladen

MINIATURE PAINTERS, SCULPTORS AND GRAVERS, ROYAL SOCIETY OF (1895), Burwood House, 15 Union Street, Wells, Somerset BA5 2PU. Tel: 01749-674472. *Executive Secretary,* Mrs S. M. Burton

MINING AND METALLURGY, THE INSTITUTION OF (1892), 44 Portland Place, London WIN 4BR. Tel: 0171-580 3802. *Secretary,* M. J. Jones

MINING ENGINEERS, INSTITUTION OF (1889), Danum House, 6A South Parade, Doncaster, S. Yorks DN1 2DY. Tel: 01302-320486. *Secretary,* Dr G. J. M. Woodrow

MISSING PERSONS HELPLINE, NATIONAL (1992), Roebuck House, 284–286 Upper Richmond Road West, London SW14 7JE. Tel: 0181-392 2000. Helpline: 0500-700700. *Chairman,* D. Winn

MISSION TO DEEP SEA FISHERMEN, ROYAL NATIONAL (1881), 43 Nottingham Place, London WIM 4BX. Tel: 0171-487 5101. *Chief Executive,* A. D. Marsden

MISSIONS TO SEAMEN, THE (1856), St Michael Paternoster Royal, College Hill, London EC4R 2RL. Tel: 0171-248 5202. *Secretary-General,* Revd Canon G. Jones

MODERN CHURCHPEOPLE'S UNION (1898), St Martin's Vicarage, 25 Birch Grove, London W3 9SP. Tel: 0181-992 2333. *General Secretary,* Revd N. Henderson

MONUMENTAL BRASS SOCIETY (1887), Lowe Hill House, Stratford St Mary, Suffolk CO7 6JX. Tel: 01206-337239/ 0181-520 5249. *Hon. Secretary,* H. M. Stuchfield

MORAVIAN MISSIONS, LONDON ASSOCIATION IN AID OF (1817), Moravian Church House, 5–7 Muswell Hill, London N10 3TH. Tel: 0181-883 3409. *Secretary,* Ms J. Morten

MOTHERS' UNION, THE (1876), Mary Sumner House, 24 Tufton Street, London SW1P 3RB. Tel: 0171-222 5533. *Chief Executive,* Mrs A. Ridler

MOTOR INDUSTRY, INSTITUTE OF THE, Fanshaws, Brickendon, Hertford SG13 8PQ. Tel: 01992-511521. *Secretary,* F. W. Janes

MOUNTBATTEN MEMORIAL TRUST (1979), 1 Grosvenor Crescent, London SW1X 7EF. Tel: 0171-235 5231. *Director,* J. Boyd-Brent

MOUNTBATTEN TRUST, THE EDWINA (1960), 1 Grosvenor Crescent, London SW1X 7EF. Tel: 0171-235 5231. *Secretary,* J. Boyd-Brent

MULTIPLE SCLEROSIS SOCIETY (1953), 25 Effie Road, London SW6 1EE. Tel: 0171-736 6267. *Chief Executive,* P. Cardy

MUNICIPAL ENGINEERS, ASSOCIATION OF, Institution of Civil Engineers, Great George Street, London SW1P 3AA. Tel: 0171-222 7722. *Director,* K. J. Marchant

MUSEUMS ASSOCIATION (1889), 42 Clerkenwell Close, London EC1R 0PA. Tel: 0171-608 2933. *Director,* M. Taylor

MUSIC HALL SOCIETY, BRITISH (1963), Brodie and Middleton Ltd, 68 Drury Lane, London WC2B 5SP. Tel: 0171-836 3289/80. *Hon. Secretary,* Mrs J. D. Masterton

MUSICIANS BENEVOLENT FUND (1921), 16 Ogle Street, London WIP 8JB. Tel: 0171-636 4481. *Secretary,* Ms H. Faulkner

MUSICIANS, INCORPORATED SOCIETY OF (1882), 10 Stratford Place, London WIN 9AE. Tel: 0171-629 4413. *Chief Executive,* N. Hoyle

MUSICIANS OF GREAT BRITAIN, ROYAL SOCIETY OF (1738), 10 Stratford Place, London WIN 9AE. Tel: 0171-629 6137. *Secretary,* Mrs M. Gibb

MUSIC INFORMATION CENTRE, BRITISH (1967), 10 Stratford Place, London WIN 9AE. Tel: 0171-499 8567. *Directors,* M. Greenall; T. Morgan

MUSIC SOCIETIES, NATIONAL FEDERATION OF (1935), Francis House, Francis Street, London SW1P 1DE. Tel: 0171-828 7320. *Chief Executive,* R. Jones

NABC – CLUBS FOR YOUNG PEOPLE (1925), 369 Kennington Lane, London SE11 5QY. Tel: 0171-793 0787. *National Director,* D. James

NACRO (NATIONAL ASSOCIATION FOR THE CARE AND RESETTLEMENT OF OFFENDERS) (1966), 169 Clapham Road, London SW9 0PU. Tel: 0171-582 6500. *Director,* Ms V. Stern

NATIONAL BENEVOLENT INSTITUTION (1812), 61 Bayswater Road, London W2 3PG. Tel: 0171-723 0021. *Secretary,* Gp Capt D. St J. Homer, MVO

NATIONAL COUNCIL FOR VOLUNTARY ORGANIZATIONS (1919), Regent's Wharf, 8 All Saints Street, London N1 9RL. Tel: 0171-713 6161. *Chief Executive,* S. Etherington

NATIONAL COUNCIL OF WOMEN OF GREAT BRITAIN (1895), 36 Danbury Street, London N1 8JU. Tel: 0171-354 2395. *President,* Mrs J. Clark

NATIONAL DEMOCRATS (formerly National Front) (1967), PO Box 2269, London E6 3RF. Tel: 0181-471 6872. *Chairman,* I. Anderson

NATIONAL EXTENSION COLLEGE (1963), 18 Brooklands Avenue, Cambridge CB2 2HN. Tel: 01223-316644. *Director,* Dr R. Morpeth

NATIONAL LISTENING LIBRARY, 12 Lant Street, London SE1 1QH. Tel: 0171-407 9417. *Executive Director*, G. A. Hepworth

NATIONAL SOCIETY, THE, (1811), Church House, Great Smith Street, London SW1P 3NZ. Tel: 0171-222 1672. For promoting religious education. *General Secretary*, G. Duncan

NATIONAL SOCIETY FOR THE PREVENTION OF CRUELTY TO CHILDREN (NSPCC) (1884), 67 Saffron Hill, London EC1N 8RS. Tel: 0171-242 1626. *Director*, C. Brown

NATIONAL TRUST, THE (1895), 36 Queen Anne's Gate, London SW1H 9AS. Tel: 0171-222 9251. *Chairman*, Lord Chorley; *Director-General*, M. Drury

NATIONAL TRUST FOR SCOTLAND (1931), 5 Charlotte Square, Edinburgh EH2 4DU. Tel: 0131-226 5922. *Chairman*, H. L. Melville; *Director*, D. Dow, CB

NATIONAL UNION OF STUDENTS (1922), Nelson Mandela House, 461 Holloway Road, London N7 6LJ. Tel: 0171-272 8900. *National President*, J. Murphy

NATIONAL VIEWERS' AND LISTENERS' ASSOCIATION (1964), All Saints House, High Street, Colchester CO1 1UG. Tel: 01206-561155. *Chairman*, Revd G. Stevens

NATIONAL WOMEN'S REGISTER (1960), 3A Vulcan House, Vulcan Road North, Norwich NR6 6AQ. Tel: 01603-406767. *National Organizer*, Ms J. Ross

NATURALISTS' ASSOCIATION, BRITISH (1905), 1 Bracken Mews, Chingford, London E4 7UT. *Hon. Membership Secretary*, Mrs Y. H. Griffiths

NATURE CONSERVATION, ROYAL SOCIETY FOR, *see* RSNC

NAUTICAL RESEARCH, SOCIETY FOR (1911), c/o National Maritime Museum, Greenwich, London SE10 9NF. *Hon. Secretary*, Lt.-Cdr. W. G. R. Gardner

NAVAL, MILITARY AND AIR FORCE BIBLE SOCIETY (1780), Radstock House, 3 Eccleston Street, London SW1W 9LZ. Tel: 0171-730 2155. *General Secretary*, Lt.-Cdr. J. M. Hines

NAVAL ARCHITECTS, ROYAL INSTITUTION OF (1860), 10 Upper Belgrave Street, London SW1X 8BQ. Tel: 0171-235 4622. *Secretary*, J. Rosewarn

NAVIGATION, ROYAL INSTITUTE OF (1947), 1 Kensington Gore, London SW7 2AT. Tel: 0171-589 5021. *Director*, Gp Capt D. W. Broughton, MBE

NAVY RECORDS SOCIETY (1893), Barclays de Zoete Wedd Ltd, Ground Floor, Minster House, 12 Arthur Street, London EC4R 9AB. *Hon. Secretary*, A. J. McMillan

NCH ACTION FOR CHILDREN (1869), 85 Highbury Park, London N5 1UD. Tel: 0171-226 2033. *Principal and Chief Executive*, T. White, CBE

NEEDLEWORK, ROYAL SCHOOL OF (1872), Apartment 12A, Hampton Court Palace, East Molesey, Surrey KT8 9AU. Tel: 0181-943 1432. *Principal*, Mrs E. Elvin

NEWCOMEN SOCIETY (1920), The Science Museum, London SW7 2DD. Tel: 0171-589 1793. For the study of the history of engineering and technology. *Executive Secretary*, C. Ellam

NEWSPAPER PRESS FUND (1864), Dickens House, 35 Wathen Road, Dorking, Surrey RH4 1JY. Tel: 01306-887511. *Director*, P. W. Evans

NEWSVENDORS' BENEVOLENT INSTITUTION (1839), PO Box 306, Dunmow, Essex CM6 1HY. Tel: 01371-874198. *Director*, B. Buckingham

NOISE ABATEMENT SOCIETY (1959), PO Box 518, Eynsford, Dartford, Kent DA4 0LL. Tel: 01322-862789. *Chairman*, J. Connell, OBE

NON-SMOKERS, NATIONAL SOCIETY OF, *see* QUIT

NORWOOD CHILD CARE (1795), Norwood House, Harmony Way, Victoria Road, London NW4 2DR. Tel: 0181-203 3030. *Executive Director*, S. Brier

NOTARIES' SOCIETY (1907), 7 Lower Brook Street, Ipswich IP4 1AF. Tel: 01473-214762. *Secretary*, A. G. Dunford

NUCLEAR ENERGY SOCIETY, BRITISH (1962), 1–7 Great George Street, London SW1P 3AA. Tel: 0171-839 9838. *Executive Officer*, P. Bacos

NUFFIELD FOUNDATION (1943), 28 Bedford Square, London WC1B 3EG. Tel: 0171-631 0566. *Director*, A. Tomei

NUFFIELD PROVINCIAL HOSPITALS TRUST (1939), 59 New Cavendish Street, London W1M 7RD. Tel: 0171-485 6632. *Secretary*, Prof. A. Maynard

NUMISMATIC SOCIETY, BRITISH (1903), c/o Hunterian Museum, Glasgow University, Glasgow G12 8QQ. Tel: 0141-330 4221. *Hon. Secretary*, Dr J. D. Bateson

NUMISMATIC SOCIETY, ROYAL (1836), c/o Department of Coins and Medals, The British Museum, Great Russell Street, London WC1B 3DG. Tel: 0171-323 8585. *Hon. Secretaries*, J. E. Cribb; R. G. Bland

NURSES' NATIONAL HOME, RETIRED (1934), Riverside Avenue, Bournemouth BH7 7EE. Tel: 01202-396418. *Chairman*, G. J. Rowlett

NURSES, ROYAL NATIONAL PENSION FUND FOR, Burdett House, 15 Buckingham Street, London WC2N 6ED. Tel: 0171-839 6785. *General Manager*, V. G. West

NURSING, MIDWIFERY AND HEALTH VISITING, ENGLISH NATIONAL BOARD FOR, Victory House, 170 Tottenham Court Road, London W1P 0HA. Tel: 0171-388 3131. *Chief Executive Officer*, A. P. Smith

NURSING, MIDWIFERY AND HEALTH VISITING, UK CENTRAL COUNCIL FOR, 23 Portland Place, London W1N 3AF. Tel: 0171-637 7181. *Registrar and Chief Executive*, Ms S. Norman

NURSING, MIDWIFERY AND HEALTH VISITING, WELSH NATIONAL BOARD FOR, Floor 13, Pearl Assurance House, Greyfriars Road, Cardiff CF1 3AG. Tel: 01222-395535. *Chief Executive*, D. A. Ravey

NURSING, MIDWIFERY AND HEALTH VISITING FOR NORTHERN IRELAND, NATIONAL BOARD FOR, Centre House, 79 Chichester Street, Belfast BT1 4JE. Tel: 01232-238152. *Chief Executive*, Dr O. D'A. Slevin

NURSING, MIDWIFERY AND HEALTH VISITING FOR SCOTLAND, NATIONAL BOARD FOR, 22 Queen Street, Edinburgh EH2 1NT. Tel: 0131-226 7371. *Chief Executive*, Mrs E. Mitchell

NURSING, ROYAL COLLEGE OF (1916), 20 Cavendish Square, London W1M 0AB. Tel: 0171-409 3333. *General Secretary*, Miss C. Hancock

NUTRITION FOUNDATION, BRITISH (1967), High Holborn House, 52–54 High Holborn, London WC1V 6RQ. Tel: 0171-404 6504. *Director-General*, Dr B. A. Wharton

NUTRITION SOCIETY (1941), 10 Cambridge Court, 210 Shepherds Bush Road, London W6 7NJ. Tel: 0171-602 0228. *Hon. Secretary*, Dr R. F. Grimble

OBSTETRICIANS AND GYNAECOLOGISTS, ROYAL COLLEGE OF (1929), 27 Sussex Place, London NW1 4RG. Tel: 0171-262 5425. *Secretary*, P. A. Barnett

OCCUPATIONAL PENSIONS ADVISORY SERVICE (1982), 11 Belgrave Road, London SW1V 1RB. Tel: 0171-233 8080. *Chief Executive*, D. Hall

OCCUPATIONAL SAFETY AND HEALTH, INSTITUTION OF (1946), The Grange, Highfield Drive, Wigston, Leics LE18 1NN. Tel: 0116-257 1399. *Chief Executive*, J. R. Barrell

OFFICERS' ASSOCIATION, THE (1920), 48 Pall Mall, London SW1Y 5JY. Tel: 0171-930 0125. *General Secretary*, Brig. P. D. Johnson

OFFICERS' PENSIONS SOCIETY LTD (1946), 68 South Lambeth Road, London SW8 1RL. Tel: 0171-820 9988. *General Secretary*, Maj.-Gen. Sir Laurence New, CB, CBE

OIL PAINTERS, ROYAL INSTITUTE OF (1883), 17 Carlton House Terrace, London SW1Y 5BD. Tel: 0171-930 6844. *Secretary*, O. Warman

OILSEED, OIL AND FEEDINGSTUFFS TRADES BENEVOLENT ASSOCIATION, c/o Baltic Exchange, 14–20 St. Mary Axe, London EC3A 8BH. Tel: 0171-369 1643. *Secretary*, D. A. Painter

ONE-PARENT FAMILIES, NATIONAL COUNCIL FOR, 255 Kentish Town Road, London NW5 2LX. Tel: 0171-267 1361. *Director*, Ms K. Pappenheim

OPEN-AIR MISSION, THE (1853), 19 John Street, London WC1N 2DL. Tel: 0171-405 6135. *Secretary*, A. J. Greenbank

OPEN SPACES SOCIETY (1865), 25A Bell Street, Henley-on-Thames, Oxon RG9 2BA. Tel: 01491-573535. *General Secretary*, Miss K. Ashbrook

OPERATIC AND DRAMATIC ASSOCIATION, NATIONAL (1899), NODA House, 1 Crestfield Street, London WC1H 8AU. Tel: 0171-837 5655. *General Administrator*, M. Thorburn

OPSIS (National Association for the Education, Training and Support of Blind and Partially Sighted People) (1992), Gretton House, 43 Hatton Garden, London EC1N 8EE. Tel: 0171-405 6697. *Secretary-General*, Sir Anthony Walker, KCB

OPTICAL COUNCIL, GENERAL (1958), 41 Harley Street, London W1N 2DJ. Tel: 0171-580 3898. *Registrar*, R. Wilshin

OPTOMETRISTS, THE COLLEGE OF, 10 Knaresborough Place, London SW5 0TG. Tel: 0171-373 7765. *General Secretary*, P. D. Leigh

ORDERS AND MEDALS RESEARCH SOCIETY (1942), 123 Turnpike Link, Croydon CR0 5NU. Tel: 0181-680 2701. *General Secretary*, N. G. Gooding

ORIENTAL CERAMIC SOCIETY, THE (1921), 30B Torrington Square, London WC1E 7LJ. Tel: 0171-636 7985. *Secretary*, Mrs J. Martin

ORNITHOLOGISTS' CLUB, SCOTTISH (1936), 21 Regent Terrace, Edinburgh EH7 5BT. Tel: 0131-556 6042. *Secretary*, Ms S. Laing

ORNITHOLOGISTS' UNION, BRITISH (1858), c/o Natural History Museum, Akeman Street, Tring, Herts HP23 6AP. Tel: 01442-890080. *Administrative Secretary*, Mrs G. Bonham

ORNITHOLOGY, BRITISH TRUST FOR (1932) National Centre for Ornithology, The Nunnery, Thetford, Norfolk IP24 2PU. Tel: 01842-750050. *Director of Services*, A. Elvin

ORTHOPAEDIC ASSOCIATION, BRITISH (1918), c/o The Royal College of Surgeons, 35–43 Lincoln's Inn Fields, London WC2A 3PN. Tel: 0171-405 6507. *Hon. Secretary*, I. J. Leslie, FRCS

OSTEOPATHIC MEDICINE, LONDON COLLEGE OF, 8–10 Boston Place, London NW1 6QH. Tel: 0171-262 1128/5250. *Secretary*, W. R. MacDonald

OSTEOPATHS, GENERAL COUNCIL AND REGISTER OF (1936), 56 London Street, Reading, Berks RG1 4SQ. Tel: 01734-576585. *Secretary*, Lt.-Col. G. P. Blaker

OSTEOPOROSIS SOCIETY, NATIONAL (1986), PO Box 10, Radstock, Bath BA3 3YB. Tel: 01761-471771. *General Secretary*, Miss H. Wollacott

OUTWARD BOUND TRUST LTD (1941), PO Box 1219, Windsor, Berks SL4 1XR. Tel: 01754-731005. *Director*, M. Hobbs, CBE

OVERSEAS DEVELOPMENT INSTITUTE (1960), Regent's College, Inner Circle, Regent's Park, London NW1 4NS. Tel: 0171-487 7413. *Director*, Prof. J. Howell

OVERSEAS SERVICE PENSIONERS' ASSOCIATION (1960), 138 High Street, Tonbridge, Kent TN9 1AX. Tel: 01732-363836. *Secretary*, D. Le Breton, CBE

OVERSEAS SETTLEMENT (1925), Church of England Board for Social Responsibility, Great Smith Street, London SW1P 3NZ. Tel: 0171-222 9011. *Administration Secretary*, Miss P. J. Hallett

OXFAM (1942), 274 Banbury Road, Oxford OX2 7DZ. Tel: 01865-311311. *Director*, D. Bryer

OXFORD PRESERVATION TRUST (1927), 10 Turn Again Lane, St Ebbes, Oxford OX1 1QL. Tel: 01865-242918. *Secretary*, Mrs M. Haynes

OXFORD SOCIETY (1932), 41 Wellington Square, Oxford OX1 2JF. Tel: 01865-270088. *Secretary*, Dr H. A. Hurren

PAEDIATRIC ASSOCIATION, BRITISH (1928), 5 St Andrew's Place, London NW1 4LB. Tel: 0171-486 6151. *Hon. Secretary*, Dr K. Dodd

PAINTER-PRINTMAKERS, ROYAL SOCIETY OF (1880), Bankside Gallery, 48 Hopton Street, London SE1 9JH. Tel: 0171-928 7521. *President*, Prof. D. Carpanini

PAINTERS IN WATER COLOURS, ROYAL INSTITUTE OF (1831), 17 Carlton House Terrace, London SW1Y 5BD. Tel: 0171-930 6844. *Secretary*, R. Spurrier

PALAEONTOLOGICAL ASSOCIATION (1957), c/o Lapworth Museum, School of Earth Sciences, University of Birmingham, Edgbaston, Birmingham B15 2TT. Tel: 0121-414 4173. *Secretary*, Dr P. Smith

PARENTS AT WORK (1985), 77 Holloway Road, London N7 8JZ. Tel: 0171-700 5771. *Director*, Mrs L. Daniels

PARKINSON'S DISEASE SOCIETY (1969), 22 Upper Woburn Place, London WC1H 0RA. Tel: 0171-383 3513. *Chief Executive*, B. A. Brooking

PARLIAMENTARY AND SCIENTIFIC COMMITTEE (1939), 16 Great College Street, London SW1P 3RX. Tel: 0171-222 7085. *Secretary*, Dr A. Whitehouse

PASTORAL PSYCHOLOGY, GUILD OF (1936), PO Box 1107, London W3 6ZP. Tel: 0181-993 8366. *Administrator*, Mrs N. Stanley

PATENT AGENTS, CHARTERED INSTITUTE OF (1882), Staple Inn Buildings, High Holborn, London WC1V 7PZ. Tel: 0171-405 9450. *Secretary*, M. C. Ralph

PATENTEES AND INVENTORS, INSTITUTE OF (1919), Suite 505A, Triumph House, 189 Regent Street, London W1R 7WF. Tel: 0171-242 7812. *Secretary*, R. Magnus

PATHOLOGISTS, ROYAL COLLEGE OF, 2 Carlton House Terrace, London SW1Y 5AF. Tel: 0171-930 5861. *Secretary*, K. Lockyer

PATIENTS ASSOCIATION (1963), 8 Guilford Street, London WC1N 1DT. Tel: 0171-242 3460. *Directors*, Mrs L. Lamont; S. Merricks

PEACE COUNCIL, NATIONAL (1908), 88 Islington High Street, London N1 8EG. Tel: 0171-354 5200. *Co-ordinator*, Ms L. Peck

PEAK AND NORTHERN FOOTPATHS SOCIETY (1894), 15 Parkfield Drive, Tyldesley, Manchester M29 8NR. Tel: 0161-790 4383. *Hon. General Secretary*, D. Taylor

PEARSON'S HOLIDAY FUND, PO Box 123, Bishops Waltham, Southampton, Hants SO32 1ZE. Tel: 01489-893260. *General Secretary*, R. Heasman

PEDESTRIANS ASSOCIATION (1929), 126 Aldersgate Street, London EC1A 4JQ. Tel: 0171-490 0750. *Chairman*, Ms F. Lawson

PEN, INTERNATIONAL (1921), 9–10 Charterhouse Building, Goswell Road, London EC1M 7AT. Tel: 0171-253 4308. World association of writers. *International Secretary*, A. Blokh

PENSION FUNDS LTD, NATIONAL ASSOCIATION OF (1923), 12–18 Grosvenor Gardens, London SW1W 0DH. Tel: 0171-730 0585. *Director-General*, Dr A. Robinson

PEOPLE'S DISPENSARY FOR SICK ANIMALS (PDSA) (1917), Whitechapel Way, Priorslee, Telford, Shropshire TF2 9PQ. Tel: 01952-290999. *Director-General*, M. R. Curtis, MBE

PERFORMING RIGHT SOCIETY LTD (1914), 29–33 Berners Street, London W1P 4AA. Tel: 0171-580 5544. *General Manager*, J. Axon

PERIODICAL PUBLISHERS ASSOCIATION LTD (1913), Imperial House, 15–19 Kingsway, London WC2B 6UN. Tel: 0171-379 6268. *Chief Executive*, I. Locks

PESTALOZZI CHILDREN'S VILLAGE TRUST (1959), Sedlescombe, Battle, E. Sussex TN33 0RR. Tel: 01424-870444. *Director*, M. Phillips

PETROLEUM, INSTITUTE OF (1913), 61 New Cavendish Street, London W1M 8AR. Tel: 0171-467 7100. *Director-General*, I. Ward

PHARMACEUTICAL SOCIETY OF GREAT BRITAIN, ROYAL (1841), 1 Lambeth High Street, London SE1 7JN. Tel: 0171-735 9141. *Secretary and Registrar*, J. Ferguson, OBE

PHARMACOLOGICAL SOCIETY, BRITISH (1931), 16 Angel Gate, City Road, London EC1V 2PT. Tel: 0171-417 0113. *Hon. General Secretary*, Prof. N. G. Bowery

PHILOLOGICAL SOCIETY (1842), School of Oriental and African Studies, University of London, Thornhaugh Street, London WC1H 0XG. Tel: 0171-637 2388. *Hon. Secretary*, Prof. R. J. Hayward

PHILOSOPHY, ROYAL INSTITUTE OF (1925), 14 Gordon Square, London WC1H 0AG. Tel: 0171-387 4130. *Director*, Prof. A. Phillips Griffiths

PHOTOGRAPHY, BRITISH INSTITUTE OF PROFESSIONAL (1901), Fox Talbot House, Amwell End, Ware, Herts SG12 9HN. Tel: 01920-464011. *Chief Executive*, A. Mair

PHYSICAL RECREATION, CENTRAL COUNCIL OF (1935), Francis House, Francis Street, London SW1P 1DE. Tel: 0171-828 3163. *General Secretary*, P. Lawson

PHYSICIANS, ROYAL COLLEGE OF (1518), 11 St Andrew's Place, London NW1 4LE. Tel: 0171-935 1174. *Secretary*, D. B. Lloyd

PHYSICIANS AND SURGEONS OF GLASGOW, ROYAL COLLEGE OF (1599), 234–242 St Vincent Street, Glasgow G2 5RJ. Tel: 0141-221 6072. *Hon. Secretary*, Dr S. Slater

PHYSICIANS OF EDINBURGH, ROYAL COLLEGE OF (1681), 9 Queen Street, Edinburgh EH2 1JQ. Tel: 0131-225 7324. *Secretary*, Dr J. St J. Thomas

PHYSICS, INSTITUTE OF (1874), 47 Belgrave Square, London SW1X 8QX. Tel: 0171-235 6111. *Chief Executive*, Dr A. Jones

PHYSIOLOGICAL SOCIETY (1876), PO Box 506, Oxford OX1 3XE. Tel: 01865-798498. *Hon. Secretary*, Dr C. A. R. Boyd

PHYSIOTHERAPY, CHARTERED SOCIETY OF (1894), 14 Bedford Row, London WC1R 4ED. Tel: 0171-306 6666. *Secretary*, T. Simon

PIG ASSOCIATION, BRITISH (1884), 7 Rickmansworth Road, Watford, Herts WD1 7HE. Tel: 01923-234377/234021. *Chief Executive*, G. E. Welsh

PILGRIM TRUST, THE (1930), Fielden House, Little College Street, London SW1P 3SH. Tel: 0171-222 4723. *Secretary*, Hon. A. Hoyer Millar

PILGRIMS OF GREAT BRITAIN, THE (1902), Savoy Hotel, London WC2R 0EU. Tel: 0171-222 0232. *Hon. Secretary*, M. P. S. Barton

PLANT ENGINEERS, INSTITUTION OF, 77 Great Peter Street, London SW1P 2EZ. Tel: 0171-233 2855. *Secretary*, P. F. Tye

PLAYING FIELDS ASSOCIATION, NATIONAL (1925), 25 Ovington Square, London SW3 1LQ. Tel: 0171-584 6445. *Director*, Ms E. Davies

PLUNKETT FOUNDATION (1919), 23 Hanborough Business Park, Long Hanborough, Oxford OX8 8LH. Tel: 01993-883636. *Director*, E. Parnell

POETRY SOCIETY, THE (1909), 22 Betterton Street, London WC2H 9BU. Tel: 0171-240 4810. *Director*, C. Meade

POLICY STUDIES INSTITUTE (1978), 100 Park Village East, London NW1 3SR. Tel: 0171-468 0468. *Director*, Ms P. Meadows

POLIO FELLOWSHIP, BRITISH (1939), Ground Floor, Unit A, Eagle Office Centre, The Runway, South Ruislip, Middx HA4 6SE. Tel: 0181-842 1898. *General Secretary*, M. Drake

POLITE SOCIETY, THE (1986), 6 Norman Avenue, Henley-on-Thames, Oxon RG9 1SG. Tel: 01491-572794. *Hon. Secretary*, Miss G. Mackenzie

PORTRAIT PAINTERS, ROYAL SOCIETY OF (1891), 17 Carlton House Terrace, London SW1Y 5BD. Tel: 0171-930 6844. *Secretary*, J. Stultiens

POST OFFICE USERS' NATIONAL COUNCIL (1970), 6 Hercules Road, London SE1 7DN. Tel: 0171-928 9458. *Secretary*, K. Hall

PRAYER BOOK SOCIETY, THE (1975), St James Garlickhythe, Garlick Hill, London EC4V 2AL. Tel: 0181-958 8769. *Hon. Secretary*, Mrs. M. Thompson

PRECEPTORS, COLLEGE OF (1846), Coppice Row, Theydon Bois, Epping, Essex CM16 7DN. Tel: 01992-812727. *Chief Executive Officer*, T. Wheatley

PRE-SCHOOL LEARNING ALLIANCE, 69 Kings Cross Road, London WC1X 9LL. Tel: 0171-833 0991. *Chief Executive Officer*, Ms M. Lochrie

PRESS UNION, COMMONWEALTH (1909), Studio House, 184 Fleet Street, London EC4A 2DU. Tel: 0171-242 1056. *Director,* R. MacKichan

PREVENTION OF ACCIDENTS, THE ROYAL SOCIETY FOR THE (1916), Cannon House, The Priory Queensway, Birmingham B4 6BS. Tel: 0121-200 2461. *Chief Executive,* A. Edwards

PRINCESS LOUISE SCOTTISH HOSPITAL (Erskine Hospital) (1916), Bishopton, Renfrewshire PA7 5PU. Tel: 0141-812 1100. For disabled ex-servicemen and women. *Commandant,* Col. M. F. Gibson, OBE

PRINCESS ROYAL TRUST FOR CARERS (1990), 16 Byward Street, London EC3R 5BA. Tel: 0171-480 7788. *Chief Executive,* Dr E. Nelson

PRINCE'S SCOTTISH YOUTH BUSINESS TRUST, THE (1989), 6th Floor, Mercantile Chambers, 53 Bothwell Street, Glasgow G2 6TS. Tel: 0141-248 4999. *Director,* D. W. Cooper

PRINCE'S TRUST, THE (1976) and THE ROYAL JUBILEE TRUSTS (1935, 1977), 8 Bedford Row, London WC1R 4BA. Tel: 0171-430 0524. *Director,* T. Shebbeare

PRINCE'S YOUTH BUSINESS TRUST, THE, 5 Cleveland Place, London SW1Y 6JJ. Tel: 0171-321 6500. *Chief Executive,* R. Street

PRINTERS' CHARITABLE CORPORATION (1827), Victoria House, Harestone Valley Road, Caterham, Surrey CR3 6HY. Tel: 01883-345331. *Director,* H. J. Court

PRINTING HISTORICAL SOCIETY (1964), St Bride Institute, Bride Lane, London EC4Y 8EE. *Hon. Secretary,* J. H. Bowman

PRINTING, INSTITUTE OF (1961), 8 Lonsdale Gardens, Tunbridge Wells, Kent TN1 1NU. Tel: 01892-538118. *Secretary-General,* D. Freeland

PRISONERS ABROAD (1978), 72–82 Rosebery Avenue, London EC1R 4RR. Tel: 0171-833 3467. *Director,* Ms J. Johnstone

PRISON VISITORS, NATIONAL ASSOCIATION OF (1922), 46B Hartington Street, Bedford MK41 7RP. Tel: 01234-359763. *General Secretary,* Mrs A. G. McKenna

PRIVATE LIBRARIES ASSOCIATION (1957), Ravelston, South View Road, Pinner, Middx HA5 3YD. *Hon. Secretary,* F. Broomhead

PROCURATORS IN GLASGOW, ROYAL FACULTY OF (1600), 12 Nelson Mandela Place, Glasgow G2 1BT. Tel: 0141-552 3422. *Clerk,* A. J. Campbell

PROFESSIONAL CLASSES AID COUNCIL (1921), 10 St Christopher's Place, London W1M 6HY. Tel: 0171-935 0641. *Secretary*

PROFESSIONAL ENGINEERS, UK ASSOCIATION OF (1969), Hayes Court, West Common Road, Bromley BR2 7AU. Tel: 0181-462 7755. *National Secretary,* J. M. Dalgleish

PROFESSIONAL FOOTBALLERS' ASSOCIATION, 2 Oxford Court, Bishopsgate, Manchester M2 3WQ. Tel: 0161-236 0575. *Chief Executive,* G. Taylor

PROFESSIONS SUPPLEMENTARY TO MEDICINE, THE COUNCIL FOR, Park House, 184 Kennington Park Road, London SE11 4BU. Tel: 0171-582 0866. *Registrar (acting),* Dr P. Burley

PROTECTION OF UNBORN CHILDREN, SOCIETY FOR THE (1967), 7 Tufton Street, London SW1P 3QN. Tel: 0171-222 5845. *National Director,* Mrs P. Bowman

PROTESTANT ALLIANCE, THE (1845), 77 Ampthill Road, Flitwick, Bedford MK45 1BD. Tel: 01525-712348. *General Secretary,* Dr S. J. Scott-Pearson

PSORIASIS ASSOCIATION (1968), 7 Milton Street, Northampton NN2 7JG. Tel: 01604-711129. *National Secretary,* Mrs L. Henley

PSYCHIATRISTS, ROYAL COLLEGE OF (1971), 17 Belgrave Square, London SW1X 8PG. Tel: 0171-235 2351. *Secretary,* Mrs V. Cameron

PSYCHICAL RESEARCH, SOCIETY FOR (1882), 49 Marloes Road, London W8 6LA. Tel: 0171-937 8984. *Secretary,* Ms E. O'Keefe

PSYCHOLOGICAL SOCIETY, BRITISH (1901), St Andrews House, 48 Princess Road East, Leicester LE1 7DR. Tel: 0116-254 9568. *Executive Secretary,* C. V. Newman, PH.D.

PUBLIC FINANCE AND ACCOUNTANCY, CHARTERED INSTITUTE OF (1885), 3 Robert Street, London WC2N 6BH. Tel: 0171-895 8823. *Director,* N. P. Hepworth, OBE

PUBLIC HEALTH AND HYGIENE, ROYAL INSTITUTE OF (1937), 28 Portland Place, London W1N 4DE. Tel: 0171-580 2731. *Secretary,* Gp Capt. R. A. Smith

PUBLIC RELATIONS, INSTITUTE OF (1948), The Old Trading House, 15 Northburgh Street, London EC1V 0PR. Tel: 0171-253 5151. *Executive Director,* J. B. Lavelle

PUBLIC TEACHERS OF LAW, SOCIETY OF (1908), All Souls College, Oxford OX1 4AL. Tel: 01865-279338. *Hon. Secretary,* Prof. P. B. H. Birks, QC

PURCHASING AND SUPPLY, CHARTERED INSTITUTE OF (1967), Easton House, Easton on the Hill, Stamford, Lincs PE9 3NZ. Tel: 01780-56777. *Director-General,* P. Thomson

PURE WATER ASSOCIATION, NATIONAL (1960), Meridan, Cae Goody Lane, Ellesmere, Shrops SY12 9DW. Tel: 01691-623015. *Secretary,* N. Brugge

QUAKER SOCIAL RESPONSIBILITY AND EDUCATION, Friends House, Euston Road, London NW1 2BJ. Tel: 0171-387 3601. *General Secretary,* Ms B. Smith

QUALITY ASSURANCE, INSTITUTE OF, PO Box 712, 61 Southwark Street, London SE1 1SB. Tel: 0171-401 7227. *Secretary-General,* D. Campbell

QUARRIER'S HOMES (1871), Quarrier's Village, Bridge of Weir, Renfrewshire PA11 3SX. Tel: 01505-612224. *Director,* G. E. Lee

QUARRYING, INSTITUTE OF (1917), 7 Regent Street, Nottingham NG1 5BS. Tel: 0115-941 1315. *Secretary,* M. J. Arthur

QUEEN ELIZABETH'S FOUNDATION FOR DISABLED PEOPLE (1967), Leatherhead Court, Leatherhead, Surrey KT22 0BN. Tel: 01372-842204. *Director,* M. B. Clark, PH.D.

QUEEN'S ENGLISH SOCIETY, THE (1972), 104 Drive Mansions, Fulham Road, London SW6 5JH. Tel: 0171-371 7530. *Hon. Membership Secretary,* M. Plumbe

QUEEN'S NURSING INSTITUTE (1887), 3 Albemarle Way, London EC1V 4JB. Tel: 0171-490 4227. *Director,* Mrs P. Bagnall

QUEEN VICTORIA CLERGY FUND (1897), Church House, Dean's Yard, London SW1P 3NZ. Tel: 0171-222 5261. *Secretary,* C. D. L. Menzies

QUEEN VICTORIA SCHOOL (1908), Dunblane, Perthshire FK15 0JY. Tel: 01786-822288. *Headmaster,* B. Raine

QUEKETT MICROSCOPICAL CLUB (1865). *Hon. Business Secretary,* B. Scott, 237 Petts Hill, Northolt, Middx UB5 4NR

QUIT (NATIONAL SOCIETY OF NON-SMOKERS) (1926), Victory House, 170 Tottenham Court Road, London WIP OHA. Tel: 0171-388 5775. *Director,* P. McCabe

RADAR (ROYAL ASSOCIATION FOR DISABILITY AND REHABILITATION) (1977), 12 City Forum, 250 City Road, London ECIV 8AF. Tel: 0171-250 3222. *Director,* B. Massie, OBE

RADIOLOGISTS, ROYAL COLLEGE OF (1934), 38 Portland Place, London WIN 4JQ. Tel: 0171-636 4432. *Secretary,* A. J. Cowles

RADIOLOGY, BRITISH INSTITUTE OF (1897), 36 Portland Place, London WIN 4AT. Tel: 0171-580 4317. *Chief Executive,* Ms M. A. Piggott

RAIL USERS' CONSULTATIVE COMMITTEE, CENTRAL (1948), 1st Floor, Golden Cross House, Duncannon Street, London WC2N 4JF. Tel: 0171-839 7338/930 1304. *Secretary,* M. Patterson

RAILWAY AND CANAL HISTORICAL SOCIETY, 17 Clumber Crescent North, The Park, Nottingham NG7 IEY. Tel: 0115-941 4844. *Hon. Secretary,* G. H. R. Gwatkin

RAILWAY BENEVOLENT INSTITUTION (1858), Pullman House, Railway Technical Centre, London Road, Derby DE24 8UP. Tel: 01332-264205. *Director,* R. B. Boiling

RAINER FOUNDATION (1876), 89 Blackheath Hill, London SEIO 8TJ. Tel: 0181-694 9497. Provides community-based services for young people who are homeless, offending or in difficulty with their families. *Director,* Dr R. Kay

RAMBLERS' ASSOCIATION (1935), 1–5 Wandsworth Road, London SW8 2XX. Tel: 0171-582 6878. *Director,* A. Mattingly

RARE BREEDS SURVIVAL TRUST (1973), National Agricultural Centre, Kenilworth, Warks CV8 2LG. Tel: 01203-696551. *Executive Director,* L. Alderson

RATHBONE COMMUNITY INDUSTRY (1919), 1st Floor, The Excalibur Building, 77 Whitworth Street, Manchester MI 6EZ. Tel: 0161-236 5358. Advice Line: 0161-236 1877. Helps people with learning difficulties. *Chief Executive,* Ms A. Weinstock, CBE

RECORD SOCIETY, SCOTTISH (1897), Department of Scottish History, University of Glasgow, Glasgow GI2 8QH. Tel: 0141-339 8855, ext. 5682. *Hon. Secretary,* J. Kirk, PH.D.

RECORDS ASSOCIATION, BRITISH (1932), 18 Padbury Court, London E2 7EH. Tel: 0171-729 1415. *Hon. Secretary,* S. Shaw

RED CROSS SOCIETY, BRITISH, *see* BRITISH RED CROSS

RED POLL CATTLE SOCIETY (1888), The Market Hill, Woodbridge, Suffolk IPI2 4LU. Tel: 01394-380643. *Secretary,* P. Ryder-Davies

REFRIGERATION, INSTITUTE OF (1899), Kelvin House, 76 Mill Lane, Carshalton, Surrey SM5 2JR. Tel: 0181-647 7033. *Secretary,* M. J. Horlick

REFUGEE COUNCIL, BRITISH (1981), Bondway House, 3–9 Bondway, London SW8 ISJ. Tel: 0171-582 6922. *Director,* M. Hardwick

REGIONAL STUDIES ASSOCIATION (1965), Wharfdale Projects, 15 Micawber Street, London NI 7TB. Tel: 0171-490 1128. *Director,* Mrs S. Hardy

REGULAR FORCES EMPLOYMENT ASSOCIATION (1885), 25 Bloomsbury Square, London WCIA 2LN. Tel: 0171-637 3918. *General Manager,* Maj.-Gen. M. F. L. Shellard, CBE

RELATE: NATIONAL MARRIAGE GUIDANCE (1938), Herbert Gray College, Little Church Street, Rugby, Warks CV2I 3AP. Tel: 01788-573241. *Director,* D. French

RENT OFFICERS, INSTITUTE OF (1966), Beaufort House, Hamble Lane, Bursledon, Southampton SO3 8BR. Tel: 01703-403716. *Hon. Secretary,* A. E. Corcoran

RESEARCH DEFENCE SOCIETY (1908), 58 Great Marlborough Street, London WIV IDD. Tel: 0171-287 2818. *Executive Director,* Dr M. Matfield

RESIDENTS' ASSOCIATIONS, NATIONAL UNION OF (1921), 35 Clement Way, Upminster, Essex RMI4 2NX. *Hon. General Secretary,* Mrs B. Reith

RETIREMENT PENSIONS ASSOCIATIONS, NATIONAL FEDERATION OF (1938), 14 St Peter Street, Blackburn BB2 2HD. Tel: 01254-52606. *General Secretary,* R. Stansfield

REVENUES, RATING AND VALUATION, INSTITUTE OF (1882), 41 Doughty Street, London WCIN 2LF. Tel: 0171-831 3505. *Director,* C. Farrington

RICHARD III SOCIETY (1924), 4 Oakley Street, London SW3 5NN. *Secretary,* Miss E. M. Nokes

ROAD SAFETY OFFICERS, INSTITUTE OF (1971), 31 Heather Grove, Hollingworth, via Hyde, Cheshire SKI4 8JL. Tel: 0161-474 4876. *Secretary,* B. Wilkinson

ROAD TRANSPORT ENGINEERS, INSTITUTE OF (1945), 22 Greencoat Place, London IPR. Tel: 0171-630 1111. *Chief Executive,* A. F. Stroud

ROMAN STUDIES, SOCIETY FOR PROMOTION OF (1910), 31–34 Gordon Square, London WCIH OPP. Tel: 0171-387 8157. *Secretary,* Dr H. M. Cockle

ROTARY INTERNATIONAL IN GREAT BRITAIN AND IRELAND (1914), Kinwarton Road, Alcester, Warks B49 6BP. Tel: 01789-765411. *Secretary,* D. Morehen

ROUND TABLES OF GREAT BRITAIN AND IRELAND, NATIONAL ASSOCIATION OF (1927), Marchesi House, 4 Embassy Drive, Edgbaston, Birmingham BI5 ITP. Tel: 0121-456 4402. *General Secretary,* R. H. Renold

ROYAL AIR FORCE BENEVOLENT FUND (1919), 67 Portland Place, London WIN 4AR. Tel: 0171-580 8343. *Controller,* Air Chief Marshal Sir Roger Palin, KCB, OBE

ROYAL AIR FORCES ASSOCIATION (1943), 43 Grove Park Road, London W4 3RX. Tel: 0181-994 8504. *Secretary-General,* J. G. Hargreaves, CBE

ROYAL ALEXANDRA AND ALBERT SCHOOL (1758), Gatton Park, Reigate, Surrey RH2 OTW. Tel: 01737-642576. *Secretary,* Wg Cdr. N. J. Wright

ROYAL ALFRED SEAFARERS' SOCIETY (1865), Weston Acres, Woodmansterne Lane, Banstead, Surrey SM7 3HB. Tel: 01737-352231. *General Secretary,* A. R. Quinton

ROYAL ARMOURED CORPS WAR MEMORIAL BENEVOLENT FUND (1946), c/o RHQ RTR, Bovington Camp, Wareham, Dorset BH20 6JA. Tel: 01929-403331. *Secretary,* Maj. A. Henzie, MBE (retd)

ROYAL ARTILLERY ASSOCIATION, Artillery House, Front Parade, Royal Artillery Barracks, Woolwich, London SEI8 4BH. Tel: 0181-781 3003. *General Secretary,* Lt.-Col. M. J. Darmody

ROYAL ASIATIC SOCIETY (1823), 60 Queen's Gardens, London W2 3AF. Tel: 0171-724 4741/2. *Secretary,* Miss L. Collins

ROYAL BRITISH LEGION, *see* BRITISH LEGION, ROYAL

ROYAL CALEDONIAN SCHOOLS (1815), Aldenham Road, Bushey, Watford, Herts wd2 3ts. Tel: 01923-226642. *Chief Executive,* J. Horsfield

ROYAL CELTIC SOCIETY (1820), 23 Rutland Street, Edinburgh eh1 2rn. Tel: 0131-228 6449. *Secretary,* J. G. Cameron, ws

ROYAL CHORAL SOCIETY (1871), at Cazenove & Co., 12 Tokenhouse Yard, London ec2r 7an. Tel: 0171-972 9442. *Administrator,* G. Tonge (Moving Oct. 1995)

ROYAL ENGINEERS ASSOCIATION, RHQ Royal Engineers, Brompton Barracks, Chatham, Kent me4 4ug. Tel: 01634-847005. *Controller,* Lt.-Col. J. W. Ray (retd)

ROYAL ENGINEERS, INSTITUTION OF (1875), Brompton Barracks, Chatham, Kent me4 4ug. Tel: 01634-842669. *Secretary,* Col. R. I. Reive, obe

ROYAL HIGHLAND AND AGRICULTURAL SOCIETY OF SCOTLAND (1784), Royal Highland Centre, Ingliston, Edinburgh eh28 8nf. Tel: 0131-333 2444. *Secretary,* J. R. Good

ROYAL HORTICULTURAL SOCIETY (1804), PO Box 313, 80 Vincent Square, London sw1p 2pe. Tel: 0171-834 4333. *Secretary,* D. P. Hearn

ROYAL HOSPITAL FOR NEURO-DISABILITY (1854), West Hill, London sw15 3sw. Tel: 0181-788 4511. *Chief Executive,* Brig. V. J. Beauchamp

ROYAL HUMANE SOCIETY (1774), Brettenham House, Lancaster Place, London wc2e 7ep. Tel: 0171-836 8155. *Secretary,* Maj. A. J. Dickinson

ROYAL INSTITUTION, THE (1799), 21 Albemarle Street, London w1s 4bs. Tel: 0171-409 2992. *Director,* Prof. P. Day, frs

ROYAL LIFE SAVING SOCIETY UK (1891), Mountbatten House, Studley, Warks b80 7nn. Tel: 01527-853943. *Director-General,* S. Lear

ROYAL LITERARY FUND (1790), 144 Temple Chambers, Temple Avenue, London ec4y 0da. Tel: 0171-353 7150. *Secretary,* Mrs F. M. Clark

ROYAL MEDICAL BENEVOLENT FUND (1836), 24 King's Road, London sw19 8qn. Tel: 0181-540 9194. *Secretary,* Mrs G. A. R. Wells

ROYAL MEDICAL SOCIETY (1737), Students Centre, 5/5 Bristo Square, Edinburgh eh8 9al. Tel: 0131-650 2672. *Secretary,* Mrs P. E. Strong

ROYAL MICROSCOPICAL SOCIETY (1839), 37–38 St Clements, Oxford ox4 1aj. Tel: 01865-248768. *Administrator,* P. B. Hirst

ROYAL MUSICAL ASSOCIATION (1874), Faculty of Music, St Aldates, Oxford ox1 1db. Tel: 01865-276146. *Secretary,* J. Wagstaff

ROYAL NATIONAL INSTITUTE FOR THE BLIND (1868), 224 Great Portland Street, London w1n 6aa. Tel: 0171-388 1266. *Director-General,* I. Bruce

ROYAL NATIONAL LIFEBOAT INSTITUTION (1824), West Quay Road, Poole, Dorset bh15 1hz. Tel: 01202-671133. *Director,* Lt.-Cdr. B. Miles, cbe, rd

ROYAL NAVAL AND ROYAL MARINES CHILDREN'S TRUST (1834), HMS *Nelson,* Portsmouth, po1 3hh. Tel: 01705-817435. *Secretary,* Mrs M. Bateman

ROYAL NAVAL ASSOCIATION (1950), 82 Chelsea Manor Street, London sw3 5qj. Tel: 0171-352 6764. *General Secretary,* Capt. J. W. Rayner, rmr

ROYAL NAVAL BENEVOLENT SOCIETY (1739), 1 Fleet Street, London ec4y 1bd. Tel: 0171-353 4080. *Secretary,* Cdr P. J. F. Moore, rn

ROYAL NAVAL BENEVOLENT TRUST (1922), Castaway House, 311 Twyford Avenue, Portsmouth, Hants po2 8pe. Tel: 01705-660296/690112. *Chief Executive,* Cdr. J. Owens

ROYAL NAVY OFFICERS, ASSOCIATION OF (1920), 70 Porchester Terrace, London w2 3tp. Tel: 0171-402 5231. *Secretary,* Lt.-Cdr. I. M. P. Coombes

ROYAL OVER-SEAS LEAGUE (1910), Over-Seas House, Park Place, St James's Street, London sw1a 1lr. Tel: 0171-408 0214. *Director-General,* R. F. Newell

ROYAL PATRIOTIC FUND CORPORATION (1854), Golden Cross House, Duncannon Street, London wc2n 4jr. Tel: 0171-930 9370. *Secretary,* Brig. T. G. Williams, cbe

ROYAL PHILATELIC SOCIETY, THE (1869), 41 Devonshire Place, London w1n 1pe. Tel: 0171-486 1044. *Hon. Secretary,* Prof. B. Jay

ROYAL PHOTOGRAPHIC SOCIETY (1853), The Octagon, Milsom Street, Bath ba1 1dn. Tel: 01225-462841. *Secretary-General,* B. Lane

ROYAL PINNER SCHOOL FOUNDATION, 110 Old Brompton Road, London sw7 3ra. Tel: 0171-373 6168. *Secretary,* D. Crawford

ROYAL SAILORS' RESTS (1876), 2a South Street, Gosport, Hants po12 1es. Tel: 01705-589551. *General Secretary,* A. A. Lockwood

ROYAL SIGNALS INSTITUTION (1950), 56 Regency Street, London sw1p 4ad. Tel: 0171-414 8421. *Secretary,* Col. A. N. de Bretton-Gordon

ROYAL SOCIETY FOR ASIAN AFFAIRS (1901), 2 Belgrave Square, London sw1x 8pj. Tel: 0171-235 5122. *Secretary,* Mrs H. McKeag

ROYAL SOCIETY FOR THE ENCOURAGEMENT OF ARTS, MANUFACTURES AND COMMERCE (RSA) (1754), 8 John Adam Street, London wc2n 6ez. Tel: 0171-930 5115. *Director,* P. Cowling

ROYAL SOCIETY FOR THE PREVENTION OF CRUELTY TO ANIMALS (RSPCA) (1824), Causeway, Horsham, W. Sussex rh12 1hg. Tel: 01403-264181. *Director-General,* P. R. Davies, cb

ROYAL SOCIETY FOR THE PROTECTION OF BIRDS (1889), The Lodge, Sandy, Beds sg19 2dl. Tel: 01767-680551. *Chief Executive,* Miss B. Young

ROYAL SOCIETY OF HEALTH, THE (1876), RSH House, 38 St George's Drive, London sw1v 4bh. Tel: 0171-630 0171. *Chief Executive,* A. J. Byrne

ROYAL SOCIETY OF LITERATURE (1823), 1 Hyde Park Gardens, London w2 2lt. Tel: 0171-723 5104. *Secretary,* Miss M. Parham

ROYAL SOCIETY OF MEDICINE (1805), 1 Wimpole Street, London w1m 8ae. Tel: 0171-290 2901. *Chief Executive,* Dr J. T. Green

ROYAL SOCIETY OF ST GEORGE (1894), Dartmouth House, 37 Charles Street, London w1x 8ab. Tel: 0171-499 5430. *Chairman,* Sir Peter Herbert; *General Secretary,* Cdr. R. Walker, lvo

ROYAL STAR AND GARTER HOME FOR DISABLED SAILORS, SOLDIERS AND AIRMEN (1916), Richmond, Surrey tw10 6rr. Tel: 0181-940 3314. *Chief Executive,* I. Lashbrooke

ROYAL STATISTICAL SOCIETY (1834), 25 Enford Street, London WIH 2BH. Tel: 0171-723 5882. *Executive Secretary,* I. Goddard

ROYAL TANK REGIMENT BENEVOLENT FUND (1919), RHQ RTR Centre, Bovington Camp, Wareham, Dorset BH20 6JA. Tel: 01929-403331. *Regimental Secretary,* Maj. A. Henzie, MBE

ROYAL TELEVISION SOCIETY (1927), Holborn Hall, 100 Gray's Inn Road, London WCIX 8AL. Tel: 0171-430 1000. *Executive Director,* M. Bunce

ROYAL UNITED KINGDOM BENEFICENT ASSOCIATION (1863), 6 Avonmore Road, London W14 8RL. Tel: 0171-602 6274. *Director,* W. Rathbone

RURAL ENGLAND, COUNCIL FOR THE PROTECTION OF (CPRE) (1926), Warwick House, 25 Buckingham Palace Road, London SWIW OPP. Tel: 0171-976 6433. *Director,* Ms F. Reynolds

RURAL SCOTLAND, ASSOCIATION FOR THE PROTECTION OF (1926), 3rd Floor, Gladstone's Land, 483 Lawnmarket, Edinburgh EHI 2NT. Tel: 0131-225 7012/3. *Manager,* Mrs E. J. Garland

RURAL WALES, CAMPAIGN FOR THE PROTECTION OF (1928), Tŷ Gwyn, 31 High Street, Welshpool, Powys SY21 7JP. Tel: 01938-552525. *Director,* M. Williams

SAILORS' FAMILIES' SOCIETY, THE (1821), Newland, Hull HU6 7RJ. Tel: 01482-42331. *General Secretary,* G. J. Powell

SAILORS' SOCIETY, BRITISH AND INTERNATIONAL (1818), 3 Orchard Place, Southampton, SO9 7SS. Tel: 01703-337333. *General Secretary,* G. Chambers

ST DEINIOL'S RESIDENTIAL LIBRARY (1902), Hawarden, Deeside, Clwyd CH5 3DF. Tel: 01244-532350. *Warden and Chief Librarian,* Revd Dr P. J. Jagger

ST DUNSTAN'S, PO Box 4XB, 12–14 Harcourt Street, London WIA 4XB. Tel: 0171-723 5021. For men and women blinded in the Services. *Secretary,* G. B. J. Frost

ST JOHN AMBULANCE (1887), 1 Grosvenor Crescent, London SWIX 7EF. Tel: 0171-235 5231. *Executive Director,* Dr D. L. Macphie

ST JOSEPH'S SOCIETY FOR THE RELIEF OF THE AGED POOR (1708), St Joseph's House, 42 Brook Green, London W6 7BW. Tel: 0171-603 9817. *Secretary,* S. Dolan

SALES AND MARKETING MANAGEMENT, INSTITUTE OF (1966), Georgian House, 31 Upper George Street, Luton LUI 2RD. Tel: 01582-411130. *Director-General,* K. Williams

SALMON AND TROUT ASSOCIATION (1903), Fishmongers' Hall, London EC4R 9EL. Tel: 0171-283 5838. *Director,* C. W. Poupard

SALTIRE SOCIETY (1936), 9 Fountain Close, 22 High Street, Edinburgh EHI ITF. Tel: 0131-556 1836. *Administrator,* Mrs K. Munro

SAMARITANS, THE (1953), 10 The Grove, Slough SLI 1QP. Tel: 01753-532713. Telephone numbers in local telephone directories. *Chief Executive,* S. Armson

SAMUEL PEPYS CLUB (1903), 26 Gloucester Street, Faringdon, Oxon SN7 7HY. *Secretary,* P. L. Gray

SANE: THE MENTAL HEALTH CHARITY (1986), 199–205 Marylebone Road, London NWI 5QP. Tel: 0171-724 6520. *Saneline:* 0171-724 8000/0345-678000. *Chief Executive,* Ms M. Wallace, MBE

SAVE BRITAIN'S HERITAGE (1975), 68 Battersea High Street, London SWII 3HX. Tel: 0171-228 3336. *Secretary,* Miss E. Phillips

SAVE THE CHILDREN FUND, THE (1919), 17 Grove Lane, London SE5 8RD. Tel: 0171-703 5400. *Director-General,* M. Aaronson

SCHIZOPHRENIA FELLOWSHIP, NATIONAL (1970), 28 Castle Street, Kingston upon Thames, Surrey KTI ISS. Tel: 0181-547 3937. *Chief Executive,* B. Mehta

SCHOOL LIBRARY ASSOCIATION (1937), Liden Library, Barrington Close, Liden, Swindon SN3 6HF. Tel: 01793-617838. *Executive Secretary,* Ms V. Fea

SCHOOLMASTERS, SOCIETY OF (1798), Dolton's Farm, Woburn, Milton Keynes MKI7 9HX. Tel: 01525-290093. *Secretary,* Mrs D. J. Skipper

SCHOOLMISTRESSES AND GOVERNESSES BENEVOLENT INSTITUTION (1843), Queen Mary House, Manor Park Road, Chislehurst, Kent BR7 5PY. Tel: 0181-468 7997. *Director,* L. I. Baggott

SCIENCE AND LEARNING, SOCIETY FOR THE PROTECTION OF (1933), 20–21 Compton Terrace, London NI 2UN. *Secretary,* Ms E. Fraser

SCIENCE, BRITISH ASSOCIATION FOR THE ADVANCEMENT OF (1831), 23 Savile Row, London WIX 2NB. Tel: 0171-973 3500. *Executive Secretary,* Dr P. Briggs

SCIENCE EDUCATION, ASSOCIATION FOR (1963), College Lane, Hatfield, Herts ALIO 9AA. Tel: 01707-267411. *General Secretary,* Dr D. S. Moore

SCOPE (formerly The Spastics Society) (1952), 12 Park Crescent, London WIN 4EQ. Tel: 0171-636 5020. *Chief Executive,* R. P. Brewster

SCOTCH WHISKY ASSOCIATION, THE (1919), 20 Atholl Crescent, Edinburgh EH3 8HF. Tel: 0131-229 4383. *Director-General,* H. Morison

SCOTTISH CHIEFS, THE STANDING COUNCIL OF (1952), Hope Chambers, 52 Leith Walk, Edinburgh EH6 5HW. Tel: 0131-554 6321. *General Secretary,* G. A. Way of Plean

SCOTTISH CHURCH HISTORY SOCIETY (1922), St Serf's Manse, 1 Denham Green Terrace, Edinburgh EH5 3PG. Tel: 0131-552 4059. *Hon. Secretary,* Revd P. H. Donald, PH.D.

SCOTTISH CORPORATION, ROYAL (1611), 37 King Street, London WC2E 8JS. Tel: 0171-240 3718. *Chief Executive,* Wg Cdr. A. Robertson

SCOTTISH COUNTRY DANCE SOCIETY, ROYAL (1923), 12 Coates Crescent, Edinburgh EH3 7AF. Tel: 0131-225 3854. *Secretary,* Miss G. S. Parker

SCOTTISH GENEALOGY SOCIETY (1953), Library and Family History Centre, 15 Victoria Terrace, Edinburgh EHI 2JL. Tel: 0131-220 3677. *Hon. Secretary,* Miss J. P. S. Ferguson

SCOTTISH HISTORY SOCIETY (1886), Department of Scottish History, University of Edinburgh, Edinburgh EH8 9YL. *Hon. Secretary,* Dr E. P. D. Torrie

SCOTTISH LANDOWNERS' FEDERATION (1906), 25 Maritime Street, Edinburgh EH6 5PW. Tel: 0131-555 1031. *Director,* S. Fraser

SCOTTISH LAW AGENTS SOCIETY, 79 West Regent Street, Glasgow G2 2AW. Tel: 0141-332 5537. *Secretary,* D. C. Clapham

SCOTTISH NATIONAL INSTITUTION FOR THE WAR BLINDED (1915), PO Box 500, Gillespie Crescent, Edinburgh EHIO 4HZ. Tel: 0131-229 1456. *Secretary,* J. B. M. Munro

SCOTTISH NATIONAL WAR MEMORIAL (1927), The Castle, Edinburgh EH1 2YT. Tel: 0131-226 7393. *Secretary*, Lt.-Col. I. Shepherd

SCOTTISH SOCIETY FOR THE PREVENTION OF CRUELTY TO ANIMALS (1839), Braehead Mains, 603 Queensferry Road, Edinburgh EH4 6EA. Tel: 0131-339 0222. *Chief Executive*, J. Morris, CBE

SCOTTISH SOCIETY FOR THE PROTECTION OF WILD BIRDS (1927), Foremount House, Kilbarchan, Renfrewshire PA10 2EZ. Tel: 01505-702419. *Secretary*, Dr J. A. Gibson

SCOTTISH WILDLIFE TRUST (1964), Cramond House, Kirk Cramond, Cramond Glebe Road, Edinburgh EH4 6NS. Tel: 0131-312 7765. *Director*, D. J. Hughes Hallett

SCOUT ASSOCIATION, THE (1907), Baden-Powell House, Queen's Gate, London SW7 5JS. Tel: 0171-584 7030. *Chief Scout*, W. G. Morrison, CBE; *Chief Executive Commissioner*, A. E. N. Black, OBE

SCRIBES AND ILLUMINATORS, SOCIETY OF (1921), 6 Queen Square, London WC1N 3AR. *Hon. Secretary*, Ms C. Turvey

SCRIPTURE GIFT MISSION INCORPORATED (1888), Radstock House, 3 Eccleston Street, London SW1W 9LZ. Tel: 0171-730 2155. *International Director*, R. Kennedy

SCRIPTURE UNION (1867), 130 City Road, London EC1V 2NJ. Tel: 0171-782 0013. *General Director*, G. D. Q. Carr

SCULPTORS, ROYAL SOCIETY OF BRITISH (1904), 108 Old Brompton Road, London SW7 3RA. Tel: 0171-373 5554. *President*, Ms P. Davidson Davis

SEA CADETS (1895), 202 Lambeth Road, London SE1 7JF. Tel: 0171-928 8978. *General Secretary*, Cdr P. J. Grindal, CBE

SEAMEN'S BOYS' HOME, BRITISH (1863), Grenville House, Berry Head Road, Brixham, Devon TQ5 9AF. Tel: 01803-882129. *Secretary*, Capt. E. M. Marks, RD, RNR

SEAMEN'S CHRISTIAN FRIEND SOCIETY (1846), 48 South Street, Alderley Edge, Cheshire SK9 7ES. Tel: 01625-590010. *General Secretary*, M. J. Wilson

SEAMEN'S PENSION FUND, ROYAL (1919), 65 High Street, Ewell, Epsom, Surrey KT17 1RX. Tel: 0181-393 5873. *Secretary*, D. Barker

SECRETARIES AND ADMINISTRATORS, CHARTERED INSTITUTE OF (1891), 16 Park Crescent, London W1N 4AH. Tel: 0171-580 4741. *Chief Executive and Secretary*, M. J. Ainsworth

SECULAR SOCIETY LTD, NATIONAL (1866), Bradlaugh House, 47 Theobald's Road, London WC1X 8SP. Tel: 0171-404 3126. *General Secretary*, T. Mullins

SEEABILITY (formerly Royal School for the Blind) (1799), 56–66 Highlands Road, Leatherhead, Surrey KT22 8NR. Tel: 01372-373086. *Chief Executive*, R. M. Perkins

SELDEN SOCIETY (1887), Faculty of Laws, Queen Mary and Westfield College, Mile End Road, London E1 4NS. Tel: 0171-975 5136. To encourage the study and advance the knowledge of the history of English law. *Secretary*, V. Tunkel

SENSE (THE NATIONAL DEAF-BLIND AND RUBELLA ASSOCIATION) (1955), 11–13 Clifton Terrace, London N4 3SR. Tel: 0171-272 7774. *Chief Executive*, R. Clark

SHAFTESBURY HOMES AND *Arethusa* (1843), 3 Rectory Grove, London SW4 0EG. Tel: 0171-720 8709. *Director*, Capt. N. C. Baird-Murray, CBE, RN

SHAFTESBURY SOCIETY, THE (1844), 16 Kingston Road, London SW19 1JZ. Tel: 0181-542 5550. Cares for physically and mentally handicapped, elderly and socially deprived people. *Chief Executive*, Ms F. Beckett

SHELLFISH ASSOCIATION OF GREAT BRITAIN (1904), Fishmongers' Hall, London Bridge, London EC4R 9EL. Tel: 0171-283 8305. *Director*, E. Edwards, OBE, PH.D.

SHELTER (THE NATIONAL CAMPAIGN FOR HOMELESS PEOPLE) (1966), 88 Old Street, London EC1V 9HU. Tel: 0171-505 2000. *Director*, C. Holmes

SHERLOCK HOLMES SOCIETY OF LONDON (1951), 64 Graham Road, London SW19 3SS. Tel: 0181-540 7657. *General Secretary*, T. J. K. Owen

SHIPBROKERS, INSTITUTE OF CHARTERED (1911), 3 Gracechurch Street, London EC3V 0AT. Tel: 0171-283 1361. *Secretary*, Mrs B. Fletcher

SHIRE HORSE SOCIETY (1878), East of England Showground, Peterborough PE2 6XE. Tel: 01733-390696. *Secretary*, T. Gibson, OBE

SHRIEVALTY ASSOCIATION (1971), Office of the High Sherrifs, Duncombe Place, York YO1 2DY. Tel: 01904-634771. *Secretary*, J. H. N. Towers

SIGHT SAVERS INTERNATIONAL (Royal Commonwealth Society for the Blind) (1950), Grosvenor Hall, Bolnore Road, Haywards Heath, W. Sussex RH16 4BX. Tel: 01444-412424. *Executive Director*, R. Porter

SIMPLIFIED SPELLING SOCIETY (1908), Clare Hall, Chapel Lane, Chigwell, Essex IG7 6JJ. *Chairman*, C. J. H. Jolly

SIR OSWALD STOLL FOUNDATION (1916), 446 Fulham Road, London SW6 1DT. Tel: 0171-385 2110. *Director*, R. C. Brunwin

SMALL BUSINESSES, FEDERATION OF (1974), Parliamentary Office, 140 Lower Marsh, London SE1 7AE. Tel: 0171-928 9272. *National Chairman*, Mrs P. McAlester

SMALL FARMERS' ASSOCIATION, THE (1979), PO Box 18, Woodbridge, Suffolk IP13 0QP. *Chairman*, J. Morford

SOCIALIST PARTY OF GREAT BRITAIN (1904), 52 Clapham High Street, London SW4 7UN. Tel: 0171-622 3811. *General Secretary*, A. Buick

SOCIAL WORKERS, BRITISH ASSOCIATION OF (1970), 16 Kent Street, Birmingham B5 6RD. Tel: 0121-622 3911. *General Secretary*, D. N. Jones

SOLDIERS' AND AIRMEN'S SCRIPTURE READERS ASSOCIATION, THE (1838), Havelock House, Barrack Road, Aldershot, Hants GU11 3NP. Tel: 01252-310033. *General Secretary*, Lt.-Col. M. Hitchcott

SOLDIERS', SAILORS' AND AIRMEN'S FAMILIES ASSOCIATION (SSAFA) (1885), 19 Queen Elizabeth Street, London SE1 2LP. Tel: 0171-403 8783. *Controller*, Maj.-Gen. C. R. Grey, CBE

SOLDIERS' WIDOWS, ROYAL CAMBRIDGE HOME FOR (1851), 82–84 Hurst Road, East Molesey, Surrey KT8 9AH. Tel: 0181-979 3788. *Superintendent*, Mrs I. O. Yarnell

SOLICITORS IN THE SUPREME COURTS OF SCOTLAND, SOCIETY OF (1784), 2 Abercromby Place, Edinburgh EH3 6JZ. Tel: 0131-556 4070. *Secretary*, A. R. Brownlie, OBE

SOROPTIMIST INTERNATIONAL OF GREAT BRITAIN AND IRELAND (1923), 127 Wellington Road South, Stockport, Cheshire SK1 3TS. Tel: 0161-976 6568. *Executive Officer*, Ms K. Heward

SOS SOCIETY, THE, *see* 2CARE

SOUTH AMERICAN MISSION SOCIETY (1844), Allen Gardiner House, Pembury Road, Tunbridge Wells, Kent TN2 3QU. Tel: 01892-538647. *General Secretary*, Rt. Revd D. Evans

SOUTH WALES INSTITUTE OF ENGINEERS (1857), Empire House, Mount Stuart Square, Cardiff CF1 6DN. Tel: 01222-481726. *Hon. Secretary*, R. E. Lindsay

SPEAKERS CLUBS, THE ASSOCIATION OF (1971), 28 High Street, Auchterarder, Perthshire PH3 1DF. Tel: 01764-662457. *National Secretary*, D. Williams

SPINA BIFIDA AND HYDROCEPHALUS, ASSOCIATION FOR (ASBAH), 42 Park Road, Peterborough PE1 2UQ. Tel: 01733-555988. *Executive Director*, A. Russell

SPORTS MEDICINE, INSTITUTE OF (1963), Burlington House, Piccadilly, London W1V 0LQ. Tel: 0171-287 5269. *Hon. Secretary*, Dr W. T. Orton

SPURGEON's CHILD CARE (1867), 74 Wellingborough Road, Rushden, Northants NN10 9TY. Tel: 01933-412412. *Chief Executive*, D. C. Culwick

STANDING CONFERENCE OF NATIONAL AND UNIVERSITY LIBRARIES (SCONUL) (1950), 102 Euston Street, London NW1 2HA. Tel: 0171-387 0317. *Secretary*, A. J. C. Bainton

STATISTICIANS, INSTITUTE OF, *see* ROYAL STATISTICAL SOCIETY

STATUTE LAW SOCIETY (1968), Onslow House, 9 The Green, Richmond, Surrey TW9 1PU. Tel: 0181-940 0017. *Hon. Secretary*, N. Frudd

STEWART SOCIETY (1899), 17 Dublin Street, Edinburgh EH1 3PG. Tel: 0131-557 6824. *Hon. Secretary*, Mrs M. Walker

STRATEGIC PLANNING SOCIETY, THE (1967), 17 Portland Place, London W1N 3AF. Tel: 0171-636 7737. *Chief Executive*, D. Firnberg

STRATEGIC STUDIES, INTERNATIONAL INSTITUTE FOR (1958), 23 Tavistock Street, London WC2E 7NQ. Tel: 0171-379 7676. *Director*, Dr J. Chipman

STROKE ASSOCIATION, THE (1899), CHSA House, Whitecross Street, London EC1Y 8JJ. Tel: 0171-490 7999. *Director-General*, Dr S. McLauchlan

STRUCTURAL ENGINEERS, INSTITUTION OF (1908), 11 Upper Belgrave Street, London SW1X 8BH. Tel: 0171-235 4535. *Chief Executive and Secretary*, Dr J. W. Dougill

STUDENT CHRISTIAN MOVEMENT (1889), Mary Burnie House, Westhill College, 14–16 Weoley Park Road, Selly Oak, Birmingham B29 6LL. Tel: 0121-440 3000. *Administrator*

SUFFOLK HORSE SOCIETY (1878), The Market Hill, Woodbridge, Suffolk IP12 4LU. Tel: 01394-380643. *Secretary*, P. Ryder-Davies

SURGEONS OF EDINBURGH, ROYAL COLLEGE OF (1505), Nicolson Street, Edinburgh EH8 9DW. Tel: 0131-556 6206. *Secretary*, I. B. MacLeod, FRCSED.

SURGEONS OF ENGLAND, ROYAL COLLEGE OF (1800), 35–43 Lincoln's Inn Fields, London WC2A 3PN. Tel: 0171-405 3474. *Secretary*, R. H. E. Duffett

SURVEYORS, ROYAL INSTITUTION OF CHARTERED (1868), 12 Great George Street, London SW1P 3AD. Tel: 0171-222 7000. *Chief Executive*, Ms C. Makin

SURVIVAL INTERNATIONAL (1969), 11–15 Emerald Street, London WC1N 7QT. Tel: 0171-242 1441. *Director*, S. Corry

SUZY LAMPLUGH TRUST (1986), 14 East Sheen Avenue, London SW14 8AS. Tel: 0181-392 1839. *Executive Secretary*, P. Lamplugh

SWEDENBORG SOCIETY (1810), 20–21 Bloomsbury Way, London WC1A 2TH. Tel: 0171-405 7986. *Secretary*, Ms M. G. Waters

TALKING BOOKS FOR THE HANDICAPPED AND HOSPITAL PATIENTS, *see* NATIONAL LISTENING LIBRARY

TAVISTOCK INSTITUTE, THE (1947), 30 Tabernacle Street, London EC2A 4DE. Tel: 0171-417 0407. *Secretary*, Ms C. Turnbull

TAXATION, CHARTERED INSTITUTE OF (1930), 12 Upper Belgrave Street, London SW1X 8BB. Tel: 0171-235 9381. *Secretary-General*, R. A. Dommett

TEACHERS OF HOME ECONOMICS AND TECHNOLOGY, NATIONAL ASSOCIATION OF (1896), Hamilton House, Mabledon Place, London WC1H 9BJ. Tel: 0171-387 1441. *Secretary*, G. Thompson

TEACHERS OF MATHEMATICS, ASSOCIATION OF (1952), 7 Shaftesbury Street, Derby DE3 8YB. Tel: 01332-346599. *Hon. Secretary*, Ms M. Gorman

TEACHERS OF THE DEAF, BRITISH ASSOCIATION OF (1977). *Hon. Secretary*, Mrs A. Underwood, 41 The Orchard, Leven, Beverley, N. Humberside HU17 5QA. Tel: 01964-544243

TEACHERS' UNION, ULSTER (1919), 94 Malone Road, Belfast BT9 5HP. Tel: 01232-662216. *General Secretary*, D. Allen

TELECOMMUNICATIONS USERS' ASSOCIATION (1965), 48 Percy Road, London N12 8BU. Tel: 0181-445 0996. *Executive Chairman*, W. E. Mieran

TEMPERANCE SOCIETIES:

British National Temperance League (1834), Westbrook Court, Sharrow Vale Road, Sheffield S11 8YZ. Tel: 0114-267 9976. *Executive Director*, A. Willis

National Council for Social Concern, 59 Catherine Place, London SW1E 6DY. Tel: 0171-630 7046. *Director*, P. Carlin

National United Temperance Council (1880), 176 Blackfriars Road, London SE1 8ET. Tel: 0171-928 1538. *General Secretary*, Revd B. Kinman

Order of the Sons of Temperance Friendly Society (1855), 5 Ashbourne Road, Derby DE22 3FQ. Tel: 01332-341672. *Secretary*, D. Newbury

Royal Naval Temperance Society (1876) (auxiliary of Royal Sailors' Rests), 2A South Street, Gosport, Hants PO12 1ES. Tel: 01705-589551. *General Secretary*, A. A. Lockwood

United Kingdom Alliance (1863), 176 Blackfriars Road, London SE1 8ET. Tel: 0171-928 1538. *General Secretary*, Revd B. Kinman

TEMPLETON FOUNDATION (1973), 18 Eastgate Gardens, Taunton, Somerset TA1 1RD. Tel: 01823-324522. *UK Representative*, Mrs N. Pearse

TERRENCE HIGGINS TRUST (1982), 52–54 Grays Inn Road, London WC1X 8JU. Tel: 0171-831 0330. *Helpline*, 0171-242 1010. *Chairman*, N. Partridge

TERRITORIAL, AUXILIARY AND VOLUNTEER RESERVE ASSOCIATIONS, COUNCIL OF (1908), Duke of York's HQ, London SW3 4SG. Tel: 0171-730 6122. *Secretary*, Maj.-Gen. W. A. Evans, CB

TEXTILE INSTITUTE, THE (1910), International HQ, 10 Blackfriars Street, Manchester M3 5DR. Tel: 0161-834 8457. *Chief Executive*, R. G. Denyer

THEATRE RESEARCH, SOCIETY FOR (1948), c/o The Theatre Museum, 1E Tavistock Street, London WC2E 7PA. *Joint Hon. Secretaries*, Ms E. Cottis; Ms F. Dann

THEATRES TRUST, THE (1976), 22 Charing Cross Road, London WC2H OHR. Tel: 0171-836 8591. *Director,* J. Earl

THEATRICAL FUND, ROYAL (1839), 11 Garrick Street, London WC2E 9AR. Tel: 0171-836 3322. *Secretary,* Mrs R. M. Oliver

THEOSOPHICAL SOCIETY IN ENGLAND (1875), 50 Gloucester Place, London WIH 4EA. Tel: 0171-935 9261. *General Secretary,* Miss L. Storey

THISTLE FOUNDATION, THE (1945), 27A Walker Street, Edinburgh EH3 7HX. Tel: 0131-225 7282. *Director,* P. Croft

THOMAS CORAM FOUNDATION FOR CHILDREN (formerly The Foundling Hospital) (1739), 40 Brunswick Square, London WCIN IAZ. Tel: 0171-278 2424. *Director and Secretary,* Dr C. Hanvey

TIDY BRITAIN GROUP, THE (1953), The Pier, Wigan WN3 4EX. Tel: 01942-824620. *Director-General,* Prof. G. Ashworth, CBE

TOC H (1915), Headquarters, 1 Forest Close, Wendover, Aylesbury, Bucks HP22 6BT. Tel: 01296-623911. *Director,* M. Lyddiard

TOURIST BOARD, ENGLISH, Thames Tower, Black's Road, London W6 9EL. Tel: 0181-846 9000. *Chief Executive,* J. East

TOURIST BOARD, NORTHERN IRELAND, St Anne's Court, 59 North Street, Belfast BTI INB. Tel: 01232-231221. *Chief Executive,* I. G. Henderson

TOURIST BOARD, SCOTTISH (1969), 23 Ravelston Terrace, Edinburgh EH4 3EU. Tel: 0131-332 2433. *Chief Executive,* D. D. Reid

TOURIST BOARD, WALES, Brunel House, 2 Fitzalan Road, Cardiff CF2 IUY. *Chief Executive,* P. Loveluck

TOWN AND COUNTRY PLANNING ASSOCIATION (1899), 17 Carlton House Terrace, London SWIY 5AS. Tel: 0171-930 8903. *Director,* D. Hall, MBE

TOWN PLANNING INSTITUTE, ROYAL (1914), 26 Portland Place, London WIN 4BE. Tel: 0171-636 9107. *Secretary-General,* D. Fryer

TOWNSWOMEN'S GUILDS (1929), Chamber of Commerce House, 75 Harborne Road, Birmingham B15 3DA. Tel: 0121-456 3435. *National Secretary,* Mrs P. Wilkes

TOYNBEE HALL, The Universities' Settlement in East London (1884), 28 Commercial Street, London EI 6LS. Tel: 0171-247 6943. *Chief Executive,* A. Prescott

TRADE MARK AGENTS, INSTITUTE OF (1934), Canterbury House, 2–6 Sydenham Road, Croydon CRO 9XE. Tel: 0181-686 2052. *Secretary,* Mrs M. J. Tyler

TRADING STANDARDS ADMINISTRATION, INSTITUTE OF (1881), 3–5 Hadleigh Business Centre, 351 London Road, Hadleigh, Essex SS7 2BT. Tel: 01702-559922. *Chief Executive,* A. J. Street

TRANSLATION AND INTERPRETING, INSTITUTE OF (1986), 377 City Road, London ECIV INA. Tel: 0171-713 7600. *Chairman,* S. Slade

TRANSPORT ADMINISTRATION, INSTITUTE OF (1944), 32 Palmerston Road, Southampton SO14 ILL. Tel: 01703-631380. *Director,* Wg Cdr. P. F. Green

TRANSPORT, CHARTERED INSTITUTE OF (1919), 80 Portland Place, London WIN 4DP. Tel: 0171-636 9952. *Director,* Mrs S. Gross

TRAVEL AGENTS, ASSOCIATION OF BRITISH (ABTA) (1950), 55–57 Newman Street, London WIP 4AH. Tel: 0171-637 2444. *President,* C. Trigger

TREE COUNCIL (1974), 51 Catherine Place, London SWIE 6DY. Tel: 0171-828 9928. *General Secretary,* R. Osborne

TREE FOUNDATION, INTERNATIONAL (formerly Men of the Trees) (1922), Sandy Lane, Crawley Down, W. Sussex RHIO 4HS. Tel: 01342-712536. *Chairman,* S. Keys

TROPICAL MEDICINE AND HYGIENE, ROYAL SOCIETY OF (1907), Manson House, 26 Portland Place, London WIN 4EY. Tel: 0171-580 2127. *Hon. Secretaries,* Dr D. C. Barker; Dr W. R. C. Weir

TURNER SOCIETY (1975), BCM Box Turner, London WCIN 3XX. *Chairman,* E. Joll

2CARE (formerly The SOS Society) (1929), 13 Harwood Road, London SW6 4QP. Tel: 0171-371 0118. Residential homes for the elderly, and psychiatric rehabilitation centres. *Chief Executive,* Miss E. C. R. O'Sullivan

UFAW (UNIVERSITIES FEDERATION FOR ANIMAL WELFARE) (1926), 8 Hamilton Close, South Mimms, Potters Bar, Herts EN6 3QD. Tel: 01707-658202. *Director,* R. Ewbank

UK INDEPENDENCE PARTY, 80 Regent Street, London WIR 5PE. Tel: 0171-434 4559. *Secretary,* G. Batten

UNITED NATIONS ASSOCIATION OF GREAT BRITAIN AND NORTHERN IRELAND (1945), 3 Whitehall Court, London SWIA 2EL. Tel: 0171-930 2931. *Director,* M. C. Harper

UNITED REFORMED CHURCH HISTORY SOCIETY (1972), 86 Tavistock Place, London WCIH 9RT. Tel: 0171-916 2020. *Hon. Secretary,* Revd Dr S. Orchard

UNITED SOCIETY FOR CHRISTIAN LITERATURE (1799), Robertson House, Leas Road, Guildford, Surrey GUI 4QW. Tel: 01483-577877. *General Secretary,* Dr A. Marriage

UNITED SOCIETY FOR THE PROPAGATION OF THE GOSPEL (USPG) (1701), Partnership House, 157 Waterloo Road, London SEI 8XA. Tel: 0171-928 8681. *Secretary,* Revd. Canon P. Price

UNIVERSITIES OF THE UNITED KINGDOM, COMMITTEE OF VICE-CHANCELLORS AND PRINCIPALS OF THE (1918), 29 Tavistock Square, London WCIH 9EZ. Tel: 0171-387 9231. *Chief Executive,* Ms D. Warwick

UNIVERSITY AND COLLEGE LECTURERS, ASSOCIATION OF (1973), 104 Albert Road, Southsea, Hants PO5 2SN. Tel: 01705-818625. *Chief Executive,* Ms C. Cheesman

VALUERS AND AUCTIONEERS, INCORPORATED SOCIETY OF (1968), 3 Cadogan Gate, London SWIX OAS. Tel: 0171-235 2282. *Chief Executive,* H. Whitty

VEGAN SOCIETY, THE (1944), Donald Watson House, 7 Battle Road, St Leonards-on-Sea, E. Sussex TN37 7AA. Tel: 01424-427393. *Information Officer,* Ms A. Rofe

VEGETARIAN SOCIETY OF THE UNITED KINGDOM LTD, Parkdale, Dunham Road, Altrincham, Cheshire WAI4 4QG. Tel: 0161-928 0793. *Chief Executive,* Ms T. Fox

VENEREAL DISEASES, MEDICAL SOCIETY FOR THE STUDY OF (1922), c/o Royal Society of Medicine, 1 Wimpole Street, London WIM 8AE. Tel: 0171-290 2968. *Hon. Secretary,* Dr T. McManus

VERNACULAR ARCHITECTURE GROUP (1953), 16 Falna Crescent, Coton Green, Tamworth, Staffs B79 8JS. Tel: 01827-69434. *Hon. Secretary,* R. Meeson

VETERINARY ASSOCIATION, BRITISH (1881), 7 Mansfield Street, London WIM OAT. Tel: 0171-636 6541. *Chief Executive,* J. H. Baird

VETERINARY SURGEONS, ROYAL COLLEGE OF (1844),
Belgravia House, 62–64 Horseferry Road, London
SW1P 2AF. Tel: 0171-222 2001. *President*, D. J. Thompson,
OBE; *Registrar*, P. E. Woolley, OBE

VICTIM SUPPORT (NATIONAL ASSOCIATION OF VICTIM
SUPPORT SCHEMES) (1979), Cranmer House, 39 Brixton
Road, London SW9 6DZ. Tel: 0171-735 9166. *Director*,
Ms H. Reeves, OBE

VICTORIA CROSS AND GEORGE CROSS ASSOCIATION,
2 Ripley Courtyard, Old Admiralty Building,
Whitehall, London SW1A 2BL. Tel: 0171-930 3506.
Chairman, Col. B. S. T. Archer, GC, OBE

VICTORIA INSTITUTE, THE (Philosophical Society of
Great Britain), 41 Marne Avenue, Welling, Kent
DA16 2EY. Tel: 0181-303 0465. *Chairman of Council*,
T. C. Mitchell

VICTORIAN SOCIETY (1958), 1 Priory Gardens, Bedford
Park, London W4 1TT. Tel: 0181-994 1019. *Director*,
Dr W. Filmer-Sankey

VICTORY (SERVICES) ASSOCIATION LTD AND CLUB
(1907), 63–79 Seymour Street, London W2 2HF. Tel:
0171-723 4474. *General Manager*, G. F. Taylor

VIKING SOCIETY FOR NORTHERN RESEARCH (1892),
Department of Scandinavian Studies, University
College, Gower Street, London WC1E 6BT. Tel: 0171-380
7176. *Hon. Secretaries*, Prof. M. P. Barnes; Dr J. Jesch

VOLUNTARY ORGANIZATIONS, NATIONAL COUNCIL FOR
(1919), Regent's Wharf, 8 All Saints Street, London
N1 9RL. Tel: 0171-713 6161. *Chief Executive*,
S. Etherington

VSO (VOLUNTARY SERVICE OVERSEAS) (1958),
317 Putney Bridge Road, London SW15 2PN. Tel: 0181-
780 2266. *Director*, D. Green

WAR ON WANT (1952), 37–39 Great Guildford Street,
London SE1 0ES. Tel: 0171-620 1111. *Director*,
G. Alhadeff

WATER AND ENVIRONMENTAL MANAGEMENT,
CHARTERED INSTITUTION OF (1987), 15 John Street,
London WC1N 2EB. Tel: 0171-831 3110. *Executive Director*,
R. A. Bispham

WATERCOLOUR SOCIETY, ROYAL (1804), Bankside
Gallery, 48 Hopton Street, London SE1 9JH. Tel: 0171-
357 0674. *President*, R. Seddon; *Secretary*, Ms J. Dixey

WELDING INSTITUTE, THE, Abington Hall, Cambridge
CB1 6AL. Tel: 01223-891162. *Chief Executive*,
A. B. M. Braithwaite

WELLBEING (1964), 27 Sussex Place, London NW1 4SP.
Tel: 0171-262 5337. *Director*, Mrs R. Barnes

WELLCOME TRUST (1936), The Wellcome Building, 183
Euston Road, London NW1 2BE. Tel: 0171-611 8888.
Director, Dr B. Ogilvie

WELLS SOCIETY, H. G. (1961). *Hon. Secretary*, Dr S. Hardy,
English Department, Nene College, Moulton Park,
Northampton NN2 7AL. Tel: 01604-735500, ext. 2133

WESLEY HISTORICAL SOCIETY (1893), 34 Spiceland Road,
Northfield, Birmingham B31 1NJ. Tel: 0121-475 4914.
General Secretary, Dr E. D. Graham

WEST LONDON MISSION (1887), 19 Thayer Street,
London W1M 5LJ. Tel: 0171-935 6179. *Superintendent*,
Revd D. S. Cruise

WESTMINSTER FOUNDATION FOR DEMOCRACY (1992),
Clutha House, 10 Storey's Gate, London SW1P 3AY. Tel:
0171-976 7565. *Chief Executive*, Ms D. Warwick

WES WORLD-WIDE EDUCATION SERVICE LTD (1888),
Canada House, 272 Field End Road, Eastcote, Ruislip,
Middx HA4 9NA. Tel: 0181-866 4400. *Head of Consultancy*,
Mrs T. Mulder-Reynolds

WILDFOWL AND WETLANDS TRUST (1946), The New
Grounds, Slimbridge, Glos GL2 7BT. Tel: 01453-890333.
Director-General, Dr M. Owen

WILDLIFE TRUSTS, THE (1912), The Green, Witham
Park, Waterside South, Lincoln LN5 7JR. Tel: 01522-
544400. *Managing Director*, M. Gough

WILLIAM MORRIS SOCIETY AND KELMSCOTT
FELLOWSHIP (1918), Kelmscott House, 26 Upper Mall,
London W6 9TA. Tel: 0171-741 3735. *Hon. Secretary*,
D. Baker

WINE AND SPIRIT ASSOCIATION OF GREAT BRITAIN AND
NORTHERN IRELAND (*c.* 1825), Five Kings House,
1 Queen Street Place, London EC4R 1XX. Tel: 0171-248
5377. *Director*, P. Lewis

WOMEN, SOCIETY FOR PROMOTING THE TRAINING OF
(1859), The Rectory, Main Street, Great Casterton,
Stamford, Lincs PE9 4AP. Tel: 01780-64036. *Hon.
Secretary*, Revd B. Harris

WOMEN ARTISTS, SOCIETY OF (1855), Westminster
Gallery, Westminster Central Hall, Storey's Gate,
London SW1H 9NU. *President*, Prof. B. Tate

WOMEN GRADUATES, BRITISH FEDERATION OF (1907),
4 Mandeville Courtyard, 142 Battersea Park Road,
London SW11 4NB. Tel: 0171-498 8037. *Secretary*,
Mrs A. B. Stein

WOMEN'S ENGINEERING SOCIETY (1920), Imperial
College of Science and Technology, Department of
Civil Engineering, Imperial College Road, London
SW7 2BU. Tel: 0171-594 6025. *Secretary*,
Mrs C. MacGillivray

WOMEN'S INSTITUTES, NATIONAL FEDERATION OF
(1915), 104 New Kings Road, London SW6 4LY. Tel:
0171-371 9300. *General Secretary*, Ms J. Osborne

WOMEN'S INSTITUTES OF NORTHERN IRELAND,
FEDERATION OF (1932), 209–211 Upper Lisburn Road,
Belfast BT10 0LL. Tel: 01232-301506/601781. *General
Secretary*, Mrs I. A. Sproule

WOMEN'S INTERNATIONAL LEAGUE FOR PEACE AND
FREEDOM (British Section) (1915), 7A Hepburn Road,
Bristol BS2 8UD. Tel: 0117-942 7878. *President*,
Ms C. Lowden

WOMEN'S NATIONWIDE CANCER CONTROL CAMPAIGN
(1964), Suna House, 128–130 Curtain Road, London
EC2A 3AR. Tel: 0171-729 4688. *Helpline*, 0171-729 2229.
Administrator, Ms J. Harding

WOMEN'S ROYAL NAVAL SERVICE BENEVOLENT TRUST
(1942), 311 Twyford Avenue, Portsmouth, Hants
PO2 8PE. Tel: 01705-655301. *General Secretary*,
Mrs J. Russell

WOMEN'S ROYAL VOLUNTARY SERVICE (WRVS),
234–244 Stockwell Road, London SW9 9SP. Tel: 0171-
416 0146. *National Chairman*, Mrs E. Toulson

WOMEN'S RURAL INSTITUTES, SCOTTISH (1917),
42 Heriot Row, Edinburgh EH3 6ES. *General Secretary*,
Mrs A. Peacock

WOMEN'S TRANSPORT SERVICE (FANY) (1907),
Mercury House, Duke of York's HQ, London SW3 4RX.
Tel: 0171-730 2058. *Corps Commander*,
Mrs A. Whitehead

WOODLAND TRUST, THE (1972), Autumn Park, Dysart Road, Grantham, Lincs NG31 6LL. Tel: 01476-74297. *Chief Executive,* J. D. James

WOOD PRESERVING AND DAMP-PROOFING ASSOCIATION, BRITISH (1930), 6 The Office Village, 4 Romford Road, London E15 4EA. Tel: 0181-519 2588. *Director,* Dr C. R. Coggins

WORKERS' EDUCATIONAL ASSOCIATION, 17 Victoria Park Square, London E2 9PB. Tel: 0181-983 1515. *General Secretary,* R. Lochrie

WORLD EDUCATION FELLOWSHIP (1921), International Headquarters, 33 Kinnaird Avenue, London W4 3SH. Tel: 0181-994 7258. *General Secretary,* Mrs R. Crommelin

WORLD ENERGY COUNCIL (1924), 34 St James's Street, London SW1A 1HD. Tel: 0171-930 3966. *Secretary-General,* I. D. Lindsay

WORLD MISSION, COUNCIL FOR (1977), Livingstone House, 11 Carteret Street, London 9DL. Tel: 0171-222 4214. *General Secretary,* D. P. Niles, PH.D.

WORLD SHIP SOCIETY (1946), 101 The Everglades, Hempstead, Gillingham, Kent ME7 3PZ. Tel: 01634-372015. *Secretary,* J. Poole

WORLD SOCIETY FOR THE PROTECTION OF ANIMALS (1981), 2 Langley Lane, London SW8 1TJ. Tel: 0171-793 0540. *Chief Executive,* A. Dickson

WRITERS TO HM SIGNET, SOCIETY OF (1532), 16 Hill Street, Edinburgh EH2 3LD. Tel: 0131-225 4923. *Clerk,* A. M. Kerr

WWF UK (World Wide Fund for Nature) (1961), Panda House, Weyside Park, Godalming, Surrey GU7 1XR. Tel: 01483-426444. *Director,* Dr R. Pellew

YEOMANRY BENEVOLENT FUND (1902), 10 Stone Buildings, Lincoln's Inn, London WC2A 3TG. Tel: 0171-831 6727. *Secretary,* Mrs C. W. Chrystie

YORKSHIRE AGRICULTURAL SOCIETY (1837), Great Yorkshire Showground, Hookstone Oval, Harrogate, N. Yorks HG2 8PW. Tel: 01423-561536. *Chief Executive,* R. Keigwin

YORKSHIRE SOCIETY, THE (1812), 35 Waldorf Heights, Camberley, Surrey GU17 9JH. Tel: 01276-36342. Educational trust making grants to students of all ages. *Secretary,* G. G. Prince, TD

YOUNG FARMERS' CLUBS, NATIONAL FEDERATION OF, YFC Centre, National Agricultural Centre, Stoneleigh Park, Kenilworth, Warks CV8 2LG. Tel: 01203-696544. *Secretary,* T. Shields, MBE

YOUNG MEN'S CHRISTIAN ASSOCIATION (YMCA) (1844), National Council of YMCAs, 640 Forest Road, London E17 3DZ. Tel: 0181-520 5599. *National Secretary,* N. Nightingale

YOUNG WOMEN'S CHRISTIAN ASSOCIATION OF GREAT BRITAIN (YWCA) (1855), 52 Cornmarket Street, Oxford OX1 3EJ. Tel: 01865-726110. *Chief Executive,* Ms G. Tishler

YOUTH ACTION, NORTHERN IRELAND (1944), Hampton, Glenmachan Park, Belfast BT4 2PJ. Tel: 01232-760067. *Director,* P. Graham

YOUTH CLUBS UK (1911), 11 St Bride Street, London EC4A 4AS. Tel: 0171-353 2366. *Chief Executive,* J. Bateman

YOUTH HOSTELS ASSOCIATION (ENGLAND AND WALES) (1930), Trevelyan House, 8 St Stephen's Hill, St Albans, Herts AL1 2DY. Tel: 01727-855215. *Chief Executive,* C. Logan

YOUTH HOSTELS ASSOCIATION OF NORTHERN IRELAND (1931), 22 Donegall Road, Belfast BT12 5JN. Tel: 01232-324733. *Hon. Secretary,* N. O'Reilly

YOUTH HOSTELS ASSOCIATION, SCOTTISH (1931), 7 Glebe Crescent, Stirling FK8 2JA. Tel: 01786-451181. *General Secretary,* J. Martin

ZOOLOGICAL SOCIETY, NORTH OF ENGLAND (1934), Chester Zoo, Upton by Chester, Chester CH2 1LH. Tel: 01244-380280. *Director,* Dr G. McGregor Reid

ZOOLOGICAL SOCIETY OF LONDON (1826), Regent's Park, London NW1 4RY. Tel: 0171-722 3333. *President,* Sir Martin Holdgate, CB, FIBIol; *Clerk to the Council,* P. H. Denton

ZOOLOGICAL SOCIETY OF SCOTLAND, ROYAL (1913), Scottish National Zoological Park, Corstorphine Road, Edinburgh EH12 6TS. Tel: 0131-334 9171. *Director,* Prof. R. J. Wheater, OBE, FRSE

LOCAL HISTORY AND ARCHAEOLOGICAL SOCIETIES

ENGLAND

Berkshire: BERKSHIRE ARCHAEOLOGICAL SOCIETY. *Hon. Secretary,* L. J. Over, 43 Laburnham Road, Maidenhead, Berks SL6 4DE. Tel: 01628-31225

Buckinghamshire: BUCKINGHAMSHIRE ARCHAEOLOGICAL SOCIETY. *Hon. Secretary,* Dr R. P. Hagerty, County Museum, Church Street, Aylesbury, Bucks HP20 2QP.

Cambridgeshire: CAMBRIDGE ANTIQUARIAN SOCIETY. *Hon. Secretary,* Dr M. Hesse, 39 Highsett Hills Road, Cambridge CB2 1NZ.

Cheshire: CHESTER ARCHAEOLOGICAL SOCIETY. *Secretary,* Dr D. J. P. Mason, FSA, Ochr Cottage, Porch Lane, Hope Mountain, Caergwrle, Clwyd LL12 9LS. Tel: 01978-760834

Cornwall: CORNWALL ARCHAEOLOGICAL SOCIETY. *Hon. Secretaries,* Mr and Mrs B. Hammond, 7 Porthmeor Road, Holmbush, St Austell, Cornwall PL25 3LT. Tel: 01726-74763

Cumberland and Westmorland: CUMBERLAND AND WESTMORLAND ANTIQUARIAN AND ARCHAEOLOGICAL SOCIETY. *Hon. Secretary,* R. Hall, 2 High Tenterfell, Kendal, Cumbria LA9 4PG. Tel: 01539-728288

Derbyshire: DERBYSHIRE ARCHAEOLOGICAL SOCIETY. *Hon. Secretary,* I. Mitchell, 159 Draycott Road, Sawley, Long Eaton, Nottingham NG10 3BX. Tel: 0115-972 9029

Devonshire: DEVON ARCHAEOLOGICAL SOCIETY, Royal Albert Memorial Museum, Queen Street, Exeter EX4 3RX. Tel: 01392-265858. *Hon. Secretary,* H. Bishop

Dorset: DORSET NATURAL HISTORY AND ARCHAEOLOGICAL SOCIETY, Dorset County Museum, Dorchester, Dorset DT1 1XA. Tel: 01305-262735. *Secretary,* R. de Peyer

Durham: DURHAM AND NORTHUMBERLAND ARCHITECTURAL AND ARCHAEOLOGICAL SOCIETY. *Hon. Secretary,* A. Lloyd-Wallis, 53 Brook Terrace, Darlington, Co. Durham DL3 6PJ. Tel: 01325-359772

Essex: ESSEX SOCIETY FOR ARCHAEOLOGY AND HISTORY, Hollytrees Museum, High Street, Colchester CO1 1UG. *Secretary,* N. P. Wickendon

Gloucestershire: BRISTOL AND GLOUCESTERSHIRE ARCHAEOLOGICAL SOCIETY. *Hon. Secretary,* D. J. H. Smith, FSA, 22 Beaumont Road, Gloucester GL2 0EJ. Tel: 01452-302610

Hampshire: HAMPSHIRE FIELD CLUB AND ARCHAEOLOGICAL SOCIETY. *Hon. Secretary,* D. Allen, Andover Museum, 6 Church Close, Andover SP10 1DP. Tel: 01264-366283

Herefordshire: WOOLHOPE NATURALISTS' FIELD CLUB. *Hon. Secretary,* J. W. Tonkin, FSA, Chy an Whyloryon, Wigmore, Leominster, Herefordshire HR6 9UD. Tel: 01568-770356

Hertfordshire: EAST HERTFORDSHIRE ARCHAEOLOGICAL SOCIETY. *Hon. Secretary,* Mrs M. C. Readman, 1 Marsh Lane, Stanstead Abbots, Ware, Herts SG12 8HH. Tel: 01920-870664

ST ALBANS AND HERTFORDSHIRE ARCHITECTURAL AND ARCHAEOLOGICAL SOCIETY. *Hon. Secretary,* B. E. Moody, 24 Rose Walk, St Albans, Herts AL4 9AF

Isle of Wight: ISLE OF WIGHT NATURAL HISTORY AND ARCHAEOLOGICAL SOCIETY. *Hon. Secretary,* Mrs T. Goodley, Island Countryside Centre, Rylstone Gardens, Shanklin, IOW PO37 6RG. Tel: 01983-867016

Kent: KENT ARCHAEOLOGICAL SOCIETY. *Hon. General Secretary,* A. Moffatt, Three Elms, Woodlands Lane, Shorne, Gravesend, Kent DA12 3HH. Tel: 01474-822280

Leicestershire: LEICESTERSHIRE ARCHAEOLOGICAL AND HISTORICAL SOCIETY, The Guildhall, Leicester LE1 5FQ. *Hon. Secretary,* Dr A. D. McWhirr

London and Middlesex: CITY OF LONDON ARCHAEOLOGICAL SOCIETY. *Hon. Secretary,* Ms M. Bowen, 34 College Cross, London N1 1PR. Tel: 0171-609 2930

LONDON AND MIDDLESEX ARCHAEOLOGICAL SOCIETY. *Hon. Secretary,* M. Curtis, 34 Alexander Road, London SW19 7JZ. Tel: 0181-879 7109

Norfolk: NORFOLK AND NORWICH ARCHAEOLOGICAL SOCIETY. *Hon. General Secretary,* R. Bellinger, 30 Brettingham Avenue, Norwich NR4 6XG. Tel: 01603-455913

Northumberland and Tyne and Wear: SOCIETY OF ANTIQUARIES OF NEWCASTLE UPON TYNE, Black Gate, Castle Garth, Newcastle upon Tyne NE1 1RQ. Tel: 0191-261 5390. *Secretary,* D. Cutts

SUNDERLAND ANTIQUARIAN SOCIETY. *Hon. Secretary,* Mrs V. M. Stevens, 16 Grizedale Court, Seaburn Dene, Sunderland SR6 8JP. Tel: 0191-548 7541

Oxfordshire: OXFORDSHIRE ARCHITECTURAL AND HISTORICAL SOCIETY. *Hon. Secretary,* Dr A. J. Dodd, 53 Radley Road, Abingdon, Oxon OX14 3PN. Tel: 01235-525960

Shropshire: SHROPSHIRE ARCHAEOLOGICAL AND HISTORICAL SOCIETY. *Chairman,* J. B. Lawson, Westcott Farm, Pontesbury, Shrewsbury SY5 0SQ. Tel: 01743-790531

Somerset: SOMERSET ARCHAEOLOGICAL AND NATURAL HISTORY SOCIETY, Taunton Castle, Taunton, Somerset TA1 4AD. Tel: 01823-272429. *Hon. Secretary,* Dr I. J. Sinclai

Staffordshire: CITY OF STOKE-ON-TRENT MUSEUM ARCHAEOLOGICAL SOCIETY, City Museum and Art Gallery, Hanley, Stoke-on-Trent ST1 3DW. Tel: 01782-202173. *Chairman,* E. E. Royle

Suffolk: SUFFOLK INSTITUTE OF ARCHAEOLOGY AND HISTORY. *Hon. Secretary,* E. A. Martin, Oak Tree Farm, Finborough Road, Hitcham, Ipswich IP7 7LS. Tel: 01449-741266

Surrey: SURREY ARCHAEOLOGICAL SOCIETY, Castle Arch, Guildford, Surrey GU1 3SX. Tel: 01483-32454. *Hon. Secretaries,* Mr and Mrs K. D. Graham

Sussex: SUSSEX ARCHAEOLOGICAL SOCIETY, Bull House, 92 High Street, Lewes, E. Sussex BN7 1XH. Tel: 01273-486260. *Chief Executive,* J. Manley

Warwickshire: BIRMINGHAM AND WARWICKSHIRE ARCHAEOLOGICAL SOCIETY, c/o Birmingham and Midland Institute, Margaret Street, Birmingham B3 3BS. Tel: 0121-236 3591. *Hon. Secretary,* A. J. Wilson

Wiltshire: WILTSHIRE ARCHAEOLOGICAL AND NATURAL HISTORY SOCIETY, The Museum, 41 Long Street, Devizes, Wilts SN10 1NS. Tel: 01380-727369. *Secretary,* P. M. Coston

Worcestershire: WORCESTERSHIRE ARCHAEOLOGICAL SOCIETY. Queen Elizabeth House, Trinity Street, Worcester WR1 2PW. Tel: 01905-722369. *Hon. Secretary,* T. J. Bridges

Yorkshire: YORKSHIRE ARCHAEOLOGICAL SOCIETY. *Hon. Secretary,* N. Cookson, ph.D., Claremont, 23 Clarendon Road, Leeds LS2 9NZ. Tel: 0113-240 9523

HALIFAX ANTIQUARIAN SOCIETY. *Hon. Secretary,* Dr J. A. Hargreaves, 7 Hyde Park Gardens, Haugh Shaw Road, Halifax, W. Yorks HX1 3AH. Tel: 01422-250780

THORESBY SOCIETY. *Hon. Secretary,* B. Harrison, Claremont, 23 Clarendon Road, Leeds LS2 9NZ

SCOTLAND

AYRSHIRE ARCHAEOLOGICAL AND NATURAL HISTORY SOCIETY. *Hon. Secretary,* Dr T. Mathews, 10 Longlands Park, Ayr KA7 4RJ. Tel: 01292-441915

DUMFRIESSHIRE AND GALLOWAY NATURAL HISTORY AND ANTIQUARIAN SOCIETY. *Hon. Secretary,* Mrs J. Muir, North Wing, Carzield House, Kirmahoe, Dumfriesshire DG1 1SY. Tel: 01387-710216

HAWICK ARCHAEOLOGICAL SOCIETY. *Hon. Secretary,* I. W. Landles, Orrock House, Stirches Road, Hawick, Roxburghshire TD9 7HF. Tel: 01450-375546

INVERNESS FIELD CLUB. *Hon. Secretary,* Miss I. McLean, 6 Drumblair Crescent, Inverness IV2 4RG

WALES

Dyfed: CEREDIGION ANTIQUARIAN SOCIETY. *Hon. Secretary,* Mrs M. Burdett-Jones, Skomer, Llanbadarn Road, Aberystwyth, Dyfed SY23 3QW. Tel: 01970-612342

Powys: POWYSLAND CLUB. *Hon. Secretary,* Miss P. M. Davies, Llygad y Dyffryn, Llanidloes, Powys SY18 6JD. Tel: 01686-412277

CHANNEL ISLANDS

SOCIÉTÉ JERSIAISE, ARCHAEOLOGICAL SECTION, La Hougue Bie Museum, Grouville, Jersey. Tel: 01534-58314. *Hon. Secretary,* Dr R. A. H. Nichols

International Organizations

ASSOCIATION OF SOUTH EAST ASIAN NATIONS
70 A. Jl. Sisingamangaraja Kebayoran Baru, Jakarta Selatan, PO Box 2072, Jakarta, Indonesia

Formed in 1967, the main aims of the Association of South East Asian Nations (ASEAN) are the acceleration of economic growth, social progress and cultural development, the promotion of collaboration and mutual assistance in matters of common interest, and the continuing stability of the South East Asian region.

The heads of government of the member countries are the highest authority and give directions to ASEAN as and when necessary. The main policy-making body is the annual meeting of foreign ministers of the member countries. The founding members are Brunei, Indonesia, Malaysia, the Philippines, Singapore and Thailand. Vietnam joined in 1995 and Laos has had observer status since 1992.

In 1992 it was agreed to create an ASEAN free trade area within 15 years. Progress towards this began in 1993 with the introduction of a common preferential tariff. In 1993 it was decided to establish the ASEAN regional forum on security to prevent potential conflicts in the Asia-Pacific area.
Secretary-General, Dato' Ajit Singh (Malaysia)

BANK FOR INTERNATIONAL SETTLEMENTS
Centralbahnplatz 2, 4002 Basle, Switzerland

The objectives of the Bank for International Settlements (founded in 1930) are to promote the co-operation of central banks; to provide facilities for international financial operations; and to act as trustee or agent in international financial settlements entrusted to it. The London agent is the Bank of England, and the Governor of the Bank of England is a member of the Board of Directors, in which administrative control is vested.
Chairman of the Board of Directors and President of the Bank for International Settlements, Dr W. F. Duisenberg (Netherlands)

CAB INTERNATIONAL
Wallingford, Oxon OX10 8DE
Tel 01491-832111

CAB International (formerly the Commonwealth Agricultural Bureau) was founded in 1929. The organization generates, disseminates and applies scientific knowledge in support of sustainable development, with an emphasis on agriculture, forestry, human health and the management of natural resources, and with particular attention to the needs of developing countries. The organization is owned and governed by its 37 member governments, each represented on an Executive Council. A Governing Board provides expert guidance to management on policy issues.

CABI has four institutes, covering mycology, entomology, parasitology and biological control. These undertake taxonomic research, offer pest and disease diagnostic services, characterize biodiversity, develop sustainable crop protection practices, test new drugs against human diseases and provide training. The organization publishes books, journals and newsletters and produces bibliographic databases on agriculture, forestry, allied disciplines and aspects of human health, as well as undertaking contracted scientific research and providing consultancy services.
Director-General, J. Gilmore

CARIBBEAN COMMUNITY AND COMMON MARKET
PO Box 10827, Georgetown, Guyana

The Caribbean Community and Common Market (CARICOM) was established in 1973 with three objectives: economic co-operation through the Caribbean Common Market, the co-ordination of foreign policy among the independent member states, and the provision of common services and co-operation in matters such as health, education, culture, communications and industrial relations. The supreme organ is the Conference of Heads of Government, which determines policy, takes strategic decisions and is responsible for resolving conflicts and all matters relating to the founding treaty. The Caribbean Community Council consists of ministers of government with special responsibility for CARICOM affairs and is responsible for the operational planning, resource allocation, development and smooth running of the Common Market and for the settlement of any problems arising out of its functioning. The principal administrative arms are the Secretariat, based in Guyana, and the Bureau of the Conference.

The 14 member states are Antigua and Barbuda, The Bahamas (which is not a member of the Common Market), Barbados, Belize, Dominica, Grenada, Guyana, Jamaica, Montserrat, St Christopher and Nevis, St Lucia, St Vincent and the Grenadines, Suriname and Trinidad and Tobago. The British Virgin Islands and the Turks and Caicos Islands are associate members. The Dominican Republic, Haiti, Mexico, Puerto Rico and Venezuela have observer status.
Secretary-General, Edwin W. Carrington

THE COMMONWEALTH

The Commonwealth is a voluntary association of 51 sovereign independent states together with their associated states and dependencies. All of the states were formerly parts of the British Empire, or League of Nations (later UN) mandated territories.

The status and relationship of member nations were first defined by the Inter-Imperial Relations Committee of the 1926 Imperial Conference, when the six existing dominions (Australia, Canada, the Irish Free State, Newfoundland, New Zealand and South Africa) were described as 'autonomous Communities within the British Empire, equal in status, in no way subordinate one to another in any aspect of their domestic or external affairs, though united by a common allegiance to the Crown and freely associated as Members of the British Commonwealth of Nations'. This formula was given legal substance by the Statute of Westminster 1931.

This concept of a group of countries owing allegiance to a single Crown changed in 1949 when India decided to become a republic. Her continued membership of the Commonwealth was agreed by the other members on the basis of her 'acceptance of The King as the symbol of the free association of its independent member nations and as such the head of the Commonwealth'. This paved the way for other republics to join the association in due course. Member nations agreed at the time of the accession of Queen Elizabeth II to recognize Her Majesty as the new Head of the Commonwealth. However, the position is not vested in the British Crown.

THE MODERN COMMONWEALTH

With the membership of India and Pakistan in 1947, Ceylon (later Sri Lanka) in 1948 and Ghana in 1957, the character of the Commonwealth changed fundamentally. The grouping of all-white dominions gave way to a modern, multi-racial association of equal, sovereign nations and their peoples as Britain granted independence to almost all of her colonies in Africa, Asia, the Caribbean and the Pacific. Virtually all of these newly-independent countries joined the Commonwealth.

In its modern form, the Commonwealth increasingly focused its attention on promoting development and racial equality. The Commonwealth played an important role in the resolution of the Rhodesian crisis ending with the independence of Zimbabwe, strongly supported the independence of Namibia, and from the late 1970s took concerted action, including sporting and economic sanctions, against the South African government over its policy of apartheid.

THE HARARE DECLARATION

As progress was made towards ending apartheid and introducing democracy in South Africa, the Commonwealth set itself new goals at its heads of government meeting in Harare, Zimbabwe, in 1991. Outlined in the Harare Commonwealth Declaration, these goals include the promotion of the Commonwealth's fundamental political values, such as democracy, the rule of law, good government and human rights; the promotion of equality for women; the provision of universal access to education; the promotion of sustainable development and the allevi- ation of poverty; action against disease and illegal drugs; help for small Commonwealth states; and support of the UN in the quest for international consensus on key issues.

At the heads of government meeting in Cyprus in 1993 the goals and principles of the Harare Declaration were transformed into membership rules for the Common- wealth for new members and for the four remaining non- democratic members (The Gambia, Nigeria, Sierra Leone, Uganda). South Africa was invited to rejoin the Common- wealth after the 1994 multi-racial election and Cameroon invited to join when it has fulfilled the Harare principles.

MEMBERSHIP

Membership of the Commonwealth involves acceptance of the association's basic principles and is subject to the approval of existing members. There are 51 members at present. (The date of joining the Commonwealth is shown in parenthesis.)

*Antigua and Barbuda (1981)	Nigeria (1960)
*Australia (1931)	Pakistan (1947)
*The Bahamas (1973)	*Papua New Guinea (1975)
Bangladesh (1972)	*St Christopher and Nevis
*Barbados (1966)	(1983)
*Belize (1981)	*St Lucia (1979)
Botswana (1966)	*St Vincent and the
Brunei (1984)	Grenadines (1979)
*Canada (1931)	Seychelles (1976)
Cyprus (1961)	Sierra Leone (1961)
Dominica (1978)	Singapore (1965)
The Gambia (1965)	*Solomon Islands (1978)
Ghana (1957)	South Africa (1931)
*Grenada (1974)	Sri Lanka (1948)
Guyana (1966)	Swaziland (1968)
India (1947)	Tanzania (1961)
*Jamaica (1962)	Tonga (1970)
Kenya (1963)	Trinidad and Tobago
Kiribati (1979)	(1962)
Lesotho (1966)	*Tuvalu (1978)
Malawi (1964)	Uganda (1962)
Malaysia (1957)	*United Kingdom
The Maldives (1982)	Vanuatu (1980)
Malta (1964)	Western Samoa (1970)
Mauritius (1968)	Zambia (1964)
Namibia (1990)	Zimbabwe (1980)
Nauru (1968)	
*New Zealand (1931)	*Realms of Queen Elizabeth II

Nauru and Tuvalu are special members, with the right to participate in all functional Commonwealth meetings and activities, but not to attend meetings of Commonwealth heads of government.

Countries which have left the Commonwealth
Fiji (1987)
Republic of Ireland (1949)
Pakistan (1972, rejoined 1989)
South Africa (1961, rejoined 1994)

Of the 51 member states, 16 have Queen Elizabeth II as head of state, 30 are republics, and five are indigenous monarchies.

In each of the realms where Queen Elizabeth II is head of state (except for the United Kingdom), she is personally represented by a Governor-General, who holds in all essential respects the same position in relation to the administration of public affairs in the realm as is held by Her Majesty in Britain. The Governor-General is appointed by The Queen on the advice of the government of the state concerned.

INTERGOVERNMENTAL AND OTHER LINKS

The main forum for consultation is the Commonwealth heads of government meetings held biennially to discuss international developments and to consider co-operation among members. New Zealand is the venue of the November 1995 meeting. Decisions are reached by consensus, and the views of the meeting are set out in a communiqué. There are also annual meetings of finance ministers and frequent meetings of ministers and officials in other fields, such as education, health, labour, law, women's affairs, agriculture, youth and science. Inter- governmental links are complemented by the activities of some 300 Commonwealth non-governmental organiza- tions linking professionals, sportsmen and sportswomen, and interest groups, forming a 'people's Commonwealth'. The Commonwealth Games take place every four years.

Assistance to other Commonwealth countries normally has priority in the bilateral aid programmes of the association's developed members (Australia, Britain, Canada and New Zealand), who direct about 30 per cent of their aid to other member countries. Developing Commonwealth nations also assist their poorer partners, and many Commonwealth voluntary organizations promote development.

Many of the smaller Commonwealth countries are party to the Lomé Convention, which accords preferential access to the European Union (EU) for developing countries of Africa, the Caribbean and the Pacific, and provides for them to receive EU aid.

COMMONWEALTH SECRETARIAT

The Commonwealth has a secretariat, established in 1965 in London, which is funded by all member governments. This is the main agency for multilateral communication between member governments on issues relating to the Commonwealth as a whole. It promotes consultation and co-operation, disseminates information on matters of common concern, organizes meetings including the biennial summits, co-ordinates Commonwealth activities, and provides technical assistance for economic and social development through the Commonwealth Fund for Technical Co-operation.

The Commonwealth Foundation was established by Commonwealth governments in 1966 as an autonomous body with a board of governors representing Commonwealth governments that fund the Foundation. It promotes and funds exchanges and other activities aimed at strengthening the skills and effectiveness of professionals and non-government organizations. It also promotes culture, rural development, social welfare and the role of women.

COMMONWEALTH SECRETARIAT, Marlborough House, Pall Mall, London SW1Y 5HX. Tel: 0171-839 3411.

Secretary-General, Chief Emeka Anyaoku (Nigeria)

COMMONWEALTH FOUNDATION, Marlborough House, Pall Mall, London SW1Y 5HY. Tel: 0171-930 3783.

Director, Dr Humayun Khan (Pakistan)

COMMONWEALTH INSTITUTE, Kensington High Street, London W8 6NQ. Tel: 0171-603 4535.

Director-General, S. Cox

COMMONWEALTH OF INDEPENDENT STATES

The Commonwealth of Independent States (CIS) is a multilateral grouping of 12 sovereign states which were formerly constituent republics of the USSR. It was formed by Russia, Ukraine and Belorussia on 8 December 1991, the remaining republics, apart from the Baltic states and Georgia, joining on 21 December. Georgia joined in December 1993. Azerbaijani and Moldovan membership effectively lapsed, because of non-ratification, until September 1993 and April 1994 respectively.

The CIS acts as a co-ordinating mechanism for foreign, defence and economic policies, and is a forum for addressing those problems which have specifically arisen from the break-up of the USSR. These matters are addressed in more than 50 inter-state, intergovernmental co-ordinating and consultative statutory bodies and not by central institutions. The two supreme CIS bodies are the Council of Heads of State, and the Council of Heads of Government. The Council of Heads of State is the highest organ of the CIS and meets not less than twice yearly; it is chaired by the heads of state of the members in (Russian)

alphabetical order. The Council of Heads of Government meets not less than once every three months and carries out the co-ordination of military and economic activity in the CIS. Other important bodies are the Council of Heads of Collective Security (defence ministers), the Joint Staff for co-ordinating the CIS member states military co-operation, the CIS Inter-Parliamentary Assembly, the Economic Arbitration Court and the Co-ordinating Consultative Committee. Administrative support is provided by the Executive Secretariat based in Minsk. The chairmanship rests with Tajikistan in 1995 and Turkmenistan in 1996.

OPERATION

In practice the CIS did not in 1992 and the first half of 1993 work as well as had been hoped and became a mechanism for attempting to ameliorate conflicts between the former republics of the USSR. However, it failed to solve the underlying political reasons for these conflicts, the organization being constantly undermined by divisions between republics over issues such as the Armenia–Azerbaijan war over Nagorno-Karabakh, Ukrainian nuclear weapons, the Black Sea Fleet, the pace of economic reform, the control of oil, gas and natural resources, inter-state debts, the separatist conflict with ethnic Russians in Moldovia, and Russian support for the Abkhazian separatists in Georgia.

In January 1993 seven states (Russia, Armenia, Belarus, Kazakhstan, Uzbekistan, Tajikistan, Kyrgyzstan) attempted to increase economic and defence co-operation with the signing of the CIS Charter, which formally established CIS functions and the obligations of member states. It was not, however, until the summer of 1993 that the CIS began to function and co-ordinate more effectively, with Russia using its economic power, aid, natural resources and military influence to force or entice some of the other republics to curb their attempts at economic or military independence. Since September 1993 Azerbaijan, Georgia and Moldova have joined or rejoined the CIS and Russia has pacified conflicts in Georgia and Tajikistan on its own terms. Economic and monetary co-operation have increased with the signing of a Treaty on Economic Union (September 1993), the creation of a Free Trade Zone (April 1994) and the establishment of an Interstate Economic Committee (October 1994). Defence co-operation has increased with the entering into force of the Treaty on Collective Security (signed May 1992) and an agreement on joint CIS defence forces for Tajikistan under Russian command and control.

DEFENCE CO-OPERATION

On becoming member states of the CIS, the 11 original states agreed to recognize their existing borders, respect one another's territorial integrity and reject the use of military force or other forms of coercion to settle disputes between them. Agreement was also reached on fulfilling all the international treaty obligations of the former USSR, and on a unified central control for nuclear weapons and other strategic forces, together with the establishment of CIS joint armed forces. However, implementation of these agreements has proved problematic because of disputes and even open warfare between republics.

The members agreed on a central CIS command for all nuclear weapons, and when President Gorbachev resigned in December 1991 he handed control of nuclear weapons to the CIS commander-in-chief Marshal Shaposhnikov. All tactical nuclear weapons had been transferred to the Russian republic by May 1992. An agreement was reached with the USA in May 1992 by the four republics with strategic nuclear weapons (Russia, the Ukraine, Belarus, Kazakhstan) on implementing the strategic arms reduction talks (START) treaty previously signed by the USA and USSR, and the START I treaty was ratified by the five parties between October 1992 and February 1994. Under this agreement the Ukraine, Belarus and Kazakhstan agreed to eliminate all their strategic nuclear weapons over a seven-year period and Russia has agreed to reduce its strategic nuclear weapons over the same period to such an extent that there will be a 38 per cent reduction in the overall former Soviet arsenal. In March 1994 Ukraine began transferring its strategic nuclear weapons to Russia for disposal and reprocessing, in return for US aid for dismantlement and for the highly enriched uranium of the warheads, and fuel-grade uranium for Ukraine's civilian nuclear reactors. In December 1994 Ukraine, Kazakhstan and Belarus signed the Nuclear Non-Proliferation Treaty.

At the non-nuclear level, the situation remained confused in 1992–3. While all member states formed their own armed forces, a CIS high command and joint armed forces were also established in early 1992 and the Treaty on Collective Security signed in May 1992 by six member states. Nine states also agreed in June 1992 on the establishment of joint peacemaking forces to intervene in CIS conflicts. Deployment of these forces is conditional on consensus in the Council of Heads of State. Forces have been deployed in Moldova and Tajikistan.

However, the fear and resentment of Russian domination by some states (Ukraine, Moldova, Turkmenistan) frustrated the defence co-operation efforts of the remaining members and led to the downgrading in August 1993 of the CIS high command into the Joint Staff for military co-operation. The member states interested in further defence co-operation led by Russia have since summer 1993 engaged in a series of bilateral and multilateral agreements under the supervision of the Council of Heads of Collective Security (established August 1993). Russia has established bilateral defence agreements with Tajikistan, Turkmenistan, Kyrgyzstan, Armenia, Kazakhstan and Georgia, together with multilateral agreements on a common air defence system, joint CIS armed forces to protect the former USSR borders of the Central Asian states, and joint peacekeeping forces in Tajikistan. Russia has gradually increased its influence since 1993, converting the bilateral and multilateral agreements into CIS ones under the umbrella of the Treaty on Collective Security, and forced several states into military co-operation. The effect has been to legitimize the stationing of Russian forces and peace-keeping troops in ten of the other 11 states (not Ukraine) and grant Russian forces control of virtually all of the former USSR's external borders. Only Ukraine and Moldova remain outside the defence co-operation framework and have not signed the Treaty on Collective Security. The division of the former Soviet Black Sea Fleet between Russia and Ukraine and its basing in Sevastopol remains unresolved.

ECONOMIC CO-OPERATION

As it became clear that the Soviet Union was disintegrating in October 1991, nine republics signed a treaty forming an economic community, and were joined by two other republics in November 1991. The principles of the treaty were embodied within the CIS and formed the basis of its economic co-operation in 1992 and the first half of 1993. Members agreed to refrain from economic actions that would damage each other and to co-ordinate economic and monetary policies. A Co-ordinating Consultative Committee, an economic arbitration court and an inter-state bank were established. A single monetary unit, the rouble, was originally agreed upon by all member states, and the members recognized that the basis of recovery for their economies was private ownership, free enterprise and

competition. Throughout 1992 and early 1993 economic co-operation failed to function effectively because of the differing pace of economic reform and the introduction of separate currencies by member states.

Russia effectively forced the collapse of the rouble zone in July 1993 by withdrawing all pre-1993 roubles and forcing the remaining states using roubles to accept Russian monetary control or introduce their own currencies, which all did apart from Tajikistan. The resulting economic collapse of the non-Russian economies led to renewed interest in economic co-operation and the signing of a Treaty on Economic Union in September 1993. The 11 CIS members who have signed the Treaty (Ukraine is an associate member of the economic union) are committed to a common market without internal barriers to trade, common fiscal policies and an eventual currency union with currencies semi-fixed against the rouble. In order to facilitate faster economic integration 11 states (not Turkmenistan) agreed in October 1994 to establish an Interstate Economic Committee, and in May 1995 a monetary committee to facilitate payments in different currencies was agreed. Belarus has withdrawn its currency and rejoined Russia and Tajikistan in the rouble zone. As the first step to a common market, the creation of a Free Trade Zone has been agreed involving the lifting of customs duties, but so far only Russia, Belarus and Kazakhstan are proceeding to form a customs union.

Originally the main advantage of economic co-ordination by the CIS members was the granting of large amounts of aid by Western countries and international organizations, which made it clear that economic aid was dependent on CIS co-ordination in accepting responsibility for the former USSR's debt, abiding by all the former USSR's international obligations (such as nuclear and conventional arms reductions), and having a secure, central control and command of nuclear weapons. As a result of CIS co-ordination members have gained extensive grants, loans, credits, trade agreements and technological, business and planning expertise and guidance.

THE COUNCIL OF EUROPE
67075 Strasbourg, France

The Council of Europe was founded in 1949. Its aim is to achieve greater unity between its members to safeguard their European heritage and to facilitate their economic and social progress through discussion and common action in economic, social, cultural, educational, scientific, legal and administrative matters, and in the maintenance and furtherance of pluralist democracy, human rights and fundamental freedoms.

The 34 members are Andorra, Austria, Belgium, Bulgaria, Cyprus, Czech Republic, Denmark, Estonia, Finland, France, Germany, Greece, Hungary, Iceland, the Republic of Ireland, Italy, Latvia, Liechtenstein, Lithuania, Luxembourg, Malta, Netherlands, Norway, Poland, Portugal, Romania, San Marino, Slovakia, Slovenia, Spain, Sweden, Switzerland, Turkey and the UK. 'Special guest status' has been granted to Albania, Belarus, Bosnia-Hercegovina, Croatia, Macedonia (Former Yugoslav Republic of), Moldova, the Russian Federation and Ukraine. Turkey's membership was suspended in April 1995 over its military offensive in northern Iraq against Kurdish guerrillas.

The organs are the Committee of Ministers, consisting of the foreign ministers of member countries, who meet twice yearly, and the Parliamentary Assembly of 239 members, elected or chosen by the national parliaments of member countries in proportion to the relative strength of political parties. There is also a Joint Committee of Ministers and Representatives of the Parliamentary Assembly.

The Committee of Ministers is the executive organ. The majority of its conclusions take the form of international agreements (known as European Conventions) or recommendations to governments. Decisions of the Ministers may also be embodied in partial agreements to which a limited number of member governments are party. Member governments accredit Permanent Representatives to the Council in Strasbourg, who are also the Ministers' Deputies. The Committee of Deputies meets every month to transact business and to take decisions on behalf of Ministers.

The Parliamentary Assembly holds three week-long sessions a year at which it debates reports on matters of concern and reports received annually from the other European organizations and certain agencies of the United Nations. Its 13 permanent committees meet once or twice between each public plenary session of the Assembly. The Congress of Local and Regional Authorities of Europe each year brings together mayors and municipal councillors in the same numbers as the members of the Parliamentary Assembly.

One of the principal achievements of the Council of Europe is the European Convention on Human Rights (1950) under which was established the European Commission and the European Court of Human Rights. Because of an increasing workload, the European Commission and European Court of Human Rights were merged into a single permanent body in 1993. The reorganized European Court of Human Rights sits usually in chambers of seven judges and exceptionally as a grand chamber of 17 judges. Litigants must still exhaust legal processes in their own country before bringing cases before the court.

Among other conventions and agreements are the European Social Charter, the European Cultural Convention, the European Code of Social Security, the European Convention on the Protection of National Minorities, and conventions on extradition, the legal status of migrant workers, torture prevention, conservation, and the transfer of sentenced prisoners. Most recently the specialized bodies of the Venice Commission and Demosthenes have been set up to assist in developing legislative, administrative and constitutional reforms in central and eastern Europe.

Non-member states take part in certain Council of Europe activities on a regular or *ad hoc* basis; thus the Holy See participates in all the educational, cultural and sports activities. The European Youth Centre is an educational residential centre for young people from all over Europe and further afield. The European Youth Foundation provides youth organizations with funds for their international activities.

Secretary-General, Daniel Tarschys (Sweden)
Permanent UK Representative, His Excellency Roger Beetham, CMG, LVO, *apptd* 1993

THE ECONOMIC COMMUNITY OF WEST AFRICAN STATES
6 King George V Road, PMB 12745, Lagos, Nigeria

The Economic Community of West African States (ECOWAS) was founded in 1975 and came into operation in 1977. It aims to promote the cultural, economic and social development of West Africa through mutual co-

operation. A revised ECOWAS Treaty was signed in 1993 which also makes the prevention and control of regional conflicts an aim of ECOWAS. The Treaty also provides for the establishment of a regional parliament, an economic and social council, and a court of justice.

Measures undertaken by ECOWAS include the gradual elimination of barriers to the movement of goods, people and services between member states and the improvement of regional telecommunications and transport.

The supreme authority of ECOWAS is vested in the annual summit of heads of government of all 16 member states. A Council of Ministers, two from each member state, meets biannually to monitor the organization and make recommendations to the summit. ECOWAS operates through a Secretariat, headed by the Executive Secretary. In addition there is a financial controller, an external auditor, the Disputes Tribunal and the Defence Council.

A Fund for Co-operation, Compensation and Development, situated at Lomé, Togo, finances development projects and provides compensation to member states who have suffered losses as a result of ECOWAS's policies, particularly trade liberalization.

In 1989–90 ECOWAS attempted to mediate in the Liberian civil war and sent an ECOWAS Monitoring Group (ECOMOG) peacekeeping force to the country in 1990. The force succeeded in establishing an interim government and preventing further conflict in 1991 but fighting broke out again in late 1992. ECOMOG forces remain in the country until a peace agreement reached in early 1994 is implemented.

Executive Secretary, Edouard Benjamin

THE EUROPEAN BANK FOR RECONSTRUCTION AND DEVELOPMENT
1 Exchange Square, London EC2A 2EH

The charter of the European Bank for Reconstruction and Development (EBRD) was signed by 40 countries, the European Commission and the European Investment Bank on 29 May 1990 and the EBRD was inaugurated on 15 April 1991.

The aim of the EBRD is to assist the transformation of the states of central and eastern Europe (Albania, Bulgaria, Czech Republic, Estonia, Hungary, Latvia, Lithuania, Poland, Romania, Slovakia, the republics of the former USSR and former Yugoslavia) from centrally-planned economies to free market economies, with particular regard for strengthening democratic institutions, promoting private and entrepreneurial initiative, and respect for human rights and the environment. The EBRD provides technical assistance, training and investment in the upgrading of infrastructure; privatization; the strengthening of legal systems; gaining foreign direct investment; the creation of modern financial systems; nuclear safety; tourism; the exploitation of natural resources; and the restructuring of state industries. The EBRD's assistance is weighted towards the private sector; no more than 40 per cent of its investment can be made in state-owned concerns. It works in co-operation with its members, private companies, and international organizations such as the OECD, the IMF, the World Bank and the UN specialized agencies.

The EBRD has an initial subscribed capital of 10 billion ECU, of which 30 per cent is paid in, and is also able to borrow on world capital markets. The major subscribers are the USA, 10 per cent; Britain, France, Germany, Italy and Japan, 8.5 per cent each; central and eastern European states, 11.9 per cent. The EBRD offers a range of financing instruments including loans, equity investments and guarantees. In 1994 the EBRD approved 91 projects, totalling ECU 1,900m; the total number of projects approved since its establishment is 259 in 19 states, involving ECU 5,700m of EBRD funds.

The EBRD has 59 members. The highest authority is the Board of Governors; each member appoints one Governor and one alternate. The Governors delegate most powers to a 23-member Board of Directors; the Directors are responsible for the EBRD's operations and budget, and are appointed by the Governors for three-year terms. The Governors also elect the President of the Board of Directors, who acts as the Bank's president, for a four-year term. A Secretary-General liaises between the Directors and EBRD staff.

President of the Board of Directors, Jacques de Larosière (France)
UK Executive Director, Robert Graham-Harrison
Secretary-General, Antonio Maria Losta (Italy)

EUROPEAN FREE TRADE ASSOCIATION
9–11 rue de Varembé, 1211 Geneva 20, Switzerland

The European Free Trade Association (EFTA) was established in 1960, by Austria, Denmark, Norway, Portugal, Sweden, Switzerland and the UK, and was subsequently joined by Finland, Iceland and Liechtenstein. Six members have left to join the European Union: Denmark and the UK (1972), Portugal (1985), Austria, Finland and Sweden (1994). The remaining members are Iceland, Liechtenstein, Norway and Switzerland (not an EEA member).

The first objective of EFTA was to establish free trade in industrial goods between members; this was achieved in 1966. Its second objective was the creation of a single market in western Europe and in 1972 EFTA signed a free trade agreement with the EC covering trade in industrial goods; the remaining tariffs on industrial products were abolished in 1984.

Exploratory talks on the free movement of goods, services, capital and labour throughout the EC–EFTA area led to negotiations on the establishment of a European Economic Area (EEA) encompassing all 19 EC and EFTA countries. These concluded with the signing of the EEA Agreement in 1992. The EEA was intended to enter into force at the same time as the EC single market in 1993 but this proved impossible when the Swiss electorate rejected ratification of the EEA Agreement in a referendum in December 1992. The other EFTA states and the EC negotiated a protocol to the EEA Agreement which was signed in March 1993 and the EEA Agreement entered into force on 1 January 1994 for the six remaining countries (except Liechtenstein, which joined on 1 May 1995 after adapting its customs union with Switzerland) after its ratification by all 18 states.

The EEA is controlled by regular ministerial meetings and by a joint EU-EFTA committee and will develop alongside EU legislation. Apart from single market measures, there will also be co-operation in education, research and development, consumer policy and tourism. An EFTA Court of Justice has been established in Geneva and an EFTA Surveillance Authority in Brussels to supervise the implementation of the EEA Agreement.

EFTA has expanded its relations with other non-EU states in recent years and free trade agreements have been signed with Turkey (1991), Israel, Poland and Romania (1992), Bulgaria, Hungary, Czech Republic and Slovakia (April 1993). In addition, EFTA has signed declarations of economic co-operation with Estonia, Latvia and Lithuania (1991), Slovenia and Albania (1992).

The Council of EFTA is the principle organ of the Association. It generally meets once a week at the level of heads of the permanent national delegations to the EFTA Secretariat in Geneva and twice a year at ministerial level. The chairmanship of the Council rotates every six months. Each state has a single vote and recommendations must normally be unanimous; decisions of the Council are binding on member countries.

Secretary-General, Kjartan Jóhannsson (Iceland)

EUROPEAN ORGANIZATION FOR NUCLEAR RESEARCH (CERN)
CH-1211 Geneva 23, Switzerland

The Convention establishing the European Organization for Nuclear Research (CERN) came into force in 1954. The organization promotes European collaboration in high energy physics of a purely scientific nature. It is not concerned with research of a military nature.

The member countries are Austria, Belgium, Czech Republic, Denmark, Finland, France, Germany, Greece, Hungary, Italy, Netherlands, Norway, Poland, Portugal, Slovak Republic, Spain, Sweden, Switzerland and the UK. Israel, the Russian Federation, Turkey, Yugoslavia (suspended), the EU Commission and UNESCO have observer status.

The Council is the highest policy-making body and is made up of two delegates from each member state. There is also a Committee of the Council comprising a single delegate from each member state (who is also a Council member) and the chairmen of the scientific policy and finance advisory committees. The Council is chaired by a President who is elected by the Council in Session. The Council also elects the Director-General, the person responsible for the internal organization of CERN. The Director-General heads a workforce of approximately 3,000, including physicists, craftsmen, technicians and administrative staff. At present over 6,000 physicists use CERN's facilities.

The member countries contribute to the budget in proportion to their net national revenue. The 1995 budget was SFr 918 million.

President of the Council, Prof. Hubert Curien (France)
Director-General (1994–9), Prof. Christopher Llewellyn-Smith (UK)

EUROPEAN SPACE AGENCY
8–10 rue Mario Nikis, 75738 Paris, France

The European Space Agency (ESA) was set up in 1975. It was formed from two earlier organizations – the European Space Research Organization (ESRO) and the European Launcher Development Organization (ELDO). Its aims include the advancement of space research and technology, the implementation of a long-term European space policy and the co-ordination of national space programmes.

The member countries are Austria, Belgium, Denmark, Finland, France, Germany, Republic of Ireland, Italy, Netherlands, Norway, Spain, Sweden, Switzerland and the United Kingdom. Canada is a co-operating state.

The agency is directed by a Council composed of the representatives of the member states, and its chief officer is the Director-General.

Director-General, Jean-Marie Luton, *apptd* 1990

FOOD AND AGRICULTURE ORGANIZATION OF THE UNITED NATIONS
Viale delle Terme di Caracalla, 00100 Rome, Italy

The Food and Agriculture Organization (FAO) is a specialized UN agency, established in 1945. It assists rural populations by raising levels of nutrition and living standards, and by encouraging greater efficiency in food production and distribution. In addition, it collects, analyses and disseminates information on agriculture and natural resources. FAO also advises governments on national agricultural policy and planning; its Investment Centre, together with the World Bank and other financial institutions, helps to prepare development projects. FAO's field programme covers a range of activities, including strengthening crop production, rural and livestock development, and conservation.

FAO's top priorities are sustainable agriculture, rural development and food security. The Organization attempts to ensure the availability of adequate food supplies, stability in the flow of supplies and the securing of access to food by the poor. FAO keeps a special watch on areas where famine can occur. The Office for Special Relief Operations channels emergency aid from governments and other agencies, and assists in rehabilitation. The Technical Co-operation Programme provides schemes for countries facing agricultural crises.

FAO had 170 members (169 states and the EU) and one associate member (Puerto Rico) as at January 1995. It is governed by a biennial conference of all its members which sets the forthcoming programme and budget. The budget for 1994–5 was US$673 million, funded by member countries in proportion to their gross national products. FAO also receives substantial additional funding from the UN Development Programme, donor governments and other institutions.

The Conference elects a Director-General and a 49-member Council, which governs between conferences. The Regular and Field Programmes are administered by a Secretariat, headed by the Director-General. Five regional, five sub-regional and 80 country offices help administer the Field Programme.

Director-General, Jacques Diouf (Senegal)
UK Representative, D. Sands Smith, British Embassy, Rome

INTERNATIONAL ATOMIC ENERGY AGENCY
Vienna International Centre, Wagramerstrasse 5, PO Box 100, 1400 Vienna, Austria

---

The International Atomic Energy Agency (IAEA) was established in 1957 as a consequence of the UN International Conference on the Peaceful Uses of Atomic Energy held the previous year. Although it operates under the aegis of, and reports annually to, the UN, the IAEA is not a specialized agency.

The IAEA aims to accelerate and enlarge the contribution of atomic energy to peace, health and prosperity, and to ensure that any assistance provided by it or under its supervision is not used for military purposes. It establishes atomic energy safety standards and offers services to its member states for the safe operation of their nuclear facilities and for radiation protection. It is the central point for the International Convention on early notification of a nuclear accident. The IAEA also encourages research and training in nuclear power. It is additionally charged with drawing up safeguards and verifying their use in accordance with the Nuclear Non-Proliferation Treaty (NPT) 1968, the Treaty for the Prohibition of Nuclear Weapons in Latin America (Tlatelolco Treaty) 1968 and the Treaty on a South Pacific Nuclear Free Zone (Rarotonga Treaty). Together with the Food and Agriculture Organization and the World Health Organization, the IAEA established an International Consultative Group on Food Irradiation in 1983.

In line with its responsibilities with regard to the Nuclear Non-Proliferation Treaty, the IAEA has for the past few years attempted to verify that the North Korean nuclear programme is non-military. In June 1994 the IAEA informed the UN Security Council that North Korea was in violation of its treaty obligations by attempting to produce nuclear weapons and suspended all technical aid to North Korea. North Korea resigned from the IAEA on 14 June 1994, but rejoined in October 1994 under the terms of a US-North Korean agreement which ended North Korea's nuclear weapons production and enabled the IAEA to resume safeguards inspections in North Korea.

The IAEA had 122 members as at May 1995. A General Conference of all its members meets annually to decide policy, a programme and a budget (1995, US$200 million), as well as electing a Director-General and 35-member Board of Governors. The Board meets four times a year to execute policy which is implemented by the Secretariat under a Director-General.

Director-General, Hans Blix (Sweden)
Permanent UK Representative, C. Hulse, Jaurésgasse 12, 1030 Vienna, Austria

---

INTERNATIONAL CIVIL AVIATION ORGANIZATION
1000 Sherbrooke Street West, Montreal, Quebec, Canada H3A 2R2

The International Civil Aviation Organization (ICAO) was founded with the signing of the Chicago Convention on International Civil Aviation in 1944, and became a specialized agency of the United Nations in 1947. It sets international technical standards and recommended practices for all areas of civil aviation, including airworthiness, air navigation, traffic control and pilot licensing. It encourages uniformity and simplicity in ground regulations and operations at international airports, including immigration and customs control. The ICAO also promotes regional air navigation, plans for ground facilities, and collects and distributes air transport statistics worldwide. It is dedicated to improving safety and to the orderly development of civil aviation throughout the world.

The ICAO had 183 members as at 20 February 1995. It is governed by an assembly of all its members which meets at least once every three years. A Council of 33 members is elected, taking into account the leading air transport nations as well as ensuring representation of less developed countries. The Council elects the President, appoints the Secretary-General and supervises the organization through subsidiary committees, serviced by a Secretariat.

President of the Council, Dr Assad Kotaite (Lebanon)
Secretary-General, Dr Philippe Rochat (Switzerland)

UK Representative, D. S. Evans, CMG, Suite 928, 1000
Sherbrooke Street West, Montreal, Quebec, Canada
H3A 3G4

INTERNATIONAL CONFEDERATION OF
FREE TRADE UNIONS
Boulevard Emile Jacqmain 155 B1, B-1210
Brussels, Belgium

Formed in 1949, the International Confederation of Free
Trade Unions (ICFTU) was created to promote free trade
unionism world-wide. It aims to establish, maintain and
promote free trade unions, and to promote peace with
economic security and social justice.

Affiliated to the ICFTU are 187 individual unions and
representative bodies in 134 countries and territories. On 9
December 1994 there were 126 million members.

The supreme authority of the organization is the
Congress which convenes at least every four years. It is
composed of delegates from the affiliated trade union
organizations. The Congress elects an Executive Board of
49 members which meets not less than once a year. The
Board establishes the budget and receives suggestions and
proposals from affiliates as well as acting on behalf of the
Confederation. The Congress also elects the General
Secretary.

General Secretary, Bill Jordan (UK)
UK Affiliate, TUC, Congress House, 23–28 Great Russell
Street, London WC1B 3LS. Tel: 0171-636 4030

INTERNATIONAL CRIMINAL POLICE
ORGANIZATION
50 quai Achille Lignon, 69006 Lyon, France

The International Criminal Police Commission (Interpol)
was set up in 1923 to establish an international criminal
records office and to harmonize extradition procedures. In
1956 a revised constitution was adopted and the organization adopted its present name. On 1 January 1995 the
organization comprised 174 member states.

Interpol's aims are to ensure and promote mutual
assistance between all criminal police authorities, and to
support government agencies concerned with combating
crime, whilst respecting the national sovereignty of
members. Interpol is financed by annual contributions
from the governments of member states.

Interpol's policy is decided by the General Assembly
which meets annually; it is composed of delegates
appointed by the member states. The 13-member Executive Committee is elected by the General Assembly from
among the member states' delegates, and is chaired by the
President, who has a four-year term of office. The
permanent administrative organ is the General Secretariat,
headed by the Secretary-General, who is appointed by the
General Assembly.

Secretary-General, Raymond Kendall, QPM (UK)
UK OFFICE, NCIS-Interpol, Spring Gardens, Tinworth
Street, London SE11 5EH
UK Representative, A. Pacey, CBE, QPM

INTERNATIONAL ENERGY AGENCY
Chateau de la Muette, 2 rue André-Pascal, 75775
Paris, France

The International Energy Agency (IEA), founded in 1974,
is an autonomous agency within the framework of the
Organization for Economic Co-operation and Development (OECD). The IEA had 23 member countries at
January 1995.

The IEA's objectives include improvement of energy
supply and demand worldwide, increased efficiency,
development of alternative energy sources and the
promotion of relations between oil producing and oil
consuming countries. The IEA also maintains an emergency system to alleviate the effects of severe oil supply
disruptions.

The main decision-making body is the Governing
Board composed of senior energy officials from member
countries. Various standing groups and special committees
exist to facilitate the work of the Board. The IEA
Secretariat, with a staff of energy experts, carries out the
work of the Governing Board and its subordinate bodies.
The Executive Director is appointed by the Board.

Executive Director, Robert Priddle (UK)

INTERNATIONAL FUND FOR
AGRICULTURAL DEVELOPMENT
107 Via del Serafico, 00142 Rome, Italy

The establishment of the International Fund for Agricultural Development (IFAD) was proposed by the 1974
World Food Conference and IFAD began operations as a
UN specialized agency in 1977. Its purpose is to mobilize
additional funds for agricultural and rural development
projects in developing countries that benefit the poorest
rural populations. The organization's lending policy is
based on using its resources to support projects which: raise
food production; provide employment and additional
income for poor farmers; reduce malnutrition; and
improve food distribution systems.

IFAD had 158 members as at 25 January 1995. Membership is divided into three categories: category I, with 22
members, the developed countries (OECD); category II,
with 12 members, the oil-exporting developing countries
(OPEC); category III, with 124 members, the remaining
developing countries. The three groups have equal voting
rights in IFAD's governing structure. All powers are vested
in a Governing Council of all member countries. It elects
an 18-member Executive Board (with 17 alternate
members) responsible for IFAD's operations. The Council
meets at least once annually and elects a President who is
also chairman of the Board. He is assisted by a Vice-
President and three Assistant Presidents.

At the end of December 1994 IFAD's loan portfolio
comprised commitments of US$4,489 million for 395
approved projects in 102 developing countries. The
operational budget for 1993 was US$122.4 million.

President, Fawzi H. Al-Sultan (Kuwait)

INTERNATIONAL LABOUR
ORGANIZATION
4 route des Morillons, 1211 Geneva 22, Switzerland

The International Labour Organization (ILO) was established in 1919 as an autonomous body of the League of

Nations and became the UN's first specialized agency in 1946. The ILO aims to increase employment, improve working conditions, raise living standards and encourage democratic development. It sets minimum international labour standards through the drafting of international conventions. Member countries are obliged to submit these to their domestic authorities for ratification, and thus undertake to bring their domestic legislation in line with the conventions. Members must report to the ILO periodically on how these regulations are being implemented. The ILO plays a major role in helping developing countries achieve economic stability and job expansion through its wide-ranging programme of technical co-operation. The ILO is also the world's principal resource centre for information, analysis and guidance on labour and employment. The organization aims to improve working and living conditions throughout the world and to support the transition to democracy and market economics under way in many states.

The ILO had 171 members as at June 1995. It is composed of the International Labour Conference, the Governing Body and the International Labour Office. The Conference of members meets annually, and is attended by national delegations comprising two government delegates, one worker delegate and one employer delegate. It formulates international labour conventions and recommendations, provides a forum for discussion of world employment and social issues, and approves the ILO's programme and budget (1995–6, US$466,510,000).

The 56-member Governing Body, composed of 28 government, 14 worker and 14 employer members, acts as the ILO's executive council. Ten governments, including Britain, hold seats on the Governing Body because of their industrial importance. There are also various regional conferences and advisory committees. The International Labour Office acts as a secretariat and as a centre for operations, publishing and research.

Director-General, Michel Hansenne (Belgium)
UK OFFICE, Vincent House, Vincent Square, London SW1P 2NB. Tel: 0171-828 6401

INTERNATIONAL MARITIME ORGANIZATION
4 Albert Embankment, London SE1 7SR

The International Maritime Organization (IMO) was established as a UN specialized agency in 1948. Owing to delays in treaty ratification it did not commence operations until 1958. Originally it was called the Inter-Governmental Maritime Consultative Organization (IMCO) but changed its name in 1982.

The IMO fosters inter-governmental co-operation in technical matters relating to international shipping, especially with regard to safety at sea. It is also charged with preventing and controlling marine pollution caused by shipping and facilitating marine traffic. The IMO is responsible for calling maritime conferences and drafting marine conventions. Additionally, it provides technical aid to countries wishing to develop their activities at sea.

The IMO had 151 members as at May 1995. It is governed by an Assembly comprising delegates of all its members. It meets biennially to make policy, decide the budget (1994–5, £34 million), vote on specific recommendations on pollution and maritime safety and elect the Council. The Council fulfils the functions of the Assembly between sessions and appoints the Secretary-General. It consists of 32 members; eight from the world's largest shipping nations, eight from the nations most dependent on

seaborne trade, and 16 other members to ensure a fair geographical representation. The Maritime Safety Committee, working through various sub-committees, makes reports and recommendations to the Council and the Assembly. There are a number of other specialist subsidiary committees, including one for marine environmental protection.

The IMO acts as the secretariat for the London Convention (1972) which regulates the disposal of land-generated waste at sea.

Secretary-General, William A. O'Neil (Canada)

INTERNATIONAL MOBILE SATELLITE ORGANIZATION
99 City Road, London EC1Y 1AX

Inmarsat (the International Mobile Satellite Organization) was founded in 1978 as the International Maritime Satellite Organization and began operations in 1982. Inmarsat is an internationally-owned co-operative which operates a system of satellites to provide global mobile communications at sea, in the air and on land. Inmarsat satellite terminals are used world-wide on ships, in aircraft and on land for telephone, facsimile, telex and e-mail data, as well as maritime safety, position reporting and distress communications.

Inmarsat comprises three bodies: the Assembly, the Council and the Directorate. The Assembly is composed of representatives of all 77 member countries, each with one vote. It meets every two years to review activities and objectives, and to make recommendations to the Council. The Council is the main decision-making body and consists of representatives of the 18 members with the largest investment shares. Four others who represent the interests of developing countries are elected to the Council on the basis of geographical representation. Members have voting powers equal to their investment shares. The Council meets at least three times a year and oversees the activities of the directorate, the permanent staff of Inmarsat.

Director-General, Olof Lundberg (Sweden)

INTERNATIONAL MONETARY FUND
700 19th Street NW, Washington DC 20431, USA

The International Monetary Fund (IMF) was established in 1944, at the UN Monetary and Financial Conference held at Bretton Woods, New Hampshire. Its Articles of Agreement entered into force in 1945 and it began operations in 1946. The IMF exists to promote international monetary co-operation, the expansion of world trade, and exchange stability, and to eliminate foreign exchange restrictions. The IMF advises members on their economic and financial policies; promotes policy co-ordination among the major industrial countries; and gives technical assistance in central banking, balance of payments accounting, taxation, and other financial matters. The IMF serves as a forum for members to discuss important financial and monetary issues and seeks the balanced growth of international trade and, through this, high levels of employment, income and productive capacity. As at April 1995 the IMF had 179 members; Sudan's and Zaire's voting rights have been suspended.

Upon joining the IMF, a member is assigned a 'quota', based on the member's relative standing in the world economy and its balance of payments position, that determines its capital subscription to the Fund, its access to IMF resources, its voting power, and its share in the allocation of Special Drawing Rights (SDRs). Quotas are reviewed every five years and adjusted accordingly. Since the Ninth General Review of quotas in 1994, total Fund quotas stand at SDR 144.8 billion. The SDR, an international reserve asset issued by the IMF, is calculated daily on a basket of usable currencies and is the IMF's unit of account; on 30 April 1995, SDR 1 equalled US$1.4944. SDRs are allocated at intervals to supplement members' reserves and thereby improve international financial liquidity.

IMF financial resources derive primarily from members' capital subscriptions, which are equivalent to their quotas. In addition, the IMF is authorized to borrow from official lenders. It may also draw on a line of credit of SDR 18.5 billion from various countries under the so-called General Arrangements to Borrow (GAB). Periodic charges are also levied on financial assistance. At the end of April 1995, total outstanding IMF credits amounted to SDR 32.1 billion; borrowings amounted to SDR 4.6 billion.

The IMF is not a bank and does not lend money; it provides temporary financial assistance by selling a member's SDRs or other members' currencies in exchange for the member's own currency. The member can then use the purchased currency to alleviate its balance of payments difficulties. The IMF's credit under its regular facilities is made available to members in tranches or segments of 25 per cent of quota. For first credit tranche purchases, members are required to demonstrate reasonable efforts to overcome their balance of payments difficulties. There are no performance criteria and the total amount is repaid in three and a quarter to five years. Upper credit tranche purchases are normally associated with stand-by arrangements. These typically cover periods of one to two years. They focus on macroeconomic policies aimed at overcoming balance of payment difficulties and are required to meet certain performance criteria. Repurchases are made in three and a quarter to five years.

The IMF supports long-term efforts at economic reform and transformation, such as the re-establishment of market economies in the countries of eastern Europe and the former Soviet Union. In addition, the IMF supports medium-term programmes under the extended Fund facility, which generally runs for three years (sometimes up to four years) and is aimed at overcoming balance of payments difficulties stemming from macroeconomic and structural problems. Members experiencing a temporary balance of payments shortfall have access to the compensatory and contingency financing facility. The IMF also offers credits to low-income countries engaged in economic reform through its structural adjustment facility and enhanced structural adjustment facility. As of 30 April 1995, SDR 7.9 billion has been disbursed under arrangements with 45 countries. Under its buffer stock financing facility, the IMF provides resources to help members' contributions to approved buffer stocks. In 1993, the IMF adopted a new contingency facility, the systemic transformation facility, designed to extend financial assistance to members experiencing severe disruptions in their trade and payments arrangements due to a shift from significant reliance on trading at nonmarket prices to multilateral, market-based trade.

The IMF is headed by a Board of Governors, comprising representatives of all members, which meets annually. The Governors delegate powers to 24 Executive Directors, five appointed and 19 elected. The Executive Directors operate the Fund on a daily basis under a Managing Director, whom they elect. The appointed directors represent France, Germany, Japan, UK and USA.
Managing Director, Michel Camdessus (France)

UK Executive Director, Huw Evans, Room 11-120, IMF, 700 19th Street NW, Washington DC 20431

INTERNATIONAL RED CROSS AND RED CRESCENT MOVEMENT
17 avenue de la Paix, 1211 Geneva, Switzerland

The International Red Cross and Red Crescent Movement is composed of three elements. The International Committee of the Red Cross (ICRC) is the founding body of the Red Cross and was formed in 1863. It is a neutral intermediary negotiating between warring factions, working throughout the world to protect and assist victims of armed conflict. It also ensures the application of the Geneva Conventions with regard to prisoners of war and detainees.

The International Federation of Red Cross and Red Crescent Societies, founded in 1919, is the body which exists to contribute to the development of the humanitarian activities of national societies, to co-ordinate their relief operations for victims of natural disasters, and to care for refugees outside areas of conflict. There are national Red Cross and Red Crescent Societies in 163 countries, with a total membership of 250 million.

The International Conference of the Red Cross and Red Crescent meets every four years, bringing together delegates of the ICRC, the International Federation and the national societies, as well as representatives of nations bound by the Geneva Conventions.
President of the ICRC, Cornelio Sommaruga
BRITISH RED CROSS, 9 Grosvenor Crescent, London SW1X 7EJ. *Director-General*, Michael R. Whitlam

INTERNATIONAL TELECOMMUNICATIONS SATELLITE ORGANIZATION
3400 International Drive NW, Washington DC 20008–3098, USA

Formed in 1964, the International Telecommunications Satellite Organization (Intelsat) owns and operates the world-wide commercial communications satellite system. The system is composed of a network of over 20 satellites and more than 2,000 antennas which link together over 180 countries, territories and dependencies.

Intelsat provides international telephone services, international television services, the Intelsat Business Service (IBS), Intelnet (a digital service designed for data collection and distribution), domestic telecommunications services and the Vista service providing telecommunications to remote communities.

Each of the 136 member states contributes to the capital costs of the organization in proportion to its investment share. The investment share is based on the relative usage of the system by member countries.

There is a four-tier hierarchy. The Assembly of Parties to the agreement meets every two years to consider long-term objectives and is composed of representatives of the member governments. The Meeting of Signatories annually considers the financial, technical and operational aspects of the system. The Board of Governors has 27 members; the executive organ is the permanent staff of Intelsat and is headed by a Director-General who reports to the Board of Governors.
Director-General, Irving Goldstein (USA)

INTERNATIONAL TELECOMMUNICATION UNION
Place des Nations, 1211 Geneva 20, Switzerland

The International Telecommunication Union (ITU) was founded in Paris in 1865 as the International Telegraph Union and became a UN specialized agency in 1947. It promotes international co-operation and sets standards and regulations for the interconnection of telecommunications systems of all kinds. It assists the development of telecommunications in developing countries by providing technical assistance, management, investment financing and network installation. The ITU adopts international regulations and treaties to allocate the radio frequency spectrum and registers radio frequency assignments in order to avoid harmful interference between radio stations of different countries. It also governs and allocates the use of the geostationary-satellite orbit and collects and disseminates telecommunications information.

The ITU had 184 member states and 363 members (scientific and industrial companies, broadcasters, public and private operators, and international organizations) as at 30 January 1995. The supreme authority is the Plenipotentiary Conference, composed of representatives of all the members, which meets once every four years. It elects the Administrative Council of 46 members which meets annually to supervise the Union and set the budget (1995, SFr 164 million). The Conference also elects the Secretary-General, who heads the General Secretariat. The ITU is structured into three sectors: the radiocommunication sector, including world and regional radiocommunication conferences, radiocommunication assemblies and the Radio Regulations Board; the telecommunication standardization sector; and the telecommunication development sector.

Secretary-General, Dr P. Tarjanne (Finland)

LEAGUE OF ARAB STATES
Maidane Al-Tahrir, Cairo, Egypt

The purpose of the League of Arab States, founded in 1945, is to ensure co-operation among member states and protect their independence and sovereignty, to supervise the affairs and interests of Arab countries, to control the execution of agreements concluded among the member states, and to promote the process of integration among them. The League considers itself a regional organization and has observer status at the United Nations.

Member states are Algeria, Bahrain, Comoros, Djibouti, Egypt, Iraq, Jordan, Kuwait, Lebanon, Libya, Mauritania, Morocco, Oman, Palestine, Qatar, Saudi Arabia, Somalia, Sudan, Syria, Tunisia, United Arab Emirates and the Republic of Yemen.

Member states participate in various specialized agencies of the League whose role is to develop specific areas of co-operation between Arab states. These include: the Arab Organization for Mineral Resources; the Arab Monetary Fund; the Arab Satellite Communications Organization; the Arab Academy of Maritime Transport; the Arab Bank for Economic Development in Africa; the Arab League Educational, Cultural and Scientific Organization, and the Council of Arab Economic Unity.

Secretary-General, Dr Ahmed Esmat Abdel-Meguid (Egypt)
UK OFFICE, 52 Green Street, London WIY 3RH

NORDIC COUNCIL
Tyrgatan 7, Box 19506, Stockholm 10432, Sweden

The Nordic Council was established in March 1952 as an advisory body on economic and social co-operation, comprising parliamentary delegates from Denmark, Iceland, Norway and Sweden. It was subsequently joined by Finland (1955), and representatives from the Faröes (1970), the Åland Islands (1970), and Greenland (1984).

Co-operation is regulated by the Treaty of Helsinki signed in 1962. This was amended in 1971 to create the Nordic Council of Ministers, which discusses all matters except defence and foreign affairs. Matters are given preparatory consideration by a Committee of Co-operation Ministers' Deputies and joint committees of officials. Decisions of the Council of Ministers, which are taken by consensus, are binding, although if ratification by member parliaments is required, decisions only become effective following parliamentary approval. The Council of Ministers is advised by the Nordic Council, to which it reports annually. There are Ministers for Nordic Co-operation in every member government.

The Nordic Council, comprising 87 voting delegates nominated from member parliaments and about 80 non-voting government representatives, meets twice a year in plenary sessions. The full Council chooses an 11-member Praesidium, comprising two delegates from each sovereign member and one party group-nominated delegate, which conducts business between sessions. A Secretariat, located in Stockholm and headed by a Secretary-General, liaises with the Council of Ministers and provides administrative support, as well as acting as a publishing house and information centre. The Council of Ministers has a separate Secretariat, based in Copenhagen.

SECRETARIAT TO THE NORDIC COUNCIL, Tyrgatan 7, S-10432 Stockholm, Sweden. *Secretary-General*, Anders Wenström (Sweden)

SECRETARIAT OF NORDIC COUNCIL OF MINISTERS, Store Strandgade 18, 1255 Copenhagen K, Denmark. *Secretary-General*, Per Stenback (Finland)

NORTH ATLANTIC TREATY ORGANIZATION
Brussels 1110, Belgium

The North Atlantic Treaty (Treaty of Washington) was signed in 1949 by Belgium, Canada, Denmark, France, Iceland, Italy, Luxembourg, the Netherlands, Norway, Portugal, the UK and USA. Greece and Turkey acceded to the Treaty in 1952, the Federal Republic of Germany in 1955 (the reunited Germany acceded in October 1990), and Spain in 1982. The North Atlantic Treaty Organization (NATO) is the structural framework for a defensive political and military alliance designed to provide common security for its members through co-operation and consultation in political, military and economic as well as scientific and other non-military fields. With the demise of the Warsaw Pact and the end of the Cold War in 1990, the Alliance has adapted its structures and policies to meet new security challenges, including contributing to peacekeeping operations and co-operating closely with the countries of central and eastern Europe. The Alliance is now committed to promoting security and stability throughout Europe and to playing a major role in support of UN and OSCE operations. NATO is involved in supporting the UN peacekeeping effort in the former Yugoslavia, supplying a naval force to monitor compliance with the UN embargo, a headquarters for the UNPROFOR II force in Bosnia-Hercegovina, and aircraft to monitor and enforce the UN air exclusion zone over Bosnia-Hercegovina and to protect and defend UN personnel and UN-designated safe areas under attack.

The North Atlantic Council, chaired by the Secretary-General, is the highest authority of the Alliance and is composed of permanent representatives of the 16 member countries. It meets at ministerial level (foreign ministers) at least twice a year. The permanent representatives (ambassadors) head national delegations of advisers and experts. Defence matters are dealt with by the Defence Planning Committee (DPC), composed of representatives of all member countries except France. The DPC also meets at ministerial level (defence ministers) at least twice a year. Nuclear matters are dealt with in the Nuclear Planning Group (NPG), composed of representatives of all countries except France (Iceland being an observer). The NPG meets regularly at Permanent Representatives level and twice a year at ministerial level (defence ministers). The NATO Secretary-General chairs the Council, the DPC and the NPG.

The Council and DPC are forums for constant inter-governmental consultation and are the main decision-making bodies within the Alliance. They are assisted by an International Staff, divided into five divisions: political affairs; defence planning and policy; defence support; infrastructure, logistics and civil emergency planning; scientific and environmental affairs.

The senior military authority in NATO, under the Council and DPC, is the Military Committee composed of the Chief of Defence Staffs of each member country except France and Iceland. The Military Committee, which is assisted by an integrated international military staff, also meets in permanent session with permanent military representatives and is responsible for making recommendations to the Council and DPC on measures considered necessary for the common defence of the NATO area and for supplying guidance on military matters to the major NATO commanders. The Chairman of the Military Committee, elected for a period of two to three years, represents the committee on the Council.

The strategic area covered by the North Atlantic Treaty is divided between two major NATO commands (MNCs), European and Atlantic; and three major subordinate commands (MSCs) within Allied Command Europe, South, Central and North-West. There is also a Regional Planning Group (Canada and the United States).

The major NATO commanders are responsible for the development of defence plans for their respective areas, for the determination of force requirements and for the deployment and exercise of the forces under their command. The major NATO commanders report to the Military Committee. From 1995 the reorganized NATO force structure will consist of three components: the Allied Rapid Reaction Corps of four divisions, with air and sea components (the majority of which will be British forces); the main defence force of four corps (one Danish-German, one Dutch-German, two US-German); and the augmentation forces of reserves and territorials.

At the 1990 London summit NATO heads of state and government redefined the goals and strategy of the organization in the light of the end of the Cold War. A Declaration of Peace and Co-operation was issued in 1991 and a new strategic concept was published, introducing major changes in the organization of NATO forces and overall reductions of around 30 per cent. The new strategic concept also provides for a reduced dependence on nuclear weapons; greater mobility, flexibility and adaptability of forces; greater use of multinational formations; active involvement in international crisis management and peacekeeping operations; increased co-ordination and co-operation with international institutions such as the UN, OSCE and WEU; and a streamlining of NATO's military command structure. The 1994 Brussels summit endorsed the development of a European Security and Defence Identity through Combined Joint Task Forces (CJTFs), whereby NATO equipment assets, principally from the USA, will be available for use by European nations and the WEU in military operations in which the USA is not involved.

A North Atlantic Co-operation Council (NACC) was established by the 1991 Rome summit within a framework of dialogue, co-operation and partnership between the member countries of the Alliance and states of eastern Europe and the former Soviet Union. The NACC has 38 member states and one observer (Finland). Its role is to facilitate closer official and informal ties on security and related issues between the members. It focuses on the particular areas of peacekeeping, defence planning, defence industry conversion, defence management and force structuring, and the democratic concepts of civilian-military relations. An NACC *ad hoc* group on co-operation in peacekeeping has also been established with participation by the 38 NACC members, Austria, Finland and Sweden.

The potential for destabilizing conflicts in central and eastern Europe has, however, led to the states of eastern Europe and the former Soviet Union being dissatisfied with the level of security and co-operation offered by NATO through the NACC and at the 1994 Brussels summit NATO launched its Partnerships for Peace (PFP) programme, inviting neutral, central and eastern European and former Soviet states to become official partners of the NATO Alliance. The PFP programme offers gradual progress towards full membership of NATO. The 26 partner states have representative offices in the NATO headquarters at Brussels and a Partnership Co-ordination Cell has been established at NATO military headquarters (SHAPE) at Mons. Partner states will be involved in NATO military planning, joint military exercises (the first took place in Poland in autumn 1994) and eventually NATO peacekeeping, search and rescue and humanitarian operations, as well as receiving aid and advice towards meeting their partnership commitments of transparent military budgets and democratic civilian control of their armed forces. NATO will consult with any partner state which perceives a direct threat to its security, territorial integrity or political independence.

Secretary-General and Chairman of the North Atlantic Council, of the DPC and of the NPG, Willy Claes (Belgium)
UK Permanent Representative on the North Atlantic Council, John Goulden, CMG
Chairman of the Military Committee, Field Marshal Sir Richard Vincent, GBE, KCB, DSO (UK)
Supreme Allied Commander, Europe, Gen. George Joulwan (USA)
Supreme Allied Commander, Atlantic, Gen. John Sheehan (USA)

ORGANIZATION FOR ECONOMIC CO-OPERATION AND DEVELOPMENT
2 rue André-Pascal, 75116 Paris

Formed in 1961, the Organization for Economic Co-operation and Development (OECD) replaced the Organization for European Economic Co-operation. The OECD is the instrument for international co-operation among industrialized member countries on economic and social policies. Its objectives are to assist its member governments in the formulation and co-ordination of policies designed to achieve high, sustained economic growth while maintaining financial stability, to contribute to world trade on a multilateral basis and to stimulate members' aid to developing countries.

The members are Australia, Austria, Belgium, Canada, Denmark, Finland, France, Germany, Greece, Iceland, Republic of Ireland, Italy, Japan, Luxembourg, Mexico, the Netherlands, New Zealand, Norway, Portugal, Spain, Sweden, Switzerland, Turkey, UK and USA. The OECD is considering membership applications from the Czech Republic, the Slovak Republic, Poland, Hungary and the Republic of Korea.

The Council is the supreme body of the organization. Composed of one representative for each member country, it meets at permanent representative level under the chairmanship of the Secretary-General, or at ministerial level (usually once a year) under the chairmanship of a minister elected annually. Decisions and recommendations are adopted by mutual agreement of all members of the Council. Fourteen members of the Council are chosen annually to form an executive committee to assist the Council. However, most of the OECD's work is undertaken in over 200 specialized committees and working parties. Five autonomous or semi-autonomous bodies are related in varying degrees to the Organization: the Nuclear Energy Agency, the International Energy Agency, the Development Centre, the Centre for Educational Research and Innovation, and the European Conference of Ministers of Transport. These bodies, the committees and the Council are serviced by an international Secretariat headed by the Secretary-General.

Secretary-General, Jean-Claude Paye (France)
UK Permanent Representative, Peter Vereker, 19 rue de Franqueville, Paris 75116

ORGANIZATION FOR SECURITY AND CO-OPERATION IN EUROPE
Kärntner Ring 5−7, A-1010 Vienna, Austria

The Organization for Security and Co-operation in Europe (OSCE) was launched in 1975 (as the Conference on Security and Co-operation in Europe (CSCE)) under the Helsinki Final Act. This established agreements between NATO members, Warsaw Pact members, and neutral and non-aligned European countries covering security in Europe; economic, scientific, technological and environmental co-operation; and humanitarian principles and co-operation. Further conferences were held at Belgrade (1977−8), Madrid (1980−3) and Vienna (1986−9).

With the end of the Cold War, it was decided that the CSCE should be changed from a continuous conference with periodic formal meetings and institutionalized to provide a new security framework for Europe. The Charter of Paris for a New Europe was signed on 21 November 1990, committing members to support for multi-party democracy, free-market economics, the rule of law, and human rights. The signatories also undertook to enhance political consultation, agreeing on regular meetings of heads of government, ministers and officials. The CSCE held its first institutionalized heads of state and government summit in Helsinki in December 1992, at which they adopted the Helsinki Document 1992. This declared the CSCE to be a regional organization in the sense of Chapter VIII of the UN Charter and defined the structures of the organization. The summit also appointed a High Commissioner on National Minorities. The December 1994 summit changed its name to the Organization for Security and Co-operation in Europe.

Three structures have been established: the Ministerial Council of Foreign Ministers, the central decision-making and governing body, which meets at least once a year; the Senior Council, which prepares work for the Council, carries out its decisions and is responsible for the overview, management and co-ordination of OSCE activities and meets at least three times a year; and the Permanent Council, which is responsible for the day-to-day operational tasks of the OSCE and is the regular body for political consultation, meeting weekly. The chairmanship of the Ministerial Council, Senior Council and Permanent Council rotates among participating states with the Senior Council meeting in Prague and the Permanent Council in Vienna. The OSCE is also underpinned by four permanent institutions: a Secretariat (Vienna); a Forum for Security Co-operation (Vienna), which meets weekly to discuss arms control, disarmament and security-building measures; an Office for Democratic Institutions and Human Rights (Warsaw), which is tasked with furthering human rights, democracy and the rule of law; and an office of the High Commissioner on National Minorities (The Hague), which identifies ethnic tensions that might endanger peace and promotes their resolution. There is also a documentation and conference centre in Prague. An OSCE Parliamentary Assembly has also been formed, with a secretariat based in Copenhagen. A Court of Conciliation and Arbitration is being established in Geneva to settle disputes submitted to it by OSCE states.

In June 1991 the CSCE agreed upon new crisis prevention mechanisms to prevent or manage violent conflict between and within member countries. In an attempt to put these mechanisms into place, the OSCE has established monitoring missions in eight areas of potential or actual conflict, and has co-ordinated the enforcement of sanctions against Serbia and Montenegro, together with sending a peacekeeping mission to Nagorno-Karabakh. A Joint Consultative Group of the OSCE promotes the objectives and implementation of the Conventional Armed Forces in Europe (CFE) Treaty (1990) which limits conventional ground and air forces.

The OSCE has 53 participating states: Albania, Armenia, Austria, Azerbaijan, Belarus, Belgium, Bosnia-Hercegovina, Bulgaria, Canada, Croatia, Cyprus, Czech Republic, Denmark, Estonia, Finland, France, Georgia, Germany, Greece, Hungary, Iceland, Ireland, Italy, Kazakhstan, Kyrgyzstan, Latvia, Liechtenstein, Lithuania, Luxembourg, Malta, Moldova, Monaco, the Netherlands, Norway, Poland, Portugal, Romania, the Russian Federation, San Marino, Slovakia, Slovenia, Spain, Sweden, Switzerland, Tajikistan, Turkey, Turkmenistan, UK, Ukraine, USA, Uzbekistan, the Vatican and Yugoslavia (suspended from activities July 1992). The Former Yugoslav Republic of Macedonia is an observer.

Chair of the OSCE (1995), Hungary
Secretary-General of the OSCE, Wilhelm Hoÿnck (Germany)
Director of the Office for Democratic Institutions and Human Rights, Audrey Glover (UK)
OSCE High Commissioner on National Minorities, Max van der Stoel (Netherlands)

ORGANIZATION OF AFRICAN UNITY
PO Box 3243, Addis Ababa, Ethiopia

The Organization of African Unity (OAU) was established in 1963 and has 53 members; Morocco suspended its participation in 1985 in protest at the Polisario-proclaimed

Saharan Arab Democratic Republic (SADR), representing Western Sahara, being admitted as a member. It aims to further African unity and solidarity, to co-ordinate political, economic, social and defence policies, and to eliminate colonialism in Africa.

The chief organs are the Assembly of heads of state or government, which is the supreme organ of the OAU and meets once a year to consider matters of common African concern and to co-ordinate the Organization's policies; the Council of foreign ministers, which is the Organization's executive body responsible for the implementation of the Assembly's policies, and which meets twice a year; and the Commission of Mediation, Conciliation and Arbitration which promotes the peaceful settlement of disputes between member countries. The main administrative body is the General Secretariat, based in Addis Ababa, headed by a Secretary-General who is elected by the Assembly for a four-year term.

Substantial budgetary arrears due to delays in the payment of national contributions has meant that the OAU continually faces difficulties in furthering its aims. Most OAU programmes were suspended in November 1994 after unpaid contributions reached US$77 million. In June 1991 the Assembly adopted an African Economic Community Treaty which envisages establishment of the Economic Community after ratification by two-thirds of the OAU's membership. In June 1993 a mechanism was created for conflict prevention, management and resolution, and a peace fund was established.

Secretary-General, Salim Ahmed Salim (Tanzania)

ORGANIZATION OF AMERICAN STATES
17th Street and Constitution Avenue NW, Washington DC 20006, USA

Originally founded in 1890 for largely commercial purposes, the Organization of American States (OAS) adopted its present name and charter in 1948. The charter entered into force in 1951 and was amended in 1967 and 1985; the 1992 Protocol of Washington and the 1993 Protocol of Managua will enter into force upon ratification by two-thirds of member states. Its aims are to strengthen the peace and security of the continent; to promote and consolidate representative democracy with due respect for the principle of non-intervention; to prevent possible causes of difficulties and to ensure the pacific settlement of disputes that may arise among the member states; to provide for common action on the part of those states in the event of aggression; to seek the solution of political, judicial and economic problems that may arise among them; to promote, by co-operative action, their economic, social and cultural development; and to achieve an effective limitation of conventional weapons that will make it possible to devote the largest amount of resources to economic and social development. The OAS is a regional organization within the United Nations.

Policy is determined by the annual General Assembly. Meetings of Consultation of foreign minsters consider urgent problems, and advise in cases of armed attack and threats to peace. A Permanent Council, comprising one representative from each member state, meets at OAS headquarters throughout the year to implement the decisions of both the senior OAS organs. The General Secretariat is the central administrative organ. Other organs are the Inter-American Juridical Committee, the Inter-American Commission on Human Rights, the Inter-American Economic and Social Council, and the Inter-American Council for Education, Science and Culture.

The 35 member states are Antigua and Barbuda, Argentina, Bahamas, Barbados, Belize, Bolivia, Brazil, Canada, Chile, Colombia, Costa Rica, Cuba, Dominica, Dominican Republic, Ecuador, Grenada, Guatemala, Guyana, Haiti, Honduras, Jamaica, Mexico, Nicaragua, Panama, Paraguay, Peru, St Christopher and Nevis, St Lucia, St Vincent and the Grenadines, El Salvador, Suriname, Trinidad and Tobago, Uruguay, USA and Venezuela.

Secretary-General, Dr César Gaviria Trujillo (Colombia)

ORGANIZATION OF ARAB PETROLEUM EXPORTING COUNTRIES
PO Box 20501, Safat 13066, Kuwait

The Organization of Arab Petroleum and Exporting Countries (OAPEC) was founded in 1968. The objectives of the organization are to promote co-operation in economic activities, to safeguard members' interests, to unite efforts to ensure the flow of oil to consumer markets, and to create a favourable climate for the investment of capital and expertise.

The Ministerial Council is composed of oil ministers from the member countries and meets twice a year to determine policy, to direct activities and to approve the budgets and accounts of the General Secretariat and the Judicial Tribunal. The Judicial Tribunal is composed of seven part-time judges who rule on disputes between member countries and disputes between countries and oil companies. The executive organ of OAPEC is the General Secretariat.

The members are Algeria, Bahrain, Egypt, Iraq, Kuwait, Libya, Qatar, Saudi Arabia, Syria and the United Arab Emirates. Tunisia's membership has been inactive since 1987.

Secretary-General, Abdel-Aziz A. Al-Turki

ORGANIZATION OF THE ISLAMIC CONFERENCE
PO Box 178, Jeddah 21411, Saudi Arabia

The Organization of the Islamic Conference (OIC) was established in 1971 with the purpose of generating solidarity and co-operation among all the Islamic countries of the world. It also has the specific aims of co-ordinating efforts to safeguard the Muslim holy places, supporting the Palestine cause and the formation of a Palestinian state, assisting member states to maintain their independence, co-ordinating the views of member states in international forums such as the UN, and improving co-operation in the economic, cultural and scientific fields.

The OIC has three central organs, supreme among them the Conference of the Heads of State which meets once every three years to discuss issues of importance to Islamic states. The Conference of Foreign Ministers meets annually to prepare reports for the Conference of Heads of State. The General Secretariat carries out administrative tasks. It is headed by a Secretary-General who is elected by the Conference of Foreign Ministers for a non-renewable four-year term.

In addition to this structure, the OIC has several subsidiary bodies and specialized bodies. These include the Islamic Solidarity Fund, to aid Islamic institutions in member countries, and the Islamic Development Bank, to finance development projects in poorer member states. An

Islamic Court of Justice is planned. The Organization runs various offices to organize the economic boycott of Israel.

The achievement of the Organization's aims has often been prevented by political rivalry and conflicts between member states, such as the Iran-Iraq war and the Iraqi invasion of Kuwait. Egypt's membership was suspended from 1979 to 1984 because of its peace treaty with Israel. Saudi Arabia, the main source of funding, exercises great influence within the Organization. Since 1991 the Organization has become more united and has spoken out against violence against Muslims in India, the Occupied Territories and Bosnia-Hercegovina. Since 1993 the OIC has co-ordinated the offering of troops to the UN by Muslim states to protect Muslim areas of Bosnia-Hercegovina.

The Organization has 51 members (50 sovereign Muslim states in Africa, the Middle East, central and south-east Asia and Europe, plus the Palestine Liberation Organization) and one observer, Turkish Northern Cyprus. It has an annual budget of £5 million.

Secretary-General, Hamid Algabid (Niger)

ORGANIZATION OF THE PETROLEUM EXPORTING COUNTRIES
Obere Donaustrasse 93, 1020 Vienna, Austria

The Organization of the Petroleum Exporting Countries (OPEC) was created in 1960 as a permanent intergovernmental organization with the principal aims of unifying and co-ordinating the petroleum policies of members, determining the best means of protecting their interests individually and collectively, and ensuring the stabilization of prices in international oil markets with a view to eliminating unnecessary fluctuations. Since 1982 OPEC has attempted (only partially successfully) to impose overall production limits and production quotas in an attempt to maintain stable oil prices. In the third quarter of 1995 the overall production quota was 24,520,000 barrels per day.

The supreme authority is the Conference of Ministers of oil, mines and energy of member countries, which meets at least twice a year and formulates policy. The Board of Governors, nominated by member countries, directs the management of OPEC and implements conference resolutions. The Secretariat carries out executive functions under the direction of the Board of Governors.

The members are Algeria, Gabon, Indonesia, Iran, Iraq, Kuwait, Libya, Nigeria, Qatar, Saudi Arabia, UAE and Venezuela. Ecuador withdrew from OPEC in 1992.

Secretary-General, Rilwanu Lukman (Nigeria)

SOUTH PACIFIC COMMISSION
BP D5, Nouméa Cedex, New Caledonia

The South Pacific Commission is a technical assistance agency with programmes in agriculture and plant protection, fisheries and marine resources, community health, socio-economic and statistical services, and community education services. The organization is run by a management committee headed by the Secretary-General. The other committee members are the Director of Services and the Director of Programmes.

The South Pacific Commission (SPC) was established in 1947 by the governments of Australia, France, the Netherlands, New Zealand, the UK and the USA. The aim was to promote the economic and social stability of the islands in the region. The SPC now numbers 27 member

states and territories: the five remaining founder states (the Netherlands has withdrawn), in which no programmes are run, and the other 22 states and territories of Melanesia, Micronesia and Polynesia.

Since 1967 the South Pacific Conference has met annually to discuss and adopt the SPC's work programme, to adopt the budget and to nominate the officers of the Commission.

Secretary-General, Ati George Sokomanu (Vanuatu)
Director of Programmes, Mafaitu'uga Vaasatia Poloma Komiti (W. Samoa)
Director of Services, Fusi Vave Caginavanua (Fiji)

THE UNITED NATIONS
UN Plaza, New York, NY 10017, USA

The United Nations is a voluntary association of states, dedicated through signature of the UN Charter to the maintenance of international peace and security and the solution of economic, social and political problems through international co-operation. The UN is not a world government and has no right of intervention in the essentially domestic affairs of states.

The UN was founded as a successor to the League of Nations and inherited many of its procedures and institutions. The name 'United Nations' was first used in the Washington Declaration 1942 to describe the 26 states which had allied to fight the Axis powers. The UN Charter developed from discussions at the Moscow Conference of the foreign ministers of China, the UK, the USA and the Soviet Union in 1943. Further progress was made at Dumbarton Oaks, Washington, in 1944 during talks involving the same states. The role of the Security Council was formulated at the Yalta Conference in 1945. The Charter was formally drawn up by 50 allied nations at the San Francisco Conference between April and 26 June 1945, when it was signed. Following ratification the UN came into effect on 24 October 1945, which is celebrated annually as United Nations Day. The UN flag is light blue with the UN emblem centred in white.

The principal organs of the UN are the General Assembly, the Security Council, the Economic and Social Council, the Trusteeship Council, the Secretariat and the International Court of Justice. The Economic and Social Council and the Trusteeship Council are auxiliaries, charged with assisting and advising the General Assembly and Security Council. The official languages used are Arabic, Chinese, English, French, Russian and Spanish. Deliberations at the International Court of Justice are in English and French only.

MEMBERSHIP

Membership is open to all countries which accept the Charter and its principle of peaceful co-existence. New members are admitted by the General Assembly on the recommendation of the Security Council. The original membership of 51 states has grown to 185:

Afghanistan	Azerbaijan
Albania	The Bahamas
Algeria	Bahrain
Andorra	Bangladesh
Angola	Barbados
Antigua and Barbuda	*Belarus
*Argentina	*Belgium
Armenia	Belize
*Australia	Benin
Austria	Bhutan

*Bolivia
Bosnia-Hercegovina
Botswana
*Brazil
Brunei
Bulgaria
Burkina
Burundi
Cambodia
Cameroon
*Canada
Cape Verde
Central African Rep.
Chad
*Chile
*China
*Colombia
Comoros
Congo
*Costa Rica
Côte d'Ivoire
Croatia
*Cuba
Cyprus
*Czech Republic
*Denmark
Djibouti
Dominica
*Dominican Republic
*Ecuador
*Egypt
Equatorial Guinea
Eritrea
Estonia
*Ethiopia
Federated States of
   Micronesia
Fiji
Finland
*France
Gabon
Gambia
Georgia
Germany
Ghana
*Greece
Grenada
*Guatemala
Guinea
Guinea-Bissau
Guyana
*Haiti
*Honduras
Hungary
Iceland
*India
Indonesia
*Iran
*Iraq
Ireland, Republic of
Israel
Italy
Jamaica
Japan
Jordan
Kazakhstan
Kenya
Korea, D.P.Rep. (North)
Korea, Rep. of (South)
Kuwait

Kyrgyzstan
Laos
Latvia
*Lebanon
Lesotho
*Liberia
Libya
Liechtenstein
Lithuania
*Luxembourg
Macedonia (The Former
   Yugoslav Republic of)
Madagascar
Malawi
Malaysia
The Maldives
Mali
Malta
Marshall Islands
Mauritania
Mauritius
*Mexico
Moldova
Monaco
Mongolia
Morocco
Mozambique
Myanmar (Burma)
Namibia
Nepal
*Netherlands
*New Zealand
*Nicaragua
Niger
Nigeria
*Norway
Oman
Pakistan
Palau
*Panama
Papua New Guinea
*Paraguay
*Peru
*Philippines
*Poland
Portugal
Qatar
Romania
*Russian Federation
Rwanda
St Christopher and Nevis
St Lucia
St Vincent and the
   Grenadines
*El Salvador
San Marino
São Tomé and Príncipe
*Saudi Arabia
Senegal
Seychelles
Sierra Leone
Singapore
*Slovak Republic
Slovenia
Solomon Islands
Somalia
*South Africa
Spain
Sri Lanka
Sudan

Suriname
Swaziland
Sweden
*Syria
Tajikistan
Tanzania
Thailand
Togo
Trinidad and Tobago
Tunisia
*Turkey
Turkmenistan
Uganda
*Ukraine

United Arab Emirates
*United Kingdom
*United States of America
*Uruguay
Uzbekistan
Vanuatu
*Venezuela
Vietnam
Western Samoa
Yemen
*Yugoslavia (suspended)
Zaire
Zambia
Zimbabwe

*Original member (i.e. from 1945). From 25 October 1971 'China' was taken to mean the People's Republic of China. Czechoslovakia was an original member in 1945 and a member until 31 December 1992. The successor states of the Czech Republic and the Slovak Republic were admitted as members in January 1993

The Russian Federation took over the membership of the Soviet Union in the Security Council and all other UN organs on 24 December 1991. Belarus (formerly Belorussia) and the Ukraine on becoming independent sovereign states continued their existing memberships of the UN, both having been granted separate UN membership in 1945 as a concession to the Soviet Union.

OBSERVERS

Permanent observer status is held by the Vatican City State and Switzerland. The Palestine Liberation Organization has special observer status.

NON-MEMBERS

A number of countries are not members, usually due to their small size and limited financial resources. Notable exceptions include Switzerland, which follows a policy of absolute neutrality, and Taiwan, which was replaced by the People's Republic of China in 1971. The others are Kiribati, Nauru, Tonga, Tuvalu, Vatican City State.

THE GENERAL ASSEMBLY
UN Plaza, New York, NY 10017, USA

The General Assembly is the main deliberative organ of the UN. It consists of all members, each entitled to five representatives but having only one vote. The annual session begins on the third Tuesday of September, when the President is elected, and usually continues until mid-December. Special sessions are held on specific issues and emergency special sessions can be called within 24 hours.

The Assembly is empowered to discuss any matter within the scope of the Charter, except when it is under consideration by the Security Council, and to make recommendations. Under the 'uniting for peace' resolution, adopted in 1950, the Assembly may also take action to maintain international peace and security when the Security Council fails to do so because of a lack of unanimity of its permanent members. Important decisions, such as those on peace and security, the election of officers, the budget, etc., need a two-thirds majority. Others need a simple majority. The Assembly has effective power only over the internal operations of the UN itself; external recommendations are not legally binding.

The work of the General Assembly is divided among six main committees, on each of which every member has the right to be represented: disarmament and international security; economic and financial; social, humanitarian and cultural; special political issues and decolonization (including non-self governing territories); administrative and budgetary; legal. In addition, the General Assembly appoints *ad hoc* committees to consider special issues, such as human rights, peacekeeping, disarmament and international law. All committees consider items referred to them by the Assembly and recommend draft resolutions to its plenary meeting.

The Assembly is assisted by a number of functional committees. The General Committee co-ordinates its proceedings and operations, while the Credentials Committee verifies the credentials of representatives. There are also two standing committees, the Advisory Committee on Administration and Budgetary Questions and the Committee on Contributions, which suggests the scale of members' payments to the UN.

President of the General Assembly (1994), Amara Essy (Côte d'Ivoire)

The Assembly has created a large number of specialized bodies over the years, which are supervised jointly with the Economic and Social Council. They are supported by UN and voluntary contributions from governments, non-governmental organizations and individuals. These organizations include:

The Conference on Disarmament (CD)
Palais des Nations, 1211 Geneva 10, Switzerland
Established by the UN as the Committee on Disarmament in 1962, the CD is the single multilateral disarmament negotiating forum. The present title of the organization was adopted in 1984. There were 40 members as at June 1994.

The Conference holds three regular sessions per year, from January to March, May to June, and July to August. The work of the Conference is conducted both in public plenary meetings and in private *ad hoc* committees set up with the consent of all members to deal with specific items of the agenda. After 25 years of negotiations, a Chemical Weapons Convention was finally agreed and opened for signing in Paris in 1993. The Convention will come into force six months after it has been ratified by 65 states. It bans the use, production, stockpiling and transfer of all chemical weapons. All US and Russian weapons must be destroyed within 15 years of the Convention entering into force, and all other states' weapons must be destroyed within ten years.

Secretary-General, Vladimir Petrovsky (Russia)
UK Representative, N. C. R. Williams, CMG, 37–39 rue de Vermont, 1211 Geneva 20, Switzerland

The International Seabed Authority
Kingston, Jamaica
Established in 1994 on the entry into force of the 1982 Law of the Sea Convention, the organization is responsible for overseeing the recovery of minerals from the seabed by adjudicating on disputes between states and mining companies.

The United Nations Children's Fund (UNICEF)
3 UN Plaza, New York, NY 10017, USA
Established in 1947 to assist children and mothers in the immediate post-war period, UNICEF now concentrates on developing countries. It provides primary health-care and health education. In particular, it conducts programmes in oral hydration, immunization against leading diseases, child growth monitoring, and the encouragement of breast-feeding. Its operations are often conducted in co-operation with the World Health Organization (WHO).
Executive Director, Carol Bellamy (USA)

The United Nations Development Programme (UNDP)
1 UN Plaza, New York, NY 10017, USA
Established in 1966 from the merger of the UN Expanded Programme of Technical Assistance and the UN Special Fund, UNDP is the central funding agency for economic and social development projects around the world. Much of its annual expenditure is channelled through UN specialized agencies, governments and non-governmental organizations.
Administrator, James G. Speth (USA)

The United Nations High Commissioner for Refugees (UNHCR)
Centre William Rappard, 154 rue de Lausanne, PO Box 2500, 1211 Geneva 2, Switzerland
Established in 1951 to protect the rights and interests of refugees, it organizes emergency relief and longer-term solutions, such as voluntary repatriation, local integration or resettlement.
High Commissioner, Sadako Ogata (Japan)
UK OFFICE, 76 Westminster Palace Gardens, London SWIP IRL. Tel: 0171-222 3065

The UN Relief and Works Agency for Palestine Refugees in the Near East (UNRWA)
Vienna International Centre, Wagramerstrasse 5, PO Box 100, 1400 Vienna, Austria
Established in 1949 to bring relief to the Palestinians displaced by the Arab-Israeli conflict.
Commissioner-General, Ilter Turkman (Turkey)

The United Nations High Commissioner for Human Rights
Established in 1993 to secure respect for, and prevent violations of human rights by engaging in dialogue with governments and international organizations. Responsible for the co-ordination of all UN human rights activities.
High Commissioner, José Ayala Lasso (Ecuador)

Other bodies include:

The UN Centre for Human Settlements (Habitat), PO Box 30030, Nairobi, Kenya
The UN Conference on Trade and Development (UNCTAD), Palais des Nations, 1211 Geneva 10, Switzerland
The Department of Humanitarian Affairs (DHA), Palais des Nations, 1211 Geneva 10, Switzerland
The UN Environment Programme (UNEP), PO Box 30552, Nairobi, Kenya
The UN Population Fund (UNFPA), 220 East 42nd Street, New York, NY 10017, USA
The UN Institute for the Advancement of Women (INSTRAW), PO Box 21747, Santo Domingo, Dominican Republic
The UN University (UNU), Toho Seimei Building, 15–1, Shibuya, 2-Chome, Shibuya-ku, Tokyo 150, Japan
The World Food Council (WFC), Via delle Terme di Caracalla, 00100 Rome, Italy
The World Food Programme (WFP), Via delle Terme di Caracalla, 00100 Rome, Italy

Budget of the United Nations
The budget adopted for the biennium 1996–7 was US$2,510 million. The scale of assessment contributions of 88 UN members is set at the minimum 0.01 per cent. The ten largest assessments are: USA, 25 per cent; Japan, 12.45; Germany, 8.93; Russia, 6.91; France, 6.00; UK, 5.02; Italy, 4.29; Canada, 3.11; Spain, 1.98; Australia, 1.51.

THE SECURITY COUNCIL
UN Plaza, New York, NY 10017, USA

The Security Council is the senior arm of the UN and has the primary responsibility for maintaining world peace and security. It consists of 15 members, each with one representative and one vote. There are five permanent members, China, France, Russia, UK and USA, and ten non-permanent members. Each of the non-permanent members is elected for a two-year term by a two-thirds majority of the General Assembly and is ineligible for immediate re-election. Five of the elective seats are allocated to Africa and Asia, one to eastern Europe, two to Latin America and two to western Europe and remaining countries. Procedural questions are determined by a simple majority vote. Other matters require a majority inclusive of the votes of the permanent members; they thus have a right of veto. The abstention of a permanent member does not constitute a veto. The presidency rotates each month by state in (English) alphabetical order. Parties to a dispute, other non-members and individuals can be invited to participate in Security Council debates but are not permitted to vote. In 1995 the ten non-permanent members were: Argentina, Czech Republic, Nigeria, Oman, Rwanda (*term expires 31 December 1995*), Botswana, Germany, Honduras, Indonesia, Italy (*term expires 31 December 1996*).

The Security Council is empowered to settle or adjudicate in disputes or situations which threaten international peace and security. It can adopt political, economic and military measures to achieve this end. Any matter considered to be a threat to or breach of the peace or an act of aggression can be brought to the Security Council's attention by any member state or by the Secretary-General. The Charter envisaged members placing at the disposal of the Security Council armed forces and other facilities which would be co-ordinated by the Military Staff Committee, composed of military representatives of the five permanent members. The Security Council is also supported by a Committee of Experts, to advise on procedural and technical matters, and a Committee on Admission of New Members.

Owing to superpower disunity, the Security Council rarely played the decisive role set out in the Charter; the Military Staff Committee was effectively suspended from 1948 until 1990, when a meeting was convened during the Gulf Crisis on the formation and control of UN-supervised armed forces. However, at an extraordinary meeting of the Security Council in January 1992, heads of government laid plans to transform the UN in light of the changed post-Cold War world. The Secretary-General was asked to draw up a report on enhancing the UN's preventive diplomacy, peacemaking and peacekeeping ability. The report, *An Agenda for Peace*, was produced in June 1992 and centred on the establishment of a UN army composed of national contingents on permanent standby, as envisaged at the time of the UN's formation.

PEACEKEEPING FORCES

The Security Council has established a number of peace-keeping forces since its foundation, comprising contingents provided mainly by neutral and non-aligned UN members. Current forces include: the UN Truce Supervision Organization (UNTSO), Israel, 1948; the UN Military Observer Group in India and Pakistan (UNMOGIP), 1949; the UN Peacekeeping Force in Cyprus (UNFICYP), 1964; the UN Disengagement Observer Force (UNDOF), Golan Heights, Syria, 1974; the UN Interim Force in Lebanon (UNIFIL), 1978; the UN Iraq-Kuwait Observation Mission (UNIKOM), 1991; the UN

Mission for the Referendum in Western Sahara (MINURSO), 1991; the UN Protection Force (UNPROFOR), Bosnia-Hercegovina, 1992; the UN Observer Mission in Georgia (UNOMIG), 1993; the UN Observer Mission in Liberia (UNOMIL), 1993; the UN Mission in Haiti (UNMIH), 1993; the UN Assistance Mission for Rwanda (UNAMIR), 1993; the UN Observer Mission in Guatemala (MINUGA), 1994; the UN Observer Mission in Tajikistan (UNMOT), 1994; the UN Angola Verification Mission III (UNAVEM III), 1995; the UN Confidence Restoration Operation in Croatia (UNCRO), 1995; the UN Preventive Deployment Force (UNPREDEP), Former Yugoslav Republic of Macedonia, 1995.

THE ECONOMIC AND SOCIAL COUNCIL
UN Plaza, New York, NY 10017, USA

The Economic and Social Council is responsible under the General Assembly for the economic and social work of the UN and for the co-ordination of the activities of the 15 specialized agencies and other UN bodies. It makes reports and recommendations on economic, social, cultural, educational, health and related matters, often in consultation with non-governmental organizations, passing the reports to the General Assembly and other UN bodies. It also drafts conventions for submission to the Assembly and calls conferences on matters within its remit.

The Council consists of 54 members, 18 of whom are elected annually by the General Assembly for a three-year term. Each has one vote and can be immediately re-elected on retirement. A President is elected annually and is also eligible for re-election. One substantive session is held annually and decisions are reached by simple majority vote of those present.

The Council has established a number of standing committees on particular issues and several commissions. Commissions include: Statistical, Human Rights, Social Development, Sustainable Development, Status of Women, Crime Prevention and Criminal Justice, Narcotic Drugs, Science and Technology for Development, and Population; and Regional Economic Commissions for Europe, Asia and the Pacific, Western Asia, Latin America and Africa.

THE TRUSTEESHIP COUNCIL
UN Plaza, New York, NY 10017, USA

The Trusteeship Council supervised the administration of territories within the UN Trusteeship system inherited from the League of Nations. It consists of the five permanent members of the Security Council. With the independence of the Republic of Palau in October 1994, all eleven trusteeships have now progressed to independence or merged with neighbouring states and the Trusteeship Council suspended its operations on 1 November 1994.

THE SECRETARIAT
UN Plaza, New York, NY 10017, USA

The Secretariat services the other UN organs and is headed by a Secretary-General elected by a majority vote of the General Assembly on the recommendation of the Security Council. He is assisted by an international staff, chosen to represent the international character of the organization. The Secretary-General is charged with bringing to the attention of the Security Council any matter which he considers poses a threat to international peace and security. He may also bring other matters to the attention of the General Assembly and other UN bodies and may be entrusted by them with additional duties. As chief administrator to the UN, the Secretary-General is present in person or via representatives at all meetings of the other five main organs of the UN. He may also act as an impartial mediator in disputes between member states.

The power and influence of the Secretary-General has been determined largely by the character of the office-holder and by the state of relations between the superpowers. The thaw in these relations since the mid-1980s has increased the effectiveness of the UN, particularly in its attempts to intervene in international disputes. It helped to end the Iran-Iraq war and sponsored peace in Central America. Following Iraq's invasion of Kuwait in 1990 the UN took its first collective security action since the Korean War. UN action to protect the Kurds in northern Iraq has widened its legal authority by breaching the prohibition on its intervention in the essentially domestic affairs of states. Currently the UN is involved in peacekeeping, aid distribution and negotiations in the former Yugoslavia; and is addressing the global problems of Aids and environmental destruction.

Secretary-General, Boutros Boutros-Ghali, apptd 1992 (Egypt)
Under-Secretaries-General:
Internal Oversight Services, Karl-Theodor Paschke (Germany)
Political Affairs, Marrack Goulding (UK)
Peacekeeping Operations, Kofi Annan (Ghana)
Development Support and Management Services, Ji Chaozhu (China)
Legal Affairs, Hans Axel Valdemar-Corell (Sweden)
Humanitarian Affairs, Peter Hansen (Denmark)
Administration and Management, Joseph Connor (USA)
Policy Co-ordination and Sustainable Development, Nitin Desai (India)
Economic and Social Information and Policy Analysis, Jean-Claude Milleron (France)
Special Advisers to the Secretary-General, Ismat Kittani (Iraq); Chinmaya Gharekhan (India)

Former Secretaries-General
1946–53   Trygve Lie (Norway)
1953–61   Dag Hammarskjöld (Sweden)
1961–71   U Thant (Burma)
1971–81   Kurt Waldheim (Austria)
1981–91   Javier Pérez de Cuéllar (Peru)

INTERNATIONAL COURT OF JUSTICE
The Peace Palace, 2517 KJ The Hague, The Netherlands

The International Court of Justice is the principal judicial organ of the UN. The Statute of the Court is an integral part of the Charter and all members of the UN are *ipso facto* parties to it. The Court is composed of 15 judges, elected by both the General Assembly and the Security Council for nine-year terms which are renewable. Judges may deliberate over cases in which their country is involved. If no judge on the bench is from a country which is a party to a dispute under consideration, that party may designate a judge to participate *ad hoc* in that particular deliberation. If any party to a case fails to adhere to the judgment of the Court, the other party may have recourse to the Security Council.
President, Mohammed Bedjaoui (Algeria) (2000)
Vice-President, Stephen M. Schwebel (USA) (1997)
Judges, Geza Herczegh (Hungary) (2003); Sir Robert Jennings (UK) (2000); Jens Evensen (Norway) (1997); Vladen S. Vereshchetin (Russia) (1997); Gilbert Guillaume (France) (2000); Mohammed Shahabuddeen (Guyana) (1997); Andrés Aguilar Mawdsley (Venezuela) (2000); Christopher G. Weeramantry (Sri Lanka) (2000); Raymond Ranjeva (Madagascar) (2000); Shi Jiuyong (China) (2003); Abdul Koroma (Sierra

Leone) (2003); Carl-August Fleischauer (Germany) (2003)

INTERNATIONAL WAR CRIMES TRIBUNAL FOR THE FORMER YUGOSLAVIA
Churchill Plein 1, PO Box 13888, 2501 EW The Hague, The Netherlands

By resolution 808 of 22 February 1993, the Security Council voted to establish a war crimes tribunal for the former Yugoslavia. This tribunal hears cases covering grave breaches of the Geneva Conventions and crimes against humanity. The Court was inaugurated in November 1993 in the Hague with 11 member judges elected by the UN General Assembly from 11 states, divided into two trial chambers of three judges each and an appeal chamber of five judges. The court is unable to force suspects to stand trial but is empowered to pass verdicts in the absence of suspects and can put suspects under an 'act of accusation' which prevents them from leaving their own country.

The first indictment was issued by the court in November 1994 against a Bosnian Serb who was extradited from Germany to the Hague in April 1995 to stand trial along with 20 absent Bosnian Serbs on charges of murder, torture and rape. In April 1995 the tribunal announced that it was investigating the Bosnian Serb leaders Radovan Karadzic and Gen. Ratko Mladic for suspected war crimes.
President, Antonio Cassesse (Italy)
Chief Prosecutor, Mr Justice Goldstone (South Africa)

INTERNATIONAL CRIMINAL TRIBUNAL FOR RWANDA
By resolution 955 of 8 November 1994, the UN Security Council voted to establish a tribunal to try those responsible for genocide and other violations of international humanitarian law in Rwanda between 1 January and 31 December 1994. The tribunal is based in Arusha, Tanzania, and is empowered to try the 100 most senior people responsible for the massacre of 500,000, mainly ethnic Tutsis, in Rwanda in 1994.
Chief Prosecutor, Mr Justice Goldstone (South Africa)

SPECIALIZED AGENCIES
Fifteen independent international organizations, each with its own membership, budget and headquarters, carry out their responsibilities in co-ordination with the UN under agreements made with the Economic and Social Council. An entry for each appears elsewhere in the International Organizations section. They are: the Food and Agriculture Organization of the UN; International Civil Aviation Organization; International Fund for Agricultural Development; International Labour Organization; International Maritime Organization; the International Monetary Fund; International Telecommunications Union; UN Educational, Scientific and Cultural Organization; UN Industrial Development Organization; Universal Postal Union; World Bank (International Bank for Reconstruction and Development, International Development Agency, International Finance Corporation); World Health Organization; World Intellectual Property Organization; and World Meteorological Organization. The International Atomic Energy Agency and the General Agreement on Tariffs and Trade/World Trade Organization are linked to the UN but are not specialized agencies.

UK MISSION TO THE UNITED NATIONS
One Dag Hammarskjöld Plaza, 885 Second Avenue, New York, NY 10017, USA
Permanent Representative to the United Nations and Representative on the Security Council, Sir John Weston, KCMG, apptd 1995
Deputy Permanent Representative, S. J. Gomersall

UK MISSION TO THE OFFICE OF THE UN AND OTHER
INTERNATIONAL ORGANIZATIONS IN GENEVA
37–39 rue de Vermont, 1211 Geneva 20, Switzerland
Permanent UK Representative, N. C. R. Williams, CMG *apptd*
1993
Deputy Permanent Representatives, E. G. M. Chaplin, OBE
(*Head of Chancery*); Miss A. E. Stoddart (*Economic Affairs*)

UK MISSION TO THE INTERNATIONAL ATOMIC ENERGY
AGENCY, THE UN INDUSTRIAL DEVELOPMENT
ORGANIZATION AND THE UNITED NATIONS OFFICE AT
VIENNA
Jaurèsgasse 12, 1030 Vienna, Austria
Permanent UK Representative, C. Hulse, CMG, OBE *apptd* 1993
Deputy Permanent Representative, S. H. Innes

UN OFFICE AND INFORMATION CENTRE
18 Buckingham Gate, London SWIE 6LB
Tel 0171-630 1981

UNITED NATIONS EDUCATIONAL,
SCIENTIFIC AND CULTURAL
ORGANIZATION
7 place de Fontenoy, 75352 Paris 07sp, France

The United Nations Educational, Scientific and Cultural
Organization (UNESCO) was established in 1946. It
promotes collaboration among its member states in
education, science, culture and communication. It aims to
further a universal respect for human rights, justice and the
rule of law, without distinction of race, sex, language or
religion, in accordance with the UN Charter.

UNESCO runs a number of programmes to improve
education and extend access to it. It provides assistance to
ensure the free flow of information and its wider and better
balanced dissemination without any obstacle to freedom of
expression, and to maintain cultural heritage in the face of
development. It fosters research and study in all areas of the
social and environmental sciences.

UNESCO had 183 member states as at July 1995. There
are three associate members. The General Conference,
consisting of representatives of all the members, meets biennially to decide the programme and the budget (1994–5,
US$455,490,000). It elects the 51-member Executive
Board, which supervises operations, and appoints a
Director-General who heads a Secretariat responsible for
carrying out the organization's programmes. In most
member states national commissions liaise with UNESCO
to execute its programme.

The UK withdrew from UNESCO in 1985. It was
granted observer status in 1986.
Director-General, Federico Mayor Zaragoza (Spain)

UNITED NATIONS INDUSTRIAL
DEVELOPMENT ORGANIZATION
Vienna International Centre, Wagramerstrasse 5,
PO Box 300, A-1400 Vienna, Austria

The United Nations Industrial Development Organization (UNIDO) was established as an organ of the UN
General Assembly in 1966, replacing the Centre for
Industrial Development. It became a UN specialized
agency in 1985 with the aims of co-ordinating industrial
activities within the UN system and promoting the
industrialization of developing countries, with special
emphasis upon the manufacturing sector. To this end it
provides technical assistance and advice, provides invest-

ment promotion and helps with planning. UNIDO assists
both public and private sectors and has made its services
available to former centrally planned economies in
transition to a market economy.

UNIDO had 167 members as at January 1995. It is
funded by the UN Development Programme, other UN
bodies, assessed contributions from member states'
governments and non-governmental organizations. A
General Conference of all the members meets biennially
to discuss strategy and policy, set a budget (1993–4,
US$196,310,300) and elect the Industrial Development
Board. This executive body is composed of members from
53 member states and reviews implementation of the
regular work programme and of General Conference
decisions. There is a subsidiary Programme and Budget
Committee. A Secretariat administers UNIDO under a
Director-General, appointed by the Conference.
Director-General, Mauricio de Maria y Campos (Mexico)
Permanent UK Representative, C. Hulse, CMG, OBE, British
Embassy, Vienna

UNIVERSAL POSTAL UNION
Weltpoststrasse 4, 3000 Berne 15, Switzerland

The Universal Postal Union (UPU) was established by the
Treaty of Berne 1874, taking effect from 1875, and became
a UN specialized agency in 1947. The UPU is an
intergovernmental organization which exists to form and
regulate a single postal territory of all member countries,
for the reciprocal exchange of correspondence without
discrimination. It also assists and advises on the improvement of postal services.

The UPU had 189 members as at June 1995. A Universal
Postal Congress of all the members is the UPU's supreme
authority and meets every five years to review the Treaty.
A Council of Administration composed of 41 members was
established by the 1994 Congress. It meets annually to
ensure continuity between congresses, study regulatory
developments and broad policies, approve the budget and
examine proposed Treaty changes. A Postal Operations
Council also meets annually to deal with specific technical
and operational issues. The three UPU bodies are served
by the International Bureau, a secretariat headed by a
Director-General.

Funding is provided by members according to a scale of
contributions drawn up by the Congress. The Council sets
the annual budget (1995, SFr 32,165,490) within a five-year
figure decided by the Congress.
Director-General, Thomas E. Leavey (USA)

WESTERN EUROPEAN UNION
4 rue de la Régence, 1000 Brussels, Belgium

The Western European Union (WEU) originated as the
Brussels Treaty Organization (BTO) established under
the Treaty of Brussels, signed in 1948 by Belgium, France,
Luxembourg, the Netherlands and UK, to provide
collective self-defence and economic, cultural and social
collaboration amongst its signatories. With the collapse of
the European Defence Community and the decision of
NATO to incorporate the Federal Republic of Germany
into the Western security system, the BTO was modified
to become the WEU in 1954 with the admission of West
Germany and Italy. However, owing to the overlap with
NATO and the Council of Europe, the Union became
largely defunct.

From the late 1970s onwards efforts were made to add a security dimension to the EC's European Political Co-operation. Opposition to these efforts from Denmark, Greece and Ireland led the remaining EC countries, all WEU members, to decide to reactivate the Union in 1984. Members committed themselves to harmonizing their views on defence and security and developing a European security identity, while bearing in mind the importance of transatlantic relations. Portugal and Spain joined the WEU in 1988, and Greece became a full member in 1995.

After much debate about its future, the EC Maastricht Treaty designated the WEU as the future defence component of the European Union. WEU foreign ministers agreed in the Petersberg Declaration 1992 to assign forces to WEU command for 'peacemaking' operations in Europe. In November 1992 the WEU's role as the common security dimension of the EU was enhanced when WEU ministers signed a declaration with remaining European NATO members to give them various forms of WEU membership. Iceland, Norway and Turkey became associate members; Ireland, Denmark and, on 1 January 1995, Austria, Finland and Sweden became observer members. In 1994 the WEU reached agreements with nine eastern European states (Estonia, Latvia, Lithuania, Poland, Czech Republic, Slovak Republic, Hungary, Romania and Bulgaria) under which they all became associate partners.

The WEU acts in accordance with positions adopted within the Atlantic Alliance, and relations between the WEU and NATO are developing on the basis of transparency and complementarity. WEU foreign ministers stated in the Luxembourg Declaration 1993 that the WEU is ready to participate in the future work of the NATO Alliance as its European pillar, and to co-operate to prevent the duplication of WEU and NATO actions.

Building on past experience of joint actions in the Gulf (1988–90), the WEU jointly operates with NATO a naval patrol force in the Adriatic Sea and an embargo enforcement mission on the River Danube, as well as a police force in Mostar, as part of the European peace initiatives in the former Yugoslavia.

The formation of a 'Eurocorps' based on the Franco-German brigade as a force answerable to the WEU was announced in 1992. The 'Eurocorps' was inaugurated in Strasbourg in 1993 and became fully operational in 1995 with a strength of 51,000 troops comprising French, German, Belgian, Luxembourg and Spanish forces.

A Council of Ministers (foreign and defence) meets biannually in the capital of the presiding country; the presidency rotates biannually. A Permanent Council of the member states' permanent representatives meets weekly in Brussels. Associate members have the right to attend Permanent Council meetings. The Permanent Council is chaired by the Secretary-General and serviced by the Secretariat. A planing cell has been established to draw up contingency plans in the areas of humanitarian relief, peacekeeping and crisis management. The Assembly of the WEU is composed of 115 parliamentarians of member states and meets twice annually in Paris to debate matters within the scope of the revised Brussels Treaty.

Presidency (1995), Belgium, Germany
Secretary-General, José Cutileiro (Portugal)
UK Representative on the Permanent Council, John Goulden, CMG
ASSEMBLY, 43 avenue du Président Wilson, 75775 Paris Cedex 16, France

THE WORLD BANK
1818 H Street NW, Washington DC 20433, USA

The World Bank, more formally known as the International Bank for Reconstruction and Development (IBRD), is a specialized agency of the UN. It developed from the international monetary and financial conference held at Bretton Woods, New Hampshire, in 1944 and was established by 44 nations in 1945 to encourage economic growth in developing countries through the provision of loans and technical assistance to their respective governments. The IBRD now has 178 members.

The Bank is owned by the governments of member countries and its capital is subscribed by its members. It finances its lending primarily from borrowing in world capital markets, and derives a substantial contribution to its resources from its retained earnings and the repayment of loans. The interest rate on its loans is calculated in relation to its cost of borrowing. Loans generally have a grace period of five years and are repayable within 20 years. The loans made by the Bank since its inception to 30 June 1994 totalled US$333,806.8 million to 110 countries. Total capital is US$170,003 million.

Originally directed towards post-war reconstruction in Europe, the Bank has subsequently turned towards assisting less-developed countries with the establishment of two affiliates, the International Finance Corporation (IFC) in 1956 and the International Development Association (IDA) in 1960. The IFC aids developing member countries by promoting the growth of the private sector of their economies and by helping to mobilize domestic and foreign capital for this purpose. The IFC's subscribed share capital was US$2,251 million at 30 June 1994. It is also empowered to borrow up to two and half times the amount of its unimpaired subscribed capital and accumulated earnings for use in its lending programme. At 30 June 1994, the IFC had committed financing totalling more than US$14,316,215 million in about 162 countries.

The IDA performs the same function as the World Bank but primarily to less developed countries and on terms that bear less heavily on their balance of payments than IBRD loans. Eligible countries typically have a per capita gross national product of less than US$835 (1994). Funds (called credits to distinguish them from IBRD loans) come mostly in the form of subscriptions and contributions from the IDA's richer members and transfers from the net income of the IBRD. The terms for IDA credits, which bear no interest and are made to governments only, are ten-year grace periods and 35- or 40-year maturities. By 30 June 1994, the IDA had extended development credits totalling US$87,880 million to 157 countries.

The IBRD and its affiliates are financially and legally distinct but share headquarters. The IBRD is headed by a Board of Governors, consisting of one Governor and one alternate Governor appointed by each member country. Twenty-four Executive Directors exercise all powers of the Bank except those reserved to the Board of Governors. The President, elected by the Executive Directors, conducts the business of the Bank, assisted by an international staff. Membership in both the IFC (162 members) and the IDA (157 members) is open to all IBRD countries. The IDA is administered by the same staff as the Bank; the IFC has its own personnel but draws on the IBRD for administrative and other support. All share the same President.

In 1988 a third affiliate, the Multilateral Investment Guarantee Agency (MIGA) was formed. MIGA encourages foreign investment in developing states by providing investment guarantees to potential investors

and advisory services to developing member countries. At 30 December 1994 128 countries were members of MIGA.
President (IBRD, IFC, IDA, MIGA), James D. Wolfensohn (USA)
UK Executive Director, H. Evans, Room 11-120, IMF, 700 19th Street NW, Washington DC 20431
EUROPEAN OFFICE, 66 avenue d'Iena, 75116 Paris, France
JAPAN OFFICE, Kokusai Building 916, 1-1 Marunouchi 3-Chomse, Chiyoda-ku, Tokyo 100, Japan
UK OFFICE, New Zealand House, Haymarket, London SWIY 4TQ

THE WORLD COUNCIL OF CHURCHES
PO Box 2100, 1211 Geneva 2, Switzerland

The World Council of Churches (WCC) was constituted in 1948 to promote unity among the many different Christian churches. The 324 member churches of the WCC have adherents in more than 100 countries. With the exception of Roman Catholicism, virtually all Christian traditions are included in the WCC membership.

The policies of the Council are determined by delegates of the member churches meeting in Assembly, about every seven years; the seventh Assembly was held in Canberra, Australia, in February 1991. More detailed decisions are taken by a 151-member Central Committee which is elected by the Assembly and meets, with the eight WCC Presidents, annually. The Central Committee in turn appoints a smaller Executive Committee and also nominates commissions to guide the various programmes.
General Secretary, Dr Konrad Raiser (Germany)

WORLD HEALTH ORGANIZATION
20 avenue Appia, 1211 Geneva 27, Switzerland

The UN International Health Conference held in 1946 established the World Health Organization (WHO) as a UN specialized agency, with effect from 1948. It is dedicated to attaining the highest possible level of health for all. It collaborates with member governments, UN agencies and other bodies to develop health standards, control communicable diseases and promote all aspects of family and environmental health. It seeks to raise the standards of health teaching and training, and promotes research through collaborating research centres worldwide. Its other services include the *International Pharmacopoeia*, epidemiological surveillance, and the collation and publication of statistics. WHO activities are orientated to achieving 'Health for all by the year 2000', i.e. a level of health allowing the world's citizens to lead socially and economically productive lives.

WHO had 190 members as at May 1995. It is governed by the annual World Health Assembly of members which meets to set policy, approve the budget (1996–7, US$1,900 million), appoint a Director-General, and adopt health conventions and regulations. It also elects 39 members who designate one health-qualified person to serve in a personal capacity on the Executive Board. The Board effects the programme, suggests initiatives and is empowered to deal with emergencies. A Secretariat, headed by the Director-General, supervises the health activities of six regional offices.
Director-General, Dr H. Nakajima (Japan)

WORLD INTELLECTUAL PROPERTY ORGANIZATION
34 chemin des Colombettes, 1211 Geneva 20, Switzerland

The World Intellectual Property Organization (WIPO) was established in 1967 by the Stockholm Convention, which entered into force in 1970. In addition to that Convention, WIPO administers 18 treaties, the principal ones being the Paris Convention for the Protection of Industrial Property and the Berne Convention for the Protection of Literary and Artistic Works. WIPO became a UN specialized agency in 1974.

WIPO promotes the protection of intellectual property throughout the world through co-operation among states, and the administration of various 'Unions', each founded on a multilateral treaty and dealing with the legal and administrative aspects of intellectual property.

Intellectual property comprises two main branches: industrial property (inventions, trademarks, industrial designs and appellations of origin); and copyright (literary, musical, photographic, audiovisual and artistic works, etc.). WIPO also assists creative intellectual activity and facilitates technology transfer, particularly to developing countries. It administers various conventions, most importantly the Berne and Paris Conventions.

WIPO had 155 members as at June 1995. The biennial session of all its governing bodies sets policy, a programme and a budget (1994–5, SFr 230 million). WIPO has three governing bodies: the General Assembly, composed of WIPO members who are also members of the Paris or Berne conventions; the Conference, composed of all WIPO members; and the Co-ordination Committee, composed of member states elected by members of WIPO and the Paris and Berne conventions. The General Assembly elects a Director-General, who heads the International Bureau (secretariat).

A separate International Union for the Protection of New Varieties of Plants (UPOV), established by convention in 1961, is linked to WIPO. It has 27 members.
Director-General, Dr Arpad Bogsch (USA)

WORLD METEOROLOGICAL ORGANIZATION
41 avenue Giuseppe Motta, PO Box 2300, 1211 Geneva 20, Switzerland

The World Meteorological Organization (WMO) was established as a UN specialized agency in 1950, succeeding the International Meteorological Organization founded in 1873. It facilitates co-operation in the world-wide establishment of networks for making meteorological, climatological, hydrological and geophysical observations, as well as their exchange, processing and standardization, and assists technology transfer, training and research. It also fosters collaboration between meteorological and hydrological services, and furthers the application of meteorology to aviation, shipping, environment, water problems, agriculture, etc.

The WMO had 178 member states and five member territories, as at 30 June 1995. The supreme authority is the World Meteorological Congress of member states and member territories, which meets every four years to determine general policy, make recommendations and set a budget (1992–5, SFr 236.1 million). It also elects 26 members of the 36-member Executive Council, the other members being the President and three Vice-Presidents of the WMO, and the Presidents of the six regional associations, who are ex-officio members. The Council supervises the implementation of Congress decisions, initiates studies and makes recommendations on matters needing international action. The WMO functions through six regional associations and eight technical commissions. Each of the regional associations has responsibility for co-ordinating meteorological activities within its region. The technical commissions study meteorological and hydrological problems, lay down the necessary methodologies and procedures, and make recommendations to the Executive Council and Congress. The Secretariat is headed by a Secretary-General, appointed by the Congress.

Secretary-General, G. O. P. Obasi (Nigeria)

WORLD TRADE ORGANIZATION
Centre William Rappard, 154 rue de Lausanne, 1211 Geneva 21, Switzerland

---

The World Trade Organization was established on 1 January 1995 as the successor to the General Agreement on Tariffs and Trade (GATT), with which it operates concurrently until 31 December 1995. GATT was established in 1948 as an interim agreement until the charter of a new international trade organization could be drafted by a committee of the UN Economic and Social Council and ratified by member states. The charter was never ratified and GATT became the only regime for the regulation of world trade, evolving its own rules and procedures.

GATT was dedicated to the expansion of non-discriminatory international trade and progressively extended free trade via 'rounds' of multilateral negotiations. Eight 'rounds' were concluded: Geneva (1947), Annecy (1948), Torquay (1950), Geneva (1956), Dillon (1960-1), Kennedy (1964-7), Tokyo (1973-9) and Uruguay (1986-94). By the time that the measures of the Uruguay Round are fully implemented in 2002 the average duties on manufactured goods will have been reduced from 40 per cent in the 1940s to 3 per cent. The Final Act of the Uruguay Round was signed by trade ministers from the 123 GATT negotiating states and the EU in Marrakesh, Morocco, on 15 April 1994. It established the World Trade Organization (WTO) to supersede GATT and implement the Uruguay Round measures.

The WTO is the legal and institutional foundation of the multilateral trading system. It provides the contractual obligations determining how governments frame and implement trade policy and provides the forum for the debate, negotiation and adjudication of trade problems. The WTO's principal aims are to liberalize world trade and place it on a secure basis, and it seeks to achieve this partly by an agreed set of trade rules and market access agreements and partly through further trade liberalization negotiations. The WTO also administers and implements a further 29 multilateral agreements in fields such as agriculture, textiles and clothing, services, government procurement, rules of origin and intellectual property.

There are three principal differences between the WTO and GATT. The WTO is a permanent international organization with a much more coherent framework than the provisional basis of GATT; it has a stronger and faster trade compliance and enforcement mechanism and dispute settlement system; it has a wider remit under the Uruguay Round than GATT's trade in merchandise goods, covering also agriculture, services, textiles and clothing, and intellectual property rights.

The highest authority of the WTO is the Ministerial Conference composed of all members which meets at least once every two years. The General Council meets as required and acts on behalf of the Ministerial Conference in regard to the regular working of the WTO. Composed of all members, the General Council also convenes in two particular forms: as the Dispute Settlement Body, dealing with disputes between members arising from the Uruguay Round Final Act; and as the Trade Policy Review Body, conducting regular reviews of the trade policies of members. A secretariat of 450 staff headed by a Director-General services WTO bodies and provides trade performance and trade policy analysis.

As at 15 June 1995 there were 97 WTO members, and a further 32 GATT contracting parties were completing joining procedures. The WTO budget for 1995 was SFr 105 million, with members' contributions calculated on the basis of their share of the total trade conducted by WTO members. The official languages of the WTO are English, French and Spanish.

Director-General, Renato Ruggiero (Italy)

Permanent UK Representative, N. C. R. Williams, CMG, 37–39 rue de Vermont, 1211 Geneva 20

The European Union

MEMBERS

STATE	ACCESSION DATE	POPULATION (million)	GNP (US$ million)	GDP PER HEAD‡	COUNCIL VOTES	EP SEATS
Austria	1 January 1995	8.00	183,530	112	4	21
Belgium	1 January 1958†	10.55	213,435	112	5	25
Denmark	1 January 1973	5.23	137,610	114	3	16
Finland	1 January 1995	5.03	96,220	92	3	16
France	1 January 1958†	56.89	1,289,235	110	10	87
Germany	1 January 1958*†	81.08	1,902,995	108	10	99
Greece	1 January 1981	10.26	76,698	62	5	25
Ireland	1 January 1973	3.53	44,906	83	3	15
Italy	1 January 1958†	57.05	1,134,980	102	10	87
Luxembourg	1 January 1958†	0.39	14,233	158	2	6
Netherlands	1 January 1958†	15.24	316,404	102	5	31
Portugal	1 January 1986	9.86	77,749	68	5	25
Spain	1 January 1986	38.87	533,986	77	8	64
Sweden	1 January 1995	8.64	216,294	98	4	22
UK	1 January 1973	58.19	1,042,700	101	10	87
TOTAL		368.81	7,280,975		87	626

* Federal Republic of Germany (West) 1952/1958; German Democratic Republic (East) acceded on German reunification (3 October 1990)
† Acceded to the European Coal and Steel Community (ECSC) on its formation in 1952
‡ Expressed as purchasing power parities: EU average = 100
EP European Parliament

DEVELOPMENT

1950 Robert Schuman (French foreign minister) proposes that France and West Germany pool their coal and steel industries under a supranational authority (Schuman Plan)

1951 Paris Treaty signed by France, West Germany, Belgium, Italy, Luxembourg and the Netherlands, establishing European Coal and Steel Community (ECSC)

1952 The ECSC treaty enters into force

1955 ECSC members discuss further moves towards economic integration

1957 25 March: The Treaty of Rome signed by the six, establishing the European Economic Community (EEC) and the European Atomic Energy Authority (EURATOM). Treaty intended to create a customs union; remove obstacles to free movement of capital, goods, people and services; establish common external trade policy and common agricultural and fisheries policies; co-ordinate economic policies; harmonize social policies; co-operate in nuclear research

1958 1 January: EEC and EURATOM begin operation. Joint Parliament and Court of Justice established for all three communities, and the Commission, Council of Ministers, Economic and Social Committee and Investment Bank for the EEC

1962 The Common Agricultural Policy (CAP) agreed (see pages 775–6)

1963 The first Yaoundé Convention signed with African, Caribbean and Pacific (ACP) associated states

1967 The EEC, ECSC and EURATOM merge to form the European Communities (EC), with a single Council of Ministers and Commission

1968 EEC customs union completed
Implementation of CAP completed

1969 Second Yaoundé Convention signed

1970 Foreign policy co-ordination begins

1971 The Common Fisheries Policy comes into operation

1972 European Social Fund established
Norway rejects EC membership in referendum

1973 Accession of Denmark, Ireland and UK

1974 Regular heads of governments summits begin

1975 'Own resources' funding of EC budget introduced (see page 775)
First Lomé Convention signed with ACP states
UK renegotiates its terms of accession
European Regional Development Fund created

1979 European Monetary System (EMS) comes into operation (see page 776)
First direct elections to European Parliament (June)

1981 Accession of Greece

1984 Fontainebleau summit settles UK annual budget rebate and agrees first major CAP reform
European Parliament elections (June)

1985 Greenland withdraws from EC

1986 Accession of Portugal and Spain
The Single European Act (SEA) signed (see pages 776–7)
European Political Co-operation (EPC) established (see page 776)

1988 Second major CAP reform

1989 European Parliament elections (June)

1990 Accession of former East Germany

1991 11 December: The Maastricht Treaty agreed (see page 777)

1992   31 December: Single internal market programme completed
1993   September: the exchange rate mechanism (ERM) of the EMS effectively suspended
        1 November: The Maastricht Treaty enters into force, establishing the European Union (EU)
1994   1 January: European Economic Area (EEA) agreement comes into operation (*see* page 777)
        Norway rejects EU membership in referendum
1995   Accession of Austria, Finland and Sweden

ENLARGEMENT AND EXTERNAL RELATIONS

The procedure for accession to the EU is laid down in the Treaty of Rome; states have to be European and stable democracies governed by the rule of law with free market economies. When a state applies for membership, its application is studied by the Commission, which produces an opinion. If the opinion is positive, negotiations may be opened leading to an Accession Treaty which must be approved by all member state governments, the European Parliament, all member state parliaments and the applicant state's government and parliament.

Applicants: Morocco (applied 1987/rejected 1987), Turkey (applied 1987/negative opinion 1989), Cyprus (applied 1990/rejected 1993), Malta (applied 1990/negative opinion 1993), Switzerland (applied 1992/no opinion yet), Hungary (applied 1994/no opinion yet), Poland (applied 1994/no opinion yet).

Apart from the EEA Agreement (*see* page 777), the EU has three types of agreements with other European and CIS states. 'Europe' Agreements commit the EU and signatory states to long-term political and economic integration, a free trade zone (apart from agriculture and labour movement) and eventual EU membership. Government representatives from the signatory states are entitled to attend one summit and two finance and foreign council meetings a year. 'Europe' agreements have been signed with Poland and Hungary (Dec. 1991), Romania (Feb. 1993), Bulgaria (March 1993) Czech Republic and Slovak Republic (Oct. 1993), Estonia, Latvia and Lithuania (June 1995). Association agreements include a commitment to EU financial aid and to eventual membership; agreements have been signed with Malta (April 1971), Cyprus (Dec. 1972) and Turkey (Dec. 1974). Partnership and co-operation agreements are based on regulating and improving political and economic relations and mutual trade concessions but exclude any possibility of membership. Agreements have been signed with Ukraine (March 1994), Russia (June 1994), Moldova (Nov. 1994), Kyrgyzstan (Feb. 1995) and Belarus (March 1995).

THE COMMUNITY BUDGET

The principles of funding the European Community Budget were established by the Treaty of Rome and remain with modifications to this day. There is a legally binding limit on the overall level of resources (known as 'own resources') that the Community can raise from its member states; this limit is defined as a percentage of gross national product (GNP). Budget revenue and expenditure must balance and there is therefore no deficit financing. The own resources decision, which came into effect in 1975, states that there are four sources of Community funding under which each member state makes contributions: levies charged on agricultural imports into the Community; customs duties on imports from non-member states; contributions based on member states' shares of a notional Community harmonized VAT base; and contributions based on member

states' shares of Community GNP. The latter is the budget-balancing item and covers the difference between total expenditure and the revenue from the other three sources. Since 1984 the UK has had an annual rebate equivalent to 66 per cent of the difference between what the UK contributes to the budget and what it receives. This was introduced to compensate the UK for disproportionate contributions caused by its high proportion of agricultural and non-agricultural imports from non-member states and its relatively small receipts from the Common Agricultural Policy, the most important portion of Community expenditure.

BUDGET 1994

	Billion ECU*	As % of total
Agriculture	37.5	51
Regional and Social	23.4	32
Foreign Aid	4.2	6
Administration	3.9	5
Research and Development	2.6	3.5
Industry, Internal Market, Education	1.8	2.5
TOTAL	73.4	100

*1 ECU = £0.82 as at 14 September 1995

EC BUDGET BY MEMBER STATE 1993 (*billion ECU**)

	Contributions		Receipts	Net gain‡
Germany	19.42	(29.8%)	7.38	−12.04
France	11.75	(18.0%)	10.71	−1.04
Italy	10.45	(16.0%)	8.90	−1.55
UK	7.76	(11.9%)	4.58	−3.18
Spain	5.28	(8.1%)	8.41	+3.13
Netherlands	4.10	(6.3%)	2.75	−1.35
Belgium	2.44	(3.7%)	2.50	+0.06
Denmark	1.23	(1.9%)	1.61	+0.38
Greece	1.03	(1.6%)	5.24	+4.21
Portugal	0.93	(1.4%)	3.48	+2.55
Ireland	0.57	(0.9%)	2.99	+2.42
Luxembourg	0.17	(0.3%)	0.45	+0.28
Allocation n/a†	—	—	6.13	—
TOTAL	65.13	(99.9%)	65.13	—

*1 ECU = £0.82 as at 14 September 1995
† Foreign development aid and administrative expenditure not received by any single member state
‡ Net contributor (−)/net recipient (+)
Under the Edinburgh summit agreement (December 1992) the EC budget will rise in stages from 1.2 per cent of Community (Union) GNP in 1992 to 1.27 per cent in 1999

THE COMMON AGRICULTURAL POLICY

The Treaty of Rome established the Common Agricultural Policy (CAP) to increase agricultural production, provide a fair standard of living for farmers and ensure the availability of food at reasonable prices. This aim is achieved by a number of mechanisms:
– import levies (the EC sets a target price for a particular product in the Community, the world price is monitored and if it falls below the guide price, an import levy can be imposed equivalent to the difference between the two)
– intervention purchase (if the price of a product falls below the level indicated by the Council, member states must purchase supplies of the product, provided that they are of suitable quality)
– export subsidies (the EC pays a food exporter a subsidy equivalent to the difference between the price at which the product is bought in the EC and the lower sale price on the world market)

These measures had the required effect of stimulating production but also placed increasing demands on the EC budget. The increase in the number of EC members and the greater use of modern technology has further increased production and exacerbated EC budgetary problems; CAP now accounts for over 50 per cent of EC expenditure. To surmount these problems reforms were agreed in 1984, 1988 and 1992.

The 1984 reforms created the system of co-responsibility levies; farm payments to the EC by volume of product sold. This system was supplemented by national quotas for particular products, such as milk. The 1988 reforms emphasize set aside, whereby farmers are given direct grants to take land out of production as a means of reducing surpluses. Originally aimed at cereal farmers, who were allowed to set aside between 15 per cent and 100 per cent of their land, the set aside reforms were extended in 1993 for another five years and to every farm in the EC, which must set aside at least 15 per cent of their land. The 1992 reforms are based on the reduction of target prices for cereals, beef and dairy produce. These are being reduced by 29 per cent, 15 per cent and 5 per cent respectively, and the amount of money spent by the EC on the three mechanisms will fall. Production is also expected to fall because EC prices will be much closer to world price levels. Under the Uruguay round agreement of GATT concluded in December 1993, the EC must, over a six-year period from 1 January 1995, reduce its import levies by 36 per cent, reduce its domestic subsidies by 20 per cent, reduce its export subsidies by 36 per cent in value, and reduce its subsidized exports by 21 per cent in volume.

EUROPEAN POLITICAL CO-OPERATION

The framework for European political co-operation (EPC) dates from an initiative at the Hague summit in 1969. In the resultant Luxembourg Report (1970), EC foreign ministers decided to harmonize and co-ordinate their foreign policy positions and achieve common actions where possible. Although the Single European Act obliged EC members to consult each other on foreign policy and the Commission participates in deliberations, EPC is an inter-governmental system operating parallel to, but outside, the Community.

The EPC system is headed by the European Council, which provides general lines of policy. Specific policy decisions are taken by the Council of Foreign Ministers, which meets at least four times a year. The foreign minister of the state holding the EC presidency initiates action, manages EPC and represents it abroad. He is supported by a secretariat based in Brussels and is advised by the past and future holders of the presidency, forming a so-called troika. The Council of Ministers is supported by the Political Committee which meets each month, or within 48 hours if there is a crisis, to prepare for ministerial discussions. A group of correspondents, designated diplomats in each member's foreign ministry, provides day-to-day contact.

THE EUROPEAN MONETARY SYSTEM

The European monetary system (EMS) began operation on 13 March 1979 with three main purposes. The first is to establish monetary stability in Europe, initially in exchange rates between EC member state currencies, and in the longer term to be part of a wider stabilization process, overcoming inflation and budget and trade deficits. The second purpose is to overcome the constraints resulting from the interdependence of EC economies, and the third is to aid the long-term process of European monetary integration. All EC member state currencies have been members of the EMS from its beginning (the Belgian and Luxembourg francs are one single currency).

The EMS has three components: the ECU; the exchange rate mechanism (ERM); and the credit mechanisms. The ECU is a monetary unit, the value of which is calculated as a basket of set amounts of each Community currency. The relative weighting given to each currency in the ECU basket is proportional to the size of an EC member's economy and the state's share of EC trade. The German Deutsche Mark (DM) has the largest weighting of 32 per cent. The ECU is used for officially fixing the central rates in the ERM and as a means of settlement among central banks in the EMS.

The exchange rate mechanism is the central component of the EMS. Officially all member currencies of the ERM have a central rate against the ECU, the anchor of the mechanism. In practice, the Deutsche Mark has become the anchor currency, with all other currencies' central rates expressed against the DM. Central banks are obliged to maintain their currencies within set margins of their central rate (either 2.25 per cent or 6 per cent above or below) by intervening in the foreign currency markets. Currencies may be revalued or devalued by up to 10 per cent by agreement with all other ERM members.

To do this, central banks co-ordinate their actions and can use the credit mechanisms to borrow money from each other and from the Central European Monetary Co-operation Fund where they each deposit 20 per cent of their reserves. Financial assistance is available to central banks over very short-term, short-term and medium-term periods.

Five currencies (Deutsche Mark, French franc, Belgian franc, Dutch guilder, Danish krone) joined the ERM with 2.25 per cent fluctuation margins, and two currencies (Irish punt and Italian lira) with 6 per cent margins in March 1979. Subsequently the punt and lira reduced to 2.25 per cent margins. The Spanish peseta (Oct. 1989), UK pound sterling (Oct. 1990) and Portuguese escudo (April 1992) joined the ERM with 6 per cent margins. The pound and the lira were forced out of the mechanism by speculation in September 1992. Speculation forced the widening of the fluctuation margins to 15 per cent from 1 August 1993 for six of the remaining ERM member currencies (the Deutsche Mark and Dutch Guilder remain within 2.25 per cent margins). By April 1994 the French franc, Belgian franc, Irish punt, Danish krone were informally operating within 2.25 per cent fluctuation margins again. The Austrian schilling joined the ERM in January 1995, operating within 15 per cent margins.

THE SINGLE MARKET

Throughout the 1970s and early 1980s, EC members became concerned at the slow growth of the European economy. Although tariffs and quotas had been removed between member states, the EC was still separated into a number of national markets by a series of non-tariff barriers. It was to overcome these internal barriers to trade that the concept of the Single Market was developed. The measures to be undertaken were outlined in the Cockfield report (1985) and codified in the Single European Act (SEA) 1986, which came into force in 1987 with a target date of 31 December 1992 for completion.

The SEA includes articles removing obstacles that distort the internal market: the elimination of frontier controls; the mutual recognition of professional qualifications; the harmonization of product specifications, largely by the mutual recognition of national standards; open tendering for public procurement contracts; the free movement of capital; the harmonization of VAT and excise duties; and the reduction of state aid to particular industries. The SEA changed the legislative process within the EC, particularly with the introduction of qualified majority voting in the Council of Ministers for some policy areas, and the introduction of the assent procedure in the European Parliament, requiring the approval of an absolute majority of MEPs for other policy areas. The SEA also extends EC competence into the fields of technology, the environment, regional policy, monetary policy and external policy. The Single Market came into effect on 1 January 1993, at which time some 90–95 per cent of the necessary legislation had been agreed and passed by all member parliaments. The Single Market is expected to result in at least a 5 per cent increase in the collective GNP of EC member states. The full implementation of the elimination of frontier controls between member states has, however, been repeatedly delayed.

THE EUROPEAN ECONOMIC AREA (*see also* EFTA entry)

The EC Single Market programme spurred European non-member states to open negotiations with the EC on preferential access for their goods, services, labour and capital to the Single Market. Principal among these states were European Free Trade Association (EFTA) members who opened negotiations on extending the Single Market to EFTA by the formation of the European Economic Area (EEA) encompassing all 19 EC and EFTA states. Agreement was reached in May 1992 but the operation of the EEA was delayed by its rejection in a Swiss referendum, necessitating an additional protocol, agreed by the remaining 18 states. The EEA came into effect on 1 January 1994 after ratification by 17 member states (Liechtenstein joined on 1 May 1995 after adapting its customs union with Switzerland).

Austria, Finland and Sweden joined the EU itself on 1 January 1995, leaving only Norway, Iceland and Liechtenstein as the non-EU EEA members. Under the EEA agreement, the three states are to adopt the EU's *acquis communautaire*, apart from in the fields of agriculture, fisheries, and coal and steel. The EEA is controlled by regular ministerial meetings and by a joint EU–EFTA consultative committee, and will develop alongside the EU.

THE SCHENGEN AGREEMENT

Representatives from France, Germany, Belgium, Luxembourg and the Netherlands met in Schengen, Luxembourg, in June 1985 to discuss abolishing border controls between their countries and improving police co-operation. The resulting Schengen Accord committed the five states to abolishing their internal border controls and to erecting tough external frontiers against illegal immigrants, drug traffickers, terrorists and organized crime. However, implementation of the Accord was repeatedly delayed because of disagreements between the states, leading to a strengthened Schengen Agreement being signed in June 1990. Under the Agreement, a Schengen Information System (SIS) database has been established in Strasbourg which contains information on over 700,000 criminals and undesirables and is linked to the national police databases in each of the signatory states. The Agreement also requires all airports and ports in 'Schengenland' to be modified to separate internal and external arrivals and Schengen and non-Schengen nationals.

Subsequently signed by Spain and Portugal, the Agreement was ratified by the seven signatory states and entered into force on 26 March 1995 with the removal of frontier passport, customs and immigration controls. Austria joined the Agreement in April 1995, and Italy and Greece had to do so by the end of 1995. Provisional agreement was reached in June 1995 between the signatory states and the Nordic Union on a merger of the two frontier-free zones to enable Denmark, Finland and Sweden to join the Schengen Agreement in the near future.

THE MAASTRICHT TREATY

The impetus given to the EC by the Single European Act and Single Market led to further moves towards European integration. Intergovernmental conferences on political and economic and monetary union began in 1990 and culminated at the Maastricht European Council in December 1991, where a new Treaty on European Union, divided into an Economic and Monetary Union section and a Political Union section was agreed. After a long and acrimonious ratification process in the 12 member states, including its rejection in the first of two Danish referendums, the Maastricht Treaty came into force on 1 November 1993.

The Maastricht Treaty established a European Union (EU) composed of three 'pillars'. The first is the existing European Community (EC) with its established institutions and decision-making processes. The second and third 'pillars' are new and have decision-making processes based on the Council of Ministers with minimal roles for the other institutions. The second 'pillar' deals with a common foreign and security policy and is based on the European Political Co-operation framework (*see* page 776). The Maastricht Treaty enshrines moves towards common foreign and defence policies, with the WEU eventually becoming the defence component of the EU. The third 'pillar' deals with justice and interior affairs; the Council of Ministers will co-ordinate policies on asylum, immigration, conditions of entry, cross-border crime, drug trafficking and international terrorism.

A common European citizenship for the nationals of all EU member states was established by the Maastricht Treaty. The Treaty also introduced into the EC the principle of subsidiarity whereby decisions are taken at the most appropriate level: national, regional or local. The Treaty extends EC competence into the areas of environmental policy, industrial policy, consumer affairs and protection, health, and education and training. The use of qualified majority voting in the Council of Ministers is extended to cover areas which previously required a unanimous vote. The power of the European Parliament is significantly increased by the Maastricht Treaty, with greater control over the budget and the Commission. The use of the co-operation procedure is extended to new policy areas, but most importantly the Treaty establishes a new co-decision procedure whereby the European Parliament can, for the first time, override decisions of the Council of Ministers.

The Treaty lays down a timetable and criteria for Economic and Monetary Union (EMU) and an eventual single currency. Stage three of EMU, with irreversibly locked exchange rates for a majority of the EU currencies which have converged sufficiently, will begin by 31 December 1996. A European Central Bank will be established by 1 July 1998 and a single currency will be introduced by 1 January 1999. A special protocol was agreed allowing the UK to 'opt out' of a single currency if it so wishes in January 1999. Denmark also secured an 'opt out' from the single currency, European citizenship, common defence policy, and the justice and interior affairs 'pillar' in order to obtain a vote in favour of ratifying Maastricht in a second referendum. A separate protocol to the Maastricht Treaty on social policy was adopted by 11 member states but not the UK. The Maastricht Treaty is to be reviewed at a series of intergovernmental conferences in 1996–7.

THE LEGISLATIVE PROCESS

The core of the EC policymaking process is a dialogue between the Commission, which initiates and implements policy, and the Council of Ministers, which takes policy decisions. A degree of democratic control is exercised by the European Parliament.

The original legislative process is known as the consultative procedure. The Commission drafts a proposal which it submits to the Council and to the Parliament. The Council then consults the ESC and the Parliament; the Parliament may request that amendments are made. With or without these amendments, the proposal is then adopted by the Council and becomes law.

Under the Single European Act, changes were made to the legislative process, particularly in strengthening the role of the Parliament by the introduction of the co-operation procedure. The Parliament now has a second reading of proposals in some fields, and after the second reading its rejection of a proposal can only be overturned by a unanimous decision of the Council. The Maastricht Treaty extends the scope of the co-operation procedure, which now applies to Single Market laws and harmonization, trans-European networks, development policy, the social fund, and some aspects of transport, environment, research, social policy and competition policy.

The SEA introduced the assent procedure, whereby an absolute majority of the European Parliament must vote to approve laws in certain fields before they are passed. Issues covered by the assent procedure include foreign treaties, accession treaties, international agreements with budgetary implications, citizenship, residence rights, the CAP, and regional and structural funds.

The Maastricht Treaty introduced the co-decision procedure; if, after the Parliament's second reading of a proposal, the Council and Parliament fail to agree, a conciliation committee of the two will reach a compromise. If a compromise is not reached, the Parliament can reject the legislation by the vote of an absolute majority of its members. This procedure applies in the areas of education and training, health, consumer protection, culture, research frameworks, and general environment programmes.

The Council issues the following legislation:
– Regulations, which are binding in their entirety and directly applicable to all member states; they do not need to be incorporated into national law to come into effect
– Directives, which are less specific, binding as to the result to be achieved but leaving the method of implementation open to member states; a directive thus has no force until it is incorporated into national law
– Decisions, which are also binding but are addressed solely to one or more member states or individuals in a member state
– Recommendations
– Opinions, which are merely persuasive.

THE COUNCIL OF THE EUROPEAN UNION
175 rue de la Loi, 1048 Brussels, Belgium

The Council of the European Union (Council of Ministers) consists of ministers from the government of each of the member states. It formally comprises the foreign ministers of the member states but in practice the minister depends on the subject under discussion, e.g. when EC environment matters are under discussion, the meeting is informally known as the Environment Council. Council decisions are taken by qualified majority vote (in which members' votes are weighted) or by unanimity. Council meetings are prepared by the Committee of

Permanent Representatives (COREPER) of the member states, which acts as the 'gatekeeper' between national governments and the supranational EC, often negotiating on proposals with the Commission during the legislative process.

Unanimity votes are taken on issues such as taxation, budgets, foreign policy, the accession of new members, European Parliament electoral law, rights of free movement and residence, and some environment and transport policies. Qualified majority votes are taken on Single Market laws and harmonization, environment policy, health and safety, transport policy, overseas aid, research and development, culture, consumer protection, education and training, the development of a single currency and social policy. Member states have weighted votes in the Council loosely proportional to their relative population sizes (see introductory table), with a total of 87 votes. For a proposal from the Commission to pass it must receive 62 votes; 26 votes are necessary to block a proposal. For other proposals to be passed they must receive 62 votes cast by at least ten member states.

The European Council, comprising the heads of government of the member states, meets twice a year to provide overall policy direction. The presidency of the EC is held in rotation for six-month periods, setting the agenda for and chairing all Council meetings. The presidency provides the incumbent nation with an opportunity to pursue its own policy priorities. The European Council holds a summit in the country holding the presidency at the end of its period in office. The holders of the presidency for the years 1995–7 are:

1995 France, Spain
1996 Italy, Ireland
1997 Netherlands, Luxembourg

OFFICE OF THE UNITED KINGDOM PERMANENT REPRESENTATIVE TO THE EUROPEAN COMMUNITIES
Rond-point Robert Schuman 6, 1040 Brussels, Belgium
Ambassador and UK Permanent Representative, John Stephen Wall, CMG, LVO, *apptd* 1995
Minister and Deputy Permanent Representative, D. R. C. Durie

THE EUROPEAN COMMISSION
200 rue de la Loi, 1049 Brussels, Belgium

The Commission consists of 20 Commissioners, two each from France, Germany, Italy, Spain and the UK, and one each from the remaining member states. The members of the Commission are appointed for five-year renewable terms by the agreement of the member states; the present Commission came into office on 23 January 1995 and in future the five-year term will run concurrently with the term of the European Parliament. The President and Vice-Presidents are elected by the Commissioners from among their number. The Commissioners pledge sole allegiance to the EC. The Commission initiates and implements EC legislation and is the guardian of the EC treaties. It is the exponent of Community-wide interests rather than the national preoccupations of the Council. Each Commissioner is supported by advisers and oversees whichever of the 23 departments, known as Directorates-General (DGs), is assigned to him. Each Directorate-General is headed by a Director-General. The Commission has a total staff of around 20,000 civil servants.

COMMISSIONERS *as at July 1995*
President
Secretariat-General; Forward Studies Unit; Inspectorate-General;

Legal Services; Spokesman's Service; Joint Interpreting and Conference Service; Security Office; Overall responsibility for monetary matters, common foreign and security policy, institutional questions and intergovernmental conference, Jacques Santer (Luxembourg)

Vice-Presidents

External Relations with the Mediterranean, the Middle East, Latin America and parts of Asia, Manuel Marin (Spain)
External Relations with North America, Australia, Japan, New Zealand, China, South Korea, Taiwan, Hong Kong, Macao, Common Commercial Policy, Relations with the OECD and WTO, Sir Leon Brittan (UK)

Members

Industrial Affairs, Information Technology and Telecommunications, Martin Bangemann (Germany)
Immigration, Interior and Judicial Affairs, Financial Control, Anti-Fraud Measures, Relations with the Ombudsman, Anita Gradin (Sweden)
Agriculture and Rural Development, Franz Fischler (Austria)
Budget, Personnel and Administration, Translation, Erkki Liikanen (Finland)
Economic and Financial Affairs, Monetary matters, Credit and Investments, Statistical Office, Yves-Thibault de Silguy (France)
Energy and Euratom Supply Agency, Small and Medium Enterprises, Tourism, Christos Papoutis (Greece)
Institutional Questions, Intergovernmental Conference, Relations with the European Parliament, Culture and Audiovisual, Publications Office, Openness, Communications and Information, Marcelino Oreja (Spain)
Transport, Neil Kinnock (UK)

Regional Policy, Relations with the Committee of the Regions, Cohesion Fund, Monika Wulf-Mathies (Germany)
Science, Research and Development, Joint Research Centre, Human Resources, Education, Training and Youth, Edith Cresson (France)
Competition, Karel Van Miert (Belgium)
External Relations with Central and Eastern Europe, the former Soviet Union and other European states, Common Foreign and Security Policy, External Service, Hans van den Broek (Netherlands)
External Relations with African, Caribbean and Pacific states, Lomé Convention, João de Deus Pinheiro (Portugal)
Social Affairs and Employment, Relations with the Economic and Social Committee, , Padraig Flynn (Ireland)
Fisheries, Consumer Policy, EC Humanitarian Office, Emma Bonino (Italy)
Environment, Nuclear Safety, Ritt Bjerregaard (Denmark)
Internal Market, Financial Services, Customs, Taxation, Mario Monti (Italy)
Secretary-General, D. Williamson (UK)

THE EUROPEAN PARLIAMENT

The European Parliament originated as the Common Assembly of the ECSC; it acquired its present name in 1962. Members (MEPs) were initially appointed from the membership of national parliaments. Direct elections to the Parliament were first held in 1979. Elections to the Parliament are held on differing bases throughout the EC; British MEPs are elected on a first-past-the-post system, except in Northern Ireland which uses proportional

EUROPEAN PARLIAMENT POLITICAL GROUPINGS

	PES	EPP	ELDR	EUL/NGL	FE	EDA	Green	ERA	EN	Ind.	Total
Austria	8	6	1	–	–	–	1	–	–	5	21
Belgium	6	7	6	–	–	–	2	1	–	3	25
Denmark	3	3	5	1	–	–	–	–	4	–	16
Finland	4	4	6	1	–	–	1	–	–	–	16
France	15	13	1	7	–	14	–	13	13	11	87
Germany	40	47	–	–	–	–	12	–	–	–	99
Greece	10	9	–	4	–	2	–	–	–	–	25
Ireland	1	4	1	–	–	7	2	–	–	–	15
Italy	18	12	6	5	29	–	4	2	–	11	87
Luxembourg	2	2	1	–	–	–	1	–	–	–	6
Netherlands	8	10	10	–	–	–	1	–	2	–	31
Portugal	10	1	8	3	–	3	–	–	–	–	25
Spain	22	30	2	9	–	–	–	1	–	–	64
Sweden	11	6	3	1	–	–	1	–	–	–	22
UK	63	19	2	–	–	–	–	2	–	1	87
TOTAL	221	173	52	31	29	26	25	19	19	31	626

PES   Party of European Socialists (including British Labour Party, Northern Ireland Social Democratic and Labour Party, Italian Democratic Left Party) Socialist, Social Democratic and Labour parties
EPP   European People's Party (including British Conservative Party, Northern Ireland Official Unionist Party, Spanish Popular Party, French UDF, Irish Fine Gael) Christian Democrats and Conservatives
ELDR   European Liberal Democratic and Reformist Group (including British Liberal Democratic Party, Italian Northern League, Portuguese Social Democrats) centre and liberal parties
EUL/ NGL   Confederal Group of the European United Left/Nordic Green Left (French, Greek, Spanish and Portuguese Communist Parties, Italian Refounded Communist Party, some Spanish regionalists, Danish, Swedish, Finnish Green/Left parties)

FE   Forza Europa (Forza Italia Party)
EDA   European Democratic Alliance (French Gaullists, Irish Fianna Fáil, Greek Political Spring Party, Portuguese Centre Party)
Green   Green and Ecologist parties
ERA   European Radical Alliance (Scottish National Party, French Radicals of the Left, Italian Radical Party, Belgian Flemish and Spanish regionalists)
EN   Europe of the Nations Group (French Other Europe Group, Dutch and Danish Euro-sceptics)
Ind   Independents (Italian National Alliance, French National Front, Belgian Vlaams Blok, Northern Ireland Democratic Unionist Party)

representation. The latest elections were held in June 1994, when the Parliament expanded to 567 seats from the previous 518 to include representatives from the former East Germany and concurrent increases in other member states' representatives. It expanded to 626 seats on 1 January 1995 with the accession of Austria, Finland and Sweden to the EU. Their MEPs are designated representatives who will hold their seats until elections are held by January 1997. For total number of seats per member and political groupings, see table on page 779. MEPs serve on 20 committees, which scrutinize draft EC legislation and the activities of the Commission. Plenary sessions are held in Strasbourg, committees meet in Brussels and the Secretariat's headquarters is in Luxembourg.

The EP has gradually expanded its influence within the EC through the Single European Act, which introduced the co-operation procedure, and the Maastricht Treaty, which extended the co-operation procedure and introduced the co-decision procedure (see Legislative Process). It has general powers of supervision over the Commission, and consultation and co-decision with the Council; it votes to approve a newly appointed Commission and can dismiss it at any time by a two-thirds majority. Under the Maastricht Treaty it has the right to be consulted on the appointment of the new Commission and can veto its appointment. It can reject the EC budget as a whole, alter non-compulsory expenditure not specified in the EC primary legislation, and can question the Commission's management of the budget and call in the Court of Auditors. Although the EP cannot directly initiate legislation, its reports can spur the Commission into action. Under the Maastricht Treaty the EP is to appoint an Ombudsman to provide citizens with redress against maladministration by EU institutions.

The Parliament's organization is deliberately biased in favour of multi-national political groupings, recognition of a political grouping in the parliament entitling it to offices, funding, representation on committees and influence in debates and legislation. A political grouping with members from only one country needs a minimum of 29 members for recognition, whereas one with members from two countries needs 23 members, a grouping with members from three countries needs 18 members, and a grouping with members from four or more countries needs only 14 members.

PARLIAMENT, Palais de l'Europe, 67006 Strasbourg Cedex, France; 97–113 rue Belliard, 1040 Brussels, Belgium
SECRETARIAT, Centre Européen, Kirchberg, 2929 Luxembourg
President, Klaus Hänsch (Germany)
(For a full list of British MEPs, see pages 272–3)

THE ECONOMIC AND SOCIAL COMMITTEE
2 rue Ravenstein, 1000 Brussels, Belgium

The Economic and Social Committee is an advisory and consultative body. The ESC has 222 members, who are nominated by member states. It is divided into three groups: employers, workers, and other interest groups such as consumers, farmers and the self-employed. It issues opinions on draft EC legislation and can bring matters to the attention of the Commission, Council and Parliament; it has a key role in providing specialist and technical input.
President, Carlos Ferrer (Spain)

THE COURT OF AUDITORS
12 rue A. De Gasperi, L-1615 Luxembourg

The Court of Auditors, established in 1977, is responsible for the audit of the legality and regularity as well as of the sound financial management of the resources managed by the European Communities and Community bodies. The Court may also submit observations on specific questions and deliver opinions. The Court draws up an annual report and a statement of assurance on the accounts and underlying operations of the Communities. The Maastricht Treaty designated the Court as a full institution of the European Union, enabling it to take other institutions to the Court of Justice. It has 15 members appointed for six-year terms by the Council of Ministers following consultation with the European Parliament.
President, André Middelhoek (Netherlands)

COURT OF JUSTICE OF THE EUROPEAN COMMUNITIES
L–2925 Luxembourg

The European Court superseded the Court of Justice of the ECSC and is common to the three European Communities. It exists to safeguard the law in the interpretation and application of the Community treaties, to decide on the legality of decisions of the Council of Ministers or the Commission, and to determine violations of the treaties. Cases may be brought to it by the member states, the Community institutions, firms or individuals. Its decisions are directly binding in the member countries, and the Maastricht Treaty enhanced the Court's powers by permitting it to impose fines on member states. The 15 judges and eight advocates-general of the Court are appointed for renewable six-year terms by the member governments in concert. During 1994, 354 new cases were lodged at the court and 188 judgments were delivered.

Composition of the Court, in order of precedence, with effect from 25 January 1995:
G. C. Rodriguez Iglesias (*President*); F. A. Schockweiler (*President of the 2nd and 6th Chambers*); F. G. Jacobs (*First Advocate-General*); P. J. G. Kapteyn (*President of the 4th Chamber*); M. C. Gulmann (*President of the 3rd and 5th Chambers*); P. Jann (*President of the 1st Chamber*); G. F. Mancini; C. N. Kakouris; C. O. Lenz (*Advocate-General*); J. C. Moitinho De Almeida; G. Tesauro (*Advocate-General*); J. L. Murray; D. A. O. Edward; A. M. La Pergola (*Advocate-General*); M. G. Cosmas (*Advocate-General*); J. P. Puissochet; M. P. Leger (*Advocate-General*); G. Hirsch; M. B. Elmer (*Advocate-General*); H. Ragnemalm; L. Sevón; N. Fennelly (*Advocate-General*); D. Ruiz-Jarabo Colomer (*Advocate-General*); R. Grass (*Registrar*)

COURT OF FIRST INSTANCE
L-2925 Luxembourg

Established under powers conferred by the Single European Act, the Court of First Instance started to exercise its functions at the end of October 1989. It had jurisdiction to hear and determine certain categories of cases brought by natural or legal persons, in particular cases brought by European Community officials, or cases on competition law. By a Council decision of 1993 the court had its jurisdiction enlarged to hear and determine all actions brought by natural or legal persons. During 1994, 409 new cases were lodged at the court and 60 judgments were delivered.

Composition of the Court, in order of precedence, for the judicial year 1994–5:
J. L. Cruz Vilaca (*President of the Court and of the 1st Chamber*); B. Vesterdorf (*President of the 2nd Chamber*); J. Biancarelli (*President of the 3rd Chamber*); K. Lenaerts (*President of the 4th Chamber*); D. P. M. Barrington; A. Saggío; H. Kirschner; R. Schintgen; C. P. Briët; R. García-Valdecasas y Fernandez; C. W. Bellamy; A. Kalogeropoulos; V. Tiili; P. Lindh; J. Azizi; H. Jung (*Registrar*)

THE EUROPEAN INVESTMENT BANK
100 Boulevard Konrad Adenauer, L-2950 Luxembourg

The European Investment Bank (EIB) was set up in 1958 under the terms of the Treaty of Rome to finance capital investment projects promoting the balanced development of the European Community.

It grants long-term loans to private and public enterprises, public authorities and financial institutions, to finance projects which further the economic development of less advanced regions (Assisted Areas); improvement of European communications; environmental protection; attainment of the Community's energy policy objectives; modernization of enterprises, co-operation between undertakings in the different member states, and the activities of small and medium-sized enterprises.

EIB activities have also been extended outside member countries as part of the Community's development co-operation policy, under the terms of different association or co-operation agreements with 12 countries in the Mediterranean region, six in central and eastern Europe, 30 in Latin America and Asia, and, under the Lomé Conventions, 70 in Africa, the Caribbean and the Pacific. The Bank has also been asked to extend its activity to Albania, Estonia, Latvia, Lithuania, Slovenia and South Africa.

The Bank's total financing operations in 1994 amounted to 19,928 million ECU, of which 17,682 million was for investment in the European Community and 2,246 million for investment outside the Community. Between 1990 and 1994 the EIB made available a total of £8,060 million for investment in the UK.

The members of the European Investment Bank are the 15 member states of the European Union, who have all subscribed to the Bank's capital of 62,013 million ECU. The bulk of the funds required by the Bank to carry out its tasks are borrowed on the capital markets of the Community and non-member countries, and on the international market.

As it operates on a non-profit-making basis, the interest rates charged by the EIB reflect the cost of the Bank's borrowings and closely follow conditions on world capital markets.

The Board of Governors of the European Investment Bank consists of one government minister nominated by each of the member countries, usually the finance minister, who lay down general directives on the policy of the Bank and appoint members to the Board of Directors (24 nominated by the member states, one by the European Commission), which takes decisions on the granting and raising of loans and the fixing of interest rates. A Management Committee, composed of the Bank's President and six Vice-Presidents, also appointed by the Board of Governors, is responsible for the day-to-day operations of the Bank. The President and Vice-Presidents also preside as Chairman and Vice-Chairmen at meetings of the Board of Directors.
President, Sir Brian Unwin, KCB

Vice-Presidents, Wolfgang Roth; Panagiotis-Loukas Gennimatas; Massimo Ponzellini; Louis Martí; Ariane Obolensky; Rudolf de Korte
UK OFFICE: 68 Pall Mall, London SW1Y 5ES. Tel: 0171-343 1200

NEW INSTITUTIONS AND AGENCIES

The Maastricht Treaty, together with the 1993 Brussels Council summit, established a number of new institutions and agencies:

THE COMMITTEE OF THE REGIONS
2 rue Ravenstein, 1000 Brussels, Belgium
The Committee of the Regions is an advisory and consultative body established under the Maastricht Treaty to redress the lack of a role for regional and local authorities in the EU democratic system. The COR is composed of 220 appointed and indirectly elected members, of whom half are from large regions and half are from small local authorities. It delivers opinions on policies affecting regions, such as trans-border transport links, economic and social cohesion, education and training, social policy, culture and regional policy.
President, Jacques Blanc (France)

THE EUROPEAN MONETARY INSTITUTE
29 Kaiserstrasse, 60311 Frankfurt-am-Main, Germany
The European Monetary Institute was established under the Maastricht Treaty to co-ordinate member states' monetary policy during stage II of economic and monetary union (EMU), which began on 1 January 1994; to oversee preparation for a transfer to a single currency; and to create the right conditions for the third and final stage of EMU. The EMI consists of the governors of the central banks of the 15 EU member states, who form the EMI Council, and support staff. The council meets monthly to assess how well member governments are meeting the criteria laid down by the Maastricht Treaty for achieving economic convergence.
President, Baron Alexandre Lamfalussy (Belgium)

THE EUROPEAN DRUGS AGENCY (EUROPOL)
Raamweg 47, 2596HN The Hague, The Netherlands
The European Drugs Agency (EUROPOL) was established under the Maastricht Treaty as an information clearing house engaged in surveillance of drug trafficking. It is staffed by 80 personnel seconded from member states' police, gendarmeries and customs forces, housed in 15 national liaison offices linked to their respective national police computers; the working language is English. Its remit has been expanded from co-ordinating cross-border drug-trafficking investigations to include combating illegal immigration rackets, trade in nuclear materials, cross-border car theft and any associated money laundering. EUROPOL has no legal powers of its own and can only operate through member states' police and customs forces. At present it operates on an *ad hoc* basis as its convention has yet to be agreed and ratified by the member states.
Co-ordinator, Juergen Storbeck (Germany)

Other bodies include:
THE EUROPEAN MEDICINE EVALUATION AGENCY, London
THE EUROPEAN TRADEMARK OFFICE, Alicante
THE EUROPEAN AGENCY FOR HEALTH AND SAFETY AT WORK, Bilbao
THE EUROPEAN OFFICE FOR VETERINARY AND PLANT HEALTH INSPECTION, Dublin

The European Drugs Observatory, Lisbon
The European Foundation for Training, Turin
The European Centre for the Development of
  Vocational Training, Salonika
The European Environment Agency, Copenhagen
The European Translation Agency, Luxembourg

EUROPEAN COMMUNITY INFORMATION

The European Commission maintains representative offices in:

England, 8 Storey's Gate, London swip 3at. Tel: 0171-973 1992

Scotland, 9 Alva Street, Edinburgh eh2 4hp. Tel: 0131-225 2058

Wales, 4 Cathedral Road, Cardiff cf1 9sg. Tel: 01222-371631

Northern Ireland, Windsor House, 9–15 Bedford Street, Belfast bt2 7eg. Tel: 01232-240708

Republic of Ireland, 39 Molesworth Street, Dublin 2

USA, 2100 M Street NW (Suite 707), Washington dc 20037; 1 Dag Hammarskjöld Plaza, 254 East 47th Street, New York, ny 10017

Canada, Inn of the Provinces, Office Tower (Suite 1110), 350 Sparks Street, Ottawa, Ontario, kir 7sa

Australia, 18 Alakana Street, Yarralumia, act 2600, and a number of other cities

UK European Parliament Information Office
2 Queen Anne's Gate, London swih 9aa. Tel: 0171-222 0411

There are European Information Centres, set up to give information and advice to small businesses, in 24 British towns and cities. A number of universities maintain European Documentation Centres.

Countries of the World

WORLD AREA AND POPULATION

The total population of the world in mid-1990 was estimated at 5,292 million, compared with 3,019 million in 1960 and 2,070 million in 1930.

Continent, etc.	Area sq. miles '000	sq. km '000	Estimated population mid-1990
Africa	11,704	30,313	642,000,000
North America[1]	8,311	21,525	276,000,000
Latin America[2]	7,933	20,547	448,000,000
Asia[3]	10,637	27,549	3,113,000,000
Europe[4]	1,915	4,961	498,000,000
Former USSR	8,649	22,402	289,000,000
Oceania[5]	3,286	8,510	26,500,000
TOTAL	52,435	135,807	5,292,000,000

[1] Includes Greenland and Hawaii
[2] Mexico and the remainder of the Americas south of the USA
[3] Includes European Turkey, excludes former USSR
[4] Excludes European Turkey and former USSR
[5] Includes Australia, New Zealand and the islands inhabited by Micronesian, Melanesian and Polynesian peoples
Source: UN Demographic Yearbook 1990 (pub. 1992)

A United Nations report *The Sex and Age Distribution of the World Populations* (revised 1994) puts the world's population in the late 20th and the 21st centuries at the following levels (medium variant data):

1995	5,716.4m	2030	8,670.6m
2000	6,158.0m	2040	9,318.2m
2010	7,032.3m	2050	9,833.2m
2020	7,887.8m		

The population by continents as forecast for the years 2000 and 2050 were:

Continent	Estimated population (million) 2000	2050
Africa	831.596	2,140.844
North America[1]	306.280	388.997
Latin America[2]	523.875	838.527
Asia	3,753.846	5,741.005
Europe	729.803	677.764
Oceania	30.651	46.070
TOTAL	6,158.051	9,833.207

[1] Includes Bermuda, Greenland, and St Pierre and Miquelon
[2] Mexico and the remainder of the Americas south of the USA

AREA AND POPULATION BY CONTINENT

No complete survey of many countries has yet been achieved and consequently accurate area figures are not always available. Similarly, many countries have not recently, or have never, taken a census. The areas of countries given below are derived from estimated figures published by the United Nations. The conversion factors used are:
(i) to convert square miles to square km, multiply by 2.589988
(ii) to convert square km to square miles, multiply by 0.3861022
Population figures for countries are derived from the most recent estimates available. Accurate and up-to-date data for the populations of capital cities are scarce, and definitions of cities' extent differ. The figures given below are the latest estimates available, and where it is known that the figure applies to an urban agglomeration this is indicated.

* latest census figure
Ψ seaport
u.a. urban agglomeration

AFRICA

COUNTRY/TERRITORY	AREA sq. miles	sq. km	POPULATION	CAPITAL	POPULATION OF CAPITAL
Algeria	919,595	2,381,741	26,346,000	Ψ Algiers	3,250,000
Angola	481,354	1,246,700	10,609,000	Ψ Luanda	3,000,000
Benin	43,484	112,622	5,047,000	Ψ Porto Novo	208,258
Botswana	224,607	581,730	1,326,796	Gaborone	133,458
Burkina	105,869	274,200	9,490,000	Ouagadougou	441,514
Burundi	10,747	27,834	5,786,000	Bujumbura	235,440
Cameroon	183,569	475,442	12,198,000	Yaoundé	635,670
Cape Verde Islands	1,557	4,033	384,000	Ψ Praia	57,748*
Central African Republic	240,535	622,984	3,173,000	Bangui	473,817
Chad	495,755	1,284,000	5,961,000	Ndjaména	402,000
Comoros	838	2,171	585,000	Moroni	17,267*
Congo	132,047	342,000	2,368,000	Brazzaville	596,200*
Côte d'Ivoire	124,503	322,463	12,190,000	Yamoussoukro	106,786
Djibouti	8,494	22,000	520,000	Ψ Djibouti	340,700
Egypt	386,662	1,001,449	57,850,000	Cairo	13,000,000
Equatorial Guinea	10,830	28,051	369,000	Ψ Malabo	30,418
Eritrea	36,170	93,679	3,500,000	Asmara	275,000
Ethiopia	471,778	1,221,900	51,617,000	Addis Ababa	3,500,000
Gabon	103,347	267,667	1,237,000	Ψ Libreville	251,000
Gambia	4,361	11,295	908,000	Ψ Banjul (*u.a.*)	109,986

Country/Territory	Area sq. miles	sq. km	Population	Capital	Population of Capital
Ghana	92,100	238,537	15,959,000	Ψ Accra (u.a.)	1,781,100
Guinea	94,926	245,857	6,116,000	Ψ Conakry	763,000
Guinea-Bissau	13,948	36,125	1,006,000	Ψ Bissau	109,214*
Kenya	224,961	582,646	25,700,000	Nairobi	1,400,000
Lesotho	11,720	30,355	1,836,000	Maseru	288,951*
Liberia	43,000	111,369	2,580,000	Ψ Monrovia	425,000
Libya	679,362	1,759,540	4,875,000	Ψ Tripoli	1,000,000
Madagascar	226,669	587,041	12,827,000	Antananarivo	1,250,000
Malawi	45,747	118,484	8,823,000	Lilongwe	233,973*
Mali	478,791	1,240,000	9,818,000	Bamako	658,275
Mauritania	397,955	1,030,700	2,143,000	Nouakchott	850,000
Mauritius	790	2,045	1,082,998	Ψ Port Louis	144,250
Mayotte (Fr.)	144	372	94,410	Mamoundzou	12,000
Morocco	172,414	446,550	27,575,000	Ψ Rabat	1,494,000
Western Sahara	102,703	266,000	183,000	Laayoune	96,784*
Mozambique	309,495	801,590	14,872,000	Ψ Maputo	1,150,000
Namibia	318,261	824,292	1,534,000	Windhoek	110,000
Niger	489,191	1,267,080	8,252,000	Niamey	410,000
Nigeria	356,669	923,768	115,664,000	Abuja	378,671
Réunion (Fr.)	969	2,510	617,000	St Denis	122,000
Rwanda	10,169	26,338	7,526,000	Kigali	156,000
St Helena (UK)	47	122	5,644	Ψ Jamestown	1,332
Ascension Island	34	88	1,110	Ψ Georgetown	—
Tristan da Cunha	38	98	295	Ψ Edinburgh	—
São Tomé and Príncipe	372	964	124,000	Ψ São Tomé	25,000
Senegal	75,750	196,192	7,736,000	Ψ Dakar	1,000,000
Seychelles	108	280	72,000	Ψ Victoria	24,324
Sierra Leone	27,699	71,740	4,376,000	Ψ Freetown	470,000
Somalia	246,201	637,657	9,204,000	Ψ Mogadishu	1,000,000
South Africa	471,445	1,221,031	40,049,000	Pretoria (u.a.)	822,925
				Ψ Cape Town (u.a.)	1,911,521
Sudan	967,500	2,505,813	26,656,000	Khartoum (u.a.)	3,000,000
Swaziland	6,704	17,363	792,000	Mbabane	38,290
Tanzania	364,900	945,087	28,359,000	Dodoma	88,474
Togo	21,925	56,785	3,763,000	Ψ Lomé	366,476
Tunisia	63,170	163,610	8,401,000	Ψ Tunis	1,394,749
Uganda	91,259	236,036	18,674,000	Kampala (u.a.)	750,000
Zaire	905,567	2,345,409	39,882,000	Kinshasa	2,778,281*
Zambia	290,586	752,614	8,638,000	Lusaka (u.a.)	1,000,000
Zimbabwe	150,804	390,580	10,583,000	Harare	681,000

AMERICA

North America

Canada	3,849,646	9,970,537	29,248,100	Ottawa (u.a.)	313,987*
Greenland (Den.)	840,004	2,175,600	55,117	Ψ Godthåb	8,425
Mexico	761,605	1,972,547	89,538,000	Mexico City (u.a.)	14,987,051
St Pierre and Miquelon (Fr.)	93	242	6,300	Ψ St Pierre	—
United States	3,787,318	9,809,108	259,681,000	Washington DC	585,221

Central America and the West Indies

Anguilla (UK)	35	91	8,800*	The Valley	1,400
Antigua and Barbuda	170	440	65,962	Ψ St John's	30,000
Aruba (Neth.)	75	193	59,000	Ψ Oranjestad	25,000
Bahamas	5,380	13,935	262,000	Ψ Nassau	171,000*
Barbados	166	431	259,000	Ψ Bridgetown	7,466
Belize	8,867	22,965	205,000	Belmopan	3,739
Bermuda (UK)	20	53	60,075	Ψ Hamilton	2,277
Cayman Islands (UK)	100	259	31,200	Ψ George Town	15,000
Costa Rica	19,575	50,700	3,194,000	San José (u.a.)	296,625
Cuba	42,804	110,861	10,811,000	Ψ Havana	2,119,000
Dominica	290	751	72,000	Ψ Roseau	15,850
Dominican Republic	18,816	48,734	7,459,000	Ψ Santo Domingom (u.a.)	1,313,172*
Grenada	133	344	95,000	Ψ St George's	10,000
Guadeloupe (Fr.)	687	1,779	408,000	Ψ Basse-Terre	14,000

Country/Territory	Area sq. miles	sq. km	Population	Capital	Population of Capital
Guatemala	42,042	108,889	9,745,000	Guatemala City	1,675,589
Haiti	10,714	27,750	6,764,000	Ψ Port au Prince	1,000,000
Honduras	43,277	112,088	4,915,900	Tegucigalpa	670,100
Jamaica	4,244	10,991	2,460,700	Ψ Kingston (u.a.)	696,300
Martinique (Fr.)	425	1,102	371,000	Ψ Fort de France	101,540
Montserrat (UK)	38	98	11,000	Ψ Plymouth	2,500
Netherlands Antilles (Neth.)	371	961	197,000	Ψ Willemstad	50,000
Nicaragua	50,193	130,000	4,131,000	Managua	615,000
Panama	29,762	77,082	2,631,013	Ψ Panama City	1,063,565
Puerto Rico (USA)	3,435	8,897	3,336,000	Ψ San Juan (u.a.)	437,745
St Christopher and Nevis	101	261	42,000	Ψ Basseterre	15,000
St Lucia	238	616	137,000	Ψ Castries	56,000
St Vincent and the Grenadines	150	388	117,000	Ψ Kingstown	33,694
El Salvador	8,124	21,041	5,376,000	San Salvador	497,644
Trinidad and Tobago	1,981	5,130	1,239,908	Ψ Port of Spain	50,878
Turks and Caicos Is. (UK)	166	430	14,000	Ψ Grand Turk	4,000
Virgin Islands:					
British (UK)	59	153	16,108*	Ψ Road Town	3,983*
US (USA)	132	342	101,809	Ψ Charlotte Amalie	11,756
South America					
Argentina	1,068,302	2,766,889	32,370,298*	Ψ Buenos Aires	2,960,976
Bolivia	424,165	1,098,581	6,440,000*	La Paz	1,115,000*
Brazil	3,286,488	8,511,965	156,275,000	Brasilia	1,596,274
Chile	292,258	756,945	13,599,000	Santiago	5,443,000
Colombia	439,737	1,138,914	33,392,000	Bogotá	5,000,000
Ecuador	109,484	283,561	10,741,000	Quito	1,387,887
Falkland Islands (UK)	4,700	12,173	2,121	Ψ Stanley	1,643
French Guiana (Fr.)	35,135	91,000	131,000	Ψ Cayenne	41,000
Guyana	83,000	214,969	808,000	Ψ Georgetown	187,056
Paraguay	157,048	406,752	4,519,000	Asunción (u.a.)	729,307
Peru	496,225	1,285,216	22,465,000	Lima (u.a.)	6,483,901
South Georgia (UK)	1,580	4,092	—	—	—
Suriname	63,037	163,265	438,000	Ψ Paramaribo (u.a.)	182,100
Uruguay	68,037	176,215	3,116,802	Ψ Montevideo	1,383,660
Venezuela	352,144	912,050	20,249,000	Caracas (u.a.)	2,784,000

ASIA

Country/Territory	Area sq. miles	sq. km	Population	Capital	Population of Capital
Afghanistan	250,000	647,497	19,062,000	Kabul	2,000,000
Bahrain	240	622	533,000	Ψ Manama	108,684*
Bangladesh	55,598	143,998	108,000,000	Dhaka	6,537,308
Bhutan	18,147	47,000	650,000	Thimphu	15,000
Brunei	2,226	5,765	260,863	Bandar Seri Begawan	46,229
Cambodia	69,898	181,035	9,054,000	Ψ Phnom Penh	920,000
China[1]	3,705,408	9,596,961	1,200,000,000	Beijing (Peking) (u.a.)	10,860,000
Hong Kong (UK)	416	1,074	6,150,0000	—	—
India	1,269,346	3,287,590	846,302,688	Delhi	8,375,188
Indonesia	735,358	1,904,569	191,170,000	Ψ Jakarta	7,885,519
Iran	636,296	1,648,000	66,000,000	Tehran	6,042,584
Iraq	167,925	434,924	19,290,000	Baghdad	3,841,286
Israel[2]	8,019	20,770	5,090,000	Tel Aviv	1,781,500
West Bank and Gaza Strip	2,406	6,231	1,635,000	Gaza City	120,000
Japan	145,834	377,708	124,764,215	Tokyo (u.a.)	11,935,700
Jordan	37,738	97,740	4,095,579	Amman	1,270,000
Kazakhstan	1,049,155	2,716,626	16,963,600	Alma-Ata	1,500,000
Korea, DPR (North)	46,540	120,538	22,618,000	Pyongyang	2,000,000
Korea, Rep. of (South)	38,025	98,484	43,663,000	Seoul	10,920,000
Kuwait	6,880	17,818	1,000,000	Ψ Kuwait (city)	400,000
Kyrgyzstan	76,642	198,501	4,500,000	Biskek	616,000
Laos	91,429	231,800	4,469,000	Vientiane	120,000
Lebanon	4,015	10,400	2,838,000	Ψ Beirut	1,500,000
Macao (Port.)	6	16	374,000	Ψ Macao	—
Malaysia	127,317	329,749	19,959,000	Kuala Lumpur	1,231,500
Maldives	115	298	246,000	Ψ Malé	46,334
Mongolia	604,250	1,565,000	2,156,000	Ulan Bator	600,500

Country/Territory	Area sq. miles	sq. km	Population	Capital	Population of Capital
Myanmar (Burma)	261,218	676,552	43,668,000	Ψ Yangon (Rangoon) (u.a.)	3,973,872
Nepal	54,342	140,747	20,577,000	Kathmandu	300,000
Oman	82,030	212,457	2,000,000	Ψ Muscat	400,000
Pakistan	341,026	883,254	119,107,000	Islamabad (u.a.)	350,000
Philippines	115,831	300,000	64,259,000	Ψ Manila	1,876,195
Qatar	4,247	11,000	453,000	Ψ Doha	220,000
Saudi Arabia	830,000	2,149,640	16,929,294	Riyadh	2,000,000
Singapore	247	639	2,873,800	—	—
Sri Lanka	25,332	65,610	17,619,000	Ψ Colombo	2,026,000
Syria	71,498	185,180	12,958,000	Damascus	1,451,000
Tajikistan	55,251	143,100	5,513,400	Dushanbe	595,000
Taiwan	13,800	35,742	20,894,522	Taipei	2,719,659
Thailand	198,457	514,000	58,336,072	Ψ Bangkok	5,572,712
Turkey[3]	301,382	780,576	58,775,000	Ankara	3,236,626
Turkmenistan	188,456	488,100	3,808,900	Ashkhabad	407,000
United Arab Emirates	32,278	83,600	2,310,000	Abu Dhabi	450,000
Uzbekistan	172,742	447,229	21,206,800	Tashkent	2,073,000
Vietnam	127,242	329,556	71,267,000	Hanoi	2,150,000
Yemen	203,850	527,696	15,800,000	Sana'a	972,000

[1] Including Tibet
[2] Including East Jerusalem, the Golan Heights and Israeli citizens on the West Bank
[3] Including Turkey in Europe

EUROPE

Albania	11,099	28,748	3,363,000	Tirana	244,153
Andorra	180	468	64,311	Andorra La Vella	22,387
Armenia	11,306	29,271	3,645,000	Erevan	1,254,000
Austria	32,374	83,849	8,015,000	Vienna	1,539,848*
Azerbaijan	33,436	86,565	7,409,900	Baku	1,149,000
Belarus	80,300	207,897	10,280,000	Minsk	1,589,000
Belgium	11,781	30,513	10,068,319	Brussels (u.a.)	950,339
Bosnia–Hercegovina	19,735	51,129	4,400,000	Sarajevo	453,324
Bulgaria	42,823	110,912	8,963,000	Sofia	1,114,925
Croatia	21,823	56,538	4,760,344	Zagreb	950,000
Cyprus	3,572	9,251	725,000	Nicosia	181,000
Czech Republic	30,372	78,664	10,302,000	Prague	1,215,076
Denmark	16,629	43,069	5,180,614	Ψ Copenhagen (u.a.)	1,339,395
Faroe Islands	540	1,399	47,287	Ψ Tórshavn	10,726
Estonia	17,413	45,082	1,526,177	Talinn	452,840
Finland	130,500	338,000	5,078,000	Ψ Helsinki	508,600
France	211,208	547,026	57,218,000	Paris (u.a.)	9,318,800
Georgia	26,911	69,673	5,401,000	Tbilisi	1,211,000
Germany	137,738	365,755	81,075,000	Berlin	3,454,200
Gibraltar (UK)	2	6	28,051	Ψ Gibraltar	—
Greece	50,944	131,944	10,256,464	Athens (u.a.)	3,096,775
Hungary	35,919	93,030	10,278,000	Budapest	2,004,000
Iceland	39,768	103,000	266,786	Ψ Reykjavik (u.a.)	103,036
Ireland, Republic of	27,136	70,283	3,525,719	Ψ Dublin	478,389
Italy	116,304	301,225	56,777,000	Rome (u.a.)	2,693,383
Latvia	24,695	63,935	2,529,600	Riga	840,000
Liechtenstein	61	157	30,310	Vaduz	5,072
Lithuania	26,173	67,761	3,724,000	Vilnius	579,000
Luxembourg	998	2,586	395,200	Luxembourg	75,800
Macedonia	9,925	25,713	1,936,877	Skopje	448,229
Malta	122	316	369,845	Ψ Valletta	9,149
Moldova	13,912	36,018	4,359,000	Kishinev	665,000
Monaco	0.4	1	29,972	Monaco-Ville	1,151
Netherlands	15,770	40,844	15,240,000	Ψ Amsterdam (u.a.)	1,034,562
Norway[1]	125,181	324,219	4,324,815	Ψ Oslo	477,515
Poland	120,725	312,677	38,300,000	Warsaw	1,655,063
Portugal[2]	35,553	92,082	9,862,700	Ψ Lisbon	2,128,000
Romania	91,699	237,500	22,760,449	Bucharest	2,064,474
Russia[3]	6,593,391	17,070,289	148,300,000	Moscow	8,700,000
San Marino	23	61	24,801	San Marino	—

Country/Territory	Area sq. miles	sq. km	Population	Capital	Population of Capital
Slovak Republic	18,932	49,035	5,336,455	Bratislava	448,785
Slovenia	7,816	20,251	1,989,477	Ljubljana	269,972
Spain[4]	194,897	504,782	38,872,268	Madrid (u.a.)	4,947,555
Sweden	173,732	449,964	8,745,109	Ψ Stockholm (u.a.)	1,532,803
Switzerland	15,943	41,293	6,907,959	Berne	135,600
Ukraine	233,090	603,700	52,100,000	Kiev	2,577,000
United Kingdom[5]	94,248	244,101	58,191,000	Ψ London (u.a.)	6,934,500
England	50,351	130,410	48,533,000	—	—
Wales	8,015	20,758	2,906,000	Ψ Cardiff	298,700
Scotland	30,420	78,789	5,120,000	Ψ Edinburgh	443,600
Northern Ireland	5,461	14,144	1,632,000	Ψ Belfast (u.a.)	287,200
Vatican City State	0.2	0.44	1,000	Vatican City	—
Yugoslavia, Fed. Rep. of	39,506	102,350	10,410,000	Belgrade	1,455,000

[1] Excludes Svalbard and Jan Mayen Islands (approx. 24,101 sq. miles (62,422 sq. km) and 3,000 population)
[2] Includes Madeira (314 sq. miles) and the Azores (922 sq. miles)
[3] Includes Russia in Asia
[4] Includes Balearic Islands, Canary Islands, Ceuta and Melilla
[5] Excludes Isle of Man (221 sq. miles (572 sq. km), 69,788* population), and Channel Islands (75 sq. miles (194 sq. km), 142,949* population)

OCEANIA

	Area sq. miles	sq. km	Population	Capital	Population of Capital
Australia	2,967,909	7,686,848	17,938,500	Canberra	328,000
Norfolk Island	14	36	1,912	Ψ Kingston	—
Fiji	7,055	18,274	746,000	Ψ Suva	69,665
French Polynesia (Fr.)	1,544	4,000	204,000	Ψ Papeete	24,200
Guam (USA)	212	549	132,152	Agaña	—
Kiribati	281	728	74,000	Tarawa	17,921
Marshall Islands	70	181	50,000	Majuro	20,000
Micronesia, Fed. States of	271	701	110,000	Palikir	—
Nauru	8	21	10,000	Ψ Nauru	—
New Caledonia (Fr.)	7,358	19,058	175,000	Ψ Noumea	65,000
New Zealand	103,736	268,676	3,494,300	Ψ Wellington (u.a.)	329,000
Cook Islands	91	236	18,300	Avarua	—
Niue	100	259	2,239	Alofi	—
Ross Dependency[1]	286,696	750,310	—	—	—
Tokelau	5	12.9	1,700	—	—
Northern Mariana Islands (USA)	184	476	43,555	Saipan	39,090
Palau (USA)	192	497	15,122	Koror	10,493
Papua New Guinea	178,260	461,691	3,847,000	Ψ Port Moresby	173,500
Pitcairn Islands (UK)	1.9	5	54	—	—
Samoa, Eastern (USA)	76	197	46,773	Ψ Pago Pago	3,075
Solomon Islands	10,983	28,446	328,723	Ψ Honiara	40,000
Tonga	270	699	97,000	Ψ Nuku'alofa	30,000
Tuvalu	10	25	12,000	Ψ Funafuti	2,856
Vanuatu	4,706	12,190	159,800	Ψ Port Vila	26,100
Wallis and Futuna Islands (Fr.)	106	274	13,705	Ψ Mata-Utu	—
Western Samoa	1,097	2,842	158,000	Ψ Apia	36,000

[1] Includes permanent shelf ice

THE ANTARCTIC

The Antarctic is generally defined as the area lying within the Antarctic Convergence, the zone where cold northward-flowing Antarctic sea water sinks below warmer southward-flowing water. This zone is at about latitude 50° S. in the Atlantic Ocean and latitude 55°–62° S. in the Pacific Ocean. The continent itself lies almost entirely within the Antarctic Circle, an area of about 14.25 million sq. km (5.5 million sq. miles), 99 per cent of which is permanently ice-covered. The average thickness of the ice is 2,450 m (7,100 ft) but in places exceeds 4,500 m (14,500 ft). Some mountains protrude, the highest being Vinson Massif, 4,897 m (16,067 ft). The ice amounts to some 30 million cubic km (7.2 million cubic miles) and represents more than 90 per cent of the world's fresh water.

Along one-third of the Antarctic coastline, land-ice flowing outwards forms extensive ice shelves, fragments of which break off to form tabular icebergs, leaving ice-cliffs up to 50 m (150 ft) high. Much of the sea freezes in winter, forming fast ice which breaks up in summer and drifts north as pack ice.

The most conspicuous physical features of the continent are its high inland plateau (much of it over 3,000 m (10,000 ft)), the Transantarctic Mountains (which together with the large embayments of the Weddell Sea and Ross Sea mark the approximate boundary between East and West Antarctica), and the mountainous Antarctic Peninsula and off-lying islands which extend northwards towards South America. The continental shelf averages about 32 km (20 miles) in width (half the global mean, and in places it is non-existent) and reaches exceptional depths (390–780 m (1,300–2,600 ft)), which is three to six times the global mean).

CLIMATE

On land, summer temperatures range from just below freezing around the coast to −34° C (about −30° F) on the plateau, and in winter from −20° C (about −4° F) on the coast to −65° C (about −85° F) inland. Over a large area the maxima do not exceed −15° C (+5° F).

Precipitation is scanty over the plateau but amounts to 25–76 cm (10–30 in) (water equivalent) along the coast and some scientific stations are permanently buried by snow. Some rain falls over the more northerly areas in summer. Gravity winds on the plateau slopes and cyclonic storms further north can both exceed 160 km/h (100 m.p.h.) and gusts have been known to reach 240 km/h (150 m.p.h.). Visibility can be reduced to zero in blizzards.

FLORA AND FAUNA

Although a small number of flowering plants, ferns and clubmosses occur on the sub-Antarctic islands, only two (a grass and a pearlwort) extend south of 60° S. Antarctic vegetation is dominated by lichens and mosses, with a few liverworts, algae and fungi. Most of these occur around the coast or on islands, but lichens and some mosses also occur inland.

The only land animals are tiny insects and mites with nematodes, rotifers, and tardigrades in the mosses, but large numbers of seals, penguins and other sea-birds go ashore to breed in the summer. The emperor penguin is the only species which breeds ashore throughout the winter. By contrast, the Antarctic seas abound with life, a wide variety of invertebrates (including krill) and fish providing food for the seals, penguins and other birds, and a residual population of whales.

In 1994 the International Whaling Commission agreed to establish a whale sanctuary around Antarctica in which commercial whaling will be banned for ten years. The sanctuary will cover all sea areas south of 60°S. latitude, apart from the south-west Atlantic and south-east Pacific where it will be south of 40°S. latitude.

POTENTIAL RESOURCES

In the 180 years from Captain James Cook's circumnavigation of the Antarctic in 1772–5 to the mid-1950s, expeditions to the Antarctic made major contributions to geographical and scientific knowledge of the area.

Increasing pressure on the world's food and mineral supplies has stimulated interest in the potential resources even in the extremely hostile polar environment. Minerals may be present in great variety but not in commercially exploitable concentrations in accessible localities. There are indications that off-shore hydrocarbons may be present but mostly below great depths of stormy, ice-infested seas.

Currently, the chief interest is in marine protein, including the shrimp-like krill already fished commercially by Japan and Poland. Research to ensure management of stocks of this organism is being continued by international groups, but it is estimated that they could sustain a yield equal to the present total annual world fish catch.

THE ANTARCTIC TREATY

The International Geophysical Year 1957–8 gave great impetus to Antarctic research, increasing the number of stations from 17 to 44 and the number of nations involved in research from four to 12 by 1957. The co-operative scientific effort proved so fruitful that the 12 nations involved (Argentina, Australia, Belgium, Chile, France, Japan, New Zealand, Norway, South Africa, the Soviet Union, the UK and the USA) pledged themselves to promote scientific and technical co-operation unhampered by politics, and the Antarctic Treaty was signed by the 12 states in 1959.

The 12 signatories to the treaty agreed to establish free use of the Antarctic continent for peaceful scientific purposes; to freeze all territorial claims and disputes in the Antarctic; to ban all military activities in the area; and to prohibit nuclear explosions and the disposal of radioactive waste. Since then additional agreements have been reached to promote conservation and restrict tourism, waste disposal and pollution.

The Antarctic Treaty was defined as covering areas south of latitude 60° S., excluding the high seas but including the ice shelves, and came into force in 1961. It has since been signed by a further 28 states, 14 of which are active in the Antarctic and have therefore been accorded consultative status, bringing the number of consultative parties to 26. In 1991 a protocol to the treaty was adopted by the signatory states which introduced a range of measures to protect Antarctica's environment and prohibit mineral exploitation and mining for at least 50 years.

TERRITORIAL CLAIMS

Under the provisions of the Antarctic Treaty all territorial claims and disputes were frozen without the acceptance or denial of the claims of the various claimants. The US and Soviet governments also made it clear that although they had not made any specific territorial claims, they did not relinquish the right to make such claims.

Seven states have made claims in the Antarctic: Argentina claims the part of Antarctica between 74° W. and 25° W.; Chile that part between 90° W. and 53° W.; Britain claims the British Antarctic Territory, an area of 1,810,000 sq. km (700,000 sq. miles) between 20° and 80° W. longitude; France claims Adélie Land, 432,000 sq. km (166,800 sq. miles) between 136° and 142° E.; Australia claims the Australian Antarctic Territory, 6,120,000 sq. km (2,320,000 sq. miles) between 160° and 45° E. longitude excluding Adélie Land; Norway claims Queen Maud Land between 20° W. and 45° E.; and New Zealand claims the Ross Dependency, 450,000 sq. km (175,000 sq. miles) between 160° E. and 150° W. longitude. The Argentinian, British and Chilean claims overlap while the part of the continent between 90° W. and 150° W. is unclaimed by any state.

SCIENTIFIC RESEARCH

There are over 40 permanently occupied stations operated by the following nations: Argentina (6), Australia (4), Brazil (1), Chile (3), China (2), France (4), Germany (1), India (1), Japan (2), New Zealand (2), Poland (1), Russia (5), South Africa (3), South Korea (1), Uruguay (1), UK (4), USA (3, including one at the South Pole).

The staff of these stations and summer field-workers are the only people present on the continent and off-lying islands. There are no indigenous inhabitants.

LARGEST CITIES OF THE WORLD

In most cases figures refer to urban agglomerations (Ψ seaport)

	Population		Population
Mexico City, Mexico	14,987,051	Moscow, Russia	8,700,000
Cairo, Egypt	13,000,000	Delhi, India	8,375,188
Ψ Shanghai, China	12,760,000	Ψ Jakarta, Indonesia	7,885,519
Ψ Bombay, India	12,571,720	Ψ New York, USA	7,322,564
Tokyo, Japan	11,718,720	Ψ Istanbul, Turkey	7,309,190
Seoul, South Korea	10,920,000	Ψ Karachi, Pakistan	7,183,000
Ψ Calcutta, India	10,916,272	Ψ London, UK	6,934,500
Beijing, China	10,860,000	Manila, Philippines	6,720,050
São Paulo, Brazil	9,480,427	Dhaka, Bangladesh	6,537,308
Paris, France	9,318,800	Lima, Peru	6,483,901

Currencies of the World

AND EXCHANGE RATES AGAINST £ STERLING

Franc CFA = Franc de la Communauté financière africaine
Franc CFP = Franc des Comptoirs français du Pacifique

COUNTRY/TERRITORY	MONETARY UNIT	AVERAGE RATE TO £ 2 September 1994	AVERAGE RATE TO £ 1 September 1995
Afghanistan	Afghani (Af) of 100 puls	Af 4014.40	Af 6896.21
Albania	Lek (Lk) of 100 qindarka	Lk 154.400	Lk 177.063
Algeria	Algerian dinar (DA) of 100 centimes	DA 59.5468	DA 80.6524
American Samoa	Currency is that of USA	US$ 1.5448	US$ 1.5525
Andorra	French and Spanish currencies in use	—	—
Angola	New Kwanza (Kz) of 100 lwei	Kz 146577.5	Kz 5005.26
Anguilla	East Caribbean dollar (EC$) of 100 cents	EC$ 4.1688	EC$ 4.1918
Antigua and Barbuda	East Caribbean dollar (EC$) of 100 cents	EC$ 4.1688	EC$ 4.1918
Argentina	Peso of 10,000 australes	Pesos 1.5107	Pesos 1.5517
Armenia	Dram of 100 couma	—	Dram 635.097
Aruba	Aruban florin	Florins 2.7638	Florins 2.7790
Australia	Australian dollar ($A) of 100 cents	$A 2.0804	$A 2.0714
Austria	Schilling of 100 Groschen	Schilling 17.0657	Schilling 15.9756
Azerbaijan	Manat of 100 gopik	—	Manat 6823.24
Bahamas	Bahamian dollar (B$) of 100 cents	B$ 1.5448	B$ 1.5525
Bahrain	Bahrain dinar (BD) of 1,000 fils	BD 0.5824	BD 0.5853
Bangladesh	Taka (Tk) of 100 poisha	Tk 61.0177	Tk 61.7895
Barbados	Barbados dollar (BD$) of 100 cents	BD$ 3.1054	BD$ 3.1226
Belarus	Rouble of 100 kopeks	Roubles 1.0821	Roubles 17853.8
Belgium	Belgian franc (or frank) of 100 centimes (centiemen)	Francs 49.6638	Francs 46.7225
Belize	Belize dollar (BZ$) of 100 cents	BZ$ 3.0880	BZ$ 3.1050
Benin	Franc CFA	Francs 826.440	Francs 784.440
Bermuda	Bermuda dollar of 100 cents	$ 1.5448	$ 1.5525
Bhutan	Ngultrum of 100 chetrum (Indian currency is also legal tender)	Ngultrum 48.4588	Ngultrum 49.5403
Bolivia	Boliviano ($b) of 100 centavos	$b 7.2140	$b 7.5141
Bosnia-Hercegovina	Dinar of 100 paras	—	—
Botswana	Pula (P) of 100 thebe	P 4.2208	P 4.3551
Brazil	Real of 100 centavos	Real 1.3687	Real 1.4740
British Virgin Islands	US dollar (US$) (£ sterling and EC$ also circulate)	US$ 1.5448	US$ 1.5525
Brunei	Brunei dollar of 100 sen (fully interchangeable with Singapore currency)	$ 2.3168	$ 2.2061
Bulgaria	Lev of 100 stotinki	Leva 87.5216	Leva 105.469
Burkina	Franc CFA	Francs 826.440	Francs 784.440
Burundi	Burundi franc of 100 centimes	Francs 382.60	Francs 393.171
Cambodia	Riel of 100 sen	Riel 5404.00	Riel 3570.75
Cameroon	Franc CFA	Francs 826.440	Francs 784.440
Canada	Canadian dollar (C$) of 100 cents	C$ 2.1115	C$ 2.0858
Cape Verde	Escudo Caboverdiano of 100 centavos	Esc 130.337	Esc 128.811
Cayman Islands	Cayman Islands dollar (CI$) of 100 cents	CI$ 1.2661	CI$ 1.2858
Central African Republic	Franc CFA	Francs 826.440	Francs 784.440
Chad	Franc CFA	Francs 826.440	Francs 784.440
Chile	Chilean peso of 100 centavos	Pesos 642.693	Pesos 610.676
China	Renminbi Yuan of 10 jiao or 100 fen	Yuan 13.2138	Yuan 12.9156
Christmas Island	Currency is that of Australia	$A 2.0804	$A 2.0714
Cocos (Keeling) Islands	Currency is that of Australia	$A 2.0804	$A 2.0714
Colombia	Colombian peso of 100 centavos	Pesos 1266.23	Pesos 1474.56
Comoros	Franc CFA/Franc	Francs 612.837	Francs 588.476
Congo	Franc CFA	Francs 826.440	Francs 784.440
Cook Islands	Currency is that of New Zealand	NZ$ 2.5527	NZ$ 2.3755
Costa Rica	Costa Rican colón (₡) of 100 céntimos	₡ 242.779	₡ 286.343
Côte d'Ivoire	Franc CFA	Francs 826.440	Francs 784.440

Country/Territory	Monetary Unit	Average Rate to £ 2 September 1994	Average Rate to £ 1 September 1995
Croatia	Kuna of 100 lipas	Kuna 8.9762	Kuna 8.3241
Cuba	Cuban peso of 100 centavos	Pesos 1.1694	Pesos 1.5525
Cyprus	Cyprus pound (C£) of 100 cents	C£ 0.7400	C£ 0.7114
Czech Republic	Koruna (Kčs) of 100 haléřu	Kčs 43.6830	Kčs 41.8570
Denmark	Danish krone of 100 øre	Kroner 9.5243	Kroner 8.8252
Djibouti	Djibouti franc of 100 centimes	Francs 274.400	Francs 275.911
Dominica	East Caribbean dollar (EC$) of 100 cents	EC$ 4.1688	EC$ 4.1918
Dominican Republic	Dominican Republic peso (RD$) of 100 centavos	RD$ 20.2882	RD$ 21.4245
Ecuador	Sucre of 100 centavos	Sucres 3223.87	Sucres 3890.57
Egypt	Egyptian pound (£E) of 100 piastres or 1,000 millièmes	£E 5.2322	£E 5.2770
Equatorial Guinea	Franc CFA	Francs 826.440	Francs 784.440
Eritrea	Ethiopian currency is in use	EB 8.4766	EB 9.0045
Estonia	Kroon of 100 sents	Kroons 19.4760	Kroons 18.2251
Ethiopia	Ethiopian birr (EB) of 100 cents	EB 8.4766	EB 9.0045
Falkland Islands	Falkland pound of 100 pence	*at parity with £ sterling*	*at parity with £ sterling*
Faroe Islands	Currency is that of Denmark	Kroner 9.5243	Kroner 8.8252
Fiji	Fiji dollar (F$) of 100 cents	F$ 2.2315	F$ 2.1971
Finland	Markka (Mk) of 100 penniä	Mk 7.7933	Mk 6.8109
France	Franc of 100 centimes	Francs 8.2644	Francs 7.8444
French Guiana	Currency is that of France	Francs 8.2644	Francs 7.8444
French Polynesia	Franc CFP	Francs 148.566	Francs 142.661
Gabon	Franc CFA	Francs 826.440	Francs 784.440
Gambia	Dalasi (D) of 100 butut	D 14.9768	D 14.9040
Georgia	Georgian Coupon	—	—
Germany	Deutsche Mark (DM) of 100 Pfennig	DM 2.4101	DM 2.2717
Ghana	Cedi of 100 pesewas	Cedi 1505.40	Cedi 1870.76
Gibraltar	Gibraltar pound of 100 pence	*at parity with £ sterling*	*at parity with £ sterling*
Greece	Drachma of 100 leptae	Drachmae 368.655	Drachmae 365.723
Greenland	Currency is that of Denmark	Kroner 9.5243	Kroner 8.8252
Grenada	East Caribbean dollar (EC$) of 100 cents	EC$ 4.1688	EC$ 4.1918
Guadeloupe	Currency is that of France	Francs 8.2644	Francs 7.8444
Guam	Currency is that of USA	US$ 1.5448	US$ 1.5525
Guatemala	Quetzal (Q) of 100 centavos	Q 8.8369	Q 9.0919
Guinea	Guinea franc of 100 centimes	Francs 1508.01	Francs 1536.04
Guinea-Bissau	Guinea-Bissau peso of 100 centavos	Pesos 18983.5	Pesos 26001.3
Guyana	Guyana dollar (G$) of 100 cents	G$ 217.395	G$ 223.250
Haiti	Gourde of 100 centimes	Gourdes 29.3360	Gourdes 29.4975
Honduras	Lempira of 100 centavos	Lempiras 13.7416	Lempiras 14.6867
Hong Kong	Hong Kong dollar (HK$) of 100 cents	HK$ 11.9364	HK$ 12.0176
Hungary	Forint of 100 fillér	Forints 165.736	Forints 201.771
Iceland	Icelandic króna (Kr) of 100 aurar	Kr 105.31	Kr 101.906
India	Indian rupee (Rs) of 100 paisa	Rs 48.4588	Rs 49.5403
Indonesia	Rupiah (Rp) of 100 sen	Rp 3361.61	Rp 3519.91
Iran	Rial	Rials 2682.50	Rials 4657.50
Iraq	Iraqi dinar (ID) of 1,000 fils	ID 0.4800	ID 0.9315
Ireland, Republic of	Punt (IR£) of 100 pence	IR£ 1.0086	IR£ 0.9774
Israel	Shekel of 100 agora	Shekels 4.6645	Shekels 4.7219
Italy	Lira of 100 centesimi	Lire 2432.83	Lire 2523.90
Jamaica	Jamaican dollar (J$) of 100 cents	J$ 51.7240	J$ 51.2325
Japan	Yen of 100 sen	Yen 153.541	Yen 151.237
Jordan	Jordanian dinar (JD) of 1,000 fils	JD 1.0798	JD 1.1054
Kazakhstan	Tenge	—	—
Kenya	Kenya shilling (Ksh) of 100 cents	Ksh 84.0399	Ksh 85.8533
Kiribati	Australian dollar ($A) of 100 cents	$A 2.0804	$A 2.0714
Korea, North	Won of 100 jun	Won 3.3196	Won 3.3379
Korea, South	Won of 100 jeon	Won 1236.96	Won 1200.32
Kuwait	Kuwaiti dinar (KD) of 1,000 fils	KD 0.4607	KD 0.4697
Kyrgyzstan	Som	—	—
Laos	Kip (K) of 100 at	K 1111.68	K 1428.30
Latvia	Lats of 100 santimes	Lats 0.8481	Lats 0.8339
Lebanon	Lebanese pound (L£) of 100 piastres	L£ 2580.51	L£ 2504.96
Lesotho	Loti (M) of 100 lisente	M 5.5260	M 5.6802
Liberia	Liberian dollar (L$) of 100 cents	L$ 1.5448	L$ 1.5525

Country/Territory	Monetary Unit	Average Rate to £ 2 September 1994	Average Rate to £ 1 September 1995
Libya	Libyan dinar (LD) of 1,000 dirhams	LD 0.4717	LD 0.5519
Liechtenstein	Swiss franc of 100 rappen (or centimes)	Francs 2.0260	Francs 1.8588
Lithuania	Litas	Litas 6.1760	Litas 6.2100
Luxembourg	Luxembourg franc (LF) of 100 centimes (Belgian currency is also legal tender)	LF 49.6638	LF 46.7225
Macao	Pataca of 100 avos	Pataca 12.3275	Pataca 12.3984
Macedonia, Former Yugoslav Rep.	Dinar of 100 paras	—	Dinars 61.0139
Madagascar	Franc malgache (FMG) of 100 centimes	FMG 5430.25	FMG 6908.63
Malawi	Kwacha (K) of 100 tambala	K 12.4717	K 23.6878
Malaysia	Malaysian dollar (ringgit) (M$) of 100 sen	M$ 3.9415	M$ 3.8743
Maldives	Rufiyaa of 100 laaris	Rufiyaa 17.9104	Rufiyaa 18.2730
Mali	Franc CFA	Francs 826.440	Francs 784.440
Malta	Maltese lira (LM) of 100 cents or 1,000 mils	LM 0.5731	LM 0.5559
Marshall Islands	Currency is that of USA	US$ 1.5448	US$ 1.5525
Martinique	Currency is that of France	Francs 8.2644	Francs 7.8444
Mauritania	Ouguiya (UM) of 5 khoums	UM 189.047	UM 200.257
Mauritius	Mauritius rupee of 100 cents	Rs 27.5218	Rs 28.2788
Mayotte	Currency is that of France	Francs 8.2644	Francs 7.8444
Mexico	Peso of 100 centavos	Pesos 5.2283	Pesos 9.7187
Moldova	Leu	—	Leu 7.0383
Monaco	French franc of 100 centimes	Francs 8.2644	Francs 7.8444
Mongolia	Tugrik of 100 möngö	Tugriks 617.600	Tugriks 697.228
Montserrat	East Caribbean dollar (EC$) of 100 cents	EC$ 4.1688	EC$ 4.1918
Morocco	Dirham (DH) of 100 centimes	DH 13.9873	DH 13.3586
Mozambique	Metical (MT) of 100 centavos	MT 9680.70	MT 14908.7
Myanmar (Burma)	Kyat (K) of 100 pyas	K 8.9904	K 8.8421
Namibia	Namibian dollar of 100 cents	—	at parity with SA Rand
Nauru	Australian dollar ($A) of 100 cents	$A 2.0804	$A 2.0714
Nepal	Nepalese rupee of 100 paisa	Rs 76.0420	Rs 78.2305
Netherlands	Gulden (guilder) or florin of 100 cents	Guilders 2.7041	Guilders 2.5461
Netherlands Antilles	Netherlands Antilles guilder of 100 cents	Guilders 2.7638	Guilders 2.7790
New Caledonia	Franc CFP	Francs 148.566	Francs 142.661
New Zealand	New Zealand dollar (NZ$) of 100 cents	NZ$ 2.5527	NZ$ 2.3755
Nicaragua	Córdoba (C$) of 100 centavos	C$ 10.5526	C$ 11.9061
Niger	Franc CFA	Francs 826.440	Francs 784.440
Nigeria	Naira (N) of 100 kobo	N 33.9845	N 34.1519
Niue	Currency is that of New Zealand	NZ$ 2.5527	NZ$ 2.3755
Norfolk Island	Currency is that of Australia	$A 2.0804	$A 2.0714
Northern Mariana Islands	Currency is that of USA	US$ 1.5448	US$ 1.5525
Norway	Krone of 100 øre	Kroner 10.5718	Kroner 9.9360
Oman	Rial Omani (OR) of 1,000 baiza	OR 0.5948	OR 0.5978
Pakistan	Pakistan rupee of 100 paisa	Rs 47.2993	Rs 48.5758
Palau	Currency is that of USA	US$ 1.5448	US$ 1.5525
Panama	Balboa of 100 centésimos (US notes are also in circulation)	Balboa 1.5448	Balboa 1.5525
Papua New Guinea	Kina (K) of 100 toea	K 1.4212	K 2.1209
Paraguay	Guaraní (Gs) of 100 céntimos	Gs 2945.18	Gs 3046.78
Peru	New Sol of 100 cénts	New Sol 3.4865	New Sol 3.5009
Philippines	Philippine peso (P) of 100 centavos	P 40.7043	P 40.3185
Poland	Złoty of 100 groszy	Złotys 35506.1	Złotys 3.8393
Portugal	Escudo (Esc) of 100 centavos	Esc 247.191	Esc 236.570
Puerto Rico	Currency is that of USA	US$ 1.5448	US$ 1.5525
Qatar	Qatar riyal of 100 dirhams	Riyals 5.6202	Riyals 5.6527
Réunion	Currency is that of France	Francs 8.2644	Francs 7.8444
Romania	Leu (Lei) of 100 bani	Lei 2616.00	Lei 3221.44
Russia	Rouble of 100 kopeks	Roubles 1.0821	Roubles 0.9717
Rwanda	Rwanda franc of 100 centimes	Francs 216.20	Francs 496.490
St Christopher and Nevis	East Caribbean dollar (EC$) of 100 cents	EC$ 4.1688	EC$ 4.1918

COUNTRY/TERRITORY	MONETARY UNIT	AVERAGE RATE TO £ 2 September 1994	AVERAGE RATE TO £ 1 September 1995
St Helena	St Helena pound (£) of 100 pence	*at parity with £ sterling*	*at parity with £ sterling*
St Lucia	East Caribbean dollar (EC$) of 100 cents	EC$ 4.1688	EC$ 4.1918
St Pierre and Miquelon	Currency is that of France	Francs 8.2644	Francs 7.8444
St Vincent and the Grenadines	East Caribbean dollar (EC$) of 100 cents	EC$ 4.1688	EC$ 4.1918
El Salvador	El Salvador colón (₡) of 100 centavos	₡ 13.5100	₡ 13.5999
San Marino	Italian currency is in circulation	Lire 2432.83	Lire 2523.90
São Tomé and Príncipe	Dobra of 100 centavos	Dobra 1060.02	Dobra 1953.56
Saudi Arabia	Saudi riyal (SR) of 20 qursh or 100 halala	SR 5.7935	SR 5.8229
Senegal	Franc CFA	Francs 826.440	Francs 784.440
Seychelles	Seychelles rupee of 100 cents	Rs 7.6737	Rs 7.5110
Sierra Leone	Leone (Le) of 100 cents	Le 903.240	Le 1133.33
Singapore	Singapore dollar (S$) of 100 cents	S$ 2.3168	S$ 2.2061
Slovak Republic	Koruna (Kčs) of 100 haléřu	Kčs 48.5255	Kčs 47.2737
Slovenia	Tolar (SIT) of 100 stotin	Tolars 186.886	Tolars 190.849
Solomon Islands	Solomon Islands dollar (SI$) of 100 cents	SI$ 5.0392	SI$ 4.6488
Somalia	Somali shilling of 100 cents	Shillings 4045.28	Shillings 4067.55
South Africa	Rand (R) of 100 cents	R 5.5260	R 5.6802
Spain	Peseta of 100 céntimos	Pesetas 200.200	Pesetas 194.893
Sri Lanka	Sri Lankan rupee of 100 cents	Rs 76.0712	Rs 78.4323
Sudan	Sudanese dinar (SD) of 10 pounds	SD 48.0184	SD 80.8543
Suriname	Suriname guilder of 100 cents	Guilders 282.737	Guilders 763.831
Swaziland	Lilangeni (E) of 100 cents (South African currency also in circulation)	E 5.5260	E 5.6802
Sweden	Swedish krona of 100 öre	Kronor 11.8205	Kronor 11.3549
Switzerland	Swiss franc of 100 rappen (or centimes)	Francs 2.0260	Francs 1.8588
Syria	Syrian pound (S$) of 100 piastres	S£ 31.6520	S£ 65.1274
Taiwan	New Taiwan dollar (NT$) of 100 cents	T$ 40.5312	NT$ 42.6914
Tajikistan	Rouble of 100 kopeks	Roubles 1.0821	Roubles 0.9717
Tanzania	Tanzanian shilling of 100 cents	Shillings 810.986	Shillings 939.263
Thailand	Baht of 100 satang	Baht 38.6265	Baht 38.8747
Togo	Franc CFA	Francs 826.440	Francs 784.440
Tokelau	Currency is that of New Zealand	NZ$ 2.5527	NZ$ 2.3755
Tonga	Pa'anga (T$) of 100 seniti	T$ 2.0804	T$ 2.0714
Trinidad and Tobago	Trinidad and Tobago dollar (TT$) of 100 cents	TT$ 8.6078	TT$ 8.8570
Tunisia	Tunisian dinar of 1,000 millimes	Dinars 1.5266	Dinars 1.4746
Turkey	Turkish lira (TL) of 100 kurus	TL 52676.1	TL 74892.7
Turkmenistan	Manat	—	—
Turks and Caicos Islands	US dollar (US$)	US$ 1.5448	US$ 1.5525
Tuvalu	Australian dollar ($A) of 100 cents	$A 2.0804	$A 2.0714
Uganda	Uganda shilling of 100 cents	Shillings 1397.32	Shillings 1490.40
Ukraine	Karbovanets (Ka)	Ka 31668.5	Ka 253057.7
United Arab Emirates	UAE dirham of 100 fils	Dirham 5.6759	Dirham 5.7024
United Kingdom	Pound sterling (£) of 100 pence	£ 1.00	£ 1.00
United States of America	US dollar (US$) of 100 cents	US$ 1.5448	US$ 1.5525
Uruguay	New Uruguayan peso of 100 centésimos	Pesos 8.1755	Pesos 10.1223
Uzbekistan	Sum	—	—
Vanuatu	Vatu of 100 centimes	Vatu 175.329	Vatu 174.269
Vatican City State	Italian currency is legal tender	Lire 2432.83	Lire 2523.90
Venezuela	Bolívar (Bs) of 100 céntimos	Bs 262.276	Bs 263.591
Vietnam	Dông of 10 hào or 100 xu	Dông 16965.5	Dông 17105.5
Virgin Islands (US)	Currency is that of USA	US$ 1.5448	US$ 1.5525
Wallis and Futuna Islands	Franc CFP	Francs 148.566	Francs 142.661
Western Samoa	Tala (WS$) of 100 sene	WS$ 3.8991	WS$ 3.8968
Republic of Yemen	Riyal of 100 fils	Riyals 88.30	Riyals 78.0132
Yugoslavia, Federal Rep.	Dinar of 100 paras	—	—
Zaïre	Zaïre of 100 makuta	Zaïre 1992.50	Zaïre 8419.52
Zambia	Kwacha (K) of 100 ngwee	K 1049.92	K 1459.23
Zimbabwe	Zimbabwe dollar (Z$) of 100 cents	Z$ 12.6376	Z$ 13.4408

Time Zones

Standard time differences from the Greenwich meridian

+   hours ahead of GMT
−   hours behind GMT
*   varies from standard time at some part of the year (Summer Time or Daylight Saving Time)
h   hours
m   minutes

	h	m
Afghanistan	+ 4	30
*Albania	+ 1	
Algeria	+ 1	
*Andorra	+ 1	
Angola	+ 1	
Anguilla	− 4	
Antigua and Barbuda	− 4	
Argentina	− 3	
*Armenia	+ 3	
Aruba	− 4	
Ascension Island	0	
*Australia	+10	
Broken Hill area (NSW)	+ 9	30
Northern Territory	+ 9	30
*South Australia	+ 9	30
Western Australia	+ 8	
*Austria	+ 1	
Azerbaijan	+ 4	
*Azores	− 1	
*Bahamas	− 5	
Bahrain	+ 3	
Bangladesh	+ 6	
Barbados	− 4	
*Belarus	+ 2	
*Belgium	+ 1	
Belize	− 6	
Benin	+ 1	
*Bermuda	− 4	
Bhutan	+ 6	
Bolivia	− 4	
*Bosnia-Hercegovina	+ 1	
Botswana	+ 2	
Brazil		
Acre	− 5	
*eastern, including all coast and Brasilia	− 3	
*western	− 4	
British Indian Ocean Territory	+ 5	
Diego Garcia	+ 6	
British Virgin Islands	− 4	
Brunei	+ 8	
*Bulgaria	+ 2	
Burkina	0	
Burundi	+ 2	
Cambodia	+ 7	
Cameroon	+ 1	
Canada		
*Alberta	− 7	
*British Columbia	− 8	
British Columbia NE	− 7	
*Labrador	− 4	
*Manitoba	− 6	
*New Brunswick	− 4	
*Newfoundland	− 3	30

	h	m
*Northwest Territories		
east of 68° W.	− 4	
63° W.–85° W.	− 5	
85° W.–102° W.	− 6	
west of 102° W.	− 7	
*Nova Scotia	− 4	
Ontario		
*east of 90° W.	− 5	
west of 90° W.	− 6	
*Prince Edward Island	− 4	
*Quebec		
east of 63° W.	− 4	
west of 63° W.	− 5	
*Saskatchewan	− 6	
*Yukon	− 8	
*Canary Islands	0	
Cape Verde	− 1	
Cayman Islands	− 5	
Central African Republic	+ 1	
Chad	+ 1	
*Chile	− 4	
China	+ 8	
Christmas Island (Indian Ocean)	+ 7	
Cocos Keeling Islands	+ 6	30
Colombia	− 5	
Comoros	+ 3	
Congo	+ 1	
Cook Islands	− 10	
Costa Rica	− 6	
Côte d'Ivoire	0	
*Croatia	+ 1	
*Cuba	− 5	
*Cyprus	+ 2	
*Czech Republic	+ 1	
*Denmark	+ 1	
Djibouti	+ 3	
Dominica	− 4	
Dominican Republic	− 4	
Ecuador	− 5	
*Egypt	+ 2	
Equatorial Guinea	+ 1	
Eritrea	+ 3	
*Estonia	+ 2	
Ethiopia	+ 3	
*Falkland Islands	− 4	
*Faroe Islands	0	
Fiji	+12	
*Finland	+ 2	
*France	+ 1	
French Guiana	− 3	
French Polynesia	−10	
Marquesas Islands	− 9	30
Gabon	+ 1	
The Gambia	0	
*Georgia	+ 3	
*Germany	+ 1	
Ghana	0	
*Gibraltar	+ 1	
*Greece	+ 2	
Greenland		
*Angmagssalik and west coast	− 3	
Danmarkshavn	0	
Mesters Vig		
*Scoresby Sound	− 1	
*Thule area	− 4	
Grenada	− 4	

	h	m
Guadeloupe	− 4	
Guam	+ 10	
Guatemala	− 6	
Guinea	0	
Guinea-Bissau	0	
Guyana	− 4	
*Haiti	− 5	
Honduras	− 5	
Hong Kong	+ 8	
*Hungary	+ 1	
Iceland	0	
India	+ 5	30
Indonesia		
Bali	+ 8	
Irian Jaya	+ 9	
Java	+ 7	
Kalimantan (south and east)	+ 8	
Kalimantan (west and central)	+ 7	
Molucca Islands	+ 9	
Sulawesi	+ 8	
Sumatra	+ 7	
Tanimbar	+ 9	
Timor	+ 8	
*Iran	+ 3	30
*Iraq	+ 3	
*Ireland, Republic of	0	
*Israel	+ 2	
*Italy	+ 1	
Jamaica	− 5	
Japan	+ 9	
*Jordan	+ 2	
*Kazakhstan	+ 6	
Kenya	+ 3	
Kiribati		
Banaba	+12	
Gilbert Islands	+12	
Kiritimati Island	−10	
Phoenix Islands	−11	
Korea, North	+ 9	
Korea, South	+ 9	
Kuwait	+ 3	
*Kyrgyzstan	+ 5	
Laos	+ 7	
*Latvia	+ 2	
*Lebanon	+ 2	
Lesotho	+ 2	
Liberia	0	
Libya	+ 2	
*Liechtenstein	+ 1	
*Lithuania	+ 2	
*Luxembourg	+ 1	
Macao	+ 8	
*Macedonia (former Yug. Rep.)	+ 1	
Madagascar	+ 3	
*Madeira	0	
Malawi	+ 2	
Malaysia	+ 8	
Maldives	+ 5	
Mali	0	
*Malta	+ 1	
Marshall Islands	+12	
Ebon Atoll	−12	
Martinique	− 4	
Mauritania	0	
Mauritius	+ 4	

	h	m
Mexico	− 6	
central	− 7	
western	− 8	
Micronesia		
Caroline Islands	+10	
Kosrae	+11	
Pohnpei	+11	
*Moldova	+ 2	
*Monaco	+ 1	
*Mongolia	+ 8	
Montserrat	− 4	
Morocco	0	
Mozambique	+ 2	
Myanmar	+ 6	30
*Namibia	+ 1	
Nauru	+12	
Nepal	+ 5	45
*Netherlands	+ 1	
Netherlands Antilles	− 4	
New Caledonia	+11	
*New Zealand	+12	
Nicaragua	− 6	
Niger	+ 1	
Nigeria	+ 1	
Norfolk Island	+11	30
*Norway	+ 1	
Oman	+ 4	
Pakistan	+ 5	
Palau	+ 9	
Panama	− 5	
Papua New Guinea	+10	
*Paraguay	− 4	
Peru	− 5	
Philippines	+ 8	
*Poland	+ 1	
*Portugal	+ 1	
Puerto Rico	− 4	
Qatar	+ 3	
Réunion	+ 4	
*Romania	+ 2	
*Russia		
Zone 0	+ 2	
Zone 1	+ 3	
Zone 2	+ 4	
Zone 3	+ 5	
Zone 4	+ 6	
Zone 5	+ 7	
Zone 6	+ 8	
Zone 7	+ 9	
Zone 8	+10	
Zone 9	+11	
Zone 10	+12	
Rwanda	+ 2	
St Helena	0	
St Kitts and Nevis	− 4	
St Lucia	− 4	
*St Pierre and Miquelon	− 3	
St Vincent and the		
Grenadines	− 4	
El Salvador	− 6	
Samoa, American	−11	
*San Marino	+ 1	
São Tomé and Príncipe	0	
Saudi Arabia	+ 3	
Senegal	0	
Seychelles	+ 4	
Sierra Leone	0	
Singapore	+ 8	
*Slovak Republic	+ 1	

	h	m
*Slovenia	+ 1	
Solomon Islands	+11	
Somalia	+ 3	
South Africa	+ 2	
South Georgia	− 2	
*Spain	+ 1	
Sri Lanka	+ 5	30
Sudan	+ 2	
Suriname	− 3	
Swaziland	+ 2	
*Sweden	+ 1	
*Switzerland	+ 1	
*Syria	+ 2	
Taiwan	+ 8	
Tajikistan	+ 5	
Tanzania	+ 3	
Thailand	+ 7	
Togo	0	
Tonga	+13	
Trinidad and Tobago	− 4	
Tristan da Cunha	0	
Tunisia	+ 1	
*Turkey	+ 2	
Turkmenistan	+ 5	
*Turks and Caicos Islands	− 5	
Tuvalu	+12	
Uganda	+ 3	
*Ukraine	+ 2	
United Arab Emirates	+ 4	
Uruguay	− 3	
United States		
*Alaska, east of		
169° 30′ W.	− 9	
*Aleutian Islands, west		
of 169° 30′ W.	−10	
eastern time	− 5	
*central time	− 6	
Hawaii	−10	
*mountain time	− 7	
*Pacific time	− 8	
Uzbekistan	+ 5	
Vanuatu	+11	
*Vatican City State	+ 1	
Venezuela	− 4	
Vietnam	+ 7	
Virgin Islands (US)	− 4	
Western Samoa	−11	
Yemen	+ 3	
*Yugoslavia (Fed. Rep.)	+ 1	
Zaire		
East	+ 2	
West	+ 1	
Zambia	+ 2	
Zimbabwe	+ 2	

Source: reproduced with permission from data produced by HM Nautical Almanac Office.

Countries of the World: A–Z

SOURCES: sources of statistical data specific to one country are credited in that country's entry. Sources of statistical data used throughout the Countries of the World section include *UN Demographic Yearbook, UN Statistical Yearbook* (pub. UN), *UNESCO Statistical Yearbook* (pub. UNESCO), *World Bank Atlas, World Bank World Tables* (pub. World Bank), *World Mineral Statistics* (pub. British Geological Survey), *The Military Balance* (pub. IISS).

Other sources of information include the Foreign and Commonwealth Office Research Department and the diplomatic representatives and information offices in London of overseas countries, whom Whitaker's wishes to thank for their assistance.

AFGHANISTAN
Da Afghanistan Jamhuriat

Afghanistan is bounded on the west by Iran, on the south by Pakistan, on the north by Tajikistan, Uzbekistan and Turkmenistan, and on the east by Pakistan and China. The estimated area is 250,000 sq. miles (647,497 sq. km).

Mountains, chief among which are the Hindu Kush, cover three-quarters of the country, the elevation being generally over 4,000 feet. There are three great river basins, the Oxus, Helmand, and Kabul. The climate is dry, with extreme temperatures.

The population is 19,062,000 (1992 UN estimate). It is estimated that 3.5 million refugees fled to Pakistan and two million to Iran during the Soviet occupation, and that one million died in the war between the mujahidin and the Soviet and Afghan armed forces. About 1.5 million refugees have returned since 1992. The most numerous race is the Pushtuns who form about half of the population and predominate in the south and west, the Tajiks, a Persian-speaking people, Uzbeks and Turkomans in the north, Hazaras in the centre, Baluchis in the south-west and Nuristanis, who live near the Chitral border. All are Sunni Muslims, except the Hazaras and Kizilbashes, who belong to the Shia sect.

CAPITAL – Kabul (1,424,400 in 1988 but much reduced since due to fighting). The chief commercial centres are Kabul and Kandahar (225,500). Other provincial capitals are (UN estimates) Herat (177,300), Mazar-i-Sharif (130,600), Jalalabad (55,000).

CURRENCY – Afghani (Af) of 100 puls.

FLAG – Three horizontal stripes of green, white, black with the national arms in the centre in gold.

NATIONAL ANTHEM – Soroud-e-Melli.

NATIONAL DAY – 19 August.

GOVERNMENT

The constitutional monarchy, introduced by the 1964 constitution, was overthrown by a coup in 1973. The country was ruled by presidential decree until 1977 when a constitution was approved and Mohammad Daoud was elected President. He was overthrown in 1978 by the armed forces and power was handed to the People's Democratic Party of Afghanistan (PDPA). In December 1979 Soviet troops invaded Afghanistan and installed Babrak Karmal as head of state. Armed Islamic resistance groups, the mujahidin, aided by western arms and Arab

finance, fought a brutal war against Soviet and Afghan armed forces. A peace agreement in April 1988 led to the withdrawal of Soviet troops, which was completed by February 1989. Mujahidin resistance to the Homeland Party (formerly PDPA) government continued until the government collapsed in April 1992. Mujahidin forces overran Kabul on 25 April 1992, bringing an end to the war, and declared an Islamic state.

The Pakistan-based government-in-exile returned to Kabul and appointed Burnahuddin Rabbani as interim president. The coalition of ten mujahidin groups (seven Sunni and three Shia) broke down over the election of a permanent president and fighting broke out in the Kabul area in December 1992. The fighting was mainly between the Hezb-i-Islami (mainly Pushtun) led by Gulbardin Hekmatyar, supported by the Hezb-i-Wahdat forces (Shia), trying to force their way into Kabul, which was controlled by the Jamiat-i-Islami led by Ahmad Shah Massoud, supported by fellow Tajik and Uzbek forces from the north. Fighting stopped in March 1993 with the signing of a peace agreement under which interim President Rabbani remained President and Hekmatyar became head of a transitional government until elections in June 1994.

However, the peace agreement collapsed in October 1993 and fighting broke out around Kabul between the forces of Hekmatyar and those of Rabbani and Massoud. The fighting spread through the north of the country after the Uzbek militia leader General Rashid Dostum allied his forces with Hekmatyar's. Hekmatyar's and Dostum's forces were finally forced out of Kabul by Rabbani and Massoud's militia at the end of June 1994. No elections have been held and fighting continues. Between September 1994 and March 1995 the Hezb-i-Islami and the Hezb-i-Wahdat forces were defeated by Taliban forces (armed Islamic students). The Taliban forces controlled nine provinces in the south-west and west of the country by mid-1995 but Rabbani and Massoud's forces had gained control of all of Kabul and had pushed back Taliban forces to the south of the city. The warfare since April 1992 has become a battle to reassert traditional Pushtun political dominance, broken by Rabbani and Massoud's Tajiks and Uzbeks.

HEAD OF STATE
President of the Islamic State of Afghanistan, Prof. Burhanuddin Rabbani, *elected* 30 December 1992

EMBASSY OF THE ISLAMIC STATE OF AFGHANISTAN
31 Prince's Gate, London SW7 1QQ
Tel 0171-589 8891
Ambassador Extraordinary and Plenipotentiary, new appointment awaited
Minister-Counsellor and Chargé d'Affaires, Ahmad Wali Masud

BRITISH EMBASSY
Karte Parwan, Kabul
Staff were withdrawn from post in February 1989.
Ambassador is now resident in Islamabad.

DEFENCE

After the fall of the PDPA government the Afghan army disintegrated, with large numbers defecting to local mujahidin groups. The Northern Army Command was formed into the National Islamic Movement under the Uzbek militia leader General Dostum and numbers around 65,000 men. The Jamiat-i-Islami forces of Rabbani and

Massoud number 60,000 men, while Hekmatyar's Hezb-i-Islami forces number 50,000. Five other Sunni Muslim mujahidin groups have forces of 113,000 personnel and the Shia Hezb-i-Wahdat coalition of forces have 116,000 men under arms. The strength of the Taliban forces is unknown. The former Afghan Air Force has been divided between Dostum's and Rabbani's forces.

ECONOMY

The economy has been devastated by the political upheavals of the last 15 years. Agriculture and sheep raising have been the principal industries. There are generally two crops a year, one of wheat (the staple food), barley or lentils, the other of rice, millet, maize and dal. Sugar beet and cotton are grown. Afghanistan is rich in fruits. Sheep, including the Karakuli, and transport animals are bred. Silk, woollen and hair cloths and carpets are manufactured. Salt, silver, copper, coal, iron, lead, rubies, lapis lazuli, gold, chrome, barite, uranium, and talc are found.

TRADE

Trade is currently limited but in the past exports have been mainly Persian lambskins (Karakul), dried fruits, nuts, cotton, raw wool, carpets, spice and natural gas, while the imports are chiefly oil, cotton yarn and piece goods, tea, sugar, machinery and transport equipment.

Trade with UK	1993	1994
Imports from UK	£5,915,000	£7,830,000
Exports to UK	4,310,000	4,096,000

COMMUNICATIONS

Main roads run from Kabul to Kandahar, Herat, Maimana via Mazari-Sharif and Faizabad via Khanabad. Roads cross the border with Pakistan at Chaman and via the Khyber Pass, and there are roads from Herat to the borders of Central Asia and Iran. A network of minor roads fit for motor traffic in fine weather links up important towns and districts.

In 1982 the Afghan and Uzbek shores of the River Oxus were linked by a road and rail bridge which joins the Afghan port of Hairatan and the Uzbek port of Termez.

CULTURE

The principal languages of the country are Dari (a form of Persian) and Pushtu, although a number of minority languages are also spoken in various provinces. All schoolchildren learn both Persian and Pushtu. Education is free and nominally compulsory, elementary schools having been established in most centres; there are secondary schools in large urban areas and four universities, in Kabul (established 1932), Jalalabad (established 1962), Balkh and Herat (both established 1988).

ALBANIA
Republika Shqipërisë

Situated on the Adriatic Sea, Albania is bounded on the north by Montenegro, on the east by Serbia and Macedonia and on the south by Greece. The area is estimated at 11,099 sq. miles (28,748 sq. km), with a population (1992 UN estimate) of 3,363,000. After many years as an officially atheist country, the Albanian population is now estimated to be 65 per cent Muslim, 20 per cent Orthodox and 10 per cent Roman Catholic.

CAPITAL – Tirana, population (1990) 244,153.
CURRENCY – Lek (Lk) of 100 qindarka.
FLAG – Black two-headed eagle on a red field.
NATIONAL DAY – 11 January.

GOVERNMENT

Albania was under Turkish suzerainty from 1468 until 1912, when independence was declared. After a period of unrest, a republic was declared in 1925, and in 1928 a monarchy. The King went into exile in 1939 when the country was occupied by the Italians; Albania was liberated in November 1944. Elections in 1945 resulted in a Communist-controlled Assembly; the King was deposed in absentia and a republic declared in January 1946.

From 1946 to 1991 Albania was a one-party, Communist state. In March 1991 multiparty elections were held and were won by the Socialist Party (the renamed Communist Party of Labour). A coalition government was formed in June 1991, but in December 1991 the Democratic Party withdrew from the government and new elections were held in March 1992. These elections were won overwhelmingly by the Democratic Party, which formed a coalition government with the Social Democrat and Republican parties. In April 1992 the Democratic Party leader Dr Sali Berisha was elected by parliament as Albania's first non-Communist President. A draft constitution defining Albania as a parliamentary republic was rejected in a national referendum in November 1994.

HEAD OF STATE
President, Dr Sali Berisha, *elected* April 1992

COUNCIL OF MINISTERS *as at June 1995*
Prime Minister, Aleksander Meksi
Deputy Prime Minister responsible for economic reform, Bashkim Kopliku
Deputy Prime Minister, Finance, Dylber Vrioni
Minister without Portfolio, Rexhep Uka
General Secretary, Vullnet Ademi
Foreign Affairs, Alfred Serreqi
Justice, Hektor Frasheri
Trade, Transport and Industry, Albert Brojka
Defence, Safet Zhulali
Interior, Agron Musaraj
Construction and Tourism, Dashamir Shehu
Health and Environment, Maksim Cikuli
Education, Xhezair Teliti
Culture, Youth and Sports, Teodor Laco
Labour, Engjell Dakli
Chairman of the Committee of Science and Technology, Maskim Konomi
Chairman of the Control Commission, Blerim Cela
Public Order, Agron Musaraj
Agriculture and Food, Hassan Halili

EMBASSY OF THE REPUBLIC OF ALBANIA
6 Wilton Court, 59 Ecclestone Square, London SW1V 1PH
Tel 0171-976 5295
Ambassador Extraordinary and Plenipotentiary, His Excellency Pavli Qesku, apptd 1993

BRITISH AMBASSADOR – His Excellency Sir Patrick Fairweather, KCMG, resident in Rome
Chargé d'Affaires, S. Nash (resident in Tirana). Tel: Tirana 42 42849

DEFENCE

Albania has a total active armed forces strength of some 73,000 personnel (22,800 conscripts). Conscripts serve for a term of 18 months. The Army has a strength of 60,000 (20,000 conscripts).

The Navy has a strength of 3,000 (1,000 conscripts) and the Air Force has a strength of 10,000 personnel (1,800 conscripts).

ECONOMY

Much of the country is mountainous and nearly a half is covered by forest. There are fertile areas along the Adriatic coast and the Koritza Basin and there have been land reclamation and irrigation programmes. The main crops are wheat, maize, sugar-beet, potatoes and fruit. There are large chromium deposits.

The principal industries are agricultural product processing, textiles, oil products and cement. Exports include crude oil, minerals (bitumen, chrome, nickel, copper), tobacco, fruit and vegetables. The government is committed to economic reform, privatization and the creation of a market economy. Most agriculture has been privatized and land redistributed, with a consequent increase in production. Most housing and 2,780 small and medium-sized enterprises have been privatized.

Since April 1992 the government has introduced severe economic measures, cut the budget to reduce deficits and brought down inflation to around 16 per cent a year. The currency has stabilized, with economic growth of 11 per cent of GDP in 1993 and 8 per cent in 1994, signalling a recovery from the economic collapse of 1988–92. Commerce and the service sectors have expanded, and agricultural production has increased. The country is now self-sufficient in food production, producing 470,000 tonnes of wheat in 1993 after most land had been privatized. Remittances from 500,000 overseas workers remain an important source of revenue. Albania has received $1 billion in aid from Western donors.

Trade with UK	1993	1994
Imports from UK	£5,406,000	£5,607,000
Exports to UK	465,000	220,000

ALGERIA
Al-Jumhuriya al-Jazairiya ad-Dimuqratiya ash-Shabiya

Algeria lies between 8° 45′ W. and 12° E. longitude, 27° 6′ N. to a southern limit about 19° N. and has an area of 919,595 sq. miles (2,381,741 sq. km). The population (1987 census) was 22,971,558. A 1992 UN estimate gives a figure of 26,346,000.

CAPITAL – ΨAlgiers, population 3,250,000 (approx). It is one of the principal ports of the Mediterranean as well as an important industrial centre. Other towns include ΨOran; Constantine; ΨAnnaba; Blida; Setif; Sidi-Bel-Abbès; Tlemcen; ΨMostaganem; ΨSkikda; ΨBejaia and Tizi Ouzou.

CURRENCY – Algerian dinar (DA) of 100 centimes.

FLAG – Divided vertically green and white with a red crescent and star over all in the centre.

NATIONAL ANTHEM – Qassaman.

NATIONAL DAY – 1 November.

GOVERNMENT

Algiers surrendered to a French force in 1830, and Algeria was annexed to France in 1842. From 1881 the three northern departments of Algiers, Oran and Constantine formed an integral part of France. The Southern Territories of the Sahara, formerly a separate colony, became an integral part of Algeria on the attainment of independence. An armed rebellion against French rule led by the (Arab) Front de Liberation Nationale (FLN) broke out in 1954. French control of Algeria came to an end when President de Gaulle declared Algeria independent on 3 July 1962. By 1965 more than 80 per cent of the French population had left Algeria.

Ben Bella was elected President of the republic in September 1963, but was deposed; a Council of the Revolution presided over by Col. Boumediène assumed power in June 1965. In December 1976 President Boumediène was elected for a six-year term of office. Following his death in December 1978, Chadli Bendjedid was elected President in February 1979.

A new constitution was agreed by referendum in February 1989 which moved Algeria away from a one-party socialist system to a pluralist system. Local elections in June 1990 were won by the opposition Islamic Salvation Front (FIS) which campaigned on a radical 'Islamist' platform. The FIS emerged as the clear winner of the first round of legislative elections in December 1991. However before the second round of the elections was held, the Army forced President Bendjedid to resign and the elections were abandoned. A Higher Committee of State (HCS) was formed, backed by the armed forces, to govern the country. The former FLN veteran Mohammed Boudiaf returned from 25 years in exile to head the HCS. The HCS declared a state of emergency in February 1992, which was extended indefinitely in February 1993, and the FIS was banned in March 1992 but continues its activities underground. In June 1992 President Boudiaf was assassinated by suspected FIS supporters.

In 1993–4 the HCS and armed forces attempted unsuccessfully to reach agreement with non-Islamic political parties on a common anti-Islamic front. A national reconciliation conference in January 1994 was boycotted by the FIS and other political parties, but nevertheless it appointed General Liamine Zeroual as President to replace the HCS, which disbanded itself. In 1994–5 President Zeroual has attempted unsuccessfully to reach a political agreement with the FIS. The regime has stated that there will be a presidential election by the end of 1995.

INSURGENCY

Since the cancelling of the second round of legislative elections in early 1992, the FIS-backed Islamic Salvation Army (AIS) and the more extreme Armed Islamic Group (GIA) have waged an armed campaign against the military regime in favour of an Islamic state. The two groups have targeted the military and security forces, their secular supporters in the population, and foreign expatriates; the military has killed and detained thousands of Islamic militants and sentenced hundreds to death. Some 30,000–40,000 have died in the fighting so far, including 85 foreigners.

HEAD OF STATE
President, Gen. Liamine Zeroual, *appointed* January 1994

GOVERNMENT *as at July 1995*
Prime Minister, Mokdad Sifi
Defence, The President
Foreign Affairs, Mohamed Salah Dembri
Interior, Abderrahmane Meziane Cherif
Finance, Ahmed Benbitour
Justice, Mohammed Adani
Communications, Lamine Bechichi
Education, Amar Sakhri
Universities and Scientific Research, Bourbekear Beibouzid
War Veterans, Mohamed Said Abadou

Industrial Restructuring, Mourad Benachnhou
Energy and Industry, Amar Mekhloufi
Equipment, Cherif Rahmani
Commerce, Sassi Aziza
Agriculture, Noureddine Bahbouh
Religious Affairs, Sassi Lamouri
Housing, Mohamed Meghlaoui
Health and Population, Yahia Kaidoum
Labour and Social Protection, Mohamed Laichoubi
Vocational Training, Hacene Laskri
Culture, Slimane Cheikh
Youth and Sport, Sid Ali Lebib
Post and Telecommunications, Tahar Allan
Transport, Mohamed Arezki Isli
Small and Medium-sized Enterprises, Redha Hamiani
Tourism and Handicrafts, Mohamed Bensalem

ALGERIAN EMBASSY
54 Holland Park, London WII 3RS
Tel 0171-221 7800
Ambassador Extraordinary and Plenipotentiary, His Excellency
    Amar Bendjama, apptd 1994

BRITISH EMBASSY
7 Chemin des Glycines,
BP43, Alger-Gare 16000, Algiers
Tel: Algiers 622411
Ambassador Extraordinary and Plenipotentiary, His Excellency
    Christopher Donald Crabbie, CMG, apptd 1994

DEFENCE

Algeria has a total active armed forces strength of 121,700 personnel, of which 90,000 are conscripts. Conscripts serve only in the Army and for a period of 18 months.

The Army has a strength of 105,000 (90,000 conscripts) with 960 main battle tanks, 1,375 armoured personnel carriers and armoured infantry fighting vehicles, 120 reconnaissance vehicles and 715 artillery pieces.

The Navy has a strength of 6,700 in four main bases. It is equipped with two submarines, three frigates and 22 patrol and coastal vessels. The Air Force has a strength of 10,000 personnel with 193 combat aircraft and 63 armed helicopters.

In addition, there are 41,000 personnel in the paramilitary Gendarmerie and National Security Forces. All military and paramilitary forces are heavily engaged in fighting the insurgency.

ECONOMY

Development from 1965 to 1989 was regulated by a series of national development plans. The economy was centrally planned and state-controlled in most sectors. Economic reform began in 1987 with the break-up of state farms into smaller units. Following riots in 1988, reform was speeded up and now includes the industrial and financial sectors. In April 1994 the government finally accepted full economic reform and liberalization under a reform programme agreed with the IMF to gain US$1,000 million necessary for balance of payments support. The government has cut the budget deficit, devalued the currency and freed price controls. In April 1995 the IMF lent Algeria a further US$1,800 million towards restructuring the economy.

The main industry is the hydrocarbons industry. Oil and natural gas are pumped from the Sahara to terminals on the coast before being exported; the gas is first liquefied at liquefaction plants at Skikda and Arzew, although pipelines serve Libya and Italy direct.

Other major industries include a steel industry, motor vehicles, building materials, paper making, chemical products and metal manufactures. Most major industrial enterprises are still under state control.

TRADE WITH UK	1993	1994
Imports from UK	£56,162,000	£47,257,000
Exports to UK	187,081,000	182,853,000

Exports are worth around US$12,000 million annually, mainly from crude oil and liquefied natural gas. The country's external debt is US$27,000 million, which was rescheduled with IMF agreement in April 1995 to half the debt service ratio.

COMMUNICATIONS

Algeria has a rapidly expanding network of roads and railways. Considerable sums are also being spent on the development of the state airline, the national shipping company and telecommunications.

ANDORRA
Principat d'Andorra

A small, neutral principality formed by a treaty in 1278, Andorra is situated on the southern slopes of the Pyrenees between Spain and France. It is surrounded by mountains of 6,500 to 10,000 feet. It has an approximate area of 175 sq. miles (468 sq. km), and population (estimate 1994) of 64,311, less than one-quarter of whom are native Andorrans. The official language of the country is Catalan, but French and Spanish (Castilian) are also spoken. The established religion is Roman Catholicism.

CAPITAL – Andorra la Vella (population 22,387).
CURRENCY – French francs and Spanish pesetas are both in use.
FLAG – Three vertical bands, blue, yellow, red; Andorran coat of arms frequently imposed on central (yellow) band but not essential.
NATIONAL DAY – 8 September.

GOVERNMENT

A new constitution was promulgated on 4 May 1993 under which Andorra is an independent, democratic parliamentary co-principality, with the state's sovereignty vested in the people rather than in the two co-princes, as was previously the case. The constitution enables Andorra to establish an independent judiciary for the first time and to carry out its own foreign policy, whilst its people may now join trade unions and political parties. The two co-princes, the President of the French Republic and the Spanish Bishop of Urgel, remain heads of state but now only have the power to veto treaties with France and Spain which affect the state's borders and security. The co-princes are represented by Permanent Delegates of whom one is the French Prefect of the Pyrenees Orientales Department at Perpignan and the other is the Spanish Vicar-General of the Diocese of Urgel. They are in turn represented in Andorra la Vella by two resident Viguiers known as the Viguier Français and the Viguier Episcopal.

Andorra has a unicameral legislature of 28 members known as the *Consell General de las Valls d'Andorra* (Valleys of Andorra General Council). Fourteen members are elected on a national list basis and 14 in seven dual-member constituencies based on Andorra's seven parishes. The Council appoints the head of the executive government, who designates the members of his government.

The first elections under the new constitution were held in December 1993, and on 20 January 1994 the first sovereign government of Andorra took office.

Viguier Français, Jean Ive Caullet
Viguier Episcopal, Nemesi Marqués

EXECUTIVE COUNCIL *as at June 1995*
President, Marc Forné Molné
Foreign Affairs, Manel Mas Ribó
Economy, Joan Tomàs Roca
Finance, Susagna Arasanz Serra
Social Affairs and Culture, Pere Canturri Montanya
Education, Youth and Sports, Carme Sala Sansa
Territorial Administration, Lluis Montanya Tarrés
Interior, Olivier Montel Monteret
Health, Lidia Magallon Font

Sindic (President) of General Council, Josep Dalleres

ANDORRAN DELEGATION, 63 Westover Road, London SW18 2RF. Tel: 0181-874 4806
BRITISH AMBASSADOR – His Excellency David Brighty, CMG, CVO, resident at Madrid

ECONOMY

The estimated national revenue (1992) was US$1,231 million, with a per capita income of US$19,988.

Potatoes are produced in the highlands and tobacco in the valleys. The mountain slopes have been developed for skiing, and it is estimated that 10 million tourists visit the valleys during the year. The economy is largely based on tourism, banking, commerce, tobacco, construction and forestry; a third of the country is classified as forest, in which pine, fir, oak, birch and box-tree predominate. Andorra has negotiated a customs union with the European Community which came into force in 1991. Andorra's very low consumer taxes enticed 12 million shopping tourists to the state in 1992. The economy is now diversifying rapidly into offshore financial services.

TRADE WITH UK	1993	1994
Imports from UK	£18,680,000	£12,070,000
Exports to UK	89,000	298,000

COMMUNICATIONS

A road into the valleys from Spain is open all year round, and that from France is closed only occasionally in winter. An airport at Seo d'Urgell just outside Andorra provides limited air connections. There are two radio stations in Andorra, one privately owned and Radio Andorra, operated by the government.

ANGOLA
República de Angola

Angola, which has an area of 481,354 sq. miles (1,246,700 sq. km), lies on the western coast of Africa. To the north and east lies Zaïre, to the east Zambia and to the south Namibia. The enclave of Cabinda is separated from the rest of Angola by Zaïre and also borders on the Congo. The population in 1991 was estimated by the UN at 10,609,000.

CAPITAL – ΨLuanda, population estimate 1993, 3,000,000.
CURRENCY – New Kwanza (Kz) of 100 lwei.
FLAG – Red and black with a yellow star, machete and cogwheel.
NATIONAL ANTHEM – Angola Avante.
NATIONAL DAY – 11 November (Independence Day).

GOVERNMENT

After a Portuguese presence of five centuries, and an anti-colonial war since 1961, Angola became independent on 11 November 1975 in the midst of civil war. Soviet-Cuban military assistance to the Popular Movement for the Liberation of Angola (MPLA) enabled it to defeat its rivals early in 1976. However, the MPLA government remained under pressure from the UNITA guerrilla movement (led by Dr Jonas Savimbi) which by the mid 1980s was operating freely. In August 1988 a ceasefire between South African, Cuban and Angolan forces took place. In December 1988 an agreement providing for the withdrawal of South African and Cuban troops by July 1991 was signed in New York. In May 1991 a peace agreement was signed between the government and UNITA. Multiparty presidential and legislative elections took place in September 1992, the MPLA winning 129 seats and UNITA 70. In the first round of the presidential election, MPLA leader President Dos Santos won 49.5 per cent of the vote to Savimbi's 40 per cent, necessitating a second round. Savimbi and UNITA refused to accept the election results and rising tension led to outbreaks of fighting throughout November and December 1992 and a return to civil war in January 1993.

Fierce fighting continued throughout most of 1993 and 1994, until UNITA and the MPLA government signed a peace agreement (the Lusaka Protocol) under UN mediation on 20 November 1994. By this stage UNITA's position had significantly deteriorated, so that it controlled only 20 per cent of the country and no major towns or cities. Under the Lusaka Protocol the 1992 presidential election will be completed, the 70 UNITA MPs will take their seats in parliament, UNITA forces and personnel are to be incorporated into the police, civil service and judiciary, and UNITA are to be awarded 11 ministerial and deputy ministerial posts. A renewed and expanded UN operation (UNAVEM III) to oversee the peace process was mandated in February 1995, with the first of 7,600 UN troops arriving in April 1995.

The MPLA, formerly a Marxist-Leninist party, was the sole legal party until early 1991 when a multi-party system was adopted. The constitution declares Angola to be a democratic state and provides for a President, who appoints a Council of Ministers to assist him, and a 220-

member National Assembly. The present MPLA-dominated government also includes several minor parties and was sworn in after the elections in November 1992.

SECESSION

In the northern enclave of Cabinda, the Front for the Liberation of the Cabinda Enclave (FLEC) has been fighting for independence against government forces since 1975, and has a strength of some 600, armed with light arms. Cabinda is rich in oil and is separated from the rest of Angola by Zaïre.

HEAD OF STATE
President, Jose Eduardo Dos Santos, *re-elected* 30 September 1992

COUNCIL OF MINISTERS *as at June 1995*

Prime Minister, Dr Marcolino Jose Carlos Moco
Defence, Pedro Tonho Pedale
Interior, Santana Andre Pitra
Foreign, Dr Venancio de Moura
Territorial Administration, Jose Anibal Rocha
Finance, Augusto Da Silva Tomas
Industry, Dr Isalino Manuel Mendes
Agriculture and Rural Development, Isaac Maria dos Anjos
Fisheries, Maria de Fatima Jardin
Geology and Mines, Jose Antonio Dias
Public Works and Urban Affairs, Dr Mateus de Brito Junior
Transport and Communications, Dr Andre Luis Brandao
Commerce and Tourism, Celestino Dias
Health, Dr Martinho Sanches Epalanga
Education, Dr Joao Manuel Bernardo
Planning, Jose Pedro de Morais
Assistance and Social Reintegration, Albino Malungo
Culture, Ana Maria de Oliveira
Youth and Sports, José Da Rocha de Castro
Justice, Dr Paulo Tjipilica
Public Administration, Employment and Social Welfare, Dr Antonio Domingos Costa Neto
Governor of Cabinda, José Amaro Tati

EMBASSY OF ANGOLA
98 Park Lane, London WIY 3TA
Tel 0171-495 1752
Ambassador Extraordinary and Plenipotentiary, His Excellency António DaCosta Fernandes, apptd 1993

BRITISH EMBASSY
Rua Diogo Caõ 4 (Caixa Postal 1244), Luanda
Tel: Luanda 334582
Ambassador Extraordinary and Plenipotentiary, His Excellency Anthony Richard Thomas, CMG, apptd 1993

DEFENCE

Under the 1991 peace agreement, the armed forces of the MPLA and UNITA were to have merged to form a 50,000 strong National Army shortly after the elections of September 1992. To this end, large proportions of MPLA and UNITA forces were in UN containment camps or had been demobilized by September 1992. However, with the return to civil war, both sides remobilized.

Government active armed forces number 82,000. The Army has 75,000 personnel with 200 main battle tanks, 200 armoured infantry fighting vehicles and armoured personnel carriers and 350 artillery pieces. The Navy has a strength of 2,000 with 17 patrol and coastal craft. The Air Force has a strength of 5,500 personnel with 79 combat aircraft and 40 armed helicopters. In addition there are 40,000 paramilitary internal security police. UNITA forces number 55,000. Equipment numbers include about

80 main battle tanks and numerous captured armoured personnel carriers, artillery, mortar and anti-aircraft guns.

ECONOMY

The government is attempting to reform the socialist economy by free market reforms but is making little progress, with high inflation and a collapsing economy, together with the loss of most diamond-producing areas to UNITA. The total foreign debt in 1994 was US$10,000 million.

Angola has valuable oil and diamond deposits and exports of these two commodities account for over 90 per cent of total exports.

Principal agricultural crops are cassava, maize, bananas, coffee, palm oil and kernels, cotton and sisal. Coffee, sisal, maize and palm oil are exported; exports also include mahogany and other hardwoods from the tropical rain forests in the north of the country.

TRADE WITH UK	1993	1994
Imports from UK	£27,512,000	£23,681,000
Exports to UK	21,202,000	12,173,000

ANTIGUA AND BARBUDA
State of Antigua and Barbuda

Antigua and Barbuda comprises the islands of Antigua (108 sq. miles (279 sq. km)), Barbuda (62 sq. miles (160 sq. km)) 25 miles north of Antigua, and Redonda ($\frac{1}{2}$sq. mile (1.2 sq. km)) 25 miles south-west of Antigua. Antigua is part of the Leeward Islands in the eastern Caribbean and lies 17° 3′ N. and 61° 48′ W. It is distinguished from the rest of the Leeward group by its absence of high hills and forest, and a drier climate than most of the West Indies. Barbuda, formerly a possession of the Codrington family, is very flat, mainly scrub-covered, with a large lagoon.

The total population (official census 1991) is 65,962; Antigua had a population of 64,562, Barbuda 1,400, and Redonda was uninhabited.

CAPITAL – ΨSt John's. Population, 30,000. The town of Barbuda is Codrington.
CURRENCY – East Caribbean dollar (EC$) of 100 cents.
FLAG – Red with an inverted triangle divided black over blue over white, with a rising gold sun on the white band.
NATIONAL ANTHEM – Fair Antigua and Barbuda.
NATIONAL DAY – 1 November (Independence Day).

GOVERNMENT

Antigua was first settled by the English in 1632, and was granted to Lord Willoughby by Charles II. It became internally self-governing in 1967 and fully independent on 1 November 1981, as a constitutional monarchy with The Queen as Head of State, represented by the Governor-General. There is a Senate of 17 appointed members and a House of Representatives of 17 members elected every five years. The Attorney-General may be appointed.

The Antigua Labour party won the general election of 8 March 1994 and a fifth successive term of office with 11 seats in the House of Representatives compared to five seats for the United Progressive Party.

Governor-General, His Excellency Sir James Carlisle, GCMG

CABINET *as at June 1995*

Prime Minister, Foreign Affairs, Social Affairs, Hon. Lester Bird
Justice, Legal Affairs and Attorney-General, Hon. Clare Roberts

Finance and Social Security, Hon. Molwyn Joseph
Home Affairs and Health, Hon. Hilroy Humphreys
Education, Youth, Sports, Community Development, Hon. Dr
  Rodney Williams
Agriculture, Fisheries, Commerce, Industry and Consumer Affairs,
  Hon. John St Luce
Tourism, Culture and Environment, Hon. Bernard Percival
Labour, Civil Service, Co-operatives, Hon. Adolphus Freeland
Public Utilities, Communications, Transportation and Energy,
  Hon. Robin Yearwood
Housing, Leader of the Senate, Sen. Hon. Henderson Simon

HIGH COMMISSION FOR ANTIGUA AND BARBUDA
15 Thayer Street, London WIM 5LD
Tel 0171-486 7073
High Commissioner, His Excellency James Thomas, CMG,
  apptd 1987

BRITISH HIGH COMMISSION
11 Old Parham Road (PO 483), St John's
Tel: St John's 462 0008/9
High Commissioner, His Excellency Emrys Thomas Davies,
  CMG, resident at Bridgetown, Barbados
Resident Representative, R. G. Baylis, MVO (*Acting High
  Commissioner*)

ECONOMY

Tourism is the main sector of the economy. Tourism and
related services account for 60 per cent of GDP and
employ 40 per cent of the workforce.

For many years sugar was the dominant crop but is no
longer produced. Agricultural production includes livestock, sea island cotton, mixed market gardening and
fishing.

FINANCE	1992*	1993*
Revenue	EC$251,331,799	EC$255,893,891
Expenditure		
(recurrent)	278,084,340	306,663,306
*estimated		

TRADE WITH UK	1993	1994
Imports from UK	£17,752,000	£24,177,000
Exports to UK	2,524,000	2,166,000

ARGENTINA
República Argentina

Argentina occupies the greater portion of the southern part
of the South American continent, and extends from Bolivia
to Cape Horn, a total distance of nearly 2,300 miles; its
greatest breadth is about 930 miles. It is bounded on the
north by Bolivia, on the north-east by Paraguay, Brazil and
Uruguay, on the south-east and south by the Atlantic, and
on the west by Chile, from which it is separated by the
Cordillera de los Andes. On the west the mountainous
Cordilleras, with their plateaux, extend from the northern
to the southern boundaries; on the east are the great plains.

The area is 1,068,302 sq. miles (2,766,889 sq. km.), with a
population (census 1991) of 32,370,298. The language is
Spanish.

CAPITAL – ΨBuenos Aires, population (1991),
  metropolitan area 2,960,976; with suburbs, 10,686,163.
  Other large towns are: ΨRosario (894,645), Córdoba
  (1,148,305), ΨLa Plata (640,344), ΨMar del Plata
  (519,707), San Miguel de Tucumán (622,348), and
  Mendoza (773,559).
CURRENCY – Peso.

FLAG – Horizontal bands of blue, white, blue; gold sun in
  centre of white band.
NATIONAL ANTHEM – Oid Mortales! (Hear, oh mortals!).
NATIONAL DAY – 25 May.

GOVERNMENT

The estuary of La Plata was discovered in 1515 by Juan
Díaz de Solís, but it was not until 1536 that Pedro de
Mendoza founded Buenos Aires. This city was abandoned
and later re-founded by Don Juan de Garay in 1580. Spain
ruled the territory from the 16th century until 1810, when
Spanish rule was defied. In 1816, after a long campaign of
liberation conducted by General José de San Martín, the
independence of Argentina was declared by the Congress
of Tucumán.

In 1946 Juan Domingo Perón became President until
overthrown in 1955. There followed eighteen years of
political and economic instability until in 1973, Perón was
recalled from exile. Elected President he died within a year
and was succeeded by his widow, Vice-President María
Estela Martínez de Perón. However, warring factions in the
Perónist movement and increasing terrorist activity led to
a coup by the armed forces in 1976. A Junta, consisting of
the three commanders of the armed forces, was established,
with one of their number as President. Following the
Falkland Islands defeat in 1982 the President, Gen.
Galtieri, resigned and the Army appointed Gen. Bignone
as President. Elections for a civilian government to replace
the military one were held in 1983 and a civilian President
was elected. Presidential elections in 1989 were won by the
Justicialist Party (Perónist) candidate Carlos Menem.

The 1853 constitution was amended by constitutional
assembly in 1994. Power is vested in the President who
appoints the Cabinet and is directly elected for a once-
renewable four-year term. A presidential candidate must
win at least 45 per cent of the vote, or 40 per cent with a 10
per cent lead over the nearest challenger, to gain victory.
The legislature consists of a 72-member (three for each
province) Senate and a 259-member Chamber of Deputies. A third of the Senate is elected every three years and
half of the Chamber of Deputies is elected every two years.
Senators serve for a nine-year term and Deputies for a
four-year term. After the most recent elections in May
1995 the Justicialist Party held 135 seats in the Chamber of
Deputies.

The republic is divided into 23 provinces, each with an
elected Governor and legislature, and one federal district
(Buenos Aires), with an elected mayor and autonomous
government.

HEAD OF STATE
President, Dr Carlos Saúl Menem, *elected* May 1989, *re-
  elected* 14 May 1995
Vice-President, Dr Carlos Ruckauf

CABINET *as at June 1995*

Interior, Carlos Corach
Foreign Affairs, Dr Guido Di Tella
Labour, Armando Caro-Figueroa
Economy and Public Works, Dr Domingo Cavallo
Education, Jorge Alberto Rodriguez
Defence, Dr Oscar Camillión
Health and Social Welfare, Dr Alberto Mazza
Justice, Rodolfo Barra

EMBASSY OF THE ARGENTINE REPUBLIC
53 Hans Place, London SWIX OLA
Tel 0171-584 6494

Ambassador Extraordinary and Plenipotentiary, His Excellency Rogelio Pfirter, apptd 1995

BRITISH EMBASSY
Dr Luis Agote 2412, 1425 Buenos Aires
Tel: Buenos Aires 803-7070/1
Ambassador Extraordinary and Plenipotentiary, His Excellency Sir Peter Hall, KBE, CMG, apptd 1994
Deputy Ambassador, Minister and Consul-General, David Reddaway, CMG
Defence and Military Attaché, Col. R. J. Lawson
First Secretary (Commercial), vacant
Cultural Attaché and British Council Representative, Michael Potter, Martcelo T. de Alvear 590, 1058 Buenos Aires

BRITISH CHAMBER OF COMMERCE, Av. Corrientes 457, 10 piso, 1043 Buenos Aires

ECONOMY

The Menem government introduced a successful economic reform programme in 1991 which has involved the privatization of most state-owned industries, widespread deregulation, exchange-rate stabilization and lower trade barriers. This has led to economic growth (33 per cent of GDP in 1990–4), increased foreign investment (US$17 billion in 1993) and much lower inflation (5 per cent annually in 1994–5), which has transformed the economy, although unemployment remains at 12 per cent.

Argentina's foreign debt has been reduced from US$50,000 million in 1988 to US$32,000 million in 1995 by an April 1993 debt reduction agreement with creditors and by privatization receipts, which also enabled the introduction of a balanced budget in February 1994. An austerity programme was introduced in April 1995, following the Mexican economic crisis, to maintain the exchange rate parity between the peso and the US dollar which is maintained by gold and foreign currency reserves.

AGRICULTURE
Of a total land area of about 700 million acres, farmland occupies 425 million, of which 60 per cent is pasture, 10 per cent annual crops, 5 per cent permanent crops and the remaining 25 per cent forest and wasteland. A large proportion of the land is still held in large estates devoted to cattle raising but the number of small farms is increasing. The principal crops are wheat, maize, oats, barley, rye, linseed, sunflower seed, alfalfa, sugar, fruit and cotton. Argentina is pre-eminent in the production of beef, mutton and wool, and pastoral and agricultural products provide about 85 per cent of Argentina's exports.

MINERAL PRODUCTION
Oil is found in various parts of the republic and the production of oil is of great importance. Total petroleum output for 1991 was 484,000 b.p.d. There is a refinery in San Lorenzo (Santa Fé province). Natural gas is also produced in a number of provinces.

Coal, lead, zinc, tungsten, iron ore, sulphur, mica and salt are the other chief minerals being exploited. There are small worked deposits of beryllium, manganese, bismuth, uranium, antimony, copper, kaolin, arsenate, gold, silver and tin. Coal is produced at the Rio Turbio mine in the province of Santa Cruz. The output of other materials is not large but greater attention is now being paid to the development of these natural resources, especially copper, for which the Government and private companies are carrying out exploration.

INDUSTRIES
Meat-packing is one of the principal industries; flour-milling, sugar-refining, and the wine industry are also important. In recent years progress has been made by the textile, plastic and machine tool industries and engineering, especially in the production of motor vehicles and steel manufactures.

TRADE WITH UK	1993	1994
Imports from UK	£179,259,000	£224,942,000
Exports to UK	141,143,000	170,970,000

COMMUNICATIONS

The 25,386 miles of railway are state-owned. Plans are in hand for complete reorganization of the railways in order to improve their operating efficiency and reduce a large financial deficit. The combined national and provincial road network totals approximately 137,000 miles of which 23,180 miles are surfaced. There are air services between Argentina and all the neighbouring republics, Europe, Asia, Canada, the USA and South Africa.

DEFENCE

Total active armed forces number 69,800 personnel (18,400 conscripts). Conscripts serve between seven and 14 months. Reserves total 377,000. The Army numbers 40,400, including about 13,400 conscripts, and has 250,000 reserves.

The Navy numbers 20,500, including 3,500 conscripts and 4,000 marines, with a further 77,000 reserves. The Air Force has a strength of 8,900 (1,200 conscripts) with 50,000 reserves. There is a paramilitary gendarmerie of 18,000 personnel under Ministry of Defence control.

Argentina currently deploys one 853-strong infantry battalion with UN forces in Croatia and one 375-strong infantry battalion with UN forces in Cyprus.

EDUCATION

Education is compulsory for the seven grades of primary school (six to 13). Secondary schools (14 to 17+) are available in and around Buenos Aires and in most of the important towns in the interior of the country. Most secondary schools are administered by the Central Ministry of Education in Buenos Aires, while primary schools are administered by the Central Ministry or by Provincial Ministries of Education. Private schools, of which there are many, are also loosely controlled by the Central Ministry. The total number of universities is over 50 with 24 national, 25 private and a small number of provincial universities.

CULTURE

The literature of Spain is part of the culture. There is little indigenous literature before the break from Spain, but all branches have flourished since the latter half of the 19th century. About 450 daily newspapers are published in Argentina, including seven major ones in the city of Buenos Aires. The English language newspaper is the *Buenos Aires Herald* (daily). There are several other foreign language newspapers.

ARMENIA
Hayastany Hanrapetoutioun

Armenia has an area of 11,306 sq. miles (29,800 sq. km) and lies between the Black and Caspian Seas, occupying the south-western part of the Caucasus region of the former Soviet Union. It is bordered on the east and south-west by Azerbaijan, on the north by Georgia, on the south by Iran and on the west by Turkey. It is a very mountainous country consisting of several vast tablelands surrounded by ridges. The climate is continental, dry and cold, but the Araks valley has a long, hot and dry summer.

The population (1995 estimate) is 3,645,000, concentrated in the low-lying part of Armenia, the Aras valley and the Erevan hollow. Armenians form 93 per cent of the population, Kurds 1.7 per cent and Russians 1.6 per cent. Azerbaijanis formed 2.6 per cent of the population, but most fled or were expelled after the outbreak of war with Azerbaijan. There are also Ukrainians, Greeks and Assyrians. The Armenian diaspora numbers some 5,300,000, including 1,500,000 in the former Soviet states, one million in the USA and 400,000 in France.

Armenian is the official language, though Russian is widely spoken and understood. The main religion is Armenian Orthodox Christian (Armenian Church centred in Etchmiadzin). Armenia adopted Christianity as its official religion in AD 301, the first state in the world to do so.

CAPITAL – Erevan. Population 1,254,000 (1990).
CURRENCY – Dram of 100 louma.
FLAG – Three horizontal stripes of red, blue and orange.
NATIONAL DAY – 21 September (Independence Day).

GOVERNMENT

Armenia was an ancient society, first mentioned in the ninth century BC. The country was first united in 95 BC but was divided between the Persian and Byzantine Empires in AD 387 and then conquered in the 11th century by the Seljuk Turks and the Mongols. In the 16th century most of Armenia was incorporated into the Ottoman Empire. In 1639 the country was divided again, the eastern-most portions, now the republic of Armenia, becoming part of the Persian Empire. In 1828 eastern Armenia became part of the Russian Empire while western Armenia remained under Ottoman rule. The Ottomans launched pogroms against the Armenians from 1894 onwards, and in 1915 to 1918 massacred 1,500,000 Armenians.

After the 1917 Russian revolution, Armenia declared its independence as a republic on 28 May 1919, but was crushed and divided between Turkish and Soviet forces in 1920, with the area under Soviet control proclaimed a Soviet Socialist Republic on 29 November 1920. The Soviet government was overthrown by a nationalist revolt in 1921 but reinstated by the Red Army a few months later. In early 1922 Armenia acceded to the USSR.

Gorbachev's reform policies slowly filtered through to Armenia in 1987 when demonstrations against pollution caused by Soviet industrialization in the republic and against local Communist Party corruption developed into political opposition to Communist rule, focussed by support for the self-determination of the autonomous region of Nagorny-Karabakh in Azerbaijan which was predominantly Armenian populated. Throughout 1988–90 the Soviet authorities were perceived as supporting Azerbaijan over Nagorny-Karabakh, and an Armenian nationalist movement evolved which swept to power in national elections in mid-1990. In a referendum in September 1991, 99 per cent of the electorate voted for independence. Armenia declared independence from the Soviet Union on 21 September 1991.

The war between the (ethnic Armenian) Nagorno-Karabakh forces supported by Armenia and the Azeri government over the disputed enclave of Nagorny-Karabakh simmered from February 1988 and erupted into all-out war in May 1992, when Nagorno-Karabakh forces breached Azerbaijan's defences to form a land bridge to Armenia. By the end of summer 1992 all of Nagorny-Karabakh was under Armenian control. Continued

victories over Azeri forces in late 1992 and 1993 brought all Azeri territory that separated Nagorny-Karabakh from Armenia and all mountainous Azeri territory around Nagorny-Karabakh under the control of Nagorny-Karabakh Armenians, an estimated 10 per cent of Azeri territory. Armenia claims this territory as historically Armenian land arbitrarily given to Azerbaijan by Stalin in 1921–2. A ceasefire agreement between Armenia, Azerbaijan and Nagorny-Karabakh was reached in Moscow in May 1994 and has held since; a CSCE peacekeeping force is to be deployed.

Legislative elections are due in late 1995. There have been clashes between opposition supporters, who claim that their candidates are being obstructed, and security forces.

Armenia is divided into 37 Administrative Districts.

HEAD OF STATE
President, Levon Ter-Petrosyan, *elected* 16 October 1991

CABINET *as at July 1995*
Prime Minister, Grant Bagratian
Deputy Prime Minister, Vigen Chitechian
Minister of State (Industry and Energy), Sepuh Tashjian
Minister of State (Agriculture and Food), Gagik Shakhbazian
Minister of State (Construction), Gagik Martirossian
Ministers of State: Rafael Bagoyan; Armenak Ghazarian
Defence, Mickael Haroutiunian
Interior, Vano Siradegyan
Higher Education and Science, Vardkes Gnuni
Public Health, Ara Babloyan
Foreign Affairs, Vagan Papazian
Culture, Hakob Movses
Light Industry, vacant
Material Resources, Vagan Melkonyan
Environment, Souren Avetissian
Industry, Ashot Safarian
Education, Ashot Bleyan
Food, David Zadoyan
Communications, Grigor Pokhpatyan
Agriculture, Ashot Voskahyan
Trade, vacant
Transport, Genrikh Kochinyan
Labour, Ashot Yessayan
Finance, Levon Barhudaryan
Economics, Armen Yeghiazarian
Justice, Vage Stepanyan
National Security, Serje Sarkissian

Chairman of the Supreme Soviet, Babken Ararktsyan

EMBASSY OF THE REPUBLIC OF ARMENIA
25 Cheniston Gardens, London W8 6TG
Tel 0171-938 5345
Ambassador Extraordinary and Plenipotentiary, His Excellency Prof. Armen Sarkissian, apptd 1993

BRITISH EMBASSY
Erevan
Ambassador Extraordinary and Plenipotentiary, His Excellency David Miller, OBE, apptd 1995

DEFENCE

Armenia maintains an army of 32,700 regular personnel, including conscripts who serve 18-month terms, and paramilitary forces of some 1,000. Both these forces are heavily involved in supplying and supporting the Nagorno-Karabakh forces. These number 20,000 personnel, equipped with light and medium weapons and artillery, while Armenian forces supply small numbers of tanks and helicopters. The regular army has 120 main battle tanks, 410 armoured personnel carriers and infantry fighting vehicles, 210 artillery pieces and 30 armed helicopters.

Russia maintains 5,000 army personnel in Armenia.

ECONOMY

The Armenian economy has been badly affected by the 1988 earthquake which devastated much of the country, and by the Azeri economic embargo which has been in place since 1988. The Azeri embargo is almost total, as the neighbouring states of Turkey and Iran generally support Azerbaijan, leaving the only remaining land supply routes and gas supplies through Georgia, where they are vulnerable to terrorism and sabotage. Energy supplies from Russia via Georgia remain insufficient, leading to an erratic electricity supply.

Armenia has a strong agricultural sector in low-lying areas, where industrial and fruit crops are grown. Grain is grown in the hills and the country is also noted for its wine and brandy. There are large copper ore and molybdenum deposits and other minerals. The country also has a developed chemicals, industrial vehicles and textiles industries.

The government introduced a programme of economic reforms in November 1994 with IMF support, including the liberalization of prices, stabilization of the currency, privatization, and reducing the budget deficit.

TRADE WITH UK	1993	1994
Imports from UK	£5,346,000	£4,371,000
Exports to UK	18,000	27,000

CULTURE

The Armenian alphabet was established in AD 391 and had a fully written form in the fifth century. Major writers include the poets Frick (13th century), Naapet Kuchak (16th century) and Saat-Nova (18th century). The composer Aram Khachaturian (1903–78) was Armenian.

AUSTRALIA
The Commonwealth of Australia

AREA AND POPULATION*

States and Territories	Area (sq. km)	Resident population 31 December 1994p
New South Wales (NSW)	801,600	6,081,200
Queensland (Qld.)	1,727,200	3,233,900
South Australia (SA)	984,000	1,471,900
Tasmania (Tas.)	67,800	472,600
Victoria (Vic.)	227,600	4,487,000
Western Australia (WA)	2,525,500	1,715,300
Australian Capital Territory (ACT)	2,400	301,700
Northern Territory (NT)	1,346,200	172,200
Total	7,682,300	17,938,500

* estimated
p preliminary

POPULATION OF ABORIGINAL AND TORRES STRAIT ISLANDER ORIGIN (*1991 census*)

	Number	% of state population
New South Wales	70,019	1.20
Queensland	70,124	2.40
South Australia	16,232	1.14

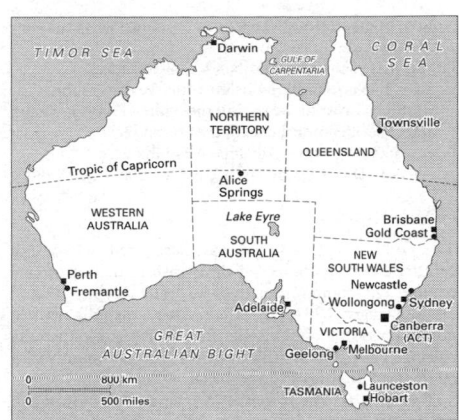

Tasmania	8,885	0.20
Victoria	16,735	0.40
Western Australia	41,779	2.54
Australian Capital Territory	1,775	0.63
Northern Territory	39,916	22.70
Total	265,459	1.60

BIRTHS, DEATHS, MARRIAGES AND DIVORCES *year ended 31 December*

	1993	1994p
Births	260,229	258,247
Deaths	121,599	126,709
Marriages	113,255	111,174
Divorces	48,324	48,256

p preliminary

MIGRATION *year ended 30 June*

	1993	1994
Permanent arrivals	76,330	69,770
Permanent departures	27,910	27,280

GEOGRAPHY

Australia lies between latitudes 10°41′ S. and 43°39′ S. and longitudes 113°09′ E. and 153°39′ E. The western half of the continent consists mainly of a great plateau 300–600 metres in altitude. The interior lowland includes the channel country of south-west Queensland (drainage to Lake Eyre) and the Murray-Darling river system to the south. The eastern uplands consist of a broad belt of varied width extending from north Queensland to Tasmania and composed largely of tablelands, ranges and ridges with only a few mountain areas above 1,000 metres. The highest point is Mt. Kosciusko (2,228 m) and the lowest, Lake Eyre (−15 m).

Climatic conditions range from the alpine to the tropical. Two-thirds of the continent is arid or semi-arid although good rainfalls (over 800 mm annually) occur in the northern monsoonal belt and along the eastern and southern highland regions. Fifty per cent of Australia has a medium rainfall of less than 300 mm per year and 80 per cent has less than 600 mm. The effectiveness of the rainfall is greatly reduced by marked alternations of wet and dry seasons, unreliability from year to year, high temperatures and high potential evaporation.

FEDERAL CAPITAL – Canberra, in the Australian Capital Territory. Estimated population at 30 June 1994 was 328,000. It has been the seat of government since 1927. The Australian Capital Territory was surrendered by

New South Wales to the Commonwealth Government in 1911.

CURRENCY – Australian dollar ($A) of 100 cents.

FLAG – The British Blue Ensign with five stars of the Southern Cross in the fly and the white Commonwealth Star of seven points beneath the Union Jack.

NATIONAL ANTHEM – Advance Australia Fair.

NATIONAL DAY – 26 January (Australia Day).

GOVERNMENT

The continent of Australia was discovered in the 18th century and was colonized by the British, initially as a penal colony. The Commonwealth of Australia was inaugurated on 1 January 1901, at which time Australia gained dominion status within the British Empire. Australia became independent within the British Commonwealth by the 1931 Statute of Westminster.

The government is that of a federal Commonwealth within the British Commonwealth, the executive power being vested in the Sovereign (through the Governor-General), assisted by a federal government. Under the constitution the federal government has acquired and may acquire certain defined powers as surrendered by the states, residuary legislative power remaining with the states. The right of a state to legislate on any matter is not abrogated except in connection with matters exclusively under federal control, but where a state law is inconsistent with a law of the Commonwealth the latter prevails to the extent of the inconsistency.

The 1993 Native Title Act restores land rights to the Aborigines which were lost after British settlement, establishing a system of tribunals that may give land title to indigenous people who can show customary use over the land.

GOVERNOR-GENERAL

Governor-General, His Excellency the Hon. Bill Hayden, AC, *assumed office,* 16 February 1989

CABINET *as at June 1995*

Prime Minister, Hon. Paul Keating
Deputy Prime Minister, Finance, Hon. Kim Beazley
Leader of the Government in the Senate and Foreign Affairs, Senator Hon. Gareth Evans, QC
Deputy Leader of the Government in the Senate and Defence, Senator Hon. Robert Ray
Treasurer, Hon. Ralph Willis
Housing and Regional Development, Hon. Brian Howe
Employment, Education and Training, Hon. Simon Crean
Health and Human Services, Hon. Dr Carmen Lawrence
Environment, Sport and Territories, Senator Hon. John Faulkner
Trade, Senator Hon. Robert McMullan
Immigration and Ethnic Affairs, Senator Hon. Nick Bolkus
Primary Industries and Energy, Senator Hon. Robert Collins
Industry, Science and Technology, Senator Hon. Peter Cook
Communications, Tourism and the Arts, Hon. Michael Lee
Industrial Relations and Transport, Hon. Laurence Brereton
Attorney-General, Hon. Michael Lavarch
Social Security, Hon. Peter Baldwin

AUSTRALIAN HIGH COMMISSION

Australia House, Strand, London WC2B 4LA
Tel 0171-379 4334
High Commissioner, His Excellency The Hon. Neal Blewett, apptd 1994
Deputy High Commissioner, D. Goss
Ministers, I. Wilcock (*Political*); R. Murray (*Economic*); D. Richard (*Commercial*); M. Fitzpatrick (*Industry, Science and Technology*)

Defence Adviser and Head of Defence Staff, Brig. P. L. McGuiness
Consul-General, Ms J. Harrhy (*Manchester*)

BRITISH HIGH COMMISSION

Commonwealth Avenue, Yarralumla, Canberra, ACT 2600
Tel: Canberra (6) 270 6666
High Commissioner, His Excellency Sir Roger John Carrick, KCMG, LVO, apptd 1995
Deputy High Commissioner, Head of Chancery, D. W. Fall
Counsellor, T. H. Byrne (*Director, Trade Promotion*)
Defence and Naval Adviser and Head of British Defence Liaison Staff, Cdre B. J. Adams
Consuls-General, J. C. Durham, LVO (*Brisbane*); G. Finlayson (*Melbourne*); A. J. Abott (*Perth*); R. S. Reeve (*Sydney*)
Cultural Adviser and British Council Representative, J. Potts, OBE, Edgecliff Centre, 203–233 New South Head Road (PO Box 88), Edgecliff, Sydney, NSW 2027

LEGISLATURE

Parliament consists of The Queen, the Senate and the House of Representatives. The constitution provides that the number of members of the House of Representatives shall be, as nearly as practicable, twice the number of senators. Members of the Senate are elected for six years by universal suffrage, half the members retiring every third year. Each of the six states returns 12 senators, and the Australian Capital Territory and the Northern Territory two each. The House of Representatives, similarly elected for a maximum of three years, contains members proportionate to the population, with a minimum of five members for each state. There are now 148 members in the House of Representatives, including one member for the Northern Territory and two for the Australian Capital Territory.

President of the Senate, Senator Hon. Kerry Sibraa
Speaker, House of Representatives, Hon. Stephen Martin, MP

JUDICATURE

The High Court, composed of a Chief Justice and six Justices, exercises jurisdiction over all matters arising from the constitution, all matters arising between the states and between residents of different states, matters to which the Commonwealth of Australia is a party, and treaties and foreign representatives in Australia. The High Court also hears appeals from the Federal Court and from the Supreme Courts of states and territories.

The Federal Court of Australia was established in 1977 as a superior court of record. It has jurisdiction over important industrial, trade practices, intellectual property, administrative law and bankruptcy matters. It also acts as a court of appeal for decisions from the Australian Capital Territory Supreme Court and certain decisions of state Supreme Courts exercising federal jurisdiction.

Each state has its own judicature of supreme, superior and minor courts for criminal and civil cases.

Chief Justice of the High Court of Australia, Hon. Sir Gerard Brennan, AC, KBE
Chief Justice of the Federal Court of Australia, Hon. M. E. J. Black
Chief Justice of the Australian Capital Territory, Hon. J. A. Miles

DEFENCE

Total defence expenditure was $A10,200 million in 1994. The total active armed forces number 61,600 personnel, with reserves numbering 29,400 personnel. All service is voluntary. The Army has a strength of 28,600 and is organized into one regular and one reservist division (reserves number 26,200). Equipment includes 103 main battle tanks, 795 armoured personnel carriers and armoured infantry fighting vehicles, 355 artillery pieces, 22 aircraft and 125 helicopters, of which 25 are armed.

The Navy has a strength of 14,800 with a further 1,600 reservists, and has four main bases at Sydney, Cockburn Sound, Cairns and Darwin. It has four submarines, three destroyers, nine frigates and 16 patrol and coastal craft with 23 armed helicopters.

The Air Force has a strength of 18,200, together with 1,600 reserves, and 155 combat aircraft organized into two ground attack/reconnaissance, three air defence, two maritime reconnaissance and seven transport squadrons with training and support units.

One Army infantry company and one Air Force detachment are stationed in Malaysia. US Navy and Air Force personnel numbering 370 are stationed at communications facilities in Australia.

FINANCE

COMMONWEALTH GOVERNMENT FINANCE

Outlays and revenue of the Commonwealth Government were ($A million):

	1993–4	1994–5
Current outlays	114,400	122,433
Capital outlays	1,026	2,449
Total revenue	100,737	110,283

STATE GOVERNMENT FINANCE 1994–5* ($A million)

	Outlay (current and capital)	Revenue and grants received	Net financing requirement
NSW	26,000	24,410	762
Victoria	18,685	17,424	369
Queensland	13,510	13,309	−210
S. Australia	7,307	6,646	584
W. Australia	7,539	7,442	−96
Tasmania	2,435	2,256	148
NT	1,554	1,440	129
ACT	1,273	1,195	46
Total	77,932	73,751	1,731

* estimated

ECONOMY

In 1993, 59.9 per cent of land area consisted of agricultural establishments, the remainder being urban areas, state forests, mining leases and unoccupied land. Crop-growing areas constituted around 2.25 per cent of the total agricultural establishments, emphasizing the relative importance of the livestock industries (sheep in the warm, temperate, semi-arid lands and beef cattle in the tropics).

The wide range of climatic and soil conditions has resulted in a diversity of crops. Generally, cereal crops (excluding rice and sorghum) are grown in all states over wide areas, while other crops are confined to specific locations in a few states. However, scanty or erratic rainfall, limited potential for irrigation and unsuitable soils or topography have restricted intensive agriculture.

GROSS VALUE OF AGRICULTURAL COMMODITIES 1992–3

	$A million
Crops	10,554.5
Livestock slaughterings and other disposals	6,023.5
Livestock products	5,205.3
Total agriculture	21,836.4

LIVESTOCK NUMBERS *at 31 March 1992*

	Thousands
Cattle	23,880
Sheep	148,203
Pigs	2,792
Poultry	55,743

Significant mineral resources include bauxite, coal, copper, crude petroleum, gems, gold, ilmenite, iron ore, lead, limestone, manganese, nickel, rutile, salt, silver, tin, tungsten, uranium, zinc and zircon. Geological exploration has significantly increased mineral resources and a number of oilfields are in production.

In 1992–3 the total value of all minerals produced was $A29,191 million. In 1992–3 mine production of black coal was 222,801,000 tonnes, crude oil (including condensate) was 30,592 megalitres and natural gas 16,631 gigalitres. Production of principal metals in 1992 was (tonnes):

Iron ore	115,703,000
Copper	330,000
Lead	525,000
Gold	240

In 1991–2 there were in Australia 41,480 manufacturing establishments, employing 906,900 persons; wages paid amounted to $A27,068 million; and turnover $A168,019 million.

TRADE

Of total exports in the year 1994–5, the largest category was iron ore concentrates worth $A7,313m followed by: coal, $A6,731m; gold, $A4,623m; and textile fibres, $A4,528m.

The largest category of imports was transport equipment, worth $A8,268m. This was followed by office and automatic data processing machines, $A5,414m; road vehicles, $A4,593m; industrial machinery $A4,063m; petrol and oils $A3,400m.

	1993–4	1994–5
Imports	$A63,242m	$A71,419m
Exports	63,542m	65,960m

In 1994–5, 24.5 per cent of total exports went to Japan. The Republic of Korea received 7.5 per cent, USA 7, New Zealand 7, Singapore 5.5, Taiwan 4.5, China 4.5, Hong Kong 4, UK 3.5.

Of total imports in 1994–5, 21 per cent came from the USA, 18 from Japan, 6 Germany, 6 UK, 5 New Zealand, 5 China and 3.5 Taiwan.

Trade with UK	1993	1994
Imports from UK	£1,598,359,000	£1,914,442,000
Exports to UK	996,153,000	1,063,253,000

COMMUNICATIONS

There are six government-owned railway systems, operated by the State Rail Authority of NSW, Victorian Railways, Queensland Government Railways, Western Australian Government Railways, the State Transport Authority of Southern Australia, and the Australian National Railways Commission. The ANRC incorporates the former Commonwealth Railways system, and the Tasmanian and non-metropolitan South Australian railways (urban rail services in Southern Australia remain the responsibility of the State Transport Authority). In 1990 there were 35,486 route-kilometres open.

In 1992–3 there were 401.4 million passenger train-kilometres travelled on government railways and 178.1 million tonnes of goods and livestock carried.

At 30 June 1993, there were 10,217,100 motor vehicles registered in Australia and 288,800 motor cycles.

Figures for domestic and overseas civil aviation services in 1992 are as follows:

	Domestic	Overseas
Paying passengers	18,577,600	9,758,265
Freight (tonnes)	144,100	432,810

At 30 June 1993 there were 7,328 ships registered in Australia of which 4,255 were for recreational purposes, 2,089 were fishing vessels and 41 were government-owned.

THE NORTHERN TERRITORY

The Northern Territory has a total area of 519,770 sq. miles (1,346,200 sq. km), and lies between 129°–138° E. longitude and 11°–26° S. latitude. The estimated population in the Northern Territory at 30 June 1993 was 175,000, of which about a quarter are Aboriginals.

GOVERNMENT

The administration was taken over by the Commonwealth on 1 January 1911 from the State of South Australia. The Northern Territory (Self-Government) Act 1978 established the Northern Territory as a body politic from 1 July 1978, with Ministers having control over and responsibility for Territory finances and the administration of the functions of government as specified by the federal government by regulations made pursuant to the Act. Proposed laws passed by the Legislative Assembly in relation to a transferred function require the assent of the Administrator. Proposed laws in all other cases may be assented to by the Administrator or reserved by the Administrator for the Governor-General's pleasure. The Governor-General may disallow any laws assented to by the Administrator within six months of the Administrator's assent.

The Northern Territory elects one member to the federal House of Representatives and two members to the Senate.

SEAT OF ADMINISTRATION – Darwin

Administrator, His Hon. the Honourable Austin Asche, AC, QC

Chief Minister, Hon. Shane Stone

Chief Justice of the Supreme Court of the Northern Territory, Hon. B. F. Martin

ABORIGINAL LANDS

Various Aboriginal Land Trusts hold title to land previously called Reserves, totalling about one-fifth of the Northern Territory. The Aboriginal Land Rights (NT) Act of 1976 provides for the investigation and determination of Aboriginal traditional claims to vacant Crown land or land already owned by or on behalf of Aboriginals. Successful land claims to date have increased Aboriginal ownership to 42 per cent of the Northern Territory and a further 6 per cent is the subject of claims.

A number of major Aboriginal communities previously administered by church mission societies and the federal government are now controlled by the Aboriginal people through local Aboriginal Councils. A recent phenomenon is the voluntary movement of some Aboriginals to their traditional homeland areas where they feel that their culture will be better preserved.

ECONOMY

Northern Territory's economy is based on the exploitation of its natural resources of minerals, land and fisheries and on tourist attractions. Following the introduction of a number of government measures designed to expand and diversify primary production, the Territory's agricultural and horticultural industries are also beginning to contribute an increasing amount to Territory output. The beef cattle industry continues to be the major user of pastoral lands.

Mining and energy resource development has played a major part in the development of the Northern Territory and in 1992–3 the total value of production was $A1.66 billion. The Territory is a leading uranium producer and contains 20 per cent of the developed world's low-cost uranium reserves. Large-scale production of zinc-lead concentrate commenced in 1994. In 1992–3 more than one million tonnes of manganese was sold, with a total value of about $A135 million. Gold production for 1992–3 was estimated at $A292 million. The value ex mines of bauxite sales exceeded $A131 million and alumina production was valued at $A392 million. The value of oil and gas production for 1992–3 was $A675 million.

Tourism is a major growth industry and generates over $A603 million annually.

COMMUNICATIONS

The Northern Territory has three main ports; Darwin, managed by the Darwin Port Authority, and the private mining ports of Gove and Groote Eylandt.

The standard gauge rail link between Southern Australia and Alice Springs opened in 1980. The link between Alice Springs and Darwin is provided by a fully co-ordinated rail-road service.

The main population centres are linked by the Stuart Highway, which connects Alice Springs to Darwin via Tennant Creek and Katherine. Of special interest to the Northern Territory is the operation of 'road trains'. These are massive trucks hauling two or three trailers, having a net capacity of about 100 tonnes and measuring up to 45 metres in length.

EXTERNAL TERRITORIES

ASHMORE AND CARTIER ISLANDS

Ashmore Islands (known as Middle, East and West Islands) and Cartier Island are situated in the Indian Ocean 850 km and 790 km west of Darwin respectively. The islands are uninhabited.

Great Britain took formal possession of the Ashmores in 1878 and Cartier was annexed in 1909. In 1931 the islands were placed under the authority of the Commonwealth of Australia, and were accepted in 1933 under the name of the Territory of Ashmore and Cartier Islands. The territory is administered by the Commonwealth Government. In 1983 Ashmore Reef was declared a national nature reserve.

THE AUSTRALIAN ANTARCTIC TERRITORY

The Australian Antarctic Territory was established in 1933 by an Order in Council which placed under the government of the Commonwealth of Australia all the islands and territories, other than Adélie Land, which are situated south of the latitude 60° S. and lying between 160° E. longitude and 45° E. longitude. The Order came into force in 1936. The territory is administered by the Antarctic Division of the Department of the Environment, Sport and Territories, which, since 1948, has organized yearly expeditions to Antarctica, known as Australian National Antarctic Research Expeditions (ANARE).

Scientific research is carried out at Mawson Station in MacRobertson Land, Davis Station in Princess Elizabeth Land and Casey Station, and a station on Macquarie Island, about 900 miles north of the Antarctic Continent. Summer stations have been established at Cape Denison, Commonwealth Bay in the Bunger Hills, the Larsemann Hills, the Prince Charles Mountains, and on Heard Island.

CHRISTMAS ISLAND

Christmas Island is situated in the Indian Ocean about 1,408 km NW of North West Cape in Western Australia, and has an area of 135 sq. km. Population (1991 census) is 1,275, largely consisting of employees of Phosphate Resources NL, and employees of the Christmas Island Administration, the Christmas Island Shire Council, and their families. There is no indigenous population. The island became an Australian territory in 1958, having previously been administered as part of the colony of Singapore.

The Administrator is responsible to the Australian Minister for the Environment, Sport and Territories in Canberra. The Christmas Island Shire Council has nine elected members. The Council is responsible for municipal functions and services on the island.

The island had extensive deposits of phosphates, the extraction of which has traditionally been the major economic activity. The deposits of low grade phosphate ore are now being extracted by a private mining company, Phosphate Resources NL. Alternative economic development is being encouraged. The principal current development is a hotel complex.

Administrator, M. Grimes

COCOS (KEELING) ISLANDS

The Cocos (Keeling) Islands are two separate atolls (North Keeling Island and, 24 km to the south, the main atoll) comprising some 27 small coral islands with a total area of about 14 sq. km, situated in the Indian Ocean in latitude 12° 5' S. and longitude 96° 53' E. The main islands of the southern atoll are West Island (about 9 km in length) on which are the administrative centre, the aerodrome, and the Australia-based employees of government departments; Home Island, where the Cocos Malay community live; Direction Island, Horsburgh and South Island. The population as at 30 June 1991 was 647.

The islands were declared a British possession in 1857. All land in the islands was granted to George Clunies-Ross and his heirs by Queen Victoria in 1886. In 1955 the islands, which had been governed through the British colonies of Ceylon (from 1878), the Straits Settlements (1886) and Singapore (1903), were accepted as a Territory of Australia. In 1978 the Australian Government purchased all Clunies-Ross land and property interests except for the family home and grounds. Between 1979 to 1984 most of the land was transferred to the Cocos (Keeling) Islands Council, the local government body established in 1979. In 1993 the federal government purchased the last of the remaining grounds.

The Cocos (Keeling) Islands Act 1955 provided the legal framework for the political and administrative arrangements in the territory. On 6 April 1984 the Cocos community, in a UN supervised Act of Self-Determination, chose to integrate with Australia. The islands are administered by the Australian Government through the Department of the Environment, Sport and Territories in Canberra.

The territory has a limited economic base. In 1986–7 the copra industry suffered severe losses and in 1987 ceased production. Tourism is being developed.

Administrator, John Read

CORAL SEA ISLANDS TERRITORY

The Coral Sea Islands Territory lies east of Queensland between the Great Barrier Reef and longitude 156° 06' E., and between latitudes 12° and 24° S. It comprises scattered islands, spread over a sea area of 780,000 sq. km. The islands are formed mainly of coral and sand, and most are extremely small, with no permanent fresh water. There is a manned meteorological station in the Willis Group but the remaining islands are uninhabited. Large populations of sea birds nest and breed in the area, and two national nature reserves were designated in the Territory in 1982.

The Australian Government bases its claim to the islands on numerous acts of sovereignty since early this century and enacted the Coral Sea Islands Act 1969 which declares the islands a territory of the Commonwealth of Australia. The Department of the Environment, Sport and Territories, Canberra, is responsible for the administration of the territory.

HEARD ISLAND AND MCDONALD ISLANDS

The Heard and McDonald islands, about 4,100 km south-west of Fremantle, comprise all the islands and rocks lying between 52° 30' and 53° 30' S. latitude and 72° and 74° 30' E. longitude. Sovereignty over the islands was transferred from the UK to the Commonwealth of Australia in 1947. The Heard Island and McDonald Islands Act 1953 provides for the government of the islands as one territory. The islands are administered by the Department of the Environment, Sport and Territories. Under the Environment Protection and Management Ordinance 1987, a permit system regulates entry to the territory and a range of activities there.

NORFOLK ISLAND

Norfolk Island is situated in the South Pacific Ocean at latitude 29° 02' S. and longitude 167° 57' E. It is about 8 km long by 5 km wide, with an area of 3,455 hectares. The climate is mild and subtropical. Resident population at the 1991 census was 1,912.

The island, discovered by Captain Cook in 1774, served as a penal colony from 1788 to 1814 and 1825 to 1855. In 1856, 194 descendants of the *Bounty* mutineers accepted an invitation to leave Pitcairn and settle on Norfolk Island, which led to Norfolk Island becoming a separate settlement under the jurisdiction of the Governor of New South Wales. In 1897 Norfolk Island became a dependency of NSW and in 1914 a territory of Australia. From that date, Norfolk Island has been regarded as an integral part of Australia.

In 1979 Norfolk Island gained a substantial degree of self-government. Wide powers are exercised by a nine-member Legislative Assembly. The Act preserves the Commonwealth's responsibility for Norfolk Island as a territory under its authority, with the Minister for the Environment, Sport and Territories as the responsible Minister.

The island is a popular tourist resort, and a large proportion of the population depends on tourism and its ancillaries for employment. In 1992–3 there were 27,376 tourist arrivals on the Island.

The seat of government and administration offices are in Kingston.

Administrator, A. G. Kerr

AUSTRALIAN STATES

NEW SOUTH WALES

New South Wales is situated entirely between the 28th and 38th parallels of S. latitude and 141st and 154th meridians of E. longitude, and comprises an area of 309,433 sq. miles

(801,427 sq. km) (exclusive of 939 sq. miles of Australian Capital Territory which lies within its borders). The preliminary estimated resident population at 30 June 1994 was 6,051,400.

STATE CAPITAL – ΨSydney, on the shores of Port Jackson. Sydney Harbour extends inland for 21 km; the total area of water is about 55 sq. km. The preliminary estimated resident population in 1994 of the Sydney statistical division was 3,738,500. The Newcastle and Wollongong statistical subdivisions contain populations of 460,210 and 251,390 respectively.

TOWNS – The populations of other principal municipalities are: Albury 41,450, Greater Taree 43,670, Hastings 53,850, Lismore 44,420, Shoalhaven 76,160, Wagga Wagga 56,670.

GOVERNMENT

New South Wales was first colonized as a British possession in 1788, and after progressive settlement a partly elective legislature was established in 1843. In 1855 responsible government was granted, the present constitution being founded on the Constitution Act of 1902. New South Wales federated with the other states of Australia in 1901.

The executive authority is vested in a Governor (appointed by the Crown), assisted by a Council of Ministers. The legislature consists of the Legislative Council of 42 members, elected by popular vote, and the Legislative Assembly of 99 members elected for a maximum period of four years. After the last election on 25 March 1995 the Assembly was composed of: Australian Labor Party 50, Liberal-National Alliance 47, Independents 2.

Governor of New South Wales, His Excellency Rear-Adm. Peter Sinclair, AO, RAN, *assumed office* August 1990

Lt.-Governor and Chief Justice of NSW, The Hon. Mr Justice Gleeson, AC

Premier, Hon. Bob Carr, MP

President of the Legislative Council, Hon. M. Willis, MLC

Speaker, Legislative Assembly, Hon. J. Murray, MP

NEW SOUTH WALES GOVERNMENT OFFICE IN LONDON, 75 King William Street, London EC4N 7HA. Tel: 0171-283 2166.

EDUCATION

Education is compulsory between the ages of six and 15 years. It is non-sectarian and free at all government schools. The enrolment in 1994 in 2,187 government and 862 non-government schools was 1,051,849. The nine universities, together with advanced education colleges, had an enrolment of 174,000 in 1993. Students enrolled in technical and further education colleges in 1993 numbered 423,600.

ECONOMY

A large area is suitable for sheep-raising, the principal breed of sheep being the merino, which was introduced in 1797.

The principal minerals are coal, lead, zinc, gold, rutile, copper and zircon. The total value of minerals extracted in 1993–4 was $A4,249 million. The average number of persons employed in the mining industry during 1993–4 was 19,483. In 1993–4, 84,014,000 tonnes of coal were produced.

In 1991–2 there were 9,588 manufacturing establishments (employing four or more persons). The number of persons employed at 30 June 1991 was 309,124.

LORD HOWE ISLAND

Lord Howe Island, which is part of New South Wales, is situated 702 kilometres north-east of Sydney, in 31° 33' 4" S. latitude and 159° 4' 26" E. longitude. Area 6.37 sq. miles (16.5 sq. km.). Population, 1994, 350. The island is of volcanic origin, Mount Gower reaching an altitude of 866 m. The affairs of the Island are administered by the Lord Howe Island Board.

QUEENSLAND

The state, including islands, is situated in 9° 14'–29° S. latitude and 138°–154° 7' E. longitude and comprises the whole north-eastern portion of the Australian continent. Queensland possesses an area (including offshore islands) of 668,997 sq. miles (1,732,700 sq. km). At 30 June 1994 the estimated resident population numbered 3,196,934.

STATE CAPITAL – ΨBrisbane is situated on the Brisbane River. The estimated resident population of the Brisbane statistical division at 30 June 1994 was 1,454,774. This area includes the cities of Brisbane (786,442), Ipswich (77,619), Logan (158,794) and Redcliffe (49,519).

CITIES – Other cities with population at 30 June 1994, are: ΨTownsville 88,855; Gold Coast 145,770; Toowoomba 89,455; ΨRockhampton 62,333; ΨCairns 43,129; ΨCaloundra 60,574; Mackay 68,607.

GOVERNMENT

Queensland was constituted a separate colony with responsible government in 1859, having previously formed part of New South Wales. The executive authority is vested in a Governor (appointed by the Crown), aided by an Executive Council of 18 members. Parliament consists of a Legislative Assembly of 89 members, elected by all persons aged 18 years and over. The Assembly, as at 30 June 1995, was composed of: Australian Labor Party, 54; National Party of Australia, 26; Liberal Party of Australia, 9.

Governor of Queensland, Her Excellency Mrs Mary Marguerite Leneen Forde, AC

Premier, Hon. W. K. Goss, MLA

Speaker, Legislative Assembly, Hon. D. Fouras, MLA

AGENT-GENERAL'S OFFICE IN LONDON, 392 Strand, London WC2R 0LZ. Tel: 0171-836 1333. *Agent-General*, R. T. Anderson

EDUCATION

Education is compulsory, secular and free between the ages of five and 15. At July 1994, there were 1,001 government primary schools, 74 primary/secondary, and 189 secondary schools with 262,499 primary students, and 140,735 secondary students. There were also 238 primary, 86 primary/secondary and 80 secondary non-government schools with 75,223 primary students and 70,074 secondary students.

Post-secondary education involves technical and further education (TAFE) and higher education. During 1993, 189,817 students were enrolled in TAFE courses, excluding 81,479 enrolled in adult education courses. At 31 March 1994 there were 55,575 full-time, 24,420 part-time, and 17,042 external students enrolled in higher education courses.

ECONOMY

Total Queensland-sawn timber produced in 1993–4 amounted to 735,306 cubic metres (gross volume measure).

There are rich deposits of both metal and non-metal ores. Coal is mined extensively in central Queensland and on a lesser scale in the Ipswich district.

In 1993–4 there were 6,068 manufacturing establishments employing 124,300 persons, with a turnover of $A23,642 million. Much of the production was the processing of foodstuffs, minerals and chemical, petroleum and coal products. Other factory production included the products from engineering, transport equipment, timber, basic and fabricated metal, cement, paper and textile mills and oil refineries.

In recent years the economy has diversified from its original base of agriculture and mining into high technology manufacturing and tourism. The labour force was 1.65 million strong in May 1995.

SOUTH AUSTRALIA

South Australia is situated between 26° and 38° S. latitude and 129° and 141° E. longitude, the total area being 380,070 sq. miles (984,376 sq. km). At 30 June 1994, the resident population was estimated to be 1,469,800.

STATE CAPITAL – ΨAdelaide, estimated resident population on 30 June 1994, 1,076,400 inclusive of suburbs. Other centres (with 1994 populations) are: ΨWhyalla (24,649); ΨMt Gambier (22,730); ΨPort Pirie (14,671); ΨPort Augusta (14,561).

GOVERNMENT

South Australia was proclaimed a British province in 1836, and in 1851 a partially elective legislature was established. The present constitution rests upon a law of 24 October 1856, the executive authority being vested in a Governor appointed by the Crown, aided by a Council of 13 Ministers.

Parliament consists of a Legislative Council of 22 members elected for eight years, one half retiring every four years; and a House of Assembly of 47 members, elected for a maximum duration of four years. Election is by ballot, with universal adult suffrage for both the Legislative Council and the House of Assembly. The representation in the House of Assembly is 36 Liberals and 11 Labor.

Governor of South Australia, Her Excellency the Hon. Dame Roma Mitchell, AC, DBE, *assumed office* 1991
Lt.-Governor, The Hon. Dr Basil Hetzel, AC, *assumed office* 1992
Premier, Hon. Dean Craig Brown, MP
President of the Legislative Council, Hon. H. P. K. Bruce, MLC
Speaker of the House of Assembly, Hon. G. Gunn, MP

AGENT-GENERAL'S OFFICE IN LONDON, 115 Strand, London WC2R OAJ. *Agent-General,* G. Walls

EDUCATION

Education at the primary and secondary level is available at government schools controlled by the Education Department and at non-government schools, most of which are denominational. In 1994 there were 674 government schools with 181,640 students, and 189 independent schools with 64,371 students. Tertiary education is available through universities, and technical and further education colleges.

The three universities had, in 1993, a total enrolment of 44,445 students, of which 26,471 were full-time.

TASMANIA

Tasmania is an island state situated in the Southern ocean off the south-eastern extremity of the mainland. It is separated from the mainland by Bass Strait and incorporates King Island and the Furneaux group of islands which are in the strait. It lies between 40° 38'–43° 39' S. latitude and 144° 36'–148° 23' E. longitude, and has an area of 26,383 sq. miles (68,331 sq. km). Macquarie Island, situated at 54° 30' S. and 158° 57' E., about 900 miles north of the Antarctic Continent, is a dependency of Tasmania. The estimated resident population at 30 June 1994 was 471,450.

STATE CAPITAL – ΨHobart, founded 1804. Population (30 June 1994) (metropolitan area), 194,167. Other towns (with population at 30 June 1994) are ΨLaunceston (metropolitan area, 97,918), ΨBurnie-Devonport (79,035).

GOVERNMENT

The island was first settled by a British party from New South Wales in 1803, becoming a separate colony in 1825. In 1851 a partly elective legislature was inaugurated, and in 1856 responsible government was established. In 1901 Tasmania became a state of the Australian Commonwealth. Executive authority is vested in a Governor appointed by the Crown, but is exercised by Cabinet Ministers responsible to the legislature, of which they are members. Parliament consists of a Legislative Council of 19 members, elected for six years (three retiring annually, in rotation, except in every sixth year, when four retire), and a House of Assembly of 35 members, elected by proportional representation for four years in five seven-member constituencies. All Tasmanians of 18 years and over who have resided continuously in the State for at least six months may vote in elections to both houses. Elections for the Assembly are held every four years.

The February 1992 election resulted in a victory for the Liberal Party, with 19 Liberal, 11 Labor and 5 Tasmanian Green members of the House of Assembly. The state of the parties in the Legislative Council following the election was Independent 17, Liberal 1, Labor 1.

Governor of Tasmania, His Excellency Gen. Sir Phillip Bennett, AC, KBE, DSO
Premier, Hon. Raymond J. Groom, MHA
President of the Legislative Council, vacant
Speaker of the House of Assembly, Hon. G. R. Page, MHA

EDUCATION

Government schools are of three main types: primary, secondary and secondary colleges. On 1 July 1994 there were 64,061 students enrolled in 233 government schools. There were also 68 independent schools with an enrolment of 21,298. The University of Tasmania with campuses in Hobart and Launceston, had 8,185 full-time students and 3,845 part-time students in 1994.

ECONOMY

Tasmania produces the most electrical energy per head of population of the Australian states. Most of it is derived from water power, with a total installed generator capacity of 2,435,000 kW at 30 June 1993. By reason of its low-cost electricity, Tasmania has large plants producing ferro-manganese and newsprint. An aluminium plant is situated at Bell Bay and Tasmania is the source of the bulk of Australian requirements of zinc and fine papers.

The quantity of timber (excluding firewood) of various species cut in 1993–4 was 4,349,200 cubic metres, including 3,448,800 cubic metres for woodchip and wood-pulp. The chief ores mined are those containing copper, tin, iron, silver, zinc and lead.

The chief manufactures for export are refined metals, preserved fruit and vegetables, butter, cheese, meat, seafood, textiles, paper, confectionery, wood chips and sawn timber. As at 30 June 1992, 858 manufacturing establishments employed 23,500 persons.

VICTORIA

Victoria comprises the south-east corner of Australia, at the part where its mainland territory projects furthest into the southern latitudes; it lies between 34°–39° S. latitude and 141°–150° E. longitude. Its area is 87,876 sq. miles (227,600 sq. km). The estimated resident population at 30 December 1993 was 4,468,300.

STATE CAPITAL – ΨMelbourne had a resident population at 30 December 1993 estimated at 3,189,201. Other urban centres are ΨGeelong 151,900; Ballarat 81,216; Bendigo 71,274.

GOVERNMENT

Victoria was originally known as the Port Phillip District of New South Wales and was created a separate colony in 1851, with a partially elective legislature. In 1855 responsible government was conferred.

The executive authority is vested in a Governor, appointed by the Crown, aided by an Executive Council of Ministers. Parliament consists of a Legislative Council of 44 members, elected for the 22 Provinces for two terms of the Legislative Assembly, one half retiring every four years at a general election; and a Legislative Assembly of 88 members, elected for a maximum duration of four years. Voting is compulsory.

The state of parties in the Legislative Council (July 1995) is Liberal Party 24, Australian Labour Party 14, National Party 6. The state of parties in the Legislative Assembly (elected 3 October 1992) is Liberal Party 52, Australian Labour Party 27, National Party 9.

Governor of Victoria, His Excellency the Hon. Richard E. McGarvie, *assumed office* 23 April 1992
Lt.-Governor, The Hon. Sir John McIntosh Young, KCMG, AO, *apptd* 1974
Premier, Hon J. G. Kennett, MLA
President of the Legislative Council, Hon. Bruce Chamberlain, MLC
Speaker of the Legislative Assembly, Hon. John Delzoppo, MLA

AGENT-GENERAL'S OFFICE IN LONDON, Victoria House, Melbourne Place, Strand, London WC2B 4LG. *Agent-General,* K. C. Crompton

EDUCATION

State education is compulsory, secular and free between the ages of six and 15. At 30 June 1994 there were 1,731 schools, attended by 521,039 students. In addition there were 665 non-government schools with 252,148 students. Victoria has 29 technical and further education colleges and eight universities with 38 campuses.

ECONOMY

Minerals raised include oil and natural gas, brown coal, limestone, clays and stone for construction material. Production of brown coal in 1992–3 was 47,898 million tonnes.

In 1965 natural gas was discovered in commercial quantities in the offshore waters of the Gippsland Basin in eastern Victoria and in 1966–7 three valuable oilfields were located in the same general area. Production from Victorian natural gas and crude oil fields in 1993–4 was 16,602 megalitres of crude oil and 6,048 million cubic metres of natural gas.

At 30 June 1993 there were 11,600 manufacturing establishments in which total employees numbered 281,000. The main manufacturing sectors are textiles, clothing and footwear, paper, automotive and transport products, chemicals, fabricated metals and food and beverages.

WESTERN AUSTRALIA

Western Australia includes all that portion of the continent west of 129° E. longitude, the most westerly point being in 113° 9' E. longitude and from 13° 44' to 35° 8' S. latitude. Its area is 975,920 sq. miles (2,527,621 sq. km). At 30 June 1994 the estimated resident population was 1,701,879.

STATE CAPITAL – ΨPerth, on the north bank of the Swan River estuary, 12 miles from Fremantle. Estimated resident population (30 June 1994) of Perth statistical division, including the port of ΨFremantle, 1,239,436.

GOVERNMENT

Western Australia was first settled in 1829, and in 1870 it was granted a partially elective legislature. In 1890 responsible government was granted. The present constitution rests upon the Constitution Act 1889, the Constitution Acts Amendment Act 1899, and amending Acts.

The executive is vested in a Governor appointed by the Crown and aided by a Council of responsible Ministers. Parliament consists of a Legislative Council and a Legislative Assembly, elected by adult suffrage subject to qualifications of residence and registration. There are 34 members in the Legislative Council elected for a period of four years. The Legislative Assembly has 57 members, who are elected for a term of four years. The Legislative Assembly (elected 6 February 1993) is composed of Liberal Party 26, Australian Labor Party 23, National Party of Australia 6, Independent Liberal 2.

Governor of Western Australia, His Excellency the Hon. Maj.-Gen. Michael Jeffrey, AO, MC
Lt.-Governor and Administrator, The Hon. D. K. Malcolm, AC
Premier, Hon. Richard Court, MLA
President of the Legislative Council, Hon. C. E. Griffiths, MLC
Speaker of the Legislative Assembly, Hon. J. Clarko, MLA

AGENT-GENERAL'S OFFICE IN LONDON, Western Australia House, 115 Strand, London WC2R 0AJ. *Agent-General,* W. R. B. Hassell

EDUCATION

In 1993 there were 766 government and 249 non-government primary and secondary school campuses with 222,451 and 74,288 full-time students respectively. The principal higher education institutions are the University of Western Australia (12,795 enrolments in 1994), Murdoch University (8,830), Curtin University (20,617) and Edith Cowan University (17,216).

ECONOMY

There were 3,386 manufacturing establishments at 30 June 1993. The total number of persons employed (including working proprietors) by these establishments at the end of June 1993 was 61,473.

The forests contain some of the finest hardwoods in the world. The total quantity of sawn timber produced during 1992–3 was 3,081,000 cubic metres.

There are large deposits of a wide range of minerals, many of which are being mined or are under development for production. The ex-mine value of all minerals (excluding construction materials) produced during 1993–4 was $A12,600 million.

AUSTRIA
Republik Österreich

Austria lies in central Europe, bounded on the north by the Czech Republic and the Slovak Republic, on the south by

Italy and Slovenia, on the east by Hungary, on the north-west by Germany and on the west by Switzerland and Liechtenstein. Its area is 32,367 sq. miles (83,855 sq. km), and its population is 8,015,000 (estimate 1994). The predominant religion is Roman Catholicism. The language is German, but the rights of the Slovene- and Croat-speaking minorities in Carinthia, Styria and Burgenland are protected.

CAPITAL – Vienna, on the Danube, population 1,539,848 (census 1991). Other larger towns are Graz (237,810), Linz (203,044), Innsbruck (118,112), Salzburg (143,978), and Klagenfurt (89,415).

CURRENCY – Schilling of 100 Groschen.

FLAG – Three equal horizontal stripes of red, white, red.

NATIONAL ANTHEM – Land der Berge, Land am Strome (Land of mountains, land on the river).

NATIONAL DAY – 26 October.

GOVERNMENT

The Republic of Austria was established in 1918 on the break-up of the Austro-Hungarian Empire. In March 1938, as a result of the *Anschluss*, Austria was incorporated into Nazi Germany under the name *Ostmark*. After the liberation of Vienna in 1945, the Republic of Austria was reconstituted within the frontiers of 1937 and a freely-elected government took office in December 1945. The country was divided at this time into four zones occupied respectively by the UK, USA, USSR and France, while Vienna was jointly occupied by the four Powers. In 1955 the Austrian State Treaty was signed in Vienna by the foreign ministers of the four Powers and of Austria. This treaty recognized the re-establishment of Austria as a sovereign, independent and democratic state, having the same frontiers as on 1 January 1938. Austria acceded to the European Union on 1 January 1995.

There is a bicameral national assembly; the lower house (*Nationalrat*) has 183 members and the upper house (*Bundesrat*) has 64 members. There is a 4 per cent qualification for parliamentary representation. After the general election of 9 October 1994 the Social Democrats and the People's Party formed a coalition government. The state of the parties in the Nationalrat as at July 1995 was: Social Democrat Party, 65; People's Party (Conservative), 52; Freedom Party (Liberal-Nationalist), 42; Green, 13; Liberal Forum, 11. In the Bundesrat in May 1994 the People's Party held 27 seats, the Social Democrat Party 26 and the Freedom Party 11.

There are nine provinces: Burgenland, Carinthia, Lower Austria, Upper Austria, Salzburg, Styria, Tyrol, Vienna, and Vorarlberg.

HEAD OF STATE
President of the Republic of Austria, Dr Thomas Klestil, *took office* 8 July 1992

CABINET *as at July 1995*

Chancellor, Dr Franz Vranitzky (SPÖ)
Vice-Chancellor, Foreign Affairs, Dr Wolfgang Schüssel (ÖVP)
Women's Affairs, Helga Konrad (SPÖ)
Economic Affairs, Dr Johannes Ditz (ÖVP)
Employment and Social Affairs, Franz Hums (SPÖ)
Finance, Dr Andreas Staribacher (SPÖ)
Health, Consumer Protection and Sport, Christa Krammer (SPÖ)
Interior, Caspar Einem (SPÖ)
Justice, Dr Nikolaus Michalek (Ind.)
Defence, Dr Werner Fasslabend (ÖVP)
Agriculture and Forestry, Wilhelm Molterer (ÖVP)

Environment, Dr Martin Bartenstein (ÖVP)
Education and Culture, Elisabeth Gehrer (ÖVP)
Public Economy and Transport, Viktor Klima (SPÖ)
Youth and Family Affairs, Dr Sonja Moser (ÖVP)
Science and Research, Dr Rudolf Scholten (SPÖ)
Ministers of State, Brigitte Ederer (SPÖ) (*European Union*); Karl Schloegl (SPO) (*Civil Service*); Dr Gerhard Schaeffer (ÖVP) (*Co-ordination*); Dr Benita Ferrero-Waldner (ÖVP) (*Foreign Affairs*)

SPÖ Social Democrats; ÖVP People's Party (Conservatives)

AUSTRIAN EMBASSY
18 Belgrave Mews West, London SW1X 8HU
Tel: 0171–235 3731
Ambassador Extraordinary and Plenipotentiary, His Excellency Dr Georg Hennig, LVO, apptd 1993
Minister-Counsellor, Dr Herbert Krauss
Defence Attaché, Brig. H. Rüdiger Sulzgruber
Consul-General, G. R. Widor
Commercial Counsellor and Trade Commissioner, Dr Gerhard Kernthaler

BRITISH EMBASSY
Jaurèsgasse 12, 1030 Vienna
Tel: Vienna 7131575/9
Ambassador Extraordinary and Plenipotentiary, His Excellency Terence Wood, CMG, apptd 1992
Deputy Ambassador, Counsellor and Consul-General, J. W. Forbes-Meyler, OBE
Defence Attaché, Lt.-Col. P. W. L. Hughes, MBE
First Secretary (Commercial), P. J. W. Le Breton

BRITISH CONSULAR OFFICES – There is a consular office at Vienna, and Honorary Consulates at Bregenz, Graz, Innsbruck and Salzburg.

BRITISH COUNCIL REPRESENTATIVE, David Handforth, Schenkenstrasse 4, 1010 Vienna

EDUCATION

Education is free and compulsory between the ages of six and 15 and there are good facilities for secondary, technical and professional education. There are 12 state-maintained universities and six colleges of art with a combined registered student population of around 205,000 in 1993–4.

COMMUNICATIONS

Internal communications are partly restricted because of the mountainous nature of the country, although there is now a network of 1,567 km of *Autobahn* between major cities which also links up with the German and Italian networks. The railways (ÖBB) are state-owned and in 1993 had 5,605 km of track, 58.8 per cent of which is electrified. Of the 425 km of waterways, 350 km are navigable and there is considerable trade through the Danube ports by both local and foreign shipping. There are six commercial airports catering for 4,644,439 passengers in 1993.

There are four national radio and two national television channels, together with three national and twelve regional newspapers which have a combined daily circulation of 2,528,998.

DEFENCE

The total active strength of the armed forces numbers 51,250 (25,000 conscripts). In addition, there are 119,000 reserves ready at 72 hours notice. Conscripts serve for six months and then either for an extra two months or they can choose to undertake two months refresher training over a

15-year period. Each year 66,000 reservists undergo refresher training.

The Army has an active strength of 44,000 (19,500 conscripts) with 170 main battle tanks, 465 armoured personnel carriers, and 945 artillery pieces and anti-tank heavy guns. The Air Force has an active strength of 7,250 (2,400 conscripts) with 54 combat aircraft. Austria deploys one infantry battalion of 347 troops with UN forces in Cyprus and one infantry battalion of 461 troops on the Golan Heights in Syria.

ECONOMY

GDP by sector in 1994 was as follows (Schilling billion):

Agriculture and forestry	50.6
Manufacturing and mining	534.0
Energy and water supply	60.7
Construction	173.8
Commerce, hotels, restaurants	354.2
Transport and communications	141.1
Asset management	434.3
Other services and producers	263.1
Import duties and other items	209.8

The total value of GDP in 1994 was Schilling 2,244.8 billion.

Austria is self-sufficient in agricultural production, with about 267,444 agricultural units. The arable land produces wheat, rye, barley, oats, maize, potatoes, sugar beet, turnips, and miscellaneous crops. Many varieties of fruit trees flourish and the vineyards produce excellent wine. The pastures support horses, cattle and pigs and large numbers of chickens are also produced. Timber forms a valuable source of Austria's indigenous wealth, about 47 per cent of the total land area consisting of forest areas. Coniferous species predominate (75 per cent of afforested area).

In 1994, 19,092,213 foreign tourists visited Austria. Foreign exchange receipts from tourism were a major contribution to the balance of payments.

FINANCE	1993	1994
Federal Budget (Schilling)		
Revenue	601,473m	628,611m
Expenditure	699,713m	709,311m
Gross Budget Deficit	98,240m	80,701m

Total federal public debt in 1994 was Schilling 1,225.6 billion.

TRADE

Main exports are processed goods (iron and steel, other metal goods, textiles, paper and cardboard products), machinery and transport equipment, other finished goods (including clothing), raw materials, chemical products and foodstuffs. Main imports are machinery and transport equipment, processed goods, chemical products, foodstuffs, fuel and energy.

	1992	1993
Imports	Schilling 594,000m	564,909m
Exports	488,000m	467,171m

Over 80 per cent of trade is with other European countries, EU countries accounting for about 70 per cent, eastern Europe for about 8 per cent and EFTA members for 6 per cent. By far the most important trading partner is Germany, with which around 40 per cent of Austrian trade is conducted.

Trade with UK	1993	1994
Imports from UK	£911,611,000	£1,034,899,000
Exports to UK	971,124,000	1,017,879,000

AZERBAIJAN
Azarbaijchan Respublikasy

Azerbaijan has an area of 33,436 sq. miles (86,600 sq. km) and occupies the eastern part of the Caucasus region of the former Soviet Union, on the shore of the Caspian Sea. It is bordered on the south by Iran, on the west by Armenia and on the north by Georgia and Russia. The north-eastern part of the republic is taken up by the south-eastern end of the main Caucasus ridge, its south-western part by the smaller Caucasus hills, and its south-eastern corner by the spurs of the Talysh Ridge. Its central part is a depression irrigated by the River Kura and the lower reaches of its tributary the Araks. Sheltered by the mountains from the humid west winds blowing from the Black Sea, Azerbaijan has a continental climate.

Azerbaijan has 64 administrative districts and also includes the Nakhichevan Autonomous Republic, which is geographically separated from the rest of Azerbaijan by Armenia and borders on Iran and Turkey, and the Nagorno-Karabakh Autonomous Province.

According to a 1993 estimate, Azerbaijan has a population of 7,400,900, of which 83 per cent are Azeri, 6 per cent Russian and 6 per cent Armenian. There are also Kurds, Jews, Georgians and Turks. There are more Azeris in Iran than in Azerbaijan.

The population is predominantly Shia Muslim although it was heavily secularized during the Soviet era. Azeri in the Latin script was adopted as the official language in December 1992. Closely related to Turkish, Azeri was previously written in the Russian script.

CAPITAL – ΨBaku. Population 1,149,000 (1990).

CURRENCY – Manat of 100 gopik.

FLAG – Three horizontal stripes of blue, red and green with a white crescent and eight-pointed star in the centre.

NATIONAL DAY – 28 May (Independence Day).

GOVERNMENT

The territory that is now Azerbaijan was fought over many times between the ninth and first centuries BC, being successively part of the Assyrian, Persian, Median and Greek empires. With the influx of Huns and Khazars in the first century BC, the Turkic Azerbaijani people evolved and formed an independent state. This was invaded by the Arab Caliphates in the seventh century AD and under their 300-year rule Islam was introduced and became the dominant religion. In the 16th century Azerbaijan was again invaded by Persia and became a Persian province. The country was divided during the Russo-Persian wars of the early 19th century, the northern portion (the present-day Azerbaijan) becoming part of the Russian Empire and the southern portion remaining Persian and subsequently Iranian.

Following the Russian Revolution of 1917, a Soviet government was set up in Azerbaijan in 1918. This was overthrown by Allied forces a few months later but when Allied forces withdrew in 1920, the Soviet government was restored and Azerbaijan acceded to the USSR in 1922.

In January 1990, the Azerbaijani Popular Front took power from the local Communist Party and declared independence from the Soviet Union, partly because of the Soviet government's decision in 1989 to take control of the Nagorno-Karabakh region away from Azerbaijan and to impose direct rule upon it to stop Azeri-Armenian fighting there. Soviet troops overthrew the Popular Front regime the day after it took power and restored the Communist regime under President Ayaz Mutalibov. This government declared Azerbaijan's independence from the Soviet

Union in August 1991. Mutalibov won the presidential election held in September 1991, but he was forced to resign by widespread civil unrest at his perceived pro-Moscow stance and the poor conduct of the war with Armenia. At the presidential election in June 1992 the Popular Front leader Abulfaz Elchibey was elected and pledged to withdraw from the CIS and align the country more closely with Turkey.

Azerbaijan withdrew from the CIS in October 1992 when its parliament (*Milli Majlis*) rejected membership. The war (*see* Secession) continued to go badly in 1992–3, the defeats leading to political crisis. President Elchibey declared a state of emergency but discontent with his rule grew in parliament and military rebels overthrew President Elchibey and his Popular Front government in June 1993. The former Azerbaijani Communist Party General Secretary Heidar Aliyev took over the presidency and the rebel leader Col. Husseinov the premiership. The new regime was confirmed in office in a referendum in August and Aliyev won the presidential election in October 1993 with 99 per cent of the vote.

The government has sought to tread a middle path between Russia, Turkey and other states interested in investing in its oil industry. It rejoined the CIS in September 1993, but in March 1995 announced that a new oil pipeline will be built across Turkey to the Black Sea. Internal tension over relations with Russia and Turkey led to unsuccessful coup attempts against President Aliyev's government in October 1994 and March 1995, the former led by Prime Minister Husseinov.

SECESSION

In 1988 fighting broke out in the predominantly Armenian-populated region of Nagorny-Karabakh between Soviet Azerbaijani forces and ethnic Armenians demanding unification with Armenia. Fighting continued through the breakup of the Soviet Union and reached its peak in late 1993 when Nagorno-Karabakh forces captured all of the region, together with all Azeri territory separating the region from Armenia (20 per cent of Azeri territory). Azeri forces pushed back the Nagorno-Karabakh forces in early 1994 before a ceasefire agreement was signed in Moscow in May 1994. The ceasefire has held since then, with a CSCE peacekeeping force due to be deployed. Ten per cent of Azeri territory remains under the control of Nagorno-Karabakh forces. Between 500,000 and one million Azeris have been displaced by the fighting.

HEAD OF STATE

President, Heidar Aliyev, *assumed office* 18 June 1993, *elected* 3 October 1993

GOVERNMENT *as at July 1995*

Prime Minister (acting), Fuad Guliev
Deputy Prime Ministers, Abbas Abbasov; Tofig Azizov; Elchin Efendiev; Samed Sadykhov
Foreign Affairs, Gasan Gasanov
Interior, Ramil Usubov
Housing and Communal Services, Suddgedin Abdullaev
Culture, Byul-byul Polad
Material Resources, Faruh Zeinalov
Land Improvement and Water Conservancy, Salekh Gadzhiyev
Local Industry, Agabba Abdulaev
Education, Lidiya Rasulova
National Security, Namig Abbasov
Defence, Lt.-Gen. Safar Abuyev
Information, Cabir Rustamhanly
Communications, Sirus Abbasbeily
Agriculture and Foodstuffs, Ershad Aliev
Trade, Miri Ganbarov

Economics, Samed Sadyhov
Justice, Ilyas Ismailov
Public Health, Ali Insanov
Finance, Fikret Usifor
Chairman of the Supreme Soviet, Rasul Guliev

AZERBAIJANI EMBASSY
London House, 19 Old Court Place, London W8 4PL
Tel: 0171-938 2222
Ambassador Extraordinary and Plenipotentiary, His Excellency Mahmud Mamed-Kuliyev, apptd 1994

BRITISH EMBASSY
c/o Old Intourist Hotel Room 214, Baku
Tel: Baku 924 813
Ambassador Extraordinary and Plenipotentiary, His Excellency Thomas Young, apptd 1993

DEFENCE

The total active strength of the armed forces is 56,000 personnel, with conscripts serving 17-month terms. The Army has a strength of 49,000, with 280 main battle tanks, 800 armoured personnel carriers and infantry fighting vehicles and 350 artillery pieces. The Navy is based at Baku, with a share of the former Soviet Caspian Fleet Flotilla, comprising one frigate and 15 patrol and coastal combatants, together with 3,000 personnel. The Air Force is 2,000 strong with 48 combat aircraft. All forces, together with 20,000 paramilitary personnel, are engaged in the conflict around Nagorny-Karabakh, where they face a force some 20,000 strong.

ECONOMY

Azerbaijan was heavily industrialized as part of the Russian Empire, with railways, commercial shipping on the Caspian Sea, and, most importantly, the oil industry. In the late 19th and early 20th centuries Baku was the most important oil-producing centre in the world.

Industry is still dominated by oil and natural gas extraction and related chemical and engineering industries centred on Baku and Sumgait and the large oil deposits in the Caspian Sea, estimated at 3–4,000 million barrels. The oil industry is at the centre of political debate within the country and of relations with other states. An agreement to explore and exploit three oilfields in the Caspian Sea was signed in September 1994 with a consortium of western oil firms, in which the consortium will gain a 70 per cent stake in the contract, Azerbaijan 20 per cent and the Russian Lukoil company 10 per cent. Russia still questions the validity of the deal, in an attempt to influence Azerbaijan to build a new pipeline across its territory rather than Turkey.

The republic is also rich in mineral resources, with iron, copper, lead and salt, and is important as a cotton-growing area and a silkworm breeding area.

However, the Azeri economy has been devastated by the war and the attempt to resettle up to one million refugees. The war in Chechenia has also closed the railway to Russia along which the majority of Azeri imports and exports travelled.

TRADE WITH UK	1993	1994
Imports from UK	£2,965,000	£5,803,000
Exports to UK	823,000	1,517,000

CULTURE

Azerbaijan was the birthplace of the prophet Zoroaster, who founded one of the first monotheistic religions in the world. The country has witnessed a succession of three religions; Zoroastrianism, Christianity and Islam.

Azeri is one of the Turkic languages. In the 18th and 19th centuries Azerbaijani literature produced the poets and dramatists Vagif, Vazekhi, Zakir, Akhundov and Vezirov, who all introduced ideas of progressive Russian culture.

THE BAHAMAS
The Commonwealth of The Bahamas

The Bahama Islands are an archipelago lying in the North Atlantic Ocean between 20° 55′–25° 22′ N. latitude and 72° 35′–79° 35′ W. longitude. They extend from the coast of Florida on the north-west almost to Haiti on the south-east. The group consists of 700 islands, of which 30 are inhabited, and 2,400 cays comprising an area of more than 5,832 sq. miles. The principal islands include: Abaco, Acklins, Andros, Berry Islands, Bimini, Cat Island, Crooked Island, Eleuthera, Exumas, Grand Bahama, Harbour Island, Inagua, Long Island, Mayaguana, New Providence (on which is located the capital, Nassau), Ragged Island, Rum Cay, San Salvador and Spanish Wells. San Salvador was the first landfall in the New World of Christopher Columbus on 12 October 1492. The population (UN estimate 1992) is 262,000.

CAPITAL – ΨNassau, population (census 1990) 171,000.
CURRENCY – Bahamian dollar (B$) of 100 cents.
FLAG – Horizontal stripes of aquamarine, gold and aquamarine, with a black equilateral triangle on the hoist.
NATIONAL ANTHEM – March on, Bahamaland.
NATIONAL DAY – 10 July (Independence Day).

GOVERNMENT

The Bahamas were settled by the British when the islands were deserted and became a Crown colony in 1717. Taken over in 1782 by the Spanish, the Treaty of Versailles in 1783 restored them to the British. The Bahamas gained independence on 10 July 1973. The head of state is HM Queen Elizabeth II, represented in the islands by a Governor-General. There is an appointed Senate of 16 members and an elected House of Assembly of 49 members. A general election held on 19 August 1992 was won by the Free National Movement, defeating the Progressive Liberal Party, which had held power since independence. The Free National Movement won 33 seats in the House of Assembly and the Progressive Liberal Party 16 seats.

Governor-General, His Excellency Sir Orville Turnquest, GCMG, QC, apptd 1994

CABINET *as at June 1995*
Prime Minister and Minister of Finance and Planning, Rt. Hon. Hubert A. Ingraham
Deputy Prime Minister, Tourism, Hon. Frank H. Watson
Foreign Affairs, Hon. Janet W. Bostwick
Social Development, Hon. Maurice E. Moore
Education, Senator the Hon. Dame Ivy Dumont, DCMG
Public Safety and Immigration, Hon. Cornelius A. Smith
Attorney-General, Senator the Hon. Theodore Brent Symonette
Transport, Hon. Tennyson R. G. Wells
Public Works, Hon. Arlington G. Butler
Youth and Culture, Hon. Algernon Allen
Health and Environment, Hon. Theresa M. Moxey-Ingraham

Finance and Planning, Hon. William C. Allen
Agriculture and Fisheries, Hon. Pierre V. Dupuch

President of the Court of Appeal, Kenneth Henry
Chief Justice, Sir Joaquim Gonsalves-Sabola, KCMG

BAHAMAS HIGH COMMISSION
Bahamas House, 10 Chesterfield Street, London WIX 8AH
Tel 0171-408 4488
High Commissioner, His Excellency Arthur A. Foulkes, apptd 1992

BRITISH HIGH COMMISSION
PO Box N-7516, Nassau
Tel: Nassau 325-7471/2/3
High Commissioner, His Excellency Brian Attewell, apptd 1992

ECONOMY

Tourism is the most important economic sector, employing about two-thirds of the labour force. It provides about two-thirds of government revenue and about half the country's foreign exchange earnings. International banking and trust business is also important. The Bahamas' absence of any direct taxation and internal stability have enabled the country to become one of the world's leading offshore financial centres. Confidence in both the tourist and financial industries dropped, however, after widespread allegations of corruption during the 25 years of PLP government surfaced in 1992–3.

Agricultural production is mainly of fresh vegetables, fruit, meat and eggs for the domestic market, and crawfish, mostly for export. Reserves of aragonite, limestone and salt are being commercially exploited. Freeport is the country's leading industrial centre, with a pharmaceutical and chemicals plant, an oil trans-shipment and storage terminal, and port and bunkering facilities. There are also a brewery and a rum distillery on New Providence.

TRADE
The imports are chiefly foodstuffs, manufactured articles, building materials, vehicles and machinery, chemicals and petroleum. The chief exports are rum, petroleum, hormones, salt, crawfish and aragonite.

Trade with UK	1993	1994
Imports from UK	£41,662,000	£30,580,000
Exports to UK	25,163,000	25,628,000

EDUCATION

Education is compulsory between the ages of five and 14. More than 59,500 students are enrolled in Ministry of Education and independent schools in New Providence and the Family Islands.

COMMUNICATIONS

The main ports are Nassau (New Providence), Freeport (Grand Bahama), Mathew Town (Inagua). International air services are operated from Abaco, Bimini, Eleuthera, Exuma, Grand Bahama and New Providence. About 50 smaller airports and landing strips facilitate services between the islands, the services being mainly provided by Bahamasair, the national carrier. There are roads on the larger islands, and roads are under construction on the smaller islands. There are no railways. Wireless and telephone services are in operation to all parts of the world.

BAHRAIN
Dawlet al-Bahrein

Bahrain consists of a group of low-lying islands situated about half-way down the Gulf, some 20 miles off the east coast of Saudi Arabia. The largest of these, Bahrain island, is about 30 miles long and 10 miles wide at its broadest, with the capital, Manama, situated on the north shore. The second largest, Muharraq, with the town and Bahrain International Airport, is connected to Manama by a causeway 1½ miles long. Bahrain is connected by causeway to Saudi Arabia.

The climate is humid all the year round, with rainfall of about 3 inches, concentrated in the mild winter months, December to March, in summer, May to October, temperatures can exceed 110°F (44°C).

The population (1992 UN estimate) is 533,000, of whom about 70 per cent are Bahraini. About 40 per cent of the Bahrainis are Sunni Muslims, the remaining 60 per cent being Shias; the ruling family and many of the most prominent merchants are Sunnis.

CAPITAL – ΨManama, population (1981 census) 108,684.
CURRENCY – Bahrain dinar (BD) of 1,000 fils.
FLAG – Red, with vertical serrated white bar next to staff.
NATIONAL DAY – 16 December.

GOVERNMENT

Bahrain has been a fully independent state since 1971, when British protectorate status was ended. Government takes the form of a constitutional monarchy, in which traditional consultative procedures continue to play an important role. The 1973 constitution provides for a National Assembly but this was dissolved in 1975. In December 1992 the Amir announced plans to set up a consultative council, which was established with 30 members in January 1993 and dominated by the business community. There were clashes in late 1994 and early 1995 between security forces and Shia protestors demanding the establishment of the National Assembly.

HEAD OF STATE
HH The Amir of Bahrain, Shaikh Isa bin Sulman Al Khalifa, GCMG, *born* 1932; *acceded* 16 December 1961
Crown Prince (and C.-in-C., Bahrain Defence Force), HE Shaikh Hamad bin Isa Al Khalifa, KCMG

CABINET *as at June 1995*
Prime Minister, HE Shaikh Khalifa bin Sulman Al Khalifa
Foreign Affairs, Shaikh Mohammed bin Mubarak Al Khalifa
Defence, Maj.-Gen. Shaikh Khalifa bin Ahmed Al Khalifa
Justice and Islamic Affairs, Shaikh Abdullah bin Khalid Al Khalifa
Development and Industry, Yusuf Ahmad Shirawi
Education, Dr Ali Fakhro
Health, Jawad Salim Al-Arayyed
Transportation, Shaikh Ali bin Khalifa bin Sulman Al Khalifa
Interior, Shaikh Mohammed bin Khalifa Al Khalifa
Information, Tariq Abdulrahman Al Moayed
Labour and Social Affairs, Shaikh Isa bin Alibin Hamad al-Khalifa
Works, Power and Water, Majid Jawad Al-Jishi
Housing, Shaikh Khalid bin Abdullah Al Khalifa
Finance and National Economy, Ibrahim Abdul Karim
Commerce and Agriculture, Habib Ahmed Kassim
Minister of State, Legal Affairs, Dr Hussain Al-Baharna
Minister of State, Cabinet Affairs, Mohammed Al Mutawa

Chairman of the Consultative Council, Ibrahim Mohammed Humaidan

EMBASSY OF THE STATE OF BAHRAIN
98 Gloucester Road, London SW7 4AU
Tel 0171–370 5132/3/4/5
Ambassador Extraordinary and Plenipotentiary, His Excellency Karim Ebrahim Al Shakar, apptd 1990

BRITISH EMBASSY
21 Government Avenue, Manama 306, PO Box 114
Tel: Manama 534404
Ambassador Extraordinary and Plenipotentiary, His Excellency Hugh Tunnell, apptd 1992

BRITISH COUNCIL REPRESENTATIVE, John Shorter, AMA Centre, PO Box 452, Manama 356

ECONOMY

The largest sources of revenue are oil production and refining. The Bahrain field, discovered in 1932, is wholly owned by the Bahrain National Oil Co. The Sitra refinery derives about 70 per cent of its crude oil by submarine pipeline from Saudi Arabia. Bahrain also has a half share with Saudi Arabia in the profits of the offshore Abu Sa'afa field. A reservoir of unassociated gas has recently been developed on Bahrain island.

Heavy industry is currently limited to the Aluminium Bahrain (ALBA) smelter, the Gulf Petrochemical Industries Co. (GPIC) producing ammonia and methanol, the Gulf Aluminium Rolling Mill (GARMCO), and the Arab Shipbuilding and Repair Yard (ASRY), operating dry dock facilities up to 500,000 tons. There are a number of small to medium-size industrial units.

The state has developed as a financial centre. Apart from several commercial banks, many international banks have been licensed as offshore banking units; there are also money brokers and merchant banks.

TRADE WITH UK	1993	1994
Imports from UK	£151,093,000	£150,378,000
Exports to UK	51,712,000	25,380,000

COMMUNICATIONS

Bahrain International airport is one of the main air traffic centres of the Gulf; it is the headquarters of Gulf Air, and a stopping point on routes between Europe and Australia and the Far East for other airlines. A causeway links Bahrain to Saudi Arabia.

A world-wide telephone and telex service, by satellite and cable, is operated by Bahrain Telecommunications Company.

BANGLADESH
Ghana Praja Tantri Bangladesh

The People's Republic of Bangladesh has an area of 55,598 sq. miles (143,998 sq. km) in the region of the Gangetic delta. The country is crossed by a network of rivers, including the eastern arms of the Ganges, the Jamuna (Brahmaputra) and the Meghna, flowing into the Bay of Bengal. The climate is tropical and monsoon; hot and extremely humid during the summer, and mild and dry during the short winter. The rainfall is heavy, varying from 50 inches to 135 inches in different districts and the bulk of it falls during the monsoon season from June to September.

The population (1991 census) was 108 million. The faith of 88 per cent of the population is Islam and 10.5 per cent

Hinduism. Islam has been declared the state religion of Bangladesh.

The state language is Bengali. Use of Bengali is compulsory in all government departments. English is understood and is used widely as an unofficial second language.

CAPITAL – Dhaka, population (1991 census) 6,537,308.
CURRENCY – Taka (Tk) of 100 poisha.
FLAG – Red circle on a bottle-green ground.
NATIONAL ANTHEM – Amar Sonar Bangla.
NATIONAL DAY – 26 March (Independence Day).

GOVERNMENT

Prior to becoming East Pakistan, Bangladesh had been the province of East Bengal and the Sylhet district of Assam of British India. The territory acceded to Pakistan in October 1947, which became a republic on 23 March 1956.

By a proclamation of 26 March 1971, Bangladesh purported to secede from the central government, and a government-in-exile, led by Sheikh Mujibur Rahman of the Awami League, was set up which formally declared independence on 17 April. Bangladesh achieved its independence on 16 December 1971, following the conclusion of the Indo-Pakistan war. Pakistan and Bangladesh accorded one another mutual recognition in 1974.

In 1975 the constitution was amended and a one-party presidential system was introduced, with Prime Minister Sheikh Rahman assuming the presidency under martial law until he was assassinated in 1975. A presidential election was held in 1978 and won by Maj.-Gen. Zia Rahman, who lifted martial law and introduced a multi-party presidential system of government. Zia was assassinated in 1981 in an unsuccessful coup. He was replaced by Justice Abdus Sattar, who was overthrown in 1982 in a coup led by the then Chief of Army Staff, Gen. Ershad. Following parliamentary elections in 1986, which were boycotted by several opposition parties, a civilian cabinet was appointed and Gen. Ershad was elected President. Popular unrest forced Gen. Ershad's resignation in December 1990 and parliamentary elections were held in February 1991. The Bangladesh Nationalist Party (BNP) won the largest number of seats and, after a series of by-elections, gained a parliamentary majority. The BNP leader, Begum Khaleda Zia, was sworn in as Prime Minister in March 1991. In August 1991 Parliament approved a constitutional amendment returning Bangladesh to parliamentary rule. BNP nominee Abdur Rahman Biswas was elected President.

Under the new constitution there is a unicameral parliament (*Jatiya Sangshad*) of 330 members which can amend the constitution by a two-thirds majority. The country is divided into six administrative divisions, subdivided into 64 districts.

HEAD OF STATE
President, Abdur Rahman Biswas, *sworn in* 8 October 1991

CABINET *as at June 1995*
Prime Minister, Defence, Establishment, Cabinet Division,
  Begum Khaleda Zia
Law, Justice and Parliamentary Affairs, Mirza Golam Hafiz
Education, Zamiruddin Sircar
Irrigation, Flood Control and Water Resources, M. Mazid Ul-Haq
Foreign Affairs, A. S. M. Mustafizur Rahman
Finance, Saifur Rahman
Local Government, Rural Development and Co-operatives, Abdus Salam Talukder
Communications, Col. Oli Ahmed (retd.)

Commerce and Information, M. Shamsul Islam
Post and Telecommunications, Tariqul Islam
Health and Family Welfare, Chowdhury Kamal Ibne Yusuf
Food and Agriculture, Abdul Mannan Bhuiyan
Home Affairs, Abdul Matin Chowdhury
Religious Affairs, Keramat Ali
Shipping, M. K. Anwar
Jute, A. S. M. Hannan Shah
Environment and Forest, Col. Akbar Hossain (retd.)
Power, Energy and Mineral Resources, Dr. Khandakar Mosharraf Hossain
Works, Rafiqul Islam Miah
Labour and Manpower, Lt.-Gen. Mir Shawkat Ali (retd.)
Fisheries and Livestock, Abdullah Al-Noman

BANGLADESH HIGH COMMISSION
28 Queen's Gate, London SW7 5AJ
Tel: 0171–584 0081/2/3/4
High Commissioner, His Excellency Dr A. F. M. Yusuf, apptd 1992
Defence Adviser, Brig. A. M. Zaman
Minister, M. M. Reza (*Economic*)

BRITISH HIGH COMMISSION
United Nations Road, Baridhara Dhaka
PO Box 6079, Dhaka-12
Tel: Dhaka 882705
High Commissioner, His Excellency Peter James Fowler, CMG, apptd 1993
Deputy High Commissioner, J. R. Nicols
Defence Adviser, Col. E. D. Powell-Jones, OBE
First Secretary (Economic), P. D. Grant

BRITISH COUNCIL REPRESENTATIVE, K. Burd, OBE, 5 Fuller Road (PO Box 161), Dhaka 1000

EDUCATION

Primary education is free and planned to be universal by 2000. There are 50,314 primary schools, mostly managed by the Government. There are 11,094 secondary schools and 980 colleges offering general and technical education. There are 11 universities with a total enrolment of 52,620 students. In 1991 the literacy rate was estimated to be 32.4 per cent (38.9 per cent male and 25.5 per cent female).

COMMUNICATIONS

Principal seaports are Chittagong and Mongla. The Bangladesh Shipping Corporation has been set up by the Government to operate the Bangladesh merchant fleet. The principal airports are Dhaka (Zia International) and Chittagong. The international airline, Bangladesh Biman, serves Europe, the Middle East, South and South-East Asia, and an internal network.

There are about 6,880 miles of roads in Bangladesh; 4,724 miles are metalled. There are 1,680 miles of railway track.

Radio Bangladesh is the main national broadcasting service. A television service was introduced in 1965 and colour transmissions began in 1980.

ECONOMY

Since 1991 the BNP government has been implementing an IMF economic reform plan which has delivered stable prices and inflation and brought down the budget deficit from 8 per cent of GDP in 1989 to 5.3 per cent in 1993.

Bangladesh is a principal producer of raw jute. Other agricultural products are rice, wheat, tobacco, tea, oil seeds, pulses and sugar cane. The chief industries are jute, cotton, tea, leather, pharmaceuticals, fertilizer, sugar, prawn fishing, natural gas and garment manufacture. Remittances sent home by Bangladeshi workers abroad are of considerable support to the economy.

Bangladesh is a major recipient of bilateral and multilateral development aid. The total aid pledged for 1994 from international donors formed into a consortium led by the World Bank was US$2,100 million.

TRADE WITH UK	1993	1994
Imports from UK	£54,274,000	£55,678,000
Exports to UK	140,114,000	156,004,000

BARBADOS

Barbados, the most easterly of the Caribbean islands, is situated in 13° 14′ N. latitude and 59° 37′ W. longitude with a total area of 166 sq. miles (430 sq. km); the land rises in a series of terraced tablelands to the highest point, Mt Hillaby (1,116 ft). It is nearly 21 miles long by 14 miles broad. The annual average temperature is 26.6°C (79.8°F) with rainfall varying from a yearly average of 75 inches in the high central district to 50 inches in the low-lying coastal areas.

The population (1992 UN estimate) was 259,000. There are 11 administrative areas (parishes): St Michael, Christ Church, St Andrews, St George, St James, St John, St Joseph, St Lucy, St Peter, St Philip and St Thomas.

CAPITAL – ΨBridgetown (population, estimated April 1980, 7,466) in the parish of St Michael. There are three other towns, Oistins in Christ Church, Holetown in St James and Speightstown in St Peter.
CURRENCY – Barbados dollar (BD$) of 100 cents.
FLAG – Three vertical stripes, dark blue, gold and dark blue, with a trident head on gold stripe.
NATIONAL ANTHEM – In Plenty and in Time of Need.
NATIONAL DAY – 30 November (Independence Day).

GOVERNMENT

The first inhabitants of Barbados were Arawak Indians but the island was uninhabited when first settled by the British in 1627. It was a Crown Colony from 1652 until it became an independent state within the Commonwealth on 30 November 1966. The legislature consists of the Governor-General, a Senate and a House of Assembly. The Senate comprises 21 Senators appointed by the Governor-General, of whom 12 are appointed on the advice of the Prime Minister, two on the advice of the Leader of the Opposition and seven by the Governor-General at his/her discretion to represent religious, economic or social interests or such other interests as the Governor-General considers ought to be represented. The House of Assembly comprises 28 members elected every five years by adult suffrage. The last general election took place on 6 September 1994 and seats in the House of Assembly were distributed as follows: Barbados Labour Party 19, Democratic Labour Party 8, National Democratic Party 1.

Governor-General, Her Excellency Dame Nita Barrow, GCMG, DA, apptd 1990

Cabinet as at June 1995
Prime Minister, Finance and Economic Affairs, Civil Service, Hon. Owen Arthur
Deputy Prime Minister, Foreign Affairs, Tourism and International Transport, Hon. Billie Miller
Attorney-General and Home Affairs, Hon. David Simmons, QC
Agriculture and Rural Development, Hon. Rawle Eastmond
Education, Youth and Culture, Hon. Mia Mottley

Health and Environment, Hon. Elizabeth Thompson
Labour, Community Development and Sport, Hon. Rudolph Greenidge
Public Works, Transport and Housing, Hon. George Payne
Industry and Commerce, Sen. Hon. Reginald Farley
International Trade, Sen. Hon. Phillip Goddard
Minister of State, Prime Minister's Office, Sen. Hon. Glyne Murray

BARBADOS HIGH COMMISSION
1 Great Russell Street, London WC1B 3JY
Tel 0171–631 4975
High Commissioner, His Excellency Peter Simmonds, apptd 1995
Deputy High Commissioner, H. Yearwood
First Secretary (Commercial), K. Campbell

BRITISH HIGH COMMISSION
Lower Collymore Rock, PO Box 676, Bridgetown C
Tel: Bridgetown 436 6694
High Commissioner, His Excellency Richard Thomas, CMG, apptd 1994
Deputy High Commissioner, J. A. Noakes
Defence Adviser, Col. C. S. Faith, OBE
First Secretary (Chancery), S. R. Morley

JUDICATURE

There is a Supreme Court of Judicature consisting of a High Court and a Court of Appeal. In certain cases a further appeal lies to the Judicial Committee of the Privy Council. The Chief Justice and Puisne Judges are appointed by the Governor-General on the recommendation of the Prime Minister and after consultation with the Leader of the Opposition.

Chief Justice, The Hon. Sir Denys Williams, KCMG

ECONOMY

The economy is based on tourism, sugar and light manufacturing. In 1993, 395,979 tourists visited Barbados and 428,611 cruise ship passengers. Chief exports are sugar and its by-products, chemicals, electronic components and clothing.

FINANCE	1993–4*
Current revenue	BD$1,009,900,000
Current expenditure	1,136,200,000
Deficit	126,300,000
*estimated	

TRADE WITH UK	1993	1994
Imports from UK	£28,229,000	£30,992,000
Exports to UK	25,079,000	15,906,000

EDUCATION

Primary and secondary education is free in government schools. There are 105 primary schools, 21 government secondary schools and 15 approved government secondary schools.

COMMUNICATIONS

Barbados has some 965 miles of roads, of which about 917 miles are asphalted. The Grantley Adams International airport is situated at Seawell, 12 miles from Bridgetown, and frequent scheduled services connect Barbados with the major world air routes. Bridgetown, the only port of entry, has a deep-water harbour with berths for eight ships, but oil is pumped ashore at Spring Gardens and at an Esso installation on the West Coast. Barbados has a colour television service, three radio broadcasting services, and a wired broadcasting service.

BELARUS
Respublika Belarus

Belarus (formerly Byelorussia) has an area of 80,300 sq. miles (207,600 sq. km) and is situated in the western part of the European area of the former USSR. It is bordered on the north by Latvia and Lithuania, on the east by Russia, on the south by the Ukraine and on the west by Poland. Much of the land is a plain, with many lakes, swamps and marshy areas. The main rivers are the upper reaches of the Dnieper, of the Niemen and of the Western Dvina.

The climate is continental with mild, humid winters and relatively cool and rainy summers.

The population (1995 official estimate) is 10,280,000, of which 78 per cent are Belarusian, 13 per cent Russian, 4 per cent Polish and 3 per cent Ukrainian, with smaller numbers of Jews and Lithuanians. Most of the population are Roman Catholics, with a large minority of Russian Orthodox.

Belarusian, one of the Slavonic family of languages, is the first official language; the alphabet is similar to the Russian one. Russian remains the dominant language and is the second official language.

CAPITAL – Minsk. Population 1,589,000 (1989). The city is the administrative centre of the CIS. Other important cities are Gomel, Vitebsk, Brest and Grodno.
CURRENCY – Rouble of 100 kopeks.
FLAG – Three horizontal stripes of white, red, white.
NATIONAL ANTHEM – The former Soviet national anthem but with the words omitted.
NATIONAL DAY – 27 July (Independence Day).

HISTORY

In the early ninth century AD the Kievan Rus state was a unified state encompassing all the Russian, Ukrainian and Belarusian populations. After being absorbed into Lithuania in the 13th and 14th centuries, the Belarusian nationality, language and culture flourished until it came under Polish rule in the mid-16th century. Two hundred years of Polish rule followed until Belarus was re-absorbed into the Russian Empire.

Much of Belarus was under German control at the time of the Russian revolution and it was not until German forces withdrew that a Byelorussian Soviet Socialist Republic was declared on 1 January 1919. Western Belarus was ceded to Poland after the Soviet defeat in the Polish-Soviet war of 1919–20, and was not recovered until Soviet forces occupied the area under the 1939 Nazi-Soviet Pact. Belarus was devastated by the German invasion in the Second World War and had to be rebuilt after the war, in which 25 per cent of the population was killed and thousands deported.

Belarus issued a Declaration of State Sovereignty on 27 July 1990 and declared its independence from the Soviet Union after the failed coup in Moscow in August 1991.

GOVERNMENT

After the failed Moscow coup, Stanislav Shuskevich replaced Nikolai Dementi, one of the coup leaders, as Belarusian leader, at the head of an informal coalition of Communists and democrats. Until 1994, however, parliament and the government remained under the control of former Communists, who thwarted the economic and political reform efforts of Shuskevich and his democratic

nationalist allies. Shuskevich was forced to resign in January 1994 after losing a no-confidence vote in the Supreme Soviet. Gen. Mecheslav Grib replaced Shuskevich as head of state and continued to resist economic and political reform, instead pursuing closer political, economic and trade relations with Russia. An economic and monetary union agreement with Russia collapsed as the two economies had diverged because of Russian economic reform.

A maverick populist Alexander Lukashenko defeated Gen. Grib in a July 1994 presidential election and appointed a reformist government to undertake economic reform. A referendum on 14 May 1995 overwhelmingly approved a renewed economic union with Russia, gave the Russian language equal official status and extended the President's powers over parliament. Legislative elections held in May 1995 were inconclusive and filled less than half of the parliamentary seats; another round is to be held in late 1995.

A new constitution came into effect on 30 March 1994 under which a directly elected President serving a maximum of two five-year terms was instituted. The President appoints the cabinet and directs government policy. Legislative power is held by a directly elected 300-seat Supreme Soviet. The republic is divided into six regions: Brest, Gomel, Grodno, Minsk, Mogilev and Vitebsk.

HEAD OF STATE
President, Alexander Lukashenko, *elected*, 10 July 1994

CABINET *as at July 1995*
Prime Minister, Mikhail Chigir
First Deputy Prime Minister, Mikhail Myasnikovich
Deputy Prime Ministers, Vladimir Rustakevich; Vladimir Garkun; Sergei Ling
Foreign Affairs, Hryoriy Navitsky
Interior, Yuri Zakharenko
Defence, Anatoly Kostenko
Justice, Leonid Dashuk
Trade, Valentin Baidak
Economy, Badzey Pyatrovich
Finance, Stephan Yanchuk
Public Health, Vasily Kazakov
Information, Anatoly Butevich
Education, Victor Gaisenok
Culture, Yevgeny Voitovich
Agriculture, Fyodor Mirochinsky
Transport and Communications, Stephan Shkapich
Social Welfare, Tamara Krutovtsova
Construction, Nikolai Novitsky

EMBASSY OF THE REPUBLIC OF BELARUS
1 St Stephens Crescent, London W2 5QT
Tel 0171-221 3941
Ambassador Extraordinary and Plenipotentiary, His Excellency Vladzimir Shchasny, apptd 1995

BRITISH EMBASSY
UL Zacharova 26, Minsk 220034
Tel: Minsk 368687
Ambassador Extraordinary and Plenipotentiary, His Excellency John Everard, apptd 1993

DEFENCE

Belarus has on its territory 54 SS-25 Intercontinental Ballistic Missiles which it is obliged to return to Russia for destruction under the terms of the START 1 Treaty, which it ratified in 1993 along with the Nuclear Non-Proliferation Treaty.

The total active armed forces number 92,500 personnel (which is being reduced to 90,000) with a term of conscription of 18 months. The Army has 52,500 personnel, the Air Force has 27,600 personnel (including 11,800 Air Defence). In addition there are 8,000 parliamentary border guards. Russia maintains 20,000 Air Force personnel in Belarus, with 150 combat aircraft.

ECONOMY

The collapse of the Soviet centrally planned economic system hit Belarusian industry badly. Belarus had many factories manufacturing products such as tractors, textiles and metal workings from raw materials sent from the rest of the former USSR. The country could not afford to pay market prices for oil, gas and raw materials, bringing the economy close to collapse by mid-1994. Since then economic reform and privatization has been introduced and in May 1995 a customs union agreement with Russia took effect under which Balarus will receive supplies of Russian oil and gas at subsidized prices. Belarus has also been given large-scale financial aid by Russia.

Belarusian agriculture, based on the meat and dairy industries, is relatively efficient and will cushion the republic from the worst of any food shortages, but rationing for some goods has been enforced since late 1992.

TRADE WITH UK	1993	1994
Imports from UK	£10,506,000	£11,097,000
Exports to UK	4,105,000	12,035,000

BELGIUM
Royaume de Belgique

A kingdom of western Europe, with a total area of 11,781 sq. miles (30,513 sq. km), Belgium is bounded on the north by the Netherlands, on the south by France, on the east by Germany and Luxembourg, and on the west by the North Sea. The Meuse and its tributary, the Sambre, divide it into two distinct regions, that in the west being generally level and fertile, while the tableland of the Ardennes, in the east, has mostly poor soil. The polders near the coast, which are protected by dykes against floods, cover an area of 193 sq. miles. The highest hill, Signal de Botranges, is 2,276 feet, but the mean elevation of the whole country does not exceed 526 feet. The principal rivers are the Scheldt and the Meuse.

The population (1993) was 10,068,319: Greater Brussels 950,339; Flanders 5,824,628; Wallonia 3,293,352, of whom 68,471 are German-speaking. The majority of Belgians are Roman Catholic.

Belgium is divided between those who speak Dutch (the Flemings) and those who speak French (the Walloons). Dutch is recognized as the official language in the northern areas and French in the southern (Walloon) area and there are guarantees for the respective linguistic minorities. Brussels is officially bi-lingual. There is a small German-speaking area (Eupen and Malmedy) along the German border, east of Liège.

CAPITAL – Brussels, population (1993) 950,339. Other towns are ΨAntwerp, the chief port (932,269); Liège (594,091); ΨGhent (489,883); Louvain (439,112); Charleroi (428,182); Namur (274,287); Mons (258,408); Bruges (226,440).
CURRENCY – Belgian franc of 100 centimes (centiemen).
FLAG – Three vertical bands, black, yellow, red.
NATIONAL ANTHEM – La Brabançonne.
NATIONAL DAY – 21 July (Accession of King Leopold I, 1831).

GOVERNMENT

The kingdom formed part of the Low Countries (Netherlands) from 1815 until 14 October 1830, when a National Congress proclaimed its independence. On 4 June 1831, Prince Leopold of Coburg was chosen as the hereditary king. The separation from the Netherlands and the neutrality and inviolability of Belgium were guaranteed by a Conference of the European powers, and by the Treaty of London 1839. On 4 August 1914 the Germans invaded Belgium, in violation of the terms of the treaty, and this led the Allies to declare war. The kingdom was again invaded by Germany in 1940 and was occupied by Nazi troops until liberated by the Allies in September 1944.

CONSTITUTION

According to the 1831 constitution the form of government is a constitutional representative and hereditary monarchy with a bicameral legislature, consisting of the King, the Senate and the Chamber of Deputies. The parliamentary term is four years.

Since 1968 separatist and regionalist political tension between the Dutch-speaking Flemish population and the French-speaking Walloons has grown considerably. This led to constitutional amendments in 1971, 1980, 1988 and 1993 intended to devolve power to the regions. The 1993 constitutional amendments state that Belgium is a federal state and devolve many powers from the national government to the community and regional governments. The national government retains competence only in the areas of foreign and defence policy, the national budget and monetary policy, social security, and the judiciary, legal and penal systems. The King loses his power to dissolve parliament and the Senate loses mosts of its power, becoming a limited revising chamber secondary to the Chamber of Representatives. The Senate has been reduced to 71 seats, of which 40 are directly elected (25 Flemish and 15 French), 21 indirectly elected (ten from Flemish Community Council, ten from Francophone Community Council and one from Germanophone Community Council), and ten co-opted by the Flemish and Francophone Communities. The Chamber of Representatives has been reduced to 150 seats. The national government is limited to 15 ministers.

The last general election was held on 21 May 1995. The results were as follows (seats):
Chamber of Deputies: CVP 29; PS 21; VLD (Flemish Liberals and Democrats) 21; SP 20; PRL-FDF (Liberal

Reform Party-Democratic Front (Francophone)) 18; PSC 12; Vlaams Blok (Flemish Nationalist Party) 11; Ecolo (Francophone Ecology Party) 6; Agalev (Flemish Environmental Party) 5; VU (Flemish People's Union) 5; Front National (FN) 2.

Senate: (directly elected): CVP 7; SP 6; VLD 6; PRL-FDF 5; PS 5; PSC 3; Vlaams Blok 3; VU 2; Ecolo 2; Agalev 1. A further 31 Senators are indirectly elected or co-opted (*see* above).

HEAD OF STATE

HM The King of the Belgians, King Albert II, *born* 6 June 1934; *succeeded* 9 August 1993, after the death of his elder brother, King Baudouin, on 31 July 1993; *married* 2 July 1959, Donna Paola Ruffo di Calabria, and has *issue* Prince Philippe (*see* below); Princess Astrid, *b.* 5 June 1962; Prince Laurent, *b.* 20 October 1963
Heir, HRH Prince Philippe Léopold Louis Marie, *born* 15 April 1960

CABINET *as at June 1995*

Prime Minister, Jean-Luc Dehaene (CVP)
Deputy Prime Minister, Economic Affairs and Telecommunications, Elio di Rupo (PS)
Deputy Prime Minister, Interior, Johan Vande Lanotte (SP)
Deputy Prime Minister, Defence, Melchoir Wathelet (PSC)
Deputy Prime Minister, Budget, Herman Van Rompuy (CVP)
Finance and Foreign Trade, Philippe Maystadt (PSC)
Social Affairs, Magda de Galan (PS)
Scientific Policy, Yvan Ylieff (PS)
Pensions and Public Health, Marcel Colla (SP)
Small and Medium-Sized Enterprises and Agriculture, Karel Pinxten (CVP)
Foreign Affairs and Development Co-operation, Eric Derycke (SP)
Transport, Michael Daerdan (PS)
Justice, Stefaan De Clerck (CVP)
Civil Service, André Flahaut (PS)
Employment and Equality, Miet Smet (CVP)

CVP Christian Social Party (Flemish); PS Socialist Party (Francophone); SP Socialist Party (Flemish); PSC Christian Social Party (Francophone)

BELGIAN EMBASSY
103 Eaton Square, London SW1W 9AB
Tel 0171–235 5422
Ambassador Extraordinary and Plenipotentiary, His Excellency Jonkheer Prosper Thuysbaert, apptd 1994
Minister-Counsellor, A. Querton (*Political*), J. M. Veranneman
Military, Naval and Air Attaché, Col. J. Bouzette
First Secretary (Economic), C. Peeters

BRITISH EMBASSY
rue d'Arlon 85, 1040 Brussels
Tel: Brussels 287 6211
Ambassador Extraordinary and Plenipotentiary, His Excellency Sir John Gray, KBE, CMG, apptd 1993
Deputy Ambassador, Counsellor and Consul-General, E. C. Glover
Counsellor (Commercial/Economic), N. R. Jarrold
Defence and Military Attaché, Gp Capt. D. C. Hencken
There are British Consular Offices at Brussels, Antwerp and Liège.
BRITISH COUNCIL REPRESENTATIVE TO BELGIUM AND LUXEMBOURG – Dr Ken Churchill, OBE, rue Joseph II 30, 1040 Brussels
BRITISH CHAMBER OF COMMERCE FOR BELGIUM AND LUXEMBOURG (INC.), rue Joseph II 30, 1040 Brussels

REGIONAL GOVERNMENT

The constitutional amendment packages of 1980, 1988 and 1993 make provision for four levels of sub-national government in Belgium: community, regional, provincial, and communal.

There are four defined communities: Flemish; Francophone; Brussels; Germanophone. Each community has its own assembly with powers in the areas of language, culture, media, sport, tourism, education, social welfare and public health. The assemblies each elect their own community government. At this level, Flanders is covered by the Flemish Community Assembly; Brussels is covered by its Joint Community Commission as well as the Flemish and Francophone Community Assemblies; most of Walloonia is covered by the Francophone Community Assembly and the remainder of Walloonia in the German-speaking communities of Eupen and Malmedy (ceded by Germany under the Versailles Treaty 1919) is covered by the Germanophone Community Assembly.

At regional level, Belgium is divided into the regions of Walloonia, Brussels and Flanders. Each region has its own assembly and government with powers over areas such as the environment, housing, energy, employment, transport, agriculture, regional economic policy and foreign trade. The Walloonia regional assembly is directly elected with 75 members, the Brussels regional assembly is directly elected with 75 members, and the Flemish regional assembly has 118 directly elected members and six nominated by the Flemish in Brussels.

There are ten provinces in Belgium, of which five are French-speaking and in Walloonia (Hainault, Liège, Luxembourg, Namur and French Brabant) and five are Dutch-speaking and in Flanders (Antwerp, East Flanders, West Flanders, Limbourg and Flemish Brabant). In addition, Belgium has 589 communes as the lowest level of local government.

The main consequence of the constitutional amendments has been the increase in political power of the regional governments at the expense of both the community and national levels. As a result the Francophone Community Assembly and Government is gradually losing power to the Walloon and Brussels regional governments, whilst the Flemish have amalgamated their community and regional governments to form one increasingly powerful Flanders government.

An Arbitration Court was set up in 1984 to resolve conflicts between laws made by the various legislative bodies.

Minister-President of the Flemish Government, Luc Van den Brande (CVP)
Minister-President of the Walloon Regional Government, Robert Collignon (PS)

DEFENCE

The total active armed forces number 49,700 with 228,800 reservists who have served within the last three years. Conscription was abolished in 1995.

The Army has a strength of 35,000 with 335 main battle tanks, 133 light tanks, 1,450 armoured personnel carriers and armoured infantry fighting vehicles, 230 artillery pieces and 84 helicopters.

The Navy has a strength of 2,600 with two frigates and seven mine warfare vessels. The Air Force is 12,100 strong with 133 combat aircraft and another 95 in store.

Belgium maintains 10,300 troops in Germany as part of its NATO commitment. It also maintains 600 troops in Croatia and 420 in Bosnia as part of the UN forces. The headquarters of NATO, SHAPE and the Western

European Union Military Planning Cell are in Belgium; 1,400 US personnel are stationed in the country.

ECONOMY

Belgium is a manufacturing country. With no natural resources except coal, production of which has now ceased, industry is based largely on the processing for re-export of imported raw materials. Principal industries are steel and metal products, chemicals and petrochemicals, textiles, glass, and foodstuffs.

In an attempt to meet the Maastricht Treaty criteria for economic and monetary union, the government introduced a series of austerity packages in 1993–5 to try to reduce Belgian public debt of 140 per cent of GDP, which is the highest in the developed world.

FINANCE

Budget	1993	1994
Revenue	BFr.1,934,200m	BFr.2,131,300m
Expenditure	2,538,800m	2,796,400m

TRADE

External trade figures relate to Luxembourg as well as Belgium since the two countries formed an economic union in 1921.

	1992	1993
Total imports	BFr.4,024,000m	BFr.4,021,000m
Total exports	3,768,000m	4,191,000m

Trade with UK (Belgium and Luxembourg)

	1993	1994
Imports from UK	£6,597,146,000	£7,111,693,000
Exports to UK	6,270,295,000	6,886,191,000

CULTURE

The literature of France and the Netherlands is supplemented by an indigenous Belgian literary activity in both French and Dutch. Maurice Maeterlinck (1862–1949) was awarded the Nobel Prize for Literature in 1911. Emile Verhaeren (1855–1916) was a poet of international standing. Of contemporary Belgian writers, the most celebrated was Georges Simenon (1903–89).

EDUCATION

Nursery schools provide free education for children from two and a half to six years. There are over 8,000 primary schools (6 to 12 years) of which approximately 5,000 are administerd by the local Communities. The remainder are free institutions (predominantly Roman Catholic). There are more than 1,100 secondary schools offering a general academic education slightly over half of which are free institutions (predominantly Roman Catholic but subsidized by the state) and the remainder official institutions. The official school-leaving age is 18.

COMMUNICATIONS

The railways are operated by the Belgian National Railways. Ship canals include Ghent-Terneuzen (18 miles, half in the Netherlands) by which ships up to 60,000 tons reach Ghent; Willebroek Rupel-Brussels (20 miles, by which ships drawing 18 ft reach Brussels from the sea); Bruges (from Zeebrugge on the North Sea to Bruges, 6¼ miles); Albert (79 miles), Liège to Antwerp for barges up to 1,350 tons. The River Meuse from the Dutch to the French frontiers, the River Sambre betwen Namur and Monceau, the River Scheldt from Antwerp to Ghent and the Brussels-Charleroi Canal are being widened or deepened to take barges up to 1,350 tons. Most maritime trade is carried in foreign shipping.

In 1986 there were 14,260 km of trunk road, of which about 1,550 km were motorways. The Belgian national airline Sabena operates regular services between Brussels and European centres, as well as intercontinental services worldwide.

BELIZE

Belize lies on the east coast of Central America, bounded on the north and north-west by Mexico, and on the west and south by Guatemala. The total area (including offshore islands) is about 8,867 sq. miles (22,965 sq. km.).

The coastal areas are mostly flat and swampy with many islets but the country rises gradually towards the interior, which is mainly forest. The northern and western districts are hilly, and in the south the Maya Mountains and the Cockscombs form the backbone of the country, reaching a height of 3,700 feet at Victoria Peak. The climate is subtropical, with a mean annual temperature of 20°C, but is tempered by sea breezes. There are two dry seasons (February–May and August–September) and occasional hurricanes.

The population is 205,000 (1993 census), of which the main racial groups are Mestizo (Maya-Spanish), 44 per cent; Creole, 30 per cent; Maya, 11 per cent; plus a number of East Indian and Spanish descent. The races are now inter-mixed. The majority of the population is Christian, about 58 per cent Catholic and 34 per cent Protestant. The official language and language of instruction is English. Spanish is also widely spoken and English Creole is the vernacular. There are also Garifuna and Maya speakers.

CAPITAL – Belmopan (1993 census 3,739). The largest city and former capital is ΨBelize City (population, 1993 census 46,342). Other towns are Corozal (7,420), San Ignacio (9,417), Dangriga (6,761), Orange Walk (11,573).

CURRENCY – Belize dollar (BZ$) of 100 cents. The Belize dollar is tied to the US dollar, BZ$2 = US$1.

FLAG – Blue ground with red band along top and bottom edges, and in centre a white disc containing the coat of arms surrounded by a green garland.

NATIONAL ANTHEM – Land of the Free.

NATIONAL DAY – 21 September (Independence Day).

GOVERNMENT

The early history of Belize is little known, although the numerous ruins in the area indicate that it was heavily populated by the Maya Indians. The first British settlement was established in 1638 but was subject to repeated attacks by the Spanish, who claimed sovereignty over the area, until the decisive defeat of Spanish forces by the Royal Navy and settlers in the battle of St George's Caye in 1798. In 1871 the area was recognized by Britain as a colony and called British Honduras. In 1973 the colony was renamed Belize, and was granted independence on 21 September 1981. The long-standing territorial dispute with Guatemala, which had delayed independence earlier, was provisionally resolved in November 1992 when the Guatemalan Congress and Supreme Court voted to recognize Belize and establish diplomatic relations. Guatemala still retains its claim, subject to arbitration by the International Court of Justice. The Guatemalan constitutional crisis and overthrow of President Serrano in May and June 1993 caused concern in Belize over the new Guatemalan government's policy towards Belize.

Queen Elizabeth II is head of state, represented in Belize by a Governor-General. There is a National Assembly, comprising a House of Representatives (29 members elected for five years) and a Senate (nine members appointed by the Governor-General). Executive power is vested in the Cabinet, which is responsible to the National Assembly.

The National Assembly was dissolved in June 1993 and in the ensuing elections the People's United Party government was defeated by the United Democratic Party.

Governor-General, His Excellency Sir Colville Norbert Young, GCMG, apptd 17 November 1993

THE CABINET *as at July 1995*

Prime Minister, Minister of Finance and Economic Development, Rt. Hon. Manuel Esquivel

Deputy PM, Attorney-General, Minister of Foreign Affairs and National Security, Hon. Dean Barrow

Natural Resources, Hon. Edwardo Juan

Agriculture and Fisheries, Hon. Russell Garcia

Tourism and Environment, Hon. Henry Young

Home Affairs and Labour, Hon. Elito Urbina

Science, Technology and Transportation, Hon. Joseph Cayetano

Health and Sports, Hon. Ruben Campos

Education and Public Service, Hon. Elodio Aragon

Housing, Urban Development and Co-operatives, Hon. Hubert Elrington

Trade and Industry, Hon. Salvador Fernandez

Youth Development, Women's Affairs and Human Resources, Hon. Philip Goldson

Works, Hon. Melvin Hulse

Ministers of State:

Housing, Urban Development and Co-operatives, Hon. Michael Finnegan

Youth Development, Women's Affairs and Human Resources, Hon. Faith Babb

Works, Hon. Wilfred Dennis Usher

BELIZE HIGH COMMISSION
22 Harcourt House, 19 Cavendish Square, London W1M 9AD
Tel 0171-499 9728
High Commissioner, Her Excellency Dr Ursula Barrow, apptd 1993

BRITISH HIGH COMMISSION
PO Box 91, Belmopan
Tel: Belmopan 22146/7
High Commissioner, His Excellency Gordon Baker, apptd 1994

ECONOMY

About 30 per cent of the population is engaged in agriculture. Corn (maize), rice, red kidney beans, root crops and fruit are the main food crops, although main agricultural exports are sugar, bananas and citrus products. The country is more or less self-sufficient in fresh beef, pork and poultry, but processed meat and dairy products are imported. About 25 per cent of timber production (mostly mahogany) is exported, and there is a large US market for lobster, conch and scale fish. Tourism is also a valuable source of income.

TRADE	1992	1993
Total imports	BZ$548.3m	BZ$545.3m
Total exports	231.1m	228.6m

Trade with UK	1993	1994
Imports from UK	£16,642,000	£12,767,000
Exports to UK	37,405,000	42,504,000

EDUCATION

Education is compulsory from six to 14 years of age. In 1992 primary education was provided by 241 schools, most of which are government-aided. Enrolment totalled 48,612. Secondary education is provided by 40 secondary and post-secondary institutions with an enrolment of 10,647. A University College of Belize has been established. The Government also offers scholarships for students to go abroad. There is an extra-mural faculty of the University of the West Indies, with a resident tutor.

COMMUNICATIONS

There is a government-operated radio service and three privately-owned radio stations but no official television service in the country. An automatic telephone service operated by Belize Telecommunications Ltd covers the whole country.

The principal airport is at Belize City and various airlines operate international flights to the USA and other Central American states. The main port is also Belize City, which has deep water quays. Several inland waterways are also navigable. There are 1,865 miles of road, including four main highways, but there is no railway system.

BENIN
République du Benin

A republic situated in West Africa, between 2° and 3° W. and 6° and 12° N., Benin (formerly known as Dahomey) has a short coastline of 78 miles on the Gulf of Guinea but extends northwards inland for 437 miles. It is flanked on the west by Togo, on the north by Burkina and Niger, and on the east by Nigeria. The four main regions, running horizontally, are a narrow sandy coastal strip, a succession of inter-communicating lagoons, a clay belt and a sandy plateau in the north. It has an area of 43,484 sq. miles (122,622 sq. km), and a population of 5,047,000 (UN 1992 estimate). The official language is French. Although poor in resources, Benin is one of the most heavily populated areas in West Africa, with a high standard of education.

CAPITAL – ΨPorto Novo, population (1982 estimate) 208,258. Principal commercial town and port, ΨCotonou (487,020).

CURRENCY – Franc CFA of 100 centimes.

FLAG – Two horizontal stripes of yellow over red with a vertical green band in the hoist.

NATIONAL DAY – 30 November.

GOVERNMENT

The first treaty with France was signed by one of the kings of Abomey in 1851 but the country was not placed under French administration until 1892. Benin became an independent republic within the French Community in December 1958; full independence outside the Community was proclaimed on 1 August 1960. Between 1963 and 1972 successive governments were overthrown by the military after only short terms in office until a coup d'état in 1972 brought to power a Marxist-Leninist military government headed by Lt.-Col. Kerekou.

In response to mounting unrest, the government dropped Marxism-Leninism as the official ideology in 1989. Following a 'National Conference of Active Forces of the Nation,' the constitution was revoked in March 1990 and the country's official name was changed from the People's Republic of Benin to the Republic of Benin. The

Revolutionary National Assembly (legislature) was dissolved and replaced by a High Council of the Republic (HCR). A new pluralistic constitution was adopted by referendum in December 1990. Legislative and presidential elections were held in February and March 1991. Nicéphore Soglo was sworn in as the new President and appointed a provisional government. The lack of a clear majority in the legislature for the Benin Renaissance Party (PRB) of President Soglo meant the government had to rely on an unstable alliance of independents in the 64-member National Assembly. Legislative elections to the 83-seat National Assembly in March 1995 gave the PRB and allies 32 seats and opposition parties 49 seats.

HEAD OF STATE
President and Head of the Armed Forces, HE Nicéphore Soglo, *sworn in* 4 April 1991

CABINET *as at June 1995*

The President
Minister of State and National Defence, Desire Vieyra
Interior, Public Security and Territorial Administration, Antoine Alabi Gbegan
Foreign Affairs and Co-operation, Robert Dossou
Finance, Paul Dossou
Planning and Economic Reconstruction, Robert Tagnon
Rural Development, Mama Adamou N'Diaye
Public Works and Transport, Lazare Kpatokpa
Industry, Small and Medium Enterprises, Rigobert Ladikpo
Energy, Mines and Hydraulic Resources, Aurelien Houessou
Culture and Communications, Marius Francisco
National Education, Karim Dramane
Youth and Sports, Alassance Idriss
Civil Service and Administrative Reform, Timothee Adahui
Labour, Employment and Social Welfare, Kapuoe Koumourade Osseni
Public Health, Véronique Lawson
Environment, Housing and Town Planning, Roger Ahoyo
Parliamentary Relations and Government Spokesman, Theodore Holo
Commerce and Tourism, Yacoumo Kpatashi
Justice and Legislation, Pierre Nevi

EMBASSY OF THE REPUBLIC OF BENIN
87 Avenue Victor Hugo, 75116 Paris, France
Tel: Paris 45009882
Ambassador Extraordinary and Plenipotentiary, His Excellency Richard Adjaho
HONORARY CONSULATE, 16 The Broadway, Stanmore, Middx HA7 4DW. Tel: 081–954 8800. *Honorary Consul,* L. Landau

BRITISH AMBASSADOR, His Excellency Sir Christopher MacRae KCMG, resident at Lagos, Nigeria

ECONOMY

In early 1994 the IMF approved a three-year enhanced structural adjustment facility credit of US$72.6m to underpin economic reforms.
The principal exports are cotton, palm products, groundnuts, shea-nuts, and coffee. Small deposits of gold, iron and chrome have been found; oil production started in 1983.

TRADE WITH UK	1993	1994
Imports from UK	£31,014,000	£30,352,000
Exports to UK	1,436,000	3,820,000

BHUTAN
Druk-yul

Bhutan is a small kingdom in the Himalayas with Tibet to the north and India to the west, south and east. The total area is about 18,147 sq. miles (47,000 sq. km), with a mountainous northern region which is infertile and sparsely populated, a central zone of upland valleys where most of the population and cultivated land is found, and in the south the densely forested foothills of the Himalayas, which are mainly inhabited by Nepalese settlers and indigenous tribespeople.
The population is estimated at 650,000, about 80 per cent of whom are Buddhists. The remainder (mostly the Nepali Bhutanese) are Hindu. The official language, for administrative and religious purposes, is Dzongkha, a variant of Tibetan, which functions as a lingua franca amongst a variety of languages and dialects. From 1990 it has been government policy to make the study of Dzongkha compulsory in schools. However, Nepali remains a recognized language and English remains the medium of instruction and the working language of the administration.

CAPITAL – Thimphu, population estimate (1987) 15,000.
CURRENCY – Ngultrum (Nu) of 100 chetrums. Indian currency is also legal tender.
FLAG – Saffron yellow and orange-red divided diagonally, with dragon device in centre.
NATIONAL DAY – 17 December.

GOVERNMENT

Under a 1949 treaty Bhutan is guided by the advice of India in regard to its external relations. It retains its own diplomatic representatives and is a member of the UN. It also receives from India an annual payment of Rs500,000 as compensation for portions of its territory annexed by the British Government in India in 1864.
Bhutan has a 150-member National Assembly which meets twice a year. The ten-member Royal Advisory Council, nominated by the King and the National Assembly, acts as a consultative body when the National Assembly is not in session. The King is also assisted by a Council of Ministers. There are no political parties.
In January 1989 the King introduced a code of national etiquette designed to protect the national culture and language from Nepali encroachment. These measures, together with the granting of citizenship only to Nepalis settled in Bhutan before 1958, has led to an exodus of ethnic Nepalis from the south of the country to Nepal, where about 80,000 live in camps. A low-level insurgency has been waged in the south of the country against the King's policies by ethnic Nepalis since 1990. Talks between the Nepali and Bhutan governments cotinue in an attempt to resolve the fate of the refugees.

HEAD OF STATE
HM The King of Bhutan, Jigme Singye Wangchuk, *born* 11 November 1955; *succeeded his father,* July 1972; *crowned,* 2 June 1974
Heir, Crown Prince Jigme Gesar Namgyal Wangchuk, *designated,* 31 October 1988

COUNCIL OF MINISTERS *as at 30 June 1995*

Chairman of Council of Ministers, HM The King
HM Representative in Ministry of Finance, HRH Ashi Sonam Chhoden Wangchuk

HM Representative in Ministry of Agriculture, HRH Ashi Dorji
W. Wangchuk
Home Affairs, HRH Namgyel Wangchuk
Finance, Dorji Tshering
Foreign Affairs, Dawa Tshering
Communications and Social Services, Dr Tashi Tobgyel
Trade, Industry and Tourism, Om Pradhan
Planning, Chenkhap Dorji
*Deputy Minister of Defence, Chief Operations Officer of Royal
Bhutan Army,* Maj.-Gen. Lam Dorji
Speaker of the National Assembly, Chief Justice, Sangye Penjor

ECONOMY

The seventh five-year plan (1992–7) envisages a doubling
of internal revenues to Nu2,000m. Economic emphasis is
on the infrastructure, especially roads and telecommunications, and hydro-electric power.

The economy is based on agriculture and animal
husbandry, which engage over 90 per cent of the workforce
in what is largely a self-sufficient rural society. The
principal food crops are rice, wheat, maize and barley.
Vegetables and fruit are also produced. Bhutan is the
world's largest producer of cardamom, which forms its
principal export to countries other than India. Agriculture
is, however, limited by the country's mountainous topography and 60 per cent forest cover. The mountains
contain rich deposits of limestone, gypsum, dolomite and
graphite and small amounts of coal, which are exported to
India. A modest industrial base is being developed. A
distillery and cement, chemicals and food-processing
plants are in production; a forestry industries complex is
being expanded. Tourism and postage stamps are increasingly important sources of foreign exchange.

TRADE

Over 90 per cent of foreign trade is with India. Principal
exports are agricultural products, timber, cement and coal;
main imports are textiles, cereals and consumer goods.
Bhutan's airline, Druk Air, flies between Paro, New Delhi
and Calcutta.

Trade with UK	1993	1994
Imports from UK	£2,263,000	£1,631,000
Exports to UK	1,642,000	857,000

BOLIVIA
República de Bolivia

Bolivia extends between 10° and 23° S. latitude and 57° 30′
and 69° 45′ W. longitude. It has an area estimated at
424,165 sq. miles (1,098,581 sq. km) and is landlocked.

The chief topographical feature is the great central
plateau over 500 miles in length, at an average altitude of
12,500 feet above sea level, between the two great chains of
the Andes, which traverse the country from south to north.
The total length of the navigable rivers is about 12,000
miles, the principal rivers being the Itenez, Beni, Mamore
and Madre de Dios.

The population (1992 census) was 6,440,000, of which
12 per cent is of white European descent, 30 per cent
mestizo (mixed European-Indian), 25 per cent Quechua
Indian and 17 per cent Aymará Indian. The official
language is Spanish, which is spoken by around 60 per
cent of the population, with Quechua spoken by 25 per
cent and Aymará by 15 per cent. Roman Catholicism was
the state religion until disestablishment in 1961.

CAPITAL – La Paz (population, 1,115,000). Other large
centres are Cochabamba (512,000), Oruro (183,000),
Santa Cruz (694,000), Potosí (112,000), Sucre, the legal
capital and seat of the judiciary (131,000) and Tarija
(90,000).
CURRENCY – Boliviano ($b) of 100 centavos.
FLAG – Three horizontal bands; red, yellow, green.
NATIONAL ANTHEM – Bolivianos, El Hado Propicio (Oh
Bolivia, our long-felt desires).
NATIONAL DAY – 6 August (Independence Day).

GOVERNMENT

Bolivia won its independence from Spain in 1825 after a
war of liberation led by Simon Bolivar (1783–1830), from
whom the country derives its name. From 1964 to 1982
Bolivia was ruled by military juntas until civilian rule was
restored. The constitution provides for a directly elected
executive President who appoints the Cabinet. The
legislature (Congress) consists of a 27-member Senate and
a 130-member Chamber of Deputies. Both the President
and Congress are elected for four-year terms.

Congressional and presidential elections were held in
June 1993 with Gonzalo Sánchez of the opposition
National Revolutionary Movement (MNR) winning the
largest share of the vote in the presidential election but as
no candidate won more than 50 per cent, the new President
was chosen by Congressional vote in August, when
Gonzalo Sánchez was elected. The MNR emerged as the
largest party in Congress, winning 52 out of 130 seats, and
formed a government in coalition with the Civic Solidarity
Union (20 seats) and the Free Bolivia Movement (7 seats).

HEAD OF STATE
President of the Republic, Gonzalo Sánchez de Lozada,
inaugurated 5 August 1993
Vice President, Victor Hugo Cardenas

CABINET *as at June 1995*
Foreign Affairs and Worship, Antonío Araníbar Quiroga
Interior, Carlos Sanchez Berzain
National Defence, Raúl Tovar Píerola
Presidency, José Guillermo Sandoval
Economic Development and Finance, Fernando Alvaro Cassio
Education and Culture, Fernando Romero Moreno
Labour, Marcelo Cespedes Gutierrez
Human Development, Enrique Ipiña Melgar
Information, Ernesto Machicado
Justice, René Blattman
Privatization, Alfonso Revollo
Sustainable Development, vacant
Minister without Portfolio, Jaime Villalobos

BOLIVIAN EMBASSY
106 Eaton Square, London SW1W 9AD
Tel 0171–235 2257/4248
Ambassador Extraordinary and Plenipotentiary, His Excellency
Carlos Morales-Landívar, apptd 1995

BRITISH EMBASSY
Avenida Arce 2732, (Casilla 694) La Paz
Tel: La Paz 357424
Ambassador Extraordinary and Plenipotentiary, His Excellency
David Ridgway, OBE, apptd 1995
Deputy Ambassador, Consul and First Secretary (Commercial),
I. Davies

There is an Honorary Consulate at Santa Cruz.

EDUCATION

Elementary education is compulsory and free and there are
secondary schools in urban centres. Provision is also made

for higher education; in addition to St Francisco Xavier's University at Sucre, founded in 1624, there are seven other universities, the largest being the University of San Andres at La Paz, and ten private universities.

ECONOMY

Mining, natural gas, petroleum and agriculture are the principal industries. The ancient silver mines of Potosí are now worked chiefly for tin, but gold, partly dug and partly washed, is obtained on the Eastern Cordillera of the Andes. The tin output, together with other minerals (copper, tungsten, antimony, lead, zinc, asbestos, wolfram, bismuth salt and sulphur), provides over one-third of exports. Small quantities of oil are produced for internal consumption, and gas (currently providing about a quarter of export income) is piped to Argentina; there are plans to build a pipeline to São Paulo, Brazil. Agricultural produce consists chiefly of soya, sorghum, beef, rice, barley, oats, wheat, sugar-cane, maize, cotton, indigo, rubber, cacao, potatoes, cinchona bark, medicinal herbs, brazil nuts etc.

The economy deteriorated badly in the late 1970s and early 1980s, with disappointing petroleum reserves, a large external debt, and the collapse of world tin prices. In the mid-1980s free market economic reforms were introduced by the government with privatization of some state-owned firms and the encouragement of foreign investment. Tin prices began to increase from April 1989, but most of the tin industry remains uneconomic or has closed down. Many workers took to growing coca which has now become a significant export.

The peso was replaced in 1987 with the Boliviano of 1,000,000 old pesos in a successful effort to stem hyper-inflation and had brought the inflation rate down to 9 per cent in 1993. The economy and currency have stabilized and the foreign debt (US$3,700 million in 1993) is being repaid. GDP in 1992 was US$5,994 million. The new government is committed to continuing the reforms, including privatization of most state firms, and in December 1994 received a US$147 million loan from the IMF to support economic reform.

TRADE

Mineral exports represent about 35 per cent of total trade. Bolivia has now developed its own smelters and is exporting metals. The chief imports are wheat and flour, iron and steel products, machinery, vehicles and textiles.

Trade with UK	1993	1994
Imports from UK	£7,997,000	£10,147,000
Exports to UK	13,144,000	16,780,000

COMMUNICATIONS

There are 2,200 miles of railways in operation including the lines from Corumbá to Santa Cruz (312 miles). There is direct railway communication to the sea at Antofagasta (32 hours), Arica (10 hours), and Mollendo (2 days), and also to Buenos Aires (3½ days). Communication with Peru is by road from La Paz via Copacabana and thence to the railhead at Puno. In 1993 Bolivia and Peru signed an agreement granting Bolivia a concession of 162 hectares at the southern Peruvian port of Ilo for 98 years to construct a free trade zone.

Commercial aviation is conducted by the national airline, Lloyd Aereo Boliviano and Transporte Aereo Militar between the major towns, and Lloyd Aereo Boliviano and a number of foreign airlines provide international flights to the USA, South and Central America and Europe.

Most towns have radio, telephone or telegraph communication with the main cities. There are nine principal daily newspapers.

BOSNIA-HERCEGOVINA

Bosnia-Hercegovina is bounded by Serbia on the east, Montenegro on the south-east and Croatia on the north and west, apart from a narrow 20 km coastline on the Adriatic at Neum. It has an area of 19,735 sq. miles (51,129 sq. km). The population (1991 census) was 4.4 million, of whom some 44 per cent were Muslims, 31 per cent Serbs and 17 per cent Croats. The current population is estimated to be 2.9 million of whom 1,270,000 are Muslims, 892,000 are ethnic Serbs and 512,000 are ethnic Croats.

CAPITAL – Sarajevo, population (1991) 453,324. Other major cities include Tuzla, Banja Luka, Zenica, Vitez and Mostar.

CURRENCY – Bosnian dinar.

FLAG – White flag bearing a blue shield with a white diagonal and six gold fleurs-de-lys.

NATIONAL DAY – 1 March (anniversary of 1992 declaration of independence).

HISTORY

The country was settled by Slavs in the seventh century and conquered by the Ottoman Turks in 1463. Ruled by the Turks for over 400 years, the country came under Austro-Hungarian control in 1878. Austria-Hungary's annexation of Bosnia-Hercegovina in 1908 was never accepted by Serbia because of the large ethnic Serb population in the country, and the assassination of the heir to the Austro-Hungarian throne in Sarajevo by an ethnic Serb precipitated the First World War. Bosnia-Hercegovina became part of the 'Kingdom of Serbs, Croats and Slovenes' (renamed Yugoslavia in 1929) under the Versailles Treaty 1919. It was occupied by German and Axis forces between 1941 and 1945, when there was heavy resistance by partisans in the mountains. At the end of the war Bosnia-Hercegovina came under Communist rule as part of the Socialist Federal Republic of Yugoslavia, which eventually collapsed with the secession of Slovenia and Croatia in 1991.

The Bosnia-Hercegovina government issued a declaration of sovereignty in October 1991 against the wishes of the ethnic Serb Democratic Party. Independence was declared on 1 March 1992 following a referendum on the subject boycotted by the Bosnian Serbs. Bosnia-Hercegovina was recognized as an independent state by the EC and USA in April 1992 and admitted to UN membership in May 1992.

THE WAR

Independence was supported by the Muslims and Croats in Bosnia but rejected by the Serbs, who wanted to form a Greater Serbia with the Serbian republic. Fighting between Muslims and Serbs broke out in March 1992 and the predominantly Serbian Federal Yugoslav Army (JNA) intervened against the poorly-armed Muslims. By May 1992 Serbian forces had overrun the majority of the republic and Croat forces much of the rest, leaving the legitimate Bosnian government forces besieged in Sarajevo, the central area of the republic, and a few other enclaves. By May international pressure forced Serbia to withdraw the JNA from Bosnia, but the JNA handed over most of its weapons to Bosnian Serb forces. At the end of May the UN imposed a total trade embargo and economic sanctions on Serbia and Montenegro, but the war in Bosnia continued, evidence of 'ethnic cleansing' and Serb-run concentration camps emerging in August 1992. The UN authorized the use of troops to keep Sarajevo airport open for relief flights, and then forced all the warring participants to attend the London peace conference at the end of August.

By this time 70 per cent of Bosnia was controlled by Bosnian Serb forces and 20 per cent by Bosnian Croat forces. The mainly Muslim forces of the Bosnian government were in an uneasy alliance with Croatian and Bosnian Croat forces, who were trying to cut Serbian supply lines to Serb enclaves in Croatia. At the conference all sides signed an agreement to end the war, respecting Bosnia's international boundaries and rejecting the use of force to gain land. However, the Bosnian Serbs would not give up the land that they had gained and the Muslims would not settle for peace without winning back land.

Muslim-Bosnian Serb fighting in the second half of 1992 in central and eastern Bosnia led Western nations to deploy troops under UN auspices to secure humanitarian aid supplies as winter began.

The joint EC-UN peace negotiating team reconvened the peace conference in Geneva in January 1993 and presented the Vance–Owen peace plan. The plan was accepted by the Bosnian government and Bosnian Croats, and the Bosnian-Serb leader Radovan Karadzic eventually signed the peace plan on 2 May after the UN imposed total trade, sporting and diplomatic isolation in April 1993 on the rump Yugoslav state (a naval blockade had been imposed in November 1992). The Bosnian Serb Parliament, however, rejected the plan in defiance of international pressure. On 22 May the USA, EC and Russia agreed on the 'Joint Action Programme' for future peace negotiations, its basis being the acceptance of territorial gain by force.

Meanwhile, in early 1993 the war divided into two conflicts, one between government and Bosnian Serb forces, and one between government and Bosnian Croat forces. Bosnian Serb forces starved and shelled Muslim enclaves in eastern Bosnia and Sarajevo, causing the UN and Western governments to intervene by instituting supply drops by air in February, demilitarizing Srebrenica

in April, declaring the Muslim enclaves of Srebrenica, Zepa, Gorazde, Sarajevo, Tuzla and Bihac UN 'safe areas' in May, and forcing Bosnian Serb forces to stop shelling Sarajevo by the threat of air strikes in August. When the Bosnian government accepted the principle of the ethnic division of Bosnia in August, the peace process was given an impetus and fighting between Bosnian Serb and government forces decreased.

The heaviest fighting of 1993 was between Bosnian government and Bosnian Croat forces in central Bosnia and Mostar, in which government forces captured the towns of Zenica and Travnik but UN aid distribution was greatly inhibited. Hostilities ended on 25 February 1994 after a US-brokered Muslim-Croat Federation was agreed (see below) and government and Bosnian Croat forces re-formed their alliance of 1992 and early 1993. Some 5,000 UN troops were despatched to Bosnia in March to patrol the government-Bosnian Croat ceasefire lines.

The peace process between the government and Bosnian Serbs collapsed in December 1993 over the ethnic division of Bosnia, leading to increased fighting and shelling of Sarajevo and government-held enclaves. A Bosnian Serb artillery attack on a Sarajevo market in February 1994 killed 68 and caused international outrage. Subsequently the UN and NATO successfully imposed a 12 mile (20 km) heavy weapons exclusion zone and local ceasefire around Sarajevo. However, Bosnian Serb forces launched an offensive in April against the eastern enclave of Gorazde, most of which they captured before halting, despite NATO air strikes. This led NATO to widen its threat of air strikes to all UN 'safe areas' and galvanized the USA, Britain, France, Germany and Russia to form the Contact Group (CG) to co-ordinate peace efforts. The CG brought about a ceasefire on 10 June 1994 and on 6 July presented its peace plan, concentrating on a 51:49 division of Bosnia-Hercegovina between the Muslim-Croat Federation and the Bosnian Serbs.

The Contact Group peace plan was accepted by the Muslim-Croat Federation but rejected by the Bosnian Serbs, leading to a CG diplomatic strategy to isolate the Bosnian Serbs. To this end Serbian President Milosevic agreed to close the Serbian-Bosnian border, imposing a blockade on the Bosnian Serbs, except for essential food and medicines, in August. In return the UN lifted cultural, sporting and transport sanctions against the rump federal Yugoslav state. Fighting intensified in late 1994 as the Bosnian Serbs refused to accept the peace plan and the Muslim-Croat Federation took advantage of their increasing supplies of armaments and better organized forces. Goverment and Bosnian Croat forces captured the town of Kupres from Bosnian Serb forces in November and broke out of the Bihac enclave for the first time in the war before being driven back by attacks on the enclave from Croatia by Croatian Serbs. NATO air strikes in December on Bosnian Serb anti-aircraft missile batteries resulted in a crisis as Bosnian Serb forces took over 350 UN peacekeepers hostage to stop the air strikes. The former US President Jimmy Carter brokered the release of the hostages and a four-month ceasefire between Muslim-Croat and Bosnian Serb forces which began on 1 January 1995.

The first half of 1995 has seen the CG attempt to persuade Serbian President Milosevic to recognize Bosnia-Hercegovina (and so end Bosnian Serb hopes of forming a Greater Serbia) in return for the lifting of remaining UN sanctions on the rump federal Yugoslav state. However, increased fighting frustrated diplomacy, government forces gaining ground in central Bosnia from March onwards. Bosnian Serb forces retaliated with artillery attacks on Sarajevo, effectively ending the heavy weapons exclusion zone agreement, and leading NATO to bomb Bosnian Serb artillery and ammunition dumps. Another hostage crisis ensued in May as 400 UN peace-keepers were taken hostage by the Bosnian Serbs to deter NATO air strikes; the UK and France announced the deployment of a 12,500 strong Rapid Reaction Force. The UN withdrew from weapons collection points around Sarajevo as the last hostages were released in June.

In July 1995, as the Rapid Reaction Force was being deployed, the Bosnian Serbs ignored NATO air strikes and overran the eastern enclaves of Srebrenica and Zepa, transporting the Muslim population out of the enclaves. The Bosnian Serbs were also poised to attack Gorazde. No UN convoys were delivering aid to Bosnian Serb-held areas and only limited supplies were reaching Sarajevo. *See also* Events of the Year.

GOVERNMENT

Results of the elections held in November and December 1990 for the 240-seat bicameral Assembly were: the Party of Democratic Action (Muslim) 86 seats, the Democratic Party (Serbian) 72, and the Croat Democratic Union 44.

In December 1990 Alija Izetbegovíc (Muslim) was elected President at the head of a seven-man collective presidency formed of two Muslims, two ethnic Serbs, two ethnic Croats and one other. Throughout the war Izetbegovic has held this office although it was originally to be rotated among the collective. The Bosnian Serb leadership under Radovan Karadzic declared their own 'Republic of Srpska' in August 1992 with its capital at Pale, and the Bosnian Croats established the 'Republic of Herceg-Bosna' in August 1993 with its capital at Mostar. The mainly Muslim Bosnian government has remained in Sarajevo.

After a Muslim-Croat cease-fire was agreed in February 1994, the Bosnian, Bosnian Croat and Croatian governments signed the Washington agreement which provided for a Bosnian Muslim-Croat Federation and a confederation of this entity with Croatia. Under the Federation constitution, a federal presidency and a joint federal-republican government and constituent assembly have been established. The Federation is based on a cantonal system, each canton having authority over the police, education, housing, public services, broadcasting and culture. The federal government has authority in the fields of foreign affairs, defence, trade and the economy. A Constitutional Court with Muslim, Croat and inter-national judges has been established. Four of the eight cantons have a Muslim majority, two a Croat majority and two Muslim-Croat parity. A federal government has been established and a Bosnian Croat president and Muslim vice-president were elected by the Constituent Assembly on 31 May 1994 to serve for six months until federal elections could be held.

In practice the Federation's operation has proved difficult, and the Presidency has not rotated. In February 1995 the Muslims and Croats agreed to appoint an international arbiter to help resolve their differences and in March agreed to form a joint military command. Since July 1994 Mostar has been under EU administration as part of the Federation agreement to aid its reconstruction.

HEAD OF STATE
President: (Republican), Alija Izetbegovic, *elected* December 1990; (*Federation*), Kresimir Zubak, *elected* 31 May 1994
Vice President (Republican and Federation), Ejup Ganic, *elected* 31 May 1994

CABINET (JOINT REPUBLICAN AND FEDERAL) *as at July 1995*
Prime Minister, Haris Silajdzic
Deputy Prime Minister, Defence, Jadranko Prlic
Foreign Affairs, Mohammed Sacirbey
Interior, Bakir Alispalic
Finance, Neven Tomic
Justice, Mate Tadic
Energy and Communications, Faruk Smalbegovic
Transport, Ibrahim Koludar
Environment, Munever Imamovic
Trade, Nikola Graborac
Social Welfare and Refugees, Muharem Cero
Health, Bozo Ljubic
Education, Culture and Science, Enes Karic
Ministers without Portfolio, Stjepo Andrijic; Hasan Muratovic; Nedeljko Despotovic

EMBASSY OF THE REPUBLIC OF BOSNIA-HERCEGOVINA
40–41 Conduit Street, London WIR 9FB
Tel 0171-743 3758
Chargé d'Affaires, Mugdim Pasic

BRITISH EMBASSY
8 Mustafa Golubica, Sarajevo
Tel: Sarajevo 444429
Ambassador Extraordinary and Plenipotentiary, His Excellency Robert Barnett, OBE, apptd 1994

TRADE WITH UK	1993	1994
Imports from UK	£3,494,000	£3,120,000
Exports to UK	70,000	191,000

BOTSWANA
The Republic of Botswana

Botswana (formerly the British Protectorate of Bechuanaland) lies between 18° and 26° S. latitude and 20° and 28° W. longitude and is bounded by South Africa on the south and east, by Zimbabwe, the rivers Zambezi and Chobe (Linyanti) on the north and north-east, and by Namibia on the west. It has a total area of 224,607 sq. miles (581,730 sq. km).

A plateau at a height of about 4,000 feet divides Botswana into two main topographical regions. To the east of the plateau streams flow into the Marico, Notwani and Limpopo rivers; to the west lies a flat region comprising the Kgalagadi Desert, the Okavango Swamps and the Northern State Lands area. Large areas of the country support only herds of game. The climate of the country is generally sub-tropical, but varies considerably with latitude and altitude.

Botswana has a population (1991 census) of 1,326,796. The national language is Setswana and the official language is English..

CAPITAL – Gaborone, population (1991 census) 133,458. Other centres are Francistown (55,244), Lobatse (26,052), and Selebi-Phikwe (39,772).
CURRENCY – Pula (P) of 100 thebe.
FLAG – Light blue with a horizontal black stripe fimbriated in white across the centre.
NATIONAL ANTHEM – Fatshe La Rona.
NATIONAL DAY – 30 September.

GOVERNMENT

On 30 September 1966, Bechuanaland became a republic within the Commonwealth under the name Botswana. The

President is head of state and is elected by an absolute majority in the National Assembly. He appoints as Vice President a member of the National Assembly who is leader of government business in the National Assembly. The Assembly consists of the President, 40 members elected every five years on a basis of universal adult suffrage, four specially elected members, the Attorney-General (non-voting) and the Speaker. Presidential and legislative elections are held every five years. There is also a 15-member House of Chiefs which considers legislation affecting the constitution and chieftaincy matters. The last general election on 15 October 1994 was won by the Botswana Democratic Party with 26 seats to the Botswana National Front's 13 seats.

HEAD OF STATE

President, His Excellency Sir Ketumile Masire, GCMG, *re-elected* 17 October 1994 for a third five-year term

CABINET *as at June 1995*

The President
Vice President, Finance and Development Planning, Hon. Festus Mogae
Presidential Affairs, Public Administration, Hon. Ponatshengo Kedikilwe
Local Government, Lands and Housing, Hon. Patrick Balopi
External Affairs, Hon. Lt.-Gen. Mompati Merafhe
Mineral Resources and Water, Hon. David Magang
Commerce and Industry, Hon. George Kgoroba
Agriculture, Hon. Roy Blackbeard
Works, Transport and Communications, Hon. Daniel Kwelagobe
Health, Hon. Chapson Butale
Education, Hon. Dr Gaositwe Chiepe
Labour and Home Affairs, Hon. Bahiti Temane
Assistant Ministers: Finance and Development Planning, Hon. J. Mothibamele; *Local Government, Housing and Lands*, Hon. B. Mokgothu, Hon. M. Nasha; *Agriculture*, Hon. R. Sebego

BOTSWANA HIGH COMMISSION
6 Stratford Place, London WIN 9AE
Tel 0171–499 0031
High Commissioner, His Excellency Alfred Uyapo Majaye Dube, apptd 1993

BRITISH HIGH COMMISSION
Private Bag 0023, Gaborone
Tel: Gaborone 352841
High Commissioner, His Excellency David Beaumont, apptd 1994

BRITISH COUNCIL REPRESENTATIVE , T. A. Jones, MBE (*Cultural Attaché*)

ECONOMY

Botswana is predominantly a pastoral country. The national herd is around 2.2 million cattle and one million sheep and goats. Cattle rearing accounts for about 85 per cent of agricultural output and livestock products, particularly beef, are a major source of foreign exchange earnings. The government has a number of programmes to improve land use and cattle and crop production, and schemes to provide financial assistance for farmers.

Mineral extraction and processing is now the major source of income following the opening of large mines for diamonds and copper-nickel. Botswana is one of the largest producers of diamonds in the world, with diamonds accounting for 70 per cent of export revenue since they were discovered in the early 1970s. Large deposits of coal have been discovered and are now being mined. Much of

the country has yet to be fully prospected. Manufacturing industry is growing but it is still a small sector of the economy. The economy expanded by an average 9 per cent a year in the 1980s.

FINANCE	1992–3	1993–4
Revenue	P4,114m	P3,907m
Expenditure	4,224m	4,476m

TRADE

Principal exports are diamonds, copper-nickel matte, and beef and beef products.

	1992	1993
Imports	P3,970m	P4,297m
Exports	3,675m	4,179m

Trade with UK	1993	1994
Imports from UK	£20,555,000	£22,461,000
Exports to UK	26,051,000	19,618,000

EDUCATION

There are 657 primary schools (enrolment 305,500), 163 community junior secondary schools (enrolment 62,634) and 23 government and government-aided senior secondary schools (enrolment 22,604). Total enrolment in the tertiary sector (teacher training establishments, colleges of education and the University of Botswana) numbers 6,923.

COMMUNICATIONS

The railway from Cape Town to Zimbabwe passes through eastern Botswana. The main roads are the north-south road, which closely follows the railway, and the road running east–west that links Francistown and Maun. A road from Nata to Kazungula provides a direct link to Zambia from Botswana. Air services are provided on a scheduled basis between the main towns.

BRAZIL
República Federativa do Brasil

Brazil is bounded on the north by the Atlantic Ocean, the Guianas, Colombia and Venezuela; on the west by Peru, Bolivia, Paraguay, and Argentina; on the south by Uruguay; and on the east by the Atlantic Ocean. It extends between 5° 16′ N. and 33° 45′ S. latitude and 34° 45′ and 73° 59′22″ W. longitude and has an area of 3,286,488 sq. miles (8,511,965 sq. km). The population (official estimate 1992) is 156,275,000. Portuguese is the language of the country, but Italian, Spanish, German, Japanese and Arabic are also spoken by minorities.

The north is mainly wide, low-lying, forest-clad plains. The central areas are principally plateau land and the east and south are traversed by successive mountain ranges interspersed with fertile valleys. The principal ranges are Serra do Mar, the Serra da Mantiqueira and the Serra do Espinhaco along the east coast.

The River Amazon flows from the Peruvian Andes to the Atlantic. Its principal tributaries are the Rio Branco, Rio Negro, Japurá, Juruá, Purus, Madeira, Tapajós and Xingú. Other major rivers are the Tocatins, Araguaia, Parnaiba, São Francisco and Paraguai.

CAPITAL – Brasilia (inaugurated 1960). Population (1991 census) 1,596,274. Other important centres are São Paulo (9,480,427); the former capital ΨRio de Janeiro (5,336,179); Belo Horizonte (2,048,861); ΨRecife

(1,290,149); ΨSalvador (2,056,013); ΨFortaleza (1,758,334).

CURRENCY – Real of 100 centavos.

FLAG – Green with a yellow lozenge containing a blue sphere studded with white stars, and crossed by a white band with the motto *Ordem e Progresso*.

NATIONAL ANTHEM – Ouviram do Ipirangasàs Margens Placidas (From peaceful Ypiranga's banks).

NATIONAL DAY – 7 September (Independence Day).

GOVERNMENT

Brazil was discovered by the Portuguese navigator Pedro Alvares Cabral in 1500 and colonized by Portugal in the early part of the 16th century. In 1822 it became an independent empire under Dom Pedro, son of King Joao VI of Portugal, who had been forced to flee to Brazil during the Napoleonic Wars. In 1889, Dom Pedro II was dethroned and a republic was proclaimed. In 1985 Brazil returned to democratic rule after two decades of military government.

The Federal Republic of Brazil is made up of the federal district and 26 states. Under the 1988 constitution the President, who heads the executive, is directly elected for a single four-year term. The Congress consists of an 81-member Senate (three senators per state elected for an eight-year term) and a 517-member Chamber of Deputies which is elected every four years; the number of deputies per state depends upon the state's population. Each state has a Governor, and a Legislative Assembly with a four-year term.

Fernando Cardoso of the Social Democratic Party, part of the Liberal Front coalition, was elected outright in the first round of the presidential election on 3 October 1994. In the November 1994 legislative elections the Liberal Front won 33 Senate seats, 175 seats in the Chamber of Deputies and nine state governorships.

HEAD OF STATE
President, Fernando Henrique Cardoso, *sworn in* 1 January 1995
Vice President, Marco Antonio de Oliveira Maciel

CABINET *as at July 1995*
Foreign Affairs, Luiz Felipe Lampreia
Planning, José Serra
Finance, Pedro Malan
Education, Paulo Renato Souza
Agriculture, José Eduardo de Andrade Vieira
Justice, Nelson Jobim
Mines and Energy, Raimundo Mendes de Brito
State Reform, Luiz Carlos Bresser Pereira
Industry, Trade and Tourism, Dorothea Werneck
Health, Adib Domingos Jatene
Science and Technology, José Israel Vargas
Transport, Odacir Klein
Labour, Paulo Paiva
Culture, Francisco Correira Weffort
Communications, Sergio Vieira da Motta
Environment, Gustavo Krause
Sport, Edson Arantes do Nascimento (Pélé)
Navy, Adm. Mauro Cesar Rodrigues Pereira
Army, Gen. Zenildo Zoroastro de Lucena
Air Force, Brig. Mauro José Gandra
Armed Forces' Chief of Staff, Gen. Benedito Bezerra Leonel

BRAZILIAN EMBASSY
32 Green Street, London WIY 4AT
Tel 0171-499 0877
Ambassador Extraordinary and Plenipotentiary, His Excellency Rubens Antonio Barbosa, LVO, apptd 1994

Minister-Counsellors, S. Moreira Lima; E. dos Santos
Defence Attachés, Capt. O. S. de Almeída (*Naval*); Col. A. A. Filho (*Army*); Gp Capt C. Costa (*Air*)

There is also a Brazilian Consulate-General in London and honorary consular offices at Cardiff and Glasgow.

BRITISH EMBASSY
Setor de Embaixadus Sul, Quadra 801, Conjunto K, CEP 70.408 Brasilia DF
Tel: Brasilia 225–2710
Ambassador Extraordinary and Plenipotentiary, His Excellency Keith Haskell, CMG, CVO, apptd 1995
Deputy Ambassador, Consul-General, P. R. Jenkins
Defence Attaché, D. M. Black
First Secretary (Commercial), P. B. Yaghmourian

There are British Consulates-General at Rio de Janeiro and São Paulo.

BRITISH COUNCIL REPRESENTATIVE, Patric Early, OBE, SCRN, 708/9 Bloco F Nos 1/3 (Caixa Postal 6104), 70740-780 Brasilia DF. Regional directors in *Recife, Rio de Janeiro* and *São Paulo*

BRITISH AND COMMONWEALTH CHAMBER OF COMMERCE IN SÃO PAULO, Rua Barão de Itapetininga 275, 7th Floor, 01042, São Paulo (*Postal Address*, PO Box 1621, 01000 São Paulo) and Rua Real Grandeza 99, 22281 Rio de Janeiro

ECONOMY

Since the return to civilian rule in 1985 successive Brazilian governments have introduced economic and financial plans to curb high inflation and large budget deficits. The most radical and successful plan so far was introduced in February 1994 when the government and Congress agreed the first balanced budget in 20 years and created a US$16 billion social emergency fund as the first stage to financial stability. An interim currency pegged to the US dollar, known as the Real Unit Value, was introduced in March 1994 as the second stage. In July 1994 a new non-inflationary currency, the real, was introduced. By mid-1995 inflation had been reduced to 2,000 per cent annually to two per cent per month, bringing about economic stabilization and an increase in foreign exchange reserves to US$40,000 million. In February 1995 the privatization programme was reactivated and the oil industry, telecommunications, electricity supplies, gas distribution and coastal shipping have been privatized. In April 1994 Brazil signed an agreement to reschedule its US$52,000 million debt to 750 foreign commercial banks.

There are large and valuable mineral deposits including iron ore (hematite), manganese, bauxite, beryllium, chrome, nickel, tungsten, cassiterite, lead, gold, monazite (containing rare earths and thorium) and zirconium. Diamonds and precious and semi-precious stones are also found. The iron ore deposits of Minas Gerais are exceeded by those of the Amazon region, principally in the Carajás areas where deposits are estimated at 35,000 million tonnes. Mining operations began in February 1985.

Electric power production in 1994 was 52,000 m Kwh. In 1993, the total output of steel was 25.2 million tonnes and production of oil was 732 thousand barrels a day. The main agriculture products are coffee, cassava, maize, soya, rice, wheat, black beans, potatoes, cotton, cocoa, tobacco and peanuts.

TRADE

Principal imports are fuel and lubricants, machinery, mineral products, chemicals, wheat, metals and metal manufactures. Principal exports are industrial goods, coffee, iron ore, soya, meat, steel and orange juice. In 1994 the Brazilian automobile industry produced 1,400,000 vehicles. Of these, 374,000 vehicles were exported.

	1994
Total imports	US$33,168m
Total exports	43,558m

Trade with UK	1993	1994
Imports from UK	£415,070,000	£525,240,000
Exports to UK	903,531,000	919,360,000

DEFENCE

The total strength of the active armed forces is 336,800 (133,500 conscripts). Conscripts serve for 12 months and there are 400,000 reservists subject to immediate recall.

The Army has a strength of 219,000, of which 126,500 are conscripts. The Navy has a strength of 58,400 personnel (2,000 conscripts) including 15,000 marines, with one aircraft carrier, four submarines, six destroyers, 13 frigates and 28 patrol and coastal craft, together with some 13 armed helicopters.

The Air Force is 59,400 strong (5,000 conscripts). It deploys 272 combat aircraft and 46 armed helicopters. In addition there is the 385,600 strong Public Security Forces paramilitary unit.

EDUCATION

Primary education is compulsory and is the responsibility of state governments and municipalities. At this level approximately 12 per cent attend private schools. Secondary education is largely the responsibility of state and municipal governments, although a small number of very old foundations (the Pedro II Schools) remain under direct federal control. Over 33 per cent of all pupils at this level attend private schools. Higher education is available in federal, state, municipal and private universities and faculties.

COMMUNICATIONS

In 1990 there were 1,670,148 km of highways and the route-length of railways was 30,129 km. Internal air services are highly developed. There are 21,944 miles of navigable inland waterways. Rio de Janeiro and Santos are the two leading ports.

BRUNEI
Negara Brunei Darussalam

Brunei is situated on the north-west coast of the island of Borneo, and has a total area of 2,226 sq. miles (5,765 sq. km). The population is 260,863 (1991), of whom 68 per cent are of Malay, 18 per cent Chinese and 5 per cent other indigenous races. The majority are Sunni Muslims. The country has a humid tropical climate.

CAPITAL – Bandar Seri Begawan, with a population of 46,229 (1991).
CURRENCY – Brunei dollar (B$) of 100 sen. It is fully interchangeable with the currency of Singapore.
FLAG – Yellow with diagonal stripes of white over black and the arms in red all over the centre.
NATIONAL ANTHEM – Allah Selamatkan Sultan (O God, long live our Majesty the Sultan).
NATIONAL DAY – 23 February.

GOVERNMENT

In 1959 the Sultan of Brunei promulgated the first written constitution, which provides for a Privy Council, a Council of Ministers and a Legislative Council. On 1 January 1984 Brunei resumed full independence from Britain. A ministerial system of government was established at independence, the ministers being appointed by the Sultan and responsible to him. The Sultan presides over the Privy Council and the Council of Ministers. The Legislative Council was disbanded in 1984. The Sultan effectively rules by decree as a state of emergency has been in effect since a revolt in 1962.

HEAD OF STATE
HM The Sultan of Brunei, HM Sultan Haji Hassanal Bolkiah Mu'izzaddin Waddaulah, Sultan and Yang Di-Pertuan, GCB, *acceded* 1967, *crowned* 1 August 1968

THE COUNCIL OF MINISTERS *as at July 1995*
Prime Minister, Minister of Defence, HM The Sultan
Foreign Affairs, HRH Prince Mohammed
Finance, HRH Prince Jefri
Special Adviser to the Sultan and Minister for Home Affairs, Pehin Dato Haji Isa
Education, Pehin Dato Abdul Aziz
Law, Pengiran Bahrin
Industry and Primary Resources, Pehin Dato Abdul Rahman
Religious Affairs, Pehin Dato Mohammed Zain
Development, Pengiran Dato Dr Ismail
Culture, Youth and Sports, Pehin Dato Haji Hussein
Health, Dato Dr Johar
Communications, Dato Haji Zakaria

BRUNEI DARUSSALAM HIGH COMMISSION
19–20 Belgrave Square, London SW1X 8PG
Tel 0171-581 0521
High Commissioner, His Excellency Dato Kassim Daud, apptd 1993

BRITISH HIGH COMMISSION
Hong Kong and Shanghai Bank Building (3rd Floor), Jalan Pemancha, PO Box 2197 Bandar Seri Begawan
Tel: Bandar Seri Begawan 222231
High Commissioner, His Excellency Ivan Callan, CMG, apptd 1994

BRITISH COUNCIL REPRESENTATIVE , Susan Mathews, PO Box 3049, Bandar Seri Begawan 1930

ECONOMY

The economy is based on the extraction and production of oil and natural gas from onshore and offshore fields by Brunei Shell Petroleum, and the liquification of natural gas at the plant at Lamut. Royalties and taxes from these operations form the bulk of government revenue and have enabled the construction of free health, education and welfare services. The country has eight hospitals, 350 schools and one university. Brunei's main road connects the capital with Kuala Belait in the centre of the oil fields. Brunei International Airport has been extensively redeveloped and expanded, and Royal Brunei Airlines operates scheduled flights to the UK, Australia and throughout the Far East. Radio Television Brunei broadcasts one colour television and three radio channels from the capital.

TRADE WITH UK	1993	1994
Imports from UK	£324,432,000	£417,540,000
Exports to UK	307,552,000	294,186,000

BULGARIA
Republika Bulgaria

Bulgaria is bounded on the north by Romania, on the west by Serbia and the former Yugoslav republic of Macedonia, on the east by the Black Sea, and on the south by Greece and Turkey. The total area is 42,823 sq. miles (110,912 sq. km), with a population (UN estimate 1992) of 8,963,000. The predominant religion is the Greek Orthodox Church.

The language is Bulgarian, a Southern Slavonic tongue closely allied to Serbo-Croat and Russian with local admixtures of modern Greek, Albanian and Turkish words. The alphabet is Cyrillic.

CAPITAL – Sofia, population (1992), 1,114,925. Other important centres are ΨVarna (308,432), on the Black Sea; ΨBourgas (195,686), on the Black Sea; Plovdiv (341,058), Rousse (170,038), Pleven (130,812), Stara Zagora (150,518), Sliven (106,212) and Dobrich (104,494).

CURRENCY – Lev of 100 stotinki.
FLAG – 3 horizontal bands, white, green, red.
NATIONAL DAY – 3 March.

HISTORY

A principality of Bulgaria was created by the Treaty of Berlin 1878 and in 1885 Eastern Roumelia was added to the principality. In 1908 the country was declared an independent kingdom. In 1912–13 the war of the Balkan League against Turkey increased the size of the kingdom, but in August 1913 a short campaign against the remaining members of the League led to the surrender of Southern Dobrudja to Romania. In October 1915, Bulgaria entered the First World War on the side of the Central Powers; Bulgaria made an unconditional surrender in September 1918, and in November 1919 signed the Treaty of Neuilly, which ceded to the Allies the Thracian territories (later handed over to Greece) and some territory on the western frontier to Yugoslavia.

Bulgaria declared for the Axis powers in 1941 when it declared war on the Soviet Union. In August 1944 the government declared Bulgaria to be neutral in the Russo-German war and sought terms of peace from Britain and the USA. The Soviet Union refused to recognize the so-called neutrality until Bulgaria declared war on Germany on 7 September. An armistice with the Allies was signed in October 1944 and a peace treaty was signed on 22 February 1947. It recognized the return of Southern Dobrudja to Bulgaria.

In September 1944 a coup d'état gave power to the Fatherland Front, a coalition of Communists, Agrarians, Social Democrats, and officers and intellectuals. In August 1945, the main body of Agrarians and Social Democrats left the government. A referendum in September 1946 led to the abolition of the monarchy and the setting up of a republic.

The post-war period was dominated by the Communist Party (BCP), led by Todor Zhivkov. After he was forced to resign in November 1989, further leadership changes and reforms culminated, in January 1990, in the National Assembly voting to abolish the BCP's constitutional guarantee of power. Multiparty elections to a Grand National Assembly (parliament) were held in June 1990 and won by the BCP, renamed the Bulgarian Socialist Party in April. A BSP-dominated government formed in September 1990 was brought down two months later by a combination of industrial strikes and opposition pressure. A multiparty government was formed in December 1990

which began to implement a programme of economic and political reform.

GOVERNMENT

A new constitution, enshrining democracy and the free market was adopted by the Grand National Assembly on 12 July 1991.

After legislative elections in October 1991 a coalition government of the Union of Democratic Forces (UDF) and the Turkish Movement for Rights and Freedom Party (MRF) was formed with a pledge to stabilize the economy and defeat inflation. The government was unable to carry out its reforms before it was brought down in a vote of no confidence and replaced in December 1992 by a weak government of non-party technocrats lacking parliamentary support. This goverment was also brought down over its plans for economic reform and privatization. The BSP won the ensuing general election on 18 December 1994 and formed a government with the Agrarian National Union (ANU). The state of the parties in the 240-seat National Assembly is BSP 125, UDF 69, ANU 18, MRF 15, Bulgarian Business Block (BBB) 13.

HEAD OF STATE
President, Zhelyu Zhelev, *elected* 1 August 1990, *re-elected* 19 January 1992

COUNCIL OF MINISTERS *as at July 1995*
Prime Minister, Zhan Videnov
Deputy PM, Regional Development and Construction, Doncho Konakchiev
Deputy PM, Trade and Foreign Economic Co-operation, Kiril Tsochev
Deputy PM, Economic Development, Roumen Gechev
Deputy PM, Svetoslav Shivarov
Foreign Affairs, Georgi Pirinski
Agriculture, Vassil Chichibaba
Environment, Georgi Dimitrov Georgiev
Culture, Georgi Kostov Georgiev
Transport, Stamen Stamenov
Justice, Mladen Chervenyakov
Labour and Social Affairs, Mihcno Aralski
Public Health, Mimi Vitkova
Interior, Lyubomir Nachev
Industry, Kliment Vouchev
Educatiion, Science and Technology, Ilcho Dimitrov
Finance, Peter Kostov
Defence, Dimiter Pavlov

EMBASSY OF THE REPUBLIC OF BULGARIA
186–188 Queen's Gate, London SW7 5HL
Tel 0171–584 9400/9433
Ambassador Extraordinary and Plenipotentiary, His Excellency Stefan Tafrov, apptd 1995
Counsellor (Commercial/Economic), D. Georgiev
Consul-General, B. Zaimov

BRITISH EMBASSY
Boulevard Vassil Levski 65–67, Sofia 1000
Tel: Sofia 885361/2
Ambassador Extraordinary and Plenipotentiary, His Excellency Roger Short, MVO, apptd 1994
Deputy Ambassador, Consul and First Secretary, J. Buchanan
Defence Attaché, Col. R. A. F. Pearson, MVO
First Secretary (Commercial), J. C. Northover

BRITISH COUNCIL REPRESENTATIVE
David Stokes, 7 Tulovo Street, 1504, Sofia

DEFENCE

Bulgaria has a total active armed forces strength of 101,900 including 51,300 conscripts. Conscripts serve for 18 months. The Army has a strength of 51,600 personnel, including 33,300 conscripts. The Navy has a strength of 3,000 personnel (2,000 conscripts). The Air Force has a strength of 21,600 (16,000 conscripts). In addition, there are 34,000 paramilitary border guards, security police and railway and construction troops.

EDUCATION

Education is free and compulsory for children from seven to 15 years inclusive. Government policy emphasizes the need to democratize the education system, to remove the former ideological basis and to encourage private education. There are three universities (at Sofia, Plovdiv and Veliko Turnovo), an American University and 21 higher educational establishments.

ECONOMY

Under Communism about 90 per cent of the country's agriculture was turned over to co-operatives, and a smaller proportion mechanized. Land is currently being handed over to its previous owners. The principal crops are wheat, maize, beet, tomatoes, tobacco, oleaginous seeds, fruit, vegetables and cotton. The livestock includes cattle, sheep, goats, pigs, horses, asses, mules and water buffaloes.

There is a substantial engineering industry and considerable production of ferrous and non-ferrous metals. There are mineral deposits of varying importance. Heavy industry includes steel, chemicals, petro-chemical and metallurgical centres. The Soviet-designed nuclear power station at Kozlodui, comprising five reactors, accounts for over 40 per cent of electrical generating capacity.

Successive post-Communist governments have attempted to introduce mass privatization programmes but have so far been unsuccessful due to the lack of widespread political support. So far only 30 to 40 large and medium-sized enterprises have been privatized. The overall lack of radical economic reform has hampered the economy; annual inflation in 1994–5 was 120 per cent and unemployment 20 per cent.

TRADE

Since 1989 the pattern of foreign trade has altered significantly. Before 1989, 79 per cent of Bulgaria's foreign trade was within the Soviet bloc. By 1994 only one-third of trade was with eastern Europe and former Soviet states and more trade was conducted with European Union and industrialized states. In 1993 Bulgaria signed an Association Agreement with the EC under which EC duties on Bulgarian industrial goods were abolished by the end of 1994 and levies on agricultural goods significantly lowered.

The principal imports are fuels, minerals and metals, engineering goods and industrial equipment. The principal exports are agricultural produce, engineering goods and industrial equipment, industrial consumer goods, chemicals and fuels, minerals and metals.

Trade with UK	1993	1994
Imports from UK	£84,229,000	£86,138,000
Exports to UK	76,218,000	69,927,000

BURKINA FASO
République Populaire de Burkina

Burkina Faso (formerly Upper Volta) is an inland savanna state in West Africa, situated between 9° and 15°N. latitude and 2°E. and 5°W. longitude, with an area of 105,869 sq. miles (274,200 sq. km). It borders Mali on the west, Niger and Benin on the east and Togo, Ghana and the Côte d'Ivoire on the south.

The population (UN estimate 1992) is 9,490,000. The largest tribe is the Mossi whose king, the Moro Naba, still wields a certain moral influence. The official language is French.

CAPITAL – Ouagadougou (441,514). Other principal towns; Bobo-Dioulasso (228,668) and Koudougou (30,000).
CURRENCY – Franc CFA.
FLAG – Equal bands of red over green, with a yellow star in centre.
NATIONAL DAY – 11 December.

GOVERNMENT

Burkina Faso was annexed by France in 1896 and between 1932 and 1947 was administered as part of the Colony of the Ivory Coast. It decided on 11 December 1958 to remain an autonomous republic within the French Community; full independence outside the Community was proclaimed on 5 August 1960.

The 1960 constitution provided for a presidential form of government with a single chamber National Assembly, but in 1966 the Army assumed power. A new constitution allowing for a partial return to civilian rule but with the Army still in effective control was adopted in 1970, but in 1974 this was suspended. Full legislative and presidential elections were held again in 1978.

Following a number of military coups, Capt. Blaise Compaoré took power in 1987, also by coup. A new constitution was adopted in 1991. Presidential elections were held in December 1991 and won by Capt. Compaoré in the face of a boycott by the main opposition parties, who were unhappy with the new constitution. Opposition parties also boycotted the legislative elections held in May 1992, which were consequently won by Compaoré's Organization for Popular Democracy-Labour Movement (ODP-MT) party, which formed the government in coalition with several smaller parties.

HEAD OF STATE
President, Blaise Compaoré, *assumed office,* October 1987, *elected* December 1991

COUNCIL OF MINISTERS *as at July 1995*
Prime Minister, Roch Marc Christian Kabore
Minister of State, Defence, Kanidoua Naboho
Minister of State, Integration and African Solidarity, Herman Yameogo
Presidential Special Envoy, Salif Diallo
Economy, Finance and Planning, Zéphirín Diabre
Foreign Affairs, Ablasse Oudraogo
Territorial Administration, Vincent Kabre
Public Works, Housing and Urban Areas, Joseph Kabore
Industry, Commerce and Mines, Souley Mohamed
Secondary and Higher Education, Scientific Research, Mélégué Traore
Justice, Yarga Larba
Culture, Communications, Government Spokesman, Claude Somda

Water, Joseph Ouedraogo
Employment, Works and Social Security, Ardiouma Ouedraogo
Transport, Ouala Koutiebou
Parliamentary Relations, Thomas Sanon
Primary Education and Literacy, Alice Tiendrebeogo
Environment and Tourism, Anatole Tiendrebeogo
Agriculture and Animal Husbandry, Jean-Paul Sawadogo
Civil Service and Administrative Reform, Juliette Bonkoungou
Health, Christophe Dabire
Youth and Sport, Ibrahim Traore
Social Action and the Family, Akila Belembaogo

EMBASSY OF BURKINA FASO
16 Place Guy d'Arezzo, 1060 Brussels, Belgium
Tel: Brussels 3459912
Ambassador Extraordinary and Plenipotentiary, His Excellency
   Youssouf Ouedraogo, apptd 1995, resident in Brussels
HONORARY CONSULATE, 5 Cinnamon Row, Plantation
   Wharf, London SW11 3TW. Tel: 0171-738 1800. *Honorary*
   Consul-General, S. G. Singer

BRITISH AMBASSADOR, Her Excellency Margaret
   Rothwell, CMG, resident at Abidjan, Côte d'Ivoire

ECONOMY

The principal industry is the rearing of cattle and sheep and
the chief exports are livestock, groundnuts, millet and
sorghum. Small deposits of gold, manganese, copper,
bauxite and graphite have been found.

TRADE WITH UK	1993	1994
Imports from UK	£5,077,000	£6,107,000
Exports to UK	477,000	851,000

BURUNDI
République de Burundi

Situated on the east side of Lake Tanganyika, Burundi has
an area of 10,747 sq. miles (27,834 sq. km). The population
(UN estimate 1992) is 5,786,000, 83 per cent Hutu and 15
per cent Tutsi. The official languages are Kirundi, a Bantu
language, and French. Kiswahili is also used.

CAPITAL – Bujumbura (formerly Usumbura), with 235,440
   (1990 estimate) inhabitants. Kitega (18,000 inhabitants)
   is the only other sizeable town.
CURRENCY – Burundi franc of 100 centimes.
FLAG – Divided diagonally by a white saltire into red and
   green triangles; on a white disc in the centre three red
   six-pointed stars edged in green.
NATIONAL DAY – 1 July.

GOVERNMENT

Formerly a Belgian trusteeship under the United Nations,
Burundi became independent as a constitutional monarchy on 1 July 1962. However, the monarchy was overthrown in 1966 and the country became a republic. In 1987
the government was overthrown by a Military Committee
of National Redemption led by Maj. Pierre Buyoya.

Although most of the population is Hutu, political and
military power has traditionally rested with the Tutsi
minority. Hutu attempts to overthrow Tutsi rule resulted
in ethnic massacres in 1965, 1969, 1972 and 1988. It
was against a background of continuing Tutsi-Hutu
violence that the ruling National Unity and Progress party
(UPRONA) of President Buyoya attempted to introduce multiparty non-tribal politics in 1991–2. This was
approved by national referendum in March 1992.

Tutsi dominance appeared to be broken by the election
of Melchior Ndadaye, a Hutu, as President in June 1993
and the success of the opposition Front for Democracy in
Burundi (FRODEBU) in the legislative elections the same
month. However, the identification of the FRODEBU
government with Hutu interests led the Tutsi-dominated
army to attempt a coup in October 1993 in which President
Ndadaye and six cabinet ministers were killed. The
remainder of the government survived and regained
control in December but two months of inter-racial
fighting left 50,000–100,000 dead and 500,000, mainly
Hutu, refugees in neighbouring states. Ndadye was succeeded by Cyprien Ntaryamira (Hutu) , but he was killed
in a rocket attack on the plane of President Habyarimana of
Rwanda in April 1994.

FRODEBU and UPRONA agreed to form a coalition
government in February 1994 with a Tutsi as Prime
Minister, and interim President Ntibantunganya (Hutu)
was appointed to the post permanently by a convention of
government in September 1994. The convention incorporated into the constitution that the 25-member cabinet
must include ten Tutsi, ten Hutu and five neutral
ministers. However, the government has been unable to
halt continued fighting between the Tutsi-dominated
army and Hutu militias. In June 1995 the army forced all
Hutu militias from Bujumbura into the Hutu-controlled
countryside.

HEAD OF STATE
President, Sylvestre Ntibantunganya, *sworn in* 1 October
   1994

COUNCIL OF MINISTERS *as at July 1995*
Prime Minister, Antoine Nduwayo
Minister of State, Development Planning and Reconstruction,
   Gerard Niyibigira
Minister of State, Foreign Affairs and Co-operation, Jean-Marie
   Ngendahayo
Minister of State, Interior and Public Security, Gabriel Sinarinzi
Finance, Salvator Toyi
National Defence, Lt.-Col. Firmin Sinzoyiheba
Justice, Melchior Ntahobama
Reintegration and Resettlement of Displaced Persons, Claudine
   Matuturu
Agriculture and Livestock, Pierre-Claver Nahimana
Primary Education and Adult Literacy, Nicephore
   Ndimurukundo
Secondary and Higher Education, Liboire Ngendahayo
Labour and Professional Training, Venerand
   Bakevyumusaya
Civil Service, Vincent Ndikumasabo
Communal Development, Séverin Mfatiye
Commerce and Industry, Astere Nzisibira
Energy and Mines, vacant
Ports and Telecommunications, Innocent Nimpagaritse
Public Works and Equipment, Bernard Barandereka
Lands, Ignace Bankamwabo
Communications, Germain Nkhshimana
Human Rights and Women's Development, Marcienne
   Mujawaha
Public Health, Charles Batungwanayo
Culture, Youth and Sports, Alphonse Rugambarara
Relations with the National Assembly, Terence Sinunguruza

EMBASSY OF THE REPUBLIC OF BURUNDI
Square Marie Louise 46, 1040 Brussels, Belgium
Tel: Brussels 2304535
Ambassador Extraordinary and Plenipotentiary, vacant
   (resident in Brussels)
BRITISH AMBASSADOR, His Excellency Edward Clay,
   CMG, resident at Kampala, Uganda

ECONOMY

The chief crop is coffee, representing about 80 per cent of Burundi's export earnings. Cotton is the second most important crop. Mineral, tea, hide and skin exports are also important.

TRADE WITH UK	1993	1994
Imports from UK	£2,267,000	£3,288,000
Exports to UK	1,968,000	4,251,000

CAMBODIA

Cambodia is situated in Indochina, with Thailand to the west and north, Laos to the north, Vietnam to the east and south, and the Gulf of Thailand to the south-west. The area is 69,898 sq. miles (181,035 sq. km), of which 50 per cent is forest or jungle. Around the Tonlé Sap lake and along the Mekong river, which traverses the country, there is ample fertile land. The climate is tropical monsoon with a rainy season from May to October.

The population (UN estimate 1992) is 9,054,000. The state religion is Buddhism of the 'Little Vehicle' which was suppressed by the Khmer Rouge. The national language is Khmer.

CAPITAL – Phnom Penh, population 920,000 (1993 estimate).

CURRENCY – Riel of 100 sen.

FLAG – Three horizontal stripes of blue, red, blue, with the blue of double width and containing a representation of the temple of Angkor in white.

NATIONAL ANTHEM – Nokoreach.

NATIONAL DAY – 9 November (Independence Day).

HISTORY

Once a powerful kingdom, which, as the Khmer Empire, flourished between the tenth and 14th centuries, Cambodia became a French protectorate in 1863 and was granted independence within the French Union as an Associate State in 1949. Full independence was proclaimed on 9 November 1953. From 1955 the political life of the country was dominated by Prince Norodom Sihanouk, first as king, then as head of government after he had abdicated in favour of his father and finally (following his father's death in 1960) as head of state. In March 1970 Prince Sihanouk was deposed and a republic was declared in October 1970, when the name of the country was changed to the Khmer Republic.

In April 1975 Phnom Penh fell to the North Vietnamese-backed Khmer Rouge after a five-year civil war. A new constitution was promulgated in 1976, a government led by Pol Pot, the leader of the Khmer Rouge (Communist) party, was appointed and the state was renamed Democratic Kampuchea. During the years of Khmer Rouge rule hundreds of thousands of Cambodians fled into exile and an estimated one million were killed in the 'killing fields'.

In December 1978 Vietnamese troops invaded Cambodia, capturing Phnom Penh on 7 January 1979. The following day the Cambodian National United Front for National Salvation established a People's Revolutionary Council. The state was renamed The People's Republic of Kampuchea (PRK); in April 1989 it became the State of Cambodia (SOC). With support from the Vietnamese army PRK forces gained control of most of the country, containing the challenge from the guerrilla forces of the Coalition Government of Democratic Kampuchea

(CGDK), formed in June 1982 by the Khmer Rouge and two non-Communist groups. Following the Vietnamese withdrawal in 1989, the resistance forces regained ground inside Cambodia.

In September 1990, the SOC and the CGDK established a Supreme National Council to embody Cambodian sovereignty and to help implement a peace settlement. A permanent cease-fire began on 23 June and peace agreements were signed on 23 October 1991. In March 1992 the United Nations Transitional Authority for Cambodia (UNTAC) began to take over the administration of the country from the SOC government in the run-up to elections. UNTAC was hampered throughout 1992 and early 1993 by Khmer Rouge attacks and SOC obstructiveness. Despite this, UNTAC stabilized the country to the extent that 95 per cent of the Cambodian electorate registered to vote in the May 1993 elections. All 330,000 refugees in Thailand were repatriated to Cambodia under UNTAC supervision by 30 March 1993.

GOVERNMENT

Multiparty elections under UNTAC supervision were held on 23–28 May 1993 for 120 seats in a National Assembly. The Royalist FUNCINPEC party won 45 per cent of the vote and 58 seats and the Cambodian People's Party (CPP) (the former ruling SOC party) won 38 per cent of the vote and 51 seats. Prince Sihanouk brokered a coalition government agreement between FUNCINPEC and the CPP under which he became head of state and FUNCINPEC and CPP leaders Prince Ranariddh and Hun Sen became co-chairmen of the coalition government. This agreement was accepted by UNTAC and officially approved by the new National Assembly on 1 July. The National Assembly adopted a new constitution on 21 September under which Cambodia became a pluralist liberal democracy with a constitutional monarchy. On 23 September the new constitution was promulgated, marking the end of the UNTAC mission and the restoration of Cambodian sovereignty. Prince Sihanouk was elected king and he appointed a new government. Legislative power is vested in the National Assembly, executive power in the Royal Government, with the King having the power only to make appointments and declare a state of emergency, in consultation with the government.

The Khmer Rouge remain unreconciled to the new government and continue their guerrilla and sabotage campaign, mainly in the north and east of the country, where they control 10 per cent of territory along the border with Thailand. In July 1994 the Royal Government outlawed the Khmer Rouge, which responded by declaring a provisional government in the territory it holds. A six-month government amnesty for defecting Khmer Rouge guerrillas ended in January 1995 with the defection of around half of the the Khmer Rouge personnel, leaving it with about 7,000 guerrillas.

HEAD OF STATE

HM *The King of Cambodia,* Norodom Sihanouk, *elected by the Council of the Throne,* 23 September 1993

ROYAL GOVERNMENT *as at July 1995*

First Prime Minister, Prince Norodom Ranariddh
Second Prime Minister, Hun Sen
Vice-Prime Ministers, Ing Huot (*Foreign Affairs and International Co-operation*); Sar Kheng (*Interior*); Ing Kiet (*Public Works and Transport*)
State Minister, Finance and Economy, Rehabilitation and Development, Keat Chhon
State Minister, Inspection, Ung Phan
State Minister, Cultural Affairs and Urbanization, Van Molivan
State Minister, Justice, Chem Snguon
State Minister, Finance and Economy, Sam Rangsi
Ministers in the Office of the Council of Ministers, Sok An; Veng Sereivut
Agriculture, Forestry, Wildlife and Fisheries, Tau Senghuo
Interior, Yu Hokkri
Education, Youth Affairs and Sports, Tol Loah
Tourism, Veng Sereivut
National Defence, Tie Banh
Industry, Minerals and Energy, Ith Prang
Planning, Chea Chanto
Public Health, Chhea Thang
Culture, Nut Narang
Rural Development, Hong Sun-huot
Commerce, Cham Prasit
Environmental Management, Mok Maret
Chairman of the National Assembly, Chea Sim

BRITISH EMBASSY

29, Street 75, Phnom Penh
Tel: Phnom Penh 855 2327124
Ambassador Extraordinary and Plenipotentiary, His Excellency Paul Reddicliffe, apptd 1994

ECONOMY

The economy is based on agriculture, fishing and forestry, the bulk of the population being rice-growing farmers. In addition to rice, which is the staple crop, the major products are rubber, livestock, maize, timber, pepper, palm sugar, fresh and dried fish, kapok, beans, soya and tobacco. Rice and rubber used to be the main exports though production was brought to a standstill by the hostilities.

Following the Khmer Rouge victory, the populations of the towns were forcibly evacuated to the country to work on the land, and re-establish plantations producing such crops as cotton, rubber and bananas. Following the Vietnamese invasion of 1978 the towns were repopulated and factories, in particular textile mills, iron smelting works and cement works, were put back in production.

Cambodia is heavily dependent on foreign aid to rebuild its economy and US$1,485 million has been given since the 1991 Paris peace agreements and a further US$1,350 million pledged in March 1995. In addition, all Cambodia's debts to the IMF have been paid by other states and US$160 million of debt was written off in February 1995. However, foreign investors have been unenthusiastic because of insecurity, corruption, and the lack of a firm legal basis for business. In August 1994 a new investment law was passed.

TRADE WITH UK	1993	1994
Imports from UK	£3,113,000	£2,327,000
Exports to UK	711,000	1,672,000

COMMUNICATIONS

The country had over 5,000 kilometres of roads, of which nearly half were hard-surfaced and passable in the rainy season, although now in a state of disrepair. There are two railways, one from Phnom Penh to the Thai border, the other from Phnom Penh to Kampot and Sihanoukville (Kompong Som), but operations and repairs are hindered by occasional Khmer Rouge attacks. Phnom Penh is on a river capable of receiving ships of up to 2,500 tons all the year round. The deep water port at Sihanoukville (Kompong Som) on the Gulf of Thailand can receive ships up to 10,000 tons. The port is linked to Phnom Penh by a modern highway.

CAMEROON
République du Cameroun

Cameroon lies on the Gulf of Guinea between Nigeria to the west, Chad and the Central African Republic to the east and Congo and Gabon and Equatorial Guinea to the south. It has an area of 183,569 sq. miles (475,442 sq. km).

The population is 12,198,000 (UN estimate 1992). French and English are both official languages and enjoy equal status.

CAPITAL – Yaoundé, population estimate (1986) 653,670.
ΨDouala (1,029,736) is the commercial centre.
CURRENCY – Franc CFA of 100 centimes.
FLAG – Vertical stripes of green, red and yellow with single five-pointed yellow star in centre of red stripe.
NATIONAL ANTHEM – O Cameroun, Berceau de Nos Ancêtres (O Cameroon, thou cradle of our forefathers).
NATIONAL DAY – 20 May.

GOVERNMENT

The German colony of the Cameroons, established in 1884, was captured by British and French forces in 1916 and divided into the League of Nations-mandated territories (later UN trusteeships) of East (French) and West (British) Cameroon. On 1 January 1960 East Cameroon became independent as the Republic of Cameroon. This was joined on 1 October 1961 by the southern part of West Cameroon after a plebiscite held under United Nations auspices; the northern part joined Nigeria. Cameroon became a federal republic with separate East and West Cameroon state governments. After a plebiscite held in 1972, Cameroon became a unitary republic and a one-party state.

After extensive unrest, multiparty elections were held in March 1992, although they were boycotted by two of the main opposition parties. The ruling People's Democratic Movement emerged short of a parliamentary majority but formed a coalition government with a small opposition party, the Movement for the Defence of the Republic.

Presidential elections were held in October 1992 and won by the incumbent Paul Biya. The results were disputed by the runner-up Fru Ndi, two opposition parties and foreign observers, who accused the authorities of widespread malpractice. Opposition parties tried unsuccessfully through the Supreme Court and violent protest to annul the election result. In November a new coalition government was formed with the two parties of the previous government being joined by the Union for Democracy and Progress and the Union of Peoples of Cameroon. In May 1993 President Biya published a draft bill on constitutional reform providing for a Council of State, Senate and a Constitutional Court but rejecting a return to a federal state. However, there has been no progress towards finalizing a new constitution.

HEAD OF STATE
President and Commander in Chief of the Armed Forces, Paul Biya, *acceded* 6 November 1982, *elected* 14 January 1984, *re-elected* 24 April 1988, 10 October 1992, *sworn in* 3 November 1992

CABINET *as at July 1995*
Prime Minister, Simon Achidi Achu
Deputy PM, Territorial Administration, Gilbert Andze-Tsoungui
Deputy PM, Housing and Town Planning, Hamadou Mustapha
Minister of State, Posts and Telecommunications, Dakole Daissala
Minister of State, Agriculture, Planning and Regional Development, Augustin Frederic Kodock
Minister of State, Communications, Augustin Koutchou Kouomegni
Defence, Edouard Akame Mfoumou
External Relations, Ferdinand Leopold Oyono
Justice, Douala Moutome
Animal Husbandry and Fisheries, Titus Edzoa
Higher Education, Peter Agbortabi
Public Health, Joseph Owona
Labour and Social Insurance, Simon Mbila
Industrial and Commercial Development, Pierre Eloundou Mani
Economy and Finance, Justin Naioro
Public Service and State Controls, Adjoudi Hamadjoda
Women and Social Affairs, Aissatou Yaou
Public Works, Jean-Baptiste Bokam
Scientific Research, Joseph Mbede
Tourism, Pierre Souman
Environment and Forests, Dr Djingoer Bava
Youth and Sports, Joseph Marie Bipoun Woum
National Education, Dr Robert Mbella
Mines, Water Resources and Energy, Andre Bello Mbelle
Transport, Issa Bakary Tchiroma
Culture, Toko Mangan

EMBASSY OF THE REPUBLIC OF CAMEROON
84 Holland Park, London WII 3SB
Tel 0171–727 0771/3
Ambassador Extraordinary and Plenipotentiary, His Excellency Samuel Libock Mbei, apptd 1995

BRITISH EMBASSY
Avenue Winston Churchill, BP 547 Yaoundé
Tel: Yaoundé 220545
Ambassador Extraordinary and Plenipotentiary, His Excellency William E. Quantrill, apptd 1991
There is also a British Consulate at Douala.
BRITISH COUNCIL DIRECTOR, Terrence Humphreys, Avenue Charles de Gaulle (BP 818), Yaoundé

ECONOMY
The main emphasis is on agricultural development, through encouraging small-scale peasant agriculture and developing large-scale agro-industrial complexes, with the aim of making the country agriculturally self-sufficient and a major food exporter.

Principal products are cocoa, coffee, bananas, cotton, timber, groundnuts, aluminium, rubber and palm products. There is an aluminium smelting plant at Edéa with an annual capacity of 50,000 tons. Oil is also one of Cameroon's principal products, with an estimated production of 7.31 million tonnes during 1989.

In 1993 President Biya's government was accused of economic incompetence and most foreign donors suspended aid after an IMF structural adjustment plan lapsed in 1992. The IMF agreed to resume support of an improved economic reform programme with a US$114 million standby credit in March 1994.

TRADE WITH UK	1993	1994
Imports from UK	£16,565,000	£15,452,000
Exports to UK	17,878,000	34,889,000

CANADA

AREA AND POPULATION

Provinces or Territories (with official contractions)	Area (sq. miles)	Population estimate 1994
Alberta (Alta.)	255,290	2,716,200
British Columbia (BC)	365,946	3,668,400
Manitoba (Man.)	250,946	1,131,100
New Brunswick (NB)	28,355	759,300
Newfoundland and Labrador (Nfld.)	156,648	582,400
Nova Scotia (NS)	21,425	936,700
Ontario (Ont.)	412,579	10,927,800
Prince Edward Island (PEI)	2,185	134,500
Quebec (Que.)	594,857	7,281,100
Saskatchewan (Sask.)	251,865	1,016,200
Yukon Territory (YT)	186,660	30,100
Northwest Territories (NWT)	1,322,902	64,300
Total	3,849,658	29,248,100

Area figures include land and water area

BIRTHS, DEATHS AND MARRIAGES 1991

Province	Births	Deaths	Marriages
Alberta	42,776	14,451	18,612
British Columbia	45,612	23,977	23,691
Manitoba	17,282	8,943	7,032
New Brunswick	9,497	5,469	4,521
Newfoundland	7,166	3,798	3,480
Nova Scotia	12,016	7,255	5,845
Ontario	151,478	72,917	72,938
Prince Edward Island	1,885	1,188	876
Québec	97,310	49,121	28,922
Saskatchewan	15,304	8,098	5,923
Yukon	568	114	196
NW Territories	1,634	237	215
Total	402,528	195,568	172,251

Canada's birth rate per 1,000 population (1991) 14.9; death rate 7.2; marriage rate 6.4. Divorces were 77,031 in 1991.

Of the total immigration of 252,537 in 1992, 14,722 were from the Caribbean, 7,512 from the UK and Ireland, and 7,155 from the USA.

MOTHER TONGUES OF THE POPULATION 1991

Single Responses

English	16,516,180
French	6,505,565
Non-official languages	3,549,305
Cree	77,355
Inuktitut	24,030
Ojibway	21,225

Multiple Responses

English and French	216,585
English and non-official language(s)	405,080
French and non-official language(s)	47,270
English, French and non-official language(s)	29,155
Non-official languages	27,715
Total Population	27,296,860

PHYSIOGRAPHY

Canada occupies the whole of the northern part of the North American continent, with the exception of Alaska, from 49° N. latitude to the North Pole and from the Pacific to the Atlantic Ocean. In eastern Canada, the southernmost point is Middle Island in Lake Erie, at 41° 41′ N.

Canada has six main physiographic divisions: the Appalachian-Acadian region, the Canadian shield, the St Lawrence-Great Lakes lowland, the interior plains, the Cordilleran region and the Arctic archipelago.

The Canadian shield comprises more than half the country. The interior as a whole is an undulating, low plateau (general level 1,000 to 1,500 feet), with water or muskeg-filled depressions separated by irregular hills and ridges, 150 to 200 feet in elevation. The St Lawrence-Great Lakes lowland varies from 500 feet in the east to 1,700 feet south of Georgian Bay. The interior plains, comprising the Pacific provinces, slope eastward and northward a few feet per mile. The descent from west to east is made from 5,000 feet to less than 1,000 feet in three distinct levels, each marked by an eastward-facing conteau or scarp.

The Cordilleran region has coastal ranges, largely above 5,000 feet with deep fjords and glaciated valleys; an interior plateau, around 3,500 feet and comparatively level; the Selkirk ranges, largely above 5,000 feet; the Rocky Mountains with their chain of 10,000 to 12,000 feet peaks; and the Peace River or Tramontane region with its rolling diversified country.

The Arctic archipelago, with its plateau-like character has an elevation between 500 and 1,000 feet, though in Baffin Land and Ellesmere Island the mountain ranges rise to 8,500 and 9,500 feet. Two tremendous waterway systems, the St Lawrence and the Mackenzie, occupy a broad area of lowland with their dominant axis following the edge of the shield.

The climate of the eastern and central portions presents greater extremes than in corresponding latitudes in Europe, but in the south-western portion of the prairie region and the southern portions of the Pacific slope the climate is milder.

FEDERAL CAPITAL – Ottawa, on the south bank of the Ottawa river, and connected with Lake Ontario by the Rideau Canal. The city population was 313,987 at the 1991 census and the population of the metropolitan area of Ottawa–Hull was estimated at 1,010,300 in 1994.
CURRENCY – Canadian dollar (C$) of 100 cents.
FLAG – Red maple leaf with 11 points on white square, flanked by vertical red bars one-half the width of the square.
NATIONAL ANTHEM – O Canada.
NATIONAL DAY – 1 July (Dominion Day).

HISTORY

Canada was originally discovered by Cabot in 1497 but its history dates from 1534, when the French took possession of the country. The first permanent settlement at Port Royal (now Annapolis), Nova Scotia, was founded in 1605, and Quebec was founded in 1608. In 1759 Quebec was captured by British forces under General Wolfe and in

1763 the whole territory of Canada became a possession of Great Britain by the Treaty of Paris 1763. Nova Scotia was ceded in 1713 by the Treaty of Utrecht, the provinces of New Brunswick and Prince Edward Island being subsequently formed out of it. British Columbia was formed into a Crown colony in 1858, having previously been a part of the Hudson Bay Territory, and was united to Vancouver Island in 1866.

The constitution of Canada has its source in the British North America Act of 1867 which formed a Dominion, under the name of Canada, of the four provinces of Ontario, Quebec, New Brunswick and Nova Scotia. To this federation the other provinces have subsequently been admitted: Manitoba (1870), British Columbia (1871), Prince Edward Island (1873), Alberta and Saskatchewan (1905) and Newfoundland (1949). Canada came into being on 1 July 1867, and the Statute of Westminster 1931 removed all limitations with regard to the legislative autonomy of Canada and the provinces, except that the British North America Act could be amended in important respects only by Acts of the British Parliament.

Agreement was reached in 1981 between the federal and provincial governments (except Quebec) to patriate the constitution so that it was amendable only in Canada. At the request of the Canadian Parliament, legislation was passed at Westminster and the constitution formally patriated on 17 April 1982.

To reconcile Quebec to the new constitution the Canadian federal government and the ten provincial governments signed the Meech Lake Accord in 1987. This transferred certain powers to the provinces and specifically recognized Quebec as 'a distinct society'. However, the provincial legislatures of Manitoba and Newfoundland refused to approve the Accord by the 1990 deadline so it did not come into effect.

GOVERNMENT

In September 1992 the federal and provincial governments reached agreement on a new federal constitution, the Charlottetown Accord. The agreement guaranteed Quebec a special status within Canada as a 'distinct society', reserved 25 per cent of House of Commons seats for the province, and proposed a directly elected Senate with equal provincial representation. The Accord was defeated by 54 per cent to 46 per cent in a national referendum in October 1992, and rejected by six provincial electorates. Canada now remains in constitutional limbo with no constitutional discussions taking place at the moment.

Executive power is vested in a Governor-General appointed by the Sovereign on the advice of the Canadian government.

Parliament consists of a Senate and a House of Commons. The Senate consists of 104 members, nominated by the Governor-General, the seats being distributed between the various provinces.

The House of Commons has 295 members and is elected every five years at longest. Representation by provinces is at present: Newfoundland 7, Prince Edward Island 4, Nova Scotia 11, New Brunswick 10, Quebec 75, Ontario 99, Manitoba 14, Saskatchewan 14, Alberta 26, British Columbia 32, Yukon 1, Northwest Territories 2.

The state of the parties in the Senate as at July 1995 was Progressive Conservatives 51, Liberals 42, Bloc Québécois 8, Reform Party 1, Independent 1, vacant 1.

The Liberal Party defeated the Progressive Conservative Party in the federal general election on 25 October 1993. The state of parties in the House of Commons as at July 1995 was Liberals 178, Bloc Québécois 54, Reform

Party 52, New Democracy 8, Progressive Conservatives 2, Independents 1.

GOVERNOR-GENERAL
Governor-General and Commander-in-Chief, His Excellency the Rt. Hon. Roméo Le Blanc, PC, CC, CMM, CD

CABINET *as at July 1995*
Prime Minister, Rt. Hon. Jean Chrétién
Deputy Prime Minister, Environment, Hon. Sheila Copps
Justice, Attorney-General, Hon. Allan Rock
Finance, Regional Development, Hon. Paul Martin
External Affairs, Hon. André Ouellet
Defence, Veteran's Affairs, Hon. David Collenette
Treasury Board President, Infrastructure, Hon. Arthur Eggleton
Agriculture and Agri-Food, Hon. Ralph Goodale
Government Leader in the Senate, Literacy, Hon. Joyce Fairburn
Atlantic Opportunities and Public Works, Hon. David Dingwall
International Trade, Hon. Roy MacLaren
Western Economic Diversification and Human Resources Development, Hon. Lloyd Axworthy
National Review, Hon. David Anderson
Fisheries and Oceans, Hon. Brian Tobin
Immigration and Citizenship, Hon. Sergio Marchi
Solicitor-General, Government Leader in the House of Commons, Hon. Herbert Gray
Transport, Hon. Douglas Young
Indian Affairs and Northern Development, Hon. Ron Irwin
Health, Hon. Diane Marleau
Natural Resources, Hon. Anne McLellan
Industry, Hon. John Manley
Intergovernmental Affairs and Public Services Renewal, Hon. Marcel Massé
Heritage, Hon. Michel Dupuy
Speaker of the Senate, The Hon. Guy Charbonneau, QC
Speaker of the House of Commons, Hon. Gilbert Parent, MP

CANADIAN HIGH COMMISSION
Macdonald House, 1 Grosvenor Square, London WIX OAB
Tel 0171–258 6600
High Commissioner, His Excellency Royce Frith, QC, apptd 1994
Deputy High Commissioner, Serge April
Ministers, J. Wright (*Political and Public Affairs*); R. Burchill (*Commercial/Economic*)
Defence Adviser, Col. G. H. Adamson
Counsellors, G. Berry (*Economic*); D. Stimpson (*Consular*); J.-M. Roy (*Commercial*); C. Latour (*Commercial*); W. G. Hughes (*Commercial*)

BRITISH HIGH COMMISSION
80 Elgin Street, Ottawa KIP 5K7
Tel: Ottawa 237 1530
High Commissioner, His Excellency Sir Nicholas Bayne KCMG, apptd 1992
Deputy High Commissioner, B. H. Dinwiddy
Counsellors, W. B. McCleary (*Economic and Commercial*); A. E. Lewis
Defence and Military Adviser, Brig. A. P. Naughton
First Secretary, R. O. Arrowsmith (*Management and Consular*)
There are also Consulates-General at Montreal, Toronto, and Vancouver and Consulates at Halifax, St John's and Winnipeg
BRITISH COUNCIL DIRECTOR, J. Harniman, OBE (*Cultural Attaché*)
BRITISH COUNCIL REPRESENTATIVE IN QUEBEC, S. Dawbarn, 1000 ouest rue de la Gauchetière, Montreal, Quebec H3B 4W5

JUDICATURE

The judicature is administered by judges following the civil law in Quebec province and common law in other provinces. Each province has its Court of Appeal. All superior, county and district court judges are appointed by the Governor-General, the others by the Lieutenant-Governors of the provinces.

The highest federal court is the Supreme Court of Canada, which exercises general appellate jurisdiction throughout Canada in civil and criminal cases, and which usually holds three sessions each year. There is one other federally constituted court, the Federal Court of Canada, which has jurisdiction on appeals from its trial division, from federal tribunals and reviews of decisions and references by federal boards and commissions. The trial division has jurisdiction in claims by or against the Crown, its officers or servants or federal bodies. It also deals with inter-provincial and federal-provincial disputes.

Chief Justice of Canada, Rt. Hon. A. Lamer, PC
Chief Justice, Federal Court, vacant

FINANCE

Federal government gross general revenue and expenditure was:

	1993–4	1994–5*
Total revenue	C$129,365m	C$136,230m
Total expenditure	171,039m	175,527m
*estimated		

	1993	1994
DEBT		
Gross public debt	C$515,794m	C$558,701m
Net public debt	461,685m	503,766m

DEFENCE

The Canadian armed forces are unified and organized into three functional commands: Mobile Command; Maritime Command; Air Command. The Canadian armed forces number 78,100 personnel and are an all-volunteer force.

Land forces comprise 20,000 personnel with 115 main battle tanks, 370 reconnaissance vehicles, 1,405 armoured personnel carriers and 330 artillery pieces.

Maritime forces number 12,500 personnel with four destroyers, 11 frigates, three submarines and 12 patrol and coastal craft. Air forces number 20,600 personnel with 198 combat aircraft and 128 armed helicopters. In addition, there are 25,000 personnel not identified in any of the above three services.

Canada deploys a 790-strong infantry battalion with UN forces in Bosnia, a 1,660-strong infantry battalion in Croatia, and a 200-strong logistics battalion on the Golan Heights in Syria.

ECONOMY

About 7.3 per cent of the total land area is farmed. Over 60 per cent of this is under cultivation, the remainder being predominantly classified as unimproved pasture. More than 80 per cent of the cultivated land is in the prairie region of western Canada.

Farm cash receipts from the sale of farm products in 1994 were C$25,450 million. Livestock and animal products contributed C$12,430 million; field crops C$11,411 million; grain and oilseed C$7,800 million.

In July 1994 the livestock included 14,036,600 cattle, 11,254,100 pigs, 962,700 sheep and lambs and 22,158,000 chickens (layers).

Canada in 1993–4 produced pelts valued at C$57 million. Wildlife pelts made up 40.4 per cent of the total, with a value of C$23 million.

The marketed value of fish catches in 1993 was C$3,017 million (preliminary).

About 42 per cent of the total land area is considered as inventoried forest area. The value of shipments and other revenue from forestry-related industries in 1992 was: logging $8,358.5 million; sawmill and planing mill products $9,215.0 million; shingle and shake $268.3 million; veneer and plywood $1,004.4 million; and paper and allied products $20.824.7 million.

In 1993, Canada was the world's largest producer of zinc, potash and uranium, the second largest of nickel, asbestos, cadmium and elemental sulphur. The country is also rich in many other minerals, including gold, copper, lead, molybdenum, platinum group metals, gypsum, cobalt, titanium concentrates, and aluminium. The total value of mineral production in 1994 was C$39.883.8 million.

Production of gold was 157,554,000 kg in 1992 and of silver 1,147,000 kg. Uranium production in 1992 was 9,057,000 kg.

TRADE

Merchandise imports in 1994 were valued at C$202,020 million and merchandise exports (including re-exports) at C$226,607 million. The main exports in 1994 were passenger automobiles and chassis, motor vehicle parts, trucks, truck tractors and chassis, lumber and sawmill products, newsprint paper, industrial and agricultural machinery, metals and alloys, chemicals, plastics and fertilizers. Trade with the USA accounts for about 75.1 per cent of total trade in merchandise.

Trade with UK	1993	1994
Imports from UK	£1,843,814,000	£1,916,664,000
Exports to UK	1,854,312,000	1,880,941,000

COMMUNICATIONS

The total track of railways in operation on 31 December 1991, was 85,563 km. In 1991 freight transportation was 261 billion tonne-kilometres, and the balance of property accounts at end 1991 was C$18,635m.

The registered shipping on 1 January 1991 including inland vessels, was 43,787 vessels with gross tonnage 4,956,845. The volume of international shipping handled at Canadian ports in 1991 was 168,030,334 metric tonnes loaded and 65,863,148 metric tonnes unloaded.

The bulk of canal shipping in Canada is handled through the two sections of the St Lawrence Seaway, which provide access to the Great Lakes for ocean-going ships. In 1992, transits on the Montreal-Lake Ontario section numbered 2,493 for a total of 31,400,000 cargo tonnes; transits in the Welland Canal section numbered 3,140 for a total of 33,200,000 cargo tonnes. Principal commodities carried were iron ore, wheat, corn, barley, soybeans, manufactured iron and steel, coal and salt.

EDUCATION

Education is under the control of the provincial governments, the cost of the publicly controlled schools being met by local taxation, aided by provincial grants. In 1992–3 there were 16,063 elementary and secondary schools with 5,287,730 pupils. Of these, 1,515 were private schools with 256,140 pupils; 383 federal schools with 55,600 pupils and 19 special schools for the blind and deaf with 2,330 pupils.

In 1992–3 there were 69 degree-granting universities with a full-time enrolment of 572,900, as well as 348,400 students in 203 other post-secondary, non-university institutions.

Source: for financial and economic statistics, Statistics Canada

YUKON TERRITORY

The area of the Territory is 205,346 sq. miles (531,842 sq. km), with a population (1991 census) of 27,797. Minerals, government and tourism are the chief industries, followed by transportation, communications and other utilities industry.

SEAT OF GOVERNMENT – Whitehorse, population (1991 census) 17,925.

The Yukon Act 1970, as amended, provides for the administration of the Territory by a Commissioner acting under instructions given by the Governor-in-Council or the Minister of Indian Affairs and Northern Development. Legislative powers, analogous to those of a provincial government, are exercised by a Legislative Assembly of 17 members elected from electoral districts in the Territory. The Executive Council of the Assembly consists of the government leader as chairman and five elected members.

Commissioner, J. K. McKinnon
Premier, Hon. John Ostashek

NORTHWEST TERRITORIES

The area of the Northwest Territories is 1,322,900 sq. miles (3,426,389 sq. km), with a population (1991 census) of 57,649. The chief industry is mining, with a total value of $637,294,000 in 1992. Lead, zinc, gold, silver, oil exploration and natural gas contributed about 19 per cent of the 1992 GDP.

The Northwest Territories are subdivided into the regions of Baffin, Fort Smith, Inuvik, Keewatin, Kitikmeot.

SEAT OF GOVERNMENT – Yellowknife, population (1991 census) 15,179.

The Northwest Territories Act 1979, as amended, provides for a Legislative Assembly of 24 elected members, of which the Executive Council under the chairmanship of the government leader is the senior decision-making body of the government in the Territory.

In 1992 a referendum in the Northwest Territories approved a plan to divide the Territories into two and to establish in one part a self-governing autonomous Inuit (Eskimo) populated territory known as Nunavat. Nunavat will be established in the east of the Northwest Territories and will comprise the present regions of Baffin, Keewatian and Kitikmeot. An agreement to establish Nunavat with self-government phased in over six years up to 1999 was signed in the new territory's capital Iqaluit on Baffin Island by the federal Prime Minister on 1 June 1993. The territory will have its own government and legislature, though neither will have the status of their provincial equivalents. It has a population of some 22,000, of which 80 per cent are Inuit, and covers some 850,000 sq. miles (2,201,500 sq. km). The agreement has yet to be ratified by the Federal Parliament.

Commissioner, D. L. Norris
Government Leader, Hon. Dennis Patterson

CANADIAN PROVINCES

ALBERTA

Alberta has an area of 661,185 sq. km (255,285 sq. miles), including about 6,485 sq. miles of water (16,796 sq. km), with a population (1 July 1994) of 2,716,200.

PROVINCIAL CAPITAL – Edmonton, city population (1994) 626,999, metropolitan area, 888,500. Other centres are Calgary (738,184), Lethbridge (64,938), Red Deer (59,826), Medicine Hat (45,892), St Albert (44,195).

GOVERNMENT

The Government is vested in a Lieutenant-Governor and Legislative Assembly composed of 83 members, elected for five years. At a provincial election held on 15 June 1993, the Progressive Conservative Party took 51 seats and the Liberal Party 32 seats.

His Hon. The Lt.-Governor, The Hon. Gordon Towers
Premier, President of Executive Council, Hon. Ralph Klein, MLA
Chief Justice, Court of Appeal, Hon. C. A. Fraser

AGENT-GENERAL'S OFFICE IN LONDON, Alberta House, 1 Mount Street, London WIY 5AA. *Agent-General,* Geoff Davey

ECONOMY

The total GDP at factor cost in 1994 amounted to C$74,958 million. Preliminary estimates for mineral production in 1994 came to C$18,925 million. Of this total, crude oil amounted to C$8,922 million, and natural gas and its by-products to C$9,056 million.

The total value of manufacturing shipments (1994) was C$24,922 million. Number of manufacturing establishments 2,635 (1991), total employees 67,312 (1991). The leading industrial products are refined petroleum and coal products, meat and meat products, chemicals and chemical products, fabricated metal products, non-metallic mineral products and primary metals.

FINANCE

Budgetary estimates	1993–4	1994–5
Revenue	C$14,337m	C$16,067m
Expenditure	16,017	15,395
Deficit (surplus)	1,680	(672)

BRITISH COLUMBIA

British Columbia has a total area estimated at 952,263 sq. km (367,669 sq. miles), with a population of 3,535,100 (July 1994).

PROVINCIAL CAPITAL – ΨVictoria, metropolitan population (1994) 312,370. Other principal cities are ΨVancouver (metropolitan population (1994) 1,774,671), Prince George, Kamloops, Kelowna and Nanaimo.

GOVERNMENT

The government consists of a Lieutenant-Governor and an Executive Council together with a Legislative Assembly of 75 members.

The New Democratic Party formed a government after a general election on 17 October 1991. The present standing in the Assembly is New Democratic Party 50, Liberal Party 15, Reform Party 4, Progressive Democratic Alliance 2, Social Credit Party 1, Independent 3.

His Hon. The Lt.-Governor, The Hon. Garde Gardom
Premier, Hon. Mike Harcourt, MLA
Chief Justice, Supreme Court, Hon. W. A. Esson

AGENT-GENERAL'S OFFICE IN LONDON, British Columbia House, 1 Regent Street, London SWIY 4NS. *Agent-General,* Paul King

FINANCE	1994–5	1995–6
Estimated revenue	C$19,244m	C$20,300m
Estimated expenditure	19,614m	20,186m

ECONOMY

Service industries generate 72 per cent of provincial GDP and account for over 76 per cent of employment. Manufacturing activity is based largely on the processing of the output of the logging, mineral, fishing and agriculture industries. The principal manufacturing centres are Vancouver, New Westminster, Victoria, North Vancouver, Kelowna and Prince George. British Columbia is the leading provincial producer of timber and sawmill products. Mining, the second most important non-service activity, is based on copper, zinc, lead, iron concentrates, molybdenum, coal, natural gas, crude petroleum, asbestos, gold and silver. Molybdenum production is approximately 96 per cent of the Canadian total.

The production levels for important industries for 1994 were: lumber 33,671,000 cu. metres; paper 2,961,000 tonnes; pulp 4,763,000 tonnes; coal 22,811,000 tonnes; natural gas 19,025,000,000 cu. metres. Solid mineral production for 1994 is estimated to be valued at C$2,635 million.

The most important agricultural products are livestock, eggs and poultry, fruits and dairy products. In 1994 farm cash receipts were valued at C$1,500.6 million. Salmon accounts for approximately 55 per cent of the value of fisheries. Other species include halibut, herring, sole, cod, flounder, perch, tuna and shellfish.

An estimated 55–60 per cent of industrial production is exported to foreign markets. Manufacturing shipments in 1994 were valued at C$30,657 million.

TRANSPORT

The province has deep water harbours which are well serviced by railways and modern highways. Vancouver has one of the finest natural harbours in the world, servicing a variety of vessels, including large bulk cargo carriers. Vancouver is also the base for regular scheduled air routes to other parts of Canada, the United States, Europe, Latin America, the Pacific, the Far East and the Middle East.

MANITOBA

Manitoba, originally the Red River settlement, is the central province of Canada. The province has a large area of prairie land but also has 645 kilometres (401 miles) of coastline on Hudson Bay, large lakes and rivers covering an area of 101,592 sq. km (39,225 sq. miles). The total area is 649,947 sq. km (250,946 sq. miles), with a population (1994 estimate) of 1,131,100.

PROVINCIAL CAPITAL – Winnipeg, population 652,355 (1991). Other cities are Brandon (38,567), Thompson (14,977), Portage la Prairie (13,186) and Flin Flon (7,119).

GOVERNMENT

The Lieutenant-Governor is The Queen's representative in Manitoba. There is a Legislative Assembly of 57 members, of which the Executive Council of Ministers are all members.

The Progressive Conservatives formed a majority government after a general election held on 25 April 1995. The standing in the House at July 1995 was: Progressive Conservatives 31, New Democratic Party 23, Liberal 3.
His Hon. The Lt.-Governor, The Hon. W. Yvon Dumont
Premier, Hon. Gary A. Filmon, MLA
Chief Justice, Court of Appeal, Hon. Richard J. Scott

ECONOMY

The projected revenue in the fiscal year 1995–6 was C$5,504 million while expenditures were forecast at C$5,455 million.

Of the total land area, 19,126,517 acres are in occupied farms. The gross value of agriculture production in 1994 was estimated at C$2,383 million.

The chief manufacturing centres are Winnipeg, Brandon, Selkirk and Portage la Prairie. The largest manufacturing industry is the food and beverage industry, followed by transportation equipment and primary metal industries.

NEW BRUNSWICK

New Brunswick is one of the eastern maritime provinces and is situated between 45°–48° N. latitude and 63° 47'–69° W. longitude. It has a total area of 73,439 sq. km (28,355 sq. miles), with a population (January 1995) of 760,600. It was first colonized by British subjects in 1761, and in 1783 by inhabitants of New England who had been dispossessed of their property in consequence of their loyalty to the British Crown.

PROVINCIAL CAPITAL – Fredericton, population (1991), 71,869. Other cities are ΨSaint John (124,981); Moncton (106,505); Bathurst (36,167); Edmundston (22,478); Campbellton (17,183).

GOVERNMENT

Government is administered by a Lieutenant-Governor, an Executive Council, and an elected Legislative Assembly of 58 members. The last provincial election was held on 23 September 1991. As of May 1995 the party standing was Liberals 43, Confederation of Regions (COR) 6, Progressive Conservatives 6, New Democratic Party 1, Independents 2.
Her Hon. The Lt-Governor, The Hon. Margaret McCain
Premier, Hon. Frank McKenna, MLA
Chief Justice, Court of Appeal, Hon. William Hoyt

ECONOMY

The estimated revenue for the year ending 31 March 1994 was C$3,739,378,086 and ordinary expenditure, $3,877,067,484.

New Brunswick's largest manufacturing sectors are the paper and allied industries and the food and wood industries. Together these accounted in 1994 for 52.1 per cent of the total value of manufacturing shipments of C$7,227 million. Saint John has an ice-free port and is the principal manufacturing centre of the province.

Farmland amounted to 926,820 acres in 1991. Dairy products and potatoes are the leading agricultural products. Farm cash receipts in 1994 totalled C$300,861,000. Fishing is an important industry, employing about 8,300 fishermen. The chief commercial fish are lobsters, herring, tuna, crab and cod. Landings reached 125,651 tonnes valued at C$143,592,000 in 1994.

Zinc, lead and copper deposits are mined in the northeastern part of New Brunswick, which is the largest zinc producer in Canada. A lead smelter, fertilizer plant and port facilities have been constructed at Belledune. Canada's only primary antimony producer is located at Lake George. Potash is produced near Sussex and Salt Springs, and a terminal has been built at the port of Saint John. Coal is mined at Grand Lake and exploration for other deposits is being undertaken. Total mineral production was valued at C$813,743,000 in 1994.

Tourism is of increasing value to the economy.

NEWFOUNDLAND AND LABRADOR

The island of Newfoundland is situated between 46° 37'–51° 37' N. latitude and 52° 44'–59° 30' W. longitude, on the north-east side of the Gulf of St Lawrence, and is separated from the North American continent by the Straits of Belle Isle on the north-west and by Cabot Strait on the south-west. The island is about 510 km long and 508 km broad and is triangular in shape. It comprises an area of 111,390 sq. km (43,008 sq. miles). The population (1994 estimate) (inclusive of Labrador) is 582,000.

Labrador forms the most easterly part of the North American continent, and extends from Point St Charles, at the north-east entrance to the Straits of Belle Isle on the south, to Cape Chidley, at the eastern entrance to Hudson's Straits on the north. It has an area of 294,328 sq. km (113,641 sq. miles), with a population (1991 census) of 30,375. Labrador is noted for its cod fisheries and also possesses valuable salmon, herring, trout and seal fisheries.

Provincial Capital – ΨSt John's (population 1991 census, Greater St John's 171,859) is North America's oldest city. It is the principal port for the island of Newfoundland. Newfoundland's second city of Corner Brook (population 1991 census, 22,410) is situated on the west coast.

Government

The government is administered by a Lieutenant-Governor, aided by an Executive Council and a Legislative Assembly of 52 members elected for a term of five years. A general election was held on 3 May 1993. The standings in the current House of Assembly are: Liberals 35; Progressive Conservatives 15, New Democrats 1, vacant 1.
His Hon. The Lt.-Governor, The Hon. Frederick W. Russell
Premier, Hon. Clyde Wells, MLA
Chief Justice, Court of Appeal, Hon. Noel H. A. Goodridge

Economy

The estimated gross capital and current account revenues for 1995–6 are C$3,545,160,000 and the gross current and capital account expenditures C$3,543,215,900.

The main primary industries are fishing, forestry and mining. In 1993 shipments of fish products were valued at C$480 million; newsprint shipments at C$419 million; and mining (mainly iron ore) plus structural materials shipments at C$728 million. Total manufacturing shipments were valued at C$1,317 million in 1993. The hydro-electric plant on the Churchill river is the largest underground plant in the world, with a capacity of 5,225,000 kW.

Over 139 wells have been drilled off Newfoundland since 1965. Oil was discovered in 1979 on the Grand Banks. Oil production is expected to begin in the 1990s, with a peak production of 110,000 barrels of oil a day.

Transport

The Trans-Canada Highway and other roads are the main transport links on the island. There is a coastal boat service that operates on the southern portion of the island and on the coast of Labrador linking isolated communities. The Quebec-North shore and Labrador Railway operates in Labrador, linking the interior with Sept-Iles, Quebec. The island is connected to mainland Canada by a ferry service that runs from Sydney, Nova Scotia, to Port Aux Basques and Argentia.

NOVA SCOTIA

Nova Scotia is a peninsula between 43° 25'–47° N. latitude and 59° 40'–66° 25' W. longitude, and is connected to New Brunswick by a low isthmus about 28 km wide. It has an area of 55,490 sq. km (21,425 sq. miles), including 2,650 sq. km of lakes and rivers and 10,424 km of shoreline. No place is more than 56 km from the Atlantic Ocean. Population (July 1994 estimate) 920,000.

Cape Breton Island has been part of Nova Scotia since 1819. It is the centre of the steel manufacturing and coal mining industries, and is noted for its lakes and coastal scenery.

Provincial Capital – ΨHalifax, including the neighbouring city of Dartmouth, has a population of 182,253. The harbour, ice-free all year round, is the main Atlantic winter port of Canada. Other cities and towns include ΨSydney (26,063), ΨGlace Bay (19,501).

Government

The government consists of a Lieutenant-Governor and a 52-member elected Legislative Assembly, from which the Executive Council is selected. The party standings in June 1995 were Liberals 40, Progressive Conservatives 8, New Democratic Party 3, vacant 1.

The Lieutenant-Governor represents The Queen and is appointed by the Governor-in-Council.
His Hon. The Lt.-Governor, The Hon. J. James Kinley
Premier, Hon. John Savage, MLA
Speaker of the House of Assembly, Hon. Paul MacEwan
Chief Justice, Supreme Court, Hon. Constance R. Glube

Economy

The revenue for the fiscal year ending 31 March 1994 was C$3,500.7 million and expenditure was C$3,872.7 million. Provincial GDP in 1994 was C$16,312 million, of which 13.6 per cent was produced by manufacturing.

Canada's first offshore oil well went into production on 6 June 1992. Total production was valued at C$131,649,000 in 1993.

The value of commodity production in 1994 was: minerals C$610,013,000; fish and shellfish C$470,362,000; farm production C$311,862,000. The total value of manufacturing shipments was C$5,484 million, of which food industries were the most important.

Forest land covers 73 per cent of the land area and most is privately owned. Forest-based industries employed an average of 8,700 in 1993, and contributed C$800 million to the Nova Scotia economy.

ONTARIO

Ontario has a total area of 1,068,472 sq. km (412,578 sq. miles), with a population (1993 estimate) of 10,746,000.

Provincial Capital – ΨToronto (metropolitan, census 1991, 3,893,046). Other major urban areas are: Ottawa, the national capital (313,987); ΨHamilton (599,760); London (381,522); ΨWindsor (262,075); Kitchener (356,421) and Sudbury (157,613).

Government

The government is vested in a Lieutenant-Governor and a Legislative Assembly of 130 members elected for five years.

The last legislative election was held on 8 June 1995 and won by the Progressive Conservatives who formed a government. The state of the parties at July 1995 was: Progressive Conservatives 82, Liberals 30, New Democrats 17, Independent 1.
His Hon. The Lt.-Governor, The Hon. Henry N. R. Jackman.
Premier, Hon. Michael Harris, MPP
Chief Justice, Court of Appeal, Hon. C. L. Dubin

Economy

Ontario is the chief manufacturing province in Canada, producing 50 per cent of all manufactured goods. Major industries are iron and steel, metal fabrication, machinery, electricals and chemicals. Toronto is also a major centre of finance and service industry.

Agricultural production had a gross value of C$6,030 million and total net farm income was C$1,180 million. Productive forested lands cover 39.9 million hectares.

Paper and allied industries are by far the most important sector of Ontario's forest industry.

Ontario's natural resources include basic minerals such as copper, iron ore, zinc, sulphur, gold, nickel and platinum. Total value of the mineral production in 1992 was estimated at C$4,800 million.

PRINCE EDWARD ISLAND

Prince Edward Island lies in the southern part of the Gulf of St Lawrence, between 46°–47° N. latitude and 62°–64° 30′ W. longitude. It is about 225 km in length, and from 6 to 64 km in breadth; its area is 5,659 sq. km (2,185 sq. miles), and its population (1994 estimate) 131,600.

PROVINCIAL CAPITAL – ΨCharlottetown (30,436), on the shore of Hillsborough Bay, which forms a good harbour.

GOVERNMENT

The government is vested in a Lieutenant-Governor, an Executive Council, and Legislative Assembly of 32 members elected for a term of up to five years, 16 as Councillors and 16 as Assemblymen. After the election of 29 March 1993 there were 31 Liberals and 1 Progressive Conservative.

Her Hon. The Lt.-Governor, The Hon. Marion L. Reid
Premier, Hon. Catherine S. Callbeck, MLA
Speaker of the Legislative Assembly, Hon. Nancy Guptill
Chief Justice, Appeal Division, Hon. Norman H. Carruthers

ECONOMY

The ordinary revenue of the province in 1993–4 was C$702.2 million and the expenditure C$772.1 million.

Approximately 46 per cent of the total area of the province is farmland. The value of farm cash receipts in 1994 was C$308.5 million, of which 54 per cent was from the sale of potatoes. Dairy, beef and hogs are also important agriculture products. Fish landings were valued at C$89.2 million in 1994 of which 72 per cent was of lobster.

The total value of manufacturing shipments was C$686.9 million in 1994, of which 69.9 per cent was in the food products industry. A major summer economic activity is tourism. Non-resident tourists spent C$154 million in the province in 1994.

QUEBEC

Quebec has an estimated area of 1,540,667 sq. km (594,855 sq. miles) with a population (1995 estimate) of 7,300,000, of which 83 per cent are French-speaking.

PROVINCIAL CAPITAL – ΨQuebec. Population (1991 census) 167,517; one of the great seaports of Canada. Other important cities are ΨMontreal (1,017,666); Laval (314,398); Sherbrooke (76,429); Montreal-Nord (85,516); La Salle (73,804); Longueuil (129,874) and Gatineau (92,284).

GOVERNMENT

The government of the province is vested in a Lieutenant-Governor, a Council of Ministers and a National Assembly of 125 members elected for five years. The last provincial election on 12 September 1994 was won by the Parti Québécois. At July 1995 the state of the parties was: Parti Québécois 77, Liberals 47, Québec Democratic Action Party 1.

His Honour The Lt.-Governor, The Hon. Martial Asselin
Prime Minister, Hon. Jacques Parizeau, MAN
Chief Justice, Court of Appeal, Hon. Pierre Michaud

AGENT-GENERAL'S OFFICE IN LONDON, 59 Pall Mall, London SW1Y 5JH. *Agent-General,* Harold Mailhot

ECONOMY

The revenue for the year 1993–4 was C$36,063.6 million; expenditure amounted to C$40,957.9 million.

Total estimated value of shipments in the manufacturing industries in 1994 was C$82,489 million. Value of 1994 shipments in the chief industries was accounted for by food, C$10,093 million; transport equipment, C$9,203 million; paper and allied industries, C$7,774 million; primary metal industries, C$7,571 million.

Forest lands cover 655,376 sq. km, of which 527,650 sq. km are productive. In 1993 total farm receipts were: crops, C$936,200,000; livestock and livestock products C$2,782,646,000; other farm receipts C$489,726,000. In 1993 58,552 tonnes of fish, to the value of C$91,560,000 were landed.

Minerals to the value of C$2,827,266,000 were mined in 1994. This included copper, C$203,425,000; asbestos, C$225,245,000; and gold, C$690,301,000.

SASKATCHEWAN

Saskatchewan lies between Manitoba to the east and Alberta to the west and has an area of 652,324 sq. km (251,864 sq. miles), of which the land area is 570,269 sq. km, or 220,182 sq. miles. The population (estimated 1993) is 1,003,100. Saskatchewan extends along the Canada–USA boundary for 632 km (393 miles) and northwards for 1,224 km (761 miles). Its northern width is 440 km (276 miles).

PROVINCIAL CAPITAL – Regina. Population (1991 census), 179,178. Other cities: Saskatoon (186,058), Moose Jaw (33,593); Prince Albert (34,181) and Yorkton (15,315).

GOVERNMENT

The government is vested in the Lieutenant-Governor, with a Legislative Assembly of 58 members. There is an Executive Council of 18 members. The Legislative Assembly is elected for five years and the state of the parties in June 1995 was: New Democratic Party 42; Liberal 11; Progressive Conservative 5.

His Hon. The Lt.-Governor, The Hon. Jack Wiebe
Premier, Hon. Roy Romanow, QC
Chief Justice, Court of Appeal, Hon. E. D. Bayda

FINANCE

Consolidated Fund and Heritage combined revenue for year ending March 1994 is C$4,631,800,000 and expenditure C$4,928,142,000.

CAPE VERDE
República de Cabo Verde

Cape Verde, off the west coast of Africa, consists of two groups of islands, Windward (Santo Antão, São Vicente, Santa Luzia, São Nicolau, Boa Vista and Sal) and Leeward (Maio, São Tiago, Fogo and Brava) with a total area of 1,557 sq. miles (4,033 sq. km). The population (UN estimate 1992) was 384,000, the majority of whom are Roman Catholic.

CAPITAL – ΨPraia, population (1980) 57,748.
CURRENCY – Escudo Caboverdiano of 100 centavos.
FLAG – Blue with three horizontal stripes of white, red, white near the bottom; over all on these near the hoist a ring of ten yellow stars.
NATIONAL DAY – 5 July (Independence Day).

GOVERNMENT

The islands, colonized c.1460, achieved independence from Portugal on 5 July 1975 under the nationalist party of Guinea Bissau and Cape Verde. A federation of the islands with Guinea Bissau was planned but this was dropped following the 1980 coup in Guinea Bissau.

The republic was a one-party state under the African Party for the Independence of Cape Verde (PAICV) until the constitution was amended in 1990. Multiparty elections, held in January 1991, were won by the opposition Movement for Democracy (MPD) which won 56 seats in the 79-seat National Assembly. António Mascarenhas Monteiro was elected President in February 1991.

HEAD OF STATE
President, António Mascarenhas Monteiro, *assumed office* 22 March 1991

COUNCIL OF MINISTERS *as at July 1995*
Prime Minister, Carlos Veiga
Minister of State, National Defence, Ulpio Fernandes
Justice, Pedro Monteiro Freire
Foreign Affairs, José Tomás Veiga
Economic Co-ordination, António Gualberto do Rosário
Sea, Helena Semedo
Infrastructure and Transport, Teofilo Silva
Health, João Medina
Education and Sport, Ondina Ferreira
Agriculture, José António Pinto Monteiro
Employment, Youth and Social Promotion, José António Reis
Cabinet Affairs, Mario Silva

EMBASSY OF THE REPUBLIC OF CAPE VERDE
44 Konninginnegracht, 2514 AD, The Hague, The Netherlands
Tel: The Hague 3469623
Ambassador Extraordinary and Plenipotentiary, new appointment awaited
BRITISH AMBASSADOR, His Excellency Alan E. Furness, CMG, resident at Dakar, Senegal
There is a British Consulate on São Vicente.

ECONOMY

The islands have little rain and agriculture is mostly confined to irrigated inland valleys. The chief products are bananas and coffee (for export), maize, sugar-cane and nuts. Fish and shellfish are important exports. Salt is obtained on Sal, Boa Vista and Maio; volcanic rock is also mined for export.

In January 1993 the government announced a programme of reform to institute a change to a market economy and to privatize most industry within four years. The main ports are Praia and Mindelo, and there is an international airport on Sal.

TRADE WITH UK	1993	1993
Imports from UK	£3,539,000	£3,763,000
Exports to UK	123,000	484,000

CENTRAL AFRICAN REPUBLIC
République Centrafricaine

The Central African Republic lies just north of the Equator between Cameroon, Chad, the southern part of Sudan, and Zaire. The area is 240,535 sq. miles (622,984 sq. km), and the population (UN estimate 1992) is 3,173,000.

CAPITAL – Bangui, near the border with Zaire, population (1984 estimate) 473,817.
CURRENCY – Franc CFA of 100 centimes.
FLAG – Four horizontal stripes, blue, white, green, yellow, crossed by central vertical red stripe with a yellow five-pointed star in top left-hand corner.
NATIONAL DAY – 1 December.

GOVERNMENT

On 1 December 1958 the French colony of Ubanghi Shari elected to remain within the French Community and adopted the title of the Central African Republic. It became fully independent on 17 August 1960. The first President David Dacko was replaced in 1966 by the then Col. Bokassa after a coup d'état. In December 1976, President Bokassa proclaimed himself Emperor and a new constitution was introduced, the country being known as the Central African Empire. In September 1979 Bokassa was deposed by David Dacko in a bloodless coup and the country reverted to a republic. President Dacko surrendered power in September 1981 to Gen. André Kolingba, who instituted military rule until September 1985, when a civilian-dominated cabinet was appointed. In November 1986 a referendum was held which approved a new constitution and the establishment of a one-party state.

Strikes and political demonstrations throughout 1991 and 1992 led to a return to multiparty politics. Multiparty presidential and legislative elections were held on 25 October 1992 but were annulled because of sabotage and irregularities. President Kolinga formed a coalition government in December 1992 and another in February 1993 in which opposition parties participated. Presidential and legislative elections were held in August and September 1993. The presidential election was won by Ange-Felix Patasse (MPLC), and the Central African People's Liberation Party (MPLC) emerged as the largest party in the National Assembly with 34 of the 85 seats. The MPLC formed a coalition government with three other former opposition parties in October 1993.

Constitutional reforms were passed in a national referendum in December 1994 which created a constitutional court, introduced elected local assemblies, extended the presidential mandate to a maximum of two six-year terms and subordinated the government to the President.

HEAD OF STATE
President, Ange-Felix Patasse, *elected* 19 September 1993

COUNCIL OF MINISTERS *as at August 1995*
Prime Minister, Gabriel Koyambounou
Finance and Budget, Emmanuel Dokouna
Defence and War Veterans, Jean Mette-Yapende
Foreign and Francophone Affairs, Prof. Simon Bedaya-Ngaro
Justice and Law Reform, Betty Maras
Education, Research and Technology, Albert Mberyo
Public Health and Population, Gabriel Fio Ngaindiro
Government Spokesman, Energy Resources and Minerals, Charles Massi
Agriculture and Livestock, Gabriel Badekara
Water, Forests, Hunting, Fishing, Laurent Ngom Baba
Industry, Commerce and Crafts, Joseph Agbo
Civil Service, Social Security and Training, Eloi Anguimate
Post and Telecommunications, Vincent Sakanga
Transport, Albert Yomba-Eyambo
Youth and Sport, Fidele Ogbami
Women's Affairs and Social Action, Marie-Noelle Koyara
Relations with Parliament, Nestor Kombot-Naguemo
Communications, Arts and Culture, Maurice Saragba
Economy, Planning and Co-operation, Dogonendji Be

Public Works, Housing and Territorial Development, Dieudonné Beket
Territorial Administration and National Security, Thierry Kiandji
Decentralization, Gerard Gaba
Environment and Tourism, Daniel Emery Dede

EMBASSY OF THE CENTRAL AFRICAN REPUBLIC
30 rue des Perchamps, 75016, Paris
Tel: Paris 42244256
Ambassador Extraordinary and Plenipotentiary, new appointment awaited
BRITISH AMBASSADOR, His Excellency William Ernest Quantrill, resident at Yaoundé, Cameroon
Honorary Consul, A. G. Perreard, PO Box 728, Bangui

ECONOMY

In an effort to revive an ailing economy, the government began in 1986 to streamline the civil service, increase tax revenues, and reduce price controls. The IMF approved a US$23 million credit to support economic reform in 1994. Cotton, diamonds, coffee and timber are the major exports.

TRADE WITH UK	1993	1994
Imports from UK	£1,487,000	£1,056,000
Exports to UK	53,000	151,000

CHAD REPUBLIC
République du Tchad

Situated in north-central Africa, the Chad Republic extends from 23° to 7° N. latitude and is flanked by Niger and Cameroon on the west, by Libya on the north, by the Sudan on the east and by the Central African Republic on the south. It has an area of 495,755 sq. miles (1,284,000 sq. km) and a population (UN estimate 1992) of 5,961,000.

The Aouzou strip was claimed by Libya, which occupied the area from 1973 to 1994. A war over the territory ended in 1987. In 1990 Chad and Libya presented their claims to the International Court of Justice, which in 1994 awarded jurisdiction over the whole of the strip to Chad.

CAPITAL – Ndjaména, south of Lake Chad (402,000).
CURRENCY – Franc CFA of 100 centimes.
FLAG – Vertical stripes, blue, yellow and red.
NATIONAL DAY – 13 April.

GOVERNMENT

Chad became a member state of the French Community in 1958, and was proclaimed fully independent on 11 August 1960. The constitution was suspended in 1975 when President Tombalbaye was killed in a military coup by Gen. Felix Malloum, who was overthrown in 1979. A Transitional Government of National Unity was replaced in 1982 by the government of Hissène Habré, but this was overthrown in 1990 in a coup led by Idriss Déby. Déby announced the adoption of a multiparty system, allowing the legalization of political parties in 1991 and 1992. A sovereign national conference held from January to April 1993 elected a Higher Transitional Council (CST) of 57 members to serve as the transitional legislature and appointed a transitional government in conjunction with President Déby until multiparty elections are held. The CST has twice extended the transitional period by one year to give the President and government sufficient time to organize elections. The CST has also adopted an electoral timetable including a constitutional referendum

in November 1995, presidential elections in February 1996 and legislative elections in April and May 1996.

HEAD OF STATE
President, Idriss Déby, *took power* December 1990

TRANSITIONAL GOVERNMENT *as at August 1995*
Prime Minister, Koibla Djimasta
Foreign Affairs, Ahmat Abderamane Haggar
Interior and Territorial Administration, Mahamat Nouri
Finance, Mahamat Saleh Alabo
Armed Forces, Ali Absakine
Civil Service and Labour, Salibou Garba
Planning and Co-operation, Nour Mariam Mahamat
Livestock and Water Resources, Mahamat Nour Malai
Justice, Maidoun Bada Abbas
Rural Development, Mahamat Adoum Kalapoum
Public Works and Transport, Gali Gatta Ngothe
Education, Nassour Waidou
Environment and Tourism, Moise Tchiete
Commerce and Industrial Production, Mahamat Ambadi
Posts and Telecommunications, Kedem Dangdi
Mines, Energy and Oil, Paul Mbainodoum
Culture, Youth and Sports, Mahamat Said Farah
Social Affairs and Women, Achta Selgue
Public Health, Dangde Laoubele
Communications, Youssouf Mboundou Mbami
Public Security, Noudjalbaye Ngaryanan
Culture, Youssouf Said Farah

EMBASSY OF THE REPUBLIC OF CHAD
Boulevard Lambermont 52, 1030 Brussels, Belgium
Tel: Brussels 2151975
Ambassador Extraordinary and Plenipotentiary, His Excellency Ramadane Barma, apptd 1994
BRITISH AMBASSADOR, His Excellency John Masefield, CMG, resident at Lagos/Abuja, Nigeria
Honorary Consul, E. Abtour, BP877, Avenue Charles de Gaulle, Ndjaména

ECONOMY

About 90 per cent of the workforce is occupied in agriculture, fishing and forestry. There is an oilfield in Kanem and salt is mined around Lake Chad, but the most important activities are cotton growing (mostly in the south) and animal husbandry (in central areas). Raw cotton and meat are the main exports.

TRADE WITH UK	1993	1994
Imports from UK	£2,006,000	£1,924,000
Exports to UK	1,471,000	1,113,000

CHILE
República de Chile

Chile lies between the Andes (5,000 to 15,000 feet above sea level) and the shores of the South Pacific, extending coastwise from the arid north around Arica to Cape Horn, between 17° 15' and 55° 59' S. latitude and 66° 30' and 75° 48' W. longitude. The extreme length of the country is about 2,800 miles, with an average breadth, north of 41°, of 100 miles. The total area is 292,258 sq. miles (756,945 sq. km).

Island possessions include the Juan Fernandez group (three islands) about 360 miles from Valparaiso; one of these islands is the reputed scene of Alexander Selkirk's (Robinson Crusoe) shipwreck. Easter Island (27° 8' S. and 109° 28' W.), about 2,000 miles away in the South Pacific

Ocean, contains stone platforms and hundreds of stone figures, the origin of which has not yet been determined. The population (UN estimate 1992) is 13,599,000. There are four main groups: indigenous Araucanian Indians, Fuegians, and Changos; Spanish settlers and their descendants; mixed Spanish Indians; and European immigrants. Because of extensive intermarriage only a few indigenous Indians are racially separate. The main religion is Roman Catholicism. The language is Spanish, with admixtures of local words of Indian origin.

CAPITAL – Santiago, population (1993 estimate) 5,443,000 (Greater Santiago). Other large towns are: ΨValparaiso (608,000), Concepción (311,000), Temuco (249,000), ΨAntofagasta (110,000), ΨValdivia (70,000). ΨPunta Arenas (50,000), on the Straits of Magellan, is the southernmost city in the world.

CURRENCY – Chilean peso of 100 centavos.

FLAG – Two horizontal bands, white, red; in top sixth a white star on blue square, next staff.

NATIONAL ANTHEM – Canción Nacional de Chile.

NATIONAL DAY – 18 September (National Anniversary).

GOVERNMENT

Chile was discovered by Spanish adventurers in the 16th century and remained under Spanish rule until 1810, when a revolutionary war, culminating in the Battle of Maipu 1818, achieved the independence of the nation.

At a general election in 1970, the Marxist candidate Dr Allende was elected President by a narrow margin. After industrial unrest and widespread violence, Allende was overthrown in a military coup in 1973.

In 1981 Gen. Pinochet was sworn in as President, to serve until 1989. Pinochet was defeated in a plebiscite in October 1988 regarding extending his term of office for a further eight years, but he initiated constitutional changes confirmed by plebiscite in July 1989. Presidential and congressional elections were held in December 1989, beginning the transition to full democracy. Gen. Pinochet remains Commander-in-Chief of the Armed Forces until 1997, before which he cannot be removed unless a two-thirds majority in both chambers of Congress agree to his removal. This has led to continued political friction between the government and armed forces.

Executive power is held by the President, legislative power is exercised by a Congress which comprises a Senate of 47 Senators (38 elected and nine appointed) and a Chamber of Deputies of 120 elected members.

Presidential and legislative elections were held in 1993. Eduardo Frei won the presidential election and his ruling Coalition for Democracy (centre and centre-left parties) won 70 Chamber of Deputies seats and 22 of the Senate seats. A joint session of Congress in 1994 reduced the presidential term from eight to six years with no possibility of re-election.

Chile is divided into 12 regions and the Metropolitan Area.

HEAD OF STATE
President of the Republic, Eduardo Frei Ruíz-Tagle, *elected* 11 December 1993, *sworn in* 11 March 1994

CABINET *as at July 1995*
Interior, Carlos Figueroa
Foreign Affairs, José Miguel Insulza
Defence, Edmundo Perez
Economy, Alvaro García
Finance, Eduardo Aninat
Education, Sergio Molina
Justice, María Soledad Alvear

Public Works, Ricardo Lagos
Agriculture, Emiliano Ortega
National Properties, Adriana del Piano
Labour, Jorge Arrate
Public Health, Carlos Massad
Mining, Benjamin Teplizky
Housing, Edmundo Ilermosilla
Transport and Communication, Narciso Irureta
General Secretary of Government, José Brunner
General Secretary of Presidency, Genaro Arriagada
Central Planning, Luis Maira
Business, Felipe Sandoval
Women's Affairs, Josefina Bilbao
Energy, Alejandro Jadresic

EMBASSY OF CHILE
12 Devonshire Street, London WIN 2DS
Tel 0171–580 6392
Ambassador Extraordinary and Plenipotentiary, His Excellency Herrán Errázuriz, apptd 1993
Minister-Counsellors, J. L. Morales; C. Lynham (*Consular*)
Military Attaché, Col. J. C. Salgado
Counsellor, H. Sotomayor (*Economic*)

BRITISH EMBASSY
Avenae El Bosque Norte 0125
Casilla 72-D, Santiago 9
Tel: Santiago 2239166
Ambassador Extraordinary and Plenipotentiary, His Excellency Frank B. Wheeler, CMG, apptd 1993
Counsellor, Head of Chancery and Consul-General, P. L. Hunt
Defence, Naval and Military Attaché, Capt. R. F. Johns, OBE, RN
First Secretary (Commercial), J. W. Ayres
There are British Consular Offices at Antofagasta, Arica, Concepción, Santiago, Punta Arenas, Valparaiso.

BRITISH COUNCIL DIRECTOR – Robin Evans (*Cultural Attaché*), Eliodoro Yañez 832, Casilla 115 Correa 55, Santiago
BRITISH-CHILEAN CHAMBER OF COMMERCE, Av. Suecia 155-C, Casilla 536, Santiago

ECONOMY

Economic reforms during the late 1970s and 1980s, with large-scale privatization and deregulation, have made Chile the most successful economy in Latin America. The economy has grown by 50 per cent in ten years, with economic growth averaging 7 per cent a year in 1987–94. In 1994 inflation was down to single figures from 30 per cent in 1990, unemployment is 5 per cent, and the country has attracted considerable foreign investment and an annual foreign trade surplus.

Cereals, vegetables, fruit, tobacco, hemp and vines are grown extensively (especially in the central zone) and livestock accounts for nearly 40 per cent of agricultural production. Sheep farming predominates in the extreme south. There are large timber tracts in the central and southern zones which produce timber, cellulose and wood for export. Industrial-scale fishing makes Chile the fifth largest producer in terms of catch.

The mineral wealth is considerable, the country being particularly rich in copper-ore, iron-ore and nitrates and having in the north the only commercial production of nitrate of soda (Chile saltpetre) from natural resources in the world. There are large deposits of high grade sulphur but mostly around extinct volcanoes in the Andes Cordillera, difficult of access. Oil and natural gas are produced in the Magallanes area from on- and off-shore wells, but domestic production is now declining. There is a steel plant at Huachipato, near Concepción. Production figures for 1993 were: coal 1,580,692 tonnes; copper 2,115,936 tonnes; crude oil 825,100 cu. metres; natural gas 4,136,200 cu. metres.

Industry is based on the processing of mineral, forestry, fish and agricultural products, and the manufacture of consumer goods.

Foreign debt at 28 February 1994 was US$20,066 million, including Central Bank obligations with the IMF of US$438 million.

TRADE

The principal exports are metallic and non-metallic minerals, timber products, metal products, fish products, vegetables, fruit and wool. The principal imports are sugar and other food products, industrial raw materials, machinery, equipment and spares, oil fuels, lubricants and transportation equipment.

	1992	1993
Total imports	US$10,125.5m	US$9,416.2m
Total exports	9,670.2m	10,771.4m

Trade with UK	1993	1994
Imports from UK	£141,773,000	£152,839,000
Exports to UK	246,826,000	194,555,000

COMMUNICATIONS

With the improvement of the roads an increasing share of internal transportation is moving by road and rail, although shipping is still important. The road system is about 65,000 km in length.

A railway line (the Longitudinal) runs from La Calera, just north of Santiago, to Iquique. Another rail line runs from Valparaiso through La Calera and Santiago to Puerto Montt. With the completion of a section of 435 miles from Corumba, Brazil, to Santa Cruz, Bolivia, the Trans-Continental Line will link the Chilean Pacific port of Arica with Rio de Janeiro on the Atlantic. A line runs from Antofagasta to Salta (Argentina).

Chile is served by over 20 international airlines. Domestic traffic is carried by Linea Aerea Nacional (LAN) and LADECO, which also operate internationally, and smaller regional carriers.

DEFENCE

Military service is compulsory for one year (Army) or two years (Navy and Air Force). The total active armed forces strength is 93,000, including 31,000 conscripts. The Army consists of 54,000 personnel (27,000 conscripts). Naval strength is 25,000 (3,000 conscripts) including 3,000 marines and 1,500 coastguard personnel. The Air Force numbers 14,000 personnel (1,000 conscripts) with 98 combat aircraft. There is a paramilitary Carabineros police force of 31,000 personnel.

EDUCATION AND CULTURE

Elementary education is free and compulsory. There are eight universities (three in Santiago, two in Valparaiso, one each in Antofagasta, Concepción and Valdivia). Recent efforts have reduced illiteracy.

The Nobel Prize for Literature was awarded in 1945 to Gabriela Mistral, for Chilean verse and prose, and in 1971 to the poet Pablo Neruda. There are over 100 newspapers and a large number of periodicals.

CHINA
Zhonghua Renmin Gongheguo – The People's Republic of China

The area is 3,705,408 sq. miles (9,596,961 sq. km).

A census (the fourth) was held in 1990 and recorded a total population of 1,130 million. The estimated population for 1994 was 1,200 million.

POPULATION OF THE PROVINCES (1991 estimates)

Anhui	57,610,000
Beijing	10,940,000
Fujian	30,790,000
Gansu	22,850,000
Guangdong	64,390,000
Guangxi Zhuang Autonomous Region	43,240,000
Guizhou	33,150,000
Hainan	6,740,000
Hebei	62,200,000
Heilongjiang	35,750,000
Henan	87,630,000
Hubei	55,120,000
Hunan	62,090,000
Jiangsu	68,440,000
Jiangxi	38,650,000
Jilin	25,090,000
Liaoning	39,900,000
Nei Monggol Autonomous Region	21,840,000
Ningxia Hui Autonomous Region	4,800,000
Qinghai	4,540,000
Shaanxi	33,630,000
Shandong	85,700,000
Shanghai	13,400,000
Shanxi	29,420,000
Sichuan	108,970,000
Tianjin	9,090,000
Tibet Autonomous Region	2,260,000
Xinjiang Uygur Autonomous Region	15,550,000
Yunnan	37,820,000
Zhejiang	42,020,000
Armed Forces	2,700,000

About 6 per cent of the population belong to around 55 ethnic minorities. Among the largest are the Zhuang of Guangxi, the Uygurs of Xinjiang, the Tibetans and the Mongols.

The indigenous religions are Confucianism (which includes ancestor worship), Taoism (originally a philosophy rather than a religion) and, since its introduction in the first century AD, Buddhism. There are also Muslims (officially estimated at about 12 million) and Christians (unofficially estimated at about 50 million). Religious freedoms, severely curtailed during the Cultural Revolution, are reviving slightly under more liberal policies. Ethnic unrest in Buddhist Tibet and Muslim Xinjiang could threaten such liberalization.

CAPITAL – Beijing (Peking), population (metropolitan area, 1990) 10,860,000 (excluding temporary residents).
MAJOR CITIES – Population of major cities in 1989 was:

ΨShanghai*	12,670,000	Harbin	2,800,000
Tianjin	5,700,000	Chengdu	2,780,000
Shenyang	4,500,000	Xian	2,710,000
Wuhan	3,710,000	Nanjing	2,470,000
Guangzhou		Taiyuan	1,900,000
(Canton)	3,540,000	Kunming	1,500,000
Chongqing	2,960,000	Lanzhou	1,480,000
*metropolitan area			

CURRENCY – The currency is called Renminbi (RMB). The unit of currency is the yuan of 10 jiao or 100 fen.
FLAG – Red, with large gold five-point star and four small gold stars in crescent, all in upper quarter next staff.
NATIONAL ANTHEM – March of the Volunteers.
NATIONAL DAY – 1 October (Founding of People's Republic).

HISTORY

China was ruled by successive imperial dynasties for over 20 centuries until the party of reform forced the Emperor to abdicate on 10 October 1911 and declared a republic. However, the new government (formed by the Chinese National People's Party (the Kuomintang)), the emergent Chinese Communist Party (CCP) after 1918, and more traditional factions were unable to provide a central unifying force or philosophy to replace the monarchy and Confucianism, or to agree on the basis for further reform. After the 1911 revolution warlords thrived and in the 1930s Japanese expansionist ambitions were irresistible, so that by the end of the 1930s Japan occupied Manchuria and all the important northern and coastal areas of China. Japan's occupation was ended by its defeat by the allies in 1945.

The Communists' initial co-operation with the Kuomintang ended in 1927, though it was revived by opposition to Japan in the late 1930s, but the Kuomintang government was unable to suppress the CCP. The CCP had successfully politicized the rural population, setting up a 'Soviet Republic' in Kiangsi in the early 1930s, but they were forced out of the area by the Kuomintang and began the 'Long March' to Shenshi in 1934. The Communists established control over large areas of China in the early 1940s and in 1945 gained control in most of the areas which Japan had occupied. Civil war lasted until 1949 when the CPP, led by Mao Zedong (Mao Tse-tung), inaugurated the Chinese People's Republic, and the Kuomintang under Chiang K'ai-shek went into exile in Taiwan. Diplomatic recognition of the People's Republic was accorded by many countries, though others, led by the USA, continued to recognize the Chiang Kai-shek regime as the rightful government of China until 1971, when the People's Republic took over China's membership of the United Nations from Taiwan.

Under Mao Zedong China was ruled on the basis of four 'cardinal principles': Marxist–Leninist–Maoist thought, the Socialist Road, the dictatorship of the proletariat, and the leadership of the Communist party. Mao's 'Great Leap Forward' (1958–61) was an attempt to industrialize rural areas which proved to be a disaster and resulted in a famine in which 30–40 million people died. The country was plunged into chaos during the cultural revolution (1966–9) when the Red Guards were used to rid the country of 'rightist elements'.

GOVERNMENT

Following the deaths of Mao Zedong and Zhou En-lai in 1976, the disgraced Deng Xiaoping was recalled. In 1977 he was elected Vice-Chairman of the CCP, becoming the dominant force within the party by eliminating leftist influence, rehabilitating fallen leaders and adjusting Maoist policies to permit economic liberalization. Deng decided economic growth was to take precedence over class struggle. The Congresses of 1982 and 1987 reaffirmed Deng's policies, and in 1987 most of the revolutionary generation were replaced in the top posts by younger, more liberal supporters of reform.

Student-led pro-democracy demonstrations in April and May 1989, centred on Tiananmen Square in Beijing, ended on 3–4 June when the army took control of Beijing, killing thousands of protesters. This strengthened the position of the hardline elements of the leadership, who readopted policies of centralization based on Marxist ideology while simultaneously pledging commitment to reform under the influence of Deng. Deng retired from his last official post as Chairman of the Central Military Commission in November 1989 but retained effective control until late 1994, when he was incapacitated by ill health.

At Deng's instigation during 1992 the emphasis switched back to economic reform and the power of the hardline elements declined again. The 14th Party Congress in 1992 endorsed Deng's calls for faster, bolder economic reforms and his 'socialist market economy'. Most of the remaining conservatives were replaced by moderate economic reformers. However, economic reforms and a series of austerity measures to combat inflation has seen official unemployment rise to around five million, with a further 50–100 million migrant labourers unemployed, causing peasant unrest. A degree of central control has been reasserted over the free-market coastal regions, especially their tax revenues, in an attempt to prevent a repetition of the political unrest of 1989.

CONSTITUTION

Under the 1982 constitution, the National People's Congress is the highest organ of state power. It is elected for a term of five years and is supposed to hold one session a year. It is empowered to amend the constitution, make laws, select the President and Vice-President and other leading officials of the state, approve the national economic plan, the state budget and the final state accounts, and to decide on questions of war and peace. The State Council is the highest organ of the state administration. It is composed of the Premier, the Vice-Premiers, the State Councillors, heads of Ministries and Commissions, the Auditor-General and the Secretary-General. Command over the armed forces is vested in the Central Military Commission.

Deputies to Congresses at the primary level are 'directly elected' by the voters 'through a secret ballot after democratic consultation'. This is now extended to county level. These Congresses elect the deputies to the Congress at the next higher level. Deputies to the National People's Congress are elected by the People's Congresses of the provinces, autonomous regions and municipalities directly under the central government, and by the armed forces.

Local government is conducted through People's Governments at provincial, municipal and county levels. Autonomous regions, prefectures and counties exist for national minorities and are described as self-governing. The system prevailing is that found elsewhere, i.e. People's Congresses and People's Governments. Beijing, Shanghai and Tianjin come directly under the central government.

HEAD OF STATE

President of the People's Republic of China, Jiang Zemin, *elected* April 1993

Vice President, Rong Yiren
Chairman of the Standing Committee of the Eighth National People's Congress, Qiao Shi
Chairman of the Central Military Commission, Jiang Zemin

STATE COUNCIL *as at August 1995*

Premier, Li Peng
Vice-Premiers, Qian Qichen; Li Lanqing; Zhu Rongji; Zou Jiahua; Wu Bangguo; Jiang Chunyun
State Councillors, Li Tieying; Chi Haotian; Song Jian; Li Guixian; Ismail Amat; Peng Peiyun; Luo Gan; Chen Junsheng

MINISTERS

Agriculture, Liu Jiang
Chemical Industry, Gu Xiulian
Civil Affairs, Doje Cering
Coal Industry, Wang Senhao
Communications, Huang Zhendong
Construction, Hou Jie
Culture, Liu Zhongde
Electronics Industry, Hu Qili
Finance, Liu Zhongli
Foreign Affairs, Qian Qichen
Foreign Trade and Economic Co-operation, Wu Yi
Forestry, Xu Youfang

Geology and Mineral Resources, Song Ruixiang
Internal Trade, Chen Bangzhu
Justice, Xiao Yang
Labour, Li Boyong
Machine Industry, He Guangyuan
Metallurgical Industry, Liu Qi
National Defence, Chi Haotian
Personnel, Song Defu
Posts and Telecommunications, Wu Jichuan
Public Health, Chen Minzhang
Public Security, Tao Siju
Radio, Film and Television, Sun Jiazheng
Railways, Han Zhubin
State Security, Jia Chunwang
Supervision, Cao Qingze
Water Resources, Niu Maosheng

MINISTERS IN CHARGE OF STATE COMMISSIONS

Economics and Trade, Wang Zhongyu
Education, Zhu Kaixuan
Family Planning, Peng Peiyun
Nationalities Affairs, Ismail Amat
Physical Culture and Sports, Wu Shaozu
Planning, Chen Jinhua
Restructuring Economy, Li Tieying
Science, Technology and Industry for National Defence, Ding Henggao
Science and Technology, Song Jian
Auditor-General, Guo Zhenqian
Secretary-General, Luo Gan

President of the People's Bank of China, Dai Xianglong

THE CHINESE COMMUNIST PARTY

General Secretary, Jiang Zemin
Politburo Standing Committee, Jiang Zemin; Li Peng; Qiao Shi; Li Ruihuan; Zhu Rongji; Liu Huaqing; Hu Jintao
Politburo of the Central Committee, Tian Jiyun; Qiao Shi; Jiang Zemin; Li Tieying; Li Ruihuan; Liu Huaqing; Zhu Rongji; Hu Jintao; Ding Guangen; Qian Qichen; Chen Xitong; Jiang Chunyun; Li Lanqing; Wei Jianxing; Wu Bangguo; Xie Fei; Yang Baibing; Zou Jiahua; Li Peng; Huang Ju (*full members*); Wen Jiabao; Wang Hanbin (*alternate members*)
Secretariat of the Central Committee, Jiang Zemin; Ding Guangen; Hu Jintao; Wei Jiangxing; Ren Jianxin; Wen Jiabao; Wu Bangguo; Jiang Chunyun (*full members*)
Discipline Inspection Commission, Wei Jianxing (*Secretary*); Xu Qing; Hou Zongbin; Chen Zuolin; Wang Deying (*Deputy Secretaries*)
Membership, 52,000,000 (1993)

EMBASSY OF THE PEOPLE'S REPUBLIC OF CHINA

49–51 Portland Place, London WIN 3AH
Tel 0171–636 9375/5726
Ambassador Extraordinary and Plenipotentiary, His Excellency Ma Yuzhen, apptd 1991
Minister-Counsellor, Lu Kexing (*Commercial*); Wang Qiliang
Defence Attaché, Maj.-Gen. Han Kaihe
Cultural Attaché, Fan Zhonghui
Consul-General, Xiao Houde

BRITISH EMBASSY

11 Guang Hua Lu, Jian Guo Men Wai, Beijing 100 600
Tel: Beijing 5321961/5
Ambassador, His Excellency Sir Leonard Appleyard, KCMG, apptd 1994
Minister, Consul-General and Deputy Head of Mission, P. A. McLean
Counsellors, N. Cox (*Political*); S. D. R. Brown (*Commercial*); M. Davidson (*Cultural, and British Council Representative*);

J. Smith-Laittan (*Head of China Trade Unit*) (resides at Hong Kong)
Defence, Military and Air Attaché, Col. K. O. Winfield
There is also a Consulate-General in Shanghai.

DEFENCE

All three military arms are parts of the People's Liberation Army (PLA). The size of this body has not been formally given, but it is estimated at approximately 2,930,000 personnel under arms (1,275,000 conscripts), with a further 1,200,000 reserves. Military service is selective, with conscripts serving three years in the Army and four years in the Air Force and the Navy.

China has 14 intercontinental and 60 intermediate range land-based, and 12 submarine-launched nuclear ballistic missiles. The Army has a strength of 2,200,000 (around 1,075,000 conscripts), with some 8,000 main battle tanks, 2,000 light tanks, 2,800 armoured personnel carriers and 14,500 artillery pieces. Organization is in ten armoured, five artillery and 78 infantry divisions, together with 15 engineer regiments and one airborne corps.

The Navy has a strength of 260,000 (40,000 conscripts), 50 submarines, 18 destroyers, 37 frigates, 870 patrol and coastal craft, one marine brigade of 5,000 men, 880 combat aircraft and 65 armed helicopters. The Air Force numbers 470,000 (160,000 conscripts) and some 5,000 combat aircraft of mainly Chinese manufacture.

ECONOMY

In 1982 China set itself the aim of quadrupling the 1980 gross agricultural and industrial output value by 2000. The focus of its reform programme was switched to industry in 1984. Reforms have been introduced to make the industrial sector more efficient by reducing central planning and broadening the role of the market. The economic reforms announced in 1993 in the 'Grand Blueprint' of the Communist Party will effectively make China a market economy over the next few years. The Central Bank is to be reorganized on a Western model; market pricing is to be extended from goods to labour, property and financial markets; small firms are to be privatized and larger ones made joint stock companies or given independent boards; a social security system is to be established and paid for by a tax on wages; a housing market is to be established; and the government is to use macroeconomic instruments, rather than administrative orders, to run the economy. The currency should become fully convertible in 1995.

Economic liberalization in the early 1980s has led to an explosion since 1984 in manufacturing, concentrated in China's coastal regions, where central government has devolved economic decision-making to provincial governments. Foreign direct investment, especially from Hong Kong and Taiwan, has mushroomed and, with low tax rates and wage levels, enabled the construction of a significant industrial base and transport infrastructure. In the coastal regions the economy has become a free market in all but name, with several stock markets and Shanghai's emergence as a financial centre. China's foreign trade has grown enormously and substantial foreign exchange reserves have been built up. The economy is prone to bouts of 'overheating', fuelled by excessive investment in capital construction, which has required austerity measures (reduced government expenditure and higher interest rates) in 1993–5 in an attempt to control inflation (24 per cent in 1994). By 1994, 50–60 per cent of industrial output was produced by private or collective firms which employed a total of 120 million people.

Agriculture remains of great importance, with 70 per cent of the population still living in rural areas.

Agricultural policies designed to give greater incentives to the rural population have meant that the responsibility for agricultural production has been devolved to individual households, whereas previously work was generally assigned on a collective basis.

Cereals, with peas and beans, are grown in the northern provinces, and rice, tea and sugar in the south. Rice is the staple food of the inhabitants. Cotton (mostly in valleys of the Yangtze and Yellow Rivers), tea (in the west and south), with hemp, jute and flax, are the most important crops. Livestock is raised in large numbers. Silkworm culture is one of the oldest industries. Cottons, woollens and silks are manufactured in large quantities.

The mineral wealth is great. Coal, iron ore, tin, antimony, wolfram, bismuth and molybdenum are abundant. Oil is produced in several northern provinces, particularly in Heilongjiang and Shandong, and off-shore deposits are being sought in co-operation with western and Japanese companies.

The State Statistical Bureau valued the GDP in 1994 at Yuan 4,380 billion, an 11.8 per cent increase over 1993. The total value of agricultural output rose by 4 per cent over the 1992 figure to Yuan 665 billion. The total value of industrial output rose by 18 per cent to Yuan 1,840 billion in 1994.

TRADE

Foreign trade and external economic relations have grown enormously since 1978. Total exports in 1994 rose 31 per cent to US$121 billion, while imports rose 11 per cent to US$115 billion. The principal exports are animals and animal products, oil, textiles, ores, metals, tea and manufactured goods. The principal imports are motor vehicles, machinery, chemical fertilizer, plants, aircraft, books, paper and paper-making materials, chemicals, metals and ores, and dyes.

Trade with UK	1993	1994
Imports from UK	£739,484,000	£844,865,000
Exports to UK	1,327,128,000	1,641,798,000

COMMUNICATIONS

Over half of the country consists of tableland and mountainous areas where communications and travel are difficult but the communications network now covers most of the country. There are more than 53,400 km of railway lines and 1,041,100 km of highway (1991). In addition, internal civil aviation has been developed, with routes now totalling more than 471,900 km.

In the past the principal means of communication east to west were by the rivers, the most important of which are the Yangtze (Changjiang) (3,400 miles), the Yellow River (Huanghe) (2,600 miles) and the West River (Xihe) (1,650 miles). These, together with the network of canals connecting them, are still much used but their overall importance has declined. Coastal port facilities are being improved and the merchant fleet expanded.

Postal services and telecommunications have developed in recent years and it is claimed that 95 per cent of all rural townships are on the telephone and that postal routes reach practically every production brigade headquarters.

EDUCATION

The Cultural Revolution of 1966 to 1969 disrupted the educational system and since 1976 attempts have been made to raise academic standards. Primary education lasts five years, and enrolment (1991) was 121,642,000 including kindergarten. Secondary education lasts five years (three years in junior middle school and two years in senior middle school). There were 52,268,000 middle school pupils in 1991. There are over 1,000 universities, colleges and institutes with an enrolment (1991) of 2 million students. In 1985 the Party announced the abolition of free higher education except for teacher training, and the aim of providing all children with junior secondary education within ten years. There are 220 million illiterates; efforts are being made to expand secondary education, particularly in the rural areas.

CULTURE

The Chinese language has many dialects, notably Cantonese, Hakka, Amoy, Foochow, Changsha, Nanchang, Wu (Shanghai) and the northern dialect. The Common Speech or *putonghua* (often referred to as Mandarin) is based on the northern dialect. The Communists have promoted it as the national language and it is taught throughout the country. As *putonghua* encourages the use of the spoken language in writing, the old literary style and ideographic form of writing has fallen into disuse.

Since 1956 simplified characters have been introduced to make reading and writing easier and there are now over 2,000 simplified characters in use. Since 1956 all Chinese newspapers and most books have characters printed horizontally from left to right, instead of reading vertically from right to left, as previously.

In 1958 the National People's Congress adopted a system of romanization known as pinyin, using 25 of the letters of the Latin alphabet (not v). This has been used within the country largely for assisting schoolchildren and others to learn the pronunciation of characters in *putonghua*, and is used for Chinese names in foreign-language publications.

Chinese literature is one of the richest in the world. Paper has been employed for writing and printing for nearly 2,000 years. The Confucian classics which formed the basis of traditional Chinese culture date from the Warring States period (fourth to third centuries BC), as do the earliest texts of Taoism. Histories, philosophical and scientific works, poetry, literary and art criticism, novels and romances survive from most periods. Many have been translated into English. With the spread of literacy in the 20th century, particularly since 1949, traditional literature has been largely superseded by modern works of a popular kind and by the classics of Marxism and modern developments from them.

The most important among the newspapers and magazines are the *People's Daily* and the twice-monthly *Qiushi*, which replaced *Red Flag* as the CCP's mouthpiece in 1989.

TIBET

Tibet is a plateau seldom lower than 10,000 feet, which forms the northern frontier of India (boundary imperfectly demarcated), from Kashmir to Burma, but is separated therefrom by the Himalayas. The area is estimated at 463,000 sq. miles with a population of 2,260,000 in 1991.

From 1911 to 1950, Tibet was virtually an independent country though its status was never officially so recognized. In 1950 Chinese Communist forces invaded eastern Tibet. In 1951 an agreement was reached whereby the Chinese army was allowed entry into Tibet, and a Communist military and administrative headquarters was set up. A series of revolts against Chinese rule over several years culminated in 1959 in a rising in Lhasa. Fighting continued for several days before the rebellion was suppressed by Chinese troops and military rule was imposed. The Dalai Lama fled to India where he and his followers were granted political asylum. The Tibetan government was replaced by the Preparatory Committee

for the Tibetan Autonomous Region, originally set up in 1955 with the Dalai Lama as chairman, which administered Tibet until it became an Autonomous Region of China in 1965.

In 1964 the Dalai Lama was declared a traitor, and both he and the Panchen Lama were dismissed. This move marked the end of the period of co-operation by the Chinese government with the traditional religious authorities and the eclipse of the latter. The Panchen Lama was rehabilitated as an official of the CPPCC, but died in 1989. The Chinese have invited the Dalai Lama to return from exile, but negotiations between the Chinese and the Dalai Lama have failed to materialize. Martial law was declared in Tibet in 1989 after serious unrest, and sporadic outbursts of unrest continue, the most recently in 1993. The Dalai Lama was awarded the Nobel Peace Prize in 1990.

COLOMBIA
República de Colombia

Colombia lies in the extreme north-west of South America, having a coastline on both the Caribbean Sea and Pacific Ocean. It is situated between 4° 13′ S. to 12° 30′ N. latitude and 68° to 79° W. longitude, with an area of 440,714 sq. miles (1,141,748 sq. km).

The country is divided by the Cordillera de los Andes into a coastal region in the north and west and extensive plains in the east. The eastern range of the Colombian Andes is a series of vast tablelands. This temperate region is the most densely peopled portion of the country. The principal rivers are the Magdalena, Guaviare, Cauca, Atrato, Caquetá, Putumayo and Patia.

The population (UN estimate 1992) is 33,392,000. The language is Spanish. Roman Catholicism is the established religion.

CAPITAL – Bogotá, population (1990 estimate) 5,000,000.
Other centres are Medellin (2,400,000); Cali (1,800,000); ΨBarranquilla (1,400,000); ΨCartagena (700,000), the major port on the Caribbean; Bucaramanga (350,000); ΨBuenaventura (130,000), the major port on the Pacific.
CURRENCY – Colombian peso of 100 centavos.
FLAG – Broad yellow band in upper half, surmounting equal bands of blue and red.
NATIONAL ANTHEM – Oh gloria inmarcesible.
NATIONAL DAY – 20 July (National Independence Day).

GOVERNMENT

The Colombian coast was visited in 1502 by Columbus, and in 1536 a Spanish expedition under Jiménez de Quesada penetrated the interior and established a government. The country remained under Spanish rule until 1819 when Simón Bolívar (1783–1831) established the Republic of Colombia, consisting of the territories now known as Colombia, Panama, Venezuela and Ecuador. In 1829–30 Venezuela and Ecuador withdrew, and in 1831 the remaining territories formed the Republic of New Granada. The name was changed to the Granadine Confederation in 1858, to the United States of Colombia in 1861 and to the Republic of Columbia in 1866. Panama seceded in 1903.

During the early 1950s Colombia suffered a period of virtual civil war between the supporters of the Conservative and the Liberal political parties. From 1957 to 1974 the country was governed under the 'National Front' agreement with an alternating presidency and ministerial posts shared equally by the parties. The alternation of the presidency ended in 1974 and parity in appointments in 1978. Thereafter, the constitution lays down that government portfolios and administrative appointments shall be divided proportionally among the two major parties in Congress.

Elections to a constitutional convention were held in 1990, in which the former guerrilla movement M19 gained 30 per cent of the vote and a new constitution was promulgated in 1991. Congressional elections to the 102-seat Senate and 163-seat House of Representatives were last held on 13 March 1994 and saw the re-emergence of the traditional parties. The Liberal Party won 89 seats, the Social Conservative Party (PSC) 56 seats and M19 two seats. In the Senate elections the Liberal Party won 52 seats, the PSC 21 seats and M19 one seat. In the second round of the 1994 presidential election the Liberal candidate Ernesto Samper narrowly defeated the PSC candidate. President Samper appointed a Liberal–PSC coalition government in August 1994.

INSURGENCY

Colombia is dogged by insurgency from left-wing guerrillas and from the drugs cartels centred on Cali. Over the 1989–94 period the government has reached peace agreements with four left-wing guerrilla groups, including M19 and the Current of Socialist Revolution (CRS), and these guerrillas have disarmed. The Simón Bolivar National Guerrilla Co-ordinating Board remains active with three main elements: the National Liberation Army (ELN) with a strength of around 3,000; the Revolutionary Armed Forces of Colombia (FARC) with a strength of 6,000; the People's Liberation Army with a strength of 500–1,000. The security threat from the Medellin drugs cartel effectively ended with the death of Pablo Escobar, the cartel leader, in December 1993. The government in 1993–5 has concentrated on combating the Cali cartel and has captured five of the seven cartel members.

HEAD OF STATE

President, Dr Ernesto Samper-Pizano, *elected* 19 June 1994, *sworn in* 7 August 1994

CABINET *as at July 1995*

Interior, Horacio Serpa Uribe
Foreign Affairs, Rodrígo Pardo Garcia-Peña
Finance, Guillermo Perry Rubio
Justice, Néstor Humberto Martínez
National Defence, Fernando Botero Zea
Transport, Juan Gómez Martínez
Labour, Maria Sol Calderón
Agriculture, Antonio Hernández Gamarra
Health, Alonso Gómez Duque
Mines and Energy, Jorge Eduardo Londoño
Communications, Armando Benedetti Jimeno
Education, Arturo Saravia Better
Development, Rodrigo Marin Bernal
Foreign Trade, Daniel Mazuera Gómez
Planning, Jesus Antonio Ocampo
Environment, Cecilia Lopez Montaño

COLOMBIAN EMBASSY

Flat 3A, 3 Hans Crescent, London SWIX OLR
Tel 0171–589 9177/5037

Ambassador Extraordinary and Plenipotentiary, Her Excellency Noemi Sanin de Rubio, apptd 1994

BRITISH EMBASSY

Torre Propaganda Sancho, Calle 98 No. 9–03 Piso 4, Bogotá
Tel: Bogota 2185111

Ambassador Extraordinary and Plenipotentiary, His Excellency Arthur L. Coltman, apptd 1994

There are British Consular Offices at Barranquilla, Bogotá, Cali and Medellin.

BRITISH COUNCIL DIRECTOR, Kate Board, Calle 87 No. 12–79, Bogotá DE
COLOMBO-BRITISH CHAMBER OF COMMERCE, Apartado Aereo 054 728, Calle 106 No. 25-41, Bogotá DE

DEFENCE

The Colombian armed forces have been occupied in recent years in fighting the armed groups of the Medellin and Cali drugs cartels and the remaining active guerrillas. The total active strength of the armed forces is 146,600 personnel (67,300 conscripts). Service is compulsory and lasts between one and two years.

The Army's strength is some 121,000 (63,800 conscripts) with 12 light tanks, 124 reconnaissance vehicles, 155 armoured personnel carriers and 130 artillery pieces. The Navy, with 18,100 personnel including 8,900 marines, has five frigates, 39 patrol and coastal craft and two submarines. The Air Force, with 7,300 personnel (3,500 conscripts), has a strength of 74 combat aircraft and 72 armed helicopters. There is also a paramilitary police force of 79,000.

ECONOMY

Coal, natural gas and hydro-electricity resources are largely unexploited, although development of coal is being given priority. Annual coal production is about 12.5 million tonnes, essentially for export, and oil exports were 472,000 b.p.d. in 1991. In 1993 oil reserves estimated to be worth US$3 billion per year when exploited were found under the eastern plains.

The hydrocarbon sector accounts for over half of the mining output, precious metals (gold, platinum and silver) and iron ore accounting for the remainder. Other mineral deposits include nickel, bauxite, copper, gypsum, limestone, phosphates, sulphur and uranium. Colombia is also the world's largest producer of emeralds and has deposits of other precious and semi-precious stones.

Because of the range of climate, a wide variety of crops are grown, principally coffee. Other major cash crops are sugar, bananas, cut flowers and cotton. Cattle are raised in large numbers, and meat and cured skins and hides are also exported.

The government has encouraged diversification to reduce dependence on coffee as the major export and this has led to the growth of new export-orientated industries, particularly textiles, paper products and leather goods. Stimulus to the economy has been provided by loans from the World Bank and IADB for project development, particularly in the power sector (in which hydroelectric projects have predominated) and for telecommunications.

Since the late 1980s the government has introduced trade liberalization and privatization measures which have effectively freed foreign exchange transactions, increased foreign competition, ended protectionism and brought down inflation. In 1994 GDP growth was 5.7 per cent.

TRADE

Principal exports are petroleum and derivatives, coffee, bananas, cut flowers, clothing and textiles, ferro-nickel and coal. Principal trading partners are USA, the EU and Latin America.

Trade with UK	1993	1994
Imports from UK	£104,592,000	£231,445,000
Exports to UK	176,094,000	191,449,000

COMMUNICATIONS

The Andes make surface transport difficult so air transport is used extensively. There are daily air services between Bogotá and all the principal towns, as well as frequent services to other countries. The 'Atlantic Railway' links the departmental lines running down to the River Magdalena, and completes the connection between Bogotá and Santa Marta. Although the railways are in a poor state, there are about 2,600 miles of rail in use at present. The road network consists of 105,201 km of roads of all types, of which 21,800 km are classified as main trunk and transversal roads.

Large appropriations have been made for modernization of the country's telecommunication system. There are over 450 radio stations and three national television channels with several regional ones.

CULTURE

State education is free. Efforts have been made in reducing illiteracy and estimates put the literacy rate at 87 per cent of those over ten years of age. There are 27 universities. There is a flourishing press in urban areas and a national literature supplements the rich inheritance from the time of Spanish colonial rule.

THE COMOROS
République Fédérale Islamique des Comores

The Comoro archipelago includes the islands of Great Comoro, Anjouan, Mayotte and Moheli and certain islets in the Indian Ocean with an area of 838 sq. miles (2,171 sq. km) and a population (UN estimate 1992) of 585,000, most of whom are Muslim.

CAPITAL – Moroni, on Great Comoro (pop. 17,267).
CURRENCY – Comorian franc of 100 centimes. The Comoros also use the Franc CFA of 100 centimes.
FLAG – Green with a white crescent and four white stars in the centre, tilted towards the lower fly.
NATIONAL DAY – 6 July (Independence Day).

GOVERNMENT

The islanders voted for independence from France in December 1974 and three islands became independent on 6 July 1975. The island of Mayotte was against independence and has remained under French administration.

A new constitution was adopted by referendum in 1992 which provides for a President directly elected for a five-year term which is renewable once only; an elected 42-member legislative assembly with a four-year term; a 15-member Senate (five from each island) chosen by an electoral college for six-year terms; and the appointment of a Prime Minister from the largest party in the legislative assembly. On 10 May 1992 President Djohar appointed a government of national unity to govern until elections were held in November. These proved inconclusive and the instability following an uprising by rebel soldiers in October 1992 continued until another legislative election was held in December 1993. This was marked by violence and allegations of rigging but brought stability as President Djohar's RDR party gained an absolute majority with 24 out of 42 seats.

Each island is administered by a Governor, assisted by up to four Commissioners whom he appoints, and has an elected Legislative Council.

HEAD OF STATE
President, Said Mohamed Djohar, *sworn in* 20 March 1990

GOVERNMENT *as at July 1995*
Prime Minister, Caabiel Yachroutou
Interior and Decentralization, Mohamed Abdouloihabi
Finance and Budget, Amadi Abdulbastu
Foreign Affairs and Co-operation, Said Mohammed Sagaf
Economy, Industry, Crafts and Planning, vacant
Public Works, Urbanization, Housing and Energy, Choudjaidine Adinane
National Education and Teaching, Mohamed Moussa Moindjie
Public Health, Manadou Boina Maecha
Transport and Tourism, Ahmed Said Issilam
Justice, Fateh Sound Mohamed
Information, Culture, Youth, Sport, Posts and Telecommunications, Nourdine Bourhane
Social Affairs, Employment and Labour, vacant

BRITISH AMBASSADOR, His Excellency Peter Smith, resident at Antananarivo, Madagascar

BRITISH CONSULATE
PO Box 986, Moroni
Honorary Consul, J. de Jaeger

ECONOMY

The most important products are vanilla, copra, cloves and essential oils, which are the principal exports; cacao, sisal and coffee are also cultivated. Great Comoro is well forested and produces some timber.

TRADE WITH UK	1993	1994
Imports from UK	£440,000	£1,272,000
Exports to UK	8,000	52,000

CONGO
République du Congo

The Congo lies on the Equator between Gabon on the west and Zaire on the east, the River Congo and its tributary the Ubangui forming most of the eastern boundary of the state. It has a short Atlantic coastline. The area is 132,047 sq. miles (342,000 sq. km), with a population of 2,368,000 (UN estimate 1992).

CAPITAL – Brazzaville (600,000); ΨPointe Noire (350,000).
CURRENCY – Franc CFA of 100 centimes.
FLAG – Divided diagonally into green, yellow and red bands.
NATIONAL DAY – 15 August.

GOVERNMENT

Formerly the French colony of Middle Congo, the Congo became a member state of the French Community on 28 November 1958 and fully independent on 17 August 1960.

In 1968, a National Council of army officers took power and created the Parti Congolais du Travail (PCT) and the People's Republic of the Congo the following year. After popular pressure, the PCT abandoned its monopoly of power and renounced Marxism in 1990. A transitional government was formed in January 1991 and a national conference convened in February which suspended the constitution, stripped President Sassou-Nguesso of all powers and formed itself into the Higher Council of the Republic (CSR). In December 1991 the CSR adopted a new multiparty constitution with a directly-elected President and a bicameral parliament. The new constitution was approved by a referendum in March 1992 and in the ensuing presidential and legislative elections in July and August the Pan-African Union for Social Democracy (UPADS) emerged as the largest party in both the Senate and the National Assembly. The lack of a parliamentary majority forced President Lissouba to call fresh elections in May and June 1993. These too were won by the UPADS but the results were disputed by opposition groups and violence broke out between the armed forces and armed supporters of the URD (Union for Democratic Renewal) - PCT opposition alliance. In a rerun of elections for 11 seats in the 125-seat National Assembly, the majority were won by the URD-PCT but UPADS still retained a parliamentary majority. Fighting between the armed forces and URD-PCT militias broke out in November and lasted until February 1994, when it was agreed to call in an international panel to examine the 1993 election results. The panel annulled the results in nine seats, for which by-elections were held in April 1995, most being won by opposition parties. A new UPADS-dominated government was appointed in January 1995 which included URD members who had left the opposition alliance.

HEAD OF STATE
President, Pascal Lissouba, *elected* 16 August 1992

CABINET *as at July 1995*
Prime Minister, Jacques-Joachim Yhombi Opango
Minister of State, Development, Martin M'Beri
Minister of State, National Defence, Maurice-Stephane Bongho-Nouarra
Minister of State, Interior, Security, Regional Development, Col. Philippe Bikinkita
Justice and Administration, Joseph Ouabari
Foreign and Francophone Affairs and Co-operation, Arsene Tsaty-Bongou
Economy and Finance, N'Guila Moungounga Nkombo
Industrial Development, Mines and Energy, Posts and Telecommunications, Esau Itachi
Equipment and Public Works, Lambert Galibali
Agriculture, Fisheries and Animal Husbandry, Jean-Prosper Koyo
Transport and Civil Aviation, Seraphin Dieken
Commerce and Small and Medium-sized Enterprises, Marius Mouambenga
Health and Social Welfare, Jean Mouyabi
Civil Service, Labour and Social Security, Anachet Tsomambet
Hydrocarbons, Benoit Koukebene
Culture, Arts, Tourism and Environment, Gabriel Matsiola
Communications, Government Spokesman, Albertine Massala
Education, Research and Technology, Martial de Paul Ikounga
Women's Development, Marie Thérèse Avemeka
Youth and Sports, Gen. Claude-Emmanuel Eta-Onka

EMBASSY OF THE REPUBLIC OF CONGO
37 bis rue Paul Valery, 75116 Paris, France
Tel: Paris 45006057
Ambassador Extraordinary and Plenipotentiary, His Excellency Alphonse Niangoula, apptd 1993

HONORARY CONSULATE, Livingstone House, 11 Carteret Street, London SWIH 9DJ. Tel: 0171-222 7575. *Honorary Consul,* L. Muzzu

BRITISH CHARGÉ D'AFFAIRES, James Lindsay, OBE, resident at Kinshasa, Zaire
There are Honorary Consulates in Brazzaville and Pointe Noire.

ECONOMY
Congo has its own oil deposits, producing about 8 million tonnes annually. It also produces lead, zinc and gold. The principal agricultural products are timber, cassava, sugar cane and yams. Imports are mainly of machinery.

TRADE WITH UK	1993	1994
Imports from UK	£12,408,000	£14,649,000
Exports to UK	4,807,000	4,061,000

COSTA RICA
República de Costa Rica

Costa Rica extends across the Central American isthmus between 8° 17' and 11° 10' N. latitude and from 82° 30' to 85° 45' W. longitude. It has an area of 19,575 sq. miles (50,700 sq. km). The republic lies between Nicaragua and Panama, and between the Caribbean Sea and the Pacific Ocean. The coastal lowlands have a tropical climate but the interior plateau, with a mean elevation of 4,000 feet, enjoys a temperate climate.

The population (1992 estimate) is 3,194,000, mainly of European origin. The language is Spanish.

CAPITAL – San José, population (estimate 1989) 296,625; Alajuela (44,358); ΨPuntarenas (37,390); ΨLimón (67,784).
CURRENCY – Costa Rican colón (₡) of 100 céntimos.
FLAG – Five horizontal bands, blue, white, red, white, blue (the red band twice the width of the others with emblem near staff).
NATIONAL ANTHEM – Himno Nacional de Costa Rica.
NATIONAL DAY – 15 September.

GOVERNMENT
For nearly three centuries (1530–1821) Costa Rica was under Spanish rule. In 1821 the country obtained its independence, although from 1824 to 1839 it was one of the United States of Central America.

In 1948 the Army was abolished, the President declaring it unnecessary. Executive power is vested in the President, who is head of state and government, with legislative power vested in the 57-member Legislative Assembly. Under the constitution both the President and the members of the Legislative Assembly are elected for a single four-year term and may not be re-elected. The main political parties are the Social Christian Unity Party (PUSC) and the National Liberation Party (PLN). The last presidential and legislative elections were held on 6 February 1994 when PLN candidate José Maria Figueres won the presidential election, and the PLN won 28 seats and the PUSC 25 seats in the Legislative Assembly.

HEAD OF STATE
President, José Maria Figueres Olsen, *took office* 8 May 1994
Vice-Presidents, Rodrigo Oreamuno; Rebecca Crynspan

MINISTERS *as at August 1995*
Minister for the Presidency, Elias Soley
Foreign Affairs, Dr Fernando Naranjo
Interior, Maureen Clarke
Justice, Enrique Castillo
Finance, Fernando Herrero
Agriculture, Marío Carvajal
Economy, Industry and Commerce, Marcos Vargas
Foreign Trade, Jose Rossi
Environment, Rene Castro

Rural Development, Roberto Solorzano
Special Projects, Dr Longino Soto
National Co-ordination, Sergio Quiros
Public Works and Transport, Bernardo Arce
Education, Marvin Herrera
Health, Dr German Weinstok
Culture, Youth and Sports, Arnoldo Mora
Labour, Farid Ayales
Planning, Leonardo Garnier
Housing, Edgar Arroyo
Security, Juan Diego Castro
Science and Technology, Roberto Dobles
Information, Florisabel Rodriguez
Tourism, Carlos Roesch

COSTA RICAN EMBASSY
Flat 1, 14 Lancaster Gate, London W2 3LH
Tel 0171-706 8844
Ambassador Extraordinary and Plenipotentiary, His Excellency
   Jorge Borbón Zeller, apptd 1994

BRITISH EMBASSY
Apartado 815, Edificio Centro Colon (11th Floor), San
José 1007
Tel: San José 2215566
*Ambassador Extraordinary and Plenipotentiary and Consul-
   General,* His Excellency Richard Michael Jackson, CVO,
   apptd 1995

ECONOMY

Agriculture is the chief industry and the principal products
are coffee, bananas, sugar and cattle (for meat). Other crops
are cocoa, rice, maize, potatoes, hemp, pineapple, casava,
ginger, chaw chaw, melon and flowers. Industrial activity is
principally in the manufacturing sector and manufactured
goods include foodstuffs, textiles and clothing, plastic
goods, pharmaceuticals, fertilizers and electrical equipment. Tourism is of growing importance and became the
main source of foreign exchange revenue in 1992.

TRADE

The chief exports are manufactured goods and other
products, coffee, bananas, cocoa and sugar. The chief
imports are machinery, including transport equipment,
manufactures, chemicals, fuel and mineral oils and foodstuffs.

	1992	1993
Total imports	US$2,461.7m	US$2,936.8m
Total exports	1,828.4m	2,064.3m
Trade with UK	1993	1994
Imports from UK	£18,473,000	£20,930,000
Exports to UK	41,286,000	76,795,000

COMMUNICATIONS

The chief ports are Limón on the Atlantic coast, through
which passes most of the coffee exported, and Caldera on
the Pacific coast, currently under construction. The railway system is 500 miles long and nationalized. LACSA is
the national airline, operating flights throughout Central
and South America, the Caribbean and USA, besides
internal flights to local airports by SANSA.

CÔTE D'IVOIRE
République de Côte d'Ivoire

Côte d'Ivoire is situated on the Gulf of Guinea between 5°
and 10° N. latitude and 3° and 8° W. longitude. It is flanked
on the west by Guinea and Liberia, on the north by Mali
and Burkina, and on the east by Ghana. It has an area of
124,503 sq. miles (322,463 sq. km). The climate is equatorial in the south and west, which are mainly forested;
tropical in the centre and east, which are savannah regions
with trees; dry and tropical in the north, which is a grassy
savannah region.
   The population of 12,190,000 (UN estimate 1992) is
divided into a large number of ethnic and tribal groups.
The official language is French. Some 39 per cent of the
population is Muslim, 28 per cent Christian (mainly
Roman Catholic) and 17 per cent maintain traditional
beliefs.

CAPITAL – Yamoussoukro (population 106,786) has been
   the political and administrative capital since 1983. The
   economic and financial capital remains Abidjan
   (population 2,700,000), which is also the largest city and
   main port.
CURRENCY – Franc CFA of 100 centimes.
FLAG – Three vertical stripes, orange, white and green.
NATIONAL ANTHEM – L'Abidjanaise.
NATIONAL DAY – 7 December.

GOVERNMENT

Although French contact was made in the first half of the
19th century, Côte d'Ivoire became a colony only in 1893
and was finally pacified in 1912. It decided on 5 December
1958 to remain an autonomous republic within the French
Community; full independence outside the Community
was proclaimed on 7 August 1960.
   Côte d'Ivoire has a presidential system of government
and a single-chamber National Assembly of 175 members.
Although the constitution provides for a multiparty
system, it was not until 1990 that any party other than the
ruling PDCI party was authorized. The PDCI won multiparty elections held in November 1990 amid allegations of
electoral fraud; opposition protests continue. After having
been President since independence in 1960, President
Houphouët-Boigny died in December 1993 and was
replaced as President by the parliamentary speaker Henri
Konan-Bédié who will serve until new elections in late
1995.

HEAD OF STATE
President, Henri Konan-Bédié, *took office* 7 December 1993

CABINET *as at August 1995*
Prime Minister, Minister of Economy and Finance, Daniel
   Kablan Duncan
Relations with Parliament, Ahoua N'Guetta Timothee
National Integration, Laurent Dona-Fologo
Defence, Leon Konan Koffi
Foreign Affairs, Amara Essy
Interior, Émile Constant Bombet
Justice, Faustin Kouame
Higher Education and Scientific Research, Salíou Toure
Agriculture and Animal Resources, Lambert Kouassi Konan
Raw Materials, Alain Gauze
National Education, Pierre Kipre
Environment and Tourism, Lancine Gon Coulibaly
Industry and Commerce, Ferdinand Kacou Angora
Mines and Energy, Mohamed Lamine Fadika

Health and Social Affairs, Maurice Kakou Guikahue
Communication, Daniele Boni-Claverie
Equipment, Transport and Telecommunciations, Ezan Akele
Construction and Town Planning, Albert Kakou Tiapani
Employment and Civil Service, Achi Atsain
Security, Gaston Ouassenan Kone
Culture, Bernard Zadi Zaourou
Women and the Family, Albertine Gnanazan Hipie
Youth and Sports, Komenan Zakpa

EMBASSY OF THE REPUBLIC OF CÔTE D'IVOIRE
2 Upper Belgrave Street, London SW1X 8BJ
Tel 0171–235 6991
Ambassador Extraordinary and Plenipotentiary, His Excellency
Gervais Yao Attoungbre, apptd 1989

BRITISH EMBASSY
Immeuble Les Harmonies, 01 BP 2581, Abidjan 01
Tel: Abidjan 226850
Ambassador Extraordinary and Plenipotentiary, Her
Excellency Margaret I. Rothwell, CMG, apptd 1990
Deputy Head of Mission, First Secretary (Commercial), Consul,
I. R. Whitting

ECONOMY

Côte d'Ivoire became wealthy in the 1970s because of the
high prices of its two principal export earners, coffee and
cocoa. In the late 1980s the economy contracted considerably as its exports deteriorated in competitiveness and its
rivals devalued their currencies while the franc CFA
remained pegged to the French franc. In early 1995 Côte
d'Ivoire had a relatively large foreign debt of US$13,100
million incurred by the infastructure programmes of the
1970s and 1980s. An economic reform and stabilization
programme began in 1989 under IMF auspices which has
brought down inflation, increased investment and led to
GDP growth. The devaluation of the CFA franc in January
1994 has increased exports considerably and restored a
trade surplus. For the 1994–6 period Côte d'Ivoire has
received US$467 million in credit support from the IMF.

The principal exports are coffee, cocoa, timber, palm oil,
sugar, rubber, pineapples, bananas, and cotton. There are a
few deposits of diamonds and minerals including manganese and iron. Oil and gas deposits began to be exploited in
1995.

TRADE WITH UK	1993	1994
Imports from UK	£33,411,000	£27,057,000
Exports to UK	67,424,000	65,958,000

CROATIA

Croatia is bounded by Slovenia, Hungary, the rump
Federal Yugoslav state and Bosnia-Hercegovina; it has an
area of 21,823 sq. miles (56,538 sq. km). It is divided into
three major geographic regions: the Pannonian region in
the north, the central mountain belt, and the Adriatic coast
region of Istria and Dalmatia which has 1,185 islands and
islets and 1,104 miles (1,778 km) of coastline.

The population (1991 census) was 4,760,344, of which
78 per cent were Croats, 12 per cent Serbs, 2 per cent
Yugoslavs and 1 per cent Muslims. The remaining
minorities were Hungarians, Italians, Albanians, Czechs,
Ukrainians and Jews. Croatia is host to some 500,000
refugees from Bosnia-Hercegovina.

About 77 per cent of the population is Roman Catholic,
11 per cent Serbian Orthodox and 1 per cent Muslim. The

majority language is Croatian in the Latin script. Serbs use
Serbian in the Cyrillic script.

CAPITAL – Zagreb, population (1991 estimate) 950,000.
Other major cities are Split (200,000), Rijeka (200,000)
and Osijek (160,000).
CURRENCY – Kuna of 100 lipas.
FLAG – Three horizontal stripes of red, white, blue, with
the national arms over all in the centre.
NATIONAL ANTHEM – Lijepa naša domovina (Our
Beautiful Homeland).
NATIONAL DAY – 30 May (Statehood Day).

HISTORY

Croatia was part of the Austro-Hungarian Empire from
1526 to 1918. On 29 October 1918 the Croatian parliament
declared Croatia independent and soon after Croatia
joined with Slovenia, Bosnia-Hercegovina, Serbia and
Montenegro to form the 'Kingdom of Serbs, Croats and
Slovenes' (renamed Yugoslavia in 1929). From 1941 to
1945 Yugoslavia was occupied by the Axis powers, with
Italy and Hungary annexing parts of Croatia and a pro-
Nazi Croat puppet state being established in the remainder
of Croatia and Bosnia-Hercegovina. The armed extremists
of this puppet state (Ustashe) engaged in fierce fighting
with Serbian royalists, Communist partisans and pro-
Allied Croat partisans.

At the end of the war Yugoslavia was re-established as a
federal republic under Communist rule but following the
death of the wartime partisan leader Josep Tito in 1980
Yugoslavia gradually disintegrated. When Croatia informed Belgrade of its independence in June 1991, the
Federal Yugoslav Army (JNA) intervened against local
defence forces to prevent the disintegration of the federation. Croatia's ethnic Serb minority, which refused to
accept Croatia's independence, formed themselves into
armed groups and fighting began in July 1991 between
Croat defence forces and armed Serbs. By September 1991
this had escalated into war between Croatia and Serbia,
which had taken over control of the JNA.

The war in Croatia continued until January 1992 when
the EC and the UN brought about a ceasefire. The JNA and
Serb forces had secured control of virtually all ethnic Serb
areas in Croatia. Four UN protected areas, Northern and
Southern Krajina and Eastern and Western Slavonia, were
created from the Serb-controlled areas in Croatia and UN
troops arrived to police the areas. The JNA withdrew from
Croatia but the ethnic Serb forces refused to disarm, apart
from placing their heaviest artillery under UN control. *See
also* Events of the Year.

GOVERNMENT

In April and May 1990 the first free, democratic elections
were held in Croatia and were won by the Croatian
Democratic Union (HDZ) of Dr Franjo Tudjman. A new
constitution was adopted by parliament in December 1990
and in a national referendum in May 1991, 94 per cent of
those who voted (the referendum was boycotted by many
ethnic Serbs) voted in favour of independence from
Yugoslavia. Croatia declared its independence on 30 May
1991.

Executive power is vested in a President and government. The President is directly elected for five-year terms.
Legislative power is vested in the bicameral parliament,
comprising the 63-member Chamber of Districts and the
138-member Chamber of Deputies.

Croatia is divided into 21 counties; each county elects
three members to the Chamber of Districts. Counties are
composed of groups of districts and function both as units

of local government and as regional offices for the central administration. There are 102 districts.

The state of the parties in August 1995 in the Chamber of Deputies is: Croatian Democratic Union (HDZ) 69; Croatian Independent Democrats Party (HND) 16; Croatian Social Liberal Party (HSLS) 14; Party of Democratic Change (SDP) 11; ethnic Serb and regionalist parties 9; Independents 6; Others 13.

SECESSION

Since 1992 the situation in the UN protected areas has remained tense. Fighting restarted in January 1993, and Croat forces managed to regain control of Zemunik airport and Maslenica bridge, and ethnic Serb forces regained their heavy weapons from UN control before a cease-fire was signed in April. Sporadic fighting continued from June to September 1993. In April 1994 a cease-fire agreement was reached under which forces and heavy weapons were withdrawn out of range of the front lines. The Croatian government maintained that the UN forces had failed to carry out their mandate of disarming ethnic Serb forces and facilitating the return of 300,000 Croatian refugees to the areas controlled by ethnic Serbs, and it refused to extend the UN mandate in March 1995. A new mandate was agreed from April 1995 for the UN Confidence Rebuilding Operation (UNCRO) controlling Croatia's borders with Bosnia-Hercegovina and Serbia under ethnic Serb control and facilitating the reintegration of ethnic Serb areas into Croatia. In early May Croatian forces captured the UN protected area of Western Slavonia from ethnic Serb forces and annulled the UN mandate in the area; ethnic Serb forces launched rocket attacks on Zagreb in retaliation. With rhe recapture of Western Slavonia, the proportion of Croatia held by ethnic Serb forces fell from 30 per cent to 20 per cent. *See also* Events of the Year.

Having voted in 1993 to establish a 'Republic of Serbian Krajina' (RSK), in January 1994 the ethnic Serbs voted in elections for a separate RSK parliament and President, the latter election being won by Milan Martic.

HEAD OF STATE
President, Franjo Tudjman, *elected* May 1990, *re-elected* 2 August 1992

CABINET *as at August 1995*
Prime Minister, Nikica Valentic
Deputy PM, Foreign Affairs, Mate Granic
Deputy PM, Development and Reconstruction, Dr Jure Radic
Deputy PMs, Ivica Kostovic; Borislav Skegro
Defence, Gojko Susak
Interior, Ivan Jarnjak
Finance, Bozo Prka
Economy, Nadan Vidoševic
Construction, Urban Planning and Housing, Marina Dropulic-Matulovic
Health, Andrija Hebrang
Education and Sports, Ljilja Vokic
Agriculture and Forestry, Ivica Gazi
Maritime Affairs, Transport and Communications, Ivica Mudrinic
Justice, Ivica Crnic
Labour and Social Welfare, Joso Skara
Tourism, Niko Bulic
Science and Technology, Branko Jeren
Culture, Zlatko Vitez
Administration, Davorin Mlakar
Privatization and Property Management, Ivan Penic
Ministers without Portfolio, Cedomir Pavlovic; Ivan Majdak; Zlatko Matesa; Juraj Njavro; Adalbert Debic
President of the Chamber of Deputies, Nedjeljko Mihanovic

EMBASSY OF THE REPUBLIC OF CROATIA
c/o 5th Floor, 18–21 Jermyn Street, London SW1Y 6HP
Tel 0171-434 2946
Ambassador Extraordinary and Plenipotentiary, Dr Ante Čičin-Šain, apptd 1994

BRITISH EMBASSY
2nd Floor, Astra Tower, Tratinska, PO Box 454, 4100 Zagreb.
Tel: Zagreb 334245
Ambassador Extraordinary and Plenipotentiary, His Excellency Gavin Hewitt, CMG, apptd 1994
There are British Consulates in Split and Dubrovnik.

BRITISH COUNCIL DIRECTOR, I. Stewart, PO Box 55, Ilica 12/1, Zagreb 41000.

DEFENCE

Croatia had to build up its armed forces rapidly to survive the 1991–2 war with ethnic Serb and federal (JNA) forces and then to support ethnic Croat forces in Bosnia-Hercegovina. Most JNA equipment in the republic was taken back to Serbia or given to ethnic Serb forces in Croatia. At present the armed forces number 105,000 active and 180,000 reserve personnel, with conscripts serving for ten months. Croatia remains constrained by the UN arms embargo on the former Yugoslavia.

The Army has some 99,600 personnel (65,000 conscripts), with 175 main battle tanks, 150 armoured personnel carriers and 225 artillery pieces. The Air Force has 4,300 personnel, mainly air defence forces, with 20 aircraft and helicopters. The Navy has 1,100 personnel with one submarine and nine patrol and coastal combatants. Paramilitary personnel include 40,000 armed police and 5,000 members of the nationalist Croatian Party of Rights (HSP) armed wing (HOS).

Opposing ethnic Serb forces number 40,000–50,000 personnel, with 240 main battle tanks, 100 armoured personnel carriers, 200 artillery pieces and 18 aircraft and helicopters. The UN deploys 8,750 troops in Croatia.

ECONOMY

Large areas of the most productive farmland were destroyed by the war or remain under Serb control. The tourist industry has been decimated by the war and by the continuing fighting in neighbouring Bosnia. Shipbuilding and fishing are major industries on the Adriatic coast. Inland there is a light manufacturing sector, food-processing industries, bauxite deposits, thermal mineral springs, hydro-electric potential, and agriculture based on grain, horticulture, livestock and tobacco. Serb control of large areas of Croatia has seriously disrupted hydro-electric supplies and transport and communications links.

TRADE WITH UK	1993	1994
Imports from UK	£42,645,000	£142,332,000
Exports to UK	30,627,000	41,238,000

CUBA
República de Cuba

Cuba, the largest island in the Caribbean, lies between 74° and 85° W. longitude, and 19° and 23° N. latitude, with a total area of 42,804 sq. miles (110,861 sq. km). The population (1992 UN estimate) was 10,811,000. The language is Spanish.

CAPITAL – ΨHavana, population estimate (1990) 2,119,000; other towns are ΨSantiago (418,000), Santa Clara (197,000), Camagüey (286,000), Holguin (232,000) and Guantánamo (203,000).

CURRENCY – Cuban peso of 100 centavos.

FLAG – Five horizontal bands, blue and white (blue at top and bottom) with red triangle, close to staff, charged with five-point star.

NATIONAL ANTHEM – Al Combate, Corred Bayameses (To battle, men of Bayamo).

NATIONAL DAY – 1 January (Day of Liberation).

GOVERNMENT

The island was visited by Columbus in 1492. Early in the 16th century the island was conquered by the Spanish, and for almost four centuries remained under Spanish rule. Separatist agitation culminated in the closing years of the 19th century in open warfare. In 1898 the USA intervened and demanded the evacuation of Cuba by Spanish forces. The Spanish–American war led to the abandonment of the island, which came under American military rule from 1899 until 1902, when an autonomous government was inaugurated with an elected President, and a legislature of two houses.

A revolution led by Dr Fidel Castro overthrew the government of Gen. Batista in 1959. In 1965 the Communist Party of Cuba was formed to succeed the United Party of the Socialist Revolution; it is the only authorized political party. A new Socialist constitution came into force in 1976 and indirect elections to the National Assembly of People's Power were subsequently held. The first direct elections to the 589-member National Assembly were held in February 1993; all candidates were officially approved by the Communist Party and ran for election unopposed. The 14 provincial assemblies were elected in the same manner.

President of Council of State, Dr Fidel Castro Ruz, *appointed* 2 November 1976, *re-elected* 15 March 1993 for a five-year term

COUNCIL OF STATE *as at July 1995*

President, Dr Fidel Castro Ruz

First Vice-President, Raúl Castro Ruz

Vice-Presidents, Juan Almeida Bosque; José Ramón Machado Ventura; Abelardo Colome Ibarra; Carlos Lage Dávila; Esteban Lazo Hernandez

Secretary, José M. Miyar Barrueco

COUNCIL OF MINISTERS *as at July 1995*

President, Dr Fidel Castro Ruz

First Vice-President, Raúl Castro Ruz

Vice-Presidents, Dr Carlos Rafael Rodríguez; Pedro Miret Prieto; José Ramón Fernández Alvarez; Osmany Cienfuegos Gorriarán; Jaime Crombet Hernández-Baquero; Aldofo Diaz Suárez

Secretary, Carlos Lage Dávila

Ministers, Alfredo Jordan Morales (*Agriculture*); Marcos J. Portal Leon (*Basic Industry*); Gen. Silvano Colás Sanchez (*Communications*); Homero Crabb (*Construction*); José M. Cañete Alvarez (*Construction Materials Industry*); Armando Enrique Hart Davalos (*Culture*); Barbara Castillo Cuesta (*Domestic Trade*); José Luis Rodriguez Garcia (*Economy and Planning*); Luis Ignacio Gomez Gutierrez (*Education*); Manuel Millares Rodriguez (*Finance and Prices*); Orlando Felipe Rodriguez Romay (*Fishing*); Alejandro Roca Iglesias (*Food Industry*); Ernesto Meléndez Bachs (*Foreign Investment and Economic Co-operation*); Roberto Robaina (*Foreign Relations*); Ricardo Cabrisas Ruiz (*Foreign Trade*); Fernando Vecino Alegret

(*Higher Education*); Gen. Abelardo Colomé Ibarra (*Interior*); Ignacio González Planas (*Iron and Steel, Machine and Electronics Industries*); Carlos Amat Fores (*Justice*); Salvador Valdes Mesa (*Labour and Social Security*); Jesus Perez Othon (*Light Industry*); Carlos Dotres Martinez (*Public Health*); Raul Castro Ruz (*Revolutionary Armed Forces*); Rosa Elena Simeón Negrín (*Science, Technology and Environment*); Nelson Torres Perez (*Sugar Industry*); Osmany Cienfuegos Gorriarán (*Tourism*); Gen. Senén Casas Regueiro (*Transport*); Wilfredo Lopez Rodriguez (*Minister without Portfolio*)

President of the National Assembly, Ricardo Alarcón de Quesada

President of the National Bank, Francisco Soberon Valdez

EMBASSY OF THE REPUBLIC OF CUBA

167 High Holborn, London WCIV 6PA

Tel 0171–240 2488

Ambassador Extraordinary and Plenipotentiary, new appointment awaited

BRITISH EMBASSY

Edificio Bolívar, Cárcel 101–103, e Morro y Prado, Apartado 1069, Havana.

Tel: Havana 33 1771

Ambassador Extraordinary and Plenipotentiary, His Excellency Philip McLean, CMG, apptd 1994

DEFENCE

Cuba has a total active armed forces strength of 106,000 personnel, including 74,500 conscripts who serve for two years. In addition, there are 135,000 ready reserves who serve for 45 days a year and a territorial militia of 1,300,000 personnel. Paramilitary Ministry of Interior personnel number 15,000.

The Army numbers 85,000 and uses reservists to man many units. The Navy has a strength of 6,000 (3,000 conscripts), including two marine battalions. The Air Force has 15,000 personnel.

The last former Soviet combat personnel left Cuba in 1993, but 810 Russian military advisers remain to operate military intelligence facilities. The United States has 2,250 naval personnel at Guantanamo Bay Naval Base, which has been leased since before the 1959 revolution.

ECONOMY

After the revolution virtually all land and industrial and commercial enterprises were nationalized. With the end of Cuba's privileged trading relationships with the Soviet bloc in 1989, the economy has deteriorated sharply. GDP has fallen by 75 per cent in 1989–94, and the economy is operating at only 25 per cent of industrial capacity. Economic difficulties have forced the government to introduce free-market economic reforms to prevent the worsening of food, fuel and mechanical parts shortages. In July 1993 the government legalized the holding of US dollars by private individuals in an attempt to gain hard currency reserves for the state. Since August 1993 individual private enterprise and small businesses have been allowed again, and state farms are being transformed into co-operatives run by private individuals who may sell produce on the open market. In May 1994 the National Assembly approved austerity measures, including reducing subsidies to loss-making state industries, price rises for selected goods and services, and the selective introduction of an income tax system. The currency is to be made convertible.

Partially successful efforts are being made to diversify the economy and encourage foreign investment, although sugar is still its mainstay and principal source of foreign exchange. In 1989–90 the harvest was 8.04 million tons but this dropped in 1993–4 to 4.0m tons owing to a lack of fuel and spare parts. Domestic oil production is rising and reached 1.3m tonnes in 1993, meeting 40 per cent of domestic demand. Production of nickel is also rising, reaching 45,000 tonnes in 1993.

The tourism industry has expanded since 1986. In 1993 544,000 tourists visited Cuba, generating US$700 million in gross income. The total foreign debt stands at US$16,000 million.

TRADE

Cuba's exports dropped from US$8.1 billion in 1989 to US$1.7 billion in 1993 while imports declined by 73 per cent. Trade between Cuba and the former socialist economies of Europe is now less than 10 per cent of pre-1989 levels. A new Russian-Cuban trade deal was signed in 1992 under which Russia promised to buy limited quantities of sugar in return for selling at world prices. The US total trade and economic embargo remains in force. Principal exports are sugar, nickel, seafood, citrus fruits, tobacco and rum.

Trade with UK	1993	1994
Imports from UK	£14,009,000	£26,456,000
Exports to UK	8,000,000	10,634,000

There are 12,700 km of railway track, of which 5,000 km are in public service. In 1986 there were 13,247 km of road. At present scheduled international air services run to Central and South American countries and Europe.

CULTURE

Education is compulsory and free. In 1964 illiteracy was officially declared to be eliminated. The press and broadcasting are under the control of the government.

CYPRUS
Kypriaki Dimokratia / Kibris Cumhuriyeti

Cyprus has an area of 3,572 sq. miles (9,251 sq. km). Its greatest length is 140 miles and greatest breadth 60 miles, situated at 35°N. latitude and 33° 30′E. longitude. It is about 40 miles from the nearest point of Asia Minor. The climate is Mediterranean, with a hot dry summer and a variable warm winter.

The population in 1994 was estimated at 725,000. There are two major communities, Greek Cypriots (81.6 per cent) and Turkish Cypriots (18.4 per cent), and minorities of Armenians, Maronites and others.

CAPITAL – Nicosia (Lefkosia), with a population of 181,000 (in the government-controlled area); the other principal towns are ΨLimassol, ΨFamagusta, ΨLarnaca, Paphos and Kyrenia.
CURRENCY – Cyprus pound (C£) of 100 cents.
FLAG – White with a gold map of Cyprus above a wreath of olive.
NATIONAL ANTHEM – Ode to Freedom.
NATIONAL DAY – 1 October (Independence Day).

GOVERNMENT

Cyprus came under British administration from 1878, and was formally annexed to Britain in 1914 on the outbreak of war with Turkey. From 1925 to 1960 it was a Crown Colony. Following the launching in 1955 of an armed campaign by EOKA in support of union with Greece, a state of emergency was declared which lasted for four years. An agreement was signed on 19 February 1959 between the United Kingdom, Greece, Turkey, and the Greek and Turkish Cypriots which provided that Cyprus would be an independent republic.

The island became independent on 16 August 1960. The constitution provided for a Greek Cypriot President and a Turkish Cypriot Vice-President elected for a five-year term by the Greek and Turkish communities respectively. The House of Representatives, elected for five years by universal suffrage of each community separately, was to consist of 35 Greek and 15 Turkish members. The constitution proved unworkable and led to intercommunal trouble. The UN Peace-Keeping Force in Cyprus (UNFICYP) was set up in 1964; its mandate was last renewed on 15 June 1995 for six months.

A general election was held for the House of Representatives (expanded to 56 Greek Cypriot and 24 vacant Turkish Cypriot seats) in 1991, resulting in the parties gaining the following seats: Democratic Rally-Liberal Party 20; AKEL (Communist) 18; Democratic Party (Centre) 16; EDEK (Socialist) 2. The last presidential election was held in 1993 and won by Glafcos Clerides of the Democratic Rally-Liberal Party.

DIVISION

In 1974, mainland Greek officers of the Greek Cypriot National Guard under instructions from the military junta in Athens launched a coup d'état against President Makarios and installed a former EOKA member, Nikos Sampson, in his place. Turkey, reserving to itself the right to maintain constitutional order and the independence and territorial integrity of the island, invaded northern Cyprus and occupied over a third of the island. In 1975 a 'Turkish Federated State of Cyprus' under Rauf Denktash was declared in this area, its constitution being approved by referendum. In 1983 a 'Declaration of Statehood' was issued which purported to establish the 'Turkish Republic of Northern Cyprus'. The declaration was condemned by the UN Security Council and only Turkey has recognized the new 'state'. In 1985 a referendum in the north of Cyprus approved a constitution for the 'Turkish Republic of Northern Cyprus', Denktash was elected President of the 'state' and a general election was held. Denktash was re-elected in 1990 and April 1995 and general elections were held in 1990 and 1993.

Since 1974 attempts to reach a settlement have focused on intercommunal talks under the auspices of the UN. In 1992 a UN plan for a bizonal bi-communal federal state, giving the Turkish community a veto over all the important decisions of the government and parliament, was approved by the UN Security Council and in principle by the Greek community but not by the Turkish.

President, Glafcos Clerides, *elected* 14 February 1993

COUNCIL OF MINISTERS *as at August 1995*
Foreign Affairs, Alecos Michaelides
Interior, Dinos Michaelides
Finance, Christodoulos Christodoulou
Education and Culture, Claire Angelidou
Justice and Public Order, Alecos Evangelou
Defence, Costas Eliades
Communications and Works, Adamos Adamides
Health, Manolis Christofides
Commerce and Industry, Kyriacos Christophy
Labour and Social Insurance, Andreas Moushouttas
Agriculture, Environment and Natural Resources, Costas Petrides

CYPRUS HIGH COMMISSION
93 Park Street, London WIY 4ET
Tel 0171-499 8272
High Commissioner, His Excellency Angelos Angelides,
apptd 1990
Counsellor and Consul-General, George Vyrides
Counsellor, A. Georghiades (*Commerce*)

BRITISH HIGH COMMISSION
Alexander Pallis Street (PO Box 1978), Nicosia
Tel: Nicosia 2-473131
High Commissioner, His Excellency David Christopher
Madden, apptd 1994
Counsellor and Deputy High Commissioner, C. B. Jennings
Defence Adviser, Col. J. A. Anderson
First Secretary (Commercial), P. J. Newman

BRITISH COUNCIL DIRECTOR, Robert Frost, PO Box
5654, 3 Museum Street, 1097 Nicosia

BRITISH SOVEREIGN AREAS
The UK retained full sovereignty and jurisdiction over two
areas of 99 square miles in all: Akrotiri–Episkopi–Paramali
and Dhekelia–Pergamos–Ayios Nicolaos–Xylophagou.
This includes use of roads and other facilities. The British
Administrator of these areas is appointed by The Queen
and is responsible to the Secretary of State for Defence.
The combined total of army and RAF personnel stationed
in the areas is 3,900.
Administrator of the British Sovereign Areas, Air Cdre P. Millar

ECONOMY

Agriculture still occupies a prime position in the economy,
employing 12 per cent of the workforce and producing 31
per cent of exports. Main products are citrus fruits, grapes
and vine products, meat, milk, potatoes and other vegetables. Manufacturing, construction, distribution and other
service industries are other major employers. Tourism is
the main growth industry with two million tourists
producing C£1,075 million in foreign exchange earnings
in 1994; it contributed 25 per cent of GDP and employed
25 per cent of the workforce. Over 5,000 foreign firms and
individuals have registered as offshore companies in
Cyprus, and 20 per cent of the world's ships are Cypriot
registered.
    Britain continues to be the most important trading
partner, taking 29 per cent of exports in 1994 and supplying
12 per cent of imports. Cyprus is seeking to diversify its
export markets away from the Middle East towards the
EU.

TRADE
There is a large visible trade deficit (C£870.9 million in
1994), which is offset by invisible earnings, particularly
from tourism. The current account in 1994 showed a
surplus of C£54.8m.

	1993	1994
Imports	C£1,116.1m	C£1,251.6m
Exports (including re-exports)	387.3m	438.3m
Trade with UK	1993	1994
Imports from UK	£235,930,000	£245,192,000
Exports to UK	136,217,000	120,857,000

CZECH REPUBLIC
Česká Republika

The Czech Republic, composed of Bohemia and Moravia,
has an area of 30,441 sq. miles (78,664 sq. km). Bohemia is
surrounded by mountain ranges while Moravian land
stretches to the Danubian basin. The republic is bordered
by Poland in the north-east, Germany in the west and
north-west, Austria in the south and Slovakia in the south-
east.
    The population (1991 census) is 10,302,000, of which 95
per cent is Czech and 3 per cent Slovak. The majority are
Roman Catholic, with a small Protestant minority. Czech is
the official language.

CAPITAL – Prague (Praha) on the Vltava (Moldau), with a
population (1991) of 1,215,076. Other major cities are
Brno (Brün) (391,093), Ostrava (331,241) and Plzeň
(174,676).
CURRENCY – Koruna (Kc) or Czech crown of 100 Haléřů
(Heller).
FLAG – White over red horizontally with a blue triangle
extending from the hoist to the centre of the flag. (The
Czech Republic retained the former Czechoslovak
federal flag.)
NATIONAL ANTHEM – Kde Domov Můj (Where is my
Motherland).
NATIONAL DAY – 28 October.

HISTORY

The area which is now the Czech Republic came under the
rule of the Habsburg dynasty in 1526 and remained part of
the Austro-Hungarian Empire until 1918. Austrian attempts to Germanize the Czech lands in the 18th and 19th
centuries led to the rise of Czech nationalism in the late
19th century. The independence of Czechoslovakia was
proclaimed on 28 October 1918 following an amalgamation of Bohemia, Moravia, Slovakia and Ruthenia and was
confirmed by the Versailles Peace Conference in 1919.
    Czechoslovakia was forced to cede the ethnic German
Sudetenland to Nazi Germany in 1938 after the Munich
Agreement. German forces invaded the Czech Republic in
March 1939 and incorporated it into Germany while
Slovakia became a puppet state. The Czech Republic was
liberated by Soviet and American forces in May 1945. The
pre-war democratic Czechoslovak state was re-established
in 1945, having ceded Ruthenia to the Soviet Union, with
the Communist Party in a strong political position. The
Communists took power in a coup in 1948 and remained in
power until 1989.
    In 1968 the Communist Party under Alexander Dubček
embarked on a political and economic reform programme
(the Prague Spring). The reforms were suppressed following an invasion by Warsaw Pact troops on the night of 20
August 1968, and were abandoned when Gustáv Husák
became leader of the Communist Party in 1969.
    Opposition to Communist Party rule gathered pace in
the late 1980s and mass protests in November 1989 led to
the resignation of the Communist Party Central Committee. The Communist Party was forced to concede its
monopoly of power and on 10 December a new government was appointed in which only half the ministers were
Communists. Husák resigned as President and was replaced by the dissident writer Václav Havel. Free elections
were held in June 1990 in which the Communist Party was
defeated.

GOVERNMENT

Legislative elections in June 1992 returned the Civic Democratic Party and the Movement for a Democratic Slovakia as the dominant parties in the Czech and Slovak republics respectively. Talks between Czech and Slovak leaders on continuing the federation broke down because of the insistence of Vladimir Meciar, the Slovak leader, on a declaration of Slovak sovereignty. An interim federal government was sworn in in July 1992 and in late 1992 the leaders of the Czech and Slovak republics agreed to dissolve the federation and form two sovereign states; this took effect on 1 January 1993.

The elections of June 1992 had returned the Civil Democratic Party (ODS) as the largest party in the Czech parliament, and it formed a coalition government with three other centre-right parties in July 1992 which was sworn in as the government of the Czech Republic on 1 January 1993. The former federal President Havel was elected President.

The Czech constitution vests legislative power in the bicameral parliament, comprising a 200-member Chamber of Deputies elected for a four-year term and an 81-member Senate elected for a six-year term, one-third being renewed every two years. The President is elected by parliament for a five-year term. Executive power is held by the Prime Minister and Council of Ministers. A two-thirds majority in parliament is necessary to amend the constitution, and federal laws remain in place unless superseded by Czech ones. A Constitutional Court has been established comprising 15 judges nominated by the President for ten-year terms with Senate approval.

HEAD OF STATE
President, Václav Havel, *elected* 26 January 1993, *sworn in* 2 February 1993

COUNCIL OF MINISTERS *as at July 1995*
Prime Minister, Vaclav Klaus (ODS)
Deputy Prime Minister, Finance, Ivan Kocarnik (ODS)
Deputy Prime Minister, Agriculture, Josef Lux (KDU-CSL)
Deputy Prime Minister, Jan Kalvoda (ODA)
Foreign Affairs, Josef Zieleniec (ODS)
Industry and Trade, Vladimir Dlouhy (ODA)
Economy, Karel Dyba (ODS)
Health, Ludek Rubas (ODS)
Interior, Jan Ruml (ODS)
Culture, Pavel Tigrid (KDU-CSL)
Education, Ivan Pilip (KDS)
Labour and Social Affairs, Jindrich Vodicka (ODS)
State Control, Igor Nemec (ODS)
Privatization, Jiri Skalicky (ODA)
Environment, Frantisek Benda (KDS)
Justice, Jiri Novak (ODS)
Economic Competition, Stanislav Belehradek (KDU-CSL)
Defence, Vilém Holáň (KDU-CSL)
Transport, Jan Strasky (ODS)

ODS Civic Democratic Party; KDU-CSL Christian Democratic Union–Czech People's Party; ODA Civic Democratic Alliance; KDS Christian Democratic Party

EMBASSY OF THE CZECH REPUBLIC
26–30 Kensington Palace Gardens, London W8 4QY
Tel 0171-243 1115
Ambassador Extraordinary and Plenipotentiary, His Excellency Karel Kühnl, apptd 1993
Minister-Counsellor, Milan Jakobec
Military Attaché, Maj.-Gen. S. Thurnvald
Counsellor (Commercial), J. Žabža

BRITISH EMBASSY
Thunovská 14, 11800 Prague 1
Tel: Prague 10439
Ambassador Extraordinary and Plenipotentiary, His Excellency Sir Michael Burton, KCVO, CMG, apptd 1994
Counsellor and Deputy Head of Mission, C. M. T. Elmes
Defence and Military Attaché, Col. W. E. Nowosielski-Slopowron
First Secretary (Commercial), J. Cummins, MBE
First Secretary (Management) and Consul, D. J. Jackson
Cultural Attaché, W. Jefferson, OBE (*British Council Director*)

ECONOMY

Under Communist rule industry was state-owned and nearly all agricultural land was cultivated by state or co-operative farms. An economic reform programme began in 1990 to produce a free-market economy, and the government of the Czech Republic has continued to follow the policies of the former federal government. This has necessitated a restrictive monetary policy to stem inflation and a restructuring of industry to be competitive, and these were major reasons for the break with Slovakia. As a result, foreign investment (US$4,000 million in 1989–94) and private enterprises have grown and reliance on trade with the former Soviet bloc countries has ended. Unemployment has risen but is still low (4 per cent), and a trade-liberalizing association agreement with the EU is in operation.

Privatization of state enterprises began in May 1993 and by late 1995 over 90 per cent of the economy had been privatized. The state continues to own and subsidize a few enterprises, such as the national airline and parts of the Skoda engineering group. Overall output dropped in 1990–2 but has grown since 1993, as has GDP (5 per cent growth in 1994). The budget and current account remain in surplus, foreign debt is small, and foreign currency reserves had risen to US$5,300 million by late 1994.

A customs union between the Czech and Slovak Republics is in place but separate currencies were introduced in February 1993 following speculation.

The Czech Republic is not rich in minerals, although significant quantities of coal and lignite are mined. Principal agricultural products are sugar-beet, potatoes and cereal crops; the timber industry is also very important. Having been the major industrial area of the Austro-Hungarian Empire, the country has long been industrialized, and machinery, industrial consumer goods and raw materials are major exports.

TRADE WITH UK	1993	1994
Imports from UK	£287,568,000	£374,453,000
Exports to UK	245,265,000	278,301,000

CULTURE

The Reformation gave a widespread impulse to Czech literature, the writings of Jan Hus (martyred in 1415 as a religious and social reformer) familiarizing the people with Wyclif's teaching. This impulse endured to the close of the 17th century when Jan Amos Komensky or Comenius (1592–1670) was expelled from the country. Under Austrian rule and with the pursuit of Germanization, there was a period of stagnation until the national revival in the 19th century. Authors of international reputation include Jaroslav Hašek (1883–1923), Jaroslav Seifert (1901–86, Nobel Prize for Literature, 1985), Václav Havel (b. 1936) and Milan Kundera (b. 1929).

EDUCATION

Education is compulsory and free for all children from the ages of six to 16. There are seven universities in the Czech Republic, of which the oldest and most famous is Charles University in Prague (founded 1348). In addition there are a considerable number of other institutions of university standing, technical colleges, agricultural colleges, etc.

DENMARK
Kongeriget Danmark

Denmark is a kingdom of northern Europe, consisting of the islands of Zealand, Funen, Lolland, etc., the peninsula of Jutland, the outlying island of Bornholm in the Baltic, and the Faröes and Greenland. It is situated between 54° 34' and 57° 45' N. latitude and 8° 4'–15° 12' E. longitude, with an area of 16,629 sq. miles (43,069 sq. km), and a population (official estimate 1993) of 5,180,614.

CAPITAL – ΨCopenhagen, population (1992) 464,566; Greater Copenhagen 1,339,395; ΨAarhus 204,139; ΨOdense 140,886; ΨAalborg 114,970; ΨEsbjerg 72,205; ΨRanders 55,358.
CURRENCY – Danish krone (Kr) of 100 øre.
FLAG – Red, with white cross.
NATIONAL ANTHEMS – Kong Kristian and Det er et yndigt land.
NATIONAL DAY – 5 June (Constitution Day).

GOVERNMENT

Under the Constitution of the Kingdom of Denmark Act 1953, the legislature consists of one chamber, the *Folketing*, of not more than 179 members, including two for the Faröes and two for Greenland, which is elected for a four-year term. The voting age is 18 with voting based on a proportional resspresentation system with a 2 per cent threshold for parliamentary representation.

On 25 January 1993 a coalition government of the Social Democrat, Centre Democrat, Social Liberal and Christian People's Party was sworn in after the previous Conservative-Liberal coalition had resigned. After the last parliamentary election on 21 September 1994, a new coalition government of the Social Democrat, Social Liberal and Centre Democrat parties was formed. The state of the parties in the Folketing is: Social Democrat Party (SD) 63; Liberals (L) 44; Conservatives (C) 28; Socialist People's Party (SP) 13; Progress Party (P) 10; Social Liberal Party (SL) 8; Red-Green Alliance 6; Centre Democrat Party (CD) 5; Independent 1.

HEAD OF STATE
HM The Queen of Denmark, Queen Margrethe II, KG, *born* 16 April 1940, *succeeded* 14 January 1972, *married* 10 June 1967, Count Henri de Monpezat (Prince Henrik of Denmark), and *has issue* Crown Prince Frederik (*see* below); Prince Joachim, *born* 7 June 1969
Heir, HRH Crown Prince Frederik, *born* 26 May 1968

CABINET *as at August 1995*
Prime Minister, Poul Nyrup Rasmussen (SD)
Business and Industry, Mimi Jakobsen (CD)
Economic Affairs and Nordic Co-operation, Marianne Jelved (SL)
Finance, Mogens Lykketoft (SD)
Foreign Affairs, Niels Helveg Petersen (SL)
Agriculture and Fisheries, Henrik Dam Christensen (SD)
Environment and Energy, Svend Auken (SD)

Education, Ole Vig Jensen (SL)
Housing and Building, Ole Løvig Simonsen (SD)
Development Co-operation, Poul Nielson (SD)
Interior and Ecclesiastical Affairs, Birthe Weiss (SD)
Labour, Jytte Andersen (SD)
Taxation, Carsten Koch (SD)
Defence, Hans Haekkerup (SD)
Cultural Affairs, Jytte Hilden (SD)
Social Affairs, Karen Jespersen (SD)
Transport, Jan Trøjborg (SD)
Justice, Bjørn Westh (SD)
Health, Yvonne Herløv Andersen (CD)
Research, Frank Jensen (SD)

ROYAL DANISH EMBASSY
55 Sloane Street, London SWIX 9SR
Tel 0171–333.0200
Ambassador Extraordinary and Plenipotentiary, His Excellency Rudolph Thorning-Petersen, apptd 1989
Minister, Mrs A. Hugau
Counsellor (Commercial), Jorgen Gulev
Defence Attaché, Capt. P. Groos

BRITISH EMBASSY
36–40 Kastelsvej, DK-2100 Copenhagen Ø
Tel: Copenhagen 35 264600
Ambassador Extraordinary and Plenipotentiary, His Excellency Hugh J. Arbuthnott, CMG, apptd 1993
Counsellor and Deputy Head of Mission, A. M. Layden
Counsellor, R. L. Owen
Defence Attaché, Cmdr. R. Kirkwood, RN
First Secretary (Management) and Consul, B. Robertson

There are Consulates at Aabenraa, Aalborg, Aarhus, Esbjerg, Fredericia, Herning, Odense, Rønne (Bornholm); at Tórshavn (Faröe Islands); and Nuuk (Godthåb) (Greenland).

BRITISH COUNCIL REPRESENTATIVE, Len Tyler, Gammel Mont 123, 1117 Copenhagen K

DEFENCE

Total active armed forces number 27,000 (8,500 conscripts). Conscripts serve for five to 12 months. Reserves number 70,000 personnel.

Army personnel number 16,300 (7,100 conscripts) but the 54,000 reservists reinforce peacetime units. Equipment includes 450 main battle tanks, 580 armoured personnel carriers and 390 artillery pieces.

The Navy has 4,600 personnel (700 conscripts) with three frigates, five submarines, 35 patrol and coastal craft and eight armed helicopters.

The Air Force numbers 6,100 personnel (700 conscripts) with 63 combat aircraft.

Denmark deploys a 975-strong infantry battalion with UN forces in Croatia, 305 troops as part of a Nordic battalion in Bosnia-Hercegovina and one frigate in the Adriatic.

ECONOMY

Of the labour force, in 1991 6 per cent was engaged in agriculture, fishing, forestry, etc.; 26 per cent in manufacturing, building and construction; 21 per cent in the retailing, transport, financial and insurance service sectors and 31 per cent in public services. The chief agricultural products are pigs, cattle, dairy products, poultry and eggs, seeds, cereals and sugar beet; manufactures are mostly based on imported raw materials but there are also considerable imports of finished goods. Denmark is self-sufficient in oil and natural gas after off-shore discoveries in recent years.

FINANCE

Budget estimates	1993	1994
Revenue	Kr307,414m	Kr334,533m
Expenditure	351,359m	388,901m

TRADE

Denmark's balance of payments on current account showed a deficit for 1993 of Kr28,700 million. The foreign debt in 1993 was Kr214,000 million.

The principal imports are industrial raw materials, consumer goods, construction inputs, machinery, raw materials, vehicles and textile products. The chief exports are miscellaneous manufactured articles, agricultural and dairy products.

Trade with UK	1993	1994
Imports from UK	£1,574,963,000	£1,771,309,000
Exports to UK	2,046,184,000	2,107,577,000

COMMUNICATIONS

Mercantile marine (ships above 250 gross tonnage) at the beginning of 1993 totalled 634 ships. In 1985 there was 2,471 km of state-owned railway and 494 km of privately-owned railway systems.

EDUCATION AND CULTURE

Education is free and compulsory. Special schools are numerous, commercial, technical and agricultural predominating. There are universities at Copenhagen (founded in 1479), Aarhus (1928), Odense (1966), Roskilde (1972) and Aalborg (1974).

The Danish language is akin to Swedish and Norwegian. Danish literature, ancient and modern, embraces all forms of expression, familiar names being Hans Christian Andersen (1805–75), Søren Kierkegaard (1813–55) and Karen Blixen (1885–1962). Some 47 newspapers are published in Denmark; nine daily papers are published in Copenhagen.

THE FARÖES

The Faröes, or Sheep Islands have an area of 540 sq. miles (1,399 sq. km) and a population (1992) of 47,287. The capital is Tórshavn.

Since 1948 the Faröes have had a degree of home rule. The islands are governed by a *Løgting* of 26 members and a *Landsstyre* of four members which deals with special Faröes affairs, and send two representatives to the *Folketing* at Copenhagen. The Faröes are not part of the EU.

The main industries are agriculture, fishing, fish-farming, whaling and the public sector; tourism is growing in importance.

Prime Minister, Edmund Joensen

TRADE WITH UK	1993	1994
Imports from UK	£7,767,000	£10,747,000
Exports to UK	52,601,000	67,936,000

GREENLAND

Greenland has a total area of 2,175,600 sq. km, of which about 16 per cent is ice-free, and a population (1993) of 55,117. It is divided into three provinces: West, North and East. The capital is Nuuk (Godthåb).

Greenland attained a status of internal autonomy on 1 May 1979 and a government (*Landsstyre*) was established. It has a *Landsting* of 31 members and sends two representatives to the *Folketing* at Copenhagen. Greenland negotiated its withdrawal from the EC, without discontinuing relations with Denmark, and left on 1 February 1985.

The traditional industries of fishing, sealing, whaling and reindeer herding are the most important sectors of the economy, together with public services and administration. Mineral and oil prospecting revealed deposits of lead, zinc, iron ore, oil, gas and uranium. Commercial exploitation of these resources has begun. The trade of Greenland is mainly under the management of the Grønlands Handel. The USA has acquired certain rights to maintain air bases in Greenland.

Premier, Lars Emil Johansen

TRADE WITH UK	1993	1994
Imports from UK	£2,209,000	£927,000
Exports to UK	5,904,000	11,295,000

DJIBOUTI
Jumhouriyya Djibouti

Djibouti is situated on the north-east coast of Africa and borders Eritrea, Ethiopia and Somalia. It has an area of 8,494 sq. miles (22,000 sq. km.). The climate is harsh and much of the country is semi-arid desert. It has a population (1991 census) of 520,000, most of which is either Afar or Issas.

CAPITAL – Ψ Djibouti, population (1991) 340,700.
CURRENCY – Djibouti franc of 100 centimes.
FLAG – Blue over green with white triangle in the hoist containing a red star.
NATIONAL DAY – 27 June (Independence Day).

GOVERNMENT

Formerly French Somaliland and then the French Territory of the Afars and the Issas, the Republic of Djibouti became independent on 27 June 1977. The sole legal party was formerly the *Rassemblement Populaire pour le Progrès* (RPP, the Popular Rally for Progress). A multiparty constitution was adopted by referendum in 1992 and subsequent multiparty elections held in December 1992 were won by the ruling RPP with 77 per cent of the vote and all 65 seats in the Chamber of Deputies. President Aptidon was re-elected for a fourth six-year term in 1993. However, less than half the electorate voted in either election and the Front for the Restoration of Unity and Democracy (FRUD) boycotted both.

INSURGENCY

Armed FRUD rebels, their support based among ethnic Afars, have been fighting the government since 1991 in protest at the concentration of political power in the hands of the Somali-speaking Issas at the expense of the nomadic Afars. FRUD gained control of most of the country in 1992 but in 1993 was driven back into the north by government forces. A formal peace agreement with the government was signed by the majority faction of FRUD in December 1994 under which FRUD will transform itself into a political party and its soldiers will be absorbed into the national army. A minority faction has condemned the agreement and continues to fight.

HEAD OF STATE

President, Hassan Gouled Aptidon, *elected* 1977, *re-elected* 1981, 1987 and 9 May 1993

CABINET *as at July 1995*

Prime Minister, Planning and Territorial Administration, Barkat Gourad Hamadou
Justice and Islamic Affairs, Moumin Bahdon Farah
Foreign Affairs and International Co-operation, Mohamed Moussa Chehem
Interior and Decentralization, Idriss Harbi Farah
National Defence, Ahmed Boulaleh Barre
Finance and Economy, Mohamed Ali Mohamed
Ports, Transport and Telecommunications, Saleh Omar Hildid
National Education, Ahmed Guirreh Waberi
Youth and Sports and Culture, Abdou Bolock Abdou
Public Health and Social Affairs, Ali Mohamed Daoud
Civil Service and Administrative Reform, Mohamed Dini Farah
Public Works, Construction and Housing, Atteyeh Ismael Waiss
Industry, Energy and Mines, Abdi Farah
Labour and Professional Organizations, Osman Robleh Daach
Agriculture and Water Resources, Ougoure Kifle Ahmed
Commerce and Tourism, Rifki Abdoulkader

EMBASSY OF THE REPUBLIC OF DJIBOUTI

26 rue Emile Ménier, 75116 Paris, France
Tel: Paris 47274922
Ambassador Extraordinary and Plenipotentiary, His Excellency Ahmed Omar Farah, apptd 1991

BRITISH AMBASSADOR, His Excellency Duncan Christopher, resides at Addis Ababa, Ethiopia

BRITISH CONSULATE

PO Box 81, 9–11 Rue de Geneve, Djibouti
Honorary Consul, J. McCauley

The French continue to maintain army, navy and air force bases in Djibouti, with a total strength of 3,800 personnel. Djibouti has an excellent port, an international airport, and a railway line runs to Addis Ababa.

TRADE WITH UK	1993	1994
Imports from UK	£21,601,000	£13,701,000
Exports to UK	1,146,000	373,000

DOMINICA
The Commonwealth of Dominica

Dominica, in the Lesser Antilles, lies in the Windward Group, between 15° 12′ and 15° 39′ N. latitude and 61° 14′ and 61° 29′ W. longitude, 95 miles south of Antigua. It is about 29 miles long and 16 miles wide, with an area of 289 sq. miles (748.5 sq. km). The island is of volcanic origin and very mountainous, and the soil is very fertile. The temperature varies, according to the altitude, from 13° to 29°C. The population is 72,000 (1992 UN estimate).

CAPITAL – ΨRoseau, on the south-west coast, population 15,850. The other principal town is Portsmouth, population 3,620.
CURRENCY – East Caribbean dollar (EC$) of 100 cents.
FLAG – Green ground with a cross overall of yellow, black and white stripes, and in the centre a red disc charged with a Sisserou parrot in natural colours within a ring of ten green stars.
NATIONAL ANTHEM – Isle of Beauty.
NATIONAL DAY – 3 November (Independence Day).

GOVERNMENT

The island was discovered by Columbus in 1493, when it was a stronghold of the Caribs, who remained virtually the sole inhabitants until the French established settlements in the 18th century. It was captured by the British in 1759 but passed back and forth between France and Britain until 1805, after which British possession was not challenged. From 1871 to 1939 Dominica was part of the Leeward Islands Colony, then from 1940 the island was a unit of the Windward Islands group. Internal self-government from 1967 was followed on 3 November 1978 by independence as a republic.

Executive authority is vested in the President, who is elected by the House of Assembly for not more than two terms of five years. Parliament consists of the President and the House of Assembly (21 representatives elected by universal adult suffrage for a five-year term) and nine Senators, five of whom are appointed on the advice of the Prime Minister and the other four on the advice of the Leader of the Opposition.

The last general election was held on 12 June 1995 and won by the Dominica United Workers' Party.

HEAD OF STATE

President, His Excellency Crispin Sorhaindo, OBE, *elected* 4 October 1993, *took office* 25 October 1993

CABINET *as at July 1995*

Prime Minister, External Affairs, Legal Affairs and Labour, Hon. Edison James
Finance, Industry and Planning, Hon. Julius Timothy
Tourism, Ports and Employment, Sen. Hon. Norris Prevost
Health and Social Security, Hon. Doreen Paul
Trade and Marketing, Hon. Norris Charles
Community Development and Women's Affairs, Hon. Gertrude Roberts
Communications, Works and Housing, Hon. Earl Williams
Agriculture and the Environment, Hon. Peter Carbon
Education, Sports and Youth Affairs, Hon. Ronald Green

HIGH COMMISSION FOR THE COMMONWEALTH OF DOMINICA

1 Collingham Gardens, London SW5 0HW
Tel 0171–370 5194/5
High Commissioner, His Excellency Ashworth Elwin, apptd 1992

BRITISH HIGH COMMISSIONER, His Excellency Richard Thomas, CMG, resides at Bridgetown, Barbados

BRITISH CONSULATE

PO Box 6, Roseau
Honorary Consul, R. W. Duckworth

ECONOMY

Agriculture is the principal occupation, with tropical and citrus fruits the main crops. Products for export are bananas, lime juice, lime oil, bay oil, copra and rum. Forestry, fisheries and agro-processing are being encouraged. The only commercially exploitable mineral is pumice, used chiefly for building purposes. Manufacturing consists largely of the processing of agricultural products.

TRADE WITH UK	1993	1994
Imports from UK	£10,226,000	£8,055,000
Exports to UK	23,534,000	18,892,000

DOMINICAN REPUBLIC
República Dominicana

The Dominican Republic, the eastern part of the island of Hispaniola (Haiti is the western part), is the oldest European settlement in America. The island lies between Cuba on the west and Puerto Rico on the east and the Dominican Republic covers an area of 18,816 sq. miles (48,734 sq. km). The climate is tropical in the lowlands and semi-tropical to temperate in the higher altitudes. The population (1992 UN estimate) is 7,459,000. Spanish is the language of the republic.

CAPITAL – Ψ Santo Domingo, population of the Capital District (1981 census) 1,313,172. Other centres, with populations (1981 census): Santiago de los Caballeros (550,372); La Vega (385,043); San Francisco De Macoris (235,544); San Juan (239,957); San Cristóbal (446,132).
CURRENCY – Dominican Republic peso (RD$) of 100 centavos.
FLAG – Divided into blue and red quarters by a white cross.
NATIONAL ANTHEM – Quisqueyanos Valientes, Alcemos (Brave men of Quisqueya, let's raise our song).
NATIONAL DAY – 27 February (Independence Day 1844).

GOVERNMENT

Santo Domingo was discovered by Columbus in 1492, and was a Spanish colony until 1821. In 1822 it was subjugated by the neighbouring Haitians who remained in control until 1844, when the Dominican Republic was proclaimed. The country was occupied by American marines from 1916 until 1924. From 1930 until 1961 (when he was assassinated) Gen. Rafael Trujillo ruled the country.
President Juan Bosch held office from December 1962 to September 1963, when he was deposed by a military junta. A left-wing revolt in favour of ex-President Bosch in April 1965 developed into civil war lasting until September the same year when Bosch's supporters were defeated by the arrival of US troops and a provisional President was elected. In November 1966 a new constitution was introduced. The last presidential election was held on 16 May 1994 and won by the incumbent President Balaguer amid allegations of violence, intimidation and vote-rigging. A national peace pact with opposition forces resulted in President Balaguer being sworn in for a term of two years and consecutive presidential terms being ended.
Executive power is vested in the President, who is directly elected for four-year terms and appoints the cabinet. Legislative power is exercised by the Congress, which has a term of four years concurrent with the presidency. The Congress comprises the Senate of 30 senators, one for each province and one for Santo Domingo, and the 120-member Chamber of Deputies.

HEAD OF STATE
President, Dr Joaquin Balaguer, *took office* 16 August 1986, *re-elected* 1990, 16 May 1994
Vice-President, Jacinto Peynado

CABINET *as at July 1995*
Presidency, Rafael Bello Andino
Finance, Florencío Lorenzo Silva
Foreign Affairs, Carlos Morales Troncoso
Education and Culture, Jacqueline Malagón
Agriculture, Luis Toral
Labour, Rafael Alburquerque
Public Health and Social Welfare, Dr Miguel A. Strepan
Industry and Trade, Juan González Pérez
Sports, Physical Education and Recreation, Cristobal Marte
Tourism, Jorge Elias
Interior and Police, Dr Atilio Guzmán Fernandez
Armed Forces, Lt.-Gen. Constantino Mato Villanueva
Without Portfolio, Domingo Gutiérrez

EMBASSY OF THE DOMINICAN REPUBLIC
17 rue La Fontaine, 75016 Paris, France
Tel: Paris 45206841
Ambassador Extraordinary and Plenipotentiary, His Excellency Dr Alfonso Canto Dinzey

HONORARY CONSULATE
6 Queen's Mansions, Brook Green, London w6 7EB
Tel: 0171-602 1885
Honorary Consul, J. de Wardener

BRITISH AMBASSADOR, His Excellency John Gerrard Flynn, CMG, resident at Caracas, Venezuela

BRITISH CONSULATE
Abraham Lincoln 552, Santo Domingo DR
Tel: Santo Domingo 5015 5010
Honorary Consul, M. Tejeda, MBE

COMMUNICATIONS

There are over 4,000 miles of roads and a direct road from Santo Domingo to Port-au-Prince, the capital of Haiti, but that part of it in the border area has fallen into disuse. The frontier has been closed since 1967, except for the section crossed by the main road linking the two capitals. A telephone system connects all the principal towns and there is a telegraph service to all parts of the world. There are more than 90 commercial broadcasting stations and six television stations.
There are two national airlines with an international airport 18 miles to the east of the capital and one near Puerto Plata on the north coast.

ECONOMY

Since 1990 the government has successfully reduced inflation from 100 per cent to 3 per cent a year and has increased output substantially. Large amounts of foreign debt have been paid off but unemployment remains high at 25 per cent. State subsidies were ended in 1995 in an attempt to reduce the budget deficit.
Sugar, coffee, cocoa, and tobacco are the most important crops. Other products are peanuts, maize, rice, bananas, molasses, salt, cement, ferro-nickel, gold, silver, cattle, sisal products, honey and chocolate. Light industry produces beer, tinned foodstuffs, glass products, textiles, soap, cigarettes, construction materials, plastic articles, shoes, papers, paint, rum, matches, peanut oil and other products.

TRADE
The chief imports are machinery, foodstuffs, iron and steel, cotton textiles and yarns, mineral oils (including petrol),

motor vehicles, chemical and pharmaceutical products, electrical equipment and accessories, construction material, paper and paper products, and rubber and rubber products. The chief exports are sugar, coffee, cocoa, tobacco, chocolate, molasses, bauxite, ferro-nickel and gold.

	1992	1993
Imports	RD$2,174.6m	RD$2,115.5m
Exports	562.4m	530.4m

Trade with UK	1993	1994
Imports from UK	£24,316,000	£24,708,000
Exports to UK	21,645,000	20,687,000

ECUADOR
República del Ecuador

Ecuador is an equatorial state of South America, extending from 1° 38′ N. to 4° 50′ S. latitude, and between 75° 20′ and 81° W. longitude, comprising an area of about 109,484 sq. miles (283,561 sq. km). It extends across the Western Andes, the highest peaks being Chimborazo (20,408 ft) and Ilinza (17,405 ft) in the Western Cordillera; and Cotopaxi (19,612 ft) and Cayambe (19,160 ft) in the Eastern Cordillera. Ecuador is watered by the Upper Amazon, and by the rivers Guayas, Mira, Santiago, Chone, and Esmeraldas on the Pacific coast. There are extensive forests.

The population (UN estimate 1992) is 10,741,000, descendants of the Spanish, aboriginal Indians, and Mestizos. Spanish is the principal language but Quechua is also a recognized language and is spoken by the majority of Indians.

CAPITAL – Quito, population (1991 estimate) 1,387,887; ΨGuayaquil (1,531,229) is the chief port; Cuenca (332,117).

CURRENCY – Sucre of 100 centavos.

FLAG – Three horizontal bands, yellow, blue and red (the yellow band twice the width of the others); emblem in centre.

NATIONAL DAY – 10 August (Independence Day).

GOVERNMENT

The former kingdom of Quito was conquered by the Incas of Peru in the latter part of the 15th century. Early in the 16th century Pizarro's conquests led to the inclusion of the present territory of Ecuador in the Spanish Vice-royalty of Quito. Independence was achieved in a revolutionary war which culminated in the battle of Mount Pichincha 1822.

After seven years of military rule, Ecuador returned to democracy in 1979. The 1978 constitution provides for an elected President and Vice-President who serve for a single four-year term. There is a unicameral National Congress which meets for two months a year and has 77 members, 12 of whom are elected on a national basis every four years and 65 on a provincial basis every two years. Voting is compulsory for all literate and voluntary for all illiterate citizens over the age of 18. The republic is divided into 21 provinces.

In the 1992 legislative election no party or coalition gained a majority but a loose agreement between various right-wing and centre-right parties enabled President Ballén to introduce a programme of economic reform, financial liberalization and privatization. This, together with reductions in state spending, caused social unrest in 1992–4 and led to the defeat of the governing parties in the May 1994 legislative elections. President Ballén has attempted to bypass a congress hostile to economic reform by constitutional changes to increase presidential power and reduce that of congress.

The border with Peru was demarcated by a 1942 treaty which was partly revoked by Ecuador in 1960 in relation to a disputed 50-mile stretch. An inconclusive four-week border war was fought with Peru in February 1995 until a ceasefire was signed on 1 March 1995.

HEAD OF STATE
President, Sixto Durán Ballén, _sworn in_ 10 August 1992
Vice-President, Alberto Dahik Garzozi

CABINET _as at August 1995_
Government Affairs, Marcelo Santos Vera
Foreign Affairs, Galo Leoro
Interior, Abraham Romero
National Defence, Jose Gallardo Roman
Education and Culture, Fausto Segovia
Finance and Public Credit, Mauricio Pinto
Public Works and Communications, Pedro Lopez Torres
Energy and Mines, Galo Abril
Industry, Commerce, Integration and Fisheries, José Vicente Maldonado
Labour, Alfredo Corral Borrero
Agriculture and Livestock, Mariano Gonzalez
Public Health, Alfredo Palacio
Social Welfare, Alberto Cárdenas Davalos
Information and Tourism, Armando Espinel Elizalde
Housing and Urban Development, Francisco Albornoz
Secretary-General of the Administration, Carlos Larreategui

EMBASSY OF ECUADOR
Flat 3B, 3 Hans Crescent, London SWIX OLS
Tel 0171–584 1367
Ambassador Extraordinary and Plenipotentiary, His Excellency Patricio Maldonado, apptd 1994

BRITISH EMBASSY
Av. Gonzalez Suarez, 111 (Casilla 314), Quito
Tel: Quito 560670
Ambassador Extraordinary and Plenipotentiary, His Excellency Richard Lavers, apptd 1993

There are British Consular Offices at Cuenca, Galápagos and Guayaquil.

BRITISH COUNCIL REPRESENTATIVE, Anthony Deyes, Av. Amazonas 1646, Orellana (Casilla 17078829), Quito

ECONOMY

Agriculture is the most important sector of the economy, supporting nearly 50 per cent of the population (particularly the poorest) and contributing 14.5 per cent of GDP and 19.5 per cent of exports. The main products for export are fish (mainly shrimps, tuna and sardines), bananas, which provide a third of agricultural exports, cocoa and coffee. Other important crops are sugar, corn, soya, rice, cotton, African palm (for oil), vegetables, fruit and timber, the temperate crops being produced mostly in the highlands. The main imports are manufactured goods and machinery.

The economy was transformed by the discovery in 1972 of major oil fields in the Oriente area and oil accounted for two-thirds of export earnings by 1981, but the fall in the price of oil has reduced economic growth. The oil is evacuated by a trans-Andean pipeline to the port of Balao (near Esmeraldas City). Ecuador withdrew from OPEC in 1992 in order to raise its production to 385,000 barrels per day by the end of 1992. The total foreign debt, estimated at US$12,500 million in early 1994, was rescheduled and reduced by the IMF in May 1994 and a US$184 million loan was also agreed.

TRADE WITH UK	1993	1994
Imports from UK	£48,269,000	£65,290,000
Exports to UK	19,855,000	22,891,000

COMMUNICATIONS

There are 23,256 km of permanent roads and 5,044 km of roads which are only open during the dry season. There are about 750 miles of railway. Ten commercial airlines operate international flights and there are internal services between all important towns. Two daily newspapers are published at Quito and four at Guayaquil.

EDUCATION

As a result of an intensive national programme more than 75 per cent of the population are now literate. Elementary education is free and compulsory. There are ten universities (three at Quito, three at Guayaquil, and one each at Cuenca, Machala, Loja and Portoviejo), polytechnic schools at Quito and Guayaquil and eight technical colleges in other provincial capitals.

GALÁPAGOS ISLANDS

The Galápagos (Giant Tortoise) Islands, forming the province of the Archipelago de Colón, were annexed by Ecuador in 1832. The archipelago lies in the Pacific, about 500 miles from the mainland. There are 12 large and several hundred smaller islands with a total area of about 3,000 sq. miles and an estimated population (1982) of 6,119. The capital is San Cristobal, on Chatham Island. Although the archipelago lies on the equator, the temperature of the surrounding water is well below average average owing to the Humboldt current. The province consists for the most part of National Park Territory, where unique marine birds, iguanas, and the giant tortoises are conserved. There is some local subsistence farming; the main industry, apart from tourism, is tuna and lobster fishing.

EGYPT
Al-Jumhuriyat Misr al-Arabiya

Egypt comprises Egypt proper, the peninsula of Sinai and a number of islands in the Gulf of Suez and Red Sea, of which the principal are Jubal, Shadwan, Gafatin and Zeberged (or St John's Island). This territory lies between 22° and 32° N. latitude and 24° and 37° E. longitude. Egypt borders the Mediterranean in the north, Sudan in the south and Libya in the west. The eastern border (of Sinai) borders on the Gaza Strip and Israel between Rafah and the Gulf of Aqaba. The total area is 386,662 sq. miles (1,001,449 sq. km).

The country is mainly flat but there are mountainous areas in the south-west, along the Red Sea coast and in the south of the Sinai peninsula; the highest peak is Mt Catherina (8,668 ft). Most of the land is desert and the Nile valley and delta were the only fertile areas until the opening of the Aswam Dam allowed areas of desert to be reclaimed by irrigation and fertilization. West of the Nile Valley is the Western desert, containing some depressions whose springs irrigate small areas (oases) of which the principal are Kharga, Dakhla, Farafra, Baharia and Siwa. The Eastern Desert between the Nile and the mountains along the Red Sea coast is mostly plateaux dissected by wadis (dry water-courses).

The population (official estimate 1994) is 57,850,000. The largest, or 'Egyptian' element, is a Hamito-Semite race, known in the rural districts as *Fellahin (fellâh,* ploughman or tiller of the soil). A second element is the *Bedouin,* or nomadic Arabs of the Western and Arabian deserts, who are now mainly semi-sedentary tent-dwellers on the outskirts of the cultivated end of the Nile Valley and the Fayûm. The third element is the *Nubian* of the Nile Valley between Aswân and Wadi-Halfa of mixed Arab and Negro blood. Over 90 per cent of the population are Muslims of the Sunni denomination, and most of the rest Coptic Christians.

CAPITAL – Cairo (population, 1994 official estimate, 13 million), stands on the Nile about 14 miles from the head of the delta. Its oldest part is the fortress of Babylon in old Cairo, with its Roman bastions and Coptic churches. The earliest Arab building is the Mosque of 'Amr (AD 643) and the most conspicuous is the Citadel (late 12th century), containing in its walls the Mosque of Mohamed Ali (19th century).
Other cities and towns are: Ψ Alexandria (population, 1994 official estimate, 3,419,000), founded 332 BC by Alexander the Great, was for over 1,000 years the capital of Egypt and a centre of Hellenic culture; Ismailia (400,000); ΨPort Said (526,000); Asyût (300,000); Faiyûm (180,000); ΨSuez (458,000).
CURRENCY – Egyptian pound (£E) of 100 piastres and 1,000 millièmes.
FLAG – Horizontal bands of red, white and black, with an eagle in the centre of the white band.
NATIONAL DAY – 23 July (Anniversary of Revolution in 1952).

HISTORY

The unification of the kingdoms of Lower and Upper Egypt under the Pharaohs *c.*3100 BC marked the establishment of the Egyptian state, with Memphis as its capital. Egypt was ruled for nearly 2,800 years by a succession of Pharaonic dynasties (31 in all), which built the pyramids at Gizeh. A period of Hellenic rule began in 332 BC, after the conquest of Egypt by Alexander the Great, followed by a period of rule by Rome (30 BC to AD 324) and then by the Byzantine Empire. In AD 640 Egypt was subjugated by Arab Muslim invaders, becoming a province of the Eastern Caliphate. In 1517 the country was incorporated in the Ottoman Empire, under which it remained until the early 19th century. A British Protectorate over Egypt lasted from 1914 to 1922, when Sultan Ahmed Fuad was proclaimed King of Egypt. In 1953 the monarchy was deposed and Egypt became a republic.

In 1956, as a result of Egypt's trade agreements with Communist countries, Britain and USA withdrew offers of financial aid and in retaliation President Nasser seized the assets of the Suez Canal Company. Egyptian occupation of the Canal Zone while repulsing an Israeli attack was used as a pretext for military action by Britain and France in support of their Suez Canal Company interests. A ceasefire and Anglo-French withdrawal were negotiated by the UN.

The Israeli invasion of 1956 overran the Sinai peninsula but six months later Israel withdrew and a UN peacekeeping force was established in the area. However, mounting tension culminated in a second invasion of Sinai (the Six Day War in June 1967) and occupation of the peninsula by Israel. Egypt's attempt to recapture the territory (the Yom Kippur War in October 1973) was unsuccessful but Sinai was returned to Egypt in 1982 under the treaty of 1979 which resulted from the Camp David talks and formally terminated a 31-year-old state of war between the two countries. The treaty with Israel caused Egypt to be ostracized by the rest of the Arab world until 1990 when its participation in the Gulf War helped to rehabilitate it.

GOVERNMENT

The constitution of 1971 provides for an executive President who appoints the Council of Ministers and determines government policy. The legislature is the People's Assembly which has 454 members, 444 of whom are elected, the remaining ten nominated by the President. The Shura Council or Consultative Assembly (258 members) has an advisory role.

The ruling National Democratic Party won the general election, boycotted by the major opposition parties, held in November and December 1990. President Mubarak was nominated by the legislature to run unopposed for a third six-year term in July 1993, and was elected in October.

INSURGENCY

Militant Muslim fundamentalists re-emerged in 1992 declaring war on the government and carrying out attacks on Coptic Christians, tourists, government ministers, civil servants and the security forces. Attacks have continued in 1993–5 and are concentrated in Upper Egypt and the Cairo area. The two main terrorist groups, the Gama'a el-Islamiya and Egyptian Islamic Jihad, extended their campaign in 1994 by ordering all foreigners to leave the country or face violent attacks. The government has reacted vigorously to the armed campaign with the arrest of 20,000 militants. By summer 1995, 750 civilians, militants and security force personnel had been killed and some 70 militants sentenced to death by military courts.

HEAD OF STATE

President, Muhammad Hosni Mubarak, *elected* 1981, re-elected 1987, 13 October 1993

COUNCIL OF MINISTERS *as at July 1995*

Prime Minister and International Co-operation, Dr Atef Muhammad Naguib Sidqi
Deputy PM and Minister of Planning, Dr Kamal Ahmed al-Ganzuri
Deputy PM and Minister of Agriculture, Animal Wealth, Fisheries and Land Reclamation, Dr Yussif Amin Wali
Defence and Military Production, Field Marshal Mohammed Hussein Tantawi
Foreign Affairs, Amre Moussa
Economy and Foreign Trade, Mohamed Mahmoud Baioumi
Finance, Dr Muhammad Ahmed el-Razzaz
Interior, Maj.-Gen. Hassan al-Alfi
Oil, Dr Hamdy El Bambi
Tourism, Mamdouh Beltagui
Justice, Farouq Saif al-Nasr
Culture, Farouq Hosni
Industry and Mineral Resources, Ibrahim Abdel-Wahed
Supply and Internal Trade, Ahmed Gueily
Public Works and Water Resources, Mohammed Abdel-Hadi Radi
Manpower and Vocational Training, Ahmed Ahmed El-Amawi
Education, Dr Hussein Kamal Baha El-Din
Transport, Communications and Civil Aviation, Suliman Metwalli Suliman
Health, Dr Ali El-Makhzangi
Information, Muhammad Safwat al-Sharif
Cabinet Affairs and Administrative Development, Ahmed Radwan Gomaa
Religious Affairs (Waqfs), Dr Muhammad Ali Mahgoub
Social Affairs and Social Insurance, Dr Amal Abdul Rahim Osman
Electricity and Energy, Mohammad Mahir Osman Abaza
Public Business, Dr Atef Mohamed Ebeid
Housing and Public Utilities, Mohammed Salaheddin Hasaballah

Local Government, Dr Mahmmoud Sherif

EMBASSY OF THE ARAB REPUBLIC OF EGYPT
26 South Street, London WIY 8EL
Tel 0171–499 2401
Ambassador Extraordinary and Plenipotentiary, His Excellency Mohamed I. Shaker, apptd 1988
Minister Plenipotentiary, Deputy Chief of Mission, Dr Mamdouh Shawky
Minister Plenipotentiary and Consul-General, Hassan Salem
Minister Plenipotentiary, Ahmed Abdel Hameed Nafeh
Defence Attaché, Comm. Nour Eldin Negm
Minister Plenipotentiary (Commercial), Amr Osman El Menshawi
Cultural Counsellor, Samir Youssef Elsayed

BRITISH EMBASSY
Ahmed Ragheb Street, Garden City, Cairo
Tel: Cairo 354–0850
Ambassador Extraordinary and Plenipotentiary, His Excellency David Blatherwick, CMG, OBE, apptd 1995
Counsellor and Deputy Head of Mission, A. F. Goulty
Counsellor, J. B. MacPherson
Defence and Military Attaché, Col. G. N. R. Sayle, OBE
First Secretary and Consul, J. M. Taylor
First Secretary (Commercial), I. S. Lockhart, MBE

There are British consular offices at Luxor, Suez and Port Said, and a Consulate-General at Alexandria.

BRITISH COUNCIL REPRESENTATIVE, Howard Thompson, OBE, 192 Sharia el Nil, Agouza, Cairo. There is also a library in Alexandria.

DEFENCE

The armed forces number 430,000 active personnel (272,000 conscripts). Selective conscription for three-year terms operates.

The Army numbers 310,000 (200,000 conscripts) with 3,235 main battle tanks, 4,090 armoured infantry fighting vehicles and armoured personnel carriers, and 1,465 artillery pieces.

The Navy has 20,000 personnel (12,000 conscripts) with one destroyer, four frigates, three submarines, 44 patrol and coastal craft, and 14 armed helicopters. The Air Force has 110,000 personnel (60,000 conscripts) with 550 combat aircraft and 79 armed helicopters. There are also 370,000 paramilitary Security Forces and National Guard personnel.

Egypt deploys an infantry battalion of 418 troops in Bosnia-Hercegovina.

ECONOMY

Egypt's foreign debt to western governments stood at US$14 billion in mid-1994, having been reduced from US$20 billion the previous year by write-offs tied to an IMF economic and financial reform programme. Economic growth has improved under the programme to 2.4 per cent of GDP in 1993–4, while inflation stood at 7.3 per cent a year in April 1994.

Despite increasing industrialization, agriculture remains the most important economic activity, employing over 45 per cent of the labour force and producing 17 per cent of exports. Output has been increased by land reclamation, more efficient methods of irrigation, fertilization and increasing mechanization. Egypt is still a net importer of foodstuffs, especially grain, and a food security programme has been set up with the aim of achieving self-sufficiency. The main cash crop is cotton, of which Egypt is one of the world's main producers. Other important crops are maize, rice, sugar cane, wheat, beans, citrus fruit and other fruits and vegetables are also grown.

With its considerable reserves of petroleum and natural gas in Sinai, the Nile delta and the Western Desert, and the hydro-electric power produced by the Aswan and High Dams, Egypt is self-sufficient in energy. Electricity has been provided to almost all of the country and there are plans to extend the natural gas network to all major cities. The production of petroleum provides 60–65 per cent of total exports, and supports a refining industry. The major manufacturing industries are food processing, motor cars, electrical goods, steel, chemical products, yarns and textiles.

TRADE

The main imports are wheat, flour, wood and trucks. The main exports are crude petroleum, cotton, cotton yarn, oranges, rice and cotton textiles.

Trade with UK	1993	1994
Imports from UK	£337,105,000	£368,000,000
Exports to UK	188,355,000	252,203,000

COMMUNICATIONS

The road and rail networks link the Nile valley and delta with the main development areas east and west of the river. The Suez Canal was reopened in 1975 and a two-stage development project begun to widen and deepen the canal to allow the passage of larger shipping and to permit two-way traffic. Port Said and Suez have been reconstructed and the port of Alexandria is being improved.

EQUATORIAL GUINEA
República de Guinea Ecuatorial

Equatorial Guinea consists of the island of Bioko, in the Bight of Biafra about 20 miles from the west coast of Africa, Annonbón Island in the Gulf of Guinea, the Corisco Islands (Corisco, Elobey Grande and Elobey Chico), and Rio Muni, a mainland area between Cameroon and Gabon. It has a total area of 10,830 sq. miles (28,051 sq. km), and a population (UN estimate 1992) of 369,000.

CAPITAL – ΨMalabo, on the island of Bioko, population (1983 estimate) 30,418. ΨBata is the principal town and port of Rio Muni.

CURRENCY – Franc CFA of 100 centimes.

FLAG – Three horizontal bands, green over white over red; blue triangle next staff; coat of arms in centre of white band.

NATIONAL DAY – 12 October.

GOVERNMENT

Formerly colonies of Spain, the territories now forming the Republic of Equatorial Guinea were constituted as two provinces of Metropolitan Spain in 1959, became autonomous in 1963 and fully independent in 1968.

In 1979 President Macias was deposed by a revolutionary military council headed by Col. Obiang Nguema. Constitutional amendments in 1982 provided for legislative elections, which were held in August 1983 and July 1988, but all candidates were presidential nominees.

A multiparty political system under a new constitution was approved by a referendum in 1991 and ten opposition parties have been legalized, operating alongside the ruling Equatorial Guinea Democratic Party (PDGE). A National Pact was agreed and signed in March 1993 but when

legislative elections were held in November they were boycotted by most of the electorate and opposition parties because of alleged election rigging by the President. The PDGE won 68 out of 80 National Assembly seats and formed a government. A presidential election is due in 1996.

HEAD OF STATE
President of the Supreme Military Council and Minister of Defence, Brig.-Gen. Teodoro Obiang Nguema Mbasogo, *took office* August 1979, *re-elected* June 1989

MINISTERS *as at August 1995*
Prime Minister, Silvestre Siale Bileka
Deputy Prime Minister, Economics and Finance, Anatolio Ndong Mba
Justice and Religion, Francisco Javier Mbengono
Public Works, Housing and Town Planning, Alejandro Envoro Ovono
Education and Science, Ricardo Mangue Obama Nfube
Labour and Social Security, Ernesto Maria Cayetano Toherida
Industry, Energy, Small and Medium-sized Enterprises, Severino Obiang Bengono
Mines and Hydrocarbons, Juan Olo Nseng
Agriculture, Fishing and Food, Alfredo Mokudi Nanga
Health and Environment, Bemabe Ngore
Social Affairs and Women, Balbina Nchama Nvo
Culture, Tourism and Francophone Affairs, Agustin Nse Nfumu
Foreign Affairs and Co-operation, Miguel Oyono Ndong

EMBASSY OF THE REPUBLIC OF EQUATORIAL GUINEA
6 Rue Alfred de Vigny, 75008, Paris
Tel: Paris 47664433
Ambassador Extraordinary and Plenipotentiary, new appointment awaited

BRITISH AMBASSADOR, His Excellency William Ernest Quantrill, resident at Yaoundé, Cameroon

ECONOMY

The chief products are cocoa, coffee and wood (which is exported almost entirely from Rio Muni). Production has declined and except for cocoa there is little commercial agriculture. The economy is heavily dependent on outside aid, principally from Spain. Oil and gas deposits exist but remain largely unexploited. Equatorial Guinea entered the 'franc zone' in 1985.

TRADE WITH UK	1993	1994
Imports from UK	£1,237,000	£387,000
Exports to UK	6,000	—

ERITREA

Eritrea is bordered on the north and north-west by Sudan, on the south and south-west by Ethiopia, on the south-east by Djibouti and on the north-east and east borders on the Red Sea. Included in its territory are the Dahlak Islands in the Red Sea. It has an area of 36,170 sq. miles (93,679 sq. km) and rises from a long, narrow, low-lying coastal strip to highlands in the centre and north which are 2,000–3,000 m (6,500–9,800 ft) high.

The population is 3,500,000 (1991 official estimate). About 50 per cent are Coptic Christian and 50 per cent Muslim. The majority of highlanders are Christian and the majority of lowlanders are Muslim. The two main languages in use for business and taught in schools are English and Arabic. There are also nine indigenous language groups: Afar; Bilen; Hadareb; Kunama; Nara; Rashida; Saho; Tigre; Tigrinya.

CAPITAL – Asmara (275,000) in the central highlands. ΨMassawa and ΨAssab are the two main ports and other major towns.

CURRENCY – The Ethiopian birr of 100 cents remains in use at present.

FLAG – Divided into three triangles; the one based on the hoist is red and bears a gold olive wreath; the upper triangle is green and the lower one light blue.

NATIONAL DAY – 24 May (Independence Day).

GOVERNMENT

Eritrea was colonized by Italy in the late 19th century and was the base for the 1936 Italian invasion of Abyssinia (Ethiopia). After the Italian defeat in East Africa in 1941 by British and Commonwealth forces, Eritrea became a British protectorate. This lasted until 15 September 1952 when, according to the wishes of the UN, Eritrea was federated with Ethiopia but retained a high degree of political autonomy. The Ethiopian Emperor Haile Selassie incorporated Eritrea as a province of Ethiopia in 1962, which provoked widespread resistance. An armed campaign for independence began in the 1970s, first against Emperor Haile Selassie's forces and from 1974 against the Mengistu regime.

In May 1991 the Mengistu government was overthrown by the Eritrean People's Liberation Front (EPLF) and the Ethiopian People's Revolutionary Democratic Front (EPRDF). In July 1991 the new EPRDF-led government in Ethiopia agreed to an Eritrean referendum on independence which was held in April 1993 and recorded a 99 per cent vote in favour. Independence was declared on 24 May 1993.

At independence the provisional government became the transitional government of Eritrea to govern for a maximum of four years while a new constitution is drafted. At the end of the transition period multiparty elections are to be held. During the transition period legislative power is vested in the National Assembly and executive power in the State Council appointed and chaired by the President. In 1994 the EPLF transformed itself into a political party, the People's Front for Democracy and Justice (PFDJ), and the National Assembly was changed for the remainder of the transition period to comprise 75 PFDJ central council members and 75 elected members. The 700,000 refugees who fled to Sudan during the war have been repatriated.

HEAD OF STATE
President, Chairman of the National Assembly, Issaias Afewerki, *elected by National Assembly* 22 May 1993

STATE COUNCIL *as at August 1995*
Chairman, The President
Local Government, Mahmoud Ahmed Sherifo
Internal Affairs, Ali Said Abdella
Defence and Health, Sebhat Ephrem
Justice, Fozia Hashim
Foreign Affairs, Petros Soloman
Culture and Information, Baraki Gebresalassie
Finance and Development, Haile Weldetensae
Trade and Industry, Ekuba Abraha
Agriculture, Tesfai Ghermazien
Marine Resources, Saleh Meki
Construction, Abraha Asfaha
Energy, Mining and Water Resources, Tesfay Gebraselassie
Education, Osman Saleh Muhammed

Transport, Giorgis Tekle Mikael
Tourism, Worku Tesfa Mikael

EMBASSY OF THE STATE OF ERITREA
382 avenue Louise, 1050 Brussels, Belgium
Tel: Brussels 644 2401
Ambassador Extraordinary and Plenipotentiary, His Excellency Ato Ghebremichael Mengistu, apptd 1993

CONSULATE
96 White Lion Street, London N1 9PF
Tel: 0171-713 0096

BRITISH AMBASSADOR, His Excellency Duncan Christopher, resides at Addis Ababa, Ethiopia

BRITISH CONSULATE
c/o Mitchell Cotts Building, Emperor Yohanes Ave 5, PO Box 5584, Asmara
Tel: Asmara 120145
Honorary Consul, Simon Bush

BRITISH COUNCIL DIRECTOR – Dr Negusse Araya, PO Box 997, Asmara

ECONOMY

The economy was devastated by the war of independence and the scorched earth policy of the retreating Ethiopian forces. Since 1991 the government has directed all its efforts into rebuilding industry, agriculture and infrastructure, especially in the highlands, where the Ethiopian army uprooted nearly all the trees, leading to serious erosion. Some 22 million tree seedlings are being grown for planting. As the agricultural and industrial sectors producing sorghum, livestock, salt, cement, fish, hides and potash are rebuilt, the government has directed large numbers of the population into infrastructure rebuilding schemes in return for daily food. The focus of the rebuilding programme are the ports of Massawa and Assab, the roads from the ports to Ethiopia, and the railway from Massawa to Sudan via Asmara. Before 1962 Eritrea was one of the most industrialized areas of Africa and some industry remains, producing textiles and footwear. The government hopes to base the rebuilding of the economy on the return of well-educated exiles, international aid and investment, the development of tourism along the coast, and the diversification of the economy away from agriculture. The reconstruction programme has, however, been hampered severely by food shortages in late 1993 and early 1994, met by foreign aid from Western donors.

TRADE WITH UK	1994
Imports from UK	£912,000
Exports to UK	—

ESTONIA
The Republic of Estonia

Estonia is situated on the eastern coast of the Baltic Sea. To the north lies the Gulf of Finland, to the east Russia, and to the south Latvia. Estonia lies between 57°30′ and 59°49′N., and between 21°46′ and 28°13′E. and has an area of 17,458 sq. miles (45,125 sq. km) including 1,500 islands in the Baltic Sea and the Gulf of Riga. Forests cover roughly 20 per cent of the country, which also has many lakes. The climate is mild and maritime.

The population is 1,526,177 (1992 estimate), of which 61.5 per cent are Estonian, 30.3 per cent Russian, 3.1 per cent Ukrainian, 1.8 per cent Belarussian. The majority religion is Lutheran, with Russian Orthodox and Baptist minorities. Estonian is the first language of 61.5 per cent and Russian of 30.3 per cent.

CAPITAL – Tallinn (population 452,840). Other cities are Tartu (109,133); Narva (80,491); Kohtla-Järve (56,141); Pärnu (52,085).

CURRENCY – Kroon (Crown) of 100 sent.

FLAG – Three horizontal stripes of blue, black, white.

NATIONAL ANTHEM – Mu Isamaa, mu õnn ja rõõm (My Fatherland).

NATIONAL DAY – 24 February (Independence Day).

HISTORY

Estonia, a former province of the Russian Empire, declared its independence from Russia on 24 February 1918. A war of independence was fought against the German army until November 1918, and then against Soviet forces until the peace treaty of Tartu was signed in February 1920. By this treaty the Soviet Union recognized Estonia's independence.

The Soviet Union annexed Estonia in 1940 under the terms of the Molotov-Ribbentrop pact with Germany. Estonia was invaded and occupied when Germany invaded the Soviet Union during the Second World War. In 1944 the Soviet Union recaptured the country from Germany and confirmed its annexation, though this was never accepted as legal by most states.

Under mounting public pressure, the Estonian Supreme Soviet in November 1989 declared the republic to be sovereign and its 1940 annexation by the Soviet Union to be illegal. In February 1990 the leading role of the Communist Party was abolished, and following multiparty elections in March 1990 a period of transition to independence was inaugurated. Independence was supported by an overwhelming majority in a March 1991 referendum and was declared on 20 August 1991. The State Council of the Soviet Union recognized the independence of Estonia on 10 September 1991.

GOVERNMENT

Under the 1992 constitution, legislative power is exercised by the unicameral *Riigikogu* of 101 members elected by proportional representation every four years. The President is elected for a five-year term by the Riigikogu by a two-thirds majority or, if no candidate receives this majority after three rounds of voting, by an electoral body composed of Riigikogu members and local government officials. Executive authority is vested in a Prime Minister and government formed from a governing majority within the parliament.

Presidential and legislative elections were held in September 1992 on the basis of special provisions different from the 1992 constitution. The President was directly elected for a four-year term and the Riigikogu for a three-year one to enable newly-naturalized citizens to be able to vote for representatives in national elections in a shorter period of time. A radical right-wing coalition government was elected which held power until losing a parliamentary vote of no confidence in September 1994. At the legislative election of March 1995 right-wing parties were defeated and a centre-left government of the Coalition and Rural People's Union and the Centre Party was formed which holds 57 of the 101 Riigikogu seats.

The majority of the ethnic Russian population was able to vote in 1995, unlike the 1992 elections when only citizens of pre-1940 Estonia and their descendants were eligible to vote. This follows the introduction of citizenship laws in July 1993 and January 1995 under which applicants for naturalization may achieve citizenship by passing language tests in the Estonian language and fulfilling a minimum residency period of five years to gain citizenship by naturalization. Tensions with ethnic Russians and Russia over citizenship have been greatly reduced by this.

Estonia is divided into six towns and 15 districts for local administration purposes.

HEAD OF STATE
President, Lennart Meri, *elected* 5 October 1992

GOVERNMENT *as at August 1995*
Prime Minister, Tiit Vähi (CRPU)
Interior, Edgar Savisaar (C)
Foreign Affairs, Riivo Sinijärv (CRPU)
Economic Affairs, Liina Tonisson (C)
Finance, Mart Opmann (CRPU)
Social Affairs, Siiri Oviir (C)
Justice, Paul Varul (CRPU)
Defence, Andrus Oovel (CRPU)
Culture and Education, Peeter Kreitzberg (C)
Agriculture, Ilmar Mändmets (CRPU)
Environment, Villu Reiljan (CRPU)
Transportation and Communications, Kalev Kallo (C)
European Affairs, Endel Lippmaa (CRPU)
Regional Affairs, Ants Leemets (CRPU)
Culture, Jack Allik (CRPU)
CRPU Coalition and Rural People's Union; C Centre Party

EMBASSY OF THE REPUBLIC OF ESTONIA
16 Hyde Park Gate, London SW7 5DG
Tel 0171-589 3428
Ambassador Extraordinary and Plenipotentiary, new appointment awaited

BRITISH EMBASSY
Kentmanni 20, Tallinn EE0100
Tel: Tallinn 313353
Ambassador Extraordinary and Plenipotentiary, His Excellency Charles De Chassiron, apptd 1994
BRITISH COUNCIL REPRESENTATIVE, Imbi Kaasik, Vana Posti 7, Tallinn

DEFENCE

Since independence Estonia has formed a small army with a total number of 2,500 active personnel. Conscripts serve 12 months and reserve forces number 6,000 militia. In addition there are 2,000 (1,200 conscripts) paramilitary and maritime border guards. The last Russian combat troops withdrew on 31 August 1994 and the last specialist support troops in September 1995 after an agreement was reached under which the Estonian government guaranteed the welfare of Russian military pensioners living in Estonia.

ECONOMY

The economy was seriously affected by the collapse of the centralized Soviet economic system. Since 1992 the government has introduced reforms to transform the economy into one based on free market principles with privatization and restructuring. To this end, and to support a strong and fully convertible currency, the IMF provided credits worth US$40 million in August 1992 and US$32 million in October 1993. Having in 1992 established a stable currency pegged to the Deutsche Mark, the economy has stabilized, with unemployment of only 2 per cent, and output is recovering from the fall experienced in 1990–2 with GDP growth of 5 per cent in 1994. Privatization, started in 1992, has gained momentum with foreign direct investment quadrupling in 1994. Estonia has no outstanding debt to Russia but is still dependent on Russian natural gas supplies.

Agriculture and dairy-farming are a major sector of the economy, the main products being rye, oats, barley, flax, potatoes, meat, milk, butter and eggs.

Light industry is the other major sector, concentrating on textiles, clothing and footwear, forestry, wood and paper products, and food and fish processing. Some heavy industry exists, mostly chemicals and the manufacture of power equipment.

TRADE

Although Estonia signed a free trade deal with Russia in September 1992, it has greatly reduced its trade with the former Soviet states. In 1994 over 70 per cent of trade was with EU and EFTA states and Estonia's trade rose by 50 per cent. Free trade and association agreements with the EU came into effect in 1995.

Trade with UK	1993	1994
Imports from UK	£8,043,000	£15,285,000
Exports to UK	20,039,000	58,830,000

COMMUNICATIONS

Freedom of the press is guaranteed in the constitution, and the state monopoly on television and radio ended soon after independence. All newspapers have been privatized and broadcasting channels are in the process of being privatized. Russian-language news and programmes are provided on Estonian Television. There are five Estonian and three Russian-language daily newspapers.

EDUCATION

Estonia has a three-tier education system, consisting of primary level (nine years), secondary level (three years) and university level (four to six years).

ETHIOPIA
Ityopia

Ethiopia is in north-eastern Africa, bounded on the north-west by the Sudan, on the south by Kenya, on the east by Djibouti and Somalia, and on the north-east by Eritrea. The area is 435,608 sq. miles (1,128,221 sq. km).

A large central plateau (average height, 6,000–7,000 ft) rises to nearly 15,000 ft at Ras Dashan in the north. The plateau drops to the Nile basin in the west, to the Ogaden desert in the east and to Eritrea and the Red Sea in the north. The chief river is the Blue Nile, issuing from Lake Tana; the Atbara and many other tributaries of the Nile also rise in the Ethiopian highlands.

The population (UN estimate 1992) is 51,617,000. About one-third are of Semitic origin (Amharas and Tigrayans) and the remainder mainly Oromos (about 40 per cent of the population), Somalis and Afar. Those of Semitic origin and many of the Oromos, are Ethiopian Orthodox Christians, whose current Patriarch is Abuna Paulos Gebre-Yohannis. The Afar people in the north and the Somalis in the south-east, as well as some Oromos, are Muslim.

There are eight major ethnic groups speaking a total of 70 languages, of which the most widely used is Amharic.

CAPITAL – Addis Ababa (population, 1994 estimate, 3,500,000). Dire Dawa is the most important commercial centre after Addis Ababa..
CURRENCY – Ethiopian birr (EB) of 100 cents.

FLAG – Three horizontal bands: green, yellow, red.
NATIONAL ANTHEM – Ityopya, Ityopya Kidemi.
NATIONAL DAY – 28 May.

GOVERNMENT

The basic Hamitic culture was heavily influenced by Semitic immigration from Arabia at about the time of Christ. Christianity was introduced in the fourth century. The empire attained a zenith in the sixth century under the Axum rulers but subsequently was checked by Islamic expansion from the east. Modern Ethiopia dates from 1855 when Theodore succeeded in establishing supremacy over the various tribes. The last Emperor was Haile Selassie who reigned from 1930, though in exile from 1936 to 1941 during the Italian occupation. After military and civil unrest, the armed forces assumed power in September 1974 and deposed the Emperor. After ten years of military rule, a Workers' Party on the Soviet model was formed in 1984, with Lt.-Col. Mengistu Haile Mariam as General Secretary. The People's Democratic Republic of Ethiopia was established under a new constitution in 1987 with Lt.-Col. Mengistu as President.

Armed insurgencies by the Eritrean People's Liberation Front (EPLF) and the Ethiopian People's Revolutionary Democratic Front (EPRDF), originating in Tigray, brought down Mengistu's government in May 1991. At a national conference in July 1991, an 87-member Council of Representatives was formed, comprising the EPRDF and a number of other opposition groups.

After three years of devolving power to regional administrations, the Council of Representatives agreed on a draft federal constitution in April 1994 and this was adopted on 8 December 1994 by an elected 547-member Constituent Assembly. The new constitution provides for a federal government which retains power in the fields of foreign affairs, defence and economic policy, and for nine regions (Tigre, Afar, Amara, Oromia, Somali, Benshangui, Gambela, Harer, Southern). Power in other fields is devolved to regional administrations, each region (except Southern) having a predominating ethnic group with the right to use its own local language and establish its own courts and schools. Each region has the right to secede.

In December 1994 the trial opened of former President Mengistu and 72 of his regime's senior officials (24, including Mengistu, in absentia). They are charged with crimes against humanity, war crimes and genocide, including the killing of 100,000 to 200,000 people.

HEAD OF STATE
President, Meles Zenawi, *elected by the Council of Representatives* 21 July 1991

FEDERAL GOVERNMENT *as at July 1995*
Prime Minister, Tamirat Layne
Justice, Mehitema Solomon
Information, Negasso Gidada
Foreign Affairs, Seyoum Mesfin
Health, Dr Adanech Kidane Mariam
Education, Genet Zewude
Industry, Asefa Kekede
Interior, Kuma Demeksa
Mines and Energy, Isedin Ali
Commerce, Tsegaye Habtenarian
State Farms, Hassan Abdalla
Defence, Seye Abraha
Agriculture and Environmental Protection, Elias Nejasa
Housing and Construction, Haile Asegde
Culture and Sports, Lieule Selassie Timamo
Labour and Social Affairs, Mebere Alenayehu
Transport, Dr Wakegera Gamechu
Finance, Alemayehu Dhaba

EMBASSY OF ETHIOPIA
17 Prince's Gate, London SW7 1PZ
Tel 0171-589 7212/3/4/5
Ambassador Extraordinary and Plenipotentiary, His Excellency
Dr Solomon Gidada, apptd 1992
Counsellor, Laine Kahsu (*Commercial*)

BRITISH EMBASSY
Fikre Mariam Abatechan Street (PO Box 858), Addis
Ababa
Tel: Addis Ababa 6112354
Ambassador Extraordinary and Plenipotentiary, His Excellency
Duncan R. Christopher, apptd 1994
Deputy Ambassador and First Secretary, C. O. Pigott
First Secretary, Dr R. Munro
BRITISH COUNCIL REPRESENTATIVE, Michael Sargent,
Artistic Building, Adwa Avenue (PO Box 1043), Addis
Ababa

ECONOMY

The post-Mengistu government has engaged in a programme of free-market economic reform. Government
spending has been brought under control and inflation
reduced. The currency has been devalued, the civil service
drastically reduced and the army cut by two-thirds.
Western states have responded with debt relief and loans
and the IMF approved a three-year loan of US$70 million
in 1992 to support economic reform.

Thousands of peasant farmers resettled by the Mengistu
regime in barren areas have returned to their own areas.
Farms remain in state ownership but farmers have been
granted security of tenure for life and agricultural policy is
now market-based. Agriculture accounts for approximately 40 per cent of GDP, 85 per cent of exports and 80
per cent of total employment. The major food crops are
teff, maize, barley, sorghum, wheat, pulses and oil seeds.
Coffee generates over 50 per cent of export earnings.
Famine conditions, which attracted world attention in
1984–5, recurred for a short period and to a lesser extent in
1992. However, agricultural liberalization has led to
dramatic progress in food production and produced a
record harvest of 7.7 million tonnes of grain and pulses in
1993.

Manufacturing industry accounts for less than 9 per cent
of GDP and is heavily dependent on agriculture. Ethiopia's
known, but as yet largely unexploited, natural resources
include gold, platinum, copper and potash. Traces of oil
and natural gas have been found.

TRADE

The chief imports by value are machinery and transport
equipment, manufactured goods and chemicals; the principal exports by value are coffee, oil seeds, hides and skins,
and pulses.

Trade with UK	1993	1994
Imports from UK	£57,660,000	£48,236,000
Exports to UK	13,011,000	13,128,000

COMMUNICATIONS

A network of roads has been built in rural areas and links the
major cities with each other, with the Sudanese and Kenyan
borders and through Eritrea to the Red Sea coast. The
Ethiopian and Eritrean governments negotiated an agreement in 1992 which guarantees Ethiopia access to the Red
Sea via the ports of Assab and Massawa. Transport links
suffered during the secessionist wars and under the heavy
burden of famine relief traffic.

There is a railway link from Addis Ababa to Djibouti.
Ethiopian Airlines maintains regular services from Addis
Ababa to many provincial towns, throughout Africa and to
Europe.

EDUCATION

Elementary education is provided by government schools
in the main centres of population; there are also mission
schools. Government secondary schools are found in Addis
Ababa and the provincial capitals. The National University
(founded 1961) co-ordinates the institutions of higher
education. There is a separate university at Alemaya
(agricultural).

Amharic was the official language of instruction, with
English as the first foreign language and main language of
instruction from secondary level upwards. Arabic is taught
in Koran schools; and Ge'ez (the ancient Ethiopic) in
Christian church schools. Language policy is now under
review by the post-Mengistu government.

FIJI
Matanitu Ko Viti – Republic of Fiji

Fiji is made up of about 332 islands (about 100 permanently
inhabited) and over 500 islets in the South Pacific, about
1,100 miles north of New Zealand. The group extends 300
miles from east to west and 300 miles north to south
between 15° 45' and 21° 10' S. latitude and 176° E. and 178°
W. longitude. The International Date Line has been
diverted to the east of the island group. Its area is 7,055 sq.
miles (18,274 sq. km). The largest islands are Viti Levu and
Vanua Levu. The main groups of islands are Lomaiviti,
Lau and Yasawas. Most of the larger islands are mountainous, but also have areas of flat land and many of the rivers
have built extensive deltas. The climate is tropical without
extremes of heat and temperatures rarely exceed 32°C or
fall below 15°C.

The population (census 1986) was 715,373, comprising
48.6 per cent Indians, 46.2 per cent Fijians, and 5.2 per cent
other races. A UN estimate (1992) gives a total figure of
746,000. Since the 1987 coup many ethnic Indians have left
and by 1994 Melanesian Fijians formed the largest
population group.

CAPITAL – ΨSuva, on the island of Viti Levu. Population
(1986) 69,665.
CURRENCY – Fiji dollar (F$) of 100 cents.
FLAG – Light blue ground with Union flag in top left
quarter and the shield of Fiji in the fly.
NATIONAL ANTHEM – God Bless Fiji.
NATIONAL DAY – 10 October (Fiji Day).

GOVERNMENT

Fiji was a British colony from 1874 until 10 October 1970
when it became an independent state and a member of the
Commonwealth.

A coalition of the left under Dr Timoci Bavadra won a
general election in April 1987. The new government,
drawing its support mainly from the Indian population, was
overthrown in a military coup on 14 May by Lt.-Col.
Sitiveni Rabuka. In the wake of the constitutional crisis an
Advisory Council was set up as an interim government, but
a second coup occurred on 25 September 1987. On 7
October Rabuka declared Fiji a republic; the Governor-
General resigned on 15 October and Fiji's Commonwealth membership lapsed. In December another interim

government was formed to work for a resolution to the political crisis.

A new constitution, promulgated in 1990, established the political dominance of the Melanesian community within the judiciary and a bicameral parliament. The parliament consists of a Senate of 34 members appointed by the President, of which 24 seats are reserved for Melanesian Fijians, one for the Polynesian island of Rotuma and nine for other races. The House of Representatives has a total of 70 seats; 37 reserved for Melanesians, 27 for Indians, one for Rotuma and five for other races. The presidency and the premiership can only be held by Melanesians. The President is elected by the Great Council of Chiefs. The Fijian Political Party led by Rabuka won the general elections in May 1992 and February 1994 and has formed a coalition government with the General Voters Party.

HEAD OF STATE
President, Ratu Sir Kamisese Mara, GCMG, KBE, *inaugurated* 18 January 1994

CABINET *as at August 1995*
Prime Minister, Constitutional Review, Maj.-Gen. Sitiveni Rabuka, OBE
Deputy PM, Agriculture, Fisheries and Forests, Ratu Timoci Vesikula
Attorney-General and Minister for Justice, Kelemedi Bulewa
Education, Women, Culture, Science and Technology, Taufa Vakatale
Finance and Economic Development, Berenado Vunibobo
Foreign Affairs, Tourism and Civil Aviation, Sen. Filipe Bole
Infrastructure and Public Works, Transport, Leo Smith
Fijian Affairs, vacant
Health and Social Welfare, Seruwaia Hong Tiy
Commerce, Industry, Trade and Public Enterprises, James Ah Koy, CBE
Regional Development and Multi-ethnic Affairs, Ratu Inoke Kabuabola
Home Affairs, Immigration, Col. Paul Manueli, OBE
Youth, Employment Opportunities and Sports, Ratu Josefa Dimuri
Lands, Mineral Resources, Energy, Local Government, Environment, Ratu Ovini Bokini
Information, Broadcasting and Telecommunications, Isimeli Bose
Labour and Industrial Relations, Ratu Jo Nacola

EMBASSY OF THE REPUBLIC OF FIJI
34 Hyde Park Gate, London SW7 5DN
Tel 0171-584 3661
Ambassador Extraordinary and Plenipotentiary, His Excellency Brig.-Gen. Ratu Epeli Nailatikau, LVO, OBE, apptd 1988

BRITISH EMBASSY
Victoria House, 47 Gladstone Road, PO Box 1355, Suva
Tel: Suva 311033
Ambassador Extraordinary and Plenipotentiary, His Excellency Michael Peart, LVO, apptd 1995
Deputy Ambassador, Consul and First Secretary, D. J. Noble

ECONOMY

The economy is primarily agrarian. The principal cash crop is sugar cane, which is the main export, followed by coconuts, ginger and copra. A variety of other fruit, vegetables and root crops are also grown, and self-sufficiency in rice is a major aim. Forestry, fishing and beef production are being encouraged in order to diversify the economy. The processing of agricultural, marine and timber products are the main industries, along with gold mining and textiles. Tourism is second only to sugar as a money-earner.

FINANCE	1993	1994
Public income	F$643m	F$685m
Public expenditure	679m	650m

TRADE

The chief imports are foodstuffs, machinery, mineral fuels, chemicals, beverages, tobacco and manufactured articles. Chief exports are sugar, coconut oil, gold, lumber, garments, molasses, ginger and canned fish.

	1993	1994
Total Imports	F$938m	F$1,209m
Total Exports	653m	800m

Trade with UK	1993	1994
Imports from UK	£8,299,000	£6,179,000
Exports to UK	86,688,000	80,642,000

COMMUNICATIONS

Fiji is one of the main aerial crossroads in the Pacific, providing services to New Zealand, Australia, Tonga, Western Samoa, Vanuatu, the Solomon Islands, Kiribati, Tuvalu, New Caledonia and American Samoa. Fiji has three ports of entry, at Suva, Lautoka and Levuka.

FINLAND
Suomen Tasavalta

Finland is situated on the Gulfs of Finland and Bothnia, with a total area of 130,500 sq. miles (338,000 sq. km), of which 69 per cent is forest, 8 per cent cultivated land and 10 per cent lakes. The population (1993 estimate) is 5,078,000. The population is predominantly Lutheran. Finnish and Swedish are both official languages, 93.6 per cent speaking Finnish as their first language and 6.2 per cent Swedish. Lapp is spoken by the Lapps who number about 2,500 and live in the far north of the country. Both Finnish and Swedish are used for administration and education.

The Åland archipelago (Ahvenanmaa), a group of small islands at the entrance to the Gulf of Bothnia, covers about 572 square miles, with a population (1993) of 25,000 (95.2 per cent Swedish-speaking). The islands have a semi-autonomous status.

CAPITAL – ΨHelsinki (Helsingfors), population (1993) 508,600; other towns are Tampere (Tammerfors), 175,000; ΨTurku (Åbo), 160,000; Espoo (Esbo), 182,679; Vantaa (Vanda), 160,000; ΨOulu (Oleåborg), 104,500; Lahti (Lahtis), 94,000; ΨPori (Björneborg), 76,500.
CURRENCY – Markka (Mk) of 100 penniä.
FLAG – White with blue cross.
NATIONAL DAY – 6 December (Independence Day).

GOVERNMENT

Finland was part of the Swedish Empire from the middle ages until it was ceded to Russia in 1809 and became an autonomous grand duchy of the Russian Empire. The country became independent after the Russian revolution of 1917, but defeats by the Soviet Union in 1939–40 and 1941–4 forced Finland to cede around one-tenth of its land to the Soviet Union and to resettle 10 per cent of its population under the Treaty of Paris 1947. The ceded land included Finland's access to the Arctic Ocean and to Lake Ladoga. A Soviet-Finnish Co-operation Treaty forced Finland to demilitarize its Soviet border, to enter into a barter trade agreement with its neighbour and to adopt a stance of neutrality. These terms lasted until the demise of the Soviet Union in 1991.

Under the constitution there is a single chamber, the *Eduskunta*, composed of 200 members elected by universal suffrage. Legislative power is vested in the Eduskunta and the President. The highest executive power is held by the President who is directly elected for a period of six years. The first direct elections for the presidency were held in 1994, the President having been elected by an electoral college before then.

The present government took office in April 1995 after legislative elections in March. The five parties in the coalition are the Social Democratic Party, the National Coalition Party (conservative), the Left-wing Alliance, the Swedish People's Party, and the Green League, with a total of 145 out of 200 seats.

Finland joined the European Union on 1 January 1995 following a referendum in October 1994 in which accession was approved by 57 per cent in Finland and by 74 per cent in a separate Åland Islands referendum.

HEAD OF STATE
President, Martti Ahtisaari, *inaugurated* 1 March 1994

CABINET *as at August 1995*

Prime Minister, Paavo Lipponen (SDP)
Deputy PM, Justice, Sauli Niinistö (NCP)
Foreign Affairs, Tarja Halonen (SDP)
Europe, Ole Norrback (SPP)
Interior, Jan-Erik Enestam (SPP)
Administration, Jouni Backman (SDP)
Defence, Anneli Taina (NCP)
Economy Iiro Viinanen (NCP)
Finance and Planning, Arja Alho (SDP)
Education, Olli-Pekka Heinonen (NCP)
Culture, Claes Anderssen (LA)
Agriculture and Forestry, Kalevi Hemilä (Ind.)
Transport, Tuula Línnaínmaa (NCP)
Trade and Industry, Antti Kalliomäki (SDP)
Health, Sinikka Mönkäre (SDP)
Social Affairs, Terttu Huttu (LA)
Labour, Liisa Jaakonsaari (SDP)
Environment, Pekka Haavisto (Green)

SDP Social Democratic Party; NCP National Coalition Party; LA Left-wing Alliance; SPP Swedish People's Party; Green Green League

EMBASSY OF FINLAND
38 Chesham Place, London SW1X 8HW
Tel 0171-838 6200
Ambassador Extraordinary and Plenipotentiary, His Excellency Leif Blomqvist, apptd 1991
Minister, L. Korpinen
Counsellor (Commercial), Olli Anttila
Defence Attaché, Co. H. Strang
Consul, Mrs T. Gallen-Kallela

BRITISH EMBASSY
Itäinen Puistotie 17, 00140 Helsinki
Tel: Helsinki 661293
Ambassador Extraordinary and Plenipotentiary, His Excellency David Burns, CMG, apptd 1995
Deputy Ambassador and Counsellor (Commercial), N. A. Thorne
First Secretary and Consul, W. Whitton
Defence Attaché, Lt.-Col. S. W. L. Strickland

There are British Consular offices at Helsinki, Jyväskylä, Kotka, Kuopio, Oulu, Pori, Tampere, Turku, Vaasa and Mariehamn.

BRITISH COUNCIL REPRESENTATIVE, Tuija Talvitie, Hakaniemenkatu 2, 00530 Helsinki

DEFENCE

The total active armed forces number some 31,200 personnel, including 23,900 conscripts, who serve for eight to 11 months. However, total mobilization strength is based on the 700,000 reservists, who are obliged to undergo between 40 and 100 days training up to age 50; 30,000 reservists undergo training each year.

The Army has a strength of 25,700 (21,600 conscripts) with 230 main battle tanks, 860 armoured infantry fighting vehicles and armoured personnel carriers, and 715 artillery pieces. The Navy has 2,500 personnel (1,000 conscripts) with 21 patrol and coastal craft. The Air Force has 3,000 personnel (1,300 conscripts) and 110 combat aircraft. There are also 4,400 Ministry of Interior Frontier Guards.

Finland deploys with UN forces abroad: one 526-strong infantry battalion in Lebanon; 222 troops in the Former Yugoslav Republic of Macedonia.

ECONOMY

Finland is a highly industrialized country producing a wide range of capital and consumer goods. Timber and timber-based products remain very important, but the importance of metal-working, shipbuilding and engineering has grown. The textile industry is well developed and the glass, ceramics and furniture industries enjoy international reputations. Other important industries are rubber, plastics, chemicals and pharmaceuticals, footwear, foodstuffs and electronic equipment.

The Finnish economy has been adversely affected by declining trade with the former Soviet bloc, together with the world-wide economic recession, causing GDP to fall by 15 per cent in 1990–3 before exports and the currency strengthened in 1994–5. Unemployment rose to 20 per cent in 1993 before declining to 17 per cent in 1995; inflation in 1995 was 1.5 per cent. The government has introduced austerity measures, raising taxes, and reducing health and social welfare spending and the large overseas development budget in order to curb the growth of public debt (60 per cent of GDP in 1994).

TRADE

The principal imports are raw materials, machinery and manufactured goods. The value of exports in 1994 was dominated by wood and paper products (38 per cent) and metal and engineering products (44 per cent). The special barter-trade relationship with the former Soviet Union collapsed in 1991 and exports to the countries of the former Soviet Union fell from 20 per cent of the total in the early 1980s to 5 per cent in 1994.

Trade with UK	1993	1994
Imports from UK	£1,129,722,000	£1,297,265,000
Exports to UK	1,904,694,000	2,253,250,000

COMMUNICATIONS

There are 9,000 km of railroad, railway connections with Sweden and Russia, and passenger boat connections with Sweden, Germany, Poland, Russia and the Baltic states. There are also passenger/cargo services between Britain and Helsinki, Kotka and other Finnish ports. External air services are maintained by most European airlines. The merchant fleet at the end of 1993 totalled 1,429,052 tons gross.

EDUCATION

Primary education (co-educational comprehensive school) is free and compulsory for children from seven to 16 years. In 1993, there were 580,800 students in comprehensive schools, 127,700 in senior secondary schools, 211,200 in vocational and professional education institutions, and 124,000 in 21 universities or other schools of similar academic level.

CULTURE

Newspapers, books, plays and films appear in both Finnish and Swedish. There is a vigorous modern literature. F. E. Sillanpää, who died in 1964, was awarded the Nobel prize for Literature in 1939. In 1994 there were 60 daily newspapers (12 Swedish).

FRANCE
La République Française

France extends from 42° 20′ to 51° 5′ N. latitude, and from 7° 85′ E. to 4° 45′ W. longitude. Its area is estimated at 211,208 sq. miles (547,026 sq. km), divided into 95 departments, including the island of Corsica, in the Mediterranean off the west coast of Italy. The principal rivers are the Seine, Loire, Garonne and Rhône. The population, according to the 1992 official estimate, is 57,218,000 (Metropolitan France), and 58,745,000 when overseas departments are included.

POPULATION OF THE REGIONS 1992
Names of Departments in brackets

Alsace (Bas-Rhin, Haut-Rhin)	1,640,000
Aquitaine (Dordogne, Gironde, Landes, Lot-et-Garonne, Pyrénées-Atlantiques)	2,825,000
Auvergne (Allier, Cantal, Haute-Loire, Puy-de-Dôme)	1,318,000
Basse-Normandie (Calvados, Manche, Orne)	1,399,000
Bourgogne (Côte-d'Or, Nièvre, Saône-et-Loire, Yonne)	1,613,000
Bretagne (Côtes-du-Nord, Finistère, Ille-et-Vilaine, Morbihan)	2,816,000
Centre (Cher, Eure-et-Loir, Indre, Indre-et-Loire, Loir-et-Cher, Loiret)	2,397,000
Champagne-Ardenne (Ardennes, Aube, Marne, Haute-Marne)	1,348,000
Corse (Corse-du-Sud, Haute-Corse)	251,000
Franche-Comté (Doubs, Haute-Saône, Jura, Territoire-de-Belfort)	1,104,000
Haute-Normandie (Eure, Seine-Maritime)	1,751,000
Île-de-France (Essonne, Hauts-de-Seine, Seine-et-Marne, Seine-St-Denis, Val-de-Marne, Val-d'Oise, Ville de Paris, Yvelines)	10,822,000
Languedoc-Roussillon (Aude, Gard, Hérault, Lozère, Pyrénées-Orientales)	2,161,000
Limousin (Corrèze, Creuse, Haute-Vienne)	720,000
Lorraine (Meurthe-et-Moselle, Meuse, Moselle, Vosges)	2,298,000
Midi-Pyrénées (Ariège, Aveyron, Haute-Garonne, Gers, Lot, Hautes-Pyrénées, Tarn, Tarn-et-Garonne)	2,458,000
Nord-Pas-de-Calais (Nord, Pas-de-Calais)	3,974,000
Pays de la Loire (Loire-Atlantique, Maine-et-Loire, Mayenne, Sarthe, Vendée)	3,093,000
Picardie (Aisne, Oise, Somme)	1,834,000
Poitou-Charentes (Charente, Charente-Maritime, Deux-Sèvres, Vienne)	1,609,000
Provence-Alpes-Côte d'Azur (Alpes-de-Haute-Provence, Alpes-Maritimes, Bouches-du-Rhône, Hautes-Alpes, Var, Vaucluse)	4,344,000
Rhône-Alpes (Ain, Ardèche, Drôme, Isère, Loire, Rhône, Savoie, Haute-Savoie)	5,442,000

CAPITAL – Paris, on the Seine. Population (census 1990) 2,152,400 (city); 9,318,800 (incl. suburbs). The largest conurbations (populations 1990) are Lyon (1,262,000); ΨMarseille (1,231,000); Lille (959,000); ΨBordeaux (696,000); Toulouse (650,000); Nice (516,000); Nantes (496,000); Toulon (437,000); Grenoble (404,000); Strasbourg (388,000). The chief towns of Corsica are ΨAjaccio (58,315) and ΨBastia (52,446).

CURRENCY – French franc of 100 centimes.

FLAG – The tricolour, three vertical bands, blue, white, red (blue next to flagstaff).

NATIONAL ANTHEM – La Marseillaise.

NATIONAL DAY – 14 July (Bastille Day 1789).

HISTORY

There are dolmens and menhirs in Brittany, prehistoric remains and cave drawings in Dordogne and Ariège, and throughout France various megalithic monuments erected by primitive tribes, predecessors of Iberian invaders from Spain (now represented by the Basques), Ligurians from northern Italy and Celts or Gauls from the valley of the Danube. Julius Caesar found Gaul 'divided into three parts' and described three political groups: Aquitanians south of the Garonne, Celts between the Garonne and the Seine and Marne, and Belgae from the Seine to the Rhine. Roman remains are plentiful throughout France in the form of aqueducts, arenas, triumphal arches, etc. The celebrated Norman and Gothic cathedrals, including Notre Dame in Paris, and those of Chartres, Reims, Amiens, Bourges, Beauvais, Rouen, etc., have survived invasions and bombardments with only partial damage, and many of the Renaissance and the 17th- and 18th-century chateaux survived the French Revolution.

CULTURE

French is the official language. The work of the French Academy, founded in 1635, has established le bon usage, equivalent to 'The Queen's English' in Britain. French authors have been awarded the Nobel Prize for Literature on 12 occasions and include R. F. A. Sully-Prudhomme (1901), Anatole France (1921), André Gide (1947), François Mauriac (1952), Albert Camus (1957), Jean Paul Sartre (1964) and Claude Simon (1985).

GOVERNMENT

The legislature consists of the National Assembly of 577 deputies (555 for Metropolitan France and 22 for the overseas departments and territories) and the Senate of 321 Senators (296 for Metropolitan France, 13 for the overseas departments and territories and 12 for French citizens abroad). One-third of the Senate is indirectly elected every three years. Following constitutional changes enacted in July 1995, the legislature will have a normal session of nine months each year, from October to June.

The Prime Minister is appointed by the President, as is the Council of Ministers on the Prime Minister's recommendation. They are responsible to the legislature, but as the executive is constitutionally separate from the legislature, ministers may not sit in the legislature and must hand over their seats to a substitute.

A Constitutional Council is responsible for supervising all elections and referenda and must be consulted on all constitutional matters and before the President of the Republic assumes emergency powers. In the event of the presidency falling vacant for any reason, the President of the Senate assumes the position until a presidential election, which must be held within 35 days.

The state of the parties in the Senate at August 1995 was: Rassemblement pour la république (RPR) 92; Socialists 67; Centrist Union (UDC) 63; Republican and Independent Union (RI) 48; Democratic and European Rally (RDE) 28; Communists 15; Independents 8.

The last elections to the National Assembly in March 1993 were won by the right-wing alliance of the Gaullist Rassemblement pour la république (RPR) and the Union pour la démocratie française (UDF) parties. At August 1995 the state of parties was: RPR 260; UDF 214; Socialists (PS) and allies 56; Communists (PCF) 23; Republic and Liberty (right-wing) 22; Independent 2.

HEAD OF STATE

President of the French Republic, Jacques Chirac, *elected* 7 May 1995, *took office* 17 May 1995

COUNCIL OF MINISTERS *as at August 1995*

Prime Minister, Alain Juppé (RPR)
Justice, Jacques Toubon (RPR)
Economy and Finance, Alain Madelin (UDF)
National and Further Education, Research and Professional Training, François Bayrou (UDF)
Town and Country Planning, Capital Works and Transport, Bernard Pons (RPR)
Foreign Affairs, Hervé de Charette (UDF)
Defence, Charles Millon (UDF)
Interior, Jean-Louis Debré (RPR)
Relations with Parliament, Roger Romani (RPR)
Labour, Social Dialogue and Participation, Jacques Barrot (UDF)
Culture, Philippe Douste-Blazy (UDF)
Economic Development and Planning, Jean Arthuis (UDF)
Administrative Reform, Decentralization and Citizenship, Claude Goasguen (UDF)
Civil Service, Jean Puech (UDF)
Public Health, Elisabeth Hubert (RPR)
Integration and the Fight against Exclusion, Eric Raoult (RPR)
Solidarity between the Generations, Colette Codaccioni (RPR)
Agriculture, Fisheries and Food, Philippe Vasseur (UDF)
Industry, Yves Galland (UDF)
Housing, Pierre-André Perissol (RPR)
Small and Medium-Sized Enterprises, Jean-Pierre Raffarin (UDF)
Posts and Information Technology, François Fillon (RPR)
Overseas Departments and Territories, Jean-Jacques de Peretti (RPR)
Environment, Corinne Lepage (Ind.)
Youth and Sport, Guy Drut (RPR)
Tourism, Françoise de Panafieu (RPR)
Veterans and War Victims, Pierre Pasquini (RPR)

President of the Senate, René Monory
President of the National Assembly, Phillipe Séguin
President of the Constitutional Council, Roland Dumas

FRENCH EMBASSY

58 Knightsbridge, London swix 7jt
Tel 0171-201 1000
Ambassador Extraordinary and Plenipotentiary, His Excellency Jean Gueguinou, apptd 1993
Minister-Counsellor, J. P. Taix
Defence Attaché, Contre-Amiral Y. de Kersauson
Cultural Counsellor, M. Lummaux
Consul-General, G. Gautier
Head of Commerce/Trade, O. Louis

BRITISH EMBASSY

35 rue du Faubourg St Honoré, 75383 Paris Cedex 08
Tel: Paris 42 66 91 42
Ambassador Extraordinary and Plenipotentiary, His Excellency Sir Christopher Mallaby, gcvo, kcmg, apptd 1993
Minister, The Hon. Michael Pakenham
Defence and Air Attaché, Air Cdre C. R. Adams, afc
Counsellor, Director of Trade Promotion and Investment, R. A. Kealy, cmg
First Secretary and Consul-General, M. E. Hunt, obe

BRITISH CONSULAR OFFICES – at Bordeaux, Biarritz,

Toulouse, Lille, Boulogne, Calais, Dunkirk, Lyon, Marseille, Nice, Paris, Cherbourg, Le Havre, Nantes and St Malo in Metropolitan France, and overseas in Cayenne (French Guiana), Papeete (French Polynesia), Fort de France (Martinique), Pointe à Pitre (Guadeloupe) and St Denis (Réunion).

BRITISH COUNCIL DIRECTOR, D. Ricks, obe, 9 rue de

Constantine, 75007 Paris

FRANCO-BRITISH CHAMBER OF COMMERCE, 8 rue Cimarosa, 75116 Paris. *President*, R. Lyon. *Vice-President*, B. Cordery, OBE

DEFENCE

The total active armed forces number 409,600 personnel (189,200 conscripts). Conscripts serve for ten months. Reserves total 339,800. Strategic nuclear forces consist of 80 submarine-launched ballistic missiles on five nuclear-powered submarines, 18 land-based intermediate range ballistic missiles, 15 (with a further 13 in store) nuclear-capable Mirage IVP aircraft and 45 Mirage 2000N aircraft, both with medium-range nuclear air-to-surface missiles.

The Army has a strength of 241,400 (136,800 conscripts) with 15 Hadès short-range nuclear missile launchers, 1,050 main battle tanks, 6,370 armoured personnel carriers and armoured infantry fighting vehicles, 925 artillery pieces and 661 helicopters. Organization is into three armoured and one motorized infantry divisions; the Rapid Action Force of four lightly armoured and air-mobile divisions; the Foreign Legion of nine regiments; 13 marine infantry regiments; and one armoured division assigned to Euro-corps, together with French elements of the Franco-German brigade.

The Navy has a strength of 64,200 (18,600 conscripts) with 38 Super Etendard aircraft (with 19 in store), capable of carrying short-range nuclear air-to-surface missiles, 13 submarines, two aircraft carriers, one cruiser, four destroyers, 36 frigates, 69 other combat aircraft and 40 armed helicopters.

The Air Force has a strength of 89,800 (33,800 conscripts) and some 761 combat aircraft. The Air Force is organized into an air defence command of four squadrons; a tactical command of nine ground attack, nine air defence, two reconnaissance, two early warning and one helicopter squadrons; an air transport command of 20 transport and five helicopter squadrons; a training command.

France deploys 55,775 armed forces personnel abroad; 15,000 in Germany; 22,200 in French Overseas Departments and Territories; 8,800 in former French colonies in Africa; and 9,775 on UN and peacekeeping duties.

There is also a paramilitary Gendarmerie with 91,800 personnel (11,700 conscripts) and 139,000 reserves.

ECONOMY

Government expenditure (ordinary and capital) in the 1994 general budget was F1,429,500 million, of which the largest components were: local government F307,300 million, education F251,300 million, defence F242,500 million. In 1994 the budget deficit was equivalent to 3.8 per cent of GDP with an unemployment rate of 12.4 per cent.

In 1993 the conservative government announced the privatization of all public sector companies apart from those in the telecommunications, utilities and gaming sectors. The programme is expected to generate F300,000 million over five years. By mid 1995 total or majority holdings in Banque National de Paris, Rhône-Poulenc (chemicals), Elf Aquitaine (oil), UAP (insurance), Usinor Sacilor (steel) and Seita (tobacco) had been sold, together with 28 per cent of Renault. Holdings in Pechiney (Aluminium), Companie Générale Maritime, Air France, Aérospatiale, Crédit Lyonnais, the remainder of Renault and a further nine companies are to follow.

In 1994 the government established the independence of the central bank, the Banque de France, with the formation of a nine-member monetary policy council to define and implement monetary policy independent of the government.

Approximately 28,114,000 hectares of land is used for agricultural purposes; 15,885,500 hectares is forested. Production in 1993 included wheat, 29,252,100 tonnes; maize, 14,843,400 tonnes; barley, 8,981,400 tonnes; and potatoes 3,556,400 tonnes.

Viniculture is extensive, regions famous for their wines including Bordeaux, Burgundy and Champagne. Production of wine in 1993 was 53,374,000 hectolitres. Cognac, liqueurs and cider are also important products.

Oil is produced from fields in the Landes area, but France is a net importer of crude oil, for processing by its important oil-refining industry. Natural gas is produced in the foothills of the Pyrenees. Electricity production was 442,000m kW in 1992.

Heavy industries include oil-refining and the production of iron and steel, and aluminium. In 1993 production of steel was 14,732,000 tonnes and cement 21,600,000 tonnes. Other important industries produce chemicals, tyres, aluminium, textiles, paper products and processed food. Engineering products include motor vehicles, and television and radio sets.

TRADE

The principal imports are raw materials for the heavy and manufacturing industries (e.g. oil, minerals, chemicals), machinery and precision instruments, agricultural products and vehicles. Raw materials, semi-manufactured and manufactured goods are also the principal exports. Other member countries of the EU are France's main trading partners.

	1992	1993
Imports	F1,217,760m	F1,095,456m
Exports	1,248,312m	1,186,656m

Trade with UK	1993	1994
Imports from UK	£11,440,344,000	£13,121,021,000
Exports to UK	12,847,093,000	14,611,129,000

COMMUNICATIONS

The length of roads in use at the end of 1992 was 915,651 km, of which 7,408 km were motorways.

The railroad system is extensive. The length of lines open for traffic at the end of 1992 was 32,731 km, of which 12,986 km were electrified.

The French mercantile marine consisted in 1992 of 221 ships of over 100 tons gross, of which 33 were passenger vessels (300,000 tons gross), 60 tankers (2,106,000 tons gross) and 128 cargo vessels (1,427,000 tons gross).

EDUCATION

The educational system is highly centralized and is administered by the Ministry of National Education. Education is compulsory, free and secular from six to 16. Schools may be single-sex or co-educational. Primary education is given in nursery schools, primary schools and *collèges d'enseignement général* (four-year secondary modern course); secondary education in *collèges d'enseignement technique, collèges d'enseignement secondaire* and *lycées* (seven-year course leading to one of the five *baccalauréats*). Special schools are numerous.

There are many *grandes écoles* in France which award diplomas in many subjects not taught at university, especially applied science and engineering. Most of these are state institutions but have a competitive system of entry, unlike the universities. There are universities in 24 towns including 13 in Paris and the immediate surrounding district.

In 1992–3 enrolment in pre-school and primary schools was 6,610,000; in secondary schools 5,458,800, and in post-secondary education 1,951,994.

In 1993 the government gave German official parity with French in Alsace schools.

OVERSEAS DEPARTMENTS

Greater powers of self-government were granted to French Guiana, Guadeloupe, Martinique and Réunion in 1982. These former colonies had enjoyed departmental status since 1946 and the status of regions since 1974. Their directly-elected Assemblies operate in parallel with the existing, indirectly constituted Regional Councils. The French government is represented by a Prefect in each.

FRENCH GUIANA – Situated on the north-eastern coast of South America, French Guiana is flanked by Suriname on the west and by Brazil on the south and east. Area, 34,749 sq. miles (90,000 sq. km). Population (1992) 131,000. Capital, ΨCayenne (41,000). Under the administration of French Guiana is a group of islands (St Joseph, Ile Royal and Ile du Diable), known as Iles du Salut.

Prefect, J.-F. Cordet

Trade with UK	1993	1994
Imports from UK	£4,807,000	£6,483,000
Exports to UK	259,000	927,000

GUADELOUPE – A number of islands in the Leeward Islands group of the West Indies, consisting of the two main islands of Guadeloupe (or Basse-Terre) and Grande-Terre, with the adjacent islands of Marie-Galante, La Désirade and Îles des Saintes, and the islands of St Martin and St Barthélemy over 150 miles to the north-west. Area, 687 sq. miles (1,779 sq. km). Population (1992) 408,000. Capital ΨBasse Terre (14,000) in Guadeloupe. Other towns are ΨPointe à Pitre (26,000) in Grande-Terre and ΨGrand Bourg (6,611) in Marie-Galante.

Prefect, A. Froute

Trade with UK	1993	1994
Imports from UK	£7,693,000	£5,772,000
Exports to UK	62,000	63,000

MARTINIQUE – An island situated in the Windward Islands group of the West Indies, between Dominica in the north and St Lucia in the south. Area, 425 sq. miles (1,102 sq. km). Population (1992) 371,000. Capital ΨFort de France (101,540). Other towns are ΨTrinité (11,214) and ΨMarin (6,104).

Prefect, M. Morin

Trade with UK	1993	1994
Imports from UK	£26,078,000	£17,417,000
Exports to UK	133,000	35,000

RÉUNION – Réunion, which became a French possession in 1638, lies in the Indian Ocean, about 569 miles east of Madagascar and 110 miles south-west of Mauritius. Area, 969 sq. miles (2,510 sq. km). Population (1992) 617,000. Capital, St Denis (122,000). Other towns are Saint-Paul (71,669) and Saint-Pierre (58,846). The smaller, unin-habited islands of Bassas da India, Europa, Îles Glorieuses, Juan de Nova and Tromelin are administered from Réunion.

Prefect, H. Fournier

Trade with UK	1993	1994
Imports from UK	£13,283,000	£14,096,000
Exports to UK	5,453,000	1,410,000

TERRITORIAL COLLECTIVITÉS

MAYOTTE – Area, 144 sq. miles (372 sq. km). Population (1991 census) is 94,410. Capital, Mamoundzou (12,000). Part of the Comoros Islands group, Mayotte remained a French dependency when the other three islands became independent as the Comoros Republic in 1975. Since 1976 the island has been a *collectivité territoriale,* an intermediate status between Overseas Department and Overseas Territory.

Prefect, A. Weil

Trade with UK	1993	1994
Imports from UK	£10,646,000	£11,086,000
Exports to UK	209,000	72,000

ST PIERRE AND MIQUELON – Area 93 sq. miles (242 sq. km). Population (1990) 6,300. Two small groups of islands off the coast of Newfoundland. Became a *collectivité territoriale* in 1985.

Prefect, R. Maurice

Trade with UK	1993	1994
Imports from UK	£1,075,000	£584,000
Exports to UK	—	—

OVERSEAS TERRITORIES

FRENCH POLYNESIA – Five archipelagos in the south Pacific, comprising the Society Islands (Windward Islands group includes Tahiti, Moorea, Makatea, Mehetia, Tetiaroa, Tubuai Manu; Leeward Islands group includes Huahine, Raiatea, Tahaa, Bora-Bora, Maupiti), the Tua-motu Islands (Rangiroa, Hao, Turéia, etc.), the Gambier Islands (Mangareva, etc.), the Tubuai Islands (Rimatara, Rurutu, Tubuai, Raivavae, Rapa, etc.) and the Marquesas Islands (Nuku-Hiva, Hiva-Oa, Fatu-Hiva, Tahuata, Ua Huka, etc.). Area, 1,544 sq. miles (4,000 sq. km). Population (1992) 204,000. Capital, ΨPapeete (24,200) in Tahiti. Economy based on tourism and exports of copra, coffee, vanilla, citrus fruits and cultured pearls.

Government Representative, M. Jau

Trade with UK	1993	1994
Imports from UK	£3,873,000	£4,028,000
Exports to UK	46,000	52,000

NEW CALEDONIA – A large island in the western Pacific, 700 miles east of Queensland. Dependencies are the Isles of Pines, the Loyalty Islands (Mahé, Lifou, Urea, etc.), the Bélep Archipelago, the Chesterfield Islands, the Huon Islands and Walpole. New Caledonia was discovered in 1774 and annexed by France in 1854; from 1871 to 1896 it was a convict settlement. A referendum in 1987 on the question of independence was boycotted by the indigenous Kanaks, and New Caledonia therefore voted to remain French. However, a new independence referendum has been promised for 1998. Area, 7,358 sq. miles (19,058 sq. km). Population (1992) 175,000. Capital ΨNoumea (65,000). It is one of the world's largest producers of nickel.

Government Delegate, A. Christnacht

Trade with UK	1993	1994
Imports from UK	£7,744,000	£7,012,000
Exports to UK	2,431,000	12,910,000

SOUTHERN AND ANTARCTIC TERRITORIES – Created in 1955 from former Réunion dependencies, the territory comprises the islands of Amsterdam (25 sq. miles) and St Paul (2.7 sq. miles), the Kerguelen Islands (2,700 sq. miles) and Crozet Islands (116 sq. miles) archipelagos and Adélie Land (116,800 sq. miles) in the Antarctic continent. The only population are members of staff of the scientific stations.

WALLIS AND FUTUNA ISLANDS – Two groups of islands (the Wallis Archipelago and the Îles de Hoorn) in the central Pacific, north-east of Fiji. Area, 106 sq. miles (274 sq. km). Population (1990 census) 13,705. Capital, Mata-Utu on Uvea, the main island of the Wallis group.
Supreme Administrator, M. Legrix.

Trade with UK	1993	1994
Imports from UK	£10,000	£4,000
Exports to UK	—	—

THE FRENCH COMMUNITY

The constitution of the Fifth French Republic, promulgated in 1958, envisaged the establishment of a French Community of States. A number of the former French states in Africa have seceded from the Community but for all practical purposes continue to enjoy the same close links with France as those that remain formally members. Most former French African colonies are closely linked to France by financial, technical and economic agreements.

Source for statistical data: *L'Annuaire Statistique de la France 1994; Tableaux de l'Economie Française 1994–5.*

GABON
République Gabonaise

Gabon lies on the Atlantic coast of Africa at the Equator and is flanked on the north by Equatorial Guinea and Cameroon, and on the east and south by Congo. It has an area of 103,347 sq. miles (267,667 sq. km) and a population (UN estimate 1992) of 1,237,000.

CAPITAL – ΨLibreville (251,000).
CURRENCY – Franc CFA of 100 centimes.
FLAG – Horizontal bands, green, yellow and blue.
NATIONAL ANTHEM – La Concorde.
NATIONAL DAY – 17 August.

GOVERNMENT

Gabon elected on 28 November 1958 to remain an autonomous republic within the French Community and gained full independence on 17 August 1960. The constitution provides for an executive President directly elected for a seven-year term, who appoints the Council of Ministers. There is a 120-member unicameral National Assembly.

Following unrest, a national conference was called in March 1990 and forced President Bongo to legalize opposition parties. Several rounds of multiparty elections were held from September to November 1990 and eventually won by the ruling Parti démocratique gabonais (PDG), amid allegations of fraud. The PDG formed a coalition government with several opposition parties but the opposition parties left the government in 1991 in protest at the domination of the PDG. Multiparty presidential elections were held in 1993 and won by the incumbent, President Bongo of the PDG, amid accusations of fraud, which led to riots in Libreville. Negotiations between the PDG government and opposition parties resulted in the Paris Agreement of September 1994 under which a new coalition government including opposition parties was formed the following month to prepare for parliamentary elections by early 1996.

HEAD OF STATE
President, El Hadj Omar Bongo, *assumed office* December 1967, *re-elected* 1973, 1979, 1986 and 5 December 1993

COUNCIL OF MINISTERS *as at August 1995*
Prime Minister, Dr Paulin Obame-Nguema
Minister of State, Equipment and Construction, Zacharie Myboto
Minister of State, Justice, Pierre-Louis Agondjo-Okawe
Minister of State, Foreign Affairs and Co-operation, Casimir Oye Mba
Minister of State, Lands, Housing, Welfare, Jean-François Ntoutoume-Emane
Minister of State, Labour, Human Resources and Training, Jean-Remy Pendy Bouyiki
Minister of State, Planning and Territorial Administration, Pierre-Claver Maganga Moussavou
Minister of State, Agriculture, Livestock and Rural Economy, Emmanuel Ondo Methogo
Public Health and Population, Dr Serge Mba Bekale
National Defence, Gen. Idriss Ngari
Communication, Culture, Arts, Education, Human Rights, Alexandre Sambat
Transport, Tourism, Merchant Marine and Fisheries, Antoine Mboumbou Miyakou
Finance, Economy and Participation, Marcel Doupambi Matoka
Civil Service and Administrative Reform, Simon Oyono Aba'a
Commerce and Industry, Andre-Dieudonne Berre
Mining, Energy and Oil, Paul Toungui
Higher Education and Scientific Research, Gaston Mozogo Ovono
Forestry, Posts and Telecommunications, Environment, Martin-Fidele Magnaga
Youth and Sports, Women's Affairs, Government Spokesperson, Paulette Missambo
Social Affairs, Sebastien Mamboundou Mouyama

EMBASSY OF THE REPUBLIC OF GABON
27 Elvaston Place, London SW7 5NL
Tel 0171–823 9986
Ambassador Extraordinary and Plenipotentiary, new appointment awaited

BRITISH AMBASSADOR, His Excellency William Quantrill, resident in Yaoundé, Cameroon.

ECONOMY

The economy is heavily dependent on oil and, to a much lesser extent, other mineral resources, including manganese and uranium. Gabon has considerable timber reserves (particularly Okoumé) with 80 per cent of the country still forested, although production has stagnated in recent years.

The economy experienced considerable growth in real terms from the mid-1970s onwards but after 1986 was adversely affected by the fall in oil prices. Revenue has increased in the 1990s following oil exploitation at Rabi-Kounga. Gabon is a full member of OPEC. The IMF approved a US$85 million credit in 1994.

TRADE WITH UK	1993	1994
Imports from UK	£21,887,000	£26,900,000
Exports to UK	6,065,000	3,851,000

THE GAMBIA
The Republic of the Gambia

The Gambia is named after the Gambia River, which it straddles for over 200 miles inland from the west coast of Africa. It is a narrow strip, surrounded by Senegal, except at the coast, lying between 13° 10′–13° 45′ N. and 13° 90′–16°

50' W. The area is 4,361 sq. miles (11,295 sq. km), of which one-fifth is the river. The climate is Sahelian, with a dry season between October and May and heavy rainfall in July and August (32–40 inches a year).

The population (UN estimate 1992) was 908,000, mainly Wolof, Mandinka and Fula peoples who originally migrated from the north and east.

CAPITAL – ΨBanjul. Population (1983 census) of the island of Banjul was 44,536; including adjacent Kombo St Mary 147,394.

CURRENCY – Dalasi (D) of 100 butut.

FLAG – Horizontal stripes of red, blue and green, separated by narrow white stripes.

NATIONAL ANTHEM – For The Gambia, Our Homeland.

NATIONAL DAY – 18 February (Independence Day).

HISTORY

The Gambia River basin was part of the region dominated in the tenth to 16th centuries by the Songhai and Mali kingdoms centred on the upper Niger. The Portuguese reached the Gambia River in 1447; English merchants began to trade along the river from 1588. Merchants from France, Courland (now Latvia) and the Netherlands also established trading posts. In 1816 the British stationed a garrison on an island at the river mouth which became the capital of a small British-administered colony. In 1889 France agreed that the British rights along the upper river should extend 10 km on either bank. British administration was extended from the Colony to this Protectorate. The Gambia became independent within the Commonwealth on 18 February 1965, and a republic on 24 April 1970.

The relationship with Senegal remains an important factor in political and economic policy. Moves towards a closer association were accelerated after an abortive coup in 1981 was put down with the help of Senegalese troops. In 1982 the Senegambia Confederation was instituted but following disagreements it was dissolved in 1989. A treaty of friendship and co-operation was signed with Senegal in 1991.

GOVERNMENT

The constitution is democratic and parliamentary, with an executive President elected for five years. The House of Representatives has 35 elected members, five elected Chiefs Representatives and up to eight nominated members plus the Attorney-General (ex-officio). The Vice-President and other ministers are appointed by the President. Parliament must be dissolved after five years.

The last general elections were held in 1992. In July 1994 junior army officers launched a military coup in protest at not being paid and at government corruption, which was blamed for squandering foreign aid. The President and some of his government fled to Senegal and the army officers formed a ruling military council. The coup leader, Lt. (later Capt.) Jammeh, assumed the presidency, the constitution was suspended and a civilian-military government was formed to rule in conjunction with the Ruling Military Council. A coup attempt in November 1994 led by Vice-President Lt. Sabally was defeated.

HEAD OF STATE
President, Chairman of the Ruling Military Council, Capt. Yayah Jammeh, *took power* 23 July 1994
Vice-President, Capt. Edward Singatey

RULING MILITARY COUNCIL *as at August 1995*
Capt. Yayah Jammeh, Capt. Edward Singatey, Capt. Yankuba Touray, Capt. Monofou Bajo, Capt. Ebou Jallow

CABINET *as at August 1995*
The President
Vice-President and Defence, Capt. Edward Singatey
Interior, Capt. Kaba Barjo
Finance, Ousman Koro-Ceesay
Justice, Mustapha Marong
Foreign Affairs, Baboucar Blaise Jagne
Tourism and Information, Capt. Mamat Omar Cham
Trade, Industry and Employment, Bala Garba Jhumpa
Local Government and Lands, Capt. Yankuba Touray
Education, Youth, Sports and Culture, Satang Jow
Public Works and Telecommunications, Mbemba Tambedu
Agriculture and National Resources, Musa Mbenga
Health, Social Welfare and Women's Affairs, Coumba Marenah-Ceesay

GAMBIA HIGH COMMISSION
57 Kensington Court, London W8 5DG
Tel 0171-937 6316
High Commissioner, His Excellency Hassan Gibril, apptd 1995

BRITISH HIGH COMMISSION
48 Atlantic Road, Fajara (PO Box 507), Banjul
Tel: Banjul 95133
High Commissioner, His Excellency Michael Hardie, OBE, apptd 1993

ECONOMY

Agriculture accounts for 75 per cent of employment and contributes 40 per cent of GDP. The chief product, groundnuts, is also the most important export item, forming over 80 per cent of domestic exports. Other crops are rice, millet, sorghum, maize and cotton. Fishing and livestock industries are being developed. Thirty per cent of the country's basic food requirements are imported. There are no significant deposits of minerals.

Manufactures are limited to groundnut processing, minor metal fabrications, paints, furniture, soap and bottling. Tourism is developing quickly. Trade through The Gambia, re-exporting imported goods to neighbouring countries, is an important element in the economy.

TRADE WITH UK	1993	1994
Imports from UK	£23,714,000	£16,521,000
Exports to UK	5,617,000	4,638,000

COMMUNICATIONS

There is an international airport at Yundum, 17 miles from Banjul, with scheduled services flying to other West African states and to the UK and Belgium. Banjul is the main port. Internal communication is by road and river. There are three broadcasting stations and a UHF telephone service linking Banjul with the principal towns in the provinces. There is no television service.

EDUCATION

There are 24 secondary schools (eight high and 16 technical) with a total enrolment of 15,635 students. Two high schools provide A-level education. Gambia College provides post-secondary courses in education, agriculture, public health and nursing. There are seven vocational training institutions with a total enrolment of 1,400. Higher education and advanced training courses are taken outside The Gambia, currently by over 200 students.

GEORGIA
Sakartvelos Respublika

Georgia has an area of 26,911 sq. miles (69,700 sq. km) and occupies the north-western part of the Caucasus region of the former Soviet Union. It is bordered on the north by Russia, on the south-east by Azerbaijan, on the south by Armenia, on the south-west by Turkey, and on the west by the Black Sea. It contains the two autonomous republics of Abkhazia and Adjaria and the autonomous province of South Ossetia.

Georgia is very mountainous, with the Greater Caucasus in the north and the Lesser Caucasus in the south. The relatively low-lying land between these two ranges is divided into western and eastern Georgia by the Surz Ridge. Western Georgia has a mild and damp climate, eastern Georgia is more continental and dry. The Black Sea shore and the Rioni lowland are subtropical.

According to a 1995 estimate, Georgia has a population of 5,401,000, of which 70 per cent are Georgian, 8 per cent Armenian, 6 per cent Russian, 6 per cent Azerbaijani and 3 per cent Ossetians, together with smaller groups of Abkhazians, Greeks, Ukrainians, Jews and Kurds. The majority religion is the Georgian Orthodox Church. There is also a small Muslim minority.

Georgian, Russian and Armenian are the most commonly used languages. Georgian is one of the oldest languages in the world to have been continually in use, the alphabet having emerged in the third century BC.

CAPITAL – Tbilisi. Population 1,260,000 (1989). Other major cities are Sukhumi (capital of Abkhazia) (125,000) and Batumi (150,000).

CURRENCY – The Georgian coupon, introduced in April 1993. In August 1993 Georgia left the rouble zone but is expected to re-enter it soon.

FLAG – Cherry red with a canton in the upper hoist divided black over white.

NATIONAL DAY – 26 May (Independence Day).

HISTORY

The Georgians are an ancient people who formed two states, Colchis and Iberia, on the edge of the Black Sea around 1000 BC. After centuries of invasions by Arabs, Turks and Khazars, Georgia entered its 'Golden Age' in the 12th century AD when trade, irrigation and communications were greatly developed. Invasions by the Khazars and Mongols led to the division of Georgia into several states. These struggled against the Turkish and the Persian Empires from the 16th to the 18th centuries, gradually turning to the Russian Empire for protection and support. Eastern Georgia signed a treaty of alliance with Russia which recognized Russian supremacy in 1783 and joined the Russian Empire in 1801, followed soon after by Western Georgia.

In the late 19th century nationalist and Marxist movements formed and competed for the limited political influence possible under autocratic Russian rule. One of the most prominent Marxist activists was Iosif Dzhugashvili (Josef Stalin). After the Russian revolution of 1917, a nationalist government came to power in Georgia supported by allied intervention forces. In 1921 Soviet forces occupied Tbilisi, and in 1922 Georgia joined the Soviet Union as part of the Transcaucasian Soviet Socialist Republic.

In March 1990 the Georgian Supreme Soviet declared illegal the treaties of 1921–2 by which Georgia had joined the Soviet Union. The Communist Party's monopoly on

power was abolished and in multiparty elections held in October and November 1990 the nationalist leader Zviad Gamsakhurdia was elected President. Georgia declared its independence from the Soviet Union in May 1991 and was admitted to UN membership on 31 July 1992.

GOVERNMENT

After independence the dictatorial attitude of Gamsakhurdia led to armed opposition to his government from late 1991 onwards. Defeat in the ensuing civil war in Tbilisi led to Gamsakhurdia's otherthrow in January 1992, with a military council taking power until March 1992, when a state council was appointed with the former Soviet foreign minister Eduard Shevardnadze as chairman. Fighting continued throughout 1992 and 1993 between the Government and supporters of Gamsakhurdia, and also Abkhazian separatists. In October 1992 Shevardnadze was elected head of state and Chairman of the Parliament, and a loose alliance of pro-Shevardnadze parties gained a majority in parliament and formed a government. No voting took place in Abkhazia or South Ossetia.

Gamsakhurdia returned to western Georgia in September 1993 to ferment rebellion after the poor conduct of the war against Abkhazian separatists, together with economic chaos and deprivations, caused the government to resign in August 1993. President Shevardnadze assumed full executive powers at the head of an emergency council, but failed to prevent the advance of the rebels from western Georgia because most government forces were engaged in Abkhazia. Shevardnadze was forced to accept Russian armaments and troops in October to defeat the rebellion the following month and in return agreed to join the CIS. Russian influence in Georgia was further increased by the signing of a ten-year Treaty of Friendship and Co-operation in February 1994 under which Russia gained a decisive say in Georgian economic policy and maintains three major military bases in the country. The Georgian parliament ratified CIS membership on 1 March 1994.

President Shevardnadze finally secured stability in Georgia in May 1995 with the disarming of the paramilitary Mkhedrioni force. This came two months after Russia pledged to secure the reintegration of Abkhazia and South Ossetia into Georgia.

SECESSION

In late 1990 the South Ossetians took up arms against Georgian rule in an attempt to join North Ossetia, itself part of Russia. The South Ossetian provincial parliament voted in November 1992 to secede from Georgia and join Russia. The province's status remains unresolved since June 1992 when fighting stopped and a joint Russian-Georgian-Ossetian peacekeeping force was put in place.

In July 1992 the Abkhazian republican parliament declared Abkhazia independent of Georgia. Fighting broke out between Georgian forces and Abkhazian separatists supported by Russian arms and irregulars; Georgian forces were defeated and had to withdraw from Abkhazia in September 1993. Negotiations under Russian auspices led to an Abkhaz-Georgian ceasefire and separation of forces agreement being signed in May 1994 and the deployment of 2,500 Russian UN peacekeepers on the Abkhaz-Georgian border. In November 1994 the Abkhaz Supreme Soviet declared Abkhazia's independence again and elected Vladislav Ardzinba as President.

HEAD OF STATE
President, Chairman of the Supreme Soviet, Eduard Shevardnadze, *elected* 11 October 1992

CABINET *as at August 1995*
Prime Minister, Otar Patsatsiya
Deputy Prime Ministers, Amiran Kadagishvili; Zurab Kervavishvili; Nicolaz Lekishvili; Avtandil Margiani; Tamas Nadareishvili; Bakur Gulua
Defence, Lt.-Gen. Vardiko Nadibaidze
National Security, Igor Georgadse
Industry, Vladimir Kereselidse
State Property, Avtandil Silagadse
Economics, Vladimir Patava
Finance, David Yakobidse
Communications, Pridon Indjia
Agriculture and Food, Georgy Kvesitadse
Environment, Shota Adamia
Education, Tamas Kvachantiradse
Culture, David Magradse
Public Health, Irakly Menagarishvili
Foreign Affairs, Alexander Chikvaidse
Interior, Shota Kviraga
Justice, Tevdore Ninidse
Social Welfare and Labour, Vaja Gudjavidse
Trade, Zurab Zankaliani

GEORGIAN AMBASSADOR, His Excellency Teimuraz Mamatsashvili, apptd 1995

BRITISH AMBASSADOR, His Excellency Stephen Nash, apptd 1995

ECONOMY

The economy was brought to the brink of collapse by civil and secessionist wars and the ending of former Soviet trading relationships. Industrial production fell by 70 per cent between 1991 and 1995 and foreign aid forms a large part of the budget, with an IMF loan of US$40 million in December 1994. Although Georgia has deposits of coal, they have not been exploited and it is desperately short of energy supplies. There were little or no supplies of gas, electricity and heating in the winter of 1994–5. It is hoped that the closer economic relations with Russia will yield cheap supplies of grain and oil. A large proportion of production is stolen by black marketers, whilst the tourist industry on the Black Sea coast has been destroyed by the fighting. The only productive sector of the economy is agriculture, with a concentration on viniculture, tea and tobacco-growing and citrus fruits. Georgia will replace its inflationary currency, the coupon, with the stronger Russian rouble when it re-enters the rouble zone.

TRADE WITH UK	1993	1994
Imports from UK	£9,166,000	£6,392,000
Exports to UK	283,000	143,000

GERMANY
Bundesrepublik Deutschland – Federal Republic of Germany

The area is approximately 138,000 sq. miles (357,050 sq km). The estimated population (March 1993) is 81,075,000, of whom 65,400,000 live in the former West and 15,700,000 in the former East Germany. In 1992 there were 28,875,000 Protestants, 27,663,000 Roman Catholics, and 1,900,000 Muslims. The number of Jews was estimated to be 41,000 in 1993.

CAPITAL – Berlin. By decision of the Bundestag, the seat of government is to be transferred from Bonn, West Germany's post-war provisional capital, to the historical capital, Berlin. The move is scheduled for completion by 2000. The *Bundesrat* (upper house) will remain in Bonn (population 297,400).

OTHER CITIES AND TOWNS – populations (1992):

Berlin	3,454,200	Stuttgart	596,900
Hamburg	1,675,200	Düsseldorf	577,400
Munich	1,241,300	Bremen	553,200
Cologne	958,600	Duisberg	538,300
Frankfurt am		Hanover	520,900
Main	660,800	Leipzig	500,000
Essen	627,800	Nuremberg	498,500
Dortmund	600,700	Dresden	483,400

CURRENCY – Deutsche Mark (DM) of 100 Pfennig.
FLAG – Horizontal bars of black, red and gold.
NATIONAL ANTHEM – Einigkeit und Recht und Freiheit (Unity and right and freedom).
NATIONAL DAY – 3 October (Anniversary of 1990 Unification).

HISTORY

The term 'deutsch' (German) probably began to be used in the eighth century and initially described the language spoken in the eastern part of the Frankish realm which reached its apogee in Charlemagne's reign; subsequently the term was transferred from the language to its speakers, and to the region they lived in. The first German realm was the Holy Roman Empire, established in AD 962 when Otto I of Saxony was crowned Emperor. The Empire endured until 1806, but from as early as the 12th century the achievement of a national state was prevented by territorial fragmentation into small principalities and dukedoms, the gradually increasing autonomy of their rulers weakening the central power.

The Holy Roman Empire was replaced by a loose association of sovereign states known as the German Confederation, which was dissolved in 1866 and replaced by the Prussian-dominated North German Federation. Prussia had translated its earlier economic predominance into political hegemony by the annexation of the duchies of Schleswig and Holstein from Denmark in 1864 and a decisive defeat of Austria in 1866 (the Seven Weeks' War) which ended Austrian influence over German politics. After the Franco-Prussian War of 1870–1 resulted in the defeat of France and the cession of Alsace and part of Lorraine, the south German principalities united with the northern federation to form a second German Empire, the King of Prussia being proclaimed Emperor in 1871.

Germany's defeat in the First World War led to the abdication of the Emperor and the princes, and the country became a republic. The Treaty of Versailles 1919 returned Alsace–Lorraine to France, large areas in the east of the country were lost to the new state of Poland, and all German colonies placed under the administration of other countries. The world economic crisis of 1929 led to the collapse of the Weimar Republic and the subsequent rise to power of the National Socialist movement of Adolf Hitler, who became Chancellor in 1933.

After concluding a Treaty of Non-Aggression with the Soviet Union in August 1939, Germany invaded Poland (1 September 1939), precipitating the Second World War, which lasted until 1945. Hitler committed suicide on 30 April 1945. On 8 May 1945, the unconditional surrender of all German forces was accepted by representatives of the Western Allied and Soviet Supreme Commanders.

THE POST-WAR PERIOD

After the surrender, the Four Powers (France, UK, USA, USSR) assumed supreme authority in Germany. Policy was agreed at the Potsdam Conference (July/August 1945) between the UK, USA and USSR. Germany was divided into American, French, British and Soviet zones of occupation. Supreme authority in each zone was exercised by the respective Commanders-in-Chief, and, in matters affecting Germany as a whole, jointly through the Control Council of the four Commanders. Berlin was placed under the joint administration of the four occupying powers. However, quadripartite control failed when differences with the USSR over the implementation of the Potsdam Agreement could not be resolved; against a background of growing international tension, the USSR withdrew from the Control Council in 1948. The rift divided Germany *de facto* into east and west.

The Federal Republic of Germany (FRG) was created out of the three western zones in 1949 when, following general elections, a federal government took office in Bonn and the Basic Law (federal constitution) came into force. A Communist government was meanwhile established in the Soviet zone (henceforth the German Democratic Republic (GDR)). The Bonn/Paris Conventions in 1955 terminated the occupation regime in West Germany and restored federal German autonomy subject to the reservation of Three Power rights and responsibilities relating to Berlin and to Germany as a whole, including the reunification of Germany and a peace settlement. The GDR became an ostensibly sovereign state in the same year.

In 1961 the Soviet zone of Berlin was sealed off, and the Berlin Wall was built along the zonal boundary, partitioning the western sectors of the city from the eastern.

Soviet-initiated reform in eastern europe during the late 1980s led to unrest in the GDR. The mass exodus of its citizens to the west via Hungary and Czechoslovakia culminated in the opening of the Berlin Wall in November 1989 and the collapse of Communist government there. The 'Treaty on the Final Settlement with respect to Germany', concluded between the FRG, GDR and the four former occupying powers in September 1990, unified Germany with effect from 3 October 1990 as a fully sovereign state occupying the territory of the former two Germanies and Berlin. Economic and monetary union preceded formal union on 1 July 1990. Unification is constitutionally the accession of Berlin and the five reformed *Länder* of the GDR to the FRG, which remains in being. The first government of the new Germany took office in January 1991 following all-German elections on 2 December 1990.

GOVERNMENT

The Basic Law provides for a President, elected by a Federal Convention (electoral college) for a five-year term, a lower house (*Bundestag*) of 672 members elected by direct universal suffrage for a four-year term of office, and an upper house (*Bundesrat*) composed of 79 members appointed by the governments of the *Länder* in proportion to *Länder* populations, without a fixed term of office.

The last election for the Bundestag was held on 16 October 1994. The distribution of seats at July 1995 is: Christian Democratic Union, 244; Social Democrats, 252; Free Democrats, 47; Christian Social Union, 50; Democratic Socialists, 30; The Greens, 49.

HEAD OF STATE
Federal President, Professor Roman Herzog, *born* 1934, *elected* 23 May 1994, *sworn in* 1 July 1994

CABINET *as at August 1995*
Federal Chancellor, Dr Helmut Kohl (CDU)
Foreign Affairs and Deputy Chancellor, Dr Klaus Kinkel (FDP)
Federal Chancellery, Friedrich Böhl (CDU)
Interior, Manfred Kanther (CDU)
Economy, Dr Günter Rexrodt (FDP)
Justice, Sabine Leutheusser-Schnarrenberger (FDP)
Finance, Dr Theodor Waigel (CSU)
Agriculture, Jochen Borchert (CDU)
Labour and Social Affairs, Dr Norbert Blüm (CDU)
Defence, Volker Rühe (CDU)
Health, Horst Seehofer (CSU)
Family and Elderly, Women and Youth, Claudia Nolte (CDU)
Transport, Matthias Wissmann (CDU)
Environment, Dr Angela Merkel (CDU)
Posts and Telecommunications, Dr Wolfgang Bötsch (CSU)
Regional Planning, Housing and Urban Development, Prof. Klaus Töpfer (CDU)
Education, Research and Technology, Dr Jürgen Rüttgers (CDU)
Economic Co-operation and Development, Carl-Dieter Spranger (CSU)

CDU Christian Democratic Union; CSU Christian Social Union; FDP Free Democratic Party.

EMBASSY OF THE FEDERAL REPUBLIC OF GERMANY
23 Belgrave Square, London SW1X 8PZ
Tel 0171-235 5033/824 1300
Ambassador Extraordinary and Plenipotentiary, His Excellency Dr Jürgen Osterhelt, apptd 1995
Minister, Dr Friedrich Kroneck

Minister-Counsellor, Gerhard Kunz
First Counsellors, Dr R. W. Ehni (*Cultural Affairs*); B. Westphal (*Economic Affairs*)
Defence Attaché, Rear-Adm. K. M. Reichert

BRITISH EMBASSY
Friedrich-Ebert-Allee 77, 53113 Bonn
Tel: Bonn 91670
Ambassador Extraordinary and Plenipotentiary, His Excellency Sir Nigel Broomfield, KCMG, apptd 1993
Minister, J. A. Shepherd, CMG
Defence Attaché, Col. P. P. Rawlens, MBE
Counsellor (Economic), Dr P. Collecott
Counsellor (Management and Consular), S. C. Johns

BRITISH CONSULATE-GENERAL
Yorck Strasse 19, 40476 Düsseldorf
Consul-General and Director-General of Trade and Investment Promotion, A. C. Hunt, CMG

BRITISH EMBASSY OFFICE, BERLIN
Unter den Linden 32/34, 0-10117 Berlin
Tel: Berlin 201 840
Minister and Head of Mission, R. J. Spencer, CMG
Counsellor, Deputy Head of Mission, D. L. Corner
First Secretary (Commercial), P. Bateman
There are British Consulates-General at Berlin, Düsseldorf, Frankfurt, Hamburg, Munich and Stuttgart and Consulates at Bremen, Hanover, Kiel and Nuremberg.

BRITISH COUNCIL REPRESENTATIVE, K. Dobson, OBE, Hahnenstrasse 6, 50667 Köln. Offices at Berlin, Leipzig, Hamburg and Munich and British Council libraries at all five centres.

BRITISH CHAMBER OF COMMERCE, Neumarkt 14, D-5000 Köln 1. *Director,* Herr Heumann

REGIONAL GOVERNMENT

Germany is a federal republic composed of 16 states (*Länder*) (ten from the former West, five from the former East and Berlin). Each *Land* has its own directly elected legislature and government led by Minister-Presidents (Prime Ministers) or equivalents. The 1949 Basic Law (federal constitution) vests executive power in the *Länder* governments except in those areas reserved for the federal government.

Land	Popu-lation (1992)	Minister-President (August 1995)
Baden-Württemberg	10.0m	Erwin Teufel (CDU)
Bavaria	11.2m	Edmund Stoiber (CSU)
Berlin	3.5m	Eberhard Diepgen (CDU)*
Brandenburg	2.7m	Manfred Stolpe (SPD)
Bremen	0.6m	Klaus Wedemeier (SPD)*
Hamburg	1.7m	Henning Voscherau (SPD)*
Hesse	5.6m	Hans Eichel (SPD)
Lower Saxony	7.2m	Gerhard Schröder (SPD)
Mecklenburg–Western Pomerania	2.0m	Berndt Seite (CDU)
North Rhine-Westphalia	17.7m	Johannes Rau (SPD)
Rhineland-Palatinate	3.9m	Kurt Beck (SPD)
Saarland	1.0m	Oskar Lafontaine (SPD)
Saxony	4.8m	Kurt Biedenkopf (CDU)
Saxony-Anhalt	2.9m	Reinhard Höppner (SPD)
Schleswig-Holstein	2.6m	Heidi Simonis (SPD)
Thuringia	2.6m	Bernhardt Vogel (CDU)

*Berlin, *Govening Mayor;* Bremen, *Mayor;* Hamburg, *First Mayor.*

JUDICATURE

Judicial authority is exercised by the Federal Constitutional Court, the federal courts provided for in the Basic Law and the courts of the Länder. The death sentence has been abolished.
President of Federal Constitutional Court, Jutta Limbach

DEFENCE

Under the terms of the Treaty of Unification the German armed forces have been limited to 370,000 active personnel since the end of 1994. The actual strength is 367,300 (154,100 conscripts), with a term of conscription of 12 months.

The Army has a strength of 254,300 including 122,800 conscripts. It deploys 4,255 main battle tanks, 1,180 artillery pieces, 6,995 armoured personnel carriers and infantry fighting vehicles, and 622 helicopters. In addition, former GDR equipment in store includes 815 main battle tanks, 2,790 armoured personnel carriers, 536 artillery pieces and 45 helicopters. The Army is organized into four armoured, three armoured infantry, one air mobile and one mountain division, with one aviation, one intelligence and one special forces brigades, eight artillery and seven air defence regiments, and eight reconnaissance battalions.

The Navy has a strength of 30,100 including 6,700 conscripts, with 20 submarines, 12 principal surface combatants and 64 combat aircraft and 17 armed helicopters. The Air Force has a strength of 82,900 including 24,600 conscripts, with 454 combat aircraft. Organization is in three commands: tactical command with one electronic counter-measures and one reconnaissance wings and seven air defence and eight ground attack squadrons; transport command with four wings; and training command.

There remain 169,700 NATO personnel in Germany (USA 103,200; UK 38,200; Belgium 10,300; France 15,000; Netherlands 3,000). The number is to be reduced to 110,000 by 2000; all remaining Russian forces left on 31 August 1994.

During 1993 both the Constitutional Court and the Bundestag agreed that German armed forces may operate outside Germany and the NATO area in UN and other peacekeeping operations for the first time since 1945. In 1994 the Constitutional Court ruled that German forces could serve in armed peacemaking missions. The wish to fulfil a stronger international role means that by August 1995 German personnel had been engaged in UN operations in Somalia, Cambodia, NATO AWACS aircraft patrols over the former Yugoslavia, NATO and WEU patrols in the Adriatic enforcing the UN blockade against the rump Yugoslav state, and were deploying a field hospital in Croatia and Tornado aircraft in Italy to support a possible UN withdrawal from Bosnia..

ECONOMY

Despite the division of Germany, which cut off the main food-producing areas of eastern Germany and some of the principal centres of light industry, West Germany became the main industrial power in Europe. The united Germany is the most economically powerful member of the European Union.

Unification costs have severely strained the German economy, also beset by widespread structural problems. Capital transfers from West to East Germany amount to around DM 180 billion a year under a massive government investment programme. After a mini-boom generated by new East German demand in 1990 and 1991, Germany entered its most severe recession since the war. Real GDP fell in the West by 1.9 per cent in 1993. The first budgetary and trade deficits in the West for over ten years resulted in tax increases, rising interest rates and serious inflationary pressures. In 1993 a 'Solidarity Pact' agreement was reached by federal and länder governments, opposition parties, and employers and trade unions, to take effect from 1995 onwards. The pact lays down the basis of future funding transfers to the East based on a 7.5 per cent rise in income taxes, wage restraint in the West, more private investment in the East, and the distribution of the funding burden between the federal and länder governments. The 'Solidarity Pact' was supplemented in August 1993 by reductions of DM 77,000 million in Western social security payments for the 1994–6 period, and in 1994 by a petrol tax levy on private motorists. A successfully restructured economy returned to export-led growth in 1994 with a GDP growth rate of 2.8 per cent and an increase in manufacturing output of three per cent. In 1993 federal GDP stood at DM 3,320,000 million and federal inflation was 3.0 per cent.

Under the impact of free market conditions East German output fell to 40 per cent of pre-unification levels. The sudden loss of established East European markets following the introduction of the Deutsche Mark, and the rapid rise of East German labour costs without corresponding increases in productivity, were largely responsible for this. Unemployment reached a peak of 15 per cent in 1993 but was much higher if job creation schemes and part-time working are taken into account. A market economic improvement began in 1994, with GDP growing by 8.9 per cent and industrial output by 20 per cent while inflation fell dramatically to 3.4 per cent and unemployment fell to 13.8 per cent.

PRODUCTION

Germany has a predominantly industrial economy. Principal industries are coal mining, iron and steel production, machine construction, the electrical industry, the manufacture of steel and metal products, chemicals, automobile production, electronics, textiles, and the processing of foodstuffs.

Annual production figures were ('000 tonnes):

All Germany	1992	1993
Hard coal	65,906	58,282
Brown coal	241,745	221,748
Crude petroleum	3,304	3,051
Pig iron	27,586	26,322
Rolled steel	28,959	29,717
Petrol	25,329	26,733
Cement	37,194	36,801
Passenger vehicles (units)	4,160,000	3,285,000

In 1992 total area of farmland was 11.5 million hectares, of which 7.3 million hectares (West Germany) and 4.2 million (East Germany) were arable land. Forest areas cover 10.4 million hectares. Crop yields were ('000 tonnes):

All Germany	1992
Rye	2,340.5
Wheat	15,541.7
Barley	12,196.5
Oats	1,314.1
Potatoes	10,897.0
Sugar beet	31,093.7
Colza and rape	2,616.8

Milk production in 1992 was 27,851,000 tonnes. Total yield of fisheries in 1992 was 211,763 tonnes, valued at DM240,556,000.

LABOUR

Labour figures, in annual averages, were:

West Germany	1993	1994
Employment	28,652,000	28,340,000
Unemployed	2,270,000	2,557,000

In 1994 the unemployment rate in the West was 8.3 per cent and in the East was 13.8 per cent, giving a federal rate of 9.9 per cent.

FINANCE

	1994	1995p
Expenditure	DM478 billion	DM484 billion
Revenue	408 billion	425 billion

p planned

TRADE (All Germany)

	1992	1993
Total imports	DM637,546m	DM566,495m
Total exports	671,203m	628,387m

Main trading partners in 1993 were (figures shown as percentage of total trade):

	Imports	Exports
France	11.2	11.7
Netherlands	8.3	7.4
Italy	8.1	7.2
USA	7.4	7.7
UK	6.1	7.7
Belgium/Luxembourg	5.7	6.6
Japan	6.3	2.6

Trade with UK	1993	1994
Imports from UK	£15,093,481,000	£16,827,931,000
Exports to UK	18,793,316,400	21,349,900,000

COMMUNICATIONS

At the end of 1991 the state-owned railways of the Federal Republic (Deutsche Bundesbahn and Reichsbahn) measured 41,525 km of which 16,285 km were electrified, and the privately owned railways totalled approximately 2,807 km. In 1991 the railways handled 418.5 million tonnes of goods. State railways rolling stock included, in 1991, 3,891 electric locomotives, 7,516 diesel locomotives and 314,325 goods wagons.

Classified roads measured 226,282 km (West and East) in 1992, of which motorways were 10,955 km. The total number of motor vehicles registered at the end of 1992 was 46.7 million.

Ocean-going shipping under the German flag in December 1991, amounted to 5,996,000 tons gross. Inland waterways were 6,929 km long in 1991.

SOCIAL WELFARE

There is compulsory insurance against sickness, accident, old age and unemployment. Children's allowances, child rearing benefits and parental leave of absence are available in respect of all children. Pension schemes for widows and orphans of public servants are in operation. Public assistance is given to persons unable to earn their living, or with insufficient income to maintain a decent standard of living.

EDUCATION

School attendance is compulsory for all children and juveniles between the ages of six and 18 and comprises nine years full-time compulsory education at primary and main schools and three years of compulsory vocational education on a part-time basis. In 1993 there were 24,095 primary and main schools (Grund und Hauptschulen) with

4,626,400 pupils. Secondary modern schools (*Realschulen*) numbered 3,527 with 1,106,000 pupils. There were 4,099 other general secondary schools (*Gymnasien* including *Gesamtschulen*) with 2,624,000 pupils.

There were also 3,389 special schools (*Sonderschulen*) for physically and mentally handicapped and socially maladjusted children with 372,200 pupils.

The secondary school leaving examination (*Abitur*) entitles the holder to a place of study at a university or another institution of higher education.

Children below the age of 18 who are not attending a general secondary or a full-time vocational school have compulsory day-release at a vocational school. In 1993 there were 3,327 full- and part-time vocational schools (*Berufsschulen*) with 1,613,700 pupils and 211 vocational extension schools (*Berufsaufbauschulen*) with 5,600 pupils, 2,627 full-time vocational schools (*Berufsfachschulen*) with 285,500 pupils, 1,337 schools for secondary technical studies (*Fachoberschulen/Fachgymnasien*) with 235,400 students.

In 1993–4 there were a total of 1,874,938 students at institutions of higher education, of whom 1,296,231 were attending universities. The largest universities are in Munich, Berlin, Hamburg, Bonn and Cologne.

CULTURE

Modern (or New High) German has developed from the time of the Reformation to the present day, with differences of dialect in Austria, Alsace, Luxembourg, Liechtenstein and the German-speaking cantons of Switzerland.

The literary language is usually regarded as having become fixed by Luther and Zwingli at the Reformation, since which time many great names occur in all branches, notably philosophy, from Leibnitz (1646–1716) to Kant (1724–1804), Fichte (1762–1814), Schelling (1775–1854) and Hegel (1770–1831); drama from Goethe (1749–1832) and Schiller (1759–1805) to Gerhart Hauptmann (1862–1946); and poetry, Heine (1797–1856). Seven German authors have received the Nobel Prize for Literature: Theodor Mommsen (1902), R. Eucken (1908), P. Heyse (1909), Gerhart Hauptmann (1912), Thomas Mann (1929), N. Sachs (1966) and Heinrich Böll (1972).

GHANA
The Republic of Ghana

Ghana is situated on the Gulf of Guinea, between 3° 07′ W. and 1° 14′ E. longitude, and extends 441 miles north from Cape Three Points (4° 45′ N.) to 11° 11′ N. It is bounded on the north by Burkina, on the west by the Côte d'Ivoire, on the east by Togo, and on the south by the Atlantic Ocean. Although tropical, Ghana is cooler than many countries in similar latitudes. It has a total area of 92,099 sq. miles (238,537 sq. km).

The population (UN estimate 1992) was 15,959,000. Most are Sudanese Negroes, although Hamitic strains are common in the north. The official language is English. The principal indigenous language group is Akan, of which Twi and Fanti are the most commonly used. Ga, Ewe and languages of the Mole-Dagbani group are common in certain regions. Most Ghanaians are Christians, although there is a substantial Muslim minority in the north.

CAPITAL – ΨAccra. Population of the Greater Accra Region (including Tema) was (1990 estimate) 1,781,100. Other towns are Kumasi, Tamale, ΨSekondi-Takoradi,

ΨCape Coast, Sunyani, Ho, Koforidua, Wa and ΨWinneba.

CURRENCY – Cedi of 100 pesewas.

FLAG – Equal horizontal bands of red over gold over green; five-point black star on gold stripe.

NATIONAL ANTHEM – God Bless our Homeland Ghana.

NATIONAL DAY – 6 March (Independence Day).

GOVERNMENT

First reached by Europeans in the 15th century, the constituent parts of Ghana came under British administration at various times, the original Gold Coast (the coastal and southern areas) being constituted in 1874; Ashanti in 1901; and the Northern Territories Protectorate in 1901. The territory of Trans-Volta-Togoland, part of the former German colony of Togo, was mandated to Britain by the League of Nations after the First World War, and remained under British administration as a United Nations Trusteeship after the Second World War. After a plebiscite in 1956, under UN auspices, the territory was integrated with the Gold Coast Colony. The former Gold Coast Colony and associated territories became the independent state of Ghana on 6 March 1957 and became a republic in 1960.

Since 1966 Ghana has experienced long periods of military rule (1966–9, 1972–9, 1982–92) interspersed with short-lived civilian governments. A coup in 1979 led to the formation of an Armed Forces Revolutionary Council chaired by Flt. Lt. Jerry Rawlings. Civilian rule was restored in 1979 but overthrown on 31 December 1981, when another coup brought Flt. Lt. Rawlings back to power.

A referendum in April 1992 approved a new multiparty constitution and the legalization of political parties. The National Democratic Congress (NDC) was established as a political party from the ruling Provisional National Defence Council. Flt. Lt. Rawlings won the presidential election in November 1992 and the National Democratic Congress won parliamentary elections in December 1992, with 189 out of 200 seats. The parliamentary election was boycotted by most opposition parties and most of the electorate, who protested at Rawlings standing for the presidency. The Fourth Republic was declared on 7 January 1993 and a new government nominated by the President and approved by parliament took office in March 1993. As executive President, Flt. Lt. (retd) Rawlings also chairs the cabinet. The presidential term is four years, renewable only once.

For political and administrative purposes Ghana is divided into ten regions, each headed by a Regional Minister who is the representative of the central government.

HEAD OF STATE
President, Flt. Lt. (retd) Jerry John Rawlings, *took power* 31 December 1981, *elected* 3 November 1992
Vice-President, Kow Nkensen Arkaah

CABINET *as at August 1995*
The President
The Vice-President
Defence, Mahama Iddrisu
Finance and Economic Planning, Dr Kwesi Botchwey
Foreign Affairs, Acting Attorney-General and Justice, Dr Obed Asamoah
Information, Kofi Quakyi
Parliamentary Affairs, J. H. Owusu-Acheampong
Interior, Col. (retd) E. M. Osei-Owusu
Trade and Industries, Emma Mitchell
Transport and Communications, Edward Salia

Mines and Energy, Richard Kwame Peprah
Education, Harry Sawyerr
Local Government and Rural Development, Kwamena Ahwoi
Food and Agriculture, Ibrahim Adams
Employment and Social Welfare, David Boateng
Environment, Christine Amoaka-Nuamah
Health, Commodore (retd) Steven Obimpeh
Lands and Forestry, Dr Kwabena Adjei

Speaker of the Legislature, Mr Justice Daniel Annan

GHANA HIGH COMMISSION
104 Highgate Hill, London N6 5HE
Tel 0181-342 8686
High Commissioner, His Excellency K. K. S. Dadzie, apptd
1994
Deputy High Commissioner, Johnson Osei-Hwedieh
Defence Adviser, Brig. H. W. K. Agbevey
Counsellor, A. K. Budu-Amoako (*Trade*)

BRITISH HIGH COMMISSION
PO Box 296, Osu Link, Accra
Tel: Accra 221665
High Commissioner, His Excellency David Walker, CVO,
apptd 1992
Deputy High Commissioner, D. Wyatt
Defence Adviser, Lt.-Col. A. R. Gale, MBE
First Secretary (Management/Consular), D. J. Walker
First Secretary (Commercial), S. S. Strong

BRITISH COUNCIL DIRECTOR, T. Cowin, Liberia Road
(PO Box 771), Accra. There is also an office in Kumasi.

ECONOMY

Agriculture is the basis of the economy, employing 70 per
cent of the work-force. Crops include cocoa, the largest
single source of revenue, rice, cassava, avocado pears,
oranges and pineapples, groundnuts, corn, millet, oil
palms, yams, maize and vegetables. Livestock is raised in
the uncultivated areas. Attempts are being made to
diversify agricultural production, with cash crops such as
coffee and tobacco being extensively cultivated for export
and to provide raw materials for local industry. Fishing is
important in coastal areas and in the Volta lake and river
system.

The area within a 60-mile radius of Dunkwa produces
90 per cent of Ghana's mineral exports. Manganese
production ranks among the world's largest and industrial
diamonds and bauxite are also produced. The Ashanti
Goldfields Corporation is one of the world's largest
producers and was privatized in 1994 with estimated gold
reserves of 20.3 million ounces. Some 30,000 persons are
employed by the mining companies.

Small-scale traditional industries include tailoring,
goldsmithing and carpentry. Priority has been given in
recent years to establishing a number of 'pioneer industries' including timber products, vehicle and refrigerator
assembly, cigarettes, boatbuilding, food processing, cotton
textiles, clothing, footwear, printing and other light industries. A modern industrial complex is growing in the Accra-
Tema area. Tourism is also of growing importance.

Since 1966 the Volta Dams at Akosombo and Kpong
have generated hydro-electric power for the processing of
bauxite and fed a power transmission network for most of
Ghana, Togo and Benin.

Under the Economic Recovery Programme (ERP) in
place since 1983, the Ghanaian economy has achieved a
growth rate of 6 per cent a year for the past decade and paid
off a large proportion of its foreign debt; debt servicing had
fallen to 30 per cent of export earnings in 1991. IMF and
World Bank support for the ERP's free market and
deregulatory restructuring has gained Ghana US$3,600

million in soft loans and grants in the past decade and
enabled the diversification of agricultural and industrial
production.

TRADE

Principal exports are cocoa, timber, minerals and gold.
Principal imports are road vehicles, manufacturing equipment, petroleum and raw materials.

Trade with UK	1993	1994
Imports from UK	£214,081,000	£190,625,000
Exports to UK	71,814,000	138,814,000

COMMUNICATIONS

The Kotoka Airport at Accra is an international airport and
Ghana Airways is the national airline. There are also
internal airports at Takoradi, Kumasi, Sunyani, and
Tamale.

There are 20,000 miles of motorable roads, of which
2,335 miles are bituminized. There are 600 miles of
railway, linking Accra and the principal ports of Takoradi
and Tema with their hinterlands, the mining centres and
with each other.

Takoradi Harbour consists of seven quay berths: one is
leased specially for manganese exports. Tema Harbour has
ten berths for larger ocean-going vessels and the largest dry
dock on the West African coast. An oil berth has also been
built to serve the refinery at Tema.

GREECE
Elliniki Dimokratia

Greece is a maritime state in the south-east of Europe,
bounded on the north by Albania, the Former Yugoslav
Republic of Macedonia and Bulgaria, on the south and west
by the Ionian and Mediterranean seas, and on the east by
Turkey and the Aegean Sea. It has an estimated area of
50,944 sq. miles (131,944 sq. km).

The main areas are: Macedonia (which includes Mt
Athos and the island of Thasos), Thrace (including the
island of Samothrace), Epirus, Thessaly, Continental
Greece (which includes the island of Euboea and the
Sporades), Crete and the Peloponnese. The main island
groups are the Sporades (of which the largest is Skyros), the
Dodecanese or Southern Sporades (Rhodes, Astypalaia,
Karpathos, Kassos, Nisyros, Kalymnos, Leros, Patmos,
Kos, Symi, Khalki, Tilos), the Cyclades (about 200,
including Syros, Andros, Tinos, Mykonos, Naxos, Paros,
Santorini, Milos and Serifos), the Ionian Islands (Corfu,
Paxos, Levkas, Ithaca, Cephalonia, Zante and Cerigo), the
Aegean Islands (Chios, Lesbos, Limnos and Samos). In
Crete from about 3000 to 1400 BC a civilization flourished
which spread its influence throughout the Aegean, and the
ruins of the palace of Minos at Knossos afford evidence of
astonishing comfort and luxury.

The population at the 1991 census was 10,256,464. Over
97 per cent are adherents of the Greek Orthodox Church,
which is the state religion, all others being tolerated. The
Church of Greece recognizes the spiritual primacy of the
Ecumenical Patriarch of Constantinople, but is otherwise a
self-governing body administered by the Holy Synod
under the presidency of the Archbishop of Athens and All
Greece. The separate Church of Crete, has a degree of
autonomy under the Ecumenical Patriarch, while the
monastic community of Mount Athos and the Church in
the Dodecanese come directly under the Ecumenical
Patriarch.

CAPITAL – Athens, population (including ΨPiraeus and suburbs), 3,096,775 (1991 census). Other large towns are (1991) ΨThessaloniki (Salonika) (739,998); ΨPatras (172,763); ΨHeraklion (Crete) (127,600); ΨVolos (115,732); Larissa (113,426); ΨCanea (Crete) (65,519); ΨKavalla (58,576); ΨRhodes (43,619).

CURRENCY – Drachma of 100 leptae.

FLAG – Blue and white stripes with a white cross on a blue field in the canton.

NATIONAL ANTHEM – Imnos Eis Tin Eleftherian (Hymn to Freedom).

NATIONAL DAY – March 25 (Independence Day).

GOVERNMENT

Greece was under Turkish rule from the mid 15th century until a war of independence (1821–2) led to the establishment of a Greek kingdom in the Peloponnese in 1829. The remainder of Greece gradually became independent in stages until the Dodecanese were returned by Italy in 1947. After heavy resistance to the Nazi German occupation of 1941–5, a civil war between monarchist and Communist groups lasted from 1946 to 1949, and tension between right-wing and radical groups continued after 1949. In 1967 right-wing elements in the army seized power and established a military regime (the 'Greek Colonels'). The King went into voluntary exile in 1967; in 1974 the monarchy was abolished and a republic established.

Unrest in Athens in 1973–4 intensified after the government was involved in the overthrow of President Makarios of Cyprus in July 1974, and led the Colonels to surrender power. Konstantinos Karamanlis (Prime Minister 1955–63) returned from exile to form a provisional government, and the first elections for ten years were held in November 1974. The constitutional position of the King, who was still in exile, remained unsettled until 8 December, when the restoration of the monarchy was rejected by 69.2 per cent to 30.8 per cent and Greece became a republic.

A new constitution came into force in 1975. In 1986 most executive power was transferred from the President to the government and the President became a ceremonial figure. The unicameral 300-member Chamber of Deputies is elected for a four-year term by universal adult suffrage under a system of proportional representation, with a three per cent threshold for parliamentary representation.

The most recent general election was held on 10 October 1993 with the Panhellenic Socialist Party (PASOK) winning 170 seats, the New Democracy Party (Christian Democrats) 111 seats, the Political Spring Party ten seats and the Communist Alliance nine seats. In February 1994 the government imposed a trade embargo on and sealed its border with the Former Yugoslav Republic of Macedonia over its alleged territorial claim to northern Greece.

HEAD OF STATE

President of the Hellenic Republic, Constantine Stephanopoulos, *elected by parliament* 8 March 1995

CABINET *as at August 1995*

Prime Minister, Andreous Papandreou
Minister to the PM, Ioannis Pottakis
Foreign Affairs, Karolos Papoulias
Interior, Constantine Skandalides
National Defence, Gerasimos Arsenis
Justice, Anastasios Peponis
National Economy, Yiannos Papantoniou
Merchant Marine, Georgios Katsifaras
Agriculture, Georgios Moraitis
Finance, Alexandros Papadoupoulos
Labour, Ioannis Skoularikis
Health, Welfare and Social Security, Dimitrios Kremastinos
Education and Religious Affairs, Georgios Papandreou
Culture, Thanos Mikroutsikos
Public Order, Sifis Valypakis
Macedonia and Thrace, Konstantinos Triaridis
Environment, Town Planning and Public Works, Constantine Laliotis
Industry, Commerce, Energy and Technology, Constantine Simitis
Transport and Communications, Athanassious Tsouras
Aegean, Antonios Kotsakas
Press and Mass Media, Government Spokesman, Evangelos Venizelos

EMBASSY OF GREECE
1A Holland Park, London WII 3TP
Tel 0171-229 3850
Ambassador Extraordinary and Plenipotentiary, His Excellency Elias Gounaris, apptd 1993
Deputy Ambassador, A. Scopelitis
Defence Attaché, Capt. A. Economou
Consul-General, G. Costoulas
Counsellor, A. Missa-Kerkentzes (*Economic Affairs*)

There are Honorary Consulates at Belfast, Birmingham, Edinburgh, Falmouth, Glasgow, Leeds and Southampton.

BRITISH EMBASSY
1 Ploutarchou Street, 10675 Athens
Tel: Athens 7236211
Ambassador Extraordinary and Plenipotentiary, His Excellency Oliver Miles, CMG, apptd 1993
Deputy Head of Mission, Counsellor and Consul-General, C. J. Denne, CMG
Defence and Military Attaché, Brig. N. M. Prideaux
First Secretary (Commercial), N. J. Bowie

BRITISH CONSULAR OFFICES – There are British Consular Offices at Athens, Corfu, Patras, Kos, Rhodes, Salonika, Heraklion (Crete) and Syros.

BRITISH COUNCIL DIRECTOR, Dr J. L. Munby, OBE, 17 Plateia Philikis Etairias (PO Box 3488), Kolonaki Square, Athens 10210. There is also an office at Salonika.

BRITISH-HELLENIC CHAMBER OF COMMERCE, 25 Vas. Sofias Avenue, GR-106 74 Athens. Tel: 72 10 361

DEFENCE

The total active armed forces number 159,300 personnel (122,300 conscripts); conscripts serve between 19 and 23 months. The strength of the Army is 113,000 (100,000 conscripts), in addition there are 34,000 in the National Guard. Equipment includes 2,720 main battle tanks, 2,510 armoured personnel carriers and armoured infantry fighting vehicles, and 1,245 artillery pieces. The Navy consists of 19,500 men (7,900 conscripts) and is equipped with eight submarines, six destroyers and eight frigates with 12 armed helicopters. The Air Force consists of 26,800 men (14,400 conscripts) and has a total of 355 combat aircraft.

Greece maintains 2,250 army personnel in Cyprus. There is also a paramilitary Gendarmerie of 26,500 personnel. Some 760 US personnel are stationed in Greece.

ECONOMY

The 1989–93 New Democracy government followed an IMF-recommended austerity programme of privatization and reduction of the overmanned public sector. This has been partially reversed by the PASOK government, which has slowed privatization. Despite significant European Union capital transfers the economy remains in poor condition, with inflation at 10 per cent, the budget deficit 13 per cent of GDP, public debt at 120 per cent of GDP, large-scale tax evasion and a huge black economy.

Though there has been a substantial measure of industrialization, agriculture still employs about a fifth of the working population. The most important agricultural products are tobacco, wheat, cotton, sugar, rice, fruit (olives, peaches, vines, oranges, lemons, figs, almonds and currant-vines). Exports of fresh fruit, currants and vegetables are an important contributor to the economy.

The principal minerals are nickel, bauxite, iron ore, iron pyrites, manganese magnesite, chrome, lead, zinc and emery, and prospecting for petroleum is being carried on. The chief industries are textiles (cotton, woollen and synthetics), chemicals, cement, glass, metallurgy, shipbuilding, domestic electrical equipment and footwear, the production of aluminium, nickel, iron and steel products, tyres, chemicals, fertilizers and sugar (from locally-grown beet). Food processing and ancillary industries have also grown up throughout the country.

The development of the country's electric power resources, irrigation and land reclamation schemes, and the exploitation of lignite resources for fuel and industrial purposes are also being carried out. Tourism has developed rapidly, with over 10 million visitors in 1994.

Trade	1992	1993
Total imports	US$19,902m	US$17,615m
Total exports	6,008m	5,034m

Trade with UK	1993	1994
Imports from UK	£875,698,000	£908,837,000
Exports to UK	310,186,000	347,634,000

COMMUNICATIONS

The 2,650 km of railways are state-owned, with the exception of the Athens–Piraeus Electric Railway. Roads total over 35,500 km, of which about 25 per cent are national highways and just under 30,000 km are provincial roads. In March 1994 the Greek mercantile fleet numbered 1,864 ships over 100 tons gross with a total tonnage of 53,778,128 tons gross. Athens has direct airline links with Australasia, North America, most countries in Europe, Africa and the Middle East.

EDUCATION

Education is free and compulsory from the age of six to 15 and is maintained by state grants. There are ten universities: Athens, Thessaloniki, Patras, Thrace, Ioannina, Piraeus, Aegean, Ionian, Thessaly and Crete. There are several other institutes of higher learning, mostly in Athens.

CULTURE

Greek civilization emerged c. 1300 BC and the poems of Homer, the blind poet of Chios, which were probably current c. 800 BC, record the struggle between the Achaeans of Greece and the Phrygians of Troy (1194 to 1184 BC).

The spoken language of modern Greece is descended from the Common Greek of Alexander the Great's empire. *Katharevousa*, a conservative literary dialect evolved by Adamantios Corais (Diamant Coray) (1748–1833) and used for official and technical matters, has been phased out. Novels and poetry are mostly in *dimotiki*, a progressive literary dialect which owes much to John Psycharis (1854–1929). The poets Solomos, Palamas, Cavafy and Sikelianos have won a European reputation. Giorgis Seferis (1963) and Odysseus Elytis (1979) have won the Nobel Prize for Literature.

GRENADA
The State of Grenada

Grenada is situated between 12°13′–11° 58′ N. latitude and 61° 20′–61° 35′ W. longitude, and is about 90 miles north of Trinidad, 68 miles south-south-west of St Vincent, and about 120 miles south-west of Barbados. The island is about 21 miles long and 12 miles wide, with an area of 133 sq. miles (344 sq. km). Also a part of Grenada are some of the Grenadines islets, the largest of which is Carriacou, 13 square miles in area. The country is mountainous.

The population is 95,000 (1992 census).

CAPITAL – ΨSt George's (population 10,000) on the south-west coast, has a good harbour.

CURRENCY – East Caribbean dollar (EC$) of 100 cents.

FLAG – Divided diagonally into yellow and green triangles within a red border containing six yellow stars, a yellow star on a red disc in the centre and a nutmeg on the green triangle in the hoist.

NATIONAL DAY – 7 February (Independence Day).

GOVERNMENT

Discovered by Columbus in 1498, and named Conception, Grenada was originally colonized by France and was ceded to Great Britain by the Treaty of Versailles 1783. It became an Associated State in 1967 and an independent nation within the Commonwealth on 7 February 1974.

The government was overthrown in 1979 by the New Jewel Movement and a People's Revolutionary Government was set up. In October 1983 disagreements within the PRG led to violence and the death of Prime Minister Maurice Bishop, whose government was replaced by a Revolutionary Military Council. These events prompted the intervention of Caribbean and US forces. The Governor-General installed an advisory council to act as an interim government until a general election was held in December 1984. A phased withdrawal of US forces was completed by June 1985.

The Queen is head of state and is represented by a Governor-General. Legislative power is vested in a bicameral parliament consisting of an elected 15-member House of Representatives and a nine-member Senate appointed by the Governor-General. The most recent general election was held on 20 June 1995 and won by the New National Party led by Dr Keith Mitchell, with eight seats in the House of Representatives to the National Democratic Congress's five seats. At the time of going to press a new government had yet to be formed.

Governor-General, His Excellency Sir Reginald Palmer, GCMG, apptd 1993

GRENADA HIGH COMMISSION
1 Collingham Gardens, London SW5 OHW
Tel 0171–373 7809
High Commissioner, new appointment awaited.

BRITISH HIGH COMMISSION
14 Church Street, St George's
Tel: St George's 3222
High Commissioner, His Excellency Emrys Davies, CMG, resides at Bridgetown, Barbados
Resident Representative, M. R. Eastburn *(Acting High Commissioner)*

JUDICIARY

Justice is administered by the Organization of Eastern Caribbean States (OECS) Supreme Court, which is composed of a High Court of Justice and a two-tier Court of Appeals, and by Magistrates' Courts. The final court of appeal remains the UK Privy Council.

ECONOMY

The economy is principally agrarian, with cocoa, nutmegs and bananas the major crops. Fruit and vegetables are grown and a little livestock raised for domestic consumption. The fishing industry is being developed. Manufacturing consists of processing agricultural products and the production of textiles, concrete, aluminium and handicrafts.

Tourism has prospered since the opening of the Point Salines International Airport in 1984. A hotel expansion programme is taking place. The number of cruise ship calls to Grenada in 1993 was 382, bringing 200,061 visitors out of a total of 300,602 tourists.

TRADE

In 1993 total exports amounted to US$20.4 million, of which 84 per cent were agricultural products, mainly nutmeg, cocoa, bananas and mace. Total imports were US$118.4 million, mainly machinery and manufactured goods. The total external debt in 1993 was US$66.4 million.

Trade with UK	1993	1994
Imports from UK	£6,628,000	£7,335,000
Exports to UK	3,919,000	2,707,000

GUATEMALA
República de Guatemala

Guatemala, in Central America, is situated in 13° 45' to 17° 49' N. latitude and 88° 12' 49" to 92°13' 43" W. longitude and has an area of 42,042 sq. miles (108,889 sq. km). The country is traversed from west to east by mountains containing volcanic summits rising to 13,000 feet above sea level; earthquakes are frequent. There are numerous rivers. The climate is hot and malarial near the coast, temperate in the higher regions.

The population (estimate 1992) is 9,745,000. The language is Spanish, but 40 per cent of the population speak an Indian language.

CAPITAL – Guatemala City, population estimate (1990), 1,675,589. Quezaltenango has a population of over 100,000. Other towns are ΨPuerto Barrios (23,000), Mazatenango (21,000), and Antigua (30,000).
CURRENCY – Quetzal (Q) of 100 centavos.
FLAG – Three vertical bands, blue, white, blue; coat of arms on white stripe.
NATIONAL ANTHEM – Guatemala Feliz (Guatemala be praised).
NATIONAL DAY – 15 September.

GOVERNMENT

Guatemala was under Spanish rule from 1524 to 1821 when it became independent. It formed part of the Confederation of Central America from 1823 to 1839, when the Confederation dissolved.

After military coups in 1963, 1982 and 1983, civilian rule was restored with the election of a Constituent Assembly in 1984 and the promulgation of a new constitution in 1985.

In May 1993 President Serrano partially suspended the constitution, dissolved Congress and the Supreme Court and attempted to rule by decree until a new constitution was drafted to combat state corruption. However, he failed to gain the support of military, political and business leaders and was effectively ousted by the Army on 1 June when he fled the country. Ramiro de León Carpio, was elected President by Congress to serve out Serrano's term to January 1996.

President de León continued the attempt to end political corruption and in November 1993 forced Congress and the Supreme Court to dissolve themselves and to agree to constitutional changes, including reducing the presidential term to four years, which were ratified by a referendum in January 1994. Legislative elections to a smaller 80-seat Congress were held in August 1994 and the new Congress elected 13 new Supreme Court judges in October 1994.

Executive power is vested in the directly elected President, who appoints the Cabinet and is assisted by the Vice-President. Legislative authority is vested in the National Congress.

The republic is divided into 22 departments.

INSURGENCY

Since 1960 the armed forces have been fighting insurgency by the left-wing, mainly Mayan Indian, guerrillas of the Guatemalan Revolutionary National Unity Movement (URNG). Some 100,000 have been killed in the fighting, which reached its peak in the Army's 1979–82 counter-insurgency campaign. Government-URNG negotiations began in 1991 and have continued since, leading to a reduction in fighting and agreements in 1993 on the return of 45,000 refugees from Mexico and in 1994 on the resettlement of one million internal refugees. In March 1994 a human rights accord was reached under which a 300-strong UN Observer Mission (MINUGUA) was established in November 1994 to supervise the implementation of government–URNG accords. An accord recognizing the rights of the indigenous population was signed in March 1995. Peace talks continue and the URNG has shrunk to around 2,000 guerrillas.

HEAD OF STATE

President, Ramiro de León Carpio, *elected by Congress* 5 June 1993
Vice-President, Arturo Herbruger Asturias

GOVERNMENT *as at August 1995*
The President
The Vice-President
Foreign Affairs, Maritza Ruíz de Vielman
Interior, Carlos Enrique Reynoso
Defence, Gen. Mario Enríquez Morales
Finance, Ana Ordoñez de Molina
Economy and Foreign Trade, Eric Meza Duarte
Communications and Public Works, Ernesto Ramirez Pereira
Education, vacant
Energy and Mines, Julio Barrios
Agriculture, Luis del Valle García
Labour and Social Work, Gladys Morfín Mansilla
Health, Gustavo Hernández Polanco
Attorney-General, Acisclo Valladares

EMBASSY OF GUATEMALA
13 Fawcett Street, London SW10 9HN
Tel 0171-351 3042
Ambassador Extraordinary and Plenipotentiary, His Excellency
  Edmundo Nanne, apptd 1992

BRITISH EMBASSY
Centro Financiero Torre II (7th Floor), Seventh Avenue
5–10, Zone 4, Guatemala City
Tel: Guatemala City 321601
Ambassador Extraordinary and Plenipotentiary, His Excellency
  Peter Newton, apptd 1995
There is also a consulate at Puerto Barrios.

ECONOMY

The central government revenue in 1992 was Quetzales
5,483 million, and expenditure Quetzales 5,756 million.
The principal export is coffee, other articles being manufactured goods, sugar, bananas, cotton, beef and essential
oils. The chief imports are petroleum, vehicles, machinery
and foodstuffs.
  The chief seaports are San José de Guatemala and
Champerico on the Pacific and Santo Tomás de Castilla
and Puerto Barrios on the Atlantic side.

TRADE WITH UK	1993	1994
Imports from UK	£25,966,000	£22,686,000
Exports to UK	16,708,000	14,683,000

GUINEA
République de Guinée

Formerly part of French West Africa, Guinea has a
coastline on the Atlantic Ocean between Guinea-Bissau
and Sierra Leone, and in the interior is adjacent to Senegal,
Mali, Côte d'Ivoire, Liberia and Sierra Leone. The area is
94,926 sq. miles (245,857 sq. km). The population (UN
estimate 1992) is 6,116,000, mostly of the Fullah, Malinké
and Soussou tribes.

CAPITAL – ΨConakry (763,000). Other towns are Kankan,
  which is connected with Conakry by a railway, Kindia,
  N'Zérékoré, Mamou, Siguiri and Labé.
CURRENCY – Guinea franc of 100 centimes.
FLAG – Three vertical stripes of red, yellow and green.
NATIONAL DAY – 2 October (Anniversary of Proclamation
  of Independence).

GOVERNMENT

Guinea was separated from Senegal in 1891 and administered by France as a separate colony until 1958. On 2
October 1958 Guinea became an independent republic.

M. Sékou Touré assumed office as head of the new
government, and was elected President in 1961. President
Sékou Touré died in 1984; a few days later there was a
military coup. Guinea was ruled by a military government
directed by a Military Committee for National Recovery
(CMRN). A new constitution, providing for the end of
military rule and the introduction of a two-party system
within five years, was approved by referendum in 1990.
  In January 1991 the CMRN was dissolved and a mixed
civilian-military Transitional Committee for National
Recovery (CTRN) was established which appointed a
new government in February. Disturbances throughout
1991 led by trade unions and opposition parties caused the
government to introduce a full multiparty system in April
1992, since when 40 opposition parties have been legalized.
A presidential election was held in 1993 and won by the
incumbent President Conté with 51 per cent of the vote
amid opposition claims of electoral fraud. Legislative
elections were held in June 1995 and won by President
Conté's Party of Unity and Progress (PUP), which gained
71 of the 114 National Assembly seats.

HEAD OF STATE
President and Minister of Defence, Maj.-Gen. Lansana Conté,
  took power 3 April 1984, *elected* 19 December 1993

COUNCIL OF MINISTERS as at August 1995
The President
Foreign Affairs and Co-operation, Kozo Zomanigui
Minister at the Presidency in charge of National Defence, Lt.-Col.
  Abdourahmane Diallo
Interior and Security, Alseny René Gomez
Planning and Co-operation, Michel Kamano
Justice, Salifou Sylla
Finance, El Hadj Camara
Agriculture and Animal Resources, Makale Kamara
Energy and Environment, Assifat Dorank
Higher Educational and Scientific Research, Alioune Banire
  Diallo
Health, Kandjoura Drame
Youth, Arts and Sports, Toumani Dakoum Sako
Administrative Reform, Germaine Dualamu
Trade and Industry, Seku Konate
Transport, Maj. Ibrahim Sylla
Economy, Kazaliou Balde
Mines and Geology, Facinet Fofana
Urban Affairs and Housing, Lt.-Col. Jean Traore
Secondary Education, Aicha Bah Diallo
Public Works, Cellon Dalen Diallo
Fishing, Mamadi Diare
Labour and Social Affairs, Josephine Guilavo
Post and Telecommunications, Emmanuel Gnan
Childhood, Yvonne Conde

EMBASSY OF THE REPUBLIC OF GUINEA
51 rue de la Faisanderie, 75061 Paris, France
Tel: Paris 47048148
Ambassador Extraordinary and Plenipotentiary, His Excellency
  Lamine Kamara, apptd 1994

BRITISH CONSULATE
BP 834 Conakry, Guinea
British Ambassador, His Excellency Alan Furness, CMG,
  resident at Dakar, Senegal

ECONOMY

The principal products are bauxite, alumina, ironore,
palm kernels, millet, rice, coffee, bananas, pineapples
and rubber. At Sangaredi in the mountainous hinterland
large deposits of bauxite are mined. Deposits of iron ore,
gold, diamonds and uranium have also been discovered.

Principal imports are cotton goods, manufactured goods, tobacco, petroleum products, sugar, rice, flour and salt; exports, bauxite, alumina, iron-ore, diamonds, coffee, hides, bananas, palm kernels and pineapples.

TRADE WITH UK	1993	1994
Imports from UK	£11,059,000	£22,307,000
Exports to UK	593,000	1,675,000

GUINEA-BISSAU
República da Guiné-Bissau

Guinea-Bissau, formerly Portuguese Guinea, lies in western Africa, between Senegal and Guinea; it has an area of 13,948 sq. miles (36,125 sq. km), and a population (UN estimate 1992) of 1,006,000. The main ethnic groups are the Balante, Malinké, Fulani, Mandjako and Pepel.

CAPITAL – ΨBissau, population (census 1979) 109,486, is also the chief port.
CURRENCY – Guinea-Bissau peso of 100 centavos.
FLAG – Horizontal bands of yellow over green with vertical red band in the hoist charged with a black star.
NATIONAL DAY – 24 September (Independence Day).

GOVERNMENT

Guinea-Bissau achieved independence on 24 September 1974. Following a coup led by Maj. (now Brig.-Gen.) Vieira in 1980, the Assembly was suspended and a Revolutionary Council was established. Under a new constitution adopted in 1984, the Revolutionary Council became a 15-member Council of State and an Assembly of 150 members was set up. The ruling African Party for the Independence of Guinea and Cape Verde (PAIGC) voted to introduce a multiparty system in January 1991. Ten opposition parties have been legalized since November 1991. Legislative elections to a new 100-seat legislature were held on 3 July 1994 and won by the PAIGC, which took 64 seats. Brig.-Gen. Vieira won the second round of the presidential election on 7 August 1994 with 52 per cent of the vote.

HEAD OF STATE
Chairman of the Council of State, C.-in-C. of the Armed Forces,
Brig.-Gen. João Bernardo Vieira, *took power* November 1980, *elected* June 1989, *re-elected for a five-year term* 7 August 1994

COUNCIL OF MINISTERS *as at August 1995*
Prime Minister, Manuel Saturnino da Costa
Foreign Affairs and Co-operation, Ansumane Mane
Justice, Daniel Ferreira
Finance, Rui Dia de Sousa
Rural Development and Agriculture, Isaac Monteiro
Fisheries, Artur Silva
Energy and Industry, Natural Resources, Joao Cardoso
Commerce and Industry, Zeca Martins
Health, Eugenia Saldanha
Youth, Culture and Sport, Paulo Silva
Social and Women's Affairs, Nharebat N'incaia N'tchasso
Public Works, Abubacar Balde
Transport and Communications, Fernando Delfim da Silva
Defence, Arafan Mane
Interior, Luis Oliveir Sanca

EMBASSY OF THE REPUBLIC OF GUINEA-BISSAU
94 Rue St Lazare, Paris 9, France
Tel: Paris 45261851
Ambassador Extraordinary and Plenipotentiary, His Excellency Leonel Sebastiao Vieira, apptd 1995

BRITISH CONSULATE
Mavegro Int., CP100, Bissau
British Ambassador, His Excellency Alan Furness, CMG, resident at Dakar, Senegal

ECONOMY

The country produces rice, coconuts, groundnuts and palm oil products. Cattle are raised, and there are bauxite deposits in the south. The government has started to introduce free market reforms to the economy and in January 1995 agreed a three-year loan of US$14 million with the IMF to support continuing reforms.

TRADE WITH UK	1993	1994
Imports from UK	£1,260,000	£4,016,000
Exports to UK	9,000	4,000

GUYANA
The Co-operative Republic of Guyana

Guyana (formerly British Guiana) is situated on the north-east coast of South America, bordering Venezuela, Brazil and Suriname. It has a total area of 83,000 sq. miles (214,969 sq. km).

There is a narrow alluvial coastal belt ten to 40 miles deep, mainly below sea level, which is drained and irrigated by canals constructed by the Dutch. Mountainous dense rain forest lies behind this, reaching its highest point at Mount Roraima (9,000 ft) on the junction of the Guyana–Brazil–Venezuela borders. In the south-west lies the open savanna of the Rupununi. The country is intersected by numerous large rivers and has many water-falls, notably the Kaieteur Fall on the Potaro River, the Horse Shoe Falls on the Essequibo and the Marina Fall on the Ipobe. There are two dry seasons: mid-February to end April and mid-August to end November.

The population (UN estimate 1992) is 808,000.

CAPITAL – ΨGeorgetown. Estimated population, including environs, 185,000. Other towns are: Linden (29,000); ΨNew Amsterdam (23,000); Corriverton (17,000).
CURRENCY – Guyana dollar (G$) of 100 cents.
FLAG – Green with a yellow, white-bordered triangle based on the hoist and surmounted by a red, black-bordered triangle.
NATIONAL ANTHEM – Dear Land of Guyana.
NATIONAL DAYS – 26 May (Independence Day); 23 February (Republic Day).

GOVERNMENT

Guyana became independent on 26 May 1966, with a Governor-General appointed by The Queen. It became a republic on 23 February 1970. The Independence constitution was replaced by a new constitution promulgated in 1980. It provides for an Executive President who serves a five-year term, a First Vice-President and Prime Minister, and a National Assembly of 65 members, of which 53 are elected nationally by proportional representation and 12 are regional representatives.

Presidential and general elections were held on 5 October 1992 after proper voter registration lists and electoral machinery had finallly been established after many years. In the presidential election Dr Cheddi Jagan defeated the incumbent Desmond Hoyte and in the legislative election Jagan's People's Progressive Party (PPP) defeated the People's National Congress (PNC) which had governed since independence. In the National Assembly the state of the parties at August 1994 was: PPP 36, PNC 26, Working People's Alliance 2, United Force 1.

HEAD OF STATE
Executive President, Dr Cheddi Bharrat Jagan, *elected* 5 October 1992, *sworn in* 9 October 1992

CABINET as at August 1995

The Executive President
First Vice-President, Prime Minister, Public Works, Communications, and Regional Development, Samuel Hinds
Attorney-General and Minister of Legal Affairs, Bernard De Santos
Senior Ministers:
Agriculture, Reepu Daman Persaud
Finance, Asgar Ally
Foreign Affairs, Clement Rohee
Health, Gail Teixeira
President's Office, vacant
Education and Cultural Development, Dale Bisnauth
Labour, Human Services and Social Security, Henry Jeffrey
Home Affairs, Feroze Mohamed
Trade, Industry and Tourism, Shree Chand
Ministers:
Public Works, Communications and Regional Development, Harripersaud Nokta
Agriculture, Clinton Collymore
Labour, Human Services and Social Security, Indra Chandarpaul
Amerindian Affairs, Vibert D'Souza
President's Office, George Fung-On

GUYANA HIGH COMMISSION
3 Palace Court, Bayswater Road, London W2 4LP
Tel 0171-229 7684
High Commissioner, His Excellency Laleshwar Singh, apptd 1993

BRITISH HIGH COMMISSION
44 Main Street (PO Box 10849), Georgetown
Tel: Georgetown 65881/4
High Commissioner, His Excellency David J. Johnson, CMG, CVO, apptd 1993

JUDICATURE

The Supreme Court of Judicature consists of a Court of Appeal and a High Court. There are also Courts of Summary Jurisdiction. The Court of Appeal consists of the Chancellor as President, the Chief Justice and Justices of Appeal.

The High Court consists of the Chief Justice, as President, and nine Puisne Judges. It is a court with unlimited jurisdiction in civil matters and exercises exclusive jurisdiction in probate, divorce and admiralty, and certain other matters.
Chancellor, K. M. George
Chief Justice, Aubrey Bishop

ECONOMY

The economy is based almost entirely on the main export items of Demerara sugar, rice, bauxite and alumina. Diamonds and gold are also mined, timber and rum are produced. There is some cattle ranching in the savanna country, and oil deposits have been found there. The fishing industry is being expanded. Industry is fairly small-scale. Much emphasis is now being placed on eco-tourism.

TRADE WITH UK	1993	1994
Imports from UK	£34,218,000	£26,922,000
Exports to UK	75,001,000	71,717,000

COMMUNICATIONS

Georgetown and New Amsterdam are the principal ports, though bauxite ships also sail to Linden, on the Demerara, and Everton, on the Berbice. There are no public railways and the few roads are confined mainly to the coastal areas. Air transport is the easiest form of communication between the coast and the interior.

There is a state-owned radio broadcasting station which operates two channels and a fledgling television service.

EDUCATION

The government assumed total control of the education system in 1976 and made education free. The government trains teachers for primary and secondary schools at its own institutions.

Approximately 1,800 students were enrolled at the University of Guyana in degree programmes and certificate and diploma courses in 1990. The government instituted fees for study at the University in 1994.

There are several technical and vocational institutions, as well as some 30 adult education schools (with an enrolment of 13,500). There are also a number of technical and vocational institutions not under the aegis of the Ministry of Education.

HAITI
République d'Haiti

The Republic of Haiti occupies the western third of the Caribbean island of Hispaniola. The area, including off-shore islands, is 10,714 sq. miles (27,750 sq. km), of which about three-quarters is mountainous. The climate is tropical with high humidity and an almost constant temperature.

The population (UN estimate 1992) is 6,764,000, of which 90 per cent are black and 10 per cent mulatto (mixed race). Both French and Creole are regarded as official languages. French is the language of government and the press but it is only spoken by the educated mulatto minority. The usual language is Creole.

CAPITAL – ΨPort-au-Prince. Population estimated at about 1 million. Other centres are: ΨCap Haitien (54,691); Gonaives (36,736); Les Cayes (27,222); Jérémie (25,117).
CURRENCY – Gourde of 100 centimes.
FLAG – Horizontally blue over red.
NATIONAL ANTHEM – La Dessalinienne.
NATIONAL DAY – 1 January.

GOVERNMENT

Haiti was a French slave colony under the name of Saint-Domingue from 1697 until 1791, when French rule was overthrown in a revolt led by Toussaint L'Ouverture, who made himself Governor-General. French rule was restored by Napoleon in 1802 but in 1803 French forces surrendered to a British naval blockade and on 1 January 1804 the colony was declared independent as Haiti by Jean Jacques Dessalines. Dessalines became Emperor of Haiti but was assassinated in 1806.

Haiti was under US military occupation from 1915 to 1934. Dr François 'Papa Doc' Duvalier was elected in 1957 and became life President in 1964. He was succeeded in 1971 by his son Jean-Claude 'Baby Doc' Duvalier who continued his father's brutal methods of maintaining power. Jean-Claude Duvalier fled to France in 1986 in the face of sustained popular unrest. Five years of political instability and military government followed until Father Jean-Bertrand Aristide, leader of the National Front for Change and Democracy, won a free presidential election in 1990.

Father Aristide launched an anti-corruption campaign, removing from power the last supporters of the Duvalier dictatorships and purging the military leadership. This led to a military coup in September 1991 which ousted Aristide, who escaped to the USA. The Organization of American States (OAS) imposed a trade embargo on Haiti to force the military to accept the return of Aristide as President, but without immediate result.

Efforts to resolve the situation continued throughout 1992–4, led by the UN and OAS who increased international pressure on the military to accept Aristide's return. In June 1993 the UN imposed an oil and arms embargo and froze the military élite's foreign assets, which forced the military government to negotiate the Governor's Island Agreement with Aristide in July 1993. The Agreement provided for Aristide's return by 30 October 1993 and led to the lifting of UN sanctions, but in September 1993 the military reneged on the agreement and violently suppressed internal dissent by Aristide supporters. The UN reimposed sanctions and imposed a naval blockade, followed by a total economic, trade and travel ban in May 1994 as violence and human rights abuses by the military regime continued. Finally, on 31 July 1994, the UN Security Council authorized the use of force to overthrow the military regime, as the number of pro-democracy activists killed by the regime since Aristide's overthrow passed 4,000 and thousands of Haitians were fleeing the country in makeshift boats, causing a refugee crisis in the Caribbean.

As the USA began preparations for an invasion, President Clinton sent a negotiating team to Haiti which on 18 September 1994 reached an agreement with the military regime on President Aristide's return and the flight of the military junta members abroad. US troops began arriving the following day and disarmed the militia and other paramilitaries. The UN sanctions were lifted on 26 September and Aristide returned on 15 October after the military junta members had left the country. President Aristide appointed a new government and the Army and police were demobilized and began retraining by US personnel to form a smaller Army and civilian police force. UN forces of the UNMIH (UN Mission in Haiti) took over responsibility for internal security and retraining Army personnel on 31 March 1995. Elections to the 27-member Senate and 83-member Chamber of Deputies were held in June 1995 and a presidential election is due in December 1995.

HEAD OF STATE
President, Jean-Bertrand Aristide, *elected* 16 December 1990, *sworn in* 7 February 1991

CABINET *as at August 1995*

Prime Minister, Smarck Michel
Interior, Mondésir Beaubrun
Defence, Gen. (retd) Wilthan Lhérisson
Foreign Affairs, Claudette Werleigh
Finance, Marie-Michelle Rey
Co-operation, Jean-Marie Cherestal
Trade and Industry, Maurice Lafortune
Agriculture, François Severin
Public Works, Georges Anglade
Public Administration, Anthony Barbier
Justice, Jean-Joseph Exume
Health, Jean-Joseph Moliere
Social Affairs, Enold Joseph
Education, Emmanuel Buteau
Culture, Jean-Claude Bajeux

Information, Henri-Claude Ménard
Women's Affairs, Lise-Marie Dejean
Environment, Antoine Verdier
Haitians Abroad, Fritzner Casseus

BRITISH AMBASSADOR, His Excellency Derek Milton, CMG, resident at Kingston, Jamaica

ECONOMY

UN sanctions led to a sharp decline in economic activity, with industry particularly badly hit by the shortage of fuel. US aid increased dramatically, however, under the September 1994 agreement with the military regime, with US$550 million in emergency aid for food and fuel and the establishment of a US$1,000 million reconstruction fund. The new government has initiated a programme of economic reform supported by an IMF loan of US$31 million.

Agricultural production declined after the ending of the colonial plantation scheme. Measures had been taken with the aim of a gradual restoration of productivity. Coffee accounts for about 32 per cent of total exports. Cocoa is the second largest export earner. Corn, sorghum and rice are also grown. Increased production of tropical fruits and vegetables is being encouraged.

Items such as leather goods, textiles, electronic components and sports equipment are manufactured, using imported raw materials, for re-export. Principal imports are raw materials for the export assembly sector, foodstuffs, machinery, vehicles, mineral oils and textiles.

TRADE WITH UK	1993	1994
Imports from UK	£10,199,000	£7,754,000
Exports to UK	932,000	539,000

COMMUNICATIONS

The main roads are asphalted and secondary roads are fair. Air services are maintained between the capital and the principal provincial towns and to the USA and Caribbean and South American countries. The principal towns and villages are connected by telephone and/or telegraph. There are several commercial radio stations and two television stations at Port-au-Prince. Most services remain disrupted and are under reconstruction.

EDUCATION

Education is free but estimates of illiteracy are as high as 85 per cent.

HOLY SEE, *see* VATICAN CITY STATE

HONDURAS
República de Honduras

Honduras, in Central America, lies between 13° and 16° 30′ N. latitude and 83° and 89° 41′ W. longitude, with a seaboard of about 375 miles on the Caribbean Sea and 63 miles on the Pacific. It borders on Guatemala, Nicaragua and El Salvador and has a total area of 43,277 sq. miles (112,088 sq. km). The country is mountainous, being traversed by the Cordilleras, with peaks rising to 1,500 and 2,400 metres above sea level. Rainfall is seasonal, May to October being wet and November to April dry.

The population is 4,915,900 (1991 estimate) and of mixed Spanish and Indian blood. The Garifunas in the north are of West Indian origin. The language is Spanish, although English is the first language of many in the islands and on the north coast.

CAPITAL – Tegucigalpa, population (1991 estimate) 670,100; other towns are San Pedro Sula (325,900), ΨLa Ceiba (77,100), ΨPuerto Cortes (32,500), Choluteca (63,200) and ΨTela (24,000).

CURRENCY – Lempira of 100 centavos.

FLAG – Three horizontal bands, blue, white, blue (with five blue stars on white band).

NATIONAL ANTHEM – Tu Bandera Es Un Lampo De Cielo (Your flag is a heavenly light).

NATIONAL DAY – 15 September.

GOVERNMENT

Discovered and settled by the Spanish in the 16th century, Honduras formed part of the Spanish American dominions until 1821 when independence was proclaimed. Under military government from 1972, Honduras returned to civilian rule in 1981 with an executive Presidency, a 128-seat unicameral Congress, and a multi-party system based on the Liberal Party and the National Party. The last presidential and legislative elections were held on 28 November 1993 and won by the Liberal Party, which formed a new government in January 1994.

The country is divided into 18 departments.

HEAD OF STATE
President of the Republic, Carlos Roberto Reina, *elected* 28 November 1993, *sworn in* 27 January 1994
Vice-Presidents, Walter López Reyes; Juan de la Cruz Avelar; Guadalupe Jerezano

CABINET *as at August 1995*
Interior and Justice, Efraín Moncada Silva
Foreign Affairs, Delmer Urbizo Panting
Defence, Gen. Reynolds Andino Flores
Education, Zenobia Rodas de Léon Gómez
Finance, Juan Ferrera
Economic Planning, Guillermo Molina Chocano
Communications and Public Works, German Aparicio
Health, Dr Enrique Samayoa
Labour and Social Security, Cecilio Zavala Méndez
Natural Resources, Dr Ramon Villeda Bermúdez
Culture, Rodolfo Pastor Fasquelle
Economy, Gustavo Adolfo Aguilar
Environment, Carlos Medina
Director of National Agrarian Institute, Ubodoro Arriaga Iraheta
President of the Central Bank of Honduras, Dr Hugo Noé Pino

EMBASSY OF HONDURAS
115 Gloucester Place, London WIH 3PJ
Tel 0171–486 4880
Ambassador Extraordinary and Plenipotentiary, Her Excellency Celia de Cabañas

BRITISH EMBASSY
Apartado Postal 290, Tegucigalpa
Tel: Honduras 32–0612/18
Ambassador Extraordinary and Plenipotentiary, His Excellency Patrick Morgan, apptd 1992
There is a British Consulate in San Pedro Sula.

ECONOMY

Three-quarters of the country is covered by pine forests. Agriculture and cattle raising is mainly confined to the fertile coastal plain on the Caribbean and the extensive valleys in the Comayagua and Olancho regions of the interior. The Mosquitia tropical forest covers the area from the coast to the border with Nicaragua and provides valuable reserves of timber. Lead, zinc and silver are mined on a small scale.

The chief exports are coffee, bananas, frozen meat and timber, the most important woods being pine, mahogany and cedar. Other products are tobacco, beans, maize, rice, cotton, palm oil, sugar cane, cement, shrimps, lobsters and tropical fruits.

In July 1994 the IMF approved a three-year loan of US$58 million in support of the government's 1992–5 economic reform programme.

TRADE WITH UK	1993	1994
Imports from UK	£14,124,000	£13,861,000
Exports to UK	12,313,000	19,157,000

COMMUNICATIONS

There are about 1,004 km of railway in operation, chiefly to serve the banana plantations and the Caribbean ports. There are 17,947 km of roads, of which 2,613 km are paved. There are 33 smaller airstrips and four international airports, Tegucigalpa, San Pedro Sula, La Ceiba and Roatan (Bay Island).

The chief ports are Puerto Cortes, Tela and La Ceiba on the north coast, through which passes the bulk of the trade with the USA and Europe. Puerto Castilla is being developed as a deep-water container port, and San Lorenzo is also experiencing rapid growth.

EDUCATION

Primary and secondary education is free, primary education being compulsory, and the government has launched a campaign to eradicate illiteracy.

HUNGARY
Magyar Köztársaság

Hungary lies in eastern Europe and is bordered by the Slovak Republic to the north, Ukraine and Romania to the east, the rump Yugoslav Federal state and Croatia to the south, and Slovenia and Austria to the west. The area is 35,919 sq. miles (93,030 sq. km) with a population (1993) of 10,278,000. There are minorities of gypsies (4.8 per cent), ethnic Germans (1.9 per cent) and Slovaks (0.9 per cent). About two-thirds of the population are Roman Catholic and the remainder mostly Calvinist.

CAPITAL – Budapest, on the Danube; population (1992) 2,004,000. Other large towns are: Miskolc (192,000); Debrecen (215,000); Szeged (177,000) and Pécs (169,000).

CURRENCY – Forint of 100 fillér.

FLAG – Red, white, green (horizontally).

NATIONAL ANTHEM – Isten Aldd Meg A Magyart (God Bless the Hungarians).

NATIONAL DAYS – 15 March, 20 August, 23 October.

GOVERNMENT

Hungary, reconstituted as a kingdom in 1920 after having been declared a republic on 17 November 1918, joined the Anti-Comintern Pact in February 1939 and entered the Second World War on the side of Germany in 1941. On 20 January 1945 a Hungarian provisional government of liberation signed an armistice under the terms of which the frontiers of Hungary were withdrawn to the 1937 limits.

After the liberation, a coalition of the Smallholder, National Peasant, Social Democrat and Communist parties carried out land reform and nationalization. By 1949 the Communists had succeeded in gaining a monopoly of power and by 1952 practically the entire economy had been 'socialized'.

Divisions within the Communist Party and popular unrest in favour of free elections and Soviet troop withdrawals grew from July 1956 onwards. A national revolution broke out on 23 October with fighting between demonstrators and factory workers, and the State Security Police. Soviet forces intervened in strength early the next morning, but by 30 October had withdrawn from Budapest and on 3 November an all-party coalition government under Imre Nagy was formed. This government was overthrown and the revolution suppressed by a renewed attack by Soviet forces on Budapest on 4 November. The formation of a new Hungarian Revolutionary Worker Peasant (Communist) government under János Kádár was announced the same day.

From 1968 the government gradually introduced economic reforms and some political liberalization. Kádár was forced to resign in May 1989. In October 1989 the National Assembly (*Országgyülés*) approved an amended constitution which described Hungary as an independent, democratic state. The 386-seat National Assembly is elected on a mixed first past the post and proportional representation basis with a five per cent threshold for representation. The first free multiparty elections took place in March and April 1990 and were won by the (conservative) Hungarian Democratic Forum.

The last general election was held in May 1994 and won by the former ruling Communist Party, reconstituted as the Hungarian Socialist Party, as voters showed their dissatisfaction at the fall in living standards since 1990. A coalition government of the Hungarian Socialist Party and the Alliance of Free Democrats was sworn in on 15 July 1994. The government promised to continue economic reforms but with significantly increased welfare support and guarantees. The composition of the National Assembly in August 1995 was: Hungarian Socialist Party (HSP) 209, Alliance of Free Democrats (AFD) 70, Hungarian Democratic Forum 37, Independent Smallholders Party 26, Christian Democratic People's Party 22, Federation of Young Democrats 20.

HEAD OF STATE
President, Árpád Göncz, *sworn in* 3 August 1990, *re-elected by parliament* 19 June 1995

CABINET AS AT AUGUST 1995
Prime Minister, Gyula Horn (HSP)
Deputy Prime Minister, Interior, Gábor Kuncze (AFD)
Agriculture, László Lakos (HSP)
Justice, Pál Vastagh (HSP)
Industry and Trade, Imre Dunai (HSP)
Transport, Telecommunications and Water Management, Károly Lotz (AFD)
Foreign Affairs, László Kovács (HSP)
Defence, György Keleti (HSP)
Environment and Regional Policy, Ferenc Baja (HSP)
Labour, Magda Kósa (HSP)
Education and Culture, Gábor Fodor (AFD)
Health and Public Welfare, György Szabó (HSP)
Finance, Lajos Bokros (HSP)
Ministers without Portfolio, István Nikolits (HSP); Tamas Suchman (HSP) (*Privatization*)

HSP Hungarian Socialist Party; AFD Alliance of Free Democrats

EMBASSY OF THE REPUBLIC OF HUNGARY
35 Eaton Place, London SW1X 8BY
Tel 0171–235 4048/7191

Ambassador Extraordinary and Plenipotentiary, His Excellency
Tádé Alföldy, apptd 1995
Minister Plenipotentiary, József Hajgató
Counsellors, I. Gerelyes (*Consul*); P. Kallós (*Press*); J. Hámori
(*Commercial*); G. Körösi; I. Takács
Defence and Military Attaché, Col. L. Hajdú

BRITISH EMBASSY
Harmincad Utca 6, Budapest V
Tel: Budapest 266–2888
Ambassador Extraordinary and Plenipotentiary, His Excellency
Christopher Long, CMG, apptd 1995
Counsellor and Deputy Head of Mission, C. Prentice
Defence and Military Attaché, Lt.-Col. H. Stephens
First Secretary (Commercial), D. Taylor
First Secretary (Management) and Consul, S. MacTaggart, LVO

BRITISH COUNCIL DIRECTOR, Dr John Grote, OBE,
Benczur Utca 26, H–1068 Budapest VI

DEFENCE

Hungary has a total armed forces active strength of
74,500 (53,400 conscripts). Conscripts serve for 12
months. The Army has a strength of 56,500 (41,000
conscripts) with 1,191 main battle tanks, 1,645 armoured
personnel carriers and armoured infantry fighting vehicles
and 773 artillery pieces. The Air Force has a strength of
18,000 (12,300 conscripts), with 171 combat aircraft. As
Hungary is landlocked it has no navy but the Army
maintains a small Danube Flotilla with six mine counter-
measure vessels. In addition there are 2,230 paramilitary
border guards.

ECONOMY

After 1968 the Hungarian economy was allowed more
decentralized decision-making than most eastern European countries. The 1990–4 government embarked upon
the privatization of state-owned concerns, the deregulation
of the command economy and the return of nationalized
land to its former owners. The IMF in 1992–3 suspended a
three-year loan of US$1,621 million because of the
government's inability to meet agreed criteria, especially
the budget deficit, until an austerity budget was introduced
and the loan reactivated. In 1994–5 the IMF has again
suspended its loan because the new HSP-AFD government virtually stopped the privatization and economic
reform programmes and increased the budget deficit and
foreign debt (US$28,000 million in 1994). The new
government finally introduced an austerity budget cutting
the equivalent of 3 per cent of GDP and devaluing the forint
by 9 per cent in March 1995.

The economy has found the transition to a market
economy and the loss of export markets in the former
Soviet Union and former Yugoslavia difficult. The budget
deficit reached 7.2 per cent of GDP in 1995, with GDP
falling substantially in 1991–3 before beginning to rise in
1994, and unemployment at 10.8 per cent and inflation at 19
per cent in mid-1995. Privatization and the establishment
of small businesses proved successful in 1990–4, aided
by large-scale foreign investment of US$7,000 million
in 1990–4. Some 40 per cent of state enterprises have
been privatized and they produced 55 per cent of GDP in
1994.

Industry is mainly based on imported raw materials but
Hungary has its own coal (mostly brown), bauxite,
considerable deposits of natural gas (some not yet under
full exploitation), some iron ore and oil. Output figures in
1993 were (1,000 tons): coal 14,121; aluminium 6,328;
rolled steel 1,835; crude oil 1,709. Natural gas production
totalled 5,325 million cubic metres.

Agriculture accounts for 14 per cent of GDP and 23 per
cent of exports. In 1993, 6 per cent of the land area was
owned by state farms and 47 per cent was within co-
operative farms, which will remain a feature of Hungarian
agriculture. Production is concentrated on maize, wheat,
sugar beet, barley, rye and oats.

TRADE (Forints)	1993	1994
Imports	1,162,500m	1,395,000m
Exports	819,900m	967,482m

Trade with UK	1993	1994
Imports from UK	£205,692,000	£259,189,000
Exports to UK	152,209,000	240,075,000

EDUCATION

There are five types of schools under the Ministry of
Education: kindergartens for age three to six, general
schools for age six to 14 (compulsory), vocational schools
(15–18), secondary schools (15–18), universities and adult
training schools (over 18).

CULTURE

Magyar, or Hungarian, is one of the Finno-Ugrian
languages. Hungarian literature began to flourish in the
second half of the 16th century. Among the greatest writers
of the 19th and 20th centuries are Mihály Vörösmarty
(1800–55), Sándor Petöfi (1823–49), János Arany (1817–
82), Imre Madách (1823–64), Kálmán Mikszáth (1847–
1910), Endre Ady (1877–1918), Attila József (1905–37),
Mihály Babits (1883–1941), Dezsö Kosztolányi (1885–
1936), Gyula Illyes (1902–83), János Pilinszky (1921–81)
and Sándov Weöres (1913–89).

ICELAND
Island

Iceland is a large volcanic island in the North Atlantic
Ocean, extending from 63° 23' to 66° 33' N. latitude, and
from 13° 22' to 24° 35' W. longitude, with an estimated area
of 39,768 sq. miles (103,000 sq. km). The population was
266,786 on 1 December 1994. Some 92.2 per cent of the
population are members of the (Lutheran) Church of
Iceland.

CAPITAL – ΨReykjavík, population (1 December 1994),
103,036. Other centres are ΨAkureyri, Kópavogur,
ΨHafnarfjördur, Keflavík, Westmann Islands, Akranes,
Isafjördur and ΨSiglufjördur.
CURRENCY – Icelandic króna (Kr) of 100 aurar.
FLAG – Blue, with white-bordered red cross.
NATIONAL ANTHEM – O Gud Vors Lands (Our Country's
God).
NATIONAL DAY – 17 June.

GOVERNMENT

Iceland was uninhabited before the ninth century, when
settlers came from Norway. For several centuries a form of
republican government prevailed, with an annual assembly
of leading men called the *Althing,* but in 1241 Iceland
became subject to Norway, and later to Denmark. During
the colonial period, Iceland maintained its cultural integrity but a deterioration in the climate, together with
frequent volcanic eruptions and outbreaks of disease, led to
a serious fall in the standard of living and to a decline in the
population to little more than 40,000. In the 19th century a

struggle for independence began which led to home rule in 1918 and to independence as a republic in 1944.

The parliamentary (*Althing*) elections on 8 April 1995 gave the Independence Party 25 seats, Progressives 15, Social Democratic Party 7, People's Alliance 9, Awakening of the Nation 4, and Women's Alliance 3. A coalition government of the Independence Party and the Progressive Party was formed after the election.

HEAD OF STATE
President, Vigdís Finnbogadóttir, *born* 1930, *elected* 29 June 1980, *re-elected* 1984, 1988 and June 1992

CABINET *as at August 1995*

Prime Minister, Minister for the Statistical Bureau of Iceland, David Oddsson (IP)
Foreign Affairs and External Trade, Halldór Ásgrímsson (PP)
Finance, Fridrik Sophusson (IP)
Fisheries, Justice and Ecclesiastical Affairs, Thorsteinn Pálsson (IP)
Education and Culture, Björn Bjarnason (IP)
Social Affairs, Páll Pétursson (PP)
Health and Social Security, Ingibjörg Pálmadóttir (PP)
Trade and Industry, Finnur Ingólfsson (PP)
Communications, Halldór Blöndal (IP)
Agriculture and Environment, Gudmundur Bjarnason (PP)

IP Independence Party; PP Progressive Party

EMBASSY OF ICELAND
1 Eaton Terrace, London SW1W 8EY
Tel 0171–730 5131/2
Ambassador Extraordinary and Plenipotentiary, His Excellency Benedikt Ásgeirsson, apptd 1995

BRITISH EMBASSY
Laufásvegur 49, 101 Reykjavík
Tel: Reykjavík 15883/4
Ambassador Extraordinary and Plenipotentiary and Consul-General, His Excellency Michael S. Hone, OBE, apptd 1993

There is also a consulate at Akureyri.

ECONOMY

Iceland has considerable resources of hydro-electric and geothermal energy. It is estimated that exploitation of these two resources (4,540 Gigawatt hours in 1992) represents only about 9 per cent of that economically exploitable. Heavy industry includes an aluminium smelter, a nitrogen fertilizer factory, a cement factory, a diatomite plant and a ferro-silicon plant.

In 1994 Iceland had a total labour force of 149,000. The major sectors of the economy are fishing and fish processing, manufacturing, agriculture, energy production, government and the public sector, and tourism, which is of growing importance with 157,926 visitors in 1993.

As a member of the European Free Trade Association (EFTA), Iceland has become a member of the European Economic Area (EEA) which extends most of the provisions of the EU's single market to EFTA states.

TRADE

The principal exports are frozen fish fillets, salt fish, stock fish, fresh fish on ice, frozen scampi, fishmeal and oil, ferro-silicon and aluminium; the chief imports are consumer durables, capital goods, petroleum products, transport equipment, textiles, foodstuffs, animal feeds, timber, and alumina.

	1992	1993
Exports	Kr87,833m	Kr94,569m
Imports	96,895m	91,307m

Trade with UK	1993	1994
Imports from UK	£146,891,000	£109,693,000
Exports to UK	249,705,000	239,275,000

COMMUNICATIONS

At 1 January 1992, the mercantile marine consisted of 1,107 registered vessels (187,217 gross tons), of which 1,000 (140,349 gross tons) are decked fishing vessels. There are regular shipping services between Reykjavík and Felixstowe, Humber ports, Europe and the USA.

A regular air service is maintained by Icelandair between Glasgow and London and Reykjavík. There are also air services to Scandinavia, USA, Germany, France and Luxembourg.

Road communications are adequate in summer but greatly restricted by snow in winter. Only roads in town centres and key highways are metalled, the rest being of gravel, sand and lava dust. The climate and terrain make first-class surfaces for highways out of the question. There are no railways.

There are three television channels (one public, two private) and several private and public radio stations.

CULTURE

The ancient Norraena (or Northern tongue) has close affinities to Anglo-Saxon and as spoken and written in Iceland today differs little from that introduced into the island in the ninth century. There is a rich literature with two distinct periods of development, from the mid-11th to the late 13th century and from the early 19th century to the present.

INDIA
The Republic of India

India has an area of 1,269,346 sq. miles (3,287,590 sq. km), and three well-defined regions: the mountain range of the Himalayas, the Indo–Gangetic plain, and the southern peninsula. The main mountain ranges are the Himalayas (over 29,000 feet) and the Western and Eastern Ghats (over 8,000 feet). Major rivers include the Ganges, Indus, Krishna, Godavari and Mahanadi.

There are four seasons: cold (December–March); hot (April–May); rainy (June–September); and retreating south-west monsoon (October–November). Temperatures vary over the country between averages of about 10°C and 33°C, reaching over 38°C in some parts during the hot season. There are similar variations in rainfall, from only a few inches a year falling in the western Thar Desert to over 400 inches in Meghalaya.

The population at the 1991 census was 846,302,688. The majority are Hindu (82.6 per cent), the rest being Muslim (11.4 per cent), Christian (2.4 per cent), Sikh (2.0 per cent), Buddhist (0.7 per cent) and Jain (0.5 per cent).

The official languages are Hindi in the Devanagari script and English, though 17 regional languages also are recognized for adoption as official state languages.

CAPITAL – Delhi (population in 1991 was 8,375,188).
Populations of other principal cities (1991 figures) were Ahmedabad 3,297,655; Bangalore 4,086,548; ΨBombay (Mumbai) 12,571,720; ΨCalcutta 10,916,272; Hyderabad 4,280,261; Kanpur 2,111,284; Lucknow 1,642,134; ΨMadras 5,361,468; Pune 2,485,014.
CURRENCY – Indian rupee (Rs) of 100 paisa.

FLAG – A horizontal tricolour with bands of deep saffron, white and dark green in equal proportions. In the centre of the white band appears an Asoka wheel in navy blue.
NATIONAL ANTHEM – Jana-gana-mana.
NATIONAL DAY – 26 January (Republic Day).

HISTORY

The Indus civilization was fully developed by *c.*2500 BC but collapsed *c.*1750 BC, subsequently being replaced by an Aryan civilization spread from the west. Arab invasions of the north-west began in the seventh century and Muslim, Hindu and Buddhist states developed until the establishment of the Mogul dynasty in 1526. The British East India Company established settlements throughout the 17th century; clashes with the French and native princes led to the British government taking control of the company in 1784 and gradually gaining control of the whole sub-continent. The separate dominions of India and Pakistan became independent within the Commonwealth on 15 August 1947 and India became a republic in 1950.

India and Pakistan have fought three major wars since independence, in 1947–8, 1965 and 1971. Since 1985 they have continued a low-level war at altitude for control of the Siachen glacier in Kashmir.

GOVERNMENT

Under the 1950 constitution, executive power is vested in the President, elected for a five-year term by an electoral college consisting of the elected members of the Union and State legislatures. He appoints the Prime Minister and, on the latter's advice, the ministers, and can dismiss them. The Council of Ministers is collectively responsible to the *Lok Sabha* (lower house). The Vice-President is ex-officio chairman of the *Rajya Sabha* (upper house).

Legislative power rests with the President, the Rajya Sabha (245 members serving six-year terms) and the Lok Sabha (545 members). Twelve members of the Rajya Sabha are Presidential nominees, the rest are indirectly elected representatives of the State and Union Territories. The 530 members of the Lok Sabha representing the States are

directly elected by universal adult franchise, and 15 representatives of the Union Territories are chosen, for a maximum term of five years. Subject to the provisions of the constitution, the Union Parliament can make laws for the whole of India and the State legislatures for their respective units.

India has been ruled by the Congress (I) Party for all but four years since independence (March 1977–January 1980, November 1989–June 1991). The Congress (I) Party has been led by members of the Nehru-Gandhi dynasty for most of the post-independence period: Prime Ministers Jawaharlal Nehru (1947–64), Indira Gandhi (1966–1977, 1980–84) and Rajiv Gandhi (1984–89). Indira Gandhi was assassinated by Sikh extremists seeking an independent Sikh state in Punjab, who continue their insurgency but at a lower level than in the early 1980s. Her son Rajiv was assassinated by Sri Lankan Tamils. Inter-communal violence between Hindus and Muslims swept India in 1992–3 following the destruction of the mosque at Ayodhya by Hindu fundamentalists; about 1,200 were killed and 5,000 injured.

The last parliamentary elections to the Lok Sabha were held in June 1991 and won by Congress (I) which formed a government with the support of independents.

SECESSION

The Hindu Maharaja of the state of Kashmir signed his state's instrument of accession to India in October 1947, two months after India and Pakistan became independent. This was not accepted by Pakistan, on the basis that the majority of the state's population was Muslim, and the UN Security Council ordered a plebiscite on the question of whether Kashmir should accede to India or Pakistan, but this has never been held. After three Indian-Pakistani wars over the state, a line of control was agreed under the 1972 Simla agreement (China has also occupied some of Kashmir since the 1962 Sino-Indian war). The line of control has not been accepted by a significant part of the Muslim population, who since 1989 have formed armed groups fighting either for unification with Pakistan or Kashmiri independence. The armed groups have waged a campaign of violence against the Hindu population of Kashmir and against Indian troops and police in the state. India claims that the rebels are armed and supplied by Pakistan.

During 1994–5 the 200,000-strong Indian security forces in the state have gained the upper hand in fighting against the 3,800 militants, who have lost support amongst the Muslim population due to violence and intimidation. Only around 30 of the previous 70 armed militant groups remain active and only six are considered a serious security threat. The state remains under direct rule but state assembly elections are planned for late 1995. Since 1989, 12,000 to 13,000 people have died in the fighting, including 3,400 militants, and 16,000 militants have been arrested.

HEAD OF STATE
President of the Republic of India, Dr Shankar Dayal Sharma, *elected* 16 July 1992
Vice-President, K. R. Narayanan, *elected* 19 August 1992

COUNCIL OF MINISTERS *as at August 1995*

Prime Minister, Minister of Personnel, Public Grievances and Pensions, Science and Technology, Electronics, Atomic Energy, Rural Development, Non-Conventional Energy Sources, Law, Justice and Company Affairs, Space, Ocean Development, Defence and Industry, Jammu and Kashmir Affairs, P. V. Narasimha Rao
Finance, Dr Manmohan Singh
Agriculture, Balram Jakhar

Human Resources Development, Madhavrao Scindia
Urban Development, Sheila Kaul
Railways, C. K. Jaffer Sharief
Power, N. K. P. Salve
Civil Supplies, Consumer Affairs and Public Distribution, Buta
    Singh
Home Affairs, S. B. Chavan
External Affairs, Pranab Mukherjee
Welfare, Sitarem Kesri
Food, Ajit Singh
Water Resources and Parliamentary Affairs, V. C. Shukla
Civil Aviation, Ghulam Nabi Azad
Commerce, P. Chidambaram
Fertilizers and Chemicals, Ram Lakhan Singh Yadav
Labour, P. A. Sangma
Textiles, G. Venkataswamy
Minister without Portfolio, Dinesh Singh
In addition there are 25 ministers of state and three deputy
ministers, making a total of 47 in the Council of Ministers.

INDIAN HIGH COMMISSION
India House, Aldwych, London WC2B 4NA
Tel 0171–836 8484
High Commissioner, His Excellency Dr L. M. Singhvi, apptd
    1991
Deputy High Commissioner, P. K. Singh
Minister, A. Bhatnagar (*Economic*); R. Banerji (*Consular*),
    G. Gandhi (*Culture*)
Military Adviser, Brig. R. Dhir

BRITISH HIGH COMMISSION
Chanakyapuri, New Delhi 21, 1100–21.
Tel: New Delhi 601371
High Commissioner, His Excellency Sir Nicholas Fenn,
    GCMG, apptd 1991
Deputy High Commissioner and Minister, H. N. H. Synnott
Deputy High Commissioners, T. D. Curran (*Bombay*);
    A. B. N. Morey, CBE (*Calcutta*); S. H. Palmer (*Madras*)
Defence and Military Adviser, Brig. A. F. Gordon, CBE
Counsellor (Economic and Commercial), J. E. Holmes
*Minister for Cultural Affairs and British Council Representative
    in India*, C. W. Perchard, OBE
Offices also at Bombay, Calcutta and Madras. There are
British Council libraries at these four centres and British
libraries at Ahmedabad, Bangalore, Bhopal, Hyderabad,
Lucknow, Patna, Pune, Ranchi and Trivandrum.

STATES AND TERRITORIES OF THE UNION

There are 25 States and seven Union Territories. Each
State is governed by a Governor, who is appointed by the
President and holds office for five years, and by a Council of
Ministers. All States have a Legislative Assembly, and
some have also a Legislative Council, elected directly by
adult suffrage for a maximum period of five years.

The Union Territories are administered, except where
otherwise provided by Parliament, by the President acting
through an Administrator or Lieutenant-Governor, or
other authority appointed by him.

(Capital in parenthesis)	Area (sq. km)	Population (1991 census)
STATES		
Andhra Pradesh (Hyderabad)	275,100	66,304,854
Arunachal Pradesh (Itanagar)	83,700	858,392
Assam (Dispur)	78,400	22,414,322
Bihar (Patna)	173,900	86,374,465
Goa (Panaji)	3,700	1,168,622
Gujarat (Gandhinagar)	196,000	41,309,582
Haryana (Chandigarh)	44,200	16,463,648
Himachal Pradesh (Shimla)	55,700	5,170,877
Jammu and Kashmir*		
(Srinagar/Jammu)	222,200	5,987,389
Karnataka (Bangalore)	191,800	44,977,201
Kerala (Trivandrum)	38,900	29,011,237
Madhya Pradesh (Bhopal)	443,500	66,135,862
Maharashtra (Bombay)	307,700	78,937,187
Manipur (Imphal)	22,300	1,826,714
Meghalaya (Shillong)	22,400	1,774,778
Mizoram (Aizawl)	21,100	686,217
Nagaland (Kohima)	16,600	1,209,549
Orissa (Bhubaneswar)	155,700	31,659,736
Punjab (Chandigarh)	50,400	20,190,795
Rajasthan (Jaipur)	342,200	44,005,990
Sikkim (Gangtok)	7,100	405,550
Tamil Nadu (Madras)	130,100	55,638,318
Tripura (Agartala)	10,500	2,744,827
Uttar Pradesh (Lucknow)	294,400	139,112,287
West Bengal (Calcutta)	88,800	67,982,732
UNION TERRITORIES		
Andaman and Nicobar Is.		
(Port Blair)	8,200	280,661
Chandigarh	114	642,015
Dadra and Nagar Haveli		
(Silvassa)	500	138,477
Daman and Diu	112	101,586
Delhi	1,500	9,420,644
Lakshadweep (Kavaratti)	30	51,681
Pondicherry	500	807,785

* The area figure includes those parts occupied by Pakistan and
China, which are claimed by India, but the population figure
excludes the population of these areas, where the census was not
taken. The state's capital is at Srinagar in summer and Jammu in
winter.

JUDICATURE

The Supreme Court consists of the Chief Justice and not
more than 25 other judges, appointed by the President. It is
the highest court in respect of all constitutional matters and
the final Court of Appeal and is situated in New Delhi.
Each state or group of states also has a High Court with a
hierarchy of subordinate courts. The judges of the High
Court of a state are appointed by the President.
Chief Justice, M. N. Venkatachaliah

DEFENCE

Total active armed forces strength numbers 1,265,000.
Service is voluntary. India exploded its first nuclear
weapon in 1974 and is since believed to have acquired a
stockpile of nuclear arms. In 1993–4 India successfully
test-fired its intermediate-range 'Agni' and short-range
'Prithvi' ballistic missiles.

The Army has a total strength of 1,100,000, with 3,400
main battle tanks; 1,060 armoured infantry fighting
vehicles and armoured personnel carriers; 3,580 artillery
pieces and 200 helicopters. The Army is organized into 11
corps and deploys two armoured, one mechanized, ten
mountain and 22 infantry divisions, with a further 23
independent brigades.

The Navy has a strength of 55,000 personnel and
consists of two aircraft carriers, 15 submarines, five
destroyers, 18 frigates, 40 patrol and coastal craft, 65
combat aircraft and 75 armed helicopters. The Air Force
has a strength of 110,000 with 800 combat aircraft and 36
armed helicopters. It is organized into 22 ground attack, 20
air defence, eight maritime attack, four reconnaissance, two
attack helicopter and 23 transport squadrons.

In addition, there are 906,700 personnel in 12 paramilitary organizations.

ECONOMY

Agriculture is the chief industry, supporting about 70 per cent of the population, and providing nearly 32 per cent of GDP. The area under cultivation has been increased by irrigation schemes but most holdings are less than five acres. Production has grown by 3 per cent each year since 1951, remaining slightly ahead of the 2 per cent increase necessary to keep pace with the rising population. Food crops occupy three-quarters of the total cultivated area and production of food grains amounted to 186 million tonnes in 1994–5. There are three main crop seasons each year, in which different crops are grown. The main food crops are rice, cereals (principally wheat) and pulses. The major cash crops include sugar cane, jute, cotton and tea. Other products include oil seeds, spices, groundnuts, soya bean, tobacco, rubber and coffee. Livestock is raised, principally for dairy purposes or for the hides: cattle (an estimated 181 million), goats (71 million), sheep (45.7 million) and pigs (10 million). In 1992–3 milk production was 58.6 million tonnes, egg production reached 22 billion, wool production 44,000 tonnes and fish caught totalled 4.1 million tonnes.

Industry is based on the exploitation and processing of mineral resources, principally coal, oil and iron, and on the production of textiles. The coal industry reached an output in 1991–2 of 244 million tonnes. Production of crude oil from the main fields in Assam and from offshore drilling was about 30.4 million tonnes in 1991–2. Steel production is mainly in the hands of the public sector, with five public and one private sector integrated steel plants producing 12 million tonnes of ingot steel in 1991–2. The engineering industry, heavy and light, is also primarily in the hands of the public sector, but is increasingly being privatized.

The manufacture of paper, cement, pharmaceuticals, chemicals, fertilizers, petrochemicals, motor vehicles and commercial vehicles has been expanded. Other principal manufactures are those derived from agricultural products, textiles, jute goods, sugar, leather, which along with tea, tobacco, rubber, fish, and iron ore and concentrates are major exports.

Faced with the need to obtain loans from the World Bank and assistance from the IMF, India abandoned centralized planning in 1991 after 40 years and introduced free market reforms. Subsidies are being cut, state corporations privatized and the economy opened up to foreign competition and investment. To take India into the international trading system proper, budgets have been passed in 1993–5 which have floated the rupee, cut interest rates and duties on imports, reduced subsidies to farmers, restructured the taxation system, removed industrial controls and dismantled protectionist structures. The budgets are in line with IMF proposals and prompted foreign and international donors to pledge US$7,400 million to support economic reforms in 1993–4 and US$6,000 million in 1994–5. The reforms have been successful, producing US$10,000 million in foreign investment since 1991, a fall in inflation from 17 to 9 per cent, a 21 per cent increase in exports, a rise in foreign currency reserves from US$1,000 million to US$21,000 million, an average GDP growth of 4 per cent per year, improved agricultural efficiency and an increase in the average annual industrial growth rate from 1 per cent to 4 per cent.

FINANCE

The budget estimates for 1995–6 placed total expenditure at Rs 1,721,500 million. Total revenue (excluding States' shares) was Rs 1,671,500 million.

TRADE WITH UK	1993	1994
Imports from UK	£1,129,998,000	£1,311,495,000
Exports to UK	1,088,837,000	1,288,939,000

COMMUNICATIONS

The International Airports Authority manages five international airports: Palam (Delhi), Sahar (Bombay), Dum Dum (Calcutta), Meenambakkam (Madras) and Trivandrum. The other 88 aerodromes are controlled and operated by the Civil Aviation Department of the Government. The national airlines are Indian Airlines (internal) and Air India (international).

The railways are grouped into nine administrative zones, Southern, Central, Western, Northern, North-Eastern, North-East Frontier, Eastern, South-Eastern and South-Central with a total track length of 62,458 km, about 17 per cent of which is electrified. The total length of the road network is 1,998,434 km of which 964,072 km is surfaced.

The chief seaports are Bombay, Calcutta, Haldia, Madras, Mormugao, Cochin, Visakhapatnam, Kandla, Paradip, Mangalore and Tuticorin. There are 139 minor working ports with varying capacity. On 31 December 1992, 430 ships totalling 6,275,000 gross tons were on the Indian Register.

INDONESIA
Republik Indonesia

Indonesia is situated between 6° N. and 11° S. latitude and between 95° and 141° E. longitude, and comprises the islands of Java, Madura, Sumatra, the Riouw-Lingga archipelago, Bangka and Billiton, part of the island of Borneo (Kalimantan), Sulawesi (formerly Celebes) Island, the Molucca Islands, the islands of Bali, Lombok, Sumbawa, Sumba, Flores, Timor and others comprising the provinces of East and West Nusa Tenggara and the western half of the island of New Guinea (Irian Jaya), with a total area of 735,358 sq. miles (1,904,569 sq. km), and a population (UN estimate 1992) of 191,170,000.

CAPITAL – ΨJakarta (population 7,885,519). Other important centres are: (Java) ΨSurabaya (2,027,913), ΨSemarang (1,026,671), Bandung (1,462,637); (Sumatra) Palembang (787,187), Medan (1,378,955); (Sulawesi) ΨUjung Pandang (709,038); (Kalimantan) Banjarmasin (381,286), ΨPontianak (304,778), (Moluccas) Ambon (208,898); (Nusa Tenggara) Kupang (329,371); (Irian Jaya) Jayapura (107,164).
CURRENCY – Rupiah (Rp) of 100 sen.
FLAG – Equal bands of red over white.
NATIONAL ANTHEM – Indonesia Raya (Great Indonesia).
NATIONAL DAY – 17 August (Anniversary of Proclamation of Independence).

GOVERNMENT

From the early part of the 17th century much of the Indonesian archipelago was under Dutch rule. Following the Second World War, during which the archipelago was occupied by the Japanese, a strong nationalistic movement formed and after sporadic fighting all the former Dutch East Indies except western New Guinea became independent as Indonesia on 27 December 1949. Western New Guinea became part of Indonesia in 1963 under the name West Irian (now Irian Jaya), this interpretation being confirmed in an 'Act of Free Choice' in July 1969, of which the United Nations took note in November 1969.

Following a three-week period of unrest and violent student demonstrations, the Army Minister Gen. Suharto took over effective political power in March 1966. Gen. Suharto was appointed President in 1968 and has been reappointed by the People's Consultative Assembly (composed of the House of People's Representatives together with 500 government, regional and party appointees) at each presidential election since. The House of People's Representatives is composed of 400 elected members and 100 military appointees. The military has effectively ruled since 1966 through its political organization Golkar.

In the 1992 general election, Golkar obtained 281 seats, the Muslim United Development Party 63 seats and the Indonesian Democratic Party 56 seats.

SECESSION

Apart from East Timor (*see* page 906), there are two armed secessionist movements based on ethnic and nationalist groups, which are fighting perceived Javanese domination of the country. In Western New Guinea (Irian Jaya) government forces are fighting the Papua Independent Organization (OPM) guerrillas who claim the 1969 referendum was flawed and rigged. In northern Sumatra the Free Aceh Movement is active.

HEAD OF STATE

President, Gen. Suharto, *appointed Acting President* March 1967; *confirmed as President* 28 March 1968, *re-elected* 1973, 1978, 1983, 1988 and March 1993
Vice-President, Try Sutrisno, *elected* March 1993

CABINET *as at August 1995*

Co-ordinating Ministers, Gen. (retd) Soesilo Soedarman (*Political and Security Affairs*); Saleh Afiff (*Economy, Finance, Industry and Development Supervision*); Maj.-Gen. Azwar Anas (*Public Welfare*); Ir Hartarto (*Industrial and Trade Affairs*)
Ministers, Lt.-Gen. (retd) Yogi Memet (*Internal Affairs*); Ali Alatas (*Foreign Affairs*); Gen. Edi Sudrajat (*Defence and Security*); Oesman Oetojo (*Justice*); Mr Harmoko (*Information*); Mar'ie Muhammad (*Finance*); Satrio Yudono (*Trade*); Tungki Arinibowo (*Industry*); Sjarifuddin Baharsyah (*Agriculture*); Lt.-Gen. Ida Bagus Sujana (*Mines and Energy*); Radinal Mochtar (*Public Works*); Haryanto Dhanutirto (*Communications*); Abdul Latief (*Manpower*); Siswono Yudohusodo (*Transmigration*); Joop Ave (*Tourism, Posts and Telecommunications*); Wardiman Joyonegoro (*Education and Culture*); Dr Suyudi (*Health*); Tarmizi Taher (*Religious Affairs*); Prof. Endang Suweno (*Social Affairs*); Jamaludin Suryohadikasumo (*Forestry*); Subiakto Cakrawerdaya (*Co-operatives and Small Businesses*); Dr Murdiono (*Minister and State Secretary*)
In addition there are 14 ministers of state.

INDONESIAN EMBASSY

38 Grosvenor Square, London WIX 9AD
Tel 0171–499 7661
Ambassador Extraordinary and Plenipotentiary, His Excellency Junus Habibie, apptd 1993
Minister, H. Sudirman (*Deputy Chief of Mission*)
First Secretary, B. Moniaga (*Commercial*)
Defence Attaché, Lt.-Col. Sudrajat

BRITISH EMBASSY

Jalan M. H. Thamrin 75, Jakarta 10310
Tel: Jakarta 330904

Ambassador Extraordinary and Plenipotentiary, His Excellency
   Graham Burton, apptd 1994
Deputy Ambassador, Counsellor and Consul-General,
   J. C. R. Gray
Counsellor (Commercial/Development), P. J. Bacon
Defence Attaché, Col. I. J. Hellberg, OBE

BRITISH CONSULAR OFFICES – There are British Consular
   Offices at Jakarta, Medan and Surabaya.
BRITISH COUNCIL DIRECTOR, Dr Neil Kemp, S Widjojo
   Centre, Jalan Jenderal Sudirman 71, Jakarta 12190.

DEFENCE

The armed forces have a total active strength of 276,000
with selective conscription of two years. The Army has a
strength of 214,000 with 305 light tanks, 750 armoured
personnel carriers, 180 artillery pieces and 41 helicopters.
The Navy has 42,000 personnel (including 12,000
marines), two submarines, 13 frigates, 42 patrol and coastal
craft, 24 combat aircraft and 23 armed helicopters. The Air
Force has 20,000 personnel and 80 combat aircraft. There
are 174,000 paramilitary police personnel.

ECONOMY

Nearly 70 per cent of the population is engaged in
agriculture and related production. Copra, kapok, nutmeg,
pepper and cloves are produced, mainly by smallholders;
palm oil, sugar, fibres and cinchona are produced by large
estates. Rubber, tea, coffee and tobacco are produced by
both in large quantities. Rice is a staple food and Java,
Sulawesi and Sumatra are important producers. Production has risen rapidly in recent years and the country is
now self-sufficient.
   Oil and liquefied natural gas are the most important
assets, the export of which constitutes around 80 per cent of
export earnings. However, dependence on these has made
the economy vulnerable to depressed international
markets and weak oil prices. Timber is the second largest
foreign exchange earner after oil.
   Indonesia is rich in minerals, particularly tin, of which
the country is the world's third biggest producer; coal,
nickel and bauxite are the other principal mineral products.
There are also considerable deposits of gold, silver,
manganese phosphates and sulphur. Aid to Indonesia is
channelled through the Indonesian Consultative Group
(ICG). Indonesia received about US$5,400 million in
1994–5.
   Indonesia is aiming to diversify its economy to reduce its
dependence on oil and gas exports, with particular
emphasis on agriculture, heavy engineering (shipbuilding)
and high technology (aerospace). The past decade has been
economically successful, with annual average GDP growth
rates of 6 per cent. However, public and private sector debt
has grown substantially to around US$104,000 million.
   Principal exports are oil and natural gas, rubber, timber,
non-ferrous metals, clothing, tea, coffee, spices, vegetable
oils and fats. Imports are mainly of machinery, transport
equipment, electrical equipment and chemicals.

TRADE WITH UK	1993	1994
Imports from UK	£331,094,000	£366,035,000
Exports to UK	700,535,000	782,546,000

COMMUNICATIONS

There are railway systems in Java and Sumatra linking the
main towns. There are about 50,000 miles of roads.
   Sea communications are maintained by the state-run
shipping companies Djakarta-Lloyd (ocean-going) and
Pelni (coastal and inter-island) and other small concerns.

Transport by small craft on the rivers of the larger islands
plays an important part in trade.
   Air services are operated by Garuda Indonesian Airways
and other local airlines, and Jakarta is served by various
international services.

EAST TIMOR

The territory of East Timor comprises the eastern half of
the mountainous island of Timor, together with an enclave
on the north coast of western Timor. The island is the
largest and most easterly of the Lesser Sundas group and is
situated across the Timor Sea from northern Australia. East
Timor was a Portuguese colony from 1702 until Portuguese control collapsed in 1974–5 following the 1974 coup
in Portugal. An independence war against Portuguese rule
waged by the Marxist Fretilin (Revolutionary Front for an
Independent East Timor) developed into a civil war
between Fretilin and local conservative forces in autumn
1975. After gaining control, Fretilin declared East Timor
independent on 27 November 1975 and this was recognized by Portugal. Indonesian forces invaded East Timor
on 7 December 1975, claiming that they had been invited
by non-Fretilin forces. In July 1976 Indonesia declared
East Timor its 27th province.
   Since 1975 the East Timorese people have resisted
integration with Indonesia and Fretilin has waged an
armed campaign for independence. Resistance has left
200,000 East Timorese dead through starvation or killings
by the Indonesian army. About 150,000 Muslims have been
settled in East Timor to dilute resistance from the
predominantly Roman Catholic population (80 per cent
in 1975). The United Nations refuses to accept Indonesia's
annexation of East Timor and considers Portugal to
exercise sovereignty still. The international community
was outraged by the massacre of pro-independence
demonstrators in the capital, Dili, in 1991. Fighting
between Fretilin and the Indonesian army continues;
Fretilin has about 800 guerrillas, armed with light weapons
and based in the island's mountainous interior. Fretilin's
leader, Xanana Gusmao, was captured and jailed by the
Indonesians in 1993. Sporadic demonstrations and strikes
against Indonesian rule continue in East Timor, and in
February 1995 Portugal brought a case to the International Court of Justice challenging the legality of
Indonesian–Australian treaties exploiting oil resources
under the Timor Sea.

IRAN
Jomhuri-e-Islami-e-Iran

Iran has an area of 636,296 sq. miles (1,648,000 sq. km). It is
mostly an arid tableland, encircled, except in the east, by
mountains, the highest in the north rising to 18,934 ft. The
central and eastern portion is a vast salt desert.
   The population (1995 estimate) is 66,000,000, of which
the majority are Shia Muslims with small minorities of
Zoroastrians, Bahais, Sunni Muslims, Jews, and Armenian
and Assyrian Christians.
   Persian or Farsi is an Indo-European language with
many Arabic elements added; the alphabet is mainly
Arabic, with writing from right to left. Among the great
names in Persian literature are those of Abu'l Kásim
Mansúr, or Firdausi (AD 939–1020), Omar Khayyám, the
astronomer-poet (died AD 1122), Muslihu'd-Din, known as
Sa'di (born AD 1184), and Shems-ed-Din Muhammad, or
Hafiz (died AD 1389).

CAPITAL – Tehran, population (1990 UN estimate) 6,042,584. Other large towns are Tabriz, Isfahan, Meshed, Shiraz, Resht, Kerman, Hamadan, Yazd, Kermanshah and Ahwaz.

CURRENCY – Rial.

FLAG – Three horizontal stripes of green, white, red, with the slogan *Allahu Akbar* repeated 22 times along the edges of the green and red stripes, and the national emblem in the centre.

NATIONAL ANTHEM – Sorood-e Jomhoori-e Eslami.

NATIONAL DAY – 11 February.

GOVERNMENT

Iran was ruled from the end of the 18th century by Shahs of the Qajar dynasty. After the First World War, the subsequent troubles and the signature of the Soviet-Iranian Treaty 1921, a vigorous Prime Minister, Reza Khan, re-established general order. In 1925 the last of the Qajar dynasty, Sultan Ahmed Shah, was deposed in his absence by the National Assembly, which handed executive power to Prime Minister Reza Khan. Reza Khan was elected Shah as Reza Shah Pahlavi by the Constituent Assembly in December 1925. In 1941 Reza Shah abdicated in favour of the Crown Prince, who ascended the throne as Mohammed Reza Shah Pahlavi.

Following persistent opposition to his regime, the Shah left Iran in January 1979. Ayatollah Khomeini, the spiritual leader of the Shia Muslims, returned from exile on 1 February. Following a national referendum, an Islamic Republic was declared on 1 April 1979. A new constitution, providing for a President, Prime Minister and Consultative Assembly, and also for overall leadership by Ayatollah Khomeini, was approved by referendum in December 1979. The government's severe measures suppressed violent opposition. In June 1989 Khomeini died and President Khamenei was appointed Leader of the Islamic Republic. Rafsanjani was elected President in July 1989, and the post of prime minister was abolished. In 1992 elections to the Majlis (consultative assembly), candidates supporting President Rafsanjani won over 200 of the 270 seats. However, in the 1993 presidential election, President Rafsanjani received only 63 per cent of the vote (compared with 94 per cent in 1989) and only 56 per cent of the electorate voted. This reflects growing discontent with economic hardship caused by the economic reforms introduced by Rafsanjani.

Iran was at war with Iraq following the Iraqi invasion of Iran in September 1980. International efforts to end the fighting resulted in a ceasefire in August 1988. In August 1990 Iraq accepted Iran's conditions for settling the conflict, including a return to the 1975 border, but a formal peace treaty has not been signed.

Leader of the Islamic Republic, Ayatollah Seyed Ali Khamenei, *appointed* June 1989
President, Hojjatoleslam Ali Akbar Hashemi Rafsanjani, *elected* 28 July 1989, *re-elected* 11 June 1993

CABINET *as at August 1995*

Agriculture, Issa Kalantari
Commerce, Yahya Al-Eshaq
Construction Crusade, Gholam Reza Forouzesh
Defence, Mohammed Forouzandeh
Economy and Finance, Mohammed Khan
Education, Mohammad Ali Najafi
Culture and Higher Education, Dr Hashemi Golpeygani
Energy, Bizhan Namdar Zanganeh
Islamic Culture and Guidance, Mostafa Mir-Salim
Foreign Affairs, Ali Akbar Velayati
Health, Ali Reza Marandi

Housing and Urban Development, Abbas Ahmad Akhundi
Industries, Mohammad Reza Nematzadeh
Intelligence, Ali Fallahian
Interior, Ali Mohammad Besharati
Justice, Mohammad Esmail Shoushtari
Labour and Social Affairs, Hossein Kamali
Mines and Metals, Mohammad Hossein Mahloujchi
Oil, Gholamreza Aghazadeh
Posts, Telephones and Telegraphs, Mohammad Gharrazi
Roads and Transport, Akbar Torkan
Co-operatives, Gholem Reza Shafei

EMBASSY OF THE ISLAMIC REPUBLIC OF IRAN
16 Prince's Gate, London SW7 1PT
Tel 0171-225 3000
Chargé d'Affaires, G. Ansari

BRITISH EMBASSY
143 Ferdowsi Avenue, PO Box 11365–4474, Tehran 11344
Tel: Tehran 675011
Counsellor and Chargé d'Affaires, Jeffrey R. James, apptd 1993
First Secretary (Commercial), M. A. Hilton

DEFENCE

The Iranian armed forces number 473,000 active personnel. The conscription term is 24 months, with conscripts serving almost exclusively in the Army. The Army has a strength of 345,000 (including 250,000 conscripts) with 1,245 main battle tanks, 1,000 armoured personnel carriers and armoured infantry fighting vehicles, 2,320 artillery pieces and 100 attack helicopters.

The Navy is 18,000 strong, with two submarines, two destroyers, three frigates, 45 patrol and coastal craft, and nine armed helicopters. The Air Force has 30,000 personnel, with some 295 combat aircraft, of which only about 50 per cent are serviceable due to the US armaments embargo, in operation since 1979.

The Islamic Revolutionary Guards Corps numbers some 120,000, of which 100,000 are ground and 20,000 naval forces.

EDUCATION

Since 1943 primary education has been compulsory and free. There are 22 universities in Iran (eight in Tehran, 14 in the provinces). The educational system has been reformed following the revolution. The literacy rate is 74.1 per cent.

ECONOMY

The economy has been badly affected by the fall in world oil prices in recent years, which has exacerbated the hardship caused by the loss of subsidies on all but the most basic foodstuffs following free market reforms. Privatization began in 1991 but since 1993 its pace has been much reduced by the government because of the job losses it caused. A full trade and investment embargo was placed on Iran by the USA in June 1995 in retaliation for Iran's support for international terrorism and its alleged nuclear weapons programme. In 1994 the total foreign debt reached US$30,000 million, with inflation at 30 per cent a month.

Agricultural output is rising following the end of the Iran–Iraq war and an attempt is being made to reduce dependence on food imports. Wheat is the principal crop; other important crops are barley, rice, cotton, sugar beet, fruit, nuts and vegetables. Wool is also a major product.

The oilfields, which lie in south-western Iran, were nationalized in 1951. From 1957 until the 1979 revolution a consortium of eight foreign oil companies was responsible for the production, refining and sale of oil but in July 1979 the National Iranian Oil Company assumed full control of the oil industry. In addition to that extracted from the onshore wells, oil is also produced from a number of off-shore oilfields. Oil production is around 3.6 million b.p.d., of which some 2.5 million b.p.d. is exported. Iran is a member of OPEC.

Apart from oil, the principal industrial products are carpets, textiles, sugar, cement and other construction materials, ginned cotton, vegetable oil and other food products, leather and shoes, metal manufactures, pharmaceuticals, motor vehicles, fertilizers and plastics. Industrial output was severely curtailed by the 1979 revolution, and by the Iran–Iraq war, but the private sector is now being encouraged again.

TRADE

Over 80 per cent of export earnings come from oil, but an effort is being made to increase non-oil exports. The level of finance for imports depends largely on the international oil price and Iran has recently had a deficit in foreign trade partly because of the depressed state of world oil prices. Tighter import controls were introduced in 1994.

Imports are mainly industrial and agricultural machinery, motor vehicles and motor vehicle components for assembly, iron and steel (including manufactures), electrical machinery and goods, meat, various other foods, and certain textile fabrics and yarns.

The principal exports, apart from oil, are cotton, carpets, dried fruit, nuts, hides and skins, mineral ores, wool, gums, caviare, cumin seed and spices. Germany and Japan are Iran's leading suppliers.

Trade with UK	1993	1994
Imports from UK	£496,555,000	£289,062,000
Exports to UK	244,851,000	132,650,000

COMMUNICATIONS

Tehran is at the centre of a network of highways linking the capital with other major towns, the ports, the Caspian Sea and the country's frontiers.

The Trans-Iranian Railway runs from Bandar Turcoman, on the Caspian Sea, via Tehran to Bandar Khomeini, on the Persian Gulf. Other lines link Tehran with Tabriz and Mashad; Tabriz to Julfa; Zahedan to Quetta; Ahwaz to Khorramshahr; Qom to Kerman; and Bandar Turcoman to Gorgan. The rail system is linked to the Turkish system via Van, and is to be linked also to Turkmenistan.

There is an international airport at Tehran (Mehrabad), and airports at all the major provincial centres. The national airline, Iranair, is government-owned and operates international and domestic routes.

IRAQ
Al-Jumhouriya al-'Iraqia

Iraq extends between 37½° to 48½° E. longitude, and 37½° to 30° N. latitude, from Turkey on the north and north-east to the Gulf on the south and south-east, and from Iran on the east to Syria and the Arabian Desert on the west. In 1993 the border between Iraq and Kuwait was formally demarcated, moving a few hundred metres northwards and giving part of the port of Umm Qasr to Kuwait. The area of Iraq is 167,925 sq. miles (434,924 sq. km), of which 37 per cent is desert. The rivers Euphrates (1,700 miles) and Tigris (1,150 miles) rise in Turkey and traverse Iraq to their

junction at Qurna, from where the Euphrates flows the 70 miles to the Gulf.

The population at the census of October 1987 was 16,278,316. The 1992 UN estimate was 19,290,000. The official language is Arabic. Minority languages include Kurdish (about 15 per cent), Turkic and Aramaic.

CAPITAL – Baghdad. Population of the governorate (1987 census) 3,841,286. Other towns of importance are ΨBasra, Mosul and Kirkuk.

CURRENCY – Iraqi dinar (ID) of 1,000 fils.

FLAG – Three horizontal stripes of red, white, black; on the white stripe three stars and the slogan *Allahu Akbar* all in green.

NATIONAL DAY – 17 July (Revolution Day).

HISTORY

Iraq is the site of the remains of several ancient civilizations: one site at Tel Hassuna, near Shura, dates back to 5000 BC; Tel Abu Shahrain near 'Ur of the Chaldees' is the site of the Sumerian city of Eridu; the ancient city of Hillah, 70 miles south of Baghdad, is near the site of Babylon and the Tower of Babel. Mosul governorate covers a great part of the ancient kingdom of Assyria, the ruins of Ninevah, the Assyrian capital, being visible on the banks of the Tigris, opposite Mosul. Qurna, at the junction of the Tigris and Euphrates, is traditionally supposed to be the site of the Garden of Eden.

Under the Treaty of Lausanne 1923, Turkey renounced sovereignty over Mesopotamia. A provisional government was set up in 1920, and in 1921 the Emir Faisal was elected King of Iraq. The country was a monarchy until July 1958, when King Faisal II was assassinated. From 1958 Iraq has been under the rule of the Ba'ath Party.

Iraq invaded Iran in September 1980 and was at war until the August 1988 cease-fire. In 1990 Iraq accepted Iran's conditions for peace, including a return to the 1975 border, but a formal peace treaty has not been signed.

Iraq invaded Kuwait on 2 August 1990 and declared Kuwait a province of Iraq. The UN Security Council declared the annexation void. After months of diplomatic attempts to secure an Iraqi withdrawal from Kuwait, an alliance of NATO and Middle East countries launched an offensive in January 1991 and liberated Kuwait in February 1991.

GOVERNMENT

According to the provisional constitution, the highest state authority is the Revolutionary Command Council (RCC), which elects the President from among its members. The President appoints the Council of Ministers. Legislative authority is shared by the RCC and the 250-member National Assembly, which is elected every four years by universal adult suffrage. Following general elections in 1989 the Arab Ba'ath Socialist Party holds the majority of the Assembly seats, the remainder being held by the state-sponsored National Progressive Patriotic Front.

As a result of the Iraqi invasion of Kuwait, the UN Security Council passed resolution 661 (August 1990) which imposed a total trade ban on Iraq, froze Iraqi assets abroad and established a standing committee to monitor compliance. Following the liberation of Kuwait three further UN Security Council resolutions have been passed which establish criteria for Iraq to meet before economic and trade sanctions are lifted: 687 (August 1991) demands the destruction of all Iraqi weapons of mass destruction and their means of production, the establishment of a long-term weapons monitoring programme, and establishes Iraqi liability for reparations; 688 (August 1991) demands adherence by the Iraqi regime to human rights norms in dealing with Kuwaiti detainees, Shias and Kurds; 833 (May 1993) demands Iraqi acceptance of Kuwait's sovereignty and independence and the validity of the Iraqi–Kuwaiti border redrawn by the UN in 1993.

In 1991–3 these demands met with defiance by Iraq, with Iraq violating the air exclusion zones (*see* below), provoking retaliatory air strikes by allied forces. The regime also obstructed the work of UN weapons inspection teams overseeing the destruction of Iraqi weapons of mass destruction. In retaliation, the UN Security Council voted in October 1992 to seize all Iraqi assets in foreign banks and use the money to compensate Gulf war victims, finance UN weapons inspection teams and fund relief operations to Kurdish and Shia areas. In January and June 1993 the USA destroyed an Iraqi nuclear weapons plant and the headquarters of the Iraqi intelligence service in retaliation for, respectively, Iraqi refusals to allow UN weapons inspection teams entry and an Iraqi attempt to murder ex-President Bush.

Since late 1993 the economic hardship caused by sanctions and the oil embargo has led to several assassination attempts on Saddam Hussein, an attempted coup, a military revolt, and government reshuffles. The regime has co-operated increasingly with UN weapons inspection teams in an attempt to have economic sanctions lifted. In November 1993 the regime agreed to the destruction of all its weapons of mass destruction and the means of manufacturing them. In February 1994 all remaining plutonium and enriched uranium was removed by the UN; in March all remaining chemical weapons were destroyed; in June all production facilities for nuclear, chemical and biological weapons and missiles were destroyed; in July a nationwide network of cameras and sensors was installed to ensure production of weapons was not restarted.

In October 1994, however, Iraq moved 70,000 men to the Kuwaiti border and withdrew only after the deployment of US and British forces in the Gulf. In November Iraq finally accepted Kuwait's sovereignty and independence and the redrawn 1993 Iraq–Kuwait border. Doubts remained over Iraq's biological weapons programme, with its refusal to disclose details of the programme until July 1995, and over its missile programme, with the discovery of machines capable of making ballistic missile parts in July 1995. UN sanctions are to remain in place until Iraq stops withholding information about its weapons programmes and returns Kuwaiti property and hundreds of Kuwaiti detainees.

SECESSION

Following the allied victory in Kuwait in February 1991, rebellion against the government broke out in the Kurdish north and the Shi'ite south. Although the revolt was suppressed by the end of April, Iraqi attacks on Kurdish civilians and the plight of the resultant Kurdish refugees led western governments to set up a security zone and a UN safe haven in northern Iraq to protect them. An air exclusion zone north of the 36th parallel was also established, patrolled by US, British and French aircraft based in Turkey. Allied ground forces were withdrawn in July. Saddam Hussein withdrew his administration from Kurdish northern Iraq in October 1991 and imposed an economic embargo on the territory. The Kurds established a *de facto* administration with its capital at Arbil and control over certain northern areas, which have a population of 3.5 million. In May 1992 the Kurds voted in free elections for a 100-seat parliament and a 'political leader'. The Kurdish Democratic Party (KDP) and the Patriotic Union of Kurdistan (PUK) both gained 50 seats and a Kurdish government was formed in July with party leaders Masoud

Barzani and Jalal Talabani as joint leaders of the territory. The Iraqi economic embargo has caused great hardship, and the neighbouring states of Syria, Iran and Turkey have been reluctant to trade with the Kurdish administration as they all have their own Kurdish minorities. Continued fuel and food shortages and land disputes have led to fighting for most of 1994–5 between KDP and PUK forces which has left 2,000 dead and the administration and parliament defunct.

Although the Shia revolt in southern Iraq was defeated in April 1991, a low-level insurgency continued in the southern marshlands. Continued Iraqi bombing of Shia refugees in these areas led to an air exclusion zone being established south of the 32nd parallel in August 1992, patrolled by US, British and French aircraft. Since August 1992 the Iraqi regime has systematically drained the southern marshes by canal construction and river diversion; with continued gound offensives, this had effectively ended the Shia rebellion by late 1994.

HEAD OF STATE

President, Chairman of the Revolutionary Command Council, Prime Minister, Saddam Hussein, *assumed office* 16 July 1979
Vice Presidents, Taha Yassin Ramadhan; Taha Mohieddin Maaruf

REVOLUTIONARY COMMAND COUNCIL

Chairman, Saddam Hussein
Vice-Chairman, Izzat Ibrahim
Head of the Presidential Office, Hatim Hamdan al-Azawi
Members, Taha Yassin Ramadhan; Tariq Aziz; Mohammed Hamza al-Zubeidi; Gen. Ali Hassan al-Majeed; Mizban Khider Hadi; Taha Mohieddin Maaruf

CABINET *as at August 1995*

Prime Minister, Saddam Hussein
Deputy Prime Ministers, Tariq Aziz; Taha Yassin Ramadhan; Mohammed Hamza al-Zubeidi
Interior, Muhammad Zimam Abdul-Razzaq
Defence, Lt.-Gen. Sultan Hashim Ahmed
Foreign Affairs, Mohammed Saaed al-Sahhaf
Finance, Ahmad Hussein al-Khodair
Culture and Information, Hamad Youssef Hammadi
Justice, Shabib al-Maliki
Agriculture and Irrigation, Khalid Abdul-Muneim Rasheed
Industry and Minerals, Lt.-Gen. Hussein Kamil Hassan
Oil, Lt.-Gen. Amir Muhammad Rashid
Education, Hikmat Abdullah al-Bazzaz
Labour and Social Affairs, Latif Nassif Jassem
Health, Umeed Madhat Mubarak
Planning, Samal Majid Faraj
Higher Education and Scientific Research, Humam Abdel-Khaliq Ghafaras
Housing and Construction, Mahmoud Diyab Al-Ahmad
Transport and Communications, Ahmed Murtada Ahmed Khalil
Religious Endowments and Religious Affairs, Abdul-Muneim Ahmed Saleh
Trade, Muhammed Mahdi Salih

IRAQI DIPLOMATIC MISSION IN LONDON

Since Iraq's breach of diplomatic relations with Britain in February 1991, the Jordanian Embassy has handled Iraqi interests in this country.

BRITISH DIPLOMATIC REPRESENTATION

The British Embassy was closed in January 1991. Since the breach of diplomatic relations, the Russian Embassy has handled British interests in Iraq.

DEFENCE

The Iraqi armed forces were decimated in the defeat by the allied coalition which drove them from Kuwait but have reorganized and now have around 382,000 active personnel (compared to a pre-war total of one million). Reservists number 650,000 personnel, of whom around 100,000 are on permanent recall to the Army. Conscripts serve 18 to 24 months.

The Army has a strength of around 350,000, with around 2,200 main battle tanks (5,300 pre-war); 4,200 reconnaissance vehicles, armoured personnel carriers and armoured infantry fighting vehicles (6,300 pre-war); 1,970 artillery pieces (3,150 pre-war) and 120 armed helicopters. The Army is organized into eight Republican Guard and 19 regular divisions with 10 specialized counterinsurgency brigades. The Navy has a strength of around 2,000 with one frigate and 11 patrol and coastal craft. The Air Force has a strength of around 30,000 with 320 combat aircraft (570 pre-war). In addition, there are 24,800 paramilitary frontier guards and security troops.

Since the end of the war, UN weapons inspection teams have destroyed or dismantled nuclear, chemical and biological weapons, Scud missiles and their launchers, and the superguns. By mid-1995 it was believed that nearly all these weapons and their means of production had been destroyed and a long-term monitoring operation was under way to ensure production did not restart.

In opposition to Iraqi forces there are 37,000 armed Kurdish guerrillas, with a further 36,000 support personnel. These are armed with captured Iraqi tanks, artillery and mortars, and small arms. There is also a brigade-sized armed Shia opposition force based in Iran.

ECONOMY

In August 1990, the UN imposed economic sanctions on Iraq, including a world-wide ban on its oil exports. Resolutions passed in August 1991 permitted Iraq to sell 20 per cent of pre-war oil production; the proceeds to be allocated to a special UN account for the purchase of food and other essential supplies, and for the funding of war reparations. However, Iraq has refused to make use of this and also rejected a more generous proposal in April 1995. These refusals have caused considerable economic hardship in Iraq.

Apart from oil revenues, agricultural production is also important, with two harvests usually gathered in a year, depending on rainfall. Salinity and soil erosion, caused by a high water table, inadequate irrigation and drainage, and traditional farming methods are the major problems being addressed by development planners.

Increasing industrialization is taking place but industrial production has been greatly reduced because of war damage and sanctions. Iraq's major industry is oil production. It was nationalized in 1972 and usually accounts for approximately 98 per cent of the total government revenue and 45 per cent of GNP. Production was 3.5 million barrels per day in 1979 but has been reduced by war damage from the Iran–Iraq and Gulf wars, the closure of Syrian, Turkish and Saudi pipelines and UN economic sanctions.

TRADE

The principal imports are normally iron and steel, cement and other building materials, mechanical and electrical machinery, motor vehicles, textiles and clothing, essential foodstuffs, grain, tinned foods and raw industrial materials. The chief exports are normally crude petroleum, dates, raw wool, raw hides and skins and raw cotton.

Trade with UK	1993	1994
Imports from UK	£11,956,000	£9,581,000
Exports to UK	39,000	122,000

COMMUNICATIONS

The port of Basra has not been used since the outbreak of hostilities with Iran in 1980. Continuous dredging of the Shatt-al-Arab has also been suspended by hostilities and the channel has seriously silted. The port of Umm Qasr on the Kuwaiti border, which was developed for freight and sulphur handling and includes a container terminal, was opened in late 1993. All external borders, except that of Jordan, are closed to Iraqi traffic.

There is an international airport at Baghdad. Iraqi Airways provided flights between Baghdad and London, and other international airlines operated to Europe. Iraqi Republican Railways provided regular passenger and goods services between Basra, Baghdad and Mosul. There is also a metre gauge rail line connecting Baghdad with Khanaqin, Kirkuk and Arbil.

Iraqi communications were greatly affected by the Gulf War; large numbers of bridges were destroyed and the railway system extensively disrupted.

IRELAND

Ireland lies in the Atlantic Ocean between 51° 26' and 55° 21' N. latitude and 5° 25' and 10° 30' W. longitude. It is separated from Scotland by the North Channel and from England and Wales by the Irish Sea and St George's Channel. The area of the island is 32,588 sq. miles (84,402 sq. km). The greatest length of the island, from north-east to south-west (Torr Head to Mizen Head), is 302 miles, and the greatest breadth, from east to west (Dundrum Bay to Annagh Head), is 174 miles. On the north coast of Achill Island (Co. Mayo) are the highest cliffs in the British Isles, 2,000 feet sheer above the sea.

The island is mostly a central plain with an elevation 50 to 350 ft above mean sea level, and with isolated mountain ranges near the coastline. The highest point is Carrantuohill (3,414 ft), which drains the central plain. The Slaney flows into Wexford Harbour, the Liffey to Dublin Bay, the Boyne to Drogheda, the Lee to Cork Harbour, the Blackwater to Youghal Harbour, and the Suir, Barrow and Nore to Waterford Harbour.

The principal hydrographic feature is the loughs; the Shannon chain of Allen, Boderg, Forbes, Ree and Derg, and the Erne chain of Gowna, Oughter, Lower Erne, and Erne; Melvin, Gill, Gara and Conn in the north-west; and Corrib and Mask (joined by a hidden channel) in the west. In Co. Kerry are the famous lakes of Killarney.

Although little is known about the earliest inhabitants of Ireland, there are traces of neolithic man throughout the island. In the later Bronze Age a Celtic race of Goidels appears to have invaded the island, and in the early Iron Age Brythons from south Britain are believed to have effected settlements in the south-east, while Picts from north Britain established similar settlements in the north. Towards the close of the Roman occupation of Britain, the dominant tribe in the island was that of the Scoti, who afterwards established themselves in Scotland.

Hibernia was visited by Roman merchants but never by Roman legions, and little is known of the history of the country until the invasions of Northmen (Norwegians and Danes) towards the close of the eighth century AD. The outstanding events in the encounters with the Northmen are the Battle of Tara (980), at which the Hy Neill king Maelsechlainn II defeated the Scandinavians of Dublin and the Hebrides under the king Amlaib Cuarán; and the Battle of Clontarf (1014) by which the Scandinavian power was completely broken.

After Clontarf the supreme power was disputed by the O'Briens of Munster, the O'Neills of Ulster, and the O'Connors of Connaught, with varying fortunes. In 1152 Dermod MacMurrough (Diarmit MacMurchada), the deposed king of Leinster, sought assistance in his struggle with Rauidhri O'Connor (the high king of Ireland) from Henry II of England. Henry authorized him to obtain armed support in England for the recovery of his kingdom, and Dermod enlisted the services of Richard de Clare, the Norman Earl of Pembroke afterwards known as Strongbow, who landed at Waterford in 1170 with 200 knights and 1,000 other troops for the reconquest of Leinster, where he eventually settled after marriage with Dermod's daughter.

In 1172 Henry II himself landed in Ireland. He received homage from the Irish kings and established his capital at Dublin. The invaders subsequently conquered most of the island and a feudal government was created. In the 14th and 15th centuries, the Irish recovered most of their lands, while many Anglo-Irish lords became virtually independent, royal authority being confined to the Pale, a small district round Dublin. Though, under Henry VII, Sir Edward Poynings, as Lord Deputy, had passed at the Parliament of Drogheda (1494) the act later known as Poynings' Law, subordinating the Irish legislature to the Crown, the Earls of Kildare retained effective power until Henry VIII began the reconquest of Ireland in 1534. Parliament in 1541 recognized him as King of Ireland and by 1603 English authority was supreme.

REPUBLIC OF IRELAND
Poblacht Na hEireann

The Republic of Ireland has a land area of 27,136 sq. miles (70,283 sq. km), divided into four provinces of 26 counties: Leinster (Carlow, Dublin, Kildare, Kilkenny, Laoighis, Longford, Louth, Meath, Offaly, Westmeath, Wexford and Wicklow); Munster (Clare, Cork, Kerry, Limerick, Tipperary and Waterford); Connacht (Galway, Leitrim, Mayo, Roscommon and Sligo); and part of Ulster (Cavan, Donegal and Monaghan).

The population of the Republic (1991 census) was 3,525,719. Figures also showed 49,456 births, 15,728 marriages and 31,656 deaths in 1993 (provisional). At the census of 1991 religious adherence was: Roman Catholic, 3,228,327; Church of Ireland, 89,187; Presbyterians, 13,199; Methodists, 5,037; others, 189,969. Irish is the first official language and English is recognized as a second official language. English is more commonly used.

CAPITAL – ΨDublin (*Baile Atha Cliath*), population (1991 census) 478,389. Other county boroughs, with their population figures at the 1991 census, are ΨCork (127,253); ΨLimerick (52,083); ΨWaterford (40,328); and Ψ Galway (50,853).
CURRENCY – Punt (Irish pound) of 100 pence.
FLAG – Equal vertical stripes of green, white and orange.
NATIONAL ANTHEM – Amhrán na BhFiann (The Soldier's Song).
NATIONAL DAY – 17 March (St Patrick's Day).

GOVERNMENT

The 1937 constitution declares the national territory to be the whole island of Ireland, but that, pending the reinteg-

ration of the national territory, laws enacted by Parliament will apply in the area which constituted the Irish Free State, i.e. not in the six counties of Northern Ireland.

The President (*Uachtarán na hEireann*) is directly elected for a term of seven years, and is eligible for a second term. The President is aided and advised by a Council of State.

The National Parliament (*Oireachtas*) consists of the President, a House of Representatives (*Dáil Éireann*) and a Senate (*Seanad Éireann*). Dáil Éireann is composed of 166 members elected for a five-year term by adult suffrage on a basis of proportional representation by means of the single transferable vote. Seanad Éireann is composed of 60 members, of whom 11 are nominated by the Taoiseach and 49 are elected, six by institutions of higher education and 43 from panels of candidates established on a vocational basis.

Executive power is vested in the government subject to the constitution. The government is responsible to the Dáil. The Taoiseach is appointed by the President on the nomination of the Dáil. The other members of the government are appointed by the President on the nomination of the Taoiseach with the previous approval of the Dáil. The Taoiseach appoints a member of the government to be his deputy (the *Tánaiste*).

The last general election was on 25 November 1992. The composition of the Dáil Eireann in August 1995 was: Fianna Fáil 67; Fine Gael 47; Labour 32; Progressive Democrats 8; Democratic Left 6; Green 1; Independent 4. The present coalition government was formed by Fine Gael (FG), the Labour Party (L) and the Democratic Left (DL) on 15 December 1994.

HEAD OF STATE
President, Mary Robinson, *assumed office* 3 December 1990

CABINET *as at August 1995*

Taoiseach (*PM*), John Bruton (FG)
Tánaiste (*Deputy PM*), *Minister for Foreign Affairs*, Dick Spring (L)
Finance, Ruarí Quinn (L)
Employment and Enterprise, Richard Bruton (FG)
Justice, Nora Owen (FG)

Agriculture, Forestry and Food, Ivan Yates (FG)
Social Welfare, Proinsias De Rossa (DL)
Environment, Brendan Howlin (L)
Health, Michael Noonan (FG)
Education, Niamh Bhreathnach (L)
Defence and Marine, Sean Barrett (FG)
Transport, Energy and Communications, Michael Lowry (FG)
Tourism and Trade, Enda Kenny (FG)
Equality and Law Reform, Mervyn Taylor (L)
Arts, Culture and the Gaeltacht, Michael Higgins (L)

IRISH EMBASSY
17 Grosvenor Place, London SW1X 7HR
Tel 0171-235 2171
Ambassador Extraordinary and Plenipotentiary, new
   appointment awaited
Counsellor, J. Timbs (*Economic and Commercial*)

BRITISH EMBASSY
31 Merrion Road, Dublin 4
Tel: Dublin 2695211
Ambassador Extraordinary and Plenipotentiary, His Excellency
   David E. S. Blatherwick, CMG, OBE, apptd 1991
Counsellor and Deputy Head of Mission, J. A. Dew
Defence Attaché, Col. S. D. Lambe
First Secretary (Commercial), J. F. Pepper

BRITISH COUNCIL REPRESENTATIVE, Harold Fish, OBE,
   22 Lower Mount Street, Dublin 2

JUDICIAL SYSTEM

The judicial system comprises courts of first instance and a court of final appeal called the Supreme Court (*Cúirt Uachtarach*). The courts of first instance include a High Court (*Ard-Chúirt*) and courts of local and limited jurisdiction, with a right of appeal as determined by law. The High Court alone has original jurisdiction to consider the question of the validity of any law having regard to the provisions of the constitution. The Supreme Court has appellate jurisdiction from decisions of the High Court.
Chief Justice, Hon. Liam Hamilton
President of the High Court, Hon. Declan Costello
Attorney-General, Dermot Gleeson

DEFENCE

There is a Permanent Defence Force in which enlistment is voluntary. The minimum term of enlistment is five years, followed by seven years in the Reserve Defence Force. Enlistment in the Reserve Defence Force is also voluntary; minimum term of enlistment is three years. The defence estimate for the year ending 31 December 1995 provides for an expenditure of IR£373,662,000.

The total active armed forces number 13,000 personnel with 16,150 reserves. The Army has a strength of 11,200 personnel. The Navy has a strength of 1,000, with seven patrol and coastal vessels. The Air Corps has a strength of 800, with 16 combat aircraft and 15 armed helicopters. Ireland deploys an infantry battalion of 679 troops with UN forces in South Lebanon.

ECONOMY

Although industry has expanded greatly since Ireland's entry into the European Community in 1973, agriculture remains of importance to the economy; in 1992, 13 per cent of the workforce was employed in agriculture. The main crops are wheat, barley, potatoes, sugar beet, oats and turnips. Animal products, dairy products and livestock, especially pigs and cows, are major exports. Agriculture has benefited considerably from the EC Common Agricultural Policy and support funds, which have been used to modernize farming methods and machinery, but agriculture has suffered from the drift of the rural population to urban areas and abroad.

Industry has recently overtaken agriculture as the most important sector of the economy, benefiting from significant European investment. The traditional brewing, spirits and food-processing sectors have expanded and have been joined by the manufacture of textiles, chemical, pharmaceuticals, electronics, office machinery and transportation equipment. Waterford glass and crystal has gained a worldwide reputation. Tourism is the most important part of the service sector and in recent years has provided substantial revenue, with over three million visitors in 1992.

The difficulties posed by the lack of energy resources have been transformed over the past 15 years by the discovery of the Kinsale Head and Ballycotton natural gas fields off the south coast, which now supply all the country's natural gas needs, and by the opening of seven government-funded milled peat power-generating stations which use the country's large peat resources. Hydro-electric power from the Shannon barrage and other schemes is also important but Ireland still must import significant quantities of oil and coal for power generation.

Metal content of ores raised (1993) was lead, 53,700 tonnes; zinc, 194,500 tonnes; silver 17,300,000 grammes. An estimated 15,470 persons were employed in the fisheries in 1994. Total value of all fish landed in 1994 was IR£109.16 million.

FINANCE

	1994	1995
Total current revenue	IR£10,203m	IR£11,542m
Total current expenditure	11,852m	11,188m

The gross debt at end 1993 was IR£28,357.2 million.

TRADE	1992	1993
Imports	IR£13,194,772,000	IR£14,748,203,000
Exports	16,628,836,000	19,641,804,000
Trade balance	3,434,064,000	4,893,601,000

Trade with UK	1993	1994
Imports from UK	£6,421,450,000	£6,947,834,000
Exports to UK	5,125,285,000	5,647,543,000

EDUCATION

Primary education is directed by the state, with the exception of 74 private primary schools with an enrolment of 8,329 in 1993–4. There were 3,317 state-aided primary schools with an enrolment of 505,883.

In 1993–4 there were 461 recognized secondary schools with 224,035 pupils under private management (mainly religious orders), and 248 vocational schools with 94,760 pupils. Vocational schools are controlled by 38 statutory local Vocational Education Committees. There were 16 state comprehensive schools in 1993–4 with a total enrolment of 9,363 students, and 57 community schools with an enrolment of 39,487 students. There were also other miscellaneous second-level schools and the total full-time enrolment at second-level for 1993–4 was 371,792.

Third-level education is catered for by seven university colleges, and also by third-level courses offered by the technical colleges and regional technical colleges and other miscellaneous third-level institutions. There were 92,595 full-time third-level students in 1993–4, of whom 50,662 were attending university courses.

The estimated state expenditure on education in 1995, excluding administration and inspection, is: first-level IR£650,034,000; second-level IR£746,187,000. The vote for third-level education amounted to IR£402,480,000.

COMMUNICATIONS

In the year ended 31 December 1993, there were 1,944 km of railway operated by *Iarnród Eireann*; the receipts were IR£81,917,000 and expenditure IR£175,783,000.

In 1993 road motor vehicles carried 231,833,000 passengers, the gross receipts being IR£164,814,000.

In 1993 the number of ships with cargo which arrived at Irish ports was 13,199 (36,408,000 net registered tons); of these 1,829 (4,604,000 net registered tons) were of Irish nationality.

Shannon Airport, Co. Limerick, is on the main transatlantic air route. In 1994 the airport handled 1,534,432 passengers. Dublin Airport serves the cross-channel and European services operated by the Irish national airline Aer Lingus and other airlines. In 1994 the airport handled 6,980,983 passengers. Cork Airport serves the cross-channel and European services operated by Aer Lingus and other airlines. In 1994 the airport handled 800,188 passengers.

ISRAEL
Medinat Israel

Israel lies at the eastern edge of the Mediterranean Sea, between 29° 30′ to 33° 15′ N. latitude and 34° 15′ to 35° 40′ E. longitude. It is bordered by Lebanon on the north, Syria on the north-east, Jordan and the West Bank on the east, and the Gaza Strip and the Egyptian province of Sinai on the south-west. The area is estimated at 8,019 sq. miles (20,770 sq. km).

Israel comprises the hill country of Galilee and parts of Judea and Samaria, rising to heights of nearly 4,000 ft; the coastal plain from the Gaza strip to north of Acre, including the plain of Esdraelon running from Haifa Bay to the south-east which divides the hill region; the Negev, a semi-desert triangular-shaped region, extending from a base south of Beersheba, to an apex at the head of the Gulf of Aqaba; and parts of the Jordan valley, including the Hula region, Tiberias and the south-western extremity of the Dead Sea.

The principal river is the Jordan, which rises from three main sources in Israel, the Lebanon and Syria, and flows through the Hula valley, Lake Tiberias/Kinneret (Sea of Galilee) and the Jordan Valley into the Dead Sea, falling 1,517 ft from Hulata to the Dead Sea. The other principal rivers are the Yarkon and Kishon. The Dead Sea is a lake (shared between Israel, the West Bank and Jordan), 1,286 ft below sea-level; it has no outlet, the surplus being carried off by evaporation.

The climate is variable, modified by altitude and distance from the sea, with hot summers and rainy winters.

The population (estimate 1992) including East Jerusalem and Jewish settlers in the Occupied Territories is 5,090,000. Of these 4,175,000 are Jewish (82 per cent); 700,000 Arab Muslims (13.8 per cent); 130,000 Christians (2.5 per cent), of which 90 per cent are Arab, and 85,000 Druze (1.7 per cent). During the upheavals of 1948–9 a large number of Arabs left the country as refugees and settled in neighbouring countries and the Occupied Territories.

Since independence Israel has had a policy of granting an immigration visa to every Jew who expresses a desire to settle in Israel. Between 1948 and 1992, 2.3 million immigrants had entered Israel from over 100 different countries.

Hebrew and Arabic are the official languages. Arabs are entitled to transact all official business with government departments in Arabic.

CAPITAL – Most of the government departments are in Jerusalem, population (1993 estimate) 556,400. A resolution proclaiming Jerusalem as the capital of Israel was adopted by the *Knesset* in 1950. It is not, however, recognized as the capital by the UN because East Jerusalem is part of the Occupied Territories captured in 1967. The UN and international law continues to reject the Israeli annexation of East Jerusalem and considers the pre-1950 capital Tel Aviv (population, with district, 1,781,500) to be the capital. Other principal towns (1990) are ΨHaifa and district (432,900) and Beersheba and district (122,000).

CURRENCY – New Shekel of 100 agora.

FLAG – White, with two horizontal blue stripes, the Shield of David in the centre.

NATIONAL ANTHEM – Hatikvah (The Hope).

GOVERNMENT

The Ottoman Empire province of Palestine was captured by British forces in 1917, the same year that the British Government issued the Balfour Declaration which 'viewed with favour the establishment of a national home for the Jewish people in Palestine'. The Balfour Declaration's terms were enshrined in Britain's League of Nations mandate over Palestine, leading to steady Jewish immigration in the inter-war years and a post-1945 flood by Nazi concentration camp survivors. The Arab Palestinian population revolted against Jewish immigration from 1936 onwards, while Jewish groups conducted a terrorist campaign against the British administration from 1945 onwards.

914   Countries of the World

In 1947 Britain announced its withdrawal from Palestine with effect from May 1948, handing over to the UN responsibility for solving the conflict between Arabs and Jews. Both sides ignored the UN partition plan; on the withdrawal of British forces on 14 May 1948 the State of Israel was proclaimed and the first Arab-Israeli war began. By the time of the January 1949 cease-fire Israeli forces controlled all of the former mandate territory apart from the West Bank (and East Jerusalem) and the Gaza Strip, which had come under Jordanian and Egyptian control respectively.

During the 1967 Six-Day War Israel captured the West Bank and the Gaza Strip, together with Sinai from Egypt and the Golan Heights from Syria, and annexed East Jerusalem. Israel held onto its gains in the 1973 Yom Kippur War. The Golan Heights were annexed in 1981; Sinai was returned to Egypt in 1982 in accordance with the 1979 Israeli–Egyptian peace treaty, and the South Lebanon Security Zone was established after the 1982–5 invasion of Lebanon. The annexations of East Jerusalem and the Golan Heights remain unrecognized internationally.

Israel is a sovereign democratic republic with executive power vested in a Prime Minister and Cabinet, and legislative power in a unicameral legislature (*Knesset*) of 120 members elected by proportional representation for a maximum term of four years. The President is head of state and is elected by the Knesset for a maximum of two five-year terms. A coalition government of the Labour, Meretz and Shas parties came to power after the general election of June 1992, the present Labour, Meretz and Yi'ud coalition forming in December 1994.

A peace process started in October 1991 in Madrid led to agreements with the Palestine Liberation Organization (*see* page 915), and with Jordan on 14 September 1993. A full peace agreement with Jordan was signed on 26 October 1994 and provides for the return to Jordan of land occupied by Israel since 1967 in the southern Araba valley; the establishment of full diplomatic and economic relations; the prevention of terrorist attacks on each other; the sharing of the Jordan and Yarmouk rivers; and King Hussein's custodianship of Muslim sites in Jerusalem. Direct telephone links have been established, the first border crossing has opened, and negotiations on water rights, environmental and economic co-operation continue.

HEAD OF STATE
President of Israel, Ezer Weizmann, *elected* 24 March 1993, *inaugurated* 13 May 1993

CABINET *as at August 1995*
Prime Minister, Defence, Yitzhak Rabin (L)
Deputy Prime Minister, Foreign Affairs, Shimon Peres (L)
Deputy Prime Minister, Transport, Yisrael Kessar (L)
Police, Moshe Shachal (L)
Communications, Science and Technology, Shulamit Aloni (M)
Health, Ephraim Sneh (L)
Industry and Trade, Michael Harish (L)
Finance, Avraham Shochat (L)
Economics and Planning, Yossi Beilin (L)
Agriculture, Yaacov Tsur (L)
Immigration Absorption, Yair Tsaban (M)
Tourism, Uzi Baram (L)
Justice, David Libai (L)
Education and Culture, Amnon Rubinstein (M)
Housing, Binyamin Ben-Eliezer (L)
Environment, Yossi Sarid (L)
Labour and Social Affairs, Ora Namir (L)
Energy Infrastructure, Gonen Segev (Y)
Religious Affairs, Shimon Shetreet (L)

Interior, Ehud Barack (L)
L Labour Party; M Meretz; Y Yi'ud

EMBASSY OF ISRAEL
2 Palace Green, Kensington, London w8 4QB
Tel 0171–957 9500
Ambassador Extraordinary and Plenipotentiary, His Excellency Moshe Raviv, apptd 1993
Minister Plenipotentiary, G. Meir
Defence Attaché, Brig.-Gen. A. Nevo
Minister, M. Hacohen (*Consular*)
Counsellor, A. Wohl (*Commercial*)

BRITISH EMBASSY
192 Hayarkon Street, Tel Aviv 63405
Tel: Tel Aviv 5249171
Ambassador Extraordinary and Plenipotentiary, His Excellency Robert A. Burns, CMG, apptd 1992
Counsellor, Consul-General and Deputy Ambassador, C. J. White
Defence and Military Attaché, Col. C. S. Wakelin, OBE
First Secretary (Commercial), P. A. Connolly
There are British consular offices in Tel Aviv and Eilat and a Consulate-General in East Jerusalem (Occupied Territories).

BRITISH COUNCIL DIRECTOR, Harley Brookes,
140 Hayarkon Street, PO Box 3302, Tel Aviv 61032.
There are also libraries in West Jerusalem and Nazareth.

ISRAEL-BRITISH CHAMBER OF COMMERCE, 76 IBN Guirol Street, Tel Aviv 64162

DEFENCE

The Israeli defence forces have a total active strength of 172,000 (including 138,500 conscripts). Since its inception, however, Israel has based its defence on a large and highly-trained reserve, which numbers at present 430,000 personnel. Conscripts serve for periods of four years (officers), three years (men) or two years (women). Reserves serve for one month a year and are eligible for call-up until age 54 (men) and age 24 or marriage (women). Israel is widely believed to have a nuclear capacity of around 100 warheads which could be delivered by aircraft and Jericho I and II missiles.

The Army has an active strength of 134,000 (114,700 conscripts) and a strength of 598,000 on mobilization, with 3,895 main battle tanks, 9,500 armoured personnel carriers and 1,784 artillery pieces. The Army is organized into three regular armoured and three regular infantry divisions, with a further four regular mechanized infantry brigades. Reserve units comprise nine armoured divisions, one air mobile division and ten infantry and four artillery brigades.

The Navy has an active strength of 7,000 (3,000 conscripts) and 12,000 on mobilization, with three submarines and 55 patrol and coastal craft. The Air Force has a strength of 32,000 (21,800 conscripts) and 37,000 on mobilization, with 728 combat aircraft and 117 armed helicopters. The Air Force comprises 13 ground attack/air defence and two ground attack squadrons, together with one transport wing and reconnaissance, airborne early warning, tanker and training units. There is also a paramilitary force of 6,000 border police.

EDUCATION AND CULTURE

Education from six to 16 years is free and compulsory. The law also provides for working youth age 16–18, who for some reason have not completed their education, to be exempted from work in order to do so. There are seven universities including two engineering and technological institutes.

Important historic sites in Israel include: *Jerusalem* – the Church of the Holy Sepulchre, the Al Aqsa Mosque and Dome of the Rock standing on the remains of the Temple Mount of Herod the Great of which the Western (wailing) Wall is a fragment, the Church of the Dormition and the Coenaculum on Mount Zion, Ein Karem, Church of the Visitation, Church of St John the Baptist; *Galilee* – the Sea, Church and Mount of the Beatitudes, ruins of Capernaum and other sites connected with the life of Christ; *Mount Tabor* – Church of the Transfiguration; *Nazareth* – Church of the Annunciation, and other Christian shrines associated with the childhood of Christ; there are also numerous sites dating from biblical and medieval days, such as Ascalon, Caesarea, Atlit, Massada, Megiddo and Hazor.

COMMUNICATIONS

Israel State Railways serves Haifa, Tel Aviv, Jerusalem, Lod, Nahariya, Beersheba, Dimona, Ashdod and intermediate stations with a network of 528 km. There were 12,823 km of paved road in 1986.

Israel's merchant marine had reached a total of 2,805,000 tons deadweight by December 1985. The chief ports are Haifa and Ashdod on the Mediterranean, and Eilat on the Red Sea; Acre has an anchorage for small vessels. The chief international airport is Ben Gurion between Tel Aviv and Jerusalem.

ECONOMY

The country is generally fertile with crops ranging from the temperate to the subtropical. Water supply for irrigation limits greater production. The area under cultivation is 1.1 million acres, of which 0.6 million is under irrigation. Agriculture accounts for 5 per cent of GNP and 4 per cent of exports.

The famous 'Jaffa' orange is produced in large quantities for export, along with other summer fruits, seasonal vegetables and glasshouse crops, such as flowers, tomatoes and strawberries. Olives are cultivated, mainly for the production of oil. The main winter crops are wheat, barley and various kinds of pulses, while in summer sorghum, millet, maize, sesame and summer pulses are grown. Beef, cattle and poultry farming have been developed and the production of mixed vegetables and dairy produce has greatly increased. Tobacco and medium staple cotton are now grown. Fishing production (mostly from fish farms) was 12,200 tons in 1993.

In value polished diamonds account for about 23 per cent of total exports. Amongst the most important industries are textiles, foodstuffs, chemicals (mainly fertilizers and pharmaceuticals). Metal-working and science-based industries are sophisticated and technologically advanced and include the aircraft and military industries. Other important manufacturing industries include plastics, rubber, cement, glass, paper and oil refining. Industry accounts for 30 per cent of GNP and 60 per cent of exports.

TRADE

The principal imports are foodstuffs, crude oil, machinery and vehicles, iron, steel and manufactures thereof, and chemicals. The principal exports are metal machinery, electronic goods, chemicals, rubber, plastics, textiles, food and beverages, minerals, citrus produce and polished diamonds.

Trade with UK	1993	1994
Imports from UK	£876,330,000	£1,031,644,000
Exports to UK	550,200,000	572,375,000

PALESTINIAN AUTONOMOUS AREAS

The total area is 2,406 sq. miles (6,231 sq. km). The area which is fully autonomous is 159 sq. miles (412 sq. km), of which the Gaza Strip is 136 sq. miles (352 sq. km) and the Jericho enclave 23 sq. miles (60 sq. km). The partially autonomous area is the remainder of the West Bank, some 2,247 sq miles (5,819 sq. km). The UN and the international community also recognize East Jerusalem as part of the Occupied Territories.

The population (1992 estimate) is 1,635,000, of whom 660,000 live in the Gaza Strip, 40,000 in Jericho, and 935,000 in the remainder of the West Bank. In addition there are 141,000 Jewish settlers in the West Bank and 4,000 in the Gaza Strip who remain under Israeli administration and jurisdiction. Some 90 per cent of Palestinians are Muslim (the vast majority Sunni) and 10 per cent are Christians.

CAPITAL – Although Palestinians claim East Jerusalem as their capital, the administrative capital has been established in Gaza City (120,000). Other major towns are Khan Yunis and Rafah in the Gaza Strip and Nablus, Hebron, Jericho, Ramallah and Bethlehem on the West Bank.

FLAG – Three horizontal stripes of black, white, green with a red triangle based on the hoist (the PLO flag).

NATIONAL ANTHEM – Biladi, Biladi (My Country, My Country).

GOVERNMENT

Israel captured the Gaza Strip, East Jerusalem and the West Bank during the 1967 Six-Day War and annexed East Jerusalem. After the war the Israeli government began to establish security settlements in the Occupied Territories and religious groups later established further settlements. Palestinian resistance to Israeli rule was led by the Palestine Liberation Organization (PLO) established in 1964, which carried out armed attacks, bombings and aircraft hijackings against Israeli targets around the world. Frustration at continued Israeli occupation led to the start of the *intifada* in 1987, a campaign of sustained unrest in the Occupied Territories which left 1,400 Palestinians and 230 Jews dead by early 1995. When the 1991 Madrid peace process stalled, Israeli and PLO officials engaged in secret negotiations in Norway in 1993 leading to the signing of the 'Declaration of Principles on Interim Self-Government Arrangements' on 13 September 1993. Under this agreement the PLO renounced terrorism and recognized Israeli's right to exist in secure borders, while Israel recognized the PLO as the legitimate representative of the Palestinian people.

The Declaration of Principles established a timetable for progress towards a final settlement: negotiations leading to an Israeli military withdrawal from the Gaza Strip and Jericho by 13 April 1994, when power was to be transferred to a nominated Palestinian National Authority (PNA); elections to a new Palestinian Council, which would also exercise control over six policy areas in the rest of the West Bank (culture, tourism, health, education, social welfare, direct taxation), and the Israeli military administration dissolved by 13 July 1994; negotiations on a permanent settlement, including Jewish settlers and East Jerusalem, to begin by 13 April 1996; and a permanent settlement to be in place by 13 April 1999.

The timetable has slipped, with the Israeli military not finally redeploying in the Gaza Strip and withdrawing from Jericho until 18 May 1994, when the five-year period of interim self-government under the PNA began. The Israeli military remains responsible for all Jewish settlements and road links in the Gaza Strip and Jericho, while the 9,000 Palestinian policemen are responsible for security and law and order for the majority of the Gaza Strip and Jericho. In the rest of the West Bank and at border crossings with Jordan and Egypt the Israeli military remains in full control and the PNA has only exercised authority in the six policy areas since December 1994.

At the time of going to press, negotiations continued on redeploying Israeli forces away from Palestinian towns and on holding elections for a new Palestinian Council so that the Israeli military administration in the West Bank can be dissolved. The timetable is now over a year behind schedule and intense negotiations in 1994–5 have so far proved unsuccessful because of three main issues: Israeli retention of thousands of Palestinian prisoners; continued expansion of Jewish settlements in the West Bank; and a series of bomb attacks in Israel by Palestinian extremists opposed to the peace process, which caused the Israelis to suspend the peace process on several occasions until the PNA clamped down on the extremists. The autonomous area has issued its own travel documents and postage stamps and has established a broadcasting service.

PALESTINIAN NATIONAL AUTHORITY *as at August 1995*

President, Interior, Yasser Arafat
Economy and Industry, Abu Ala'a
Planning and Economic Co-operation, Nabil Shaath
Finance, Agriculture, Muhammed Nashashibi
Jerusalem, Feisal Husseini
Education, Yasser Amru
Art and Culture, Yasser Abd Rabbu
Social Affairs, Intisar al-Wazir
Justice, Freih Abu Middein
Labour, Samir Ghosheh
Housing, Zakaria al-Agha
Local Government, Saeb Erikat
Tourism, Elias Freij
Health, Riad Za'anoun
Youth and Sports, Azmi Shuaibi
Communications, Abdul Hafez Ashab
Transport, Abdul Aziz Ahmed
Civil Affairs and Liaison with Israel, Jamil Tarifi
Religious Affairs and Waqfs, Sheikh Hasan Tahbub
Government Secretary-General, Tayeb Abdul Rahim
Minister without Portfolio, Munib Masri

BRITISH CONSULATE-GENERAL
19 Nashashibi Street, PO Box 19690, East Jerusalem 97200
Consul-General, R. J. Dalton

BRITISH COUNCIL DIRECTOR, Peter Skelton, 2 Abu Obeida Street, PO Box 19136, Jerusalem.

ITALY
Repubblica Italiana

Italy consists of a peninsula, the large islands of Sicily and Sardinia, the island of Elba and about 70 other small islands. It is bounded on the north by Switzerland and Austria, on the south by the Mediterranean Sea, on the east by the Adriatic Sea and Slovenia, and on the west by France and the Ligurian and Tyrrhenian Seas. The total area is about 116,304 sq. miles (301,225 sq. km).

The peninsula is for the most part mountainous, but between the Apennines, which form its spine, and the east coastline are two large fertile plains: Emilia/Romagna in the north and Apulia in the south. The Alps divide Italy from France, Switzerland, Austria and Slovenia. Partly within the Italian borders are Monte Rosa (15,217 ft), the

Matterhorn (14,780 ft) and several peaks from 12,000 to 14,000 ft. The chief rivers are the Po (405 miles), flowing through Piedmont, Lombardy and the Veneto; the Adige (Trentino and Veneto); the Arno (Florentine plain); the Tiber (flowing through Rome to Ostia).

The population (UN estimate 1992) was 56,777,000. The language is Italian, a Romance language derived from Latin. It is spoken in its purest form in Tuscany, but there are numerous dialects, showing variously French, German, Spanish and Arabic influences. Sard, the dialect of Sardinia, is accorded by some authorities the status of a distinct Romance language.

CAPITAL – Rome. Population of the commune (1991 census) 2,693,383. The Eternal City was founded, according to legend, by Romulus in 753 BC. It was the centre of Latin civilization and capital of the Roman Republic and Roman Empire. The other principal cities and towns (population of the commune, 1991 census) are Milan 1,371,008; ΨNaples 1,054,601; Turin 961,916; ΨGenoa 675,639; Bologna 404,322; Florence 402,316; *Sicily*, ΨPalermo 697,162; *Sardinia*, ΨCagliari 203,254.
CURRENCY – Lira of 100 centesimi.
FLAG – Vertical stripes of green, white and red.
NATIONAL ANTHEM – Inno di Mameli.
NATIONAL DAY – 2 June.

HISTORY
Italian unity was accomplished under the House of Savoy after a struggle from 1848 to 1870 in which Mazzini (1805–72), Garibaldi (1807–82) and Cavour (1810–61) were the principal figures. It was completed when Lombardy was ceded by Austria in 1859 and Venice in 1866, and through the evacuation of Rome by the French in 1870. In 1871 the King of Italy entered Rome, and that city was declared to be the capital.

The fascist regime came to power in 1922 under Benito Mussolini, known as *Il Duce* (The Leader), who was Prime Minister from 1922 until 25 July 1943, when the fascist regime was abolished. Mussolini was captured by Italian partisans while attempting to escape across the Swiss frontier and killed on 28 April 1945.

In fulfilment of a promise given in April 1944 that he would retire when the Allies entered Rome, a decree was signed in June 1944 by King Victor Emmanuel III under which Prince Umberto, his son, became Lieutenant-General of the Realm. The King remained head of the House of Savoy and retained the title King of Italy until his abdication in May 1946, when he was succeeded by the Crown Prince. A general election was held in June 1946, together with a referendum on the future of the monarchy, in which a majority favoured a republic and the royal family left the country.

GOVERNMENT

The 1947 constitution provides for the election of the President for a seven-year term by an electoral college which consists of the two houses of the parliament (the Chamber of Deputies and the Senate) sitting in joint session, together with three delegates from each region (one in the case of the Valle d'Aosta). The President, who must be over 50 years of age, has numerous carefully defined powers, the main one of which is the right to dissolve one or both houses after consultation with the Speakers. Members of both houses were elected wholly by proportional representation until 1993. Now 75 per cent (232) of the 315 elected seats in the Senate are elected on a first-past-the-post basis and the remaining elected seats are filled by proportional representation. In addition there are 11 life senators, who are past presidents and prime ministers. In the Chamber of Deputies 75 per cent (472) of seats are elected on a first-past-the-post basis, and 25 per cent (158) by proportional representation, with a 4 per cent threshold for parliamentary representation.

Political instability (50 governments since 1947) and widespread political and business corruption, often with Mafia links, led to public disillusion with the major political parties. Their support collapsed in the April 1992 general election, which produced a great increase in support for Northern League and anti-Mafia parties. Disillusionment with the established parties was confirmed in regional and local elections when the governing parties lost most of their local power and the Northern League, Democratic Left and anti-Mafia La Rête parties progressed. Meanwhile, the so-called 'clean hands' investigation into corruption and Mafia links that began in Milan in February 1992 has led to the arrest by magistrates of thousands of politicians and businessmen.

Between 1992 and 1994 the political and economic systems have been transformed to increase political stability, improve the economy and reduce corruption. In addition to constitutional reform, governments have acted to privatize state industries, to reduce the budget deficit and inflation with an austerity budget, to reorganize and reduce the civil service, and to reorganize and increase democracy in local government.

The first general election under the new electoral system, on 27–28 March 1994, resulted in victory for the right-wing Freedom Alliance composed of the new Forza Italia party, the Northern League and the National Alliance (based on the neo-fascist MSI party). The Freedom Alliance won 366 seats in the Chamber of Deputies, the left-wing Progressive Alliance 213 seats and the Centre Coalition 46 seats. The Forza Italia leader and millionaire businessman Silvio Berlusconi formed a government in May 1994. Berlusconi's coalition government proved unstable and collapsed on 21 December 1994 when the majority of the Northern League ministers withdrew from the government over Berlusconi's indictment on charges of bribery and corruption. The independent Treasury minister Lamberto Dini formed a government of technocrats in January 1995 with a mandate to carry out four major reforms: significantly reduce public spending and the

budget deficit; reform the regional electoral system; continue to reform the bloated state pension system; and ensure equal political access to television. By mid-1995 only legislation concerning the last reform had still to be put into practice.

HEAD OF STATE
President, Oscar Luigi Scalfaro, *elected by electoral college* 25 May 1992

COUNCIL OF MINISTERS *as at August 1995*
Prime Minister, Treasury, Lamberto Dini
Foreign Affairs, Susanna Agnelli
Interior, Giovanni Coronas
Justice, Filippo Mancuso
Defence, Domenico Corcione
Finance, Augusto Fantozzi
Budget, Rainer Masera
Health, Elio Guzzanti
Education, Giancarlo Lambardi
Industry and Trade, Alberto Clo
Agriculture, Walter Lucchetti
Employment, Tiziano Treu
Transport, Giovanni Caravale
Public Works and Environment, Paolo Baratta
Posts and Telecommunications, Agostino Gambino
Universities and Scientific Research, Georgio Salvini
Culture, Antonio Paolucci
Public Administration and Regional Affairs, Franco Frattini
Institutional Reform, Giovanni Motzo
Family, Adriano Ossicini

ITALIAN EMBASSY
14 Three Kings Yard, Davies Street, London WIY 2EH
Tel 0171-312 2200
Ambassador Extraordinary and Plenipotentiary, His Excellency Dr Paolo Galli, apptd 1995
Minister-Counsellor, A. Armellini
Defence Attaché, P. Rizzo
Cultural Attaché, Prof. F. Villari
Consul-General, L. Brofferio
First Counsellor, G. Ardizzone (*Commercial*)
There are also consular offices in Bedford, Edinburgh and Manchester.

BRITISH EMBASSY
Via XX Settembre 80A, 00187 Rome
Tel: Rome 482-5441
Ambassador Extraordinary and Plenipotentiary, His Excellency Sir Patrick Fairweather, KCMG, apptd 1992
Minister, D. H. Colvin, CMG
Defence and Military Attaché, Brig. J. H. Thoyts
Director-General for British Trade Development in Italy and Consul-General, P. H. Wetton, CMG (*Milan*)
Counsellor (Economic and Commercial), T. G. Paxman

BRITISH CONSULAR OFFICES – There are Consulates-General at Milan and Naples and Consulates offices at Rome, Genoa, Florence, Venice, Trieste, Bari and Turin.

BRITISH COUNCIL REPRESENTATIVE, K. Hunter, OBE, Palazzo del Drago, Via Quattro Fontane 20, 00184 Rome. There are British Council Offices at Milan, Bologna and Naples, each with a library.

BRITISH CHAMBER OF COMMERCE, Via San Paolo 7, 20121 Milan.

DEFENCE

Total active armed forces personnel number 322,300 (including 197,100 conscripts who serve for 12 months).

Reserves number 584,000, with an obligation to age 25 or 45 (Air Force), 45 (Army), 39 or 73 (Navy).

The Army has a strength of 205,000 (154,000 conscripts), with 1,210 main battle tanks, 3,020 armoured personnel carriers and 1,230 artillery pieces. Organization consists of a Field Army and Territorial Defence forces. The Field Army has three mechanized, four mountain, one armoured cavalry and two armoured brigades, seven artillery regiments, two armoured cavalry, five anti-aircraft and two aviation regiments. Territorial Defence forces comprise eight mechanized and one airborne brigades, a Rapid Intervention Force of two brigades, and one infantry, five armoured cavalry and four engineer regiments.

The Navy has a strength of 44,000 (including 17,600 conscripts), with nine submarines, one helicopter carrier, one cruiser, four destroyers and 23 frigates with 30 armed helicopters. The Air Force has a strength of 73,300 (25,500 conscripts) with 363 combat aircraft. Organization is into seven air defence, nine ground attack, three transport, two reconnaissance, two maritime reconnaissance, one electronic warfare, two communications and six training squadrons.

In addition to the regular armed forces there is the 111,800-strong paramilitary Carabinieri. There are several NATO bases in Italy with 12,600 US armed forces personnel stationed in the country, together with 171 aircraft and support forces from Britain, France, the Netherlands, Turkey and USA for operations over the former Yugoslavia.

ECONOMY

The governments of 1992–4 introduced economic reforms to reduce corruption and the budget deficit and national debt. In October 1992 the government significantly reduced public expenditure by reforming the pensions system, civil service and health service. In March 1993 further welfare reductions were made, privatization began and the tradition of annual wage indexation to inflation was ended. This was followed in April by a referendum in which the electorate voted to reform the state's participation in industry, and in July the government announced the beginning of large-scale privatization. The IMI banking group, banks Credito Italiano and Banca Commerciale Italiana, and INA insurance have been transferred to the private sector. One of the economy's major problems is the large budget deficit which in 1995 was still around 8 per cent of GDP despite four successive austerity budgets in 1993–5. The national debt remains high, at 120 per cent of GDP, as does unemployment at 11.5 per cent in 1994.

The state-owned sector of Italian industry is still important, dominated by the holding companies IRI (mechanical, steel, airlines), ENI (petrochemicals), STET (telecommunications) and ENEL (electricity). Industry accounted for 30.2 per cent of GDP in 1991. It is centred around Milan (steel, machine tools, motor cars), Turin (motor cars, steel, roller bearings, textiles), Rome (light industries), Venice (shipbuilding, paper, mechanical equipment, electrical goods, woollens), Bologna/Florence (food industry, footwear and textiles, reproduction furniture, glassware, pottery, ceramics), Naples, Bari (valves, vehicle bodies, tyres), Taranto (steel, oil refining), Trieste (shipbuilding) and Cagliari (aluminium production, petrochemicals).

Italy is generally poor in mineral resources but deposits of natural methane gas and oil have been discovered, mainly south of Sicily, and rapidly exploited. Production of lignite has also increased. Other minerals include iron ores and pyrites, mercury (over one-quarter of the world production), lead, zinc and aluminium. Marble is a traditional product of the Massa Carrara district.

Agriculture accounted for 3.8 per cent of GDP in 1991. Production is concentrated in Tuscany, Emilia and Romagna, Sicily and the whole of the southern third of the country. The principal products are wine, tobacco, citrus fruits, tomatoes, almonds, sugar beet, wheat and maize.

Tourism is a major sector of the economy, with over 50 million foreign tourists a year. Tourism is centred on Rome, Florence, Venice, the Alps, Sicily, the Adriatic coast and the Bay of Naples. The commercial and banking services are concentrated in Rome and in Milan, where the stock market is located.

TRADE WITH UK	1993	1994
Imports from UK	£5,761,242,000	£6,617,827,000
Exports to UK	6,467,666,000	7,181,993,000

COMMUNICATIONS

The main railway system is state-run by the *Ferrovia dello Stato*. A network of motorways (*autostrade*) covers the country, built and operated mainly by the IRI state holding company and ANAS, the state highway authority. Alitalia, the principal international and domestic airline, is also state-controlled by the IRI group. Other smaller companies, including ATI (an Alitalia subsidiary) and Air Mediterranea, operate on domestic routes. Genoa is the major port, handling about one-third of Italy's foreign trade.

CULTURE

Florence, the capital of Tuscany, was one of the greatest cities in Europe from the 11th to the 16th centuries, and the cradle of the Renaissance. Under the Medici family in the 15th century flourished many of the greatest names in Italian art, including Filippo Lippi, Botticelli, Donatello and Brunelleschi, and in the 16th century Michelangelo and Leonardo da Vinci.

Italian literature (in addition to Latin literature, which is the common inheritance of western Europe) is one of the richest in Europe, particularly in its golden age (Dante, 1265–1321; Petrarch, 1304–74; Boccaccio, 1313–75) and in the Renaissance (Ariosto, 1474–1533; Machiavelli, 1469–1527; Tasso, 1544–95). Notable in modern Italian literature are Manzoni (1785–1873), Carducci (1835–1907) and Gabriele d'Annunzio (1864–1938). The Nobel Prize for Literature has been awarded to Italian authors on five occasions: G. Cariducci (1906), Signora G. Deledda (1926), Luigi Pirandello (1934), Salvatore Quasimodo (1959) and Eugenio Montale (1975).

EDUCATION

Education is free and compulsory between the ages of six and 14; this comprises five years at primary school and three in the 'middle school', of which there are about 8,000. Pupils who obtain the middle school certificate may seek admission to any 'senior secondary school', which may be a lyceum with a classical or scientific or artistic bias, or an institute directed at technology (of which there are eight different types), trade or industry (including vocational schools), or teacher-training. Courses at the lyceums and technical institutes usually last for five years and success in the final examination qualifies for admission to university. In 1990–1 there were 3,056,000 students at elementary school, 2,266,000 at middle school and 2,861,000 at senior secondary school.

There are 35 state and 14 private universities, some of ancient foundation; those at Bologna, Modena, Parma and Padua were started in the 12th century. University education is not free, but entrants with higher qualifications are charged reduced fees according to a sliding scale. In 1990–1 there were 1,381,000 students at university.

In general, schools, lyceums and universities are financed by local taxation and central government grants.

ISLANDS

PANTELLERIA ISLAND (part of Trapani Province) in the Sicilian Narrows; area 31 sq. miles; population 9,601.

THE PELAGIAN ISLANDS (Lampedusa, Linosa and Lampione) are part of the province of Agrigento; area 8 sq. miles; population 4,811.

THE TUSCAN ARCHIPELAGO (including Elba); area 293 sq. km; population 31,861.

PONTINE ARCHIPELAGO, including Ponza; area 10 sq. km; population 2,515.

FLEGREAN ISLANDS, including Ischia; area 60 sq. km; population 51,883.

CAPRI.

EOLIAN ISLANDS, including Lipari; area 116 sq. km; population 18,636.

TREMITI ISLANDS; area 3 sq. km; population 426.

JAMAICA

Jamaica is situated in the Caribbean Sea south-east of Cuba and lies between 17° 43' and 18° 32' N. latitude and 76° 11' and 78° 21' W. longitude. It is 4,244 sq. miles (10,991 sq. km) in area and is divided into three counties (Surrey, Middlesex and Cornwall) and 14 parishes. The island consists mainly of coastal plains, divided by the Blue Mountain range in the east and the hills and limestone plateaux in the central and western areas of the interior. The central chain of the Blue Mountains is over 6,000 feet above sea level, and the Blue Mountain Peak is 7,402 feet. The population (UN estimate 1992) was 2,460,700.

CAPITAL – ΨKingston, the largest town and seaport (estimated population of the corporate area of Kingston and St Andrew in 1982, 696,300). Other main towns are ΨMontego Bay, Ocho Rios, Spanish Town, Mandeville and May Pen.

CURRENCY – Jamaican dollar (J$) of 100 cents.

FLAG – Gold diagonal cross forming triangles of green at top and bottom, triangles of black at hoist and in fly.

NATIONAL ANTHEM – Jamaica, Land We Love.

NATIONAL DAY – First Monday in August (Independence Day).

GOVERNMENT

The island was discovered by Columbus in 1494, and occupied by Spain from 1509 until 1655 when a British expedition under Admiral Penn and General Venables captured the island. In 1670 it was formally ceded to England by the Treaty of Madrid. Jamaica became an independent state within the Commonwealth on 6 August 1962.

HM Queen Elizabeth II is the head of state, represented by the Governor-General. The legislature consists of a Senate of 21 nominated members and a House of Representatives consisting of 60 members elected by universal adult suffrage.

At the general election of 30 March 1993, the People's National Party won 52 seats and the Jamaica Labour Party won 8.

Governor-General, His Excellency Howard Felix Hanlon Cooke, apptd 1991

CABINET *as at 15 August 1995*

Prime Minister, Defence, Rt. Hon. Percival J. Patterson, QC
Deputy Prime Minister, Foreign Affairs and Trade, Hon. Seymour Mullings
Tourism, Hon. John Junior
Public Utilities, Transport and Energy, Hon. Robert Pickersgill
Housing and the Environment, Hon. Easton Douglas
Industry, Investments and Commerce, Hon. Dr Paul Robertson
Education, Youth and Culture, Hon. Burchell Whiteman
Health, Sen. the Hon. Peter Phillips
Labour, Social Security and Sports, Hon. Portia Simpson
Local Government and Works, Hon. Roger Clarke
National Security and Justice, Hon. K. D. Knight
Minister without Portfolio, Hon. Maxine Henry-Wilson
Legal Affairs, Hon. David Coore
Agriculture and Mining, Hon. Horace Clarke
Finance and Planning, Hon. Omar Davies

JAMAICAN HIGH COMMISSION
1–2 Prince Consort Road, London SW7 2BZ
Tel 0171-823 9911
High Commissioner, His Excellency Derek Heaven, apptd 1994
Deputy High Commissioners, Mrs M. Roberts; J. K. Pringle, CBE (*Trade*)
Minister-Counsellor, S. H. Parris (*Consular Affairs*)
Defence Adviser, Col. T. D. Lewis

BRITISH HIGH COMMISSION
PO Box 575, Trafalgar Road, Kingston 10
Tel: Kingston 926 9050
High Commissioner, His Excellency Derek Francis Milton, CMG, apptd 1989
Deputy High Commissioner, A. White
Defence Adviser, Col. J. J. Dumas, OBE
First Secretary (Management/Consular), J. McLeod

BRITISH COUNCIL REPRESENTATIVE IN THE CARIBBEAN, Andrew Norris, 3rd Floor, PCMB Building, 64 Knutsford Boulevard, Kingston 5.

JUDICATURE

Chief Justice, Rt. Hon. Edward Zacca
President of the Court of Appeal, Hon. Carl Rattray
Judges of the Court of Appeal, Hons. M. L. Wright; I. X. Forte; H. E. Downer; U. D. Gordon; B. M. Carey; C. Patterson; L. Wolfe

ECONOMY

Since 1989 the PNP government has introduced economic reforms including the abolition of price subsidies, the removal of foreign exchange controls and the introduction of a 10 per cent consumption tax. The IMF in 1992 approved a credit facility of US$153 million for a three-year period. Jamaica is a popular tourist resort, attracting 1,563,097 visitors during 1992. Actual foreign exchange receipts from tourism amounted to US$850 million in 1992.

Alumina, bananas, bauxite and sugar are the main exports. Earnings from sugar in 1992 amounted to US$82.5 million, bauxite and alumina US$560 million and bananas US$39.6 million. Other exports include garments, processed food products, limestone and ornamental horticultural products.

TRADE	1991	1992
Merchandise imports	US$1,828.6m	US$1,692.8m
Merchandise exports	1,150.7m	1,052.8m

Trade with UK	1993	1994
Imports from UK	£56,257,000	£56,354,000
Exports to UK	121,623,000	133,963,000

COMMUNICATIONS

There are several excellent harbours, Kingston being the principal port. The island has 2,944 miles of main roads and 7,264 miles of subsidiary roads.

There are two international airports, the Norman Manley International Airport on the south coast serving Kingston, and Sangster Airport on the north coast serving the major tourist areas. In addition there are licensed aerodromes at Port Antonio, Ocho Rios, Mandeville and Negril. There are 16 privately owned, seven public and two military airstrips. Air Jamaica, the national airline, operates international services; Trans-Jamaica Airlines operates scheduled internal and regional services.

JAPAN
Nihon Koku – Land of the Rising Sun

Japan consists of four large islands: *Honshū* (or Mainland) 88,839 sq. miles (230,448 sq. km), *Shikoku*, 7,231 sq. miles (18,757 sq. km), *Kyūshū*, 16,170 sq. miles (42,079 sq. km), *Hokkaido*, 30,265 sq. miles (78,508 sq. km), and many small islands (including Okinawa) situated in the north Pacific Ocean between 128° 6′ and 145° 49′ E. longitude and between 26° 59′ and 45° 31′ N. latitude, with a total area of 145,834 sq. miles (377,708 sq. km).

The coastline is deeply indented, so that few places are far from the sea. The interior is very mountainous, and crossing the mainland from the Sea of Japan to the Pacific is a group of volcanoes, mainly extinct or dormant. Mount Fuji, the most sacred mountain of Japan, is 12,370 ft high and has been dormant since 1707, but volcanoes which are active include Mount Aso in Kyūshū. There are frequent earthquakes, mainly along the Pacific coast near the Bay of Tokyo. The climate varies from sub-tropical in the south to cool temperate in the north.

The population (1993 estimate) is 124,764,215. The principal religions are Mahayana Buddhism and Shinto. About 1 per cent of Japanese are Christians.

CAPITAL – Tokyo, population (December 1989) 11,718,720. The other chief cities had the following populations (1994): ΨYokohama (3,265,000); ΨOsaka (2,481,000); ΨNagoya (2,091,000); Sapporo (1,719,000); ΨKobé (1,479,000); Kyoto, the ancient capital (1,391,000); ΨFukuoka (1,221,000).
CURRENCY – Yen of 100 sen.
FLAG – White, charged with sun (red).
NATIONAL ANTHEM – Kimigayo.
NATIONAL DAY – 23 December (the Emperor's Birthday).

GOVERNMENT

According to Japanese tradition, Jimmu, the first Emperor of Japan, ascended the throne on 11 February 660 BC. Under the *Meiji* constitution (1889), the monarchy is hereditary in the male heirs of the Imperial house.

After the unconditional surrender to the allied nations (14 August 1945), Japan was occupied by Allied forces under General MacArthur. A Japanese peace treaty became effective on 28 April 1952. Japan then resumed her status as an independent power.

Under the 1947 constitution, legislative authority rests with the elected Diet, which is bicameral, consisting of a 511-member House of Representatives and a 252-member House of Councillors. The House of Councillors, whose powers are subordinate to the House of Representatives, elects half its members every three years. Executive authority is vested in the Cabinet which is responsible to the legislature.

The (conservative) Liberal Democratic Party (LDP) governed Japan almost without interruption from the Second World War until 1993. During the 1990s growing public disgust at political corruption led to a loss of support for the LDP and in 1992 a group of LDP MPs broke away to form the Japan New Party (JNP). After several attempts at political reform to end corruption failed, the LDP government was brought down by its own rebel MPs in a no confidence motion in the Diet in June 1993. Two new groups of LDP MPs broke away to form the Japan Renewal Party (JRP) (Shinseito) and the Sakigate (Harbinger) Party and support for the new parties caused the LDP to lose its majority at the election in July. After the election the three new parties formed a coalition with the opposition Komeito, Social Democratic (SDPJ), Democratic Socialist (DSP) and United Social Democratic (USDP) (Shaminren) parties, and the new government was sworn in on 9 August 1993.

The seven-party coalition government led by Morihiro Hosokawa (JNP) was unable to push anti-corruption and electoral reforms bills through the Diet undiluted because of LDP control of the House of Councillors. Eventually a compromise was reached with the LDP and in January 1994 laws were passed to limit corporate donations to individual MPs' funds and to ban them after five years, to introduce state subsidies for political parties, and to change the first-past-the-post electoral system with multi-member constituencies to a system with 200 MPs elected by proportional representation and 300 single-member, first-past-the-post constituencies (with effect from the next general election). After corruption scandals and coalition manoeuvrings the governments of Hosokawa and his successor Tsutoma Hata were brought down and the LDP returned to power in June 1994 in coalition with the SDPJ and Sakigate parties, with SDPJ leader Tomiichi Murayama becoming Japan's first socialist Prime Minister. The five reformist opposition parties (JNP, JRP, Komeito, DSP, USDP) merged in November 1994 to form the New Frontier Party (NFP) (Shinshinto) as a rival centre-right conservative party to the LDP, and appointed former LDP Prime Minister Toshiki Kaifu as its leader.

In August 1995 the strength of the parties in the House of Representatives was: Liberal Democratic Party 200; New

Frontier Party (Shinshinto) 187; Social Democratic Party 73; Sakigate 21; Japan Communist Party 15; Independents 13; vacant 2.

In August 1995 the strength of the parties in the House of Councillors was: Liberal Democratic Party 110; New Frontier Party (Shinshinto) 56; Japan Socialist Party 38; Japan Communist Party 11; Sakigate 3; others 34.

HEAD OF STATE

His Imperial Majesty The Emperor of Japan, Emperor Akihito, *born* 23 December 1933; *succeeded* 8 January 1989; *enthroned* 12 November 1990; *married* 10 April 1959, Miss Michiko Shoda, and has *issue*: the Crown Prince; Prince Akishino, *born* 30 November 1965, and Princess Sayako, *born* 18 April 1969

Heir, HRH Crown Prince Naruhito Hironomiya, *born* 23 February 1960, *married* 9 June 1993 Miss Masako Owada

CABINET *as at August 1995*

Prime Minister, Tomiichi Murayama (SDPJ)
Deputy PM, Foreign Affairs, Yohei Kono (LDP)
Justice, Isao Maeda (LDP)
Finance, Masayoshi Takemura (Sakigate)
Education, Yoshinobu Shimamura (LDP)
Health and Welfare, Shoichi Ide (Sakigate)
Agriculture, Forestry and Fisheries, Taichiro Okawara (LDP)
International Trade and Industry, Ryutaro Hashimoto (LDP)
Transport, Shizuka Kamei (LDP)
Posts and Telecommunications, Shun Oide (SDPJ)
Labour, Manso Hamamoto (SDPJ)
Construction, Koken Nosaka (SDPJ)
Home Affairs, Hiromu Nonaka (LDP)

MINISTERS OF STATE

Chief Cabinet Secretary, Kozo Igarashi (SDPJ)
Director-General, Management and Co-ordination Agency, Tsuruo Yamaguchi (SDPJ)
Director-General, Hokkaido and Okinawa Development Agencies, Sadatoshi Ozato (LDP)
Director-General, Defence Agency, Tokuichiro Tamazawa (LDP)
Director-General, Science and Technology Agency, Makiko Tanaka (LDP)
Director-General, Environment Agency, Sohei Miyashita (LDP)
Director-General, Economic Planning Agency, Masahiko Komura (LDP)
Director-General, National Land Agency, Kiyoshi Ozawa (LDP)

SDJP Social Democratic Party of Japan; LDP Liberal Democratic Party.

EMBASSY OF JAPAN
101–104 Piccadilly, London WIV 9FN
Tel 0171-465 6500
Ambassador Extraordinary and Plenipotentiary, His Excellency Hiroaki Fujii, apptd 1994
Ministers, Sadaaki Numata; Takayuki Kimura; Keisuke Takanishi (*Commercial*); Yoshihiko Matsuo (*Financial*); Kyoji Komachi (*Consul-General*)
Defence Attaché, Capt. Kazuo Tohyama
Counsellor (*Culture*), Haruhisa Takeuchi

BRITISH EMBASSY
No. 1 Ichiban-cho, Chiyoda-ku, Tokyo 102
Tel: Tokyo 3265-5511
Ambassador Extraordinary and Plenipotentiary, His Excellency Sir John Boyd, KCMG, apptd 1992
Ministers, C. T. W. Humfrey (*Deputy Head of Mission*); J. E. W. Kirby (*Financial*)

Counsellors, D. A. Warren (*Commercial*); P. V. Rollitt (*Management and Consul-General*)
Defence and Naval Attaché, Capt. N. D. V. Robertson

There are British Consulates General at Tokyo and Osaka, and Honorary Consulates at Fukuoka, Hiroshima and Nagoya.

BRITISH COUNCIL REPRESENTATIVE, Michael Barrett, OBE, 2 Kagurazaka 1-Chome, Shinjuku-ku, Tokyo 162. There is also an office and library in Kyoto.

BRITISH CHAMBER OF COMMERCE, No. 16 Kowa Building, 1–9–20 Akasaka, Minato-ku, Tokyo 107

ECONOMY

Owing to the mountainous nature of the country less than 20 per cent of its area can be cultivated and only 14 per cent is used for agriculture; 67 per cent is wooded. The soil is only moderately fertile but intensive cultivation secures good crops. Tobacco, tea, potato, rice, maize, wheat and other cereals are all cultivated. Rice is the staple food of the people, about 13,255,000 tonnes being produced in 1992. Fruit is abundant, including the mandarin, persimmon, loquat and peach, apples, strawberries, pears, grapes and figs. Pigs and chickens are widely reared.

The country has mineral resources, including gold, silver, copper, lead, zinc, iron chromite, white arsenic, coal, sulphur, petroleum, salt and uranium. However, iron ore, coal and crude oil are among the principal imports to supply deficiencies at home.

Japan is one of the most highly industrialized nations in the world, with the whole range of modern light and heavy industries, including steel, aerospace, computers, office machinery, motor vehicles, electronics, metals, machinery, chemicals, textiles (cotton, silk, wool and synthetics), cement, pottery, glass, rubber, lumber, paper, oil refining and shipbuilding.

The labour force in 1993 (average) was 64,500,000, of which around 2.5 per cent were unemployed. Of the total labour force, over 15 per cent are over 65 and this rate is increasing. Industrial, manufacturing and services workers numbered 60,694,000 and agricultural, forestries and fisheries workers 3,806,000 in 1993. In 1992 primary industry accounted for 2.2 per cent of GDP, manufacturing, mining and construction for 41.1 per cent of GDP, and services for 59.1 per cent. Japan's GDP of US$4,190,399 million in 1993 made its economy the second largest in the world.

FINANCE

The budget for the financial year 1994 for revenue and expenditure on the general account was Yen 73,000,000 million.

TRADE

Being deficient in natural resources, Japan has had to develop a complex foreign trade. Principal imports in 1993 consisted of machinery and equipment (19.4 per cent), foodstuffs (16.4 per cent), petroleum (11.6 per cent), chemicals (7.5 per cent), metal ores and scrap (2.9 per cent). Principal exports consist of machinery and equipment (76 per cent, of which motor vehicles comprise (16.1 per cent), iron and steel (4.0 per cent), chemicals (5.6 per cent), textile goods (2.3 per cent) and ships (1.4 per cent).

	1992	1993
Total imports	US$232,698m	US$240,670m
Total exports	339,762m	360,911m

Trade with UK	1993	1994
Imports from UK	£2,653,575,000	£2,991,159,000
Exports to UK	8,536,146,000	8,841,577,000

COMMUNICATIONS

Japan National Railways was privatized in 1987 and is known as Japan Railways (JR). There are six regional companies and one goods company. Shinkansen (bullet train) tracks are currently being expanded. The opening in 1988 of the Seikan rail tunnel and the Seto Ohashi rail bridge means that the four major islands are now linked for the first time.

The merchant fleet had a shipping capacity of 25.4 million gross tons and 10,091 vessels in 1992, making it the largest in the world in terms of number of vessels and third in terms of tonnage.

DEFENCE

After the unconditional surrender of August 1945 the Imperial Army and Navy were disarmed and disbanded. Although the constitution prohibits the maintenance of armed forces, internal security forces came into being in 1950 and 1952. In 1954 the mission of the forces was extended to include the defence of Japan against direct and indirect aggression. Legislation passed in 1992 allows a maximum of 2,000 troops to take part in UN peacekeeping missions overseas, limited to non-front line activities; legislation passed in 1994 allows the armed forces to enter foreign conflicts in order to rescue Japanese nationals.

The total active armed forces strength is 237,700. The Ground Self-Defence Force (GSDF) has a strength of 150,000 and is organized into 12 infantry and one armoured division, together with two composite, one airborne, one artillery, two air defence, five engineer and one helicopter brigades. Equipment includes 1,160 main battle tanks, 1,030 armoured personnel carriers and infantry fighting vehicles, 890 artillery pieces and 90 attack helicopters.

The Maritime Self-Defence Force (MSDF) has a strength of 43,000 personnel, with 15 submarines and 62 destroyers and frigates, 110 combat aircraft and 100 armed helicopters.

The Air Self-Defence Force (ASDF) has a strength of 44,500 personnel with 440 combat aircraft organized into ten air defence, three ground attack, five transport, one airborne early warning, one reconnaissance and ten training squadrons.

The USA at present stations 44,800 personnel in Japan: Army 1,900; Navy 7,300; Marines 20,000; Air Force 15,600.

EDUCATION

Education at elementary (six-year course) and lower secondary (three-year course) schools is free, compulsory and co-educational. The (three-year) upper secondary schools are attended by 96.7 per cent of the age group. They have courses in general, agricultural, commercial, technical, mercantile marine, radio communication and home economics education, etc.

Of the population aged between 18 and 21, 32.7 per cent were enrolled in higher education in 1992. There are two- or three-year junior colleges and four-year universities. Some of the universities have graduate schools. In 1993 there were 1,129 universities and junior colleges, the vast majority of which are privately maintained. The most prominent universities are the seven state universities of Tokyo, Kyoto, Tohoku (Sendai), Hokkaido (Sapporo), Kyushu (Fukuoka), Osaka and Nagoya, and the two private universities of Keio and Waseda.

CULTURE

Japanese is said to be one of the Uro-Altaic group of languages and remained a spoken tongue until the fifth to seventh centuries AD, when Chinese characters came into use. Japanese who have received school education (99.8 per cent of the population) can read and write the Chinese characters in current use (about 1,800 characters) and also the syllabary characters called Kana. English is the best known foreign language. It is taught in all middle and high schools and universities. There are 125 daily newspapers in Japan.

JORDAN
Al-Mamlaka al Urduniya al-Hashemiyah

The Hashemite Kingdom of the Jordan, which covers 37,738 sq. miles (97,740 sq. km), is bounded on the north by Syria, on the west by Israel, on the south by Saudi Arabia and on the east by Iraq.

The population on the East Bank of the Jordan (1994 census) was 4,095,579. The majority are Sunni Muslims and Islam is the religion of the state; however, freedom of belief is guaranteed by the constitution.

CAPITAL – Amman, population (1994 estimate) 1,270,000.
CURRENCY – Jordanian dinar (JD) of 1,000 fils.
FLAG – Three horizontal stripes of black, white, green and a red triangle based on the hoist, containing a seven-pointed white star.
NATIONAL ANTHEM – Long Live the King.
NATIONAL DAY – 25 May (Independence Day).

HISTORY

After the defeat of Turkey in the First World War, the Amirate of Transjordan was established in the area east of the River Jordan as a state under British mandate. The mandate was terminated after the Second World War and the Amirate, still ruled by its founder the Amir Abdullah, became the Hashemite Kingdom of Jordan. Following the 1948–9 war between Israel and the Arab states, that part of Palestine remaining in Arab hands (the West Bank and East Jerusalem, but excluding Gaza) was, with Palestinian agreement, incorporated into the Hashemite Kingdom. King Abdullah was assassinated in 1951; his son Talal ruled briefly but abdicated in favour of King Hussein in 1952.

The West Bank has been under Israeli occupation since its capture from Jordan in the 1967 war, and East Jerusalem was annexed by Israel in 1967. In 1988 Jordan severed its legal and administrative ties with the occupied West Bank, but did not formally renounce sovereignty over the area. As a result of the wars of 1948–9 and 1967 there are about one million Palestinian refugees and displaced persons living in East Jordan, about 200,000 of whom live in refugee and displaced persons camps established by the UN Relief and Works Agency (UNRWA). In addition there are 300,000 self-supporting Palestinians in East Jordan.

GOVERNMENT

The 1952 constitution provides for a senate of 40 members (all appointed by the King) and an elected House of Representatives. Until 1988, the House of Representatives had 60 members representing both the East and West Banks. Legislation passed in 1989 stipulated that in future elections seats would be contested on the East Bank only. The first parliamentary elections since 1967 took place in 1989 to a new 80-member House of Representatives.

The King appoints the members of the Council of Ministers. Crown Prince Hassan normally acts as regent when King Hussein is away from Jordan. In 1991 a new national charter was agreed between the King and political parties in a National Conference in which the ban on political parties, imposed in 1957 after a left-wing coup attempt, was lifted in return for allegiance to the monarchy. The first multiparty parliamentary elections since 1956 were held in 1993, traditionalists and centrists winning 59 seats and the Islamic Action Front 16 seats.

The Middle East peace process begun in 1991 led to Jordan signing an agreement on a 'common agenda' for peace with Israel in 1993. Intensive bilateral negotiations continued throughout 1993–4 with Israel agreeing to return two narrow strips of territory in the Arava desert seized in 1967 and a border commission being established. On 25 July 1994 King Hussein and the Israeli Prime Minister signed a framework agreement for peace which ended the state of war existing since 1948. The first Israeli–Jordanian border crossing was opened between Eilat and Aqaba in August 1994. A full peace treaty was signed on 26 October 1994 which established full and normal diplomatic and economic relations between the two states. It included agreements on sharing water from the Jordan and Yarmouk rivers; co-operating in the fields of commerce, transport, tourism, communications, energy and agriculture; and granted King Hussein custodianship of Islamic holy sites in Jerusalem. Israeli forces completed their withdrawal from Jordanian land in the Arava valley on 9 February 1995.

HEAD OF STATE

His Majesty The King of the Jordan, King Hussein, GCVO, *born* 14 November 1935, *succeeded* on the abdication of his father, King Talal, 11 August 1952, *assumed constitutional powers,* 2 May 1953, on coming of age
Crown Prince, Prince Hassan, third son of King Talal of Jordan, *born* 1947, *appointed Crown Prince,* 1 April 1965

COUNCIL OF MINISTERS *as at August 1995*

Prime Minister and Minister of Defence, Field Marshal Sharif Zeid bin Shaker
Deputy PM, Education, Abdul Raouf al-Rawabdeh
Deputy PM, Information, Khaled Karaki
Foreign Affairs, Abdul Karim Kabariti
Finance, Basel Jardaneh
Interior, Salameh Hammad
Agriculture, Mansour Tarif
Culture, Samir Habashneh
Higher Education, Rateb Saoud
Energy and Mineral Resources, Samih Darwazeh
Health, Aref Bataineh
Justice, Hisham Tel
Labour, Nader Abu Sha'ar
Municipal, Rural and Environmental Affairs, Nader Thuheirat
Planning, Rima Khalaf
Public Works and Housing, Abdul Razzaq Ensour
Religious Affairs, Abdul Salam al-Abbadi
Social Development, Salwa Damen-Masri
Supply, Adel Qudah
Tourism and Antiquities, Abdul Ilah Khatib
Trade and Industry, Ali Abul Ragheb
Transport, Samir Kawar
Water and Irrigation, Saleh Irsheidat
Youth, Awad Khleifat
Communications and Posts, Jamal Sarayireh
Administrative Development, Moheiddin Toq

EMBASSY OF THE HASHEMITE KINGDOM OF JORDAN
6 Upper Phillimore Gardens, London W8 7HB
Tel 0171-937 3685
Ambassador Extraordinary and Plenipotentiary, His Excellency Fouad Ayoub, apptd 1991
Counsellor, S. Lash
Defence Attaché, Brig. A. Maytah
Consul, S. N. Faris, MBE

Commercial Attaché, G. Malhas
Information Bureau: 11–12 Buckingham Gate, London SW1E 6LB. Tel: 0171-630 9277

BRITISH EMBASSY
Abdoun (PO Box 87), Amman
Tel: Amman 823100
Ambassador Extraordinary and Plenipotentiary, His Excellency Peter R. M. Hinchcliffe, CMG, CVO, apptd 1994
Counsellor, J. W. Watt (*Deputy Head of Mission and Consul-General*)
Defence Attaché, Col. B. A. C. Duncan, MBE
First Secretary, D. G. Tunstall (*Management*)
BRITISH COUNCIL DIRECTOR, Dr David Burton, Rainbow Street (PO Box 634), Amman 11118

DEFENCE

The total active armed forces strength is 98,600 personnel, with selective conscription of two-year terms in operation. Reserves number a further 35,000. The Army has a strength of 90,000, with 1,140 main battle tanks, 150 reconnaissance vehicles, 1,160 armoured personnel carriers and armoured infantry fighting vehicles, and 495 artillery pieces.

The Navy has 600 personnel in its Aqaba base with five patrol craft. The Air Force has a strength of 8,000 personnel with 102 combat aircraft and 24 armed helicopters. In addition, there is a paramilitary civil militia of 200,000 personnel.

ECONOMY

The main agricultural areas are the Jordan Valley, the hills overlooking the valley, and the flatter country to the south of Amman and around Madaba and Irbid. However, several large farms, which depend for irrigation on water pumped from deep aquifers, have been established in the southern desert area. The rest of the country is desert and semi-desert. The principal crops are wheat, barley, vegetables, olives and fruit (mainly grapes and citrus fruits). Agricultural production has increased considerably in recent years due to improvements in production and irrigation techniques, and exports are increasing.

Important industrial products are raw phosphates (1994, 4.2 million tons) and potash (1994, 1.6 million tons), most of which is exported, together with fertilizers and pharmaceuticals. The Trans-Arabian oil pipeline (Tapline) runs through north Jordan from Saudi Arabia to the Lebanese port of Sidon. A branch pipeline, together with oil trucked by road from Iraq, feeds a refinery at Zerqa (production 1994, 2.9 million tons) which meets most of Jordan's requirements for refined petroleum products. Sufficient reserves of natural gas have been discovered in the north-east to produce electricity for the national grid since 1989. No significant reserves of oil have been found.

Tourism has steadily developed, principally in Amman, Aqaba, Zerka Ma'in and on the shores of the Dead Sea. The peace agreement with Israel has enabled planning to begin of new coastal resorts spanning the border between Aqaba and Israel. Following the peace agreement, the US and UK governments wrote off most of the bilateral debt owed by Jordan.

TRADE WITH UK	1993	1994
Imports from UK	£140,083,000	£114,716,000
Exports to UK	21,520,000	24,034,000

COMMUNICATIONS

The trunk road system is good. Amman is linked to Aqaba, Damascus, Baghdad and Jeddah by roads which are of considerable importance in the overland trade of the Middle East.

The former Hejaz Railway runs from Syria through Jordan, and is used mainly for freight between Amman and Damascus. The Aqaba railway carries phosphate rock from the mines of al Hasa and al Abiad to Aqaba. A total of 2,485 vessels called at Aqaba in 1994, and 10,572,300 tons of cargo were handled.

The Royal Jordanian Airline operates from Amman to Aqaba and has an extensive network of routes to the Middle East, Europe, North America and the Far East.

KAZAKHSTAN
Kazak Respublikasy

Kazakhstan has an area of 1,049,155 sq. miles (2,717,300 sq. km) and occupies the northern part of what was Soviet Central Asia. It stretches from the Volga and the Caspian Sea in the west to the Altai and Tienshan mountains in the east. It is bordered on the west by the Caspian Sea and Russia, on the south by Turkmenistan, Uzbekistan and Kyrgyzstan, on the east by China and on the north by Russia. The country consists of arid steppes and semi-deserts, flat in the west, hilly in the east and mountainous in the south-east (Southern Altai and Tienshan mountains). The main rivers are the Irtysh, the Ural, the Syr-Darya and the Ili. The climate is continental and very dry.

The population (1994 estimate) is 16,963,600, of which 43 per cent are Kazakhs, 36 per cent Russians, 5 per cent Ukrainians and 4 per cent ethnic Germans, with smaller numbers of Tatars, Uzbeks, Koreans and Belarusians. The Russian population is concentrated in the north of the country, where it forms a significant majority, and in Alma-Ata. By the end of 1995 all non-Kazakh residents will have to decide whether to acquire Kazakh citizenship or not.

The majority of ethnic Kazakhs are Sunni Muslims, and this is the main religion of the republic. Kazakh (one of the Turkic languages) became the official language in 1993 and Russian was given a special status as the 'social language between peoples'. Otherwise each ethnic group uses its own language.

CAPITAL – Alma-Ata (Almaty). Population 1,500,000 (1994). The Kazakh parliament in 1994 voted to move the capital to the central town of Akmola by 2000. The other major city is Chimkent, population 400,000 (1992).

CURRENCY – Tenge.

FLAG – Dark blue with a sun and a soaring eagle in the centre all in gold, and a red vertical ornamentation stripe near the hoist.

NATIONAL DAY – 16 December (Republic Day).

HISTORY

For centuries Kazakhstan was inhabited by nomadic tribes before being invaded by Ghenghiz Khan and incorporated into his empire in 1218. After his empire disintegrated feudal towns emerged based on large oases. These towns affiliated and established a Kazakh state in the late 15th century which engaged in almost continuous warfare with the marauding Khanates on its southern border. After appealing to Russia for aid and protection, in 1731 Kazakhstan acceded to the Russian Empire under a voluntary act of accession.

The First World War brought privation to Kazakhstan, leading to an uprising in 1916 against the conscription of male Kazakhs. After the 1917 Russian revolution, Kazakh-stan came under the control of White Russian forces until 1919. On 26 August 1920 a constitution was signed under which Kazakhstan became a Soviet Socialist Republic. Under Soviet rule in the 1920s and 1930s there was rapid industrial development and the traditional nomadic way of life disappeared. The Kazakhs suffered greatly in the Stalinist purges, the merchant and religious classes being murdered and thousands dying in the desert on collective farms. Other nationalities, such as Tatars and Germans, were forceably transported to Kazakhstan by Stalin. Kazakhstan was the last of the former USSR republics to declare its independence (16 December 1991).

GOVERNMENT

Under the constitution adopted on 28 January 1993, executive power is vested in the President and government. The President must be a Kazakh speaker and has the power to appoint the Prime Minister, other senior ministers and all ambassadors. The parliament does not have the power to impeach the President but the President can dissolve parliament. The legislature is the 177-member Supreme Kenges.

Elections to a new Supreme Kenges were held on 7 March 1994 and won by the Congress of People's Unity of Kazakhstan (SNEK), which is derived from the former Communist Party and supported by most ethnic Kazakhs. SNEK gained a majority in the Supreme Kenges despite claims of fraud by the ethnic Russian-supported LAD party which were supported by international election observers. The Supreme Kenges was dissolved by President Nazarbaev in March 1995 after the Supreme Court had ruled that the 1994 elections were invalid. The President also dismissed the government but retained it as an interim administration until new elections are held. The President has taken the power to rule by decree and his almost absolute power was confirmed in a national referendum in April 1995 which extends his term of office until 2000.

President Nazarbaev has maintained a delicate balance between ethnic Kazakhs and Russians, though tensions between the two nationalities remain and the language compromise is disliked by many. Ethnic Russians dominate the state's economy and the north of the country, and Nazarbaev knows he needs their co-operation for the country's successful development. However, many Russians have emigrated to Russia as the economic situation has worsened during the transition to a market economy. Unrest continues, with the LAD party calling for the north of the country to secede. In an attempt to calm the unrest, Nazarbaev signed an agreement in January 1995 with President Yeltsin securing the legal status of Russian and Kazakh citizens in each other's countries and simplifying the acquisition of citizenship in each other's countries. Nazarbaev has also signed agreements with Russia regarding the space launch site centre at Baikonur, which Russia will rent for 20 years at US$115 million per year, and the nuclear testing ground at Semipalatinsk.

HEAD OF STATE
President, Nursultan Nazarbaev, *elected* 1 December 1991, *confirmed in office until 2000 by referendum* 29 April 1995

BRITISH EMBASSY
Ul Furmanova 173, Alma-Ata
Tel: Alma-Ata 506191
Ambassador Extraordinary and Plenipotentiary, His Excellency Noel Jones, apptd 1993

DEFENCE

Kazakhstan retains close defence relations with Russia but in 1993–4 established its own armed forces from forces that were formerly under joint CIS control with Russia. The CIS mutual defence treaty of 1993, to which Kazakhstan is a signatory, retains a common air defence force, while Kazakh forces also take part in the CIS peacekeeping force along the Tajikistan-Afghanistan border. Kazakhstan ratified the Start 1 Treaty in 1992 and signed the Nuclear Non-Proliferation Treaty in December 1994. In December 1994, when the Start 1 Treaty came into effect, Kazakhstan began to transfer its strategic nuclear forces of 104 SS-18 intercontinental ballistic missiles and 40 nuclear-capable Tu-95H bombers to Russia.

The army numbers 25,000 personnel with 1,100 main battle tanks, 1,550 artillery pieces and 2,340 armoured personnel carriers. The Caspian Sea Flotilla, which Kazakhstan shares with Russia and Turkmenistan, operates under Russian command. The air force has a strength of 15,000 personnel, with 178 combat aircraft and 48 attack helicopters. In addition, paramilitary internal security, border guard and republican guard forces number 34,500.

ECONOMY

In March 1993 the government announced a privatization programme for 1993–6 under which most state-owned enterprises (37 large and 3,500 medium-sized enterprises) are to be sold by means of a voucher system. Outside the programme, small businesses and retail outlets have been sold at auction since 1992. Foreign investment from western states has been significant since 1992, with US$500 million invested so far. Foreign aid pledged in 1993–4 reached US$1,000 million, including US$396 million from the USA to dismantle nuclear weapons and US$255 million from the IMF to aid the transformation to a market economy. The economy has been weakened by the less preferential trading links to other CIS states since the end of the Soviet Union, with GDP falling each year since 1991. An agreement on forming a customs union with Russia was signed in February 1995, however.

Kazakhstan is rich in minerals, with copper, lead, gold, uranium, chromium, silver, zinc, iron ore, coal, oil and natural gas. In 1993 production of coal was 60 million tonnes and iron ore was 20 million tonnes, while reserves of gold were estimated at 60 million tonnes. The oil and gas industry, concentrated in the west of the country, is being expanded by western investment, which is also being used to explore two large fields in the Caspian Sea: Karachaganak (gas), with reserves of 16,000 million cubic feet; and Tengiz (oil), with reserves of 6,000–9,000 million barrels. Oil production in 1993 was 470,000 barrels per day with estimated reserves of 35,000 million barrels. Industry is dominated by food processing and mining and metals production; textiles, steel and tractors are also produced. The main centres of the metal industry are in the Altai mountains, in Chimkent, north of Lake Balkhash and in central Kazakhstan.

Agriculture, including stock-raising, is highly developed, particularly in the central and south-west of the republic. Grain is grown in the north and north-east, and cotton and wool produced in the south and south-east. A record grain crop was grown in 1992 and 1.5 million tonnes of meat produced in 1993.

TRADE WITH UK	1993	1994
Imports from UK	£14,943,000	£40,699,000
Exports to UK	57,915,000	70,576,000

KENYA
Jamhuri ya Kenya

Kenya is bisected by the equator and extends approximately from 4° N. to 4° S. latitude and from 34° E. to 41° E. longitude. The Indian Ocean and Somalia lie to the east, Ethiopia to the north, Sudan to the north-west, Uganda and Lake Victoria to the west, and Tanzania to the south. The total area is 224,961 sq. miles (582,646 sq. km), including 5,171 square miles of water. The country is divided into eight provinces (Central, Coast, Eastern, Nairobi, Nyanza, North Eastern, Rift Valley, Western).

The population is 25,700,000 (1992 UN estimate). The main tribal groups are the Kikuyu, Luhya, Luo, Kalenjin, Kamba and Masai. The official languages are Swahili, which is generally understood throughout Kenya, and English; numerous indigenous languages are also spoken.

CAPITAL – Nairobi, population 1,400,000 (1989 estimate).
CURRENCY – Kenya shilling (Ksh) of 100 cents.
FLAG – Horizontally black, red and green with the red fimbriated in white, and with a shield and crossed spears all over in the centre.
NATIONAL ANTHEM – Kenya, Land of the Lion.
NATIONAL DAY – 12 December (Independence Day).

GOVERNMENT

Kenya became an independent state and a member of the British Commonwealth on 12 December 1963 and a republic in 1964. In 1982 the government introduced amendments to the constitution making the country a one-party state, with Kenya African National Union (KANU) as the ruling party. In December 1991 the government yielded to internal and international pressure and introduced a multiparty democracy.

Multiparty presidential and legislative elections were held in December 1992 which were won by President Moi and KANU respectively, amid opposition claims that the elections were not free and fair which were supported by the Commonwealth observers monitoring the election. In the unicameral National Assembly of 200 seats, KANU has 107 seats (95 elected and 12 nominated by the President) and the three major opposition parties have 85 seats between them. KANU formed a new government on 13 January 1993 and parliament reopened on 22 March 1993 but was boycotted by two of the main opposition parties for three months. In May the government reached agreement with the IMF and World Bank on anti-corruption and economic reform measures and the IMF resumed aid to Kenya, suspended in November 1991.

Ethnic clashes in the Rift Valley since 1991 between the Kikuyus, the Luo and the Luhya tribes on the one hand, who mainly support opposition parties, and the smaller government-supporting tribes of the Kalenjin, Masai and Pokot have left some 1,500 dead and 300,000 displaced. Government-opposition fighting, government clampdowns on opposition political activities, continued human rights abuses, and the failure to keep promises of political reform caused international organizations and western donor states to end or drastically cut aid to Kenya in mid-1995.

HEAD OF STATE
President and C.-in-C. Armed Forces, Hon. Daniel T. arap Moi, *took office* 14 October 1978, *re-elected* 1979, 1983, 1988 and 29 December 1992

CABINET *as at August 1995*
The President
Vice-President and Minister for Planning and National Development, Hon. Prof. George Saitoti
Foreign Affairs, Hon. Stephen Musyoka
Finance, Hon. Wycliffe Mudavadi
Agriculture, Livestock Development and Marketing, Hon. Simon Nyachae
Land Reclamation, Regional and Water Development, Hon. Hussein Maalim Mohammed
Environment and Natural Resources, Hon. John Sambu
Transport and Communication, Hon. Dalmas Otieno
Energy, Hon. Darius Mbela
Commerce and Industry, Hon. Kirugi M'mukindia
Tourism and Wildlife, Hon. Katana Ngala
Health, Hon. Joshua Angatia
Local Government, Hon. William Ntimana
Home Affairs and National Heritage, Hon. Francis Lotodo
Lands and Urban Planning, Hon. Jackson Mulinge
Labour and Manpower Development, Hon. Phillip Masinde
Information and Broadcasting, Hon. Johnstone Makau
Cultural and Social Services, Hon. Nyiva Mwendwa
Co-operative Development, Hon. Kamwithi Munyi
Public Works and Housing, Hon. Jonathan N'geno
Research and Technical Training, Hon. Zachary Onyonka
Attorney-General, Hon. Amos Wako

KENYA HIGH COMMISSION
45 Portland Place, London WIN 4AS
Tel 0171-636 2371
High Commissioner, His Excellency Joseph K. A. Ruto, apptd 1993
Defence Attaché, Col. E. Sifuma
Commercial Attaché, D. Mbogua

BRITISH HIGH COMMISSION
Bruce House, Standard Street, PO Box 30465 Nairobi
Tel: Nairobi 335944
High Commissioner, His Excellency Simon Nicholas Hemans, CMG, CVO, apptd 1995
Deputy High Commissioner, R. A. Pullen
Defence and Military Adviser, Col. R. D. Vellacott, OBE
First Secretary (Commercial), D. L. Littlefield
First Secretary (Consular), A. Summers
There are consular offices in Nairobi, Mombasa and Malindi.

BRITISH COUNCIL REPRESENTATIVE, Bill Harvey, (PO Box 40751) ICEA Building, Kenyatta Avenue, Nairobi. There are offices at Kisumu and Mombasa.

ECONOMY

Agriculture provides about 52 per cent of total export earnings (excluding processed oil products). The great variation in altitude and ecology provide conditions under which a wide range of crops can be grown. These include wheat, barley, pyrethrum, coffee, tea, sisal, coconuts, cashew nuts, cotton, maize and a wide variety of tropical and temperate fruits and vegetables. The total area of well-farmed land on which concentrated mixed farming can be practised is small and the remainder is arid or semi-arid country but population pressure and the need to increase agricultural production for export has led to attempts to develop such areas.

Mineral production consists of soda ash, salt and limestone. Hydro-electric power has been developed, particularly on the Upper Tana River. Kenya is now almost self-sufficient in electric power generation but the connection with Owen Falls in Uganda is still in being.

There has been considerable industrial development over the last 15 years and Kenya has a variety of industries

processing agricultural produce and manufacturing products from local and imported raw materials. New industries are steel, textile mills, dehydrated vegetable processing and motor tyre manufacture. Smaller schemes have added to the country's consumer goods manufacturing base. There is an oil refinery in Mombasa supplying both Kenya and Uganda, and a fuel pipeline now connects Mombasa and Nairobi.

TRADE

Principal exports are coffee and tea, which account for 33 per cent of total export earnings. Also exported are fruit, vegetables, and crude animal and vegetable material. Petroleum products account for about 37 per cent of imports; other imports are manufactured goods, particularly machinery, transport equipment, metals, pharmaceuticals and chemicals.

Trade with UK	1993	1994
Imports from UK	£152,208,000	£195,880,000
Exports to UK	172,680,000	167,152,000

COMMUNICATIONS

The Kenya Railways Corporation has 1,700 miles of railway open to traffic. There are also 39,000 miles of road, of which 5,000 are bitumen surfaced. Trans-border links with Tanzania were reopened in 1985 with rail services for freight and steamer services for passengers and freight.

The principal port is Mombasa, operated by the Kenya Ports Authority. International air services operate from airports at Nairobi and Mombasa.

KIRIBATI
Ribaberikin Kiribati

Kiribati, the former Gilbert Islands, became an independent republic in 1979. Kiribati comprises 36 islands, the Gilberts Group (17) including Banaba (formerly Ocean Island), the Phoenix Islands (8), and the Line Islands (11), which are situated in the south-west central Pacific around the point at which the International Date Line cuts the Equator. The total land area of 281 sq. miles (728 sq. km) is spread over some 2 million square miles of ocean. Few of the atolls are more than half a mile in width or more than 12 feet high. The vegetation consists mainly of coconut palms, breadfruit trees and pandanus. The population (UN estimate 1992) is 74,000, and predominantly Christian.

CAPITAL – Tarawa, population estimated at 17,921.
CURRENCY – Kiribati uses the Australian dollar ($A) of 100 cents.
FLAG – Red, with blue and white wavy lines in base, and in the centre a gold rising sun and a flying frigate bird.
NATIONAL ANTHEM – Teirake Kain Kiribati (Stand Kiribati).
NATIONAL DAY – 12 July (Independence Day).

GOVERNMENT

The President is head of state as well as head of government and and is elected nationally. There is a House of Assembly of 41 members (39 elected and two appointed: the Attorney-General and a representative of Banaba Island). Executive authority is vested in the Cabinet. The last legislative election was held in July 1994, and the last presidential election, on 30 September 1994, was won by Teburoro Tito.

HEAD OF STATE
President, Teburoro Tito, *sworn in* 1 October 1994
Vice-President, Tewareka Tentoa

CABINET *as at August 1995*
President, Foreign Affairs, Trade, Teburoro Tito
Vice-President, Home Affairs, Rural Development, Tewareka
  Tentoa
Education, Science and Technology, Willie Tokataake
Finance and Economic Planning, Benjamina Tinga
Environment and Natural Resources, Anote Tong
Health, Family Planning and Social Welfare, Katoike Tekee
Transport, Communications and Tourism, Manroai Kaiea
Commerce, Industry and Employment, Tanieru Awerika
Works and Energy, Emile Schutz
Line and Phoenix Islands, Teiraoi Tetabea

HONORARY CONSULATE
c/o Faith House, 7 Tufton Street, London SW1P 3QN
Tel 0171-222 6952
Honorary Consul, M. Chandler, CBE

BRITISH HIGH COMMISSIONER, His Excellency Michael
Peart, CMG, LVO, apptd 1995, resident at Suva, Fiji.

ECONOMY

Most people still practise a semi-subsistence economy, the
main staples of their diet being coconuts and fish.
  The principal imports are foodstuffs, consumer goods,
machinery and transport equipment. The principal exports
are copra and fish. Total value of exports in 1990 was
$A3,681,000.

TRADE WITH UK	1993	1994
Imports from UK	£327,000	£300,000
Exports to UK	2,000	13,000

COMMUNICATIONS

Air communication exists between most of the islands and
is operated by Air Tungaru, a statutory corporation. Air
Marshall Islands operates a weekly service between
Majuro, Tarawa, Funafuti and Nandi, and Air Nauru
between Tarawa, Nauru and Nandi. Inter-island shipping
is operated by a statutory corporation, the Shipping
Corporation of Kiribati.

SOCIAL WELFARE

The government maintains a teacher training college and a
secondary school. Five junior secondary schools are
maintained by missions. Throughout the republic there
are about a hundred primary schools. The total enrolment
of children of school age is about 16,000. The Marine
Training School at Tarawa trains seamen for service with
overseas shipping lines.
  There is a general hospital at Tarawa. The other
inhabited islands have dispensaries.

KOREA

Korea is situated between 124° 11″ and 130° 57′ E. longitude, and between 33° 7′ and 43° 1″ N. latitude. It has an
area of 84,565 sq. miles (219,022 sq. km).
  The population (UN estimate 1992) is 66,281,000. The
southern and western coasts are fringed with innumerable
islands, of which the largest, forming a province of its own,
is Cheju. The Korean language is of the Ural-Altaic Group.
Its script, Hangul, was invented in the 15th century; prior to

this Chinese characters alone were used. Despite the great
cultural influence of the Chinese, Koreans have developed
and preserved their own cultural heritage.

HISTORY

The last native dynasty (Yi) ruled from 1392 until 1910
when Japan formally annexed Korea. The country remained part of the Japanese Empire until the defeat of
Japan in 1945, when it was occupied by troops of the USA
and the USSR, the 38th parallel being fixed as the boundary
between the two zones of occupation.
  The US government endeavoured to reach agreement
with the Soviet government for the creation of a Korean
government for the whole country and the withdrawal of
all Soviet and American troops. These efforts met with no
success, and in September 1947 the US government
referred the future of Korea to the UN General Assembly.
The Assembly in November 1947 resolved that elections
should be held in Korea for a National Assembly under the
supervision of a UN temporary commission and that the
National Assembly when elected should set up a government. The Soviet government refused to allow the
Commission to visit the Soviet-occupied zone and therefore it could only operate south of the 38th parallel.
  A general election was held on 10 May 1948 and the first
National Assembly met in Seoul on 31 May. The Assembly
passed a constitution on 12 July and on 15 August 1948 the
republic was formally inaugurated and American military
government came to an end. Meanwhile, in the Soviet-
occupied zone north of the 38th parallel the Democratic
People's Republic had been set up with its capital at
Pyongyang. A Supreme People's Soviet was elected in
September 1948, and a Soviet-style constitution adopted.

THE KOREAN WAR

The country remained effectively divided into two along
the 38th parallel until June 1950, when North Korean
forces invaded South Korea. In response to Security
Council recommendations, 16 nations, including the USA
and the UK, came to the aid of the Republic of Korea. China
entered the war on the side of North Korea in November
1950. The fighting was ended by an armistice agreement
signed on 27 July 1953. By this agreement (which was not
signed by the Republic of Korea), the line of division
between North and South Korea remained in the neighbourhood of the 38th parallel, and a Military Armistice
Commission (MAC) was established to monitor the cease-
fire. North Korea and China withdrew from the MAC in
1994.
  Talks between North and South Korea on the reunification of the country have taken place intermittently. A non-
aggression accord was signed between the North and South
in 1991 and an agreement on the denuclearization of the
Korean peninsula was reached in 1992. In June 1994 an
agreement was reached on a July summit of North and
South Korean Presidents but Kim Il-sung died before it
could take place.

REPUBLIC OF KOREA
Daehanminkuk

The Republic of Korea has long been officially recognized
by most governments but not by any former Communist
bloc country until 1989, and not by the People's Republic
of China until 1992.
  The population (UN estimate 1992) is 43,663,000.
There is freedom of religion; the largest religion is

Buddhism (13 million), with large minorities of Christians (8 million Protestants, 2.2 million Roman Catholics) and Confucianists (4.7 million).

CAPITAL – Seoul, population (1993) 10,920,000. Other main centres are ΨPusan (3,654,097), Taegu (2,165,954) and ΨInchon (1,526,435).
CURRENCY – Won of 100 jeon.
FLAG – White with a red and blue yin-yang in the centre, surrounded by four black trigrams.
NATIONAL ANTHEM – Aegukka.
NATIONAL DAY – 15 August (Independence Day).

GOVERNMENT

Following extensive political unrest in 1987, a new constitution was adopted in 1988. The President, who is head of state, chief of the executive and commander-in-chief of the Armed Forces, is directly elected for a single term of five years. He appoints the Prime Minister with the consent of the National Assembly, and members of the State Council (Cabinet) on the recommendation of the Prime Minister. The President is also empowered to take wide-ranging measures in an emergency, including the declaration of martial law, but must obtain the agreement of the National Assembly. The National Assembly of 299 members is directly elected for a four-year term.

The most recent elections to the National Assembly were held in March 1992 and won by the ruling Democratic Liberal Party (DLP) with 159 seats to the Democratic Party's (DP) 96 seats. In the most recent presidential election of December 1992, long-time opposition leader Kim Young-sam was victorious. In February 1993 he named the first wholly civilian government in 32 years. In 1993–5 the government of President Kim Young-sam has implemented an anti-corruption programme against the bureaucracy and armed forces, and also has begun the deregulation of the economy with plans for mass privatization and tax cuts.

HEAD OF STATE
President, Kim Young-sam, *elected* 18 December 1992, *took office* 25 February 1993

CABINET *as at August 1995*
Prime Minister, Yi Hong-ku
Deputy PM, Finance, Economic Planning Board, Hong Chae-hyong
Deputy Prime Minister, National Unification, Na Ung-pae
Foreign Affairs, Kong No-myong
Home Affairs, Kim Yong-tae
Justice, An U-man
Defence, Yi Yang-ho
Education, vacant
Agriculture and Fisheries, Choi In-kee
Environment, Kim Chung-wi
Trade and Industry, Pak Chae-yun
Construction and Transportation, Oh Myung
Health and Social Affairs, So Sang Mok
Labour, Yi Hong-ku
Communications, Kyong Sang-hyon
Culture and Sports, Chu Ton-sik
Information, Oh In-hwan
Government Administration, So Sok-chae
Science and Technology, Chung Kun-mo
Patriot's and Veteran's Administration, Hwang Chang-pyung
First Minister for Political Affairs, Kim Yun-hwan
Second Minister for Political Affairs, Kim Chang-suk
Director, National Security Planning Agency, Kwon Yong-Lae

EMBASSY OF THE REPUBLIC OF KOREA
4 Palace Gate, London w8 5NF
Tel 0171–581 0247
Ambassador Extraordinary and Plenipotentiary, His Excellency Chang-Hee Roe, apptd 1993
Defence Attaché, Capt. Jang Kil Joo
Consul, Han Gon Lee
Commercial Attaché, Young Sang Yoo

BRITISH EMBASSY
No. 4, Chung-Dong, Chung-Ku, Seoul 100
Tel: Seoul 735–7341/3
Ambassador Extraordinary and Plenipotentiary, His Excellency Thomas George Harris, CMG, apptd 1994
Counsellor (Economic), Consul-General and Deputy Ambassador, T. C. Holmes
Defence and Military Attaché, Brig. C. D. Parr, OBE
First Secretary (Commercial), A. C. Stephens

There is a Trade Office and an Honorary British Consul at Pusan.

BRITISH COUNCIL REPRESENTATIVE, Terry Toney, Anglican Church Annex, 3–7 Chung Dong, Choongku, Seoul 100–120. There is also an office at Pusan.

BRITISH CHAMBER OF COMMERCE, c/o Chartered Bank, 1st and 2nd Floors, Samsung Building, 50, 1-Ka Ulchi Ro, Chung-Ku, Seoul.

DEFENCE

The Republic of Korea has total active armed forces of 633,000 personnel. Conscripts serve for 26 months (army) or 30 months (navy and air force) and then in reserve forces until age 33. Reserves number 4,500,000 personnel.

The army has a strength of 520,000 personnel, with 1,900 main battle tanks, 2,000 armoured personnel carriers and armoured infantry fighting vehicles, 4,540 artillery pieces and 135 armed helicopters. The regular army is organized into three mechanized infantry and 19 infantry divisions together with two infantry and ten special forces brigades. The reserves comprise 23 infantry divisions.

The navy has a strength of 60,000 (19,000 conscripts) including 25,000 marines, with two submarines, eight destroyers and 32 frigates, 122 patrol and coastal craft, 15 combat aircraft and 47 armed helicopters. The air force has a strength of 53,000, with 447 combat aircraft, organized into eight ground attack, four air defence, one counterinsurgency, one reconnaissance and three transport squadrons.

The USA maintains 36,250 personnel in the country, divided into 26,500 army and 9,750 air force personnel.

ECONOMY

The soil is fertile but arable land is limited by the mountainous nature of the country. Staple agricultural products are rice, barley and other cereals, beans, tobacco and hemp. Fruit-growing, sericulture and the growing of the medicinal root ginseng are also practised. The fishing industry is a major contributor to both food supply and exports.

The Republic of Korea is deficient in mineral resources, except for deposits of coal on the east coast and tungsten. There are some prospects of discovering oil in the sea between Korea and Japan.

Since the 1960s South Korea has followed the Japanese model of a government-business partnership controlling the economy. Rapid industrialization has also taken place since the 1960s, on the basis of the model of the Japanese income-doubling plan concentrating on expanding exports. Major industries now include shipbuilding, construction, iron and steel, textiles, electrical and electronic goods, footwear, passenger vehicles and railway rolling stock. The 1994–8 five-year economic plan includes the liberalization of foreign exchange rates and capital markets, the deregulation of interest rates and the easing of regulations on foreign exchange holdings by companies.

FINANCE

The 1994 budget totals Won 43,250,000 million. From 1962 a series of successful five-year plans resulted in real economic growth averaging around 10 per cent a year. However, GDP growth fell to 8.5 per cent in 1991 and to 4.8 per cent in 1992 before rising to 8.4 per cent in 1994. Annual per capita GNP is US$8,483 (1994).

TRADE WITH UK	1993	1994
Imports from UK	£769,380,000	£970,978,000
Exports to UK	1,077,735,000	1,096,209,000

COMMUNICATIONS

In 1989 there were 37,493 km of paved road. Seoul and Pusan have subway systems and there are national railway and airline systems. Korean Air operates regular flights to Europe, the USA, the Middle East and south-east Asia. Pusan and Inchon are the major ports with Pusan serving the industrial areas of the south-east. Inchon, 28 miles from Seoul, serves the capital, but development and operation at Inchon are hampered by a tidal variation of 9–10 metres.

EDUCATION

Primary education is compulsory for six years from the age of six. Secondary and higher education is extensive with the option of middle school to age 15 and high school to age 18. The national illiteracy rate is among the lowest in Asia.

DEMOCRATIC PEOPLE'S REPUBLIC OF KOREA
Chosun Minchu-chui Inmin Kongwa-guk

The area is 46,540 sq. miles (120,538 sq. km), with a population (UN estimate 1992) of 22,618,000.

CAPITAL – Pyongyang, approximate population, 2,000,000.

CURRENCY – Won of 100 chon.

FLAG – Red with white fimbriations and blue borders at top and bottom; a large red star on a white disc near the hoist.

NATIONAL ANTHEM – A Chi Mun Bin No Ra I Gang San (Shine bright, oh dawn, on this land so fair).

NATIONAL DAY – 8 September.

GOVERNMENT

The constitution of the Democratic People's Republic of Korea provides for a Supreme People's Assembly, presently consisting of 687 deputies, which is elected every five years by universal suffrage. The Assembly elects a President for a five-year term, and the Central People's Committee. In turn, the Central People's Committee directs the Administrative Council which implements the policy formulated by the Committee. The Administrative Council (51 members), the government of North Korea, includes the Prime Minister and various ministers. In practice, however, the country is ruled by the Korean Workers' Party which elects a Central Committee; this in turn appoints a Politburo. The senior ministers of the Administrative Council are all members of the Communist Party Central Committee and the majority are also members of the Politburo. Kim Il-sung, who had been head of the state, party and military since the country's inception in 1948, died on 8 July 1994. His son Kim Jong-il has not yet assumed his father's positions but is expected to do so eventually.

In 1992–4 North Korea's attempts to develop nuclear weapons in secret brought it into conflict with western countries. As a signatory of the Nuclear Non-Proliferation Treaty (NPT), North Korea is legally required to open its nuclear facilities to inspection by the International Atomic Energy Authority (IAEA). After repeatedly blocking special inspections of its facility at Yongbyon, in April 1993 North Korea was reported to the UN Security Council, which ordered it to allow special inspections. It refused and announced its decision to withdraw from the NPT by 12 June 1993. After negotiations with the USA, it announced on 11 June that it would remain in the NPT and allow partial IAEA inspections. After continued negotiations with the USA and IAEA in late 1993 and early 1994, IAEA inspectors visited all seven nuclear sites in March 1994 but the inspections were of limited scope and regularity. In May 1994 the IAEA informed the UN Security Council that North Korea was in violation of NPT by attempting to reprocess plutonium for nuclear weapons. A crisis ensued, with North Korea announcing its withdrawal from the IAEA in June and international pressure for sanctions until, after Kim Il-sung's death, a provisional agreement was reached by the USA and North Korea in August, and a full agreement was signed on 21 October 1994.

Under the agreement North Korea will remain a party to the IAEA and the NPT; switch from its present graphite nuclear reactors to two light-water reactors which are unsuitable for the production of weapons grade plutonium; forgo the reprocessing of spent fuel rods; allow full IAEA inspections of all its nuclear facilities; and reveal the details of its nuclear weapons programme. In return the USA will establish liaison offices, move to establish diplomatic and economic relations, and organize and pay for oil shipments to North Korea to meet its energy needs until the new reactors are built. IAEA inspectors verified the halting of North Korea's nuclear programme in November 1994 and the first oil shipments were delivered in January 1995. However, the agreement remained in the balance until June 1995 when North Korea finally accepted that the two light-water reactors could be built by South Korea.

HEAD OF STATE
President, Commander-in-Chief, General Secretary of the Party, vacant

Vice-Presidents, Kim Yong-ju; Kim Pyong-sik; Pak Song-ch'ol; Yi Chong-ok

Politburo of the Central Committee, Kim Jong-il (*full member and member of the presidium*); Kim Yong-ju; Yi Chong-ok; Pak Song-chol; Kim Yong-nam; Kye Ung-tae; Kang Song-san; So Yun-sok; Chon Pyong-ho; Choe Kwang; Han Song-yong (*full members*); Kang Hui-won; Kim Pok-sin; Hong Si-hak; Hong Song-nam; Choe Tae Pok; Kim Chol-man; Choe Yong-nim; Ying Hyong-sop; Yon Hyong-muk; Hong Sok-hyong (*alternate members*)

Secretariat of the Central Committee, vacant (*General Secretary*); Kim Chong-il; Hwang Chang-yop; So Kwan-hui; Pak Nam-ki; Kim Chung-nin; Kye Ung-tae; Chon Pyong-ho; Choe Tae-pok; Han Song-yong; Yun Ki-pok; Kim Yong-sun; Kim Kuk-tae; Kim Ki-nam

Premier of Administrative Council, Kang Song-san, *appointed* 11 December 1992

DEFENCE

It is believed that North Korea has manufactured a very small number of nuclear weapons or has the technology and raw materials to do so. In 1993 the Rodong 1 intermediate range missile with a range of 1,000 km and the ability to carry nuclear, chemical or biological weapons was successfully tested.

The total active armed forces number remains high, at 1,128,000 personnel, and is a destabilizing factor in the region. Conscripts serve for three to four years (air force), five to eight years (army) or five to ten years (navy), followed by service in the reserves to age 40 and the Red Guard to age 60.

The army has an active strength of 1 million personnel, with 3,700 main battle tanks, 3,000 armoured personnel carriers and 9,080 artillery pieces. Personnel are organized into one armoured, one artillery, one special forces, four mechanized and eight infantry corps. Reserves number 1,200,000 divided into 23 infantry divisions and six infantry brigades. The navy is 46,000 strong, with 25 submarines, three frigates and 390 patrol and coastal vessels. The air force has a strength of 82,000 personnel, with 770 combat aircraft and 50 armed helicopters, organized into three bomber, six ground attack, and ten air defence regiments, with attendant transport and training units. In addition, paramilitary troops of the Ministry of Public Security number 115,000 personnel.

ECONOMY

North Korea is rich in minerals and industry was developed, but the economy has stagnated for many years because of poor planning and a shortage of foreign exchange. Since the collapse of the Soviet Union in 1991, the economy has been in crisis because of the ending of barter trade, severe fuel shortages and the end of Soviet aid. China has also stopped supplying oil and grain at subsidized prices. Industrial output has collapsed, with industry only operating at one-third of capacity and agricultural production also badly affected. The economy has been sustained by foreign exchange sent by ethnic Koreans in Japan.

Under the nuclear agreement, North Korea is to receive 500,000 tons of oil a year and is hoping to export manganese to the USA; it has lifted the embargo on the import of US commodities. In May 1995 North Korea admitted it could not feed its population and appealed to Japan for rice, which was refused, although South Korea sent a shipment but stopped when its ship was forced to fly the North Korean flag.

TRADE WITH UK	1993	1994
Imports from UK	£5,928,000	£23,134,000
Exports to UK	249,000	158,000

KUWAIT
Dowlat al-Kuwait

Kuwait extends along the shore of the Persian Gulf from Iraq to Saudi Arabia, with an area of 6,880 sq. miles (17,818 sq. km). In 1993 the UN decided on the border dispute between Kuwait and Iraq, moving the border some few hundred metres northwards and Kuwait has since completed a 130-mile ditch, sand wall and barbed wire system along its border.

Kuwait has a dry, desert climate with summer extending from April to September. The mean temperature varies between 29–45°C in summer, and 8–18°C in winter.

Humidity rarely exceeds 60 per cent except in July and August.

At the 1985 census the population was 1,695,128, of which about 40 per cent were Kuwaiti citizens, the remainder being other Arabs, Iranians, Indians and Pakistanis. The total European and American population was about 12,500. The Iraqi occupation of Kuwait led to a substantial emigration of nationals and foreign residents. The population was estimated to have returned to over one million in January 1992, including 425,000 foreigners. It is the government's intention to keep the proportion of foreigners down to 40 per cent.

Islam is the official religion, though religious freedom is constitutionally guaranteed. The official language is Arabic, and English is widely spoken as a second language.

CAPITAL – Ψ Kuwait, population (excluding suburbs) 400,000.

CURRENCY – Kuwaiti dinar (KD) of 1,000 fils.

FLAG – Three horizontal stripes of green, white and red, with black trapezoid next to staff.

NATIONAL DAY – 25 February.

GOVERNMENT

Although Kuwait had been independent for some years, the 'exclusive agreement' of 1899 between the Sheikh of Kuwait and the British Government was formally abrogated by an exchange of letters dated 19 June 1961. Iraq invaded Kuwait on 2 August 1990 and it was liberated in February 1991 by an alliance of western and Arab forces. Iraq built up its armed forces on Kuwait's border in October 1994, until it was deterred by the arrival of US and British forces. Iraq formally recognized the sovereignty and territorial integrity of Kuwait as well as the UN-demarcated border in November 1994. Hundreds of Kuwaitis are still held in Iraq.

Under the constitution legislative power is vested in the Amir and the 50-member National Assembly, and executive power in the Amir and the Cabinet. The sixth National Assembly was dissolved in July 1986. Following popular pressure after the liberation, elections for a new National Assembly were held on 5 October 1992. The electorate consists of all Kuwaiti male nationals over 21 whose families have lived in the Emirate since before 1921.

HEAD OF STATE
HH The Amir of Kuwait, Sheikh Jabir al-Ahmad al Jabir Al-Sabah, *born* 1928, acceded 1 January 1978
Crown Prince, HH Sheikh Saad al-Abdullah al-Salim al-Sabah

CABINET *as at August 1995*
Prime Minister, HH The Crown Prince
First Deputy Prime Minister and Minister for Foreign Affairs, Sheikh Sabah al-Ahmad al-Jabir al-Sabah
Second Deputy Prime Minister, Finance, Nasir al-Rowdhan
Education and Higher Education, Dr Ahmad al-Rubie
Defence, Sheikh Ahmad Hamoud al-Jabir al-Sabah
Interior, Sheikh Ali Sabah al-Salim al-Sabah
Information, Sheikh Saoud Nasir al-Sabah
Social Affairs and Labour, Ahmed Khalid al-Kulaib
Communications, Electricity and Water, Jasim Muhammed al-Awn
Public Health, Dr Abdul Rahman Saleh al-Mehilan
Public Works and Housing, Habib Jawhar Hayat
Oil, Abdel-Mohsen al-Mudej
Awqaf and Islamic Affairs, Dr Ali Fahd al-Zumai
Commerce and Industry, Hilal Meshari al-Mutairi
Planning and Cabinet Affairs, Abdul-Aziz al-Dakheel
Justice and Administrative Affairs, Mishari Jassim al-Anjari

Speaker of the National Assembly, Ahmad Abdul-Aziz al-Saadoun

EMBASSY OF THE STATE OF KUWAIT
45–46 Queen's Gate, London SW7 5JN
Tel 0171-589 4533
Ambassador Extraordinary and Plenipotentiary, His Excellency Khaled al-Duwaisan, apptd 1993
Attachés, Abdul-Rahman Saleh Al-Radi (*Consular Affairs*); Dr Jasem Karam (*Cultural*)

BRITISH EMBASSY
PO Box 2 Safat, 13001 Safat, Kuwait
Tel: Kuwait 2403334/6
Ambassador Extraordinary and Plenipotentiary, His Excellency William Hugh Fullerton, CMG, apptd 1992
Counsellor and Deputy Ambassador, J. Jenkins, LVO
First Secretaries, F. Thompson (*Management and Consul*); C. R. Winter, MBE (*Commercial*)
Defence Attaché, T. V. Merritt, OBE

BRITISH COUNCIL REPRESENTATIVE, A. Broderick, 2 al Arabi Street (PO Box 345), 13004 Safat, Mansouriyah.

ECONOMY

Despite the desert terrain, 8.4 per cent of land is under cultivation, fruit and vegetables being the main crops. Shrimp fishing is becoming important.

The oil industry was brought into government ownership in 1975. Since reorganization in 1980, the national industry has been run by the Kuwait Petroleum Corporation. The centre of oil production is at Burgan, south of Kuwait City. Oil is also lifted in the Kuwait/Saudi Arabia Partitioned Zone (Wafra) south of the state. Oil is exported through a specially constructed port at Mina al Ahmadi.

Oil installations were extensively damaged during the Iraqi occupation. Oil exports were resumed in July 1991 and production (including output from the neutral zone) reached 2,000,000 barrels per day in December 1993, in line with the quota allocated to it by OPEC (compared to a production capacity of 2,200,000 barrels per day before the Iraqi invasion). Capacity is 2,500,000 barrels per day.

Before the Iraqi invasion Kuwait had six power stations capable of generating 7,200 MW of electricity. Associated desalination capacity, on which the country largely depends for water, was 118 million gallons a day; reserves stored up to 2,000 million barrels. All six power stations were damaged during the Iraqi occupation. Essential services were restored after liberation and after substantial investment electricity and water distillation capacity was restored to pre-invasion levels in 1995.

FINANCE

Expected revenue for the financial year 1994–5 was KD2,537m and expenditure KD4,390m. Oil revenues constitute about 90 per cent of total revenue. The cost of paying allied nations for the war and of rebuilding the country (now complete) has severely affected public finances, but the government aims to return the budget to balance by 2000 by raising indirect taxes and privatizing assets. The banking system is controlled by the Central Bank of Kuwait.

TRADE

Oil is the major export. Non-oil exports, mainly to Asian countries and the Indian sub-continent, have included chemical fertilizers, ammonia and other chemicals, metal pipes, shrimps and building materials. Re-exports to neighbouring states traditionally accounted for a major proportion of non-oil exports but were brought to a halt by the Iraqi invasion. Major trading partners are Japan, the USA and Western Europe.

Trade with UK	1993	1994
Imports from UK	£311,669,000	£312,037,000
Exports to UK	236,480,000	239,359,000

COMMUNICATIONS

Ports and airport were damaged during the Iraqi occupation, but have reopened since liberation. There is a network of dual-carriageway roads and more are under construction. Telecommunications and postal services are conducted by the government. Its earth satellite station and telecommunications network were severely damaged during the Iraqi occupation but domestic and international telephone services have been fully restored.

SOCIAL WELFARE

The government invested its considerable oil revenues in comprehensive social services. Education and medical treatment are free. Kuwait University opened in 1966, and in 1987–8 had 15,602 students. In 1987–8 there were over 489,000 pupils at government and private schools. These numbers have declined along with the total population since the Iraqi invasion and a number of schools did not reopen after Kuwait's liberation.

KYRGYZSTAN
Kyrgyz Respublikasy

Kyrgyzstan (formerly Kirghizia) has an area of 76,642 sq. miles (198,500 sq. km) and occupies the central eastern part of the former Soviet Central Asia. It is bordered on the north by Kazakhstan, on the east by China, on the south and south-west by Tajikistan and on the west by Uzbekistan. The country is mountainous, the major part being covered by the ridge of the Central Tienshan, while the Pamir-Altai system occupies its southern part. There are a number of spacious mountain valleys, the Alai, Susamyr and others. Kyrgyzstan is divided into six administrative regions.

The population (1994 estimate) is 4,500,000, of which 52.4 per cent are Kirghiz (Turkic origin), 21.5 per cent are Russian and 12.9 per cent Uzbek, with smaller numbers of Ukrainians, Germans, Tatars and Kazakhs. The majority of the population is concentrated in plains lying at the foot of the mountains. Islam is the main religion.

Kirghiz is a Turkic language which was given an alphabet in the 1930s and became the official language after independence. Russian is an equal official language in the fields of science, industry and the health service, and in all regions where there is a large Russian population. Otherwise the ethnic groups use their own languages.

CAPITAL – Bishkek. Population 616,000 (1989 census).
CURRENCY – Som (introduced on 10 May 1993 at rate of 1:200 against the Rouble).
FLAG – Red with a rayed sun containing a representation of a yurt, all in gold.
NATIONAL DAY – 31 August (Independence Day).

GOVERNMENT

The Kirghiz people were first mentioned in Chinese chronicles in the second millenium BC. They are a merger of two ethnic groups, a Turkic-speaking people driven into the area by the Mongols from the River Yenisei area of Central Asia, and indigenous peoples who spoke a similar language. After a long period under Mongol, Chinese and

Persian rule, the Kirghiz became part of the Russian
Empire in the 1860s and 1870s. Kyrgyzstan became part of
the Soviet Union in 1920 and underwent some industrialization.

Kyrgyzstan declared independence from the Soviet
Union just after the failed Moscow coup on 31 August 1991.
A new constitution was adopted on 5 May 1993 by the *Uluk
Kenesh* (parliament) which requires the country's adherence to moral and international principles of law and
human rights and to the values of Islam. President Akaev
transferred the role of head of government from himself to
the Prime Minister.

Ethnic tensions between the rural nomadic Kirghiz, the
urban Russians and the wealthy Uzbeks who own many
businesses and form the majority in the second largest town
of Osh, are never far from the surface. By presidential
decree the sphere of official usage of the Russian language
has been expanded to encourage Russians to remain, and a
treaty on dual citizenship has been signed with Russia. The
government is also committed to the fair representation of
ethnic Russians in the civil service.

President Akaev had difficulty in introducing economic
reforms because of obstruction by the bureaucracy and the
Uluk Kenesh over the reforms enshrined in the constitution. The President won a referendum on his plans for
greater economic reform in January 1994. A second
referendum in October 1994 overwhelmingly supported
the abolition of the Uluk Kenesh and its replacement by a
smaller bicameral parliament composed of a 35-member
Legislative Assembly and a 70-member People's
Assembly. Elections to the new parliament, the *Zhogorku
Kenesh*, were held in February 1995.

HEAD OF STATE
President, Askar Akaev, *elected* 12 October 1991

GOVERNMENT *as at August 1995*

Prime Minister, Apas Jumagulov
First Deputy Prime Minister, Almanat Mutabrimov
Deputy Prime Ministers, Osmanakul Ibraimov; Dgungalbek
    Amanbaev; Essengul Omuraliev; Andrey Iordan
    (*Industry, Material Resources and Trade*); Yan Fisher
Interior, Medalbek Moldoshev
Foreign Affairs, Rosa Otunbayeva
Finance, Kemelbek Nanaev
Communications, Emil Bektenov
Economics, Kamchibek Shakirov
Justice, Mukar Cholponbaev
Agriculture, Bekbolot Talgarbekov
Education, Askar Kakeev
Defence, Myrsykan Subanov
Transport, Sykdykbek Ablesov
Culture, Cholponbek Basarbaev
Health, Naken Kasiyev
Labour and Social Affairs, Zafar Hakimov
Water Conservancy and Land Improvement, Meirazhdin
    Zulpuyev
Chairman of the Legislative Assembly, Mukar Cholponbaev

BRITISH AMBASSADOR, His Excellency Noel Jones;
    resident at Alma-Ata, Kazakhstan.

ECONOMY

The government introduced the som in May 1993 to break
the link with the depreciating rouble, the cause of high
inflation in 1992 and early 1993. The IMF has provided a
US$62 million credit to support the currency reform and a
loan of US$26 million to support privatization. In July 1993
the IMF announced a further three-year loan of US$104
million to support the 1994–7 economic and financial

reform programme. The President and government have
also made the Central Bank independent of government
and parliamentary control. However, the country needs
direct foreign investment desperately and has had most of
its trading links with other Central Asian republics reduced
because of their refusal to accept payments in soms,
although this has been ameliorated by the signing of an
economic union agreement with Kazakhstan and Uzbekistan in February 1994. Subsidized goods supplies from
Russia have also been reduced.

Agriculture is the main sector of the economy, with
sugar beet, cotton and sheep the main products. Industry is
concentrated in the food-processing, textiles, timber and
mining fields. Hydro-electric power is abundant and
Kyrgyzstan has reserves of gold, coal, mercury and
uranium, although only gold has so far been exploited and
is the country's largest export.

TRADE WITH UK	1993	1994
Imports from UK	£7,629,000	£6,729,000
Exports to UK	331,000	2,600,000

CULTURE

Until the 1930s the Kirghiz language had an oral tradition
of literature which included the epic poem *Manas*, which
tells the history of the Kirghiz people. Internationally, one
of the best-known writers of the former Soviet Union is the
Kirghiz writer Chingiz Aitmatov (1928–).

LAOS
Satharanarath Pasathipatai Pasason Lao

Laos is in the northern part of Indo-China, with China and
Vietnam on the north and east, Myanmar (Burma) and
Thailand on the west, and Cambodia to the south. The area
of the country is 91,429 sq. miles (231,800 sq. km), with a
population (UN estimate 1992) of 4,469,000.

CAPITAL – Vientiane, population (estimated 1984)
    120,000.
CURRENCY – Kip (K) of 100 at.
FLAG – Blue background with a central white circle,
    framed by two horizontal red stripes.
NATIONAL DAY – 2 December.

GOVERNMENT

The kingdom of Lane Xang, the Land of a Million
Elephants, was founded in the 14th century but broke up
at the beginning of the 15th century into the separate
kingdoms of Luang Prabang and Vientiane and the
principality of Champassac, which together came under
French protection in 1893. In 1945 the Japanese executed a
coup and suppressed the French administration. In 1947
Laos became a constitutional monarchy under King
Sisvang Vong, and an independent sovereign state in
1953. The next 22 years in Laos were marked by power
struggles and civil war, eventually won by the North
Vietnamese-backed Pathet Lao, a Communist-dominated
organization.

The Lao People's Democratic Republic was proclaimed
in December 1975 following victory by the Pathet Lao and
the abdication of the King. A President and Council of
Ministers were installed, and a 45-member Supreme
People's Council was appointed to draft a constitution,
which was approved in 1991. The Lao People's Revolutionary Party (LPRP) is the sole legal political organization. A general election to the 85-member National

Assembly established by the 1991 constitution was held on 20 December 1992; all the candidates were approved by the LPRP. The President, Prime Minister and Council of Ministers were confirmed in their posts by the National Assembly on 22 February 1993.

HEAD OF STATE
President, Nouhak Phonmsavan, *elected by Supreme People's Assembly* 25 November 1992

COUNCIL OF MINISTERS *as at August 1995*
Prime Minister, Gen. Khamtai Siphandone
Deputy PM and President of State Committee for Planning and Co-operation, Khamphoui Keoboualapha
Deputy Prime Minister, Phoun Sipaseut
National Defence and Supreme Commander of the Lao People's Army, Lt.-Gen. Choummali Sayqnasone
Minister, and Head of the Office of the Council of Ministers, Khamsai Souphanouvong
Foreign Affairs, Somsavat Lengsavat
Interior, Asang Laoli
Justice, Khamouane Boupha
Health, Vannareth Rasapho
Agriculture and Forestry, Sisavat Keobounphan
Industry, Soulivong Dalavong
Communications, Transport, Posts and Construction, Phao Bounnaphon
Finance, Saysomphone Phonvihane
Education, Phimmasone
Commerce, Sompadith Volasane
Information and Culture, Osakan Thammatheva
Governor of the National Bank, Boutsabong Souvannavong
Labour and Social Welfare, Thongloun Sisoulith
Head of the President's Office, Thongdam Chanthapon
President of the Supreme People's Assembly, Samane Vignaket

EMBASSY OF THE LAO PEOPLE'S DEMOCRATIC REPUBLIC
74 Avenue Raymond-Poincaré 75116 Paris
Tel: Paris 45530298
Ambassador Extraordinary and Plenipotentiary, new appointment awaited

BRITISH AMBASSADOR, His Excellency Christian Adams, CMG, resident at Bangkok, Thailand

ECONOMY

A 'new economic management' programme was introduced in 1986 which began the liberalization of the Laotian economy, with greater autonomy for state enterprises, the relaxation of price controls and the encouragement of private business and investors. These reforms have produced a market-orientated economic system which has led to economic growth of 5 per cent annually and a decline in inflation from 68 per cent in 1989 to 12 per cent in 1993. The economy is dominated by the agricultural sector, which contributed 59 per cent of real GDP in 1992, when 1.5 million tons of paddy rice was produced. Although Laos has a balance of payments problem, exports have recently been increasing.

Although Laos is one of the poorest states in the world, there is potential for increased hydro-electric power exports to Thailand and there are unexploited deposits of iron ore, gold, bauxite and lignite. Foreign capital investment in infrastructure began with the 1994 opening of the Friendship Bridge over the Mekong river border with Thailand which links road routes from Singapore to China. Hydroelectric power is the main export, followed by wood.

TRADE WITH UK	1993	1994
Imports from UK	£1,486,000	£1,308,000
Exports to UK	87,000	1,804,000

LATVIA
The Republic of Latvia

Latvia is situated in northern Europe on the eastern coast of the Baltic sea. To the north lies Estonia, to the south Lithuania and Belarus, and to the east the Russian Federation. The area is 63,935 sq. km (24,695 sq. miles). Latvia is low-lying with occasional chains of hills. Forests cover more than 20 per cent of the total territory. The climate is continental and temperate, influenced by maritime winds.

The population is 2,529,600 (1995), of which 54.8 per cent is Latvian, 32.8 per cent Russian, 4.0 per cent Belarusian, with small Ukrainian and Polish minorities. The main religions are Lutheran, Roman Catholic and Russian Orthodox.

The majority (54.8 per cent) have Latvian as their first language and 32.8 per cent Russian. Education is in Latvian and Russian. Public sector employees must pass language tests in Latvian to a level commensurate with the nature of their employment. The right of minorities to use their mother tongue has been acknowledged.

CAPITAL – Riga (population (1995) 840,000). Other major cities are: Daugavpils (120,200); Liepaja (100,200); Jelgava (71,100); Jurmala (59,300); and Ventspils (47,000).
CURRENCY – Lats of 100 santimes.
FLAG – Crimson, with a white horizontal stripe across the centre.
NATIONAL ANTHEM – Dievs, svētī Latviju (God bless Latvia).
NATIONAL DAY – 18 November (Independence Day 1918).

HISTORY

Latvia came under the control of the German Teutonic Knights at the end of the 13th century. During the next few centuries the country endured sporadic invasions by the Swedes, Poles and Russians. By 1795 Latvia was entirely under Russian control. On 18 November 1918 Latvia declared its independence and this was confirmed by the Versailles Treaty in 1919. Several years of fighting with the new Soviet Union ensued until a peace treaty was signed under which the Soviet Union renounced all claims to Latvian territory.

The Soviet Union annexed Latvia in 1940 under the terms of the Molotov–Ribbentrop pact with Germany. Latvia was invaded and occupied when Germany invaded the Soviet Union during the Second World War. In 1944 the Soviet Union recaptured the country from Germany and confirmed its annexation, though this was never accepted as legal by most states.

In 1988 the Popular Front of Latvia was formed to campaign for greater sovereignty and democracy for Latvia. The Popular Front won the elections to the Supreme Council in 1989, and on 4 May 1990 the Supreme Council declared the independent republic of Latvia to be, *de jure*, still in existence. Agitation in Latvia against Soviet rule led in 1990 and early 1991 to clashes between independence supporters and Latvian Communists and the Soviet military. Violence reached a peak in January 1991 with deaths caused by Soviet Interior Ministry troops and attacks on Baltic border posts. A national referendum was held in March 1991 in which 73 per cent voted in favour of independence, and this was declared on 21 August 1991. The State Council of the Soviet Union recognized the independence of Latvia on 10 September 1991.

GOVERNMENT

Democratic government and a unicameral parliament were restored after multiparty elections in June 1993. The 1922 constitution was restored in July 1993 and the laws of the pre-war republic are gradually being restored. Executive authority is vested in a Prime Minister and Cabinet of Ministers. Legislative power is exercised by the unicameral parliament (*Saeíma*), which consists of 100 deputies elected for three-year terms by proportional representation with a 4 per cent threshold for parliamentary representation. The deputies elect a President of State, who in turn appoints the Prime Minister. The Prime Minister appoints, and the Saeíma approves, the Cabinet of Ministers. The electorate and citizenship has been restricted to those whose forefathers had been Latvian citizens before the 1940 Soviet occupation and to those who can pass the required Latvian language tests. Former Soviet and Russian security service and armed forces personnel have been barred from citizenship; around half of the ethnic Russian population has been unable to vote and this has caused tension with the Russian government.

After the June 1993 general election eight political parties were represented in the Saeíma. No party had a clear majority, but a coalition of Latvia's Way and the Peasants' Union formed a government. This government resigned in July 1994 after the Peasants' Union withdrew its support and in September 1994 a new coalition government of Latvia's Way, the Political Union of Economists and independents was formed which held 49 seats in parliament.

HEAD OF STATE
President, Guntis Ulmanis, *elected* 7 July 1993

COUNCIL OF MINISTERS *as at August 1995*
Prime Minister, Defence, Māris Gailis
Deputy PM, Foreign Affairs, Valdis Birkavs
Deputy PM, Welfare, Andris Bērziņš
Deputy PM, Transport, Andris Gūtmanis
Finance, Indra Sāmīte
Education and Science, Jānis Gaigals
Justice, Romāns Apsītis
Economy, Jānis Zvanītajs
Agriculture, Ārijs Ūdris
Interior, Jānis Ādamsons
Environment and Regional Development, Juris Iesalnieks
Culture, Jānis Dripe

EMBASSY OF THE REPUBLIC OF LATVIA
45 Nottingham Place, London WIM 3FE
Tel 0171-312 0040
Ambassador Extraordinary and Plenipotentiary, His Excellency Jānis Lūsis, apptd 1992

BRITISH EMBASSY
5, Alunana Iela Street, Riga LV1010
Tel: Riga 7338 126
Ambassador Extraordinary and Plenipotentiary, His Excellency Richard Ralph, CVO, apptd 1993

BRITISH COUNCIL DIRECTOR, Arthur Sanderson, MBE, Lazaretes iela 3, Riga 226010

DEFENCE

Since independence Latvia has sought to form its own armed forces. Total active armed forces number 6,850 personnel with conscripts serving for 18 months. The army has 1,500 personnel, formed into one engineer, one infantry and one reconnaissance battalions. The army reserve of the Home Guard numbers 18,000 personnel. The navy is 900 strong, with 14 patrol craft. The air force is 150 strong, with a few transport aircraft and helicopters. The paramilitary border guard numbers 4,300 personnel, organized into nine battalions.

All remaining Russian forces withdrew from Latvia on 31 August 1994 except for those stationed at the anti-ballistic missile early-warning radar at Skrunda, which will continue to operate until 1999.

ECONOMY

Since independence Latvia has pressed ahead with transition from a command economy to a market economy system. It has also attempted to achieve economic independence from the CIS. The government has initiated a privatization process which has made many industrial facilities available for purchase both by Latvian and foreign private investors. By the end of 1993 20 per cent of economic production and 40 per cent of agricultural production had been privatized.

Latvia is an agricultural exporter, specializing in cattle and pig breeding, dairy farming and crops, including sugar beet, flax, cereals and potatoes. Natural resources include limestone, gypsum, peat and timber.

Industry was organized to contribute to the centralized Soviet economy and is specialized in certain areas. These include the production of electric and diesel trains, telephones, telephone exchange equipment, food processing, agricultural machinery, and timber and paper products.

Tourism is being developed, capitalizing on its beach resorts, nature reserves and parks. Latvia is also geographically well-placed for the development of transport services.

TRADE

Russia remains one of the most important trading partners for Latvia. In 1994, 41 per cent of exports went to the CIS, 40 per cent to the European Union and EFTA states, and 6 per cent to Lithuania and Estonia. Of total imports, 38 per cent came from the CIS, 17 per cent from the EU, 13 per cent from Lithuania and Estonia, 11 per cent from EFTA states. The main imports are oil and energy, and the main exports are wood and wood products, artificial fibres, meat, dairy products and rolled ferrous metals.

Trade with UK	1993	1994
Imports from UK	£15,823,000	£30,696,000
Exports to UK	69,254,000	222,378,000

COMMUNICATIONS

Latvia has a reasonably well-developed railway (2,397 km) and road (18,834 km) system, along which a significant proportion of exports from CIS republics are transported to western Europe. Latvia is also being developed as a transportation route from Scandinavia to central and southern Europe. Several warm-water ports exist, of which two, Riga and Ventspils, are developed for commercial transport. The national airline, Latvijas Aviolinijas, operates regular flights to Russia, Scandinavia and Europe.

CULTURE

The Latvian language belongs to the Baltic branch of the Indo-European languages, and as such is distinct from Russian. The Latin alphabet is used. Independent Latvian literature appeared in the late 18th and early 19th century and played a role in the fight for independence in 1918.

There are 15 higher education institutions, of which four are universities.

LEBANON
Al-Jumhouriya al-Lubnaniya

Lebanon forms a strip about 120 miles long and between 30 and 35 miles wide along the Mediterranean littoral. It extends from the Israeli frontier in the south to the Nahr al Kebir (15 miles north of Tripoli) in the north; its eastern boundary runs down the Anti-Lebanon range and then down the great central depression, the *Beqa'a*, from which flow the rivers Orontes and Litani. It is divided into five districts, North Lebanon, Mount Lebanon, Beirut, South Lebanon and Beqaa. The seaward slopes of the mountains have a Mediterranean climate and vegetation. The inland range of Anti-Lebanon has the characteristics of steppe country. The area is 4,015 sq. miles (10,400 sq. km).

The population (UN estimate 1992) was 2,838,000. It is a mixture of Christians, Muslims and Druses. Arabic is the official language, and French and English are also widely used.

CAPITAL – Ψ Beirut (population 1,500,000). Other towns are Ψ Tripoli (200,000), Ψ Sidon (100,000), Ψ Tyre (70,000), Zahlé (30,000).
CURRENCY – Lebanese pound (L£) of 100 piastres.
FLAG – Horizontal bands of red, white and red with a green cedar of Lebanon in the centre of the white band.
NATIONAL ANTHEM – Kulluna Lil Watan Lil'ula Lil'alam (We all belong to the homeland).
NATIONAL DAY – 22 November.

GOVERNMENT

Lebanon became an independent state in 1920, administered under French mandate until 22 November 1943. Powers were transferred to the Lebanese government from January 1944 and French troops were withdrawn in 1946.

In 1975, fighting broke out in Beirut between members of the predominantly Christian Phalangist Party and predominantly Muslim militias, later supported by Palestinian guerrillas based in Lebanon. In the autumn of 1976 the Arab Deterrent Forces, composed mainly of Syrian troops, imposed a ceasefire but fighting began again subsequently and continued until the end of the civil war in 1990. In 1978 Israeli forces invaded but withdrew some months later, handing over their positions, except for a belt in the south, to the UN Interim Force in Lebanon (UNIFIL). In 1982 Israeli forces again invaded the country, penetrating as far as Beirut. Following negotiations, Palestinian officials and fighters left Beirut for various Arab countries. Although the bulk of Israeli troops withdrew from southern Lebanon in 1985, a buffer zone controlled by the Israeli-backed South Lebanon Army (SLA), a Christian militia, was established along the Israeli-Lebanon border. Syrian forces are deployed in west Beirut and in the north and the east of the country.

The Taif Accord 'for national conciliation', drawn up by an Arab League-appointed committee, gained the approval of a majority of Lebanese MPs in 1989, but was resisted by Gen. Aoun, who insisted on an immediate Syrian troop withdrawal. The Lebanese government acted with the backing of Syrian troops to oust Gen. Aoun in October 1990 and a new government which included the main militia leaders was formed in December 1990. Since then the government has moved to clear the militias from the Greater Beirut area and has restored its authority throughout most of the country. The Beqa'a valley remains under Syrian control and the South Lebanon Security Zone under Israeli control. All militias have been disarmed apart from Hezbollah and the SLA. Since 1993 the Lebanese Army has deployed in southern villages alongside UNIFIL forces but has not disarmed Hezbollah forces, who are financed, armed and trained by Syria and Iran to continue fighting against Israel and the SLA. This fighting has continued throughout 1993–5. By the end of 1994 the government had resettled 200,000 refugees in the country.

The first parliamentary elections since 1972 were held between August and October 1992. The 128-seat unicameral parliament was directly elected by universal suffrage and divided equally between Christians and Muslims. The polls were widely boycotted in Christian areas because of the continuing presence of Syrian troops, in breach of the Taif Accord. A government was formed under Prime Minister Rafiq Hariri in October 1992 which has focused on the economy and reconstruction.

In October 1991 Lebanon began to participate in the bilateral sessions of the Middle East peace talks, but so far has, with Syria, boycotted the multilateral rounds.

HEAD OF STATE
President of the Republic of Lebanon, Elias Hrawi, *took office* 25 November 1989

CABINET *as at August 1995*
Prime Minister and Finance, Rafiq Hariri
Deputy PM, Interior, Michel Murr
Foreign and Expatriate Affairs, Fares Bouez
Justice, Bahij Tabbara
Health, Marwan Hamadeh
Defence, Mohsen Dalloul
Labour, Ali Hrajli
Posts and Telecommunications, El-Fadl Chalak
Education, Youth and Sports, Robert Ghanem
Economy and Trade, Yasser Jaber
Information, Farid Mkari
Agriculture, Chawki Fakhoury
Public Works, Assaad Hardan
Industry and Oil, Chahe Barsoumian
Municipal and Rural Affairs, Hagop Demirdjian
Refugee Affairs, Walid Jumblatt
Housing and Co-operatives, Mohammad Abu Hamdan
Tourism, Nicolas Fattoush
Hydroelectricity Resources, Ilyas Hubayqah
Culture and Higher Education, Michel Edde
Transport, Omar Meskaoui
Vocational and Technical Education, Abdel-Rahim Mrad
Environment, Pierre Pharaon
Emigrants, Ali El-Khalil
Social Affairs, Estephan Doueyhi
National Assembly Speaker, Nabih Berri

LEBANESE EMBASSY
21 Kensington Palace Gardens, London W8 4QM
Tel 0171–229 7265/6
Ambassador Extraordinary and Plenipotentiary, His Excellency Mahmoud Hammoud, apptd 1990

BRITISH EMBASSY
Autostrade Jal El Dib, Coolrite Building (PO Box 60180), Beirut
Tel: Beirut 406330

Ambassador Extraordinary and Plenipotentiary, Her
Excellency Maeve Fort, CMG, apptd 1992

BRITISH COUNCIL DIRECTOR, Ann Malamah-Thomas,
MBE, Sidani Street, Azar Building, Beirut

ECONOMY

A ten-year plan has been initiated to repair war damage and
to restore Lebanon's position as a regional financial
services and light industrial centre. The 1993–2002
reconstruction plan is estimated to cost US$12,900 million
in total, of which US$7,600 million is to come from foreign
loans and grants and US$5,300 million from budget
surpluses. It is to concentrate on rebuilding housing,
transport, utilities, services, education and health services,
and aiding industry and agriculture.

Economic recovery has been impressive, with GDP
growth of 6 per cent in 1994, inflation reduced to 9 per cent
(from 131 per cent in 1992) and foreign exchange reserves
increased to US$4,000 million. A plan to reconstruct the
commercial centre of Beirut has been started, with the issue
in January 1994 of US$650 million shares in the US$1,800
million Solidère company which will reconstruct the 400-
acre site. The government has also obtained US$1,600
million in loans and grants for its national reconstruction
programme, mainly from Arab states and international
agencies.

Fruits are the most important products and include
citrus fruit, apples, grapes, bananas and olives. There is
some light industry, mostly for the production of consumer
goods, but most factories are still in need of reconstruction
because of the civil war.

TRADE

Principal imports are gold and precious metals, machinery
and electrical equipment, textiles and yarns, vegetable
products, iron and steel goods, and motor vehicles. There
had been a gradual decline in the overall amount of imports
as a result of continued instability.

Principal exports include gold and precious metals,
fruits and vegetables, textiles, building materials, furniture,
plastic goods, foodstuffs, tobacco and wine.

At one time there was a considerable transit trade
through Beirut into the Arab hinterland. Lebanon is the
terminal for two oil pipelines, one formerly belonging to
the Iraq Petroleum Company, debouching at Tripoli, the
other belonging to the Trans Arabian Pipeline Company,
at Sidon. These lines have not functioned for some years.

Trade with UK	1993	1994
Imports from UK	£136,372,000	£138,616,000
Exports to UK	11,436,000	7,282,000

COMMUNICATIONS

The railways are not functioning as a result of the civil war.
There is an international airport at Beirut, served by the
national carrier MEA and other airlines. An internal service
operates from Beirut to Tripoli.

ARCHAEOLOGY

Lebanon has some important historical remains, notably
Baalbek (Heliopolis) which contains the ruins of first- to
third-century Roman temples and Jbeil (Byblos), one of the
oldest continuously inhabited towns in the world, and
ancient Tyre.

EDUCATION

There are six universities in Beirut, the American and the
French universities, and the Lebanese National University, the Beirut University College, the Kaslik Saint Esprit
University and the Arab University, with the University of
Balamond situated near Tripoli. There are several institutions for vocational training, and there is a good provision
throughout the country of primary and secondary schools,
among which are a great number of private schools.
Education at all levels has been severely disrupted by the
civil war.

LESOTHO
'Muso oa Lesotho

Lesotho is a landlocked mountainous state entirely surrounded by South Africa. Of the total area of 11,720 sq.
miles (30,355 sq. km), about one-third, in the west and
south, is lowland, between 5,000 and 6,000 ft above sea
level. The remaining two-thirds are foothills and highlands, rising to 11,425 ft. The population (UN estimate
1992) is 1,836,000.

CAPITAL – Maseru, population (1986 census) 288,951.

CURRENCY – Loti (M) of 100 lisente.

FLAG – Diagonally white over blue over green with the
white of double width, and an assegai and knobkerrie on
a Basotho shield in brown in the upper hoist.

NATIONAL ANTHEM – Pina ea Sechaba.

NATIONAL DAY – 4 October (Independence Day).

GOVERNMENT

Lesotho (formerly Basutoland) became a constitutional
monarchy within the Commonwealth on 4 October 1966.
The independence constitution was suspended in 1970 and
the country was governed by a Council of Ministers
headed by Leabua Jonathan until the establishment of a
nominated National Assembly in 1974.

Jonathan's government was overthrown in 1986, and
executive and legislative powers were conferred upon the
King, to be advised by the Military Council and Council of
Ministers led by Maj.-Gen. Justin Lekhanya. In March
1990 King Moshoeshoe II's powers were formally revoked
and in November the King was deposed and replaced by
his son, who assumed the title of Letsie III. Maj.-Gen.
Lekhanya was overthrown in 1991 in a coup led by Col.
Elias Ramaema. Elections promised for 1992 were eventually held in March 1993 and the Basotho Congress Party
(BCP) won all 65 seats in the new National Assembly. The
BCP government led by Ntsu Mokhele was sworn in on
2 April 1993, at which time King Letsie III swore allegiance to a new multiparty democratic constitution and the
Military Council was dissolved.

Sections of the military remained opposed to the BCP
government and launched two unsuccessful coup attempts
in 1994 which were defeated after heavy fighting. On 17
August 1994 King Letsie III and sections of the military
launched a coup attempt and announced the dismissal of
the government and the dissolution of parliament until
new elections. After mediation by South Africa, Zimbabwe
and Botswana, the government, which had refused to leave
office, was restored by the King. King Letsie also
announced his intention to abdicate voluntarily in favour
of his father, Moshoeshoe II, who was restored on 25
January 1995.

The country is divided into ten administrative districts.
In each district there is a district secretary who co-
ordinates all government activity in the area, working in
co-operation with hereditary chiefs.

HEAD OF STATE
King, HM King Moshoeshoe II, *acceded* 30 April 1965, *deposed* November 1990, *restored* 25 January 1995
Crown Prince, HH Prince Letsie

COUNCIL OF MINISTERS *as at August 1995*
Prime Minister, Public Service, Dr Ntsu Mokhehle
Deputy PM, Education and Training, Manpower Development and Youth Affairs, Pakalitha Mosisili
Foreign Affairs, Mpho Malie
Trade, Industry, Tourism, Sports and Culture, Shakhane Robong Mokhehle
Agriculture, Co-operatives and Marketing, Ntsukunyane Mphanya
Home Affairs, Lesao Lehohla
Health and Social Welfare, Dr Khauhelo Ralitapole
Natural Resources, Tseliso Makhakhe
Transport, Post and Telecommunications, David Mochochoko
Information and Broadcasting, Lira Motete
Justice, Human Rights, Law and Constitutional Affairs, Kelebone Maope
Employment and Labour, Not'si Molopo
Works, Molapo Qhobela
Defence, Sephiri Motanyane

HIGH COMMISSION FOR THE KINGDOM OF LESOTHO
7 Chesham Place, London SW1X 8HN
Tel 0171-235 5686
High Commissioner, His Excellency M. K. Tsekoa, apptd 1989

BRITISH HIGH COMMISSION
PO Box 521, Maseru 100
Tel: Maseru 313961
High Commissioner, His Excellency James Roy Cowling, apptd 1992

BRITISH COUNCIL REPRESENTATIVE, P. Thompson, Hobson's Square, PO Box 429, Maseru 100

JUDICIARY

The courts of law consist of the court of appeal, the High Court, magistrates' courts, judicial commissioners' court, central and local courts. Magistrates' and higher courts administer the law and also adjudicate appeals from the judicial commissioners' and subordinate courts.
Chief Justice, Hon. J. L. Kheola

ECONOMY

The economy is based on agriculture and animal husbandry, and the adverse balance of trade (mainly consumer and capital goods) is offset by the earnings of the large numbers of the population who work in South Africa. Apart from some diamonds, Lesotho has few natural resources and only small-scale industrial development. The Lesotho National Development Corporation was set up to promote the development of industry, mining, trade and tourism. Work has commenced on the Highlands Water Scheme designed to provide water for the Vaal industrial zone in South Africa and hydroelectricity for Lesotho. Drilling is being carried out for oil. A National Park has been established at Sehlabathebe in the Maluti mountains. A number of light manufacturing and processing industries have recently been established.

The main sources of revenue are customs and excise duty. The IMF approved a US$12 million loan in September 1994 to support the government's 1994–5 economic reform programme.

TRADE WITH UK	1993	1994
Imports from UK	£908,000	£665,000
Exports to UK	2,343,000	1,605,000

COMMUNICATIONS

A tarred road links Maseru to several of the main lowland towns, and this is being extended in the south of the country. The mountainous areas are linked by tarred, gravelled and earth roads and tracks. Roads link border towns in South Africa with the main towns in Lesotho. Maseru is also connected by rail with the main Bloemfontein–Natal line of the South African Railways. Scheduled international air services are operated daily between Maseru and Johannesburg and other scheduled international flights are to Gabarone, Harare, Manzini and Maputo. There are around 30 airstrips. Internal scheduled services are operated by the Lesotho Airways Corporation.

The telephone network is fully automated in all urban centres. Radio telephone communication is used extensively in the remote rural areas.

EDUCATION

Most schools are mission-controlled, the government providing grants for salaries and buildings. There are over 1,000 primary and over 100 secondary schools; few areas lack a school and there is a literacy rate of about 70 per cent. Increasing emphasis is being laid on agricultural and vocational education. The National University of Lesotho at Roma was established as a university in 1975.

LIBERIA
Republic of Liberia

An independent republic of West Africa, occupying that part of the coast between Sierra Leone and the Côte d'Ivoire which is between the rivers Mano in the north-west and Cavalla in the south-east, a distance of about 350 miles, and extending to the interior to latitude 8° 50', a distance of 150 miles from the seaboard. The area is about 43,000 sq. miles (111,369 sq. km). The population at the census of 1974 was 1,481,524; a 1992 UN estimate put the figure at 2,580,000. The official language is English. Over 16 ethnic languages are spoken.

CAPITAL – ΨMonrovia, population estimate (1984) 425,000. Other ports are ΨBuchanan, ΨGreenville (Sinoe) and ΨHarper (Cape Palmas).
CURRENCY – Liberian dollar (L$) of 100 cents.
FLAG – Alternate horizontal stripes (five white, six red), with five-pointed white star on blue field in upper corner next to flagstaff.
NATIONAL ANTHEM – All Hail, Liberia, Hail.
NATIONAL DAY – 26 July.

GOVERNMENT

Liberia was founded by the American Colonization Society in 1822 as a colony for freed American slaves, and has been recognized since 1847 as an independent state.

William V. S. Tubman, President since 1944, died in 1971 and was succeeded by Dr Tolbert. The constitution was suspended following a military coup in 1980 during which Tolbert was killed. M/Sgt. Samuel Doe assumed power as chairman of a military council. A new constitution was endorsed by a referendum in 1984. Doe and his party, the National Democratic Party of Liberia (NDPL) won the elections held in 1985, amid allegations of electoral fraud, and a civilian government was formally installed in 1986.

CIVIL WAR

A rebel incursion launched in 1989 by the National Patriotic Front of Liberia (NPFL) led by Charles Taylor developed into a full-scale civil war in 1990. A five-nation ECOWAS peacekeeping force (known as ECOMOG) landed in Monrovia in an effort to end the conflict but in September 1990 President Doe was killed, having refused to step down. The Interim Government of National Unity (IGNU) was formed in August 1990 in The Gambia and arrived in Monrovia in November. An agreement to establish a ceasefire and confine troops to barracks under ECOMOG supervision broke down in October 1992 when the NPFL attempted to seize Monrovia. In response ECOMOG was enlarged to 15,000 personnel and assumed a more offensive role, driving NPFL forces out of Monrovia's suburbs. By March 1993 the NPFL had been driven into eastern parts of Liberia and peace negotiations between the warring factions had begun. Under UN-sponsored negotiations a peace agreement was signed by the IGNU, NPFL and another rebel group ULIMO on 25 July 1993 which brought about a ceasefire on 1 August. Interim President Amos Sawyer was due to be replaced within one month by a five-member Council of State to govern the country during a transitional period, together with a 35-member transitional legislature including members from all three factions. The Council of State and the transitional legislature did not actually take power until March 1994 and the transitional government of IGNU, NPFL and ULIMO members not until May 1994. Continued fighting and the fracturing of the three factions to form more factions led to further negotiations and an agreement in December 1994 on a new Council of State and the holding of legislative elections by November 1995. Intermittent fighting continued into 1995 in a civil war that has left 150,000 people dead and 80 per cent of the country's population displaced, with 750,000 as refugees in neighbouring states.

COUNCIL OF STATE *as at August 1995*
Chairman, David Kpormakor (IGNU)
First Deputy Chairman, Mohammed Sherif (ULIMO)
Second Deputy Chairman, Issac Moussa (NPFL)
Members, Phillip Banks (IGNU); Dexter Taylor (NPFL)
IGNU Interim Government of National Unity; ULIMO United Liberation Movement for Democracy; NPFL National Patriotic Front of Liberia.

EMBASSY OF THE REPUBLIC OF LIBERIA
2 Pembridge Place, London W2 4XB
Tel 0171-221 1036
Minister-Counsellor, Chargé d'Affaires, Ishmael Grant

BRITISH EMBASSY
The British Embassy in Monrovia was closed in March 1991.

ECONOMY

Before the civil war began principal exports were iron ore, crude rubber, timber, uncut diamonds, palm kernels, cocoa and coffee, but the civil war has resulted in the suspension of most economic activity.

TRADE WITH UK	1993	1994
Imports from UK	£9,549,000	£8,510,000
Exports to UK	56,000	254,000

COMMUNICATIONS

The artificial harbour and free port of Monrovia was opened in 1948. There are nine ports of entry, including three river ports. Robertsfield International Airport is under NPFL control and not yet in use. Spriggs Payne airfield, on the outskirts of Monrovia, normally used for internal flights, is currently being used for flights to other West African countries.

LIBYA

Al-Jamahiriya Al-Arabiya
Al-Libiya Al-Shabiya Al-Ishtirakiya Al-Uthma

Libya, on the Mediterranean coast of Africa, is bounded on the east by Egypt and Sudan, on the south by Chad and Niger, and on the west by Algeria and Tunisia. It consists of the three former provinces of Tripolitania, Cyrenaica and the Fezzan, with an area of 679,362 sq. miles (1,759,540 sq. km).

Vast sand and rock deserts, almost completely barren, occupy the greater part of Libya. The southern part of the country lies within the Sahara Desert. There are few rivers and as rainfall is irregular outside parts of Cyrenaica and Tripolitania, good harvests are rare.

The population (UN estimate 1992) is 4,875,000. The people of Libya are principally Arab with some Berbers in the west and some Tuareg tribesmen in the Fezzan. Islam is the official religion of Libya, but other religions are tolerated. The official language is Arabic.

The ancient ruins in Cyrenaica, at Cyrene, Ptolemais (Tolmeta) and Apollonia, are outstanding, as are those at Leptis Magna, 70 miles east, and at Sabratha, 40 miles west of Tripoli. An Italian expedition found in the south-west of the Fezzan a series of rock-paintings more than 5,000 years old.

CAPITAL – ΨTripoli, population estimate (1991) 1,000,000. The principal towns are: ΨBenghazi (500,000); ΨMisurata (200,000); Sirte (100,000).
CURRENCY – Libyan dinar (LD) of 1,000 dirhams.
FLAG – Libya uses a plain emerald green flag.
NATIONAL DAY – 1 September.

GOVERNMENT

Libya was occupied by Italy in 1911–12 in the course of the Italo-Turkish War, and under the Treaty of Ouchy 1912 sovereignty over the province was transferred by Turkey to Italy. In 1939 the four provinces of Libya (Tripoli, Misurata, Benghazi and Derna) were incorporated in the national territory of Italy as *Libia Italiana.* After the Second World War Tripolitania and Cyrenaica were placed provisionally under British and the Fezzan under French administration, and in conformity with a resolution of the UN General Assembly in 1949, Libya became on 24 December 1951 the first independent state to be created by the United Nations. The monarchy was overthrown by a revolution in 1969 and the country was declared a republic. It was ruled by the Revolutionary Command Council (RCC) under the leadership of Colonel Muammar Gadhafi.

In 1977 a new form of direct democracy, the 'Jamahiriya' (state of the masses) was promulgated and the official name of the country was changed to Socialist People's Libyan Arab Jamahiriya. At local level authority is now vested in about 1,500 Basic and 14 Municipal People's Congresses which appoint Popular Committees to execute policy. Officials of these congresses and committees, together with representatives from unions and other organizations, form the General People's Congress, which normally meets for about a week each year. In addition, a number of extraordinary sessions are held throughout the year. This is the highest policy-making body in the country.

The General People's Congress appoints its own General Secretariat and the General People's Committee, whose members head the government departments which execute policy at national level. The Secretary of the General People's Committee has functions similar to those of a Prime Minister.

Since a reorganization in 1979 neither Col. Gadhafi nor his former RCC colleagues have held formal posts in the administration. Gadhafi continues to hold the ceremonial title 'Leader of the Revolution'.

Leader of the Revolution and Supreme Commander of the Armed Forces, Col. Muammar al-Gadhafi

SECRETARIAT OF THE GENERAL PEOPLE'S CONGRESS *as at August 1995*

Secretary, Zanati Muhammad al-Zanati
Assistant Secretary, Abu Zayd Umar Durdah
Secretary, Affairs of People's Congresses, Ali al-Sha'iri
Secretary, Affairs of People's Committees, Mahmud al-Hitki
Secretary, Trade Unions, Ali al-Shamikh
Secretary, Women's Affairs, Salmah Rashid
Secretary, Foreign Affairs, Sa'ad Mujbir

GENERAL PEOPLE'S COMMITTEE (CABINET)

Secretary-General (Premier), Abd al-Majid al-Qa'ud
Foreign Liaison, Omar al-Muntasir
Unity, Jum'a al-Mahdi al-Fazzani
Justice and Public Order, Mohammed Mahmud al-Hijazi
Animal Resources, Messaoud Abousoud
Information and Culture, Fawzia Bashir Challabi
Marine Resources, Miftah Muhammad Ka'aybah
Industry and Mining, Mufta Azzouz
Energy, Abdullah Salem al-Badri
Planning and Finance, Dr Muhammad Bayt al Mal
Education, Youth and Sports, Training and Scientific Research, Ma'tug Muhammad Ma'tug
Health and Social Security, Dr Baghdadi Ali al-Mahmudi
Public Works and Housing, Mubarak Abdullah al-Shamikh
Public Accounting and Control, Mahmud Badji
Economy and Trade, Tahir al-Jihimi
Transport and Communications, Izz al-Din al-Hinshiri
Great Man-Made River Project, Jadallah Azzouz el-Talhi
Tourism, Boukhari Hawda

LIBYAN DIPLOMATIC MISSION IN LONDON

Since the break of diplomatic relations with Libya in April 1984, the Royal Embassy of Saudi Arabia has handled Libyan interests in Britain.

BRITISH EMBASSY

British interests are currently handled by the British Interests Section of the Italian Embassy, Sharia Uahran 1 (PO Box 4206), Tripoli.

DEFENCE

Libya has a total active armed forces of 70,000, with selective conscription of two years. The army has a strength of 40,000 (25,000 conscripts), with 2,350 main battle tanks, 2,670 armoured infantry fighting vehicles and armoured personnel carriers, and some 1,770 artillery pieces. The navy has a strength of 8,000 personnel, with four submarines, two frigates, 36 patrol and coastal vessels, and 30 armed helicopters. The air force has 22,000 personnel, with 406 combat aircraft and 65 armed helicopters.

As part of the UN economic sanctions imposed in April 1992 there is a total embargo on arms sales to Libya.

ECONOMY

Economic sanctions were imposed on Libya in April 1992 under UN Security Council Resolution 748 following Libya's failure to hand over to the USA or Britain two suspects in the bombing of Pan-Am flight 103 over Lockerbie, Scotland, in 1988. The UN imposed additional sanctions in December 1993, including freezing assets abroad and restricting imports of spare parts and equipment for the oil and aviation sectors. All the sanctions remain in place and are renewed every 120 days by the UN Security Council.

Agriculture is confined mainly to the coastal areas of Tripolitania and Cyrenaica, where barley, wheat, olives, almonds, citrus fruits and dates are produced, and to the areas of the oases, many of which are well supplied with springs supporting small fertile areas. Among the important oases are Jaghbub, Ghadames, Jofra, Sebha, Murzuq, Brak, Ghat, Jalo and the Kufra group in the south-east.

The main industry is oil and gas production. There are pipelines from Zelten to the terminal at Mersa Brega, from Dahra to Ras-es-Sider, from Amal to Ras Lanuf, and from the Intisar field to Zuetina. In 1994 average production of crude oil was about 1.38 million barrels per day. A major petrochemical complex has been built at Ras Lanuf where a refinery and ethylene plant began operations in 1985. The construction of an iron and steel plant at Misurata has been completed. Economic constraints have delayed some projects, particularly since Libya decided in 1983 to go ahead with a major irrigation scheme, the 'Great Man-Made River'.

Libya has technical assistance agreements with a number of countries, and also employs large numbers of foreign labourers and experts.

TRADE

Exports are dominated by crude oil, but some wool, cattle, sheep and horses, olive oil, and hides and skins are also exported. Principal imports are foodstuffs, including sugar, tea and coffee, and most construction materials and consumer goods. After the revolution the private sector was virtually eliminated and Libya became a state trading country with imports controlled by state monopolies. In 1988, however, reforms were implemented which have allowed a small private sector to be re-established.

Trade with UK	1993	1994
Imports from UK	£274,051,000	£194,905,000
Exports to UK	156,542,000	148,151,000

COMMUNICATIONS

The coastal road running from the Tunisian frontier through Tripoli to Benghazi, Tobruk and the Egyptian border serves the main population centres. Main roads also link the provincial centres, and the oil-producing areas of the south with the coastal towns.

There are airports at Tripoli and Benghazi (Benina), Tobruk, Mersa Brega, Sebha, Ghadames and Kufra regularly used by commercial airlines. Since April 1992 a UN embargo on air links with Libya has been in force.

LIECHTENSTEIN
Fürstentum Liechtenstein

Liechtenstein is a principality on the Upper Rhine, between Vorarlberg (Austria) and Switzerland, with an area of 61 sq. miles (158 sq. km), and a population in 1993 of 30,310. The language of the principality is German.

CAPITAL – Vaduz, population (1993) 5,072.
CURRENCY – Swiss franc of 100 rappen (or centimes).
FLAG – Equal horizontal bands of blue over red; gold crown on blue band near staff.
NATIONAL ANTHEM – Oben am Jungen Rhein (High on the Rhine).
NATIONAL DAY – 15 August.

GOVERNMENT

The Patriotic Union and Progressive Citizens' parties have governed the country in coalition since 1938. There is a threshold of 8 per cent for parties to gain representation in the Landtag. At the general election on 24 October 1993 the Progressive Citizens' Party won 11 seats, the Patriotic Union Party 13 seats and the Free List (Environmentalist) grouping, 1 seat.

HEAD OF STATE

HSH The Prince of Liechtenstein, Hans Adam II, *born* 14 February 1945; *succeeded* 13 November 1989; *married* 30 July 1967, Countess Marie Kinsky; and has *issue*: Prince Alois (*see* below); Prince Maximilian, *b.* 16 May 1969; Prince Constantin, *b.* 15 March 1972; Princess Tatjana, *b.* 10 April 1973
Heir, HSH Prince Alois, *b.* 11 June 1968, *married* 1993 Duchess Sophie of Bavaria; and has *issue*: Prince Wenzel, *b.* 24 May 1995

MINISTRY *as at August 1995*

Prime Minister, Dr Mario Frick (*Head of Government 'Presidium', Finance, Justice*)
Deputy PM, Thomas Büchel (*Interior, Agriculture, Forestry and Environment, Education*)
Government Councillors, Cornelia Gassner-Matt (*Construction, Traffic*), Andrea Willi (*Foreign Affairs, Culture, Youth and Sport*), Michael Ritter (*Economy, Family, Welfare, Health*)

DIPLOMATIC REPRESENTATION

Liechtenstein is represented in diplomatic and consular matters in the United Kingdom by the Swiss Embassy.

BRITISH CONSUL-GENERAL, D. Bell, Dufourstrasse 56, 8008 Zürich

ECONOMY

The main industries are high and ultra-high vacuum engineering, the semi-conductor industry, roller bearings, fastenings and securing systems, artificial teeth, heating and hot water equipment, synthetic fibres, woollen and homespun fabrics.

In 1991 Liechtenstein became a member of the European Free Trade Association, and as such is a party to the European Economic Area (EEA) Agreement with the EU which came into force on 1 January 1994. In December 1992 in separate referenda, Switzerland voted against EEA membership while Liechtenstein voted in favour. After adapting its customs union with Switzerland, and again voting in favour of joining the EEA in a referendum on 9 April 1995, Liechtenstein joined the EEA on 1 May 1995.

FINANCE	1992	1993
Revenue	F426,805,387	F449,165,116
Expenditure	430,531,696	441,383,850

LITHUANIA
Lietuva

Lithuania lies on the eastern coast of the Baltic Sea between 53° 54' and 56° 27' N., and 20° 56' and 26° 51' E. To the north lies Latvia, to the east and south lies Belarus, to the south-west lie Poland and the Kaliningrad region of the Russian Federation. The area is 25,170 sq. miles (65,200 sq. km).

The country lies in the middle and lower basin of the river Nemunas. Along the coast is a lowland plain which rises inland to form uplands in east and central Lithuania. These uplands, the Middle Lowlands, give way to the Baltic Highlands in east and south-east Lithuania; the highest point is 294 m (965 ft). The country has a network of rivers and over 2,800 lakes, which mainly lie in the east of the country. The climate varies between maritime and continental.

The population is 3,724,000 (1994), of which 80.6 per cent are Lithuanian, 8.7 per cent Russian, 7.1 per cent Polish, 1.6 per cent Belarusian, 1.1 per cent Ukrainian. The majority are Roman Catholic, with Russian Orthodox and Lutheran minorities. Lithuanian is the state language, spoken by 80 per cent, with Russian, Polish and Belarusian minorities.

CAPITAL – Vilnius (population 579,000). Other major cities are Kaunas (419,000), Klaipéda (203,000), Siauliai (147,000).
CURRENCY – Litas.
FLAG – Three horizontal stripes of yellow, green, red.
NATIONAL ANTHEM – Tautiška Giesmé (The National Song).
NATIONAL DAY – 16 February (Independence Day).

HISTORY

The first independent Lithuanian state emerged as the Kingdom of Lithuania in 1251, and over the next few centuries acted as a buffer state between Germans to the west and Mongols and Tartars to the east. After forming a joint Commonwealth and Kingdom with Poland in 1561, Lithuania was taken over by the Russian Empire in the partitions of Poland that occurred in 1772, 1792 and 1795.

Lithuania declared its independence from the Russian Empire on 16 February 1918 and then fought against German and Soviet forces until its independence was recognized by the Versailles Treaty 1919 and the peace treaty signed with the Soviet Union on 12 July 1920. The Soviet Union annexed Lithuania in 1940 under the terms of the Molotov–Ribbentrop pact with Germany. Lithuania was invaded and occupied when Germany invaded the Soviet Union during the Second World War. In 1944 the Soviet Union recaptured the country and confirmed its annexation, though this was never accepted as legal by most states.

In December 1989 public pressure forced the Lithuanian Communist Party to agree to multiparty elections, which were held in February 1990. These were won by the nationalist Sajudis movement, and the Supreme Council (parliament) declared the restoration of the independence of Lithuania on 11 March 1990. Clashes occurred throughout 1990 between the Lithuanian population and Soviet military forces, culminating in January

1991 with the killing of Lithuanians at the television centre in Vilnius. Over 90 per cent of the population voted for independence in a referendum in February 1991. The Soviet Union recognized the independence of Lithuania on 10 September 1991.

GOVERNMENT

Under the 1992 constitution, executive authority is vested in the government, consisting of the Prime Minister, who is appointed by the President with the approval of the Seimas, and ministers appointed upon the recommendation of the Prime Minister. The government is accountable to the Seimas, and presidential powers are under strict parliamentary control.

Legislative power is exercised by the Seimas, which is a one-chamber parliament of 141 members elected for four-year terms. Seventy-one members are elected in first-past-the-post constituencies and 70 by proportional representation, with a 4 per cent threshold for representation. The constitution bans an alignment of Lithuania with any post-Soviet eastern alliance.

In the parliamentary elections of October and November 1992, a majority of seats in the Seimas were won by the Lithuanian Democratic Labour Party (DLP) (the former Lithuanian Communist Party), which formed a government under Bronislovas Lubys. The DLP leader Algirdas Brazauskas was elected Chairman of the Seimas and acting President of Lithuania until direct presidential elections, which he won in February 1993. The Sajudis leader and former Chairman of the Supreme Council, (President) Vytautas Landsbergis, became leader of the opposition in Parliament. On 10 March 1993 President Brazauskas appointed as Prime Minister Adolfas Šleževičius, who formed a new government on 16 March. In August 1995 the state of the parties in the Seimas was: DLP 73; Sajudis 30; Christian Democratic Party 18; Social Democratic Party 8; others 12.

LOCAL GOVERNMENT

Lithuania is divided into 11 cities and 44 rural districts. Each has a municipal council elected by the local population for a period of five years.

HEAD OF STATE

President, Algirdas Brazauskas, *elected* 14 February 1993 for a five-year term

GOVERNMENT *as at August 1995*

Prime Minister, Adolfas Šleževičius
Agriculture, Vytautas Einoris
Housing and Urban Development, Julius Laiçonas
Communication and Information, Gintautas Žintelis
Culture, Juozas Nekrošius
Economics, vacant
Education and Science, Vladislavas Domarkas
Energy, Arvydas Lěščinskas
Finance, Reinoldijus Šarkinas
Foreign Affairs, Povilas Gylys
Forestry, Albertas Vasiliauskas
Health, Antanas Vinkus
Industry and Trade, Kazimieras Klimašauskas
Interior, Romasis Vaitiekunas
Justice, Jonas Prapiestis
Social Security and Labour, Mindaugas Mikaila
Transportation, Jonas Biržiškis
Defence, Linas Linkevičius
Environment Protection, Bronius Bradauskas
Administrative Reform and Municipal Affairs, Laurynas Stankevičius

EMBASSY OF THE REPUBLIC OF LITHUANIA
17 Essex Villas, London W8 7BP
Tel 0171-938 2481
Ambassador Extraordinary and Plenipotentiary, His Excellency Raimundas Rajeckas, apptd 1994

BRITISH EMBASSY
2 Antakalnio, Gatve, PO Box 863, 2055 Vilnius
Ambassador Extraordinary and Plenipotentiary, His Excellency Thomas Macan, apptd 1994

BRITISH COUNCIL REPRESENTATIVE, Virginija Ziukiene, Vilniaus 39, Vilnius

JUDICIAL SYSTEM

The judicial system comprises the Constitutional Court (consisting of nine judges appointed for terms of nine years), the Supreme Court, Court of Appeal, district and local courts. For the investigation of administrative, labour, family and other litigations, specialized courts may be established pursuant to law. Supreme legal supervision is exercised by the Prosecutor-General and by local prosecutors under his supervision.

DEFENCE

Lithuania has gradually developed its defence forces since independence from the Soviet Union. Total active armed forces personnel stands at 8,900. Authorized conscription for 12 month terms operates and the reserve National Guard numbers a further 12,000 personnel. The army has an active strength of 4,300 personnel organized into a rapid reaction brigade. The navy numbers 350 personnel with two frigates and seven patrol and coastal craft. The air force has 250 personnel, whilst the paramilitary border guard numbers 4,000. The last Russian troops withdrew on 31 August 1993.

ECONOMY

The economy was an agricultural one that was heavily and rapidly industrialized by the Soviet Union in the 1940s and 1950s. The transition of the economy from a centralized system to a free-market one has taken place against the background of a decline in GDP in 1992 of 35 per cent before GDP began to grow again in 1994. The major obstacles met by the programme of privatization begun in September 1991 concern the restitution of agricultural land ownership and large state-owned industrial enterprises that need fundamental technological renovation, but progress in the sale of small enterprises has been quick and successful. By the end of 1993 nearly all housing and agricultural enterprises had been privatized. In October 1994 the IMF approved a three-year loan of US$201 million to support economic stabilization and reform.

Agriculture and forestry are still major sectors of the economy, the chief products being beef, pork, rye, oats, wheat, flax, barley, sugar beet and potatoes. The main industries are chemicals and petrochemicals, food processing, wood products, building materials, textiles, leather goods, machinery, machine tools and household appliances. Lithuania is capitalizing on its clean beaches and picturesque countryside to develop a tourism industry attractive to western visitors.

TRADE

In 1994 trade with western states (51.4 per cent) overtook trade with the CIS (48.6 per cent). The Lithuanian economy is still heavily dependent on Russian supplies of oil, gas and metals.

Trade with UK	1993	1994
Imports from UK	£13,746,000	£24,080,000
Exports to UK	143,377,000	155,387,000

COMMUNICATIONS

Lithuania has a relatively well-developed railway system of 1,240 miles (2,000 km) running east-west and north-south and linking the major towns with Vilnius and Klaipéda, the main international port. Vilnius has an international airport and there are smaller ones at Kaunas, Palanga and Siauliai.

CULTURE

Lithuanian culture and literature are closely linked to the national liberation movements of the 19th and early 20th centuries, and the underground literature of the Soviet occupation era.

There are national television and radio stations and several privately-owned radio stations.

SOCIAL WELFARE

Lithuania re-established a national education system in 1990. There are 2,147 schools of general education with 517,000 pupils (1991). Education begins at age 6–7 years, with the system comprising elementary schools (four years), nine-year schools (five years), and secondary schools (three years). The language of instruction is predominantly Lithuanian, but there are also Russian and Polish schools. There are 108 vocational schools and 65 colleges. Lithuania has six universities and eight other institutes of higher education. Vilnius University, founded in 1579, is one of the oldest universities in eastern Europe.

In 1991 there were 202 hospitals with 45,900 beds, 16,800 physicians and 44,000 paramedical personnel. A national social security system exists which comprises compulsory state social insurance, and social benefits provided by the state. The retirement age is 60 years for men and 55 years for women.

LUXEMBOURG
Grand-Duché de Luxembourg

Luxembourg is a grand duchy in western Europe, bounded by Germany, Belgium and France. The area is 998 sq. miles (2,586 sq. km), the population of 395,200 (1993) is nearly all Roman Catholic. The country is well wooded, with many deer and wild boar. The officially designated 'national language' is Letzebuergesch (Luxembourgish), a mainly spoken language which is a dialect of German with many French admixtures. French and German are the official languages for written purposes, and French is the language of administration.

CAPITAL – Luxembourg, population (1993) 75,800, is a dismantled fortress.
CURRENCY – Luxembourg franc (LF) of 100 centimes. Belgian currency is also legal tender. The Luxembourg franc is linked in a currency union with the Belgian franc.
FLAG – Three horizontal bands, red, white and blue.
NATIONAL ANTHEM – Ons Hémécht (Our homeland).
NATIONAL DAY – 23 June.

GOVERNMENT

Established as an independent state under the sovereignty of the King of the Netherlands as Grand Duke by the Congress of Vienna in 1815, Luxembourg formed part of the Germanic Confederation from 1815 to 1866, and was included in the German 'Zollverein'. In 1867 the Treaty of London declared it a neutral territory. On the death of the King of the Netherlands in 1890 it passed to the Duke of Nassau.

The territory was invaded and overrun by the Germans at the beginning of the war in 1914 but was liberated in 1918. By the Treaty of Versailles 1919, Germany renounced its former agreements with Luxembourg and in 1921 an economic union was made with Belgium. The Grand Duchy was again invaded and occupied by Germany in 1940, and liberated in 1944.

The constitution was modified in 1948 and the stipulation of permanent neutrality was abandoned. Luxembourg is now a signatory of the Brussels and North Atlantic Treaties, and also a member of the European Union. Luxembourg is a member of the Belgium-Netherlands-Luxembourg Customs Union (Benelux 1960).

There is a Chamber of 60 deputies, elected by universal suffrage for five years. Legislation is submitted to the Council of State. The last general election was held on 12 June 1994 and a coalition government was subsequently installed.

HEAD OF STATE
HRH The Grand Duke of Luxembourg, Grand Duke Jean, KG, *born* 5 January 1921; *succeeded* (on the abdication of his mother) 12 November 1964; *married* 9 April 1953 Princess Joséphine-Charlotte of Belgium, and has *issue,* three sons and two daughters
Heir, HRH Prince Henri, *born* 16 April 1955, *married* 14 February 1981, Maria Teresa Mestre, and has *issue,* Prince Guillaume, *b.* 11 November 1981; Prince Felix, *b.* 3 June 1984; Prince Louis, *b.* 3 August 1986; Princess Alexandra, *b.* 2 February 1991; Prince Sébastien, *b.* 16 April 1992.

CABINET *as at August 1995*
Prime Minister, Minister of State, Employment, Finance and Treasury, Jean-Claude Juncker (CD)
Deputy PM, Foreign Affairs, Trade, Overseas Aid and Development, Jacques Poos (SOC)
Agriculture, Rural Development, Small Businesses, Housing and Tourism, Fernand Boden (CD)
Justice, Budget, Relations with Parliament, Marc Fischbach (CD)
Family, Women and the Disabled, Marie-Josée Jacobs (CD)
Education, Cultural and Religious Affairs, Erna Hennicot-Schoepges (CD)
Home Affairs, Civil Service and Administrative Reforms, Michel Wolter (CD)
Economy, Public Works, Energy, Robert Goebbels (SOC)
Environment, Health, Johny Lahure (SOC)
Land Planning, Defence, Youth and Sports, Alex Bodry (SOC)
Social Security, Transport, Post and Communication, Mady Delvaux-Stehres (SOC)
CD Christian Social People's Party; SOC Luxembourg Socialist Worker's Party

EMBASSY OF LUXEMBOURG
27 Wilton Crescent, London SW1X 8SD
Tel 0171-235 6961
Ambassador Extraordinary and Plenipotentiary, His Excellency Joseph Weyland, apptd 1993

BRITISH EMBASSY
14 Boulevard F. D. Roosevelt, L-2450 Luxembourg Ville
Tel: Luxembourg 229864
Ambassador Extraordinary and Plenipotentiary, His Excellency John N. Elam, CMG, apptd 1994

DEFENCE

Luxembourg has a total active armed forces strength of 800 personnel organized into one light infantry battalion. For legal reasons, NATO's squadron of 18 E-3A Sentry airborne early warning aircraft is registered in Luxembourg. The paramilitary gendarmerie number 560 personnel.

ECONOMY

The country has an important iron and steel industry and is an important financial centre. Government revenue for 1994 was estimated at LF 133 million, expenditure LF 135 million.

TRADE WITH UK
(Belgium and Luxembourg)

	1993	1994
Imports from UK	£6,597,146,000	£7,111,693,000
Exports to UK	6,270,295,000	6,886,191,000

MACEDONIA (FORMER YUGOSLAV REPUBLIC OF)

Macedonia is a mountainous landlocked republic situated in the southern Balkans and bordered on the north by the Federal Republic of Yugoslavia (Serbia), on the east by Bulgaria, on the south by Greece and on the west by Albania. It has an area of 9,925 sq. miles (25,713 sq. km).

According to the 1994 census the population is 1,936,877, of whom 66.5 per cent are Macedonian, 22.9 per cent Albanian, 4.0 per cent ethnic Turks, 2.3 per cent gypsies, 2.3 per cent Serbs and 0.4 per cent Vlachs. The census results are disputed by the ethnic Albanians and Serbs.

Macedonian Orthodox Christianity is the majority religion, with a Muslim minority. The main language is Macedonian (a south Slavic language), with Albanian a minority language. Macedonian is written in the Cyrillic script.

CAPITAL – Skopje, population (1991 census) of 448,229.
    Other major towns are Bitola (84,002), Prilep (70,152) and Kumanova (69,231).
CURRENCY – Macedonian Denar.
FLAG – Red with a gold star of sixteen rays in the centre.
NATIONAL ANTHEM – Today over Macedonia.

GOVERNMENT

From the ninth to the 14th centuries AD Macedonia was ruled alternately by the Bulgars and the Byzantine Empire. In the middle of the 14th century the area was conquered by the Turks and remained under the Ottoman Empire for over 500 years. After the defeat of Turkey in the two Balkan wars of 1912–13 the geographical area of Macedonia was divided, the major part becoming Serbian (the areas of the present-day Macedonia) and the remainder given to Greece and Bulgaria. In 1918 on the formation of the Kingdom of the Serbs, Croats and Slovenes (later Yugoslavia), Serbian Macedonia was incorporated into Serbia as South Serbia. When Yugoslavia was reconstituted in 1944 as a Communist federal republic under President Tito, Macedonia became a constituent republic.

Multiparty elections for the 120-seat assembly held in November and December 1990 produced the first non-Communist government since the Second World War. The electorate overwhelmingly approved Macedonian sovereignty and independence in a referendum on 8 September 1991 and Macedonia declared its independence from Yugoslavia on 18 September 1991. A new constitution was adopted in November 1991 and then amended at the EC's request to make it clear that Macedonia had no territorial claim on its neighbours. Macedonia applied for EC recognition in December 1991 but was refused because of Greece's objections to the state's name, flag and currency which, according to the Greek government, amounted to a territorial claim on the Greek province of Macedonia. The peaceful withdrawal of the Yugoslav Army (JNA) from Macedonia was completed in April 1992.

The inability of the government to secure Macedonia's international recognition, which denied it access to international aid, trade and investment, and the effect on the economy of UN trade sanctions against Serbia and Montenegro, caused the downfall of the government in July 1992 and its replacement in September. Tensions between Macedonia and its neighbours grew in late 1992, with Greece imposing a virtual economic blockade and Albania alleging discrimination against ethnic Albanians. Fearing conflict over Macedonia, the UN sent 1,000 peacekeepers in 1992–3 to man border posts with Serbia and Albania. A full UN peacekeeping force, the UN Preventive Deployment Force (UNPREDEP) was established in March 1995.

Macedonia gained UN membership on 8 April 1993 following a compromise with Greece by which it is temporarily known as the 'Former Yugoslav Republic of Macedonia' (FYROM). Following the FYROM compromise Greece reopened its border to Macedonian trade in September 1993, but reimposed its economic blockade and embargo in February 1994 after the majority of EU states established diplomatic relations with Macedonia in December 1993. Greece has been taken to the European Court of Justice by the European Commission over its unilateral embargo.

Presidential and parliamentary elections were held in October 1994, and the presidential election was won by the incumbent, Kiro Gligorov, in the first round. The parliamentary elections to the 120-seat Sobranje (National Assembly) was marred by allegations of ballot-rigging and partially boycotted by the Democratic Party and the nationalist UMRO party. The elections were won by the ruling Alliance for Macedonia (a coalition of the Social Democrat, Liberal and Socialist parties) with 95 seats; the ethnic Albanian parties won 19 seats, and independents six. A coalition government was formed in December 1994 by the Alliance for Macedonia and the Albanian Party for Democratic Prosperity.

Despite the coalition government, ethnic tensions continue between Macedonians and Albanians over the constitution, which Albanians claim to be discriminatory; the 1994 census, which ethnic Albanians partially boycotted; the forbidding of the use of the Albanian language on identity cards and passports; and the Albanian-language university at Tetovo which opened in February 1995 but was forcibly closed by the government, leading to violent clashes and deaths.

HEAD OF STATE
President, Kiro Gligorov, *elected* 27 January 1991, *re-elected* 16 October 1994

GOVERNMENT *as at August 1995*
Prime Minister, Branko Crvenkovski
Deputy PM, Foreign Minister, Stevo Crvenkovski
Interior, Ljubomir Danailov-Frckovski
Defence, Blagoja Handziski
Justice, Vlado Popovski
Economy, Risto Ivanov

Finance, Jane Miljovski
Health, Dr Ilija Filipce
Science, Dr Sofija Todorova
Education and Physical Culture Emilija Simovska
Development, Bekir Zuta
Urbanism, Civil Engineering, Traffic and Environment, Jorgo
  Sundovski
Agriculture, Ivan Angelov
Labour and Social Policy, Ilijaz Sabriu
Culture, Estref Aliu
Ministers without Portfolio, Ljube Trpevski; Guner Ismail;
  Sasko Stefkov

EMBASSY OF THE FORMER YUGOSLAV REPUBLIC OF
MACEDONIA
10 Harcourt House, 19A Cavendish Square, London
WIM 9AD
Tel 0171-499 5152
Ambassador Extraordinary and Plenipotentiary, His Excellency
  Risto Nikovski, apptd 1994

BRITISH EMBASSY
Veljko Vlahović 26, 9100 Skopje
Tel: Skopje 116 772
Ambassador Extraordinary and Plenipotentiary, His Excellency
  Tony Millson, apptd 1994

ECONOMY

Economic activity has been decimated by the UN trade
sanctions against the rump Yugoslav Federal Republic
(Serbia and Montenegro), with which Macedonia previously conducted 60 per cent of its trade. The Greek
economic blockade has deprived Macedonia of most of its
oil supplies and industry has survived on imports from
Turkey and Bulgaria via the one remaining major transportation route, the road from the Bulgarian port of Burgas
to Skopje. Macedonia is attempting to transform its
economy to a market-orientated one and introduce
privatization under an IMF stabilization programme
which began in 1994 with loans totalling US$97 million.
Foreign debt, mostly inherited from the former Yugoslavia, stands at US$846 million, although western donors
have paid off debts to the World Bank. In early 1995
unemployment was 45 per cent and annual inflation 57 per
cent. Output and GDP have fallen significantly since 1990.
Foreign investment has been minimal because of the lack
of international recognition.
  In 1991 41.2 per cent of GDP was produced by industry
and mining and 14 per cent by agriculture. Mineral
resources include nickel, lead, zinc, manganese and iron
ore. The main industrial sectors are basic metal industries,
chemicals, textiles and food processing. Important agricultural crops are wheat, tobacco, rice, wine, lamb, cotton and
sugar beet.

TRADE WITH UK	1993	1994
Imports from UK	£47,612,000	£14,166,000
Exports to UK	41,005,000	5,897,000

MADAGASCAR
Repoblika n'i Madagaskar

Madagascar lies 240 miles off the east coast of Africa and is
the fourth largest island in the world. It has an area of
226,669 sq. miles (587,041 sq. km), and a population (UN
estimate 1992) of 12,827,000. The people are of mixed
Malayo-Polynesian, Arab and African origin. There are
sizeable French, Chinese and Indian communities. The
official languages are Malagasy and French.

CAPITAL – Antananarivo, population estimate 1,250,000.
  Other main towns are the chief port ΨToamasina
  (230,000); ΨMahajanga (200,000); Fianarantsoa
  (300,000); ΨAntsiranana (220,000).
CURRENCY – Franc Malgache (Malagasy franc) (FMG) of
  100 centimes.
FLAG – Equal horizontal bands of red (above) and green,
  with vertical white band by staff.
NATIONAL DAY – 26 June (Independence Day).

GOVERNMENT

Madagascar (known from 1958 to 1975 as the Malagasy
Republic) became a French protectorate in 1895, and a
French colony in 1896 when the former queen was exiled.
Republican status was adopted on 14 October 1958, and
independence was proclaimed on 26 June 1960.
  The post-independence civilian government was re-
placed by a military government in 1975 and the following
month martial law was declared. A Supreme Council of the
Revolution under Capitaine de Frégate (subsequently
Admiral) Didier Ratsiraka was established.
  In November 1991, after six months of strikes and
agitation against his one-party socialist rule, President
Ratsiraka relinquished executive power to a new Prime
Minister, Guy Razanamasy. However, the President
retained his official position and the main opposition
grouping, the *Forces Vives,* established a rival government
led by Albert Zafy. In December 1991 a transitional
government including Forces Vives and Razanamasy
supporters was formed to draft a new constitution which,
after continued instability and Ratsiraka attempting to
regain executive power, was approved by referendum in
August 1992. Presidential elections were held in two
rounds in November 1992 and February 1993, Albert Zafy
emerging victorious with 67 per cent of the vote. He
became the first President of the Third Republic, which
also came into being at the same time. A legislative election
held in June 1993 was won by Forces Vives and allied
parties, with Forces Vives member Francisque Ravony
being elected Prime Minister by parliament in August
1993. The new constitution declares Madagascar to be a
unitary state and reduces the executive powers of the
President.

HEAD OF STATE
President, Professor Albert Zafy, *elected* 10 February 1993

COUNCIL OF MINISTERS *as at August 1995*
Prime Minister, Finance and Budget, Francisque Ravony
Agriculture and Rural Development, Emmanuel Rakotovahiny
Foreign Affairs, Jacques Sylla
Civil Service, Labour and Social Legislation, Henri
  Rakotovololona
Economy, Town Planning and Social Recovery, Tovonanahary
  Rabetsitonta
Industrial Promotion and Craftsmanship, Gedeon Rajohnson
Interior and Decentralization, Charles Clement
Energy and Mining, Bruno Betiana
Transport and Meteorology, Daniel Ramaromisa
Regional Planning, vacant
Culture and Communications, Tsilavina Ralaindimby
Research and Development, Roger Andrianasolo
Public Works, Royal Raoelfils
Police, Bertin Razafindrazaka
Armed Forces, Gen. Charles Rabenja
Secondary and Basic Education, Falgence Fanony
Public Health, Damasy Andriambo
Justice, Ramanoelison Rabendrainy

Higher Education, Adolphe Rakotomanga
Trade and Supplies, Jerome Sambalis
Tourism, Alphonse Ralison
Environment, Georges Aldine Rabelaza
Population, Youth and Sports, Thérèse Ravao
Posts and Telecommunications, Nyhasina Andriamanjato

EMBASSY OF THE REPUBLIC OF MADAGASCAR
4 avenue Raphael, 75016 Paris, France
Tel: Paris 45046211
Ambassador Plenipotentiary and Extraordinary, new
  appointment awaited

HONORARY CONSULATE OF THE REPUBLIC OF
MADAGASCAR
16 Lanark Mansions, Pennard Road, London W12 8DT
Tel 0181-746 0133
Honorary Consul, Stephen Hobbs

BRITISH EMBASSY
1st Floor, Immeuble 'Ny Havana', Cite de 67 Ha,
BP 167, Antananarivo
Tel: Antananarivo 277 49
Ambassador Extraordinary and Plenipotentiary, His Excellency
  Peter John Smith, CBE, apptd 1992

ECONOMY

The economy is still largely based on agriculture, which
accounts for three-quarters of its exports. Development
plans have placed emphasis on increasing agricultural and
livestock production, the improvement of communications, the exploitation of mineral deposits and the creation
of small industries.

TRADE WITH UK	1993	1994
Imports from UK	£5,418,000	£7,881,000
Exports to UK	10,747,000	18,785,000

MALAWI
Dziko La Malawi

Malawi lies in south-eastern Africa. Its neighbours are
Tanzania to the north-east, Zambia to the west, and
Mozambique, which surrounds the southern part of the
country. Much of the eastern border of Malawi is formed
by Lake Malawi (formerly Lake Nyasa), which covers
nearly half of the north of the country. The valley of the
River Shire runs south from the lake, its watershed with the
Zambezi lying on the western border with Mozambique
and its tributary, the Ruo, with lakes Chinta and Chirwa,
lying on the eastern border with Mozambique. The north
and centre are plateaux, and the south highlands. The total
area is 45,747 sq. miles (118,484 sq. km).

According to a UN estimate (1992), the population was
8,823,000. The official languages are Chichewa and
English.

CAPITAL – Lilongwe, population (1987) 223,973. The
city of Blantyre in the south, incorporating Blantyre
and Limbe (population (1987) 331,588), is the major
commercial and industrial centre. Other main centres
are: Mzuzu, Thyolo, Mulanje, Mangochi, Salima,
Dedza and Zomba, the former capital.
CURRENCY – Kwacha (K) of 100 tambala.
FLAG – Horizontal stripes of black, red and green, with
rising sun in the centre of the black stripe.
NATIONAL ANTHEM – O God Bless Our Land of Malawi.
NATIONAL DAY – 6 July (Independence Day).

GOVERNMENT

Malawi (formerly Nyasaland) assumed internal self-
government on 1 February 1963, and became independent
on 6 July 1964. It became a republic on 6 July 1966.

There is a Cabinet consisting of the President and other
ministers. The National Assembly consists of 177 members, each elected by universal suffrage, and usually meets
three times a year. A new multiparty constitution took
effect on 17 May 1994. It ends the idea of the Life
Presidency, reduces presidential powers, establishes the
posts of First and Second Vice-President and provides for a
Senate, to come into being by May 1999.

In late 1991 and the first half of 1992 Life President
Hastings Banda, who had ruled since independence, came
under increasing international and internal pressure to
move towards a multiparty democratic system of government. In May 1992 aid donors tied new loans to improvements in the country's human rights record and moves to
multiparty democracy. A referendum was held on the
adoption of a multiparty democracy in June 1993 and
approved by 63 per cent of voters. President Banda and the
Malawi Congress Party refused to resign but parliament
passed a law to amend the constitution to allow multiparty
politics and Banda announced a political amnesty to allow
exiles to return. Multiparty presidential and legislative
elections were held in May 1994 and won by Bakili Muluzi
and the United Democratic Front (UDF) respectively.
Foreign and multilateral aid has since been restored. A
coalition UDF-AFORD government has been formed. In
August 1995 the state of the parties in parliament was
United Democratic Front (UDF) 84 seats, Malawi Congress Party (MCP) 55 seats, Alliance for Democracy
(AFORD) 36 seats.

HEAD OF STATE
President, Bakili Muluzi, *elected* 17 May 1994, *sworn in* 21
  May 1994
First Vice-President, Justin Malewezi
Second Vice-President, Chakufwa Chihana

CABINET *as at August 1995*
The President
Defence, The First Vice-President
Irrigation, The Second Vice-President
Finance, Economic Planning and Development, Aleka Banda
Tourism, Patrick Mbewe
External Affairs, Edward Bwanali
Information and Broadcasting, Posts and Telecommunications,
  Brown James Mpinganjira
Home Affairs, Wenham Nakanga
Education, Cassim Chilumpha
Justice and Attorney-General, Collins Chizumira
Transport and Civil Aviation, Dr George Ntafu
Agriculture and Livestock Development, Mapopa Chipeta
Health and Population, Sam Mpasu
Local Government and Rural Development, Dr Nasembo
  Mzunda
Lands and Valuation, Alhaji Shaiba Itimu
Energy and Mining, Revd Dr Jombo Lemani
Youth, Sports and Culture, Kamangadadzi Chambalao
Labour and Manpower Development, Richard Sembenuka
Physical Planning and Surveys, Peter Fachi
*Women, Children's Affairs, Community Development and Social
  Welfare,* Edda Chitolo
Relief and Rehabilitation Affairs, Rolph Patel
Natural Resources, Zililo Chibambo
Housing, Timothy Mangwazu
Works and Supplies, Dr Mponda Mkandawire
Research and Environment, Bethwell Kaonga

Commerce and Industry, Peter Kalilombe
Without Portfolio, Harry Thompson

MALAWI HIGH COMMISSION
33 Grosvenor Street, London WIX ODE
Tel 0171-491 4172/7
High Commissioner, His Excellency Jake Muwamba, apptd
1995

BRITISH HIGH COMMISSION
PO Box 30042, Lilongwe 3
Tel: Lilongwe 782400
High Commissioner, His Excellency John Francis Martin,
CMG, apptd 1993

BRITISH COUNCIL REPRESENTATIVE, James Kennedy,
PO Box 30222, Lilongwe 3. There is also a library at
Blantyre.

ECONOMY

The economy is largely agricultural, with maize the main
subsistence crop. Tobacco, sugar, tea, groundnuts and
cotton are the main cash crops and principal exports. There
are two sugar mills and total production in 1989 was 157
million kg. A number of light manufacturing industries
have been established, mainly in agricultural processing,
clothing/textiles and building materials. In November
1994 the IMF approved a US$22 million loan to support
economic reform.

TRADE WITH UK	1993	1994
Imports from UK	£18,021,000	£19,594,000
Exports to UK	21,714,000	25,816,000

COMMUNICATIONS

A single-track railway runs from Mchinji on the Zambian
border, through Lilongwe and Salima on Lake Malawi
(itself served by two passenger and a number of cargo
boats) through to Blantyre. The route south to the
Mozambican port of Beira was severed by the Mozambican
civil war, but the route to Nacala in Mozambique is open
again. There are 12,215 km of roads in Malawi of which
about 21.8 per cent are bituminized. There is an international airport 26 km from Lilongwe, which handles
regional and intercontinental flights.

EDUCATION

Primary education is the responsibility of local authorities
in both urban and rural areas, although policy, curricula
and inspection are the responsibility of the Ministry of
Education and Culture. The Ministry is also responsible
for secondary schools, technical education and primary
teacher training. Religious bodies, with government assistance, still play an important part in these fields. The
University of Malawi was opened in 1965 and has five
constituent colleges.

MALAYSIA
Persekutuan Tanah Malaysia

Malaysia, comprising the 11 states of peninsular Malaya
plus Sabah and Sarawak, lies between 1° and 7° N. latitude
and 100° and 119° E. longitude. It occupies two distinct
regions, the Malay peninsula which extends from the
isthmus of Kra to the Singapore Strait, and the north-west
coastal area of the island of Borneo. Each is separated from
the other by the South China Sea. The total area of
Malaysia is about 127,317 sq. miles (329,749 sq. km).

The year is commonly divided into the south-west and
north-west monsoon seasons. Rainfall averages about 100
inches throughout the year. The average daily temperature varies from 21° C to 32° C, though in higher areas
temperatures are lower and vary widely.

The population was 16,921,300 (1988 census),
19,959,000 official estimate (1995). The principal racial
groups are the Malays (53 per cent), the Chinese (35 per
cent), and those of Indian and Sri Lankan origin, as well as
the indigenous races of Sarawak and Sabah. Bahasa
Malaysia (Malay) is the sole official language, but English,
various dialects of Chinese, and Tamil are also widely
spoken. There are a few indigenous languages widely
spoken in Sabah and Sarawak.

Islam is the official religion of Malaysia, each ruler being
the head of religion in his state (except in Sabah and
Sarawak). The Yang di-Pertuan Agung is the head of
religion in Melaka and Penang. The constitution guarantees religious freedom.

CAPITAL – Kuala Lumpur was proclaimed federal
   territory in 1974. Its population (1990) is 1,231,500.
CURRENCY – Malaysian dollar (ringgit) (M$) of 100 sen.
FLAG – Equal horizontal stripes of red (seven) and white
   (seven); 14-point yellow star and crescent in blue
   canton.
NATIONAL ANTHEM – Negara-Ku.
NATIONAL DAY – 31 August (*Hari Kebangsaan*).

GOVERNMENT

The Federation of Malaya became an independent coun-
try within the Commonwealth on 31 August 1957. On 16
September 1963 the federation was enlarged by the
accession of the states of Singapore, Sabah (formerly
British North Borneo) and Sarawak, and the name of
Malaysia was adopted from that date. On 9 August 1965
Singapore seceded from the federation.

The constitution was designed to ensure the existence of
a strong federal government and also a measure of
autonomy for the state governments. It provides for a
constitutional Supreme Head of the Federation (HM the
Yang di-Pertuan Agung) and a Deputy Supreme Head (HRH
Timbalan Yang di-Pertuan Agung) to be elected for a term of
five years by the rulers from among their number. The
Malay rulers are either chosen or succeed to their position
in accordance with the custom of the particular state. In
other states of Malaysia, choice of the head of state is at the
discretion of the Yang di-Pertuan Agung after consultation
with the Chief Minister of the state.

The Federal Parliament consists of two houses, the
Senate and the House of Representatives. The Senate
(*Dewan Negara*) consists of 68 members, 26 elected by the
Legislative Assemblies of the States (two from each) and 42
appointed by the Yang di-Pertuan Agung. The House of
Representatives (*Dewan Rakyat*) consists of 192 members
elected by universal adult suffrage with a common
electoral roll.

The constitution provides that each state shall have its
own constitution not inconsistent with the federal constitution, with the ruler or Governor acting on the advice of an
Executive Council appointed on the advice of the Chief
Minister and a single-chamber Legislative Assembly. The
Legislative Assemblies are fully elected on the same basis
as the Federal Parliament.

The National Front (Barisan Nasional) Coalition led by
Dr Mahathir Muhammad won a fourth term in office in a
general election held on 25 April 1995, winning 161 of the
192 seats.

HEAD OF STATE

Supreme Head of State, HM Tuanku Jaafar Ibni Al-Marhum Tuanku Abdul Rahman (Yang Dipertuan Besar of Negeri Sembilan), *sworn in* 26 April 1994, *crowned* 22 September 1994.

Deputy Supreme Head of State, HRH Sultan Salahuddin Abdul Aziz Shah Al-Haj ibni Almarhum Sultan Hishamuddin Alam Shah Al-Haj (Sultan of Selangor)

CABINET *as at August 1995*

Prime Minister, Minister of Home Affairs, Hon. Datuk Seri Dr Mahathir Muhammad
Deputy Prime Minister, Minister for Finance, Hon Datuk Seri Anwar Ibrahim
Transport, Hon. Datuk Seri Dr Ling Liong Sik
Energy, Telecommunications and Posts, Hon. Datuk Leo Moggie Anak Irok
Primary Industries, Hon. Datuk Seri Dr Lim Keng Yaik
Works, Hon. Datuk Seri S. Samy Vellu
International Trade and Industry, Hon. Datuk Seri Rafidah Aziz
Education, Hon. Datuk Seri Najib Tun Razak
Agriculture, Hon. Datuk Dr Sulaiman Daud
Rural Development, Senator Datuk Haji Annuar bin Musa
Domestic Trade and Consumer Affairs, Hon. Datuk Haji Abu Hassan bin Haji Omar
Health, Hon. Chua Jui Meng
Foreign Affairs, Hon. Datuk Abdullah bin Haji Ahmad Badawi
Defence, Hon. Datuk Syed Hamid Albar
Information, Hon. Datuk Mohamed bin Rahmat
Culture, Arts and Tourism, Hon. Datuk Sabbaruddin bin Chik
National Unity and Community Development, Hon. Datin Paduka Zaleha Ismail
Entrepreneur Development, Hon. Datuk Mustapa Mohamed
Human Resources, Hon. Datuk Lim Ah Lek
Science, Technology and Environment, Hon. Datuk Law Hieng Ding
Housing and Local Government, Hon. Datuk Dr Ting Chew Peh
Land and Co-operative Development, Hon. Osu bin Haji Sukam
Youth and Sports, Hon. Tan Sri Muhyiddin Yassin
Prime Minister's Department, Hon. Datuk Abang Abu Bakar bin Datu Bandar Abang Haji Mustapha; Hon. Dr Abdul Hamid Othman; Senator Datuk Chong Kah Kiat

NOTE: Tunku/Tengku, Tun, Tan Sri, and Datuk are titles. Tunku/Tengku is equivalent to Prince. Tun denotes membership of a high order of Malaysian chivalry and Tan Sri and Datuk (Datuk Seri in Perak and Datu in Sabah) are each the equivalent of a knighthood. The wife of a Tun is styled Toh Puan, that of a Tan Sri is styled Puan Sri and of a Datuk, Datin. The honorific Tuan or Encik is equivalent to Mr and the honorific Puan is equivalent to Mrs.

MALAYSIAN HIGH COMMISSION
45 Belgrave Square, London SW1X 8QT
Tel 0171-235 8033
High Commissioner, His Excellency Dato Kamarudin Abu, apptd 1992
Deputy High Commissioner, Muhammad Noh
Defence Attaché, Col. Muhammad Yunus
Counsellor (Commercial), Z. M. Perai

BRITISH HIGH COMMISSION
185 Jalan Ampang (PO Box 11030), 50450 Kuala Lumpur
Tel: Kuala Lumpur 2482122
High Commissioner, His Excellency David Moss, CMG, apptd 1994
Deputy High Commissioner, T. N. Byrne

Counsellor (Commercial/Economic), I. R. Murray
Defence Adviser, Col. J. L. Seddon-Brown

BRITISH COUNCIL DIRECTOR, T. Edmundson, PO Box 10539, Jalan Bukit Aman, Kuala Lumpur 50916. There are also offices at Johore Bahru, Kota Kinabalu (Sabah) and Kuching (Sarawak), and a library in Penang.

STATES

The 13 states of the Federation of Malaysia are:

State	Capital	Population (1988 census)
ΨJohore	Johore Bahru	2,007,300
Kedah	Alor Setar	1,353,500
Kelantan	Kota Bahru	1,150,400
ΨMelaka	Melaka	560,700
Negri Sembilan	Seremban	694,100
ΨPahang	Kuantan	1,001,200
ΨPenang	Georgetown	1,103,200
Perak	Ipoh	2,143,200
Perlis	Kangar	179,700
ΨSabah	Kota Kinabalu	1,371,000
ΨSarawak	Kuching	1,591,000
ΨSelangor	Shah Alam	1,878,300
ΨTerengganu	Kuala Terengganu	705,200
Federal Territories		
Kuala Lumpur		} 1,182,700
Labuan		

JUDICATURE

The judicial system consists of a Supreme Court and two High Courts, one in peninsular Malaysia and one for Sabah and Sarawak. The Supreme Court comprises a President, the two Chief Justices of the High Courts and other judges. It possesses appellate, original and advisory jurisdiction.

Each of the High Courts consists of a Chief Justice and not less than four other judges. In peninsular Malaysia the subordinate courts consist of the sessions courts and the magistrates' courts. In Sabah/Sarawak the magistrates' courts constitute the subordinate courts.

DEFENCE

Total active armed forces personnel number 114,500, with volunteer service in operation. The Army has a strength of 90,000 personnel, with 26 light tanks, 388 reconnaissance vehicles, 745 armoured personnel carriers and 200 artillery pieces. Reserve army personnel number 55,000. The Royal Malaysian Navy has a strength of 12,000, with four frigates, 37 patrol and coastal craft and 12 armed helicopters. The Royal Malaysian Air Force has a strength of 92 combat aircraft and 12,500 personnel.

The paramilitary police field force has a strength of 18,000 personnel in 21 battalions, together with marine police (2,100) and air wing units. Border scouts in North Borneo number 1,200.

Malaysia deploys 1,504 infantry in Bosnia-Hercegovina. Australia maintains an infantry company and an air force detachment in Malaysia.

ECONOMY

From being an agriculturally-based economy reliant on raw materials exports at independence, Malaysia has undergone an industrialization programme and now produces clothing, textiles, rubber goods, electronics, office equipment, cars, household appliances, semi-conductors, food processing and chemicals. Under the New Economic Policy of 1970–90, the economy grew at an average rate of

6.7 per cent a year. The National Development Policy 1990–2000 is seen as the second stage in making Malaysia a fully-developed industrial state by 2020. Economic growth in 1990–5 has averaged 8.0 per cent a year. In 1993 44 per cent of GDP was produced by services, 30 per cent by manufacturing and 16 per cent by agriculture.

FINANCE	1992	1993*
Revenue	M$38,106m	M$41,231m
Expenditure	42,414m	41,036m
*estimated		

TRADE

Malaysia is the largest exporter of natural rubber, tin, palm oil and tropical hardwoods. Other major export commodities are manufactured and processed products, petroleum, oil, and other minerals, palm kernel oil, tea and pepper. Exports of major commodities were (1993): manufactured goods 71 per cent, agricultural products 13 per cent, minerals, oil and gas 9 per cent. Imports consist mainly of machinery and transport equipment, manufactured goods, foods, mineral fuels, chemicals and inedible crude materials.

	1992	1993
Imports (c.i.f.)	M$105,805m	M$113,639m
Exports (f.o.b.)	104,608m	120,225m

Trade with UK	1993	1994
Imports from UK	£964,985,000	£1,305,201,000
Exports to UK	1,396,413,000	1,204,026,000

THE MALDIVES
Divehi Jumhuriya

The Maldives are a chain of coral atolls 400 miles to the south-west of Sri Lanka, stretching north for about 600 miles from just south of the Equator. There are about 20 coral atolls comprising over 1,200 islands, 202 of which are inhabited. The total area of the islands is 115 sq. miles (298 sq. km). No point in the entire chain of islands is more than 8 feet above sea-level.

The population of the islands (official estimate 1994) is 246,000. The people are Sunni Muslims and the Maldivian (Dhivehi) language is akin to Elu or old Sinhalese.

CAPITAL – ΨMalé, population (1985) 46,334. There is an international airport at Malé.
CURRENCY – Rufiyaa of 100 laaris.
FLAG – Green field bearing a white crescent, with wide red border.
NATIONAL ANTHEM – Qawmee Salaam.
NATIONAL DAY – 26 July.

GOVERNMENT

Until 1952 the islands were a sultanate under the protection of the British Crown. Internal self-government was achieved in 1948 and full independence in 1965. The Maldives became a special member of the Commonwealth in 1982 and a full member in 1985.

The Maldives form a republic which is elective. There is a legislature, the *Citizens' Majlis*, with representatives elected from all the atolls. The life of the Majlis is five years. The government consists of a Cabinet, which is responsible to the Majlis.

HEAD OF STATE
President, His Excellency Maumoon Abdul Gayoom, *elected* 1978, *re-elected* 1983, 1989, 1 October 1993

CABINET *as at August 1995*
Defence and National Security, The President
Foreign Affairs, Fathulla Jameel
Justice, Mohamed Rasheed Ibrahim
Home Affairs and Sports, Abdulla Jameel
Finance, Maumoon Abdul Gayoom
Education, Mohamad Latheef
Health and Welfare, Ahmed Abdulla
Fisheries and Agriculture, Hassan Sobir
Atolls Administration, Abdul Rasheed Hussain
Trade and Industries, Abdulla Yameen
Tourism, Ibrahim Hussain Zaki
Planning and Environment, Ismail Shafeen
Transport and Shipping, Ahmed Zahir
Minister at the President's Office, Mohamed Zahir Hussain

BRITISH HIGH COMMISSIONER, His Excellency Edward Field, CMG, resides at Colombo, Sri Lanka

ECONOMY

The vegetation of the islands is coconut palms with some scrub. Hardly any cultivation of crops is possible and nearly all food to supplement the basic fish diet has to be imported. The principal industry is fishing and considerable quantities of fish and dried fish are exported to Japan and Sri Lanka. The tourist industry is expanding rapidly (278,000 visitors in 1994). Fishing and tourism together account for about 30 per cent of GDP. The Maldives National Ship Management Ltd (MNSML) has a fleet of nine merchant ships.

TRADE WITH UK	1993	1994
Imports from UK	£4,968,000	£2,580,000
Exports to UK	8,996,000	7,404,000

MALI
République du Mali

Mali, an inland state in north-west Africa, has an area of 478,791 sq. miles (1,240,000 sq. km), and a population (UN estimate 1992) of 9,818,000. The principal rivers are the Niger and the Senegal.

CAPITAL – Bamako (1987 census, 658,275). Other towns are Gao, Kayes, Mopti, Sikasso, Segou and Timbuktu (all regional capitals).
CURRENCY – Franc CFA of 100 centimes.
FLAG – Vertical stripes of green (by staff), yellow and red.
NATIONAL DAY – 22 September.

GOVERNMENT

Formerly the French colony of Soudan, the territory elected on 24 November 1958 to remain an autonomous republic within the French Community. It associated with Senegal in the Federation of Mali, which was granted full independence on 20 June 1960. The Federation was effectively dissolved in August 1960 by the secession of Senegal. The title of the Republic of Mali was adopted in September 1960.

The regime of Modibo Keita was overthrown in 1968 by a group of army officers who formed a National Liberation Committee and appointed a Prime Minister. Moussa Traoré assumed the functions of head of state. A new civil constitution came into being in 1979.

After several months of pro-reform protests, often leading to riots, President Traoré was overthrown in March 1991 by troops led by Lt.-Col. Toure. A military National Reconciliation Committee joined with democratic parties to form a Transitional Committee for the Salvation of the People which suspended the constitution and dissolved the Mali People's Democratic Union (UPDM), formerly the sole party. A transitional government was formed in April. A new constitution was approved by a national conference in August 1991 and by a national referendum in January 1992. The new constitution provided for a multiparty political system, and legislative elections were held in February and March 1992 with the Alliance for Democracy in Mali (ADEMA) emerging victorious. Alpha Konare, the ADEMA leader, won the presidential elections in April 1992 and appointed a government in June dominated by ADEMA members. The government resigned in April 1993 after political unrest in Bamako led by students. On 12 April the President appointed a new cabinet, again dominated by ADEMA, but this was replaced by another ADEMA-dominated cabinet in February 1994.

HEAD OF STATE
President, Alpha Oumar Konare, *elected* 28 April 1992, *sworn in* 8 June 1992

CABINET *as at August 1995*

Prime Minister, Ibrahim Boubacar Keita
Minister of State, Foreign Affairs, Malians Abroad and African Integration, Dioncounda Traore
Mines, Energy and Water Resources, Cheickna Seydou Diawara
Civil Service, Labour and Employment, Boubacar Diarra
Public Works and Transport, Mohamed Ag Erlaf
Finance and Commerce, Soumeyla Cisse
Youth and Sports, Boubacar Coulibaly
Tourism and Crafts, Fatou Haidara
Health, Solidarity and Pensioners, Modibo Sidibe
Territorial Administration and Security, Lt.-Col. Sada Samake
Primary Education, Adama Sammassekou
Rural Development and Environment, Modibo Traore
Justice, Cheikna Kamissoko
Secondary and Higher Education and Scientific Research, Moustapha Dicko
Culture and Communications and Government Spokesman, Bakary Koniba Traore
Armed Forces and Veterans, Momedou Ba
Urbanization and Housing, Sy Kadiatou Sow

EMBASSY OF THE REPUBLIC OF MALI
Avenue Molière 487, 1060 Brussels, Belgium
Tel: Brussels 3457432
Ambassador Extraordinary and Plenipotentiary, His Excellency N'Tiji Traoré, apptd 1993; resident at Brussels
BRITISH AMBASSADOR, His Excellency Alan Furness, CMG, resident at Dakar, Senegal
There is a Consulate in Bamako.

ECONOMY

Mali's principal exports are gold, groundnuts (raw and processed), cotton fibres, meat and dried fish. Mali rejoined the CFA Franc Zone in 1984. In March 1994 the IMF approved a US$41 million credit to support a free market economic reform programme intended to enhance foreign investment and combat the problems of drought and national debt.

TRADE WITH UK	1993	1994
Imports from UK	£9,455,000	£10,841,000
Exports to UK	1,561,000	477,000

MALTA
Repubblika Ta'Malta

Malta lies in the Mediterranean Sea, 58 miles (93 km) from Sicily and about 180 miles (288 km) from the African coast. It is about 17 miles (27 km) in length and 9 miles (14.5 km) in breadth, and has an area of 94.9 sq. miles (246 sq. km). Malta includes also the islands of Gozo (area 25.9 sq. miles (67 sq. km)), Comino and minor islets.

The estimated population in March 1995 was 369,845. The Maltese are mainly Roman Catholic. The Maltese language is of Semitic origin and held by some to be derived from the Carthaginian and Phoenician tongues. Maltese and English are the official languages of administration. Maltese is the official language in all the courts of law and the language of general use in the islands.

CAPITAL – ΨValletta. Population (census 1993), 9,149.
CURRENCY – Maltese lira (LM) of 100 cents and 1,000 mils.
FLAG – Two equal vertical stripes, white at the hoist and red at the fly. A representation of the George Cross is carried edged with red in the canton of the white stripe.
NATIONAL ANTHEM – L-Innu Malti.
NATIONAL DAYS – 31 March (Freedom Day); 8 September (Lady of Victories); 7 June; 21 September (Independence Day); 13 December (Republic Day).

GOVERNMENT

Malta was in turn held by the Phoenicians, Carthaginians, Romans and Arabs. In 1090 it was conquered by Count Roger of Normandy and in 1530 handed over to the Knights of St John, who made it a stronghold of Christianity. In 1565 it sustained the famous siege, when the Turks were successfully withstood by Grandmaster La Valette. The Knights fortified the islands and built Valletta before being expelled by Napoleon in 1798. The Maltese rose against the French garrison soon afterwards and the island was subsequently blockaded by the British fleet. The Maltese people freely requested the protection of the British Crown in 1802 on condition that their rights and privileges would be preserved and respected. The islands were finally annexed to the British Crown by the Treaty of Paris 1814.

Malta was again closely besieged in the Second World War. From June 1940 to the end of the war, 432 members of the garrison and 1,540 civilians were killed by enemy aircraft, and about 35,000 houses were destroyed or damaged. The island was awarded the George Cross for gallantry on 15 April 1942.

On 21 September 1964 Malta became an independent state within the Commonwealth, and on 13 December 1974 a republic within the Commonwealth.

Elections are held for the unicameral Parliament of 65 members every five years by a system of proportional representation. Seats are obtained by the highest number of votes in the respective districts. The party with the highest number of votes forms the government, with extra members being co-opted if necessary.

Malta applied for EC membership in 1990 and in June 1993 the Commission issued its opinion that Malta should be accepted as a member once it had carried out a series of economic reforms to restructure its economy in line with

EU policies. In June 1995 the European Council confirmed that most of the reforms were being carried out successfully and that accession negotiations would be opened in 1997.

HEAD OF STATE
President, Dr Ugo Mifsud Bonnici, *took office* 4 April 1994

CABINET *as at August 1995*

Prime Minister, Dr Edward Fenech Adami
Deputy PM and Minister of Foreign Affairs, Prof. Guido de Marco
Education and Human Resources, Michael Falzon
Social Development, Dr Louis Galea
Economic Services, Prof. Josef Bonnici
Environment, Dr Francis Zammit Dimench
Food, Agriculture and Fisheries, Censu Galea
Home Affairs, Tonio Borg
Justice and the Arts, Dr Michael Refalo
Transport, Communications and Technology, Dr Michael Frendo
Gozo, Anton Tabone
Finance, John Dalli

MALTA HIGH COMMISSION
Malta House, 36–38 Piccadilly, London WIV OPQ
Tel 0171-292 4800
High Commissioner, His Excellency Saviour Stellini, apptd 1991

BRITISH HIGH COMMISSION
7 St Anne Street, Floriana (PO Box 506)
Tel: Floriana 233134/8
High Commissioner, His Excellency Graham Archer, apptd 1995

BRITISH COUNCIL REPRESENTATIVE, Anne Bradley, c/o British High Commission

ECONOMY

Agriculture and fisheries contributed 3 per cent of GDP in 1993 and employed 2.4 per cent of the workforce. Principal products are animal products, vegetables, fruit (especially grapes), flowers and cuttings.

The island's leading industry is the state-owned Malta Drydocks, employing about 3,329 people. The main port of Grand Harbour handled traffic of 1.75 million tonnes in 1993. Malta Freeport was opened in 1990 in the southern port of Marsaxlokk and comprises a container distribution centre, an oil products terminal and warehouse facilities. A second container terminal is being built.

In 1993 manufacturing employed 27.7 per cent of the workforce and accounted for 24 per cent of GDP. Industries include food processing, textiles, footwear and clothing, plastics and chemical products, electronic equipment, machinery and components. The gross output of the manufacturing industry in 1993 was LM708.9 million, of which LM475.6 million were export sales.

Tourism has assumed primary importance, with 1,176,223 tourists visiting the island in 1994, and Marsamxett Harbour has been further developed by the extension of a yacht centre. The number of cruise liners calling at the Grand Harbour has increased considerably. Gross income from this industry stood at LM241.6 million in 1994. In 1994 2,565,000 passengers passed through Malta airport.

FINANCE

	1992	1993
Revenue	LM395,036,000	LM428,310,000
Expenditure	388,032,000	455,972,000

TRADE

The principal imports are foodstuffs (mainly wheat, meat and bullocks, milk and fruit), fodder, beverages and tobacco, fuels, chemicals, textiles and machinery (industrial, agricultural and transport). The chief exports are processed food, electronics, textiles, and other manufactures.

	1992	1993
Imports	LM747,770,000	LM830,920,000
Exports	490,903,000	518,325,000

Trade with UK	1993	1994
Imports from UK	£206,113,000	£205,463,000
Exports to UK	62,961,000	75,096,000

EDUCATION

In 1994 there were 65 government kindergarten centres with 7,850 pupils, 81 government primary schools with 23,614 pupils, 34 secondary and junior lyceum schools with a total of 19,426 pupils, and 10 post-secondary upper lyceum schools with 5,000 students.

The government also runs several technical/trade schools (with an enrolment of 3,685 students). Tertiary education is available at the University of Malta, which had 5,500 students in 1994.

There are 94 private schools (67 run by the Roman Catholic Church) with 25,040 students. Education is compulsory from five to sixteen years and is free from kindergarten to university in both private and government sectors.

MARSHALL ISLANDS
Republic of the Marshall Islands

The Republic of the Marshall Islands consists of 29 atolls and five islands in the central Pacific Ocean lying between 4° and 19° N., and 160° and 175° E. The islands and atolls are scattered over 1,294,500 sq. km (500,000 sq. miles), forming two parallel chains running north-west to south-east: the Ratak (Sunrise) chain and the Ralik (Sunset) chain. The total land area is 70 sq. miles (181 sq. km). The largest atoll is Kwajalein in the Ralik chain. The atolls are coral and the islands are volcanic. None of the islands rises more than a few metres above sea level. The climate is hot and humid with little seasonal variation in temperature. The typhoon season lasts from December to March.

The population is 50,000 (1992 UN estimate), of which 99 per cent are Micronesian. Over half the population is under 15. About 60 per cent of the population is concentrated on the two atolls of Majuro and Kwajalein.

The population is Christian, primarily Protestant but with a substantial Catholic minority. The principal Protestant denomination is the United Church of Christ. Marshallese and English are the official languages.

CAPITAL – Majuro (population 20,000). The other major town is Ebeye (9,200).
CURRENCY – US Dollar.
FLAG – Blue with a diagonal ray divided white over orange running from the lower hoist to the upper fly; in the canton a white sun.
NATIONAL DAY – 21 October (Compact Day).

GOVERNMENT

The Marshall Islands were claimed by Spain in 1592 but were left undisturbed by the Spanish Empire for 300 years. In 1886 the Marshall Islands formally became a German protectorate. On the outbreak of the First World War in 1914, Japan took control of the islands on behalf of the Allied powers, and after the war administered the territory as a League of Nations mandate. During the Second World War US armed forces took control of the islands from the Japanese after intense fighting. In 1947 the USA entered into agreement with the UN Security Council to administer the Micronesia area, of which the Marshall Islands are a part, as the UN Trust Territory of the Pacific Islands.

The islands became internally self-governing in 1979, and the US Trusteeship administration came to an end on 21 October 1986, when a Compact of Free Association between the USA and the Republic of the Marshall Islands came into effect. By this agreement the USA recognized the Republic of the Marshall Islands as a fully sovereign and independent state. The UN Security Council terminated the UN Trust Territory of the Pacific in relation to the Marshall Islands and recognized its independence in December 1990.

The republic is a democracy based on a parliamentary system of government. Under the 1979 constitution, the executive is under the leadership of the President, who is elected by the *Nitijela* from among its members. The President serves for a four-year term. The legislature has two chambers, the Council of Iroij of 12 members and the Nitijela of 33 members. The Nitijela is the law-making chamber, to which the President and government are accountable. The Council of Iroij has an advisory role.

There are 24 local government districts, each of which usually consists of an elected council, a mayor and appointed local officials.

The Republic of the Marshall Islands has no defence forces. The Compact of Free Association places full responsibility for defence of the Marshall Islands on the USA. The US Department of Defence retains control of islands within Kwajalein Atoll where it has a missile test range.

HEAD OF STATE

President, Hon. Amata Kabua, *elected* 1979, *re-elected* 1984, 1988, 1992

THE GOVERNMENT *as at August 1995*

The President
Finance, Ruben Zackras
Foreign Affairs, Phillip Muller
Transport and Communications, Kunio Lemari
Resources and Development, Lomes McKay
Education, Evelyn Konou
Social Services, Christopher Loeak
Public Works, Hiroshi Yamamura
Health and Environment, Thomas Kijner
Justice, Luckner Abner
Internal Affairs, Brenson Wase

BRITISH AMBASSADOR, His Excellency Michael Peart, CMG, LVO, resident at Suva, Fiji

JUDICIARY

There are four court levels: the Supreme Court; the High Court; the district and community courts; and the traditional rights courts. Trial is by jury. Jurisdiction of the traditional rights courts is limited to cases involving titles or land rights and other disputes arising from customary law and traditional practice.

ECONOMY

The economy is a mixture of subsistence and a service-based sector. About half the working population is engaged in agriculture and fishing, with coconut oil and copra production comprising 90 per cent of total exports. The service sector is based in Majuro and Ebeye and concentrated in banking and insurance, construction, transporta-

tion and tourism. Direct US aid under the Compact accounts for two-thirds of the islands budget. The islands charge large foreign (mainly Japanese) fishing fleets licences for fishing tuna in the waters around the islands. Japanese fleets pay some US$3 million a year. The USA and Japan are the major trading partners.

The GDP was (1988) US$68 million and GDP per head (1988) was US$1,600.

TRADE WITH UK	1993	1994
Imports from UK	£1,666,000	£2,403,000
Exports to UK	—	76,000

COMMUNICATIONS

Air Marshall Islands provides air services within the islands and to Hawaii. Continental Air Micronesia serves Majuro and Kwajalein with flights to Hawaii and Guam. Majuro also has shipping links to Hawaii, Australia, Japan and throughout the Pacific.

SOCIAL WELFARE

The state school system provides education up to age 18, but only 25 per cent of students proceed beyond elementary level because of inadequate resources.

Majuro and Ebeye have hospitals run by the government with aid from the US Public Health Service. Each outer island community has a health assistant.

MAURITANIA
République Islamique de Mauritanie

Mauritania lies on the north-west coast of Africa. It is bounded on the south by Senegal, on the south and east by Mali, and on the north by Algeria and the Western Sahara. The area is 397,955 sq. miles (1,030,700 sq. km). The population (UN estimate 1992) is 2,143,000. The official languages are French and Arabic.

CAPITAL – Nouakchott (850,000).
CURRENCY – Ouguiya of 5 khoums.
FLAG – Yellow star and crescent on green ground.
NATIONAL DAY – 28 November.

GOVERNMENT

Mauritania elected on 28 November 1958 to remain within the French Community as an autonomous republic. It became fully independent on 28 November 1960. In 1972 Mauritania left the Franc Zone.

Mauritania and Morocco occupied the Western Sahara territory in February 1976 when Spain formally relinquished it and in April 1976 agreed on a new frontier dividing the territory between them. In August 1979, Mauritania relinquished all claim to the southern sector of the Western Sahara after a three-year war against Polisario Front guerrillas.

After a military coup in 1978, Mauritania was ruled by a Military Committee for National Salvation (CMSN). Having previously rejected reform, in April 1991 President Ould Taya announced a political amnesty and a referendum on the constitution, followed by multiparty elections for a reconvened Senate and National Assembly. The constitution was approved in July. Multiparty elections to the Senate and National Assembly were held in March 1992 and won by the Republican Democratic and Social Party (PRDS) led by President Ould Taya. The President appointed a cabinet of PRDS members in April 1992 but the legitimacy of the new government was undermined by the boycott of the elections by the main opposition grouping, the Union of Democratic Forces (UDF). Tension continues between the Arab-dominated government and the African minority in the south of the country.

HEAD OF STATE

President, Col. Maaouya Ould Sidi Ahmed Taya, *took power* 12 December 1984, *elected* 17 January 1992

CABINET *as at August 1995*

Prime Minister, Sidi Mohammed Ould Boubaker
Foreign Affairs and Co-operation, Mohammed Salem Ould Lekhel
Defence, Abdallahi Ould Abdi
Justice, Adema Samba Sow
Interior, Posts and Telecommunications, Lemrabet Cheikh Ahmed
Finance, Sidi Mohammed Ould Biya
Planning, Ch'Bih Ould Cheikh Melainine
Fisheries and Maritime Economy, Cheikh Afia Ould Mohammed Khouna
Commerce, Handicrafts and Tourism, Digana Moussa
Mines and Industry, N'Gaide Lamine
Secretary-General of the Presidency, Col. Ahmed Ould Minnih
Civil Service, Labour, Youth and Sports, Sidi Mohammed Ould Mohammed Fall
Equipment and Transport, Sow Mohammed Deina
Education and Literacy, Louleid Ould Weddad

EMBASSY OF THE ISLAMIC REPUBLIC OF MAURITANIA
5 rue de Montevideo, Paris XVIe, France
Tel: Paris 45048854
Ambassador Extraordinary and Plenipotentiary, His Excellency Muhammad Al-Hanchi Ould Muhammad Saleh, apptd 1989, resident at Paris

BRITISH AMBASSADOR, His Excellency Sir Allan Ramsay, KBE, CMG, resident at Rabat, Morocco

ECONOMY

The main source of potential wealth lies in rich deposits of iron ore around Zouérate, in the north of the country, and rich fishing grounds off the coast.

In October 1992 Mauritania agreed a four-year economic restructuring programme with the IMF to reduce inflation and the country's external debt. In late 1992 the IMF announced a US$47 million loan to support the government's economic and financial reform programme up to September 1995, with further loans of US$23 million announced in January 1994 and US$63 million in January 1995.

	1993	1994
TRADE WITH UK		
Imports from UK	£8,418,000	£9,949,000
Exports to UK	15,071,000	10,978,000

MAURITIUS

Mauritius is an island group lying in the Indian Ocean, 550 miles east of Madagascar, between 57° 17′ and 57° 46′ E. longitude and 19° 58′ and 20° 33′ S. latitude. Mauritius and Rodrigues with the other outer islands comprise an area of 790 sq. miles (2,045 sq. km). The climate is sub-tropical and maritime, with a wide range of rainfall and temperature resulting from the mountainous nature of the island. Humidity is high throughout the year.

The population (1994 estimate, excluding Rodrigues and the outer islands) was 1,082,998, made up of Asiatic races (Hindus 51.8 per cent, Muslims 16.5 per cent,

Chinese 2.8 per cent), and persons of European (mainly French) extraction, mixed and African descent (28.6 per cent). English is the official language but French may be used in the National Assembly and lower law courts. However, Creole is the most commonly used language and several Indian languages are also used.

CAPITAL – ΨPort Louis, population (1993) 144,250; other centres are Beau Bassin-Rose Hill (95,966); Curepipe (76,133); Vacoas-Phoenix (92,846) and Quatre Bornes (72,999).
CURRENCY – Mauritius rupee of 100 cents.
FLAG – Red, blue, yellow and green horizontal stripes.
NATIONAL ANTHEM – Glory to thee, Motherland.
NATIONAL DAY – 12 March.

GOVERNMENT

Mauritius was discovered in 1511 by the Portuguese; the Dutch visited it in 1598 and named it Mauritius after Prince Maurice of Nassau. From 1638 to 1710 it was held as a Dutch colony and in 1715 the French took possession but did not settle it until 1721. Mauritius was taken by a British force in 1810 and became a Crown Colony. Mauritius became an independent state within the Commonwealth on 12 March 1968 and a republic on 12 March 1992.

The President is head of state and is elected by the members of the National Assembly. The Prime Minister, appointed by the President, is the member of the National Assembly who appears to the President best able to command the support of the majority of members of the Assembly. Other ministers are appointed by the President acting in accordance with the advice of the Prime Minister.

The National Assembly has a normal term of five years and consists of 62 elected members (the island of Mauritius is divided into 20 three-member constituencies and Rodrigues returns two members), and eight specially-elected members. Of the latter, four seats go to the 'best loser' of whichever communities in the island are under-represented in the Assembly after the general election and the four remaining seats are allocated on the basis of both party and community.

The last general election was held on 15 September 1991. The present government is a coalition of the Mouvement Socialiste Militant (MSM), Renouveau Militant Mauricien (RMM), the Mouvement Travailliste Democrate (MTD) and the Parti Mauricien Social Democrate (PMSD) which holds a total of 43 seats.

HEAD OF STATE

President, Cassam Uteem, *elected* June 1992

COUNCIL OF MINISTERS *as at August 1995*

Prime Minister, Minister of Defence and Internal Security, Institutional Reform and the Outer Islands, Rt. Hon. Sir Anerood Jugnauth, KCMG, QC
Deputy PM, Minister for Economic Planning and Development, Information, and Internal and External Communications, Hon. Dr Paramhamsa Nababsing
External Affairs, Hon. Ramduthsing Jaddoo
Finance, Hon. Ramakrishna Sithanen
Education and Science, Hon. Armoogum Parsuramen
Trade and Shipping, Hon. Dwarkanath Gungah
Energy, Water Resources, Scientific Research and Technology, and Postal Services, Hon. Ahmud Swaley Kasenally
Housing, Lands and Town and Country Planning, Hon. Louis Darga
Social Security and National Solidarity, Hon. Dharmanand Goopt Fokeer
Women's Rights, Child Development and Family Welfare, Hon. Sheilabhai Bappoo

Rodrigues, Hon. Serge Clair
Co-operatives and Handicrafts, Hon. Jagdishwar Goburdhun
Agriculture and Natural Resources, Hon. Keertee Coomar
   Ruhee
Tourism, Industry and Industrial Technology, Hon. Sir Gaëtan
   Xavier Duval, KCMG
Works, Hon. Anil Kumar Bachoo
Local Government, Hon. Premdut Koonjoo
Civil Service Affairs and Employment, Hon. Ashok Kumar
   Jugnauth
Environment and Quality of Life, Hon. Ahmud Khodabux
Manpower Resources, Vocational and Technical Training, Hon.
   Noel Ah-Quret Lee Cheong Lem
Health, Hon. Jean Regis Finette
Fisheries and Marine Resources, Hon. Mathieu Ange Laclé
Arts, Culture and Youth Development, Hon. Mookhesswur
   Choonee
Labour and Industrial Relations, Hon. Karl Auguste Offman
Attorney-General, Justice, Hon. Sir Maurice Louis Rault,
   KCMG

MAURITIUS HIGH COMMISSION
32–33 Elvaston Place, London SW7 5NW
Tel 0171-581 0294
High Commissioner, His Excellency Babooram Mahadoo,
   apptd 1992

BRITISH HIGH COMMISSION
Les Cascades Building, Edith Cavell Street, Port Louis
(PO Box 1063)
Tel: Port Louis 211 1361
High Commissioner, His Excellency John Clive Harrison,
   apptd 1993

BRITISH COUNCIL DIRECTOR, M. Bootle, PO Box 111,
   Foondun Building, 2nd Floor, Royal Road, Rose Hill.

ECONOMY

About 55 per cent of the total sugar crop is produced on plantations, while smaller owners (cultivating less than ten acres) cultivate about 24 per cent of the land under cane. Tea and tobacco are also grown commercially but on a smaller scale than sugar. Production in 1994 was: sugar, 500,209 tonnes; tea (manufactured), 5,089 tonnes; tobacco (leaves), 1,025 tonnes. In 1994 production of molasses, mainly for export, was 138,421 tonnes. Other products include alcohol, rum, denatured spirits, perfumed spirits and vinegar.

The bulk of the island's requirements in manufactured products still has to be imported. However, the Mauritius Export Processing Zone (MEPZ) scheme, introduced in 1971, has attracted investment from overseas and the number of export-orientated enterprises had risen from ten in 1971 to 509 at the end of 1994, employing 83,862 people. The biggest firms are in clothing manufacture, particularly woollen knitwear, but the range of goods produced includes toys, plastic products, leather goods, diamond cutting and polishing, watches, television sets and telephones.

Tourism is a major source of income, with an estimated 400,000 tourists in 1994. Earnings from tourism in 1994 are estimated to be Rs.6,052 million. France is the most important source of tourists, followed closely by the neighbouring French island of Réunion.

FINANCE

The main sources of government revenue are private and company income tax, customs and excise duties, mainly on imports but also on sugar exports.

	1993	1994
Public revenue	Rs.12,937m	Rs.13,800m
Public expenditure (recurrent)	13,250m	14,290m

TRADE

Most foodstuffs and raw materials have to be imported from abroad. Apart from local consumption (about 36,500 tonnes a year), the sugar produced is exported, mainly to Britain.

	1993	1994
Total imports	Rs.30,319m	Rs.34,473m
Total exports	23,522m	24,697m
Trade with UK	1993	1994
Imports from UK	£73,335,000	£75,182,000
Exports to UK	281,362,000	292,504,000

COMMUNICATIONS

Port Louis, on the north-west coast, handles the bulk of the island's external trade. A bulk sugar terminal capable of handling the total crop began operating in 1980. The international airport is located at Plaisance about five miles from Mahébourg. There are four daily newspapers and 15 weeklies, mostly in French, and two Chinese daily papers and one weekly paper. The Mauritius Broadcasting Corporation operates television and radio broadcasting in the country. There is a satellite communications ground station near Port Louis.

EDUCATION

Primary and secondary education are free and primary education is compulsory. In 1994 212,748 children were in education, with 123,167 children at 279 primary schools. At secondary level there were a total of 89,581 students attending 127 secondary schools; fees and teachers' salaries in the private secondary schools are paid by government. There are a number of training facilities offering vocational training. The Institute of Education is responsible for training primary and secondary schoolteachers and for curriculum development. The University of Mauritius had 2,186 students in 1994–5. Estimated expenditure on education in 1994–5 was Rs.2,062,875,000.

RODRIGUES AND DEPENDENCIES

Rodrigues, formerly a dependency but now part of Mauritius, is about 350 miles east of Mauritius, with an area of 40 square miles. Population (1994) 34,652. Cattle, salt fish, sheep, goats, pigs, maize and onions are the principal exports. The island is administered by an Island Secretary.

Island Secretary, B. Juggoo

The islands of Agalega and St Brandon are dependencies of Mauritius. Total population (1989) 500.

MEXICO
Estados Unidos Mexicanos

Mexico occupies the southern part of North America, with an extensive seaboard to both the Atlantic and Pacific Oceans, extending from 14° 33' to 32° 43' N. latitude and 86° 46' to 117° 08' W. longitude. It covers an area of 761,605 sq. miles (1,972,547 sq. km).

The Sierra Nevada, known in Mexico as the Sierra Madre, and Rocky Mountains continue south from the northern border with the USA, running parallel to the west and east coasts. The interior consists of an elevated plateau between the two ranges. In the west is the peninsula of Lower California, separated from the mainland by the Gulf of California. The main rivers are the Rio Grande (Rio Bravo) del Norte, which forms part of the northern boundary and is navigable for about 70 miles from its mouth in the Gulf of Mexico, and the Rio Grande de Santiago, the Rio Balsas and Rio Papaloapan.

At the 1990 census, the population was 81,140,922; a 1992 UN estimate gives a figure of 89,538,000. Spanish is the official language and is spoken by about 95 per cent of the population. In addition, there are five main groups of Indian languages (Náhuatl, Maya, Zapotec, Otomí, Mixtec) and 59 dialects derived from them. The poet Octavio Paz won the Nobel Prize for Literature in 1991.

CAPITAL – Mexico City, population of metropolitan area (1990 census) 14,987,051. Other cities (1990 census) are:

Guadalajara	2,846,000	Puebla	1,454,526
Monterrey	2,521,697	León	956,070
Torreón	876,456	Ciudad Juarez	797,679
Toluca	827,339	Tijuana	742,686

CURRENCY – Peso of 100 centavos.

FLAG – Three vertical bands in green, white, red, with the Mexican emblem (an eagle on a cactus devouring a snake) in the centre.

NATIONAL ANTHEM – Mexicanos, Al Grito De Guerra (Mexicans, to the war cry).

NATIONAL DAY – 16 September (Proclamation of Independence).

HISTORY

The present Mexico and Guatemala were once the centre of a civilization which flowered in the periods from AD 500 to 1100 and 1300 to 1500 and collapsed before the little army of Spanish adventurers under Hernán Cortés in the years following 1519. Pre-Columbian Mexico was divided between different but connected Indian cultures, each of which has left distinctive archaeological remains. The best-known of these are Chichén Itzá, Uxmal, Bonampak and Palenque, in Yucatán and Chiapas (Maya); Teotihuacon, renowned for the Pyramid of the Sun in the Valley of Mexico (Teotihuacáno); Monte Albán and Mitla, near Oaxaca (Zapotec); El Tajín in the state of Veracruz (Totonac); and Tula in the state of Hidalgo (Toltec). The last and most famous Indian culture, the Aztec, based on Tenochitlán, suffered more than the others from the Spanish and very few Aztec monuments remain.

After the conquest, the Spanish appointed a Viceroy to rule their new dominions, which they called New Spain. The country was largely converted to Christianity and a distinctive colonial civilization, representing a marriage of Indian and Spanish traditions, developed. In 1810 a revolt began against Spanish rule. This was finally successful in 1821, when a precarious independence was proclaimed.

Friction with the USA in Texas led to the war of 1845–8, at the end of which Mexico was forced to cede the northern provinces of Texas, California and New Mexico. In 1862 Mexican insolvency led to invasion by French forces which installed Archduke Maximilian of Austria as Emperor. The empire collapsed with the execution of the Emperor in 1867 and the austere reformer Juárez restored the republic. Juárez's death was followed by the dictatorship of Porfirio Díaz, which saw an enormous increase in foreign, particularly British and American, investment in the country. In 1910 began the Mexican Revolution which reformed the social structure and the land system, curbed the power of foreign companies and ushered in the independent industrial Mexico of today. In 1986 Mexico joined GATT

and began a liberalization programme of privatization and administrative reform.

GOVERNMENT

Under the 1917 constitution (as subsequently amended), Congress consists of a Senate of 128 members, elected for six years, and of a Chamber of Deputies, at present numbering 500, elected for three years. Presidents, who wield full executive powers, are elected for six years; they cannot be re-elected.

There are nine registered political parties, of which the largest and most influential is the Partido Revolucionario Institucional (PRI) which for more than 60 years has constituted the governing party despite constant allegations of electoral fraud. The main opposition parties are Partido de Acción Nacional (PAN) and Partido de la Revolución Democrática (PRD). In June 1995 the state of the parties in the Chamber of Deputies was: PRI 302, PAN 123, PRD 69, other parties six. In the Senate the state of the parties was PRI 95, PAN 25, PRD 8.

In 1988–94 President Salinas de Gortari reformed Mexico's political, economic and social systems. Economic reforms have brought about significant economic growth, whilst political reform has reduced corruption and the autocratic control by the PRI. However, certain areas of the country and sections of the population remain untouched by the reforms. An armed revolt of Zapatista peasant Indians in the southern state of Chiapas in January 1994 highlighted continuing charges against the PRI of corruption and fraud at national and local level, and these continued up to the 21 August 1994 presidential and Congressional elections. Although fraud and irregularities in the elections were confirmed, they were considered to be on a much smaller scale than in the past. PRI candidate Ernesto Zedillo won the presidential election with 50 per cent of the vote.

A further armed revolt by the Zapatista National Liberation Army (ZNLA) in Chiapas from December 1994 to February 1995 caused a crisis of confidence in the government and economy by foreign investors and a run on the peso. Insolvency and defaulting on the foreign debt was only averted by a US$50,000 million loan package from the USA and international institutions. President Zedillo responded to the political crisis by introducing political reforms agreed with the PAN and PRD, making the electoral commission fully independent and providing for the re-examination of contentious elections by impartial observers. Negotiations were also opened with the ZNLA in Chiapas province, where the PRI governor was removed.

The country is divided into 31 states and the federal district of Mexico City.

HEAD OF STATE
President, Dr Ernesto Zedillo Ponce de León, *elected* 4 June 1994, *took office* 1 December 1994

CABINET *as at August 1995*

Interior, Emilio Chauyffet Chemor
Foreign Affairs, José Angel Gurria
Finance and Public Credit, Guillermo Ortiz
Defence, Gen. Enrique Cervantes Aguirre
Navy, Adm. José Ramón Lorenzo Franco
Energy, Ignacio Pichardo Pagaza
Trade and Industry, Herminio Blanco
Agriculture, Rural Development and Livestock, Francisco Ochoa
Communications and Transport, Carlos Ruiz Sacristán
Education, Miguel Limón Rojas
Social Development, Carlos Rojas
Health, Juan Ramón Ramirez

Employment and Social Welfare, Santiago Laborde
Agrarian Reform, Arturo Warman
Tourism, Silvia Hernández
Fishing, Environment and Natural Resources, Julia Caravias
Attorney-General, Antonio Lozano
Attorney-General of Federal District, José Antonio Fernández
Comptroller-General, Norma Samaniego
Mayor of Mexico City, Oscar Espinoza Villarreal

MEXICAN EMBASSY
42 Hertford Street, London WIY 7TF
Tel 0171-499 8586
Ambassador Extraordinary and Plenipotentiary, His Excellency
Andrés Rozental, apptd 1995
Minister, Deputy Ambassador, J. Brito-Moncada
Military Attaché, Gen. Rafael Ramos-Padilla
Minister, Consul-General, J. Ibarra
Counsellor, F. Estandia (*Commercial*)

BRITISH EMBASSY
Calle Río Lerma 71, Colonia Cuauhtémoc,
06500 Mexico City
Tel: Mexico City 207 20 89
Ambassador Extraordinary and Plenipotentiary, His Excellency
Adrian John Beamish, CMG, apptd 1994
Deputy Ambassador and Counsellor, G. Berg
Defence Attaché, Col. S. R. Daniell
First Secretary (*Commercial*), M. H. McIntosh

There are British Consular Offices at Mexico City,
Acapulco, Cancun, Guadalajara, Mérida, Monterrey,
Tampico, Tijuana, Veracruz, and Cuidad Juarez.

BRITISH COUNCIL DIRECTOR, Dr Frank Edwards,
Maestro Antonio Caso 127, Col. San Rafael (PO Box
30-588), Mexico 06470 DF.

BRITISH CHAMBER OF COMMERCE, British Trade Centre,
Rio de la Plata 30, Col. Cuauhtemoc, CP 06500,
Mexico City DF, *Manager*, Stephen Grant.

DEFENCE

The total armed forces number some 175,000, including
60,000 conscripts. Conscription is decided by lottery and is
for a one-year period. The Army has a strength of 130,000
(including 60,000 conscripts), with 350 reconnaissance
vehicles, 110 armoured personnel carriers, 120 artillery
pieces.

The Navy has a strength of 37,000 personnel, including
8,000 marines, with three destroyers, two frigates, 104
patrol and coastal vessels, and nine combat aircraft. The Air
Force is 8,000 strong, with 101 combat aircraft and 25
armed helicopters.

ECONOMY

Political and economic uncertainty in late 1994 caused an
economic crisis and a collapse in the value of the peso until
supported by international loans. Since January 1995 the
government has introduced two austerity packages, increasing interest rates and petrol taxes, curbing pay levels
and reducing public expenditure in an attempt to keep
inflation and debt levels under control and to rein back a
runaway trade deficit. Inflation has risen to 14 per cent
(from 7 per cent in 1994) and unemployment is rising.
Mexico joined the OECD in 1994.

In 1991 26 per cent of GDP was produced by commerce,
23 per cent by manufacturing, 33.6 per cent by services, 5
per cent by construction, 7.4 per cent by agriculture, 3.5 per
cent by mining and 1.5 per cent by public utilities. Direct
foreign investment at the end of 1991 was a cumulative
US$33.9 billion, of which over 60 per cent was American.
Privatization has been successful, with only 208 public

enterprises remaining in 1991 (1,155 in 1982). Agriculture
has been reformed to allow communal farmers to buy and
sell their own plots.

The principal crops are maize, beans, rice, wheat, sugar
cane, coffee, cotton, tomatoes, chili, tobacco, chick-peas,
groundnuts, sesame, alfalfa, vanilla, cocoa and many kinds
of fruit. The maguey, or Mexican cactus, yields several
fermented drinks, mezcal and tequila (distilled) and pulque
(undistilled). Another species of the plant supplies sisal-
hemp (henequen). The forests contain mahogany, rose-
wood, ebony and chicle trees. Agriculture employs an
estimated 20 per cent of the working population.

The principal industries are mining and petroleum,
although there has been considerable expansion of both
light and heavy industries; exports of manufactured goods
now average about 56 per cent of total exports. The steel
industry expanded steadily until recently and current
production is around 7.9m tons. In 1991, 989,000 motor
vehicles were produced of which 365,000 were for export.

The mineral wealth is great, and principal minerals are
gold, silver, copper, lead, zinc, quicksilver, iron and
sulphur. Substantial reserves of uranium have been found.
Mexico produces 25 per cent of the world's supply of
fluorspar.

Oil exports were 1.37 million barrels per day in 1991.
Daily production of natural gas is approximately 3 billion
cubic feet. Oil reserves have increased substantially due to
discoveries in the Gulf of Campeche. A refinery at Tula is
the nation's largest; and new refineries in Monterrey, State
of Nuevo Leon, and Salina Cruz, State of Oaxaca, are
under construction.

TRADE

Major imports include computers, auto assembly material,
electrical parts, auto and truck parts, powdered milk, corn
and sorghum, transport, sound-recording and power-
generating equipment, chemicals, industrial machinery,
pharmaceuticals and specialized appliances. Principal exports include oil, automobiles, auto engines, fruits and
vegetables, shrimps, coffee, computers, cattle, glass, iron
and steel pipes, and copper. The main trading partners are
the USA (65.6 per cent), EC (15 per cent), Latin America
(5.2 per cent) and Japan (5 per cent). The North American
Free Trade Agreement, to which Mexico is a signatory,
came into effect on 1 January 1994, significantly increasing
Mexico's trade.

Trade with UK	1993	1994
Imports from UK	£335,872,000	£389,299,000
Exports to UK	165,743,000	239,740,000

COMMUNICATIONS

Veracruz, Tampico and Coatzacoalcos are the chief ports
on the Atlantic, and Guaymas, Mazatlán, Puerto Lázaro
Cárdenas, Acapulco, Salina Cruz and Puerto Madero on
the Pacific. Work is proceeding on the reorganization and
re-equipment of the whole rail system. Total track length
of the railways was 240,186 km in 1990. Mexico City may
be reached by at least three highways from the USA, and
from the south from Yucatán as well as on two principal
highways from the Guatemalan border.

There are 1,113 airports and landing fields in Mexico, of
which 18 are equipped to handle long-distance flights.
There are 166 airline companies, including two of the
major, now private, national airlines, Mexicana de Avia-
ción and Aeroméxico.

Teléfonos de México, now privatized, controls about 98
per cent of all telephone services.

EDUCATION

Education is divided into primary, secondary and superior levels. In 1990 there were 18,061,000 in the first level, 6,599,000 in the second and 1,236,000 in the third.

FEDERATED STATES OF MICRONESIA

The Federated States of Micronesia comprise more than 600 islands extending 2,900 km (1,800 miles) across the archipelago of the Caroline Islands in the western Pacific Ocean. The islands are located between the Equator and 9° N., and 138° and 168° E. Pohnpei island is 4,670 km (2,900 miles) south-west of Honolulu and 1,610 km (1,100 miles) south-east of Guam. The area is 700 sq. km (270 sq. miles). The islands vary geologically from mountainous islands to low coral atolls. The climate is tropical. Storms are common between August and December, and typhoons between July and November.

The population (1992 UN estimate) of 110,000 is Micronesian and predominantly Christian.

Pohnpei: population, 31,000; capital, Kolonia
Chuuk (Truk): population, 52,000; capital, Moen
Yap: population, 12,000; capital, Colonia
Kosrae: population, 6,500; capital, Lelu

English (official) and eight other languages are used in different parts of the Federated States: Yapese, Ulithian, Woleaian, Ponapean, Nukuoran, Kapingamarangi, Trukese and Kosraen.

CAPITAL – The federal capital is Palikir, on Pohnpei island.

FLAG – United Nations blue with four white stars in the centre.

HISTORY

The Spanish Empire claimed sovereignty over the Caroline Islands until 1899, when Spain withdrew from her Pacific territories and sold her possessions in the Caroline Islands to Germany. The Caroline Islands became a German protectorate until the outbreak of the First World War in 1914, when Japan took control of the islands on behalf of the Allied powers. After the war Japan continued to administer the territory under a League of Nations mandate. During the Second World War, US armed forces took control of the islands from the Japanese. In 1947 the USA entered into agreement with the UN Security Council to administer the Micronesia area, of which the Federated States of Micronesia were a part, as the UN Trust Territory of the Pacific Islands.

The US Trusteeship administration came to an end on 3 November 1986, when a Compact of Free Association between the USA and the Federated States of Micronesia came into effect. By this agreement the USA recognized the Federated States of Micronesia as a fully sovereign and independent state. The independence of the Federated States of Micronesia was recognized by the UN in December 1990.

GOVERNMENT

The Federated States of Micronesia is a federal republic of four constituent states: Chuuk, Kosrae, Pohnpei, Yap. The constitution separates the executive, legislative and judicial branches. There is a bill of rights and provision for traditional rights.

The executive comprises a federal President and Vice-President, both of whom must be chosen from amongst the four nationally-elected senators. There is a one-chamber legislature of 14 members, four members elected on a nation-wide basis and ten members elected from congressional districts apportioned by population.

Each of the constituent states has its own government and legislative system.

The Compact of Free Association places full responsibility for the defence of the Federated States of Micronesia on the USA.

HEAD OF STATE
President, Bailey Olter (Pohnpei), *elected by parliament* 11 May 1991
Vice-President, Jacob Nina (Kosrae)

CABINET *as at August 1995*
External Affairs, Resio Moses
Finance, Aloysius Tuuth
Human Resources, Eliuel Pretrick
Resources and Development, Asterio Takesy
Transportation and Communications, Robert Weilbacher
Administrative Services, Kohne Ramon
Budget, Patrick MacKenzie
Planning and Statistics, Marcelino Actouka
Attorney-General, Camillo Noket
Postmaster-General, Henry Bethwel

BRITISH AMBASSADOR, His Excellency Michael Peart, CMG, LVO, resident at Suva, Fiji

JUDICIARY

The judiciary is headed by the Supreme Court, which is divided into trial and appellate divisions. Below this, each state has its own judicial system.

ECONOMY

The economy is dependent mainly on subsistence agriculture and government spending. Copra and fish are the two main exports. The majority of the working population is engaged in government administration, subsistence farming, fishing, copra production and the growing tourist industry.

TRADE WITH UK	1993	1994
Imports from UK	£116,000	£106,000
Exports to UK	27,000	—

CULTURE

Each of the four states has an indigenous culture, and these differ considerably from one another. Recognition of the role of traditional leaders and customs is common to all, though Kosrae has no traditional leaders.

MOLDOVA

Republica Moldovenească

Moldova has an area of 13,912 sq. miles (33,700 sq. km) and occupies the extreme south-western corner of the former USSR. To the north, east and south-east it is bordered by Ukraine, and to the west by Romania. The border with Romania is formed by the Pruth (Prut) river, but the main river of the republic is the Dniester, navigable along its whole course. The north consists of flat steppe lands, in the centre there are woody hills, and in the south low-lying steppe lands. Forests skirt the Dniester. The climate is moderate.

The population (official estimate 1994) is 4,359,000, of which 65 per cent are Moldovan, 14.2 per cent Ukrainian and 13 per cent Russian, together with smaller numbers of Gagauz (ethnic Turks), Jews and Bulgarians. Most of the population are adherents of the Romanian Orthodox Church.

Moldovan was made the official language (written in the Latin script) in 1989 but the use of Russian and Ukrainian in official business is permitted.

CAPITAL – Kishinev. Population 665,000 (1989 census).

CURRENCY – Leu (plural lei) which replaced the rouble in November 1993.

FLAG – Vertical stripes of blue, yellow, red, with the national arms in the centre.

NATIONAL DAY – 27 August (Independence Day).

GOVERNMENT

A Moldovan feudal state was established in the 14th century when Slavic tribes who had previously lived under Roman and Byzantine rule integrated with Slavic tribes from further east. In the 15th century a Moldovan principality was formed which entered into military and political alliances with Muscovy before being conquered and absorbed into the Turkish Empire in the 16th century. Moldova became the site of many Russo-Turkish battles and skirmishes in the 18th century before the area between the Dniester and Prut rivers (later known as Bessarabia) was annexed to the Russian Empire by the Bucharest Peace Treaty 1812.

After the Russian Revolution in 1917, Bessarabia was under the control of White Russian forces and was annexed to Romania under the Versailles Peace Treaty 1919. In 1924 the Moldavian Autonomous Soviet Socialist Republic (ASSR) was established on the east bank of the Dniester river as part of Soviet Ukraine. In August 1940 the Soviet Union forced Romania to cede Bessarabia and the Moldavian Soviet Socialist Republic was formed from the fusion of the majority of Bessarabia (the southernmost parts were incorporated into the Ukraine) with the Moldavian ASSR.

When Moldova (formerly Moldavia) declared its independence from the USSR in August 1991, the majority ethnic Romanian (Moldovan) population expressed a wish to rejoin Romania. This alienated the ethnic Ukrainian and Russian populations, who form a majority east of the Dniester. After failed negotiations and several armed clashes, the Ukrainian and Russian populations declared their independence from Moldova as the Transdniester republic in December 1991. The Moldovan government refused to recognize this and in the first half of 1992 a war was waged between government forces and Transdniester forces, who were supported by the 30,000-strong former Soviet 14th Army stationed in Transdniester and by Cossack volunteers from Russia.

A mainly Russian CIS peacekeeping force (later changed to a joint Russian-Moldovan-Transdniester force) was deployed in July 1992 and a ceasefire has held since August 1992. Although no political solution has been finalized and a state of armed truce remains, the Moldovan government in February 1994 agreed to a CSCE plan for the Transdniester area to have a high degree of autonomy within Moldova but no independent or federal status. Negotiations on the CSCE plan continue, while in October 1994 the Russian and Moldovan presidents signed an agreement on the withdrawal of the 14th Army over a three-year period.

The idea of reunification with Romania was defeated by a 90 per cent vote against in a national referendum on 6 March 1994, following which the Moldovan parliament in April 1994 voted to ratify the CIS agreement and joined the organization. In July 1994 the Moldovan parliament adopted a new constitution which defines Moldova as a 'presidential parliamentary republic' based on political pluralism. It also provides for autonomous status for the Gagauz and Transdniester regions, with the Gagauz region having its own elected National Assembly.

The Moldovan Popular Front government which came to power in the 1990 legislative elections to the 380-seat Supreme Soviet was replaced in July 1992 by a government of national accord led by the Peasant Democratic Party, which began an economic reform programme in 1993. The former Communists of the Agrarian Democratic Party were brought back to power in the legislative election of February 1994 and formed a coalition government with the Socialist Party. Parliament now has 104 seats and is elected by proportional representation.

HEAD OF STATE
President, Mircea Snegur, *elected* 8 December 1991

GOVERNMENT *as at August 1995*
Prime Minister, Andrei Sangeli
Deputy PMs, Ion Gutzu, Grigoire Ojugu, Valeriu Bulgar, Valentin Kunev
Minister of State, Gheorghe Gusac
National Economy, Valerian Boboutac
Agriculture and Foodstuffs, Vitali Gorincioi
Industry, Grigore Triboi
Transport and Roads, Vasile Iouv
Foreign Economic Relations, Andrei Keptine
Information, Science and Communications, Ion Cassian
Public Health, Timofei Mosneaga
Culture, Mihail Cebotari
Justice, Vasile Sturza
Internal Affairs, Maj.-Gen. Constantin Antoci
Foreign Affairs, Mihai Popov
National Security, Col. Vasile Calmoi
Defence, Maj.-Gen. Pavel Creanga
Finance, Valeriu Chitan
Education, Pavel Gauges
Relations with Parliament, Victor Pascas
Utilities, Mihai Severovan
Social Protection, Dumitru Nidelcu
Privatization, Ceslav Ciobanu
Power Engineeering, Valentin Chumak

BRITISH AMBASSADOR, His Excellency Andrew Wood, CMG, resident at Moscow

ECONOMY

The main sector is agriculture, especially viniculture, fruit-growing and market gardening. Industry is small and concentrated east of the Dniester. Severe drought in 1992, the severance of most trading ties with former Soviet republics, war damage and reductions in Russian fuel deliveries paralysed the economy from 1992 to 1994. Entry into the CIS and its economic union in April 1994 should, however, improve trading ties with other former Soviet republics and increase Russian fuel supplies. An economic reform programme began in summer 1993 and is being supported by IMF credits of US$225 million. A privatization programme began in March 1995 in which 1,450 enterprises are to be sold by direct sale and vouchers.

TRADE WITH UK	1993	1994
Imports from UK	£2,243,000	£1,686,000
Exports to UK	325,000	793,000

MONACO
Principauté de Monaco

A small principality on the Mediterranean, with land frontiers joining France at every point, Monaco is divided into the districts of Monaco-Ville, La Condamine, Fontvielle and Monte Carlo. The principality comprises a narrow strip of land about two miles long with an area of approximately 195 hectares, and 29,972 inhabitants (1992).

CAPITAL – Monaco-Ville, population (1992) 1,151.
CURRENCY – The French franc is legal tender.
FLAG – Two equal horizontal stripes, red over white.
NATIONAL ANTHEM – Hymne Monegasque.
NATIONAL DAY – 19 November.

GOVERNMENT

The principality, ruled by the Grimaldi family since the late 13th century, was abolished during the French Revolution and re-established in 1815 under the protection of the kingdom of Sardinia. In 1861 Monaco came under French protection.

The 1962 constitution, which can be modified only with the approval of the National Council, maintains the traditional hereditary monarchy and guarantees freedom of association, trade union freedom and the right to strike. Legislative power is held jointly by the Prince and a unicameral, 18-member National Council elected by universal suffrage. Executive power is exercised by the Prince and a four-member Council of Government, headed by a Minister of State. The judicial code is based on that of France.

HEAD OF STATE
HSH The Prince of Monaco, Prince Rainier III Louis-Henri-Maxence Bertrand, *born* 31 May 1923, *succeeded* 9 May 1949; *married* 19 April 1956, Miss Grace Patricia Kelly (died 14 September 1982) and *has issue* Prince Albert (*see* below); Princess Caroline Louise Marguerite, *born* 23 January 1957; and Princess Stephanie Marie Elisabeth, *born* 1 February 1965
Heir, HRH Prince Albert Alexandre Louis Pierre, *born* 14 March 1958

President of the Crown Council, Jean-Charles Marquet
President of the National Council, Dr Jean-Louis Campora
Minister of State, Paul Dijoud, *appointed* 1994

CONSULATE-GENERAL OF MONACO
4 Cromwell Place, London SW7 2JE
Tel 0171-225 2679
Consul-General, I. B. Ivanovic.

BRITISH CONSUL-GENERAL, P. Yarnold, apptd 1995, resident at Marseilles, France

ECONOMY

The whole available ground is built over so that there is no cultivation, though there are some notable public and private gardens. The economy is based on real estate revenues, the financial sector and tourism (over 250,000 visitors a year). Monaco has a small harbour (30 ft alongside quay) and the import duties are the same as in France.

MONGOLIA
State of Mongolia

Mongolia lies in northern Asia, bordered by Russia to the north and China to the south. Its area is 604,250 sq. miles (1,565,000 sq. km). Mongolia, which is almost nowhere below 1,000 metres above sea level, forms part of the central Asiatic plateau and rises towards the west in the mountains of the Mongolian Altai and Hangai ranges. The Hentai range, situated to the north-east of the capital Ulan Bator, is less high. The Gobi region covers much of the southern half of the country and contains sand deserts interspersed with semi-desert. There are several long rivers and many lakes but good water is scarce as much of the lake water is salty. The climate is harsh, with a short mild summer giving way to a long winter when temperatures can drop as low as −50°C.

The population (1992 estimate) is 2,156,000; this total constitutes only part of the Mongolians of Asia, a number of whom are to be found in China and in the neighbouring regions of Russia, especially the Mongolian Buryat Autonomous Region.

CAPITAL – Ulan Bator (Ulaanbaator), population (1993) 600,500.
CURRENCY – Tugrik of 100 möngö.
FLAG – Vertical tri-colour red, blue, red and in the hoist the traditional Soyombo symbol in gold.
NATIONAL DAY – 11 July.

GOVERNMENT

Mongolia, under Genghis Khan the conqueror of China and much of Asia, was for many years a buffer state between Tsarist Russia and China, although it was under general Chinese suzerainty. The Chinese Revolution in 1911 led to a declaration of autonomy under Chinese suzerainty which was confirmed by the Sino-Russian Treaty of Kiakhta 1915 but cancelled by a unilateral Chinese declaration in 1919. Later the country became a battleground of the Russian civil war, and Soviet and Mongolian troops occupied Ulan Bator in 1921; this was followed by another declaration of independence. In 1924 the Soviet Union in a treaty with China again recognized the latter's sovereignty over Mongolia, but this was never properly exercised because of China's preoccupation with internal affairs and later by the war with Japan. The Mongolian People's Republic was formally established in 1924. Under the Yalta Agreement, Chiang Kai-shek agreed to a plebiscite, held in 1945, in which the Mongolians declared their desire for independence and this was formally recognized by China.

The Mongolian People's Revolutionary Party (MPRP) was the sole political party from 1924 to 1990. Demonstrations in favour of political and economic reform began in December 1989 and led to changes in the MPRP leadership in March 1990. The MPRP's constitutionally guaranteed monopoly of power was subsequently relinquished, and the introduction of a multiparty system was approved by the Great People's Hural (parliament). The MPRP won the first multiparty elections, held in July 1990. Since then, and following Moscow's lead, Mongolia has embarked on a programme of political and economic reforms.

A new constitution was approved in January 1992 which enshrines the concepts of democracy, a mixed economy, free speech and neutrality in foreign affairs. The Great and Little Hurals were abolished, and a new unicameral Great Hural became the legislative body of the country. Elections were held in June 1992 which were won by the MPRP with 57 per cent of the vote and 71 out of 76 seats. The country's first direct presidential election was held in 1993 and won by the incumbent Punsalmaagiyn Orchirbat, who stood as an opposition candidate after the MPRP refused to endorse him as its candidate.

The last remaining former Soviet armed forces personnel were withdrawn in late 1992.

The country and three city districts (Ulan Bator, Darkhan and Erdenet) are divided into 21 *aimaks* (provinces) and beneath these into 258 *somons* (districts), and these form the basis of the state organization of the country.

HEAD OF STATE
President, Punsalmaagiyn Ochirbat, *elected* June 1993

CABINET *as at August 1995*

Prime Minister, Puntsagiyn Jasray
Deputy PM, Administration, Lhamsurengiyn Enebish
Deputy PM, Choyjilsurengiyn Purevdorj
Defence, Maj.-Gen. Shagalyn Jadambaa
Minister of State and Chairman of National Development Board,
Chultemiyn Ulaan
Agriculture and Food, Tseveenjavyn Oold
Foreign Relations, Tserenpiliyn Gombosuren
Culture, Nambaryn Enhbayar
Demography and Labour, Erdeniyn Gormbojav
Finance, Dalrain Davaasambun
Energy, Geology and Minerals, Byambyn Jigjid
Law, Narnsraijavyn Luvsanjav
Infrastructure Development, Razdakyn Sandalhaan
Science and Education, Nadmidyn Olziihutag
Trade and Industry, Tsevegmediyn Tsogt
Health, Pagvajavyn Nyamdavaa
Nature and the Environment, Zambyn Batjargal
Chairman of the Great Hural, Natsagiyn Bagabandi

EMBASSY OF MONGOLIA
7 Kensington Court, London W8 5DL
Tel 0171-937 0150
Ambassador Extraordinary and Plenipotentiary, His Excellency
Choisurengyn Baatar, apptd 1991

BRITISH EMBASSY
30 Enkh Taivny Gudamzh (PO Box 703), Ulan Bator 13
Tel: Ulan Bator 358133
Ambassador Extraordinary and Plenipotentiary, His Excellency
Ian Sloane, apptd 1994

ECONOMY

The country has been experiencing transitional problems in its attempt to establish a market economy, with food and fuel shortages, inflation, and unemployment. Western countries, Japan and the IMF have provided loans of US$287 million in 1993–5 to aid its economic restructuring. In April 1994 Mongolia signed a treaty of friendship and mutual assistance with China to gain aid and economic and technological co-operation.

Traditionally the Mongolians led a nomadic life tending flocks of sheep, goats, horses, cows and camels. With the coming of the Communist regime, and especially after 1952, great efforts were made to settle the population but a proportion still live nomadically or semi-nomadically in the traditional *ger* (circular tent). Collectivization at the end of the 1950s into huge *negdels* (co-operatives) and state farms hastened the process of settlement, but within these the herdsmen and their families still move with their *gers* from pasture to pasture as the seasons change. Total livestock was 25 million in 1993.

The semi-desert areas of the Gobi region provide pasture for sheep, goats, camels, horses and some cattle. In the steppe areas to the north of the Gobi pasturage is better and livestock more abundant. Even further north, in the better-watered provinces, grain, fodder and vegetable crops are grown.

Although the economy remains predominantly based on the herds of animals, factories have started up, coal, copper and molybdenum are mined and the electricity industry has been developed. Ulan Bator and Darkhan are the main seats of industry. Industries include lime, cement and building materials, a flour mill and a power station. Choibalsan is also being developed industrially.

Mongolia's fundamental difficulty is its very small population and labour force, and its basic infastructure. Communication is still difficult in the country as there are very few tarmac roads and horses are still the characteristic means of transport for the rural population. The trans-Mongolian railway links Mongolia with both China and Russia.

TRADE

Foreign trade was formerly dominated by the Soviet Union and other eastern bloc countries. Following the collapse of the CMEA, trade with western countries, Japan and South Korea is increasing. Since January 1991, trade is in hard currency, causing particular strain. The principal exports are animal by-products (especially wool, hides and furs) and cattle.

Trade with UK	1993	1994
Imports from UK	£1,659,000	£2,637,000
Exports to UK	2,284,000	1,680,000

MOROCCO
Al-Mamlaka Al-Maghrebia

Morocco is situated in the north-west of the African continent between 27° 40′ and 36° N. latitude and 1° and 13° W. longitude with an area estimated at 172,414 sq. miles (446,550 sq. km). It is traversed in the north by the Rif mountains and, in a south-west to north-east direction, by the Middle Atlas, the High Atlas, the Anti-Atlas and the Sarrho ranges. Much of the country is desert. The north-westerly point of Morocco is the peninsula of Tangier dominated by the Jebel Mousa which, with the rocky eminence of Gibraltar, was known to the ancients as the Pillars of Hercules, the western gateway of the Mediterranean.

The population (1990 estimate) is 27,575,000. Arabic is the official language. Berber is the vernacular, mainly in the mountain regions. French and Spanish are also spoken, mainly in the towns. Islam is the state religion.

CAPITAL – ΨRabat, population (including Salé)
1,494,000. Regional capitals, with municipal population figures as at 1991, are: ΨCasablanca (2,990,000); Marrakesh (644,000); Fez (719,000); Oujda (646,000); Meknes (484,000); ΨAgadir (420,000).
CURRENCY – Dirham (DH) of 100 centimes.
FLAG – Red, with green pentagram (the Seal of Solomon).
NATIONAL DAY – 3 March (Anniversary of the Throne).

GOVERNMENT

Morocco became an independent sovereign state in 1956, following joint declarations made with France on 2 March 1956 and with Spain on 7 April 1956. The Sultan of

Morocco, Sidi Mohammad ben Youssef, adopted the title of King Mohammad V.

The 1992 constitution states that Morocco is a democratic constitutional monarchy. The King nominates the Prime Minister and, on the latter's recommendation, appoints the members of the Council of Ministers. The government is responsible both to parliament and to the King. The unicameral legislature (Chamber of Representatives) has 333 members, 222 elected by direct universal suffrage (including five representing overseas workers) and 111 members elected by electoral colleges representing local government, industry, agriculture, professional and trade union groups.

Effective political power remains with the King despite the constitutional changes of October 1992 enhancing the Prime Minister's and legislature's powers. Legislative elections were held in June–September 1993, with the centre-right four-party Entente National coalition winning 154 seats and the leftist six-party Bloc Démocratique winning 120 seats. After both coalitions had been unable to form a government, King Hassan appointed a government of technocrats and independents in November 1993. In February 1995 the King replaced this with a government of the Entente National and technocrats. Diplomatic relations with Israel were opened in September 1994.

HEAD OF STATE
HM The King of Morocco, King Hassan II (Moulay Hassan Ben Mohammed), *born* 9 July 1929; *acceded* 3 March 1961
Heir, HRH Crown Prince Sidi Mohamed, *born* 21 August 1963

COUNCIL OF MINISTERS *as at August 1995*
Prime Minister, Foreign Affairs and Co-operation, Abdellatif Filali
Minister of State, Moulay Ahmed Alaoui
Minister of State, Interior, Driss Basri
Justice, Abderrahmane Amalou
National Education, Rachid Ben Mokhtar
Public Health, Ahmed Alami
Religious Endowments and Islamic Affairs, Abdelkebir Alaoui M'Daghri
Public Works, Abdelaziz Meziane Belfkih
Finance and Foreign Investments, Mohamed Kabbaj
Transport, Said Ameskane
Energy and Mines, Abdelatif Gurraoui
Youth and Sport, Ahmed Meziane
Sea Fisheries and the Merchant Marine, Mustapha Sahel
Secretary-General of the Government, Abdessadek Rabiah
Culture, Abdellah Azmani
Housing, Driss Toulali
Posts and Telecommunications, Hamza Kettani
Agriculture and Agricultural Investment, Hassan Abouyoub
Trade, Industry and Handicrafts, Driss Jettou
Employment and Social Affairs, Amine Demnati
Foreign Trade, Mohammad Alami
Tourism, Mohammad Alaoui M'Hamdi
Communications, Government Spokesman, Driss Alaoui M'daghri
Privatization, Abderrahmane Saaidi
Higher Education and Scientific Research, Driss Khalil
Environment, Dr Noureddine Benomar Alami
Vocational Training, Abdessalam Beroual

EMBASSY OF THE KINGDOM OF MOROCCO
49 Queen's Gate Gardens, London SW7 5NE
Tel 0171–581 5001/4
Ambassador Extraordinary and Plenipotentiary, His Excellency Khalil Haddaoui, apptd 1991

BRITISH EMBASSY
17 Boulevard de la Tour Hassan (BP 45), Rabat
Tel: Rabat 7209 05/6
Ambassador Extraordinary and Plenipotentiary, His Excellency Sir Allan Ramsay, KBE, CMG, apptd 1992
There is a British Consulate-General/Commercial Office at Casablanca and Consulates at Agadir, Marrakesh and Tangier.

BRITISH COUNCIL DIRECTOR, Tony O'Brien, BP 427, 36 rue Tanger, Rabat
BRITISH CHAMBER OF COMMERCE, 1st Floor, 185 Boulevard Zerktouni, Casablanca. Tel: 256920

DEFENCE

The armed forces have a total active strength of 195,500, including authorized conscripts who serve 18-month terms. Total reserves number 150,000. The Army has a strength of 175,000 (100,000 conscripts), the majority of whom have been deployed in southern Morocco and Western Sahara fighting the Polisario Front. It is equipped with 555 main battle tanks, 100 light tanks, 345 reconnaissance vehicles, 900 armoured infantry fighting vehicles and armoured personnel carriers, and 320 artillery pieces.

The Navy has a strength of 7,000, with one frigate, and 27 patrol and coastal combatant craft, together with a marine battalion. The Air Force has a strength of 13,500, with 95 combat aircraft and 24 armed helicopters. In addition, there are a paramilitary Gendarmerie Royale of 12,000 and an Auxiliary Force of 30,000 paramilitaries.

Morocco deploys 2,000 troops in the United Arab Emirates. The UN has some 310 personnel in Western Sahara pending the referendum. Polisario deploys 3,000–6,000 troops in Western Sahara with Algerian-supplied and captured Moroccan tanks, armoured personnel carriers, anti-tank and anti-aircraft weapons.

ECONOMY

Morocco's main sources of wealth are agricultural and mineral. The latest development plan (1987 onwards) emphasizes social improvement, industrial development, agriculture, fisheries and tourism. Economic reform has also been pursued over the past few years, to reduce debt and inflation. A large-scale privatization programme has brought in substantial foreign investment, but inflation remains high at 17 per cent.

Agriculture employs more than 40 per cent of the working population and accounts for about 36 per cent of exports. The main agricultural exports are fruit and vegetables, with cereals and sugar beet produced and sheep reared for domestic consumption. Cork and wood-pulp are the most important commercial forest products. Esparto grass is also produced. There is a fishing industry and substantial quantities of canned fish, mainly sardines and fishmeal, are exported.

For a developing country Morocco has a large industrial sector, which accounts for about 70 per cent of exports (including mineral exports). The main sectors are chemicals, textiles and leather goods, food processing and cement production. Manufacturing industries are centred in Casablanca, Fez, Tangier and Safi.

Morocco's mineral exports are phosphates, fluorite, barite, manganese, iron ore, lead, zinc, cobalt, copper and antimony. Morocco possesses nearly three-quarters of the world's estimated reserves of phosphates. There are oil refineries at Mohammedia and Sidi Kacem handling about four million tonnes of crude oil per year, but no significant quantities of hydrocarbons have been found.

Tourism is of increasing importance to the economy, with development concentrated in Agadir and Marrakesh. In 1992, 3,252,062 foreign tourists visited Morocco and tourism accounted for 3–4 per cent of GDP. Workers' remittances, US$1,959 million in 1993, are also very important to the economy.

TRADE

The main imports are petroleum products, motor vehicles, building materials, agricultural and other machinery, chemical products, sugar, green tea and other foodstuffs. The EU, led by France and Spain, is Morocco's largest trading partner. The main exports are textiles, phosphates and phosphoric acid, fertilizers, citrus fruits, and fish and seafoods.

	1992	1993
Imports	US$7,389m	US$6,643m
Exports	3,995m	3,680m
Trade with UK	1993	1994
Imports from UK	£168,303,000	£193,665,000
Exports to UK	182,378,000	200,583,000

COMMUNICATIONS

Railroads cover 1,175 miles (1,893 km), linking the major towns. An extensive network of 9,880 miles (15,900 km) of well-surfaced roads covers all the main towns. There are air services between Casablanca, Tangier, Agadir (seasonal), Marrakesh and London, and also between Tangier and Gibraltar connecting with London. Royal-Air-Maroc operates internal services and services to 36 states in Europe, Africa and Asia.

EDUCATION

There are government primary, secondary and technical schools. In 1991 there were 4,890 government schools with a total of 3,608,757 pupils. At Fez there is a theological university of great repute in the Muslim world. There is a secular university at Rabat. A total of 206,725 students studied at 13 universities in 1991. Schools for special denominations, Jewish and Catholic, are permitted and may receive government grants. American schools operate in Rabat and Casablanca.

WESTERN SAHARA

Formerly the Spanish Sahara, the territory was split between Morocco and Mauritania in 1976 after Spain withdrew in December 1975. In 1976 the Polisario Front (Frente Popular para la Liberación de Saguia y Río de Oro) declared Western Sahara to be an independent state, the Saharan Arab Democratic Republic, and formed a government led by Bouchraya Bayoune which remains in exile. The Polisario Front has been recognized as the legitimate government of Western Sahara by over 70 states and the Organization of African Unity. In 1979 Mauritania renounced its claim to its share of the territory, which was added by Morocco to its area. Morocco's annexation has been opposed by Polisario guerrillas, who want the territory to become an independent state.

In 1988, Morocco and the Polisario Front accepted a UN peace plan under which a ceasefire came into effect in September 1991. A referendum to determine the future of the area was to have been held in January 1992 but has not yet taken place because the Moroccan government and Polisario have not agreed on the referendum terms or who should be eligible to vote. The UN Security Council intervened to break the impasse, passing resolution 809 (March 1993) which stipulates that the referendum should

be a straight choice between independence or integration with Morocco. UN Security Council resolution 907 (March 1994) mandated the UN to establish a new voter registration list by means of a voter identification commission. The voter identification operation began in August 1994 but has yet to be completed because of continued disagreement on who is eligible to vote.

MOZAMBIQUE
República de Moçambique

Mozambique lies on the east coast of Africa, and is bounded by Swaziland in the south, South Africa in the south and west, Zimbabwe in the west, Zambia and Malawi in the north-west and Tanzania in the north. It has an area of 309,495 sq. miles (801,590 sq. km), with a population (1992 UN estimate) of 14,872,000. The official language is Portuguese.

CAPITAL – Ψ Maputo, estimated population (1990), 1,150,000. Other main ports are ΨBeira and ΨNacala.
CURRENCY – Metical (MT) of 100 centavos.
FLAG – Horizontally green, black, yellow with white fimbriations; a red triangle based on the hoist containing the national emblem.
NATIONAL DAY – 25 June (Independence Day).

GOVERNMENT

Mozambique, discovered by Vasco de Gama in 1498 and colonized by Portugal, achieved independence from Portugal on 25 June 1975. The country was a Marxist one-party (Frelimo) state until a multiparty system was adopted in 1990. The legislative assembly has 250 members.

Following two years of negotiations, the (Frelimo) Mozambican government and rebel Mozambican National Resistance (Renamo) signed a peace agreement in August 1992 which ended 16 years of civil war. Under the peace agreement the Frelimo government and Renamo troops assembled at designated points around the country within one month of parliamentary ratification of the peace accord (which occurred on 9 October 1992) and began to hand over their weapons to UN monitors. The majority of troops were to be demobilized and the remainder integrated to form a 30,000-strong Army and police force. However, the process was soon behind schedule, with arguments over demobilization and the late arrival of UN forces. The UN Operation for Mozambique (ONUMOZ) was approved by the Security Council on 16 December 1992, but the first of 6,000 UN troops and civilian police only arrived in May 1993. Multiparty presidential and legislative elections planned for June 1993 were postponed. The demobilization of government and Renamo forces took place between January and August 1994 and the formation of the unified Mozambican Defence Armed Forces (FADM) is under way. Meanwhile the 1.7 million refugees in neighbouring states were repatriated.

Presidential and legislative elections were finally held on 27–29 October 1994, with a Renamo boycott only being rescinded on the 28th. The incumbent, Joaquim Chissano of Frelimo, won the presidential election in the first round with 53 per cent of the vote. Frelimo also won the legislative election, gaining 129 seats to Renamo's 112 seats and the Democratic Union's 9 seats. President Chissano was sworn in for a five-year term on 23 December with his new Frelimo government. The last ONUMOZ troops left in January 1995.

HEAD OF STATE
President, Joaquim Alberto Chissano, *sworn in* November 1986, *elected* 29 October 1994

COUNCIL OF MINISTERS *as at August 1995*
Prime Minister, Pascoal Mocumbi
Foreign Affairs and Co-operation, Leonardo Simão
National Defence, Aguiar Real Mazula
State Administration, Alfredo Gamito
Education, Arnaldo Nhavoto
Interior, Manuel Macananda
Transport and Communications, Paulo Muxanga
Finance, Tomas Salomao
Health, Aurelio Zihao
Agriculture and Fisheries, Carlos Rosario
Industry, Trade and Tourism, Oldemiro Baloi
Mineral Resources and Energy, John Kachamila
Justice, José Abudo
Culture, Youth and Sports, Jose Mateus Katupha
Labour, Guilherme Mavila
Environment, Bernardo Ferraz
Social Affairs, Alcinda de Abreu
Construction and Housing, Roberto White
Ministers in the President's Office, Eneias Comiche (*Economic and Social Affairs*); Francisco Madeira (*Parliamentary Affairs*); Almerindo Manheje (*Defence and Security Affairs*)

EMBASSY OF THE REPUBLIC OF MOZAMBIQUE
21 Fitzroy Square, London WIP 5HJ
Tel 0171–383 3800
Ambassador Extraordinary and Plenipotentiary, His Excellency Lt.-Gen. Armando Alexandre Panguene, apptd 1988

BRITISH EMBASSY
Av. Vladimir I Lenine 310, CP 55, Maputo
Tel: Maputo 420111/2/5/6/7
Ambassador Extraordinary and Plenipotentiary, His Excellency Richard J. Edis, CMG, apptd 1992

BRITISH COUNCIL DIRECTOR, Gail Liesching, PO Box 4178, Maputo

ECONOMY

The basis of the economy is subsistence agriculture, but there is an industrial sector based mainly in Beira and Maputo. There are substantial coal deposits in Tete province and an offshore gas field at Pande. After giving priority to the development of collective farms and state enterprises in all sectors, the government is now encouraging the private sector and foreign investment, particularly in agriculture and consumer goods production. An IMF economic reform programme is being followed, with subsidies on basic foods having been removed. Mozambique has a range of aid and co-operation agreements with a number of countries and following the signing of the peace accord US$520 million in aid has been pledged for reconstruction. An agreement of non-aggression and good neighbourliness with South Africa was signed in 1984 (the Nkomati Accord), and in June 1994 a joint Mozambican-South African Chamber of Commerce was formed. In March 1995 the Paris club of donor states pledged US$780 million in loans and grants to reform the economy and reduce poverty. A five-year plan has been launched with the priorities of rural development, education, health and land reform.

TRADE

The main exports are sugar, cashew nuts, prawns, copra, cotton, tea and sisal.

Trade with UK	1993	1994
Imports from UK	£21,717,000	£35,489,000
Exports to UK	1,568,000	2,903,000

MYANMAR
Pyidaungsu Myanma Naingngandaw – Union of Myanmar

Myanmar (Burma) forms the western portion of the Indo-Chinese part of Asia, lying between 9° 58' and 28° N. latitude and 92° 11' and 101° 9' E. longitude, with an extreme length of approximately 1,200 miles and an extreme width of 575 miles. It has a sea coast on the Bay of Bengal to the south and west, and a frontier with Bangladesh along the Naaf River and with India to the north-west. In the north and east the country borders China and there is a short frontier with Laos in the east, while the long finger of Tenasserim stretches southwards along the west coast of the Malay peninsula, forming a frontier with Thailand to the east. The total area is 261,218 sq. miles (676,552 sq. km).

Mountains enclose the Union on three sides. The principal river systems are the Kaladan-Lemro in Arakan, the Irrawaddy-Chindwin and the Sittang in central Myanmar, and the Salween which flows through the Shan Plateau.

The population (UN estimate 1992) is 43,668,000. The indigenous inhabitants are of similar racial types and speak languages of the Tibeto-Burman, Mon-Khmer and Thai groups. The three significant non-indigenous elements are Indians, Chinese and those from Bangladesh. Burmese is the official language, but minority languages include Shan, Karen, Chin, Kayah and the various Kachin dialects. English is spoken in educated circles.

Buddhism is the religion of 85 per cent of the people, with 5 per cent Animists, 4 per cent Muslims, 4 per cent Hindus and less than 3 per cent Christians.

CAPITAL – ΨYangon (Rangoon). Population (1983): Yangon District 3,973,872; city population 2,458,712. The other major cities are Mandalay, population (1983): Mandalay district 4,580,923; city 532,985; Mawlamyine (Moulmein) 219,991 and Pathein (Bassein) 144,092. Pagan, on the Irrawaddy, contains many sacred buildings.
CURRENCY – Kyat (K) of 100 pyas.
FLAG – Red, with a canton of dark blue, inside which are a cogwheel and two rice ears surrounded by 14 white stars.
NATIONAL DAY – 4 January.

GOVERNMENT

The Union of Burma (the name was officially changed to the Union of Myanmar in 1989) became an independent republic outside the British Commonwealth on 4 January 1948 and remained a parliamentary democracy for 14 years. In 1962 the army took power and suspended the parliamentary constitution. A Revolutionary Council of senior officers under Gen. Ne Win took measures to create a socialist state.

After months of popular demonstrations and rioting and a series of presidents during the summer of 1988, Gen. Saw Maung, leader of the armed forces, assumed power in September 1988. The People's Assembly, the Council of State and the Council of Ministers were abolished and replaced by the State Law and Order Restoration Council (SLORC). The constitution was effectively abrogated.

A People's Assembly Election Law was published in 1989 committing the SLORC to hold multiparty elections.

These were held on 27 May 1990, resulting in a majority for the National League for Democracy (NLD) even though its leader Aung San Suu Kyi had been under house arrest since July 1989. The SLORC refused to transfer power to a civilian government and large numbers of NLD MPs and supporters were detained. Others fled to the border areas with Thailand where they established an exile government led by Sein Win which is known as the National Coalition Government of the Union of Burma (NCGUB). However, following the replacement of Saw Maung by Than Shwe as SLORC Chairman and Prime Minister in April 1992, the government began a dialogue with some elements of the opposition. A Constitutional Convention of delegates appointed by the SLORC to discuss a future constitution convened in January 1993 and has continued fitfully since, but with minimal progress because the majority of the delegates refuse to accept the leading role in politics demanded by the armed forces. The SLORC has released about 2,000 political detainees including on 10 July 1995 Aung San Suu Kyi (who won the Nobel Peace Prize in 1991), but many others remain in detention or under house arrest.

Myanmar is comprised of seven states (Chin, Kachin, Kayin (Karen), Kayah, Mon, Rakhine, Shan) and seven divisions (Irrawaddy, Magwe, Mandalay, Pegu, Yangon (Rangoon), Sagaing, Tenasserim).

INSURGENCY

Since independence in 1948 the government has fought various armed insurgent groups, mostly ethnic minorities seeking greater autonomy or independence. The largest

insurgent forces were dreived from the Kachin, Karen, Karenni, and Wa ethnic groups but the Shan, Mon, Arakan and Chin ethnic minorities have also formed armed groups. In 1989 Wa insurgents signed an agreement with the government ending their insurgency, but in 1990 the fleeing NLD and pro-democracy supporters allied themselves to the remaining ethnic insurgent groups to form the Democratic Alliance of Burma (DAB) based at Mannerplaw near the Thai border, which was also the NCGUB base. Since 1992, as a result of government offensives, 13 armed ethnic groups have signed cease-fire agreements with the government, including the Kachin Independence Army in February 1994, the Karenni National People's Liberation Front in May 1994, the Shan State Liberation Organization in October 1994, and Mon rebels in July 1995. A government offensive from December 1994 to February 1995 captured the rebel headquaters at Mannerplaw and forced the Karen National Union forces, together with armed pro-democracy supporters across the Thai border. The only remaining armed rebel forces are the Karen forces along the Thai border, Karenni rebels in Kayah state, and the forces of the drugs warlord Khun Sa, known as the Mong Tai army, in Shan state.

CABINET *as at August 1995*

Chairman of SLORC, Prime Minister and Minister of Defence,
  Gen. Than Shwe
Deputy Prime Ministers, Vice-Adm. Maung Maung Khin;
  Lt.-Gen. Tin Tun
Agriculture, Maj.-Gen. Myint Aung
Border Areas, Maj.-Gen. Maung Thint
Communications, Posts and Telegraphs, U Soe Tha
Construction, Maj.-Gen. Saw Tun
Co-operatives, U Than Aung
Culture, Brig.-Gen. Thaung Myint
Education, Pan Aung
Energy, U Khin Maung Thein
Finance and Revenue, Brig.-Gen. Win Tin
Foreign Affairs, U Ohn Gyaw
Forestry, Lt.-Gen. Chit Swe
Health, Rear-Adm. Than Nyunt
Home, Maj.-Gen. Mya Thinn
Hotels and Tourism, Maj.-Gen. Kyaw Ba
Immigration and Population, Lt.-Gen. Maung Hla
Industry, Lt.-Gen. Sein Aung; Maj.-Gen. Kyaw Than
Information, Maj.-Gen. Aye Kyaw
Labour, Maj.-Gen. Aye Thoung
Livestock Breeding and Fisheries, Brig.-Gen. Maung Maung
Mines, Maj.-Gen. Kyaw Min
Office of the Prime Minister, Brig.-Gen. Lun Maung
Planning and Finance, Brig.-Gen. Do Abel
Rail and Transportation, U Win Sein
Religious Affairs, Maj.-Gen. Myo Nyunt
Social Welfare, Maj.-Gen. Soe Myint
Trade, Maj.-Gen. Tun Kyi
Transport, Maj.-Gen. Thein Win

EMBASSY OF THE UNION OF MYANMAR
19A Charles Street, Berkeley Square, London WIX 8ER
Tel 0171-629 6966
Ambassador Extraordinary and Plenipotentiary, His Excellency
  U Hla Maung, apptd 1992

BRITISH EMBASSY
80 Strand Road (Box No. 638), Rangoon
Tel: Rangoon 95300
Ambassador Extraordinary and Plenipotentiary, His Excellency
  Julian Hartland-Swann, CMG, apptd 1990
Cultural Attaché and British Council Director, Chris Harrison

ECONOMY

The chief sources of revenue are profits on state trading, taxes and duties; the chief heads of expenditure are defence, education and police. The budget estimates for 1992–3 were: revenue K53,867 million; expenditure, K57,203 million.

Three-quarters of the population depend on agriculture; the chief products are rice, oilseeds (sesamum and groundnut), maize, millet, cotton, beans, wheat, grain, tea, sugar-cane, tobacco, jute and rubber.

Myanmar is rich in minerals, including petroleum, lead, silver, tungsten, zinc, tin, wolfram and gemstones. Of these, petroleum products are the most important. Oil is produced from oilfields in Myanaung, Prome and Shwepyitha and at Chauk, Yenangyaung, Mann, and Letpando. Production of crude oil in 1991–2 totalled 5,500,000 US barrels. There are refineries at Chauk, the main oilfield, Syriam and Mann. There has been a steady decline in oil production in recent years and the country is no longer self-sufficient. Onshore exploration continues. There has also been some offshore oil exploration on a small scale. Major reserves of natural gas have been discovered in the Martaban Gulf, which Myanmar is hoping to develop. Timber production is also an important industry and timber is a major export.

All industrial activity of any size is in the public sector. Under development plans, projects completed or under construction with overseas financial and technical assistance include the production of cement, bricks and tiles, sheet glass, steel sections, jute bags and twine, cotton yarns and cloth, pharmaceuticals, sugar, paper, plywood, urea fertilizers, soda ash, tractors and tyres; also a hydroelectric scheme and various irrigation works.

A new ministry was established in 1992 with the task of attracting 500,000 tourists; less than 10,000 visited in 1991 but visitors and revenues are increasing.

In 1993 the military government began to open the economy to foreign investment, signing 50 joint ventures in the fields of oil and gas exploration, hotel construction and forestry. Mild economic liberalization, including the legalization of small-scale private enterprises, has so far failed to gain the country IMF loans, but the first foreign hotels have opened in Rangoon and Mandalay.

TRADE WITH UK	1993	1994
Imports from UK	£19,274,000	£13,011,000
Exports to UK	9,100,000	14,004,000

COMMUNICATIONS

The Irrawaddy and its chief tributary, the Chindwin, are important waterways, the main stream being navigable 900 miles from its mouth and carrying much traffic. The chief seaports are Yangon (Rangoon), Mawlamyine (Moulmein), Akyab (Sittwe) and Pathein (Bassein).

The railway network covers 2,764 route miles, extending to Myitkyina on the Upper Irrawaddy. There are 2,452 miles of highways and 11,767 miles of other main roads. The airport at Mingaladon, about 13 miles north of Yangon (Rangoon), only handles limited international air traffic.

EDUCATION

The literacy rate is high compared to other Asian countries. Most children attend primary school, and about four million are currently enrolled; in middle and high schools, enrolment is about 11 million. There are five universities, at Yangon (Rangoon), Mandalay, Taunggyi, Sagaing and Mawlamyine (Moulmein). Under the universities are three affiliated degree colleges and the Workers' College,

Yangon. There are also 14 two-year colleges affiliated to the universities, spread throughout the country.

Vocational training is provided at 16 teachers' training institutes, seven government technical institutes, 14 technical high schools, 15 agricultural institutes and schools, and 34 vocational schools for handicrafts, etc.

NAMIBIA
The Republic of Namibia

Namibia lies on the south-west coast of Africa. It is bordered in the north by Angola (17° 23′ S. latitude), in the south by the Northern Cape region of South Africa, in the east by Botswana, and on the west lies the Atlantic Ocean. In addition the Caprivi Strip in the north-east of the country borders on Zambia and Zimbabwe. Namibia has an area of 318,261 sq. miles (824,292 sq. km), including the area of Walvis Bay (434 sq. miles). The average rainfall over 70 per cent of the country is below 400 mm a year.

The population was estimated by the UN at 1,534,000 in 1992. The main population groups are: Ovambo (587,000), Kavango (110,000), Damara (89,000), Herero (89,000), whites (78,000), Nama (57,000), coloured (48,000), Caprivians (44,000), Bushmen (34,000), Rehoboth Baster (29,000), Tswana (7,000). English is the official language, with Afrikaans, German and local languages also in use.

CAPITAL – Windhoek (population, 1987 estimate, 110,000). Other major towns are Grootfontein, ΨWalvis Bay, ΨLüderitz, Karasburg and Keetmanshoop.

CURRENCY – Namibian Dollar of 100 cents, introduced in September 1993 at parity to South African rand (the previous currency).

FLAG – Divided diagonally blue, red and green with the red fimbriated in white; a gold twelve-rayed sun in the upper hoist.

NATIONAL DAY – 21 March (Independence Day).

HISTORY

The German protectorate of South West Africa from 1880 to 1915, Namibia was administered until the end of 1920 by the Union of South Africa. Under the terms of the Treaty of Versailles, the territory was entrusted to South Africa with full powers of administration and legislation over the territory. After the dissolution of the League of Nations and in the absence of a trusteeship agreement, South Africa informed the United Nations that it would continue to administer South West Africa.

In 1971 the International Court of Justice at The Hague delivered a majority opinion that the continued presence of South Africa was illegal, and that it was to withdraw its administration from Namibia immediately, putting an end to its occupation of the territory. The South African government rejected this opinion, but accepted the principle that the territory should attain independence. In 1977 the five Western members of the UN Security Council drew up a plan, later incorporated into Security Council Resolution 435, for a peaceful settlement. Implementation of Resolution 435 began in April 1989 and elections for 72 seats in Namibia's first nationally elected body took place under UN supervision on 7–11 November 1989. The South West Africa People's Organization (SWAPO) won 41 seats, the Democratic Turnhalle Alliance 21 seats, the United Democratic Front 4 seats, Action Christian National 3, Namibia Patriotic Front 1, Federal Convention of Namibia 1, and Namibia National Front 1.

Independence was declared on 21 March 1990. Namibia joined the Commonwealth upon independence.

Previously a British and South African colony separate from German South West Africa/Namibia, Walvis Bay was governed from August 1992 by the joint South African-Namibian Walvis Bay Administrative Body until 28 February 1994, when South Africa renounced its claim to sovereignty over the enclave and it became part of Namibia.

GOVERNMENT

Constitutionally defined as a multiparty, secular, democratic republic, Namibia has an executive President as head of state who exercises the functions of government with the assistance of a Cabinet headed by a Prime Minister. The President is directly elected for a maximum of two five-year terms. Legislative authority lies with the National Assembly, which is the lower house of a bicameral parliament; an upper house (National Council) representing regional councils was elected in November 1992 and inaugurated in January 1993. Each of the 13 regional councils appoints two representatives to the National Council. The main function of the National Council is to review and consider legislation from the National Assembly. Under a system of proportional representation, elections to the National Assembly are to take place every five years, or earlier if decided by the President. Members of the National Council hold their seats for six years. The constitution can only be changed by a two-thirds majority in the National Assembly.

Presidential and legislative elections were held on 7–8 December 1994 and won by the incumbent, Sam Nujoma, and by SWAPO respectively. In the 72-seat National Assembly SWAPO has 53 seats, the Democratic Turnhalle Alliance 15 seats, and other parties four seats.

HEAD OF STATE
President, Dr Sam Nujoma, *elected* 16 February 1990,
   re-elected 8 December 1994

CABINET *as at August 1995*
Home Affairs, The President
Prime Minister, Hon. Hage Geingob
Deputy Prime Minister, Hon. Revd. Hendrik Witbooi
Foreign Affairs, Hon. Theo-Ben Gurirab
Defence, Hon. Phillemon Malima
Finance, Hon. Helmut Angula
Tertiary Education and Vocational Training, Hon. Nahas
   Angula
Information and Broadcasting, Hon. Ben Amathila
Health and Social Services, Hon. Dr Nicky Iyambo
Labour and Manpower Development, Hon. Moses Garoeb
Mines and Energy, Hon. Andimba Toivo Ya Toivo
Justice, Hon. Ngarikutuke Tjiriange
Regional and Local Government and Housing, Hon. Libertine
   Amathila
Agriculture, Water and Rural Development, Hon. Nangolo
   Mbumba
Trade and Industry, Hon. Hidipo Hamutenya
Environment and Tourism, Hon. Gert Hanekom
Works, Transport, and Communication, Hon. Hampie Plichta
Lands, Resettlement and Rehabilitation, Hon. Richard
   Kapelwa-Kabajani
Youth and Sport, Hon. Pendukeni Iithana
Fisheries and Marine Resources, Hon. Hifikepunye Pohamba
Prisons and Correctional Services, Marco Hausiku
Basic Education and Culture, John Mutorwa

HIGH COMMISSION OF THE REPUBLIC OF NAMIBIA
6 Chandos Street, London WIM OLQ
Tel 0171-636 6244

High Commissioner, His Excellency Veiccoh K. Nghiwete,
   apptd 1991

BRITISH HIGH COMMISSION
116 Robert Mugabe Avenue, Windhoek 9000
Tel: Windhoek 223022
High Commissioner, His Excellency Henry George Hogger,
   apptd 1992

BRITISH COUNCIL REPRESENTATIVE, Phillip Mitchell,
   PO Box 24224, 74 Bülowstrasse, Windhoek 9000

ECONOMY

Mining (mainly diamonds and uranium), agriculture and fisheries account for over 40 per cent of GDP. Most of the labour force is employed in the agricultural sector. Large deposits of diamonds along the coast and offshore along the sea bed are estimated at between 1,500 and 3,000 million carats. Walvis Bay and Lüderitz are the main ports.

TRADE WITH UK	1993	1994
Imports from UK	£6,214,000	£4,530,000
Exports to UK	23,641,000	26,723,000

NAURU
The Republic of Nauru

Nauru is an island 8.2 sq. miles (21 sq. km) in area, situated in 166° 55′ E. longitude and 0° 32′ S. of the Equator. It had a population (census 1983) of 8,042: Nauruans 4,964; other Pacific Islanders 2,134; Asians 682; Caucasians 262. The UN estimated a total population of 10,000 in 1992. About 43 per cent of Nauruans are adherents of the Nauruan Protestant Church and there is a Roman Catholic mission on the island. The main languages are English and Nauran.

CURRENCY – Nauru uses the Australian dollar ($A) of 100
   cents as legal tender.
FLAG – Twelve-point star (representing the 12 original
   Nauruan tribes) below a gold bar (representing the
   Equator), all on a blue ground.
NATIONAL DAY – 31 January (Independence Day).

GOVERNMENT

From 1888 until the First World War Nauru was administered by Germany. In 1920 it became a British Empire-mandated territory under the League of Nations, administered by Australia. A trusteeship superseding the mandate was approved in 1947 by the UN and Nauru continued to be administered by Australia until it became independent on 31 January 1968. It was announced in November 1968 that a special form of membership of the Commonwealth had been devised for Nauru at the request of its government.

Parliament has 18 members including the Cabinet and Speaker. Voting is compulsory for all Nauruans over 20 years of age, except in certain specified instances. Elections are held every three years. The Cabinet is chosen by the President, who is elected by the Parliament from amongst its members, and comprises not fewer than five nor more than six members including the President.

HEAD OF STATE
*President and Minister for External Affairs, Island Development
   and Industry, Civil Aviation Authority and the Public Service,*
   Bernard Dowiyogo *elected by parliament* December 1989,
   re-elected November 1992

CABINET *as at August 1995*

Internal Affairs, Works and Community Services and Minister Assisting the President, Vinson Detenamo
Finance, Vinci Clodumar
Education, Nimes Ekewona
Justice, Derog Gioura
Health, Ludwig Scotti
BRITISH HIGH COMMISSIONER, His Excellency Michael Peart, CMG, CVO, resident at Suva, Fiji

JUDICIARY

A Supreme Court of Nauru is presided over by the Chief Justice. The District Court, which is subordinate to the Supreme Court, is presided over by a Resident Magistrate. Both the Supreme Court and the District Court are courts of record. The Supreme Court exercises both original and appellate jurisdiction.

ECONOMY

The only fertile areas are the narrow coastal belt and local requirements of fruit and vegetables are mostly met by imports. The economy is heavily dependent on the extraction of phosphate, of which the island has one of the world's richest deposits. About one million tonnes of phosphate are mined each year, providing employment for over 1,000 people. The industry has been run since 1970 by the Nauru Phosphate Corporation. Considerable investments have been made abroad with the royalties on phosphate exports to provide for a time when production declines. In 1993 an agreement was signed with Australia for compensation to cover damage caused by phosphate mining during the Australian mandate and trusteeship periods. The compensation package is worth some £50 million (a portion of which will be paid by the UK and New Zealand governments), composed of a £33 million payment and a 20-year package of health and education programmes.

The Nauru Pacific Line owns six ships; the government-owned Air Nauru operates air services throughout the Pacific region and to Australia, New Zealand, Japan, Singapore and the Philippines.

TRADE WITH UK	1993	1994
Imports from UK	£185,000	£837,000
Exports to UK	35,000	—

SOCIAL SERVICES

Nauru has a hospital service and other medical and dental services. There is also a maternity and child welfare service.

Education is available in nine primary and two secondary schools on the island with a total enrolment of about 1,600 pupils receiving primary education and 500 secondary education.

NEPAL

Nepal lies between India and the Tibet Autonomous Region of China on the slopes of the Himalayas, and includes Mount Everest (29,028 ft). It has a total area of 54,342 sq. miles (140,747 sq. km).

The southern region, the Terai, was covered with jungle but has been more widely cultivated recently. It forms about 23 per cent of the total land area and nearly 44 per cent of the population live there. The central belt of the country is hilly, but with many fertile valleys, leading up to

the snowline at about 16,000 feet. The hills account for 42 per cent of the area of the country and about 48 per cent of the population. The remainder of the country, the Himalayan region, consists of high mountains which are sparsely inhabited. The country is drained by three great river systems rising within and beyond the Himalayan mountain ranges and eventually flowing into the Ganges in India.

The population (UN estimate 1992) was 20,577,000. The inhabitants are of mixed stock, with Mongolian characteristics prevailing in the north and Indian in the south. The official religion is Hinduism: 89.5 per cent of the population are Hindus and 6 per cent are Buddhist. Gautama Buddha was born in Nepal.

CAPITAL – Kathmandu, population (1989) 300,000. Other towns of importance are Biratnagar (94,000), Lalitpur (81,000), Bhaktapur (50,500), and Pokhara (48,500).
CURRENCY – Nepalese rupee of 100 paisa.
FLAG – Double pennant of crimson with blue border on peaks; white moon with rays in centre of top peak; white quarter sun, recumbent in centre of bottom peak.
NATIONAL ANTHEM – May Glory Crown Our Illustrious Sovereign.
NATIONAL DAYS – 18 February (National Democracy Day); 28 December (The King's Birthday).

GOVERNMENT

Nepal was originally divided into numerous hill clans and petty principalities but emerged as a nation in the middle of the 18th century when it was unified by the warrior Raja of Gorkha, Prithvi Narayan Shah, who founded the present Nepalese dynasty. In 1846 power was seized by Jung Bahadur Rana after a massacre of nobles, and he was the first of a line of hereditary Rana Prime Ministers who ruled Nepal for 104 years. During this time the role of the monarchs was mainly ceremonial.

In 1950–1 a revolutionary movement broke the hereditary power of the Ranas and restored the monarchy to its former position. After ten years, during which various parties and individuals tried their hand at government, King Mahendra proscribed all political parties and assumed direct powers in 1960, with the object of leading a united country to democracy. In 1962 he introduced a new constitution embodying a tiered, partyless system of panchyat (council) democracy.

Mass agitation for political reform led in April 1990 to the lifting of the ban on political parties and the abolition of the panchyat system. A new constitution was promulgated in November 1990 establishing a multiparty, parliamentary system of government and a constitutional monarchy. The King retains joint executive power with the Council of Ministers. A bicameral legislature was set up, consisting of a 205-member House of Representatives and a 60-member National Council, including ten royal nominees. Elections in May 1991 were won by the Nepali Congress Party, which formed a government. This was brought down by a no-confidence vote in July 1994 on charges that the economy had worsened and corruption increased during its rule. Elections in November 1994 resulted in no overall control for any party and the United Marxist Leninist Party formed a minority government as the largest party. This government was brought down by a no-confidence vote in June 1995 and another election is planned for November 1995.

HEAD OF STATE
HM The King of Nepal, King Birendra Bir Bikram Shah Dev, *born* 28 December 1945; *succeeded* 31 January 1972; *crowned* 24 February 1975; *married* February 1970, HM Queen Aishwatya Rajya Laxmi Devi Shah

Heir, HRH Crown Prince Dipendra Bir Bikram Shah Dev, *born* 27 June 1971

ROYAL NEPALESE EMBASSY
12A Kensington Palace Gardens, London w8 4QU
Tel 0171–229 1594/6231
Ambassador Extraordinary and Plenipotentiary, His Excellency Surya Prasad Shrestha, apptd 1992
Minister-Counsellor, Madhab Prasad Khanal

BRITISH EMBASSY
Lainchaur Kathmandu, PO Box 106
Tel: Kathmandu 410583
Ambassador Extraordinary and Plenipotentiary, His Excellency Timothy George, CMG, apptd 1990

BRITISH COUNCIL REPRESENTATIVE, Sarah Ewans, (PO Box 640), Kantipath, Kathmandu

ECONOMY

The budget for the fiscal year 1995–6 is estimated at NRs. 52,894.6 million, of which NRs. 22,342.8 million was allocated to regular and NRs. 30,551.7 million to development expenditures. Revenue was estimated at NRs. 31,782.5 million, foreign aid and grants NRs. 14,573.6 million, and domestic borrowing NRs. 2,300 million.

In October 1992 the IMF approved a three-year loan of US$49 million to support Nepal's medium-term economic reform programme. In February 1993 the rupee was floated and made fully convertible.

Nepal exports carpets, jute, handicrafts, garments, hides and skins, medicinal herbs, cardamom, pulses, tea, etc., and imports textiles, machinery and parts, transport equipment, medicine, construction materials etc. Tourism is the single largest commercial earner of foreign exchange.

Trade with UK	1993	1994
Imports from UK	£11,920,000	£9,419,000
Exports to UK	6,440,000	6,877,000

COMMUNICATIONS

The total length of roads is 6,525 km. Most of the major roads have been built since the 1960s, often with aid from India and China. Kathmandu is connected by road with India and Tibet. Internally, the road network links Kathmandu to Kodari and Pokhara, and Pokhara to Sunauli. A road between Mugling and Naryanghat has further improved communications between Kathmandu and the Terai. The East–West Highway (Mahendra Raj Marg) running along the entire length of the country is complete except for the Banbasa-Mahakali section.

Royal Nepal Airlines operates an extensive network of domestic flights, and there are international flights to Europe, the Middle East and throughout Asia.

Telecommunication services, both domestic and international, are available. Television was introduced in 1984.

THE NETHERLANDS
Koninkrijk der Nederlanden

The kingdom of the Netherlands is a maritime country of western Europe, situated on the North Sea, in 50° 46' to 53° 34' N. latitude and 3° 22' to 7° 14' E. longitude, consisting of 12 provinces (Eastern and Southern Flevoland being amalgamated to form the twelfth province) and containing a total area of 15,770 sq. miles (40,844 sq. km). The land is generally flat and low, intersected by numerous

canals and connecting rivers. The principal rivers are the Rhine, Maas, Yssel and Scheldt.

The population (1991 estimate) is 15,240,000. The language is Dutch, a West Germanic language of Saxon origin closely akin to Old English and Low German. It is spoken in the Netherlands and the northern part of Belgium (Flanders). It is also used in the Netherlands Antilles.

CAPITAL – ΨAmsterdam, population 1,031,000 (urban agglomeration), 713,407 (city) (1992).
SEAT OF GOVERNMENT – The Hague (Den Haag or, in full, 's-Gravenhage), population 445,287 (1992).
Other principal cities (1992) ΨRotterdam 589,707; Utrecht, 232,705; Eindhoven, 193,966; Haarlem 149,788; Groningen 169,387; Tilburg 160,618.
CURRENCY – Netherlands guilder of 100 cents.
FLAG – Three horizontal bands of red, white and blue.
NATIONAL ANTHEM – Wilhelmus.

GOVERNMENT

In 1815 the Netherlands became a constitutional kingdom under King William I, a descendant of the house of Orange-Nassau which had taken a leading part in the affairs of the nation since the 16th century.

The States-General consists of the *Eerste Kamer* (First Chamber) of 75 members, elected for four years by the Provincial Council; and the *Tweede Kamer* (Second Chamber) of 150 members, elected for four years by voters of 18 years and upwards. Members of the *Tweede Kamer* are paid. The most recent election to the Second Chamber was held on 3 May 1994 and resulted in a three-party centre-left coalition of the Labour Party, People's Party and Democrats 66. The state of the parties as at August 1995 was: Labour Party (PvdA) 37; Christian Democratic Appeal (CDA) 34; People's Party for Freedom and Democracy (VVD) 31; Democrats 66 (D66) 24; Protestants Alliance 7; General League of the Elderly 6; Greens 5; others 6.

HEAD OF STATE
HM The Queen of the Netherlands, Queen Beatrix Wilhelmina Armgard, KG, GCVO, *born* 31 January 1938; *succeeded* 30 April 1980, upon the abdication of her mother Queen

Juliana; *married* 10 March 1966, HRH Prince Claus
George Willem Otto Frederik Geert of the Netherlands,
Jonkheer van Amsberg; and has *issue*, Prince Willem (*see*
below); Prince Johan Friso, *b.* 25 September 1968; Prince
Constantijn Christof, *b.* 11 October 1969
Heir, HRH Prince Willem Alexander, *b.* 27 April 1967

CABINET *as at August 1995*

Prime Minister, Minister of General Affairs, Wim Kok (PvdA)
Deputy P.M and Home Affairs, Hans Dijkstal (VVD)
Deputy P.M and Foreign Affairs, Hans van Mierlo (D66)
Finance, Gerrit Zalm (VVD)
Development Co-operation, Jan Pronk (PvdA)
Defence, Netherlands Antilles and Aruba Affairs, Joris
    Voorhoeve (VVD)
Economic Affairs, G. J. Wijers (D66)
Justice, Winnie Sorgdrager (D66)
Agriculture, Nature Management and Fisheries, J. van Aartsen
    (VVD)
Education, Culture and Science, Prof. Dr Jo Ritzen (PvdA)
Social Affairs and Employment, Ad Melkert (PvdA)
Transport, Water Management, and Public Works, Annemarie
    Jorritsma-Lebbink (VVD)
Housing, Physical Planning and Environment, M. De Boer
    (PvdA)
Welfare, Health and Sport, Dr E. Borst-Eilers (D66)

VVD People's Party for Freedom and Democracy;
    D66 Democrats 66; PvdA Labour Party

ROYAL NETHERLANDS EMBASSY
38 Hyde Park Gate, London SW7 5DP
Tel 0171–584 5040
Ambassador Extraordinary and Plenipotentiary, His Excellency
    Jan Herman van Roijen, apptd 1990
Ministers Plenipotentiary, M. H. R. Loudon; A. J. Quanjer
    (*Economic*)
Consul-General, H. Nijenhuis
Defence, Naval and Air Attaché, Capt. J. J. Blok

BRITISH EMBASSY
Lange Voorhout 10, The Hague, 2514 ED
Tel: The Hague 427 0427
Ambassador Extraordinary and Plenipotentiary, His Excellency
    Sir David Miers, KBE, CMG, apptd 1993
Counsellors, P. S. Dimond (*Deputy Head of Mission*);
    C. W. Robins (*Commercial*)
Defence and Naval Attaché, Capt. P. J. Organ, RN
Consul-General, D. H. Doble (resides at Amsterdam)

There is a Consulate-General at Amsterdam, a Consulate
at Willemstad (Curaçao) and a Vice-Consulate at Philips-
burg (St Maarten) (both Netherlands Antilles).

BRITISH COUNCIL DIRECTOR, Iain Frater, Keizersgracht
    343, 1016 EH Amsterdam

NETHERLANDS-BRITISH CHAMBER OF COMMERCE, The
    Dutch House, 307–308 High Holborn, London WC1V
    7LS

UK OFFICE IN THE HAGUE, Holland Trade House,
    Bezuidenhoutseweg 181, 2594 AH The Hague

DEFENCE

The armed forces are almost entirely committed to
NATO. Total armed forces number 70,900, which includes 29,500 conscripts. In addition there are 130,600
reservists. There is compulsory military service of nine
months. In 1993 the government announced plans to
abolish conscription in 1998.
    The Army has a strength of 43,300 (24,700 conscripts)
with 740 main battle tanks, 1,975 armoured infantry

fighting vehicles and armoured personnel carriers, and
420 artillery pieces.
    The Navy has a strength of 14,300, including 2,930
marines and 1,000 conscripts. It maintains a force of six
submarines, four destroyers, 14 frigates with 33 patrol and
coastal craft, 13 combat aircraft and 22 armed helicopters.
    The Air Force has a strength of 9,000 (3,300 conscripts),
with 183 combat aircraft.
    As part of its NATO commitment, the Netherlands
maintains 3,000 Army personnel in Germany and is the
base for HQ Allied Forces Central Europe, and for 1,350
US personnel. One frigate, marine and aircraft detachments are deployed in the Netherlands Antilles; 1,675
troops are deployed with UN forces in Bosnia; 17 aircraft
and 360 personnel are deployed in Italy for NATO
operations over Bosnia; one frigate is deployed in the
Adriatic.
    There is also a paramilitary Royal Military Constab-
ulary of 3,600 personnel (500 conscripts).

ECONOMY

Of a total GNP of US$279.1 billion in 1990, industry
accounted for around 31 per cent, agriculture for 4 per cent
and services 65 per cent. Inflation was 2.1 per cent in 1995.
    The chief agricultural products are potatoes, wheat, rye,
barley, sugar beet, cattle, pigs, milk and milk products,
cheese, butter, poultry, eggs, beans, peas, vegetables, fruit,
flower bulbs, plants and cut flowers and there is an
important fishing industry.
    Among the principal industries are engineering, elec-
tronics, nuclear energy, petrochemicals and plastics, road
vehicles, aircraft and defence equipment, shipbuilding
repair, steel, textiles of all types, electrical appliances,
metal ware, furniture, paper, cigars, sugar, liqueurs, beer,
clothing etc.

TRADE

The Dutch are traditionally a trading nation. Trade,
banking and shipping are of particular importance to the
economy. The geographical position of the Netherlands, at
the mouths of the Rhine, Meuse and Scheldt, brings a large
volume of transit trade to and from the interior of Europe
to Dutch ports. Principal trading partners are Germany,
Belgium/Luxembourg and France.

	1991	1992
Imports	Guilders 118,194m	Guilders 117,526m
Exports	124,862m	126,119m

Trade with UK	1993	1994
Imports from UK	£7,909,232,000	£9,314,331,000
Exports to UK	8,535,619,000	9,745,362,000

COMMUNICATIONS

The total extent of navigable rivers including canals, was
5,046 km in 1992, and of metalled roads 104,831 km. The
total length of the railway system amounted to 2,780 km, of
which 1,939 km were electrified. The mercantile marine in
1992 consisted of 410 ships of total 2,890,000 gross
registered tons. The total of kilometres flown by KLM
(Royal Dutch Airlines) in 1991–2 was 188 million km.
    There are six national papers, four of which are morning
papers, and there are many regional daily papers.

EDUCATION

Primary and secondary education is given in both denominational and state schools. Attendance at primary school is
compulsory.

The principal universities are at Leiden, Utrecht, Groningen, Amsterdam (two), Nijmegen, Maastricht and Rotterdam, and there are technical universities at Delft, Eindhoven, Enschede and Wageningen (agriculture).

OVERSEAS TERRITORIES

ARUBA

Aruba covers an area of 75 sq. miles (193 sq. km) and has a population (1994) of 71,000. The island was from 1828 part of the Dutch West Indies and from 1845 part of the Netherlands Antilles. On 1 January 1986 it became a separate territory within the Kingdom of the Netherlands. The 1983 Constitutional Conference agreed that Aruba's separate status would last for ten years from 1986, after which the island would become fully independent. In 1994 this decision was changed and it was decided that Aruba will retain its separate status within the Kingdom of the Netherlands.
Governor, O. L. Koolman
Prime Minister, J. H. A. Eman

CAPITAL – ΨOranjestad (population 25,000); and Sint Nicolaas (17,000).
CURRENCY – Aruban florin.

ECONOMY – The economy of Aruba is based largely on tourism. In 1994 there were 582,136 tourists.

TRADE WITH UK	1993	1994
Imports from UK	£41,930,000	£47,748,000
Exports to UK	80,000	5,417,000

NETHERLANDS ANTILLES

The Netherlands Antilles comprise the islands of Curaçao, Bonaire, part of St Martin, St Eustatius, and Saba in the West Indies. The islands cover an area of 308 sq. miles (800 sq. km) with a population (1993) of 197,000 (Curaçao 146,800, Bonaire 11,400, St Martin 35,800, St Eustatius 1,840, Saba 1,180). The Netherlands Antilles, which have a 22-member federal parliament, are largely self-governing under the terms of the Realm Statute which took effect in 1954.
Governor, Dr Jaime Saleh
Prime Minister, Miguel Pourier

CAPITAL – ΨWillemstad (on Curaçao) (pop. 50,000).
CURRENCY – Netherlands Antilles guilder of 100 cents.

ECONOMY – The economy of the Netherlands Antilles is based on small manufacturing industries. The soil is too poor to permit large-scale agriculture and most products for consumption and industrial raw materials must be imported. Tourism is also important, with 753,000 tourists and 866,000 cruise-ship day trippers in 1993.

TRADE WITH UK	1993*	1994*
Imports from UK	£17,024,000	£17,831,000
Exports to UK	28,871,000	28,633,000
*Curaçao		

NEW ZEALAND

AREA AND POPULATION

Islands	Area (sq. miles)	Population at 31 March 1993
North Island	44,281	2,604,200
South Island	58,093	890,100
Other islands	1,362	
Total	103,736	3,494,300
Territories		
Tokelau	5	1,700 (a)
Niue	100	2,239
Cook Islands	93	18,300 (b)
Ross Dependency	175,000	
(a) 1994		
(b) 1991		

Of the total population of New Zealand, some 79 per cent is of European stock, 13 per cent Maori and 5 per cent other Pacific Islanders.

The main religion is Christianity. In 1991 the principal denominations were Anglican 22.1 per cent, Presbyterian 16.3 per cent, Roman Catholic 15 per cent, Methodist 4.2 per cent, Baptist 2.1 per cent.

GEOGRAPHY

New Zealand consists of a number of islands in the South Pacific Ocean, and has also administrative responsibility for the Ross Dependency in Antarctica. The two larger islands, North Island and South Island, are separated by a relatively narrow strait. The remaining islands are very much smaller and are dispersed over a considerable expanse of ocean. The boundaries, inclusive of the most outlying islands and dependencies, range from 33° to 53° S. latitude, and from 162° E. longitude to 173° W. longitude.

Much of the North and South Islands is mountainous. The principal range is the Southern Alps, extending the entire length of the South Island and having its culminating point in Mount Cook (12,349 ft). The North Island mountains include several volcanoes, two of which are active. Of the numerous glaciers in the South Island, the Tasman (18 miles long by 1½ wide), the Franz Josef and the Fox are the best known. The North Island is noted for its hot springs and geysers. The more important rivers include the Waikato (270 miles in length), Wanganui (180), and Clutha (210) and lakes include Taupo, 234 sq. miles in area; Wakatipu, 113; and Te Anau, 133.

New Zealand includes, in addition to North and South Islands: Chatham Islands (Chatham, Pitt, South East Islands and some rocky islets, combined area, 965 sq. km (373 sq. miles), largely uninhabited; Stewart Island (area 1,746 sq. km (674 sq. miles), largely uninhabited); the Kermadec Group (Raoul or Sunday, Macaulay, Curtis Islands, L'Esperance, and some islets; population 9–10, all government employees at a meteorological station); Campbell Island, used as a weather station; the Three Kings (discovered by Tasman on the Feast of the Epiphany); Auckland Islands; Antipodes Group; Bounty Islands; Snares Islands and Solander.

New Zealand has a temperate marine climate, but with abundant sunshine. The mean temperature ranges from 15°C in the north to about 9°C in the south. Rainfall in the North Island ranges from 35 to 70 inches and in the South Island from 25 to 45 inches.

CAPITAL – ΨWellington, in the North Island. Population (March 1994 estimate) of Wellington urban area, 329,000. Other large urban areas: ΨAuckland 929,300; ΨChristchurch 318,100; ΨDunedin 112,400; Hamilton 153,800; Ψ Napier-Hastings 110,200.

CURRENCY – New Zealand dollar (NZ$) of 100 cents.

FLAG – Blue ground, with Union Flag in top left quarter, four five-pointed red stars with white borders on the fly.

NATIONAL ANTHEM – God Save The Queen/God Defend New Zealand.

NATIONAL DAY – 6 February (Waitangi Day).

GOVERNMENT

The discoverers and first colonists of New Zealand were Polynesian people, ancestors of the Maori of today. Whether there was a single colonization or many is not known but the ninth century is generally considered to be the date of the first settlement. By the 13th or 14th century there were well-established Maori settlements. The first European to discover New Zealand was a Dutch navigator, Abel Tasman, who sighted the coast in 1642 but did not land. It was the British explorer James Cook who circumnavigated New Zealand and landed in 1769. Largely as a result of increased British emigration, the country was annexed by the British government in 1840. The British Lieutenant-Governor, William Hobson, proclaimed sovereignty over the North Island by virtue of the Treaty of Waitangi, signed by him and many Maori chiefs, and over the South Island and Stewart Island by right of discovery.

In 1841 New Zealand was created a separate colony distinct from New South Wales. In 1907 the designation was changed to 'The Dominion of New Zealand'. The constitution rests upon the Constitution Act 1852 and other imperial statutes. A 1986 Constitution Act brought a number of statutory constitutional provisions. The Statute of Westminster was formally adopted by New Zealand in 1947.

The executive authority is entrusted to a Governor-General appointed by the Crown and aided by an Executive Council, within a unicameral legislature, the House of Representatives. The House of Representatives consists of 99 members elected for three years. There are four Maori electorates. In a referendum in 1992 the electorate voted in favour of the introduction of a mixed-member proportional representation system to replace the first-past-the-post system. From the 1996 elections onwards there will be 120 House of Representatives seats, of which 65 will be elected by the first-past-the-post system and 55 by proportional representation on a party list basis. The number of Maori electorates will be increased to five.

Following the general election of 6 November 1993, the state of the parties in the House of Representatives is National 49, Labour 44, The Alliance 2, New Zealand First 2, Future New Zealand 1, Right of Centre Party 1.

In December 1994 the government offered NZ$1,000 million over a ten-year period to Maori tribes to settle outstanding land claims. The first agreement, with the Tainui tribe, was signed in May 1995 for NZ$170 million.

GOVERNOR-GENERAL

Governor-General and Commander-in-Chief, Her Excellency Dame Catherine Tizard, GCMG, DBE, *sworn in* November 1990

THE EXECUTIVE COUNCIL *as at August 1995*

The Governor-General

Prime Minister, Minister in Charge of the New Zealand Security Intelligence Service, Rt. Hon. J. B. Bolger.

Deputy PM, Foreign Affairs and Trade, Pacific Island Affairs, Leader of the House, Rt. Hon. D. C. McKinnon

Finance, Rt. Hon. W. F. Birch

Health and Women's Affairs, Hon. Jenny Shipley

Attorney-General, Hon. Paul East

Agriculture and Forestry, Hon. John Falloon

Employment, Hon. Wyatt Creech

Commerce, Industry and Trade Negotiations, State-Owned Enterprises, Railways, Hon. Philip Burdon

Environment, Research, Science and Technology, Hon. Simon Upton

Local Government, Tourism, Recreation and Sport, Hon. John Banks

Social Welfare, Senior Citizens, Hon. Peter Gresham

Defence, Interior, Hon. Warren Cooper

Justice, Disarmament and Arms Control, Treaty of Waitangi Negotiations, Culture, Hon. Douglas Graham

Education, Hon. Dr Lockwood Smith

Labour, Fisheries and Energy, Hon. Doug Kidd

Housing, Customs, Hon. Murray McCully

Conservation and Lands, Hon. Denis Marshall

Police, Maori Affairs, Hon. John Luxton

Transport, Communications, Broadcasting, Statistics, Hon. Maurice Williamson

Insurance, Radio and Television, Hon. Bruce Cliffe

Speaker of the House of Representatives, Hon. Peter Tapsell

NEW ZEALAND HIGH COMMISSION

New Zealand House, Haymarket, London SW1Y 4TQ Tel 0171-930 8422

High Commissioner, His Excellency John Collinge, apptd 1994

Deputy High Commissioner, M. Chilton

Minister, J. Charles (*Commercial*)

Head, Defence Staff, Cdre J. Peddie

First Secretary, Ms S. Craig (*Cultural Affairs*)

Consul-General, B. M. Burrows

BRITISH HIGH COMMISSION

44 Hill Street (PO Box 1812), Wellington 1 Tel: Wellington 4726-049

High Commissioner, His Excellency Robert Alston, CMG, apptd 1994

Deputy High Commissioner, A. Heath

Counsellor, A. W. Turquet

Defence Adviser, Col. P. R. Barry

First Secretary, M. Capes (*Commercial*)

Consul-General and Director of Trade Promotion, J. F. Holding (*resides at Auckland*)

There is a Consulate-General at Auckland and a Consulate in Christchurch.

BRITISH COUNCIL DIRECTOR, Francis King (*Cultural Attaché*)

BRITISH CHAMBER OF COMMERCE FOR AUSTRALIA AND NEW ZEALAND, PO Box 141, Manuka, ACT 2603, Australia; UK OFFICE, Suite 615, 6th Floor The Linen Hall, 162–168 Regent Street, London W1R 5TB.

JUDICATURE

The judicial system comprises a High Court, a Court of Appeal and district courts having both civil and criminal jurisdiction.

Chief Justice, Rt. Hon. Sir Thomas Eichelbaum, GBE, PC.

President, Court of Appeal, Rt. Hon. Sir Robin Cooke, KBE.

DEFENCE

The total active armed forces personnel is 10,000, with a further 7,850 reserves. The Army has a strength of 4,500 personnel, with 26 light tanks, 78 armoured personnel carriers and 44 artillery pieces. The Navy has a strength of 2,200, with four frigates, four patrol and support craft, and five armed helicopters. The Air Force has a strength of 3,300 personnel with 37 combat aircraft. A support unit of 20 troops is maintained in Singapore. In 1994 250 troops were dispatched to serve under UK command with UN forces in Bosnia-Hercegovina.

FINANCE

Revenue and expenditure for the year ended 30 June 1994 was: revenue NZ$29,598 million, expenditure NZ$29,174 million. Taxation receipts in 1993–4 for all purposes amounted to NZ$28,203 million. The principal items of expenditure were social services NZ$10,528 million, education NZ$4,631 million, health NZ$4,103 million, debt services NZ$3,557 million and administration NZ$2,979 million.

ECONOMY

Since 1984 economic reforms have changed the economy from a highly regulated, nationalized and protected economy with a large welfare state to an economy at the forefront of market economics. Finance market and labour market deregulation, privatization, VAT reform, the introduction of private sector principles in the civil service, health service and education, the ending of agricultural subsidies and the near elimination of import tariffs have all occurred. The Reserve Bank has been made independent, with a contract to keep inflation below 2 per cent. Centralized wage-bargaining has ended and widespread means-testing has been introduced throughout the welfare state, so that only the very poor receive free or subsidized healthcare and other benefits. In 1994 economic growth was five per cent and the net public debt began to be reduced after public spending had been brought under control during the previous few years.

GROSS VALUE OF AGRICULTURAL PRODUCTION
to year ended March (NZ$ million)

	1992
Gross output	9,014
Sheep	833
Wool	782
Cattle	1,423
Dairy products	2,203
Fruit, nuts, oilseeds	821
Agricultural services	742
Sales of live animals	701

AGRICULTURAL AND PASTORAL PRODUCTION

	1992	1993
‡Meat, metric tons	1,142,000	1,098,000
*Wool, metric tons	221,000	193,000
†Butter, metric tons	271,000	267,000
†Cheese, metric tons	137,000	143,000

*Year ended 30 June
†Year ended 31 May
‡Year ended 30 September

Livestock on farms at 30 June 1994 included 3,600,000 dairy cattle, 4,800,000 beef cattle and 1,500,000 deer and goats. Sheep numbered 50,000,000.

The output of sawn timber for 1993–4 was 2,800,000 cubic metres, of which 90 per cent was radiata pine.

Non-metallic minerals such as coal, clay, limestone and dolomite are more important than metallic ones. Coal output in 1993 was 3,100,000 tonnes. Of the metals, the most important are gold and ironsand. Natural gas deposits in the offshore Taranaki Maui field and onshore fields are

increasingly being exploited and used for electricity generation and as a premium fuel. Hydroelectric power is used to generate 96 per cent of the country's electricity.

Manufacturing has become increasingly important to the economy over the past decade and is based on food processing, machinery production, motor vehicle assembly, chemicals, electrical and electronic goods, and paper and printing. Tourism is the fastest growing sector of the economy, with 1,263,000 visitors in 1993–4 earning New Zealand NZ$3,500 million in foreign exchange.

TRADE	1992–3	1993–4
Imports (c.i.f.)	NZ$17,333m	NZ$18,469m
Exports (f.o.b.)	18,971m	19,808m

New Zealand's largest trading partners are Australia, Japan, USA and the UK. New Zealand exports to the UK include butter and cheese, wool, lamb, hides, skins and leather.

Trade with UK	1993	1994*
Imports from UK	£332,897,000	£412,865,000
Exports to UK	496,357,000	539,830,000

*Includes Niue, Tokelau and Cook Islands

COMMUNICATIONS

The national railway system is owned and operated by the privately-owned New Zealand Rail Ltd. In March 1993, there were 4,251 route km of railway in operation. At 31 March 1993 there were 2,379,417 licensed motor vehicles operating on the road network of 93,322 km.

During 1991–2 the vessels entered from overseas ports numbered 3,282 (gross tonnage 27,983,000) and those cleared for overseas 3,298 (gross tonnage 27,508,000).

Domestic flights in 1990 carried 4,502,000 passengers and 47,700 tonnes of freight. International flights carried 3,129,000 passengers, 134,074 tonnes of freight and 5,082 tonnes of mail.

EDUCATION

Schools are free and attendance is compulsory between the ages of six and 15. In 1991 there were 403,435 pupils attending public primary schools, and 12,649 pupils attending registered private primary schools. Secondary education is carried on in 314 state secondary schools and 21 registered private secondary schools. The total number of pupils receiving full-time secondary education in July 1992 was 227,912. There were seven universities with a total of 93,182 students in 1992.

TERRITORIES

TOKELAU (OR UNION ISLANDS)

Tokelau is a group of atolls, Fakaofo, Nukunonu and Atafu, with a total land area of 5 sq. miles and a population of 1,700 (1994). It was proclaimed part of New Zealand as from 1 January 1949. A Council of Faipule, composed of one elected representative from each atoll, was established in August 1992 to govern Tokelau when the council of elders (General Fono) was not in session. The position of Ulu-o-Tokelau (leader) was also established in 1992 and is rotated among the three Faipale members annually. Administrative responsibility for Tokelau lies with the Administrator but in January 1994 his powers were delegated to the General Fono and Council of Faipale. New Zealand provides substantial aid ($5.0 million in year ended 30 June 1994), to meet administrative, social, economic and development requirements. Tokelau receives revenue from the granting of fishing rights in its economic zone.
Administrator, Lindsay Watt
Ulu-o-Tokelau (1995) Lepaio Simi

THE ROSS DEPENDENCY

The Ross Dependency, placed under the jurisdiction of New Zealand in 1923, is defined as all the Antarctic islands and territories between 160° E. and 150° W. longitude which are situated south of the 60° S. parallel, including Edward VII Land and portions of Victoria Land. Since 1957 a number of research stations have been established in the Dependency.

ASSOCIATED STATES

COOK ISLANDS

Included in the realm of New Zealand since June 1901, the Cook Islands group consists of the islands of Rarotonga, Aitutaki, Mangaia, Atiu, Mauke, Mitiaro, Manuae, Takutea, Palmerston, Penrhyn or Tongareva, Manihiki, Rakahanga, Suwarrow, Pukapuka or Danger, and Nassau. The total population of the group was 18,300 in 1991.

The Queen has a representative on the islands, as does the New Zealand government. Since 1965 the islands have been in free association with New Zealand and enjoyed complete internal self-government, executive power being in the hands of a Cabinet consisting of the Prime Minister and 12 other ministers. There is a 25-member Legislative Assembly. New Zealand has residual responsibility for foreign affairs and defence. The New Zealand citizenship of the Cook Islanders is embodied in the constitution.

The chief industries are tourism, financial services and the production of fruit juice, clothing, copra, bananas, citrus fruit and pulp, and black pearls. The New Zealand Government continues to give budget support and development aid to the Cook Islands.

HM Representative, Apenera Short, OBE
Prime Minister, Sir Geoffrey Henry, KBE
New Zealand High Commissioner, Darryl Dunn

NIUE

The population of Niue was 2,239 at the November 1991 census. A New Zealand High Commissioner is stationed at Niue, which since 1974 has been self-governing in free association with New Zealand. New Zealand is responsible for external affairs and defence, and continues to give financial aid. Executive power is in the hands of a Premier and a Cabinet of three drawn from the Assembly of 20 members. The Assembly is the supreme legislative body.

New Zealand High Commissioner, W. Searell

NICARAGUA
República de Nicaragua

Nicaragua is the largest state of Central America, with a long seaboard on both the Atlantic and Pacific Oceans, situated between 10° 45' and 15° N. latitude and 83° 40' and 87° 38' W. longitude. It has an area of 50,193 sq. miles (130,000 sq. km).

There is a population (UN estimate 1992) of 4,131,000, of whom about three-quarters are of mixed blood. Another 15 per cent are white, mostly of pure Spanish descent, and the remaining 10 per cent are West Indians or Indians. The latter group includes the Misquitos, who live on the Atlantic coast. The official language is Spanish and the majority are Roman Catholic, although the English language and the Moravian Church are widespread on the Atlantic coast.

CAPITAL – Managua, population 615,000. Other centres are León, 158,577; Granada, 72,640; Masaya, 78,308; Chinandega, 144,291.

CURRENCY – Córdoba (C$) of 100 centavos.

FLAG – Horizontal stripes of blue, white and blue, with the Nicaraguan coat of arms in the centre of the white stripe.

NATIONAL ANTHEM – Salve A Ti Nicaragua (Hail, Nicaragua).

NATIONAL DAY – 15 September.

GOVERNMENT

The eastern coast of Nicaragua was touched by Columbus in 1502, and in 1518 was overrun by Spanish forces. It formed part of the Spanish Captaincy-General of Guatemala until 1821, when its independence was secured. In 1927 Augusto Cesar Sandino began a guerrilla war against the occupation of Nicaragua by US Marines, which continued until they were expelled in 1933. Sandino was assassinated by Anastasio Somoza, director of the National Guard, and in 1936 Somoza assumed the presidency. He was succeeded in power by his sons Luis and Anastasio Somoza, until 1979 when the family and the National Guard were overthrown by guerrillas of the Sandinista National Liberation Front (FSLN).

After ten years in power and a ten-year civil war against US-backed Contra guerrillas, the Sandinistas lost their parliamentary majority in elections held in February 1990. A coalition of former opposition parties, Unión Nacional de Oposirora (UNO), gained 51 seats to the Sandinistas' 39 seats in the 92-seat National Assembly and formed a government, with UNO leader Violeta Chamorro becoming President. With the defeat of the Sandinistas, the civil war came to an end.

President Chamorro and the UNO found that they had to compromise with the still-powerful Sandinistas, who controlled the trade unions, and to leave the armed forces and police under Sandinista control. Resentment among the UNO coalition at the compromises came to a head in December 1992 when UNO deputies tried to topple Chamorro from power. In response Chamorro ordered the police to seize the National Assembly and negotiated a new governing majority in the National Assembly of 39 Sandinistas and nine loyal UNO deputies, forcing the remaining 42 UNO deputies and Vice-President Godoy into opposition. A further 19 UNO deputies formed the Democratic Christian Union (UDC) in January 1994, which joined the governing coalition and enabled constitutional reforms to be passed affecting civil and political rights, the national economy, legislature and defence.

In the north of the country from late 1992 to early 1994 government forces fought re-armed Contra and Sandinista groups disgruntled at the lack of land and jobs. The last of the groups disarmed in April 1994 after offers of jobs in the police force. The government has initiated negotiations with political, business and church leaders to try to strengthen democracy and national security further through reforms to the judiciary and the executive.

In November 1994 the National Assembly passed constitutional reforms transferring most executive power from the presidency to the legislature. President Chamorro has refused to promulgate the changes and a constitutional deadlock has ensued.

HEAD OF STATE

President, Violeta Barrios de Chamorro, *inaugurated* 25 April 1990

Vice-President, Virgilio Godoy

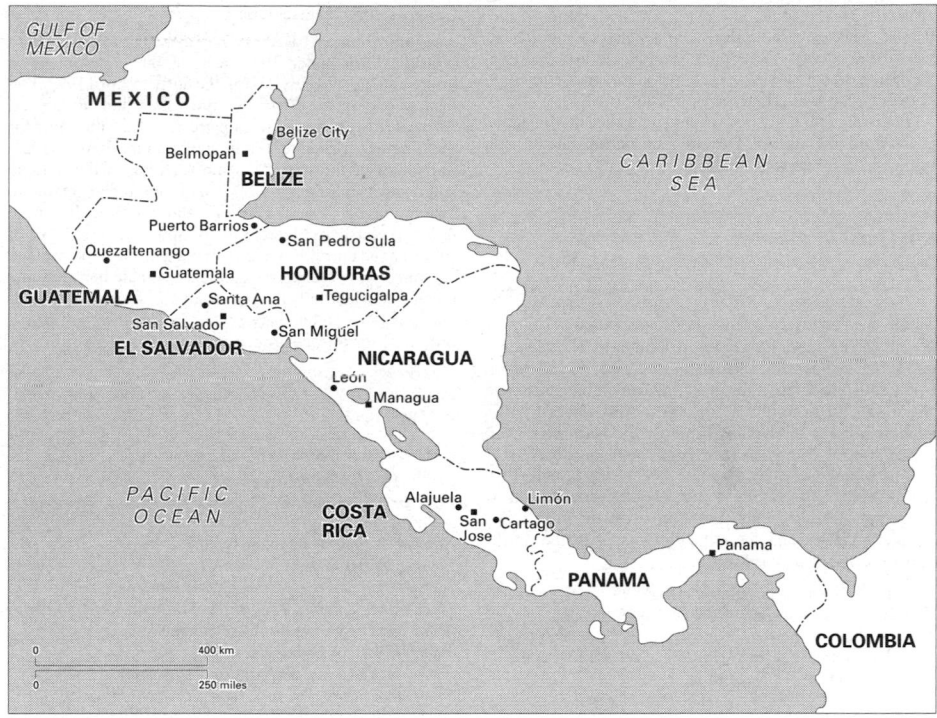

GULF OF
MEXICO

MEXICO

Belize City

Belmopan ■

BELIZE

Puerto Barrios ●

Quezaltenango

■ Guatemala

HONDURAS

●San Pedro Sula

CARIBBEAN
SEA

GUATEMALA

Santa Ana

San Salvador ■

■Tegucigalpa

EL SALVADOR

●San Miguel

NICARAGUA

León

Managua

PACIFIC
OCEAN

Alajuela

**COSTA
RICA**

San
Jose

●Cartago

Limón

Panama

PANAMA

COLOMBIA

0   400 km

0   250 miles

COUNCIL OF MINISTERS *as at August 1995*
Defence, The President
Minister to the Presidency, Antonio Lacayo
External Relations, Ernesto Leal
Interior, Sergio Narvaez
Finance, Emilio Pereira
Foreign Co-operation, Erwin Krugger
Construction and Transport, Pablo Vigil
Health, Marta Palacio
Agriculture, Dionisio Cuadra
Labour, Francisco Rosales
Economy and Planning, Pablo Pereira
Education, Humberto Belli Pereira
Tourism, Fernando Guzman
Environment and Natural Resources, Milton Caldera

EMBASSY OF NICARAGUA
2nd Floor, 36 Upper Brook Street, London WIY IPE
Tel 0171-409 2536
Ambassador Extraordinary and Plenipotentiary, Her
   Excellency Veronica Lacayo de Gómez, apptd 1995

BRITISH EMBASSY
PO Box A-169, El Reparto 'Los Robles', Primera Etapa,
Entrada Principal de la Carretera a Masaya, Managua,
Nicaragua.
Tel: Managua 780014
Ambassador and Consul-General, His Excellency John
   Howard Culver, apptd 1992

DEFENCE

Under the Sandinista government, Nicaragua maintained
armed forces of over 120,000 personnel. Since 1990, active
armed forces personnel has fallen to 15,200 and service is
now voluntary. The Army has 13,500 personnel. The Navy

has a strength of 500, with ten patrol and coastal vessels.
The Air Force has 1,200 personnel.

ECONOMY

Since the end of the civil war the UNO government has
begun to transform the Sandinistas' socialist economy into
a free-market one. An agreement was reached with the IMF
in April 1994 which provided US$662 million in credits to
stabilize the economy and refinance some debt.
   The country is mainly agricultural. The major crops are
peanuts, cotton, coffee, sugar-cane, tobacco, sesame and
bananas. Beans, rice, maize and ipecacuanha, livestock and
timber production are also important. However, fishing,
forestry, grain and cattle production are still recovering
from the civil war in the main growing areas. Nicaragua
possesses deposits of gold and silver.

TRADE

Considerable quantities of foodstuffs are imported as well
as cotton goods, jute, iron and steel, machinery and
petroleum products. The chief exports are peanuts, sesame
seed, cotton, coffee (30 per cent of total export earnings),
beef, gold, sugar, cottonseed and bananas.

Trade with UK	1993	1994
Imports from UK	£4,369,000	£3,969,000
Exports to UK	1,857,000	5,185,000

COMMUNICATIONS

Transport, except on the Pacific slope, is still difficult but
many new roads have been opened. The Inter-American
Highway runs between the Honduras and the Costa Rican
borders; the inter-oceanic highway runs from the Corinto
on the Pacific coast via Managua to Rama, where there is a
natural waterway to Bluefields on the Atlantic. The main

airport is at Managua. The chief port is Corinto on the Pacific. There are 252 miles of railway, all on the Pacific side of the country. There are 51 radio stations and five television stations in Managua. An automatic telephone system has been installed in major cities.

There are four daily newspapers published at Managua, apart from the official Gazette (*La Gaceta*). There are universities at León and Managua.

NIGER
République du Niger

Situated in central west Africa, between 12° and 24° N. and 0° and 16° E., Niger has common boundaries with Algeria and Libya in the north, Chad in the east, Nigeria and Benin in the south, Mali and Burkina in the west. It has an area of about 489,191 sq. miles (1,267,000 sq. km). Apart from a small region along the Niger Valley in the south-west near the capital, the country is entirely savannah or desert.

The population (UN estimate 1992) is 8,252,000. The main ethnic groups are the Hausa (54 per cent) in the south, the Songhai and Djerma in the south-west, the Fulani, the Beriberi–Manga, and the nomadic Tuareg in the north. The official language is French.

CAPITAL – Niamey, population 410,000.

CURRENCY – Franc CFA of 100 centimes.

FLAG – Three horizontal stripes, orange, white and green with an orange disc in the middle of the white stripe.

NATIONAL DAY – 18 December.

GOVERNMENT

The first French expedition arrived in 1891 and the country was fully occupied by 1914. It decided on 18 December 1958 to remain an autonomous republic within the French Community; full independence outside the Community was proclaimed on 3 August 1960.

The 1960 constitution provided for a presidential system of government and a single-chamber National Assembly. In 1974 Lt.-Col. Seyni Kountché seized power, suspended the constitution, dissolved the National Assembly and suppressed all political organizations. He set up a Supreme Military Council with himself as President. President Kountché died in 1987 and was succeeded peacefully by his cousin, Col. Ali Saibou, who restored a measure of normal political life.

In August 1991, a national conference of all groups voted to suspend the constitution and stripped President Saibou of all powers. A transitional government held office until a legislative election was held in February 1993. The former ruling party, the National Movement for a Development Society (MNSD), emerged as the largest party, with 29 seats in the 83-seat National Assembly. The opposition Alliance of Forces for Change (AFC) gained 50 seats, however, and formed the government. Mahamane Ousmane of the AFC won the presidential election in March, when the Third Republic also came into being.

The defection of one of the main AFC parties from the government in late 1994 led to a parliamentary election in January 1995 which was won by the MNSD and allied parties, with 43 seats to the AFC's 40 seats. Political deadlock followed until Hama Amadou of the MNSD was able to form a government in February 1995. The cohabitation between President and government of different parties has caused further political instability.

INSURGENCY

An ethnic Tuareg-based insurgency began in the north of Niger in November 1991, leading the government to impose a state of emergency in the north in April 1992. The insurgency by the Front for the Liberation of Aïr and Azawad (FLAA) aimed to gain greater local autonomy for the Tuaregs, a change to regional boundaries, the demilitarization of the north and the teaching of the Tuareg language, Tamashek. In 1993 two groups, the Front for the Liberation of Tamoust (FLT) and the Revolutionary Army of Northern Niger (RANN) split from the FLAA in protest at its entry into negotiations with the government. An interim peace agreement was signed between the government and all Tuareg groups in Ouagadougou in October 1994, and a peace accord ending the conflict and providing for a peace process was signed on 24 April 1995.

HEAD OF STATE
President of the Third Republic, Mahamane Ousmane, *elected* March 1993

CABINET *as at August 1995*
Prime Minister, Hama Amadou
Minister of State, Industry, Commerce, Handicrafts, Tourism, Sidiki Oumarou
National Defence, Mahamane Dobi
Interior, Moussa Ibrahim
Foreign Affairs and Co-operation, Mohamed Bazoum
Finance and Planning, Almustapha Soumaila
Mines and Energy, Issoufou Assoumane
Public Health, Amstrong Karna
Equipment and Transport, Ahmoud Ousmane
Social Development, Population and Promotion of Women, Aissatou Dambo Dodo
National Education and Government Spokesman, Ali Bouli Diallo
Civil Service, Labour and Employment, Zahouri Ousmane
Communications, Culture, Youth and Sport, Kaka Amadou
Justice, Ibrahim Baidou
Agriculture and Livestock, Alitor Mano
Water Resources and Environment, Sani Bawa
Higher Education, Research and Technology, Mouke Dji

EMBASSY OF THE REPUBLIC OF NIGER
154 rue de Longchamp, 75116, Paris
Tel: Paris 45048060
Ambassador Extraordinary and Plenipotentiary, His Excellency Sandi Yacouba, apptd 1990

BRITISH AMBASSADOR, Her Excellency Margaret Rothwell, CMG, resident at Abidjan, Côte d'Ivoire

ECONOMY

The cultivation of groundnuts and the production of livestock are the main industries and provide two of the main exports. A company formed by the government, the French Atomic Energy Authority and private interests is exploiting uranium deposits at Arlit, and this is the main export. There is also some oil exploration which has found signs of oil in the eastern desert. Gold deposits exist north-west of Niamey.

TRADE WITH UK	1993	1994
Imports from UK	£5,317,000	£3,853,000
Exports to UK	3,495,000	4,312,000

NIGERIA
Federal Republic of Nigeria

Nigeria is situated on the west coast of Africa. It is bounded on the south by the Gulf of Guinea, on the west by Benin, on the north by Niger and on the east by Cameroon. It has an area of 356,669 sq. miles (923,768 sq. km). A belt of mangrove swamp forest lies along the entire coastline. North of this there is a zone of tropical rain forest and oil-palms. North of the rain forest, the country rises and the vegetation changes to open woodland and savannah. In the extreme north the country is semi-desert. The Niger, Benue, and Cross are the main rivers. The climate is tropical. The rainy season is from about April to October. During the dry season the cool *harmattan* wind blows from the desert.

The population (UN estimate 1992) is 115,664,000; Nigerian census result (1991) 88,514,501. The main ethnic groups are Hausa/Fulani, Yoruba and Ibo, and the principal languages are English, Hausa, Yoruba and Ibo. Over half the population are Muslim, these being concentrated in the north and west. In the southern areas in particular there are many Christians.

CAPITAL – ΨAbuja, estimated population 378,671, declared the federal capital in December 1991. Other important towns are the former capital Lagos, Ibadan, Kaduna, Kano, Benin City, Enugu and ΨPort Harcourt.
CURRENCY – Naira (N) of 100 kobo.
FLAG – Three equal vertical bands, green, white and green.
NATIONAL ANTHEM – Arise, O Compatriots.
NATIONAL DAY – 1 October (Independence Day).

GOVERNMENT

The Federation of Nigeria attained independence as a member of the Commonwealth on 1 October 1960 and became a republic in 1963. Originally regional in structure, the Federation is now divided into 30 states and the Federal Capital Territory.

In 1966 the military took power; in 1979 civil rule was restored after elections at national and state level. After similar elections in 1983 the new administration was overthrown by the military on 31 December, this regime itself being overthrown in August 1985. A 28-member Armed Forces Ruling Council (AFRC) was sworn in and governed in conjunction with a Council of Ministers until January 1993, when the AFRC and Council of Ministers were replaced by a National Defence and Security Council (NDSC) and a civilian Transitional Council respectively to govern the country until a handover to civilian government. A presidential election was held on 11 June and is generally believed to have been won by Chief Moshood Abiola of the SDP but the military government refused to release the results and had the election declared invalid. The military tried to organize a new election but widespread rioting and support for Chief Moshood Abiola prevented this. The military government resigned on 26 August, handing power to the Transitional Council.

Continued strikes in support of Abiola and a High Court ruling that the interim government was illegal threatened to bring down the government and led Defence Minister Gen. Sanni Abacha to launch a military coup on 17 November 1993 and install himself as head of state. A (military) Provisional Ruling Council and (civilian) Federal Executive Council were established to govern the country until a new constitution is passed. Strikes and pro-democracy demonstrations continued in 1994 in support of

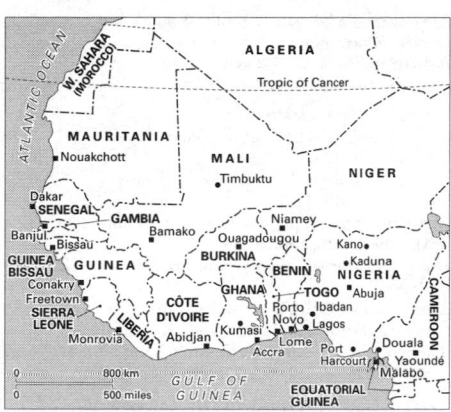

Chief Moshood Abiola, who returned from exile in June 1994 to establish a rival government, for which he has been arrested and put on trial for treason.

The National Constitutional Conference (NCC) convened by Gen. Abacha in June 1994 announced in January 1995 that Gen. Abacha should have an open-ended term of office. An attempted coup was defeated in March 1995 and political activity was restored in June, when the NCC presented the draft of a new constitution to Gen. Abacha. Chief Abiola remains in prison but the case against him has been suspended.

HEAD OF STATE
Chairman of the Provisional Ruling Council and Federal Executive Council, Commander-in-Chief of the Armed Forces, Gen. Sanni Abacha, *took power* 17 November 1993

FEDERAL EXECUTIVE COUNCIL *as at August 1995*
Chairman, Minister of Defence, Gen. Sanni Abacha
Vice-Chairman, Chief of General Staff, Lt.-Gen. D. O. Diya
Federal Capital Territory, Lt.-Gen. J. Useni
Education, Mohammad Liman
Industries, Lt.-Gen. Muhammadu Haladu
Works and Housing, Maj.-Gen. Abdulkarim Adisa
Finance, Chief Anthony Ani
Petroleum Resources, Chief Dan Etete
Power and Steel, Bashir Dalhatu
Health, Ikechukwa Madubuike
Foreign Affairs, Chief Tom Ikimi
Interior, Babagana Kingibe
Communications, Maj.-Gen. Tajudeen Olarenwaju
Labour, Uba Ahmed
Agriculture, Gambo Jimata
Information and Culture, Walter Ofonagoro
Justice and Attorney-General, Michael Agbamuche
Commerce and Tourism, Rear Adm. Isaac Ariola
Aviation, Air Cdre. Nsikak Eduok
Water Resources, Aliyu Yelwa
Science and Technology, Brig.-Gen. Samuel Momah
Planning, Ayo Ogunlade
Solid Mineral Resources, Kaloma Ali
Transport, Maj.-Gen. Ibrahim Gumel
Women's and Social Affairs, Judith Attah
Youth and Sports, Chief Jim Nwobodo

NIGERIA HIGH COMMISSION
9 Northumberland Avenue, London WC2N 5BX
Tel 0171-839 1244
High Commissioner, His Excellency Alhaji Abubakar Alhaji, KBE, apptd 1992
Deputy High Commissioner, T. A. B. Sodipo

Ministers, U. O. Okeke; A. A. Ella; A. K. Sambo
Defence Attaché, vacant
Information Attaché, O. Oyawale
Head of Commerce/Trade, B. A. Ameh

BRITISH HIGH COMMISSION
Shehu Shangari Way (North), Maitama, Abuja
Tel: Abuja 5232011
11 Eleke Crescent, Victoria Island, Lagos
Tel: Lagos 2619531
High Commissioner, His Excellency John Thorold
  Masefield, CMG, apptd 1994
Deputy High Commissioner and Minister-Counsellor, G. S.
  Hand
Defence Adviser, Col. J. R. D. Andrew, OBE
Counsellor (Economic and Commercial), E. A. Burner
There are liaison offices at Kaduna, Kano, Port Harcourt
  and Ibadan.

BRITISH COUNCIL DIRECTOR, Dr John Hawkins, 11
  Kingsway Road, Ikoyi (PO Box 3702), Lagos. Branch
  offices at Enugu, Ibadan, Kaduna and Kano City.

DEFENCE

Nigeria has a total active armed forces of 76,500 personnel,
all of whom are volunteers. The Army is 62,000 strong,
with 178 main battle tanks, 810 armoured personnel
carriers and reconnaissance vehicles and 460 artillery
pieces. The Navy has 5,000 personnel, with one frigate, 53
patrol and coastal vessels and two armed helicopters. The
Air Force numbers 9,500 personnel, with 92 combat
aircraft and 15 armed helicopters.
  Nigeria deploys 10,000 personnel in Liberia as part of
the ECOMOG peacekeeping force, 800 troops in Sierra
Leone, and a 70-strong training unit in the Gambia.

EDUCATION

A programme was introduced in 1976 intended to achieve
universal primary education. There are 37 universities (24
federal, 12 state and one military).

COMMUNICATIONS

The Nigerian railway system, which is controlled by the
Nigerian Railway Corporation, has 2,178 route miles of
lines. The principal international airlines operate from
Lagos, Kano and Port Harcourt. A network of internal air
services connects the main centres. The principal seaports
are served by a number of shipping lines, including the
Nigerian National Line. A nationwide television and radio
network is being developed, with each state eventually
having its own television and radio station.

ECONOMY

Nigeria was a predominantly agricultural country until the
early 1970s when oil became the principal source of export
revenue (over 90 per cent). Since 1981 oil revenues have
fallen to half their peak level and austerity measures were
introduced in 1982. Recent governments have attempted
to stimulate greater self-reliance in the economy by
encouraging non-oil exports and the use of local rather
than imported raw materials. Even so the country has a
foreign debt of US$30,000 million which it takes 30 per
cent of annual foreign exchange earnings to service. The
1994 budget deficit was equivalent to 12 per cent of GDP,
while inflation in 1994 was 70 per cent. In response to these
problems the government introduced economic reforms in
January 1995, including lifting exchange controls and
ending foreign investment controls in Nigerian or jointly-
owned firms.

Three oil refineries are in operation at Port Harcourt,
Warri and Kaduna, and steel plants at Warri and Ajaokuta.
Other projects include natural gas liquifaction, petrochemicals, fertilizers, power stations and irrigation
schemes. Tin and calumbite mining on the Jos plateau,
textiles and coal mining are also important.

TRADE

The principal exports are oil, groundnuts, palm products,
tin, cocoa, rubber and timber.

Trade with UK	1993	1994
Imports from UK	£634,688,000	£457,916,000
Exports to UK	112,375,000	124,577,000

NORWAY
Kongeriket Norge

Norway is a kingdom in the northern and western part of
the Scandinavian peninsula, 1,752 km in length, its greatest
width about 430 km. The length of the coastline is
2,650 km, and the frontier between Norway and the
neighbouring countries of Sweden, Finland and Russia is
2,542 km. It has an area of 149,405 sq. miles (386,958 sq.
km), of which Svalbard and Jan Mayen have a combined
area of 24,355 sq. miles (63,080 sq. km).
  The coastline is deeply indented with numerous fjords
and fringed with rocky islands. The surface is mountainous, consisting of elevated and barren tablelands separated
by deep and narrow valleys. At the North Cape the sun
does not appear to set from the second week in May to the
last week in July, causing the phenomenon known as the
Midnight Sun; conversely, there is no apparent sunrise
from about 18 November to 23 January. During the long
winter nights are seen the Northern Lights or Aurora
Borealis.
  The population (1994) is 4,324,815. The Norwegian
language in both its present forms is closely related to other
Scandinavian languages. Independence from Denmark
(1814) and resurgent nationalism led to the development
of 'new Norwegian' based on dialects, which now has equal
official standing with 'bokmål', in which Danish influence
is more obvious. This was formed in the time of the
Reformation. Ludvig Holberg (1684–1754) is regarded as
the father of Norwegian literature, though the modern
period begins with the writings of Henrik Wergeland
(1808–45). Some of the famous names are Henrik Ibsen
(1828–1906), Bjørnstjerne Bjørnson (1832–1910), Nobel
Prizewinner in 1903, and the novelists Jonas Lie
(1833–1908), Alexander Kielland (1849–1906), Knut
Hamsun (1859–1952) and Sigrid Undset (1882–1949), the
latter two also Nobel Prizewinners. Old Norse literature is
among the most ancient and richest in Europe.

CAPITAL – ΨOslo (including Aker), population (1994)
  477,515. Other towns are ΨTrondheim 142,015;
  ΨBergen 219,810; ΨStavanger 102,539; ΨKristiansand
  67,864.
CURRENCY – Krone of 100 øre.
FLAG – Red, with white-bordered blue cross.
NATIONAL ANTHEM – Ja, Vi Elsker Dette Landet (Yes,
  we love this country).
NATIONAL DAY – 17 May (Constitution Day).

GOVERNMENT

The kingdom of Norway was founded in AD 872. From
1397 to 1814 Norway was united with Denmark and from
1814 with Sweden. The union with Sweden was dissolved

Industry, Petroleum and Energy, Jens Stoltenberg
Defence, Jorgen Kosmo
Local Government and Labour, Gunnar Berge
Government Administration, Nils Olav Totland
Agriculture, Gunhild Øyangen
Justice, Grete Faremo
Fisheries, Jan Henry Olsen
Environment, Thorbjørn Berntsen
Transport and Communications, Kjell Opseth
Health, Werner Christie
Church, Education and Research, Gudmund Hernes
Trade and Shipping, Grete Knudsen
Family and Children's Affairs, Grete Berget
Cultural Affairs, Åse Kleveland
Finance, Sigbjørn Johnsen
Development Co-operation, Kari Nordheim Larsen
Social Affairs Hill-Marta Solberg

ROYAL NORWEGIAN EMBASSY
25 Belgrave Square, London SW1X 8QD
Tel 0171-235 7151
Ambassador Extraordinary and Plenipotentiary, His Excellency
Tom Vraalsen, GCVO, apptd 1994
Minister, Truls Hanevold
Defence Attaché, Capt. T. Seim
First Secretary, Inger Brusell (Consular)
Counsellor, T. Gulli (Commercial)

BRITISH EMBASSY
Thomas Heftyesgate 8, 0244 Oslo
Tel: Oslo 22 55 24 00
Ambassador Extraordinary and Plenipotentiary, His Excellency
  Mark Elliott, CMG, apptd 1994
Counsellor, E. J. Hughes (Deputy Head of Mission and Consul-
  General)
First Secretary, N. S. Archer (Economic and Commercial)
Defence and Naval Attaché, Cdr. G. S. Pearson, RN
BRITISH CONSULAR OFFICES – There is a British
  Consular Office at Oslo and Honorary Consulates at
  Bergen, Tromsø, Alesund, Kristiansund (North),
  Stavanger, Trondheim, Kristiansand (South),
  Haugesund and Harstad.

BRITISH COUNCIL REPRESENTATIVE, Rosalind Olsen,
  Fridtjof Nansens Plass 5, 0160, Oslo 1

on 7 June 1905 when Norway regained complete independence. Under the 1814 constitution, the 165-member Storting elects one-quarter of its members to constitute the Lagting (Upper Chamber), the other three-quarters forming the Odelsting (Lower Chamber).

The centre-right coalition government collapsed in October 1990 because of a dispute over whether to apply for membership of the European Community and was replaced by a minority Labour government. This was returned to power in the general election held on 13 September 1993. The state of the parties as at August 1995 was Labour 67, Centre Party 32, Conservatives 28, Christian Democrats 13, Socialist Left 13, Progress Party 10, Liberal Party 1.

The Storting voted in November 1992 to apply to join the European Community. Negotiations with the EU concluded on 1 March 1994 with a proposed accession date of 1 January 1995, subject to parliamentary and national referendum ratifications. However, in a national referendum on 28 November 1994 the electorate voted against joining the EU by 52.4 per cent to 47.6 per cent.

HEAD OF STATE

HM The King of Norway, King Harald V, GCVO, born 21 February 1937; succeeded 17 January 1991, on the death of his father King Olav V; married 29 August 1968, Sonja Haraldsen, and has issue, Prince Haakon Magnus (see below), and Princess Martha Louise, born 22 September 1971

Heir, HRH Crown Prince Haakon Magnus, born 20 July 1973

CABINET as at August 1995

Prime Minister, Gro Harlem Brundtland
Foreign Affairs, Björn Tore Godal

DEFENCE

Norway is a member of NATO and the headquarters of Allied Forces Northern Europe is situated near Oslo. The total active armed forces number 33,500 (22,100 conscripts). Reserve forces number 282,000. The Army has a strength of 18,000 (14,000 conscripts), with 170 main battle tanks, 223 armoured infantry fighting vehicles and armoured personnel carriers, and 405 artillery pieces. The Navy has a strength of 6,600, including 4,000 conscripts, with 12 submarines, four frigates, and 30 patrol and coastal combatants. The Air Force has a strength of 7,900 (4,100 conscripts), with 79 combat aircraft. The period of compulsory national service is 12 months.

Norway deploys 843 troops with UN forces in Lebanon and 393 in Bosnia-Hercegovina, with one frigate in the Adriatic.

ECONOMY

The cultivated area is about 10,826 sq. km, 3.5 per cent of the total surface area. Forests cover nearly 23 per cent; the rest consists of highland pastures or uninhabitable mountains. The chief agricultural products are grain, potatoes, root vegetables, milk, furs and timber.

The Gulf Stream causes the sea temperature to be higher than the average for the latitude, which brings shoals of herring and cod into the fishing grounds. The quantity of fish caught by Norwegian fishing vessels is greater than that of any other European country except Russia. In 1993 the total catch amounted to 2,374,840 tonnes.

The chief industries are oil production and transport, construction, electricity supply, manufactures, agriculture and forestry, fisheries, mining, production of metals and ferro-alloys, and shipping. Industries providing both manufactured products and services for the development of North Sea oil and gas resources have become increasingly important. In 1994 129,321,000 tons of crude oil were produced, of which 111,336,000 tons were exported. Manufactures are aided by great resources of hydroelectric power. Actual production in 1993 amounted to 120,000 GWh. In 1993, the total workforce was 2,004,000 of which 5.6 per cent were employed in agriculture, forestry and fishing, 22.8 per cent in industry, construction and mining, and 71.6 in services.

FINANCE	1994
Total revenue	K344,521,000,000
Total expenditure	373,443,000,000

TRADE

The chief imports are raw materials, motor vehicles, chemicals, ships and machinery, foods and textiles. Exports consist chiefly of crude oil and gas, manufactured goods, fish and fish products (as canned fish, whale oils), pulp, paper, iron ore and pyrites, nitrate of lime, stone, calcium carbide, aluminium, ferro-alloys, zinc, nickel, cyanamides, etc. Norway's major trading partners are members of the EU.

	1992	1993
Total imports	K251,748m	K267,800m
Total exports	303,034m	317,600m

Trade with UK	1993	1994
Imports from UK	£1,519,473,000	£2,020,878,000
Exports to UK	4,170,275,000	3,709,666,000

EDUCATION

Education from seven to 16 is free and compulsory in the 'basic schools', and free from 16 to 19 years. The majority of the pupils receive post-compulsory schooling at 'upper secondary' schools, regional colleges akin to polytechnics (98), universities (four) and six other university-level specialist colleges. In 1994–5 there were 160,000 students at universities and university-level institutions.

COMMUNICATIONS

The total length of railways open at the end of 1993 was 4,023 km, excluding private lines. There are 89,737 km of public roads in Norway (including urban streets). Scheduled internal air services are operated by Scandinavian Airlines System (SAS) on behalf of Det Norske Luftfartselskap (DNL), by Braathens South American and Far East Airtransport (SAFE), and by Widerőes Flyveselskap AS. The mercantile marine in 1994 consisted of 1,642 vessels of 21,745,000 gross tons (vessels above 100 gross tons, excluding fishing boats, floating whaling factories, tugs, salvage vessels, icebreakers and similar types of vessel). In 1993 there were 149 daily newspapers.

TERRITORIES

SVALBARD

The Svalbard archipelago lies between 74° and 81° N. and between 10° and 35° E., with an estimated area of 24,295 sq. miles. The archipelago consists of the main island, Spitsbergen (15,200 sq. miles), North East Land, the Wiche Islands, Barents and Edge Islands, Prince Charles Foreland, Hope Island, Bear Island and many islands in the neighbourhood of the main group. Glaciers cover 60 per cent of the land area. South Cape is 355 miles from the Norwegian coast. Transit from Tromsø to Green Harbour takes two to three days.

The sovereignty of Norway over the archipelago was recognized by other nations in 1920 and in 1925 Norway assumed sovereignty. The 3,700 inhabitants are mainly engaged in coal-mining, but the islands are also visited by hunters for seals, foxes and polar bears.

JAN MAYEN ISLAND

Jan Mayen, an island in the Arctic Ocean (70° 49' to 71° 9' N. and 7° 53' to 9° 5' W.) was joined to Norway by law in 1930.

NORWEGIAN ANTARCTIC TERRITORIES

BOUVET ISLAND (54° 26' S. and 3° 24' E.) was declared a dependency of Norway in 1930.
PETER THE FIRST ISLAND (68° 48' S. and 90° 35' W.), was declared a dependency of Norway in 1931.
PRINCESS RAGNHILD LAND (from 70° 30' to 68° 40' S. and 24° 15' to 33° 30' E.) has been claimed as Norwegian since 1931.
QUEEN MAUD LAND – In 1939 the Norwegian Government declared the area between 20° W. and 45° E., adjacent to Australian Antarctica, to be Norwegian territory.

OMAN
The Sultanate of Oman

Oman lies at the eastern corner of the Arabian peninsula, bordered on the west by Yemen, Saudi Arabia and the UAE. To the north lies the Gulf of Oman and to the east the Arabian Sea, giving a coastline of nearly 1,000 miles. Sharjah and Fujairah (UAE) separate the main part of Oman from the northernmost part of the state, a peninsula extending into the Strait of Hormuz. The area has been estimated at 82,030 sq. miles (212,457 sq. km).

The north and the south of Oman are divided by nearly 400 miles of desert. The Batinah, the coastal plain, is fertile. The Hajjar is a mountain spine running from north-west to south-east and for the most part barren, but valleys penetrate the central massif which are irrigated by wells or a system of underground canals called *falajs* which tap the water table. The two plateaus leading from the western slopes of the mountains descend to the Empty Quarter of the Arabian Desert. Dhofar, the southern province, is the only part of the Arabian peninsula to be touched by the south-west monsoon. Temperatures are more moderate than in the north.

The population (1992 census) is 2,000,000. The inhabitants of the north are mostly Arab, though there are large communities of Hindus, Khojas and Baluch, in addition to Omanis of Zanzibari origin, especially around Salalah. However, in the mountains the inhabitants are either of pure Arab descent or belong to tribes of pre-Arab origin, the Qarra and Mahra, who speak their own dialects of Semitic origin.

CAPITAL – Ψ Muscat, estimated population 400,000. The commercial centre has grown around Mutrah, three miles away and the main port, and Ruwi. The main towns on the northern coast are ΨSur, ΨBarka and ΨSohar. The main town of Dhofar is Salalah.
CURRENCY – Rial Omani (OR) of 1,000 baiza.
FLAG – Red with a white panel in the upper fly and a green one in the lower fly; in the canton the national emblem in white.
NATIONAL DAY – 18 November.

GOVERNMENT

A State Consultative Council established in 1981 was replaced by Sultanic decree in 1991 by a *Majlis A' shura*, or State Advisory Council. This body, meeting twice a year, consists of a representative from each of the 59 wilayats, or governorates, of the Sultanate. The Council has the right to review legislation, question ministers and make policy proposals. Effective political power remains with the Sultan, who rules by decree and is advised by the Cabinet, which he appoints.

HEAD OF STATE
HM *The Sultan of Oman*, Sultan HM Qaboos Bin-Said, *succeeded* on deposition of Sultan Said bin Taimur, 23 July 1970

COUNCIL OF MINISTERS *as at August 1995*
Prime Minister, Foreign Affairs, Defence and Finance, The Sultan
Personal Representative of HM The Sultan, HH Sayyid Thuwainy bin Shihab Al Said
Deputy PM for Security and Defence, HH Sayyid Fahr bin Taimur al Said
Deputy PM for Legal Affairs, HH Sayyid Fahad bin Mahmood al Said
Deputy PM for Financial and Economic Affairs, HE Qais bin Abdul Munem al Zawawi
Minister of State and Governor of Dhofar, HE Sayyid Mussellam bin Ali Al Busaidi
Minister of State and Governor of Muscat, HE Sayyid Al Mutassim bin Hamoud Al Busaidi
National Heritage and Culture, HH Sayyid Faisal bin Ali al Said
Agriculture and Fisheries, HE Mohammed bin Abdallah bin Zaher al Hinai
Electricity and Water, HE Shaikh Mohammed bin Ali Al Qatabi
Water Resources, HE Hamed bin Said Al Aufi
Justice, Awqaf and Islamic Affairs, HE Hamoud bin Abdullah Al Harthi
Health, HE Dr Ali bin Mohammed bin Moosa
Petroleum and Minerals, HE Said bin Ahmed bin Said al Shanfari
Housing, HE Malik bin Suleiman al Ma'amari
Civil Services, HE Ahmed bin Abdul Nabi Macki
Communications, HE Salim bin Abdullah Al Ghazali
Education and Youth Affairs, HE Saud bin Ibrahim bin Saud al-Busa'di
Higher Education, HE Yahya bin Mahfoodh al Manthri
Interior, HE Sayyid Badr bin Sa'oud bin Hareb al Busaidi
Information, HE Abdul Aziz bin Mohammed al Rowas
Regional Municipalities and Environment, HE Shaikh Amer bin Shuwain al Hosni
Minister of State for Foreign Affairs, HE Yousuf bin Alawi bin Abdullah
Commerce and Industry, HE Maqbool bin Ali bin Sultan
Social Affairs and Labour, HE Ahmed bin Mohammed bin Salim Al Isa'ee

Posts, Telegraphs and Telephones, HE Ahmed bin Sweidan al Baluchi
Secretary-General at the Ministry of Defence, HE Saif bin Hamad al Batashi
Diwan of Royal Court, HE Sayyid Saif bin Hamed bin Sa'oud
Palace Office Affairs, HE Gen. Ali bin Majid Al Ma'amari

EMBASSY OF THE SULTANATE OF OMAN
167 Queen's Gate, London SW7 5HE
Tel 0171-225 0001
Ambassador Extraordinary and Plenipotentiary, new appointment awaited
First Secretary and Deputy Head of Mission, Mahmood bin Mohamed Al-Raeesy
Military Attaché, Capt. Mohammed bin Ali Al-Farsi

BRITISH EMBASSY
PO Box 300, Muscat
Tel: Muscat 738501/5
Ambassador Extraordinary and Plenipotentiary, His Excellency Richard John Muir, CMG, apptd 1994
Counsellor, N. J. Guckian (*Deputy Head of Mission*)
Defence Attaché, H. D. Duncan, MBE
First Secretary (Commercial), P. Nessling
Consul, V. I. Milton

BRITISH COUNCIL DIRECTOR, Clive Bruton, PO Box 73, Muscat, Oman. There are also offices at *Salalah* and *Sohar*.

DEFENCE

The total active armed forces strength is 42,900 personnel. Service is voluntary. The Army has a strength of 25,000 personnel, with 73 main battle tanks, 43 light tanks and 96 artillery pieces. The Navy has 4,200 personnel, and 12 patrol and coastal vessels. The Air Force has 3,500 personnel and 58 combat aircraft. The Royal Household has 6,500 personnel formed into a Royal Guard brigade, two special forces regiments, the Royal Yacht Squadron and the Royal Flight. In addition there is the paramilitary home guard (*Firqat*) of 3,500 personnel. Some 3,700 hired and seconded personnel (many British) serve in the Omani armed forces.

ECONOMY

Although there is considerable cultivation in the fertile areas and cattle are raised on the mountains, the backbone of the economy is the oil industry. Petroleum Development (Oman) Ltd (owned 60 per cent by Oman Government and 34 per cent by Shell) began exporting oil in 1967. Concessions (off and on shore) are held by several major international companies. The current level of oil production is about 650,000 barrels per day, planned to increase to 700,000.
A gas turbine power station operates at Rusail, where there is also a 200-plot industrial estate. There is a power station and a desalination plant near Muscat and flour, animal feed, cement and copper production facilities.

TRADE

Trade is mainly with the UAE, UK, Japan, the Netherlands, USA, Germany, France and India. Chief imports are machinery, cars, building materials, food and telecommunications equipment.

Trade with UK	1993	1994
Imports from UK	£305,592,000	£362,129,000
Exports to UK	82,664,000	78,273,000

COMMUNICATIONS

Port Qaboos at Matrah has eight deep-water berths which have been constructed as part of the harbour facilities. A modern telecommunications service to the main population centres and an international service are operated by the General Telecommunications Organization. There are good tarmac roads linking most main population centres of the country with the coast and with the towns of the UAE, though only a trunk road links the north and south of Oman.

SOCIAL WELFARE

For many years the Sultanate was a poor country but the advent of oil revenues and the change of regime in 1970 led to the initiation of a wide-ranging development programme, especially concerned with health, education and communications. There are now nearly 50 hospitals with around 3,400 beds; 823 schools, with 387,000 pupils, were in operation in 1992.

PAKISTAN
Islami Jamhuriya-e-Pakistan

Pakistan is situated in the north-west of the Indian sub-continent, bordered by Iran, Afghanistan, China, the disputed territory of Kashmir, and India. It covers a total area (including Pakistan-controlled Kashmir) of 341,026 sq. miles (883,254 sq km). Running through Pakistan are five great rivers, the Indus, Jhelum, Chenab, Ravi and Sutlej. The upper reaches of these rivers are in Kashmir, and their sources in the Himalayas.

The census in 1981 showed a population figure of 83,780,000 (1992 UN estimate, 119,107,000). Of these, about 95 per cent are Muslims, 3.5 per cent Christians, about 1 per cent Hindus, and 0.5 per cent Buddhists. Urdu is the national language, but is only spoken by a small minority of the population. The most widely used language is Punjabi, followed by Sindi and Pushto. English is used in business, government and higher education.

CAPITAL – Islamabad, population 350,000. ΨKarachi (estimated population 7,183,000) is the largest city and seaport; Lahore has a population of 4,072,000.
CURRENCY – Pakistan rupee of 100 paisa.
FLAG – Green with a white crescent and star, and a white vertical strip in the hoist
NATIONAL ANTHEM – Quami Tarana.
NATIONAL DAYS – 23 March (Pakistan Day), 14 August (Independence Day).

GOVERNMENT

Pakistan was constituted as a Dominion under the Indian Independence Act 1947, becoming a republic on 23 March 1956. Until 1972 Pakistan consisted of two geographical units, West and East Pakistan, separated by about 1,100 miles of Indian territory. East Pakistan's insistence on complete autonomy led to civil war, which broke out on 25 March 1971 and continued until December 1971 when a ceasefire was arranged. The independence of East Pakistan as Bangladesh was proclaimed in April 1972. Under the 1972 Simla Agreement with India, a line of control was established in Kashmir; Pakistan controls an area of 33,653 sq. miles (87,159 sq. km) to the north and west of the line. The armed forces under Gen. Zia-ul-Haq assumed power in 1977 and martial law was in force from July 1977 to March 1985. Gen. Zia declared himself President in

September 1978. Zia was killed in a plane crash in August 1988. The Pakistan People's Party won the election to the National Assembly and Benazir Bhutto became Prime Minister. In August 1990 the President dissolved the National Assembly and dismissed the Bhutto cabinet. Elections were held in October 1990 and won by the Islamic Democratic Alliance, led by Mian Muhammad Nawaz Sharif.

In late 1992 and early 1993 a power struggle between President Ishaq Khan and Prime Minister Sharif developed, in which the Army eventually intervened in July 1993, forcing both Khan and Sharif to resign and replacing them with a caretaker President and Cabinet until new elections were held in October. These were won by the Pakistan People's Party (PPP) and Benazir Bhutto resumed the premiership. The PPP and allies gained majorities in the National Assembly and in the provincial assemblies of the Punjab, Sind and North-West Frontier, with no party controlling the Baluchistan provincial assembly. The PPP candidate Farooq Leghari was elected President by an electoral college of the National and provincial assemblies.

INSURGENCY

Since early 1994 there has been fighting and civil disorder in areas of Sind province, especially in Karachi, in two conflicts: armed militants of the Mohajir Qaumi Movement (MQM) Party, which represents Urdu-speaking Indian Muslims who fled from India at partition and their descendants, are fighting for an autonomous Karachi province against local Sindis; and there is an armed conflict between Shia and Sunni fundamentalists. Some 750 people were killed in the fighting in 1994 and 1,200 in 1995 before the Army and security forces intervened in July 1995 to clear MQM militants from their strongholds in Karachi suburbs. The MQM and the government have had talks in an attempt to end the fighting but it continues in Karachi at a reduced level.

HEAD OF STATE
President, Farooq Ahmad Khan Leghari, *elected* 13 November 1993

FEDERAL CABINET *as at August 1995*
Prime Minister, Minister of Finance, Benazir Bhutto
Defence, Aftab Shahban Mirani
Foreign Affairs, Aseff Ahmad Ali
Industries and Production, Muhammad Asghar
Interior, Maj.-Gen. Nasirullah Khan Babar
Kashmir and Northern Affairs, Muhammad Afzal Khan
Law and Justice, Prof. N. D. Khan
Social Welfare and Special Education, Dr Sher Afghan Khan Niazi
Petroleum and Natural Resources, Anwar Saifullah Khan
Information and Broadcasting, Khalid Ahmad Khan Kharal
Education, Khurshid Ahmed Shah
Works, Makhdoom Mohammed Amin Fahin
Food, Agriculture and Livestock, Mohammed Yousef Talpur
Water and Power, Ghulam Mustafa Khar
Commerce, Chaudhry Ahmed Mukhtar
Population Welfare, Julius Salik
Minister without Portfolio, Abdul Qadir Jilani

HIGH COMMISSION FOR PAKISTAN
35–36 Lowndes Square, London SW1X 9JN
Tel 0171-235 2044
High Commissioner, His Excellency Wajid Shamsul Hassan, apptd 1994
Minister and Deputy High Commissioner, M. J. Naim
Minister, K. Shafi

Consul-General, M. Nisar
Defence and Naval Attaché, Cdre M. J. Akhtar
Counsellor, M. A. Tahir (*Commercial*)

BRITISH HIGH COMMISSION
Diplomatic Enclave, Ramna 5, PO Box 1122, Islamabad
Tel: Islamabad 822131/5
High Commissioner, His Excellency Sir Christopher
MacRae, KCMG, apptd 1994
Deputy High Commissioners, A. J. F. Caie (*Islamabad*); E. W.
Callway (*Karachi*)
Counsellor (Economical and Comercial), S. N. Evans, OBE
Counsellor, T. A. Willasey-Wilsey
Defence and Military Adviser, Brig. R. D. O'Lone

There is a British Deputy High Commission at Karachi
and a Consulate at Lahore.

BRITISH COUNCIL REPRESENTATIVE, Peter Elborn, OBE,
PO Box 1135, Islamabad. There are offices at Karachi,
Lahore and Peshawar.

DEFENCE

In 1993 the former Pakistani Army Chief-of-Staff Gen.
Aslam Beg confirmed that since 1987 Pakistan has had the
capability to construct nuclear weapons at short notice and
that Pakistan would use this capability if its conventional
forces faced defeat in a war with India. In August 1994
former Prime Minister Nawaz Sharif stated that Pakistan
had constructed a nuclear weapon. Pakistan has Chinese
manufactured M11 (range 185 miles) and M9 (range 370
miles) missiles capable of delivering nuclear warheads.

Pakistan has a total armed forces active strength of
587,000 personnel, with a further 313,000 reserves. The
Army has a strength of 520,000 personnel, with 2,000 main
battle tanks, 820 armoured personnel carriers, 1,850
artillery pieces and 20 attack helicopters. The Navy has
22,000 personnel, with six submarines, three destroyers, six
frigates, 13 patrol and coastal vessels, four combat aircraft
and 16 armed helicopters. The Air Force has 45,000
personnel, and 430 combat aircraft. In addition, there are
277,000 paramilitary personnel in four organizations.
Pakistan deploys 677 personnel with the UN peacekeeping
force in Bosnia.

ECONOMY

The economy is based on agriculture. The principal crops
are cotton, rice, wheat, sugar cane, maize and tobacco.
Pakistan has one of the longest irrigation systems in the
world. The total area irrigated is 33 million acres. There
are large deposits of rock salt.

Pakistan also produces hides and skins, leather, wool,
fertilizers, paints and varnishes, soda ash, paper, cement,
fish, carpets, sports goods, surgical appliances and engineering goods, including switchgear, transformers, cables
and wires.

An agreement was reached in 1993 with the IMF for a
three-year loan of US$1,300 million in return for the
implementation of an austerity and structural adjustment
programme. The programme has led to the lowering of the
foreign debt, reductions in inflation and in the budget
deficit (5.8 per cent of GDP in 1994). Privatization and
economic deregulation begun under Bhutto's 1988–90
government has continued. There was US$5,000 million of
foreign investment in 1994.

TRADE

Principal imports are petroleum products, machinery,
fertilizers, transport equipment, edible oils, chemicals and
ferrous metals. Principal exports are raw cotton, cotton

yarn and cloth, carpets, rice, petroleum products, synthetic
textiles, leather, and fish.

Trade with UK	1993	1994
Imports from UK	£338,581,000	£355,058,000
Exports to UK	324,335,000	358,879,000

COMMUNICATIONS

The main seaport is Karachi. The main airports are at
Karachi, Islamabad, Lahore, Peshawar and Quetta. Pakistan International Airlines operates air services between
the principal cities within the country as well as abroad.
Post and telegraph facilities are available to every country
in the world.

EDUCATION

Education consists of five years of primary education (five
to nine years), three years of middle or lower secondary
(general or vocational), two years of upper secondary, two
years of higher secondary (intermediate) and two to five
years of higher education in colleges and universities.
Education is free to upper secondary level.

PALAU
Republic of Palau

The Republic of Palau consists of 340 islands and islets in
the western Pacific Ocean, of which eight are inhabited.
Part of the Caroline Islands group, the Palau archipelago
stretches over 400 miles (644 km) between 2° and 8°N., and
131° and 138°E. Koror island is about 810 miles (1,300 km)
south-west of Guam and about 530 miles (852 km) south-
east of Manila. The total land area is 177 sq. miles (458 sq.
km), and Babelthaup is by far the largest island. The islands
vary in terrain from the highly mountainous to low coral
atolls. The climate is tropical with a rainy season lasting
from June to October; the average temperature is 27°C
(80°F).

The population (1990 census) is 15,122, of which 13,900
live on Koror and Babelthaup. The population is Micronesian, and predominantly Roman Catholic with a Protestant minority. Both Palauan and English are official
languages.

CAPITAL – Koror, population 10,493.
CURRENCY – US dollar.
FLAG – Light blue with a yellow disc set neat the hoist.

HISTORY

Spain acquired sovereignty over the Caroline Islands, of
which the Palau archipelago is part, in 1886. After defeat in
the Spanish-American war of 1898, Spain sold its remaining Pacific possessions, including Palau, to Germany in
1899. On the outbreak of the First World War in 1914
Japan took control of Palau on behalf of the Allied powers,
and Japanese administration was confirmed in a League of
Nations mandate in 1921. During the Second World War
Allied forces gained control of the archipelago after intense
fighting. In 1947 the USA entered into agreement with the
UN Security Council to administer the Micronesia area,
including Palau, as the UN Trust Territory of the Pacific
Islands.

In July 1978 the Palau electorate voted in a referendum
not to join the new Federated States of Micronesia and
instead became a separate part of the UN Trust Territory.
A popularly approved constitution came into effect on 1
January 1981 which prohibited the stationing of US

nuclear weapons and the storage of nuclear waste in Palau. However, Palau and the USA signed a Compact of Free Association in 1982 allowing the entry of US nuclear waste and weapons into Palau. A succession of referenda to allow changes to the constitution to allow the Compact to come into effect failed to gain the required three-quarters majority. In November 1992 the majority necessary to change the constitution was changed to a simple majority in three-quarters of Palau's 16 component states, and a national referendum in November 1993 brought the constitution into agreement with the Compact. Implementation of the Compact of Free Association took place on 1 October 1994 after legal objections by opponents of the Compact had been rejected by the Palau courts. Under this agreement the USA recognized the Republic of Palau as a fully sovereign and independent state and the UN Trust Territory of the Pacific Islands was terminated. Palau was admitted to UN membership in December 1994.

GOVERNMENT

Under the 1981 constitution, Palau is a democracy with separate executive, legislative and judicial branches of government. Executive power is vested in the President and Vice-President, who are elected for four-year terms; the President appoints the cabinet. There is a bicameral legislature (*Olbiil Era Kekulau*) composed of the 16-member House of Delegates (one member elected from each of the 16 constituent states) and the 14-member Senate. There is also a Council of Chiefs to advise the President on matters concerning traditional law and customs. The judiciary consists of a Supreme Court, a National Court and lesser courts. Each of the 16 component states have their own elected governors and legislatures. The last presidential and legislative elections were held in November 1992.

Palau maintains no defence forces. The Compact of Free Association places responsibility for the defence of Palau on the USA for 50 years.

HEAD OF STATE
President, Kuniwo Nakamura, *elected* 4 November 1992
Vice-President, Tommy Remengesau

ECONOMY

The economy remains heavily dependent on US financial support, which the USA is committed to giving under the Compact. Fisheries, tourism, subsistence agriculture and government service are the main areas of employment. Agricultural products include coconuts and copra, and Palau earns significant revenue from the sale of fishing licences to foreign fleets fishing for tuna. Phosphate mining, introduced under the Germans and Japanese, is no longer carried out at a significant level. Tourism is being developed; there were 26,000 visitors in 1989.

The USA carried out an infrastructure improvement programme in the 1970s and 1980s. There are now three airports on Koror, Peleliu and Angaur which have daily flights from Guam operated by Continental Air Micronesia. Ocean freight services to Palau are provided by two shipping lines to the port at Koror. A communications centre on Arakabesang Island handles international telephone, telex, cable and facsimile communications. There is a privately owned television station and a government-operated radio station.

SOCIAL WELFARE

There is a free public school system which, together with independent missionary schools, provides primary and secondary education. A tertiary technical school has been established on Koror since 1969. General medical and dental care is provided by a public hospital and a medical clinic.

PANAMA
República de Panama

Panama lies on the isthmus of that name which connects North and South America. The area is 29,762 sq. miles (77,082 sq. km), the population (1995 estimate) 2,631,013. Spanish is the official language.

CAPITAL – ΨPanama City, population (1990) 1,064,221.
CURRENCY – Balboa of 100 centésimos (at parity with the US dollar). US$ notes are also in circulation.
FLAG – Four quarters; white with blue star (top, next staff), red (in fly), blue (below, next staff) and white with red star.
NATIONAL ANTHEM – Alcanzamos Por Fin La Victoria (Victory is ours at last).
NATIONAL DAY – 3 November.

GOVERNMENT

After a revolt in 1903, Panama declared its independence from Colombia and established a separate government. After 1968, control of Panama was increasingly taken over by Gen. Omar Torrijos, commander of the National Guard, following a military coup. In 1978 Gen. Torrijos withdrew from the government, and Dr Aristides Royo was elected President by the Assembly of Representatives.

An attempt in February 1988 by President Delvalle to remove Gen. Noriega as Commander of the Defence Forces failed. Noriega ousted Delvalle and replaced him with Manuel Solis Palma. Presidential elections were held in May 1989 but Noriega annulled the results, which appeared to give victory to the opposition and on 15 December he assumed power formally as head of state. On 20 December US troops invaded Panama to oust Noriega. Guillermo Endara, believed to have won the May elections, was installed as President. In December 1991 the Legislative Assembly approved a change to the constitution which abolished the armed forces.

Legislative power is vested in a unicameral Legislative Assembly of 72 members; executive power is held by the President, assisted by two elected Vice-Presidents and an appointed Cabinet. Elections are held every five years under a system of universal and compulsory adult suffrage. The last presidential election was held on 8 May 1994 and won by Ernesto Pérez Balladares of the Democratic Revolutionary Party (PRD) who appointed the government.

HEAD OF STATE
President, Ernesto Pérez Balladares, *elected* 8 May 1994, *sworn in* 1 September 1994
First Vice-President, Tomas Gabriel Altamirano Duque
Second Vice-President, Felipe Alejandro Virzi

CABINET *as at August 1995*

Interior and Justice, Raul Montenegro
Foreign Affairs, Gabriel Lewis Galindo
Public Works, Luis Blanco
Finance and Treasury, Olmedo Miranda
Education, Dr Pablo Thalassinos
Labour and Social Welfare, Mitchel Doens
Health, Aida de Rivera
Commerce and Industry, Nitzia de Villareal
Housing, Dr Francisco Sanchez Cardenas
Agricultural Development, Carlos Sousa-Lennox

Economy and Planning, Dr Guillermo Chapman
Presidency, Raul Arango

EMBASSY OF THE REPUBLIC OF PANAMA
48 Park Street, London WIY 3PD
Tel 0171-493 4646
Ambassador Extraordinary and Plenipotentiary, His Excellency
    Aquilino Boyd de la Guardia, apptd 1994

BRITISH EMBASSY
Torre Swiss Bank, Calle 53 (Apartado 889) Zona 1,
Panama City, Panama 1
Tel: Panama City 269-0866
Ambassador Extraordinary and Plenipotentiary, His Excellency
    Thomas Malcomson, apptd 1992

ECONOMY

The soil is moderately fertile, but nearly one-half of the
land is uncultivated. The chief crops are bananas, sugar,
coconuts, cacao, coffee and cereals. The shrimping industry plays an important role in the economy. In 1992 tourism
became the principal foreign currency earner, ahead of
bananas. A railway joins the Atlantic and Pacific oceans.
    Education is compulsory and free from seven to 15 years.

TRADE

Imports are mostly manufactured goods, machinery,
lubricants, chemicals and foodstuffs. Exports are bananas,
petroleum products, shrimps, sugar, meat and fishmeal.

Republic of Panama	1992	1993
Imports	US$2,108,424m	US$2,187,376m
Imports	480,912m	507,606m
Colon Free Zone		
Imports	US$4,364,054m	US$4,495,687m
Re-Exports	4,826,386m	5,150,552m
Trade with UK†	1993	1994
Imports from UK	£53,367,000	£48,614,000
Exports to UK	12,674,000	7,139,000

†Including Colon Free Zone

THE PANAMA CANAL ZONE

With effect from 1 October 1979 the Canal Zone (647 sq.
miles) was disestablished, with all areas of land and water
within the Zone reverting to Panama. By the 1977 treaty
with the USA, the USA is allowed the use of operating bases
for the Panama Canal, together with several military bases,
but the Republic of Panama is sovereign in all such areas.
Control of the Canal will revert to Panama at noon on 31
December 1999.

DEPENDENCIES

Taboga Island (area 4 sq. miles) is a popular tourist resort
some 12 miles from the Pacific entrance to the Panama
Canal.
    Tourist facilities have also been developed in the Las
Perlas Archipelago in the Gulf of Panama, particularly on
the island of Contadora.
    There is a penal settlement at Guardia on the island of
Coiba (area 19 sq. miles) in the Gulf of Chiriqui.

PAPUA NEW GUINEA

Papua New Guinea extends from the Equator to Cape
Baganowa in the Louisiade Archipelago at 11° S. latitude
and from the border with Irian Jaya to 160° E. longitude.

The total area is 178,260 sq. miles, (461,691 sq. km), of
which approximately 152,420 sq. miles form the mainland
on the island of New Guinea. The country has many island
groups, principally the Bismarck Archipelago, a portion of
the Solomon Islands, the Trobriands, the D'Entrecasteaux
Islands and the Louisade Archipelago. The main islands of
the Bismarck Archipelago are New Britain, New Ireland
and Manus. Bougainville is the largest of the Solomon
Islands within Papua New Guinea.
    Papua New Guinea lies within the tropics and has a
typically monsoonal climate. Temperature and humidity
are uniformly high throughout the year.
    The population in 1992 (UN estimate) was 3,847,000.

CAPITAL – ΨPort Moresby. Estimated population (1990),
    173,500. Other major towns are Lae, Rabaul, Madang,
    Wewak, Goroka and Mount Hagen.
CURRENCY – Kina (K) of 100 toea.
FLAG – Divided diagonally red (fly) and black (hoist); on
    the red a soaring Bird of Paradise in yellow and on the
    black five white stars of the Southern Cross.
NATIONAL ANTHEM – Arise All You Sons.
NATIONAL DAY – 16 September (Independence Day).

GOVERNMENT

New Guinea was sighted by Portuguese and Spanish
navigators in the early 16th century, but remained largely
isolated from the rest of the world. In 1884 a British
Protectorate, British New Guinea, was proclaimed over
the southern coast of New Guinea (Papua) and the adjacent
islands, which were annexed outright in 1888. In 1906 the
Territory of British New Guinea was placed under the
authority of Australia.
    In 1884 Germany had formally taken possession of
certain northern areas, later to be known as the Trust
Territory of New Guinea. In 1914 the German areas were
occupied by Australian troops and remained under military administration until 1921, when they became a League
of Nations mandate administered by Australia. New
Guinea was administered under the mandate and Papua
under the Papua Act until the invasion by the Japanese in
1942 when the civil administration was suspended until the
surrender of the Japanese in 1945.
    From 1970 there was a gradual assumption of powers by
the Papua New Guinea government, culminating in
formal self-government in December 1973. Papua New
Guinea achieved full independence within the Commonwealth on 16 September 1975.
    Elections are held every five years. The Parliament
comprises 109 elected members, 20 from regional electorates, the remainder from open electorates. There are 19
provinces, which have their own provincial governments
with certain legislative and administrative powers.

SECESSION

Bougainville witnessed separatist tensions at the time of
independence and in 1989 a secessionist movement, the
Bougainville Revolutionary Army (BRA), began an insurrection on Bougainville. In March 1990 the Papua New
Guinean security forces withdrew from the island and the
BRA declared an independent republic in May 1990. In
January 1991 a peace accord was signed between the two
sides; the question of Bougainville's future status was
deferred. However, fighting has continued, with Papua
New Guinea security forces returning to the island in
October 1992. Raids by Papua New Guinean forces on
islands in the Solomons chain to destroy supply routes to
the rebels led to protests by the Solomon Islands government and clashes between Papuan and Solomon Islands
patrol boats in April 1993. By late 1993 Papua New

Guinean security forces were in control of the island's port and airport and the capital, Arawa. In August 1994 the Panguna copper and gold mine was recaptured from the BRA and the following month a ceasefire agreement was signed by the government and the BRA. The agreement provided for a neutral peacekeeping force to be deployed on the island while peace negotiations were to begin in October. The BRA, however, boycotted the peace negotiations and the peacekeeping force was withdrawn when fighting restarted.

Governor-General, His Excellency Sir Wiwa Korowi, GCMG, *appointed* 18 November 1991

NATIONAL EXECUTIVE COUNCIL *as at August 1995*
Prime Minister, Foreign Affairs and Trade, Rt. Hon. Sir Julius Chan, GCMG, KBE
Deputy PM, Finance and Planning, Hon. Chris Haiveta
Provincial Affairs and Village Development, Hon. Castan Maibawa
Works, Hon. Peter Yana
Transport, Hon. Andrew Baing
Fisheries, Hon. Titus Philemon
Public Services, Hon. Bart Philen
Lands, Hon. Sir Albert Kipalan, KBE, CMG
Mining and Petroleum, Hon. John Giheno
Forests, Hon. Andrew Posai
State Affairs, Hon. Paul Tohian
Justice, Hon. Robert Timo Nagele
Agriculture and Livestock, Hon. Bernard Narakobi
Environment and Conservation, Hon. Parry Zeipi
Commerce and Industry, Hon. David Mai
Labour and Employment, Hon. Jerry Nalau
Defence, Hon. Mathias Ijape
Education, Hon. Joseph Onguglo
Health, Hon. Peter Baster
Housing, Hon. Dick Mune
Home Affairs, Hon. Nakikus Konga
Communications, Hon. John Momis
Energy and Science, vacant
Police, Hon. Paul Mambei
Tourism and Civil Aviation, Hon. Paul Pora
Correctional Services, Hon. Sylvanius Siembo

PAPUA NEW GUINEA HIGH COMMISSION
3rd Floor, 14 Waterloo Place, London SWIR 4AR
Tel 0171-930 0922/7
High Commissioner, His Excellency Noel Levi, CBE, apptd 1991

BRITISH HIGH COMMISSION
PO Box 4778, Boroko, Port Moresby
Tel: Port Moresby 251677
High Commissioner, His Excellency Robert Low, CBE, apptd 1994

ECONOMY

Until the 1970s the economy was based almost entirely on agriculture, principally copra, cocoa, tea, coffee, palm oil, rubber, groundnuts, spices and timber. A variety of commercial agricultural developments co-exist with the traditional rural economy.

There are extensive mineral deposits throughout Papua New Guinea, including copper, gold, silver, nickel, chromite, bauxite and possibly commercial deposits of oil and gas. In 1972, Bougainville Copper Pty Ltd (BCL) began mining in the North Solomons province, producing copper, silver and gold. The Bougainville copper mine closed indefinitely in 1989 because of the unrest on the island. The most important new developments are the exploitation of large copper and gold deposits on the Ok

Tedi, in the Western province and the development of a gold mine on Lihir island with an estimated reserve of 42.5 million ounces, where production is planned to begin in 1997.

Industry includes processing of primary products, and brewing, bottling and packaging, paint, plywood, and metal manufacturing and the construction industries.

TRADE WITH UK	1993	1994
Imports from UK	£10,858,000	£9,074,000
Exports to UK	53,690,000	56,981,000

COMMUNICATIONS

Air Niugini (the national airline) operates regular air services to other countries in the region. Internal air services are operated by Air Niugini, Douglas Airways, and Talair. Several shipping companies operate cargo services to Australia, Europe, the Far East and USA. There are very limited cargo and passenger services between Papua New Guinea main ports, outports, plantations and missions. Road communications are very limited, the most important road being that linking Lae with the populous highlands. Papua New Guinea is linked by international cable to Australia, Guam, Hong Kong, Kota Kinabalu, the Far East and USA. Telecommunications are widely available.

PARAGUAY
República del Paraguay

Paraguay is an inland subtropical state of South America, situated between Argentina, Bolivia and Brazil. The area is estimated at 157,048 sq. miles (406,752 sq. km). It is a country of grassy plains and forested hills. In the angle formed by the Paraná-Paraguay confluence are extensive marshes, one of which, known as Neembucú (or endless) is drained by Lake Ypoa, a large lagoon south-east of the capital. The Chaco, lying between the rivers Paraguay and Pilcomayo and bounded on the north by Bolivia, is a flat plain, rising uniformly towards its western boundary to a height of 1,140 feet; it suffers much from floods and still more from drought, but the building of dams and reservoirs has converted part of it into good pasture for cattle.

The population (1992 UN estimate) is 4,519,000. Spanish is the official language of the country but outside the larger towns Guarani, the language of the largest single group of original Indian inhabitants, is widely spoken, and is also an official language.

CAPITAL – Asunción, population (1985 census) 729,307; other centres are Ciudad del Este (98,491); Encarnación (31,445); Concepción (25,607); P. Juan Caballero (41,475).
CURRENCY – Guaraní (Gs) of 100 céntimos.
FLAG – Three horizontal bands, red, white, blue with the National seal on the obverse white band and the Treasury seal on the reverse white band.
NATIONAL ANTHEM – Paraguayos, Republica O Muerte (Paraguayans, republic or death).
NATIONAL DAY – 15 May.

GOVERNMENT

In 1535 Paraguay was settled as a Spanish possession. In 1811 it declared its independence from Spain.

The constitution provides for a two-chamber legislature consisting of a 45-member Senate and an 80-member Chamber of Deputies. Deputies are elected on a regional basis, the number of seats allocated to each regional department being directly proportional to the department's population. Voting is compulsory for all citizens over 18. The President is elected for a single five-year term and may not be re-elected. The Vice-President may only put himself forward for presidential elections if he resigns his post six months before the election. The President appoints the Cabinet, which exercises all the functions of government.

Gen. Alfredo Stroessner, dictator from 1954, was overthrown in February 1989 by Gen. Andrés Rodriguez, who was elected President in May 1989. In May 1991, the first free municipal elections were held, and elections to the parliament were held in December 1991. Amendments to the constitution came into effect in June 1992. The last presidential and legislative elections were held on 9 May 1993. The presidential election was won by Juan Carlos Wasmosy (Colorado Party). In the legislative election, the distribution of seats in the senate was: the ruling Colorado Party (ANR-PC) 20; Authentic Radical Liberal Party (PLRA) 17; National Encounter (EN) eight. In the Chamber of Deputies, the distribution of seats was: ANR-PC 40, PLRA 32, EN eight. After his inauguration, President Wasmosy moved to subjugate the military to civilian control.

HEAD OF STATE
President, Juan Carlos Wasmosy, *elected* 9 May 1993, *sworn in* 15 August 1993

CABINET *as at August 1995*
Foreign Affairs, Luis Maria Ramirez Boetther
Interior, Carlos Podesta
Finance, Orlando Bareiro
Education, Nicanor Duarte Frutos
Agriculture and Livestock, Arseuio Vascoucellos
Public Works and Communications, Carlos Facetti
National Defence, Hugo Estigarribia Elizeche
Public Health and Social Welfare, Andrés Vidovich
Justice and Labour, Juan Manuel Morales
Industry and Commerce, Ubaldo Scavone

EMBASSY OF PARAGUAY
Braemar Lodge, Cornwall Gardens, London SW7 4AQ
Tel 0171-937 1253
Ambassador Extraordinary and Plenipotentiary, new
appointment awaited

BRITISH EMBASSY
Calle Presidente Franco 706 (PO Box 404), Asunción
Tel: Asuncíon 444472
Ambassador Extraordinary and Plenipotentiary and Consul-General, His Excellency Graham Pirnie, apptd 1995

ECONOMY

President Rodriguez introduced an economic liberalization programme and this has been continued by the Wasmosy government, which has managed to bring the foreign debt under control and to attract foreign investment. About three-quarters of the population are engaged in agriculture and cattle raising. Cassava, sugar cane, soya, corn, cotton and wheat are the main agricultural products. The forests contain many varieties of timber which find a good market abroad.

Paraguay's rivers give it considerable hydroelectric capacity. There is a hydroelectric power station at Acaray which exports surplus power to Argentina and Brazil. Joint hydroelectric projects have been undertaken with Brazil, on a hydroelectric dam at Itaipú (the largest in the world), and with Argentina, at Yacyretá.

TRADE
The chief imports are machinery; fuels and lubricants; transport and accessories; and drinks and tobacco. The chief exports are soya bean, cotton fibres, meat and coffee.

Trade with UK	1993	1994
Imports from UK	£35,797,000	£48,935,000
Exports to UK	3,113,000	3,321,000

COMMUNICATIONS

There are direct shipping services from Asunción to Europe and the USA, and river steamer services for internal transport and to Argentina. Eight airlines operate services from Asunción. There are 27,741 km (1990) of asphalted roads in Paraguay, connecting Asunción with São Paulo (26 hours) via the Bridge of Friendship and Foz de Yguazú, and with Buenos Aires (24 hours) via Puerto Pilcomayo, and about 4,050 miles of earth roads in fairly good condition but liable to be closed or to become impassable in wet weather. A 1,000 km road links Asunción with the Bolivian border. Rail services, with train ferries, provide internal and international links. Four daily and five weekly newspapers are published in Asunción.

EDUCATION

Education is free and compulsory. In 1990 there were 4,641 government primary schools with 694,972 pupils and 27,477 teachers. There were 809 secondary schools with 155,339 pupils and 8,112 teachers. The National University in Asunción had 20,343 students in 1984. The Catholic University had 10,971 students.

PERU
República del Peru

Peru is a maritime republic of South America, situated between 0° 00' 48" and 18° 21' 00" S. latitude and between 68° 39' 27" and 81° 20' 13" W. longitude. The area is 496,225 sq. miles (1,285,216 sq. km). The country is traversed throughout its length by the Andes, running parallel to the Pacific coast. There are three main regions, the Costa, west of the Andes, the Sierra or mountain ranges of the Andes, which include the Punas or mountainous wastes below the region of perpetual snow, and the Montaña or Selva, which is the vast area of jungle stretching from the eastern foothills of the Andes to the eastern frontiers of Peru. The coastal area, lying upon and near the Pacific, is not tropical though close to the Equator, being cooled by the Humboldt Current.

The population (1992 estimate) is 22,465,000. Spanish, the language of the original Spanish stock from which the governing and professional classes are mainly recruited is an official language, together with Quechua and Aymará. Quechua and Aymará are spoken by more than half the population.

CAPITAL – Metropolitan Lima (including ΨCallao), population census (1993) 6,483,901. Other major cities are: Arequipa (820,471) and Trujillo (508,715).
CURRENCY – Nuevo Sol 100 cents.
FLAG – Three vertical stripes of red, white, red.
NATIONAL ANTHEM – Somos Libres, Seámoslo Siempre (We are free, let us remain so forever).
NATIONAL DAY – 28 July (Anniversary of Independence).

GOVERNMENT

Peru was conquered in the early 16th century by Francisco Pizarro (1478–1541). He subjugated the Incas (the ruling caste of the Quechua Indians), who had started their rise to power some 500 years earlier, and for nearly three centuries Peru remained under Spanish rule. A revolutionary war of 1821–4 established its independence, declared on 28 July 1821. A military junta ruled Peru from 1968 until 1980 when civilian government was restored. In April 1992 President Fujimori, faced with increasing terrorist violence, with the support of the armed forces suspended the constitution, dissolved Congress and began to govern with absolute powers. A programme of market-orientated economic reform, new measures in the anti-terrorist war, and a streamlining of the executive, legislative and judicial institutions was undertaken. In November 1992 a legislative general election was held to an 80-seat Democratic Constituent Congress (CCD) which was installed as an interim legislature and constituent assembly to write a new constitution. Parties supporting Fujimori's suspension of the constitution gained a majority in the CCD. In January 1993 the 1979 constitution was re-established and the CCD declared Fujimori constitutional head of state. The CCD produced a new constitution which was passed in a national referendum in October 1993. The constitution, promulgated in December 1993, provides for the President to be able to serve two terms rather than one, as previously; the introduction of the death penalty for terrorists; and the formation of a new 120-member unicameral Congress.

Parliamentary and presidential elections were held on 9 April 1995, with President Fujimori winning the first round of the presidential election outright and his Cambio 90-Nueva Mayoria Party winning 58 out of 120 seats in the new Congress.

INSURGENCY

Since the late 1970s the government has faced violence from drug organizations and insurgencies from two leftist guerrilla movements, the Maoist Sendero Luminoso (Shining Path) and the Movimiento Revolucionario Tapac Amaru (MRTA). Some areas of the country remain under states of emergency, but the capture of the leaders of both groups in 1992 and the anti-terrorist clampdown in 1992–4 has drastically reduced the size and resources of both groups and reduced violence considerably. The Shining Path continues to launch attacks on security forces and the country's infrastructure and has engaged in mass intimidation and execution campaigns in rural and jungle areas, with fighting so far having left 27,000 dead. In mid 1995 the Shining Path joined forces with drugs organizations in the north of the country as a means of continuing to fund their guerrillas.

HEAD OF STATE

President of the Republic, Alberto Fujimori, *assumed office* 28 July 1990, *re-elected* 9 April 1995

CABINET *as at August 1995*

Prime Minister and Minister of Foreign Affairs, Efraín Goldenberg Schreiber
Economy and Finance, Jorge Camet Dickman
Interior, Gen. Juan Briones Dávila
Justice, Dr Fernando Vega Santa Gadea
Defence, Gen. Victor Malca Villanueva
Education, Dante Córdoba
Health, Dr Eduardo Yong Motta
Labour and Social Promotion, Dr Augusto Antoniolli Vásquez
Agriculture, Absalon Vásquez Villanueva
Energy and Mines, Amado Yataco

Transport and Communications, Housing and Construction, Juan Castilla Meza
Fisheries, Jaime Augustin Sobero Taira
Industry, Commerce, Tourism, Integration and International Commercial Negotiations, Liliana Canale Novella
Minister of the Presidency, Manuel Vara Ochoa

EMBASSY OF PERU

52 Sloane Street, London SWIX 9SP
Tel 0171-235 1917/2545/3802
Ambassador Extraordinary and Plenipotentiary, new appointment awaited

BRITISH EMBASSY

Edificio El Pacifico Washington, Piso 12, Plaza Washington (PO Box 854), Lima 100
Tel: Lima 334735
Ambassador Extraordinary and Plenipotentiary, His Excellency John Illman, apptd 1994
First Secretary (Commercial), R. G. Church (*Deputy Head of Mission*)

There is a British Consular Office at Lima and Honorary Consulates in Arequipa, Cusco, Iquitos, Piura and Trujillo.

BRITISH COUNCIL DIRECTOR, Chris Brown, PO Box No. 14-0114, Calle Alberto Lynch 110, San Isidro, Lima 27

DEFENCE

The armed forces have a total active strength of 115,000 (65,500 conscripts), with selective conscription of two years duration. The Army has a strength of 75,000 (50,000 conscripts) and is heavily engaged in combating the Shining Path and MRTA guerrilla movements. It has 300 main battle tanks, 110 light tanks, 440 reconnaissance and armoured personnel carriers and 248 artillery pieces. The Navy has 25,000 personnel (13,500 conscripts), divided into the Pacific, Lake Titicaca and Amazon River force areas. It has a strength of six submarines, two cruisers, five destroyers and four frigates, seven patrol and coastal vessels, seven combat aircraft and 14 armed helicopters. The Air Force has a strength of 15,000 personnel (2,000 conscripts), with 94 combat aircraft and 15 armed helicopters. In addition there is the paramilitary National Police, 60,000 strong, who also play a major role in counter-insurgency operations.

ECONOMY

Since 1990 the government has launched a radical free-market restructuring programme which has rebuilt the country's foreign exchange reserves from virtually zero, reduced inflation from 7,600 per cent a year in 1990 to 10 per cent in 1995, cut subsidies and import tariffs, freed interest rates, privatized most state firms, and seen the economy grow by 12 per cent of GDP in 1994. Foreign investment has been encouraged and has grown dramatically; in June 1993 US$900 million was gained in credits from foreign donors. In March 1993 Peru cleared its arrears with the World Bank and IMF of US$1,700 million, enabling it to gain access to a new IMF loan of US$1,395 million over three years. The total foreign debt in 1994 stood at US$23,200 million.

The chief products of the coastal belt are cotton, sugar and petroleum. There are large tracts of land suitable for cultivation and stock-raising (cattle, sheep, llamas, alpacas and vicuñas) on the eastern slopes of the Andes, and in the mountain valleys maize, potatoes and wheat are grown. The jungle area is a source of timber and petroleum. Other major crops are fruit, vegetables, rice, barley, grapes and coffee. The mountains contain rich mineral deposits and mineral exports include lead, zinc, copper, iron ore and silver. Peru is normally the world's largest exporter of fishmeal.

TRADE

The principal imports are machinery and chemicals and pharmaceutical products. The chief exports are minerals and metals, fishmeal, sugar, cotton and coffee.

Trade with UK	1993	1994
Imports from UK	£33,031,000	£44,580,000
Exports to UK	126,482,000	112,911,000

COMMUNICATIONS

In recent years the coastal and sierra zones have been opened up by means of roads and air routes. There is air communication, as well as communication by protracted land routes, with the tropical and eastern zones which lie east of the Andes towards the borders of Brazil. The Andean Highway forms a link between the Pacific, the Amazon and the Atlantic. The Pan-American Highway runs along the Peruvian coast connecting it with Ecuador and Chile. The Inter-Ocean Corridor linking the port of Matarani and Buenos Aires will be opened soon.

The railway is administered by the government. There is also steam navigation on the Ucayali and Huallaga, and in the south on Lake Titicaca. Air services are maintained throughout Peru, and many international services call at Lima.

EDUCATION

Education is compulsory and free between five and 16.

THE PHILIPPINES
Repúblika ng Pilipinas

The Philippines are situated between 21° 20'–4° 30' N. latitude and 116° 55'–126° 36' E. longitude, and are about 500 miles from the south-east coast of the continent of Asia. The total land area of the country is 115,831 sq. miles (300,000 sq. km). There are eleven larger islands and 7,079 other islands. The principal islands are:

	sq. miles		sq. miles
Luzon	40,422	Mindoro	3,759
Mindanao	36,538	Leyte	2,786
Samar	5,050	Cebu	1,703
Negros	4,906	Bohol	1,492
Palawan	4,550	Masbate	1,262
Panay	4,446		

Other groups are the Sulu islands (capital, Jolo), Babuyanes and Batanes; the Calamian islands; and Kalayaan Islands.

The population (UN estimate 1992) is 64,259,000. The inhabitants are basically of Malay stock, with a considerable admixture of Spanish and Chinese blood in many localities. The Chinese minority is estimated at 500,000, with smaller numbers of Spanish, American and Indian. About 90 per cent are Christian, predominantly Roman Catholics. Most of the remainder are Muslims, in the south, and indigenous animists, mainly in Luzon and parts of Mindanao.

The official languages are Filipino and English. Filipino is based on Tagalog, one of the Malay–Polynesian languages and is spoken by 29.66 per cent of the total number of households (and understood by nearly 90 per cent of the population), but local languages and dialects are strong and Cebuano is spoken by 24.2 per cent of total

households. English, which is the language of government and of instruction in secondary and university education, is spoken by at least 44 per cent of the population. Spanish, which ceased to be an official language in 1973, is now spoken by a very small minority. Eighty-nine per cent of the population are literate.

CAPITAL – ΨManila, on the island of Luzon, estimated population (1990) City area 1,876,195; Manila with suburbs (incl. Quezon City, Pasay City, Caloocan City, Makati, Parañaque, San Juan Mandaluyong, Malabon, Valenzuela, Peteros, Las Piñas, Taguig, Muntinlupa and Navotas) 6,720,050. The next largest cities are (1989 estimate) ΨCebu (613,184), ΨDavao (819,525), ΨIloilo (287,711), ΨZamboanga (433,328), and Bacolod (328,648).

CURRENCY – Philippine peso (P) of 100 centavos.

FLAG – Equal horizontal bands of blue (above) and red; gold sun with three stars on a white triangle next staff.

NATIONAL ANTHEM – Bayang Magiliw.

NATIONAL DAY – 12 June (Independence Day 1898).

GOVERNMENT

The Portuguese navigator Magellan came to the Philippines in 1521 and was killed by the natives of Mactan, a small island near Cebu. In 1565 Spain undertook the conquest of the country, which was named Filipinas after Philip II of Spain, then heir apparent. In 1896 the Filipinos revolted against Spanish rule and declared their independence on 12 June 1898. In the Spanish–American War of 1898, Manila was captured by American troops with the help of Filipinos and the islands were ceded to the USA by the Treaty of Paris 1898. Despite a rebellion against US rule between 1899 and 1902, the Americans remained in control of the country until 1946. The Republic of the Philippines came into existence on 4 July 1946.

Ferdinand Marcos was President from 1965 to 1986. Although he gained a majority of votes in the official count of a presidential election in February 1986, the election was marred by widespread electoral abuse and his rival, Mrs Corazon Aquino, launched a campaign of non-violent civil disturbance which gained wide support. On 25 February Marcos, his family and aides left for Hawaii. Mrs Aquino took over as President and survived seven coup attempts.

A new constitution was approved by referendum in 1987 and came into force that July. Legislative authority is vested in a bicameral elected Congress comprising a House of Representatives of 250 members and a 24-member Senate. Fidel Ramos was elected President on 11 May 1992 and has overcome the problems that plagued President Aquino, namely military coup attempts and legislative obstructiveness. Legislative elections to both houses of Congress were held on 8 May 1995 when the coalition of the Lakas ng Edsa, National Union of Christian Democrats and Laban ng Demokratikong Pilipino won majorities in both houses.

INSURGENCY

Muslim insurgents, the Moro National Liberation Front (MNLF) have since 1968 operated in central and western Mindanao and the Sulu archipelago. The Communist New People's Army (NPA), has maintained a presence in eastern Mindanao, Negros, Samar, Bicol, the mountains of northern Luzon, and Bataan. Open warfare in the 1970s between the MNLF and the government left 50,000 dead but the effectiveness of the MNLF has been declining for several years. In November 1993 the government and the MNLF signed an interim ceasefire agreement including a three-year cessation of hostilities while negotiations continue. The strength and activity of the NPA has also declined and in December 1993 a government-NPA ceasefire was agreed. The NPA maintains 8,000 armed personnel and the MNLF 3,300 but the most active insurgents are now 3,400 who broke away from the MNLF and 900 in the Islamic fundamentalist Abu Sayyaf group. Over 100 people were killed by the Abu Sayyaf group in an attack on Ipil in April 1995.

HEAD OF STATE
President, Fidel V. Ramos, *assumed office* 30 June 1992
Vice-President, Joseph Estrada

CABINET SECRETARIES *as at August 1995*

Foreign Affairs, Domingo Siazon
Finance, Roberto de Ocampo
Justice, Teofisto Guingona
Agriculture, Roberto Sebastian
Public Works and Highways, Gregorio Vigilar
Education, Culture and Sport, Ricardo Gloria
Labour and Employment, Jose Brillantes
National Defence, Gen. Renato de Villa
Health, Hilarion Ramiro
Trade and Industry, Rizalino Navarro
Social Welfare and Development, Lina Laigo
Agrarian Reform, Ernesto Garilao
Interior and Local Government, Rafael Alunan
Tourism, Eduardo Pilapil
Environment and Natural Resources, Victor Ramos
Budget and Management, Salvador Enriquez
Transport and Communications, Jesus Garcia
Science and Technology, William Padolina
Director-General, Socio-Economic Planning Authority, Cielito Habito
Energy, Francisco Viray
Press and Presidential Spokesman, Hector Villanueva

EMBASSY OF THE PHILIPPINES
9A Palace Green, London w8 4QE
Tel 0171-937 1600
Ambassador Extraordinary and Plenipotentiary, His Excellency Jesus P. Tambunting, apptd 1993
Minister-Counsellor, George B. Reyes
Defence Attaché, Col. E. Abu
Counsellor and Consul-General, E. Castro
Commercial Counsellor, P. Sales

BRITISH EMBASSY
Locsin Building, 6752 Ayala Avenue, Corner Makati Avenue, 1226 Makati, Metro Manila (PO Box 2927 MCPO)
Tel: Manila 816-7116
Ambassador Extraordinary and Plenipotentiary, His Excellency Adrian Thorpe, apptd 1995
Deputy Ambassador, D. B. Merry
Defence Attaché, Col. J. L. Seddon-Brown (resides at Kuala Lumpur)
First Secretary, C. B. Glynn (*Commercial*)

BRITISH COUNCIL DIRECTOR, Dr Kate Bailey, 7, 3rd Street, New Manila, PO Box AC 168, Cubao, Quezon City, Metro Manila.

DEFENCE

The Philippine armed forces number 106,500 active personnel with a further 131,000 reserves, and have been engaged for some years in combating insurgent forces. The Army has an active strength of 68,000 personnel, with 41 light tanks, 380 armoured personnel carriers and armoured infantry fighting vehicles and 240 artillery pieces. The Navy has 23,000 personnel, including 8,500 marines, and deploys one frigate, 44 patrol and coastal vessels, eight

combat aircraft and ten marine battalions. The Air Force has some 15,500 personnel, with 43 combat aircraft and 104 armed helicopters. The paramilitary Philippine National Police number 40,500 personnel and there is a part-time militia of 60,000 personnel.

ECONOMY

The Philippines has been bypassed by the economic growth of most of the rest of south-east Asia since the 1960s, mainly because of the incompetence and corruption of Marcos' rule. President Ramos has, however, restored economic growth, which was 5.1 per cent in 1993, and increased electricity generation to solve the energy crisis, which reached its peak in 1993. An economic reform programme of liberalization and deregulation has also been put into place and has led to increased exports, increased foreign investment, a reduction in inflation to 5.1 per cent in 1994, and brought the debt service ratio down to 16 per cent of GDP. Total foreign debt in 1994 was US$42,000 million. In June 1994 the IMF approved a US$684 million loan over three years to support the economic reform programme.

The Philippines is a predominantly agricultural country, the chief products being rice, coconuts, maize, coffee, sugar-cane, abaca (manila hemp), fruits, tobacco and lumber. There is, however, an increasing number of manufacturing industries and it is the policy of the government to diversify its economy. There are also deposits of nickel, iron, copper, gold and silver.

TRADE
Principal exports are sugar, coconut oil, copper concentrate, lumber and copra, together with increasingly important manufactured exports such as electronics products and clothing. The major trading partners are the USA, Japan, Taiwan and Hong Kong.

	1992	
Total imports	US$10,580m	
Total exports	7,150m	

Trade with UK	1993	1994
Imports from UK	£306,146,000	£355,131,000
Exports to UK	276,820,000	244,346,000

COMMUNICATIONS

The highway system covers about 161,709 kilometres. The Philippine National Railway used to operate 1,282 km of track, but a greater part of this is being rebuilt. There are 94 ports of entry and 164,404 vessels of various types totalling 50,467,000 tons are engaged in inter-island traffic. There are 82 national airports and 137 privately operated airports. Philippine Air Lines have regular flights throughout the Far East, to the USA and Europe, in addition to inter-island services.

EDUCATION

Secondary and higher education is extensive and there are 37 private universities recognized by the government, including the Dominican University of Santo Tomas (founded in 1611). There are also 296 state-supported colleges and universities, including the University of the Philippines, founded 1908.

POLAND
Rzeczpospolita Polska

Poland adjoins Germany in the west, the boundary being formed by the rivers Oder and Neisse, the Czech Republic and Slovakia in the south, and Belarus, Ukraine, Lithuania and the Kaliningrad region of Russia in the east. To the north is the Baltic Sea. The country has an area of 120,725 sq. miles (312,677 sq. km), and a population (official estimate 1991) of 38,300,000. Roman Catholicism is the religion of 95 per cent of the inhabitants.

CAPITAL – Warsaw, on the Vistula, population (1989) 1,655,063. Other large towns are Lódź (851,690); Kraków (748,356); Wroclaw (642,234); Poznan (588,715); Gdansk (464,649); Szczecin (412,000); Katowice (367,041); Bydgoszcz (380,385).
CURRENCY – New Zloty of 100 groszy (equal to 10,000 old Zloty). Both old and new are legal tender until 31 December 1996.
FLAG – Equal horizontal stripes of white (above) and red.
NATIONAL ANTHEM – Jeszcze Polska Nie Zginela (Poland has not yet been destroyed).
NATIONAL DAY – 3 May.

GOVERNMENT

The Polish Commonwealth ceased to exist in 1795 after three successive partitions in 1772, 1793 and 1795 in which Prussia, Russia and Austria shared. The Republic of Poland, reconstituted within the limits of the old Polish Commonwealth, was proclaimed at Warsaw in November 1918, and its independence guaranteed by the signatories of the Treaty of Versailles.

German forces invaded Poland on 1 September 1939; on 17 September, Russian forces invaded eastern Poland, and on 21 September 1939 Poland was declared by Germany and Russia to have ceased to exist. At the end of the war a coalition government was formed in which the Polish Workers' Party played a large part. In December 1948, the Polish Workers' Party and the Polish Socialist Party merged to form the Polish United Workers' Party (PUWP). A new constitution modelled on the Soviet constitution was adopted in 1952, and was modified in 1976.

Strikes in 1980 over steep rises in food prices forced the government to agree to allow independent trade unions, the right to strike, the easing of censorship and other political and economic demands. The independent trade union movement Solidarity, led by Lech Walesa, became a powerful force but many of its leaders, including Walesa, were detained and union activity suspended when martial law was declared in December 1981. Initially there was some passive resistance to martial law, which was suspended in December 1982 and finally lifted in July 1983.

A wave of strikes resulted in talks between Walesa and the PUWP early in 1989. By April plans for political and economic reforms had been drawn up. Multiparty parliamentary elections were held in the summer of 1989, following which the PUWP ceased to be the ruling party. The post-Communist governments have introduced a market economy but political divisions, economic difficulties and a fragmented Parliament of over 20 parties led to a succession of short-lived governments in the early 1990s. Elections were held on 19 September 1993 and resulted in six parties gaining representation in the 460-seat Sejm: Democratic Left Alliance (SLD) 171 seats; Polish Peasant Party (PSL) 132 seats; Freedom Union (UW) 74 seats; Labour Union (UP) 41 seats; Confederation

for an Independent Poland (KPN) 22 seats; Reform Bloc 16 seats; German minority parties 4 seats. In the 100-member Senate the results were: SLD 37; PSL 36; Solidarity 10; UW 4; others 13. The SLD (the largest section of which is the Social Democratic grouping formed in 1990 by reformist members of the Communist (PUWP) Party) returned to power after four years by forming a coalition government with the PSL and UP parties, as a result of the electorate's backlash against the hardships caused by economic reform. The government has promised to increase subsidies to industry, increase welfare spending and reduce unemployment.

The cohabitation between a left-wing government and the former Solidarity leader and anti-Communist President Lech Walesa has caused political tension over the scale and pace of economic reform in 1993–5. PSL Prime Minister Waldemar Pawlak was forced to resign by President Walesa in February 1995 under the threat of a dissolution of parliament because he was considered to be obstructing economic reform. He was replaced by Józef Oleksy of the SLD, who formed a new government in March 1995.

Disagreement over a post-Communist constitution ended in November 1992 when President Walesa signed a 'small constitution' approved by the parliament which defines the division of powers between the President and government. The President has the right to be consulted over the appointment of the foreign, defence and interior ministers. There is a 5 per cent threshold for representation for parties in the Sejm and 8 per cent for alliances (except for minority groups). The Senate is elected on a provincial basis.

HEAD OF STATE
President, Lech Walesa, *elected* 9 December 1990 *for a five-year term*

COUNCIL OF MINISTERS *as at August 1995*
Prime Minister, Józef Oleksy (SLD)
Deputy PM, Finance, Prof. Grzegorz Kolodko (Ind)
Deputy PM, Agriculture, Roman Jagieliński (PSL)
Deputy PM, Head of the Scientific Research Committee, Aleksander Luczak (PSL)
Head of the Council of Ministers' Office, Marek Borowski (SLD)
Foreign Affairs, Wladyslaw Bartoszewski (Ind)
Internal Affairs, Andrzej Milczanowski (Ind)
National Defence, Zbigniew Okoński (Ind)
Justice, Jerzy Jaskiernia (SLD)
Head of the Central Planning Office, Miroslaw Pietrewicz (PSL)
Foreign Economic Relations, Jacek Buchacz (PSL)
Transport and Maritime Economy, Boguslaw Liberadzki (Ind)
Environment Protection, Natural Resources and Forestry, Stanislaw Zelichowski (PSL)
Labour and Social Policy, Leszek Miller (SLD)
Culture, Kazimierz Dejmek (PSL)
Health, Ryszard Zochowski (SLD)
Industry and Trade, Klemens Ścierski (Ind)
Regional Planning and Construction, Barbara Blida (SLD)
Communication, Andrzej Zieliński (Ind)
Privatization, Wieslaw Kaczmarek (SLD)
National Education, Ryszard Czarny

PSL Polish Peasant Party; SLD Democratic Left Alliance; Ind Independent

EMBASSY OF THE REPUBLIC OF POLAND
47 Portland Place, London WIN 3AG
Tel 0171-580 4324/9

Ambassador Extraordinary and Plenipotentiary, His Excellency
Ryszard Stemplowski, apptd 1994
Defence Attaché, Cdr. R. Szlegier
Consul-General, Dr J. Kochanowski
Minister, R. Szuniewicz (*Commercial*)

BRITISH EMBASSY
No. 1 Aleja Róz, 00-556 Warsaw
Tel: Warsaw 6281001
Ambassador Extraordinary and Plenipotentiary, His Excellency
Michael J. Llewellyn-Smith, CMG, apptd 1991
Counsellor, W. A. Harrison (*Deputy Head of Mission*)
Defence and Air Attaché, Gp. Capt. H. Delve, MBE
First Secretary (*Commercial*), A. J. Gooch
There are Honorary Consulates at Katowice, Poznan and
Gdansk.

BRITISH COUNCIL DIRECTOR, Edward Pugh, Al.
Jerozolimskie 59, 00-697 Warsaw

DEFENCE

The total active armed forces number 283,600 personnel
(160,000 conscripts) with a further 465,500 reserves. Conscripts serve in all services for 18 months. The Army
numbers 185,900 (105,000 conscripts) with 2,110 main
battle tanks, 510 reconnaissance vehicles, 2,295 armoured
infantry fighting vehicles and armoured personnel carriers
and 1,460 artillery pieces. The Navy has a strength of
19,000 including 10,300 conscripts, with three submarines,
one destroyer, one frigate, 32 patrol and coastal vessels, 35
combat aircraft and 11 armed helicopters. The Air Force is
78,700 strong (44,700 conscripts), with 398 combat aircraft
and 30 attack helicopters. The Paramilitary Border Guards
and Police Prevention Units number 23,400 personnel
(1,400 conscripts). Poland deploys 567 troops with UN
forces in Lebanon and 357 troops on the Golan Heights in
Syria with UN forces.

ECONOMY

Until recently over 99 per cent of Polish industry was
stated to be 'socialized', but 68 per cent of agricultural land
was privately farmed. Legislation passed in July 1990
provided for 80 per cent of the economy to be transferred
from the state to the private sector. In 1991 the IMF and
western banks suspended co-operation and lending because the government had exceeded agreed budget deficit
and inflation limits. The IMF-prescribed 'shock therapy'
for the economy was resumed in 1992 with reforms to allow
bankruptcy and the ending of state subsidies to reduce the
budget deficit. After the passing of a budget in March 1993,
which kept the deficit to 5.5 per cent of GDP, and a mass
privatization bill for 600 state-owned firms, passed by
parliament in April, the IMF and the banks provided more
credit to enable reforms to continue. The third stage of
privatization of some 444 firms began in October 1994 and
by January 1995 2,500 out of 8,400 state enterprises had
been privatized or liquidated.

The transition to a market economy has been painful,
with unemployment in 1994 reaching 16 per cent. Privatization continues, and GDP grew in 1994 by 4.5 per cent.
The budget deficit fell from 5 per cent of GDP in 1993 to
2.8 per cent in 1994, while annual inflation was 29.5 per
cent. Agreements were also reached in 1994 to cancel 30
per cent of Poland's US$33,000 million debt to foreign
governments and US$6,900 million of US$14,000 million
debt to commercial banks. Some 60 per cent of the
workforce is now employed in the private sector and 55
per cent of Poland's GDP is produced by the private sector.

TRADE WITH UK	1993	1994
Imports from UK	£717,802,000	£702,711,000
Exports to UK	449,320,000	544,928,000

EDUCATION

Elementary education (ages seven to 15) is compulsory and
free. Secondary education is optional and free. There are
universities at Kraków, Warsaw, Poznan, Lódź, Wroclaw,
Lublin and Toruń and a number of other towns.

CULTURE

Polish is a western Slavonic tongue, the Latin alphabet
being used. Major writers include Henryk Sienkiewicz
(1846–1916), Nobel Prizewinner for Literature in 1905;
Boleslaw Prus (1847–1912); Stanislaw Reymont
(1868–1925), Nobel Prizewinner in 1924; Czeslaw
Milosz, Nobel Prizewinner in 1980.

The state monopoly on radio and television broadcasting ended in October 1992.

PORTUGAL
República Portuguesa

Portugal occupies the western part of the Iberian Peninsula, covering an area of 34,317 sq. miles (88,880 sq. km). It
lies between 36° 58′ and 42° 12″ N. latitude and 6° 11′ 48″
and 9° 29′ 45″ W. longitude. It is 362 miles in length from
north to south, and averages about 117 miles in breadth
from east to west.

The population (census 1991) is 9,862,700 (including
the Azores and Madeira). The language is Portuguese, a
Romance language with admixtures of Arabic and other
idioms.

CAPITAL – ΨLisbon, population estimate (1989)
2,128,000. ΨOporto 1,683,000.
CURRENCY – Escudo (Esc) of 100 centavos.
FLAG – Divided vertically into unequal parts of green and
red with the national emblem over all on the line of
division.
NATIONAL ANTHEM – A Portuguesa.
NATIONAL DAY – 10 June.

GOVERNMENT

From the 12th century until 1910 Portugal was a monarchy, but in 1910 an armed rising in Lisbon drove King
Manuel II into exile and a republic was set up. A period of
political instability ensued until eventually the military
stepped in and abolished political parties in 1926. The
constitution of 1933 gave formal expression to the cor-
porative 'Estado Novo' (New State) inspired and headed
by Dr Salazar, Prime Minister 1932–68. Dr Caetano
succeeded Salazar as Prime Minister in 1968 but his failure
to liberalize the regime or to conclude the wars in the
African colonies resulted in his government's overthrow by
a military coup on 25 April 1974. There was great political
turmoil between April 1974 and July 1976 but with the
failure of an attempted coup by the extreme left in
November 1975 the situation became more stable.

Under the 1976 constitution, amended in 1982 and 1989,
the President, elected for a five-year term by universal
adult suffrage, appoints the Prime Minister and, on the
latter's recommendation, the members of the Council of
Ministers. Legislative authority is vested in the 230-
member Assembly of the Republic, elected by a system of
proportional representation every four years. The

President retains certain limited powers to dismiss the government, dissolve the Assembly or veto laws.

In the general election held on 6 October 1991, the Social Democratic Party (PSD) won 135 seats; the Socialist Party (PS) 72 seats; the Communist Party (PCP) 17 seats, the Christian Democrats (CDS) 5 seats and the National Solidarity Party 1 seat.

HEAD OF STATE
President of the Republic, Dr Mario Soares, *elected* 1986, *re-elected* 13 January 1991

COUNCIL OF MINISTERS *as at August 1995*

Prime Minister, Prof. Anibal Cavaco Silva
Defence, Rui Figueiredo Lopes
Justice, Dr Alvaro Laborinho Lucio
Parliamentary Affairs, Luis Marques Mendes
Finance, Eduardo Catroga
Planning and Territorial Administration, Luis Valente de Oliveira
Home Affairs, Manuel Dias Loureiro
Foreign, José Durão Barroso
Agriculture and Sea, António Duarte Silva
Industry and Energy, Luis Mira Amaral
Education, Manuela Ferreira Leite
Public Works, Transport and Communications, Joaquim Ferreira do Amaral
Health, Paulo Mendo
Labour and Social Security, José Falcão e Cunha
Commerce and Tourism, Fernando Faria de Oliveira
Environment and Natural Resources, Teresa Gouveia

PORTUGUESE EMBASSY
11 Belgrave Square, London SWIX 8PP
Tel 0171-235 5331
Ambassador Extraordinary and Plenipotentiary, His Excellency Antonio Costa Lobo, apptd 1995
Minister-Plenipotentiary and Consul-General, A. de Almeida Ribeiro
Minister-Counsellor, F. Xavier-Esteves
Defence Attaché, Cdr. R. Telles-Palhinha, CBE
Counsellors, M. Quartin-Bastos, LVO (*Economic*); M. do Céu Hespanha (*Commercial*)

BRITISH EMBASSY
35–37 Rua de S. Domingos à Lapa, 1200 Lisbon
Tel: Lisbon 3961191
Ambassador Extraordinary and Plenipotentiary, His Excellency Roger Westbrook, CMG, apptd 1995
Deputy Ambassador, Counsellor, A. F. Smith
Defence Attaché, Cdr. R. Wykes-Sneyd, AFC
First Secretaries, P. Shaw (*Commercial*); D. J. Ferguson (*Consul*)

There are British Consulates in Oporto, Portimão, Funchal (Madeira), Ribeira Grande (Azores) and Macao

BRITISH COUNCIL DIRECTOR, Patrick Jackson, Rua de Sao Marçal 174, 1294 Lisbon. There are also offices at Cascais, Coimbra and Oporto.
BRITISH PORTUGUESE CHAMBER OF COMMERCE, Rua da Estrela 8, 1200 Lisbon and Rua Sa de Bandeira 784–20E, Frente, 4000 Oporto.

DEFENCE

The armed forces have a total active strength of 50,700 (17,600 conscripts) with reserves of 210,000. Conscripts serve four to 18 months. The present strength of the Army is 27,200 (15,000 conscripts), with 210 main battle tanks, 505 armoured personnel carriers and reconnaissance vehicles, and 150 artillery pieces. The Navy consists of 12,500 personnel (800 conscripts), including 1,850 marines,

with three submarines, 11 frigates and 30 patrol and coastal vessels. The strength of the Air Force is 11,000 (1,800 conscripts), including 1,800 paratroops, with 83 combat aircraft plus helicopters and transport and training aircraft. The paramilitary National Republican Guard, Public Security Police and Border Security Force number a total of 49,800 personnel.

Lisbon is the base of the NATO Iberian Atlantic Command and the USA maintains 1,155 personnel in mainland Portugal and on the Azores. Portugal maintains one frigate in the Adriatic enforcing the former Yugoslavia weapons embargo.

ECONOMY

Since joining the EC (EU) in 1986 Portugal has been adjusting its economy to the European single market, and to the criteria for membership of a future economic and monetary union as laid down in the Maastricht Treaty. The escudo joined the ERM in April 1992 and the budget deficit has been reduced to 5.8 per cent of GDP in 1995; inflation in 1994 was 5.5 per cent and unemployment 7.1 per cent.

The chief agricultural products are cork, potatoes, maize, wheat, rice, vegetables, olives, olive oil, figs, citrus fruits, almonds, timber, port wine and table wines. There are extensive forests of pine, cork, eucalyptus and chestnut covering about 20 per cent of the total area of the country. The principal mineral products are pyrites, wolfram, uranium, iron ores, copper and sodium and calcium minerals.

The country is moderately industrialized. The principal manufactures are textiles, clothing and footwear, machinery (including electric machinery and transport equipment), pulp and paper, pharmaceuticals, foodstuffs, chemicals, fertilizers, wood, cork, furniture, cement, glassware and pottery. There are a modern steelworks and two large shipbuilding and repair yards at Lisbon and Setúbal, working mainly for foreign shipowners. There are several hydroelectric power stations and a new thermal power station.

TRADE

The principal imports are cereals, meat, raw and semi-manufactured iron and steel, industrial machinery, chemicals, crude oil, motor vehicles and raw materials for textiles. The principal exports are textiles, footwear, timber, pulp, automotive parts, cork, electrical and other machinery, and chemicals.

	1991	1992
Total imports	Esc3,811,076,000m	Esc4,087,577,000m
Total exports	2,354,083,000m	2,475,202,000m
Trade with UK	1993	1994
Imports from UK	£1,325,193,000	£1,226,872,000
Exports to UK	1,189,352,000	1,253,541,000

COMMUNICATIONS

There are international airports at Lisbon and Oporto, and at Faro in the Algarve. Four morning and one evening daily newspapers are published in Lisbon and four morning newspapers in Oporto, and six main weekly newspapers.

EDUCATION

Education is free and compulsory for nine years from the age of six. Secondary education is mainly conducted in state lyceums, commercial and industrial schools, but there are also private schools. There are also military, naval, technical, polytechnic and other special schools. There are universities at Coimbra (founded in 1290), Oporto, Lisbon, Braga, Aveiro, Vila Real, Faro, Evora and in the Azores.

AUTONOMOUS REGIONS

Madeira and The Azores are two administratively autonomous regions of Portugal, having locally elected assemblies and governments.

MADEIRA

Madeira is a group of islands in the Atlantic Ocean about 520 miles south-west of Lisbon, and consists of Madeira, Porto, Santo and three uninhabited islands (Desertas). The total area is 314 sq. miles (813 sq. km), with a population of 271,400 (1989). ΨFunchal in Madeira, the largest island (270 sq. miles), is the capital (population 44,111); Machico (10,905).

THE AZORES

The Azores are a group of nine islands (Flores, Corvo, Terceira, São Jorge, Pico, Faial, Graciosa, São Miguel and Santa Maria) in the Atlantic Ocean, with a total area of 922 sq. miles (2,387 sq. km), and a population of 255,100 (1989). ΨPonta Delgada, on São Miguel, is the capital of the group (population 137,700). Other ports are ΨAngra, in Terceira (55,900) and ΨHorta (16,300).

OVERSEAS TERRITORY

MACAO

Macao, situated at the mouth of the Pearl River, comprises a peninsula and the islands of Coloane and Taipa, having an area of six sq. miles (15.5 sq. km), with a population (UN estimate 1992) of 374,000. Macao became a Portuguese colony in 1557; in a Sino-Portuguese treaty of 1887 China recognized Portugal's sovereignty over Macao. Following the Sino-British Joint Declaration on Hong Kong in 1984, Sino-Portuguese negotiations on the transfer of administration began in 1986 and an agreement on the transfer of the administration of Macao to the Chinese authorities was signed on 13 April 1987. Macao will become a 'special administrative region' (SAR) of China when transferred on 20 December 1999. The final session of the Macao SAR Basic Law Drafting Committee was held in Beijing in January 1993 and approved the Basic Law which will serve as Macao's constitution after 1999.

Macao is subject to Portuguese constitutional law but otherwise enjoys autonomy. The Governor is appointed by the Portuguese President and there is a 23-member legislative assembly, which has a three-year term. The assembly comprises seven members appointed by the Governor; eight directly elected, and eight indirectly elected by business associations.

Macao's major industry is textile manufacturing which accounts for 62 per cent of all exports. Most government revenue, however, comes from gambling, which attracts many Hong Kong and Chinese visitors. Port Macao is served by British, Portuguese and Dutch shipping lines and has regular services to Hong Kong, some 35 miles away.

Governor, Rocha Vieira.

TRADE WITH UK	1993	1994
Imports from UK	£12,835,000	£15,591,000
Exports to UK	37,141,000	55,208,000

QATAR
Dawlat Qatar

The state of Qatar covers the peninsula of Qatar in the Gulf from approximately the northern shore of Khor al Odaid to the eastern shore of Khor al Salwa. The area is about 4,247 sq. miles (11,000 sq. km).

The population (UN estimate 1992) is 453,000. Most of the population is concentrated in the urban district of Doha. Only a small minority still pursue the traditional life of the semi-nomadic tribesmen and fisherfolk.

CAPITAL – ΨDoha, population (estimated) 220,000. Other towns include Khor, Dukhan, Wakra and ΨUmm Said.

CURRENCY – Qatar riyal of 100 dirhams.

FLAG – White and maroon, white portion nearer the mast; vertical indented line comprising 17 angles divides the colours.

NATIONAL DAY – 3 September.

GOVERNMENT

Qatar was one of nine independent emirates in the Gulf in special treaty relations with the UK until 1971, when the special treaty relations were terminated. On 2 April 1970 a provisional constitution for Qatar was proclaimed, providing for the establishment of a Council of Ministers and for the formation of a Consultative Council to assist the Council of Ministers in running the affairs of the state. There are no political parties or legislature. The Amir, who had ruled since 22 February 1972, was overthrown on 27 June 1995 by his son and heir, who assumed power as Amir the same day.

HEAD OF STATE
HH Amir of Qatar, Sheikh Hamad bin Khalifa Al Thani, KCMG, *assumed power* 27 June 1995

COUNCIL OF MINISTERS *as at August 1995*
Prime Minister, Minister of Defence and Commander-in-Chief of Armed Forces, The Amir
Deputy PM, Interior, HE Sheikh Abdullah bin Khalifa Al Thani
Minister of State, Amiri Diwan Affairs, HE Sheikh Hamad bin Suhaim Al-Thani
Finance, Economy and Trade, HE Sheikh Mohammed bin Khalifa Al-Thani
Foreign Affairs, HE Sheikh Hamad bin Jassem bin Jabr Al-Thani
State, HE Sheikh Ahmed bin Saif Al Thani
Minister of State for Defence Affairs, Deputy C.-in-C. of Armed Forces, HE Sheikh Hamad bin Abdulah Al-Thani
Endowments and Islamic Affairs, HE Sheikh Abdullah bin Khalid Al-Thani
Municipal Affairs and Agriculture, HE Sheikh Ahmed bin Hamad Al-Thani
Cabinet Affairs, HE Sheikh Mohammed bin Khalid Al-Thani
Labour, Social Affairs and Housing, HE Abdulrahman Saad Al Dirham
Communications and Transport, HE Abdulla bin Saleh Al Manei
Public Health, HE Ali Saeed Al-Khayareen
Information and Culture, HE Dr Hamad Abdulaziz Al-Kawari
Education, HE Abdulaziz Abdullah Turki
Electricity and Water, HE Ahmed Mohamed Ali Al-Subaie
Energy and Industry, HE Abdulla bin Hamad Al-Attiyah
Justice, HE Dr Najib Mohammed Al-Nuaimi

Minister of State for Foreign Affairs, HE Ahmed Abdulla Al-Mahmoud

EMBASSY OF THE STATE OF QATAR
1 South Audley Street, London WIY 5DQ
Tel 0171-493 2200
Ambassador Extraordinary and Plenipotentiary, His Excellency Ali Al-Jaidha, apptd 1993

BRITISH EMBASSY
PO Box 3, Doha
Tel: Doha 421991
Ambassador Extraordinary and Plenipotentiary, His Excellency Patrick F. Wogan, CMG, apptd 1993
First Secretary, J. McGuire (*Commercial*)

BRITISH COUNCIL DIRECTOR, Brian Austin, Ras Abu Aboud Road (PO Box 2992), Doha

ECONOMY

Although Qatar is a desert country, there are gardens and smallholdings near Doha and to the north, and encouragement is being given to the development of agriculture.

The Qatar General Petroleum Corporation is the state-owned company controlling Qatar's interests in oil, gas and petrochemicals. The corporation is responsible for Qatar's oil production onshore and offshore. The production level for Qatar agreed in OPEC is currently 364,000 b.p.d. Explorations continue for further oil. The large reserves of natural gas in the North Field came into production in September 1991. A 50,000 b.p.d. oil refinery was commissioned in 1984 to increase domestic refinery capacity.

Current industries include a steel mill, a fertilizer plant, a cement factory, a petrochemical complex and two natural gas liquids plants. With the exception of the cement works at Umm Bab, all these industries are at Umm Said, about 30 miles south of Doha. Qatar is also expanding its infrastructure, including electrical generation and water distillation, roads, houses, and government buildings, although reduced demand for crude oil in international markets has led to a downturn in the economy and a slower rate of development than hitherto.

TRADE WITH UK	1993	1994
Imports from UK	£143,021,000	£127,575,000
Exports to UK	20,464,000	7,499,000

COMMUNICATIONS

Regular air services provided by Gulf Air and Qatar Airways connect Qatar with the other Gulf states, the Middle East, the Indian sub-continent, Africa and Europe. The Qatar Broadcasting Service transmits on medium, shortwave, and VHF. Regular television transmissions in colour began in 1974 and a second channel opened in 1982.

ROMANIA
România

Romania is a republic of south-eastern Europe, formerly the classical Dacia and Scythia Pontica. The area is 91,699 sq. miles (237,500 sq. km).

The population (1992 census) is 22,760,449. Romanians number 21,559,910 (88 per cent), there is a Hungarian minority of 1,714,000 (7.9 per cent), a dwindling German minority of 359,000 (1.6 per cent) and 227,000 gypsies (1.1 per cent). The leading religion is that of the Romanian Orthodox Church; the Roman Catholic and some Protestant denominations are of importance numerically.

Romanian is a Romance language with many archaic forms and with admixtures of Slavonic, Turkish, Magyar and French words. There is a wealth of folk-songs and folklore, transmitted orally through many centuries and collected in the 19th century.

CAPITAL – Bucharest, on the Dimbovita, population (1992 census) 2,064,474.
Other large towns are:

Braşov	323,835	Ψ Galati	325,788
Constanţa	350,476	Craiova	303,520
Cluj-Napoca	328,008	Ploiesti	252,073
Iasi	342,994	Ψ Brăila	234,706
Timisoara	334,278		

CURRENCY – Leu (*plural* Lei) of 100 bani.
FLAG – Three vertical bands, blue, yellow, red.
NATIONAL ANTHEM – Desteapta-te, romane.
NATIONAL DAY – 1 December.

GOVERNMENT

Romania has its origin in the union of the Danubian principalities of Wallachia and Moldavia under the Treaty of Paris 1856. Although under nominal Turkish suzerainty, the principalities achieved effective unification and independence in 1859 when Alexander Cuza had himself proclaimed ruler of both principalities. The new country adopted the name Romania in 1862. Cuza was deposed and replaced by Prince Karl von Hohenzollern in 1864. By the Treaty of Berlin 1878 the principality was recognized as an independent state, and part of the Dobrudja (which had been occupied by the Romanians) was incorporated; on 27 March 1881 it was recognized as a kingdom. The First World War added Bessarabia, the Bukovina, the Banat and Crisana-Maramures, these additions of territory being confirmed by the Versailles Treaty in 1919. Following the break-up of the Austro-Hungarian Empire, a National Assembly was held in Transylvania on 1 December 1918 which proclaimed the union of all Romanians in one state. In June 1920 Transylvania was formally acquired from Hungary under the Treaty of Trianon. In June 1940, in compliance with an ultimatum from USSR, Bessarabia and Northern Bukovina were ceded to the Soviet Union, and in August 1940 Romania ceded to Bulgaria the portion of southern Dobrudja taken from Bulgaria in 1913.

In 1947 King Michael was forced to abdicate and Romania became 'The Romanian People's Republic' in December 1947. The leading political force from the Second World War until 1989 was the Romanian Communist Party. A revolution in December 1989 led to the overthrow of Nicolae Ceauşescu, President since 1967. A provisional government was formed which abolished the leading role of the Communist Party and held free elections in May 1990. A new constitution was adopted in 1991 and formally makes Romania a multiparty democracy and endorses human rights and a market economy. There is a Senate of 143 members and a 341-member Assembly of Deputies (of which 13 seats are reserved for ethnic minorities other than Hungarians).

Presidential and parliamentary elections took place in September and October 1992. President Ilieseu was re-elected and his Democratic National Salvation Front (DNSF), renamed the Social Democracy Party of Romania (PSDR) in July 1993, gained the largest number of seats in both houses of parliament and formed a minority government with the support of nationalist parties and the ex-Communists. Throughout 1992–4 the government, which included many members of the Ceauşescu regime, remained antagonistic to economic reform. The worsening economic situation caused the PSDR to press for political support and in March 1994 it formed a coalition government with the nationalist Party of Romanian National Unity (PRNU). In January 1995 a protocol was signed by these two parties and the Greater Romanian Party (GRP) and the ex-Communist Socialist Labour Party (SLP) which states the basis under which the latter three parties will continue to support the PSDR.

HEAD OF STATE
President of the Republic, Ion Iliescu, *elected* May 1990, re-elected 11 October 1992

GOVERNMENT *as at August 1995*

Prime Minister, Nicolae Vacaroiu
Minister of State, Foreign Affairs, Teodor Melescanu
Minister of State, Finance, Florin Georgescu
Minister of State, Labour and Social Protection, Dan Popescu
Minister of State, Economic Reform and Strategy, Mircea Cosea
Defence, Gheorghe Tinca
Industry, Dumitru Popescu.
Interior, Ioan Taracila
Justice, Iosif Chiuzbaian
Communications, Adrian Turicu
Parliamentary Relations, Valer Dorneanu
Public Works, Marin Cristea
Research and Technology, Doru Palade
Education, Liviu Maior
Culture, Viorel Marginean
Agriculture and Food Industry, Valeriu Tabara
Environment, Forestry and Water, Aurel Ilie
Health, Iulian Mincu
Tourism, Matei Dan
Trade, Petru Crisan
Transport, Aurel Novac
Youth and Sports, Alexandru Mironov

EMBASSY OF ROMANIA
Arundel House, 4 Palace Green, London W8 4QD
Tel 0171-937 9666
Ambassador Extraordinary and Plenipotentiary, His Excellency Sergiu Celac, apptd 1990
Defence Attaché, Lt.-Col. Vasile Huica
First Secretary, C. Turturea (*Economic*)
Third Secretary, A. Gheorghe (*Consular*)

BRITISH EMBASSY
24 Strada Jules Michelet, 70154 Bucharest
Tel: Bucharest 3120 303/4/5/6
Ambassador Extraordinary and Plenipotentiary, His Excellency Andrew Bache, CMG, apptd 1992
Counsellor, Deputy Head of Mission, R. M. Publicover.
Defence Attaché, Lt.-Col. R. J. F. Owen, OBE
First Secretary (Commercial), W. J. Preston

BRITISH COUNCIL DIRECTOR, Claus Henning, Calea Dorobantilor 14, Bucharest

DEFENCE

Romania has a total active armed forces strength of 230,500 personnel (125,000 conscripts) with a further 427,000 reserves. Conscripts serve 12 months (Army and Air Force) and 18 months (Navy). The Army has a strength of 160,500 (105,000 conscripts) with 2,395 main battle tanks, 251 assault guns, 2,450 armoured infantry fighting vehicles and armoured personnel carriers and 1,840 artillery pieces. The Navy has a strength of 19,000 personnel (10,000 conscripts) including 1,000 coastal defence and 8,000 marines. It deploys one submarine, one destroyer, five frigates and 82 patrol and coastal vessels. The Air Force has 27,400 personnel (10,000 conscripts) with 382 combat aircraft and 37 armed helicopters. Paramilitary Border Guards, Security Guards and Gendarmerie number 72,100 personnel.

ECONOMY

Wallachia, Moldavia and Transylvania are among the most fertile areas in Europe, and agriculture and sheep and cattle raising are the principal industries of Romania. The principal cereal crops are vegetables, flax and hemp. Vines and fruits are also grown. The forests of the mountainous regions are extensive, and the timber industry is important. Collectivization of agriculture was achieved in 1962. Since December 1989 agricultural workers have sold produce on the open market and since 1991 private ownership of plots up to 10 hectares in size has been permitted. Allocation of land and distribution of ownership certificates continues to take place, though in many areas it is virtually complete.

There are plentiful supplies of natural gas, together with various mineral deposits including coal, iron ore, bauxite, lead, zinc, copper and uranium in quantities which allow a substantial part of the requirements of industry to be met from local resources. Production of crude oil was 6,600,000 tonnes in 1992.

The economy faced increasing problems from the late 1970s as a result of over-investment in heavy industry and neglect of agriculture. The effects of these policies were aggravated by the international recession and by high interest rates, and Romania was severely in debt by the early 1980s. The Ceauşescu government aimed to completely repay the foreign debt by reducing borrowing, cutting imports and increasing exports. After the 1989 revolution the government pursued only a limited programme of economic reform and liberalization, mainly because of the opposition of the large ex-Communist element within the PSDR. Subsidies for fuel, food and other goods continued, as did those for uneconomic state firms, wages were indexed to prices and privatization delayed. In early 1994, after inflation had reached over 300 per cent annually and unemployment 10 per cent, the government and parliament agreed to an IMF austerity package to gain loans of US$700 million. Most consumer subsidies and price controls have since been lifted, interest and exchange rates have been freed and the free-marketing restructuring of state enterprises has begun. In July 1994 the government announced a mass privatization programme, with foreign ownership of up to 100 per cent permitted. This programme was approved by parliament in March 1995 with the aim of privatizing 3,000 enterprises by spring 1996. Only 900 smaller firms have been privatized so far.

TRADE

Imports are chiefly semi-manufactured goods, raw materials, fuel, machinery and metals. Exports consist principally of maize, wheat, barley, oats, petroleum, timber, cattle, meat, machines and industrial equipment.

Trade with UK	1993	1994
Imports from UK	£93,843,000	£127,059,000
Exports to UK	93,289,000	146,375,000

COMMUNICATIONS

In 1990 there were 11,348 km of railway open for traffic. The mercantile marine had a gross tonnage of 12,140,000 tons in 1990. The principal ports are Constanta (on the Black Sea), Sulina (on the Danube Estuary), Galati, Braila, Giurgiu and Turnu Severin. The Danube and the Black Sea are linked by a canal completed in 1984.

EDUCATION

Education is free and nominally compulsory. There are state universities in seven cities, 66 private universities, six polytechnics, two commercial academies, and five agricultural colleges. An education bill adopted in July 1995 was opposed by the ethnic Hungarian community who claimed that it would reduce the provision for education in the Hungarian language agreed in 1993.

RUSSIA
Rossiiskaya Federatsiya – Russian Federation

Russia has an area of 6,593,391 sq. miles (17,075,400 sq. km) and occupies three-quarters of the land area of the former Soviet Union. In the west it is bordered by Norway, the Gulf of Finland, Finland, Estonia, Latvia, Belarus and the Ukraine; the Kaliningrad enclave borders Lithuania and Poland. To the south Russia is bordered in Europe by Georgia, Azerbaijan, the Black Sea and the Caspian Sea, and in Asia by Kazakhstan, China, Mongolia and North Korea. In the east it meets the North Pacific (where its nearest point is only a few miles from Japan), and the Bering Strait (where its nearest point is only a few miles from Alaska). To the north is the Arctic Ocean and the Barents Sea.

The Russian Federation comprises 89 members: 49 regions (*oblast*) – Amur, Archangel, Astrakhan, Belgorod, Bryansk, Chelyabinsk, Chita, Irkutsk, Ivanovo, Kaliningrad, Kaluga, Kamchatka, Kemerovo, Kirov, Kostroma, Kurgan, Kursk, Leningrad, Lipetsk, Magadan, Moscow, Murmansk, Nizhny Novgorod, Novgorod, Novosibirsk, Omsk, Orel, Orenburg, Penza, Perm, Pskov, Rostov, Ryazan, Sakhalin, Samara, Saratov, Smolensk, Sverdlovsk, Tambov, Tomsk, Tula, Tver, Tyumen, Ulyanovsk, Vladimir, Volgograd, Vologda, Voronezh, Yaroslavl; six autonomous territories (*krai*) – Altai, Khabarovsk, Krasnodar, Krasnoyarsk, Primorye, Stavropol; 21 republics – Adygeia, Altai, Bashkortostan, Buryatia, Chechen, Chuvash, Daghestan, Ingush, Kabardin-Balkar, Kalmykia, Karachaevo-Cherkess, Karelia, Khakassia, Komi, Mari-El, Mordovia, North Ossetia (Alania), Sakha, Tatarstan, Tyva, Udmurt; ten autonomous areas – Agin-Buryat, Chukot, Evenki, Khanty-Mansi, Komi-Permyak, Koryak, Nenets, Taimyr, Ust-Ordyn-Buryat, Yamalo-Nenets; two cities of federal status – Moscow, St Petersburg; and one autonomous Jewish region, Birobidjan.

There are three principal geographic areas: a low-lying flat western area stretching eastwards up to the Yenisei and divided in two by the Ural ridge; the eastern area between the Yenisei and the Pacific, consisting of a number of tablelands and ridges; and a southern mountainous area. Russia has a very long coast-line, including the longest Arctic coastline in the world (about 17,000 miles). The most important rivers are the Volga, the Northern Dvina and the Pechora, the Neva, the Don and the Kuban in the European part, and in the Asiatic part, the Ob, the Irtysh, the Yenisei, the Lena and the Amur, and, further north, Khatanga, Olenek, Yana, Indigirka, Kolyma and Anadyr. Lakes are abundant, particularly in the north-west. The huge Baikal Lake in eastern Siberia is the deepest lake in the world. There are also two large artificial water reservoirs within the Greater Volga canal system, the Moscow and Rybinsk 'Seas'. Climatically, Russia extends from Arctic and tundra belts to the subtropical in the south.

The 1994 estimate gave a population of 148,300,000, of which about 87.5 per cent are Russian, 3.5 per cent Tatar, 2.7 per cent Ukrainian, 1.3 per cent ethnic German, 1.1 per cent Chavash, 0.9 per cent Bashkir, 0.7 per cent Belarusian and 0.7 per cent Mordovian. There are another six minorities with populations of over half a million and more than 130 nationalities in total.

The Russian Orthodox Church is the predominant religion, though the Tatars are Muslims and there are Jewish communities in Moscow and St Petersburg.

Russian is a branch of the Slavonic family of languages and is written in the Cyrillic script.

CAPITAL – Moscow (population 8,700,000 (1994)), founded about 1147, became the centre of the rising Moscow principality and in the 15th century the capital of the whole of Russia (Muscovy). In 1325 it became the seat of the Metropolitan of Russia. In 1703 Peter the Great transferred the capital to St Petersburg, but on 14 March 1918 Moscow was again designated as the capital. ψ St Petersburg (from 1914 to 1924 Petrograd and from 1924 to 1991 Leningrad) has a population of 4,952,000 (1993).

Other towns with populations (1990) exceeding one million are:

Nizhny-Novgorod (Gorky)	1,438,000
Novosibirsk (Novonikolayevsk)	1,436,000
Yekaterinburg (Sverdlovsk)	1,367,000
Samara (Kuibyshev)	1,257,000
Omsk	1,148,000
Chelyabinsk	1,143,000
Ufa	1,083,000
Perm (Molotov)	1,091,000
Kazan	1,094,000
Rostov-on-Don	1,020,000

CURRENCY – Rouble of 100 kopeks.
FLAG – Three horizontal stripes of white, blue, red.
NATIONAL ANTHEM – The Patriotic Song.
NATIONAL DAY – 12 June (Independence Day).

HISTORY

The Gregorian calendar was not introduced until 14 February 1918. For the events surrounding the 1917 revolutions the dates given here are the Gregorian calendar dates in use in the rest of the world at the time, with the dates in the Julian calendar (os) in parenthesis.

Russia was formally created from the principality of Muscovy and its territories by Tsar Peter I (The Great) (1682–1725), who initiated its territorial expansion, introduced western ideas of government and state organization and founded St Petersburg. By the end of Peter the Great's reign, the Baltic territories (modern-day Estonia and Latvia) had been annexed from Sweden and Russia had become the dominant military power of north-eastern Europe. In the 18th century the partitions of Poland and wars with Turkey brought the territories of modern-day Lithuania, Belarus, Ukraine and the Crimea under Russian control, and the colonization of Siberia east of the Urals began in earnest. Russia overran the Caucasus region (modern-day Armenia, Azerbaijan and Georgia) in the early 19th century, seized Finland from Sweden in 1809 and Bessarabia from Turkey in 1812. Throughout the remainder of the 19th century Russia subdued and annexed the independent Muslim states which later formed the five Central Asian republics.

It was as a multinational empire covering a huge geographical area, in which the monarch and nobility held almost absolute power (an ineffectual parliament, the Duma, was created in 1905), that the Russian Empire entered the First World War in 1914. Discontent caused by autocratic rule, the poor conduct of the military campaign and wartime privation led to a revolution which broke out on 12 March (27 February os) 1917. Tsar Nicholas II abdicated three days later and a provisional government was formed; a republic was proclaimed on 14 September (1 September os) 1917. A political power struggle ensued between the provisional government and the Bolshevik Party which controlled the Soviets (councils) set up by workers, soldiers and peasants. This led to a second revolution on 7 November (25 October os) 1917 in which the Bolsheviks, led by Lenin, seized power.

The Bolshevik (Communist) Party withdrew from the First World War under the Treaty of Brest-Litovsk (March 1918), surrendering large areas of territory. Armed resistance to Communist rule developed into an all-out civil war between 'red' Bolshevik forces and 'white' monarchist and anti-Communist forces which lasted until the end of 1922. During the civil war, Russia had been declared a Soviet Republic and other Soviet republics had been formed in the Ukraine, Byelorussia and Transcaucasia. These four republics merged to form the Union of Soviet Socialist Republics (USSR) on 30 December 1922.

The Nazi-Soviet pact of August 1939 and the Second World War resulted in further territorial expansion, regaining much of the territory lost in or after 1918, as well as extending Soviet influence to the countries of eastern Europe liberated by Soviet troops. The USSR lost 26 million combatants and civilians in the war.

After an internal Communist Party power struggle following Lenin's death in 1924, Joseph Stalin emerged in 1928 as the undisputed party leader. He initiated a series of reorganizations of the USSR, introduced a policy of rapid industrialization under a series of five-year plans, brought all sectors of industry under government control, abolished private ownership and enforced the collectivization of agriculture. He eliminated potential political opponents through purges and show trials, and total political repression lasted until his death in 1953.

Repression lessened under Khruschev and Brezhnev, but the Communist Party remained dominant in all walks of life. This was the state of affairs when Mikhail Gorbachev became Soviet leader in March 1985. Gorbachev introduced the policies of *perestroika* (complete restructuring) and *glasnost* (openness) in order to revamp the economy, which had stagnated since the 1970s, to root out corruption and inefficiency, and to end the Cold War and its attendant arms race. Private ownership was allowed, individual expression and limited private enterprise were tolerated, political prisoners released and the guaranteed leading role of the Communist Party abolished. The political openness and the retreat from total control by the Communist Party unleashed ethnic and nationalist tensions. Events came to a head on 19 August 1991 when a coup was attempted against President Gorbachev by hardline elements of the Communist Party, the armed forces and the state security service (KGB) in order to reimpose Communist control on the USSR. The coup was defeated by reformist and democratic political groupings supported by the majority of the population, who took to the streets of Moscow and other large cities under the leadership of Russian President Yeltsin. The coup leaders were arrested and imprisoned, and Mikhail Gorbachev returned to Moscow. However, it became clear that effective political power was in the hands of the republican leaders, especially Russian President Yeltsin, and the Soviet Union began to break up as the constituent republics declared their independence. Mikhail Gorbachev resigned as Soviet President on 25 December 1991 and on 26 December 1991 the USSR formally ceased to exist.

GOVERNMENT

Russia was recognized as an independent state by the EC and USA in January 1992, and it inherited the Soviet Union's seat at the UN on 24 December 1991.

A new Russian Federal Treaty was signed on 13 March 1992 between the central government and the autonomous republics. Tatarstan refused to sign the Treaty and in April 1992 declared its 'independence'. In February 1994 Tatarstan signed its own agreement with the federal government on the basis of being a 'state united with Russia'. Similarly, after declaring its 'independence' in March 1992, Bashkortostan signed a treaty with the Federation in August 1994 giving it considerable legislative and economic autonomy. In November 1992 President Yeltsin imposed direct rule in the autonomous republics of Ingush and North Ossetia after Ingush forces attacked North Ossetia; a state of emergency was declared by President Yeltsin in the two autonomous republics in March 1993; it remains in place in both republics.

Throughout 1992–3 President Yeltsin's government and reformist political groups faced opposition to constitutional political and economic reform from the bureaucracy, some of the military, influential heads of major state enterprises and the Supreme Soviet and the Congress of People's Deputies, led by its speaker Ruslan Khasbulatov. Despite an overwhelming victory for President Yeltsin in an April 1993 referendum on continuing socio-economic reform, parliamentary hardliners continued to block reform. Events came to a head on 21 September 1993 when President Yeltsin dissolved parliament and called new elections. The hardline parliamentary forces led by Khasbulatov and Rutskoi declared the move a coup d'état, formed a rival government and occupied the White House. After several days of fighting in Moscow between parliamentary and government forces, the parliamentary hardline forces attempted a coup which was put down by the army. After the hardline defeat, President Yeltsin's government suspended the constitutional court, clamped down on broadcasting and press organizations that had supported the coup attempt, and held new elections in all 89 regions and republics. Elections to the Federal Assembly were held on 12 December 1993 and resulted in the pro-reform Russia's Democractic Choice bloc emerging as the largest party in the State Duma, but the anti-reform neo-fascist Liberal Democratic Party gained the largest share of the vote in the proportional representation section. The strong showing of the anti-reform Communist and Agrarian parties and the splintered nature of the resulting parliament led to a more centrist government being formed and the ending of radical economic reforms. The state of the major parties in the State Duma as at August 1995 was: Russia's Democratic Choice 103; Liberal Democratic Party 66; Communist Party 62; Agrarian Party 47; Yabloko 33; Party of Unity and Accord 27; Women of Russia 25; Democratic Party 21; Civic Union 18. The next State Duma election is scheduled for 17 December 1995.

Constitution

The present constitution came into force on 22 December 1993 after approval in a national referendum. It enshrines the right to private ownership and the freedoms of press, speech, association, worship and travel, and states that Russia is a multiparty democracy. The President is given strong powers under the constitution, being head of state, head of government, head of the Security Council and commander-in-chief of the armed forces. The President is pre-eminent in foreign and defence policies and may declare war on foreign states or declare a state of emergency or martial law in Russia (subject to confirmation by the Federation Council). He may chair cabinet meetings, determine basic government policy, veto parliamentary legislation, issue decrees and directives, call referendums, dismiss the government, nominate senior judges, the prosecutor-general and the Central Bank Governor. The President nominates the Prime Minister and Deputy Prime Ministers, who must be approved by the State Duma. If the President's nominees are rejected once or twice by the State Duma he may ignore it; on the third rejection he may dismiss the State Duma and call new elections. The President is directly elected for a maximum of two four-year terms, and may only be impeached on the grounds of treason or serious crime after rulings in both the Supreme and Constitutional Courts and two-thirds majorities in both houses of parliament. The Prime Minister takes over from the President in the event that he is unable to fulfil his duties.

Legislative power is vested in the Federal Assembly, comprising the Federation Council (upper house) of 178 members, two elected by each of the 89 members of the Russian Federation; the State Duma (lower house) of 450 members, of which 225 are elected by constituencies on a first-past-the-post basis and 225 by proportional representation, with a 5 per cent threshold for representation.

The Federation Council maintains jurisdiction over central-local government matters, and its approval is needed for economic and defence legislation to be passed. The State Duma, elected for four-year terms, oversees government appointments, has the power to reject the government's fiscal and monetary policies, may pass votes of no confidence in the government (which the President may ignore on the first vote), and cannot be dissolved less than one year after its election.

The main clauses of the constitution may only be changed with the agreement of the President and with a three-quarters vote in the Federation Council, a two-thirds vote in the State Duma, and the agreement of two-thirds of the Russian Federation's 89 members. A transitional period is in operation with the present Federal Assembly having a two-year term, and President Yeltsin a five-year term until June 1996.

The judicial system consists of a Constitutional Court of 19 members appointed for a 12-year term which protects and interprets the constitution and decides if laws are compatible with it. The Supreme Court adjudicates in criminal and civil laws cases. The Arbitration Court deals with commercial disputes between companies. The new code of civil law came into force in January 1995.

Secession

The Chechen republic declared its 'independence' in November 1991 after a nationalist coup in the republic which brought former Soviet Air Force General Dudayev to power as republican President. Chechenia refused to sign the Russian Federal Treaty in March 1992 and a constitutional stalemate ensued. Civil war began in early 1994 between Gen. Dudayev's forces and armed opposition forces of the 'Provisional Chechen Council', tacitly supported by the Russian government. After Russian forces surrounded Chechenia in September 1994 to stop the conflict overspilling the borders, President Yeltsin ordered fighting in the republic to stop and the laying down of arms by the rival groups on 29 November. When this request was refused Russian aircraft began to bomb the Chechen capital Grozny and on 9 December President Yeltsin ordered the Russian military ro retake the republic and disarm all armed groups. Russian army and interior ministry forces entered Chechenia two days later and after heavy fighting against strong Chechen rersistance managed to capture the presidential palace in Grozny on 19 January 1995. Chechen forces were finally forced out of Grozny in early February and by mid-May Chechen forces had been pushed back into the Caucasus mountains in the southern third of the republic, while Russian forces controlled the plains of the north and centre.

After Chechen forces had taken over 1,000 hostages in the southern Russian town of Budyonnovsk on 14 June, Russian Prime Minister Chernomyrdin took control of negotiations with the Chechens which led to the release of the hostages, the safe return of the Chechens to Chechenia and a cease-fire agreement on 22 June. Fighting resumed on 4 July but negotiations continued, leading to the signing of an accord to end the fighting on 30 July. The accord provides for the phased disarmament of Chechen fighters; the partial withdrawal of Russian forces; the withdrawal of both sides from conflict lines by three miles; the exchange of all prisoners of war. The first Chechen weapons were handed over to Russian forces on 16 August after a Russian ultimatum to do so or face renewed fighting. However, sporadic fighting continued at the end of August, putting the agreement at risk. The political and constitutional status of Chechenia remains unresolved. (*See also* Events of the Year).

HEAD OF STATE
President, Boris Yeltsin, *elected* 12 June 1991

GOVERNMENT *as at August 1995*
Prime Minister, Viktor Chernomyrdin
First Deputy PM (Economy and Privatization), Anatoly Chubais
First Deputy PM, Oleg Soskovets
Deputy PMs, Oleg Davydov (*Foreign Economic Relations*); Sergei Shakhrai; Alexei Bolshakov (*CIS relations*); Yuri Yarov (*Social Policy*)
Foreign Affairs, Andrei Kozyrev
Defence, Marshal Pavel Grachev
Interior, Col.-Gen. Anatoly Kulikov
Justice, Valentin Kovalev
Finance, Vladimir Panskov
Economics, Yevgeny Yasin
Privatization, Sergei Belyayev
Education, Yevgeny Tkachenko
Labour, Gennady Melikyan
Ecology and Natural Resources, Viktor Danilov-Danilyan
Public Health, Eduard Nechaev
Communications, Vladimir Bulgak
Transport, Vitaly Yefimov
Fuel and Energy, Yuri Shafranik
Agriculture and Foodstuffs, Alexander Nazachuk
Railways, Gennady Fadeyev
Culture and Tourism, Yevgeny Sidorov
Nuclear Power, Viktor Mikhailov
Science, Technology and Higher Education, Boris Saltykov
Social Welfare, Lyudmila Bezlepkina
Civil Defence, Sergei Shoigu
Construction, Yefim Basin
Nationalities and Regional Policy, Vyacheslav Mikhailov
Co-operation with CIS states, Valery Serov
Minister without Portfolio, Nikolai Travkin
Speaker of the Federation Council, Vladimir Shumeiko
Speaker of the State Duma, Ivan Rybkin
Chairman of the Constitutional Court, Vladimir Tumanov

EMBASSY OF THE RUSSIAN FEDERATION
13 Kensington Palace Gardens, London w8 4QX
Tel 0171-229 3628
Ambassador Extraordinary and Plenipotentiary, His Excellency Anatoly Adamishin, apptd 1994
Minister-Counsellor, Aleksandr Kudinov; G. Gventsadze
Defence Attaché, Lt.-Gen. V. N. Pronin
Trade Representative, N. B. Teliatnikov.

BRITISH EMBASSY
Moscow 72, Sosiiskaya Naberezhnaya 14
Tel: Moscow 230 6333
Ambassador Extraordinary and Plenipotentiary, His Excellency Sir Andrew Wood, KCMG, apptd 1995
Minister and Deputy Head of Mission, A. Carter
Minister-Counsellor, M. B. Nicholson
Defence and Air Attaché, Air Cdre P. J. Wilkinson, CVO
Counsellors (Commercial), A. R. Brenton (Moscow); C. P. Winnington-Ingram (St Petersburg)
Consuls-General: I. Kydd (Moscow); S. D. Jack (St Petersburg)
There is a British Consulate-General in St Petersburg.

BRITISH COUNCIL DIRECTOR, M. Evans, CVO, Ul Nikoloyamskaya 1, Moscow 109189. There is also an office at St Petersburg.

DEFENCE (*see also* CIS entry, pages 753–4)

Since the demise of the Soviet Union the Russian armed forces have been considerably reduced but remain some of the most powerful in the world. The total active armed forces number 1,714,000 personnel (including 950,000 conscripts serving for 18- or 24-month periods and 150,000 Ministry of Defence staff). Reserves number 2,400,000 personnel.

The Strategic Nuclear Forces are centrally controlled, number 167,000 personnel and have 700 nuclear missiles in 46 submarines; 1,161 inter-continental ballistic missiles based on land; 158 long-range nuclear bombers; 100 anti-ballistic missiles with related satellites, radar and long-range early warning systems.

The Navy has a strength of 282,000 personnel (including 180,000 conscripts, 45,000 naval aviation, 12,000 naval infantry and 17,500 coastal defence and artillery personnel). It deploys 127 tactical submarines; one fixed-wing and one V/STOL aircraft carriers; 25 cruisers; 22 destroyers; 112 frigates; 145 patrol and coastal craft; 193 mine warfare vessels; and 600 support ships. Naval Aviation has 783 combat aircraft and 251 armed helicopters whilst the infantry and coastal defence forces deploy 960 main battle tanks, 1,810 armoured vehicles and 1,120 artillery pieces. The Navy is organized into four fleets: Northern, Baltic, Pacific and Black Sea (which is to be divided, with 81 per cent of the fleet becoming Russian and 19 per cent Ukrainian); and one flotilla (Caspian Sea) operated jointly with Kazakhstan and Turkmenistan.

The Army numbers 780,000 personnel (450,000 conscripts) organized into 90 divisions and 149 brigades. Equipment includes 19,500 main battle tanks; 37,000 armoured infantry fighting vehicles and armoured personnel carriers; 16,300 artillery pieces; 500 surface-to-surface missiles; 1,000 attack helicopters. The Air Force has a strength of 356,000 personnel (including 185,000 conscripts) with 220 long-range bombers, 775 ground attack aircraft, 1,825 air defence fighters, 350 transport aircraft, 325 reconnaissance aircraft and 2,100 training aircraft. Paramilitary forces number 280,000, including 100,000 Frontier Forces and 180,000 internal security troops.

The Russian withdrawal from eastern Europe was completed on 31 August 1994, except for 600 troops in Latvia to operate and then dismantle the Skrunda radar base over five and a half years, and 200 in Estonia to dismantle the Paldiski nuclear submarine base by late 1995. In the rest of the CIS, Russia maintains a joint air defence force with the five Central Asian republics, maintains joint armed forces of 34,000 personnel with Turkmenistan, and is to establish a joint armed forces with Kazakhstan by the end of 1995. It also deploys forces in Armenia (5,000), Georgia (20,000), Moldova (10,000), Tajikistan (12,000), Belarus (30,000). In addition, Russia deploys 575 troops with UN peacekeeping forces in Bosnia-Hercegovina; 3,000 as a UN peacekeeping force in Abkhazia in Georgia; and 600 in South Ossetia in Georgia.

ECONOMY

Under the Soviet regime, an essentially agricultural economy in 1917 was transformed by the early 1960s into the second strongest industrial power in the world. However, by the early 1970s the concentration of resources on the military-industrial complex was causing the civilian economy to stagnate. This was exacerbated by the bureaucratic inefficiency of the centrally planned economic system and the extremely poor distribution system. It was in an attempt to solve the problems of the centrally planned economic system that Gorbachev introduced economic restructuring (*perestroika*). After attempts to reform the economy within the restraints of the centrally planned system had failed, an increasing number of free market reforms were introduced, including the legalization of small private businesses in August 1990, the reduction of state control over the economy in October 1990, and denationalization and privatization measures in July 1991. In May 1992 most state subsidies were abolished and price liberalization was introduced. The first stage of mass privatization of state industries began in October 1992 and the central distribution system was abolished with effect from 1 January 1993.

However, the abolition of central planning before a fully free market system was in place, and continued argument over reform between radicals and centrists in the government in 1992–4 resulted in economic confusion. Economic reform and the continuation of western aid were thrown into doubt in January 1993 when Prime Minister Chernomyrdin signalled the re-introduction of price controls on some goods; but President Yeltsin returned to economic reform policies soon afterwards. By the end of the first stage of mass privatization in June 1994 an estimated 35–40 per cent of enterprises had been privatized (about 85,000, including 15,000 large and medium-sized enterprises employing 70 per cent of industrial workers); 45 per cent of the workforce worked in the private sector, which produced 40 per cent of GDP; and an estimated 40 million Russians owned shares. This added to the 30,000 small enterprises and shops and 184,000 agricultural holdings privatized in 1992. On 27 October 1993 President Yeltsin issued a decree allowing the unrestricted buying and selling of land for the first time since 1917. The second stage of mass privatization was launched on 1 July 1994 and consists of the sale of residual government shares in most companies which will be used to finance government expenditure. By mid-1995, 50 per cent of GDP was produced by the private sector, and some 280,000 agricultural holdings had been privatized.

While privatization has been a success, the restructuring of state industries and enterprises has not, because of the continued obstruction of economic reform. In January 1992 the radical reform government introduced economic 'shock therapy' to end hyperinflation and restore government reserves by liberalizing prices and restructuring firms to end their reliance on state subsidies. The result would have been reduced inflation and money supply levels, the stabilization of production levels and improved budget and trade positions, but the shock therapy was only partially implemented in 1992–4 because of parliamentary control over the Central Bank until summer 1993 and parliamentary insistence on large budget deficits to support credits to enterprises which were bankrupt. The result was that industrial production fell further (18 per cent in 1992, 15.5 per cent in 1993), hyperinflation (900 per cent in 1993) continued and the rouble fell further (90 per cent against the US dollar in 1992–4) than necessary. In early 1994 the economic situation stabilized, with industrial output growing, inflation at 8 per cent a month, a budget deficit of 6 per cent of GDP, and a trade surplus of US$20,900 million for 1993, which had helped to raise government foreign currency reserves to US$10,000 million. GDP in 1993 was 170,320,000 million roubles and foreign investment was US$5,000 million.

1994–5 has seen a stabilization of the Russian economy, with economic reforms judged to have passed the point where they can be reversed and the economy no longer needing to rely on western financial support for its survival. Although industrial output and GDP fell by 21 per cent and 15 per cent respectively in 1994, the government finally gained control of the money supply in October 1994 with the resignation of the Central Bank governor Viktor Geraschenko. Subsidies to coal, agriculture and the military-industrial complex have since been reduced, inflation has been brought under control and the rouble stabilized (although both were severely tested by the effects of the Chechen war). The main economic battle of 1994–5 has been over the budget; the government finally forced the legislature to pass an IMF-approved budget which keeps the budget deficit down to 7.8 per cent of GDP and aims for an inflation rate of 2 per cent per month. The foreign trade surplus in 1994 was US$19,800 million, while by February 1995 the total official and commercial debt owed by Russia to foreign creditors had risen to US$120,000 million. GDP in 1994 was 630,000,000 million roubles.

Russia has received considerable international aid since 1993. In April 1993 a rescheduling of Russia's US$80 billion foreign debt was announced, which saved US$15 billion in repayments; in June 1994 a further US$7 billion was rescheduled. The G7 summit in Tokyo in April 1994 pledged aid of US$43 billion for structural reform and rouble stabilization, conditional on political and economic reforms. Since 1992 the IMF has provided US$4,000 million under its systemic transformation facility to bring about a market economy. In 1995 the IMF provided US$6,800 million in standby credit to cover part of the budget deficit.

Russia has some of the richest mineral deposits in the world. Coal is mined in the Kuznetsk area, in the Urals, south of Moscow, in the Donets basin and in the Pechora area in the north. Oil is produced in the northern Caucasus, between the Volga and the Urals, and in western Siberia, which also has large deposits of natural gas. Coal and gas deposits in Siberia and the far east (especially Yakutia) are currently being developed. The Ural mountains contain high-quality iron ore, manganese, copper, aluminium, gold, platinum, precious stones, salt, asbestos, pyrites, coal, oil, etc. Iron ore is also mined near Kursk, Tula, Lipetsk, in several areas in Siberia and in the Kola Peninsula. Non-ferrous metals are found in the Altai, in eastern Siberia, in the northern Caucasus, in the Kuznetsk basin, in the far east and in the far north.

The vast area and the great variety in climatic conditions cause great differences in the structure of agriculture from north to south and from west to east. In the far north reindeer breeding, hunting and fishing are predominant. Further south, timber industry is combined with grain growing. In the southern half of the forest zone and in the adjacent forest-steppe zone, the acreage under grain crops is larger and the structure of agriculture more complex. Between the Volga and the Urals cericulture is predominant (particularly summer wheat), followed by cattle breeding. Beyond the Urals is another important grain-growing and stock-breeding area in the southern part of the western Siberian plain. The southern steppe zone is the main wheat granary of Russia, containing also large acreages under barley, maize and sunflowers. In the extreme south cotton is cultivated. Vine, tobacco and other southern crops are grown on the Black Sea shore of the Caucasus.

Moscow and St Petersburg are still the two largest industrial centres in the country, but new industrial areas have been developed in the Urals, the Kuznetsk basin, in Siberia and the far east. Most of the oil produced in the former USSR came from Russia; half the annual output comes from Tyumen Oblast in western Siberia. All industries are represented in Russia, including iron and steel and engineering.

TRADE

Foreign trade in 1993 was worth US$76,200 million, the main trading partners being other CIS states, the USA, Germany, Japan, UK, France and Italy.

Trade with UK	1993	1994
Imports from UK	£551,873,000	£707,599,000
Exports to UK	822,125,000	804,817,000

COMMUNICATIONS

The European area of Russia is well served by railways, St Petersburg and Moscow being the two main focal points of rail routes. The centre and south have a good system of north-south and east-west lines, but the eastern part (the Volga lands), traversed by trunk lines between Europe and Asia, lacks north-south routes. In Asia, there are still large areas, notably in the far north and Siberia, with few or no railways. In the northern part of European Russia, the North Pechora Railway has been completed, while in the far east a second Trans-Siberian line (the Baikal-Amur Railway) is partially in use; it follows a more northerly alignment than the earlier Trans-Siberian and terminates in the Pacific port of Sovetskaya Gavan.

The most important ports (Taganrog, Rostov and Novorossiisk) lie around the Black Sea and the Sea of Azov. The northern ports (St Petersburg, Murmansk and Archangel) are, with the exception of Murmansk, icebound during winter. Several ports have been built along the Arctic Sea route between Murmansk and Vladivostok and are in regular use every summer. The far eastern port of Vladivostok, the Pacific naval base of Russia, is kept open by icebreakers all the year round.

Inland waterways, both natural and artificial, are of great importance in the country, although some of them are icebound in winter (from two and a half months in the south to six months in the north). The great rivers of European Russia flow outwards from the centre, linking all parts of the plain with the chief ports, an immense system of navigable waterways which carried about 690 million tons of freight in 1988. They are supplemented by a system of canals which provide a through traffic between the White, Baltic, Black and Caspian Seas. The most notable are the White Sea-Baltic Canal, the Moscow-Volga Canal and the Volga-Don Canal linking the Baltic and the White Seas in the north to the Caspian Sea, the Black Sea and the Sea of Azov in the south.

CULTURE

Before the westernization of Russia under Peter the Great (1682–1725), Russian literature consisted mainly of folk ballads (*byliny*), epic songs, chronicles and works of moral theology. The 18th and 19th centuries saw the development of poetry and fiction. Poetry reached its zenith with Alexander Pushkin (1799–1837), Mikhail Lermontov (1814–41), Alexander Blok (1880–1921), the 1958 Nobel Prize laureate Boris Pasternak (1890–1960), Vladimir Mayakovsky (1893–1930) and Anna Akhmatova (1888–1966). Fiction is associated with the names of Nikolai Gogol (1809–52), Ivan Turgenev (1818–83), Fyodor Dostoevsky (1821–81), Leo Tolstoy (1828–1910), Anton Chekhov (1860–1904), Maxim Gorky (1868–1936), Ivan Bunin (1870–1953), Mikhail Bulgakov (1891–1940), Mikhail Sholokhov (1905–84) and Alexander Solzhenitsyn (b. 1918).

Great names in music include Glinka (1804–57), Borodin (1833–87), Mussorgsky (1839–81), Rimsky-Korsakov (1844–1908), Rubinstein (1829–94), Tchaikovsky (1840–93), Rachmaninov (1873–1943), Skriabin (1872–1915), Prokofiev (1891–1953), Stravinsky (1882–1971), Shostakovich (1906–75) and Alfred Schnittke (b. 1934).

RWANDA
Republika y'u Rwanda

Rwanda, formerly part of the Belgian-administered trusteeship of Ruanda-Urundi, has an area of 10,169 sq. miles (26,338 sq. km), and a population (UN estimate 1992) of 7,526,000, with the Hutu tribe (90 per cent), with Tutsi (9 per cent) and Twa (pygmy) (1 per cent) minorities.

CAPITAL – Kigali (156,000).
CURRENCY – Rwanda franc of 100 centimes.
FLAG – Three vertical bands, red, yellow and green with letter R on yellow band.
NATIONAL DAY – 1 July.

GOVERNMENT

The majority Hutu population rebelled against Tutsi feudal rule (under the Belgian colonial authority) in 1959–61, leading to the massacre of thousands of Tutsis. Large numbers fled into exile in Uganda. A referendum held in September 1961 showed the majority of the population were opposed to the retention of the monarchy, which was abolished in October 1961. Rwanda became an independent republic on 1 July 1962, with Gregoire Kayibanda as head of state. He was deposed in 1973 and replaced by a military government under Maj.-Gen. Juvénal Habyarimana, who established a one-party state.

Armed Tutsi exiles repeatedly attempted to invade Rwanda in the 1960s and 1970s but were defeated by the Hutu army, leading to a series of massacres of Tutsis remaining in the country by Hutus, and continued Hutu-Tutsi conflict which left hundreds of thousands dead over a period of 30 years. In October 1990 Rwanda was invaded by the Rwandan Patriotic Front of exiled Tutsis and moderate Hutus, who were sufficiently strong to force the one-party MRND (National Revolutionary Movement for Development) government to end its monopoly of power and introduce a multiparty constitution in 1991. After the government reneged on a 1992 peace agreement, the RPF advanced on the capital Kigali and forced the government to restart negotiations, which led to the August 1993 Arusha peace accord. The accord provided for a transitional period under a broad-based government including the RPF until 1995 elections, with UN forces in the country throughout the period.

The transitional period was proceeding, albeit with a degree of inter-racial violence, when President Habyarimana, who had retained the interim presidency, died on 6 April 1994 in a plane crash widely believed to have been caused by a rocket attack by extremist sections of the Hutu army. The Hutu army and armed militia, the *interahamwe*, then carried out a preplanned act of genocide against the Tutsi minority and moderate Hutus; 500,000 people were massacred in three months. The civil war restarted and the RPF gradually put an end to the massacres as it took control of the country, forcing the defeated government forces and two million Hutu refugees into Zaire, Burundi and Tanzania, while another 1.2 million Hutus fled to the French 'safe zone' in the south-west. On 18 July 1994 the RPF declared victory in the civil war and established a broad-based government of national unity in which moderate Hutus were given the presidency and premiership and the RPF took eight of the 22 seats.

Some 50,000–60,000 Hutu refugees died of disease in refugee camps in eastern Zaïre in August–September 1994 before sufficient international aid arrived. The majority of refugees have since been prevented from returning to Rwanda by the extremist Hutu army and militia forces, who have gained control of the refugee camps. French troops withdrew from their 'safe zone' in the south-west of Rwanda in September 1994 and were replaced by RPF forces who gradually returned most Hutu refugees in the zone to their homes in the rest of the country, while UN forces (UNAMIR II) were deployed to moderate any revenge attacks by Tutsis on Hutus. However, by April 1995 200,000 Hutu refugees remained in camps in the south-west controlled by armed Hutu militia members who prevented their return. RPF forces attacked the camps, most importantly at Kibeho, and broke the Hutu militia control in fighting in which hundreds of Hutu militia and refugees were killed before the return of refugees was completed. In August the Zaïrean government began the forcible repatriation of some of the over one million Hutu refugees who, it felt, were destabilizing the east of Zaïre. However, after thousands had fled to the countryside rather than return to Rwanda, international pressure forced the Zaïrean government to agree to a voluntary repatriation programme organized and run by the UN High Commissioner for Refugees (UNHCR). In November 1994 the UN Security Council established the International Criminal Tribunal for Rwanda to prosecute those responsible for genocide and other international humanitarian law violations between 1 January and 31 December 1994. An estimated 200,000 Tutsi refugees who fled to Uganda in the 1960s and 1970s have returned to Rwanda.

The 70-member Transitional National Assembly provided for by the Arusha agreement began operation on 12 December 1994 with the extremist Hutu MRND excluded. However, tensions between Tutsis and moderate Hutus in the government remain, with Prime Minister Twagiramungu and four other ministers being dismissed in August 1995 after criticizing the lack of power-sharing by the RPF and the security situation in the country.

HEAD OF STATE
President, Pasteur Bizimungu, *sworn in* 19 July 1994
Vice-President, Gen. Paul Kagame

GOVERNMENT OF NATIONAL UNITY *as at August 1995*
The President
Defence, The Vice-President
Prime Minister, Pierre Claver Rwigema
Deputy PM, Alexis Kanyarungwe
Foreign Affairs, Anastase Gasana
Interior, vacant
Justice, vacant
Primary and Secondary Education, Pierre Rwigema
Finance, Marc Rugenera
Health, Dr J. Kalemera
Transport, vacant
Social Affairs, P. Mugabo
Environment and Tourism, Jean Nayinzira
Public Works, C. Ntakirutinka
Youth, P. Mazimhaka
Rehabilitation, Dr J. Bihozagara

EMBASSY OF THE REPUBLIC OF RWANDA
42 Aylmer Road, London N2
Ambassador Extraordinary and Plenipotentiary, Gideon Kayinamura, apptd 1995

BRITISH AMBASSADOR , His Excellency Edward Clay, CMG, resident at Kampala, Uganda

ECONOMY

Coffee, tea and sugar are grown. Tin, hides, bark of quinine and extract of pyrethrum flowers are also exported.

In 1987 total imports were valued at US$351.7 million; total exports, US$112.3 million. Coffee accounted for 90 per cent of export earnings in 1989.

Trade with UK	1993	1994
Imports from UK	£3,337,000	£2,542,000
Exports to UK	1,892,000	1,666,000

ST CHRISTOPHER AND NEVIS
The Federation of St Christopher and Nevis

The state of St Christopher and Nevis is located at the northern end of the eastern Caribbean. It comprises the islands of St Christopher (St Kitts) (68 sq. miles) and Nevis (36 sq. miles). The central area of St Christopher, 17° 18′ N. and 62° 48′ W., is forest-clad and mountainous, rising to the 3,792 ft. Mount Liamuiga. Nevis, 17° 10′ N. and 62° 35′ W., is separated from the southern tip of St Christopher by a strait two miles wide and is dominated by Nevis Peak, 3,232 ft. The combined population (UN estimate 1992) was 42,000.

CAPITAL – ΨBasseterre (estimated population, 15,000). The chief town of Nevis is ΨCharlestown (population 1,200), which is a port of entry.
CURRENCY – East Caribbean dollar (EC$) of 100 cents.
FLAG – Three diagonal bands, green, black and red; each colour separated by a stripe of yellow. Two white stars on the black band.
NATIONAL ANTHEM – Oh Land of Beauty.
NATIONAL DAY – 19 September (Independence Day).

GOVERNMENT

St Christopher was the first island in the British West Indies to be colonized (1623). The Territory of St Christopher and Nevis became a State in Association with Britain in 1967. The State of St Christopher and Nevis became an independent nation on 19 September 1983.

Under the constitution, The Queen is head of state, represented in the islands by the Governor-General. There is a central government with a ministerial system, the head of which is the Prime Minister of St Christopher and Nevis, and a National Assembly located on St Christopher. The National Assembly is composed of the Speaker, three senators (nominated by the Prime Minister and the Leader of the Opposition) and 11 elected representatives. On Nevis there is a Nevis Island Administration, the head being styled Premier of Nevis, and a Nevis Island Assembly of five elected and three nominated members.

Governor-General, His Excellency Sir Clement Athelston Arrindell, GCMG, GCVO, QC, apptd 1983

CABINET *as at August 1995*

Prime Minister and Minister of Finance, National Security, Planning, Information and Foreign Affairs, Hon. Dr Denzil Douglas
Deputy PM, Trade and Industry, Caricom Affairs, Youth, Sports and Community Affairs, Hon. Sam Condor
Agriculture, Lands and Housing, Hon. Timothy Harris
Health and Women's Affairs, Hon. Dr Earl Asim Martin
Culture, Environment and Tourism, Hon. G. A. Dwyer Astaphan
Education, Labour and Social Security, Hon. Rupert Herbert
Communications, Works, Public Utilities and Posts, Hon. Cedric Liburd

HIGH COMMISSION FOR ST CHRISTOPHER AND NEVIS
10 Kensington Court, London W8 5DL
Tel 0171-937 9522
High Commissioner for the Eastern Caribbean States, His
Excellency Aubrey Hart, apptd 1994

BRITISH HIGH COMMISSIONER , His Excellency Richard
Thomas, CMG, resident at Bridgetown, Barbados

ECONOMY

The economy of the islands has been based on sugar for
over three centuries. Tourism (88,264 visitors in 1992) and
light industry, concentrating on brewing and food processing, are now being developed. The economy of Nevis
centres on small peasant farmers, but a sea-island cotton
industry is being developed for export.

FINANCE	1991	1992
Revenue	EC$93,300,000	EC$108,900,000
Expenditure	97,500,000	105,000,000

TRADE WITH UK	1993	1994
Imports from UK	£8,735,000	£6,915,000
Exports to UK	8,996,000	6,505,000

COMMUNICATIONS

Basseterre is a port of registry and has deep water harbour
facilities. Golden Rock airport, on St Kitts, can take most
large jet aircraft; Newcastle airstrip on Nevis can take small
aircraft and has night landing facilities. The sea ferry route
from Basseterre to Charlestown is 11 miles.

ST LUCIA

St Lucia, the second largest of the Windward group,
situated in 13° 54′ N. latitude and 60° 50′ W. longitude, is
27 miles in length, with an extreme breadth of 14 miles. It
comprises an area of 238 sq. miles (616 sq. km), with a
population (1992 UN estimate) of 137,000. It is mountainous, its highest point being Mt Gimie (3,145 ft) and for the
most part it is covered with forest and tropical vegetation.

CAPITAL – ΨCastries (population 1989, 56,000).
CURRENCY – East Caribbean dollar (EC$) of 100 cents.
FLAG – Blue, bearing in centre a device of yellow over
black over white triangles having a common base.
NATIONAL ANTHEM – Sons and Daughters of Saint Lucia.
NATIONAL DAY – 22 February (Independence Day).

GOVERNMENT

Possession of St Lucia was fiercely disputed and it
constantly changed hands between the British and the
French. It became independent within the Commonwealth
on 22 February 1979. The head of state is The Queen,
represented in the island by a St Lucian Governor-
General, and there is a bicameral legislature. The Senate
has 11 members, six appointed by the ruling party, three by
the Opposition and two by the Governor-General. The
House of Assembly, which has a life of five years, has 17
elected Members and a Speaker, who may be elected from
outside the House.

Governor-General, His Excellency Sir Stanislaus James,
KCMG, OBE

CABINET *as at August 1995*
*Prime Minister, Minister of Finance, Planning, Development,
    Information and Broadcasting*, Rt. Hon. John G. M.
    Compton
*Deputy PM and Minister of Home Affairs, Foreign Affairs, Trade
    and Industry*, Hon. George Mallet
Communications, Works and Transport, Hon. Gregory Avril
Tourism, Public Utilities and National Mobilization, Hon.
    Romanus Lansiquot
*Youth, Community Development, Social Affairs, Sports and
    Co-operatives*, Hon. Desmond Braithwaite
Attorney-General and Minister for Legal Affairs, Hon. Senator
    Lorraine Williams
Agriculture, Lands, Fisheries and Forestry, Hon. Ira
    D'Auvergne
Education, Culture and Labour, Hon. Louis George
Health and Local Government, Hon. Stephenson King
Minister of State, Housing, Urban Development and Renewal,
    Hon. Senator Michael Pilgrim
Minister of State, Youth, Sports and Co-operatives, Hon. Edward
    Innocent
Minister of State, Trade and Industry, Hon. Rufus Bousquet

ST LUCIA HIGH COMMISSION
10 Kensington Court, London W8 5DL
Tel 0171-937 9522
High Commissioner for the Eastern Caribbean States, His
Excellency Aubrey Hart, apptd 1994

OFFICE OF THE BRITISH HIGH COMMISSION
Derek Walcott Square, PO Box 227, Castries
Tel: Castries 4522484
High Commissioner, His Excellency Richard Thomas, CMG,
resident at Bridgetown, Barbados
Acting High Commissioner, A. Ferguson

ECONOMY

The economy is mainly agrarian, with manufacturing
based on the processing of agricultural products. Principal
crops are bananas, coconuts, cocoa, mangoes, avocado
pears, breadfruit, spices, root crops such as cassava and
yams, and citrus fruit. Attempts are being made to diversify
the economy, in particular through greater industrialization. Tourism is also of increasing importance, with
204,000 visitors to the island in 1989.

TRADE

The principal exports are bananas, coconut products
(copra, edible oils, soap), cardboard boxes, beer, and textile
manufactures. The chief imports are flour, meat, machinery, building materials, motor vehicles, cotton piece goods,
petroleum and fertilizers.

Trade with UK	1993	1994
Imports from UK	£19,559,000	£42,496,000
Exports to UK	53,663,000	41,294,000

ST VINCENT AND THE GRENADINES

The territory of St Vincent includes certain of the
Grenadines, a chain of small islands stretching 40 miles
across the Caribbean Sea between Grenada and St Vincent,
some of the larger of which are Bequia, Canouan, Mayreau,
Mustique, Union Island, Petit St Vincent and Prune Island.
The whole territory extends 150 sq. miles (388 sq. km). The
main island, St Vincent, is situated between 13° 6′ and 14°
35′ N. latitude and 61° 6′ and 61° 20′ W. longitude. The

island has an area of 133 sq. miles (344 sq. km), and a population (1992 UN estimate) of 109,000.

CAPITAL – ΨKingstown, estimated population 33,694.
CURRENCY – East Caribbean dollar (EC$) of 100 cents.
FLAG – Three vertical bands, of blue, yellow and green, with three green diamonds in the shape of a 'V' mounted on the yellow band.
NATIONAL ANTHEM – St Vincent, Land So Beautiful.
NATIONAL DAY – 27 October (Independence Day).

GOVERNMENT

St Vincent was discovered by Christopher Columbus in 1498. It was granted by Charles I to the Earl of Carlisle in 1627 and after subsequent grants and a series of occupations alternately by the French and English, it was finally restored to Britain in 1783. St Vincent achieved full independence within the Commonwealth as St Vincent and the Grenadines on 27 October 1979.

The Queen is head of state, represented by a Governor-General. The House of Assembly consists of 15 elected members and four Senators appointed by the government and two by the Opposition. It is presided over by a Speaker elected by the House from within or without it. The governing New Democratic Party won 12 seats and the United Labour Party three seats at the election held in February 1994.

Governor-General, His Excellency Sir David Jack, GCMG, MBE, *sworn in* 20 September 1989.

CABINET *as at August 1995*

Prime Minister, Minister of Finance and Planning, Rt. Hon. Sir James Mitchell, KCMG
Deputy PM, Attorney-General and Minister of Justice and Information, Hon. Parnell Campbell, CVO
Culture, Education, Youth and Women's Affairs, Hon. John Horne
Agriculture, Industry and Labour, Hon. Allan Cruickshank
Foreign Affairs and Tourism, Hon. Alpian Allen
Health and the Environment, Hon. Yvonne Gibson
Trade and Consumer Affairs, Hon. Bernard Wyllie
Housing, Local Government, Community Development, Hon. Louis Jones
Communications and Works, Hon. Jeremiah Scott
Ministers of State, Hon. Stephanie Browne (*Communications and Works*); Hon. Monty Roberts (*PM's Office*).

ST VINCENT AND THE GRENADINES HIGH COMMISSION
10 Kensington Court, London W8 5DL
Tel 0171-937 9522
High Commissioner for the Eastern Caribbean States, His Excellency Aubrey Hart, apptd 1994

BRITISH HIGH COMMISSION
Granby Street (PO Box 132), Kingstown
Tel: St Vincent 4571701
High Commissioner, His Excellency Richard Thomas, CMG, resident at Bridgetown, Barbados
Acting High Commissioner, A. Ferguson

ECONOMY

This is based mainly on agriculture but tourism (155,068 visitors in 1992) and manufacturing industries have been expanding. The main products are bananas, arrowroot, coconuts, cocoa, spices and various kinds of food crops. The main imports are foodstuffs (meat, rice, beverages), textiles, lumber, cement and other building materials, fertilizers, motor vehicles and fuel.

TRADE WITH UK	1993	1994
Imports from UK	£7,959,000	£7,652,000
Exports to UK	25,891,000	14,312,000

EL SALVADOR
República de El Salvador

El Salvador extends along the Pacific coast of Central America for 160 miles, with an area of 8,124 sq. miles (21,041 sq. km). The surface of the country is very mountainous, many of the peaks being extinct volcanoes. Much of the interior has an average altitude of 2,000 feet. The climate varies from tropical to temperate. There is a wet season from May to October, and a dry season from November to April. Earthquakes have been frequent, the most recent being in October 1986.

The population (1991 estimate) was 5,376,000. The language is Spanish.

CAPITAL – San Salvador (497,644, 1989 estimate). Estimated population of metropolitan area, 2,000,000. Other towns are Santa Ana (417,000), San Miguel (157,838), Ψ La Union (Cutuco), Ψ La Libertad and Ψ Acajutia.
CURRENCY – El Salvador colón (₡) of 100 centavos.
FLAG – Three horizontal bands, sky blue, white, sky blue; coat of arms on white band.
NATIONAL ANTHEM – Saludemos La Patria Orgullosos (Let us proudly hail the Fatherland).
NATIONAL DAY – 15 September.

GOVERNMENT

El Salvador was conquered in 1526 by Pedro de Alvarado, and formed part of the Spanish viceroyalty of Guatemala until 1821. It is divided into 14 Departments.

Decades of military rule ended in March 1982 when a Constituent Assembly was elected. Subsequent presidential and parliamentary elections were boycotted by the FMLN (Farabundo Martí National Liberation Front) guerrilla movement. Conflict between the guerrillas and the government continued throughout the 1980s until negotiations culminated in a peace plan signed in January 1992. A cease-fire took effect on 1 February and began a nine-month transition period which ended in December 1992 when the FMLN finished its disarmament and became a political party. A 'Truth Commission', established under UN auspices to investigate and report on human rights abuses in the 1980–91 period, reported in March 1993. The report caused a political crisis when it declared that 15 senior army commanders should be removed by the government. The government was reluctant to do so but came under economic pressure from the USA, which withheld aid for reconstruction until the officers were dismissed on 1 July 1993.

The UN Observer Mission in El Salvador (ONUSAL) monitored the 1992–4 transition process, overseeing the final destruction of FMLN arms in August 1993 and the presidential, parliamentary and local elections held in March and April 1994. Armando Calderón Sol of the ruling right-wing ARENA party won the presidential election, defeating the FMLN's Ruben Zamora. ARENA won 39 of the Legislative Assembly's 84 seats and formed a government with other right-wing parties; the FMLN won 21 seats. The ONUSAL mandate was extended to 30 April 1995 after the UN Security Council expressed concern that the reform of the police and the transfer of land as agreed under the peace process had yet to take place.

HEAD OF STATE
President, Armando Calderón Sol, *assumed office* 1 June 1994
Vice-President, Enrique Borgo Bustamante

CABINET *as at August 1995*
Minister of the Presidency, The Vice President
Foreign Affairs, vacant
Planning, Ramón González
Interior, Mario Acosta Oertel
Justice, Dr Rubén Antonio Mejía Peña
Economy, Eduardo Zablah Touche
Education, Cecilia Gallardo de Cano
Defence, Col. Humberto Corado Figueroa
Labour and Social Security, Dr Juan Sifontes
Agriculture, Oscar Gutiérrez
Public Health, Dr Eduardo Interiano
Public Works, Jorge Sansivirini
Finance, Manuel Hinds
Public Security, Hugo Cesar Barrera

EMBASSY OF EL SALVADOR
5 Great James Street, London WCIN 3DA
Tel 0171-430 2141
Ambassador Extraordinary and Plenipotentiary, His Excellency
Don Ernesto Trigueros Alcaine, apptd 1994

BRITISH EMBASSY
PO Box 1591, San Salvador
Tel: San Salvador 2981763
Ambassador Extraordinary and Plenipotentiary, His Excellency
Ian Gerken, LVO, apptd 1995

ECONOMY

El Salvador has received substantial aid to rebuild the country's war-damaged infrastructure and services. The USA has written off 75 per cent of El Salvador's debt and in May 1993 the IMF agreed a standby credit facility for El Salvador of US$49 million over 10 months.

The principal cash crops are coffee, cotton, sugar-cane and shrimps. However, cotton and sugar production have decreased as a result of the civil war. Also cultivated are maize, sesame, indigo, rice, balsam, etc. In the lower altitudes towards the east, sisal is produced and used in the manufacture of coffee and cereal bags. The Salvadorean Coffee Company, sugar exports and the banking system are being privatized.

Existing factories make textiles, clothing, constructional steel, furniture, cement and household items. In 1989 GDP amounted to US$4,808 million (US$874 per capita).

TRADE

Chief exports are coffee, cotton, sugar, shrimps, sisal balsam, meat, towels, hides and skins. The chief imports are chemicals, fertilizers, pharmaceutical goods, petroleum, manufactured goods, industrial and electronic machinery and equipment, vehicles and consumer goods.

Trade with UK	1993	1994
Imports from UK	£15,160,000	£19,217,000
Exports to UK	8,895,000	7,200,000

COMMUNICATIONS

The Executive Autonomous Port Commission (CEPA) administers the ports of Cutuco, La Union, Acajutla, and the railways through FENADESAL. The roads are paved and in good condition but some bridges are temporary structures following guerrilla action. There are good roads between Acajutla and the capital (60 miles), and between the capital and Guatemala City. The Pan-American Highway from the Guatemalan frontier follows this route and

continues to the Honduran frontier. The El Salvador international airport can receive jet aircraft with daily flights to other Central American capitals, Mexico, and five US cities. There are 100 broadcasting stations and six television stations. Five daily newspapers are published in San Salvador and four in the provinces.

EDUCATION

The illiteracy rate has risen to 68.1 per cent (1985) since 1980 when the figure was 30.5 per cent. Primary education is nominally compulsory, but the number of schools and teachers available is too small to enable education to be given to all children of school age.

SAN MARINO
Repubblica di San Marino

San Marino is a small republic in the hills near Rimini, on the Adriatic, founded, it is said, by a pious stonecutter of Dalmatia in the fourth century. The republic resisted Papal claims and those of neighbouring dukedoms during the 15th to 18th centuries, and its integrity and sovereignty is recognized and respected by Italy. The area is approximately 23 sq. miles (61 sq. km.) and the population (1995) is 24,801.

CITY – San Marino, on the slope of Monte Titano, has three towers, a fine church and Government palace, a theatre and museums.
CURRENCY – San Marino and Italian currencies are in circulation.
FLAG – Two horizontal bands, white, blue (with coat of arms of the republic in centre).
NATIONAL DAY – 3 September.

The republic is governed by a Congress of State of ten members, under the presidency of two heads of state, who are elected at six-monthly intervals (every March and October). The Great and General Council, a legislative body of 60 members, is elected by universal suffrage for a term of five years. A Council of Twelve forms in certain cases a Supreme Court of Justice. A coalition government of the Christian Democratic Party and the Socialist Party took office in March 1992, and was returned in the general election of 31 May 1993.

The principal products are wine, cereals, and cattle, and the main industries are tourism, ceramics, lime, concrete, cotton yarns, colour and paints.

HEADS OF STATE
Regents, Two 'Capitani Reggenti'

CONGRESS OF STATE *as at August 1995*
Foreign and Political Affairs, Gabriele Gatti
Finance and Budget, Planning and Information, Clelio Galassi
Interior and Justice, Antonio Volpinari
Environment and Agriculture, Emma Rossi
Industry and Handicrafts, Fiorenzo Stolfi
Education and Culture, Pier Menicucci
Labour and Co-operation, Claudio Podeschi
Health and Social Security, Sante Canducci
Communications, Transport, Tourism and Sport, Augusto Casali
Commerce and Relations with Local Councils, Ottaviano Rossi

CONSULATE-GENERAL IN LONDON
166 High Holborn, London WCIV 6TT
Tel 0171-836 7744
Consul-General, The Lord Forte
BRITISH CONSUL-GENERAL, M. Holmes, OBE, resident at
  Florence, Italy

TRADE

Trade with UK	1994
Imports from UK	£4,312,000
Exports to UK	711,000

SÃO TOMÉ AND PRÍNCIPE
República Democrática de São Tomé e Príncipe

The islands of São Tomé and Príncipe are situated in the Gulf of Guinea, off the west coast of Africa. They have an area of 372 sq. miles (964 sq. km), and a population (UN estimate 1992) of 124,000.

CAPITAL – ΨSão Tomé (25,000).
CURRENCY – Dobra of 100 centavos.
FLAG – Horizontal stripes of green, yellow, green, the yellow of double width and bearing two black stars; and a red triangle in the hoist.
NATIONAL DAY – 12 July (Independence Day).

GOVERNMENT

The islands became independent on 12 July 1975. A multi-party constitution was approved by referendum in August 1990. The Movement for the Liberation of São Tomé and Príncipe-Social Democratic Party (MLSTP-PSD), which had been the sole legal party since independence, was defeated by the opposition Democratic Convergence Party (PCD) in legislative elections held on 20 January 1991. Miguel Trovoada, an independent, was elected President on 3 March 1991. The President dismissed governments in 1992 and 1994 because of mounting criticism of economic reforms. A legislative election on 2 October 1994 was won by the MLSTP-PSD with 27 seats in the 55-seat National Assembly to the PCD's 14 seats. The MLSTP-PSD formed a government but this was dismissed on 15 August 1995 after five junior army officers launched a bloodless military coup, arrested the President and suspended parliament and the constitution. The EU threatened to suspend all aid and the officers relinquished power on 21 August after Angolan mediation. The President, government, parliament and constitution were restored and the officers were granted an amnesty.

HEAD OF STATE
President and Commander-in-Chief of the Armed Forces, Miguel Trovoada, *elected* 3 March 1991

COUNCIL OF MINISTERS *as at August 1995*
Prime Minister, Dr Carlos da Graça
Minister to the PM, Amindo vaz d'Almeida
Foreign Affairs and Co-operation, G. Posser da Costa
Economy, Joaquim Rafael Branco
Finance and Planning, Carlos Batista de Sousa
Defence and Interior, Alberto Paulino
Justice and Social Security, Manuel vaz Alonso Fernandes
Education and Sport, G. O. Viegas d'Abreu
Health, Fernando da Conceicao Silveira
Príncipe, Zelerino vas dos Prazeres
Social Affairs, Alcino M. de Barros Pinto

EMBASSY OF THE DEMOCRATIC REPUBLIC OF SÃO TOMÉ
AND PRÍNCIPE
42 avenue Brugman, Brussels 1060, Belgium
Tel: Brussels 3475375
Ambassador Extraordinary and Plenipotentiary, new
  appointment awaited

HONORARY CONSULATE
42 North Audley Street, London WIA 4PY
Tel 0171-499 1995
Honorary Consul, W. S. Wilder

BRITISH CONSULATE
c/o Hull Blythe (Angola) Ltd, BP 15, São Tomé
British Ambassador, His Excellency Anthony Thomas,
  resident at Luanda, Angola
Honorary Consul, J. Gomes

ECONOMY

The economy is heavily dependent on tourism and agriculture, with cacao being the main product. In 1995 the total foreign debt was US$255 million, annual inflation was 40 per cent and unemployment 38 per cent.

TRADE WITH UK	1993	1994
Imports from UK	£3,433,000	£2,313,000
Exports to UK	—	3,000

SAUDI ARABIA
Al Mamlaka al Arabiya as-Sa'udiyya

Saudi Arabia comprises almost the whole of the Arabian peninsula, with the exception of Yemen in the extreme south, Oman and the UAE in the south-east and Qatar in the east. In the north-west it borders Jordan and in the north-east Iraq and Kuwait, while to the west lies the Red Sea and to the east the Gulf where a causeway links the Eastern Province with Bahrain. The Nejd ('plateau') extends over the centre of the peninsula, including the Nafud and Dahna deserts. The Hejaz ('the boundary') extends along the Red Sea coast to Asir and contains the holy towns of Mecca (Makkah) and Medina (Madinah). Asir ('inaccessible') is named for its mountainous terrain, and, with the coastal plain of the Tihama, lies along the southern Red Sea coast from the Hejaz to the border with Yemen. It is the only region to enjoy substantial rainfall. The east and south-east of the country are lower-lying and largely desert. The total area is about 830,000 sq. miles (2,149,640 sq. km), with a population (1992 census) of 16,929,294. Islam is the only permitted religion.

Mecca (Al-Makkah), about 60 km east of Jeddah, is the birthplace of the Prophet Muhammad, and contains the Great Mosque, within which is the Kaaba (*Ka'abah*) or sacred shrine of the Muslim religion. This is the focus of the annual Hajj ('pilgrimage'). Medina (Al-Madinah) Al Munawwarah ('The City of Light'), some 300 km north of Mecca, is celebrated as the first city to embrace Islam and as the Prophet Muhammad's burial place.

CAPITAL – Riyadh, population (1992) about 2 million.
  Other major centres are Jeddah (estimated population
  1.5 million), Buraydah, Dammam, Hofuf, Mecca,
  Medina and Tabuk.
CURRENCY – Saudi riyal (SR) of 20 qursh or 100 halala.
FLAG – Green oblong, white Arabic device in centre:
  'There is no God but God and Muhammad is the
  Prophet of God,' and a white scimitar beneath the
  lettering.
NATIONAL ANTHEM – Long live our beloved King.

NATIONAL DAY – 23 September (proclamation and unification of the Kingdom, 1932).

GOVERNMENT

In the 18th century Nejd was an independent state governed from Diriya and the stronghold of the Wahhabis, a puritanical Islamic sect. It subsequently fell under Turkish rule; in 1913 Abdul Aziz Ibn Saud threw off Turkish rule and captured the Turkish province of Al Hasa. In 1920 he captured the Asir and in 1921 the Jebel Shammar territory of the Rashid family. In 1925 he completed the conquest of the Hejaz. Great Britain recognized Abdul Aziz Ibn Saud as an independent ruler, King of the Hejaz and of Nejd and its Dependencies, in 1927. The name was changed to the Kingdom of Saudi Arabia in September 1932.

Saudi Arabia is a hereditary monarchy, ruled by the sons and grandsons of Abdul Aziz Ibn Saud, in accordance with the *Shari'ah* law of Wahhabi Islam. The line of succession passes from brother to brother according to age, although several sons of Ibn Saud renounced their right to the throne. All sons and grandsons of Ibn Saud must be consulted before a new king accedes the throne.

In 1992 King Fahd announced a new Basic Law for the system of government based on *Shari'ah* law and including rules to protect personal freedoms. The constitution of the country is defined as the Holy Koran (*Qur'an*) and the *Sunnah* (the teachings and sayings of the Prophet Muhammad). The King and the Council of Ministers (established in 1953) retain executive power. A consultative council (*Majlis-al-Shura*) of a chairman and 60 members appointed by the King was set up to share power with, and question, the government and to make recommendations to the King. The Majlis-al-Shura began meeting in December 1993 and debates government policy in the areas of the budget, defence, foreign and social affairs. Members of the ruling Al-Saud family are excluded from membership of the Council, which has a four-year term and takes decisions by majority vote. Cabinet ministers have terms of four years, with the possibility of a two-year extension.

In 1993 the country's provinces were reorganized into 13 provinces: Riyadh; Mecca (Makkah); Medina (Madinah); Al Qasim; Eastern; Asir; Tabuk; Hail; Northern Border; Jizan; Najran; Baha; Jouf. Each province has a governor appointed by the King and a council of prominent local citizens to advise the governor on local government, budgetary and planning issues.

The judicial system is based on the *Shari'ah* (Islamic law), administered by the Justice Ministry through the *Shari'ah* courts: general courts, courts of first instance, the High *Shari'ah* Court and the Appeals Court. Labour, social affairs and commercial disputes may be dealt with by the Board of Grievances or by special courts. The highest court of appeal is the Council of Ministers whose decision, signed by the King, is final and absolute.

HEAD OF STATE

Custodian of the Two Holy Mosques and HM The King of Saudi Arabia, King Fahd bin Abdul Aziz Al Saud, *born* 1921, *ascended the throne* 1 June 1982
HRH Crown Prince, Prince Abdullah bin Abdul Aziz Al Saud

COUNCIL OF MINISTERS *as at August 1995*

Prime Minister, HM The King
First Deputy Prime Minister and Commander of the National Guard, HRH The Crown Prince
Second Deputy Prime Minister, Defence and Aviation, HRH Prince Sultan bin Abdul Aziz Al Saud
Public Works and Housing, HRH Prince Mit'ab bin Abdul Aziz Al Saud
Interior, HRH Prince Naif bin Abdul Aziz Al Saud
Foreign Affairs, HRH Prince Saud al-Faisal bin Abdul Aziz
Finance and National Economy, Muhammad Aba al-Khail
Agriculture and Water, Dr Abdul Rahman bin Abdul Aziz bin Hassan Al al-Shaikh
Municipal and Rural Affairs, Muhammad al-Shaikh
Justice, Dr Abdallah bin Ibrahim al-Shaikh
Commerce, Dr Sulaiman al-Solaim
Communications, Dr Hussain Mansouri
Petroleum and Mineral Resources, Ali bin Ibrahim al-Nouaimi
Planning, Abdul Wahab al-Attar
Labour and Social Affairs, Dr Mohamed Ali al-Faiz
Information, Ali Sha'er
Health, Faisal bin Abdul Aziz al Hejailan
Islamic Affairs, Awqafs and Guidance, Abdul Mohsen Al-Turki
Pilgrimage, Dr Mahmoud Safr
Education, Dr Abdul Aziz Al-Abdullah al-Khuwaiter
Higher Education, Khalid al-Angari
Posts, Telegraphs and Telecommunications, Dr Alawi Darwish Kayyal
Industry and Electricity, Abdul Aziz al-Zamil
Chairman of the Consultative Council, Sheikh Mohammed bin Ibrahim al Jubeir
Chairman of the Board of Grievances, Sheikh Nasir bin Hamad al-Rashid
Chairman of the Supreme Judicial Council, Sheikh Salih Bin Muhammad al-Lihaydan
Grand Mufti of Saudi Arabia, Sheikh Abdul Aziz bin Baz
Royal Court Adviser, Sheikh Abdul Wahhab Ahmad Abdul Wasi

ROYAL EMBASSY OF SAUDI ARABIA

30 Charles Street, London WIX 7PM
Tel 0171-917 3000
Ambassador Extraordinary and Plenipotentiary, His Excellency Dr Ghazi Algosaibi, apptd 1992
Minister-Counsellor, Dr Mohammed Rajah Al-Hussainy
Defence Attaché, Brig. A. H. Al-Bassam
Cultural Attaché, A. M. Al-Nasser
Commercial Attaché, M. A. Al-Sheddi

BRITISH EMBASSY

PO Box 94351, Riyadh 11693
Tel: Riyadh 488 0077
Ambassador Extraordinary and Plenipotentiary, His Excellency The Hon. David Gore-Booth, CMG, apptd 1993

Counsellors, W. C. Patey (*Deputy Head of Mission and Consul-General*); C. M. J. Sugar (*Commercial*); J. H. Bunney *Defence and Military Attaché*, Brig. W. E. Strong *First Secretary and Consul*, T. C. Lamb

CONSUL-GENERAL, L. E. Walker, OBE, LVO, PO Box 393, Jeddah 21411. There is also a trade office in Dhahran/Al Khobar (PO Box 88, Dhahran Airport 31932).

BRITISH COUNCIL DIRECTOR, Anthony Lewis, Olaya Main Road, Al Mousa Centre, Tower B (PO Box 58012), Riyadh 11594. There are also offices in Jeddah, Dammam and Jubail.

DEFENCE

Total active armed forces number 161,000 personnel, service being voluntary. The Army numbers 70,000 personnel, with 770 main battle tanks, 2,855 armoured infantry fighting vehicles and armoured personnel carriers and 460 artillery pieces. The Navy has 12,000 personnel including two battalions of 1,500 marines. It deploys eight frigates, 29 patrol and coastal combatants and 20 armed helicopters. The Air Force has 22,000 personnel, including 4,000 air defence forces, and deploys 292 combat aircraft of US and UK manufacture. The National Guard, which is directly under royal command, has 57,000 active personnel and 20,000 tribal levies, with 1,100 armoured personnel carriers and 70 artillery pieces. In addition, the paramilitary Frontier Force and Coast Guard number 15,000 personnel. Saudi Arabia is base to the Gulf Co-operational Council Peninsula Shield Force of 7,000 troops. The USA, UK and France station aircraft and support units in the country to patrol the air exclusion zone in southern Iraq.

ECONOMY

Saudi Arabia's revenue has been lower since the drop in world oil prices from the mid-1980s onwards, and in the 1990s financial reserves have been used up to meet budget deficits. In addition the country has had the cost of the 1990–1 Gulf War, estimated at US$60,000 million. The 1995 budget was in deficit by SR15,000 million, or 4.0 per cent of GDP, following spending cuts of 20 per cent in 1994 and increases in local petrol and utilities prices in an attempt to achieve a balanced budget. GDP in 1992 was US$113,000 million.

Outside the manufacturing centres which have grown up around many towns, most of the population are engaged in agriculture. The productivity of traditional dryland farming is supplemented by extensive irrigation, desalination and use of aquifers, so that agricultural production has increased greatly over the past 20 years.

The principal industry is oil extraction and processing, which produced 33 per cent of GDP in 1992. Oil was first found in commercial quantities in 1938. About 97 per cent of the total is extracted by Saudi Aramco, formerly the Arabian–American Oil Company. Aramco's 66-year lease will terminate in 1999 but the company was effectively nationalized in 1980. Proven oil reserves at 260,100 million barrels account for about one-quarter of the world's proven reserves. The country is the world's largest oil exporter and supplied 12 per cent of world demand in 1993. Recoverable gas reserves of 181.65 trillion cubic feet, in fields, associated with crude oil and those separate from it, are beginning to be exploited. Mineral exploitation of gold, silver, copper and other minerals is also beginning, with gold production of 5.5 tons in 1992.

The government, in a series of five-year development plans since 1970, has actively encouraged the establishment of manufacturing industries in the country. Industries have developed in the fields of construction materials, metal fabrication, simple machinery and electrical equipment, food and beverages, textiles, chemicals and plastics. Investment in industrial gases, intermediate petrochemicals, light engineering and machinery is encouraged.

Eight industrial centres have been established, the principal ones at Jubail and Yanbu, financed by the state agency Saudi Arabian Basic Industries Corporation. Linked by gas and oil pipelines, both have petrochemical complexes producing ethylene and methanol; six of the seven plants on-stream are joint ventures with American and Japanese companies.

The state agency Petromin operates nine refineries with a capacity of 1,800,000 b.p.d., producing petrol, fuel and diesel oil, liquefied petroleum gas, jet fuel, kerosene and asphalt.

TRADE

Oil remains the main source of receipts in the balance of payments. The leading suppliers of imports are USA, Japan, Germany, the UK, Italy and France and the chief customers for exports are Japan, France, USA and Singapore. There is a total ban on the importation of alcohol, pork products, firearms, and items regarded as non-Islamic or pornographic.

Trade with UK	1993	1994
Imports from UK	£1,826,121,000	£1,515,252,000
Exports to UK	£1,274,480,000	£739,601,000

COMMUNICATIONS

There is one railway line from Damman on the Gulf of Riyadh which was opened in 1951 and is operated by the Saudi Government Railway Organization, carrying around 400,000 passengers and 1.8 million tons of goods per year. The line is being extended to the port of Jubail on the Gulf. A network of 80,000 miles of roads, including an expressway system, connects all the cities and main towns. There are 21 ports, of which the five major ones are Damman and Jubail (Gulf) and Jeddah, Yanbu and Jizan (Red Sea). The total of 179 berths moved 73 million tons of cargo in 1992. The 15.5 mile-long King Fahd Causeway completed in 1986 connects the Eastern Province to the state of Bahrain.

The government-owned Saudi Arabian Airlines (Saudia) operate scheduled services to 22 domestic airports. There are international airports at Dhahran (King Fahd), Jeddah (King Abdul Aziz), and Riyadh (King Khalid). Saudia have an extensive overseas operation, and a large number of international airlines operate into the country.

Telecommunications are being rapidly expanded with 1.64 million telephone lines in 1992 and seven earth stations linked to the Intelsat system, allowing direct dialling to 185 countries.

EDUCATION

With the exception of a few schools for expatriate children, all schools are government-supervised and are segregated for boys and girls. There are universities in Jeddah, Mecca, Riyadh (branches in Abha and Qassim), Dammam (branch at Hofuf) and Dhahran, and there are Islamic universities in Medina and Riyadh together with 83 tertiary colleges with a total of 142,000 students. There is great emphasis on vocational training, provided at literacy and artisan skill training centres and more advanced industrial, commercial and agricultural education institutes. Education from kindergarten to university is free, with 18,000 schools and 926,000 pupils in 1992.

SENEGAL
République du Sénégal

Senegal lies on the west coast of Africa between Mauritania in the north, Mali in the east, and Guinea-Bissau and Guinea in the south. It entirely surrounds the Gambia, except for its sea-coast. Senegal has an area of 75,750 sq. miles (196,192 sq. km), and a population (UN estimate 1992) of 7,736,000.

CAPITAL – ΨDakar (1,000,000).
CURRENCY – Franc CFA of 100 centimes.
FLAG – Three vertical bands, green, yellow and red; a green star on the yellow band.
NATIONAL DAY – 4 April.

GOVERNMENT

Formerly a French colony, Senegal elected in 1958 to remain within the French Community as an autonomous republic. It became independent as part of the Federation of Mali in June 1960 and seceded to form the Republic of Senegal in September 1960. A border dispute with Mauritania was defused in early 1992 when the border was reopened and diplomatic relations restored. There is an insurgent separatist movement (Movement of Democratic Forces of Casamance (MFDC)) in the southern Casamance region. A ceasefire between the government and MFDC was signed in July 1993 but a political agreement has still to be reached.

In 1963 a new constitution was approved giving executive powers to the President. There are 16 officially recognized political parties. A general election for the National Assembly of 120 seats (70 elected by proportional representation and 50 on a majority basis) is held every five years.

President Diouf was re-elected in the first round of presidential elections in February 1993 with 58.4 per cent of the vote. The legislative election in May 1993 was won by the ruling Parti Socialiste (PS), which secured 84 seats, with the Parti Démocratique Sénégalais (PDS) winning 27 seats, and other parties nine seats. A coalition PS-PDS government was formed in March 1995 to settle political instability.

HEAD OF STATE
President, Abdou Diouf, *installed* 1981, *re-elected* 1988, 21 February 1993

GOVERNMENT *as at August 1995*

Prime Minister, Habib Thiam
Minister of State, Moustapha Niasse (*Foreign Affairs and Expatriates*); Robert Sagna (*Agriculture*); Ousmane Dieng (*Presidential Services*); Abdoulaye Wade (*Presidency*)
Justice, Jacques Baudin
Interior, Abdourahmane Sow
Armed Forces, Cheikh Hamidou
Economy, Finance and Planning, Papa Sakho
Environment and Protection of Nature, Abdoulaye Bathily
Urban Planning and Housing, Amath Dansokho
National Education, André Sonko
Energy, Mines and Industry, Magued Diouf
Modernization, Nene Babacar Mbaye
Communications, Serigne Diop
Culture, Abdoulaye Kane
Public Health and Social Action, Ousmane Ngom
Employment, Labour and Professional Training, Assane Diop
Commerce and Handicrafts, Idrissa Seck
Women, Children and Family Welfare, Aminata Ndiaye

Equipment and Land Transport, Landing Sané
Youth and Sports, Ousmane Paye
Fisheries and Sea Transport, Alassawne Dialy N'diaye
Tourism and Air Transport, Tidiane Sylla
Water Resources, Mamadou Faye
Towns, Daour Cisse
Scientific Research and Technology, Marie-Louise Corea

EMBASSY OF THE REPUBLIC OF SENEGAL
11 Phillimore Gardens, London w8 7QG
Tel 0171-937 0925/6
Ambassador Extraordinary and Plenipotentiary, His Excellency Gabriel Alexandre Sar, apptd 1993

BRITISH EMBASSY
BP 6025, Dakar
Tel: Dakar 237392
Ambassador Extraordinary and Plenipotentiary, His Excellency Alan Furness, CMG, apptd 1993

BRITISH COUNCIL REPRESENTATIVE, Donald Munro, 34–36 Blvd. de la Republique, Immeuble Sonatel, BP 6232, Dakar

TRADE

Senegal's principal exports are groundnuts (raw and processed) and phosphates. Tourism is also of growing importance as a revenue earner.

Trade with UK	1993	1994
Imports from UK	£14,615,000	£20,933,000
Exports to UK	4,012,000	7,625,000

SEYCHELLES
The Republic of Seychelles

Seychelles, in the Indian Ocean, consists of 115 islands with a total land area of 176 sq. miles (456 sq. km), spread over 400,000 sq. miles of ocean. There is a relatively compact granitic group, 32 islands in all, with high hills and mountains (highest point about 2,972 ft), of which Mahé is the largest and most populated (90 per cent of the population live on Mahé); and the outlying coralline group, for the most part only a little above sea-level. Although only 4° S. of the Equator, the climate is pleasant though tropical.

The population is 72,000 (1992 UN estimate).

CAPITAL – ΨVictoria (population, 1987, 24,324), on Mahé.
CURRENCY – Seychelles rupee (Rs) of 100 cents.
FLAG – Red over green, divided by wavy white band.
NATIONAL ANTHEM – Fyer Seselwa (Proud Seychellois).
NATIONAL DAY – 5 June.

GOVERNMENT

Proclaimed French territory in 1756, the Mahé group was settled as a dependency of Mauritius from 1770, was captured by a British ship in 1794, and changed hands several times between 1803 and 1814, when it was finally assigned to Great Britain. In 1903 these islands, together with the coralline group, were formed into a separate colony. On 29 June 1976, the islands became an independent republic within the Commonwealth. A coup d'état took place in 1977. Seychelles was a one-party state from 1979 until 1991, when a multiparty democratic system was proposed by the President. A new constitution was adopted in a referendum in June 1993. Under the new constitution multiparty politics was institutionalized, a National Assembly of 33 members (22 elected by constituencies, 11 by proportional representation) was established and the presidential mandate was set at five years, renewable three times. In presidential and legislative elections held in July 1993, President René was re-elected and the Seychelles People's Progressive Front formed a government after winning 27 of the National Assembly seats, to the Democratic Party's five.

HEAD OF STATE

President, France Albert René, *assumed office* 5 June 1977; *elected* 1979; *re-elected* 1984, 1989, 27 July 1993

COUNCIL OF MINISTERS *as at August 1995*

Finance, Information and Defence, James Michel
Administration and Manpower, Joseph Belmont
Industry, Ralph Adam
Environment, Planning and Foreign Affairs, Danielle de St Jorre
Health, Jacqueline Dugasse
Agriculture and Fisheries, Esme Juneau
Employment and Social Affairs, William Herminie
Tourism and Transport, Testa Simone
Local Government, Youth and Sports, Sylvette Frichot
Education and Culture, Patrick Pillay
Community Development, Dolor Ernesta

SEYCHELLES HIGH COMMISSION
Box No. 4PE, 2nd Floor, Eros House, 111 Baker Street, London WIM IFE
Tel 0171-224 1660
High Commissioner, His Excellency John P. Mascarenhas, apptd 1993

BRITISH HIGH COMMISSION
Victoria House, PO Box 161 Victoria, Mahé
Tel: Victoria 225225
High Commissioner, His Excellency Peter Thomson, CVO, apptd 1994

ECONOMY

The economy is based on tourism, fishing, small-scale agriculture and manufacturing, and the re-export of fuel for aircraft and ships. Deep sea tuna fishing by foreign fleets under licence, improved trans-shipment and other port facilities at Victoria, exports from a tuna canning factory and the export of fresh and frozen fish, attract growing revenues. The government is attempting to reduce the reliance on tourism, which generates 70 per cent of foreign exchange earnings, by promoting the country as an offshore haven for financial services.

TRADE

The principal imports are foodstuffs, beverages, tobacco, mineral fuels, manufactured items, building materials, machinery and transport equipment.

Trade with UK	1993	1994
Imports from UK	£17,821,000	£20,065,000
Exports to UK	6,598,000	9,159,000

SIERRA LEONE
The Republic of Sierra Leone

Sierra Leone, with a total land area of 27,699 sq. miles (71,740 sq. km), is on the west coast of Africa, between Guinea and Liberia.

The population (1992 UN estimate) is 4,376,000. The south is inhabited by peoples whose languages fall into the Mende group; the north by the Temne and smaller groups such as the Limba, Loko, Koranko and Susu.

CAPITAL – ΨFreetown (population, 1985 census, 470,000).
CURRENCY – Leone (Le) of 100 cents.
FLAG – Three horizontal stripes of leaf green, white and cobalt blue.
NATIONAL ANTHEM – High We Exalt Thee, Realm of the Free.
NATIONAL DAY – 27 April (Independence Day).

GOVERNMENT

In the late 18th century a project was begun to settle destitute Africans from England on Freetown peninsula. In 1808 the settlement was declared a Crown colony and became the main base in West Africa for enforcing the 1807 Act outlawing the slave trade. The colony was also used as a settlement for Africans from North America and the West Indies, and Africans rescued from slave ships also settled there. In 1896 a Protectorate was declared over the hinterland.

In 1951 a new constitution was set up that united the colony of Freetown and the Protectorate and on 27 April 1961 Sierra Leone became a fully independent state within the Commonwealth. In 1971 a republican constitution was adopted and Dr Siaka Stevens became the first Executive President. In 1978 Sierra Leone became a one-party state, following approval by Parliament and a referendum.

In September 1991 a new multiparty constitution was adopted and an interim government formed until a general election could be held. This government was overthrown because of alleged corruption by a coup on 29 April 1992. Captain Valentine Strasser became head of state, the House of Representatives was dissolved and all political activity was suspended. A cabinet was appointed to govern the country until promised multiparty elections. In July 1992 Strasser abolished the cabinet and appointed a Council of State Secretaries to co-ordinate the day-to-day running of government. This is subordinate to a military Supreme Council of State (SCS). The military government has announced a timetable to put an elected civilian government in power by the end of 1995.

INSURGENCY

Since May 1991 government forces have been fighting the Revolutionary United Front (RUF) led by Foday Sankoh whose aim is to force all foreigners out of the country and to nationalize the important mining sector. The poor conduct of the campaign against the RUF, based in the south-east of the country, was part of the reason for the 1992 military coup. Since the coup the military government has successfully retaken some of the territory controlled by the RUF but many areas in the east remain under RUF control. South African mercenaries, paid for by foreign mining concerns, are training the government's forces and improving their effectiveness. The conflict has left 10,000 people dead and one-quarter of the population displaced.

HEAD OF STATE
President, Capt. Valentine Strasser, *sworn in* 3 May 1992

SUPREME COUNCIL OF STATE *as at August 1995*

Chairman, Defence, The President
Vice-Chairman, Lt. Julius Bio
Labour, Energy, Power, Trade and Industry, State Enterprises, Lands, Housing and Environment, Lt. Samuel Kambo
Transport, Communications, Tourism, Mines and Works, Lt. Charles M'Bayo

COUNCIL OF STATE SECRETARIES *as at August 1995*
Chief Secretary of State, Health and Social Services, Lt.-Col. A. A. Gibril
Youth, Sports and Social Mobilization, Sulaiman Banja Tejan Sie
Chairman's Office, Col. (retd) S. B. Jumu
Finance, Dr John Karimu
Development and Planning, Victor Brandon
Foreign Affairs, Abass Bundu
Transport and Communications, Hindolo Trye
Agriculture and Forestry, Lesley Scott
Mineral Resources, Lt.-Col. S. F. Koroma
Trade, Industry and State Enterprises, Dr Alusine Fofana
Works, Lt.-Col. J. P. Gbondo
Information, Broadcasting and Culture, Arnold Bishop-Gooding
Energy and Power, Sylvanus Taylor Lewis
Education, Christina Thorpe
Attorney-General, Claude Campbell
Lands, Housing and Environment, Mohammed Samura
Interior and Rural Development, Col. (retd) A. Kamara
Tourism, Maj. (retd) Gabriel Turay
Marine Resources, Ernest Ndomoihina
Eastern Region, Lt. S. Nyuma
Northern Region, Maj. Fallah Sewah
Southern Region, Lt. Idris Kamara

SIERRA LEONE HIGH COMMISSION
33 Portland Place, London WIN 3AG
Tel 0171-636 6483/4/5/6
High Commissioner, His Excellency Alhaji Harom Buhari, apptd 1995

BRITISH HIGH COMMISSION
Spur Road, Freetown
Tel: Freetown 223963
High Commissioner, His Excellency Ian McCluney, CMG, apptd 1993

BRITISH COUNCIL DIRECTOR, Peter Hilken, PO Box 124, Tower Hill, Freetown

ECONOMY

The military government has cracked down on corruption, liberalized the foreign exchange system and reduced inflation from 120 per cent to 25 per cent. The government's economic and financial reform programme for 1994–6 has been approved by the IMF, which has provided a credit of US$163 million to support it.

On the Freetown peninsula, farming is largely confined to the production of cassava and crops such as maize and vegetables for local consumption. In the hinterland the principal agricultural product is rice, which is the staple food of the country, and cash crops such as cocoa, coffee, palm kernels and ginger.

The economy depends largely on mineral exports; mainly diamonds, gold, bauxite and rutile, the production of which has been disrupted by the insurgency. Diamond exports provided Le1,254.5m in 1989. Total imports for 1989 were to the value of Le10,901.8m and exports were Le8,269.5m.

TRADE WITH UK	1993	1994
Imports from UK	£20,169,000	£20,241,000
Exports to UK	16,219,000	19,743,000

COMMUNICATIONS

Since the phasing out of the railway system in 1974 the road network has been developed considerably and there are now 5,000 miles of roads in the country, over 2,000 miles being surfaced. A bridge has been constructed over the Mano River linking Sierra Leone and Liberia.

The Freetown international airport is situated at Lungi. The main port is Freetown, which has one of the largest natural harbours in the world, and where there is a deep water quay. There are smaller ports at Pepel, Bonthe and Niti.

Radio is operated by the government. Broadcasts are made in several of the indigenous languages, in addition to English and French.

EDUCATION

In 1989 there were 2,554 primary schools in Sierra Leone and 201 secondary schools. Technical education is provided in the two government technical institutes, situated in Freetown and Kenema, in two trade centres and in the technical training establishments of the mining companies. Teacher training is carried out at the University of Sierra Leone, six colleges in the provinces and in the Milton Margai Training College near Freetown.

SINGAPORE

Singapore consists of the island of Singapore and 59 islets, covering a total area of 244 sq. miles (639 sq. km). Singapore island is 26 miles long and 14 miles in breadth and is situated just north of the Equator off the southern extremity of the Malay peninsula, from which it is separated by the Straits of Johore. A causeway crosses the three-quarters of a mile to the mainland. The climate is hot and humid. Rainfall averages 240 cm a year and temperature ranges from 24° to 32° C (76°–89° F).

In 1993 the population was 2,873,800, which comprised 2,228,600 (77.5 per cent) Chinese, 407,600 (14.2 per cent) Malays, 204,100 (7.1 per cent) Indians (including those of Pakistani, Bangladeshi and Sri Lankan origin) and 33,500 (1.2 per cent) from other ethnic groups. Malay, Mandarin, Tamil and English are the official languages. At least eight Chinese dialects are used. Malay is the national language and English is the language of administration.

CURRENCY – Singapore dollar (S$) of 100 cents.
FLAG – Horizontal bands of red over white; crescent with five five-point stars on red band near staff.
NATIONAL ANTHEM – Majulah Singapura.
NATIONAL DAY – 9 August.

GOVERNMENT

Singapore, where Sir Stamford Raffles first established a trading post under the East India Company in 1819, was incorporated with Penang and Malacca to form the Straits Settlements in 1826. The Straits Settlements became a Crown colony in 1867. Singapore fell into Japanese hands in 1942 and civil government was not restored until 1946, when it became a separate colony. Internal self-government was introduced in 1959. Singapore became a state of Malaysia when the Federation was enlarged in September 1963, but left Malaysia and became an independent sovereign state within the Commonwealth on 9 August 1965. Singapore adopted a republican constitution from that date. There is a Cabinet collectively responsible to an 87-member (81 elected and six nominated by the President) Parliament. In November 1991 the constitution was amended to provide for a directly-elected President, elected for a six-year term, with enlarged powers and the ability to veto government decisions in certain instances relating to internal security, the budget, financial reserves and the appointment of senior civil servants. The President appoints the Prime Minister and, on his advice, the members of the Cabinet.

After the general election of 31 August 1991 the People's Action Party (PAP) had 77 seats in Parliament. The Singapore Democratic Party (SDP) won three seats and the Workers' Party won one seat.

HEAD OF STATE
President, Ong Teng Cheong, *elected* 28 August 1993, *took office*, 2 September 1993

CABINET *as at August 1995*
Prime Minister, Hon. Goh Chok Tong
Senior Minister, PM's Office, Hon. Lee Kuan Yew, GCMG, CH
Deputy PM, Foreign, Trade, Defence, Hon. Lee Hsien Loong
Trade and Industry, Hon. Yeo Cheow Tong
Education, Hon. Lee Yock Suan
Environment and Communications, Hon. Mah Bow Tan
Law and Foreign Affairs, Hon. Prof. S. Jayakumar
Finance, Hon. Dr Richard Hu Tsu Tau
Labour, Hon. Lee Boon Yang
Muslim Affairs and Community Development, Hon. Abdullah Tarmugi
Health, Information and The Arts, Hon. George Yeo
Home Affairs, Hon. Wong Kan Seng
National Development, Hon. Lim Hng Kiang
Without Portfolio, Hon. Lim Boon Heng

HIGH COMMISSION FOR THE REPUBLIC OF SINGAPORE
9 Wilton Crescent, London SW1X 8SA
Tel 0171-235 8315
High Commissioner, His Excellency Abdul Aziz Mahmood, apptd 1988
Counsellor (Defence Procurement), Col. Hung Khiang Puah
First Secretary, F. Tay (*Commercial*)

BRITISH HIGH COMMISSION
Tanglin Road, Singapore 1024
Tel: Singapore 4739333
High Commissioner, His Excellency Gordon Duggan, apptd 1990
Deputy High Commissioner and Counsellor (Economic/Commercial), J. P. Freeman
Defence Adviser, Gp Capt J. M. Collier

BRITISH COUNCIL DIRECTOR, J. Davies, 30 Napier Road, Singapore 1025

ECONOMY

Historically Singapore's economy was based on the sale and distribution of raw materials from surrounding countries and on entrepot trade in finished products. However an industrialization programme was launched in 1968 and manufacturing industries have been established, including shipbuilding and repairing, iron and steel, transport equipment, textiles, footwear, wood products, microelectronics, televisions, computers, telecommunications equipment, office machinery, audio equipment, scientific instruments, detergents, confectionery, pharmaceuticals, petroleum products, etc. Singapore has also become an important financial services centre with significant insurance and foreign exchange markets, a stock exchange, 132 commercial banks and 75 merchant banks and an oil-refining centre. The economy grew by 9.9 per cent of GDP in 1993. Singapore's major trading partners are the USA, Malaysia, the EU, Hong Kong and Japan.

FINANCE (estimates)	1992	1993
Revenue	S$17,219m	S$19,527m
Expenditure	12,270m	12,550m

TRADE	1992	1993
Total imports	S$117,529m	S$137,603m
Total exports	103,351m	119,473m

Trade with UK	1993	1994
Imports from UK	£1,429,660,000	£1,768,541,000
Exports to UK	1,615,210,000	1,896,892,000

COMMUNICATIONS

Singapore is one of the largest and busiest seaports in the world, with six terminals, deep water wharves and ship repairing facilities. Ships also anchor in the roads, unloading into lighters. In 1993, the total volume of cargo handled was 274,000,000 tonnes. More than 500 shipping lines use the port, with 92,600 ship arrivals in 1993.

The international airport is at Changi, in the east of the island, with Singapore Airlines operating flights to 80 countries and 19,987,000 passengers using the airport in 1993. There are 67 km of metre gauge railway connected to the Malaysian rail system by the causeway across the Straits of Johore, and 2,989 km of roads.

There are nine radio and three television channels operated by the Singapore Broadcasting Corporation in the four official languages, and three private broadcasting stations.

SLOVAKIA
Slovenská Republika – The Republic of Slovakia

Slovakia has an area of 18,940 sq. miles (49,035 sq. km). It is situated in central Europe and is bordered to the north by Poland, to the east by the Ukraine, to the south by Hungary, to the south-west by Austria and to the west by the Czech Republic. The Tatry (Tatras) mountains in the centre and north of the country reach heights of 2,600 m (8,530 ft). The major river is the Váh which flows from the Tatry mountains to join the Danube at the Hungarian border. The climate is continental.

The population (1993) is 5,336,455, of which 85.7 per cent are ethnic Slovaks, 10.8 per cent ethnic Hungarians, 1.4 per cent gypsy, 1.1 per cent Czech, with smaller numbers of Ruthenians, Ukrainians and Germans. The population is mainly Christian, some 60 per cent Roman Catholic and 6 per cent Protestant.

The main languages are Slovak (85.7 per cent), Hungarian (10.8 per cent), Czech (1.1 per cent). Slovak is the official language but the law safeguards the right to use minority languages in dealing with public authorities in areas where the minority forms 20 per cent or more of the population.

CAPITAL – Bratislava, on the Danube, population (1993) 448,785. Other major cities are: Košice (238,454); Žilina (97,537); Prešov (89,000); Banská Bystríca (78,321).
CURRENCY – Slovak Koruna (SK) (Crown).
FLAG – Three horizontal stripes of white, blue, red with the arms all over near the hoist.
NATIONAL ANTHEM – Nad Tatrou sa blýska (Storm over the Tatras).
NATIONAL DAYS – 1 January (Establishment of Slovak Republic); 5 July (Day of the Slav Missionaries); 29 August (Slovak National Uprising); 1 September (Constitution Day).

GOVERNMENT (*see also* Czech Republic)

At the end of the 11th century Slovakia became part of the Hungarian state when the Magyars gained control of the area. After the Hungarians were defeated at the battle of Moháč in 1526, most of Hungary (including part of Slovakia) was occupied by the Turks, with the remainder of Hungary and Slovakia being incorporated into the Austrian Empire. With the establishment of the Austro-Hungarian monarchy in 1867, Slovakia again came under Hungarian control. The attempted Magyarization of Slovakia gave impetus to the national revival which had begun in 1848–9, and when the First World War came many Slovaks fought with the allies. Amalgamated into the republic of Czechoslovakia on 28 October 1918, Slovakia became independent in March 1939 as a Nazi puppet state when Germany invaded the Czech lands. Slovakia was liberated by Soviet forces in 1945 and returned to Czechoslovakia. The formation of a federal republic between the Czech lands and Slovakia was the only Prague Spring reform to survive the Soviet invasion of 1968. Following the collapse of Communist rule at federal and republic level in 1989, nationalist feeling grew even stronger and the Czech and Slovak republics began to negotiate the dissolution of the federation into two sovereign states in 1992. Dissolution took effect on 1 January 1993.

The constitution vests legislative power in the National Council of 150 members elected for a four-year term by proportional representation with a five per cent threshold for parliamentary representation. The President is elected for a five-year term by the National Council; executive power is held by the Prime Minister and Cabinet. Minority rights are enshrined in the constitution but discrimination is claimed by the ethnic Hungarian population.

A coalition government of the Movement for a Democratic Slovakia (HZDS) and Slovak National Party (SNS) was sworn in on 12 January 1993 but lost its majority in the National Council when the SNS left the government. Increasing criticism of the economic policy and authoritarian style of the HZDS government led ten HZDS members to break away and form a new party which, in alliance with three other parties, brought down the government by a parliamentary no-confidence vote in March 1994. The four-party coalition then formed a government which was approved by President Kovac on 16 March 1994.

Legislative elections on 30 September and 1 October 1994, however, returned the HZDS to power at the head of a three-party coalition with the Association of Slovak Workers (ZRS) and the Slovak National Party (SNS) which took office on 13 December 1994. Meanwhile, the previous government's privatization contracts were cancelled by a parliamentary vote in November 1994. The new government announced the indefinite suspension of the privatization programme in late December, its lukewarm attitude to economic reform caused by the inclusion in the coalition of extreme left- and right-wing parties.

The state of the parties in the National Council as at August 1995 was: HZDS 61; Democratic Left Party (SDL) 18; Christian Democratic Movement (KDH) 17; Hungarian Coalition 17; Democratic Union (DU) 15; ZRS 13; SNS 9.

HEAD OF STATE
President, Michal Kovac, *elected* 15 February 1993

COUNCIL OF MINISTERS *as at August 1995*
Prime Minister, Vladimir Mečiar (HZDS)
Deputy PM, Legislature and Media, Katarina
    Tóthová (HZDS)
Deputy PM, Economy and Finance, Sergej Kozlík (HZDS)
Deputy PM, Social, Industrial and Trade Union Relations, Jozef
    Kalman (ZRS)

Foreign Affairs, Juraj Schenk (HZDS)
Defence, Ján Sitek (SNS)
Economy, Ján Ducký (HZDS)
Privatization, Peter Bisák (ZRS)
Interior, Ludovít Hudek (HZDS)
Labour, Social Affairs and Family, Oľga Keltošová (HZDS)
Culture, Ivan Hudec (HZDS)
Justice, Jozef Liščák (ZRS)
Education and Science, Eva Slavkovská (SNS)
Health, Ľabomír Javorský (HZDS)
Agriculture, Peter Baco (HZDS)
Transport and Communications, Alexander Rezes (HZDS)
Environment, Jozef Zlocha (ZRS)
Minister without Portfolio, Ján Mráz (ZRS)

HZDS Movement for a Democratic Slovakia; ZRS Association of Slovak Workers; SNS Slovak National Party

Chairman, Slovak National Council, Ivan Gašparovič.

EMBASSY OF THE SLOVAK REPUBLIC
25 Kensington Palace Gardens, London w8 4QY
Tel 0171-243 0803
Ambassador Extraordinary and Plenipotentiary, His Excellency
    Jan Vilikovsky, apptd 1992

BRITISH EMBASSY
4th Floor, Grosslingova 35, 81109 Bratislava
Tel: Bratislava 364459
Ambassador Extraordinary and Plenipotentiary, His Excellency
    Peter Harborne, apptd 1995
BRITISH COUNCIL DIRECTOR, Susan Wallace-Shaddad,
    PO Box 68, Panska 17, 81499 Bratislava

ECONOMY

From independence until mid-1994 Slovakia faced economic difficulties because of the structure of its centrally-planned and inefficiently managed economy, reliant on state-subsidized heavy industries with low productivity, and because of the ambivalent attitude to reform of the HZDS government. The HZDS faced increasing problems in 1993 as output, exports and foreign currency reserves fell and unemployment and inflation increased. In July 1993 the Slovak Crown was devalued by 10 per cent in return for an IMF loan of US$89 million. Economic reform policies, including macro-economic stabilization, price liberalization, currency convertibility and extensive privatization were continued, though at a slower rate than in the Czech Republic. Firms have been privatized by a voucher system, transfer, public auction, restoration to former owners, or transformation into joint-stock companies.

In mid-1994, however, the economic situation stabilized as the Moravčik government, more committed to reform, speeded up the privatization process with a second round of privatization. The budget deficit was brought down to 3.8 per cent of GDP, the trade balance was brought into surplus, while the foreign debt was reduced and foreign exchange reserves increased significantly. In 1994 unemployment (15 per cent) and inflation (11.7 per cent) were reduced and foreign investment is increasing and beginning to offset the loss of subsidies from the former Czechoslovak federation. In July 1994 the IMF approved a US$263 million credit to support the economic reform programme. GDP grew by four per cent in 1994, but the election of a new HZDS-led government in October 1994 has put future economic reform in doubt. Natural resources include brown coal, natural gas, iron ore, antimony, lead, zinc and magnesite.

TRADE WITH UK	1993	1994
Imports from UK	£10,628,000	£44,666,000
Exports to UK	2,392,000	56,654,000

SLOVENIA
Republika Slovenija

Slovenia is a small mountainous state which was the most northerly of the former Yugoslav republics. It has an area of 7,819 sq. miles (20,251 sq. km) and is bordered on the north by Austria, on the north-east by Hungary, on the east and south by Croatia and on the west by Italy. The two major rivers are the Sava and the Drava. There is a short coastline in the south-west 25 miles (40 km) in length on the Adriatic. The climate is a mixture of Mediterranean, continental and alpine.

The population (1994) is 1,989,477 and is mostly Slovenian. There are small Hungarian (0.5 per cent) and Italian (0.1 per cent) minorities, together with a Romany population. About 30,000 refugees from the former Yugoslavia remain in Slovenia.

The main religion is Roman Catholicism. Slovene is the official language, together with Hungarian and Italian in ethnically mixed regions.

CAPITAL – Ljubljana, population (1994) 269,972. Other major towns (1994) are: Maribor (103,113); Celje (39,782); Kranj (36,770) and ΨKoper (24,495), the only port.

CURRENCY – Slovene Tolar (SIT) of 100 stotin.

FLAG – Three horizontal stripes of white, blue, red, with the arms in the upper hoist.

NATIONAL ANTHEM – Zdravljica (A Toast).

NATIONAL DAY – 25 June (Independence Day).

GOVERNMENT

The area that is now Slovenia came under the control of the Habsburg Empire in the 15th century and remained so until the defeat of the Austro-Hungarian Empire in 1918. On 27 October 1918 Slovenia became part of the state of Slovenes, Croats and Serbs (later Yugoslavia) and this was confirmed by the Versailles Treaty 1919. Slovenia was reduced in size, however, by the Italian annexation of the western third of the country and the Austrian annexation of parts of the north. In 1941 Yugoslavia was invaded by German forces and Slovenia was divided between Germany, Italy and Hungary. Slovenia was reformed as a constituent republic of the federal Yugoslav state in May 1945. After a dispute with Italy and nine years of international administration, the Adriatic coast and hinterland were returned to Slovenia in 1954 and Italy retained Trieste.

Slovenian fears of Serbian dominance led the Slovene Assembly in 1989 to amend the republican constitution to lay the basis of a sovereign state. In a referendum in December 1990, 88 per cent of the electorate voted for independence, which was declared on 25 June 1991. A tenday war with the Yugoslav National Army followed before the Army called off hostilities and withdrew.

A new constitution was adopted in December 1991. Executive power is vested in the Prime Minister and Cabinet of Ministers. Legislative authority is held by the bicameral National Assembly, composed of the 90-member State Chamber (lower house) and 40-member State Council (upper house). The State Chamber is elected on a proportional representation basis, with one seat each reserved for the Italian and Hungarian minorities. The State Council has 22 elected and 18 appointed members (six by non-profit making organizations, four by employers, four by employees and four by farmers, small businessmen and independent professionals). Presidential and legislative elections were held on 6 December 1992, with incumbent President Milan Kučan being re-elected and the Liberal Democratic Party emerging as the largest party in parliament. A coalition government led by the Liberal Democrats was formed in January 1993.

HEAD OF STATE
President, Milan Kučan, *elected* April 1990, *re-elected for a five-year term* 6 December 1992

CABINET *as at August 1995*
Prime Minister, Janez Drnovšek (LDS)
Deputy PM, Foreign Affairs, Zoran Thaler (LDS)
Finance, Mitja Gaspari (LDS)
Economy, Development, Janko Deželak (SKD)
Education and Sports, Slavko Gaber (LDS)
Justice, Meta Zupančič (Ind.)
Internal Affairs, Andrej Šter (SKD)
Transport and Communications, Igor Umek (SKD)
Agriculture and Forestry, Jože Osterc (SKD)
Health, Božidar Voljč (LDS)
Science and Technology, Rado Bohinc (ZL)
Labour, Family and Social Affairs, Rina Klinar (ZLSD)
Culture, Sergij Pelhan (ZL)
Economic Activities, Maks Tajnikar (ZL)
Environment, Dr Pavle Gantar (LDS)
Defence, Jelko Kacin (LDS)

LDS Liberal Democratic Party; SKD Slovenian Christian Democrats; ZL United List; ZLSD Associated List of Social Democrats.

EMBASSY OF SLOVENIA
11–15 Wigmore Street, London WIH 9LA
Tel 0171-495 7775
Ambassador Extraordinary and Plenipotentiary, His Excellency Matjaž Šinkovec, apptd 1992

BRITISH EMBASSY
4th Floor, Trg Republike 3, 61-000 Ljubljana
Tel: Ljubljana 1257191
Ambassador Extraordinary and Plenipotentiary, His Excellency Gordon Johnston, apptd 1992

BRITISH COUNCIL DIRECTOR, Francis King, Stefanova 1/III, 61000 Ljubljana

ECONOMY

Although still with problems, Slovenia's economy has emerged as the most stable of the former Yugoslav economies and the least affected by the end of central planning. Although it has lost its captive export market and cheap supplies of raw materials from Serbia, the country is one of the richest of the former Communist countries. It has successfully re-orientated its exports towards western markets, with 70 per cent of exports going to EU states in 1994. By mid-1995, 88 per cent of companies were in the private sector. Trade surpluses have been recorded in 1992–4 (US$475 million in 1994), with foreign currency reserves of US$3.2 billion in mid-1995 and foreign debt at US$2.49 billion. Inflation has been gradually reduced to around 18 per cent and the tolar is stable and convertible, while GDP grew in 1993 and 1994.

In 1994 GDP was US$14,037 million, of which agriculture, forestry and fishing produced 5 per cent. The main products are potatoes, wheat, corn, apples, wine, meat and milk. Mining and manufacturing produced 55 per cent of GDP, the major sectors being metal-working, electronics, textiles, automotive parts, chemicals, glass products and food-processing. Tourism (worth US$750 million in 1993) and transport are major export earners, with 1,400,000 tourists visiting in 1991. Foreign investment is being attracted, with US$1,300 million invested by the end of 1993.

TRADE WITH UK	1993	1994
Imports from UK	£56,713,000	£89,690,000
Exports to UK	53,344,000	93,529,000

COMMUNICATIONS

Important road and rail communications cross the country from west to east (Milan–Ljubljana–Budapest), and north to south (Munich–Ljubljana–Zagreb–Belgrade–Athens). There are international airports at Ljubljana, Maribor and Portoroz (Adriatic Coast). The port of Koper is an important shipment point for goods from Austria, Hungary, the Czech Republic and Slovakia.

EDUCATION

Education is compulsory and free between the ages of seven and 14. There are 821 primary schools (age seven–14), 152 secondary or middle schools (age 14–19), 30 colleges and two universities (Ljubljana and Maribor).

SOLOMON ISLANDS

Forming a scattered archipelago of mountainous islands and low-lying coral atolls, the Solomon Islands stretches about 900 miles in a south-easterly direction from the Shortland Islands to the Santa Cruz islands. The archipelago covers an area of about 249,000 sq. miles, with a land area of 10,938 sq. miles (28,446 sq. km), between 155° 30' and 170° 30'E. longitude and 5° 10' and 12° 45'S. latitude. The six biggest islands are Choiseul, New Georgia, Santa Isabel, Guadalcanal, Malaita and Makira. They are characterized by thickly-forested mountain ranges intersected by deep, narrow valleys.

The total population was 328,723 at the 1991 census. English is the official language; there are over 80 local languages.

CAPITAL – ΨHoniara, population (1991) 40,000.
CURRENCY – Solomon Islands dollar (SI$) of 100 cents.
FLAG – Blue over green divided by a diagonal yellow band, with five white stars in the top left quarter.
NATIONAL ANTHEM – God Bless our Solomon Islands.
NATIONAL DAY – 7 July (Independence Day).

GOVERNMENT

The origin of the present Melanesian inhabitants is uncertain. European discovery of the islands began in the mid-16th century and continued intermittently for about 300 years, when the inauguration of sugar plantations in Queensland and Fiji (which created a need for labour) and the arrival of missionaries and traders led to increased European interest in the region. Great Britain declared a Protectorate in 1893 over the Southern Solomons, adding the Santa Cruz group in 1898 and 1899. The islands of the Shortland groups were transferred from Germany to Great Britain by treaty in 1900.

The Solomon Islands achieved internal self-government in 1976, and became independent in July 1978. The Solomon Islands is a constitutional monarchy, The Queen being represented locally by the Governor-General. Legislative power is vested in a unicameral

National Parliament of 47 members, elected for a four-year term. Executive authority is exercised by the Cabinet. A four-party National Coalition government led by Francis Billy Hilly took power after winning 24 of the 47 seats in the legislative election of 26 May 1993. Hilly was, however, forced to resign as Prime Minister in October 1994 after his coalition lost its parliamentary majority. On 7 November the National Parliament elected Solomon Mamaloni as Prime Minister and he formed a new government.

Governor-General, His Excellency Sir Moses Pitakaka, GCMG, apptd 1994

CABINET *as at August 1995*

Prime Minister, Hon. Solomon Mamaloni
Deputy PM, Home Affairs, Hon. Dennis Lulei
Agriculture and Fisheries, Hon. Edmond Adresen
Commerce, Employment and Trade, Hon. George Luilamo
Development Planning, Hon. David Sitai
Culture and Tourism, Hon. William Haomae
Education and Training, Hon. Alfred Martin
Finance, Hon. Christopher Abe
Health and Medical Services, Hon. Gordon Mars
Foreign Affairs, Hon. Danny Philip
Justice, Hon. Oliver Zapo
Provincial Government and Rural Development, Hon. Allan Qurucu
Post and Communication, Hon. John Masuota
Transport, Works and Utilities, Hon. John Fieango
Lands and Housing, Hon. Francis Orodani
Forestry, Environment and Conservation, Hon. Allan Kemakeza
Energy, Minerals and Mines, Hon. Eric Serl
Sports, Youth and Women's Development, Hon. Brown Beu
Police and National Security, Hon. Victor Ngele

HIGH COMMISSION OF THE SOLOMON ISLANDS
Avenue de l'Yser 13, BTE 3, 1040 Brussels
Tel: Brussels 2732 7085
High Commissioner, His Excellency Levi Malau Laka, apptd 1995

HONORARY CONSULATE
19 Springfield Road, London SW19 7AL
Tel 0181-296 0232
Honorary Consul, Edward Nielsen, OBE

BRITISH HIGH COMMISSION
Telekon House, Mendana Avenue (PO Box 676), Honiara
Tel: Honiara 21705/6
High Commissioner, His Excellency Raymond F. Jones, OBE, apptd 1991

COMMUNICATIONS

Solomon Airlines operates international services to other Pacific states and Australia. Air Niugini flies from Port Moresby to Honiara. There are about 52 miles of secondary and minor roads in the urban areas of Honiara, Auki and Gizo. In the rural areas there are some 800 miles of road, including those in private plantations, forestry areas and roads built and maintained by councils. Telekom, a company jointly owned by Cable and Wireless and the Solomon Islands government, operates the international and domestic telephone circuits from a ground station in Honiara via the Intelsat Pacific Ocean communication satellite.

TRADE

The main imports are foodstuffs, consumer goods, machinery and transport materials. Principal exports are timber, fish, copra, and palm oil. Fisheries exports for 1992 totalled SI$88.1m, timber SI$110.4m and copra SI$22.7m. Other exports include cocoa and marine shells.

Trade with UK	1993	1994
Imports from UK	£1,681,000	£1,059,000
Exports to UK	2,339,000	2,719,000

SOMALIA
Jamhuuriyadda Diimoqraadiga ee Soomaaliya

Somalia occupies part of the north-east horn of Africa, with a coastline on the Indian Ocean extending from the boundary with Kenya (2° S. latitude) to Cape Guardafui (12° N.), and on the Gulf of Aden to the boundary with Djibouti. Somalia is bounded on the west by Djibouti, Ethiopia and Kenya and covers an area of about 246,201 sq. miles (637,657 sq. km). The population, of which a large proportion is nomadic, is 9,204,000 (UN estimate 1992).

CAPITAL – ΨMogadishu, population (estimated 1987), 1,000,000. Other towns are Hargeisa (20,000), Boroma (65,000), ΨKisimayu (60,000), ΨBerbera (15,000) and Burao (15,000).

CURRENCY – Somali shilling of 100 cents.

FLAG – Five-pointed white star on blue ground.

NATIONAL DAY – under review.

GOVERNMENT

British rule in Somaliland lasted from 1887 until 1960, except for a short period in 1940–1 when the Protectorate was occupied by Italian forces. Somalia, formerly an Italian colony, was occupied by British forces in 1941. In 1950 it was placed under Italian administration by a resolution of the UN; this trusteeship lasted until the British protectorate and the trust territory became independent as the Somali Democratic Republic on 1 July 1960. In 1969, the armed forces took over the government and a Revolutionary Council under Siad Barre assumed control of the country.

Siad Barre was overthrown in January 1991 by rebel movements. One group, the United Somali Congress, took control in Mogadishu and formed an interim administration in February 1991 with the USC leader, Ali Mahdi Mohammed, as president. However, the USC government failed to establish its authority over the other, clan-based movements, the Somali Salvation Democratic Front (SSDF), the Somali Patriotic Movement (SPM) and the Somali Democratic Movement (SDM). In the north of the country, the Somali National Movement (SNM) refused to participate in negotiations and formed a government under SNM leader Abourahman Ahmed Ali.

Fighting erupted in the summer of 1991 between supporters of Ali Mahdi Mohammed and supporters of the Somali National Alliance (SNA) of Gen. Mohammed Aideed. The fighting degenerated into civil war in 1991, devastating Mogadishu and large parts of the south of the country. The UN intervened in April 1992 with food aid to prevent starvation. In August 1992 the UN Security Council approved the dispatch of the UN Operation in Somalia (UNOSOM) force to protect relief convoys, while the USA initiated an emergency food airlift. However, the UN force proved ineffective in securing aid distribution routes from the armed factions. On 9 December 1992, with UN authority, a US-led United Task Force (UNITAF) intervened to create a safe environment for the delivery of aid. Distribution routes were secured by the end of December and UNITAF turned its attention to confiscating and destroying the weapons of the armed factions, which provoked clashes with armed gunmen in the Mogadishu area in early 1993.

On 4 May 1993 UNITAF handed over to a 28,000-strong UN force (UNOSOM II) mandated to maintain a secure environment and promote political reconciliation. Fighting between Gen. Aideed's SNA forces and UN troops attempting to destroy the SNA's weapons, arrest Aideed and broker a political settlement took place between June and November 1993, and left 90 UN troops and 2,000 Somalis dead. From November 1993 onwards the UN focused its efforts on political reconciliation between the various Somali factions, but this remained elusive despite a March 1994 ceasefire agreement between Gen. Aideed and Ali Mahdi Mohammed. With the withdrawal of US and other western troops from the UN operation in March 1994, the remaining UN troops of around 20,000 were composed of less well-equipped troops from India, Pakistan and Egypt. The Somali factions took advantage of this; fighting broke out again and attacks on UN troops increased.

Accepting that the UN troops were unable to carry out their mandate, the UN Security Council voted on 4 November 1994 to withdraw UN forces and terminate UNOSOM II's mandate by March 1995. The last UN forces withdrew from Mogadishu on 2 March 1995 and Gen. Aideed's militia took over the city's port and airport. Factional fighting continued. On 12 June Gen. Aideed was ousted as SNA leader by Osman Ali Ato, splitting the SNA into two factions; Gen. Aideed responded by declaring himself President on 15 June and forming a government, but this remains ineffective. Political authority remains in the hands of clan leaders; there is no national government. About 350,000 are believed to have died from starvation or in the fighting.

SECESSION

Civil war broke out in May 1988 between the government and the opposition Somali National Movement (SNM) in the north of the country. With the downfall of Siad Barre, the SNM took control of the north-west (the former British Somaliland Protectorate) and in May 1991 declared unilateral independence as the 'Somaliland Republic'. A government and legislature was formed which elected Mohamed Ibrahim Egal as President in May 1993.

SOMALI DIPLOMATIC REPRESENTATION

The Embassy closed in January 1992.

BRITISH DIPLOMATIC REPRESENTATION

The British Embassy in Mogadishu closed in January 1991.

ECONOMY

Livestock raising is the main occupation and there is a modest export trade in livestock, skins and hides. Italy, the Gulf States and Saudi Arabia import the bulk of the banana crop, the second biggest export. Due to UN aid and pacification of the countryside, the harvest improved from 10 per cent of normal in 1992 to 50 per cent in 1993.

TRADE WITH UK	1993	1994
Imports from UK	£3,540,000	£7,502,000
Exports to UK	246,000	1,508,000

SOUTH AFRICA
Republiek van Suid-Afrika

South Africa occupies the southernmost part of the African continent from the courses of the Limpopo, Marico, Molopo, Nosop and Orange Rivers (34° 50′ 22″ S.) to the Cape of Good Hope, with the exception of Lesotho, Swaziland and the extreme south of Mozambique. It has a total area of 471,445 sq. miles (1,221,031 sq. km) and borders on Namibia in the north-west, Botswana and Zimbabwe in the north, Mozambique and Swaziland in the north-east, and Lesotho, which it completely surrounds. To the west, east and south lie the south Atlantic and southern Indian Oceans. Some 1,192 miles (1,920 km) to the south-east of Capetown lie Prince Edward and Marion Islands, part of South Africa since 1947.

Ranges of hills run parallel to the coast along much of the southern and eastern coastline, rising in steps towards the interior. Most of the ranges are of no great height, the exception being the Drakensberg (11,000 ft) running south-west to north-east in the east of the country. Between the ranges of hills and in the interior in the north-east are plateaux, such as the Great Karoo in the south. In the north and centre are grassy plains with occasional hills or kopjes. The Orange, with its tributary the Vaal, is the principal river, rising in the Drakensberg and flowing into the Atlantic near the border with Namibia. The Limpopo, or Crocodile River, in the north, rises in the Transvaal and flows into the Indian Ocean through Mozambique. Most of the remaining rivers are furious torrents after rain, with partially dry beds at other seasons.

The climate is subtropical, dry and sunny moderated by the warm temperate winds from the Atlantic and Indian Oceans. Moist hot air masses from the Indian Ocean are the chief source of rainfall for most of the country.

The official population estimate for 1993, excluding Bophuthatswana, Ciskei, Transkei and Venda, was 32,589,000, comprising 23,016,000 Blacks, 5,149,000 Whites, 3,402,000 Coloureds, and 1,022,000 Indians. The population of the four homelands (now reincorporated into

South Africa) was 7,460,000, which was overwhelmingly black, giving a total estimated population of 40,049,000. The population in May 1995 was estimated as: 75.6 per cent Black; 13 per cent White; 8.7 per cent Coloured; 2.7 per cent Indian.

The interim constitution designates 11 official languages: Afrikaans; English; Ndebele; Sesotho sa Leboa; Sesotho; Si Swati (Swazi); Tsonga; Tswana; Venda; Xhosa; Zulu. Afrikaans and English are to remain the languages of record although any citizen may correspond official business in his own language. Afrikaans is descended from old Dutch and is the language of the Afrikaner and Coloured populations.

CAPITAL – The administrative seat of the government is Pretoria, Gauteng; population (1985 estimate) 822,925; the seat of the legislature is ΨCape Town, Western Cape, population (1985) 1,911,521; the seat of the judiciary is Bloemfontein, Orange Free State (232,984). Other large towns (1985 figures) are Johannesburg, Gauteng (1,609,408); ΨDurban, Kwazulu/Natal, the largest seaport (634,301); ΨPort Elizabeth, Eastern Cape (651,993); ΨEast London, Eastern Cape (167,992); and Pietermaritzburg, Kwazulu/Natal (192,417).

CURRENCY – Rand (R) of 100 cents.

FLAG – Divided red over blue by a horizontal white-fimbriated green Y; in the hoist a black triangle fimbriated in yellow.

NATIONAL ANTHEMS – Die Stem Van Suid-Afrika (The Call of South Africa); Nkosi Sikelel'i Afrika (God Bless Africa).

NATIONAL DAY – To be decided.

HISTORY

The colony of the Cape of Good Hope was founded by the Dutch at Cape Town in 1652 and remained a Dutch colony until 1795 when Britain took possession of it in 1795. Restored to Dutch rule in 1803, it was again taken by Britain in 1806 and this was confirmed by the London Convention of 1814. Increasing Anglicization of the colony led to the movement of a large proportion of the descendants of Dutch settlers (known as Boers) north-eastwards in the years following 1834. This 'Great Trek' led to the foundation of the Orange Free State and Transvaal republics by the Boers, which were recognized by Britain in 1853–4. Natal was annexed to Cape Colony by the British in 1844 and then formed as a separate colony in 1856, to which Zululand was added in 1897 after the British victory in the Zulu wars. Transvaal and the Orange Free State (renamed the Orange River Colony) became British colonies after the Boer defeat in the Second Boer War 1899–1902. The self-governing colonies of the Cape of Good Hope, Natal, the Transvaal and the Orange River Colony became united in 1910 under the name of the Union of South Africa. Independence within the Commonwealth was gained in 1931 under the Statute of Westminster. South Africa left the Commonwealth and became a republic on 31 May 1961, largely as a result of international condemnation of apartheid and of the Sharpeville massacre.

From 1948, when the Afrikaner National Party came to power, South Africa's social and political structure was based on apartheid, a policy of racial segregation. Opposition protests culminated in the Sharpeville massacre in 1960; the African National Congress and other opposition groups were subsequently banned. A new wave of opposition climaxed in 1976 with uprisings in Soweto, in which hundreds were shot dead. In 1984 renewed rioting in the black townships and continuing unrest led to the declaration of a state of emergency in July 1985 in 36 districts, and nationwide from 12 June 1986; it was renewed annually until 1990.

As part of its policy of apartheid, the government established a number of black 'homelands'. Six areas (Gazankulu, Lebowa, KwaNdebele, KaNgwane, Qwaqwa and KwaZulu) were designated as self-governing states. A further four (Bophuthatswana, Ciskei, Transkei and Venda) were regarded as independent republics by the South African government but never recognized as such by the UN.

Moves to Democracy

The first moves to reform apartheid came into effect in 1984, when a new constitution extended the franchise to the Coloured and Indian populations. Coloured and Indians elected members to a three-house parliament, Coloured and Indian houses being added to the existing white chamber. However, whites retained effective political power and blacks remained excluded.

In 1989, F. W. de Klerk became President of South Africa and accelerated the process of reform. In 1990, the ban on the ANC and restrictions on other anti-apartheid groups were lifted; Nelson Mandela, the main ANC political detainee, was released. In 1991 the laws implementing apartheid were effectively abolished. In 1992 a referendum amongst the white electorate on continued political reform and a new constitution reached by negotiation was approved by 69 per cent to 31 per cent.

Negotiations continued between various groups to establish a non-racial democracy. These negotiations led to the opening in Johannesburg on 20 December 1991 of the Convention on a Democratic South Africa (CODESA) talks between the government, the ANC, the Inkatha Freedom Party and other political, business and church groups. The talks took place against an escalating level of violence involving mainly ANC and Inkatha supporters, but also the security forces, white extremists and Pan-Africanist Congress (PAC) supporters. After the Boipatong massacre in June 1992 the ANC withdrew from the talks, which broke down. Violence, strikes and campaigns of mass action escalated, culminating in the massacre at Bisho, Ciskei, in September 1992.

The continuing violence led the government and the ANC to resume negotiations on 25 September. Agreements were reached in January and February 1993 on establishing an interim multiracial administration in the latter half of 1993 and on the formation of a five-year coalition government after the multiracial election. On 1 April full CODESA negotiations resumed, attended for the first time by the right-wing Conservative Party and by

the PAC. Progress towards the establishment of a Transitional Executive Council (TEC) in June 1993 was disrupted by the assassination of the senior ANC member Chris Hani by white extremists on 10 April. Negotiations reached an impasse in June and subsequently the Conservative Party and Inkatha and some homelands leaders left the talks in protest at the refusal of the government and ANC to grant in an interim constitution a degree of regional autonomy that could not be removed when a full constitution was agreed.

The remaining CODESA delegations agreed on 7 September 1993 upon the formation of the multiparty TEC which, together with the independent media and electoral commissions, became effective in December 1993. An interim constitution was agreed on 17 November and adopted by parliament on 22 December. The TEC was boycotted and the interim constitution rejected by the powerful Freedom Alliance (FA) composed of Inkatha, the homeland governments of KwaZulu, Ciskei and Bophuthatswana, and the Afrikaner Volksfront (AVF), itself composed of the Conservative Party, the neo-Nazi AWB and the Afrikaner Volksunie. Throughout late 1993 and early 1994 the government and ANC were involved in intense negotiations with the FA and its constituent parts to accept the interim constitution and take part in the April general election. By the time of the election, the majority of groups had agreed to participate after amendments to the interim constitution had been made.

GOVERNMENT

The interim constitution establishes South Africa as a democratic multiparty state which will be governed by the interim constitution for a period of two to five years. The final constitution will be decided by the Constituent Assembly (composed of the National Assembly and Senate) by two-thirds majorities in both houses by 27 April 1996. If that is not achieved, it will be approved by a 60 per cent vote in a national referendum, and if that fails it will wait until after the 1999 general election for approval.

Under the interim constitution the ten homelands have been reincorporated in South Africa. Executive power is vested in a President and Cabinet, with the President elected by parliament; at least two deputy Presidents appointed by parties with over 20 per cent of the vote; and a Cabinet and government of national unity to last five years composed of all parties gaining over 5 per cent of the vote. Legislative power is vested in a bicameral parliament, a directly elected 400-member National Assembly elected by proportional representation, and an indirectly elected 90-member Senate composed of ten members elected by each of the nine regional legislatures.

The four former provinces (Cape Province, Natal, Orange Free State, Transvaal) have been replaced by nine new regions (Western Cape, Northern Cape, Eastern Cape, Orange Free State, North-West, KwaZulu/Natal, Gauteng, Northern Transvaal, Eastern Transvaal). Each region has its own Prime Minister, a legislature of between 30 and 100 seats elected by proportional representation, and its own constitution. At local government level, new multiracial municipal councils have their seats allocated on a 30 per cent white, 30 per cent non-white and 40 per cent non-racial basis.

The interim constitution also established, in February 1995, a constitutional court of 11 members to adjudicate in disputes between the three tiers of government, to interpret and certify amendments to the constitution, to ensure that all executive, legislative and judicial actions conform to the new Bill of Rights, to decide on the validity of the final constitution, and to protect all rights and freedoms.

In the country's first multiracial general election held on 26–29 April 1994 the results were (National Assembly seats): African National Congress (ANC) 62.7 per cent (252), National Party (NP) 20.4 per cent (82), Inkatha Freedom Party (IFP) 10.5 per cent (43), Freedom Front (FF) 2.2 per cent (9), Democratic Party (DP) 1.7 per cent (7), Pan Africanist Congress (PAC) 1.3 per cent (5), African Christian Democratic Party 0.4 per cent (2). In the Senate the ANC gained 60 seats, the NP 17, IFP 5, FF 5, DP 3. In the regional elections the ANC won control of seven regional legislatures: Gauteng, Northern Transvaal, Eastern Transvaal, North-West Northern Cape, Eastern Cape, Orange Free State. The National Party won control in the Western Cape and the IFP in KwaZulu/Natal.

Since its election the new Parliament has passed two significant pieces of legislation to settle the legacy of the apartheid era. In November 1994 the Restitution of Land Rights Act was passed which established a Land Claims Commission and a Land Claims Court to restore the rights of those dispossessed of their land since the 1913 Land Act. In June 1995 the Promotion of National Unity and Reconciliation Act was passed which established a Truth Commission covering the apartheid era, with a remit to assess confessions, grant amnesties for political crimes and set compensation for victims.

Against a background of ANC-IFP violence in KwaZulu/Natal which has left 1,600 people dead since the April 1994 election, there has been continuous ANC-IFP argument over the final constitution. The IFP is demanding more autonomy for KwaZulu/Natal in the final constitution than exists at present and than the ANC is prepared to accept.

HEAD OF STATE
President, Nelson Rolihlahla Mandela, OM, *elected by parliament* 9 May 1994, *sworn in* 10 May 1994
First Deputy President, Thabo Mbeki (ANC)
Second Deputy President, Frederick de Klerk (NP)

CABINET *as at August 1995*

Justice, Dullah Omar (ANC)
Defence, Joe Modise (ANC)
Safety and Security, Sydney Mufamadi (ANC)
Education, Sibusiso Bhengu (ANC)
Trade, Industry and Tourism, Trevor Manuel (ANC)
Foreign Affairs, Alfred Nzo (ANC)
Labour, Tito Mboweni (ANC)
Post, Telecommunications and Broadcasting, Pallo Jordan (ANC)
Health, Nkosazana Zuma (ANC)
Transport, Mac Maharaj (ANC)
Provincial Affairs and Constitutional Development, Roelf Meyer (NP)
Land Affairs, Derek Hanekom (ANC)
Public Enterprises, Stella Sigcau (ANC)
Public Services and Administration, Zola Skweyiya (ANC)
Housing, Sankie Nkondo (ANC)
Public Works, Jeff Radebe (ANC)
Correctional Services, Sipho Mzimela (IFP)
Finance, Christo Liebenberg (Ind.)
Agriculture, Kraai Van Niekerk (NP)
Sports and Recreation, Steve Tshwete (ANC)
Home Affairs, Mangosuthu Buthelezi (IFP)
Water and Forestry, Kader Asmal (ANC)
Environmental Affairs, Dawie de Villiers (NP)
Mines and Energy, Pik Botha (NP)
Welfare and Population Development, Abe Williams (NP)
Arts, Culture, Science and Technology, Ben Ngubane (IFP)
Reconstruction and Development, Jay Naidoo (ANC)
General Services, Chris Fismer (NP)

In addition there are 13 deputy ministers, of whom nine are ANC, three are NP and one is IFP.

President of the Senate, Dr Kobie Coetsee
Speaker of the National Assembly, Dr Frene Ginwala
President of the Constitutional Court, Arthur Chaskalson

HIGH COMMISSION OF THE REPUBLIC OF SOUTH AFRICA
South Africa House, Trafalgar Square, London WC2N 5DP
Tel 0171-930 4488
High Commissioner, His Excellency Mendi Msimang, apptd 1995
Deputy High Commissioner, G. J. Grobler
Minister (*Economic*), P. M. Pullen
Counsellors, B. H. Knoefel; S. Morkel; D. J. Cloete; T. Eygelaar (*Consul-General*)
Defence Attaché, Col. G. A. Hallowes
First Secretary, S. Singh (*Cultural*)

BRITISH HIGH COMMISSION
255 Hill Street, Pretoria 0002
Tel: Pretoria 4333121
91 Parliament Street, Cape Town 8001
Tel: Cape Town 4617220
High Commissioner, His Excellency Sir Anthony Reeve, KCMG, apptd 1991
Counsellor, Deputy High Commissioner, Dr D. Carter, CVO
Counsellor (*Political*), A. Hardie, OBE
Defence Attaché, Brig. J. W. Parker, CBE
Consul-General and Director of Trade Promotion (*Johannesburg*), P. Longworth

There is a British Consulate-General at Johannesburg (PO Box 10101, Johannesburg 2000), Consulates at Cape Town and Durban, and Honorary Consuls at Port Elizabeth and East London.

Cultural Attaché and British Council Representative, Les Phillips, OBE, 76 Juta Street, (PO Box 30637), Braamfontein 2017, Johannesburg. There is also an office in Cape Town.

DEFENCE

The armed forces are engaged in the formation of a new South African National Defence Force (SANDF) from the merger of the South African Defence Forces (SADF), the Umkhonto we Sizwe (MK) armed wing of the ANC, the Azanian People's Liberation Army (APLA) of the PAC, and the defence forces of the four former independent homelands. White conscription is being phased out and the SANDF will be a fully professional force.

The total active armed forces strength of the former SADF numbers 78,500 (35,400 white conscripts). Total reserves number 635,000 personnel. The active Army strength is 58,000 personnel, of whom 12,000 are white and 46,000 other races. Equipment includes 250 main battle tanks, 1,700 reconnaissance vehicles, 3,160 armoured personnel carriers and infantry fighting vehicles and 550 artillery pieces.

The Navy has a strength of 4,500 with three submarines and 12 patrol and coastal combatants. The Air Force has a strength of 10,000 with 245 combat aircraft and 14 armed helicopters. In addition the paramilitary South African Police number 110,000 personnel, with 37,000 reserves. MK forces number 6,000 personnel, the APLA 200 and the former homeland defence forces 7,000 personnel.

COMMUNICATIONS

There are international airports at Johannesburg, Durban and Cape Town. South African Airways operates international services to Europe, South America, the Far East,

Africa, Australia and the USA, and it is the principal operator of domestic flights. The largest seaport is Durban, Natal. Other major ports are Cape Town, Port Elizabeth, East London, Saldanha Bay and Mossel Bay in Cape Province and Richards Bay, Natal. The national railway system, and most long-distance passenger and freight road transport are run by independent companies. The six landlocked states of Botswana, Lesotho, Swaziland, Zimbabwe, Zambia and Malawi make extensive use of South African Railways for foreign trade.

ECONOMY

The economy has suffered in recent years from recession, industrial unrest, drought, the fall in the world gold price and foreign disinvestment. With the end of financial sanctions the government hopes that investors will return in their previous numbers. The price of gold has recovered somewhat and the drought ended but industrial unrest continues because of black workers' increased expectations. An austerity programme launched in 1985 brought the national debt down to 70 per cent of GDP and enabled the government in September 1993 to announce the repayment of the US$5,000 million foreign debt over an eight-year period.

The first budget of the new government in June 1994 envisaged expenditure of R135,100 million and revenue of R104,300 million, with a one-off 5 per cent levy on corporations and wealthy individuals. Although the budget was well-received, subsequent argument over the cost of the ANC's reconstruction and development programme (RDP), including increased spending on education, health care, new homes and electrification, led to a run on the rand and a crisis in foreign exchange and gold reserves, necessitating a scaling-down of planned RDP expenditure. Some R2,500 million has been spent in 1994–5 on the RDP, with a projected R10,000 million to be spent over ten years. The RDP is partly to be paid for by cuts in government administration and defence, the sale of state enterprises and a state lottery. The March 1995 budget envisaged expenditure of R153,300 million and revenue of 125,200 million, and a budget deficit of 6.4 per cent of GDP, to be paid for mainly by foreign loans. The economy grew by 2 per cent in 1994 with a surge of foreign capital and investment and the lessening of industrial strikes. Foreign exchange reserves have been increased and inflation kept down to 10 per cent, but unemployment remains high at 3,600,000.

Mining is of great importance, producing 10.0 per cent of GDP and 60 per cent of exports in 1993 and minerals to the value of R39,376 million. The principal minerals produced are gold, coal, diamonds, copper, iron ore, manganese, lime and limestone, uranium, platinum, fluorspar, andalusite, zinc, zirconium, vanadium, titanium, nickel, lead and chrome ore. South Africa is the world's largest producer of gold, platinum, diamonds, chrome ore, manganese and vanadium, and has the world's largest reserves of chrome ore, manganese, vanadium and andalusite.

Agriculture, forestry and fishing account for about 5 per cent of GDP. Over 50 per cent of land is pasture so livestock farming is widespread and meat and wool important products. Principal crops are maize, sugar-cane, fruits and vegetables, wheat, sorghum, sunflower seed and groundnuts. Cotton is widely grown because of its suitability to the climate, and viticulture is also widespread.

Industries, concentrated most heavily around Johannesburg, Pretoria and the major ports, process foodstuffs, metals and non-metallic mineral products, produce oil from coal, and also produce beverages and tobacco, motor vehicles, chemicals and chemical products, machinery, textiles and clothing, and paper and paper products.

Manufacturing industry contributed 24.0 per cent of GDP in 1994.

Energy production is based upon coal and natural gas and the production of synthetic liquid fuel from coal. One nuclear power station is in operation and others are planned. South Africa exports electricity through its electric grid connections to all states in southern Africa.

TRADE

Principal exports are gold, base metals and metal products, coal, diamonds, food (especially fruit), chemicals, machinery and transport equipment, and wool. Principal imports are machinery, chemicals, motor vehicles, metals and metal products, food, inedible raw materials and textiles.

American and EC sanctions, in place since 1986, were lifted in July 1991 and January 1992 respectively. The longer-standing UN finance, oil and arms embargoes were lifted in October 1993, December 1993 and April 1994 respectively.

Trade with UK	1993	1994
Imports from UK	£1,124,424,000	£1,410,878,000
Exports to UK	998,437,000	970,718,000

SPAIN
España

Spain occupies most of the Iberian Pensinsula, between 36° and 43° 45′ N., and 4° 25′ E. and 9° 20′ W. It is bounded on the south and east by the Mediterranean, on the west by the Atlantic and Portugal, and on the north by the Bay of Biscay and France. It comprises a total area of 194,897 sq. miles (504,782 sq. km), with a population (1991 census) of 38,872,268.

The interior of the Iberian peninsula consists of an elevated tableland surrounded and traversed by mountain ranges: the Pyrenees, the Cantabrian Mountains, the Sierra Guadarrama, Sierra Morena, Sierra Nevada, Montes de Toledo, etc. The principal rivers are the Duero, the Tajo, the Guadiana, the Guadalquivir, the Ebro and the Miño.

CAPITAL – Madrid, population (1991) 4,947,555. Other large cities are ΨBarcelona (4,654,407), ΨValencia (2,117,972), Seville (1,619,703), Alicante (1,292,563), ΨMálaga (1,160,843), Bilbao (1,179,148); Murcia (1,045,601).
CURRENCY – Peseta of 100 céntimos.
FLAG – Three horizontal stripes of red, yellow, red, with the yellow of double width.
NATIONAL ANTHEM – Marcha Real Española.
NATIONAL DAY – 12 October.

GOVERNMENT

Spain was a monarchy until 1931, when King Alfonso XIII left the country and a republic was proclaimed. A provisional government, drawn from the various republican and socialist parties, was formed. In July 1936 a counter-revolution broke out in military garrisons in Spanish Morocco and spread throughout Spain. The principal leader was Gen. Franco, leader of the Military-Fascist fusion, or *Falange*. Civil war ensued until March 1939, when the Popular Front governments in Madrid and Barcelona surrendered to the Nationalists (as Gen. Franco's followers were then named). Gen. Franco became President and ruled the country until his death in 1975, when, according to his wishes, he was succeeded as head of state by Prince Juan Carlos of Bourbon (grandson of Alfonso XIII) and

Spain again became a monarchy. The first free election was held on 15 June 1977.

Under the 1978 constitution there is a bicameral *Cortes Generales* comprising a 350-member Congress of Deputies elected for a maximum term of four years by universal adult suffrage; and a Senate consisting of 208 directly elected representatives of the provinces, islands, and Ceuta and Melilla, and 44 representatives appointed by the assemblies of the autonomous regions. At the general election on 6 June 1993, PSOE (Spanish Socialist Workers' Party) won 159 seats; the PP (Popular Party) 141; the (Communist) United Left Party 18; Catalan Nationalists 17; Basque Nationalists (PNV) 5; others 10. The PSOE formed a minority government with the support of the Catalan and Basque nationalists in July. Throughout 1994–5 the Socialist government has been plagued by resignations and scandals, most notably the anti-terrorist GAL scandal, which caused the Catalan Nationalists to announce in July 1995, that they would withdraw their support from the government at the end of Spain's EU presidency in December 1995.

REGIONS

Since the promulgation of the 1978 constitution, 17 autonomous regions have been established, with their own parliaments and governments. These are Andalucia, Aragon, Asturias, Balearics, the Basque country, Canaries, Castilla-La Mancha, Castilla-Leon, Cantabria, Cataluña, Extremadura, Galicia, Madrid, Murcia, Navarre, La Rioja and Valencia. In addition Madrid and Barcelona have special autonomous status, but not the same degree of autonomy as the autonomous regions. In February 1995 statutes of autonomy for Ceuta and Melilla were approved by the Cortes, giving them similar autonomous status to Madrid and Barcelona. They will each have a mayor, a council of government and an elected legislative assembly.

SECESSION

The Basque separatist terrorist organization ETA (*Euzkadi ta Azkatasuna* – Basque Nation and Liberty) has since its formation in 1959 carried out a terrorist campaign of bombings, shootings and kidnappings against the Spanish state and its security forces in an attempt to gain independence for the Basque country. ETA rejected regional autonomy for the Basque country in 1979 as insufficient and continued its campaign, but increased co-operation between French and Spanish security forces and an alleged illegal anti-terrorist campaign organized by the Spanish state under the acronym GAL (*Grupos Antiterroristas de*

Liberación) had greatly weakened ETA by the early 1990s. Most of its leaders were caught and jailed in 1992; the conflict has left 700–800 dead and 600 ETA members in jail.

HEAD OF STATE

HM The King of Spain, King Juan Carlos I de Borbón y Borbón, KG, GCVO, *born* 5 January 1938, *acceded to the throne* 22 November 1975, *married* 14 May 1962, Princess Sophie of Greece *and has issue*, Infante Felipe (*see* below); Infanta Elena Maria Isabel Dominga, *born* 20 December 1963; and Infanta Cristina Federica Victoria Antonia, *born* 13 June 1965

Heir, HRH The Prince of the Asturias (Infante Felipe Juan Pablo Alfonso y Todos los Santos), *born* 30 January 1968

CABINET *as at August 1995*

Prime Minister, Felipe González Márquez
Deputy PM, Relations with the Cortes and Government Secretariat, Alfredo Pérez Rubalcaba
Foreign Affairs, Javier Solana Madariaga
Justice and Interior, Juan Alberto Belloch
Defence, Gustavo Pertierra
Economy and Finance, Pedro Solbes Mira
Public Works and Town Planning and Transport, José Borrell Fontelles
Education and Science, Joan Lerma
Labour and Social Security, José Griñán Martínez
Industry, Juan Eguiagaray Ucelay
Trade and Tourism, Javier Gómez Navarro
Agriculture, Food and Fisheries, Luis Maria Atienza
Public Administration, Jerónimo Saavedra Acevedo
Culture, Carmen Alboroch
Health and Consumer Affairs, Angeles Amador Millán
Social Affairs, Cristina Alberdi Alonso

SPANISH EMBASSY

39 Chesham Place, London SW1X 8QA
Tel 0171-235 5555
Ambassador Extraordinary and Plenipotentiary, His Excellency Don Alberto Aza Arias, apptd 1993
Minister-Plenipotentiary, Don Pablo Barrios Almanzor
Defence Attaché, Capt. J. M. Pery
Minister, Dr D. de Lario (*Cultural*)
Minister, Don L. E. Valera (*Consul*)
Counsellor, J. G. Valverde (*Commercial*)

BRITISH EMBASSY

Calle de Fernando el Santo, 16, 28010 Madrid
Tel: Madrid 319 0200
Ambassador Extraordinary and Plenipotentiary, His Excellency Anthony David Brighty, CMG, CVO, apptd 1994
Minister, Deputy Ambassador, Dr E. Jones Parry, CMG
Counsellors, M. H. Conner (*Commercial*); C. J. Ingham (*Economic and Community Affairs*); D. C. Ankerson
Defence and Naval Attaché, Capt. J. Gozzard RN
Consuls-General, D. R. McIntyre (*Madrid*); M. Perceval (*Barcelona*); M. McLoughlin (*Bilbao*)

There are Consulates-General in Madrid, Barcelona, Bilbao; Consulates in Tenerife, Alicante, Seville, Malaga, Palma de Mallorca, Las Palmas; Vice-Consulates in Ibiza and Menorca; Honorary Consulates in Santander, Tarragona, Vigo.

BRITISH COUNCIL DIRECTOR, Peter Taylor, OBE, Paseo del General Martinez, Campos 31, 2800 Madrid. There are offices in Barcelona, Bilbao, Las Palmas, Palma, Segovia, Seville and Valencia.

BRITISH CHAMBER OF COMMERCE, Plaza de Santa Barbara 10, 1st Floor, 28004 Madrid; Paseo de Gracia 11, Barcelona 7; Alameda de Mazaredo 5, Bilbao 1.

DEFENCE

The armed forces have a total active strength of 206,500 (133,200 conscripts) with a nine-month period of conscription. The Army has 145,000 personnel (102,500 conscripts), with 1,010 main battle tanks, 440 reconnaissance vehicles, 1,990 armoured personnel carriers, 911 artillery pieces, and 28 combat helicopters. The Army is organized into eight regional commands and a General Reserve Force.

The Spanish Navy has a strength of 33,100 (18,600 conscripts), including 7,150 marines, and consists of eight submarines, one V/STOL aircraft carrier, 16 frigates, 31 patrol and coastal combatants, 28 armed helicopters and 20 Harrier aircraft. The Air Force has a strength of 28,400 (12,100 conscripts) and has 150 combat aircraft. The paramilitary Guardia Civil with 72,000 personnel (2,200 conscripts) operates as a gendarmerie in rural areas under the control of the Ministry of Defence and has been actively engaged in combating Basque terrorism.

Spain deploys an infantry battalion group of 1,220 troops with UN forces in Bosnia and two frigates in the Adriatic enforcing the weapons embargo on the former Yugoslavia. The USA maintains 4,100 naval and 400 air force personnel in Spain.

ECONOMY

The expansion of the economy and accession to the EC have led to changes in Spanish agriculture. It accounts for over 5 per cent of GDP and employs over 10 per cent of the working population. The country is generally fertile, and fruits such as olives, oranges, lemons, almonds, pomegranates, bananas, apricots, tomatoes, peppers, cucumbers and grapes are cultivated. Other agricultural products include wheat, barley, oats, rice, hemp and flax. The vine is cultivated widely; in the south-west, around Jerez, sherry and tent wines are produced. The fishing industry is important.

Spain's mineral resources of coal, iron, wolfram, copper, zinc, lead and iron ores are variously exploited. Output of coal in 1988 was 15.5 million tonnes; output of steel (1988) 11.9 million tonnes.

The principal industrial goods are cars, steel, ships, manufactured goods, textiles, chemical products, footwear and other leather goods. Tourism is a major industry; in 1993 an estimated 57,259,000 tourists visited Spain.

The government is attempting to reform the economy so that it will meet the convergence criteria laid down for entry into a future EU economic and monetary union. The budget deficit is being reduced from 6.7 per cent of GDP in 1994 to 5.9 per cent in 1995. However, inflation (4.5 per cent), public debt (64 per cent of GDP) and unemployment (25 per cent) all remained high in 1994. The weak peseta had to be devalued by 7 per cent in the exchange rate mechanism in March 1995.

TRADE

The principal imports are cotton, tobacco, cellulose, timber, coffee and cocoa, food products, fertilizers, dyes, machinery, motor vehicles and agricultural tractors, wool and petroleum products. The principal exports include cars, petroleum products, iron ore, cork, salt, vegetables, fruits, wines, olive oil, potash, mercury, pyrites, tinned fruit and fish, tomatoes and footwear.

Trade with UK	1993*	1994
Imports from UK	£4,124,367,000	£4,996,135,000
Exports to UK	3,044,042,000	3,630,298,000

*Excluding the Canary Islands, Ceuta and Melilla

EDUCATION

Education is free for those aged six to 18, and compulsory up to the age of 14. Private schools (30 per cent of primary and 60 per cent of secondary schools) have to fulfill certain criteria to receive government maintenance grants. There are 33 public sector universities, the oldest of which, Salamanca, was founded in 1218. Other ancient foundations are Valladolid (1346), Barcelona (1430), Zaragoza (1474), Santiago (1495), Valencia (1500), Seville (1505), Madrid (1508), Granada (1531), Oviedo (1604). Private universities are Deusto in Bilbao, Navarra in Pamplona, one in Madrid and one in Salamanca. Student numbers in the universities in 1989–90 totalled 1,067,874.

CULTURE

Castilian is the language of more than three-quarters of the population of Spain. Basque, said to have been the original language of Iberia, is spoken in Vizcaya, Guipuzcoa and Alava. Catalan is spoken in Provençal Spain, and Galician, spoken in the north-western provinces, is akin to Portuguese. The governments of these regions actively encourage use of their local languages.

The literature of Spain is one of the oldest and richest in the world, the *Poem of the Cid*, the earliest of the heroic songs of Spain, having been written about 1140. The outstanding writings of its golden age are those of Miguel de Cervantes Saavedra (1547–1616), Lope Felix de Vega Carpio (1562–1635) and Pedro Calderón de la Barca (1600–81). The Nobel Prize for Literature has five times been awarded to Spanish authors: J. Echegaray (1904), J. Benavente (1922), Juan Ramón Jiménez (1956), Vicente Aleixandre (1977) and Camilo José Cela (1989).

ISLANDS AND ENCLAVES

The Balearic Isles form an archipelago off the east coast of Spain. There are four large islands (Majorca, Minorca, Ibiza and Formentera), and seven smaller (Aire, Aucanada, Botafoch, Cabrera, Dragonera, Pinto and El Rey). The total area is 1,935 sq. miles (5,011 sq. km), with a population of 685,088. The archipelago forms a province of Spain, the capital being ΨPalma in Majorca, pop. 304,422.

The Canary Islands are an archipelago in the Atlantic, off the African coast, consisting of seven islands and six mostly uninhabited islets. The total area is 2,807 sq. miles (7,270 sq. km), with a population of 1,444,626. The Canary Islands form two provinces of Spain: Las Palmas, comprising Gran Canaria, Lanzarote (38,500), Fuerteventura (19,500) and the islets of Alegranza, Roque del Este, Roque del Oeste, Graciosa, Montaña Clara and Lobos, with seat of administration at ΨLas Palmas (366,454) in Gran Canaria; and Santa Cruz de Tenerife, comprising Tenerife, La Palma (76,000), Gomera (31,829), and Hierro (10,000), with seat of administration at ΨSanta Cruz in Tenerife, population estimate 190,784.

Isla de Faisanes is an uninhabited Franco-Spanish condominium, at the mouth of the Bidassoa in La Higuera bay.

ΨCeuta is a fortified post on the Moroccan coast, opposite Gibraltar. The total area is 5 sq. miles (13 sq. km), with a population of 70,864.

ΨMelilla is a town on a rocky promontory of the Rif coast, connected with the mainland by a narrow isthmus.

Population 58,449. Ceuta and Melilla are parts of Metropolitan Spain.

OVERSEAS TERRITORIES

Spanish settlements on the Moroccan seaboard are:
Peñón de Alhucemas, a bay including six islands, population 366
Peñón de la Gomera (or *Peñón de Velez*), a fortified rocky islet, population 450
The Chaffarinas (or *Zaffarines*), a group of three islands near the Algerian frontier, population 610

SRI LANKA
Sri Lanka Prajatantrika Samajawadi Janarajaya

Sri Lanka (formerly Ceylon) is an island in the Indian Ocean, off the southern tip of India and separated from it by the narrow Palk Strait. Situated between 5° 55' and 9° 50' N. latitude and 79° 42' and 81° 52' E. longitude, it has an area of 25,332 sq. miles (65,610 sq. km), including 33 sq. miles of inland water. Forests, jungle and scrub cover the greater part of the island. In areas over 2,000 ft above sea level grasslands (*patanas* or *talawas*) are found. One of the highest peaks in the central massif is Adam's Peak (7,360 ft), a place of pilgrimage for Buddhists, Hindus and Muslims.

The climate is warm throughout the year, with a high relative humidity. The two main monsoon seasons are mid-May to September (south-west) and November to March (north-east).

The population (1993 estimate) was 17,619,000, of which 74 per cent were Sinhalese, 12.6 per cent Sri Lankan Tamils, 5.6 per cent Indian Tamils, 7.1 per cent Sri Lankan Moors and 0.7 per cent Burghers, Malays and others. The religion of the majority is Buddhism (69.3 per cent), then Hinduism (15.5 per cent), Islam (7.6 per cent), and Christianity (7.5 per cent). The national languages are Sinhalese, Tamil and English.

CAPITAL – ΨColombo, population (1993) 2,026,000.
Other principal towns are ΨJaffna (879,000), Kandy (1,269,000), ΨGalle (971,000), and ΨTrincomalee (323,000).
CURRENCY – Sri Lankan rupee (Rs) of 100 cents.
FLAG – On a dark red field, within a golden border, a golden lion passant holding a sword in its right paw, and a representation of a *bo*-leaf, issuing from each corner; and to its right, two vertical stripes of saffron and green also placed within a golden border, to represent the minorities of the country.
NATIONAL ANTHEM – Namo Namo Matha (We all stand together).
NATIONAL DAY – 4 February (Independence Commemoration Day).

GOVERNMENT

The Portuguese landed in Ceylon in the early 16th century and founded settlements, eventually conquering much of the country. Portuguese rule lasted 150 years; in 1658 it gave way to that of the Dutch East India Company until 1796. The maritime provinces of Ceylon were ceded by the Dutch to the British in 1798, becoming a British Crown Colony in 1802. With the annexation of the Kingdom of Kandy in 1815, all Ceylon came under British rule.

Ceylon became a self-governing state and a member of the British Commonwealth on 4 February 1948. A republican constitution was adopted in 1972 and the country was renamed Sri Lanka (meaning 'Resplendent Island'). In 1978 a new constitution introduced a system of proportional representation. Legislative power is exercised by the National State Assembly, executive power being exercised by the President and Cabinet.

Eight provincial councils were set up in 1988 under the Indo-Sri Lankan peace accord in an attempt to diffuse ethnic tension. Since then, except for the temporarily merged North-East province, all provinces have had elected provincial councils. In the south of the country during the 1980s 100,000 people were killed in fighting between government forces and Sinhalese armed extremists.

In the general election of 16 August 1994 the ruling United National Party (UNP) was defeated by the opposition People's Alliance led by Chandrika Bandaranaike Kumaratunga. The People's Alliance won 105 seats; the United National Party 94 seats; and other parties, mainly Muslim and moderate Tamils, 26 seats. The People's Alliance formed a government with the support of the Sri Lankan Muslim Congress and moderate Tamil parties. Prime Minister Kumaratunga won the presidential election on 9 November 1994 with 62 per cent of the vote after the UNP candidate Gamini Dissanayake was assassinated by Tamil Tiger terrorists in a bomb attack which killed 50 people. President Kumaratunga handed over the premiership to her mother, the former Prime Minister Sirimavo Bandaranaike.

In August 1995 the government announced a package of constitutional proposals intended to form a federal state with eight autonomous regions (one covering the Tamil north-east). Each region would have its own elected legislature, executive and judicial branch of government, a police force, and powers devolved from the central government. The package must be passed by a two-thirds parliamentary majority and a national referendum.

SECESSION

The Liberation Tigers of Tamil Eelam (LTTE) guerrilla group has been fighting Sri Lankan forces for control of the Tamil majority areas in the north and east of the country since 1983. They were suppressed by Indian peacekeepers in 1987–90 but grew in strength after the Indians left. They are now virtually confined to the Jaffna peninsula by Sri Lankan forces, but a Tamil suicide bomber assassinated President Premadasa on 1 May 1993. Some 40,000–50,000 have been killed in 12 years of fighting, including 1,000 in November 1993 when the Tamil Tigers' attempt to break out of the Jaffna peninsula was defeated by government forces.

The People's Alliance government came to power on a platform of negotiating a peaceful settlement with the LTTE, to include full autonomy for the Tamil-majority areas in the north and east. It began by allowing the ten-year-old state of emergency to lapse throughout the country, apart from the east and north, and by relaxing the economic blockade on the Jaffaa peninsula in September 1994. Peace negotiations were opened the same month, leading to a formal cease-fire with the LTTE which began on 8 January 1995. However, fighting resumed in April 1995 after the LTTE had unilaterally broken the cease-fire and negotiations had broken down. The economic blockade was reimposed and fighting since April has left around 1,000 dead as LTTE attempts to break out of the peninsula have again been defeated. The LTTE has a strength of around 4,000 personnel and runs its own administration in the Jaffna peninsula, which has a population of around 800,000.

HEAD OF STATE
President, Chandrika Bandaranaike Kumaratunga, *elected*
9 November 1994, *sworn in* 12 November 1994

CABINET *as at August 1995*
Finance and Defence, The President
Prime Minister, Sirimavo Bandaranaike
Public Administration, Local Government, Plantations, Ratnasiri
    Wickremanayke
Power and Energy, Irrigation, Col. Anuruddha Ratwatte
Home Affairs, Provincial Councils and Co-operatives, Amarasiri
    Dodangoda
Foreign Affairs, Laksham Kadirgamar
Cultural and Religious Affairs, Laksham Jayakody
Science, Technology and Human Resources Development, Bernard
    Soysa
Agriculture, Lands and Forests, D. M. Jayaratna
Labour and Vocational Training, Mahinda Rajapakse
Shipping, Ports, Rehabilitation and Reconstruction, M. H. M.
    Ashraff
Information, Tourism and Aviation, Dharmasiri Senanayake
Trade, Commerce and Food, Kingsley Wickremaratna
Industrial Development, C. V. Gunaratna
Education and Higher Education, Richard Pathirana
Housing, Construction and Public Utilities, Nimal Siripala De
    Silva
Posts and Telecommunications, Mangala Samaraweera
Youth Affairs, Sports and Rural Development, D. S. M. B.
    Dissanayaka
Transport, Highways, Environment and Women's Affairs,
    Srimani Athulathmudali
External Trade, Justice and Constitutional Affairs, G. L. Peiris
Health and Social Services, A. H. M. Fowzie
Fisheries, Indika Gunawardena

HIGH COMMISSION FOR THE DEMOCRATIC SOCIALIST
REPUBLIC OF SRI LANKA
13 Hyde Park Gardens, London W2 2LU
Tel 0171-262 1841
High Commissioner, His Excellency Sarath
    Wickremesinghe, apptd 1995
Deputy High Commissioner, G. S. Munasinghe
Minister-Counsellors, Mrs S. Rajapakse (*Consular*); K. J.
    Weerasinghe (*Commercial*)
First Secretary, N. De Silva Gunatilleke (*Defence*)

BRITISH HIGH COMMISSION
Galle Road 190, Kollupitiya (PO Box 1433), Colombo 3
Tel: Colombo 437336
High Commissioner, His Excellency Edward John Field,
    CMG, apptd 1991
Deputy High Commissioner, P. C. Gregory-Hood
First Secretary (*Commercial*), I. M. Dallas

BRITISH COUNCIL DIRECTOR, Peter Ellwood, 49 Alfred
    House Gardens, PO Box 753, Colombo 3. Library also in
    Kandy.

ECONOMY

The staple products of the island are tea, rubber, copra,
spices and gems. There is increasing emphasis on local
production of food, especially rice, and plans for the large-
scale production of sugar-cane, cotton and citrus fruits.
    The manufacturing sector has grown considerably over
the past few years and produces ceramic ware, vegetable
oils and by-products, paper, tobacco, tanning and leather
goods, plywood, cement, chemicals, beverages, sugar,
flour, salt, textiles and garments, ilmenite, tiles, tyres,
fertilizers, clothing, jewellery and hardware and there is a
petroleum refinery. Foreign investment in manufacturing
is increasing considerably and, together with the tourism

sector (400,000 visitors in 1994), has contributed to an
economic growth rate of 5 per cent of GDP in 1994.

TRADE WITH UK	1993	1994
Imports from UK	£126,243,000	£153,850,000
Exports to UK	142,478,000	185,784,000

COMMUNICATIONS

There are over 15,660 miles of roads in Sri Lanka and a
government-run railway system with 984 miles of lines. A
satellite earth station at Padukka provides telecommunication links world-wide. The principal airport is at Katu-
nayake, 19 miles north of Colombo. Air Lanka operates 69
flights weekly to the Gulf States, the Maldives, western
Europe and throughout the Far East.

SUDAN
Al-Jamhuryat es-Sudan Al-Democratia

Sudan lies in north-east Africa, between 22° and 3°36' N.
latitude, and 21° 49' and 38° 35' E. longitude. To the north
lies Egypt, to the east the Red Sea, Eritrea and Ethiopia, to
the south Kenya, Uganda and Zaire, and to the west the
Central African Republic, Chad, and Libya. The area is
about 967,500 sq. miles (2,505,813 sq. km).
    The White Nile, as the Bahr el Jebel, flows through
Sudan from Nimule to Wadi Halfa. The Blue Nile flows
from Lake Tana on the Ethiopian plateau through Sudan to
join the White Nile at Khartoum. The next confluence of
importance is at Atbara where the main Nile is joined by
the River Atbara. Between Khartoum and Wadi Halfa lie
five of the six cataracts.
    The population is 26,656,000 (UN estimate 1992). Arab
and Nubian peoples populate the north and centre, Nilotic
and Negro peoples the south. Arabic is the official language
and Islam the state religion, although the Nilotics of the
Bahr el Ghazal and Upper Nile valleys are generally
Animists or Christians.

CAPITAL – Khartoum. The combined population of
    Khartoum, Khartoum North and Omdurman (excluding
    refugees and displaced people) is estimated at 3,000,000.
CURRENCY – Sudanese Dinar of 10 pounds.
FLAG – Three horizontal stripes of red, white and black
    with a green triangle next to the hoist.
NATIONAL ANTHEM – Nahnu Djundullah (We are the
    army of God).
NATIONAL DAY – 1 January (Independence Day).

GOVERNMENT

The Anglo-Egyptian Condominium over Sudan was
established in 1899 and ended when the Sudan House of
Representatives, on 19 December 1955, declared Sudan a
fully independent sovereign state. A republic was proclaimed on 1 January 1956, and was recognized by Great
Britain and Egypt. Sudan was under military rule from
1958 to 1964; under the rule of a revolutionary council
headed by Col. Gaafar Mohamed El Nimeri from 1969
until April 1985 when the army command deposed
Nimeri; and experienced a third military coup in June
1989 when the civilian government, in power since 1986,
was overthrown by Brig.-Gen. Omar Hassan Ahmad al-
Bashir. The constitution was suspended and parliament
was replaced by a 15-member ruling junta (Revolutionary
Command Council) who exercised control over a cabinet.
The ruling junta appointed Gen. al-Bashir as head of state

on 16 October 1993 and then dissolved itself, paving the way for presidential and legislative elections in 1995.

The government has developed close relations with Iran and is believed by western states to support international terrorism and have Iranian Revolutionary Guards' bases on its territory. Supported and dominated by the National Islamic Front (NIF), the government has since 1989 turned Sudan into an Islamic state. In August 1993 the USA placed Sudan on a list of countries sponsoring terrorism and suspended all trade apart from humanitarian goods. In 1995 Sudan's relations with its neighbours, notably Egypt, Eritrea and Uganda, deteriorated as they consider that Sudan is arming Islamic and insurgent groups in their states.

SECESSION

Nearly 17 years of insurrection in the southern provinces ended in 1972 with the signing of an agreement recognizing southern regional autonomy within the Sudanese state. However, insurrection broke out again in 1983 and since then there has been civil war in the regions of Eastern and Western Equatoria in the south of the country between government forces and the Christian and Animist majority in the area, organized into the Sudan People's Liberation Army (SPLA). Although the Islamic government has officially stated that it is not attempting to introduce Sharia law in the south, the Sharia affects the two million Christians in northern areas. In 1991–4 the SPLA was split into four factions based on different tribal groups. The two principal factions were SPLA-Torit led by the original SPLA leader John Garang, and SPLA-United led by Riek Machar. The SPLA lost the control that it had exercised over most of the south to government forces because of fighting between the SPLA factions, three of whom were armed by government forces to fight the SPLA-Torit faction. By early 1994 government forces controlled most of the towns and roads in the region and launched the largest offensive since 1983 against the secessionist forces. The SPLA factions resorted to guerrilla tactics and then regrouped and joined forces against the government in November 1994, making some advances. The warfare has left an estimated one million dead, including 300,000 who died in the war-induced famine in 1988 and thousands in a similar situation in 1994. Some three million refugees have fled the fighting, either to the north, to neighbouring states or to the far south near the Ugandan border. The fighting has left large areas of the south desolate and uninhabitable.

HEAD OF STATE

President, Minister of Defence, Lt.-Gen. Omar Hassan Ahmad al-Bashir, *appointed* 16 October 1993
First Vice-President, Maj.-Gen. Zubir Mohammed Saleh
Second Vice-President, George Kengor Arop

CABINET *as at August 1995*

Interior, El Tayyib Ibrahim Mohammed Kheir
Presidential Affairs, Brig. Abd al-Rahim Hussain
Federal Administration, Dr Ali al-Hajj Muhammad
Foreign Affairs, Ali Uthman Taha
Justice and Attorney-General, Abdel-Aziz Shiddo
Culture and Information, Abdel-Basit Sahdarat
Planning and Investment, Mohammed Khair al-Zubeir
Agriculture and Natural Resources, Abdul-Gasim Shammo
Peace and Development, Abdallah Deng Niyal
Local Government and Co-ordination of Provincial Affairs, Natali Yanku Ambu
Irrigation, Yacoub Abu Shura Musa
Energy and Mining, Salah al-Din Karrar
Industry, Badr Eddin Suleiman
Social Planning, Mohammed Osman Khalifa

Housing, Construction and Public Utilities, Osman Abdoul Gadir Abdul Latif
Higher Education and Scientific Research, Dr Ibrahim Ahmed Omer
Tourism and Environment, Mohammed Tahir Eilla
Commerce, Tag al-Sir Mustafa
Education, Kabosho Kuku
Aviation and Survey, Al Tigania Adam Tahir
Transport, Al-Fatih Mohammed
Roads and Communications, Uthman Abd al-Qadir al-Latif
Labour and Administrative Reform, Gen. Dominic Kassiano
Health, Lt.-Col. Galwuk Deng Garang

EMBASSY OF THE REPUBLIC OF THE SUDAN
3 Cleveland Row, London SWIA IDD
Tel 0171-839 8080
Ambassador Extraordinary and Plenipotentiary, new appointment awaited

BRITISH EMBASSY
(PO Box 801), Khartoum
Tel: Khartoum 70760
Ambassador Extraordinary and Plenipotentiary, His Excellency Alan Goulty, apptd 1995

BRITISH COUNCIL DIRECTOR, Don Sloan, 14 Abu Sin Street (PO Box 1253), Khartoum.

ECONOMY

Agriculture provides employment for over half the labour force and contributes over one-third of GDP. It is based on large and medium-sized public sector irrigation projects with small-scale private irrigation schemes providing mostly fruit and vegetables. Mechanized and traditional agriculture is practised in areas of sufficient rainfall. The principal grain crops are *dura* (great millet) and wheat, the staple food of the population. Sesame and groundnuts are other important food crops, which also yield an exportable surplus, and a promising start has been made with castor seed. The principal export crop is cotton, both long-staple cotton and short and medium-staple cotton. Sudan also produces the bulk of the world's supply of gum arabic. Sugar is an increasingly important crop, although Sudan still has to achieve self sufficiency in its production.

Livestock is the mainstay of the nomadic Arab tribes of the desert and the Negro tribes of the swamp and wooded grassland country in the south. Production has, however, been affected by drought, famine and civil war.

The manufacturing sector contributes less than 8 per cent to GDP and provides employment for 4 per cent of the work force. The main manufacturing enterprises are food processing, textiles, shoes, cigarettes and batteries.

Sudan's voting rights at the IMF were suspended in August 1993 after its persistent failure to fulfil its obligations regarding overdue amounts of US$1,700 million.

TRADE

The principal exports are cotton, livestock, gum arabic and other agricultural produce. The chief imports are petroleum goods and other raw materials, machinery and equipment, transport and equipment, medicines and chemicals.

Trade with UK	1993	1994
Imports from UK	£45,399,000	£45,603,000
Exports to UK	8,174,000	7,301,000

COMMUNICATIONS

The railway system, adversely affected by the civil war, has a route length of about 3,200 miles. Nile river services between Khartoum and Juba have been interrupted by the

SUD – SWA **1025**

southern insurrection. Port Sudan is the country's main seaport. Sudan Airways fly services from Khartoum to other parts of the Sudan and to other African states, Europe and the Middle East.

EDUCATION

School education is free for most children but not compulsory, beginning with six years primary education, followed by three years secondary education at general secondary schools, the more academic higher secondary schools or vocational schools. The medium of instruction is Arabic. English is no longer taught in schools since new Arabization legislation came into effect in 1991.

Khartoum University has ten faculties. There is a branch of Cairo University in Khartoum, an Islamic University at Omdurman and universities at Wad Medani and Juba. In addition to the universities there are various technical post-secondary institutes as well as professional and vocational training establishments.

SURINAME
Republiek Suriname

Suriname is situated on the north coast of South America and is bounded by the Atlantic in the north, French Guiana in the east, Brazil in the south and Guyana in the west. It has an area of 63,037 sq. miles (163,265 sq. km), with a population (UN 1992 estimate) of 438,000. The official language is Dutch, the native language Sranang Tongo, and other widely-used languages are Hindustani and Javanese.

CAPITAL – ΨParamaribo, population (1971) 110,000.
CURRENCY – Suriname guilder (gulden) of 100 cents.
FLAG – Horizontal stripes of green, white, red, white, green, with a five-pointed yellow star in the centre.
NATIONAL DAY – 25 November.

GOVERNMENT

Formerly known as Dutch Guiana, Suriname remained part of the Netherlands West Indies until 25 November 1975, when it achieved complete independence from the Netherlands. The civilian government was ousted in 1980 by the military who appointed a predominantly civilian government in 1982. According to the 1987 constitution, a National Assembly of 51 members elects the President.

President Shankar was overthrown in a military coup, instigated by Lt.-Col. Desi Bouterse, in December 1990; Johan Kraag, a supporter of Bouterse, was installed as President. Elections to the National Assembly were held in May 1991. The New Front for Democracy and Development, a coalition comprising opposition groups, won 30 of the 51 seats, but failed to gain the necessary two-thirds majority to appoint the President. In September 1991 a special sitting of a United People's Assembly elected New Front leader Ronald Venetiaan as President and he formed a government which amended the constitution in April 1992 to limit the power of the military. In August 1992 the government and the two largest guerrilla groups signed a peace agreement under which the guerrillas will be integrated into the police force.

HEAD OF STATE
President, Dr Ronald Venetiaan, *elected* 7 September 1991

CABINET *as at August 1995*
Vice-President, Prime Minister, Jules Ajodhia
Labour, Jack Kross

Foreign Affairs, Subhas Mungra
Defence, Siegfried Gilds.
Finance, Humphrey Hildenberg
Economics, Richard Kalloe
Justice and Police, Soeshiel Girjasing
Natural Resources, Franco Demon
Education, Gerard Hiwat
Public Works, Radj Koemar Randjietsingh
Planning and Development, Edwin Sedoc
Regional Affairs, Romeo van Russel
Agriculture and Fisheries, Johan Sisal
Transport, Communications and Tourism, John Defares
Public Health, Mohamed Khudabux
Interior, Saban Sabiran
Social Affairs, W. Soemita

EMBASSY OF THE REPUBLIC OF SURINAME
2 Alexander Gogelweg, The Hague, The Netherlands
Tel: The Hague 3650844
Ambassador Extraordinary and Plenipotentiary, His Excellency Evert Guillaume Azimullah, apptd 1994

BRITISH AMBASSADOR, His Excellency David Johnson, CVO, resident at Georgetown, Guyana
BRITISH CONSULATE, c/o VSH United Buildings, Van't Hogerhuystraat, PO Box 1300, Paramaribo. *Honorary Consul,* J. J. Healy, MBE

ECONOMY

Suriname has large timber resources. Rice and sugar-cane are the main crops. Bauxite is mined, and is the principal export. Principal trading partners are the Netherlands, USA and Norway.

TRADE WITH UK	1993	1994
Imports from UK	£6,289,000	£9,163,000
Exports to UK	14,232,000	17,447,000

SWAZILAND
Umbuso we Swatini

Swaziland is a small, land-locked country surrounded by South Africa on its northern, western and southern borders and by Mozambique to the east. The broken mountainous Highveld along the western border, with an average altitude of 4,000 ft, is densely forested, mainly with conifers and eucalyptus; the Middleveld, averaging about 2,000 ft, is a mixed farming area including cotton and pineapples; and the Lowveld in the east was mainly scrubland until the introduction of large sugar-cane plantations. Four rivers, the Komati, Usutu, Mbuluzi and Ngwavuma, flow from west to east. The total area of Swaziland is 6,704 sq. miles (17,363 sq. km), and the population (UN estimate 1992) is 792,000.

CAPITAL – Mbabane (population 1986, 38,290). Other main townships are Manzini (estimated population, 30,000), Big Bend, Mhlambanyati, Mhlume, Nhlangano, Pigg's Peak and Simunye.
CURRENCY – Lilangeni (E) of 100 cents. South African currency is also in circulation. Swaziland is a member of the Common Monetary Area and its unit of currency *Emalangeni* (singular *Lilangeni*) has a par value with the South African rand.
FLAG – Blue with a wide crimson horizontal band bordered in yellow across the centre, bearing a shield and two spears horizontally.
NATIONAL ANTHEM – Ingoma Yesive.
NATIONAL DAY – 6 September (Independence Day).

GOVERNMENT

The Kingdom of Swaziland came into being on 25 April 1967 under a self-government constitution and became an independent kingdom, headed by HM Sobhuza II, in membership of the Commonwealth on 6 September 1968.

A new government system was introduced in 1978 and amended in 1992–3 under which the King, assisted by his appointed Cabinet, holds considerable executive, legislative and judicial authority. In addition, there is a bicameral legislative body comprising a Senate and a House of Assembly. Each of the 55 traditional *Tinkhundla* (chieftaincies) are directly elected and become members of the House of Assembly. The King appoints ten members to the House of Assembly, making 65 in all, who then elect ten members of their own number to the Senate. To these are added 20 senators appointed by the King, bringing the full membership of the Senate to 30. All political parties are banned under the 1978 constitution.

HEAD OF STATE
King of Swaziland, HM King Mswati III, *inaugurated* 25 April 1986

CABINET *as at August 1995*
Prime Minister, Rt. Hon. Prince Mbilini
Deputy Prime Minister, Hon. Dr Sishayi Nxumalo
Foreign Affairs, Hon. Solomon Dlamini
Justice, Hon. Chief Maweni Simelane
Home Affairs, Hon. Prince Sobandla
Finance, Hon. Dr Derrick von Wissel
Education, Hon. Khoza Arthur
Works and Construction, Hon. Prince Mahlalengangeni
Health, Hon. Muntu Mswane
Agriculture and Co-operatives, Hon. Chief Dambuza Lukhele
Commerce and Industry, Hon. Majahenkaba Dlamini
Labour and Public Service, Hon. Albert Shabangu
Natural Resources and Energy, Hon. Revd Absalom Dlamini
Housing and Urban Development, Hon. John Carmichael
Economic Planning and Development, Hon. Themba Masuku
Transport and Communications, Hon. Ephraem Magagula
Broadcasting, Information and Tourism, Hon. Prince Khuzulwandle

KINGDOM OF SWAZILAND HIGH COMMISSION
20 Buckingham Gate, London SW1E 6LB
Tel 0171-630 6611
High Commissioner, His Excellency Revd Percy S. Mngomezulu, apptd 1994

BRITISH HIGH COMMISSION
Allister Miller Street, Mbabane
Tel: Mbabane 42581
High Commissioner, His Excellency Richard Gozney, apptd 1993

BRITISH COUNCIL DIRECTOR, Dr Patrick Brazier (*Cultural Attaché*)

ECONOMY

In the 1989–90 budget, total expenditure, including debt repayment, was projected at E447 million. A surplus of E12.5 million was predicted due to increase in revenue. Manufacturing was announced to have replaced agriculture as the dominant sector in 1988.

TRADE WITH UK	1993	1994
Imports from UK	£2,887,000	£3,287,000
Exports to UK	42,187,000	42,034,000

COMMUNICATIONS

Swaziland's railway is about 150 miles long and connects with the Mozambique port of Maputo and the South African railway network to Richards Bay. A rail line to the north-west border provides a link to Komatipoort. Most passenger and goods traffic is carried by privately-owned motor transport services. There are scheduled air services by Royal Swazi National Airways to southern and eastern Africa. International telecommunications and television services are provided through a satellite earth station, and there is also a national telephone network.

SWEDEN
Konungariket Sverige

Sweden occupies the eastern area of the Scandinavian peninsula in north-west Europe with a total area of 173,732 sq. miles (449,964 sq. km), and population of 8,745,109 (1993 census). The state religion is Lutheran Protestant, to which over 95 per cent officially adhere.

CAPITAL – ΨStockholm. Population (1993): City 692,954; Greater Stockholm, 1,532,803; ΨGothenburg (Göteborg) (437,313); ΨMalmö (237,438); Uppsala (178,011).
CURRENCY – Swedish krona of 100 öre.
FLAG – Yellow cross on a blue ground.
NATIONAL ANTHEM – Du Gamla, Du Fria (Thou ancient, thou freeborn).
NATIONAL DAY – 6 June (Day of the Swedish Flag).

GOVERNMENT

Sweden is a constitutional monarchy, with the monarch retaining purely ceremonial functions as head of state. Under the Act of Succession 1810 (with amendments) the throne is hereditary in the House of Bernadotte. The constitution is based upon the Instrument of Government 1974, which amended the 1810 Act and removed from the monarch the roles of appointing the Prime Minister and signing parliamentary bills into law. A 1979 amendment vested the succession in the monarch's eldest child irrespective of sex.

Executive power is vested in the Prime Minister and Council of Ministers. There is a unicameral legislature (*Riksdag*) of 349 members elected by universal suffrage on a proportional representation basis (with a 4 per cent threshold for representation) for four years. The Council of Ministers (*Statsråd*) is responsible to the *Riksdag*. In the general election held on 18 September 1994 the four-party centre-right coalition of the Moderate, Liberal, Centre and Christian Democratic Parties was defeated by the Social Democrats, who formed a minority government. (The Social Democratic Party has been in government, either alone or in coalition, continuously since 1932, apart from 1936, 1976–82 and 1991–4.) The state of the parties in the legislature in August 1995 was: Social Democrats 161; Moderates 80; Centre 27; Liberals 26; Left Party 22; Greens 18; Christian Democrats 15.

Sweden applied for European Community membership in July 1991 and negotiations on entry were successfully concluded on 1 March 1994. The Accession Treaty to the European Union was ratified in a national referendum on 13 November 1994 by 52.3 per cent to 46.8 per cent and by a parliamentary vote on 15 December, enabling Sweden to accede to the EU on 1 January 1995.

Sweden is divided into 24 counties (*län*) and 288 municipalities (*kommun*).

HEAD OF STATE

HM The King of Sweden, Carl XVI Gustaf, KG, *born* 30 April 1946, *succeeded* 15 September 1973, *married* 19 June 1976 Fräulein Silvia Renate Sommerlath and has *issue*, Crown Princess Victoria (*see* below); Prince Carl Philip Edmund Bertil, Duke of Värmland, *born* 13 May 1979; Princess Madeleine Thérèse Amelie Josephine, Duchess of Hälsingland and Gästrikland, *born* 10 June 1982
Heir, HRH Crown Princess Victoria Ingrid Alice Désirée, Duchess of Västergötland, *born* 14 July 1977

COUNCIL OF MINISTERS *as at August 1995*

Prime Minister, Ingvar Carlsson
Deputy Prime Minister, Equality Issues, Mona Sahlin
Co-ordination, Jan Nygren
Justice, Laila Freivalds
Foreign Affairs, Lena Hjelm-Wallén
Defence, Thage Petersson
Transport and Communications, Ines Uusmann
Finance, Göran Persson
Education, Carl Tham
Agriculture, Margareta Winberg
Labour, Anders Sundström
Industry and Commerce, Sten Heckscher
Public Administration, Marita Ulvskog
Environment and Physical Planning, Anna Lindh
Culture, Margot Wallström
International Development Co-operation, Pierre Schori
European Union Affairs and Foreign Trade, Mats Hellström
Health and Social Affairs, Ingela Thalén
Schools and Adult Education, Ylva Johansson
Refugee and Immigration Policy, Leif Blomberg
Housing and Energy Policy, Jörgen Andersson

SWEDISH EMBASSY
11 Montagu Place, London WIH 2AL
Tel 0171-917 6400
Ambassador Extraordinary and Plenipotentiary, His Excellency Lars-Åke Nilsson, apptd 1995
Minister (Economic), Mårten Grunditz
Defence and Naval Attaché, Cdr. Count Gustaf Taube
Consul-General, G. Naessén
Trade Commissioner, A. Lundwall

BRITISH EMBASSY
Skarpögatan 6–8, S115 93 Stockholm
Tel: Stockholm 671 9000
Ambassador Extraordinary and Plenipotentiary, His Excellency Robert Bone, apptd 1995
Counsellor (Political) and Consul-General, Dr V. Caton
Counsellor (Economic and Commercial), A. R. Murray
Defence and Air Attaché, Wg Cdr. P. McCullum

There are British Consular Offices at Stockholm and Gothenburg, and Honorary Consulates at Luleå, Gothenburg, Malmö and Sundsvall.

BRITISH COUNCIL REPRESENTATIVE , Ann Hellström, Strandagen 57A, S-111 523 Stockholm
BRITISH-SWEDISH CHAMBER OF COMMERCE, Grevgatan 34, 11453 Stockholm.

ECONOMY

Following the election of a centre-right government in 1991 there was drastic change in the Swedish socio-economic system. Free market economic policies of privatization, deregulation, the ending of state subsidies, trade union legislation, floating the exchange rate, central bank independence, tax reform, and welfare and spending cuts have been introduced. Austerity packages were introduced in November 1992 and April 1993 to overcome budget deficits, improve competitiveness and stabilize the currency. The restructuring of industry, together with the world recession, caused unemployment to rise to 9.5 per cent (together with a further 4 per cent on workfare schemes) in 1994, before falling to 8.3 per cent in 1995; manufacturing output fell 15 per cent between 1989 and 1992, and GDP fell by 5 per cent from 1990 to 1993. The 1995 budget deficit remained high at 11.2 per cent of GDP, with the national debt reaching 90 per cent of GDP in the same year. Further budget cuts and reductions in the public sector, local government, and the welfare state, together with tax increases, were announced in the new Social Democratic government's first budget in January 1995. The aim is to reduce the unsustainable levels of public spending and reduce the budget deficit to 5 per cent of GDP by 1998.

Industrial prosperity is based on natural resources: forests, mineral deposits and water power. The forests cover about half the total land surface and sustain timber, finished wood products, pulp and paper milling industries. The mineral resources include iron ore, lead, zinc, sulphur, granite, marble, precious and heavy metals (the latter not exploited) and extensive deposits of low grade uranium ore. Industries based on mining are important but it is the general engineering industry that provides the basis of Sweden's exports, especially specialized machinery and systems, motor vehicles, aircraft, electrical and electronic equipment, pharmaceuticals, plastics and chemical industries. The relative importance of agriculture has declined and in 1993 only 3.5 per cent of the labour force was engaged in farming, compared to 26 per cent in mining, manufacturing and construction, 41 per cent in services and 29.5 per cent in government.

Apart from water power (hydroelectricity supplies 15 per cent of energy needs) Sweden has no significant indigenous resources of conventional hydrocarbon fuels and relies for 50 per cent of its energy needs upon imported oil and coal. Around half of Sweden's electricity is generated by nuclear power but as a result of a referendum in 1980 the nuclear programme is to be discontinued by 2010. However, this decision is now being debated once more and could be reversed. Small supplies of natural gas are imported from Denmark into southern Sweden, with the pipeline being extended to Gothenburg.

FINANCE	1993	1994
Revenue	Kronor 878,600m	Kronor 895,700m
Expenditure	1,071,600m	1,063,900m

TRADE
About 45 per cent of industrial output is exported, mainly in the form of cars, trucks, machinery, electrical and communications equipment. Sweden conducts 70 per cent of its trade with EFTA and the rest of the EU.

	1992	1993
Imports	Kronor 289,923m	Kronor 420,500m
Exports	326,008m	473,100m

Trade with UK	1993	1994
Imports from UK	£2,892,123,000	£3,348,029,000
Exports to UK	3,622,621,000	4,159,883,000

COMMUNICATIONS

The total length of railroads is 11,745 km. The road network is over 400,000 km in length. The mercantile marine amounted in 1992 to 3,037,000 gross tonnage. Regular domestic air traffic is maintained by the

Scandinavian Airlines System and by Linjeflyg. Regular European and inter-continental air traffic is maintained by the Scandinavian Airlines System.

DEFENCE

Sweden has a policy of non-alignment in peace and neutrality in war, and it maintains a 'total defence' which includes peacetime organizations for civil, economic and psychological defence. All men aged 18–47 are eligible for conscription, with the initial term being seven to 15 months for the Army and Navy and eight to 12 months for the Air Force. Men are obliged to serve in the reserves until age 47 with a commitment to five periods of refresher training.

The armed forces have a total active strength of 64,000 (36,600 conscripts), with reserves of 729,000 (Army 586,000; Navy 66,000; Air Force 77,000). The Army has an active strength of 43,500 (27,000 conscripts), and on mobilization a strength of 630,000. Equipment includes 630 main battle tanks, 210 light tanks, 505 armoured infantry fighting vehicles, 715 artillery pieces and 20 combat helicopters. The Navy has 12 submarines, 41 patrol and coastal vessels, 29 mine warfare craft, six coast artillery brigades, 10 combat helicopters and a strength of 9,000 (4,100 conscripts). The Air Force has 481 combat aircraft and a strength of 11,500 (5,500 conscripts). Sweden deploys some 495 troops in Lebanon, 121 in Macedonia and 1,150 in Bosnia with UN forces.

CULTURE

Swedish belongs, with Danish and Norwegian, to the North Germanic language group. Swedish literature dates back to King Magnus Eriksson, who codified the old Swedish provincial laws in 1350. With his translation of the Bible, Olaus Petri (1493–1552) formed the basis for the modern Swedish language. Literature flourished during the reign of Gustavus III, who founded the Swedish Academy in 1786. Notable Swedish writers include Almquist (1795–1866), Strindberg (1849–1912) and Lagerlöf (1858–1940), Nobel Prizewinner in 1909. Contemporary authors include Lagerquist (1891–1974), Nobel Laureate in 1951, Martinson (1904–78) and Johnson (1900–76), Nobel Laureates jointly in 1974. The Swedish scientist Alfred Nobel (1833–96) founded the Nobel Prizes for literature, science and peace.

EDUCATION

The state system provides nine years' free and compulsory schooling from the age of seven to 16 in the comprehensive elementary schools. Over 90 per cent continue into further education of two to four years' duration in the upper secondary schools and a unified higher education system administered in six regional areas containing one of the universities: Uppsala (founded 1477); Lund (1668); Stockholm (1878); Gothenburg (1887); Umeå (1963) and Linköping (1967). At present there are 33 institutions of higher education including three technical universities in Stockholm, Gothenburg and Luleå, and the Karolinska Institute in Stockholm, which specializes in medicine and dentistry.

SWITZERLAND
Schweizerische Eidgenossenschaft – Confédération Suisse – Confederazione Svizzera

Switzerland, the Helvetia of the Romans, lies in central Europe, situated between 45° 50' and 47° 48' N. latitude and 5° 58' and 10° 30' E. longitude. It comprises a total area

of 15,943 sq. miles (41,293 sq. km), with a population (1992 estimate) of 6,907,959. Of the total population in 1991, 46.1 per cent was Roman Catholic, 40 per cent Protestant, 5 per cent other religions and 8.9 per cent without religion. The official languages are German (the first language of 63.7 per cent), French (19.2 per cent), Italian (7.6 per cent) and Romansch (0.6 per cent).

Switzerland is the most mountainous country in Europe. The Alps, from 5,000 to 15,217 ft in height, occupy its southern and eastern frontiers and the chief part of its interior; the Jura mountains rise in the north-west. The Alps occupy 61 per cent, and the Jura mountains 12 per cent of the country. The highest peak, Mont Blanc, Pennine Alps (15,782 ft) is partly in France and Italy; Monte Rosa (15,217 ft) and Matterhorn (14,780 ft) are partly in Switzerland and partly in Italy. The highest wholly Swiss peaks are Dufourspitze (15,203 ft), Finsteraarhorn (14,026), Aletschhorn (13,711), Jungfrau (13,671), Mönch (13,456), Eiger (13,040), Schreckhorn (13,385), and Wetterhorn (12,150) in the Bernese Alps, and Dom (14,918), Weisshorn (14,803) and Breithorn (13,685). The Swiss lakes include Lakes Maggiore, Zürich, Lucerne, Neuchâtel, Geneva, Constance, Thun, Zug, Lugano, Brienz and the Walensee. There are also many artificial lakes.

CAPITAL – Berne, population (1991 census) 135,600 (city). Other large towns are (1991) Zürich (345,200), Basle (173,800), Geneva (169,600), Lausanne (124,800), Winterthur (86,800), St Gallen (74,500), Lucerne (60,500).
CURRENCY – Swiss franc of 100 centimes or rappen.
FLAG – Square and red, bearing a couped white cross.
NATIONAL ANTHEM – Trittst im Morgenrot Daher (Radiant in the morning sky).
NATIONAL DAY – 1 August.

GOVERNMENT

Switzerland is a federal republic. There are 23 cantons, three of which are subdivided, making 26 in all. Each canton has its own government.

The federal government consists of the Federal Assembly of two chambers, a National Council (*Nationalrat*) of 200 members, and a States Council (*Ständerat*) of 46 members (two from each canton and one from each demicanton). Members of the National Council are elected for four years, elections taking place in October. The executive power is in the hands of a Federal Council (*Bundesrat*) of seven members, elected for four years by the Federal Assembly and presided over by the President of the Confederation. Each year the Federal Assembly elects from the Federal Council the President and the Vice-

President. Not more than one of the same canton may be elected a member of the Federal Council; however, there is a tradition that Italian and French-speaking areas should between them be represented on the Federal Council by at least two members.

The Federal Council voted in 1992 to apply for European Community membership. The European Economic Area (EEA) Treaty between the EC and EFTA, which extends the provisions of the EC single internal market to EFTA states, was defeated in a national referendum on 6 December 1992. Switzerland is consequently the only EFTA state outside the EEA.

FEDERAL COUNCIL

President of the Swiss Confederation (1995) *and Head of Defence*, Kaspar Villiger

Vice-President (1995) *and Public Economy*, Jean-Pascal Delamuraz

Transport, Communications and Energy, Adolf Ogi

Foreign Affairs, Flavio Cotti

Justice and Police, Arnold Koller

Home Affairs, Ruth Dreifuss

Finance, Otto Stich

EMBASSY OF SWITZERLAND
16–18 Montagu Place, London WIH 2BQ
Tel 0171-723 0701

Ambassador Extraordinary and Plenipotentiary, His Excellency François Nordmann, apptd 1994

Minister, R. Reich

Defence Attaché, Col. Walter Ritzmann

Consul-General, E. Jaun

Counsellor, J. de Watteville (*Economic and Financial*)

There is a Swiss Consulate-General in Manchester.

BRITISH EMBASSY
Thunstrasse 50, 3005 Berne
Tel: Berne 3525021/6

Ambassador Extraordinary and Plenipotentiary, His Excellency David Beattie, CMG, apptd 1992

Counsellor and Deputy Head of Mission, I. Knight-Smith

Consul-General and Director of British Export Promotion, D. M. Bell (*Zurich*)

Consul-General, P. J. Priestley (*Geneva*)

Defence Attaché, Lt.-Col. The Lord Crofton

BRITISH COUNCIL DIRECTOR , Caroline Morrissey, Thunstrasse 50, PO Box 265, Berne 15

BRITISH CONSULAR OFFICES – There is a Consular section at the Embassy in Berne; Consulates-General at Zürich and Geneva and Consular offices at Lugano, Valais and Montreux. The Directorate of British Export Promotion in Switzerland is in the Consulate-General Office, Dufourstrasse 56, 8008 Zürich.

BRITISH-SWISS CHAMBER OF COMMERCE, Freiestrasse 155, 8032 Zürich

SWISS-BRITISH SOCIETIES: Berne, *President*, Dr H. Beriger; Zürich, *President*, J.-P. Müller; Basle, *President*, Dr C. Grey

DEFENCE

All Swiss males must undertake military service in the Army or the Air Corps, which is part of the Army. The total active armed forces number some 1,800 regulars with 28,000 each year for recruit training. Conscription takes the form of 17 weeks recruit training at age 20 and 30 weeks of regular reservist refresher training up to age 42, with some 390,000 reservists attending training each year. The Army has a strength on mobilization of 565,000 with 810 main

battle tanks, 1,250 armoured personnel carriers and armoured infantry fighting vehicles, and 1,095 artillery pieces. The Air Corps has a strength on mobilization of 60,000 with 216 combat aircraft. In addition, there are the paramilitary civil defence forces, with 300,000 fully-trained personnel.

ECONOMY

Agriculture is followed chiefly in the valleys and the central plateau, where cereals, flax, hemp, and tobacco are produced, and fruits and vegetables as well as grapes are grown. Dairying and stock-raising are the principal industries, about 3,000,000 acres being under grass for hay and 2,000,000 acres pasturage. The forests cover about 28 per cent of the whole surface.

The chief manufacturing industries comprise engineering and electrical engineering, metal-working, chemicals and pharmaceuticals, textiles, watchmaking, woodworking, foodstuffs, printing and publishing, and footwear. Banking, insurance and tourism are major industries.

Some 5.9 per cent of the work-force is employed in agriculture, 34.7 per cent in industry and 59.4 per cent in services.

FINANCE	1993
Revenue	SFr35,000m
Expenditure	39,700m

TRADE

The principal imports are machinery, electrical and electronic equipment, textiles, motor vehicles, non-ferrous metals, chemical elements, clothing, food, medicinal and pharmaceutical products. The principal exports are machinery, chemical elements, non-ferrous metals, watches, electrical and electronic equipment, textiles, dyeing, tanning and colouring equipment.

	1991	1992
Total imports	SFr95,032m	SFr96,271m
Total exports	87,946m	95,306m
†Trade with UK	1993	1994
Imports from UK	£2,273,423,000	£2,455,847,000
Exports to UK	4,721,923,000	4,817,153,000
†Including Liechtenstein		

COMMUNICATIONS

There were in 1992, 5,029 km of railway tracks (Swiss Federal Railways, 2,990 km; privately owned railways 2,039 km). At the end of 1992 the total length of motorways was 1,515 km. The merchant marine consisted at June 1990 of 20 vessels with a total gross tonnage of 287,487 tonnes. In 1989, goods handled at Basle Rhine ports amounted to 8,845,162 tonnes. In 1990, 163 lake and river vessels (excluding the Rhine) transported 12 million passengers and 500 tonnes of freight. Swiss airlines have a network covering 348,762 km (1990) and in 1990 carried 17,100,000 passengers. Swissair, the national airline, flies to and from the airports at Zürich, Geneva and Basle.

The Swiss electorate voted in a February 1994 referendum for a ban on foreign lorries using alpine roads, which will be phased in over ten years. From 2005 onwards foreign lorries will have to use two new north-south road-rail tunnels.

EDUCATION

Education is controlled by cantonal and communal authorities. Primary education is free and compulsory. School age varies, generally seven to 14, with secondary education from age 12 to 15. Special schools make a feature of commercial and technical instruction. Universities are Basle (founded 1460), Berne (1834), Fribourg (1889), Geneva (1873), Lausanne (1890), Zürich (1833), and Neuchâtel (1909), the technical universities of Lausanne and Zürich and the economics university of St Gall.

CULTURE

There are four national languages: French, German, Italian and Romansch. German is the dominating language in 19 of the 26 cantons; French in Fribourg, Jura, Geneva, Neuchâtel, Valais and Vaud; Italian in Ticino; and Romansch in parts of the Grisons.

Modern authors who have achieved international fame include Karl Spitteler (1845–1924) and Hermann Hesse (1877–1962), awarded the Nobel Prize for Literature in 1919 and 1946 respectively.

In 1992 there were 99 daily newspapers published (78 German, 17 French, four Italian).

SYRIA
Al-Jamhouriya Al-Arabia as-Souriya

Syria is in the Levant, bounded by the Mediterranean and Lebanon on the west, Israel and Jordan on the south-west, Iraq on the east and Turkey on the north. It has an estimated area of 71,498 sq. miles (185,180 sq. km). The Orontes flows northwards from the Lebanon range across the northern boundary to Antakya (Antioch, Turkey). The Euphrates crosses the northern boundary near Jerablus and flows through north-eastern Syria to the boundary of Iraq.

The population (UN estimate 1992) is 12,958,000, most of whom are Muslim. Arabic is the principal language, but Kurdish, Turkish and Armenian are spoken among significant minorities and a few villages still speak Aramaic, the language spoken by Christ and the Apostles. English has taken over from French as the main foreign language.

The region is rich in historical remains. Damascus (Dimishq ash-Sham) is said to be the oldest continuously inhabited city in the world (although Aleppo disputes this claim), having existed as a city for over 4,000 years. The city contains the Omayed Mosque, the Tomb of Saladin, and the 'street which is called Straight' (Acts 9:11), while to the north-east is the Roman outpost of Dmeir and further east is Palmyra. On the Mediterranean coast at Amrit are ruins of the Phoenician town of Marath, and also ruins of Crusaders' fortresses at Markab, Sahyoun, and Krak des Chevaliers. At Tartous the cathedral of Our Lady of Syria, built by the Knights Templars in the 12th and 13th centuries, has been restored as a museum. One of the oldest alphabets in the world has been discovered at Ugarit (Ras Shamra), a Phoenician village near the port of Latakia. Hittite cities dating from 2000 to 1500 BC, have been explored on the west bank of the Euphrates at Jerablus and Kadesh.

CAPITAL – Damascus, population (1992 estimate) 1,451,000. Other important towns are Aleppo, Homs and Hama, and the principal port is ΨLatakia.

CURRENCY – Syrian pound (S£) of 100 piastres.

FLAG – Red over white over black horizontal bands, with two green stars on central white band.

NATIONAL DAY – 17 April.

GOVERNMENT

Once part of the Ottoman Empire, following the First World War Syria came under French mandate. Syria became an independent republic during the Second World War; the first independently elected Parliament met in August 1943, but foreign troops were in part occupation until April 1946. Syria remained an independent republic until 1958, when it became part, with Egypt, of the United Arab Republic. It seceded from the United Arab Republic in September 1961.

A new constitution was promulgated in 1973. This declared that Syria is a democratic, popular socialist state, and that the Arab Socialist Renaissance (Ba'ath) Party, which has been the ruling party since 1963, is the leading party in the state and society. Elections to the 250-seat People's Council in August 1994 resulted in a large majority for the National Progressive Front which won 167 seats and is dominated by the Ba'ath Party, its allies being the Arab Socialist Union, Socialist Unionist Movement, Arab Socialist Party and Syrian Communist Party. Independents won 83 seats.

HEAD OF STATE
President, Lt.-Gen. Hafez el Assad, *assumed office* 14 March 1971, *re-elected*, 1978, 1985, 3 December 1991
Vice-Presidents, Abdul Halim Khaddam, Rifaat Al Assad, Zuhair Mashariqa

MINISTERS *as at August 1995*
Prime Minister, Mahmoud Al Zubi
Deputy PM and Minister for Defence, Gen. Mustafa Tlass
Deputy PM for Public Services, Rashid Akhtarini
Deputy PM for Economic Affairs, Dr Salim Yassin
Education, Ghassan Halabi
Higher Education, Salha Sankar
Interior, Mohammad Harbah
Transport, Mufeed Abdul-Karim
Information, Mohammad Salman
Local Administration, Yahya Abu Asali
Supply and Internal Trade, Nadim Akkash
Economy and Foreign Trade, Mohammad al-Imadi
Culture, Najah al-Attar
Foreign Affairs, Farooq al-Shara
Tourism, Amin Abul-Shamat
Health, Iyad al-Shatti
Waqfs (Religious Endowments), Abdel-Majid Tarabulsi
Irrigation, Abd ar-Rahman Madani
Electricity, Munib Daher
Oil and Mineral Resources, Nadir Nabulsi
Construction, Majid Ezzou Ruhaybani
Housing and Utilities, Hosam al-Safadi
Agriculture and Agrarian Reform, As'ad Mustafa
Finance, Khaled al-Mahayni
Industry, Ahmad Nizan al-Din
Communications, Redwan Martini
Justice, Hussein Hassun
Presidential Affairs, Wahib Fadil
Labour and Social Affairs, Ali Khalil

EMBASSY OF THE SYRIAN ARAB REPUBLIC
8 Belgrave Square, London SWIX 8PH
Tel 0171-245 9012
Ambassador Extraordinary and Plenipotentiary, His Excellency Mohammed Khodor, apptd 1991

BRITISH EMBASSY
Quartier Malki, 11 rue Mohammad Kurd Ali, Imm. Kotob, Damascus (PO Box 37)
Tel: Damascus 3712561
Ambassador Extraordinary and Plenipotentiary, His Excellency Adrian John Sindall, CMG, apptd 1994
There is also a consulate in Aleppo.

BRITISH COUNCIL DIRECTOR, Dr Peter Clark, OBE, Ground Floor, Tasheen Tabaa' Building, Abd Almalek Bin Marwan Street, Malki, PO Box 33105, Damascus.

DEFENCE

The total active armed forces have a strength of 408,000. There is a conscription period of 30 months, with a reserve commitment to age 45; reserves number 400,000 personnel. The Army has a strength of 300,000 (200,000 conscripts), with 4,500 main battle tanks, 1,000 reconnaissance vehicles, 3,800 armoured personnel carriers and infantry fighting vehicles and 2,560 artillery pieces. The Navy has a strength of 8,000 personnel, with three submarines, two frigates, 29 patrol and coastal combatants and 29 armed helicopters. The Air Force (including the Air Defence Command) has a strength of some 100,000 combat aircraft and 100 armed helicopters of Soviet manufacture, together with 22 Air Defence brigades with surface-to-air missiles. Syria maintains a force of some 30,000 men in Lebanon; 1,035 UN troops are deployed on the Golan Heights.

ECONOMY

Agriculture is the principal source of production; wheat and barley are the main cereal crops, but the cotton crop is the highest in value. Tobacco is grown in the maritime plain in Sahel, the Sahyoun and the Djebleh district of Latakia. Large areas are coming under cultivation in the north-east of the country as a result of irrigation from the Thawra dam. There are an increasing number of light assembly plants as Syria's industrialization programme develops. Skins and hides, leather goods, wool and silk, textiles, cement, vegetable oil, glass, soap, sugar, plastics and copper and brass utensils are produced. Oil has been found at Karachuk and other parts in the north-eastern corner of the country and production of high quality reserves is proceeding in the region of Deir ez Zor. Syria produces nearly 400,000 barrels per day at present. A pipeline has been built to the Mediterranean port of Banias, via Homs. Two oil refineries are in production at Homs and Banias. Syria also has gas reserves, deposits of phosphate and rock salt, and produces asphalt.

TRADE

The principal imports are foodstuffs (fruit, vegetables, cereals, meat and dairy products, tea, coffee and sugar), mineral and petroleum products, yarn and textiles, iron and steel manufactures, machinery, chemicals, pharmaceuticals, fertilizers and timber. Exports include raw cotton, oil, cereals, fruit, phosphates, cement, livestock and dairy products, other foodstuffs, textiles and raw wool.

Trade with UK	1993	1994
Imports from UK	£74,551,000	£101,988,000
Exports to UK	105,311,000	97,990,000

COMMUNICATIONS

Although railway lines run from Damascus to both Beirut and Amman, train services go only to Amman as much of the Lebanese line has been dismantled. A track has been opened connecting Homs with Damascus. A track links Homs, Hamah, Aleppo, Deir ez Zor and Qamishliye to the Iraq frontier. Branch lines connect the ports of Tartous and Latakia to the system and another line runs from Aleppo down the Euphrates valley to Deir ez Zor and thence north to Qamishliye, with a branch going to the Euphrates dam. All the principal towns in the country are connected by roads which vary from modern dual carriageways to narrow country lanes. An internal air service operates between all major towns. The main international airport is at Damascus and there are also flights from Aleppo.

There are three daily newspapers and several periodicals in Arabic published in Damascus, and also a daily newspaper in English.

EDUCATION

Education is under state control and although a few of the schools are privately owned, they all follow a common syllabus. Elementary education is free at state schools and is compulsory from the age of seven. Secondary education is not compulsory and is free only at the state schools. Because of the shortage of places, entry to the state schools is competitive. There are universitites at Damascus, Aleppo, Tishrin, Latakia and the Ba'ath University, Homs. Approximately 10 per cent of all students receive scholarships, and the rest pay fees.

TAIWAN (REPUBLIC OF CHINA)
Chung-hua Min-kuo

An island of some 13,800 sq. miles (35,742 sq. km) in the China Sea, Taiwan, formerly Formosa, lies 90 miles east of the Chinese mainland in 21° 45′ to 25° 56′ N. latitude. The eastern part of the main island is mountainous and forested. Mt Morrison (Yu Shan) (13,035 ft) and Mt Sylvia (Tz'ukaoshan) (12,972 ft) are the highest peaks. The western plains are watered by many rivers.

Territories include the Pescadores Islands (50 sq. miles), some 35 miles west of Taiwan, as well as Quemoy (68 sq. miles) and Matsu (11 sq. miles) which are only a few miles from the mainland.

The population (1993) is 20,894,522, almost entirely Chinese. About two million mainlanders came to the island with Chiang Kai-shek in 1947–9. Mandarin Chinese has been the official language since 1949. Now Taiwanese, spoken by 85 per cent of the population, is growing in importance.

CAPITAL – Taipei, population (1990) 2,719,659. Other towns are ΨKaohsiung (1,386,723); Tainan (667,622); Taichung (730,376); and ΨKeelung (348,672).
CURRENCY – New Taiwan dollar (NT$) of 100 cents.
FLAG – Red, with blue quarter at top next staff, bearing a 12-point white sun.
NATIONAL DAY – 10 October.

GOVERNMENT

Settled for centuries by the Chinese, the island was ceded by China to Japan in 1895 and remained part of the Japanese empire until Japan's defeat in 1945. Nationalist Kuomintang leader Gen. Chiang Kai-shek withdrew to Taiwan in 1949, towards the end of the war against Communist regime in mainland China, after which the territory continued under his presidency until his death in 1975. He was succeeded as President by his son Gen. Chiang Ching-kuo who ruled until his death in 1988, when Vice-President Lee Teng-hui was appointed President. Taiwan (Nationalist China) held China's seat on the UN Security Council until 25 October 1971 when it was replaced by the People's Republic of China. Martial law was lifted in 1987 after 38 years.

In 1991, President Lee announced that the 'period of Communist rebellion' on the Chinese mainland was over, recognizing *de facto* the People's Republic of China. The announcement also ended emergency measures which had frozen political life on Taiwan since 1949. In 1991–2 power shifted away from mainlanders to native Taiwanese with the forcible retirement of the 'Senior Parliamentarians' who had retained their seats since being elected on the mainland in 1948. The new parliament, the Legislative Yuan, gained control of the budget, of law-making and of the appointment of the Prime Minister. A general election to the Legislative Yuan in December 1992 was won by the Nationalist Kuomintang (KMT) with 96 of the 161 seats; the opposition Democratic Progressive Party won 50 seats, and independents and minor parties the remaining 15 seats. During 1993–4 the KMT was weakened by the defection of a number of senior figures who established the China New Party, which largely represents mainlanders and their descendants who wish to retain the claim on the mainland.

Constitutional reforms passed by the Legislative Yuan in July 1994 provide for the President and Vice-President to be directly elected for four-year terms (previously the President was elected by parliament). The first direct elections are to be held in March 1996.

HEAD OF STATE
President, Lee Teng-hui, *appointed* 13 January 1988, *elected by parliament* 21 March 1990
Vice-President, Li Yuan-zu

EXECUTIVE YUAN *as at August 1995*
Prime Minister, Lien Chan
Deputy PM, Hsu Li-teh
Secretary-General, Shih Chi-yang
Interior, Huang Kun-hui
Foreign Affairs, Chien Fu
Finance, Lin Chen-kuo
Education, Kuo Wei-fan
Economic Affairs, P. K. Chiang
Justice, Ma Ying-jeou
National Defence, Gen. Chiang Chung-ling
Transportation and Communications, Liu Chao-shiuan
Ministers without Portfolio, Chiu Hung-ta; Kuo Wan-jung; Wang Chau-ming; Hsia Han-min; Huang Shih-cheng

Chairs of Councils:
Mainland Affairs, Hsiao Wan-chang
Atomic Energy, Hsu Yih-yun
Research, Wang Jen-hung
Agriculture, Sun Ming-hsien
Labour Affairs, Hsien Sheng-shan
Economic Planning and Development, H Su Li-teh
Overseas Chinese Affairs, Chang Hsiao-yen
Youth, Yin Shih-hao
Science, Kuo Nan-hung
Culture, Shen Hsueh-yung
Mongolian and Tibetan Affairs, Li Hou-kao
Health, Chang Po-ya

BRITISH COUNCIL REPRESENTATIVE, Mark Rawson, 7th Floor, Fu Key Building, 99 Jen Al Road, Section 2, Taipei 10625.

DEFENCE

The total active armed forces number 425,000 personnel, with conscripts serving for two-year terms. Reserves number 1,657,500 with an obligation until the age of 30. The Army is 289,000 strong with 510 main battle tanks, 905 light tanks, 1,175 armoured infantry fighting vehicles and armoured personnel carriers, 1,375 artillery pieces and 112 helicopters. The Navy has a strength of 68,000, including 30,000 marines, with four submarines, 22 destroyers, 11 frigates, 97 patrol and coastal combatants, 32 combat aircraft and 22 armed helicopters. The Air Force has 68,000 personnel, with 459 combat aircraft. Paramilitary security groups under Ministry of Defence control number 25,000 personnel.

ECONOMY

Over the past 30 years Taiwan has transformed itself from a mainly agricultural country to one of the fastest growing industrial economies in Asia. A series of six-year plans has expanded the industrial base; important sectors are steel, shipbuilding, chemicals, cement, machinery, plastic and rubber goods, electrical equipment and textiles. In 1990–4 economic growth averaged 6 per cent and inflation 3.6 per cent. GNP in 1994 was US$244,200 million. Continued trade surpluses have led to one of the largest foreign exchange reserves of any country in the world (US$97,930 million in early 1995).

The soil is very fertile, producing sugar, rice, sweet potatoes, tea, bananas, pineapples and tobacco. Mineral resources are meagre. Taiwan produces one-tenth of its coal needs and some natural gas. There are important fisheries. The principal seaports are ΨKeelung and ΨKaohsiung situated in the north and south of the island.

TRADE

The principal exports are electronic goods, machinery, metal goods, textiles, plastic products and toys and games. The main imports are oil, chemicals, machinery and natural resources. The main trading partners are the USA, Japan, Hong Kong, Germany, UK, Canada.

Trade with UK	1993	1994
Imports from UK	£667,765,000	£735,287,000
Exports to UK	1,617,418,000	1,580,880,000

TAJIKISTAN
Respublika i Tojikiston

Tajikistan has an area of 55,251 sq. miles (143,100 sq. km) and occupies the extreme south-east of former Soviet Central Asia. It is bordered on the west and north-west by Uzbekistan, on the north-east by Kyrgyzstan, on the east by China and on the south by Afghanistan. The republic includes the Gorno-Badakhstan Autonomous Province and the Kulyab, Kurgan-Tyubinsk and Khodzhent Provinces. The country is mountainous with the Pamir highlands in the east and the high ridges of the Pamir-Altai system in the centre. Plains are formed by wide stretches of the Syr-Darya valley in the north and of the Amu-Darya in the south. The country has areas prone to earthquakes, and a continental climate.

The population (1989 census) is 5,093,000, of which 62 per cent are Tajiks, 23 per cent Uzbeks and 8 per cent Russians, with smaller numbers of Tatars, Kirghiz, Germans and Ukrainians. The estimated population in 1995 was 5,513,400. The people are predominantly Sunni Muslim. The main languages are Tajik (62 per cent), Uzbek (23 per cent), Russian (8 per cent). Tajik is close to the Farsi spoken in Iran.

CAPITAL – Dushanbe. Population 595,000 (1989).
CURRENCY – Rouble of 100 kopeks.
FLAG – Three horizontal stripes of red, white and green with the white of double width and charged with a crown and seven stars, all in gold.
NATIONAL DAY – 9 September (Independence Day).

GOVERNMENT

The area that is now Tajikistan had a highly developed culture when it was invaded and conquered by Alexander the Great in the fourth century BC. The area remained under Greek and Greco-Persian rule for 200 years until the

Kingdom of Kusha was established, based on Bacharia (Bukhara). Tajikistan was invaded by the Arabs in the seventh century AD and by the Samanid Persians in the ninth century AD. The Tajik cities of Bukhara and Samarkand became two of the most important cultural and educational centres in the Islamic world.

The Tajiks lived under the control of various feudal emirates until the area which is now Tajikistan was subsumed within the Russian Empire in 1868. At the time of the Russian revolution in 1917 the central Asian emirates attempted to re-establish their independence. Soviet power was re-established in northern Tajikistan by 1 April 1918, when the Turkestan Soviet Socialist Republic was formed, and the Bukhara emirate was overthrown by Soviet forces in 1920. In 1924 the Tajikistan Autonomous Soviet Socialist Republic was formed as part of the Uzbek Republic before Tajikistan was given full republican status within the Soviet Union in 1929. Stalin deprived the Tajiks of Bukhara and Samarkand, which remained in Uzbekistan, and during Soviet rule 1,000,000 Uzbeks and 800,000 Russians were settled in Tajikistan.

Tajikistan declared independence from the Soviet Union on 9 September 1991 and became a UN member on 2 March 1992. Tension between President Nabiev's supporters and the opposition Islamic and democratic groups led to demonstrations and armed clashes in the capital Dushanbe in 1992 and Nabiev was forced to resign on 7 September 1992 as he tried to flee the capital. The Islamic-Democratic alliance formed a government in September but civil war broke out as forces loyal to the former Communist regime rebelled against the new government. By early November pro-Communist forces controlled virtually all the country and the Islamic-Democratic forces were driven out of Dushanbe on 11 December. The Supreme Soviet installed Imamoli Rakmanov as its Speaker and head of state. Fighting continued in the mountainous east and south of the country, but by March 1993 the Islamic-Democratic forces had been defeated by government and Russian Army units and driven across the border into Afghanistan.

However, fighting restarted in July between Russian and Tajik government forces and the Afghan-based rebels, leading to the establishment of a CIS peacekeeping force on the Tajik-Afghan border to contain continuing rebel attacks. Throughout 1993-4 fighting continued along the border and there were terrorist and guerrilla attacks inside Tajikistan. Negotiations between the government and opposition began in April 1994 in Moscow, bringing about a cease-fire in October 1994 to allow for presidential and parliamentary elections. The elections were, however, boycotted by most opposition groups and fighting restarted along the Afghan border in early 1995, with rebel attacks on Russian and Tajik border posts. In retaliation Russian forces launched air attacks on rebel bases in Afghanistan in April.

A new democratic constitution which re-established the presidency was approved by parliament in July 1994 and by the electorate in a national referendum on 6 November 1994. On the same day the presidential election was won by acting head of state Imomali Rakmonov amid a boycott by most opposition parties. Legislative elections to the new 181-seat Supreme Assembly (*Madjlisi Oli*) were held on 26 February 1995 and won by the ruling (former Communist) People's Party of Tajikistan amid another opposition boycott. The election was condemned as undemocratic by the OSCE monitoring team. Administratively Tajikistan is divided into two regions and one autonomous region.

HEAD OF STATE
President, Imomali Rakmonov, *elected by Supreme Soviet* 19 November 1992, *elected* 6 November 1994

GOVERNMENT *as at August 1995*
Prime Minister, Jamshed Karimov
First Deputy PM, Makhmasaid Ubaidullaev
Deputy PMs, Okil Okilov; Kholisjon Temurjanov; Jamoliddin Mansurov; Kadriddin Glyasov
Interior, Yakub Salimov
Foreign Affairs, Talbak Nazarov
Culture and Information, Bobkhon Makhmadov
Defence, Maj.-Gen. Aleksandr Shishlyannikov
Industry, Shavkat Umarov
Finance, Anvarzho Muzaffarov
Justice, Shavkat Ishmoilev
Agriculture, Kurbon Turaiev
Economy and Foreign Economic Relations, Rustam Mirzoiev
Communications, Ibrahim Usmanov
Transport, Fariddun Muhiddinov
Trade and Material Resources, Khakim Saliyev
Health, Alamkhon Ahmedov
Environmental Protection, Ismail Davlatov
Land Improvement and Water Conservancy, Ismat Eshmirzoev
Social Security, Abdusayer Jaburov
Chair of State Property Committee, Davlatov
Ambassador to Russia, Ramazan Mirzoyev
Education, Munira Inoyatova
Labour, Shukurgan Zukhurov
Bakery, Bekmurod Urakov

BRITISH AMBASSADOR, His Excellency Alexander Paul Bergne, OBE, apptd 1994, resident in Tashkent, Uzbekistan

ECONOMY
In January 1994 Tajikistan entered into a monetary union with Russia and exchanged its old roubles for post-1993 new Russian roubles. Effectively monetary control was handed over to the Russia central bank and a large amount of economic sovereignty to the Russian government in exchange for a US$100 million loan from Russia. This was needed to prevent an economic collapse caused by 40 per cent of the budget being spent on the civil war. The economy is being reformed and privatization undertaken in order to attract foreign investment.

Agriculture is the major sector of the economy, concentrating on cotton-growing and cattle-breeding. Tajikistan also has rich mineral deposits of lead, zinc and oil, is a source of uranium, and has estimated gold reserves of 16 million ounces. Industry specializes in the production of clothing and textiles.

TRADE WITH UK	1993	1994
Imports from UK	£19,486,000	£4,266,000
Exports to UK	157,000	142,000

TANZANIA
Jamhuri ya Muungano wa Tanzania

Tanzania comprises Tanganyika, on the mainland of east Africa between 1° and 11° 45′ S. latitude and 29° 20′ and 40° 38′ E. longitude, and the island of Zanzibar. The mainland part is bounded on the north by Kenya and Uganda; on the south by Mozambique; on the south-west by Lake Malawi, Malawi and Zambia; on the west by Rwanda, Burundi and Zaire; and on the east by the Indian Ocean. Tanzania has an area of 364,900 sq. miles (945,087 sq. km). The greater part of the country is occupied by the central African plateau from which rise, among others, Mt Kilimanjaro (19,340 ft), the highest point on the continent of Africa, and Mt Meru (14,974 ft). The Serengeti National Park covers an area of 6,000 sq. miles in the Arusha, Mwanza and Mara Regions.

Zanzibar was formerly ruled by the Sultan of Zanzibar and was a British Protectorate until 10 December 1963. It consists of the islands of Zanzibar, Pemba and Mafia. The area is 2,461 sq. km, and the population (1992 estimate) is 687,634. ΨZanzibar (population, 133,000) is the chief town and seaport of the island.

The total population was (UN estimate 1992) 28,359,000. Africans form a large majority, with European, Asian, and other non-African minorities. The African population consists mostly of tribes of mixed Bantu race. Swahili is the national and official language. The use of English is widespread both for educational and government purposes.

CAPITAL – Dodoma (population 88,474, 1988 estimate). The economic and administrative centre is ΨDar es Salaam (population 1,096,000, 1985 estimate). Other towns (1985 population) are ΨTanga (172,000), Mwanza (252,000), Mbeya (194,000).

CURRENCY – Tanzanian shilling of 100 cents.

FLAG – Green (above) and blue; divided by diagonal black stripe bordered by gold, running from bottom (next staff) to top (in fly).

NATIONAL ANTHEM – Mungu Ibariki Afrika (God Bless Africa).

NATIONAL DAY – 26 April (Union Day).

GOVERNMENT

Tanganyika became an independent state and a member of the British Commonwealth on 9 December 1961, and a republic within the Commonwealth on 9 December 1962. On 10 December 1963, Zanzibar became an independent state within the Commonwealth and on 26 April 1964, Tanganyika united with Zanzibar to form the United Republic of Tanzania.

There are a President and two Vice-Presidents, one the President of Zanzibar and the other the Prime Minister. If the President comes from Zanzibar the Prime Minister will be the First Vice-President and must come from Tanganyika. If the President comes from Tanganyika the President of Zanzibar will be the First Vice-President. The President may only serve two terms.

The National Assembly contains 255 members, of whom 130 are elected from mainland constituencies and 50 from Zanzibar, 25 are ex-officio, 15 nominated by the President and 35 indirectly elected. The Speaker may either be elected from among the members or be an additional member. Constituency members are elected by popular vote at a general election held at a maximum of five-yearly intervals.

Although Zanzibar has its own President, government and 75-member House of Representatives, Tanganyika is governed by the government of the Union. The sole legal political party from 1977 to 1992 was the Chama Cha Mapinduzi (CCM) (a merger of two parties which were the sole legal political parties in Tanganyika and Zanzibar from 1965 to 1977). In 1992 President Mwinyi and the CCM leadership agreed to amend the constitution to allow multiparty politics. In June 1992 President Mwinyi endorsed a bill legalizing multiparty politics, with the stipulation that all parties must be active in both the mainland and in Zanzibar and that parties must not be formed on regional, religious, tribal or racial grounds. The first multiparty presidential and parliamentary elections will be held in late 1995 after which a constitutional change will become effective whereby the President of Zanzibar ceases to be a Union Vice-President.

HEAD OF STATE
President of the United Republic, HE Hon. Ali Hassan Mwinyi, *elected* 1985; *re-elected* 28 October 1990
First Vice-President of the United Republic and Prime Minister, Hon. Cleopa D. Msuya
Second Vice-President of the United Republic and President of Zanzibar, HE Dr Salmin Amour

CABINET *as at August 1995*
The President (also Minister of Defence)
The First Vice-President and Prime Minister
The Second Vice-President
Minister of State, President's Office, Hon. H. Diria
Foreign Affairs and International Co-operation, Hon. Joseph Rwegasira
Agriculture, Livestock and Co-operatives, Hon. Frederick Sumaye
Education, Culture, Communications and Transport, Hon. Prof. Phillemon Sarungi
Works, Hon. Nalaila Kiula
Energy, Minerals and Water, Hon. Jackson Makweta
Finance, Hon. Jakaya Kikwete
Health, Hon. Amran Mayagila
Industry and Trade, Hon. Prof. Kighoma Malima
Information and Broadcasting, Hon. Philip S. Marmo
Labour and Youth, Hon. Basil Mramba
Community Development, Women and Children, Hon. Anna Makinda
Tourism, Natural Resources, Environment, Hon. Juma Omar Juma
Science, Technology and Higher Education, Hon. Benjamin Mkapa
Ministers without Portfolio, Hon. K. Ngombale Mwiru; Hon. John Malecela

HIGH COMMISSION FOR THE UNITED REPUBLIC OF TANZANIA
43 Hertford Street, London WIY 8DB
Tel 0171-499 8951/2/3/4
High Commissioner, His Excellency Ali S. Mchumo, apptd 1991

BRITISH HIGH COMMISSION
Hifadhi House, Samora Avenue (PO Box 9200), Dar es Salaam
Tel: Dar es Salaam 29601-5
High Commissioner, His Excellency Alan Montgomery, apptd 1995
BRITISH COUNCIL DIRECTOR, Robert Sykes, Ohio Samora Avenue (PO Box 9100), Dar es Salaam

ECONOMY

The economy is based mainly on the production and export of primary produce and the growing of foodstuffs for local consumption. The islands of Zanzibar and Pemba produce a large part of the world's supply of cloves and clove oil; and coconuts, coconut oil and copra are also produced. The mainland's chief export crops are coffee, cotton, sisal, tea, tobacco, cashew nuts and diamonds. The most important minerals are diamonds. Hides and skins are another valuable export. Industry is largely concerned with the processing of raw material for either export or local consumption. There are also secondary manufacturing industries, including factories for the manufacture of leather and rubber footwear, knitwear, razor blades, cigarettes and textiles, and a wheat flour mill.

TRADE WITH UK	1993	1994
Imports from UK	£108,943,000	£82,312,000
Exports to UK	25,633,000	22,452,000

COMMUNICATIONS

The main ports are Dar es Salaam, Tanga, Mtwara, Zanzibar, Mkoani and Wete, in addition to Mwanza, Musoma and Bukoba on Lake Victoria and Kigoma on Lake Tanganyika. Coastal shipping services connect the mainland to Zanzibar, and lake services are operated on Lake Tanganyika and Lake Malawi with neighbouring countries. The principal international airports are Dar es Salaam and Kilimanjaro. Other airports include Zanzibar, Arusha, Mwanza and Tanga. There are two railway systems; one connecting Dar es Salaam to Zambia, and the second having two main lines running from Dar es Salaam, one to northern Tanzania and Kenya and the other to Lake Tanganyika and Victoria.

EDUCATION

The school system is administered in Swahili but the government is making efforts to improve English standards for the purposes of secondary and higher education. All Tanzanian secondary schools are expected to include practical subjects in the basic course. For higher education Tanzanian students go to the University of Dar es Salaam, Sokoine University of Agriculture in Morogoro, other African universities, or to universities and colleges outside Africa.

THAILAND
Prathes Thai

Thailand, formerly known as Siam, has an area of 198,457 sq. miles (514,000 sq. km). It has a common boundary with Malaysia in the south, is bounded on the west by Myanmar (Burma) and on the north-east and east by Laos and Cambodia. Thailand is divided geographically into four: the centre is a plain; to the north-east there is a plateau area and to the north-west mountains. The south of Thailand consists of a narrow mountainous peninsula. The principal rivers are the Chao Phraya in the central plains, and the Mekong on the northern and north-eastern borders.

The population (1993 census) is 58,336,072. The principal language is Thai, a monosyllabic, tonal language of the Indo-Chinese linguistic family, with a vocabulary strongly influenced by Sanskrit and Pali. It is written in an alphabetic script derived from ancient Indian scripts. Significant minorities speak Chinese (in urban areas), Lao (in the north-east), Khmer (in the east) and Malay (in the far south).

The principal religion is Buddhism (94.37 per cent), with 3.95 per cent Muslims, 0.53 per cent Christians and 1.15 per cent other religions.

CAPITAL – ΨBangkok, at the mouth of the River Chao Phraya, population (metropolitan area) (1993) 5,572,712. Other centres are Chiang Mai, Phitsanulok, Chon Buri, Korat, Khon Kaen, Surat Thani, Hat Yai and ΨPhuket.
CURRENCY – Baht of 100 satang.
FLAG – Five horizontal bands, red, white, dark blue, white, red (the blue band twice the width of the others).
NATIONAL ANTHEM – Pleng Chart.
NATIONAL DAY – 5 December (The King's Birthday).

GOVERNMENT

Thailand became a constitutional monarchy in 1932. The 1978 constitution (as amended) provides for a National Assembly consisting of a 240-member Senate appointed by the monarch and a 360-member House of Representatives elected by universal adult suffrage for a term of four years. Following a military coup in February 1991, a new constitution was approved in December 1991 under which the military would appoint the members of the Senate and so enshrine its place in Thai politics. Parties aligned with the military won the general election in March 1992, but opposition to the military-controlled government grew and mass demonstrations held in Bangkok from 17 to 20 May eventually, with the help of the King, forced the government from power. Military power was curbed, the 1978 constitution was restored and the interim government sacked military chiefs.

Parliamentary elections in September 1992 resulted in a majority for 'democratic parties', i.e. those not allied with the military. Chuan Leekpai became Prime Minister at the head of a five-party governing coalition which implemented a series of reforms in education, land tenure and the constitution. Some 600,000 families have been granted land title rights, the voting age has been reduced to 18, the appointed Senate reduced to a maximum of two-thirds of the number of House of Representatives' seats and anti-corruption laws introduced. However, the coalition government lost power in May 1995 when one of the main parties withdrew over corruption allegations. In the ensuing general election on 2 July 1995 the opposition and military-aligned Chart Thai party emerged as the largest party and entered into talks with other parties to form a new coalition government; this had yet to be named at the time of going to press.

HEAD OF STATE
HM The King of Thailand, King Bhumibol Adulyadej, *born* 1927; *succeeded his brother*, 9 June 1946; *married* 28 April 1950 Princess Sirikit Kitiyakara; *crowned* 5 May 1950; and has *issue*, Princess Ubolratana, *born* 6 April 1951; Crown Prince Vajiralongkorn (*see* below); Princess Maha Chaki Sirindhorn, *born* 2 April 1955; Princess Chulabhorn, *born* 4 July 1957
Heir, HRH Crown Prince Vajiralongkorn, *born* 28 July 1952; *married* 3 January 1977 Soamsawali Kitiyakra

ROYAL THAI EMBASSY
29–30 Queen's Gate, London SW7 5JB
Tel 0171-589 2944
Ambassador Extraordinary and Plenipotentiary, His Excellency Vidhya Rayananonda, apptd 1994
Minister and Deputy Head of Mission, P. Phrombubpha
Defence Attaché, Gp Capt. A. Ganchanahirun
Minister Counsellor, S. Jaovisidha (*Commercial*)

BRITISH EMBASSY
Wireless Road, Bangkok 10330
Tel: Bangkok 253 0191 9
Ambassador Extraordinary and Plenipotentiary, His Excellency Charles C. Adams, CMG, apptd 1992
Deputy Ambassador and Counsellor, R. T. Fell
Defence Attaché, Col. J. D. Fielden, MBE
Counsellor (Commercial), M. J. Greenstreet
Consul, J. C. Sharpe, OBE
There is a British Consulate at Chang Mai

BRITISH COUNCIL DIRECTOR, Dr John Richards, 428 Rama 1 Road, Siam Square Soi 2, Pathumwan, Bangkok 10330. There is also an office in Chiang Mai

BRITISH CHAMBER OF COMMERCE, BP Building 18th Floor, Unit 1810, 54 Asoke Road (Sukhumvit 21) Bangkok 10110

DEFENCE

Total active armed forces number 256,000 personnel, with conscription terms of two years. Reserves number a further 200,000 personnel. The Army numbers 150,000 (80,000 conscripts) with 250 main battle tanks, 510 light tanks, 970 armoured personnel carriers, 410 artillery pieces and four attack helicopters. The Navy has 63,000 personnel (26,000 conscripts), with nine frigates, 62 patrol and coastal combatants, 21 combat aircraft, eight armed helicopters and a 20,000-strong marine division. The Air Force has 43,000 personnel, with 191 combat aircraft. Six para-military forces, including four police forces, have a total strength of 161,500 personnel.

ECONOMY

The agricultural sector provides just under half the national income and employs 67.5 per cent of the labour force. Rice remains the most important crop, accounting for 60 per cent of the area planted. The other main crops are sugar, maize, sorghum, cassava, rubber, tobacco, kenaf and jute. In recent years the production of livestock and poultry, especially pigs and chickens for export, has gained importance. There is a large fishing industry with more than 20,000 vessels registered. Fish and prawn farming is popular in many inland areas. A ban on hardwood export has resulted in the decline of the forestry industry.

Onshore oil and offshore gas were discovered in the late 1970s; crude oil production began in 1983. The predicted surplus of natural gas has led the government to designate an area on the east coast as the future centre of the petrochemical industry. Another energy resource is lig-nite, which is found mainly in the north and is being used increasingly for electricity production. Mineral resources are mainly tin, tungsten, lead, antimony and iron. Among these tin is the most important. In addition, a zinc refinery was opened in 1984.

Since 1960 the government has actively promoted industrial investment by means of tax relief and other incentives to local and foreign investors; in 1985, 74.6 per cent of this investment was in Thai projects. Initially industries established under this scheme were import-substituting but the emphasis has shifted now to export-oriented industries. Important sectors are textiles, trans-portation vehicles and equipment, construction materials, brewing, petroleum refining, electrical appliances, plastics, computers and parts, and integrated circuits. Manufactur-ing now accounts for about 21.8 per cent of the national income, and the rapid growth of manufacturing exports since 1985 meant that by 1994 manufacturers provided 81 per cent of exports. The service sector is large, the banking system contributing greatly to the economy, and since 1982 tourism has been the main foreign exchange earner.

In 1994 the economy grew by 8.5 per cent, inflation was 5.0 per cent, the government budget had a surplus of 1.8 per cent of GDP and foreign currency reserves stood at US$25,500 million.

TRADE

Thailand's main exports are rice, tapioca and tapioca products, garments, rubber, computers and parts, cars, integrated circuit boards, precious stones, pearls and other ornaments, maize, canned sea food, fabrics, sugar and tin. Main imports are crude oil, chemicals and pharmaceut-icals, electrical and non-electrical machinery and spare parts, industrial machinery, iron and steel, diesel oil and other fuel oil, vehicle and transport equipment.

	1993	1994
Total imports	Bhat 1,151,000m	Bhat 1,352,425m
Total exports	909,000m	1,088,073m
Trade with UK	1993	1994
Imports from UK	£659,376,000	£745,587,000
Exports to UK	770,677,000	913,135,000

EDUCATION

Primary education is compulsory and free, and secondary education in government schools is free. Private univer-sities and colleges are playing an increasing role in higher education. Out of 43 universities and other similar higher institutes of learning, 21 are private.

COMMUNICATIONS

The road network, totalling 56,903 km in 1993, reaches all parts of the country. Most of the smaller towns and bigger villages are now served by paved roads. Navigable water-ways have a length of about 1,100 km in the dry season and 1,600 km in the wet season. About 4,450 km of state-owned railways were open to traffic in 1989. Main lines run from Bangkok to the Cambodian border, the ferry terminal on the River Mekong opposite Vientiane, Chiang Mai and to Hat Yai, whence lines run down both sides of the Malay peninsula to Singapore. A new line to Sattahip on the east coast is being constructed. Bangkok is the international airport, though airports at Chiang Mai, Phuket and Hat Yai also receive international flights. Most major provincial towns have airports. The THAI airline is state-owned.

There are two important ports in the country. Bangkok, which is a river port, can serve vessels up to 27 ft draught. The deep-sea port at Sattahip caters for larger vessels. Phuket and Songkhla deep-water ports have already been completed and are the first to be managed privately under a ten-year concession. Construction of Laem Chabang deep-water port started in 1988.

TOGO
République Togolaise

Togo is situated in West Africa between 0° and 2° W. and 6° and 11° N., with a coastline 35 miles long on the Gulf of Guinea. It extends northwards inland for 350 miles and is flanked on the west by Ghana, on the north by Burkina and in the east by Benin. It has an area of 21,925 sq. miles (56,785 sq. km), and a population (UN estimate 1992) of 3,763,000, including people of several African races. The official language is French; Ewe is spoken by about 47 per cent.

CAPITAL – ΨLomé, population (1983) 366,476.

CURRENCY – Franc CFA of 100 centimes.

FLAG – Five alternating green and yellow horizontal stripes; a quarter in red at top next staff bearing a white star.

NATIONAL DAY – 13 January (National Liberation Day).

GOVERNMENT

The first President of Togo, Sylvanus Olympio, was assassinated in 1963. His successor was overthrown by an army coup d'état in 1967 and the army commander Lt.-Col. (later Gen.) Eyadéma named himself President. President Eyadéma came under increasing popular pressure to introduce reforms in 1990 and in October the Rassemblement du peuple togolais (RPT), the sole legal party, approved plans for a new constitutional conference after pro-democracy riots. Riots broke out again in March 1991 in protest at the slow pace of reform, and in April the government was forced to concede a political amnesty, the introduction of a multiparty constitution and a national conference. In August 1991 the national conference stripped President Eyadéma of all powers, banned the RPT and elected Kokou Koffigoh as Prime Minister of an interim government. The national conference set a date of 9 February 1992 for a referendum on a new constitution.

However, from the second half of 1991 onwards the political situation became progressively more unstable. Troops loyal to President Eyadéma three times attempted to overthrow the Koffigoh government (October, November and December 1991) but were frustrated by pro-democracy supporters. Continued political violence in 1992 between the army and pro-democracy groups and among rival opposition parties forced the postponement of the referendum until September 1992, when a new multiparty constitution was agreed. In November Eyadéma, who had regained the position of head of state in August 1992, ordered the Army to crush civil unrest and a general strike against his rule. In February 1993, as political violence continued, Koffigoh and Eyadéma agreed on the formation of a crisis government, which the national conference and the Collective Democratic Opposition-2 (COD-2) declared illegal.

President Eyadéma won a presidential election in August 1993 that was boycotted by opposition parties and declared rigged by international monitors. Legislative elections to the 81-seat National Assembly were held in February 1994 and won by the opposition alliance of the Action Committee for Renewal (CAR) (36 seats) and the Togolese Union for Democracy (UTD) (7 seats), while the RPT and allied parties won 38 seats. However, Eyadéma persuaded UTD leader Edem Kodjo to form a coalition UTD-RPT government in April 1994, the RPT retaining a majority of cabinet seats.

HEAD OF STATE
President, Gen. Gnassingbé Eyadéma, *assumed office* 14 April 1967; *re-elected* 1986, August 1993

GOVERNMENT *as at August 1995*
Prime Minister, Edem Kodjo
Economy and Finance, Elome Dadzie
Foreign Affairs and Co-operation, vacant
Planning, Yandjia Yentchabre
Equipment, Tchamdja Andjo
Justice, Kagni Gabriel
Security, Seyi Memene
Communications and Culture, Atsutse Agbobli
Tourism, Rural Development and Environment, Yao Do Felli
Health, Afatbao Amédomé
Welfare and Solidarity, Were Gazaro
Defence, Alfa Abalo
Industry, Payadowa Boukpessi
Youth and Sport, Kouami Agbogboli Ihou
Education and Scientific Research, Komlavi Seddoh
Commerce, Price Control and Transport, Dedevi Michele Ekue
Interior and Decentralization, Kodjo Sagbo
Human Rights and Relations with Parliament, Djovi Gally
Energy, Anato Agbodouhoue

EMBASSY OF TOGO – The Embassy of Togo closed in September 1991

BRITISH AMBASSADOR, His Excellency David Walker, CVO, resident in Accra, Ghana

There is a Consulate (BP 20050) and a Commercial Office (BP 60958 BE) in Lomé.

ECONOMY

Although the economy remains largely agricultural, exports of phosphates have superseded agricultural products as the main source of export earnings. Other exports include palm kernels, copra and manioc. The production of phosphates entirely for export was taken over completely by the government in February 1974. The IMF approved a loan of US$95 million in September 1994 to support the 1994–7 economic reform programme.

TRADE WITH UK	1993	1994
Imports from UK	£4,769,000	£7,278,000
Exports to UK	901,000	3,176,000

TONGA
Kingdom of Tonga

Tonga, or the Friendly Islands, comprises a group of islands situated in the southern Pacific some 450 miles east-south-east of Fiji, with an area of 270 sq. miles (699 sq. km), and population (1992 UN estimate) of 97,000. The largest island, Tongatapu, was discovered by Tasman in 1643. Most of the islands are of coral formation, but some are volcanic (Tofua, Kao and Niuafoou or 'Tin Can' Island). The limits of the group are between 15° and 23° 30′ S., and 173° and 177° W.

CAPITAL – ΨNuku'alofa (population estimate 30,000), on Tongatapu.
CURRENCY – Pa'anga (T$) of 100 seniti.
FLAG – Red with a white canton containing a couped red cross.
NATIONAL ANTHEM – E, 'Otua Mafimafi (Oh, Almighty God Above).
NATIONAL DAY – 4 June (Independence Day).

GOVERNMENT

The Kingdom of Tonga is an independent constitutional monarchy within the Commonwealth. Prior to 4 June 1970 it had been a British-protected state for 70 years. The constitution provides for a government consisting of the Sovereign, an appointed privy council which functions as a cabinet, a legislative assembly and a judiciary. The 30-member legislative assembly comprises the King, the 11-member privy council, nine hereditary nobles elected by their peers, and nine popularly elected representatives who hold office for three years. The most recent election took place on 4 February 1993 and six of the nine seats were won by candidates wishing to reduce the power of the King and nobles and to strengthen democracy.

HEAD OF STATE
King of Tonga, HM King Taufa'ahau Tupou IV, GCMG, GCVO, KBE, *acceded* 16 December 1965
Heir, HRH Crown Prince Tupouto'a

CABINET *as at August 1995*
Prime Minister, Minister of Agriculture, Fisheries, Forests, and Marine, Baron Vaea of Houma
Deputy Prime Minister, Minister of Education, Works and Civil Aviation, Hon. Dr S. Langi Kavaliku
Finance, Labour, Commerce and Industry, Hon. Tutoatasi Fakafanua
Police, Prisons and Fire Services, Hon. George 'Akau'ola
Health, Hon. Dr S. Tapa

Foreign Affairs and Defence, HRH Crown Prince Tupouto'a
Attorney-General, Justice, Hon. Tevita P. Tupou
Minister without Portfolio, Hon. Ma'afu Tuku'i'aulahi
Minister of Lands, Survey, and Natural Resources, Hon.
   Dr S. Ma'afu Tupou
Governor of Ha'apai, Hon. Fakafanua
Governor of Vava'u, Hon. Tu'i'afitu

TONGA HIGH COMMISSION
36 Molyneux Street, London WIH 6AB
Tel 0171-724 5828
High Commissioner, His Excellency Sione Kité, apptd 1992

BRITISH HIGH COMMISSION
PO Box 56, Nuku'alofa
Tel: Nuku'alofa 21020
High Commissioner, His Excellency Andrew James Morris,
   apptd 1994

ECONOMY

The economy is primarily agricultural; the main crops are
coconuts, bananas, vanilla, yams, taro, cassava, groundnuts,
squash pumpkins and other fruits. Fish is an important
staple food, though recent shortfalls have led to canned fish
being imported. Industry is based on the processing of
agricultural produce, and the manufacture of foodstuffs,
clothing and sports equipment.

TRADE

The principal exports are copra, squash, other coconut
products, tropical root crops, bananas, knitwear, leather
goods and fibreglass boats.

Trade with UK	1993	1994
Imports from UK	£1,463,000	£686,000
Exports to UK	55,000	341,000

TRINIDAD AND TOBAGO
The Republic of Trinidad and Tobago

Trinidad, the most southerly of the West Indian islands,
lies seven miles off the north coast of Venezuela. The
island is situated between 10° 2' and 11° 12' N. latitude
and 60° 30' and 61° 56' W. longitude, and is about 50 miles
in length by 37 miles in width, with an area of
1,864 sq. miles (4,828 sq. km). Two mountain systems, the
Northern and Southern Ranges, stretch across almost its
entire width and a third, the Central Range, lies diagonally
across its middle portion; otherwise the island is mostly flat.
   Tobago lies between 11° 9' and 11° 21' N. latitude and
between 60° 30' and 60° 50' W. longitude, 19 miles north-
east of Trinidad. The island is 32 miles long at its widest
point, and 11 wide, and has an area of 116 sq. miles
(300 sq. km).
   Corozal Point and Icacos Point, the north-west and
south-west extremities of Trinidad, enclose the Gulf of
Paria. West of Corozal Point lie several islands, of which
Chacachacare, Huevos, Monos and Gaspar Grande are the
most important.
   The climate is tropical. There is a dry season from
December to May, and a wet season from June to
November broken by a short dry season (the *Petite Careme*)
in September and October.
   The population (1992 estimate) was 1,239,908; Toba-
go's population is about 45,000. The language is English.
Roman Catholicism, Protestantism, Hinduism and Islam
are all practised.

CAPITAL – ΨPort of Spain (population (1990) 50,878) is
the administrative centre of the islands. San Fernando
(population 34,300) is emerging as the industrial centre
of Trinidad. The main town of Tobago is
ΨScarborough.
CURRENCY – Trinidad and Tobago dollar (TT$) of 100
cents.
FLAG – Black diagonal stripe bordered with white stripes,
running from top by staff, all on a red field.
NATIONAL DAYS – 31 August (Independence Day); 24
September (Republic Day).

GOVERNMENT

Trinidad was discovered by Columbus in 1498, was
colonized in 1532 by the Spaniards, capitulated to the
British in 1797, and was ceded to Britain under the Treaty
of Amiens 1802. Tobago was discovered by Columbus in
1498. Dutch colonists arrived in 1632; Tobago subsequently changed hands numerous times until it was
ceded to Britain by France in 1814 and amalgamated with
Trinidad in 1888.
   The Territory of Trinidad and Tobago became an
independent state and a member of the British Commonwealth on 31 August 1962, and a republic in 1976. The
President is elected for five years by all members of the
Senate and the House of Representatives. The House of
Representatives has 36 members, elected by universal
adult suffrage, and the Senate has 31, of whom 16 are
appointed on the advice of the Prime Minister, six on the
advice of the Leader of the Opposition and nine at the
discretion of the President. Legislation was passed in
September 1980 which afforded Tobago a degree of self-
administration through the 15-member Tobago House of
Assembly.
   The most recent general election on 16 December 1991
was won by the People's National Movement, which took
21 out of 36 seats and formed a government.

HEAD OF STATE
President, His Excellency Noor Mohammed Hassanali,
   elected 1987, *re-elected* February 1992

CABINET *as at August 1995*
Prime Minister, Hon. Patrick Manning
Foreign Affairs, Public Administration and Information, Sen. the
   Hon. Gordon Draper
Finance and Tourism, Hon. Wendell Mottley
Attorney-General, Hon. Keith Sobion
Energy and Energy Industries, Sen. the Hon. Barry Barnes
Trade and Industry, Hon. Kenneth Valley
National Security, Hon. John Eckstein
Public Utilities, Hon. Ralph Maraj
Sport and Youth Affairs, Hon. Jean Pierre
Health, Hon. Linda Baboolal
Local Government, Works and Transport, Hon. Colm Imbert
Education, Hon. Augustus Ramrekersingh
*Science, Technology, Higher Education, Planning and
   Development*, Sen. the Hon. Lenny Saith
Labour and Co-operatives, Hon. Kenneth Collis
Community Development, Culture and Women's Affairs, Sen. the
   Hon. Joan Yuille-Williams
Agriculture, Lands and Marine Resources, Hon. Dr Keith
   Rowley
Housing and Settlements, Hon. Dr Vincent Lasse
Consumer Affairs, Sen. the Hon. Camille Robinson-Regis
Social Development, Sen. the Hon. Russell Huggins

HIGH COMMISSION OF THE REPUBLIC OF TRINIDAD AND TOBAGO
42 Belgrave Square, London SWIX 8NT
Tel 0171-245 9351
High Commissioner, His Excellency Rabindranath Permanand, apptd 1993

BRITISH HIGH COMMISSION
19 St Clair Ave, St Clair, Port of Spain
Tel: Port of Spain 6222748
High Commissioner, His Excellency Richard Neilson, CMG, LVO, apptd 1994

ECONOMY

Trinidad and Tobago's main source of revenue is from oil. Production of domestic crude was 55 million barrels in 1990. Trinidad has large reserves of natural gas, and reserves are estimated to be in the region of 100 years at the current rates of production. An integrated steel plant, an anhydrous ammonia plant and a methanol plant have been constructed at Point Lisas. An industrial complex, including an iron and steel production, is developing around San Fernando.

Fertilizers, tyres, clothing, soap, furniture and foodstuffs are manufactured locally while motor vehicles, radios, TV sets, and electro-domestic equipment are assembled from parts, mainly from Japan. The main agricultural products are sugar, cocoa, coffee, horticultural products, and teak.

TRADE	1991	1992
Imports	TT$7,084.8m	TT$6,081.1m
Exports	8,436.4m	7,942.9m
Trade with UK	1993	1994
Imports from UK	£70,700,000	£72,270,000
Exports to UK	43,077,000	48,287,000

EDUCATION

Education is free at all state-owned and government-assisted denominational schools and certain faculties at the University of the West Indies. In addition there are various private teaching establishments. Attendance is compulsory for children aged six to 12 years, after which attendance at free secondary schools is determined by success in the common entrance examination at 11 years. There are three technical institutes, two teachers' training colleges, and one of the three branches of the University of the West Indies is located in Trinidad. A medical teaching complex at Mt Hope operates in collaboration with the University of the West Indies.

COMMUNICATIONS

There are some 6,436 km of all-weather roads in Trinidad and Tobago. The only general cargo port is Port of Spain but there are specialized port facilities elsewhere for crude oil, refinery products, sugar, bauxite and cement. Regular shipping services call and many inter-island craft use the port. Another rapidly growing port is at Port Lisas where new industries powered by local natural gas are located. International scheduled airlines, including the national airline, Trinidad and Tobago Airways (BWIA) Corporation, use Piarco International Airport, Port of Spain. The airline also flies between Piarco and Crown Point Airport in Tobago.

Three commercial broadcasting stations and one commercial television station operate in Trinidad and Tobago. The internal telephone system and the external telephone and telegraph connections are operated by partly state-owned companies.

TUNISIA
Al-Djoumhouria Attunusia

Tunisia lies between Algeria and Libya and extends southwards to the Sahara Desert, with a total area of 164,150 sq. km, and a population (UN estimate 1992) of 8,401,000.

CAPITAL – Ψ Tunis had a population (1984) of 1,394,749. The ruins of ancient Carthage lie a few miles from the city. Other towns of importance are: Ψ Sfax (577,992); Ψ Sousse (322,491); Ψ Bizerta (394,670); Kairouan; Gabes; Menzel Bourguiba.
CURRENCY – Tunisian dinar of 1,000 millimes.
FLAG – Red with a white disc containing a red crescent and star.
NATIONAL ANTHEM – Himat Al Hima.
NATIONAL DAY – 20 March.

GOVERNMENT

A French Protectorate from 1881 to 1956, Tunisia became an independent sovereign state on 20 March 1956. In 1957 the Constituent Assembly abolished the monarchy and elected M. Bourguiba President of the Republic. In March 1975 the National Assembly proclaimed M. Bourguiba as President for life but he was deposed on 7 November 1987 and succeeded by President Zine el-Abidine Ben Ali. Presidential and legislative elections were held in April 1989. The Rassemblement Constitutionnel Démocratique (RCD) won all 141 seats in the National Assembly, which were contested by seven parties; President Ben Ali was elected with 99 per cent of the vote. Electoral changes enacted in September 1993 provide for opposition parties to be represented in the National Assembly; the Assembly has been expanded to 163 seats, 19 of which are reserved, on a proportional basis, for those parties not winning any of the 144 first-past-the-post seats. Presidential and legislative elections held in March 1994 were won by President Ben Ali, the only candidate, and the RCD, which won all 144 constituency seats. Diplomatic relations were opened with Israel in October 1994.

The country is divided into 23 regions (*gouvernorats*) each administered by a governor.

HEAD OF STATE
President, Zine el-Abidine Ben Ali, *took office* 7 November 1987, *elected* 2 April 1989, *re-elected* 21 March 1994

CABINET *as at August 1995*
Prime Minister, Hamed Karoui
Minister of State, Special Presidential Adviser, Abdallah Kallel
Justice, Sadok Chaabane
Director of Presidential Office, Mohamed el Jeri
Foreign Affairs, Habib ben Yahia
Defence, Abdelaziz Ben Dhia
Interior, Mohammed Jegham
Finance, Nouri Zorgati
Economic Development, Mustapha Nabli
International Co-operation and Foreign Investment, Mohammed Ghannouchi
Agriculture, M'Hamed Ben Rajab
State Property, Mustapha Bouaziz
Equipment and Housing, Ali Chaouch
Transport, Mondher Zenaidi
Tourism and Handicrafts, Slaheddine Maaoui
Communications, Habib Ammar
Education, Hatem Ben Othman
Culture, Salah Baccari

Health, Hedi Henni
Social Affairs, Sadok Rabah
Environment and Land Development, Mohamed Mehdi Melika
Vocational Training and Employment, Moncer Rouissi
Youth and Childhood Welfare, Abderrahim Zouari
Secretary-General of the Government, Ridha Grira
Religious Affairs, Ali Chebbi
Higher Education, Dali Jazi
Family and Women's Affairs, Neziha Zarrouk
Trade, Slaheddine Ben M'Barek
Industry, Slaheddine Bouguerra

TUNISIAN EMBASSY
29 Prince's Gate, London SW7 1QG
Tel 0171-584 8117
Ambassador Extraordinary and Plenipotentiary, His Excellency Mohamed Lessir, apptd 1992

BRITISH EMBASSY
5 Place de la Victoire, Tunis 1015 RP
Tel: Tunis 1341444
Ambassador Extraordinary and Plenipotentiary and Consul-General, His Excellency Michael Tait, CMG, LVO, apptd 1992
First Secretary, B. England (*Deputy Head of Mission*)
There is a Consulate at Sfax.

BRITISH COUNCIL DIRECTOR, C. Stevenson (*Cultural Attaché*)

ECONOMY

The valleys of the northern region support large flocks and herds and contain rich agricultural areas in which wheat, barley, and oats are grown. Vines and olives are extensively cultivated. Some oil has been discovered and crude oil production in 1989 was 4.8 million tons. Gas has also been discovered off the east coast but exploitation is not viable at present. Tourists numbered 3,540,000 in 1992 and tourism is the main foreign exchange earner.

TRADE

The chief exports are crude oil, phosphates, olive oil, finished textiles, and fruit. The chief imports are machinery and equipment, foodstuffs, petroleum products, and textiles. France remains the main trading partner.

Tunisia became an associate of the EC early in 1969 and signed a new agreement with the EC in 1976. In May 1995 a new EU-Tunisian partnership agreement was signed which aims to modernize Tunisia's economy and improve its competitiveness with a view to creating a future free trade zone with the EU.

Trade with UK	1993	1994
Imports from UK	£62,210,000	£81,056,000
Exports to UK	39,383,000	46,000,000

TURKEY
Türkiye Cumhuriyeti

Turkey lies partly in Europe and partly in Asia. The total area is 814,578 sq. km, of which 790,200 sq. km is in Asia and 24,378 sq. km is in Europe. Turkey in Europe consists of Eastern Thrace, including the cities of Istanbul and Edirne, and is separated from Asia by the Bosporus at Istanbul and by the Dardanelles (about 40 miles in length with a width varying from one to four miles), the political neighbours being Greece and Bulgaria on the west. Turkey in Asia comprises the whole of Asia Minor or Anatolia and extends

from the Aegean Sea to the western boundaries of Georgia, Armenia and Iran, and from the Black Sea to the Mediterranean and the northern boundaries of Syria and Iraq.

Population at the 1990 census was 56,473,035. The 1992 UN estimate is 58,775,000. Islam ceased to be the state religion in 1928 but 98.99 per cent of the population are Muslim. The main religious minorities, which are concentrated in Istanbul and on the Syrian frontier, are Greek Orthodox, Armenian, Syrian Christian, and Jewish.

CAPITAL – Ankara (Angora), in Asia, population (1990) 3,236,626. Ankara (or Ancyra) was the capital of the Roman Province of *Galatia Prima*, and a marble temple (now in ruins), dedicated to Augustus, contains the *Monumentum* (*Marmor*) *Ancyranum*, inscribed with a record of the reign of Augustus Caesar. ΨIstanbul (7,309,190), in Europe, is the former capital. The Roman city of Byzantium, it was selected by Constantine the Great as the capital of the Roman Empire about AD 328 and renamed Constantinople. Istanbul contains the celebrated church of St Sophia, which, after becoming a mosque, was made a museum in 1934. It also contains Topkapi, former palace of the Ottoman Sultans, which is also a museum. Other cities are ΨIzmir (2,694,770); Adana (1,934,907); Bursa (1,603,137); Gaziantep (1,140,549); and Konya (1,750,303).

CURRENCY – Turkish lira (TL) of 100 kurus.

FLAG – Red, with white crescent and star.

NATIONAL ANTHEM – Istiklal Marşi (The Independence March).

NATIONAL DAY – 29 October (Republic Day).

GOVERNMENT

On 29 October 1923 the National Assembly declared Turkey a republic and elected Gazi Mustafa Kemal (later known as Kemal Ataturk) President. In 1945 a multiparty system was introduced but in 1960 the government was overthrown by the armed forces. A new constitution was adopted in 1961 and, after a general election, a civilian government took office. Civilian governments remained in power until September 1980 when mounting problems with the economy and terrorism led to a military takeover.

A new constitution, extending the powers of the President, was approved in 1982. It provided for the separation of powers between the legislature, executive and judiciary, and the holding of free elections to the unicameral Grand National Assembly, which now has 450 members elected every five years. Following the general election in November 1983 the military leadership handed over power to a civilian government. The last election was held in October 1991. Süleyman Demirel, leader of the True Path Party, formed a coalition government with the Social Democrat Populist Party. President Özal died on 17 April 1993 leading to the election by parliament of Süleyman Demirel as President. Tansu Çiller was elected party chairman by the True Path Party and formed a government which was sworn in on 25 June by President Demirel, when Çiller became the first woman Turkish Prime Minister. The Social Democrat Populist Party merged with the Republican People's Party (CHP) in February 1995 when the CHP became the junior coalition party.

Turkey is divided for administrative purposes into 76 *il* with subdivisions into *ilçe* and *nahiye*. Each *il* has a governor (*vali*) and elective council.

SECESSION

Since 1984 Turkey has been fighting armed guerrillas of the Marxist Kurdish Workers Party (PKK) in the south-east of the country where Kurds are the majority population. The PKK has an estimated strength of 10,000 operating from bases in Lebanon, northern Iraq and Syria, with the latter giving tacit support and finance. The southeast remains under martial law and about 15,000 have died in the 11 years of warfare. Since the end of a two-month PKK cease-fire in May 1993, the Turkish army has attempted to destroy the PKK by launching land and air raids against PKK bases in Syria and northern Iraq. The largest land incursion occurred in northern Iraq from March to May 1995 when 35,000 Turkish troops, backed by tanks and aircraft, destroyed PKK bases and supply routes and killed about 500 guerrillas. The PKK has unsuccessfully attempted to gain the Kurdish population's support by intimidating and executing hundreds of those who oppose it. Turkish security forces have razed villages suspected of harbouring PKK guerrillas. Some 1,500,000 Kurds have been driven from their homes by the fighting and 200,000 Turkish troops are engaged in the conflict.

HEAD OF STATE
President, Süleyman Demirel, *elected by parliament for a seven-year term,* 16 May 1993

GOVERNMENT *as at August 1995*
Prime Minister, Prof. Tansu Çiller (DYP)
Deputy Prime Minister, Hikmet Çetin (CHP)
Ministers of State, Necmettin Cevheri; Yildirim Aktuna;
    Bekir Sami Daçe; Esat Kiratlioğlu; Nafiz Kurt; Aykon
    Doğan; Abdulbaki Ataç; Ayvaz Gökdemir; Şükrü Erdem
    (DYP); Onur Kumbaracibaşi; Algan Hacaloğlu; Aysel
    Baykal (CHP)
Justice, Mehmet Mogultay (CHP)
National Defence, Mehmet Gölhan (DYP)
Interior, Nahit Menteşe (DYP)
Foreign, Erdal Inönü (CHP)
Finance and Customs, Ismet Atilla (DYP)
Education, Nevzat Ayaz (DYP)
Public Works and Housing, Erman Şahin (CHP)
Health, Dogan Baran (DYP)
Communications, Ali Şevki Erek (DYP)
Labour and Social Security, Ziya Halis (CHP)
Trade and Industry, Hasan Akyol (CHP)
Agriculture and Rural Affairs, Refaiddin Şahin (DYP)
Energy and Natural Resources, Veysel Atasoy (DYP)
Culture, Ismail Cem (CHP)
Tourism, Irfan Gürpinar (CHP)
Forestry, Hasan Ekinci (DYP)
Environment, Riza Akçali (DYP)
DYP True Path Party; CHP Republican People's Party

TURKISH EMBASSY
43 Belgrave Square, London SW1X 8PA
Tel 0171-393 0202
Ambassador Extraordinary and Plenipotentiary, His Excellency
    Özdem Sanberk, apptd 1995
Minister Counsellor, Cinar Aldemir
Defence Attaché, Col. A. Backlacioglu
Consul-General, A. Ünlütürk
Counsellor, T. F. Baran (*Commercial*)

BRITISH EMBASSY
Sehit Ersan Caddesi 46/A, Cankaya, Ankara
Tel: Ankara 4686230
Ambassador Extraordinary and Plenipotentiary, His Excellency
    Sir Kieran Prendergast, KCVO, CMG, apptd 1994
Counsellor, Deputy Head of Mission, N. A. Ling
First Secretary, D. T. Healy (*Commercial*)
Defence and Military Attaché, Brig. The Hon. S. J. T.
    Coleridge
Consul-General (*Istanbul*), M. E. Cook

BRITISH CONSULAR OFFICES, There is a Consulate-
General at Istanbul, a Vice-Consulate at Izmir and
Honorary Consulates at Antalya, Bodrum, Iskenderun,
Mersin and Marmaris.

BRITISH COUNCIL DIRECTOR, David Marler, OBE,
Kirklangic Sokak 9, Gazi Osman Pasa, Ankara 06700.
There is also a centre and library at Istanbul.

BRITISH CHAMBER OF COMMERCE OF TURKEY INC.,
Mesrutiyet Caddessi No. 34, Tepebasi Beyoğlu,
Istanbul (*postal address,* PO Box 190 Karaköy, Istanbul).

DEFENCE
The armed forces have a total active strength of 503,800 (410,200 conscripts), with a term of conscription of 15 months. Reserves number 952,300 with commitment to age 41. The Army has an active strength of 393,000 (345,000 conscripts) with 4,920 main battle tanks, 3,360 armoured personnel carriers and 2,430 artillery pieces. The Navy has 54,000 personnel (36,500 conscripts) including 3,000 marines, with 15 submarines, 5 destroyers, 16 frigates, 45 patrol and coastal craft, 21 combat aircraft and 17 armed helicopters. The Air Force has a strength of 56,800 (28,700 conscripts), with 555 combat aircraft. Paramilitary Gendarmerie and National Guard forces number 70,000 active and 50,000 reserve personnel.

Between 150,000 and 200,000 troops are stationed in the south-east of the country fighting Kurdish guerrillas.

Since its invasion of Cyprus in 1974, Turkey has maintained forces in the north of the island and at present has 30,000 men in two infantry divisions stationed there. Turkey has also deployed one infantry battalion of 1,534 troops with UN forces in Bosnia, one frigate in the Adriatic to patrol the weapons embargo on the former Yugoslavia, and an air force detachment of 18 aircraft in Italy for NATO operations over Bosnia.

As a member of NATO, Turkey is host to the Headquarters Allied Land Forces South-Eastern Europe and the Sixth Allied Tactical Air Force Headquarters. US (3,400 personnel), UK (260 personnel) and French (150 personnel) air force detachments are based at Incirlik air base in southern Turkey to patrol the air exclusion zone over northern Iraq.

ECONOMY
Agricultural production accounts for some 16 per cent of GDP at constant factor prices. About 50 per cent of the working population are in the rural sector. The principal crops are wheat, barley, rice, tobacco, sugar beet, tea, olives, grapes, figs and hazelnuts. With the exception of wheat, which is mostly grown on the arid central Anatolian plateau, most of the crops are grown on the fertile littoral. Tobacco, sultana and fig cultivation is centred around Izmir, where substantial quantities of cotton are also grown. The main cotton area is in the Cukurova plain around Adana. The forests that lie between the littoral plain and the Anatolian plateau contain beech, pine, oak, elm, chestnut, lime, plane, alder, box, poplar and maple. In 1990 28 per cent of the land area was forest.

After agriculture, Turkey's most important industry is based on the considerable mineral wealth which is, however, comparatively unexploited. The main export minerals are chromite and boron. Production in 1990 was (tons):

Coal	5,628,000
Lignite	46,892,000
Crude petroleum	3,753,000
Crude iron	4,928,000
Boron minerals	2,062,000

The bulk of the country's requirements in sugar, cotton, woollen and silk textiles, and cement, is produced locally. Other industries include vehicle assembly, paper, glass and glassware, iron and steel, leather and leather goods, sulphur refining, canning and rubber goods, soaps and cosmetics, pharmaceutical products, and prepared foodstuffs.

Steep rises in oil prices from 1973 onwards led to a succession of economic crises culminating in January 1980 in the introduction of an economic stability programme. Exports have since risen dramatically, topping US$11,846 million in 1988, but since 1988 imports have risen dramatically too, creating a significant trade gap. Inflation remains high (60 per cent in 1993). GNP growth for 1992 was 5.2 per cent and unemployment remains high. The total foreign debt in 1992 stood at US$54,700 million and the budget deficit in 1993 was equivalent to 9 per cent of GDP.

The government of Tansu Çiller has announced radical measures to deregulate, liberalize and transform the economy. The government effectively gained the power to issue decrees to run the economy without parliamentary approval in June 1992. About 100 large state-owned firms are debt-ridden and seen as a source of inflation, which reached an annual rate of 130 per cent in 1995. A large-scale privatization programme is under way, which is designed to raise some US$26,000 million in revenue. An austerity package of price rises, new taxes and job cuts in state industries was introduced in April 1994 to curb inflation and reduce the budget deficit. At the same time a standby agreement was reached with the IMF for loans of US$690 million over three years in return for a devaluation of the lira by 28 per cent; a further loan of US$742 million was approved in July 1994 in support of the 1994-5 economic reform programme.

TRADE

The main imports are machinery, crude oil and petroleum products, iron and steel, vehicles, medicines and dyes, chemicals, fertilizers and electrical appliances. Agricultural commodities (cotton, tobacco, fruits, nuts, livestock) represent 47 per cent of total exports. Other exports are minerals, textiles, glass and cement.

	1989	1991
Total imports	US$15,762.6m	US$22,302m
Total exports	11,627.3m	12,959m
Trade with UK	1993	1994
Imports from UK	£1,046,504,000	£813,522,000
Exports to UK	532,007,000	628,109,000

COMMUNICATIONS

The rail network is run by the State Railways Administration. The total length of lines in operation (1989) is 10,369 km. At the end of 1988 there were 59,128 km of roads (31,149 of which were national). The Bosporus is spanned by two bridges; plans are being drawn up for a third fixed link between the two continents. By the end of 1988 the number of ships over 18 gross tons was 3,805. The state airline (THY) operates all internal services and has services to Europe, the Far East, Africa, North America and the Middle East. Most of the leading European airlines operate services to Istanbul and some also to Ankara.

EDUCATION

Education is free, secular and compulsory at primary level. There are elementary, secondary and vocational schools. There are 27 universities in Turkey, including six in Istanbul, five in Ankara, two in Izmir, and one each in Erzurum and Trabzon.

CULTURE

Turkish was written in Arabic script until 1926 when a version of the Roman alphabet reflecting Turkish phonetics was substituted for use in official correspondence and in 1928 for universal use, with Arabic numerals as used throughout Europe. The revolution of 1908 led to the introduction of native literature free from foreign influences and adapted to the understanding of the people.

The leading Turkish newspapers are centred in Istanbul and Ankara, although most provincial towns have their own daily papers. There are foreign language papers in French, Greek, Armenian and English and numerous magazines and weeklies.

TURKMENISTAN
Turkmenostan Respublikasy

Turkmenistan has an area of 188,456 sq. miles (488,100 sq. km) and occupies the extreme south of the former Soviet Central Asia between the Caspian Sea and the Amu-Darya river. To the west it is bordered by the Caspian Sea, to the south by Iran, to the south-east by Afghanistan, to the east and north by Uzbekistan and to the north-west by Kazakhstan. The republic comprises five regions: Ashkhabad; Chardjou; Krasnovodsk; Mary; and Tashauz. The country is a low-lying plain fringed by hills in the south. Ninety per cent of the plain is taken up by the Obe Kara-Kum (Black Sands) desert. The climate is hot and dry.

The population (1995 estimate) is 3,808,900, of which 72 per cent are Turkomans, 9.5 per cent Russians and 9 per cent Uzbeks, together with smaller numbers of Kazakhs, Tatars, Ukrainians and Armenians. Most of the population are Sunni Muslims. The main languages are Turkmenian (72 per cent), Russian (9 per cent), Uzbek (9 per cent). Turkmenian is one of the Turkic languages.

CAPITAL – Ashkhabad. Population 407,000 (1990).
CURRENCY – Manat.
FLAG – Green with a vertical carpet pattern near the hoist in black, white and wine-red; in the upper hoist a crescent and five stars, all in white.
NATIONAL DAY – 27 October (Independence Day).

GOVERNMENT

Situated at the cross-roads of Central Asia, the area that is now Turkmenistan has been invaded and occupied by many empires: Persian; Greek under Alexander the Great; Parthian; Mongol. A Turkmenian nation was established in the 15th century but remained riven with dissent and divided between warring emirates. From the early 19th century until 1886 Turkmenistan was gradually incorporated into the Russian Empire. Soviet control over Turkmenistan was established on 30 April 1918 when it became an Autonomous Soviet Socialist Republic. The banks, cotton refineries and oil and gas fields were nationalized before a civil war broke out in July 1918, sparked by the intervention of British troops from Iran and India. The war ended in 1920 with the withdrawal of the interventionist forces and Turkmenistan became a full republic of the Soviet Union in February 1925.

Turkmenistan declared its independence from the Soviet Union on 27 October 1991 and gained UN membership on 2 March 1992. The constitution passed on 18 May 1992 makes the President head of state and government and provides for a bicameral legislature of the existing Supreme Soviet (renamed the *Majlis*) and a 60-member (50 directly elected and ten appointed) supervisory upper house, the *Khalk Maslakhaty* (People's Council).

The autocratic government of President Niyazov has prevented any effective political opposition or free press through harassment and the continuation of Soviet authoritarianism. The political leadership has rejected political pluralism and instead a cult of personality has developed around President Niyazov. The Supreme Soviet voted on 30 December 1993 to extend the term of President Niyazov to 2002 and this was confirmed by a 99.99 per cent vote in a referendum on 15 January 1994. The Communist Party, renamed the Democratic Party, remains in power. Legislative elections to the *Khalk Maslakhaty* were won by the Democratic Party.

In 1991–2 there were fears of inter-ethnic tension and conflict with Russia because the constitution abolished the use of Russian as the official language of inter-ethnic communication. However, these fears have failed to materialize and in 1993–4 Turkmenistan's relations with Russia and the CIS improved. In 1992 joint Turkmen–Russian armed forces of 34,000 army and air force personnel were established and remain in operation. In late 1993 Turkmen–Russian agreements were signed allowing Russian troops to protect the borders with Iran and Afghanistan; Russian citizens to undergo military training in Turkmenistan; Turkmen officers to train in Russia; and Turkmenistan to bear the cost of Russian forces in the country. Agreement on dual citizenship for ethnic Russians in Turkmenistan was also reached. In December 1993 Turkmenistan signed the CIS charter to become a full CIS member and in January 1994 became a member of the CIS economic union.

HEAD OF STATE

President, Saparmurad Niyazov, *elected* 27 October 1990, *re-elected* 21 June 1992, *appointed head of government* 18 May 1992, *elected by referendum for an eight-year term* 15 January 1994

COUNCIL OF MINISTERS *as at August 1995*

Prime Minister, The President
Deputy PM, Foreign Affairs, Boris Shikmuradov
Deputy PM, Interior, National Security, Justice, Batyr Sarjayev
Deputy PM, Construction, Transport and Communications, Yagmur Ovezov
Deputy PMs, Orasgeldy Ajdogdyev; Matkarim Rajapov; Reedjep Saparov; Klekhim Ishanov; Batyr Ovezov
Defence, Dangatar Kopekov
Trade, Halnazar Agakhanov
Economy and Finance, Muhamed Abalakov
Justice, Tagandurdy Khallyev
Culture and Tourism, Geldymurad Nurmukhamedov
Health, Gurbangeldy Kadamov
Communications, Anmanmurad Djummiev
Oil and Gas, Aman Ezenov
Agriculture and Foodstuffs, Tagandurdy Nuryev
Social Affairs, Khalykberdy Ataiev
Construction and Architecture, Allaberdy Tekaiev
Education, Rejepdurdye Karaev
Water Conservancy, Amannazar Ilamanov
Automobile Transport and Roads Maintenance, Senkuly Rakhmanov
Foreign Economic Relations, Chary Kuliev
Environment, Dortkuli Kurbanov
Industry, Khalmukhamed Orazsakhatov
Consumer Goods, Ashir Ataiev

Grain Products, Amageldy Chariyarov
Power Engineering and Industry, Saparmurad Nuryev

BRITISH EMBASSY
Ashkhabad
Ambassador Extraordinary and Plenipotentiary, His Excellency Neil Hook, MVO, apptd 1995

ECONOMY

The large reserves of natural gas and the foreign revenue that they earn make the country economically viable and have enabled the government to maintain low stable prices for all basic commodities and utilities.

Cotton cultivation, stock-raising and mineral extraction are the principal industries, together with the natural gas production and the long-established silk industry. Some fisheries exist along the Caspian sea coast. Arable land is irrigated by the Niyazov canal, which cuts through the Kara Kum desert. There are estimated reserves of some 700 million tonnes of oil and 8,000,000 million cubic metres of natural gas. Natural gas is exported by pipeline to Ukraine and western Europe and another pipeline is being built through Iran and Turkey to Europe.

Agreements have been reached with Iran to build rail links so that the Persian Gulf and Mediterranean can be reached.

TRADE WITH UK	1993	1994
Imports from UK	£14,619,000	£4,382,000
Exports to UK	25,000	837,000

TUVALU

Tuvalu comprises nine coral atolls situated in the southwest Pacific around the point at which the International Date Line cuts the Equator. The total land area is about 10 sq. miles. Few of the atolls are more than 12 ft above sea level or more than half a mile in width. The vegetation consists mainly of coconut palms.

The resident population in 1985 was 8,229, but it is estimated that about 1,500 Tuvaluans work overseas, mostly in Nauru, or as seamen. The UN estimated that the population was 12,000 in 1992. The people are almost entirely Polynesian. The principal languages are Tuvaluan and English. The entire population is Christian, predominantly Protestant.

CAPITAL – ΨFunafuti, estimated population 2,856. The capital has a grass strip airfield from which a service operates regularly to Fiji and Kiribati, and is also the only port.
CURRENCY – Tuvalu uses the Australian dollar ($A) of 100 cents as legal tender. In addition there are Tuvalu dollar and cent coins in circulation.
FLAG – Blue ground with Union Flag in top left quarter and nine five-pointed gold stars in the fly (under review).
NATIONAL ANTHEM – Tuvalu Mo Te Atua (Tuvalu for the Almighty).
NATIONAL DAY – 1 October (Independence Day).

GOVERNMENT

Tuvalu, formerly the Ellice Islands, formed part of the Gilbert and Ellice Islands Colony until 1 October 1975, when separate constitutions came into force. Separation from the Gilbert Islands was implemented on 1 January 1976. On 1 October 1978 Tuvalu became a fully independent state within the Commonwealth.

The constitution provides for a Prime Minister and four other Ministers, who must be members of the 12-member elected Parliament. The Prime Minister presides at meetings of the Cabinet, which consists of the five Ministers, and is attended by the Attorney-General. Local government services are provided by elected Island Councils.

Governor-General, His Excellency Tulaga Manuella

CABINET *as at August 1995*

Prime Minister, Foreign Affairs and Economic Planning, Hon. Kamuta Latasi
Deputy Prime Minister, Natural Resources, Home Affairs and Rural Development, Hon. Otinielu Tausi
Labour, Works and Communications, Hon. Houati Iele
Health and Human Resource Development, Hon. Faimalaga Luka, OBE
Finance, Trade, Commerce, Public Corporations, Koloa Talake
BRITISH HIGH COMMISSIONER, His Excellency Michael Peart, CMG, LVO, resides at Suva, Fiji

SOCIAL WELFARE

There are eight primary schools in Tuvalu and a church secondary school run jointly with the Government. A maritime training school caters for 60 boys a year. There is a 30-bed hospital at Funafuti. All islands are served by a dispensary and a primary school.

ECONOMY

Most people still practise a subsistence economy, the main staples of the diet being coconuts and fish. The main imports are foodstuffs, consumer goods and building materials. The only export is copra, though philatelic sales provide a major source of revenue and handicraft sales are increasing. However, Tuvalu is almost entirely dependent on foreign aid.

TRADE WITH UK	1993	1994
Imports from UK	£74,000	£134,000
Exports to UK	£1,000	£1,000

UGANDA
Republic of Uganda

Uganda is situated in eastern Africa, flanked by Zaire, Sudan, Kenya and on the south by Tanzania and Rwanda. Large parts of Lakes Victoria, Edward and Albert (Mobuto) are within its boundaries, as are Lakes Kyoga, Kwania, George and Bisina (formerly Salisbury) and the course of the River Nile from its outlet from Lake Victoria to the Sudan border at Nimule. Uganda has an area of 91,259 sq. miles (236,036 sq. km) (water and swamp 16,400 sq. miles) and a population (1992 UN estimate) of 18,674,000. The official language is English. The main local vernaculars are of Bantu, Nilotic and Hamitic origins. Ki-Swahili is generally understood.

Despite its tropical location, the climate is tempered by its situation some 3,000 ft above sea level, and well over that altitude in the highlands of the Western and Eastern Regions. Uganda has three National Parks and a fourth (Lake Mburo) has been designated.

CAPITAL – Kampala (estimated population of Greater Kampala, 1990, 750,000). Other principal towns are Jinja (45,000), Mbale (28,000) and Masaka (29,000).
CURRENCY – Uganda shilling of 100 cents.

FLAG – Six horizontal stripes of black, yellow, red, with a white disc in the centre containing the badge of a crested crane.
NATIONAL ANTHEM – Oh Uganda.
NATIONAL DAY – 9 October (Independence Day).

GOVERNMENT

Uganda became an independent state within the Commonwealth on 9 October 1962, after some 70 years of British rule. A republic was instituted in 1967, under an executive President assisted by a Cabinet of Ministers.

Early in 1971 an army coup took place and Maj.-Gen. Idi Amin, the army commander, proclaimed himself head of state. In 1979, following risings and military intervention by Tanzania, President Amin was overthrown. Dr Milton Obote became President in 1980 but was ousted by a military coup in 1985. A military council was installed but the National Resistance Movement led by Yoweri Museveni captured Kampala in January 1986, securing control of the rest of the country in the following few months. Yoweri Museveni was sworn in as President in January 1986; subsequently a National Resistance Council (NRC) was appointed to draw up a constitution. A draft constitution was published in February 1993. Elections to a constituent assembly to amend the draft constitution were held in March 1994, the assembly having 214 elected and 66 appointed seats. The National Resistance Movement won the majority of the seats; the assembly plans to debate the draft constitution. The ban on political party activity in the interest of stability will continue until 2000.

HEAD OF STATE
President, Yoweri Museveni, *sworn in* 29 January 1986
Vice-President, Speciosa Wandira Kazibwe

CABINET *as at August 1995*

Defence, The President
Gender and Community Development, The Vice-President
Prime Minister, Kintu Musoke
First Deputy PM, Eriya Kategaya
Second Deputy PM, Public Service, Paul Ssemogerere
Third Deputy PM, Lands, Housing and Urban Development, Eric Adriko
Interior, Crispus Kiyonga
Foreign Affairs, Ruhakana Rugunda
Finance and Economic Planning, Joshua Mayanja-Nkangi
Agriculture, Animal Industry and Fisheries, Mrs Victoria Ssekitoleko
Commerce, Industry and Co-operatives, Richard Kaijuka
Local Government, Jaberi Bidandi-Ssali
Educational and Sports, Amanya Mushega
Information, Paul Etiang
Labour and Social Affairs, Stephen Chebrot
Works, Transport and Communications, Ali Kirunda Kivejinja
Tourism, Wildlife and Antiquities, Brig. Moses Ali
Health, James Makumbi
Natural Resources, Henry Kajura
Justice, Joseph Ekemu

UGANDA HIGH COMMISSION
Uganda House, 58–59 Trafalgar Square, London WC2N 5DX
Tel 0171–839 5783
High Commissioner, His Excellency Prof. George Kirya, apptd 1990
Deputy High Commissioner, D. Ssozi
Financial Attaché, A. Bamweyana

BRITISH HIGH COMMISSION
10–12 Parliament Avenue, PO Box 7070, Kampala
Tel: Kampala 257054/9

High Commissioner, His Excellency Edward Clay, CMG, apptd 1993
Deputy High Commissioner, J. O. Atkinson
Defence Adviser, Lt.-Col. N. P. C. Lewis, MBE
First Secretary (Commercial), P. L. D. Byrde

BRITISH COUNCIL DIRECTOR, Roger Wilkins (*Cultural Attaché*)

EDUCATION

Education is a joint undertaking by the government, local authorities and voluntary agencies. In 1988 Uganda had an estimated 7,905 primary schools with 2,638,100 children, 774 secondary schools with 240,834 students; and 7,291 students in various technical training institutions. There are four universities, Makerere University in Kampala, the Uganda Martyrs University, and at Mbale and Mbarara.

COMMUNICATIONS

There is an international airport at Entebbe, and eight other airfields around the country. Having no sea coast, Uganda is dependent upon rail and road links to Mombasa and Dar es Salaam for its trade. Over 5,000 km of the country's roads are currently being rehabilitated. A railway network joins the capital to the western, eastern and northern centres.

ECONOMY

Since 1988 the government has been successful in implementing an IMF recovery programme. The civil service and army have been reduced in size, foreign investment encouraged, and property returned to Asians expelled by Idi Amin. Annual growth since 1988 has averaged 6 per cent, inflation has been reduced to 3 per cent a year and aid donors in June 1993 gave £550 million of aid. In October 1994 the IMF approved a US$175 million loan to support the government's economic reform programme over the next three years. In February 1995 the Paris Club of bilateral official aid donors agreed to write off two-thirds of Uganda's debt to them.

The principal export earner is coffee, over 90 per cent of all exports. Attempts are being made to increase production of tobacco, cocoa, cotton and tea for export. Hydroelectricity is produced from the Owen Falls power station, some of which is exported to Kenya. The principal food crops are plantains, bananas, cassava, sweet potatoes, potatoes, maize and sorghum; livestock raising and inshore fishing are also important.

TRADE WITH UK	1993	1994
Imports from UK	£30,439,000	£40,779,000
Exports to UK	7,601,000	15,491,000

UKRAINE
Ukraina

Ukraine has an area of 233,090 sq. miles (603,700 sq. km) and lies in the south-west of the European part of the former Soviet Union. It is bordered on the north by Belarus and Russia, on the east by Russia, on the south by the Black Sea, on the south-west by Romania and Moldova and on the west by Hungary, Slovakia and Poland. The area of the present Ukraine is larger than that of the Ukrainian Soviet Republic formed in 1917–19 because of the westward territorial expansion of the former Soviet Union in the 1939–45 period and the addition of the Crimea from Russia in 1954. The Ukraine now consists of 25 regions:

Cherkassy, Chernigov, Chernovtsy, Crimea, Dnepropetrovsk, Donetsk, Ivano-Frankovsk, Kharkov, Kherson, Khmelnitsky, Kiev, Kirovograd, Lugansk, Lvov, Nikolayev, Odessa, Poltava, Rovno, Sumy, Ternopol, Transcarpathia, Vinnitsa, Volhynia, Zaporozhye and Zhitomir.

Most of the Ukraine forms a plain with small elevations. The Carpathian mountains lie in the south-western part of the republic. The main rivers are the Dnieper with its tributaries, the Southern Bug and the Northern Donets (a tributary of the Don). The climate is moderate with relatively mild winters (particularly in the south-west) and hot summers.

The population (1989 census) was 51,471,000, of which 73 per cent are Ukrainian and 22 per cent Russian, with smaller numbers of Jews, Belarusians, Moldovans, Tatars, Poles, Hungarians and Greeks. The 1995 estimate put the population at 52,100,000.

The two main religions are Roman Catholicism and Orthodox. The Orthodox rite is divided between the Russian Orthodox Church with its Patriarch in Moscow and the Autocephalous Orthodox Church of the Ukraine with its own Patriarch in Kiev. There are also large numbers of Reformed Protestants in the Transcarpathian region and a sizeable Jewish community in Kiev.

The main languages are Ukrainian (73 per cent) and Russian (22 per cent). Ukrainian is an Eastern Slavonic language related to Russian and Belarusian.

CAPITAL – Kiev. Population 2,577,000 (1989). Other major cities (1990) are Kharkov (1,611,000); Dnepropetrovsk (1,179,000); ΨOdessa (1,115,000); Donetsk (1,110,000).
CURRENCY – Coupons called Karbovanets were introduced in November 1992 and are fully convertible to the rouble.
FLAG – Two horizontal stripes of blue over yellow.
NATIONAL DAY – 24 August (Independence Day).

GOVERNMENT

The earliest Russian state was formed in the middle reaches of the Dnieper River with its capital at Kiev in the ninth century AD. The state united the two large Slav states of Kiev and Novgorod and established the first common Russian language and nationality. The state lasted until Kiev fell to the Mongols in 1240. For the next four centuries the Ukraine was invaded and ruled by Tatars, Turks, Poles, Hungarians and Lithuanians. In 1648 the Ukrainians threw off Polish rule to become independent and increasingly allied with Russia (formerly Muscovy). During the reign of Catherine the Great of Russia (1763–96) the Ukraine and the Crimea came under Russian control.

By the time of the Treaty of Brest-Litovsk in March 1918, most of the Ukraine had been occupied by German and Austrian forces. The Treaty forced the Soviet government in Moscow to cede parts of western Ukraine to Germany and Austria-Hungary and accept the independence of the remainder. After the defeat of Germany in 1918, the Ukraine became a battleground in the Russian civil war before the imposition of Soviet rule in 1922. The Ukraine became a constituent republic of the USSR on 30 December 1922. The 1920s saw the collectivization of agriculture, which led to a famine in which millions died, and the Stalinist purges caused thousands more to be killed. The Ukraine was again devastated in the Second World War and millions of Ukrainians died. The country was rebuilt and heavily industrialized in the post-war period.

The Ukraine declared itself independent of the Soviet Union, subject to a referendum, after the failed Moscow coup in August 1991. The referendum was held on 1 December 1991 and 90 per cent of the electorate voted for independence. Simultaneously, the former Ukrainian Communist leader Leonid Kravchuk was elected President of the Republic. Political power in the Ukraine in 1991–4 rested with the former Communists, led by the President, in loose alliance with the Rukh nationalist party. This has limited political and economic change, although Leonid Kuchma, Prime Minister 1992–3, began to introduce economic reforms in December 1992, with privatization and the partial liberalization of price controls. Kuchma resigned in September 1993 after the Supreme Council obstructed his reform programme and President Kravchuk effectively took over the government. Economic chaos due to strikes forced the President to call early legislative and presidential elections.

In the legislative elections, by a first-past-the-post system, to the 450-seat Supreme Council in March to November 1994, the western regions of Ukraine voted for nationalist and reformist candidates while the eastern regions voted for Communist and allied ones; the result was a majority of Communist and allied candidates, plus 'independents' who were mainly agricultural and industrial managers tied to the status quo. In the June 1994 presidential election Kuchma defeated President Kravchuk.

A power struggle over who should appoint and control the cabinet and over economic reform soon developed between President Kuchma and the Supreme Council. Kuchma inherited the government of his predecessor President Kravchuk and was only finally able to appoint his own government in March 1995. This reformist government lost a no confidence vote in the Supreme Council but President Kuchma refused to dismiss it, and in June 1995 secured the passing of a 'constitutional treaty' by the Supreme Council. This gives the President the power to appoint and dismiss the government without reference to the Supreme Council and allows greater presidential power to rule by decree in certain policy areas.

The situation of the Crimea with its ethnic Russian majority has caused concern, as the Crimean parliament voted to make the Crimea an autonomous republic in September 1991, which was accepted by Kiev, but then voted for independence in May 1992, which was not accepted and was suspended. A Russian nationalist, Yuri Meshkov, was elected President of Crimea in January 1994 and the Crimean parliament in May 1994 restored the suspended 1992 constitution declaring sovereignty. A constitutional and political crisis in the Crimea caused by a power struggle between President Meshkov and the Crimean parliament from September 1994 onwards was solved by Ukrainian intervention in March 1995. The Supreme Council voted to suppress the Crimean constitution and abolish the Crimean presidency, removing the Crimea's autonomous status and reducing it to a region of the Ukraine. This was confirmed in a presidential decree by President Kuchma on 3 April when the Crimean government was subordinated to the Ukrainian Cabinet.

A referendum in June 1994 in the Donbass region of eastern Ukraine in favour of closer economic ties with Russia and making Russian an official language was overwhelmingly passed, as was one in the Crimea in favour of dual Russian–Ukrainian citizenship.

HEAD OF STATE
President, Leonid Kuchma, *elected* 10 July 1994, *sworn in* 19 July 1994

CABINET *as at August 1995*

Prime Minister, Evgeny Marchuk
First Deputy PM, Pavel Lazarenko

Deputy PM, Security, Emergencies and Combating Organized Crime, Vasili Durdinets
Deputy PM, Industry, Anatoly Kinakh
Deputy PM, Humanitarian Policy, Ivan Kuras
Deputy PM, Agro-Industries, Pyotr Sabluk
Deputy PM, Economy, Roman Shpek
Foreign Economic Relations and Trade, Sergei Osyka
Interior, Yuri Kravchenko
Health, Vladimir Bobrov
Foreign Affairs, Gennadi Yudovenko
Defence, Valeri Shmarov
Environment, Yuri Kostenko
Education, Mikhail Zgurovsky
Industry, Valeri Mazur
Communications, Oleg Prozhivalsky
Agriculture, Yuri Karasik
Social Security, Arkady Yershov
Transport, Orest Klimpush
Labour, Mikhail Kaskevich
Finance, Petr Germanchuk
Economics, Vasili Gureiev
Justice, Vasili Onopenko
Youth and Sport, Valeri Borzov
Nationalities, Alexander Yemets
Press and Information, Mikhail Onufriychuk
Construction, Yuri Serbin
Forestry, Valeri Samoplavsky
Power Engineering, Vilen Semenyuk
Military Industry, Viktor Petrov

Chairman of the Supreme Council, Alexander Moroz

UKRAINIAN EMBASSY
78 Kensington Park Road, London WII 2PL
Tel 0171-727 6312
Ambassador Extraordinary and Plenipotentiary, His Excellency Prof. Sergui Komisarenko, apptd 1992
Minister-Counsellor, Prof. M. Bilooussov
Counsellor (Economic and Commercial), Dr B. Savchuk

BRITISH EMBASSY
252025 Kiev Desyatinna 9
Tel: Kiev 228 0504
Ambassador Extraordinary and Plenipotentiary, His Excellency Roy Reeve, apptd 1995
Consul-General and Deputy Head of Mission, R. T. Jenkins, OBE
Defence Attaché, Capt. L. P. C. Merrick, RN
First Secretary (Commercial), T. Abbott-Watt
BRITISH COUNCIL DIRECTOR – John Day, 9/1
Bessarabska Ploshcha, Flat 9, Kiev 252004.

DEFENCE

Since the demise of the Soviet Union, Russia and Ukraine have clashed over defence issues. All strategic nuclear weapons were placed under a central CIS command in December 1991, but on the abolition of the central command in July 1993 the government claimed possession of all nuclear weapons on its territory. Despite international pressure, the Supreme Council only ratified the START I Treaty in February 1994 and the Nuclear Non-Proliferation Treaty in November 1994.

Under a January 1994 USA–Russia–Ukraine Treaty, the Ukrainian nuclear arsenal will be transferred to Russia for dismantling over a seven-year period. This includes all the warheads in Ukraine's 166 inter-continental ballistic missiles and carried by its 42 nuclear-capable bombers (some 1,800 warheads in total). In return Ukraine has received a territorial guarantee by Russia, a cancellation of a large part of its debt to Russia, and nuclear security guarantees from Russia and the USA. Ukraine will also receive lower grade uranium from Russia for use in its power stations; economic and technical aid from the USA; US$300 million from the USA to pay for dismantling the weapons; and US$1,000 million to buy some of the enriched uranium from the warheads. The first warheads were transferred to Russia in March 1994.

Agreement between Ukraine and Russia over the division of the former Soviet Black Sea Fleet was reached in June 1995. The fleet is to be divided 81:19 Russian: Ukrainian, with Russia retaining the use of and the control of the fleet base at Sevastopol. The fleet remains under joint Russian–Ukrainian control, with a strength of 48,000 personnel (including 2,000 marines), 20 submarines, one helicopter carrier, four cruisers, five destroyers, 21 frigates, 241 combat aircraft and 85 combat helicopters.

The total armed forces number 517,000 personnel (including 47,000 central staff but excluding Navy), with conscripts serving 24 months. The Army numbers 308,000 personnel, with 5,380 main battle tanks, 7,260 armoured personnel carriers and armoured infantry fighting vehicles and 3,060 artillery pieces. The Air Force and air defence forces have 146,000 personnel, with 995 combat aircraft, 305 attack helicopters and 825 surface-to-air missiles. The paramilitary National Guard and Border Guard number 66,000 personnel.

Ukraine deploys an infantry battalion of 580 troops with UN forces in Bosnia.

ECONOMY

Throughout 1991–4 the Communist-led government and legislature obstructed economic reform and economic mismanagement resulted. The economy came close to collapse because of hyperinflation caused by the printing of money to support uneconomic enterprises and to pay strikers' wage demands. Industrial output and GDP fell considerably, while Russia threatened to cut all oil and gas supplies as Ukraine could not pay in hard currency. Ukraine has joined the CIS economic union as an associate member and is likely to seek full membership for access to better trading relations with Russia. In March 1995 Ukrainian debt to Russia was US$5,000 million.

President Kuchma has, since September 1994, introduced a wide-ranging economic reform programme. Price controls on food and rents have been lifted, as have currency and export controls; subsidies to industries are being reduced; agricultural reform has begun; mass privatization has started. The economic reform programme has been supported by US$2,700 million in aid and loans, while a large proportion of Ukraine's debt to Russia has been paid by granting Russian enterprises shares in Ukrainian firms which are to be privatized; the remainder of the debt has been rescheduled. Under economic reform the exchange rate has stabilized and inflation has fallen to 10 per cent a month. Some 8,000 enterprises are to be privatized in 1995–6.

The southern part of the country contains a coal-mining and iron and steel industrial area which was the largest in the former Soviet Union. The Ukraine also contains engineering and chemical industries and ship-building yards on the Black Sea coast. Ukrainian agricultural production is good with large areas under cultivation with wheat, cotton, flax and sugar beet; stock-raising is very important. There are large deposits of coal and salt in the Donets Basin, of iron ore in Krivoy Rog and near Kerch in the Crimea, of manganese in Nikopol, and of quicksilver in Nikitovka.

The major ports are Odessa, Nikolayev, Kerch and Sevastopol.

TRADE WITH UK	1993	1994
Imports from UK	£73,091,000	£86,284,000
Exports to UK	12,462,000	18,072,000

UNITED ARAB EMIRATES
Al-Imarat Al-Arabiya Al-Muttahida

The United Arab Emirates are situated in the south-east of the Arabian peninsula. Six of the emirates lie on the shore of the Gulf between the Musandam peninsula in the east and the Qatar peninsula in the west while the seventh, Fujairah, lies on the Gulf of Oman. The climate varies between hot and humid in May to September and mild with erratic rainfall in October to April. The approximate area is 32,278 sq. miles (83,600 sq. km), and the population (1993 estimate) is 2,310,000, of which 75 per cent are expatriates. The official language is Arabic, and English is widely spoken. The established religion is Islam.

CAPITAL – Abu Dhabi. Population (city) 450,000.
CURRENCY – UAE dirham (Dh) of 100 fils.
FLAG – Horizontal stripes of green over white over black with vertical red stripe in the hoist.
NATIONAL DAY – 2 December.

GOVERNMENT

The United Arab Emirates (formerly the Trucial States) is composed of seven emirates (Abu Dhabi, Ajman, Dubai, Fujairah, Ras al-Khaimah, Sharjah and Umm al-Qaiwain) which came together as an independent state on 2 December 1971 when they ended their individual special treaty relationships with the British Government (Ras al-Khaimah joined the other six on 10 February 1972). On independence the Union Government assumed full responsibility for all internal and external affairs apart from some internal matters that remained the prerogative of the individual emirates.

Overall authority lies with the Supreme Council of the seven emirate rulers, each of whom also governs in his own territory. The President and Vice-President are elected every five years by the Supreme Council from among its members. The Supreme Council appoints the Council of Ministers. A 40-member Federal National Council, drawn proportionately from each emirate and composed of appointees of the rulers, studies draft laws referred to it by the Council of Ministers. Each emirate also has its separate government, with Abu Dhabi having an executive council chaired by the Crown Prince.

The legal system consists of both secular and religious courts guided by the Islamic philosophy of justice. Individual emirates retain their own penal codes and courts alongside a federal court system and penal code.

Relations with Iran remain strained over Iran's illegal occupation of three UAE islands in the Gulf (Abu Musa and the Two Tunbs).

HEAD OF STATE
President, HH Sheikh Zayed bin Sultan al-Nahyan (*Abu Dhabi*), *elected* 1971, *re-elected* 1976, 1981, 1986, October 1991
Vice-President, HH Sheikh Maktoum bin Rashid al-Maktoum (*Dubai*), *elected* October 1991

SUPREME COUNCIL *as at August 1995*
President, HH Sheikh Zayed bin Sultan al-Nahyan (*Abu Dhabi*)
Vice-President, HH Sheikh Maktoum bin Rashid al-Maktoum (*Dubai*)

HH Sheikh Sultan bin Mohammed al-Qassimi (*Sharjah*)
HH Sheikh Saqr bin Mohammed al-Qassimi (*Ras Al-Khaimah*)
HH Sheikh Hamid bin Mohammed al-Sharqi (*Fujairah*)
HH Sheikh Humaid bin Rashid al-Nuaimi (*Ajman*)
HH Sheikh Rashid bin Ahmed al-Mualla (*Umm al-Qaiwain*)

COUNCIL OF MINISTERS *as at August 1995*
The President
Prime Minister, The Vice-President
Deputy Prime Minister, Sheikh Sultan bin Zayed al-Nahyan
Finance and Industry, HH Sheikh Hamdan bin Rashid al-Maktoum
Defence, HH Lt.-Gen. Sheikh Mohammed bin Rashid al-Maktoum
Interior, Lt.-Gen. Dr Mohammed Saeed al-Badi
Foreign Affairs, Rashid Abdullah al-Nuaimi
Communications, Mohammed Saeed al-Mulla
Planning, Sheikh Humaid bin Ahmed al-Mu'alla
Islamic Affairs and Endowments, Sheikh Mohammed bin Ahmed al Khazraji
Water and Electricity, Humaid bin Nasser al-Owais
Economy and Commerce, Saeed Ghobash
Agriculture and Fisheries, Saeed al-Ragabani
Labour and Social Affairs, Saif al-Jarwan
Information and Culture, Khalfan bin Mohammed al-Roumi
Education, Hamad Abdul Rahman al-Madfa
Higher Education, HH Sheikh Nahyan bin Mubarak al-Nahyan
Justice, Dr Abdullah bin Omran Taryam
Health and Environment, vacant
Petroleum and Mineral Resources, Ahmed bin Saeed al-Badi
Public Works and Housing, Rakkad bin Salem bin Rakkad
Youth and Sports, Sheikh Faisal bin Khaled al-Qassimi
Minister of State for Cabinet Affairs, Saeed al-Ghaith
Minister of State for Financial and Industrial Affairs, Ahmed bin Humaid al-Tayer
Minister of State for Foreign Affairs, Sheikh Hamdan bin Zayed al-Nahyan
Minister of State for Supreme Council Affairs, Sheikh Mohammed bin Saqr al-Qassimi

EMBASSY OF THE UNITED ARAB EMIRATES
30 Prince's Gate, London SW7 1PT
Tel 0171–581 1281
Ambassador Extraordinary and Plenipotentiary, His Excellency Easa Saleh Al-Gurg, CBE, apptd 1991
Minister-Plenipotentiary, Khalid Abdul-Latif Al-Bassam
Military Attaché, Lt.-Col. M. A. M. Al-Mehrizi
Cultural Attaché, A. A. M. Al-Marri

BRITISH EMBASSIES
PO Box 248, Abu Dhabi
Tel: Abu Dhabi 326600
Ambassador Extraordinary and Plenipotentiary, His Excellency Anthony David Harris, CMG, LVO, apptd 1994
First Secretary, Consul and Deputy Head of Post, W. R. Henderson, LVO
First Secretary (Commercial), J. P. R. Girdlestone
Defence Attaché, Col. C. J. Copeland

PO Box 65, Dubai
Tel: Dubai 521070
Counsellor and Consul-General, C. E. J. Wilton
Deputy Head of Post, Consul and First Secretary (Commercial), J. C. Fisher

BRITISH COUNCIL REPRESENTATIVES
Abu Dhabi – David Latta (*Cultural Attaché*).
Dubai – A. Mackay, PO Box 1636, Dubai
There is also an office at Al Ain

DEFENCE

The armed forces of the emirates were merged in 1976, although Dubai still retains some independent units. The total active armed forces strength is 61,500, of which around 30 per cent are hired or seconded foreign nationals. The Army is 57,000 strong including 12,000 Dubai forces, and is equipped with 125 main battle tanks, 76 light tanks, 160 reconnaissance vehicles, 605 armoured personnel carriers and armoured infantry fighting vehicles and 235 artillery pieces. The Navy has a strength of 2,000 personnel, with 19 patrol and coastal vessels. The Air Force is 2,500 strong, including 700 Dubai forces, with 97 combat aircraft and 39 armed helicopters. Some 2,000 Moroccan troops are stationed in the UAE.

ECONOMY

The UAE is the Gulf's third largest oil producer after Saudi Arabia and Iran, producing 3 million barrels per day (bpd) in 1993, and with oil reserves of 200,000 million barrels and gas reserves of 200,000,000 million cubic feet. Oil production in 1993 accounted for 40 per cent of GDP. Other important sectors of the economy are government, re-exporting, construction, manufacturing (aluminium, cement, chemicals, fertilizers, ship repair), finance and insurance services, and transport and communications. Tourism is growing in importance. Agricultural production (vegetables, dates, fruit, milk, eggs, poultry, flowers, olives, animal husbandry) has increased significantly due to large-scale water desalination and irrigation projects, with 280,000 hectares of agricultural land in 1993. There is no personal or corporate taxation apart from on oil companies and foreign banks.

Fourteen major ports, of which nine are modern container terminals, handled 35 million tonnes of cargo in 1993. Six international airports (Dubai, Abu Dhabi, Sharjah, Ras al-Khaimah, Fujairah, Al Ain) are in operation.

Oil revenues over the past 30 years have enabled the government to invest heavily in education, health and social services, housing, transport and communications infrastructure, and agriculture, and enabled the UAE's citizens to have one of the highest GDPs per capita in the world.

TRADE	1993
Exports	Dhs 85,200m
Imports	67,700m

Trade with UK	1993	1994
Imports from UK	£1,314,578,000	£1,113,578,000
Exports to UK	251,453,000	230,670,000

SOCIAL WELFARE

In 1993 there were 300,000 pupils studying at the 580 government schools, where education is free; some 150,000 (many expatriates) attended 300 private schools. The Emirates University at Al Ain (Abu Dhabi) had 10,900 students in 1993, and the three Colleges of Technology (Abu Dhabi, Dubai, Al Ain) had 1,800 students. There are 29 government and six private hospitals, 96 government health centres and 500 private clinics with a total of 4,300 beds.

ABU DHABI

Abu Dhabi is by far the largest emirate, with an area of 30,888 sq. miles (80,000 sq. km) stretching from Khor al-Odaid in the west to the borders with Dubai in the Jebel Ali area. It includes six villages in the Buraimi oasis, the other three being part of the Sultanate of Oman, and a number of settlements in the Liwa oasis system. Following negotiations with Saudi Arabia, some adjustment of the border has now been made in the Khor al-Odaid region, but the agreement has not yet been ratified. The population of the Emirate (1990) is 889,000

The Abu Dhabi government controls oil, gas and petrochemical operations in the emirate through the Supreme Petroleum Council. This body in turn issues instructions to the Abu Dhabi National Oil Company (ADNOC) which has majority shareholdings in the oil operating and gas treatment companies, and in oil industry-related companies covering drilling, refining, distribution, chemical manufacture and investment. Production began offshire in 1962 and onshore in 1963. Crude oil production in 1990 was approximately 1.65 million barrels per day. With its oil wealth the emirate has seen a period of growth (which is currently slowing down), in Abu Dhabi, Al-Ain in the Buraimi oasis and in the new petro-chemical city at Ruwais.

AJMAN AND UMM AL-QAIWAIN

Ajman (100 sq. miles, 259 sq. km) and Umm al-Qaiwain (300 sq. miles, 777 sq. km) are the smallest emirates in area; they have populations (1990) of 92,000 and 21,000 respectively. Both lie on the Gulf coast although Ajman has two inland enclaves at Manama and Masfut. Exploration work continues in both emirates for oil and gas but so far only Umm al-Qaiwain has experienced any success, with the offshore discovery of natural gas, but the field has yet to be commercially developed. The discovery of onshore gas in nearby Sharjah has increased hopes of similar discoveries in both Ajman and Umm al-Qaiwain.

DUBAI

Dubai is the second largest emirate both in size (1,506 sq. miles, 3,900 sq. km) and in population, which is (1990) 559,000. The town of Dubai is the main port for the UAE. Dubai's prosperity was established by this trade long before the discovery of oil in 1966; production began in 1969. The producer in Dubai's offshore oilfields is Dubai Petroleum Company, operated by CONOCO. Production is in excess of 350,000 b.p.d. In 1982 an extensive gas and condensate field was discovered onshore. A small amount of condensate is produced from the onshore Margam field. Oil income has been used to finance Dubai's infrastructure. The port of Jebel Ali, at the heart of an industrial complex, and its immediate area is a free trade zone which is expected to attract more industry.

FUJAIRAH

Fujairah, with an area of 502 sq. miles (1,300 sq. km) and a population (1990) of 76,000, is the most remote of the seven emirates, lying on the Gulf of Oman coast and only connected by a metal road to the rest of the country. Largely agricultural, its population is spread between the slopes of the inland Hajar mountain range and the town of Fujairah itself, together with a number of smaller settlements on the comparatively fertile plain on the coast. Although exploration work continues, there have been no hydrocarbon discoveries in the emirate. However, there are some chrome and other mineral deposits and a free trade zone has been established.

RAS AL-KHAIMAH

Ras al-Khaimah has an area of 656 sq. miles (1,700 sq. km) and a population (1990) of 159,000, of whom more than half live in the town. An ancient sea-port, near to which archaeological remains have been found, Ras al-Khaimah

is the most agricultural of the emirates, producing vegetables, dates, fruit and tobacco. In 1982 oil and gas were discovered offshore and this field currently produces approximately 5,000 b.p.d. An industrial area has been developed to the north of the emirate, and the infrastructure has been developed. It is hoped that more industry will be attracted to the emirate.

SHARJAH

Sharjah, with an area of 1,004 sq. miles (2,600 sq. km) and a population (1990) of 377,000, has declined from its former position as principal town in the area. Oil production began in 1974 and gas discoveries were made in 1982; production now stands at about 55,000 b.p.d. Sharjah is connected by metalled roads to all the other northern emirates. A container port has been constructed on the Gulf of Oman at Khor Fakkan. A free trade zone has been established.

UNITED STATES OF AMERICA

The United States of America occupies nearly all of the North American continent between the Atlantic and Pacific Oceans, in 25° 07' to 49° 23' N. latitude and 66° 57' to 124° 44' W. longitude, its northern boundary adjoining Canada and the southern boundary Mexico. The separate state of Alaska reaches a latitude of 71' 23° N., at Point Barrow. The coastline has a length of about 2,069 miles on the Atlantic, 7,623 miles on the Pacific, 1,060 miles on the Arctic, and 1,631 miles on the Gulf of Mexico.

The principal river is the Mississippi-Missouri-Red (3,710 miles long), traversing the whole country to its mouth in the Gulf of Mexico; its main affluents are the Yellowstone, Platte, Arkansas, and Ohio rivers. The chain of the Rocky Mountains separates the western portion of the country from the remainder. West of these, bordering the Pacific coast, the Cascade Mountains and Sierra Nevada form the outer edge of a high tableland, consisting in part of stony and sandy desert and partly of grazing land and forested mountains, and including the Great Salt Lake, which extends to the Rocky Mountains. In the eastern states large forests still exist, the remnants of the forests which formerly extended over all the Atlantic slope. The highest point is Mount McKinley (20,320 ft) in Alaska, and the lowest point of dry land is in Death Valley (Inyo, California), 282 ft below sea-level.

AREA AND POPULATION

	Total land area 1990 (sq. miles)	Population census 1990
The United States (a)	3,536,278	248,709,873
Outlying areas under US jurisdiction	4,043	3,847,309
Territories	4,027	3,847,116
Puerto Rico	3,427	3,522,037
Guam	210	133,152
US Virgin Islands	134	101,809
American Samoa	77	46,773
Northern Mariana Is.	179	43,345
Other possessions	16	193
Population abroad (b)	–	925,845
TOTAL	3,540,321	253,483,027

(a) the 50 states and the Federal District of Columbia
(b) excludes US citizens temporarily abroad on business

The total population was estimated at 259,681,000 on 1 January 1994

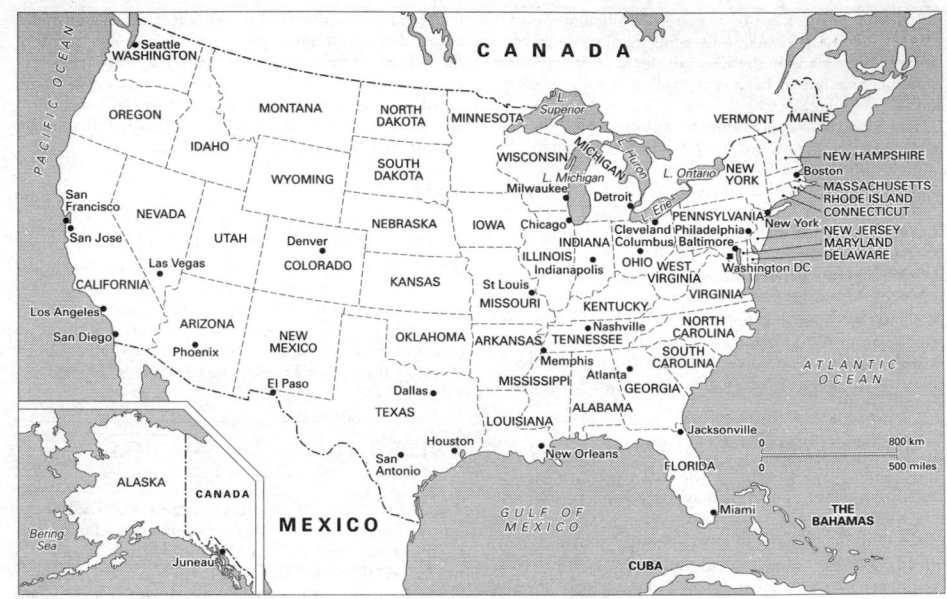

RESIDENT POPULATION BY RACE 1990 (*Thousands*)

White	199,686.1
Black	29,986.1
*American Indian	1,959.2
Chinese	1,645.5
Filipino	1,406.8
Japanese	847.6
Asian Indian	815.4
Korean	798.8
Vietnamese	614.5
Other Asian	780.0
Pacific Islander	365.0
All other races	9,804.8
†Hispanic origin	22,354.1
Cuban	1,043.9
Mexican	13,495.9
Puerto Rican	2,727.8
Other Hispanic	5,086.4
TOTAL	248,709.9

*Includes Eskimo and Aleut
†Persons of Hispanic origin may be of any race

IMMIGRATION

From 1820 to 1994, 61,503,866 immigrants were admitted to the United States. Total number of immigrants in 1994 was 804,416, of which 319,603 came from North and South America (111,398 from Mexico), 292,589 from Asia and 160,916 from Europe.

VITAL STATISTICS

In 1993 (provisional figures) live births were 4,039,000, a rate of 15.7 per 1,000 of population. Deaths were 2,268,000, a rate of 8.8 per 1,000 of population. In 1993 marriages were 2,334,000, a rate of 9.0 per 1,000 of population. Divorces were approximately 1,187,000, a rate of 4.6 per 1,000 of population.

LARGEST CITIES 1992 *estimate*

ΨNew York, NY	7,311,966
ΨLos Angeles, California	3,489,779
ΨChicago, Illinois	2,768,483
ΨHouston, Texas	1,690,180
ΨPhiladelphia, Pennsylvania	1,552,572
ΨSan Diego, California	1,148,851
Dallas, Texas	1,022,497
Phoenix, Arizona	1,012,230
ΨDetroit, Michigan	1,012,110
San Antonio, Texas	966,437

Ψ seaport

CAPITAL

The federal capital is the City of Washington in the District of Columbia. It is situated on the west central edge of Maryland, opposite the state of Virginia, on the left bank of the Potomac at its confluence with the Anacostia. The area of the District of Columbia (with which the City of Washington is considered co-extensive) is 61 sq. miles, with a resident population (mid-1992 estimate) of 585,221. The population of the metropolitan area in 1992 was estimated at 4,360,349. The District of Columbia is governed by an elected mayor and City Council.

CURRENCY – The dollar ($) of 100 cents.

FLAG – Thirteen horizontal stripes, alternately red and white, with blue canton in the fly showing 50 white stars in nine horizontal rows of six and five alternately (known as the Star-Spangled Banner).

NATIONAL ANTHEM – The Star-Spangled Banner.
NATIONAL DAY – 4 July (Independence Day).

GOVERNMENT

The United States of America is a federal republic consisting of 50 states and the federal District of Columbia and of organized territories. Of the present 50 states, 13 are original states, seven were admitted without previous organization as territories, and 30 were admitted after such organization.

THE STATES OF THE UNION

STATE (with date and *order* of admission)	LAND AREA sq. m.	POPULATION (1990 census)	CAPITAL	GOVERNOR (term of office in years, and expiry year)
Alabama (Ala.) (1819) (*22*)	50,750	4,040,587	Montgomery	Fob James (*R*) (4 – 1999)
Alaska (1959) (*49*)	570,374	550,043	Juneau	Tony Knowles (*D*) (4 – 1998)
Arizona (Ariz.) (1912) (*48*)	113,642	3,665,228	Phoenix	Fife Symington (*R*) (4 – 1999)
Arkansas (Ark.) (1836) (*25*)	52,075	2,350,725	Little Rock	Jim Guy Tucker (*D*) (4 – 1999)
California (Calif.) (1850) (*31*)	155,973	29,760,021	Sacramento	Pete Wilson (*R*) (4 – 1999)
Colorado (Colo.) (1876) (*38*)	103,729	3,294,394	Denver	Roy Romer (*D*) (4 – 1999)
Connecticut (Conn.)§(1788) (*5*)	4,845	3,287,116	Hartford	John Rowland (*R*) (4 – 1999)
Delaware (Del.) § (1787) (*1*)	1,955	666,168	Dover	Tom Carper (*D*) (4 – 1997)
Florida (Fla.) (1845) (*27*)	53,997	12,937,926	Tallahassee	Lawton Chiles (*D*) (4 – 1999)
Georgia (Ga.) § (1788) (*4*)	57,919	6,478,216	Atlanta	Zell Miller (*D*) (4 – 1999)
Hawaii (1959) (*50*)	6,423	1,108,229	Honolulu	Ben Cayetano (*D*) (4 – 1998)
Idaho (1890) (*43*)	82,751	1,006,749	Boise	Phil Batt (*R*) (4 – 1999)
Illinois (Ill.) (1818) (*21*)	55,593	11,430,602	Springfield	Jim Edgar (*R*) (4 – 1999)
Indiana (Ind.) (1816) (*19*)	35,870	5,544,159	Indianapolis	Evan Bayh (*D*) (4 – 1997)
Iowa (1846) (*29*)	55,875	2,776,755	Des Moines	Terry Branstad (*R*) (4 – 1999)
Kansas (Kan.) (1861) (*34*)	81,823	2,477,574	Topeka	Bill Graves (*R*) (4 – 1999)
Kentucky (Ky.) (1792) (*15*)	39,732	3,685,296	Frankfort	Brereton C. Jones (*D*) (4 – 1996)
Louisiana (La.) (1812) (*18*)	43,566	4,219,973	Baton Rouge	Edwin Edwards (*D*) (4 – 1996)
Maine (Me.) (1820) (*23*)	30,865	1,227,928	Augusta	Angus King (*I*) (4 – 1999)
Maryland (Md.) § (1788) (*7*)	9,775	4,781,468	Annapolis	Parris Glendening (*D*) (4 – 1999)
Massachusetts (Mass.) § (1788) (*6*)	7,838	6,016,425	Boston	William Weld (*R*) (4 – 1999)
Michigan (Mich.) (1837) (*26*)	56,809	9,295,297	Lansing	John Engler (*R*) (4 – 1999)
Minnesota (Minn.) (1858) (*32*)	79,617	4,375,099	St Paul	Arne Carlson (*R*) (4 – 1999)
Mississippi (Miss.) (1817) (*20*)	46,914	2,573,216	Jackson	Kirk Fordice (*R*) (4 – 1996)
Missouri (Mo.) (1821) (*24*)	68,898	5,117,073	Jefferson City	Mel Carnahan (*D*) (4 – 1997)
Montana (Mont.) (1889) (*41*)	145,556	799,065	Helena	Marc Raciot (*R*) (4 – 1997)
Nebraska (Neb.) (1867) (*37*)	76,878	1,578,385	Lincoln	Ben Nelson (*D*) (4 – 1999)
Nevada (Nev.) (1864) (*36*)	109,806	1,201,833	Carson City	Robert J. Miller (*D*) (4 – 1999)
New Hampshire (NH) § (1788) (*9*)	8,969	1,109,252	Concord	Steve Merrill (*R*) (2 – 1997)
New Jersey (NJ) § (1787) (*3*)	7,419	7,730,188	Trenton	Christine Whitman (*R*) (4 – 1998)
New Mexico (NM) (1912) (*47*)	121,365	1,515,069	Santa Fé	Gary Johnson (*R*) (4 – 1999)
New York (NY) § (1788) (*11*)	47,224	17,990,455	Albany	George Pataki (*R*) (4 – 1999)
North Carolina (NC) § (1789) (*12*)	48,718	6,628,637	Raleigh	James B. Hunt, jun. (*D*) (4 – 1997)
North Dakota (ND) (1889) (*39*)	68,994	638,800	Bismarck	Edward Schafer (*R*) (4 – 1997)
Ohio (1803) (*17*)	40,953	10,847,115	Columbus	George Voinovich (*R*) (4 – 1999)
Oklahoma (Okla.) (1907) (*46*)	68,679	3,145,585	Oklahoma City	Frank Keating (*R*) (4 – 1999)
Oregon (Ore.) (1859) (*33*)	96,003	2,842,321	Salem	John Kitzhaber (*D*) (4 – 1999)
Pennsylvania (Pa.) § (1787) (*2*)	44,820	11,881,643	Harrisburg	Tom Ridge (*R*) (4 – 1999)
Rhode Island (RI) § (1790) (*13*)	1,045	1,003,464	Providence	Lincoln Almond (*R*) (2 – 1997)
South Carolina (SC) § (1788) (*8*)	30,111	3,486,703	Columbia	David Beasley (*R*) (4 – 1997)
South Dakota (SD) (1889) (*40*)	75,896	696,004	Pierre	William Janklow (*R*) (4 – 1999)
Tennessee (Tenn.) (1796) (*16*)	41,220	4,877,185	Nashville	Don Sundquist (*R*) (4 – 1999)
Texas (1845) (*28*)	261,914	16,986,510	Austin	George W. Bush (*R*) (4 – 1999)
Utah (1896) (*45*)	82,168	1,722,850	Salt Lake City	Mike Leavitt (*R*) (4 – 1997)
Vermont (Vt.) (1791) (*14*)	9,249	562,758	Montpelier	Howard Dean (*D*) (2 – 1997)
Virginia (Va.) § (1788) (*10*)	39,598	6,187,358	Richmond	George Allen (*R*) (4 – 1998)
Washington (Wash.) (1889) (*42*)	66,581	4,866,692	Olympia	Mike Lowry (*D*) (4 – 1997)
West Virginia (W. Va.) (1863) (*35*)	24,087	1,793,477	Charleston	Gaston Caperton (*D*) (4 – 1997)
Wisconsin (Wis.) (1848) (*30*)	54,314	4,891,769	Madison	Tommy Thompson (*R*) (4 – 1999)
Wyoming (Wyo.) (1890) (*44*)	97,105	453,588	Cheyenne	Jim Geringer (*R*) (4 – 1999)
Dist. of Columbia (DC) (1791)	61	606,900	—	Marion Barry (*D*) (*Mayor*)

OUTLYING TERRITORIES AND POSSESSIONS

American Samoa	77	46,773	Pago Pago	A. P. Lutati (*D*) (4 – 1997)
Guam	210	133,152	Agaña	Carl Gutierrez (*D*) (4 – 1999)
Northern Mariana Islands	179	43,345	Saipan	Froilan C. Tenorio (*D*) (4 – 1998)
Puerto Rico	3,427	3,522,037	San Juan	Dr Pedro J. Rossello (*PNP*) (4 – 1997)
US Virgin Islands	134	101,809	Charlotte Amalie	Roy Schneider (*I*) (4 – 1999)

§The 13 original states
D Democratic Party; *I* Independent; *PNP* New Progressive Party; *R* Republican Party

By the constitution of 17 September 1787 (to which amendments were added in 1791, 1798, 1804, 1865, 1868, 1870, 1913, 1920, 1933, 1951, 1961, 1964, 1967, 1971 and 1992), the government of the United States is entrusted to three separate authorities: the executive (the President and Cabinet), the legislature (Congress) and the judicature.

The President is indirectly elected every four years. There is also a Vice-President, who, should the President die, becomes President for the remainder of the term. The tenure of the presidency is limited to two terms.

The President, with the consent of the Senate, appoints the Cabinet officers and all the chief officials. He makes recommendation of a general nature to Congress, and when laws are passed by Congress he may return them to Congress with a veto. But if a measure so vetoed is again passed by both Houses of Congress by two-thirds majority in each House, it becomes law, notwithstanding the objection of the President. The President must be at least 35 years of age and a native citizen of the United States.

Presidential elections

Each state elects (on the first Tuesday after the first Monday in November of the year preceding the year in which the presidential term expires) a number of electors, equal to the whole number of Senators and Representatives to which the state may be entitled in the Congress. The electors for each state meet in their respective states on the first Monday after the second Wednesday in December following, and vote for a President by ballot. The ballots are then sent to Washington, and opened on 6 January by the President of the Senate in the presence of Congress. The candidate who has received a majority of the whole number of electoral votes cast is declared President for the ensuing term. If no one has a majority, then from the highest on the list (not exceeding three) the House of Representatives elects a President, the votes being taken by states, the representation from each state having one vote. A presidential term begins at noon on 20 January.

President of the United States, William Jefferson Blythe IV Clinton, *born* 19 August 1946, *sworn in* 20 January 1993. Democrat
Vice-President, Albert Gore, jun., *born* 31 March 1948, *sworn in* 20 January 1993

THE CABINET *as at August 1995*

Secretary of State, Warren Christopher
Secretary of the Treasury, Robert Rubin
Secretary of Defence, William Perry
Attorney-General, Janet Reno
Secretary of the Interior, Bruce Babbit
Secretary of Agriculture, Daniel Glickman
Secretary of Commerce, Ron Brown
Secretary of Labour, Robert Reich
Secretary of Health and Human Services, Donna Shalala
Secretary of Housing and Urban Development, Henry Cisneros
Secretary of Transportation, Federico Pena
Secretary of Energy, Hazel O'Leary
Secretary of Education, Richard Riley
Secretary of Veterans' Affairs, Jesse Brown
Ambassador to the UN, Madeleine Albright
US Trade Representative, Mickey Kantor
Administrator, Environmental Protection Agency, Carol Browner
Director, Office of Management and Budget, Alice Rivlin
National Security Adviser, Anthony Lake
White House Chief of Staff, Leon Panetta

Other senior positions:
Director of CIA, John Deutsch

Director, Office of National Drug Control Policy, Lee Brown
Director of FBI, Louis Freeh
Chairman, Federal Reserve Board of Governors, Alan Greenspan

UNITED STATES EMBASSY
24 Grosvenor Square, London WIA IAE
Tel 0171-499 9000
Ambassador Extraordinary and Plenipotentiary, The Honourable Adm. William J. Crowe jun., apptd 1994
Minister, T. E. Deal
Defence and Naval Attaché, Capt. J. E. Hart
Minister-Counsellors, T. H. Gewecke (*Economic*); M. F. O'Brien (*Cultural*); N. S. Baskey, jun. (*Administrative*); C. A. Ford (*Commercial*); E. A. Swift (*Consular*)

BRITISH EMBASSY
3100 Massachusetts Avenue NW, Washington DC 20008
Tel: Washington DC 462 1340
Ambassador Extraordinary and Plenipotentiary, His Excellency Sir John Kerr, KCMG, apptd 1995
Ministers, H. P. Evans (*Economic*); S. Webb (*Defence Equipment*); D. B. Logan, CMG; C. H. Mak, E. B. Wiggam, CBE (*Hong Kong Economic and Trade Affairs*)
Head of British Defence Staff and Defence Attaché, Rear-Adm. D. A. Blackburn, LVO, RN
Counsellor, H. Parkinson (*Management and HM Consul-General*)
Consul-General (*New York*) *and Director-General of Trade and Investment*, Sir Alistair Hunter, KCMG
Cultural Attaché and British Council Director, David Evans

BRITISH CONSULATES-GENERAL – Atlanta, Boston, Chicago, Houston, Los Angeles, New York and San Francisco.
BRITISH CONSULATES – Anchorage, Charlotte, Cleveland, Dallas, Denver, Kansas City, Miami, Minneapolis, New Orleans, Orlando, Philadelphia, Portland, St Louis, Salt Lake City, Seattle and Puerto Rico.

BRITISH-AMERICAN CHAMBER OF COMMERCE, 275 Madison Avenue, New York 10016; UK OFFICE, Suite 201, High Holborn, London WCIV 6RR

THE CONGRESS

Legislative power is vested in two houses, the Senate and the House of Representatives. The Senate has 100 members, two Senators from each state, elected for the term of six years, and each Senator has one vote. Representatives are chosen in each state, by popular vote, for two years.

The House of Representatives consists of 435 Representatives, a resident commissioner from Puerto Rico and a delegate each from American Samoa, the District of Columbia, Guam and the Virgin Islands.

Members of the 104th Congress were elected on 2 November 1994. The 104th Congress is constituted as follows:

Senate – Republicans 54; Democrats 46; total 100
House of Representatives – Republicans 233; Democrats 201; Independent 1; total 435 (August 1995)

President of the Senate, The Vice-President
Senate Majority Leader, Robert Dole (*R*), *Kansas*
Speaker of the House of Representatives, Newton Gingrich (*R*), *Georgia*
Secretary of the Senate, Kelly D. Johnson, *Virginia*
Clerk of the House of Representatives, Robin H. Carle, *Virginia*

THE JUDICATURE

The federal judiciary consists of three sets of federal courts: the Supreme Court at Washington DC, consisting of a Chief Justice and eight Associate Justices, with original jurisdiction in cases where a state is a party to the suit, and with appellate jurisdiction from inferior federal courts and from the judgments of the highest courts of the states; the United States Courts of Appeals, dealing with appeals from district courts and from certain federal administrative agencies, and consisting of 168 circuit judges within 13 circuits; the 94 United States district courts served by 575 district court judges.

THE SUPREME COURT

US Supreme Court Building, Washington DC 20543

Chief Justice, William H. Rehnquist, *Arizona*, apptd 1986

Associate Justices
John Paul Stevens, *Illinois*, apptd 1975
Sandra Day O'Connor, *Arizona*, apptd 1981
Antonin Scalia, *Virginia*, apptd 1986
Anthony M. Kennedy, *California*, apptd 1988
David H. Souter, *New Hampshire*, apptd 1990
Clarence Thomas, *Georgia*, apptd 1991
Ruth Bader Ginsburg, *New York*, apptd 1993
Stephen Breyer, *Massachusetts*, apptd 1994

Clerk of the Supreme Court, William K. Suter

CRIMINAL STATISTICS *Number of offences*

	1992	1993
Murder and non-negligent manslaughter	23,760	24,526
Forcible rape	109,062	106,014
Robbery	672,478	659,757
Aggravated assault	1,126,974	1,135,099
Burglary	2,979,884	2,834,808
Larceny – theft	7,915,199	7,820,909
Thefts of motor vehicles	1,610,834	1,561,047
Total	14,438,191	14,142,160

DEFENCE

Each military department is separately organized and functions under the direction, authority and control of the Secretary of Defence. The Air Force has primary responsibility for the Department of Defence space development programmes and projects.

Secretary of Defence (in the Cabinet), Dr William Perry
Chairman, Joint Chiefs of Staff, Gen. John Shalikashvili

STRENGTHS *as at 30 May 1995*
The US Army had a strength of 527,514. The strength of the Navy was 445,902 active duty personnel. The strength of the Marine Corps was 171,928 active duty personnel. The Air Force had 409,127 officers and airmen on active duty.

DEPLOYMENT

Under strategic command the USA has 384 submarine-launched ballistic missiles, 705 inter-continental ballistic missiles and 200 heavy nuclear-capable bombers, together with multiple intelligence satellites, radars and early warning systems throughout the world. The Army deploys 14,524 main battle tanks, 125 light tanks, 35,080 armoured infantry fighting vehicles and armoured personnel carriers, 5,960 artillery pieces, 386 aircraft and 1,490 armed helicopters. The Navy deploys 17 strategic (SLBM) submarines, 85 tactical submarines, 13 aircraft carriers, 34 cruisers, 41 destroyers, 51 frigates, 24 patrol and coastal combatants, 184 amphibious and support ships, 1,675

combat aircraft and 390 armed helicopters. The Marine Corps has 287 main battle tanks, 1,960 armoured vehicles, 1,050 artillery pieces, 495 combat aircraft and 242 armed helicopters. The Air Force deploys 200 long-range and 3,330 tactical combat aircraft and 3,165 transport, tanker and training aircraft. The major deployments of US personnel overseas are: Germany (103,900); UK (14,550); Italy (12,600); Mediterranean (17,000); Japan (44,800); South Korea (36,250); Panama (7,100); Spain (4,500); Turkey (3,400).

FINANCE

BUDGET

	1993	1994
Total receipts	$1,153.2 bn	$1,257.2 bn
Total outlay	1,408.5 bn	1,460.6 bn
Defence	291.1 bn	281.5 bn
Social security	304.6 bn	319.6 bn
Income security	207.3 bn	214.0 bn
Debt interest	198.8 bn	203.0 bn

SOCIAL WELFARE EXPENDITURE 1992

	Total	Per capita
Social insurance	$616,975 m	$2,369
Education	292,199 m	1,126
Public aid	207,945 m	801
Health and medical	71,035 m	274
Veterans' programmes	34,767 m	130
Other social welfare	21,532 m	83
Housing	20,617 m	79
TOTAL	1,265,070 m	4,863

PUBLIC DEBT

At the end of September 1992 the total gross federal debt stood at US$4,002,815 million.

ECONOMY

GROSS DOMESTIC PRODUCT BY INDUSTRY 1993

	US$ millions
Private industries	5,559,454
Agriculture, forestry, fisheries	107,299
Mining	89,378
Construction	234,225
Manufacturing	1,118,298
Transportation and public utilities	559,283
Wholesale trade	413,110
Retail trade	592,389
Finance, insurance, and real estate	1,180,627
Services	1,264,845
Government and government enterprises	781,598
Statistical discrepancy	2,303
TOTAL	6,343,355

AGRICULTURE

The total number of farms in 1994 was 2,040,410, with a total area of land in farms of 974,800,000 acres, and an average acreage per farm of 478 acres. The total number of people employed on farms during the week of 9–15 April 1995 was 2,822,000, of whom 386,000 were unpaid workers, 822,000 hired workers and 214,000 agricultural service workers. Principal crops are corn for grain, soybeans, wheat hay, cotton, tobacco, grain sorghums, potatoes, oranges and barley.

Livestock on farms on 1 January 1994 and 1995 was:

	1994	1995
Cattle and calves	100,988,000	103,265,000
Milk cows	9,528,000	9,532,000
Sheep and lambs	9,742,000	8,895,000
Hogs and pigs	57,904,000	59,992,000
Chickens	379,640,000	383,779,000

Gross income from farming in 1994 was US$213,700 million, of which cash receipts from marketing were US$190,700 million and government payments US$7,800 million. Cash income from all crops in 1994 was US$91,600 million and from livestock and livestock products US$88,300 million.

MINERALS

The value of non-fuel raw mineral production in 1993 totalled an estimated US$31,844 million compared with US$32,012 million in 1992. Mineral exports in 1993 were valued at US$26,904 million, and imports at US$41,583 million.

Production ('000 metric tons)	1992	1993
Iron ore	55,593	55,661
Phosphate rock	46,965	35,494
Zinc ore	523	488
Refined copper	1,765	1,801
Refined lead	305	335

ENERGY

Production in 1994 was 70.43 quadrillion BTU, principally coal, natural gas and crude oil. Coal accounted for almost half of energy exports of 4.09 quadrillion BTU. Imports were 22.41 quadrillion BTU, of which crude oil was 15.26 quadrillion BTU, to meet consumption of 88.45 quadrillion BTU (quadrillion=10^{15}).

LABOUR

The civilian labour force was 131,869,000 in June 1995. Unemployment was estimated at 7,384,000 in June 1995 (5.6 per cent) (6.1 per cent in June 1994).

TRADE	1991	1992
General imports		
c.i.f. value	US$510,168m	US$553,335m
customs value	488,453	532,665
Exports and re-exports		
†f.a.s. value	421,853	447,471
Trade balance		
f.a.s. exports: c.i.f.		
imports	−88,315	−105,864
f.a.s. exports: customs		
imports	−65,723	−84,501

†excluding military aid

Principal sources of imports were Asian countries (of which Japan contributed 41 per cent), north and central America (of which Canada 68 per cent), Europe (of which EC countries 83 per cent). Principal destinations for exports and re-exports were Asian states (of which Japan took 34 per cent), north and central America (of which Canada 63 per cent), Europe (of which EC 83 per cent).

Trade with UK	1993	1994
Imports from UK	£15,354,306,000	£16,792,741,000
Exports to UK	16,357,928,000	17,728,209,000

COMMUNICATIONS

Revenue, etc., of class I line-haul railroads (US$ thousands):

	1991	1992
Operating revenue		
Total	27,845,000	28,349,000
Freight	26,949,000	27,508,000
Passenger	962,300	933,200
Total operating expenses	28,061,000	25,325,000
Railroad track (miles)	234,000	227,000
Average number of		
employees	206,000	197,000

In 1992 there were 3.9 million miles of public roads and streets, of which 3.12 million miles were in rural areas and 785,160 miles were in urban areas. Surfaced roads and streets account for 58.8 per cent of the total. An estimated total of US$80,012 million was spent in 1992 on roads and streets in the United States. In 1992 there were 39,235 deaths caused by motor vehicle accidents. The death rate per 100 million vehicle-miles of travel was 1.75 in 1992 compared with 1.91 in 1991.

The ocean-going merchant marine on 1 April 1995 consisted of 540 vessels of 1,000 gross tons and over, of which 351 were privately-owned and 189 were government-owned ships. There were 138 ships in the National Defence Reserve Fleet of inactive government-owned vessels.

According to preliminary figures, US domestic and international scheduled airlines in 1994 carried 528,715,417 passengers over 519,036,589,000 revenue passenger miles. Air cargo ton-miles were distributed as follows: freight and express 18,961,259,583; and air mail 2,540,743,616. Total operating revenues of all US scheduled airlines were US$87,338,617,000 in 1994. Total operating expenses rose to US$84,578,460,127 in 1994. Scheduled operations showed a net operating loss of US$2,760,156,873 in 1994, compared with a net operating loss of US$1,443,619,545 in 1993.

EDUCATION

All the states and the District of Columbia have compulsory school attendance laws. In general, children are obliged to attend school from seven to 16 years of age. In the autumn of 1994, 49,610,000 children were enrolled in regular elementary and secondary day schools, of whom 5.58 million or 11.2 per cent attended private schools.

During the 1992–3 school year, the average daily attendance in regular public elementary and secondary day schools was 39,567,978. In the 1993–4 school year 2,225,000 students graduated from regular public high schools and 254,000 graduated from private high school. In addition an estimated 498,000 received high school equivalency certificates. Public school teachers numbered 2,505,075, with an average salary of US$35,819.

Most of the revenue for public elementary and secondary school purposes comes from federal, state, and local governments. Less than one per cent comes from gifts and from tuition and transportation fees. Revenue receipts during 1992–3 amounted to US$248,500 million; 6.9 per cent from the federal government, 45.6 per cent from state governments, and 47.4 per cent from local sources. Estimated current expenditure in the 1992–3 school year was US$221,400 million; for sites, buildings, furniture and equipment expenditures, US$22,700 million; for interest on school debt US$5,439 million.

HIGHER EDUCATION

In the autumn of 1994, total enrolment in universities, colleges, professional schools, and two-year schools numbered 14,300,000.

During 1992–3 the major fields for bachelor's degrees were business and management (256,842), social sciences (135,703), education (107,781) and engineering (61,973). First-profession degrees in law (40,302) and medicine (15,531) predominated. Master's degrees were heavily concentrated in education (96,028) and business and management (89,615). The most popular fields of study for doctorates were education (7,030) and engineering (5,823). Total expenditures for colleges and universities during the 1992–3 academic year were US$165,241 million.

Among the better-known universities are: Harvard, founded at Cambridge, Mass. in 1636, and named after John Harvard of Emmanuel College, Cambridge, England, who bequeathed to it his library and a sum of money in 1638; Yale, founded at New Haven, Connecticut, in 1701; Princeton, NJ, founded 1746.

US TERRITORIES, ETC

Responsibility for territorial affairs generally is centred in the Office of the Assistant Secretary, Territorial and International Affairs, Department of the Interior, Washington DC.

As well as the territories mentioned below, the USA also exercises sovereignty over the following:

Johnston Atoll – two small islands, less than 1 sq. mile in area, to the south-west of Hawaii; administered by the US Air Force.

Midway Islands – two islands (area, 3 sq. miles), at the western end of the Hawaiian chain; administered by the US Navy.

Wake Islands – area about 3 sq. miles and average elevation of less than 3 metres, lying about 2,300 miles west of Hawaii; administered by the US Air Force.

Certain small guano islands, rocks or keys, considered as appertaining to the USA.

THE COMMONWEALTH OF PUERTO RICO

Puerto Rico (Rich Port) is an island of the Greater Antilles group in the West Indies, and lies between 17° 50' and 18° 30' N. latitude and 65° 30' and 67° 15' W. longitude, with a total area of 3,427 sq. miles (8,875 sq. km), and a population (1994 estimate) of 3,600,000. The 1990 census put the population at 3,522,037. The majority of the inhabitants are of Spanish descent, and Spanish and English are the official languages.

Puerto Rico was discovered in 1493 by Columbus and explored by Ponce de Léon in 1508. It was a Spanish possession until 1898, when the USA took formal possession as a result of the Spanish-American War.

The 1952 constitution establishes the Commonwealth of Puerto Rico with full powers of local government. The Legislative Assembly consists of two elected houses; the Senate of 27 members and the House of Representatives of 51 members. The term of the Legislative Assembly is four years. The Governor is popularly elected for a term of four years. Residents of Puerto Rico are US citizens. Puerto Rico is represented in Congress by a Resident Commissioner, elected for a term of four years, who has a seat in the House of Representatives but not a vote, although he has a right to vote on those committees of which he is a member.

A plebiscite on the future constitutional status of Puerto Rico was held on 14 November 1993 in which 48 per cent voted to maintain the existing Commonwealth status, 46 per cent voted for full US statehood and 4 per cent for independence. The existing Commonwealth status continues which gives Puerto Rico the benefit of a common market with the USA and leaves it without the burden of federal taxes.

Preliminary 1994 figures for the Commonwealth government's budget were receipts, US$12,627 million. Manufacturing added US$13,183 million to net Commonwealth income in 1993 (preliminary figures), trade US$3,834 million, finance, insurance and real estate US$4,000 million and agriculture US$468 million. Principal crops are sugar cane, coffee, vegetables, fruits and tobacco. Most valuable areas of manufacturing are chemicals and allied products, metal products and machinery, and food processing.

CAPITAL – ΨSan Juan, population of the municipality (1990), 437,745; Other major towns are: Bayamón (220,262); ΨPonce (187,749); and Carolina (177,806).

Governor, Dr Pedro J. Rossello

TRADE	1992	1993
Total Imports	US$19,677m	US$19,133m
Total Exports	21,051m	19,791m
Trade with UK	1992	1993
Imports from UK	£188,417,000	£309,154,000
Exports to UK	107,113,000	77,236,000

GUAM

Guam, the largest of the Mariana Islands in the north Pacific Ocean, lies in 13° 26' N. latitude and 144° 39' E. longitude and has an area of about 210 sq. miles (544 sq. km). The population (1990 estimate) is 133,152, mostly of Chamorro stock mingled with Filipino and Spanish blood. The Chamorro language belongs to the Malayo-Polynesian family, but with considerable admixture of Spanish. Chamorro and English are the official languages and most residents are bilingual.

Guam was occupied by the Japanese in December 1941 but was recaptured by US forces in 1944. Under the Organic Act of Guam 1950, Guam has statutory powers of self-government, and Guamanians are US citizens. A 21-member unicameral legislature is elected biennially. The Governor and Lieutenant-Governor are popularly elected. A non-voting Delegate is elected to serve in the US House of Representatives. There is also a District Court of Guam, with original jurisdiction in cases under federal law.

Guam's two main sources of revenue are tourism and US military spending.

CAPITAL – Agaña. Port of entry, ΨApra.

Governor, Carl Gutierrez
Lt.-Governor, Frank Blas

AMERICAN SAMOA

American Samoa consists of the islands of Tutuila, Anu'u, Ofu, Olesega, Ta'u, Rose and Swains Islands, with a total area of 77 sq. miles (199 sq. km). Tutuila, the largest of the group, has an area of 52 sq. miles and a magnificent harbour at Pago Pago. The remaining islands have an area of about 24 sq. miles. The population (1990 estimate) is 46,773. Tuna and copra are the chief exports.

American Samoans are US nationals, but some have acquired citizenship through service in the United States armed forces or other naturalization procedure. The 1960 constitution grants American Samoa a measure of self-government, with certain powers reserved to the US Secretary of the Interior. There is a bicameral legislature with popularly elected Representatives and Governors and a popularly elected Governor. A non-voting Delegate is elected to serve in the US House of Representatives.

SEAT OF GOVERNMENT – Fagatogo.

Governor, A. P. Lutali
Lt.-Governor, Tauese P. Sunia

THE VIRGIN ISLANDS

The US Virgin Islands were purchased from Denmark and proclaimed US territory in 1917. The total area of the islands is 134 sq. miles (347 sq. km), with a population (1990) of 101,809. There are three main islands, St Thomas (28 sq. miles), St Croix (84 sq. miles), St John (20 sq. miles) and about 50 small islets or cays, mostly uninhabited.

Under the provisions of the Revised Organic Act of the Virgin Islands 1954, legislative power is vested in the Legislature, a unicameral body composed of 15 senators popularly elected for two-year terms. The Governor is popularly elected. Virgin Islanders are US citizens. A non-voting Delegate is elected to serve in the US House of Representatives. A referendum is to take place at a future date to determine the future political status of the islands.

CAPITAL – ΨCharlotte Amalie on St Thomas. Population (1980) 11,756.

Governor, Roy Schneider
Lt.-Governor, Derek M. Hodge

TRADE WITH UK	1993	1994
Imports from UK	£5,311,000	£178,500,000
Exports to UK	488,000	365,000

NORTHERN MARIANA ISLANDS

The land area of the Northern Mariana Islands is 179 sq. miles (464 sq. km) with an estimated population (1990) of 43,345. The USA administered the islands as part of a UN Trusteeship until the trusteeship agreement was terminated in 1986 bringing fully into effect a 1976 congressional law establishing a commonwealth of the Northern Mariana Islands. Most of the residents became US citizens. There is a popularly elected bicameral legislature and a popularly elected Governor.

SEAT OF GOVERNMENT – Saipan.
Population (1990 estimate) 39,090.

Governor, Froilan C. Tenorio
Lt.-Governor, Benjamin M. Manglona

THE PANAMA CANAL

As a result of the Panama Canal Treaty 1977, the Canal Zone was disestablished, with all jurisdiction over the former Canal Zone reverting to Panama with effect from 1 October 1979. Under the treaty, the United States is allowed the use of operating areas for the Panama Canal, together with several military bases, although the Republic of Panama is sovereign in all such areas. The Panama Canal Commission, an arm of the US Government, will continue to operate the canal until noon on 31 December 1999.

In the fiscal year 1994, the total number of transits by ocean-going commercial traffic was 12,337; canal net tons totalled 194,289,433; cargo tons totalled 170,538,437.

URUGUAY
República Oriental del Uruguay

Uruguay is situated on the east coast of the Rio de la Plata in South America, in 30° to 35° S. latitude and 53° 15' to 57° 42' W. longitude, with an area of 68,037 sq. miles (176,215 sq. km). The country consists mainly of undulating grassy plains. The principal river is the Rio Negro (with its tributary the Yi), flowing from north-east to south-west into the Rio Uruguay. The climate is temperate.

The population (1992) is 3,116,802, predominantly of Spanish and Italian descent. Spanish is the official language. Many Uruguayans are Roman Catholics. There is no established church.

CAPITAL – ΨMontevideo, population (1992) 1,383,660.
Other centres are Salto, ΨPaysandu, Mercedes, Minas, Melo, Rivera and Punta del Este.

CURRENCY – New Uruguayan peso of 100 centésimos.

FLAG – Four blue and five white horizontal stripes surcharged with sun on a white ground in the top corner, next flagstaff.

NATIONAL ANTHEM – Orientales, La Patria O La Tumba (Uruguayans, the fatherland or death).

NATIONAL DAY – 25 August (Declaration of Independence, 1825).

GOVERNMENT

Uruguay (or the *Banda Oriental*, as the territory lying on the eastern bank of the Uruguay River was then called) resisted all attempted invasions of the Portuguese and Spanish until the early 17th century; 100 years later the Portuguese settlements were captured by the Spanish. From 1726 to 1814 the country formed part of Spanish South America. In 1814 the armies of the Argentine Confederation captured the capital and annexed the province; afterwards it was annexed by Portugal and became a province of Brazil. In 1825, the country threw off Brazilian rule. This action led to war between Argentina and Brazil which was settled by the mediation of the United Kingdom, Uruguay being declared an independent state in 1828. In 1830 a republic was inaugurated.

Under the constitution the President (who may serve only a single term) appoints a council of 11 ministers and a Secretary (Planning and Budget Office), and the Vice-President presides over Congress. The Congress consists of a Chamber of 99 deputies and a Senate of 30 members (plus the Vice-President), elected for five years by proportional representation. General elections held in 1984 marked the return to civilian rule after 11 years of presidential rule with military support. The first fully free presidential and legislative elections since 1971 were held in 1989, and were won by the Partido Nacional Blanco. After the 1994 elections a coalition government of the Colorado Party and the Partido Nacional Blanco was appointed by President Sanguinetti (Colorado Party).

The republic is divided into 19 Departments, each with an elected governor and legislature.

HEAD OF STATE
President, Dr Julio Maria Sanguinetti, *elected* 27 November 1994, *took office* 1 March 1995
Vice-President, Dr Hugo Batalla

CABINET *as at August 1995*

Interior, Dr Didier Operti
Foreign Affairs, Alvaro Ramos
Economy and Finance, Luis Mosca

Transport and Public Works, Lucio Caceres
Public Health, Dr Alfredo Solari
Labour and Social Security, Ana Lía Piñeyrua
Livestock, Agriculture and Fisheries, Carlos Gasparri
Education and Culture, Samuel Lichtensztejn
National Defence, Dr Raúl Iturria
Industry and Energy, Federico Slinger
Tourism, Benito Stern
Housing, Territorial Regulation and Environment, Juan
  Chiruchi
Secretary, Planning and Budget Office, Ariel Davrieux

EMBASSY OF THE ORIENTAL REPUBLIC OF URUGUAY
2nd Floor, 140 Brompton Road, London SW3 1HY
Tel 0171-584 8192; *Consulate* 0171-589 8835
Ambassador Extraordinary and Plenipotentiary, His Excellency
  Juan Enrique Fischer, apptd 1993

BRITISH EMBASSY
Calle Marco Bruto 1073, Montevideo 11300 (PO Box
16024)
Tel: Montevideo 623650
Ambassador Extraordinary and Plenipotentiary, His Excellency
  Robert Hendrie, apptd 1994

BRITISH-URUGUAYAN CHAMBER OF COMMERCE,
  Avenida Labertador Brig. Gen., Lavalleja 1641, P2-OF
  201, Montevideo

ECONOMY

The economy is based on agriculture, primarily livestock.
There are just over 9 million cattle and just under 24
million sheep. Wheat, barley, maize, linseed, sunflower
seed and rice are cultivated. In addition to wool, meat
packing, other foodstuffs (citrus, wine, beer), fishing and
textile industries are of importance.

Industrial development continues and, in addition to the
greatly augmented textile industry, includes tyres, sheet-
glass, three-ply wood, cement, leather-curing, beet-sugar,
plastics, household consumer goods, edible oils and the
refining of petroleum and petroleum products. There are
some ferrous minerals, not extracted at present. Non-
ferrous exploited minerals include clinker, dolomite,
marble and granite.

The external debt in 1993 was US$4,200 million.
Central Bank reserves (1992) were US$1,711 million,
while GNP was (1991) US$9,480,000m, inflation (1992)
58.9 per cent, unemployment (1992) 8.3 per cent and
budget deficit (1992) was 0.7 per cent of GDP.

FINANCE	1991	1992
Revenue	US$1,839,075m	US$1,990,373m
Expenditure	1,800,733m	1,959,930m

TRADE

The major exports are meat and by-products, wool and by-
products, hides and bristle and agricultural products. The
principal imports are raw materials, construction materials,
oils and lubricants, automotive vehicles, kits and machinery. Principal trading partners are Brazil, USA and
Argentina.

	1991	1992
Total exports	US$1,604,700m	US$1,702,500m
Total imports	$1,636,400m	2,058,000m
Trade with UK	1993	1994
Imports from UK	£45,674,000	£51,546,000
Exports to UK	47,394,000	52,173,000

COMMUNICATIONS

There are about 11,300 km of national highways, and
2,993 km of standard gauge railway in use. Passenger rail
services were cancelled in 1988 and services are now
limited to cargo transport; services are state-run. A state-
owned airline, PLUNA, provides international services,
and internal passenger and limited freight services are
provided by TAMU, another state-owned airline, using
principally military aircraft and personnel. The international airport of Carrasco lies 12 miles outside Montevideo.
The River Uruguay is navigable from its estuary to Salto,
200 miles north, and the Negro is also navigable for a
considerable distance.

Six daily newspapers are published in Montevideo and
most of them are distributed throughout the country.

EDUCATION

Primary and secondary education is compulsory and free,
and technical and trade schools and evening courses for
adult education are state controlled. The university at
Montevideo (founded in 1849) has ten faculties and a new
university has been built at Salto.

UZBEKISTAN
Ozbekiston Respublikasy

Uzbekistan has an area of 172,742 sq. miles (447,400 sq. km)
and occupies the south-central part of former Soviet
Central Asia, lying between the high Tienshan Mountains
and the Pamir highlands in the east and south-east and
sandy lowlands in the west and north-west. It is bordered
on the north by Kazakhstan and the Aral Sea, on the east by
Kyrgyzstan and Tajikistan, on the south by Afghanistan
and Turkmenistan, and on the west by Kazakhstan.
Uzbekistan consists of the Kara-Kalpak Autonomous
Republic and 12 regions: Andizhan, Bokhara, Dzhizak,
Ferghana, Kashkadar, Khorezm, Namangan, Navoi,
Samarkand, Surkhan-Darya, Syr-Darya and Tashkent.
Most of the country is a plain with huge waterless deserts,
and several large oases which form the main centres of
population and economic life. The climate is continental
and dry.

The population (1995 estimate) is 21,206,800, of which
71 per cent are Uzbeks, 8 per cent Russians, 5 per cent
Tajiks and 4 per cent Kazakhs, with smaller numbers of
Tatars, Kara-Kalpaks, Koreans, Ukrainians and Kirghiz.
The predominant religion is Sunni Muslim. Islam is
tolerated within strict bounds; it is allowed to play no part
in politics.

The principal language is Uzbek (71 per cent) with
Russian (8 per cent), Tajik (5 per cent) and Kazakh (4 per
cent). Uzbek is one of the Turkic group of languages. In
June 1994 the government approved a six-year programme
for the transfer of the Uzbek language to a Latin script.

CAPITAL – Tashkent. Population 2,073,000 (1992).
  Samarkand (388,000) contains the Gur-Emir
  (Tamerlane's Mausoleum) completed 1400 by Ulugbek,
  Tamerlane's astronomer grandson.
CURRENCY – Sum (Som) of 100 tiyin.
FLAG – Three horizontal stripes of blue, white, green, with
  the white fimbriated in red; on the blue near the hoist a
  crescent and twelve stars, all in white.
NATIONAL DAY – 1 September (Independence Day).

GOVERNMENT

Between the sixth and fourth centuries BC the area that is now Uzbekistan was under the control of the Persians and then Alexander the Great. In the 14th century the area became the centre of a great Muslim empire under Tamerlane and then his grandson Ulugbek, following whose murder the state disintegrated. By the beginning of the 19th century three independent Khanates, Khiva, Kokand and Bukhara, existed in what is now Uzbekistan. These were gradually annexed to the Russian Empire by the middle of the 19th century. In November 1917 a Communist revolution broke out in Tashkent and parts of Uzbekistan were included in the Turkestan Soviet Republic at its formation in 1918. The remainder of Uzbekistan was under the rule of the independent states of Khiva and Bukhara, which had re-emerged in 1918, until they were defeated by the Red Army and Soviet rule was established throughout the area in 1921. Under Soviet rule a massive land irrigation programme was implemented to allow the cultivation of cotton.

Uzbekistan declared its independence from the Soviet Union on 1 September 1991 after the failed Moscow coup. Its independence was confirmed in a referendum on 29 December and recognized internationally. A new constitution was adopted by the Supreme Soviet in December 1992 under which the President and government hold executive power. The President may serve a maximum of two five-year terms and has the power to dissolve the 250-member Supreme Assembly (*Oliy Majilis*), which may not remove or impeach the President. Elections to the new *Oliy Majilis* were held on 25 December 1994 and won by the ruling People's Democratic Party and its allies with a total of 205 seats.

The government of President Karimov is formed by the former Communist Party, which has renamed itself the People's Democratic Party. Despite the constitutionally guaranteed freedom of religion and thought and respect for human rights and multiparty democracy, censorship is still widely used and little political opposition is tolerated. The main opposition parties, Erk (Freedom) and Birlik (Unity) nationalist party, have been continually banned since the introduction of the multi-party constitution in December 1992. In March 1995 President Karimov's hold on power was confirmed when his term of office was extended to 2000 by a national referendum. Uzbek forces have been deployed in Tajikistan since late 1992 to help maintain the government and defeat the Islamic forces.

Uzbek nationalism has caused violent clashes with Tajiks in the Ferghana valley in recent years. The ability to speak Uzbek is now a condition of appointment to government posts, and those not able to speak it are being dismissed. This has severely disrupted the civil service and public sector, mostly staffed by ethnic Russians. President Karimov is attempting to form close ties with Turkey in the cultural and business spheres, and in 1994 began to strengthen economic ties with Russia again.

HEAD OF STATE

President, Islam Karimov, *elected* 29 December 1991, *elected by referendum for a five-year term* 26 March 1995.

CABINET *as at August 1995*

Chairman of the Cabinet, The President
Prime Minister, Abdulkhashim Mutalov
First Deputy Prime Minister, Agro-industrial Complex, Ismail Djurabekov
Deputy PMs, Dilbar Gulamova (*Women*); Kayim Khakkulov (*Industry, Fuel and and Power*); Bakhtiyar Khamidov (*Finance and Economy*); Utkir Sultanov (*Foreign Economic Relations*); Viktor Chzhen (*State Property and Privatization*); Yuri Paigin; Saidmukhtar Saidkasymov;

Mirabror Usmanov; Murat Sharifkhoyaiev; Rustam Yunusov
Interior, Zokirjon Almatov
Foreign Affairs, Abdulaziz Komilov
Defence, Lt.-Gen. Rustam Akhmedov
Justice, Alisher Mardiev
Health, Shavkat Karimov
Education, Djura Yuldashev
Industry and Construction, Inom Iskanderov
Agriculture, Rasulmat Khusanov
Communications, Kamilzhan Rakhimov
Labour, Okitjan Obidov
Higher Education, Akil Salimov
Public Utilities, Viktor Mikhailov
Culture, Erkin Khaitvaiev
Land Improvement, Rim Giniyatullin
Social Security, Bakhodir Umarzakov
Power Engineering, Valeri Ataiev
Construction, Adilzhan Aripov
Bread, Rakhmatull Akhmedov

Chairman of the Oliy Majilis, Erkin Khalilov

EMBASSY OF THE REPUBLIC UZBEKISTAN
72 Wigmore Street, London WIH 9DL
Tel: 0171-935 1899
Ambassador Extraordinary and Plenipotentiary, new appointment awaited

BRITISH EMBASSY
Flats 84–85, Murtazaeva Street 6, Tashkent
Tel: Tashkent 891288
Ambassador Extraordinary and Plenipotentiary, Her Excellency Barbara Hay, MBE, apptd 1995

ECONOMY

Uzbekistan is attempting to integrate its economy with that of Kazakhstan, with which it signed an economic agreement in January 1994 to allow the free circulation of goods, services and capital and the co-ordination of credit and finance policies, budgets, taxation and customs duties. Uzbekistan is also a member of the CIS economic union and in March 1994 signed an economic treaty with Russia to provide for mutually convertible currencies and enhance private business links. In 1994–5 the government has also embarked on an economic reform programme under which subsidies on foodstuffs and transport were abolished and those on public utilities reduced. Peasant farmers have been granted private plots of land and inflation has been reduced. In January 1995 the IMF approved a US$75 million loan to support the economic reform programme.

Uzbekistan's economy is based on intensive agricultural production, and especially cotton production, made possible by extensive irrigation schemes. In addition there are some agricultural and textile machinery plants and several chemical combines. Large and previously underdeveloped mineral resources have begun to be exploited; these include gold, natural gas, oil, copper, lead, zinc and coal. A sizeable oilfield was discovered in the Ferghana Valley in 1992. The Muruntao mine is the largest open-cast gold mine in the world, producing 75 million tonnes per year. Foreign direct investment of US$2,000 million has been pledged in the fields of mining, exploration and vehicle assembly plants.

TRADE WITH UK	1993	1994
Imports from UK	£8,363,000	£17,297,000
Exports to UK	282,000	3,493,000

VANUATU
Ripablik Blong Vanuatu

Vanuatu is situated in the South Pacific Ocean, between 13° and 21° S. and 166° and 170° E. It includes 13 large and some 70 small islands, of coral and volcanic origin, including the Banks and Torres Islands in the north, and has a total land area of 4,706 sq. miles (12,190 sq. km). The principal islands are Vanua Lava, Espiritu Santo, Maewo, Pentecost, Ambae, Malekula, Ambrym, Epi, Efate, Erromango, Tanna and Aneityum. Most islands are mountainous and there are active volcanoes on several. The climate is oceanic tropical, moderated by the south-east trade winds which blow between May and October. At other times winds are variable and cyclones may occur.

The population (1993 estimate) is 159,800. About 95 per cent are Melanesian, the rest being mostly Micronesian, Polynesian and European. The national language is Bislama, but English and French are also official languages.

SEAT OF ADMINISTRATION – ΨPort Vila, Efate,
   population (1993) 26,100. The only other town is
   Luganville (population, 1993, 8,800), on Espiritu Santo.
CURRENCY – Vatu of 100 centimes.
FLAG – Red over green with a black triangle in the hoist,
   the three parts being divided by fimbriations of black and
   yellow, and in the centre of the black triangle a boar's
   tusk overlaid by two crossed fern leaves.
NATIONAL ANTHEM – Nasonal sing sing blong Vanuatu.
NATIONAL DAY – 30 July (Independence Day).

GOVERNMENT

Vanuatu, the former Anglo-French Condominium of the New Hebrides, became an independent republic within the Commonwealth on 30 July 1980. Parliament consists of 46 members elected for a term of four years. A Council of Chiefs advises on matters of custom. Executive power is held by the Prime Minister (elected from and by parliament) and a Council of Ministers who are responsible to parliament. The President is elected for a five-year term by the presidents of the six provincial governments and the members of parliament.

HEAD OF STATE
President, His Excellency Jean-Marie Leye, *elected* 2 March
   1994

COUNCIL OF MINISTERS *as at August 1995*
Prime Minister and Minister of Foreign Affairs, Public Service,
   Planning and Statistics, Police, Media and Language Services,
   Hon. Maxime Carlot Korman
Deputy Prime Minister and Minister for Justice, Culture and
   Women's Affairs, Hon. Sethy John Regenvanu
Home Affairs, Hon. Charlie Nako
Finance, Commerce and Industry, Hon. Willie Jimmy
Economic Affairs and Tourism, Hon. Serge Vohor
Transport, Public Works, Ports and Marine and Urban Water
   Supply, Hon. Amos Bangabiti
Natural Resources, Hon. Paul Telukluk
Education, Hon. Romain Batick
Health and Rural Water Supply, Hon. Dr. Edward Tambisari
Agriculture, Livestock, Forestry and Fisheries, Hon. Thomas
   Faratia
Postal Services, Telecommunications and Meteorology, Hon.
   Cecil Singer

Chief Justice, Charles Vaudin D'Imecourt
Attorney-General, Hon. Patrick Ellum

HIGH COMMISSIONER TO GREAT BRITAIN, vacant,
   resident at Port Vila, Vanuatu

BRITISH HIGH COMMISSION
PO Box 567, Port Vila
Tel: Vila 23100
High Commissioner, His Excellency James Daly, CVO, apptd
   1995

ECONOMY

Most of the population is employed on plantations or in subsistence agriculture. Subsistence crops include yams, taro, manioc, sweet potato and breadfruit; principal cash crops are copra, cocoa and coffee. Large numbers of cattle are kept on the plantations and beef is the second largest export. Principal exports are copra, meat (frozen, tinned and chilled), timber and cocoa.

Tourism is an important revenue earner, and the absence of direct taxation has led to growth in the finance and associated industries.

TRADE WITH UK	1993	1994
Imports from UK	£220,000	£383,000
Exports to UK	1,484,000	1,618,000

VATICAN CITY STATE
Stato della Città del Vaticano

The office of the ecclesiastical head of the Roman Catholic Church (Holy See) is vested in the Pope, the Sovereign Pontiff. For many centuries the Sovereign Pontiff exercised temporal power but by 1870 the Papal States had become part of unified Italy. The temporal power of the Pope was in suspense until the treaty of 1929 which recognized the full and independent sovereignty of the Holy See in the City of the Vatican. The area of the Vatican City is 108 acres and its population in 1989 was about 1,000.

CURRENCY – Italian currency is legal tender.
FLAG – Square flag; equal vertical bands of yellow (next
   staff), and white; crossed keys and triple crown device on
   white band.
NATIONAL DAY – 22 October (Inauguration of present
   Pontiff).

Sovereign Pontiff, His Holiness Pope John Paul II (Karol
   Wojtyla), *born* at Wadowice (Krakow, Poland), 18 May
   1920, *elected* Pope in succession to Pope John Paul I, 16
   October 1978
Secretary of State, Cardinal Angelo Sodano, *appointed*
   December 1990

APOSTOLIC NUNCIATURE
54 Parkside, London SW19 5NF
Tel 0181-946 1410
Apostolic Nuncio, His Excellency Archbishop Luigi
   Barbarito, apptd 1986

BRITISH EMBASSY TO THE HOLY SEE
91 Via Condotti, I–00187 Rome
Tel: Rome 678 9462
Ambassador Extraordinary and Plenipotentiary, Her
   Excellency Maureen Macglashen, apptd 1995

TRADE WITH UK	1993	1994
Imports from UK	£869,000	£1,138,000
Exports to UK	53,000	1,000

VENEZUELA
República de Venezuela

Venezuela is a South American republic, situated approximately between 0° 45′ S. and 12° 12′ N. latitude and 59° 45′ and 73° 09′ W. longitude. It has a total area of 352,144 sq. miles (912,050 sq. km) and is bounded on the north by the Caribbean Sea, west by Colombia, east by Guyana, and south by Brazil. Included in the area of the republic are 72 islands off the coast, with a total area of about 14,650 sq. miles, the largest being Margarita (area, about 400 sq. miles), which is politically associated with Tortuga, Cubagua and Coche to form the state of Nueva Esparta. The mountains are the Eastern Andes and Maritime Andes, running south-west to north-east. The main range is known as the Sierra Nevada de Merida, and contains Pico Bolivar (16,411 ft) and Picacho de la Sierra (15,420 ft). The principal river is the Orinoco, with innumerable affluents, the main river exceeding 1,600 miles in length. The upper waters of the Orinoco are united with those of the Rio Negro (a Brazilian tributary of the Amazon) by a natural river or canal, known as the Casiquiare. The coastal regions contain many lagoons and lakes, of which Maracaibo (area 8,296 square miles) is the largest lake in South America. The climate is tropical, except where modified by altitude or tempered by sea breezes.

The population (UN estimate 1992) is 20,249,000, of which 67 per cent are Mestizo, 21 per cent white, 10 per cent black and 2 per cent Indian. Spanish is the language of the country. About 96 per cent of the population is Roman Catholic.

CAPITAL – Caracas, population 2,784,000. Other principal towns are ΨMaracaibo (1,364,000), Barquisimeto (602,000), Valencia (903,000), Maracay (354,000), San Cristobal (230,000), Cumaná (212,000) and Ciudad Guayana (536,506).

CURRENCY – Bolivar (BS) of 100 céntimos.

FLAG – Three horizontal stripes of yellow, blue, red with an arc of seven white stars on the blue stripe.

NATIONAL ANTHEM – Gloria Al Bravo Pueblo (Glory to the brave people).

NATIONAL DAY – 5 July.

GOVERNMENT

Venezuela gained independence from Spain in 1830. Under the 1961 constitution, executive power is held by the President, who also appoints the Council of Ministers. Legislative power is exercised by a bicameral National Congress, comprising a 201-member Chamber of Deputies and a Senate of 49 elected members plus the former presidents of constitutional governments as life members. The President and National Congress are directly elected for concurrent five-year terms.

Carlos Andrés Pérez of the (Social Democratic) Democratic Action (AD) party won the December 1988 presidential election and the AD emerged as the largest party in both houses in the Congressional elections. President Pérez's government successfully introduced a series of free market economic reforms which led to impressive economic growth but increasing social problems. Two military coup attempts in 1992 were defeated but President Pérez resigned in May 1993 after the Supreme Court indicted him on corruption charges. Former President Rafael Caldera won the ensuing presidential election in December 1993 but his National Convergence coalition of 17 parties failed to gain majorities in either house of Congress, where the traditional AD and COPEI (Social

Christian) parties remained strong. President Caldera took office with his new government in February 1994 and announced an economic austerity programme and the revival of privatization.

Venezuela is divided into 22 states, one federal territory and a federal district.

HEAD OF STATE
President, Rafael Caldera Rodríguez, *elected* 5 December 1993, *sworn in* 2 February 1994

COUNCIL OF MINISTERS *as at August 1995*
Interior, Ramón Escovar Salom
Foreign Affairs, Miguel Angel Burelli
Finance, Luis Raul Matos
Defence, Gen. Orozco Graterol
Transport and Communications, Ciro Zaa
Urban Development, Francisco Gonzalez
Energy and Mines, Erwin José Arrieta
Environment and Natural Resources, Roberto Pérez Lecuna.
Health and Social Security, Carlos Walter
Agriculture and Livestock, Raul Alegrett
Education, Antonio Luis Cardenas
The Family, Mercedes Pulido
Justice, Ruben Creixems
Presidential Secretariat, Andres Caldera
Decentralization, José Guillermo Andueza
Culture, Oscar Sambrano
Industrial Development and Commerce, Werner Corrales
Minister, Guyana Corporation of Venezuela, Alfredo Gruber
Federal District Governor, Asdrubal Aguiar
Labour and Employment, Juan Garrido
Central Planning Office, Edgar Paredes Pizani
Venezuelan Tourist Corporation, Hermann Soriano
Information, Guillermo Alváraz
Higher Education, Science and Technology, Guido Arnal Arroyo
Venezuelan Investment Fund, Carlos Bernardez
State Reform, Ricardo Combellas

VENEZUELAN EMBASSY
1 Cromwell Road, London SW7 2HW
Tel 0171-584 4206/7
Ambassador Extraordinary and Plenipotentiary, His Excellency Dr Ignacio Arcaya, apptd 1992
Defence Attaché, Capt. Juan B. Leoni
Cultural Attaché, G. Carnevali

BRITISH EMBASSY
Apartado 1246, Caracas 1010–A
Tel: Caracas 9934111
Ambassador Extraordinary and Plenipotentiary, His Excellency John G. Flynn, CMG, apptd 1993
Counsellor, P. Ware, LVO (*Deputy Head of Mission*)
Defence Attaché, Capt. K. Ridland, RN
First Secretary (Commercial), S. S. Calder

There are British Consular Offices at Caracas, Maracaibo, Margarita and Mérida.

BRITISH COUNCIL DIRECTOR, Paul de Quincey, Apartado 65131, Caracas 1065

BRITISH-VENEZUELAN CHAMBER OF COMMERCE, Apartado 5713, Caracas 1010. Torre Británica, Piso 10, Letra E, Av. José Félix Sosa, Altamira Sur, Caracas 1060

DEFENCE

The total active armed forces strength is 79,000 personnel, including 31,000 conscripts, who serve for 30 months. Conscription is selective. The Army has 34,000 personnel (27,000 conscripts), with 70 main battle tanks, 161 light tanks, 330 armoured personnel carriers, 127 artillery pieces and five attack helicopters. The Navy has 15,000 personnel (4,000 conscripts), including 5,000 marines, with two submarines, six frigates, six patrol and coastal vessels, four combat aircraft and eight armed helicopters. The Air Force is 7,000 strong, with 119 combat aircraft and 27 armed helicopters. The National Guard has 23,000 internal security personnel, with 194 armoured infantry fighting vehicles and armoured personnel carriers, mortar, aircraft, helicopters and inshore patrol craft.

EDUCATION

Education is free and compulsory between the ages of five and 14. There are ten universities in Venezuela, five in Caracas and the others in Maracaibo, Mérida, Valencia, Cumaná and Barquisimeto.

ECONOMY

The government of President Caldera, despite introducing an austerity budget, has promised to moderate the free market reforms which provided impressive GDP growth in 1990–2 but saw recession in 1993–4. The oil industry accounted for 21.3 per cent of GNP in 1992, manufacturing 16.8 per cent, commerce 11.7 per cent, government 8.7 per cent and construction 7.4 per cent. A banking crisis in 1994 which necessitated a government rescue of private banks caused the budget deficit to increase drastically, inflation to soar and the currency to collapse. In response, the government announced a two-year economic stabilization programme, reintroducing exchange and currency controls, raising taxes and domestic petrol prices, attracting foreign investment, reactivating the privatization programme and reducing government spending. It is hoped that these measures will stabilize the economy by reducing inflation and the budget deficit.

Products of the tropical forest region include orchids, wild rubber, timber, mangrove bark, balata gum and tonka beans. Agricultural products include corn, bananas, cocoa beans, coffee, cotton, rice, maize, sugar, sesame, groundnuts, potatoes, tomatoes, other vegetables, sisal and tobacco. There is an extensive beef and dairy farming industry. Despite substantial improvements in agriculture, Venezuela is heavily reliant upon food imports, which constitute about 60 per cent of total consumption.

The principal industry is that of petroleum, which in 1988 contributed 81 per cent of Venezuela's foreign exchange income and 52 per cent of government revenues. Daily production in the oilfields (nationalized 1976) has steadily declined since 1973 in line with Venezuela's conservation policies. There are eight refineries. The Orinoco heavy oil belt is being developed; estimates put recoverable resources at 70,000 million barrels in the Orinoco region.

Aluminium is the second highest source of foreign exchange after petroleum. The Venezuelan state holds the majority stake in both the principal producing companies, Venalum and Alcasa, and is moving towards a consolidation of the industry. Rich iron ore deposits in eastern Venezuela have been developed. The government-owned steel mill at Matanzas uses local iron ore and obtains its electric power from hydro-electric installations on the Caroní River. A mill at Ciudad Guayana produces centrifugally-cast iron pipe. Other industry includes a wide variety of manufacturing and component assembly, principally petrochemicals, gold, diamonds, clothing and foodstuffs.

TRADE

Apart from oil the main exports are bauxite, iron ore, agricultural products and basic manufactures. The main imports are machinery and transport equipment, chemicals and foodstuffs. Some 50 per cent of trade is conducted with the USA.

	1992	1993
Total imports	US$11,240m	US$11,013m
Total exports	14,000m	14,226m

Trade with UK	1993	1994
Imports from UK	£226,769,000	£196,787,000
Exports to UK	125,492,000	133,589,000

COMMUNICATIONS

There are about 93,471 km of roads, 29,954 km of them paved. The state has now acquired all but a very few of the railway lines, whose total length is only some 363 km. Road and river communications have made railways of negligible importance in Venezuela except for carrying iron ore in the south-east, though the government is expanding the network.

The Orinoco is navigable for ocean-going ships (up to 40 ft draught) for 150 miles upstream, by large steamers for 700 miles, and by smaller vessels some 900 miles upstream. There are seven Venezuelan airlines which between them have a comprehensive network of internal and international flights. There are ten television stations, one of which is government controlled.

VIETNAM
Công Hòa Xã Hội Chu Nghĩa Việt Nam

Vietnam has an area of 127,242 sq. miles (329,556 sq. km), and an estimated population (1993) of 71,267,000. It is bordered on the north by China and the west by Laos and Cambodia.

CAPITAL – Hanoi, population (1993) 2,150,000. Other cities are Ho Chi Minh City (3,169,000) and Hai Phong (456,000).
CURRENCY – Dông of 10 hao or 100 xu.
FLAG – Red, with yellow five-point star in centre.
NATIONAL ANTHEM – Tien Quan Ca (The troops are advancing).
NATIONAL DAY – 2 September.

GOVERNMENT

Following the end of the war in Vietnam in 1975, North and South Vietnam were reunified in 1976 under the name of the Socialist Republic of Vietnam. The national flag, anthem and capital of North Vietnam were adopted, and Saigon was renamed Ho Chi Minh City. Effective power lies with the Vietnamese Communist Party (VCP), its highest executive body being the Central Committee, elected by a Party Congress on a national basis. The Politburo and the Secretariat of the Central Committee exercise the real power.

A new constitution was adopted in June 1992 which reaffirmed Communist Party rule but also formalized free market economic reforms. The constitution increased the powers of the President and replaced the Council of Ministers by a Prime Minister and Cabinet. A new National Assembly of 365 members was elected in August 1992 and convened in September when it elected Le Duc

Anh as President and, in October, approved the composition of the new government headed by Vo Van Kiet.

HEAD OF STATE
President, Le Duc Anh, *elected by National Assembly,* 23 September 1992
Vice President, Nguyen Thi Binh

CABINET *as at August 1995*
Prime Minister, Vo Van Kiet
First Deputy PM, Phan Van Khai
Deputy PM, Nguyen Kanh; Tran Duc Luong
National Defence, Doan Khue
Foreign Affairs, Nguyen Manh Cam
Interior, Bui Thien Ngo
Chairman, State Planning Commission, Do Quoc Sam
Chairman, State Inspectorate, Nguyen Ky Cam
Chairman, Ethnic Minorities and Mountain Region Commission, Hoang Duc Nghi
Chairman, National Population Committee, Mai Ky
Finance, Ho Te
Governor, State Bank, Cao Sy Kiem
Commerce and Tourism, Le Van Triet
Labour, War Invalids and Social Affairs, Tran Dinh Hoan
Construction, Ngo Xuan Loc
Communications and Transport, Bui Danh Luu
Heavy Industry, Tran Lum
Energy, Thai Phung Ne
Agriculture, Nguyen Cong Tan
Forestry, Nguyen Quang Ha
Water Conservancy, Nguyen Canh Dinh
Marine Products, Nguyen Tan Trinh
Culture and Information, Tran Hoan
Public Health, Nguyen Trong Nhan
Education and Training, Tran Hong Quan
Justice, Nguyen Dinh Loc
Population and Family Planning, Mai Ky
Children, Tran Thi Thanh Thanh

VIETNAMESE COMMUNIST PARTY
Politburo of the Central Committee, Do Muoi (*General Secretary*); Le Duc Anh; Vo Van Kiet; Dao Duy Tung; Doan Khue; Vu Oanh; Le Phuoc Tho; Pham Van Khai; Bui Thien Ngo; Nong Duc Manh; Pham The Duyet; Nguyen Duc Binh; Vo Tran Chi; Nguyen Manh Cam; Le Kha Phieu; Do Quang Thang; Nguyen Ha Phan (*full members*)

EMBASSY OF THE SOCIALIST REPUBLIC OF VIETNAM
12–14 Victoria Road, London w8 5RD
Tel 0171-937 1912/8564
Ambassador Extraordinary and Plenipotentiary, His Excellency Huynh Ngoc An, apptd 1994

BRITISH EMBASSY
16 Pho Ly Thuong Kiet, Hanoi
Tel: Hanoi 25 2349
Ambassador Extraordinary and Plenipotentiary, His Excellency Peter Williams, CMG, apptd 1990
There is also a Consulate-General in Ho Chi Minh City.
BRITISH COUNCIL DIRECTOR, Muriel Kirton (*Cultural Attaché*)

DEFENCE

Total active armed forces number 572,000 personnel, with conscripts serving between two and three years. Reserves number three to four million. The Army has 500,000 personnel, with 1,300 main battle tanks, 600 light tanks, 1,500 armoured infantry fighting vehicles and armoured personnel carriers and 3,060 artillery pieces. The Navy is 42,000 strong, including 30,000 naval infantry, and deploys

seven frigates and 55 patrol and coastal vessels. Air Force strength is 15,000, with 190 combat aircraft and 33 armed helicopters. The Air Defence Force has 15,000 personnel, with surface-to-air missiles.

ECONOMY

Vietnam experienced economic difficulties following the imposition of socialist reforms in the south after 1975. These were exacerbated by reductions in western aid as a result of Vietnam's invasion and occupation of Cambodia, border hostilities with China, and the allocation of resources to military expenditure. The economy has also been adversely affected by the sharp decrease in aid from the former Soviet Union. However, economic reforms, known as 'Doi Moi' liberalization, were instituted after the Sixth Party Congress (1986) and have had significant success. Inflation had been brought down to 4 per cent a year in 1994, but rose to 14 per cent in 1995; the exchange rate has been rationalized, subsidies removed, much greater private economic activity allowed and average economic growth of 7 per cent a year in 1991–3 attained (8.8 per cent in 1994). The state's share of control has fallen to 60 per cent of industry, 40 per cent of services and 2 per cent of agriculture, which is now mainly run by family farms. This has led to a significant improvement in agricultural production, with Vietnam becoming a major rice exporter.

Foreign investment has been actively encouraged, with US$5,300 million invested in 1988–93. This level is growing since the USA dropped its opposition to IMF and World Bank loans and aid to Vietnam in July 1993 and ended its trade embargo in February 1994. Investment will be further boosted by the US decision in July 1995 to establish full diplomatic and economic relations and by Vietnam's accession to ASEAN in August 1995. International aid donors, the IMF and the World Bank approved a loan and grant package of US$1,860 million in November 1993 and US$2,535 million in November 1994 to support economic reform. A bankruptcy law has been passed, which has led to increasing unemployment and fears for social stability. Oil production (mainly offshore) has increased to 110,000 barrels per day and large natural gas reserves have been found offshore, though these are also claimed by China.

TRADE WITH UK	1993	1994
Imports from UK	£16,950,000	£62,915,000
Exports to UK	22,104,000	66,389,000

WESTERN SAMOA
Malotuto'atasi o Samoa i Sisifo

Western Samoa lies in the south Pacific Ocean between 13° and 15° S. latitude and 171° and 173° W. longitude. It consists of the islands of Savai'i (662 sq. miles), Upolu, Apolima, Manono, Fanuatapu, Namua, Nuutele, Nuulua and Nuusafee, and has an area of 435 sq. miles (1,714 sq. km). All the islands are mountainous. Upolu, the most fertile, contains the harbours of Apia and Saluafata, and Savai'i the harbours of Asau and Salelologa.

The population (1989 census) was 162,000, the largest numbers being on Upolu (114,980) and Savai'i (43,150); a 1992 UN estimate put the figure at 158,000. The Samoans are a Polynesian people, though the population also includes other Pacific Islanders, Euronesians, Chinese and Europeans. The main languages are Samoan and English. The islanders are Christians of different denominations.

CAPITAL – ΨApia, on Upolu (population, 1989 census, 36,000). Robert Louis Stevenson died and was buried at Apia in 1894.
CURRENCY – Tala (WS$) of 100 sene.
FLAG – Red with a blue canton bearing five white stars of the Southern Cross.
NATIONAL ANTHEM – The Banner of Freedom.
NATIONAL DAY – 1 June (Independence Day).

GOVERNMENT

Formerly administered by New Zealand (latterly with internal self-government), Western Samoa became fully-independent on 1 January 1962. The state was treated as a member country of the Commonwealth until its formal admission on 28 August 1970.

The 1962 constitution provides for a head of state to be elected by the 49-member legislative assembly, the *Fono*, for a five-year term. Initially two of the four Paramount chiefs jointly held the office of head of state for life. When one of the chiefs died in April 1963, Malietoa Tanumafili II became head of state for life. The head of state's functions are analogous to those of a constitutional monarch. Executive government is carried out by a Cabinet of Ministers.

Suffrage was made universal following a referendum held in 1990. After elections held on 7 March 1991, the seats in the *Fono* were: Human Rights Protection Party 30; Samoan National Development Party 16; Independents 3.

Head of State, HH Malietoa Tanumafili II, GCMG, CBE, *since* 15 April 1963
Deputy Head of State, Hon. Mataafa Faasuamaleaui Puela

CABINET *as at August 1995*
Prime Minister, Minister for Foreign Affairs, Hon. Tofilau Eti Alesana
Finance, Hon. Tuilaepa Sailele
Justice, Hon. Fuimanono Lotomau
Education, Hon. Fiame Naomi
Health, Hon. Sala Vaimili Uili II
Post and Telecommunications, Hon. Toi Aukuso
Agriculture, Fisheries and Transport, Hon. Misa Telefoni
Public Works, Hon. Leafa Vitale
Lands and Environment, Hon. Faasooatuloa Pati
Civil Aviation, Hon. Jack Netzler
Interior, Women's Affairs, Hon. Polatavao Fosi
Youth, Sports and Culture, Hon. Pule Lameko
Labour, Vui Viliamu

WESTERN SAMOA HIGH COMMISSION
Avenue Franklin D. Roosevelt 123, 1050 Brussels
Tel: Brussels 6608454
High Commissioner, His Excellency Afamasaga Toleafoa, apptd 1990

BRITISH HIGH COMMISSIONER, His Excellency Robert Alston, CMG, resident at Wellington, New Zealand
There is an Honorary Consulate (PO Box 2029) in Apia.

ECONOMY

Agriculture is the basis of the economy, the principal cash crops (and exports) being coconuts (copra), cocoa and bananas. Other agricultural exports include coffee, timber, tropical fruits and seeds. Efforts are being made to develop fishing on a commercial scale. Manufacturing is very small in scope and concerned largely with processing agricultural products, but is being encouraged by the government. Tourism is increasing rapidly.

TRADE WITH UK	1993	1994
Imports from UK	£1,297,000	£1,115,000
Exports to UK	23,000	12,000

REPUBLIC OF YEMEN
Al-Jamhuriya Al-Yamaniya

Yemen lies in the extreme south-west of the Arabian peninsula. Bounded on the west by the Red Sea, on the north by Saudi Arabia, on the east by Oman and on the south by the Gulf of Aden, Yemen has an estimated area of 203,850 sq. miles (527,969 sq. km) and a population (1995 census) of 15,800,000. Included in the state are the offshore islands of Perim and Kamaran in the Red Sea, and Socotra in the Gulf of Aden. The border with Saudi Arabia is unclear and remains in dispute; only the north-west corner of it is delineated, by the 1934 Taif Accord. The highlands and central plateau, and the highest portions of the maritime range in the south, form the most fertile part of Arabia, with abundant but irregular rainfall. The north is largely composed of mountains and desert, and rainfall is generally scarce.

CAPITAL – Sana'a, population (1995) 972,000. Ψ Aden (562,000) is the other main city and the former capital of South Yemen.
CURRENCY – Yemeni Riyal of 100 fils.
FLAG – Horizontal bands of red, white and black.
NATIONAL DAY – 22 May.

GOVERNMENT

Turkish occupation of North Yemen (1872–1918) was followed by the rule of the Hamid al-Din dynasty until a revolution in 1962 overthrew the monarchy and the Yemen Arab Republic was declared. The People's Republic of South Yemen was set up in 1967 when the British government ceded power to the National Liberation Front, bringing to an end 129 years of British rule in Aden and some years of protectorate status in the hinterland. Negotiations towards merging the two states began in 1979 and unification was proclaimed on 22 May 1990. The constitution was approved by referendum in May 1991. A five-member Presidential Council comprising former senior government figures of the separate states was formed for the period of transition.

A general election for the House of Representatives took place on 27 April 1993. Of the total of 301 seats, 122 were won by the General People's Congress (GPC, former ruling party in the North), 62 by the Islamic Islah (Alliance for reform) party and 56 by the Yemini Socialist Party (YSP, former ruling party in the South). The three parties formed a coalition government and the House of Representatives asked the Presidential Council to remain in office.

Continued political tensions and a power struggle between the former Northern and Southern Yemen elites in mid-1993, coupled with arguments over the distribution of oil revenues and the alleged assassination of Southern ministers led YSP leaders to withdraw to Aden in August 1993. A reconciliation pact signed in February 1994 by President Saleh and Vice-President al-Beedh was never implemented and, after sporadic clashes, a civil war broke out on 5 May 1994 between the unmerged Northern and Southern forces. The Southern leadership declared secession on 20 May but fled when Aden was captured by victorious Northern forces on 7 July, bringing the civil war to an end.

After the civil war a coalition government of the General People's Congress and the Islamic Islah was formed, an amnesty for the secessionists declared (with the exception of key YSP leaders) and the constitution amended. The Presidential Council was abolished and will be replaced from 1999 with a directly elected President. Gen. Saleh was elected President by the House of Representatives for a five-year term. Multiparty democracy, a free market economy and Shari'a-based Islamic law are enshrined in the constitution.

HEAD OF STATE
President, Gen. Ali Abdullah Saleh, *took office* 22 May 1990, *elected* 1 October 1994
Vice-President, Maj. Gen. Abd Rabbah Mansour Hadi

COUNCIL OF MINISTERS *as at August 1995*
Prime Minister, Abdel Aziz Abdel-Ghani
Deputy PM, Abdel-Wahab Ali al-Ounsi
Deputy PM, Foreign Affairs, Abdul Ali Karim al-Iryani
Deputy PM, Industry, Oil and Mineral Resources, Mohammed Said al-Attar
Deputy PM, Planning and Development, Abdul-Qader Ba Jammal
Interior, Hussein Mohammed Arab
Finance, Mohammed Ahmad al-Junayd
Information, Abdurahman al-Akawaa
Transport, Ahmad Musa'id Husayn
Communications, Ahmad Mohammed al-Unsi
Culture and Tourism, Yahya Husayn al-Arashi
Social Affairs and Labour, Mohammed Abdullah al-Batani
Legal and Parliamentary Affairs, Abdullah Ahmad Ghanim
Civil Administration, Sadiq Amin Abu Ras
Supply and Trade, Mohammed Ahmad Afendi
Health, Najib Ghanem
Local Government, Mohammed Hassan Damaj
Religious Guidance, Ghaleb Abdul-Kafi al-Quirshi
Fisheries, Abdul-Rahman al-Qadar Bafadl
Justice, Abd al-Wahhab Lufti al-Daylami
Defence, Brig. Abd al-Malik Ali al-Sayyani
Agriculture, Ahmad Salim al-Jabali
Housing and Urban Planning, Ali Hamid Sharaf
Education, Abduh Ali al-Qudati
Youth and Sports, Abd al-Wahhab Rawih
Electricity and Water Resources, Abdallah Muhsin al-Akwa
Speaker of the House of Representatives, Shaikh Abdullah bin Husain al-Ahmar

EMBASSY OF THE REPUBLIC OF YEMEN
57 Cromwell Road, London SW7 2ED
Tel 0171-584 6607
Ambassador Extraordinary and Plenipotentiary, His Excellency Dr Hussein Abdullah Al-Amri, apptd 1995

BRITISH EMBASSY
PO Box 1287, Sana'a
Tel: Sana'a 1215630
Ambassador Extraordinary and Plenipotentiary, His Excellency Douglas Scrafton, apptd 1995

BRITISH COUNCIL DIRECTOR, Brendan McSharry, OBE, As-Sabain Street No. 7 (PO Box 2157), Sana'a

ECONOMY

The civil war has seriously damaged the country's economy, already weakened since 1991 by the loss of US$2,000 million in annual remittances from 800,000 Yemini workers in Saudi Arabia, who were sent home because of Yemen's support for Iraq in the Gulf War. However, the war had little effect on oil production, which averages 180,000 barrels per day (bpd) from the Marib field and 150,000 bpd from the Masila field, on stream since August 1993. The refinery at Aden was damaged in the civil war and is working at reduced capacity. Despite the production of oil Yemen remains one of the poorest states in the world. The critical economic situation obliged the

government in 1995 to begin implementing a series of IMF and World Bank-prescribed reforms to combat the 100 per cent inflation, 50 per cent unemployment and US$9,000 million external debt.

Agriculture is the main occupation of the inhabitants. This is largely of a subsistence nature, sorghum, sesame and millets being the chief crops, with wheat and barley widely grown at the higher elevations. Exports include cotton, coffee, hides and skins.

TRADE WITH UK	1993	1994
Imports from UK	£85,484,000	£74,177,000
Exports to UK	16,065,000	5,081,000

YUGOSLAVIA
Federativna Republika Jugoslavije – Federal Republic of Yugoslavia

The area of the two remaining Yugoslav republics (Serbia and Montenegro) is 39,506 sq. miles (102,350 sq. km). The rump Federal Yugoslav state, which is not internationally recognized as the successor state to the former Socialist Federal Republic of Yugoslavia, is bordered to the north by Hungary, to the east by Romania and Bulgaria, to the south by the Former Yugoslav Republic of Macedonia, to the south-west by Albania and the Adriatic Sea, and to the west by Bosnia-Hercegovina and Croatia. The climate is continental. Montenegro and southern Serbia are extremely mountainous, while the north is dominated by the low-lying plains of the Danube. The major rivers are: the Danube, which flows through the north of Serbia to Romania and Bulgaria; the Sava, which flows eastwards from Bosnia to join the Danube at Belgrade; the Drina, which flows along most of the Serbian–Bosnian border to join the Sava; and the Morava, which flows from the extreme south to join the Danube in the north.

The last (federal) estimate of 1988 gave a population of 10,410,000, of which 66 per cent are Serbs and Montenegrins, 18 per cent Albanian, 8 per cent Muslim, 4 per cent Hungarian, with smaller numbers of Yugoslavs (no ethnic group), Croats and Bulgarians. The majority religion is Serbian Orthodox, with significant Muslim and small Roman Catholic minorities.

The main language is Serbian (Serbo-Croat) (74 per cent), with Albanian and Hungarian minorities. Serbo-Croat is a South Slav language written in the Cyrillic script.

CAPITAL – (federal and Serbian) Belgrade, on the Danube (population 1,455,000). Other major cities are (1981): Novi Sad (257,685); Niš (230,711); Priština (210,040); Kragujevac (164,823); Subotica (154,611); Podgorica (132,290), the capital of Montenegro.
CURRENCY – Dinar of 100 paras.
FLAG – Three horizontal stripes of blue, white, red.
NATIONAL ANTHEM – Hej, Slaveni, Jošte Živi Reö Našíh Dedova (Oh! Slavs, our ancestors' words still live).
NATIONAL DAY – 29 November.

GOVERNMENT

Serbia emerged from the rule of the Byzantine Empire in the 13th century to form a large and prosperous state in the Balkans. Defeat by the Turks in 1389 led to almost 500 years of Turkish rule. After gaining autonomy within the Ottoman Empire in 1815, Serbia became fully independent in 1878 and a kingdom in 1881. Montenegro was part of the Serbian state before it was conquered by the Turks in 1355; it became independent in 1851. At the end of the First

World War Serbia and Montenegro joined with the former Austro-Hungarian provinces of Slovenia, Croatia and Bosnia-Hercegovina to form the 'Kingdom of Serbs, Croats and Slovenes' which was proclaimed on 1 December 1918 under the rule of the Serbian royal house. The state was renamed Yugoslavia in 1929. In 1941–5 Yugoslavia was occupied by Axis forces which were fought by Communist and royalist Chetnik partisans supplied by Allied forces. In 1945 with the defeat of Nazi Germany, Yugoslavia was reformed as a Communist federal republic under the presidency of partisan leader Josip Tito.

Increasing pressure from the non-Serbian nationalities for more political power were met by Tito in the post-war period by new constitutions in 1963 and 1974 which devolved power to the republics (Slovenia, Croatia, Bosnia-Hercegovina, Serbia, Montenegro, Macedonia). Tito died in 1980 and the delicate political balance of a rotating federal presidency was unable to contain the gradually growing nationalist movements after his death. The Catholic, western-looking, more prosperous republics of Slovenia and Croatia began to break away from the other, predominantly Orthodox and Muslim, Balkan republics; Communism was widely rejected. Efforts by the six republican Presidents to end inter-communal conflict and negotiate a new federal or confederal structure for the country failed in 1991. On 25 June 1991 Slovenia and Croatia declared their independence from Yugoslavia. Intervention by the Federal Yugoslav Army (JNA) against local defence forces to prevent the disintegration of the Yugoslav federation failed and within two months the ethnically homogeneous Slovenia had negotiated its independence.

The situation in Croatia differed because its ethnic Serb minority comprised 12 per cent of the population. These ethnic Serbs refused to accept Croatia's independence and fighting began in July 1991 between Croat Defence Forces and Serbian guerrillas backed by the JNA. By September 1991 this had escalated into war between Croatia and Serbia. In October the last vestiges of the power of the Federation ended when the federal presidency was usurped by Serbia and its ally Montenegro. The war in Croatia continued until January 1992 when, after constant attempts, the EC and the UN were able to bring about a ceasefire that held (*see* Croatia).

Bosnia-Hercegovina adopted a memorandum on state sovereignty on 15 October 1991. Independence was affirmed in a referendum on 1 March 1992. Independence was supported by the ethnic Muslims and Croats but rejected by the ethnic Serbs, who formed 33 per cent of the population and wanted to form a Greater Serbia with the Serbian republic. Fighting between Muslims and Serbs broke out on 2 March 1992 and the JNA intervened against the poorly-armed Muslims. In May 1992, after intense international pressure, the JNA withdrew to Serbia and Montenegro, but left its weapons with Bosnian Serb forces.

On 27 April 1992 the two remaining republics of the former Socialist Federal Republic of Yugoslavia, Serbia and Montenegro, announced the formation of a new Yugoslav federation, which they invited Serbs in Croatia and Bosnia-Hercegovina to join. The new federation remains unrecognized internationally because of continued ethnic Serb aggression in Bosnia, and is seen as a Serbian attempt to inherit the rights of the former federation. Continued Serbian aid and supplies to the ethnic Serb forces in the Bosnian war has led to increasing international pressure and the imposition by the UN in May 1992 of a trade embargo, economic sanctions and a ban on air and sporting links. In April 1993 a total blockade was imposed.

In October 1993 the UN Security Council imposed the condition that ethnic-Serb held territories in Croatia must be integrated into Croatia before sanctions on the rump Yugoslav state would be lifted. In July 1994 after the Bosnian Serbs had rejected the International Contact Group's (ICG's) peace plan and map for Bosnia-Hercegovina, the ICG announced that new sanctions (including a ban on all Serbian officials and military travelling abroad; a directive to neighbouring states to erect physical barriers at their borders; permission for countries to sell frozen Yugoslav assets; a ban on Danube river traffic stopping at Serbian ports; and a ban on all traffic crossing Yugoslav borders) would be implemented if the Bosnian Serbs did not agree to the plan. To stave off these sanctions, President Milosevic severed all political and economic ties to the Bosnian Serb leadership and in September 1994 closed the Yugoslav-Bosnian border to all trade except food and medicines. International monitors were deployed on the Yugoslav-Bosnian border and verified that it had been closed, leading the UN Security Council to suspend the ban on sporting, cultural, air and sea links with Yugoslavia in October. Despite increasing doubt as to the extent to which the border is closed, and what supplies are reaching the Bosnian Serbs, the UN Security Council has continued to renew the suspension of the ban every 100 days.

The Federal Republic has a bicameral parliament with a 138-seat (108 Serbian, 30 Montenegrin) lower house, the Chamber of Citizens, and a 40-seat (20 Serbian, 20 Montenegrin) upper house, the Chamber of Republics. Executive power is vested in a Federal President and government but has effectively been usurped by the authoritarian Serbian Socialist (former Communist) Party leader and Serbian President Slobodan Milosevic. The last federal legislative elections were held in December 1992 and were universally considered flawed and unfair. The Serbian Socialist Party emerged as the largest party in the federal legislature and formed a coalition government with the extreme nationalist Serbian Radical Party. This government was replaced in March 1993 by a coalition of the Serbian Socialist Party and the Montenegrin Social Democratic Party.

HEAD OF STATE

Federal President, Zoran Lilic, *elected by parliament* 25 June 1993

FEDERAL GOVERNMENT *as at August 1995*

Prime Minister, Radoje Kontic
Deputy Prime Ministers, Jovan Zebic (*Finance*); Nikola Sainovic (*Economy*); Uros Klikovac (*Justice*)
Foreign Affairs, Milan Milutinovic
Interior, Vukasin Jokanovic
Defence, Pavle Bulatovic

Transport and Communications, Zoran Vujovic
Labour, Health and Social Policy, Miroslav Ivanesevic
Development, Science and Environment, Djanko Radulovic
Information, Dragutin Brcin
Trade, Djordje Siradovic
Agriculture, Kiviljko Lovre
Sport, Zoran Bingulac
Human and Minority Rights, Margit Savovic
Without Portfolio, Tomislav Rajicevic; Vuk Ognjanovic
Government Secretary-General, Mladen Vukcevic

EMBASSY OF YUGOSLAVIA
5 Lexham Gardens, London w8 5JJ
Tel 0171-370 6105
Chargé d'Affairs, R. Bogojevic
Defence Attaché, Capt. M. Ladicorbic
Consul-General, R. Jengic
Second Secretary, L. Raspopovic (*Economic*)

BRITISH EMBASSY
Generala Ždanova 46, 11000 Belgrade
Tel: Belgrade 645055
Chargé d'Affaires, Counsellor and Consul-General, I. A. Roberts, CMG
Defence and Military Attaché, Col. A. M. Moody
First Secretary (Political), A. Crombie

BRITISH COUNCIL REPRESENTATIVE, J. McGrath,
Generala Ždanova 34-Mazanin (Post Fah 248), 11001 Belgrade

MONTENEGRO

Montenegro has an area of 5,331 sq. miles (13,812 sq. km) and a population of 615,000, of whom 62 per cent are Montenegrins, 14.5 per cent Muslims, 6.5 per cent Albanians and 3 per cent Serbs. The capital is Podgorica with a population (1981) of 132,290. The Montenegrin Social Democrat Party (former Communists) won multiparty elections in December 1992 for the 85-seat republican assembly and formed a government.

President, Momir Bulatovic, *elected* 11 January 1993
Prime Minister, Milo Djukanović

SERBIA

Serbia has a total area of 34,175 sq. miles (88,538 sq. km) and a total population of 9.3 million, of whom 66 per cent are Serbs. The capital is Belgrade with a population (1981) of 1,455,000. It includes the provinces of Kosovo (population 1.6 million), of great historic importance to Serbs, and Vojvodina (population 2 million); the autonomy of both was ended in September 1990. Kosovo, with its capital at Priština, is predominantly Albanian (90 per cent). In defiance of the Serbian authorities, ethnic Albanians held parliamentary and presidential elections in May 1992, which were won respectively by the Democratic League of Kosovo and its leader Ibrahim Rugova. Tension between Albanians and Serbs remains very high. Vojvodina, with its capital at Novi Sad, has a large Hungarian minority (21 per cent).

The Socialist Party of Serbia (SPS) (formerly the Communists) emerged as the largest party in multiparty elections for the 250-seat National Assembly, held in December 1992 and formed a coalition government with the extreme nationalist Serbian Radical Party (SRS). The coalition broke down in September 1993 when the SRS called for a parliamentary vote of no confidence in the government, forcing President Milosevic to dissolve parliament. In the ensuing parliamentary election on 19 December 1993 the SPS gained 123 seats; the People's Assembly Party (NSS) 45 seats; SRS 39 seats; Democratic Party 29 seats; Democratic Party of Serbia 7 seats;

Democratic Community of Hungarians in the Vojvodina 5 seats; Albanian coalition 2 seats. The SPS, three seats short of a majority, formed a minority government in March 1994, and has unsuccessfully sought the support of centrist opposition parties.

President, Slobodan Milosevic, *elected* 20 December 1992
Prime Minister, Mirko Marjanovic

ECONOMY

Since 1991 the economy has been devastated by the wars in Croatia and Bosnia-Hercegovina, by the UN economic sanctions and trade embargo, and because of the lack of free-market reforms. Most factories have closed. Only the evasion of UN sanctions and the country's agricultural self-sufficiency has kept it alive. In 1993 hyperinflation became rampant because the government continued to print money to finance the wars and subsidize industries. By December 1993 inflation had reached 21,000 per cent a month, the tax system had collapsed, output was one-third of pre-war levels, industry was working at one-quarter of capacity and the dinar had been devalued ten times. In January 1994 a successful economic stabilization package was introduced with a new superdinar pegged at one-to-one parity with the Deutsche Mark. This reduced monthly inflation from 313 million per cent in January to 1 per cent in February. The package is based on the use of state and private individuals' gold and foreign currency reserves to maintain the value of the dinar, an increasingly leaky economic embargo which is allowing in significant amounts of goods and supplies (and creating a powerful class of criminals), and an economy based on barter rather than money. Industrial production remains extremely low and unemployment high, and it is doubtful how long the package can be maintained.

TRADE WITH UK	1993	1994
Imports from UK	£3,652,000	£4,253,000
Exports to UK	2,000	44,000

ZAIRE
République du Zaïre

Situated between 12° and 31° E. longitude and 5° N. and 13° S. latitude, Zaïre comprises an area of 905,567 sq. miles (2,345,409 sq. km). Apart from the coastal district in the west which is fairly dry, the rainfall averages between 60 and 80 inches. The average temperature is about 27°C, but in the south the winter temperature can fall nearly to freezing point. Extensive forest covers the central districts.

The population was 34,671,607 at the 1985 census. A 1992 UN estimate put it at 39,882,000. It is composed almost entirely of Bantu groups, divided into semi-autonomous tribes. Minorities include Sudanese, Nilotes, Pygmies and Hamites, as well as refugees from Angola.

Swahili, a Bantu dialect with an admixture of Arabic, is the nearest approach to a common language in the east and south, while Lingala is the language of a large area along the river and in the north, and Kikongo of the region between Kinshasa and the sea. French is the language of administration.

CAPITAL – Kinshasa (formerly Leopoldville), population (1985 census) 2,778,281. Principal towns, Lubumbashi (formerly Elisabethville) (403,623); Kisangani (formerly Stanleyville) (310,705); Likasi (146,394); Kananga (601,239); ΨMatadi (143,598); and Mbandaka (134,495).
CURRENCY – Zaïre of 100 makuta.

FLAG – Dark brown hand and torch with red flame in yellow roundel on green background.
NATIONAL DAY – 24 November.

GOVERNMENT

The state of the Congo, founded in 1885, became a Belgian colony in 1908 and was administered by Belgium until independence in 1960. Mobutu Sésé Seko, formerly commander-in-chief of the Congolese National Army, came to power in a coup in 1965 and was elected President in 1970. Legislative power was vested in a unicameral National Legislative Council, elected for a five-year term by compulsory direct and universal suffrage with candidates proposed by the sole legal political party, Mouvement Populaire de la Révolution (MPR).

Following mounting tension, political reforms were announced in April 1990 and President Mobutu called a National Conference to draft a new constitution in April 1991. The conference convened in August but the government refused to grant it sovereign status, causing the main opposition parties to form a 'Sacred Union' to bring down the transitional government. Mobutu accepted an opposition-dominated government under Prime Minister Etienne Tshisekedi in October 1991. His attempts to replace this with MPR-dominated governments failed and the National Conference confirmed the Tshisekedi government as the legitimate one in August 1992.

In 1992–5 President Mobutu and the opposition have been locked in a power struggle. In December 1992 the National Conference adopted a draft constitution and elected an interim legislature, the High Council of the Republic (HCR). Throughout 1993 the Tshisekedi government attempted to transfer the President's powers to the HCR, while President Mobutu unsuccessfully attempted to dismiss the HCR and Tshisekedi government, and then used the Army to intimidate them while a rival pro-Mobutu government was established. A constitutional limbo existed until January 1994 when President Mobutu dissolved the pro-Mobutu government and the HCR and endorsed the formation of a new High Council of the Republic–Parliament of Transition (HCR–PT) with a mandate of choosing a new Prime Minister. On 9 April 1994 President Mobutu promulgated a Transitional Constitutional Act endorsed by the HCR–PT which regulated a 15-month period of transition to democracy. During the period the HCR–PT oversees the activities of a transitional government while a constitutional referendum and presidential and legislative elections are held. On 17 June 1994 President Mobutu appointed Kengo Wa Dondo as Prime Minister after he had been elected by the HCR–PT; Tshisekedi's candidacy was excluded, leading to opposition unrest. Prime Minister Dondo named a cabinet and government equally divided between opposition parties and Mobutu-supporting MPR members, but Tshisekedi's supporters refused to join the government. In July 1995 the HCR–PT voted to extend the transition period by a further two years.

There are 11 regions, each under a Governor and provincial administration: Bas-Zaïre (provincial capital, Matadi); Bandundu (Bandundu); Equateur (Mbandaka); Haut-Zaïre (Kisangani); Kinshasa (Kinshasa); Maniema (Kindu); Nord-Kivu (Goma); Sud-Kivu (Bukavu); Shaba (Katanga) (Lubumbashi); East Kasai (Mbuji-Mayi); West Kasai (Kananga).

SECESSION

Since 1992 ethnic Katangans have been forcing ethnic Kasai mineworkers and their families out of the southern region of Shaba (Katanga) in a wave of ethnic violence which is a repeat of the Katanga secessionist war in 1960. In December 1993 the Governor of Shaba declared total autonomy from the rest of Zaïre and announced the reversion of the region's name to Katanga.

HEAD OF STATE

President of the Republic and National Security, Marshal Mobutu Sésé Séko, *assumed office* 25 November 1965; *elected* 5 November 1970; *re-elected* 1977, 1984, *remained in power when term ended* 1991

CABINET *as at August 1995*

Prime Minister, Leon Kengo Wa Dondo
Deputy Prime Ministers, Gustave Malumba Mbangula (*Interior*); Adm. Mavua Mudima (*National Defence*); Kamanda Wa Kamanda (*Foreign Affairs, Justice and Institutional Reform*); Mozagba Ngbuka (*International Co-operation*)
Press and Information, Masegabio Nzanzu
Planning, Kiawama Kia Kiziki
Finance, Pay Pay Wa Syakassighe
Budget, Bahati Lukwebo
Agriculture, Landu Kavidi
National Economy, Industry and Small and Medium-sized Enterprises, Katanga Mukumadi
Mines, Mutombo Bakafwa
Energy, Kisanga Kabongelo
Public Works, Territorial Administration and Housing, Mwando Nsimba
Transport and Communication, Nyindu Kitenge
Foreign Trade, Jibi Ngoy
Land Affairs, Mangwanda Gifugu
Education, Sekimonyo Wa Magangu
Social Affairs, Soki Fuani Eyenga
Labour and Social Welfare, Omba Pene Djunga
Civil Service, Bolenge Mekesombo
Posts and Telecommunications, Pierre Lumbi
Environment, Conservation and Tourism, Kisimba Ngoy
Sport and Leisure, Bofassa Djema
Culture and Arts, Lukonzala Munyangwa
Without Portfolio, Assea Mindre

EMBASSY OF THE REPUBLIC OF ZAIRE
26 Chesham Place, London SW1X 8HH
Tel 0171-235 6137
Ambassador Extraordinary and Plenipotentiary, new appointment awaited

BRITISH EMBASSY
Avenue des Trois 'Z', Gombe, Kinshasa
Tel: Kinshasa 34775
Chargé d'Affaires and Consul, J. G. Lindsay, OBE

There is a British Consulate at Kisangani.

ECONOMY

The cultivation of oil palms is widespread, palm oil being the most important agricultural cash product though it is no longer exported. Coffee, rubber, cocoa and timber are the most important agricultural exports. The production of cotton, pyrethrum and copal is increasing. The country is rich in minerals, particularly Shaba (Katanga) province. Copper is widely exploited, and industrial diamonds and cobalt are also produced. Oil deposits are exploited off the Zaïre estuary and reef-gold is mined in the north-east of the country.

There is a wide variety of small secondary industries, the main products being foodstuffs, beverages, tobacco, textiles, leather, wood products, cement and building materials, metallurgy, small river craft and bicycles. There are reserves of hydro-electric power and the Inga dam on the river Zaïre supplies electricity to Matadi, Kinshasa and Shaba.

Rampant hyper-inflation and corruption have left the economy and the state's finances in a parlous state. Multilateral and bilateral aid has also been greatly reduced because of President Mobutu's refusal to leave office. In June 1994 Zaïre's voting rights at the IMF were suspended over its failure to pay its financial arrears.

TRADE

The chief exports are copper, crude oil, coffee, diamonds, rubber, cobalt, gold, cassiterite, zinc and other metals.

Trade with UK	1993	1994
Imports from UK	£16,941,000	£12,058,000
Exports to UK	7,138,000	10,973,000

COMMUNICATIONS

There are approximately 20,500 km of roads (earth-surfaced) of national importance, and 6,000 km of railways. The country has four international and 40 principal airports.

ZAMBIA
Republic of Zambia

Zambia lies on the plateau of Central Africa between 22° and 33° 33' E. longitude and 8° 15' and 18° S. latitude. It has an area of 290,586 sq. miles (752,614 sq. km) and a population (UN estimate, 1992) of 8,638,000. With the exception of the valleys of the Zambezi, the Luapula, the Kafue and the Luangwa rivers, and the Luano valley, elevations vary from 3,000 to 5,000 feet above sea level, but in the north-east the plateau rises to occasional altitudes of over 6,000 feet. Although Zambia lies within the tropics, and fairly centrally in the African land mass, its elevation relieves it from extremely high temperatures and humidity.

CAPITAL – Lusaka, population (1989 estimate) 1 million. Other centres are Livingstone, Kabwe, Chipata, Mazabuka, Mbala, Kasama, Solwezi, Mongu, Mansa, Ndola, Luanshya, Mufulira, Chingola, Chililabombwe, Kalulushi and Kitwe, the last six towns being the main centres on the copper belt.

CURRENCY – Kwacha (K) of 100 ngwee.

FLAG – Green with three small vertical stripes, red, black and orange (next fly); eagle device on green above stripes.

NATIONAL ANTHEM – Stand and Sing of Zambia, Proud and Free.

NATIONAL DAY – 24 October (Independence Day).

GOVERNMENT

Northern Rhodesia came under British rule in 1889. It achieved internal self-government when the Federation of Rhodesia and Nyasaland was dissolved in 1963 and became an independent republic within the Commonwealth on 24 October 1964 under the name of Zambia.

The country was a one-party state (the United National Independence Party) from 1973 until 1990, when pressure from opposition groups led to a new constitution (August 1991) and multiparty legislative and presidential elections in October 1991. The Movement for Multiparty Democracy (MMD) won 125 of the 150 seats in parliament, and the MMD candidate Frederick Chiluba defeated Kaunda, who had ruled since independence, in the presidential election. The MMD government has begun the transformation of the state-controlled economy into a free market system with the sale and privatization of large sectors of the economy. Aid and investment have poured into the country, foreign exchange controls have been removed, the Kwacha floated and prices freed. A state of emergency was in force between March and May 1993 after the discovery of a coup plot by UNIP. Continued allegations of corruption by government ministers led first to the resignation of 15 MMD MPs from the party and then ministerial resignations, under pressure from foreign aid donors in 1993–4.

HEAD OF STATE
President, Hon. Frederick J. Chiluba, *elected* 31 October 1991
Vice-President, Hon. Brig. Godfrey Miyanda

CABINET *as at August 1995*
Defence, Hon. Benjamin Mwila
Foreign Affairs, Hon. Gen. Christon Tembo
Finance, Hon. Ronald Penza
Home Affairs, Hon. Chitalou Sampa
Local Government and Housing, Hon. Ben Mwiinga
Health, Hon. Michael Sata
Education, Hon. Alfeyo Hambayi
Commerce, Trade and Industry, Hon. Dipak Patel
Community Development and Social Welfare, Hon. Paul Kapinga
Labour and Social Security, Hon. Newstead Zimba
Communications and Transport, Hon. Dawson Lupunga
Energy and Water Development, Hon. Edith Nawakwi
Agriculture, Food and Fisheries, Hon. Suresh Desai
Lands, Hon. Luminzu Shimaponda
Environment and Natural Resources, Hon. William Harrington
Information and Broadcasting, Hon. Amusa Mwanawambwa
Mines and Mineral Development, Hon. Kelly Walubita
Technical Education and Vocational Training, Hon. Dr Kabunda Kayongo
Sport, Youth and Child Development, Hon. Lt.-Col. Patrick Kafumukache
Tourism, Hon. Gabriel Maka
Works and Supply, Hon. Simon Zukas

HIGH COMMISSION FOR THE REPUBLIC OF ZAMBIA
2 Palace Gate, London w8 5LS
Tel 0171-589 6655
High Commissioner, His Excellency Love Mtesa, apptd 1992
Deputy High Commissioner, A. M. Mwale
Consul-General, M. C. Mwanambale
First Secretary, J. Chikwenda (*Information/Tourism*)

BRITISH HIGH COMMISSION
Independence Avenue (PO Box 50050), 15 101 Ridgeway, Lusaka
Tel: Lusaka 251133
High Commissioner, His Excellency Patrick Nixon, CMG, OBE, apptd 1993
Deputy High Commissioner, B. S. Jones, LVO
First Secretary (Commercial/Consular), K. A. Neill

BRITISH COUNCIL DIRECTOR, Adrian Greer, Heroes Place, Cairo Road (PO Box 34571), Lusaka. There is also a library in Ndola.

ECONOMY

The free market economic reforms introduced since 1991 by the MMD government have revolutionized the economy, which had been highly regulated and protected from competition. Price subsidies and tariffs have been lowered or abolished and public sector wages frozen but inflation and interest rates have increased, causing hardships. Increased imports have affected manufacturing and agricultural production.

Principal products are maize, sugar, groundnuts, cotton, livestock, vegetables and tobacco. Mineral production was valued at K8,390 million in 1987, of which copper production (of 483,100 tonnes) accounted for K6,870 million.

Following the reforms initiated by the government, the US government wrote off K59,000 million of debt in April 1993.

TRADE WITH UK	1993	1994
Imports from UK	£73,548,000	£44,523,000
Exports to UK	12,056,000	13,038,000

ZIMBABWE
Republic of Zimbabwe

Zimbabwe, the former Southern Rhodesia, lies south of the Zambezi river and borders Zambia and Mozambique on the north, South Africa and Botswana on the south and west, and Mozambique on the east. It has a total area of 150,804 sq. miles (390,580 sq. km), and a population (UN estimate 1992) of 10,583,000.

CAPITAL – Harare (formerly Salisbury) situated on the Mashonaland plateau, population (July 1983) 681,000. Bulawayo is the largest town in Matabeleland, population (July 1983) 429,000. Other centres are Chitungwiza, Mutare, Gweru, Kadoma, Kwe Kwe, Masvingo and Hwange.

CURRENCY – Zimbabwe dollar (Z$) of 100 cents.

FLAG – Seven horizontal stripes of green, yellow, red, black, red, yellow, green; a white, black-bordered, triangle based on the hoist containing the national emblem.

NATIONAL ANTHEM – Ngaikomberarwe Nyika Ye Zimbabwe (Blessed be the country of Zimbabwe).

NATIONAL DAY – 18 April (Independence Day).

GOVERNMENT

Southern Rhodesia was granted responsible government in 1923. An illegal declaration of independence on 11 November 1965 was finally terminated on 12 December 1979. Following elections in February 1980 the country became independent on 18 April 1980 as the Republic of Zimbabwe, a member of the British Commonwealth.

The independence constitution was amended in 1987, making the presidency an executive post. The President is popularly elected for a six-year term, appoints the Cabinet and can veto parliamentary bills. The legislature became unicameral in 1990 and the House of Assembly has 150 members, 120 elected, 20 appointed by the President and ten appointed by traditional chiefs. A merger agreement between the ZANU (PF) and ZAPU parties was signed in 1987 with a view to the eventual creation of a one-party state. The new party is known as ZANU-PF. The latest general election was held in April 1995 and ZANU-PF won 118 of the 120 elective seats.

The country is divided into eight provinces: Manicaland, Masvingo, Matabeleland North, Matabeleland South, Midlands, Mashonaland West, Central and East.

HEAD OF STATE
Executive President, Hon. Robert Gabriel Mugabe, *elected* 30 December 1987, *re-elected* March 1990

CABINET *as at August 1995*
The President
Vice-Presidents, Hon. Simon Muzenda; Hon. Dr Joshua Nkomo
National Security, Hon. Dr Sidney Sekeramayi
Finance, Hon. Ariston Chambati
Planning, Hon. Richard Hove
National Affairs, Employment Creation and Co-operatives, Hon. Florence Chitauro
Local Government, Rural and Urban Development, Hon. John Nkomo
Agriculture, Hon. Denis Norman
Foreign Affairs, Hon. Dr Stanislaus Mudenge
Justice, Legal and Parliamentary Affairs, Hon. Emmerson Munangagwa
Defence, Hon. Moven Mahachi
Higher Education, Hon. Ignatius Chombo
Education, Hon. Thenjive Lesabe
Home Affairs, Hon. Dumiso Dabengwa
Public Construction and National Housing, Hon. Enos Chikowore
Lands and Water Resources, Hon. Kumbirai Kangai
Information, Posts and Telecommunications, Hon. David Karimanzira
Labour, Public Service and Social Welfare, Hon. Dr. Nathan Shamuyarira
Industry and Commerce, Hon. Dr Herbert Murerwa
Mines, Hon. Dr Eddison Zvobgo
Transport and Energy, Hon. Simon Moyo
Health and Child Welfare, Hon. Dr Timothy Stamps
Environment and Tourism, Hon. Chen Chimutingwende
Sports, Recreation and Culture, Hon. Dr Witness Mangwende
President's Office, Hon. Ceplas Msipa

HIGH COMMISSION OF THE REPUBLIC OF ZIMBABWE
Zimbabwe House, 429 Strand, London WC2R 0SA
Tel 0171-836 7755
High Commissioner, His Excellency Dr Ngoni Togarepi Chideya, apptd 1993
Minister-Counsellors, A. Nyazika; J. Mupamhanga
Defence Adviser, Lt.-Col. E. Zabanyana
Counsellor, S. Undenge (*Commercial*)

BRITISH HIGH COMMISSION
Stanley House, Samora Machel Avenue (PO Box 4490), Harare
Tel: Harare 793781
High Commissioner, His Excellency Richard Dales, CMG, apptd 1992
Deputy High Commissioner, R. S. Dewar
Defence Adviser, Col. A. R. Screen, OBE
First Secretaries, M. K. Page (*Commercial*); G. M. Johnson (*Consular*)

BRITISH COUNCIL DIRECTOR, Dr Jerry Eyres, OBE, 23 Jason Moyo Avenue (PO Box 664), Harare. There is also a library at Bulawayo.

ECONOMY

Ten years of socialism and central planning in 1980–90, coupled with a period of drought, brought the economy to crisis point before free market economic reforms were introduced in 1990 under the auspices of a World Bank-enhanced structural adjustment programme. This has involved the removal of food subsidies, the floating of the currency, opening the market to imports, and reducing subsidies. The programme has been partly implemented but the economy remains highly regulated and the civil service and armed forces have not been reduced sufficiently, leading to a budget deficit of around 10 per cent of

GDP. The foreign debt is £2,000 million and costs one-third of export revenue to service. Inflation remains high at 20 per cent and the economic restructuring programme has caused unemployment to rise to 40 per cent as the government lays off public sector workers. The compulsory purchase of white-owned commercial farms by the government in 1993–4 has caused a scandal as the land has been given to senior government officials rather than the landless black peasants it was intended for, and the farmers given compensation in worthless government bonds. This policy means agricultural production is set to decline.

The country is endowed with minerals, water, forests, wildlife and other resources. The agricultural sector is well-developed, accounts for 68 per cent of GDP and employs 70 per cent of the workforce. Tobacco remains the most important crop in terms of export (Zimbabwe is the largest exporter in the world), and maize the most important for domestic consumption. Agriculture has diversified in recent years with horticultural products (especially roses and tulips), fruit and vegetables becoming important export earners. Other crops include wheat, cotton, and sugar. Beef is exported to the EU.

The manufacturing sector is very dependent on the agricultural sector for raw materials. Industry is also dependent on imports e.g. fuel oil, steel products and chemicals, as well as heavy machinery and items of transport. The mining sector, although contributing a relatively small portion to GDP, is important to the economy as a foreign exchange earner. Almost all mineral production is exported. Gold is the most important mineral, others are asbestos, diamonds, silver, nickel, copper, chrome ore, tin, iron ore and cobalt. There is a successful ferro-chrome industry and a substantial steel works which has been heavily subsidized by government. Platinum mining is about to begin following a £160 million investment by an Australian firm.

Tourism is of growing importance, with 800,000 visitors in 1994.

Trade with UK	1993	1994
Imports from UK	£83,114,000	£104,690,000
Exports to UK	121,500,000	145,640,000

EDUCATION

Since independence, a policy of free primary education and accelerated expansion at secondary level has resulted in rapidly expanding enrolment. Over 80 per cent of schools are government-aided schools. The University of Zimbabwe was founded in 1955.

British Dependent Territories

ANGUILLA

Anguilla is a flat coralline island, about 16 miles in length, three and a half miles in breadth at its widest point and its area is about 35 sq. miles (91 sq. km). It lies approximately 18° N. latitude and 63° W. longitude, to the north of the Leeward Islands group. The island is covered with low scrub and fringed with white coral-sand beaches. The climate is pleasant, with temperatures in the range of 24-30° C throughout the year.

POPULATION – The population (1992 census) is 8,960.
CAPITAL – The Valley (population 1,400).
CURRENCY – East Caribbean dollar (EC$) of 100 cents.
FLAG – British Blue Ensign with the shield of arms in the fly.

GOVERNMENT

Anguilla has been a British colony since 1650. For much of its history it was linked administratively with St Christopher, but three months after the Associated State of Saint Christopher (St Kitts)-Nevis-Anguilla came into being in 1967, the Anguillans repudiated government from St Kitts. A Commissioner was installed in 1969 and in 1976 Anguilla was given a new status and separate constitution. Final separation from St Kitts and Nevis was effected on 19 December 1980 and Anguilla reverted to a British dependency. A new constitution was introduced in 1982, providing for a Governor, an Executive Council comprising four elected Ministers and two ex-officio members (the Attorney-General and Permanent Secretary, Finance), and an 11-member legislative House of Assembly presided over by a Speaker.

The 1982 Constitution (Amendment) Order 1990 came into operation on 30 May 1990. Among the new constitutional provisions are a Deputy Governor (who replaces the Permanent Secretary (Finance) in the Executive Council and the Legislature), a Parliamentary Secretary, Leader of Opposition and Deputy Speaker.

Governor, His Excellency Alan Shave, CVO, OBE, *apptd* 1992
Deputy Governor, Henry McCrory, LVO, OBE, *apptd* 1991

EXECUTIVE COUNCIL *as at June 1995*

Chief Minister and Minister of Lands, Agriculture and Fisheries, Hon. Hubert Hughes
Social Services, Hon. Edison Baird
Communications, Public Utilities and Works, Hon. Albert Hughes
Finance and Economic Development, Hon. Victor Banks
Attorney-General, Hon. Kurt De Freitas

ECONOMY

Low rainfall limits agricultural output and export earnings are mainly from sales of lobsters. Tourism has developed rapidly in recent years and accounts for most of the island's economic activity. In 1993 there were 37,658 tourists and a further 73,692 day visitors.

FINANCE	1992	1993
Revenue	EC$34,810,000	EC$36,554,029
Expenditure	31,895,000	34,183,714

TRADE WITH UK	1993	1994
Imports from UK	£1,501,000	£1,320,000
Exports to UK	118,000	86,000

ASCENSION
— *see* St Helena

BERMUDA

The Bermudas, or Somers Islands, are a cluster of about 100 small islands (about 20 of which are inhabited) situated in the west of the Atlantic Ocean, in 32° 18' N. latitude and 64° 46' W. longitude, the nearest point of the mainland being Cape Hatteras in North Carolina, about 570 miles distant. The total area is approximately 20.59 sq. miles (53 sq. km), which includes 2.3 sq. miles leased to the USA.
POPULATION – The civil population (1994) is 60,075.
CAPITAL – ΨHamilton (population 1993, 2,277).
CURRENCY – Bermuda dollar of 100 cents.
FLAG – British Red Ensign with the shield of arms in the fly.

GOVERNMENT

The colony derives its name from Juan Bermudez, a Spaniard, who sighted it before 1515. No settlement was made until 1609 when Sir George Somers, who was shipwrecked there on his way to Virginia, colonized the islands.

Internal self-government was introduced on 8 June 1968. There is a Senate of 11 members and an elected House of Assembly of 40 members. The Governor retains responsibility for external affairs, defence, internal security and the police, although administrative matters for the police service have been delegated to the Minister of Home Affairs.

The last general election was held on 5 October 1993. The United Bermuda Party holds 22 seats, and the Progressive Labour Party 18 seats.

Governor and Commander-in-Chief, His Excellency The Lord Waddington, GCVO, PC, QC, *apptd* 1992
Deputy Governor, Peter Willis

CABINET *as at June 1995*

Premier, Hon. Sir John Swan, KBE
Deputy Premier and Minister of Labour and Home Affairs, Hon. J. Irving Pearman
Health, Social Services and Housing, Hon. Quinton Edness
Environment, Senator Hon. Gerald D. E. Simons
Education, Dr the Hon. Clarence Terceira
Youth, Sport and Recreation, Hon. Pamela Gordon
Works and Engineering, Hon. Leonard O. Gibbons
Tourism, Hon. C. V. Jim Woolridge
Transport, Hon. Maxwell Burgess
Finance, Dr the Hon. David Saul
Management and Technology, Senator Dr the Hon. E. Grant Gibbons

Human Affairs and Information, Hon. C. Jerome Dill
Community and Cultural Affairs, Hon. Wayne L. Furbert
President of the Senate, Hon. A. S. Jackson, MBE
Speaker of the House of Assembly, Hon. Ernest DeCouto
Chief Justice, Hon. Austin Ward, QC

ECONOMY

The islands' economic structure is based on tourism, the major industry, and international company business, attracted by the low level of taxation and sophisticated telecommunications system. In 1994 a total of 482,227 visitors arrived by air and cruise ship.

Locally manufactured concentrates, perfumes, cut flowers and pharmaceuticals are the colony's leading exports. Little food is produced except vegetables and fish, other foodstuffs being imported.

FINANCE	1993–4	1994–5
Public revenue	$360,801,000	$385,112,000
Public expenditure	334,787,000	358,112,000

TRADE WITH UK	1993	1994
Imports from UK	£23,344,000	£23,512,000
Exports to UK	1,687,000	6,309,000

COMMUNICATIONS

One daily and three weekly newspapers are published in Bermuda. Three commercial companies operate radio and television services, including a cable-television system which started service in July 1988. The Bermuda Telephone Company and Cable and Wireless provide telecommunications links to more than 140 countries.

EDUCATION

Free elementary education was introduced in 1949. Free secondary education was introduced in 1965 for those children in the aided and maintained schools who were below the upper limit of the statutory school age of 16 (from 1969 onwards).

THE BRITISH ANTARCTIC TERRITORY

The British Antarctic Territory was designated in 1962 and consists of the areas south of 60°S. latitude which were previously included in the Falkland Islands Dependencies. The territory lies between longitudes 20° and 80°W., south of latitude 60°S. and includes the South Orkney Islands, the South Shetland Islands, the mountainous Antarctic Peninsula (highest point Mount Jackson, 13,620 ft, in Palmer Land) and all adjacent islands, and the land mass extending to the South Pole. The territory has no indigenous inhabitants and the British population consists of the scientists and technicians who man the British Antarctic Survey stations. The number averages about 60 to 70 in winter, but increases considerably in the summer months with the arrival of field workers. Argentina, Brazil, Chile, China, Korea (South), Poland, USA, Russia and Uruguay also have scientific stations in the territory.

The first two British Antarctic Survey stations were established in the South Shetland Islands in 1944, and by 1956 the number of stations had risen to 12. Due to the completion of field work in some areas and increased mobility, the number has now been reduced to four. These are Rothera (Adelaide Island), Halley (Caird Coast) and, in summer only, Fossil Bluff (George VI Sound) and Signy

(Signy Island, South Orkney Islands). Fifteen other stations have been established but are at present unoccupied.

The territory is administered by a Commissioner, resident in London.

Commissioner (non-resident), Anthony J. Longrigg, *apptd* 1995

THE BRITISH INDIAN OCEAN TERRITORY

The British Indian Ocean Territory was established by an Order in Council in 1965 and included islands formerly administered from Mauritius and the Seychelles. The islands of Farquhar, Desroches and Aldabra became part of the Seychelles when it became independent in 1976; since then the Territory has consisted of the islands of the Chagos Archipelago only.

The Chagos Archipelago consists of six main groups of islands situated on the Great Chagos Bank and covering some 21,000 sq. miles (54,389 sq. km). The largest and most southerly of the Chagos Islands is Diego Garcia, a sand cay with a land area of about 17 sq. miles approximately 1,100 miles east of Mahé, used as a joint naval support facility by Britain and USA.

The other main island groups of the archipelago, Peros Banhos (29 islands with a total land area of 4 sq. miles) and Salomon (11 islands with a total land area of 2 sq. miles) are uninhabited. The islands have a tropical maritime climate, with average temperatures between 25° C and 29° C in Diego Garcia, and rainfall in the whole archipelago of 90–100 inches a year.

FLAG – Divided horizontally into blue and white wavy stripes, with the Union Flag in the canton and a crowned palm-tree over all in the fly.

Commissioner, David Ross MacLennan, *apptd* 1994
Administrator, D. J. Smith

TRADE WITH UK	1993	1994
Imports from UK	£701,000	£1,557,000
Exports to UK	28,000	5,000

THE BRITISH VIRGIN ISLANDS

The Virgin Islands are a group of islands at the eastern extremity of the Greater Antilles, divided between Great Britain and the USA. Those of the group which are British number 46, of which 11 are inhabited, and have a total area of about 59 sq. miles, (153 sq. km). The principal are Tortola, the largest (situated in 18° 27′ N. lat. and 64° 40′ W. long., area, 21 sq. miles, Virgin Gorda (8¼ sq. miles), Anegada (15 sq. miles) and Jost Van Dyke (3½ sq. miles).

Apart from Anegada, which is a flat coral island, the British Virgin Islands are hilly, being an extension of the Puerto Rico and the US Virgin Islands archipelago. The highest point is Sage Mountain on Tortola which rises to a height of 1,780 feet.

The islands lie within the trade winds belt and possess a sub-tropical climate. The average temperature varies from 22°–28° C in winter to 26°–31° C in summer. Average annual rainfall is 53 inches.

POPULATION – The 1991 census showed a total population of 16,108: Tortola (13,225); Virgin Gorda (2,431); Anegada (162); Jost Van Dyke (140); and other islands (144).

CAPITAL – ΨRoad Town, on the south-east of Tortola. Population 3,983.
CURRENCY – The US dollar (US$) of 100 cents is legal tender.
FLAG – British Blue Ensign with the shield of arms in the fly.

GOVERNMENT

Under the 1977 constitution the Governor, appointed by the Crown, remains responsible for defence and internal security, external affairs and the civil service but in other matters acts in accordance with the advice of the Executive Council. The Executive Council consists of the Governor as Chairman, one ex-officio member (the Attorney-General), the Chief Minister and three other ministers. The Legislative Council consists of a Speaker chosen from outside the Council, one ex-officio member (the Attorney-General), and 13 elected members returned from 13 one-member electoral districts.

Governor, His Excellency David Patrick Mackilligin, CMG, *apptd* 1995
Deputy Governor, E. Georges, OBE

THE EXECUTIVE COUNCIL *as at 30 June 1995*
Chairman, The Governor
Chief Minister and Minister of Finance, Hon. Ralph O'Neal, OBE
Natural Resources and Labour, Hon. Oliver Cills
Communications and Works, Hon. Alvin Christopher
Health, Education and Welfare, Hon. Alred Frett
Attorney-General, Hon. Dancia Penn

Puisne Judge (resident), Justice Ephraim Georges

ECONOMY

Tourism is the main industry but the financial centre is growing steadily in importance. Other industries include a rum distillery, three stone-crushing plants and factories manufacturing concrete blocks and paint. The major export items are fresh fish, gravel, sand, fruit and vegetables; exports are largely confined to the US Virgin Islands. Chief imports are building materials, machinery, cars and beverages.

FINANCE	1993	1994
Revenue	US$70,538,000	US$77,125,000
Expenditure	66,945,000	76,475,000

TRADE WITH UK	1993	1994
Imports from UK	£2,597,000	£5,935,000
Exports to UK	1,316,000	3,716,000

COMMUNICATIONS

The principal airport is on Beef Island, linked by bridge to Tortola, and an extended runway of 3,600 ft enables larger aircraft to call. There is a second airfield on Virgin Gorda and a third on Anegada. There are direct shipping services to the United Kingdom and the United States and fast passenger services connect the main islands by ferry.

THE CAYMAN ISLANDS

The Cayman Islands, between 79° 44' and 81° 26' W. and 19° 15' and 19° 46' N., consist of three islands, Grand Cayman, Cayman Brac, and Little Cayman, with a total area of 100 sq. miles (259 sq. km). About 150 miles south of Cuba, the islands are divided from Jamaica, 180 miles to the

south-east, by the Cayman Trench, the deepest part of the Caribbean. The nearest point on the US mainland is Miami in Florida, 450 miles to the north. Cooled by trade winds, the annual average temperature and rainfall are 27.2° C and 50.7 inches respectively.
POPULATION – Population (estimate 1993) 31,200, of which the vast majority live on Grand Cayman.
CAPITAL – ΨGeorge Town, in Grand Cayman, population (estimate 1992) 15,000.
CURRENCY – Cayman Islands dollar (CI$) of 100 cents, which is fixed at CI$ = US$1.20.
FLAG – British Blue Ensign with the arms on a white disc in the fly.

GOVERNMENT

The colony derives its name from the Carib word for the crocodile, 'caymanas', which appeared in the log of the first English visitor to the Cayman Islands, Sir Francis Drake. Although tradition has it that the first settlers arrived in 1658, the first recorded settlers arrived in 1666–71. The first recorded permanent settlers followed the first land grant by Britain in 1734. The islands were placed under direct control of Jamaica in 1863. When Jamaica became independent in 1962, the islands opted to remain under the British Crown.

The constitution provides for a Governor, a Legislative Assembly and an Executive Council, and effectively allows a large measure of self-government. Unless there are exceptional reasons, the Governor accepts the advice of the Executive Council, which comprises three official members and five ministers elected from the 15 elected members of the Assembly. The official members also sit in the Assembly. The Governor has responsibility for the police, civil service, defence and external affairs. The Governor handed over the presidency of the Legislative Assembly to the Speaker in 1991. The normal life of the Assembly is four years, with a general election next due in November 1996.

Governor, His Excellency John Wynne Owen, MBE, *apptd* 1995

EXECUTIVE COUNCIL *as at 30 June 1995*
President, The Governor
Chief Secretary, Hon. J. Ryan, OBE
Attorney-General, Hon. R. H. Coles
Financial Secretary, Hon. G. A. McCarthy, OBE
Tourism, Aviation and Commerce, Hon. T. C. Jefferson, OBE
Community Development, Sports, Youth Affairs and Culture, Hon. W. M. Bush
Education and Planning, Hon. T. M. Bodden, OBE
Health, Drug-abuse Prevention and Rehabilitation, Hon. A. S. Eden
Communications, Works, Agriculture and Environment, Hon. J. McLean, OBE
Speaker of Legislative Assembly, Mrs S. I. McLaughlin, MBE

LONDON OFFICE
Cayman Islands Government Office, 6 Arlington Street, London SW1A 1RE. Tel: 0171-491 7772. *Government Representative,* T. Russell, CMG, CBE

ECONOMY

With a complete absence of direct taxation, the Cayman Islands have become successful over the past 25 years as an offshore financial centre. With representation from 62 countries, there were, at the end of 1994, 592 banks and trust companies, of which local offices were maintained by 84. In addition, there were 352 licensed offshore insurance companies and 28,344 registered companies at the end of

1994. Tourism, with an emphasis on scuba diving, has also been developed successfully. There were 341,491 visitors by air and 599,387 cruise ship callers in 1994.

The two industries support a heavy imbalance in trade resulting from the need to import most of what is consumed and used on the islands, and have created a thriving local economy in which the GNP reached US$783.6m (US$27,480 per capita) in 1992. Import duty and fees from financial centre operations have provided revenue enabling the government to undertake heavy investment in education (which is provided free to all four to 16 year olds), health and other social programmes.

FINANCE	1994	1995*
Revenue	CI$152.0m	CI$172.0m
Expenditure	156.9m	178.0m
*estimated		

TRADE	1992	1993
Total imports	CI$278.4m	CI$261.1m
Total exports	3.7m	1.8m

TRADE WITH UK	1993	1994
Imports from UK	£7,136,000	£6,780,000
Exports to UK	1,268,000	2,575,000

FALKLAND ISLANDS

The Falkland Islands, the only considerable group in the South Atlantic, lie about 300 miles east of the Straits of Magellan, between 52° 15'–53° S. latitude and 57° 40'–62° W. longitude. They consist of East Falkland (area 2,610 sq. miles; 6,759 sq. km), West Falkland (2,090 sq. miles; 5,413 sq. km) and over 100 small islands. Mount Usborne (E. Falkland), the loftiest peak, rises 2,312 feet above the level of the sea. The islands are chiefly moorland.

The climate is cool. At Stanley the mean monthly temperature varies between 9° C in January and 2° C in July.

POPULATION – The population, excluding the British garrison, was 2,121 at 5 March 1991.

CHIEF TOWN – ΨStanley, population (1991) 1,643. Stanley is about 8,103 miles from Britain.

CURRENCY – Falkland pound of 100 pence.

FLAG – British Blue Ensign with the arms on a white disc in the fly.

GOVERNMENT

The Falklands were sighted first by Davis in 1592, and then by Hawkins in 1594; the first known landing was by Strong in 1690. A settlement was made by France in 1764; this was subsequently sold to Spain, but the latter country recognized Great Britain's title to a part at least of the group in 1771. After Argentina declared independence from Spain, the Argentine government in 1820 proclaimed its sovereignty over the Falklands and a settlement was founded in 1826. The settlement was destroyed by the Americans in 1831. In 1833 occupation was resumed by the British for the protection of the seal-fisheries, and the islands were permanently colonized. Argentina continued to claim sovereignty over the islands (known to them as las Islas Malvinas), and in pursuance of this claim invaded the islands on 2 April 1982 and also occupied South Georgia. A naval and military force dispatched from Great Britain recaptured South Georgia on 25 April and after landing at San Carlos Bay on 21 May, recaptured the islands from the Argentines, who surrendered on 14 June 1982. A British naval and military garrison of 1,700 personnel remains in

the area. A military zone of 55 miles (previously 80) remains around the islands within which Argentinian naval and air forces may not intrude.

Under the 1985 constitution, the Governor is advised by an Executive Council consisting of three elected members of the Legislative Council and two ex-officio members, the Chief Executive and the Financial Secretary. The Legislative Council consists of eight elected members and the same two ex-officio members.

Governor and Chairman of the Executive Council, His Excellency David Everard Tatham, CMG, *apptd* 1992
Chief Executive, Hon. A. M. Gurr
Financial Secretary, Hon. D. F. Howatt
Commander, British Forces, Falkland Islands, Cdr. A. S. Backus
Attorney-General, D. G. Lang, QC

LONDON OFFICE
Falkland Islands Government Office, Falkland House, 14 Broadway, London SW1H 0BH. Tel: 0171-222 2542. *Government Representative*, Miss S. Cameron

ECONOMY

The economy was formerly based solely on agriculture, principally sheep-farming with a little dairy farming for domestic requirements and crops for winter fodder. Since the 1982 war the UK government has provided some £46 million to restore the economy. Since the establishment of an interim conservation and management fishing zone around the islands and the consequent introduction in 1987 of a licensing regime for vessels fishing within the 200 mile zone, the economy has diversified and income from the associated fishing activities, mainly for illex squid, is now the largest source of revenue. The dramatic increase in government revenue from fishing licences has led to the establishment of a substantial health, education and welfare system with a well-equipped hospital in Stanley, free education until the age of 16 and further education in the UK paid for by the Falklands government. The islands are now self-financing except for defence. Chief imports are provisions, alcoholic beverages, timber, clothing and hardware. Tourism is a small but expanding industry. Most important, the Falkland Islands Government in 1993 announced a 200-mile oil exploration zone around the islands. Early seismic surveys suggest substantial reserves capable of producing 500,000 barrels per day.

FINANCE	1992–3	1993–4
Public revenue	£40,500,000	£38,000,000
Expenditure	34,500,000	33,500,000

TRADE WITH UK	1993	1994
Imports from UK	£10,380,000	£9,360,000
Exports to UK	4,317,000	4,516,000

GIBRALTAR

Gibraltar is a rocky promontory with a total area of 2½ sq. miles (6.5 sq km) and a height of 1,396 ft at its greatest elevation. It juts southwards from the south-east coast of Spain, with which it is connected by a low isthmus. It is about 20 miles (32 km) from the opposite coast of Africa. The town stands at the foot of the promontory on the west side.

POPULATION – The population at the end of 1993 was 28,051.

CURRENCY – Gibraltar pound of 100 pence.
FLAG – White with a red stripe along the lower edge; over all a red castle with a key hanging from its gateway.

GOVERNMENT

Gibraltar was captured in 1704, during the war of the Spanish Succession, by a combined Dutch and English force, and was ceded to Great Britain by the Treaty of Utrecht 1713. Several attempts have been made to retake it, the most celebrated being the great siege of 1779 to 1783, when General Eliott held it for three years and seven months against a combined French and Spanish force. The Treaty of Utrecht stipulates that if Britain ever relinquishes its colonial rights over Gibraltar the colony would return to Spain. In a 1967 referendum on the colony's status, 12,000 voted to remain a British Dependent Territory and 44 voted to join Spain. Spain closed the border with Gibraltar from 1969 to 1985 and refused to engage in any trade.

The 1969 constitution makes provision for certain domestic matters to devolve on a local government of ministers appointed from among elected members of the House of Assembly. The House of Assembly consists of an independent Speaker, 15 elected members, the Attorney-General and the Financial and Development Secretary.

The Governor retains responsibility for external affairs, defence, internal security and financial security, while the local government is responsible for other domestic matters. However, the Gibraltar government has recently been agitating for more local autonomy and responsibility, especially in the colony's relations with the EU, and this has led to tension with the UK and Spanish governments. Gibraltar is part of the EU (with the UK government responsible for enforcing EU directives affecting Gibraltar) but is not a fully-fledged member. In recent years Spain has insisted on excluding Gibraltar's airport from the air liberalization directive of the EC Single Market programme, while the Gibraltar government has been slow in implementing EU directives against drug and tobacco smuggling and money-laundering, which has primarily impacted on Spain. After an ultimatum from the British government in May 1995 that it would use its residual constitutional power to assume executive power, the Gibraltar government agreed to act against tobacco smuggling and money-laundering and implement the directives.

Governor and Commander-in-Chief, His Excellency Field Marshal Sir John Chapple, GCB, CBE
Flag Officer, Gibraltar, and Admiral Superintendent, HM Naval Base, Gibraltar, Maj.-Gen. S. J. Pack
Deputy Governor, A. Carter
Financial and Development Secretary, B. Traynor
Attorney-General, K. Dawson
Chief Justice, A. Kneller
Chief Minister, Hon. Joe Bossano
Speaker, Mayor R. J. Peliza, OBE

ECONOMY

Gibraltar enjoys the advantages of an extensive shipping trade and is a popular shopping centre. The chief sources of revenue are the port dues, the rent of the Crown estate in the town, and duties on consumer items. The free port tradition of Gibraltar is still reflected in the low rates of import duty. The gradual change from a fortress city to a holiday centre has led to a flourishing tourist trade. A financial services industry is expanding, based on Gibraltar's status as an offshore financial centre. However,

many jobs have been lost over the past few years as a result of reductions in the British naval and military presence.

A total of 4,026 merchant ships (53.5 million gross registered tons aggregate) entered the port during 1994. There are 49.9 km of roads.

FINANCE	1991–2	1992–3
Revenue	£86,700,000	£72,735,000
Expenditure	83,683,000	77,916,000

TRADE	1992	1993
Total imports	£327.5m	£370.9m
Total exports	370.9m	161.4m

TRADE WITH UK	1993	1994
Imports from UK	£103,402,000	£74,866,000
Exports to UK	3,693,000	4,819,000

EDUCATION

Education is compulsory and free for children between the ages of four and 15 whose parents are ordinarily resident in Gibraltar. Scholarships are available for higher education in Britain. The total enrolment in government schools was 4,696 in December 1994.

HONG KONG

Hong Kong, consisting of more than 230 islands and of a portion of the mainland (Kowloon and the New Territories) on the south-east coast of China, is situated at the eastern side of the mouth of the Pearl River, between 22° 9' and 22° 37' N. latitude and 113° 52'–114° 30' E. longitude. The total area of the territory (including recent reclamation) is 418 sq. miles (1,083 sq. km).

The island of Hong Kong is about 11 miles (18 km) long and from two to five miles (three to eight km) broad, with a total area of 30 sq. miles (77.6 sq. km); at the eastern entrance to the harbour it is separated from the mainland by a narrow strait.

The climate is sub-tropical, tending towards the temperate for nearly half the year. The mean monthly temperature ranges from 16° C to 29° C. The average annual rainfall is 2,214 mm, of which nearly 80 per cent falls between May and September. Tropical cyclones occur between May and November, causing high winds and heavy rain.

POPULATION – Population at the end of 1994 was 6,150,000.
CURRENCY – Hong Kong dollar (HK$) of 100 cents.
FLAG – British Blue Ensign with the arms on a white disc in the fly.

GOVERNMENT

The island of Hong Kong was first occupied by Great Britain in 1841 and formally ceded by the Treaty of Nanking in 1842. Kowloon was acquired by the Peking Convention of 1860 and the New Territories, consisting of a peninsula in the southern part of the Guangdong province together with adjacent islands, by a 99-year lease signed on 9 June 1898.

Hong Kong is administered by the Hong Kong government, at the head of which is the Governor. The Governor governs aided by an Executive Council and a Legislative Council. The Executive Council consists of three ex-officio members (the Chief Secretary, the Financial Secretary and the Attorney-General) together with ten other members, including one member who is an official and appointed by the Governor with the approval of the British Foreign Secretary. The Legislative Council consists of 60 members all of whom (from the September 1995 election) are elected: 20 directly elected by geographical constituencies; 30 indirectly elected by functional constituencies, including nine new functional constituencies with large working population electorates; and ten indirectly elected by an election commission whose members are directly elected members of the Regional and Urban Councils. The President of the Legislative Council is elected to that office by the members.

The Urban Council provides services relating to public health and sanitation, culture and recreation in the urban area. From the March 1995 elections the Urban Council consists of 41 members, of whom 32 are directly elected from district constituencies and nine are representative members from the urban district boards. A Regional Council was also set up in 1986 to provide similar services in the New Territories. Of the 39 Regional Council seats, 27 are directly elected from district constituencies and nine are elected as representatives of the nine district boards within the Regional Council area. The remaining three are ex-officio members, being the chairman and the two vice-chairmen of the Heung Yee Kuk (a statutory advisory body which represents the indigenous population of the New Territories). There are also 18 district boards (nine in the urban areas and nine in the New Territories) which are statutory bodies that provide a forum for public consultation and participation in the administration of the districts. There are 346 directly elected members and 27 ex-officio members who are rural committee chairmen.

HANDOVER TO CHINA

Under the terms of the Joint Declaration of the British and Chinese governments, which came into force on 27 May 1985, Hong Kong will become, with effect from 1 July 1997, a Special Administrative Region of the People's Republic of China. However, the social and economic systems in the SAR will remain unchanged for 50 years. The Declaration guarantees: the free movement of goods and capital; the retention of Hong Kong's free port status, separate customs territory and freely convertible currency; the protection of property rights and foreign investment; the right of free movement to and from Hong Kong; Hong Kong's autonomy in the conduct of its external commercial relations and its own monetary and financial policies; and judicial independence. The British and Chinese governments have, since the entry into force of the agreement, been involved in consultations on the implementation of the agreement via the Joint Liaison Group.

China is demanding an increasing voice in Hong Kong affairs as the handover approaches. This has led to friction between the British and Hong Kong authorities on one side and the Chinese government on the other. Central to the acrimonious disputes in 1992 to 1995 has been Governor Patten's plan for an extension of democracy in Hong Kong first presented in October 1992.

The plan outraged the Chinese government, which believes it agreed in the 1985 Joint Declaration to only 20 directly-elected seats on the Legislative Council and 40 appointed (or pliant pro-Beijing) members. The Chinese government suspended meetings of the Joint Liaison Group and talks on the new airport in late 1992. Talks resumed in June 1993 but after 17 rounds of fruitless negotiations between the UK and Chinese governments and no progress in the Joint Liaison Group meetings, the Legislative Council passed Governor Patten's democratic reform package in two stages in February and June 1994. The reforms established the constituencies, and direct and indirect elections to the legislative, Regional and Urban

Councils for the 1995 elections (*see* above); introduced single-member constituencies; reduced the voting age from 21 to 18; replaced corporate voting by individual voting in the existing functional constituencies; and established independent boundary and election commissions.

The Chinese government refuses to accept the reforms and says that it will dismantle all the elected councils and replace them with its own arrangements after it assumes sovereignty. Meanwhile, it has adopted flexible positions on 'non-political' issues, allowing the Joint Liaison Group to reach agreement on: the stationing of Chinese defence forces in Hong Kong after 1 July 1997; the establishment of a new body to manage the new airport; and the establishment of a Court of Final Appeal to replace the UK Privy Council after July 1997.

Governor, His Excellency The Rt. Hon. Christopher Patten, *sworn in* 9 July 1992
Chief Justice, The Hon. Sir Ti Liang Yang

CIVIL ESTABLISHMENT *as at June 1995*
Chief Secretary, Hon. Mrs Anson Chan, CBE
Commander, British Forces, Maj.-Gen. B. Dutton, CBE
Financial Secretary, Hon. Donald Tsang, OBE
Attorney-General, Hon. J. F. Mathews, CMG
Civil Service, Hon. Michael Sze, ISO
Constitutional Affairs, Hon. Nicholas Ng
Planning, Environment and Lands, Hon. Bowen Leung
Transport, Hon. Haider Barma, ISO
Education and Manpower, Hon. Joseph Wong
Economic Services, Hon. Gordon Siu
Home Affairs, Hon. Michael M. Y. Suen
Health and Welfare, Hon. Mrs Katherine Fok, OBE
Security, Hon. Peter Lai
Financial Services and Economic Analysis, Hon. Rafael Hui
Recreation and Culture, Hon. Chau Tak-hay, CBE
Trade and Industry, Hon. Denise Yue
Works, Hon. Kwong Hon-sang
Political Adviser, Robert Peirce
Commissioner of Police, Eddie Hui Ki-on
Treasury, Kwong Ki-chi
*ex-officio member of the Executive Council

BRITISH COUNCIL REPRESENTATIVE, T. Buchanan, Easey Commercial Building, 225 Hennessy Road, Wanchai, Hong Kong.

LONDON OFFICE
Hong Kong Government Office, 6 Grafton Street, London WIX 3LB. Tel: 0171-499 9821. *Commissioner,* Sir David Ford, KBE, LVO, *apptd* 1993

ECONOMY

Over the past 30 years Hong Kong has become one of the world's major trade, manufacturing and financial centres. In 1994 it had an unemployment rate of 1.9 per cent, an annual inflation rate of 8.1 per cent, a GDP growth rate of 5.5 per cent, and a budget surplus of HK$15 billion. Increasingly tied economically to China, Hong Kong firms are the largest investors in China and China has invested some HK$20 billion in Hong Kong, which is also the main trade and investment entry point into China.

The main economic sector is the services industry, especially financial services, and it employs about 75 per cent of the workforce. The manufacturing sector contributes about 11.4 per cent to the GDP and accounts for about 15.3 per cent of total employment. Up to 80 per cent of manufacturing output is eventually exported. Light consumer goods, such as electronics, plastics, electrical products, watches and clocks, accounted for 27 per cent of total domestic exports in 1994. Textiles and clothing, Hong Kong's traditional leading industries, accounted for 40 per cent of exports in 1994.

Diversification in terms of products and markets continues to be the main feature of recent industrial development, as are industrial partnerships with overseas companies. The economy is based on export rather than the domestic market.

FINANCE	1993–4	1994–5
Public revenue	HK$166,602m	HK$173,561m
Public expenditure	155,207m	170,852m

TRADE

In 1993 the total value of visible trade (including domestic exports, re-exports and imports) amounted to 277 per cent of GDP. Hong Kong's visible trade account had in 1994 a deficit of HK$80,695 million. Taking visible and invisible trade together, there was a combined surplus of HK$18,739 million, compared with HK$61,436 million in 1993. In 1994, Hong Kong's principal customers for its domestic products, in order of value of trade, were USA, China, Germany, Singapore, Japan, the UK, and Taiwan. China was its principal supplier.

	1993	1994
Total exports	HK$1,046,250m	HK$1,170,013m
Total imports	1,072,597m	1,250,709m

Trade with UK	1993	1994
Imports from UK	£2,170,115,000	£2,297,561,000
Exports to UK	2,997,774,000	3,079,611,000

COMMUNICATIONS

Hong Kong has one of the world's finest natural harbours, and it is the busiest container port in the world, with eight terminals, as well as large modern cargo and liner terminals. Dockyard facilities include eight floating drydocks, the largest being capable of docking vessels up to 150,000 tonnes deadweight. In 1994 some 383,900 ocean-going and river-trade vessels called at Hong Kong and loaded and discharged more than 147 million tonnes of cargo.

Hong Kong International Airport, Kai Tak, situated to the east of the Kowloon peninsula, is regularly used by over 63 international airlines, providing nearly 3,000 scheduled passenger and cargo services each week. During 1994, over 143,324 aircraft on international flights arrived and departed, carrying 25.3 million passengers and 1,293,000 tonnes of freight. A new international airport is being built on reclaimed land off Lantau Island at Chek Lap Kok and is planned to become operational by 1997.

EDUCATION

In the school year 1994–5 there were 2,355 day schools with 1,157,219 pupils. Free education for children up to the age of 15 is compulsory. Post-secondary education is provided by six universities and one college; total student numbers were 72,154 in December 1994. The Open Learning Institute of Hong Kong provides university education to about 18,400 students. There are also seven technical institutes and the Hong King Institute of Education.

MONTSERRAT

Situated in 16° 45′ N. latitude and 61° 15′ W. longitude, 27 miles south-west of Antigua, Montserrat is about 11 miles long and seven miles wide, with an area of 38 sq. miles (98 sq. km). Fertile and green, it is volcanic with several hot springs. About two-thirds of the island is mountainous, the rest capable of cultivation.

POPULATION – Population (estimate 1991) was 11,000.
CHIEF TOWN – ΨPlymouth, population 2,500.
CURRENCY – East Caribbean dollar (EC$) of 100 cents.
FLAG – British Blue Ensign with the shield of arms in the fly.

GOVERNMENT

Discovered by Columbus in 1493, Montserrat became a British colony in 1632. The first settlers were predominantly Irish indentured slaves from St Kitts. The island was captured by the French in 1664, 1667 and 1782 but the island reverted to Britain within a few years on each occasion and was finally assigned to Great Britain in 1783.

A ministerial system was introduced in Montserrat in 1960. The Executive Council is presided over by the Governor and is composed of four elected members (the Chief and three other Ministers) and two ex-officio members (the Attorney-General and the Financial Secretary). The four Ministers are appointed from the members of the political party holding the majority in the Legislative Council. The Legislative Council consists of the Speaker, two ex-officio members (the Attorney-General and the Financial Secretary), two nominated members and seven elected members.

Governor, His Excellency Frank Savage, LVO, OBE, *apptd* 1993

EXECUTIVE COUNCIL *as at July 1995*
President, The Governor
Chief Minister and Minister of Finance and Economic Development, Hon. Reuben T. Meade
Communications and Works, Hon. Nowell Tuitt
Agriculture, Trade and the Environment, Hon. Charles T. Kirnon
Education, Health, Community Services and Labour, Hon. Lazelle Howes
Attorney-General, Hon. Gertel Thom
Financial Secretary, Hon. C. T. John, OBE

Speaker of the Legislative Council, Dr the Hon. H. A. Fergus, CBE

ECONOMY

The economy is dominated by tourism, related construction activities and offshore business services. There is some light industry and efforts are being made to increase agricultural exports and establish an agro-processing industry.

FINANCE	1991	1992
Revenue	EC$44,443,000	EC$39,273,000
Expenditure	39,216,000	39,056,000

TRADE WITH UK	1993	1994
Imports from UK	£2,141,000	£2,651,000
Exports to UK	65,000	15,000

PITCAIRN ISLANDS

Pitcairn, a small volcanic island 1.9 sq. miles (5 sq. km) in area, is the chief of a group of islands situated about midway between New Zealand and Panama in the South Pacific Ocean at longitude 130° 06' W. and latitude 25° 04' S. The island rises in cliffs to a height of 1,100 feet and access from the sea is possible only at Bounty Bay, a small rocky cove, and then only by surf boats. The other three islands of the group (Henderson lying 105 miles east-north-east of Pitcairn, Oeno lying 75 miles north-west and Ducie lying 293 miles east) are all uninhabited. Henderson Island, a UNESCO World Heritage Site, is occasionally visited by the Pitcairn Islanders to obtain supplies of 'miro' wood which is used for their carvings. Oeno is visited for excursions of about a week's duration every two years or so.

Mean monthly temperatures vary between 66° F (19° C) in August and 75° F (24° C) in February and the average annual rainfall is 80 inches. With an equable climate, the island is very fertile and produces both tropical and sub-tropical trees and crops.

POPULATION – At 31 December 1994 the population was 54. Since 1887 the islanders have all been adherents of the Seventh-day Adventist Church.

FLAG – British Blue Ensign with the arms in the fly.

GOVERNMENT

First settled in 1790 by the Bounty mutineers and their Tahitian companions, Pitcairn was left uninhabited in 1856 when the entire population was resettled on Norfolk Island. The present community are descendants of two parties who, not wishing to remain on Norfolk, returned to Pitcairn in 1859 and 1864 respectively.

Pitcairn became a British settlement under the British Settlement Act 1887, and was administered by the Governor of Fiji from 1952 until 1970, when the administration was transferred to the British High Commission in New Zealand and the British High Commissioner was appointed Governor. The local Government Ordinance of 1964 provides for a Council of ten members of whom six are elected.

Governor of Pitcairn, Henderson, Ducie and Oeno Islands, His Excellency Robert John Alston, CMG (*British High Commissioner to New Zealand*)
Island Magistrate and Chairman of Island Council, J. Warren

ECONOMY

The islanders live by subsistence gardening and fishing, and their limited monetary needs are satisfied by the manufacture of wood carvings and other handicrafts which are sold to passing ships and to a few overseas customers. Other than small fees charged for gun and driving licences there are no taxes and government revenue is derived almost solely from the sale of postage stamps and income from investments. Communication with the outside world is maintained by cargo vessels travelling between New Zealand and Panama which call at irregular intervals, and by means of a satellite service providing telephone, telex and fax facilities.

SOCIAL WELFARE

Education is compulsory between the ages of five and 15. Secondary education in New Zealand is encouraged by the Administration which provides scholarships and bursaries for the purpose. Medical care is provided by a registered nurse when a doctor is not present.

ST HELENA AND DEPENDENCIES

ST HELENA

St Helena is situated in the South Atlantic Ocean, 955 miles south of the Equator, 702 miles south-east of Ascension, 1,140 miles from the nearest point of the African continent, 1,800 miles from the coast of South America, 1,694 miles from Cape Town, in 15° 55' S. latitude and 5° 42' W. longitude. It is 10½ miles long, 6½ broad, and encloses an area of 47 sq. miles (122 sq. km).

St Helena is of volcanic origin, and consists of numerous rugged mountains, the highest rising to 2,700 feet (820 m), interspersed with picturesque ravines. Although within the tropics, the south-east trade winds keep the temperature mild and equable.

POPULATION – The population (1987) is 5,644.
CAPITAL– ΨJamestown. Population (1987) 1,332.
CURRENCY – St Helena pound (£) of 100 pence.
FLAG – British Blue Ensign with the shield of arms in the fly.

GOVERNMENT

St Helena was discovered by the Portuguese navigator, Juan da Nova Castella, in 1502 (probably on St Helena's Day) and remained unknown to other European nations until 1588. It was used as a port of call for vessels of all nations trading to the East until it was annexed by the Dutch in 1633. It was never occupied by them, however, and the English East India Company seized it in 1659. From 1815 to 1821 the island was lent to the British government as a place of exile for the Emperor Napoleon Bonaparte who died in St Helena on 5 May 1821, and in 1834 it was ceded to the British Crown.

The government of St Helena is administered by a Governor, with the aid of a Legislative Council, consisting of a Speaker, three ex-officio members (Chief Secretary, Financial Secretary and Attorney-General) and 12 elected members. Five committees of the Legislative Council are reponsible for general oversight of the activities of government departments and have in addition a wide range of statutory and administrative functions. The Governor is also assisted by an Executive Council of the three ex-officio members and the chairmen of the Council committees.

Governor, His Excellency David Leslie Smallman, LVO, *apptd* 1995
Chief Secretary, J. G. Perrott
Financial Secretary, R. Perrott, OBE
Attorney-General, D. Jeremiah
Deputy Secretary, E. C. Yon
Chief Medical Officer, Dr J. L. Sharp
Chief Agriculture and Forestry Officer, C. Lomas
Chief Education Officer, B. George
Chief Engineer, D. Johnston
Chief Social Services and Employment Officer, J. Young
Chief Personnel Officer, S. I. Ellick
Chief Development Officer, R. I. Ellick
Chief Finance Officer, D. H. Wade
Chief Justice, G. W. Martin, OBE

ECONOMY

The only significant export is canned and frozen fish. The other exports are a small amount of high quality coffee and cottage industry products (including lace, decorative woodwork and beadwork). St James's Bay, on the north-west of the island, possesses a good anchorage. There is as yet no airport or airstrip.

FINANCE	1991–2	1992–3
Local revenue	£4,384,626	£3,545,407
Budgetary	3,424,000	3,526,100
Recurrent expenditure	6,756,049	6,816,429
Development aid	1,397,531	1,614,478

TRADE	1991–2	1992–3
Total imports	£6,543,088	£6,100,400
Total exports	90,095	169,525

TRADE WITH UK	1993	1994
Imports from UK	£6,564,000	£10,423,000
Exports to UK	412,000	496,000

ASCENSION

The small island of Ascension lies in the South Atlantic (7° 56′ S., 14° 22′ W.) some 700 miles north-west of the island of St Helena. It is a rocky peak of purely volcanic origin. The highest point (Green Mountain), some 2,817 ft, is covered with lush vegetation and has a farm of some ten acres, producing vegetables and livestock. The island is famous for turtles, which land on the beaches from January to May to lay their eggs. It is also a breeding area for the sooty tern, or wideawake, large numbers of which settle on the south-western coast every tenth month to hatch their eggs. Other wildlife on the island includes feral donkeys and cats, rabbits and francolin partridge. All wildlife except rabbits and cats is protected by law. The ocean surrounding the island contains shark, barracuda, tuna, bonito and many other fish.

POPULATION – The resident population in March 1995 totalled 1,110, of whom 757 were from St Helena, 135 from the UK and 218 from the USA. The residents consist of the employees and families of the British organizations, of the contractors of the US Air Force (Computer Sciences Raytheon) and of the St Helena government.

British forces returned to the island in April 1982 in support of operations in the Falkland Islands. At present there are over 100 RAF personnel on the island supporting the air link to the Falklands.

CAPITAL – Georgetown.

GOVERNMENT

Ascension is said to have been discovered by Juan da Nova Castella on Ascension Day 1501 and two years later was visited by Alphonse d'Albuquerque, who gave the island its present name. It was uninhabited until the arrival of Napoleon in St Helena in 1815 when a small British naval garrison was stationed on the island. It remained under the supervision of the Board of Admiralty until 1922, when it was made a dependency of St Helena.

The British Foreign Secretary appoints the Administrator who is responsible to the Governor resident in St Helena. There is a small police force and post office. The British organizations through Ascension Island Services (AIS) provide and operate various common services for the island (school, hospital, public works etc).

Administrator, Roger Huxley, *apptd* 1995

COMMUNICATIONS

Cable and Wireless PLC operates the international telephone and cable services and maintains an internal telephone service. The BBC opened its Atlantic relay station broadcasting to Africa and South America in 1967.

TRISTAN DA CUNHA

Tristan da Cunha is the chief island of a group of islands in the South Atlantic which lies in latitude 37° 0′ S. and longitude 12° 2′ W., some 1,260 nautical miles (2,333 km) south-south-west of St Helena. It has an area of 38 sq. miles (98 sq. km). Inaccessible Island lies 20 nautical miles south-west and has an area of 4 sq. miles (10 sq. km), and the three Nightingale Islands lie 20 nautical miles south of Tristan da Cunha and have an area of three-quarters of a sq. mile (2 sq. km). Gough Island lies some 230 nautical miles south-south-east of Tristan da Cunha in latitude 40° 20′ S. and longitude 9° 58′ W. and has an area of 35 sq. miles (91 sq. km).

All the islands are volcanic and steep-sided with cliffs or narrow beaches. Tristan itself has a single volcanic cone rising to 6,760 feet (2,060 m) and a narrow north-western coastal plain on which the settlement of Edinburgh is situated.

Inaccessible Island is a lofty mass of rock with sides two miles in length; the island is the resort of penguins and sea-birds. Cultivation was started in 1937 but has been abandoned.

The Nightingale Islands are three in number, of which the largest is one mile long and three-quarters of a mile wide, and rises in two peaks, 960 and 1,105 feet above sea level respectively. The smaller islands, Stoltenhoff and Middle Isle, are little more than huge rocks. Seals, innumerable penguins, and vast numbers of sea-birds visit these islands.

Gough Island is about eight miles long and four miles broad. It is the resort of penguins, sea-elephants, fur seals and sea-birds and has valuable guano deposits.

Gough and Inaccessible islands are nature reserves and access is strictly limited.

The islands have a warm-temperate oceanic climate which is damp and windy. Rainfall averages 66 inches a year on the coast of Tristan da Cunha.

POPULATION – Population in 1992 was 295, in the settlement of Edinburgh on Tristan da Cunha. In addition, there is a meteorological station maintained on Gough Island by the South African government and manned by South Africans. Inaccessible Island and the Nightingale Islands are uninhabited.

CAPITAL – Edinburgh.

CURRENCY – Pound sterling.

HISTORY

Tristan da Cunha was discovered in 1506 by a Portuguese admiral (Tristão da Cunha) after whom it was named. In 1760 a British naval officer visited the group of islands and gave his name to Nightingale Island. In 1816 the group was annexed to the British Crown and a garrison was placed on Tristan da Cunha, but this force was withdrawn in 1817. Corporal William Glass remained at his own request with his wife and two children. This party, with two others, formed a settlement. In 1827 five women from St Helena, and afterwards others from Cape Colony, joined the party.

Due to its position on a main sailing route the colony thrived, with an economy based on trading with whalers, sealers and other passing ships. However, the replacement of sail by steam and the opening of the Suez Canal in the late 19th century led to decline.

In October 1961 a volcano, believed to have been extinct for thousands of years, erupted and the danger of further volcanic activity led to the evacuation of inhabitants to the United Kingdom. An advance party returned to Tristan da Cunha in 1963 and subsequently the main body of the islanders returned to the island.

GOVERNMENT

In 1938 Tristan da Cunha and the neighbouring islands of Inaccessible, Nightingale and Gough were made dependencies of St Helena and this remains their status today. They are administered by the Governor of St Helena through a resident Administrator, with headquarters at Edinburgh. Under a constitution introduced in 1985, the Administrator is advised by an Island Council of eight elected members, of whom one must be a woman, and three appointed members. There is universal suffrage at 18.

Administrator, Brendan Dalley, *apptd* 1994

ECONOMY

The main industries are crayfish fishing, fish-processing and agriculture, with the shore-based fishing industry having been developed with the construction of the boat harbour in 1967 and the re-establishment of the lobster factory in 1966. There are no taxes, income being derived from the royalties from the rock lobster fishery around the islands, interest from the reserve fund, and the sales of stamps and handicrafts. Apart from the fishing industry, the other main employer is the Administration itself. There is one hospital with a resident medical officer, and a school catering for those up to age 15. Healthcare and education are free for the islanders.

COMMUNICATIONS

The island is isolated and scheduled visits are restricted to about six calls a year by fishing vessels from Cape Town and annual calls of the RMS *St Helena* and the *SA Agulhas*, also from Cape Town. A wireless station on the island is in daily contact with Cape Town and a radio-telephone service was established in 1969, the same year that electricity was introduced to all the islanders' homes. A marine satellite system providing direct dialling telephone, telex and fax facilities was installed in 1992.

SOUTH GEORGIA AND THE SOUTH SANDWICH ISLANDS

South Georgia is an island 800 miles east-south-east of the Falkland group, with an area of 1,450 sq. miles. The population comprises a small military garrison and a civilian harbour master at King Edward Point, and staff of the British Antarctic Survey at Bird Island, to the north-west of South Georgia.

The South Sandwich Islands lie some 470 miles south-east of South Georgia. The group is a chain of uninhabited, actively volcanic islands about 150 miles long, with a wholly Antarctic climate.

The present constitution came into effect in 1985. It provides for a Commissioner who, for the time being, is the officer administering the government of the Falkland Islands.

In 1993 the UK government decreed an extension of Crown sovereignty and jurisdiction from 12 miles around South Georgia and the South Sandwich Islands to 200 miles around each in order to preserve marine stocks.

Commissioner for South Georgia and the South Sandwich Islands, David Everard Tatham, CMG, *apptd* 1992

TURKS AND CAICOS ISLANDS

The Turks and Caicos Islands are situated between 21° and 22° N. latitude and 71° and 72° W. longitude, about 50 miles south-east of the Bahamas of which they are geographically an extension. There are over 30 islands, of which eight are inhabited, covering an estimated area of 166 sq. miles (430 sq. km). The principal island and seat of government is Grand Turk.

The islands lie in the trade wind belt. The average temperature varies from 24°–27° C in the winter to 29°–32° C in the summer and humidity is generally low. Average rainfall is 21 inches a year.

POPULATION – The population in 1995 was estimated to be 14,000 (Grand Turk 4,000).

FLAG – British Blue Ensign with the shield of arms in the fly.

GOVERNMENT

A constitution was introduced in 1988, and amended in 1993, which provides for an Executive Council and a Legislative Council. The Executive Council is presided over by the Governor and comprises the Chief Minister and five elected Ministers, together with the ex-officio Chief Secretary and Attorney-General.

At the general election of 31 January 1995, the People's Democratic Movement won eight seats and the Progressive National Party five seats in the Legislative Council.

Governor, His Excellency Martin Bourke, *apptd* 1993

EXECUTIVE COUNCIL *as at 15 June 1995*

President, The Governor
Chief Secretary, Hon. R. Cousins
Attorney-General, Hon. D. F. Ballantyne
Chief Minister, Hon. D. H. Taylor
Other Ministers, Hon. S. Harvey; Hon. O. Skippings; Hon. H. Ewing; Hon. C. Selver; Hon. S. Rigby

ECONOMY

FINANCE	1992–3	1993–4*
Local revenue	US$25,745,720	US$25,981,350
Expenditure	31,557,206	28,615,287
*estimate		

The most important industries are fishing, tourism and offshore finance.

TRADE WITH UK	1993	1994
Imports from UK	£758,000	£1,492,000
Exports to UK	528,000	104,000

COMMUNICATIONS

The principal airports are on the islands of Grand Turk, Providenciales and South Caicos. There is an air service between Miami, Providenciales and Grand Turk, between South Caicos and the Bahamas, and between Providenciales and Grand Turk and Haiati and the Dominican Republic. An internal air service provides a twice daily service between the principal islands. There are direct shipping services to the USA (Miami). A comprehensive telephone and telex service is provided by Cable and Wireless (WI) Ltd.

Events of the Year

1 September 1994 to 31 August 1995

BRITISH AFFAIRS

SEPTEMBER 1994

2. Ros Hepplewhite resigned as chief executive of the Child Support Agency. 5. The TUC conference opened in Blackpool. 7. Malaysia lifted the ban on British firms bidding for public sector contracts imposed in February 1994. 9. A British soldier was killed when an armoured personnel carrier crashed near Gorazde, Bosnia. 10. A prison guard was shot and injured when five IRA prisoners attempted to escape from Whitemoor prison, Cambs, the Home Secretary (Michael Howard) set up an independent inquiry into the incident. On 22 September two pounds of Semtex and three detonators were found inside the prison. On 19 December the inquiry report was published and severely criticized security arrangements and the management of the prison up to ministerial level; the Home Secretary rejected calls for his resignation but announced a full inquiry into prison security headed by Gen. Sir John Learmont. 11. The Archbishop of Canterbury arrived in China for an 11-day visit. 12. Bank base rates rose by half a per cent to $5\frac{3}{4}$ per cent. Three British soldiers were killed when their vehicle ran down a mountainside in Gorazde, Bosnia. A man was seriously injured after climbing into the lions' den at London Zoo. 18. The Prince of Wales and thousands of veterans and war widows attended a service at Oosterbeek war cemetery to mark the 50th anniversary of the Battle of Arnhem. 19. The Prime Minister arrived in South Africa for a three-day visit. The Liberal Democrat annual conference opened in Brighton. 24. President Yeltsin of Russia arrived in Britain for talks with the Prime Minister. 28. The RMT and Railtrack settled the four-month-old pay dispute.

OCTOBER 1994

3. The Labour Party annual conference opened in Blackpool. On 4 October the Labour Party leader Tony Blair called for the party's constitution, including clause four relating to public ownership, to be rewritten; on 6 October delegates voted to retain the clause. A book was published in which a former army officer, James Hewitt, said that he had had an affair with the Princess of Wales. 8. The *Sunday Times* alleged that Lady Thatcher's son Mark had received £12 million commission from a £20 billion arms deal with Saudi Arabia negotiated while she was prime minister. 9. Violence broke out in Hyde Park and Oxford Street, London, after a

demonstration against the Criminal Justice Bill. 11. The Conservative Party conference opened in Bournemouth. 17. The Queen and the Duke of Edinburgh arrived in Russia for a four-day state visit, the first by a reigning British monarch. 19. In the House of Commons the Labour MP Stuart Bell accused two junior government ministers, Tim Smith and Neil Hamilton, of accepting payment to ask parliamentary questions on behalf of a Westminster lobbying company. On 20 October Mr Smith resigned as a minister in the Northern Ireland Office. Mr Hamilton denied any impropriety but after further allegations he resigned as a trade and industry minister at the request of the Prime Minister on 25 October. The seven Labour MPs on the House of Commons privileges committee resigned in protest at the decision to hold the committee's inquiry into similar allegations made against two Conservative MPs in July 1994 in private. The MPs returned to the committee on 1 November to attempt to negotiate a compromise. Tony Benn, MP, announced that he would publish minutes of the meeting, which therefore adjourned without taking evidence. On 12 December MPs voted to remove Mr Benn from the committee. 20. The new Shadow Cabinet was announced. 24. The social justice commission set up by the late Labour leader John Smith in 1992 published its recommendations for reforming the welfare state. 25. The Prime Minister published the report of an investigation by the Cabinet Secretary (Sir Robin Butler) into allegations of impropriety made against government ministers by the chairman of Harrods, Mohammed Al Fayed. He said that a file on Mr Al Fayed had been passed to the Director of Public Prosecutions; on 25 November the Crown Prosecution Service said that no charges would be brought against Mr Al Fayed. The Prime Minister also announced an independent inquiry headed by Lord Nolan into standards in public life. 27. The Chief Secretary to the Treasury (Jonathan Aitken) denied allegations made in the *Guardian* that he had misled Sir Robin Butler about the payment of a bill at the Ritz hotel in Paris. The editor of the *Guardian* (Peter Preston) later admitted that House of Commons notepaper had been used to forge a letter from Mr Aitken in order to protect the newspaper's source; after an emergency debate in the House of Commons on 2 November he was ordered to appear before the privileges committee. A deputy chairman of the Conservative Party, Dame Angela Rumbold, resigned as an executive director of a lobbying company after allegations connected with the Government's choice of a Channel Tunnel rail link station. **31.** Three British tourists were kidnapped by Kashmiri rebels in New Delhi; they were freed unharmed on 1 November. The Prince of Wales left Britain for a five-day official visit to Los Angeles, followed by an official visit to Hong Kong. The Milk Marketing Board was abolished.

NOVEMBER 1994

1. Cambodian officials confirmed that three Western tourists kidnapped in July 1994, including a Briton, Mark Slater, had been murdered by the Khmer Rouge. **3.** The Government's abandoned its plans to privatize the Post Office. **8.** The Employment Secretary (Michael Portillo), who had cited EC rules as the reason for withdrawing the priority suppliers scheme (designed to promote the employment of disabled people) in August 1994, restored an amended version of the scheme. **9.** The Court of Appeal ruled that the Home Secretary (Michael Howard) had acted unlawfully in introducing a new criminal injuries compensation scheme in April 1994 without parliamentary approval. **10.** The High Court ruled that the Foreign Secretary had acted unlawfully in authorizing £234 million in aid for the Pergau dam project in Malaysia in 1991. The Government published a new version of the national curriculum. **14.** The Eurostar passenger rail service between London and Paris was launched. The National Lottery was launched; the first draw took place on 19 November. **15.** The Duke of York arrived in Argentina for a five-day official visit. **16.** The state opening of Parliament took place. The Prime Minister said that he would regard a planned vote to increase Britain's contribution to the European Union as a vote of confidence in the Government; on 23 November the Chancellor of the Exchequer said that the Cabinet would resign if the vote were lost (*see* 28 November). **20.** A 75 per cent pay rise awarded to the chief executive of British Gas provoked widespread criticism. **22.** The Princess Royal arrived in South Africa for a four-day official visit. **28.** The Government's bill to increase Britain's contribution to the EU was passed by a majority of 285; eight Conservative MPs abstained and had the whip withdrawn. On 29 November Sir Richard Body resigned the whip in protest at the Government's tactics. **29.** The Chancellor of the Exchequer presented his Budget to the House of Commons (*see* pages 1163–4).

DECEMBER 1994

6. An Opposition motion paving the way for a vote to rescind the planned rise in VAT on domestic fuel to 17.5 per cent was passed in the House of Commons by a majority of eight; fifteen Conservative MPs supported the motion or abstained. The Chancellor of the Exchequer said that VAT on domestic fuel would remain at 8 per cent; on 8 December Mr Clarke raised duties on petrol, alcohol and tobacco in order to make up the £1.5 billion shortfall caused by the decision on VAT. **7.** Bank base rates rose by half a per cent to 6¼ per cent. **10–11.** Severe flooding

hit the west of Scotland; three men drowned. **13.** The winner of a national lottery jackpot of £17.9 million was identified in spite of having requested anonymity; on 14 December the High Court lifted an injunction preventing newspapers from naming him. The Shadow Home Secretary (Jack Straw) complained to the Press Complaints Commission about the role of the national lottery operator, Camelot, in the incident. **15.** The Dudley West by-election took place. **19.** MPs voted to end late-night Parliamentary sittings. The Government announced that 270 road schemes would be reviewed after a report showed that new roads generate more traffic. **20.** Following a House of Lords ruling the Employment Secretary announced that part-time workers would be given the same compensation rights for redundancy and unfair dismissal as full-time workers. **22.** Britain's trade figures showed a surplus of exports over imports for the first time since 1987. **27–28.** Heavy rain and strong winds caused flooding in many parts of Britain.

JANUARY 1995

2–7. Animal rights protesters clashed with police during demonstrations against the export of calves from Shoreham harbour, W. Sussex. Similar demonstrations were held at Brightlingsea, Essex, later in the month. On 19 January the Shoreham port trust said that the export of live animals from the port would cease. **2.** About 70 prisoners rioted at Everthorpe prison, Humberside. **3.** Three prisoners escaped from Parkhurst prison, Isle of Wight; they were captured on 8 January. On 10 January the governor of the prison, John Marriott, was moved to other duties pending the outcome of an independent inquiry into the escape. Rioting broke out again at Everthorpe prison. **15.** The Prince of Wales's valet, Ken Stronach, was suspended after details of the Prince's personal life were published in the *News of the World*; on 23 January he resigned. **17.** The Nolan inquiry into standards in public life held its first public hearings; on 19 January Lord Nolan proposed the introduction of an independent element into MPs' self-regulation of their financial interests. **19.** Eight of the whipless Conservative MPs published a policy statement calling for a reduction in the powers of the EU. **20.** Members of the NUT voted to abandon their boycott of national curriculum testing. **23.** The Social Security Secretary (Peter Lilley) announced radical reforms of the Child Support Agency (*see* page 1174). **26.** At least four people died when heavy snow fell in northern England. **27.** The accident and emergency unit at St Bartholomew's Hospital, London, closed.

FEBRUARY 1995

1. An animal rights protester was killed when she fell under the wheels of a lorry carrying veal calves for export at Coventry airport. Heavy rain and melting snow caused severe flooding in parts of northern England. **2.** Bank base rates rose by half a per cent to 6¾ per cent. **5.** The Princess of Wales arrived in

Tokyo for a four-day visit as a charity ambassador. 7. Allan Stewart resigned as a junior minister after allegations that he had brandished a pickaxe at a man protesting against a motorway extension in Glasgow on 5 February. 9. Air Chief Marshal Sir Sandy Wilson resigned from the RAF at the request of the Secretary of State for Defence (Malcolm Rifkind) after controversy over a £387,000 refurbishment of his official residence. 11. Charles Wardle resigned as a junior minister on the grounds that the Single European Act could lead to uncontrolled immigration into Britain. 15. Lord Lester of Herne Hill alleged that many peers were accepting payment for asking questions in the House of Lords. 16. The Islwyn by-election took place. 26. The merchant bank Barings went into receivership after dealings in derivatives by its Singapore office resulted in losses of more than £500 million and a rescue attempt led by the Bank of England failed; on 27 February the Chancellor of the Exchequer announced an inquiry into the collapse. A trader in the Singapore office, Nick Leeson, was arrested and held for questioning in Frankfurt on 2 March. On 6 March Barings was bought by the Dutch banking and insurance group ING. 28. Five parishes in Norfolk opted out of Church of England control after their vicar, who offered his resignation because he planned to marry for a third time, was sacked.

MARCH 1995

1. The former Chancellor Norman Lamont voted for an Opposition motion in the House of Commons criticizing the Government's handling of policy relating to the EU; the motion was defeated by 319 votes to 314. Pentos, the parent company of the Dillons bookshop and Rymans stationery chains, went into receivership. On 2 March Dillons was bought by Thorn EMI and on 18 March Rymans was bought by NAG Telecom. 2. Sir John Banham resigned as chairman of the Local Government Commission at the request of the Environment Secretary (John Gummer); he was replaced by Sir David Cooksey. 6. Robert Hughes resigned as a junior minister after admitting an extra-marital affair. The Government sold its remaining shares in PowerGen and National Power, raising £4 billion. 7. The value of shares in PowerGen and National Power fell after the Director-General of Electricity Supply (Prof. Stephen Littlechild) said that he was considering new controls on electricity prices. 11. The Prince of Wales arrived in Cairo at the beginning of a seven-day official visit to Egypt and Morocco. 12. The Prime Minister arrived in Jerusalem at the beginning of a four-day visit to the Middle East. 13. The national executive of the Labour Party voted in favour of a new clause four of the constitution. After pressure from the homosexual group OutRage, the Bishop of London (David Hope) said that his sexuality was 'ambiguous' and condemned the group's intimidatory tactics. 19. The Queen and the Duke of Edinburgh arrived in South Africa for a six-day state visit.

21. The deputy governor of the Bank of England, Rupert Pennant-Rea, resigned after press revelations about an extra-marital affair. 29. The Chief Secretary to the Treasury (Jonathan Aitken) denied that he had known that a company of which he was a non-executive director had broken the Government's arms embargo by selling guns to Iran via Singapore in the 1980s.

APRIL 1995

1-3. Four thousand people were evacuated from their homes in Portland, Dorset, while an unexploded war-time bomb found was defused. 4. The Prime Minister met President Clinton for talks in Washington. Two Labour MPs, Ann Clwyd and Jim Cousins, were sacked from the Opposition foreign affairs team for taking an unauthorized trip abroad and missing votes in the House of Commons. 5. The Health Secretary (Virginia Bottomley) was criticized in the House of Commons by the Opposition and by Conservative back-benchers after confirming plans for the reorganization of hospitals in London, including the closure of St Bartholomew's. 6. In local elections in Scotland the Conservatives failed to win control of any of the 29 unitary authorities to be established in April 1996. 9. Richard Spring, MP, resigned as parliamentary private secretary to the Northern Ireland Secretary after newspaper revelations about his private life. 10. Jonathan Aitken announced his intention to sue the *Guardian* over its reports about his business activities and later sued Granada Television over a *World in Action* programme which made further allegations. 11. The Bishop of London, David Hope, was appointed Archbishop of York from August 1995. 12. Two High Court judges ruled that bans by ports or airports on the export of live animals for slaughter were illegal. There were further clashes between police and demonstrators at Brightlingsea, Essex, when the exports resumed on 18 April. 20. The Conservative MPs David Tredinnick and Graham Riddick were suspended from the House of Commons without pay for 20 days and ten days respectively for accepting money in exchange for tabling questions in the House when approached by a *Sunday Times* reporter in July 1994. Six Britons held hostage by the Revolutionary United Front in Sierra Leone were released. 24. The whip was restored to eight Conservative MPs from whom it had been withdrawn in November 1994. 26. A row broke out after the pre-1945 papers of Sir Winston Churchill were bought from the Churchill family for £12.5 million with funds from the National Lottery. 29. At a special conference, Labour Party delegates voted in favour of the new clause four of the party's constitution.

MAY 1995

3. The Prince of Wales visited Hamburg to mark the 50th anniversary of VE Day. 4. In the local council elections in England and Wales the Conservatives lost more than 2,000 seats, retaining control of only

eight councils. **6–8.** Events were held throughout the UK to mark the 50th anniversary of VE Day. On 6 May The Queen Mother opened three days of celebrations in Hyde Park and The Queen and other members of the royal family attended a banquet for more than 50 heads of state at the Guildhall, London. On 7 May The Queen, other members of the royal family and the heads of state attended a service at St Paul's Cathedral and a ceremony of peace and reconciliation in Hyde Park. On 8 May The Queen, The Queen Mother and Princess Margaret appeared on the balcony at Buckingham Palace and watched a flypast of Second World War aircraft. At sunset on 8 May two minutes' silence was observed before The Queen lit a beacon in Hyde Park; other beacons were lit throughout the country. **8–9.** The Prime Minister attended VE Day anniversary ceremonies in Paris and Moscow. **9.** The first award of the Conspicuous Gallantry Cross was made, to Cpl Wayne Mills, The Duke of Wellington's Regiment. The pound fell to a record low against the Deutsche Mark and other leading European currencies. **9–10.** The Prince of Wales attended events in the Channel Islands to mark the 50th anniversary of Liberation Day. **11.** The Nolan Committee on Standards in Public Life published its first report (*see* page 1175). On 18 May the Prime Minister announced that the recommendations, to which many Conservative MPs had expressed opposition, would be referred to a parliamentary committee. **13.** Alison Hargreaves became the first woman to climb Mount Everest alone and without oxygen. **15.** The Government announced that rail fares would be capped for seven years from 1996. **16.** The Conservative MP Sir Jerry Wiggin was reported to have tabled an amendment to a bill in which he had a financial interest, using the name of another MP and without the MP's knowledge or permission; on 22 May Sir Jerry apologized to the House. **23.** The Emir of Kuwait arrived in Britain for a three-day state visit. A report strongly criticized the management of the social services department of Islington council in north London between 1982 and 1992 and its failure to investigate allegations of child abuse and misconduct against council staff. **24.** The former Prime Minister Lord Wilson of Rievaulx died. **25.** The Perth and Kinross by-election took place. **28.** Thirty-three British soldiers were taken hostage by the Bosnian Serbs in Gorazde. The Prime Minister held emergency talks at Downing Street and announced that 1,200 troops would be sent to the area immediately; a further 5,500 troops were put on standby. On 31 May Parliament was recalled to discuss the crisis. **31 May–1 June.** The Prince of Wales paid an official visit to the Republic of Ireland.

JUNE 1995

2. Eleven of the British soldiers taken hostage in Bosnia were released. **3.** Britain agreed to send 5,500 troops to Bosnia as part of the new UN rapid

intervention force. **5.** Draft extracts from the report of the Scott inquiry into the export of defence equipment to Iraq between 1984 and 1990 were leaked to the press; the Agriculture Minister, William Waldegrave, was criticized for misleading MPs. Further extracts leaked on 19 June said that the Government had deliberately misled Parliament and the public. **6.** A further 17 British soldiers were released in Bosnia. **10.** Rioting broke out for a second successive night in Bradford, W. Yorks. **12.** In a television interview, Baroness Thatcher criticized John Major for his policies on Europe and other issues. **13.** The President of the Board of Trade (Michael Heseltine) announced an inquiry into an alleged breach of the arms embargo to Iran in the late 1980s by BMARC, a company of which the Chief Secretary to the Treasury (Jonathan Aitken) was then a director. The remaining British hostages in Bosnia were released. **14.** Pauline Clare was appointed chief constable of the Lancashire Constabulary, becoming the first female chief constable in Britain. **15.** The North Down by-election took place. **20.** The Labour Party suspended all 17 Labour councillors on Monklands district council after allegations of corruption. **22.** The Prime Minister resigned as leader of the Conservative Party in order to force a leadership election; he challenged his critics in the party to 'put up or shut up'. EU countries agreed on uniform controls for the transport of live animals from 1997. **23.** Douglas Hurd announced that he would resign as foreign secretary after the leadership election. The Prince of Wales visited the Shankill Road, Belfast. **26.** John Redwood resigned as Secretary of State for Wales in order to contest the Conservative Party leadership election.

JULY 1995

4. In the election for the leadership of the Conservative Party, John Major received 218 votes and John Redwood 89; there were 20 abstentions or spoiled ballot papers and two MPs failed to vote. Two British tourists and an American were taken hostage by Kashmiri militants in southern Kashmir. **5.** In a Cabinet reshuffle, Michael Heseltine was appointed First Secretary of State and Deputy Prime Minister and Malcolm Rifkind replaced Douglas Hurd as Foreign Secretary. The Department of Employment was disbanded, with the bulk of its responsibilities moved to the Department for Education, renamed the Department for Education and Employment. Two British and two American tourists were kidnapped by Kashmiri militants in northern India. **5–6.** Two nights of rioting broke out in Luton, Beds. **7.** The Metropolitan Police Commissioner, Sir Paul Condon, was criticized for saying that most muggings in London are carried out by young black men. **10.** Police said that a man had been arrested after firing a starting pistol at the Prime Minister on 18 June. **14.** Train drivers held the first of two 24-hour strikes over pay. **17.** A committee headed by Sir Richard Greenbury published a code of practice for executive salaries and benefits in listed companies, including the recommendation that executive share options should be taxed as income rather than capital gains; the Chancellor of the Exchequer announced that the change would be implemented in all cases with immediate effect. After widespread criticism, the Chancellor announced on 27 July that the change would not apply to members of existing schemes. **18.** The Board of Banking Supervision presented to Parliament its report on the collapse of Barings Bank; it blamed the collapse on the activities of the trader Nick Leeson, but was highly critical of the bank's management and of the failure of its auditors, Coopers and Lybrand, and the Bank of England to detect the problems. **21.** After an international meeting in London on the crisis in Bosnia, the Prime Minister said that there would be a 'substantial and decisive' response if the Bosnian Serbs attacked the UN-protected area of Gorazde. **27.** The Littleborough and Saddleworth by-election took place. The Government announced that an education association would take over the management of Hackney Downs School, east London. **28.** A report was published which highlighted corruption, fraud and incompetence in the running of Lambeth council, London, in the 1970s and 1980s.

AUGUST 1995

6. Sunday licensing laws in England and Wales were relaxed. **8.** The Labour Party suspended its district party organization in Walsall amid allegations that it had exceeded its powers and was seeking to dictate the policies of the ruling Labour group on Walsall council. **13.** Alison Hargreaves and six fellow climbers were killed while descending from the summit of K2. **15.** Ceremonies were held throughout Britain to mark the 50th anniversary of VJ Day. **18.** The largest traditional stone Hindu temple outside India opened in Neasden, north-west London. **19.** A service led by the Archbishop of Canterbury and attended by The Queen, the Duke of Edinburgh, other members of the Royal Family and thousands of veterans was held at the Royal Victoria Memorial to mark the 50th anniversary of VJ Day. After a two-minute silence a Lancaster bomber showered more than a million poppies onto the assembled crowds. The Queen then took the salute as the veterans marched down The Mall. In the evening The Queen and The Duke of Edinburgh sailed down the Thames to board the Royal Yacht *Britannia* which was moored in the Pool of London. A flypast of historic planes was followed by a firework display from five bridges to celebrate the anniversary of the end of the war. **19.** Services were held throughout the country to mark the anniversary of VJ Day, including a Service of Remembrance attended by the Duke of Edinburgh at St Paul's Cathedral. In the evening ceremonies were held at Horse Guard's Parade, Cardiff Castle, Edinburgh Castle and Carrickfergus Castle. After the two-minute silence The Queen led a procession from Horse Guard's Parade to Buckingham Palace, where hymns were sung. Four British soldiers in the Rapid Reaction Force in the former Yugoslavia were killed when their helicopter crashed off the coast of Croatia. **21.** The Government published a document, *Water Conservation - Government Action*, which proposed new by-laws to cut domestic consumption and said that water companies should extend the use of metering as far and as quickly as possible. The Office of Water Services started an inquiry into the failure of some water companies to provide essential water supplies to homes during the long spell of hot weather. **25.** The Revd Chris Brain, a priest in the Sheffield diocese of the Church of England, was admitted to a psychiatric hospital and barred from practising as a minister after allegations of sexual abuse and corruption. **26.** It was reported that a soldier working at the British embassy in Bogota, Colombia, had been kidnapped by left-wing guerrillas. **28.** James Molyneaux announced his resignation as leader of the Ulster Unionists. **31.** The Meteorological Office said that August 1995 had been the hottest August since records began in 1659.

ACCIDENTS AND DISASTERS

SEPTEMBER 1994

1. An earthquake registering 7.2 on the Richter scale hit the coast of northern California, USA. **8.** All 132 people on board a Boeing 737 were killed when the plane crashed at Pittsburgh, USA. **12.** An earthquake registering 6.0 on the Richter scale hit northern California and Nevada, USA. **14.** Six people were killed and seven seriously injured when a walkway collapsed at Ramsgate ferry terminal, Kent. **18.** Two women and three girls were killed when a double-decker bus drove under a low bridge in Glasgow. **19-24.** More than 94,00 people were left homeless when the volcanoes Vulcan and Tavurvur erupted at Rabaul, Papua New Guinea. **26.** Twenty-six people were killed when a Russian plane crashed near Vanavara, Siberia. **28.** At least 909 people drowned when the ferry *Estonia* sank in the Baltic Sea.

OCTOBER 1994

4. At least nine people were killed and hundreds injured when an earthquake registering 7.9 on the Richter scale occurred in the Pacific Ocean 14 miles from the Kurile Islands off northern Japan. **12.** All 66 people on board an Iranian airliner were killed when it crashed in central Iran. **15.** Five people were killed and at least 11 injured when two trains crashed in thick fog near Cowden, Kent. **21.** At least 32 people were killed when a bridge over the river Han collapsed in Seoul, South Korea. Excavations for an underground rail link caused a landslip at Heathrow airport. **23.** Up to 4,000 people were reported to have died in an outbreak of cerebral malaria in India. **31.** All 68 people on board a commuter plane were killed when it crashed near Chicago, USA. A Russian factory ship, the *Pionersk*, ran aground and broke up off Shetland; the crew were rescued.

NOVEMBER 1994

2-3. At least 460 people were killed when storms hit southern Egypt and a fuel depot was struck by lightning. 5-6. At least 64 people died in flooding caused by torrential rain in the Piedmont region of north-west Italy. 13. A keeper was mauled to death by a tiger at Howletts Zoo near Canterbury, Kent. 14. At least 350 people were killed when a tropical storm hit Haiti. 22. At least 31 people were killed and 100 injured when Mount Merapi erupted in Java, Indonesia. 27. A fire in a discotheque in north-east China killed 233 people. 30. Two people were killed in a fire on the Italian cruise liner *Achille Lauro* off the coast of Somalia; 980 people abandoned ship and were rescued.

DECEMBER 1994

2. At least 147 people were presumed drowned when a ferry sank after being hit by a freighter in Manila Bay, the Philippines. 9. More than 300 people, mainly schoolchildren, were killed in a fire in a cinema in north-west China. 21. An Air Algerie cargo aircraft crashed on the edge of a housing estate near Coventry airport, W. Midlands; all five people on board were killed. 26. Four people were killed when a light aircraft crashed at Stapleford flying club, Essex. A circus acrobat, Neville Campbell, was killed in an accident while performing at the Blackpool Tower Circus. 27. Five people were drowned when a speedboat sank in Strangford Lough, Co. Down. 29. At least 50 people died when a Turkish Airlines Boeing 737 crashed near Van, Turkey.

JANUARY 1995

2. The main debating chamber of the former Northern Ireland parliament at Stormont, Belfast, was destroyed by fire. 12. Fifty-two people were killed when a DC9 aircraft crashed near Cartagena, Colombia. 16. At least 5,100 people were killed and nearly 27,000 injured when an earthquake registering 7.2 on the Richter scale hit the Kobe area, Japan. At least 183 people were killed by an avalanche in the foothills of the Himalayas in Kashmir. 31. A train conductor was killed and 23 people were injured when two trains collided at Aisgill Summit, Cumbria. 31 January-2 February. At least 26 people died and 250,00 people were evacuated from their homes as flooding hit north-west Europe.

FEBRUARY 1995

8. At least 38 people were killed and more than 230 injured when an earthquake registering 6.4 on the Richter scale hit western Colombia.

MARCH 1995

31. All 59 people on board a Romanian airbus were killed when it crashed near Bucharest.

APRIL 1995

17. The catamaran ferry *St Malo* struck rocks off the Jersey coast; 58 people were injured. 27. A fractured gas pipeline exploded in Ukhta, northern Russia, causing a fireball. 28. At least 100 people were killed when a gas explosion destroyed a road in Taegu, S. Korea. A charter plane crash-landed at Manchester Airport; there were no casualties.

MAY 1995

11. Over 100 gold miners were killed when the underground lift they were in was crushed by a locomotive in the Transvaal, South Africa. 13. Five children and a man died in a house fire at Farnborough, Hants. 23. Thirteen people on a Royal British Legion outing were killed in a coach crash on the M4 near Bristol. 24. All 12 people on board were killed when an aircraft crashed during a thunderstorm soon after taking off from Leeds-Bradford airport, W. Yorks. 28. About 1,600 people were killed when an earthquake registering 7.5 on the Richter scale hit Neftegorsk on the Russian island of Sakhalin. 30. The world's oldest working square-rigged vessel, the 137-year-old *Maria Asumpta*, was wrecked off the coast of north Cornwall with the loss of three lives.

JUNE 1995

7. Southend pier was badly damaged by fire. 15. At least 21 people were killed when an earthquake registering 6.1 on the Richter scale hit the northern Peloponnese, Greece. 17. Three Scottish tourists were killed in a coach crash in Turkey. 29. A shopping complex collapsed in Seoul, S. Korea, killing 640 people.

JULY 1995

5. Nine people were killed and at least 22 seriously injured when a coach crashed on the A40 at Raglan, Gwent. 7. The death toll from flooding in central China reached 1,200. One person was killed and five others injured when an explosion caused by a gas leak destroyed a block of flats in Ilkeston, Derbys.

AUGUST 1995

6. The president of the British Mountaineering Council, Paul Nunn, was killed in an avalanche on Haramosh 2 in the Karakoram range of mountains in northern Pakistan. 20. At least 350 people were killed when an express train crashed into a stationary train in Uttar Pradesh, India.

ARTS, SCIENCE AND MEDIA

SEPTEMBER 1994

2. Following a controversial decision by the National Heritage Secretary (Stephen Dorrell) to extend the deadline for raising the funds needed to prevent Canova's statue *The Three Graces* being sold

to the Getty Museum in California, Baron Hans Heinrich Thyssen-Bornemisza donated £800,000 to the campaign; the statue was subsequently purchased by the Victoria and Albert Museum and the National Gallery of Scotland. **14.** After two years' research an international art group said that the National Gallery's painting *The Entombment,* attributed to Michelangelo, was more likely to be the work of Baccio Bandinelli. **21.** Craigie Aitchison won the first Jerwood Painting Prize, worth £30,000. **26.** The publishing company Hodder Headline withdrew from the Net Book Agreement. **29.** An investment group led by the film directors Ridley and Tony Scott bought Shepperton film studios.

October 1994

1. Genetic tests proved that Anna Anderson, who died in 1984, was not, as she had claimed, Grand Duchess Anastasia, the daughter of the last tsar of Russia. **6.** John Galliano was named British Fashion Designer of the Year. **19.** Ealing Studios went into receivership. **24.** Sotheby's announced that the manuscript of Schumann's second symphony had been discovered in a private collection. Seven works by Picasso were stolen from a private art gallery in Zurich. **25.** Klaus Tennstedt, the conductor laureate of the London Philharmonic Orchestra, announced his retirement.

November 1994

2. The Globe Theatre in London was renamed the Gielgud Theatre in honour of Sir John Gielgud. A team of astronomers announced that a new galaxy, Dwingeloo 1, had been discovered behind the Milky Way. **11.** Leonardo da Vinci's *Codex Hammer* was sold at Christie's in New York for £19.2 million. **22.** The sculptor Anthony Gormley won the Turner Prize for modern art.

December 1994

8. Art treasures from Houghton Hall, Norfolk, were sold for £21.2 million at Christie's. A *Guardian* journalist, Richard Gott, resigned after admitting that he had accepted hospitality from the KGB in the 1980s. **15.** Granada Television was fined £500,000 by the Independent Television Commission for plugging brand-name products in its show *This Morning.* **20.** Vladimir Ashkenazy resigned as music director of the Royal Philharmonic Orchestra when the orchestra said that it wished to offer the post to Daniele Gatti. Leonard Ingrams, the organizer of the Garsington opera festival in Oxfordshire, was fined £1,000 for causing noise pollution; on 3 May the conviction was overturned.

January 1995

13. The Radio 1 disc jockey Steve Wright announced his resignation; he was later replaced by Chris Evans. **17.** The controversial Radio 4 programme *Anderson Country* was axed. **19.** The Royal Astronomical Society said that the signs of the zodiac used by astrologers are inaccurate.

February 1995

14. A stained-glass window in memory of Oscar Wilde was unveiled in Poet's Corner, Westminster Abbey. Britain's third national commercial radio station, Talk Radio, went on the air. **15.** The BBC published the results of its programme strategy review, including plans to make its output more widely accessible. **20.** The actor Stephen Fry withdrew from a starring role in the West End play *Cell Mates* after only three performances. **27.** An exhibition of works of art seized by Russia at the end of the Second World War opened in Moscow. On 29 March a similar exhibition opened in St Petersburg.

March 1995

9. The director of the Bolshoi Ballet, Yuri Grigorovich, resigned. **15.** The Council of Europe voted to condemn any closer trade or political links with Iran until the lifting of the *fatwa* against Salman Rushdie. **17.** The Minister of Public Service and Science (David Hunt) launched National Science Week. **22.** Colin Rowe was awarded the 1995 Royal Gold Medal for Architecture.

April 1995

3. The Court of Session in Edinburgh ruled that a *Panorama* interview with John Major should not be broadcast in Scotland before the local elections.

May 1995

12. The managing director of the London Philharmonic Orchestra, Christopher Lawrence, resigned in protest at a proposed merger with the Royal Philharmonic Orchestra. **23.** The Government announced proposals for new rules on cross-media ownership (*see* page 1176).

June 1995

1. Uppark House, W. Sussex, which was destroyed by fire in 1989, reopened. Ealing Studios were sold to the National Film and Television School. **2.** The magazine *The Modern Review* closed. **9.** The artistic director of the Royal Shakespeare Company (Adrian Noble) announced that the company would vacate its base at the Barbican Centre, London, for six months a year from 1997 to tour the provinces. **10.** The South Bank Centre announced that the Philharmonia Orchestra would join the London Philharmonic Orchestra in co-residency from 1997. **18.** A Swedish mezzo-soprano, Katarina Karneus, won the Cardiff Singer of the World competition. **27.** The actor Hugh Grant was arrested in Los Angeles and charged with lewd conduct with a prostitute in a public place. **30.** The Virgin Group bought the MGM cinema chain for £200 million.

July 1995

13. The controversial youth programme *The Word* was axed by Channel 4. **17.** The Government published a White Paper on privacy and media intrusion (*see* page 1177). **20.** The Royal Opera House was awarded £55 million of National

Lottery funds for a redevelopment scheme. **30.** The proposed merger of the London Philharmonic Orchestra and the Royal Philharmonic Orchestra was scrapped.

AUGUST 1995

10. The Government published proposals to create new television and radio channels using digital technology (*see* page 1177). **17.** The London *Evening Standard* apologized to the former Shadow Cabinet member Bryan Gould for publishing an article under his name attacking the Labour leader Tony Blair; the article was in fact written by the son of the Home Secretary, Michael Howard. **23.** Microsoft launched its new computer operating system, Windows 95. **25.** At the Edinburgh Television Festival, Janet Street-Porter, head of the cable channel Live TV, attacked the management of British television as being male, middle-class and out of touch. **30.** The National Gallery bought Bermejo's *St Michael Triumphant over the Devil* from Luton Hoo.

CRIMES AND LEGAL AFFAIRS

SEPTEMBER 1994

12. Carol Wardell, the assistant manageress of a building society, was found murdered in Nuneaton, Warks, after a robbery from her branch; her husband was found bound and gagged at their home but was later charged with the murder. **14.** At the Central Criminal Court the trial of Colin Stagg, who had been charged with the murder of Rachel Nickell on Wimbledon Common in July 1992, was halted when the judge strongly criticized the undercover police operation which led to his arrest. **19.** The European Commission of Human Rights ruled that Ernest Saunders, the former chief executive of Guinness who was convicted in 1990 of theft and conspiracy to defraud, had not received a fair trial because he was denied the right to remain silent during interviews with DTI inspectors. **27.** At the Central Criminal Court 17-year-old Francis Casey was sentenced to eight terms of life imprisonment for the murder of 88-year-old Lillian Notley and eight other offences of assault and robbery of elderly people. **29.** A surgeon, Umesh Gaud, was sentenced at Southwark Crown Court to one year's imprisonment for performing operations knowing that he was a carrier of the hepatitis B virus. **30.** The leading racehorse trainer Alex Scott was found shot dead at his home near Newmarket; a former employee was charged with the murder.

OCTOBER 1994

4. Lloyd's Names won damages estimated at £504 million in the High Court after alleging that negligence on the part of underwriters had led to losses of £629 million on the insurance market. The widow and three children of the actor Roy Kinnear, who was killed in a stunt accident while filming in Spain in 1988, were awarded £650,000 damages in the High Court. **4–6.** Fifty-three members of the Order of the Solar Temple religious sect were found dead in burnt-out houses in Switzerland and Canada. **13.** The footballer John Fashanu and his former club Wimbledon agreed to pay £70,000 in settlement of a High Court action brought by John O'Neill, who was forced to retire from the game in 1987 after being injured in a tackle by Fashanu. **14.** A British couple, Adrian and Bernadette Mooney, were sentenced in Romania to 28 months' imprisonment for buying a baby and attempting to smuggle it out of the country; on 16 November the sentence was suspended by the Romanian appeal court. **19.** A GP, Donald Mackay, was stabbed to death in his surgery in Airdrie, Scotland. **20.** A British woman, Patricia Hussain, was sentenced in Thailand to life imprisonment for trafficking in heroin. **21.** Gerard Mackin and Derek Doherty were sentenced at the Central Criminal Court to 25 years' imprisonment each for taking part in IRA bombing campaigns in London. **23.** A British tourist was shot dead in southern Egypt. **24.** George Walker, the former chairman of the leisure group Brent Walker, was cleared at Southwark Crown Court of charges of false accounting and theft of £17 million. **26.** An American, Curtis Howard, was sentenced at the Central Criminal Court to life imprisonment after admitting the manslaughter of a British student, Catherine Ayling, in May 1991.

NOVEMBER 1994

1. A 14-year-old boy suffering from Asperger's syndrome, a rare psychiatric disorder, was ordered at Winchester Crown Court to be detained indefinitely for the manslaughter of an 85-year-old woman in March 1994. **3.** An assistant store manager was stabbed to death at Woolworth's in Teddington, Middx. **8.** Two 19-year-old students, James Petrolini and Richard Elsey, were sentenced at the Central Criminal Court to life imprisonment for the motiveless murder of Mohammed El-Sayed in January 1994. Feilim O'Hadhmaill was sentenced at the Central Criminal Court to 25 years' imprisonment for his part in planning an IRA bombing campaign in Britain. **11.** A shop manager at Littlewoods in Cardiff was stabbed to death by a shoplifter; on 24 May 1995 Carl Hughes was sentenced to life imprisonment for the murder. **24.** At Sheffield Crown Court 16-year-old Errol Donaldson was ordered to be detained at Her Majesty's pleasure for murdering 17-year-old Grant Jackson with a bayonet in April 1993. **28.** The serial killer Jeffrey Dahmer was beaten to death in prison in Wisconsin, USA. **29.** Eleven-year-old Nayntara Ali, who went missing on 4 November, was found murdered in Forest Gate, east London. Six-year-old Rikki Neave, who went missing on 28 November, was found murdered in Peterborough, Cambs.

ANNIVERSARY OF THE END OF THE WAR
The 50th anniversaries of VE Day and VJ Day were celebrated and those who died in the Second World War were commemorated in May and August 1995 *(Camera Press)*

NORTHERN IRELAND
Although the peace process continued, Pte Clegg's release from prison and the start of the marching season led to rioting in July 1995 *(Press Association)*

ANIMAL RIGHTS DEMONSTRATIONS
Demonstrations against the export of live animals were held at ports throughout Britain in early 1995 *(Rex Features)*

THE QUEEN IN RUSSIA
The Queen paid the first-ever state visit to Russia by a reigning British monarch in October 1994 *(Rex Features)*

CROATS RECAPTURE KRAJINA
Croatia regained control of the Serb-held region of Krajina, causing thousands of Croatian Serbs to flee to Serbia and Serb-held Bosnia *(Rex Features)*

BOSNIA
Bosnian Serbs took UN peacekeeping troops hostage in July 1995 to stop NATO bombing Bosnian Serb positions *(Popperfoto)*

BOSNIA
NATO began attacking key Bosnian Serb military and communications sites on 30 August to eliminate threats to UN safe zones *(Associated Press)*

CHECHENIA
Russia attempted to re-establish control over the breakaway republic of Chechenia in December 1994 and became embroiled in war *(Rex Features)*

ISLAMIC TERRORISM
Violence by Islamic extremists in Algeria spilled over into France with a hijacking and several bombings in 1994–5 *(Rex Features)*

THE MIDDLE EAST
The peace process made progress despite Palestinian suicide bombings in Israel and the resistance of Israeli settlers on the West Bank *(Popperfoto)*

KOREA DISASTER
Shoddy construction was blamed for the collapse of a department store in Seoul in June 1995 which killed 640 people *(Rex Features)*

EARTHQUAKE IN JAPAN
Over 5,000 people were killed in an earthquake which flattened most of Kobe in January 1995 *(Rex Features)*

OKLAHOMA BOMBING
A car bomb exploded outside a government building in Oklahoma City in April 1995, killing 168 people and injuring over 400 *(Rex Features)*

TOKYO UNDERGROUND GAS ATTACK
Nerve gas attacks during the rush hour in March 1995 left 12 dead and over 5,000 in need of treatment *(Associated Press)*

WEATHER EXTREMES
Huge areas of north-west Europe were flooded in early 1995 (top, *Rex Features*), while a dry summer led to serious water shortages in Britain *(Press Association)*

FOOTBALLER ATTACKS FAN
Manchester United star Eric Cantona was fined by the Football Association and banned for the rest of the season after attacking an abusive spectator in January 1995 *(Rex Features)*

OBITUARIES
Deaths included (left to right): (top) Burt Lancaster, Harold Wilson, Odette Hallowes, Peter Cook; (bottom) John Osborne, Jean Muir, Keith Joseph, Harold Larwood *(Rex Features, Allsport/Hulton Deutsch)*

Alison Hargreaves (right) conquered Everest in May 1995 but died on K2 in August *(Alison Jane Hargreaves)*.
Ginger Rogers (left, with Fred Astaire) died in April *(Rex Features)*

RUGBY UNION WORLD CUP
Jonah Lomu and the All Blacks denied England a place in the World Cup final in June 1995 but lost the final to South Africa *(Allsport)*

RUGBY LEAGUE GRAND SLAM
Wigan won the Challenge Cup (for the eighth successive year), premiership, league championship and Regal Trophy in the 1994–5 season *(Allsport)*

ATHLETICS RECORD
Jonathan Edwards set a new world triple jump record at the 1995 World Championships *(Allsport)*

CRICKET TRIUMPH
Dominic Cork took seven wickets for 43 runs in his Test début in June 1995 and took the first Test hat trick by an English player since 1957 in July *(Allsport)*

DECEMBER 1994

6. Roger Severs was sentenced at Nottingham Crown Court to life imprisonment for the murder of his parents in Hambleton, Leics, in November 1993. **7.** Thomas Bourke, a garage owner, was sentenced at Manchester Crown Court to life imprisonment for murdering two MoT inspectors at his garage in Stockport in November 1993. A retired police superintendent, Gordon Anglesea, accepted libel damages of £375,000 against newspapers which had alleged that he had sexually abused boys at a children's home in Wrexham, Clwyd. **8.** Peter Kite, the managing director of the activity centre in Lyme Regis which ran a canoeing trip on which four teenagers died in March 1993, was convicted at Winchester Crown Court of their manslaughter and sentenced to three years' imprisonment. Fifteen people were stabbed by a man in a department store in Birmingham; he was arrested and charged with attempted murder. **9.** At Nottingham Crown Court Julie Kelley, who abducted a baby, Abbie Humphries, from a maternity ward in Nottingham in July 1994, was put on probation for three years on the condition that she receive in-patient psychiatric care. **14.** An elderly couple were found strangled at their home in Bramford, Suffolk. On 20 December another man was found murdered in the village; his son, who had escaped from a mental hospital, was arrested and charged with the murders. **17.** Deith Bridges and Paul Tubbs were sentenced at the Central Criminal Court to life imprisonment for plotting the murder of Graeme Woodhatch in May 1992; Te Rangimaria Ngarimu, a Maori woman who was hired to commit the murder, was later sentenced to life imprisonment. **19.** The European Human Rights Commission ruled that the Home Secretary's discretionary powers to decide when juvenile murderers should be released on licence violate the European Human Rights Convention. Keith Mann, a member of the Animal Liberation Front, was sentenced at the Central Criminal Court to 14 years' imprisonment for incitement to commit arson and criminal damage in relation to attacks on businesses in 1990–1. **24.** An Air France Airbus was hijacked in Algiers by four members of an Algerian fundamentalist Islamic group; two passengers were shot dead and about 20 were released. On 25 December another passenger was shot dead and about 40 were released. On 26 December the plane was flown to Marseilles airport. It was stormed by French commandos, who shot dead the hijackers and released the remaining passengers and crew; about 25 people were injured. On 27 December four priests were murdered in revenge in Algeria. **25.** A woman died after being doused with petrol and set on fire by two men in a churchyard in Eaton, Cheshire. **27.** A Wild West enthusiast was shot dead by police at his home in Huddersfield after he fired blanks at them from a replica pistol. An Asian taxi driver was stabbed to death during a fight between more than 20 taxi drivers in Luton, Beds.

JANUARY 1995

1. The alleged serial killer Frederick West was found hanged in his cell at Winson Green prison, Birmingham. **4.** Ronnie Knight, the former husband of the actress Barbara Windsor, was sentenced at the Central Criminal Court to seven years' imprisonment for handling part of the proceeds of a £5.9 million robbery in 1983. **7.** A painting by Titian was stolen from Longleat House, Wilts. **12.** Four couples from Bishop Auckland, Co. Durham, were cleared at Newcastle upon Tyne Crown Court of sexually abusing five children. **19.** Fifteen-year-old Claire Hood was found murdered in woodland near her home in St Mellons, Cardiff. **20.** Two IRA members, Robert Fryers and Hugh Jack, were sentenced at the Central Criminal Court to 25 years' and 20 years' imprisonment respectively for conspiracy to cause explosions. Robert Eades was sentenced at the Central Criminal Court to life imprisonment for the murder of a police sergeant in February 1994. **27.** Enda Doyle was sentenced at the Central Criminal Court to nine years' imprisonment for the manslaughter of two women neighbours in May 1994 by starting a fire under their flat after they had complained about noise. **29.** A woman and her six children died in a fire deliberately started at their home in south London.

FEBRUARY 1995

1. Amine Akanour, a Moroccan student, was sentenced at Winchester Crown Court to life imprisonment for the murder of his former girlfriend's parents in Southsea in December 1993. Paul Agutter was sentenced at the High Court in Edinburgh to 12 years' imprisonment for attempting to murder his wife in August 1994 by adding the poison atropine to her drink and contaminating bottles of Safeway tonic water to avert suspicion. **2.** Leslie Beattie was sentenced at Durham Crown Court to ten years' imprisonment for setting fire to his wife during a row at their home in December 1993. **5.** Armed raiders stole jewellery worth £250,000 from Garrards in Regent Street, London. **7.** The Princess of Wales reached an out-of-court settlement with Bryce Taylor and Mirror Group Newspapers to prevent further publication of photographs taken secretly of her exercising in a gymnasium in 1993. Four members of the Parachute Regiment were each sentenced at Winchester Crown Court to 200 hours' community service for badly injuring a man in a drunken assault in Aldershot in September 1993. **9.** Leroy Smith was sentenced at the Central Criminal Court to 25 years' imprisonment for the attempted murder of a policeman in March 1994. **10.** Three-day-old Lydia Owens was abducted from a hospital near Rhyl, north Wales; she was found on 11 February. On 9 June Susan Brooke was sentenced to three years' imprisonment for the abduction. Graeme West was sentenced at the Central Criminal Court to life imprisonment for the contract killing of a businessman in January 1993. A woman was murdered while walking near her home at

Burton Fleming, Humberside. **16.** Colin Middleton was sentenced at Birmingham Crown Court to life imprisonment for the murder of his former manager in Nuneaton, Warks, in January 1994. **17.** Melanie Myers was sentenced at the Central Criminal Court to life imprisonment for the murder of a taxi driver in April 1994. **18.** Seven-year-old Jonathan Copley and his 15-year-old babysitter Rachel Rooney were found murdered at his home in Bradford, W. Yorks. **20.** PC Michael Seear was cleared at the Central Criminal Court of raping a female colleague after a party. **23.** An American, Michael Austin, was sentenced at Carlisle Crown Court to life imprisonment for ordering the murder of an accountant in March 1992. **24.** A GP, Patrick Alesworth, was ordered at Reading Crown Court to be detained in a psychiatric hospital after admitting the manslaughter of his daughter in April 1994. **27.** The High Court in Edinburgh ruled that eight children had been wrongly taken into care in Ayrshire in 1990 after allegations of ritual sexual abuse and that they should be allowed home. **28.** Milton Wheeler was sentenced at the Central Criminal Court to life imprisonment for the manslaughter of an elderly couple at their home in April 1994. A policeman hanging onto the bonnet of a stolen car in Barnes, London, shot and seriously wounded the driver, who later died.

MARCH 1995

3. The actor Craig Charles was cleared at Southwark Crown Court of raping a female friend in July 1994. **10.** The Court of Appeal overturned a High Court ruling that Cambridge Health Authority did not have the right to refuse treatment to a 10-year-old girl dying from leukaemia. An anonymous donor paid for the girl to be treated privately. **12.** A 75-year-old woman was stabbed to death by a burglar at her home in Greater Manchester. **16.** Five law lords ruled that the presumption that a child aged between ten and 14 cannot commit a criminal offence unless it is proved that the child knew the act to be seriously wrong should stand, but they called for the law to be reviewed by Parliament; the ruling overturned a High Court ruling of March 1994. The law lords also ruled that receivers appointed to failed companies between 1986 and 1994 were liable to pay all the contractual benefits due to employees still employed 14 days after the start of the insolvency. **17.** A man was shot dead in Wallsend, Tyneside, while trying to protect his 17-year-old son from attackers. **20.** Twelve people died and 5,500 were taken ill when nerve gas was released on the underground rail system in Tokyo, Japan. **22.** A fraud trial at Newport Crown Court collapsed after six months when the judge ruled that the evidence was too complicated for the jury to understand. **27.** David Lauwers was sentenced at the Central Criminal Court to life imprisonment for the manslaughter of 11 men in an arson attack on a sex cinema in London in February 1994.

APRIL 1995

6. Kevin Callan, who was sentenced to life imprisonment in January 1992 for the murder of his girlfriend's four-year-old daughter, was released after the Court of Appeal quashed his conviction in the light of medical evidence produced by Mr Callan's study of neurology while in prison. Jonathon Jones was sentenced at Newport Crown Court to life imprisonment for the murder of his girlfriend's parents in Llanharry, Mid Glamorgan, in July 1993. A woman was found dead near Middleton-on-the-Wolds, Humberside; she was later identified as the wife of Martin Link, who committed suicide at his home in Edgbaston on 9 April. **7.** Nicholas Ingram, a Briton convicted of murder in the USA in 1983, was executed in Jackson, Georgia, after losing a final appeal against his sentence. A verdict of unlawful killing was returned at an inquest into the *Marchioness* riverboat disaster on the Thames in August 1989. **10.** The world's first national computerized DNA database was set up by the Forensic Science Service in Birmingham to assist police in criminal investigations. **11.** A woman was found murdered at her home near Radnage, Bucks. Maxine Robinson was sentenced at Sheffield Crown Court to two terms of life imprisonment for suffocating her children, aged 19 months and five months, in June 1993. **12.** The body of 13-year-old Lindsay Rimer, who went missing from her home in Hebden Bridge, W. Yorks, in November 1994, was found in the Rochdale canal. **18.** A policeman was shot dead and another wounded while investigating a robbery at a house in Ilford, Essex. Police confirmed that the remains of nine-year-old Daniel Handley, who went missing from his home in London in October 1994, had been found near Bristol. **19.** At least 167 people were killed when a 1,000 lb car bomb exploded outside a federal government building in Oklahoma City, USA. Over 300 people were treated in hospital after inhaling fumes at Yokohama underground station, Japan.

MAY 1995

10. Three children who had been stabbed to death by their mother were found at their home in Thetford, Norfolk; their mother was later found drowned nearby. **11.** Susan Cawthorne, a registered childminder, was sentenced at Sheffield Crown Court to four years' imprisonment for the manslaughter of eight-month-old Helen Sangar in October 1993. **19.** Anthony Williams, a former Scotland Yard finance officer, was sentenced at the Central Criminal Court to 7½ years' imprisonment for stealing £5 million from the Metropolitan Police. David and Patricia Whitehead were sentenced at Winchester Crown Court to four months' and two months' imprisonment respectively for perverting the course of justice by lying to police about a road accident in August 1994; Mrs Whitehead was released on 22 May after appealing against the sentence. **21.** Fourteen-year-old Janet Swanson was found strangled in Leeds, W. Yorks; a 15-year-old boy was later charged with the murder. **23.** The founders of the London Marathon, Chris Brasher and John Disley, were awarded libel damages of £1.1 million in the High Court against Channel 4 and the *New Statesman* over allegations that they had improperly and fraudulently used the event to enrich themselves. **25.** Ryan James, a veterinary surgeon, was sentenced at Stafford Crown Court to life imprisonment for the murder of his wife, whom he poisoned in January 1994. **26.** A 23-year-old New Zealander, Louise Crowe, was stabbed to death near an underground station in London.

JUNE 1995

2. Sir Nicholas Scott, MP was arrested and bailed after a road accident in London involving a three-year-old child. **14.** Det. Sgt Linda Evans and PC Colin Whitby were cleared at the Central Criminal Court of the manslaughter of Joy Gardner, an illegal immigrant who died after a struggle to arrest her in July 1993. **15.** The football manager Graeme Souness was awarded libel damages of £750,000 against Mirror Group Newspapers over an article in the *People* newspaper in May 1994 which alleged that he had behaved like a 'dirty rat' to his former wife and children. **16.** A report by Lord Woolf proposing radical changes to the civil justice system was published (*see* pages 1176–7). **21.** A hijacker held 365 people hostage on a Boeing 747 at Hakodate Airport, Japan. The plane was stormed by Japanese police on 22 June; all the hostages were released and the hijacker was arrested. Garnet Bell was sentenced at Antrim Crown Court to six terms of life imprisonment for a flame-thrower attack on pupils at his former school in June 1994. **28.** Donna Maguire was sentenced at a court in Celle, Germany, to nine years' imprisonment for the attempted bombing of a British Army barracks in Osnabruck in 1989; she was released because she had spent nearly six years in prison on remand. **30.** Matthew Pearce and Darren Jones were sentenced at Winchester Crown Court to life imprisonment for the kidnap and murder of an accountant, Grant Price, who was stabbed to death on a deserted beach near Lymington in January 1994.

JULY 1995

6. Graeme Alderton was sentenced at Teesside Crown Court to ten years' imprisonment for the manslaughter of his three children, who died when he set fire to their home in Peterlee, Co. Durham, in February 1994. Michael Allen was sentenced at Newcastle upon Tyne Crown Court to life imprisonment for beating his wife to death in July 1994 and hiding her body in a freezer. **7.** Emma Humphreys, a former teenage prostitute who had served ten years of a life sentence for stabbing her lover to death after six months of physical and mental abuse, was released when the Court of Appeal substituted a manslaughter conviction on the grounds that the trial judge had attached insufficient importance to

the ill-treatment in relation to her defence of provocation. The former leader of the Labour Party, Michael Foot, won 'substantial' damages in the High Court against the *Sunday Times* over allegations published in February 1995 that the KGB had regarded him as an 'agent of influence'. Jason Mitchell, a paranoid schizophrenic, was sentenced at Ipswich Crown Court to three terms of life imprisonment for murdering three people, including his father, in December 1994. **13.** Szymon Serafinowicz was charged at Epsom magistrates' court with murdering four Jews in Nazi-occupied Belarussia in 1941 and 1942. **19.** The dean of Lincoln, the Very Revd Brandon Jackson, was cleared by a Church of England consistory court of commiting adultery with a former cathedral verger. **20.** Ian Kay, who had absconded while on home leave from prison, was sentenced at the Central Criminal Court to life imprisonment for the murder of a Woolworths shop manager in Teddington, Middx, in November 1994. **24.** Phillip Manning was sentenced at Cardiff Crown Court to life imprisonment for the murder of his ex-wife in Abertillery, Gwent, on Christmas Day 1994. **26.** Chuon Mean was sentenced in Cambodia to 15 years' imprisonment for the murders of two Britons and an Australian woman in April 1994. **27.** Shaun Armstrong was sentenced at Leeds Crown Court to life imprisonment for the murder of three-year-old Rosie Armstrong in Hartlepool, Cleveland in June 1994. **28.** William O'Brien was sentenced at Norwich Crown Court to life imprisonment for the murder of the racehorse trainer Alex Scott in September 1994. Susan Hagan and Sally Croft were convicted at a court in Oregon, USA, of plotting to murder the state attorney in 1985 when they were members of the Bhagwan Shree Rajneesh sect. Sara Thornton, who was sentenced to life imprisonment in 1990 for the murder of her violent husband, was released on bail pending an appeal. Susan Smith was sentenced at a court in South Carolina, USA, to life imprisonment for drowning her two children in a lake in October 1994. **29.** Twelve-year old Robert Gee and 13-year-old Paul Barker were found stabbed to death at Eastham Rake, near Ellesmere Port, Merseyside; on 2 August a man was charged with the murders. Seven-year-old Sophia Hook was found murdered in Craigside, Llandudno; on 3 August a man was charged with the murder. **31.** The Court of Appeal ruled that the law in force between 1985 and 1991 requiring people to work for an employer for two years before being entitled to claim unfair dismissal was incompatible with the principle of equal treatment enshrined in European law because fewer women than men met the requirement.

AUGUST 1995

1. Six executives of the Co-op supermarket chain were sentenced at Coventry Crown Court to terms ranging from six months' to four years' imprisonment for their parts in a £5.6 million fraud.

3. Thirteen-year-old Darren Fawns was found murdered near Lough Neagh, Co. Antrim. 5–6. Five men were murdered in separate incidents in Glasgow. 14. Fifteen-year-old Louise Sellars was found strangled in a field near Wigan, Lancs. 15. A British student, Trevor Catton, who was kidnapped in Colombia on 24 June, was found murdered. 18. Vikki Thompson, who had been attacked while walking her dog near Ascott-under-Wychwood on 12 August, died of her injuries. 25. David Kang, who fired shots from a starting pistol near the Prince of Wales in Sydney, Australia, in January 1994, was sentenced in Sydney to 500 hours' community service. 29. A ten-year-old boy was charged with manslaughter after a woman was killed by a lump of concrete dropped from a tower block in Kirkstall, Leeds. 31. A teacher was found murdered at her home in Dalton, Huddersfield.

ENVIRONMENT

SEPTEMBER 1994

8. A CIA report said that the wetlands of southern Iraq had been transformed into desert after a campaign of drainage and burning by President Saddam Hussein. 30. A Friends of the Earth survey showed that more than 700 Sites of Special Scientific Interest in England and Wales were under threat from pollution or other sources.

OCTOBER 1994

4. The World Meteorological Organization said that damage to the ozone layer over the Antarctic reached a record level in September 1994. 25. The transport select committee of the House of Commons called for super-unleaded petrol to be banned because of its high level of carcinogens; on 17 March 1995 the Government rejected this recommendation. Greenpeace Russia reported a spillage of about 280,000 tonnes of crude oil near Usinsk; local officials said the spillage was 14,000 tonnes. 26. The Royal Commission on Environmental Pollution recommended that the price of petrol should double over the next ten years and that public funds should be switched from road building to public transport. 27. The Natural Environment Research Council published research findings showing that vehicle emissions have affected air quality even in rural areas of Britain.

NOVEMBER 1994

1. The House of Commons environment select committee recommended a moratorium on the building of out-of-town superstores and further restrictions on retail warehouses. 16. The Government announced plans to set up an Environment Agency to take over the work of HM Inspectorate of Pollution and the National Rivers Authority and the waste regulation functions of local authorities. 25. The captain of a Greenpeace ship was arrested after

blocking the River Clyde in an attempt to stop the Trident submarine *Vanguard* loading nuclear warheads.

DECEMBER 1994

2. Thousands of fish were killed by a cyanide spillage into the River Wye, Bucks. 7. Eleven sperm whales died after beaching themselves in the Orkneys; eight killer whales were guided back to sea after beaching themselves in the Shetlands.

JANUARY 1995

4. Berkshire County Council granted temporary planning permission for exploratory drilling for oil to take place in Windsor Great Park. 13. Two drums of nuclear waste were found dumped on a farm near Rushden, Northants. 31. The Sizewell B nuclear plant in Suffolk began to generate power.

FEBRUARY 1995

6. The National Trust for Scotland banned fox hunting on its land. The Environment Secretary (John Gummer) launched an initiative, 'Going for Green', to increase awareness of sustainable development issues. 27. The British Antarctic Survey said that a massive iceberg had broken away from Antarctica and that almost every ice sheet on the Antarctic coast was melting.

MARCH 1995

3. In a vote on the second reading of a Private Member's Bill in the House of Commons, MPs voted to ban all forms of hunting. 17. The Court of Appeal ruled that a ban on deer hunting imposed by Somerset County Council in August 1993 was unlawful.

APRIL 1995

6. The Government agreed to give up the right to carry out underground nuclear test explosions. 7. At a UN conference on global warming in Berlin, an agreement was reached requiring industrial nations to cut their fossil fuel emissions after the year 2000. 26. The National Trust for Scotland confirmed that a £10 million grant from the National Lottery had enabled it to buy the Mar Lodge estate in the Cairngorms. An injured killer whale was destroyed after beaching itself twice near Ramsgate.

MAY 1995

1. An operation began to evict protesters who had built a tree-top 'village' blocking the path of the M65 extension at Stanworth Woods, Lancs. 22. Shell UK failed in an attempt to board the disused Brent Spar oil platform in the North Sea which had been occupied by Greenpeace protesters since late April in protest at plans to sink disused rigs in the Atlantic; the protest ended on 23 May.

JUNE 1995

8. The Government was criticized at the North Sea Conference in Denmark for allowing Shell to sink

disused rigs. **16.** Two Greenpeace protesters were dropped by helicopter onto the Brent Spar platform as it was being towed to a dumping site in the Atlantic. **20.** Shell abandoned plans to sink the rig and said that it would seek a licence to dismantle it onshore.

JULY 1995

5. The Government gave approval for the building of a controversial bypass through protected countryside around Newbury, Berks. **9.** French commandos seized the Greenpeace ship *Rainbow Warrior II* after it had entered French waters off Mururoa atoll where France planned to resume nuclear testing in September 1995. **17.** About 20 tons of hydrochloric acid escaped from a storage tank in Hailsham, E. Sussex; part of the spillage leaked into a tributary of the River Cuckmere. **19.** The Environment Secretary (John Gummer) announced stricter planning rules for out-of-town shopping centres.

AUGUST 1995

1. The Transport Minister (Robert Jones) appealed to people to use their cars as little as possible because of air pollution exacerbated by the heatwave. **4.** The sea wall at Tollesbury Fleet on the Essex coast was breached, flooding 20 hectares of marsh, to relieve pressure on other coastal defences in the area. **30.** The Tamar valley was designated an area of outstanding natural beauty.

NORTHERN IRELAND AFFAIRS

SEPTEMBER 1994

1. A Roman Catholic man was shot dead by the UFF in north Belfast. Four IRA prisoners were transferred from England to prisons in Northern Ireland; the director-general of the prison service said that the transfers were not connected with the IRA cease-fire and that he regretted their politically insensitive timing. **4.** A large car bomb exploded outside the Sinn Fein press office in west Belfast. **6.** The Irish Taoiseach (Albert Reynolds) met the president of Sinn Fein (Gerry Adams) in Dublin; they issued a joint statement pledging their 'total and absolute commitment' to democratic and peaceful methods of resolving the political future of Northern Ireland. The Prime Minister (John Major) cut short a meeting with the leader of the Democratic Unionists, Ian Paisley, at Downing Street after Mr Paisley refused to say that he would accept Mr Major's word that no deal had been struck with the IRA. **7.** The US Vice-President Al Gore met the Taoiseach in Shannon and pledged the USA's support for the peace process. The Prime Minister called on the IRA to confirm that the cease-fire was permanent. The Northern Ireland Secretary (Sir Patrick Mayhew) said that security would be scaled down in Northern Ireland. **8.** The Combined Loyalist

Military Command (comprising elements of the UFF, the UVF and the Red Hand Commandos) issued a statement setting out six preconditions for a cease-fire, including a guarantee that Northern Ireland would remain within the UK. **12.** Two women were injured when the detonator of a bomb planted by the UVF exploded on a Belfast to Dublin train. **16.** The Prime Minister lifted the ban on broadcasting the voices of members of Sinn Fein imposed in 1988 and said that there would be a referendum in Northern Ireland on the outcome of political talks.

OCTOBER 1994

13. The Combined Loyalist Military Command announced a cease-fire from midnight. **21-22.** The Prime Minister visited Northern Ireland and announced that the Government was prepared to assume that the IRA cease-fire was permanent; he said that exploratory talks could begin with Sinn Fein before the end of the year, that paramilitaries on both sides should hand in their weapons and explosives, that all cross-border roads would be re-opened, that exclusion orders on Gerry Adams and Martin McGuinness would be lifted, and that proposals would be put forward for a local assembly in Northern Ireland. **24.** British troops were withdrawn from the streets of Londonderry. **28.** The inaugural meeting of a Forum for Peace and Reconciliation initiated by the Irish government was held in Dublin.

NOVEMBER 1994

7. The Republic of Ireland's Justice Minister (Maire Geoghegan-Quinn) said that some IRA prisoners serving their sentences in the Republic would be released before Christmas. **10.** A Roman Catholic man was shot dead in an armed robbery by IRA gunmen at a postal depot in Newry, Co. Down. The IRA later said that the operation had not been sanctioned by its leaders, apologised to the victim's family and restated its commitment to the peace process. The Irish government cancelled the early release of IRA prisoners. **14.** The Prime Minister said that representatives of loyalist paramilitaries would be invited to exploratory talks before the end of 1994. **17.** Gerry Adams visited London and gave a press conference at Westminster.

DECEMBER 1994

9. Formal talks took place at Stormont between government representatives and a Sinn Fein delegation. **14.** The Prime Minister attended an international investment conference in Belfast. **18.** A 2 lb Semtex bomb was defused at Enniskillen, Co. Fermanagh, after a telephone warning; the IRA denied responsibility. **24.** Thirty-nine IRA prisoners serving their sentences in the Republic of Ireland were granted temporary parole; on 18 January nine of the prisoners were released permanently. Five loyalist men were sentenced at Belfast Crown Court to life imprisonment for the murder of a Roman Catholic woman in February 1992.

JANUARY 1995

12. The chief constable of the RUC (Sir Hugh Annesley) said that troops would be withdrawn from the streets of Belfast during daylight hours from 15 January. 27. Sean Kelly was sentenced at Belfast Crown Court to nine terms of life imprisonment for murdering nine people in the IRA bombing in the Shankill Road in October 1993. 31. *The Times* published leaked details of a joint framework consultation document drawn up by the British and Irish governments which included proposals for a powerful cross-border executive authority accountable to the Irish government and a Northern Ireland assembly.

FEBRUARY 1995

1. The Prime Minister made a television broadcast to appeal for support for the peace process and reaffirmed that a referendum would be held in Northern Ireland on any proposed constitutional changes. 3. The Irish government released five IRA prisoners. 8. Trooper Andrew Clarke was sentenced at Belfast Crown Court to ten years' imprisonment for the attempted murder of a mourner at the wake of Thomas Begley, who was killed planting the Shankill Road bomb in October 1993. 10. Two Scots Guards were sentenced at Belfast Crown Court to life imprisonment for the murder of a teenager in north Belfast in September 1992. 21. The Ulster Unionists published a proposed framework for talks which would lead to an interim elected assembly in Northern Ireland. The Democratic Unionists published their proposals for a Northern Ireland constitutional convention which would lead to a devolved assembly. 22. In Belfast the Prime Minister and the Irish Taoiseach (John Bruton) launched *A New Framework for Agreement* on the future of Northern Ireland and Mr Major launched *A Framework for Accountable Government in Northern Ireland* (*see* below); the Prime Minister said that the proposals were not immutable and other ideas could be considered alongside them. The SDLP, Sinn Fein and British and Irish politicians welcomed the initiative; the Ulster Unionists and the Democratic Unionists reaffirmed their opposition to the framework document. 24. Four members of the UFF were each sentenced at Belfast Crown Court to eight terms of life imprisonment for the murder of eight Roman Catholics at the Rising Sun pub in Greysteel, Co. Londonderry, in October 1993; one also received four life sentences for murdering four Roman Catholic men in Castlerock, Co. Londonderry, in March 1993.

A New Framework for Agreement
– a North-South body to be set up, composed of elected representatives of the Northern Ireland Assembly and the Irish Parliament, with executive powers over areas including EU programmes, the

environment and heritage, and consultative and harmonizing functions on a wide range of issues
– the Republic to abandon the territorial claim to Northern Ireland in its constitution
– the British government to amend or replace the Government of Ireland Act to recognize the right of the people of Northern Ireland to decide their future
– a new intergovernmental conference to be established
– both governments to guarantee to protect civil, political, social and cultural rights of all the citizens of Northern Ireland
– referendums to be held in Northern Ireland and the Republic, with majorities needed for the proposals to be implemented

A Framework for Accountable Government in Northern Ireland
– a 90-member single-chamber assembly to be elected by proportional representation for a fixed term of four or five years and to have wide-ranging legislative and executive powers
– a panel of three representatives to be elected by proportional representation to oversee the work of the assembly
– a system of committees constituted in proportion to party strengths to oversee the work of the Northern Ireland departments; committee chairmen to be required to serve on the North-South body
– a system of checks and balances to ensure adequate representation of the nationalist minority

MARCH 1995

9. The Queen visited Belfast and Armagh and restored city status to Armagh. 11. Gerry Adams arrived in the USA for a ten-day fund-raising tour, for which permission had been granted in spite of the disapproval of the British government; on 16 March he met President Clinton and on 17 March he attended a St Patrick's Day reception at the White House. 14. Loyalist prisoners rioted at the Maze prison, Belfast. The Secretary of State for Northern Ireland announced that 400 troops would leave the province by the end of March. 16. Gerry Adams accused Britain of 'dirty tricks' after a bomb containing 2 lb of Semtex was found and defused in Newry, Co. Down. 24. Routine night army patrols in the greater Belfast area ended.

APRIL 1995

4. After talks at the White House President Clinton praised the Prime Minister's handling of the peace process. 12. The Secretary of State for Northern Ireland announced the departure of a second army unit from the province. 13. A cache of loyalist arms and ammunition was seized by police at Holywood, Co. Down; more weapons were later found in Ouston, Co. Durham. 24. The Government said that it would hold formal ministerial talks with Sinn Fein.

MAY 1995

3. Rioting broke out during a republican demonstration held as the Prime Minister visited Londonderry. **4.** Rioting broke out after an Orange Order march in east Belfast. **10.** The Northern Ireland minister Michael Ancram met a Sinn Fein delegation led by Martin McGuinness for formal talks at Stormont. **24.** Sir Patrick Mayhew met Gerry Adams in private before an investment conference in Washington DC; on 25 May President Clinton addressed the conference and urged all paramilitary groups in Northern Ireland to disarm. **28.** Rioting broke out in the Shankill Road area of Belfast.

JUNE 1995

12. Sir Patrick Mayhew announced an extension of compassionate leave arrangements for prisoners in Northern Ireland. **17.** Gerry Adams said that there was no question of the IRA decommissioning its weapons before substantive political talks and that exploratory talks with the Government were at an end.

JULY 1995

3. Pte Lee Clegg, a paratrooper who was convicted of the murder of a joyrider at an army checkpoint in Belfast in 1990, was released from prison; rioting broke out in nationalist areas of Belfast and Londonderry, and Sinn Fein called for the early release of republican prisoners. **9.** More than 1,000 Orangemen refused to accept a police ban on their marching through a nationalist area of Portadown, Co. Armagh; a stand-off ensued, and on 10 July violence broke out. On 11 July the Orangemen were permitted to march through the area but without their fife and drum bands. **22.** The Government admitted that it had held talks in private with Sinn Fein leaders during the previous week. Another private meeting was held on 27 July. **24.** Sir Patrick Mayhew said that British and Irish ministers were considering setting up an international commission to deal with the issue of decommissioning arms. **30.** Twelve IRA prisoners in the Republic of Ireland were released early. Martin McGuinness, a leading Sinn Fein spokesman, said that there was no possibility of the IRA decommissioning its arms before a negotiated settlement.

AUGUST 1995

12. Rioting broke out in Londonderry and in the Lower Ormeau Road area of Belfast. **25.** Sir Patrick Mayhew said that more troops would be withdrawn from Northern Ireland in the autumn if the cease-fire held, and that legislation would be introduced to restore remission rates for prisoners convicted of terrorist offences to 50 per cent.

SPORT

SEPTEMBER 1994

7. The International Motor Sport Association (FIA) cleared the Benetton team of tampering with refuelling equipment before the German grand prix in July 1994. **8.** Fighting broke out between groups of rival boxing fans during a WBC title fight in Birmingham. **14.** The baseball world series in the USA was cancelled because of a players' strike. **18.** Warwickshire became the first side to win the Cricket County Championship, the Benson and Hedges Cup and the Sunday League title in one season. **23.** The Welsh rugby union international Scott Quinnell joined the rugby league club Wigan. **24.** Lennox Lewis lost his WBC heavyweight title to Oliver McCall of the USA at Wembley Arena, London. **27.** Blackburn Rovers were knocked out of the UEFA Cup in the first round by the semi-professional Swedish side Trelleborgs. The flat-race jockey Kieran Fallon was banned from racing for six months by the Jockey Club for pulling another jockey from his horse after crossing the finishing line in a race at Beverley on 14 September. Chad Hunderby set a new record time of 7 hours 17 minutes for swimming the English Channel.

OCTOBER 1994

12. Neil Jenkins set a new record of 308 points scored for Wales in rugby union internationals. **14.** Ffyona Campbell became the first woman to walk around the world when she arrived at John O'Groats. **22.** The Great Britain captain Shaun Edwards was sent off in the first rugby league international against Australia at Wembley. **27.** Hong Kong set a world record score in international rugby union when they beat Singapore 164–13 in Kuala Lumpur. **31.** The International Amateur Athletic Federation won its appeal against the record damages awarded in December 1992 by a court in the USA to Butch Reynolds, the world 400 metres record holder, who had been suspended for drug abuse.

NOVEMBER 1994

1. The Football Association expressed their support for the England coach Terry Venables after allegations concerning his business dealings were made in a *Panorama* programme; on 4 November the Serious Fraud Office decided not to launch an investigation. Osvaldo Ardiles was sacked as manager of Tottenham Hotspur FC. **6.** The 45-year-old former world champion George Foreman became the oldest world champion in professional boxing when he beat Michael Moorer to win the IBF and WBA titles in Las Vegas. **8.** The *Sun* published allegations that the Southampton and former Liverpool goalkeeper Bruce Grobbelaar had taken bribes to fix Premier League match results; Grobbelaar denied the allegations and issued libel writs. On 14

November he was charged by the FA with bringing the game into disrepute. **11.** Gerry Francis resigned as manager of Queen's Park Rangers FC; on 15 November he was appointed manager of Tottenham Hotspur and Ray Wilkins was appointed player-manager of QPR. **13.** Michael Schumacher won the world motor racing championship after a collision with Damon Hill in the Adelaide grand prix forced both drivers to retire from the race. **15.** Martina Navratilova played the last singles match of her career at Madison Square Garden, New York. **24.** John Toshack was sacked as manager of Real Sociedad. **25.** The England and Arsenal footballer Paul Merson admitted that he used cocaine; on 1 December he was suspended by the FA. **29.** It was reported that seven Chinese swimmers and four Chinese athletes had failed drugs tests at the Asian Games in October and been stripped of their medals. The Doncaster rugby league player Jamie Bloem was suspended for two years after testing positive for anabolic steroids.

DECEMBER 1994

7. The Chinese world swimming champion Lu Bin was banned for two years by the International Swimming Federation after testing positive for drugs on 30 September. **9.** An independent arbitration tribunal restored to Tottenham Hotspur FC the six Premier league points deducted by the Football Association as a punishment for making irregular payments to players and reinstated the club in the FA Cup (*see* Whitaker's Almanack 1995). **11.** Damon Hill was voted BBC Sports Personality of the Year. **14.** The former 800 metres Commonwealth champion Diane Modahl was banned for four years by the British Athletic Federation after testing positive for drugs in June 1994; on 16 December the International Amateur Athletic Federation nullified the results of the British women's team at the World Cup in September 1994 because Modahl's victory in a race after the positive drugs test had enabled the team to qualify for the event. **15.** A Premier League commission of inquiry was set up after allegations that the Arsenal manager, George Graham, had accepted money in relation to a transfer deal.

JANUARY 1995

3. Darren Gough took six wickets for 49 runs for England in the Test match against Australia in Sydney. **4.** The Plymouth Argyle football manager Peter Shilton was suspended after failing to pay an outstanding £50,000 tax debt; on 11 January he resigned. **10.** The striker Andy Cole was transferred from Newcastle United to Manchester United for a record £7 million. **15.** The first Sunday horseracing meeting with legal on-course betting was held at Tweseldown, Hants. **25.** The Manchester United footballer Eric Cantona launched a flying kick at an abusive spectator after being sent off in a match against Crystal Palace. He was banned by Manchester United until the end of the season; the FA

fined him £10,000 and suspended him from all football until 30 September. On 27 February the spectator was charged with two public order offences. On 23 March Cantona was sentenced by magistrates to two weeks' imprisonment; the sentence was reduced on appeal to 120 hours' community service. On 24 May the Manchester Utd captain Paul Ince was cleared of assaulting a spectator in the same incident. **30.** England won their first Test match in Australia for eight years.

FEBRUARY 1995

8. Crowd trouble broke out after a football match between Chelsea and Milwall at Stamford Bridge; 11 policemen were injured and 38 arrests were made. **11.** Two Australian cricketers said that they were offered bribes to throw a Test match in Karachi in November 1994. **15.** A football match between the Republic of Ireland and England in Dublin was abandoned after 25 minutes when some English supporters began fighting and throwing missiles; about 20 people were injured. **19.** Linford Christie set a new indoor 200 metres world record of 20.25 seconds at a meeting in Lievin, France. **21.** The Arsenal manager George Graham was sacked; on 23 February a Premier League inquiry revealed that he had received £425,000 following transfers of European players to the club in 1991 and 1992. **25.** The American boxer Gerald McClellan underwent an emergency brain operation after being knocked out in a world championship fight against Nigel Benn in London. **27.** More than 140 Chelsea football fans were deported from Belgium after violent incidents the day before a match against Bruges; hundreds more fans were rounded up on 28 February and deported.

MARCH 1995

4. Andy Cole scored five goals for Manchester United in their 9-0 defeat of Ipswich in a Premier League match at Old Trafford. **6.** The yacht *oneAustralia* sank during an America's Cup race off San Diego, USA. **7.** Salim Malik and Intikhab Alam were sacked as captain and manager respectively of the Pakistan cricket team. **8.** Keith Fletcher was sacked as manager of the England cricket team and replaced by the chairman of selectors, Ray Illingworth. **13.** The Chelsea and England footballer Dennis Wise was sentenced at Horseferry Road Magistrates' Court to three months' imprisonment for assaulting a taxi driver in October 1994; his appeal against conviction was upheld on 2 June. **14.** Three Premier League footballers, Bruce Grobbelaar, John Fashanu and Hans Segers, were arrested and questioned about alleged match-fixing; they were released on 15 March. **16.** Kim Bailey and Norman Williamson became the first trainer and jockey pairing since 1950 to win the Champion Hurdle and the Cheltenham Gold Cup in the same year. **18.** England won the rugby union grand slam for the third time in five years. Chris Eubank lost his WBO super-middleweight title to Steve Collins. **26.**

Michael Schumacher and David Coulthard were disqualified for using irregular fuel after finishing first and second in the Brazilian grand prix; they were reinstated on 13 April but Benetton and Williams were excluded from the result and fined $200,000 each. **27.** Alan Davies resigned as the Wales rugby union coach.

APRIL 1995

9. The Rugby Football League voted to accept a News Corporation proposal for an Anglo-French Super League from March 1996 to replace the current structure of the sport. A Crystal Palace football supporter was killed in fighting in Walsall between rival fans before an FA Cup semi-final against Manchester United at Villa Park. In the replay on 12 April Roy Keane of Manchester United and Darren Patterson of Crystal Palace were sent off for fighting; the FA charged them with bringing the game into disrepute and on 26 May Keane was fined £5,000. **19.** The World Professional Billiards and Snooker Association held an inquiry into allegations of match-fixing after betting had been suspended on a match between Jimmy White and Peter Francisco at the World Championship on 16 April; Jimmy White was cleared of any involvement but on 8 May Peter Francisco was banned from competition for five years. The national heritage select committee of the House of Commons criticized the Rugby Football Union for discriminating against former rugby league players. **27.** At the world snooker championships Stephen Hendry scored a maximum break of 147 points in a semi-final match against Jimmy White. **29.** Wigan won the Rugby League Challenge Cup for the eighth successive year. **30.** Stephen Hendry won the world snooker championship for the fourth successive year.

MAY 1995

3. West Indies lost a Test series at home for the first time since 1973 when Australia won the fourth Test at Kingston, Jamaica. **4.** The England rugby union captain Will Carling called the Rugby Football Union '57 old farts' and said that there should be an openly professional structure to the game; on 6 May he was stripped of the England captaincy but on 8 May he was reinstated after apologizing to the RFU. **7.** Betting shops opened on a Sunday for the first time. **11.** The Tottenham Hotspur striker Jurgen Klinsmann said that he was returning to Germany after only one season with the club. **14.** Blackburn Rovers won the football league championship for the first time since 1914. **21.** Wigan became the first club in the modern era to complete the rugby league grand slam when they won the Premiership in addition to the league championship, the Challenge Cup and the Regal Trophy. **23.** Nigel Mansell left the McLaren motor racing team. **25.** The rugby union World Cup opened in South Africa. The Everton footballer Duncan Ferguson was sentenced at Glasgow Sheriff Court to three months' impri-

sonment for head-butting an opponent during a match in April 1994; he was released pending an appeal against the sentence. **26.** Gavin Hastings scored 44 points in Scotland's 89-0 victory over Ivory Coast in the rugby union World Cup. **30.** The Dutch footballer Ruud Gullit signed for Chelsea.

JUNE 1995

3. At the rugby union World Cup an Ivory Coast player, Max Brito, was left paralysed by an accidental blow to the back of his head during a match against Tonga. Three players were sent off for fighting during a match between Canada and South Africa; five of the players involved were suspended by the World Cup directors. **4.** At the rugby union World Cup New Zealand beat Japan 145-17, Simon Culhane scoring 45 points on his debut for the All Blacks. **5.** The Ethiopian runner Haile Gebresilasie set a new world record of 26 minutes 43.53 seconds for the 10,000 metres. **9.** The Derby was held on a Saturday for the first time since 1952. **11.** At the rugby union World Cup England beat Australia in the quarter-finals with a last-minute dropped goal by Rob Andrew. **12.** The world and Olympic 100 metres champion Linford Christie said that he would retire at the end of the season; Christie later said he would compete on the international circuit in 1996 but would not defend his Olympic title. **18.** At the rugby union World Cup England conceded a record 45 points in their 29-45 defeat by New Zealand in the semi-final; the All Black Jonah Lomu scored four tries. **23.** News Corporation signed a ten-year £340 million broadcasting contract with the rugby unions in New Zealand, Australia and South Africa. **24.** South Africa won the rugby union World Cup. **25.** At a meeting in Lille Jonathan Edwards jumped a wind-assisted 18.43 metres in the triple jump, 48 cm longer than the world record. **26.** England beat the West Indies in a Test match at Lord's for the first time since 1957; Dominic Cork took seven wickets for 43 runs on his Test debut. **28.** Mike Smith was sacked as manager of the Wales football team. The British tennis players Tim Henman and Jeremy Bates were disqualified at Wimbledon after a ball struck in anger by Henman hit a ball girl on the head during a doubles match; on 29 June Henman was fined £1,950. The Nottingham Forest footballer Stan Collymore signed for Liverpool for a record £8.5 million. **29.** Lisa Clayton arrived at Dartmouth, Devon, in her yacht *Spirit of Birmingham*, becoming the first woman to circumnavigate the globe from the northern hemisphere non-stop and unassisted.

JULY 1995

1. The American tennis player Jeff Tarango left the court after a row with the umpire during a third-round match at Wimbledon; his wife then slapped the umpire; on 3 July Tarango was fined £10,000, and in August he was fined a further £31,000 and suspended from two Grand Slam tournaments, including Wimbledon 1996. **3.** The West Indies suffered their worst-ever defeat against a county cricket side when they were beaten by Sussex by an innings and 121 runs. The American tennis player Murphy Jensen failed to turn up for his mixed doubles match at Wimbledon; he was fined £650. **8.** Steffi Graf won the ladies' singles title at Wimbledon for the sixth time after beating Arantxa Sanchez Vicario in three sets; there were 13 deuces in the penultimate game of the match. England were all out for 89 runs in their second innings in the second Test against the West Indies. **9.** Pete Sampras won the men's singles title at Wimbledon for the third successive year. **10.** The England football captain David Platt signed for Arsenal from Sampdoria for £4.75 million. The footballer Paul Gascoigne signed for Rangers for £4.3 million from Lazio. **12.** The former Arsenal football manager George Graham was found guilty by the FA of misconduct for accepting payments as part of the transfer of two players to the club in 1991-2; on 13 July he was banned from football for a year. Noureddine Morceli set a new 1,500 metres world record of 3 minutes 27.37 seconds. **15.** The 110 metres hurdles world champion Colin Jackson withdrew from the AAA Championships in Birmingham after the first heat, citing injury; a row broke out when he raced in Padua, Italy, the following day. On 21 July Jackson withdrew from the world championships in Gothenburg in August. **18.** The Italian Olympic champion cyclist Fabio Casartelli was killed in a crash during the Tour de France. Jonathan Edwards set a new triple jump world record of 17.98 metres. **24.** Bruce Grobbelaar, John Fashanu and Hans Segers were charged with accepting money to fix matches; they were bailed to appear in court on 11 October. **26.** Diane Modahl won her appeal against the four-year ban imposed by the British Athletic Federation in December 1994; on 31 July the International Amateur Athletics Federation referred the decision to an arbitration panel. **29.** The former tennis champion Monica Seles played her first match since being stabbed on court in Hamburg, Germany in April 1993. Ivan Pedroso set a new world long jump record of 8.96 metres. **30.** In the fourth Test against the West Indies, Dominic Cork became the first Englishman to take a Test hat-trick since 1957.

AUGUST 1995

7. Jonathan Edwards set a new triple jump world record of 18.29 metres at the world championships. **11.** Kim Batten set a new women's 400 metres hurdles record of 52.61 seconds. **16.** Haile Gebresilasie set a new 5,000 metres world record of 12 minutes 44.39 seconds. Moses Kiptanui set a new 3,000 metres steeplechase world record of 7 minutes 59.18 seconds. **17.** Bobby Gould was appointed manager of the Wales football team. **20.** The former world boxing champion Mike Tyson beat Peter McNeeley in 89 seconds in Las Vegas, USA, in his first fight since being released from jail. **27.** The International Rugby Football Board announced that the amateur rules governing rugby union would be abolished and players would be able to receive payment for participating in the sport at all levels.

APPOINTMENTS AND RESIGNATIONS

In addition to those mentioned above, the following appointments and resignations were announced:

1994

2 September: Phil Walker was appointed editor of the *Daily Star*

12 September: Giles Shepard resigned as managing director of the Savoy hotels group; Rodney Walker was appointed chairman of the Sports Council

26 October: Arthur Miller was appointed professor of contemporary theatre at Oxford University for 1995

3 November: Tiny Rowland resigned as deputy chairman and chief executive of Lonrho from the end of 1994

16 November: John Witherow was appointed editor of the *Sunday Times* from the end of 1994

1995

12 January: Peter Preston, the editor of the *Guardian*, was appointed editor-in-chief of the *Guardian* and the *Observer*; Jonathan Fenby resigned as editor of the *Observer*

24 January: Alan Rusbridger was appointed editor of the *Guardian*

27 January: David Gordon resigned as chief executive of ITN

7 February: Andrew Jaspan was appointed editor of the *Observer*

7 March: Chris Green was appointed chief executive of English Heritage

11 March: Baroness O'Cathain resigned as managing director of the Barbican Centre, London; on 26 July she was replaced by John Tusa

25 March: Ian Jack resigned as editor of the *Independent on Sunday*; he was replaced by Peter Wilby

19 May: Dr Alan Borg, the director of the Imperial War Museum, was appointed director of the Victoria and Albert Museum from September 1995

22 June: Georgina Nayler resigned as director of the National Heritage Memorial Fund

19 July: Adair Turner was appointed director-general of the CBI from September 1995

1 August: Mark Rylance was appointed artistic director of the reconstructed Globe Theatre from the summer of 1996

30 August: Piers Morgan, the editor of the *News of the World*, was appointed editor of the *Daily Mirror*

AFRICA

SEPTEMBER 1994

14. King Letsie of Lesotho restored to power Prime Minister Ntsu Mokhehle and his government, which he had attempted to overthrow in August. **15.** The ECOMOG intervention force shelled the Liberian presidential palace after rebel Liberian troops took control of it in a coup attempt.

OCTOBER 1994

29. The first free presidential and parliamentary elections in Mozambique since independence were won by the incumbent president Joachim Chissano and the ruling Frelimo party. **31.** The Angolan government and UNITA initialled a UN-brokered peace agreement.

NOVEMBER 1994

6. Algerian security forces killed 112 armed Islamic fundamentalists in a five-day offensive. **7.** The UN Security Council voted to establish an international war crimes tribunal to deal with the genocidal massacres in Rwanda. **10.** The UNITA headquarters and the city of Huambo were captured by government forces, leading UNITA to declare invalid the peace treaty initialled in October. **20.** Representatives of the Angolan government and UNITA signed a UN-mediated peace treaty.

DECEMBER 1994

11. The South West Africa People's Organization (SWAPO) and its leader President Nujoma won Namibia's first parliamentary and presidential elections since independence. **13.** The trials for war crimes of 3,000 members of the former Marxist Dergue regime opened in Ethiopia. **27.** Armed Islamic extremists killed four Roman Catholic priests in Algeria in revenge for the killing of four Algerian Islamic hijackers by French security forces (*see* page 1089).

JANUARY 1995

5. Malawi's former President for life Hastings Banda and a former aide, John Tembo, were arrested on charges of ordering the murder of four government ministers in 1983. **19.** Ten Europeans, including five Britons, were kidnapped from mining areas in Sierra Leone by the Revolutionary United Front. **25.** King Letsie of Lesotho abdicated in favour of his father King Moshoeshoe II, who had been deposed in a military coup in 1990. **30.** A car bomb left by Islamic fundamentalists outside the central police station in Algiers exploded killing 38 people and wounding 256.

FEBRUARY 1995

8. The UN Security Council voted to approve the establishment of a 7,000 strong peacekeeping force to oversee the implementation of the Angolan peace agreement. **14.** President Mandela inaugurated South Africa's new constitutional court. **21.** The Inkatha Freedom Party led by Chief Buthelezi suspended its participation in the South African Parliament, claiming that the ANC and the National Party had reneged on a pre-election agreement to establish international mediation of constitutional differences. **22.** Ninety-five Islamic fundamentalists were killed by security forces in an attempt to break out of an Algerian prison. **27.** A force of 2,500 US and 500 Italian marines arrived in

Mogadishu to protect the withdrawal of the remaining UN troops from Somalia.

MARCH 1995

2. The last UN troops were evacuated from Mogadishu. **5.** The Inkatha Freedom Party (IFP) ended its two-week boycott of the South African parliament but set the government a one-month deadline to establish international constitutional mediation or the IFP would withdraw from the constitutional assembly. **26.** Fighting in the Burundi capital of Bujumbura between the Tutsi-dominated army and Hutu gangs left 500 dead. **27.** President Mandela dismissed his estranged wife Winnie from her post as a deputy government minister because of her continued criticism of the government and involvement in financial scandals; she had to be reinstated on 12 April because of a legal technicality but was dismissed again by President Mandela on 14 April.

APRIL 1995

8. The Inkatha Freedom Party suspended its involvement in the South African constitutional assembly after the ANC failed to involve international mediators in preparing a new constitution. **9.** President Mugabe's ZANU-PF party won 118 of the 120 contested seats in Zimbabwe's general election. **16.** British troops arrived in the Angolan port of Lobito as the first contingent of a 7,000-strong UN peacekeeping force. **18.** The Rwandan government closed its border with Zaire to stop food aid reaching Hutus in refugee camps in eastern Zaire, and surrounded Kibeho refugee camp in southern Rwanda. **22.** Three hundred Hutu refugees in Kibeho camp were killed and hundreds more wounded by government soldiers after they attempted to break out of the army cordon around the camp. **23.** Between two and three thousand Hutu refugees and militia were killed and 600 injured when the Rwandan army forcibly emptied Kibeho camp after it had been used as a militia base to attack surrounding villages.

MAY 1995

5. Islamic militants killed five foreign workers in retaliation for a recent offensive by Algerian security forces in which hundreds of militants had been killed. **11.** The Zairean government sealed off the capital Kinshasa from the neighbouring province of Bandundu where 48 people had died in an outbreak of the Ebola virus.

JUNE 1995

5. President Mandela was questioned by the country's police chief George Fivaz over his admission in the Senate the previous week that in March 1994 he had ordered ANC security guards to fire upon and kill Zulu marchers in Johannesburg. **7.** The mainly Tutsi Burundian army seized control of the last Hutu suburb in Bujumbura after defeating Hutu militia. **28.** The South African Parliament passed the

Promotion of National Unity and Reconciliation Bill, establishing a Truth Commission to investigate the apartheid period.

AUGUST 1995

10. The Kenyan opposition leader Dr Richard Leakey and a group of supporters and journalists were beaten by members of the ruling KANU party as they tried to establish an opposition party office in the Rift Valley area. 15. Five army officers took power in São Tomé and Príncipe in a bloodless coup; the President and government were restored to power six days later when the officers relinquished power after a parliamentary amnesty was granted. 19. Zairean forces began forcibly repatriating several thousand Rwandan Hutu refugees in eastern Zaire. 22. Zairean troops destroyed several Rwandan refugee camps in eastern Zaire; 85,000 Hutu refugees fled in to the surrounding hills rather than return to Rwanda. 24. Zaire stopped forcibly repatriating Rwandan refugees after agreement was reached with the UN on a voluntary repatriation programme.

THE AMERICAS

SEPTEMBER 1994

9. The USA and Cuba reached an agreement to end the sea-borne flight of thousands of Cubans to Florida; the USA pledged to admit at least 20,000 Cuban immigrants a year and Cuba agreed to end unsafe departures. 12. The separatist Parti Quebecois won the Quebec provincial parliamentary election and promised to hold a referendum on secession from Canada within ten months. 15. In a nation-wide television address President Clinton issued an ultimatum to the Haitian military junta to leave Haiti or be forced from power. 18. A US negotiating team (former President Carter, Senator Nunn and Gen. Colin Powell) reached agreement with the Haitian military junta for their resignation by 15 October, the return of President Aristide and the deployment of a US and later a UN peace-keeping force. 19. The first US troops began arriving in Haiti to ensure a peaceful transition period until democracy was restored. 22. US troops began destroying the Haitian army's heavy weapons in an attempt to prevent further military coups. 25. US marines killed ten Haitian military police in a gunfight in the city of Cap Haitien. 28–29. Two days of fighting in Port-au-Prince between pro-Aristide demonstrators and paramilitaries left 11 people dead.

OCTOBER 1994

2. The Haitian military and US forces began to disarm Haitian paramilitaries; US forces began arresting militiamen the following day. 3. Fernando Henrique Cardoso won the Brazilian presidential election outright in the first round. 3. The US

Agriculture Secretary Mike Espy resigned over allegations that he had broken government rules on the receipt of corporate gifts. 7. The Haitian parliament voted to grant an amnesty to the military junta but could not agree on its extent. 15. The Haitian President Jean-Bertrand Aristide returned to Port-au-Prince after three years in exile. 16. The UN formally lifted its economic sanctions against Haiti. 29. A man was arrested in Washington after firing an automatic weapon at the White House.

NOVEMBER 1994

8. The Democratic Party was heavily defeated in Congressional and state gubernatorial elections, the Republicans gaining majorities in both the Senate and the House of Representatives for the first time since 1954. 27. Julio Maria Sanguinetti of the opposition Colorado party was elected President of Uruguay.

DECEMBER 1994

6. The former Associate Attorney-General in the Clinton administration, Webster Hubbell, pleaded guilty to charges of tax evasion and fraud brought by the Whitewater investigation special prosecutor; on 28 June Hubell was sentenced to 21 months' imprisonment. 9. President Clinton dismissed the US Surgeon-General Jocelyn Elders over comments recommending masturbation to young people. 20. A man running towards the White House in Washington wielding a knife was shot and seriously wounded by police. 21. A fire-bomb exploded on a crowded New York subway train, injuring 37 people. 28. The director of the CIA, James Woolsey, resigned over criticism of the CIA's ability to detect moles in its organization.

JANUARY 1995

4. The 104th US Congress was sworn in. 5. In a 14-hour opening session, the US House of Representatives voted to end Congress's exemption from federal laws, order an independent audit of Congress for waste and fraud, make a 60 per cent vote in Congress necessary for any income tax rises, limit the terms of the Speaker and committee chairmen, eliminate 28 Congressional committees, 26 caucuses and 600 staff, and open all committee hearings to the public. 26. The US House of Representatives passed a constitutional amendment requiring the government to balance its budget by 2002. 29. Several days of border clashes between Peruvian and Ecuadorian armed forces over a disputed 50-mile stretch of the border developed into open warfare.

FEBRUARY 1995

7. President Clinton nominated Gen. Michael Carns as director of the CIA. 10. The Mexican army launched an offensive against Zapatista guerrillas in the south of the country; security forces found arms caches in Mexico City and Veracruz. 14. Peru and Ecuador both claimed victory in their three-week

border conflict; both countries claimed control of three border posts in the disputed area and announced unilateral cease-fires. **17.** Peru and Ecuador signed a peace agreement under which negotiations on the border would be held and the disputed area demilitarized.

MARCH 1995

2. The Republicans failed to gain the necessary two-thirds majority in the US Senate to approve a balanced budget constitutional amendment when the measure was approved by only 65 votes to 35. **7.** New York became the 38th US state to restore capital punishment. **11.** President Clinton's nominee as CIA director, Gen. Michael Carns, was forced to withdraw over his family's employment of an illegal immigrant. President Clinton nominated Deputy Defence Secretary John Deutsch as CIA director. **12.** Canada seized a Spanish fishing trawler in internatonal waters off Newfoundland, sparking off a two-month dispute with the European Union (*see* pages 1110–1). **24.** The US House of Representatives passed a welfare reform bill which included the denial of state benefits to immigrants, unmarried teenage mothers and those who refuse to work. The Senate voted to grant President Clinton and future presidents a line item veto power over the US federal budget.

APRIL 1995

2. Shining Path insurgents killed 15 soldiers and civilians in two attacks on remote areas of Peru in an attempt to disrupt the country's general election. **5.** A Republican Party bill cutting taxes by US$189,000 million over five years was passed by the US House of Representatives. **9.** President Fujimori was re-elected for a second term in the first round of Peru's presidential election, the Cambio 90-Nueva Mayoria party won the parliamentary elections. **19.** A 1,000 lb car bomb exploded outside a US federal government building in Oklahoma City, killing at least 167 people. **20.** The legislative building of the Canadian province of Prince Edward Island was damaged by a bomb while the legislature was in session. **21.** Two men wanted for the Oklahoma bombing, Timothy McVeigh and Terry Nichols, were arrested by the FBI.

MAY 1995

9. The US Senate confirmed John Deutsch as CIA director. **14.** Carlos Menem was re-elected in the first round of Argentina's presidential election. **24.** An armed intruder who entered the White House grounds in Washington DC was shot and wounded by secret service agents. **25.** The US Senate passed a bill to reduce government spending over the next seven years and balance the federal budget by 2002.

JUNE 1995

7. President Clinton used his veto to block a Congressional bill to reduce federal government spending by US$16,400 million in the present financial year. **7.** Jim Tucker, who replaced Bill Clinton as the governor of Arkansas, was indicted on three charges of illegal land-dealing by a federal jury investigating the Whitewater affair. **8.** The Progressive Conservative Party won the Ontario provincial legislative election. **10.** A bomb exploded in the Colombian city of Medellin, killing 28 people, a day after a leader of the Cali cocaine cartel, Gilberto Rodriguez Orejuela, was arrested by police. **12.** In a test case, the US Supreme Court narrowed the circumstances when positive discrimination in favour of ethnic minorities and women could be justified, overturning years of race- and gender-based affirmative action programmes. **22.** The US Senate voted to block the approval of President Clinton's nominee, Henry Foster, as Surgeon-General because he admitted that he had carried out abortions. **29.** The US House of Representatives passed a budgetary plan to reduce government spending and eliminate the federal budget deficit by 2002. The US Supreme Court ruled that US states could not redraw Congressional boundaries to ensure the election of ethnic minority candidates.

JULY 1995

18. The US Senate reopened investigative hearings into the Whitewater affair (President Clinton's land dealings in Arkansas) and the death of deputy White House counsel Vincent Foster in 1993. **23.** President and Mrs Clinton were interviewed by Whitewater special prosecutor Kenneth Starr; a Congressional hearing was told that Mrs Clinton impeded the investigation of the death of Vincent Foster in 1993.

AUGUST 1995

6. The leader of the Cali cocaine cartel, Miguel Rodriguez Orejuela, was arrested by Colombian police, leaving only one of the seven cartel members at large. **8.** The US House of Representatives' banking committee heard from three federal regulators that the Clinton administration systematically and repeatedly intervened to stop investigation of the Whitewater loans and land development project. **10.** Timothy McVeigh and Terry Nichols were formally charged by a federal grand jury with bombing the federal buildings in Oklahoma City in April. **16.** President Samper of Colombia declared a state of emergency as the national security situation worsened, with a spate of kidnappings and attacks by left-wing guerrillas. **17.** The electorate of Bermuda voted by 74 per cent to 26 per cent to reject independence and to retain its British status. **17.** President and Mrs Clinton's former business partners in the Whitewater project, James and Susan McDougal, were indicted by the Whitewater special prosecutor on multiple fraud and conspiracy charges; the Arkansas governor Jim Tucker was indicted on further fraud charges.

ASIA

SEPTEMBER 1994

18. Independent and pro-democracy candidates won most of the seats in elections to the District Boards in Hong Kong. 20. Members of the ruling military council in Myanmar held talks with the pro-democracy movement leader Aung San Suu Kyi for the first time since she was placed under house arrest in 1990. 21. Three hundred people were killed in seven days of fighting between rival mujahidin groups in the Afghan capital Kabul. 23. Thousands of people fled from the Indian city of Surat after an outbreak of pneumonic plague caused 110 deaths. 29. The government of the Delhi region ordered the closure of all schools and cinemas after the pneumonic plague spread to the Indian capital.

OCTOBER 1994

21. The USA and North Korea signed a treaty under which North Korea agreed to end its military and civilian nuclear programmes and allow international inspections of its nuclear sites, in return for diplomatic and economic relations with the USA and new nuclear reactors for non-military use. 23. The presidential candidate of the Sri Lankan opposition United National Party, Gamini Dissanayake, was assassinated in a bombing which killed 50 people.

NOVEMBER 1994

7. South Korea announced that it would lift its ban on business contacts with North Korea. 9. Prime Minister Chandrika Kumaratunga won the Sri Lankan presidential election, becoming the country's first woman president. 18. Pro-independence protesters clashed with Indonesian soldiers in East Timor's capital Dili.

DECEMBER 1994

17. A US helicopter was shot down by North Korean troops after straying into North Korean airspace. One of the pilots was killed; the other pilot was released by North Korea on 30 December. 21. Myanmar troops launched an offensive against the border base of the ethnic Karen and pro-democracy opposition.

JANUARY 1995

5. The Sri Lankan President signed a truce with the Tamil Tigers separatists which came into effect from 8 January. 20. The USA partially lifted its 45-year-old sanctions against North Korea. 27. Myanmar forces captured the opposition headquarters at Mannerplaw.

FEBRUARY 1995

21. Myanmar forces captured the last remaining opposition base at Kawmoora. 26. Thirty people died in ethnic and sectarian clashes in the Pakistani

city of Karachi after a Shi'ite mosque was attacked by Sunni Muslims.

MARCH 1995

6. Afghan government forces launched an offensive to drive opposition forces from their last remaining stronghold in Kabul. 6. Pro-democracy parties won most of the seats in elections to Hong Kong's Regional and Urban Councils. 8. Two US consular diplomats were killed and one wounded in a gun attack in Karachi. 10. Eleven people were killed and 24 injured by a car bomb outside a mosque in Karachi. 14. Right-wing Hindu extremist parties led by the Shiv Sena and Bharatya Janata Party (BJP) defeated the ruling Congress (I) Party in state elections in northern India. 19. Afghan government forces defeated armed militant Islamic students and forced them beyond rocket range of Kabul. 20. Twelve people died and 5,500 were taken ill when the nerve gas sarin was released on the Tokyo underground system. 22. Japanese police raided several properties of the Aum Shinrikyo religious sect and found chemicals used in the manufacture of the nerve gas sarin. 29. The chief of Japan's National Police Agency, who was investigating the sarin gas attack, was shot and seriously wounded.

APRIL 1995

4. Armed Muslim insurgents attacked Ibil in the southern Philippines, killing 47 and injuring hundreds. 8. Suspected Tamil Tiger guerrillas shot dead Sri Lankan soldiers in the Jaffna peninsula, breaking the truce in place since January. 19. Over 300 people were treated in hospital after a gas attack at Yokohama underground station, Japan. 19. Eleven Sri Lankan sailors were killed in an attack by Tamil Tiger guerrillas on navy patrol boats as the Tamil Tigers ended peace talks with the Sri Lankan government; the government reimposed an economic embargo on the Tamil-held Jaffna peninsula. 25. The governing National Front Coalition won the Malaysian general election.

MAY 1995

11. Fighting between Indian security forces and 70 Pakistani gunmen in the Kashmiri town of Chari-i-Sharif led to the destruction of an ancient Muslim shrine, the death of 35 gunmen and the imposition of a curfew in the area. 15. Japanese police arrested members of the Aum Shinrikyo sect, including the leader Shoko Asahara, for involvement in the sarin gas attacks on the Tokyo underground. 21. Twenty-two people were killed in Kashmir as security forces fought with protesters against Indian rule.

JUNE 1995

9. Britain and China reached agreement on the establishment of a court of final appeal for Hong Kong to replace the UK Privy Council after the handover to China. 21. Japanese riot police stormed an aircraft at Hakodate airport in northern Japan and released 365 people who had been held hostage for

15 hours by an armed man demanding the release of the leader of the Aum Shinrikyo sect. **28.** More than 140 guerrillas and government soldiers were killed in a series of attacks by the Tamil Tigers in north and east Sri Lanka. **30.** Britain and China signed an agreement on funding the new Hong Kong airport and associated railway after six years of argument.

JULY 1995

2. The opposition Chart Thai party emerged as the largest party in legislative elections to the Thai House of Representatives; a coalition government was formed with Chart Thai leader Banharn Sipla-archa as Prime Minister. **9.** The Sri Lankan government launched an offensive against the Tamil-held Jaffna peninsula, capturing an important causeway held by the rebels for eight years. **10.** The State Law and Order Restoration Council released the Burmese pro-democracy leader and 1991 Nobel Peace Prize winner Aung San Suu Kyi, who had spent six years under house arrest. **23.** In elections to Japan's upper house of parliament, the House of Councillors, the ruling coalition retained a majority. **28.** A Tamil Tiger offensive against four Sri Lankan army bases near the Jaffna peninsula was defeated, leaving 180 guerrillas dead.

AUGUST 1995

3. Fighting in Karachi between security forces and armed rebels of the Mohajir Qaumi Movement left 24 dead. **7.** A Tamil suicide bomb attack in the Sri Lankan capital Colombo killed 21 people. **24.** China expelled the dissident Harry Wu, now a US citizen, after sentencing him to 15 years in jail on a spying charge relating to his researches into the Chinese prison system. **31.** The chief minister of the Indian state of Punjab, Beant Singh, was killed, in a car bomb attack in Chandigarh.

AUSTRALASIA AND THE PACIFIC

SEPTEMBER 1994

5. John Newman, a member of the New South Wales state legislature and an anti-crime campaigner, was shot dead. **23.** Rabaul in Papua New Guinea was buried in three feet of ash caused by the eruption of two nearby volcanoes, leaving over 90,000 people homeless.

OCTOBER 1994

31. The Prime Minister of the Solomon Islands, Francis Billy Hilly resigned 18 days after he was dismissed by the Governor-General.

NOVEMBER 1994

7. The National Parliament of the Solomon Islands elected opposition leader Solomon Mamaloni Prime Minister.

FEBRUARY 1995

6. New Zealand's traditional Waitangi Day celebrations were abandoned after they were disrupted by Maori protesters, who fought with police and spat at the Governor-General.

MARCH 1995

25. The Labor Party won the state legislative elections in New South Wales.

JULY 1995

9. French commandos seized the Greenpeace ship *Rainbow Warrior II* as it entered an exclusion zone around the nuclear testing ground of Muroroa atoll in French Polynesia.

AUGUST 1995

21. New Zealand asked the International Court of Justice in the Hague to reopen the legal action filed in 1973 to stop France conducting nuclear tests in French Polynesia.

EUROPE

SEPTEMBER 1994

2. The Bulgarian government resigned; the parliament accepted the resignation on 8 September. **8.** British, French and American troops withdrew from Berlin after 49 years. **18.** The Social Democratic Party won Sweden's general election but without a majority. **21.** The Social Democratic-led coalition government lost its majority in the Danish general election but retained power with the support of socialist and Communist parties. **26.** The Estonian Prime Minister Mart Laar was forced to resign after a parliamentary vote of no-confidence.

OCTOBER 1994

1. The Movement for a Democratic Slovakia emerged as the largest party in the Slovak parliamentary election with 35 per cent of the vote. **9.** The governing coalition of the Socialist and People's Parties retained their parliamentary majority in the Austrian general election but lost seats to the Freedom Party. **14.** The French industry minister Gerard Longuet resigned over allegations of corruption. **14.** There was a general strike in Italy against proposed government budget cuts. **16.** The coalition government won the German general election but with a much reduced parliamentary majority.

NOVEMBER 1994

8. The Italian government declared a state of emergency in six northern regions after three days of flooding left 64 people dead and 5,000 homeless. Security forces detained 95 suspected Islamic militants in raids throughout France which also uncovered arms caches and equipment for forging identity papers. **13.** The French Minister for Overseas Co-operation, Michel Roussin, resigned and was put under investigation for illicit party funding. **15.** Helmut Kohl was re-elected as German Chancellor by the Bundestag by only one vote more than the absolute majority required. **16.** The Italian government won a parliamentary vote of confidence on a proposed austerity budget. **17.** The Irish Prime Minister Albert Reynolds resigned after the Labour Party withdrew from the coalition government over the delay in extraditing a paedophile priest to Northern Ireland. **18.** President Mitterrand of France and the British Prime Minister John Major announced the establishment of a combined Anglo-French air force command for peacekeeping and humanitarian operations. **22.** The Italian Prime Minister Silvio Berlusconi was placed under investigation by Milan magistrates on suspicion of bribery and corruption.

DECEMBER 1994

6. Attempts to preserve the Irish coalition government were ended by Labour leader Dick Spring because of the contentious appointment of a new President of the High Court. **8.** Judge Antonio Di Pietro, the Milan magistrate leading the three-year-old national political corruption investigation, resigned in protest at government interference in the investigation. **11.** A new Slovak government was formed by the nationalist Movement for a Democratic Slovakia (HZDS) and extreme left and right-wing parties, with HZDS leader Vladimir Meciar as Prime Minister. **13.** Silvio Berlusconi was questioned by Milan magistrates over suspected illegal payments to tax inspectors investigating his Finnivest holding company. **15.** A new coalition government of the Fine Gael, Labour and Democratic Left parties was formed in the Irish Republic with Fine Gael leader John Bruton as Prime Minister. **18.** The Bulgarian Socialist Party won the country's general election. **21.** Four of the five Northern League ministers in the Italian government resigned as the Northern League, together with opposition parties, initiated a parliamentary debate of no confidence in Silvio Berlusconi's government. **22.** Silvio Berlusconi resigned after his coalition government collapsed over a corruption investigation into his Finnivest business. **26.** Four Algerian Islamic militants were killed when the Air France aircraft they had hijacked was stormed by French commandos at Marseille airport.

JANUARY 1995

13. President Scalfaro appointed Lamberto Dini Prime Minister-designate of Italy. **17.** Lamberto Dini's government of non-political technocrats was sworn in. **20.** Jean-Claude Juncker was sworn in as Prime Minister of Luxembourg to replace Jacques Santer, who had become President of the European Commission. **25.** The new Italian government won a vote of confidence in the lower house of the Italian

parliament; MPs loyal to Silvio Berlusconi abstained.

FEBRUARY 1995

6. President Walesa told the Polish government to resign because they were obstructing economic reform or he would dissolve parliament; Prime Minister Waldemar Pawlak resigned the following day.

MARCH 1995

2. The former Italian Prime Minister Giulio Andreotti was charged in Sicily with membership of the Cosa Nostra. **5.** In Estonia's general election the Centrist coalition emerged as the largest party. **8.** Costis Stephanapoulos was elected President of Greece by the parliament. **14.** Seven former East German politburo members were charged with the manslaughter of 47 people killed while trying to escape to the former West Germany. **16.** The Italian Chamber of Deputies approved the emergency budget in what was also a vote of confidence in the government. **19.** The opposition Social Democratic party emerged as the largest party in the Finnish parliament after the general election. **22.** The Belgian Deputy Prime Minister and Foreign Minister Frank Vandenbroucke resigned after he admitted knowledge of a bribe paid by the helicopter manufacturer Augusta to the Flemish and Walloon socialist parties in 1988 to secure a defence contract.

APRIL 1995

13. Paavo Lipponen became Prime Minister of Finland at the head of a five-party coalition government. **23.** The first round of the French presidential election was won by Lionel Jospin (Socialist) with 23.2 per cent of the vote; Jacques Chirac (Gaullist) came second with 20.1 per cent.

MAY 1995

7. Jacques Chirac was elected President of France, defeating Lionel Jospin in the second round of the presidential election. **15.** The former French minister Bernard Tapie was jailed for one year for illegal match-fixing when he was president of Olympique-Marseille football club. **17.** Jacques Chirac succeeded Francois Mitterrand as President of France and appointed Alain Juppé Prime Minister. **21.** The four-party coalition government retained power in the Belgian general election. **28.** The right-wing Popular Party defeated the ruling Socialist Party in regional and municipal elections throughout Spain.

JUNE 1995

11. The Italian electorate voted in a series of referenda to reject proposals intended to reduce the control of Silvio Berlusconi over Italian broadcasting. **18.** In French municipal elections the right-wing National Front won control of Toulon, Orange and Marignane, and a National Front-allied candidate won the mayorship of Nice. **20.** French police and security forces arrested 140 Algerian and Tunisian Islamic militants and recovered weapons and explosives in a series of raids across France. **28.** Spain's Deputy Prime Minister Narcis Serra and Defence Minister Julian Garcia Vargas resigned over allegations that the Spanish military intelligence service had bugged leading politicians and businessmen, including King Juan Carlos.

JULY 1995

9. After high-speed launches were seized in Gibraltar to curb tobacco smuggling, protests at the seizures degenerated into rioting. **25.** A bomb exploded on a train at the St Michel metro station in Paris, killing seven people. **28.** German police stormed a hijacked tourist bus in Cologne, killing the hijacker, who had killed the driver and one passenger.

AUGUST 1995

10. Spanish security forces arrested three suspected ETA terrorists who were plotting to kill King Juan Carlos. **17.** A bomb exploded near the Arc de Triomphe in Paris, injuring 17 people. **24.** The trial opened in Berlin of eight former East German military officers charged with the manslaughter of people killed while trying to escape to the former West Germany,

COMMONWEALTH OF INDEPENDENT STATES

SEPTEMBER 1994

11. President Meshkov of the autonomous Ukrainian republic of Crimea suspended the Crimean parliament and denounced its vote to reduce his constitutional powers. The suspension was lifted two days later after the parliament agreed to restore the powers.

OCTOBER 1994

7. President Aliyev of Azerbaijan dismissed Prime Minister Surat Husseinov for his alleged involvement in a coup attempt and appointed Faud Huliyev to replace him. **27.** The Russian government survived a vote of no confidence in the State Duma.

NOVEMBER 1994

6. President Imomali Rakmonov was re-elected in the Tajik presidential election. **25.** Forces loyal to President Dudayev of the breakaway Chechen republic in Russia defeated an armed opposition attack on the Chechen capital, Grozny. **29.** President Yeltsin warned the warring factions in Chechenia to stop fighting or a state of emergency would be declared in the republic within 48 hours; Russian warplanes bombed Grozny airport.

DECEMBER 1994

11. Russian armoured columns entered Chechenia and moved towards Grozny in an attempt to over-

throw the regime of President Dudayev. **16.** After five days of intermittent fighting against irregular Chechen forces, a Russian armoured column reached the heights to the north of Grozny; two other columns were blocked by civilians. **17.** Russian forces bombarded Chechen forces after President Dudayev refused to disarm his forces in accordance with an ultimatum from President Yeltsin. **19.** Russian troops began to surround Grozny, facing fierce Chechen resistance, as warplanes continued their bombardment of the city. **20.** Russia sealed Chechenia's borders with Azerbaijan and Georgia and closed all air links; Russian troops encountered fierce resistance to their attempts to surround Grozny. **31.** After days of intense fighting on the outskirts of the city, Russian forces began to move towards the centre of Grozny, encountering stiff resistance.

JANUARY 1995

2. Chechen forces defeated a Russian thrust towards the centre of Grozny, destroying many Russian tanks and armoured vehicles. **8.** Fresh Russian forces composed of paratroops, marines and special forces units, plus intensive air and artillery bombardments, pushed Chechen forces back into the centre of Grozny. **10.** Fighting in Grozny decreased with the implementation of a unilateral 48-hour cease-fire by Russian forces. **11.** President Yeltsin announced that the general staff of the Russian armed forces would henceforth come under his direct control as commander-in-chief and would be removed from Ministry of Defence control. **12.** Russian forces resumed air, artillery and armoured attacks on Grozny, pushing Chechen forces further towards the city centre. **19.** Russian troops captured the Chechen forces' headquarters in the presidential palace in the centre of Grozny, forcing Chechen forces to withdraw to eastern parts of the city.

FEBRUARY 1995

1. The Russian Prosecutor-General formally charged the Chechen secessionist leader Gen. Dzhokhar Dudayev with terrorism, treason and crimes against the state. **3.** Russian armoured forces broke through Chechen defences south of Grozny, encircling the remaining Chechen fighters in the city. **6.** Russian forces crossed the Sunzha river in Grozny and completed the capture of the centre of the city, Chechen forces being driven into an enclave in the south-east of the city. **7.** Chechen forces began withdrawing from Grozny and re-grouping to the south and east as Russian troops advanced throughout the city. **13.** Russian and Chechen commanders agreed a partial cease-fire to enable the exchange of prisoners and the return of the dead. **21.** Russian forces launched ground and air strikes on towns and villages to the south of Grozny and seized the town of Alkhan-Yurt from Chechen fighters.

MARCH 1995

2. President Yeltsin dismissed Moscow's police chief and public prosecutor for incompetence after the murder two days earlier of the popular television journalist Vladislav Listyev. 10. Russia and the International Monetary Fund reached agreement on a £4,000 million loan to Russia to support its 1995 economic reform programme. 17. Azerbaijani troops defeated a rebellion and attempted coup by paramilitary police in Baku. 17. The Ukrainian parliament voted to abolish the presidency and constitution of the autonomous republic of Crimea and sent troops to disarm the Crimean President's bodyguards. 22. Russian forces bombarded the Chechen stronghold of Shali south of Grozny after surrounding the town. 23. Russian forces captured the towns of Argun and Shali; the Chechen defenders retreated southwards towards the Caucasus mountains. 26. The Uzbek electorate approved the extension of President Karimov's term of office until 2000 in a national referendum.

APRIL 1995

2. President Kuchma issued a decree that abolished the autonomous status of the Crimean republic and gave him the right to appoint the Crimean Prime Minister. 4. The Ukrainian parliament passed a vote of no confidence in the reformist government. 9. Russian forces captured the town of Samashki in western Chechenia after a two-day massacre of Chechen civilians by Russian forces. 9. Russian and Tajik border guards were killed in a weekend of cross-border raids from Afghanistan by Tajik Muslim rebels. 13. Russian aircraft bombed the Afghan border town of Taloqan, killing 100 people, in an attempt to hit the Tajik rebel bases. 20. Russian forces withdrew from the Chechen town of Bamut after heavy fighting with Chechen guerrillas. 27. President Yeltsin ordered a unilateral cease-fire by Russian troops to take effect at midnight and last until 11 May. 30. President Nazarbaev of Kazakhstan had his term of office extended by four years to 2000 in a national referendum.

MAY 1995

15. The Russian armed forces relaunched their offensive against Chechen separatists after a two-week cease-fire. 15. In a national referendum the electorate of Belarus voted in favour of President Lukashenko's proposals to reintegrate the country's economy with Russia and to give the Russian language equal status. 23. President Yeltsin vetoed an electoral bill passed by the State Duma which proposed that half of its members should be elected by proportional representation and half in first-past-the-post constituencies.

JUNE 1995

7. The Ukrainian parliament agreed to President Kuchma's 'constitutional treaty' giving the President the power to appoint the government without reference to parliament and greater powers to issue decrees. 9. President Yeltsin and President Kuchma signed an agreement on the division of the former Soviet Black Sea fleet giving Russia 81 per cent of the vessels and allowing Russia to continue basing its vessels in the Ukrainian port of Sevastopol. 14. Chechen guerrillas entered southern Russia and seized between 300 and 1,500 hostages in Budyonnovsk. 17. Russian security forces freed 200 hostages in an attack on the hospital in Budyonnovsk where the Chechen rebels were holding Russian hostages, but failed to dislodge the rebels. 18. The Chechen rebels left Budyonnovsk and headed towards Chechenia with 150 hostages in a convoy of buses after the Russian government agreed to the rebels' demands for a cease-fire in Chechenia and the resumption of negotiations; the hostages were released on 19 June when the convoy reached south-east Chechenia. 21. The Russian State Duma passed a non-binding vote of no confidence in the government over its handling of the Budyonnovsk hostage crisis. 30. President Yeltsin accepted the resignations of the Interior Minister, the head of the Federal Security Service, and the Nationalities Minister over the handling of the Budyonnovsk hostage crisis.

JULY 1995

4. Fighting broke out between Russian and Chechen forces in southern Chechenia after peace negotiations ended without agreement. 30. A military accord to end the fighting in Chechenia was signed by Russian and Chechen negotiators; it included a phased disarmament of Chechen guerrillas, an exchange of prisoners and a potential withdrawal of Russian forces. 31. The Chechen leader Gen. Dudayev rejected the peace agreement with Russian forces, leading to renewed fighting in the south of the republic.

AUGUST 1995

2. Gen. Dudayev accepted the cease-fire agreement of 30 July; the first exchange of Russian and Chechen prisoners took place. 16. Some Chechen forces began handing over their weapons to Russian forces. Other groups continued to clash with Russian forces, leading to a Russian air attack on the south-west of the republic on 17 August. 21–22. In a two-day battle in Argun, Russian troops crushed an attempt by Chechen forces to seize the town. 24. The Georgian parliament adopted a new constitution, renamed South Ossetia as Tskhinvali and gave the breakaway Abkhazia region the status of an autonomous republic. 29. The Georgian President Eduard Schevardnadze was injured in a failed assassination attempt when a car bomb exploded outside the Georgian parliament.

THE FORMER YUGOSLAVIA

SEPTEMBER 1994

4. Bosnian Serb authorities expelled 800 Muslim and Croat civilians from Bjeljina to Muslim-held

Tuzla. **9.** The rump Yugoslav state agreed to allow international civilian monitors to verify the closure of its border with Serb-held areas of Bosnia in return for an easing of UN sanctions; the monitors began to arrive on 14 September. **9.** One British soldier was killed and three injured when their armoured personnel carrier crashed near Gorazde. **9.** Ethnic Serb forces from Croatia joined a Bosnian Serb offensive against the Muslim-held Bihac pocket. **12.** A new bridge across the river Neretva was opened by the European Union Commissioner for Mostar, Hans Koschnik. **12.** Three British troops were killed and five wounded when their vehicle left the road and rolled down a mountainside near Gorazde. **18.** An outbreak of fighting in Sarajevo, the heaviest since the February cease-fire, caused UN commander Lt.-Gen. Sir Michael Rose to threaten to use NATO air strikes to stop it. **22.** Two RAF aircraft destroyed a Bosnian Serb tank within the 20 km heavy weapons exclusion zone around Sarajevo after it had fired on UN troops. **23.** The UN Security Council voted to suspend cultural, sporting and air travel sanctions against the rump Yugoslav state for a period of 100 days after monitors reported that the Yugoslav-Bosnian border had been sealed. At the same time sanctions on the Bosnian Serbs were tightened.

OCTOBER 1994

3. International monitors reported that the Yugoslav-Bosnian border had been sealed; the next day UN sanctions were lifted for a period of 100 days. **6.** The bodies of 20 Bosnian Serb soldiers were found with their throats cut by UN troops on Mt Igman, close to Sarajevo; 128 Bosnian Serbs and 166 Muslim prisoners were exchanged in Sarajevo. **7.** UN peacekeeping troops forced Bosnian government troops out of the demilitarized zone around Sarajevo. **27.** Bosnian government forces drove back Bosnian Serb forces from 80 sq. miles of territory in the Bihac pocket.

NOVEMBER 1994

3. Combined Bosnian Muslim and Bosnian Croat forces captured the town of Kupres from Bosnian Serb forces. **6.** Bosnian Serb and government forces exchanged artillery fire in and around Sarajevo; fighting grew heavier near Bihac and Kupres. **8.** Four people were killed by renewed Bosnian Serb shelling and sniper fire in Sarajevo. **9.** Bosnian Serb and Croatian Serb forces counterattacked the Muslim-held Bihac enclave. **12.** The USA ended its enforcement of the UN arms embargo against the Bosnian government. **16.** Bosnian Serb forces reached the town of Velika Kladusa in the Bihac enclave after recapturing most of the land lost to government forces three weeks before. **18.** Croatian Serb aircraft attacked the Bihac pocket with napalm bombs. **19.** The town of Cazin in the Bihac pocket was bombed by Croatian Serb aircraft; the UN Security Council authorized air strikes on Croatian Serb air bases. **21.** NATO aircraft bombed the

Croatian Serb air base at Udbina and rendered the runway unusable. **22.** Bosnian Serb forces fired surface-to-air missiles at two British aircraft patrolling over Bosnia and continued attacking the Bihac enclave; NATO aircraft bombed the Bosnian Serb missile sites the following day. **23.** Bosnian Serb forces entered the UN safe area of Bihac and reached the outskirts of the town. **24.** Bosnian Serb forces entered Bihac town; NATO ministers failed to agree to a US proposal to prevent the enclave being overrun. **27.** Rebel Muslim forces led by Fikret Abdic retook the town of Velika Kladusa in the Bihac enclave from Bosnian government forces. About 400 UN peacekeepers were held by Bosnian Serb forces to prevent NATO air strikes. **30.** Bosnian Serb forces released 42 British UN troops whose convoy had been held in eastern Bosnia for five days.

DECEMBER 1994

2. The Croatian government and the rebel Serbs of the Krajina region of Croatia signed an agreement to restore electricity and water supplies, fuel deliveries, roads and telephone lines. Russia vetoed a UN Security Council resolution to restrict fuel and supplies reaching Bosnian Serbs through Serb-held areas of Croatia. **4.** Two UN convoys were released by Bosnian Serb forces in eastern Bosnia. **8.** Bosnian Serb forces released UN troops held hostage near Sarajevo and allowed a UN convoy to reach the Bihac enclave. **11.** Bosnian Serb forces announced the indefinite refusal of passage to armour-escorted UN aid convoys through areas under their control; they also released 180 UN troops. **15.** A Royal Navy helicopter made an emergency landing near Kiseljak after being hit by Bosnian Serb anti-aircraft and rifle fire. **18.** Former US President Jimmy Carter arrived in Sarajevo to meet Bosnian government and Bosnian Serb leaders in an attempt to mediate in the Bosnian conflict. **29.** The Bosnian Serb parliament voted in favour of Carter's proposal to negotiate a comprehensive peace agreement based on the International Contact Group's peace plan. **31.** The Bosnian President Alija Izetbegovic and the Bosnian Serb leader Radovan Karadzic signed a UN-brokered four-month cease-fire agreement intended to enable formal peace negotiations to begin.

JANUARY 1995

1. The cease-fire came into effect throughout Bosnia. **11.** President Tudjman announced that the UN mandate in Croatia would be terminated on 31 March 1995 because of the UN's failure to force rebel Serbs to disarm or to enable the return of refugees to their homes. **15.** Bosnian government forces gained ground around the Bihac pocket. **20.** The UK announced it was sending additional helicopters, ground crew and military observers to Bosnia to police the cease-fire. **22.** Lt.-Gen. Sir Michael Rose ended his term as UN commander in Bosnia-Hercegovina and was replaced by Lt.-Gen. Rupert Smith.

FEBRUARY 1995

6. As part of the cease-fire agreement, Bosnian Serb forces opened routes out of Sarajevo for civilian traffic for the first time since July 1994. **13.** The international tribunal on war crimes in the former Yugoslavia charged 21 Bosnian Serb guards from the Omarska concentration camp with torture, rape and murder.

MARCH 1995

6. Croatia, the Bosnian Croats and the Bosnian government agreed to form a joint military command to counter a joint Bosnian and Croatian Serb command. **12.** President Tudjman agreed to let a smaller UN peacekeeping force remain in Croatia with a redefined mandate. **15.** A British UN patrol was pinned down for several hours by Bosnian Serb forces in the UN safe area of Gorazde until rescued by reinforcements. **20.** Bosnian Serb forces shelled Tuzla to counter an offensive eastwards from Tuzla by government forces. **21.** Bosnian Serb forces seized artillery pieces, anti-aircraft guns and a heavy mortar weapon from a UN depot near Sarajevo, violating the heavy weapons exclusion zone. **24.** Bosnian government forces captured a Bosnian Serb communications tower on Mt Vlasic, near the town of Travnik. **26.** Bosnian Serb forces shelled Gorazde, Tuzla, Bihac and Sarajevo in retaliation for Bosnian government offensives around Tuzla and Travnik.

APRIL 1995

4. Bosnian government forces captured Mt Vlasic from Bosnian Serb forces. **9.** Bosnian Serb forces shelled Sarajevo, killing three civilians. **13.** Bosnian Serb forces shelled the airport and outskirts of the Croatian port of Dubrovnik. **18.** Bosnian government and Bosnian Serb forces exchanged mortar fire in and around Sarajevo. **24.** Bosnian Serb leaders Radovan Karadzic and Ratko Mladic were named as suspected war criminals by the international tribunal on war crimes.

MAY 1995

1. Fighting broke out in Croatia as Croatian forces attempted to regain land held by Croatian Serbs, who took UN peacekeepers hostage. The UN Secretary-General's special envoy to the former Yugoslavia, Yasushi Akashi, failed to get the Bosnian government and the Bosnian Serbs to agree to extend the four-month cease-fire, which expired at midday. **2.** Croatian forces captured the towns of Pakrac and Okucani and the remainder of the Western Slavonia UN-protected area from Croatian Serb forces, liberating UN peacekeepers held hostage by the Croatian Serbs and forcing Croatian Serb refugees to flee to Bosnia. **2–3.** Croatian Serb forces launched rocket attacks on Zagreb, killing six. **3.** The UN brokered a cease-fire between Croatian forces and Croatian Serbs under which all Serb forces and ethnic Serbs wishing to leave the Western Slavonia area would be evacuated to Serb-held areas of Bosnia. **7.** Bosnian Serbs shelled

a supply route into Sarajevo, killing nine. **14.** Bosnian Serb forces reduced gas supplies to Sarajevo and continued to prevent UN aircraft landing at the airport; Bosnian Serb and Bosnian Croat forces engaged in heavy fighting around Orasje in northern Bosnia. **16.** The UN rejected a Bosnian government appeal for air strikes as Sarajevo was hit by hundreds of shells, killing five. **22.** Bosnian Serb snipers killed three people in Sarajevo; Bosnian Serb forces took heavy weapons from UN weapons protection points around the city. **24.** The UN commander in Bosnia, Lt.-Gen. Rupert Smith, issued an ultimatum to Bosnian Serb and government forces to return heavy weapons to UN weapon collection points or to remove them from the 20 km exclusion zone around Sarajevo, or face NATO air strikes. **25.** NATO planes bombed a Bosnian Serb ammunition dump at Pale near Sarajevo after Bosnian Serb forces failed to return artillery pieces to UN collection points; in retaliation Bosnian Serb forces shelled Sarajevo and Tuzla, killing 71 people. **26.** NATO planes repeatedly bombed Bosnian Serb ammunition dumps near Pale because of the Bosnian Serb forces' refusal to return artillery pieces to UN collection points and their shelling UN safe areas. Bosnian Serb forces took 38 UN troops hostage, chaining them up at potential bombing targets, and surrounded a further 200 UN troops. **27.** Bosnian Serbs and French UN troops fought for control of a bridge in Sarajevo; two UN soldiers died and 12 were taken hostage. **28.** Thirty-three British UN troops in Gorazde were taken hostage by Bosnian Serb forces; the number of UN personnel held hostage rose to 372. The British government announced the dispatch of 1,200 British troops to Bosnia. **29.** The Bosnian Serbs announced the cancellation of all agreements with UNPROFOR forces. **31.** Lord Owen resigned as the European Union's peace envoy to the former Yugoslavia. Britain announced the formation of a new mobile Theatre Reserve Force in Bosnia of British, French, Dutch, Canadian and New Zealand forces.

JUNE 1995

1. Bosnian Serb forces took hostage five UN personnel and engaged in fierce fighting with Bosnian government forces in Gorazde. **2.** The Bosnian Serbs released 121 UN hostages, but they took a further 63 UN personnel hostage and shot down a US aircraft. **3.** Defence ministers and chiefs of staff from 15 NATO and Scandinavian states agreed at an emergency meeting in Paris to reinforce UN forces in Bosnia-Hercegovina. **6.** The Bosnian Serbs released 108 hostages. **7.** Bosnian government and Bosnian Serb forces engaged in heavy shelling in and around Sarajevo. **8.** The US pilot shot down six days earlier was rescued by US marines. **9.** EU heads of government chose the former Swedish Prime Minister Carl Bildt as the new EU peace envoy to the former Yugoslavia. **13.** Bosnian Serb forces released 130 hostages, including the six remaining Britons. **15.** Bosnian government forces launched an artillery and infantry offensive against Bosnian Serb forces to the north and west of Sarajevo in an attempt to weaken the Bosnian Serb siege of the city. **16.** Government forces captured several strategic hills around Sarajevo and cut two Bosnian Serb supply routes. Bosnian Serb forces shelled Sarajevo in retaliation, killing nine. **16.** The UN Security Council approved resolution 998 authorizing an increase of 12,500 troops for UN forces in Bosnia-Hercegovina to accommodate the Anglo-French rapid reaction force. **18.** The remaining 26 UN hostages held by the Bosnian Serbs were released in exchange for four Bosnian Serb soldiers held by the UN and the withdrawal of UN forces from weapons collection points around Sarajevo. **21.** The first UN aid convoy for a month reached Sarajevo. **28.** Bosnian Serb forces shelled Sarajevo, killing eight people, as Bosnian government forces continued their attempt to break the siege of the city. **30.** The German Bundestag approved the deployment of a field hospital and support troops in Croatia and aircraft in Italy to cover a possible withdrawal of UN forces.

July 1995

1-2. Bosnian Serb artillery and rocket attacks on Sarajevo, in which UN buildings were deliberately targeted for the first time, killed 13 people. **4.** UN peacekeeping troops began to use the Mt Igman route to transport food supplies into Sarajevo and to return fire if Bosnian Serbs fired at the convoy. **5.** A Croatian Serb aircraft attacked the only electricity generating station in Bihac, in defiance of the UN air exclusion zone. **6.** Fighting erupted in and around Srebrenica after Bosnian Serb forces repeatedly shelled the town. **9.** Bosnian Serb forces took hostage 32 Dutch UN peacekeepers in their advance on Srebrenica. **11.** Bosnian Serb forces captured Srebrenica; NATO destroyed two Bosnian Serb tanks but failed to stop the offensive. **12.** Bosnian Serb forces took a further 22 Dutch UN troops hostage. **13.** Bosnian Serb forces transported all Muslim women, children and old men from Srebrenica to government-held areas and took all Muslim men between 16 and 65 to the Bosnian Serb town of Bratunac. **14.** Bosnian Serb forces began advancing on Zepa. **18.** Bosnian government forces surrounded the UN base in Zepa, saying that they would use the UN troops as human shields against the continuing Bosnian Serb attack. In Gorazde Bosnian government forces took the weapons, equipment and money of UN troops. **20.** Bosnian Serb forces shelled Zepa after the Bosnian government rejected Bosnian Serb terms for the surrender of the enclave. **22.** Bosnian Serb forces killed two French UN peacekeepers in an attack on a UN aid convoy in Sarajevo. **23.** The UN Rapid Reaction Force began deploying to Mt Igman near Sarajevo to secure the only aid route into the city from Bosnian Serb attacks. **24.** Bosnian Serb, Croatian Serb and renegade Muslim forces attacked Bihac from three sides in a

co-ordinated offensive. **25.** Bosnian Serb forces captured Zepa and began transporting Muslim women and children to government-held areas; government troops and Muslim men took to the hills to avoid capture. **26.** The US Senate voted to require the US government to lift the arms embargo against the Bosnian government within 12 weeks of the Bosnian government asking for the withdrawal of UN peacekeepers. **26.** The UN Secretary-General delegated UN command of air strikes to the UNPROFOR commander Gen. Bernard Janvier. **28.** Bosnian Croat forces supported by Croatian army brigades captured the strategically important towns of Glamoc and Bosansko Grahovo in western Bosnia from Bosnian Serb forces.

August 1995

1. Croatian Serb forces shelled the Croatian-held town of Gospic and attacked Croatian army positions with three aircraft from the Udbina airbase. The US House of Representatives voted to require the US government to lift the UN arms embargo against the Bosnian government unilaterally; the measure was vetoed by President Clinton on 11 August. **3.** Bosnian Serb forces shelled the outskirts of the Croatian port of Dubrovnik. **4.** Croatia launched an offensive against the ethnic Serb-held Krajina region of Croatia, capturing the town of Drnis and damaging the Krajina capital of Knin. **5.** Croatian forces captured Knin and the town of Benkovac, forcing thousands of ethnic Serbs to flee into Bosnian Serb areas of Bosnia. Bosnian government forces broke out of Bihac and crossed into Krajina to link up with Croatian forces and divide ethnic Serb-held territory in Croatia. **6.** Croatian forces captured the ethnic Serb-held towns of Petrinja and Slunj, and the town and airbase of Udbina. **7.** The Croatian offensive against Krajina ended as the last significant ethnic Serb force surrendered at Topusko. **7.** Bosnian government forces from Bihac defeated the rebel Muslim forces led by Fikret Abdic. **8.** Sporadic Serb resistance continued in Krajina around the towns of Dvor and Glina. Ethnic Serb refugees and troops were trapped around Dvor as Bosnian government forces prevented them entering Bosnia. **9.** The remaining Croatian Serb forces surrendered; refugees fled to Serbia. **10.** The US government presented to the UN Security Council satellite photographs of what it claimed were the mass graves of thousands of Muslim men murdered by Bosnian Serb forces after the capture of Srebrenica. **10.** Muslim-Croat Federation forces launched a new offensive in central Bosnia to capture Bosnian Serb territory and form a territorial link to the Bihac enclave. The UN announced the beginning of the withdrawal of most of its peacekeepers in Croatia. **13.** Bosnian government and Bosnian Croat forces launched an offensive in central Bosnia to capture the Bosnian Serb-held town of Donji Vakuf. Croatian and Bosnian Serb forces engaged in fighting around Dubrovnik as Croatian forces attempted to push

Bosnian Serb forces out of artillery range of the city. **18.** The UN began withdrawing its troops from Gorazde to prevent their possible future capture by Bosnian Serb forces. **22.** The UN Rapid Reaction force on Mt Igman fired at Bosnian Serb forces after they had shelled Sarajevo, killing six people. **23.** After producing a report on the Bosnian Serb capture of Srebrenica and Zepa which stated that the Bosnian Serbs carried out mass executions and rapes of the captured Muslims, the UN Human Rights Investigator for the former Yugoslavia, Tadeusz Mazowiecki, resigned in protest at the lack of international action on the report. **25.** British UN troops began withdrawing from Gorazde after repulsing an attack by renegade Bosnian government soldiers in the enclave; all remaining UN troops in the enclave withdrew three days later. **28.** A Bosnian Serb artillery attack on the crowded main market in central Sarajevo killed 37 people. **30.** NATO aircraft and UN Rapid Reaction Force artillery on Mt Igman launched waves of air attacks and artillery bombardments on Bosnian Serb ammunition dumps, air defence radars, communications sites, missile batteries and command centres around Sarajevo, Gorazde, Tuzla, Zepa and Mostar in an attempt to destroy Bosnian Serb capability to shell civilians in Sarajevo and other safe areas. The UN told the Bosnian Serbs that they would have to withdraw all heavy weapons from within 12 miles of Sarajevo and sign an agreement on the secession of hostilities before the attacks would stop. **31.** NATO aircraft and the Rapid Reaction Force artillery on Mt Igman bombarded Bosnian Serb artillery positions and infantry barracks around Sarajevo, and command and control centres around Pale to enforce the UN ultimatum.

THE EUROPEAN UNION

SEPTEMBER 1994

22. The British Employment Secretary (Michael Portillo) exercised Britain's opt out from the social protocol to the Maastricht Treaty over paternity leave and workers' councils.

OCTOBER 1994

16. The Finnish electorate voted to ratify Finland's accession to the European Union. **29.** The President-designate of the European Commission, Jacques Santer, allocated the portfolios to the 21 Commissioners.

NOVEMBER 1994

13. The Swedish electorate voted to join the European Union in a referendum. **14.** The European Court of Auditors published its annual report, which stated that fraud and waste cost the European Union between £600 million and £4,000 million in 1993. **18.** The Finnish parliament ratified Finland's accession to the European Union. **28.** The Norwegian electorate voted against membership of the European Union in a referendum.

DECEMBER 1994

6. In a European Council meeting the British Employment Secretary vetoed a proposed European directive extending the statutory rights of full-time workers to part-time staff. **10.** The European Union heads of government summit in Essen, Germany, ended with agreement to reduce employment and welfare benefits in order to cut unemployment; to seek a negotiated rather than a military solution to the Bosnian conflict; to provide EU aid for Northern Ireland; to structure preparation for membership of the six east European states. **21.** The European Commission fined ten EU member states a total of £1,170 million for allowing agricultural fund fraud by their farmers.

JANUARY 1995

1. The European Union increased from 12 to 15 member states with the accession of Austria, Finland and Sweden. **18.** The European Parliament endorsed the new European Commission.

FEBRUARY 1995

1. Sir Leon Brittan (UK) and Manuel Marin (Spain) were elected Vice-Presidents of the European Commission. **9.** Greece reversed its earlier conditional acceptance of an agreement on a customs union between the EU and Turkey and vetoed the agreement. **15.** Jacques Santer presented the European Commission's programme for 1995 to the European Parliament and stressed the concepts of subsidiarity, transparency and effective decision-making and a more limited agenda of legislative proposals.

MARCH 1995

6. The European Union and Turkey signed a customs union agreement after Greece withdrew its veto in return for a commitment to open accession negotiations with Cyprus in 1997. **6.** The central rates of the Spanish peseta and the Portuguese escudo in the exchange rate mechanism of the European monetary system were devalued by 7 per cent and 3½ per cent respectively. **13.** The EU suspended all political dialogue with Canada in protest at Canada's seizure of a Spanish fishing trawler in international waters off Newfoundland the previous day; the trawler was released by Canada two days later after its captain and crew had been charged with illegal fishing. **21.** Belgian police raided offices at the European Commission headquarters to search for evidence of an alleged misuse of funds by EU tourist officials. **26.** The Schengen Agreement (signed by Belgium, France, Germany, Luxembourg, Netherlands, Portugal and Spain) came into effect, abolishing frontier controls between signatory states. **28.** Canadian coastguard vessels cut the nets of a Spanish fishing trawler in international waters off Newfoundland; the Canadian government displayed in New York undersized fishing nets from the Spanish trawler held two weeks earlier. **29.** Britain vetoed a proposed EU protest to Canada over its action against Spanish fishing vessels operating in the North Atlantic.

APRIL 1995

6. Britain and Sweden vetoed a proposed EU resolution which condemned the alleged cutting of the nets of Spanish trawlers by Canadian patrol vessels. **9.** European Union finance ministers agreed on the size and colour of eight coins and seven notes for the future single European currency. **14.** Spain and Portugal vetoed a draft EU-Canadian agreement on fishing quotas in the north-west Atlantic designed to end the disputes in the area. **16.** Agreement was reached between the EU and Canada over the Atlantic fishing dispute; Canada rescinded its jurisdiction over the whole of the Grand Banks area in return for satellite tracking and international monitoring of fishing trawlers, and a reduction in EU fish quotas from 44,000 to 12,000 tons.

MAY 1995

31. The European Commission presented its green paper on European monetary union, stating that exchange rates would be fixed one year after heads of government agree to implement monetary union and that a single currency would replace national currencies three years later.

JUNE 1995

3. The inaugural meeting began in Messina, Italy, of the EU group planning the agenda for the intergovernmental conference on the Maastricht Treaty in 1996; it comprises representatives of the 15 member governments, the European Commission and the European Parliament. **16.** The Schengen group of EU states reached agreement with the Nordic Union states to merge their border control-free areas, allowing Denmark, Finland and Sweden to join the Schengen zone. **19.** EU finance ministers agreed to abandon the target date of 1 January 1997 for the introduction of a single currency and set a new target date of 1 January 1999. **27.** The Cannes summit of EU heads of government ended with a compromise agreement allowing Europol to expand its operations and an agreement on foreign aid for the 1995-9 period. **30.** The French government refused to abolish border controls permanently, as required under the Schengen Agreement, stating that it was dissatisfied by the failure to strengthen inter-state police co-operation.

THE MIDDLE EAST

SEPTEMBER 1994

1. Israel and Morocco established low-level diplomatic relations, Morocco opening a liaison office in Tel Aviv.

OCTOBER 1994

1. Israel and Tunisia established low-level diplomatic relations. The Gulf Co-operation Council states (Saudi Arabia, Kuwait, Bahrain, Qatar, Oman and the UAE) ended their boycott of firms dealing with Israel. **6.** The UN weapons inspection team in Iraq began monitoring Iraq's weapons manufacturing plants to ensure that weapons of mass destruction are not built. **7.** President Clinton warned Iraq not to invade Kuwait after two Iraqi divisions moved close to the Kuwaiti border. **9.** The USA and Britain sent troops, aircraft and naval forces to Kuwait and the Gulf as Iraqi troops massed near Kuwait's border. **12.** Iraqi forces began to withdraw from their positions close to the Kuwaiti frontier as US and British military deployments continued. **14.** Israeli forces stormed the house in which an Israeli soldier was being held by Islamic militants; he was killed, along with three militants and another Israeli soldier. **15.** The UN Security Council passed a resolution ordering Iraq to withdraw all troops deployed near the Kuwaiti border back to their original positions. **19.** A Hamas suicide bomber blew himself up in Tel Aviv, killing 22 other people. **26.** The final Israeli-Jordanian peace treaty was signed by King Hussein and Prime Minister Rabin on the Israeli-Jordanian border in the presence of President Clinton.

NOVEMBER 1994

10. Iraq formally recognized the sovereignty, independence and borders of Kuwait, ending its long-standing claim to the country. **10.** King Hussein of Jordan made his first public visit to Israel to exchange legal documents which ratified the Israeli-Jordanian peace treaty. **11.** An Islamic Jihad suicide bomber killed three Israeli soldiers at a checkpoint on the Israeli-Gaza Strip border. **19.** Fifteen people were killed and 250 injured in two days of street battles in the Gaza Strip between Palestinian police and Islamic fundamentalists. **27.** Jordan and Israel established full diplomatic relations and announced that ambassadors would be exchanged on 10 December.

JANUARY 1995

2. Three Palestinian police officers were killed in a gun battle with Israeli soldiers on the border between Israel and the Gaza Strip. **22.** Nineteen Israelis, mainly soldiers, were killed and 60 injured at a bus stop near Tel Aviv by two suicide bombers belonging to Islamic Jihad.

FEBRUARY 1995

2. The leaders of Egypt, Israel, Jordan and the Palestine Liberation Organization held a summit in Cairo at which they agreed to condemn terrorism and violence and to continue with the peace process. 9. The Israeli Prime Minister Yitzhak Rabin and the PLO chairman Yasser Arafat held a crisis meeting at which they failed to agree on the holding of Palestinian elections, the redeployment of Israeli troops or the opening of the West Bank and Gaza Strip border crossings into Israel. 16. Mr Rabin and Mr Arafat agreed to a gradual lifting of the ban on Palestinian workers from the Occupied Territories entering Israel. 23. The chief UN weapons inspector accused Iraq of failing to provide complete details of its biological weapons programme. 27. A car bomb exploded in the town of Zakho in Kurdish-controlled northern Iraq, killing 70 people.

MARCH 1995

9. Yasser Arafat and the new Israeli Prime Minister Shimon Peres agreed a target date of 1 July 1995 for the start of the implementation of the second stage of the Israeli-Palestinian peace process. 20. Turkish troops crossed into northern Iraq to destroy bases of the separatist Kurdistan Worker's Party (PKK).

APRIL 1995

9. Seven Israeli soldiers and Jewish settlers were killed in two suicide bomb attacks in the Occupied Territories by Islamic Jihad. 10. UN weapons inspectors reported to the UN Security Council that Iraq refused to disclose the extent of its past biological weapons programme. 14. Iraq rejected a UN plan to allow the export of US$2,000 million worth of Iraqi oil over six months in order to raise funds for food, medicine, Iraqi Kurds and reparations to Kuwait. 25. Turkey withdrew some of the troops deployed in northern Iraq in the campaign against the PKK.

MAY 1995

5. Turkey announced the end of its six-week offensive in northern Iraq against the PKK. 17. The USA vetoed a UN Security Council resolution which declared invalid the Israeli decision to expropriate Arab land in East Jerusalem. 22. The Israeli government suspended its expropriation of land in East Jerusalem rather than face certain defeat in a no-confidence vote on the measure in the Knesset.

JUNE 1995

14–15. A battalion of Iraqi troops rebelled against the regime of Saddam Hussein, attacking Baghdad Radio transmitters and Saddam Hussein's private heliport before being defeated by loyal troops in fighting which left most of the rebels dead; three days later 150 rebel soldiers were executed. 18. Three Israeli soldiers were killed in an attack on their patrol in the South Lebanon Security Zone by Hezbollah guerrillas. 26. President Mubarak of

Egypt survived an assassination attempt by Islamic fundamentalists at an OAU summit in Addis Ababa. 27. The Amir of Qatar, Sheikh Khalifa bin Hamad Al Thani, was overthrown in a bloodless coup by his son, the Crown Prince Sheikh Hamad bin Khalifa Al Thani.

JULY 1995

6. Turkish forces re-entered northern Iraq to attack PKK guerrillas and killed about 60 guerrillas. 16. President Saadam Hussein of Iraq released two Americans, William Barloon and David Daliberti, who had been sentenced to eight years imprisonment for straying across the border from Kuwait in March. 24. Six Israelis were killed when a Hamas suicide bomber exploded a bomb on a bus in Tel Aviv. Two weeks of fighting between the Kurdish Democratic Party and the Patriotic Union of Kurdistan for control of the Kurdish areas in northern Iraq left 200 dead.

AUGUST 1995

10. President Saadam Hussein's two daughters and their husbands, Gen. Hussein Hassan, the Industry Minister and Gen. Saadam Kamel, the personal bodyguard and military adviser of Saadam Hussein, and 30 Iraqi officers were granted political asylum after fleeing to Jordan. 13. The Iraqi Deputy Prime Minister Tariq Aziz admitted that Iraq had withheld information about its weapons-building programmes and invited UN officials to discuss the weapons programmes, in an attempt to pre-empt any revelations by defector Gen. Hussein Hassan. 13. A Palestinian man was shot dead by Israeli settlers on the West Bank as Palestinians attempted to dismantle illegal Jewish encampments on Palestinian land. 21. Five Israelis were killed when a Hamas suicide bomber exploded a bomb on a bus in Jerusalem. The Israeli government suspended peace negotiations with the Palestinians and sealed off the West Bank and Gaza Strip from Israel. 27. Israel and the Palestinian National Authority signed an agreement which transferred civilian power in the West Bank over industry, trade, gas, petrol, postal services, agriculture, insurance, labour and municipal affairs to the PNA.

INTERNATIONAL RELATIONS

SEPTEMBER 1994

4. President Yeltsin of Russia and President Jiang Zemin of China signed treaties retargeting their nuclear weapons away from each other's territory and demarcating the western section of their border. 5. The UN population conference opened in Cairo with disagreement over abortion between the Vatican and many Muslim states on the one hand and Western states on the other. 12. The first of NATO's Partnership for Peace military exercises began in Poland with units from six NATO states and seven

former Warsaw Pact members participating. **13.** The UN population conference in Cairo ended with agreement by nearly all states and delegations to a 20-year plan to limit world population growth by extending women's education and family planning facilities and encouraging sustainable development. **28.** President Clinton and President Yeltsin agreed to increase the speed of destruction of US and Russian nuclear warheads under the START treaties. **29.** The Belgian Foreign Minister Willy Claes was appointed Secretary-General of NATO.

OCTOBER 1994

4. The USA lifted trade sanctions on China imposed in August 1993 after China agreed that it would not export missiles in contravention of the Missile Technology Control Regime.

NOVEMBER 1994

8. The UN tribunal for war crimes in the former Yugoslavia held its first public hearing in The Hague. **11.** The Japanese parliament passed a bill allowing the country's armed forces to enter foreign conflicts in order to rescue endangered Japanese nationals. **15.** Heads of state of the Asia-Pacific Economic (APEC) Forum agreed to form a free trade area by 2020. **16.** The Ukrainian parliament finally ratified Ukraine's adherence to the Nuclear Non-Proliferation Treaty. **22.** A court in Copenhagen found a Bosnian Muslim guilty of war crimes committed at a Bosnian Croat prison camp and sentenced him to eight years' imprisonment. **23.** A three-day UN conference on fighting international organized crime ended with agreement to establish an international task force of magistrates and police, and to tighten laws on banking secrecy and money-laundering.

DECEMBER 1994

1. The US Senate voted to ratify the Uruguay round of the GATT Treaty; it had been approved by the House of Representatives in November. The Russian Foreign Minister Andrei Kozyrev refused to approve a plan for Russia's participation in NATO's Partnership for Peace programme in protest at NATO plans to bring forward the membership of east European states. **5.** President Yeltsin and President Clinton clashed publicly over the eastward expansion of NATO at a CSCE summit in Budapest; Ukraine, Belarus and Kazakhstan signed the Nuclear Non-Proliferation Treaty. **6.** The two-day CSCE conference ended with failure to agree a statement on Bosnia after a Russian veto of a statement condemning Serbian aggression. The Conference agreed to change its name to the Organization for Security and Co-operation in Europe.

JANUARY 1995

13. The Algerian government announced its decision to accede to the Nuclear Non-Proliferation Treaty.

FEBRUARY 1995

5. The USA and China announced the imposition, after a three-week period, of punitive tariffs on each other's imports after China failed to meet a US deadline to ensure the protection of US intellectual property rights in China. **22.** The French government asked for the withdrawal of five US diplomats said to be CIA agents. **26.** China and the USA reached agreement over intellectual copyright protection.

MARCH 1995

20. The members of the Organization for Security and Co-operation in Europe signed a Pact for Stability in Europe which emphasized democratic principles and settling differences by negotiation.

APRIL 1995

7. The two-week UN conference on climatic change in Berlin ended with agreement on a climatic convention to reduce emissions of greenhouse gases after stabilizing emission levels in 2000. **21.** Negotiations between the USA and North Korea on the implementation of the accord ending North Korea's nuclear weapons programme broke down over North Korea's refusal to accept South Korean-built nuclear reactors. **27.** The Council of Europe suspended Turkey from membership because of Turkey's armed incursion against Kurdish guerrillas in northern Iraq. Turkey announced a boycott of the organization.

MAY 1995

11. The signatories of the Nuclear Non-Proliferation Treaty voted to extend the treaty indefinitely and make its provisions a permanent part of international law. **15.** The Western European Union accepted an offer by France, Italy, Portugal and Spain to create a joint military and naval rapid reaction force for Mediterranean operations. **16.** The USA announced that it would impose a 100 per cent tariff on Japanese luxury car imports unless Japan agreed to open its market to US car exports by the end of June. **31.** The Russian foreign minister Andrei Kozyrev signed Russia's Partnership for Peace agreement with NATO and an agreement on enhanced dialogue with NATO on issues such as peacekeeping and nuclear decommissioning.

JUNE 1995

13. France announced that it would resume nuclear testing at Mururoa Atoll in French Polynesia in September. **13.** North Korea and the USA reached agreement on the supply of South Korean-built nuclear reactors to North Korea. **28.** The USA and Japan reached agreement on increasing Japanese purchases of US car parts and increasing the number of Japanese dealers selling US cars. **29.** The US space shuttle *Atlantis* successfully docked with the Russian space station *Mir.*

JULY 1995

11. The USA restored full diplomatic relations with Vietnam. **25.** The International War Crimes Tribunal for the former Yugoslavia formally charged the Bosnian Serb leaders Radovan Karadzic and Gen. Ratko Mladic, the Croatian Serb president Milan Martic, and 21 others with genocide and crimes against humanity. **28.** Vietnam was admitted as a member of the Association of South East Asian Nations.

AUGUST 1995

11. President Clinton announced that the USA would end its nuclear testing in an attempt to improve the chances of concluding a comprehensive nuclear test ban treaty. **15.** The Japanese Prime Minister Tomiichi Murayama made a statement on the 50th anniversary of VJ Day in which he apologized for Japan's aggression and the suffering it caused, the first time since the end of the war that a Japanese public figure had made an apology. It was unclear, however, whether this was a personal or government apology and the Japanese government continued to refuse to accept any responsibility for financial compensation.

Obituaries

1 SEPTEMBER 1994 TO 31 AUGUST 1995

Abbott, George, American playwright, director, producer and actor, aged 107 – 31 January 1995

Adrian, 2nd Baron, FRCP, FRS, physiologist, Master of Pembroke College, Cambridge 1981–92, Vice-Chancellor of the University of Cambridge 1985–7, aged 67 – 4 April 1995

Albu, Austen, Labour MP for Edmonton 1948–74, aged 91 – 23 November 1994

Alfvén, Hannes, Swedish physicist and Nobel laureate, aged 86 – 2 April 1995

Alston, Rex, sports broadcaster and journalist, aged 93 – 8 September 1994

Andrews, Michael, painter, aged 66 – 19 July 1995

Alfinsen, Christian, American biochemist and Nobel laureate, aged about 78 – 15 May 1995

Baverstock, Donald, former television producer and BBC and ITV executive, aged 71 – 17 March 1995

Baxter, William, GC, aged 87 – 4 April 1995

Beaton, Norman, actor, aged 60 – 13 December 1994

Begg, Admiral of the Fleet Sir Varyl, GCB, DSO, DSC, First Sea Lord 1966–8, aged 86 – 13 July 1995

Benson, Lord (Henry), GBE, accountant and former adviser to the Governor of the Bank of England, aged 85 – 5 March 1995

Berens, Harold, radio comedian and screen actor, aged 92 – 10 May 1995

Bird, Mynah, Nigerian-born model, aged 43 – March 1995

Blackburn, John, ph.D., MP, Conservative MP for Dudley West since 1979, aged 61 – 12 October 1994

Bolt, Robert, CBE, dramatist and screenwriter, aged 70 – 20 February 1995

Bonham-Carter, Lord, publisher and politician, aged 72 – 4 September 1994

Brimelow, Lord, GCMG, OBE, head of the Diplomatic Service 1973–5, aged 79 – 2 August 1995

Broadhurst, Air Chief Marshal Sir Harry, GCB, KBE, DSO and bar, DFC and bar, AFC, Second World War fighter ace, Commander Allied Air Forces Central Europe 1959–61, aged 89 – 29 August 1995

Brophy, Brigid, novelist, critic and campaigner for public lending rights for authors, aged 66 – 7 August 1995

Bruce Lockhart, John, CB, CMG, OBE, senior M16 officer, university administrator and academic, aged 80 – 7 May 1995

Buckton, Ray, general secretary of the Associated Society of Locomotive Engineers and Firemen 1970–87, aged 72 – 7 May 1995

Burden, 2nd Lord, aged 79 – 25 June 1995

Butenandt, Adolf, German chemist and Nobel laureate, aged 91 – 18 January 1995

Calloway, Cab, American jazz bandleader and singer, aged 86 – 18 November 1994

Campbell of Eskan, Lord, businessman, aged 82 – 26 December 1994

Camrose, 2nd Viscount, TD, deputy chairman of the *Daily Telegraph* 1939–87, Conservative MP for Hitchin 1941–5, aged 85 – 15 February 1995

Carlisle, 12th Earl, MC, former forestry commissioner, aged 71 – 28 November 1994

Carter, Raich, footballer, aged 80 – 9 October 1994

Castle, Roy, OBE, comedian, musician and dancer, aged 62 – 3 September 1994

Chacksfield, Frank, orchestra leader and composer, aged 81 – 9 June 1995

Chandrasekhar, Subrahmanyan, astrophysicist and Nobel laureate, aged 84 – 21 August 1995

Clancarty, 8th Earl, author of books on UFOs, aged 83 – 18 May 1995

Clavell, James, author and scriptwriter, aged 69 – 6 September 1994

Cook, Peter, comic writer and entertainer, aged 57 – 9 January 1995

Cook, Elisha, jun., American film actor, aged 92 – 18 May 1995

Cooper, Susie, OBE, ceramic designer, aged 92 – 28 July 1995

Cork and Orrery, 13th Earl, a former Deputy Chairman of Committees, House of Lords, aged 85 – 8 August 1995

Cowdray, 3rd Viscount, president of the Pearson Group, aged 84 – 19 January 1995

Cradock, Fanny, television cook, aged 85 – 27 December 1994

Crosby, Prof. Theo, RA, architect, aged 69 – 12 September 1994

Crozier, Eric, OBE, librettist, opera producer and writer, aged 79 – 7 September 1994

Cvitanovich, Frank, documentary film-maker, aged 67 – 12 August 1995

Davies, David, oldest man in Britain, aged 108 – April 1995

de Grey, Sir Roger, KCVO, RA, artist and President of the Royal Academy 1984–93, aged 76 – 14 February 1995

Dell, Alan, radio presenter, aged 71 – 18 August 1995

Denbigh (11th) and Desmond (10th), Earl, former Liberal Democrat spokesman on arts and transport, aged 51 – 23 March 1995

Derby, 18th Earl, MC, aged 76 – 28 November 1994

Desai, Morarji, follower of Mahatma Gandhi and Prime Minister of India, 1977–9, aged 99 – 10 April 1995

Dickens, Geoffrey, MP, Conservative MP for Huddersfield West 1979–83 and for Littleborough and Saddleworth since 1983, aged 63 – 17 May 1995

Dickson, Alec, founder of Voluntary Service Overseas (VSO) and Community Service Volunteers (CSV), aged 80 – 23 September 1994

Drake, Ted, England and Arsenal footballer and Chelsea manager, aged 82 – 29 May 1995

Dundas, Sir Hugh, CBE, DSO and bar, wartime fighter pilot, journalist, chairman of Rediffusion 1978–85, BET 1982–7, Thames Television 1981–7, aged 74 – 10 July 1995

Durrani, Lt.-Col. Mahmood Khan, GC, wartime intelligence agent, aged 81 – 20 August 1995

Durrell, Gerald, OBE, naturalist and writer, aged 70 – 30 January 1995

Easton, Jack, GC, wartime bomb disposal officer, aged 88 – 30 November 1994

Edwards, Ronald ('Buster'), one of the Great Train robbers in 1963, aged 62 – 29 November 1994

Eisenstaedt, Alfred, photographer, aged 96 – 23 August 1995

Elphinstone, 18th Lord, aged 41 – 19 December 1994

Elton, Prof. Sir Geoffrey, FBA, historian, aged 73 – 4 December 1994

Emson, Air Marshal Sir Reginald, KBE, CB, AFC, aged 83 – 27 March 1995

English, Arthur, comedian and actor, aged 75 – 16 April 1995

Ennals, Lord, PC, Labour MP for Dover 1964–70 and Norwich North 1974–83, Secretary of State for Social Services 1976–9, aged 72 – 17 June 1995

Erskine of Rerrick, 2nd Baron, aged 69 – 8 June 1995

Ervine-Andrews, Lt.-Col. Marcus, VC, aged 83 – 30 March 1995

Everett, Kenny, disc jockey and television comedian, aged 50 – 4 April 1995

Fairbairn, Sir Nicholas, QC, MP, Conservative MP for Perth and Kinross since 1974 and Solicitor-General for Scotland 1979–82, aged 61 – 19 February 1995

Fangio, Juan Manuel, Argentinian racing driver, aged 84 – 17 July 1995

FitzGeorge-Balfour, Gen. Sir Victor, KCB, CBE, DSO, MC, aged 81 – 28 December 1994

Flemyng, Robert, OBE, MC, actor, aged 83 – 22 May 1995

Fowler, William, American astrophysicist and winner of Nobel Prize for physics 1983, aged 83 – 14 March 1995

Fulbright, William, US senator for Arkansas 1945–74, founder of Fulbright scholarships, aged 89 – 9 February 1995

Furness, 2nd Viscount, businessman and theatrical producer, aged 66 – 1 May 1995

Gabor, Eva, Hungarian-born actress, aged 76 – 4 July 1995

Gibson, Sir Alexander, CBE, founder and former artistic and music director of Scottish Opera, aged 68 – 14 January 1995

Giles, Carl, OBE, cartoonist, aged 78 – 27 August 1995

Glentoran, 2nd Baron, KBE, PC(NI), former Speaker in the Northern Ireland Senate and Lord Lieutenant of Belfast 1976–85, aged 83 – 22 July 1995

Goad, William, GC, aged 72 – 25 December 1994

Godunov, Alexander, Russian ballet dancer and film actor, aged 45 – found dead 18 May 1995

Gonzales, Pancho, American tennis player, aged 67 – 3 July 1995

Goodman, Lord, CH, solicitor, chairman of the Arts Council 1965–72, Master of University College, Oxford 1976–86, aged 81 – 12 May 1995

Gort, 8th Viscount, aged 78 – 6 April 1995

Grant, James, executive director of UNICEF since 1980, aged 72 – 28 January 1995

Grantchester, 2nd Baron, CBE, QC, a Deputy Chairman of Committees, House of Lords since 1988 and Deputy Speaker since 1990, aged 73 – 12 August 1995

Grantley, 7th Baron, MC, Lloyd's broker and underwriter, aged 71 – 24 June 1995

Grayson, Larry, comedian, aged 71 – 7 January 1995

Hallowes, Odette, GC, MBE, wartime heroine of Special Operations Executive, aged 82 – 13 March 1995

Hamilton, Adm. Sir John, GBE, CB, aged 84 – 27 October 1994

Hardy, Bert, photographer, principally with *Picture Post*, aged 82 – 3 July 1995

Hargreaves, Alison, mountaineer, aged 33 – 13 August 1995

Herriot, James (J. A. Wight, OBE, FRCVS), veterinary surgeon and author, aged 78 – 23 February 1995

Hewison, Rebecca, oldest woman in Britain, aged 112 – 22 September 1994

Highsmith, Patricia, American crime writer, aged 74 – 4 February 1995

Hordern, Sir Michael, CBE, actor, aged 83 – 2 May 1995

Hudleston, Air Chief Marshal Sir Edmund, GCB, CBE, aged 85 – 14 December 1994

Irving, Sir Charles, Conservative MP for Cheltenham 1974–92, aged 71 – 30 March 1995

Ives, Burl, American folk singer and actor, aged 85 – 14 April 1995

Jackson-Stops, Gervase, OBE, architectural adviser to the National Trust, writer, exhibition organizer, aged 48 – 2 July 1995

Jerne, Prof. Niels, FRS, immunologist and winner of Nobel prize for medicine 1984, aged 82 – 7 October 1994

Johnson, James, Labour MP for Rugby 1950–9 and Kingston-upon-Hull 1964–83, aged 86–31 January 1995

Joseph, Lord (Sir Keith Joseph), CH, PC, Conservative MP for Leeds North-East 1956–87 and Cabinet minister 1962–4, 1970–4, 1979–86, aged 76 – 10 December 1994

Julia, Raul, Puerto Rican actor, aged 54 – 24 October 1994

Kagan, Lord, textile manufacturer, creator of the Gannex raincoat, aged 79 – 17 January 1995

Kennedy, Rose, matriarch of the Kennedy family, aged 104 – 22 January 1995

Kilfedder, Sir James, MP, Ulster Popular Unionist Party MP for Down North since 1970, aged 66 – 20 March 1995

Kindersley, David, MBE, stone-carver and typeface designer, aged 79 – 2 February 1995

Köhler, Georges, German immunologist and winner of Nobel prize for physiology 1984, aged 48 – April 1995

Kray, Ronnie, London gangland killer, aged 61 – 17 March 1995

Kroger, Peter, American spy for Soviet Union, aged 85 – 23 June 1995

Lageson, Air Marshal Sir Philip, KCB, DFC, AFC, aged 71 – 9 October 1994

Lancaster, Burt, American film actor, aged 80 – 20 October 1994

Larwood, Harold, Nottinghamshire and England cricketer, aged 90 – 22 July 1995

Lever of Manchester, Lord, PC, Labour MP for Manchester Exchange/Cheetham/Central 1945–79 and Chancellor of the Duchy of Lancaster 1974–9, aged 81 – 6 August 1995

Lipton, Sydney, dance band leader, aged 89 – 19 July 1995

Lo, Kenneth, Chinese chef and restaurateur, aged 81 – 11 August 1995

Lock, Tony, former England and Surrey bowler, aged 65 – 30 March 1995

Lovat, Brig. 15th Lord, DSO, MC, TD, landowner and soldier, aged 83 – 16 March 1995

Lupino, Ida, film actress and producer, aged 77 – 3 August 1995

Lyttleton, Prof. Raymond, FRS, astronomer, aged 84 – 16 May 1995

McAloney, William, GC, OBE, aged 85 – 31 August 1995

McClure, Doug, American film and television actor, aged 59 – 5 February 1995

Maconchy, Dame Elizabeth, DBE, composer, aged 87 – 11 November 1994

MacPherson, Stewart, Canadian radio commentator, aged 86 – 16 April 1995

Maczek, Gen. Stanislaw, CB, DSO, commander of Polish forces during Second World War, aged 102 – 11 December 1994

May, Peter, CBE, England cricket captain 1955–61 and chairman of selectors 1982–8, aged 64 – 27 December 1994

May, Phillip, GC, aged 72 – 15 December 1994

Medley, Robert, CBE, RA, painter, aged 88 – 20 October 1994

Messervy, Sir Godfrey, chairman and chief executive of Lucas Industries 1980–7, aged 70 – 22 July 1995

Miller, John, GC, wartime mine disposal expert and African government administrator, aged 91 – 14 December 1994

Montagu, Victor (disclaimed Earldom of Sandwich in 1964), Conservative MP for South Dorset 1941–62, aged 88 – 25 February 1995

Morgan, Geraint, QC, Conservative MP for Denbigh 1959–83, aged 74 – 2 July 1995

Morrison, Rt. Hon. Sir Peter, Conservative MP for Chester 1974–92, former parliamentary private secretary to Margaret Thatcher, aged 51 – 13 July 1995

Morton of Shuna, Lord, a Senator of the College of Justice since 1988, aged 65 – 26 April 1995

Moschino, Franco, Italian fashion designer, aged 44 – 18 September 1994

Muir, Jean, CBE, fashion designer, aged 66 – 28 May 1995

Mulley, Lord (Fred), PC, Labour MP for Sheffield, Park 1950–83 and Cabinet Minister, aged 76 – 15 March 1995

Napley, Sir David, solicitor, aged 79 – 24 September 1994

Needham, Joseph, CH, FRS, FBA, scientist, Sinologist, Master of Gonville and Caius College, Cambridge 1966–76, aged 94 – 24 March 1995

Nelson of Stafford, 2nd Baron, FEng., chairman of GEC 1968–83, aged 79 – 19 January 1995

Osborne, John, playwright, actor and author, aged 65 – 24 December 1994

O'Shea, Tessie, music-hall artiste and actress, aged 82 – 21 April 1995

Parish, Sister, American interior designer, aged 84 – 8 September 1994

Parsons, Geoffrey, OBE, concert accompanist, aged 65 – 26 January 1995

Perry, Fred, lawn and table tennis player, three times Wimbledon singles champion, aged 85 – 2 February 1995

Phelps Brown, Sir Henry, MBE, FBA, economist, aged 88 – 15 December 1994

Pilkington, Sir Alastair, FRS, inventor of the float-glass process, chairman of Pilkington PLC 1973–80, philanthropist, Chancellor of Liverpool University since 1994, aged 75 – 5 May 1995

Pitt of Hampstead, Lord (David), doctor and politician, aged 81 – 18 December 1994

Place, Rear-Adm. Godfrey, VC, CB, CVO, DSC, aged 73 – 27 December 1994

Pleasence, Donald, OBE, actor, aged 75 – 2 February 1995

Pope-Hennessy, Sir John, CBE, FBA, FSA, art historian, director of the Victoria and Albert Museum 1967–73 and the British Museum 1974–6, aged 80 – 31 October 1994

Popper, Sir Karl, CH, FRS, philosopher, aged 92 – 17 September 1994

Porter, Eric, actor, aged 67 – 15 May 1995

Powell, Dilys, film critic, aged 93 – 3 June 1995

Raney, Jimmy, jazz guitarist, aged 67 – 10 May 1995

Rathcavan, 2nd Baron, PC(NI), Ulster Unionist MP for North Antrim at Westminster 1952–9 and Stormont 1959–72, aged 85 – 20 December 1994

Reigate, Lord, PC, Conservative MP for Reigate 1950–70, aged 89 – 26 January 1995

Rich, Charlie, American singer and songwriter, aged 62 – 25 July 1995

Rie, Dame Lucie, DBE, potter, aged 93 – 1 April 1995

Risman, Gus, rugby league footballer, aged 83 – 17 October 1994

Robinson, Harold, OBE, rocket scientist and space programme administrator, aged 70 – 4 January 1995

Rodger, George, photographer, aged 87 – 24 July 1995

Rogers, Ginger, actress and dancer, aged 83 – 25 April 1995

Rusk, Dean, KBE (HON.), American Secretary of State 1961–9, aged 85 – 20 December 1994

Russell, Sir Archibald, CBE, FRS, FEng., joint chairman, Concorde committee of directors 1965–9, aged 90 –29 May 1995

Salk, Jonas, American developer of first effective polio vaccine, aged 80 –23 June 1995

Sarton, May, American novelist, poet and autobiographer, aged 83 – 16 July 1995

Schon, Lord, industrialist and chairman of the National Research Development Corporation 1969–79, aged 82 – 7 January 1995

Scott-Hopkins, Sir James, Conservative MP for North Cornwall 1959–66, Derbyshire West 1967–79 and MEP 1973–94 (for Hereford and Worcester 1979–94), aged 73 – 11 March 1995

Selkirk, 10th Earl, KT, GCMG, GBE, AFC, AE, PC, QC, former government minister and diplomat, aged 88 – 24 November 1994

Serraillier, Ian, writer, aged 82 – 28 November 1994

Shackleton, Lord, KG, OBE, FRS, PC, Labour politician, aged 83 – 22 September 1994

Shaw, Sebastian, actor, aged 89 – 23 December 1994

Siad Barre, Mohamed, President of Somalia 1969–91, aged 75 officially, but believed to be about 85 – 1 January 1995

Slovo, Joe, anti-apartheid activist from 1950s to 1994, South African housing minister since 1994, aged 68 – 6 January 1995

Somers, 8th Baron, aged 87 – 15 February 1995

Somes, Michael, CBE, ballet dancer, aged 77 – 19 November 1994

Soukop, Willi, RA, sculptor, aged 88 – 9 February 1995

Souphanouvong, Prince, former Pathet Lao leader and President of Laos 1975–86, aged 82 – 9 January 1995

Speed, Doris, MBE, Annie Walker in *Coronation Street*, aged 95 – 16 November 1994

Spender, Sir Stephen, CBE, poet, aged 86 – 16 July 1995

Stewart, J. I. M., novelist (as Michael Innes) and university don, aged 88 – 12 November 1994

Stockwood, Rt. Revd Mervyn, Bishop of Southwark 1959–80, aged 81– 13 January 1995

Symons, Julian, crime writer and biographer, aged 82 – 19 November 1994

Tandy, Jessica, actress, aged 85 – 11 September 1994

Taylor of Hadfield, Lord, civil engineer, life president of the Taylor Woodrow Group, aged 90 – 15 February 1995

Thomas, Dr Roger, Labour MP for Carmarthen 1979–87, aged 68 –1 September 1994

Thurso, 2nd Viscount, landowner, founder of Caithness Glass, and Lord Lieutenant of Caithness since 1973, aged 72 – 29 April 1995

Townsend, Gp Capt. Peter, CVO, DSO, DFC and bar, Battle of Britain pilot, equerry to King George VI 1944–52 and to The Queen 1952–3, aged 80 – 19 June 1995

Traherne, Sir Cennydd, KG, TD, Lord Lieutenant of Glamorgan 1952–85, aged 84 – 26 January 1995

Trevor, Elleston, author (also as Adam Hall), aged 75 – 21 July 1995

Turner, Lana, American film actress, aged 75 – 29 June 1995

Tynan, Kathleen, writer, aged 57 – 10 January 1995

Upham, Charles, VC and bar, aged 86 – 21 November 1994

Waldegrave, 12th Earl, KG, GCVO, TD, agriculturist, Conservative junior minister 1958–62, chairman of the Forestry Commission 1963–5, Lord Warden of the Stannaries 1965–76, aged 89 – 23 May 1995

Waley, His Honour Judge Felix, VRD, QC, Judge Advocate of the Fleet since 1986, aged 69 – 16 April 1995

Walton, Ernest, nuclear physicist and Nobel laureate 1951, aged 91 – 25 June 1995

Waring, Richard, television scriptwriter, aged 69 – 5 December 1994

Western, David, GC, aged 57 – 12 March 1995

White of Hull, Lord (Gordon), KBE, co-founder of Hanson PLC and chairman of Hanson Industries since 1983, aged 72 – 23 August 1995

Wigner, Eugene, American nuclear physicist and Nobel laureate, aged 92 – 1 January 1995

Wilson, Gordon, Northern Ireland peace campaigner and Republic of Ireland senator, aged 67 – 27 June 1995

Wilson of Rievaulx, Lord (Harold Wilson), KG, OBE, PC, FRS, Labour MP 1945–83, entered the Cabinet 1947, elected leader of the Labour Party 1963, Prime Minister 1964–70 and 1974–6, aged 79 – 24 May 1995

Woods, Peter, journalist and television newsreader, aged 64 – 22 March 1995

Wright, Billy, CBE, footballer, captained England 1948–60, aged 70 – 3 September 1994

Wright, Peter, CBE, former M15 officer and author of *Spycatcher*, aged 78 – 27 April 1995

Wyatt, R. E. S. (Bob), former England cricket captain, aged 93 – 20 April 1995

Wykeham, Air Marshal Sir Peter, KCB, DSO, DFC, AFC, aged 79 – 23 February 1995

Archaeology

Sites of Palaeolithic date in which flint tools and animal bones are found together are rare in Europe and especially rare in Britain. Only one site of the Late Upper Palaeolithic was known, at Uxbridge, excavated in 1987–8, until a second was found at Staines in Surrey. The site is a gravel pit at Church Lammas where about 10,000 years ago a large animal was hunted down and butchered. According to the report in *British Archaeology* (number 4, May 1995) 'The site contains vertebrae and ribs but no long bones – the classic assemblage of a killing site, where the animal's meat-bearing leg bones were chopped off by Palaeolithic hunters and carried back to camp, to avoid dragging the full weight of the carcass over a distance perhaps of several miles.' In addition to the discarded bone there are 'a large number of flint tools of the distinctive Late Upper Palaeolithic "long-blade industry", including long blades, crested blades, hammer stones, burins, long-blade cores and "bruised" blades, so-called because they seem to have been damaged by chopping up antler and bone. The flint pieces can be refitted together, suggesting the blades were made on the spot for the act of butchery and then abandoned.' Because the site at Staines is only a few miles south of Uxbridge further research will endeavour to discover whether or not there is a connection between the two sites.

THE PICT'S KNOWE

Threats to the survival of ancient monuments take different forms; at the henge monument in Scotland known as the Pict's Knowe, some two miles south-west of Dumfries, the problem was rabbits! This henge monument, a ditch surrounded by a low external bank, had been so damaged by cattle-trampling and rabbit-burrowing that excavation was required. The work is described in *Current Archaeology* (number 141, December 1994/January 1995) and attention is drawn to a find of particular interest, namely an ard plough, recovered from the ditch where it may have been deliberately placed. It is reported that 'The ard is composed of a single member, evidently made from a branch of a tree and a part of the trunk, which forms a bulbous weight at one end. The beam is flattened and perforated in three places: once to allow attachment to some means of traction, once for a steering stilt, and once for a wooden spike or share, found in position.' The potential significance of this find is that: 'The ards discovered hitherto in Britain have all been of Iron Age or Roman date, but this new discovery in a henge monument suggests a much earlier date. While any pronouncement must await forthcoming accelerator radio-carbon dates, the ard is quite possibly the oldest in the British Isles and is potentially older than any from Europe north of

the Swiss lake villages. We know that the plough must have existed earlier than this in northern Europe because ard marks have been recognized in a series of old land surfaces.'

BRONZE AGE TRACKWAYS

As redevelopment proceeds along the north bank of the River Thames and in the London Docklands Development Corporation area, important discoveries have been made in excavations into the water-logged subsoil on sites scheduled for housing and retail development. An account is given, with details of the various sites in Rainham, Barking, Dagenham, Beckton and Silvertown, in *Current Archaeology* (number 143, June 1995). It explains that 'Timber trackways have been discovered in east London in the former marshlands leading down to the River Thames. Over the last 10,000 years the south-east of England has been sinking and as a result the level of the River Thames has been rising. The basic subsoil is gravel: behind the flood plain is a gravel terrace along which runs the modern A13 road from London to Tilbury. Along the foreshore the gravels are often covered by up to 10 metres of deposits. First comes a layer of peat: the build-up began in the Mesolithic/Neolithic transition, and is often 2–4 metres thick. It is within this peat that the trackways have now been discovered, often towards the top, and have been radiocarbon-dated to the Middle Bronze Age, the dates clustering between 1,600 and 1,000 BC (calibrated).' After a description of the various sites and their differing characteristics, there is a summary of the work to date: 'Seventeen sites in this area have now been excavated, of which ten have produced remains, six of them from the Bronze Age. At least four different methods of construction have been recorded, ranging from the brush-wood types, the cradle supported trackways through to the cut planks of Silvertown, the metalled causeway with fire-cracked flints at the Hays storage site at Dagenham. Their purpose remains obscure: the pollen evidence suggests that this was a period of agricultural intensification, with a dramatic change in the dominant vegetation from trees to grasses. Were they used for taking cattle down onto the marshes for summer grazing? In the Middle Ages there is a suggestion that the marshes were particularly favoured for fattening sheep because a parasite that lived on the marshes caused the sheep to grow unnaturally fat: was a similar phenomenon noted in the Bronze Age? Already these remarkable discoveries throw new light on London in the Bronze Age: there is, no doubt, more evidence to come.'

ROMAN LONDON

Lord Palumbo devoted many years to acquiring properties to the west of Bank underground station in the City of London with the intention of carrying out a major redevelopment, the plans for which created considerable public controversy. The granting of planning permission resulted in the opportunity to investigate No. 1 Poultry which is described in *Current Archaeology* (number 143, June 1995) as 'the biggest single archaeological excavation in the City of London in many years'. As the report explains 'Archaeologically, the Poultry site is very interesting. It lies on the western bank of the Walbrook, the small stream that divided Roman London into two low hills, about 100 metres north of the Mithraeum excavated by Prof. W. F. Grimes in 1954. Roman London's main east-west road crossed the site – it is sometimes called the *Via Decumana* though it could perhaps be described as part of Roman Watling Street.' In advance of excavation a number of test pits in the form of timber-shored shafts were dug in the basements of the Victorian building and the account in *Current Archaeology* summarizes the results. 'The first shaft, in the north-west, was on the highest and therefore the driest part of the site. Here evidence was found for an early mill on the Walbrook, for in the lowest part of the sequence there were post holes packed with quern stones. The second shaft, in the north-east, revealed more of what the site is expected to be all about, that is "wet" archaeology with wood well-preserved. At the bottom of the sequence was a series of early Roman timber revetted drains sealed by Roman timber buildings. The third shaft, in the southern part of the site, was deliberately placed on the predicted northern edge of Roman Watling Street – which was duly discovered, its position confirmed. The fourth shaft was located to the east, at the apex of the triangular site. This was expected to be the wettest part of the area, right on the edge of the Walbrook stream. A Victorian basement here had removed all the medieval material, but a great depth of Roman stratigraphy still survived. The evidence suggested that the Walbrook had been riveted with timber from a very early stage in its use. Most surprisingly the early-Roman Walbrook channel was sealed by a hollowed-out tree-trunk which formed a water-pipe bringing fresh water to the area – perhaps the first-century Walbrook had already become polluted. The most spectacular find also came from this shaft, a bronze hanging lamp complete with its chain and crescent-shaped bronze spacer which kept it from the wall.'

Work has also continued on another complex London site, that of the two amphitheatres at the Guildhall, concentrating on the Roman features outside the amphitheatres on the east of the site. An account is given in the *London Archaeologist* (volume 7, number 10, winter 1994) in which it is noted that amongst the backfill of an abandoned drainage system was 'one of the least-expected discoveries of the site. This was the largest single deposit of Roman glass ever found in the north-western provinces of the Empire. The glass is all cullet: fragments of up to 1,000 vessels, as well as glass-blowing waste and window glass. It was collected by the Romans for a reworking which never happened. Most fragments are small, and the waste contained filaments as fine as hair. All the deposits containing the glass were therefore painstakingly sieved to maximize retrieval: more than 60 kg were collected. The deposits do not appear to represent activity *in situ*: there was no evidence for glass-working in this precise location, though there was plenty of re-deposited associated material including furnace fragments. It is not likely, however, that the deposits had come from far, and glass-working in the upper Walbrook valley is well known.'

In *British Archaeology* (number 5, June 1995) is a note concerning another important discovery in the capital, namely, 'a massive late Roman church, possibly London's first cathedral, has been found by archaeologists on Tower Hill. The fourth-century church is almost identical in design to the church of St Thecla in Milan – the biggest church in what was then the capital of the Roman Empire – but the London church is larger.' Apparently 'built between AD 350 and AD 400 out of masonry reused from other buildings. It was decorated in part by a veneer of black marble, its walls were painted red, white, grey, pink and yellow and its floor was made of broken tiles in cement. The church may have been built by Magnus Maximus, who used Britain as a power base to become western Emperor between AD 383 and AD 388. It was burned down in the fifth century.'

EARLY CHRISTIANITY

A monastery at Llandough, near Penarth in South Glamorgan, previously known only from documentary sources, has been located and is described in *British Archaeology* (number 2, March 1995). It is reported that 'a cemetery has now been found there containing over 800 burials dating from late Roman times to the 11th century. The cemetery lies close to the site of a 2nd–4th century Roman villa, and contains several Christian burials of late Roman date, suggesting the monastery may have developed out of a late Roman Christian centre. Examples of ecclesiastical continuity from Roman times are common on the continent but extremely rare in Britain. The number of burials, and the discovery of high-status imported pottery, confirmed the cemetery as the site of Llandough monastery,' although no traces of the structure itself were found and it is thought to be beneath the present churchyard. 'The pottery, from olive-oil amphorae made in the eastern Mediterranean dating from *c.* AD 475–550, belongs to a type found at only a handful of sites in Britain – among them the early medieval royal centre at Dinas Powys 2 km to the south-west.

In *British Archaeology* (number 4, May 1995) it is reported that 'The skeleton of a man who may have been one of Ireland's first Christians has been found on a hilltop south-east of Ballyhaunis on the Roscommon Mayo border.' Buried east-west following Christian practice and without grave goods 'It has been radiocarbon-dated to AD 418–442 (at a

68 per cent probability) or AD 406–532 (95 per cent probability), consistent with the dates of St Patrick, patron saint of Ireland, who traditionally began his missionary work in AD 432.' Apparently 'it is the only certain fifth-century skeleton in Ireland, and the earliest Irish burial known to be aligned east-west. The location of the burial – at the foot of a standing stone, with a cremation and a traditional late Iron Age ring barrow cemetery nearby – suggests it took place at the point of transition between the pagan and Christian eras in Ireland.'

New Castle at Exeter

In *Current Archaeology* (number 141, December 1994/January 1995) it is reported that 'Exeter has acquired a new castle – thanks to South West Water Services. The castle, which was probably built in 1136, was thought to have been destroyed in 1852 when a new reservoir was built to supply water to Exeter.' When that reservoir was taken out of commission, the original castle was found in one corner complete with 11th/12th-century pottery which was found upon excavation. 'In 1136 Exeter and its principal castle at Rougemont in the corner of the medieval walls was held by Baldwin de Redvers. King Stephen gained admittance to the city and besieged Rougemont Castle for three months, building at the same time a siege castle 300 yards to the north of Rougemont Castle. It is this siege castle that has been rediscovered. It soon became clear that the Victorian water engineers had merely levelled off the tops of the circular embankment, thrown the spoil into the centre, but had otherwise left the castle intact.'

Hereford Cathedral

The public debate over the proposal that Hereford Cathedral should sell the *Mappa Mundi*, a unique medieval map of the world, has had archaeological consequences. The proposed sale was abandoned and a scheme devised to form a trust to raise money to display the map and the equally famous chained library. It was decided to build a two-storey building near the west end of Hereford Cathedral where both could be housed, the construction of the basement requiring archaeological excavation. The results of this work are reported in *Current Archaeology* (number 142, March/April 1995); it is explained that 'The importance of the site can be considered under three general headings: the burials, the evidence for the Saxon topography of the city, and the problems of excavation associated with a site of this nature.' Hereford is in origin Saxon, the Roman predecessor settlement being at Kenchester, about five miles to the west. 'The regular street plan of central Hereford has long been considered to represent a planned Saxon town and various defensive lines had been postulated.' Because of this regularity it had long been predicted that 'the line of Widemarsh Street, the main road from the north, if projected to the south, would meet up with the best ford across the River Wye, passing the edge of the Cathedral Close

on its way.' Excavations showed this prediction to be true in that 'a well-made road with four or five layers of cobbling running north and south' was found, together with a well-built drain running along one side. The most substantial discoveries lay between the Saxon road and the cathedral. These included burials interpreted as dating from a cemetery which had perhaps surrounded the postulated Saxon cathedral, as well as buildings between the road and the cathedral cemetery, the purpose of which is unknown. What is certain is that they did not serve their purpose for long because 'the basement was eventually used as a cess pit in which over a metre of waste matter accumulated. Amongst this unsavoury deposit were the bones of dogs and cats, but the most remarkable object was a late Saxon sword. This appeared to be still perfectly usable but presumably whoever had dropped it must have felt that the cost of recovery from the murky depths would exceed its value: it was left for the archaeologists. There was no apparent ceiling to the pit and the next event was when a pit was dug which destroyed the south side of the cellar.' It is suggested that this pit was probably dug to provide gravel for the building of the new cathedral sometime between 1107 and 1115. The pit was reused as a convenient place in which to put bones disturbed when the foundations of the new cathedral were made. This Hereford charnel pit was 'totally chaotic. It is estimated that there could have been 5,000 re-interred there. An effort had been made to place about two skulls at the west end, but otherwise the bones were all higgledy piggledy. Gruesomely, in among this vast array of bones were 23 fully or partially articulated bodies. It was apparent that some had been in a state of decay, presumably having been re-interred shortly after their original burial. But there were several articulated burials correctly oriented which were presumably added to this mass grave while the bones were still being moved. In one case there was even an attempt to make a proper grave with pillow stones around the head and elsewhere five children were laid out side by side. In each case the bodies were laid on charnel and more charnel was then dumped on top. A trackway leading up to the south of the pit may have been where the carts had come bringing their loads of bones to be thrown in. The whole process can be worked out. When the foundations for the new cathedral were being dug, the soil was sieved, the bones were then put onto a cart and taken to the charnel pit while the soil was put to one side. This was eventually dumped over the top of the charnel forming a 2 metre-thick layer still containing the very small bones typically from hands and feet.' Subsequently the pit was levelled and the area became a proper cemetery in which nearly 1,000 graves were excavated. 'There was, however, yet more excitement for the archaeologists, for cut into this cemetery were three carefully dug rectangular pits used as mass graves – probably for plague burials. One contained 120 bodies; there were 50 from the second and 12 from the third – but only parts of these pits fell within the excavated area. They appeared to date to the late 14th or early 15th centuries, which would fit in well with the Black Death. Once again the grim rite can be appreciated. We should imagine the bodies being brought in by the cartload. The pit had already been dug and as far as possible the bodies were laid in carefully: but time was short, and if the bodies were too long, the legs were flexed in order to fit; some were put in the wrong way round. After each cartload, a layer of distinctive red clay was laid over the bodies, presumably to prevent disease and smell.' The site continued as a cemetery until the early 16th century and then became a garden and in 1741 a timber yard. The archaeologists were able to establish the sequence of developments of the site until the 1850s when the Close was landscaped.

THE HEMINGTON BRIDGES

'The largest known medieval timber structure in eastern England after the roof of Lincoln Cathedral has recently been discovered in a former bed of the River Trent. These were the remains of three medieval bridges recently unearthed in a gravel quarry at Hemington near Castle Donington.' Thus begins an account of these remarkable discoveries in *Current Archaeology* (number 140, September/November 1994) in which it is explained that the three bridges are of 11th-century, early 13th-century and mid 13th-century date, with the last being the first to be found. While all the bridges are of the greatest interest, particular note may be taken of the earliest three planks, which were given a preliminary felling date of AD 1096. It is noted that 'This was a very unusual form of bridge structure and is unique on several counts. It is the only surviving example of an 11th-century bridge across a major river, and employs previously unknown structural forms and jointing. The remains consisted of two diamond-shaped pier bases laid onto the riverbed, each made out of four massive squared beams with internal horizontal braces to form a base frame. In the four corners of the frames were braced upright posts, holding together planked revetments – essentially forming wooden boxes, 8 × 5 metres across, looking not unlike log cabins. The bases had been filled with several tonnes of sandstone rubble to provide ballast and stability.' The significance of this earliest bridge lies in the fact that 'It combines the "earth-fast" (set in the ground) building techniques of Anglo-Saxon England with the timber-framed technology which was to become commonplace in the 12th century. Since no 11th-century timber buildings survive above ground, this bridge provides unique information about the development and construction of buildings at this time.'

MEDIEVAL WESTMINSTER

Archaeological investigations in advance of tunnelling and other works associated with the construction of the Jubilee Line are already showing interesting results. In the *London Archaeologist* (spring 1995) a report is given on the discovery of a previously unknown medieval building in Parliament Square, Westminster. It is reported that 'The stone structure was constructed across the line of an earlier ditch which ran parallel to it. This ditch included a large post hole and may have been a late 12th-century boundary ditch, possibly defining the northern edge of the Abbey precinct. Only the northern and southern walls of the building were found; the east and west walls remain unexcavated.' It is estimated that the whole building could have been perhaps 89 feet long, while 'The two walls were constructed from ragstone, greensand, caen-stone and some chalk; the northern wall contained at least one piece of Roman brick.' As to the dating of the walls, it is reported that 'Both construction cuts contained pottery dating to 1230–1530. Both walls were cut into an alluvial clay layer though not definitely at the same time. Two rubbish pits, contemporary with the buildings' construction were cut into the alluvial clay. One, containing domestic refuse at the base and building waste at the top, was dated to 1150–1300; the other to 1200–1250. Sealing the pits was a floor laid in crushed greensand.' It is further noted that this floor 'had a thin plaster skim and was sealed by a later clay floor which also had a hard plaster skim. These were sealed by three successive layers of occupation material interleaved with two areas of floor patching, and were predominantly dated to 1150–1350 or 1230–1350. The occupation layers contained animal bone, charcoal and fragments of white plaster painted with red stripes, some of which were also found in a dumped layer against the north wall. This suggests that the walls were originally plastered.' The account in the *London Archaeologist* describes the development of the building and surrounding area until the former was demolished in about 1800.

JEWISH CEMETERY

As so often in archaeology, the true significance of a site is only apparent after extensive research and publication of the report. So it is with the publication by the York Archaeological Trust of the results of the excavation of the Jewbury Cemetery, York, in 1980. According to *Current Archaeology* (number 140, September/November 1994) 'This was the excavation of the Jewish burial ground at York, excavated in 1980, in something of a hurry in advance of redevelopment by Sainsburys. The Jewish authorities were not altogether happy about this and no sooner were the excavations completed than they insisted that all the bones should be reburied. The Trust and its collaborators had just three weeks to complete all the post-excavation measurements and analysis. Work went on day and night and in the event it just enabled them to finish measuring the bones in time. It was the burial ground not only for the Jews of York but also, until they got their own cemetery, for the Jews of Lincoln whose bodies often arrived in York somewhat the worse for the delay. There are lots of interesting similarities and differences with the Christian cemeteries of medieval York. (The main comparison is with St Helen's, a poor Christian cemetery excavated by the Trust: they would now like to excavate a medieval cemetery in a rich quarter of York for a full comparison). The Jews were buried in wooden coffins nailed together with iron nails, quite contrary to modern Jewish practice which forbids the use of iron. However, the cemetery was extremely neatly laid out with none of the inter-cutting of earlier burials that is a feature of the Christian cemeteries. Medieval writers often refer to Jewish cemeteries as being the 'Garden of the Jews' – *Hortus Iudeorum* – immaculately kept by a garden keeper and it is clear that the York burial ground lived up to this high standard.'

AIR POLLUTION

Those concerned with the quality of the air we breathe may be surprised to learn that the problem is not specifically a modern one. In a report in *British Archaeology* (number 2, March 1995) it is stated that 'Medieval air pollution was severe enough to damage the health of people living in towns, according to a study of sinusitis in medieval skeletons. The study of more than 2,000 skeletons from urban and rural sites found significantly more maxillary sinusitis in urban populations, which the researchers attribute to the effects of living in a smoky atmosphere polluted by industrial fumes. Infection of the maxillary sinuses is caused by environmental pollutants and dental disease, and chronic infection leaves its mark on bone. Skeletons were studied from the pre-urban site at Raunds (AD 850–1150), the village of Wharram Percy (AD 900–1600) and the poor urban parish of St Helen-on-the-Walls in York (AD 1000–1600).'

BERSHAM IRONWORKS

Interest in sites of industrial archaeological importance continues and one such to be investigated is the Bersham Ironworks near Wrexham in north Wales. Probably established in the middle of the 17th century, the ironworks was producing cannons and steam cylinders by the end of the 18th and some of the 12-pounder cannon on board HMS *Victory* at the Battle of Trafalgar were made at Bersham. The old works closed in 1812. *Current Archaeology* (number 141, December 1994/January 1995) explains that investigations included 'The oldest railway excavation in the world.' The significance lies in the fact that 'the first railways were wooden railways, called waggonways, and were initially constructed entirely out of wood and have therefore not survived. The discovery of a 40-metre length at Bersham … came as quite a surprise. It had been preserved because the wood had carbonized, and included a primitive set of points, which were lifted for eventual display. The waggonway appears to have been built to bring coal and iron ore to the blast furnace at the Bersham works.' It is suggested that it dates to the decade between 1753 and 1763.

'Waggonways can be divided into two separate traditions, each with a distinctive gauge: the Newcastle tradition gauge varied between four and five feet, while the gauge of the Coalbrookedale (Shropshire) tradition was mostly around 3ft 6in. It has been suggested that the difference is due to the different methods of operation. In the north-east the mines were deep, the coal was brought to the surface up vertical shafts and then transferred into wagons to be taken to its eventual destination. In Coalbrookedale the mines were often adits cut horizontally into the side of the hill, so that the waggonways could go directly up the coalface itself resulting in the waggons, and therefore the gauge, being smaller than their northern counterparts. The Bersham waggonway gauge of 4ft suggests that it was built under northern influence.'

HAMPTON COURT GARDENS

The Privy Garden at Hampton Court Palace was formally reopened by the Prince of Wales. After a major fire in 1986, the Historic Royal Palaces Agency decided to restore King William III's Privy Garden, which was laid out with the palace. For the first time in 200 years it is now possible to view the façade of Wren's palace as it was intended to be seen. The trees in the garden have been clipped so that the palace is once more visible from the river. The positions of paths, lawns, steps and statue bases have been identified and the original flower beds dug into the river terrace gravel have been discovered.

Architecture

OFFICES FOR THE INLAND REVENUE
Nottingham
Architect: Michael Hopkins & Partners

This new headquarters office complex for the Inland Revenue is the result of a limited architectural competition held in 1992 after a government building project already under construction had been abandoned. The potential for disruption in the relocation process that had been set in train led to a demand for a speedy construction period. The architects' winning design divided the 40,000 square metres of accommodation into a number of separate buildings, which also assisted a phased occupation as groups of workers became available to move in.

The six office buildings occupy a site on the south bank of the Nottingham Canal, overlooked by Nottingham Castle. They are disposed in a roughly symmetrical arrangement of two quadrangle blocks and four L-shaped buildings. These create a pattern of interconnecting streets and define a central space alongside the canal which is occupied by a dramatic tented amenity building. The streets are treated as tree-lined boulevards, the central one laid out on a long curved line connecting the canal's edge at one end to the town at the other.

The design of the predominantly four-storey quadrangle blocks was dictated by the client's requirement for an energy-saving approach which avoided the use of air-conditioning and artificial cooling and maximized the use of ambient energy. The client also required an internal environment capable of a degree of control by its users, with as many as possible able to open their windows if desired. The solution is a building of substantial mass with loadbearing precast piers faced with a red brick matching the traditional Nottingham brick colour, and precast concrete floor units formed as shallow vaults that span the building to create column-free space.

The structural arrangement is expressed on the exterior, giving rise to a rhythmical treatment in which the projecting brick piers, which decrease in width at each ascending floor level by means of a tapered concrete capital, are linked by the shallow curves of the exposed ends of the concrete vaults. The concrete capitals are shaped to receive the projecting ends of the vaults so that the pieces interlock visually and structurally. The uppermost storey cantilevers forwards from the main plane; here the vaulted soffits of the concrete floor units are clearly expressed, resolving gracefully to a thin horizontal band supporting the glazed wall of the attic storey.

Perhaps the most memorable features of the design are the cylindrical towers placed at each external corner of the office buildings. These contain spiral staircases for internal access and escape, and are constructed in steel frame infilled entirely with glass blocks. Rising above the general roof line, the towers have shallow-domed oversailing roofs which can be automatically raised and lowered. They act as thermal chimneys, utilizing the stack-effect to draw the hot air that accumulates under the exposed vaulted soffits through the offices into the stair towers and out at the top.

The attic storey is roofed with a pitched steel truss structure fully expressed beneath a prefabricated panelled roofing system. Here the internal environment is controlled by a bank of extract louvres placed along both sides of a central linear skylight. This also allows daylight into the centre of the office space, which, being cantilevered over the lower floors, has an internal span of 18 metres rather than the 13.6-metre span of the lower floors.

As the structural bays of the perimeter are almost completely infilled with glazing, a variety of solar control measures had to be developed to avoid excessive solar heat gain. The most obvious is the horizontal projecting glass light-shelves placed at the head of the full-height opening windows just below the springing point of the expressed concrete vaults. The shelves have a reflective upper surface, so that daylight bounces off through a clerestory window containing a Venetian blind fixed at a 45° angle and up onto the shallow curved surfaces of the concrete vaults, thus diffusing natural light into the interior off the pale concrete surfaces. The lower surface of each glass light shelf is 'fritted' to reduce the amount of light that can fall directly onto the windows.

The vertical windows are also shaded by an external steel balustrade of angled slats spanning between the projecting brick piers. The attic storey windows are protected by a *brise-soleil* (sun-break) projecting at eaves level, again with angled slats on projecting brackets that support a pressed metal gutter section. These devices all contribute to a richly detailed exterior façade of substantial weight and dignity.

All the non-office functions have been placed in the central amenity building, which is a large tented structure roofed with an expansive translucent membrane. It is laid out as two shallow curving wings of accommodation either side of a timber-floored multi-purpose games court, with the reception area placed centrally at the front. A crèche is located at the rear overlooking the canal, and the upper levels of accommodation are given over to a bar, cafeteria and restaurant for staff use.

The great tented roof is supported via suspension cables from four huge masts set at an outward-leaning angle from pin-joint bases atop stubby columns rising through the ground floor. The edges of the main roof and the lower side canopies are in turn supported off shorter, narrower-angled struts tied to counterweight footings at ground level. The roof shape itself is segmented, the curving panels separated by thin wedges of glazing which allow light into the sports hall below.

The development officially opened in May 1995 and is sure to prove a high-quality and user-friendly workplace, visually stimulating and of noticeably human scale despite its overall size. It is also a landmark in the quest for a more environmentally-conscious and energy-efficient form of office building.

PRIVATE RESIDENCE
Baggy Point, N. Devon
Architect: Anthony Hudson Architects

Baggy Point is a rocky promontory on the North Devon coast sticking out into the Bristol Channel, and the setting for an unusual and striking new house. Located on the site of a 19th-century hotel which was demolished to make way for the new building, Baggy House provides a holiday home with ample accommodation for both family and guests, arranged to take full advantage of the exposed coastal setting.

The site is defined by an existing stone wall to the east and by a long hedge that immediately borders the coastal path above the cliffs. In order to ensure unobstructed views over the hedge, the principal living areas have been placed at first-floor level. The numerous level changes between them and the adjoining spaces reflects the general slope of the ground as it rises away from the path. The plan form is complex and irregular, an ingeniously adapted series of interlocking and overlapping L-shapes derived from a tartan grid, but without the rigidity and regularity that a grid implies. To the north and east the exterior is solid and opaque, a geometric jumble of battered white-rendered walls with a few small window openings and a modest bay window overlooking a sheltered garden terrace, as the building tucks itself obliquely into the rising ground beneath a series of pitched slate roofs that echo vernacular forms. To the south and west living rooms step down towards a raised terrace, and large expanses of glazing under a sweeping copper-clad canopy frame panoramic views of the sea.

Entry to the house is from the driveway to the east. A huge sloping-sided chimney marks the position of the front door, which is flanked by the solid block of the kitchen and guest bedrooms to one side and the garage with its garden terrace to the right. Inside, the hall swells out round a free-standing granite column as a slate staircase curves away to the upper levels. Further steps lead down towards the playroom tucked under the main living space and thence out to the lower terrace beyond. The kitchen and utility rooms are immediately to the left through doors opening off a small recess.

This is the beginning of a complex pattern of interconnecting spaces and changes in level. From the kitchen and breakfast area, steps lead down into the playroom in the centre of the house and up into the dining room, with its south-facing sweep of windows overlooking a narrow paved terrace atop a grassy bank. At the far end of the dining room a curved dusky pink wall encloses a small private garden room, with glazed screens projecting forwards to the south-west corner. The terrace sweeps round this protected vantage point and back to the dining room, from where a further short flight of steps leads up into the main living room. This has an open balustrade along the side overlooking the dining area, and windows looking out over the playroom terrace below. At the opposite side an opening leads into a corridor connecting with the west-facing suite of family bedrooms, and back to the first floor landing of the spiral stair ascending from the entrance hall.

From the first floor landing, a door opens onto the small garden courtyard over the garage, and in one corner steps lead up to the set of guest bedrooms placed at ascending levels over the kitchen and living areas. Two short flights and a quarter landing lead to the lowest of the three bedrooms which has a small open terrace tucked against the sheer white walls just outside. Ascending further, a flight of glass steps with open risers giving glimpses of the kitchen below leads on up to the second floor level. Here the square white-walled form of the two further bedrooms and a bathroom rises out of the complex of roof shapes below, and a long narrow terrace extends out into space. Yet below, in the open-plan living area, the only indication of this strong cubic form is in the L-shape of the canopy shading the outside terraces, and a single tapering laminated timber column, thickening towards the ceiling to take the load from the floors above at the outer corner.

Separated from the walls above by a narrow slot of glazing, the canopy is constructed from a plywood stressed skin glued and stapled to a series of aerofoil-shaped plywood ribs. Clad on the leading edges and underside with pre-patinated copper sheeting, which gives it its bright greenish-blue colour, it is provided with a continuous recess for a roller shutter box on the line of the windows and a recessed gutter along the rear upper edge. Three circular porthole-like openings are cut through the centre of the canopy to let light through to the rooms below.

The glazed walls below the canopy are in fact a series of vertically-sliding glazed screens, which can be fully retracted with the aid of motorized jacking devices into a chamber set directly below the external terrace, so that in fine weather the windows can not just be opened but removed from sight altogether. The vertically-sliding screens are constructed in three horizontal sections. The lowest section comprises glazed sliding doors on a cedar cill, which is fixed to the main steel section support.

The topmost section terminates in a tapering section clad in copper on the underside and capped with a cedar headpiece that acts as a threshold when the screens are fully retracted.

This disappearing glass wall is typical of the confident and dynamic handling of materials, forms and spaces evident throughout the entire building. The design contrasts angular cubic geometry with soft curving surfaces, and homely vernacular materials with technological constructions while playing an inventive and complicated three-dimensional game with its component parts. This is an exceptional house, possessing not only the complexity, quality and range of facilities required by a family residence, but also the vitality, informality and flexibility appropriate to a holiday home.

STUDENT HOUSING
St John's College, Oxford
Architect: MacCormac Jamieson Prichard

St John's Garden Court is a new student residence on a long narrow site bordering Parks Road, with accommodation in study bedrooms for about 50 undergraduates and a range of communal facilities. Defined by the centuries-old high stone wall that encloses the Fellows' Garden to the south and by existing squash courts and sports buildings to the north and west, the site previously contained a group of 19th-century buildings. Of these, the only one to be retained is a small terraced building fronting the street, which has been adapted and incorporated into the new complex to provide the main entrance to the Court and its porters' lodge.

The architects have displayed considerable ingenuity and imagination in the way they have layered the spaces vertically so as to achieve in effect two ground levels, thus making maximum use of the very cramped site. This device has created a contrast between the cave-like 'underworld' that contains the major communal facilities, and the formal garden court above which is the setting for the pavilions and towers of the tightly clustered bedroom blocks. The two worlds connect in numerous ways via interconnecting staircases, and daylight floods down into the undercroft through small glazed pavilion-like roof-light structures and a large central oculus which is open to the sky.

The retained 19th-century building facing the street defines the eastern edge of a small intimate courtyard between it and the bulk of the new building. At one end of this courtyard stands a small detached two-storey building that contains a suite of small music rooms. The main four-storey range of study bedrooms forms the northern edge of the new building, with narrower wings extending southwards at each end to contain and define the south-facing garden court. The garden court extends across three-quarters of the site area, its southern boundary set back from the Fellows' Garden wall to reveal the paved and landscaped lower levels.

Below the leading edge of the garden an open-sided cloister walk leads from the entrance courtyard into the heart of the building. The plan form at ground level is based on three large square spaces, that nearest the entrance enclosing the reception and dining hall, with the furthest away providing an auditorium with raked seating. The central space is the open 'atrium', with its large open oculus defining the precise centre point of the whole complex composition. The cloister route opens onto the south side of this space, with staircases rising on either side to the paved terraces above. Around the perimeter of the courtyard intricate glass screens, designed by the artist Alexander Beleschenko, frame the timber-slatted pairs of doors which lead into the adjoining rooms. On the central axis of this space a new, narrow opening has been cut into the old stone boundary wall to form another entrance, guarded by a wrought iron gate designed by Wendy Ramshaw.

The forms and spaces of the lowest level have a robust, over-scaled quality, with heavy clusters of chains suspended through small apertures from above to guide the flow of rainwater, and a detailed but monumental precast concrete structure that supports the garden court and buildings above.

It quickly becomes apparent that this building represents a triumph of precast concrete technology, employing a variety of finely engineered forms and a range of specialized finishes to impart the sculptural and textural qualities characteristic of traditional load-bearing stone buildings in the Classical style. The three major ground floor spaces are typical of this expertise, utilizing a structural grid 10.8 metres square and based on the plan concept of a square within a square. Four elongated L-shaped corner columns, rusticated above a plinth and textured by means of heavy point tooling, define the outer square, and by implication a smaller square at each corner, on the free corner of which sits a cluster of four square columns also rising from a plinth defining the four corners of the inner square. These provide the twin support points for a series of precast corner arch beams spanning away from the corners which in turn support central keystone-like sections to complete the square.

Set within the corners of this structural arched square are four precast pendentive sections supporting an *in situ* concrete dome 8.6 metres in diameter, pierced with a central opening into the glazed lanterns above, except in the central space where the covering dome is omitted. The finished structure is a composite one in that the individual precast forms were set up on site on timber formwork and centring, and then tied together using steel reinforcement bars and *in situ* concrete infill to create a continuous two-way spanning structure.

Above this compressed yet monumental undercroft, the construction, and the architecture, takes on progressively lighter forms. The massing of the study bedroom blocks reflects the underlying square-based geometry, with three heavily articulated sections responding to the format of the ground-floor plan and addressing the tripartite layout of the garden court, set out around the central oculus and the two counter-balancing lantern structures. Each section comprises two projecting wings, each of which rises beyond a central two-storey linking section to form a free-standing tower.

Here the construction is in load-bearing brick-work and masonry supporting *in situ* concrete floors, with individual column and wall elements highly articulated to give a very strong 'constructed' appearance. The creamy-buff brickwork is inter-rupted at floor levels by a double string course and masonry feature panels at the centres and corners. Each tower element terminates in a double-height room, with translucent clerestory panels and small gable roof-lights set within a system of masonry frames. The frames are articulated on each face by withdrawing each corner post away from its corner, a device repeated in the brick walls below, where adjacent brick jambs define a tall slit window in each corner.

Each pair of towers is joined together by a spiral staircase entered from the garden and featuring finely finished precast concrete open treads lit from the top by a glazed skylight. These stairs serve as the focal point for clusters of study bedrooms, each with communal kitchen and bathroom facilities opening off the landing. The study bedrooms sometimes appear as glazed boxes projecting out between adjacent towers to enjoy views over the court and surrounding gardens.

This complex building is an intimate and self-contained environment which unfolds its many subtleties only upon exploration. Spatial inter-relationships emerge, linking and separating the communal areas of the undercroft, the semi-public/semi-private courtyard garden, and the private study bedrooms in their lofty towers. The architec-ture is strong, positive and muscular, the detailing intricate and painstaking, the materials carefully selected and beautifully finished. This building demonstrates clearly that the traditions of collegiate life can still be the basis for imaginative and rewarding architecture.

WELSH WILDLIFE CENTRE
Near Cardigan, Dyfed, Wales
Architect: Niall Phillips Architects

Demand for all-purpose visitor centres has in-creased greatly in recent years with the growing interest in the countryside and environmental issues. The concept of visitor centres has received many different architectural interpretations, often dependent on local influences for the selection of materials and appropriate forms of construction. A limited design competition was held when Dyfed Wildlife Trust ac-quired a tract of land adjacent to the established Teifi Marshes nature reserve near Cardigan in 1992. The choice of site for the building was left to the architect, but the brief established a requirement for exhibition areas, a shop and restaurant, classroom and field laboratory, as well as a staff rest room, offices and ancillary accommodation. The selected scheme developed by Niall Phillips Architects placed the new building centrally within the re-serve, just to one side of a long ridge running east–west. The siting and building form have clearly taken into consideration the varied topography of the landscape and the needs of the functions housed in the centre. To the north of the ridge the land slopes down to River Teifi, while to the south a long grassy meadow lines a narrow valley defined by a further wooded east–west ridge.

The building utilizes the steep fall on the south side of the ridge to minimize the amount of land built over. It is tucked close in to the slope and arranged on three floor levels, enabling the topmost floor to emerge above the ridge line so that only one storey is visible from the reed beds to the north. On plan the building is arranged with a long curved spine of service accommodation following the line of the ridge. This contains the kitchen, lavatory facilities, stores, plant and offices. It is detailed in a traditional and solid way with a timber structural frame of Douglas fir, oak boarding for the external cladding, which is left untreated, and a curving pitched roof clad in cedar shingles, with exposed rafter ends. Windows are kept to a minimum, except at the upper level where the cladding is replaced by windows giving outlook from the café and a simple timber balustrade to an open observation deck at the east end.

The shop, exhibition and restaurant areas are arranged along the southern side of this range in a dramatic double-height glazed enclosure, giving dramatic views up and down the valley. The glazed wall follows the curve of the longer timber clad range, which projects beyond the return line of glazing at each end. It is a relatively sophisticated piece of construction in planar glass, supported by clear glass fins and metal patch fixings at the corners of individual panes, and is restrained laterally at eaves level. The roof is curved on section as well as on plan, and employs a series of curved laminated Douglas fir lattice trusses supported, by means of inserted steel connector plates, on a braced frame-work of Douglas fir columns and diagonal struts.

The restaurant balcony is set back from the line of glazing and is cantilevered out from the service range via a secondary row of timber columns. The horizontal bars of the balustrade are supported by flat steel plates that curve prominently on the outer face. The effect is of being in a very sophisticated tree-house.

The lower ground storey is set back below the cantilevered edge of the glazed pavilion structure. A battered natural slate base wraps around the ends of the office and the staff rest room, and is cut away in the centre to provide the teaching space with a bank of windows overlooking the valley floor. The slabs of slate are laid flat and roughly coursed, with a core of blockwork and a similar slate finish internally. However, they are not structural, the upper floors being supported on tubular metal columns and a blockwork spine wall, and this is recognized by the thin glazed strip inserted between the top of the slate wall and the soffit of the exhibition space floor.

Each of the floor levels is directly accessible from the surrounding landscape, although the decision to create three levels has required the inclusion of a lift. At the lowest level a long curved corridor has doors at each end connecting to paths at valley level. The principal entrance to the ground floor is set centrally in the rear elevation of the curved service spine, where another path leading from the car park passes between the building and the sloping valley side. This entrance position coincides with a bridge which spans from the centre of the top floor out to the top of the ridge to provide a third point of entry to the centre.

The centre was completed in March 1994 at a total cost of £600,000. Despite the use of traditional materials it is a contemporary building, full of contrasts between openness and solidity, traditional and modern forms of construction, concealment and display, yet sympathetically integrated into the landscape.

HEADQUARTERS BUILDING FOR CHANNEL 4 TELEVISION
Horseferry Road, London
Architect: Richard Rogers Partnership

Channel 4's decision to house its 550 staff in a single building led to the acquisition of a site in Horseferry Road, London, which was originally designated for housing. Permission was granted for the use of the site by Channel 4 provided an element of housing was retained, and a design for the new building was sought by means of a limited architectural competition held in 1991.

The new £35 million building maintains the integrity of the existing street pattern by placing what is predominantly office accommodation in two adjoining wings along the north and west sides of the site. Two blocks of housing are then placed along the other two sides, creating a large open space in the middle. The housing has been separately designed and developed. The rectangular wings of the new L-shaped building meet at the corner of Horseferry Road and Chadwick Street, and are joined by a recessed arc of vertical glazing flanked by dramatic tower elements, which focus onto a small paved piazza and frame the main entrance to the building.

The two towers, each markedly different in form and function, provide a dramatic sculptural statement. A stack of meeting rooms constructed as shiny metal and glass boxes hung from an externally expressed portal frame structure, and flanked by the smooth curved aluminium cladding of a stair tower, stands forward from the office wing to the left of the entrance. To the right, a much taller and thinner

tower contains the lift lobbies to three wall-climber lifts which are exposed externally to the street. The lifts are surmounted by lift gear machinery in three modular enclosures and coolers for the air-handling system. Boiler and extract flues rise up independently between the lift lobbies and a second metal-clad staircase tower. The whole composition is terminated by a tapering red communications mast capped with transmitting antennae and satellite dishes.

The approach to the main entrance is made on the diagonal through the centre line of the 'knuckle' between the two wings, where a delicate glazed canopy floats forward from the curved glass wall of the entrance lobby or 'atrium'. Entry to the building is gained by crossing a glass-floored bridge which spans a circular opening in the floor. This too is glazed, and is in fact a circular skylight lighting the lobby to the preview theatre located at basement level.

At the end of the bridge two glass revolving doors set into the glazed screen give entry to the reception foyer, a tall narrow curved space following the arc of the glazed screen and with a glazed rear wall which gives views out over the landscaped central garden. The spectacular entrance hall is given further dramatic impetus by projecting balcony walkways at each floor level linking the two wings of office accommodation. Metal brackets painted dark grey support a continuous metal fascia and a metal floor perforated with holes which are filled with glass disks. From these atrium galleries there are dramatic views towards Westminster Cathedral.

The most striking feature of this dramatic space is the curved arc of glass rising sheer through nearly five storeys. It is in fact a suspended façade, hung from the top by a radiating structure of steel fingers which spring from three large metal bosses located on top of three of the main structural concrete columns. The red-painted metal fingers are I-section members swelling in the middle and tapered at the ends, and their outer ends are supported by tie rods hung from steel masts which project upwards from the bosses. At each point of connection between the glazed wall and radiating supports, large spring fixings are positioned to allow for differential movement between the glass and the supporting steelwork. Jacks are incorporated at the junction of the steel supports and the concrete columns to permit adjustment to be made for longer term settlement movement.

Compared with the entrance and its marker towers, the main wings of the building are relatively restrained. They comprise an elegant aluminium window system in charcoal grey, providing floor to ceiling glazing, with the expressed bays divided into four horizontal strips between solid recessed spandrel panels. The upper and lower strips of glazing are shielded from the sun by means of grey-painted aluminium expanded mesh screens set in frames, which assist privacy and reduce solar heat gain. At ground level the cladding is recessed just behind the line of the round *in-situ* concrete perimeter columns to establish a single storey arcade.

This feature occurs again at the rear, where the curved glass façade of the restaurant overlooking the inner garden is pulled back from the main face of the 'knuckle' of offices overhead to provide a shaded terrace. The top storey of the curved knuckle, where the executive offices and board room are located, is also recessed to form a wide timber-decked roof terrace, which is partially shaded by a wide canti-levered band of louvres.

Internally the office interiors are fairly conven-tional air-conditioned spaces, the typical layout incorporating cellular offices around the perimeters and open-plan offices in the interior. Glazed parti-tions and translucent doors provide a measure of daylight and glimpses of views out for the internal offices.

Channel 4's main role is the commissioning and publishing of programmes as opposed to hands-on production, and so there is only one production studio in the building. This is a substantial black box buried in the basement, where the broadcasting and production-related facilities are also located. At this level also is the preview theatre, a totally enclosed space set under the paved corner forecourt. Access to this space is gained from the main foyer by means of a curved staircase following the inner line of the glazed entrance wall down to a circular foyer space with a glazed rooflight. This is the glazed well which the entrance bridge spans, and affords yet more dramatic glimpses of the soaring glass façade above.

This is an eye-catching and visually stimulating building that provides a very apposite reflection of Channel 4's public image and appears to satisfy the varying demands of the activities which it has to accommodate.

The Seven Wonders of the World

I THE PYRAMIDS OF EGYPT

The pyramids are found from Gizeh, near Cairo, to a southern limit 60 miles (96 km) distant. The oldest is that of Zoser, at Saqqara, built *c.*2650 BC. The Great Pyramid of Cheops (built *c.*2580 BC) covers 13.12 acres (756 × 756 ft (230.4 × 230.4 m) at the base) and was originally 481 ft (146.6 m) in height

II THE HANGING GARDENS OF BABYLON

These adjoined Nebuchadnezzar's palace, 60 miles (96 km) south of Baghdad. The terraced gardens, ranging from 75 ft to 300 ft (25–90 m) above ground level, were watered from storage tanks on the highest terrace

III THE TOMB OF MAUSOLUS

Built at Halicarnassus, in Asia Minor, by the widowed Queen Artemisia about 350 BC. The memorial originated the term mausoleum

IV THE TEMPLE OF ARTEMIS AT EPHESUS

Ionic temple erected about 350 BC in honour of the goddess and burned by the Goths in AD 262

V THE COLOSSUS OF RHODES

A bronze statue of Apollo, set up about 280 BC. According to legend it stood at the harbour entrance of the seaport of Rhodes

VI THE STATUE OF ZEUS

Located at Olympia in the plain of Elis, and constructed of marble inlaid with ivory and gold by the sculptor Phidias, about 430 BC

VII THE PHAROS OF ALEXANDRIA

A marble watch tower and lighthouse on the island of Pharos in the harbour of Alexandria, built *c.*270 BC

Bequests to Charity

The alphabetical list below represents some of the principal charitable bequests from wills published since the last edition. Other bequests, expenses and inheritance tax have to be deducted from the net value of each estate shown below, so the exact amount bequeathed to the charities is uncertain.

The largest bequests to charity this year were mostly made by women: Dorothy Turner left £7.8 million; Ruth Agutter left the bulk of £6.2 million; Alice Hawkins left £4.8 million; Winifred Bassham and Rosi Schilling both left over £3 million; and Essie Elliot left £2.5 million.

Well-known personalities in this list include Phyllis Whitby-Cradock, better known as the TV cook Fanny Cradock, who left the residue of her estate to the Institute of Child Health's 'Help a Child to See' fund. Arthur Perry was the founder of the theatrical production company H. M. Tennent, with the late Hugh 'Binkie' Beaumont. Lady Du Cros was one of the first women to ferry aircraft from factories to the squadrons in the Second World War. William Ward was a former director of education in Mauritius and adviser at the Colonial Office, while Alexander Birch was a former Deputy High Commissioner in Australia.

Those who left their whole estate to charity included New Zealander David Burns, the medievalist Dr Margaret Gibson, and Ruby Sedgwick. Florence Masters left all her estate to the National Trust, who also benefitted by receiving the residues of the estates of Phyllis Paine and Alice Robinson. The Army Benevolent Fund was left the residues of the estates of Edith Gorlinsky and Ernest Johnson.

The church architect Stephen Dykes Bower left large bequests to St Paul's Cathedral Choir School and the Royal College of Organists, and the residue of his estate to extend, embellish or repair Bury St Edmunds Cathedral, or any other charitable purpose his trustees determined. Alec Jessop left most of his estate betwen his local church at Bridlington, Beverley Minster and York Minster, all for restoration purposes. Stanley Lord left a large part of his estate to Chester Cathedral Fabric Fund, and Richard Wall left much of his estate among churches in Northamptonshire, Leicestershire and Shropshire. Wilfred Hadfield, the traffic control expert who invented the yellow line parking system, left half the residue of his estate to Jesus College, Cambridge, part to be used to assist engineering students; and Kathleen Verney, the sister of the pianist Harriet Cohen, left a large number of charitable bequests for musical purposes, including her sister's Memorial Trust, and the residue of her estate, including her Bluthner grand piano, to Somerville College, Oxford. Margery Maplethorpe made bequests to Jesus College, Oxford, and London University to establish fellowships in pharmacy.

Two unusual bequests not listed below were those of Norah Dearsley of Eastbourne who left some £100,000 betwen St Paul's Cathedral, for its cleaning and maintenance, and the Secretary of State for the Environment for the cleaning and maintenance of the Houses of Parliament. Elsie Bushen of Torquay left nearly £2 million, and, after bequests of just £2,000, left the rest for the relief of the National Debt because 'it has throughout my long life been a privilege which I have appreciated to be a citizen of the United Kingdom'.

Ruth Pattinson Agutter, of Sheringham, Norfolk, £6,252,861 – the residue equally between the RSPCA, Leukaemia Research Fund and Age Concern

Kathlyn Angell, of Castlenau, London sw13, £1,243,539 – the residue equally between the RNLI, National Anti-Vivisection Society, Donkey Sanctuary, Sidmouth, International League for the Protection of Horses, PDSA, Horses and Ponies Protection Society, Bransby Home of Rest for Horses, British Union for the Abolition of Vivisection, and the RSPCA, for the use of the special investigation department in regard to horses sent abroad for slaughter

Richard Raymond Archer, of Colyton, Devon, £726,493 – the residue equally between the Imperial Cancer Research Fund and Cancer Research Campaign

Winifred Mabel Bassham, of Norwich, £3,844,137 – the residue equally between the British Heart Foundation, Imperial Cancer Research Fund and Age Concern

Gladys Edith Bates, of Boscombe, Dorset, £573,404 – one sixth of the residue each to the Save the Children Fund and Cheshire Foundation, and one ninth of the residue each to the RSPCA, International League for the Protection of Horses, Crusade Against All Cruelty to Animals, RSPB, International Fund for Animal Welfare and the Greek Animal Welfare Fund

Pauline Beaumont, of Bexhill, E. Sussex, £435,620 – seven-tenths of the residue to the British Diabetic Association and three-tenths of the residue to the Cancer Research Campaign

Alexander Hope Birch, of Clevedon, Avon, £244,831 – his entire estate equally between the Institute of Cancer Research, Distressed Gentlefolk's Aid Association and the Diplomatic Service Welfare Fund

Marjorie Birnie Boothman, of Blackburn, Lancs, £692,972 – the residue equally between the Blackburn Support Group at Honresfield Cheshire Home, Littleborough, NSPCC, Children's Socity, Barnardo's and Imperial Cancer Research Fund

Stephen Ernest Dykes Bower, of Quendon, Essex, £2,092,522 – the residue for any extension to Bury St Edmunds Cathedral, the embellishment or repair of its fabric or for such other charitable purposes as his trustees determine

Edith Mary Brewer, of Stratford-upon-Avon, Warks, £2,443,983 – 5 per cent of the residue each to Gifford House, Worthing, Counsel and Care for the Elderly, Cancer Research Campaign, Imperial Cancer Research Fund, BLESMA, League of Remembrance,

Not Forgotten Association, Cheshire Foundation, Royal Star and Garter Home, Richmond, Alexandra Rose Day, Age Concern England and National Benevolent Institution, and 4 per cent of the residue each to the Royal School for the Blind, Leatherhead, Methodist Homes for the Aged, Burma Star Association, Salvation Army, British Heart Foundation, Arthritis and Rheumatism Council, National Canine Defence League, Royal British Legion, National Benevolent Fund for the Aged and RUKBA

Edna Mary Brun, of Great Barr, W. Midlands, £841,183 – the residue equally between the Alzheimers Disease Society, and the Elizabeth Svendsen Trust for Children and Donkeys, Sidmouth

David Joseph Burns, of Onehunga, New Zealand, £2,235,980 in England and Wales – all his estate in the UK to the Jewish Philanthropic Association for Israel and the Middle East

Emmeline Nora Waley Cohen, of Cambridge, £1,483,487 – three-eighths of the residue each to the Cambridge Hearing Trust, and the Aurological Department of Addenbrookes Hospital, Cambridge

Phyllis Nan Sortain Whitby-Cradock, of Hailsham, East Sussex, £199,899 – the residue to the Help a Child to See fund at the Institute of Child Health

Eric Melville Batting Dashwood, of Croydon, Surrey, £427,326 – his entire estate equally between the RNLI, Cancer Reasearch Campaign, RNIB, Royal Association in Aid of the Deaf and Dumb, and Distressed Gentlefolk's Aid Association

Betty Florence Deasley, of Beckenham, Kent, £1,059,932 – the residue equally between the Imperial Cancer Research Fund, NSPCC and British Heart Foundation

Dorothy Deighan, of Macclesfield, Cheshire, £328,552 – the residue to UNICEF

Lady Rosemary Theresa Du Cros, of Parkham, Bideford, Devon, £548,497 – one-third of the residue each to the RSPCA and Japan Animal Welfare Society, and one-sixth of the residue each to SPANA and British Union for the Abolition of Vivisection

Essie Joan Elliot, of Bocking Braintree, Essex, £2,542,446 – the residue to the Essex Naturalists Trust

Constance Augusta Fletcher, of Bexhill, E. Sussex, £307,439 – the residue to the National Trust

Wilfred Ivan Madge-Forman, of Canford Cliffs, Dorset, £1,161,189 – £1,000 and one-eighth of the residue each to the Seamen's Friendly Society of St Paul, Shipwrecked Fishermen and Mariners Benevolent Society, SPANA and RSPB, and one-eighth of the residue to the International Fund for Animal Welfare

Margaret Gertrude Fulks, of Bexhill, E. Susex, £544,224 – the residue equally between Shelter, British Red Cross Society and Oxfam

Margaret Templeton Gibson, of Oxford, £165,674 – her entire estate to the University of London, for the Warburg Institute

Edith Winifred Gorlinsky, of Grosvenor Square, London w1, £1,698,246 – the residue to the Army Benevolent Fund

Wilfred Hadfield, of Windsor, Berks, £549,913 – 50 per cent of the residue to Jesus College, Cambridge, 10 per cent of the residue each to Holy Trinity Church, Windsor, Thames Valley Hospice, Windsor, Gardeners Royal Benevolent Society and Intermediate Technology, and 5 per cent of the residue each to the Children's Society and Age Concern England

Miles Aubrey Handy, of Morebath, Tiverton, Devon, £729,887 – one-fifth of the residue each to the Devon Gardens Trust, National Trust, RSPB and Leukaemia Research Fund

Helen Elizabeth Hanson, of Parbold, Lancs, £1,589,429 – half the residue equally between the parish of Parbold, LEPRA, Wildfowl and Wetlands Trust, Council for the Protection of Rural England, Lancashire Trust for Nature Conservation, NSPCC, Oxfam, RNID, Royal Commonwealth Society for the Blind, Cancer Research Campaign, Imperial Cancer Research Fund, Salvation Army and Puppet Centre Trust

Adrienne Karin Harker, of Woolton, Liverpool, £920,726 – the residue equally between the RSPB, RNIB, RSPCA, Association for International Cancer Research, Royal Society for Nature Conservation, and Liverpool Area Health Authority for the cardio-thoracic unit at Broadgreen Hospital

William Harris, of Copt Heath, Solihull, W. Midlands, £1,048,335 – half the residue to the RSPCA, and one-quarter of the residue each to Birmingham Dogs Home, and the Donkey Sanctuary, Sidmouth

Alice Elizabeth Margaret Hawkins, of Southbourne, Dorset, £4,851,520 – the residue equally between Age Concern England, Blue Cross, British and Foreign Bible Society, British Red Cross Society, Christian Aid, Cheshire Foundation, Barnardo's, Donkey Sanctuary, Sidmouth, Guide Dogs for the Blind Association, Help the Aged, British Heart Foundation, Home of Rest for Horses, Aylesbury, Imperial Cancer Research Fund, International Fund for Animal Welfare, Missions to Seamen, RNIB, NSPCC, Oxfam, PDSA, RNLI, RSPCA, Salvation Army, Save the Children Fund, USPG, Spastics Society, St Dunstan's, RSPB, British Union for the Abolition of Vivisection, John Grooms Association for Disabled People, and World Wide Fund for Nature

Margaret Elsie Herod, of Budleigh Salterton, Devon, £994,500 – £5,000 and half the residue to the RSPCA, and her home and half the residue to the RNLI

Elliot Howard Joseph Hillyer, of Bourne Avenue, London N14, £578,592 – £50,000, some effects and one-quarter of the residue to the Church Army, and £50,000 and one-quarter of the residue each to the Children's Society, National Children's Homes and Salvation Army

Muriel Grace Howlett, of Rowlands Castle, Hants, £202,056 – one 12th of the residue each to the British Red Cross Society, Guide Dogs for the Blind Association, Spastics Society and NSPCC

Alec Jessop, of Bridlington, N. Humberside, £1,786,193 – the residue equally between the Priory Church, Bridlington, Beverly Minster and York Minster

Ernest Freeman Johnson, of Princes Gate, London sw7, £806,296 – the residue to the Army Benevolent Fund

Catherine Mary Judson, of East Sheen, London sw14, £1,257,172 – the residue equally between St Martin-in-the-Fields Social Care Unit, London, Salvation Army and Barnardo's

Betty Maud Kelsey, of Bexhill, East Sussex, £502,537 – the residue for charitable purposes in accordance with her known wishes

Phyllis Oswald Kerr, of Polegate, E. Sussex, £1,023,222 – £5,000 and half the residue to the RSPCA, and £2,000 and half the residue to the Animal Health Trust

Lady Yvonne Kleinwort, of Hove, E. Sussex, £302,685 – the residue to the Disabled Housing Trust, of Ernest Kleinwort Court, Burgess Hill

Minnie Hetta Lewis, of Oak Hill Park, London NW3, £1,615,606 – £500,000 to the Maisie and Raphael Lewis Charitable Trust

Ida Vera Longman, of Ferring, W. Sussex, £1,939,562 – the residue equally between Battersea Dogs Home, St Dunstan's, Atkinson Morley Hospital, London, Salvation Army, International League for the Protection of Horses, Blue Cross and Cancer Relief MacMillan Fund

Stanley Tutton Lord, of Wallasey, Merseyside, £633,083 – £3,000, his silver cross and chalice and half the residue to Chester Cathedral, and half the residue to the RSPCA for the Wallasey Branch

Roy Leslie Maggs, of Kingswood, Avon, £567,886 – the residue equally between the Imperial Cancer Research Fund, RNIB, RSPCA, NSPCC, and Donkey Sanctuary, Sidmouth

Margery Bessie Maplethorpe, of Hertford, £2,547,001 – £238,000 to the Margery Maplethorpe Trust, £200,000 to Jesus College, Oxford, for research fellowships, half the residue to London University for fellowships, and half the residue to St Hugh's College, Oxford, for postgraduate facilities

Lilian Mary May Marks, of Park Road, London NW1, £1,156,133 – two-thirds of the residue equally between the Royal London Society for the Blind, National Benevolent Fund for the Aged, and the Cheshire Foundation

Florence Evelyn May Masters, of Bexhill, E. Sussex, £224,986 – her entire estate to the National Trust

Paul Leon Mechulam, of Elstree, Herts, £969,423 – the residue for such charities and individuals at the discretion of his trustees in accordance with his wishes, and any balance equally between the Mayhew Home, London NW10, and Age Concern

Josephine Petronella Cornelia Miles, of Westbourne, Dorset, £842,640 – the residue equally between the Marie Curie Memorial Foundation, Malcolm Sargent Cancer Fund for Children, National Society for Cancer Relief, and Sue Ryder Foundation

Joan Culver Mott, of Oxford, £1,045,231 – one 12th of the residue each to Cheltenham Ladies College, Newnham College, Cambridge, and Wolfson College, and one 12th of the residue for such charitable purposes and institutions as her trustees think fit

Ida Mary Nicoll, of Westella, N. Humberside, £1,784,910 – the residue equally between the North Humberside Hospice Project, Hull, RNLI, Arthritis and Rheumatism Council, and Salvation Army

Louis Stanham Potter Norris, of Luton, Beds, £532,127 – £2,000 and half the residue to the National Trust, and half the residue to the Baptist World Alliance

Phyllis Newell Paine, of Prestbury, Macclesfield, Cheshire, £1,302,405 – the residue to the National Trust

Ray Winifred Parry, of East Cholderton, Hants, £1,152,598 – £55,000 and one 13th of the residue to the National Canine Defence League, £10,000 and one 13th of the residue each to St Mary's Church, Amport, Andover, the PALS Animal Sanctuary, Newton Toney, Salisbury, PDSA, RSPCA, RSPB, Animal Health Trust, Donkey Sanctuary, Sidmouth, and the National Trust, £5,000 and one 13th of the residue each to the Lady Brecknock Hospice at Andover Hospital, Barnardo's and Marie Curie Memorial Foundation, and £500 and one 13th of the residue to the 2nd Andover Scout Group

Amy Rebecca Pateman, of St Neots, Cambs, £1,089,325 – the residue equally between the Cancer Research Campaign, Marie Curie Memorial Foundation, PDSA, British Heart Foundation, National Kidney Research Fund, Guide Dogs for the Blind Association, RNLI, RNIB, British Diabetic Association, and Arthritis and Rheumatism Council

Arthur John Perry, of Heydon, Herts, £297,616 – the residue to the Actors Charitable Trust

Alice Robinson, of Monyash, Derbyshire, £1,106,170 – the residue to the National Trust

Rosi Schilling, of Edgware, Middx, £3,184,570 – one-third of the residue to Jewish old age homes, one-third of the residue to non-Jewish old age homes, and one-third of the residue to Hammersmith Hospital for research into blood diseases

Marjorie Rose Schwab, of Maidenhead, Berks, £1,313,295 – one-fifth of the residue to the Salvation Army, for the benefit of the homeless

Ruby May Sedgwick, of Plymouth, Devon, £609,218 – her entire estate to the radiotherapy and oncology unit at Freedom Fields Hospital, Plymouth

Freda Phyllis Selby, of Colyton, Devon, £1,070,968 – the residue equally between the Baptist Union Housing for Retired Ministers and their Wives, Baptist Union, Baptist Missionary Society, West Ham Central Mission, Barnardo's, Leprosy Mission, Marie Curie Memorial Foundation, Bible Society, Royal Commonwealth Society for the Blind, and Salvation Army

Adolphus Henry Siminson, of Westgate on Sea, Kent, £1,166,835 – the residue equally between Stoke Mandeville Hospital, Save the Children Fund, Guide Dogs for the Blind Association, Help the Aged, Royal Hospital and Home for Incurables, Putney, National Society for Cancer Relief, Salvation Army, British Heart Foundation, RSPCA, and Leukaemia Research Fund

Stanley Stein, of Rutland Gate, London SW7, £1,842,041 – half the residue to the Stanley Stein Charitable Trust

Dorothy Alice Turner, of Warwick, £7,839,519 – the residue equally between the Cancer Research Campaign and British Heart Foundation

Kathleen Irene Myra Verney, of Gurney Drive, London N2, £897,604 – £20,000, her Bluthner grand piano, other effects and the residue to Somerville College, Oxford

David Frank Vissenga, of Wilmington, Honiton, Devon, £999,626 – the residue equally between the Friends of the Elderly and Gentlefolk's Help, National Trust and British Red Cross Society

Millicent Walker, of Middleton-on-Sea, W. Sussex, £1,211,395 – the residue equally between the Distressed Gentlefolk's Aid Association, RSPB, RNLI, RSPCA and World Wildlife Fund

Richard Gittins Wall, of Kelmarsh, Northants, £1,295,607 – two-fifths of the residue to Kelmarsh Church, one-fifth of the residue to Market Harborough Parish Church, one-tenth of the residue each to Clare College, Cambridge, Baschurch Parish Church, Salop, and Peterborough Diocesan Board of Finance, to augment clergy stipends, three 50ths of the residue to the League of Friends of Market Harborough Hospitals, and one 50th of the residue each to Petton Parish Church, Salop, and the Railway Benevolent Institution

William Ernest Frank Ward, of Banstead, Surrey, £674,837 – one 13th of the residue each to St Andrew's United Reformed Church, Cheam, Save the Children Fund, Christian Aid, Barnardo's, National Trust, Royal Commonwealth Society for the Blind, Imperial Cancer Research Fund, Woodland Trust, Shelter, RSPCA, NSPCC, and Lincoln College, Oxford

Winifred May Webster, of Hyde Park Square, London W2, £1,507,434 – the residue to the Salvation Army

Cyril Gordon Wicks, of Blackheath Village, London SE3, £894,721 – his entire estate equally between the Greater London Fund for the Blind, Marie Curie Memorial Foundation and British Deaf Association

Reginald Bolton Wilson, of Hastings, E. Sussex, £553,891 – the residue to the National Trust

Leslie Philip Woolf, of Franklins Row, London SW3, £1,301,883 – half the residue to the Reform Club, and one-quarter of the residue each to the Imperial Cancer Research Fund and Kidney Research Aid Fund

Broadcasting

TELEVISION

The year was dominated by concern that the increasingly fierce battle for ratings between Britain's four terrestrial television networks was compromising programme quality. ITV came under fire from advertisers and the Independent Television Commission (ITC) for relying too much on proven, long-running drama series and not investing enough money in new shows. Critics and programme-makers were worried that the BBC's flagship service, BBC1, was sacrificing risk-taking and originality for predictable, populist programming. Thanks to the success of a third weekly episode of *EastEnders*, shown on Mondays, *National Lottery Live*, launched in November, and several much-needed popular drama hits, BBC1's ratings improved at the expense of ITV, the market leader. Channel 4 was criticized by commentators for what appeared to be an ever greater emphasis on high-profile, themed programming designed to generate publicity and arouse controversy.

In April the ITC pinpointed the central dilemma facing ITV as it attempted to come to terms with increased competition. 'The network's undoubted popularity with viewers appeared to inhibit new scheduling and commissioning initiatives,' it said. 'This was especially evident in the most commercially significant areas of the schedule – drama, entertainment and comedy.' In drama ITV continued to win big audiences with its long-running staples *Peak Practice*, *Heartbeat* and *Soldier, Soldier*.

However, the year's surprise hit was a controversial new serial set in Bradford's red light district, *Band of Gold*, written by Kay Mellor. Critics welcomed *Band of Gold* for its gritty realism, a refreshing change to the formulaic dramas evident elsewhere on ITV. The second series of *Cracker*, starring Robbie Coltrane as a police psychologist, was also saluted. Unusually, the ITC went out of its way to praise the programme. 'In several episodes *Cracker* achieved a quality of writing, performance and direction unsurpassed elsewhere,' the Commission said. 'Some viewers found it too strong even after 9pm, but a later scheduling would have denied it the large audience it deserved.' *The Governor*, featuring Janet McTeer as a hard-pressed prison governor, was another edgy ITV series to generate controversy. Reviewers were divided over its merits. 'Lynda La Plante's new series will stand or fall on the performance of Janet McTeer and, after the introductory episode, I have to say things look a little unsteady', the *Independent*'s Thomas Sutcliffe said.

She's Out, a sequel to the 1980s drama *Widows*, failed to match the impact of its predecessor. The critics were more approving of *Bramwell*, a medical saga based on the tribulations of a young female Victorian doctor determined to combat the prejudices of the male-dominated hospital establishment. *Bramwell* was one of ITV's few attempts at costume drama, a genre much in evidence on the BBC following the success of *Middlemarch* in the winter of 1994. Another departure for ITV was a quirky new comedy drama, *Moving Story*, created by Jack Rosenthal and set in the world of the removal man.

Despite these innovations, the feeling persisted that by relying so much on tried-and-tested drama series, ITV was in danger of boring audiences with the sameness of the fare. In January Andrew Davies, the award-winning writer who adapted *Middlemarch* and created *A Very Peculiar Practice*, accused channel controllers of trying to 'narcotise the viewing population' with series based on worn-out formulas. 'Shows that seemed fresh, bright and sparky when we first saw them are flogged relentlessly until the last dodgy plot possibility flops exhausted on the living room carpet to bleed to death', Davies said. Another complaint was that there was no longer any room in the schedule for risk or experiment.

ITV's safety-first attitude was also evident in comedy and entertainment. The news that *Spitting Image* was to be axed after 11 years on air was welcomed by critics, who had felt for some time that the series was past its prime. *Blind Date*, which celebrated its tenth anniversary in December, received a mild rebuke from the ITC for its 'increasingly obvious sexual innuendo'. More serious for the network was ITV's continued failure to add to its diminishing roster of successful situation comedies. Ironically, one of the BBC's biggest comic hits of the year was *Men Behaving Badly*, originally shown on ITV but dropped after one series because it was not an instant success. The BBC persevered with *Men Behaving Badly*, which achieved critical acclaim as well as ratings.

Much of ITV's factual programming seemed designed to win high ratings at all costs. There was criticism for series such as *Blues and Twos* and *The Day I Nearly Died* because of their tendency to concentrate unduly on stories emphasizing disaster, crisis or suffering, summed up by one critic as an excess of 'flashing blue lights'. Responding to earlier ITC comment that ITV had not shown enough distinguished documentaries of late, the network took the unprecedented step of screening a week-long season of programmes examining the arms trade, *The War Machine*, broadcast in November. Observers agreed that one of the highlights was the drama-documentary *The Dying Of The Light*.

Not all the rebukes for ITV came from outsiders. In November Andy Allan, Carlton UK's chief executive, mounted an outspoken attack on ITV's daytime programmes. He accused them of being predictable, repetitive and unadventurous. 'Watching the shows is like being in a tank robbed of all sensory perceptions,' Allan said. His comments were all the more remarkable given that ITV's daytime schedule was far more popular with viewers than the BBC's.

BBC REVIVAL

For years the BBC had lagged behind ITV in popular drama but 1994–5 saw a revival in this key area of programming. *EastEnders* and *Casualty* continued to play well for the Corporation but several new drama series also achieved decent audiences and were recommissioned. There were two new police-based shows, *Hamish Macbeth* and *Dangerfield*. Based on the life and loves of a police doctor in rural Warwickshire, many critics dismissed *Dangerfield* as a clone of ITV's *Peak Practice*. Writing in the *Daily Telegraph*, Stephen Pile said, 'You can just imagine the excitement when the idea for *Dangerfield* came into the office. "It's about a country GP who also does police work". Brilliant, this means we can have little cars and new wave rough-house police detectives in black leather jackets in the same series'.

Bugs, co-created by Brian Clemens, who had helped mastermind *The Avengers*, provided BBC1 with a long-overdue Saturday night drama hit But despite the care taken with special effects and endless high-tech gadgetry, most reviewers gave the series the thumbs down. In the *Financial Times*, Christopher Dunkley wondered why the BBC bothered to make a show that seemed more in keeping with ITV's approach to drama. The answer was the increasingly fierce battle for ratings. In several speeches the National Heritage Secretary Stephen Dorrell emphasized that the Corporation must achieve high audiences to justify the licence fee. But with its public service obligations, the BBC also had to continue to make and screen shows of quality and distinction, the kind of fare not readily available on commercial channels.

With BBC2 axing the post-*Newsnight* arts and media show *The Late Show*, the demise of the avant garde arts series *Arena*, and a more populist BBC1, some commentators wondered if the BBC was in danger of betraying its Reithian past. Responding to the debate over what many regarded as a lacklustre BBC1 Christmas schedule, Brenda Maddox, writing in *The Times*, argued that the Corporation should stop fighting ITV and start to once again produce programmes that challenge and stimulate audiences. 'There is intelligent life out there; a nationwide audience for radio and television, which does not expect costume dramas on Himalayan peaks, yet expects the BBC to be risk-taking, the national leader not in "accessibility" but in presenting modern English well used,' Maddox said. 'That is the BBC's classic brand image at home, and it is not

produced by committees and "referral upwards" '. Alan Yentob, controller of BBC1, denied there had been any lurch downmarket. 'It's just that some things are beginning to work that didn't work before,' Yentob said in July. 'If you look at the range of factual programmes, there are far more of them in the schedule than when I took over.'

Despite having more success with new drama series, BBC1 screened several new series that backfired. The much-publicized family saga *Seaforth*, set in the Second World War, was not renewed. The new, twice-weekly soap *Castles*, originally developed for Channel 4, was a critical and ratings disaster. Reviewers suggested that *Castles'* middle-class, suburban world was too tame for the high melodrama that keeps *EastEnders*, *Coronation Street* and *Brookside* alive.

On the plus side, BBC2 followed up its acclaimed adaptation of *Middlemarch* with a triumphant serialization of Dickens' *Martin Chuzzlewit*. Critics praised Tom Wilkinson's performance as Pecksniff. A film based on Jane Austen's *Persuasion* was said to be of a similarly high calibre. Reviewers even forgave the BBC taking liberties with the original text by adding a climactic kiss absent from Austen's novel. There was criticism that BBC2 screened *Persuasion* at 10p.m. on Easter Sunday, too late for many viewers to watch a 90-minute film.

The BBC's renewed enthusiasm for literary drama came unstuck with *The Buccaneers*. Controversy erupted when it emerged that screenwriter Maggie Wadey had spiced up Edith Wharton's unfinished novel by writing in scenes depicting rape and homosexuality. For many reviewers, *The Buccaneers* turned out to be a crinoline too far. 'Baywatch with bustles,' commented the *Financial Times'* Christopher Dunkley. The fashion for period pieces was also notable in the BBC1 Sunday afternoon teatime slot. Audiences and critics responded well to adaptations of *Just William* and *Little Lord Fauntleroy*. In its original work for television, the BBC scored with *Pat and Margaret*, reuniting Victoria Wood with Julie Walters, and written by Wood. On BBC2 critics hailed *Takin' Over The Asylum*, created by new television dramatist Donna Franceschild. The serial tackled the difficult subject of mental health. It was not a ratings success, however. In drama, BBC2's biggest hit of the year was the cult paranormal series *The X-Files*, imported from America. The *Daily Mail's* Marcus Berkman described *The X-Files* as 'a science fiction series of unusual subtlety and intelligence'.

LOTTERY MANIA

BBC1's success in securing the contract to screen the results of the National Lottery live on Saturday evenings and the subsequent furore over what many saw as the show's initial amateurishness added more fuel to the debate over declining programme quality. The *Sun's* Garry Bushell summed up the feeling of many when he described the first week's lottery coverage as 'diabolical'. In the *Evening*

Standard, Milton Shulman said it was 'a parochial no-talent show'. Mr Yentob demanded changes and the programme became more polished, although many sensed that the BBC was still uncomfortable with such a blatantly populist programme.

The lottery helped to increase BBC1's ratings. The first show drew more than 20 million viewers. As the lottery became less of a novelty, audiences dropped back to an average of around 15 million. By July BBC1's audience share was stable at just over 32 per cent. ITV, on the other hand, lost viewers; its average share had decreased by approximately three per cent since 1992. Moreover, BBC1 could point to a list of acclaimed documentaries unmatched by the commercial opposition. There was universal praise for Sir David Attenborough's latest natural history blockbuster, *The Private Life of Plants*. The series used state-of-the-art cameras to show how apparently inanimate plants can be as deadly as any meat-eating animal. Documentary series such as *Watergate* and *25 Bloody Years*, marking a quarter-century of troubles in Northern Ireland, were also considered outstanding. There was praise too for the BBC's coverage of the fiftieth anniversary of D-Day; Charles Wheeler's contributions were thought to be excellent. One of the year's new television 'discoveries' was Jeremy Clarkson, presenter of BBC2's *Motorworld*. Observers regarded him as a small screen natural with the flair of an Attenborough or an Alan Whicker. Critics also welcomed the return of *University Challenge* with Jeremy Paxman as the new quiz-master.

In comedy the BBC also out-pointed the opposition. Repeats of *Fawlty Towers* and *Blackadder* were welcomed. Contemporary talent such as Steve Coogan featured in the acclaimed chat show spoof *Knowing Me, Knowing You … With Alan Partridge*, a transfer from Radio 4. Other successes included *Harry Enfield and Chums*, the final series of *Absolutely Fabulous*, and a new situation comedy vehicle for Dawn French, *The Vicar of Dibley*, written by Richard Curtis, creator of *Four Weddings and A Funeral*.

NEWS AND CURRENT AFFAIRS

Television's coverage of Westminster's political activities will never satisfy all politicians. But as the electoral battle intensified between the Government and an invigorated Opposition led by Tony Blair, attention turned to how the broadcasters reflected the national debate. As usual, it was the BBC that had to defend itself against attacks of bias from ministers. Many Corporation journalists felt their job of grilling the people's representatives was not made any easier by a speech made by John Birt, the BBC director-general, in February.

Speaking at the annual Independent Newspaper Lecture in Dublin, Mr Birt appeared to be reprimanding tough inquisitors in the Jeremy Paxman and John Humphrys mould when he criticized 'overbearing interviewers who sneer disdainfully at their interviewees'. Mr Birt went on, 'We in broadcasting should be aware of interviewers who feel more self-important than the subject matter at hand, who like the disorientating opening question – the rabbit-punch – designed to destabilize, to knock off-balance. On occasion, such an approach can goad an interviewee into making an interesting response, but the result is more often a battle of wits which goes nowhere.' However, when in March Government minister Jonathan Aitken accused *Today's* John Humphrys of anti-government bias and the BBC of being 'the Blair Broadcasting Corporation', Mr Birt defended his journalists.

The following month another, more significant row involving BBC news and current affairs coverage erupted. A *Panorama* interview with the Prime Minister, due to be broadcast three days before local elections in Scotland, led to embarrassment for the Corporation after a Scottish court decided it would be wrong to transmit it so close to polling day. Opposition parties argued that screening the interview would infringe the BBC's own impartiality rules. Many, including Michael Grade, the head of Channel 4, felt the Corporation had made an editorial error in scheduling the interview with Mr Major on the eve of Scottish elections. Others expressed concern that the successful court action could set a precedent whereby politicians might regularly use the law as a way of suppressing programmes whose content they disagreed with. The BBC's governors acknowledged the Corporation had made a mistake by showing 'insufficient sensitivity to the Scottish dimension'.

CHANNEL 4

In June the controversy over what many saw as Channel 4's obsession with sex and breaking accepted boundaries of taste and decency took centre-stage when Paul Johnson, writing in the *Daily Mail*, described Channel 4's Michael Grade as Britain's 'pornographer in chief'. Much of the debate regarding the station's apparent determination to shock audiences centred on *The Word*, the late-night Friday youth show. The ITC had reprimanded Channel 4 on several occasions for controversial items featured in the series but in June the station received a formal warning following stunts included in *The Word*. A month later Channel 4 announced that the series would not be recommissioned but said its decision had nothing to do with the criticism.

There was also outrage over Dyke TV, 15 hours of late-night programming aimed at lesbians, and The Red Light Zone, a late-night season about the sex industry. The Archdeacon of York accused the channel of a 'silly undergraduate attempt to shock'; Lord Annan said Mr Grade was 'a jackanapes', and Lord Elton called on the ITC to penalize Channel 4 for blasphemy after screening Martin Scorsese's film *The Last Temptation of Christ*. Mr Grade was unrepentant and defended his editorial policy. 'People are fascinated by sex,' he said. 'It's a question of whether you take a healthy interest and explore that in a serious-minded way or whether you do it in an unhealthy way, which is to exploit people'. Pot

Night, a celebration of cannabis, added to the disquiet.

Another criticism levelled at the station was what some regarded as its retreat from high-quality serious drama. There was, however, praise for *The Politician's Wife*, Paula Milne's story of a Government minister's adultery and his wife's revenge. 'Juliet Stevenson's superlative acting raised *The Politician's Wife* to a higher level than schlock,' was the verdict of the *Daily Telegraph's* Hugh Massingberd. *ER*, the fast-moving American hospital drama created by Michael Crichton, added to Channel 4's stable of hit American shows.

Brookside continued to make headlines. The Jordache murder story involving a body under the patio became a national talking point. When Mandy and Beth Jordache were finally jailed for the murder of Mandy's violent husband Trevor, Channel 4 helplines were jammed with calls from battered wives. The shock death of Beth increased *Brookside's* audience by two million. In documentary programmes the station continued to make waves. One of the most harrowing was *Secret Asia: The Dying Rooms*, an expose of Chinese orphanages. Critics also praised *Lockerbie: The Maltese Double Cross*, an investigation of the Lockerbie bombing. In comedy and entertainment, it was felt that Channel 4 had not lived up to its previous high standards. *Paris*, a new situation comedy starring Alexei Sayle as a Bohemian artist, met with poor reviews. New series of *Drop The Dead Donkey* and *Rory Bremner ... Who Else?* retained their form, however.

Throughout the year, Channel 4 stepped up its campaign to break its final financial links with ITV. In 1995 the station handed over £57.3 million to ITV as part of a complex subsidy arrangement. But despite support from several eminent figures, including Jeremy Isaacs, the station's founder, there was no sign of the Government changing the law to end the funding arrangement.

SATELLITE AND CABLE

By July 1995 almost one in five British homes had access to the extra television channels provided by satellite and cable operators. British Sky Broadcasting, the Rupert Murdoch-backed satellite station, announced in March it was planning to launch up to 120 extra channels in 1996. It is likely that many of the 'new' channels will be used to screen existing material, such as feature films, at different times of the day, perhaps at 15-minute intervals. This would give audiences greater flexibility. But commentators were sceptical that BSkyB would meet its timetable.

Of more immediate concern to BSkyB's rivals was the growing strength of the operation's film and sports subscription business. The success of pay-TV led writer and broadcaster Melvyn Bragg, speaking in September 1994, to predict that British television might degenerate into a two-tier system, 'telly for cash and a telly for trash'. 'Look at sport,' Bragg

added. 'The best of it is already cut off from millions of fans because they cannot afford it.'

This was an exaggeration, but the BBC and ITV were becoming increasingly vexed over BSkyB signing exclusive deals to screen key sports, including boxing, golf and a proposed rugby super-league. Satellite's success also had an impact on cable. After years of false dawns, the number of UK homes taking cable TV had grown to 1,152,000 by July 1995. Nevertheless, pundits argued that if cable was ever to be a force to be reckoned with, it needed to offer more exclusive programming in order to compete effectively with satellite.

With this in mind, several cable-only channels were launched during the year. These included Channel One, financed by Associated Newspapers, Live TV, masterminded by Janet Street-Porter and backed by the Mirror Group, and SelectTV, the production company responsible for such hit shows as *Birds of a Feather* and *Goodnight Sweetheart*. Doubts, however, were expressed regarding the ability of these channels to offer programmes of real merit and originality.

In January the much-heralded commercial partnership between the BBC and Pearson, owners of the *Financial Times*, bore fruit with the launch of two pan-European channels, BBC Prime and BBC World, designed for satellite and cable viewers in continental Europe. The Corporation's charter prohibits it from offering the channels at home. The BBC's plans to launch an entertainment-based cable channel in America were postponed.

DIGITAL TRANSMISSION

The explosion of new services is possible because of digital technology. This enables broadcasters to provide a greatly increased number of services, and the possibility of CD quality sound and improved picture reproduction. Signals can be squashed so that more than one can be sent along the same frequency channel simultaneously. This is impossible with traditional analogue technology.

Throughout the year, broadcasters became increasingly excited at the prospects for digital services. In November the BBC announced plans to start a digital radio service in September 1995. Digital Audio Broadcasting promised trouble-free radio reception with no interference, even in cars, though new radio sets would be needed to receive the service. The plan was to introduce it gradually throughout the UK. Sixty per cent coverage within four years was predicted. More ambitious still was the announcement in August by Virginia Bottomley, the new National Heritage Secretary, of at least 18 new terrestrial television channels to be delivered digitally. Mrs Bottomley hailed the emergence of digital services as 'perhaps the most significant technological and commercial step forward for television and radio since the development of the cathode ray tube'. However, it was unclear how these proposed new channels, the first of which could be on air by late 1997, would generate enough revenue to provide programmes of a high enough quality to persuade people to watch. Unlike satellite TV, no dish aerial would be required but viewers would have to pay up to £500 for new, set-top boxes.

Even advocates of the technology admitted that the four terrestrial channels would remain the most watched networks well into the digital age. Writing in the *Guardian*, Steve Barnett expressed doubts over the plan, concluding that the initiative would be stillborn.

It was unclear how the digital 'revolution' affected the chances for Channel 5, the terrestrial network due on air by 1997. The franchise was re-advertised during the year and in May four groups announced their bids. Many had predicted Rupert Murdoch would walk away with the licence, to be awarded to the highest bidder, subject to meeting ITC criteria on programme quality and business viability. However, the Murdoch-backed New Century TV was the lowest bidder, offering £2 million for the franchise. There was amazement that two groups, Virgin TV and Channel 5 Broadcasting, made identical bids of £22 million. The winner of the auction will be announced by late 1995.

RADIO

The dynamic growth in the number of new radio stations continued throughout the year. On 14 February Talk Radio UK, Britain's third national commercial network, was launched. There was immediate controversy over the station's 'shock jocks', disc jockeys specializing in insulting and provoking audiences with strong language and explicit sexual material. After three weeks on air, the Radio Authority had received 26 complaints from listeners offended by Talk's programmes. In April a new programme director, Jerry Thomas, was appointed following the departure of several key managers and disc jockey Wild Al Kelly.

Despite curbing the sleaze and swearing, and seeing audiences rise to half a million listeners after disappointing initial listening figures, Talk failed to prove a serious threat to any of the BBC's five national radio networks. Other new stations launched during 1994–5 included several London-only stations such as Viva!, aimed at female listeners, Heart FM, offering adult contemporary music, Premier, the UK's first Christian radio station, and Country 1035 specializing in country music. Virgin, the Richard Branson-backed rock station, finally began broadcasting to London on the FM waveband, a move which helped to increase audience figures to more than four million.

Despite the activity in the commercial sector, the changing fortunes of Radio 1 attracted the most attention from commentators. After two years of alarming decline, when five million listeners deserted the station, audiences began to return to Radio 1. The weekly audience grew from 10.5 million in the first quarter of 1995 to 11.05 million in the second. Some observers were sceptical about the increase and wondered if the station could sustain it in the coming months. The improvement came after a particularly painful period for the network; two new signings, Danny Baker and Emma Freud, left the network after failing to make an impact with listeners. Steve Wright, Radio 1's most popular presenter, announced his resignation in January.

The increase in listening levels was attributed largely to the arrival of Wright's successor, Chris Evans, who began hosting the breakfast show on 24 April. The manic Evans, best known for presenting Channel 4's *The Big Breakfast* and *Don't Forget Your Toothbrush*, became one of Britain's highest-paid radio presenters; his eight-month contract with Radio 1 was reputedly worth £500,000. This was considerably less than the £2 million spent by the BBC on an advertising campaign promoting the station's new, more youthful image personified by Evans and other new recruits such as Lisa l'Anson. But not all the critics were impressed. After listening to Evans' debut, the *Daily Telegraph*'s Gillian Reynolds said the programme lacked originality, and called for 'a mind stretch and a mouthwash'.

The BBC's other national radio networks also had good news to report. In May it was revealed that BBC Radio had regained a narrow lead over the commercial sector (the latter had moved ahead of the Corporation for the first time in late 1994). By the summer commercial radio was once more in the lead with a 50.1 per cent audience share compared with the BBC's 47.9 per cent; the remainder of listening was accounted for by audiences tuning in to pirate stations. Despite increased commercial competition, Radios 2, 3, and 4 sustained their audiences while Radio 5 Live continued to grow. Mr Birt hailed Radio 5 Live as a triumph for the BBC. 'It is rare for a media launch to achieve instant success but the BBC's new network, Radio 5 Live, did just that,' he said. Most critics agreed.

The director-general was particularly gratified by the success of Radio 5 Live because its programmes were popular with younger, less middle-class audiences, listeners and viewers who traditionally shun the BBC in favour of commercial broadcasters. Elsewhere, the BBC's core constituency of supporters made their presence felt. In November it emerged that Radio 4 was to axe *Anderson Country*, the afternoon magazine show seen by network loyalists as an inelegant attempt to cater for a younger, more downmarket audience. Christopher Dunkley, host of Radio 4's *Feedback* series, said, 'It's certainly the most hated programme . . . The feeling was "This is not what we expect on Radio 4" '.

There was also opposition to suggestions that the BBC was planning to close or merge more than 20 of its local radio stations. The Corporation denied this was the case. Various options were under consideration as part of a ten-year plan for regional broadcasting, officials said.

Conservation and Heritage

BIODIVERSITY CONVENTION

The UN Convention on Biological Diversity which was agreed at the Earth Summit in Rio in 1992 was formally ratified by the UK in June 1994. The Convention places obligations on the signatory states to 'protect and sustainably use' their biological resources. It also requires each nation to produce a plan setting out exactly how it intends to meet this challenge. The Government's document *Biodiversity: the UK Action Plan*, was published in January 1994 (*see* Whitaker's Almanack 1995). To put its intentions into practice, the Government has appointed a Biodiversity Steering Group including representatives from four conservation bodies. Its initial task is to prepare action plans for sustainable fisheries and transport policies.

The well-informed (and increasingly political) conservation charities and non-official bodies have in fact made most of the running so far. In January 1995 a revised version of the voluntary sector's document *Biodiversity Challenge* was presented to the Environment Secretary (John Gummer) by Sir David Attenborough. Using the Government's own language of targets and costings, it presents 600 'priority species' of wild animals and plants, and 35 'key habitats' in the UK. The report has been described as the most detailed 'audit' of the UK's wildlife ever published. It is also a reminder that global biodiversity is only the sum of local biodiversities, and that global action begins in one's own back yard.

CONSERVATION OF NATURAL HABITATS

The 1992 EC directive on the conservation of natural habitats and of wild flora and fauna, known as the Habitats Directive, requires member states to identify sites of 'Community interest' on their territory and designate them as 'Special Areas of Conservation' (SACs). Such habitats include yew woods, active raised and blanket bogs, dune grassland and heath, Caledonian pine forest, limestone pavement, and submerged sea caves. The plants and animals listed include the Scottish wild cat, dormouse, great crested newt, sand lizard, marsh fritillary butterfly, bottle-nosed dolphin, early gentian and all 14 species of bat. Although many of these are protected already, the directive extends this protection to their 'breeding sites or resting places'.

In Britain the directive became law in June 1994 and regulations to put it into effect were approved by Parliament in October 1994. The four official nature conservation agencies in England, Scotland, Wales and Northern Ireland, co-ordinated by the Joint Nature Conservation Committee (JNCC), were charged with recommending proposed SACs. The list of 280 sites was published on 31 March 1995, and includes 123 in England, 108 in Scotland, 38 in Wales and and 17 in Northern Ireland. They include such extensive areas of land as the Cairngorms, Snowdonia, the Broads, Salisbury Plain and the New Forest. The directive allows each member state a degree of flexibility in the 'forms and methods' of designating SACs. In Britain the mechanism will be the existing one of Sites of Special Scientific Interest (SSSI); most of the recommended SACs are already SSSIs. After prolonged deliberation, the Government decided not to introduce new legislation, preferring to rely on planning guidelines and by-laws. It has allowed itself a number of legal loopholes, for example exempting Acts of Parliament from the requirements of the directive, and interpreting habitat 'damage' narrowly so as to exclude gradual deterioration.

The list of SACs met with broad approval, although Friends of the Earth (FoE) pointed out that it surprisingly omits sites like Carmel Wood, perhaps (it suggested) because they are threatened by quarrying or other destructive development. Greater reservation has been expressed over the use of the SSSI mechanism, which is relatively weak; FoE have documented 1,005 cases of habitat loss or damage on SSSIs over the past seven years, but only nine prosecutions. Furthermore, there is no existing framework to designate marine SACs, apart from the moribund mechanism of Marine Nature Reserves.

Once they are designated – and this will take several years – the SACs are expected to join the existing SPAs (Special Protection Areas for wild birds) in a pan-European network of protected areas to be called Natura 2000.

ROADS

The Royal Commission on Environmental Pollution published a report condemning current transport policy, proposing improvements, including the better integration of transport and other land-use policies, and calling for a reassessment of the way in which the Department of Transport matches expected demand with more highways.

The report's conclusions were supported by the Government's own standing advisory committee on trunk road assessment, which criticized the Department for failing to comprehend that new roads generate more traffic, and for neglecting alternative forms of transport. As a result, the Department is reviewing all major road schemes still at the planning stage, and has cancelled plans to build 14-lane link roads on the M25.

In spite of these developments, the then Transport Secretary, Brian Mawhinney, announced in July 1995 that the long-delayed Newbury bypass would go ahead without modification. The £77 million bypass, which would complete a 'Euroroute' connecting Britain, France and Spain, will damage part of Snelsmore Common, an SSSI and country park, meadows along the Rivers Lambourne and Kennet, and archaeological sites, including two Civil War battlefields. Many residents are in favour of the bypass because it would relieve severe congestion in the town, but even the Department's own consultants agree that it will be 'massively destructive of a largely intimate countryside, unable to absorb the impact of a major highway'. Protesters have taken their case to the European Commission on the technical grounds of damage to the habitat of protected dormice, nightjars and bats.

Waiting in the wings is a £330 million motorway whose 'preferred route' crosses the Gwent Levels near Newport. As one of the best-preserved areas of unimproved wet grassland in Britain, much of the Levels is scheduled as SSSI. It is feared that the intricate network of drainage dikes, known as reens, would be vulnerable to pollution from motorway run-off.

The Government's transport policy is now in some disarray; a Green Paper is promised later in 1995.

SUPER-QUARRY ON HARRIS

A public inquiry heard evidence over a period of eight months for and against the construction of a super-quarry by Redland Aggregates near the southern tip of Harris in the Outer Hebrides. Over the next 60 years, the company wishes to extract 600 million tonnes of rock from the mountain of Roineabhal (which would disappear in the process) between the coastal communities of Lingarabay and Leverburgh. The quarry would meet the expected demand for anorthosite, a hard rock particularly suited for road-building.

The company presented the development in terms of the jobs and prosperity it claimed it would bring to Harris. It was supported at the public inquiry by the Western Isles Island Council, which had given planning permission for the development. A referendum held in April 1993 had shown that the islanders themselves were evenly split over the proposal. By 1995, another poll showed that opinion had hardened against it. Evidently the inquiry had revealed to many for the first time the full scale of the development. Fears of noise and pollution, of the impact of incomers on island life, and indignation at the possible violation of the Sabbath, which is faithfully observed in this corner of Britain, all helped to change local peoples' minds. As a consequence, the Island Council made a sudden U-turn and has now voted 21-8 against the development.

At the inquiry, Scottish Natural Heritage (SNH) produced evidence that exposed Redland's environmental assessment as perfunctory. For example, the assessment recorded only 11 species of moss and liverwort at the site, while SNH's expert found no fewer than 164, making it a nationally important site for these organisms. Research also showed that the site is of importance for otters, golden eagles and golden plovers, all species protected under EC directives.

The result of the inquiry is expected towards the end of 1995.

CONSERVATION CUTS

The budget of the Countryside Council for Wales (CCW) was cut by 20 per cent for the year 1995-6. The Council reportedly incurred the displeasure of the then Welsh Secretary, John Redwood, by revealing in its accounts that a third of its budget went on staff salaries. Although this is unexceptional, more 'streetwise' organizations rarely present salaries as separate expenditure.

In May 1995, Mr Redwood published an 'action plan for the Countryside Council for Wales' which proposes to transfer some of its activities to local authorities and the Welsh Office, though without allocating extra funds to these bodies. Furthermore, CCW has been stripped of its right to intervene and comment on planning applications except in 'special cases'. The cuts will result in redundancies at the CCW and will have knock-on effects through the likely reduction of grant-aid to the voluntary conservation bodies in Wales. In a separate decision, Mr Redwood refused to endorse planning guidelines used in England, preferring fewer controls on activities such as outdoor recreation and tourism-related developments. These decisions mean that conservation practice in England and Wales has diverged, which is exactly what many predicted would happen when the Nature Conservancy Council was broken up in 1991.

The budget of Scottish Natural Heritage (SNH), CCW's sister organization in Scotland, is now under review and its chairman has spoken of the need for a 'leaner, fitter, better' organization. Some fear that 'leaner and fitter' may be a euphemism for 'smaller and cheaper'.

MAMMAL CENSUS

For the first time, zoologists have assessed the population size of all 65 native or well-established British mammals. In some cases, like red and fallow deer and seals, the numbers are known with a high degree of accuracy. With others there is a high level of uncertainty. In a report published by the JNCC and written by a team headed by Professor Steven Harris of Bristol University, the mammals are censused in rank order. The commonest species turns out to be the field vole, which, with about 75 million individuals, is the only wild mammal exceeding *Homo sapiens* in numbers. Also in excess of the ten million are the common shrew, wood mouse, rabbit, bank vole and mole. At the opposite end of the scale, the mouse-eared bat is extinct, and the coypu successfully exterminated. There are believed to be only 1,300 ship rats left, mainly on Lundy and the Shiant Islands in the Inner Hebrides. Serious declines have been detected in the water vole, brown hare, wild cat, red squirrel and many species of bat.

The report confirms that Britain is a significant refuge for several mammals, with 78 per cent of Europe's grey seals, 40 per cent of common seals, 40 per cent of fallow deer, 30 per cent of red deer, 17 per cent of badgers, and a 'significant' proportion of Europe's otters. More neglected are Britain's feral populations of wild sheep (2,100) and goats (3,565+), which are believed to be unique descendants of Neolithic farm stock.

The animal causing greatest concern is the brown hare, which has declined by four-fifths since the turn of the century. The report's estimate of between 680,000 and 954,000 adult individuals is, however, disputed by the Game Conservancy Trust, which reckoned there were about two million hares in 1991. The hare's habit of sitting tight when threatened makes it vulnerable to cutting machines, and it is also vulnerable to the use of pesticides.

The review may help to stimulate more work on British mammals. Its main value is as a benchmark against which to evaluate future change. It is a significant step forward in bringing our relatively neglected mammal fauna into line with existing surveys of wild birds.

NEW SPECIES

Since there are only six native amphibians in Britain the news that we may have a seventh is exciting. The pool frog, *Rana lessonae*, has been recorded in Britain since the 1770s. It has been much confused with the introduced edible frog, which is now known to be a hybrid of the pool frog and the marsh frog. Until recently pool frogs have been assumed to be introductions. However, contemporary records studied by Charles Snell suggest that 18th-century naturalists regarded it as a native species. Further evidence came to light in 1995 when bones identified as belonging to pool frogs were discovered at a Bronze Age site in Cambridgeshire and at Saxon sites in Norfolk and Lincolnshire. It seems probable, therefore, that the pool frog is an overlooked native species of small pools and marshes in The Fens. If so, it is not only our most recently discovered native amphibian, but also our rarest. While it has been introduced in a number of places, only one site is known which is believed to house native pool frogs. The numbers are believed to be small, and the exact site is a secret. It is hoped that the population can be safeguarded, and perhaps used to reintroduce the frog to some of its old fenland haunts.

A very different species has been the subject of considerable press attention: the 'French or Median Wasp' (*Dolichovespula media*). This large wasp began to colonize Britain from the European mainland in the late 1980s and by 1995 it had reached northern England. Its nest, suspended from branches or the sides of buildings, is easily recognized by its long spout-like extension. Press reports of wasps attacking and stinging gardeners led to exaggerated stories of 'French killer wasps' and 'super-wasps'. Experts are, however, convinced that it is no more dangerous or aggressive than any other kind of wasp, though its large size and the all-black colour of some of the worker males perhaps make it seem more fearful. Its rapid colonization of England could be further evidence of climatic warming.

BRINGING BACK THE BEAVER

In response to the UK Action Plan on Biodiversity (*see* above), Scottish Natural Heritage has produced a list of 200 species of plants and animals as candidates for survey and research. The European beaver, which has been extinct in Britain since the Middle Ages, has been successfully reintroduced to several European countries, and SNH proposed a study to investigate the practicality of introducing the beaver to Scotland. The proposal follows recommended international guidelines in assessing the suitability of the habitat and the likely environmental impact of such an introduction. If it passes the first hurdle, the proposal would then go to public consultation.

THREATS AND RESCUES

In 1994 Friends of the Earth published *Losing Interest: a Survey of Threats to SSSIs in England and Wales*, which revealed threats to 700 SSSIs, most frequently from pollution by farm waste or sewage, from acid precipitation or from road-building. The following four cases attracted public attention during 1995.

In Windsor Great Park there is a prominent avenue of mature trees known as Queen Anne's Ride. Planted in 1720, these trees are now considered to be past their prime, and too 'untidy' to fulfil their role as a dramatic landscape feature. In wildlife terms, on the other hand, these trees are just reaching their prime, and the Great Park is among the most celebrated sites for the lichens, fungi and invertebrates of old trees. The Duke of Edinburgh has ordered the estate to fell the trees and replace them with saplings. He is fully within his rights, since the Great Park is Crown property and exempt from the laws that protect trees. This is an unusual case where landscape interests appear to conflict with those of wildlife.

What may be the largest colony of great crested newts in Britain was discovered in shallow flooded brick pits near Peterborough, Cambs. Unfortunately the area is schedule for a major housing development, the Peterborough Southern Township. The best arrangement English Nature could make is to relocate the estimated 30,000 newts to a site nearby. Some herpetologists have expressed scepticism, pointing out that newts have homing instincts.

Carmel Woods in Dyfed has in recent years been a battleground between the local wildlife trust and Wimpey-Hobbs, who want to extend their nearby quarry workings into the area. This ancient wood contains five habitats of European importance, including the Pantyllyn Furlough, a seasonal lake unique in Britain. For technical reasons the site was not included in the proposed list of European SACs, which seemed to be its best hope for protection. Hydrological studies indicate that quarrying would drain the lake and destroy its interest. The legal battle is continuing.

Selar Farm in South Wales is an SSSI which contains a large population of the marsh fritillary butterfly, a rare species listed by the EC Habitats Directive as in need of special protection. However, Celtic Energy obtained planning permission to turn the site into an open-cast coal mine, and the Welsh Secretary refused to call-in the application for a public inquiry, claiming that the SSSI was only 'of local interest'. As a sop to conservationists, sods of earth containing the butterfly's foodplant are to be translocated to a new site nearby.

There have also been several large purchases in the year under review. The 31,360-hectare Mar Lodge estate in the Cairngorms was purchased by the National Trust for Scotland with funding from the National Heritage Memorial Fund. Conservation bodies had failed in their bid to buy the site in 1993 when the Scottish Office refused its support. The estate will now be managed to encourage forest regeneration, with advice and financial support from Scottish Natural Heritage.

The RSPB purchased the 7,123-hectare Forsinard Estate in Eastern Sutherland to safeguard the area and its rare birds from afforestation. This vast wilderness of moorland and bog is the second largest nature reserve owned by RSPB. English Nature extended its Ribble Marshes reserve by some 2,000 hectares, renaming it the Ribble Estuary National Nature Reserve.

Better News for Bitterns

The bittern has been in steady decline during the past 40 years. In 1994 only 16 booming males were recorded, compared with about 80 in the 1950s. Since the nest is built deep inside dense reed-beds, calling males are used as the only practicable way of assessing breeding numbers. The decline is attributed to the drying of reed-beds, partly due to the failure to maintain waterways, once the responsibility of reed harvesters. Pollution, including pesticides, is a secondary cause.

The conservation of bitterns is now the number one priority of the RSPB. Together with English Nature, the RSPB has undertaken a programme of research to learn more about this secretive bird's life and needs. The long-term objective is to provide enough habitat for at least 100 males – about 1,200 hectares of wet reed-bed. The goal is ambitious and its achievement will be expensive.

Preparatory work during 1995 was on two fronts. Firstly, reeds were planted on a nine-hectare trial plot on former peat cuttings at Ham Wall on the Somerset Levels. If successful, the RSPB intends to extend this to 100 hectares in an attempt to encourage bitterns to stay and breed. Secondly, it has been restoring old waterways through the reed-beds at Minsmere, with encouraging results – in 1995 booming males there doubled their numbers from two to four. The RSPB also has plans to create new reed-beds in Anglesey and on the Solway, while English Nature and the Broads Authority are trying to improve conditions in the bittern's former stronghold on the Broads.

THE BUILT ENVIRONMENT

The most spectacular manifestation of 1994–5 was the success of the National Lottery. The Heritage Lottery Fund, a section within the National Heritage Memorial Fund, had received about £167 million for distribution by 1 August 1995 and had made awards to the value of £48.254 million. This compared with the £10.5 million that the NHMF had to spend in 1993–4, the last year in which it operated under the terms of the National Heritage Act 1980. The 1993–4 funding permitted grants for the repair of the The Crescent at Buxton, Derbys; the purchase by Westminster Abbey of 21 drawings by Nicholas Hawksmoor indicating his plans for the west front; the acquisition by the National Trust for Scotland of Alexander 'Greek' Thomson's Glasgow villa of 1857 and conservation work on the paintings by Sir James Thornhill at St Andrew's Church in Chinnor, Oxon, recently identified as the cartoons for the stained glass in the great rose window of the north front of Westminster Abbey.

In 1994–5 the Heritage Lottery Fund has enabled the NHMF to be more bountiful. Almost £3 million was allocated to the repair of Highcliffe Castle at Christchurch, Dorset, the subject of several earlier applications to demolish. Some £10.2 million was allocated to the endowment of Mar Lodge, Grampian, for the National Trust for Scotland. The money did not just go to historic buildings; the largest and the most controversial donation was the £12.5 million which secured the archives of Sir Winston Churchill for Churchill College, Cambridge. Schemes for the conservation of historic buildings are also eligible for help from the Millenium Commmission, and among the schemes mooted is one for the reinstatement of the three lost spires of Lincoln Cathedral.

English Heritage, having previously been the largest single distributor of public money towards historic buildings, now finds itself with a budget much smaller than that of the Heritage Lottery Fund. Nevertheless, its annual report for 1993–4 records substantial grants, including £325,000 to the De La Warr Pavilion at Bexhill-on-Sea, E. Sussex;

£400,000 to the Clapton Park United Reformed Church in Hackney, London, to enable it to become a centre for the performing arts; and £1 million each to The Crescent at Buxton, Derbys, and Pell Wall Hall, Shropshire, the last house designed by Sir John Soane.

Among properties in the direct care of English Heritage, repair programmes were completed at Clun Castle and Lilleshall Priory, both in Shropshire. The conservation programme at the mid-Victorian Brodsworth Hall, near Doncaster, bequeathed to EH in 1990, was completed on time and the Hall was opened in July 1995.

LISTING

One of English Heritage's principal roles is to advise the Secretary of State for National Heritage on revisions to the statutory lists of buildings of special architectural and historic interest. By 31 December 1994 the total number of listed buildings was 447,043, of which 6,078 were Grade 1 listed. Areas recently resurveyed include the city of Bristol, and spot-listings in 1994–5 have protected structures as various as the summerhouse in Anglesey where the first meeting of the Women's Institute was held in 1915, one of England's earliest cinemas (dating back to 1910) at Brighton, and the house in Worcestershire built by the Duc d'Orleans in 1897, the year he inherited the claim as pretender to the French throne.

On 8 March 1995 the then Secretary of State, Stephen Dorrell (who was succeeded in July 1995 by Virginia Bottomley), announced potentially radical changes. He proposed that the ongoing programme of thematic surveys of particular building types should be subject to public consultation. The owners as well as the general public are now being invited to comment on the projected listings before they are confirmed. This experiment, on which the Government will consult further in a Green Paper expected in the autumn of 1995, began with post war industrial and commercial buildings and 19th-century textile mills in Manchester. Mr Dorrell also announced the final abolition of Crown exemption from listed building consent controls, and a new policy encouraging government departments to dispose of surplus building stock of historic value to the most appropriate user rather than the highest bidder.

The listing of historic parks and gardens remains advisory rather than statutory, although their protection was enhanced in June 1995 when directions came into force requiring that applications affecting sites on the Register of Historic Parks and Gardens should be referred to English Heritage and to the Garden History Society. English Heritage also published its first register of historic battlefields. More than 40 sites have been identified, ranging from Maldon, Essex, where swords were crossed in AD 991 to Sedgemoor, Somerset, the scene of the collapse of the rebellion of the Duke of Monmouth in 1685.

Listing does not guarantee preservation in perpetuity, although it establishes a presumption against demolition. Buildings threatened in the course of the year included Barrington Park (Grade I listed) in Great Barrington, Glos, where a proposal to demolish the substantial wings of 1870 was rejected; St Elizabeth's Church in Eastbourne, E. Sussex, which contains a 130-feet mural in its crypt by Hans Feibusch, who is still painting at the age of 95; Ansley Hall, Warks, which has been derelict for more than three decades; Neuadd Fawr at Cilycwm, Dyfed, an impressive ruined neo-Classical house of 1831 and the Grade II* listed Bethesda Baptist Church in Prince of Wales Road, Swansea (application refused).

Sites are also regularly added to the lists of Scheduled Ancient Monuments, and one of the more unusual recent additions is a medieval rabbit warren in Bedfordshire. The warren, on Dunstable Downs, is one of about 2,000 surviving medieval warrens in England, and is thought to have been built in the 13th century to supply meat and pelts for the monks at the nearby Augustinian priory. The site consists of two 'pillow mounds' surrounded by shallow drainage ditches. One of the mounds is over 32 metres long, 5 metres wide and about 1 metre high.

NATIONAL TRUST

In the summer of 1995 the Grade I listed late 17th-century house Uppark in Sussex was reopened to the public by the National Trust after a £20 million reconstruction following a disastrous fire. The press was generally complimentary and to many visitors the old and new sections shaded into an indistinguishable architectural whole. The reopening of Uppark was an appropriate manifestation of the National Trust's commitment to its buildings in its centenary year. Since its foundation in 1895 the NT has grown to a membership of 2.5 million, an acreage of 570,000, staff levels of around 2,800 and a total expenditure in 1992 of nearly £128 million. It was one of the great regrets of the centenary year that it was marked by the death in July 1995 at the age of 48 of Gervase Jackson-Stops, the NT's respected expert on country houses.

Two of Cumbria's more notable historic buildings succumbed to fire in the course of the year. The partly Georgian, partly Victorian, parish church of St Michael at Workington was gutted late in 1994, and the remarkable Belle Isle on Windermere, a rotunda of 1774, went up in flames at Christmas 1994.

LEGAL CHANGES

Increased controls within conservation areas came into force in June 1995, after which date district councils were able to increase controls without first seeking clearance from the Department of the Environment. In Wales a proposal which would have handed back listed building consent powers to local authorities was rejected in March 1995 in light of the disorganization occasioned by local government reform and after protests by conservationists at the track record of many planning authorities in Wales. It remains necessary for most listed building consents issued by local planning authorities to be cleared by the Welsh Office.

In 1994 the Department of the Environment and the National Heritage Department issued *Planning Policy Guidance: Planning and the Historic Environment, PPG15*. Although the title seems designed to put readers off, it is a very important restatement and amplification of government policy, replacing the earlier DoE circular 8/87. It reintroduces a 'general presumption in favour of the preservation of listed buildings', which had been deleted at draft stage, and states that 'subjective claims for the architectural merits of proposed replacement buildings should not in themselves be held to justify the demolition of any listed building', a policy which, if in force, would have prevented the demolition of nine listed buildings at the No. 1 Poultry site in the City of London. These were demolished in 1994 and archaeological examination and redevelopment continued in 1995.

CHURCHES

Churches are no longer exempt from listed building consent and conservation area consent controls, since Ecclesiastical Exemption was abolished in 1994. The Open Churches Trust, founded by Sir Andrew Lloyd Webber in 1994, launched pilot projects in Liverpool, London and rural Suffolk, and in April 1995 offered its first grants to pay for the expenses of a roster of guides or attendants. The intention is to allow more churches to stay open to the public by taking realistic security measures: a similar scheme has been set up in Scotland. Save Our Parsonages is another new group established in 1994-5 to stem the now well-advanced programme of disposal by the church authorities of mostly historic rectories and parsonages.

Organizations which exist to protect churches once they have closed also grew in strength in 1994-5. The Historic Chapels Trust, concerned with all non-Anglican buildings, negotiated to acquire its first synagogue, in Spitalfields, and took into its care the Dissenters' Chapel of 1834 at Kensal Green Cemetery, London, and a late 18th-century Roman Catholic chapel at Netherton on the outskirts of Liverpool. Peter Brooke, MP, became chairman of the Churches Conservation Trust (formerly the Redundant Churches Fund), which acquired the medieval parish church of All Saints at Langport, Somerset, St Martin's, Colchester, and St Stephen's at Copley, W. Yorks.

Dr David Hope, the outgoing Bishop of London, rejected in July 1995 the recommendation of the Templeman Commission, which he established to consider the future of the 37 Anglican churches within the City of London, that 24 of the churches should be reduced to 'reserve' status. He promoted instead a City Churches Trust to tap support and enthusiasm from outside the congregations of the churches.

WALES

The 1993-4 annual report of Cadw: Welsh Historic Monuments, published on 1 November 1994, recorded the offer of grants of £3,021,000 towards listed buildings and £266,000 for the conservation of ancient monuments. Cadw's 131 sites earned £3,102,000 through gate receipts, an impressive record and proportionately better than that achieved by English Heritage. One-third of the historic buildings grants went to properties owned by the National Trust, the largest sums being offered to Chirk Castle and the Conwy Suspension Bridge. A total of £500,000 went to churches, £400,000 to local authority projects, including the restoration of the Newport Transporter Bridge, and £600,000 to private owners and charitable bodies. The most significant ancient monument grant went to support the programme of Pembrokeshire Coast National Park at Carew Castle: a grant of £286,000 towards the castle for 1993-8 has been agreed in principle. Cadw's holding of sites increased by two with the passing into guardianship of the motte and bailey castle at Wiston, Dyfed, and St Quintin's Castle, Llanblethian, near Cowbridge, the latter after the threat of a compulsory purchase order.

The report also announced the launch of a non-statutory register of historic landscapes in Wales, and a target date of December 1996 for the completion of the county registers of historic parks and gardens.

SCOTLAND

Historic Scotland's annual report for 1994-5, published on 18 July 1995, records the successful move by that organizaton into its new headquarters at Longmore House, Edinburgh, a listed building constructed as a hospital in 1874. Historic Scotland brought the total of scheduled sites in Scotland to 6,108, and completed the target of 150 survey units in additions to the statutory lists of protected buildings. Resurveys of Dundee, Peebles, Duns, Banff and Buchan, and Leith were all completed during the year. A total of £11.4 million was paid out in grants, that expenditure generating an estimated £40 million worth of repair work. The major project of the year was the restoration, at a cost of £2.5 million, of Duff House, which opened to the public in April 1995. Among properties owned directly by Historic Scotland, £1 million went towards the restoration and conversion of Argyll's Lodging in Stirling, which involved collaboration with the University of Stirling's recently established Institute of International Scottish Studies.

Dance

The Royal Ballet continued to attract both praise and opprobium in the year under review. The standard of dancing in the company cannot be faulted but the company's repertoire and management received constant criticism. The company's director, Anthony Dowell, could in part blame bad luck for the problems which beset the company in the early part of 1995. The acclaimed modern dance choreographer Michael Clark had been commissioned to produce a new work, and the prospect of the Royal Ballet-trained *provocateur* finally returning to work with the company aroused enormous curiosity and anticipation. Unfortunately, the work was cancelled shortly before its première due to Clark's self-professed inability to tailor himself to the tight rehearsal schedule. The other eagerly awaited première of the season was a work by the Frankfurt-based choreographer William Forsythe, whose aggressive classicism had been surprisingly well assimilated by the Royal Ballet's dancers in recent seasons. Shortly before the scheduled première, Forsythe announced that he could no longer create works on unfamiliar dancers and that he had moved on so far from the classicism of his earlier work that he could not work successfully with the Royal's classically-trained dancers. He offered to create a ten-minute piece as a consolation, and to give the company his 1985 piece *Steptext*. In the event, he worked with two of his Frankfurt collaborators to produce about 25 minutes of movement entitled *Firstext*. Unfortunately it did not bear comparison with *Steptext*, an exciting and strongly classical work in which the leading role was stunningly danced by Deborah Bull; *Firstext* was a dull and predictable piece which even Sylvie Guillem could not redeem.

In a move caused not by bad luck but by bad planning, a revival of MacMillan's *Prince of the Pagodas* had to be cancelled due to lack of rehearsal time. This was apparently brought about by the company's need to maximize box-office income by performing extra shows of *Swan Lake* over Christmas. The company's new production of *The Sleeping Beauty*, premièred in the USA in the spring of 1994, proved highly controversial, the overpowering designs largely swamping both the dancers and the choreography. The new designs for Ashton's *Rhapsody* were also criticized, and the general timidity of the repertoire was lamented. In a completely inexplicable decision, the widely admired principal dancer Fiona Chadwick was deemed by Anthony Dowell to be superfluous to requirements; she left the company in May 1995. Another departure was the retirement of the company's much loved senior ballerina, Lesley Collier, who has taken up a teaching post at the Royal Ballet School after 30 years with the company.

In November 1994 the Royal Ballet's former principal male dancer Michael Somes died after a short illness. He was a famous partner to Margot Fonteyn, and a teacher, coach and repetiteur to the company for many years. He safeguarded in particular the Ashton repertoire, and had mounted *Enigma Variations* on Birmingham Royal Ballet a month before his death. In spite of a preponderance of Ashton works in the Royal Ballet's repertoire this season, concern has been expressed about the security of his legacy. The increasing influence of Russian training in the Royal Ballet School and therefore in the company has led to fears that the English style of ballet, all but created by Ashton, is being irrevocably eroded. An Ashton conference was held at the Roehampton Institute in November at which proposals for an Ashton Foundation were warmly received.

The new director of Birmingham Royal Ballet, David Bintley, is one of the strongest opponents of the drift to a bland and uniform international style of ballet. He took over from Sir Peter Wright in the summer of 1995. Wright's last season with BRB after 18 years as director was characteristically successful; he mounted an excellent new production of *Coppélia* as well as bringing Massine's *Le Tricorne* (The Three-Cornered Hat) and Tudor's *Pillar of Fire* into the repertoire. The latter gave the company's senior ballerina Marion Tait another opportunity to show her great dramatic talents; she retired at the end of the season but will continue to work with the company as ballet mistress. Sir Peter Wright was made director laureate of the company after a farewell gala at the Birmingham Hippodrome.

For Derek Deane, the director of English National Ballet, an international style of ballet is evidently acceptable. In fact, in spite of its name, the company is notable for its dearth of English dancers. It has always welcomed dancers from many different countries and traditions but can never before have been so resolutely international. Deane considers the technical competence of British students to be unacceptably low and has made scathing comments about teaching standards. He and others have expressed anger about the inadequacy of the system of discretionary grants for dance (and drama) training in the UK. The Labour Party started a consultation process in the autumn of 1994 which could lead it to adopt a policy of accrediting a number of dance and drama schools so that students accepted at the schools would receive mandatory grants. English National Ballet's season was notable mainly for a new production of *Giselle* set in a luxury hotel resort in 1920s Austria, and for a revival of Rudolf Nureyev's dramatic version of *Romeo and Juliet*.

Northern Ballet Theatre mounted two big new productions, both evidently successful with audiences but attracting critical derision. *Swan Lake* was given with new choreography by Christopher Gable and Michael Barrett-Pink; it was generally judged to be a musical and dramatic travesty of the ballet. Gillian Lynne choreographed a full-length ballet based on the life of the Brontë family (*The Brontës*), which was over-ambitious and choreographically and structurally weak.

London City Ballet's productions are more conventional than those favoured by Northern Ballet Theatre. It offers scaled-down but generally traditional productions of the classics and tours them (and one-act ballets) to small venues throughout the country. Its production of *Giselle*, by Galina Samsova with designs by Peter Farmer, is an excellent one. The company has always attracted good dancers; Kim Miller is a much-admired current principal and Clair Thomas a possible future star. It is, however, arguable whether the company is wise to offer its productions in London, where larger-scale (and more expensive) versions are readily available.

Scottish Ballet also mounted a new production of *Swan Lake*, to a better (although not wildly enthusiastic) critical reception. It was designed by Jasper Conran and therefore received a good deal of attention. However, the pretty designs were largely blamed for weakening the drama of the ballet.

CONTEMPORARY DANCE

Rambert Dance Company was officially relaunched in the autumn of 1994 under Christopher Bruce's directorship. His aim is to win back audiences by offering a mixture of revivals of popular works from the company's past and high-quality new works, with the particular object of presenting works which span the divide between classical ballet and modern dance. This was a very promising first season which presented works by Bruce himself, Jiri Kylian (the respected choreographer and director of Netherlands Dance Theatre) and others. In May 1995 the company was invited to perform at the San Francisco Dance Festival which was held to celebrate the 50th anniversary of the signing of the UN Charter in the city. Bruce choreographed a highly successful new work, *Meeting Point*, for the occasion.

Following the demise of London Contemporary Dance Theatre, a small company was set up in the autumn of 1994 under the directorship of Richard Alston. Called simply Richard Alston Dance Company, it is intended to be a vehicle for his choreography. Alston also has an expanded role at The Place in London, establishing it as a choreographic centre and integrating the activities of the Contemporary Dance Trust. The four works offered in the company's inaugural season (two recent and two new works) were all of a high quality and offer a welcome contrast to the avowedly more theatrical approach of Rambert Dance Company.

One of the most ambitious ventures in the season under review was the Woking Dance Umbrella

Festival. It presented a wide range of companies at a variety of venues in the town in the spring of 1995. Participants included Scottish Ballet, CandoCo, V-Tol Dance Company, Laurie Booth, the Jiving Lindy Hoppers (celebrating their tenth anniversary), the tap musical *Hot Shoe Shuffle*, and the classical Indian dancer Nahid Saddiqui. The biggest draw of the season was the Mark Morris Dance Group, who started their first British tour at the Festival. Mark Morris is currently riding the crest of a wave of critical and popular enthusiasm. His work is accessible, musical, intelligent, unpretentious and very entertaining. His tastes and imagination are wide-ranging, and the music he uses encompasses Bach, Brahms, country and western, Gershwin and contemporary composers. He himself is a highly-praised and distinctive performer and his company won universal plaudits.

The contemporary dance festival Dance Umbrella offered its usual impressive array of performers in the autumn of 1994. Particularly welcome was the long overdue London début of the Lucinda Childs Dance Company from New York. Childs's choreography is unrepentantly minimalist, to the point where some critics have wondered if there is anything there at all. Her dance vocabulary is restricted and repetitive, but it achieves moments of great formal beauty. The London repertoire included a rare revival of her 1983 work *Available Light*, to music by John Adams and with designs by the architect Frank Gehry. Other participants in the festival included Matthew Hawkins, Stephen Petronio, Mark Baldwin, Angelin Preljocaj (the French-Albanian choreographer whose programmes included a highly-praised version of *Les Noces*) and Siobhan Davies. Dance Umbrella won the Prudential Award for Dance, worth £25,000, for the second time in two years. Other major contemporary dance festivals were Spring Loaded, a 12-week season at The Place in London in the spring of 1995, including the Cholmondeleys, Yolande Snaith, Bunty Mathias, and a new work by Shobana Jeyasingh entitled *Raid*; and The Turning World, a season also organized by The Place and featuring ten overseas companies.

Siobhan Davies, who received an MBE in the Queen's Birthday Honours, toured a new work, *Wild Translations*, in the spring and summer of 1995 in a programme with her successful 1994 piece *The Glass Blew In*. *Wild Translations* is set to a string quartet by Kevin Volans into which recorded sounds from an African village are introduced by the composer. This is a richly rewarding work, beautifully performed by seven dancers. Kim Brandstrup, whose *Orfeo* won the 1990 Olivier Award, created a new work entitled *Saints and Shadows*, inspired by the Mexican Day of the Dead, for his Arc Dance Company in March 1995. Another notable première was Nigel Charnock's *Hell Bent* in February 1995. This was the final part in a trilogy of powerful self-exploratory works of dance-theatre (often more theatre than dance) by the former member of DV8 Physical Theatre.

VISITORS

The Royal Swedish Ballet came to London for the first time in their 200-year history in July 1995; the company performed Nureyev's production of *Don Quixote* and was generally well-received. Monte Carlo Ballet also made its London début, in May 1995, and proved to be a talented young company. The Royal Danish Ballet made a rare visit to London, performing Flemming Flindt's *Caroline Mathilde* at the Royal Opera House in August–September 1995. Lindsay Kemp presented his 'Gothic operetta' version of *Cinderella* at Sadler's Wells in January–February 1995 as part of the London International Mime Festival; it was a grotesque and completely spellbinding production. Maurice Béjart's Ballet Lausanne performed two programmes at Sadler's Wells in the spring of 1995; one featured the music of Stravinsky and the other was billed as 'The Essence of Béjart – the Art of *pas de deux*'. Sylvie Guillem, a favourite Béjart dancer, guested in a gala to open the season.

Guillem also guested with the Kirov Ballet at the London Coliseum during a season in the summer of 1995. The visit threatened to be overshadowed by internal ructions at the Kirov, where the long-standing artistic director, Oleg Vinogradov, seemed on the point of being ousted. One of the company's star dancers, Farukh Ruzimatov, has been appointed deputy director and Vinogradov's days would appear to be numbered. (The Kirov's rival company in Moscow, the Bolshoi, also underwent a series of crises during the year, culminating with the appointment of the former rebel dancer Vladimir Vasiliev to replace Yuri Grigorovich as director in April 1995.) In the event the season was an undoubted success, especially for the company's incomparable *corps de ballet*.

SECOND-CLASS DANCE

In January 1995 a report commissioned by the Arts Council of England reviewed the provision of theatres for opera and dance in London. It stated that 'it is essential that we move from the current "second class citizenry" provision [for dance] to one in which the dance community has access as of right to suitable facilities'. It came to the conclusion that this could best be achieved not by a dedicated dance house, which would be costly and unlikely to fulfil the diverse needs of dance companies, but by a network of theatres, including one whose main activity would be the provision of dance. It discussed the merits of various theatres for this purpose, with Sadler's Wells being the most favoured. It also said that grand opera was over-provided for, and that English National Opera should refocus its activities to include more small-scale work at different venues, thus freeing the London Coliseum for large-scale dance performances. It also recognized the need for a venue for smaller-scale dance companies.

The report was criticized in some quarters for concentrating on the current level of demand for dance and underestimating the potential growth in audiences should high-quality dance be regularly provided in suitable venues. However, it provided a boost to the redevelopment plans in progress at Sadler's Wells, which also received £1.5 million of National Lottery funding in May 1995. More controversially, the Royal Opera House received £55 million from the same source in July 1995 towards its ambitious £213 million redevelopment plans. Although it came with the proviso that some ticket prices should be reduced and that education activities should be increased, it provoked a storm of protest. In an unfortunate piece of timing, the Royal Opera House announced a few days later that its schools' opera matinées would be cancelled in the 1995–6 season due to lack of sponsorship. The Royal Opera House will close for the refurbishment in the middle of 1997; a final decision has yet to be taken about a temporary home for its companies.

PRODUCTIONS

ROYAL BALLET
Founded 1931 as the Vic-Wells Ballet
Royal Opera House, Covent Garden, London WC2E 9DD

World premières:
All Things Considered (William Tuckett), 24 January 1995. A solo given at the Orchard Theatre, Dartford, as part of the 'Dance Bites' tour. Music, Jimmy Davis, Roger Ramirez, Jimmy Sherman. Dancer, Leire Ortueta

Two or Three Dialogues (Ashley Page), 24 January 1995. A *pas de deux* given at the Orchard Theatre, Dartford, as part of the 'Dance Bites' tour. Music, Brian Eno; costumes, Flora McLean. Dancers, Ann de Vos, William Trevitt

Ebony Concerto (Ashley Page), 30 March 1995. A one-act ballet. Music, Stravinsky; costumes, Antony McDonald. Dancers, Deborah Bull, Ann de Vos, Adam Cooper, Tetsuya Kumakawa

Firstext (Dana Caspersen, William Forsythe, Antony Rizzi), 27 April 1995. A one-act work. Music, Thom Willems; set, William Forsythe; costumes, Naoki Takizawa (Miyake Design Studio) and Raymond Dragon Design Inc. Cast, Sylvie Guillem, Adam Cooper, Peter Abegglen, Matthew Dibble, Matthew Hart, Benazir Hussein

Company premières:
Duo Concertant (Balanchine), 24 January 1995. Given at the Orchard Theatre, Dartford, as part of the 'Dance Bites' tour. Music, Stravinsky. Cast, Viviana Durante, Bruce Sansom, Philip Gammon (piano), Yuri Torchinsky (violin)

A Shropshire Lad (William Tuckett), 24 January 1995. Given at the Orchard Theatre, Dartford, as part of the 'Dance Bites' tour. Music, George Butterworth, E. J. Moeran. Cast, Gary Avis, Belinda Hatley, Adam Cooper, William Trevitt

Solo (Matthew Hart), 24 January 1995. Given at the Orchard Theatre, Dartford, as part of the 'Dance Bites' tour. Music, Shostakovich. Dancer, Ricardo Cervera

Steptext (William Forsythe), 27 April 1995. Music, Bach; designs, Raymond Dragon Design Inc./William Forsythe.

Cast, Deborah Bull, Zoltan Solymosi, Tetsuya Kumakawa, Peter Abegglen

Full length ballets from the repertoire: *The Sleeping Beauty* (Petipa, prod. Dowell 1994), *Cinderella* (Ashton, 1948), *Swan Lake* (Petipa/Ivanov, prod. Dowell 1987), *Giselle* (Coralli/Perrot, prod. Wright 1985), *Romeo and Juliet* (MacMillan, 1965).

One-act ballets and *pas de deux* from the repertoire: *La Valse* (Ashton, 1958), *Birthday Offering pas de deux* (Ashton, 1956), *Sylvia pas de deux* (Ashton, 1967), *Symphonic Variations* (Ashton, 1946), *Daphnis and Chloë* (Ashton, 1951, with new designs by Martyn Bainbridge), *Fearful Symmetries* (Page, 1994), *Herman Schmerman* (Forsythe, 1992), *Symphony in C* (Balanchine, 1947), *The Dream* (Ashton, 1964), *Façade* (Ashton, 1931), *Air pas de deux* from *Homage to the Queen* (Ashton, 1953), *La Chatte metamorphosée en femme* (Ashton, 1985), *Meditation* from *Thaïs* (Ashton, 1971), *Raymonda pas de deux* (Ashton, 1962), *Danses Concertantes* (MacMillan, 1955), *Petrushka* (Fokine, 1911), *Rhapsody* (Ashton, 1980, with new designs by Patrick Caulfield), *La Ronde* (Tetley, 1987).

In addition to performances at the Royal Opera House, the company toured to S. Korea (Seoul), Japan (Tokyo and a regional tour) and the USA (San Francisco and Los Angeles) in May–July 1995. The performances in San Francisco were part of the San Francisco Dance Festival celebrating the 50th anniversary of the signing of the UN Charter in the city in June 1945. The repertoire on the tour was *Giselle*, *The Sleeping Beauty*, *Swan Lake*, *Herman Schmerman*, *Fearful Symmetries*, *A Month in the Country*, *La Valse*, *Raymonda pas de deux*, *Sylvia pas de deux* and *Meditation* from *Thaïs*.

A group of Royal Ballet dancers performed in Dartford, Cambridge, Leicester and Newcastle upon Tyne in January–February 1995 on the second 'Dance Bites' tour. They performed the world premières of *All Things Considered* and *Two or Three Dialogues*, the company premières of *Duo Concertant*, *A Shropshire Lad* and *Solo*, together with *Meditation* from *Thaïs* and *Herman Schmerman*.

BIRMINGHAM ROYAL BALLET
Founded 1946 as the Sadler's Wells Opera Ballet
Birmingham Hippodrome, Thorp Street, Birmingham B5 4AU

World premières:
Coppélia (Petipa, Cecchetti and Peter Wright, prod. Wright), 3 March 1995. Music, Delibes; design, Peter Farmer. Cast led by Sandra Madgwick, Sergiu Pobereznic and John Auld
    Libramenta (Oliver Hindle), 10 March 1995. Music, Bartók; design, Lakis Yenethli. Cast included Sergiu Pobereznic, Monica Zamora, Duncan de Gruchy, Catherine Batcheller, Andrea Tredinnick

Company premières:
Le Tricorne (Massine), 11 October 1994. Music, de Falla; design, Picasso. Cast led by Joseph Cipolla, Monica Zamora and David Morse
    Enigma Variations (Ashton), 11 October 1994. Music, Elgar; design, Julia Trevelyan Oman. Cast led by Desmond Kelly, Sherilyn Kennedy, Sandra Madgwick, Leslie Edwards, Ravenna Tucker, Alain Dubreuil, Michael O'Hare, Edwin Mota, Kevin O'Hare, Jessica Clarke, Duncan de Gruchy, Catherine Batcheller
    Pillar of Fire (Tudor), 10 March 1995. Given as part of the 'Towards the Millennium' festival's celebrations of the 1940s. Music, Schoenberg; design, Jo Mielziner. Cast led by Marion Tait, Kevin O'Hare, Sherilyn Kennedy and Simone Clarke

Full length ballets from the repertoire: *Romeo and Juliet* (MacMillan, 1965), *La fille mal gardée* (Ashton, 1960), *The Nutcracker* (Ivanov, prod. Wright, additional choreography

by Vincent Redmon, 1990), *The Sleeping Beauty* (Petipa, prod. Wright 1984), *Swan Lake* (Petipa/Ivanov, prod. Wright and Samsova 1981).

One-act ballets from the repertoire: *Galanteries* (Bintley, 1992), *Street* (Hart, 1993), *Prodigal Son* (Balanchine, 1929), *Pineapple Poll* (Cranko, 1951), *Theme and Variations* (Balanchine, 1947), *Las Hermanas* (MacMillan, 1963), *Choreatium* (Massine, 1933).

In addition to four seasons at Birmingham Hippodrome, the company toured to Edinburgh, Bradford (two seasons), Bristol, Plymouth (two seasons), London (one season each at the London Coliseum, Sadler's Wells Theatre and the Royal Opera House), Sunderland, Liverpool and Southampton. It also toured to Germany (Stuttgart, Frankfurt and Ludwigshafen) in May 1995, with a repertoire of *Enigma Variations*, *Pillar of Fire*, *Choreatium* and *Swan Lake*.

On 1 July 1995 a farewell gala for Sir Peter Wright was held at the Birmingham Hippodrome. The programme included *Serenade* (Balanchine, 1934), *Theme and Variations* and extracts from *Job* (de Valois, 1931), *Hobson's Choice* (Bintley, 1989), *The Mirror Walkers* (Wright, 1963) and *Romeo and Juliet*. An all-star cast performed *Façade* (Ashton, 1931) and the Royal Ballet School performed *Valse Fantaisie* (Balanchine, 1953).

ENGLISH NATIONAL BALLET
Founded 1950 as London Festival Ballet
Markova House, 39 Jay Mews, London SW7 2ES

World premières:
Giselle (Coralli/Perrot, prod. Deane), 31 October 1994. Music, Adam; design, Charles Cusick-Smith. Cast led by Agnes Oaks and Thomas Edur
    Symphonic Dances (Mauro Bigonzetti), 25 April 1995. Music, Rachmaninov; design, Enrico Coveri. Dancers, Ambra Vallo, Giuseppe Picone, Sarah McIlroy, Daniel Jones, Lucy Smith, David Dawson, Marta Barahona, Christopher Hampson, Rachael Hunt, Fabio Caracci

Full-length ballets from the repertoire: *Swan Lake* (Petipa/Ivanov, prod. Struchkova 1993), *The Nutcracker* (Ivanov, prod. Stevenson 1972), *Romeo and Juliet* (Nureyev, 1977), *Coppélia* (Petipa and Cecchetti, prod. Hynd 1985).

One-act ballets from the repertoire: *Graduation Ball* (Lichine, 1940), *Square Dance* (Balanchine, 1957), *Dances from Napoli* (Bournonville), *Grand Pas* from *The Sleeping Beauty* (Petipa), *X. N. Tricities* (Bigonzetti, 1994), *Grand Pas* from *Paquita* (Petipa/Deane).

The full company toured to Manchester (two seasons), Leeds, Liverpool, Southampton (two seasons), Nottingham, London (two seasons at the Royal Festival Hall) and Bristol. In April–May 1995 the company split into two groups and went on two small-scale tours. One had piano accompaniment and a repertoire of *Square Dance*, *Graduation Ball* and *Symphonic Dances*. The other toured with an orchestra and performed *Dances from Napoli*, the *Grand Pas* from *The Sleeping Beauty*, *X. N. Tricities* and the *Grand Pas* from *Paquita*. The small-scale tours visited Dartford, Crewe, High Wycombe, Barrow-in-Furness, Tunbridge Wells, Basingstoke, Barnstaple, Cambridge, Leicester and Darlington.

In June 1995 the company toured to South Korea with a repertoire of *Swan Lake* and *Coppélia*.

RAMBERT DANCE COMPANY
Founded 1926 as the Marie Rambert Dancers
94 Chiswick High Road, London W4 1SH

World premières:
Meeting Point (Christopher Bruce), 9 May 1995, as part of the San Francisco Dance Festival. Music, Michael Nyman; design, Marian Bruce

Jupiter is Crying (Per Jonsson), 17 May 1995. Score, Sven-David Sandström; design, Per Jonsson
Dancing Attendance on the Cultural Chasm (Matthew Hawkins), 28 June 1995. Music, Rameau; design, Pearl

Company premières:
Petite Mort (Jiri Kylian), 21 October 1994. Music, Mozart; design, Joke Visser
Axioma 7 (Ohad Naharin), 21 October 1994. Music, Bach; design, Ohad Naharin
Rooster (Christopher Bruce), 1 March 1995. Music, The Rolling Stones; design, Marian Bruce
Swansong (Christopher Bruce), 12 April 1995. Music, Philip Chambon; design, Christopher Bruce

Works from the repertoire: *Sergeant Early's Dream* (Bruce, 1984), *The Garden of Earthly Delights* (Clarke, 1984), *Crossing* (Bruce, 1994), *Land* (Bruce, 1985), *Banter Banter* (Baldwin, 1994).
    The company performed in Edinburgh (two seasons), Swansea, Dartford, Sheffield, Liverpool, Newcastle upon Tyne, Leeds, Oxford, Northampton, Brighton, Canterbury, Norwich, Swindon and Ashton-under-Lyne. It also performed at the Oldenburg Festival, Germany, and in Denmark (Copenhagen and Aarhus) in March 1995, with a repertoire of *Crossing, Petite Mort* and *Rooster.*
    Dancers from the company took part in two gala performances by London Musici at St John's Smith Square, London. On 20 April 1995 Mark Baldwin choreographed excerpts from the world première of *Odi et Amo* by Roxanna Panufnik (dancers, Hope Muir and Steven Brett) and on 12 July 1995 Didy Veldman collaborated with the composer Adam Gorb on the world première of *Kol Simcha* (dancers, Patricia Hines, Paul Liburd, Christopher Powney and Sarah Warsop).

RICHARD ALSTON DANCE COMPANY
Founded 1994
The Place, 17 Duke's Road, London WC1H 9AB

World premières:
Something in the City, 17 November 1994. Music, Man Jumping; costumes, Jane Beckley
Shadow Realm, 17 November 1994. Music, Simon Holt

Company premières:
Movements from Petrushka, 17 November 1994. Music, Stravinsky
Lachrymae (originally entitled *Sad Eyes*), 17 November 1994. Music, Benjamin Britten; design, Belinda Ackermann
    The company performed in Warwick, London (The Place), Manchester, Swindon, Crewe, Nottingham, Edinburgh, Inverness, Dundee, Glasgow, Stirling, Aberdeen, Sheffield, Perth, Blackpool, Hayes, and at the Dublin Festival in June 1995.

SCOTTISH BALLET
Founded 1956 as the Western Theatre Ballet
261 West Princes Street, Glasgow G4 9EE

World premières:
Swan Lake (Petipa/Ivanov, prod. Samsova), 2 March 1995. Music, Tchaikovsky; design, Jasper Conran. Cast led by Yurie Shinohara, Campbell McKenzie and Robert Hampton
Haydn Pieces (Mark Baldwin), 14 June 1995. Music, Haydn; design, Marian Bruce. Dancers, Daria Klimentova, Vladislav Bubnov, Nicci Theis, Christopher Giles, Ruth Robinson, Robin Bernadet, Leesa Sparkes, Oliver Rydout, Claire Mahon
Full-length ballets from the repertoire: *Cinderella* (Darrell, 1979), *The Nutcracker* (Darrell after Ivanov, 1973).

One-act ballets from the repertoire: *Chéri* (Darrell, 1980), *Les Sylphides* (Fokine, 1907), *Shoals of Herring* (Maldoom, 1983), *pas de trois* from *The Fairy Doll* (Nikolai and Sergei Legat, 1903), *L'Après-Midi d'un Faune* (Uboldie), *The Flower Festival pas de deux* (Bournonville, 1858).
    The full company performed in Edinburgh (two seasons), Newcastle upon Tyne (two seasons), Aberdeen (two seasons), Glasgow, Woking, Inverness, Hull and Belfast. In June 1995 it split into three groups and staged three small-scale tours with a repertoire of *Chéri, L'Après-Midi d'un Faune, Les Sylphides, pas de trois* from *The Fairy Doll, The Flower Festival pas de deux, Haydn Pieces* and *Shoals of Herring.* The tours visited Dumfries, Irvine, Falkirk, Stranraer, Fort William, Wick, Kirkcaldy, Dunoon, Dornoch, Oban, Inverurie, Perth, Fraserburgh, Cumbernauld, Aboyne, Galashiels, Montrose, Dundee and Greenock. The company also performed *The Nutcracker* in Seville, Spain, in January 1995.

Film

The centenary of cinema was celebrated in 1995 – except in Britain, where the official anniversary is 1996, marking the first public screenings of films in this country. It is impossible to put an exact date on the birth of cinema; inventors in France, Britain and the USA were all developing motion picture cameras in the 1890s, but the Lumière Brothers' claim has become institutionalized, in part, perhaps, because their earliest films survive. It is the date of their première exhibition in Paris – 28 December 1895 – which gave the cinema world a chance to celebrate and to take stock. (As Jean-Luc Godard noted drily, it is telling that the centenary should be marked not by the invention of the process, nor by the first filming, but by the first time people paid to see a film.)

Looking back on the first 100 years of cinema, what is most striking is how the USA has dominated this industry and art form in a way that would have been unimaginable in the first 40 years of the medium. Strong local industries do exist in parts of the world western critics too often neglect – in Japan, Hong Kong, and especially Bombay – but Hollywood's global reach is without parallel and the American studios' grip has continued to tighten in 1994–5, making significant inroads in China, the former Soviet bloc and India.

ALL-TIME GREATS

The domination of the USA was reflected in poll after poll of international critics, film-makers and film-goers. The clear consensus was that the greatest films ever made are *Citizen Kane*, *The Godfather*, *La Règle du Jeu*, *Vertigo*, *Seven Samurai*, *Lawrence of Arabia*, *Raging Bull*, *Touch of Evil*, *Tokyo Story* and *L'Atalante*. Honourable mentions go to *Night of the Hunter*, *Casablanca*, and *Les Enfants du Paradis*. The American influence is even clearer in the lists of the greatest actors and directors: Marlon Brando, Charlie Chaplin, Cary Grant, James Stewart and Robert De Niro; Katharine Hepburn, Barbara Stanwyck, Bette Davis, Meryl Streep and Jodie Foster; Alfred Hitchcock, Orson Welles, Jean Renoir, Martin Scorsese, David Lean, Stanley Kubrick, Howard Hawks and John Ford. (The first 35 years of cinema's century were typically ignored or forgotten, with the exceptions of Chaplin, Buster Keaton, and D. W. Griffith.)

If 1994–5 holds out any promise for film-makers outside Hollywood, it is amongst the young and in the East. China is likely to emerge as the largest single market for films in the next decade. Ironically, the most established of the local film-makers, Zhang Yimou and Chen Kaige, increasingly look to the West for finance and critical acceptance. Zhang's humanist fable *To Live* was acclaimed at the 1994 Cannes Festival, where it won a Best Actor award for

Ge You and shared the Grand Jury Prize with Nikita Mikhalkov's sly evocation of the Stalinist era, *Burnt by the Sun* (which later won the Oscar for Best Foreign Film). Although *To Live* focussed on the trials and tribulations of everyday life, its chronicle of Chinese Communism was deemed insidious in Beijing, and Zhang was forced to apologize before he was permitted to shoot his next film, the glamorous 1930s gangster picture *Shanghai Triad*. Younger and surprisingly provocative independent film-makers are gradually emerging in China, including He Yi (*Postman*), Zhang Yuan (*Beijing Bastards*) and Wang Xiaoshuai (*The Days*).

Taiwan's Edward Yang and Hou Hsiaohsien, two of the most promising film-makers of the 1980s, continue to make astute, rich films, including *A Confucian Confusion* and *Good Men, Good Women*, but are proving too esoteric to make a significant impact elsewhere. In Hong Kong, the most successful supplier of Asian films, production is currently standing at less than half the 200 films a year it produced in 1993. While there is obvious nervousness about the implications of Chinese rule from 1997, especially in terms of censorship, there has been no mass exodus of film talent as yet.

The Hong Kong industry is arguably even more commercial than Hollywood, an unedifying mixture of slapstick comedies, supernatural romances and martial arts thrillers. Wong Kar-Wai is an exception and one of the most exciting talents to emerge on the art film scene for a long time. He is one of cinema's great romantics, a purveyor of heartbreak and elegy. His 1989 masterpiece *Days of Being Wild* was only noticed by western distributors in 1994, after the unveiling of his long-awaited epic *Ashes of Time*, which was followed almost immediately by *Chungking Express*, an invigorating urban love story made in just three months. Both films have firmly established Wong as a man to watch.

EYES DOWN

This was a good year for Australasian cinema. A new generation of young directors has emerged to fill the void left by Peter Weir, Bruce Beresford and Fred Schepisi, who have all moved to Hollywood. Stephen Elliott's *The Adventures of Priscilla, Queen of the Desert*, a comedy about three drag queens driving across the outback, is far removed from the tasteful period pieces which were typical of Australian cinema 15 years ago. P. J. Hogan's *Muriel's Wedding* was equally bold and brash, an ugly duckling romance which was loud, anarchic and very popular. From New Zealand, Peter Jackson's *Heavenly Creatures* caused a stir with its vividly imaginative reconstruction of a notorious 1950s matricide. Jackson takes us into the confused minds of two teenage girls, hopelessly besotted with each other and utterly at odds with the repressive society around them. (Lesbian killers were much in vogue this year, having *Fun* in America, and sharing a *Butterfly Kiss* in Britain.) Lee Tamahori's *Once Were Warriors* was an even more controversial adaptation of a best-selling autobiographical novel which portrayed contemporary Maoris as boorish, chauvinist drunks. A hard-hitting, aggressively stylized film, *Once Were Warriors* made more money in New Zealand than *Jurassic Park*. However, history may be on the verge of repeating itself in Australasia. Hollywood still exerts a strong siren call and Tamahori has since shot *Mulholland Falls* in America with Nick Nolte and Melanie Griffith.

The year under review was a mixed one for British cinema. Activity remained low but *The Madness of King George*, *Tom and Viv* and *Carrington* all won accolades in America and at Cannes, where Britain was also represented by Ken Loach with the impressive Spanish Civil War drama *Land and Freedom*, Terence Davies, whose *Neon Bible* received mixed reviews, and honorary Englishman James Ivory with the disappointing *Jefferson in Paris*. Mike Newell followed *Four Weddings and a Funeral* with a sour, half-achieved adaptation of Beryl Bainbridge's bittersweet backstage reminiscence *An Awfully Big Adventure*. The role of a homosexual, sadistic and pretentious director was never going to please Hugh Grant's new legion of fans, and so it proved. It was a miserable year for the English heart-throb: the media's already keen interest in his relationship with Liz Hurley exploded when he was arrested for 'lewd behaviour' with a prostitute on Sunset Boulevard, just weeks before the release of his mainstream romantic comedy *Nine Months*.

THE LUCK OF THE DRAW

The year produced first feature films from four stage and television directors: Nicolas Hytner's triumphant *The Madness of King George*, Antonia Bird's *Priest*, Paula Milne's *Captives* and Danny Boyle's *Shallow Grave*, which captured significant British audiences. Box-office business slumped in the first half of 1995, down 11 per cent on 1994 in the first quarter; this was the first fall in attendance since 1984. The National Lottery was just one of the factors that was blamed. The Secretary of State for National Heritage (Stephen Dorrell, replaced by Virginia Bottomley in July 1995) redirected some of the National Lottery funds to film-makers, in the form of £10 million a year for the next seven years, but disappointed the industry by not providing the kind of tax incentives which have proved so successful in Ireland.

Ireland was the principal beneficiary of Hollywood's current swashbuckler fad, as represented by Liam Neeson in *Rob Roy*, Mel Gibson in *Braveheart* and Richard Gere in *First Knight*. British production facilities were nevertheless much in demand; *Judge Dredd*, *Mary Shelley's Frankenstein* and *Mission Impossible* were all shot in Britain. The Scott brothers,

Tony and Ridley, were sufficiently confident to spend £12 million to acquire Shepperton studios.

The British Board of Film Classification (BBFC) finally released *Reservoir Dogs* on video, uncut, after a delay of 18 months. *Pulp Fiction* followed without a hitch, and *Bad Lieutenant* – though this was discreetly censored.

If Hollywood remains the mecca of the film world, it is a mecca with a crisis in prospect. Under political fire once more with the rise of the New Right, and in a period of corporate transition, the studios have a vulnerable air. The new Speaker of the House of Representatives, Newt Gingrich, turned his fire on liberals in general and the Public Broadcasting Service in particular, but Republican presidential front-runner Bob Dole hit even closer to home, attacking the Time-Warner corporation for backing 'nightmares of depravity' like *Natural Born Killers*, directed by Oliver Stone from a script by Quentin Tarantino. The most controversial film of the year, *NBK*, as it became known, caused a storm within days of its release when media reports began to link the film to real crime sprees. In essence a re-run of the familiar story of two misunderstood lovers on the run from society who become famous (cf. *Bonnie and Clyde*, *Badlands*), *Natural Born Killers* upped the ante with hyperbolic violence – the death toll is ludicrously high – and a disorientating multimedia visual aesthetic incorporating 35 mm and 16 mm film, video, black and white and colour, and even some animation; this stylistic overload caused Tarantino to disown the film, though not on moral grounds. Stone claimed he was satirizing the media, but the media were largely unimpressed, especially in Europe. Scheduled for a November 1994 release in Britain, the film was initially denied a certificate by the BBFC after the press claimed that there had been ten copycat killings in the USA. The film was released uncut in February 1995 after the BBFC investigated these cases and found that the link had been given no credence by the police agencies involved.

CRITICAL SUCCESS

Hollywood did not have a great deal to boast about in 1994–5. There were a handful of prestigious movies, but they often were not produced by the major studios and they did not make money. The film that received the best reviews was Robert Redford's *Quiz Show*, an intelligent picture about the rigging of the television show *Twenty-One* in the 1950s. With a subtly nuanced screenplay by Paul Attanasio and a wonderful cast including Ralph Fiennes, John Turturro, Paul Scofield, Rob Morrow and David Paymer, this was an unusually sophisticated entertainment. However, the film struggled to make more than $30 million in the USA, despite a full relaunch before the Academy Awards.

It was a similar story with *The Shawshank Redemption*, *Nobody's Fool* and *Ed Wood*. Adapting a short story by Stephen King, writer-director Frank

Darabont cast Tim Robbins in *The Shawshank Redemption* as a man falsely convicted of murder who puts his accounting skills to good use inside the Shawshank prison. Morgan Freeman deserved his Oscar nomination for his portrayal of Robbins' pal, Red, one of seven nominations the film received. The reviews were great but the audiences stayed away. *Nobody's Fool* was a charming smalltown drama with a very funny Oscar-nominated performance from Paul Newman as Sully, an ageing freelance labourer trying to get by on his own who finds he is actually at the hub of his family and community. This was a return to form for writer-director Robert Benton, with revelatory acting support from Bruce Willis and Melanie Griffith, but it cost $30 million to make and barely surpassed that at the box-office. (As a rule of thumb studios reckon the US box-office must double the production cost if the film is to make a profit after advertising and distribution costs.)

Directed by Tim Burton (*Beetlejuice*, *Edward Scissorhands* and the first two *Batman* films), *Ed Wood* made less than $10 million. Burton received the best reviews of his career for his affectionate black and white tribute to the late and not-so-great director Ed Wood. Played by Johnny Depp as an innocent *auteur* with a penchant for tight-fitting angora sweaters, Wood made a handful of low-budget horror films in the 1950s, including *Plan Nine from Outer Space*, which commonly features on lists as the worst film ever made. Wood had no talent, but he never knew it – that was his tragedy, suggests Burton, and his salvation. Martin Landau won the best supporting actor Oscar with his devastating portrayal of *Dracula* star Bela Lugosi.

Oscars

Despite the quality of these films and the British Oscar contenders *The Madness of King George* (which earned nominations for Nigel Hawthorne and Helen Mirren), *Tom and Viv* (Miranda Richardson and Rosemary Harris) and *Four Weddings and a Funeral* (best picture, best original screenplay), the Academy likes to reward success and this year that effectively narrowed the field to two films, *Pulp Fiction* and *Forrest Gump*.

Pulp Fiction, directed by Quentin Tarantino, was released in the autumn of 1994 after winning the *Palme D'Or* at the Cannes festival. It was the first substantial hit to come from the generation who grew up idolizing Scorsese and watching films on video, and then started to make them on Hollywood's independent fringe inspired by the examples of Spike Lee and Jim Jarmusch. It was produced by Miramax, combined flip humour and casual violence, and played out post-modern structural conundrums in the form of three overlapping generic tales: the bodyguard who falls for the boss's wife; the boxer who refuses to throw a fight; and two hit men out on a job. However, unlike most independent films it had an all-star cast (John Travolta, Samuel L. Jackson, Bruce Willis, Uma Thurman, Harvey

Keitel, Tim Roth, Eric Stoltz, Rosanna Arquette and Christopher Walken) and it took more than $100 million at the American box-office. In the event, despite seven nominations, the film only picked up the Oscar for best screenplay. However, Tarantino was the writer-director every actor wanted to work with. He collaborated with Robert Rodriguez, Alexandre Rockwell and Allison Anders on the portmanteau film *Four Rooms*, and again with Rodriguez to produce, script and co-star in *From Dusk Til Dawn*, but refused to be drawn on what his next feature film project would be. A new distribution deal with Miramax, whereby he can bring over four Asian films a year on his own label, put the imprimatur on his success. His influence as a director is already visible in recent independent thrillers like Bryan Singer's masterly *The Usual Suspects* and *Things to Do in Denver When You're Dead* (both acclaimed at the 1995 Cannes Festival), and his significance as a figure-head for young filmmakers can scarcely be over-estimated.

Much of what was bold and exciting in American film-making in 1994–5 came out of the independent sector: the astonishingly successful ghetto documentary *Hoop Dreams*, Richard Linklater's *Dazed and Confused* and *Before Sunrise*, David O. Russell's *Spanking the Monkey*, Kevin Smith's *Clerks*, James Gray's *Little Odessa*, Hal Hartley's *Amateur*, John Dahl's *The Last Seduction* and Boaz Yakin's aptly-named *Fresh*. These films seemed all the fresher for the staleness of big budget studio productions like *Batman Forever*, *Judge Dredd*, *Casper* and *Tank Girl*, films which lack any engagement with the real world.

Gump is Innocent – OK?

If Tarantino is the great white hope of the 'New' Hollywood, then *Forrest Gump* stands for the status quo: a $50 million paean to escapism. Tom Hanks played the eponymous simpleton, who conducted the audience on what amounted to a virtual reality tour of American history from the 1960s to the present day. Gump walks through the desegregation riots, Vietnam and Watergate utterly oblivious to what is going on around him, and director Robert Zemeckis confers on this ignorance the grace of innocence. The film became a national phenomenon in the USA where its politics were hotly debated – some found it platitudinous and politically correct, while others pointed out the reactionary tendency by which the counter-culture came to signify a creeping social malaise. Gumpisms were all the rage: 'Life is like a box of chocolates, you never know what you're going to get'; 'Simple is as simple does' and so forth. The box-office gross surpassed $600 million world-wide, and *Forrest Gump* dominated the Academy Awards, winning best picture, best actor (the second year running for Hanks), and best director.

The scale of the success was a reminder of how high the stakes have become for film-makers. With increasingly sophisticated merchandising and marketing tie-in arrangements, the continuing growth of ancillary markets (satellite, cable, video and television sales), and the ever-expanding foreign box-office reaches, blockbuster films are more lucrative than ever before. Ironically, the sheer scale of operations may be undermining Hollywood's competitiveness. Actors, directors, even script-writers, are all demanding a bigger share. After just two hits, *Ace Ventura: Pet Detective* and *The Mask*, the comedian Jim Carrey commanded a salary of $7 million for *Dumb and Dumber* (half its budget), and then $20 million for the forthcoming *Cable Guy*. The novelist John Grisham was paid $6 million for the film rights to *A Time To Die*. Joe Eszterhas, who scripted *Basic Instinct* and *Jagged Edge*, earned a reported $4 million for a four-page outline of a film which will probably never be made. These costs are pushing budgets so high that even relatively straightforward dramas need to be blockbusters to turn in a profit, and this necessarily inhibits the production of more challenging material. More-over, if a film does not deliver immediately, in its opening weekend, the distributors can no longer wait to see if it will build an audience on the strength of word of mouth. Again, this mitigates against anything that cannot be sold on its name alone, and that includes literate, middle-brow fare. Films by major directors, like Barry Levinson's *Jimmy Holly-wood*, Bill Forsyth's *Being Human* and James L. Brooks' *I'll Do Anything* all went straight to video in the UK after disappointing box-office in the USA. *Blue Sky* won the best actress Oscar for Jessica Lange but it only played a token week in London before its video release.

DEEP WATERS

The dangers of this climate even for the purveyors of blockbusters are amply illustrated by the saga of *Waterworld*. Kevin Costner starred in this futuristic action picture set in a world flooded because of global warming. An initial budget of $70 million was quickly revised upwards to $120 million as the difficulties of filming on water began to sink in. Even this proved optimistic, but the studio, Universal, had no option but to keep bailing the film out until it finally came in at a cost of some $170 million. When advertising costs come into play, that makes *Water-world* the first $200 million film. Universal is part of the MCA conglomerate owned by Matsushita, who sold 80 per cent of their interests to Seagrams shortly before the film opened. Meanwhile Pioneer wrote off $90 million in losses from their invest-ment in Carolco, and Sony wiped $3.2 billion from the value of SPE (Columbia-TriStar) which it had acquired only five years before. All this bad news was overshadowed by more glamorous corporate manoeuvering – Disney's takeover of ABC and distribution deals with Miramax and Merchant-Ivory, and the establishment of the first major new studio since Twentieth Century Fox in 1935: Dreamworks SKG, founded by multi-millionaires David Geffen, Steven Spielberg, and ex-Disney

production head Jeffrey Katzenberg. Nevertheless, the writing is on the wall: Hollywood intends to spend its way out of trouble, but in trying to be all things to all people, it could end up satisfying no-one.

FILM AWARD WINNERS

ACADEMY AWARDS 1994
Best Picture – *Forrest Gump*
Best Director – Robert Zemeckis, *Forrest Gump*
Best Actor – Tom Hanks, *Forrest Gump*
Best Actress – Jessica Lange, *Blue Sky*
Best Supporting Actor – Martin Landau, *Ed Wood*
Best Supporting Actress – Dianne Wiest, *Bullets Over Broadway*
Best Original Screenplay – Quentin Tarantino, Roger Avary, *Pulp Fiction*
Best Adapted Screenplay – Eric Roth, *Forrest Gump*
Best Foreign Language Film – *Burnt by the Sun* (Russia)
Best Original Score – Hans Zimmer, *The Lion King*
Best Original Song – Elton John, Sir Tim Rice, 'Can You Feel the Love Tonight?', *The Lion King*
Best Cinematography – *Legends of the Fall*
Best Art Direction – *The Madness of King George*
Best Costume Design – *The Adventures of Priscilla, Queen of the Desert*
Best Film Editing – *Forrest Gump*
Best Sound – *Speed*
Best Sound Effects Editing – *Speed*
Best Visual Effects – *Forrest Gump*
Best Make-up – *Ed Wood*
Best Animated Short – *Bob's Birthday*
Best Documentary Feature – *Maya Lin: A Strong Clear Vision*
Best Short Documentary – *A Time for Justice*
Best Live Action Short (tie) – *Franz Kafka's It's A Wonderful Life*, *Trevor*
Irving G. Thalberg Memorial Award – Clint Eastwood
Jean Hersholt Humanitarian Award – Quincy Jones
Honorary Award – Michaelangelo Antonioni

BAFTA AWARDS 1995
Best Film – *Four Weddings and a Funeral*
Best Director – Mike Newell, *Four Weddings and a Funeral*
Best Actor – Hugh Grant, *Four Weddings and a Funeral*
Best Actress – Susan Sarandon, *The Client*
Best Supporting Actor – Samuel L. Jackson, *Pulp Fiction*
Best Supporting Actress – Kristin Scott Thomas, *Four Weddings and a Funeral*
Alex Korda Award (British film of the year) – *Shallow Grave*
Best Film not in English – *To Live*
Most Popular Film – *Four Weddings and a Funeral*

CANNES FESTIVAL 1995
Palme d'Or – *Underground*
Best Director – Mathieu Kassovitz, *La Haine*
Best Actor – Jonathan Price, *Carrington*
Best Actress – Helen Mirren, *The Madness of King George*
Grand Jury Prize – *Ulysses' Gaze* (Theo Angelopoulos)
Special Jury Prize – Christopher Hampton, *Carrington*

BERLIN FESTIVAL 1995
Golden Bear – *L'Appât*
Special Jury Prize – *Smoke*
Best Director – Richard Linklater, *Before Sunrise*
Best Actor – Paul Newman, *Nobody's Fool*
Best Actress – Josephine Siao, *Summer Snow*

Literature

The shortlist for the 1994 Booker Prize, memorably described as the 'Mogadon list', failed to excite the public and the winner, *How Late It Was, How Late* by Glaswegian novelist James Kelman, was never going to replicate the runaway success of the 1993 winner *Paddy Clarke Ha Ha Ha*, which set new records with sales of 350,000. But the book itself and the manner of its choosing caused more than the usual amount of controversy. Rabbi Julia Neuberger, one of the judges, castigated chairman John Bayley for his handling of the final session, which over-ran into the Guildhall dinner itself and produced a far from unanimous verdict. Neuberger called it 'a disgrace', the book itself 'inaccesible', and dissociated herself from the choice even before the ceremonies had been properly concluded. James Wood, another of the judges, was unapologetic, comparing Kelman to Beckett, Joyce, Camus and many besides. For his part Bayley, in an eve-of-prize outburst, dismissed modern fiction as 'an ordeal ... at best ambitious and, at worst, pretentious'. Victoria Glendinning, a previous Booker chairman, countered that he had missed the point; new fiction was ambitious or it was nothing.

A few weeks later, presiding over the annual Crime Writers Association awards ceremony where the Gold Dagger went to Minette Walters for *The Scold's Bridle*, Neuberger praised crime writing as 'often the best form of moral and philosophical debate, tackling issues in a way literary fiction often fails to do', and encouraged publishers to enter more genre fiction for the Booker.

Happily William Trevor's winning of both the *Sunday Express* Book of the Year Award and the Whitbread with *Felicia's Journey* was something upon which everyone could agree, though at the announcement of the five Whitbread category winners poetry judge Auberon Waugh lamented declining standards while Clare Francis, speaking of the biography entries, noted that editing appeared to be a dying art; books were frequently over-long and riddled with errors. Trevor donated his £21,000 prize money to the homeless, the subject of his 'brilliant, shocking masterpiece'.

Another popular prize-winner was Alan Bennett, whose *Writing Home* was named Book of the Year at the annual British Book Awards. A runaway success from the moment it was published in October 1994, it was the nation's favourite Christmas present and continued to sell well in 1995, notching up a total of 200,000 copies in hardback in the UK.

Other bestsellers of 1994–5 included Nelson Mandela, whose memoir *A Long Walk To Freedom* reprinted before publication and went on to sell 100,000 copies, Delia Smith, whose *Summer Collection* occupied a place in the top 20 for two years with sales to date of over one million copies, and sports-men Graham Gooch and Brian Clough. Fittingly, in a year that included Britain's first National Poetry Day, poetry too had its place in the sun; the film *Four Weddings and a Funeral* propelled *Tell Me The Truth About Love*, an Auden anthology, into the bestseller lists.

ROYAL REVELATIONS

The book to hit the headlines, however, was *Princess in Love*, Anna Pasternak's account of Major James Hewitt's alleged affair with the Princess of Wales, published by Bloomsbury. More Mills and Boon than *Dr Zhivago* (though Dame Barbara Cartland, the Princess's step-grandmother, was quick to say that *she* would never write such tosh, and anyway it was most ungallant of the Major), it was variously described as 'racy', 'torrid', 'breathless' and 'gushing'. The tabloid newspapers went through prepublication paroxysms of panic, each fearing they were about to miss out on The Big One. When copies were finally released, a feeding frenzy ensued, with every newspaper devoting column upon column to the story even as some of them condemned this latest invasion of privacy. Hewitt, they decided, may have been an officer but he was no gentleman. Bloomsbury's share price took a tumble and Sir William Rees-Mogg sniffily declared company chairman Nigel Newton, a former colleague, to be 'a chancer.'

The hype resulted in impressive sales in the days following publication but then the public got bored. O'Mara Books judiciously leaked nuggets from *Diana: Her New Life*, Andrew Morton's sequel to *Diana: Her True Story*. However, when finally it was published, it was clear that rather more had been promised than was delivered and domestic sales, though impressive, failed to live up to expectations.

A counter-attack from Diana's estranged husband came in the form of Jonathan Dimbleby's *The Prince of Wales: An Intimate Portrait*, an authorized account which, conversely, delivered more than it had originally promised after Charles decided to make personal correspondence available to the author. The *Sunday Times*'s three prepublication extracts each dominated the day's news agenda and were debated across the media and around dinner tables, changing perceptions of the main protagonists. In the wake of Dimbleby, opinion polls revealed that many thought Charles unfit to be king.

From across the Atlantic, Kitty Kelley, the tell-all biographer of Nancy Reagan and Frank Sinatra, let it be known that the most damning book on the British royal family was yet to come. Her book, about the entire family, is expected in 1996. British publishers who not long ago declared the book 'too hot to handle' are now much more positive about the project, explaining that *Diana: Her True Story* had extended the horizon of what is publishable.

Perhaps in an attempt to raise the tone of 'royal' publishing, Prince Charles assembled a personal selection of Shakespeare favourites, *The Prince's Choice*, for the Christmas market, adding to a published *oeuvre* that includes a children's book, a broadside fired at modern architecture and a volume of advocacy of traditional farming. On an accompanying cassette, the Prince played Prince Hal to Robert Stephens' Falstaff in *Henry IV*.

An antidote to such temporal excitement was provided by Pope John Paul II. Random House were rumoured to have paid $4 million for *Crossing the Threshold of Hope* and their faith was rewarded by UK sales in excess of 250,000 copies. A prominent member of his flock, Mother Teresa of Calcutta, agreed a contract with Ebury Press to offer some spiritual guidance of her own. *A Simple Path* was published in October 1995 to mark the 45th anniversary of the founding of her mission. The former Bishop of Durham, David Jenkins, also turned his attention to books, signing with Sinclair-Stevenson for an autobiography and an enquiry into the nature of society and politics, a subject on which he famously disagreed with Margaret Thatcher.

CELEBRITY AUTHORS

Sometimes it seems that everyone wants to write a book, be it a novel or a memoir, or the latter thinly disguised as the former. Having a well-known name can give a head-start in winning a publishing contract, though it also exposes the celebrity author to greater criticism if the book does not come up to scratch. Supermodel Naomi Campbell's much talked-of novel, *Swan*, a catwalk *roman à clef* ghostwritten by Carly McIntyre, turned into something of an ugly duckling. The hype never translated into sales and the publicity descended into farce when Campbell was reluctant to declare unequivocally that she had actually read the novel. Wisely, fellow-models Claudia Schiffer and Kate Moss confined themselves to picture books. Other celebrities to try their hand, some more successfully than others, included globetrotter, actor and former Monty Python star Michael Palin (*Hemingway's Chair*), journalist and broadcaster Libby Purves (*Casting Off*), actress Jill Gascoine (*Addicted*) and Wimbledon champion Martina Navratilova, whose tennis circuit thriller, *The Total Zone*, acknowledged the efforts of co-writer Liz Nickles.

A trio of powerful women teamed up to write *Splash*, a novel about ambition, friendship and sex in a media setting. Authors Val Corbett, Joyce Hopkirk and Eve Pollard have pursued colourful careers in television, magazines and newspapers and their literary début, bought by Headline for around £250,000, bore more than a passing resemblance to real life.

Among the few other first novels to command high prices, the greatest excitement was generated by an unassuming screenwriter who, down on his luck, decided to take a crack at fiction. Nicholas Evans's *The Horse Whisperer* was bought by Bantam Press (UK and Commonwealth rights) for £357,000. The still unfinished manuscript set new records: £355,000 in Germany, £330,000 in Italy, £108,000 in France, and $3,150,000 in the USA. Hollywood was no less excited, with Evans agreeing a $3 million deal with Robert Redford, the producer-director he felt to be most in sympathy with the spirit of the novel.

Established authors fared well; though few as well as Jeffrey Archer, whose three-book deal with HarperCollins was rumoured to be worth up to £22 million. Kingsley Amis also moved to Harper-Collins, receiving £270,000 for two novels. There he was soon joined by his son, Martin, who quit Cape after they declined to pay the £500,000 asking price for his novel *The Information*.

CONTROVERSY

The demands of Amis *fils* were soon public knowledge, as was the fact that he had dropped his longtime London literary agent, Pat Kavanagh, in favour of New Yorker Andrew Wylie. The swap caused a rift with Julian Barnes, Kavanagh's husband and Amis's friend and tennis partner, newspapers and magazines in both Britain and the USA chronicling the falling-out at length. Malcolm Edwards, HarperCollins' publishing director, commented 'We expect to make a profit out of the deal.' However, most editors felt the figures simply did not add up. Novelist A. S. Byatt publicly condemned what she saw as mere 'male turkey-cocking'. Such greed would ultimately deprive other writers with more modest needs. Predictably, when *The Information* was published its price tag made clear-eyed literary criticism difficult and most reviewers agreed that the book was good, but not that good.

Other books and authors to make headlines included Margaret Thatcher, who inevitably launched the second (and last) volume of her memoirs, *The Path to Power*, with an attack on the Government, and Betty Maxwell. *A Mind of My Own*, her memoir of life with the late, unlamented tycoon, raised more questions than it answered – not least why she remained married to such a tyrant. In a lighter vein, rock star Boy George published his autobiography *Take It Like a Man*, while *Oz* founder Richard Neville recalled the ups and downs of the 1960s in *Hippie Hippie Shake*.

PRICE WARS

Despite such successes, booksellers continued to feel the chill of recession, added to which there was renewed anxiety about the Net Book Agreement (NBA), referred by the Office of Fair Trading for a preliminary review which could lead to a full-scale hearing in the Restrictive Practices Court. The likely costs of defence inevitably prompted publishers to reconsider their position on the issue but Clive Bradley, chief executive of the Publishers Association, declared there would be no problem putting together a £1 million fighting fund. Within days, however, Hodder Headline announced their intention to discount some of their books as of 26 December 1994. Discounting, said group chief executive Tim Hely Hutchinson, was a necessary weapon in the battle for sales and market share.

In the run-up to Christmas 1994, a price war in Dublin gave the trade a foretaste of what could happen in Britain if the NBA disappeared. Taking advantage of a European Commission judgment that the agreement was technically unenforceable in the Republic of Ireland (though publishers there have always tended to support it), the Hodges Figgis and Waterstone's bookshops traded discounts and insults across Dawson Street. But other shops did not join what was seen as 'another English battle on Irish soil'. In January 1995, the European Court of Justice decreed that the European Commission had been wrong in its ruling, so boosting the pro-NBA case.

Come the spring and the agreement was subject to the scrutiny of a House of Commons select committee. However, after hearing evidence from all interested parties, chairman Gerald Kaufman – a seeming abolitionist who praised America's price promotion-led bookstores – was not persuaded that 'abrogation of the NBA would result in greater benefit to the public than its retention.' Change, he said, should evolve from within the book trade, without the intervention of Parliament.

Meanwhile, John le Carré's latest novel, *Our Game*, published in May, became the first serious test of Hodder Headline's denetting policy. Independent booksellers protested as Safeway and Asda piled 'em high and sold 'em cheap at £8.49, half price. W. H. Smith, an upholder of the NBA, sold the book at its £16.99 recommended price while Menzies knocked £5 off. Hodder claimed the price promotion would enable them to double sales of the hardback, though many observers felt that only meant they would lose out on paperback sales. Either way, all indications were that the book sold well but not as well as its publishers hoped. When, later in the summer, W. H. Smith elected to participate in the price promotion of another Hodder Headline title, Rosamunde Pilcher's novel *Coming Home*, by giving the book free to customers spending in excess of £15, the Publishers Association and independent booksellers were quick to express their concern. Smiths responded by saying the heavily-advertised campaign had nothing to do with the NBA. 'All we want to do is increase the traffic in our stores in an attempt to increase our profits.' Hit by the slump, the store group had earlier in the year issued a profits warning which sent shares tumbling and resulted in changes in top management.

Smiths' concern for its profits was understandable after the troubles at Pentos, owners of the Dillons bookshop chain, earlier in the year. Despite the best efforts of the new management installed in 1993 following the ousting of Terry Maher, by the end of 1994 the group's Athena stores were in receivership and in March 1995 Pentos itself was in administration. With Dillons' debt to publishers and other creditors estimated at £30 million, the book trade was relieved that buyers Thorn EMI agreed a deal giving publishers upwards of 65p in the pound.

ELECTRONIC BOOKS

Meanwhile, mainstream publishers seeking ways to increase turnover and profits looked beyond the traditional to audiobooks and the brave new world of multimedia. Few embraced the latter with the enthusiasm of Dorling Kindersley which, through DK Multimedia, published its first four titles on CD-Rom in the autumn of 1994. Other publishers sought to develop projects in partnership with outside specialists. HarperCollins, the BBC and Attica Cybernetics joined forces to produce a range of titles for the school and home markets. *The Guinness Book of Records* appeared on CD-Rom, and Penguin released an electronic version of Peter James's 'techno-terror' novel *Host*. With both hardware and software becoming more financially accessible, the market is expected to grow rapidly.

Children's publishing celebrated a half-century of Thomas the Tank Engine, and his 84-year-old creator, the Revd Awdry, was the subject of a biography, Brian Sibley's *The Thomas the Tank Engine Man*. Sadly, it also mourned the passing of illustrator Janet Ahlberg at the early age of 50. With her husband Allan, she created such modern classics as *The Jolly Postman* and *Each Peach Pear Plum*. In the 1994 British Book Awards, the Ahlbergs were named Children's Author of the Year.

Neither was children's publishing devoid of controversy; tabloid coverage of the Carnegie Medal, awarded to the year's most outstanding children's book, accused the 1994 winner Robert Swindells of dishing out 'sorrow and cynicism to young people' in his novel *Stone Cold*. Set on the streets of King's Cross, it was a thriller about London's down-and-outs, written in angry reaction to a housing minister's comment that the homeless were 'the sort of people you step over when you come out of the opera'.

James Herriot's tales of a Yorkshire vet were appreciated by all ages and made him one of Britain's bestselling authors. At his death in February 1995, total sales of his 12 books was over 15 million copies, while six of them had each sold more than one million. Said Jacqueline Korn, the agent who represented him for 25 years, 'He was a natural writer who had a real gift – it just flowed from the first book'.

PENGUIN 60

Most notably, 1995 was Penguin's sixtieth birthday year. Twenty-five years after the death of founder Sir Allen Lane, Penguin remains 'a remarkable and distinguished publishing house,' observed novelist and former editor Jeremy Lewis in one of the innumerable anniversary assessments, 'but its titles often look indistinguishable from those of the upstart imprints with which they now jostle for space in the shops and the publication of each month's new titles is no longer the event it was some 30 years ago.' Lane, who was once so outraged by a book of Siné cartoons published by his then heir-apparent that he raided the warehouse in dead of night and removed the offending books to his garden where they were burned, must surely spin in his grave at some of the books which now bear the Penguin imprimatur. But to the generation weaned on its once-distinctive green, orange and blue liveries, when the very name was synonymous with paperbacks, it is still special.

Lane's first books cost just sixpence, so it was fitting that Penguin marked their anniversary by publishing *Penguin 60s*, 60 miniature books selling at just 60 pence each. In bookshops across the land and in the bestseller lists, the likes of John Grisham, Maeve Binchy and Jeffrey Archer were forced to battle it out with Marcus Aurelius, Anaïs Nin, Sigmund Freud and Anton Chekhov, as the public rushed to buy *Meditations*, *The Model*, *Five Lectures on Psychoanalysis* and *The Black Monk*. By mid-summer, the series, which also includes such authors as Spike Milligan, Elizabeth David, Oscar Wilde, Virginia Woolf, Albert Camus, John Updike and Camille Paglia, had sold 13 million copies world-wide and Penguin was considering expanding the range and making it a permanent feature.

Penguin and the public were delighted; other publishers were not. In August 1995, when 21 of the top 25 paperbacks in the bestseller lists were *Penguin 60s*, a number of publishers complained about their unfair inclusion in the lists, saying it was impossible for their own authors to compete. In 1935, when Lane launched the paperback revolution, so bringing literature to the masses, George Orwell observed, 'Penguin books are splendid value for sixpence, so splendid that if other publishers had any sense, they would combine against them and suppress them.' *Plus ça change, plus c'est la même chose . . .*

LITERARY AWARDS

Nobel Prize 1994 – Kenzaburo Oe
Commonwealth Writers Prize 1994 – Vikram Seth, *A Suitable Boy*
David Cohen British Literature Prize 1995 (biennial) – Harold Pinter
Prix Goncourt 1994 – Didier van Cauwelaert, *Un aller simple (A One-Way Ticket)*
Booker Prize 1994 – James Kelman, *How Late It Was, How Late*
   1995 shortlist: *The Ghost Road*, Pat Barker; *In Every Face I Meet*, Justin Cartwright; *The Moor's Last Sigh*, Salman Rushdie; *Morality Play*, Barry Unsworth; *The Riders*, Tim Winton
Whitbread Prize 1994:
   Novel – William Trevor, *Felicia's Journey*
   First novel – Fred D'Aguiar, *The Longest Memory*

Biography – Brenda Maddox, *A Married Man: A Life of D. H. Lawrence*
Poetry – James Fenton, *Out of Danger*
Children's novel – Geraldine McCaughrean, *Gold Dust*
David Higham Prize 1994 – Fred D'Aguiar, *The Longest Memory*
Sunday Express Prize 1994 – William Trevor, *Felicia's Journey*
Forward Prize 1994 (poetry) – Alan Jenkins, *Harm*
   First collection – Kwame Dawes, *Progeny of Air*
Catherine Cookson Prize 1994 – Susanna Kearsley, *Marianna*
William Hill Sports Book of the Year 1994 – Simon Kuper, *Football Against the Enemy*
Smarties Prize 1994 (children's books) – Hilary McKay, *The Exiles at Home*
   Age 0–5 – Trish Cook, Helen Oxenbury, *So Much*
   Age 6–8 – Henrietta Branford, *Dimanche Diller*
   Age 9–11 – Hilary McKay, *The Exiles at Home*
Crime Writers Association 1994:
   Diamond Dagger – Reginald Hill
   Gold Dagger (fiction) – Minette Walters, *The Scold's Bridle*
   Silver Dagger (fiction) – Peter Hoeg, *Miss Smilla's Feeling for Snow*
British Books Awards 1995 – Author of the Year, Alan Bennett
AT T Award (formerly NCR Award) 1995 (non-fiction) – Mark Hudson, *Coming Back Brockens*
Somerset Maugham Prize 1995 – Patrick French, Simon Garfield, Kathleen Jamie, Laura Thompson
Betty Trask Prize 1995 – Robert Newman, *Dependence Day* (£10,000); Mark Behr, *The Smell of Apples* (£8,000); Martina Evans, *Midnight Feast* (£3,000)
McKitterick Prize 1995 (first novel by a writer over 40) – Christopher Bigsby, *Hester*
Hawthornden Prize 1995 – James Michie, *Collected Poems*
W. H. Smith Prize 1995 – Alice Munro, *Open Secrets*
Mail on Sunday/John Llewellyn Rhys Prize 1995 – Jonathan Coe, *What a Carve Up!*
Encore Prize 1995 (second novel) – Dermot Healy, *A Goat's Song*
Cholmondeley Award 1995 (poetry) – U. A. Fanthorpe, Christopher Reid, C. H. Sisson, Kit Wright
Romantic Novel of the Year 1995 – Charlotte Bingham, *Change of Heart*
Carnegie Prize 1995 (children's) – Theresa Breslin, *Whispers in the Graveyard*
Kate Greenaway 1995 (children's illustrated) – Gregory Rogers, *Way Home* by Libby Hathorn

Nobel Prizes

For prize winners for the years 1901–91, *see* earlier editions of *Whitaker's Almanack*.

The Nobel Prizes are awarded each year from the income of a trust fund established by the Swedish scientist Alfred Nobel, the inventor of dynamite, who died on 10 December 1896 leaving a fortune of £1,750,000. The prizes are awarded to those who have contributed most to the common good in the domain of:

Physics
 awarded by the Royal Swedish Academy of Sciences
Chemistry
 awarded by the Royal Swedish Academy of Sciences
Physiology or Medicine
 awarded by the Karolinska Institute
Literature
 awarded by the Swedish Academy of Arts
Peace
 awarded by a five-person committee elected by the Norwegian Storting
Economic Sciences (instituted 1969)
 awarded by the Royal Swedish Academy of Sciences

The first awards were made in 1901 on the fifth anniversary of Nobel's death. The prizes are awarded every year on 10 December, the anniversary of Nobel's death.

The Trust is administered by the board of directors of the Nobel Foundation, Stockholm, consisting of five members and three deputy members. The Swedish Government appoints a chairman and a deputy chairman, the remaining members being appointed by the awarding authorities.

The awards have been distributed as follows:
Physics
American 58, British 20, German 19 (1948–90, West German 8), French 11, Soviet 7, Dutch 6, Swedish 4, Austrian 3, Danish 3, Italian 3, Japanese 3, Canadian 2, Chinese 2, Swiss 2, Indian 1, Irish 1, Pakistani 1
Chemistry
American 39, German 27 (1948–90, West German 10), British 23, French 7, Swiss 5, Swedish 4, Canadian 3, Dutch 2, Argentinian 1, Austrian 1, Belgian 1, Czech 1, Finnish 1, Hungarian 1, Italian 1, Japanese 1, Norwegian 1, Soviet 1
Physiology or Medicine
American 72, British 23, German 14 (1948–90, West German 4), French 7, Swedish 7, Danish 5, Swiss 5, Austrian 4, Belgian 4, Italian 3, Australian 2, Canadian 2, Dutch 2, Hungarian 2, Russian 2, Argentinian 1, Japanese 1, Portuguese 1, South African 1, Spanish 1
Literature
French 12, American 10, British 8, Swedish 7, German 6 (1948–90, West German 1), Italian 5, Spanish 5, Danish 3, Norwegian 3, Soviet 3, Chilean 2, Greek 2, Irish 2, Japanese 2, Polish 2, Swiss 2, Australian 1, Belgian 1, Colombian 1, Czech 1, Egyptian 1, Finnish 1, Guatemalan 1, Icelandic 1, Indian 1, Israeli 1, Mexican 1, Nigerian 1, South African 1, Trinidadian 1, Yugoslav 1, Stateless 1
Peace
American 17, Institutions 16, British 9, French 9, Swedish 5, German 4 (1948–90, West German 1), South African 4, Belgian 3, Israeli 3, Swiss 3, Argentinian 2, Austrian 2, Norwegian 2, Soviet 2, Burmese 1, Canadian 1, Costa Rican 1, Danish 1, Dutch 1, Egyptian 1, Guatemalan 1, Irish 1, Italian 1, Japanese 1, Mexican 1, Palestinian 1, Polish 1, Tibetan 1, Vietnamese 1, Yugoslav 1
Economics
American 23, British 6, Norwegian 2, Swedish 2, Dutch 1, French 1, German 1, Soviet 1

Prize	1992	1993	1994
Physics	Prof. G. Charpak (French)	Dr R. Hulse (American) Dr J. Taylor (American)	Prof. B. Brockhouse (Canadian) Prof. C. Shull (American)
Chemistry	Prof. R. Marcus (American)	Prof. M. Smith (Canadian) Dr K. Mullis (American)	Prof. G. Olah (American)
Physiology or Medicine	Dr E. Krebs (American) Dr E. Fisher (American)	R. Roberts (British) Prof. P. Sharp (American)	Dr A. Gilman (American) Dr M. Rodbell (American)
Literature	D. Walcott (Trinidadian)	Ms T. Morrison (American)	K. Oe (Japanese)
Peace	Sra R. Menchú (Guatemalan)	N. Mandela (South African) Pres. F. W. de Klerk (South African)	Y. Rabin (Israeli) Y. Arafat (Palestinian) S. Peres (Israeli)
Economics	G. S. Becker (American)	Prof. R. Fogel (American) Prof. D. North (American)	J. Harsanyi (American) J. Nash (American) R. Selten (German)

Opera

Most British opera companies applied for money from the National Lottery to fund their capital projects. The Royal Opera House heard in July 1995 that it would receive £55 million towards the redevelopment of Covent Garden, with the promise of a further £23 million later. Meanwhile, the 1994–5 season at the Royal Opera House was artistically one of the most interesting for many years. A new *Ring* cycle conducted by Bernard Haitink, directed by Richard Jones and designed by Nigel Lowery, was inaugurated in September with *Das Rheingold* and *Die Walküre*. The highly original staging won the 1994 Evening Standard Award for outstanding opera production. *Siegfried*, equally well-received, followed early in 1995, and the cycle will be completed next season with *Götterdämmerung.*

Jonathan Miller directed a new production of *Così fan tutte*, designing the set himself with the aid of Covent Garden's technical staff and with costumes from the latest Giorgio Armani collection. This was Jonathan Miller's very belated début with the Royal Opera. A revival of *Peter Grimes* to mark the 50th anniversary of Britten's opera was not very successful, but the new production of his *Billy Budd*, finely directed by Francesca Zambello, made more than adequate amends. The original four-act version of the opera was restored, with the magnificent ensemble at the end of Act I reinstated.

The tricentenary of Henry Purcell's death was marked by a complete performance of the 'dramatick opera' *King Arthur, or The British Worthy*, with text by John Dryden. The conductor William Christie and his ensemble, Les Arts Florissants, were joined by solo singers, dancers, and actors. At over four hours, the performance was something of an endurance test, but it provided a welcome opportunity to see and hear the work in its entirety. The Covent Garden season ended with the first of seven instalments of the Royal Opera's Verdi Festival. The company will stage all the composer's operas, with earlier or later variants given in concert, by the year 2001, the centenary of his death. This year's instalment included revivals of *Stiffelio*, *Un ballo in maschera*, *La traviata* and *Simon Boccanegra*, as well as a new production of *I due Foscari*. There were concert performances of the original version of *Simon Boccanegra*, and of *Aroldo* (a later version of *Stiffelio*). The artistic merit of these performances varied, but taken together they were a magnificent achievement, particularly for Edward Downes, who conducted many of the operas and deserves much of the credit for planning the festival.

English National Opera applied for lottery money to restore the London Coliseum to the full Edwardian glory envisaged by its architect, Frank Matcham. Dennis Marks, the general director, also put forward other options, such as building a new theatre for the company on the South Bank, which might well be cheaper in the long run. ENO's new staging by Francesca Zambello of Mussorgsky's epic *Khovanshchina* won the Laurence Olivier Award for best new opera production. It received special praise for the contribution made by the chorus which has greatly improved in recent years. A new production of *King Priam* celebrated Sir Michael Tippett's 90th birthday. The British première of Victor Schnittke's controversial *Life with an Idiot* – a joint production with Scottish Opera – was not much liked by either critics or public, although the text, adapted by Victor Erofeyev from his own short story, was notable for the savage irony of its depiction of life in the Soviet Union.

BRITTEN'S DREAM

Robert Carsen's staging of Britten's *A Midsummer Night's Dream*, which had been enormously successful in France, divided critical opinion; however, audiences loved it, and Declan Donnellan's production of the Brecht/Weill *Rise and Fall of the City of Mahagonny* was equally popular. In line with ENO's aim of renewing the core repertory over the next few years, the season began with a new production of *Tosca*, staged by Keith Warner and conducted by Sir Alexander Gibson, who was returning after some years absence to the company of which he was musical director in the 1950s. Gibson died on 14 January 1995, aged 68.

After studying at the Royal Scottish Academy of Music, Glasgow, Alexander Gibson worked at Sadler's Wells from 1951 to 1959, for the last three years as musical director. In 1962 he founded and became first musical director of Scottish Opera. For 25 years he conducted an amazing variety of operas, including *Pelléas et Mélisande*, Gluck's *Orfeo* and *Alceste*; *Otello*, *Falstaff* and other Verdi operas; a *Ring* cycle, *Tristan and Isolde* and *Die Meistersinger*; *Fidelio*, *Oberon*, *Der Rosenkavalier*, *The Rake's Progress*, *Wozzeck* and Henze's *Elegy for Young Lovers*; *Madama Butterfly* and other Puccini operas; and Mozart's three Da Ponte comedies. His finest achievement was probably the first complete performance of Berlioz' *Les Troyens*, with Janet Baker as a memorable Dido.

If Cardiff Bay Opera House Trust is successful in its application for money from the Millennium Commission, Welsh National Opera should have its own theatre for the first time in its history by 2000. Zaha Hadid's beautiful designs, at first disliked by the people of Cardiff, were accepted after some modification. Carlo Rizzi has extended his contract as WNO's music director until 2000. Anthony Friend, who succeeded Matthew Epstein as general director in September 1994, was forced to make cuts in the repertory to balance the budget, but on the whole WNO maintained its high standards.

Opera North also underwent management changes when Ian Ritchie resigned as general director and was succeeded by Richard Mantle. Perhaps the most interesting of the new productions was William Walton's *Troilus and Cressida*, not staged since the Covent Garden revival of 1976, when the composer made substantial cuts in the score and lowered the part of Cressida from soprano to mezzo for Janet Baker. This production reverted to a soprano heroine, but did not, as many had hoped, restore the cuts. *Oberto*, Verdi's first opera, was staged by the bass John Tomlinson (his first attempt at direction), who also sang the title role with tremendous authority and assurance. This production will eventually be part of the Royal Opera's Verdi Festival.

GLYNDEBOURNE HONOURS

The architect of the new Glyndebourne Festival Theatre, Michael Hopkins, was knighted in the Queen's 1995 Birthday Honours, and Sir George Christie was awarded the 1994 Evening Standard Award for Outstanding Achievement in Opera. The second season in the new theatre was as successful as the first. Rossini's 'opera seria', *Ermione*, receiving its British stage première, was convincingly directed by Graham Vick and opened up a whole new category of operas suitable for the Festival. Harrison Birtwistle's *The Second Mrs Kong*, premièred by Glyndebourne Touring Opera last year, was successfully transferred to the main company. The much-praised series of Janáček operas, directed by Nicholas Lehnhoff, continued with *The Makropulos Case*, which was notable for an amazing performance of the central role, Emilia Marty, by the soprano Anya Silja. GTO's new production this year was Britten's *Owen Wingrave*. Written for BBC television in 1971 and staged at Covent Garden in 1973, the opera was receiving only its second British production, which was directed by Robin Philips.

Opera Factory gave the first performance of Nigel Osborne's *Sarajevo* at Queen Elizabeth Hall on 23 August 1994. A three-part music-theatre tribute to the city, it comprised a shortened translation of Euripides' *The Trojan Women*, a section of musical settings of diaries, letters and news reports, and an oratorio-style setting of a text by Craig Raine. Pimlico Opera gave the British stage première of Shostakovich's operetta, *Cheryomushki*, in October 1994 at the Lyric Theatre, Hammersmith, in a translation by David Pountney. First performed in Moscow in 1958, the piece takes its title from a huge housing estate in the Moscow suburbs.

The première of *Powder her Face*, the first opera by the immensely gifted 24-year-old composer, Thomas Adès, was given at the Cheltenham Festival, now under the direction of Michael Berkeley, on July 1; it then moved to the Almeida Theatre in Islington. Philip Hensher's caustic libretto, based on the life of Margaret, Duchess of Argyll, helped to make the work an outstanding success. On 13 July Almeida Opera gave the première of Ian Mac-

Queen's *East and West*, with a text by Jonathan Moore, which deals with racial tensions caused by a Bosnian family living in Germany. The Aldeburgh Festival gave the first performance of Nicola Lefanu's opera, *The Wildman*, with a libretto by Kevin Crossley-Holland, on 9 June. The opera is set in Orford, not far from Aldeburgh on the Suffolk coast, and based on a local legend about a naked, wordless man hauled from the sea in a fisherman's net in medieval times. The theme of this year's Buxton Festival was Venice: Monteverdi's *Il ritorno d'Ulisse in patria* and Britten's *The Turn of the Screw* were both premièred in the Italian city. The productions derived from Opera North.

EDINBURGH 1995

The 1995 Edinburgh International Festival gave Scottish Opera's new production of Dvořák's rarely heard *The Jacobin* as part of its Dvořák season. The American 'docu-opera', *I was Looking at the Ceiling and then I saw the Sky*, a collaboration between composer John Adams, poet June Jordan and director Peter Sellers which charted the impact of the 1994 Los Angeles earthquake on the lives of seven young Californians, received its British première. The Kirov Opera from St Petersburg offered Rimsky-Korsakov's *The Legend of the Invisible City of Kitezh* and *Sadko*, and a concert performance of Glinka's *Russlan and Ludmila*, all conducted by Valery Gergiev, the company's artistic director.

Open-air country-house opera continued to be popular. Cancellation of the 1995 Garsington season appeared likely after South Oxfordshire District Council prosecuted Leonard Ingrams, owner of Garsington Manor, for breach of the noise conditions of his public entertainment licence. Magistrates at Thame found Ingrams guilty, but this judgement was overturned on appeal and the festival was able to go ahead. It gave its now familiar programme of an opera each by Rossini, Haydn and Richard Strauss, whose *Daphne* was the outstanding production of the festival. Broomhill, near Tonbridge Wells, offered *Il trittico*, Puccini's three one-act operas (*Il tabarro*, *Suor Angelica* and *Gianni Schicchi*).

Dame Elizabeth Maconchy, the English composer of Irish descent, died in November 1994 aged 87. Her operas included three one-acters: *The Sofa* (1959) and *The Departure* (1962) were first performed by the New Opera Workshop at Sadler's Wells; *The Three Strangers* (1968), based on one of Thomas Hardy's Wessex Tales, was commissioned and premièred by Bishop's Stortford College. It was broadcast by the BBC in 1970 and then staged by the Royal College of Music, where Maconchy had studied with Ralph Vaughan Williams. He, together with Béla Bartók, was one of the chief influences on her musical style.

The English composer Hugo Cole, who died in March 1995 aged 68, wrote several successful operas for children and young people. In 1960 he won a competition organized by the John Lewis Partnership Music Society for an opera to inaugurate the auditorium of their new Oxford Street store. *The Tunnel*, for which, as usual, he wrote his own text, dealt with a disaster during the railway construction boom of the 1840s.

The English baritone John Heddle Nash, who died aged 67 in September 1994, appeared with Carl Rosa and Sadler's Wells Opera in the 1950s and 1960s. The son of Heddle Nash, the famous tenor of the inter-war years, he was a stylish singer with a fine stage presence in roles such as Don Giovanni, Figaro in *The Barber of Seville*, Dr Malatesta in *Don Pasquale* and Falke in *Die Fledermaus*. The Scottish tenor Murray Dickie, who died aged 71 in June 1995, spent 25 years as a member of the Vienna State Opera, but early in his career he sang frequently at Covent Garden and Glyndebourne. A specialist in character roles, he had a large and very varied repertory. He created the Curé in Arthur Bliss's *The Olympians* in 1949 at Covent Garden, and sang Sellem the Auctioneer in the British première of Stravinsky's *The Rake's Progress* with Glyndebourne at Edinburgh in 1953. His outstanding role was David in *Die Meistersinger*.

PRODUCTIONS

In the summaries of company activities shown below, the dates in brackets indicate the year that the current production entered the company's repertory.

ROYAL OPERA
Founded 1946
Royal Opera House, Covent Garden, London WC2E 9DD

Productions from the repertory: *Turandot* (1984), *La Cenerentola* (1990), *Otello* (1987), *Der Rosenkavalier* (1984), *La bohème* (1974), *Peter Grimes* (1975), *Un ballo in maschera* (1975), *Stiffelio* (1993), *Simon Boccanegra* (1991).

New productions:
Das Rheingold (Wagner), 13 October 1994. Conductor, Bernard Haitink; director, Richard Jones; designer, Nigel Lowery. Rita Cullis (Freia), Jane Henschel (Fricka), Birgitta Svendén (Erda), Paul Charles Clarke (Froh), Robert Tear (Loge), Peter Sidhom (Donner), John Tomlinson (Wotan), Robin Leggate (Mime), Ekkehard Wlaschiha (Alberich), Gwynne Howell (Fasolt), Carsten Sabell (Fafner)
Die Walküre (Wagner), 14 October 1994. Conductor, Bernard Haitink; director, Richard Jones; designer, Nigel Lowery. Ulla Gustafsson (Sieglinde), Deborah Polaski (Brünnhilde), Jane Henschel (Fricka), Poul Elming (Siegmund), John Tomlinson (Wotan), Matthias Holle (Hunding)
Roméo et Juliette (Gounod), 28 October 1994. Conductor, Charles Mackerras; director, Nicolas Joel; designer, Carlo Tommasi. Leontina Vaduva (Juliet), Anne-Marie Panzarella (Stephano), Sarah Walker (Gertrude), Roberto Alagna (Romeo), Paul Charles Clarke (Tybalt), François Le Roux (Mercutio), Robert Lloyd (Fr Lawrence)
La traviata (Verdi), 25 November 1994. Conductor, Georg Solti; director, Richard Eyre; designer, Bob Crowley. Angela Gheorghiu (Violetta), Leah-Marian Jones (Flora), Frank Lopardo (Alfredo), Leo Nucci (Germont), Richard Van Allan (Baron Douphol)
Così fan tutte (Mozart), 19 January 1995. Conductor, Evelino Pido; director/set designer, Jonathan Miller; costume designer, Giorgio Armani. Amanda Roocroft (Fiordiligi), Susan Graham (Dorabella), Ann Murray

(Despina), Bruce Ford (Ferrando), Simon Keenlyside (Guglielmo), Thomas Allen (Don Alfonso)
Salome (R. Strauss), 11 March 1995. Conductor, Christoph von Dohnanyi; director, Luc Bondy; designers, Erich Wonder (set), Susanne Raschig (costumes). Catherine Malfitano (Salome), Anja Silja (Herodias), Robin Leggate (Narraboth), Kenneth Riegel (Herod), Bryn Terfel (Jokanaan)
Siegfried (Wagner), 27 March 1995. Conductor, Bernard Haitink; director, Richard Jones; designer, Nogel Lowery. Anne Evans (Brünnhilde), Linda Kitchen (Forest bird), Birgitta Svendén (Erda), Graham Clark (Mime), Siegfried Jerusalem (Siegfried), John Tomlinson (Wanderer), Carsten Stabell (Fafner), Ekkehard Wlaschiha (Alberich)
King Arthur (Purcell), 3 May 1995. Conductor, William Christie; director, Graham Vick; designer, Paul Brown. Veronique Gens (Venus), Sandrine Piau (She), Susannah Waters (Cupid), Claron McFadden (Philidel/Honour), Mark Padmore, Iain Paton (tenors), Petteri Salomaa (Cold Genius/Aeolus), Jonathan Best (Grimbald/He), François Bazola (Pan), Les Arts Florissants
Billy Budd (Britten), 30 May 1995. Conductor, Robert Spano; director, Francesca Zambello; designer, Alison Chitty. Graham Clark (Captain Vere), Rodney Gilfry (Billy Budd), David Wilson-Johnson (Mr Redburn), Roderick Earle (Lt Ratcliffe), Gidon Saks (Mr Flint), Mark Tucker (Novice), John Connell (Dansker), John Tomlinson (John Claggart)
I due Foscari (Verdi), 24 June 1995. Conductor, Daniele Gatti; director, August Everding; designer, Michael Goden. June Anderson (Lucrezia), Dennis O'Neill (Jacopo), Vladimir Chernov (Francesco), Miguel Angel Zapater (Loredano)

ENGLISH NATIONAL OPERA
Founded 1931
London Coliseum, St Martin's Lane, London WC2N 4ES

Productions from the repertory: *The Mikado* (1986), *The Magic Flute* (1988), *Ariadne auf Naxos* (1983), *Figaro's Wedding* (1991), *Rigoletto* (1982), *Madam Butterfly* (1984), *The Cunning Little Vixen* (1988), *Così fan tutte* (1994), *The Force of Destiny* (1992).

New productions:
Tosca (Puccini), 12 September 1994. Conductor, Alexander Gibson; director, Keith Warner; designer, John Conklin. Rosalind Plowright (Tosca), David Rendall (Cavaradossi), Henk Smit (Scarpia)
Don Quixote (Massenet), 8 October 1994. Conductor, Emmanuel Joel; director, Ian Judge; designers, John Gunter (set), Deirdre Clancy (costumes). Louise Winter (Dulcinea), Alan Opie (Sancho), Richard Van Allan (Don Quixote)
Khovanshchina (Mussorgsky), 24 November 1994. Conductor, Sian Edwards; director, Francesca Zambello; designer, Alison Chitty. Catherine Pope (Emma), Anne-Marie Owens (Marfa), Kim Begley (Prince Vasily), Alan Woodrow (Prince Andrey), Willard White (Prince Ivan), Paul Whelan (Shaklovity), Gwynne Howell (Dosifey)
King Priam (Tippett), 3 February 1995. Conductor, Paul Daniel; director/designer, Tom Cairns. Janice Cairns (Hecuba), Jean Rigby (Helen), Susan Bickley (Andromache), Christopher Ventris (Paris), Thomas Randle (Achilles), Christopher Booth-Jones (Hector), Andrew Shore (King Priam)
Don Giovanni (Mozart), 15 March 1995. Conductor, Markus Stenz; director, Guy Joosten; designers, Johannes Leiacker (set), Sven Use (costumes). Penelope Walmsley-Clark (Donna Anna), Janice Watson (Donna Elvira), Nerys Jones (Zerlina), John Hudson (Don Ottavio), Peter

Coleman-Wright (Don Giovanni), Urban Malmberg (Leporello), Andrew Slater (Masetto), John Connell (Commendatore)

Life with an Idiot (Schnittke), British première 1 April 1995. Conductor, Richard Armstrong; director, Jonathan Moore; designer, David Blight. David Barrell ('I'), Louisa Kennedy-Richardson (Wife), Alasdair Elliott (Vova), Quentin Hayes (Proust)

A Midsummer Night's Dream (Britten), 17 May 1995. Conductor, Steuart Bedford; director, Robert Carsen; designer, Michael Levine. Lilian Watson (Tytania), Christopher Robson (Oberon), Emil Wolk (Puck), Susan Chilcott (Helena), Eirian James (Hermia), John Graham-Hall (Lysander), Christopher Booth-Jones (Demetrius), Peter Rose (Bottom), Christopher Gillett (Flute)

The Rise and Fall of the City of Mahagonny (Weill), 8 June 1995. Conductor, Sian Edwards; director, Declan Donnellan; designer, Nicholas Ormerod. Lesley Garrett (Jenny), Sally Burgess (Begbick), Adrian Thompson (Fatty), Brian Matthews (Trinity Moses), Robert Brubaker (Jim), John Daszak (Jake/Toby), Riccardo Simonetti (Bill), Richard Angas (Joe)

OPERA NORTH
Founded 1978
Grand Theatre, 46 Briggate, Leeds LS1 6NU

Productions from the repertory: *The Magic Flute* (1994), *Le Roi malgré lui* (1994), *The Secret Marriage* (1993), *Tosca* (1988), *The Pearl Fishers* (1988), *Orpheus in the Underworld* (1992).

New productions:
Il trovatore (Verdi), 1 October 1994. Conductor, Paul Daniel; director, Inga Levant; designers, Charles Edwards (set), Brigitte Reiffenstuel (costumes). Katerina Kudriavchenko (Leonora), Sally Burgess (Azucena), Edmund Barham (Manrico), Ettore Kim (Di Luna), Clive Bayley (Fernando)

Oberto (Verdi), 15 December 1994. Conductor, David Porcelijn; director, John Tomlinson; designer, Russell Craig. Rita Cullis (Leonora), Linda Finnie (Cuniza), David Maxwell-Anderson (Riccardo), John Tomlinson (Oberto)

Troilus and Cressida (Walton), 14 January 1995. Conductor, Richard Hickox; director, Matthew Warchus; designer, Neil Warmington, Judith Howarth (Cressida), Yvonne Howard (Evadne), Arthur Davies (Troilus), Nigel Robson (Pandarus), Alan Opie (Diomede), Clive Bayley (Calkas)

Pelléas et Mélisande (Debussy), 15 May 1995. Conductor, Paul Daniel; director, Richard Jones; designers, Anthony McDonald (set), Nicky Gillibrand (costumes). Joan Rodgers (Mélisande), Catherine Wyn-Rogers (Geneviève), William Dazeley (Pelléas), Robert Hayward (Golaud), Clive Bayley (Arkel)

Performances were given at the Grand Theatre, Leeds, and on tour in Sheffield, Nottingham, Manchester, London (Royal Opera House), Hull, Norwich and York.

SCOTTISH OPERA
Founded 1962
39 Elmbank Crescent, Glasgow G2 4PT

Productions from the repertory: *Madama Butterfly* (1987), *Fidelio* (1994), *Tristan und Isolde* (1994), *Iolanthe* (1986), *La forza del destino* (1990).

New productions:
Maria Stuarda (Donizetti), 7 October 1994. Conductor, Richard Armstrong; director/designer, Stefanos Lazaridis; Yvonne Kenny (Mary Stuart), Michie Nakamaru (Elisabeth I), Peter Bronder (Leicester), David Ellis (Talbot), Stafford Dean (Cecil)

The Marriage of Figaro (Mozart), 24 January 1995.

Conductor, Nicholas McGegan; director, David Leveaux; designers, Vicki Mortimer (set), Deirdre Clancy (costumes). Claire Rutter (Countess), Lisa Milne (Susanna), Claire Bradshaw (Cherubino), Fiona Kimm (Marcellina), Alasdair Elliott (Don Basilio), Stephen Gadd (Count), Paul Whelan (Figaro), Jonathan Veira (Dr Bartolo)

Life with an Idiot (Schnittke), 11 May 1995. Conductor, Richard Armstrong; director, Jonathan Moore; designer, David Blight. David Barrell ('I'), Louisa Kennedy-Richardson (Wife), Alasdair Elliott (Vova), Quentin Hayes (Proust)

The Jacobin (Dvořák), 14 August 1995 (Edinburgh). Conductor, Richard Armstrong; director, Christine Mielitz; designer, Reinhart Zimmermann. Rita Cullis (Julie), Alasdair Elliott (Benda), Claire Rutter (Terinka), Richard Coxon (Jiri), Donald Maxwell (Filip), Stafford Dean (Count Vilem), Robert Hayward (Adolf)

Performances were given at the Theatre Royal, Glasgow, and on tour in Newcastle, Edinburgh and Aberdeen.

WELSH NATIONAL OPERA
Founded 1946
John Street, Cardiff CF1 4SP

Productions from the repertory: *La traviata* (1987), *Turandot* (1994), *The Makropulos Case* (1978), *Le nozze di Figaro* (1987), *Elektra* (1992).

New productions:
Beatrice and Benedict (Berlioz), 15 September 1994. Conductor, John Nelson; director, Elijah Moshinsky; designers, Michael Yeargan (set), Dona Granata (costumes). Sara Fulgoni (Beatrice), Rebecca Evans (Hero), Patricia Bardon (Ursula), Donald Kaasch (Benedict), Karl Morgan Daymond (Claudio), Donald Maxwell (Somarone)

The Yeomen of the Guard (Sullivan), 13 December 1994. Conductor, Gareth Jones; director, Tim Hopkins; designers, Peter J. Davison (set), Nicky Gillibrand (costumes). Alwyn Mellor (Elsie), Felicity Palmer (Dame Carruthers), Neill Archer (Colonel Fairfax), Peter Savidge (Sir Richard), Richard Suart (Jack Point)

Così fan tutte (Mozart), 20 May 1995. Conductor, Mark Wigglesworth; director, Tim Hopkins; designer, Anthony Baker. Alwyn Mellor (Fiordiligi), Ann Taylor-Morley (Dorabella), Gail Pearson (Despina), Neill Archer (Ferrando), Nathan Berg (Guglielmo), Peter Sidhom (Don Alfonso)

Performances were given at the New Theatre, Cardiff, and on tour in Plymouth, Oxford, Liverpool, Nottingham, Birmingham, Bristol, Llandudno, Southampton, Swansea and London (Royal Opera House and Sadler's Wells).

GLYNDEBOURNE FESTIVAL OPERA
Founded 1934
Glyndebourne, Lewes, East Sussex BN8 5UU

The Festival ran from 22 May to 27 August 1995. *La clemenza di Tito* (1991), *The Queen of Spades* (1992) and *Don Giovanni* (1994) were revived.

New productions:
Ermione (Rossini), 22 May 1995. Conductor, Andrew Davis; director, Graham Vick; designer, Richard Hudson. Anna Catarina Antonacci (Hermione), Diana Montague (Andromache), Bruce Ford (Orestes), Jorge Lopez-Yanez (Pyrrhus), Paul Austin Kelly (Pylades)

The Second Mrs Kong (Birtwistle), 23 May 1995. Conductor, Elgar Howarth; director/designer, Tom Cairns. Helen Field (Pearl), Phyllis Cannan (Inanna), Michael Chance (Orpheus), Omar Ebrahim (Vermeer), Philip Langridge (Kong), Steven Page (Anubis)

The Makropulos Case (Janáček), 28 June 1995. Conductor,

Andrew Davis; director, Nikolaus Lehnhoff; designer, Tobias Hoheisal. Anja Silja (Emilia Marty), Manuela Kriscak (Kristina), Kim Begley (Grègor), Victor Braun (Jaroslav Prus), Christopher Ventris (Janek), Andrew Shore (Kolenatý), Nigel Douglas (Hauk-Šendorf)

GLYNDEBOURNE TOURING OPERA performed *La bohème* (1991), *Don Giovanni* (1994) and a new production of *Owen Wingrave* (Britten) at Glyndebourne, Southampton, Plymouth, Norwich, Oxford, Woking, Manchester and Northampton from 9 October to 14 December 1995.

ENGLISH TOURING OPERA
Founded 1980 as Opera 80

Orpheus and Eurydice and *La bohème* were toured to Richmond, Basingstoke, Bath, Weston-super-Mare, Dartford, Buxton, York and High Wycombe from 19 October to 2 December 1994.

 The Barber of Seville and *Orpheus and Eurydice* were toured to London (Sadler's Wells), Poole, Coventry, Reading, Brighton, Crawley, Yeovil, Exeter, Ipswich, Cambridge, Lincoln, Darlington, Carlisle, Ulverston, Preston and Swindon from 21 February to 2 June 1995.

OPERA FACTORY
Founded 1982
South Bank Centre, London SE1

First performance of *Sarajevo* (Nigel Osborne), 23 August 1994. Conductor, Nicholas Kok; director, David Freeman; designer, David Roger. With Marie Angel, Claire Daniels, Andrew Burden, and three actors from the former Yugoslavia.

OPERA NORTHERN IRELAND
Founded 1985
181A Stranmillis Road, Belfast BT9 5DU

Autumn season at Grand Opera House, Belfast:
Don Giovanni (Mozart), 16 September 1994. Conductor, Roy Goodman; director, Roman Terleckyj; designers, David Myerscough-Jones (set), John Pascoe (costumes). Ingrid Attrot (Donna Anna), Elizabeth Gale (Donna Elvira), Yvonne Barclay (Zerlina), Eric Ashcraft (Ottavio), Johannes Mannov (Don Giovanni), Christopher Purves (Leporello), Jonathan May (Masetto)

 Yevgeny Onegin (Tchaikovsky), 17 September 1994. Conductor, Kenneth Montgomery; director, Ion Carmitru; designer, Maria Miu. Melanie Armistead (Tatyana), Kate McCarney (Olga), Enid Hartle (Filipyevna), Mark Beudert (Lensky), Kimm Julian (Onegin), John Hall (Prince Gremin)

Spring season at Grand Opera House, Belfast:
L'elisir d'amore (Donizetti), 4 March 1995. Conductor, Kenneth Montgomery; director, Javier Lopez Pinon; designer, Jan Klatter. Mary Hegerty (Adina), Richard Coxon (Nemorino), Karl Morgan Daymond (Sgt Belcore), Jonathan Veira (Dr Dulcamare)

Masters of the Queen's (King's) Music

'Master of the King's Music' was the title given to the official who presided over the court band during the reign of Charles I. The first Master was appointed in 1626. Today the Master is expected to organize the music for state occasions and to write new music for them, although there are no fixed duties. The post is held for life and the Master receives an annual honorarium of £100.

Nicholas Lanier (1588–1666), appointed 1626
Louis Grabu (?–1674), appointed 1666
Nicholas Staggins (1650–1700), appointed 1674
John Eccles (1668–1735), appointed 1700
Maurice Greene (1695–1755), appointed 1735
William Boyce (1710–79), appointed 1755

John Stanley (1713–86), appointed 1779
Sir William Parsons (1746–1817), appointed 1786
William Shield (1748–1829), appointed 1817
Christian Kramer (?–1834), appointed 1829
François (Franz) Cramer (1772–1848), appointed 1834
George Anderson (?–1870), appointed 1848
Sir William Cusins (1833–93), appointed 1870
Sir Walter Parratt (1841–1924), appointed 1893
Sir Edward Elgar (1857–1934), appointed 1924
Sir Henry Walford Davies (1869–1941), appointed 1934
Sir Arnold Bax (1883–1953), appointed 1941
Sir Arthur Bliss (1891–1975), appointed 1953
Malcolm Williamson (1931–), appointed 1975

Parliament

The House of Lords returned from the summer recess on 10 October, and the House of Commons on 17 October, when the Secretary of State for Transport (Dr Brian Mawhinney), in response to a private notice question from Labour's transport spokesman (Frank Dobson), announced the setting-up of an independent inquiry into the train crash at Cowden in Kent on 15 October in which five people had been killed.

On 19 October, during Commons consideration of Lords amendments to the Criminal Justice and Public Order Bill, the Government overturned earlier defeats in the Lords on the use of secure training units for persistent young offenders and on the moving-on of gypsies from legal gypsy sites. On 20 October it overturned another Lords defeat attempting to reinstate the old Criminal Injuries Compensation Scheme. The Lords accepted these reverses on 25 October and the bill received royal assent on 3 November. In the Lords on 20 October peers approved minor but detailed changes to their procedures, as outlined in the second and third reports of the procedure committee.

On 25 October the Prime Minister (John Major) announced that following the resignations of two government ministers over unsubstantiated allegations of impropriety, he had ordered the publication of the Cabinet Secretary's report into various allegations made by Mohammed Al Fayed and the setting-up of a committee on standards in public life under Lord Nolan to examine current concerns and make recommendations as to any changes. The Leader of the Opposition (Tony Blair) welcomed the new body as 'plainly sensible and necessary' and expressed the hope that the inquiry would be comprehensive, covering 'past malpractice, present practice and future rules'.

On 31 October the deputy leader of the Labour Party (John Prescott) introduced a motion calling for the sittings of the privileges committee looking into the 'cash for questions' issue to be held in public. The Leader of the House (Tony Newton) moved a government amendment calling for the decision to be left to the committee itself. During the debate a senior member of the committee, Tony Benn (Lab.) said he would produce his own version of the proceedings if the motion was defeated and deliberation took place in private. The motion was defeated and the government amendment passed by 299 votes to 259.

On 1 November the Speaker of the House (Betty Boothroyd) said she would accept an emergency motion for debate on the following day on the specific issue of the falsification of a facsimile on House of Commons letterhead paper sent by the *Guardian* newspaper to the Ritz Hotel in Paris. The emergency debate on the *Guardian* on 2 November was on a motion introduced by David Wilshire (C.) to refer the matter to the committee of privileges and this was approved by 313 votes to 38. In the Lords further changes to procedure and sittings of the House were approved.

QUEEN'S SPEECH 1994

The 1993–4 session ended on 3 November and The Queen opened the 1994–5 session of Parliament on 16 November. The speech outlined 13 major bills, including seven intended to improve the supply side of the economy and three to take forward social welfare reform:

- a measure to reform benefits and give unemployed people better help into work (Jobseeker's Bill)
- a measure to promote greater competition in the gas industry (Gas Bill)
- legislation to provide for a high-speed rail link between London and the Channel Tunnel (Channel Tunnel Rail Link Bill)
- improvements to security and choice in non-state pensions, and making the state pension age the same for men and women (Pensions Bill)
- legislation to tackle discrimination against disabled people (Disability Discrimination Bill)
- measures to improve management in the National Health Service (Health Authorities Bill)
- a bill to provide for people with serious mental disorder discharged from hospital to be cared for under supervision (Mental Health (Patients in the Community) Bill)

The programme also provided for bills:

- to simplify and improve enforcement of environmental policy (Environment Bill)
- to carry through important law reforms (Criminal Justice (Scotland) Bill)
- on domestic violence and occupation of the family home (Family Homes and Domestic Violence Bill)
- on the hearsay rule in civil proceedings (Civil Evidence Bill)
- on the effect of divorce on wills (Law Reform (Succession) Bill)
- on distribution on intestacy in the areas of the 'hotch potch' rule, survivorship provisions and application for provision out of the estate of cohabitants (Distribution of Estates Bill)

John Major said 'over the past four years, I have consistently pursued a number of long-term objectives ... supply side reform for lasting growth, a better quality of life for all our citizens, a higher standard of public service and a lasting peace in Northern Ireland. They remain at the centre of my objectives for this year and the future. This programme will take those objectives forward.' Tony

Blair felt the programme 'shows a Government who are out of touch and out of steam' and was 'the hallmark of this Government: dogma tempered only by dithering ... there is a case for action on behalf of the people of Britain and it will be put by the Opposition. We know what needs to be done – the people of Britain know what needs to be done – because we share the hopes and ambitions of our people ... we share something more – their shame at what has happened to Britain under the Conservative government.' The Liberal Democrat leader (Paddy Ashdown) thought that 'the programme illustrates clearly that this Administration are not the masters of events but are at the mercy of them. They are led by a Prime Minister to whom things happen, rather than by one who makes things happen. He is a weak Prime Minister who cannot command a wilful Cabinet or reunite a divided party. The Government have lost both the trust of the nation and confidence in themselves. They cannot go too soon.' During the usual six days of debate a Labour amendment critical of the Government's treatment of the National Health Service in general and the Health Secretary (Virginia Bottomley) in particular was defeated by 309 votes to 272, and a further Labour amendment critical of the Government's economic record was defeated by 312 votes to 266. A Liberal Democrat amendment also criticizing economic policy was defeated by 311 votes to 25; the speech itself was approved without division.

On 21 November the Secretary of State for Defence (Malcolm Rifkind) reported to the Commons on the decision by the UN Security Council to order an air strike against the Bosnian Serb airfield at Udbina, following Serbian aggression in the area around Bihac. Labour's defence spokesperson (Dr David Clark) recognized that 'the action was justified, in accordance with UN Resolution 958'. On 24 November Brian Mawhinney made a statement on the Government's intention to privatize Railtrack within the lifetime of this Parliament using the powers provided by the Railways Act 1993. Labour's transport spokesperson (Michael Meacher) made it clear 'without equivocation that Labour remains wholly committed to a publicly-owned rail system'. Later that day the Commons agreed to the setting-up of a select committee on deregulation and also approved a motion to increase the pay of Ministers in line with the agreed formula linking it to Civil Service pay, by 179 votes to 13.

The European Communities (Finance) Bill to approve the United Kingdom's contribution to the increase in the European Union budget agreed at the Edinburgh summit in 1992 was given a second reading in the Commons on 28 November. The Prime Minister had made the clear passage of this bill a matter of confidence. The Shadow Chancellor (Gordon Brown) tabled an amendment declining to approve any increase in UK contributions until stronger action had been taken against EU fraud. The amendment was defeated by 330 votes to 303

and the second reading was approved by 329 votes to 44. Seven Conservative MPs (Nicholas Budgen, Christopher Gill, Teresa Gorman, Tony Marlow, Richard Shepherd, Sir Teddy Taylor and John Wilkinson) abstained in the first vote and had the whip withdrawn for failing to vote with the Government. Another Conservative MP, Michael Carttiss, abstained on the second vote and also had the whip withdrawn. One further Conservative MP, Sir Richard Body, resigned the whip of his own accord. The committee of the whole House was held on 7 December, when no amendments were passed, and on the same day the third reading was approved by 295 votes to 23. The bill received an unopposed second reading in the Lords on 9 January and its remaining stages in the Lords were completed without amendment on 10 January. The bill received royal assent on 16 January.

The Criminal Justice (Scotland) Bill to make the Scottish legal system more responsive to the needs of victims, witnesses and jurors and to increase the capacity of the system to deal with offenders, was given an unopposed second reading in the Lords on 29 November. In the Commons the Labour Party tabled an amendment declining to give the bill a second reading on 27 February as it was neither an acceptable nor effective measure. This was defeated by 282 votes to 207. The third reading was passed without division on 6 June and the bill received royal assent on 19 July.

THE BUDGET

The Chancellor (Kenneth Clarke) presented his second Budget on 29 November. He said that the Budget was designed to 'ensure that the improvements in the public finances announced in 1993 are delivered and to produce further structural reforms to make the economy work better'. The main points were:

Fiscal outlook
 – government spending plans in 1995–6 to be reduced by £7,200 million, with further reductions of £9,000 million in 1996–7 and £9,800 million in 1997–8 to reflect the fall in the projected levels of inflation and government savings
 – control total reduced to £249,600 million in 1994–5, some £1,300 million below forecast. This would rise to £255,700 million in 1995–6 (some £6,900 million lower than forecast)
 – total government spending projected to fall from 44 per cent to 41 per cent of national output over the next three years
 – taxes and social security revenues to rise from 33.75 per cent of GDP in 1993–4 to 35.25 per cent in 1994–5
 – public sector borrowing requirement (PSBR) to fall from £34,400 million in 1994–5 to £21,500 million in 1995–6, then to fall to £13,000 million in 1996–7 and £5,000 million in 1997–8, and then return to balance at the end of the decade

Taxation
- no change to Advance Corporation Tax, Corporation Tax or capital allowances; small businesses' VAT threshold increased to £46,000; 30 per cent increase in threshold for monthly PAYE payments; business rates rises as a result of revaluation to be limited to 10 per cent for large businesses and 7.5 per cent for smaller ones
- no change in basic rates of income tax but 20p lower band extended to £3,200; full indexation of personal allowances and the threshold of higher rates tax; personal allowances for the over-65s up £430; Capital Gains Tax exempt amount increased to £6,000 a year; Inheritance Tax threshold raised to £154,000
- no change in plans for VAT; second tranche of VAT on domestic fuel to come into effect in April 1995; package of help to lessen impact of VAT on fuel to be extended with increases in home energy efficiency scheme grants, cold weather payments and pensions
- TESSAs to be extended beyond January 1996; existing five-year holders able to renew accounts with tax-free interest on amounts up to £9,000; PEPs to be extended to cover specified corporate bonds
- road fuel duties to increase by a real 5 per cent a year in future budgets; petrol up by 2.5 pence a litre; diesel up by 3 pence a litre; vehicle excise duty increased to £135; tobacco duties to increase by a real 3 per cent a year in future budgets; packet of 20 cigarettes up 10 pence; no change in alcohol duties; amusement machines to be taxed in line with gaming machines

Spending
- public sector pay controls to remain tight; increase in pay to be offset by increased efficiency; total Civil Service numbers to fall below 500,000 over next four years
- central government costs to remain constant in cash terms for next four years, a 10 per cent fall in real terms
- local government total standard spending in 1995-6 to increase by 2.2 per cent
- education spending to increase by almost 1 per cent in real terms in 1995-6; student loans and grants to increase in line with inflation
- Urban Regeneration Grant given an extra £800 million in 1996-7
- employers taking on anyone unemployed for more than two years to be exempt from National Insurance contributions for a year; employer NI contributions for the low-paid to be reduced 0.6 per cent a year from April 1995; family credit to be increased for those in full-time work; payment of housing benefit and family credit to be speeded up for people taking jobs; jobfinder's grants to be introduced; schemes such as Workstart to be extended; training budget for 1995-6 to be reduced to £578 million

- health budget to increase by £1,300 million (1 per cent) in 1995-6; further initiatives to attract private finance for health construction projects
- spending on police up by 3 per cent in 1995-6, with Chief Constables given more control over their budgets; further initiatives to attract private finance into prisons
- rules covering housing benefit changed so that local authorities will not be reimbursed fully for rents significantly higher than local averages; state support for mortgage payments in case of sickness/unemployment to be reduced; further initiatives against fraud announced
- spending on motorways and trunk roads to be reduced but more encouragement for private sector investment; London Underground to get £1,000 million in 1995-6 but also expected to attract considerable private finance

Forecast
- inflation to remain low; expected to reach a plateau at 2.5 per cent in 1995 and then to fall
- stronger growth predicted, with GDP set to rise by over 4 per cent during 1994 with a forecast for 1995 of a 3.25 per cent increase; the current account to improve by £6,000 million in 1994-5.

DEBATE ON THE BUDGET

Kenneth Clarke said, 'This Budget keeps Britain firmly on track for real economic growth that can last. This Budget concentrates on strengthening British business. It will help to create more jobs. And it will lay the foundations for sustained rises in prosperity.' Tony Blair accused the Government of breaking their specific election pledge that they would never raise VAT 'and they will never be trusted again'; he added that Labour would table an amendment allowing MPs to vote specifically on the VAT rise. He accused the Chancellor of producing tax increases in his two Budgets that amounted to 'seven pence on the standard rate of income tax. That is a betrayal that the British people will never forget'. He criticized the Budget for being 'silent on how to invest in our people at school and at work, to motivate them, extend their potential and treat them fairly as proper partners in the enterprise of the country'. The Liberal Democrat Treasury spokesperson (Malcolm Bruce) poured scorn on the Chancellor's idea that the UK was on the road to long-term recovery: 'the reality is that no-one believed him. People know that he is taking more taxes out of our pockets today – seven additional taxes in the current financial year totalling more than £6,000 million – and that he intends to hang on to them to cut tax in advance of the next general election ... The Budget will fool no-one.'
On the second day of the debate on the Budget, the Shadow Chancellor (Gordon Brown) formally moved an amendment to repeal the second tranche of the imposition of VAT on domestic fuel. During the five days of debate two Conservative MPs (Nicholas Winterton and David Sumberg) said they

would vote against the Government and for the Labour amendment and two more (Phil Gallie and Sir Teddy Taylor) said they would abstain. In his summing-up speech on 6 December, Kenneth Clarke offered a further £20 million for the Home Energy Efficiency Scheme and an extra £100 million to assist pensioners in a last-ditch attempt to appease those Conservative back-bench rebels who had threatened to support the Labour amendment. Although it appeared that this might be sufficient, in the event the Opposition amendment was passed by 319 votes to 311. Seven Conservative MPs voted against the Government (Michael Carttiss, David Sumberg, Paul Marland, Richard Shepherd, Tony Marlow, Ann Winterton and Nicholas Winterton) and eight abstained (Sir Richard Body, Sir Rhodes Boyson, Phil Gallie, Christopher Gill, Teresa Gorman, William Powell, Sir Teddy Taylor and John Wilkinson). Two other potential rebels (Geoffrey Dickens and Sir Nicholas Fairbairn) were absent sick for the vote. The rest of the Budget statement was approved by 324 votes to 297. As a result of this defeat Kenneth Clarke announced that the Government would not be bringing forward the second tranche of the VAT increase, even though the vote itself would not directly have caused that, and that he would make a further statement to the House on 8 December. In that statement he announced that he would be making up the £1,500 million shortfall that this change caused in the Budget by increasing excise duties:

– tobacco to be increased by 4 per cent
– fuel to be increased by 1 pence a litre
– alcohol to be increased by 4 per cent

However, the increased package of compensation measures previously announced would not be implemented. Gordon Brown commented 'this latest Budget statement shows a Government who have been stumbling from crisis to crisis, from panic measure to panic measure – a Government who are to their core incompetent and unfair. They are no longer fit to be in charge of our nations' finances.' Malcolm Bruce said the Chancellor 'is simply demonstrating the politics of pique, and the pain and anguish could have been avoided if he had only listened to the people in the first place'. These changes were approved by a series of votes on 13 December.

On 30 November the Secretary of State for Social Security (Peter Lilley) made the annual statement on social security benefits uprating as a result of the Budget, in which he reiterated the details of the Chancellor's VAT compensation package (later dropped) and other measures. He said he was introducing further measures to curb the growth of social security expenditure and to help people get off benefit. In particular he outlined intended changes to income support for mortgage interest.

On 7 December the Foreign Secretary (Douglas Hurd) reported on the deteriorating situation in Bosnia and the outcome of the Contact Group meeting on 2 December and the CSCE summit on 5–6 December. He confirmed that the Government wanted the UN force to be able to continue its peacekeeping mission and for the British contingent to continue to play a major part, but this would depend on a lasting ceasefire. Labour's foreign affairs spokesperson (Robin Cook) expressed appreciation for the fortitude and persistence which continued to be shown by British troops in Bosnia. On 12 December John Major reported back on the outcome of the European Council meeting held in Essen on 9–10 December. A motion to remove Tony Benn from the committee on privileges because he refused to allow proceedings to be held in camera was approved by 181 votes to 52.

On 13 December Douglas Hurd announced that the Government would not be appealing against the judgement in the Divisional Court on illegal payments from the Overseas Aid Budget to Malaysia for the Pergau dam project. Labour's overseas aid spokesperson (Joan Lestor) wanted to know whether the money already spent on the project (£34.5 million) would be repaid 'since those funds have clearly been misappropriated'.

ENVIRONMENT BILL

The bill to establish an Environment Agency for England and Wales and to set up a Scottish Environment Protection Agency and other measures to improve the protection and management of the environment was given an unopposed second reading in the Lords on 15 December. In seven days in committee in January and February, the Government suffered a defeat on clause 58 (purpose of National Parks) on 2 February when an amendment moved by Lord Norrie (C.) designed to protect 'quiet enjoyment and understanding' was passed by 129 votes to 121. It was also defeated on third reading on 20 March on clause 57 (amendments to Water Resources Act) when an amendment moved by Lord Stanley of Alderley (C.) covering polluted water spilling from abandoned mines was passed by 108 votes to 100. The bill received an unopposed second reading in the Commons on 18 April. In committee in April, May and June the Government added clauses to include a specific definition of contaminated land and to cover local authority air quality standards. The third reading was passed without a vote and the bill received royal assent on 19 July.

On 19 December the Home Secretary (Michael Howard) made a statement on the publication of the report by Sir John Woodcock on the escape attempt from Whitemoor Prison, revealing several major lapses of security. He announced the setting-up of a comprehensive and independent review of security throughout the prison service to be headed by General Sir John Learmont. Labour's home affairs spokesperson (Jack Straw) felt the report 'reveals a catalogue of incompetence and negligence on a truly monumental scale, which has been compounded by buck-passing by the Secretary of State and his failure to recognize his responsibility for this appalling state of affairs'. The Commons approved the recommendations of the Jopling report on sittings of the House to ensure that there would be fewer late-night sittings and introducing the concept of not sitting on eight Fridays to discuss Private Members' business but sitting on eight Wednesday mornings instead as an experiment. A motion calling for shorter speeches was also approved.

When the Commons returned from the Christmas recess on 10 January, the Minister for Agriculture, Fisheries and Food (William Waldegrave) made a statement in response to a private notice question from David Harris (C.) on the outcome of the EU fisheries council meeting on 22 December, when proposals to integrate the Spanish and Portuguese fishing fleets into the EU common fisheries policy had been agreed; restrictions in the Irish box would be relaxed so as to allow up to 40 Spanish vessels to fish in certain parts, although not in the Irish Sea or the Bristol Channel. Labour's agriculture spokesperson (Gavin Strang) said the deal was 'a disaster for our fishing communities and represents a wholesale failure by the Government'. Michael Howard made a statement on the escape of three prisoners from Parkhurst prison, disturbances at Eversthorpe prison and the suicide of Frederick West in Birmingham prison. Jack Straw felt it 'wholly fails to meet public anxieties about the lamentable sequence of events'.

The Jobseekers' Bill, introducing the new jobseeker's allowance to replace unemployment benefit and income support and improving incentives to work, was given a second reading in the Commons on 10 January. The third reading was approved on 23 March. In the Lords the bill had to be recommitted to the committee on 11 May (after it had finished in committee) to discuss clause 6 (regulations to require attendance at interviews) following a report from the new delegated powers scrutiny committee suggesting that the procedure for dealing with these regulations should be the affirmative procedure. The bill received royal assent on 28 June.

The Channel Tunnel Rail Link Bill, the hybrid bill to allow for the construction of the link, was given an unopposed second reading in the Commons on 16 January. A special select committee of five MPs to look at objections was set up but a Labour amendment calling for compensation for people affected by the link in Islington was defeated. The special select committee was still sitting as the Commons rose for the summer recess.

FINANCE BILL

The bill to enact the provisions of the (revised) Budget was given a second reading in the Commons on 17 January by 318 votes to 277. The committee of the whole House on 23, 25 and 30 January dealt with VAT on fuel, excise duties, venture capital trusts and pensions. During the remaining stages debate on 3 and 4 April, the Government added new clauses covering pool betting duty and accepted a new clause on deferment of balancing charges in respect of ships; the bill was given a third reading without division. The Lords considered the bill on 28 April and it received royal assent on 1 May.

On 18 January during a debate on a Labour motion condemning the recent EU fisheries agreement, William Waldegrave announced an extra £28 million for the compensation package available to UK fishermen. Despite this, nine Conservative MPs voted against the Government (seven of the 'whipless rebels' plus Rupert Allason and David Harris) and seven abstained (the two other 'rebels' plus Bill Cash, Toby Jessel, Norman Lamont, Sir Trevor Skeet and Anthony Steen); the motion was defeated by 312 votes to 294. On 20 January Diana Maddock (LD), who had won first place in the ballot for Private Members' Bills, gained an unopposed second reading for her Home Energy Conservation Bill which would give local authorities the duty to survey the energy efficiency of properties. The bill was similar to one which had been introduced in the previous session but which the Government had blocked. This time the Parliamentary Under-Secretary of State at the Department of the Environment (Robert Jones) welcomed many aspects of the measure, although with some reservations which he said he would seek to resolve in committee. The bill received royal assent on 28 June.

The Disability Discrimination Bill to provide a right for disabled people not to be discriminated against in employment, to place a duty on employers to make reasonable adjustments to working practices and environment to overcome practical difficulties, and to establish a National Disability Council, was given a second reading in the Commons on 24 January. Labour tabled an amendment declining to give a second reading because of the shortcomings of the bill but this was defeated by 307 votes to 280. During the remaining stages debate on 27 and 28 March the Government announced proposals for a new funding scheme to improve access for disabled pupils at school, new concessions to protect people with a history of disability, and plans to bring forward amendments in the Lords to set minimum access requirements for new passenger transport vehicles. In the Lords the Government was defeated in committee on 15 June when an amendment to clause 12 (discrimination in relation to goods, facilities and services) moved by Baroness Hollis (Lab.) redefining disability as regards the provision of goods and services was passed by 94 votes to 50. The bill completed its report stage in the Lords on 20 July.

PENSIONS BILL

The bill to improve security, equality and choice in occupational pensions and to equalize the state pension age at 65 for both sexes was given a second reading in the Lords on 24 January. In the five days in committee in the Lords in February, the Minister of State at the Department of Social Security (Lord Mackay of Ardbrecknish) promised to look again at the issue of pension rights being taken into account in divorce settlements in England and Wales. On 20 February the Government was defeated by 105 votes to 61 on an amendment to schedule 4 (Equalization) moved by Baroness Hollis (Lab.) concerning the averaging of SERPS not over the whole of one's working life but to allow for the dropping of the five 'worst' years from the equation. On report on 14 March the Government was defeated when an amendment moved by Lord Freyberg (Ind.) to allow war widows who lose their pensions rights on remarriage to have them restored if they are widowed a second time or divorced, was passed by 191 votes to 145. The Government also announced measures to force divorced husbands to pay up to half their pension to an ex-wife. On second reading in the Commons on 24 April, Peter Lilley announced that the Government would not seek to overturn the Lords amendments on war widows or give powers to courts to introduce 'deferred maintenance' orders. An amendment by Labour was defeated by 267 votes to 228 and the second reading was similarly passed. The bill was given an un-opposed third reading on 5 July and received royal assent on 19 July.

The first of the new Wednesday morning sessions of Parliament was on 25 January, with a number of balloted back-bench debates from 10.00 a.m. to 2.30 p.m. On 26 January Dale Campbell-Savours (Lab.) was named by the Speaker and barred from the House for the rest of the day for refusing to withdraw remarks concerning alleged 'criminal' activities and Lord Archer of Weston-super-Mare.

On 27 January David Jamieson (Lab.) gained an unopposed second reading for his Activity Centres (Young Person's Safety) Bill, to raise standards of safety for those who provide adventure holidays for people under 18. The Minister of State at the Department for Employment (Eric Forth) accepted the thrust of the bill. It received royal assent on 28 June.

On 30 January Brian Mawhinney responded to a private notice question from Michael Meacher concerning reports in the *Observer* about inadequate security arrangements for the Eurostar and Euro-tunnel trains. On 1 February the Northern Ireland Secretary (Sir Patrick Mayhew) made a statement on the leak of a document to *The Times* suggesting that the setting-up of an all-Ireland assembly had been agreed secretly. Whilst he admitted that he 'recognized a few phrases, lifted highly selectively ... I do not recognize the conclusions ... drawn'. He would not be drawn into premature publication of a document still under negotiation that had not been agreed by the two governments: 'the process is too important ... to be further damaged in such a way.' The Prime Minister went on national television later that evening to explain the situation. On 3 February two Private Members' Bills, the Proceeds

of Crime Bill (Sir John Hannam (C.)), to give greater powers to courts to recover the proceeds of crime from so-called 'lifestyle criminals' and the Road Traffic (New Drivers) Bill (Michael Clark (C.)), to introduce a two-year probationary period for all new drivers were given second readings. They both received royal assent on 28 June.

On 10 February Harry Barnes (Lab.), who had come fourth in the ballot for Private Members' Bills, succeeded in getting a second reading for his Civil Rights (Disabled Persons) Bill by 175 votes to nil, but the Minister for Disabled People (William Hague), although supporting the objective of ending discrimination against disabled people, said he could not support this bill (although he would not vote against it) as it would not be workable, preferring instead the government bill that was already in committee. The Government tabled numerous amendments in committee, delaying its progress. The debate on the report stage of the bill was adjourned on 14 July.

On 13 February a Liberal Democrat motion calling for a referendum before any substantial alteration of the present constitutional settlement between the EU and its member states was rejected by both the Government and the Labour Party. But as MPs from the two major parties did not vote, the motion was technically passed by 47 votes to 3. On 15 February the Parliamentary Under-Secretary of State for Corporate Affairs (Jonathan Evans) responded to a private notice question from Labour's trade and industry spokesperson (Dr Jack Cunningham) on the future ownership of the regional electricity companies in the light of the decision not to refer the bid by Trafalgar house for Northern Electric to the Monopolies and Mergers Commission. Jack Cunningham felt that the public interest had been ignored by not making a reference.

The Licensing (Sunday Hours) Bill to extend the opening of off-licences, pubs and clubs on Sundays and also on Christmas Day and Easter Sunday, was given a second reading in the Commons on 15 February on a free vote by 304 votes to 116. During the remaining stages debate on 5 April the Government introduced amendments deleting Christmas Day from the provisions of the bill. In the committee stage in the Lords on 18 May amendments were accepted covering off-licence opening hours on Good Friday. The bill received royal assent on 19 July.

On 22 February John Major made a statement on the long-awaited publication of the framework documents on the future of Northern Ireland (*see* page 1094). He stressed that nothing in the documents would be imposed; it was for discussion and negotiation with the parties in Northern Ireland. Publication was welcomed by Tony Blair who said that whatever party was in power, the process would continue, pursued with the same patience and determination and motivated by the same desire for peace.

The Family Homes and Domestic Violence Bill, to reform the discretionary remedies in family law to deal with the protection of one member of a family against violence from another and the occupation of the family home when a relationship has broken down by the introduction of 'non-molestation orders' and 'occupation orders', was given an unopposed second reading in the Lords on 23 February. The bill was dealt with under the simplified Jellicoe procedures, which meant that a special public committee was constituted in the Lords when public evidence was taken during March and April. In the Commons a second reading committee was constituted which discussed the bill on 3 July.

On 27 February Kenneth Clarke made a statement on the collapse of the merchant bank Barings following speculation on the derivatives market in the Far East by one of its traders; he announced the setting-up of an inquiry by the Board of Banking Supervision. Gordon Brown said the collapse demonstrated the need for 'better supervision, stronger safeguards and more adequate investor protection … through international co-operation'. On 28 February Brian Mawhinney made a statement on the Government's response to the Donaldson report into the prevention of pollution from merchant shipping. The Government accepted 86 of the 103 recommendations in full and was still considering the majority of the others; it had rejected only four.

On 1 March there was a debate on a Labour motion, introduced by Tony Blair, refusing to support the Government's policy towards the EU as it did not promote the interests of the British people. John Major spoke to a government amendment rejecting the policy of the Opposition. The motion was defeated by 319 votes to 314 but nine Ulster Unionists and one Conservative MP (Norman Lamont) voted against the Government, and five of the 'whipless rebels' and one other Conservative MP (Bill Cash) abstained. On 2 March the Secretary of State for the Environment (John Gummer) reported on progress in the review of the local government structure in England; he had accepted all but two of the recommendations of the Commission for 17 of the counties but he had accepted only some of the recommendations for changes in Bedfordshire, Buckinghamshire and Durham. He also announced that Sir John Banham was standing down as chairman of the Commission and that he would be seeking a new chairman to look again at some areas. On 3 March John McFall (Lab.), who had come seventh in the ballot for Private Members' Bills, gained a second reading for his Wild Mammals (Protection) Bill, which would *inter alia* outlaw the hunting of foxes with hounds, by 253 votes to nil. Because it was so low on the list, committee discussion was not held until July. Mr McFall then deleted all the references to fox-hunting so that further progress could be made. As a result the report stage was passed on 14 July.

CRIMINAL APPEAL BILL

The bill to improve the system of dealing with miscarriages of justice had an unopposed second reading in the Commons on 6 March and an unopposed third reading on 26 April. On report in the Lords on 26 June, the Government was defeated when an amendment moved by Lord Ackner (Ind.) and backed by the Lord Chief Justice (Lord Taylor) and other law lords to reform the system for fixing the 'tariff' period for mandatory life sentences for murder was passed by 142 votes to 126. On third reading on 3 July the Minister of State at the Home Office (Baroness Blatch) moved technical government amendments as a result of this defeat but stressed that this did not necessarily mean that the Government would not seek to overturn the original amendments in the Commons. On 17 July during Commons consideration of Lords amendments, the Government did reject these amendments, by 254 votes to 225. The Lords accepted this reverse on 18 July and the bill received royal assent on 19 July.

On 8 March the Commons debated a motion to approve the draft Prevention of Terrorism (Temporary Provisions) Act 1989 (Continuance) Order 1995. Michael Howard announced the lifting of some 50 exclusion orders. Jack Straw explained why Labour would continue to vote against this annual order but the motion was passed by 314 votes to 212. The Commons did not sit on 10 March as this was the first of their 'constituency Fridays'.

On 13 March the Fisheries Minister (Michael Jack) responded to a private notice question from Peter Shore (Lab.) on UK policy over the seizure by the Canadian government of a Spanish trawler in the international waters near Newfoundland. Gavin Strang said the dispute was an example of a wider problem, 'the inadequacy of the international arrangements which are unable effectively to conserve stocks outwith national limits'.

The Gas Bill, allowing greater competition in the domestic gas market, was given a second reading in the Commons on 13 March. An amendment moved by Labour to deny a second reading because the bill failed to give adequate safeguards to consumers was defeated by 318 votes to 244 and the second reading approved by 312 votes to 22. The third reading on 16 May was passed by 297 votes to 228. The bill finished in committee in the Lords on 28 June.

The Child Support Bill to improve the system of child support, streamline the operations of the Child Support Agency and encourage greater compliance, was given a second reading in the Commons on 20 March. An amendment moved by Labour to deny a second reading as the bill in its present form was unacceptable was defeated by 290 votes to 258. An amendment moved on second reading in the Lords on 5 June by Lord Simon of Glaisdale (Ind.) regretting that the bill did not fully obviate the hardships and injustices caused by the 1991 Act was defeated. The bill received royal assent on 19 July.

On 21 March John Gummer made a statement on the last stage of the local government review, covering the twelve remaining counties. He had broadly accepted the Commission's recommendations for nine of them (although he felt there should be further study done on the future of Rutland) but he had not fully accepted the recommendations for Hampshire, Dorset and Berkshire. He also announced that Sir David Cooksey would be the next chairman of the Commission. Later there was a debate on EU agricultural prices, with a Labour amendment stressing that the CAP was still failing consumers and accusing the Government of failing to do enough to make fundamental changes. Although the amendment was defeated by 305 votes to 278 and the government motion passed, the Ulster Unionist MPs abstained on both votes and of the Conservative 'whipless rebels', one (Nicholas Budgen) voted with the Government on both votes with the other eight abstaining on the government motion, and all bar one (Sir Teddy Taylor) voted with the Government on the Labour amendment. Another Conservative MP, David Porter, abstained on both votes.

On 28 March William Waldegrave responded to a private notice question from Gavin Strang on the dispute between the EU and Canada over fishing rights. He said that the UK was uniquely positioned as a member of both the EU and the Commonwealth to broker a resolution and added that the UK would not be able to support any EU sanctions against Canada. On 31 March the Attorney-General (Sir Nicholas Lyell) made a statement on the way ahead for the investigation and prosecution of serious and complex fraud following the Graham and Dowie reports; in essence the Serious Fraud Office will be retained but thoroughly overhauled.

On 3 April Brian Mawhinney made a statement about measures to promote the use of rail and other transport infrastructure to meet the diverse needs of both private and business travellers using London's airports. He announced that plans for a 14-lane M25 motorway had been scrapped. Michael Meacher accused government transport policy of being 'in tatters, because, while roads are being cut, it says little or nothing about proposals for alternative public transport systems'. Before rising for the Easter recess on 5 April, the Secretary of State for Health (Virginia Bottomley) responded to a private notice question from Peter Brooke (C.) on the announcement of the proposed changes to the National Health Service in London, affecting St Thomas' and Guys, the Queen Elizabeth Military Hospital, Greenwich, the closure of Barts Hospital and the Accident and Emergency Unit at Edgware Hospital, and in particular how this had been announced by means of a written answer rather than a ministerial statement. Mrs Bottomley faced considerable back-bench criticism from her own party, which was echoed that evening when several Conservative MPs spoke in an adjournment debate on Edgware General Hospital criticizing the

decisions taken by the Department of Health. Later Brian Mawhinney made a statement on the outcome of the Marine Safety Agency inquiry into ferry safety, following the *Estonia* disaster, which showed that fitting transverse bulkheads to sea ferries would improve buoyancy. The Government would try to persuade the International Maritime Organization to tighten the current regulations but failing that the UK might act unilaterally. He also published a list of the ferries using UK ports that failed to meet current standards.

CASH FOR QUESTIONS

Returning from the Easter recess on 18 April, William Waldegrave, responding to a private notice question from Sir Teddy Taylor, brought MPs up-to-date on the agreement reached between the EU and Canada over fishing and the subsequent representations made by the Spanish government to the UK. On 20 April the Commons approved a motion from the privileges committee concerning the punishment of the two Conservative MPs in the 'cash for questions' row; this led to the suspension from the House of Graham Riddick for ten days and of David Tredinnick for 20 days. Both MPs apologized to the House and the motion was passed without division. MPs then considered a motion moved by Tony Newton to ensure that MPs not on a committee could not disrupt the workings of that committee (this followed an incident with Dale Campbell-Savours (Lab.) and the select committee on members' interests), which was passed by 135 votes to 35. On 21 April the Government announced it would broadly accept the thrust of the Carers' (Recognition and Services) Bill, a Private Member's Bill introduced by Malcolm Wicks (Lab.), and added amendments to ensure that children as carers were specifically covered; it received royal assent on 28 June.

On 3 May Douglas Hurd, responding to a private notice question from Robin Cook, made a statement on the resumption of hostilities in Bosnia and the UN reaction to it. A full day's debate on the former Yugoslavia was held on 9 May. On 10 May there was a debate on a Labour motion criticizing the Government's health reforms in London. Although the motion was defeated by 320 votes to 308, two Conservative MPs (Peter Brooke and John Marshall) voted against the Government and two others (Sir Rhodes Boyson and Hugh Dykes) abstained. On 11 May the President of the Board of Trade (Michael Heseltine) made a statement on the future of the Post Office. He announced changes to the financial regime (particularly the external financing limit), the adoption of a more strategic corporate plan process, and the removal of the limit on capital expenditure, plus a willingness to consider requests by the Post Office to extend its activities into adjacent markets.

On 16 May Michael Howard announced proposals for reforming the law on disclosure of evidence in criminal cases. On 18 May the Commons debated the Nolan Report (*see* page 1175). The Chancellor of the Duchy of Lancaster (David Hunt) welcomed the report and its recommendations and broadly accepted the restrictions on ministers taking jobs on leaving office and new rules on the membership of quangos. Tony Newton announced the setting-up of a committee of senior MPs to examine in detail the proposals in the report, thus giving Parliament the final say on the matter. The Shadow Leader of the House (Ann Taylor) said 'if we are to begin to restore public confidence in our democracy, our parliamentary system and the House of Commons we must get on with it as quickly as possible'.

On 22 May Sir Jerry Wiggin (C.) made a personal statement to the House apologizing for having tabled amendments to the Gas Bill in standing committee in the name of another MP (Sebastian Coe) but without his knowledge, which had come to light after a television documentary. On 23 May Michael Heseltine made a statement about the proposed acquisition of VSEL by either British Aerospace (BAe) or GEC. He had accepted the Monopolies and Mergers Commission clearance of the BAe bid but had rejected the majority MMC recommendation to block the GEC bid and had instead endorsed the minority MMC report to allow that bid to proceed as well. He recognized that this was unusual but decided that the public interest would be best served by allowing the market to determine future ownership. Jack Cunningham welcomed the statement but was saddened that the Government 'has taken no strategic view on the maintenance of jobs or skills in our defence industries nor ... on maintaining our defence capability for the future'.

The Criminal Injuries Compensation Bill to provide for the establishment of a scheme for compensation for criminal injuries had its second reading in the Commons on 23 May. Labour tabled an amendment declining a second reading because the new measure would cut the cash available to victims; this was defeated by 274 votes to 229. The Labour Party also tabled an amendment objecting to the third reading on 29 June but this was defeated by 260 votes to 202. It had an unopposed second reading in the Lords on 19 July.

Business in both Houses was cancelled on 24 May as a mark of respect following the death of the former Labour Prime Minister Harold Wilson. Short tributes were paid in both Houses.

Parliament was recalled from the spring recess on 31 May to discuss the worsening situation in Bosnia. John Major described the situation, the Government's decision to reinforce the UK contingent and the taking of UN troops (including British soldiers) as hostages by the Bosnian Serbs. 'I have indicated that I wish our forces to stay there, and I wish the UN protection force as a whole to stay there to carry out the job for which it was sent. That job is not yet concluded. I hope it will be possible for it to remain.' Tony Blair offered his support to the Prime

Minister: 'I believe that the more united the House can be on this issue, the better.' He went on to say that 'talk of withdrawal in Bosnia in response to the taking of hostages is deeply unhelpful at this time. It is hardly a message of firm resolve in the face of what is effectively an act of coercive blackmail.' Paddy Ashdown agreed that 'the sending of reinforcements will be a signal to the Bosnian Serbs of the seriousness of our intent ... we must be clear that it will always be preferable to take sides against aggression than to run away in the face of it'.

On 8 June Robert Jackson (C.), in his capacity as Kevin Maxwell's local MP, introduced a motion asking for papers relating to the enquiry into the Maxwell fraud case held by the select committee on social security to be released to the court; the motion was withdrawn. On 9 June the Financial Secretary to the Treasury (Sir George Young) responded to a private notice question from Gordon Brown on the inquiry into the sale of shares in PowerGen and National Power, following the release of a letter from the Stock Exchange to the Treasury asking them to examine further the circumstances surrounding the sale. Sir George confirmed that the Treasury would undertake such an inquiry and that the results would be published. Gordon Brown called the response 'wholly inadequate .. [and] no answer to the charge that damage has been done to the City's financial reputation and ... there is an urgent need to repair that reputation'.

On 12 June the Commons approved the draft Northern Ireland (Emergency and Prevention of Terrorism Provisions) (Continuance) Order 1995 by 286 votes to 190; the Labour Party continued to oppose adoption. On 13 June Michael Heseltine made a statement on the outcome of his inquiry into the Department of Trade and Industry's relationship with the defence manufacturer BMARC and the export of naval guns and ammunition during the late 1980s. Jack Cunningham suggested that 'not because of any honesty on the part of the Government, or because of any desire for openness, and certainly not because of any competence on their part, the House and the country have learnt of yet another scandal – another piece of unvarnished Government duplicity'.

On 19 June John Major reported on the outcome of the G7 summit in Halifax, Nova Scotia, followed by the brief G8 meeting (including Boris Yeltsin). There was a debate on a Labour motion calling for an independent inquiry into the BMARC affair which was defeated by 291 votes to 267. On 22 June William Waldegrave reported on the outcome of the EU agriculture council meeting on 19-22 June, when agreement had finally been reached on a comprehensive framework of law covering the welfare of animals transported throughout the EU, with maximum limits on travel times for all journeys. Elliot Morley, one of Labour's agriculture team, welcomed the progress towards a European-wide structure for animal welfare and journey times but regretted that in many cases the maximum time for European journeys had been increased compared to the standards laid down in UK law and that there would be no review for three years.

On the same day John Major called a surprise press conference to announce that he was standing down as leader of the Conservative Party so as to force an election for the post, in which he would be a candidate, and so end speculation about his leadership. On 26 June the Secretary of State for Wales (John Redwood) announced his intention to stand against the Prime Minister. On 28 June John Major reported on the outcome of the EU summit in Cannes on 26–27 June. On a single currency, it had been acknowledged that a move towards it by some member states would have serious practical and economic consequences for the future operations of the Union, and Finance Ministers had been asked to look again at this and report back. He had also held a separate bilateral meeting with John Bruton, the Irish Taoiseach.

On 4 July John Major was re-elected as leader of the Conservative Party, receiving 218 votes to John Redwood's 89, with 12 abstentions, eight spoilt papers and two MPs not voting. On 5–6 July John Major reshuffled his ministerial team. On 6 July the Secretary of State for Education and Employment (Gillian Shephard) made a statement on plans to introduce vouchers worth up to £1,100 for the parents of all four-year-olds to spend on their children's pre-school nursery education. After a pilot scheme, it would be introduced nationwide in April 1997. Labour's education spokesperson (David Blunkett) called the proposal 'a con-trick on children and on parents. It is an experiment in offering a paper promise without providing a single extra place in a nursery class in this country.'

On 10 July Labour MPs boycotted Welsh question time in the Commons in protest at the appointment of William Hague, an English MP, as Secretary of State; inevitably Conservative MPs christened this a 'boyo-cott'. On 12 July the Foreign Secretary (Malcolm Rifkind) made a statement on the capture of Srebrenica by the Bosnian Serbs, despite the use of NATO airstrikes in an attempt to stop the attack on this UN 'safe area', and the withdrawal of UN troops from the area.

On 17 July the President of the Board of Trade (Ian Lang) made a statement on the publication of the report by the CBI committee chaired by Sir Richard Greenbury, chief executive of Marks and Spencer, on directors' remuneration. The Government had immediately accepted one of the recommendations and announced that executive share options would now be taxed as income. (After a week of arguments, Kenneth Clarke announced a compromise position on 27 July.) Jack Cunningham thought the report had some welcome proposals but felt that it 'will not be welcomed outside the House by consumers who are fed up with being exploited and fed up with the Government's failure to act'. On 18 July Kenneth Clarke reported on the outcome of the Bank of England inquiry into the collapse of Barings Bank, which concluded that there had been a failure of the Baring's internal system and deceit by Nick Leeson, the trader involved. He did not, therefore, intend to change the regulatory system. Gordon Brown thought the report highlighted failures that reflected 'not just incompetence, but a flawed structure of regulation' and asked for a review to be set up to consider wider changes to the system. The Chancellor of the Duchy of Lancaster (Roger Freeman) announced the publication of the Government's response to the Nolan Committee report, accepting that ministers should be brought within the scope of the Advisory Committee on Business Appointments, like senior civil servants, a move welcomed by Labour. On 19 July the Commons approved government motions setting up a Parliamentary Commissioner for Standards and a new select committee on standards and privileges, and endorsing the principle of a code of conduct for MPs. Labour amendments on disclosure of earnings from consultancies and a bar on any consultancies with lobbying companies were defeated, as was a Liberal Democrat amendment on disclosure of details in the register of members' interests.

The House of Commons rose for the summer recess on 19 July and the Lords on 21 July.

PUBLIC ACTS OF PARLIAMENT

This list is of those Public Acts which received the royal assent after August 1994. The date stated after each Act is the date on which it came into operation; c. indicates the chapter number of each Act

Sale of Goods (Amendment) Act 1994, c. 32, 3 January 1995
 Abolishes market overt

Criminal Justice and Public Order Act 1994, c. 33, various dates
 Makes new provisions in many areas of criminal justice and public order, including the sentencing of juvenile offenders; bail; reform of the right of silence; police powers to take samples; measures against trespassers, squatters and illegal camping; anti-terrorism; obscenity; and the contracting out of prisons and prison escorts. Applies in part to Scotland

Marriage Act 1994, c. 34, various dates
 Enables civil marriages to be solemnized on premises approved by local authorities; and for related purposes

Sale and Supply of Goods Act 1994, c. 35, 3 January 1995
 Amends the law in the UK relating to the sale of goods by, *inter alia*, providing for an implied term

in a contract that goods supplied in the course of a business are of satisfactory quality and giving rights for examination and partial rejection; modifies the law in England and Wales with regard to rejection for breach of condition in non-consumer cases and provides in Scotland for remedies for breach of contract and for matters connected with the sale of goods there

Law of Property (Miscellaneous Provisions) Act 1994, c. 36, day or days to be appointed
Introduces reforms to simplify and clarify the law of property in two areas: obligations or covenants for title which are implied by statute on certain dispositions of property; and certain technical and legal problems in dealing with property following the owner's death

Drug Trafficking Act 1994, c. 37, 3 February 1995
Consolidates the 1986 Act and certain provisions of the Criminal Justice (International Co-operation) Act 1990 relating to drug trafficking

European Union (Accession) Act 1994, c. 38, 3 November 1994
Amends the European Communities Act 1972 by extending the definitions of 'the Treaties' and 'the Community Treaties' to include the treaty dealing with the accession of Norway, Austria, Finland and Sweden to the European Union; and to approve that treaty for certain purposes

Local Government etc. (Scotland) Act 1994, c. 39, various dates
Makes provision for the creation of a unitary structure of local government in Scotland comprising 32 councils, and for connected purposes, such as elections and transfers of property and staff to such councils; provides for the creation of three new authorities to be the water and sewerage authorities in Scotland and for the requisite powers and duties; provides for the creation of the Scottish Water and Sewerage Customers Council

Deregulation and Contracting Out Act 1994, c. 40, various dates
Provides an order-making power to amend or repeal legislation for the purpose of reducing or removing a burden and also for a number of deregulatory amendments to or repeals of legislation; amends and clarifies the law relating to goods and public service vehicles operator licensing; and for various connected purposes

Consolidated Fund (No. 2) Act 1994, c. 41, 16 December 1994
Applies funds from the Consolidated Fund to the service of the years ending 31 March 1995 and 1996

European Communities (Finance) Act 1995, c. 1, 16 January 1995
Amends the definition of 'the Treaties' and 'the Community Treaties' in the 1972 Act to include the Council's decision of 31 October 1994 on the Communities' system of own resources and to remove a spent provision

Consolidated Fund Act 1995, c. 2, 23 March 1995
Applies funds out of the Consolidated Fund to the service of the years ending 31 March 1994 and 1995

South Africa Act 1995, c. 3, 23 March 1995
Makes provision relating to the re-admission of South Africa as a member of the Commonwealth on 1 June 1994

Finance Act 1995, c. 4, 1 May 1995
Grants certain duties, alters others and amends the law relating to the National Debt and public finance, *inter alia* it provides for the reduced rate of VAT on domestic fuel, extends the tax relief for TESSAs, brings in many changes relating to self assessment of income tax

Building Societies (Joint Account Holders) Act 1995, c. 5, 1 May 1995
Secures the rights of second-named account holders in building society accounts

Civil Evidence (Family Mediation) (Scotland) Act 1995, c. 6, day to be appointed
Makes provision for the inadmissibility as evidence in civil proceedings in Scotland of information as to what occurred during family mediation

Requirements of Writing (Scotland) Act 1995, c. 7, 1 August 1995
Reforms Scottish law relating to the requirements for writing for certain matters and the formal validity of contractual and other documents; abolishes any rule of law restricting the proof of any matter to writ or oath and the procedure of reference to oath

Agricultural Tenancies Act 1995, c. 8, 1 September 1995
Sets out a new framework of law for new agricultural tenancies (to be known as farm business tenancies) in England and Wales other than those created under the statutory succession provisions of the Agricultural Holdings Act 1986

Commonwealth Development Corporation Act 1995, c. 9, 28 June 1995
Increases the limits under the 1978 Act; makes provision in relation to interest on advances to the Corporation and to the remuneration pensions and compensation of its members

Home Energy Conservation Act 1995, c. 10, various dates to be appointed

Makes provision for the drawing up of local energy conservation reports in relation to residential accommodation; and for connected purposes

Proceeds of Crimes Act 1995, c. 11, various dates

Makes further provision for and in relation to the recovery of the proceeds of criminal conduct; for facilitating enforcement of overseas forfeiture and restraint orders; and for connected purposes

Carers (Recognition and Services) Act 1995, c. 12, 1 April 1996

Provides for the assessment of the ability of carers to provide care; and for connected purposes

Road Traffic (New Drivers) Act 1995, c. 13, day or days to be appointed

Makes provision in relation to newly qualified drivers who commit certain offences, including provisions concerning tests of competence to drive

Land Registers (Scotland) Act 1995, c. 14, day to be appointed

Provides for the appropriate prepayment of statutory fees as a condition for acceptance of writs for recording in the Register of Sasines and of applications for registration in the Land Register of Scotland

Activity Centres (Young Person's Safety) Act 1995, c. 15, 28 August 1995

Makes provision for the regulation of centres and providers of facilities where children and young persons under the age of 18 engage in adventure activities, including provision for the imposition of requirements relating to safety

Prisoners (Return to Custody) Act 1995, c. 16, day or days to be appointed

Makes provision by the creation of an offence and the conferring of powers of entry for the punishment and return to lawful custody of persons unlawfully at large

Health Authorities Act 1995, c. 17, various dates

Abolishes Regional Health Authorities, District Health Authorities and Family Health Service Authorities; requires the establishment of Health Authorities and makes provision in relation to Health Authorities and Special Health Authorities; and for connected purposes

Jobseekers Act 1995, c. 18, day or days to be appointed

Provides for jobseekers' allowances and makes other provision to promote employment of the unemployed and for the assistance of persons without a settled way of life

Appropriation Act 1995, c. 19, 19 July 1995

Applies a sum out of the Consolidated Fund to the service of the year ending 31 March 1996; appropriates the supplies granted in this session of Parliament; and repeals certain Consolidated Fund and Appropriation Acts

Criminal Justice (Scotland) Act 1995, c. 20, day or days to be appointed

Amends the criminal justice system of Scotland in respect to criminal proceedings, investigation of offences, sentences and other disposals applicable in respect of certain offences, legal aid for certain appeals, and the treatment of offenders; amends the law of Scotland in relation to confiscation of the proceeds of, and the forfeiture of property used in, crime; and as regards jury lists for both civil and criminal trials; and for connected purposes

Merchant Shipping Act 1995, c. 21, 1 January 1996

Consolidates the 1894–1994 Acts and other enactments relating to shipping

Shipping and Trading Interests (Protection) Act 1995, c. 22, 1 January 1996

Consolidates certain enactments for the protection of shipping and trading interests

Goods Vehicles (Licensing of Operators) Act 1995, c. 23, various dates

Consolidates Part V of the Transport Act 1968 and related provisions concerning the licensing of operators of certain goods vehicles

Crown Agents Act 1995, c. 24, 19 July 1995

Provides for the vesting of property rights and liabilities of the Crown Agents in a company nominated by the Foreign Secretary and for the subsequent dissolution of the Crown Agents; and for connected purposes

Environment Act 1995, c. 25, various dates

Provides for the establishment of the Environment Agency and the Scottish Environment Protection Agency; and for related and connected purposes

Pensions Act 1995, c. 26, various dates

Amends the law about pensions and for connected purposes

Geneva Conventions (Amendments) Act 1995, c. 27, day to be appointed

Makes provision for the amendment of the 1957 Act to enable effect to be given to the protocols additional to the 1949 Conventions done at Geneva on 10 June 1977; and for connected purposes

Sale of Goods (Amendment) Act 1995, c. 28, 19 September 1995

Amends the law relating to the sale of unascertained goods forming part of an identified bulk and the sale of undivided shares in goods

Insurance Companies (Reserves) Act 1995, c. 29, various dates
Provides for the maintenance by insurance companies of reserves in respect of certain classes of business; and for connected purposes

Landlord and Tenant (Covenants) Act 1995, c. 30, day to be appointed
Makes provision for persons bound by covenants of a tenancy to be released from such covenants on the assignment of the tenancy and makes other provisions with respect to the rights and liabilities arising under such covenants; restricts in certain circumstances the operation of rights of re-entry, forfeiture and disclaimer; and for connected purposes

National Health Service (Amendment) Act 1995, c. 31, day or days to be appointed
Makes provision in relation to persons disqualified or subject to proceedings for disqualification under the 1977 Act and for the tribunal set up under that section; corresponding provision for Scotland; and for connected purposes

Olympic Symbol etc. (Protection) Act 1995, c. 32, day to be appointed
Makes provision about the use for commercial purposes of the Olympic symbol and certain words associated with the Olympic Games

Licensing (Sunday Hours) Act 1995, c. 33, day to be appointed
Amends provisions of the Licensing Act 1964 concerning permitted hours in licensed premises and clubs on Sundays and Good Fridays; and for connected purposes

Child Support Act 1995, c. 34, day or days to be appointed
Makes provision with respect to child support maintenance and other maintenance; and to provide for a child maintenance bonus as part of income support or jobseeker's allowance

Criminal Appeal Act 1995, c. 35, various dates
Amends provisions relating to appeals and references to the Court of Appeal in criminal cases; establishes a Criminal Cases Review Commission and confers functions on and makes other provision concerning the Commission; amends section 142 of the Magistrates' Courts Act 1980; and for connected purposes

Children (Scotland) Act 1995, c. 36, day or days to be appointed
Reforms the law of Scotland concerning children and young persons who as children have been in local authority care; makes provision for the relationship between parent and child and guardian and child in Scotland; and for residential establishments for children; and for connected purposes

WHITE PAPERS, ETC.

The white paper *Jobseeker's Allowance* was presented to Parliament by the Social Security Secretary (Peter Lilley) and the Employment Secretary (Michael Portillo) on 24 October 1994. It included the following proposals, for implementation in April 1996:
  – a means-tested jobseeker's allowance to replace unemployment benefit and income support; those who have paid National Insurance contributions only to be means tested after six months
  – a compulsory jobseeker's agreement to be introduced, under which the Employment Service will agree with each claimant an individual programme to find them a job; claimants in breach of the agreement to incur a temporary loss of benefit
  – claimants to be required to be available for at least 40 hours' work a week, unless they are ill or disabled or having caring responsibility
  – job centre staff to be given powers to order claimants to improve their skills or do community work
  – the Employment on Trial scheme to be available to claimants after three rather than six months

  – a 'back to work bonus' of up to £1,000 to be introduced for claimants with part-time jobs moving off benefit into full-time employment
  – a National Insurance credit to be given for any work undertaken by claimants

The white paper *Improving Child Support* was presented to Parliament by the Social Security Secretary (Peter Lilley) on 23 January 1995. Its main proposals were:
  – assessment of cases not involving benefit claimants to be postponed indefinitely
  – a limited right of appeal to be introduced
  – 'clean-break' divorce settlements, travel costs and all housing costs to be taken into account in assessments
  – no absent parent to have to pay more than 30 per cent of their net income in child maintenance
  – maximum extra payment by better-off absent parents to be reduced to £250 a week
  – a maintenance 'credit' of up to £5 a week to be paid to parents with custody who return to working more than 16 hours a week

A command paper, *The Civil Service: Taking Forward Continuity and Change*, was published on 26 January 1995. The main proposals announced by the

Chancellor of the Duchy of Lancaster (David Hunt) were:
- a code of practice to be introduced detailing the duties and responsibilities of civil servants and defining their relationship with the Government
- the role of the Civil Service Commission to be enhanced and to include responsibility for hearing appeals relating to alleged breaches of the code
- the First Civil Service Commissioner to be responsible for monitoring senior internal appointments and to be appointed from outside the Civil Service

The white paper *Looking to the Future: Mediation and the Ground for Divorce* was presented to Parliament by the Lord Chancellor (Lord Mackay of Clashfern) on 27 April 1995. Its main proposals were:
- irretrievable breakdown of a marriage to be the sole ground for divorce
- the partner initiating the proceedings to attend a compulsory information session about the nature of divorce and the options available; the other partner may attend voluntarily but would only be compelled to do so if he/she wishes to make an application relating to children, property or money
- divorce to be granted after one year, during which couples would have the chance to take part in mediation sessions to discuss arrangements concerning children, property and money; these arrangements normally to be finalized by the time of the divorce

The white paper *The Prospects for Nuclear Power in the UK* was presented to Parliament by the President of the Board of Trade (Michael Heseltine) on 9 May 1995. Its main proposals were:
- seven advanced gas-cooled reactors and the pressurized water reactor at Sizewell to be privatized in 1996 as wholly-owned subsidiaries of a single holding company based in Scotland
- Magnox stations to remain in the public sector and to be decommissioned by BNFL over the next 15 years
- the fossil fuel levy on electricity bills (for nuclear decommissioning) to be largely abolished; a reduced levy to be retained to support windmill farms and waste-burning plants; the premium price paid to Scottish Nuclear (which does not receive levy funds) to be cut at the same time
- the new company to set aside separate funds to cover the cost of decommissioning its plants

The white paper *Tackling Drugs Together, A Strategy for England 1995–8* was presented to Parliament by the Home Secretary (Michael Howard) on 10 May 1995. Its main proposals were:
- drugs-related crime to be targeted as a major police objective
- the police, probation and prison services to devise anti-drugs strategies by March 1996
- £8.8 million to be provided over the next three years for a network of drug action teams in

England to develop co-ordinated local strategies to combat drug abuse
- £5.9 million to be provided in 1995–6 for drug education programmes in schools
- the Home Office drugs prevention initiative to be expanded
- drugs-testing to be mandatory in prisons from autumn 1996
- a 24-hour national help-line to be operated for 18 months
- a needle exchange scheme to be set up for drug users
- health and safety measures to be provided by club owners and rave organizers

The Nolan Committee on Standards in Public Life published its first report on 11 May 1995. It concluded that although there was no evidence of systematic corruption in British public life, urgent remedial action was needed to clarify the boundaries of acceptable conduct. The main recommendations were:
- an independent Parliamentary Commissioner for Standards to be appointed to oversee new, clearer rules on MPs' interests, including a ban on working for firms engaged in lobbying
- MPs to be obliged to disclose full details of consultancy contracts and the payments and benefits in kind received under them
- a code of conduct to be drawn up for MPs and a clearer code of conduct to be drawn up for ministers
- ex-ministers to be obliged to seek advice about jobs they propose to take within two years of leaving office, with an automatic waiting period of three months for ex-Cabinet ministers
- special advisers to be subject to the same restrictions on moving to private-sector jobs as civil servants
- confidential routes to be provided for civil servants to report impropriety, corruption or waste
- a Public Appointments Commissioner to be appointed to ensure propriety in appointments to quangos
- public bodies to draw up codes of conduct incorporating the principles of selflessness, integrity, objectivity, accountability, openness, honesty and leadership
- more independent scrutiny of public bodies and better guidance and training

The House of Commons select committee on standards in public life, set up to implement the changes recommended by the Nolan inquiry, in July 1995 recommended the following:
- training in ethics for all new MPs
- an ethics ombudsman, to investigate allegations of breaches of the rules on conduct
- a standards committee, to hold public hearings into alleged breaches of the rules
- MPs facing allegations to be allowed legal advice

– MPs to declare financial interests when tabling Commons questions

The committee felt further consideration was needed of the proposals that MPs should declare their earnings from consultancy and that MPs should be barred from working for lobbying companies before recommendations could be made.

The white paper *Forging Ahead* was presented to Parliament by the President of the Board of Trade (Michael Heseltine) on 22 May 1995. It reviewed progress made on the recommendations of the 1994 white paper on competitiveness (*see* Whitaker's Almanack 1995) and made 70 further proposals, including the following:

– £100 million extra to be provided for Business Links
– £70 million to be provided for technology transfer and scientific innovations
– £40 million to be provided to encourage new exporters
– more challenging national training and education targets to be agreed and consultation to be carried out on learning credits
– further deregulation to be encouraged

A green paper, *Media Ownership: the Government's Proposals* was published by the Secretary of State for National Heritage (Stephen Dorrell) on 23 May 1995. It proposed the following long-term measures, on which comments were invited by 31 August 1995:

– no company to be allowed to own more than 10 per cent of the total market
– no company to be allowed to own more than 20 per cent of the market in any region
– no company to be allowed to own more than 20 per cent of each sectoral market (i.e. television, newspapers or radio)
– an independent media regulator to examine whether existing concentrations above these levels are in the public interest

In advance of the above measures the document proposed several minor measures to be introduced immediately through secondary legislation, and the following main measures to be introduced through primary legislation by January 1997:

– newspaper groups with less than 20 per cent of the national market to be allowed to own ITV companies outright, except where a group's regional titles account for more than 30 per cent of the regional newspaper circulation in the relevant ITV region
– ITV companies with less than 15 per cent of the total television audience to be allowed to buy national newspapers
– the restrictions on ownership between terrestrial, satellite and cable television services to be abolished, subject to a 15 per cent limit of the total television audience and, except for satellite and cable companies, where a national newspaper above the 20 per cent national circulation

threshold already has more than a 20 per cent stake

– no group to be allowed to own more than two ITV companies or more than 15 per cent of the sector
– no group to be allowed to own more than one national radio licence
– the upper limit on ownership of local radio licences to be removed, subject to a limit of 15 per cent of the sector
– the Independent Television Commission and the Radio Authority to have the power to restrict any transactions deemed not to be in the public interest

The Secretary of State for National Heritage (Stephen Dorrell) announced a package of measures relating to the British film industry on 6 June 1995. The main measures were:

– more than £80 million of National Lottery money from the Arts Council of England to support film production and distribution over the next five years
– start-up funding for a new London Film Commission
– a grant of £180,000 for Cinema 100, an organization set up by the film industry to celebrate cinema's centenary
– a new advisory committee to examine the financing of independent film production and film-makers' access to capital
– discussions on further support for training in the film industry
– a study into the feasibility of establishing a West End showcase dedicated to screening British films

An interim report covering the first stage of a two-year review of the civil justice system by Lord Woolf was published on 16 June 1995. The main proposals were:

– the small claims court to be expanded to deal with claims up to £3,000
– a fast-track system for claims between £3,000 and £10,000, with capped costs and a fixed timetable; cases to be brought to trial in 20–30 weeks and trial hearings to be limited to three hours
– a multi-track system for claims over £10,000, with a team of judges controlling progress
– a new post of Head of Civil Justice to be created, with responsibility for all civil courts; the post to be filled by a senior judge
– judges to be responsible for managing cases, setting timetables and controlling costs
– encouragement and incentives to be provided to settle cases early or to pursue other ways of resolving disputes
– solicitors to be obliged to explain to clients how their charges are calculated and to estimate the overall costs of a case; notice to be given if this estimate is about to be exceeded
– simplified procedural rules and a single method for starting all claims

– improved access to information, especially for those conducting their own litigation, and greater use of information technology

The white paper *Our Future Homes – Opportunities, Choice, Responsibility* was presented to Parliament by the Secretary of State for the Environment (John Gummer) on 27 June 1995. Its main proposals were:
– all new housing association tenants to have the right to buy their home
– existing housing associations to have the option of giving their tenants the right to buy
– 180,000 new homes for the public sector over the next three years
– improved access to hostels for homeless people
– one-year probationary tenancies for new council tenants; anti-social behaviour to be penalized
– the homeless, including single mothers, no longer to receive automatic priority in the allocation of council accommodation
– the private sector to be encouraged to buy, refurbish and run council estates, subject to a vote of tenants
– government properties to be auctioned within six months of being vacated
– tax incentives to encourage investment in the creation of housing trusts
– simplified letting arrangements for small landlords to enable easier eviction of tenants who do not pay their rent
– an improved housing advice service

A policy statement, *Sport – Raising the Game* was published by the Department of National Heritage on 14 July 1995. The main proposals were:
– a British Academy of Sport, to be funded by National Lottery funds
– greater emphasis on traditional team games and competitive sport in schools, with a target of four hours of extra-curricular sport provision
– an extra £1 million to be provided by the Sports Council for coaching teachers
– a £2 million fund to be provided by the Sports Council for promoting links between schools and clubs
– schools to be encouraged to attract sponsors
– action to prevent the further loss of playing fields
– a working group to advise on increasing sports scholarships in higher education
– a better system of financial support for top sports men and women

The white paper *Privacy and Media Intrusion* was presented to Parliament by the Secretary of State for National Heritage (Virginia Bottomley) on 17 July 1995. It stated that the Government had decided not to introduce legislation to curb invasions of privacy by the media but that press self-regulation would be tightened. The main proposals were:
– a tighter code of practice for the newspaper industry, with representatives from the general public involved in its drafting

– a rapid and direct line of communication between the Press Complaints Commission and newspaper editors to pre-empt abuses of the code
– better public information about the PCC
– a compensation fund for people who have suffered an invasion of privacy

The white paper *Better Accounting for the Taxpayer's Money* was presented to Parliament by the Chancellor of the Exchequer (Kenneth Clarke) on 26 July 1995. Its main proposals were:
– resource accounting systems to replace the present system of cash planning in central government departments by April 1998
– resource budgeting to be introduced in 2000, when commercial-style accounts will become the basis for planning and controlling public expenditure

The white paper *Digital Terrestrial Broadcasting: the Government's Proposals* was published by the Secretary of State for National Heritage (Virginia Bottomley) on 10 August 1995. The main proposals were:
– six separate frequency channels ('multiplexes') to be made available for digital terrestrial television, each able to carry at least three television channels
– the existing television broadcasters to be offered guaranteed access to digital frequencies
– at least 80 per cent of the programmes broadcast on existing analogue channels to be broadcast also on the equivalent digital services
– seven multiplexes to be made available for digital radio broadcasting, each able to carry at least six stereo programme services
– one radio multiplex has already been allocated to the BBC; one to be allocated for independent national radio; four to be reserved for local radio services; the use of the final channel to remain under consideration
– multiplex operators to be required to make payments to the Exchequer once their operation becomes profitable (with a possible waiver for the first licence period)
– the first multiplex licences to be issued for a period of 12 years
– no single company to be allowed to control more than two multiplexes (further views were sought on this proposal)

The Queen's Awards

The Queen's Award for Export Achievement and The Queen's Award for Technological Achievement were instituted by royal warrant in 1976. The two separate awards took the place of The Queen's Award to Industry, which had been instituted in 1965. In 1992 the scheme was extended with the launch of a third award, The Queen's Award for Environmental Achievement.

The export and technological awards are designed to recognize and encourage outstanding achievements in exporting goods or services from the United Kingdom and in advancing process or product technology. The purpose of the environmental award is to recognize and encourage product and process development which has major benefits for the environment and which is commercially successful.

The awards differ from a personal royal honour in that they are given to a unit as a whole, management and employees working as a team. They may be applied for by any organization within the United Kingdom, the Channel Islands or the Isle of Man producing goods or services which meet the criteria for the awards. Eligibility is not influenced in any way by the particular activities of the unit applying, its location, or size. Units or agencies of central and local government with industrial functions, as well as research associations, educational institutions and bodies of a similar character, are also eligible, provided that they can show they have contributed to industrial efficiency.

Each award is formally conferred by a grant of appointment and is symbolized by a representation of its emblem cast in stainless steel and encapsulated in a transparent acrylic block.

Awards are held for five years and holders are entitled to fly the appropriate award flag and to display the emblem on the packaging of goods produced in this country, on the goods themselves, on the unit's stationery, in advertising and on certain articles used by employees. Units may also display the emblem of any previous current awards during the five years.

Awards are announced on 21 April (the birthday of The Queen) and published formally in a special supplement to the London Gazette.

Awards Office

All enquiries about the scheme and requests for application forms (completed forms must be returned by 31 October) should be made to: The Secretary, The Queen's Awards Office, Bridge Place, 88–89 Eccleston Square, London SW1V 1PT. Tel: 0171–222 2277.

EXPORT ACHIEVEMENT

The criterion upon which recommendations for an award for export achievement are based is a substantial and sustained increase in export earnings to a level which is outstanding for the products or services concerned and for the size of the applicant unit's operations. Account will be taken of any special market factors described in the application. Applicants for the award will be expected to explain the basis of the achievement (e.g. improved marketing organization or new initiative to cater for export markets) and this will be taken into consideration. Export earnings considered will include receipts by the applicant unit in this country from the export of goods produced in this country, and the provision of services to non-residents. Account will be taken of the overseas expenses incurred other than marketing expenses. Income from profits (after overseas tax) remitted to this country from the applicant unit's direct investments in its overseas branches, subsidiaries or associates in the same general line of business will be taken into account, but not receipts from profits on other overseas investments or by interest on overseas loans or credits.

In 1995, The Queen's Award for Export Achievement was conferred on the following concerns:

Rotherham and Bradford Branch of AES Engineering Ltd, Rotherham, S. Yorks
APV Baker Ltd (FES Division), Confectionery, Cereal & Snack Division, Peterborough, Cambs
AT&T Global Information Solutions (Scotland) Ltd, Dundee
Allen and Heath Ltd, Penryn, Cornwall
Ano-Coil Ltd, Milton Keynes, Bucks
Apollo Fire Detectors Ltd, Havant, Hants
Armabord Ltd, Burnley, Lancs
Ove Arup Partnership, London, W1
Aviall Ltd, t/a Aviall Caledonian Engine Services, Prestwick, Ayrshire
Baillie Gifford Overseas Ltd, Edinburgh
Balfour Beatty Construction International Ltd, Thornton Heath, Surrey
J. Barbour & Sons Ltd, South Shields, Tyne and Wear
Biological Crop Protection Ltd, Ashford, Kent
Microscopy Division of Bio-Rad Microscience Ltd, Hemel Hempstead, Herts
Boss Industrial Mouldings Ltd, Mildenhall, Suffolk
British Aerospace Defence Ltd, Military Aircraft Division, Preston, Lancs
Brompton Bicycle Ltd, London W4
Caledonian Paper PLC, Irvine, Ayrshire
Carron Bathrooms Ltd, Falkirk
Carron Phoenix Ltd, Falkirk
Cash Bases GB Ltd, Newhaven, E. Sussex
Caterpillar (UK) Ltd, Desford, Leics
Chase Research PLC, Basingstoke, Hants
Chilprufe Ltd, Leicester
The Chivas and Glenlivet Group, Paisley
Jane Churchill Ltd, London W1
Toby Churchill Ltd, Cambridge
Ciba Grimsby, Grimsby, S. Humberside

Cincinnati Milacron UK Ltd, Machine Tool Division, Birmingham
Claremont Fabrics, Glossop, Derbys
COBE Laboratories Manufacturing, a division of COBE Laboratories Ltd, Quedgeley, Glos
Cookson Entek Ltd, Newcastle upon Tyne
Copeland & Jenkins Ltd, Wellingborough, Northants
Cray Systems Space Division, Bristol, Avon
Crosrol Ltd, Halifax, W. Yorkshire
Crowson Fabrics Ltd, Uckfield, E. Sussex
Cummins Engine Company Ltd – Daventry, Daventry, Northants
Densitron Microwave Ltd, Southend, Essex
Dents Manufacturing, Warminster, Wilts
Derwent Information Ltd, London WC2
Desurvey PLC, Birkenhead, Merseyside
Devro Ltd, Glasgow
Diamond Power Specialty Ltd, Dumbarton
Donvand Ltd, t/a Gulliver's Travel Agency, London EC1
A. C. Egerton Ltd, Orpington, Kent
Electrolux (Floor Care Division), a division of Emaco Ltd, Luton, Beds
EMI Music Publishing – UK, London WC2
Ethicon Ltd, Edinburgh
Euro Iseki Ltd, Stratford-upon-Avon, Warks
EuroTalk Ltd, London SW6
Farr Vintners Ltd, London SW1
W. Fein and Sons Ltd, Bradford, W. Yorkshire
Filofax Group PLC, London W1
Financial Engineering Ltd, London W1
Financial Times Group Ltd, London SE1
Fireater Ltd, Great Yarmouth, Norfolk
Sir Norman Foster and Partners Ltd, London SW11
Foster Wheeler Energy Ltd, Reading, Berks
Franklin Hodge Industries Ltd, Hereford
International Division of Freemans PLC, London SW99
Peter Geeson Ltd, Long Eaton, Notts
Glaxo PLC, London W1
Bakery Division of Golden West Foods Ltd, Hemel Hempstead, Herts
Gossard, Leighton Buzzard, Beds
John Guest Ltd, West Drayton, Middx
E. C. Harris International Ltd, London WC1
Haven Country Classics, Horncastle, Lincs
J. M. Heaford Ltd, Altrincham, Cheshire
James H. Heal and Company Ltd, Halifax, W. Yorkshire
Heraeus Noblelight Ltd, Cambridge
Hewlett-Packard Ltd, Bracknell, Berks
Horton Kirby Paper Mills Ltd, Dartford, Kent
Domnick Hunter Ltd, Birtley, Co. Durham
ICI 'Saffil' Business, Widnes, Cheshire
IOP Publishing Ltd, Bristol, Avon
The Information & Technology Publishing Company Ltd, Hitchin, Herts
International Combustion Ltd, Derby
Interopa Holidays Ltd, London W2
K Shoes, Kendal, Cumbria
King's College London, University of London, London SE1
Kodak Ltd, Hemel Hempstead, Herts
Lambie-Nairn & Company Ltd, London W1
Lightning Export Ltd, Enfield, Middx
Lloyd Loom Furniture Ltd, Spalding, Lincs
Lloyd's Register of Shipping, London EC3
Longwall AFC Ltd, Worcester
Loughborough Sound Images PLC, Loughborough, Leics
Lyson Ltd, Stockport, Cheshire
Mackie International Ltd, Belfast
Cameron Mackintosh Ltd, London WC1
Marks and Spencer PLC, London W1

Masons Overseas Ltd, London W3
Masterfil Ltd, Aylesbury, Bucks
Meltog Ltd, Birstall, W. Yorkshire
The Mezzanine Floor Company Ltd, Tonbridge, Kent
Midland Cosmetic Sales PLC, Birmingham, W. Midlands
Samuel Montagu & Co Ltd, Export & Project Finance Department, London EC3
Motorola Ltd, European Cellular Infrastructure Division (ECID), Swindon, Wilts
Motorola Ltd, European Cellular Subscriber Division, Bathgate, West Lothian
Munradtech Industrial Generators Ltd, Loughborough, Leics
New Holland Ford Ltd, Basildon, Essex
The North of England Protecting and Indemnity Association Ltd, Newcastle upon Tyne
Optical Fibres, Deeside, Clwyd
Pan Liner Agencies Ltd, Solihull, W. Midlands
Parallax Software Ltd, London W1
Pilkington Architectural Division, Pilkington Glass Products Ltd, St Helens, Merseyside
Pitney Bowes Ltd, Harlow, Essex
Polaroid (UK) Ltd, Dumbarton
Precision Disc Castings Ltd, Poole, Dorset
Psion PLC, London NW8
RBR Armour Ltd, London SE1
RSR Ltd, Cardiff, S. Glamorgan
Rotary (International) Ltd, Mallusk, Co. Antrim
Sandon Flexographic Printing Rollers Ltd, Runcorn, Cheshire
R. P. Scherer Ltd, Swindon, Wilts
SEOS Displays Ltd, Burgess Hill, W. Sussex
Severn-Lamb Ltd, Alcester, Warks
Shield Diagnostics Ltd, Dundee
Slingsby Aviation Ltd, Kirkbymoorside, N. Yorkshire
Paul Smith Ltd, Nottingham
Smith & Nephew Medical Ltd, Hull, N. Humberside
Sony Manufacturing Company UK, Pencoed, M. Glam
Specialist Refractory Services Ltd, Riddings, Derbys
Spectrum Technologies Ltd, Bridgend, M. Glam
Strix Ltd, Ronaldsway, Isle of Man
Synpac Chemicals Ltd, Bedlington, Northumberland
Tadmod Ltd, Maldon, Essex
Trademade International Ltd, Bromley, Kent
TRAK Microwave Ltd, Dundee
Trimat Ltd, Brierley Hill, W. Midlands
Trinity College London, London W1
Edwin Trisk Systems Ltd, Sunderland
UES Bright Bar Ltd, Tipton, W. Midlands
Ultra Hydraulics Ltd, Mobile Products Division, Cheltenham, Glos
Vita Fibres Ltd, Alpha Flock Division, Nr. Port Talbot, W. Glam
Walker Filtration Ltd, Washington, Tyne and Wear
Westwind Air Bearings Ltd, Poole, Dorset
The Wrigley Company Ltd, Plymouth, Devon
Yuasa Battery (UK) Ltd, Ebbw Vale, Gwent
Zeneca Pharmaceuticals, Macclesfield, Cheshire

TECHNOLOGICAL ACHIEVEMENT

The criterion upon which recommendations for an award for technological achievement are based is a significant advance, leading to increased efficiency, in the application of technology to a production or development process in British industry or the production for sale of goods which incorporate new and advanced technological qualities. An award is only granted for production or development processes which have achieved commercial success.

In 1995 The Queen's Award for Technological Achievement was conferred on the following concerns:

ABT Industries Ltd, Peterborough, Cambs – *ABT live service insertion and sealing systems*

Applied Vision Ltd, Whitwick, Leics – *plasma-sputtered ophthalmic coatings*

Blackhawk Automotive Ltd, Ashford, Kent – *'Shark' computerized measuring system*

Borden (UK) Ltd, European Resins Group, Southampton, Hants – *foundry sand binders*

James Dewhurst Ltd, Dewtex Division, Accrington, Lancs – *Dewtex: a technique for manufacturing non-woven 'laid' reinforcement scrim products*

Marconi Instruments Ltd, St Albans, Herts – *RF frequency synthesis using fractional-N techniques*

McKechnie Vehicle Components Extrusion Operation, Milton Keynes, Bucks – *revolutionary method of assembling and forming thermoplastic*

MediSense Inc., Abingdon, Oxon – *technological innovation in blood glucose monitoring*

Messier-Dowty Ltd, Gloucester – *large landing-gear structures*

Novamedix Ltd, Andover, Hants – *A-V Impulse System: technological innovation in blood circulation enhancement*

Quantel Ltd, Newbury, Berks – *the 'Henry' concurrent editing system*

Racal Instruments Ltd, Slough, Berks – *test systems for GSM and DCS 1800 base transceiver stations*

Renishaw Transducer Systems Division of Renishaw PLC, Wotton-under-Edge, Glos – *QC10: Renishaw Ballbar*

STC Submarine Systems Ltd, London SE10 – *submarine telecommunications systems employing erbium-doped fibre amplifiers*

Snell & Wilcox Ltd, Petersfield, Hants – *electronic film transfer equipment*

Stanhay Webb Ltd, Newmarket, Suffolk – *multi-line pneumatic seed planter*

Underwater Excavation Ltd, Portlethen, Aberdeenshire – *jet prop underwater excavation systems*

ENVIRONMENTAL ACHIEVEMENT

The criterion upon which recommendations for an award for environmental achievement are based is a significant advance in the application by British industry of the development of products, technology or processes which offer major benefits in environmental terms compared to existing products, technology or processes. An award is only granted for products, technology or processes which have achieved commercial success.

In 1995 The Queen's Award for Environmental Achievement was conferred on the following concerns:

BP Exploration Operating Company Ltd, Poole, Dorset – *onshore development of Wytch Farm oilfield*

Devon Valley Industries, Exeter, Devon – *coloured papers for decorative laminates*

ICI Autocolor, Slough, Berks – *aquabase waterborne basecoat for car repair*

United Distillers Operations, Edinburgh – *light-weight spirit bottles*

United Glass Ltd, St Albans, Herts – *light-weight spirit bottles*

Vortoil Separation Systems Ltd, Gloucester – *liquid/liquid hydrocyclone*

Science and Discovery

SUNSPOTS AND GLOBAL WARMING

One school of thought claims that sunspot activity has a pronounced effect on our weather but others believe that the correlation used in support of this theory is purely coincidental. Recent work has, however, produced strong evidence for a link and American astronomers now claim that the correlation is genuine.

Sallie Baliunas and Willie Soon of the Harvard-Smithsonian Center for Astrophysics have examined data from 18 stars whose colour and age are similar to that of the Sun. Since 1966 these stars have been monitored using the amount of light emitted by singly ionized calcium, a set of frequencies strongly recorded from sunspots. The results show that most of the stars have starspot cycles ranging from seven to 21 years, and that the stars with shorter cycles have stronger calcium emission. It appears that the increased starspots correlate with increased stellar brightness, with shorter cycles coming from stars which are brighter than the average. On our Sun, the average length of a cycle is about 11 years, but over the last 250 years the value has varied irregularly between nine and 14 years.

In 1991 it was claimed that the shorter sunspot cycles were associated with a warming of the Earth; by implication, fewer sunspots should have a cooling effect. This idea is strengthened by the fact that there was an exceptionally cool period called the Maunder Minimum from 1645 to 1715, when the Sun had very few spots. Over the last few centuries the shorter than average cycles have given rise to warmer than average weather. During the Maunder Minimum, it is implied that a cycle of about 23 years existed and that the brightness of the Sun was 0.4 per cent less than it is today. This would explain the very cold spell, often referred to as the 'Little Ice Age'.

OCEAN CURRENTS AND THE WEATHER

Much research has been conducted on the effect of the disruption of surface currents in the Pacific Ocean, known as El Nino, which causes drought and floods in areas bordering the Pacific Ocean. Now it has been discovered that there exist smaller but similar disruptions in the Indian and Atlantic Oceans.

These new discoveries were announced at an international climate conference held in Melbourne in April 1995 to mark the end of the World Meteorological Organization's 10-year Tropical Ocean Global Atmosphere (TOGA) experiment. The pattern of rainfall recorded in regions bordering the Indian and Atlantic Oceans was linked to changes in the temperature of the sea surface in those oceans. TOGA and another international study, the World Ocean Circulation Experiment, co-operated in the sea temperature measurements, using data collected from satellites, moored and drifting buoys, and merchant ships.

The results have shown similar effects to El Nino but on a more limited scale. The study of the Indian Ocean has confirmed the phenomenon, first suspected in the early 1980s when a link was found between the surface temperature of the ocean and rainfall across the Australian deserts. The original network was set up to provide a detailed study of the behaviour of El Nino. Under normal conditions trade winds push water from east to west across the Pacific towards the warm regions surrounding Indonesia. When an El Nino occurs, the surface temperature of this warm pool drops, causing a weakening of the trade winds. This allows the warmer water to flow eastwards, dragging with it tropical storms. These changes produce floods in Peru and drought in eastern Australia. In the Indian Ocean, cold water pushes northwards the prevailing west to east winds. The cold winds carried by this airstream interact with the warm tropical air, forming cloud banks over north-west Australia. These travel across the continent in a south-easterly direction, bringing rain to a normally dry area. A similar effect has been recorded in the southern Atlantic, affecting rainfall in Brazil.

UNDERSTANDING TYPHOONS

Trying to forecast accurately the route of a typhoon has long baffled meteorologists. Modern weather forecasting depends heavily on complicated computer models which are based on data collected from many stations around the world. Data such as temperature, atmospheric pressure and wind direction are fed into the computer and the model then predicts how a particular weather pattern will develop. Much of the necessary data comes from ships but these, understandably, alter course to avoid typhoons and the storms which accompany them, depriving meteorologists of data for computer models and so making the behaviour of typhoons difficult to predict.

To overcome this lack of information, meteorologists have tried to generate models covering the area surrounding the storms by using a series of bogus observations of wind and pressure around an idealized typhoon. These attempts were not very successful until a chance meeting of two scientists in China brought about a sudden improvement. Two years ago Julian Hunt, chief executive of the Met Office, gave a talk on typhoon forecasting in Beijing. After the talk, Johnnie Chan, a meteorologist at Hong Kong Polytechnic, told Hunt that he could improve the accuracy of the forecasts by altering the bogus observations around the centre of the typhoon from a circular, symmetrical pattern of the winds to an asymmetric one.

These ideas have been developed and now the average error in forecasting of where the centre of the storm will be in 24 hours time has been reduced to about 100 km from the previous accuracy of about 200 km. Over longer periods of time the improvement in accuracy is even greater. In October 1994, Typhoon Wilda headed towards the Philippines for a couple of days, then moved back on itself and veered northwards towards Japan. It then turned east and headed out to sea. On this occasion the Met Office was able to forecast Wilda's twists and turns with surprising accuracy.

BIRTH OF AN OCEAN

Oceans form when continental plates become stretched and thinned, forming a rift valley. The rift may form on the sea-bed but if it forms on land, it will subsequently be drowned as the plate thins and subsides. The drowned valley then thins to a point where the molten rock underneath can break through, forming an ocean floor. The two sides of the original continental rock are gradually forced apart, producing an ever-widening ocean. This is how the Atlantic Ocean was born some 200 million years ago.

The rifts that start these processes have always been assumed to occur in a slow, progressive fashion but the discovery of a spreading rift on the sea-bed near Papua New Guinea, the Woodlark basin, is making geologists think again about the whole process. Brian Taylor and colleagues at the University of Hawaii have found that a rift does not progress steadily along a line of weakness but jumps from one site to another. This mode of formation necessitates a rethink about the strength of the Earth's crust and the forces that break it apart.

The new discovery has been made possible by the fact that, unlike cases such as the Gulf of California where the actual rift is masked by overlying sediments, the Woodlark basin is not covered by sediment and the actual progression of continental rifting and the initiation of seafloor-spreading can be clearly seen. A section some 500 km long, situated about 750 km from where the split had already occurred, has suddenly broken open. It can be likened to a zip that bursts open in the middle whilst it is only partially unfastened. According to the scientists, it requires more force to rupture a continental plate than to tear it apart, so at the moment it is not obvious how the Earth can produce the force necessary to achieve this rupturing. Alternatively, it may be that geologists have overestimated the strength of the crust.

MID-ATLANTIC CHIMNEYS

Hydrothermal vents are undersea 'chimneys' which give off gases and toxic metals at a temperature of about 350°C. They are often referred to as black smokers. A recent expedition led by Chris German of the Institute of Oceanic Sciences Deacon Laboratory in Wormley, Surrey, has shown that hydrothermal vents along the Mid-Atlantic Ridge might be ten times more common than originally thought. The project involved towing an instrument known as BRIDGET along the sea floor for over 240 km. The chemical sensors continuously tested the water for sulphides and metals, resulting in the identification of seven new sites. Earlier investigations had tested the sea-bed every 24 km and consequently missed many of the vents. The new finds indicate that the vents are spaced roughly every 30 km along the ridge, at a latitude of 36° to 38°N. In this region the sea-bed is 3,000 metres below the surface. One of the new vents, said German, was the biggest of its kind in the Atlantic and one of the largest in the world. He announced his findings at the annual meeting of the British Mid-Atlantic Ridge Project (BRIDGE), saying that he estimated that there were ten times more smokers than previously thought.

Accurate data of the rate at which toxic metals escape from the smokers can be used to assess the amount being put into the oceans by human activity. Although the natural emission is less than 10 per cent, the problem needs to be reinvestigated. Hydrothermal vents are considered to be the source for the loss of heat from the Earth's interior and this new data fits well with current observations of how quickly the Earth is cooling. The new data also helps to explain how animals can spread between sites. At 3,000 metres the sea is sparsely inhabited but the vents are a haven for strange creatures such as blind shrimps, echinoderms and metal-digesting bacteria. If the vents were, as previously believed, several hundred kilometres apart, scientists were puzzled about the way animals migrated from one site to another. This puzzle vanishes if the sites are only 30 to 50 km apart.

THE KOBE EARTHQUAKE

The Kobe earthquake in January 1995 occurred along a fault system where no large tremors had been reported for over a thousand years. It happened along a strike-slip fault, where sections of the Earth's crust scrape passed each other horizontally. The epicentre lay between Kobe on the mainland and Awaji, an Island few kilometres to the south-west.

Data provided by Japan's Meteorological Agency has shown that this earthquake, which devastated the town of Kobe, was the strongest ever recorded in Japan. The maximum horizontal acceleration of the ground during the tremor was 8.17 metres per second per second, about 80 per cent of the acceleration due to gravity. This horizontal acceleration was more than twice that of the maximum vertical acceleration. Ground acceleration is a measure of the intensity of shaking and varies considerably from place to place. At Kobe, it has been estimated that the maximum acceleration was twice that recorded during the 1923 Kanto earthquake which killed 140,000 people and destroyed two-thirds of Tokyo. The intensity of the lateral shaking has surprised seismologists. Parts of some of the islands just off the coast near Kobe moved sideways by as much as 4 metres, compared with the normal movement of 10 to 20 centimetres. The Agency has upgraded the event for most of Kobe from six to seven, the maximum on the Japanese Shindo Scale, which grades intensity of shaking rather than the overall energy of the tremor measured on the better-known Richter scale.

It is suspected that the high lateral shaking was due to seismic waves bouncing off firmer rock below, as was the case during the Mexico City earthquake in 1985, the echo waves being strongest when strong horizontal waves occur. The echo waves travel more slowly and surface structures can suffer greater damage when they are hit by both waves. Japanese seismologists say that the Kobe tremor has provided the clearest example yet of this type of phenomenon. The initial seismic wave echoed off the solid mountains and increased the duration of the lateral shaking on the softer ground. The high intensity of the shock has raised questions for Japanese engineers. Most highways in Japan are built to resist accelerations of 3.5 metres per second per second, less than half that experienced at Kobe. A panel has been set up to see if standards should be tightened.

THE TUNGUSKA IMPACT

Ever since the first visits to the region to study the impact which occurred over the Tunguska region of Siberia in 1908, debate has taken place as to whether the impacting object was a meteoroid or a comet. During the last few decades, evidence has swung in favour of a cometary impact but this is now being questioned in the light of new discoveries.

Evidence in support of a meteoroid is mounting because of the discovery of solid particles in tree resin at the impact site; these particles have a composition typical of a stony meteorite. The object which caused the impact exploded and vapourized some 5 to 10 km above the forest. The area was pelted with countless particles, some of which stuck to the resin exuded by the conifers. These particles have remained trapped with the resin in the same way that insects have been found caught in amber.

A team of scientists, led by Guiseppe Longo and Menotti Galli of the University of Bologna, used a scanning electron microscope to examine thousands of particles trapped in the resin between 1885 and 1930, these dates being determined by the counting of three rings. They found an unusually large number of particles trapped in 1908. These particles contained iron, calcium, gold, copper, titanium and other elements associated with normal meteorites.

If the asteroidal origin is confirmed, it supports many earlier investigations indicating such an origin but there are still two main questions to be clarified. No evidence for impact craters have been found and no major meteorite fragments have been collected. Until these mysteries have been settled satisfactorily, the quest for a true explanation of the event will be pursued.

ANCIENT BACTERIA

There have been many claims in the past for microbial spores surviving for thousands and even millions of years but many of these claims have not been substantiated, mainly due to the lack of data. Some recent work pushes the time back some 40 million years and on this occasion the evidence is well-documented.

Raul Cano and Monica Borucki of California Polytechnic State University have carried out research on bees entombed in amber for up to 40 million years. They withdrew a tiny sample of the stomach of a bee entombed in amber from the Dominican Republic. They isolated bacterial spores and added them to a growth medium, where the bacteria started to reproduce. The bacterium was identified by its shape and by the sequence of its ribosomal DNA. It was found that the sequence was similar to that of *Bacillus sphaericus*, found in bees flying today. There were small differences which could be explained by mutations over the intervening years.

Like all research, it is not possible to realize the full implementations of the results obtained, but the purpose of recreating past microbial conditions is to find new chemicals that may be useful in the pharmaceutical industry. Raul Cano and Robin Steele set up a company called Ambergene in 1992 specifically for this purpose. Steele said that the primary metabolism of these ancient organisms is similar to modern metabolisms so it is possible to grow them. But the secondary metabolism, that which adapts to the environment, is very different and offers chemical conditions that are hard to generate synthetically. Ambergene scientists have already begun testing new chemicals from ancient organisms for antibacterial, antifungal and anti-tumour effects and they claim that they have made significant progress.

Earlier work in this field was queried by many scientists, who suspected contamination with modern DNA, but the tightly controlled conditions of this latest work should allay such fears.

FIRST STEPS ON LAND

The recent discovery of tracks in ancient sedimentary rocks in the Lake District indicate that the first creatures to come out of the sea onto dry land did so some 50 million years earlier than previously thought. A team led by Eric Johnston from the British Geological Survey in Newcastle has examined the tracks and suggests that they could have been made by animals similar to modern centipedes and millipedes, living in shallow, fresh water that had dried out. Each of the tracks consisted of two closely spaced parallel lines, separated by less than 1 cm. Some tracks contained individual imprints just a few millimetres in size but others showed the prints merging together into continuous trails. The tracks were found in rocks which were formed when volcanic ash settled into sediments in shallow water some 450 million years ago, in the late Ordovician period.

Derek Bridges and Jill Wright of Bristol University carried out experiments to see if they could produce the two types of track using woodlice walking over sand of varying degrees of wetness. They showed that the same animal could produce both types of track. The woodlice left clear footprints on dry sand but on wet sand the individual prints merged together to form a continuous trail.

It had been thought that complex multicellular animals existed only in the sea during the Ordovician period, but these finds suggest that some animals were living in lakes and rivers and were also capable of surviving out of water. The tracks showed that the animals walked on several pairs of legs and that these were strong enough to lift the body clear of the ground. This indicates that the animals were not soft-bodied creatures like worms but had hard external skeletons similar to modern centipedes. Unfortunately, this cannot be verified because no fossils of the actual creatures have been found.

DINOSAUR EVOLUTION THEORY

The discovery of the oldest-known member of a family of ostrich-like dinosaurs in Spain is causing palaeontologists to rethink their idea about the evolution of these creatures. Until this discovery Pelicanimimus was known only in Asia and North America in the Cretaceous period, from about 100 to 65 million years ago. The new fossil is the first evidence for its existence in Europe and, even more intriguing, it is 115 million years old.

Diego Rasskin-Gutman and colleagues at the Independent University of Madrid found the upper part of the animal's body in limestone deposited in an ancient lake. The skull was crushed but sufficient remained for a thorough examination. The impressions of the skin were preserved, including folds that resemble the mouth pouch of a pelican, hence the name 'pelican mimic' given to the fossil. The creature had an array of 220 small teeth. This has surprised scientists because later members of the Pelicanimimus family had bird-like toothless beaks. The manner in which the teeth disappeared in the evolution of this dinosaur could provide evidence about the evolution of another bird-like dinosaur. Ostrich dinosaurs, or ornithomimosaurs, were theropods, a group made up of predators that walked on two legs. These included the allosaurus and tyrannosaurus. From the theropods evolved the first bird, archaeopteryx, about 150 million years ago. Several theropod families evolved in the late Cretaceous period, but their inter-relationships are not clear.

It had been though that ornithomimosaurs became the only toothless dinosaurs by evolving in such a way that the number of teeth gradually decreased. This latest find suggests an alternative theory. The number of teeth could have gradually increased and at the same time became smaller until they became one long cutting edge. This idea cannot be checked at present because the Spanish discovery is the only theropod with an extremely elongated snout and high tooth count.

EARLIER MAN DISCOVERED

A team of scientists from the USA, Japan and Ethiopia have recently found fossils of early man (hominids) in a barren region called the Middle Awash, in the Afar Depression in northern Ethiopia. These fossils are of the earliest known hominids, having an age of 4.4 million years. They have been given the name *Australopithecus ramidus* after a word meaning 'root' in the language of the Afar people. The species falls in the gap between the earliest known hominids (australopithecines) and the last common ancestor of the African apes and humans.

The new species is distinct from the well-known 'Lucy' and her kin (*Australopithecus afarensis*) which lived between 3.9 and 2.9 million years ago, the date given for Lucy being 3.1 million years. It had been thought that human and African ape lineages diverged between 8 and 6 million years ago, but no fossils from this period have ever been found. This new fossil, however, together with molecular evidence, now places the divergence at about 6 million years.

The site for this new find is about 75 km southwest of Hadar, where Lucy and several other *A. afarensis* fossils were found. In 1992–3 the team found fragmentary fossil specimens from about 17 individuals. Pieces of a skull, a jawbone, many teeth and broken arm bones were collected, but no hip or leg bones were found. It is therefore not certain whether the hominids walked on two legs. However, the team found that the foramen magnum, the main opening at the back of the skull through which the brain is connected to the spinal cord, is farther forward than it is in apes, suggesting that the head was balanced on the backbone. This and other features distinguish *A. ramidus* from extinct and living apes. Overall there is a tendency to think that this new hominid was bipedal.

There are a lot of theories being put forward about how this new find fits into a satisfactory evolutionary tree but until more fossils have been found and examined it is difficult to place much confidence in any of them.

MOUSE LEMURS

Madagascar is the home of several unique species of lemur and there has been considerable research into these strange creatures. Of particular interest are the mouse lemurs. These seem to have their own distinctive territories. The brown mouse lemur, *Microcelus rufus*, lives in the rain forests in the northern and eastern regions of the island, whilst the slightly larger grey mouse lemur, *Microcebus murinus*, is dominant in the drier deciduous forests in the south and west. In addition to these, the existence of a third species, a pygmy mouse lemur, *M. myoxinus*, has been suspected since it was first described in 1852. For the past century there has been confusion over the proper status of this lemur. Occasionally a reddish brown mouse lemur was observed living alongside a grey mouse lemur but it was assumed that this was either an immature creature or a sub-species of the other two. In 1992 Jutta Schmid and Peter Kappeler of the German Primate Centre in Gottingen captured a little, reddish-coloured animal in western Madagascar. It weighed only 30 grams, about half that of the other species. Until this find, scientists had more or less written off the existence of a third species but further searching revealed more of the very small creatures. A detailed study has shown that the creatures have several distinctive features, sufficient to confirm *M. myoxinus* as a distinct and separate species.

Army Ant Trails

One of the puzzles of the animal world is how army ants, which are totally blind, travel in columns when out foraging and find their way through even the densest jungle. Light has been thrown on the problem by David Morgan and Neil Oldham of Keele University, working in conjunction with a team of zoologists at the Catholic University of Leuven in Belgium led by Johan Billen.

The researchers collected worker ants of the species *Aenictus* from Hong Kong's New Territories. The Belgian team dissected samples of glandular tissue from some of the ants and sent them to Keele for chemical analysis. It was found that the ants would follow artificial trails made with extracts taken from a gland in the ant's stomach. The pheromones present were sufficiently powerful for the ants to respond even when the solution containing the pheromones was diluted a hundred times. But the ants ignored trails made using extracts from glands in the head of the thorax.

Morgan and Oldham analysed the glandular secretions to identify the chemical involved, using mass spectrometric techniques. The first results seem to indicate that there was one important component, methyl anthranilate, used in grape flavouring, but the ants failed to react to trails containing this. Further work identified another compound, methyl nicotinate, present in the gland extract at 1 per cent of the quantity of the anthrailate. Trails using the nicotinate also failed to interest the ants, but the ants responded immediately to trails containing both chemicals, reacting in the same way as they would have done to the natural trails.

It is unclear why army ants require the presence of two pheromones whilst many other insects require the presence of just one. In the case of the ants, it appears that methyl nicotinate acts as a relatively long-lasting primer, lasting possibly as long as six hours, to make the ants follow the trails until they were exhausted.

Vitamin B12 Synthesized

A team of chemists led by Ian Scott of Texas A. and M. University have developed a method of making vitamin B12 which is more efficient than the natural process. They isolated some of the enzymes that are used by bacteria to create vitamin B12 naturally and then mixed them back again. This produced a system of chemicals which, after a series of steps, transformed relatively simple organic molecules into an advanced precursor of vitamin B12 known as corrin. Although the structure of vitamin B12 was discovered over 50 years ago, there has been a problem unravelling each stage in the synthesis and identifying the enzymes that catalyse each step. The vitamin is made by only a few micro-organisms and the team chose one of these to manufacture the enzymes. The genes of the bacterium *Pseudomonas denitrificans* were modified so that it made the enzymes in larger quantities and then 12 of these were mixed in a flask with the simple natural starting compound 5-amino-laevulinic acid (ALA). The process was monitored by using ALA containing carbon-13 and the reactions were stopped at intervals to identify the intermediate products. The 12 enzymes made 17 modifications to the starting material. In the micro-organisms that produce the vitamin naturally, the intermediate products are diverted into reactions needed to keep the cell alive. However, in the laboratory experiments the only enzymes present were those needed to make the vitamin, so the process turned out to be more efficient than that occurring naturally. The yield for the whole process was 20 per cent, indicating that the average efficiency of each of the intermediate transformations was about 90 per cent.

Improving Catalyst Efficiency

The rate at which certain chemicals react can be speeded up dramatically by using a catalyst. These catalysts are not used up in the reactions but efficiency falls off because continual use causes the catalysts to disintegrate and become virtually useless. Disintegrated remains interfere with the reaction and consequently have to be removed. The catalyst often includes precious metals and these can be recycled, a process requiring much time, effort and expense, so any technique which can eliminate the disintegration has many advantages.

Craig Hill and Xuan Zhang of Emory University in Atlanta, Georgia, carried out research into the behaviour of catalysts but instead of trying to find catalysts which did not break down easily, they investigated the possibility of finding ones which would be self-fixing when they started to disintegrate. They used the basic reactions of adding oxygen to simple hydrocarbon molecules called alkenes to synthesize epoxides, used in the manufacture of polymers and resins. The catalyst used was a complex molecule containing cobalt, tungsten and a phosphate. They spent months carrying out the reactions under precise conditions of temperature, acidity and a range of chemicals in the hope of getting the catalyst to recombine after use. The chemists finally succeeded by making the catalyst under acidic conditions before transferring it to the reaction vessel. This contained chloroform and a detergent-like molecule. The mixture was kept at room temperature under an atmosphere of argon and stirred continuously. Close examination of the reaction mixture showed that the catalyst molecules were rejuvenated as soon as they began to disintegrate. This opens up the possibility of widespread use of similar techniques for many of the important chemical processes which depend on the use of catalysts.

AGE OF THE UNIVERSE

In October 1994 information from the Hubble space telescope caused a stir in cosmological circles. The data showed that the Universe was younger than its oldest stars. At first it was thought that there must be something wrong with the figure for the age of the Universe, a figure based on the standard model of the Big Bang. A closer scrutiny by British and American astronomers has suggested that the figures for the age of the older stars may be wrong.

Astronomers from the National Optical Astronomy Observatory in Tucson, Arizona, and the University of Cambridge have used more accurate techniques for assessing the age of relatively young clusters of stars. The figures obtained differ considerably from the earlier estimates, suggesting that the well-established technique of measuring ages is less reliable than originally thought. The method used involves measuring the temperatures of white dwarfs, stars which have exhausted their nuclear fuel and are gradually dying and fading from view. The temperature of these stars gives a very reliable value of how long ago the star formed. Until recently it was not possible to use white dwarfs for measuring ages of star clusters because the individual stars were in general too faint to be seen from ground-based observatories. But by using data from the Hubble space telescope, it is possible to measure stars as faint as magnitude +25, about 100 million times fainter than stars visible to the naked eye.

The established value for the age of a star cluster known as NGC2477 was 500 million years but the new value indicates a much greater age, somewhere in the region of 1.25 billion years. Work on some of the oldest clusters in our Galaxy have shown that the accepted ages have been overestimated but if the data overall shows an under-estimate, the standard model for the Big Bang will be drastically undermined.

MISSING MASS DISCOVERED?

Cosmologists claim that there should be two to three times more mass in the Universe than is accounted for by the gas clouds, stars and galaxies that have been catalogued so far. Many explanations have been put forward to explain this discrepancy but until now none have withstood the test of time. In a recent attempt to solve this problem, a team of astronomers from Arizona's Steward Observatory, led by Christopher Impey, have shown that the Universe contains a multitude of faint galaxies which have not yet been catalogued. Impey says that these may contain as much material as all the previously catalogued galaxies put together.

Over a period of five years, the astronomers have scanned photographic plates covering 750 square degrees of the sky, picking out faint galaxies. Their spectra were then examined using optical telescopes in Arizona and the 305-metre radio dish at Arecibo in Puerto Rico. From this data Impey and colleagues were able to calculate the distances and brightnesses of these objects. They were able to identify more than 600 previously uncatalogued galaxies, most lying between 200 and 400 million light years away. It was concluded that there must be between 30 and 100 per cent more galaxies than previously thought.

These new objects contain all types of galaxies, ranging from shapeless dwarfs to disc-like giants three times the size of our own Galaxy. The galaxies are fainter because they contain fewer stars. They appear to be surrounded by massive haloes of dark unknown matter, its presence detected solely by its gravitational effect on nearby stars and galaxies. Impey suggests that this dark matter could make up much of the extra mass required by cosmologists to support their theories.

FEWER FAINT STARS

Observations using the Hubble space telescope indicate that the number of very faint stars is far fewer than expected. If this is the case, they cannot be the major part of the elusive dark matter which makes up most of the mass of our Galaxy. The existence of the gravitational forces associated with invisible or dark matter is required to explain how stars in our Galaxy can orbit as fast as they do without flying off into intergalactic space and also to explain why galaxies do not escape from parent clusters.

Two separate projects showed that the number of stars increased as the mass decreased down to a mass about 20 per cent that of the Sun. Below this value the number of stars fell rapidly. From a theoretical point of view the mass of a star has to be greater than 8 per cent of that of the Sun before nuclear reactions can take place in the core. Stars smaller than this critical mass are called brown dwarfs but neither survey was able to detect them. John Bahcall of the Institute for Advanced Studies at Princeton, New Jersey, surveyed stars in the outer regions of the Galaxy whilst Francesco Paresce of the Space Telescope Science Institute in Baltimore concentrated on the Globular Cluster NGC6397. Bahcall estimates that faint red dwarfs make up only 6 per cent of the mass of globular clusters and the outer regions of the Galaxy, and no more than 15 per cent of the mass of the Galactic disc.

Both Bahcall and Paresce are convinced that the rapid fall-off recorded would not be reversed for even smaller objects and so believe that brown dwarfs as well as red dwarfs can be ruled out as the source of the dark matter. They are inclined to think that the source of this matter could be in more exotic alternatives such as neutron stars, black holes or unknown massive particles.

BIG BANG GAS FOUND

The Big Bang theory predicts that some of the matter formed at the time of the Big Bang would not condense into galaxies but remain in gaseous form. Evidence of the existence of this gas has eluded astronomers for over a quarter of a century. However, its existence is now confirmed as a result of work by Arthur Davidsen of John Hopkins University. The Hopkins Ultraviolet Telescope, part of the Astro 2 mission which flew in one of the space shuttle flights, detected partly ionized helium by its absorption of light from a distant quasar. Davidsen has estimated that the intergalactic medium contains about one atom in 100 cubic metres. This is sufficient to account for about 3 per cent of the missing mass not yet identified by astronomers.

The primordial gas would have consisted mainly of hydrogen and helium. The identification of intergalactic hydrogen is difficult, but the identification of helium atoms, although not present in such great quantities can be achieved with care. Helium atoms, which have two electrons, can be partially ionized and yet still keep one electron. For the last 17 years Davidsen has been looking for the absorption lines of ionized helium in the spectra of distant quasars. His first telescope was put on board the Astro 1 in 1990 but technical problems prevented the telescope from looking at quasar targets for a long enough period of time. In 1994 the European Space Agency detected intergalactic helium absorption lines using the Hubble space telescope. Unfortunately Hubble could not observe at ultraviolet wavelengths below 120 nanometres. Although there was evidence for the presence of the gas, the results were not definite enough. However, the second Hopkins telescope flight in Astro 2 allowed Davidsen to concentrate on a close quasar and he was able to obtain confirmation of the gas's existence.

CARBON-14 IN SPACE

The radioactive isotone carbon-14 has been identified in the gas surrounding the red giant star catalogued as either CW Leonis or IRC +10216. This particular star is about 600 light years away from the Earth and contains large quantities of carbon and carbon compounds. In this mix, the radioactive carbon-14 was identified by Gregory Wright of the A. T. and T. Bell Laboratories in Holmdel, New Jersey.

Using a 7-metre radio antenna at Bell Laboratories, he studied the star on 11 different nights and recorded emissions that contained the carbon-14 isotope. He thinks the isotope was produced when helium nuclei fused together in the interior of the star. The isotope subsequently migrated into or was ejected into the surrounding atmosphere.

This is the first time carbon-14 has been definitely identified in space. It has a relatively short half-life of about 5,700 years. It will now be possible for astronomers to date relatively recent events in our Galaxy with the isotope in the same way that it is used for dating purposes on Earth.

THE EARTH'S ATMOSPHERE

One of the mysteries of the evolution of the Earth's atmosphere is why it took so long for the atmosphere to acquire the amount of oxygen that is now present. The first photosynthetic oxygen-producing organisms are thought to have evolved about 2,800 million years ago, yet until about 600 million years ago the amount of oxygen was about 10 per cent of the present-day value. John Hayes and colleagues at the Indiana University in Bloomington seem to have found a possible reason for this.

The team analysed compounds from sediments formed between 1,800 and 550 million years ago and found that the simple hydrocarbon in the sediments contained more carbon-13 than the more complex organic molecules. They have suggested that these hydrocarbons were formed by 'heterotrophic' bacteria which fed by rotting down organic material from dead photosynthetic cells. Modern heterotropic bacteria break organic matter down into molecules that are rich in carbon-13.

Heterotrophic bacteria need oxygen and the theory is that there were enough of the bacteria present in the early days to mop up most of the oxygen produced by photosynthetic organisms. Hayes claims that the huge bacterial population could only have survived if the decaying material sank very slowly from the surface. The top layers of the oceans about 1,000 million years ago were populated by a thin oxygenated layer containing photosynthetic organisms and heterotrophic bacteria. Below this, the water did not contain any oxygen but it did contain bacteria which could break down organic molecules without oxygen. About 600 million years ago, something caused a big drop in the quantity of heterotrophic bacteria. The researchers believe that the multicellular marine animals that appeared at this time ate much of the photosynthetic plankton. After being eaten the cells' remains would have been packaged into faecal pellets which would have sunk rapidly to the ocean floor, out of reach of the heterotrophic bacteria. The resulting drop in the density of the bacteria allowed the oxygen to start building up in the atmosphere and the oxygenated surface layers of the ocean would have expended to produce a much deeper layer, giving more space for marine animals to develop.

MOON MAPPING REVEALS CRATER

A huge crater, about 13 km deep and 2,500 km across, has been identified by the American lunar probe *Clementine* during its 70-day mission to compile a topographical map of the Moon's surface. Previous maps of the Moon have concentrated on the equatorial regions; this is the first detailed mapping of the whole of the lunar surface and in particular the polar regions.

The new data reveal that the differences in altitude between the highest and lowest points is over 16 km, compared with a value of less than 12 km obtained during the Apollo *Orbiter* flights some 20 years ago. In addition to this huge crater, the new maps show many other large basins caused by ancient impacts. The new crater has been named the South Pole-Aitken crater and is thought to be the largest and deepest crater in the solar system. Its diameter is roughly a quarter of the Moon's circumference and it has been calculated that an object about 200 km across was responsible for the crater. Its age is estimated to be between 3.8 and 4.3 thousand million years. To calculate the age, Maria Zuber of the NASA Goddard Space Flight Center in Maryland counted the number of smaller craters marking the surface of the crater, these indicating subsequent events. Having reasonable data for estimating the rate of impacting, the results gave a surprisingly early date for the formation of the huge crater. Research had suggested that the early lunar surface was warm and plastic, so that any impact produced a flattened crater, but the ratio of diameter to depth for the South Pole-Aitken crater is approximately the same as for much younger craters. This implies that the lunar surface cooled much faster than had been thought. The region just north of the crater is the highest point on the lunar surface and the extra volume of rock in this area is comparable to the empty space in the crater, suggesting that a glancing impact might have pushed material northwards to form this highland.

The Sun's Polar Regions

Until last year all earthbound observations of the Sun and those from satellites and space probes have been from points not far removed from the ecliptic, the plane of the Earth's orbit round the Sun. During the latter half of 1994 the European Space Agency's spacecraft *Ulysses* studied the Sun's south polar regions, reaching a point over a solar latitude of 80°.2 on 13 September.

Ulysses was launched from the space shuttle *Discovery* in October 1990 and passed within 459,000 km of Jupiter in February 1992. The course past Jupiter was such that Jupiter's strong gravitational field propelled the spacecraft out of the ecliptic and back towards the Sun in an orbit highly inclined to the ecliptic. During its passage over the Sun's south pole, the probe discovered that the solar wind originating from the polar regions travels roughly twice as fast, about 800 km per second, as that coming from the equatorial regions. It has been known for some time that within the solar corona there are areas known as coronal holes, large, cool, rarified regions where the magnetic field is weak. The high-speed solar wind experienced by *Ulysses* escapes unimpeded through a persistent coronal hole situated over the Sun's south pole. *Ulysses* has thrown light on coronal mass ejections (CMEs), sporadic ejections of gas, along with solar flares, which cause magnetic storms and aurorae on the Earth. Until the *Ulysses* information became available, the data collected about CMEs suggested that their speeds were independent of solar latitude, but this latest data shows that the CMEs detected at high latitudes are moving much faster than those encountered on Earth.

Ulysses will pass over the north polar regions during the latter half of 1995 and then speed outwards from the Sun. The return visit to the Sun will occur in 2000 and 2001, when the spot cycle will be at a maximum. If the probe is still working then, it could provide a comparison of the conditions existing at sunspot maximum and minimum.

Blind Spots on Mars

Conditions on Mars have altered drastically since the *Viking* spacecraft landed on the surface in 1976. The atmosphere is now known to be 20° cooler than it was 20 years ago. This temperature change has caused the formation of large quantities of high altitude cirrus cloud, which has removed the water vapour from the atmosphere, making it much drier. There has also been a three-fold increase since 1992 in the amount of ozone in the Martian atmosphere. Planetary scientists say that these changes are linked to the fall in the number of dust-storms recorded. The suspended dust absorbs solar radiation, thus warming the planet, but the lack of dust has allowed the planet to cool.

Scientists from the California Institute of Technology and the Jet Propulsion Laboratory have discovered an area of about one million square kilometres in the equatorial region of the planet which does not reflect radar waves. This was discovered in 1988 during the compilation of a radar map of the planet. However, the possibility that this blind area was reflecting the signals in another direction could not be ruled out. More recent scans in 1992 and 1993 revealed a second blind region in the southern hemisphere. This time the planet was farther away, which allowed astronomers to view it from different angles. Results confirmed that the radar signals were absorbed and not reflected.

At visible wavelengths, both blind regions look similar to the rest of the Martian surface but at 3.5 cm wavelengths they stand out as dark areas. This indicates that their surface layers contain few rocks and have a very low density, roughly 1 gram per cubic centimetre, compared to roughly twice this value for the normal surface. It is thought that the absorbing regions consist of volcanic ash or pumice. Radar studies of volcanic ash fields in Hawaii and the Galapagos Islands show that they reflect radar waves very weakly. It is thought that the dust covering the larger area was blown in from volcanoes in the Tharsis Ridge to the east of the area.

The small region in the southern hemisphere, in the Argyre Basin, also lies near to volcanoes.

VENUS UNVEILED

On 11 October 1994 the *Magellan* spacecraft plunged to its death on the barren surface of Venus after five years' systematic scanning of the surface with powerful microwave radar. More than 80 per cent of its surface was found to be covered with lava flows, fractured plains and other volcanic features. The radar image showed huge volcanoes 4 to 5 km high, plus hundreds of smaller ones. A 1,000 km rift valley, Devava Chasma, cuts the crust where powerful internal forces have torn it apart. Mountain chains were identified, one of them containing the solar system's highest peak, the 12,000-metre Maxwell Mons, some 3,000 metres higher than Everest. In spite of the detailed scanning, scientists failed to find any current volcanic activity.

Investigations of conditions on the planet have continued since the demise of *Magellan*. Larry Esposito of the University of Colorado, using the Goddard high-resolution spectrometer on board the Hubble space vehicle, identified changes in the amount of sulphuric acid in the atmosphere. Using the ultraviolet region of the spectrum, there appears to be just one-tenth of the amount of the acid present in 1978, when it was measured by the *Pioneer Venus* spacecraft. The experimenters believe that just before the *Pioneer* mission there was a massive volcanic eruption which flung huge quantities of sulphuric acid into the atmosphere, and over the intervening years this acid will have gradually rained on to the surface of the planet. It is thought that the volcano responsible was Maat Mons, shown by the *Magellan* data to be surrounded by very recent lava flows.

THE OUTER PLANETS

The *Voyager* spacecraft passed the outer planets of the solar system a few years ago, sending back detailed information that made astronomers rethink their ideas about these planets. A second batch of detailed data has come from cameras on board the Hubble spacecraft. These photographs are unaffected by atmospheric turbulence and overturn accepted theories about the solar system.

During its flight past Neptune in 1989, *Voyager*'s cameras showed a world of hurricane winds and huge storms. One of these, called the Great Dark Spot, which could have swallowed the Earth, was likened to the Great Red Spot on Jupiter. Six years later, Hubble found that it had disappeared, but recorded a similar spot in the northern hemisphere. Hubble also found that the cloud features could change drastically in just a few days. Scientists are inclined to think that some internal heat source is driving the dynamic atmosphere.

Uranus, on the other hand, seems to be relatively quiet and very little has been observed, mainly, it thought, because Uranus is so far away at present. Nevertheless, Hubble has been able to confirm the presence of high altitude haze over the south pole and has also observed two large cloud plumes in the southern hemisphere. It has photographed the motions of small chunks of rock less than 80 km in diameter orbiting just outside the ring system.

Hubble has also obtained the best views yet of Pluto, the outermost planet, and its moon Charon. Although no surface features have identified, the pictures show that Charon is bluer than Pluto, suggesting that the two bodies are entirely different. A bright highlight on Pluto indicates that it might have an icy surface which is behaving like a smooth mirror.

Over the past five years Hubble has recorded two vast storms which have erupted in the pale yellow clouds of Saturn. The one in September 1994 was as large as the Earth but the 1990 storm was even larger. According to *Voyager*, Saturn's moon, Titan, is covered in a dense cloud layer of hydrocarbons. However, the Hubble instruments, using a near infra-red wavelength, were able to penetrate the haze to show a pattern of light and dark patches, the origins of which are unknown at present.

CIGAR-SHAPED PLANET

Although two minor planets (951 Gaspra and 243 Ida) have been successfully photographed from spacecraft, they both belong to the main belt of asteroids in orbit round the Sun which he between the orbits of Mars and Jupiter. So the opportunity was taken to learn more about Earth-crossing asteroids when the minor planet 1620 Geographos passed within 0.034 AU (astronomical units) (5.1 million km) of the Earth in August 1994. 1620 Geographos was discovered in 1951 at the Palomar Observatory and extensive photometric and polarimetric observations were made at a subsequent approach in 1969. They showed very high oscillations in the brightness curves. Astronomers speculated that the object was cigar-shaped, hence the drive to confirm these ideas.

During the recent pass, ground-based radar observations were made using the Goldstone dish for seven days. Hundreds of silhouette images were obtained and from the data an extraordinary picture emerged. Geographos is the most elongated body yet identified in the solar system. Although approximately 5 km long, its width is only about 1.8 km. These figures agree closely with the light curves obtained independently. The results also support the belief derived from the spacecraft images of Gaspra and Ida that shape models based on well-determined light curves can be used to produce reliable shapes for future studies.

Why Geographos has such an extraordinary shape has yet to be determined. Small asteroids are thought to be the product of several generations of collisions but there is no satisfactory explanation for the production of such an elongated body.

NEWLY DISCOVERED GALAXIES

The Local Group of galaxies includes, amongst other smaller associations of stars, our own Milky Way, the Andromeda Galaxy (M31) and the two Magellanic Clouds. Over the years, astronomers have identified 70 galaxies within a distance of 10 million light years, but during the last two years, two important discoveries have been made which may answer questions such as why the Andromeda Galaxy is the only one moving towards us.

An international team led by Renée Kraan-Korteweg of the Kapteyn Astronomical Institute identified a large spiral galaxy about 10 million light years away in the constellation of Cassiopeia in what is known as the Zone of Avoidance, a part of the sky obscured by dust in the plane of the Milky Way. It was detected using the 25-metre radio dish at Dwingeloo in the Netherlands. Their find was confirmed at red and infra-red wavelengths. It has been called Dwingeloo 1 and is a barred spiral about a quarter the size of the Milky Way. But for the dust, the galaxy would be one of the brightest objects in the sky. Within a year, the team discovered a second galaxy in the same part of the sky about 20 minutes of arc to the west-north-west of Dwingeloo 1. This new object, named Dwingeloo 2, is about a tenth the size of its companion and has a recessional velocity identical to it. There is evidence of a gravitational interaction between the two and both exhibit spiral-like rotation.

Radio studies of the rim of another member of the local group, Maffei 1, on the Cassiopeia-Perseus border, have recently identified two faint amorphous bodies roughly half a degree to the south. American astronomers produced change-coupled device images using the 0.6-metre Burrell Schmidt telescope at Kitt Peak. The new galaxies were visible in near-infrared wavelengths but were invisible in blue light. The larger object of the two is thought to be a barred spiral but the smaller one appears to be a dwarf irregular galaxy. If these new objects are in fact associated with Maffei 1, they lie at a distance roughly three times that of the Andromeda Galaxy.

GAMMA-RAY BURSTS

Gamma-Ray bursts, intense flashes of gamma radiation which seem to come from all directions in the sky, have long puzzled astronomers. The bursts were first detected in the 1960s from satellites designed to monitor nuclear explosions on the Earth but the data was not revealed until 1973. Data on these bursts have been collected by scientists at the California Institute of Technology in Pasadena. Their studies show that there are two main types, those that seem to originate from the same point in space and those which appear to be single events. The repeating type could be due to a normal star shedding material onto a nearby neutron star. The one-off events, by far the most common, may be linked to cosmic ray bursts (*see* below), or could be the result of the collision of two neutron stars, though there is no general agreement on the latter theory.

The bursts are very violent events, with sources situated in other galaxies. This is implied by the fact that they come from all directions. If the sources were within our Galaxy, their directions would be concentrated in a band across the sky. The fact that one burst is recorded each day and from completely random directions supports the belief of an extra-galactic origin.

If the neutron collision theory is correct, it should be possible to test it. When two such bodies collide, the energy released would be equivalent to that of 100 supernovae. Some of this energy would be in the form of neutrinos and antineutrinos, which would react to form electrons and positrons. These would annihilate each other to form gamma rays. This would account for a small percentage of the total energy released but sufficient to account for the outbursts. Another by-product of the collision could be the generation of gravity waves. If this idea is correct, it may be possible to identify a correlation between the waves and the arrival of the gamma rays.

GAMMA RAYS LINKED TO COSMIC-RAY BURSTS?

Observational evidence suggests that there may be a link between gamma-ray bursts and cosmic-ray bursts. Mordehai Milgrom and Vladimir Usov of the Weizmann Institute at Rehovot, Israel, have pointed out that the two most energetic cosmic-ray events ever recorded came from the same parts of the sky as the strong gamma-ray bursts. They are convinced that the high-energy cosmic rays and the gamma rays had the same source. If this theory is correct, the source must lie well outside our Galaxy because an explosion within our Galaxy capable of emitting such energetic cosmic rays would have destroyed part of it.

Cosmic rays are energetic particles that bombard our atmosphere, colliding with other particles and sending them as a shower to the ground, where they are detected at various establishments throughout the world. From the velocity of such particles it is possible to deduce the direction from which the original cosmic particles came, in the same way that the original path of a snooker ball can be deduced from an analysis of the paths taken by the balls hit.

Milgrom and Usov have calculated that the directions of the original particles causing the two most energetic cosmic-ray events were identical to that of two powerful gamma-ray bursts. In the first event, in October 1991, the cosmic-ray particles arrived within about five and a half months of the arrival of the gamma rays; in the second case the time difference was 11 months. Because evidence suggests that the cosmic rays consist of protons, it is thought that the sources of these events lie at distances of between 100 and 200 parsecs (326 to 652 light years) away.

EVOLUTION OF WHITE DWARFS

One of the mysteries of the evolution of white dwarfs has been solved by Martin Barstow and colleagues at Leicester University. White dwarfs originate from stars which originally had masses lying between one and eight times that of the Sun. After all the hydrogen in the core has been converted to helium, the star expands to form a red giant. The outer layers of hydrogen are ejected to form a ring and we see them as planetary nebulae. The central star collapses to form a white dwarf, which slowly cools and fades.

There are basically two types of white dwarfs, those that are helium-rich and those which contain much hydrogen. Astronomers have in the past found many examples of hydrogen-rich stars at the centres of planetary nebulae, either with temperatures of about 120,000°C or with relatively cool ones in the region of 70,000°C, but none with intermediate temperatures. The only known examples with intermediate temperatures were the helium-rich type. Barstow has identified a hydrogen-rich star, known as RE 1738+665, with a temperature of about 90,000°C. It was picked up as a source of ultraviolet light by the ROSAT satellite. The identification of the star with an intermediate temperature might have simplified the theories for the evolution of white dwarfs, although the question arises as to why only one such star has been identified. It is possibly because very hot stars cool quickly, so that at any one time there are few such objects at this stage. Further surveys are being carried out at ultraviolet wavelengths to try to identify more examples.

POLARIS STILL PULSATING

The reported behaviour of the Pole Star, Polaris, in recent years has led astronomers confidently to expect that the star would stop pulsating and become an object emitting a steady light. Polaris is a star of the type known as Cepheid Variables, in which there is a known relationship between he luminosity and the period over which the star brightens and fades. In the case of Polaris, although its period of about four days has remained roughly constant, the amplitude of the variability in its brightness has decrease from a magnitude of roughly 0.12 at the turn of the century to 0.01 by 1992, the rate of change gradually speeding up. This led some astronomers to think that the variability would vanish within the next few years but this has not proved to be the case.

Astronomers from the Harvard-Smithsonian Center for Astrophysics obtained high resolution spectra of the star through much of 1994 using the Mount Hopkins 1.5-metre telescope. They were able to detect motions in the atmosphere as low as 30 metres per second, and found that the atmosphere still expanded and contracted with a period of 3.97 days, reaching peak velocities of 850 metres per second. It appears that although the variability in the brightness has fallen to a very low value, the star is still pulsating.

The behaviour of the atmospheres of Cepheid Variables is quite involved. The atmosphere becomes alternately opaque and transparent as it expands and contracts. Consequently, either velocity shifts on the star's surface or brightness variations can be monitored. The Harvard team observed velocities corresponding to a magnitude variability of 0.03, a value confirmed by astronomers from the University of Toronto. Although the physical basis for the behaviour of Cepheid Variables is understood, it is not known why a given amplitude occurs or why, as in the case of Polaris, it changes. Polaris is under constant monitoring and it may be that some answers will be arrived at in the near future.

THE KUIPER BELT

Whenever the Hubble Space Telescope has been used to investigate a particular problem, the results obtained have been sensational. One of the mysteries of the solar system is its structure and composition in the region beyond the orbits of Neptune and Pluto. Any objects in this region, known as the Kuiper Belt, are difficult to study or even detect because they are so faint. Ground-based telescopes are capable of detecting only the brightest of these objects. These have diameters of slightly less than 100 km, a value much larger than the normal diameters of comets. Many astronomers think that the Kuiper Belt is the source of short-period comets but observational evidence has been lacking. The Hubble telescope seems to have provided the answer.

Anita Cochran and colleagues at the University of Texas used the Wide Field/Planetary camera on board the spacecraft to take 34 ten-minute exposures of a small section of the sky. Using a computer, all objects that remained in the same position on all the photographs were eliminated, leaving only the faint spots which appeared to have moved. The brightness of these spots was barely distinguishable from the measuring instrument's background noise. To ensure that these really were moving objects, the investigators checked their paths, eliminating those which had orbits far removed from the orbits of Pluto and the larger objects previously observed. The initial analysis showed that 244 objects were moving in what were described as realistic orbits and only 185 which were not. This ratio was statistically significant, showing that the team had discovered the first comet-sized bodies in the Kuiper Belt. Because the discovery relies on a statistical argument, there is an element of doubt so confirmation from direct observational techniques is awaited. This may be achieved within the next year when workers at the University of Hawaii complete their research using the 10-metre Keck telescope on Mauna Kea.

Theatre

Major announcements by the 'Big Two', the Royal National Theatre and the Royal Shakespeare Company, coloured the year. In December 1994, the artistic director of the Royal National Theatre, Richard Eyre, announced that he would retire in 1997 after ten years. His decision was greeted with regret, and admiration was expressed for his regime in spite of an unusually cautious year. It also provoked a vast number of column inches on the subject of who should be his successor. With Nicholas Hytner making waves in the film world with *The Madness of King George*, Adrian Noble committed for a further five years to the RSC and Sir Ian McKellen apparently not interested, focus centred on a new generation: Jude Kelly, the artistic director of West Yorkshire playhouse; Stephen Daldry, the artistic director of the Royal Court; Sam Mendes, currently running the Donmar Warehouse; and Jonathan Kent at the Almeida. The National Theatre's board will probably announce the name of Eyre's successor in the summer of 1996.

While Eyre's announcement was not unexpected, Adrian Noble's was a bombshell. In June 1995 he announced that from 1997 the RSC would play in the Barbican theatre for only six months of the year, instead of the present twelve; that the company's touring schedule would be substantially increased; that there would be a slight cut back on the number of new productions each year; and that another residency would be set up similar to the five-week season that the RSC presents annually in Newcastle upon Tyne. The decision was all the more unexpected since the RSC had recently negotiated a large increase in sponsorship from the Corporation of London, owners of the Barbican. Noble insisted that the decision was not provoked by dissatisfaction with the Barbican but rather out of a missionary zeal to be a truly national theatre. Noble also denied that the company was struggling to fill houses in London and, as if to prove the point, this summer the RSC extended its playing areas to include the Young Vic as well as the Barbican and the Pit. Bernard Harty, the caretaker managing director of the Barbican Arts Centre after the abrupt departure of Detta O'Cathain, admitted that he was disappointed by the news but at the same time, with half the Barbican's current subsidy to the RSC (£3.6 million) now available for other schemes, he looked forward to a new era.

London critics were for the most part apoplectic, fearing that it was the beginning of the end for one of the world's great companies. They believe that touring will erode standards, that the best actors will be reluctant to tour, and that the programming will inevitably become more conservative. They also worried about the impact on the tourist season, although the RSC claimed that the tourists only made up 2 per cent of the London audience during the summer, most going to Stratford. Others speculated on whether the regions, who were not consulted, were interested in receiving the RSC and would not prefer to be given sufficient funds to produce their own work.

REPS DECLINE

Nobody involved in theatre doubts that the regions are in trouble. At the end of 1994 three theatres, the Salisbury Playhouse, Cheltenham's Everyman and Farnham's Redgrave theatres, informed the Arts Council that they would be forced to curtail their planned programmes. The Everyman decided to embark on a series of co-productions with the Bristol Old Vic in order to cut costs. The days of a repertory company rooted in its community and producing work that reflects that community appear to be numbered. In the past it was in these repertory companies that young actors learnt their skills playing a wide range of parts with an equally wide age range. Today the most flourishing repertories are those like the Nottingham Playhouse under Ruth Mackenzie, which produces an eclectic programme including dance, performance art, comedy and co-productions with foreign companies.

Fighting to preserve the repertory system is not so easy when the public perception is that the arts are being flooded with money from the National Lottery. In reality, lottery money is only available for capital projects and not for revenue and many people in the theatre are campaigning for this rule to be changed. Even playwrights did not seem to understand the Herculean task that currently faces the reps; 87 playwrights, including Harold Pinter and Caryl Churchill, wrote to every theatre in the country demanding that they should all present at least three new plays in their main houses. Most reps responded that there was nothing that they would like better. Bill Alexander (the artistic director of Birmingham Rep), speaking of the struggle to keep going, was quoted in the *Independent* as saying, 'We walk a tightrope between regeneration and oblivion. You must take risks to revitalize, but those risks could kill you.'

Another announcement was that the actor Mark Rylance would be the artistic director of the Shakespeare Globe, an adventurous selection – especially since Rylance is not convinced that Shakespeare wrote all the plays! It reassured those who feared that the theatre, the late Sam Wanamaker's dream and now nearly completed, was in danger of becoming little more than a quaint theme park.

MUSICALS

With Andrew Lloyd Webber busy launching *Sunset Boulevard* on Broadway, British producers were tentative players in the musical field. Cameron Mackintosh's contribution to the year was not a new musical but a £3.5 million revival of *Oliver!* which opened at the London Palladium just before Christmas. Despite the topicality of Dickens' subject matter, Sam Mendes and his adventurous team fell somewhere between the stools of the cockney chirpiness of Lionel Bart's music and lyrics and the social concerns of Dickens. Jonathan Pryce's downbeat performance as Fagin was clearly inhibited by his desire to avoid playing a Jewish stereotype; more engaging were Sally Dexter's brazen Nancy and Adam Searles as the Artful Dodger. The set was infinitely more elaborate than Sean Kenny's revolutionary designs of 34 years ago; Anthony Ward's succession of London views, while not necessarily an improvement, were certainly spectacular.

In the 1980s *Fame* emerged first as a film and then as a television series, based on the New York school for the performing arts where the students are driven to succeed in 'the hardest profession in the world'. This year it was transformed into *Fame: the Musical*, the other big expensive hit of the year. Apart from the title track little remains from the film. Critics were not impressed, missing the strong story-line of its predecessor, condemning its sentimentality, and open-mouthed at lyrics that rhymed *The Lion in Winter* with Harold Pinter. But whatever the critics thought, audiences appreciated the energy and enthusiasm of the young performers and tickets were extremely hard to come by.

Knowing the dangers of mounting a musical in the West End, the producers of the American musical *Once On This Island*, a transfer from Birmingham Rep, took drastic steps, changing the name of the Royalty Theatre to the Island and redecorating the foyer as a Caribbean wonderland. The marketing could not disguise the weakness of the show, however, despite sterling performances by P. P. Arnold, Clive Rowe and Sharon D. Clarke.

Tokura Productions UK Ltd took a very different and very novel approach to launching a musical. Instead of courting publicity, the Japanese producers appeared to shun it and few people were aware of the opening of *Out of the Blue*, a 'musical drama' about the physical and emotional fall-out of the atomic bomb dropped on Nagasaki. With its echoes of *Madama Butterfly* and *Miss Saigon*, the show could not survive the critical fall-out nor its daunting subject matter, and it quickly closed.

The Japanese producer behind *Mama, I Want to Sing* proved determined to make sure that his show survived its critical roasting. With 2,400 performances off Broadway, *Mama* is America's longest running black musical, and after tours of Europe and Japan it has played to over three million people. It is based on the life of the black gospel singer Doris Troy, who appears in the show as her own mother. A shambolic, raucous affair which resembled a party more than a show, it did not look like surviving in a competitive West End but the producer kept it going and moved to the Gielgud when the run came to an end at the Cambridge.

Mama I Want to Sing was one of a number of musicals during the year that were based on the work of a musician, whether performer or composer. *Only the Lonely* drapes the songs of Roy Orbison around the story of his eventful life. There were enough Orbison fans around to admire Larry Branson's impersonation for the show still to be running a year later. *Ain't Misbehavin'*, a revival that started life at the Tricycle in Kilburn before moving into the West End, is a tribute to the larger-than-life performer Fats Waller, and a close cousin to the tribute to Louis Jordan, *Five Guys Named Moe*, that found a new lease of life in the West End after a spell on tour. Finally, Clarke Peters, a consummate performer himself and the deviser of *Five Guys*, revived *Unforgettable*, a tribute to Nat King Cole first seen and admired at the Theatre Royal Stratford East. But it looked less appealing in the West End and suffered the scorn of critics submitted to one nostalgic tribute too many.

REVIVALS

The revival that generated the most publicity was at the Hackney Empire where, amid considerable hype, Ralph Fiennes took on the role of Hamlet in a production that later transferred to Broadway. AA signs led the way to 'Hamlet at the Hackney Empire' for those who had never been so far east before, but after Fiennes' extraordinary performance in Spielberg's film *Schindler's List* there was no shortage of audiences. Much was expected, both from those who had come to Fiennes via his film work and those who remembered his Henry VI at the RSC. Jonathan Kent's production was, in many ways, an excellent one for Fiennes' fans, most of whom were seeing the play for the first time. In a version that was heavily cut the concentration was all on the story. Kent gave the play a Victorian setting and a barnstorming production to go with the Frank Matcham-designed theatre. At the centre, Fiennes was a romantic Hamlet, rattling through the speeches at a tremendous pace. But for all the excitement that this production generated, most critics felt that Stephen Dillane's sardonic, mocking Hamlet in Peter Hall's production at the renamed Gielgud, Hall's third attempt at the play, was a more original and arresting reading. It was a busy year for the Dane; although Simon Russell Beale's long-awaited Hamlet was postponed, Richard Dreyfuss directed a production for the Birmingham Old Rep. It was a long way for the American film star to come only to be panned by the critics.

Elsewhere Shakespeare's characters suffered a degree of gender changing they had not encountered since Shakespeare's own days. Cheek by Jowl's all-male production of *As You Like It* arrived in the West End, a considerable hit with both audiences and critics. At the centre was Adrian Lester's dazzling and touching Rosalind, whose feelings were no less sincere because he was playing a woman or a woman playing a man or, sometimes, a woman playing a man playing a woman. Declan Donnellan's production, helped by Nicholas Ormerod's green ribbon forest, sustained a sexual energy and a sense of sheer joy right to the end. Later in the year Fiona Shaw appeared as Richard II at the Cottesloe in an absorbing production by Deborah Warner. Shaw's Peter Pan-like performance heightened Richard's isolation, his irresponsibility and inability to make a decision, especially when cooling hot flushes with a spoon or sucking a thumb. In complete contrast but looking like Shaw's twin, David Threlfall's Bolingbroke stood at the other end of Hildegard Bechtler's traverse set in which the audience sat on either side in stalls looking down on the action. This heightened the tension in the deposition scene, with the audience as witnesses to a historical moment as Bolingbroke took the crown from a King whose power was then thought to be divine. Shaw's performance met with a mixed response but Warner's concentrated staging was much admired.

Unusually, these two productions eclipsed the RSC, where the Shakespearean work seemed more conventional. Stratford, in particular, had a sluggish opening, with Josie Lawrence making her début with the company as Kate in The Taming of the Shrew. Peter Hall returned to the main stage after an absence of 25 years with a production of Julius Caesar that confidently filled the main stage but was marred by the use of local people as the crowd, who, not being Equity members, were only allowed to mumble. Adrian Noble, whose A Midsummer Night's Dream was the highlight of the previous year in Stratford and now moved to London, could not do much with Romeo and Juliet but was gloriously on form with The Cherry Orchard. In London, Toby Stephens, son of Maggie Smith and Robert Stephens, was heralded as a new star for his brattish Coriolanus in David Thacker's Napoleonic production. In autumn 1994 foreign Shakespeare dominated at the Barbican with 'Everybody's Shakespeare', an eclectic selection of productions from around the world. In a festival that was generally disliked, most controversial of all was Peter Sellars' production of The Merchant of Venice in which Venice, Italy, was transformed into Venice Beach, California, with Paul Butler as a black Shylock and a Chinese-American Portia who discovers that her would-be husband Bassanio, a Latino yuppy, is bisexual. The production drew parallels between anti-Semitism and the LA race riots and used the play to criticize contemporary American society, with video monitors hanging over the audience depicting LA in flames. Michael Billington of the Guardian was the sole champion of this event; other critics were appalled at the way Sellars had sacrificed Shakespeare's play to his own political agenda. At the Riverside Studios, Vanessa Redgrave's first try at direction was a multiracial

Antony and Cleopatra which received poor reviews, condemned for its incoherence and inattention to the rhythm and sense of Shakespeare's text.

Non-Shakespearean revivals included Sean Matthias's production of Noel Coward's Design for Living which transferred from the Donmar to the Globe. Predictably the play's bisexual subtext was brought out, with the assumption that that was what Noel Coward would have written in 1933 if censorship had allowed. Within the relationship of the three talented artistic bohemians, Otto and Leo's sexual passion for each other is just as intense as their sexual passion for Gilda. With the help of Rupert Graves and Marcus D'Amico, Rachel Weisz's Gilda sent the temperature soaring. In complete contrast, in that no liberties were taken at all, Nigel Hawthorne made his début as a director and acted in The Clandestine Marriage, Deborah Findlay winning acclaim as the socially ambitious Miss Sterling. Gorden Kaye made a rare appearance on stage as a man who makes friends with an invisible rabbit in Harvey at the Shaftesbury, and Bernard Hill came into town from Bristol as the tortured longshoreman in A View from the Bridge.

At the National Theatre, routine productions of The Devil's Disciple, Under Milk Wood, What the Butler Saw and The Merry Wives of Windsor passed without much comment, but three other revivals were more interesting. Howard Davies' production of Lillian Hellman's 1934 play The Children's Hour was the first major London production because of a plot in which two teachers are falsely accused of lesbianism by a malicious pupil. The irony is that by the end of the play one of them realizes that there is some truth in the charge. A creaky old melodrama was redeemed by the sensitivity of Harriet Walter and Clare Higgins as the two teachers in an agonizing final scene. Rodney Ackland's Absolute Hell was long overdue for a revival. First presented as The Pink Room in 1952, it is set in 1945, just after VE Day, in a London club full of boozy squabbling egotists. When first performed, it was too much for an audience who preferred to believe that all the British had acted with true grit and courage during the war. The reception of this black comedy was so negative that Ackland never wrote another major play and declined into obscurity until Sam Walters revived the play with its new title and more forthright language at the Orange Tree, Richmond, recently. At the National, a vast cast was led by Judi Dench as the blowsy club owner, a weepy soak who cannot bear to be alone. In August 1995 the National produced its biggest hit, with Michael Gambon returning to play Volpone and Simon Russell Beale as Mosca in a magnificent staging by Matthew Warchus of Ben Jonson's cynical comedy.

New Plays

A new play in the Royal Court's tiny Theatre Upstairs generated the most controversy; 23-year-old Sarah Kane's Blasted contained scenes of masturbation, fellatio, frottage, defecation, homosexual rape, eye-gouging and cannibalism. The small audience at the first night, before publicity had made people aware of what to expect, felt their stomachs churning and became slightly hysterical as one horror piled on top of another. It was, said Paul Taylor of the *Independent* a little 'like having your face rammed into an overflowing ashtray, just for starters, and then having your whole head held down in a bucket of offal'. Confusion was caused by the fact that the play begins naturalistically with a middle-aged tabloid hack and an infantile 21-year-old in a hotel room in Leeds, before moving into fantasy as the violence that the hack reports invades the room. Kane's attack on the media's manipulation of violence created a violent reaction among the critics, moving the play off the arts pages and into the news. Unsurprisingly the run was packed out. It followed a remarkably successful season of plays by promising young playwrights like Michael Wynne, Joe Penhall and Nick Grosso.

The main house at the Royal Court started more slowly but built to a tremendous climax. Artistic director Stephen Daldry finally directed a new play, *The Editing Process* by Meredith Oakes. A well-observed small-scale satire on the state of the publishing industry was blown up by Daldry into something much more grandiose, and ultimately meaningless, on a state of the art set. The climax to the season was *Mojo* by Jez Butterworth, who won this year's George Devine award and was hailed as an exciting new discovery. His fast and furious play is set among the small-time criminals of 1950s Soho and recalls the early work of Harold Pinter and the vigorous language of David Mamet as well as the current cinema favourite Quentin Tarantino.

The play that really hit the headlines was Simon Gray's *Cell Mates*. About the escape from Wormwood Scrubs of the spy George Blake, *Cell Mates*, directed by the playwright, had a starry cast led by Stephen Fry and Rik Mayall. Audiences were enthusiastic on tour but it opened in London to only moderate reviews. Prepublicity interviews with Stephen Fry implied that he had become very sensitive to criticism both on his own behalf and that of others. A few of the reviews suggested that Fry was more of a comedian than an actor, only capable of playing himself. Three days after the opening Fry failed to turn up for a performance and disappeared, leaving a series of notes. After initial anxiety that he might have committed suicide, he sent a supposedly reassuring note from Bruges saying that he had been a 'silly old fool'. This infuriated both Gray and the producer Duncan Weldon, one of whom stood to lose a great deal of prestige and the other, responsible to those who had invested in the show, a great deal of money. Simon Ward nobly stepped into the breach but the show soon closed in spite of all the publicity. Fry was forced to creep back into the country to get a doctor's certificate and Gray has since written a controversial account of the whole affair and a legal case is pending. A misconception arose that Fry had been slaughtered by the critics,

provoking a nervous breakdown. This fuelled a backlash against those who spend night after night sitting in the stalls. Tony Slattery used the Olivier awards, usually an anodyne affair, to express his feelings about the critical fraternity and was wildly applauded.

One play that the critics almost unanimously praised was David Hare's *Skylight* at the Cottesloe. This three-hander was a great contrast to Hare's massive trilogy exploring the Church, the judiciary and party politics performed in the much larger Olivier in 1993–4, but it had as much to say about the state of the nation. A fierce mix of passion and political comment, it pinpointed a divided nation as two ex-lovers, one an idealist living in a dump in Kensal Rise and teaching in an East End comprehensive, and the other a successful restaurateur, rekindle their feelings for each other and exasperate each other as they attempt to come to terms with each other's values and life-styles. Another hit in the Cottesloe was Patrick Marber's first stage play *Dealer's Choice*, which he also directed, in which he explored a father–son relationship within the context of a game of poker. It was a well-made play that was also funny and full of suspense and it was no surprise when it transferred to the West End.

Another transfer, the first to go straight from the Theatre Upstairs into the West End without first appearing in the Royal Court's main house, was *My Night with Reg*, one of a string of so-called gay plays. Kevin Elyot's intricately structured, delicate and funny play was an exploration of love, sex and death, with David Bamber heading the cast as the friend everybody confides in and nobody fancies.

Dame Maggie Smith made a welcome return to the stage in Edward Albee's powerful Pulitzer prize-winning drama *Three Tall Women*, in which Smith portrayed a dying old woman visited by Frances de la Tour and Astrid Hille, playing the same woman at 52 and 26 respectively and depicting the disappointments that soured her life. At first a grim account of the humiliations of old age, it slowly develops into a more humane acceptance of death. *Indian Ink*, not exactly a new Tom Stoppard play since it was a reworking of his outstanding radio play *In The Native State*, opened at the Aldwych. A literate piece of theatre rather betraying its radio origins, it was welcomed for its wit and its sensitive explor-ation of the relationship between India and Britain, but without the same enthusiasm that greeted *Arcadia*. Like *Arcadia*, however, there was an emotional depth to the play that was not to be found in Stoppard's early plays.

The RSC tends to concentrate more on the classics these days but the other outstanding play of the year, along with *Mojo* and *Skylight*, and David Edgar's most eloquent to date, was *Pentecost*. A challenging play of ideas and intricate debate, it explores art and politics, the fate of eastern Europe after the collapse of Communism and the nature of nationalism.

IN THE REGIONS

In September 1994 Bill Bryden directed *The Big Picnic* in the Harland and Wolff engine shed in Govan, Glasgow, with a 250 foot-long set and a £1 million budget. For almost four hours, *The Big Picnic* described a group of Govan workers who joined up at the beginning of the First World War. The audience either promenaded or travelled on mobile seating about designer William Dudley's recreation of the muddy wasteland of the Western Front. A piece of epic popular theatre, the size of the staging did not quite compensate for its dramatic short-comings. Theatre Clwyd, Mold, attracted Anthony Hopkins to make his début as a director with Julian Mitchell's *August*, an adaptation of Chekhov's *Uncle Vanya* transposed to Wales with Hopkins as Uncle Ieuan. The West Yorkshire Playhouse produced a new Sharman MacDonald play, *The Winter Guest*, in conjunction with the Almeida, with another actor, Alan Rickman, making his directorial début. Mac-Donald's haunting, sharply-observed mood play had little plot but a great atmosphere. Again at the West Yorkshire Playhouse, Antony Sher appeared in a joint Market Theatre Johannesburg and National Theatre Studio production of *Titus Andronicus* which, with its South African setting and use of Afrikaner accents, proved highly controver-sial in Johannesburg. In Mold Julie Christie re-turned to the stage after a 20-year absence in a revival of Harold Pinter's *Old Times* which later transferred to the West End. There were big changes in Chichester, where the West End impre-sario Duncan Weldon and the actor Sir Derek Jacobi took control. Jacobi began his regime by playing the lead in a revival of Peter Luke's *Hadrian VII*, but more favourably received was a revival of Harold Brighouse's Mancunian comedy *Hobson's Choice* with Leo McKern as the tyrannical shoe-shop proprietor and Nichola McAuliffe as his strong-minded daughter. In the studio Harold Pinter directed Ronald Harwood's *Taking Sides*, based on the life of Wilhelm Furtwängler, chief conductor of the Berlin Philharmonic during the Third Reich. Michael Pennington played Major Arnold, sent to investi-gate possible Nazi sympathisers before the denazifi-cation tribunals. Anderson is unimpressed by Furt-wängler's reputation, ignorant of music and deeply disturbed by what he has witnessed liberating concentration camps. Daniel Massey's Furtwängler believes that art can bring solace to people in a time of trouble. He defends himself eloquently but at the same time reveals a tortured soul. The production moved later to the West End.

FESTIVAL

The biennial London International Festival of Theatre opened in June 1995. Visitors included companies from South Africa, Germany, India, Australia and Bali. The directors of LIFT also invite British artists to participate, setting their work, often more experimental than usual, alongside the com-panies from abroad. This year one of the highlights

was Deborah Warner's St Pancras Project, in which the 'audience' consisted of one individual every 20 minutes who wandered alone through the ruined gothic grandeur of the St Pancreas Hotel, passing down long-deserted corridors in which Edwardian shoes and breakfast trays sat forlornly on the floor and glimpsing in the distance bellboys running up and down the stairs and maids in their black and white uniforms. The death of Barney Simon, the artistic director of the Market Theatre in Johannes-burg and a long-time opponent of apartheid, was much mourned, particularly in the light of his production of *The Suit*, an adaptation of a bitter short story of the 1950s by the black journalist Can Themba. Another major event was a difficult, unsettling piece *Murx den Europaer! Murx Ihn!...*, produced by the Volkesbuhne Theatre in Berlin and directed by Christophe Marthaler. The pro-duction took place in a former brewery on Three Mills Island in order to accommodate the huge set depicting a waiting-room with strip lighting, a stopped clock, a lift, clanking radiators and a vast ominous boiler. A group of grotesque, badly-dressed people sit in the hall waiting and just occasionally bursting into sublime singing, drawing on music from the German repertoire and from the recent Nazi and Communist regimes. It proved to be a profound and emotional examination of the psyche of post-Communist Europe of a kind that perhaps only theatre can achieve.

PRODUCTIONS
August 1994 to August 1995

LONDON PRODUCTIONS

ADELPHI, WC2. *Sunset Boulevard*, since July 1993

ALBERY, WC2 (13 December 1994) *The Rivals* (Sheridan), transferred from the Chichester Festival Theatre. (25 January 1995) *As You Like It*, a Cheek by Jowl production. (16 February 1995) *Cell Mates* (Simon Gray) with Rik Mayall, Stephen Fry/Simon Ward; director, Simon Gray. (3 April) *One Fine Day*, transferred from Liverpool Playhouse. (25 May) *Five Guys Named Moe*, revival of Lyric Theatre production

ALDWYCH, WC2 (27 February 1995) *Indian Ink* (Stoppard) with Felicity Kendal, Margaret Tyzack, Art Malik, Colin Stinton; director, Peter Wood

ALMEIDA, N1 (5 September 1994) *The Playboy of the Western World* (Synge) with Aiden Gillen, Aisling O'Sullivan; director, Lynne Parker. (3 November) *Molly Sweeney* (Friel) with Catherine Byrne, Mark Lambert, T. P. McKenna; director, Brian Friel. (17 January 1995) *The Dance of Death* (Strindberg) with John Neville, Gemma Jones, Anthony O'Donnell; director, Peter Stormare. (14 March) *The Winter Guest*, transferred from Leeds. (10 May) *The Silver Tassie* (O'Casey) with Stuart Graham; director, Lynne Parker

AMBASSADORS, WC2 (21 September 1994) *900 Oneonta*, transferred from Old Vic theatre. (26 April 1995) *The Killing of Sister George* (Frank Marcus) with Miriam Margolyes, Serena Evans, Josephine Tewson; director, Mark Raymond

APOLLO, W1 (3 October 1994) *Neville's Island* (Tim Firth) with Tony Slattery, Jonathan Coy, Michael Siberry, Paul Raffield; director, Jeremy Sams. (6 March 1995) *In Praise of Love* (Rattigan) with Peter Bowles, Lisa Harrow; director, Richard Olivier. (17 July) *Dead Guilty* (Richard Harris) with Jenny Seagrove, Hayley Mills; director Auriol Smith

APOLLO VICTORIA, SW1. *Starlight Express*, since 1984

ARTS, WC2 (19 January 1995) *Fever Pitch* (Nick Hornby, adapt. Paul Hodson) with Stephen North; producer, David Johnson

BARBICAN, EC2 (14 September 1994) *The Hostage* (Brendan Behan) with John Woodvine; director Michael Bogdanov. (5 October) *The Venetian Twins* (Goldoni) with David Troughton, Sarah Woodward, Paul Greenwood, Jenny Quayle, Jonathan Phillips; director, Michael Bogdanov. (6 December) *A Christmas Carol* (Dickens, adapt. John Mortimer) with Clive Francis; director, Ian Judge. (31 January 1995) *Love's Labours Lost*, revival of 1994 production. (6 April) *Twelfth Night* (Shakespeare), with Emma Fielding, Desmond Barrit; director, Ian Judge. (25 April) *A Midsummer Night's Dream* (Shakespeare) with Stella Gonet, Alex Jennings, Desmond Barrit, Barry Lynch; director, Adrian Noble. (7 June) *Measure for Measure* (Shakespeare) with Stella Gonet, Alex Jennings, Michael Feast; director, Steven Pimlott. (10 August) *Coriolanus* (Shakespeare) with Toby Stephens; director, David Thacker

THE PIT (13 September 1994) *Moby Dick* (Melville, adapt. Rod Wooden) with David Calder, Christopher Hunter, David Birrell; director, Gerry Mulgrew. (4 October) *Ion* (Euripides) with Jude Law, Diana Hardcastle, Peter Guinness; director, Nicholas Wright. (29 November) *New England* (Richard Nelson) with David Burke, Angela Thorne, Mick Ford; director, Peter Gill. (25 January 1995) *Easter* (Strindberg) with Susan Brown, Adrian Rawlins, Lucy Whybrow, Philip Locke; director, Katie Mitchell. (3 April) *After Easter* (Anne Devlin) with Stella Gonet, Katharine Rogers; director, Michael Attenborough. (27 April) *The Wives' Excuse* (Thomas Southerne) with Olivia Williams, Leslie Manville, Clive Wood; director, Max Stafford-Clark. (6 June) *The Broken Heart* (Ford) with Emma Fielding, Iain Glen, Philip Voss; director, Michael Boyd. (8 August) *Spring Awakening* (Wedekind) with Andrew Falvey, Ellie Beaven, Barry Farrimond; director, Tim Supple

BUSH, W12 (16 September 1994) *The Mortal Ash* (Richard Cameron) with Paul Copley, Richard Standing, Jane Cox; director, Simon Usher. (1 November) *Two Horsemen* (Biyi Bandele-Thomas) with Leo Wringer, Colin McFarlane; director, Roxana Silbert. (25 November) *Raising Fires* (Jenny McLeod) Julie Saunders, Gary Love; director, Dominic Dromgoole. (19 January 1995) *Killer Joe* (Tracy Letts), a Hired Gun production. (17 February) *The Present* (Nick Ward) with Ewen Bremner, Katrin Cartlidge, Christopher Simon; director, Nick Ward. (31 March) *Trainspotting* (Irvin Welsh, adapt. Harry Graham) with Ewen Bremner, Malcolm Shields; director, Kenny Miller. (11 May) *True Lines* (devised play), a Bickerstaffe Theatre Company production. (9 June) *Crossing the Equator* (Jane Coles) with Paul Copley, Philip Glenister, Tessa Peake-Jones, Paul Ritter, Sophie Stanton; director, John Dove. (21 July) *Boom Bang-a-Bang* (Jonathan Harvey) with Chris Hargreaves, Jane Hazlegrove, Gary Love, Francis Lee; director, Kathy Burke

CAMBRIDGE, WC2 (20 December 1994) *Peter Pan* (Piers Chater-Robinson) with Nicola Stapleton, Ron Moody; director, Piers Chater-Robinson. (1 February 1995) *Mama,*

I Want to Sing (Vy Higginsen, Ken Wydro) with Stacy Francis, Chaka Khan, Doris Troy; directors, Vy Higginsen, Ken Wydro. (27 June) *Fame: the Musical* (Steve Margoshes, Jacques Levy, Jose Fernandez) with Scott Sherrin, Loraine Velez, Richard Dempsey, Sonia Swaby; director, Runar Borge

COCHRANE, WC1 (October 1994) *Resurrections* (Biyi Bandele-Thomas), a Talawa Theatre Company production. (13 December) *Maskarade* (Sylvia Wynter) with Cy Grant, Allister Bain, Angela Wynter; director, Yvonne Brewster. (5 April 1995) *George Dandin* (Molière), a Red Shift production

COCKPIT, NW8 (7 September 1994) *My Goat* (Michele Celeste) with Anna Savva, Jonathan Arun; director, Burt Caesar. (6 October) *The Mark* (David Ashton) with Neil McKinven, Seamus Gubbins; director, Daniel Slater. (7 November) *Tulip Futures* (John Constable) with William Chubb, Sean Baker, Anna Healy; director, Abigail Morris. (December) *Skaville* (Paul Sirett), an Abacus Arts production. (24 January 1995) *The Yiddish Trojan Women* (Carole Braverman) with Maria Charles, Joanna Foster; director, Hettie MacDonald. (21 February) *Temporary Girl* (Lisa Kolin) with Lisa Kolin

COMEDY, WC2 (19 September 1994) *The Official Tribute to the Blues Brothers* with Mark White, Giles New; director, David Leland. (7 November) *A Passionate Woman* (Kay Mellor) with Stephanie Cole; director, Ned Sherrin

CRITERION, W1 (21 November 1994) *My Night With Reg*, transferred from the Royal Court Theatre Upstairs. (3 July 1995) *Taking Sides*, transferred from the Minerva Theatre, Chichester

DOMINION, WC1. *Grease*, since July 1993

DONMAR WAREHOUSE, WC2 (26 September 1994) *Design For Living* (Coward) with Clive Owen, Paul Rhys, Rachel Weisz; director, Sean Matthias. (10 November) *True West*, transferred from Leeds. (14 December) *The Threepenny Opera* (Weill, Brecht, Jeremy Sams) with Tom Hollander, Tom Mannion, Tara Hugo; director, Phyllida Lloyd. (12 April 1995) *Our Boys* (Jonathan Lewis) with Sean Gilder, Jake Wood, Lloyd Owen, Marston Bloom; director, Niki Turner. (7 June) *Insignificance* (Terry Johnson) with Alun Armstrong, Frances Barber, Ian Hogg, Jack Klaff; director, Terry Johnson

DRURY LANE THEATRE ROYAL, WC2. *Miss Saigon*, since 1989

DUCHESS, WC2. *Don't Dress for Dinner*, since 1992

DUKE OF YORK'S, WC2 (26 September 1994) *Beautiful Thing* (Jonathan Harvey) with Zubin Varla, Richard Dormer, Amelda Brown; director, Hettie Macdonald (24 February 1995) *Broken Glass*, transferred from the National Theatre. (17 May) *The Rocky Horror Show* (Richard O'Brien) with Nicholas Parsons, Robin Cousins

FORTUNE, WC2. *The Woman in Black*, since 1989

GARRICK, WC2 (11 October 1994) *Moscow Stations* (Venedikt Yerofeev, adapt. Stephen Mulrine) with Tom Courtenay; director, Ian Brown. (7 February 1995 *The Live Bed Show* (Arthur Smith) with Caroline Quentin, Paul Merton; director, Audrey Cooke. (3 May) *The Plough and the Stars* (O'Casey) with Aideen O'Kelly, Catherine Byrne, Eamon Morrissey, Anita Reeves; director, Joe Dowling. (19 June) *Unforgettable* (Clarke Peters, Larrington Walker) with Clarke Peters; director, Clarke Peters, Larrington Walker

GATE, W11 (7 September 1994) *Black Sail, White Sail* (Hélène Cixous) with Kika Markham; director, Sue Parrish. (17 October) *Aurélie, My Sister* (Marie Laberge) with Sheila Reid, Carol Starks; director, Lawrence

Boswell. (8 November) *The Danube* (Maria Irene Fornes), a Shared Experience production. (5 December) *The Boat Plays* (Gil Vicente, trans. David Johnston) with Tony Curran, Phil McKee; director, David Farr. (13 January 1995) *Swans Flying* and *The Raft of the Medusa* (Joe Pintauro), a London Gay Theatre Company production. (8 February) *Creditors* (Strindberg), a Fusion Theatre production. (8 March) *Agamemnon's Children: Elektra, Orestes, Iphigeneia* (Euripides) with Sara Mair Thomas, Charles Daish, Barbara Flynn; director, Laurence Boswell. (7 April) *The Lovers* (Goldoni) with Nicola Walker, David Sant, Stephen Harper; director, Roxana Silbert. (5 May) *Time and the Room* (Botho Strauss) with Susannah Corbett, John Turnbull, Andrew Havill; director, Lisa Forrell. (2 June) *Amphitryon* (Kleist) with Eilidh Fraser, Simon Robson, Simon Roberts, Mark Hadfield; director, David McVicar. (July) *Hunting Scenes from Lower Bavaria* (Martin Sperr), an Act of Faith production. (31 July) *The Robbers* (Schiller) with Ian Hughes, Carol Starks; director, Lindsay Posner. (31 August) *Laundry Room at the Hotel Madrid* (Isaac Babel), an Abacus Arts production

GIELGUD (formerly the Globe) WI (4 November 1994) *Hamlet* (Shakespeare) with Stephen Dillane; director, Peter Hall. (20 February 1995) *Design for Living* with Rupert Everett, Marcus D'Amico, Rachel Weisz, transferred from the Donmar Warehouse. (14 June) *Mama, I Want to Sing*, transferred from the Cambridge theatre. (7 August) *Communicating Doors* (Ayckbourn) with Julia McKenzie, Adie Allen, Sara Markland, Ken Bones; director, Alan Ayckbourn

GREENWICH, SE10 (September 1994) *Joking Apart* (Ayckbourn) with Julia Watson, James Coombes, Crispin Letts, Liz Crowther; director, Robin Herford. (7 November) *A Song At Twilight* (Coward) with John Quentin, Lois Baxter, Alison Skilbeck; director, Tom Smith. (19 December) *A Tale of Two Cities* (Dickens, adapt. Matthew Francis) with Timothy Walker, Eleanor Tremain, Alexis Denisof; director, Matthew Francis. (13 February 1995) *The Duchess of Malfi* (Webster) with Juliet Stevenson, Simon Russell-Beale, Robert Demeger, Robert Glenister; director, Philip Franks. (6 April) *If We Are Women* (Joanna McClelland Glass) with Joan Plowright, Diana Quick, Sheila Paterson, Caroline Catz; director, Richard Olivier. (9 May) *Jeffrey* (Paul Rudnich) with Christopher Villiers; director, Tim Luscombe. (3 July) *Penny Blue* (Vanessa Brooks); director, Fiona Laird. (16 August) *Handling Bach* (Paul Barz) with David Henry, Bill Stewart; director, Matthew Francis

HACKNEY EMPIRE (28 February 1995) *Hamlet* (Shakespeare) with Ralph Fiennes; director, Jonathan Kent

HAMPSTEAD, NW3 (19 September 1994) *Poor Superman* (Brad Fraser) with Ian Gelder, Christopher Simon; director, Ian Brown. (24 October) *Gaucho* (Doug Lucie) with Tim McInnerny, Phyllis Logan; director, Doug Lucie. (13 December) *Slavs!* (Tom Kushner) with Ron Cook, Paul Jesson, Imelda Staunton, Annette Badland; director, Matthew Lloyd. (15 February 1995) *Bearing Fruit*, five short plays; director, Deborah Paige. (March) *Morning and Evening* (Astrid Saalbach) with Reece Dinsdale, Alex Kingston; director, John Dove. (27 April) *The Maiden Stone* (Rona Munro) with Frances Tomelty, Carol Ann Crawford, Alexander Morton, Paul Higgins; director, Matthew Lloyd. (24 May) *Jeff Banks Loves My Sister* with Ann Bryson; director, Audrey Cooke. (13 June) *Danti-Dan* (Gina Moxley) with Alan King, Sophie Flannery, Eileen Walsh, Dawn Bradfield, Donal Beecher; director, Lynne Parker. (19 July) *Now You Know* (Michael Frayn) with Adam Faith, Louise Lombard, Rosalind Ayres; director, Michael Blakemore

HAYMARKET THEATRE ROYAL, SW1 (25 July 1995) *Burning Blue*, transferrd from the King's Head

HER MAJESTY'S, SW1 *The Phantom of the Opera*, since 1986

KING'S HEAD, N1 (28 September 1994) *The Night Larry Kramer Kissed Me* (David Drake) with David Drake; director, Chuck Brown. (21 November) *Stairway to Heaven* (Tom Morgan, Kevin Metchear) with Gary Cady, Fiona Sinnott, Michael Medwin; director, Dan Crawford. (15 February 1995) *Mystery Bruises* (Ken Campbell) with Ken Campbell. (13 March) *Burning Blue* (D. M. W. Greer) with Antony Edridge, Robert Dirske, David Pullan; director, John T. Hickok. (17 May) *Jacques Brel is Alive and Well and Living in Paris*, a Canal Cafe Theatre production. (22 June) *The Dark Stranger* (Diana Morgan) with Ruth Madoc, Paul Raynor, Elinor Hunt; director, Stephen Rayne. (July) *The Promised Land* (Roy Smiles) with Roy Smiles, Rebecca Turner. (August) *The Effect of Gamma Rays on Man-in-the-Moon Marigolds* (Paul Zindel) with Katey Crawford Kastin, Caroline Conway, Naomi Bell

LILIAN BAYLIS, EC1 (22 November 1994) *Sir Martin Mar-All* (Dryden), a Magnificant Theatre Company production. (21 June 1995) *What About Leonardo?* (Evald Flisar) with Peter Lindford; director, Janine Wünsche

LONDON PALLADIUM, WC1 (8 December 1994) *Oliver!* (Lionel Bart) with Jonathan Pryce, James Daley/Gregory Bradley, Paul Bailey/Adam Searles; director, Sam Mendes

LYRIC, W1 (13 March 1995) *Ain't Misbehavin'*, transferred from the Tricycle Theatre

LYRIC, W6 (8 September 1994) *The Picture of Dorian Gray* (Wilde) with Benedict Bates, Tim Pigott-Smith, Maria Aitken, Bette Bourne; director, Neil Bartlett. (9 October) *Mirandolina* (Goldoni) with Caroline Quentin, Reece Dinsdale; director, Dalia Ibelhauptaite. (12 December) *The Little Match Girl* (Neill Bartlett, Nicolas Bloomfield) with Sian Reeves; director, Leah Hausman (7 February 1995) *Romeo and Juliet* (Shakespeare) with Stuart Bunce, Emily Woof; director, Neil Bartlett. (19 April) *The Mill on the Floss*, a Shared Experience production. (17 May) *Dumbstruck* (David Kane), a Tron Theatre production. (21 June) *Splendid's* (Genet) with Julian Clary, Everett Quinton, Richard Hawley, Malcolm Sinclair, David Foxxe; director, Neil Bartlett

LYRIC STUDIO (8 September 1994) *Katerina* (Leonid Andreyev), a Damned Poets production. (28 September) *Wax* (Lavinia Murray), a Paines Plough production. (18 October) *Boy* (Shaun Duggan), an Altered States production. (8 November) *Revolver* (Emily Woof) with Emily Woof. (November) *Ion* (Euripides), an Actors Touring Company production. (5 January 1995) *To the Lighthouse* (Woolf, adapt. Julia Limer) an Empty Space production. (29 March) *Lust and Comfort*, a Gay Sweatshop/Split Britches production. (August) *Something About Us* (Andrew Alty) with Simon Beresford, James Kennedy, Gregory Donaldson; director, Philip Howard

MAN IN THE MOON, SW3 (July 1995) *Oh, What a Bloody Circus* (Ionesco) with Roger McKern; director, John Burton. (August) *Brecht's Baal* (Brecht) with Karlos Coleman; director, Natasha Holmes

MERMAID, EC4 (29 November 1994) *Treasure Island* (Stevenson, adapt. Glyn Robbins) with Roy Marsden; director, John Adams

NATIONAL THEATRE, SE1, COTTESLOE (20 September 1994) *Two Weeks With The Queen* (Morris Gleitzman, adapt. Mary Morris) with Tamblyn Lord, Peter Forbes; director, Alan Ayckbourn. (8 November) *Alice's Adventures Under Ground* (Carroll, adapt. Christopher Hampton) with Sasha Hanau, Michael Maloney; director, Martha Clarke.

Theatre 1199

(23 November) *Landscape* (Pinter) with Ian Holm, Penelope Wilton; director, Harold Pinter. (4 January 1995) *Leave Taking* (Winsome Pinnock) with Jenni George, Karen Tomlin, Ginny Holder, Doreen Ingleton; director, Paulette Randall. (9 February) *Dealer's Choice* (Patrick Marber) with Nicholas Day, Tom Georgeson, Ray Winstone, David Bark-Jones, Phil Daniels; director, Patrick Marber. (30 March) *The Blue Ball* (Paul Godfrey) with Nigel Terry, Trevor Peacock, Sonia Ritter; director, Paul Godfrey. (4 May) *Skylight* (David Hare) with Michael Gambon, Lia Williams; director, Richard Eyre. (2 June) *Richard II* (Shakespeare) with Fiona Shaw, David Threlfall; director, Deborah Warner. (18 July) *Titus Andronicus* (Shakespeare), a Market Theatre of Johannesburg production with Anthony Sher. (11 August) *The Machine Wreckers* (Ernst Toller) with Colin Tierney, Declan Conlon, Ron Cook; director, Katie Mitchell

LYTTELTON (22 September 1994) *The Children's Hour* (Lillian Hellman) with Clare Higgins, Harriet Walter, Gillian Barge; director, Howard Davies. (1 December) *Out of a House Walked a Man* (Daniil Kharms), a Théâtre de Complicité production. (2 March 1995) *What the Butler Saw* (Orton) with Richard Wilson, John Alderton, Nicola Pagett, Debra Gillett; director, Phyllida Lloyd. (25 April) *The Man Who*, revival of 1994 production. (23 May) *Absolute Hell* (Rodney Ackland's *The Pink Room*) with Judi Dench, Greg Hicks; director, Anthony Page. (13 July) *La Grande Magia* (Eduardo de Filippo) with Alan Howard, Bernard Cribbins; director, Richard Eyre

OLIVIER (8 September 1994) *The Devil's Disciple* (Shaw) with Richard Bonneville, Helen McCrory, Paul Jesson, Daniel Massey, Jeremy Sinden; director, Christopher Morahan. (15 December) *The Wind in the Willows*, revival of 1990 production. (26 January 1995) *The Merry Wives of Windsor* (Shakespeare) with Denis Quilley, Brenda Bruce, Geraldine Fitzgerald, Maureen Beattie; director, Terry Hands (16 March) *Women of Troy* (Euripides) with Rosemary Harris, Jane Birkin, Josette Bushell-Mingo, Peter McEnery; director, Annie Castledine. (13 April) *Under Milk Wood* (Dylan Thomas) with Mark Lewis Jones, Shirley King, Brendan O'Hea, Nerys Hughes, Sian Rivers; director, Roger Michell. (27 July) *Volpone* (Jonson) with Michael Gambon, Simon Russell Beale; director, Matthew Warchus

NEW END, NW3 (September 1994) *The Provok'd Husband* (Vanbrugh) with John Nettles, Katherine O'Toole; director, Stuart Burge. (20 September) *Statues of Liberty* (David Hart) with Jonathan Oliver, Robert Langdon Lloyd; director, Tom Smith. (17 November) *Miss Julie* (Strindberg) with Geraldine Alexander, Rob Spendlove; director, Sue Lefton. (12 January 1995) *Leocadia* (Anouilh, trans. Timberlake Wertenbaker), a Generation X Theatre Company production. (May) *The Seven Year Itch* (George Axelrod) with Jasper Jacob, Eleanor Tremain. (July) *Reunion in Gethin* (Leon Kruczkowski) with Tom Hillier; director, Andrew Visnevski. (27 July) *The Real Don Juan* (José Zorrilla) with Shaun French; director, Anna Coombs. (24 August) *Love for Love* (Congreve); director, Jon Harris

NEW LONDON, WC2. *Cats*, since 1981

OLD VIC, SE1 (20 September 1994) *The Sisters Rosensweig*, transferred from Greenwich Theatre. (7 March 1995) *Conversations With My Father* (Herb Gardner), transferred from Scarborough. (7 July) *The Importance of Being Earnest*, transferred from Birmingham

OPEN AIR, Regent's Park, NW1 (30 May 1995) *Richard III* (Shakespeare) with Jasper Britton; director, Brian Cox. (14 June) *A Midsummer Night's Dream* (Shakespeare) with Brian

Protheroe, Harriet Thorpe, Robert Lang, Toyah Wilcox; director, John Doyle. (26 July) *The Music Man* (Meredith Wilson) with Brian Cox, Liz Robertson; director, Ian Talbot

PALACE, WC2. *Les Misérables*, since 1985

PHOENIX, WC1. *Blood Brothers*, since 1991

PICCADILLY, W1 (September 1994) *Only The Lonely* (Shirlie Roden, Jon Miller) with Larry Branson; producer, Bill Kenwright

PLAYHOUSE (13 October 1994) *On Approval* (Lonsdale) with Martin Jarvis, Anna Carteret, Simon Ward, Louise Lombard; director, Peter Hall. (8 March 1995) *Up 'n' Under* (John Godber), a Liverpool Playhouse production. (27 June) *My Night With Reg*, transferred from Criterion Theatre

PRINCE EDWARD, W1. *Crazy For You*, since March 1993

PRINCE OF WALES, W1. *Copacabana*, since June 1994

QUEENS, W1 (12 October 1994) *What A Performance* (William Humble) with David Suchet. (5 December) *The Clandestine Marriage* (Colman and Garrick) with Nigel Hawthorne, Susan Engel, Deborah Findlay, Jonathan Cullen, Elizabeth Chadwick, Simon Chandler, Christopher Benjamin; director, Nigel Hawthorne. (24 May 1995) *Hot Mikado* (Gilbert and Sullivan, adapt. David H. Bell, Rob Bowman) with Paulette Ivory, Sharon Benson, Lawrence Hamilton, Ross Lehman

RIVERSIDE, W6 (14 September 1994) *Sturm und Drang* and *Brighton Beach Scumbags* (Steven Berkoff) with Steven Berkoff, Katy Carmichael, Timothy Walker, Annette Badland, Michael Jenn. (9 November) *The Master Builder* (Ibsen) with Brian Cox, Siri Neal; directors, Brian Cox, John Crowley. (18 April 1995) *The Liberation of Skopje* (Dusan Jovanovic) with Rade Serbedzija, Vanessa Redgrave; director, Ljubisa Ristic. (25 April) *Casement* (Alex Ferguson) with Corin Redgrave. (11 May) *Antigone* (Sophocles) with Marina Matthias, Ekkehard Schall; director, Hansgunther Heyme. (23 May) *Real Writing* (Maureen Lawrence) with Kika Markham, Kate Buffery, Kate Byron; director, Corin Redgrave. (30 May) *The Fire Raisers* (Frisch) with Frances de la Tour, Malcolm Tierney, Cliff Parisi, Jonathan Barlow; director, Lenka Udovichi. (1 June) *Antony and Cleopatra* (Shakespeare) with Vanessa Redgrave, Paul Butler; director, Vanessa Redgrave

ROYAL COURT, SW1 (9 September 1994) *Babies* (Jonathan Harvey) with Lorraine Ashbourne, Melissa Wilson, Ian Dunn; director, Polly Teale. (2 November) *The Editing Process* (Meredith Oakes) with Alan Howard, Prunella Scales, Nicholas Woodeson; director, Stephen Daldry. (9 December) *The Libertine* (Stephen Jeffreys) with David Westhead, Amanda Drew; director, Max Stafford-Clark. (15 December) *The Man of Mode* (Etherege) with David Westhead, Tim Potter, Katrina Levon, Amanda Drew; director, Max Stafford-Clark. (1 March 1995) *The Strip* (Phyllis Nagy) with Cheryl Campbell, Nicholas le Prevost, Nicholas Farrell; director, Steven Pimlott. (11 April) *Simpatico* (Sam Shepard) with Ciaran Hinds, Sean McGinley, Janet McTeer, Diana Hardcastle, Tony Haygarth; director, James Macdonald. (18 July) *Mojo* (Jez Butterworth) with Tom Hollander, David Westhead, Andy Serkis, Aidan Gillen; director, Ian Rickson

THEATRE UPSTAIRS, SW1 (September 1994) *Some Voices* (Joe Penhall) with Lee Ross; director, Ian Rickson. (October) *Coming On Strong*. (November) *Peaches* (Nick Grosso) with Ben Chaplin, Holly Aird, Kate Hardie; director, James Macdonald. (5 December) *Ashes and Sand* (Judy Upton) with Susan Lynch, Nick Reding; director,

Ian Rickson. (17 January 1995) *Blasted* (Sarah Kane) with Pip Donaghy, Kate Ashfield, Dermot Kerrigan. (21 February) *The Knocky* (Michael Wynne) with Eileen O'Brien, Felicity Montague, Richard Henders; director, Brian Stirner. (14 March) *Uganda* (Judith Johnson) with David Fielder; director, Polly Teale. (4 April) *The Steward of Christendom* (Sebastian Barry) with Donal McCann; director, Max Stafford-Clark. (11 May) *Star-Gazy Pie and Sauerkraut* (James Stock) with Bridget Turner, Robin Soans; director, Mark Wing-Davey. (June) *Disappeared* (Phyllis Nagy) with Kerry Shale, Alexandra Gilbreath; director, Derek Wax

ROYALTY, WC2 (28 September 1994) *Once On This Island*, transferred from Birmingham

SADLER'S WELLS, EC1 (4 July 1995) *The Adventures of Pinocchio*, transferred from Nottingham Playhouse. (17 August) *Cavalcade* (Coward) with Jeremy Clyde, Gabrielle Drake; director, Dan Crawford

ST MARTINS, WC2. *The Mousetrap*, since 1974

SAVOY, WC2. *She Loves Me*, since July 1994

SHAFTESBURY, WC2 (23 November 1994) *Out Of The Blue* (Shun Ichi-Tokura, Paul Sand) with Simon Burke, Meredith Braun, James Graeme, Michael McCarthy; director, David Gilmore. (23 January 1995) *The Three Lives of Lucie Cabrol*, a Théâtre de Complicité production. (18 May) *Harvey* (Mary Chase) with Gorden Kaye, Rue McClanahan; director, Clifford Williams

STRAND, WC2 (25 October 1994) *The Prime of Miss Jean Brodie* (Spark, adapt. Jay Presson Allen) with Patricia Hodge; director, Alan Strachan. (7 April 1995) *The View from the Bridge*, a Bristol Old Vic production. (20 June) *Forever Tango*

THEATRE ROYAL, E15 (October 1994) *D'Yer Eat With Your Fingers* with A. J. India, Syreeta Kumar, Akbar Kurta, Paul Sharma; director, Indhu Rubasingham. (14 February 1995) *Zorro – the Musical!* (Ken Hill) with Bogdan Kominowski, Sylvester McCoy, Leigh McDonald; director, Ken Hill/Peter Rankin. (10 April) *Dusky Warriors* (Nasser Memarzia, Kulvinder Ghir) with Ashok Kumar, Janet Bamford; director, Jeff Teare

TRICYCLE, NW6 (13 September 1994) *The Day The Bronx Died* (Michael Henry Brown) with Thomas Goodridge, Ewen Cummins, Andrew Fraser; director, Gordon Edelstein. (19 October) *Come Good Rain* (George Seremba) with George Seremba. (7 November) *Matilda Liar!* (Debbie Isitt), a Snarling Beasties production. (November) *Far Above Rubies* (Robbie Gringras), a Besht Teller production. (9 January 1995) *Ain't Misbehavin'* (Fats Waller) with Ray Shell, Debby Bishop, Melanie Marshall, Dawn Hope, Sean Palmer; directors, Nicolas Kent, Gillian Gregory. (28 February) *A Night in November (An Afternoon in June)* (Marie Jones), a Dubbeljoint production. (10 April) *Uncle Vanya*, a Field Day production. (8 May) *Victor and the Ladies* (Jenny McLeod) with Rudolph Walker; director, Paulette Randall. (15 June) *The Suit* (Can Themba), a Market Theatre Company of Johannesburg production. (11 July) *Red Roses and Petrol* (Joseph O'Connor), a Pigsback Company production

VAUDEVILLE, WC2 (19 October 1994) *The Queen And I*, transferred from the Royal Court Theatre. (21 February 1995) *Killer Joe*, transferred from the Bush Theatre. (3 May) *Dealer's Choice*, transferred from the National Theatre

VICTORIA PALACE, SW1. *Buddy*, since 1989

WHITEHALL, SW1 (October 1994) *The Street of Crocodiles*, a Théâtre de Complicité production. (19 January 1995)

Dangerous Corner (J. B. Priestley) with Keith Baxter, Jean Boht, Gayle Hunnicut, Susan Penhaligon, Christopher Timothy; director, Keith Baxter

WYNDHAM'S, WC2 (September 1994) *The Miracle Worker*, transferred from the Comedy Theatre. (15 November) *Three Tall Women* (Edward Albee) with Maggie Smith, Frances de la Tour, Anastasia Hille; director, Anthony Page. (25 April) *The Duchess of Malfi*, transferred from Greenwich. (11 July) *Old Times* (Pinter) with Julie Christie, Leigh Lawson, Harriet Walter; director, Lindy Davis (a Theatre Clwyd production)

YOUNG VIC, SE1 (1 October 1994) *The Slab Boys, Cuttin' a Rug, Still Life* (John Byrne) with Stuart McQuarrie, Paul Higgins; director, Tim Supple. (7 December) *Grimm Tales* (adapt. Carol Ann Duffy) with Natasha Pope, Sarah Cameron, Alan Perrin; director, Tim Supple. (8 February 1995) *Full Moon*, transferred from Theatre Clwyd, Mold. (March) *If We Shadows* (adaptation of Shakespeare) with Jan Pearson, Tony Guilfoyle; director, Pete Brooks. (29 March) *The Mosquito Coast*, transferred from Southampton. (May) *The Counting of the Years* (created in collaboration with Pete Brooks) with Gail Ghislaine-Sixsmith, Miltos Yerolomu, Nick Sutton. (8 June) *Pentecost* (David Edgar) with Charles Kay, Jan Ravens, Linal Haft; director, Michael Attenborough. (29 June) *Bingo* (Edward Bond) with Paul Jesson; director, David Thacker. (29 June) *The Tempest* (Shakespeare) with Paul Jesson; director, David Thacker. (9 August) *Zenobia* (Nick Dear) with Penny Downie; director, Mike Ockrent

OUTSIDE LONDON

BIRMINGHAM: REPERTORY (13 September 1994) *The Tempest* (Shakespeare) with Jeffrey Kissoon, Ginny Holder, Richard McCabe, Rakie Ayola; director, Bill Alexander. (27 October) *Loot* (Orton) and *Entertaining Mr Sloane* (Orton) with Michael Cashman, Stephanie Feyerman, John Rogan; director, Gwenda Hughes. (14 February 1995) *The Servant* (Robin Maugham) with Paul Copley, James Purefoy, Fo Cullen; director, Bill Alexander. (10 March) *A View from the Bridge*, transferred from the Old Vic, Bristol. (25 April) *Pygmalion* (Shaw) with Roy Marsden, Jayne Ashbourne; director, Anthony Clark. (30 May) *The Importance of Being Earnest* (Wilde) with Roger Allam, Philip Franks, Barbara Leigh-Hunt; director, Terry Hands. (6 July) *The Red Balloon* (Anthony Clark, Mark Vibrams) with Nicky Adams; director, Anthony Clark

BRISTOL: OLD VIC (October 1994) *Twelfth Night* (Shakespeare) with Robin Weaver, Anna Rose, Guy Lankester, Richard Frost; director, Andrew Hay. (7 February 1995) *A View from the Bridge* (Miller) with Bernard Hill, Charlotte Cornwell, Alan McNaughtan; director, David Thacker. (20 April) *Flare Path* (Rattigan) with Nicky Henson, Guy Lankester, Barbara Wilshere; director, Andrew Hay. (May) *The Life and Death of a Buffalo Soldier* (David Goodland) with John Amos, Shaun Parkes, Isabel Brook; directors, Andrew Hay, Ian Hastings. (28 July) *Stone Free* (Jim Cartwright); director, Andrew Hay

CHICHESTER: FESTIVAL (4 October 1994) *Present Laughter* (Coward) with Peter Bowles, Leslie Ash, Deborah Grant, Helen Atkinson-Wood. (9 May 1995) *Hadrian VII* (Peter Luke) with Derek Jacobi; director, Terry Hands. (11 May) *Hobson's Choice* (Harold Brighouse) with Nichola McAuliffe, Leo McKern, Graham Turner; director, Frank Hauser. (10 July) *The School for Scandal* (Sheridan), transferred from Crucible Theatre, Sheffield. (2 August) *The Miser* (Molière) with Ian Richardson; director, Nicholas Broadhurst

MINERVA (22 May 1995) *Taking Sides* (Ronald Harwood) with Daniel Massey, Michael Pennington; director, Harold Pinter. (16 June) *A Word from Our Sponsors* (Ayckbourn) with Peter Forbes, Dale Rapley, Kate Arneil, Phyllida Hancock; director, Alan Ayckbourn. (18 July) *Playing the Wife* (Ronald Hayman) with Derek Jacobi, Derbhle Crotty; director, Richard Clifford. (22 August) *The Hothouse* (Pinter) with Harold Pinter, John Shrapnel, Tony Haygarth, Celia Imrey; director, David Jones

EDINBURGH: ROYAL LYCEUM (30 September 1994) *Dancing At Lughnasa* (Brian Friel); director, Kenny Ireland. (21 October) *Death And The Maiden* (Dorfman) with Alison Peebles, Michael Mackenzie, Robert McIntosh. (11 November) *Twelfth Night* (Shakespeare); director, Deborah Paige. (16 January 1995) *On Golden Pond* (Ernest Thompson) with Eileen McCallum, Thane Bettany, James Mackenzie; director, Caroline Hall. (10 March) *Waiting for Godot* (Beckett) with David Shaw-Parker, Tam Dean Burns; director, Kenny Ireland. (7 April) *The Gowk Storm* (Nancy Brysson Morrison, adapt. Colin MacDonald); director, Kenny Ireland. (20 July) *Private Lives* (Coward) with Briony McRoberts, David Robb

GLASGOW: CITIZENS (14 October 1994) *Private Lives* (Coward) with Greg Hicks, Sophie Ward, Victoria Scarborough, Rupert Everett; director, Philip Prowse. (28 October) *The Milk Train Doesn't Stop Here Any More* (Tennessee Williams) with Rupert Everett, Greg Hicks; director, Philip Prowse. (3 February) *Women Beware Women* (Middleton) with Gerrard McArthur, Victoria Scarborough, Anne Lambton; director, Philip Prowse. (10 March) *Swing Hammer Swing!* (Jeff Torrington, adapt. Giles Havergal) with Tam Clay; director, Giles Havergal. (30 March) *Betrayal* (Pinter) with Amanda Elwes, Adrian Howells, Michael Jenn, Gerrard McArthur; director, David Fielding. (18 July) *Fever Pitch* (Nick Hornby) with Robin Hodson. (27 July) *Arsenic and Old Lace*, an Arches Theatre Company production

LEEDS: WEST YORKSHIRE PLAYHOUSE (October 1994) *True West* (Sam Sheppard) with Mark Rylance, Michael Rudko; director, Matthew Warchus. (24 January 1995) *The Winter Guest* (Sharman MacDonald) with Phyllida Law, Sian Thomas, Sheila Reid, Sandra Voe; director, Alan Rickman. (7 February) *Getting On* (Bennett) with Timothy West, Christopher Strauli; director, Prunella Scales. (March) *Romeo and Juliet* (Shakespeare), transferred from the Lyric, Hammersmith. (17 May) *Coriolanus* (Shakespeare) with Steven Berkoff, Faith Brook, David Henry; director, Steven Berkoff. (17 June) *Pilgermann* (Russell Hoban, adapt. Michael Birch) with Damien Goodwin; director, Michael Birch. (20 July) *Anansi Come Back*, a National Pantomine Company of Jamaica production

COURTYARD (8 November 1994) *Mail Order Bride* (James Robson) with Timothy West, Swee-Lin; director, Jude Kelly. (November) *The Sound of Music* (Rodgers, Hammerstein) with Kathryn Evans; director, Irina Brown. (28 February 1995) *The Cracked Pot* (Kleist, adapt. Blake Morrison), a Northern Broadsides production. (2 May) *Call in the Night* (Bernard Kops) with Gary Waldhorn; director, Jude Kelly. (5 June) *Holidays* (John Harrison) with Morag Hood; directors, John Harrison, Jude Kelly. (12 July) *Titus Andronicus* (Shakespeare), a Market Theatre of Johannesburg production with Anthony Sher; director, Gregory Doran. (25 July) *Love* (Graham Reid) with Gwen Taylor, Alexandra Mathie; director, Les Waters

LEICESTER: HAYMARKET (13 September 1994) *The Cherry Orchard* (Chekov) with Susannah York, Alfred Marks;

director, Misha Mokeiev. (11 October) *Follies* (Sondheim) with Mari Gordon-Pryce, Russell Dixon, Michael Heath; director, Paul Kerryson. (22 November) *Calamity Jane*, director, Paul Kerryson. (10 February 1995) *Disappeared* (Phyllis Nagy) with Kerry Shale, Alexandra Galbreath; director, Derek Wax. (25 April) *The Taming of the Shrew* (Shakespeare) with Josette Simon, James McPherson; director, Mihai Maniutu. (23 May) *Edward II* (Marlowe) with Eddie Izzard; director, Paul Kerryson

LIVERPOOL: PLAYHOUSE (17 February 1995) *One Fine Day* (Dennis Lumborg) with Joe McGann. (3 July) *The Sound of Fury* with Danny McGall

MANCHESTER: ROYAL EXCHANGE (8 September 1994) *Julius Caesar* (Shakespeare) with Denys Hawthorne, Patrick O'Kane, Paul Gwilym, Danny Sapani; director, Robert Delamere. (26 January 1995) *Look Back in Anger* (Osborne) with Michael Sheen, Claire Skinner; director, Gregory Hersov. (6 April) *The Colleen Bawn* (Boucicault) with John Elmes, Alison McKenna, Margaret Robertson, Ingrid Craigie, Malcolm Douglas; director, Garry Hynes. (11 May) *Unidentified Human Remains and the True Nature of Love* (Brad Fraser) with Andy Serkis, Marie Francis, Gary Whitaker; director, Braham Murray. (August) *Private Lives* (Coward) with Pip Donaghy, Sian Thomas; director, Braham Murray

MOLD: THEATR CLWYD (13 September 1994) *Macbeth* (Shakespeare) with Timothy West, Alexandra Mathie; director, Helena Kaut-Howson. (21 October) *August* (Chekov's *Uncle Vanya*, adapt. Julian Mitchell) with Anthony Hopkins, Gawn Granger, Lisa Orgolini; director, Anthony Hopkins. (1995) *Full Moon* (Caradog Prichard), adapt. Helena Kaut-Howson, John A. Owen) with Jon Strickland, Simon Gregor; director, Helena Kaut-Howson. (7 March) *Mrs Warren's Profession* (Shaw) with Una Stubbs; director, Caroline Eves. (28 April) *The Rose Tattoo* (Tennessee Williams) with Kathryn Hunter, Marcello Magni, Rebecca Johnson, Benedick Bates; director, Helena Kaut-Howson. (16 May 1995) *Old Times* (Pinter) with Julie Christie, Leigh Lawson, Carol Drinkwater; director, Lindy Davies

NOTTINGHAM: PLAYHOUSE (6 September 1994) *The Comedy of Errors* (Shakespeare) with Robert Bathurst, Simon Poland, Paula Wilcox; director, Paul Clayton. (October) *Get Off My Foot!* (McDermott, Simpson) with Phelim McDermott, Lee Simpson, Linda Dobell; directors, McDermott, Simpson. (11 February 1995) *Twelfth Night* (Shakespeare) with Rebecca Egan, Tony Armatrading, Alexandra Mathie, Richard Durdon, Campbell Morrison; director, David Pountney. (24 February) *Better Late Than Never*, part-improvised drama with Sandi Toksvig. (25 March) *The Nose* (Gogol, adapt. Alistair Beaton) with Robert Bathurst, Phelim McDermott; director, Martin Duncan (22 April) *Enjoy* (Alan Bennett) with James Bolam, Anne Reid; director, Jeremy Sams. (20 May) *Vieux Carré* (Tennessee Williams) with Jonathan Cullen, Michael Fitzgerald, Andrew Woodall, Amanda Hillwood; director, Steven Pimlott. (15 June) *The Adventures of Pinocchio* (adapt. Peter Biddle), a co-production with Teatro Kismet

PLYMOUTH: THEATRE ROYAL (30 March 1995) *The Seagull* (Chekov) with Deborah Findlay, Kate Beckinsale, Aden Gillett; director, Robert Sturua

SCARBOROUGH: STEPHEN JOSEPH (25 October 1994) *Conversations With My Father* (Herb Gardner) with Judd Hirsch, Michael Mears, Jane Bertish; director, Alan Ayckbourn. (18 January 1995) *Oleanna* (Mamet); director, Malcolm Hebden. (20 April) *A Word from Our Sponsor* (Ayckbourn, John Pattison) with Peter Forbes, Sophie

Winter; director, Alan Ayckbourn. (June) *Misery* (Stephen King, adapt. Simon Moore); director, Stephen Hirst. (27 June) *For Services Rendered* (Somerset Maugham) with Peter Laird, Jan Carey, Will Tracey, Susannah Hitchings; director, Malcolm Hebden. (28 July) *Betrayal* (Pinter) with Mairead Carty, Simon Curry, Richard Derrington; director, Alan Ayckbourn. (8 August) *Let's Pretend* (Vanessa Brooks) with Ann Penfold, Timothy Knightley, Susannah Hitching, Cliff Howells, Jan Carey; director, Malcolm Hebden

SHEFFIELD: CRUCIBLE (October 1994) *Romeo and Juliet* (Shakespeare) with Jonathan Wrather, Nicola Buckingham; director, Michael Rudman. (March 1995) *When We Are Married* (Priestley) with Judy Flynn. (12 June) *The School for Scandal* (Sheridan) with Honor Blackman, Dora Bryan, Ian Carmichael, Dinsdale Landen; director, Richard Cottrell

SOUTHAMPTON: NUFFIELD (18 October 1994) *Dogspot* (Claire Luckham) with Lisa Harrow, Tilly Edwards. (15 November) *The Mosquito Coast* (Paul Theroux), a David Glass Ensemble production. (7 February 1995) *Dark Glory* (Steve Gooch) with Nicholas Gleaves; director, Patrick Sandford. (14 March) *And a Nightingale Sang* (C. P. Taylor); director, Patrick Sandford. (11 April) *A Voyage Round My Father* (John Mortimer) with Robert Lang, Lynn Farleigh, Mark Tandy; director, Laurence Boswell. (23 May) *A Going Concern* (Stephen Jeffreys)

STRATFORD: MEMORIAL (20 October 1994) *Measure for Measure* (Shakespeare) with Stella Gonet, Michael Feast, Alex Jennings; director, Steven Pimlott. (5 April) *Romeo and Juliet* (Shakespeare) with Lucy Whybrow, Zubin Varla; director, Adrian Noble. (21 April) *The Taming of the Shrew* (Shakespare) with Josie Lawrence, Michael Silberry; director, Gale Edwards. (5 July) *Julius Caesar* (Shakespeare) with John Nettles, Julian Glover, Hugh Quarshie, Christopher Benjamin; director, Peter Hall

SWAN (19 October 1994) *The Broken Heart* (Ford) with Iain Glen, Emma Fielding, Philip Voss; director, Michael Boyd. (4 April 1995) *The Devil is an Ass* (Jonson) with David Troughton, John Nettles; director, Matthew Warchus. (20 April) *The Relapse* (Vanbrugh) with Hugh Quarshie, Jennifer Ehle, Susan Tracy, Michael Gardiner, Victor Spinetti; director, Ian Judge. (4 July) *The Cherry Orchard* (Chekov) with Penelope Wilton, Alec McCowan, David Troughton; director, Alan Thacker. (26 August) *Bingo* (Bond) with Paul Jesson; director, David Thacker

THE OTHER PLACE (26 October 1994) *Pentecost* (David Edgar) with Jan Ravens, Charles Kay, Linal Half; director, Michael Attenborough. (6 July 1995) *The Painter of Dishonour* (Calderon) with John Carlisle, Jennifer Ehle, Douglas Henshall, Sophie Heyman, Clifford Rose; director, Laurence Boswell. (3 August) *Lord of the Flies* (Golding, adapt. Nigel Williams) with Daniel Brocklebank, Marc Elliot, Christopher Hudson; director, Elijah Moshinsky

WATFORD: PALACE (7 September) *Great Expectations* (Dickens, adapt. Mark Brickman) with Scott Ransome, Nina Jacques, Siobhan Wills; director, Mark Brickman. (22 March 1995) *Borders of Paradise* (Sharman Macdonald) with Pauline Turner, Kathy Kiera Clarke, Paul Sharma, Karl Collins, Tat Whalley, Mark Letheren, Tom Wisdom; director, Lou Stein. (30 May) *Good Morning, Bill* (P. G. Wodehouse); director, Martin Connor

THEATRE AWARD WINNERS

OLIVIER AWARDS 1995

Best Actor – David Bamber, *My Night with Reg*
Best Actress – Clare Higgins, *Sweet Bird of Youth*
Best Actor in a Musical – John Gordon Sinclair, *She Loves Me*
Best Actress in a Musical – Ruthie Henshall, *She Loves Me*
Best Director (Play) – Declan Donnellan, *As You Like It*
Best Director (Musical) – Scott Ellis, *She Loves Me*
Best Play – Arthur Miller, *Broken Glass*
Best Musical – *Once On This Island*
Best Comedy – *My Night with Reg*
Best Revival – *As You Like It*
Best Musical Revival – *She Loves Me*
Best Entertainment – Maria Friedman, *Special Arrangement*
Best Supporting Actor – Ken Stott, *Broken Glass*
Best Supporting Actress – Dora Bryan, *The Birthday Party*
Best Comedy Performance – Niall Buggy, *Dead Funny*
Best Supporting Performance in a Musical – Tracie Bennett, *She Loves Me*

REGIONAL THEATRE AWARDS 1994

Best Actor – Alan Cumming, *Hamlet* (on tour)
Best Actress – Sheila Hancock, *Gypsy* (West Yorkshire Playhouse)
Best Director – Anthony Clark, *The Atheist's Tragedy* and *The Playboy of the Western World* (Birmingham Repertory Theatre)
Overall Production – *The Man Who* (on tour)
Best New Play – *Hated Nightfall* (on tour)
Best Musical – *Assassins* (Library Theatre, Manchester)
Best Touring Production – *The Three Lives of Lucie Cabrol* (Théâtre de Complicité)
Best Show for Children/Young People – *Two Weeks With The Queen* (The Round, Scarborough)
Best Supporting Actor – Jude Akuwudike, *Poor Super Man* (Traverse Theatre, Edinburgh)
Best Supporting Actress – Matilda Ziegler, *The Lady from the Sea* (West Yorkshire Playhouse)
Most Outstanding Contribution – Renée Stephan

EVENING STANDARD AWARDS 1994

Best Actor – Tom Courtenay, *Moscow Stations*
Best Actress – Maggie Smith, *Three Tall Women*
Best Director – Sean Mathias, *Design for Living* and *Les Parents Terribles*
Best Play – *Three Tall Women*
Best Comedy – *My Night with Reg*
Most Promising Playwright – Jonathan Harvey, *Babies*
Special Award – Peter Brook

CRITICS CIRCLE AWARDS (LONDON THEATRE) 1995

Best New Play – *Dead Funny*
Best Musical – *She Loves Me*
Best Actor – Tom Courtenay, *Moscow Stations*
Best Actress – Clare Higgins, *The Children's Hour* and *Sweet Bird of Youth*
Best Director – Sean Mathias, *Design for Living* and *Les Parents Terribles*
Most Promising Playwright – Kevin Elyot, *My Night with Reg*
Most Promising Newcomer – Rachel Weisz, *Design for Living*

Weather bulletins are broadcast daily on BBC Radio 4 on 198 kHz (1515m), and on Radio 4 regional medium wave frequencies, at the following clock times: 0048, 0555, 1355, 1750.
  Stations whose latest reports are broadcast in the 5 minute forecast:

Br Bridlington
C   Channel Light-Vessel (auto)
D   Dover
F   Fife Ness
G   Greenwich Light-Vessel (auto)
J   Jersey
M   Malin Head
R   Ronaldsway
Sc Scilly (auto)
St Stornoway
Su Sumburgh
T   Tiree
V   Valentia

Weather

JULY 1994

Rainfall totals were generally well below normal, except in Northern Ireland where they were close to normal and some north-western areas where they were above normal. On the 1st thunderstorms occurred over southern England and the Midlands and five teenagers were struck by lightning at Kenilworth (Warks). Widespread rain and thunder occurred in southern areas on the 4th. Heavy rain fell in northern Scotland on the 5th and in south-west England on the 7th. Also on the 7th a severe storm flooded houses in Penmaenmawr (Gwynedd). Heavy rain fell in southern Scotland on the 10th, northern Scotland on the 11th and Northern Ireland and Scotland on the 12th. Heavy thunderstorms occurred over East Anglia and south-east England on the 13th. Rain fell in northern and western areas on the 21st and thunderstorms were widespread on the 24th, when 73.6 mm (2.9 in) of rain fell at Denstone (Staffs). On the same day 26 people were injured when lightning set an oil refinery on fire at Milford Haven (Dyfed), and a man was killed by lightning at Cranberry Rock (Shropshire). Hail caused a serious accident on the M4 near Swindon (Wilts). Widespread fog formed on the 25th. Rain or drizzle fell generally on the 26th. Heavy rain fell in northern and western areas on the 27th and heavy rain with thunder occurred in the south on the 28th. Heavy thunderstorms occurred over several areas of England and Wales on the 30th and 31st, with flooding in Scarborough (N. Yorks).

Monthly mean temperatures were above normal everywhere and it was the second hottest July in central England since 1659. The highest temperature recorded was 33.4°C (92.1°F) at Morley St Botolph (Norfolk) on the 12th and the lowest was 1.0°C (33.8°F) at Tomatin (Highland) on the 17th.

Sunshine totals were above average generally except in Northern Ireland. The highest monthly total was 292.6 hours at Levington (Suffolk) and the highest daily total was 16.0 hours at Fair Isle (Shetland) on the 18th.

AUGUST 1994

Rainfall totals were below normal in most of Scotland but near normal elsewhere. Fair Isle (Shetland) had its driest August since 1976. Heavy rain fell over southern England on the 2nd. The 3rd and 4th brought thunderstorms to many areas. A whirlwind damaged houses in Corbridge (Northumberland), a fisherman was struck by lightning at Cullercoats and many houses were flooded in the north-east. A docker was killed when a fuel dump was struck by lightning at Avonmouth (Avon), and a footballer was killed by lightning at Goole (Humberside);

99.7 mm (3.9 in) of rain fell at Capheaton (Northumberland). Rain, heavy in the south-west, occurred in southern areas on the 9th when 67 mm (2.6 in) fell at Penhalvean (Cornwall). Rain and drizzle affected most areas on the 10th, with heavy thunderstorms in the south-east. In London 80 mm (3.1 in) of rain fell in Holland Park and 47.6 mm (1.9 in) in Deptford in 16 minutes. Tube stations were closed, the Savoy Theatre evacuated and the Natural History Museum flooded. Heavy rain fell in East Anglia, the Midlands and southern England on the 11th. Lightning caused much damage in Kent. The 16th and 17th were generally wet days, and a herd of 22 cows was killed by lightning at Thetford (Norfolk). The 18th produced some heavy rain in western areas. Heavy rain fell in Northern Ireland on the 22nd and over northern England and southern Scotland on the 23rd. The 24th was generally wet and the 25th brought further rain, mainly in the south and west. On the 26th rain, heavy at times, affected south-western and northern areas. Further rain fell on the 30th in southern England. The 31st was very wet over England and Wales and 146.8 mm (5.8 in) of rain fell at Ditchingham (Norfolk). Severe flooding occurred in parts of Norfolk.

Monthly mean temperatures were generally above normal in England and Wales, near normal in Scotland and a little below normal in Northern Ireland. The highest temperature recorded was 31°C (87.8°F) at Heathrow (Greater London) on the 3rd and the lowest was −2.0°C (28.4°F) at Kielder Castle (Northumberland) on the 14th.

Sunshine totals were near normal everywhere. The highest daily total was 13.9 hours at Culdrose (Cornwall) on the 13th and the highest monthly total was 243.97 hours at Folkestone (Kent).

SEPTEMBER 1994

Rainfall totals were generally above normal in England and Wales and northern Scotland but below normal elsewhere. Heavy rain fell over England and Wales on the 1st, with severe flooding in many areas of the south-east and East Anglia. Rain, heavy at times, affected most areas on the 3rd and most of England and Wales on the 4th. On the 6th a whirlwind caused damage at Woolacombe (Devon). Thunderstorms were widespread on the 7th when a child was killed by lightning at Faversham (Kent). Thunderstorms were again widespread on the 8th when a whirlwind caused much damage in Penhros (Gwynedd). On the 11th heavy rain fell in the southern half of England and Wales. The 12th was again wet, particularly over northern England where flooding occurred at Sellafield (Cumbria). Heavy rain with thunderstorms affected much of England and Wales on the 13th. A man was killed by lightning near Dorchester (Dorset) and extensive flooding occurred in many areas, causing traffic chaos and accidents. The 14th and 15th brought further heavy rain to England and Wales; 72.5 mm (2.9 in) fell at Penkridge (Staffs) and 70 mm (2.8 in) at Wittering (Cambs) on the 14th. The 18th was wet in western areas. The 19th and 20th were wet everywhere and the 23rd brought rain to the south-west. Rain fell over many areas on the 24th and a whirlwind hit Burley-on-the-Hill (Leics). On the 25th heavy rain fell over northern and southern England and the far north of Scotland. The remainder of the month was generally wet over Scotland and Northern Ireland but mainly dry elsewhere. On the 29th 70.4 mm (2.8 in) of rain fell at Cape Wrath (Highland).

Monthly mean temperatures were below normal everywhere. The highest temperature recorded was 24.5°C (76.1°F) at Ballater (Grampian) on the 23rd and the lowest was −1.9°C (28.6°F) at Kielder Castle (Northumberland) on the 6th.

Sunshine totals were above normal in western Scotland and Northern Ireland but below normal elsewhere. The highest daily total was 12.6 hours at Kirkwall (Orkney), Cape Wrath (Highland), Leeds (W. Yorks) and Nottingham on the 2nd and the highest monthly total was 159.9 hours at Gorey Castle (Jersey).

OCTOBER 1994

Rainfall totals were below normal over Northern Ireland and most of Scotland but near or above normal over England and Wales. Nearly half the rain over England and Wales fell in the last four days of the month. Rain, heavy at times, fell in many areas on the 1st and 2nd. Snow fell over Scotland on the 3rd with rain or showers elsewhere. Heavy rain fell in the Shetlands on the 5th and 6th. Morning fog formed over much of England and Wales on the 9th. There was dense fog over north-east England and East Anglia on the 10th. Further fog, dense at times, formed morning and evening over most of the country from the 11th to the 14th. The 15th brought further fog in the south. Rain, heavy at times, fell over England, Wales and Northern Ireland on the 19th and 20th. The 21st was generally showery, with heavy rain in the Shetlands and on the south coast of England. Rain or showers fell everywhere on the 22nd, with 53.8 mm (2.1 in) at Ronaldsway (Isle of Man). Heavy rain fell over southern Scotland and north-west England on the 23rd. Rain or showers with hail at times fell over western areas on the 24th. The 25th was mainly wet everywhere and the 26th was showery with hail at times. Heavy rain fell in the south-west late on the 28th. The 29th brought heavy rain to many areas. Very heavy rain fell in the Midlands, Wales and southern England on the 30th. Many sheep were drowned in flooding in north Devon, where Weare Giffard and Taddiport were the worst affected areas. Flooding also occurred in and around Bristol, in Hurst (Berks) and in Wales, and 25 vehicles were involved in an accident on the M25 in Essex. Rail services between Taunton and

Exeter were cancelled because of flooding. At East Stoke (Dorset) 72 mm (2.8 in) of rain fell, with 85.2 mm (3.3 in) falling at Scorriton (Devon) and 40.8 mm (1.6 in) at Cilfynydd (Glamorgan).

Monthly mean temperatures were below normal over Scotland, Wales and England but near normal over Northern Ireland. The highest temperature recorded was 21.9°C (71.4°F) at Saunton Sands (Devon) and St Helier (Jersey) on the 15th and the lowest was −5.4°C (22.3°F) at Shap (Cumbria) on the 4th.

Sunshine totals were above normal over England, Wales and Northern Ireland but below normal over much of Scotland. Over England and Wales it was the sunniest October since 1959 and the second sunniest since 1909. The highest daily total was 11.1 hours at Portland (Dorset) on the 4th and the highest monthly total was 181.3 hours at Southsea (Hants).

NOVEMBER 1994

Rainfall totals were mainly normal, except for some areas of Northern Ireland where they were well below normal and southern Scotland where they were well above normal. On the 2nd rain occurred mainly in the west and the 3rd brought heavy rain to western areas and northern England. Heavy rain fell over England and Wales on the 4th and over northern England and Scotland on the 5th. The 6th was wet in northern Scotland and fog became persistent in central and north-eastern areas of England on the 7th. Heavy rain fell everywhere except Scotland on the 8th and over the whole of the UK on the 9th, when hundreds of acres of Somerset were flooded. Fog formed over southern England on the 10th with rain elsewhere. Heavy rain fell in the south-west on the 11th and almost everywhere on the 12th and 13th. Many areas of Wales were flooded as rivers burst their banks. Hundreds of sheep and some cattle were drowned in the Conway area of north Wales, and houses were flooded in Llanrwst, Betws-y-Coed, Penmachno and Blaenau Ffestiniog. On the 13th 113 mm (4.5 in) of rain fell at Yspytty Ifan (Gwynedd). Further heavy rain fell over southern England on the 14th and over western and central areas on the 17th. Rain, heavy at times, fell almost everywhere on the 18th and was heavy in northern areas on the 19th. Further heavy rain fell over northern England on the 20th. Fog formed over much of England on the 21st–22nd. Fog became widespread and freezing in central areas on the 29th. A gust of 101 knots (116 mph) was recorded at Cairngorm (Highland) on the 23rd.

Monthly mean temperatures were above normal everywhere and it was the mildest November in England since 1659. It was the warmest November on record in Scotland (1884) and in Northern Ireland (1865). The highest temperature recorded was 19.1°C (66.4°F) at the London Weather Centre on the 3rd and the lowest was −6.3°C (20.7°F) at Braemar (Grampian) on the 30th.

Sunshine totals were generally below normal except over Northern Ireland. Eskdalemuir

(Dumfries and Galloway) had its dullest November since 1910. The highest daily total was 8.7 hours at Tynemouth (Tyne and Wear) and Wyton (Cambs) on the 1st and at Scilly on the 4th. The highest monthly total was 82.2 hours at Hunstanton (Norfolk).

DECEMBER 1994

Rainfall totals were above normal everywhere except in parts of Scotland. At Paisley (Strathclyde) it was the wettest December since 1885. The 3rd was generally wet. The 4th was wet over England and Wales and the 5th was wet everywhere, with gales in the north and west. Gales continued in the north on the 6th, when there was rain and thunder in the west. Heavy showers with thunder and gales affected western areas on the 7th when a waterspout was observed in Morecambe Bay (Lancs). Gales and heavy rain spread to all areas on the 8th, with flooding in Devon and Cornwall. The Christmas tree in Trafalgar Square, London, was damaged and the Severn Bridge was closed by overturned vehicles. The 10th was another wet day with gales in the north-west, and the 11th was very wet in western Scotland. On the 10th–11th 109 mm (4.3 in) of rain fell at Glasgow (Strathclyde), the highest total there since records began in 1920. On the 10th 126 mm (5.0 in) fell at Mugdock Park (Central Scotland) and severe flooding occurred in Scotland. Heavy rain fell over most of England, Wales and Northern Ireland on the 13th. Freezing fog was slow to clear in eastern areas on the 15th. The 17th was wet in western areas, with gales in the north-west. On the 18th thunderstorms and gales affected the north-west, with some heavy rain over southern England. Freezing fog occurred in many places on the 21st and 22nd, and became persistent and widespread in the south on the 23rd. Heavy rain fell in Wales on the 24th. The 26th was very wet generally and 115 mm (4.5 in) of rain fell at Moel Cynnedd (Powys). Severe flooding occurred in parts of Wales and hundreds of sheep were drowned as the rivers Wye, Usk and Dovey burst their banks. Some railway lines, including the Derby to London line, were flooded and cross-channel ferries from Dover were cancelled because of gales. The 27th was again wet over England and Wales. The 28th was wet everywhere with gales in the south, and the 29th brought thunderstorms and gales in southern areas. There were gales in the north on the 30th. The 31st brought snow showers to many places with more prolonged snow over northern England.

Monthly mean temperatures were above normal everywhere. The highest temperature recorded was 17.7°C (63.9°F) at Penkridge (Staffs) on the 11th and the lowest was −10.7°C (12.7°F) at Westonbirt (Glos) on the 24th.

Sunshine totals were above normal everywhere except western Scotland. The highest daily total was 7.5 hours at Dunkeswell (Devon) on the 23rd and the highest monthly total was 84.0 hours at Hemsby (Norfolk).

THE YEAR 1994

Rainfall totals were generally higher than normal except over eastern Scotland. It was the wettest year over England and Wales since 1966. The year was warmer and sunnier than normal; over England and Wales it was the second warmest year since 1659. January was very wet and stormy. Floods over 1 m (3 ft) deep swept through Chichester, severe gales were frequent and damage to property and vehicles was great. Landslips occurred on the Isle of Wight. February was also wet, with heavy snowfall. Roads over the Pennines were blocked and flooding occurred in the West Country. Drifting snow caused chaos in Wales and lighting struck a gas main at Newcastle upon Tyne. March was the wettest on record over Scotland and gales were frequent. April was also wetter and windier than normal, with heavy snowfall. Flooding occurred in Wales, and ferry services were disrupted. May was another wet month over England and Wales, with frequent thunderstorms. Stornoway had the highest monthly sunshine total, 294 hours, ever recorded there. June was a month of thunderstorms, particularly on the 24th when floods and lightning damage occurred in many areas. July was the second warmest since 1659, but there were some thunderstorms and flooding. An oil refinery was struck by lightning and set on fire at Milford Haven (Dyfed). August also had severe thunderstorms, which caused considerable damage and several deaths. September was also wet, except over Northern Ireland and southern Scotland. Flooding occurred in many places, traffic accidents were numerous, and two people were killed by lightning. October was unusual in that almost half of the total rainfall fell in the last four days, causing severe flooding in many areas. It was the sunniest October since 1959 over England and Wales. November was the warmest on record over Scotland and Northern Ireland and the second warmest since 1659 over England. Flooding occurred in Somerset and large areas of Wales. December was also wet, with floods in Devon, Cornwall, Scotland and Wales and severe gales which caused widespread damage.

JANUARY 1995

Rainfall totals were above normal everywhere, with parts of north-west Scotland receiving twice the normal amount. Over England and Wales it was the wettest January since 1948. It was a very windy month which started with snow or sleet showers in many areas. The 3rd brought rain to the south-west and Northern Ireland and snow to south-west Scotland. On the 4th rain fell in the south and snow in the north. The 5th was wet with strong winds generally and gales in the north-west. Gales occurred over northern Scotland on the 8th and 9th when a gust of 114 knots (131.3 mph) was recorded at Cairngorm (Highland). Rain fell, mainly in the north, on both days and the 10th was wet everywhere. Precipitation then fell over various areas, becoming more widespread on the 15th when

67 mm (2.6 in) fell at Inverailort (Highland). The 16th was again wet, with gales in the south-west and north-east of England. The 17th was also wet and windy and a gust of 82 knots (94.4 mph) was recorded at Brixham (Devon). The west of Scotland had severe flooding and damage also occurred in the Isle of Man where a gust of 98 knots (113 mph) was recorded on Snaefell. Gales continued over Scotland and Northern Ireland on the 18th. Winds were again strong on the 19th and heavy rain in the south turned to snow in the north to give 13 cm (5 in) on the Pennines. There was traffic chaos all over the country because of the blizzards and driving rain. On the 20th there were thunderstorms in the south. The 21st brought heavy rain to many areas and the strong winds continued; 40 caravans were wrecked at Towyn and Merionnydd (Clwyd) and flooding occurred near Cardigan and Fishguard (Dyfed). The 22nd brought heavy rain to southern England and flooding occurred in Kent and West Sussex. Heavy rain fell in southern areas on the 24th. Heavy snow fell over northern England on the 25th and six people were killed. Snow continued on the 26th and 27th and there was heavy rain in the south. At Great Dun Fell (Cumbria) 80.5 mm (3.2 in) of rain fell on the 27th. Floods occurred in Wales and York station had to be closed. More heavy rain fell in the south on the 29th and in the west on the 30th and 31st. On the 31st 80 mm (3.1 in) of rain fell at Preston (Lancs) and flooding was extensive in many areas.

Monthly mean temperatures were near or above normal except in the far north of Scotland. The highest temperature recorded was 15.2°C (59.4°F) at Cardiff (S. Glam) on the 31st and the lowest was −15°C (5.0°F) at Dalwhinnie (Highland) on the 31st.

Sunshine totals were generally around normal. The highest daily total was 7.9 hours at Bristol (Avon) on the 12th and the highest monthly total was 77.2 hours at Folkestone (Kent).

FEBRUARY 1995

Rainfall totals were above normal everywhere and areas of central Scotland received two and a half times the normal amount. The 1st was wet in the south and the 2nd was wet in Scotland. Scattered rain then fell over many areas until the 7th when it was generally wet. The 8th and 9th were wet over England and Wales with snow in some places. The 10th was generally wet while the 11th was very wet and windy with heavy rain in many places; 49.5 mm (1.95 in) fell at Nantmor (Gwynedd). On the 12th flooding occurred in Devon. The 13th and 14th brought further heavy rain to all areas, with gales over Northern Ireland and Scotland. Thunderstorms occurred in many places on the 15th with gales in western areas. Hailstones caused some damage in Pembrokeshire. Gales continued on the 16th with heavy rain and thunder over England and Wales. Flooding caused much damage in south Wales where a gust of 72 knots (82.9 mph) was recorded. A gust of 71 knots (81.8 mph) was

recorded in Devon. Scattered thunderstorms occurred on the 17th and the River Severn burst its banks, flooding many homes. The main railway line was closed by fallen cables near Rugby. The 18th was wet and windy and a tornado damaged three houses at Bolton (Lancs). Heavy rain fell over England and Wales on the 19th and 20th. On the 21st another tornado damaged property in Bolton. The 22nd was generally wet with thunderstorms, hail and snow in many areas and gales were severe at times. Flooding occurred in North Wales and northern England. Gusts of 70 knots (80 mph) and heavy, drifting snow caused chaos in the Scottish mountains. The 23rd was wet over southern England, scattered rain or showers fell on the 24th to 26th, and the 27th was wet generally, with 59 mm (2.32 in) of rain falling at Black Mount (Strathclyde). The 28th was very wet over Scotland and Northern Ireland, with gales in the west.

Monthly mean temperatures were above normal everywhere. The highest temperature recorded was 15.1°C (59.2°F) at Dyce (Grampian) on the 6th and the lowest was −13.2°C (8.2°F) at Keith (Grampian) on the 10th.

Sunshine totals were near or above normal over England and Wales, below normal over Northern Ireland and western Scotland and above normal over eastern Scotland. The highest daily total was 10.1 hours at Bognor Regis (W. Sussex) on the 26th and the highest monthly total was 124 hours at Dyce (Grampian).

MARCH 1995

Rainfall totals were above normal over Scotland and Northern Ireland but below normal over England and Wales. The 1st brought wintry showers generally, with thunderstorms in places, and snow fell over much of the country on the 2nd, causing chaos on the roads. The 3rd brought snow to the south-west and eastern England and the 4th brought rain in the south and snow in the north. The 7th was wet in the south and flooding occurred in Suffolk, Essex and Surrey. In Brighton (E. Sussex) 50 mm (2 in) of snow fell and most south coast rail services were cancelled. The 9th, 10th and 11th brought rain to many areas. Fog affected much of England on the 13th. There were thunderstorms in the south on the 15th while the 16th was wet in western areas. The 17th brought wintry showers everywhere with gale-force winds. A gust of 84 knots (97 mph) was recorded at Cardiff (S. Glam). A gust of 76 knots (87.5 mph) was recorded in Lincolnshire and a boy was killed by a falling tree in West Sussex. The Severn Bridge was closed and many roads were blocked. The 19th was very windy over northern Scotland. Rain fell over northern Scotland on the 21st. The 23rd was wet over Northern Ireland and north-west Scotland, and the 24th was wet over Northern Ireland and Scotland. The 26th was generally wet, with snow in northern areas; 63 mm (2.48 in) of rain fell at Cassley (Highland). The 28th brought heavy snow to many areas, causing a spate of accidents. Rain fall over northern areas on the 30th.

Monthly mean temperatures were mainly below normal over Scotland and Northern Ireland and near normal over England and Wales. The highest temperature recorded was 18.8°C (65.84°F) at Hawarden Bridge (Clwyd) on the 23rd and the lowest was −14.0°C (6.8°F) at Black Mount (Strathclyde) on the 4th.

Sunshine totals were below normal over Northern Ireland and western Scotland but above normal elsewhere. The highest daily total was 12.1 hours at Weymouth (Dorset) on the 29th and the highest monthly total was 215.5 hours at Southend (Essex).

April 1995

Rainfall totals were well below normal, except in the far north of Scotland where they were above normal. Cape Wrath (Sutherland) received nearly 50 mm (2 in) of rain in the first three days of the month. Rain fell in eastern England and northern areas on the 9th. From the 10th to the 15th there was a long spell of sunshine. On the 16th 94 mm (3.7 in) of rain fell at Lentran (Highland). The 17th was wet almost everywhere with snow over Scotland. The 18th brought snow, quite heavy at times, to northern England, north Wales, Scotland and Northern Ireland, with rain elsewhere and thunderstorms in places. Two people were killed in accidents on icy roads near Sunderland (Tyne and Wear). The 19th and 20th brought further snow showers to many places, with thunderstorms at times, and the 22nd was wet everywhere. The 23rd was wet over southern England, Northern Ireland and Scotland, and the 24th was mostly wet. Thunderstorms occurred over southern England on the 26th and rain fell in western areas on the 29th.

Monthly mean temperatures were above normal everywhere except northern and western Scotland, but there were some very cold days everywhere. The highest temperature recorded was 22.1°C (71.8°F) at Malvern (Worcs) on the 25th and the lowest was −10.0°C (14.0°F) at Loch Venachar (Central Scotland) on the 22nd.

Sunshine totals were above normal everywhere except northern Scotland. The highest daily total was 13.8 hours at Saunton Sands (Devon) on the 21st and the highest monthly total was 207 hours at Teignmouth (Devon).

May 1995

Rainfall totals were generally below or near normal except in the far north of Scotland. Rain fell over Scotland on the 1st and 2nd, and there was rain in Scotland and Northern Ireland on the 6th and 7th and over northern England and Scotland on the 8th and 9th. Rain fell over southern Wales and south-west England on the 11th. The 14th brought rain to northern areas and the 16th and 17th were wet over England and Wales. On the 16th 40 mm (1.57 in) of rain fell at Moel-y-Crio (Clwyd) and on the 17th 50 mm (2 in) of snow fell over the Pennines and the

river Wye burst its banks. The 19th was wet over East Anglia. Rain fell in Scotland and Northern Ireland on the 21st and 22nd. The 23rd brought more general rain, heavy at times, with thunderstorms in the Midlands and northern England. Rain fell in the west and north on the 26th and 27th and more generally on the 28th.

Monthly mean temperatures were around normal almost everywhere in spite of a brief spell early in the month when temperatures of 22–25°C (72–77°F) were commonplace. The highest temperature recorded was 28.4°C (83.1°F) at Southampton (Hants) on the 6th and the lowest was −5.5°C (22.1°F) at Tomatin (Highland) on the 15th.

Sunshine totals were around normal in most areas. The highest daily total was 14.9 hours at Teignmouth (Devon) on the 13th and the highest monthly total was 301.3 hours at Gorey Castle (Jersey).

June 1995

Rainfall totals were below normal everywhere except in a small area of north-east Scotland. Rain, heavy at times, fell in most areas on the 3rd when flash floods occurred in Tayside. From the 6th to the 12th rain, showers or drizzle fell in many areas. The 16th and 17th brought rain to all areas, and heavy rain fell over Northern Ireland, north Wales and south-west Scotland on the 19th, when 32.5 mm (1.4 in) fell at Hillsborough (Co. Down). Further rain fell in many areas on the 20th. Drizzle occurred in many places on the 24th to 26th, but the rest of the month was mostly dry, with patches of fog at times.

Monthly mean temperatures were mostly around normal; most of the month was cool and most of the hot days were in the last week. The temperature reached 31.5°C (88.7°F) at Greenock (Strathclyde) on the 28th and 30.0°C (86.0°F) in Belfast on the 29th. The highest temperature recorded was 33.8°C (92.8°F) at Barbourne (Worcs) on the 30th and the lowest was −0.7°C (30.7°F) at Loch Glascarnoch (Highland) on the 12th.

Sunshine totals were mostly well above normal. Glasgow (Strathclyde) had its sunniest June since 1920. The highest daily total was 16.9 hours at Lerwick (Shetland) and Fair Isle on the 25th and the highest monthly total was 286.5 hours at Teignmouth (Devon).

Source: Prepared from data provided by the Met Office

AVERAGE AND GENERAL VALUES 1993–5 (June)

	Rainfall (mm)				Temperature (°C)				Bright Sunshine (hrs per day)			
	Average 1961–90	1993	1994	1995	Average 1961–90	1993	1994	1995	Average 1961–90	1993	1994	1995
ENGLAND AND WALES												
January	77	113	123	161	3.8	5.9	5.2	4.8	1.6	1.2	2.1	1.6
February	55	16	82	114	3.8	4.8	3.3	6.5	2.3	1.8	2.3	2.7
March	63	26	96	64	5.6	6.5	7.5	5.5	3.5	3.7	3.7	5.2
April	53	94	74	27	7.7	9.3	8.1	8.9	4.9	4.1	5.8	5.9
May	56	90	62	48	10.9	11.4	10.6	11.6	6.2	5.7	5.1	6.8
June	58	66	36	n/a	13.9	14.7	14.3	n/a	6.4	6.6	7.1	n/a
July	56	83	47	–	15.7	15.1	17.6	–	6.0	5.6	7.2	–
August	68	55	72	–	15.6	14.5	15.9	–	5.7	6.5	5.6	–
September	70	113	106	–	13.6	12.5	12.8	–	4.5	3.5	3.8	–
October	77	89	79	–	10.7	8.6	10.4	–	3.2	3.6	3.9	–
November	81	74	86	–	6.6	4.9	10.0	–	2.2	1.9	1.5	–
December	82	167	142	–	4.7	5.4	6.6	–	1.5	1.4	1.7	–
YEAR	796	986	1023	–	9.4	9.5	10.2	–	4.0	3.8	4.1	–
SCOTLAND												
January	117	306	215	227	3.1	4.2	3.4	2.9	1.3	0.9	1.1	1.3
February	78	67	96	207	3.1	5.6	2.3	3.9	2.3	1.3	2.2	2.4
March	94	120	250	147	4.6	5.4	4.8	3.6	3.2	3.3	3.1	3.4
April	60	116	133	67	6.5	7.5	6.4	7.0	4.8	3.6	4.5	4.3
May	67	111	29	85	9.3	9.2	8.7	9.4	5.6	4.5	7.1	5.9
June	67	72	110	n/a	12.1	12.3	11.8	n/a	5.6	3.9	4.8	n/a
July	74	113	67	–	13.6	12.7	14.7	–	4.9	3.7	5.1	–
August	92	74	101	–	13.5	12.4	13.3	–	4.6	4.0	4.4	–
September	111	76	103	–	11.5	10.9	10.9	–	3.5	3.8	3.8	–
October	120	118	110	–	9.1	7.0	8.5	–	2.6	2.6	2.6	–
November	118	76	156	–	5.3	4.3	8.5	–	1.7	2.1	1.4	–
December	116	232	245	–	3.9	2.8	4.8	–	1.0	0.9	1.2	–
YEAR	1114	1481	1615	–	7.9	7.9	8.2	–	3.4	2.9	3.4	–

Source: data provided by the Met Office

WEATHER RECORDS

WORLD RECORDS

Maximum air temperature   57.8°C/136°F
  San Louis, Mexico, 11 August 1933
Minimum air temperature   −89.2°C/−128.56°F
  Vostok, Antarctica, 21 July 1983
Greatest rainfall in one day   1870 mm/73.62 in
  Cilaos, Isle de Réunion, 16 March 1952
Greatest rainfall in one calendar month 9300 mm/366.14 in
  Cherrapunji, Assam, July 1861
Greatest annual rainfall total   22,990 mm/905.12 in
  Cherrapunji, Assam, 1861
Fastest gust of wind   201 knots/231 mph
  Mt Washington Observatory, USA, 12 April 1934

UNITED KINGDOM RECORDS

Maximum air temperature   37.1°C/98.8°F
  Cheltenham, Glos, 3 August 1990
Minimum air temperature   −27.2°C/−17°F
  Braemar, Grampian, 11 February 1895 and 10 January 1982
Greatest rainfall in one day   280 mm/11 in
  Martinstown, Dorset, 18 July 1955
Greatest annual rainfall total   6528 mm/257 in
  Sprinkling Tarn, Cumbria, 1954
Fastest gust of wind   150 knots/173 mph
  Cairngorm, Highland, 20 March 1986
Fastest low-level gust*   123 knots/141.7 mph
  Fraserburgh, Grampian, 13 February 1989
Highest mean hourly speed   92 knots/106 mph
  Great Dun Fell, Cumbria, December 1974
Highest low-level mean hourly speed*   72 knots/83 mph
  Shoreham-by-Sea, Sussex, 16 October 1987

* below 200 m/656 ft

WIND FORCE MEASURES

The *Beaufort Scale* of wind force has been accepted internationally and is used in communicating weather conditions. Devised originally by Admiral Sir Francis Beaufort in 1805, it now consists of the numbers 0–17, each representing a certain strength or velocity of wind at 10 m (33 ft) above ground in the open.

Scale no.	Wind Force	mph	knots
0	Calm	1	1
1	Light air	1–3	1–3
2	Slight breeze	4–7	4–6
3	Gentle breeze	8–12	7–10
4	Moderate breeze	13–18	11–16
5	Fresh breeze	19–24	17–21
6	Strong breeze	25–31	22–27
7	High wind	32–38	28–33
8	Gale	39–46	34–40
9	Strong gale	47–54	41–47
10	Whole gale	55–63	48–55
11	Storm	64–72	56–63
12	Hurricane	73–82	64–71
13	–	83–92	72–80
14	–	93–103	81–89
15	–	104–114	90–99
16	–	115–125	100–108
17	–	126–136	109–118

TEMPERATURE, RAINFALL AND SUNSHINE
At selected climatological reporting stations, July 1994–June 1995 and calendar year 1994

	Ht m	July 1994 °C	July 1994 Rain mm	July 1994 Sun hrs	August 1994 °C	August 1994 Rain mm	August 1994 Sun hrs	September 1994 °C	September 1994 Rain mm	September 1994 Sun hrs	October 1994 °C	October 1994 Rain mm	October 1994 Sun hrs
Abbotsinch (Glasgow)	5	15.5	63	5.2	13.9	129	5.3	11.4	53	4.0	9.1	60	2.4
Aberporth	134	15.5	55	6.7	14.8	80	6.0	12.4	116	3.6	11.1	92	4.6
Aldergrove	68	15.4	60	4.2	14.3	106	3.9	11.9	58	4.0	9.9	45	3.4
Aspatria	61	15.9	63	6.5	14.3	65	5.2	11.4	60	4.1	9.2	84	3.0
Auchincruive	48	15.3	70	5.4	13.8	91	4.9	11.5	68	3.7	9.5	57	2.5
Bala	163	14.9	45	6.0	13.5	74	4.0	11.2	135	3.2	9.3	96	3.3
Boulmer	23	15.0	19	5.4	13.9	94	5.4	11.6	56	3.5	9.4	52	4.0
Bradford	134	17.1	43	5.6	14.8	56	4.7	11.5	92	3.4	9.5	80	2.9
Braemar	339	13.9	32	5.1	12.4	42	4.6	9.4	72	3.3	6.7	83	–
Bristol	42	19.1	40	7.7	17.1	75	5.3	13.9	104	4.0	11.7	104	4.8
Bude	15	16.3	48	5.9	16.1	89	5.6	13.7	105	4.0	11.7	127	5.4
Buxton	307	16.1	51	7.0	13.7	65	5.6	10.5	164	3.6	8.0	179	3.2
Cambridge	24	19.5	23	7.2	17.5	36	5.7	13.3	72	3.4	10.9	75	3.5
Cheltenham	65	19.9	33	–	16.9	106	–	12.9	122	–	11.3	95	–
Clacton-on-Sea	16	18.8	55	8.9	17.7	74	6.5	14.2	63	4.0	11.2	67	3.9
Cleethorpes	23	17.9	55	8.5	16.3	49	7.4	12.9	94	4.1	10.0	42	3.5
Dundee	45	15.6	28	5.7	14.6	30	5.5	12.2	32	3.9	9.3	56	3.2
Durham	102	15.9	44	5.9	14.2	49	4.5	11.5	69	3.9	8.8	59	3.2
Dyce (Aberdeen)	65	15.3	35	6.0	13.9	35	4.8	11.8	65	3.9	8.4	62	3.3
East Malling	33	19.3	33	8.3	17.5	74	6.1	13.7	73	3.7	10.7	96	4.4
Edinburgh	26	15.5	39	5.5	14.3	34	5.0	12.0	33	3.5	9.2	60	3.2
Elmdon (Birmingham)	98	18.0	37	7.4	15.8	48	6.1	12.5	113	3.8	9.6	62	3.8
Eskdalemuir	242	14.1	114	4.9	12.2	141	2.9	9.8	69	3.0	7.5	88	2.3
Hastings	45	18.7	67	8.7	17.7	51	5.7	14.5	87	4.5	11.8	126	5.0
Heathrow (London)	25	20.7	17	8.6	18.3	32	5.8	14.3	86	3.7	11.5	76	4.5
Hurn (Bournemouth)	10	18.1	23	8.7	16.9	42	6.3	13.5	84	4.8	10.6	134	5.5
Inverness	4	15.9	26	5.0	14.3	80	4.2	11.5	46	4.1	8.9	40	2.5
Isle of Portland	53	17.2	17	8.5	17.1	39	6.5	14.1	67	4.7	12.3	83	5.0
Leeming	32	17.5	37	6.0	15.3	49	4.9	12.2	70	3.8	9.5	62	2.6
Lerwick	82	12.5	25	4.7	12.0	86	4.7	9.7	141	4.1	7.2	109	2.5
Long Sutton	145	18.5	12	7.0	–	38	5.0	13.1	72	3.3	10.4	120	4.4
Lowestoft	25	18.7	45	8.0	17.4	60	7.0	14.1	45	4.1	10.7	75	4.0
Manston	44	19.5	33	8.9	17.9	72	7.0	13.8	53	4.2	10.7	77	4.4
Morecambe	7	17.2	49	7.0	15.6	166	4.9	12.7	128	4.3	10.4	81	3.6
Oxford	63	19.3	54	8.0	17.1	53	6.2	13.5	63	3.8	10.5	67	4.4
Penzance	19	16.8	65	6.1	–	118	–	–	107	–	12.5	107	4.7
Plymouth	27	17.1	41	7.2	16.5	95	5.9	13.7	118	4.1	11.9	126	5.4
Presteigne	175	16.5	31	7.8	14.5	55	5.3	11.6	123	3.7	8.8	87	3.7
Rhoose	65	17.3	62	7.9	15.9	83	5.7	13.3	102	4.0	10.8	142	4.7
Ringway (Manchester)	75	17.7	71	7.2	15.5	44	5.3	12.3	115	3.9	10.1	125	3.5
Ronaldsway	16	14.6	73	6.7	14.5	72	5.7	12.5	71	4.4	10.9	99	3.9
Rustington	3	18.1	31	9.4	17.1	55	6.9	13.8	87	4.6	11.1	109	5.5
St. Mawgan	103	16.4	39	6.3	16.0	86	5.4	13.4	110	4.5	12.0	145	5.5
Shawbury	72	17.1	46	7.5	15.5	41	5.3	12.3	103	3.4	9.7	49	3.5
Sheffield	131	18.1	33	6.7	15.7	45	5.9	12.3	148	3.5	9.5	58	2.3
Skegness	5	17.9	62	8.5	16.6	48	6.9	13.2	63	4.1	10.1	51	3.4
Stornoway	15	13.6	49	4.7	12.5	105	3.5	10.8	131	4.0	8.8	64	2.5
Tenby	5	15.7	64	6.2	15.3	112	5.7	13.1	107	4.1	–	133	–
Terrington St Clement	2	18.9	48	7.7	16.7	47	5.8	13.4	94	3.9	10.1	68	3.6
Tiree	9	14.0	83	4.6	13.2	73	5.8	11.9	98	4.8	10.1	105	2.5
Torquay	8	17.2	21	8.0	17.1	86	6.2	14.1	85	3.9	12.1	118	4.5
Valley	10	15.7	46	7.0	15.3	80	5.3	13.1	82	4.3	11.5	64	4.7
Ventnor	135	18.3	13	9.4	17.5	50	7.0	14.3	79	4.7	12.7	103	5.7
Waddington	68	18.6	54	7.5	16.2	58	6.2	12.8	101	3.9	9.5	49	3.2
Watnall (Nottingham)	117	18.5	34	7.3	16.1	56	5.9	12.3	121	3.5	9.5	53	3.1
Whitby	41	16.9	37	6.8	15.3	36	5.1	12.3	78	3.6	9.7	41	3.1

Ht   height (in metres) of station above mean sea level
°C   mean air temperature
Rain   total monthly rainfall
Sun   mean daily bright sunshine (hours)
Source: data provided by the Met Office

	November 1994			December 1994			The Year 1994			January 1995			February 1995		
	°C	Rain mm	Sun hrs	°C	Rain mm	Sun hrs	°C	Rain mm	Sun hrs	°C	Rain mm	Sun hrs	°C	Rain mm	Sun hrs
Abbotsinch (Glasgow)	9.3	130	1.5	5.3	237	0.9	8.8	1261	3.5	3.5	159	2.0	4.7	160	2.5
Aberporth	10.5	100	1.5	7.5	157	1.7	10.0	1052	4.1	5.9	146	1.2	6.8	109	1.6
Aldergrove	9.3	67	1.9	5.8	101	1.6	9.1	879	3.3	4.1	85	1.3	5.3	96	2.2
Aspatria	9.6	113	1.5	6.1	195	1.1	9.0	1058	3.8	3.7	143	1.5	5.3	116	2.2
Auchincruive	9.7	119	1.5	6.0	190	1.1	9.0	–	3.3	3.9	112	1.6	5.4	113	2.1
Bala	9.5	127	1.1	6.3	211	0.8	8.9	1302	3.2	4.5	237	0.9	5.9	204	1.2
Boulmer	8.9	79	2.7	5.3	32	2.0	8.9	606	4.5	3.7	64	2.3	5.5	59	4.1
Bradford	8.8	120	1.7	5.9	148	1.6	9.4	968	3.4	–	141	1.6	5.6	123	2.8
Braemar	6.6	69	0.9	3.1	88	1.1	–	–	–	0.9	155	0.9	1.7	84	2.3
Bristol	11.7	76	0.9	8.0	183	1.4	11.6	1044	–	6.5	172	1.6	8.0	105	2.0
Bude	11.8	87	1.0	8.9	141	1.8	11.1	1081	4.2	7.3	179	1.1	8.3	106	1.7
Buxton	8.0	113	1.3	4.9	181	1.5	8.2	1477	3.6	2.7	257	1.3	4.4	162	2.5
Cambridge	9.8	27	1.2	–	42	2.1	–	547	4.1	–	87	1.8	6.5	63	3.0
Cheltenham	10.9	69	–	7.1	131	–	11.2	1024	–	5.7	135	–	7.6	108	–
Clacton-on-Sea	11.0	21	1.6	7.2	56	2.7	10.9	613	4.5	4.9	101	2.0	6.5	73	2.9
Cleethorpes	10.1	31	2.1	5.9	68	2.4	–	–	–	3.9	79	1.9	6.3	41	3.6
Dundee	8.7	81	2.0	5.0	54	2.3	9.0	–	–	3.2	63	2.0	4.5	92	–
Durham	8.3	62	2.0	5.3	67	1.9	8.8	612	4.0	3.3	75	1.9	5.5	62	3.3
Dyce (Aberdeen)	8.1	103	2.1	4.9	72	1.9	8.5	773	4.3	2.9	89	1.3	4.3	48	4.4
East Malling	10.7	29	1.4	6.8	89	2.0	11.0	752	–	5.3	141	1.9	7.7	66	2.9
Edinburgh	9.5	77	2.1	5.1	94	2.0	9.1	–	4.0	3.5	78	2.1	4.8	67	3.4
Elmdon (Birmingham)	9.4	67	1.6	6.0	116	2.0	10.0	778	4.3	4.4	105	1.9	6.2	64	2.7
Eskdalemuir	7.3	224	0.7	3.8	318	1.0	7.2	1837	2.9	1.5	258	1.4	3.3	221	1.6
Hastings	11.5	50	1.4	7.9	110	2.0	11.3	899	4.8	5.7	137	2.3	7.7	95	3.2
Heathrow (London)	11.0	43	1.4	7.3	63	2.0	11.7	631	4.6	5.5	114	1.9	7.5	72	2.5
Hurn (Bournemouth)	11.1	99	1.0	7.0	109	2.0	10.7	955	4.8	5.5	166	1.6	7.6	125	2.4
Inverness	8.9	67	1.3	5.4	110	1.4	9.0	–	3.5	3.8	98	1.1	4.3	85	2.6
Isle of Portland	12.1	73	1.0	9.3	78	2.0	–	828	4.7	7.2	122	–	–	105	–
Leeming	8.8	72	1.9	5.5	86	2.0	9.6	616	3.9	3.7	92	1.8	6.1	57	3.5
Lerwick	7.1	141	1.0	4.3	210	0.4	6.9	1458	3.4	2.9	165	0.8	2.5	133	3.1
Long Sutton	10.1	76	1.0	6.5	127	2.0	–	778	4.0	4.7	157	1.7	–	113	2.2
Lowestoft	10.1	21	1.8	6.7	52	2.0	10.7	554	4.4	4.7	98	1.6	6.2	70	3.6
Manston	10.5	18	1.7	6.9	58	2.1	11.0	570	4.0	5.1	94	2.1	7.2	53	3.0
Morecambe	10.0	129	1.7	6.5	166	1.1	10.0	1208	3.7	4.7	161	1.4	6.2	126	2.3
Oxford	10.5	56	1.6	6.7	75	2.2	11.0	704	4.6	5.5	116	2.0	7.4	66	2.7
Penzance	12.1	92	1.4	9.7	166	1.8	–	1294	–	8.3	208	1.3	9.1	125	2.5
Plymouth	11.5	117	1.1	8.7	139	1.9	11.3	1250	–	7.1	168	1.4	8.3	118	2.3
Presteigne	9.1	98	1.0	5.6	186	1.8	9.2	1038	4.3	4.1	176	1.9	5.8	122	2.6
Rhoose	11.0	123	1.1	7.6	148	1.6	10.6	1274	4.4	5.9	172	1.6	7.1	109	1.5
Ringway (Manchester)	10.0	93	1.9	6.0	112	1.5	9.9	924	3.9	4.5	137	1.8	6.1	97	2.4
Ronaldsway	10.7	85	1.8	8.1	101	1.6	9.9	887	4.0	5.7	115	1.1	6.9	97	2.4
Rustington	11.3	90	1.3	7.5	115	2.2	10.9	917	5.1	5.7	178	2.1	7.7	105	2.9
St. Mawgan	11.3	118	1.2	8.8	153	2.0	11.0	1245	4.4	7.1	186	1.2	7.9	123	2.1
Shawbury	9.5	59	1.6	5.9	96	1.6	9.7	678	4.0	4.4	105	1.7	6.2	92	2.8
Sheffield	9.3	103	1.2	6.3	104	1.0	9.9	905	3.7	4.1	158	1.1	6.2	99	2.3
Skegness	9.7	28	2.1	6.1	61	2.5	–	603	4.6	4.5	86	2.1	6.1	52	3.3
Stornoway	8.8	121	1.5	5.5	190	0.9	8.2	1288	3.5	3.9	212	1.0	3.9	155	2.1
Tenby	10.9	117	1.1	7.7	206	1.0	–	1346	–	6.4	182	1.3	–	–	–
Terrington St Clement	9.5	21	2.0	5.9	49	2.2	10.4	615	4.2	4.3	91	1.9	6.3	51	3.1
Tiree	10.2	133	1.4	6.8	205	0.8	9.1	1351	3.6	5.1	183	1.2	5.3	145	2.7
Torquay	11.6	103	1.1	8.9	168	2.2	11.8	1118	4.7	7.3	187	1.6	8.5	158	2.4
Valley	10.9	83	1.7	8.0	126	1.7	10.4	907	4.2	5.9	136	1.1	7.0	97	2.1
Ventnor	11.9	78	1.4	8.9	100	2.3	11.6	882	5.1	6.3	140	1.8	7.9	118	2.9
Waddington	9.1	44	2.1	5.8	63	2.1	10.0	615	4.4	4.0	82	2.0	6.1	53	3.1
*Watnall (Nottingham)	9.3	79	1.7	5.7	103	1.8	9.9	765	4.1	4.7	105	1.9	6.5	55	2.6
Whitby	9.3	51	2.7	6.1	96	1.9	9.7	606	4.3	4.1	91	1.5	6.1	47	3.7

*From Jan. 1995 Watnall is replaced by Sutton Bonington (ht 48 m)

TEMPERATURE, RAINFALL AND SUNSHINE *contd.*

	March 1995			April 1995			May 1995			June 1995		
	°C	Rain mm	Sun hrs	°C	Rain mm	Sun hrs	°C	Rain mm	Sun hrs	°C	Rain mm	Sun hrs
Abbotsinch (Glasgow)	4.3	98	3.6	8.3	35	5.4	10.5	62	5.3	14.0	23	9.3
Aberporth	5.5	65	4.8	8.1	27	6.1	10.9	50	6.6	13.5	13	8.7
Aldergrove	4.5	76	2.9	8.5	22	5.5	10.7	47	5.4	13.9	32	8.0
Aspatria	4.5	91	3.3	7.9	18	6.5	10.8	51	7.1	13.5	31	8.3
Auchincruive	4.5	115	3.1	7.9	38	–	10.3	50	–	13.5	21	–
Bala	4.4	90	3.6	7.7	26	5.8	9.7	73	4.7	12.3	16	7.3
Boulmer	4.5	34	4.9	7.7	44	6.0	9.7	47	7.1	11.8	33	6.6
Bradford	4.7	75	4.5	8.1	28	5.7	10.9	56	–	13.5	11	5.7
Braemar	1.3	65	3.8	5.3	–	–	8.0	–	5.5	11.9	–	8.2
Bristol	6.7	70	5.3	10.1	30	5.5	13.1	61	7.6	15.9	12	7.3
Bude	6.5	83	4.3	8.7	52	5.9	11.4	50	7.7	14.5	16	8.6
Buxton	3.5	113	4.6	7.1	41	5.7	9.9	67	6.3	12.2	36	6.3
Cambridge	5.7	51	6.0	9.2	10	5.4	12.1	24	6.5	14.0	17	5.3
Cheltenham	6.7	37	–	10.2	36	–	13.5	49	–	16.3	27	–
Clacton-on-Sea	6.3	69	6.1	9.9	20	5.5	12.7	27	7.3	14.3	28	5.8
Cleethorpes	5.6	48	5.8	8.3	16	6.1	11.1	39	7.5	–	–	–
Dundee	4.7	27	4.8	8.4	33	–	10.4	–	–	13.7	31	–
Durham	4.5	39	5.2	7.9	27	5.8	10.5	31	6.0	12.7	16	5.8
Dyce (Aberdeen)	4.3	56	4.9	6.9	56	4.3	9.3	60	6.8	12.0	48	6.6
East Malling	6.5	55	6.1	10.0	8	5.9	12.3	20	7.5	14.9	19	6.3
Edinburgh	4.7	–	4.5	8.1	21	5.4	10.5	–	6.1	13.4	24	7.6
Elmdon (Birmingham)	5.1	50	5.3	8.9	13	6.4	11.5	36	6.7	14.5	9	7.1
Eskdalemuir	2.1	173	2.7	6.3	45	4.7	8.9	93	5.5	12.9	52	7.6
Hastings	6.5	59	6.4	9.6	15	6.3	12.7	20	8.4	14.5	27	7.3
Heathrow (London)	6.6	49	6.3	10.5	17	6.7	13.6	30	7.6	15.8	11	6.3
Hurn (Bournemouth)	5.7	41	5.8	9.1	28	5.6	11.8	25	8.4	15.3	7	8.0
Inverness	4.3	42	3.7	7.5	41	3.4	10.9	–	5.4	13.2	28	4.4
Isle of Portland	7.1	31	–	–	–	–	–	–	–	–	–	–
Leeming	4.9	47	5.1	8.3	27	5.7	11.5	34	6.3	13.3	17	6.3
Lerwick	2.9	154	3.4	4.9	63	4.2	6.9	31	5.0	10.1	34	6.1
Long Sutton	5.7	55	6.2	9.3	20	6.2	12.1	21	7.4	14.4	7	5.6
Lowestoft	5.9	55	5.8	9.3	18	6.2	11.8	19	7.5	13.3	43	5.1
Manston	6.1	41	6.2	9.3	18	5.8	12.3	19	8.1	14.1	27	5.9
Morecambe	5.0	86	3.7	8.9	17	6.3	11.9	69	6.9	14.7	35	8.1
Oxford	6.3	49	6.4	9.9	19	6.3	12.8	54	7.5	15.1	7	6.5
Penzance	–	95	–	9.7	41	5.7	11.8	39	7.3	15.6	21	7.9
Plymouth	6.9	64	4.9	9.5	29	6.0	11.9	36	7.8	15.3	15	7.3
Presteigne	4.5	80	5.2	8.5	24	6.6	10.2	61	6.1	13.5	7	8.2
Rhoose	5.9	53	4.9	9.1	23	6.2	11.7	52	8.0	14.9	14	8.6
Ringway (Manchester)	5.2	65	4.4	9.1	24	5.8	11.7	45	6.4	14.5	28	7.2
Ronaldsway	6.0	41	3.6	8.6	18	6.2	10.5	58	5.6	13.7	16	9.1
Rustington	6.0	56	6.3	9.4	12	6.5	11.9	13	9.3	14.7	16	8.4
St. Mawgan	6.7	86	4.7	8.8	40	5.8	11.7	31	7.7	14.5	24	8.4
Shawbury	5.1	44	5.2	8.7	19	6.5	11.1	56	6.2	13.9	13	7.8
Sheffield	5.5	64	5.6	9.1	25	5.7	12.1	48	6.6	14.0	11	6.1
Skegness	5.2	52	5.6	8.5	13	6.0	12.0	34	6.5	12.7	20	5.6
Stornoway	3.7	135	2.9	6.5	65	3.2	8.5	60	5.0	11.3	27	6.5
Sutton Bonington	5.5	35	5.2	8.9	13	5.7	11.7	23	5.8	14.3	12	4.3
Tenby	5.9	55	4.7	8.9	28	6.3	10.7	42	7.1	14.1	15	8.2
Terrington St Clement	5.5	46	5.7	8.7	12	5.3	12.1	25	6.7	13.3	17	5.4
Tiree	4.8	156	2.8	7.5	41	4.4	9.4	65	6.9	12.2	28	8.3
Torquay	7.1	56	5.1	10.0	39	6.9	12.3	60	8.1	15.7	6	8.9
Valley	6.3	49	3.8	8.8	21	6.1	11.7	42	6.7	14.1	18	8.5
Ventnor	7.3	49	6.7	10.0	25	6.5	13.1	26	8.9	15.1	11	8.9
Waddington	5.1	31	5.9	8.8	12	5.5	11.7	44	6.4	13.6	18	6.1
Whitby	5.3	31	5.6	8.2	27	6.2	11.1	37	–	12.2	34	–

METEOROLOGICAL OBSERVATIONS London (Heathrow)

Temperature maxima and minima cover the 24-hour period 9–9 h; mean wind speed is 10 metres above the ground; rainfall is for the 24 hours starting at 9 h on the day of entry; sunshine is for the 24 hours 0–24 h; averages are for the period 1961–90
Source: data provided by the Met Office

JULY 1994

		Temperature Max. °C	Min. °C	Wind knots	Rain mm	Sun hrs
Day	1	26.6	12.8	8.4	Trace	10.7
	2	27.6	18.2	3.6	0.0	4.7
	3	28.0	14.8	2.4	4.0	9.8
	4	24.4	16.7	5.9	Trace	7.0
	5	22.5	12.1	5.5	0.1	7.4
	6	21.4	12.3	5.8	8.0	3.3
	7	22.4	11.9	4.2	1.7	11.2
	8	18.3	14.0	3.3	Trace	0.0
	9	25.0	14.0	4.5	0.0	10.1
	10	26.6	12.2	5.4	0.0	14.7
	11	30.0	13.3	3.9	0.0	15.0
	12	33.1	17.4	4.5	0.4	13.1
	13	23.4	17.4	3.4	0.0	0.9
	14	26.7	15.6	3.6	0.0	9.0
	15	23.0	13.5	3.4	Trace	4.3
	16	25.1	15.5	5.7	0.0	10.2
	17	25.1	13.9	8.5	0.0	12.2
	18	25.1	13.9	7.0	0.0	10.3
	19	26.3	13.7	4.3	0.0	11.1
	20	27.0	13.8	2.5	0.0	12.1
	21	29.3	15.5	3.0	0.0	11.3
	22	27.8	16.7	3.8	0.0	11.2
	23	28.5	15.8	5.9	0.3	12.1
	24	32.0	17.9	4.1	0.0	9.2
	25	30.2	18.4	4.8	0.2	10.5
	26	23.3	17.0	6.9	Trace	0.3
	27	27.2	18.1	3.5	1.9	7.1
	28	20.4	15.3	3.1	Trace	3.8
	29	26.3	13.1	3.6	0.0	11.6
	30	31.8	16.7	6.0	Trace	7.8
	31	26.1	20.1	5.1	0.3	4.8
Total		–	–	–	16.9	267.1
Mean		26.2	15.3	4.7	0.5	8.6
Temp °F		79.2	59.5	–	–	–
Average		22.5	13.1	7.4	46.0	198.5

AUGUST 1994

		Temperature Max. °C	Min. °C	Wind knots	Rain mm	Sun hrs
Day	1	24.5	16.6	6.4	0.0	8.1
	2	23.9	14.0	4.7	0.6	1.1
	3	31.0	17.1	6.1	Trace	8.7
	4	25.2	20.7	3.9	0.7	0.4
	5	27.4	17.3	2.2	0.0	8.0
	6	27.2	16.5	6.4	0.0	2.0
	7	23.9	16.9	8.5	0.0	2.0
	8	24.5	15.4	6.5	0.0	6.9
	9	23.8	13.7	10.4	1.4	7.3
	10	19.0	15.6	6.8	11.4	0.0
	11	18.3	15.3	3.3	4.9	0.0
	12	20.1	14.3	3.2	Trace	2.2
	13	21.6	9.9	2.5	0.0	9.7
	14	20.6	10.4	3.0	0.0	12.0
	15	23.8	9.0	2.7	0.0	11.0
	16	26.1	11.9	5.6	0.9	8.6
	17	20.8	12.4	9.0	Trace	7.1
	18	22.5	9.9	6.7	1.9	7.6
	19	23.0	14.6	6.1	0.2	6.9
	20	21.8	11.1	3.2	0.0	6.0
	21	23.1	12.8	2.3	0.0	8.2
	22	26.4	16.1	6.8	Trace	5.5
	23	22.6	15.7	4.5	0.9	2.2
	24	22.6	12.5	6.0	2.1	8.3
	25	19.9	12.9	2.5	2.5	3.4
	26	24.5	14.7	5.3	0.3	7.9
	27	21.9	15.0	6.7	0.0	9.7
	28	20.6	10.7	8.0	Trace	11.4
	29	21.1	9.5	4.5	0.0	5.0
	30	21.1	10.8	2.7	0.4	3.7
	31	18.5	13.1	4.5	4.0	0.0
Total		–	–	–	32.2	180.9
Mean		23.0	13.8	5.2	1.0	5.8
Temp °F		73.4	56.8	–	–	–
Average		22.1	12.8	7.2	51.0	186.7

SEPTEMBER 1994

		Temperature Max. °C	Min. °C	Wind knots	Rain mm	Sun hrs
Day	1	17.9	14.0	6.3	2.1	0.1
	2	22.1	9.6	5.7	0.0	12.4
	3	19.5	10.0	4.4	3.7	0.6
	4	21.7	15.3	7.8	Trace	6.0
	5	20.2	12.4	6.2	0.0	8.0
	6	17.7	9.6	4.0	Trace	0.1
	7	19.3	10.5	4.8	24.7	6.7
	8	18.7	12.1	8.6	0.2	10.1
	9	19.2	9.4	9.7	5.3	6.5
	10	17.8	9.7	10.3	0.5	8.5
	11	18.4	8.9	7.7	3.0	4.0
	12	18.7	13.4	11.5	0.1	5.2
	13	19.4	9.4	6.3	3.7	8.5
	14	18.0	12.5	6.0	15.4	0.7
	15	11.5	9.7	8.6	12.2	0.0
	16	14.4	9.3	7.6	0.0	5.5
	17	15.1	4.9	5.7	Trace	1.0
	18	14.0	9.2	2.9	6.2	0.4
	19	13.8	9.3	5.4	7.3	0.0
	20	16.5	10.9	5.7	1.4	2.3
	21	20.0	8.8	6.5	Trace	5.7
	22	19.5	11.5	8.1	0.0	6.3
	23	19.1	11.9	8.1	0.2	0.7
	24	18.6	13.5	7.7	Trace	0.1
	25	18.0	13.8	6.7	0.3	0.0
	26	18.0	13.9	3.7	Trace	0.8
	27	18.8	9.8	3.7	0.0	4.4
	28	18.3	10.2	3.6	0.0	5.1
	29	15.4	9.1	2.9	Trace	0.0
	30	14.7	12.0	3.2	Trace	0.0
	31					
Total		–	–	–	86.3	109.7
Mean		17.9	10.9	6.4	2.9	3.7
Temp °F		64.2	51.6	–	–	–
Average		19.3	10.8	7.1	51.0	144.7

OCTOBER 1994

		Temperature Max. °C	Min. °C	Wind knots	Rain mm	Sun hrs
Day	1	16.1	11.2	1.8	0.4	0.1
	2	16.2	10.0	5.0	3.6	0.0
	3	13.0	8.9	6.9	1.5	1.7
	4	11.1	1.9	3.7	0.0	10.6
	5	14.8	2.0	3.0	0.0	10.0
	6	16.0	4.0	3.9	0.0	8.3
	7	16.5	5.5	2.6	0.0	7.9
	8	16.6	5.8	2.3	0.0	7.2
	9	17.3	9.6	3.4	0.0	5.2
	10	18.8	5.0	5.1	0.0	8.5
	11	16.9	8.8	2.5	Trace	0.9
	12	16.8	7.7	4.0	0.0	7.4
	13	18.0	9.5	5.5	0.0	8.1
	14	18.8	8.8	2.0	0.0	5.7
	15	18.1	7.8	3.0	Trace	5.5
	16	13.8	8.5	6.7	Trace	0.0
	17	11.5	7.8	6.7	0.0	0.5
	18	13.3	3.1	7.9	Trace	9.5
	19	15.8	6.5	7.3	2.3	0.0
	20	14.1	10.9	5.4	3.7	0.0
	21	16.5	11.0	7.4	5.8	2.9
	22	18.3	12.4	8.2	8.5	2.5
	23	14.8	9.9	4.7	0.1	7.1
	24	14.8	7.1	4.3	5.3	6.2
	25	12.8	9.2	5.2	5.3	2.5
	26	13.7	6.6	6.0	Trace	4.7
	27	12.6	5.1	4.8	0.0	7.6
	28	13.1	3.1	4.2	6.8	8.5
	29	15.4	6.6	6.9	6.2	0.5
	30	16.5	11.0	11.3	18.6	0.0
	31	14.6	12.2	11.7	7.9	1.4
Total		–	–	–	76.0	141.0
Mean		15.4	7.7	5.3	2.5	4.5
Temp °F		59.7	45.9	–	–	–
Average		15.4	8.0	7.2	58.0	107.2

NOVEMBER 1994

Day	Temperature Max. °C	Min. °C	Wind knots	Rain mm	Sun hrs
1	13.5	6.2	5.0	Trace	8.4
2	14.4	3.5	6.1	0.1	5.0
3	18.2	6.0	8.9	2.9	1.6
4	14.9	11.5	2.7	16.7	0.9
5	11.9	11.3	2.5	3.4	0.0
6	14.5	8.5	2.9	0.0	6.6
7	13.9	5.7	6.0	0.0	3.6
8	14.8	7.6	5.9	1.2	0.9
9	12.5	10.7	6.9	4.9	0.0
10	13.5	8.0	1.7	0.1	0.6
11	12.5	10.0	1.4	3.0	0.0
12	13.2	10.2	5.3	1.7	0.0
13	15.6	6.9	7.9	0.4	0.0
14	16.4	9.8	11.5	0.1	0.0
15	14.1	10.5	8.6	Trace	6.2
16	11.4	6.0	3.7	0.1	3.9
17	12.6	5.3	5.7	2.8	4.0
18	15.2	6.8	3.0	5.3	0.0
19	16.5	10.7	7.0	0.1	0.0
20	15.6	14.2	9.0	0.1	0.0
21	12.1	7.6	1.6	Trace	0.0
22	14.0	5.0	2.1	0.0	0.2
23	14.5	9.6	4.0	0.0	0.6
24	14.0	10.3	2.1	0.2	0.0
25	13.6	10.9	2.2	0.0	0.1
26	12.6	7.8	2.1	Trace	0.0
27	11.6	9.5	1.4	0.0	0.0
28	10.3	9.2	2.2	0.0	0.1
29	9.7	6.0	5.5	0.0	0.0
30	9.0	7.0	4.1	Trace	0.0
31					
Total	–	–	–	43.1	42.7
Mean	13.6	8.5	4.7	1.5	1.5
Temp °F	56.5	47.3	–	–	–
Average	10.4	4.1	8.0	55.0	68.1

DECEMBER 1994

Day	Temperature Max. °C	Min. °C	Wind knots	Rain mm	Sun hrs
1	9.4	6.0	4.5	Trace	0.1
2	13.0	5.4	4.7	Trace	3.0
3	13.3	6.6	8.0	6.1	1.9
4	13.6	7.7	11.0	Trace	4.1
5	12.3	3.9	8.0	3.5	3.2
6	11.8	4.6	8.9	6.6	5.0
7	12.1	5.0	9.3	8.7	1.5
8	13.0	6.1	10.4	12.2	0.6
9	12.0	1.3	2.0	Trace	1.5
10	15.1	3.5	9.3	Trace	0.0
11	15.4	11.1	10.1	0.0	0.3
12	15.2	11.0	10.0	Trace	1.0
13	13.0	10.8	6.0	1.3	0.3
14	7.1	2.6	2.2	Trace	3.4
15	9.2	-4.8	3.0	0.1	5.6
16	9.7	-2.6	2.4	Trace	2.1
17	12.2	0.6	7.1	7.1	0.0
18	10.3	9.0	7.3	0.1	1.0
19	7.9	3.0	4.7	0.0	3.0
20	7.1	-0.3	2.5	0.3	6.4
21	5.8	0.3	3.0	0.1	4.1
22	6.6	0.1	2.5	0.0	6.8
23	-0.5	-3.9	1.5	Trace	1.5
24	4.8	-4.8	2.0	Trace	0.0
25	10.2	-2.7	5.5	1.7	0.0
26	13.1	4.3	8.9	2.6	1.3
27	14.0	5.5	11.8	2.5	0.0
28	14.7	12.0	14.5	2.1	0.0
29	13.2	10.9	13.0	8.1	0.8
30	8.8	6.2	13.4	0.1	0.4
31	7.2	4.0	7.4	0.1	1.9
Total	–	–	–	63.3	60.8
Mean	10.7	4.0	7.0	2.1	2.0
Temp °F	51.3	39.2	–	–	–
Average	8.0	2.3	8.1	57.0	46.2

JANUARY 1995

Day	Temperature Max. °C	Min. °C	Wind knots	Rain mm	Sun hrs
1	4.9	-2.0	6.7	0.1	4.3
2	3.2	-1.2	5.9	0.0	7.1
3	4.8	-4.4	2.7	0.0	6.9
4	6.2	-3.8	8.7	2.3	2.3
5	5.5	2.9	9.9	3.1	0.0
6	8.1	1.6	3.7	0.1	5.6
7	9.9	-0.8	2.2	Trace	0.0
8	10.5	1.2	3.7	2.5	0.0
9	10.9	0.5	7.5	0.2	0.0
10	12.5	4.2	8.8	1.6	0.1
11	5.3	2.5	5.1	0.0	6.7
12	6.1	0.4	5.6	0.0	6.6
13	7.7	0.2	2.8	Trace	0.6
14	10.9	1.4	5.7	Trace	0.3
15	11.8	7.2	7.8	0.0	0.7
16	10.0	7.4	12.9	3.3	0.0
17	10.2	7.4	15.9	11.6	0.0
18	7.8	5.2	7.0	0.6	2.0
19	10.1	1.8	10.6	15.8	0.0
20	9.7	3.3	10.7	1.1	0.6
21	10.0	3.2	11.6	13.1	0.3
22	7.5	5.3	7.3	9.0	0.0
23	8.7	2.6	12.7	Trace	5.6
24	7.5	4.5	7.2	4.7	0.0
25	12.9	4.6	7.7	11.5	0.0
26	5.2	3.8	9.7	0.2	0.0
27	12.0	-1.9	7.5	6.6	0.0
28	10.3	1.1	10.6	2.7	2.6
29	12.2	6.8	8.3	15.4	0.3
30	8.9	2.1	3.3	1.5	6.7
31	12.9	2.1	14.3	6.7	0.0
Total	–	–	–	113.7	59.6
Mean	8.9	2.3	7.9	3.7	2.0
Temp °F	48.0	36.1	–	–	–
Average	7.1	1.4	8.5	52.0	51.7

FEBRUARY 1995

Day	Temperature Max. °C	Min. °C	Wind knots	Rain mm	Sun hrs
1	10.0	8.3	6.0	4.2	0.0
2	9.1	0.8	3.0	0.0	6.2
3	10.9	2.2	8.3	Trace	0.0
4	13.2	8.4	2.7	0.0	4.1
5	11.6	2.8	4.3	Trace	0.0
6	11.8	6.7	9.3	0.0	1.2
7	10.5	8.6	5.8	5.2	0.0
8	9.9	7.3	5.0	2.5	0.0
9	7.0	2.3	6.5	3.5	0.0
10	11.9	3.3	6.4	2.8	1.2
11	12.4	6.5	10.1	2.8	0.0
12	13.2	6.5	10.7	0.3	2.9
13	11.6	7.8	6.6	7.8	0.5
14	12.3	4.7	10.0	2.8	5.2
15	12.5	6.0	12.1	1.7	3.7
16	11.1	4.2	14.3	4.7	2.4
17	10.2	4.2	9.3	Trace	6.8
18	10.8	1.6	8.0	2.7	7.7
19	11.8	5.0	8.7	1.9	0.0
20	10.8	5.5	5.8	7.6	0.0
21	8.8	6.1	8.0	2.0	5.6
22	10.3	3.5	13.6	8.8	2.3
23	8.3	1.1	6.5	3.5	4.8
24	8.2	3.3	3.2	1.2	0.1
25	9.0	4.6	4.4	Trace	5.6
26	8.1	0.7	3.5	0.0	9.5
27	10.2	-1.8	6.7	0.9	0.0
28	12.9	2.8	12.2	5.0	1.1
29					
30					
31					
Total	–	–	–	71.9	70.9
Mean	10.7	4.4	7.6	2.6	2.6
Temp °F	51.3	39.9	–	–	–
Average	7.5	1.5	8.8	35.0	67.3

MARCH 1995

Day	Temperature Max. °C	Min. °C	Wind knots	Rain mm	Sun hrs
1	9.7	8.5	14.3	1.4	6.0
2	8.4	0.1	8.4	12.5	6.4
3	6.5	-0.6	5.9	0.0	9.6
4	7.5	-3.8	5.1	2.8	8.2
5	9.7	0.0	8.8	0.0	3.3
6	7.7	3.0	8.3	Trace	6.1
7	7.7	0.1	7.0	11.8	0.4
8	9.3	0.2	5.0	0.8	6.9
9	10.2	-1.2	5.5	0.0	5.9
10	14.4	3.8	11.0	0.0	8.8
11	16.1	3.8	2.5	1.3	6.4
12	13.1	6.7	3.7	0.0	9.0
13	8.8	1.6	2.1	0.0	3.8
14	12.9	1.6	3.5	1.8	3.7
15	9.0	1.9	5.7	0.7	3.7
16	11.1	0.4	8.0	3.5	5.2
17	12.5	5.1	16.5	4.4	7.3
18	12.1	3.2	9.5	Trace	5.9
19	10.5	1.8	5.3	0.5	7.8
20	9.3	0.5	6.3	Trace	7.7
21	10.8	-1.4	2.2	0.0	9.9
22	12.8	0.9	3.9	0.0	9.1
23	16.1	0.6	3.5	0.0	11.0
24	15.9	4.4	5.6	1.5	9.1
25	14.3	7.4	7.9	Trace	5.6
26	12.6	7.5	9.0	0.9	0.2
27	7.2	2.6	9.6	Trace	7.3
28	11.4	-1.2	7.7	5.6	0.0
29	9.5	-0.1	6.1	0.0	11.2
30	12.2	-1.3	5.0	Trace	6.3
31	16.6	5.8	5.9	0.0	2.7
Total	–	–	–	49.5	194.5
Mean	11.2	2.0	6.8	1.6	6.3
Temp °F	52.2	35.6	–	–	–
Average	10.3	2.7	8.9	47.0	110.1

APRIL 1995

Day	Temperature Max. °C	Min. °C	Wind knots	Rain mm	Sun hrs
1	20.6	7.9	5.1	0.0	6.4
2	19.7	5.1	5.5	0.0	10.2
3	16.9	8.1	5.9	0.0	10.3
4	16.6	6.8	3.2	0.0	6.3
5	15.5	8.7	4.9	0.0	4.8
6	19.7	9.9	3.2	0.0	5.6
7	19.4	7.4	5.5	0.0	8.3
8	12.2	4.8	4.1	0.0	11.5
9	13.8	3.1	2.4	0.0	7.8
10	16.6	7.3	2.7	0.0	4.3
11	19.0	5.2	2.6	0.0	11.1
12	16.0	7.0	3.9	0.0	12.3
13	16.5	4.4	5.4	0.0	12.7
14	17.9	7.2	2.7	0.0	8.5
15	13.9	8.6	3.9	Trace	0.1
16	12.6	5.6	5.1	Trace	3.4
17	11.5	8.5	7.9	0.3	0.0
18	11.2	8.3	7.2	Trace	9.9
19	11.5	-1.0	2.7	Trace	9.4
20	12.4	-0.5	2.8	0.0	11.3
21	13.9	-0.3	5.0	2.1	12.1
22	12.0	5.9	10.3	0.8	2.2
23	14.1	5.7	6.6	4.2	5.0
24	13.3	7.6	5.4	0.0	0.0
25	20.7	8.1	7.1	9.2	10.7
26	9.7	7.9	8.4	0.1	0.1
27	12.5	5.1	5.3	0.0	8.7
28	12.2	5.9	5.2	0.0	6.0
29	12.5	5.6	4.5	Trace	0.0
30	16.4	7.7	1.9	Trace	0.5
31					
Total	–	–	–	16.9	199.5
Mean	15.1	6.1	4.9	0.6	6.7
Temp °F	59.2	43.0	–	–	–
Average	13.1	4.7	8.5	45.0	146.9

MAY 1995

Day	Max. °C	Min. °C	Wind knots	Rain mm	Sun hrs
1	19.9	7.5	4.0	0.0	9.1
2	24.0	9.5	3.0	0.0	10.3
3	25.3	10.1	3.8	0.0	12.7
4	26.7	9.4	2.0	0.0	13.5
5	26.8	10.4	2.4	0.0	13.9
6	26.9	11.0	1.9	0.0	12.8
7	27.1	13.0	5.1	0.0	12.6
8	18.1	11.5	5.2	0.0	11.8
9	15.9	6.3	3.8	0.0	7.9
10	16.7	4.3	4.1	Trace	8.5
11	11.0	6.5	7.0	Trace	0.0
12	10.5	4.7	7.0	0.2	0.4
13	12.6	4.0	5.8	0.0	8.6
14	14.6	3.0	3.4	0.0	8.3
15	16.4	2.8	3.3	Trace	9.2
16	15.0	6.7	6.4	8.4	0.0
17	12.0	8.5	4.8	5.0	0.1
18	14.6	3.9	3.6	Trace	11.1
19	16.5	5.2	4.3	0.8	7.3
20	15.4	6.0	3.1	0.0	0.6
21	17.1	5.2	2.9	0.0	5.1
22	19.6	7.5	4.8	0.0	9.0
23	23.0	9.7	4.5	0.0	6.7
24	20.4	10.9	5.7	Trace	3.7
25	20.5	9.6	7.0	Trace	12.2
26	20.6	9.9	6.3	0.4	11.0
27	21.2	12.2	7.8	2.1	4.7
28	21.1	13.0	10.6	Trace	7.0
29	20.2	10.5	7.8	0.5	7.0
30	18.9	10.0	2.7	12.6	1.7
31	20.4	10.9	2.7	0.0	7.6
Total	–	–	–	30.0	234.4
Mean	19.0	8.2	4.8	1.0	7.6
Temp °F	66.2	46.8	–	–	–
Average	17.0	8.0	8.1	51.0	193.7

JUNE 1995*

Day	Max. °C	Min. °C	Wind knots	Rain mm	Sun hrs
1	18.7	7.9	–	Trace	2.0
2	18.8	11.0	–	Trace	5.8
3	15.9	12.0	–	7.2	0.0
4	16.2	11.6	–	1.4	0.7
5	18.4	10.8	–	0.0	4.8
6	17.7	11.0	–	0.1	0.5
7	20.1	13.8	–	0.0	5.4
8	16.9	7.7	–	0.1	8.3
9	18.5	6.9	–	Trace	2.4
10	15.2	8.8	–	Trace	2.0
11	16.0	10.4	–	0.6	0.0
12	14.6	9.5	–	Trace	0.1
13	14.5	8.1	–	0.0	0.5
14	16.7	9.6	–	Trace	1.6
15	17.8	9.1	–	Trace	1.3
16	22.5	9.6	–	0.6	5.0
17	17.2	10.9	–	1.1	0.0
18	22.8	12.0	–	0.0	11.6
19	25.3	10.5	–	0.0	11.1
20	24.8	12.6	–	0.0	7.8
21	23.2	12.3	–	0.0	10.2
22	22.9	12.7	–	0.0	14.3
23	21.9	9.6	–	Trace	15.6
24	16.0	11.4	–	Trace	0.4
25	24.1	11.8	–	0.0	10.9
26	25.5	11.4	–	0.0	11.1
27	27.1	11.9	–	0.0	11.1
28	31.0	12.3	–	0.0	12.6
29	29.3	14.2	–	0.0	15.7
30	32.3	13.7	–	0.0	14.9
31					
Total	–	–	–	11.1	187.7
Mean	20.8	10.9	–	0.4	6.3
Temp °F	69.4	51.6	–	–	–
Average	20.4	11.0	7.6	50.0	198.5

*Wind values for June were not available at the time of going to press

Sports Results

ALPINE SKIING

WORLD CUP 1994-5

MEN

Downhill: Luc Alphand (France), 484 pts
Slalom: Alberto Tomba (Italy), 700 pts
Giant Slalom: Alberto Tomba (Italy), 450 pts
Super Giant Slalom: Peter Runggaldier (Italy), 332 pts
Overall: Alberto Tomba (Italy), 1,150 pts

WOMEN

Downhill: Picabo Street (USA), 709 pts
Slalom: Vreni Schneider (Switzerland), 560 pts
Giant Slalom: Vreni Schneider (Switzerland), 450 pts
Super Giant Slalom: Katja Seizinger (Germany), 446 pts
Overall: Vreni Schneider (Switzerland), 1,248 pts

Nations Cup: Austria, 8,862 pts

The 1995 World Championships were cancelled owing to the lack of snow at the planned venue (Sierra Nevada, Spain)

AMERICAN FOOTBALL

XXIX American Superbowl 1995 (Miami, Florida, 29 January): San Francisco 49ers beat San Diego Chargers 49–26
World Bowl 1995 (Amsterdam, 17 June): Frankfurt Galaxy beat Amsterdam Admirals 26–22
British League Division 1 final 1995: Birmingham Bowls beat London Amtrak Olympians 34–30

ANGLING

NATIONAL COARSE CHAMPIONSHIPS 1994

Division: 1
Venue: Rivers Cam and Great Ouse; *no. of teams:* 85
Individual winner: S. Ellis (Scunthorpe and District AA), 19.800 kg
Team winners: Highfield AS, 810 pts

Division: 2
Venue: River Trent; *no. of teams:* 80
Individual winner: A. Simpson (Darnall Horticultural AC), 12.870 kg
Team winners: Darnell Horticultural AC, 803 pts

Division: 3
Venue: River Witham; *no. of teams:* 83
Individual winner: G. Greaves (Woodlands Headingley), 18.490 kg
Team winners: Tightlines Cutlers, 739 pts

Division: 4
Venue: Gloucester Canal; *no. of teams:* 82
Individual winner: J. Merchant (Farringdon Social), 7.800 kg
Team Winners: Hot Rods MG, 873 pts

Division: 5
Venue: Keadby and New Junction Canals; *no. of teams:* 96
Individual winner: W. Lazenby (Yorkshire Copper Works), 13.760 kg
Team winners: Yorkshire Copper Works, 918 pts

Ladies' Championship
Venue: Suffolk Stour; *no. of competitors:* 143
Winner: L. Gunner (Billericay), 4.000 kg

WORLD CHAMPIONSHIPS 1995
Saimaa Canal, Finland, August

Individual winner: P. Jean (France), 2 pts
Team winners: France, 23 pts

ASSOCIATION FOOTBALL

LEAGUE COMPETITIONS 1994-5

ENGLAND AND WALES

Premiership
1. Blackburn Rovers, 89pts
2. Manchester United, 88 pts
Relegated: Crystal Palace, 45 pts; Norwich City, 43 pts; Leicester City, 29 pts; Ipswich Town, 27 pts

Division 1
1. Middlesbrough, 82 pts
Second promotion place: Bolton Wanderers
Relegated: Swindon Town, 48 pts; Burnley, 46 pts; Bristol City, 45 pts; Notts County, 40 pts

Division 2
1. Birmingham City, 89 pts
Second promotion place: Huddersfield Town
Relegated: Cambridge United, 48 pts; Plymouth Argyle, 46 pts; Cardiff City, 38 pts; Chester City, 29 pts; Leyton Orient, 26 pts

Division 3
1. Carlisle United, 91 pts
2. Walsall, 83 pts
Third promotion place: Chesterfield
Bottom: Exeter City, 34 pts

GM Vauxhall Conference
Champions: Macclesfield, 80 pts (not promoted because the necessary improvements to their ground had not been made by 31 December 1994)
Relegated: Merthyr Tydfil, 44 pts; Stafford Rangers, 38 pts; Yeovil Town, 37 pts
League of Wales: Bangor City, 88 pts
Women's Premier League: Arsenal

SCOTLAND

Premier Division
1. Rangers, 69 pts
2. Motherwell, 54 pts
Relegated: Dundee United, 36 pts

Division 1
1. Raith Rovers, 69 pts
2. Dunfermline Athletic, 68 pts (not promoted because lost a play-off against Aberdeen)
Relegated: Ayr United, 29 pts; Stranraer, 17 pts

Division 2
1. Greenock Morton, 64 pts
2. Dumbarton, 60 pts
Relegated: Meadowbank Thistle, 35 pts; Brechin City, 24 pts

Division 3
1. Forfar Athletic, 80 pts
2. Montrose, 67 pts
Bottom: Albion Rovers, 18 pts

NORTHERN IRELAND

Irish League Championship: Crusaders, 67 pts

CUP COMPETITIONS

ENGLAND

FA Cup final 1995 (Wembley, 20 May): Everton beat Manchester United 1–0
Coca Cola (League) Cup final 1995: Liverpool beat Bolton Wanderers 2–1
Auto Windscreens Shield final 1995: Birmingham City beat Carlisle United 1–0 after sudden-death extra time
Anglo-Italian Cup final 1995: Notts County beat Ascoli 2–1
FA Vase final 1995: Arlesey Town beat Oxford City 2–1
FA Trophy final 1995: Woking beat Kidderminster Harriers 2–1 a.e.t.
Arthur Dunn Cup final 1995: Old Salopians beat Old Foresters 2–1
Charity Shield 1995: Everton beat Blackburn Rovers 1–0
Women's FA Cup final 1995: Arsenal beat Liverpool 3–2
Women's League Cup final 1995: Arsenal beat Doncaster Belles 4–0

WALES

Welsh FA Cup final 1995: Wrexham beat Cardiff City 2–1
Welsh League Cup final 1995: Llasant Ffraid beat Ton Pentre 2–1

SCOTLAND

Scottish FA Cup final 1995 (Hampden Park, 27 May): Celtic beat Airdrieonians 1–0
B & Q Cup final 1994: Airdrieonians beat Dundee 3–2 a.e.t.
Coca Cola (League) Cup final 1994: Raith Rovers 2, Celtic 2 a.e.t. Raith Rovers won 6–5 on penalties

NORTHERN IRELAND

Irish Cup final 1995: Linfield beat Carrick 3–1

EUROPE

European Champions' Cup final 1995 (Vienna): Ajax beat AC Milan 1–0
European Cup-Winners' Cup final 1995 (Paris): Real Zaragoza beat Arsenal 2–1 a.e.t.
UEFA Cup final 1995: Parma beat Juventus 2–1 on agg.
Women's World Cup final 1995: Norway beat Germany 2–0

INTERNATIONALS

EUROPEAN CHAMPIONSHIPS QUALIFYING MATCHES

1994		
12 Oct	Vienna	Austria 1, N. Ireland 2
	Glasgow	Scotland 5, Faroe Islands 1
	Kishinev	Moldova 3, Wales 2
16 Nov	Belfast	N. Ireland 1, Rep. of Ireland 4
	Glasgow	Scotland 1, Russia 1
	Tbilisi	Georgia 5, Wales 0
14 Dec	Cardiff	Wales 0, Bulgaria 3
18 Dec	Athens	Greece 1, Scotland 0

1995		
29 March	Dublin	Rep. of Ireland 1, N. Ireland 1
	Moscow	Russia 0, Scotland 0
	Sofia	Bulgaria 3, Wales 1
26 April	Riga	Latvia 0, N. Ireland 1
	San Marino	San Marino 0, Scotland 2
	Dusseldorf	Germany 1, Wales 1
7 June	Belfast	N. Ireland 1, Latvia 2
	Cardiff	Wales 0, Georgia 1
	Tórshavn	Faroe Islands 0, Scotland 2
16 Aug	Glasgow	Scotland 1, Greece 0
3 Sept	Oporto	Portugal 1, N. Ireland 1
6 Sept	Cardiff	Wales 1, Moldova 0
	Glasgow	Scotland 1, Finland 0

FRIENDLIES

1994		
12 Oct	Wembley	England 1, Romania 1
16 Nov	Wembley	England 1, Nigeria 0

1995		
15 Feb	Dublin	match abandoned at Rep. of Ireland 1, England 0
29 March	Wembley	England 0, Uruguay 0
21 May	Hiroshima	Japan 0, Scotland 0
23 May	Edmonton	Canada 2, N. Ireland 0
26 May	Edmonton	Chile 2, N. Ireland 1
3 June	Wembley	England 2, Japan 1
8 June	Elland Road	England 3, Sweden 3
11 June	Wembley	England 1, Brazil 3
6 Sept	Wembley	England 0, Colombia 0

ATHLETICS

EUROPEAN CROSS-COUNTRY CHAMPIONSHIPS
Alnwick, 10 December 1994

MEN

Individual: Paulo Guerra (Portugal), 27 min. 43 sec.
Team result: Portugal, 20 pts

WOMEN

Individual: Catherina McKiernan (Ireland), 14 min. 29 sec.
Team result: Romania, 26 pts

GREAT BRITAIN v. RUSSIA (INDOORS)
Birmingham, 28 January 1995

MEN

	min.	sec.
60 *metres:* Colin Jackson (GB)		6.58
200 *metres:* John Regis (GB)		20.65
400 *metres:* Dmitriy Golovastov (Russia)		47.09
800 *metres:* Tom McKean (GB)	1	50.04
1,500 *metres:* Ian Grime (GB)	3	52.02
3,000 *metres:* Vyacheslav Shabunin (Russia)	8	14.49
60 *metres hurdles:* Colin Jackson (GB)		7.43
4 × 400 *metres relay:* Great Britain	3	09.22

	metres
High jump: Brendan Reilly (GB)	2.26
Pole vault: Vladimir Strogalyov (Russia)	5.20
Long jump: Barrington Williams (GB)	7.54
Triple jump: Gennadiy Markov (Russia)	17.00
Shot: Sergei Smirnov (Russia)	18.71

Team points: Great Britain 72, Russia 64

WOMEN

	min.	sec.
60 *metres:* Paula Thomas (GB)		7.29
200 *metres:* Paula Thomas (GB)		23.61
400 *metres:* Yelena Andreyeva (Russia)		52.57
800 *metres:* Yelena Afanasyeva (Russia)	2	05.14
1,500 *metres:* Ann Griffiths (GB)	4	14.74
3,000 *metres:* Klara Kashapova (Russia)	9	15.45
60 *metres hurdles:* Jackie Agyepong (GB)		8.05
4 × 400 *metres relay:* Russia	3	32.26
		metres
High jump: Tatyana Motkova (Russia)		1.98
Pole vault: Kate Staples (GB)		3.75
Long jump: Ludmila Galkina (Russia)		6.58
Triple jump: Ashia Hansen (GB)		14.17
Shot: Larissa Peleshenko (Russia)		19.57

Team points: Russia 78, Great Britain 62

AAA INDOOR CHAMPIONSHIPS
Birmingham, 3–4 February 1995

MEN

	min.	sec.
60 *metres:* Michael Rosswess (Birchfield)		6.63
200 *metres:* Solomon Wariso (Haringey)		20.87
400 *metres:* Mark Hylton (Windsor)		46.56
800 *metres:* Martin Steele (Longwood)	1	49.17
1,500 *metres:* Grant Graham (Clydesdale)	3	55.68
3,000 *metres:* Steve Green (Trafford)	8	08.71
60 *metres hurdles:* Paul Gray (Cardiff)		7.83
		metres
High jump: Geoff Parsons (Blue Circle)		2.24
Pole vault: Paul Williamson (TVH)		5.20
Long jump: Barrington Williams (Wolverhampton)		7.55
Triple jump: John Herbert (Haringey)		16.48
Shot: Lee Newman (Blackheath)		17.30

WOMEN

	min.	sec.
60 *metres:* Stephanie Douglas (Sale)		7.28
200 *metres:* Jackie Agyepong (Shaftesbury-Barnet)		24.22
400 *metres:* Melanie Neef (Glasgow)		52.82
800 *metres:* Abigail Hunte (unattached)	2	08.06
1,500 *metres:* Lynn Gibson (Oxford)	4	18.41
60 *metres hurdles:* Clova Court (Birchfield)		8.22
		metres
High jump: Lea Haggett (Croydon)		1.86
Pole vault: Kate Staples (Essex Ladies)		3.80
Long jump: Denise Lewis (Birchfield)		6.28
Triple jump: Ashia Hansen (Essex Ladies)		13.61
Shot: Judy Oakes (Croydon)		17.81

Birmingham, 18 February 1995

	min.	sec.
3,000 *metres:* Angela Davies (Basingstoke)	9	25.65

GREAT BRITAIN v. FRANCE (INDOORS)
Glasgow, 11 February 1995

MEN

	min.	sec.
60 *metres:* Linford Christie (GB)		6.56
200 *metres:* John Regis (GB)		20.67
400 *metres:* Mark Hylton (GB)		47.06
800 *metres:* Tom McKean (GB)	1	48.72
1,500 *metres:* Eric Dubos (France)	3	41.66
3,000 *metres:* Jacques Carlier (France)	7	58.03
60 *metres hurdles:* Colin Jackson (GB)		7.39
4 × 400 *metres relay:* Great Britain	3	09.28

	metres
High jump: Didier Detchenique (France)	2.23
Pole vault: Alain Andji (France)	5.30
Long jump: Kader Klouchi (France)	7.65
Triple jump: John Herbert (GB)	16.50
Shot: Mark Proctor (GB)	18.39

WOMEN

	min.	sec.
60 *metres:* Stephanie Douglas (GB)		7.21
200 *metres:* Paula Thomas (GB)		23.42
400 *metres:* Melanie Neef (GB)		53.67
800 *metres:* Patricia Djate (France)	2	02.99
1,500 *metres:* Frederique Quentin (France)	4	18.04
3,000 *metres:* Laurence Duquennoy (France)	9	20.49
60 *metres hurdles:* Jackie Agyepong (GB)		8.08
4 × 400 *metres relay:* Great Britain	3	37.60
		metres
High jump: Katell Courgeon (France)		1.86
Pole vault: Kate Staples (GB)		3.60
Long jump: Denise Lewis (GB)		6.35
Triple jump: Michelle Griffith (GB)		13.76
Shot: Judy Oakes (GB)		17.15

Team Points: Great Britain 155, France 122

WORLD INDOOR CHAMPIONSHIPS
Barcelona, 10–12 March 1995

MEN

	min.	sec.
60 *metres:* Bruny Surin (Canada)		6.46
200 *metres:* Geir Moen (Norway)		20.58
400 *metres:* Darnell Hall (USA)		46.17
800 *metres:* Clive Terrelonge (Jamaica)	1	47.30
1,500 *metres:* Hicham El Guerrouj (Morocco)	3	44.54
3,000 *metres:* Gennaro Di Napoli (Italy)	7	50.89
60 *metres hurdles:* Allen Johnson (USA)		7.39
4 × 400 *metres relay:* USA	3	07.37
		metres
High jump: Javier Sotomayor (Cuba)		2.38
Pole vault: Sergei Bubka (Ukraine)		5.90
Long jump: Ivan Pedroso (Cuba)		8.51
Triple jump: Brian Wellman (Bermuda)		17.72
Shot: Mika Halvari (Finland)		20.74
Heptathlon: Christian Plaziat (France)		6,246 pts

WOMEN

	min.	sec.
60 *metres:* Merlene Ottey (Jamaica)		6.97
200 *metres:* Melinda Gainsford (Australia)		22.64
400 *metres:* Irina Privalova (Russia)		50.23
800 *metres:* Maria Mutola (Mozambique)	1	57.62
1,500 *metres:* Regina Jacobs (USA)	4	12.61
3,000 *metres:* Gabriela Szabo (Romania)	8	54.50
60 *metres hurdles:* Aliuska Lopez (Cuba)		7.92
4 × 400 *metres relay:* Russia	3	29.29
		metres
High jump: Alina Astafei (Germany)		2.01
Long jump: Ludmila Galkina (Russia)		6.95
Triple jump: Yolanda Chen (Russia)		15.03
Shot: Larisa Peleshenko (Russia)		19.93
Pentathlon: Svetlana Moskalets (Russia)		4,834 pts

MEN'S NATIONAL CROSS-COUNTRY CHAMPIONSHIPS
Luton, 11 March 1995

Individual: Spencer Duval (Cannock), 43 min. 43 sec.
Team: Blackheath, 120 pts

WOMEN'S NATIONAL CROSS-COUNTRY CHAMPIONSHIPS
Luton, 11 March 1995

Individual: Kate McCandess (USA), 19 min. 55 sec.
Team: Parkside, 41 pts

WORLD CROSS-COUNTRY CHAMPIONSHIPS
Durham, 25 March 1995

MEN (12,020 *metres*)
Individual: Paul Tergat (Kenya), 34 min. 05 sec.
Team: Kenya, 62 pts

WOMEN (6,470 *metres*)
Individual: Derartu Tulu (Ethiopia), 20 min. 21 sec.
Team: Kenya, 26 pts

LONDON MARATHON
2 April 1995

Men: Dionicio Ceron (Mexico), 2 hr. 08 min. 30 sec.
Women: Malgorzata Sobanska (Poland), 2 hr. 27 min. 43 sec.

WORLD MARATHON CUP
Athens, 9 April 1995

MEN
Individual: Douglas Wakiihuri (Kenya), 2 hr. 12 min. 01 sec.
Team: Italy, 6 hr. 44 min. 28 sec.

WOMEN
Individual: Anuta Catuna (Romania), 2 hr. 31 min. 10 sec.
Team: Romania, 7 hr. 35 min. 05 sec.

EUROPEAN CUP
Lille, 24–25 June 1995

MEN

	min.	sec.
100 *metres:* Linford Christie (GB)		10.05
200 *metres:* Linford Christie (GB)		20.11
400 *metres:* Mark Richardson (GB)		45.43
800 *metres:* Nico Motchebon (Germany)	1	46.75
1,500 *metres:* Rudiger Stenzel (Germany)	3	42.58
5,000 *metres:* Gennaro Di Napoli (Italy)	13	45.57
10,000 *metres:* Stefano Baldini (Italy)	28	45.77
3,000 *metres steeplechase:* Alessandro Lambruschini (Italy)	8	21.94
110 *metres hurdles:* Florian Schwarthoff (Germany)		13.28
400 *metres hurdles:* Laurent Ottoz (Italy)		49.30
4 × 100 *metres relay:* Great Britain		38.73
4 × 400 *metres relay:* Great Britain	3	00.34
		metres
High jump: Steve Smith (GB)		2.31
Pole vault: Igor Trandenkov (Russia)		5.80
Long jump: Stanislav Tarasenko (Russia)		8.32
Triple jump: Jonathan Edwards (GB)		18.43
Shot: Alexander Bagach (Ukraine)		20.65
Discus: Lars Riedel (Germany)		68.76
Hammer: Ilya Konovalov (Russia)		79.66
Javelin: Raymond Hecht (Germany)		87.24

Team points: Germany 117, Great Britain 107, Russia 105, Italy 96½, Ukraine 82, Sweden 78½, Spain 67, Poland 66

WOMEN

	min.	sec.
100 *metres:* Melanie Paschke (Germany)		11.08
200 *metres:* Silke Knoll (Germany)		22.45
400 *metres:* Melanie Neef (GB)		51.35

800 *metres:* Yelena Afanasyeva (Russia)	1	59.26
1,500 *metres:* Kelly Holmes (GB)	4	07.02
5,000 *metres:* Victoriya Nenasheva (Russia)	15	16.06
10,000 *metres:* Maria Guida (Italy)	32	01.75
100 *metres hurdles:* Yulia Graudyn (Russia)		12.86
400 *metres hurdles:* Marie-José Pérec (France)		54.51
4 × 100 *metres relay:* Russia		42.74
4 × 400 *metres relay:* Russia	3	24.69
		metres
High jump: Alina Astafei (Germany)		2.00
Long jump: Heike Drechsler (Germany)		7.04
Triple jump: Ashia Hansen (GB)		14.37
Shot: Astrid Kumbernuss (Germany)		20.00
Discus: Natalya Sadova (Russia)		66.86
Javelin: Steffi Nerius (Germany)		68.42

Team points: Russia 117, Germany 100, Great Britain 85, France 75, Ukraine 75, Belarus 71, Italy 52, Poland 37

NATIONAL CHAMPIONSHIPS
Birmingham, 15–16 July 1995

MEN

	min.	sec.
100 *metres:* Darren Braithwaite (Haringey)		10.33
200 *metres:* John Regis (Belgrave)		20.37
400 *metres:* Mark Richardson (Windsor, Slough and Eton)		44.94
800 *metres:* Curtis Robb (Liverpool)	1	46.78
1,500 *metres:* John Mayock (Cannock and Stafford)	3	40.55
5,000 *metres:* Rob Denmark (Basildon)	13	37.57
3,000 *metres steeplechase:* Spencer Duval (Cannock and Stafford)	8	24.64
110 *metres hurdles:* Neil Owen (Belgrave)		13.63
400 *metres hurdles:* Rohan Robinson (Australia)		49.21
10 *km walk:* Darrell Stone (Steyning)	41	10.11
		metres
High jump: Steve Smith (Liverpool)		2.35
Pole vault: Nick Buckfield (Crawley)		5.50
Long jump: Fred Salle (Belgrave)		7.66
Triple jump: Francis Agyepong (Shaftesbury Barnet)		17.13
Shot: Mark Proctor (RAF)		18.81
Discus: Nick Sweeney (Ireland)		60.34
Hammer: Sean Carlin (Australia)		73.40
Javelin: Mick Hill (Leeds City)		80.54

WOMEN

	min.	sec.
100 *metres:* Paula Thomas (Trafford)		11.48
200 *metres:* Catherine Murphy (Shaftesbury Barnet)		23.40
400 *metres:* Melanie Neef (Glasgow)		51.63
800 *metres:* Kelly Holmes (Ealing)	1	57.56
1,500 *metres:* Yvonne Murray (Motherwell)	4	11.47
5,000 *metres:* Alison Wyeth (Parkside)	15	39.14
100 *metres hurdles:* Melanie Wilkins (Aldershot)		13.34
400 *metres hurdles:* Gowry Retchakan (Thurrock)		57.18
5,000 *metres walk:* Lisa Langford (Wolverhampton)	22	20.03
		metres
High jump: Lea Haggett (Croydon)		1.85
Pole vault: Mellisa Price (USA)		3.70
Long jump: Nicole Boegman (Australia)		6.50
Triple jump: Michelle Griffith (Windsor, Slough and Eton)		13.43
Shot: Judy Oakes (Croydon)		17.75
Discus: Lisa-Marie Vizaniari (Australia)		61.98

Hammer: Debbie Sosimenko (Australia)   65.24
Javelin: Lorna Jackson (Edinburgh)   55.48

Loughborough, 11 June 1995
10,000 *metres:* Gary Staines (Belgrave), 28 min. 49.29 sec.

Bedford, 1 July 1995
10,000 *metres:* Jill Hunter (Valli), 32 min. 26.12 sec.

WORLD CHAMPIONSHIPS
Gothenburg, Sweden, 4–13 August 1995

MEN

	hr.	min.	sec.
100 *metres:* Donovan Bailey (Canada)			9.97
200 *metres:* Michael Johnson (USA)			19.79
400 *metres:* Michael Johnson (USA)			43.39
800 *metres:* Wilson Kipketer (Denmark)		1	45.08
1,500 *metres:* Noureddine Morceli (Algeria)		3	33.73
5,000 *metres:* Ismael Kirui (Kenya)		13	16.77
10,000 *metres:* Haile Gebresilasie (Ethiopia)		27	12.95
Marathon: Martin Fiz (Spain)	2	11	41
3,000 *metres steeplechase:* Moses Kiptanui (Kenya)		8	04.16
110 *metres hurdles:* Allen Johnson (USA)			13.00
400 *metres hurdles:* Derrick Adkins (USA)			47.98
400 × 100 *metres relay:* Canada			38.31
4 × 400 *metres relay:* USA		2	57.32
20 *km walk:* Michele Didoni (Italy)	1	19	59
50 *km walk:* Valentin Kononen (Finland)	3	43	42

	metres
High jump: Troy Kemp (Bahamas)	2.37
Pole vault: Sergei Bubka (Ukraine)	5.92
Long jump: Ivan Pedroso (Cuba)	8.70
Triple jump: Jonathan Edwards (GB)	18.29
Shot: John Godina (USA)	21.47
Discus: Lars Riedel (Germany)	68.76
Hammer: Andrei Abduvalyev (Tajikistan)	81.56
Javelin: Jan Zelezny (Czech Republic)	89.56
Decathlon: Dan O'Brien (USA)	8,695 pts

WOMEN

	hr.	min.	sec.
100 *metres:* Gwen Torrence (USA)			10.85
200 *metres:* Merlene Ottey (Jamaica)			22.12
400 *metres:* Marie-José Pérec (France)			49.28
800 *metres:* Ann Quirot (Cuba)		1	56.11
1,500 *metres:* Hassiba Boulmerka (Algeria)		4	02.42
5,000 *metres:* Sonia O'Sullivan (Ireland)		14	46.47
10,000 *metres:* Fernanda Ribeiro (Portugal)		31	04.99
Marathon (*short course*): Manuela Machado (Portugal)	2	25	39
100 *metres hurdles:* Gail Devers (USA)			12.68
400 *metres hurdles:* Kim Batten (USA)			52.61
4 × 100 *metres relay:* USA			42.12
4 × 400 *metres relay:* USA		3	22.39
10 *km walk:* Irina Stankina (Russia)		42	13

	metres
High jump: Stefka Kostadinova (Bulgaria)	2.01
Long jump: Fiona May (Italy)	6.98
Triple jump: Inessa Kravets (Ukraine)	15.50
Shot: Astrid Kumbernuss (Germany)	21.22
Discus: Ellina Zvereva (Belarus)	68.64
Javelin: Natalya Shikolenko (Belarus)	67.56
Heptathlon: Ghada Shovaa (Syria)	6,651 pts

GREAT BRITAIN v. USA
Gateshead, 21 August 1995

MEN

	min.	sec.
100 *metres:* Tony McCall (USA)		10.26
200 *metres:* John Regis (GB)		20.63
400 *metres:* Marion Ramsey (USA)		44.96
800 *metres:* Terrance Herrington (USA)	1	46.52
1,500 *metres:* Paul McMullen (USA)	3	46.87
3,000 *metres:* Rob Denmark (GB)	8	02.16
3,000 *metres steeplechase:* Tom Hanlon (GB)	8	24.37
110 *metres hurdles:* Colin Jackson (GB)		13.18
400 *metres hurdles:* Danny Harris (USA)		48.70
4 × 100 *metres relay:* Great Britain		38.55
4 × 400 *metres relay:* Great Britain	3	03.16

	metres
High jump: Charles Austin (USA)	2.31
Pole vault: Scott Hoffman (USA)	5.70
Long jump: Percy Knox (USA)	7.90
Triple jump: Jonathan Edwards (GB)	17.49
Shot: Kevin Toth (USA)	20.57
Discus: Rob Weir (GB)	62.54
Hammer: David Smith (GB)	69.20
Javelin: Steve Backley (GB)	83.00

Team points: Great Britain 203, USA 182

WOMEN

	min.	sec.
100 *metres:* Paula Thomas (GB)		11.62
200 *metres:* Celena Mondie-Milner (USA)		22.99
400 *metres:* Kim Graham (USA)		51.15
800 *metres:* Amy Wickus (USA)	2	00.58
1,500 *metres:* Ruth Wysocki (USA)	4	05.03
3,000 *metres:* Yvonne Murray (GB)	8	59.80
100 *metres hurdles:* Jackie Agyepong (GB)		13.09
400 *metres hurdles:* Trevaia Williams (USA)		56.48
4 × 100 *metres relay:* USA		43.10
4 × 400 *metres relay:* USA	3	28.22

	metres
High jump: Lea Hoggett (GB)	1.88
Pole vault: Melissa Price (USA)	3.80
Long jump: Denise Lewis (GB)	6.56
Triple jump: Ashia Hansen (GB)	14.66
Shot: Connie Price-Smith (USA)	19.52
Discus: Pam Dukes (USA)	56.50
Hammer: Lorraine Shaw (GB)	59.68
Javelin: Sharon Gibson (GB)	58.10

Team points: USA 210½, Great Britain 156½

GRAND PRIX 1995 FINAL RESULTS

MEN
200 *metres:* Michael Johnson (USA)
800 *metres:* Benson Koech (Kenya)
3,000 *metres:* Haile Gebresiliasie (Ethiopia)
3,000 *metres steeplechase:* Moses Kiptanui (Kenya)
110 *metres hurdles:* Mark Crear (USA)
Pole vault: Okkert Brits (South Africa)
Long jump: Ivan Pedroso (Cuba)
Discus: Dmitri Shevchenko (Russia)
Javelin: Jan Zelezny (Czech Republic)
Overall winner: Moses Kiptanui (Kenya)

WOMEN
200 *metres:* Gwen Torrence (USA)
800 *metres:* Maria Mutola (Mozambique)
3,000 *metres:* Sonia O'Sullivan (Ireland)
400 *metres hurdles:* Kim Batten (USA)
High jump: Inga Babakova (Ukraine)
Triple jump: Anna Biryukova (Russia)

Shot: Astrid Kumbernuss (Germany)
Overall winner: Maria Mutola (Mozambique)

BADMINTON

WORLD CHAMPIONSHIPS 1995
Lausanne, May

Men's Singles: Heryanto Arbi (Indonesia) beat Park Sung
Woo (S. Korea) 15–11, 15–8
Women's Singles: Ye Zhaoying (China) beat Han Jingna
(China) 11–7, 11–0
Men's Doubles: Rexy Mainaky and Ricky Subagya
(Indonesia) beat Jon Holst-Christensen and Thomas
Lund (Denmark) 15–5, 15–2
Women's Doubles: Gil Young Ah and Jany Hyc-Ock (S.
Korea) beat Finarsih Tampi and Lili Tampi (Indonesia)
3–15, 15–11, 15–10
Mixed Doubles: Marlene Thomsen and Thomas Lund
(Denmark) beat Helene Kirkegaard and Jens Eriksen
(Denmark) 15–2, 15–6

ENGLISH NATIONAL CHAMPIONSHIPS 1995
Norwich, February

Men's Singles: Anders Nielsen beat Darren Hall 15–12,
6–15, 15–8
Women's Singles: Julia Mann beat Alison Humby 11–2,
11–6
Men's Doubles: Simon Archer and Chris Hunt beat Neil
Cottrill and John Quinn 15–4, 15–8
Women's Doubles: Julie Bradbury and Jo Wright beat
Nichola Beck and Joanne Davies 15–3, 15–5
Mixed Doubles: Jo Wright and Nick Ponting beat Julie
Bradbury and Simon Archer 15–12, 15–11

SCOTTISH NATIONAL CHAMPIONSHIPS 1995
Edinburgh, February

Men's Singles: Bruce Flockhart beat Jim Mailer 15–6,
15–12
Women's Singles: Anne Gibson beat Gillian Martin 11–5,
11–2
Men's Doubles: Russell Hogg and Kenneth Middlemiss beat
Alastair Gatt and Craig Robertson 15–5, 15–2
Women's Doubles: Elinor Allan and Jenny Allen beat Jillian
Haldane and Aileen Travers 15–2, 15–5
Mixed Doubles: Elinor Allen and Kenneth Middlemiss beat
Jillian Haldane and Gordon Haldane 18–16, 18–14

WELSH NATIONAL CHAMPIONSHIPS 1995
Cardiff, February

Men's Singles: John Leung beat Geraint Lewis 15–11, 15–5
Women's Singles: Kelly Morgan beat Katy Howell 11–0,
11–2
Men's Doubles: Lyndon Williams and Chris Rees beat
Richard Vaughan and Simon Richards 15–8, 15–9
Women's Doubles: Sarah Williams and Gail Davies beat
Katy Howell and Ruth Gardner 15–12, 18–14
Mixed Doubles: Sarah Williams and Andrew Burke beat
Nicola Hill and Julien Priestly 15–8, 15–7

ALL-ENGLAND CHAMPIONSHIPS 1995
Birmingham, March

Men's Singles: Poul-Erik Hoyer Larsen (Denmark) beat
Heryanto Arbi (Indonesia) 17–16, 15–6
Women's Singles: Lim Xiao Qing (Sweden) beat Camilla
Martin (Denmark) 11–9, 10–12, 11–3
Men's Doubles: Rexy Mainaky and Ricky Subagya
(Indonesia) beat Antonius Kantono and Denny
Kantono (Indonesia) 15–12, 18–15, 15–8

Women's Doubles: Gil Young-Ah and Jang Hye-Ock (S.
Korea) beat Elisa Zelin and Rosiana Zelin (Indonesia)
15–6, 15–3
Mixed Doubles: Marlene Thomsen and Thomas Lund
(Denmark) beat Rikke Olsen and Jon Holst-
Christensen (Denmark) 15–7, 15–7

BASKETBALL

MEN
Championship play-off final 1995: Worthing Bears beat
Manchester Giants 77–73
League Trophy final 1995: Thames Valley Tigers beat
Sheffield Sharks 74–69
National Cup final 1995: Sheffield Sharks beat Thames
Valley Tigers 89–66
National League Championship 1995: Sheffield Sharks

WOMEN
Championship play-off final 1995: Sheffield Hatters beat
Barking 76–65
National Cup final 1995: Sheffield Hatters beat Birmingham
Quality Cats 64–50
National League Championship 1995: Sheffield Hatters

BILLIARDS

World Professional Championship 1994: Peter Gilchrist
(England) beat Mike Russell (England) 1,539–645
World Professional Championship 1995: Geet Sethi (India)
beat Derendra Joshi (India) 1,661–931
UK Professional Championship 1995: Subhash Agarwal
(India) beat Peter Gilchrist (England) 1,240–1,114
British Open Championship 1995: Peter Gilchrist (England)
beat Rex Williams (England) 1,397–592

BOWLS (MEN)

WORLD INDOOR CHAMPIONSHIPS 1995
Preston, February

Singles: Andy Thomson (England) beat Richard Corsie
(Scotland) 7–2, 7–6, 7–3
Pairs: Richard Corsie and Alex Marshall (Scotland) beat
David Bryant and Tony Allcock (England) 6–7, 7–4,
7–3, 1–7, 7–4

NATIONAL CHAMPIONSHIPS 1995
Worthing, August–September

Singles: John Leeman (Craghead) beat Les Gillett
(Cheltenham) 21–13
Pairs: Swindon Westlecot beat Loxford Park, Ilford 21–20
Triples: Cheltenham beat Courtfield, Carlisle 14–12
Fours: Hollingbury Park, Brighton beat Parsons Green
18–17

NATIONAL INDOOR CHAMPIONSHIPS 1995
Melton Mowbray, April

Singles: Ian Bond (Exonia) beat Ian Wones (North
Walsham) 21–20
Pairs: Cumbria beat Tilbury 27–26
Triples: Wey Valley beat Stanley 17–14
Fours: Whiteknights beat Ipswich 17–14

BRITISH ISLES CHAMPIONSHIPS 1995
Llanelli, July

Singles: Brett Morley (England) beat Alan McCarley
(Wales) 21–5
Pairs: England beat Scotland 16–15
Triples: Wales beat Ireland 24–13
Fours: England beat Scotland 21–11

BRITISH ISLES INDOOR CHAMPIONSHIPS 1995
Nottingham, March

Singles: Mervyn King (England) beat John Price (Wales)
21–20
Pairs: England beat Ireland 16–13
Triples: Wales beat Ireland 16–12
Fours: England beat Ireland 21–17
Home International Championship 1995: Wales
Hilton Trophy (Home International Indoor Championship) 1995:
Scotland
Middleton Cup (Inter-County Championship) final 1995:
Cumbria beat Suffolk 119–107
Liberty Trophy (Inter-County Indoor Championship) final 1995:
Cumbria beat Wiltshire 131–104

BOWLS (WOMEN)

WORLD INDOOR CHAMPIONSHIPS 1995
Cumbernauld, April

Singles: Joyce Lindores (Scotland) beat Margaret Johnston
(Ireland) 7–0, 3–7, 2–7, 7–3, 7–3

NATIONAL CHAMPIONSHIPS 1995
Royal Leamington Spa, August

Singles (four woods): Janet Newman (Cornwall) beat Val
Wade (Kingsthorpe, Northampton) 21–10
Singles (two woods): Liz Shorter (Norwich County Arts)
beat Sharon Rickman (Raynes Park) 17–14
Pairs: Burnham beat Brixham 28–13
Triples: Cambridge Chesterton beat Northfleet 22–12
Fours: Marlow beat Blackwell 23–16

NATIONAL INDOOR CHAMPIONSHIPS 1995
Northampton, March

Singles: Brenda Brown (Colchester) beat Maureen
Monkton (Ilminster) 21–13
Pairs: Desborough, Maidenhead beat Angel, Tonbridge
26–5
Triples: Cherwell beat Darlington 21–9
Fours: Arun beat Thornaby 30–12

BRITISH ISLES CHAMPIONSHIPS 1995
Portrush, June

Singles: Betty Morgan (Wales) beat Margaret Johnston
(Ireland) 25–23
Pairs: Wales beat Ireland 24–15
Triples: England beat Scotland 16–14
Fours: Ireland beat England 22–13

BRITISH ISLES INDOOR CHAMPIONSHIPS 1995
Ballymoney, March

Singles: Mary Price (England) beat Doreen Rowlands
(Wales) 21–18
Pairs: Scotland beat England 32–16
Triples: Scotland beat Wales 16–10
Fours: Wales beat Scotland 22–15
Home International Championship 1995: England
Home International Indoor Championship 1995: England
Johns Trophy (Inter-County Championship) final 1995:
Wiltshire beat Sussex 125–119

Atherly Trophy (Inter-County Indoor Championship) final 1995:
Surrey beat Norfolk 116–111

BOXING

PROFESSIONAL BOXING
as at 4 September 1995

WORLD BOXING COUNCIL (WBC) CHAMPIONS

Heavy: Frank Bruno (GB)
Cruiser: Anaclet Wamba (France)
Light-heavy: Fabrice Tiozzo (France)
Super-middle: Nigel Benn (GB)
Middle: Quincey Smith (USA)
Super-welter: Terry Norris (USA)
Welter: Pernell Whitaker (USA)
Super-light: Julio Cesar Chavez (Mexico)
Light: Miguel Gonzalez (Mexico)
Super-feather: Gabriel Ruelas (USA)
Feather: Alejandro Gonzales (Mexico)
Super-bantam: Hector Acero-Sanchez (USA)
Bantam: Wayne McCullough (Ireland)
Super-fly: Hiroshi Kawashima (Japan)
Fly: Yuri Arbachakov (Russia)
Light-fly: Saman Sorjaturong (Thailand)
Straw: Ricardo Lopez (Mexico)

WORLD BOXING ASSOCIATION (WBA) CHAMPIONS

Heavy: Bruce Seldon (USA)
Cruiser: Nate Miller (USA)
Light-heavy: Virgil Hill (USA)
Super-middle: Frank Liles (USA)
Middle: Jorge Castro (Argentina)
Junior-middle: Carl Daniels (USA)
Welter: Ike Quartey (Ghana)
Junior-welter: Frankie Randall (USA)
Light: Olzubek Nazarov (Kyrgyzstan)
Junior-light: vacant
Feather: Eloy Rojas (Venezuela)
Junior-feather: Antonio Ceremeno (Venezuela)
Bantam: Daorung Chuvatana (Thailand)
Junior-bantam: Alimi Soitia (Venezuela)
Fly: Saen Sor Ploenchit (Thailand)
Light-fly: Hiyong Choi (Korea)
Straw: Chana Porpaoin (Thailand)

INTERNATIONAL BOXING FEDERATION (IBF)
CHAMPIONS

Heavy: vacant
Cruiser: Alfred Cole (USA)
Light-heavy: Henry Maske (Germany)
Super-middle: Roy Jones jun. (USA)
Middle: Bernard Hopkins (USA)
Super-welter: Vincent Pettway (USA)
Welter: Felix Trinidad (Puerto Rico)
Super-light: Konstantin Tszyu (Australia)
Light: vacant
Super-feather: Tracey Patterson (USA)
Feather: Tom Johnson (USA)
Super-bantam: Vuyani Bungu (S. Africa)
Bantam: Mbulelo Botile (S. Africa)
Super-fly: Harold Grey (Colombia)
Fly: Danny Romero (USA)
Light-fly: Saman Sorjaturong (Thailand)
Straw: Ratanapol Sovorapin (Thailand)

BRITISH CHAMPIONS

Heavy: James Oyebola

Cruiser: Terry Dunstan
Light-heavy: Crawford Ashley
Super-middle: Sam Storey
Middle: Neville Brown
Light-middle: Robert McCracken
Welter: Del Bryan
Light-welter: Ross Hale
Light: Michael Ayers
Super-feather: Floyd Havard
Feather: Michael Deveney
Super-bantam: Richie Wenton
Bantam: Draw Docherty
Fly: Francis Ampofo

EUROPEAN CHAMPIONS

Heavy: Zeljko Mavrovic (Croatia)
Cruiser: Patrice Aoussi (France)
Light-heavy: Eddy Smulders (Holland)
Super-middle: Henry Wharton (GB)
Middle: Richie Woodhall (GB)
Light-middle: Laurent Boudouani (France)
Welter: Patrick Charpentier (France)
Light-welter: Khalid Rahilou (France)
Light: Angel Mona (France)
Super-feather: Anatoly Alexandrov (Russia)
Feather: Medhi Labdouni (France)
Super-bantam: Vincenzo Belcastro (Italy)
Bantam: Johnny Armour (GB)
Fly: vacant

COMMONWEALTH CHAMPIONS

Heavy: vacant
Cruiser: Franco Wanyama (Uganda)
Light-heavy: Noel Magee (GB)
Super-middle: Henry Wharton (GB)
Middle: vacant
Light-middle: Leo Young (Australia)
Welter: Andrew Murray (Guyana)
Light-welter: Ross Hale (GB)
Light: Billy Schwer (GB)
Super-feather: Tony Pep (Canada)
Feather: Billy Hardy (GB)
Super-bantam: Neil Swain (GB)
Bantam: Johnny Armour (GB)
Fly: Daniel Ward (S. Africa)

AMATEUR BOXING

**AMATEUR BOXING ASSOCIATION (ABA) CHAMPIONSHIP
WINNERS 1995**

Super-heavy (91+ kg): Rod Allen
Heavy (91 kg): Matthew Ellis
Light-heavy (81 kg): Kelly Oliver
Middle (75 kg): Jason Matthews
Light-middle (71 kg): Chris Bessey
Welter (67 kg): Michael Hall
Light-welter (63.5 kg): Alan Vaughan
Light (60 kg): Roy Rutherford
Feather (57 kg): David Burrows
Bantam (54 kg): Noel Wilders
Fly (51 kg): Danny Costello
Light-fly (48 kg): Darren Fox

CHESS

PCA World Champion (since 1993): Garry Kasparov
(Russia)

FIDE World Champion (since 1993): Anatoly Karpov
(Russia)
Women's World Champion (since 1993): Xie Jun (China)
World Team Champions (since 1993): USA
British Champion 1995: Matthew Sadler
British Women's Champion 1995: Harriet Hunt

CRICKET

TEST SERIES

AUSTRALIA V. ENGLAND

First Test (Brisbane, 25–29 November 1994): Australia
won by 184 runs. Australia 426 and 248–8 dec.; England
167 and 323
Second Test (Melbourne, 24–29 December 1994): Australia
won by 295 runs. Australia 279 and 320–7 dec.; England
212 and 92
Third Test (Sydney, 1–5 January 1995): Match drawn.
England 309 and 255–2 dec.; Australia 116 and 344–7
Fourth Test (Adelaide, 26–30 January 1995): England won
by 106 runs. England 353 and 328; Australia 419 and
156
Fifth Test (Perth, 3–7 February 1995): Australia won by
329 runs. Australia 402 and 345–8 dec.; England 295 and
123

ENGLAND V. WEST INDIES

First Test (Headingley, 8–11 June 1995): West Indies won
by 9 wickets. England 199 and 208; West Indies 282 and
129–1
Second Test (Lord's, 22–26 June 1995): England won by 72
runs. England 283 and 336; West Indies 324 and 223
Third Test (Edgbaston, 6–8 July 1995): West Indies won
by an innings and 64 runs. England 147 and 89; West
Indies 300
Fourth Test (Old Trafford, 27–30 July 1995): England won
by 6 wickets. West Indies 216 and 314; England 437 and
94–4
Fifth Test (Trent Bridge, 10–14 August 1995): Match
drawn. England 440 and 269–9 dec.; West Indies 417
and 42–2
Sixth Test (The Oval, 24–28 August 1995): Match drawn.
England 454 and 223–4; West Indies 692–8 dec.

PAKISTAN V. AUSTRALIA (September–November 1994):
Pakistan won 1–0; two matches drawn
ZIMBABWE V. SRI LANKA (October 1994): 3 matches, all
drawn
INDIA V. WEST INDIES (November–December 1994):
India 1, West Indies 1; one match drawn
SOUTH AFRICA V. NEW ZEALAND (November
1994–January 1995): South Africa won 2–1
SOUTH AFRICA V. PAKISTAN (January 1995): South Africa
won 1–0
ZIMBABWE V. PAKISTAN (February 1995): Pakistan beat
Zimbabwe 2–1
NEW ZEALAND V. WEST INDIES (February 1995): West
Indies won 1–0; one match drawn
NEW ZEALAND V. SOUTH AFRICA (March 1995): South
Africa won 1–0
NEW ZEALAND V. SRI LANKA (March 1995): Sri Lanka
won 1–0; one match drawn
WEST INDIES V. AUSTRALIA (March–May 1995):
Australia won 2–1; one match drawn
PAKISTAN V. SRI LANKA (September 1995): Sri Lanka
won 2–1

ONE-DAY INTERNATIONALS

ENGLAND v. WEST INDIES

Trent Bridge (24–25 May 1995): West Indies won by 5 wickets. England 199–9; West Indies 201–5

The Oval (26 May 1995): England won by 25 runs. England 306–5; West Indies 281

Lord's (28 May 1995): England won by 73 runs. England 276–7; West Indies 203

World Series Cup final 1995: Australia beat Australia A 2–0

AUSTRALIA v. ENGLAND 1994–5 (Test Averages)

AUSTRALIA BATTING

	I	NO	R	HS	Av.
G. S. Blewett	4	1	249	115	83.00
M. J. Slater	10	0	623	176	62.30
S. R. Waugh	10	3	345	99*	49.28
M. A. Taylor	10	0	471	113	47.10
M. E. Waugh	10	0	435	140	43.50
I. A. Healy	10	3	249	74	35.57
D. C. Boon	10	0	246	131	24.60
T. B. A. May	5	3	31	10*	15.50
M. G. Bevan	6	0	81	35	13.50
D. W. Fleming	4	0	40	24	10.00
C. J. McDermott	8	2	42	21*	7.00
S. K. Warne	10	1	60	36*	6.66
G. D. McGrath	2	0	0	0	0.00

Played in one match: J. Angel, 11, 0; P. E. McIntyre, 0,0
*Not out

AUSTRALIA BOWLING

	O	M	R	W	Av.
M. E. Waugh	53	11	157	8	19.62
S. K. Warne	256.1	84	549	27	20.33
C. J. McDermott	232.5	56	675	32	21.09
D. W. Fleming	102.2	30	274	10	27.40
J. Angel	25.3	7	85	3	28.33
G. D. McGrath	67	16	229	6	38.16
P. E. McIntyre	27.3	3	87	2	43.50
T. B. A. May	101	30	219	1	219.00

Also bowled: M. G. Bevan, 7–1–19–0; G. S. Blewett, 24–5–91–0

ENGLAND BATTING

	I	NO	R	HS	Av.
G. P. Thorpe	10	1	444	123	49.33
G. A. Hick	6	1	208	98*	41.60
M. A. Atherton	10	0	407	88	40.70
J. P. Crawley	5	0	171	72	34.20
G. A. Gooch	10	0	245	56	24.50
D. Gough	5	1	98	51	24.50
A. J. Stewart	4	1	73	33	24.33
M. W. Gatting	9	0	182	117	20.22
P. A. J. DeFreitas	8	0	141	88	17.62
C. C. Lewis	4	0	68	40	17.00
D. E. Malcolm	7	3	50	29	12.50
A. R. C. Fraser	5	0	53	27	10.60
S. J. Rhodes	9	1	72	39*	9.00
P. C. R. Tufnell	7	3	6	4*	1.50

Played in one match: M. R. Ramprakash, 72, 42; M. J. McCague, 1, 0
*Not out

ENGLAND BOWLING

	O	M	R	W	Av.
D. Gough	152.5	33	425	20	21.25
C. C. Lewis	78.5	13	249	11	22.63
A. R. C. Fraser	129.5	25	389	14	27.78
P. A. J. DeFreitas	184	39	558	13	42.92
P. C. R. Tufnell	207.4	45	442	10	44.20
D. E. Malcolm	181.1	32	588	13	45.23
M. J. McCague	19.2	4	96	2	48.00
G. A. Gooch	25	6	74	1	74.00

Also bowled: G. A. Hick, 16–3–58–0; M. R. Ramprakash, 19–1–74–0

ENGLAND v. WEST INDIES 1995 (Test Averages)

ENGLAND BATTING

	I	NO	R	HS	Av.
M. Watkinson	4	1	156	82*	52.00
G. A. Hick	10	2	403	118*	50.37
R. C. Russell	5	1	199	91	49.75
R. A. Smith	8	1	305	90	43.57
G. P. Thorpe	12	0	506	94	42.16
M. A. Atherton	12	0	488	113	40.66
D. G. Cork	8	1	197	56*	28.14
R. K. Illingworth	8	5	69	17*	23.00
A. J. Stewart	5	0	113	37	22.60
N. V. Knight	4	0	89	57	22.25
J. P. Crawley	6	1	100	50	20.00
D. Gough	6	0	73	29	12.16
P. J. Martin	6	0	52	29	8.66
J. E. R. Gallian	4	0	32	25	8.00
C. White	4	0	26	23	6.50
A. R. C. Fraser	8	4	22	10*	5.50
M. R. Ramprakash	4	0	22	18	5.50
D. E. Malcolm	3	0	15	10	5.00

Played in one match: P. A. J. DeFreitas, 23, 1; J. E. Emburey, 8; A. P. Wells, 3, 0
*Not out

ENGLAND BOWLING

	O	M	R	W	Av.
D. G. Cork	184.2	30	661	26	25.42
A. R. C. Fraser	187.5	52	563	16	35.18
R. K. Illingworth	100	40	215	6	35.83
M. Watkinson	93	21	289	8	36.12
D. Gough	70	6	255	6	42.50
D. E. Malcolm	50.3	7	220	5	44.00
P. J. Martin	84	21	241	5	48.20
P. A. J. DeFreitas	27	3	115	2	57.50
G. A. Hick	18	4	64	1	64.00

Also bowled: J. E. R. Gallian, 12–1–56–0; C. White, 16–0–76–0; J. E. Emburey, 30–7–82–0

WEST INDIES BATTING

	I	NO	R	HS	Av.
B. C. Lara	10	1	765	179	85.00
C. O. Browne	3	2	62	34	62.00
S. Chanderpaul	3	1	103	80	51.50
S. C. Williams	2	0	92	62	46.00
S. L. Campbell	10	0	454	93	45.40
C. L. Hooper	8	1	310	127	44.28
R. B. Richardson	8	0	275	93	34.37
J. C. Adams	6	0	160	58	26.66
C. E. L. Ambrose	7	4	77	23*	25.66
K. L. T. Arthurton	7	0	172	75	24.57
K. C. G. Benjamin	6	2	74	20	18.50
J. R. Murray	6	0	84	26	14.00
C. A. Walsh	7	1	61	19	10.16
I. R. Bishop	8	1	71	16	10.14

Played in one match: O. D. Gibson, 29, 14; R. Dhanraj, 3
*Not out

WEST INDIES BOWLING

	O	M	R	W	Av.
K. C. G. Benjamin	158.2	33	506	23	22.00
I. R. Bishop	242.3	49	649	27	24.03
C. E. L. Ambrose	185.1	43	506	21	24.09
C. A. Walsh	290	57	786	26	30.23
C. L. Hooper	68	22	149	3	49.66
O. D. Gibson	34	3	132	2	66.00

Also bowled: B. C. Lara, 1–1–0–0; S. Chanderpaul, 6–0–22–0; J. C. Adams, 12–1–32–0; K. L. T. Arthurton, 33.5–6–76–0; R. Dhanraj, 55–8–191–0

COUNTY CHAMPIONSHIP TABLE 1995

Order for 1994 in brackets	P	W	L	D	Bt	Bl	Pts
Warwickshire (1)	17	14	2	1	49	64	337
Middlesex (4)	17	12	2	3	51	62	305
Northamptonshire (5)	17	12	2	3	41	57	290
Lancashire (10)	17	10	4	3	48	61	269
Essex (6)	17	8	9	0	42	58	228
Gloucestershire (12)	17	8	4	5	45	50	223
Leicestershire (2)	17	7	8	2	41	61	214
Yorkshire (13)	17	7	8	2	39	55	206
Somerset (11)	17	7	5	5	40	49	201
Worcestershire (15)	17	6	7	4	29	57	182
Nottinghamshire (3)	17	5	9	3	41	54	175
Surrey (7)	17	5	8	4	34	55	169
Hampshire (13)	17	5	8	4	32	56	168
Derbyshire (17)	17	4	10	3	39	64	167
Sussex (8)	17	4	7	6	37	51	152
Glamorgan (18)	17	3	8	6	40	57	145
Durham (16)	17	4	13	0	20	53	137
Kent (9)	17	3	10	4	40	44	132

FIRST CLASS BATTING AVERAGES 1995

	I	NO	R	HS	Av.
M. R. Ramprakash	20	32	2,258	235	77.86
M. D. Moxon	13	23	1,145	203*	76.33
A. C. Gilchrist	8	11	495	122	61.87
P. A. de Silva	16	30	1,781	255	59.36
B. C. Lara	13	20	1,126	179	59.26
S. Chanderpaul	15	25	1,003	140*	59.00
J. L. Langer	7	12	516	149	57.33
K. L. T. Arthurton	15	23	1,077	146	56.68
D. Byas	20	37	1,913	213	56.26
A. J. Lamb	16	26	1,237	166	56.22
A. Symonds	18	31	1,438	254*	55.30
T. M. Moody	18	31	1,600	168	55.17
M. G. Bevan	20	34	1,598	153*	55.10
N. Hussain	19	35	1,854	186	54.52
A. P. Wells	18	30	1,524	178	54.42
M. W. Gatting	16	22	1,139	148	54.23
R. T. Robinson	18	32	1,728	209	54.00
P. D. Bowler	19	33	1,619	196	53.96
P. C. L. Holloway	12	22	863	129*	53.93
R. A. Smith	12	23	1,117	172	53.19

*Not out

FIRST CLASS BOWLING AVERAGES 1995

	O	M	R	W	Av.
A. A. Donald	535.3	136	1,431	89	16.07
D. A. Reeve	312	118	661	38	17.39
J. Srinath	568.4	147	1,661	87	19.09
Wasim Akram	518.1	108	1,598	81	19.72
T. A. Munton	373.5	119	952	48	19.83
C. L. Cairns	375.5	89	1,035	52	19.90
D. G. Cork	586.5	111	1,800	90	20.00
R. L. Johnson	301.4	79	812	40	20.30
A. Kumble	899.4	265	2,143	105	20.40
K. C. G. Benjamin	284.1	71	923	43	21.46
A. M. Smith	415.3	104	1,275	59	21.61
P. C. R. Tufnell	678.1	207	1,634	74	22.08
M. S. Kasprowicz	175.1	42	599	27	22.18
P. J. Newport	548	148	1,551	69	22.47
P. J. Hartley	549	120	1,861	81	22.97
J. E. Emburey	708.4	198	1,701	74	22.98
D. J. Capel	358.2	70	1,206	51	23.64
M. P. Bicknell	285	65	978	41	23.85
M. C. Ilott	582.4	126	1,897	78	24.32
J. E. Benjamin	420.4	85	1,326	53	25.01

Source for averages and county championship table: TCCB/PA *Cricket Record*

OTHER RESULTS 1995

Benson and Hedges Cup final: Lancashire beat Kent by 35 runs. Lancashire 274–7; Kent 239

NatWest Trophy final: Warwickshire beat Northamptonshire by 4 wickets. Northamptonshire 200; Warwickshire 203–6

Sunday League Champions: Kent

MCC Trophy (Minor Counties knockout final): Cambridgeshire beat Herefordshire by 2 wickets. Cambridgeshire 227–8; Herefordshire 226–4

Minor Counties Championship final: Devon beat Lincolnshire by 57 runs. Devon 263–2; Lincolnshire 206–8

National Club Championship final: Chorley beat Clifton Flax Bourton by 12 runs. Chorley 239–2; Clifton Flax Bourton 227–8

National Village Championship final: Woodhouse Grange beat Tiddington by 14 runs. Woodhouse Grange 151–9; Tiddington 137–8

Varsity Match: Oxford beat Cambridge by 9 wickets. Cambridge 295 and 126; Oxford 233–9; dec. and 190–1

CYCLING

World Cup series overall winner 1994: Gianluca Bortolami (Italy), 151 pts

Tour of Italy 1995: Tony Rominger (Switzerland)
Tour de France 1995: Miguel Indurain (Spain)
Tour of Spain 1995: Laurent Jalabert (France)

World Professinal Road Race Championship 1994: Luc Leblanc (France)

World Amateur Road Race Championship 1994: Alex Pedersen (Sweden)

World Open Cyclo-Cross Championship 1995: Dieter Runkel (Switzerland)

British Road Race Championship 1995: Robert Millar
British Amateur Road Race Championship 1995: Simon Gray
British Open Cyclo-Cross Championship 1995: Barrie Clarke
British Amateur Cyclo-Cross Championship 1995: James Norfolk

Women's World Road Race Championship 1994: Monica Valvik (Norway)

Women's National Road Race Championship 1995: Marie Purvis

Women's British Open Cyclo-Cross Championship 1995: Caroline Alexander

EQUESTRIANISM

SHOW JUMPING
World Cup final 1995: Nick Skelton on Everest Dollar Girl
(GB)
European Championships 1995:
    Individual: Peter Charles on La Ina (Ireland)
    Team: Switzerland
British Jumping Derby 1995 (Hickstead): Capt. John
    Ledingham on Kilbaha (Ireland)

THREE-DAY EVENTING
European Championships 1995:
    Individual: Lucy Thompson on Welton Romance
    (Ireland)
    Team: Great Britain
Badminton Horse Trials 1995: Bruce Davidson on Eagle
    Lion (USA)
British Open Horse Trials 1995 (Gatcombe Park): William
    Fox-Pitt on Chaka (GB)
Burghley Horse Trials 1995: Andrew Nicholson on Buckley
    Province (New Zealand)

ETON FIVES

NatWest County Championship 1995: Middlesex
Amateur Championship (Kinnaird Cup) 1995: Robin Mason
    and Andrew Mole beat Edward Wass and James
    Halstead 3–1
Holmwoods Schools' Championship 1995: Highgate beat
    Shrewsbury 3–0
Barber Cup final 1995: Old Cholmeleians beat Old
    Edwardians 2–1
League Championship (Douglas Keeble Cup) 1995: Old
    Cholmeleians

FENCING (MEN)

WORLD CHAMPIONSHIPS 1995
The Hague, July

Foil: Dmitri Chevtchenko (Russia)
Epée: Eric Srecki (France)
Sabre: Grigori Kirienko (Russia)
Team Foil: Hungary
Team Epée: Germany
Team Sabre: Italy

BRITISH CHAMPIONS 1995
Foil: Paul Walsh (Sussex House)
Epée: Quentin Berriman
Sabre: Amin Zahir (Salle Frohlich)
Team Foil: Salle Paul
Team Epée: Kingston
Team Sabre: Salle Frohlich

International Epée World Cup Series 1995: Arndt Schmitt
    (Germany)
Corble Cup 1995 (international sabre tournament): Jurgen
    Scheicher (Austria)

FENCING (WOMEN)

WORLD CHAMPIONSHIPS 1995
The Hague, July
Foil: Laura Badea (Romania)

Epée: Joanna Jakimiuk (Poland)
Team Foil: Italy
Team Epée: Hungary

BRITISH CHAMPIONS 1995
Foil: Linda Strachan (Salle Paul)
Epée: Kate Houston (MPAGB)
Sabre: Sue Benny (Glastonbury)
Team Epée: London Thames

Ipswich Cup 1995 (international epée word cup series):
    Claudia Bokel (Germany)

GOLF (MEN)

THE MAJOR CHAMPIONSHIPS 1995
US Masters (Augusta, Georgia, 6–9 April): Ben Crenshaw
    (USA), 274
US Open (Shinnecock Hills, 15–18 June): Corey Pavin
    (USA), 280
The Open (The Old Course, St Andrews, 20–23 July): John
    Daly (USA), 282*
US PGA Championship (Riviera Country Club, Los
    Angeles, 10–13 August): Steve Elkington (Australia),
    267*

PGA EUROPEAN TOUR 1994
World Matchplay Championship (Wentworth): Ernie Els (S.
    Africa) beat Colin Montgomerie (Scotland) 4 and 2
Czech Open (Marienbad): Per-Ulrick Johansson (Sweden),
    237
Volvo Masters (Valderrama): Bernhard Langer (Germany),
    276
European Tour Order of Merit 1994: 1. Colin Montgomerie
    (Scotland); 2. Bernhard Langer (Germany); 3.
    Severiano Ballasteros (Spain)
World Championship 1994 (Montego Bay, Jamaica): Ernie
    Els (S. Africa), 268
World Cup 1994 (Dorado Beach, Puerto Rico): Fred
    Couples (USA), 265
World Open Championship 1994 (Chateau Elan, Georgia):
    Ernie Els (S. Africa), 273

PGA EUROPEAN TOUR 1995
Dubai Desert Classic: Fred Couples (USA), 268
Johnnie Walker Classic (Manila, Philippines): Fred Couples
    (USA), 277
Madeira Island Open: Santiago Luna (Spain), 272
Canary Islands Open (Gran Canaria): Jarmo Sandelin
    (Sweden), 282
South African PGA Championship (Johannesburg): Ernie Els
    (S. Africa), 271
Mediterranean Open (Valencia): Robert Karlsson (Sweden),
    276
Andalucian Open (Huelva): Alexander Cejka (Germany),
    278
Moroccan Open (Agadir): Mark James (England), 275
Portuguese Open (Lisbon): Adam Hunter (Scotland), 277*
Balearic Open (Majorca): Greg Turner (New Zealand), 274
Catalonia Open (Gerona): Philip Walton (Ireland), 281
Cannes Open: Andre Bossert (Switzerland), 132 (rain
    curtailed play)
Pairs Tournament (St Cloud, Paris): Severiano Ballasteros
    and José-Maria Olazábal (Spain), 256
Italian Open (Milan): Sam Torrance (Scotland), 269
International Open (St Mellion): Peter O'Malley (Australia),
    280
Spanish Open (Madrid): Severiano Ballasteros (Spain), 274

*After a play-off

PGA Championship (Wentworth): Bernhard Langer (Germany), 279

English Open (Forest of Arden): Philip Walton (Ireland), 274*

Tournament Players' Championship (Hamburg): Bernhard Langer (Germany), 270

Jersey Open (La Moye): Andrew Oldcorn (England), 273

French Open (St Quentin-en-Yvelines): Paul Broadhurst (England), 274

International Open (St Eurach, Munich): Frank Nobilo (New Zealand), 272

Irish Open (Kilkenny): Sam Torrance (Scotland), 277*

Scottish Open (Carnoustie): Wayne Riley (Australia), 276

Dutch Open (Hilversum): Scott Hoch (USA), 269

Scandinavian Masters (Malmo): Jesper Parnevik (Sweden), 270

Austrian Open (Litschau): Alexander Cejka (Germany), 267

Czech Open (Marianske Lazne): Peter Teravainen (USA), 268

German Open (Stuttgart): Colin Montgomerie (Scotland), 268

European Masters (Crans-sur-Sierre): Mathias Gronberg (Sweden), 270

Lancôme Trophy (St-Nom-la-Brêteche): Colin Montgomerie (Scotland), 269

British Masters (Collingtree, Northampton): Sam Torrance (Scotland), 270

European Open (K Club, Dublin): Bernhard Langer (Germany), 280*

Team Events

Alfred Dunhill Cup final 1994 (St Andrews, 6–9 October): Canada beat USA 2–1

World Cup 1994 (Dorado Beach, Puerto Rico): USA, 536

Ryder Cup 1995 (Oak Hill, New York State): Europe beat USA 14½–13½

Walker Cup 1995 (amateur) (Royal Porthcawl): GB and Ireland beat USA 14–10

Eisenhower Trophy (world amateur team championship) 1994 (Versailles): USA, 838

European Amateur Team Championship 1995 (Royal Antwerp): Scotland

Home International Championship 1995 (amateur) (Royal Portrush): England

Amateur Championships

British Amateur Championship 1995 (Hoylake): Gordon Sherry (Kilmarnock)

English Amateur Championship 1995 (Hunstanton): Mark Foster (Worksop)

Welsh Amateur Championship 1995 (Royal St Davids): Gary Houston (Flint)

Scottish Amateur Championship 1995 (Southerness): Simon Mackenzie (West Linton)

Brabazon Trophy (English Open Strokeplay) 1995 (Southport): = Colin Edwards (Bath) and Mark Foster (Worksop), 283

Welsh Open Strokeplay 1995 (Prestatyn): Mathew Peet (Pyle and Kenfig), 282

Scottish Open Strokeplay 1995 (Paisley and Renfrew): Stephen Gallacher (Bathgate), 282

Lytham Trophy 1995 (Royal Lytham and St Anne's): Stephen Gallacher (Bathgate), 281

Berkshire Trophy 1995 (The Berkshire): Gary Harris (Broome Manor), 275

International Match 1995 (Fairhaven): England beat Spain 14½–9½

European Amateur Championship 1995 (Barcelona): Sergio Garcia (Spain), 276

President's Putter 1995 (Rye): Andy Woolnough beat Michael MacPhee 5 and 4

Halford Hewitt Trophy 1995 (for public schools' old boys): Harrow beat Watson's 4–1

Varsity Match 1995: Oxford beat Cambridge 8–7

GOLF (Women)

US Women's Open 1995 (The Broadmoor, 13–16 July): Annika Sorenstam (Sweden), 278

Women's World Championship 1994 (Naples, Florida): Beth Daniel (USA), 274

WPG European Tour 1994

French Open (St Endreol): Julie Forbes (Scotland), 213*

European Tour Order of Merit 1994: 1. Liselotte Neumann (Sweden); 2. Helen Alfredsson (Sweden); 3. Laura Davies (England)

WPG European Tour 1995

Costa Azul Open (Setubal, Portugal): Marie-Laure de Lorenzi (France), 205

Ford Classic (Chart Hills, Kent): Lora Fairclough (England), 277

Evian Masters: Laura Davies (England), 271

Austrian Open (Zell am See): Annika Sorenstam (Sweden), 270

European Masters (Antwerp): Lora Fairclough (England), 206

Hennessy Cup (Cologne): Annika Sorenstam (Sweden), 271

Irish Open (Dublin): Laura Davies (England), 267

Scottish Open (Dalmahoy): Alison Nicholas (England), 272

Welsh Open (St Pierre): Laura Davies (England), 278

British Open (Woburn): Karrie Webb (Australia), 278

Danish Open (Vejle): Caroline Hall (England), 201

English Open (The Oxfordshire): Laura Davies (England), 279

Trygg-Hansa Open (Haninge): Liselotte Neumann (Sweden), 281

Dutch Open (Rijk van Nijmegen): Marie-Laure de Lorenzi (France), 201

Maredo Open (Treudelberg): Rachel Hetherington (Australia), 275

Italian Open (Il Picciolo): Deni Booker (Australia), 284

Team Events

Solheim Cup 1994 (The Greenbrier, West Virginia, 21–23 October): USA beat Europe 13–7

Home International Championship 1994 (amateur) (Huddersfield): England

Espirito Santo Trophy (world amateur team championship) 1994: USA

European Amateur Team Championship 1995 (Milan): Spain

Amateur Championships

British Open Championship 1995 (Royal Portrush): Julie Hall (Felixstowe Ferry)

English Amateur Championship 1995 (Ipswich): Julie Hall (Felixstowe Ferry)

Welsh Amateur Championship 1995 (Aberdovey): Lisa Dermott (Royal Liverpool)

Scottish Amateur Championship 1995 (Portpatrick): Hilary Monaghan (Longniddry)

British Strokeplay 1995 (Sandwich): Maria José Pons (Spain), 289

English Strokeplay 1995 (Hallamshire): Lisa Walton (Calcot Park), 289

Welsh Strokeplay 1995 (Newport): Fiona Brown (Heswall), 221*

---

*After a play-off

Scottish Strokeplay 1995 (Portland and Royal Troon): Maria Hjorth (Sweden), 219
European Amateur Championship 1995 (Berlin): Maria Hjorth (Sweden), 284

GREYHOUND RACING

Grand Prix 1994 (Walthamstow): Redwood Girl
St Leger 1994 (Wembley): Ballarue Minx
Television Trophy 1995 (Oxford): Last Action
Grand National 1995 (Hall Green): Elegant Brandy
Greyhound Derby 1995 (Wimbledon): Moaning Lad
Scurry Gold Cup 1995 (Catford): Demesne Bear
The Masters 1995 (Reading): Longvalley Manor
The Regency 1995 (Brighton): Suncrest Sail
Gold Collar 1995 (Catford): Alan's Rose

GYMNASTICS (Men)

World Team Champions 1994: China

BRITISH CHAMPIONSHIPS 1994
British Champion: Lee McDermott (Sutton)
British Individual Apparatus Champions:
    Floor: Criag Heap
    Pommell Horse: Lee McDermott (Sutton)
    Rings: Lee McDermott (Sutton)
    Vault: Andrew Minshall (Liverpool)
    Parallel Bars: = Lee McDermott (Sutton) and Craig Heap (Lilleshall)
    High Bar: Lee McDermott (Sutton)
British Team Champions 1995 (Adam Shield): City of Liverpool

GYMNASTICS (Women)

World Team Champions 1994: Romania
World Rhythmics Champion 1994: Maria Petrova (Bulgaria)
World Rhythmics Champion 1995: Maria Petrova (Bulgaria) and Ekaterina Serebrianskaya (Ukraine)

BRITISH CHAMPIONSHIPS 1994
British Champion: Zita Lusack (Heathrow)
British Individual Apparatus Champions:
    Floor: Annika Reeder (Loughton)
    Beam: Anna-Liese Acklam (Camberley)
    Vault: = Sonia Lawrence (Spelthorne) and Anna-Liese Acklam (Camberley)
    Asymmetric Bars: Zita Lusack (Heathrow)

BRITISH CHAMPIONSHIPS 1995
British Champion: Annika Reeder (S. Essex)
British Individual Apparatus Champions:
    Floor: Annika Reeder (S. Essex)
    Beam: Zita Lusack (Heathrow)
    Vault: Annika Reeder (S. Essex)
    Asymmetric Bars: Gemma Cuff (Heathrow)
British Team Champions 1995: Heathrow
British Rhythmics Champion 1995: Jenny McGuire

HOCKEY (Men)

National League 1995: Teddington

Hockey Association Cup final 1995: Guildford beat Teddington 4-1
National Indoor Club Championship final 1995: Old Loughtonians beat Barford Tigers 6-5
County Championship final 1995: Yorkshire beat Kent 3-2
Champions Trophy final 1995: Germany 2, Australia 2. Germany won 4-2 on penalties
World Cup final 1994: Pakistan 1, Netherlands 1. Pakistan won 4-3 on penalties
European Club Championship final 1995: Uhlenhorst (Germany) beat Amsterdam (Netherlands) 1-0
European Indoor Club Championship final 1995: Rottweis Cologne (Germany) beat Harvestehuder (Germany) 5-3
European Cup Winners' Cup final 1995: Harvestehuder (Germany) 0, HDM (Netherlands) 0. Harvestehuder won 4-1 on penalties
European Nations Cup final 1995: Germany 2, Netherlands 2. Germany won 9-8 on penalties
Varsity Match 1995: Oxford beat Cambridge 4-0

HOCKEY (Women)

National League 1995: Slough
AEWHA Cup final 1995: Hightown beat Trojans 5-0
National Indoor Club Championship 1995: Hightown
County Championship final 1995: Suffolk beat Staffordshire 1-0
Champions Trophy final 1995: Australia beat Korea 4-3
Centenary Match 1995: England 1, Germany 1
European Club Championship final 1995: SV Kampong (Netherlands) 1, Berliner (Germany) 1. SV Kampong won 2-0 on penalties
European Indoor Club Championship final 1995: Russelsheim (Germany) beat Slough (England) 7-1
European Cup Winners' Cup final 1995: Russelsheim (Germany) 1, Slough (England) 1. Russelsheim won 4-2 on penalties
European Nations Cup final 1995: Netherlands 2, Spain 2. Netherlands won 4-1 on penalties

HORSERACING

WINNING OWNERS 1994

Sheikh Mohammed	£2,683,384
Hamdan Al-Maktoum	2,636,272
Maktoum Al-Maktoum	1,138,812
Khalid Abdulla	730,145
Cheveley Park Stud	536,483
Robert Sangster	516,907
Peter Savill	354,724
Lord Howard de Walden	345,862
Jeff Smith	345,010
Sheikh Ahmed Al-Maktoum	269,133

WINNING TRAINERS 1994

Michael Stoute	£1,913,626
John Dunlop	1,667,263
Henry Cecil	1,534,330
John Gosden	1,225,889
Richard Hannon	1,128,348
Mark Johnston	924,272
Paul Cole	798,632
Luca Cumani	779,538
Jack Berry	693,955
Ian Balding	619,120

Leading Breeders 1994

	Value
Shadwell Farm Inc. & Shadwell Estate Co. Ltd	£831,416
Sheikh Mohammed	610,825
Juddmonte Farms	518,031
Cheveley Park Stud	352,567
T. J. Monaghan	331,353
Michael Poland	306,552
Gainsborough Stud Management Ltd	289,935
Shadwell Estate Co. Ltd	273,721
Shadwell Farm Inc.	270,622
Stanley Estate & Stud Co.	266,637

Winning Sires 1994

	Horses	Races won	Total value
Sadler's Wells (1981) by Northern Dancer	34	51	£1,237,989
Chief's Crown (1982) by Danzig	7	9	880,567
Green Desert (1983) by Danzig	30	53	587,383
Last Tycoon (1983) by Try My Best	20	34	520,714
Caerleon (1980) by Nijinsky	19	29	505,871
Danzig (1977) by Northern Dancer	18	26	500,628
Night Shift (1980) by Northern Dancer	29	55	419,138
Alzao (1980) by Lyphard	25	37	404,187
Warning (1985) by Known Fact	22	34	395,872
Rainbow Quest (1981) by Blushing Groom	21	30	367,444

Winning Flat Jockeys 1994

	1st	2nd	3rd	Unpl.	Total mts
Frankie Dettori	183	195	131	578	1,087
Jason Weaver	162	132	108	507	909
Pat Eddery	154	110	79	459	802
Kevin Darley	138	116	111	510	875
Richard Quinn	103	112	109	520	844
John Reid	98	86	74	435	693
Willie Carson	87	92	86	385	650
Michael Hills	85	74	64	395	618
John Carroll	81	49	67	415	612
Michael Roberts	80	72	75	538	765

Winning National Hunt Jockeys 1994–5

	1st	2nd	3rd	Unpl.	Total mts
Richard Dunwoody	160	117	102	367	746
Adrian Maguire	130	111	76	352	669
Norman Williamson	130	113	93	377	713
Jamie Osborne	111	80	66	248	505
Peter Niven	106	74	50	158	388
David Bridgwater	78	53	48	272	451
†Tony McCoy	74	63	56	276	469
Mick Fitzgerald	68	89	91	307	555
Warren Marston	66	36	46	242	390
Mark Dwyer	65	77	40	223	405

†Conditional jockey

The above statistics are the copyright of *The Sporting Life*

RESULTS

Cesarewitch
(1839) Newmarket, 2 miles and about 2 f

1991	Go South (7y), (7st 11lb), N. Carlisle
1992	Vintage Crop (5y), (9st 6lb), W. Swinburn
1993	Aahsaylad (7y), (8st 12lb), J. Williams
1994	Captain's Guest (4y), (9st 9lb), A. Clark

Champion Stakes
(1877) Newmarket, 1 mile, 2 f

1991	Tel Quel (3y), (8st 12lb), A. Fabre
1992	Rodrigo de Triano (3y), (8st 12lb), L. Piggott
1993	Hatoof (4y), (9st), W. Swinburn
1994	Dernier Empereur (4y), (9st 4lb), S. Guillot

*Hennessy Gold Cup
(1957) Newbury, 3 miles and about 2½ f

1991	Chatham (7y), (10st 6lb), P. Scudamore
1992	Sibton Abbey (7y), (10st), A. Maguire
1993	Cogent (9y), (10st 8lb), D. Fortt
1994	One Man (6y), (10st), A. Dobbin

*King George VI Chase
(1937) Kempton, about 3 miles

1991	The Fellow (6y), (11st 10lb), A. Kondrat
1992	The Fellow (7y), (11st 10lb), A. Kondrat
1993	Barton Bank (7y), (11st 10lb), A. Maguire
1994	Algan (6y), (11st 10lb), P. Chevalier

*Champion Hurdle
(1927) Cheltenham, 2 miles and about ½ f

1992	Royal Gait (9y), (12st), G. McCourt
1993	Granville Again (7y), (12st), P. Scudamore
1994	Flakey Dove (8y), (11st 9lb), M. Dwyer
1995	Alderbrook (6y), (12st), N. Williamson

*Queen Mother Champion Chase
(1959) Cheltenham, about 2 miles

1992	Remittance Man (8y), (12st), J. Osborne
1993	Deep Sensation (8y), (12st), D. Murphy
1994	Viking Flagship (7y), (12st), A. Maguire
1995	Viking Flagship (8y), (12st), C. Swan

*Cheltenham Gold Cup
(1924) 3 miles and about 2½ f

1992	Cool Ground (10y), (12st), A. Maguire
1993	Jodami (8y), (12st), M. Dwyer
1994	The Fellow (9y), (12st), A. Kondrat
1995	Master Oats (9y), (12st), N. Williamson

Lincoln Handicap
(1965) Doncaster, 1 mile

1992	High Low (4y), (8st), J. Quinn
1993	High Premium (5y), (8st 8lb), K. Fallon
1994	Our Rita (5y), (8st 5lb), D. Holland
1995	Roving Minstrel (4y), (8st 3lb), K. Darley

*Grand National
(1837) Liverpool, 4 miles and about 4 f

1992	Party Politics (8y), (10st 7lb), C. Llewellyn
1993	Race declared void. Esha Ness (J. White) first past post
1994	Miinnehoma (11y), (10st 8lb), R. Dunwoody
1995	Royal Athlete (9y), (11st 10lb), J. Titley

Record times: 8 minutes 47.8 seconds by Mr Frisk in 1990; 9 minutes 1.9 seconds by Red Rum in 1973

*National Hunt

THE CLASSICS

ONE THOUSAND GUINEAS

(1814) Rowley Mile, Newmarket, for three-year-old fillies

Year	Winner	Betting	Owner	Jockey	Trainer	No. of Runners
1992	Hatoof	5–1	M. Al-Maktoum	W. Swinburn	C. Head	14
1993	Sayyedati	4–1	Mohamed Obaida	W. Swinburn	C. Brittain	12
1994	Las Meninas	12–1	R. Sangster	J. Reid	T. Stack	15
1995	Harayir	5–1	H. Al-Maktoum	R. Hills	R. Hern	14

TWO THOUSAND GUINEAS

(1809) Rowley Mile, Newmarket, for three-year-olds

Year	Winner	Betting	Owner	Jockey	Trainer	No. of Runners
1992	Rodrigo de Triano	6–1	R. Sangster	L. Piggott	P. Chapple-Hyam	16
1993	Zafonic	5–6	K. Abdulla	P. Eddery	A. Fabre	14
1994	Mister Baileys	16–1	P. Venner	J. Weaver	M. Johnston	23
1995	Pennekamp	9–2	Sheikh Mohammed	T. Jarnet	A. Fabre	11

Record time: 1 minute 35.84 seconds, 1990

THE DERBY

(1780) Epsom, 1 mile and about 4 f, for three-year-olds

The first winner was Sir Charles Bunbury's Diomed in 1780. The owners with the record number of winners are Lord Egremont, who won in 1782, 1804, 1805, 1807, 1826 (also won five Oaks); and the late Aga Khan, who won in 1930, 1935, 1936, 1948, 1952 (also won two Oaks). Other winning owners are: Duke of Grafton (1802, 1809, 1810, 1815); Mr J. Bowes (1835, 1843, 1852, 1853); Sir J. Hawley (1851, 1858, 1859, 1868); the 1st Duke of Westminster (1880, 1882, 1886, 1899); and Sir Victor Sassoon (1953, 1957, 1958, 1960).

Record times are: 2 min. 33.80 sec. by Mahmoud in 1936; 2 min. 33.84 sec. by Kahyasi in 1988; 2 min. 33.9 sec. by Reference Point in 1987.

The Derby was run at Newmarket from 1915–18 and from 1940–5.

Year	Winner	Betting	Owner	Jockey	Trainer	No. of Runners
1992	Dr Devious	8–1	S. Craig	J. Reid	P. Chapple-Hyam	18
1993	Commander In Chief	15–2	K. Abdulla	M. Kinane	H. Cecil	16
1994	Erhaab	7–2	H. Al-Maktoum	W. Carson	J. Dunlop	25
1995	Lammtarra	14–1	S. M. Al-Maktoum	W. Swinburn	Saeed bin Suroor	15

THE OAKS

(1779) Epsom, 1 mile and about 4 f, for three-year-old fillies

Year	Winner	Betting	Owner	Jockey	Trainer	No. of Runners
1992	User Friendly	5–1	W. Gredley	G. Duffield	C. Brittain	7
1993	Intrepidity	5–1	Sheikh Mohammed	M. Roberts	A. Fabre	14
1994	Balanchine	6–1	M. Al-Maktoum	F. Dettori	H. Ibrahim	10
1995	Moonshell	3–1	M. Al-Maktoum/ Godolphin	F. Dettori	Saeed bin Suroor	10

ST LEGER

(1776) Doncaster, 1 mile and about 6 f, for three-year-olds

Year	Winner	Betting	Owner	Jockey	Trainer	No. of Runners
1992	User Friendly	7–4	W. Gredley	G. Duffield	C. Brittain	8
1993	Bob's Return	3–1	Mrs J. Smith	P. Robinson	M. Tompkins	9
1994	Moonax	40–1	Sheikh Mohammed	P. Eddery	B. Hills	8
1995	Classic Cliche	100–30	Godolphin	F. Dettori	Saeed bin Suroor	10

*WHITBREAD GOLD CUP
(1957) Sandown, 3 miles and about 5 f

1992 Topsham Bay (9y), (10st), H. Davies
1993 Topsham Bay (10y), (10st), R. Dunwoody
1994 Ushers Island (8y), (10st), C. Swan
1995 Cache Fleur (9y), (9st 10lb), R. Dunwoody

JOCKEY CLUB STAKES
(1894) Newmarket, 1½ miles

1992 Sapience (6y), (8st 12lb), R. Cochrane
1993 Zinaad (4y), (8st 9lb), W. Swinburn
1994 Silver Wisp (5y), (8st 9lb), M. Hills
1995 Only Royale (6y), (8st 11lb), F. Dettori

KENTUCKY DERBY
(1875) Louisville, Kentucky, 1¼ miles

1992 Lil E Tee, P. Day
1993 Sea Hero, J. Bailey
1994 Go for Gin, C. McCarron
1995 Thunder Gulch, G. Stevens

PRIX DU JOCKEY CLUB
(1836) Chantilly, 1½ miles

1992 Polytain (9st 2lb), F. Dettori
1993 Hernando (9st 2lb), C. Asmussen
1994 Celtic Arms (9st 2lb), G. Mossé
1995 Celtic Swing (9st 2lb), K. Darley

ASCOT GOLD CUP
(1807) Ascot, 2 miles and about 4 f

1992 Drum Taps (6y), (9st 2lb), F. Dettori
1993 Drum Taps (7y), (9st 2lb), F. Dettori
1994 Arcadian Heights (6y), (9st 2lb), M. Hills
1995 Double Trigger (4y), (9st), J. Weaver

IRISH SWEEPS DERBY
(1866) Curragh, 1½ miles, for three year olds

1992 St Jovite (9st), C. Roche
1993 Commander In Chief (9st), P. Eddery
1994 Balanchine (8st 11lb), F. Dettori
1995 Winged Love (9st), O. Peslier

ECLIPSE STAKES
(1886) Sandown, 1 mile and about 2 f

1992 Kooyonga (4y), (9st 4lb), W. O'Connor
1993 Opera House (5y), (9st 7lb), M. Kinane
1994 Ezzoud (5y), (9st 7lb), W. Swinburn
1995 Halling (4y), (9st 7lb), W. Swinburn

KING GEORGE VI AND QUEEN ELIZABETH DIAMOND STAKES
(1952) Ascot, 1 mile and about 4 f

1992 St Jovite (3y), (8st 9lb), S. Craine
1993 Opera House (5y), (9st 7lb), M. Stoute
1994 King's Theatre (3y), (8st 9lb), M. Kinane
1995 Lammtarra (3y), (8st 9lb), F. Dettori

GOODWOOD CUP
(1812) Goodwood, about 2 miles

1992 Further Flight (6y), (9st 5lb), M. Hills
1993 Sonus (4y), (9st 3lb), P. Eddery
1994 Tioman Island (4y), (9st 5lb), T. Quinn
1995 Double Trigger (4y), (9st 5lb), J. Weaver

CAMBRIDGESHIRE HANDICAP
(1839) Newmarket, 1 mile

1992 Rambo's Hall (7y), (9st 3lb), D. McKeown
1993 Penny Drops (4y), (7st 13lb), D. Harrison
1994 Halling (3y), (8st 8lb), F. Dettori
1995 Cap Juluca (3y), (9st 10lb), R. Hughes

PRIX DE L'ARC DE TRIOMPHE
(1920) Longchamp, 1½ miles

1992 Subotica (4y), (9st 4lb), T. Jarnet
1993 Urban Sea (4y), (9st 1lb), E. Saint-Martin
1994 Carnegie (3y), (8st 11lb), T. Jarnet
1995 Lammtarra (3y), (8st 11lb), F. Dettori

ICE HOCKEY

World Championship final 1995: Finland beat Sweden 4–1
British Championship final 1995: Sheffield Steelers beat
  Edinburgh Racers 7–2
League Championship 1995:
  Premier Division: Sheffield Steelers
  First Division: Slough Jets
Benson and Hedges Cup final 1994: Nottingham Panthers
  beat Cardiff Devils 7–2
Stanley Cup final 1995: New Jersey Devils beat Detroit Red
  Wings 4–0

ICE SKATING

BRITISH CHAMPIONSHIPS 1994
Hull, November–December

Men: Steven Cousins
Women: Jenna Arrowsmith
Pairs: Lesley Rogers and Michael Aldred
Ice Dance: Michelle Fitzgerald and Vincent Kyle

EUROPEAN CHAMPIONSHIPS 1995
Dortmund, January-February

Men: Ilya Kulik (Russia)
Women: Surya Bonaly (France)
Pairs: Mandy Woetzel and Ingo Steuer (Germany)
Ice Dance: Susanna Rahkamo and Petri Kokko (Finland)

WORLD CHAMPIONSHIPS 1995
Birmingham, March

Men: Elvis Stojko (Canada)
Women: Lu Chen (China)
Pairs: Radka Kovarikova and Rene Novotny (Czech
  Republic)
Ice Dance: Oksana Gritschuk and Evgeny Platov (Russia)

JUDO

WORLD CHAMPIONSHIPS 1995
Makuhari, Japan, September–October

MEN

Heavyweight (over 95 kg): David Douillet (France)
Light-heavyweight (95 kg): Pawel Nastula (Poland)
Middleweight (86 kg): Ki-Young Jeon (S. Korea)
Light-middleweight (78 kg): Toshihiko Koga (Japan)
Lightweight (71 kg): Daisuke Hideshima (Japan)
Featherweight (65 kg): Uda Quellmalz (Germany)
Bantamweight (60 kg): N. Ojeguine (Russia)
Openweight: David Douillet (France)

WOMEN

Heavyweight (over 72 kg): Angelique Seriese (Holland)
Light-heavyweight (72 kg): Castellano Luna (Cuba)
Middleweight (66 kg): Min-Sun Cho (S. Korea)
Light-middleweight (61 kg): Sung-Sook Jung (S. Korea)

Lightweight (56 kg): Driulis Gonzalez (Cuba)
Featherweight (52 kg): Marie Restoux (France)
Bantamweight (48 kg): Ryoko Tamura (Japan)
Openweight: Monique van der Lee (Holland)

BRITISH NATIONAL CHAMPIONSHIPS 1994
Meadowbank, December

MEN

Heavyweight (over 95 kg): Nick Kokotaylo
Light-heavyweight (95 kg): Chris Bacon
Middleweight (86 kg): Wayne Lakin
Light-middleweight (78 kg): Darren Warner
Lightweight (71 kg): Billy Cusack
Featherweight (65 kg): Simon Moss
Bantamweight (60 kg): Jamie Johnston

WOMEN

Heavyweight (over 72 kg): Jane Morris
Light-heavyweight (72 kg): Stacey Smith
Middleweight (66 kg): Chloe Cowan
Light-middleweight (61 kg): Diane Bell
Lightweight (56 kg): Cheryle Peel
Featherweight (52 kg): Debbie Allan
Bantamweight (48 kg): Joyce Heron

LAWN TENNIS

MAJOR CHAMPIONSHIPS 1995

AUSTRALIAN OPEN CHAMPIONSHIPS
Melbourne, 16–29 January

Men's Singles: Andre Agassi (USA) beat Pete Sampras
  (USA) 4–6, 6–1, 7–6, 6–4
Women's Singles: Mary Pierce (France) beat Arantxa
  Sánchez Vicario (Spain) 6–3, 6–2
Men's Doubles: Richey Reneberg and Jared Palmer (USA)
  beat Mark Knowles (Bahamas) and Daniel Nestor
  (Canada) 6–3, 3–6, 6–3, 6–2
Women's Doubles: Jana Novotna (Czech Republic) and
  Arantxa Sánchez Vicario (Spain) beat Gigi Fernandez
  (USA) and Natasha Zvereva (Belarus) 6–3, 6–7, 6–4
Mixed Doubles: Natasha Zvereva (Belarus) and Rick Leach
  (USA) beat Gigi Fernandez (USA) and Cyril Suk
  (Czech Republic) 7–6, 6–7, 6–4

FRENCH OPEN CHAMPIONSHIPS
Paris, 29 May–11 June

Men's Singles: Thomas Muster (Austria) beat Michael
  Chang (USA) 7–5, 6–2, 6–4
Women's Singles: Steffi Graf (Germany) beat Arantxa
  Sánchez Vicario (Spain) 7–5, 4–6, 6–0
Men's Doubles: Jacco Eltingh and Paul Haarhuis
  (Netherlands) beat Nicklas Kulti and Magnus Larsson
  (Sweden) 6–7, 6–4, 6–1
Women's Doubles: Gigi Fernandez (USA) and Natasha
  Zvereva (Belarus) beat Jana Novotna (Czech Republic)
  and Arantxa Sánchez Vicario (Spain) 6–7, 6–4, 7–5
Mixed Doubles: Larissa Neiland (Latvia) and Mark
  Woodforde (Australia) beat Jill Hetherington (Canada)
  and John-Laffnie De Jager (S. Africa) 7–6, 7–6

ALL-ENGLAND CHAMPIONSHIPS
Wimbledon, 26 June–9 July

Men's Singles: Pete Sampras (USA) beat Boris Becker
  (Germany) 6–7, 6–2, 6–4, 6–2
Women's Singles: Steffi Graf (Germany) beat Arantxa
  Sánchez Vicario (Spain) 4–6, 6–1, 7–5

Men's Doubles: Mark Woodforde and Todd Woodbridge
  (Australia) beat Rick Leach and Scott Melville (USA)
  7–5, 7–6, 7–6
Women's Doubles: Jana Novotna (Czech Republic) and
  Arantxa Sánchez Vicario (Spain) beat Gigi Fernandez
  (USA) and Natasha Zvereva (Belarus) 7–5, 5–7, 6–4
Mixed Doubles: Martina Navratilova and Jonathan Stark
  (USA) beat Gigi Fernandez (USA) and Cyril Suk
  (Czech Republic) 6–4, 6–4

US OPEN CHAMPIONSHIPS
New York, 28 August–10 September

Men's Singles: Pete Sampras (USA) beat Andre Agassi
  (USA) 6–4, 6–3, 4–6, 7–5
Women's Singles: Steffi Graf (Germany) beat Monica Seles
  (USA) 7–6, 0–6, 6–3
Men's Doubles: Todd Woodbridge and Mark Woodforde
  (Australia) beat Alex O'Brien (USA) and Sandon Stolle
  (Australia) 6–3, 6–3
Women's Doubles: Gigi Fernandez (USA) and Natasha
  Zvereva (Belarus) beat Brenda Schultz-McCarthy
  (Holland) and Renée Stubbs (Australia) 7–5, 6–3
Mixed Doubles: Meredith McGrath and Matt Lucena
  (USA) beat Gigi Fernandez (USA) and Cyril Suk
  (Czech Republic) 6–4, 6–4

Grand Slam Cup 1994: Magnus Larsson (Sweden) beat Pete
  Sampras (USA) 7–6, 4–6, 7–6, 6–4

TEAM CHAMPIONSHIPS

Davis Cup final 1994: Sweden beat Russia 4–1
LTA County Cup 1995:
  Men: Devon
  Women: Essex

NATIONAL CHAMPIONSHIPS 1994
Telford, November

Men's Singles: Jeremy Bates beat Miles Maclagan 6–4, 6–2
Women's Singles: Jo Ward beat Kaye Hand 6–0, 6–2
Men's Doubles: Paul Hand and Gary Henderson beat Nick
  Fulwood and Danny Sapsford 6–7, 6–3, 6–3
Women's Doubles: Julie Pullin and Lorna Woodroffe beat
  Valda Lake and Clare Wood 7–6, 6–2

MOTOR CYCLING

---

500 CC GRAND PRIX 1994

European (Barcelona): Luca Cadalora (Italy), Yamaha
Riders' Championship 1994: 1. Michael Doohan (Australia),
  Honda, 317 pts; 2. Luca Cadalora (Italy), Yamaha, 174
  pts; 3. John Kocinski (USA), Cagiva, 172 pts

500 CC GRAND PRIX 1995

Australian (Eastern Creek): Michael Doohan (Australia),
  Honda
Malaysian (Shah Alam): Michael Doohan (Australia),
  Honda
Japanese (Suzuka): Daryl Beattie (Australia), Suzuki
Spanish (Jerez): Albert Puig (Spain), Honda
German (Nurburgring): Daryl Beattie (Australia), Suzuki
Italian (Mugello): Michael Doohan (Australia), Honda
Dutch (Assen): Michael Doohan (Australia), Honda
French (Le Mans): Michael Doohan (Australia), Honda
British (Donington Park): Michael Doohan (Australia),
  Honda
Czech (Brno): Luca Cadalora (Italy), Yamaha
Brazilian (Rio de Janeiro): Luca Cadalora (Italy), Yamaha

Argentine (Buenos Aires): Michael Doohan (Australia), Honda

Senior Manx Grand Prix 1995: Mike Casey (Honda)
Senior TT 1995, Isle of Man: Joey Dunlop (Honda)
Junior TT 1995, Isle of Man: Iain Duffus (Honda)

MOTOR RACING

FORMULA ONE GRAND PRIX 1994

European (Jerez): Michael Schumacher (Germany), Benetton Ford
Japanese (Suzuka): Damon Hill (GB), Williams Renault
Australian (Adelaide): Nigel Mansell (GB), Williams Renault
Drivers' World Championship 1994: 1. Michael Schumacher (Germany), Benetton Ford, 92 pts; 2. Damon Hill (GB), Williams Renault, 91 pts; 3. Gerhard Berger (Austria), Ferrari, 41 pts
Constructors' World Championship 1994: 1. Williams Renault, 118 pts; 2. Benetton Ford, 103 pts; 3. Ferrari, 71 pts

FORMULA ONE GRAND PRIX 1995

Brazilian (Sao Paulo): Michael Schumacher (Germany), Benetton Renault
Argentinian (Buenos Aires): Damon Hill (GB), Williams Renault
San Marino: Damon Hill (GB), Williams Renault
Spanish (Barcelona): Michael Schumacher (Germany), Benetton Renault
Monaco: Michael Schumacher (Germany), Benetton Renault
Canadian (Montreal): Jean Alesi (France), Ferrari
French (Magny-Cours): Michael Schumacher (Germany), Benetton Renault
British (Silverstone): Johnny Herbert (GB), Benetton Renault
German (Hockenheim): Michael Schumacher (Germany), Benetton Renault
Hungarian (Budapest): Damon Hill (GB), Williams Renault
Belgian (Spa-Francorchamps): Michael Schumacher (Germany), Benetton Renault
Italian (Monza): Johnny Herbert (GB), Benetton Renault
Portuguese (Estoril): David Coulthard (GB), Williams Renault
European (Nurburgring): Michael Schumacher (Germany), Benetton Renault
Indianapolis 500 1995: Jacques Villeneuve (Canada), Reynard Ford
Le Mans 24-hour Race 1995: Yannick Dalmas (France), J.J. Lehto (Finland) and Masanori Sekiya (Japan), McLaren

MOTOR RALLYING

1994
San Remo Rally: Didier Auriol (France), Toyota Celica
RAC Rally: Colin McRae (GB), Subaru Impreza
Hong Kong-Beijing Rally: Possum Bourne (New Zealand), Subaru Impreza
Drivers' World Championship 1994: Didier Auriol (France), Toyota Celica, 116 pts
Manufacturers' World Championship 1994: Toyota, 151 pts
1995
Paris-Dakar Rally: Pierre Lartigue (France), Citroen
London-Mexico Rally: Hannu Mikkola (Finland), Ford Escort

Monte Carlo Rally: Carlos Sainz (Spain), Subaru Impreza
Swedish Rally: Kenneth Eriksson (Sweden), Mitsubishi Lancer
Portuguese Rally: Carlos Sainz (Spain), Subaru Impreza
Safari Rally: Yoshio Fujimoto (Japan), Toyoto Celica Turbo
Corsican Rally: Didier Auriol (France), Toyota Celica
Indonesian Rally: Colin McRae (GB), Subaru Impreza
New Zealand Rally: Colin McRae (GB), Subaru Impreza
1,000 Lakes Rally (Finland): Tommi Makinen (Finland), Mitsubishi Lancer
Australian Rally: Kenneth Eriksson (Sweden), Mitsubishi Lancer

NETBALL

TEST MATCHES

1994

Date	Venue	Result
2 Nov	Manchester	England 44, S. Africa 57
5 Nov	Wembley	England 36, S. Africa 55
9 Nov	Gateshead	England 46, S. Africa 58
12 Nov	Sheffield	England 45, S. Africa 46
16 Nov	Birmingham	England 47, S. Africa 52

1995

Date	Venue	Result
11 Apr	Dunedin	New Zealand 64, England 42
15 Apr	Palmerston N.	New Zealand 60, England 36
20 Apr	Auckland	New Zealand 55, England 36

INTERNATIONALS

1994

Date	Venue	Result
26 Oct	Belfast	N. Ireland 33, South Africa 63
31 Oct	Cardiff	Wales 36, South Africa 69

1995

Date	Venue	Result
28 Jan	Cardiff	Wales 22, England 67
11 Feb	Bedford	England 58, Rep. of Ireland 20
12 Feb	Glasgow	Scotland 35, Wales 45
18 Feb	Worthing	England 64, Scotland 22
25 Feb	Belfast	N. Ireland 50, Wales 49
11 Mar	Deeside	Wales 59, Rep. of Ireland 28
	Glenrothes	Scotland 46, N. Ireland 48
25 Mar	Belfast	N. Ireland 23, England 63
	Dublin	Rep. of Ireland 36, Scotland 68

World Championship final 1995: Australia beat South Africa 68–48
Inter-County Championship final 1995: Hertfordshire beat Nottinghamshire 15–10
National Clubs Championship final 1995: Astrosyn Arupians (Kent) beat Kent Club 49–42
English Counties League Championship 1995: Essex Metropolitan
National Clubs League Championship 1995: New Cambell (Essex Metropolitan)

POLO

1995
World Championships final: Brazil beat Argentina 11–10
Prince of Wales's Trophy final: Alcatel beat Ellerston White 8–7
Queen's Cup final: Labegorce beat Alcatel 9–8
Warwickshire Cup final: Royal Pahang beat Black Bears 10–9
Gold Cup (British Open) final: Ellerston White beat Black Bears 12–10
Coronation Cup final: Argentina beat England 14–8

Silver Jubilee Cup final: Labegorce beat Ellerston White 12–11
Varsity Match: Cambridge beat Oxford 5–3

RACKETS

World Singles Championship 1995: Willie Boone (GB) beat Rupert Owen-Browne (GB) 3–0
World Doubles Championship 1995: Rupert Owen-Browne (GB) and K. Nemec (Canada) beat Willie Boone (GB) and Eddy Ulmann (USA) 3–1
Professional Singles Championship final 1995: Peter Brake beat Neil Smith 3–2
British Open Singles Championship final 1995: Willie Boone (GB) beat Neil Smith (GB) 4–0
British Open Doubles Championship final 1995: Willie Boone and Tim Cockroft (GB) beat Neil Smith and Peter Brake (GB) 4–3
Amateur Singles Championship final 1994: James Male beat Willie Boone 3–1
Amateur Doubles Championship final 1995: John Prenn and James Male beat Willie Boone and Tim Cockroft 4–3
National League final 1995: Manchester beat Old Harrovians 3–2
Noel Bruce Cup final 1994 (public schools old boys' doubles championship): Eton (Willie Boone and Mark Hue Williams) beat Radley (James Male and Luke Danby) 4–0
Public Schools Singles Championship final 1994: Rugby (Richard Carter) beat Haileybury (Duncan Stahl) 3–0
Public Schools Doubles Championship final 1995: Rugby (Richard Carter and Robin Hicks) beat Eton (Neil Bailey and Patrick Wigan) 4–2
Varsity Match 1995: Cambridge beat Oxford 2–1

REAL TENNIS

World Singles Championship 1995: Robert Fahey (Australia) beat Wayne Davies (Australia) 6–2 (Davies retd injured)
Professional Singles Championship final 1995: Lachie Deuchar (Australia) beat Mike Gooding (GB) 3–2
Professional Doubles Championship final 1995: Lachie Deuchar (Australia) and Jonathan Howell (GB) beat Chris Bray and Mike Gooding (GB) 3–2
British Open Singles Championship final 1994: Julian Snow (GB) beat Lachie Deuchar (Australia) 3–1
British Open Doubles Championship final 1994: Chris Bray and Mike Gooding (GB) beat Wayne Davies and Lachie Deuchar (Australia) 3–0
Amateur Singles Championship final 1995: Julian Snow beat Nigel Pendrigh 3–0
Amateur Doubles Championship final 1995: Mike McMurrugh and Julian Snow beat James Acheson-Gray and Nigel Pendrigh 3–0
Henry Leaf Cup final 1995 (public schools old boy's doubles championship): Charterhouse (Nigel Pendrigh and James Acheson-Gray) beat Haileybury (William Hollington and Ruaraidh Gunn) 2–0
Varsity Match 1995: Oxford beat Cambridge 6–0
Women's World Singles Championship final 1995: Penny Lumley (GB) beat Sue Haswell (GB) 2–1
Women's World Doubles Championship final 1995: Sue Haswell and Penny Lumley (GB) beat Sally Jones and Lesley Ronaldson (GB) 2–1
Women's British Open Singles Championship final 1995: Penny Lumley (GB) beat Sally Jones (GB) 2–0

Women's British Open Doubles Championship final: Sally Jones and Sue Haswell (GB) beat Fiona Deuchar (Australia) and Emma Wood (GB) 2–0

ROAD WALKING

BAF MEN's 20 KM ROAD CHAMPIONSHIP
Horsham, 25 March 1995
Individual: Darrell Stone (Steyning), 1 hr. 27 min. 44 sec.
Team: Steyning, 31 pts

BAF WOMEN's 10 KM ROAD CHAMPIONSHIP
Horsham, 25 March 1995
Individual: Vicky Lupton (Sheffield), 47 min. 44 sec.
Team: Manx Harriers, 25 pts

WORLD CUP
Beijing, 29–30 April 1995
Men (20 kilometres)
Individual: Li Zewen (China), 1 hr. 19 min. 44 sec.
Team: China, 436 pts
Men (50 kilometres)
Individual: Zhao Yongshen (China), 3 hr. 41 min. 20 sec.
Team: Mexico, 426 pts
Men's Team (Overall): Mexico, 846 pts
Women (10 kilometres)
Individual: Gao Hongmiao (China), 42 min. 19 sec.
Team: China, 443 pts

RWA MEN's 20 MILES WALK
Enfield, 3 June 1995
Individual: Gareth Brown (Steyning), 2 hr. 41 min. 36 sec.
Team: Steyning, 13 pts

NATIONAL WOMEN's 5 KM WALK
Enfield, 3 June 1995
Individual: Lisa Langford (Wolverhampton), 23 min. 00 sec.
Team: Sheffield United, 17 pts

RWA 50 KM WALK
Stockport, 1 July 1995
Individual: Les Morton (Sheffield), 4 hr. 1 min. 36 sec.
Team: Sheffield United, 22 pts

WOMEN's NATIONAL 20 KM WALK
Stockport, 1 July 1995
Individual: Vicky Lupton (Sheffield), 1 hr. 42 min. 47 sec.
Team: Sheffield United, 11 pts

RWA 10 MILE WALK
Sutton Coldfield, 22 July 1995
Individual: Chris Maddocks (Plymouth), 1 hr. 9 min. 11 sec.
Team: Coventry, 35 pts

ROWING

WORLD CHAMPIONSHIPS 1995
Tampere, Finland, August

MEN
Coxed pairs: Italy
Coxless pairs: Great Britain
Coxed fours: USA
Coxless fours: Italy
Single sculls: Iztok Cop (Slovenia)
Double sculls: Denmark
Quad sculls: Italy
Eights: Germany

WOMEN

Coxless pairs: Australia
Coxless fours: USA
Single sculls: Maria Brandin (Sweden)
Double sculls: Canada
Quad sculls: Germany
Eights: USA

NATIONAL CHAMPIONSHIPS 1995
Holme Pierrepont, July

MEN

Coxed pairs: Isis B
Coxless pairs: Thames Tradesmen
Coxed fours: Lea
Coxless fours: Nottinghamshire County B
Single sculls: Simon Goodbrand (Rob Roy A)
Double sculls: Nottinghamshire County
Quad sculls: Tideway Scullers
Eights: Nottinghamshire County A

WOMEN

Coxless pairs: Thames
Coxed fours: Thames
Coxless fours: Bedford/Thames Tradesmen/University of
   London/Weybridge
Single sculls: Patricia Reid (Lea)
Double sculls: Henley/Tideway Scullers
Quad sculls: Nottinghamshire County
Eights: Tideway Scullers

THE 141st UNIVERSITY BOAT RACE

Putney–Mortlake, 4 miles 1 f, 180 yd, 1 April 1995

Cambridge beat Oxford by 4 lengths; 18 min. 4 sec.
Cambridge have won 71 times, Oxford 68 and there has
been one dead heat. The record time is 16 min. 45 sec.,
rowed by Oxford in 1984

WOMEN'S BOAT RACE 1995 (Henley): Cambridge beat
Oxford by 1⅓ lengths (6 min. 2 sec.)

HENLEY ROYAL REGATTA 1995

Grand Challenge Cup: San Diego TC (USA) beat Leander
   and Molesey by ⅓ length
Ladies' Challenge Plate: Nottinghamshire County A beat
   Princeton University (USA) by 3 lengths
Thames Challenge Cup: Imperial College London beat
   University of Washington (USA) by 3¼ lengths
Temple Challenge Cup: Oxford Brookes University beat
   Trinity College Dublin by 3¼ lengths
Princess Elizabeth Challenge Cup: Eton College beat
   Hampton School A by 1 length
Stewards' Challenge Cup: Cambridge University/Mladost
   (Croatia) beat College BC (USA) by 2¼ lengths
Prince Philip Challenge Cup: Leander A beat Leander B by 4
   lengths
Queen Mother Challenge Cup: Augusta TC (USA) beat
   Dinamo Moscow (Russia) by ¾ length
Visitors' Challenge Cup: Isis BC beat University of London
   by ¾ length
Wyfold Challenge Cup: Lea A beat University of London
   Tyrian Club by a canvas
Britannia Challenge Cup: Wallingford beat University of
   London by ⅓ length
Fawley Challenge Cup: Windsor Boys' School/Poplar,
   Blackwall and District beat Durham/Norwich, not
   rowed out
Silver Goblets and Nickalls' Challenge Cup: Steve Redgrave
   and Matthew Pinsent (Leander) beat Roger Everington
   and Mark Partridge (London/Nottinghamshire
   County) by 5 lengths

Double Sculls Challenge Cup: Markus Free and Peter Antonie
   (Australia) beat Brian Jamieson and David Gleeson
   (USA) by 2 ft
Diamond Challenge Sculls: Juri Jaanson (Estonia) beat Xeno
   Muller (Switzerland) by 2 lengths
Women's Single Sculls: Maria Brandin (Sweden) beat Silken
   Laumann (Canada) by 4¾ lengths

OTHER ROWING EVENTS

Oxford Torpids 1995: Men, Oriel; *Women,* Osler House
Cambridge Lents 1995: Men, Downing; *Women,* Emmanuel
Oxford Summer Eights 1995: Men, Pembroke; *Women,* Osler
   House
Cambridge Mays 1995: Men, Trinity Hall; *Women,*
   Emmanuel
Head of the River 1995: Men, Netherlands Rowing
   Federation; *Women,* Kingston/Thames/Tideway
   Scullers
Doggett's Coat and Badge 1995: Scott Neicho (Poplar,
   Blackwall and District)
Wingfield Sculls 1995: Peter Haining (Auriol Kensington)
Thames World Sculling Challenge 1994: Peter Haining (GB)

RUGBY FIVES

National Singles Championship final 1994: Wayne Enstone
   beat Rick Carr 15–4, 15–5
National Doubles Championship final 1995: Wayne Enstone
   and Neil Roberts beat Ian Fuller and David Hebden
   15–11, 15–11
National Club Championship final 1995: Old Bradfieldians
   beat Manchester YMCA 102–70
National Schools' Singles Championships final 1995: St
   Dunstan's (Tim Stock) beat St Paul's (Ben Thomas)
   11–7, 11–5
National Schools' Doubles Championships final 1995: St Paul's
   (Matthew Simons and Ben Thomas) beat Bradfield
   (Richard Holland and Jeremy Sinton) 11–3, 12–10
Varsity Match 1995: Oxford beat Cambridge 287–162

RUGBY LEAGUE

World Sevens final 1995 (Sydney): Manly-Warringah beat
   Fiji 36–12

INTERNATIONAL MATCHES

1994
30 Oct   Cardiff   Wales 4, Australia 46

1995
1 Feb   Cardiff   Wales 18, England 16
15 Feb   Gateshead   Wales 19, France 16
5 March Carcassonne   France 10, Wales 22

TEST MATCHES

1994
22 Oct   Wembley   Great Britain 8, Australia 4
5 Nov   Old Trafford   Great Britain 8, Australia 38
20 Nov   Elland Road   Great Britain 4, Australia 23

DOMESTIC COMPETITIONS

Challenge Cup final 1995 (Wembley, 29 April): Wigan beat
   Leeds 30–10
Premiership Trophy final 1995 (Old Trafford, 21 May):
   Wigan beat Leeds 69–12
Regal Trophy final 1995 (Huddersfield, 28 January): Wigan
   beat Warrington 40–10

Second Division Premiership final 1995: Keighley beat
Huddersfield 26-6
Stones Bitter Championship 1995: Wigan, 56 pts
Division 2 Championship 1995: Keighley, 48 pts
Varsity Match 1995: Cambridge beat Oxford 16-8

AMATEUR RUGBY LEAGUE 1994-5

County Championship: Cumbria
National Inter-League Open Age Shield Competition: Copeland
National Cup Open Age Competition: Woolston
National League Premier Division Champions: Woolston

RUGBY UNION

WORLD CUP 1995

South Africa, 25 May–24 June

FIRST ROUND
Pool A: S. Africa 9 pts; Australia 7 pts; Canada 5 pts;
Romania 3 pts
Pool B: England 9 pts; W. Samoa 7 pts; Italy 5 pts; Argentina
3 pts
Pool C: New Zealand 9 pts; Ireland 7 pts; Wales 5 pts; Japan
3 pts
Pool D: France 9 pts; Scotland 7 pts; Tonga 5 pts; Ivory
Coast 3 pts

QUARTER-FINALS
France 36, Ireland 12; S. Africa 42, W. Samoa 14; England
25, Australia 22; New Zealand 48, Scotland 30

SEMI-FINALS
France 15, S. Africa 19; England 29, New Zealand 45

THIRD PLACE PLAY-OFF
England 9, France 19

FINAL
Johannesburg, 24 June
South Africa 15, New Zealand 12 a.e.t.

FIVE NATIONS' CHAMPIONSHIP 1995

21 Jan	Dublin	Ireland 8, England 20
	Paris	France 21, Wales 9
4 Feb	Twickenham	England 31, France 10
	Murrayfield	Scotland 26, Ireland 13
18 Feb	Cardiff	Wales 9, England 23
	Paris	France 21, Scotland 23
4 Mar	Murrayfield	Scotland 26, Wales 13
	Dublin	Ireland 7, France 25
18 Mar	Twickenham	England 24, Scotland 12
	Cardiff	Wales 12, Ireland 16

	P	W	D	L	Pts F	A	Total
England	4	4	0	0	98	39	8
Scotland	4	3	0	1	87	71	6
France	4	2	0	2	77	70	4
Ireland	4	1	0	3	44	83	2
Wales	4	0	0	4	43	86	0

OTHER INTERNATIONALS

1994
17 Sept	Bucharest	Romania 9, Wales 16
12 Oct	Cardiff	Wales 29, Italy 19
5 Nov	Dublin	Ireland 26, USA 15
12 Nov	Twickenham	England 54, Romania 3
19 Nov	Murrayfield	Scotland 10, S. Africa 34
26 Nov	Cardiff	Wales 12, S. Africa 20
10 Dec	Twickenham	England 60, Canada 19

1995
21 Jan	Murrayfield	Scotland 22, Canada 6
22 Apr	Murrayfield	Scotland 49, Romania 16
6 May	Madrid	Spain 7, Scotland 62
	Treviso	Italy 22, Ireland 12
2 Sept	Johannesburg	S. Africa 40, Wales 11

DOMESTIC COMPETITIONS

English League: Division 1, Leicester, 31 pts; Division 2,
Saracens, 31 pts; Division 3, Bedford, 27 pts; Division 4,
Rotherham, 34 pts; Division 5 (north), Walsall, 21 pts;
Division 5 (south), London Welsh, 22 pts
County Championship final 1995: Warwickshire beat
Northumberland 15-9
Pilkington Cup final 1995: Bath beat Wasps 36-16
Scottish League: Division 1, Stirling County, 23 pts; Division
2, Kelso, 22 pts; Division 3, Ayr, 24 pts; Division 4,
Glenrothes, 24 pts; Division 5, Berwick, 21 pts; Division
6, Annan, 23 pts; Division 7, Garnock, 24 pts
Welsh League: Division 1, Cardiff, 36 pts; Division 2,
Aberavon, 34 pts; Division 3, Ystradgynlais, 38 pts;
Division 4, Cardiff Institute, 36 pts; Division 5, Rumney,
39 pts
Welsh Challenge (Swalec) Cup final 1995: Swansea beat
Pontypridd 17-12
Irish League: Division 1, Shannon, 20 pts; Division 2, Old
Belvedere, 16 pts; Division 3, NIFC, 18 pts; Division 4,
Bohemians, 18 pts
Ulster Cup final 1995: Dungannon beat Instonians 21-16
Hospitals' Cup final 1995: Charing Cross/Westminster beat
St Mary's 6-3
Services Championship 1995: Royal Navy beat Army 34-17;
Army beat RAF 28-26; Royal Navy beat RAF 43-19
Varsity Match 1994: Cambridge beat Oxford 26-21
Middlesex Sevens final 1995: Leicester beat Ithuba 38-19

SHOOTING

126TH NATIONAL RIFLE ASSOCIATION IMPERIAL
MEETING
Bisley, July 1995

Queen's Prize: Andrew Luckman, 289.30 pts
Grand Aggregate: Stuart Collings, 596.87 pts
Prince of Wales Prize: R. Surette, 75.13 pts
St George's Vase: Flt. Lt. Andrew Gent, 149.21 pts
Allcomers Aggregate: Glyn Barnett, 322.50 pts
National Trophy: England, 2027.219 pts
Kolapore Cup: Jersey, 1156.128 pts
Chancellor's Trophy: Cambridge University, 1137.116 pts
Musketeers Cup: London University, 580.69 pts
Vizianagram Trophy: House of Lords, 667.41 pts
County Long-Range Championship: Surrey, 444.62 pts
Mackinnon Challenge Cup: England, 1076.90 pts
The Ashburton: Uppingham School, 462 pts
The Elcho: England, 1655.149 pts
The Albert: John Bridger, 218.25 pts
Hopton Challenge Cup: Stuart Collings, 987.117 pts

CLAY PIGEON SHOOTING
International Cup (Down-the-Line) 1995: Ireland, 5916/6000
British Open Down-the-Line Championship 1995: D. Booth,
100/300*
Mackintosh Trophy 1995: Canada, 5934/6000
British Open Skeet Championship 1995: Peter Dodd, 100*

British Open Sporting Championship 1995: George Digweed, 86*

Coronation Cup 1995: Paul Chaplow, 385

*After a shoot-off

SNOOKER

1994
Dubai Classic: Alan McManus (Scotland) beat Peter Ebdon (England) 9–6
Skoda Grand Prix: John Higgins (Scotland) beat Dave Harold (England) 9–6
Benson and Hedges Championship: Mark Williams (Wales) beat Rod Lawler (England) 9–5
UK Professional Championship: Stephen Hendry (Scotland) beat Ken Doherty (Ireland) 10–5
European Open: Stephen Hendry (Scotland) beat John Parrott (England) 9–3
World Amateur Championship: Mohammed Yusuf (Pakistan) beat Johannes Johannesson (Iceland) 11–9

1995
Welsh Open: Steve Davis (England) beat John Higgins (Scotland) 9–3
Benson and Hedges Masters: Ronnie O'Sullivan (England) beat John Higgins (Scotland) 9–3
International Open: John Higgins (Scotland) beat Steve Davis (England) 9–5
Thailand Open: James Wattana (Thailand) beat Ronnie O'Sullivan (England) 9–6
Irish Masters: Peter Ebdon (England) beat Stephen Hendry (Scotland) 9–8
British Open: John Higgins (Scotland) beat Ronnie O'Sullivan (England) 9–6
World Championship: Stephen Hendry (Scotland) beat Nigel Bond (England) 18–9
European League: Stephen Hendry (Scotland) beat Ken Doherty (Ireland) 10–2
Regal Masters: Stephen Hendry (Scotland) beat Peter Ebdon (England) 9–5

Women's British Open Championship 1994: Ann-Marie Farren beat Kim Shaw 4–3
Women's Scottish Regal Masters 1994: Allison Fisher beat Kelly Fisher 4–0
Women's Welsh Regal Championship 1995: Allison Fisher beat Kim Shaw 4–1
Women's World Championship 1995: Karen Corr beat Kim Shaw 6–3
Women's UK Championship 1995: Allison Fisher beat Karen Corr 4–1
Women's British Open Championship 1995: Karen Corr beat Ann-Marie Farren 4–1

SPEEDWAY

GRAND PRIX 1995
Polish (Wroclaw): Tomasz Gollob (Poland)
Austrian (Wiener Neustadt): Billy Hamill (USA)
German (Abensberg): Tommy Knudsen (Denmark)
Swedish (Linkoping): Tommy Knudsen (Denmark)
Danish (Vojens): Hans Nielsen (Denmark)
British (London Stadium): Greg Hancock (USA)
World Champion 1995: Hans Nielsen (Denmark)
World Team Cup final 1995: Denmark
World Championship, British final 1995: Andy Smith (Coventry)

World Championship, Overseas final 1995: Ryan Sullivan (Peterborough)
British League Riders' Championship 1994: Sam Ermolenko (Wolverhampton)
British League Division 1 Championship 1994: Poole
British League Division 1 Knock-Out Cup final 1994: Eastbourne beat Cradley Heath 106–86 on agg.

SQUASH RACKETS

MEN
European Team Championship final 1995: England beat Finland 4–0
European Club Championship final 1995: OFC Ingolstadt (Germany) beat Linkoping (Sweden) 3–1

British Open Championship final 1995: Jansher Khan (Pakistan) beat Peter Marshall (England) 3–0
National Championship final 1995: Stephen Meads beat Nick Taylor 3–0

WOMEN
World Open Championship final 1995: Michelle Martin (Australia) beat Sarah Fitz-Gerald (Australia) 3–1
World Open Championship final 1994: Michelle Martin (Australia) beat Cassie Jackman (England) 3–0
World Team Championship final 1994: Australia beat England 3–0
European Team Championship final 1995: England beat Holland 3–0
European Club Championship final 1995: Edgbaston Priory (England) beat Paderborn (Germany) 2–1
British Open Championship final 1995: Michelle Martin (Australia) beat Liz Irving (Australia) 3–0
National Championship final 1995: Fiona Geaves beat Linda Charman 3–1

SWIMMING

EUROPEAN CHAMPIONSHIPS 1995
Vienna, August

MEN
50 metres freestyle: Alexander Popov (Russia)
100 metres freestyle: Alexander Popov (Russia)
200 metres freestyle: Jani Sievinen (Finland)
400 metres freestyle: Stefan Zesner (Germany)
1,500 metres freestyle: Joerg Hoffmann (Germany)
100 metres backstroke: Vladimir Selkov (Russia)
200 metres backstroke: Vladimir Selkov (Russia)
100 metres breaststroke: Frederic Deburghgraeve (Belgium)
200 metres breaststroke: Andrei Korneev (Russia)
100 metres butterfly: Denis Pankratov (Russia)
200 metres butterfly: Denis Pankratov (Russia)
200 metres medley: Jani Sievinen (Finland)
400 metres medley: Jani Sievinen (Finland)
4×100 metres freestyle relay: Russia
4×200 metres freestyle relay: Germany
4×100 metres medley relay: Russia

WOMEN
50 metres freestyle: Linda Olofsson (Sweden)
100 metres freestyle: Franziska van Almsick (Germany)
200 metres freestyle: Kerstin Kielgass (Germany)

400 metres freestyle: Franziska van Almsick (Germany)
800 metres freestyle: Julia Jung (Germany)
100 metres backstroke: Mette Jacobsen (Denmark)
200 metres backstroke: Krisztina Egerszegi (Hungary)
100 metres breaststroke: Brigitte Becue (Belgium)
200 metres breaststroke: Brigitte Becue (Belgium)
100 metres butterfly: Mette Jacobsen (Denmark)
200 metres butterfly: Michelle Smith (Ireland)
200 metres medley: Michelle Smith (Ireland)
400 metres medley: Krisztina Egerszegi (Hungary)
4×100 metres freestyle relay: Germany
4×200 metres freestyle relay: Germany
4×100 metres medley relay: Germany

NATIONAL CHAMPIONSHIPS 1995
Coventry, July

MEN

50 metres freestyle: Mark Foster (City of Cardiff)
100 metres freestyle: Simon Handley (City of Bristol)
200 metres freestyle: Paul Palmer (City of Lincoln Pentaqua)
400 metres freestyle: Ian Wilson (City of Leeds)
1,500 metres freestyle: Ian Wilson (City of Leeds)
50 metres backstroke: Neil Willey (Barnet Copthall)
100 metres backstroke: Neil Willey (Barnet Copthall)
200 metres backstroke: Adam Ruckwood (City of Birmingham)
50 metres breaststroke: James Parrack (City of Leeds)
100 metres breaststroke: James Parrack (City of Leeds)
200 metres breaststroke: Nick Gillingham (City of Birmingham)
50 metres butterfly: Mark Foster (City of Cardiff)
100 metres butterfly: Andrew Clayton (City of Leeds)
200 metres butterfly: Stephen Parry (Liverpool)
200 metres medley: Fraser Walker (Warrington Warriors)
400 metres medley: James Hickman (Stockport Metro)
4×100 metres freestyle relay: City of Sheffield
4×200 metres freestyle relay: City of Leeds
4×100 metres medley relay: City of Birmingham

WOMEN

50 metres freestyle: Susan Rolph (City of Newcastle)
100 metres freestyle: Susan Rolph (City of Newcastle)
200 metres freestyle: Karen Pickering (Ipswich)
400 metres freestyle: Sarah Hardcastle (Bracknell)
800 metres freestyle: Sarah Hardcastle (Bracknell)
50 metres backstroke: Hannah Barnes (Maxwell Chipping Norton)
100 metres backstroke: Zoe Cray (Ipswich)
200 metres backstroke: Kathy Osher (Ealing)
50 metres breaststroke: Karen Rake (City of Oxford)
100 metres breaststroke: Karen Rake (City of Oxford)
200 metres breaststroke: Marie Hardiman (City of Birmingham)
50 metres butterfly: Sarah Massey (City of Bradford)
100 metres butterfly: Caroline Foot (York City Baths)
200 metres butterfly: Helen Jepson (City of Leeds)
200 metres medley: Susan Rolph (City of Newcastle)
400 metres medley: Katie Goddard (Portsmouth Northsea)
4×100 metres freestyle relay: City of Leeds
4×200 metres freestyle relay: Portsmouth Northsea
4×100 metres medley relay: City of Leeds

TABLE TENNIS

WORLD CHAMPIONSHIPS 1995
Tianjin, China, May

Men's Singles: Kong Linghui (China) beat Liu Guoliang (China) 3–2
Women's Singles: Deng Yaping (China) beat Qiao Hong (China) 3–2
Men's Doubles: Wang Tao and Lu Lin (China) beat Zoran Primorac (Croatia) and Vladimir Samsonov (Belarus) 3–1
Women's Doubles: Deng Yaping and Qiao Hong (China) beat Liu Wei and Qiao Yunping (China) 3–1
Mixed Doubles: Liu Wei and Wang Tao (China) beat Deng Yaping and Kong Linghui (China) 3–0
Men's Team Event: China
Women's Team Event: China

World Cup final 1994: Jean-Philippe Gatien (France) beat Jean-Michel Saive (Belgium) 3–2
World Team Cup final 1994: Russia beat Germany 3–1
European Nations Cup final 1995: Sweden beat Russia 3–1

ENGLISH NATIONAL CHAMPIONSHIPS 1995
King's Lynn, March

Men's Singles: Carl Prean beat Chen Xinhua 3–0
Women's Singles: Andrea Holt beat Alison Gordon 3–2
Men's Doubles: Desmond Douglas and Alan Cooke beat Nicky Mason and Skylet Andrew 2–0
Women's Doubles: Kate Goodall and Andrea Holt beat Helen Lower and Linda Radford 2–0
Mixed Doubles: Linda Radford and Damien Holland beat Helen Lower and Clive Carthy 2–0

VOLLEYBALL

MEN

World Championship final 1994: Italy beat Holland 3–1
World League final 1995: Italy beat Brazil 3–1
National League Championship 1995: Mizuno Malory Lewisham
National Cup final 1995: Mizuno Malory Lewisham beat Wessex 3–0

WOMEN

World Championship final 1994: Cuba beat Brazil 3–0
World Grand Prix 1995: USA
National League Championship 1995: London Malory
National Cup final 1995: Sale beat Britannia Music City 3–2

YACHTING

BOC Challenge Single-Handed Round-the-World Race (started from Charleston, S. Carolina, 17 September 1994): Christophe Auguin (France) in Sceta Calberson, 121 days, 17 hours, 11 minutes and 46 seconds
Admiral's Cup 1995: Italy, 112.958 pts
Fastnet Race 1995:
   Big boat class: Group 4 Seahorse (GB)
   ILC 40 class: Brava Q8 (Italy)
   Mumm 36 class: Mumm a'Mia (Italy)
America's Cup 1995 (San Diego, May): Black Magic (New Zealand) beat Young America (USA) 5–0

Sports Records

All the world records given below have been accepted by the International Amateur Athletic Federation except those marked with an asterisk* which are awaiting homologation. Fully automatic timing to 1/100th second is mandatory up to and including 400 metres. For distances up to and including 10,000 metres, records will be accepted to 1/100th second if timed automatically, and to 1/10th if hand timing is used.

MEN'S EVENTS

Track Events	hr.	min.	sec.
100 metres			9.85
Leroy Burrell, USA, 1994			
200 metres			19.72
Pietro Mennea, Italy, 1979			
400 metres			43.29
Harry Reynolds, USA, 1988			
800 metres	1		41.73
Sebastian Coe, GB, 1981			
1,000 metres	2		12.18
Sebastian Coe, GB, 1981			
1,500 metres	3		27.37*
Noureddine Morceli, Algeria, 1995			
1 mile	3		44.39
Noureddine Morceli, Algeria, 1993			
2,000 metres	4		47.88*
Noureddine Morceli, Algeria, 1995			
3,000 metres	7		25.11
Noureddine Morceli, Algeria, 1994			
5,000 metres	12		44.39*
Haile Gebresilasie, Ethiopa, 1995			
10,000 metres	26		43.53*
Haile Gebresilasie, Ethiopa, 1995			
20,000 metres	56		55.6
Arturo Barrios, Mexico, 1991			
21,101 metres (13 miles 196 yards 1 foot)	1	00	00.0
Arturo Barrios, Mexico, 1991			
25,000 metres	1	13	55.8
Toshihiko Seko, Japan, 1981			
30,000 metres	1	29	18.8
Toshihiko Seko, Japan, 1981			
110 metres hurdles (3 ft 6 in)			12.91
Colin Jackson, GB, 1993			
400 metres hurdles (3 ft 0 in)			46.78
Kevin Young, USA, 1992			
3,000 metres steeplechase	7		59.18*
Moses Kiptanui, Kenya, 1995			

Relays		min.	sec.
4×100 metres			37.40
USA, 1992, 1993			
4×200 metres		1	19.11
Santa Monica TC, 1992			
4×400 metres		2	54.29
USA, 1993			
4×800 metres		7	03.89
GB, 1982			
4×1,500 metres		14	38.8
Federal Republic of Germany, 1977			

Field Events	metres	ft	in
High jump	2.45	8	0½
Javier Sotomayor, Cuba, 1993			
Pole vault	6.14	20	1¾
Sergei Bubka, Ukraine, 1994			
Long jump	8.95	29	4½
Mike Powell, USA, 1991			
Triple jump	18.29	60	0¼
Jonathan Edwards, GB, 1995			
Shot	23.12	75	10¼
Randy Barnes, USA, 1990			
Discus	74.08	243	0
Jürgen Schult, GDR, 1986			
Hammer	86.74	284	7
Yuriy Sedykh, USSR, 1986			
Javelin	95.66	313	10
Jan Zelezny, Czech Rep., 1993			
Decathlon†		8,891 pts	
Dan O'Brien, USA, 1992			

† Ten events comprising 100 m, long jump, shot, high jump, 400 m, 110 m hurdles, discus, pole vault, javelin, 1500 m

Walking (Track)	hr.	min.	sec.
20,000 metres	1	18	35.2
Stefan Johansson, Sweden, 1992			
29,572 metres (18 miles 660 yards)	2	00	00.0
Maurizio Damilano, Italy, 1992			
30,000 metres	2	01	44.1
Maurizio Damilano, Italy, 1992			
50,000 metres	3	41	38.4
Raul Gonzalez, Mexico, 1979			

WOMEN'S EVENTS

Track Events		min.	sec.
100 metres			10.49
Florence Griffith-Joyner, USA, 1988			
200 metres			21.34
Florence Griffith-Joyner, USA, 1988			
400 metres			47.60
Marita Koch, GDR, 1985			
800 metres		1	53.28
Jarmila Kratochvilova, Czechoslovakia, 1983			
1,500 metres		3	50.46
Qu Yunxia, China, 1993			
1 mile		4	15.61
Paula Ivan, Romania, 1989			
3,000 metres		8	06.11
Wang Junxia, China, 1993			
5,000 metres		14	36.45
Fernanda Ribeiro, Portugal, 1995			
10,000 metres		29	31.78
Wang Junxia, China, 1993			
100 metres hurdles (2 ft 9 in)			12.21
Yordanka Donkova, Bulgaria, 1988			
400 metres hurdles (2 ft 6 in)			52.61
Kim Batten, USA, 1995			

RELAYS	min.	sec.
4×100 metres		41.37
GDR, 1985		
4×200 metres	1	28.15
GDR, 1980		
4×400 metres	3	15.17
USSR, 1988		
4×800 metres	7	50.17
USSR, 1984		

FIELD EVENTS	metres	ft	in
High jump	2.09	6	10¼
Stefka Kostadinova, Bulgaria, 1987			
Pole vault	4.21	13	9¾
Daniela Bartova, Czech Republic, 1995			
Long jump	7.52	24	8¼
Galina Chistiakova, USSR, 1988			
Triple jump	15.50	50	10¼
Inessa Kravets, Ukraine, 1995			
Shot	22.63	74	3
Natalya Lisovskaya, USSR, 1987			
Discus	76.80	252	0
Gabriele Reinsch, GDR, 1988			
Hammer	68.14	223	7
Olga Kuzentova, Russia, 1995			
Javelin	80.00	262	5
Petra Felke, GDR, 1988			
Heptathlon†			7,291 pts
Jackie Joyner-Kersee, USA, 1988			

†Seven events comprising 100 m hurdles, shot, high jump, 200 m, long jump, javelin, 800 m

ATHLETICS NATIONAL (UK) RECORDS
AS AT 3 SEPTEMBER 1995

Records set anywhere by athletes eligible to represent Great Britain and Northern Ireland

MEN

TRACK EVENTS	hr.	min.	sec.
100 metres			9.87
Linford Christie, 1993			
200 metres			19.87
John Regis, 1994			
400 metres			44.47
David Grindley, 1992			
800 metres		1	41.73
Sebastian Coe, 1981			
1,000 metres		2	12.18
Sebastian Coe, 1981			
1,500 metres		3	29.67
Sebastian Coe, 1985			
1 mile		3	46.32
Steve Cram, 1985			
2,000 metres		4	51.39
Steve Cram, 1985			
3,000 metres		7	32.79
David Moorcroft, 1982			
5,000 metres		13	00.41
David Moorcroft, 1982			
10,000 metres		27	23.06
Eamonn Martin, 1988			
20,000 metres		57	28.7
Carl Thackery, 1990			
20,855 metres	1		
Carl Thackery, 1990			
25,000 metres	1	15	22.6
Ron Hill, 1965			
30,000 metres	1	31	30.4
Jim Alder, 1970			
3,000 metres steeplechase		8	07.96
Mark Rowland, 1988			
110 metres hurdles			12.91
Colin Jackson, 1993			
400 metres hurdles			47.82
Kriss Akabusi, 1992			

RELAYS	min.	sec.
4×100 metres		37.77
GB team, 1993		
4×200 metres	1	21.29
GB team, 1989		
4×400 metres	2	57.53
GB team, 1991		
4×800 metres	7	03.89
GB team, 1982		

FIELD EVENTS	metres	ft	in
High jump	2.37	7	9¼
Steve Smith, 1992, 1993			
Pole vault	5.70	18	8¼
Nick Buckfield, 1995			
Long jump	8.23	27	0
Lynn Davies, 1968			
Triple jump	18.29	60	0¼
Jonathan Edwards, 1995			
Shot	21.68	71	1½
Geoff Capes, 1980			
Discus	64.32	211	0
William Tancred, 1974			
Hammer	77.54	254	5
Martin Girvan, 1984			
Javelin	91.46	300	1
Steve Backley, 1992			
Decathlon			8,847 pts
Daley Thompson, 1984			

WALKING (TRACK)	hr.	min.	sec.
20,000 metres	1	23	26.5
Ian McCombie, 1990			
30,000 metres	2	19	18
Christopher Maddocks, 1984			
50,000 metres	4	05	44.6
Paul Blagg, 1990			
2 hours	26,037 metres (16 miles 315 yards)		
Ron Wallwork, 1971			

WOMEN

TRACK EVENTS	min.	sec.
100 metres		11.10
Kathy Cook, 1981		
200 metres		22.10
Kathy Cook, 1984		
400 metres		49.43
Kathy Cook, 1984		
800 metres	1	56.21
Kelly Holmes, 1995		
1,500 metres	3	59.96
Zola Budd, 1985		
1 mile	4	17.57
Zola Budd, 1985		
3,000 metres	8	28.83
Zola Budd, 1985		
5,000 metres	14	48.07
Zola Budd, 1985		
10,000 metres	30	57.07
Liz McColgan, 1991		

		metres	ft	in
100 metres hurdles				12.82
Sally Gunnell, 1988				
400 metres hurdles				52.74
Sally Gunnell, 1993				

RELAYS	min.	sec.
4×100 metres		42.43
GB team, 1980		
4×200 metres	1	31.57
GB team, 1977		
4×400 metres	3	22.01
GB team, 1991		
4×800 metres	8	23.8
GB team, 1971		

FIELD EVENTS	metres	ft	in
High jump	1.95	6	4¾
Diana Elliott, 1982			
Pole vault	3.80	12	5½
Kate Staples, 1995			
Long jump	6.90	22	7¾
Beverley Kinch, 1983			
Triple jump	14.66	48	1¼
Ashia Hansen, 1995			
Shot	19.36	63	6¼
Judy Oakes, 1988			
Discus	67.48	221	5
Margaret Ritchie, 1981			
Hammer	64.90	212	11
Lorraine Shaw, 1995			
Javelin	77.44	254	1
Fatima Whitbread, 1986			
Heptathlon		6,623 pts	
Judy Simpson, 1986			

SWIMMING WORLD RECORDS
AS AT 31 AUGUST 1995

MEN	min.	sec.
50 metres freestyle		21.81
Tom Jager, USA		
100 metres freestyle		48.21
Alexander Popov, Russia		
200 metres freestyle	1	46.69
Giorgio Lamberti, Italy		
400 metres freestyle	3	43.80
Kieren Perkins, Australia		
800 metres freestyle	7	46.00
Kieren Perkins, Australia		
1,500 metres freestyle	14	41.66
Kieren Perkins, Australia		
100 metres breaststroke	1	00.95
Karoly Guttler, Hungary		
200 metres breaststroke	2	10.16
Mike Barrowman, USA		
100 metres butterfly		52.32
Denis Pankratov, Russia		
200 metres butterfly	1	55.22
Denis Pankratov, Russia		
100 metres backstroke		53.86
Jeff Rouse, USA		
200 metres backstroke	1	56.57
Martin Lopez-Zubero, Spain		
200 metres medley	1	58.16
Jani Sievinen, Finland		
400 metres medley	4	12.30
Tom Dolan, USA		
4×100 metres freestyle relay	3	15.11
USA		
4×200 metres freestyle relay	7	11.95
CIS		
4×100 metres medley relay	3	36.93
USA		

WOMEN	min.	sec.
50 metres freestyle		24.51
Jingyi Le, China		
100 metres freestyle		54.01
Jingyi Le, China		
200 metres freestyle	1	56.78
Franziska van Almsick, Germany		
400 metres freestyle	4	03.85
Janet Evans, USA		
800 metres freestyle	8	16.22
Janet Evans, USA		
1,500 metres freestyle	15	52.10
Janet Evans, USA		
100 metres breaststroke	1	07.69
Samantha Riley, Australia		
200 metres breaststroke	2	24.76
Rebecca Brown, Australia		
100 metres butterfly		57.93
Mary Meagher, USA		
200 metres butterfly	2	05.96
Mary Meagher, USA		
100 metres backstroke	1	00.16
Cihong He, China		
200 metres backstroke	2	06.62
Krisztina Egerszegi, Hungary		
200 metres medley	2	11.65
Lin Li, China		
400 metres medley	4	36.10
Petra Schneider, GDR		
4×100 metres freestyle relay	3	37.91
USA		
4×200 metres freestyle relay	7	55.47
GDR		
4×100 metres medley relay	4	01.67
China		

Abbreviations

A — Associate of
AA — Alcoholics Anonymous
Anti-Aircraft
Automobile Association
AAA — Amateur Athletic Association
AB — Able-bodied seaman
ABA — Amateur Boxing Association
abbr(ev) — abbreviation
ABM — Anti-ballistic missile
abr — abridged
ac — alternating current
a/c — account
AC — Aircraftman
(*Ante Christum*) Before Christ
Companion, Order of Australia
ACAS — Advisory, Conciliation and
Arbitration Service
ACT — Australian Capital Territory
AD — (*Anno Domini*) In the year of our
Lord
ADC — Aide-de-Camp
ADC (P) — Personal ADC to The Queen
adj — adjective
Adj — Adjutant
ad lib — (*ad libitum*) at pleasure
Adm — Admiral
Admission
adv — adverb
advocate
AE — Air Efficiency Award
AEA — Atomic Energy Authority
AEEU — Amalgamated Engineering and
Electrical Union
AEM — Air Efficiency Medal
AERE — Atomic Energy Research
Establishment
AFC — Air Force Cross
Association Football Club
AFM — Air Force Medal
AFRC — Agricultural and Food
Research Council
AFV — Armoured fighting vehicle
AG — Adjutant-General
Attorney-General
AGM — air-to-ground missile
annual general meeting
AH — (*Anno Hegirae*) In the year of the
Hegira
AIDS — Acquired immune deficiency
syndrome
alt — altitude
am — (*ante meridiem*) before noon
AM — (*Anno mundi*) In the year of the
world
amplitude modulation
amp — ampere
amplifier
ANC — African National Congress
anon — anonymous
ANZAC — Australian and New Zealand
Army Corps
AO — Air Officer
Officer, Order of Australia
AOC — Air Officer Commanding
AONB — Area of Outstanding Natural
Beauty
AS — Anglo-Saxon
ASA — Advertising Standards
Authority
Amateur Swimming
Association
asap — as soon as possible
ASB — Alternative Service Book
ASEAN — Association of South East Asian
Nations

ASH — Action on Smoking and Health
ASLEF — Associated Society of
Locomotive Engineers and
Firemen
ASLIB — Association for Information
Management
ASW — anti-submarine warfare
ATC — Air Training Corps
AUC — (*ab urbe condita*) In the year from
the foundation of Rome
(*anno urbis conditae*) In the year
of the founding of the city
AUT — Association of University
Teachers
AV — Audio-visual
Authorized Version (*of Bible*)
AVR — Army Volunteer Reserve
AWOL — Absent without leave

b — born
bowled
BA — Bachelor of Arts
BAA — British Airports Authority
British Astronomical
Association
BAF — British Athletics Federation
BAFTA — British Academy of Film and
Television Arts
BAOR — British Army of the Rhine
Bart — Baronet
BAS — Bachelor in Agricultural
Science
British Antarctic Survey
BB — Boys' Brigade
BBC — British Broadcasting
Corporation
BBSRC — Biotechnology and Biological
Sciences Research Council
BC — Before Christ
British Columbia
BCCI — Bank of Credit and Commerce
International
B Ch (D) — Bachelor of (Dental) Surgery
BCL — Bachelor of Civil Law
B Com — Bachelor of Commerce
BD — Bachelor of Divinity
BDA — British Dental Association
BDS — Bachelor of Dental Surgery
B Ed — Bachelor of Education
BEM — British Empire Medal
B Eng — Bachelor of Engineering
BFI — British Film Institute
BFPO — British Forces Post Office
BL — British Library
B Litt — Bachelor of Letters *or* of
Literature
BM — Bachelor of Medicine
British Museum
BMA — British Medical Association
B Mus — Bachelor of Music
BOTB — British Overseas Trade Board
Bp — Bishop
B Pharm — Bachelor of Pharmacy
B Phil — Bachelor of Philosophy
Br — Britain
British
BR — British Rail
BRCS — British Red Cross Society
Brig — Brigadier
Brit — Britain
British
BSc — Bachelor of Science
BSC — British Steel Corporation
BSI — British Standards Institution

BST — British Summer Time
Bt — Baronet
BTEC — Business and Technology
Education Council
B Th — Bachelor of Theology
Btu — British thermal unit
BVM — (*Beata Virgo Maria*) Blessed
Virgin Mary
BVMS — Bachelor of Veterinary
Medicine and Surgery
BWB — British Waterways Board

c — (*circa*) about
C — Celsius
Centigrade
Conservative
CA — Chartered Accountant
(*Scotland*)
CAA — Civil Aviation Authority
CAB — Citizens' Advice Bureau
Cantab — (of) Cambridge
Cantuar: — of Canterbury (*Archbishop*)
CAP — Common Agricultural Policy
Capt — Captain
Caricom — Caribbean Community and
Common Market
Carliol: — of Carlisle (*Bishop*)
CB — Companion, Order of the Bath
CBE — Commander, Order of the
British Empire
CBI — Confederation of British
Industry
CC — Chamber of Commerce
Companion, Order of Canada
City Council
County Council
County Court
CCC — County Cricket Club
CCF — Combined Cadet Force
C Chem — Chartered Chemist
CD — Civil Defence
compact disc
Corps Diplomatique
Cdr — Commander
Cdre — Commodore
CDS — Chief of the Defence Staff
CE — Christian Era
Civil Engineer
C Eng — Chartered Engineer
Cento — Central Treaty Organization
Cestr: — of Chester (*Bishop*)
CET — Central European Time
Common External Tariff
cf — (*confer*) compare
CF — Chaplain to the Forces
CFC — Chlorofluorocarbon
CGC — Conspicuous Gallantry Cross
CGM — Conspicuous Gallantry Medal
CGS — Centimetre-gramme-second
(*system*)
Chief of General Staff
CH — Companion of Honour
ChB/M — Bachelor/Master of Surgery
CI — Channel Islands
The Imperial Order of the
Crown of India
CIA — Central Intelligence Agency
Cicestr: — of Chichester (*Bishop*)
CID — Criminal Investigation
Department
CIE — Companion, Order of the
Indian Empire
cif — cost, insurance and freight
C-in-C — Commander-in-Chief

CIPFA   Chartered Institute of Public Finance and Accountancy
C Lit   Companion of Literature
CLJ   Commander, Order of St Lazarus of Jerusalem
CM   (*Chirurgiae Magister*) Master of Surgery
CMG   Companion, Order of St Michael and St George
CND   Campaign for Nuclear Disarmament
c/o   care of
CO   Commanding Officer conscientious objector
COD   Cash on delivery
C of E   Church of England
COHSE   Confederation of Health Service Employees
COI   Central Office of Information
Col   Colonel
Con   Conservative
Cpl   Corporal
CPM   Colonial Police Medal
CPRE   Council for the Protection of Rural England
CPS   Crown Prosecution Service
CPVE   Certificate of Pre-Vocational Education
CRE   Commission for Racial Equality
CSA   Child Support Agency
CSCE   Conference on Security and Co-operation in Europe
CSE   Certificate of Secondary Education
CSI   Companion, Order of the Star of India
CVO   Commander, Royal Victorian Order

d   (*denarius*) penny
DBE   Dame Commander, Order of the British Empire
dc   direct current
DC   District Council District of Columbia
DCB   Dame Commander, Order of the Bath
D Ch   (*Doctor Chirurgiae*) Doctor of Surgery
DCL   Doctor of Civil Law
DCM   Distinguished Conduct Medal
DCMG   Dame Commander, Order of St Michael and St George
DCVO   Dame Commander, Royal Victorian Order
DD   Doctor of Divinity
DDS   Doctor of Dental Surgery
DDT   dichlorodiphenyl-trichloroethane
del   (*delineavit*) he/she drew it
DFC   Distinguished Flying Cross
DFEE   Department for Education and Employment
DFM   Distinguished Flying Medal
DG   (*Dei gratia*) By the grace of God Director-General
DH   Department of Health
DHA   District Health Authority
Dip Ed   Diploma in Education
Dip H E   Diploma in Higher Education
Dip Tech   Diploma in Technology
DJ   Disc jockey
DL   Deputy Lieutenant
D Litt   Doctor of Letters *or* of Literature
D Mus   Doctor of Music
DNA   deoxyribonucleic acid

DNB   *Dictionary of National Biography*
DNH   Department of National Heritage
do   (*ditto*) the same
DoE   Department of the Environment
DOS   Disk operating system (*computer*)
DP   Data processing
D Ph *or*
D Phil   Doctor of Philosophy
DPP   Director of Public Prosecutions
Dr   Doctor
D Sc   Doctor of Science
DSC   Distinguished Service Cross
DSM   Distinguished Service Medal
DSO   Companion, Distinguished Service Order
DSS   Department of Social Security
DTI   Department of Trade and Industry
DTP   Desk-top publishing
Dunelm: of Durham (*Bishop*)
DV   (*Deo volente*) God willing

E   East
Ebor: of York (*Archbishop*)
EBRD   European Bank for Reconstruction and Development
EC   European Community
ECG   Electrocardiogram
ECGD   Export Credits Guarantee Department
ECSC   European Coal and Steel Community
ECU   European Currency Unit
ED   Efficiency Decoration
EEC   European Economic Community
EEG   Electroencephalogram
EFA   European Fighter Aircraft
EFTA   European Free Trade Association
eg   (*exempli gratia*) for the sake of example
EMS   European Monetary System
ENEA   European Nuclear Energy Agency
EPSRC   Engineering and Physical Sciences Research Council
ER   (*Elizabetha Regina*) Queen Elizabeth
ERD   Emergency Reserve Decoration
ERM   Exchange Rate Mechanism
ERNIE   Electronic random number indicator equipment
ESA   European Space Agency
ESP   Extra-sensory perception
ESRC   Economic and Social Research Council
ETA   *Euzkadi ta Askatasuna* (Basque separatist organization)
et al   (*et alibi*) and elsewhere
et alii   (*et alii*) and others
etc   (*et cetera*) and the other things/and so forth
et seq   (*et sequentia*) and the following
EU   European Union
Euratom   European Atomic Energy Commission
Exon: of Exeter (*Bishop*)

f   (*forte*) loud

F   Fahrenheit Fellow of
FA   Football Association
FANY   First Aid Nursing Yeomanry
FAO   Food and Agriculture Organization (*UN*)
FBA   Fellow, British Academy
FBAA   Fellow, British Association of Accountants and Auditors
FBI   Federal Bureau of Investigation
FBIM   Fellow, British Institute of Management
FBS   Fellow, Botanical Society
FC   Football Club
FCA   Fellow, Institute of Chartered Accountants in England and Wales
FCCA   Fellow, Chartered Association of Certified Accountants
FCGI   Fellow, City and Guilds of London Institute
FCIA   Fellow, Corporation of Insurance Agents
FCIArb   Fellow, Chartered Institute of Arbitrators
FCIB   Fellow, Chartered Institute of Bankers Fellow, Corporation of Insurance Brokers
FCIBSE   Fellow, Chartered Institution of Building Services Engineers
FCII   Fellow, Chartered Insurance Institute
FCIPS   Fellow, Chartered Institute of Purchasing and Supply
FCIS   Fellow, Institute of Chartered Secretaries and Administrators
FCIT   Fellow, Chartered Institute of Transport
FCMA   Fellow, Chartered Institute of Management Accountants
FCO   Foreign and Commonwealth Office
FCP   Fellow, College of Preceptors
FD   (*Fidei Defensor*) Defender of the Faith
fec   (*fecit*) made this
FEng   Fellow, Royal Academy of Engineering
ff   (*fecerunt*) made this (*pl*)
ff   (*fortissimo*) very loud
FFA   Fellow, Faculty of Actuaries (*Scotland*) Fellow, Institute of Financial Accountants
FFAS   Fellow, Faculty of Architects and Surveyors
FFCM   Fellow, Faculty of Community Medicine
FFPHM   Fellow, Faculty of Public Health Medicine
FGS   Fellow, Geological Society
FHS   Fellow, Heraldry Society
FHSM   Fellow, Institute of Health Service Management
FIA   Fellow, Institute of Actuaries
FIBiol   Fellow, Institute of Biology
FICE   Fellow, Institution of Civil Engineers
FICS   Fellow, Institution of Chartered Shipbrokers
FIEE   Fellow, Institution of Electrical Engineers
FIERE   Fellow, Institution of Electronic and Radio Engineers
FIFA   International Association Football Federation

FIM	Fellow, Institute of Metals	FRICS	Fellow, Royal Institution of Chartered Surveyors	HBM	Her/His Britannic Majesty('s)
FIMM	Fellow, Institution of Mining and Metallurgy	FRMetS	Fellow, Royal Meteorological Society	HCF	Highest common factor
FInstF	Fellow, Institute of Fuel				Honorary Chaplain to the Forces
FInstP	Fellow, Institute of Physics	FRMS	Fellow, Royal Microscopical Society	HE	Her/His Excellency
FIQS	Fellow, Institute of Quantity Surveyors	FRNS	Fellow, Royal Numismatic Society		His Eminence
FIS	Fellow, Institute of Statisticians	FRPharmS	Fellow, Royal Pharmaceutical Society	HGV	Heavy Goods Vehicle
FJI	Fellow, Institute of Journalists			HH	Her/His Highness
fl	(*floruit*) flourished	FRPS	Fellow, Royal Photographic Society		Her/His Honour
FLA	Fellow, Library Association				His Holiness
FLS	Fellow, Linnean Society	FRS	Fellow, Royal Society	HIM	Her/His Imperial Majesty
FM	Field Marshal	FRSA	Fellow, Royal Society of Arts	HIV	Human immunodeficiency virus
	frequency modulation	FRSC	Fellow, Royal Society of Chemistry	HJS	(*hic jacet sepultus*) here lies buried
fo	folio	FRSE	Fellow, Royal Society of Edinburgh	HM	Her/His Majesty('s)
FO	Flying Officer			HMAS	Her/His Majesty's Australian Ship
fob	free on board	FRSH	Fellow, Royal Society of Health		
FPA	Family Planning Association	FRSL	Fellow, Royal Society of Literature	HMC	Headmasters' Conference
FPhS	Fellow, Philosophical Society			HMI	Her/His Majesty's Inspector
FRAD	Fellow, Royal Academy of Dancing	FRTPI	Fellow, Royal Town Planning Institute	HML	Her/His Majesty's Lieutenant
FRAeS	Fellow, Royal Aeronautical Society	FSA	Fellow, Society of Antiquaries	HMS	Her/His Majesty's Ship
FRAI	Fellow, Royal Anthropological Institute	FSS	Fellow, Royal Statistical Society	HMSO	Her/His Majesty's Stationery Office
FRAM	Fellow, Royal Academy of Music	FSVA	Fellow, Incorporated Society of Valuers and Auctioneers	HNC	Higher National Certificate
FRAS	Fellow, Royal Asiatic Society	FT	*Financial Times*	HND	Higher National Diploma
	Fellow, Royal Astronomical Society	FTI	Fellow, Textile Institute	HOLMES	Home Office Large Major Enquiry System
FRBS	Fellow, Royal Botanic Society	FTII	Fellow, Institute of Taxation	Hon	Honorary
	Fellow, Royal Society of British Sculptors	FZS	Fellow, Zoological Society		Honourable
FRCA	Fellow, Royal College of Anaesthetists			hp	horse power
				HP	Hire purchase
FRCGP	Fellow, Royal College of General Practitioners	GATT	General Agreement on Tariffs and Trade	HQ	Headquarters
FRCM	Fellow, Royal College of Music	GBE	Dame/Knight Grand Cross, Order of the British Empire	HRH	Her/His Royal Highness
FRCO	Fellow, Royal College of Organists	GC	George Cross	HSE	Health and Safety Executive
FRCOG	Fellow, Royal College of Obstetricians and Gynaecologists	GCB	Dame/Knight Grand Cross, Order of the Bath		(*hic sepultus est*) here lies buried
		GCE	General Certificate of Education	HSH	Her/His Serene Highness
FRCP	Fellow, Royal College of Physicians, London	GCHQ	Government Communications Headquarters	HTR	High temperature reactor
FRCPath	Fellow, Royal College of Pathologists	GCIE	Knight Grand Commander, Order of the Indian Empire	HWM	High water mark
FRCPE *or* FRCPEd	Fellow, Royal College of Physicians, Edinburgh	GCLJ	Knight Grand Cross, Order of St Lazarus of Jerusalem	I	Island
		GCMG	Dame/Knight Grand Cross, Order of St Michael and St George	IAAS	Incorporated Association of Architects and Surveyors
FRCPI	Fellow, Royal College of Physicians, Ireland			IAEA	International Atomic Energy Agency
FRCPsych	Fellow, Royal College of Psychiatrists	GCSE	General Certificate of Secondary Education	IATA	International Air Transport Association
FRCR	Fellow, Royal College of Radiologists	GCSI	Knight Grand Commander, Order of the Star of India	ibid	(*ibidem*) in the same place
FRCS	Fellow, Royal College of Surgeons of England	GCVO	Dame/Knight Grand Cross, Royal Victorian Order	IBRD	International Bank for Reconstruction and Development
FRCSE *or* FRCSEd	Fellow, Royal College of Surgeons of Edinburgh	GDP	Gross domestic product	ICAO	International Civil Aviation Organization
		Gen	General	ICBM	Inter-continental ballistic missile
FRCSGlas	Fellow, Royal College of Physicians and Surgeons of Glasgow	GHQ	General Headquarters	ICFTU	International Confederation of Free Trade Unions
		GM	George Medal		
		GMB	General, Municipal, Boilermakers and Allied Trades Union	ICJ	International Court of Justice
FRCSI	Fellow, Royal College of Surgeons in Ireland			ICRC	International Committee of the Red Cross
FRCVS	Fellow, Royal College of Veterinary Surgeons	GMT	Greenwich Mean Time	id	(*idem*) the same
		GNP	Gross national product	IDA	International Development Association
FREconS	Fellow, Royal Economic Society	GOC	General Officer Commanding	IDD	International direct dialling
		GP	General Practitioner	ie	(*id est*) that is
FRGS	Fellow, Royal Geographical Society	Gp Capt	Group Captain	IEA	International Energy Agency
		GSA	Girls' Schools Association	IFAD	International Fund for Agricultural Development
FRHistS	Fellow, Royal Historical Society	GSO	General Staff Officer	IFC	International Finance Corporation
				IHS	(*Iesus Hominum Salvator*) Jesus the Saviour of Mankind
FRHS	Fellow, Royal Horticultural Society			ILO	International Labour Office/Organization
				ILR	Independent local radio
FRIBA	Fellow, Royal Institute of British Architects	HAC	Honourable Artillery Company	IMF	International Monetary Fund
		HB	His Beatitude	IMO	International Maritime Organization
				Inc	Incorporated

incog	(*incognito*) unknown, unrecognized	lbw	leg before wicket	MIRAS	Mortgage Interest Relief at Source
INF	International Nuclear Force	lc	lower case (*printing*)	MLA	Member of Legislative Assembly
INLA	Irish National Liberation Army	LCJ	Lord Chief Justice		
in loc	(*in loco*) in its place	LCM	Least/lowest common multiple	MLC	Member of Legislative Council
Inmarsat	International Maritime Satellite Organization	LD	Liberal Democrat	MLitt	Master of Letters
		LDS	Licentiate in Dental Surgery	Mlle	Mademoiselle
INRI	(*Iesus Nazarenus Rex Iudaeorum*) Jesus of Nazareth, King of the Jews	LEA	Local Education Authority	MLR	Minimum lending rate
		LHD	(*Literarum Humaniorum Doctor*) Doctor of Humane Letters/ Literature	MM	Military Medal
				Mme	Madame
inst	(*instant*) current month	Lib	Liberal	MN	Merchant Navy
Intelsat	International Telecommunications Satellite Organization	Lic	(*Licenciado*) lawyer (*Spanish*)	MO	Medical Officer/Orderly
		Lic Med	Licentiate in Medicine	MoD	Ministry of Defence
		Lit	Literary	MoT	Ministry of Transport
Interpol	International Criminal Police Commission	Lit Hum	(*Literae Humaniores*) Faculty of classics and philosophy, Oxford	MP	Member of Parliament
					Military Police
IOC	International Olympic Committee	Litt D	Doctor of Letters	mph	miles per hour
		LJ	Lord Justice	MR	Master of the Rolls
IOM	Isle of Man	LLB	Bachelor of Laws	MRC	Medical Research Council
IOU	I owe you	LLD	Doctor of Laws	MS	Master of Surgery
IOW	Isle of Wight	LLM	Master of Laws		Manuscript (*pl* MSS)
IPLO	Irish People's Liberation Organization	LM	Licentiate in Midwifery		Multiple Sclerosis
		LMSSA	Licentiate in Medicine and Surgery, Society of Apothecaries	MSc	Master of Science
IQ	Intelligence quotient			MSF	Manufacturing, Science and Finance Union
IRA	Irish Republican Army				
IRC	International Red Cross	loc cit	(*loco citato*) in the place cited	MTh	Master of Theology
Is	Islands	log	logarithm	Mus B/D	Bachelor/Doctor of Music
ISBN	International Standard Book Number	Londin:	of London (*Bishop*)	MV	Merchant Vessel
		Long	Longitude		Motor Vessel
ISO	Imperial Service Order	LS	(*loco sigilli*) place of the seal	MVO	Member, Royal Victorian Order
ITC	Independent Television Commission	LSA	Licentiate of Society of Apothecaries		
				MW	medium wave
ITU	International Telecommunication Union	Lsd	(*Librae, solidi, denarii*) », shillings and pence		
		LSE	London School of Economics and Political Science	N	North
ITV	Independent Television			n/a	not applicable
		Lt	Lieutenant		not available
JP	Justice of the Peace	LTA	Lawn Tennis Association	NAAFI	Navy, Army and Air Force Institutes
		Ltd	Limited (liability)		
		LTh *or* L Theol	Licentiate in Theology	NALGO	National and Local Government Officers' Association
K	Ko«chel numeration (*of Mozart's works*)				
		LVO	Lieutenant, Royal Victorian Order	NASA	National Aeronautics and Space Administration
KANU	Kenyan African National Union				
		LWM	Low water mark	NAS/UWT	National Association of Schoolmasters/Union of Women Teachers
KBE	Knight Commander, Order of the British Empire				
		M	Member of		
KCB	Knight Commander, Order of the Bath		Monsieur	NATO	North Atlantic Treaty Organization
		MA	Master of Arts		
KCIE	Knight Commander, Order of the Indian Empire	MAFF	Ministry of Agriculture, Fisheries and Food	NB	New Brunswick
					(*nota bene*) note well
KCLJ	Knight Commander, Order of St Lazarus of Jerusalem	Maj	Major	NCC	Nature Conservancy Council
		max	maximum	NCIS	National Criminal Intelligence Service
KCMG	Knight Commander, Order of St Michael and St George	MB	Bachelor of Medicine		
		MBA	Master of Business Administration	NCO	Non-commissioned officer
KCSI	Knight Commander, Order of the Star of India			NDPB	Non-departmental public body
		MBE	Member, Order of the British Empire	NEB	New English Bible
KCVO	Knight Commander, Royal Victorian Order			nem con	(*nemine contradicente*) no one contradicting
		MC	Master of Ceremonies		
KG	Knight of the Garter		Military Cross	NERC	Natural Environment Research Council
KGB	(*Komitet Gosudarstvennoi Besopasnosti*) Committee of State Security (USSR)	MCC	Marylebone Cricket Club.		
		MCh(D)	Master of (Dental) Surgery	nes	not elsewhere specified
		MD	Managing Director	NFT	National Film Theatre
KKK	Ku Klux Klan		Doctor of Medicine	NFU	National Farmers' Union
KLJ	Knight, Order of St Lazarus of Jerusalem	MDS	Master of Dental Surgery	NHS	National Health Service
		ME	Middle English	NI	National Insurance
ko	knock out (*boxing*)		Myalgic Encephalomyelitis		Northern Ireland
KP	Knight, Order of St Patrick	MEC	Member of Executive Council	NIV	New International Version (*of Bible*)
KStJ	Knight, Order of St John of Jerusalem	MEd	Master of Education		
		mega	one million times	No	(*numero*) number
Kt	Knight	MEP	Member of the European Parliament	non seq	(*non sequitur*) it does not follow
KT	Knight of the Thistle			Norvic:	of Norwich (*Bishop*)
kV	Kilovolt			NP	Notary Public
kW	Kilowatt	MFH	Master of Foxhounds	NRA	National Rifle Association
kWh	Kilowatt hour	Mgr	Monsignor		National Rivers Authority
		MI	Military Intelligence	NS	New Style (*calendar*)
L	Liberal	micro	one-millionth part		Nova Scotia
Lab	Labour	milli	one-thousandth part		
Lat	Latitude	min	minimum		

NSPCC   National Society for the Prevention of Cruelty to Children

NSW   New South Wales

NT   National Theatre
National Trust
New Testament

NUCPS   National Union of Civil and Public Servants

NUJ   National Union of Journalists

NUM   National Union of Mineworkers

NUPE   National Union of Public Employees

NUS   National Union of Students

NUT   National Union of Teachers

NVQ   National Vocational Qualification

NWT   Northwest Territory

NY   New York

NZ   New Zealand

OAPEC   Organization of Arab Petroleum Exporting Countries

OAS   Organization of American States

OAU   Organization of African Unity

Ob *or* obit   died

OBE   Officer, Order of the British Empire

OC   Officer Commanding

ODA   Overseas Development Administration

OE   Old English
omissions excepted

OECD   Organization for Economic Co-operation and Development

OED   *Oxford English Dictionary*

Offer   Office of Electricity Regulation

Ofgas   Office of Gas Supply

OFM   Order of Friars Minor (*Franciscans*)

Ofsted   Office for Standards in Education

OFT   Office of Fair Trading

Oftel   Office of Telecommunications

Ofwat   Office of Water Services

OHMS   On Her/His Majesty's Service

OM   Order of Merit

OND   Ordinary National Diploma

op   (*opus*) work

OP   Opposite prompt side (*of theatre*)
Order of Preachers (*Dominicans*)
out of print (*books*)

op cit   (*opere citato*) in the work cited

OPCS   Office of Population Censuses and Surveys

OPEC   Organization of Petroleum Exporting Countries

OPRAF   Office of Passenger Rail Franchising

OPSS   Office of Public Service and Science

ORR   Office of the Rail Regulator

OS   Old Style (*calendar*)
Ordnance Survey

OSA   Order of St Augustine

OSB   Order of St Benedict

OST   Office of Science and Technology

O StJ   Officer, Order of St John of Jerusalem

OT   Old Testament

OTC   Officers' Training Corps

Oxon   (of) Oxford
Oxfordshire

p   page

p   (*piano*) softly

PA   Personal Assistant
Press Association

PAYE   Pay as You Earn

pc   (*per centum*) in the hundred

PC   personal computer
Police Constable
Privy Counsellor

PCC   Press Complaints Commission

PDSA   People's Dispensary for Sick Animals

PE   Physical Education

Petriburg: of Peterborough (*Bishop*)

PGA   Professional Golfers Association

PhD   Doctor of Philosophy

pinx(it)   he/she painted it

pl   plural

PLA   Port of London Authority

PLC   Public Limited Company

PLO   Palestine Liberation Organization

pm   (*post meridiem*) after noon

PM   Prime Minister

PMRAFNS   Princess Mary's Royal Air Force Nursing Service

PO   Petty Officer
Pilot Officer
Post Office
postal order

POW   Prisoner of War

pp   pages
(*per procurationem*) by proxy

PPARC   Particle Physics and Astronomy Research Council

PPS   Parliamentary Private Secretary

PR   Proportional representation
Public relations

PRA   President of the Royal Academy

Pro tem   (*pro tempore*) for the time being

Prox   (*proximo*) next month

PRS   President of the Royal Society

PRSE   President of the Royal Society of Edinburgh

Ps   Psalm

PS   (*postscriptum*) postscript

PSBR   Public sector borrowing requirement

psc   passed Staff College

PSV   Public Service Vehicle

Pte   Private

PTO   Please turn over

QARANC   Queen Alexandra's Royal Army Nursing Corps

QARNNS   Queen Alexandra's Royal Naval Nursing Service

QB   Queen's Bench

QBD   Queen's Bench Division

QC   Queen's Counsel

QED   (*quod erat demonstrandum*) which was to be proved

QGM   Queen's Gallantry Medal

QHC   Queen's Honorary Chaplain

QHDS   Queen's Honorary Dental Surgeon

QHNS   Queen's Honorary Nursing Sister

QHP   Queen's Honorary Physician

QHS   Queen's Honorary Surgeon

QMG   Quartermaster General

QPM   Queen's Police Medal

QS   Quarter Sessions

QSO   Quasi-stellar object (quasar)
Queen's Service Order

quango   quasi-autonomous non-governmental organization

qv   (*quod vide*) which see

R   (*Regina*) Queen
(*Rex*) King

RA   Royal Academy/Academician
Royal Artillery

RAC   Royal Armoured Corps
Royal Automobile Club

RADA   Royal Academy of Dramatic Art

RADC   Royal Army Dental Corps

RAE   Royal Aerospace Establishment

RAEC   Royal Army Educational Corps

RAeS   Royal Aeronautical Society

RAF   Royal Air Force

RAM   Random-access memory (*computer*)
Royal Academy of Music

RAMC   Royal Army Medical Corps

RAN   Royal Australian Navy

RAOC   Royal Army Ordnance Corps

RAPC   Royal Army Pay Corps

RAVC   Royal Army Veterinary Corps

RBA   Royal Society of British Artists

RBG   Royal Botanic Garden

RBS   Royal Society of British Sculptors

RC   Red Cross
Roman Catholic

RCM   Royal College of Music

RCN   Royal Canadian Navy

RCT   Royal Corps of Transport

RD   Refer to drawer (*banking*)
Royal Naval and Royal Marine Forces Reserve Decoration
Rural Dean

RDI   Royal Designer for Industry

RE   Religious Education
Royal Engineers

REME   Royal Electrical and Mechanical Engineers

Rep   Representative
Republican

Rev(d)   Reverend

RFU   Rugby Football Union

RGN   Registered General Nurse

RGS   Royal Geographical Society

RHA   Regional Health Authority

RHS   Royal Horticultural Society
Royal Humane Society

RI   Rhode Island
Royal Institute of Painters in Watercolours
Royal Institution

RIBA   Royal Institute of British Architects

RIP   (*Requiescat in pace*) May he/she rest in peace

RIR   Royal Irish Regiment

RL   Rugby League

RM   Registered Midwife
Royal Marines

RMA   Royal Military Academy

RMN   Registered Mental Nurse

RMT   National Union of Rail, Maritime and Transport Workers

RN   Royal Navy

RNIB	Royal National Institute for the Blind
RNID	Royal National Institute for the Deaf
RNLI	Royal National Lifeboat Institution
RNR	Royal Naval Reserve
RNVR	Royal Naval Volunteer Reserve
RNXS	Royal Naval Auxiliary Service
RNZN	Royal New Zealand Navy
Ro	(*Recto*) on the right-hand page
ROC	Royal Observer Corps
Roffen:	of Rochester (*Bishop*)
ROI	Royal Institute of Oil Painters
ROM	Read-only memory (*computer*)
RoSPA	Royal Society for the Prevention of Accidents
RP	Royal Society of Portrait Painters
rpm	revolutions per minute
RRC	Lady of Royal Red Cross
RSA	Republic of South Africa
	Royal Scottish Academician
	Royal Society of Arts
RSC	Royal Shakespeare Company
RSCN	Registered Sick Children's Nurse
RSE	Royal Society of Edinburgh
RSM	Regimental Sergeant Major
RSPB	Royal Society for the Protection of Birds
RSPCA	Royal Society for the Prevention of Cruelty to Animals
RSV	Revised Standard Version (*of Bible*)
RSVP	(*Répondez, s'il vous plaît*) Please reply
RSW	Royal Scottish Society of Painters in Watercolours
RTPI	Royal Town Planning Institute
RU	Rugby Union
RUC	Royal Ulster Constabulary
RV	Revised Version (*of Bible*)
RVM	Royal Victorian Medal
RWS	Royal Water Colour Society
RYS	Royal Yacht Squadron
s	second
	(*solidus*) shilling
S	South
SA	Salvation Army
	South Africa
	South America
	South Australia
SAE	stamped addressed envelope
Salop	Shropshire
Sarum:	of Salisbury (*Bishop*)
SAS	Special Air Service Regiment
SBS	Special Boat Squadron
SBN	Standard Book Number
ScD	Doctor of Science
SCM	State Certified Midwife
SDLP	Social Democratic and Labour Party
SDP	Social Democratic Party
SEAQ	Stock Exchange Automated Quotations system
SEN	State Enrolled Nurse
SERC	Science and Engineering Research Council
SERPS	State Earnings Related Pension Scheme
SFO	Serious Fraud Office
SHMIS	Society of Headmasters and Headmistresses of Independent Schools
SI	(*Syste'me International d'Unite¤s*) International System of Units
	Statutory Instrument

sic	So written
Sig	Signature
	Signor
SJ	Society of Jesus (*Jesuits*)
SLD	Social and Liberal Democrats
SMP	Statutory Maternity Pay
SNP	Scottish National Party
SOE	Special Operations Executive
SOS	Save Our Souls (*distress signal*)
sp	(*sine prole*) without issue
spgr	specific gravity
SPQR	(*Senatus Populusque Romanus*) The Senate and People of Rome
SRN	State Registered Nurse
SRO	Self Regulating Organizations
SS	Saints
	Schutzstaffel (Nazi paramilitary organization)
	Steamship
SSC	Solicitor before Supreme Court (*Scotland*)
SSF	Society of St Francis
SSP	Statutory Sick Pay
SSSI	Site of special scientific interest
STD	(*Sacrae Theologiae Doctor*) Doctor of Sacred Theology
	Subscriber trunk dialling
stet	let it stand (*printing*)
stp	Standard temperature and pressure
STP	(*Sacrae Theologiae Professor*) Professor of Sacred Theology
Sub Lt	Sub-Lieutenant
SVQ	Scottish Vocational Qualification
TA	Territorial Army
TB	Tuberculosis
TCCB	Test and County Cricket Board
TCD	Trinity College, Dublin
TD	Territorial Efficiency Decoration
temp	temperature
	temporary employee
TES	*Times Educational Supplement*
TGWU	Transport and General Workers' Union
THES	*Times Higher Education Supplement*
TLS	*Times Literary Supplement*
TNT	trinitrotoluene (*explosive*)
trs	transpose (*printing*)
TRH	Their Royal Highnesses
TT	Teetotal
	Tourist Trophy (*motorcycle races*)
	Tuberculin tested
TUC	Trades Union Congress
TVEI	Technical and Vocational Education Initiative
U	Unionist
UAE	United Arab Emirates
uc	upper case (*printing*)
UCAS	Universities and Colleges Admissions Service
UCATT	Union of Construction, Allied Trades and Technicians
UDA	Ulster Defence Association
UDI	Unilateral Declaration of Independence
UDM	Union of Democratic Mineworkers
UDR	Ulster Defence Regiment
UEFA	Union of European Football Associations
UFF	Ulster Freedom Fighters
UFO	Unidentified flying object

UHF	ultra-high frequency
UK	United Kingdom
UKAEA	UK Atomic Energy Authority
UN	United Nations
UNESCO	United Nations Educational, Scientific and Cultural Organization
UNHCR	United Nations High Commissioner for Refugees
UNICEF	United Nations Children's Fund
UNIDO	United Nations Industrial Development Organization
Unita	National Union for the Total Independence of Angola
UPU	Universal Postal Union
URC	United Reformed Church
US(A)	United States (of America)
USDAW	Union of Shop, Distributive and Allied Workers
USM	Unlisted Securities Market
USSR	Union of Soviet Socialist Republics
UTC	Co-ordinated Universal Time system
UVF	Ulster Volunteer Force
v	(*versus*) against
VA	Vicar Apostolic
	Victoria and Albert Order
VAD	Voluntary Aid Detachment
VAT	Value added tax
VC	Victoria Cross
VD	Venereal disease
	Volunteer Officers' Decoration
VDU	Visual display unit
Ven	Venerable
VHF	very high frequency
VIP	Very important person
Vo	(*Verso*) on the left-hand page
VRD	Royal Naval Volunteer Reserve Officers' Decoration
VSO	Voluntary Service Overseas
VTOL	Vertical take-off and landing (*aircraft*)
W	West
WCC	World Council of Churches
WEA	Workers' Educational Association
WEU	Western European Union
WFTU	World Federation of Trade Unions
WHO	World Health Organization
WI	West Indies
	Women's Institute
Winton:	of Winchester (*Bishop*)
WIPO	World Intellectual Property Organization
WMO	World Meteorological Organization
WO	Warrant Officer
WRAC	Women's Royal Army Corps
WRAF	Women's Royal Air Force
WRNS	Women's Royal Naval Service
WRVS	Women's Royal Voluntary Service
WS	Writer to the Signet
YMCA	Young Men's Christian Association
YWCA	Young Women's Christian Association
ZANU	Zimbabwe African National Union
Ψ = seaport	

Index

Abbreviations 1242–7
Aberavon, MP 265
Aberconwy 535, 563, 564
Aberdeen 535, 567, 569, 570
    airport 502
    Bishop (RC) 416
    MPs 266
    Robert Gordon University 459
    University 452
Aberdeen and Orkney, Bishop 407
Aberdeenshire 570
Aberration, constant of 75
Abertay University 452
Aberystwyth, University College 460
Abidjan 858
Abingdon, Oxford West and, MP 257
Abu Dhabi 786, 1047, 1048–9
Abuja 784, 975
Academies of art 705–6
Academies of scholarship, national 705–6
Academy awards 1151
ACAS 281–2
Accidents:
    death statistics 121
    events (1994–5) 1085–6
    insurance 633–5
    Investigation Branch (Transport) 354
    rail 504
    road 507
Accountancy, qualifying bodies 463
Accounts Commission for Scotland 288
Accra 784, 889
Achonry, Bishop (RC) 417
Achonry, Tuam, Killala and, Bishop 408
Acton (Ealing), MP 248
Acts of Parliament (1994–5) 1171–4
Actuarial science, professional
    organizations 463
Actuary, The Government 306
Addis Ababa 783, 874
Address, style of:
    Archbishops 167
    Baronesses 161, 217
    Baronets 177, 217
    Barons 152, 217
    Bishops 167
    Countesses 149, 217
    courtesy title holders 169, 217
    Dames 209, 217
    Dukes 142, 217
    Earls 144, 217
    heirs to peerage 169, 217
    Knights 177, 217
    Marquesses 143, 217
    Privy Counsellors 217
    Viscounts 149, 217
Adelaide 811
Administration, professional
    bodies 463–4
Admirals of the Fleet 387
Adopted children register 336
Adoption, legal notes 662
Adult and continuing education 446–7,
    462–3
    National Institute of 447, 462
    Welsh Committee 447
Adult education 446–7, 462–3
    Northern Ireland Council for 447
Adur 532, 549
Advent Sunday 9
    (1996-2028) 83
Advertising Standards Authority 721

Advisory, Conciliation and Arbitration
    Service 281–2
Advisory Council on Public Records 339
Advocates, Faculty of 466
AEA Technology 288
Aegean:
    Archdeacon 400
    Islands 890
Aerodromes in UK 502
Afghanistan 785, 796–7
Africa:
    area 111
    continent 110
    countries of 783–4
    events (1994–5) 1098–100
    migration to UK 119
African and Afro-Caribbean Churches,
    UK 423
African Unity, Organization of 763–4
Agaña 787, 1051, 1055
Agricultural Development, International
    Fund for 758
Agricultural Development and Advisory
    Service 284
Agricultural Land Tribunals 376
Agricultural Museum, Scotland 329, 598
Agricultural Science Agency,
    Scotland 344
Agriculture:
    CAB International 751
    Department, Scotland 344
    HM Inspectorate 310
Agriculture, Fisheries and Food:
    Minister 279, 282
    Ministry of 282–5
    regional offices 284
Agriculture Organization, Food and,
    UN 757
Aides-de-Camp to The Queen 125
Air:
    distances from London 117
    transport statistics 501
Air Accidents Investigation Branch 354
Airmail:
    rates 510
    zones 516–17
Airports in UK 502
Ajman 1049
Alabama 1051
Alaska 1051
Albania 786, 797–8
    Archbishops (RC) 417
Albert Hall, Royal 602
Alberta 838, 842
Aldermen, Corporation of London 529,
    555, 556
Alderney 575
    airport 502
Aldershot, MP 241
Aldridge-Brownhills, MP 241
Alexandra Palace 599
Algeria 783, 798–9
    Archbishop (RC) 417
Algiers 783, 798
Algol, minima (1996) 16, 20, 24, etc., 71
All Saints' Day 56
Allerdale 532, 549
Allowances:
    income tax 641–2
    social security 488–95
Alma Ata 785, 924
Alnwick 532, 549
Alofi 787

Alpine skiing 1216
Altrincham and Sale, MP 241
Alyn and Deeside 535, 563
    MP 265
Ambassadors 796–1020
Amber Valley 532, 549
    MP 241
America:
    area 111
    continent 110–11
    Southern Cone of, Anglican
        Church 411
American football 1216
American Samoa 1049, 1055–6
American States, Organization of 764
Americas 110–11
    countries of 784–5
    events (1994–5) 1100–1
    migration to UK 119
Amersham, Chesham and, MP 246
Amman 785, 922
Amsterdam 786, 967
Ancient monuments 586–92
Ancient Monuments Board:
    for Scotland 310
    for Wales 310
Andorra 786, 799–800
    map 878
Andorra La Vella 786, 799
Anglesey 535, 561, 563, 564
Anglia Polytechnic University 452
Anglican Communion 396–414
    overseas 408–14
    UK 396–408
Angling 1216
    close seasons 585
Angola 783, 800–1
    Archbishops (RC) 417
    map 800
Anguilla 784, 1071
    map 897
Angular measures 520
Angus 535, 569, 570
Angus East, MP 266
Animals (Scientific Procedure)
    Inspectorate 313
Ankara 786, 1040
Annandale and Eskdale 535, 569
Anniversaries:
    (1995) 14
    (1996) 14
Antananarivo 784, 944
Antarctic:
    area 111
    Australian 808
    British 1072
    continent 111, 788–9
    French 881
    Norwegian 978
    Survey, British 710
Antarctica 111, 788–9
Antigua and Barbuda 784, 801–2
    map 897
Antilles, Netherlands 785, 969
Antipodes Islands 969
Antrim 572
    MPs 270
Aotearoa, New Zealand and Polynesia,
    Anglican Church 408
Apia 787, 1063
Apogee (1996) 16, 20, 24, etc.
Apostolic Church 427
Apparent sidereal time 73, 74

Apparent solar time 71, 73
Appeal Courts 361, 362
  Scotland 371
Appeals Tribunals, social security 493
Appointments (1994–5) 1098
Arab Emirates, United 786, 1047–9
Arab States, League of 761
Arbitration Committee, Central 702
Archaeology, (1994–5) 1118–22
Archbishops:
  Anglican overseas 408–14
  Church of England 167, 396, 404
  Roman Catholic 415–16
Archbishops of Canterbury 429
Archbishops of York 429
Archdeacons 396–408
Arches, Court of 375
Architecture:
  (1994–5) 1123–8
  professional training 463
Arctic Ocean 110
Ardagh and Clonmacnois, Bishop
  (RC) 417
Ardagh, Kilmore, Elphin and, Bishop 408
Ards 572
Area, measurement 518, 519
Areas of Outstanding Natural
  Beauty 579–81
  England and Wales 579–80
  Northern Ireland 581
Areas of Special Scientific Interest 581–2
Arfon 535, 563
Argentina 785, 802–3
  Archbishops (RC) 417
Argyll and Bute 535, 569, 570
  MP 267
Argyll and the Isles:
  Bishop (Anglican) 407
  Bishop (RC) 416
Aries, first point of 17, 21, 25, etc. 74
Arizona 1051
Arkansas 1051
Armagh 572
  Archbishop (Anglican) 408
  Archbishop (RC) 416
  Newry and, MP 270
Armed Forces 384–95
  defence cuts 384
  Defence Staff 384–7
  deployment 384
  Minister of State 279, 384
  pay 393–5
  pay review bodies 341
  relative ranks 394
  retirement benefits 395
  strengths 384
Armenia 786, 803–5
  map 884
Arms, College of 285
Army 389–91
  colleges 464
  corps 390–1
  General Staff 385
  Museum, National 329
  regiments 390–1
  staff appointments 389–90
  strength 384
Art:
  academies 705–6
  Royal College of 461
Art Collection, Government 330
Art galleries 593–8
  national 286–7
Art Library, National 328
Arts, events (1994–5) 1086–8
Arts Boards, regional 286
Arts Council:
  of England 286
  of Northern Ireland 286
  Scottish 286
  of Wales 286

Aruba 784, 969
  map 897
Arun 532, 549
Arundel, MP 241
Arundel and Brighton, Bishop (RC) 416
Ascension Day 9, 83
  (1996–2028) 83
Ascension Island 784, 1079
ASEAN 751
Ash Wednesday 9, 83
Ashfield 532, 549
  MP 241
Ashford 532, 549
  MP 241
Ashkhabad 786, 1042
Ashmore Islands 808
Ashton-under-Lyne, MP 241
Asia:
  area 111
  continent 111
  countries of 785–6
  events (1994–5) 1102–3
  migration to UK 119
Asmara 783, 872
Assay marks 604–5
Assemblies of God in Great Britain and
  Ireland 427
Assisted Places Scheme 437–8
Associated Presbyterian Churches of
  Scotland 423
Association football 1216–17
  European cups 1217
  FA Cup finals 1217
  league results 1216–17
Association for Payment Clearing
  Services 615
Association of South East Asian
  Nations 751
Aston:
  Archdeacon 398
  Bishop Suffragan 398
  University 452
Astronomers Royal 80
Astronomical constants 75
Astronomical phenomena (1996) 16, 20,
  24, etc., 71
Astronomical predictions (1996) 16–63
Astronomical unit 75
Astronomy, Particle Physics and, Research
  Council 711
Asunción 785, 984
Atcham, Shrewsbury and 533, 552
  MP 259
Athens 786, 891
Athletics 1217–21
  records 1239–41
Atomic Energy Agency, International 757
Atomic Energy Authority, UK 288
  constabulary 383
Atomic time 74
Attendance allowance 491
Attercliffe (Sheffield), MP 259
Attorney-General 279, 321, 361
  departments 321
Auckland:
  Archdeacon 404
  Islands 969
Audit Commission for England and
  Wales 288
Audit Office, National 329–30
Australasia:
  countries of 787
  events (1994–5) 1103
  migration to UK 119
Australia 111, 787, 805–12
  Anglican Church 408
  Archbishops (RC) 417
  capital territory 805
  continent 111
  external territories 808–9

Australia continued
  map 805
  Norfolk Island 787, 809
  states 809–12
Austria 786, 812–13
  Archbishops (RC) 417
Automobile Association 723
Autumn:
  defined 15
  equinox 15, 81
Avarua 787
Avon 531, 546, 547
  Education Authority 448
Avon, Itchen, Test and, MEP 275
Avon and Somerset, Police Authority 381
Awards:
  film 1151
  literature 1155
  Queen's 1178–80
  theatre 1202
Aylesbury, MP 242
Aylesbury Vale 532, 549
Ayr, MP 267
Ayrshire:
  East 570
  North 570
  South 570
Azerbaijan 786, 814–16
  map 884
Azores 787, 992

Babergh 532, 549
Baden Württemberg 887
Badenoch and Strathspey 535, 569
Badminton 1221
BAFTA awards 1151
Baghdad 785, 908
Bahamas 784, 816
  map 897
Bahrain 785, 817
  map 1006
Baku 786, 814
Balance of payments statistics 608
Balearic Isles 1021
Bali 904
Ballet 1145–7
  Birmingham Royal 1146
  English National 1146
  Royal 1145
  Scottish 1147
Ballymena 572
Ballymoney 572
Bamako 784, 948
Banbridge 572
Banbury, MP 242
Bandar Seri Begawan 785, 832
Banff and Buchan 535, 569
  MP 267
Bangkok 786, 1035
Bangladesh 785, 817–19, 980
  Archbishop (RC) 417
Bangor:
  Bishop 407
  University College of 460
Bangui 783, 846
Banjul 783, 883
Bank base rates (1994–5) 615
Bank of England 288
  Museum 595
Bank holidays 87
  (1996) 10
  (1997) 11
Bank for International Settlements 751
Banking 615–20
  Clearing Services 615
  hours 615
  Ombudsman 614
  professional organizations 463
  services 615

Banknotes, British 611–12
Bankruptcy, High Court 363
Banks:
  authorized 616–20
  base rates (1994–5) 615
  clearing banks 615
  deposit-taking institutions 616–20
  financial results 615
Banqueting House 587
Banstead, Reigate and 533, 552
Baptist Church 423
Bar of England and Wales 466
Bar of Northern Ireland 466
Barbados 784, 819–20
  map 897
Barbican Centre 599
Barbuda, Antigua and 784, 801–2
  map 897
Barking:
  Bishop (Suffragan) 398
  MP 238, 242
Barking and Dagenham 534, 560
  Education Authority 449
Barnes, Richmond and, MP 258
Barnet 534, 560
  Education Authority 449
Barnsley 531, 548
  Education Authority 448
  MPs 242
Barnstaple, Archdeacon 399
Baronesses:
  form of address 161, 217
  Life 166–7
  in own right 161–2
Baronets 177, 178–208
  form of address 177, 217
  premier 142, 179, 184, 185
Barons:
  courtesy titles 169–70
  form of address 152, 217
  hereditary 152–61
  life 162–7
  premier 142, 155, 157
Barony, premier 155
Barristers' training 466
Barrow and Furness, MP 242
Barrow-in-Furness 532, 549
Basildon 524, 532, 549
  MP 242
Basingstoke:
  Archdeacon 398
  Bishop (Suffragan) 397
  MP 242
Basingstoke and Deane 532, 549
Basketball 1221
Basse-Terre (Guadeloupe) 784, 881
Basseterre (St Kitts) 785, 1001
Bassetlaw 532, 549
  MP 242
Bath 532, 546, 549
  Archdeacon 398
  MP 242
  University 453
Bath and North East Somerset 546
Bath, Order of 174
  Dames 209–10
  Knights 178–208
Bath, Wiltshire North and, MEP 277
Bath and Wells, Bishop 168, 398
Batley and Spen, MP 242
Battersea, MP 242
Battle, Bexhill and, MP 242
Bavaria 887
BBC 289
  future of 679
  radio 680–1
  television 679
Beaconsfield, MP 242
Bear Island 978
Bearsden, Strathkelvin and, MP 270

Bearsden and Milngavie 535, 569
Beaufort scale 1209
Beckenham, MP 242
Bedford 532, 549
  Archdeacon 402
  Bishop (Suffragan) 402
Bedfordshire 531, 546, 547
  Education Authority 448
  MEPs 273
  Mid 533, 551
  MPs 242
  Police Authority 381
  South 533, 552
Bedworth, Nuneaton and 533, 552
Beijing (Peking) 785, 849
Beirut 785, 935
Belarus 786, 820–1
  Archbishop (RC) 417
Belfast 571, 572, 787
  airports 502
  Education and Library Board 450
  MPs 270
  Queen's University 459
Belgium 786, 821–3
  Archbishop (RC) 417
  map 821
Belgrade 787, 1064, 1066
Belize 784, 823–4
  map 973
Belmopan 784, 823
Benefits:
  Agency 348
  contributory 589–90
  non-contributory 490–1
Benin 783, 824–5
  Archbishop (RC) 417
  map 975
Bequests to Charity 1129–31
Berkshire 531, 546, 547
  Archdeacon 401
  East, MP 242
  Education Authority 448
Berlin 786, 885, 887
Bermondsey, Southwark and, MP 260
Bermuda 784, 1071–2
  Bishop (Anglican) 413
Berne 787, 1028
Berwick-upon-Tweed 532, 549
  MP 242
Berwickshire 535, 569
  Roxburgh and, MP 269
Beth Din 432
Bethnal Green Museum of
  Childhood 328, 595
Bethnal Green and Stepney, MP 242
Beverley 532, 549
  Bishop (Suffragan) 404
  MP 242
Bexhill and Battle, MP 242
Bexley 534, 560
  Education Authority 449
Bexleyheath, MP 242–3
Bhutan 785, 825–6
Biggar Gasworks Museum 329
Biggin Hill airport 502
Billericay, MP 243
Billiards 1221
Billion defined 520
Bills, Parliamentary 222, 224, 225
Biological Sciences, Biotechnology and,
  Research Council 707
Biology, qualifying body 463
Biotechnology and Biological Sciences
  Research Council 707
  research units 707
Birkenhead:
  Bishop (Suffragan) 405
  MP 243
Birmingham 531, 539, 548
  airport 502

Birmingham continued
  Archbishop (RC) 416
  Archdeacon 398
  Bishop 167, 398
  Education Authority 448
  MEPs 273
  MPs 243
  Royal Ballet 1146
  University 453
  University of Central England 454
Births:
  certificates 663–4
  registration 336–7, 662–3
    Scotland 347
  statistics 119–20
Bishkek 785, 931
Bishop Auckland, MP 243
Bishops:
  Anglican, overseas 408–14
  Church of England 167–8, 396–408
  Roman Catholic 416, 417
  Suffragan 396–408
Bissau 784, 895
Blaby 532, 549
  MP 243
Blaby, Northamptonshire and, MEP 276
Black Rod:
  Gentleman Usher 126, 174, 223
  Yeoman Usher 223
Blackburn 532, 549
  Archdeacon 404
  Bishop 168, 404
  MP 243
Blackley (Manchester), MP 255
Blackpool 532, 549
  airport 502
  MPs 243
Blaenau Gwent 535, 563, 564
  MP 265
Blaydon, MP 243
Blue Rod 175
Blyth Valley 532, 549
  MP 243
Board of Trade (BOTB) 350
  President 279, 350
Boat Race, The 1235
Bodmin, Archdeacon 403
Bogotá 785, 853
Bolivia 785, 826–7
  Archbishops (RC) 417
Bolsover 532, 549
  MP 243
Bolton 531, 548
  Archdeacon 405
  Bishop (Suffragan) 405
  Education Authority 448
  MPs 243–4
Bonds:
  National Savings 626
  Premium 626
Bonn 885
Booker prize 1155
Books:
  copyright 677
  literary awards 1155
  Public Lending Right 338
  publishers 694–6
  reference 697–9
  sizes 522
Boothferry 532, 549
  MP 244
Bootle, MP 244
Bophuthatswana 1017
Border, Penrith and The, MP 25
Borders 535, 567, 570
  Education Authority 450
  Lothian and, Police Authority 382
Borneo 111, 946
Bornholm Island 864
Borough councils:
  England 548–54

Borough Councils *continued*
London 560
Metropolitan 548
Northern Ireland 572–3
political composition 531–6
Wales 563
Boroughs, Parliamentary 241–71
Bosnia-Hercegovina 786, 827–9
Archbishop (RC) 418
map 828
Boston 532, 549
Holland with, MP 252
Bosworth, MP 244
Bosworth, Hinckley and 533, 551
Botanic Gardens, Royal 341–2
Botswana 783, 829–30
Boundary Commissions 288–9
Bounty Islands 969
Bournemouth 532, 549
airport 502
MPs 244
University 453
Bouvet Island 978
Bow and Poplar, MP 244
Bowls 1221–2
Boxing 1222–3
Bracknell 524
Bracknell Forest 532, 549
Bradford 531, 539, 548
Archdeacon 404
Bishop 168, 404
Education Authority 448
MPs 238, 244
University 453
Bradwell, Bishop (Suffragan) 398
Braintree 532, 549
MP 244
Brandenburg 887
Brasilia 785, 830
Bratislava 787, 1011
Brazil 785, 830–2
Archbishops (RC) 418
Episcopal Church of 408–9
Brazzaville 783, 855
Brechin, Bishop 407
Brechou 575
Breckland 532, 549
Brecknock 535, 563
Brecon, Swansea and, Bishop 407
Brecon and Radnor, MP 265
Bremen 887
Brent 534, 560
Education Authority 449
MPs 244
Brentford and Isleworth, MP 244
Brentwood 532, 549
Bishop (RC) 416
Brentwood and Ongar, MP 244
Bridgend 564
MP 265
Bridges:
London 599
longest 115–16
Bridgetown 784, 819
Bridgnorth 532, 549
Bridgwater, MP 244
Bridlington, MP 244
Brigg and Cleethorpes, MP 244
Brighton 532, 549
MPs 244
University 453
Brighton, Arundel and, Bishop (RC) 416
Brightside (Sheffield), MP 259
Brisbane 810
Bristol 532, 539, 546, 549
airport 502
Archdeacon 398
Bishop 167, 398
MEP 273
MPs 245

Bristol *continued*
University 453
University of the West of England 460
Bristol UWE 460
Britannia Royal Naval College 464
British Academy 705
British Antarctic Survey 710
British Antarctic Territory 789, 1072
British Broadcasting Corporation 289, 679–81
British citizenship 653–4
British Coal:
Corporation 289, 498
privatization 498
British Columbia 838, 842–3
Anglican Province 409
British Council 289
British dependent territories 1071–80
British Embassies 796–1020
British Empire, Order of 176
British Film Commission 289
British Film Institute 290
British Gas 499
British Geological Survey 710
British Indian Ocean Territory 1072
British Library 321–2
Board 321
British Museum 326–7, 595
British National Space Centre 350
British Overseas Trade Board 352
British Pharmacopoeia Commission 290
British Railways 503–4
Board 290
privatization 503
British Standards Institution 290
British Summer Time 15, 70
British Telecom 512–14
British Tourist Authority 290
British Transport Police 383
British Virgin Islands 785, 1072–3
British Waterways Board 290
Brixworth, Bishop (Suffragan) 402
Broadcasting 679–84
(1994–5) 1132–6
BBC 289, 679–81
independent radio 681–4
independent television 679–80
Independent Television
Commission 317
Radio Authority 339
World Service (radio) 681
Worldwide Television (BBC) 679
Broadcasting Complaints
Commission 679
Broadcasting Standards Council 290–1
Broadgreen (Liverpool), MP 254
Broadland 532, 549
Broads, The 579
Authority 291
Bromley 534, 560
Archdeacon 402
Education Authority 449
Bromsgrove 532, 549
MP 245
Broxbourne 532, 549
MP 245
Broxtowe 532, 549
MP 245
Brunei 785, 832
map 905
Brunel University 453
Brussels 786, 821
BSI 290
BTEC 442, 444, 452
Buchan, Banff and 535, 569
MP 267
Bucharest 786, 993
Buckingham:
Archdeacon 401
Bishop (Area) 401
MP 245

Buckingham *continued*
University 444, 453
Buckingham Palace 587
Buckinghamshire 531, 546, 547
Education Authority 448
and Oxfordshire East, MEP 273
South 533, 552
Budapest 786, 899
Buddhism 430
organizations in UK 430
Budget (1994) 1163–5
Buenos Aires 785, 802
Building, qualifying bodies 463
Building Research Establishment 302
Building Societies 622–5
Commission 305
financial statistics 623–5
interest rates 623
Ombudsman 614
Buildings, tallest 115
Bujumbura 783, 835
Bulgaria 786, 833–4
Burial, legal notes 657
Burkina 783, 834–5
Archbishop (RC) 418
map 975
Burnley 532, 549
Bishop (Suffragan) 404
MP 245
Burntwood, Cannock and, MP 245
Burton, MP 245
Burundi 783, 835–6
Anglican Province 409
Archbishop (RC) 418
map 800
Bury 531, 548
Education Authority 448
MPs 245
Bury St Edmunds, MP 245
Business, qualifying bodies 463–4
Business and Technology Education
Council 442, 444, 452
Bute, Argyll and 535, 569, 570
MP 267
Buying Agency 302
By-elections, UK Parliament 238–9

CAB International 751
Cabinet:
functions of 228
members of 279
Cabinet Office 291–2
Cadw: Welsh Historic Monuments 310, 359
Caenozoic Era 94
Caernarfon, MP 265
Caernarfonshire and Merionethshire 564
Caerphilly 564
MP 265
Caicos Islands, Turks and 785, 1080
map 897
Cairo 783, 869
Caithness 535, 569
Caithness, Moray, Ross and, Bishop 407
Caithness and Sutherland, MP 267
Calder Valley, MP 245
Calderdale 531, 548
Education Authority 448
Calendars:
(1770–2033) 90
(1996) 10
(1997) 11
Chinese 88
Christian 82–3
Coptic 88
Gregorian 82
Hindu 84–5
Japanese 88
Jewish 85
Julian 82

Calendars *continued*
  Muslim 86
  Olympiads 88
  Orthodox churches 82
  perpetual 90–3
  Roman 89
  Sikh 86
  year 81
  Zoroastrian 88
California 1051
Camberley Staff College 464
Cambodia 785, 836–7
  map 836
Camborne, Falmouth and, MP 249
Cambridge 532, 539, 549
  airport 502
  MP 245
  University 453
Cambridgeshire 531, 546, 547
  East 532, 550
  Education Authority 448
  MEP 273
  MPs 245
  Police Authority 381
  South 533, 552
Camden 534, 560
  Education Authority 449
Cameroon 783, 837–8
  Archbishops (RC) 418
  map 975
Campbell Island 969
Canada 784, 838–45
  Anglican Church 409
  Archbishops (RC) 418
  map 839
  provinces 842–5
Canals, longest 116
Canary Islands 1021
Canberra 787, 805
Candlemas (term day) 9
Cannock and Burntwood, MP 245
Cannock Chase 532, 549
Canons Residentiary 396–408
Canopus 69
Canterbury 532, 539, 549
  Archdeacon 397
  MP 245
  University of Kent 455
Canterbury, Province of 397–404
  Archbishop 167, 397
  ecclesiastical courts 375
CAP 775–6
Capacity, measurement 519
Cape Breton Island 844
Cape Town 784, 1016
Cape Verde 783, 845–6
Capital cities 783–7
Capital gains tax 644–6
Capital Taxes Office 318
  Scotland 318
Caracas 785, 1060
Caradon 532, 549
Cardiff 535, 562, 563, 564, 787
  airport 502
  Archbishop (RC) 416
  MPs 265
  University College 460
Cardiganshire 564
Cardinals, College of 415
Caribbean Community and Common
  Market 751
CARICOM 751
Carlisle 532, 539–40, 549
  Archdeacon 405
  Bishop 168, 405
  MP 245
Carmarthen 535, 563
  MP 265
Carolina, North 1051
Carolina, South 1051

Caroline Islands 956
Carrick (Cornwall) 532, 549
Carrick, Cumnock and Doon Valley,
  MP 267
Carrick, Kyle and 536, 569
Carrickfergus 572
Carshalton and Wallington, MP 245
Cartier Islands 808
Cashel, Archbishop (RC) 416
Cashel and Ossory, Bishop 408
Castle Morpeth 532, 549
Castle Point 532, 549
  MP 245
Castleford, Pontefract and, MP 257
Castlereagh 573
Castles 586–92
Castries 785, 1002
Cathcart (Glasgow), MP 268
Catholic Church, *see* Roman Catholic
  Church
Caucasia, Archbishop (RC) 418
Cayenne 785, 881
Cayman Islands 784, 1073–4
  map 897
CBI 700
CCTA 292
Celestial phenomena (1996) 66
Cenotaph 599
Census results, UK (1801-1991) 118
Centenaries 14
Central Adjudication Services 292
Central Advisory Committee on War
  Pensions 349
Central Africa, Anglican Province 409
Central African Republic 783, 846–7
  Archbishop (RC) 418
  map 800
Central America 110–11, 784–5
Central Arbitration Committee 702
Central England, University of 454
Central government expenditure 606
Central Lancashire:
  New Town 524
  University 454
Central Office of Information 292–3
  regional offices 293
Central Region (Scotland) 535, 567
  Education Authority 450
  Police Authority 382
Central Science Laboratory 284–5
Central Statistical Office 293
Central Veterinary Laboratory 285
Ceredigion 535, 563
Ceredigion and Pembroke North, MP 265
CERN 756
Certificate of Pre-Vocational
  Education 439
Certification Office for Trade Unions and
  Employers' Associations 293
Certification Officer 293, 700
Ceuta 1021
Chad 783, 847
  Archbishop (RC) 418
Chaffarinas Islands 1022
Chairman of Ways and Means 224
Chamberlain, Lord 125
Chamberlain, Lord Great 325
Chancellor of the Exchequer 279, 355
Chancery Court of York 375
Chancery Division:
  High Court 361, 362–3
  Vice Chancellor 362
Channel Islands 575, 787
  airports 502
  currency 612
  Education Authorities 450
  Police Authorities 382
  population 119
Channel Tunnel 116, 504
  rail link 504

Channel Tunnel *continued*
  Safety Unit 353
  services 504
Chanucah 9
Chapels Royal 126, 127, 602
Charing Cross, Archdeacon 396
Charities 721–49
Charity Commission 293–4
Charlotte Amalie 785, 1051, 1056
Charlottetown 845
Charnwood 532, 549
Charterhouse 599
Chatham Islands 869, 969
Cheadle, MP 246
Cheam, Sutton and, MP 261
Chelmsford 532, 549
  Bishop 167, 398
  MP 246
Chelsea, MP 246
Chelsea, Kensington and 534, 560
  Education Authority 449
Chelsea Physic Garden 599
Cheltenham 532, 549
  Archdeacon 400
  MP 246
Chemistry:
  Nobel prize 1156
  qualifying body 463
Chertsey and Walton, MP 246
Cherwell 532, 549
Chesham and Amersham, MP 246
Cheshire 531, 546, 547
  Education Authority 448
  MEPs 273–4
  Police Authority 381
Chess 1223
Chester 532, 540, 549
  Archdeacon 405
  Bishop 167, 405
  MP 246
Chester-le-Street 532, 550
Chesterfield 532, 549
  Archdeacon 399
  MP 246
Chesterfield, Nottinghamshire North and,
  MEP 276
Chichester 532, 550
  Archdeacon 399
  Bishop 167, 399
  MP 246
Chief Accountancy Adviser to the
  Treasury 356
Chief Adjudication Officer 292
Chief Constables 381
Chief Rabbi 432
Chief Rabbinate 432
Chief Registrar of Friendly Societies 305
Chief Secretary to the Treasury 279, 355
Chief Whip 280
Chiefs of clans 212–13
Child benefit 491
Child Support Agency 348
Child Support Commissioners 378
Childhood, Bethnal Green Museum
  of 328, 595
Children:
  adoption 662, 665
  custody of 665, 667
  legitimacy 667
Chile 785, 847–9
  Archbishops (RC) 418
Chiltern 532, 550
Chiltern Hundreds 225
China 785, 849–53
  Archbishops (RC) 418
  map 850
  Taiwan 786, 1031–2
Chingford, MP 246
Chipping Barnet, MP 246
Chiropody, training 467

Chislehurst, MP 246
Chivalry, Orders of 174–6
Chorley 532, 550
  MP 246
Christchurch 532, 550
  MP 238, 246
Christian Scientists 423–4
Christmas Day 9
  quarter day 9
Christmas Island 809
Church of Christ, Scientist 423–4
Church Commissioners 294
Church of England 396–408
  General Synod 396
Church Estate Commissioners 294
Church of Ireland 407–8
  General Synod 407
Church of Jesus Christ of the Latter-Day
  Saints 424
Church of Scotland 414
  presbyteries 414
Church in Wales 407
  Governing Body 407
Churches 396–429
  African and Afro-Caribbean, UK 423
  Anglican 396–414
  Lutheran 425
  Methodist 425
  Orthodox 425–6
  Pentecostal 427
  Presbyterian 414, 427
  Roman Catholic 414–23
  World Council of 772
Churches for Britain and Ireland, Council
  of 726
Churches Together in England 726
Churches Together in Scotland, Action
  of 726
Churches Together in Wales 728
Chuuk 956
Cinema (1994–5) 1148–51
Cinque Ports 676
Circuit judges:
  Midland and Oxford 366
  North-Eastern 366
  Northern 366
  South-Eastern 366–7
  Wales and Chester 367
  Western 367
Circular measurement 520
Cirencester and Tewkesbury, MP 246
CIS 753–4
Ciskei 1017
Cities, largest 789
Citizens Charter Unit 291
Citizenship, legal notes 653–4
City and Guilds of London Institute 442,
  452
City of London 555–60
  Education Authority 449
  Police 382–3
City of London and Westminster South,
  MP 246
City University 454
Civic dignitaries 527
Civic Trust 726
Civil Aviation Authority 294
Civil Aviation Organization,
  International 757–8
Civil List 130, 296
Civil Service 281–360
  College 292
  Commission 292
  grading structure 281
  Minister for 279, 291
  pay review body 341
  salaries 281
Civil Service Commissioners, Office
  of 292
Civil twilight 17, 21, 25, etc., 72
Civil year 86–7

Clackmannan 535, 569, 570
  MP 267
Claims:
  social security 492–3
  war pensions 495
Clan chiefs 212–13
Clay pigeon shooting 1236–7
Clearing houses, recognized 614
Cleethorpes 532, 550
Cleethorpes, Brigg and, MP 244
Clergy, Anglican diocesan 396–7
Cleveland 531, 546, 547
  Archdeacon 404
  Education Authority 448
  Police Authority 381
Cleveland, Middlesborough and
  Redcar 546
Cleveland and Richmond, MEP 274
Clifton, Bishop (RC) 416
Clogher:
  Bishop (Anglican) 408
  Bishop (RC) 417
Clonfert, Bishop (RC) 417
Clonmacnois, Ardagh and, Bishop
  (RC) 417
Close seasons (game) 585
Cloyne, Bishop (RC) 417
Cloyne, Cork, and Ross, Bishop 408
Clubs:
  London 717–18
  provincial 718–19
  yacht 719–20
Clwyd 535, 562, 563
  Education Authority 450
  MPs 265
Clydebank 535, 569
Clydebank and Milngavie, MP 267
Clydesdale 535, 569
  MP 267
Co-ordinated universal time 73
Coal 498
  supply and consumption 498
Coal Authority 295, 498
Coal Corporation, British 289, 498
Coal and Steel Community,
  European 774
Coastguard Agency 354
Coastguard service 525
Cocos Islands 809
Coinage, British 611
Colchester 532, 550
  Archdeacon 398
  Bishop (Suffragan) 398
  MPs 246
Coleraine 573
College of Arms 285
College of Cardinals 415
College of Justice, Senators 371
Colleges:
  City Technology 433, 435
  higher education 461–2
  theological 469–70
Colne Valley, MP 246
Colombia 785, 853–5
  Archbishops (RC) 418
Colombo 786, 1022
Colorado 1051
Columbia, District of 1051
Colwyn 535, 563, 564
Commissary Office, HM 372
Commission for Local Administration:
  England 323
  Wales 323
Commission for the New Towns 524
Commission for Racial Equality 339
Commission for the Rights of Trades
  Union Members 702
Commissioner for Local Administration in
  Scotland 323
Commissioners, European Union 778–9

Commissioners, Social Security and Child
  Support 378
Commissioners of Northern
  Lighthouses 323
Common Agricultural Policy, EU 775–6
Common Entrance Examination 437
Commons Commissioners 376
Commonwealth 751–3
  member states 752
  migration to UK statistics 119
  Secretariat 753
Commonwealth Day 9
Commonwealth Development
  Corporation 295
Commonwealth of Independent
  States 753–4
Commonwealth Institute 328, 595
  Scotland 597
Commonwealth Parliamentary
  Association 271
Commonwealth War Graves
  Commission 295
Communicable Diseases Surveillance
  Centre 338
Communications Headquarters,
  Government (GCHQ) 304
Community charge 526
  Scotland 530
Community child health service,
  NHS 485
Community councils:
  Scotland 530
  Wales 529
Comoros 783, 855
Companies Court 363, 364
  Registrar 363–4
Companies House 352
Companions of Honour 176
Compass variation (magnetism) 77
Compensation Commission, Foreign 305
Conakry 784, 894
Confederation of British Industry 700
Conference on Disarmament 767
Conference on Security and Co-operation
  in Europe 763
Congleton 532, 550
  MP 246
Congleton, Staffordshire West and,
  MEP 276
Congo 783, 855–6
  Archbishop (RC) 418
  map 800
Congregational Federation 424
Connecticut 1051
Connor, Bishop 408
Connor, Down and, Bishop (RC) 417
Conservation:
  buildings 586
  environmental 578–82
  wildlife 583–5
Conservation and Heritage (1994–5)
  built environment 1140–2
  natural environment 1137–40
Conservative and Unionist Party 229
  development 229
  local representation 531–6
  MEPs 272–3
  MPs 231–7
  Whips 280
Constabulary:
  Chief Constables 381
  county 381
  HM Inspectorate of 313, 345, 380
Constants:
  astronomical 75
  tidal 96–7
Constellations 16, 20, 24, etc., 71
Constituencies:
  by-elections 238–9
  England 241–64
  European in UK 273–8

Constituencies *continued*
  Northern Ireland 270–1
  Scotland 266–70
  Wales 265–6
Constitution of UK 221–2
Consulates-General 796–1020
Consumer Council, National 330
Consumer expenditure statistics 609
Consumer law 654–6
Continents 110–11
Contributions Agency 348
Contributory benefits 489–90
Conversion table, weights and
  measures 523
Conwy, MP 265
Cook Islands 787, 969, 972
Cookstown 573
Copeland 532, 550
  MP 246
Copenhagen 786, 864
Copyright 677
  legal deposit 677
  organizations 678
Copyright Tribunal 376
Coral Sea Islands 809
Corby 524, 532, 550
  MP 246–7
Corfu 890
Cork, Cloyne and Ross, Bishop 408
Cork and Ross, Bishop (RC) 417
Cornwall 531, 546, 547
  Archdeacon 403
  Duchy of 298
  Education Authority 448
  MPs 247
  North 533, 551
Cornwall, Devon and, Police
  Authority 381
Cornwall and Plymouth West, MEP 274
Coroners' courts 362
Corporation of London 529, 555–7
  Aldermen 555, 556
  Common Council 556–7
  Lord Mayor 555
  Records Office 340–1
  Sheriffs 555
Corporation tax 649–51
Corporation of Trinity House 322–3
Corpus Christi 9, 83
Corsica 878
Cost of living 610
Costa Rica 784, 856–7
  Archbishop (RC) 418
  map 973
Côte d'Ivoire 783, 857–8
  Archbishop (RC) 418
  map 975
Cotswolds 532, 550
  MEP 274
Council for the Central Laboratory of the
  Research Councils 708
Council of Europe 754–5
Council of the European Union 778
Council tax 526–7
  England 526, 528–9, 548–54, 560
  Scotland 526, 530, 568–9
  valuation bands 526–7
  Wales 526, 530, 563
Council on Tribunals 357
Counsellors of State 221
Countesses in own right 149
  form of address 149, 217
Counties:
  England 545
  Northern Ireland 572
  Wales 562
Countries of the world 783–7, 796–1020
Countryside Commission 295
Countryside Council for Wales 295–6
County councils:
  England 526, 527–8, 546, 547

County councils *continued*
  political composition 531, 535
  Wales 562–3
Court of Arches 375
Court of Faculties 375
Court of Justice, European 780
Court of Lord Lyon 285
Court of Session 371
Courtauld Institute galleries 595
Courts:
  ecclesiastical 375
  England and Wales 361–70
  Northern Ireland 374
  Scotland 371–4
Courts administration:
  England and Wales 361–2
  Scotland 371
Courts of Vicars-General 375
Covent Garden Market Authority 296
Coventry 531, 540, 548
  airport 502
  Archdeacon 399
  Bishop 167, 399
  Education Authority 448
  MPs 247
  University 454
Coventry and Warwickshire North,
  MEP 274
CPVE 439
Craigavon 573
Cranfield University 460
Cranwell, Royal Air Force College 464
Craven 532, 550
  Archdeacon 404
Crawley 524, 532, 550
  MP 247
Crawley, Sussex South and, MEP 276
Crayford, Erith and, MP 249
Crediton, Bishop (Suffragan) 399
Cremation, legal notes 657
Crete 890
Crewe and Nantwich 532, 550
  MP 247
Cricket 1223–5
  county championship 1225
  Test series 1223
Crime, events (1994–5) 1088–92
Criminal Injuries Compensation
  Board 296
Criminal Intelligence Service,
  National 380
Croatia 786, 858–9
  Archbishops (RC) 418
  map 1065
Crofters Commission 296
Cromarty, Ross and 536, 569
Cromarty, Ross, and Skye, MP 269
Crosby, MP 247
Cross-country running (athletics) 1217,
  1218
Crown, proceedings against 656
Crown Agent, Scotland 371
Crown Agents 296
Crown Courts 365
Crown Estate Commissioners 296
Crown Estate Receiver for Scotland 296
Crown of India, Imperial Order of 175
Crown Office 324
  Scotland 371, 373
Crown Prosecution Service 370
Crown Solicitor, Northern Ireland 374
Croydon 534, 560
  Archdeacon 403
  Bishop (Area) 403
  Education Authority 449
  MPs 247
CSCE 763
Cuba 111, 784, 859–61
  Archbishops (RC) 419
  Bishop (Anglican) 414
  map 897

Cumbernauld 524
Cumbernauld and Kilsyth 535, 569
  MP 267
Cumbria 531, 546, 547
  Education Authority 448
  Police Authority 381
Cumbria and Lancashire North, MEP 274
Cumnock, Carrick, and Doon Valley,
  MP 267
Cumnock and Doon Valley 535, 569
Cunninghame 535, 569
  MPs 267
Curia (RC) 415
Currencies:
  British 611–12
  exchange rates 790–3
  world 790–3
Curriculum 438–9
  councils 451
Custody of children, legal notes 665, 667
Customs and Excise 297
  Board 297
Cyclades Islands 890
Cycling 1225
Cynon, Rhondda, Taff and 564
Cynon Valley 535, 563
  MP 265
Cyprus 786, 861–2
  Archbishop (RC) 419
  British sovereign areas 862
Czech Republic 786, 862–4
  Archbishops (RC) 419

Dacorum 532, 550
Dagenham, MP 238, 247
Dagenham, Barking and 534, 560
  Education Authority 449
Dakar 784, 1008
Dakota, North 1051
Dakota, South 1051
Damascus 786, 1030
Dames 209–10
  form of address 209, 217
Dams, tallest 115
Dance:
  (1994–5) 1143–7
  productions 1145–7
  training bodies 464
Dar-es-Salaam 1034
Darlington 532, 550
  MP 247
Dartford 532, 550
  MP 247
Dartmouth, Royal Naval College 464
Darwen, Rossendale and, MP 258
Darwin 808
Data Protection:
  Registrar 297
  Tribunal 376
Datapost 511
Daventry 532, 550
  MP 247
Davyhulme, MP 247
Day:
  apparent solar 73
  defined 81
  mean solar 73
  sidereal 69, 74
Day of Atonement 9
Days:
  names of 81
  Saints 9, 87
De Montfort University 454
Deane, Basingstoke and 532, 549
Deans, Anglican diocesan 396–408
Deaths:
  registration 336–7, 656–7
  registration, Scotland 347
  statistics 119–20, 121
Decathlon 1220

Declination 69, 72
  magnetic 77
Decorations and medals 214–16
Deer, close seasons 585
Deeside, Alyn and 535, 563
  MP 265
Deeside, Kincardine and 536, 569
  MP 269
Defence 384–95
  Air Staff 385
  Defence Council 384–5
  Defence Staff 385
  General Staff 385
  Ministers 279, 384
  Ministry of 384–7
  Naval Staff 385
  Police 383
  Procurement Executive 386–7
  restructuring 384
  Scientific Staff 385
  Secretary of State 279, 384
  strengths 384
Defence Export Services
  Organization 387
Defence Procurement, Minister of
  State 279, 384
Defence Research Agency 385
Delaware 1051
Delhi 785, 901
Delyn 535, 563
  MP 265
Democratic Unionists, financial
  support 229
Denbighshire 564
Denmark 786, 864–5
  map 864
Dental service, NHS 484
Dentistry, qualifying body 464–5
Dentists' pay review body 341
Denton and Reddish, MP 247
Dependent Territories, British 1071–80
Deposit-taking institutions 615, 616–20
Depressions, deepest 112
Deptford (Lewisham), MP 254
Derby 532, 540, 550
  Archdeacon 399
  Bishop 168, 399
  MPs 247
  University 454
Derby, Staffordshire East and, MEP 276
Derby, The 13, 1230
Derbyshire 531, 546, 547
  Education Authority 448
  MPs 247–8
  North East 533, 551
  Police Authority 381
  South 533, 552
Derbyshire Dales 532, 550
Derry 573
  Bishop (RC) 417
Derry and Raphoe, Bishop 408
Derwentside 532, 550
Deserts, largest 112
Design, registry 678
Design Council 297–8
Designated investment exchanges 614
Development Board for Rural Wales 524
Development corporations 524–5
Devizes, MP 248
Devon 531, 546, 547
  East 532, 550
  Education Authority 448
  MEPs 274, 276
  Mid 533, 551
  MPs 248
  North 533, 551
  West 534, 553
Devon and Cornwall Police
  Authority 381
Devonport (Plymouth), MP 257

Dewsbury, MP 248
Dhaka 785, 818
Diego Garcia 1072
Dietetics, professional body 465
Dinefwr 535, 563
Dioceses, Church of England 396–408
Dip-poles, magnetic 77
Diploma of Vocational Education 439–40
Diplomatic Corps:
  Marshal 126
  Vice-Marshal 304
Director of Public Prosecutions 361, 370
  Northern Ireland 374
Directorate-General of Defence
  Accounts 385
Disability living allowance 491
Disablement:
  allowances 491, 493–4
  war pensions 495
Disasters (1994–5) 1085–6
Distance of horizon 521
Distinguished Service Order 176
District councils:
  England 526, 528, 548–54
  Northern Ireland 530, 572–3
  political composition 531–6
  Scotland 530, 569
  Wales 529, 563
District Health Authorities 483
Divorce:
  legal notes 664–7
  statistics 120
Djibouti 783, 865–6
  map 1015
  town 783, 865
Doctors' pay review body 341
Dodoma 784, 1034
Dog days 81
Doggett's Coat and Badge 1235
Doha 786, 992
Domestic violence, legal notes 666, 667
Dominica 784, 866–7
  map 897
Dominical letter 9, 82
  (1500–2033) 84
Dominican Republic 784, 867–8
  Archbishops (RC) 419
  map 897
Don Valley, MP 248
Doncaster 531, 548
  Archdeacon 406
  Bishop (Suffragan) 406
  Education Authority 448
  MPs 248
Doon Valley, Carrick, Cumnock and,
  MP 267
Doon Valley, Cumnock and 535, 569
Dorchester, Bishop (Area) 401
Dorking:
  Archdeacon 400
  Bishop (Suffragan) 400
Dorset 531, 546, 547
  Archdeacon 403
  East 532, 550
  Education Authority 448
  MEPs 274
  MPs 248
  North 533, 551
  Police Authority 381
  West 534, 553
Douglas, (Isle of Man) 574
Dover 532, 550
  Bishop (Suffragan) 397
  MP 248
Down 573
  MPs 238, 270
Down and Connor, Bishop (RC) 417
Down and Dromore, Bishop 408
Downing Street 599
Drake (Plymouth), MP 257

Drama, training courses 465
Driver and Vehicle Licensing Executive
  Agency 354
Driving:
  licences 506
  tests 506
Driving Standards Executive Agency 354
Dromore, Bishop (RC) 417
Dromore, Down and, Bishop 408
Dubai 1049
Dublin 786, 911
  Archbishop (Anglican) 408
  Archbishop (RC) 416
Duchess of Gloucester 124, 129
  military titles 132
Duchess of Kent 124, 129
  military titles 133
  University Chancellorship 456
Duchess of York 123, 128
Duchy of Cornwall 298
Duchy of Lancaster 298
  Chancellor 279, 298
Dudley 531, 548
  Archdeacon 403
  Bishop (Suffragan) 403
  Education Authority 448
  MPs 238, 248
Duke of Cornwall, see Prince of Wales
Duke of Edinburgh, see Prince Philip
Duke of Gloucester 124
  Civil List 130
  family 124
  household 129
  military titles 132
  Order of St John 211
Duke of Kent 124
  Civil List 130
  family 124
  household 129
  military titles 133
  Orders of Chivalry 174, 175
  University Chancellorship 460
Duke of York 123
  Civil List 130
  family 123
  household 128
  military titles 132
Dukes 142–3
  form of address 142, 217
  premier 142
  Royal 142
Dulwich, MP 248
Dumbarton 535, 569
  MP 267
Dumbartonshire, East 570
Dumfries, MP 267
Dumfries and Galloway 535, 567, 570
  Education Authority 450
  Police Authority 382
Dunblane, St Andrews, Dunkeld and,
  Bishop 407
Dundee 535, 567, 569, 570
  MPs 267
  University 454
Dunfermline 535, 569
  MPs 267
Dungannon 573
Dunkeld, Bishop (RC) 416
Dunkeld, St Andrews, Dunblane and,
  Bishop 407
Dunwich, Bishop (Suffragan) 402
Durham (city) 532, 540, 550
  MP 248
  University 454
Durham (county) 531, 546, 547
  Education Authority 448
  MEP 274
  MPs 248
  Police Authority 381

Durham (diocese):
    Archdeacon 404
    Bishop 167, 404
Dushanbe 786, 1032
Dwyfor 535, 563
Dyfed 535, 562, 563
    Education Authority 450
Dyfed-Powys Police Authority 382

Ealing 534, 560
    Education Authority 449
    MPs 248
Earl Marshal 142, 285
Earldom, premier 149
Earls 144–9
    courtesy titles 169
    form of address 144, 217
    mier 142, 145, 148
Earth 76
    area 110
    dimensions 76, 110
    satellite 76
    velocity 110
Easington 532, 550
    MP 248
East Anglia:
    Bishop (RC) 416
    University 454
East Ayrshire 570
East Cambridgeshire 532, 550
East Devon 532, 550
East Dorset 532, 550
East Dunbartonshire 570
East Hampshire 532, 550
East Hertfordshire 532, 550
East Kilbride 524, 535, 569
    MP 267
East Lindsey 532, 550
East London University 454
East Lothian 535, 569, 570
    MP 267
East Midlands airport 502
East Northamptonshire 532, 550
East Renfrewshire 570
East Riding, Archdeacon 404
East Staffordshire 532, 550
East Sussex 531, 546, 547
    Education Authority 448
East Yorkshire 532, 550
Eastbourne 532, 550
    MP 248
Easter 9, 82–3
    (1996-2028) 83
    dominical letters (1500-2033) 84
    fixed 82–3
    Greek Orthodox 9
    law term 9
Easter Island 847–8
Eastern Europe, events (1994–5) 1105–6
Eastleigh 532, 550
    MP 238, 249
Eastwood 535, 569
    MP 267
Ebbsfleet, Bishop (Suffragan) 397
Eccles, MP 249
Ecclesiastical courts 375
Ecclesiastical Patronage, Secretary for 324
ECGD 303
Eclipses (1996) 17, 66
Economic Community of West African
    States 755
Economic and Social Research
    Council 708
    research units 708–9
Economic statistics, UK 606–10
Economics, Nobel prize 1156
Ecuador 785, 868–9
    Archbishops (RC) 419
Eddisbury, MP 249

Eden 532, 550
Edgbaston (Birmingham), MP 243
Edinburgh 535, 567, 569, 570, 787
    airport 502
    Bishop 407
    MPs 267–8
    Royal Botanical Garden 341–2
    Royal Observatory 711
    universities 454, 457
Edinburgh (Tristan da Cunha) 784, 1079
Edinburgh, St Andrews and, Archbishop
    (RC) 416
Edmonton:
    Bishop (Area) 397
    MP 249
Edmonton (Canada) 842
Education:
    administration 433–4
    adult 446–7, 462–3
    advisory bodies 450–1
    alternative provision 437
    authorities 448–50
    continuing 446–7, 462–3
    expenditure 433
    further 441–3
    higher 443–6
    HM Inspectorate, Scotland 344
    nursery 436
    Office of HM Chief Inspector 299
    Office of HM Chief Inspector in
        Wales 359
    Office for Standards in 299–300
    primary 436
    professional 463–71
    secondary 436
    special 437
    vocational 439, 441–3
Education and Employment, Department
    for 298–300
    Ministers 279, 298
    Secretary of State 279, 298
Education Department, Scottish 344
Education, Training, Enterprise and,
    Directorate 299
Education Training and Targets, National
    Advisory Council for 450
Edward VII 135, 138
    descendants 135
Edward VIII 134, 138
EEA 756, 775
EFTA 756
Egypt 783, 869–71
Eire, see Ireland, Republic of
Eisteddfod 12, 562
Elba 916
Elections:
    European Parliament 272–8
    local government 526, 528, 531–6
    Parliamentary 222, 223, 241–71
Elections Petitions Office 364
Electorate, size of 240
Electricity:
    measurement 520
    Regulation, Office of 300
    supply companies 500
    supply and consumption 500
Elim Pentecostal Church 427
Elizabeth II 123, 139
    see also Queen, HM The,
Ellesmere Port and Neston 532, 550
    MP 249
Elmbridge 532, 550
Elmet, MP 249
Elphin, Bishop (RC) 417
Elphin, Kilmore, and Ardagh, Bishop 408
Eltham, MP 249
Ely:
    Archdeacon 399
    Bishop 168, 399
Embassies:
    British 796–1020

Embassies continued
    in London 796–1020
Ember Days 83
Emergency Planning College 312
Employers' Associations 700–1
Employment:
    Appeal Tribunal 376
    legal notes 661–2
Employment, Education and, Department
    for 298–300
    Ministers 279, 298
    Secretary of State 279, 298
Employment Service 299
EMS 776
Energy Agency, International 758
Energy Efficiency Unit 301
Enfield 534, 560
    Education Authority 449
    MPs 249
Engineering:
    professional bodies 465
    Royal Academy of 705
Engineering and Physical Sciences
    Research Council 709
England:
    Church of 396–408
    counties 546, 547
    early history 538
    educational system 433–42
    flag 537
    geographical features 537
    High Sheriffs 545
    judicature 361–70
    kings and queens 136–8
    local government 526–36
    Local Government Commission 526
    Lord Lieutenants 545
    MEPs 273–8
    MPs 241–64
    museums and galleries 593–7
    Police Authorities 381
    population statistics 118–21, 537
    precedence 576
    unitary authorities 546
English Heritage 310
English National Ballet 1146
English National Opera 1159–60
English Nature 300
English Partnerships 300
English Touring Opera 1161
English Tourist Board 350
Enterprise, Education, Training and,
    Directorate 299
Entitlement Appeal Tribunals 378
Environment, events (1994–5) 1092–3
Environment, Department of 300–2
    Ministers 279, 300
    Secretary of State 279, 300
Environment Department, Scottish 344–5
Environmental Achievement, Queen's
    Awards for 1180
Environmental Pollution, Royal
    Commission on 302
Environmental Technology Centre,
    National 288
Epact 9, 88
Ephemeris time 74
Epiphany 9, 82
Episcopal Church in Scotland 407
    General Synod 407
Epping Forest 532, 550, 601
    MP 249
Epsom and Ewell 532, 550
    MP 249
Equal Opportunities Commission 302
    Northern Ireland 302
Equation of time 17, 21, 25, etc., 71, 73
Equator:
    celestial 69
    circumference 110
    diameter 110

Equator *continued*
  magnetic 77
Equatorial Guinea 783, 871
  Archbishop (RC) 419
  map 975
Equerries to the Queen 125
Equestrianism 1226
Equinoctial year 81
Equinoxes 15, 81
Erdington (Birmingham), MP 243
Erevan 786, 804
Erewash 532, 550
  MP 249
Erith and Crayford, MP 249
Eritrea 783, 871–2
  map 1015
ERM 776
ERNIE 626
Esher, MP 249
Eskdale, Annandale and 535, 569
Essex 531, 546, 547
  Education Authority 448
  MEPs 274
  Police Authority 381
  University 455
Estonia 786, 872–4
Ethiopia 783, 874–5
  Archbishop (RC) 419
  map 1015
Eton Fives 1226
Ettrick and Lauderdale 535, 569
Ettrick, Tweeddale, and Lauderdale,
  MP 270
Euratom 774
Europe:
  area 111
  Bishop Suffragan 400
  continent 111
  Council of 754–5
  countries of 786–7
  events (1994–5) 1103–11
  Gibralter in (Anglican diocese) 400
  migration to UK 119
  North-West, Archdeacon 400
European Bank of Reconstruction and
  Development 755–6
European Communities, Court of Justice
  of the 780
European Community *see* European
  Union
European Court of Human Rights 755
European Court of Justice 780
European Drugs Agency 781
European Economic Area 775, 777
European Environment Agency 782
European Investment Bank 781
European Monetary Institute 781
European monetary system 776
European Organization for Nuclear
  Research 756
European Parliament 779–80
  information office 782
  political groupings 779
  UK constituencies 273–8
  UK MEPs 272–3
European political co-operation 776
European Space Agency 756–7
European Union 774–82
  Atomic Energy Community 774
  budget 775
  Coal and Steel Community 774
  Commission 778–9
  Commissioners 778–9
  Common Agricultural Policy 775–6
  Council of Ministers 778
  Court of Auditors 780
  development 774–5
  Economic and Social Committee 780
  European political co-operation 776
  events (1994–5) 1110–11

European Union *continued*
  information offices 782
  legislation 778
  members 774
  new institutions 781
  parliament 779–80
  Presidency 778–9
  Single Market 776–7
Europol 781
Eurotunnel 504
Events, forthcoming (1996) 12–13
Events of the year (1994–5) 1081–114
  British 1081–98
  overseas 1098–114
Everest 112
Ewell, Epsom and 532, 550
  MP 249
Examinations:
  A-level 439
  A-level boards 451
  AS-level 439
  further education 442
  GCSE 439
  GCSE boards 451
  higher education 444–5
  S-level 439
  Scotland 440, 442
  secondary 439–40
Exchange rate mechanism 776
Exchange rates 790–3
Excise, Board of Customs and 297
Executive Agencies:
  Cabinet Office 292
  Department of the Environment 302
  Department of Health 309
  Department of Social Security 348–9
  Department of Trade and
    Industry 352–3
  Department of Transport 354–5
  Home Office 313, 316
  Ministry of Agriculture 284–5
  Ministry of Defence 387
  Overseas Development
    Administration 334
  Scottish Office 344–5
  Welsh Office 359–60
Exeter 532, 540–1, 550
  airport 502
  Archdeacon 409
  Bishop 167, 399
  MP 249
  University 455
Exhibition of 1851, Royal Commission
  for 342
Expectation of life table 120
Export Achievement, Queen's
  Awards 1178–9
Export Credits Guarantee
  Department 303
Export Guarantees Advisory Council 303
Exports:
  balance of payments 608
  UK statistics 608

Factories, HM Inspectorate 310
Faculties, Court of 375
Faculty of Advocates 466
Fagatogo 1056
Fair Trading, Office of 303
  Director-General 303
Falkirk 535, 569, 570
  MPs 268
Falkland Islands 785, 1074
Falmouth and Camborne, MP 249
Family credit (benefit) 492
Family Division, High Court 361, 363
  President 363
  Principal Registry 364–5
Family doctor service, NHS 483

Family law 662–70
Fareham 532, 550
  MP 249
Faröe Islands 786, 864, 865
Father of the House 226
Faversham, MP 249
Feast of Tabernacles 9
Feast of Weeks 9
Fellowship of Engineering, *see* Royal
  Academy of
Feltham and Heston, MP 249
Fencing 1226
Fenland 532, 550
Fermanagh 573
Fermanagh and South Tyrone, MP 270
Ferns, Bishop (RC) 417
Festivals:
  Christian 9, 82–3
  Hindu 9, 84–5
  Jewish 9, 85
  Muslim 9, 86
  Sikh 9, 86
Field events (athletics) 1217–21
  records 1239–41
Field Marshals 389
Fife 535, 567, 570
  Education Authority 450
  MPs 268
  North East 536, 569
  Police Authority 382
Fife, Scotland Mid and, MEP 277
Fiji 787, 875–6
Film:
  (1994–5) 1148–51
  awards 1151
Film Commission, British 289
Film Institute, British 290
FIMBRA 613
Finance:
  banking 615–20
  Budget (1994) 1163–5
  local government 526–7
  taxation 639–52
  UK statistics 606–9
Finance Corporation, International 771
Finchley, MP 249
Finland 786, 876–8
  map 877
Finsbury, Islington South and, MP 253
Fire Service College 316
Fire Service Inspectorate 312
First point of Aries 17, 21, 25, etc., 69, 73
  transit 71
First point of Libra 69
Fisheries Department, Ministry of
  Agriculture 283–4
Fisheries Protection Agency, Scottish 344
Fives:
  Eton 1226
  Rugby 1235
Flags:
  countries of world 796–1080
  days for flying 122
  England 537
  Guernsey 575
  Isle of Man 574
  Jersey 575
  Northern Ireland 571–2
  Scotland 565
  United Kingdom 122
  Wales 561
Fleet:
  merchant 508
  Royal Navy 388–9
Fleet Air Arm 389
Flegrean Islands 919
Flintshire 564
Florida 1051
Folkestone and Hythe, MP 249
Food and Agriculture Organization,
  UN 757

Food Safety Directorate 283
Food science, professional bodies 465
Football:
  American 1216
  Association 1216–17
  Rugby 1235–6
Forecast areas, shipping 1203
Forecast services, weather 515
Foreign and Commonwealth Affairs:
  Ministers 279, 303–4
  Secretary of State 279, 303
Foreign and Commonwealth
    Office 303–5
  Ministers 279, 303–4
  Secretary of State 279, 303
Foreign Compensation Commission 305
Foreign events (1994–5) 1098–114
Forest of Dean 532, 550
Forest Heath 532, 550
Forest Nature Reserves 582
Forestry Commission 305
Forestry, professional organizations 465
Formentera 1021
Fort de France 785, 881
Forthcoming events (1996) 12–13
Foyle, MP 270
France 786, 878–82
  Archbishops (RC) 419
  map 878
  overseas departments, etc. 881–2
France, Archdeacon 399
Franchise qualifications 675–6
Fredericton 843
Free Church of England 424
Free Church of Scotland 424
Free Presbyterian Church of Scotland 424
Freetown 784, 1009
French Guiana 785, 881
French Polynesia 787, 881
  Archbishop (RC) 419
Friendly Societies 621
  Chief Registrar 305
  Registry of 305–6
Friends, Religious Society of 427
Frome, Somerton and, MP 259
Front Line First, defence costs study 384
Fuel and energy, professional
    bodies 465–6
Fuel supply and consumption
    statistics 498–500
Fujeirah 1049
Fulham:
  Bishop (Suffragan) 397
  MP 249
Fulham, Hammersmith and 534, 560
  Education Authority 449
Funafuti 787, 1043
Funding Agency for Schools 452
Funding councils 452
  further education 452
  higher education 452
  schools 452
Funen Island 864
Furness, Barrow and, MP 242
Furness, Westmorland and,
    Archdeacon 405
Further education 441–3
  funding councils 452
  regional advisory councils 451
Futuna, Wallis and, Islands 787, 882
Fylde 532, 550
  MP 249

Gabon 783, 882
  Archbishop (RC) 419
Gaborone 783, 829
Gainsborough and Horncastle, MP 250
Galapagos Islands 869
Galloway, Bishop (RC) 416

Galloway, Dumfries and 535, 567, 568,
    570
  Education Authority 450
Galloway, Glasgow and, Bishop 407
Galloway and Upper Nithsdale, MP 268
Galway and Kilmacduagh, Bishop
    (RC) 417
Gambia 783, 882–3
  map 975
Gaming Board for Great Britain 306
Garscadden (Glasgow), MP 268
Garston (Liverpool), MP 254
Garter, Order of 174
Gas:
  British Gas 499
  supply and consumption 498
  Supply, Office of 306
Gasworks Museum, Biggar 329
Gateshead 531, 548
  Education Authority 448
Gateshead East, MP 250
GATT 773
Gatwick airport 502
Gaza City 785
Gaza, Palestinian Autonomous Area 915
GCE 439
GCHQ 304
GCSE 439
  examination boards 451
Gedling 532, 550
  MP 250
General Agreement on Tariffs and
    Trade 773
General election (1992):
  constituency results 241–71
  members of parliament 231–7
  party strengths 240
  small majorities 239
  statistics 240
General National Vocational
    Qualifications 440, 443
General Register Office, Scotland 347
General Synod:
  Church of England 396
  Church of Ireland 407
  Episcopal Church of Scotland 407
Gentlemen Ushers:
  Black Rod 126, 174, 223
  Orders of Chivalry 174–6
  Sword of State 126
  The Queen's Household 125–6
Geological eras 94
George V 134, 135, 138
  descendants 134
George VI 134, 138–9
George Cross 216
George Town (Cayman Islands) 784,
    1073
Georgetown (Ascension) 784, 1079
Georgetown (Guyana) 785, 895
Georgia 786, 884–5
  map 884
Georgia (USA) 1051
Germany 786, 885–9
  Archbishops (RC) 419
  map 886
Ghana 784, 889–90
  Archbishops (RC) 419
  map 975
Gibraltar 786, 1074–5
  Archdeacon 400
  Bishop 400
  map 1020
Gillingham 532, 550
  MP 250
Girls' Schools Association 479
  schools 479–82
Glaciated areas, largest 111
Glamorgan:
  Mid 535, 562, 563

Glamorgan continued
  South 535, 562, 563
  University 455
  West 535, 562, 563
Glamorgan, Vale of 535, 563, 564
  MP 266
Glanford 532, 550
Glanford and Scunthorpe, MP 250
Glasgow 535, 567, 569, 570
  airport 502
  Archbishop (RC) 416
  MEP 277
  MPs 268
  Universities 455, 459
Glasgow and Galloway, Bishop 407
Glenrothes 524
Gloucester 532, 550
  Archdeacon 400
  Bishop 168, 400
  MP 250
Gloucestershire 531, 546, 547
  Education Authority 448
  Police Authority 381
  South 546
Gloucestershire West, MP 250
Glyndebourne Festival Opera 1160–1
Glyndŵr 535, 563
GNVQ 440, 443
Godthåb 784, 865
Gold:
  coin 611
  hallmarks 604–5
Gold Stick:
  England 125
  Scotland 127
Golden Number 9, 87
Golf 1226–8
Good Friday 9
Gordon 535, 569
  MP 268
Gorton (Manchester), MP 255
Gosport 532, 550
  MP 250
Gough Island 1079
Govan (Glasgow), MP 268
Government:
  by party 229
  Cabinet 279
  constitution 221, 228
  current ministry 279–80
  finance 606–7
  local 526–36
  Prime Minister 279
  the Sovereign 221
  Whips 280
Government Actuary 306
Government Art Collection 330
Government Centre for Information
    Systems (CCTA) 292
Government Chemist, Laboratory of 352
Government Communications
    Headquarters (GCHQ) 304
Government departments 281–360
Government Hospitality Fund 306
Gower, MP 265
Gozo 949
Grampian 535, 567
  Education Authority 450
  Police Authority 382
Grand National 13, 1229
Grand Turk 785, 1080
Grantham:
  Bishop (Suffragan) 401
  MP 250
Grants, student 445–6, 447
Gravesham 532, 550
  MP 250
Gray's Inn 466, 600
Great Grimsby 532, 550
Great Yarmouth 533, 550
  MP 250

Greater Manchester 531, 548
  MEPs 274
  Police Authority 381
Greece 786, 890–2
  Archbishops (RC) 419
  map 891
Greek Orthodox Church 426
Green Park 600
Green Party 732
Green Rod 174
Greenland 111, 784, 865
Greenock and Port Glasgow, MP 269
Greenwich 534, 560
  Education Authority 449
  MP 250
  Royal Naval College 464, 600
  Royal Observatory 600, 711
  University 455
Greenwich Mean Time 73, 75
Greenwich Sidereal Time 71, 74
Grenada 784, 892–3
  map 897
Grenadines, St Vincent and the 785,
  1002–3
Greyhound racing 1228
Grimsby:
  Bishop (Suffragan) 401
  MP 250
Gross domestic product statistics 607
Guadeloupe 784, 881
  map 897
Guam 787, 1049, 1051, 1055
Guardian allowance 490
Guatemala 785, 893–4
  Archbishop (RC) 419
  map 973
Guatemala City 785, 893
Guernsey 575
  airport 502
  currency 612
  Dean 398
  Education Authority 450
  flag 575
  Police Authority 382
Guiana, French 785, 881
Guildford 533, 550
  Bishop 168, 400
  MP 250
Guilds, City of London 557–9
Guinea 784, 894–5
  Archbishop (RC) 419
  map 975
Guinea-Bissau 784, 895
  map 975
Guyana 785, 895–6
Gwent 535, 562, 563
  Education Authority 450
  Police Authority 382
Gwynedd 535, 562, 563
  Education Authority 450
Gymnastics 1228

Hackney 534, 560
  Archdeacon 397
  Education Authority 449
  MPs 250
Haiti 785, 896–8
  Archbishops (RC) 419
  map 897
Halesowen and Stourbridge, MP 250
Halifax:
  Archdeacon 406
  MP 250
Halifax (Nova Scotia) 844
Hall Green (Birmingham), MP 243
Hallam, Bishop (RC) 416
Hallam (Sheffield), MP 259
Hallmarks 604–5
Halton 533, 550
  MP 250

Hambleton 533, 550
Hamburg 887
Hamilton 535, 569
  MP 269
Hamilton (Bermuda) 784, 1071
Hammersmith, MP 250
Hammersmith and Fulham 534, 560
  Education Authority 449
Hampshire 531, 546, 547
  East 532, 550
  Education Authority 448
  MEPs 274, 277
  MPs 250
  Police Authority 381
Hampstead:
  Archdeacon 397
  Heath 601
Hampstead and Highgate, MP 251
Hampton Court Palace 588
Hanoi 786, 1061
Harare 784, 1069
Harborough 533, 550
  MP 251
Haringey 534, 560
  Education Authority 449
Harlington, Hayes and, MP 251
Harlow 524, 533, 550
  Archdeacon 398
  MP 251
Harrogate 533, 551
  MP 251
Harrow 534, 560
  Education Authority 449
  MPs 251
Hart 533, 551
Hartlepool 533, 546, 551
  MP 251
Harwich, MP 251
Hastings 533, 551
Hastings, Lewes and, Archdeacon 399
Hastings and Rye, MP 251
Hatfield 524
Havana 784, 860
Havant 533, 551
  MP 251
Havering 534, 560
  Education Authority 449
Hawaii 1051
Hayes and Harlington, MP 251
Hazel Grove, MP 251
Headmasters' Conference 437, 472
  schools 472–7
Health:
  Authorities (England) 309
  Boards (Scotland) 345–6
  Commissioners 335
  Department of 307–10
  Ministers 279, 307
  Organization, World 772
  Secretary of State 279, 307
  Service *see* National Health Service
Health and Safety:
  Commission 309–10
  Executive 310
  Inspectorates 310
Health Education Authority
  (England) 309
Health Education Board for Scotland 346
Health Visitors' pay review body 341
Heard Island 809
Heathrow airport 502
Hebrides 566
Heeley (Sheffield), MP 259
Helicopter stations 502
Helsinki 786, 876
Hemel Hempstead 524
Hemsworth, MP 251
Hendon, MPs 251
Henley, MP 251

Heptathlon 1220
Heralds 285
  Scottish 285
Hereford 533, 551
  Archdeacon 400
  Bishop 168, 400
  MP 251
Hereford and Worcester 531, 546, 547
  Education Authority 448
Herefordshire and Shropshire, MEP 274
Herefordshire, South 533, 552
Heriot-Watt University 455
Heritage Memorial Fund, National 331
Herm 575
Hertford, Bishop (Suffragan) 402
Hertford and Stortford, MP 251
Hertfordshire 531, 546, 547
  East 532, 550
  Education Authority 448
  MEPs 274
  MPs 251
  North 533, 551
  Police Authority 381
  University 455
Hertsmere 533, 551
  MP 251
Hesse 887
Heston, Feltham and, MP 249
Hexham, MP 251
Hexham and Newcastle, Bishop (RC) 416
Heywood and Middleton, MP 252
High Commissioner for Refugees,
  UN 767
High Commissioners 796–1020
High Commissions:
  British 796–1020
  in London 796–1020
High Court of Justice 362–3
  Northern Ireland 374
High Court of Justiciary 371–2
High Peak 533, 551
  MP 252
High Sheriffs 527
  England 545
  Northern Ireland 572
  Wales 562
High water (1996) 98–109
Higher education 443–6
  funding councils 443, 452
  institutions 452–62
Highgate, Hampstead and, MP 251
Highland Region (Scotland) 535, 568, 570
  Education Authority 450
Highlands and Islands:
  airports 502
  MEP 277
Highlands and Islands Enterprise 310
Highway authorities 505
Highways Agency 354
Hilary law term 9
Hillhead (Glasgow), MP 268
Hillingdon 534, 560
  Education Authority 449
Hillsborough (Sheffield), MP 259
Hinckley and Bosworth 533, 551
Hindu calendar 84–5
Hindu Temples, National Council of 431
Hinduism 430–1
  organizations in UK 431
Historic buildings 586–92
  listing 586
Historic Buildings and Monuments
  Commission for England 310
Historic Buildings Council for
  Scotland 310
Historic Buildings Council for Wales 310
Historic monuments 586–92
Historic Royal Palaces Agency 330
Historic Scotland 345

Historical Manuscripts, Royal
    Commission on 340
Historical year 86
HMSO 349
Hobart 811
Hockey 1228
Hodge Hill (Birmingham), MP 243
Hokkaido 920
Holborn and St Pancras, MP 252
Holderness 533, 551
Holland, *see* Netherlands
Holland with Boston, MP 252
Holland, South 534, 552
Holy See 414–15, 1059
Home Department, Secretary of
    State 279, 312
Home and Health Department,
    Scottish 345
Home Office 312–16
    Ministers 279, 312
    Secretary of State 279, 312
Home-Grown Cereals Authority 311
Honduras 785, 898–9
    Archbishop (RC) 419
    map 973
Hong Kong 785, 1075–7
    Archbishop (RC) 419
    map 850
Honiara 787, 1014
Honiton, MP 252
Honours Nomination Unit 292
Honshu 920
Horizon, distances of 521
Horncastle, Gainsborough and, MP 250
Hornchurch, MP 252
Hornsey and Wood Green, MP 252
Horserace Totalisator Board 316
Horseracing 1228–31
    classics 13, 1230
Horsham 533, 551
    Archdeacon 399
    Bishop (Suffragan) 399
    MP 252
Hospital trusts 485
Hospitals, NHS 485
Hotelkeeping, qualifying body 466
Houghton and Washington, MP 252
Hounslow 534, 560
    Education Authority 449
House of Commons 223–5
    constituencies 241–71
    election to 223
    Government Whips 280
    Leader of 279
    majorities (since 1970) 240
    MPs 231–7
    officers 224–5
    party strengths (since 1970) 240
    payment of MPs 224
    procedure 223–4, 225–8
    Public Information Office 228
    select committees 227
    state of parties 223
    summary (1994–5) 1162–71
House of Keys 574
House of Lords 222–3
    composition 222
    Court of Appeal 361
    Government Whips 280
    Information Office 228
    Leader of 279
    officers 222–3
    procedure 222, 225–8
    Record Office 340
    state of parties 222
    summary (1994–5) 1162–71
House of Windsor 134
Household expenditure statistics 609
Household income statistics 609
Households, Royal 125–9

Houses open to the public 586–92
Houses of Parliament 222–5, 600
Housing Corporation 316
Hove 533, 551
    MP 252
Huddersfield:
    MP 252
    University 455
Hull:
    MPs 252
    University 455
    see also Kingston upon Hull
Hulme, Bishop (Suffragan) 405
Human Fertilization and Embryology
    Authority 317
Human race, development of 94–5
Human Rights:
    European Convention on 755
    European Court of 755
Humberside 531, 546, 547
    airport 502
    Education Authority 448
    MEPs 274–5
    Police Authority 381
    University 455
Hungary 786, 899–900
    Archbishops (RC) 419
Huntingdon:
    Archdeacon 399
    Bishop (Suffragan) 399
    MP 252
Huntingdonshire 533, 551
Hyde Park 601
Hyde, Stalybridge and, MP 260
Hydrographic Office 386, 387
Hyndburn 533, 551
    MP 252
Hythe, Folkestone and, MP 249

Ibiza 1021
IBRD 771–2
Ice hockey 1231
Ice skating 1231
Iceland 111, 786, 900–1
IDA 771–2
Idaho 1051
IDD codes 516–17
IFC 771–2
ILEA 529
Ilford, MPs 252
Illegitimacy, legal notes 667–8
Illinois 1051
Imams and Mosques Council 431
IMF 759–60
Immigration:
    Appeal Tribunal 376–7
    Appellate Authorities 376–7
    into UK (1993) 119
    Service 313
Imperial Order of the Crown of India 175
Imperial Service Order 176
Imperial War Museum 328, 595
Imports:
    balance of payments 608
    UK statistics 608
IMRO 613
Inaccessible Island 1079
Incapacity benefit 489
Income support (benefit) 491–2
Income tax 639–44
    allowances 641–2
    Special Commissioners 379
Independent Commission for Police
    Complaints for Northern Ireland 317
Independent Methodist Churches 424–5
Independent radio stations:
    local 682–4
    national 681–2
    regional 682

Independent Review Service for the Social
    Fund 317
Independent schools 437–8, 472–82
    advisory bodies 450
Independent Schools, Society of
    Headmasters and Headmistresses
    of 478
Independent Television Commission 317,
    679
Independent television stations 679–80
Independent tribunal service 377
India 785, 901–4
    Archbishops (RC) 419
    map 902
    states 903
Indian Empire, Order of 175
Indian Ocean:
    Anglican Province 409
    Territory, British 1072
Indiana 1051
Indonesia 785, 904–6
    Archbishops (RC) 419
    map 905
Industrial Development Organization,
    UN 770
Industrial injuries:
    Advisory Council 317
    benefits 493–4
Industrial research associations 711–12
Industrial Tribunals 377
Industrial Tribunals and the Fair
    Employment Tribunal (Northern
    Ireland) 377
Industrial and vocational training 466
Industry:
    Confederation of British 700
    Department, Scotland 346–7
    Department of Trade and 350–3
    Queen's Awards 1178–80
Infant mortality (UK) 120
Inflation rates 610
Information, Central Office of 292–3
Information Systems, Government Centre
    for (CCTA) 292
Inheritance, legal notes 657–61
Inheritance tax 646–9
Injuries:
    Criminal, Compensation Board 296
    industrial, benefits 493–4
Inland Revenue, Board of 317–18
    Scotland 318
Inland telephones 513
Inmarsat 514, 759
Inner London Education Authority 529
Inner Temple 466, 600
Inns of Court 466, 600
Insolvency Service 352
Insurance:
    business 629–33
    companies 633–5
    Ombudsman 614
    qualifying bodies 466
Intellectual property 677–8
Intellectual Property Organization,
    World 772
Inter-Parliamentary Union 271
Interception Commissioner 319
Interception of Communications
    Tribunal 319
Interest rates:
    bank base rates 615
    building societies 623
    National Savings certificates 627–8
International Atomic Energy
    Agency 763–4
International atomic time 74
International Baccalaureate 440, 450
International Bank for Reconstruction and
    Development 771–2

International Civil Aviation
 Organization 757–8
International Confederation of Free Trade
 Unions 758
International Court of Justice 769
International Criminal Police
 Organization 758
International date line 75
International Development
 Association 771–2
International direct dialling codes 516–17
International Energy Agency 758
International Finance Corporation 771–2
International Fund for Agricultural
 Development 758
International Labour Organization 758–9
International Maritime Organization 759
International Mobile Satellite
 Organization 759
International Monetary Fund 759–60
International Petroleum Exchange 613
International Red Cross and Red Crescent
 Movement 760
International relations (1994–5) 1112–14
International Stock Exchange of the UK
 and the Republic of Ireland 636
International Telecommunications
 Satellite Organization 760
International Telecommunications
 Union 761
International telephones 514
 dialling codes 516–17
INTERPOL 758
Intervention Board 319
Intestacy, legal notes 657–61
Invalid care allowance 490
Invalidity benefit 490, 491
Inverclyde 535, 569, 570
Inverclyde, Renfrew West and, MP 269
Inverness 535, 569
Inverness, Nairn and Lochaber, MP 269
Investment Bank, European 781
Investment business regulation 613–14
Investment exchanges:
 designated 614
 recognized 613–14
Investment and Loans Office,
 National 331
Investment Ombudsman 614
Ionian Islands 890
Iowa 1051
Ipswich 533, 551
 Archdeacon 402
 MP 252
Ipswich, St Edmundsbury and,
 Bishop 167, 402
Iran 785, 906–8
 Archbishops (RC) 419
 Bishop (Anglican) 410
Iraq 785, 908–10
 Archbishops (RC) 419
 map 1006
Ireland 111
 Church of 407–8
 geography 910
 history 910–11
 map 911
 Roman Catholic Church 416–17
Ireland, Northern, see Northern Ireland
Ireland, Republic of 786, 911–13
 map 911
Irvine 524
Islam 431
 calendar 86
 organizations in UK 431
Islamabad 786, 980
Islamic Conference, Organization of 764
Islamic Cultural Centre 431
Islands:
 largest 111
 Scottish 565–6

Islands Councils (Scotland) 535, 568, 570
Isle of Man, see Man, Isle of
Isle of Wight, see Wight, Isle of
Isles, Argyll and the:
 Bishop (Anglican) 407
 Bishop (RC) 416
Isles of Scilly, see Scilly, Isles of
Isleworth, Brentford and, MP 244
Islington 534, 560
 Education Authority 449
 MPs 252–3
Islwyn 535, 563
 MP 238, 265
Israel 785, 913–16
 Archbishop (RC) 419
 map 913
 Occupied Territories 913
 Palestinian Autonomous Areas 915–16
Italy 786, 916–19
 Archbishops (RC) 419–20
 Archdeacon 400
 map 916
Itchen (Southampton), MP 259
Itchen, Test and Avon, MEP 275
ITV 679–80
Ivory Coast, see Côte d'Ivoire

Jakarta 785, 904
Jamaica 785, 919–20
 Archbishop (RC) 420
 map 897
Jamestown 784, 1078
Jan Mayen Island 787, 978
Japan 785, 920–2
 Archbishops (RC) 420
 Holy Catholic Church 409–10
 map 920
Jarrow:
 Bishop (Suffragan) 404
 MP 253
Java 904
Jersey 575
 airport 502
 currency 612
 Dean 397
 Education Authority 450
 flag 575
 Police Authority 382
Jerusalem 913
Jerusalem and the Middle East, Episcopal
 Church 410
Jethou 575
Jewish calendar 85
Jewish Museum 595
Jews, Board of Deputies of British 432
John Paul II, Pope 415, 1059
Johnston Atoll 1055
Jordan 785, 922–4
 Archbishop (RC) 420
 map 913
Journalism, training 466
Juan Fernandez Islands 847
Judaism 431–2
 calendar 85
 organizations in UK 432
Judge Advocate of the Fleet 365
Judge Advocate-General of the
 Forces 365
Judges:
 Circuit 366–7
 High Court 362–3
 Northern Ireland 374
 pay review body 341
 Scotland 371–2
Judicial Committee of the Privy
 Council 221, 361
Judo 1231–2
Julian Day 15

Julian Period 9, 87
Jupiter 69, 70, 76
 monthly data (1996) 17, 19, 21, 23, etc.
 phenomena (1996) 16, 20, 24, etc.
 satellites (1996) 70, 76
Jury service, legal notes 671
Justice, Court of 780
Justice, International Court of 769
Justices of the Peace 361
Jutland 864

Kabul 785, 796
Kampala 784, 1044
Kansas 1051
Kathmandu 786, 966
Kazakhstan 785, 924–5
 Archbishop (RC) 420
Keele University 455
Keeling Islands 809
Keighley, MP 253
Kemptown (Brighton), MP 244
Kenilworth, Rugby and, MP 258
Kennet 533, 551
Kensington:
 Bishop (Area) 397
 MP 253
Kensington and Chelsea 534, 560
 Education Authority 449
Kent 531, 546, 547
 Education Authority 448
 MEPs 275, 276
 Mid, MP 253
 Police Authority 381
 University 455
Kentucky 1051
Kenya 784, 925–6
 Anglican Province 410
 Archbishops (RC) 420
 map 1015
Kermadec Islands 969
Kerrier 533, 551
Kerry, Bishop (RC) 417
Kesteven:
 North 533, 551
 South 534, 552
Kettering 533, 551
 MP 253
Kew 601
 Palace 588
 Royal Botanic Gardens 342, 601
Khartoum 784, 1023
Kiev 787, 1045
Kigali 784, 1000
Kilbride, East 524, 535, 569
Kildare, Meath and, Bishop 408
Kildare and Leighlin, Bishop (RC) 417
Killala, Bishop (RC) 417
Killala, Achonry and Tuam, Bishop 408
Killaloe, Bishop (RC) 417
Killaloe, Limerick and, Bishop 408
Kilmacduagh, Galway and, Bishop
 (RC) 417
Kilmarnock and Loudoun 535, 569
 MP 269
Kilmore, Bishop (RC) 417
Kilmore, Elphin and Ardagh, Bishop 408
Kilsyth, Cumbernauld and 535, 569
 MP 267
Kincardine and Deeside 536, 569
 MP 269
Kings:
 British 138–9
 of England 136–8
 of Scots 139–40
Kings of Arms 285
 of Orders of Chivalry 174–6
King's Lynn and West Norfolk 533, 551
Kingston (Jamaica) 785, 919
Kingston (Norfolk Island) 787

Kingston University 455
Kingston upon Hull 533, 541, 546, 551
 Bishop (Suffragan) 404
Kingston upon Thames 534, 560
 Bishop (Area) 403
 Education Authority 449
 MP 253
Kingstown 785, 1003
Kingswood 533, 551
 MP 253
Kinross, Perthshire and 570
Kinross, Perth and 536, 569
 MP 269
Kinshasa 784, 1066
Kiribati 787, 926–7
Kirkcaldy 536, 569
 MP 269
Kirklees 531, 548
 Education Authority 448
Kishinev 786, 957
Knaresborough, Bishop (Suffragan) 406
Knighthood, Orders of 174–7
Knights:
 Bachelor 178–208
 Commander 178–208
 forms of address 177, 217
 of Garter 174
 Grand Commander 178–208
 Grand Cross 178–208
 of Thistle 174
 of Windsor, Military 211
Knowsley 531, 548
 Education Authority 449
 MPs 253
Korea 927
 Anglican Province 410
 Archbishops (RC) 420
Korea, Democratic People's Republic
 of 785, 929–31
 map 920
Korea, Republic of 785, 927–9
 map 920
Koror 787, 981
Kosrae 956
Kuala Lumpur 785, 946
Kuwait 785, 930–1
 (city) 785, 930
 map 1006
Kyle and Carrick 536, 569
Kyrgyzstan 785, 931–2
Kyushu 920

La Paz 785, 826
Laayoune 784
Laboratory of the Government
 Chemist 352
Labour, unemployment statistics 607
Labour Organization, International 758–9
Labour Party 229–30
 development 229
 financial support 229
 local government representation 531–6
 MEPs 272–3
 MPs 231–7
 Shadow Cabinet 229–30
 Whips 230
Labrador 843–4
Lady Day (quarter day) 9
Ladywood (Birmingham), MP 243
Lagan Valley, MP 270
Lakeland, South 534, 552
Lakes, largest 113–14
Lambeth 534, 560
 Archdeacon 403
 Education Authority 449
Lammas (term day) 9
Lampeter, St David's College 460
Lanarkshire:
 North 570
 South 570

Lancashire 531, 546, 547
 Central, University of 454
 Education Authority 448
 MEPs 274, 275
 North 546
 Police Authority 381
Lancashire, West 534, 553
 MP 253
Lancaster 533, 551
 Archdeacon 404
 Bishop (RC) 416
 Bishop (Suffragan) 404
 Duchy of 298
 MP 253
 University 455
Land Authority for Wales 319
Land Court, Scottish 372
Land Registers of Scotland 320
Land Registry, HM 319–20
 regional offices 319–20
Lands Tribunal 377
 Scotland 377
Langbaurgh 533, 551
 MP 253
Laos 785, 932–3
 map 836
Larne 573
Las Palmas 1021
Latvia 786, 933–5
 Archbishop (RC) 420
Lauderdale, Ettrick and 535, 569
Lauderdale, Tweeddale, Ettrick and,
 MP 270
Laurence, Captain Timothy 123
LAUTRO 613
Law:
 adoption 662
 births 662–4
 citizenship 653–4
 consumer 654–6
 custody of children 665, 667
 death 656–7
 divorce 664–7
 domestic violence 666, 667
 education and training 466
 employment 661–2
 family 662–70
 franchise 675–6
 intestacy 657–61
 jury service 671
 leases 671–3
 legal aid 673–5
 legitimacy 667–8
 marriage 663–4, 668–70
 proceedings against Crown 656
 separation 664–7
 tenancies 671–3
 town and country planning 675
 voters' qualifications 675–6
 wills 658–61
Law Commission 320
 Scottish 320
Law courts 361–74
 England and Wales 361–70
 Northern Ireland 374
 Scotland 371–4
 tribunals 376–9
Law lords 141, 162, 361
Law Officers 279, 320–1, 329–30
 departments 329–30
Law Societies 466
Law terms 9
Lawn tennis 1232
Lay magistrates 361
Leader of the Opposition 226
League of Arab States 761
Leamington, Warwick and, MP 263
Leap year 81
Leases, legal notes 671–3

Lebanon 785, 935–6
 Archbishops (RC) 420
Leeds 531, 541, 548
 airport 502
 Archdeacon 406
 Bishop (RC) 416
 Education Authority 449
 MEP 275
 MPs 253
 universities 456
Legal advice and assistance scheme 673–4
Legal affairs (1994–5) 1088–92
Legal aid 673–5
Legal Aid Board 321
 Scottish 321
Legal education and training 466
Legal Services Ombudsman 321
Legal tender 611
Legal year 86–7
Legitimacy, legal notes 667–8
Leicester 533, 541, 551
 Archdeacon 401
 Bishop 168, 400
 MEP 275
 MPs 253
 universities 454, 456
Leicestershire 531, 546, 547
 Education Authority 448
 Police Authority 381
Leicestershire North West 533, 552
 MP 254
 Nottingham and, MEP 276
Leigh, MP 254
Leighlin, Kildare and, Bishop (RC) 417
Leith (Edinburgh), MP 268
Length, measurement 518, 519
Lent 82
Leominster 533, 551
 MP 254
Lesotho 784, 936–7
 Archbishop (RC) 420
Lewes 533, 551
 Bishop (Suffragan) 399
 MP 254
Lewes and Hastings, Archdeacon 399
Lewis with Harris 566
Lewisham 534, 560
 Archdeacon 403
 Education Authority 449
 MPs 254
Leyton, MP 254
Liberal Democrats 230
 development 229
 financial support 229
 local government representation 531–6
 MEPs 273
 MPs 231–7
 spokesmen 230
 Whips 230
Liberal Party 229, 735
 development 229
Liberia 784, 937–8
 Archbishop (RC) 420
 map 975
Libra, first point of 69
Librarianship training 467
Libraries, national 321–2
Libreville 783, 882
Libya 784, 938–40
Licences:
 driving 506
 marriage 668, 670
 television 679
 vehicle 506
Licencing corporations, medical 467–8
Lichfield 533, 551
 Archdeacon 401
 Bishop 167, 401
Liechtenstein 786, 940
 map 1028

Life expectancy tables 120
Life insurance:
  business 632–3
  companies 633–5
Life peers 141, 162–7
  form of address 217
Lighthouse authorities 322–3
Lighting-up time 71, 73
Lihou 575
Lilongwe 784, 945
Lima 785, 985
Limavady 573
Limerick, Bishop (RC) 417
Limerick and Killaloe, Bishop 408
Lincoln 533, 541, 551
  Archdeacon 401
  Bishop 167, 401
  MP 254
Lincoln's Inn 466, 601
Lincolnshire 531, 546, 54/
  Education Authority 448
  North East 546
  Police Authority 381
Lincolnshire and Humberside South,
  MEP 275
Lindisfarne, Archdeacon 406
Lindsey, Archdeacon 401
Lindsey, East 532, 550
  MP 254
Lindsey, West 534, 553
Linlithgow, MP 269
Lisbon 786, 990
Lisburn 573
Lismore, Waterford and, Bishop (RC) 417
Literature:
  (1994–5) 1152–5
  awards 1155
  Booker Prize 1155
  Nobel prize 1155, 1156
Lithuania 786, 940–1
  Archbishops (RC) 420
Littleborough and Saddleworth, MP 238,
  254
Liverpool 531, 542, 548
  airport 502
  Archbishop (RC) 416
  Archdeacon 405
  Bishop 167, 405
  Education Authority 449
  MPs 254
  universities 456
Livery companies, London 557–9
Livingston 524
  MP 269
Ljubljana 787, 1013
Llandaff, Bishop 407
Llanelli 535, 563
  MP 265
Lliw Valley 535, 563
Lloyd's of London 600, 630–1
Local administration, commissions for 323
Local authorities:
  England 546–54
  government support for 607
  London 560
  Northern Ireland 572–3
  Scotland 568–9
  Wales 562–3
Local commissioners 323
Local education authorities 433–4,
  434–5, 445–6
  directory 448–50
Local government 526–36
  changes 526, 529, 530
  election results 531–6
  England 527–9
  finance 526–7, 530
  London 529
  Northern Ireland 530
  Ombudsmen 323

Local government continued
  political composition of councils 531–6
  Scotland 530
  Wales 529–30
Local Government Commission for
  England 526
Local history societies 749–50
Local Nature Reserves 582
Local radio stations:
  BBC 680–1
  independent 682–4
Locate in Scotland 347
Lochaber 536, 569
Lochaber, Inverness, Nairn and, MP 269
Lochalsh, Skye and 536, 569
Lomé 784, 1036
London:
  airports 502
  Archdeacon 397
  Bishop 167, 397
  borough councils 529, 534, 560
  capital 787
  cemeteries 599
  City of, MP 246
  civic dignitaries 555
  clubs 717–18
  Corporation of 555–7
  distances by air from 117
  education authorities 449–50
  galleries 595
  High Sheriff 545
  Lord Lieutenant 545
  Lord Mayor 555, 1279
  markets 601
  MEPs 275
  Museum of 328, 595
  museums 595–6
  parks 600–1
  places of interest 599–603
  police forces 380, 382–3
  Port of London Authority 337
  sights of 599–603
  stipendiary magistrates 370
  tourism board 603
  universities 456–7, 459, 460
London Commodity Exchange Ltd 614
London International Financial
  Futures 614
London Metal Exchange 614
London Planetarium 601
London Regional Transport 324
London Residuary Body 529
London Zoo 603
Londonderry 571, 572
Londonderry East, MP 270
Lonsdale, Westmorland and, MP 263
Lord Advocate 279, 324, 371
  Department 324
Lord Chamberlain 125
  Office 125–6
Lord Chancellor 226, 279, 324, 361
Lord Chancellor's Advisory Committee on
  Statute Law 324
Lord Chancellor's Department 324
  Visitors 364
Lord Chief Justice:
  of England 361, 363
  of Northern Ireland 374
Lord Great Chamberlain 143, 325
  Office 325
Lord High Admiral 387
Lord High Chancellor 226, 279, 324, 361
Lord High Commissioner, Church of
  Scotland 414
Lord Howe Island 810
Lord Justice Clerk 371
Lord Justice General 371
Lord Justices of Appeal 362
  Northern Ireland 374
Lord Lieutenants 527
  England 545

Lord Lieutenants continued
  Northern Ireland 572
  Scotland 567–8
  Wales 562
Lord Lyon, Court of 285
Lord Mayor:
  London 555, 1279
  office of 527
Lord Mayor's Day 9, 555
Lord Mayors 548–54, 563, 572–3
Lord President of the Council 279, 338
Lord Privy Seal 279, 325
  Office 325
Lord Steward 125, 151
Lord Warden of the Stannaries 298
Lords of Appeal in Ordinary 162, 361
Lords of Parliament 141, 152–61
Lords of Session 371
Lords-in-Waiting 125, 280
Lothian 535, 568
  Education Authority 450
  West 536, 569, 570
Lothian and Borders Police Authority 382
Lothian, East 535, 569, 570
  MP 267
Lothians, MEP 277
Loudoun, Kilmarnock and 535, 569
  MP 269
Loughborough:
  Archdeacon 401
  MP 254
  University 457
Louisiana 1051
Lower Saxony 887
Luanda 783, 800
Ludlow:
  Archdeacon 400
  Bishop (Suffragan) 400
  MP 254
Lunar cycle 87
Lunar occultations (1996) 66–7
Lundy 537
Lunesdale, Morecambe and, MP 255
Lusaka 784, 1068
Lutheran Church 425
Luton 533, 551
  airport 502
  MPs 254
  University 457
Luxembourg 786, 942–3
  Archbishop (RC) 420
  map 821
Luxembourg (city) 942
Luzon 987
Lydd airport 502
Lynn:
  Archdeacon 401
  Bishop (Suffragan) 401

Maastricht, Treaty of 774, 777, 1111
Macao 785, 992
  map 850
Macclesfield 533, 551
  Archdeacon 405
  MP 254
McDonald Islands 809
Macedonia 786, 943–4
  map 1065
Madagascar 111, 784, 944–5
  Archbishops (RC) 420
Madame Tussaud's Exhibition 601
Madeira 787, 992
Madrid 787, 1019
Magazines 687–93
Magherafelt 573
Magistrates:
  lay 361
  stipendiary 369–70, 373
Magistrates' Courts Service
  Inspectorate 324

Magnetic storms 77–8
Magnetism, terrestrial 77–8
Mahé Island 1008
Maidenhead, Windsor and 534, 553
  MP 263
Maidstone 533, 551
  Archdeacon 397
  Bishop (Suffragan) 397
  MP 255
Mail services 510–12
  airmail zones 516–17
Maine 1051
Maintenance orders, legal notes 665, 666
Majorca 1021
Majuro 787, 950
Makerfield, MP 255
Malabo 783, 871
Malawi 784, 945–6
  Archbishop (RC) 420
Malaysia 785, 946–8
  Archbishops (RC) 420
  Bishop (Anglican) 414
  map 905
Maldives 785, 948
Maldon 533, 551
Maldon, Colchester South and, MP 246
Malé 785, 948
Mali 784, 948–9
  Archbishop (RC) 420
  map 975
Malling, Tonbridge and 534, 553
  MP 261
Malta 786, 949–50
  Archbishop (RC) 420
Malvern Hills 533, 551
Mamoundzou 784, 881
Man, Isle of 574
  Archdeacon 406
  currency 612
  Education Authority 450
  flag 574
  Police Authority 382
  population 119
Management, qualifying bodies 463–4
Managua 785, 972
Manama 785, 817
Manchester 531, 542, 548
  airport 502
  Archdeacon 405
  Bishop 168, 405
  Education Authority 449
  MPs 255
  universities 457
Manchester, Greater 531, 548
  MEPs 274
  Police Authority 381
Manila 786, 987
Man, Sodor and, Bishop 406
Manitoba 838, 843
Mankind:
  development of 94–5
  Museum of 326, 595
Manpower Economics, Office of 325
Mansfield 533, 551
  MP 255
Manston airport 502
Maputo 784, 961
Mariana Islands, Northern 787, 1049,
  1051, 1056
Marine Accidents Investigation
  Branch 354
Marine Nature Reserves 582
Marine Safety Agency 354
Marinecall service 515
Maritime Museum, National 328, 595
Maritime Organization, International 759
Maritime Satellite Organization,
  International 759
Marlborough House 601

Marquesses 143–4
  courtesy titles 169
  form of address 143, 217
  premier 142, 143, 144
Marriage:
  certificates 663–4
  legal notes 663–4, 668–70
  licences 668, 670
  registration 347, 663
  statistics 120
Mars 72, 76
  monthly data (1996) 17, 18, 21, 22, etc.,
    72
  phenomena (1996) 16, 20, 24, etc.
  satellites 76
Marshall Islands 787, 950–1
Marshals of the Royal Air Force 391
Martinique 785, 881
  Archbishop (RC) 420
  map 897
Martinmas (term day) 9
Maryhill (Glasgow), MP 268
Maryland 1051
Maseru 784, 936
Masonic year 88
Mass, measurement 519
Massachusetts 1051
Master of the Horse 125, 160
Master of the Rolls 362
Master of The Queen's Music 125
Masters of The Queen's Music 1161
Mata-Utu 787, 882
Materials studies, qualifying body 467
Maternity benefits 489, 490
Maternity Pay, Statutory 489
Maundy Thursday 28, 82
Mauritania 784, 951–2
  map 975
Mauritius 784, 952–3
Maxwell Pensions Unit 348
Mayor, office of 527
Mayotte 784, 881
Mbabane 784, 1025
MCC Museum 595
Mean refraction 75
Mean sidereal time 74
Mean time 69
Measures, weights and 518–23
Meat Hygiene Service 285
Meath, Bishop (RC) 417
Meath and Kildare, Bishop 408
Mebyon Kernow party 531
Mecklenburg 887
Medals 214–16
  Albert Medal 216
  Distinguished Service Order 176
  Edward Medal 216
  Empire Gallantry Medal 216
  George Cross 216
  Victoria Cross 215
Media, events (1994–5) 1086–8
Medical Appeal Tribunals 377
Medical Research Council 709–10
Medicine:
  Nobel prize 1156
  Royal Colleges 467
  supplementary professions 467–8
Medicines, Committee on Safety of 309
Medicines Control Agency 309
Medway, MP 255
Meirionnydd 535, 563
Meirionnydd Nant Conwy, MP 266
Melanesia, Anglican Province 410
Melbourne 812
Melilla 1021–2
Melton 533, 551
  Rutland and, MP 258
Members of Parliament 231–7
  England 241–64
  European 272–3
  Northern Ireland 270–1

Members of Parliament continued
  pay 224
  Scotland 266–70
  small majorities 239
  Wales 265–6
Mendip 533, 551
Menevia, Bishop (RC) 416
Mental Health Act Commission 325
Mental Health Review Tribunal 378
Mental Welfare Commission for
  Scotland 345
Mercury 72, 76
  monthly data (1996) 17, 18, 21, 22, etc.,
    72
  phenomena (1996) 16, 20, 24, etc.
Mercury Communications 512, 513
Meriden, MP 255
Merionethshire, Caernarfonshire and 564
Merit, Order of 175
Merseyside 531, 548
  MEPs 276
  National Museums and Galleries 329,
    594
  Police Authority 381
Merthyr Tydfil 535, 563, 564
Merthyr Tydfil and Rhymney, MP 266
Merton 534, 560
  Education Authority 449
Mesozoic Era 94
Meteor showers (1996) 45, 61
Meteorological Office 387
Meteorological Organization,
  World 772–3
Methodist Church 425
Methodist Churches, Independent 424–5
Metonic cycle 87
Metrication, UK 519–20
Metropolitan councils 527–9, 531, 548
Metropolitan Police 380, 382
Mexico 784, 953–6
  Archbishops (RC) 420
  Episcopal Church of 410
Mexico City 784, 954
MI5 313
MI6 304
Michaelmas:
  law term 9
  quarter day 9
Michigan 1051
Micronesia, Federated States of 787, 956
Mid Bedfordshire 533, 551
Mid Devon 533, 551
Mid Glamorgan 535, 562, 563
  Education Authority 450
Mid Kent, MP 253
Mid Suffolk 533, 551
Mid Sussex 533, 551
Mid Ulster, MP 271
Middle East, events (1994–5) 1111–12
Middle East, Jerusalem and, Episcopal
  Church 410
Middle Temple 466, 600
Middlesbrough 533, 551
  Bishop (RC) 416
  MP 255
  Redcar and Cleveland 546
Middlesex:
  Archdeacon 397
  University 457
Middleton:
  Bishop (Suffragan) 405
  Heywood and, MP 252
Midlands, West 531, 548
  MEP 276
  Police Authority 381
Midlothian 536, 569, 570
  MP 269
Midsummer (quarter day) 9
Midway Islands 1055
Midwives' pay review body 341
Migration statistics 119

Military colleges 464
Military Knights of Windsor 211
Military Survey 387
Millennium Commission 326
Million defined 520
Milngavie, Bearsden and 535, 569
Milngavie, Clydebank and, MP 270
Milton Keynes 524, 533, 551
    MPs 255
Milton Keynes, Bedfordshire and,
    MEP 273
Mindanao 987
Mines Inspectorate, HM 310
Minima of Algol (1996) 16, 20, 24, etc., 71
Minister for the Civil Service 279, 291
Ministers of State 279
    salaries 281
Minnesota 1051
Minorca 1021
Minsk 786, 820
Mint, The Royal 342
    Master of the Mint 342
Miquelon, St Pierre and 784, 881
Mississippi 1051
Missouri 1051
Mitcham and Morden, MP 255
Mobility component, Disability Living
    Allowance 491
Moderator of the General Assembly,
    Church of Scotland 414
Mogadishu 784, 1015
Moldova 786, 956–7
Mole Valley 533, 551
    MP 255
Molucca Islands 904
Monaco 786, 958
    Archbishop (RC) 421
    map 878
Monaco-ville 786, 958
Monarchy, constitutional role 221
Monetary Fund, International 759–60
Money:
    British currency 611–12
    slang terms 612
    world currencies 790–3
Mongolia 785, 958–9
    map 850
Monklands 536, 569
    MPs 238, 269
Monmouth 535, 563
    Bishop 407
    MP 266
Monmouthshire 564
Monopolies and Mergers
    Commission 326
Monrovia 784, 937
Montana 1051
Montenegro 1066
    map 1065
Montevideo 785, 1056
Montgomery, MP 266
Montgomeryshire 535, 563
Month, defined 81
Montserrat 785, 1077
    map 897
Monument, The London 601
Monuments:
    historic 586–92
    London 601–2
Monuments Boards, Ancient 310
Moon 76
    apogee 16, 20, 24, etc., 71
    apsides 16, 20, 24, etc.
    astronomical constants 75
    conjunctions (1996) 16, 20, 24, etc.
    eclipses (1996) 66
    epact 88
    nodes 16, 20, 24, etc., 71
    occultations (1996) 66–7
    perigee 16, 20, 24, etc., 71

Moon *continued*
    phases 16, 20, 24, etc., 71
    phenomena (1996) 16, 20, 24, etc.
    rising and setting times (1996) 18, 22,
        26, etc., 65, 72
Moorlands (Staffordshire), MP 260
Moray 536, 569, 570
    MP 269
Moray, Ross and Caithness, Bishop 407
Morden, Mitcham and, MP 255
Morecambe and Lunesdale, MP 255
Morley, Leeds South and, MP 253
Mormons 424
Morocco 784, 959–61
    Archbishops (RC) 421
    Western Sahara 784, 961
Moroni 783, 855
Mortgage interest rates 623
Moscow 786, 995
Mossley Hill (Liverpool), MP 254
MOT tests 507
Mothering Sunday 83
Motherwell 536, 569
    Bishop (RC) 416
    MPs 269
Motor cycling 1232–3
Motor racing 1233
Motor rallying 1233
Motor vehicles:
    accidents 507
    insurance 629–35
    licences 506
    lighting-up time 71
Motorways 505
Mountain ranges, longest 112
Mountains, highest 112–13
Mourne, Newry and 573
Movable feasts 83
Moyle 573
Mozambique 784, 961–2
    Archbishops (RC) 421
Mull 566
Municipal elections results 531–6
Muscat 786, 979
Museum of Flight 329, 597
Museum of London 328, 595
Museum of Mankind 326, 595
Museum of the North 597
Museum of Welsh Life 329, 597
Museum of the Welsh Woollen
    Industry 597
Museums 326–30, 593–8
    England 593–7
    Northern Ireland 598
    Scotland 597–8
    Wales 597
Museums and Galleries Commission 326
Music, training colleges 468
Muslim calendar 86
Mutual societies 621–5
Myanmar 786, 962–4
    Anglican Province 410
    Archbishops (RC) 421
    map 963

Nairn 536, 569
Nairn, Inverness, and Lochaber, MP 269
Nairobi 784, 925
Namibia, Archbishop (RC) 421
Nantwich, Crewe and 532, 550
    MP 247
Napier University 457
Nassau 784, 816
National Advisory Council for Education
    Training and Targets 450
National Army Museum 329, 595
National art collections 286–7
National Art Library 328
National Audit Office 329–30
National Blood Authority 309

National Consumer Council 330
National Criminal Intelligence
    Service 380
National Curriculum 438
National Debt 619
    Office 331
National Engineering Laboratory 352
National Environmental Technology
    Centre 288
National Film Theatre 602
National flags, *see* Flags
National Galleries of Scotland 287, 597–8
National Gallery 287, 595
National Health Service 483–5
    Commissioners (Ombudsmen) 335
    community child health services 485
    dental service 484
    Department of Health 307–10
    family doctor service 483
    general practitioner practices 483
    hospital trusts 485
    ophthalmic services 484
    pay review bodies 341
    pharmaceutical service 484
    Policy Board 307
    primary health care 484
    Regional Health Authorities 309
    Special Health Authorities 309
    Supplies Authority 309
    Tribunal 378
National Health Service Executive 308
National Health Service, Scotland:
    Boards 345–6
    Management Executive 345
    Tribunal 378
National Health Service, Wales 359–60
    Health Authorities 359
National Heritage:
    Department of 330
    Secretary of State 279, 330
National Heritage Memorial Fund 331
National Insurance 486–7
    contributions 486–7
    Fund 488
    Joint Authority 331
    related benefits 489–50
    state earnings related pension
        scheme 487–8
National Investment and Loans
    Office 331
National Library of Scotland 322
National Library of Wales 322
National Lottery 286, 1133
    arts councils 286
    Charities Board 331
    Millennium Commission 326
    National Heritage Memorial Fund 331
    Office of 286
    Sports Council 349
National Maritime Museum 328, 595
National Monuments Record 311
    for Scotland 311
    for Wales 311
National Museum of Photography, Film
    and Television 327, 593
National Museum of Wales 329, 597
National museums 326–30
National Museums of Scotland 329,
    597–8
National Nature Reserves 582
National Parks 578–9
National Physical Laboratory 74
National Portrait Gallery 287, 595
    Scottish 287, 598
National Radiological Protection
    Board 332
National Railway Museum 327, 597
National Rivers Authority 332, 496
National Savings 626–8
    Bank 626

National Savings *continued*
  bonds 626
  certificates 627–8
  Department 332
  stocks 627
National Scenic Areas 581
National Sound Archive 322
National Theatre, Royal 602, 1192
  Board 342
National Trust 738
  Scotland 738
National Vocational Qualifications 442–3
National Weights and Measures
  Laboratory 353
NATO 761–2
  commands 761–2
Natural Conservation Areas 581–5
Natural Environment Research
  Council 710
  research institutes 710–11
Natural History Museum 327, 595
Natural Resources Institute 334–5
Naturalization, legal notes 653–4
Nature Conservancy Council for England
  (English Nature) 300
Nature Conservancy Council for Scotland,
  see Scottish Natural Heritage
Nature Conservation Committee,
  Joint 332
Nature reserves 582
Nauru 787, 965–6
Nautical measures 520–1
Nautical training 468
Nautical twilight (1996) 17, 21, 25, etc., 72
Naval colleges 464
Ndjaména 783, 847
Neap tides 96–7
Neath 535, 563
  MP 266
Neath and Port Talbot 564
Nebraska 1051
Nepal 786, 966–7
  map 902
Neptune 73, 76
  monthly data (1996) 19, 23, 27, etc., 73
  satellites 76
Neston, Ellesmere Port and 532, 550
  MP 249
Netball 1233
Netherlands 786, 967–9
  Archbishop (RC) 421
  map 967
  overseas territories 969
Netherlands Antilles 785, 969
  map 897
Nevada 1051
Nevis, St Christopher and 785, 1001–2
New Brunswick 838, 843
New Caledonia 787, 881
New Forest 533, 551
  area of national significance 579
  MP 255
New Guinea 111
New Hampshire 1051
New Jersey 1051
New Mexico 1051
New South Wales 805, 809–10
  Anglican Province 408
New Testament Church of God 427
New Towns 524
  Commission for 524
New Year 9, 86
  Chinese 9, 88
  Hindu 9, 84
  Islamic 9, 86
  Jewish 9, 85
  Sikh 9, 86
New York (State) 1051
New Zealand 787, 969–72
  Archbishop (RC) 421
  territories, etc. 971–2

New Zealand, Aotearoa, Polynesia and,
  Anglican Church 408
Newark:
  Archdeacon 406
  MP 255
Newark and Sherwood 533, 551
Newbury 533, 551
  MP 238, 255
Newcastle, Bishop 167, 405
Newcastle, Hexham and, Bishop (RC) 416
Newcastle under Lyme 533, 551
  MP 255
Newcastle upon Tyne 531, 542, 548
  airport 502
  Education Authority 449
  MPs 255
  universities 457–8
Newfoundland 111
Newfoundland and Labrador 838, 843–4
Newham 534, 560
  Education Authority 449
  MPs 238, 256
Newport 535, 563, 564
  MPs 266
Newry and Armagh, MP 270
Newry and Mourne 573
News agencies 693
Newspapers:
  national 685
  regional 685–6
  religious 687
  trade 690–3
  weekly 686–7
Newtownabbey 573
NHS Supplies Authority 309
Niamey 784, 974
Nicaragua 785, 972–4
  Archbishop (RC) 421
  map 973
Nicosia 786, 861
Niger 784, 974
  map 975
Nigeria 784, 975–6
  Anglican Province 410–11
  Archbishops (RC) 421
  map 975
Nightingale Islands 1079
Nithsdale 536, 569
Niue 787, 969, 972
Nobel prizes 1156
Non-contributory benefits 490–1
Nordic Council 761
Norfolk 531, 546, 547
  Archdeacon 401
  Education Authority 448
  MEPs 276
  MPs 256
  North 533, 551
    Police Authority 381
  South 534, 552
Norfolk Island 787, 809
Normanton, MP 256
North America 110–11
  countries of 784
North Atlantic Council 762
North Atlantic Treaty
  Organization 761–2
North Ayrshire 570
North Carolina 1051
North Cornwall 533, 551
North Dakota 1051
North Devon 533, 551
North Dorset 533, 551
North Down 573
North East Derbyshire 533, 551
North East Fife 536, 569
North Hertfordshire 533, 551
North Kesteven 533, 551
North Korea 929–30
  map 920

North Lanarkshire 570
North London University 458
North Norfolk 533, 551
North Rhine-Westphalia 887
North Shropshire 533, 552
North Tyneside 531, 548
  Education Authority 449
North Wales Police Authority 382
North Warwickshire 533, 552
North West Leicestershire 533, 552
North West Somerset 546
North Wiltshire 533, 552
North Yorkshire 531, 546, 547
  Education Authority 448
  Police Authority 381
North-Eastern Education and Library
  Board, Northern Ireland 450
Northampton 524, 533, 551
  Archdeacon 402
  Bishop (RC) 416
  MPs 256
Northamptonshire 531, 546, 547
  East 532, 550
  Education Authority 448
  Police Authority 381
  South 534, 553
Northamptonshire and Blaby,
  MEP 276
Northavon 533, 551
  MP 256
Northern Ireland 378
  airports 502
  Arts Council 286
  Civil Service 332–4
  Commissioner for Complaints 335
  communications 572
  constitution 571
  currency 612
  Customs and Excise 297
  educational system 433–42
  events (1994–5) 1093–5
  finance 572
  flag 571–2
  High Sheriffs 572
  judicature 374
  local government 530
  Lord Lieutenants 572
  map 911
  MEPs 278
  MPs 270–1
  museums 598
  Office of Electricity Regulation 300
  Parliamentary Commissioner for
    Administration 335
  Police Authority 382
  political parties 230
  population statistics 118–21, 571
  Privy Council 220
  production 572
  Public Record Office 340
  Social Security and Child Support
    Commissioners 378
  Tourist Board 350
  transport 572
  universities 459, 460
Northern Ireland Office 332–4
  Ministers 279, 332
  Secretary of State 279, 332
Northern Lighthouses, Commissioners
  of 323
Northern Mariana Islands 787, 1049, 1051,
  1056
Northern (Scotland) Police Authority 382
Northern Territory, Australia 805, 808
Northfield (Birmingham), MP 243
Northolt, Archdeacon 397
Northumberland 531, 546, 547
  Archdeacon 406
  Education Authority 448

Northumbria:
  MEP 276
  Police Authority 381
  University 458
Northwest Territories 838, 842
Norway 786, 976–8
  map 977
Norwich 533, 542, 552
  airport 502
  Archdeacon 401
  Bishop 167, 401
  MPs 256
  University of East Anglia 454
Norwood, MP 256
Nottingham 533, 542–3, 552
  Archdeacon 406
  Bishop (RC) 416
  MPs 256
  universities 458
Nottingham and Leicestershire North
    West, MEP 276
Nottinghamshire 531, 546, 547
  Education Authority 448
  MEPs 276
  Police Authority 381
Nouakchott 784, 951
Noumea 787, 881
Nova Scotia 838, 844
Nuclear Research, European Organization
    for 756
Nuclear Safety Inspectorate 310
Nuku'alofa 787, 1037
Nuncios, Papal 415, 416
Nuneaton, MP 256
Nuneaton and Bedworth 533, 552
Nursing:
  pay review body 341
  services (armed forces) 389, 391, 392
  training 468
Nutation 74
  constant of 75
Nutrition science, professional bodies 465
NVQs 442–3

Oadby and Wigston 533, 552
Oakham, Archdeacon 402
Oaks, The 13, 1230
Obituaries (1994–5) 1114–17
Observatories:
  magnetic 77
  Royal 711
Occultations (1996) 66–7
Occupational Health Service 292
Occupational Pensions Board 334
Occupational therapy, professional
    qualifications 467
Oceania:
  Archbishops (RC) 421
  countries of 787
Oceans, areas and depths 110
OECD 762–3
Offer 300
Office of Electricity Regulation 300
  Northern Ireland 300
Office of Gas Supply 306
Office of Public Service 291–2
  Minister 291
Office of the Social Security and Child
    Support Commissioners 378
  Northern Ireland 378
Office for Standards in
    Education 299–300, 434
Office of Telecommunications 349–50,
    512
Office of Water Services 358, 496
Official Receivers' Department 364
Official Referees 363
Official Solicitor 364
  Department 364

Ofgas 306
OFSTED 299–300, 434
Oftel 349–50, 512
Ofwat 358, 496
Ogilvy, Hon. Sir Angus 124
Ogmore, MP 266
Ogwr 535, 563
Ohio 1051
Oklahoma 1051
Old Bexley and Sidcup, MP 256
Oldham 531, 548
  Education Authority 449
  MPs 256
Olivier awards (1995) 1202
OM London Ltd 614
Omagh 573
Oman 786, 978–80
  map 1006
Ombudsmen:
  Banking 614
  Building Societies 614
  Corporate Estate Agents 730
  Insurance 614
  Investment 614
  Legal Services 321
  local government 323, 527
  National Health Service 335
  Parliamentary Commissioner 335
  Pensions 614
  Unit Trusts 614
Omsk 995
One Thousand Guineas 13, 1230
One-parent benefit 491
Ongar, Brentwood and, MP 244
Ontario 838, 844–5
  Anglican Province 409
OPEC 765
Open University 443–4, 446, 460–1
Opera:
  (1994–5) 1157–61
  English National 1159–60
  Northern Ireland 1161
  productions 1159–61
  Royal 1159
  Scottish 1160
  Welsh National 1160
Opera Factory 1161
Opera North 1160
Ophthalmic service, NHS 484
Ophthalmics, professional body 469
Opposition, Leader of 226, 229
OPS 291–2
Oranjestad 784, 969
Order of St John 211
Orders of Chivalry 174–6
Orders of Knighthood 174–7
  Central Chancery 126
Ordination of women 396
Ordnance Survey 334
Oregon 1051
Organization for Economic Co-operation
    and Development 762–3
Organization for Security and
    Co-operation in Europe 763
Organization of African Unity 763–4
Organization of American States 764
Organization of Arab Petroleum Exporting
    Countries 764
Organization of the Islamic
    Conference 764
Organization of Petroleum Exporting
    Countries 765
Orkney:
  airports 502
  Education Authority 450
  islands 565–6
  Islands Council 535, 568, 570
Orkney, Aberdeen and, Bishop 407
Orkney and Shetland, MP 269
Orpington, MP 256–7

Orthodox Church 425–6
  patriarchs 426
Orthoptics, training 467
Oscars 1151
Oslo 786, 976
Ossory, Bishop (RC) 417
Ossory, Cashel and, Bishop 408
Oswestry 533, 552
Ottawa 784, 839
Ouagadougou 783, 834
Overseas Development
    Administration 334–5
  Minister 279, 334
Oxford 533, 543, 552
  Archdeacon 401
  Bishop 167, 401
  MEPs 274
  MPs 257
  universities 458–9
Oxfordshire 531, 546, 547
  Education Authority 448
  MEPs 273
  South 534, 553
  West 534, 553

Pago Pago 787, 1051, 1055
Paisley:
  Bishop (RC) 416
  MPs 269
  University 459
Pakistan 786, 980–1
  Archbishop (RC) 421
Palaeozoic Era 94
Palau 787, 981–2
  map 905
Palestine Refugees in the Near East, UN
    Relief and Works Agency for 767
Palestinian Autonomous Areas 915–16
  map 913
Palikir 787, 956
Palm Sunday 24, 82
Palma 1021
Panama 785, 982–3
  Archbishop (RC) 421
  map 973
Panama Canal 116, 1056
Panama City 785, 982
Pantelleria Island 919
Papal ambassadors 415
Papeete 787, 881
Paper, sizes of 522
Papua New Guinea 787, 983–4
  Anglican Church 411
  Archbishops (RC) 421
Paraguay 785, 984–5
  Archbishop (RC) 421
Paramaribo 785, 1025
Paris 785, 786, 878
Parish councils 528
Parks:
  Constabulary, Royal 383
  London 600–1
  National 578–9
Parliament:
  Acts of (1994–5) 1171–4
  development 221–2
  Houses of 222–5, 600
  Members of 231–7
  officers 222–3, 224–5
  party strengths (1995) 222, 223
  procedure 222, 223–4, 225–8
  Record Office 340
  statistics 240
  summary (1994–5) 1162–71
  Whips 230, 280
Parliamentary associations 271
Parliamentary Commissioner
    (Ombudsman) 335

Parliamentary constituencies:
  England 241–64
  European in UK 273–8
  Northern Ireland 270–1
  Scotland 266–70
  Wales 265–6
Parliamentary Counsel 335
Parliamentary private secretaries 281–360
Parole Board:
  England and Wales 335
  Scotland 336
Particle Physics and Astronomy Research
  Council 711
Parties, political 229–30
  development 229
Passenger Rail Franchising, Office of 503
Passover 9, 85
Passport Agency 316
Patent (Appellate Section) Court 363
Patent Office 336, 677
Patents 677
Patriarchs:
  in communion with Roman Catholic
    Church 422–3
  Orthodox 426
Patron saints 573
Pavilion (Brighton), MP 244
Pay As You Earn 641
Pay review bodies 341
PAYE 641
PAYMASTER 336
Paymaster-General 279, 336
  Office of 336
Peace prize, Nobel 1156
Peak District, MEP 276
Peckham, MP 257
Peculiars 397, 398
  Royal 403–4
Peer, premier 142
Peerage 141–73
  courtesy titles 169–70
  disclaimed 141
  extinct (1994–5) 141
  precedence 576
Peers 141–67
  form of address 217
  hereditary 141–62
  life 141, 162–7
  minors 141
  premier, see Premier
  surnames 170–3
  women 141, 149, 161–2, 166–7
Peking (Beijing) 785, 849
Pelagian Islands 919
Pembroke, MP 266
Pembroke North, Ceredigion and,
  MP 265
Pembrokeshire 564
Pembrokeshire, Preseli 535, 563
Pembrokeshire, South 535, 563
Penarth, Cardiff South and, MP 265
Pendle 533, 552
  MP 257
Peninsulas, largest 111
Penistone, Barnsley West and, MP 242
Pennsylvania 1051
Peñon de Alhucemas 1022
Peñon de la Gomera 1022
Penrith, Bishop (Suffragan) 405
Penrith and the Border, MP 257
Pensions:
  Appeal Tribunals 378, 495
  contracted-out 488
  contributory 489–90
  earnings related scheme
    (SERPS) 487–8
  income support premiums 491–2
  industrial injuries and diseases 493–4
  non-contributory 491
  Occupational, Board 334

Pensions continued
  personal schemes 488
  war 494–5
Pensions Ombudsman 337, 614
  Office of 337, 614
Pentecost 9
  (1996-2028) 83
Pentecostal Churches 427
Pentlands (Edinburgh), MP 268
Penwith 533, 552
Perigee (1996) 16, 20, 24, etc.
Periodicals:
  consumer 687–90
  professional 690–3
Perpetual calendar 90–3
Perry Barr (Birmingham), MP 243
Perth (Western Australia) 812
Perth and Kinross 536, 569
  MP 238, 269
Perthshire and Kinross 570
Peru 785, 985–7
  Archbishops (RC) 421
Pesticides Safety Directorate 285
Peter the First Island 978
Peterborough 524, 533, 552
  Bishop 167, 402
  MP 257
Petroleum Exporting Countries:
  Organization of 765
  Organization of Arab 764
Pharmaceutical service, NHS 484
Pharmacopoeia Commission, British 290
Pharmacy, professional body 469
Phases of the Moon 16, 20, 24, etc., 71
Philippine Episcopal Church 411
Philippines 786, 987–8
  Archbishops (RC) 421
  map 905
Phnom Penh 785, 836
Photography, Film and Television,
    National Museum 327, 593
Photography, professional body 469
Physics:
  Nobel prize 1156
  qualifying body 463
Physiology prize, Nobel 1156
Physiotherapy courses 468
Pitcairn Islands 787, 1078
Plaid Cymru 230
  financial support 229
Planets 76
  conjunctions (1996) 16, 20, 24, etc.
  satellites 76
Planning Inspectorate 302
  Wales 359–60
Planning, town and country 675
  courses 471
Platinum hallmarks 604–5
Pluto 76
  satellite 76
Plymouth 533, 543, 552
  airport 502
  Archdeacon 400
  Bishop (RC) 416
  Bishop (Suffragan) 399
  MEPs 274
  MPs 257
  University 459
Plymouth (Montserrat) 785, 1077
PMRAFNS 392
Podgorica 1066
Poet Laureate 125
Pohnpei 956
Poland 786, 989–90
  Archbishops (RC) 421
Poles, magnetic 77
Police:
  Authorities 381–2
  Department, Home Office 313
  HM Inspectorate 313, 380
  HM Inspectorate, Scotland 345

INTERPOL 758
  Metropolitan 380, 382
  Ministry of Defence 383
  National Computer 313
  National Criminal Intelligence Ser-
    vice 380
  pay 380
  Royal Parks 383
  special constabulary 380
  staff associations 383
  Transport 383
  UK Atomic Energy Authority 383
Police Complaints Authority 336, 380
Police Complaints for Northern Ireland,
    Independent Commission for 317
Police Federations 383
Police Staff College 313
Political Honours Scrutiny
    Committee 336
Political parties 229–30
  development 229
  financial support 229
  in local government 531–6
Poll tax, see Community charge
Pollok (Glasgow), MP 268
Pollution:
  HM Inspectorate 301
  HM Inspectorate for Wales 359
  Royal Commission on Environmen-
    tal 302
Polo 1233–4
Polynesia, Aotearoa, New Zealand and,
    Anglican Church 408
Pontefract:
  Archdeacon 406
  Bishop (Suffragan) 406
Pontefract and Castleford, MP 257
Pontypridd, MP 266
Poole 533, 552
  MP 257
Pope John Paul II 415, 1059
Poplar, Bow and, MP 244
Population:
  countries of the world 783–7
  future estimates (world) 783
  United Kingdom 118, 119
  United Kingdom censuses (1801-
    1991) 118
Population Censuses and Surveys, Office
    of 336–7
Port au Prince 785, 896
Port Glasgow, Greenock and, MP 269
Port of London 602
  Authority 337
Port Louis 784, 952
Port Moresby 787, 983
Port of Spain 785, 1038
Port Talbot 535, 563
  Neath and 564
Port Vila 787, 1059
Portland, Weymouth and 534, 553
Porto Novo 783, 824
Portrait Gallery, National 287, 595
Portrait Gallery, Scottish National 287,
    598
Ports:
  Cinque 676
  statistics 501
Portsmouth 533, 543, 552
  Archdeacon 402
  Bishop 167, 402
  Bishop (RC) 416
  MPs 257
  University 459
Portugal 786, 990–2
  Archbishops (RC) 421
  Lusitanian Church 414
  map 1020
Post Office 337
  Board 337

Post Office *continued*
  financial results 337
  services 510–12
Postage stamps 510
Postal orders 510–11
Postal services 510–12
  airmail zones 516–17
  special delivery 511
Postal Union, Universal 770
Postgraduate education 443–4, 446
  grants 446–7
Powys 535, 562, 563, 564
  Education Authority 450
Prague 786, 862
Praia 783, 845
Precambrian Era 94
Precedence:
  England 576
  local 577
  Scotland 576–7
  women 577
Precession 69, 75
Premier:
  Baronets 143, 179, 184, 185
  Barons 154, 155, 157
  Dukes 142
  Earldom 149
  Earls 145, 148
  Marquesses 142, 143
  Peer 142
  Viscounts 150, 151
Premium bonds 626
Premiums, insurance 629–33
Presbyterian Church in Ireland 427
Presbyterian Church of Wales 427
Presbyterian Churches of Scotland,
  Associated 423
Prescription charges (NHS) 484, 485
Preseli Pembrokeshire 535, 563
President, Family Division (High
  Court) 363
Press, The 685–93
Press agencies 693
Press Complaints Commission 685
Preston 533, 552
  MP 257
Prestwick airport 502
Pretoria 784, 1016
Prime Minister 279, 291, 355
  Deputy 279
  office of 228
  residences 599
  salary 281
Prime Minister's Office 291
Prince Andrew, *see* Duke of York
Prince Andrew of Greece 135
  descendants 135
Prince Edward 123
  Civil List 130
  household 128
Prince Edward Island 838, 845
Prince Henry of Wales 123
Prince Michael of Kent 124
  family 124
  household 129
  military titles 133
Prince Philip, Duke of Edinburgh 123,
  135
  Armed Forces 387, 389, 391
  Civil List 130
  household 128
  military titles 131
  Orders of Chivalry 174, 175, 176
  University Chancellorships 453, 454
Prince of Wales 123
  Civil List 130
  Duchy of Cornwall 298
  family 123
  household 128
  military titles 132

Prince of Wales *continued*
  Orders of Chivalry 174
  taxation 130
  University Chancellorship 460
Prince William of Wales 123
Princes of Wales 140
Princess Alexandra 124
  Civil List 130
  family 124
  household 129
  military titles 133
  University Chancellorship 455
Princess Alice, Duchess of Gloucester 124
  Civil List 130
  household 129
  military titles 132
  Orders of Chivalry 175
Princess Anne, *see* Princess Royal
Princess Beatrice of York 123
Princess Eugenie of York 123
Princess Margaret 123
  Civil List 130
  family 123
  household 128–9
  military titles 132
  Orders of Chivalry 175
Princess Mary's RAF Nursing Service 392
Princess Michael of Kent 124, 129
Princess of Wales 123, 128
  military titles 132
Princess Ragnhild Land 978
Princess Royal 123
  Civil List 130
  family 123
  household 128
  military titles 132
  University Chancellorship 456
Princesses Royal 140
Príncipe, São Tomé and 784, 1005
Printing courses 469
Prison Complaints Commission,
  Scottish 347
Prison Service 313–16
  HM Inspectorate 316
  Scottish 346
Prisons 314–16
  Scottish 346
Prisons Board 313
Privy Council 218, 221
  Judicial Committee 361
  Lord President 279, 338
  members 218–20
  Northern Ireland 220
Privy Council Office 337–8
Privy Counsellors 218–20
  form of address 217
Privy Purse:
  Keeper of 125
  Office 125
  royal finances 130
Probate, legal notes 666
Probate Registrars 365
Probation Service 375
  Scotland 375
Proceedings against Crown 656
Procurator Fiscal Service 373–4
Procurator-General, HM 356
Procurement Executive, Ministry of
  Defence 386–7
Professional institutes 463–71, 721–50
Prosecution Service:
  England and Wales 370
  Scotland 373
Protected species 583–5
Protection, Court of 364
Provan (Glasgow), MP 268
Provident Societies 622
Provosts, diocesan 397–407
PSBR 607
Public expenditure statistics 606–7
Public Health Laboratory Service 338

Public holidays 87
  (1996) 10
  (1997) 11
Public Lending Right, Registrar 338
Public offices 281–360
Public Record Office 339–41
Public Records:
  Advisory Council on 339
  Corporation of London 340–1
  House of Lords 340
  Northern Ireland 340
  Scottish 340
Public schools 437, 472–82
Public sector borrowing requirement 607
Public Service, Office of 291–2
  Minister 291
Public Trust Office 338–9
Public Trustee 339
Public Works Loan Board 331
Publishers 694–6
Pudsey, MP 257
Puerto Rico 785, 1049, 1051, 1055
  Archbishop (RC) 421
  map 897
Pupil numbers 434–5, 436–7
Purbeck 533, 552
Purchasing power of pound 610
Purple Rod 176
Pursuivants 285
  Scottish 285
Putney, MP 257
Pyongyang 785, 929

QARANC 391
QARNNS 389
Qatar 786, 992–3
  map 1006
Quakers 427
Quarter days 9
Quebec (city) 845
Quebec (province) 838, 845
Queen Alexandra's Royal Army Nursing
  Corps 391
Queen Alexandra's Royal Naval Nursing
  Service 389
Queen, HM The 123, 139
  Civil List 130
  constitutional role 221
  Head of Armed Forces 387, 389, 391
  Household 125–7
  Household in Scotland 127
  military titles 131
  Official Birthday 9, 122
  Orders of Chivalry 174, 175, 176
  Private Secretary to 125
  taxation 130
Queen Elizabeth the Queen
  Mother 123–4
  Civil List 130
  household 128
  military titles 131
  Orders of Chivalry 174, 175, 176
Queen Maud Land 978
Queen Victoria 134, 138
  descendants 134–6
Queens:
  British 138–9
  of England 136–8
  of Scots 139–40
Queen's Awards 1178–80
Queen's Bench Division 361, 363
  Lord Chief Justice 363
Queen's Coroner and Attorney 364
Queen's Gallery 595
Queen's Messengers, Corps of 305
Queen's Proctor 356
Queen's Remembrancer 364
Queen's speech 1162–3
Queen's University of Belfast 459

Queensland 805, 810–11
Anglican Province 408
Quito 785, 868

Rabat 784, 959
Racial Equality, Commission for 329
Racing:
athletics 1217–21
horse 13, 1228–31
motor 1233
Rackets 1234
Radio:
(1994–5) 1136
BBC 680–1
independent stations 681–4
Radio Authority 339
Radio time-signals 74–5
Radiocommunications Agency 353
Radiography training 468
Radiological Protection Board,
National 332
Radiotherapy training 468
Radnor, Brecon and, MP 265
Radnorshire 535, 563
Rail Regulator, Office of the 339, 503
Railtrack 503
Railways:
HM Inspectorate 310
National Museum 327, 597
privatization 503
statistics 503–4
Railways Board, British 290
Rainfall:
averages 1209
records 1210–15
Rallying, motor 1233
Ramadan 9, 86
Ramsbury, Bishop (Suffragan) 403
Rangoon 962
Raphoe, Bishop (RC) 417
Raphoe, Derry and, Bishop 408
Ras al Khaimah 1049
Rates 526–7
Scotland 530
Ravensbourne, MP 257
Reading 533, 552
Bishop (Area) 401
MPs 257
University 459
Real tennis 1234
Recognized clearing houses 614
Recognized investment exchanges 614
Reconstruction and Development,
International Bank for, UN 771–2
Record offices:
Corporation of London 340–1
House of Lords 340
Public Record Office 339–40
Scottish 340
Recorders 367–9
Northern Ireland 374
Recruitment and Assessment Services 292
Red Cross and Red Crescent Movement,
International 760
Red Deer Commission 341
Red-letter days 87
Redbridge 534, 560
Education Authority 449
Redcar, Middlesborough, Cleveland
and 546
Redcar, MP 257
Reddish, Denton and, MP 247
Redditch 524, 533, 552
Refraction, Mean 75
Regent's Park 601
Regina 845
Regional Advisory Councils, further
education 451
Regional Arts Boards 286

Regional Councils, Scotland 530, 535, 568
Regional Health Authorities 309
Regional theatre awards 1202
Register Office, General 347
Registers of Scotland (agency) 320
Registrar-General 337, 662
Scotland 347
Regnal year 87
Reigate:
Archdeacon 403
MP 257
Reigate and Banstead 533, 552
Relief and Works Agency for Palestine
Refugees in the Near East (UN) 767
Religious festivals 9, 82–6
Religious Society of Friends 427
Remand centres 315–16
Remembrance Sunday 9
Removal days, Scotland 9
Renfrew 536, 569
Renfrew West and Inverclyde, MP 269
Renfrewshire 570
East 570
Repton, Bishop (Suffragan) 399
Research associations, industrial 711–12
Research Councils:
Biotechnology and Biological
Sciences 707
Council for the Central Laboratory
of 708
Economic and Social 708
Engineering and Physical Sciences 709
Medical 709–10
Natural Environment 710–11
Particle Physics and Astronomy 711
Research Institutes, Scottish Agricultural
and Biological 707–8
Resettlement Agency 349
Residuary Body, London 529
Resignations (1994–5) 1098
Restormel 533, 552
Restrictive Practices Court:
Clerk 364
members 363
Retail Price Index 610
Retirement pensions, see Pensions
Réunion 784, 881
Revenue support grant 528
Review bodies, pay 341
Reykjavik 786, 900
Rhineland Palatinate 887
Rhode Island 1051
Rhondda 535, 563
Cynon and Taff 564
MP 266
Rhuddlan 535, 563
Rhymney, Merthyr Tydfil and, MP 266
Rhymney Valley 535, 563
Ribble, South 534, 553
Ribble Valley 533, 552
MP 257–8
Richard Alston Dance Company 1147
Richborough, Bishop (Suffragan) 397
Richmond (Yorkshire):
Archdeacon 406
MP 258
Richmond and Barnes, MP 258
Richmond, Cleveland and, MEP 274
Richmond upon Thames 534, 560
Education Authority 449
Richmondshire 533, 552
Riga 786, 933
Right ascension 69, 71, 72
Ripon:
Bishop 167, 406
Skipton and, MP 259
Rivers, longest 114
Rivers Authority, National 332, 496
Riverside (Liverpool), MP 254
Riyadh 786, 1005

Road Town 785, 1073
Road walking 1234
Roads 505–7
building programme 505
landscape threat 1137
private finance 505
statistics 505–7
usage 507
Robert Gordon University 459
Rochdale 531, 548
Archdeacon 405
Education Authority 449
MP 258
Rochester:
Archdeacon 402
Bishop 168, 402
Rochester upon Medway 533, 552
Rochford 533, 552
MP 258
Rodrigues Island 953
Rogation days 83
Rogation Sunday 9, 83
Roman calendar 89
Roman Catholic Church 414–23
Apostolic Nuncio to Ireland 416
Apostolic Nuncio to the UK 415
Great Britain 415–16
Holy See 414–15, 1059
Ireland 416–17
overseas 417–23
patriarchs in communion with 422–3
Roman indiction 9, 88
Roman names of cities and towns 554
Romania 786, 993–5
Archbishops (RC) 421
Rome 786, 916
Treaty of 774
Romford, MP 258
Romsey and Waterside, MP 258
Ronaldsay airport 502
Ronaldsway (Isle of Man) 502
Roseau 784, 866
Ross, Cork and, Bishop (RC) 417
Ross, Cork, Cloyne and, Bishop 408
Ross and Cromarty 536, 569
Ross, Cromarty and Skye, MP 269
Ross Dependency 787, 969, 972
Ross, Moray and Caithness, Bishop 407
Rossendale 533, 552
Rossendale and Darwen, MP 258
Rother 533, 552
Rother Valley, MP 258
Rotherham 531, 548
Education Authority 449
MP 238, 258
Rowing 1234–5
Boat Race 12, 1235
Doggett's Coat and Badge 1235
Henley Royal Regatta 13, 1235
Roxburgh 536, 569
Roxburgh and Berwickshire, MP 269
Royal Academy 705
Academicians 706
Royal Academy of Engineering 705
Royal Air Force 391–2
Air Staff 385
aircraft, etc. 392
colleges 464
commands 392
constitution 392
Maintenance Group Agency 387
staff appointments 391–2
strength 384
Royal Air Force Museum 329, 595
Royal Air Force Staff College,
Bracknell 464
Royal Air Force Volunteer Reserve 392
Royal Albert Hall 602
Royal Almonry 125
Royal arms 133

Royal Auxiliary Air Force 392
Royal Ballet 1145
  Birmingham 1146
Royal Botanic Gardens 341–2
Royal Collection 127
Royal College of Art 461
Royal colleges (professions) 721–50
Royal Commissions:
  Ancient and Historical Monuments of
    Scotland 311
  Ancient and Historical Monuments in
    Wales 311
  Environmental Pollution 302
  Exhibition of 1851 342
  Historical Manuscripts 340
  Historical Monuments of England 311
Royal Company of Archers 127–8
Royal dukes 142
Royal family 123–4
  Civil List 130
  households 125–9
  military titles 131–3
  order of succession 124
  taxation 130
  titles 123–4
Royal Fine Art Commission 286
  Scotland 286–7
Royal Fleet Auxiliary 389
Royal Hospital Chelsea 602
Royal Houses 136–40
Royal Institution 743
Royal Marines 389
Royal Marines Reserve 389
Royal Mews Department 127
Royal Mint 342
  Master of the Mint 342
Royal Museum of Scotland 329, 597–8
Royal National Theatre 602, 1192
  Board 342
Royal Naval Reserve 389
Royal Navy 387–9
  colleges 464
  Fleet 388–9
  Naval Staff 385
  staff appointments 387–8
  strength 384
Royal Observatories 711
Royal Opera 1159
Royal Palaces Agency, Historic 330
Royal Parks:
  Constabulary 383
  Executive Agency 330
Royal Peculiars 403–4
Royal salutes 129
Royal Scottish Academy 705
Royal Shakespeare Company 1194
Royal Society 705–6
Royal societies 742–4
Royal Society of Arts 442, 452
Royal Society of Edinburgh 706
Royal Ulster Constabulary 382
Royal Victorian Chain 176
Royal Victorian Order 175
  Dames 209–10
  Knights 178–208
Royton, Oldham Central and, MP 256
RSA, see Royal Society of Arts
Rugby 533, 552
Rugby Fives 1235
Rugby and Kenilworth, MP 258
Rugby League 1235–6
Rugby Union 1236
Ruislip-Northwood, MP 258
Runcorn 524
Runnymede 533, 552
Rupert's Land, Anglican Province 409
Rural Development Commission 342
Rushcliffe 533, 552
  MP 258
Rushmoor 533, 552

Russia 786, 995–1000
  Archbishops (RC) 421
  British Embassy 998
  communications 1000
  defence 998
  economy 998–9
  government 996–7
  history 995–6
  map 996
Russian Orthodox Church 426
Rutherglen (Glasgow), MP 268
Rutland 533, 552
Rutland and Melton, MP 258
Rwanda 784, 1000–1
  Anglican Province 411
  Archbishop (RC) 421
  events (1994–5) 1098–1100
  map 800
Rye, Hastings and, MP 251
Ryedale 533, 552
  MP 258

Saarland 887
Saddleworth, Littleborough and, MP 238,
  254
Safety of Medicines, Committee on 309
Saffron Walden, MP 258
St Albans 533, 543, 552
  Archdeacon 402
  Bishop 168, 402
  MP 258
St Andrew's Day 9
St Andrews, Dunkeld and Dunblane,
  Bishop 407
St Andrews and Edinburgh, Archbishop
  (RC) 416
St Andrews University 459
St Asaph, Bishop 407
St Christopher and Nevis 785, 1001–2
  map 897
St David's, Bishop 407
St David's College, Lampeter 460
St David's Day 9
St Denis 784, 881
St Edmundsbury 533, 552
St Edmundsbury and Ipswich, Bishop 167,
  402
St George's 784, 892
St George's Day 9
St Germans, Bishop (Suffragan) 403
St Helena 784, 1078
St Helens 531, 548
  Education Authority 449
  MPs 258
St Helier 575
St Ives, MP 258
St James's Palace 602
St James's Park 601
St John, Order of 211
St John's (Antigua and Barbuda) 784, 802
St John's (Newfoundland) 844
St Kitts-Nevis, see St Christopher and
  Nevis
St Leger 1230
St Lucia 785, 1002
  Archbishop (RC) 421
  map 897
St Michael and St George, Order of 175
  Knights 178–208
St Pancras, Holborn and, MP 252
St Patrick's Day 9
St Paul's Cathedral 602
St Peter Port 575
St Pierre 784
St Pierre and Miquelon 784, 881
St Vincent and the Grenadines 785,
  1002–3
  map 897
Saints Days 9, 87

Saipan 787, 1051, 1056
Sale, Altrincham and, MP 241
Salford 531, 548
  Bishop (RC) 416
  Education Authority 449
  University 459
Salford East, MP 258
Salisbury 533, 552
  Bishop 168, 403
  MP 258
Salop, Archdeacon 401
Salvador, El 785, 1003–4
  Archbishop (RC) 421
  map 973
Salvation Army 427–8
Samoa:
  American 787, 1049, 1051, 1055–6
  Western 787, 1062–3
San Cristobal 869
San José 784, 856
San Juan 785, 1051, 1055
San Marino 786, 1004–5
  map 916
San Salvador 785, 1003
Sana'a 786, 1063
Sandhurst, Royal Military Academy 464
Sandwell 531, 548
  Education Authority 449
Santiago 785, 848
Santo Domingo 784, 867
São Tomé (town) 784, 1005
São Tomé and Príncipe 784, 1005
Sarajevo 786, 827
Sardinia 916
Sark 575
Sarum, Archdeacon 403
Saskatchewan 838, 845
Satellite television stations 680
Satellites:
  artificial 78
  launchings 78–80
  planetary 76
Saturn 76
  monthly data (1996) 17, 19, 23, etc., 73
  phenomena (1996) 16, 20, 24, etc.
  rings of 73
  satellites 76
Saudi Arabia 786, 1005–7
  map 1006
Savings, National:
  bonds 626
  certificates 627–8
Saxony 887
Saxony Anhalt 887
Scandinavia, Archdeacon 400
Scarborough 533, 552
  MP 258
Scarlet Rod 174
Scenic Areas, National 581–2
Scheduled monuments 586
Schengen Agreement 777
Schleswig Holstein 887
School Curriculum and Assessment
  Authority 451
School Teachers' Pay Review Body 341
Schools:
  curriculum 438–9
  grant-maintained 434–5
  HM Inspectorate 434
  HM Inspectorate, Scotland 344
  independent 437–8, 472–82
  maintained 434–5
  Office of HM Chief Inspector 299
  Office of HM Chief Inspector in
    Wales 359
  public 437
  pupil numbers 434–5, 436–7
  state sector 434–7
  voluntary 435

Science and Discovery 1181–91
  events (1994–5) 1086–8
Science Museum 327, 595
Scilly, Isles of 536
  airport 502
  Education Authority 450
Scotland:
  Accounts Commission for 288
  Associated Presbyterian Churches 423
  Church of 414
  clan chiefs 212–13
  Commission for Local Administration 323
  currency 612
  early history 566–7
  educational system 433–43
  Episcopal Church 407
  flag 565
  Free Church 424
  Free Presbyterian Church 424
  geographical features 565
  Inland Revenue 318
  islands 565–6
  judicature 371–4
  kings and queens 139–40
  local government changes 530, 570
  Lord Lieutenants 567–8
  MEPs 277–8
  MPs 266–70
  museums 597–8
  national galleries 287, 597–8
  National Health Service 345–6
  National Library 322
  national museums 329, 597–8
  police authorities 382
  political parties 229
  population statistics 118–21, 565
  precedence 576–7
  Queen's Household 127
  transport 501–7
  unitary authorities 530, 570
  universities 445, 452–61
Scottish Agricultural Museum 329, 598
Scottish Agricultural Science Agency 344
Scottish Arts Council 286
Scottish Ballet 1147
Scottish Enterprise 343
Scottish Fisheries Protection Agency 344
Scottish Homes 343
Scottish Law Commission 320
Scottish Legal Aid Board 321
Scottish National Gallery of Modern Art 287, 598
Scottish National Party 230
  financial support 229
Scottish National Portrait Gallery 287, 598
Scottish Natural Heritage 343
Scottish Office 343–7
  Agriculture and Fisheries Department 344
  Education Department 344
  Environment Department 344–5
  Home and Health Department 344
  Industry Department 346–7
  Ministers 279, 343
  Secretary of State 279, 343
Scottish Opera 1160
Scottish Prisons Complaints Commission 347
Scottish Record Office 340
Scottish Records Advisory Council 340
Scottish Tourist Board 350
Scottish United Services Museum 329, 598
Scottish Vocational Qualifications 442
Scunthorpe 533, 552
  Glanford and, MP 250
Sea Fish Industry Authority 347
Sea Fisheries Inspectorate 283

Seaport traffic 509
Seas, areas and depths 110
Seasons, defined 15
Second, defined 74
Secret Intelligence Service 304
Secretaries of State 279
  salaries 281
Securities and Investments Board 613
  recognized bodies 613–14
Security Council, UN 768
Security Service 313
Security Service Commissioner 347
Security Service Tribunal 347
Sedgefield 533, 552
  MP 259
Sedgemoor 533, 552
Sefton 531, 548
  Education Authority 449
Selby 533, 552
  Bishop (Suffragan) 404
  MP 259
Select committees 227
Self-regulating organizations 613
Selly Oak (Birmingham), MP 243
Senegal 784, 1008
  Archbishop (RC) 421
  map 975
Senior Salaries Review Body 341
Seoul 785, 928
Separation, legal notes 664–7
Serbia 1066
  map 1065
Serbian Orthodox Church 426
Serious Fraud Office 347
SERPS 487–8
Seven Wonders of the World 1122
Sevenoaks 533, 552
  MP 259
Seventh-Day Adventist Church 428
Severe disablement allowance 491
Seychelles 784, 1008–9
Shadow Cabinet 229–30
Sharjah 1049
Sheffield 531, 543–4, 548
  Archdeacon 406
  Bishop 167, 406
  Education Authority 449
  MEP 276
  MPs 259
  universities 459
Shepway 533, 552
Sherborne:
  Archdeacon 403
  Bishop (Suffragan) 403
Sheriff Court of Chancery 372
Sheriffs:
  Corporation of London 555
  Scotland 372–3
Sheriffs, High 527, 545, 562, 572
Sherwood:
  Bishop (Suffragan) 406
  MP 259
Sherwood, Newark and 533, 551
Shetland:
  airports 502
  Education Authority 450
  islands 566
  Islands Council 535, 568, 570
Shetland, Orkney and, MP 269
Shettleston (Glasgow), MP 268
Shikoku 920
Shipley, MP 259
Shipping:
  British registered vessels 509
  lighthouse authorities 322–3
  Lloyd's List 631
  merchant fleets 508
  passenger movement 509
  UK seaborne trade 509
Shipping forecast areas 1203

Shooting:
  Bisley 1236
  clay pigeon 1236–7
  close seasons 585
Shoreditch, Hackney South and, MP 250
Shoreham:
  airport 502
  MP 259
Show jumping 1226
Shrewsbury:
  Bishop (RC) 416
  Bishop (Suffragan) 401
Shrewsbury and Atcham 533, 552
  MP 259
Shrivenham, Royal Military College 464
Shropshire 531, 546, 547
  Education Authority 448
  North 533, 552
  North, MP 259
  South 534, 553
Shropshire, Herefordshire and, MEP 274
SI units of measurement 518
Sicily 916
Sick Pay, Statutory 489, 661
Sickness benefit 489, 490
Sidcup, Old Bexley and, MP 256
Sidereal day 74, 77
Sidereal time (1996) 17, 21, 25, etc., 69, 71, 73–4
Sidereal year 75
Sierra Leone 784, 1010
  Archbishop (RC) 421
  map 975
Sikhism 432
  calendar 86
  organizations in UK 432
Silver:
  coin 611
  hallmarks 604–5
Singapore 786, 1010–11
  Archbishop (RC) 421
  Bishop (Anglican) 414
  map 905
Single European Act 776–7
Single Market, European Union 776–7
Sirius 69, 81
Sites of Special Scientific Interest 581–2
Skating 1231
Skelmersdale 524
Skiing 1216
Skipton and Ripon, MP 259
Skopje 786, 943
Skye 566
Skye, Ross, Cromarty and, MP 269
Skye and Lochalsh 536, 569
Slough 533, 552
  MP 259
Slovak Republic 787, 1011–13
  Archbishop (RC) 421
Slovakia 1011–13
Slovenia 787, 1013–14
  Archbishop (RC) 421
  map 1065
Small Heath (Birmingham), MP 243
Snares Islands 969
Snooker 1237
Snowdon, Earl of 123, 148
Soccer 1216–17
Social and Liberal Democrats:
  local government representation 531–6
  see also Liberal Democrats *and* Liberal Party
Social Democratic and Labour Party 230
  financial support 229
Social Democratic Party:
  development 229
  local government representation 531–6
Social Fund 493
  Commissioner 317
  discretionary payments 493

Social Fund *continued*
  Independent Review Service 317
  regulated payments 493
Social Security:
  Advisory Committee 349
  benefits 491–5
  Commissioners, Office of 378
  Commissioners for Northern Ireland,
    Office of 378
  Department 347–9
  Ministers 279, 347–9
  Secretary of State 279, 347
Social Security and Child Support
    Commissioners 378
  Northern Ireland 378
Social Services Inspectorate 308
Social work, professional body 469
Societies 721–50
  archaeological 749–50
  local history 749–50
Society of Friends, Religious 427
Sodor and Man, Bishop 406
Sofia 786, 833
Solander Island 969
Solar apex 75
Solar cycle 9, 87
Solar motion 75
Solar parallax 75
Solar system 76
Solar time 71, 73
Solicitor-General 279, 321
  Scotland 279, 324
Solicitors' Complaints Bureau 466
Solicitors' Disciplinary Tribunal 379
Solicitors' training 466
Solihull 531, 548
  Education Authority 449
  MP 259
Solomon Islands 787, 1014–15
Solstices 15, 81
Somalia 784, 1015–16
  map 1015
Somerset 531, 546, 547
  Education Authority 448
  North West 546
  South 534, 553
  West 534, 553
Somerset, Avon and, Police Authority 381
Somerset House 602
Somerset and North Devon, MEP 276
Somerset North East, Bath and 546
Somerton and Frome, MP 259
South Africa 784, 1016–19
  Archbishops (RC) 421
  homelands 1017
  map 1016
South America 111
  countries of 785
South Australia 805, 811
  Anglican Province 408
South Ayrshire 570
South Bank University 459
South Bedfordshire 533, 552
South Buckinghamshire 533, 552
South Cambridgeshire 533, 552
South Carolina 1051
South Dakota 1051
South Derbyshire 533, 552
South Downs West, MEP 276
South Eastern Education and Library
    Board (Northern Ireland) 450
South Georgia 785, 1080
South Glamorgan 535, 562, 563
  Education Authority 450
South Gloucestershire 546
South Hams 534, 552
  MP 259
South Herefordshire 534, 552
South Holland 534, 552
South Kesteven 534, 552

South Korea 927–9
  map 920
South Lakeland 534, 552
South Lanarkshire 570
South Norfolk 534, 552
South Northamptonshire 534, 553
South Oxfordshire 534, 553
South Pacific Commission 765
South Pembrokeshire 535, 563
South Ribble 534, 553
  MP 260
South Sandwich Islands 1080
South Shields, MP 260
South Shropshire 534, 553
South Somerset 534, 553
South Staffordshire 534, 553
South Tyneside 531, 548
  Education Authority 449
South Tyrone, Fermanagh and, MP 270
South Wales Police Authority 382
South Yorkshire 531, 548
  Police Authority 381
Southall (Ealing), MP 248
Southampton 533, 544, 552
  airport 502
  Bishop (Suffragan) 397
  MPs 259
  University 459
Southend 533, 552
  airport 502
  Archdeacon 398
  MPs 259
Southern Africa, Anglican Province 411
Southern and Antarctic Territories
    (French) 881
Southern Cone of America, Anglican
    Church 411
Southern Education and Library Board
    (Northern Ireland) 450
Southgate (Enfield), MP 249
Southport, MP 259–60
Southwark 534, 560
  Archbishop (RC) 416
  Archdeacon 403
  Bishop 167, 403
  Education Authority 449
Southwark and Bermondsey, MP 260
Southwell, Bishop 167, 406
Space Agency, European 756–7
Space Centre, British National 350
Spain 787, 1019–22
  Archbishops (RC) 421–2
  map 1020
  overseas territories, etc. 1022
  Reformed Church 414
Spalding, Stamford and, MP 260
Sparkbrook (Birmingham), MP 243
Speaker, The:
  House of Commons 224, 227
  House of Lords 223
Speakers of the House of Commons 278
Special Commissioners of Income
    Tax 379
Special constabulary 380
Speech therapy training 469
Speedway 1237
Spelthorne 534, 553
  MP 260
Spen, Batley and, MP 242
Spitsbergen 978
Sport 1216–41
  events (1994–5) 1095–8
  fixtures (1996) 12–13
  records 1239–41
  representative bodies 713–16
  results (1994–5) 1216–38
Sports Council 349, 713
  for Northern Ireland 713
  Scottish 713
  for Wales 713

Spring:
  defined 15
  equinox 15, 81
Spring tides 96–7
Springburn (Glasgow), MP 268
Squash rackets 1237
Sri Lanka 786, 1022–3
  Archbishop (RC) 422
  map 902
Stafford 534, 553
  Bishop (Suffragan) 401
  MP 260
Staffordshire 531, 546, 547
  East 532, 550
  Education Authority 448
  MEPs 276
  MPs 260
  Police Authority 381
  South 534, 553
  University 459
Staffordshire Moorlands 534, 553
Stalybridge and Hyde, MP 260
Stamford and Spalding, MP 260
Stamp duties 637–8
Stamp Office 318
  Scotland 318
Standard time 75
  British 75
  zones 794–5
Standards Institution, British 290
Stanley 785, 1074
Stansted airport 502
Star of India, Order of 175
Stars:
  magnitude of 68
  mean places (1996) 68–9
  occultations 66
State earnings related pension
    scheme 487–8
State Veterinary Service 283
Stationery Office, HM 349
Statistical Office, Central 293
Statute Law, Advisory Committee on 324
Stepney, Bishop (Area) 397
Stepney, Bethnal Green and, MP 242
Stevenage 524, 534, 553
  MP 260
Stewart Island 969
Stewartry 536, 569
Stipendiary magistrates 369–70
  Scotland 373
Stirling 536, 569, 570
  MP 270
  University 459
Stock Exchange 636
  regulation 636
Stockholm 787, 1026
Stockport 531, 548
  Bishop (Suffragan) 405
  Education Authority 449
  MP 260
Stockton-on-Tees 534, 546, 553
  MP 260
Stoke Newington, Hackney North and,
    MP 250
Stoke-on-Trent 534, 544, 553
  Archdeacon 401
  MPs 260
Stop-press 1278–9
Storms, magnetic 77–8
Stortford, Hertford and, MP 251
Stourbridge, Halesowen and, MP 250
Stow, Archdeacon 401
Strabane 573
Strangford, MP 271
Stratford-upon-Avon 534, 553, 590
  MP 260
Strathclyde 535, 568
  Education Authority 450

Strathclyde *continued*
  MEPs 278
  Police Authority 382
  University 459
Strathkelvin 536, 569
Strathkelvin and Bearsden, MP 270
Strathspey, Badenoch and 535, 569
Streatham, MP 260
Stretford, MP 260
Stroud 534, 553
  MP 260
Structures, tallest 115
Students:
  course fees 446
  grants 446, 447
  numbers 442, 443, 447
Styles of addressing peers, etc. 217
Succession to throne 124
Sudan 784, 1023–5
  Archbishops (RC) 422
  Episcopal Church of 411–12
Sudbury, Archdeacon 402
Suez Canal 116, 869
Suffolk 531, 546, 547
  Archdeacon 402
  Education Authority 448
  MEPs 274, 276
  MPs 261
  Police Authority 381
Suffolk Coastal 534, 553
Suffolk, Mid 533, 551
Suffragan Bishops (Church of
  England) 397–407
Sulewesi 904
Sumatra 904
Sumburgh airport 502
Summer:
  defined 15
  solstice 15, 81
Summer Time 75
  British 15, 75
Sun 76
  astronomical constants 75
  eclipses (1996) 66
  rising and setting times (1996) 17, 19,
    21, 23, 25, etc., 73
Sunderland 531, 548
  Education Authority 449
  MPs 261
  University 460
Sunrise, defined 71
Sunset, defined 71
Sunshine:
  averages 1209
  records 1210–15
Supreme Court, England and Wales 361,
  362–3
  departments 364–5
  judges 362–3
  Masters 364
Supreme Court, Northern Ireland 374
Surbiton, MP 261
Suriname 785, 1025
Surrey 531, 546, 547
  Archdeacon 400
  Education Authority 448
  MEPs 275, 276
  MPs 261
  Police Authority 381
  University 460
Surrey Heath 534, 553
Surveying, professional bodies 469
Sussex:
  East 531, 546, 547
  Education Authorities 448
  MEPs 276
  Mid 533, 551
    MP 261
  Police Authority 381
  University 460
  West 531, 546, 547

Sutherland 536, 569
Sutherland, Caithness and, MP 267
Sutton 534, 560
  Education Authority 449
Sutton (Plymouth), MP 257
Sutton and Cheam, MP 261
Sutton Coldfield, MP 261
Suva 787, 875
Svalbard 787, 978
Swale 534, 553
Swansea 535, 562, 563, 564
  MPs 266
  University College 460
Swansea and Brecon, Bishop 407
Swaziland 784, 1025–6
Sweden 787, 1026–8
  map 977
Swiftair (postal service) 511
Swimming 1237–8
  records 1241
Swindon:
  Archdeacon 398
  Bishop (Suffragan) 398
  MP 261
Switzerland 787, 1028–30
  Archdeacon 400
  map 1028
Sydney 810
Synagogues, Federation of 432
Syria 786, 1030–1
  Archbishops (RC) 422
  map 913

Table tennis 1238
Taff, Rhondda, Cynon and 564
Taff-Ely 535, 563
Tahiti 881
Taipei 786, 1031
Taiwan 786, 1031–2
  Archbishop (RC) 422
  map 850
Tajikistan 786, 1032–3
Takeover Panel 614
Tallinn 786, 873
Tameside 531, 548
  Education Authority 449
Tamworth 534, 553
Tandridge 534, 553
Tanzania 784, 1033–5
  Anglican Province 412
  Archbishops (RC) 422
Tarawa 787, 926
Tariffs (GATT) 773
Tashkent 786, 1057
Tasmania 805, 811
  Anglican diocese 408
Tate Gallery 287, 595
  Liverpool 287, 594
  St Ives 287, 596
Tatton, MP 261
Taunton:
  Archdeacon 398
  Bishop (Suffragan) 398
  MP 261
Taunton Deane 534, 553
Taxation:
  Budget (1994) 1163–5
  capital gains tax 644–6
  corporation tax 649–51
  income tax 639–44
  inheritance tax 646–9
  Inland Revenue 318
  royal family 130
  stamp duties 637–8
  value added tax 651–2
Tayside 535, 568
  Education Authority 450
  Police Authority 382

Tayside North, MP 270
Tbilisi 786, 884
Teacher Training Agency 440, 452
Teachers 440–1
  changes in training 440–1
  initial training 440–1, 469
  licensed 440
  numbers 441
  pay review body 341
  salaries 441
  shortage subjects 441
Teachers Pension Agency 299
Technological Achievement, Queen's
  Awards for 1179–80
Technological research
  associations 711–12
Technology academies 435
Technology, Office of 349–50,
Teesdale 534, 553
Teesside:
  airport 502
  University 460
Tegucigalpa 785, 898
Tehran 785, 907
Teignbridge 534, 553
  MP 261
Tel Aviv 785
Telecommunications 512–14
Telecommunications, Office of 349–50,
  512
Telecommunications Satellite
  Organization, International 760
Telecommunications Union,
  International 761
Telemessage 514
Telephone services 512–14
  cards 513
  inland 513
  international 514
  international dialling codes 516–17
  licensed operators 512
  mobile systems 513
  operator services 514
Television:
  (1994–5) 1132–6
  BBC 289, 679
  independent companies 679–80
  Independent Television
    Commission 317, 679
  licences 679
  satellite 680
Telex 514
Telford 524
Temperature:
  averages 1209
  conversion 521
  measures 521
  records 1210–15
Tenancies, legal notes 671–3
Tendring 534, 553
Tenerife 1021
Tennessee 1051
Tennis 1232
Term days 9
Terrestrial magnetism 77–8
Territorial Army 391
Test (Southampton), MP 259
Test, Itchen, Avon and, MEP 275
Test series:
  forthcoming (1996) 12–13
  results (1994–5) 1223
Test Valley 534, 553
Tewkesbury 534, 553
  Bishop (Suffragan) 400
  Cirencester and, MP 246
Texas 1051
Textiles, professional body 469
Thailand 786, 1035–6
  Archbishops (RC) 422
  map 836

Thames Valley:
　MEP 276
　Police Authority 381
　University 460
Thamesdown 534, 553
Thanet 534, 553
　MPs 261
The Valley 784, 1071
Theatre:
　(1994–5) 1192–1202
　awards 1202
　productions 1196–1202
Theatre Museum 327, 596
Theological colleges 469–70
Thetford, Bishop (Suffragan) 401
Thimphu 785, 825
Thistle, Order of 174
Three Kings Islands 969
Three Rivers 534, 553
Three-day eventing 1226
Thuringia 887
Thurrock 534, 553
　MP 261
Tibet 786, 853
Tidal constants 96–7
Tidal predictions (1996) 98–109
Tigray 874
Time:
　apparent sidereal 73, 74
　apparent solar 71, 73
　atomic 74
　British Summer 15, 75
　civil 73, 74
　co-ordinated universal 73
　ephemeris 74
　geological eras 94
　Greenwich Mean 73, 75
　human development 94–5
　lighting-up 71
　mean 69
　mean solar 73
　measurements 81
　sidereal 69, 73–4
　signals 74–5
　solar 71, 73
　standard 75
　Summer 75
　universal 73
　zones 794–5
Timor 904
Tirana 786, 797
Titles:
　courtesy 169–70
　forms of address 217
　heirs to peerages 142–61
　holders of peerages 142–68
　Malaysian 947
Tiverton, MP 261
Tobago, Trinidad and 785, 1038–9
　map 897
Togo 784, 1036–7
　Archbishop (RC) 422
　map 975
Tokelau 787, 969, 971
Tokyo 785, 920
Tonbridge:
　Archdeacon 402
　Bishop (Suffragan) 402
Tonbridge and Malling 534, 553
　MP 261
Tonga 787, 1037–8
Tooting, MP 261
Top Salaries Review Body 341
Torbay 534, 553
　MP 262
Torfaen 535, 563, 564
　MP 266
Toronto 844
Torres Islands 805
Torridge 534, 553

Torridge, Devon West and, MP 248
Tórshavn 786, 865
Totalisator Board, Horserace 316
Totnes, Archdeacon 400
Tottenham, MP 262
Tourist Authority, British 290
Tourist boards:
　England 350
　London 603
　Northern Ireland 350
　Scotland 350
　Wales 350
Tower Bridge 596, 599
Tower Hamlets 534, 560
　Education Authority 449
Tower of London 590
Town and country planning 675
　courses 471
Track events (athletics) 1217–21
　records 1239–41
Trade:
　associations 700–1
　balance of payments statistics 608
　export statistics 608
　General Agreement on Tariffs and 763
　import statistics 608
　President of the Board of 279, 350
Trade and Industry, Department of 350–3
　Ministers 279, 350
　Secretary of State 279, 350
Trade marks 677–8
　registry 678
Trade unions 702–4
　International Confederation of
　　Free 758
　mergers (1994–5) 704
Trade Unions and Employers'
　Associations, Certification Office
　for 293
Trades Union Congress 12, 702
　affiliated unions 702–4
　Scottish 702
Traffic Commissioners 355, 379
Trafford 531, 548
　Education Authority 449
Training, Enterprise and Education
　Directorate 299
Transkei 1017
Transplant Regulatory Authority,
　Unrelated Live 357
Transport 501–9
　air 501–2
　Police, British 383
　professional training 471
　rail 503–4
　road 505–7
　shipping 508–9
　Tribunal 379
Transport, Department of 353–5
　Ministers 279, 353
　Secretary of State 279, 353
Transport Research Laboratory Executive
　Agency 355
Treasury 355–6
　Chancellor of the Exchequer 279, 355
　Chief Secretary 279, 355
　Economic Secretary 279, 355
　Financial Secretary 279, 355
　First Lord of 279, 355
　Lord Commissioners 280, 356
　Ministers 279, 355
　Parliamentary Secretary 280, 355
Treasury Solicitor 356
　Department 356–7
Treaties:
　Antarctic 788
　Helsinki 761
　Maastricht 774, 777, 1111
　North Atlantic 761–2
　Rome 774

Tribunal Service, Independent 377
Tribunals 376–9
　Council on 357
　Interception of Communications 319
　Medical Appeal 494
　Pensions Appeal 378, 495
　Security Service 347
　Social Security Appeal 493
Trinidad, Archbishop (RC) 422
Trinidad and Tobago 785, 1038–9
　map 897
Trinity House, Corporation of 322–3
Trinity law term 9
Trinity Sunday 9, 83
Tripoli 784, 938
Tristan da Cunha 784, 1079
Tropical year 75, 81
Truro:
　Bishop 168, 403
　MP 262
Tuam, Archbishop (RC) 417
Tuam, Killala and Achonry, Bishop 408
TUC 702
　Scottish 702
Tunbridge Wells 534, 553
　MP 262
Tunis 784, 1039
Tunisia 784, 1039–40
Tunnels, longest 116
Turkey 786, 1040–2
　Archbishops (RC) 422
Turkmenistan 786, 1042–3
Turks and Caicos Islands 785, 1080
　map 897
Tuvalu 787, 1043–4
TV see Television
Tweeddale 536, 569
Tweeddale, Ettrick and Lauderdale,
　MP 270
Twickenham, MP 262
Twilight 71–2
　monthly tables 17, 21, 25, etc.
Two Thousand Guineas 13, 1230
Tyne Bridge, MP 262
Tyne and Wear 531, 548
　MEP 277
Tynedale 534, 553
Tynemouth, MP 262
Tyneside, North 531, 548
　Education Authority 449
Tyneside, South 531, 548
　Education Authority 449
Tynwald 574
Tynwald Day 574
Tyrone 572

UAE 786, 1047–9
　map 1006
UCAS 445
Uganda 784, 1044–5
　Anglican Province 412
　Archbishop (RC) 422
Ukraine 787, 1045–6
　Archbishop (RC) 422
Ulan Bator 785, 958
Ulster:
　Mid, MP 271
　University of 460
Ulster Democratic Unionist Council,
　financial support 229
Ulster Unionist Party:
　Council 230
　financial support 229
ULTRA 357
Umm al Qaiwain 1049
UN see United Nations
Under Secretaries of State 279–80
　salaries 281

Unemployment:
  benefits 489, 490
  statistics 607
UNESCO 770
UNICEF 767
Union flag (Jack) 122
  when flown 122
Union of Welsh Independents 428
Unitarian and Free Christian
    Churches 428
Unitary authorities:
  England 546
  Scotland 570
  Wales 564
United Arab Emirates 786, 1047–9
  map 1006
United Kingdom 118–750
  churches 396–408, 414–17, 423–5
  constitution 221–2
  defence 384–92
  economic statistics 606–9
  educational system 433–47
  legal system 361–74
  local government 526–36
  population statistics 118–21
  Royal family 123–4
United Kingdom Atomic Energy
    Authority 288
United Nations 765–71
  budget 767
  Economic and Social Council 768
  General Assembly 766–7
  International Court of Justice 769
  members 765–6
  peace-keeping forces 768
  secretariat 768–9
  Security Council 768
  specialized agencies 769–70
  specialized bodies 767
  Trusteeship Council 768
  UK representation 769–70
United Nations Children's Fund 767
United Nations Development
    Programme 768
United Nations Educational, Scientific and
    Cultural Organization 770
United Nations High Commissioner for
    Refugees 767
United Nations Industrial Development
    Organization 770
United Nations Relief and Works Agency
    for Palestine Refugees in the Near
    East 767
United Reformed Church 428
United Services Museum, Scotland 329,
    598
United States of America 784, 1049–56
  agriculture 1053–4
  Archbishops (RC) 422
  British Embassy 1052
  cabinet 1052
  defence 1053
  education 1054–5
  Embassy 1052
  Episcopal Church of 412–13
  finance 1053
  government 1050–2
  judicature 1053
  map 1050
  President 1052
  state governors 1051
  states 1051
  territories, etc. 1055–6
  trade 1054
  transport 1054
Universal Postal Union 770
Universal time 73
Universities 443–6
  admissions 445
  directory 452–61

Universities continued
  finance 444
  UCAS 445
University Boat Race 12, 1235
Unrelated Live Transplant Regulatory
    Authority 357
Upminster, MP 262
Upper Bann, MP 271
Upper Nithsdale, Galloway and, MP 268
Uranus 73, 76
  monthly data (1996) 19, 23, 27, etc., 73
  satellites 76
Urban development corporations 524–5
Urban Regeneration Agency (English
    Partnerships) 300
Uruguay 785, 1056–7
  Archbishop (RC) 422
USA, see United States
Utah 1051
Uttlesford 534, 553
Uxbridge, MP 262
Uzbekistan 786, 1057–8

Vaduz 786, 940
Vale of Glamorgan 535, 563, 564
  MP 266
Vale of White Horse 534, 553
Vale Royal 534, 553
Valletta 786, 949
Valuation bands, council tax 526
Valuation Office Executive Agency 318
Valuation tribunals 379
Value added tax 651–2
  Policy Directorate 297
  tribunals 379
Vanuatu 787, 1059
VAT 651–2
Vatican City State 414–15, 787, 1059
Vauxhall, MP 262
Vehicle Inspectorate Executive
    Agency 355
Vehicles:
  licences 506
  statistics 506–7
Venda 1017
Venezuela 785, 1060–1
  Archbishops (RC) 422
Venus 69, 72, 75
  monthly data (1996) 17, 18, 21, 22, etc.,
    72
  phenomena (1996) 16, 20, 24, etc.
Vermont 1051
Vernal equinox 15, 73, 81
Veterinary Medicines Directorate 285
Veterinary Service, State 283
Vicars-General 375
  Courts of 375
Vice-Chancellor, Chancery Division
    (High Court) 362
Victoria (Australia) 805, 812
  Anglican Province 408
Victoria (British Columbia) 842
Victoria (Seychelles) 784, 1008
Victoria, Queen 134
  descendants 134–6
Victoria and Albert Museum 327–8, 596
Victoria Cross 215
Victorian Order, Royal 175
Vienna 786, 810
Vientiane 785, 932
Vietnam 786, 1061–2
  Archbishops (RC) 422
  map 836
Vilnius 786, 940
Virgin Islands:
  American 785, 1049, 1051, 1056
  British 785, 1072–3
  map 897
Virginia 1051

Viscounts 149–52
  courtesy titles 169
  form of address 149, 217
  premier 150, 151
Vocational Education, Diploma
  of 439–40
Vocational Qualifications, National
    Council for 442–3
Volcanoes 113
Volleyball 1238
Volume, measurement 519
Voters' qualifications 675–6

Wages, legal notes 661
Wake Islands 1055
Wakefield 531, 548
  Bishop 168, 406
  Education Authority 449
  MP 262
Wales:
  Archbishop 407
  Archbishop (RC) 416
  art galleries 597
  Arts Council 286
  bishops (RC) 416
  Church in 407
  Commission for Local
      Administration 323
  counties 562
  Countryside Council 295–6
  early history 561–2
  educational system 433–42
  flag 561
  geographical features 561
  High Sheriffs 562
  judicature 361–70
  Land Authority 319
  local government 529–30
  local government changes 529, 564
  Lord Lieutenants 562
  map 564
  MEPs 277
  MPs 265–6
  museums 597
  National Library 322
  National Museum 329, 597
  Police Authorities 382
  political parties 231–7
  population statistics 118–21, 561
  Presbyterian Church of 427
  Prince, see Prince of Wales
  princes 140
  tourist board 350
  transport 501–7
  unitary authorities 564
  universities 460
  Youth Agency 357
Walking (athletics) 1234
  records 1239
Wallace Collection 287, 595
Wallasey, MP 262
Wallington, Carshalton and, MP 245
Wallis and Futuna Islands 787, 882
Wallsend, MP 262
Walsall 531, 548
  Education Authority 449
  MPs 262
Waltham Forest 534, 560
  Education Authority 450
Walthamstow, MP 262
Walton, Chertsey and, MP 246
Walton (Liverpool), MP 254
Wandsworth 534, 560
  Archdeacon 403
  Education Authority 450
Wansbeck 534, 553
  MP 262
Wansdyke 534, 553
  MP 262
Wanstead and Woodford, MP 262

Wantage, MP 262
War crimes tribunals 769
War Graves Commission,
    Commonwealth 295
War pensions 494–5
    Central Advisory Committee on 349
War Pensions Agency 349
Warley, MPs 262
Warrington 524, 534, 553
    Archdeacon 405
    Bishop (Suffragan) 405
    MPs 262–3
Warsaw 786, 989
Warwick 534, 553
    Archdeacon 399
    Bishop (Suffragan) 399
    University 460
Warwick and Leamington, MP 263
Warwickshire 531, 546, 547
    Education Authority 448
    MEPs 274, 277
    Police Authority 381
Warwickshire, North 533, 552
    MP 263
Washington (state) 1051
Washington (Tyne and Wear) 524
    Houghton and, MP 252
Washington DC 784, 1050
Water:
    Directorate 302
    industry 496–7
    measurement 520
    regulatory body 358, 496
    service companies 496
Water Services, Office of 358, 496
Waterfalls, greatest 114–15
Waterford and Lismore, Bishop (RC) 417
Waterside, Romsey and, MP 258
Waterways Board, British 290
Watford 534, 553
    MP 263
Waveney 534, 553
    MP 263
Waverley 534, 553
    MP 263
Ways and Means, Chairman of 224
Wealden 534, 553
    MP 263
Wear, Tyne and 531, 548
    MEP 277
Wear Valley 534, 553
Weather:
    average and general values 1209
    forecast information services 515
    Heathrow records (1994–5) 1213–15
    monthly records (1994–5) 1210–12
    stations records (1994–5) 1210–12
    summary (1994–5) 1204–15
    wind force measures 1209
Weights and measures 518–23
    conversion tables 523
    imperial units 519
    metric units 518–19
    metrication in UK 519–20
    National Laboratory 353
    SI units 518
Wellingborough 534, 553
    MP 263
Wellington 787, 970
Wells:
    Archdeacon 398
    MP 263
Wells, Bath and, Bishop 168
Welsh Development Agency 358
Welsh Folk Museum 597
Welsh Independents, Union of 428
Welsh Industrial and Maritime
    Museum 329, 597
Welsh Life, Museum of 329, 597
Welsh National Opera 1160

Welsh Office 358–60
    Ministers 280, 358
    Secretary of State 279, 358
Welsh Slate Museum 597
Welwyn Garden City 524
Welwyn Hatfield 534, 553
    MP 263
Wentworth, MP 263
Wesleyan Reform Union 428–9
West Africa, Anglican Province 413
West Bromwich, MPs 263
West Cumberland, Archdeacon 405
West Derby (Liverpool), MP 254
West Devon 534, 553
West Dorset 534, 553
West of England, University of the 460
West Glamorgan 535, 562, 563
    Education Authority 450
West Ham, Archdeacon 398
West Indies 784–5
    Anglican Province 413
    Archbishop (RC) 422
West Lancashire 534, 553
West Lindsey 534, 553
West Lothian 536, 569, 570
West Mercia Police Authority 381
West Midlands 531, 548
    Police Authority 381
West Norfolk, King's Lynn and 533, 551
West Oxfordshire 534, 553
West Somerset 534, 553
West Sussex 531, 546, 547
    Education Authority 448
West Virginia 1051
West Wiltshire 534, 553
West Yorkshire 531, 548
    Police Authority 381
Westbury, MP 263
Western Australia 805, 812
    Anglican Province 408
Western Education and Library Board
    (Northern Ireland) 450
Western European Union 770–1
Western Isles:
    Education Authority 450
    Island Council 535, 568, 570
    MP 270
Western Sahara 784, 961
Western Samoa 787, 1062–3
Westminster, Archbishop (RC) 415
Westminster, City of 534, 560
    Education Authority 449
Westminster Abbey 603
    Dean and Chapter 404
Westminster Cathedral 603
Westminster North, MP 263
Westminster South, City of London and,
    MP 246
Westminster University 460
Westmorland and Furness,
    Archdeacon 405
Westmorland and Lonsdale, MP 263
Weston-super-Mare, MP 263
Weymouth and Portland 534, 553
Whips, parliamentary 228, 230, 280
Whit Sunday 9, 83
Whitby, Bishop (Suffragan) 404
White papers 1174–7
Whitehorse, Yukon Territory 842
Whitsunday (term day) 9
Widow's benefits 489, 490
Wigan 531, 548
    Education Authority 449
    MP 263
Wigan, Merseyside East and, MEP 276
Wight, Isle of 531, 537, 546, 547
    Archdeacon 402
    Education Authority 448
    MP 252
Wight and Hampshire South, MEP 277

Wigston, Oadby and 533, 552
Wigtown 536, 569
Wild birds, close seasons 585
Wildlife, protected 583–5
Willemstad 785, 969
Willesden, Bishop (Area) 397
Wills, legal notes 658–61
Wiltshire 531, 546, 547
    Archdeacon 403
    Education Authority 448
    Police Authority 381
Wiltshire, North 533, 552
    MP 263
Wiltshire North and Bath, MEP 277
Wiltshire, West 534, 553
Wimbledon, MP 263
Wimbledon championships 13, 1232
Winchester 534, 544, 553
    Archdeacon 398
    Bishop 167, 397
    MP 263
Wind force measures 1209
Windhoek 784, 964
Windsor:
    Castle 590
    Dean and Chapter 404
    House of 134
    Military Knights of 211
Windsor and Maidenhead 534, 553
    MP 263
Wine measurement 520
Winnipeg 843
Winter:
    defined 15
    solstice 15, 81
Winter Olympic Games (venues
    1924–98) 716
Wirral 531, 548
    Education Authority 449
    MPs 263–4
Wirral, Cheshire West and, MEP 274
Wisbech, Archdeacon 399
Wisconsin 1051
Withington (Manchester), MP 255
Witney, MP 264
Woking 534, 553
    MP 264
Wokingham 534, 554
    MP 264
Wolverhampton 531, 548
    Bishop (Suffragan) 401
    Education Authority 449
    MPs 264
    University 460
Women priests 396
Women's National Commission 359
Women's Royal Voluntary Service 748
Wood Green, Hornsey and, MP 252
Woodford, Wanstead and, MP 262
Woodspring 534, 554
    MP 264
Woolwich:
    Bishop (Area) 403
    MP 264
Worcester 534, 554
    Archdeacon 403
    Bishop 167, 403
    MP 264
Worcester, Hereford and 531, 546, 547
    Education Authority 448
Worcestershire:
    MEP 277
    MPs 264
Workers' Educational Association 447
Workington, MP 264
World, The:
    countries 783–7, 796–1070
    geographical statistics 110–16
    physical data 110
    population 783

World Bank 771–2
World Council of Churches 772
World Health Organization 772
World Intellectual Property
  Organization 677, 678, 772
World Meteorological
  Organization 772–3
World records:
  athletics 1239–40
  swimming 1241
World Service, radio 681
Worldwide Television (BBC) 679
Worsley, MP 264
Worthing 534, 554
  MP 264
Wrekin 534, 554
  MP 264
Wrexham 564
  Bishop (RC) 416
  MP 266
Wrexham Maelor 535, 563
Wychavon 534, 554
Wycombe 534, 554
  MP 264
Wyoming 1051
Wyre 534, 554
  MP 264
Wyre Forest 534, 554
  MP 264
Wythenshawe (Manchester), MP 255

Yacht clubs 719–20
Yacht races 1238

Yamoussoukro 783, 857
Yangon (Rangoon) 786, 962
Yaoundé 783, 837
Yap 956
Yardley (Birmingham), MP 243
Year:
  anomalistic 75
  bissextile 89
  calendar 81
  equinoctial 81
  Hejira 86
  Hindu 84–5
  Jewish 85
  leap 81
  length 75
  Muslim 86
  sidereal 75
  Sikh 86
  tropical 75, 81
Yellowknife, Northwest Territories 842
Yemen, Republic of 786, 1063–4
  map 1006
Yeovil, MP 264
Ynys Môn (Anglesey) 535, 563
  MP 266
Yom Kippur 9, 85
York 534, 544, 546, 554
  Archdeacon 404
  MP 264
  University 460
York, Province of 404–7
  Archbishop 167, 404
  Chancery Court 375

Yorkshire:
  East 532, 550
  East Riding 546
  Education Authorities 448
  MEPs 277
  North 531, 546, 547
  Police Authorities 381
  South 531, 548
  West 531, 548
Young offender institutions 316
Youth courts 361
Yugoslav Federal Republic 787, 1064–6
  Archbishops (RC) 422
  map 1065
Yugoslavia (former), events
  (1994–5) 1106–10
Yukon Territory 838, 842

Zagreb 786, 858
Zaïre 784, 1066–8
  Anglican Province 413
  Archbishops (RC) 422
  map 800
Zambia 784, 1068–9
  Archbishops (RC) 422
  map 800
Zanzibar 1034
Zimbabwe 784, 1069–70
  Archbishop (RC) 422
Zodiacal light (1996) 21, 25, 49
Zoological gardens (London Zoo) 603

Stop-press

CHANGES SINCE PAGES WENT TO PRESS

ROYAL HOUSE
Gen. Sir Michael Rose appointed Aide-de-Camp General to The Queen
Deputy Private Secretary to The Queen: Sir Kenneth Scott retired, replaced by R. B. Janvrin. Janvrin replaced as Assistant Private Secretary by Ms M. Francis
Extra Chaplains: Canon J. S. D. Mansel, KCVO, died

PEERAGE
Died: 2nd Baron Broughshane, 6th Baron Harris
Life peerage gazetted: Rt. Revd John Habgood – Lord Habgood
Lords Spiritual: Kenneth Stevenson elected Bishop of Portsmouth

BARONETAGE AND KNIGHTAGE
Died:
Clark, Prof. Sir Grahame, CBE, FBA
Jones, Sir James, KCB
Jones, Air Marshal Sir Laurence, KCB, AFC
Mansel, James S. D., KCVO
Peierls, Sir Rudolf, CBE, FRS
Radford, Sir Ronald, KCB, MBE
Sich, Sir Rupert, CB

PARLIAMENT
David Trimble, MP, elected Ulster Unionist Council party leader, 8 September

GOVERNMENT DEPARTMENTS AND PUBLIC OFFICES
Cabinet Office: Special Advisers to Mr Heseltine, Lady Strathnever; Dr A. Kemp

Crown Estate Commissioners: D. E. G. Griffiths appointed a Commissioner
Department of Education and Employment restructured into seven Directorates and the Employment Service:
  Director-General, Schools, P. Owen
  Director-General, Further and Higher Education and Youth Training, R. Dawe
  Director-General, Employment and Lifetime Learning, N. Stuart
  Director-General, Strategy, International and Analytical Services, G. Reid
  Director-General, Operations, J. Hedger
  Director-General, Finance, L. Lewis
  Director-General, Personnel and Support Services, D. Normington
  Chief Executive, Employment Service, M. Fogden
Home Office: Legal Adviser, D. Nissen
Imperial War Museum: Director-General, R. Crawford
London Regional Transport Board: new members, C. Hodson, CBE; (part-time, non-executive) Ms S. O'Sullivan; B. Appleton
Department of National Heritage: J. Bercow appointed special adviser to Mrs Bottomley
National Lottery Charities Board: Ms M. McWilliams, I. Clarke, Mrs S. Clarke, N. Stewart, A. Higgins appointed members
Social Security Advisory Committee: chairman (from early 1996), Sir Thomas Boyd-Carpenter, KBE
HM Procurator-General and Treasury Solicitor, and Queen's Proctor, M. L. Saunders

LAW COURTS AND OFFICES

High Court judges: M. J. Moore-Bick (Queen's Bench Division); The Hon. M. C. Hogg (Family Division) appointed

Circuit judges: Miss A. O. H. Sander, J. S. Wiggs, S. H. Lloyd, A. R. L. Ansell appointed; J. R. Main, Mrs N. M. Lowry, R. J. Lowry retired

Recorders: P. Curl; D. S. Aubrey; A. H. Edwards; B. L. Lever; C. J. Swift; R. A. Britton; Mrs J. R. Case; P. M. Farmer; D. W. Morgan

Metropolitan Stipendiary Magistrate: J. B. Coleman

DEFENCE

Air Vice-Marshal T. I. Jenner to be Assistant Chief of the Air Staff

THE CHURCH OF ENGLAND

T. Stevens, Archdeacon of West Ham (Chelmsford), to be Suffragan Bishop of Dunwich (St Edmundsbury and Ipswich)

ROMAN CATHOLIC CHURCH

Owen Swindlehurst, Auxiliary Bishop of Hexham and Newcastle, died

LOCAL GOVERNMENT

Lord Mayor of London 1995–6: Alderman John Chalstrey

Isle of Man: Lieutenant Governor, Air Marshal Sir Laurence Jones, died

COUNTRIES OF THE WORLD

Canada: Quebec to hold a referendum on independence from Canada on 30 October

The Comoros: President Djohar arrested 28 September in attempted coup

Greece: Costas Simitis resigned as industry minister 11 September

Haiti: Richard Thomas appointed (non-resident) British ambassador from October 1995

India: Prime Minister Narasimha Rao brought 15 new ministers into the government 13 September

Japan: Ryutaro Hashimoto elected President of the Liberal Democratic Party, the dominant partner in the coalition government, 22 September

Nepal: Prime Minister Man Mohan Adhikari resigned 10 September after Communist Party lost parliamentary vote of no-confidence; leader of Nepali Congress Party, Sher Bahadur Deuba, sworn in 11 September and formed coalition government

Solomon Islands: Brian Connelly appointed British High Commissioner 24 September

Spain: Catalan nationalists withdrew parliamentary support for the minority socialist (PSOE) government 9 September

Sweden: first direct elections to the European Parliament held 17 September

Turkey: Tansu Çiller resigned as Prime Minister 20 September after the People's Republican Party withdrew its support for her coalition government; President Demirel asked her to form a new administration 21 September

BRITISH DEPENDENT TERRITORIES

Anguilla: Alan Hoole appointed Governor from November 1995

Gibraltar: Adm. Sir Hugo White appointed Governor 22 September

Hong Kong: elections to the Legislative Council held 17 September; Democratic Party and its allies won largest number of seats

EVENTS

SEPTEMBER 1995

1. NATO suspended its bombing of Bosnian Serb positions in Bosnia-Hercegovina and demanded that their heavy weapons be withdrawn from around Sarajevo. 3. Four people were slightly injured when a bomb exploded in Paris. 4. The UN Fourth World Conference on Women opened in Beijing. 5. NATO resumed bombing of Bosnian Serb positions in Bosnia-Hercegovina. France exploded a nuclear device underground at Mururoa atoll in the south Pacific. 5–6. Twelve people were killed and widespread damage was caused when Hurricane Luis hit Antigua and St Martin in the Caribbean. 6–7. Anti-nuclear protesters rioted in Papeete, Tahiti. 7. Fourteen people were injured when a car bomb exploded near a Jewish school in France. 8. After talks in Geneva foreign ministers representing Bosnia, Croatia and the rump Yugoslav republic agreed an American-brokered three-point programme on the future of Bosnia-Hercegovina. President Yeltsin denounced the NATO airstrikes and said that Russia would increase humanitarian aid to the Bosnian Serbs. 10. NATO fired cruise missiles at Bosnian Serb anti-aircraft missile sites around Banja Luka. 13. Muslim-Croat forces advanced into Bosnian Serb-held western Bosnia. 14. NATO suspended its bombing of Bosnian Serb positions after securing an undertaking that Bosnian Serb heavy weapons would be withdrawn from around Sarajevo in return for disclosure of the location of Bosnian government weapons in the city and a local cease-fire. 15. Bosnian Serb heavy weapons began to be withdrawn from around Sarajevo. The UN airlift bringing humanitarian aid to Sarajevo resumed. 17. Muslim-Croat forces advanced into Bosnian Serb-held northern Bosnia. At least nine people were killed when Hurricane Marilyn hit the US Virgin Islands and Puerto Rico. 19. The cross-channel Sealink ferry *Stena Challenger* ran aground outside Calais; it was refloated on 20 September. 20. NATO airstrikes against Bosnian Serb positions were called off indefinitely. 24. Israel reached agreement with the PLO on the extension of Palestinian autonomy in the West Bank; the pact was signed at the White House in Washington DC on 28 September. Europe won the Ryder Cup for the first time since 1989. 26. Agreement was reached at the UN on constitutional principles for a revised Bosnian state divided between a Muslim-Croat federation and the Bosnian Serbs. Penguin, HarperCollins and Random House announced that they would pull out of the Net Book Agreement from 1 October; on 28 September the Publishers' Association announced that it could no longer enforce the terms of the agreement. 27. The European Court of Human Rights ruled that Britain had breached the Human Rights Convention over the shooting of three IRA members in Gibraltar in 1988. 29. The IRA ruled out any decommissioning of weapons before a political settlement in Northern Ireland.

OBITUARIES

12. Jeremy Brett, actor, aged 59

15. McCluskie, Sam, general secretary of the National Union of Seamen 1986–90, aged 63

20. Maj.-Gen. Jerrie Hulme, CB, senior logistics officer to UN High Commissioner for Refugees in the former Yugoslavia since 1992, aged 60

23. Air Marshal Sir Laurence Jones, KCB, AFC, Lieutenant Governor of the Isle of Man since 1990, aged 62

25. Dorothy Dickson, actress and musical comedy star, aged 102